RAND McNALLY

Atlas of the World
Masterpiece Edition

RAND McNALLY

Atlas of the World
Masterpiece Edition

Advisers and Consultants

The editors wish to express their special appreciation to these geographers, cartographers, and regional specialists who assisted in the refinement of the basic concepts of the atlas or who participated in the review of many of the regional maps.

International Planning Conference

DR. MANLIO CASTIGLIONI
Italy

DR. ARCH C. GERLACH
United States

DR. IR. CORNELIS KOEMAN
Netherlands

DR. ANDRÉ LIBAULT
Brazil

BRIG. D. E. O. THACKWELL
United Kingdom

ROBERT J. VOSKUIL
United States

DR. AKIRA WATANABE
Japan

Map Advisers

Europe
PROF. DR. EMIL MEYNEN
Germany

DR. SANDOR RADO
Hungary

Asia
DR. HISASHI SATO
Japan

Australia
R. O. BUCHANAN
United Kingdom

Anglo-America
DR. ARCH C. GERLACH
United States

Latin America
DR. ANDRÉ LIBAULT
Brazil

DRA. CONSUELO SOTO MORA
Mexico

DR. JORGE A. VIVÓ ESCOTO
Mexico

Metropolitan Area Maps
PROF. HAROLD M. MAYER
United States

Rand McNally Corporate Advisory Group

Thomas J. Hermes
Dennis O'Shea
Carl Mapes, Ph.D.
Bruce C. Ogilvie, Ph.D.
Paul T. Tiddens

International Atlas Staff

RAND MCNALLY

Publisher
Andrew McNally III
Andrew McNally IV

Editorial and Cartographic Direction
Russell L. Voisin
Michael W. Dobson, Ph.D.
Jon M. Leverenz

Art and Design Direction
Chris Arvetis
Gordon Hartshorne
John Nelson

Coordination
V. Patrick Healy
Arlen H. Winterfeld
John E. Zych

Geographic Research and Index
Susan Hudson
Keith Jennerjohn
Felix A. Lopez
Raymond T. Tobiaski
Richard L. Forstall (Consultant)

Cartographic Editorial
Robert K. Argersinger
Winifred V. Farbman

Cartographic Compilation
Ernest A. Dahl
Esther A. Grene
Lynn N. Jasmer
Han Sik Lee
Larry K. Tyler

Cartographic Production
Timothy J. Carter
Ronald Peters
Barbara Smith
Walter E. Erck
Joseph H. Funke
Ruthe Garner
Raymond J. Nitch

Composition and Typesetting
Sam Wilen
Rajani Veeramachaneni

Terrain Illustrators
Ivan Barcaba
Evelyn Mitchell
Mary Jo Schrader

MONDADORI MCNALLY GmbH, STUTTGART

General Manager
Helmut Schaub
and Cartographic Staff

CARTOGRAPHIA, BUDAPEST

Coordinator
Ervin Földi
and Cartographic Staff

ESSELTE MAP SERVICE, STOCKHOLM

Editorial and Cartographic Direction
Paul R. Kraske,
Jürgen Jansch,
and Cartographic Staff

GEORGE PHILIP & SON, LONDON

Editorial and Cartographic Direction
Harold Fullard,
A. G. Poynter,
and Cartographic Staff

TEIKOKU-SHOIN CO., LTD., TOKYO

Supervisor
Kimio Moriya
and Cartographic Staff

Rand McNally Atlas of the World, Masterpiece Edition

Copyright © 1993 by Rand McNally & Company

Maps and index on pages 1-288 and I·1-I·200 from *The New International Atlas*, copyright © 1993 by Rand McNally & Company.

Maps on pages 290-351, revised in 1992, are from *Atlas of the United States*, copyright © 1983 by Rand McNally & Company

Library of Congress Cataloging-in-Publication Data

Rand McNally & Company.
   Rand McNally atlas of the world.— Masterpiece ed.
      p.   cm.
   Includes index.
   ISBN: 0-528-83555-6
   1. Atlases.   I. Title   II. Title: Atlas of the world.
   G1021.R27 1992   <G&M>
   912—dc20   92-24031
                                                            CIP
                                                            MAP

Printed in the United States of America.

Title page photo by David Muench,
Bridger Wilderness, Wyoming

Foreword

The history of maps is as old as travel, discovery, and curiosity about the world. Since the earliest times, cartographers have served mariners with guidance for their explorations, monarchs with portraits of their territories, and scholars with a record of the earth's surface. Today, maps play an even more important role by providing a record of the ties that link the world's countries and peoples to one another.

The prime function of a map is to portray the earth's surface and the patterns of human occupance that have developed upon it. If a map were no more than an objective record, it would not need revision; however, a map is more than just a simple picture. Greatly reduced in scale from the reality it represents, it must abstract and generalize from that reality, selecting and interpreting the facts deemed to be of greatest significance. Thus, not only must cartography map new regions of the world, but it must also reflect a steady improvement in the techniques of portraying geographic information for the user.

This century has offered a great challenge to map makers. Not only has it witnessed the increasing demand for specialized map information from governments, teachers, and scientists, it has also seen growing numbers of non-specialists eager to use maps in their business, for travel, or simply for enjoyment.

The Editors feel, then, that a new work should be more than an updated version of older ones. The goal should be to produce an atlas of the greatest possible value and interest to a wide range of specialists and laymen. In this Foreword we call the attention of users to several aspects which are new to the traditional framework of atlas publishing. The two most significant of these are the internationality of its planning and execution, and the designing of the maps as components of six distinctive series.

The Atlas is international in concept, planning, editorial policy, and production. It is felt that important gains in source material and expertise result from the participation of organizations with previous cartographic experience in widely varying regions of the world. The advice and guidance of the senior personnel of these organizations has borne out this belief, though Rand McNally & Company as publisher has retained prime responsibility.

Editorial policies have been established with the broadest possible use. It is designed for use by English as well as for those whose native tongue is Spanish, French, German, or Portuguese. This international approach has been carried into the maps through the utilization of the metric system of measurement, and particularly by a strong emphasis on the use of local forms for geographic names. Essentially all names are in the local language, and English is used only for names of major features which extend across international borders. The names of countries appear on most of the maps both in English and in the locally official forms.

Generic terms for physical features (mountain, island, cape, etc.) also appear in their local forms, not in English. Short glossaries translating the most common of these terms appear in the margins of most maps. In the main index to the Atlas, translation of generic terms is aided by the use of a system of symbols.

The coverage of the world's regions has also been planned so that balanced world coverage will result. The space allotted to each region reflects its relative economic and cultural significance on the world scene, as well as its total population and area.

The second of the Atlas' significant new aspects is the planning of the maps as components of six separate series. Each series has a distinctive style and content. In the first of these series, the continents are portrayed at 1:24,000,000 in natural colors, as they might appear from about 4,000 miles in space. The series also includes maps of the oceans at 1:48,000,000 and the world at 1:75,000,000.

In the next series, the major world regions are uniformly portrayed at 1:12,000,000 (190 miles to the inch). These maps are primarily political in style and content. The third series covers virtually the entire inhabited area of the earth at either 1:6,000,000 (95 miles to the inch), for the less dense regions, or 1:3,000,000 (47 miles to the inch), for Europe, most of North America, and the densest portions of South and East Asia. Physical and cultural detail are given approximately equal emphasis in this series.

In the fourth series, the scale of 1:1,000,000 (16 miles to the inch) has been used to portray key regions in each continent, selected for their exceptional importance, high population density or complexity of development. The emphasis is on cultural detail, though shaded relief also appears. A fifth series maps the world's major urban areas at 1:300,000 (4.7 miles to the inch) showing details of the complex patterns characteristic of large urban areas, omitting relief portrayal.

The final series focuses on the United States and Canada by mapping individual states and provinces. Transportation networks, rivers, lakes, cities, and other features that impart special character to each state and province are shown in great detail against a background of shaded relief. An index of major places accompanies each map.

Each of the map series is comprehensive in a significant sense. The first three are territorially comprehensive, except for a few remote areas, and the last three are comprehensive for the most densely settled regions of the earth and for regions of special interest.

The sequence of maps in the Atlas begins with the series of world, continent, and ocean maps. Next are the three series of regional maps, arranged within major regions from smallest scale (1:12,000,000) to largest scale (1:1,000,000). The metropolitan map series (1:300,000) has been kept together in one section following the regional maps. The United States and Canada section is the final map element of the atlas.

The individual map layouts have usually been planned to portray geographic and economic regions rather than individual countries. Thus there are maps of the Iberian Peninsula and of Southeastern Europe, but no separate maps of Portugal or Romania. In a few instances, this has necessitated the omission of some small portion of the region or country described in the map title. Inset maps have also been avoided, though exceptions have been made to portray some isolated islands or island groups.

The map symbols used for given features (Legend to Maps, pages viii-x) are generally alike on all of the map scales, though reduced in size on smaller scales. The symbols most often used have been arranged on page viii. A special legend for the states and provinces is on 289.

No aspect of map design has shown more dramatic advances in recent years than the cartographic rendering of relief. The Editors believe that the most effective method to depict this is the bird's-eye view of hill shading technique, which uses varying tones, from light through dark, to pictorially show slope and shape of the earth's surface. This Atlas uses shaded relief on all but one of its six map series. On the 1:6,000,000 and 1:3,000,000 maps, it appears in combination with altitude tints, which show changes in elevation by a graded series of colors.

Concluding the atlas is the Index for the first five series of maps. The Index provides map location references—latitude and longitude—for more than 160,000 names. Indexes for the states and provinces are located in the margins of each map.

List of Maps

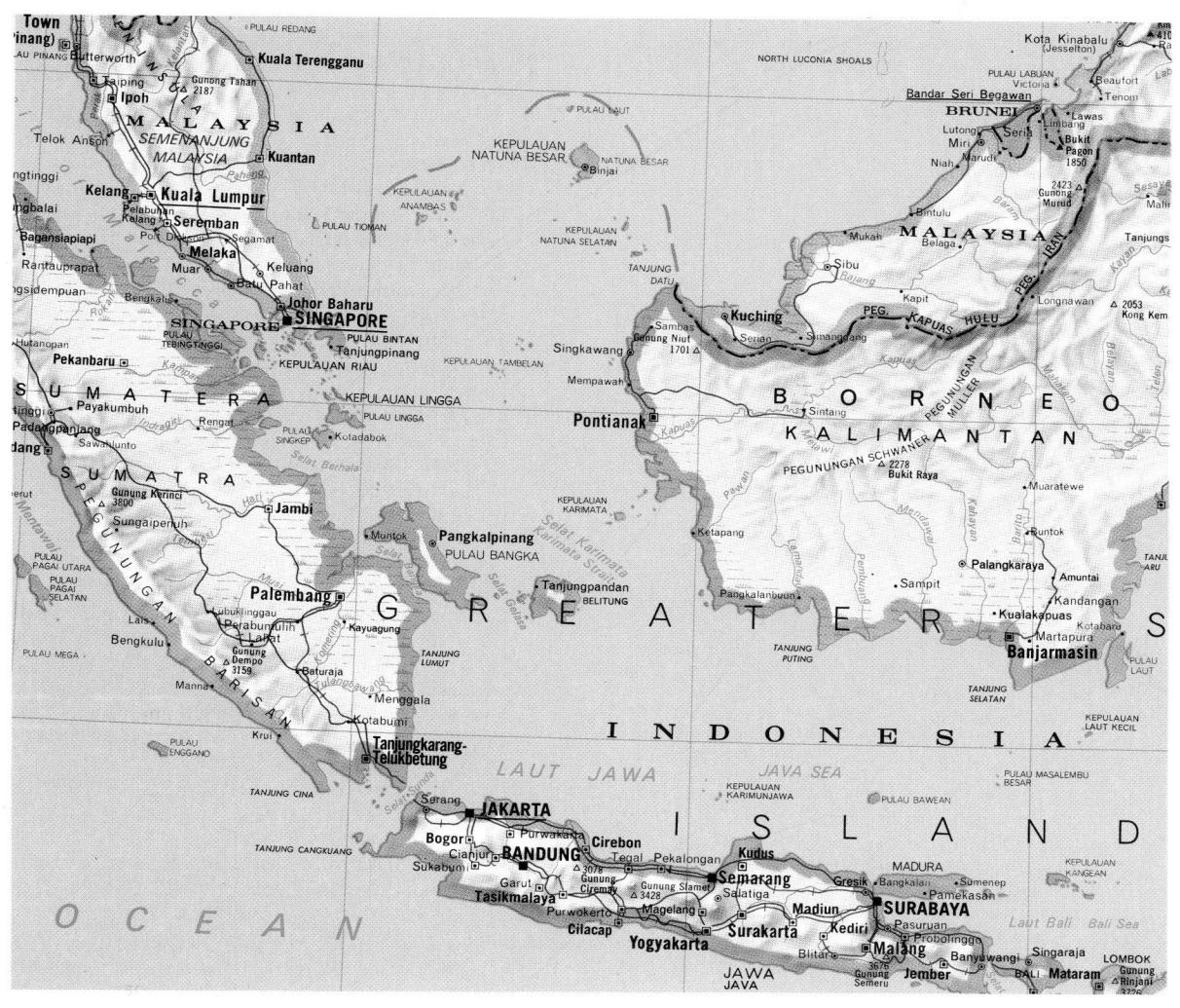

Legend to Maps/Zeichenerklärung
Leyendas Para Mapas/Légende des Cartes/Legendas dos Mapas

The design and color of the map symbols are consistent throughout the Regional and Metropolitan Area maps, although the size of the symbol varies with scale. An asterisk marks those symbols which appear only on the 1:300,000 scale maps. Symbols for inhabited localities, boundaries, and capitals are given on page xi.

The symbol 80-81→ in the margin of a map directs the reader to a map of the adjoining area.

A separate legend on page 1 identifies the land and submarine features which appear on the World, Ocean, and Continent maps.

Der Entwurf und die Farbe der Kartensymbole sind einheitlich für alle Regionalkarten und Karten von Stadtregionen, während die Grösse des Symbols sich mit dem Massstab ändert. Ein Stern kennzeichnet diejenigen Symbole, welche nur auf den Karten im Massstab 1:300 000 erscheinen. Symbole für bewohnte Orte, für Grenzen und Hauptstädte sind auf Seite xi angeführt.

Kennzeichen 80-81→ am Rande einer Karte ist ein Hinweis für den Leser, die Karte eines angrenzenden Gebietes nachzuschlagen.

Eine andere Legende auf Seite 1 identifiziert die Land- und untermeerischen Phänomene, die auf den Weltkarten, Karten der Ozeane und Erdteile erscheinen.

El diseño y el color de los símbolos cartográficos son uniformes para todas los mapas regionales y de las áreas metropolitanas, aunque el tamaño del símbolo varía según la escala. Un asterisco distingue los símbolos que aparecen sólo en los mapas a 1:300 000. Los símbolos de lugares poblados, de límites y de capitales se hallan en la página xi.

El símbolo 80-81→ al margen de un mapa dirige al lector a un mapa del área adyacente.

Otra leyenda, en la página 1, identifica la topografía terrestre y submarina que se encuentra en los mapas del Mundo, Océanos y Continentes.

La couleur et la forme des symboles cartographiques des cartes régionales et des cartes des zones métropolitaines sont identiques, bien que la grandeur des signes varie selon l'échelle. Un astérisque accompagne les symboles qui n'apparaissent que sur les cartes au

1:300 000? La légende des signes conventionnels pour les lieux habités, les frontières et les capitales se trouve à la page xi.

Le symbole 80-81→ en marge d'une carte renvoie le lecteur à une carte de la région voisine.

Pour les cartes du monde, des océans et des continents une légende séparée, à la page 1, donne le sens des symboles représentant les paysages continentaux et les formes de relief sous-marin.

A cor e a forma dos símbolos cartográficos dos mapas regionais e das áreas metropolitanas são idênticos, ainda que a dimensão do símbolo varie segundo a escala. Um asterisco distingue os símbolos que só aparecem nos mapas da escala de 1:300 000. As legendas dos símbolos convencionais dos lugares povoados, fronteiras e capitais encontram-se à pág. xi.

O símbolo 80-81→ à margem de um mapa, remete o leitor a um mapa da região vizinha.

Nos mapas do mundo, dos oceanos e dos continentes uma legenda separada, na pág. 1, indica o sentido dos símbolos representativos das paisagens continentais e das formas do relevo submarino.

Hydrographic Features / Hydrographische Objekte / Elementos Hidrográficos
Données Hydrographiques / Acidentes Hidrográficos

Shoreline/Uferlinie
Línea costanera/Trait de côte
Linha costeira

Undefined or Fluctuating Shoreline
Unbestimmte oder Veränderliche Uferlinie
Línea costanera indefinida o fluctuante
Trait de côte indéfini ou fluctuant
Linha costeira indefinida ou flutuante

River, Stream/Fluss, Strom
Río, Corriente/Rivière, Cours d'eau
Rio, curso d'água

Intermittent Stream/Periodischer Fluss
Corriente intermitente/Cours d'eau périodique
Rio, curso d'água intermitente

Rapids, Falls/Stromschnellen, Wasserfälle
Rápidos, Cascadas/Rapides, Chutes d'eau
Corredeiras, quedas d'água

Depth of Water/Wassertiefe
Profundidad del aqua/Profondeur bathymétrique
Profundidade da água

Greatest Depth (Atlantic, Indian, Pacific oceans)
Grösste Tiefe (Atlantischer, Indischer, Pazifischer Ozean)
Profundidad más grande (Océanos Atlántico, Índico, Pacífico)
Profondeur maximum (océans Atlantique, Indien, Pacifique)
Profundidade máxima (oceanos Atlântico, Índico, Pacífico)

Canal du Midi
Navigable Canal/Schiffbarer Kanal
Canal navegable/Canal navigable
Canal navegável

Irrigation or Drainage Canal
Be- oder Entwässerungskanal
Canal de irrigación o desagüe
Canal d'irrigation ou de drainage
Canal de irrigação ou drenagem

Los Angeles Aqueduct
Aqueduct/Aquädukt
Acueducto/Aqueduc
Aqueduto

Pier, Breakwater/Landungsbrücke, Wellenbrecher
Embarcadero, Rompeolas/Jetée, Brise-lames
Cais, Quebra-mar

GREAT BARRER REEF
Reef/Riff
Arrecife/Récif
Recife

Kumdah
Uninhabited Oasis/Unbewohnte Oase
Oasis deshabitado/Oasis inhabitée
Oásis desabitado

L. Victoria
Lake, Reservoir/See, Stausee
Lago, Embalse/Lac, Réservoir
Lago, reservatório (represa)

Intermittent Lake, Reservoir
Periodischer See, Stausee
Lago o Embalse intermitente
Lac ou Réservoir périodique
Lago, reservatório (represa) intermitente

Tuz Gölü
Salt Lake/Salzsee
Lago salado/Lac salé
Lago salgado

Dry Lake Bed/Trockener Seeboden
Lecho de lago seco/Fond de lac asséché
Leito de lago seco

The Everglades
Swamp/Sumpf
Pantano/Marais
Pântano

RIMO GLACIER
Glacier/Gletscher
Glaciar/Glacier
Geleira

(395)
Lake Surface Elevation
Seehöhe
Elevación del lago
Cote du niveau du lac
Altitude do nível do lago

Topographic Features / Topographische Objekte / Elementos Topográficos
Données Topographiques / Acidentes Topográficos

Matterhorn 4478 △
Elevation Above Sea Level
Höhe über dem Meeresspiegel
Elevatión sobre el nivel del mar
Cote au-dessus du niveau de la mer
Altitude acima do nível do mar

76 ▽
Elevation Below Sea Level
Höhe unter dem Meeresspiegel
Elevación bajo del nivel del mar
Cote au-dessous du niveau de la mer
Altitude abaixo do nível do mar

Mount Cook 3764 ▲
Highest Elevation in Country
Höchster Punkt des Landes
Elevación más alta en el país
Cote la plus élevée d'un pays
Altitude mais elevada de um país

133 ▼
Lowest Elevation in Country
Tiefster Punkt des Landes
Elevación más baja en el país
Cote la plus basse d'un pays
Altitude mais baixa de um país

(106)
Elevation of City
Höhenangabe einer Stadt
Elevación de ciudad
Altitude d'une ville
Altitude de uma cidade

Khyber Pass 1067 =
Mountain Pass/Pass
Paso/Col de montagne
Passo (de montanha)

*
Rock/Fels
Roca/Rocher
Rocha

Lava/Lava
Lava/Lave
Lava

Sand Area/Sandgebiet
Area de arena/Région sableuse, Erg
Região arenosa, Erg

Salt Flat/Salzebene
Salar/Dépression salée
Depressão salgada

Elevations and depths are given in meters
Höhen und Tiefen sind in Metern angegeben
Elevaciones y profundidades se dan en metros
Cotes et profondeurs sont indiqués en mètres
Altitudes e profundidades são apresentadas em metros

ANDES
KUNLUN SHAN
Mountain Range, Plateau, Valley, etc.
Gebirge, Hochebene, Tal, usw.
Sierra, Meseta, Valle, etc.
Chaîne de montagnes, Plateau, Vallée, etc.
Cadeia de montanhas. Planalto, Vale etc.

BAFFIN ISLAND
NUNIVAK ISLAND
Island
Insel
Isla
Île
Ilha

POLUOSTROV KAMČATKA
CABO DE HORNOS
Peninsula, Cape, Point, etc.
Halbinsel, Kap, Landspitze, usw.
Península, Cabo, Punta, etc.
Péninsule, Cap, Pointe, etc.
Península, Cabo, Ponta etc.

Highest Elevation and Lowest Elevation of a continent are underlined
Höchster und tiefster Punkt innerhalb eines Erdteils sind unterstrichen
Elevación más alta y más baja de un continente se subrayan
La cote la plus haute et la cote la plus basse d'un continent sont soulignées
As altitudes mais e menos elevadas de um continente são sublinhadas

Inhabited Localities / Bewohnte Orte / Lugares Poblados / Lieux Habités / Lugares Habitados

The symbol represents the number of inhabitants within the locality/Die Signatur entspricht der Einwohnerzahl des Ortes
El símbolo representa el número de habitantes dentro del lugar/Le symbole représente le nombre d'habitants de la localité
O símbolo representa o número de habitantes do lugar

1:300,000 1:1,000,000		1:12,000,000		1:24,000,000	
1:3,000,000 1:6,000,000	· 0—10,000		· 0—50,000	1:48,000,000	· 0—100,000
	∘ 10,000—25,000		⊙ 50,000—100,000		⊙ 100,000—1,500,000
	⊙ 25,000—100,000		⊡ 100,000—250,000		■ >1,500,000
	⊡ 100,000—250,000		⊟ 250,000—1,000,000		
	⊞ 250,000—1,000,000		■ >1,000,000		
	■ >1,000,000				

The size of type indicates the relative economic and political importance of the locality
Die Schriftgrösse entspricht der relativen wirtschaftlichen und politischen Bedeutung des Ortes
El tamaño del tipo de imprenta indica la relativa importancia económica y política del lugar
La dimension des caractères indique l'importance économique et politique relative d'une localité
A dimensão dos caracteres tipográficos indica a importância econômica e política relativa do lugar

Écommoy	Lisieux	Rouen
Trouville	Orléans	**PARIS**

Hollywood ▫ **Section of a City, Neighborhood/Stadtteil, Nachbarschaft**
Westminster **Sección de una ciudad, Barrio/Arrondissement, Quartier**
Seção de uma cidade, Bairro

Northland ■ * **Major Shopping Center/Haupteinkaufszentrum/Mercado principal**
Center **Centre commercial important/Centro comercial importante**

BYRD ▫ **Scientific Station/Wissenschaftliche Station/Estación científica**
Station scientifique/Estação científica

Bi'r Safājah ∘ **Inhabited Oasis/Bewohnte Oase/Oasis habitado**
Oasis habitée/Oásis habitado

Kumdah ∘ **Uninhabited Oasis/Unbewohnte Oase/Oasis deshabitado**
Oasis inhabitée/Oásis desabitado

Urban Area (area of continuous industrial, commercial, and residential development)
Stadtgebiet (ausgedehntes industrie-, Geschäfts- und Wohngebiet)
Zona urbanizada (área de desarrollo industrial, comercial y residencial)
Zone urbanisée (zone d'occupation continue par des industries, des commerces, des habitations)
Zona urbanizada (área de ocupação contínua por indústrias, estabelecimentos comerciais e habitações)

* **Major Industrial Area/Hauptindustriegebiet/Zona principal industrial**
Région industrielle importante/Zona industrial importante

* **Wooded Area/Wald/Área de bosque**
Région boisée/Área verde

* **Local Park or Recreational Area/Park oder Erholungsgebiet**
Parque municipal o área de recreo/Parc municipal ou zone de loisirs
Parque municipal ou área de lazer

Political Boundaries / Politische Grenzen / Límites Políticos / Frontières Politiques / Fronteiras e Limites

International (First-order political unit) /**Staatsgrenze** (Politische Einheit erster Ordnung)
Internacionales (Unidad política de primer orden) /**Internationales** (Entités politiques de premier ordre)
Internacionais (Unidade política de primeiro nível)

Capitals of Political Units
Hauptstädte politischer Einheiten
Capitales de Unidades Políticas
Capitales d'Entités Politiques
Capitais de Unidades Políticas

1:1,000,000	1:300,000 1:3,000,000 1:6,000,000	1:24,000,000 1:48,000,000	1:12,000,000	

━ ━ ━ ━ HUNGARY
Demarcated, Undemarcated, and Administrative
Markiert, unmarkiert, verwaltungstechnisch
Demarcado, No demarcado, y Administrativo
Délimitées, Non-délimitées, Administratives
Delimitados, Não delimitados, Administrativos

BUDAPEST **Independent Nation**
Unabhängiger Staat
Nación independiente
État indépendant
Estado independente

Disputed de facto/Umstritten de facto
Disputado de hecho/Contestées de facto
Contestados de fato

Cayenne **Dependency**
(Colony, protectorate, etc.)
Abhängiges Gebiet
(Kolonie, Protektorat, usw.)
Dependencia
(Colonia, protectorado, etc.)
Territoire dépendant
(Colonie, protectorat, etc.)
Dependência
(Colônia, protetorado, etc.)

Disputed de jure/Umstritten de jure
Disputado de derecho/Contestées de jure
Contestados de direito

Indefinite or Undefined/Unklar oder Unbestimmt
Indefinido o No determinado/Imprécises ou Non définies
Imprecisos ou Não definidos

GALAPAGOS **Administering Country**
(Ecuador) **Verwaltender Staat**
País administrador
Pays administrateur
País administrador

Demarcation Line/Demarkationslinie
Línea de demarcación/Ligne de démarcation
Linha de demarcação

Internal/Verwaltungsgrenze/Internos/Intérieures/Limites Internos

PERNAMBUCO
State, Province, etc. (Second-order political unit)
Land, Provinz, usw. (Politische Einheit zweiter Ordnung)
Estado, Provincia, etc. (Unidad política de segundo orden)
État, Province, etc. (Subdivision administrative de deuxième ordre)
Estado, Província, etc. (Unidade política de segundo nível)

Recife **State, Province, etc./Land, Provinz, usw.**
Estado, Provincia, etc./État, Province, etc.
Estado, Província, etc.

SIENA WESTCHESTER
County, Oblast, etc. (Third-order political unit)/**Grafschaft, Oblast, usw.** (Politische Einheit dritter Ordnung)
Condado, Oblast, etc. (Unidad política de tercer orden)
Comté, Oblast, etc. (Subdivision administrative de troisième ordre)
Condado, Oblast, etc. (Unidade política de terceiro nível)

Ambāla **County, Oblast, etc./Grafschaft, Oblast, usw.**
Johnstown **Condado, Oblast, etc./Comté, Oblast, etc.**
Condado, Oblast, etc.

ISERLOHN
Okrug, Kreis, etc. (Fourth-order political unit)/**Okrug, Kreis, usw.** (Politische Einheit vierter Ordnung)
Okrug, Kreis, etc. (Unidad política de cuarto orden)
Okrug, Kreis, etc. (Subdivision administrative de quatrième ordre)
Okrug, Kreis, etc. (Unidade política de quarto nível)

Iserlohn **Okrug, Kreis, etc./Okrug, Kreis, usw.**
Okrug, Kreis, etc./Okrug, Kreis, etc.
Okrug, Kreis, etc.

City or Municipality (may appear in combination with another boundary symbol)
Stadt oder Gemeinde (kann zusammen mit einem anderen Begrenzungssymbol erscheinen)
Ciudad o Municipio (puede aparecer en combinación con otro símbolo de límite)
Ville ou Municipalité (peut paraître en combinaison avec un autre symbole de limites politiques)
Cidade ou Municipalidade (Pode aparecer em combinação com outro símbolo de limite político)

NORMANDIE **Historical Region** (No boundaries indicated)
Historische Landschaft (Grenzen werden nicht gezeigt)
Región Histórica (Sin indicación de límites)
Région Historique (Sans indication de frontières)
Região Histórica (Sem indicação de fronteiras)

Legend to Maps/Zeichenerklärung
Leyendas Para Mapas/Légende des Cartes/Legendas dos Mapas

Transportation / Verkehr / Transporte / Transports / Transporte

	1:300,000	1:1,000,000	1:3,000,000 1:6,000,000	1:12,000,000

Road/Strasse/Camino/Route/Rodovia

Primary/Erster Ordnung/Principal/de premier ordre/Principal — PASSAIC EXPWY. (1-80) — PENNSYLVANIA TURNPIKE

Secondary/Zweiter Ordnung/Secundario/de second ordre/Secundária — BERLINER RING

Tertiary/Dritter Ordnung/Terciario/de troisième ordre/Terciária

Minor Road, Trail/Weg, Pfad
Rodera, Vereda/Route secondaire, Piste/Caminho, trilha

Railway/Eisenbahn/Ferrocarril/Voie ferrée/Ferrovia

Primary/Hauptbahn/Principal/Principale/Principal — CANADIAN NATIONAL — SANTA FE

Secondary/Sonstige Bahn/Secundario/Secondaire/Secundária

*Rapid Transit/Schnellverkehr/Tránsito rápido/Métro/Trânsito rápido (metrô)

Airport/Flughafen/Aeropuerto/Aéroport/Aeroporto — LONDON (HEATHROW) AIRPORT — DULLES INTERNATIONAL AIRPORT

*Rail or Air Terminal/Bahnhof oder Flughafengebäude
Terminal ferroviaria o aéro/Gare ou aérogare
Terminal ferroviário ou aéreo (estação) — SÜD-BAHNHOF

REICHS-BRÜCKE — Bridge/Brücke/Puente/Pont/Ponte

GREAT ST. BERNARD TUNNEL — Tunnel/Tunnel/Túnel/Tunnel/Túnel

Shipping Channel/Schiffahrtsrinne
Canal maritimo/Chenal maritime
Canal maritimo
Houston Ship Channel

Navigable Canal/Schiffbarer Kanal
Canal navegable/Canal navigable
Canal navegável
Canal du Midi

Intracoastal Waterway/Küstenschiffahrtsweg
Via fluvial Intracostera/Canal côtier
Via costeira interna

Ferry/Fähre
Balsadera/Bac
Balsa
TO MALMÖ

Miscellaneous Cultural Features / Sonstige Objekte / Elementos Culturales Misceláneos
Éléments Culturels Divers / Acidentes Culturais Diversos

PARQUE NACIONAL LANIN
National or State Park or Monument
National- oder Naturpark oder Denkmal
Parque o Monumento nacional o provincial
Parc ou Monument national ou régional
Parque ou Monumento nacional ou regional

EDISON NAT. HIST. SITE
National or State Historic(al) Site, Memorial
Historische Stätte, Gedenkstätte
Sitio histórico nacional o provincial, Monumento
Site historique national ou régional, Mémorial
Sítio histórico nacional ou regional, Monumento histórico

SEMINOLE IND. RES.
Indian Reservation/Indianerreservation
Reserva de indios/Réserve indienne
Reserva indígena

FORT DIX
Military Installation/Militäranlage
Instalación militar/Installation militaire
Instalação militar

GREENWOOD CEMETERY
* Cemetery/Friedhof
Cementerio/Cimetière/Cemitério

Point of Interest (Battlefield, museum, temple, university, etc.)
SORBONNE
Sehenswürdigkeit (Schlachtfeld, Museum, Tempel, Universität, usw.)
Punto de interés (Campo de batalla, museo, templo, universidad, etc.)
Curiosité (Champ de bataille, musée, temple, université, etc.)
Pontos de interesse (Campo de batalha, museu, templo, universidade, etc.)

STEPHANSDOM
Church, Monastery/Kirche, Kloster
Iglesia, Monasterio/Église, Monastère
Igreja, Mosteiro

UXMAL
Ruins/Ruinen/Ruinas/Ruines/Ruínas

WINDSOR CASTLE
Castle/Burg, Schloss/Castillo/Château/Castelo

* Lighthouse/Leuchtturm
Faro/Phare/Farol

ASWÀN DAM
Dam/Damm/Presa/Barrage
Represa (barragem)

<> * Lock/Schleuse/Esclusa
Écluse/Eclusa

Crib
* Water Intake Crib/Wasseraufnahmestation
Toma de agua/Prise d'eau/Captação de água

Quarry or Surface Mine
Steinbruch oder Tagebau
Cantera o Mina de hoyo abierto
Carrière ou Mine à ciel ouvert
Pedreira ou mina a céu aberto

Subsurface Mine/Bergwerk
Mina subterránea/Mine souterraine
Mina subterrânea

* Oil Well/Ölbohrturm
Pozo de petróleo/Puits de pétrole
Poço de petróleo

Metric-English Equivalents / Umrechnung metrischer Masse in englische Masse / Métrico-Equivalentes Ingleses
Equivalences métriques des mesures anglaises / Equivalentes métricos das medidas inglesas

Areas represented by one square centimeter at various map scales
Flächen die einem cm² in den verschiedenen Kartenmassstäben entsprechen
Áreas representados por un centímetro cuadrado a varias escalas de mapas
Surface représentée par un cm² aux échelles indiquées
Áreas representadas por cm² nas escalas indicadas nos mapas

Meter = 3.28 feet

Meter² (m²) = 10.76 square feet

Kilometer = 0.62 mile

Kilometer² (km²) = 0.39 square mile

1:300,000
9 km²
3.48 square miles

1:1,000,000
100 km²
39 square miles

1:3,000,000
900 km²
348 square miles

1:6,000,000
3,600 km²
1,390 square miles

1:12,000,000
14,400 km²
5,558 square miles

1:24,000,000
57,600 km²
22,234 square miles

1:48,000,000
230,400 km²
88,934 square miles

Elevation tints shown only on 1:3,000,000 and 1:6,000,000 scale maps
Höhenschichten erscheinen nur auf Karten im Massstab 1:3 000 000 und 1:6 000 000
Se indica las tintas de elevación sólo en los mapas de escala 1:3 000 000 y 1:6 000 000
Teintes hypsométriques exprimées seulement sur cartes à 1:3 000 000 et 1:6 000 000
Indicaram-se as graduações de cor hipsométricas somente nos mapas de escalas 1:3 000 000 e 1:6 000 000

Meters	Feet
6000	19685
4000	13124
3000	9843
2000	6562
1000	3281
500	1640
200	656
Land Below Sea Level 0	0
200	656
1000	3281
3000	9843
6000	19685
9000	29520

Alternate Names / Alternative Namensformen / Nombres Alternativos
Variantes Toponymiques / Variantes Toponímicas

MOSKVA
MOSCOW

English or second official language names are shown in reduced size lettering
Englische Namen oder Namen in einer zweiten offiziellen Sprache erscheinen in kleineren Schriftgrössen

Basel
Bâle

Los nombres en inglés o un segundo idioma oficial se muestran en tipo de imprenta mas pequeño
Les toponymes en anglais ou dans la seconde langue officielle sont indiqués en caractères plus petits
Os topônimos em inglês ou num segundo idioma oficial aparecem em tipologia menor

VOLGOGRAD
(STALINGRAD)

Historical or other alternates in the local language are shown in parentheses
Historische oder alternative Namensformen einheimischen Sprache erscheinen in Klammern

Ventura
(San Buenaventura)

Los nombres históricos y alternativos locales se muestran en paréntesis
Les noms historiques de lieux ou les variantes toponymiques locales sont mis entre parenthèses
Os topônimos históricos ou as variantes toponímicas locais aparecem entre parênteses

x

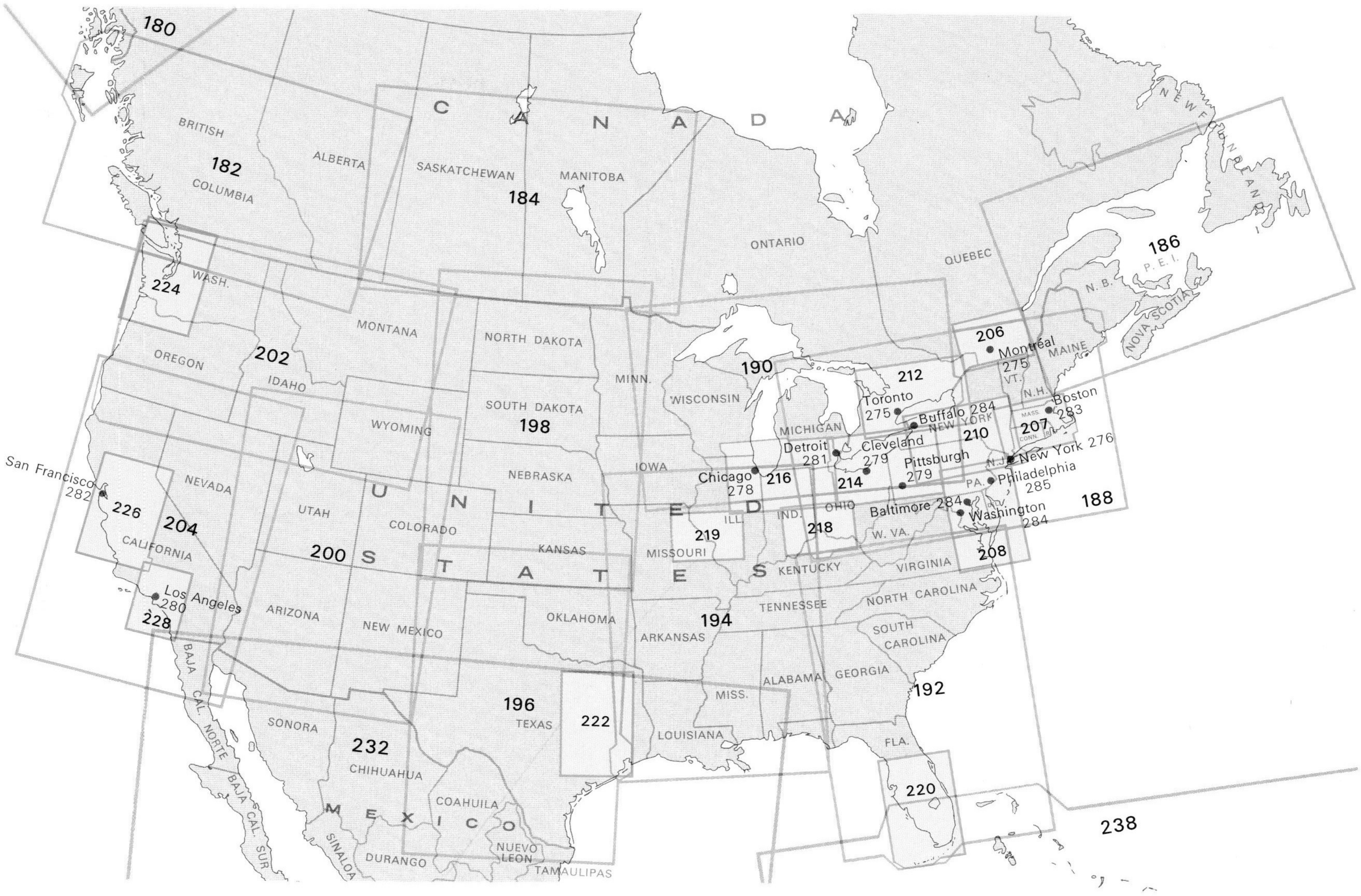
180
BRITISH
182
COLUMBIA
ALBERTA
SASKATCHEWAN
MANITOBA
184
C A N A D A
ONTARIO
QUEBEC
186
NEWFOUNDLAND
P.E.I.
N.B.
NOVA SCOTIA
WASH.
224
MONTANA
NORTH DAKOTA
OREGON
202
IDAHO
MINN.
WISCONSIN
190
212
206
Montréal
275
VT.
MAINE
N.H.
Boston
283
MASS.
CONN.
R.I.
207
Toronto
275
Buffalo 284
NEW YORK
210
SOUTH DAKOTA
198
WYOMING
MICHIGAN
Detroit
281
Cleveland
279
Pittsburgh
279
New York 276
N.J.
Philadelphia
285
188
NEBRASKA
IOWA
Chicago
278
216
214
PA.
San Francisco
282
NEVADA
226
204
UTAH
COLORADO
U N I T E D S T A T E S
ILL.
IND.
OHIO
Baltimore 284
Washington
284
DEL.
CALIFORNIA
200
KANSAS
MISSOURI
219
218
W. VA.
208
KENTUCKY
VIRGINIA
Los Angeles
280
228
ARIZONA
NEW MEXICO
OKLAHOMA
ARKANSAS
194
TENNESSEE
NORTH CAROLINA
SOUTH CAROLINA
BAJA
ALABAMA
GEORGIA
MISS.
192
196
TEXAS
222
SONORA
232
CHIHUAHUA
LOUISIANA
FLA.
CAL. NORTE
BAJA CAL. SUR
M E X I C O
COAHUILA
220
238
SINALOA
DURANGO
NUEVO LEÓN
TAMAULIPAS

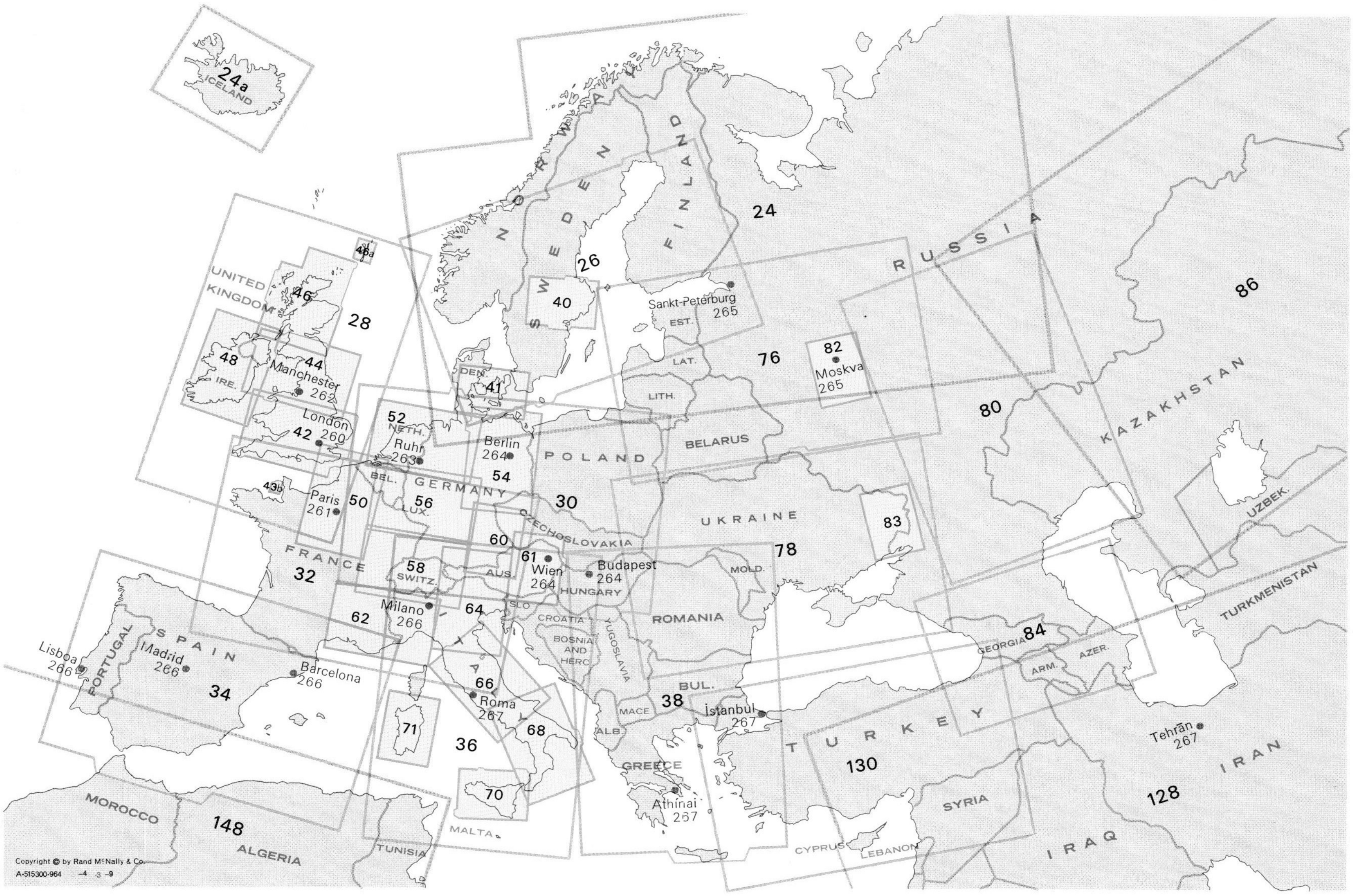
24a
ICELAND
NORWAY
SWEDEN
FINLAND
24
46a
UNITED KINGDOM
46
28
26
40
Sankt-Peterburg
265
EST.
R U S S I A
86
48
IRE.
44
Manchester
262
DEN.
41
LAT.
76
82
Moskva
265
LITH.
80
KAZAKHSTAN
London
260
42
52
NETH.
Ruhr
263
Berlin
264
54
POLAND
BELARUS
BEL.
GERMANY
43b
Paris
261
50
56
LUX.
30
CZECHOSLOVAKIA
UKRAINE
83
UZBEK.
FRANCE
32
58
SWITZ.
60
61
Wien
264
AUS.
Budapest
264
HUNGARY
MOLD.
78
TURKMENISTAN
62
Milano
266
SLO.
64
CROATIA
BOSNIA AND HERC.
YUGOSLAVIA
ROMANIA
GEORGIA
84
ARM.
AZER.
Lisboa
266
PORTUGAL
SPAIN
Madrid
266
34
Barcelona
266
66
Roma
267
ITALY
BUL.
38
İstanbul
267
MACE.
ALB.
68
71
36
TURKEY
130
Tehrān
267
IRAN
GREECE
Athínai
267
70
128
MALTA
SYRIA
CYPRUS
LEBANON
IRAQ
MOROCCO
148
ALGERIA
TUNISIA

World Index Maps / Welt Indexkarten / Indice de Mapas del Mundo
Index des Cartes du Monde / Índice de Mapas do Mundo

MAP COVERAGE / KARTENAUSSCHNITTE
CONTENIDO DEL ATLAS / TABLEAU D'ASSEMBLAGE
ABRANGÊNCIA DO MAPA

Map Scale

Manila
269 •   1:300,000

[ ]   1:1,000,000   [ ]   1:6,000,000

[ ]   1:3,000,000   [ ]   1:12,000,000

148   Page Reference / Seitenangabe
Página de Referencia / Page de Référence / Página de Referência

Enlarged maps of Anglo-America and Europe on page xiii.
Vergrösserte Karten von Anglo-Amerika und Europa auf Seite xiii.
Mapas aumentados de América Anglosajona y Europa, página xiii.
Cartes à grande échelle de l'Amérique anglo-saxonne et de l'Europe à la page xiii.
Mapas ampliados da América Anglo-saxônica e da Europa, página xiii.

World, Ocean, and Continent maps on pages 2-19.
Weltkarten, Karten der Ozeane und Erdteile auf Seiten 2-19.
Mapas del Mundo, Océanos y Continentes, páginas 2-19.
Cartes du Monde, des Océans et des Continents aux pages 2-19.
Mapas do Mundo, dos Oceanos e dos Continentes, páginas 2-19.

Additional Pacific Ocean Island maps on pages 174-175.
Zusätzliche Karten der Inseln des Pazifischen Ozeans auf Seite 174-175.
Mapas adicionales de las Islas del Océano Pacífico, páginas 174-175.
Cartes supplémentaires des Îles de l'Océan Pacifique aux pages 174-175.
Mapas suplementares das ilhas do Oceano Pacífico, páginas 174-175.

RUSSIA
24
76
80
86
KAZAKHSTAN
88
89
MONGOLIA
CHINA
92a
JAPAN
92
94
93b
98
104
105
KOREA
Beijing (Peking) 271
Seoul 271
Pacific Ocean
UKRAINE
78
BELARUS
Black Sea
84
85
TURKEY
130
TURKMENISTAN
UZBEKISTAN
KYRG.
TAJIKISTAN
Caspian Sea
Tehrān 267
IRAN
IRAQ
128
SYRIA
132
142
Al Qāhirah (Cairo) 273
EGYPT
SAUDI ARABIA
OMAN
YEMEN
Red Sea
AFGHANISTAN
PAKISTAN
123
120
NEPAL
Delhi 272
124
INDIA
Calcutta 272
126
BNGL.
Bombay 272
122
SRI LANKA
102
107
106
Shanghai 269
100
T'aipei 269
TAIWAN
Hong Kong 271
174m
175d
BURMA
LAOS
VIETNAM
THAILAND
Krung Thep (Bangkok) 269
CAMBODIA
Thanh-pho Ho Chi Minh (Saigon) 269
110
Manila 269
116
PHILIPPINES
175c
TRUK ISLANDS
175b
PALAU ISLANDS
140
SUDAN
144
ETHIOPIA
SOMALIA
KENYA
UGANDA
ZAIRE
TANZANIA
154
ZAMBIA
MALAWI
MOZAMBIQUE
ZIMBABWE
156
158
Johannesburg 273
LESOTHO
COMOROS
157a
MADAGASCAR
157b
157c
MAURITIUS
REUNION
Indian Ocean
MALAYSIA
BRUNEI
114
SUMATRA
Singapore 271
BORNEO
112
CELEBES
INDONESIA
Jakarta 269
115a
JAVA
LESSER SUNDA ISLANDS
115b
NEW GUINEA
PAPUA NEW GUINEA
164
SOLOMON ISLANDS
175e
VANUATU
175f
NEW CALEDONIA
175g
FIJI
AUSTRALIA
162
166
168a
168b
169
170
171a
171b
Sydney 274
Melbourne 274
TASMANIA
NEW ZEALAND
172

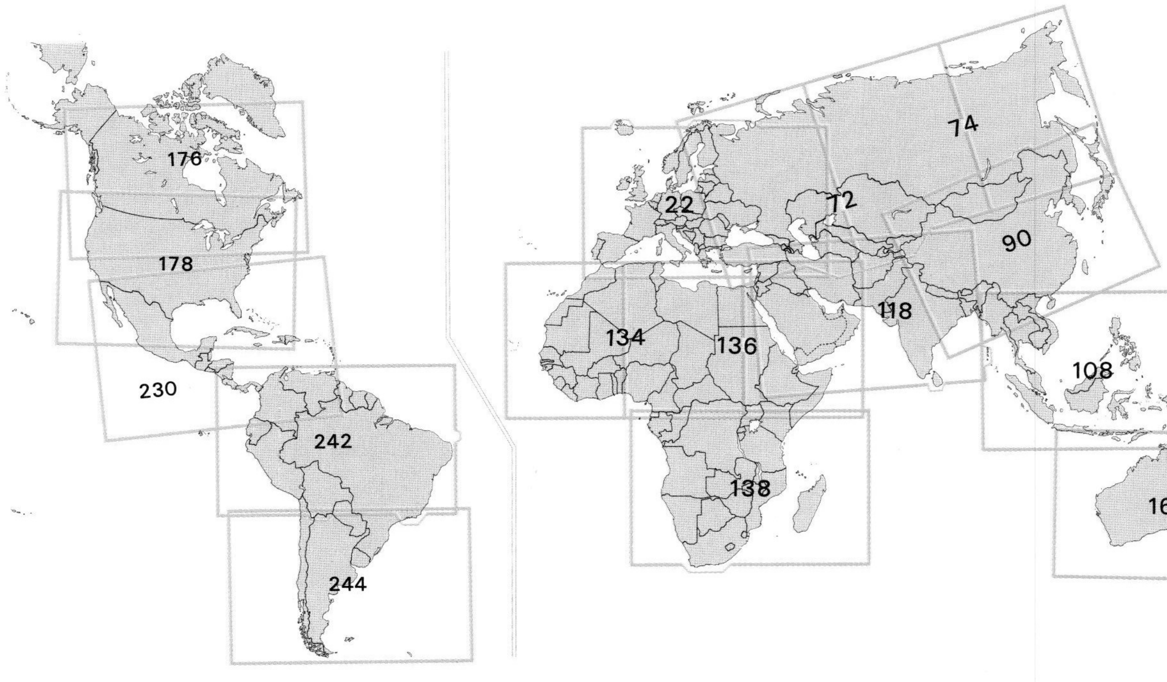
176
178
230
242
244
22
72
74
90
134
136
118
108
138
160

Using the Atlas

Maps and Atlases

Satellite images of the world (Figure 1) constantly give us views of the shape and size of the earth. It is hard, therefore, to imagine how difficult it once was to ascertain the look of our planet. Yet from early history we have evidence of humans trying to work out what the world actually looked like.

Twenty-five hundred years ago, on a tiny clay tablet the size of a hand, the Babylonians inscribed the earth as a flat disk (Figure 2) with Babylon at the center. The section of the Cantino map of 1502 (Figure 3) is an example of a portolan chart used by mariners to chart the newly discovered Americas. Handsome and useful maps have been produced by many cultures. The Mexican map drawn in 1583 marks hills with wavy lines and roads with footprints between parallel lines (Figure 4). The methods and materials used to create these maps were dependent upon the technology available, and their accuracy suffered considerably. A modern topographic map (Figure 5), as well as those in this atlas, shows the detail and accuracy that cartographers are now able to achieve. They benefit from our ever-increasing technology including satellite imagery and computer assisted cartography.

In 1589 Gerardus Mercator used the word atlas to describe a collection of maps. They have become a unique and indispensable reference for graphically defining the world and answering the question *where.* Only on a map can the countries, cities, roads, rivers, and lakes covering a vast area be simultaneously viewed in their relative locations. Routes between places can be traced, trips planned, boundaries of neighboring states and countries examined, distances between places measured, the meandering of rivers and streams and the sizes of lakes visualized—and remote places imagined.

Figure 1

Figure 2

Figure 3

Das antiguo de Nova Gallia

Figure 4

Figure 5

Sequence of the Maps

The maps in this atlas start with a section covering the world, oceans, and continents. Maps that follow the opening section are arranged in a continental sequence; Europe, Asia, Africa, Australia, North America, and South America. To allow for the inclusion of detail, each continent is broken down into a series of maps with the smallest scale first, followed by maps of larger scale. The maps are arranged so that as consecutive pages are turned, a continuous successive part of the continent is shown. A special section of metropolitan area maps and United States and Canada maps complete the coverage.

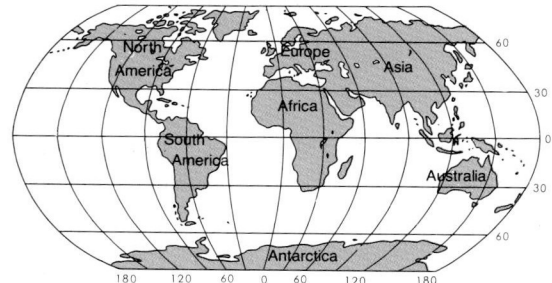

Figure 6

Getting the Information

An atlas can be used for many purposes, from planning a trip to finding hot spots in the news and supplementing world knowledge. To realize the potential of an atlas the user must be able to:

1. Find places on the maps
2. Measure distances
3. Determine directions
4. Understand map symbols

Finding Places

One of the most common and important tasks facilitated by an atlas is finding the location of a place in the world. A river's name in a book, a city mentioned in the news, or a vacation spot may prompt your need to know where the place is located. The illustrations and text below explain how to find Yangon (Rangoon), Burma.

1. Look up the place-name in the index at the back of the atlas. Yangon, Burma can be found on the map on page 110, and it can be located on the map by its latitude and longitude, expressed in degrees and minutes: 16.47 North Latitude; 96.10 East Longitude (Figure 7).

Yangmiao, Zhg.	**106**	30.51 N 120.49 E
Yangmingshan ✦ 8	**269d**	25.09 N 121.33 E
Yangming Shan ⋀	**102**	26.03 N 111.56 E
Yangmugou, Zhg.	**98**	40.36 N 124.28 E
Yangmugou, Zhg.	**104**	41.11 N 123.50 E
Yangmulin	**105**	40.06 N 115.12 E
Yangon (Rangoon)	**110**	16.47 N 96.10 E
Yangon �□ 8	**110**	16.50 N 96.10 E
Yangor	**174b**	0.31 S 166.54 E
Yangpingguan	**102**	32.51 N 106.09 E
Yangpu	**100**	27.14 N 119.08 E
Yangp'yŏng	**98**	37.30 N 127.29 E
Yangp'yŏng-ni	**98**	40.53 N 127.58 E
Yangqi	**106**	31.23 N 119.57 E
Yangquan	**102**	37.52 N 113.36 E
Yangriwan	**102**	31.37 N 110.49 E
Yangsan	**98**	35.21 N 129.03 E
Yangshan, Zhg.	**98**	41.13 N 120.24 E
Yangshan, Zhg.	**98**	35.13 N 116.13 E
Yangshan, Zhg.	**102**	24.28 N 112.38 E
Yangshigangzi	**104**	41.42 N 122.59 E
Yangshitun	**104**	42.06 N 123.44 E
Yangshu	**106**	31.39 N 120.08 E

Figure 7

2. Turn to the map of Southeastern Asia found on page 110. Note that the latitude appears in the right and left margins of the map, and the longitude in the upper and lower margins.

3. To find Yangon on the map place your left index finger in the left margin at 16 degrees, 47 minutes (between 15 and 20); and your right index finger in the top margin at 96 degrees, 10 minutes (between 95 and 100). Move your left finger across the map and your right finger down the map. Your fingers will meet in the area in which Yangon is located. (Figure 8).

(Maps of the states and provinces have the index located on each page. These use a letter and number system in the margins to locate places in the same fashion as latitude and longitude explained above.)

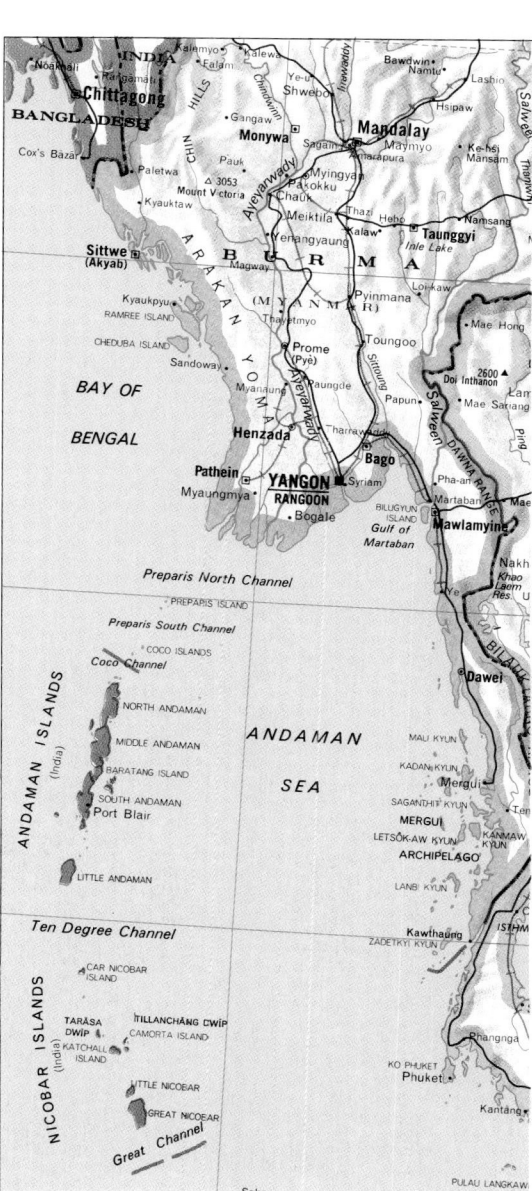

Figure 8

Measuring Distances

In planning trips, determining the distance between two places is essential, and an atlas can help in travel preparation. For instance, to determine the approximate distance between Paris and Rouen, France, follow these three steps:

1. Lay a slip of paper on the map on page 32 so that its edge touches the two cities. Adjust the paper so one corner touches Rouen. Mark the paper directly at the spot where Paris is located (Figure 9).

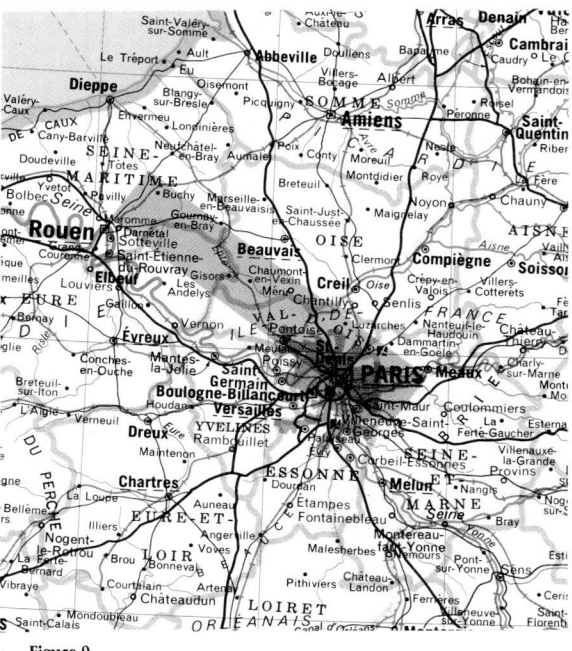

Figure 9

2. Place the paper along the scale of miles beneath the map. Position the corner at 0 and line up the edge of the paper along the scale. The pencil mark on the paper indicates Rouen is between 50 and 100 miles from Paris (Figure 10).

3. To find the exact distance, move the paper to the left so that the pencil mark is at 100 on the scale. The corner of the paper stands on the fourth 5-mile unit on the scale. This means that the two towns are 50 plus 20, or 70 miles apart (Figure 11).

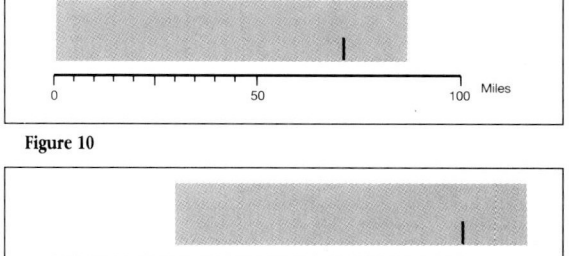

Figure 10

Figure 11

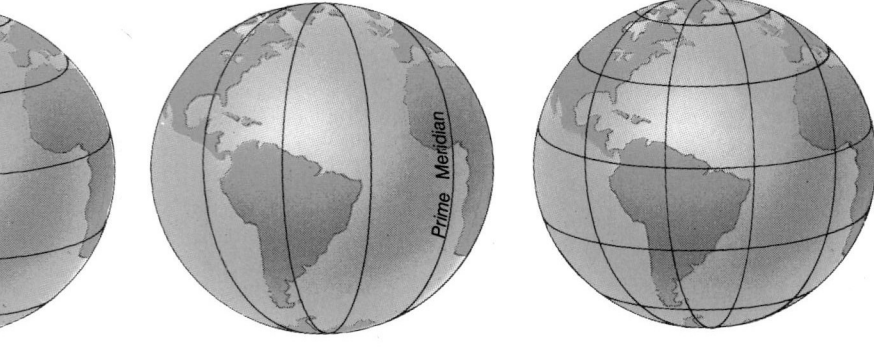

Figure 12

Determining Directions

Most of the maps in the atlas are drawn so that when oriented for normal reading, north is at the top of the map, south is at the bottom, west is at the left, and east is at the right. Most maps have a series of lines drawn across them–the lines of latitude and longitude. Lines of latitude, or parallels of latitude, are drawn east and west. Lines of longitude, or meridians of longitude, are drawn north and south (Figure 12).

Parallels and meridians appear as either curved or straight lines. For example, in the section of the map of Europe (Figure 13) the parallels of latitude appear as curved lines. The meridians of longitude are straight lines that come together toward the top of the map.

Latitude and longitude lines help locate places on maps. Parallels of latitude are numbered in degrees north and south of the Equator. Meridians of longitude are numbered in degrees east and west of a line called the Prime Meridian, running through Greenwich, England, near London. Any place on earth can be located by the latitude and longitude lines running through it.

To determine directions or locations on the map, you must use the parallels and meridians. For example, suppose you want to know which is farther north, Bergen, Norway, or Stockholm, Sweden. The map in Figure 13 shows that Stockholm is south of the 60° parallel of latitude and Bergen is north of it. Bergen is farther north than Stockholm. By looking at the meridians of longitude, you can determine which city is farther east, Bergen is approximately 5° east of the 0° meridian (Prime Meridian), and Stockholm is almost 20° east of it. Stockholm is farther east than Bergen.

Understanding Map Symbols

In a very real sense, the whole map is a symbol, representing the world or a part of it. It is a reduced representation of the earth; each of the world's features–cities, rivers, etc.–is represented on the map by a symbol. Map symbols may take the form of points, such as dots or squares (often used for cities, capital cities, or points of interest), or lines (roads, railroads, rivers). Symbols may also occupy an area, showing extent of coverage (terrain, forests, deserts). They seldom look like the feature they represent and therefore must be identified and interpreted. For instance, some of the maps in this atlas define political units by a colored line depicting their boundaries. Neither the colors nor the boundary lines are actually found on the surface of the earth, but because countries and states are such important political components of the world, strong symbols are used to represent them. The Map Symbols pages in this atlas identify the symbols used on the maps.

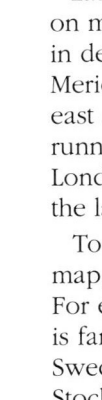

Figure 13

World, Ocean, and Continent Maps / Weltkarten, Karten der Ozeane und Erdteile
Mapas del Mundo, Océanos y Continentes / Cartes du Monde, des Océans et des Continents
Mapas do Mundo, dos Oceanos e dos Continentes

1

THIS SECTION OPENS with World Political and World Physical maps at the scale of 1:75,000,000. There follow maps of the Pacific, Indian, and Atlantic oceans at the scale 1:48,000,000, the largest scale at which the total expanse of these bodies of water could be portrayed. Finally, a series of continent relief maps at the scale of 1:24,000,000 show a global view of the earth as it would appear from about 4,000 miles in space. The Azimuthal Equal-Area projection is used for the 1:24,000,000 maps, the scale being approximately that of a globe 20 inches in diameter.

The colors of the continent maps portray the land areas as if viewed from space during the growing season, without regard to the fact that the growing seasons are not concurrent in all areas. Underwater features and varying water depths are represented by shaded relief and different color tones. The result is a strong physical portrait of the earth's major land and submarine forms. The legend below shows how these different kinds of terrain and vegetation have been represented. The names of physical features—plateaus, basins, mountain ranges, seas, rivers, lakes, gulfs, trenches, bays, islands—predominate on these maps.

DIESER KARTENTEIL BEGINNT mit politischen und physischen Weltkarten im Massstab 1:75 Millionen. Dann folgen Karten des Pazifischen, Indischen und Atlantischen Ozeans in 1:48 Millionen, dem grössten Massstab, in dem diese Wasserflächen in ihrer ganzen Ausdehnung abgebildet werden konnten. Schliesslich folgt eine Reihe von Reliefkarten der Erdteile in 1:24 Millionen. Sie geben eine Übersicht der Erde, wie sie aus einer Entfernung von ungefähr 6 400 Kilometer aus dem Weltraum gewonnen würde. Den Karten im Massstab 1:24 Millionen liegt ein flächentreuer azimutaler Entwurf zugrunde, dieser Massstab entspricht ungefähr dem eines Globus von 50 cm Durchmesser.

Die Farben der Erdteilkarten bilden jedes Landgebiet so ab, wie es in der Vegetationsperiode aus der Vogelperspektive erschiene, ohne zu berücksichtigen, dass die Vegetationsperioden nicht in allen Gebieten gleichzeitig eintreten. Die Gliederung des Meeresbodens und die unterschiedlichen Meerestiefen werden durch Schummerung und verschiedene Farbstufen dargestellt. Das Ergebnis ist eine anschauliche physische Darstellung der wichtigsten terrestrischen und untermeerischen Formen der Erde. Die untenstehende Zeichenerklärung zeigt, wie diese verschiedenen Geländeformen und Vegetationsgebiete veranschaulicht werden. Namen physischer Objekte—Hochebenen, Becken, Gebirgszüge, Meere, Flüsse, Seen, Buchten, Gräben, Inseln—herrschen in diesen Karten vor.

ESTA SECCIÓN DA PRINCIPIO con los Mapas Políticos y Físicos del Mundo, a una escala de 1:75 000 000. A continuación están los mapas de los océanos Pacífico, Indico y Atlántico a una escala de 1:48 000 000, que es la mayor escala utilizable para la representación de esas masas de agua en toda su extensión. Por último, una serie de mapas del relieve de los continentes, a una escala de 1:24 000 000, proporcionan una vista global de la tierra tal como se apreciaría desde el espacio a una distancia aproximada de 6 400 kilómetros. La proyección azimutal equiárea se usa, para los mapas de 1:24 000 000, a una escala según la cual la tierra se reduciría a un globo de unos 50 cm de diámetro.

Los colores utilizados en los mapas de los continentes representan las diversas regiones de la tierra tal como se verían desde el espacio durante la estación en que la vegetación se desarrolla, sin tomar en cuenta que este fenómeno no se produce simultáneamente en todas las áreas. Las estructuras características del fondo marino y las variaciones de profundidad de los océanos se representan mediante relieve sombreado y distintos matices de color. El resultado es una imagen elocuente de las formas terrestres y submarinas más notables del planeta. La leyenda abajo explica cómo se representan estos diferentes tipos de terreno y vegetación. En estos mapas predomina la nomenclatura de elementos físicos: mesetas, cuencas, sierras, mares, ríos, lagos, golfos, bahías, trincheras, islas.

CETTE PARTIE comprend d'abord des cartes du monde politique et du monde physique à l'échelle de 1:75 000 000. Viennent ensuite les cartes des océans Pacifique, Indien et Atlantique à l'échelle de 1:48 000 000, la plus grande échelle qui a permis la reproduction complète de ces étendues d'eau. Pour terminer, une série de cartes en relief des continents à l'échelle de 1:24 000 000 donne une vue globale de la terre, telle qu'elle apparaîtrait vue de l'espace à une distance d'environ 6 400 kilomètres.

La projection azimutale équivalente a été utilisée pour les cartes au 1:24 000 000ᵉ, dont l'échelle équivaut à celle d'un globe de 50 cm de diamètre environ.

Les couleurs des cartes font apparaître les continents tels qu'on les verrait de l'espace, pendant la saison de croissance végétale, mais sans tenir compte du fait que cette saison n'apparaît pas partout simultanément. Le relief sous-marin est représenté par un estompage et la profondeur des océans par une variation de la couleur. Il en résulte une reproduction vigoureuse des principaux paysages continentaux et des principales formes sous-marines. La légende ci-dessous indique de quelle façon ils sont cartographiés. Les noms d'éléments topographiques tels que plateaux, bassins, chaînes de montagnes, mers, cours d'eau, lacs, golfes, baies, crêtes, îles et fosses océaniques, prédominent dans ces cartes.

ESTA SEÇÃO PRINCIPIA com os mapas políticos e físicos do Mundo, em escala de 1:75 000 000. Seguem-se os mapas dos oceanos Pacífico, Índico e Atlântico na escala de 1:48 000 000, a maior escala que se pode utilizar para a representação dessas massas de água em toda a sua extensão. Finalmente, uma série de mapas de relevo dos continentes, na escala de 1:24 000 000, proporciona uma visão global da Terra tal como apareceria do espaço a uma distância aproximada de cerca de 6 400 km. A projeção azimutal equiárea foi usada para os mapas da escala de 1:24 000 000, segundo a qual a Terra se apresentaria como um globo de cerca de 50 cm de diâmetro.

As cores utilizadas nos mapas dos continentes representam as massas terrestres tal como apareceriam vistas do espaço durante a estação do crescimento vegetal, sem levar em conta que este fenômeno não se produz simultaneamente em todas as regiões. As características do fundo do mar e as variações de profundidade das águas são representadas por um relevo sombreado e por diferentes matizes de cor. O resultado proporciona uma imagem física eloquente das principais formas terrestres e submarinas da Terra. As legendas abaixo explicam como foram representados os diversos tipos de terreno e de vegetação. Nestes mapas predomina a nomenclatura dos elementos físicos: planaltos, bacias, cadeias de montanhas, mares, rios, lagos, golfos, baías, fossas, ilhas.

Land Features / Land Phänomene / Elementos de la Tierra
Paysages Continentaux / Acidentes Continentais

Submarine Features / Untermeerische Phänomene
Elementos Submarinos / Formes de Relief Sous-marin / Acidentes do Revelo Submarino

Ice and Snow
Eis und Schnee
Hielo y nieve
Glace et neige
Gelo e neve

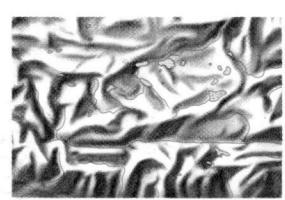

High Barren Area
Hochgebirgswüste
Alta zona árida
Région haute et aride
Alta zona árida

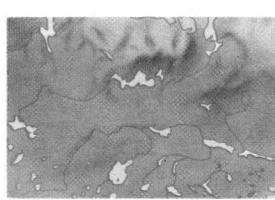

Tundra and Alpine
Tundra und Alpine Vegetation
Tundra y alpina
Toundra et végétation alpine
Tundra e vegetação alpina

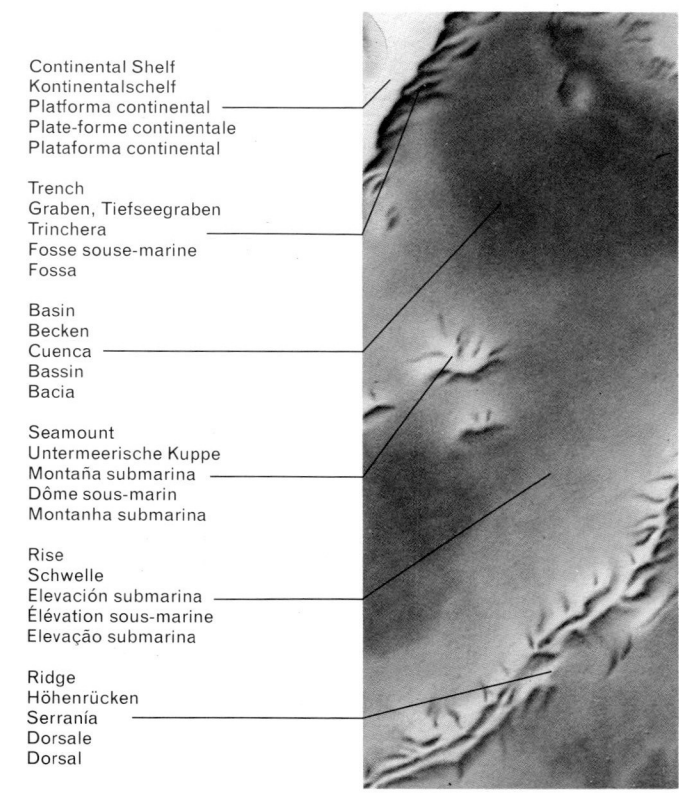

Continental Shelf
Kontinentalschelf
Platforma continental
Plate-forme continentale
Plataforma continental

Trench
Graben, Tiefseegraben
Trinchera
Fosse souse-marine
Fossa

Basin
Becken
Cuenca
Bassin
Bacia

Seamount
Untermeerische Kuppe
Montaña submarina
Dôme sous-marin
Montanha submarina

Rise
Schwelle
Elevación submarina
Élévation sous-marine
Elevação submarina

Ridge
Höhenrücken
Serranía
Dorsale
Dorsal

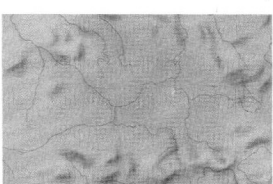

Needleleaf Trees
Nadelwälder
Conifferas
Forêt de conifères
Coníferas

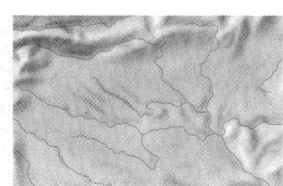

Broadleaf Trees
Laubwälder
Árboles de hojas anchas
Forêt à feuilles caduques
Árvores de folhas caducas

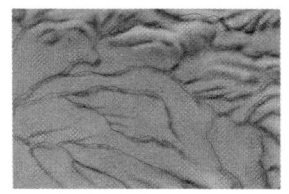

Tropical Rainforest
Tropischer Regenwald
Bosque tropical lluvioso
Forêt tropicale humide
Floresta tropical úmida

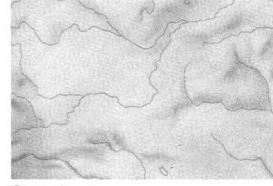

Grassland
Grasland
Pradera
Formations herbacées
Pradaria

Dry Scrub
Trockenes Buschland
Matorral
Brousse sèche
Caatinga

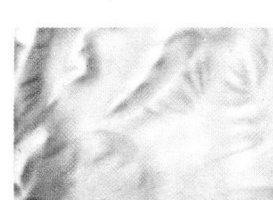

Desert
Wüste
Desierto
Désert
Deserto

World: Political / Erde: Politisch / Mundo: Político
Monde: Politique / Mundo: Político

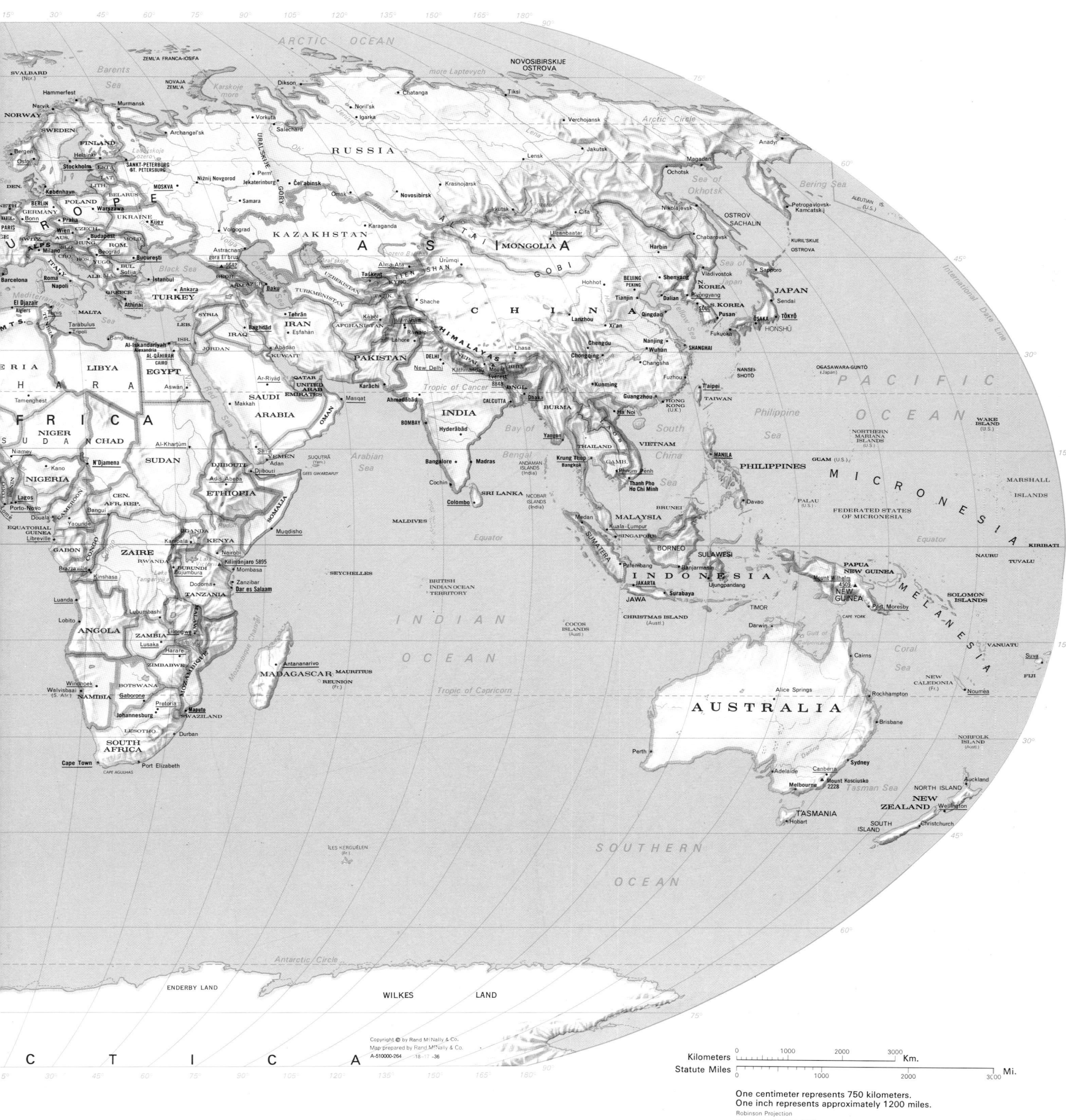

Kilometers 0   1000   2000   3000 Km.
Statute Miles 0   1000   2000   3000 Mi.

One centimeter represents 750 kilometers.
One inch represents approximately 1200 miles.
Robinson Projection
Scale 1:75,000,000

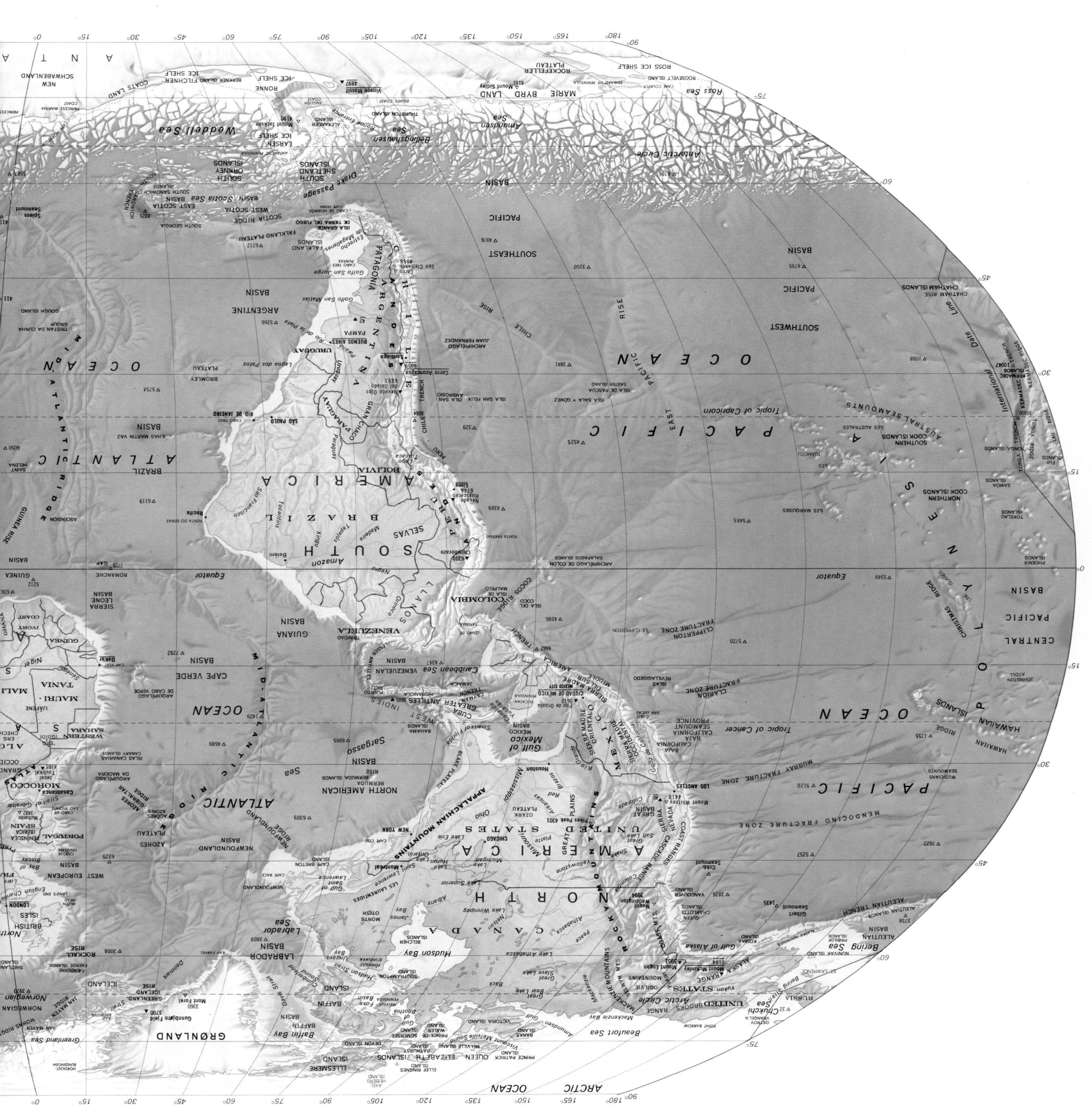

Kilometers 0 1000 2000 3000 Km.
Statute Miles 0 1000 2000 3000 Mi.

One centimeter represents 750 kilometers.
One inch represents approximately 1200 miles.
Robinson Projection
Scale 1:75,000,000

GREENLAND
ICELAND
IRELAND
UNITED KINGDOM
FRANCE
HUNGARY
ROMANIA
BULGARIA
TURKEY
ASIA MINOR
MEDITERRANEAN SEA
Black Sea
Caspian Sea
FINLAND
Barents Sea
NOVAJA ZEML'A
URAL'SKIJE GORY
URAL MOUNTAINS
KAZAKHSTAN
UKRAINE
POLAND
ZAPADNO-SIBIRSKAJA RAVNINA
SREDNESIBIRSKOJE PLOSKOGORJE
SIBERIA
R U S S I A
MONGOLIA
GOBI
C H I N A
TIEN SHAN
KUNLUN SHAN
QING ZANG GAOYUAN
HIMALAYAS
INDIA
PAKISTAN
IRAN
IRAQ
SAUDI ARABIA
ARABIAN PENINSULA
EGYPT
LIBYA
S A H A R A
Tropic of Cancer
SUDAN
ETHIOPIA
SOMALIA
KENYA
TANZANIA
ZAMBIA
ZIMBABWE
MOZAMBIQUE
BOTSWANA
SOUTH AFRICA
MADAGASCAR
A F R I C A
ARABIAN SEA
Bay of Bengal
BURMA
THAILAND
INDOCHINA
VIETNAM
MALAYSIA
SUNDA SHELF
GREATER SUNDA ISLANDS
I N D O N E S I A
PHILIPPINES
Philippine Sea
South China Sea
East China Sea
Yellow Sea
Sea of Japan
JAPAN
Sea of Okhotsk
PAPUA NEW GUINEA
A U S T R A L I A
GREAT SANDY DESERT
GREAT VICTORIA DESERT
Great Australian Bight
GREAT DIVIDING RANGE
I N D I A N O C E A N
Tropic of Capricorn
MID-INDIAN BASIN
NINETY EAST RIDGE
WHARTON BASIN
SOUTHWEST INDIAN RIDGE
MID-INDIAN RIDGE
CROZET BASIN
AGULHAS BASIN
SOUTHEAST INDIAN RIDGE
SOUTH INDIAN BASIN
ATLANTIC-INDIAN RIDGE
ATLANTIC-INDIAN BASIN
SOUTHERN OCEAN
Antarctic Circle
ENDERBY LAND
A N T A R C T I C A
WILKES LAND

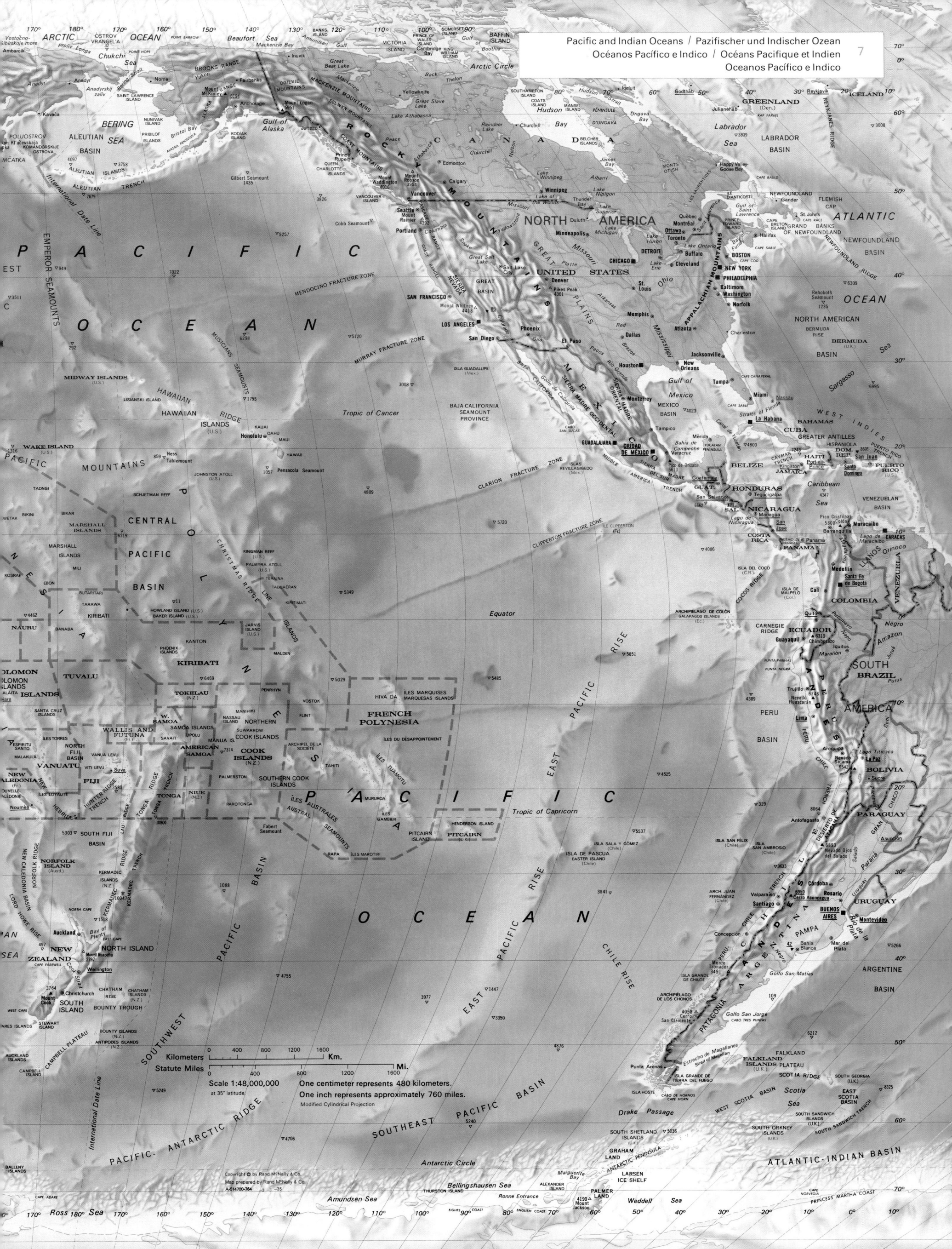

Pacific and Indian Oceans / Pazifischer und Indischer Ozean
Océanos Pacífico e Indico / Océans Pacifique et Indien
Oceanos Pacífico e Indico

7

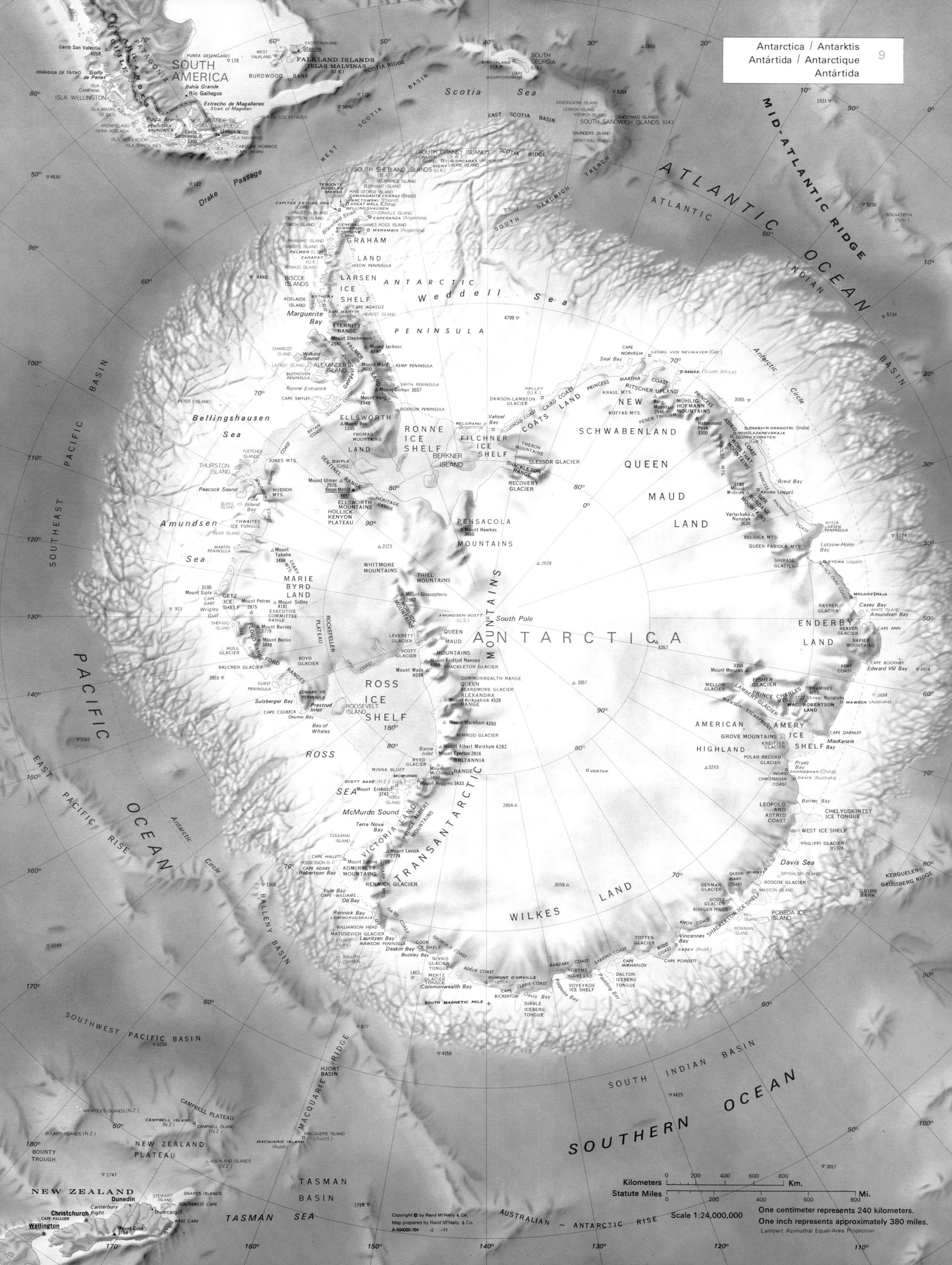

SOUTH AMERICA

ATLANTIC OCEAN

MID-ATLANTIC RIDGE

PACIFIC OCEAN

Scotia Sea

Weddell Sea

PENINSULA

GRAHAM LAND

LARSEN ICE SHELF

Bellingshausen Sea

ELLSWORTH LAND

RONNE ICE SHELF

FILCHNER ICE SHELF

COATS LAND

NEW SCHWABENLAND

QUEEN MAUD LAND

ENDERBY LAND

Amundsen Sea

MARIE BYRD LAND

ANTARCTICA

South Pole

TRANSANTARCTIC MOUNTAINS

ROSS ICE SHELF

WILKES LAND

AMERICAN HIGHLAND

AMERY ICE SHELF

MAC. ROBERTSON LAND

ROSS SEA

VICTORIA LAND

McMurdo Sound

Davis Sea

SOUTHERN OCEAN

SOUTH INDIAN BASIN

TASMAN SEA

NEW ZEALAND

Wellington

Christchurch

Dunedin

SOUTHWEST PACIFIC BASIN

Scale 1:24,000,000

Kilometers 0 200 400 600 800 Km.
Statute Miles 0 200 400 600 Mi.

One centimeter represents 240 kilometers.
One inch represents approximately 380 miles.
Lambert Azimuthal Equal-Area Projection

ATLANTIC OCEAN
MID-ATLANTIC RIDGE
WEST EUROPEAN BASIN
AZORES-GIBRALTAR RIDGE
CANARY BASIN
LABRADOR BASIN
Labrador Sea
IRMINGER BASIN
REYKJANES RIDGE
ICELAND BASIN
ROCKALL RISE
NORWEGIAN BASIN
Norwegian Sea
LOFOTEN BASIN
GREENLAND BASIN
Greenland Sea
Barents Sea
Kara Sea
Denmark Strait
Davis Strait
Arctic Circle
Tropic of Cancer
CANADA
GREENLAND (Den.)
ICELAND
FAEROE ISLANDS (Den.)
SPITSBERGEN
SVALBARD (Nor.)
NOVAJA ZEML'A
North Sea
Baltic Sea
Gulf of Bothnia
Gulf of Finland
Bay of Biscay
English Channel
Irish Sea
Mediterranean Sea
Tyrrhenian Sea
Adriatic Sea
Ionian Sea
Aegean Sea
Black Sea
Caspian Sea
Aral'skoje more
Red Sea
Persian Gulf
Gulf of Oman
IRELAND
UNITED KINGDOM
FRANCE
SPAIN
PORTUGAL
ANDORRA
GERMANY
NETH.
BEL.
LUX.
SWITZ.
ITALY
AUSTRIA
CZECHOSLOVAKIA
POLAND
DENMARK
NORWAY
SWEDEN
FINLAND
EST.
LAT.
LITH.
BELARUS
UKRAINE
MOLD.
HUNGARY
ROMANIA
SLO.
CROATIA
BOSNIA AND HERC.
YUGO.
ALBANIA
MACE.
GREECE
BULGARIA
TURKEY
ASIA MINOR
CYPRUS
NORTH CYPRUS
SYRIA
LEBANON
ISRAEL
JORDAN
IRAQ
IRAN
KUWAIT
BAHRAIN
QATAR
UNITED ARAB EMIRATES
OMAN
YEMEN
SAUDI ARABIA
ARABIAN PENINSULA
AR-RUB' AL-KHALI
GEORGIA
ARM.
AZER.
TURKMENISTAN
UZBEKISTAN
KAZAKHSTAN
RUSSIA
EUROPE
ASIA
URAL'SKIJE GORY
URAL MOUNTAINS
ZAPADNO-SIBIRSKAJA RAVNINA
BOL'ŠOJ KAVKAZ
CAUCASUS
MOROCCO
ALGERIA
TUNISIA
LIBYA
EGYPT
WESTERN SAHARA
MAURITANIA
MALI
NIGER
CHAD
CAPE VERDE
SAHARA
SUDAN
ATLAS MOUNTAINS
ALPS
CARPATHIAN MOUNTAINS
PYRENEES
APENNINO
MESOPOTAMIA
Reykjavík
Oslo
Stockholm
Helsinki
København
Tallinn
Riga
Vilnius
Minsk
MOSKVA
MOSCOW
SANKT-PETERBURG
ST. PETERSBURG
KIJEV
WARSZAWA
BERLIN
Praha
WIEN
VIENNA
BUDAPEST
BUCUREŞTI
Beograd
Sofija
Tiranë
Athínai
İSTANBUL
ANKARA
ROMA
MILANO
PARIS
LONDON
Dublin
Amsterdam
Bruxelles
Bonn
Bern
MADRID
Lisboa
BARCELONA
Gibraltar (U.K.)
Rabat
CASABLANCA
EL DJAZAÏR
ALGIERS
Tunis
Tarābulus
Tripoli
AL-QĀHIRAH
CAIRO
AL-ISKANDARĪYAH
ALEXANDRIA
Bayrūt
DIMASHQ
'Ammān
Yerushalayim
Jerusalem
BAGHDĀD
TEHRĀN
BAKU
Tbilisi
Jerevan
Al-Kuwayt
Ar-Riyāḍ
Makkah
Al-Madīnah
Jiddah
Ṣan'ā'
Al-Khartūm
Umm Durmān
Dakar
Nouakchott
Las Palmas
Santa Cruz

Europe and Africa / Europa und Afrika
Europa y África / Europe et Afrique
Europa e África

11

ARABIAN SEA

INDIAN OCEAN

ATLANTIC OCEAN

SOMALI BASIN

MASCARENE BASIN

MADAGASCAR BASIN

SOUTHWEST INDIAN RIDGE

NATAL BASIN

MOZAMBIQUE PLATEAU

AGULHAS PLATEAU

CAPE BASIN

ANGOLA BASIN

GUINEA BASIN

BRAZIL BASIN

MID-ATLANTIC RIDGE

WALVIS RIDGE

CAPE RISE

GUINEA RISE

ROMANCHE GAP

SIERRA LEONE RISE

SUDAN

ETHIOPIA

SOMALIA

DJIBOUTI

OGADEN

GREAT RIFT VALLEY

KENYA

UGANDA

RWANDA

BURUNDI

TANZANIA

ZAIRE

CONGO BASIN

CONGO

GABON

EQUAT. GUI.

CAMEROON

CENTRAL AFRICAN REPUBLIC

NIGERIA

BENIN

TOGO

GHANA

IVORY COAST

LIBERIA

SIERRA LEONE

GUINEA

GUINEA BISSAU

GAMBIA

BURKINA FASO

MALAWI

MOZAMBIQUE

ZAMBIA

ZIMBABWE

ANGOLA

NAMIBIA

BOTSWANA

SOUTH AFRICA

LESOTHO

SWAZILAND

TRANSKEI

KALAHARI DESERT

NAMIB DESERT

COMOROS

MAYOTTE (Fr.)

SEYCHELLES

MADAGASCAR

MAURITIUS

REUNION (Fr.)

MASCARENE ISLANDS

A F R I C A

SAINT HELENA (U.K.)

Adis Abeba
Nairobi
Mombasa
Dar es Salaam
Zanzibar
KAMPALA
Kigali
Bujumbura
KINSHASA
Brazzaville
Luanda
Lusaka
Harare
Bulawayo
Lilongwe
Blantyre
Beira
Maputo
Pretoria
JOHANNESBURG
Bloemfontein
Durban
Cape Town
Windhoek
Gaborone
Antananarivo
Toamasina
Libreville
Douala
Yaoundé
Bangui
N'Djamena
Lagos
Ibadan
Abidjan
Accra
Lomé
Porto-Novo
Monrovia
Freetown
Conakry
Bissau
Banjul
Bamako
Ouagadougou
Niamey

Equator

Tropic of Capricorn

Scale 1:24,000,000

One centimeter represents 240 kilometers.
One inch represents approximately 380 miles.

Lambert Azimuthal Equal-Area Projection

Kilometers
Statute Miles

Mi.

Km.

Copyright © by Rand McNally & Co.
Map prepared by Rand McNally & Co.
A-519394-264   33

ATLANTIC OCEAN
ARCTIC OCEAN
North Pole
GREENLAND (Den.)
ICELAND
Reykjavík
Greenland Sea
Norwegian Sea
Barents Sea
Kara Sea
Karskoje more
Laptev Sea
Vostočno-Sibirskoje more
East Siberian Sea
Chukchi Sea
Bering Strait
Bering Sea
UNITED STATES
ALEUTIAN ISLANDS
FAEROE ISLANDS (Den.)
SVALBARD
ZEML'A FRANCA-IOSIFA
FRANZ JOSEF LAND
SEVERNAJA ZEML'A
NOVOSIBIRSKIJE OSTROVA
OSTROV VRANGEL'A
IRELAND
Dublin
UNITED KINGDOM
LONDON
North Sea
NORWAY
Oslo
SWEDEN
Stockholm
FINLAND
Helsinki
Baltic Sea
DENMARK
København
NETHERLANDS
Amsterdam
BELGIUM
Bruxelles
GERMANY
BERLIN
POLAND
Warszawa
CZECHOSLOVAKIA
Praha
HUNGARY
BUDAPEST
ROMANIA
Bucureşti
BULGARIA
Sofija
UKRAINE
KIJEV
BELARUS
Minsk
E U R O P E
MOSKVA
SANKT-PETERBURG
R U S S I A
URAL'SKIJE GORY
URAL MOUNTAINS
ZAPADNO-SIBIRSKAJA RAVNINA
SIBERIA
SREDNESIBIRSKOJE PLOSKOGORJE
CHREBET ČERSKOGO
Sea of Okhotsk
Ochotskoje more
OSTROV SACHALIN
SAKHALIN
KURIL'SKIJE OSTROVA
KURIL ISLANDS
Black Sea
Caspian Sea
TURKEY
ASIA MINOR
ANKARA
ISTANBUL
SYRIA
IRAQ
BAGHDAD
IRAN
TEHRĀN
SAUDI ARABIA
KAZAKHSTAN
UZBEKISTAN
TURKMENISTAN
KYRGYZSTAN
TAJIKISTAN
AFGHANISTAN
Kābol
PAMIR
HINDU KUSH
TIEN SHAN
TARIM PENDI
KUNLUN SHAN
A S I A
MONGOLIA
Ulaanbaatar
GOBI
ALTAI
C H I N A
BEIJING
SHANGHAI
XI'AN
WUHAN
DA HINGGAN LING
NORTH KOREA
SOUTH KOREA
SŎUL
P'yŏngyang
J A P A N
HOKKAIDO
HONSHŪ
KYŪSHŪ
Sea of Japan
Yellow Sea
EAST CHINA SEA
Ozero Bajkal
Lake Baikal

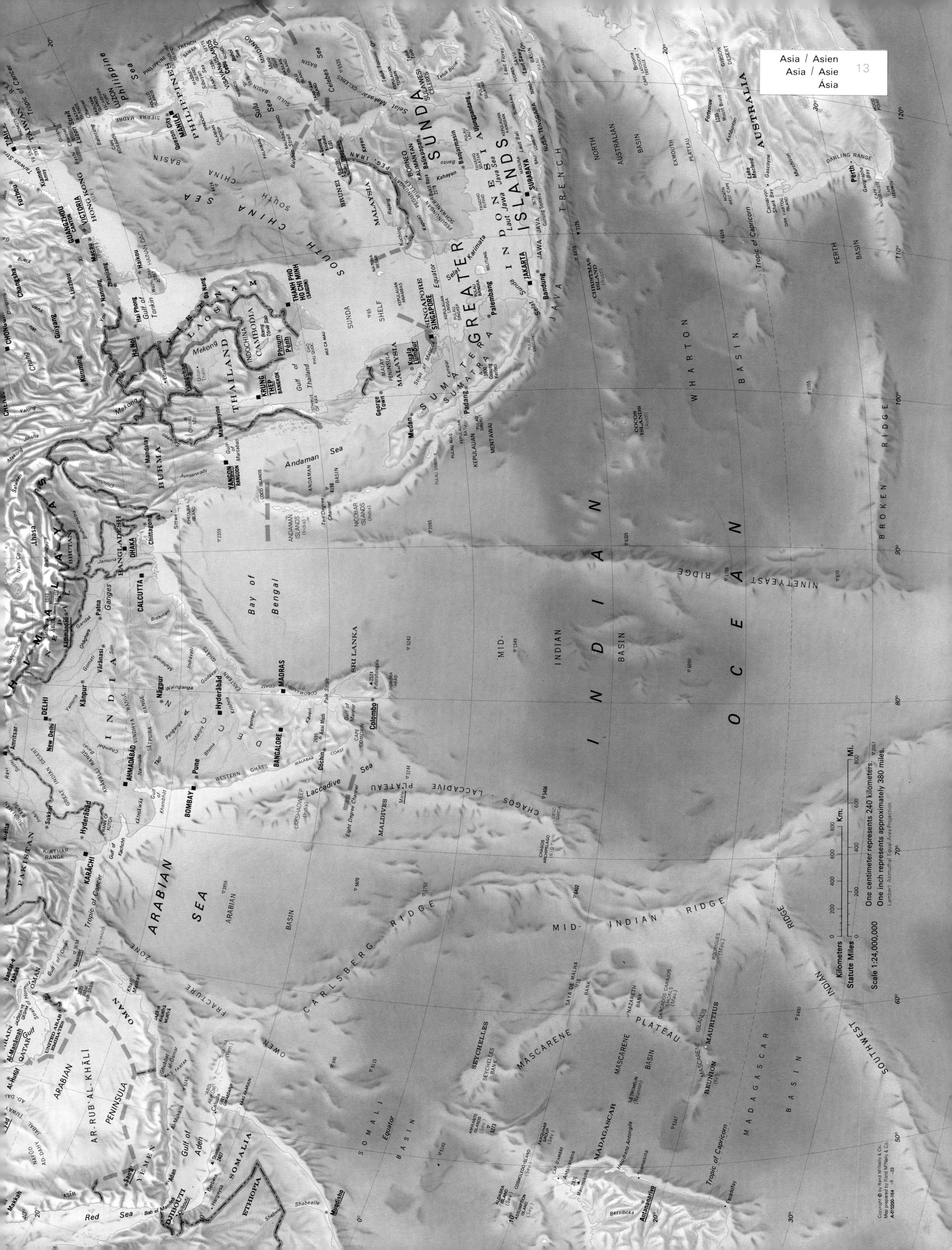
INDIAN OCEAN
ARABIAN SEA
Bay of Bengal
Andaman Sea
SOUTH CHINA SEA
Laccadive Sea
Gulf of Aden
Red Sea
Gulf of Oman
Gulf of Thailand
Gulf of Tonkin
Java Sea
Celebes Sea
Sulu Sea
Philippine Sea
INDIA
PAKISTAN
BANGLADESH
BURMA
THAILAND
LAOS
VIET NAM
CAMBODIA
MALAYSIA
INDONESIA
PHILIPPINES
AUSTRALIA
SRI LANKA
NEPAL
BHUTAN
OMAN
YEMEN
SOMALIA
ETHIOPIA
DJIBOUTI
MADAGASCAR
MAURITIUS
SEYCHELLES
MALDIVES
ARABIAN PENINSULA
AR-RUB' AL-KHĀLĪ
HIMALAYAS
GREATER SUNDA ISLANDS
SUNDA SHELF
JAVA TRENCH
WHARTON BASIN
NINETYEAST RIDGE
BROKEN RIDGE
CARLSBERG RIDGE
MID-INDIAN RIDGE
MID-INDIAN BASIN
MASCARENE PLATEAU
MASCARENE BASIN
MADAGASCAR BASIN
SOMALI BASIN
ARABIAN BASIN
CHAGOS LACCADIVE PLATEAU
SOUTHWEST INDIAN RIDGE
OWEN FRACTURE ZONE
NORTH AUSTRALIAN BASIN
PERTH BASIN
Tropic of Cancer
Equator
Tropic of Capricorn
Kilometers 0 200 400 600 800
Statute Miles 0 200 400 600 800
Scale 1:24,000,000
One centimeter represents 240 kilometers.
One inch represents approximately 380 miles.
Lambert Azimuthal Equal-Area Projection
Copyright © by Rand McNally & Co.
Map prepared by Rand McNally & Co.

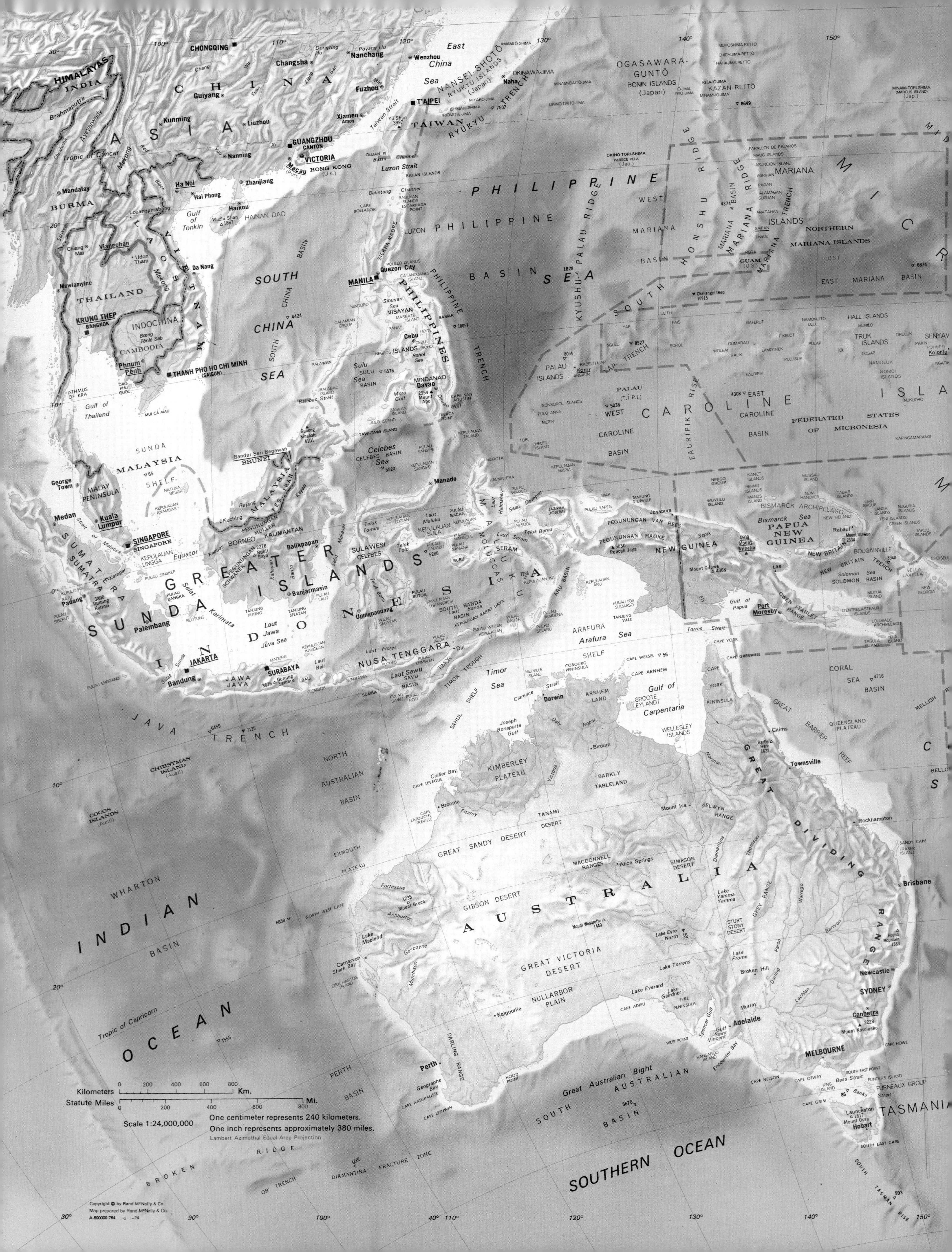

ASIA
CHINA
INDIA
HIMALAYAS
BURMA
THAILAND
INDOCHINA
CAMBODIA
LAOS
VIETNAM
MALAYSIA
PHILIPPINES
INDONESIA
GREATER SUNDA ISLANDS
NUSA TENGGARA
MALUKU
NEW GUINEA
PAPUA NEW GUINEA
AUSTRALIA
TASMANIA
CHONGQING
Nanchang
Changsha
Wenzhou
Fuzhou
Guiyang
Kunming
Liuzhou
Nanning
Xiamen
GUANGZHOU
CANTON
VICTORIA
HONG KONG (U.K.)
Macau (Port.)
T'AIPEI
TAIWAN
Mandalay
Ha Noi
Hai Phong
Zhanjiang
Haikou
HAINAN DAO
Viangchan
Da Nang
Mawlamyine
KRUNG THEP
BANGKOK
Phnum Pénh
THANH PHO HO CHI MINH (SAIGON)
MANILA
Quezon City
Cebu
Davao
Manado
Bandar Seri Begawan
BRUNEI
George Town
Medan
Kuala Lumpur
SINGAPORE
Balikpapan
Banjarmasin
Ujungpandang
Padang
Palembang
JAKARTA
Bandung
SURABAYA
Dili
Jayapura
Port Moresby
Rabaul
Darwin
Townsville
Rockhampton
Brisbane
Newcastle
SYDNEY
Canberra
MELBOURNE
Adelaide
Perth
Kalgoorlie
Hobart
East China Sea
SOUTH CHINA SEA
PHILIPPINE SEA
Sulu Sea
Celebes Sea
Java Sea
Arafura Sea
Timor Sea
Gulf of Carpentaria
CORAL SEA
Bismarck Sea
Solomon Sea
Gulf of Tonkin
Gulf of Thailand
Luzon Strait
Torres Strait
Bass Strait
Great Australian Bight
INDIAN OCEAN
SOUTHERN OCEAN
CAROLINE ISLANDS
FEDERATED STATES OF MICRONESIA
NORTHERN MARIANA ISLANDS
GUAM (U.S.)
PALAU (T.T.P.I.)
BISMARCK ARCHIPELAGO
OGASAWARA-GUNTŌ
BONIN ISLANDS (Japan)
NANSEI-SHOTŌ
RYUKYU ISLANDS (Japan)
CHRISTMAS ISLAND (Austl.)
COCOS ISLANDS (Austl.)
GREAT DIVIDING RANGE
GREAT BARRIER REEF
GREAT SANDY DESERT
GIBSON DESERT
GREAT VICTORIA DESERT
NULLARBOR PLAIN
SIMPSON DESERT
KIMBERLEY PLATEAU
BARKLY TABLELAND
MACDONNELL RANGES
JAVA TRENCH
PHILIPPINE TRENCH
MARIANA TRENCH
Challenger Deep 10915
Tropic of Cancer
Tropic of Capricorn
Equator
Kilometers 0 200 400 600 800 Km.
Statute Miles 0 200 400 600 800 Mi.
Scale 1:24,000,000
One centimeter represents 240 kilometers.
One inch represents approximately 380 miles.
Lambert Azimuthal Equal-Area Projection
Copyright © by Rand McNally & Co.
Map prepared by Rand McNally & Co.
A-590000-764 -2 -24

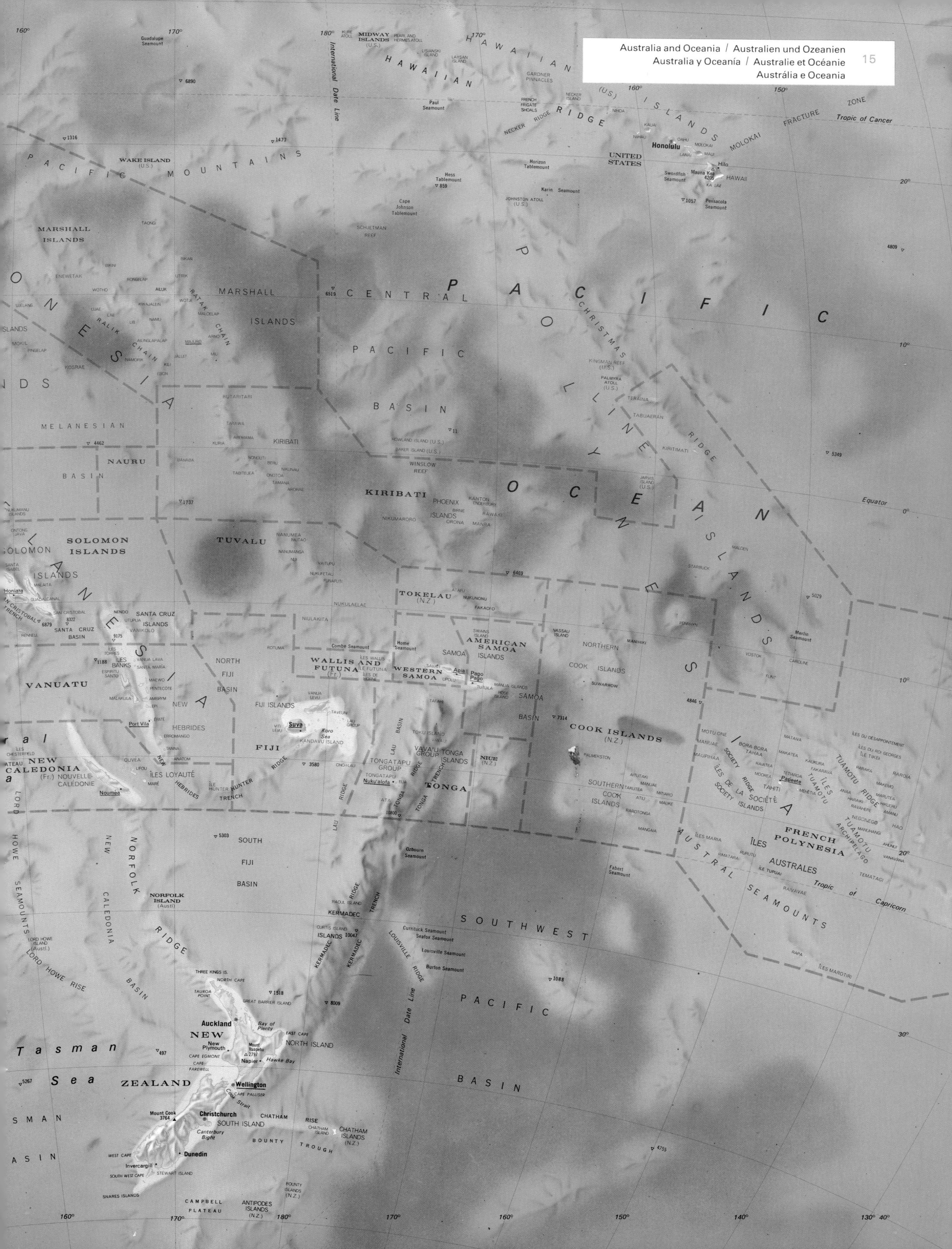

Australia and Oceania / Australien und Ozeanien
Australia y Oceanía / Australie et Océanie
Austrália e Oceania

15

ARCTIC OCEAN

North Pole

UNITED STATES

ALASKA

CANADA

GREENLAND

ICELAND

RUSSIA

SIBERIA

ASIA

EUROPE

ATLANTIC OCEAN

BERING SEA

Sea of Okhotsk

Beaufort Sea

Chukchi Sea

East Siberian Sea / Vostočno-Sibirskoje more

Laptev Sea / more Laptevych

Kara Sea / Karskoje more

Barents Sea

Greenland Sea

Norwegian Sea

North Sea

Baltic Sea

Hudson Bay

Baffin Bay

Labrador Sea

Davis Strait

Denmark Strait

Gulf of Alaska

ALEUTIAN ISLANDS

ALEUTIAN BASIN

ALEUTIAN TRENCH

BOWERS RIDGE

BROOKS RANGE

MACKENZIE MOUNTAINS

ROCKY MOUNTAINS

COAST MOUNTAINS

QUEEN ELIZABETH ISLANDS

VICTORIA ISLAND

BANKS ISLAND

MELVILLE ISLAND

ELLESMERE ISLAND

BAFFIN ISLAND

SOUTHAMPTON ISLAND

FOXE BASIN

LANCASTER SOUND

PARRY CHANNEL

GULF OF BOOTHIA

SVALBARD

SPITSBERGEN

NOVAJA ZEMLJA

ZEMLJA FRANCA-JOSIFA / FRANZ JOSEF LAND

SEVERNAJA ZEMLJA

NOVOSIBIRSKIJE OSTROVA

OSTROV VRANGELA

VERCHOJANSKIJ CHREBET

SREDINNYJ CHREBET

POLUOSTROV KAMČATKA

CHREBET ČERSKOGO

ANADYRSKOJE PLOSKOGORJE

URAL'SKIJE GORY / URAL

SIGHOTE-ALIN

GREENLAND BASIN

NORWEGIAN BASIN

LOFOTEN BASIN

LABRADOR BASIN

IRMINGER BASIN

NEWFOUNDLAND BASIN

ICELAND BASIN

REYKJANES RIDGE

MOHNS RIDGE

JAN MAYEN RIDGE

WEST JAN MAYEN RIDGE

KNIPOVIČ RIDGE

LOMONOSOV RIDGE

BARENTS TROUGH

SPITSBERGEN BANK

NORWEGIAN TRENCH

TIMANSKIJ KRJAŽ

SEVERO-SIBIRSKAJA NIZMENNOST'

Magadan

Petropavlovsk-Kamčatskij

Ochotsk

Jakutsk

Komsomol'sk-na-Amure

Chabarovsk

Norilsk

Murmansk

Archangel'sk

SANKT-PETERBURG

MOSKVA (MOSCOW)

Helsinki

Stockholm

Oslo

København

Edinburgh

Glasgow

Reykjavik

Tórshavn

Trondheim

Bergen

Minsk

Kiev

Riga

Tallinn

Vilnius

Kaliningrad

Nižnij Novgorod

Kirov

Vologda

Kazan'

Voronež

Kursk

Tula

Smolensk

Rostov-na-Donu

Doneck

Char'kov

FINLAND

NORWAY

SWEDEN

DENMARK

UNITED KINGDOM

FAEROE ISLANDS

Edmonton

Dawson Creek

Fort Nelson

Flin Flon

Churchill

St. John's

Bethel

Nome

Fairbanks

Anchorage

Barrow

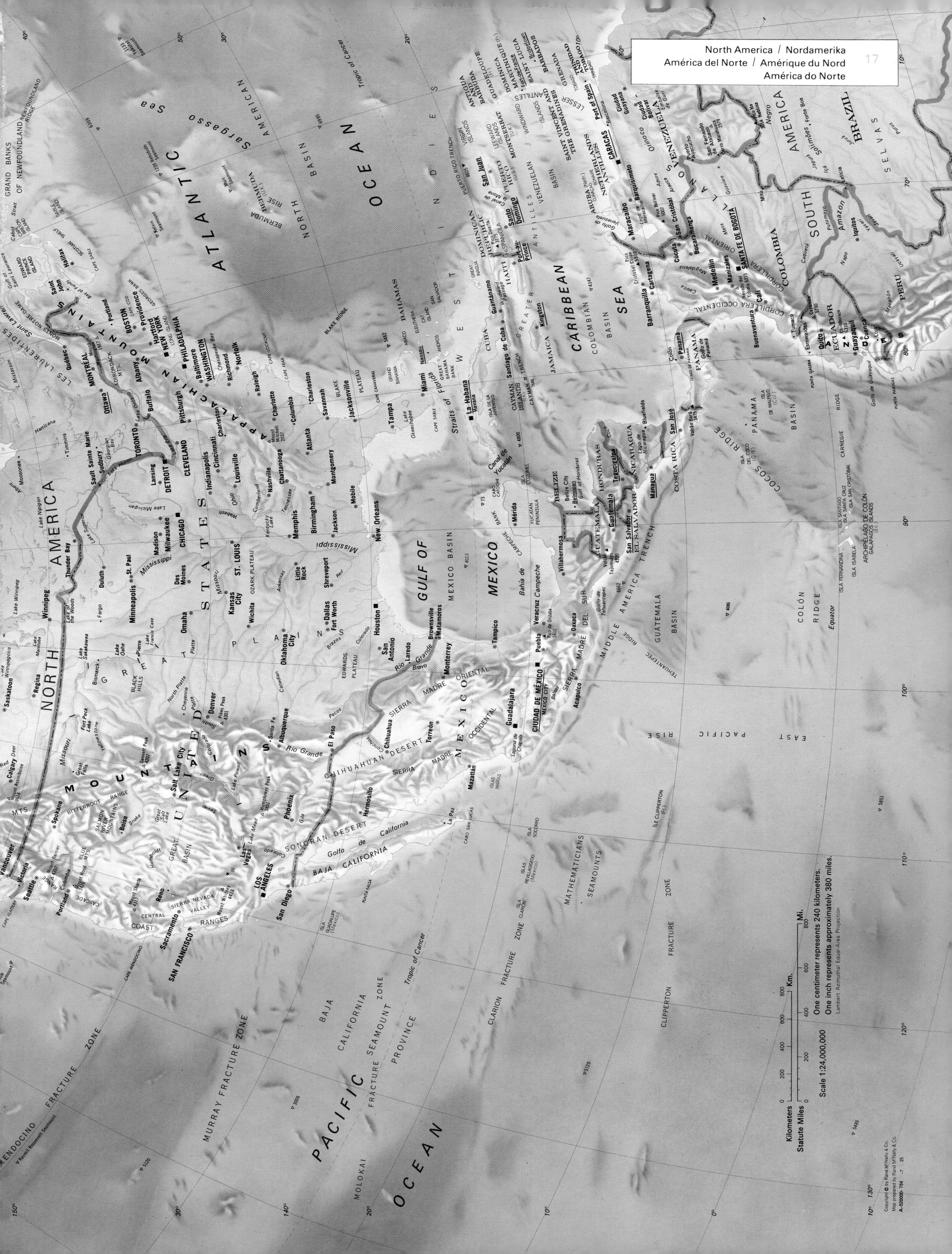

ATLANTIC OCEAN

PACIFIC OCEAN

NORTH AMERICA

UNITED STATES

GULF OF MEXICO

MEXICO

CARIBBEAN SEA

SOUTH AMERICA

BRAZIL

VENEZUELA

COLOMBIA

One centimeter represents 240 kilometers.
One inch represents approximately 380 miles.
Scale 1:24,000,000
Lambert Azimuthal Equal-Area Projection

Copyright © by Rand McNally & Co.
Map prepared by Rand McNally & Co.
A-520000-764 -7 25

NORTH AMERICA
UNITED STATES
ROCKY MTS.
GREAT PLAINS
OZARK PLATEAU
APPALACHIAN MOUNTAINS
EDWARDS PLATEAU
Omaha
Des Moines
CHICAGO
CLEVELAND
NEW YORK
LONG ISLAND
GEORGES BANK
PHILADELPHIA
Baltimore
WASHINGTON
Chesapeake Bay
Pittsburgh
Indianapolis
Cincinnati
Charleston
Louisville
Richmond
Norfolk
Raleigh
Cheyenne
Denver
Pikes Peak 4301
Kansas City
ST. LOUIS
Wichita
Oklahoma City
Santa Fe
Albuquerque
Little Rock
Nashville
Chattanooga
Memphis
Birmingham
Atlanta
Montgomery
Savannah
Charlotte
Columbia
Mt. Mitchell 2037
CAPE HATTERAS
CAPE LOOKOUT
CAPE FEAR
Fort Worth
Dallas
Shreveport
Jackson
El Paso
Mobile
Jacksonville
Houston
New Orleans
San Antonio
Laredo
Brownsville
Tampa
Lake Okeechobee
Miami
CAPE CANAVERAL
CAPE SABLE
BLAKE PLATEAU
BLAKE RIDGE
MEXICO
SIERRA MADRE ORIENTAL
SIERRA MADRE DEL SUR
Monterrey
Matamoros
Torreón
Tampico
Guadalajara
Laguna de Chapala
CIUDAD DE MÉXICO
MEXICO CITY
Puebla
Veracruz
Pico de Orizaba 5610
Oaxaca
Acapulco
Villahermosa
Mérida
YUCATAN PENINSULA
Bahía de Campeche
CAMPECHE BANK
GULF OF MEXICO
MEXICO BASIN
Straits of Florida
Canal de Yucatán
La Habana
Havana
CUBA
BAHAMAS
Nassau
GRAND BAHAMA
GREAT BAHAMA BANK
ANDROS
ELEUTHERA
CAT ISLAND
SAN SALVADOR
GREAT INAGUA
ISLA DE LA JUVENTUD
CAYMAN ISLANDS (U.K.)
CAYMAN TRENCH
Santiago de Cuba
Guantánamo
Windward Passage
JAMAICA
Kingston
HAITI
Port-au-Prince
HISPANIOLA
DOMINICAN REPUBLIC
Pico Duarte 3175
Santo Domingo
Canal de la Mona
PUERTO RICO
San Juan
PUERTO RICO TRENCH
VIRGIN ISLANDS
WEST INDIES
GREATER ANTILLES
LESSER ANTILLES
LEEWARD ISLANDS
WINDWARD ISLANDS
ANTIGUA AND BARBUDA
MONTSERRAT (U.K.)
GUADELOUPE (Fr.)
DOMINICA
MARTINIQUE (Fr.)
Fort-de-France
SAINT LUCIA
BARBADOS
Bridgetown
SAINT VINCENT AND THE GRENADINES
GRENADA
TRINIDAD AND TOBAGO
Port of Spain
CARIBBEAN SEA
COLOMBIAN BASIN
VENEZUELAN BASIN
ARUBA (Neth.)
CURAÇAO
BONAIRE
NETHERLANDS ANTILLES
BELIZE
Belize City
Belmopan
Gulf of Honduras
GUATEMALA
Guatemala
HONDURAS
Tegucigalpa
EL SALVADOR
San Salvador
NICARAGUA
Managua
Lago de Nicaragua
Bluefields
COSTA RICA
San José
Volcán Barú 3475
PANAMA
Panamá
Colón
ISTMO DE PANAMÁ
Golfo de Panamá
Golfo de Tehuantepec
MIDDLE AMERICA TRENCH
TEHUANTEPEC RIDGE
GUATEMALA BASIN
COCOS RIDGE
PANAMA BASIN
ISLA DEL COCO (C.R.)
ISLA DE MALPELO (Col.)
COLÓN RIDGE
CARNEGIE RIDGE
ARCHIPIÉLAGO DE COLÓN
GALAPAGOS ISLANDS (Ec.)
ISLA FERNANDINA
ISLA ISABELA
ISLA SANTA CRUZ
ISLA SAN CRISTÓBAL
Equator
COLOMBIA
Barranquilla
Cartagena
Maracaibo
Lago de Maracaibo
Golfo de Venezuela
Medellín
Manizales
Cali
Buenaventura
Tumaco
Bucaramanga
Cúcuta
SANTA FE DE BOGOTÁ
CORDILLERA OCCIDENTAL
CORDILLERA ORIENTAL
Nevado del Tolima 5215
LLANOS
VENEZUELA
CARACAS
Barquisimeto
Barcelona
Ciudad Bolívar
Ciudad Guayana
Pico Bolívar 5007
San Cristóbal
Orinoco
Puerto Ayacucho
San Fernando de Atabapo
Cerro Marahuaca 2579
SALTO ÁNGEL ANGEL FALLS
Mount Roraima 2875
PAKARAIMA MTS.
GUYANA
Georgetown
SURINAME
Paramaribo
FRENCH GUIANA
Cayenne
TUMUC-HUMAC MTS.
ECUADOR
Quito
Cayambe 5790
Chimborazo 6310
Guayaquil
Golfo de Guayaquil
Cuenca
Loja
Esmeraldas
PERU
Iquitos
Chiclayo
Trujillo
Cajamarca
Pucallpa
Nevado Huascarán 6746
Huaraz
Nevado Yerupaja 6634
Cerro de Pasco
LIMA
Huancayo
Cuzco
Puerto Maldonado
Lago Titicaca
Puno
La Paz
PERU-CHILE TRENCH
SOUTH AMERICA
BRAZIL
SELVAS
Manaus
Amazon
Belém
Macapá
ILHA DE MARAJÓ
São Luís
Fortaleza
Teresina
Natal
João Pessoa
Recife
Maceió
Aracaju
Salvador
Campina Grande
Caruaru
Brasília
Mato Grosso
Porto Velho
Rio Branco
Leticia
Santarém
Óbidos
Negro
Madeira
Purus
Tocantins
PLANALTO DO MATO
NORTH AMERICAN BASIN
BERMUDA (U.K.)
BERMUDA RISE
Sargasso Sea
ATLANTIC OCEAN
Tropic of Cancer
MID-ATLANTIC RIDGE
GUIANA BASIN
CAPE VERDE BASIN
AZORES PLATEAU
AÇORES AZORES (Port.)
FLORES
TERCEIRA
PICO
SÃO MIGUEL
SANTA MARIA
Great Meteor Tablemount 269
Kelvin Seamount
Rehoboth Seamount 1235
Yakutat Seamount 1133
Muir Seamount
ATOL DAS ROCAS
ILHA FERNANDO DE NORONHA (Braz.)
CABO DE SÃO ROQUE
BASIN

ATLANTIC OCEAN

BROMLEY PLATEAU

ARGENTINE BASIN

PACIFIC OCEAN

NAZCA BASIN

CHILE BASIN

CHILE RISE

GOMEZ RIDGE

EAST PACIFIC RISE

SOUTHEAST PACIFIC BASIN

SOUTH GEORGIA AND THE SOUTH SANDWICH ISLANDS

SOUTH GEORGIA (U.K.)

SOUTH SANDWICH ISLANDS

SANDWICH TRENCH

EAST SCOTIA BASIN

Scotia Sea

FALKLAND PLATEAU

Falkland Ridge

WEST SCOTIA BASIN

SOUTH ORKNEY ISLANDS

SOUTH SHETLAND ISLANDS (U.K.)

Weddell Sea

ANTARCTICA

ATLANTIC INDIAN BASIN

Antarctic Circle

Tropic of Capricorn

BRAZIL

PARAGUAY

URUGUAY

ARGENTINA

CHILE

PAMPA

PATAGONIA

ANDES

ATACAMA DESIERTO DE

CHILE TRENCH

PERU TRENCH

FALKLAND ISLANDS (U.K.)

WEST FALKLAND

EAST FALKLAND

Stanley

BURDWOOD BANK

ISLA DE LOS ESTADOS

ISLA GRANDE DE TIERRA DEL FUEGO

Drake Passage

Bellingshausen Sea

ANTARCTIC PENINSULA

GRAHAM LAND

PALMER LAND

LARSEN ICE SHELF

ALEXANDER ISLAND

THURSTON ISLAND

Ronne Entrance

ELLSWORTH LAND

São Paulo
Rio de Janeiro
Santos
Belo Horizonte
Vitória
Campos
Curitiba
Florianópolis
Porto Alegre
Santa Maria
Pelotas
Rio Grande
Montevideo
Buenos Aires
La Plata
Mar del Plata
Bahía Blanca
Rosario
Santa Fe
Córdoba
San Miguel de Tucumán
Salta
Santiago del Estero
San Juan
Mendoza
Santiago
Valparaíso
Concepción
Valdivia
Puerto Montt
Asunción
Concepción
Corrientes
Paraná
Antofagasta
Arica
Sucre
Potosí
Rawson
Viedma
Neuquén
Comodoro Rivadavia
Río Gallegos
Punta Arenas
Ushuaia

GRAN CHACO

Scale 1:24,000,000
One centimeter represents 240 kilometers.
One inch represents approximately 380 miles.
Lambert Azimuthal Equal-Area Projection

Kilometers
Statute Miles
Km.
Mi.

Copyright © by Rand McNally & Co.
Map prepared by Rand McNally & Co.
A-64000-764

THE REGIONAL MAPS consist of three basic series, each distinctive in style, but using common symbols to ensure ease of understanding (see Legend to Maps, pages x-xii). Every major land region, continent or subcontinent, is introduced by one or more maps at the scale of 1:12,000,000. There follow maps at 1:6,000,000 and 1:3,000,000 which cover the region in sections, in greater detail. Except for scale, the 1:6,000,000 and 1:3,000,000 maps are alike. Finally, selected areas of special importance in the region are shown at 1:1,000,000. Each scale is identified by a color bar, and a locater map with the same color may be found in the margin of the map page. A sample area at each of the scales, including centimeter-kilometer and inch-mile equivalents, appears on page 21.

The three basic series differ in content and emphasis. The 1:12,000,000 maps, which are primarily political, present an overview of each region. They show national boundaries and, in some cases, subordinate administrative subdivisions as well. These introductory maps make it possible to compare location, areal extent, and shape among the nations of the world. The distribution of cities, towns and metropolitan areas is shown in the context of broad physical configurations. A selection of the most important railways and highways also appears.

The 1:6,000,000 and 1:3,000,000 maps together constitute about half of the map pages and provide the basic reference coverage of the Atlas. They show sections of regions in great detail—in some cases individual countries (Japan and New Zealand), in others, parts of countries (central Mexico), in still others, larger regions (the Middle East). The more densely settled areas appear at the larger 1:3,000,000 scale, the remaining areas at 1:6,000,000. Maps at these two scales present political and cultural information against the background of a detailed physical portrait of the terrain, which is depicted by both shaded relief and a spectrum of altitude tints. Bathymetric tints are used to show offshore water depths. The transportation pattern shown includes major railways, two classes of roads, and airports that offer either international or jet service. The names and boundaries of political subdivisions are given for selected countries.

In the 1:1,000,000 series, strategic areas that are of special interest because of economic importance, dense settlement, or both, appear in even greater detail. This series is designed to show the pattern of cities, towns, roads, railways, bridges, airports, dams, reservoirs, and other interrelated features reflecting man's dense occupancy in these areas. The most important parks, places of historical interest, and recreational facilities are indicated. Three classes of highways and two classes of railways are shown, and major roads are named. All features are portrayed against a topographic background of shaded relief.

Inhabited places on the regional maps are classified in two distinct ways. Cities and towns of different *population size* are distinguished by the *size and shape of the symbol* that locates the place. The symbol reflects the population within the municipal or corporate limits, exclusive of any suburbs. In countries where the limits of a municipality include rural areas, the symbol represents only the urban or agglomerated population. The *relative political and economic importance* of a place which may be independent of the number of its inhabitants, is indicated by the *size of type* in which its name appears.

DIE REGIONALKARTEN bestehen aus drei Serien, die im Stil verschieden sind, der besseren Lesbarkeit halber aber gemeinsame Kartensignaturen verwenden (siehe "Zeichenerklärung" S. x-xii). Jede Grossregion, jeder Kontinent oder Subkontinent werden durch eine oder mehrere Karten im Massstab 1:12 Millionen eingeleitet. Es folgen sodann Karten in den Massstäben 1:6 und 1:3 Millionen, welche die Region in Teilen und grösseren Einzelheiten darstellen. Die Karten in 1:6 Millionen und 1:3 Millionen unterscheiden sich nur im Massstab. Schliesslich werden ausgewählte Gebiete von besonderer Bedeutung innerhalb der Region in 1:1 Million dargestellt. Jede Massstabsangabe ist durch ein Farbfeld gekennzeichnet, und ein Lagekärtchen in derselben Farbe erscheint am Rand der Kartenseite. Kartenausschnitte als Beispiele für jeden dieser Massstäbe mit Angabe des Verhältnisses Zentimeter zu Kilometer und Zoll ·zu Meilen sind auf Seite 21 aufgeführt.

Die drei Kartenreihen unterscheiden sich in Inhalt und Betonung. Die Karten im Massstab 1:12 Millionen, die vor allem politische Karten sind, geben einen Überblick über jede Region. Sie zeigen die Staatsgrenzen und in manchen Fällen auch die Grenzen von nachgeordneten Verwaltungseinheiten. Diese einführenden Karten ermöglichen einen Vergleich der Lage, Ausdehnung und Gestalt der Staaten der Erde. Die Verteilung der städtischen Ballungsgebiete, Grossstädte und Städte wird in ihrem Zusammenhang mit dem grossräumigen Formenschatz des Reliefs dargestellt. Gezeigt wird auch eine Auswahl der wichtigsten Eisenbahnlinien und Fernverkehrsstrassen.

Die Karten 1:6 Millionen und 1:3 Millionen machen zusammen mehr als die Hälfte der Kartenseiten aus und bilden den grundlegenden Teil des Atlas. Sie zeigen sehr inhaltsreiche Ausschnitte von Regionen—in einigen Fällen einzeln Länder (Japan und Neuseeland), in anderen Landesteile (Zentralmexiko) und wieder anderen Grossräume (Mittlerer Osten).

Die dichter besiedelten Gebiete sind im Massstab 1:3 Millionen dargestellt, die übrigen Gebiete im Massstab 1:6 Millionen. Die Karten in diesen beiden Massstäben liefern politische und kulturgeographische Informationen vor dem Hintergrund einer detaillierten Geländedarstellung, gekennzeichnet durch Reliefschummerung und eine Skala von Höhenschichten. Tiefenstufen werden verwendet, um die Meerestiefen jenseits der Küsten zu gliedern. Das abgebildete Verkehrsnetz umfasst wichtige Eisenbahnlinien, zwei Klassen von Strassen und Flughäfen, die entweder im internationalen Verkehr oder von Düsenflugzeugen angeflogen werden. Die Verwaltungsgliederung wird für eine grosse Zahl von Staaten gezeigt.

In der Kartenserie 1:1 Million sind mit noch zahlreicheren Einzelheiten zentrale Räume dargestellt, denen infolge ihrer wirtschaftlichen Bedeutung, dichten Besiedlung oder durch beide Faktoren bedingt besonderes Interesse zukommt. Diese Kartenserie wurde entwickelt, um die Verteilung der Grossstädte, Städte, Strassen, Eisenbahnen, Brücken, Flughäfen, Dämme, Stauseen und anderer Objekte zu zeigen, die Ausdruck sind für die dichte Besiedlung. Verzeichnet sind auch die wichtigsten Parks, Örtlichkeiten von historischem Interesse und Erholungsstätten. Drei Strassenklassen und zwei Klassen von Eisenbahnlinien werden unterschieden. Die Darstellung ist mit einer Reliefschummerung unterlegt.

Die Siedlungen auf den Regionalkarten sind auf zwei bestimmte Arten klassifiziert. Grossstädte und Städte unterschiedlicher *Einwohnerzahl* sind durch *Grösse und Form der Signatur* unterschieden, die den Ort lokalisiert. Die Signatur entspricht der Zahl der Einwohner innerhalb der Stadtgrenzen, schliesst also nicht eingemeindete Vororte aus. In Staaten, in denen ländliche Gebiete in die Stadtgemeinden einbezogen sind, entsprechen die Signaturen nur der in den zentralen Siedlungen ansässigen Bevölkerung. Die *relative politische und wirtschaftliche Bedeutung* eines Ortes, die von der Zahl seiner Einwohner unabhängig sein kann, ist ausgedrückt durch die *Schriftgrösse*, in welcher der Ortsname erscheint.

LOS MAPAS REGIONALES integran tres series básicas, cada una con su estilo propio; pero los símbolos usados son en todas los mismos para facilitar su comprensión (véanse las Leyendas para Mapas, páginas x-xii). Cada una de las grandes regiones, continentes o subcontinentes, se presenta a través de uno o varios mapas a la escala de 1:12 000 000. A continuación hay mapas a escalas de 1:6 000 000 y 1:3 000 000 que presentan la región correspondiente en secciones, con mayores detalles. Con excepción de su escala, los mapas de 1:6 000 000 y 1:3 000 000 tienen las mismas características. Por ultimo, aparecen a la escala de 1:1 000 000 áreas de cada región seleccionadas por su importancia. Cada escala se identifica por una barra de color, y un mapa-guía con el mismo color se presenta en el margen de la página de cada mapa. La página 21 ofrece como ejemplo un área-muestra a cada una de las escalas, incluyendo equivalentes en centímetros-kilómetros y pulgadas-millas.

Las tres series básicas son diferentes en contenido y en énfasis. Los mapas a escala de 1:12 000 000, fundamentalmente políticos, ofrecen una vista general de cada región. Indican las fronteras nacionales y, en algunos casos, las subdivisiones administrativas secundarias. Son mapas introductivos que permiten comparar la ubicación, extensión territorial y forma de las distintas naciones. La distribución de ciudades, poblados y áreas metropolitanas se aprecia en un contexto físico esbozado a grandes rasgos. Los detalles incluyen una selección de las vías férreas y las carreteras más importantes.

Las series de mapas a 1:6 000 000 y a 1:3 000 000 ocupan entre ambas cerca de la mitad de los mapas del atlas y en ellas se concentra el material de consulta básico de la obra. Los mapas muestran secciones de regiones en gran detalle: en algunos casos países enteros, como Japón y Nueva Zelandia: en otros, partes de países, como el centro de México; y en otros, regiones mas extensas, como el Medio Oriente. Las áreas con mayor densidad de establecimientos humanos se presentan a una escala mayor, la de 1:3 000 000, y las demás a la escala de 1:6 000 000. En estas dos escalas los mapas contienen información política y cultural, sobre un fondo que ilustra en detalle la configuración física del terreno, utilizando sombreado para el relieve y toda una gama de tintes para indicar las altitudes. Un colorido batimétrico señala las variaciones de profundidad en el suelo marino. El esquema de las vías de comunicación incluye las principales vías férreas, dos clases de caminos, y los aeropuertos que ofrecen servicio nacional o internacional de jets. Las subdivisiones políticas secundarias se dan para una selección de varios países.

En la serie de mapas de 1:1 000 000, las áreas estratégicas de especial interés por su importancia económica, su densidad de población, o ambos factores combinados, aparecen aún con mayor detalle. Esta serie se diseñó para mostrar la distribución de ciudades, poblados, caminos, vías férreas, puentes, aeropuertos, presas, embalses y otros elementos similares, que reflejan la densidad de la ocupación humana. También se consignan los parques más importantes, los sitios de interés histórico, los campos de recreo, tres clases de carreteras, y dos de ferrocarriles, se da los nombres de los caminos más importantes. Todos estos elementos aparecen sobre un fondo topográfico de relieve sombreado.

En los mapas regionales se hacen dos clasificaciones distintas de los lugares habitados. Las ciudades y las poblaciones *de diferente densidad de habitantes* se distinguen por la *forma y tamaño del símbolo* que las localiza en el mapa. Este símbolo refleja el tamaño de la población dentro de sus límites municipales, sin tomar en cuenta los suburbios. En los países donde los límites de una municipalidad incluyen áreas rurales, el símbolo se limita a representar el conglomerado urbano de habitantes. La *importancia económica y política de un lugar*, la cual puede ser independiente del número de sus habitantes, se indica mediante el *tamaño del tipo de imprenta* en que aparece su nombre.

LES CARTES RÉGIONALES sont de trois types principaux, chacun d'un style différent mais avec des symboles communs pour faciliter la compréhension (voir la légende des cartes pages x-xii). Chaque grande région, continent ou subcontinent, est représentée par une ou plusieurs cartes à l'échelle de 1:12 000 000ᵉ. Viennent ensuite des cartes au 1:6 000 000ᵉ et au 1:3 000 000ᵉ qui couvrent la région par sections plus détaillées; hormis la différence d'échelle, ces cartes sont semblables. Enfin, des secteurs particulièrement importants sont représentés au 1:1 000 000ᵉ. À chaque échelle correspond une bande colorée et une carte repère de même couleur, dans la marge de chaque page. Un échantillon de cartes aux diverses échelles est représenté à droite. Chaque carte est accompagnée d'une double échelle graphique donnant les rapports centimètre/kilomètre et inch/mille correspondants.

Les trois catégories de cartes diffèrent par le contenu et par ce qu'elles mettent en relief. Les cartes au 1:12 000 000ᵉ, qui sont essentiellement politiques, donnent un aperçu général de chaque région. Elles indiquent les frontières nationales et, dans certains cas, les subdivisions administratives intérieures. Ces cartes d'introduction permettent de comparer la localisation, la superficie et la forme des pays du monde. La répartition des villes et des zones métropolitaines y apparaît dans le cadre des grandes régions naturelles. Les routes et les voies ferrées les plus importantes y figurent également.

Les cartes au 1:6 000 000ᵉ et au 1:3 000 000ᵉ forment la moitié de l'Atlas et en constituent la série cartographique essentielle. Elles représentent de façon plus détaillée une partie de pays (centre du Mexique), ou encore des régions plus vestes (Moyen-Orient) ou, parfois, des pays entiers (Japon, Nouvelle-Zélande). Les régions les plus peuplées sont représentées à plus grande échelle (1;3 000 000ᵉ) que les autres (1:6 000 000ᵉ). Ces cartes offrent des informations d'ordre politique et culturel sur un fond topographique précis où le relief est indiqué à la fois par un estompage et par des variations de couleur. Différentes teintes de bleu sont utilisées pour symboliser les profondeurs marines. Les réseaux de transport représentés comprennent les principales voies ferrées, deux catégories de routes et des aéroports internationaux ou desservis par des avions à réaction. Les subdivisions politiques d'un certain nombre de pays sont aussi tracées.

Dans la série de cartes au 1:1 000 000ᵉ, des régions très importantes, soit du fait de leur densité de population, soit du fait de leur rôle économique, sont représentées d'une manière encore plus détaillée. L'objectif de cette série de cartes est de montrer la répartition des villes, routes, voies ferrées, ponts, aéroports, barrages, lacs de barrages et autres données associées qui traduisent la densité de l'occupation humaine dans ces régions. Les parcs les plus importants, les sites historiques essentiels et les centres de loisirs sont indiqués. Toutes les informations se détachent sur un fond topographique où le relief apparaît en estompage.

Les centres urbains des cartes régionales sont classés de deux manières différentes. *L'importance de la population* des villes est indiquée par *la dimension et la forme du symbole* qui les situe sur la carte. Seule la population comprise dans les limites municipales est prise en considération; dans les pays où des espaces ruraux sont inclus dans les limites d'une municipalité, seule la population urbaine entre en ligne de compte. *L'importance politique et économique relative* d'une ville, qui n'est pas nécessairement liée au nombre d'habitants, est indiquée par la dimension des caractères qui composent son nom.

OS MAPAS REGIONAIS compreendem três séries básicas, cada uma em estilo diferente, mas que empregam os mesmos símbolos para facilitar sua compreensão (Ver as *Legendas dos mapas*, pág. x-xii). Os mapas de cada uma das principais regiões terrestres, continentes ou subcontinentes, são introduzidos por um ou mais mapas na escala 1:12 000 000. Em seguida, vêm mapas, nas escalas de 1:6 000 000 e 1:3 000 000, que apresentam, com maiores detalhes, seções da região considerada. Exceto quanto à escala, os mapas de 1:6 000 000 e 1:3 000 000 têm as mesmas características. Finalmente, aparecem, na escala de 1:1 000 000, os mapas das áreas mais importantes da região considerada. A cada escala corresponde uma barra colorida e um indicador da mesma cor, que se encontra à margem da página de cada mapa. À página 21, acha-se um exemplo de cada escala, bem como a equivalência das relações centímetro/quilômetro e polegada/milha.

As três séries básicas de mapas são diferentes quanto ao conteúdo e à apresentação. Os mapas em escala de 1:12 000 000, que são essencialmente políticos, oferecem uma visão geral de cada região. Indicam as fronteiras nacionais e, em alguns casos, as subdivisões administrativas internas. Esses mapas servem de introdução e permitem avaliar e comparar a posição, superfície e forma dos países do Mundo. Neles está claramente indicada a distribuição das cidades e outros centros urbanos, bem como as principais características da configuração do solo. Encontra-se neles também uma seleção das ferrovias e rodovias mais importantes.

A série de mapas das escalas de 1:6 000 000 e de 1:3 000 000 constituem o principal material de referência do Atlas e representa cerca de metade do conjunto de mapas. Entre eles há mapas detalhados de parte de um país (centro do México), de um país inteiro (Japão e a Nova Zelândia) ou de uma região mais extensa (Oriente Médio). As áreas de maior densidade demográfica são apresentadas em escala maior, a de 1:3 000 000, e as demais, na 1:6 000 000. Nessas duas escalas, os mapas fornecem informações de ordem política e cultural sobre um fundo que indica a configuração detalhada das particularidades físicas do solo, cujo relevo se destaca por contrastes de sombras e cores. Diversos matizes do azul traduzem o mapa batimétrico da profundidade ao largo das costas. Indicam também os aeroportos internacionais, as principais ferrovias, duas categorias de rodovias. As subdivisões políticas internas de numerosos países estão igualmente assinalados.

Na série de mapas da escala de 1:1 000 000, certas áreas, de interesse estratégico conjugado à importância econômica, densidade demográfica, ou ambos os elementos combinados, aparecem em forma ainda mais detalhada. O objetivo dessa série é representar a distribuição dos grandes centros urbanos, cidades, rodovias, ferrovias, pontes, aeroportos, represas, reservatórios e outras características associadas às grandes densidades demográficas. Indicam-se, também, os parques mais importantes, os lugares de interesse histórico, as áreas de lazer, três categorias de rodovias, e duas de ferrovias; e a nomenclatura dos grandes itinerários rodoviários. Todos esses elementos destacam-se sobre um fundo topográfico do relevo, executado em matizes das diversas cores.

Nos mapas regionais, assinalam-se os centros urbanos de dois modos. A *grandeza da população* das grandes cidades e dos centros urbanos secundários é representada pela *dimensão e forma do símbolo* que as localiza no mapa. O símbolo só reflete a população situada dentro de limites administrativos, sem levar em conta os subúrbios. Nos países onde os limites de uma municipalidade incluem zonas rurais, o símbolo representa apenas a população. A *importância política e econômica* de uma cidade, que não se relaciona necessariamente com o número de seus habitantes, é indicada pela *dimensão* dos caracteres tipográficos com que se compõe o seu nome.

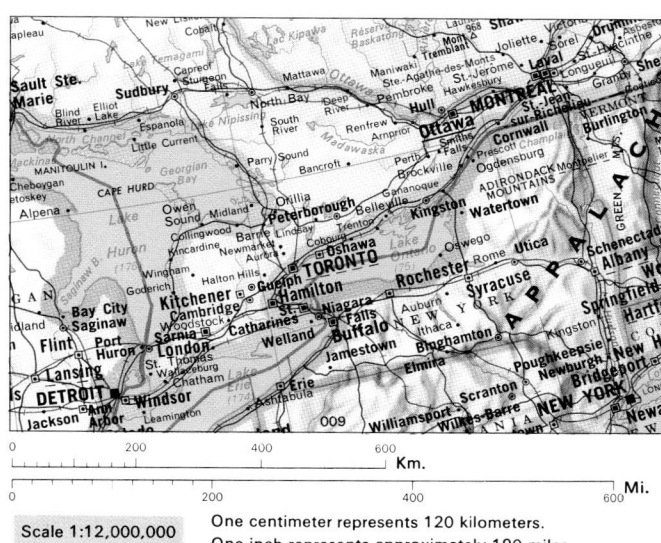

Scale 1:12,000,000

One centimeter represents 120 kilometers.
One inch represents approximately 190 miles.

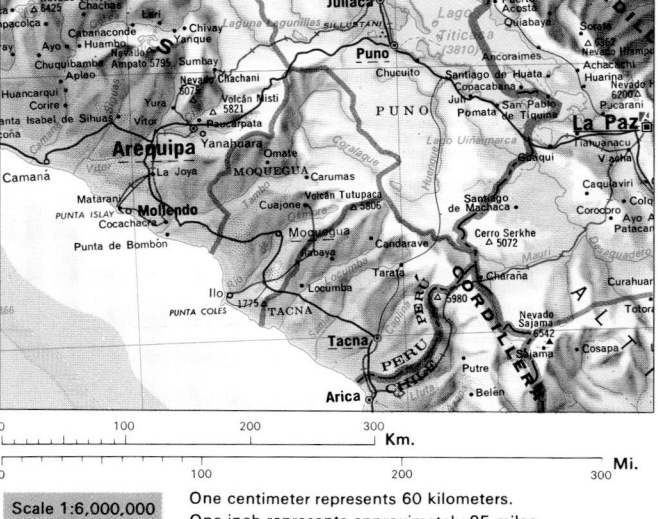

Scale 1:6,000,000

One centimeter represents 60 kilometers.
One inch represents approximately 95 miles.

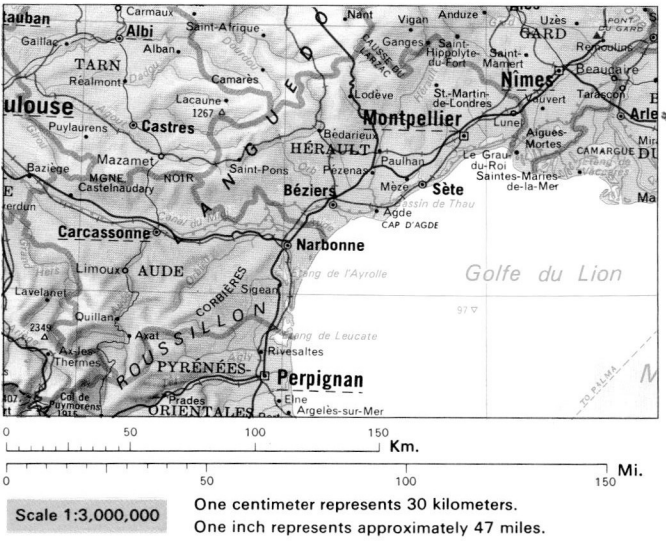

Scale 1:3,000,000

One centimeter represents 30 kilometers.
One inch represents approximately 47 miles.

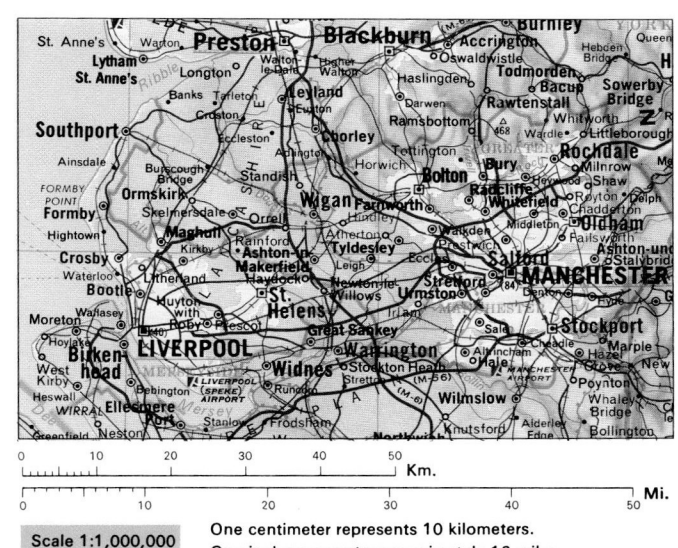

Scale 1:1,000,000

One centimeter represents 10 kilometers.
One inch represents approximately 16 miles.

Map continues pages 134-135

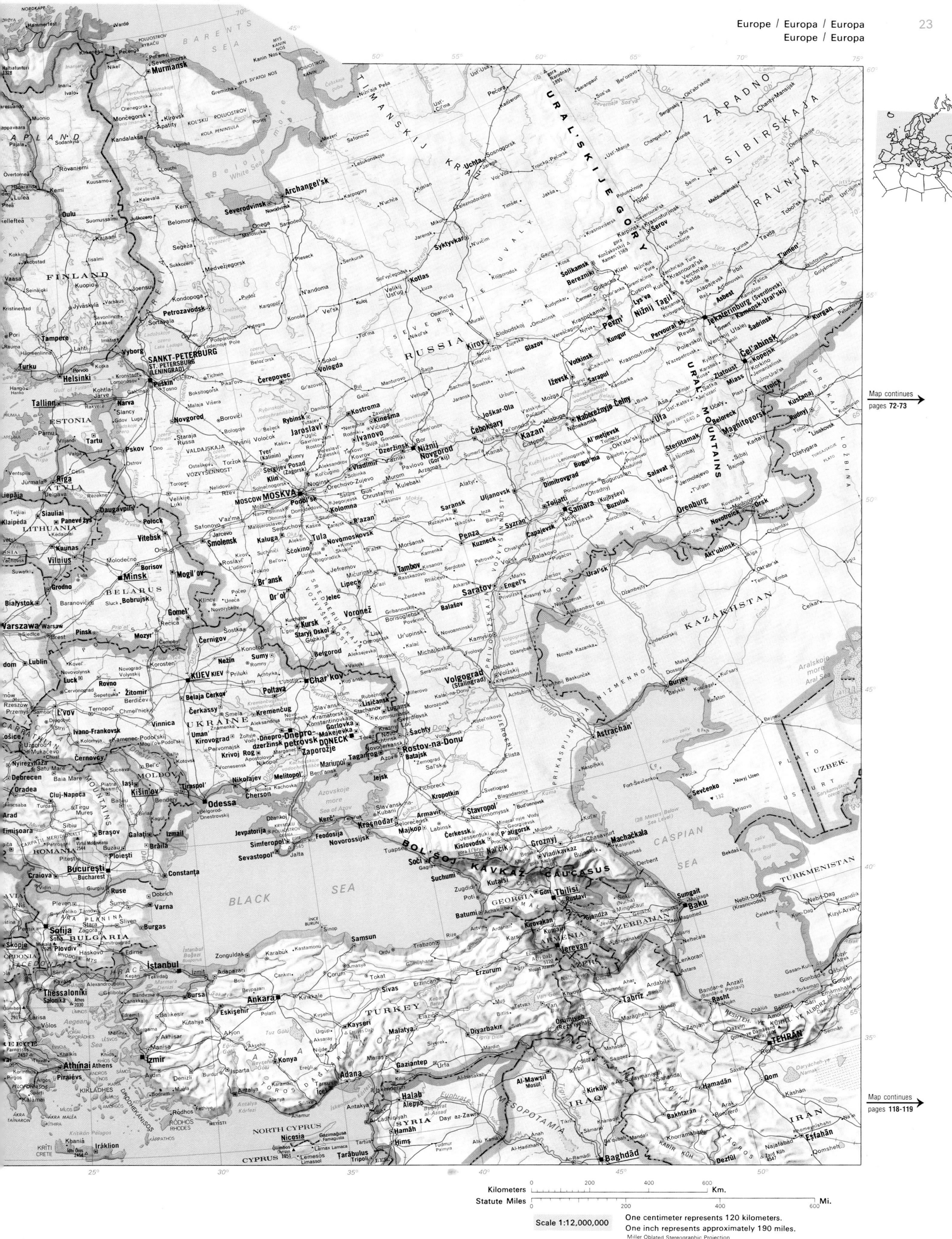

Map continues
pages 72-73

Map continues
pages 118-119

Kilometers 0   200   400   600
                              Km.
Statute Miles 0   200   400   600
                                    Mi.

Scale 1:12,000,000
One centimeter represents 120 kilometers.
One inch represents approximately 190 miles.
Miller Oblated Stereographic Projection

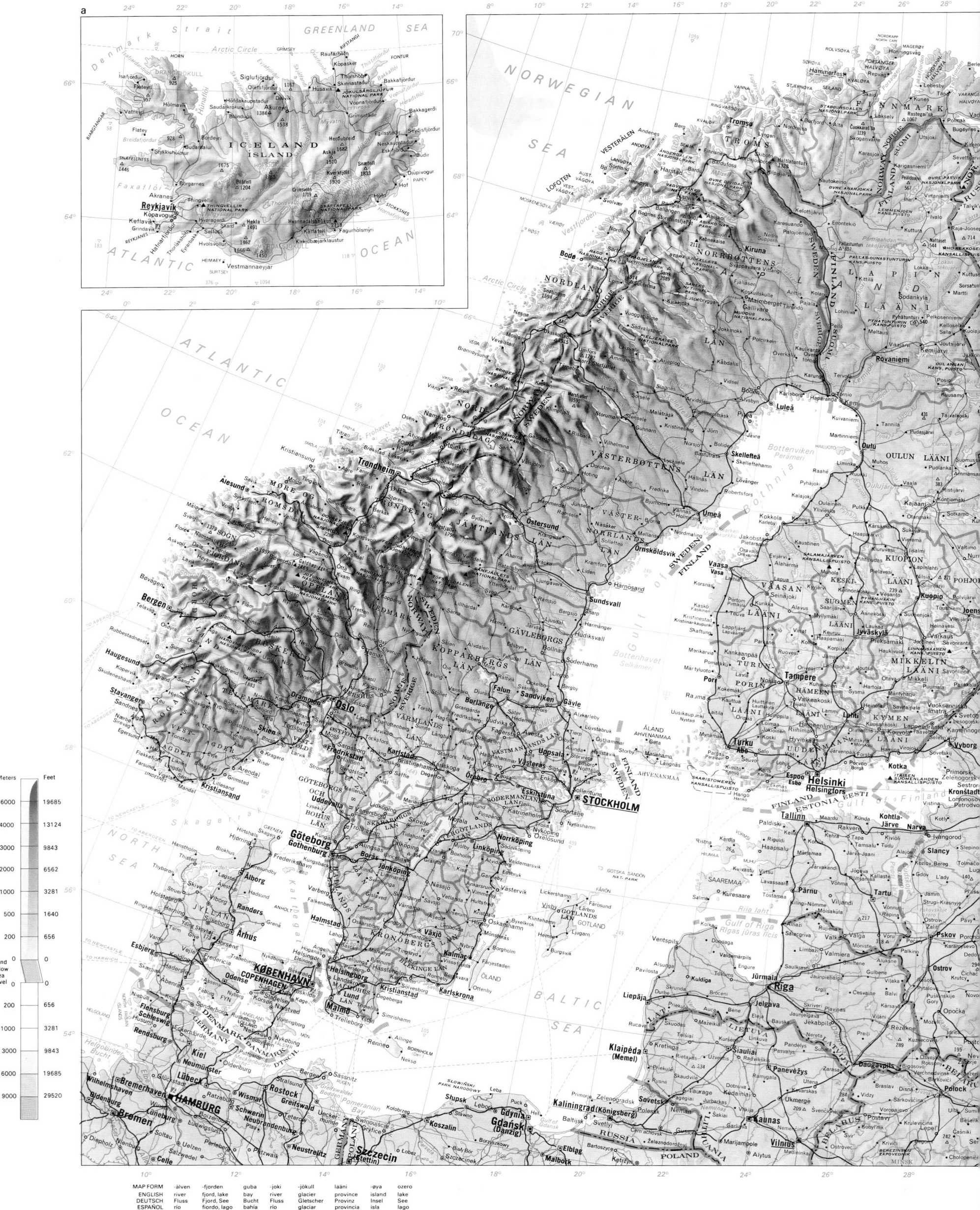

MAP FORM	-älven	-fjorden	guba	-joki	-jökull	lääni		-øya	ozero
ENGLISH	river	fjord, lake	bay	river	glacier	province		island	lake
DEUTSCH	Fluss	Fjord, See	Bucht	Fluss	Gletscher	Provinz		Insel	See
ESPAÑOL	río	fiordo, lago	bahía	río	glaciar	provincia		isla	lago
FRANÇAIS	rivière	fjord, lac	baie	rivière	glacier	province		île	lac
PORTUGUÊS	rio	fiorde, lago	baía	rio	geleira	provincia		ilha	lago

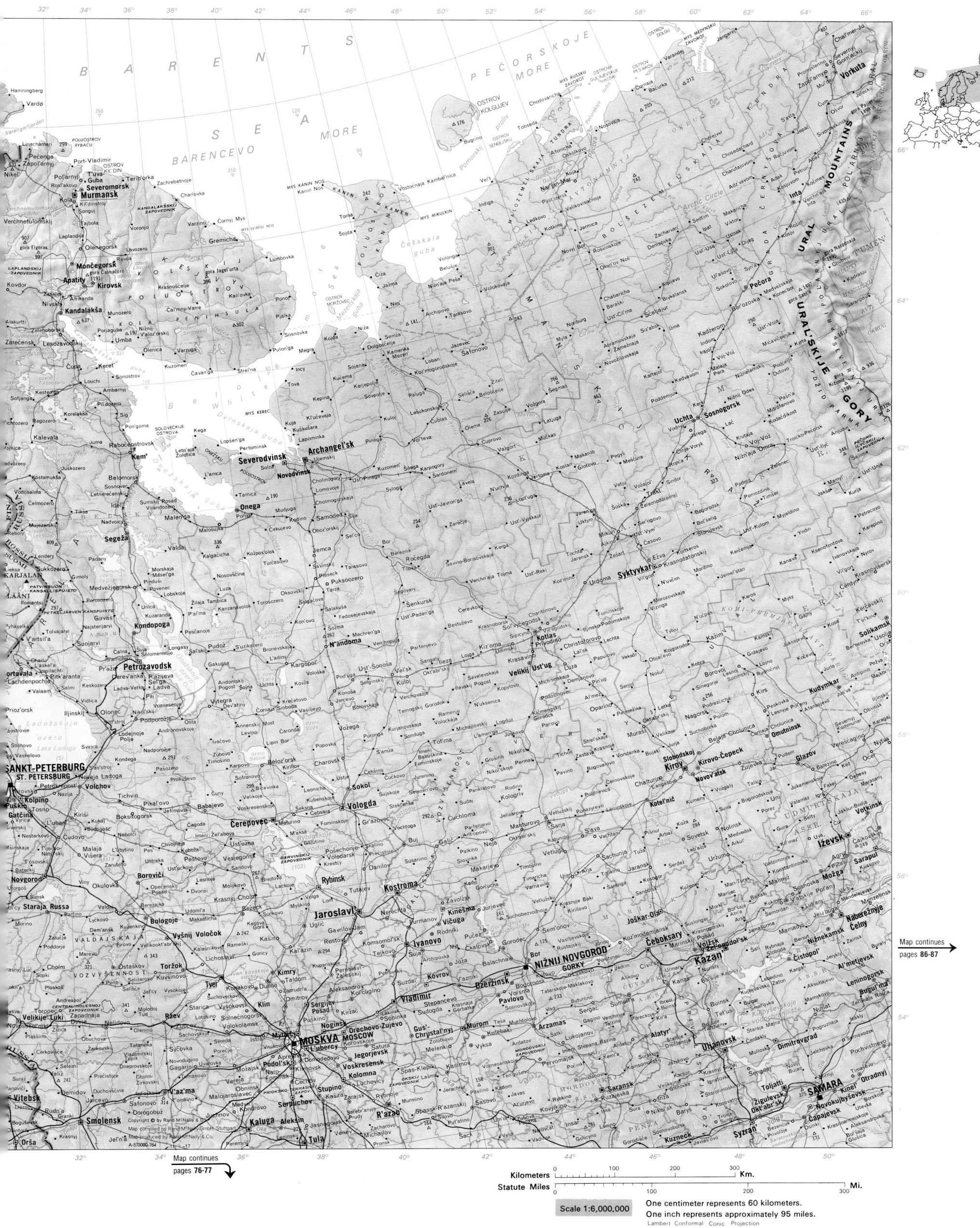

Map continues
pages 86-87

Map continues
pages 76-77

Kilometers 0   100   200   300   Km.

Statute Miles 0   100   200   300   Mi.

Scale 1:6,000,000
One centimeter represents 60 kilometers.
One inch represents approximately 95 miles.
Lambert Conformal Conic Projection

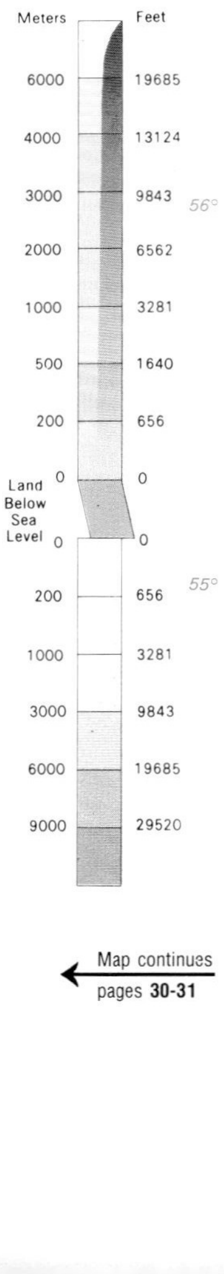

Map continues pages 30-31

MAP FORM	-älven	bugt	-fjället	-fjell	-fjorden	-järvi	-joki	-ö, -ön	-sjön	-vesi
ENGLISH	river	bay	mountain	mountain	fjord, lake	lake	river	island	lake	lake
DEUTSCH	Fluss	Bucht	Berg	Berg	Fjord, See	See	Fluss	Insel	See	See
ESPAÑOL	río	bahía	montaña	montaña	fiordo, lago	lago	río	isla	lago	lago
FRANÇAIS	rivière	baie	montagne	montagne	fjord, lac	lac	rivière	île	lac	lac
PORTUGUÊS	rio	baía	montanha	montanha	fiorde, lago	lago	rio	ilha	lago	lago

Map continues
pages 24-25

Map continues
pages 76-77

Map continues
pages 76-77

Scale 1:3,000,000

Kilometers 0 50 100 150 Km.
Statute Miles 0 50 100 150 Mi.

One centimeter represents 30 kilometers.
One inch represents approximately 47 miles.
Conic Projection, Two Standard Parallels

BALTIC SEA

Bottenviken
Perämeri

Gulf of Bothnia

Bottenhavet
Selkämeri

Gulf of Finland
Suomenlahti   Finskij zaliv

Gulf of Riga
Riia laht
Rīgas jūras līcis

SWEDEN
SVERIGE
FINLAND
SUOMI

RUSSIA
ROSSIJA

ESTONIA

LATVIA

Lake Ladoga
Ladožskoje ozero

Čudskoje ozero

Helsinki
Helsingfors

Tallinn

Riga

SANKT-PETERBURG
ST. PETERSBURG
(LENINGRAD)

Stockholm

Turku / Åbo

Tampere

Oulu

Vaasa / Vasa

Pori

Jyväskylä

Kuopio

Joensuu

Lahti

Kouvola

Lappeenranta

Imatra

Savonlinna

Sortavala

Vyborg

Novgorod

Pskov

Tartu

Pärnu

Narva

Gatčina

Sundsvall

Umeå

Örnsköldsvik

Härnösand

Skellefteå

Luleå

Boden

Kemi

Staraja Russa

Liepāja

Ventspils

Jūrmala

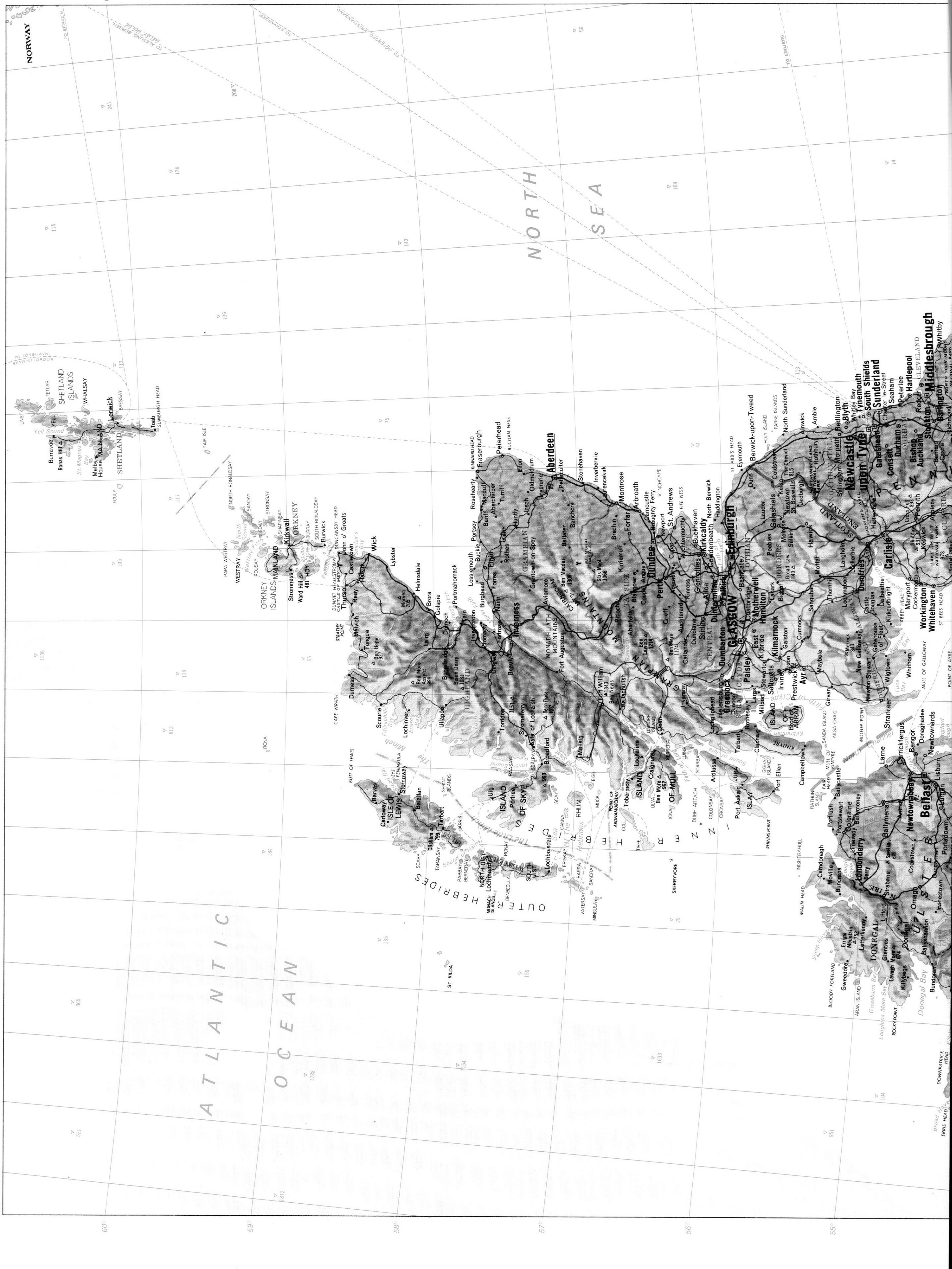
NORWAY
NORTH SEA
ATLANTIC OCEAN
SHETLAND ISLANDS
Lerwick
ORKNEY ISLANDS
Kirkwall
OUTER HEBRIDES
INNER HEBRIDES
ISLE OF LEWIS
Stornoway
ISLAND OF SKYE
ISLAND OF MULL
ST KILDA
GRAMPIAN MOUNTAINS
Aberdeen
Inverness
Dundee
Perth
Edinburgh
GLASGOW
Paisley
Greenock
Kilmarnock
Ayr
Dumfries
Carlisle
Newcastle upon Tyne
Sunderland
Middlesbrough
Belfast
Londonderry
DONEGAL
Wick
Thurso
Fraserburgh
Peterhead
Montrose
St. Andrews
Kirkcaldy
Berwick-upon-Tweed

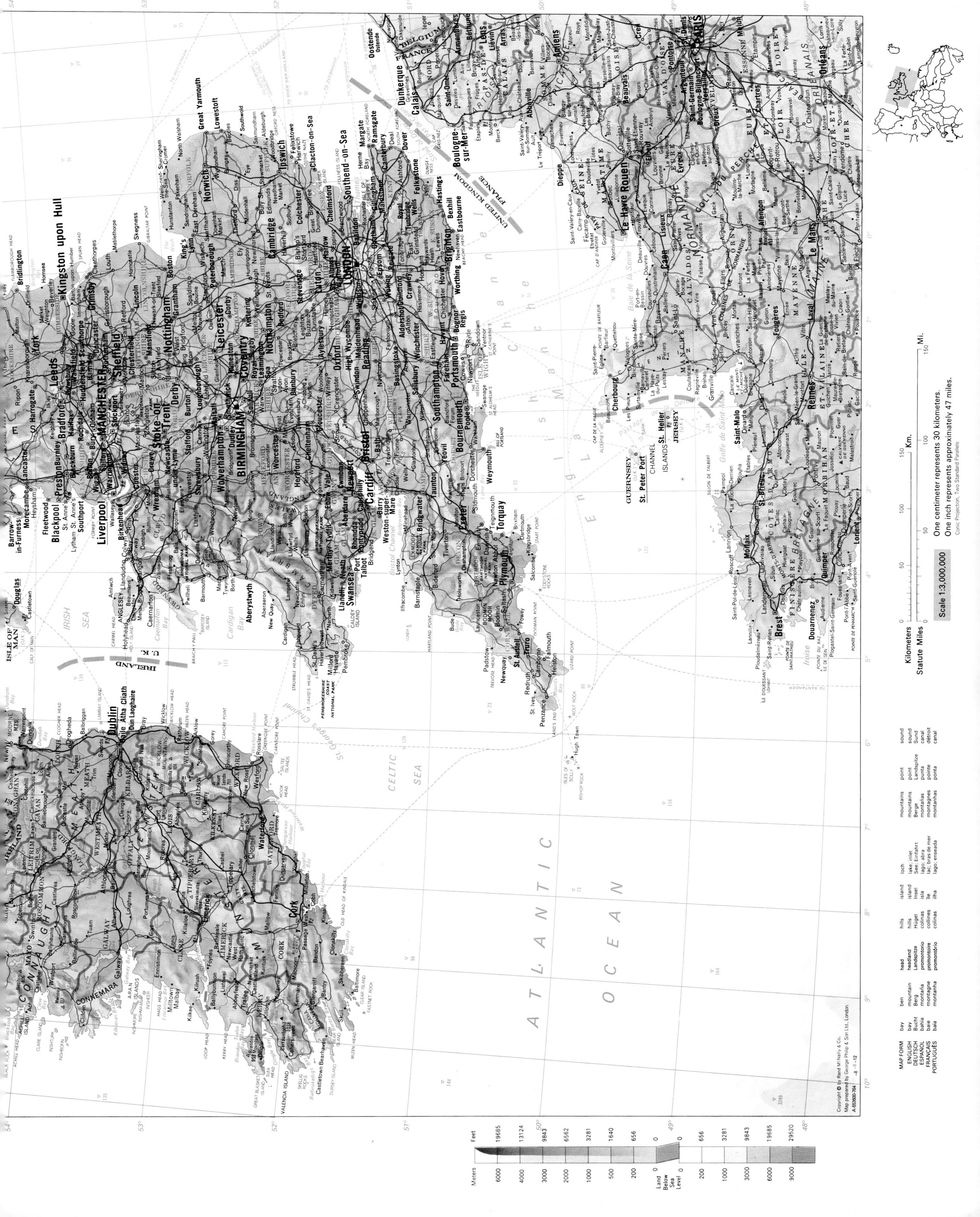
ATLANTIC OCEAN
CELTIC SEA
IRISH SEA
English Channel
LONDON
BIRMINGHAM
MANCHESTER
Liverpool
Leeds
Sheffield
Kingston upon Hull
Bristol
Cardiff
Dublin
Baile Átha Cliath
Cork
PARIS
Le Havre
Rouen
Cherbourg
Brest
Rennes
Le Mans
Caen
Amiens
Calais
Dunkerque
Boulogne-sur-Mer
Oostende
UNITED KINGDOM
FRANCE
BELGIUM
IRELAND
U.K.
Scale 1:3,000,000
One centimeter represents 30 kilometers.
One inch represents approximately 47 miles.
Conic Projection, Two Standard Parallels
Kilometers
Statute Miles
MAP FORM
ENGLISH
DEUTSCH
ESPAÑOL
FRANÇAIS
PORTUGUÊS
Copyright © by Rand McNally & Co.
Map prepared by George Philip & Son Ltd., London.
Feet
Meters
Land Below Sea Level

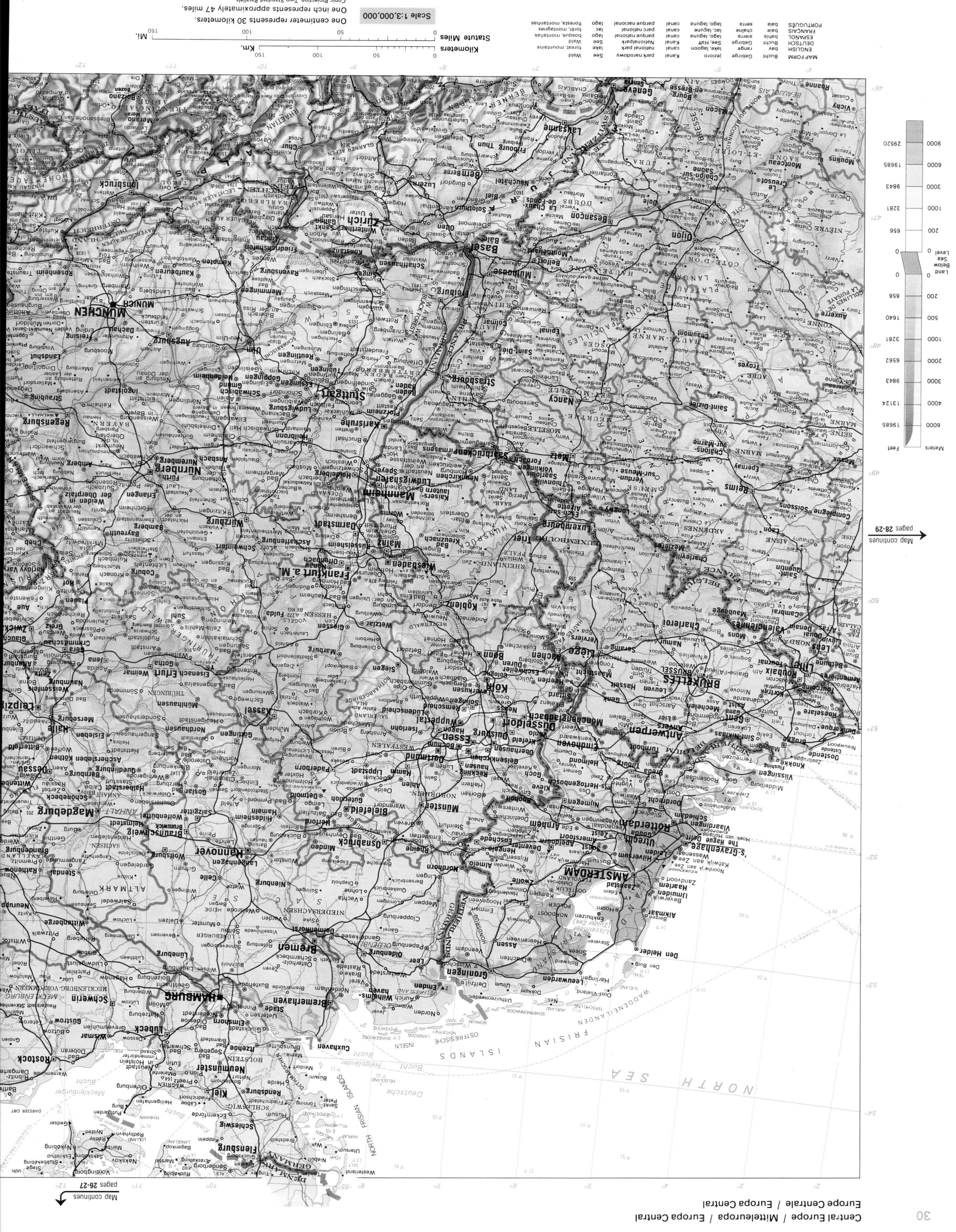

Map continues pages 26-27

Map continues pages 28-29

Scale 1:3,000,000

One centimeter represents 30 kilometers.
One inch represents approximately 47 miles.
Conic Projection, Two Standard Parallels.

MAP FORM		
ENGLISH	Gebirge	Bucht
DEUTSCH	range	bay
ESPAÑOL	sierra	bahía
FRANÇAIS	chaîne	baie
PORTUGUÊS	serra	baía

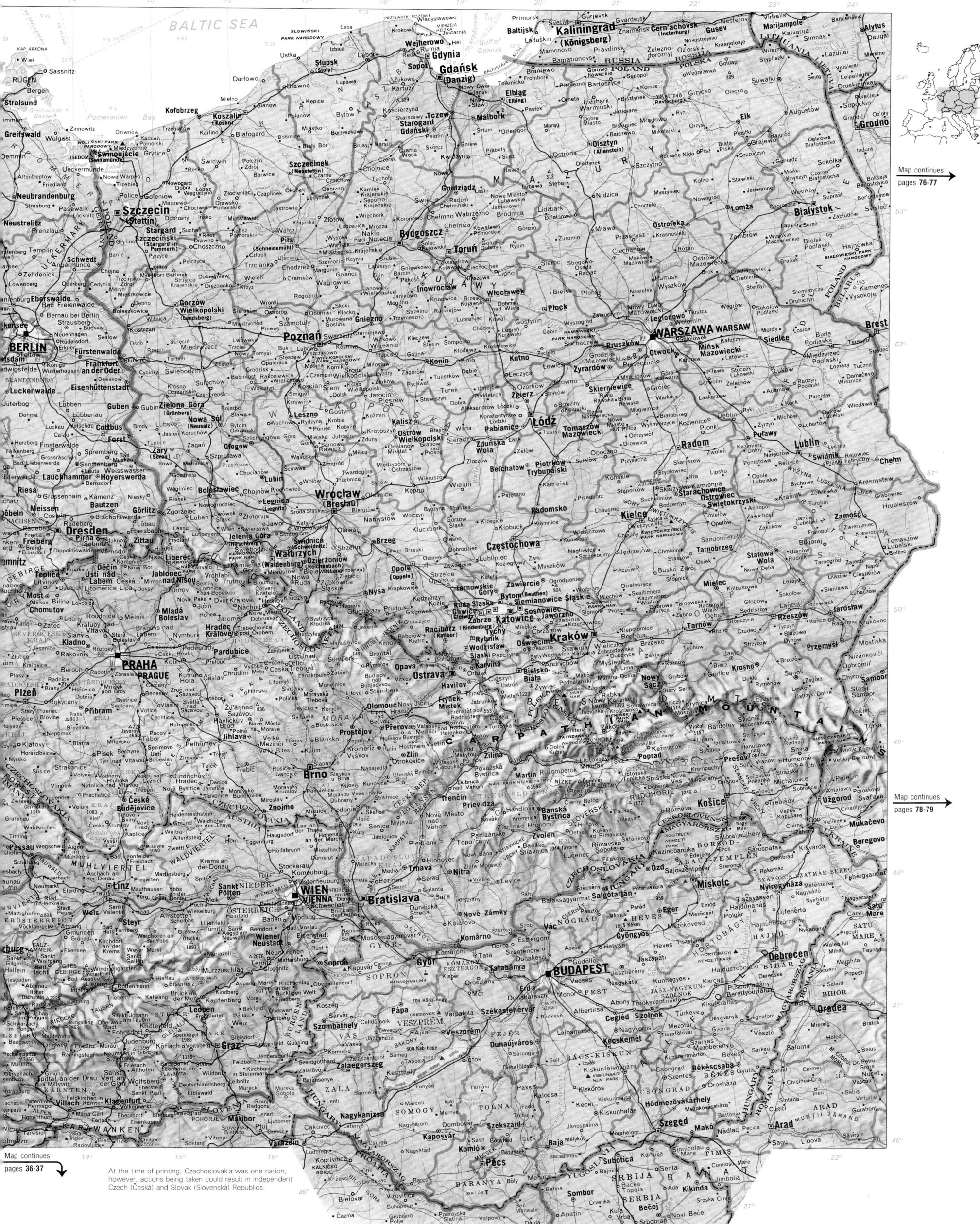

Map continues
pages 76-77

Map continues
pages 78-79

Map continues
pages 36-37

At the time of printing, Czechoslovakia was one nation,
however, actions being taken could result in independent
Czech (Česká) and Slovak (Slovenská) Republics.

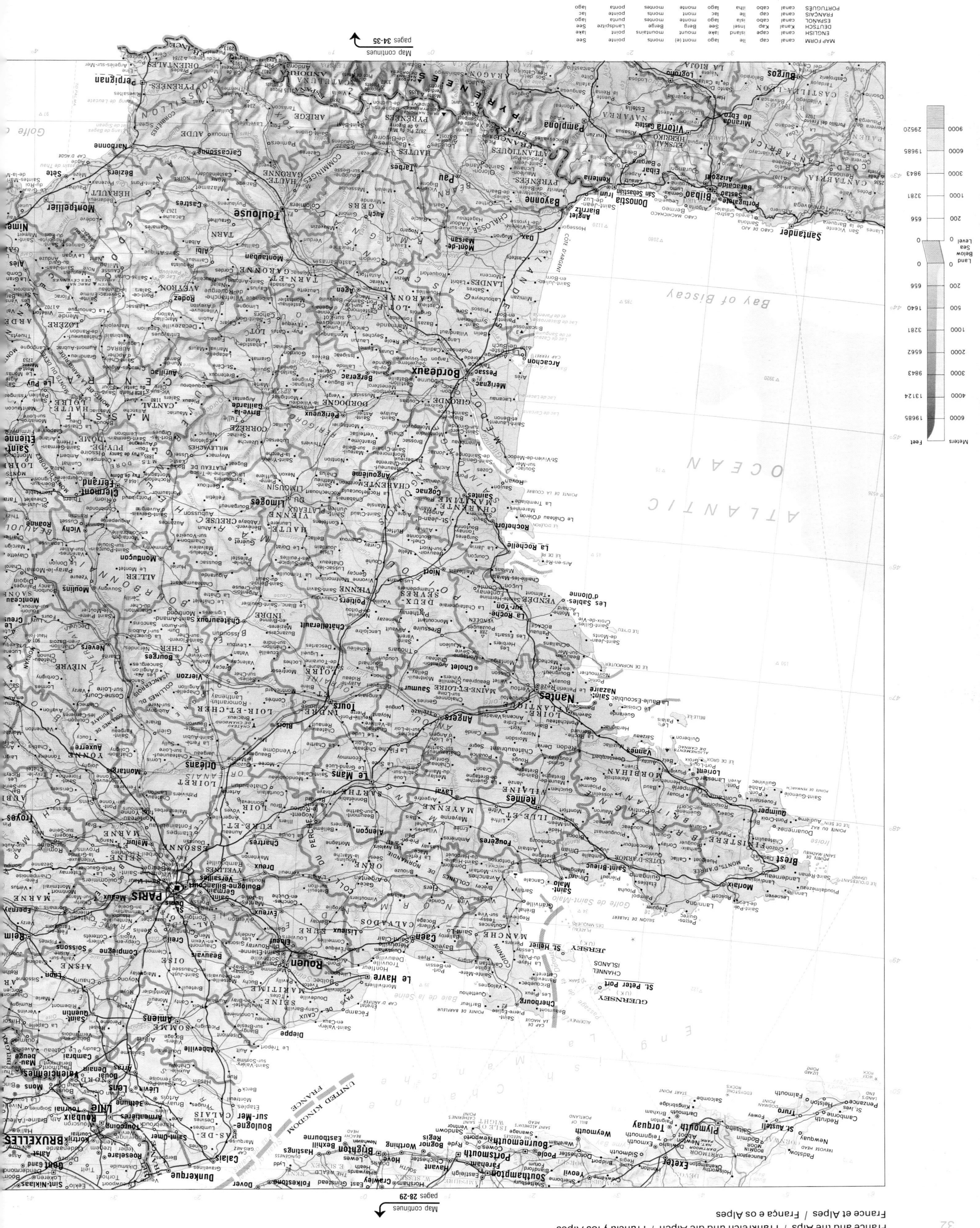

Map continues pages 34-35

Map continues pages 28-29

Map continues
pages 30-31

Map continues
pages 36-37

Copyright © Rand McNally & Co.
Map prepared by Rand McNally GmbH, Stuttgart.
A-559495-764   -8 ⊙ -15

Kilometers

Statute Miles

Scale 1:3,000,000

One centimeter represents 30 kilometers.
One inch represents approximately 47 miles.
Lambert Conformal Conic Projection

Meters	**Feet**		
6000	19685		
4000	13124		
3000	9843		
2000	6562		
1000	3281		
500	1640		
200	656		
0	0		
Land Below Sea Level			
0	0		
200	656		
1000	3281		
3000	9843		
6000	19685		
9000	29520		

Copyright © by Rand McNally & Co.
Map prepared by Rand McNally GmbH, Stuttgart.
A-659900-764 -6 -5 -12

ESPAÑOL	bahia	cabo	isla	embalse	puerto	punta	ria	sierra
ENGLISH	bay	cape	island	reservoir	port	point	estuary	mountains
DEUTSCH	Bucht	Kap	Insel	Stausee	Hafen	Landspitze	Trichtermündung	Berge
FRANÇAIS	baie	cap	île	réservoir	port	pointe	estuaire	montagnes
PORTUGUÊS	baia	cabo	ilha	reservatório	porto	ponta	estuário	serra

Map continues
pages 32-33

Map continues
pages 148-149

Kilometers 0   50   100   150 Km.

Statute Miles 0   50   100   150 Mi.

Scale 1:3,000,000

One centimeter represents 30 kilometers.
One inch represents approximately 47 miles.

Conic Projection, Two Standard Parallels

Map continues
pages 32-33

Map continues
pages 30-31

Map continues
pages 38-39

MEDITERRANEAN SEA

IONIAN SEA

TYRRHENIAN SEA
MARE TIRRENO

ADRIATIC SEA

Strait of Otranto

Golfo di Taranto

Gulf of Gioia

Golfo di Salerno

Strait of Sicily

Malta Channel

ITALY ITALIA
TUNISIA TUNISIE

ITALY ITALIA

NAPOLI NAPLES

Bari

Taranto

Brindisi

Lecce

Foggia

Salerno

Reggio di Calabria

Messina

Catania

Siracusa Syracuse

Augusta

Palermo

SICILIA
SICILY

Agrigento

Licata

Gela

Trapani

Marsala

Mazara del Vallo

Sciacca

CALABRIA

PUGLIA

CAMPANIA

SARDEGNA
SARDINIA

Cagliari

Sassari

Nuoro

Oristano

Carbonia

Iglesias

Alghero

FRANCE
ITALY

MALTA
ITALY ITALIA

Valletta

Tunis

Bizerte

Nabeul

Sousse

Kairouan

Annaba (Bône)

ALGERIA ALGÉRIE
TUNISIA TUNISIE

Map continues
pages 148-149

MAP FORM					
ENGLISH	cape	gulf	island	lake	mountain	mountains	point
DEUTSCH	Kap	Golf	Insel	See	Berg	Gebirge	Landspitze
ESPAÑOL	cabo	golfo	isla	lago	monte	montes	punta
FRANÇAIS	cap	golfe	île	lac	mont	monts	pointe
PORTUGUÊS	cabo	golfo	ilha	lago	monte	montes	ponta
	capo	golfo	isola	lago	monte	monti	punta
			otok				

Scale 1:3,000,000

One centimeter represents 30 kilometers.
One inch represents approximately 47 miles.
Conic Projection, Two Standard Parallels

Kilometers 0 50 100 150 Km.
Statute Miles 0 50 100 150 Mi.

Meters		Feet
6000		19685
4000		13124
3000		9843
2000		6562
1000		3281
500		1640
200		656
0 Land Below Sea Level 0		0
200		656
1000		3281
3000		9843
6000		19685
9000		29520

Copyright © by Rand McNally & Co.
Map prepared by Rand McNally GmbH, Stuttgart.
A-956906-764

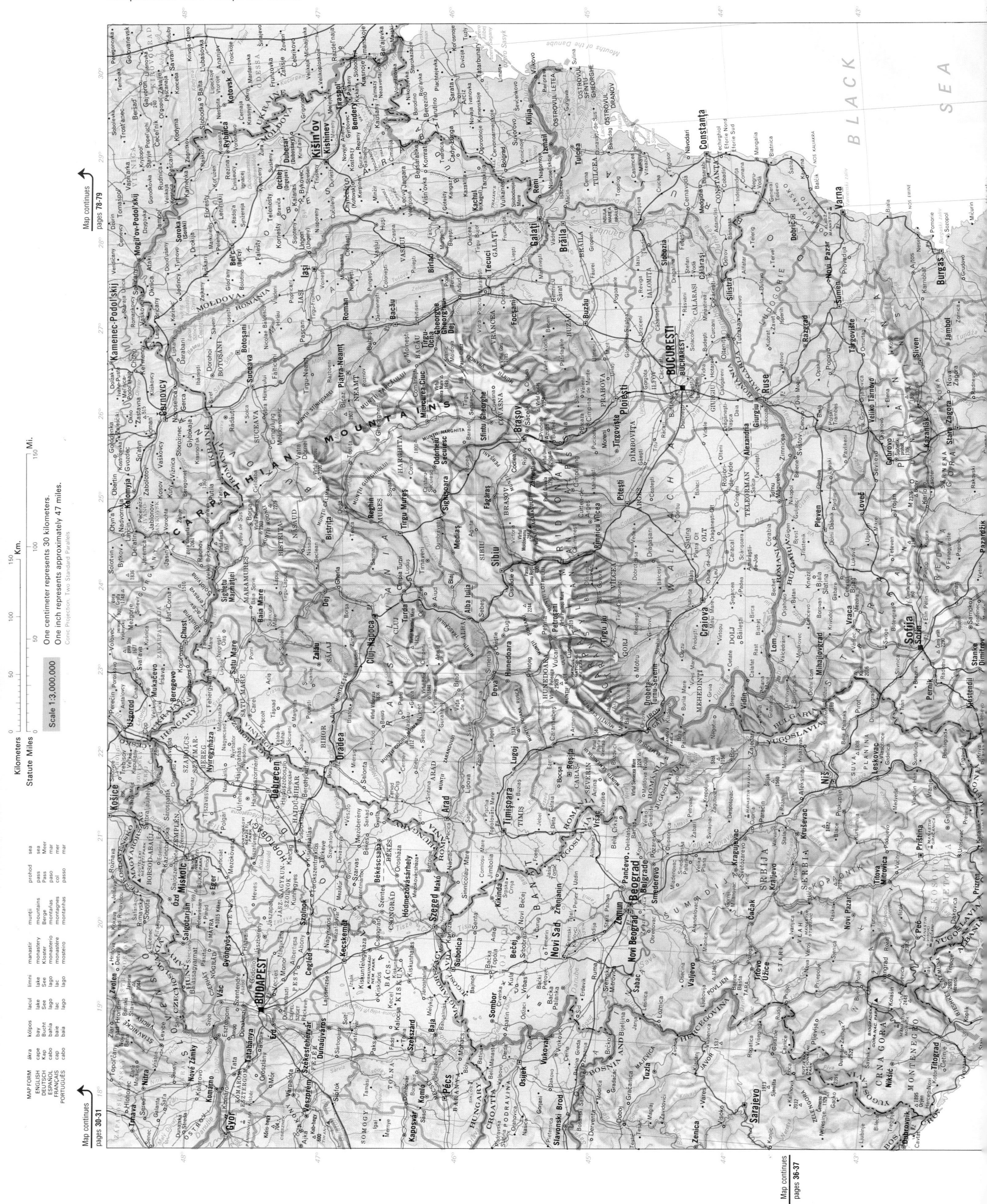

Map continues
pages 78-79

Map continues
pages 30-31

Map continues
pages 36-37

Scale 1:3,000,000

One centimeter represents 30 kilometers.
One inch represents approximately 47 miles.

Conic Projection, Two Standard Parallels

Kilometers
Statute Miles

MAP FORM							
ENGLISH	cape	bay	lake	lagoon	monastery	mountains	pass
DEUTSCH	Kap	Bucht	See	See	Kloster	Berge	Pass
ESPAÑOL	cabo	bahía	lago	lago	monasterio	montañas	paso
FRANÇAIS	cap	baie	lac	lago	monastère	montagnes	paso
PORTUGUÊS	cabo	baía	lago	lago	mosteiro	montanhas	passo
	äkra	kölpos	lacul	limni	manastir	muntii	prohod

Map continues pages 130-131

AEGEAN SEA
IONIAN SEA
MEDITERRANEAN SEA
ADRIATIC SEA
Strait of Otranto
Marmara Denizi Sea of Marmara
KIKLÁDHES CYCLADES
D'HODHEKÁNISOS DODECANESE
KRÍTI CRETE
LÉSVOS LESBOS
RÓDHOS RHODES
İSTANBUL
Bursa
İzmir (Smyrna)
Thessaloníki Salonika
ATHÍNAI ATHENS
Piraiévs Piraeus
Tiranë
Skopje
Pátrai
Lárisa
Kérkira
Iráklion
Khaniá
TURKEY TÜRKIYE
GREECE ELLÁS
ITALY
Meters
Feet
Land Below Sea Level

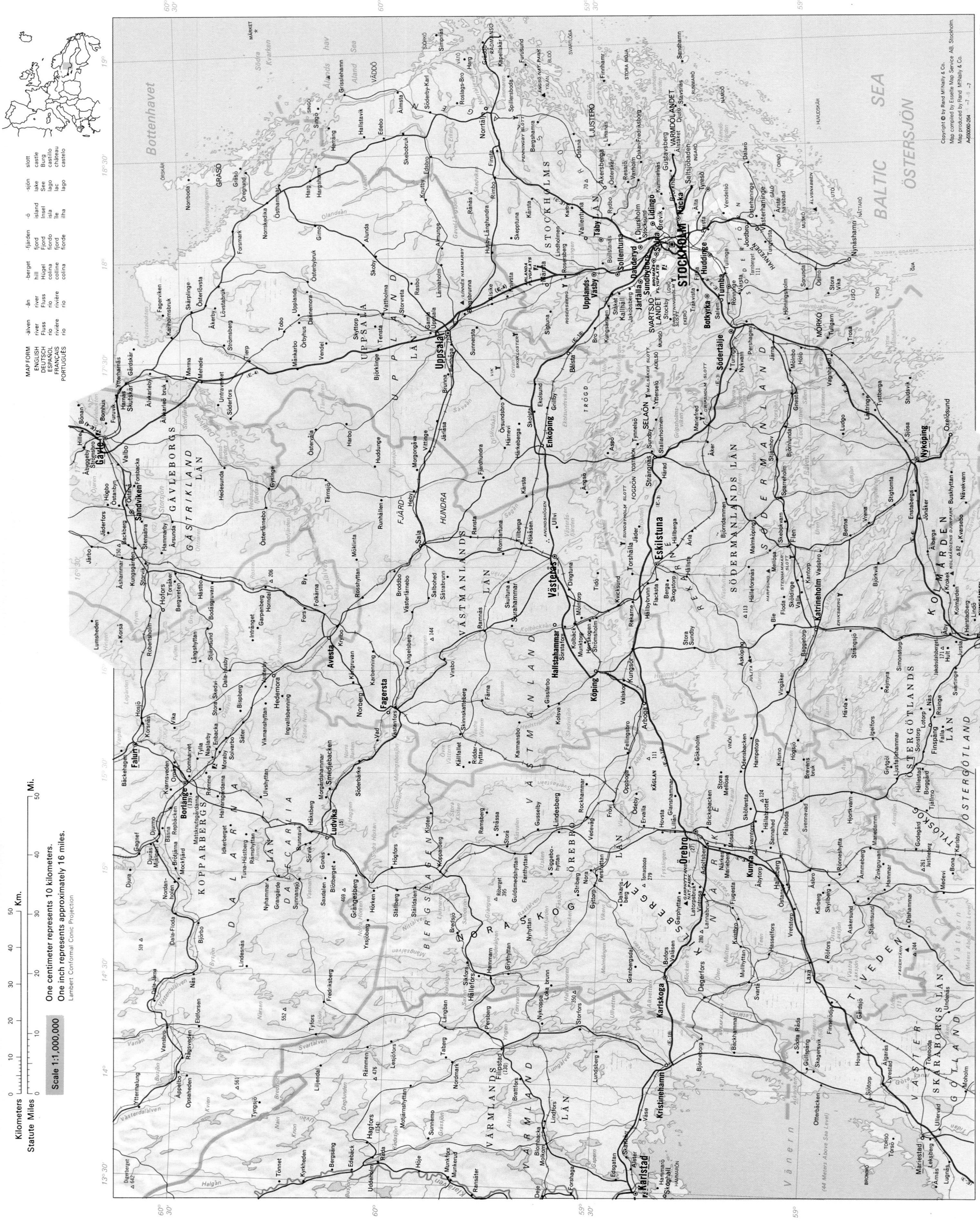
Kilometers 0 10 20 30 40 50 Km.
Statute Miles 0 10 20 30 40 50 Mi.
Scale 1:1,000,000
One centimeter represents 10 kilometers.
One inch represents approximately 16 miles.
Lambert Conformal Conic Projection
MAP FORM -älven -ån -berget -fjärden -ö -sjön slott
ENGLISH river river hill fjord island lake castle
DEUTSCH Fluss Fluss Hügel Fjord Insel See Burg
ESPAÑOL río río colina fiordo isla lago castillo
FRANÇAIS rivière rivière colline fjord île lac château
PORTUGUÊS rio rio colina fiorde ilha lago castelo
Bottenhavet
BALTIC SEA
ÖSTERSJÖN
Vänern
STOCKHOLM
Uppsala
Västerås
Örebro
Karlstad
Gävle
Falun
Eskilstuna
Norrköping
Nyköping
Södertälje
Borlänge
Sandviken
Kristinehamn
Karlskoga
VÄRMLANDS LÄN
ÖREBRO LÄN
VÄSTMANLANDS LÄN
UPPSALA LÄN
STOCKHOLMS LÄN
SÖDERMANLANDS LÄN
ÖSTERGÖTLANDS LÄN
SKARABORGS LÄN
GÄVLEBORGS LÄN
KOPPARBERGS LÄN
DALARNA
GÄSTRIKLAND
UPPLAND
SÖDERMANLAND
VÄSTMANLAND
BERGSLAGEN
KILSBERGEN
TIVEDEN
KOLMÅRDEN
Copyright © by Rand McNally & Co.
Map compiled by Esselte Map Service AB, Stockholm.
Map produced by Rand McNally & Co.
A-550000-284 -7-8-7

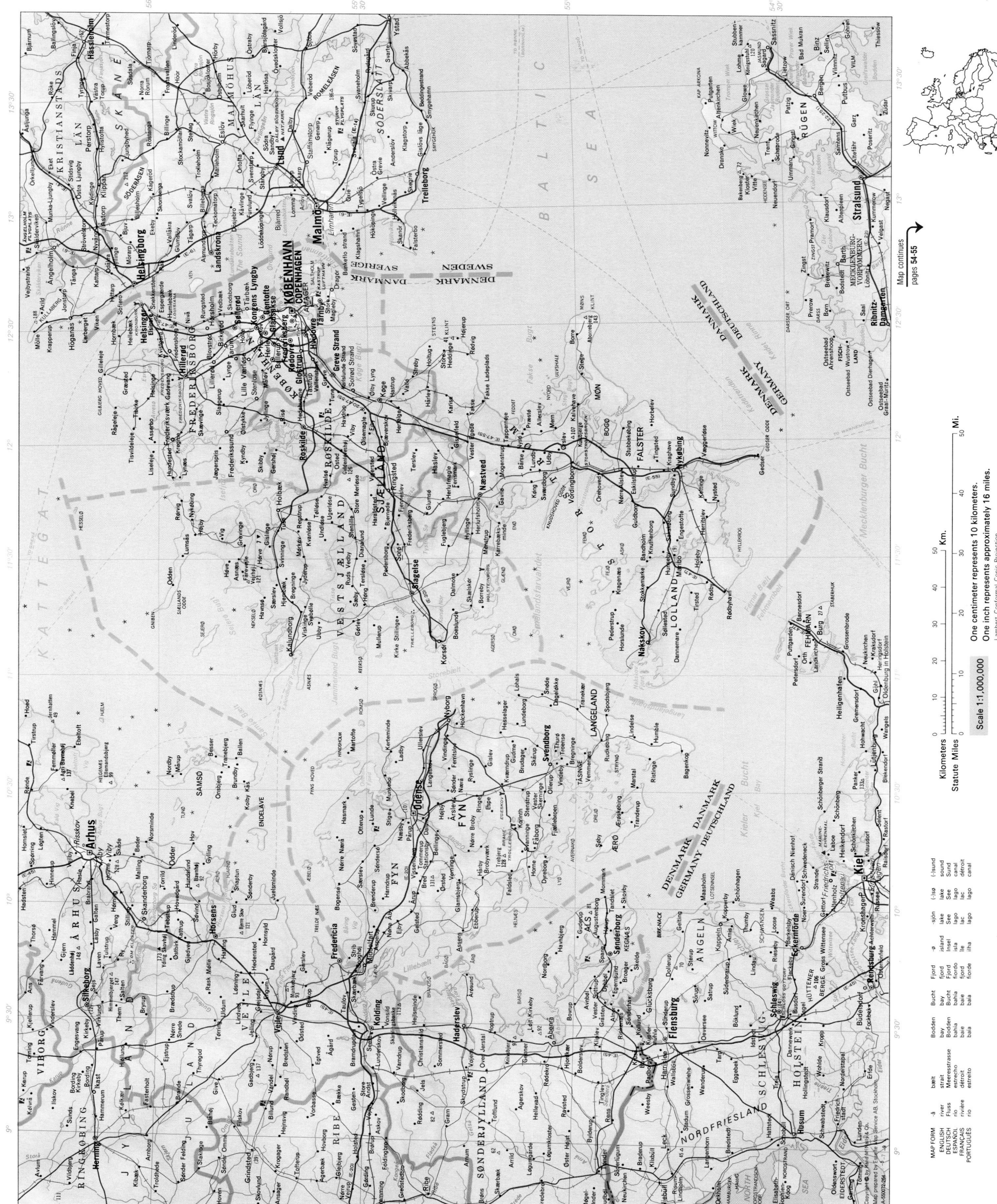

Map continues
pages 54-55

Kilometers

Statute Miles

Scale 1:1,000,000

One centimeter represents 10 kilometers.
One inch represents approximately 16 miles.

Lambert Conformal Conic Projection

MAP FORM				
ENGLISH	-å	river	bælt	strait
DEUTSCH		Fluss		Meeresstrasse
ESPAÑOL		río		estrecho
FRANÇAIS		rivière		détroit
PORTUGUÊS		rio		estreito

Map continues
pages 48-49

ENGLISH	DEUTSCH	ESPAÑOL	FRANÇAIS	PORTUGUÊS
bay	Bucht	bahía	baie	baía
drain	Abzugsgraben	acqua	drenagem	drenagem
forest	Wald	bosque	forêt	floresta
head	Landspitze	promontorio	promontoire	promontório
hill	Hügel	colina	colline	colina
isle	Insel	isla	île	ilha
marsh	Marsch	pantano	marais	pântano
point	Landspitze	punta	pointe	ponta
vale	Tal	valle	val	vale

Copyright Laurie et al Co.
Map prepared by Rand McNally & Co.
A-556900-254

ATLANTIC OCEAN

ISLES OF SCILLY

a

London — Birmingham — Cardiff

Map continues pages 44-45

Map continues pages 50-51

Kilometers 0 10 20 30 40 50 Km.

Statute Miles 0 10 20 30 40 50 Mi.

Scale 1:1,000,000

One centimeter represents 10 kilometers.
One inch represents approximately 16 miles.

Lambert Conformal Conic Projection

Map continues pages 46-47

Map continues pages 48-49

MAP FORM		
ENGLISH	bay	dale
DEUTSCH	Bucht	Tal
ESPAÑOL	bahía	valle
FRANÇAIS	baie	vallée
PORTUGUÊS	baía	vale
	head	firth
	Landspitze	Trichtermündung
	cabo	estuario
	cap	estuaire
	cabo	estuário
	head	forest
	promontorio	bosque
	promontoire	forêt
	promontório	floresta
	lake; inlet	moor
	See; Einfahrt	Moor
	lago; abra	páramo
	lac; bras de mer	lande
	lago; enseada	pántano
	water (lake, river)	loch
	See; Fluss	moor
	lago; río	páramo
	lac; rivière	lande
	lago, rio	lago, rio

IRELAND   ÉIRE
UNITED KINGDOM

WEXFORD
WICKLOW
CARLOW
KILDARE
WICKLOW MOUNTAINS
DUBLIN   BAILE ÁTHA CLIATH
MEATH
LOUTH
CAVAN
MONAGHAN
NORTHERN IRELAND
ARMAGH
DOWN
ANTRIM
TYRONE
DONEGAL
LONDONDERRY   Derry

IRISH   SEA

ISLE OF MAN   (U.K.)
Douglas

LAKE   DISTRICT   Barrow-in-Furness   Workington   Whitehaven

GALLOWAY   THE RHINS   THE GLENKENS   CARRICK   Dumfries   Ayr   Kilmarnock

ANGLESEY   Holyhead   Llandudno   Colwyn Bay   Rhyl   Bangor   Caernarfon   SNOWDONIA NATIONAL PARK   LLEYN PENINSULA

NORTH SEA

Berwick-upon-Tweed
Tweedmouth
Scremerston

HOLY ISLAND
FARNE ISLANDS
Bamburgh
Seahouses
North Sunderland

Alnwick
Lesbury
Amble
Warkworth
Amble

Widdrington Station
Ellington
Lynemouth
Newbiggin-by-the-Sea
North Seaton
Morpeth
Ashington

Blyth
Seaton Sluice
Seaton Delaval

Whitley Bay
North Shields
Tynemouth
NEWCASTLE UPON TYNE
Long Benton
Wallsend
Gosforth
South Shields
Jarrow
Hebburn

Gateshead
Sunderland
Whickham
Ryhope
Seaham

Consett
Chester-le-Street
Houghton-le-Spring
Stanley
Lanchester
Hetton-le-Hole
Durham
Easington
Peterlee
Horden
Blackhall Colliery

Hartlepool
Spennymoor
Bishop Auckland
Wingate
Trimdon
Sedgefield

Middlesbrough
Redcar
Stockton-on-Tees
Billingham
Marske-by-the-Sea
Saltburn-by-the-Sea
Darlington
Eston
Guisborough
Loftus

Barnard Castle
Middleton St. George
Great Ayton
Stokesley
Castleton

Whitby
WHITBY ABBEY
Egton
Robin Hood's Bay

NORTH YORK MOORS NATIONAL PARK
Goathland
Sleights
Burniston

Richmond
Catterick
Northallerton
Scalby
Newby
Scarborough
Eastfield

Bedale
Thirsk
Kirkbymoorside
Pickering
Ayton
Seamer
Filey
FILEY BAY

VALE OF PICKERING
Malton
Humanby
Hunmanby

Ripon
HOWARDIAN HILLS
Norton
Rillington
Burton Fleming
FLAMBOROUGH HEAD
Flamborough
Bridlington
BRIDLINGTON BAY

Boroughbridge
Easingwold
Great Driffield
Wetwang
Sledmere
Kilham

Harrogate
Knaresborough
York
Pocklington
Middleton-on-the-Wolds
Hornsea

Wetherby
Stamford Bridge
Dunnington
Market Weighton
Beverley
Leconfield
Aldbrough

Tadcaster
Cottingham
Swanland
Kingston upon Hull

Leeds
Selby
HUMBERSIDE
Hedon
Withernsea
Patrington
Bradford
Halifax
Castleford
Wakefield
Pontefract
Goole
Howden
Brough
Barton-upon-Humber
Immingham

Huddersfield
Barnsley
Thorne
Crowle
Keelby
Grimsby
SPURN HEAD
Cleethorpes
Humberston
New Waltham

Doncaster
Scunthorpe
Epworth
Caistor
North Somercotes
Saltfleet

Sheffield
Rotherham
Gainsborough
Market Rasen
Louth
Manby
Mablethorpe
Sutton on Sea

Chesterfield
Worksop
East Retford
Lincoln
Wragby
Alford
Chapel St. Leonards
Skegness

Bakewell
Mansfield
Southwell
Sleaford
Burgh le Marsh
GIBRALTAR POINT

Matlock
Sutton in Ashfield
Kirkby in Ashfield
Mansfield
Newark-on-Trent
Wainfleet All Saints

Buxton
HIGH PEAK
Belper
Arnold
Bingham
Grantham
Boston
The Wash

Stoke-on-Trent
Cheadle
Uttoxeter
Derby
Nottingham
Carlton
Long Eaton
Radcliffe
Spalding
King's Lynn

Stafford
Burton upon Trent
Swadlincote
Loughborough
Melton Mowbray
Bourne
Long Sutton

Manchester
Salford
Stockport
Ashton-under-Lyne
Stretford
Oldham
Rochdale
Bury
Bolton
Wigan

Liverpool
Birkenhead
St. Helens
Widnes
Warrington
Wilmslow
Macclesfield

Preston
Blackburn
Burnley
Nelson
Colne
Accrington
Blackpool
Lytham
St. Anne's
Southport

Lancaster
Morecambe
Heysham
Kendal
Windermere
Ambleside

Carlisle
Penrith
LAKE DISTRICT NATIONAL PARK

Hawick
Selkirk
Galashiels
Jedburgh
NORTHUMBERLAND NATIONAL PARK
The Cheviot 815

SCOTLAND
ENGLAND

Chester
Crewe
Wrexham
Nantwich
Newcastle-under-Lyme
Leek

YORKSHIRE DALES NATIONAL PARK
WENSLEYDALE
SWALEDALE
VALE OF YORK
PENNINES

Kilometers 0 10 20 30 40 Km.
Statute Miles 0 10 20 30 40 50 Mi.

Scale 1:1,000,000
One centimeter represents 10 kilometers.
One inch represents approximately 16 miles.
Lambert Conformal Conic Projection

Map continues pages 42-43

SHETLAND ISLANDS

FOULA

SHETLAND

MAINLAND

HERMA NESS
UNST
Baltasound
Haroldswick

POINT OF FETHALAND
Isbister
St. Magnus Bay
Ronas Hill △ 450
Hillswick
MUCKLE ROE
PAPA STOUR
Sandness
VAILA
Walls
Gruting
Aith
Voe
Moss bank
YELL
Gutcher
ISLE OF NOSS
BRESSAY
Burravoe

FITFUL HEAD
Brindister
WEST BURRA
Scalloway
Lerwick
Kirkabister
MOUSA
HELLI NESS
OUT SKERRIES
WHALSAY
Brae

SUMBURGH HEAD
Toab
Boddam
Sandwick

FETLAR

HEBRIDES
FLANNAN ISLANDS

MONACH ISLANDS
HASKEIR ISLANDS
Solas
NORTH UIST
Hougharry
Lochmaddy
BORERAY
PABBAY
BERNERAY
RONAY
BALESHARE
Carinish

Western Isles
HARRIS
TARANSAY
SCARP
MEALASTA ISLAND
GALLAN HEAD
Aird
Brenish
Miavig
Breasclete
Leverburgh
Rodel
KENDIBIG POINT
Tarbert
Balallan
SCALPAY
SHIANT ISLANDS
Gallain
Carloway
Callanish
Laxay
LEWIS
Bragar
Barvas
Five Penny Borve
Stornoway
W. Maldun
Cromore
Crossbost
North Tolsta
BUTT OF LEWIS
Port of Ness
Dell
TOLSTA HEAD
CELLAR HEAD
TIUMPAN HEAD
EYE PENINSULA
Portnaguran
Bayble

The Minch
Little Minch

RONA
Shieldaig
Diabaig
Torridon
Kinlochewe
Achnasheen
Opinan
Melvaig
Naast
Cove
GREENSTONE POINT
Gairloch
Melon Udrigle
Laide
Poolewe
Aultbea
SUMMER ISLES
PRIEST ISLAND
RUBHA COIGEACH
POINT OF STOER
Lochinver
Stoer
Drumbeg
Achiltibuie
Elphin
Kylesku
Scourie
HANDA
Strath Kanaird
Ullapool
Poolbain
Strath Martin
Inchnadamph
Durness
CAPE WRATH
Kinlochbervie
Rhiconich
Durine
Kyle of Durness
WHITEN HEAD
Hope
Tongue
Melvich
Talmine
Bettyhill
Coldbackie
Kinbrace
Syre
Lairg
Altnaharra
Shinness
Reay
FOREST
REAY

HIGHLAND

Kinloch
Okel Bridge
Achnaclach
Ardgay
Bonar Bridge
Rosehall
Invershin
Lairg
Golspie
Rogart
Dornoch
Embo
Tain
Fearn
Portmahomack
TARBAT NESS
Cromarty
BLACK ISLE
Dingwall
Conon Bridge
Maryburgh
Evanton
Alness
Invergordon
Balintore
Hill of Fearn
Nigg
Culloden
Fortrose
Avoch
Munlochy
Helmsdale
Brora
Loth
Kildonan
STRATH OF KILDONAN
STRATHY POINT
Armadale
Bettyhill
Kirtomy
Skerray
Skelpick
Naver
Halladale
Forsinard

Dalhalvaig
Reay
Scrabster
Thurso
DUNNET HEAD
Castletown
Dunbeath
Latheron
Lybster
Ulbster
Sarclet
Wick
Staxigoe
Keiss
Reiss
NOSS HEAD
Mybster
Watten
Halkirk
Bower
Canisbay
John o'Groats
DUNCANSBY HEAD
STROMA
CASTLE OF MEY
SWONA
Burwick
SOUTH RONALDSAY
St. Margaret's Hope
BURRAY
COPINSAY
AUSKERRY
STRONSAY
SANDAY
Whitehall
NESS OF OR
SHAPINSAY
EGILSAY
Balfour
Pierowall
WESTRAY
PAPA WESTRAY
Rackwick
HOY
Lyness
Hunda
Flotta
Longhope
Stromness
Finstown
KIRKWALL
Orphir
HOLM
Tankerness
ROUSAY
Sourin
EDAY
Backaland
Rapness
Broughton
Northwall
DENNIS HEAD
PAPA WESTRAY
Holland
NORTH RONALDSAY
MULL HEAD

ORKNEY ISLANDS

ORKNEY

PENTLAND FIRTH

Pentland Skerries

ATLANTIC OCEAN

NORTH SEA

STACK SKERRY

SULE SKERRY

Moray Firth

Nairn
Forres
Elgin
Lossiemouth
Hopeman
Burghead
Alves
Dallas
Dyke
Cawdor
Ardclach
Dulsie
Lhanbryde
Fochabers
Garmouth
Spey Bay
Portgordon
Buckie
Findochty
Portknockie
Cullen
Portsoy
Keith
Knock
Cornhill
Banff
Macduff
Gardenstown
Rosehearty
Fraserburgh
KINNAIRD HEAD
Sandhaven
Inverallochy
St. Combs
Rathen
TROUP HEAD
Pennan
New Aberdour
New Pitsligo
Maud
Strichen
Mintlaw
Peterhead
Mormond
Crimond
BUCHAN NESS
Boddam
RATTRAY HEAD

SHETLAND

FAIR ISLE

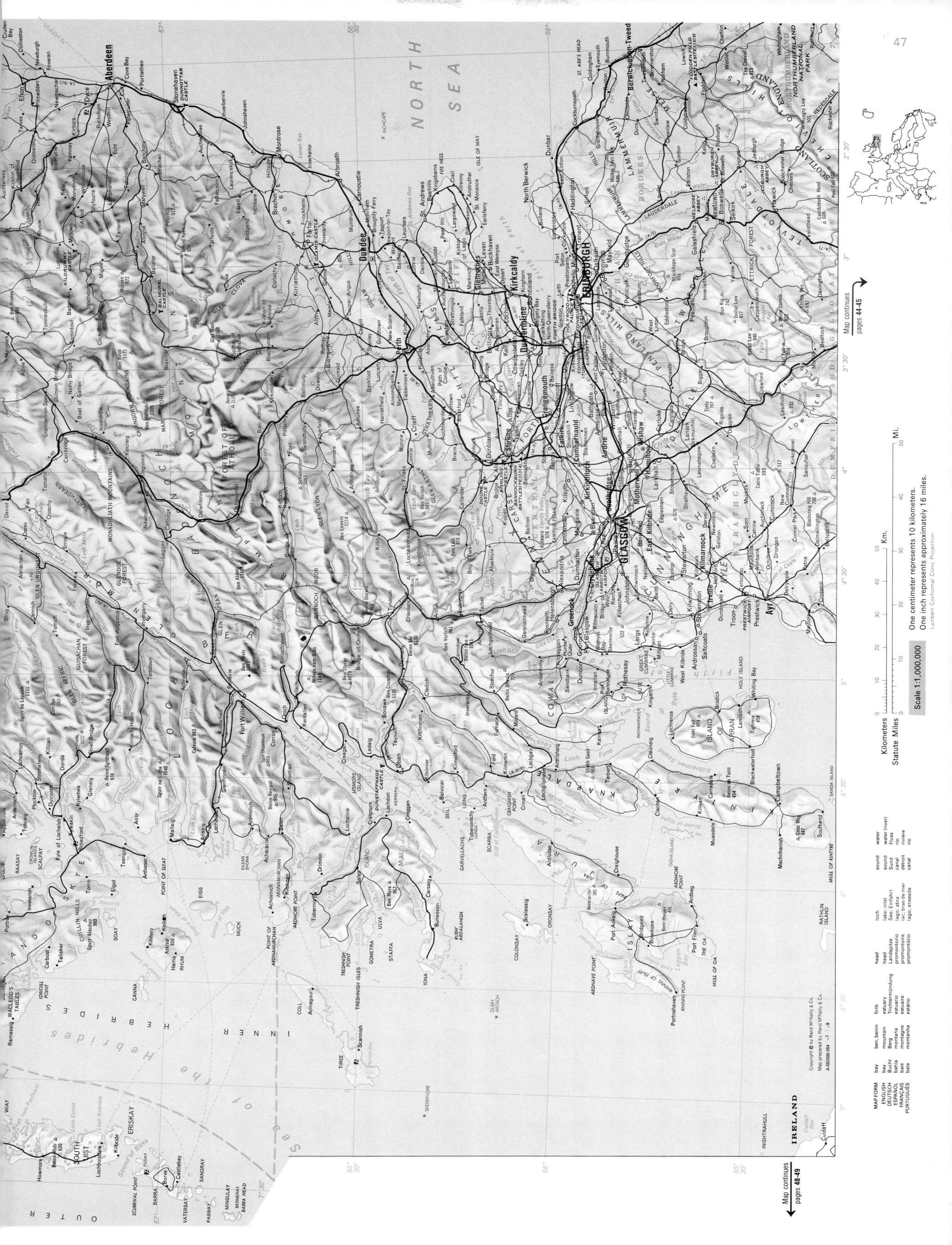

NORTH SEA

IRELAND

Map continues pages 48-49

Map continues pages 44-45

OUTER HEBRIDES

INNER HEBRIDES

GRAMPIAN MOUNTAINS

Aberdeen

Dundee

EDINBURGH

GLASGOW

Ayr

Kilmarnock

Greenock

ISLAND OF ARRAN

MULL OF KINTYRE

ISLAND OF ISLAY

MULL ISLAND

SKYE

CUILLIN HILLS

NORTHUMBERLAND NATIONAL PARK

CHEVIOT HILLS

SOUTHERN UPLANDS

PENTLAND HILLS

LAMMERMUIR HILLS

Scale 1:1,000,000

Kilometers
Statute Miles

Km.
Mi.

One centimeter represents 10 kilometers.
One inch represents approximately 16 miles.
Lambert Conformal Conic Projection

MAPFORM					
ENGLISH	bay	ben, benin	firth	head	loch
DEUTSCH	Bucht	mountain	estuary	head	lake; inlet
		Berg	Trichtermündung	Landspitze	See; Einfahrt
ESPAÑOL	bahía	montaña	estuario	promontorio	lago; abra
FRANÇAIS	baie	montagne	estuaire	promontoire	lac; bras de mer
PORTUGUÊS	baía	montanha	estuário	promontório	lago; enseada

sound	water
sound	water (river)
Sund	Fluss
estuario	canal
détroit	rivière
canal	río

Copyright © by Rand McNally & Co.
Map prepared by Rand McNally & Co.
A-850300-264 -7 -9

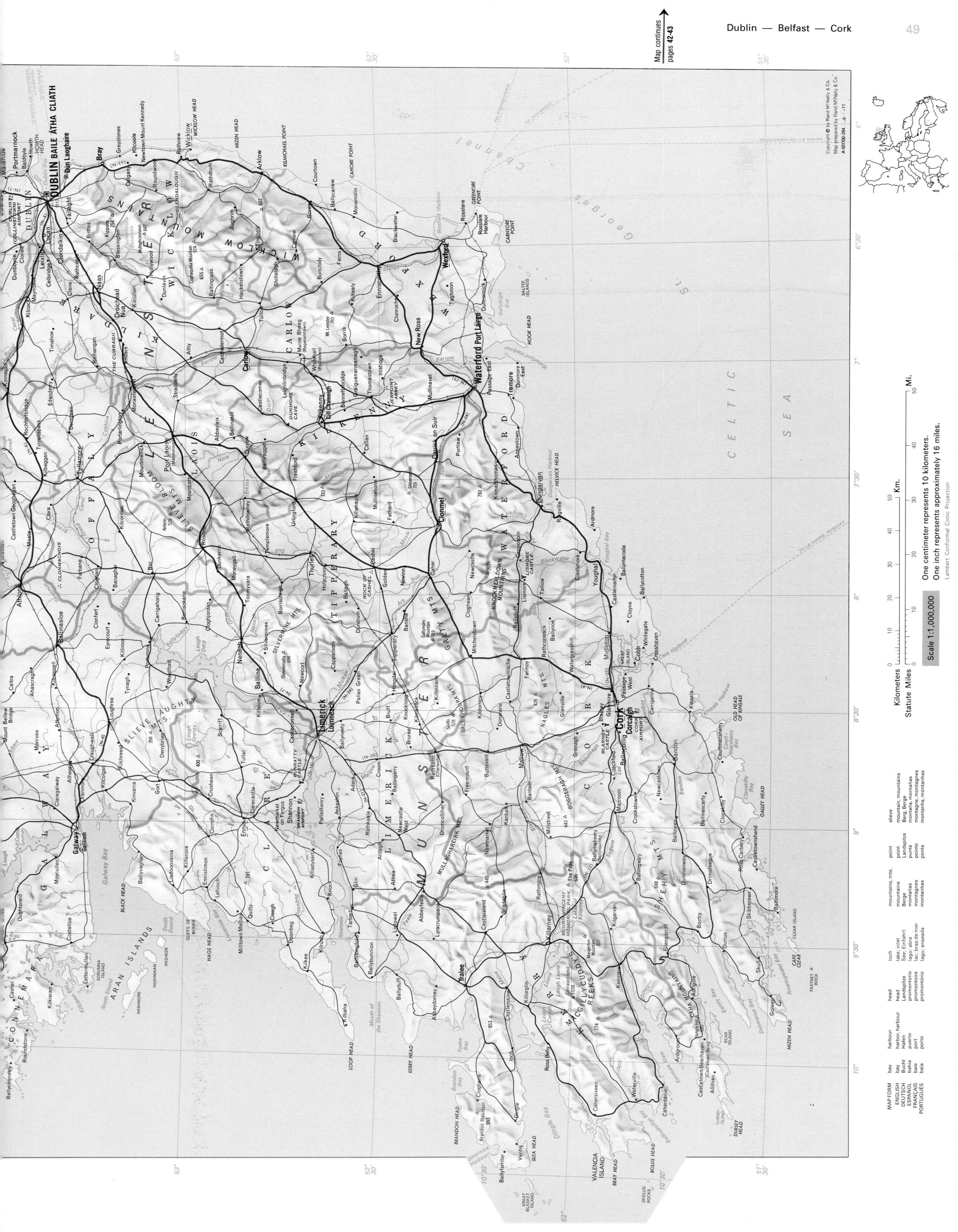

Map continues pages 42-43

Scale 1:1,000,000

Kilometers

Statute Miles

One centimeter represents 10 kilometers.
One inch represents approximately 16 miles.

Lambert Conformal Conic Projection

Km.

Mi.

MAPFORM	bay	harbour	head	loch	mountains, mts.	point	slieve
ENGLISH	bay	harbour, harbour	head	lake; inlet	mountains	point	mountain, mountains
DEUTSCH	Bucht	Hafen	Helm	See; Einfahrt	Berge	Landspitze	Berge
ESPAÑOL	bahía	puerto	Landspitze	lago; abra	montañas	punta	montaña, montañas
FRANÇAIS	baie	port	promontoire	lac; bras de mer	montagnes	pointe	montagne, montagnes
PORTUGUÉS	baía	porto	promontorio	lago; enseada	montanhas	ponta	montanha, montanhas

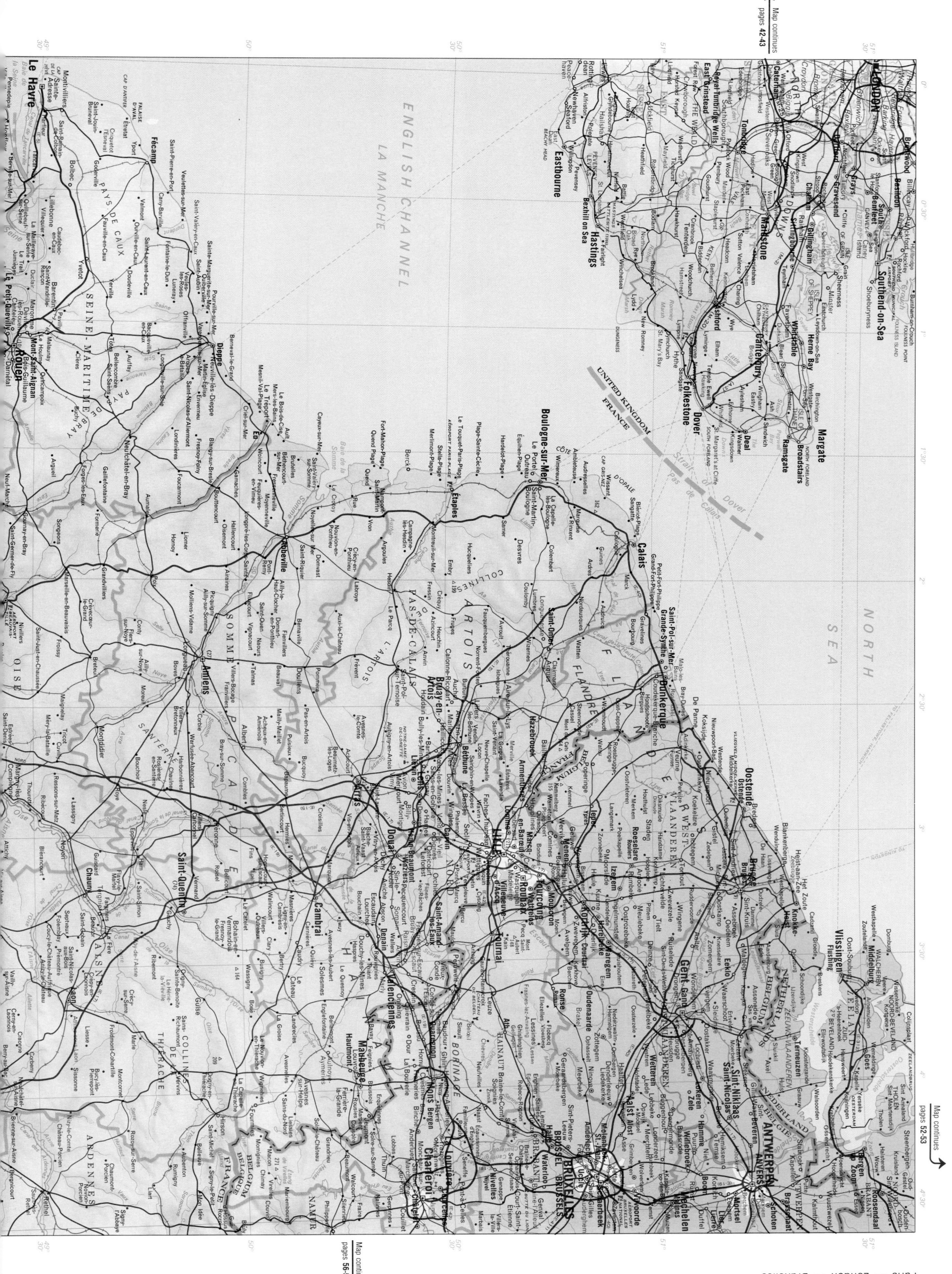

Map continues
pages 42-43

Map continues
pages 52-53

Map continues
pages 56-57

pages 58-59
Map continues

Paris — London — Bruxelles

Scale 1:1,000,000

One centimeter represents approximately 10 kilometers.
One inch represents approximately 16 miles.

Lambert Conformal Conic Projection

Kilometers
0 10 20 30 40 50 Km.

Statute Miles
0 10 20 30 40 50 Mi.

FRANÇAIS	aeroport	canal	cap	chateau	collines	reservoir, rés.
ENGLISH	airport	canal	cape	castle	hills	reservoir
DEUTSCH	Flughafen	Kanal	Kap	Burg	Hügel	Stausee
ESPAÑOL	aeropuerto	canal	cabo	castillo	colinas	embalse
PORTUGUÊS	aeroporto	canal	cabo	castelo	colinas	reservatório

NORMANDIE

CALVADOS

ORNE

EURE

EURE-ET-LOIR

MAINE

SARTHE

ANJOU

TOURAINE

INDRE-ET-LOIRE

LOIR-ET-CHER

SOLOGNE

ORLÉANAIS

LOIRET

BEAUCE

YVELINES

ESSONNE

VAL-D'OISE

ILE-DE-FRANCE

PARIS

SEINE-ET-MARNE

BRIE

BERRY

CHER

NIVERNAIS

BOURGOGNE

YONNE

AUBE

CHAMPAGNE

MARNE

CÔTE-D'OR

MORVAN

Le Mans

Chartres

Orléans

Tours

Vierzon

Dreux

Évreux

Alençon

Versailles

Melun

Fontainebleau

Montargis

Sens

Auxerre

Troyes

Romilly-sur-Seine

Châlons-sur-Marne

Épernay

Reims

Château-Thierry

Meaux

Chinon

Map continues
pages **50-51**

Map continues
pages **56-57**

DEUTSCH	Gebirge	Kanal	Moor	Naturpark	Stausee	Talsperre	Wald
ENGLISH	range	canal	moor	reserve	reservoir	dam	forest, mountains
ESPAÑOL	sierra	canal	paramo	reserva	embalse	presa	bosque, montañas
FRANÇAIS	chaîne	canal	lande	réserve	réservoir	barrage	forêt, montagnes
PORTUGUÊS	serra	canal	pântano	reserva natural	reservatório	represa	floresta, montanhas

Scale 1:1,000,000
One centimeter represents 10 kilometers.
One inch represents approximately 16 miles.
Lambert Conformal Conic Projection

Kilometers 0 10 20 30 40 50 Km.
Statute Miles 0 10 20 30 40 50 Mi.

Map continues pages 54-55

Major cities and regions:

Lübeck · HAMBURG · Cuxhaven · Bremerhaven · Wilhelmshaven · Emden · Norden · Aurich · Oldenburg · Bremen · Delmenhorst · Wittmund · Varel · Brake · Leer · Meppen · Cloppenburg · Vechta · Lüneburg · Uelzen · Celle · Burgdorf · Hannover · Braunschweig · Peine · Hildesheim · Salzgitter · Goslar · Osterode · Clausthal-Zellerfeld · Einbeck · Holzminden · Göttingen · Münden · Kassel · Mühlhausen · Bad Pyrmont · Hameln · Herford · Bielefeld · Detmold · Lemgo · Höxter · Paderborn · Gütersloh · Rietberg · Beckum · Hamm · Lippstadt · Soest · Arnsberg · Iserlohn · Hagen · Wuppertal · Solingen · Remscheid · Lüdenscheid · Bochum · Dortmund · Gelsenkirchen · Herne · Castrop-Rauxel · Recklinghausen · Marl · Münster · Osnabrück · Ibbenbüren · Rheine · Lengerich · Meppen · Haren

Regions: OSTFRIESLAND · HARLINGER LAND · JEVERLAND · OLDENBURG · WESER-EMS · OSTFRIESISCHE INSELN · LÜNEBURGER HEIDE · HANNOVER · BRAUNSCHWEIG · HARZ · SOLLING · TEUTOBURGER WALD · WIEHENGEBIRGE · WESERGEBIRGE · DEISTER · SÜNTEL · MÜNSTERLAND · NIEDERSACHSEN · NORDRHEIN-WESTFALEN · SCHLESWIG-HOLSTEIN · DITHMARSCHEN · ALTES LAND · LAND KEHDINGEN · LAND WURSTEN · HESSEN · THÜRINGEN · EICHSFELD · ROTHAARGEBIRGE · SAUERLAND · HELLWEG · HAARSTRANG

BALTIC SEA
Pomeranian Bay
Mecklenburger Bucht
RÜGEN
Stralsund
Greifswald
Rostock
Wismar
Lübeck
Kiel
HAMBURG
Schwerin
Güstrow
Neubrandenburg
Neustrelitz
Prenzlau
Szczecin (Stettin)
Świnoujście
Goleniów
Police
Stargard Szczeciński
BERLIN
Potsdam
Brandenburg
Frankfurt an der Oder
Eberswalde
Oranienburg
Lüneburg
Uelzen
Salzwedel
Stendal
Wittenberge
Wolfsburg
Gifhorn
Neuruppin
Rathenow
Parchim
Anklam
Demmin
Waren
MECKLENBURG
VORPOMMERN
UCKERMARK
PRIGNITZ
ALTMARK
WENDLAND
HAVELLAND
BARNIM
POMERANIA
POLAND
GERMANY
POLSKA
DEUTSCHLAND
SACHSEN-ANHALT
NIEDERSACHSEN
MECKLENBURG-VORPOMMERN
BRANDENBURG

Map continues page 41

Map continues pages 52-53

Map continues
page 60

Map continues
pages 56-57

Kilometers
Statute Miles

Km.
Mi.

Scale 1:1,000,000

One centimeter represents 10 kilometers.
One inch represents approximately 16 miles.
Lambert Conformal Conic Projection

DEUTSCH	Berg, Bg	Bodden	Bucht	Gebirge	Heide	Kanal	See	Talsperre
ENGLISH	mountain	bay	bay	range	heath	canal	dam	presa
ESPAÑOL	montaña	bahía	bahía	sierra	matorral	canal	lago	barrage
FRANÇAIS	montagne	baie	baie	chaîne	lande	canal	lac	represa
PORTUGUÉS	montaña	baía	baía	serra	charneca	canal	lago	

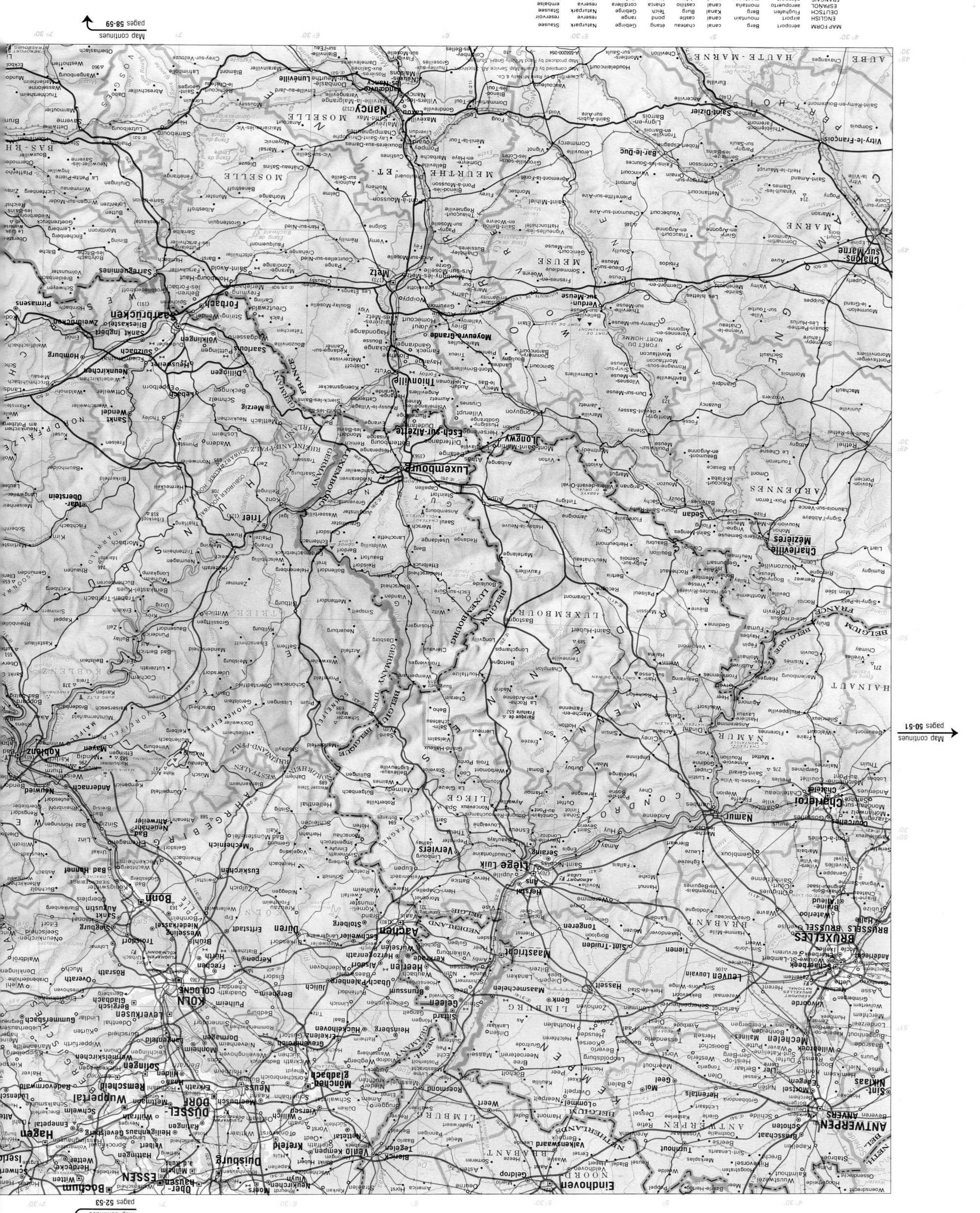

Map continues pages 50-51

Map continues pages 52-53

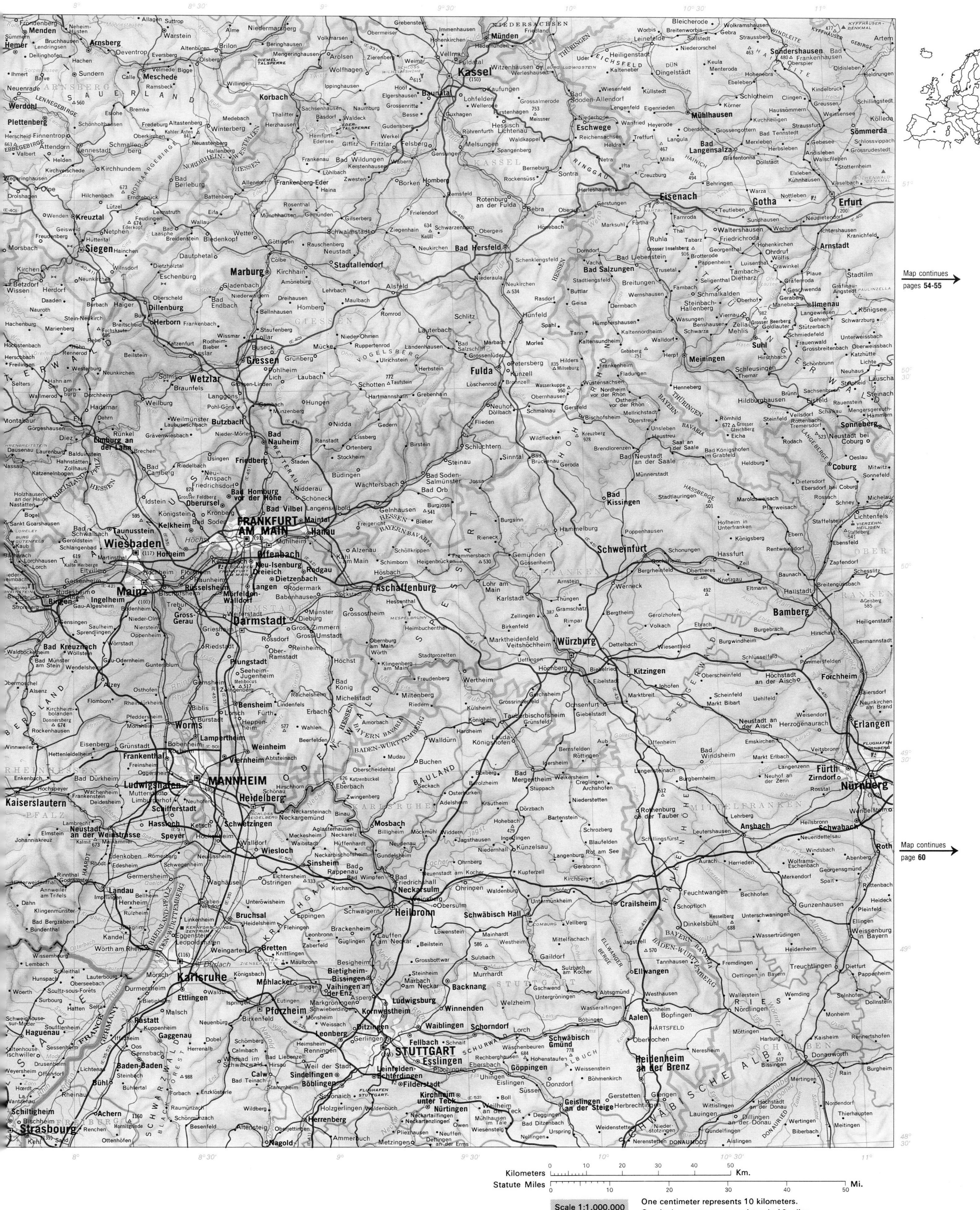

Kilometers 0 10 20 30 40 50 Km.
Statute Miles 0 10 20 30 40 50 Mi.

Scale 1:1,000,000

One centimeter represents 10 kilometers.
One inch represents approximately 16 miles.

Lambert Conformal Conic Projection

Map continues pages 54-55

Map continues page 60

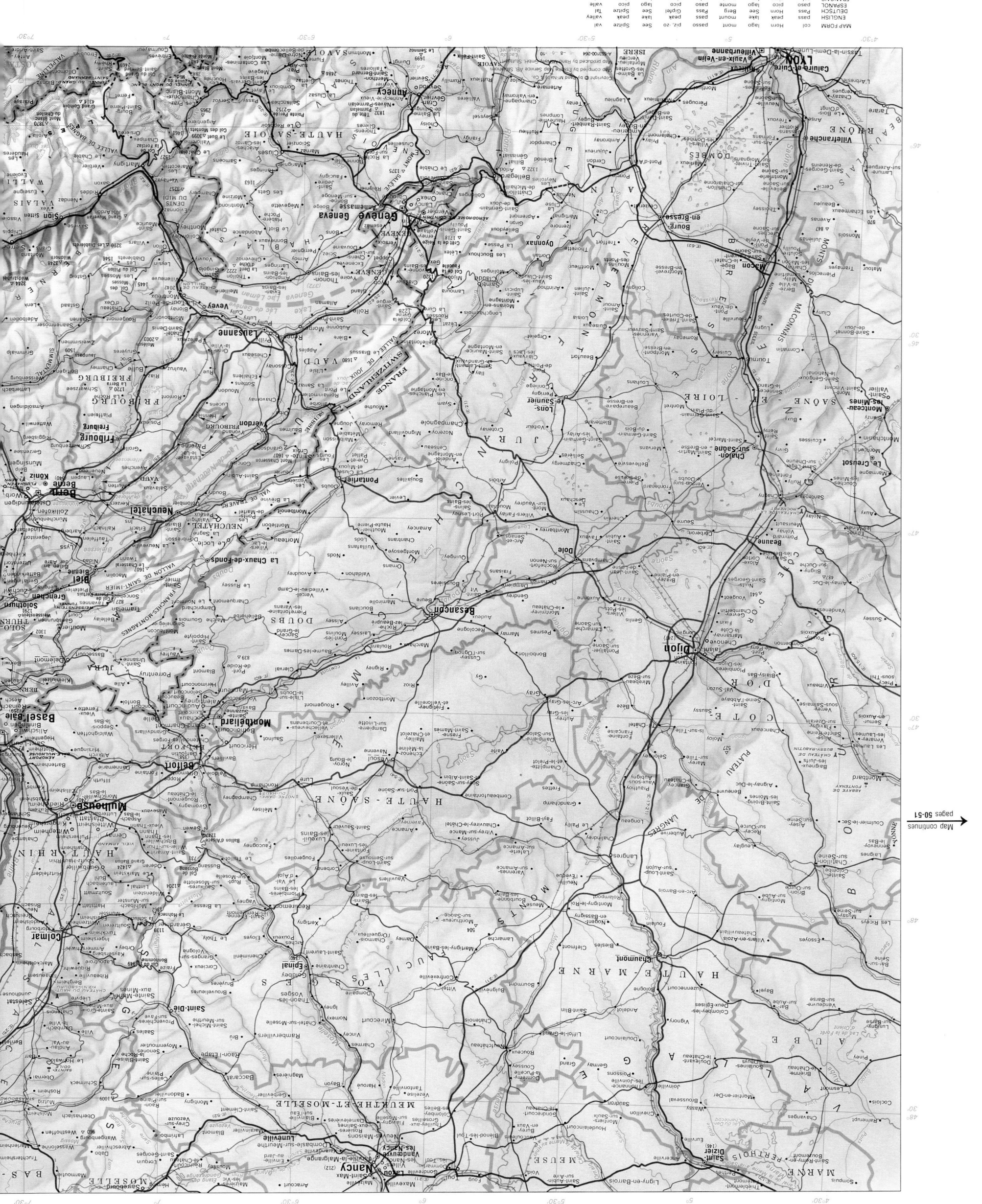

Map continues pages 50-51

MAP FORM							
ENGLISH	col	Horn	pass	peak	See	lake	passo
DEUTSCH	Pass	Horn	Pass	peak	See	Berg	passo
	col			Spitze	Tal		
FRANCAIS	col	cime	mont	passo	lac	lago	pico
ESPAÑOL	col	cime	monte	paso	lago	pico	passo
PORTUGUÊS	col	cime	monte	passo	lago	pico	passo

Map continues
pages 56-57

Map continues
page 60

Map continues
pages 64-65

Map continues
pages 62-63

Kilometers   0 10 20 30 40 50 Km.
Statute Miles   0 10 20 30 40 50 Mi.

Scale 1:1,000,000
One centimeter represents 10 kilometers.
One inch represents approximately 16 miles.
Lambert Conformal Conic Projection

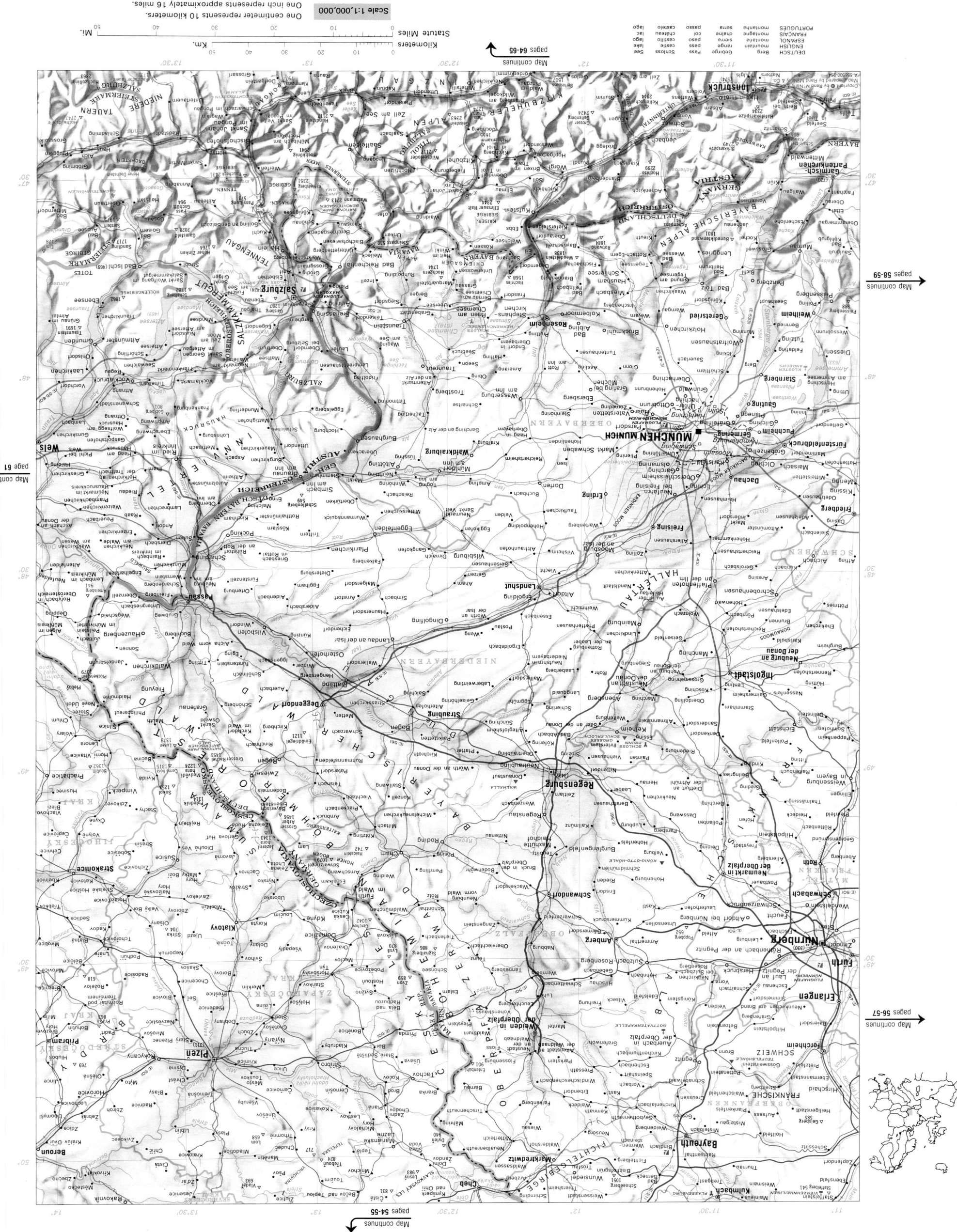

Map continues pages 64-65

Map continues pages 58-59

Map continues page 61

Map continues pages 56-57

Map continues pages 54-55

Scale 1:1,000,000
One centimeter represents 10 kilometers.
One inch represents approximately 16 miles.
Modified Polyconic Projection

DEUTSCH	ENGLISH	ESPAÑOL	FRANÇAIS	PORTUGUÊS
Berg	mountain	montaña	montagne	montanha
Gebirge	mountain range	sierra	chaîne	serra
Pass	pass	paso	col	passo
Schloss	castle	castillo	château	castelo
See	lake	lago	lac	lago

Map continues page 60

Map continues pages 64-65

DEUTSCH	Alpe, -n	Berg	Gebirge	Sattel	Schloss	Wald
ENGLISH	mountains	mountain	range	saddle	castle	forest; mountains
ESPAÑOL	montañas	montaña	sierra	paso	castillo	bosque; montañas
FRANÇAIS	montagnes	montagne	montagne	col	château	forêt; montagnes
PORTUGUÊS	montanhas	montanha	serra	passo	castelo	Floresta; montanhas

Kilometers

Statute Miles

Scale 1:1,000,000

One centimeter represents 10 kilometers.
One inch represents approximately 16 miles.

Lambert Conformal Conic Projection

Copyright © 1980, 1987 by Rand McNally & Co.
Map prepared by Rand McNally & Co.
A-556700-364

MAP FORM	ENGLISH	DEUTSCH	FRANCAIS	ESPAÑOL	PORTUGUES
abbaye	abbey	Abtei	abbaye	abadia	abadia
capo	cape	Kap	cap	cabo	cabo
île (-l)	island	Insel	île	isla	ilha
lac, l.	lake	See	lac	lago	lago
monte	mountain	Berg	montagne	montanha	montanha
pic	peak	Gipfel	cime	pico	pico
passo	pass	Pass	col	paso	passo
val (-le)	valley	Tal	vallée	valle	vale

Map continues
pages 58-59

Map continues
pages 64-65

Kilometers

Statute Miles

Scale 1:1,000,000   One centimeter represents 10 kilometers.
One inch represents approximately 16 miles.
Lambert Conformal Conic Projection

Map continues pages 58-59

Map continues page 60

Map continues page 61

München — Venezia — Firenze

SWITZERLAND
ITALY
AUSTRIA
ÖSTERREICH
DEUTSCHLAND
SLOVENIA
ITALIA

MÜNCHEN
MUNICH

Kempten
Leutkirch
Memmingen
Weingarten
Bregenz
Dornbirn
Sonthofen
Landsberg am Lech
Fürstenfeldbruck
Starnberg
Weilheim
Garmisch-Partenkirchen
Innsbruck
Rosenheim
Bad Reichenhall
Salzburg
Trento
Trento
Bolzano
Merano
Bozen
Belluno
Vittorio Veneto
Udine
Lienz
Villach
Spittal

ALPS
ALPI
DOLOMITI
DOLOMITEN
ADAMELLO
BERNINA
ORTLES
ÖTZTALER ALPEN
ZILLERTALER ALPEN
TUXER ALPEN
STUBAIER ALPEN
HOHE TAUERN
KITZBÜHELER ALPEN
CHIEMGAUER ALPEN
ALLGÄUER ALPEN
LECHTALER ALPEN
KARWENDEL
AMMER GEBIRGE
BAYERISCHE VORALPEN
CARNICHE
JULIAN ALPS
DOLOMITI BELLUNESI
TRENTINO ALTO ADIGE
VENETO
FRIULI
VORARLBERG
TIROL
OSTTIROL
SALZBURG
OBERBAYERN
NIEDERE TAUERN
RADSTÄDTER TAUERN
GURKTALER ALPEN
KÄRNTEN
STEIERMARK
SALZKAMMERGUT
TOTES GEBIRGE

Map continues
pages 66-67

Map continues
pages 62-63

Scale 1:1,000,000

One centimeter represents 10 kilometers.
One inch represents approximately 16 miles.
Lambert Conformal Conic Projection

Kilometers
Statute Miles

MAP FORM						
ENGLISH	mountains	range	mountain	peak	castle	lake
DEUTSCH	Alpen	Gebirge	Berg	Spitze	Schloss	See
ESPAÑOL	montañas	sierra	monte	pico	castillo	lago
FRANCAIS	montagnes	chaîne	montagne	pic	château	lac
PORTUGUÊS	montanhas	serra	montanha	pico	castelo	lago

Berg	cima	monte	piz	See
mountain	peak	mountain	peak	lake
montaña	pico	montaña	pico	lago
montagne	cime	montagne	cime	lac
montanha	cime	montanha	pico	lago

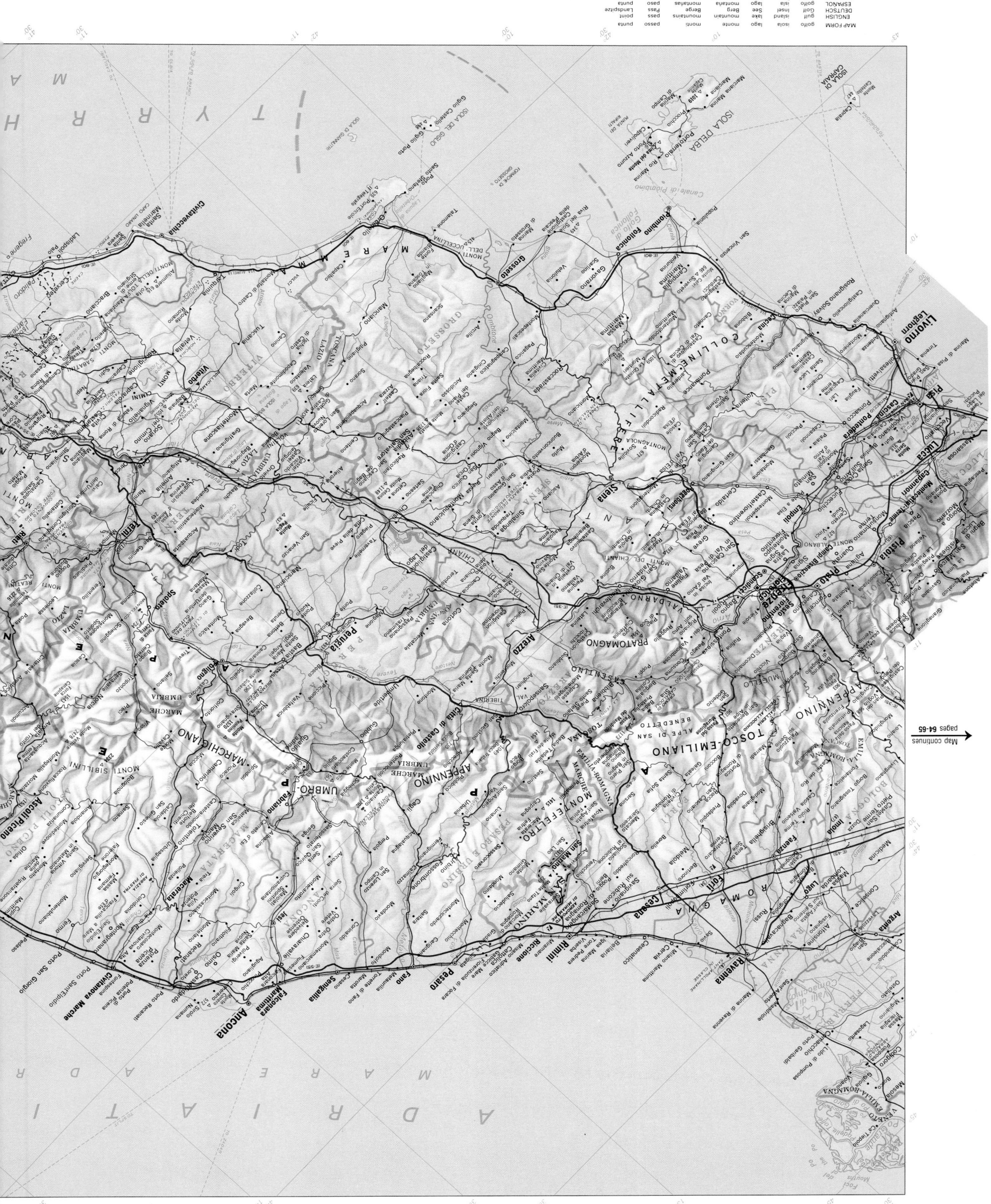

Map continues pages 64-65

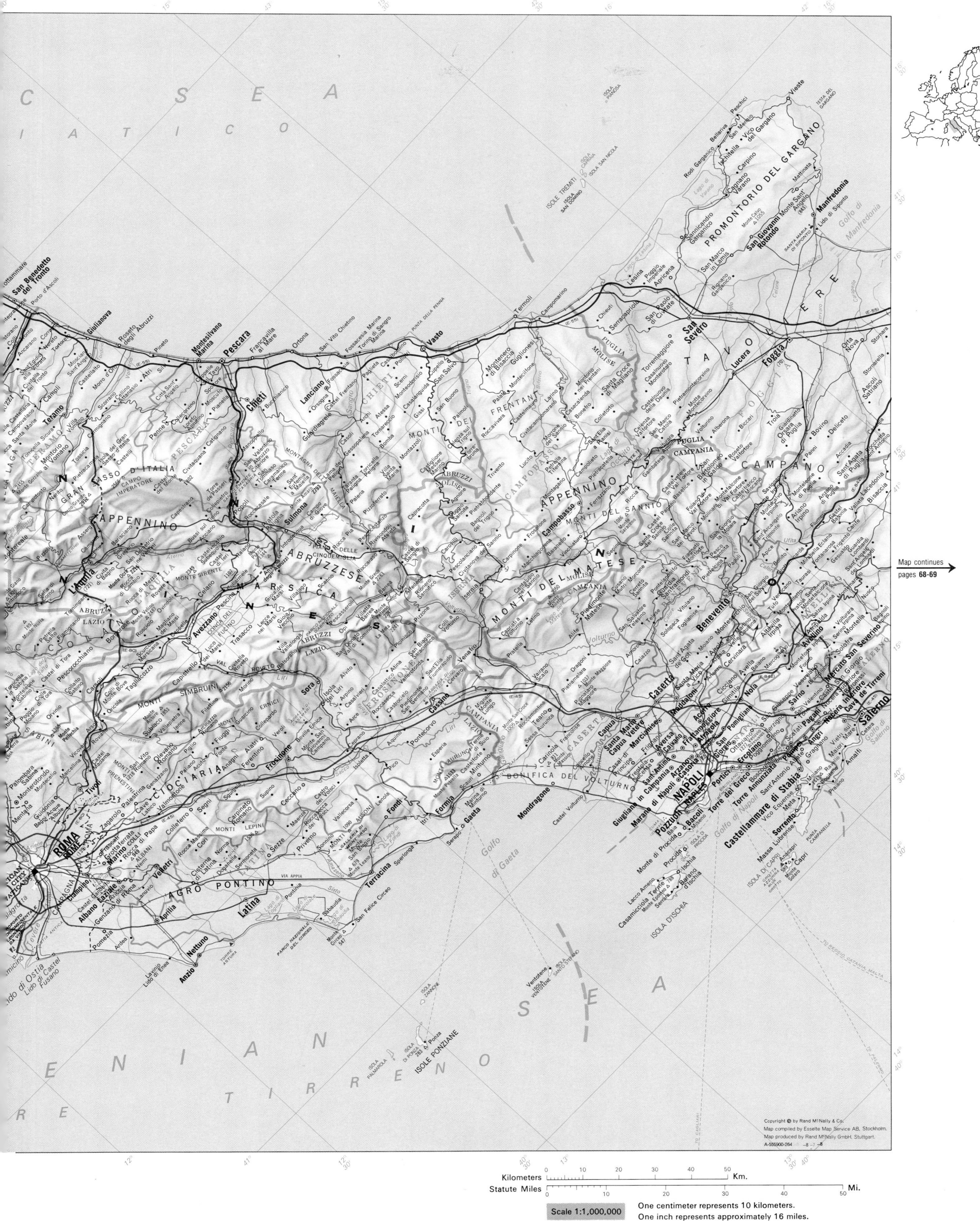

Map continues
pages 68-69 →

Kilometers ⊢⊢⊢⊢⊢⊢⊢⊢⊢⊢⊢⊢⊢⊢⊢⊢⊢⊢⊢⊢ Km.
0 10   20   30   40   50

Statute Miles ⊢⊢⊢⊢⊢⊢⊢⊢⊢⊢⊢⊢⊢⊢⊢⊢⊢ Mi.
0   10   20   30   40   50

Scale 1:1,000,000   One centimeter represents 10 kilometers.
One inch represents approximately 16 miles.
Lambert Conformal Conic Projection

Map continues pages 66–67

MAP FORM	ENGLISH	DEUTSCH	ESPAÑOL	FRANÇAIS	PORTUGUÊS
capo	cape	Kap	cabo	cap	cabo
monti	mountains	Berge	montañas	montagnes	montanhas
monte	mountain	Berg	montaña	montagne	montanha
lago	lake	See	lago	lac	lago
isola	island	Insel	isla	île	ilha
golfo	gulf	Golf	golfo	golfe	golfo
capo	cape	Kap	cabo	cap	cabo
punta	point	Landspitze	punta	pointe	ponta

TYRRHENIAN SEA

MARE ADRIATICO

ADRIATIC SEA

CROATIA · ITALY

NAPOLI
Bari
Taranto
Brindisi
Caserta
Benevento
Foggia
San Severo
Salerno
Matera
Potenza
Castellammare di Stabia
Sorrento
Barletta
Trani
Bisceglie
Molfetta
Monopoli
Gravina in Puglia
Altamura
Corato
Andria
Canosa di Puglia
Cerignola
Lucera
Manfredonia
PROMONTORIO DEL GARGANO
Golfo di Manfredonia
PIANA DEL SELE
VALLO DI DIANO
APPENNINO LUCANO
CAMPANIA
BASILICATA
PUGLIA
BARI
TARANTO
BRINDISI
ISOLA DI CAPRI
ISOLE TREMITI
Golfo di Gaeta
Golfo di Taranto

Strait of Otranto

Lecce

SALENTINE

PENISOLA SALENTINA

Golfo di Taranto

MARE TIRRENO

IONIAN SEA
MARE IONIO

Crotone

CAPO COLONNA

Catanzaro

Golfo di Squillace

Golfo di Sant'Eufemia

Golfo di Gioia

CALABRIA
SICILIA

Reggio di Calabria

SICILIA
SICILY

Messina

Map continues
page 70

Kilometers 0 10 20 30 40 50 Km.

Statute Miles 0 10 20 30 40 50 Mi.

Scale 1:1,000,000

One centimeter represents 10 kilometers.
One inch represents approximately 16 miles.

Lambert Conformal Conic Projection

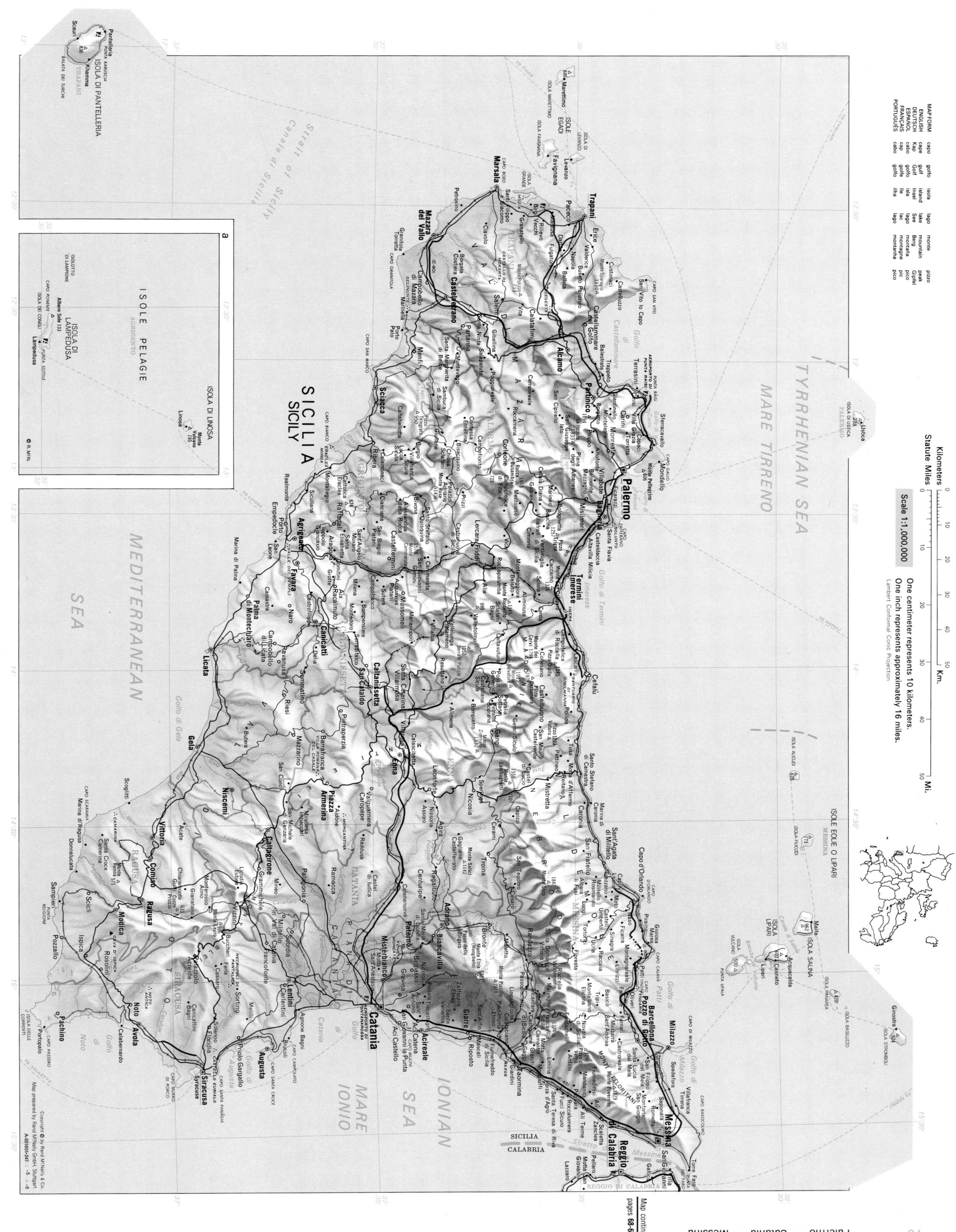

Map continues pages 68-69

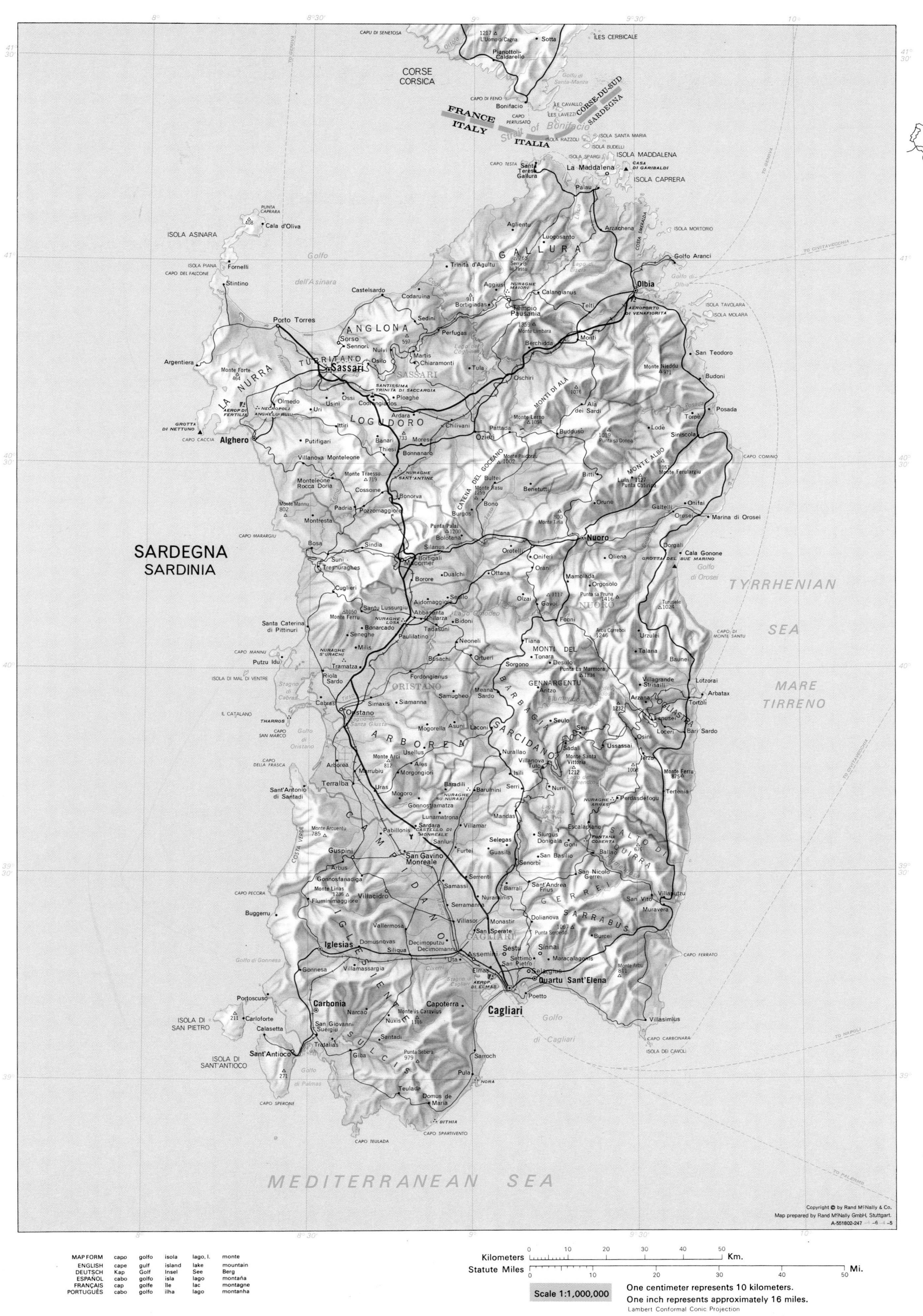

SARDEGNA
SARDINIA

CORSE
CORSICA

FRANCE
ITALY
ITALIA

MEDITERRANEAN SEA

TYRRHENIAN SEA

MARE TIRRENO

MAP FORM	capo	golfo	isola	lago, l.	monte
ENGLISH	cape	gulf	island	lake	mountain
DEUTSCH	Kap	Golf	Insel	See	Berg
ESPAÑOL	cabo	golfo	isla	lago	montaña
FRANÇAIS	cap	golfe	île	lac	montagne
PORTUGUÊS	cabo	golfo	ilha	lago	montanha

Kilometers
Statute Miles
0 10 20 30 40 50 Km.
0 10 20 30 40 50 Mi.

Scale 1:1,000,000

One centimeter represents 10 kilometers.
One inch represents approximately 16 miles.
Lambert Conformal Conic Projection

Copyright © by Rand McNally & Co.
Map prepared by Rand McNally GmbH, Stuttgart.
A-551802-247

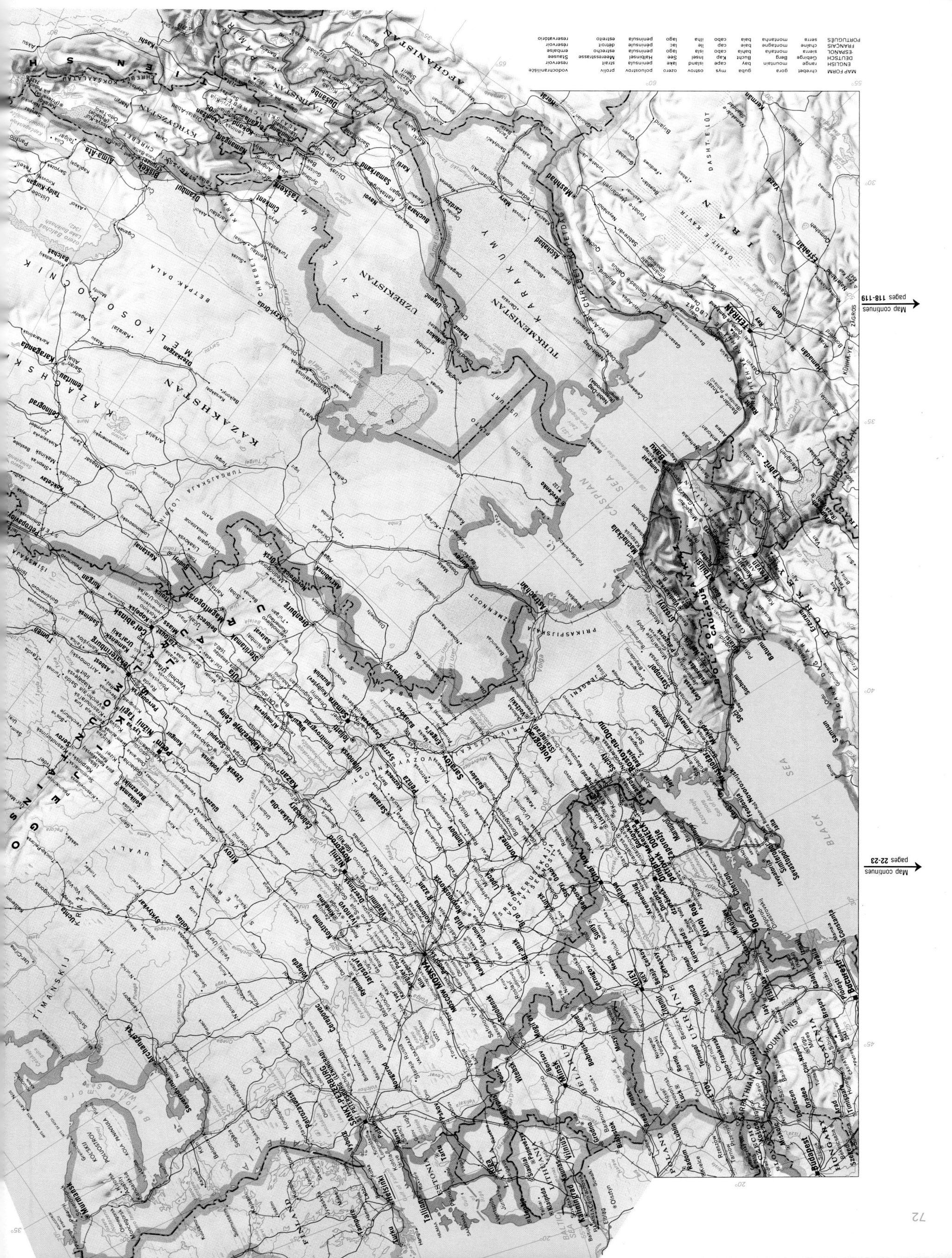

Map continues pages 118-119

Map continues pages 22-23

ENGLISH	DEUTSCH	ESPAÑOL	FRANÇAIS	PORTUGUÊS
range	Gebirge	sierra	chaîne	serra
mountain	Berg	sierra	montagne	montanha
bay	Bucht	bahia	baie	baía
cape	Kap	cabo	cap	cabo
île	lac	lago	lago	
island	Insel	isla	île	ilha
peninsula	Halbinsel	peninsula	péninsule	peninsula
lake	See	lago	lac	lago
strait	Meeresstrasse	estrecho	détroit	estreito
reservoir	Stausee	embalse	réservoir	reservatório

chrebet / gora / Gebirge / range
Bucht / guba / bay
mys / Kap / cape
ostrov / Insel / island
poluostrov / Halbinsel / peninsula
ozero / See / lake
proliv / strait
vodochranilišče / reservoir

72

Map continues
pages 74-75

Map continues
pages 90-91

Kilometers

Statute Miles

Scale 1:12,000,000

One centimeter represents 120 kilometers.
One inch represents approximately 190 miles.

Lambert Conformal Conic Projection

Copyright © by Rand McNally & Co.
Map prepared by Esselte Map Service AB, Stockholm.
A-579594-264   -9   -13 -20

Map continues
pages 72-73

Map continues
pages 90-91

MAP FORM	chrebet	gora	guba	mys	ostrov	ozero	poluostrov	proliv	vodochranilišče
ENGLISH	range	mountain	bay	cape	island	lake	peninsula	strait	reservoir
DEUTSCH	Gebirge	Berg	Bucht	Kap	Insel	See	Halbinsel	Meerestrasse	Stausee
ESPAÑOL	sierra	montaña	bahía	cabo	isla	lago	península	estrecho	embalse
FRANÇAIS	chaîne	montagne	baie	cap	île	lac	péninsule	détroit	réservoir
PORTUGUÊS	serra	montanha	baía	cabo	ilha	lago	península	estreito	reservatório

Copyright © by Rand McNally & Co.
Map prepared by Esselte Map Service AB, Stockholm
A-579395-264 -6'- -10

Kilometers 0 200 400 600 Km.
Statute Miles 0 200 400 600 Mi.

Scale 1:12,000,000
One centimeter represents 120 kilometers.
One inch represents approximately 190 miles.
Lambert Conformal Conic Projection

ALASKA
UNITED STATES

OSTROVA

VOSTOČNO-SIBIRSKOJE MORE
EAST SIBERIAN SEA

NOVOSIBIRSKIJE

OSTROVA ANŽL

OSTROV KOTEL'NYJ

SIBERIA

CHREBET

CHREBET ČERSKOGO

VERCHOJANSKIJ CHREBET

KOLYMSKAJA NIZMENNOST'

JUKAGIRSKOJE PLOSKOGORJE

MOMSKIJ CHREBET

EKIATAPSKIJ CHREBET

AN'UJSKIJ CHREBET

Chukchi Sea

Bering Sea

KORÄKSKOJE NAGORJE

ANADYRSKOJE PLOSKOGORJE

PENŽINSKIJ CHREBET

Jakutsk

Magadan

SEA OF OKHOTSK
OCHOTSKOJE MORE

POLUOSTROV KAMČATKA
KAMCHATKA

SREDINNYJ CHREBET

Petropavlovsk-Kamčatskij

KOMANDORSKIJE OSTROVA

ALDANSKOJE NAGORJE

CHREBET DŽUGDŽUR

STANOVOJ CHREBET

Komsomol'sk-na-Amure

Svobodnyj

Blagoveščensk

Chabarovsk

OSTROV SACHALIN
SAKHALIN

Južno-Sachalinsk

KURIL'SKIJE OSTROVA
KURIL ISLANDS

Habomai, Shikotan, Kunashir,
and Etorofu, occupied since
1945, are claimed by Japan
pending a final peace treaty

NEI MONGGOL ZIZHIQU
INNER MONGOLIA

DA HINGGAN LING

MANCHURIA

HEILONGJIANG

Qiqihar Tsitsihar

Harbin

Mudanjiang

Ussurijsk

Vladivostok

JILIN

Asahikawa

Kushiro

HOKKAIDO

Otaru
Sapporo

Muroran
Hakodate

Aomori
Hirosaki
Akita

JAPAN

HONSHU

SEA OF JAPAN

PACIFIC OCEAN

Baltic and Moscow Regions / Baltenland und Mittelrussland / Regiones de Báltico y de Moscú
Républiques Baltes et la Région de Moscou

76

Map continues pages 26-27
Map continues pages 30-31
MAP FORM	gr'ada	ostrov, o.	ozero, o.	vodochranilišče, vdchr.	vozvyšennost', vozv.	zaliv	zapovednik, zapov.
ENGLISH	ridge	island	lake	reservoir	upland	gulf; bay	reserve
DEUTSCH	Höhenrücken	Insel	See	Stausee	Bergland	Golf; Bucht	Reservat
ESPAÑOL	lomerío	isla	lago	embalse	tierras altas	golfo; bahía	reserva
FRANÇAIS	crête	île	lac	réservoir	hautes terres	golfe; baie	réserve
PORTUGUÊS	cordilheira	ilha	lago	reservatório	terras altas	golfo; baía	reserva

Baltic and Moscow Regions / Baltenland und Mittelrussland / Regiones de Báltico y de Moscú
Républiques Baltes et la Région de Moscou / Regiões do Báltico e de Moscou

77

Map continues
pages 24-25

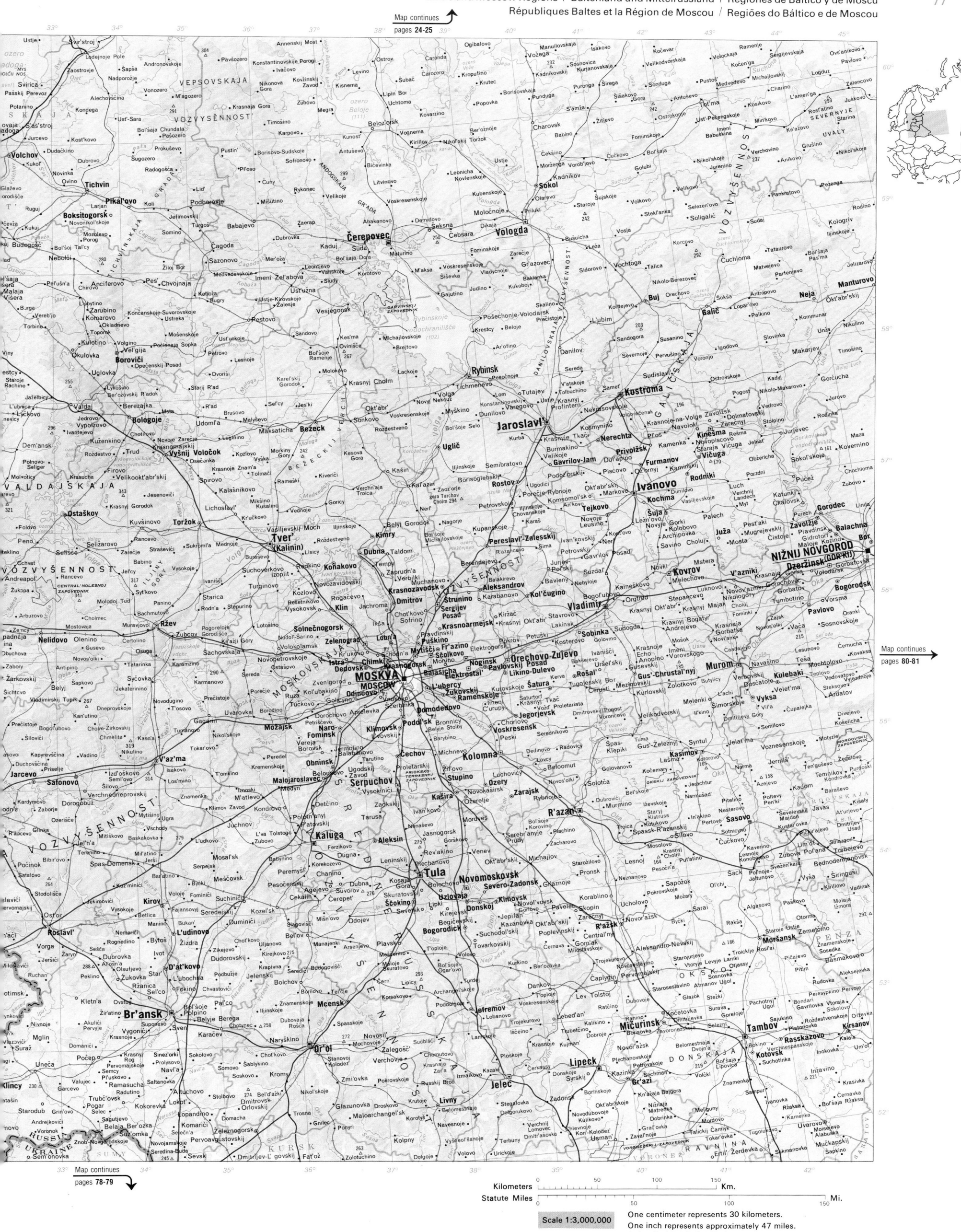

Map continues
pages 80-81

Map continues
pages 78-79

Kilometers

Statute Miles

Scale 1:3,000,000

One centimeter represents 30 kilometers.
One inch represents approximately 47 miles.

Lambert Conformal Conic Projection

Map continues pages 38-39

Map continues pages 30-31

	ENGLISH	DEUTSCH	FRANÇAIS	ESPAÑOL	PORTUGUÊS
liman	bay	Bay	baie	bahia	baía
gora	cape	Kap	cap	cabo	cabo
	upland	Bergland	hautes terres	terras altas	
	plain	Ebene	plaine	llano	planicie
	lake	See	lac	lago	lago
mys	cape	Kap	cap	cabo	cabo
	bay	Bucht	baie	bahia	baía
	mountain	Berg	montagne	montaña	montanha

MAP FORM
zaliv, ozero, 24, nizmennost', vozvyšennost', mys

Map continues pages 76-77

Map continues pages 80-81

Map continues page 84

BR'ANSK

RUSSIA / UKRAINE

Major places:

Černigov · Nežin · Konotop · Gluchov · Kursk · Voronez · Staryj Oskol · Gubkin · Belgorod · Sumy · Romny · Priluki · Lubny · Mirgorod · Achtyrka · CHAR'KOV KHARKOV · Čuguev · Kup'ansk · Svatovo · Poltava · Kremenčug · Čerkassy · Kirovograd · Krivoj Rog · DNEPROPETROVSK · Dneprodzeržinsk · Novomoskovsk · Pavlograd · Kramatorsk · Stachanov · Gorlovka · Lugansk · Kommunarsk · Makejevka · DONECK · Krasnyj Luč · Šachty · Novočerkassk · Rostov-na-Donu · Zaporožje · Nikopol' · Ordžonikidze · Marganec · Melitopol · Nikolajev · Cherson · Berd'ansk · Mariupol' · Taganrog · Azov · Batajsk · Krasnodar · Majkop · Novorossijsk · Tuapse · Soči

Sevastopol' · Simferopol' · Jalta Yalta · Jevpatorija · Saki · Bachčisaraj · Alušta · Gurzuf · Feodosija · Sudak · Kerč' · Temr'uk · Anapa

KRYMSKIJ POLUOSTROV-CRIMEA · KRYMSKAJA A.S.S.R.

Azovskoje more
Sea of Azov

BLACK SEA
ČORNOJE MORE

Scale:

Kilometers 0 50 100 150 Km.
Statute Miles 0 50 100 150 Mi.

Scale 1:3,000,000
One centimeter represents 30 kilometers.
One inch represents approximately 47 miles.
Lambert Conformal Conic Projection

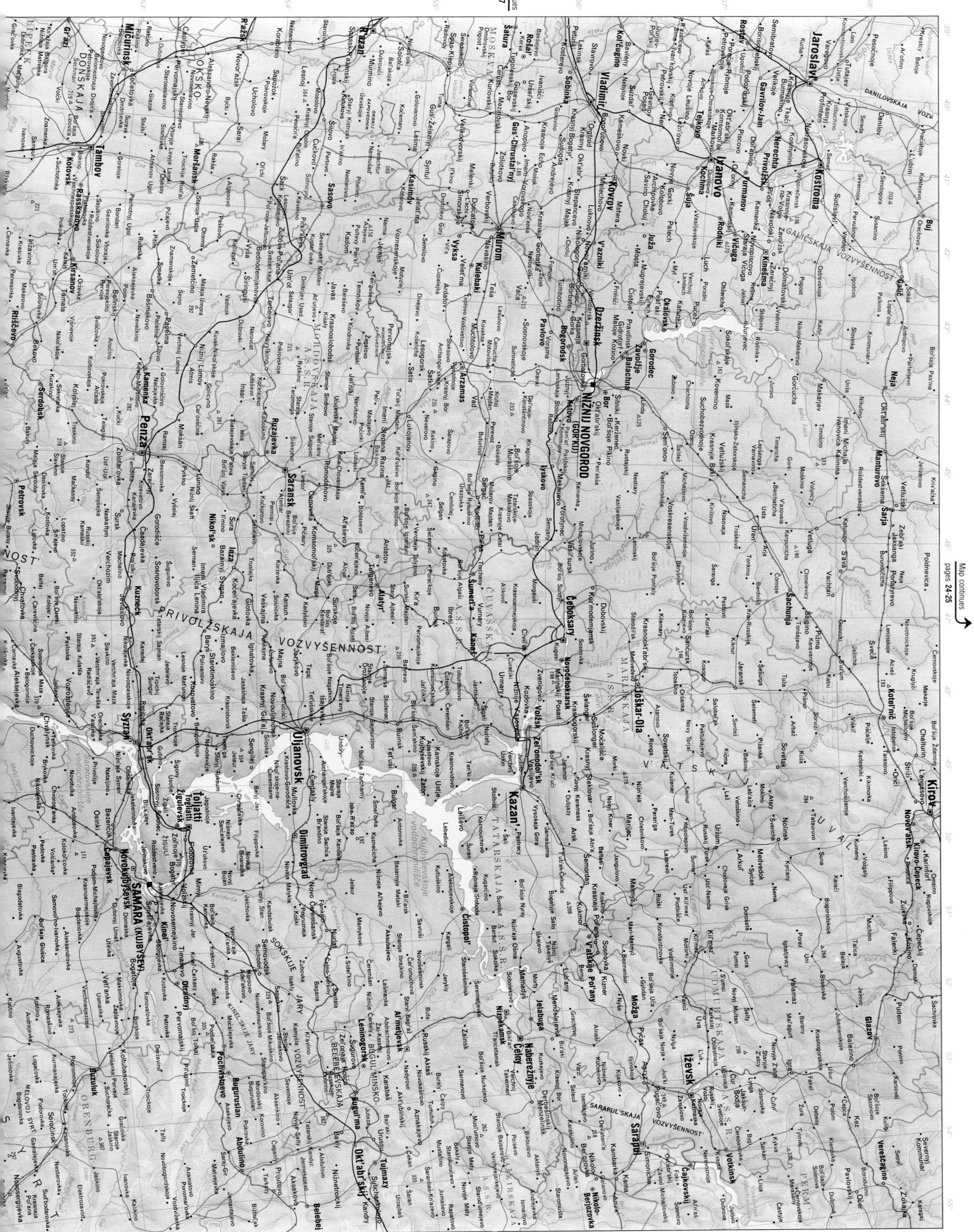

Map continues
pages 24-25

Map continues pages 86-87

Map continues pages 78-79

Map continues page 84

CASPIAN SEA
KASPIJSKOJE MORE

NIZMENNOST

PRIKASPIJSKAJA

RYN-PESKI

PESKI KOSDAULET

RYN-PESKI

MENTEKE

KAZAKHSTAN
RUSSIA ROSSIJA

K A L M Y C K A J A   A.S.S.R.

S A R P I N S K A J A

S A R S K O - M A N Y Č S K A J A

D O N

V O Z V Y Š E N N O S T'

E R G E N I

STAVROPOL

VOLGOGRAD (STALINGRAD)

Astrachan'

Saratov

Engel's

Marks

Kamyšin

Volžskij

Ačtubinsk

Ėlista

Gur'jev

Ural'sk

Jeršov

Atkarsk

Balašov

Novoanninskij

Ur'upinsk

Povorino

Borisoglebsk

Kotovo

Frolovo

Michajlovka

Morozovsk

Kalač-na-Donu

Belaja Kalitva

Volgodonsk

Sal'sk

Kotel'nikovo

Petrov Val

Serafimovič

Kalač

POLUOSTROV PEŠNOJ

OSTROVA DURNEVA

OSTROV ZJUDEV

ASTRACHANSKIJ ZAPOVEDNIK

Copyright © by Rand McNally & Co.
Map compiled by Cartographia, Budapest.
Map produced by Rand McNally & Co.
A-572000-764   -6 4 ⅄12

Scale 1:3,000,000

One centimeter represents 30 kilometers.
One inch represents approximately 47 miles.
Lambert Conformal Conic Projection

Kilometers
Statute Miles

Km.
Mi.

0   50   100   150

0   50   100   150

MAP FORM			
ENGLISH	gory	mountains	ostrov	island
DEUTSCH	Berge	Berge	Insel	Insel
ESPAÑOL	montañas	montañas	isla	isla
FRANÇAIS	montagnes	montagnes	île	île
PORTUGUÊS	montanhas	montanhas	ilha	ilha

ozero	lake	peski	desert	vodochranilišče	reservoir	vozvyšennost'	upland	zapovednik	reserve
See	lake	Wüste	desert	Stausee	reservoir	Bergland	upland	Reservat	reserve
lago	lago	desierto	desierto	embalse	embalse	tierras altas	tierras altas	reserva	reserva
lac	lake	désert	désert	réservoir	réservoir	hautes terres	hautes terres	réserve	réserve
lago	lago	deserto	deserto	reservatório	reservatório	terras altas	terras altas	reserva	reserva

Meters
6000 4000 3000 2000 1000 500 200 0

Feet
19685 13124 9843 6562 3281 1640 656 0

Land Below Sea Level

0 200 656 1000 3281 3000 9843 6000 19685 9000 29520

Tver' (Kalinin) · Moskva (Moscow) · Tula · Kaluga · Klin · Serpuchov · Kolomna · Voskresensk · Noginsk · Orechovo-Zujevo · Sergijev Posad (Zagorsk) · Dmitrov · Aleksandrov · Pereslavl'-Zalesskij · Konakovo · Dubna · Kimry · Zelenograd · Solnečnogorsk · Istra · Volokolamsk · Možajsk · Naro-Fominsk · Obninsk · Malojaroslavec · Podol'sk · Čechov · Kašira · Zarajsk · Ozery · Aleksin · Novomoskovsk · Jasnogorsk

MOSKOVSKAJA VOZVYŠENNOST' · KLINSKO-DMITROVSKAJA GRJADA · SREDNERUSSKAJA VOZVYŠENNOST'

Map compiled by Cartographia, Budapest.
Map prepared by Rand McNally GmbH, Stuttgart.
A-570311-264 -5 -7 -7

MAP FORM	gr'ada	ozero	vodochranilišče, vdchr.	vozvyšennost'	zapovednik
ENGLISH	ridge	lake	reservoir	upland	reserve
DEUTSCH	Höhenrücken	See	Stausee	Bergland	Reservat
ESPAÑOL	lomerio	lago	embalse	tierras altas	reserva
FRANÇAIS	crête	lac	réservoir	hautes terres	réserve
PORTUGUÊS	cordilheira	lago	reservatório	terras altas	reserva

Kilometers 0 10 20 30 40 50 Km.
Statute Miles 0 10 20 30 40 50 Mi.

Scale 1:1,000,000

One centimeter represents 10 kilometers.
One inch represents approximately 16 miles.
Lambert Conformal Conic Projection

MAP FORM					
ENGLISH	kosa	ostrov, o.	vodochranilišče, vdchr.	vozvyšennost', vozv.	zaliv	zapovednik, zapov
	spit	island	reservoir	upland	bay	reserve
DEUTSCH	Landzunge	Insel	Stausee	Bergland	Bucht	Reservat
ESPAÑOL	lengua de tierra	isla	embalse	tierras altas	bahía	reserva
FRANÇAIS	flèche	île	réservoir	hautes terres	baie	réserve
PORTUGUÊS	ponta de terra	ilha	reservatório	terras altas	baía	reserva

Kilometers

Statute Miles

One centimeter represents 10 kilometers.

Scale 1:1,000,000   One inch represents approximately 16 miles

Lambert Conformal Conic Projection

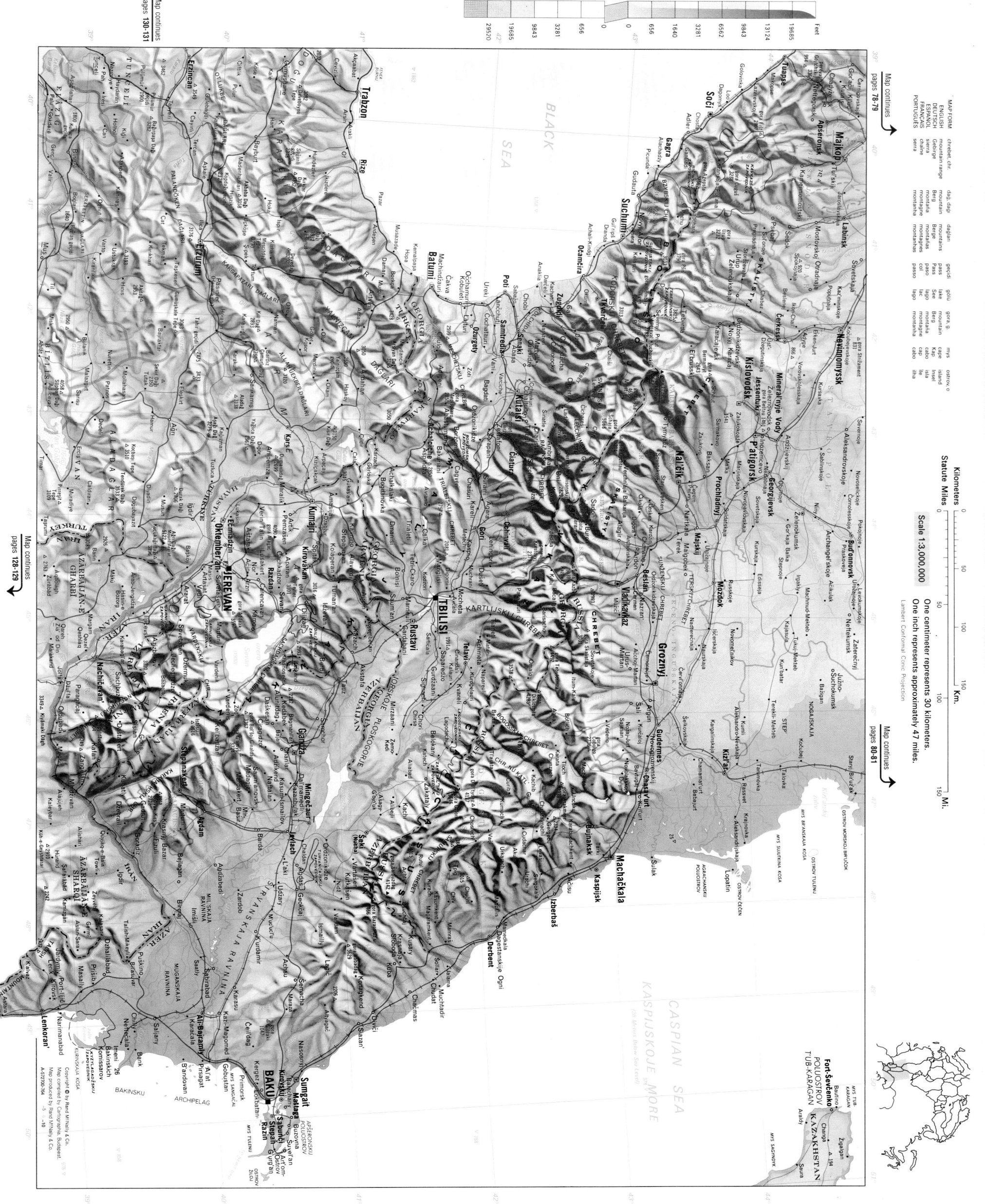

Caucasus and Transcaucasia / Kaukasus und Transkaukasien / Cáucaso y Transcaucasia
Caucasie et Transcaucasie / Cáucaso e Transcaucasia

84

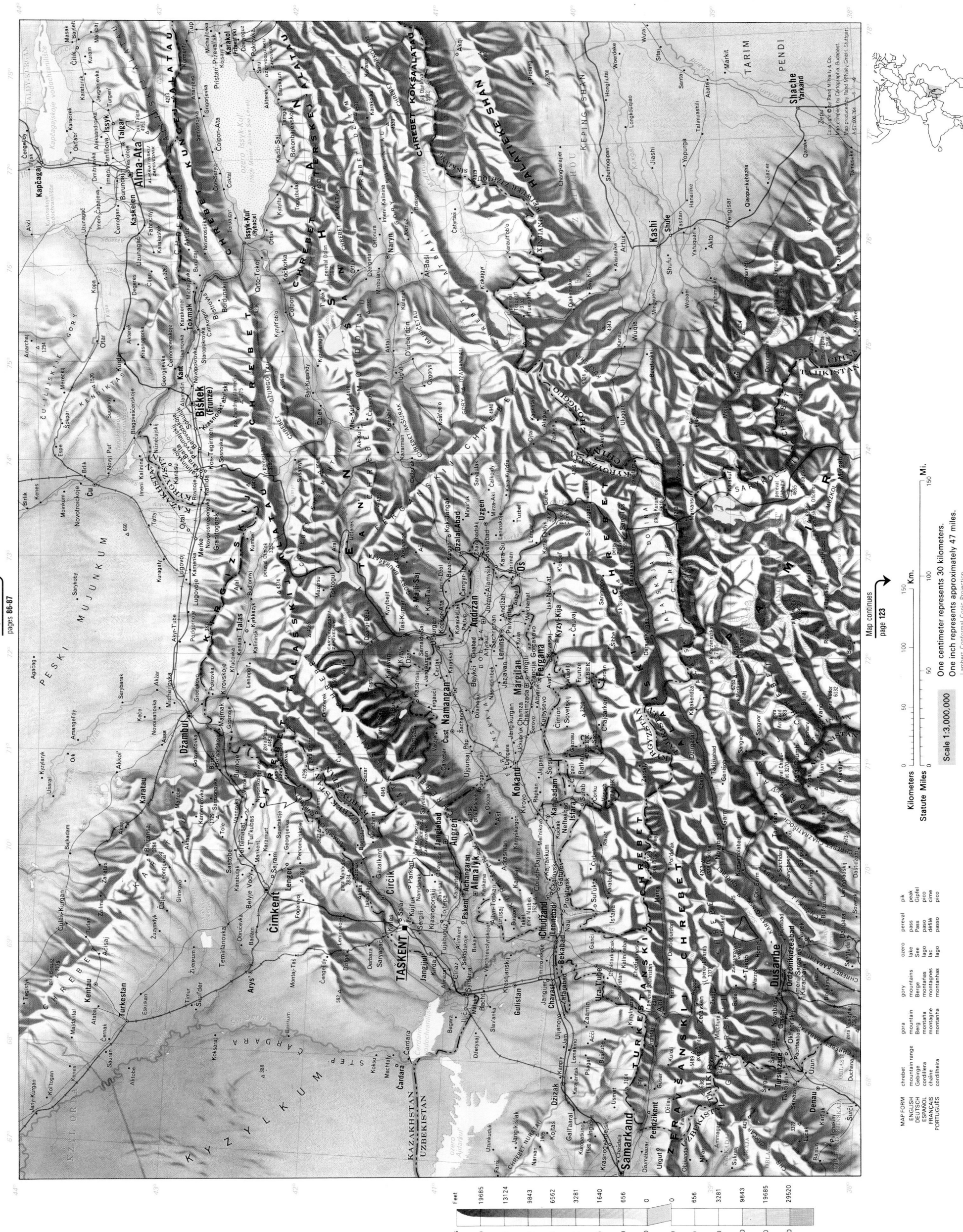

Map continues
pages 86-87

Map continues
page 123

Scale 1:3,000,000

One centimeter represents 30 kilometers.
One inch represents approximately 47 miles.
Lambert Conformal Conic Projection

MAP FORM	chrebet	gora	gory	ozero	pereval	pik
ENGLISH	mountain range	mountain	mountains	lake	pass	peak
DEUTSCH	Gebirge	Berg	Berge	See	Pass	Gipfel
ESPAÑOL	cordillera	montaña	montañas	lago	paso	pico
FRANÇAIS	chaîne	montagne	montagnes	lac	défilé	cime
PORTUGUÊS	cordilheira	montanha	montanhas	lago	passo	pico

Central Russia and Kazakhstan / Mittelrussland und Kasachstan / Rusia Central e Kazajstan
Russie Centrale et Kazakhstan / Rússia Central e Casaquistão

Map continues
pages 72-73

Map continues
pages 24-25

Map continues
pages 80-81

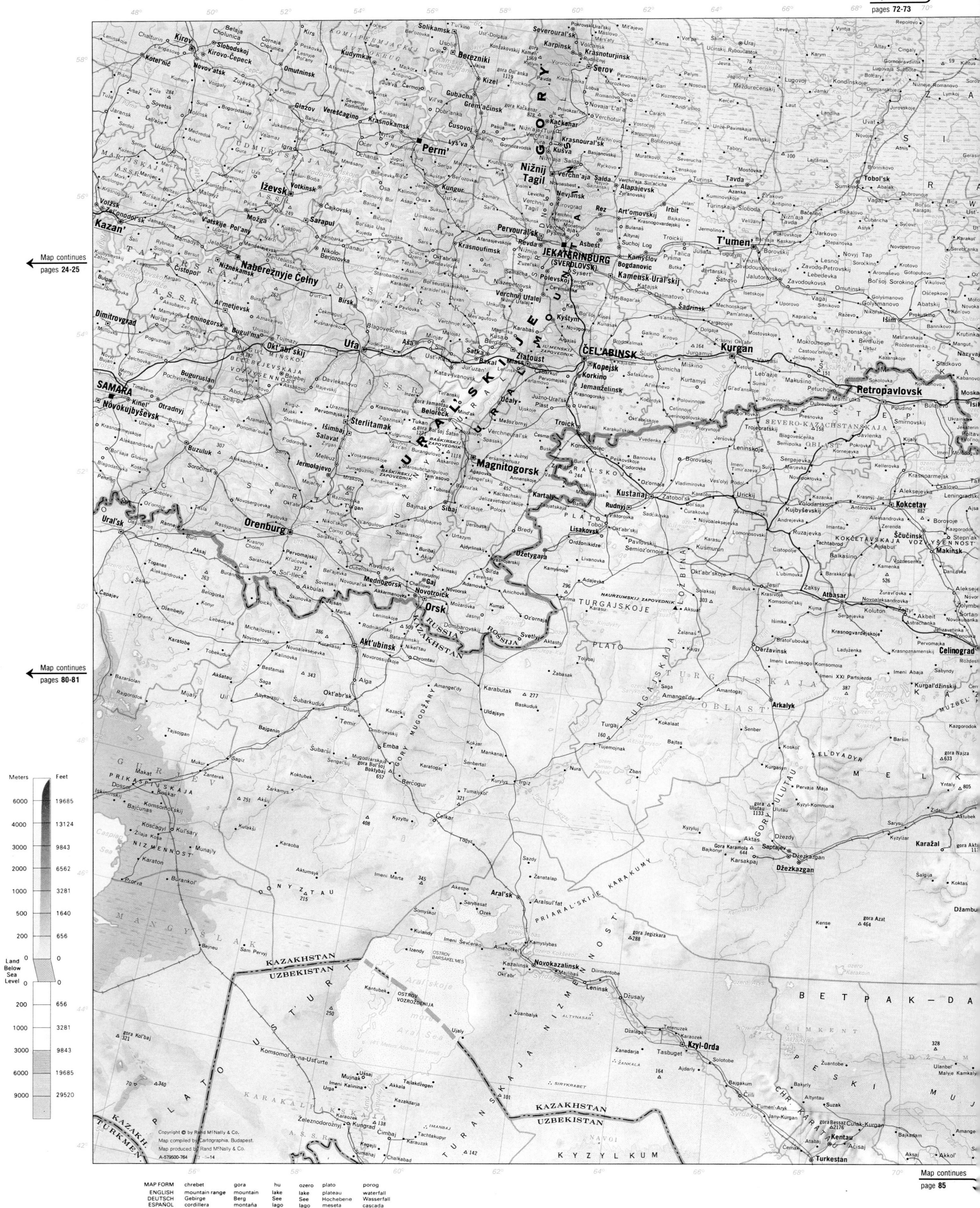

Map continues
page 85

	MAP FORM	chrebet	gora	hu	ozero	plato	porog
	ENGLISH	mountain range	mountain	lake	lake	plateau	waterfall
	DEUTSCH	Gebirge	Berg	See	See	Hochebene	Wasserfall
	ESPAÑOL	cordillera	montaña	lago	lago	meseta	cascada
	FRANÇAIS	chaîne	montagne	lac	lac	plateau	chute d'eau
	PORTUGUÊS	cordilheira	montanha	lago	lago	planalto	queda d'agua

Meters / Feet

Meters	Feet
6000	19685
4000	13124
3000	9843
2000	6562
1000	3281
500	1640
200	656
0	0
Land Below Sea Level 0	0
200	656
1000	3281
3000	9843
6000	19685
9000	29520

Central Russia and Kazakhstan / Mittelrussland und Kasachstan / Rusia Central e Kazajstan
Russie Centrale et Kazakhstan / Rússia Central e Casaquistão

87

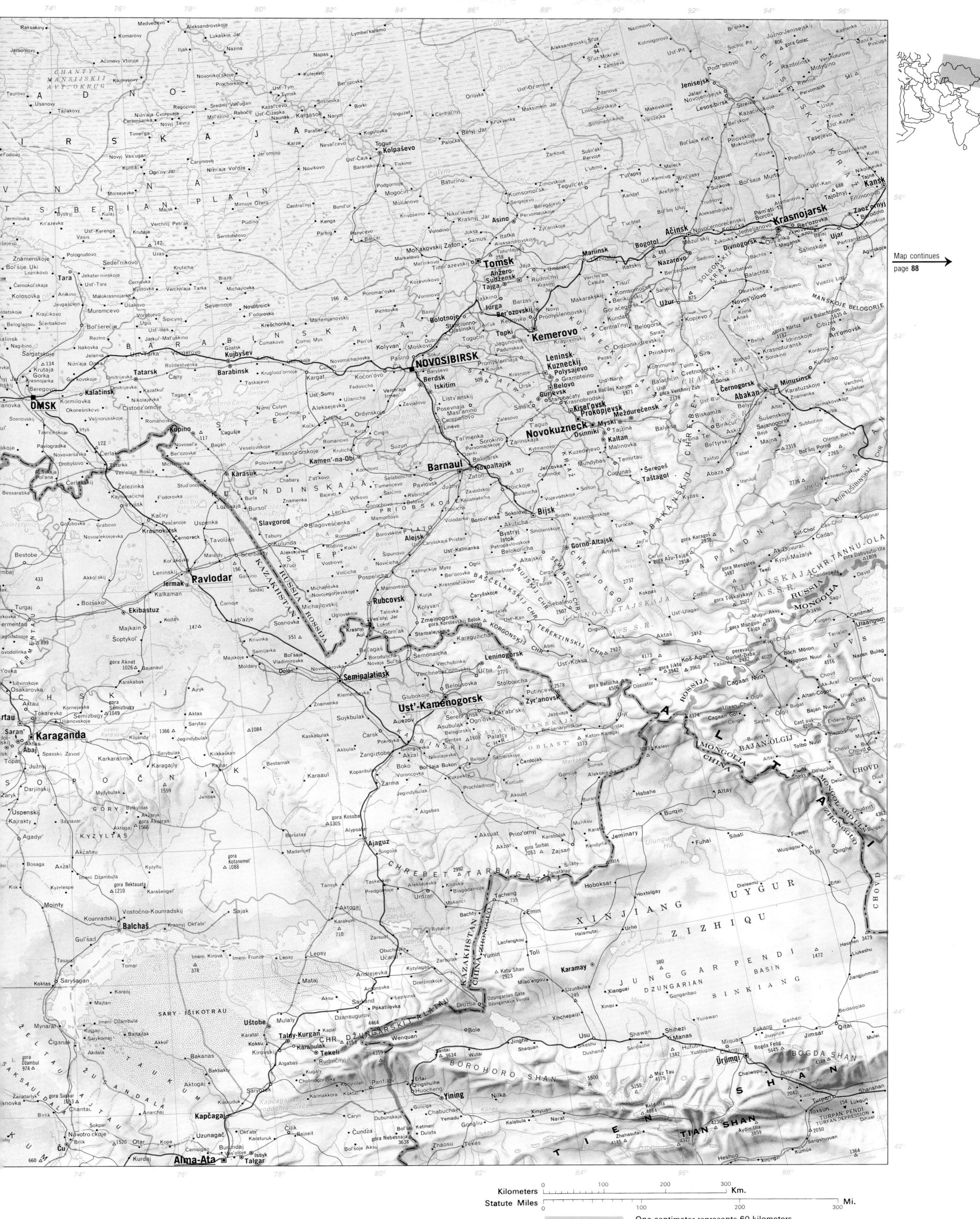

Map continues
page 88

Kilometers 0   100   200   300 Km.
Statute Miles 0   100   300 Mi.

Scale 1:6,000,000

One centimeter represents 60 kilometers.
One inch represents approximately 95 miles.

Lambert Conformal Conic Projection

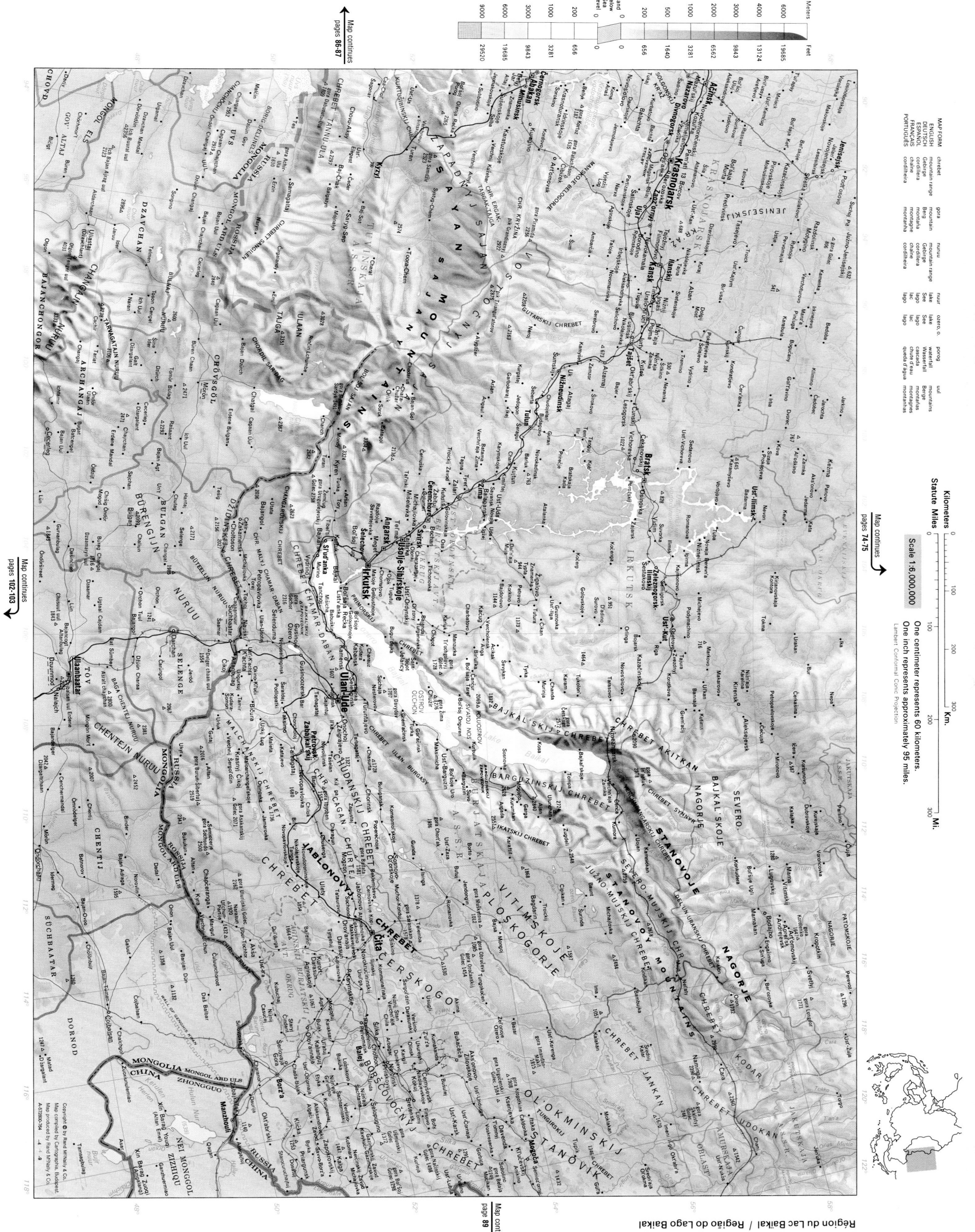

Lake Baikal Region / Baikalseegebiet / Región del Lago Baikal
Région du Lac Baïkal / Região do Lago Baikal

Map continues page 89

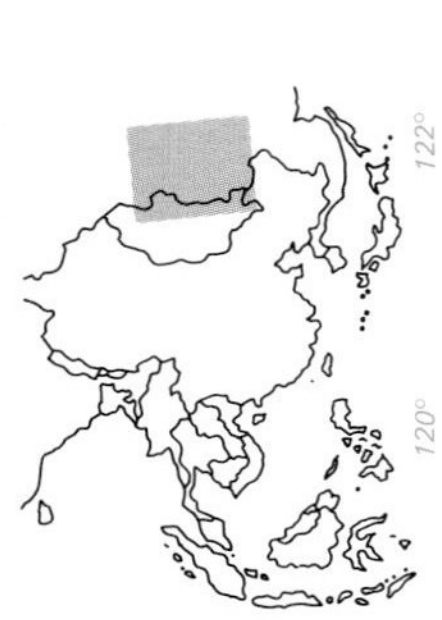

MAP FORM	chrebet	gora	nuruu	nuur	ozero, o.	porog	uul
ENGLISH	mountain range	mountain	mountain range	lake	lake	waterfall	mountains
DEUTSCH	Gebirge	Berg	Gebirge	See	See	Wasserfall	Berge
ESPAÑOL	cordillera	montaña	cordillera	lago	lago	cascada	montañas
FRANÇAIS	chaîne	montagne	chaîne	lac	lac	chute d'eau	montagnes
PORTUGUÊS	cordilheira	montanha	cordilheira	lago	lago	queda d'água	montanhas

Kilometers 0 100 200 300 Km.
Statute Miles 0 100 200 300 Mi.

Scale 1:6,000,000

One centimeter represents 60 kilometers.
One inch represents approximately 95 miles.
Lambert Conformal Conic Projection

Map continues pages 74-75

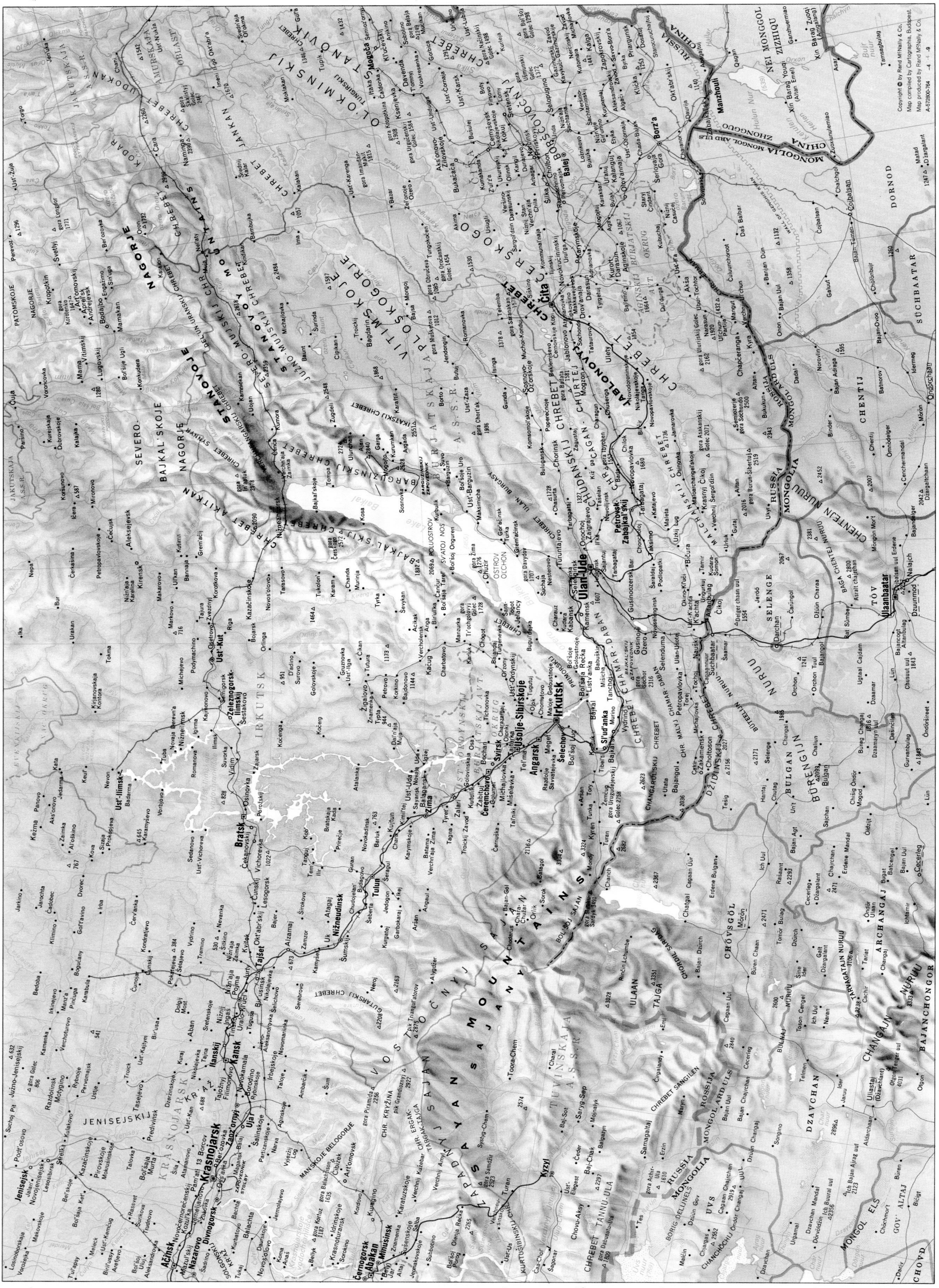

Map continues pages 102-103

Meters	Feet
6000	19685
4000	13124
3000	9843
2000	6562
1000	3281
500	1640
200	656
0	0
Land Below Sea Level 0	0
200	656
1000	3281
3000	9843
6000	19685
9000	29520

Map continues pages 86-87

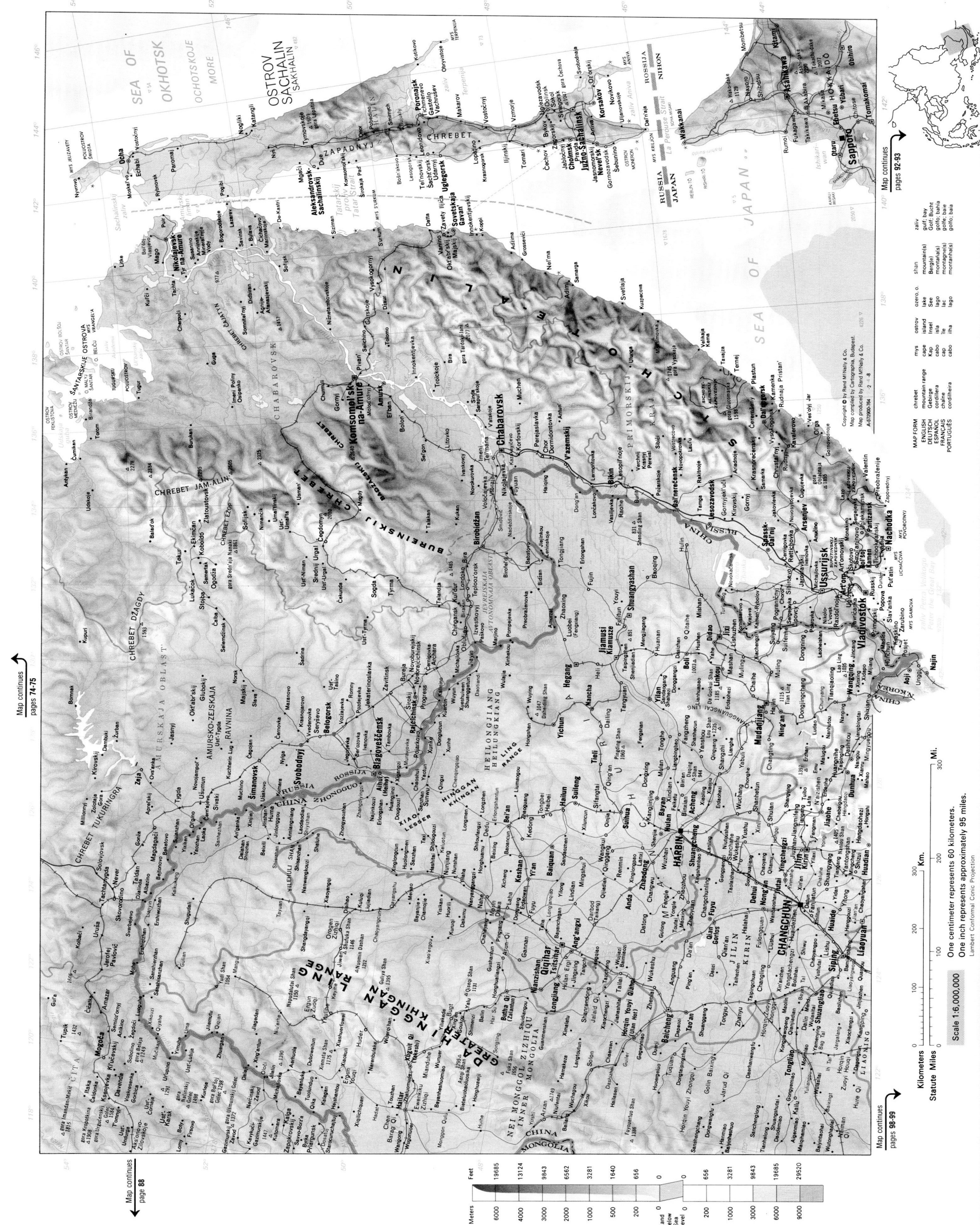

Map continues
pages 92-93

Map continues
pages 74-75

Map continues
page 88

Map continues
pages 98-99

MAP FORM		
ENGLISH	zaliv	gulf, bay
DEUTSCH	Golf, Bucht	
ESPAÑOL	golfo, bahía	
FRANÇAIS	golfe, baie	
PORTUGUÊS	golfo, baía	

ozero, o. lake
See lago
lago

ostrov island
Insel isla
ilha

mys cape
Kap cabo
cabo

shan mountain(s)
Berg(e) montaña(s)
montanha(s)

chrebet mountain range
Gebirge cordillera
cordilheira

Scale 1:6,000,000

One centimeter represents 60 kilometers.
One inch represents approximately 95 miles.

Lambert Conformal Conic Projection

Copyright © by Rand McNally & Co.
Map compiled by Cartographia, Budapest.
Map produced by Rand McNally & Co.
A-972000784

Feet 19685 13124 9843 6562 3281 1640 656 0 0 656 3281 9843 19685 29520
Meters 6000 4000 3000 2000 1000 500 200 0 200 1000 3000 6000 9000
Land Below Sea Level

Kilometers
Statute Miles

← Map continues
pages 118-119

MAP FORM	bandao	dao	hu	-jima	pendi	shan	-shima
ENGLISH	peninsula	island	lake	island	basin	mountain(s)	island
DEUTSCH	Halbinsel	Insel	See	Insel	Becken	Berg(e)	Insel
ESPAÑOL	península	isla	lago	isla	cuenca	montaña(s)	isla
FRANÇAIS	péninsule	île	lac	île	bassin	montagne(s)	île
PORTUGUÊS	península	ilha	lago	ilha	bacia	montanha(s)	ilha

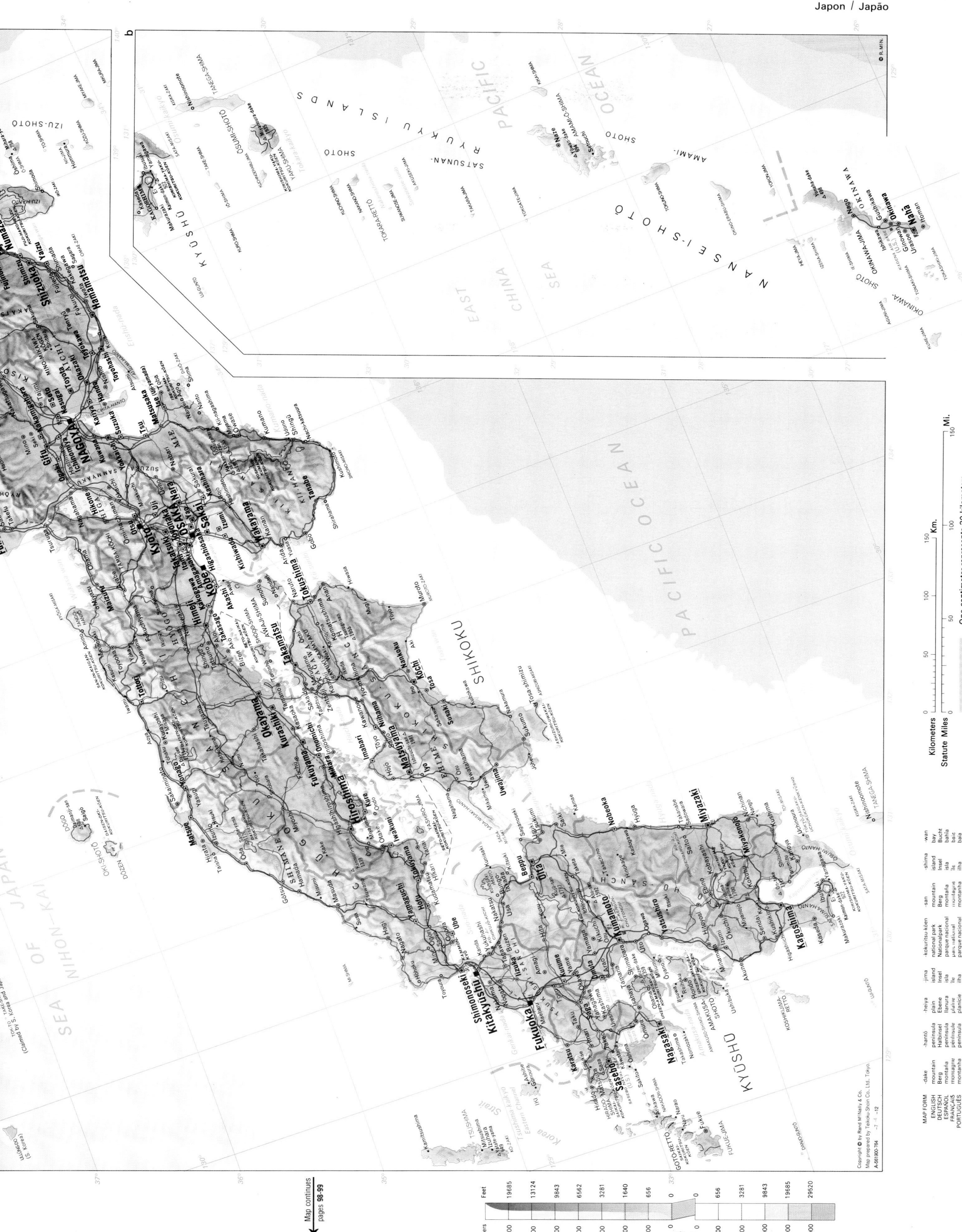

Map continues
pages 98-99

Scale 1:3,000,000

One centimeter represents 30 kilometers.
One inch represents approximately 47 miles.
Lambert Conformal Conic Projection

MAP FORM	-dake	-hantō	-heiya	-jima	-kokuritsu-kōen	-san	-shima	-wan
ENGLISH	mountain	peninsula	plain	island	national park	mountain	island	bay
DEUTSCH	Berg	Halbinsel	Ebene	Insel	Nationalpark	Berg	Insel	Bucht
ESPAÑOL	montaña	península	llanura	isla	parque nacional	montaña	isla	bahía
FRANÇAIS	montagne	péninsule	plaine	île	parc national	montagne	île	baie
PORTUGUÊS	montanha	península	planície	ilha	parque nacional	montanha	ilha	baía
Kilometers 0 50 100 150 Km.
Statute Miles 0 50 100 150 Mi.

Map continues pages 96-97

			MAP FORM
			ENGLISH
			DEUTSCH
			ESPAÑOL
			FRANÇAIS
			PORTUGUÊS
-dake	-hantō		
mountain	peninsula	-misaki	
Berg	Halbinsel	-san	-yama
montaña	peninsula	cape	mountain
montagne	péninsule	Kap	Berg
montanha	peninsula	cabo	montaña
		cap	montagne
-koku-ritsu-kōen	cabo	montanha
national park			
Nationalpark		-wan	-tōge
parque nacional		bay	pass
parc national		Bucht	Pass
parque nacional		bahía	paso
		baie	col
		baía	passo
-zaki			
point			
Landspitze			
punta			
punta			
ponta			

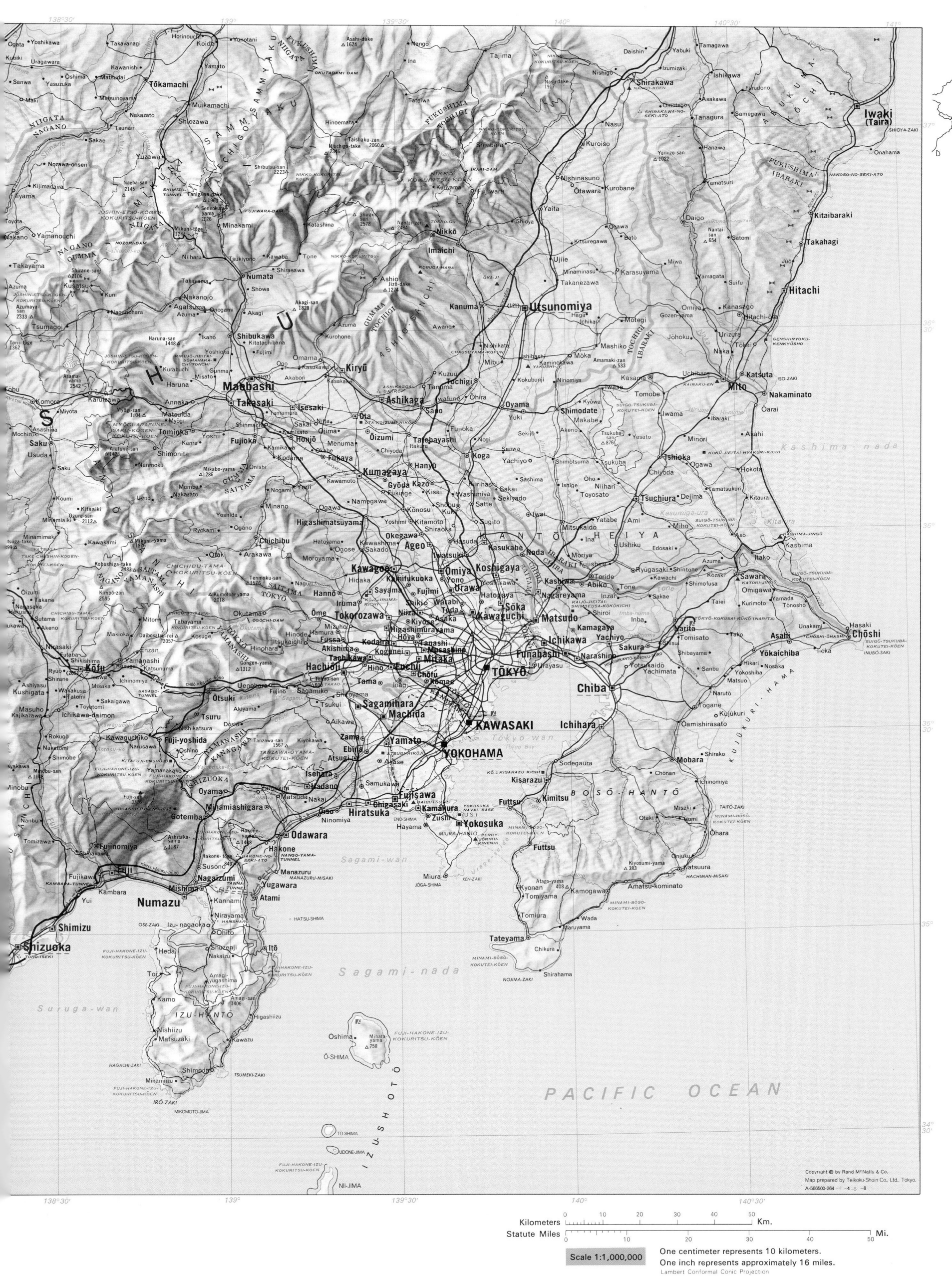

Kilometers
Statute Miles

Scale 1:1,000,000   One centimeter represents 10 kilometers.
One inch represents approximately 16 miles.
Lambert Conformal Conic Projection

MAP FORM	-jima	-misaki	-san	-sen	-shima	-tōge	-yama	-zen
ENGLISH	island	cape	mountain	mountain	island	pass	mountain	mountain
DEUTSCH	Insel	Kap	Berg	Berg	Insel	Pass	Berg	Berg
ESPAÑOL	isla	cabo	montaña	montaña	isla	paso	montaña	montaña
FRANÇAIS	île	cap	montagne	montagne	île	col	montagne	montagne
PORTUGUÊS	ilha	cabo	montanha	montanha	ilha	passo	montanha	montanha

Map continues
pages **94-95**

PACIFIC OCEAN

Kilometers 0 10 20 30 40 50 Km.
Statute Miles 0 10 20 30 40 50 Mi.

Scale 1:1,000,000

One centimeter represents 10 kilometers.
One inch represents approximately 16 miles.
Lambert Conformal Conic Projection

Copyright © by Rand McNally & Co.
Map prepared by Teikoku-Shoin Co., Ltd. Tokyo.

A-566600-264 -4 -5 -6

98

Northeast China and Korea / Nordostchina und Korea / China Nor-oriental y Corea
Nord-Est de la Chine et Corée / Nordeste da China e Coréia

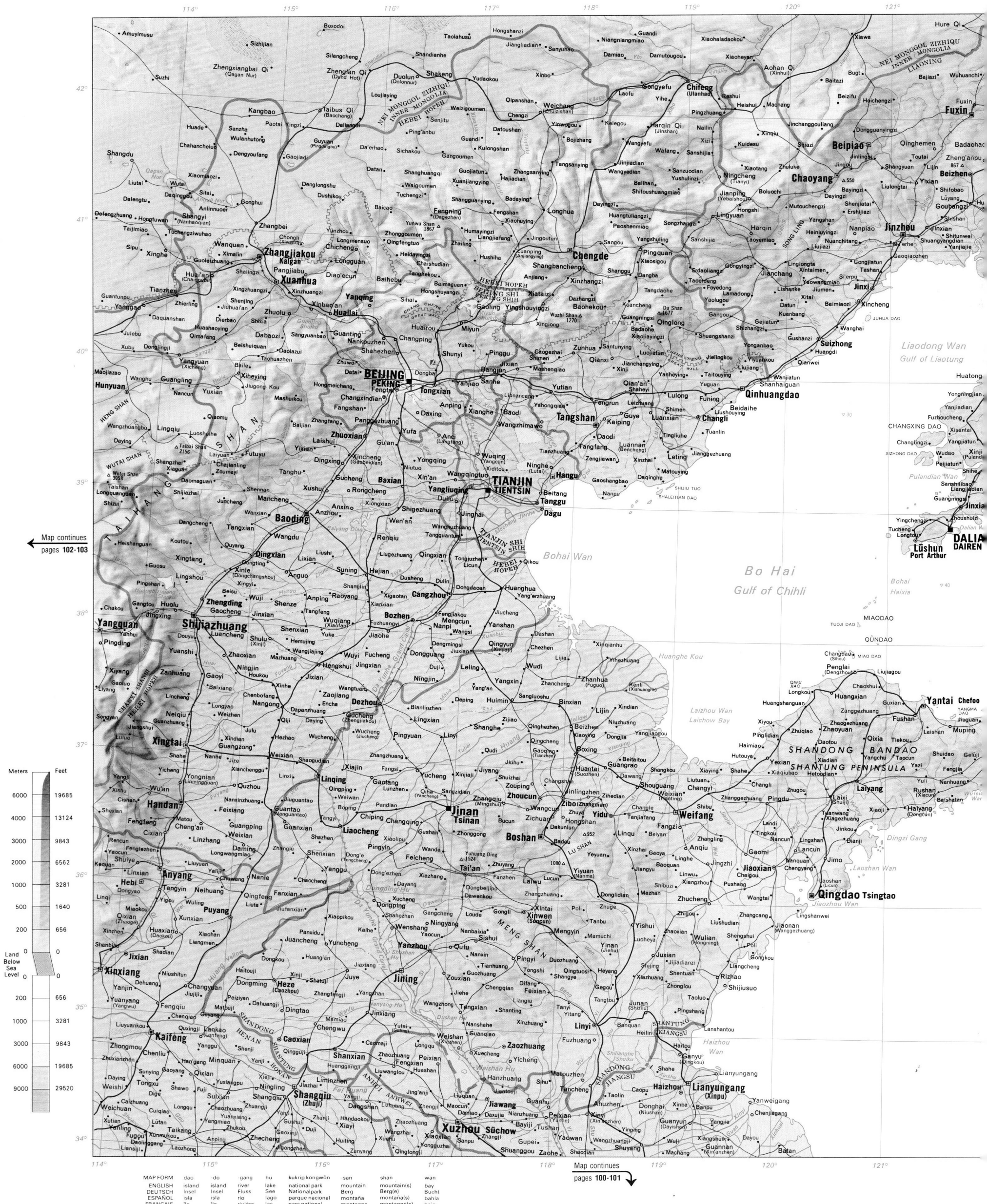

← Map continues
pages 102-103

Map continues
pages 100-101 ↓

	Meters	Feet
	6000	19685
	4000	13124
	3000	9843
	2000	6562
	1000	3281
	500	1640
	200	656
	0	0
Land Below Sea Level	0	0
	200	656
	1000	3281
	3000	9843
	6000	19685
	9000	29520

	MAP FORM	dao	-do	-gang	hu	kukrip kongwǒn	-san	shan	wan
	ENGLISH	island	island	river	lake	national park	mountain	mountain(s)	bay
	DEUTSCH	Insel	Insel	Fluss	See	Nationalpark	Berg	Berg(e)	Bucht
	ESPAÑOL	isla	isla	rio	lago	parque nacional	montaña	montaña(s)	bahia
	FRANÇAIS	île	île	rivière	lac	parc national	montagne	montagne(s)	baie
	PORTUGUÊS	ilha	ilha	rio	lago	parque nacional	montanha	montanha(s)	baia

Map continues page 89

Map continues pages 92-93

MANCHURIA

SHENYANG
MUKDEN
FUSHUN

NORTH KOREA

CHINA 中國 **ZHONGGUO**

CHAGANG-DO

YANGGANG-DO

HAMGYŎNG PUKDO

HAMGYŎNG NAMDO

Ch'ŏngjin

Kyŏngsong

Kimch'aek
(Sŏngjin)

Hamhŭng

Hŭngnam

Wŏnsan

P'YŎNGAN PUKDO

P'YŎNGAN NAMDO

P'yŏngyang

Namp'o

HWANGHAE PUKDO

HWANGHAE NAMDO

Haeju

Kaesŏng

KANGWŎN DO

NORTH KOREA
SOUTH KOREA

Ch'unch'ŏn

Kangnŭng

SŎUL
SEOUL

Inch'ŏn

Suwŏn

Wŏnju

KYŎNGGI DO

KANGWŎN DO

Ch'ungju

CH'UNGCH'ŎNG PUKDO

CH'UNGCH'ŎNG NAMDO

Ch'ŏngju

Taejŏn

KYŎNGSANG PUKDO

Andong

P'ohang

Taegu

Kyŏngju

Ulsan

Kunsan

Chŏnju

CHŎLLA PUKDO

Kwangju

CHŎLLA NAMDO

KYŎNGSANG NAMDO

Namwŏn

Chinju

Masan
Chinhae

Pusan

Mokp'o

Sunch'ŏn

Yŏsu

SEA OF JAPAN

Korea Bay

YELLOW SEA

Korea Channel
SOUTH KOREA
JAPAN 日本 NIHON

TSUSHIMA

LIAODONG BANDAO
LIAODONG PENINSULA

Anshan

Liaoyang

Benxi
Penhsi

Dandong

Sinŭiju

CHINA
RUSSIA

Yanji

Tumen

Najin

Kilometers 0 50 100 150 Km.

Statute Miles 0 50 100 150 Mi.

Scale 1:3,000,000

One centimeter represents 30 kilometers.
One inch represents approximately 47 miles.
Lambert Conformal Conic Projection

Copyright © by Rand McNally & Co.
Map compiled by Cartographia, Budapest.
Map produced by Rand McNally & Co.
A-564400-764   -5.-.5.-.11

Map continues pages 98-99 →

Major labels (provinces, ranges, cities, seas):

HUNAN · KIANGSI · JIANGXI · HUBEI · HUPEI · HENAN HONAN · ANHUI ANHWEI · KIANGSU · KIANGSI · CHEKIANG · ZHEJIANG · FUKIEN

Changsha · **Nanchang** · **Wuhan** · **Hefei** · **Nanjing** NANKING · **SHANGHAI** · **Ningbo** · **Wenzhou** · **Hangzhou** HANGCHOW · **Suzhou** SOOCHOW · **Wuxi** WUHSI · **Shaoxing** · **Jiaxing** · **Bengbu** · **Huainan** · **Xuzhou** SIUCHOW · **Shangqiu** · **Fuyang** · **Nanyang** · **Xuchang** · **Pingdingshan** · **Luohe** · **Xinyang** · **Xiping** · **Zhumadian** · **Huangshi** · **Jiujiang** · **Jingdezhen** · **Jinhua** · **Linhai** · **Haimen** · **Taizhou** · **Nantong** · **Changshu** · **Zhenjiang** · **Yangzhou** · **Changzhou** · **Dangyang** · **Liuyang** · **Fengcheng** · **Boyang** · **Leping** · **Lishui** · **Yueyang** · **Xianning** · **Xiaogan** · **Qingpu** · **Dingtai**

Mountain ranges: JIULING SHAN · MUFU SHAN · TONGBAI SHAN · TONGBAI SHAN · DABIE SHAN · FUNIU SHAN · HONG SHAN · HUAIYU SHAN · XIANXIA LING · TIANMU SHAN · KUOCANG SHAN

Rivers/lakes: Yangtze · Chang Jiang · Huai He · Poyang Hu · Tai Hu · Chao Hu · Hongze Hu · Dongting

HUANG HAI · **YELLOW SEA** · Hangzhou Wan · Zhoushan Dao · ZHOUSHAN QUNDAO

East and Southeast China / Ost- und Südostchina / Este y Sudeste de la China / Chine de l'Est et du Sud-Est / Leste e Sudeste da China

100

East and Southeast China / Ost- und Südostchina / Este y Sudeste de la China
Chine de l'Est et du Sud-Est / Leste e Sudeste da China

101

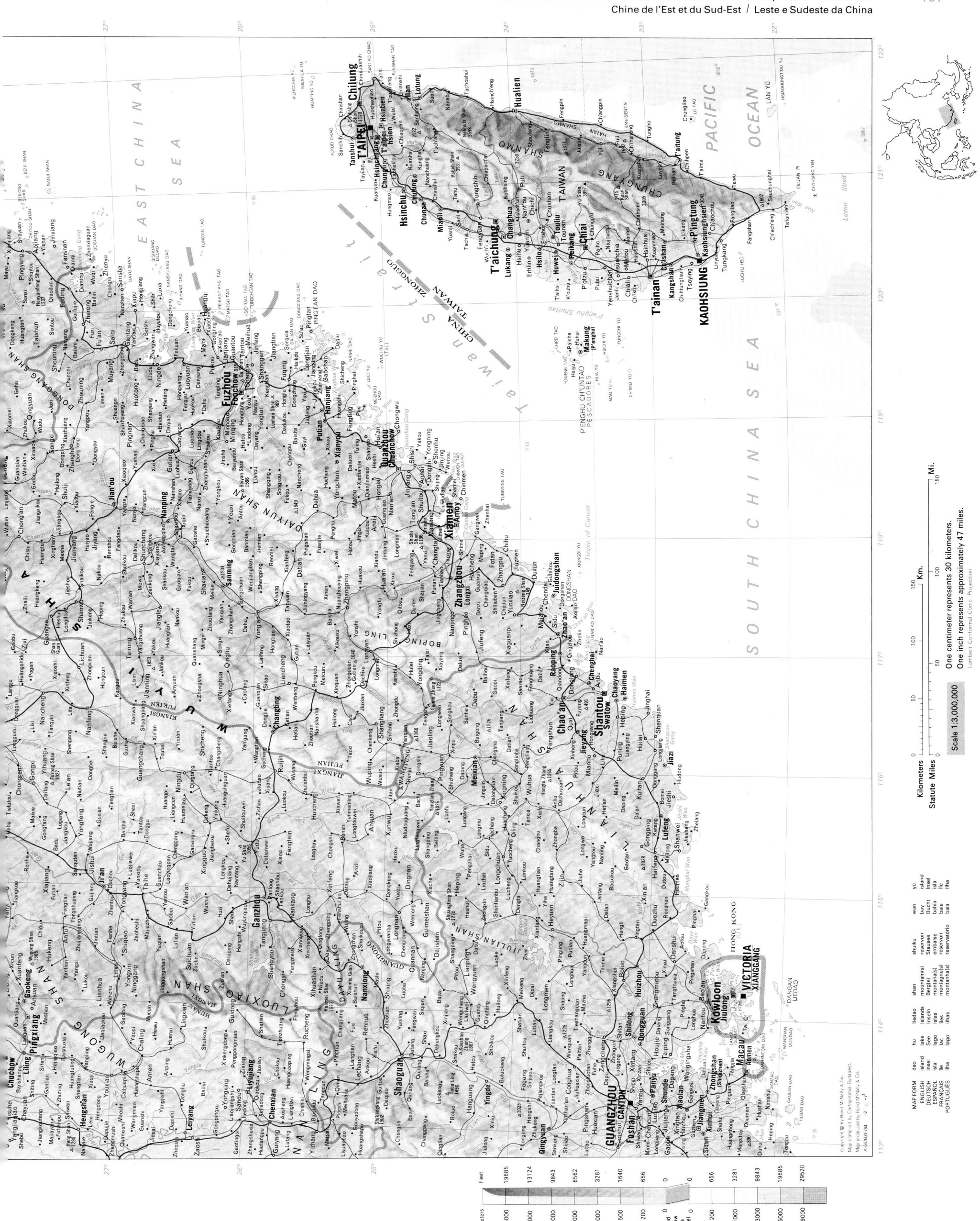

Scale 1:3,000,000

One centimeter represents 30 kilometers.
One inch represents approximately 47 miles.

Lambert Conformal Conic Projection

MAP FORM						
ENGLISH	dao	hu	liedao	shan	shuiku	wan	yü
DEUTSCH	island	lake	islands	mountain(s)	reservoir	bay	island
ESPAÑOL	Insel	See	Inseln	Berg(e)	Stausee	Bucht	Insel
FRANÇAIS	isla	lago	islas	montaña(s)	embalse	bahía	isla
PORTUGUÊS	île	lac	îles	montagne(s)	réservoir	baie	île
	ilha	lago	ilhas	montanha(s)	reservatório	baía	ilha

Map continues page 88

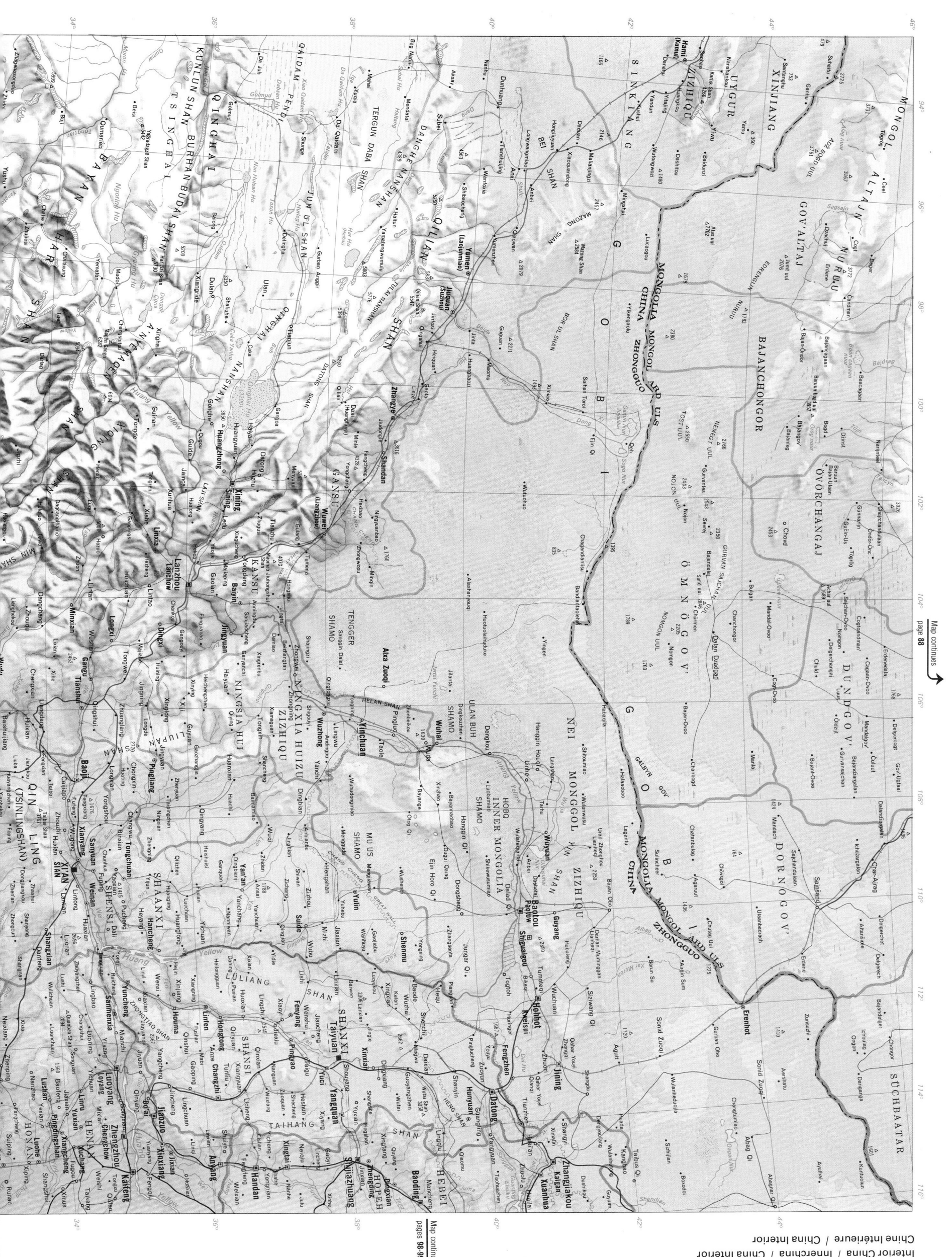
MONGOL ALTAJN NURUU
GOV'ALTAJ
BAJANCHONGOR
ÖVÖRCHANGAJ
DUNDGOV'
DORNOGOV'
SÜCHBAATAR
ÖMNÖGOV'
XINJIANG
UYGUR ZIZHIQU
SINKIANG
GOBI
MONGOLIA MONGOL ARD ULS
CHINA ZHONGGUO
NEI MONGGOL ZIZHIQU
INNER MONGOLIA
GANSU
KANSU
QINGHAI
TSINGHAI
NINGXIA HUIZU ZIZHIQU
NINGSIA HUI
SHAANXI
SHENSI
SHANXI
SHANSI
HEBEI
HOPEH
HENAN
HONAN
QILIAN SHAN
KUNLUN SHAN
QIN LING (TSINLINGSHAN)
TENGGER SHAMO
MU US SHAMO
Hami (Kumul)
Lanzhou Lanchow
Xining Sining
Yinchuan
Baotou Paotow
Hohhot Kweisui
Datong
Taiyuan
Xi'an Sian
Zhengzhou Chengchow
Shijiazhuang
Zhangjiakou Kalgan
Erenhot

Map continues pages 98-99

Map continues
pages 100-101

Map continues
pages 110-111

Map continues
pages 120-121

SOUTH CHINA SEA

Gulf of Tonkin

Scale 1:16,000,000

One centimeter represents 60 kilometers.
One inch represents approximately 95 miles.

Lambert Conformal Conic Projection

MAP FORM				
ENGLISH	dao	hu	ling	shamo
DEUTSCH	island	lake	mountains	desert
ESPAÑOL	Insel	See	Berge	Wüste
FRANÇAIS	isla	lago	montañas	desierto
PORTUGUÊS	île	lac	montagnes	désert
	ilha	lago	montanhas	deserto

shan	shuiku
mountain(s)	reservoir
Berg(e)	Stausee
montaña(s)	embalse
montagne(s)	réservoir
montanha(s)	reservatório

Kilometers
Statute Miles

Feet
19685
13124
9843
6562
3281
1640
656
0
Land Below Sea Level
656
3281
9843
19685
29520

Meters
6000
4000
3000
2000
1000
500
200
0
Land Below Sea Level
200
1000
3000
6000
9000

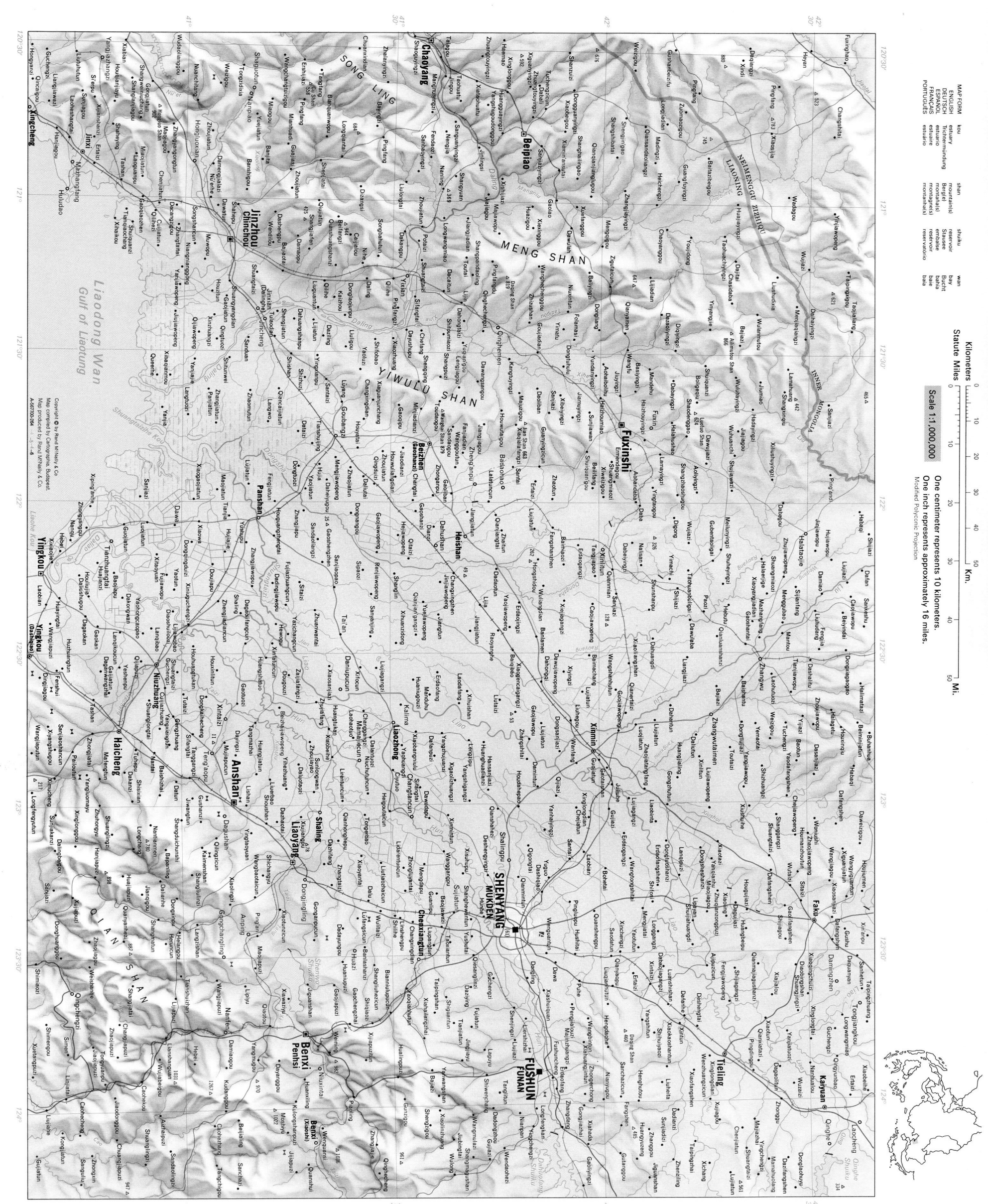

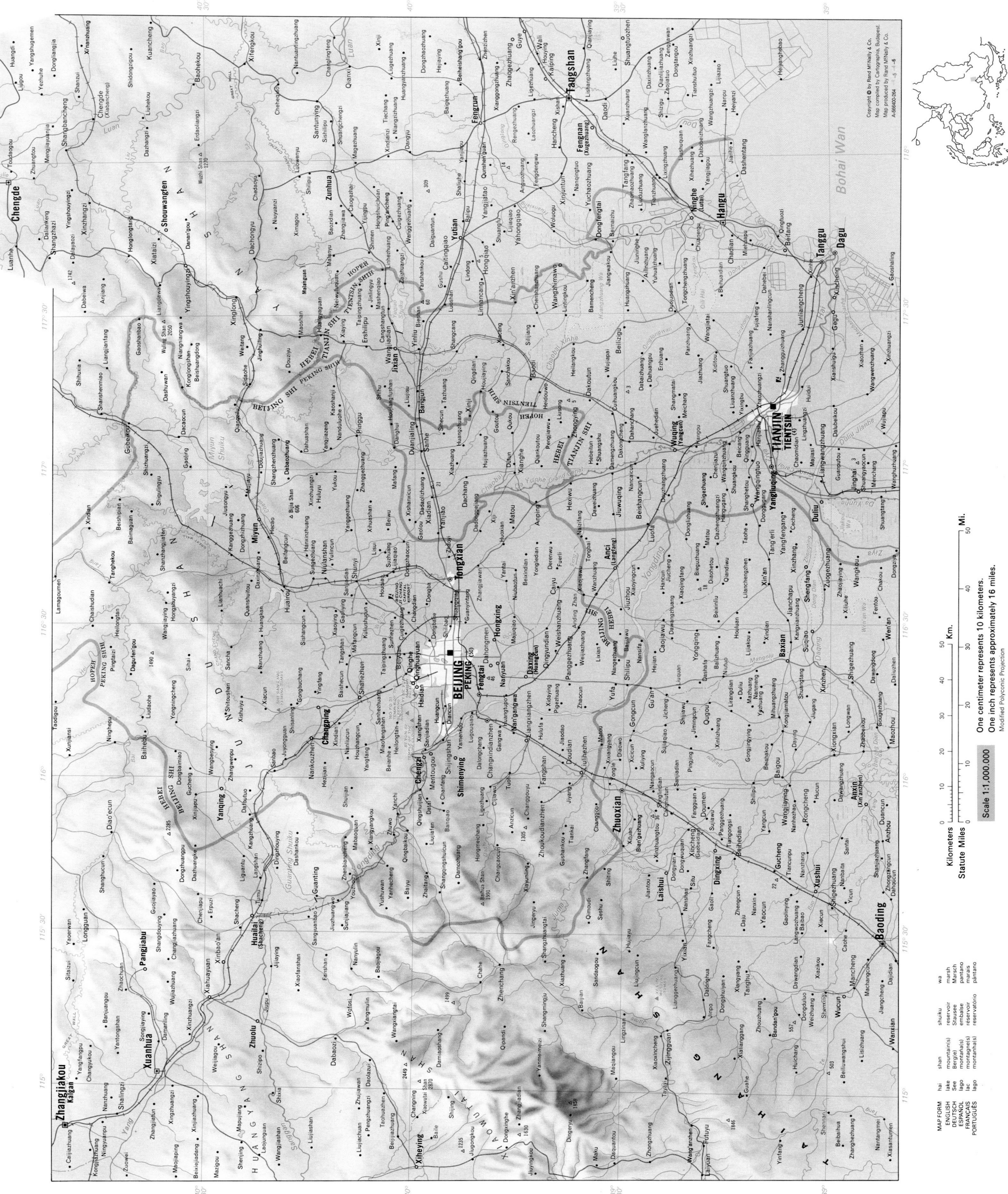

Scale 1:1,000,000

One centimeter represents 10 kilometers.
One inch represents approximately 16 miles.

Modified Polyconic Projection

MAP FORM
ENGLISH	hai	lake	shan	mountain(s)	shuiku	reservoir	wa	marsh
DEUTSCH	See		Berg(e)		Stausee		Marsch
ESPAÑOL	lago		montaña(s)		embalse		pantano
FRANÇAIS	lac		montagne(s)		réservoir		marais
PORTUGUÊS	lago		montanha(s)		reservatório		pântano

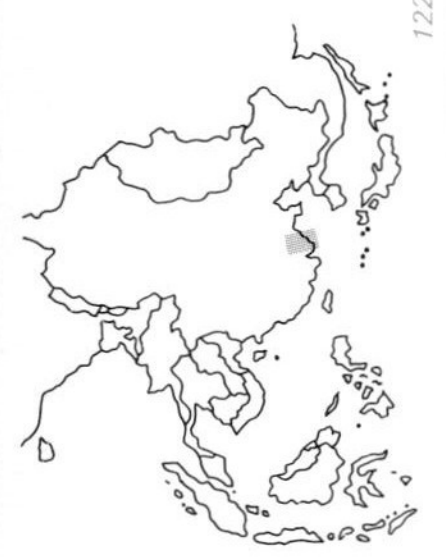

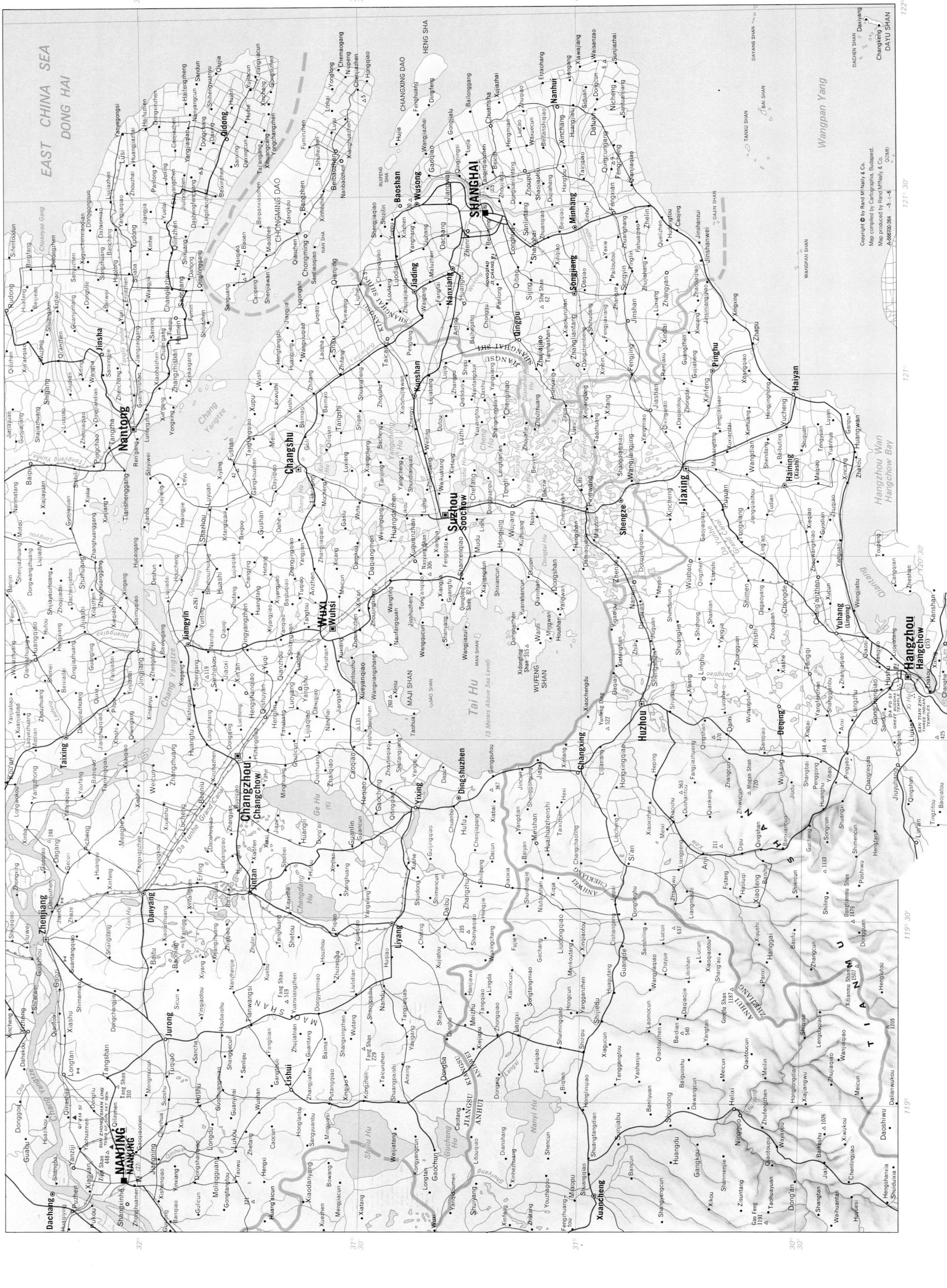
EAST CHINA SEA
DONG HAI
SHANGHAI
NANJING
NANKING
Suzhou
Soochow
Changzhou
Changchow
Hangzhou
Hangchow
Wuxi
Wuhsi
Nantong
Zhenjiang
Changshu
Jiaxing
Huzhou
Tai Hu
Hangzhou Wan
Hangchow Bay
Wangpan Yang
CHONGMING DAO
Copyright © by Rand McNally & Co.
Map compiled by Cartographia, Budapest.
Map produced by Rand McNally & Co.
A-566700-264 -5-4-6

Kilometers 0 10 20 30 40 50 Km.

Statute Miles 0 10 20 30 40 50 Mi.

Scale 1:1,000,000

One centimeter represents 10 kilometers.
One inch represents approximately 16 miles.

Lambert Conformal Conic Projection

MAP FORM	dao	hu	sha	shan	si	wan
ENGLISH	island	lake	island	mountain(s); island	temple	bay
DEUTSCH	Insel	See	Insel	Berg(e); Insel	Tempel	Bucht
ESPAÑOL	isla	lago	isla	montaña(s); isla	templo	bahía
FRANÇAIS	île	lac	île	montagne(s); île	temple	baie
PORTUGUÊS	ilha	lago	ilha	montanha(s); ilha	templo	baía

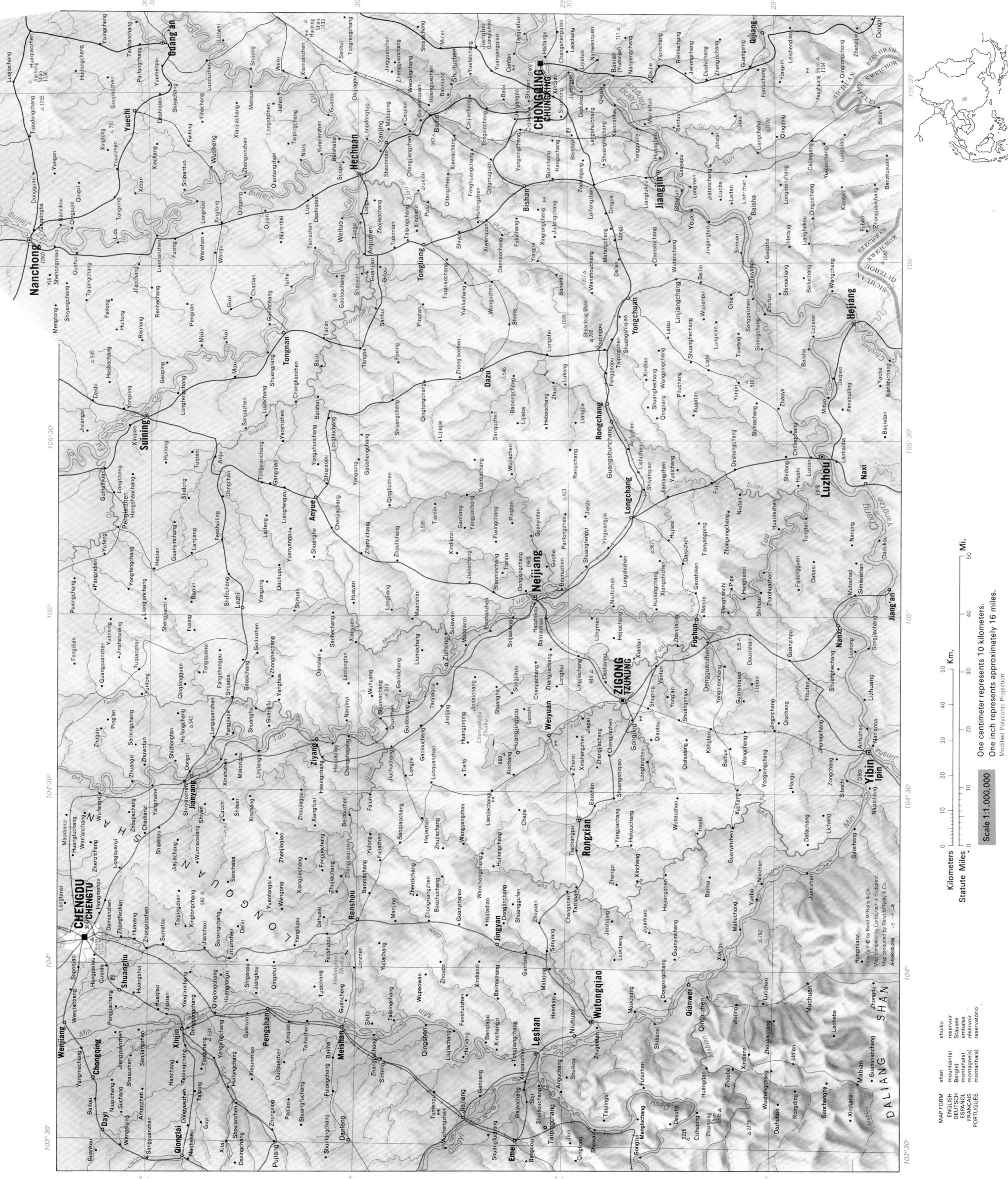

Kilometers

Statute Miles

Mi.

Km.

Scale 1:1,000,000

One centimeter represents 10 kilometers.
One inch represents approximately 16 miles.
Modified Polyconic Projection

Copyright © by Rand McNally & Co.
Map compiled by Cartographia, Budapest.
Map produced by Rand McNally & Co.
A666000-264   —4   —4   —8

MAP FORM   shan   shuku
ENGLISH   mountain(s)   reservoir
DEUTSCH   Berg(e)   Stausee
ESPAÑOL   montaña(s)   embalse
FRANÇAIS   montagne(s)   réservoir
PORTUGUÊS   montanha(s)   reservatório

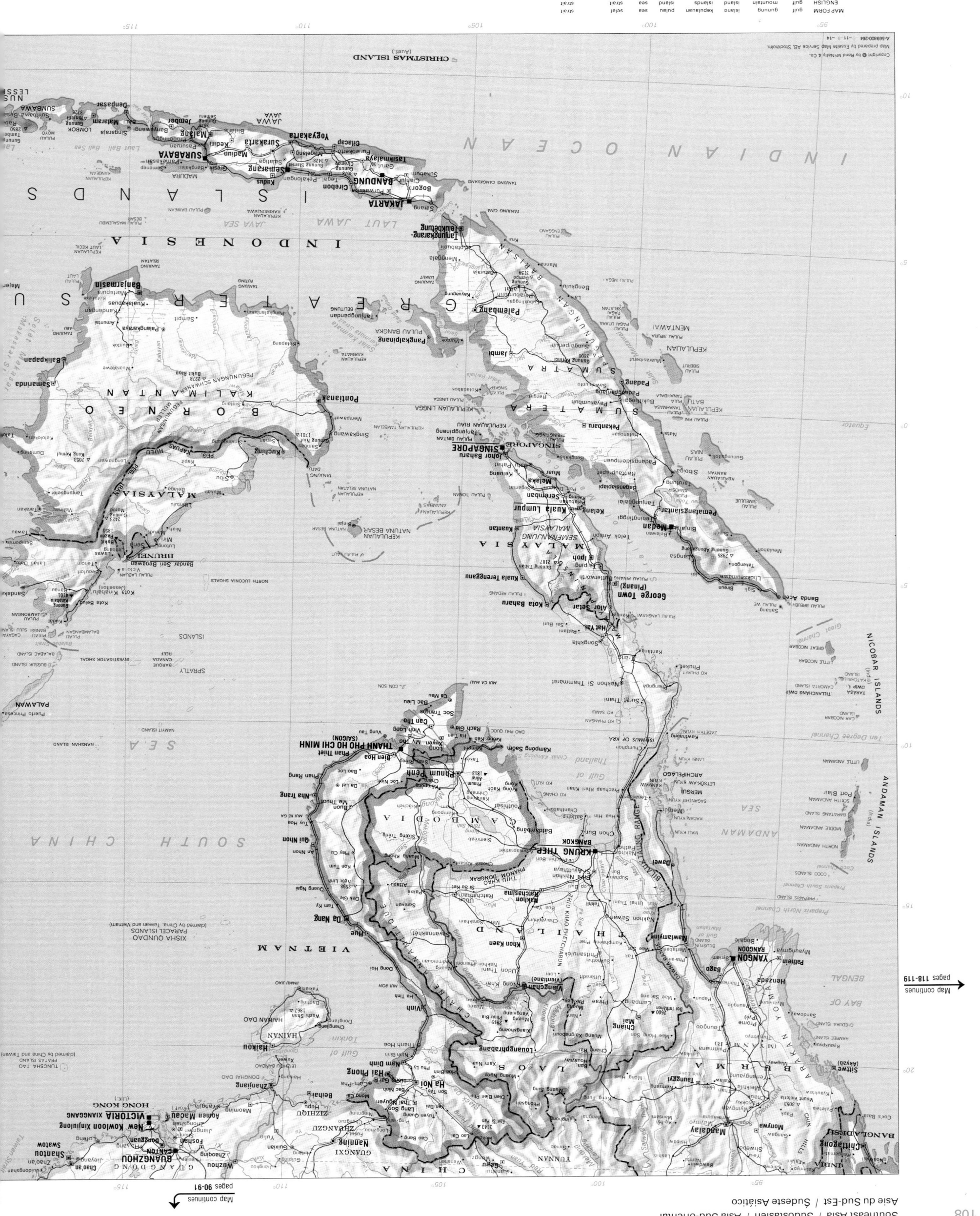

Southeast Asia / Südostasien / Asia Sud-oriental
Asie du Sud-Est / Sudeste Asiático

Map continues pages 90-91

Map continues pages 118-119

MAP FORM					
ENGLISH	gulf	mountain	island	islands	strait
DEUTSCH	Golf	Berg	Insel	Inseln	Meerestrasse
ESPAÑOL	golfo	montaña	isla	islas	estrecho
FRANÇAIS	golfe	montagne	île	îles	détroit
PORTUGUÊS	golfo	montanha	ilha	ilhas	estreito

ENGLISH	gulf	mountain	sea	sea	strait
DEUTSCH	Golf	Berg	Meer	See	Meerestrasse
ESPAÑOL	golfo	montaña	mar	mar	estrecho
FRANÇAIS	golfe	montagne	mer	mer	détroit
PORTUGUÊS	golfo	montanha	mar	mar	estreito

gunung	pulau	kepulauan	selat

INDIAN OCEAN

INDONESIA

GREATER SUNDA ISLANDS

SOUTH CHINA SEA

THAILAND

VIETNAM

CAMBODIA

LAOS

BURMA (MYANMAR)

MALAYSIA

BORNEO

SUMATRA

JAVA

Map continues
pages 160-161

Kilometers
Statute Miles

Km.
Mi.

Scale 1:12,000,000

One centimeter represents 120 kilometers.
One inch represents approximately 190 miles.
Lambert Conformal Conic Projection

Kilometers
Statute Miles
Scale 1:6,000,000
One centimeter represents 60 kilometers.
One inch represents approximately 95 miles.
Lambert Conformal Conic Projection
Map continues pages 102-103
Map continues pages 120-121
MAP FORM dao gunung island kepulauan khao kyun pulau shan
ENGLISH island mountain island islands mountain island island mountain(s)
DEUTSCH Insel Berg Insel Inseln Berg Insel Insel Berg(e)
ESPAÑOL isla montaña isla islas montaña isla isla montaña(s)
FRANÇAIS île montagne île îles montagne île île montagne(s)
PORTUGUÊS ilha montanha ilha ilhas montanha ilha ilha montanha(s)

Burma, Thailand and Indochina / Burma, Thailand und Indochina / Birmania, Siam e Indochina
Birmanie, Thaïlande et Indochine / Birmânia, Tailândia e Indochina

111

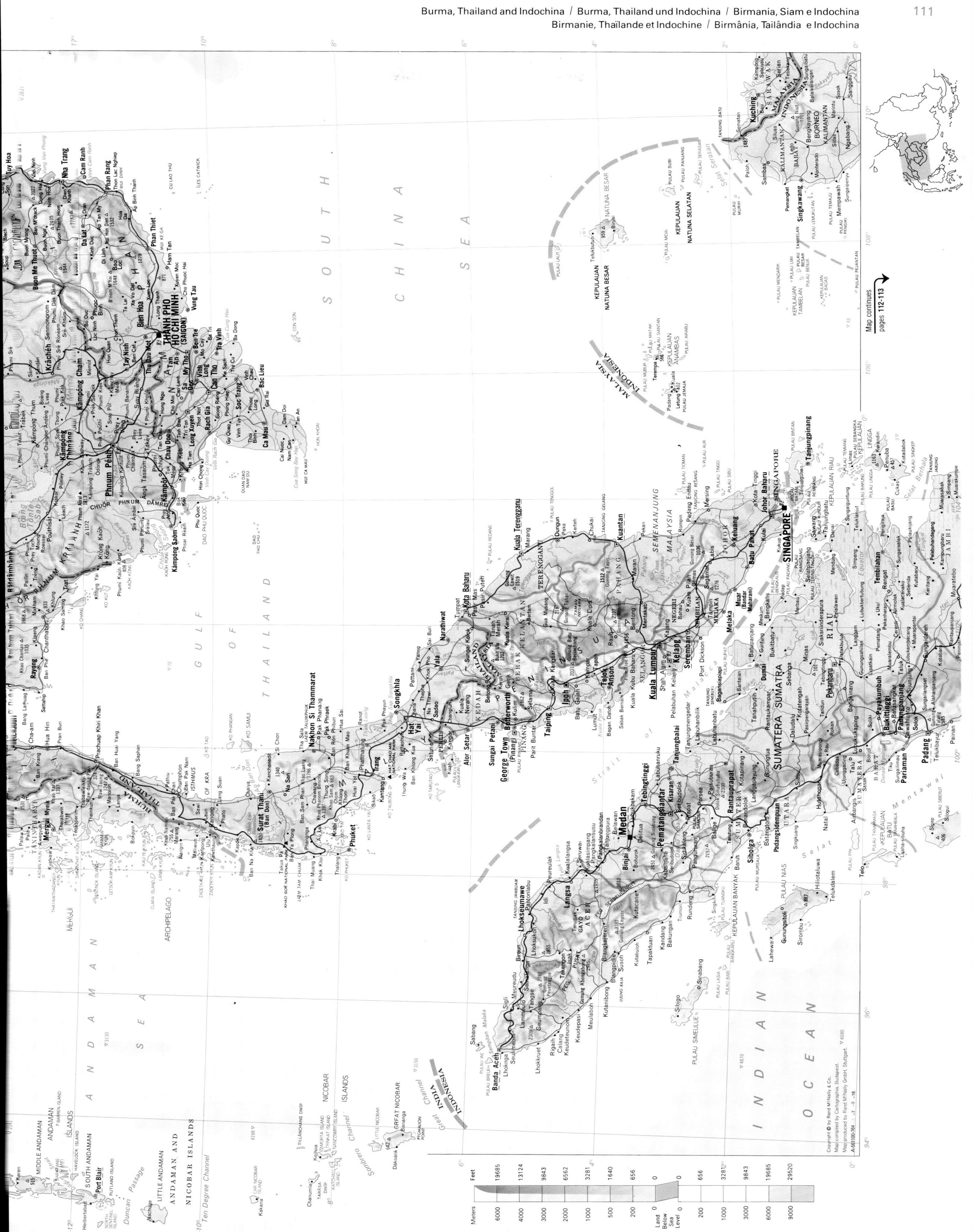

Map continues
pages 112-113

Meters		Feet
6000		19685
4000		13124
3000		9843
2000		6562
1000		3281
500		1640
200		656
0	Land Below Sea Level	0
200		656
1000		3281
2000		9843
6000		19685
9000		29520

Malaysia and Western Indonesia / Malaysia und westliches Indonesien / Malasia e Indonesia Occidental
Malaisie et Indonésie Occidentale / Malásia e Indonésia Ocidental

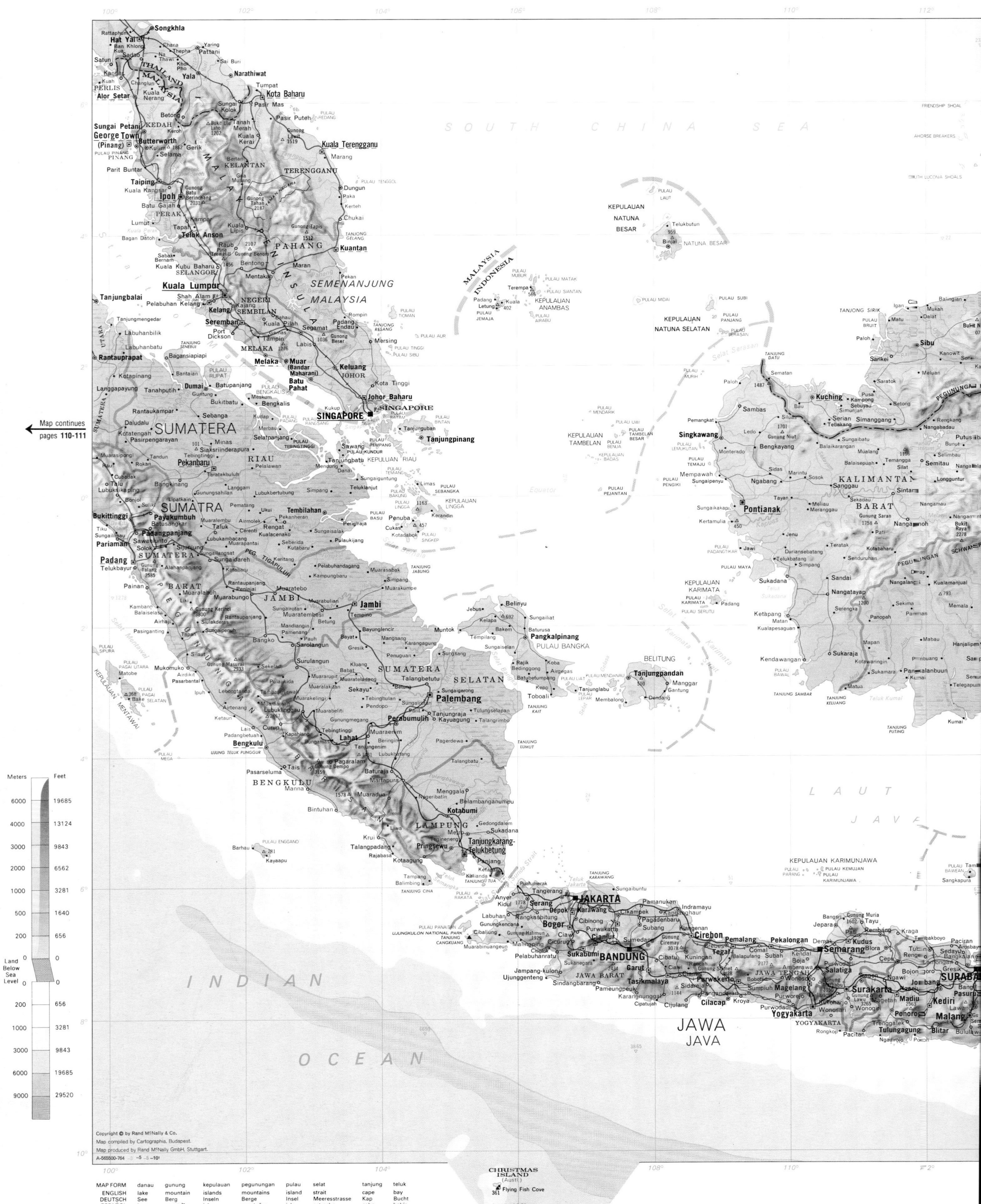

← Map continues
pages 110-111

Meters	Feet
6000	19685
4000	13124
3000	9843
2000	6562
1000	3281
500	1640
200	656
Land 0 Below Sea Level 0	0 0
200	656
1000	3281
3000	9843
6000	19685
9000	29520

MAP FORM	danau	gunung	kepulauan	pegunungan	pulau	selat	tanjung	teluk
ENGLISH	lake	mountain	islands	mountains	island	strait	cape	bay
DEUTSCH	See	Berg	Inseln	Berge	Insel	Meeresstrasse	Kap	Bucht
ESPAÑOL	lago	montaña	islas	montañas	isla	estrecho	cabo	bahía
FRANÇAIS	lac	montagne	îles	montagnes	île	détroit	cap	baie
PORTUGUÊS	lago	montanha	ilhas	montanhas	ilha	estreito	cabo	baia

Malaysia and Western Indonesia / Malaysia und westliches Indonesien
Malasia e Indonesia Occidental / Malaisie et Indonésie Occidentale
Malásia e Indonésia Ocidental

113

Map continues
pages 116-117

Map continues
pages 164-165

PHILIPPINES
MALAYSIA
INDONESIA

SULU SEA
CELEBES SEA
JAWA SEA
LAUT BANDA / BANDA SEA
LAUT FLORES / FLORES SEA
LAUT MALUKU / MOLUCCA SEA
MAKASAR STRAIT / Selat Makassar
TIMOR SEA
LAUT SAWU
Teluk Tomini
Teluk Tolo
Teluk Bone
MALUKU

BRUNEI
Bandar Seri Begawan
Miri
SARAWAK
SABAH
Kota Kinabalu (Jesselton)
Sandakan
Tawau
Lahad Datu

BORNEO
KALIMANTAN
KALIMANTAN TIMUR
KALIMANTAN TENGAH
KALIMANTAN SELATAN
Samarinda
Balikpapan
Banjarmasin
Martapura
Palangkaraya
Tarakan

SULAWESI
CELEBES
SULAWESI UTARA
SULAWESI TENGAH
SULAWESI SELATAN
SULAWESI TENGGARA
Manado
Gorontalo
Palu
Poso
Palopo
Parepare
Singkang
Watampone (Bone)
Ujungpandang (Makasar)
Kendari
Baubau

Davao
MINDANAO
Zamboanga
Koronadal
General Santos
Jolo

PULAU BUTON
PULAU MUNA
PULAU KABAENA
KEPULAUAN TOGIAN
KEPULAUAN BANGGAI
KEPULAUAN SULA
KEPULAUAN TUKANGBESI
BURU

MADURA
Pamekasan
JAWA TIMUR
Situbondo
Probolinggo
Jember
Banyuwangi
BALI
Singaraja
Denpasar
Mataram
LOMBOK
SUMBAWA
NUSA TENGGARA BARAT
NUSA TENGGARA TIMUR
FLORES
Ende
SUMBA
Waingapu
TIMOR
TIMOR TIMUR
Kupang
Dili
PULAU WETAR
PULAU ROTI

Equator

Kilometers | 0 | 100 | 200 | 300 | Km.
Statute Miles | 0 | 100 | 200 | 300 | Mi.

Scale 1:6,000,000
One centimeter represents 60 kilometers.
One inch represents approximately 95 miles.
Mercator Projection

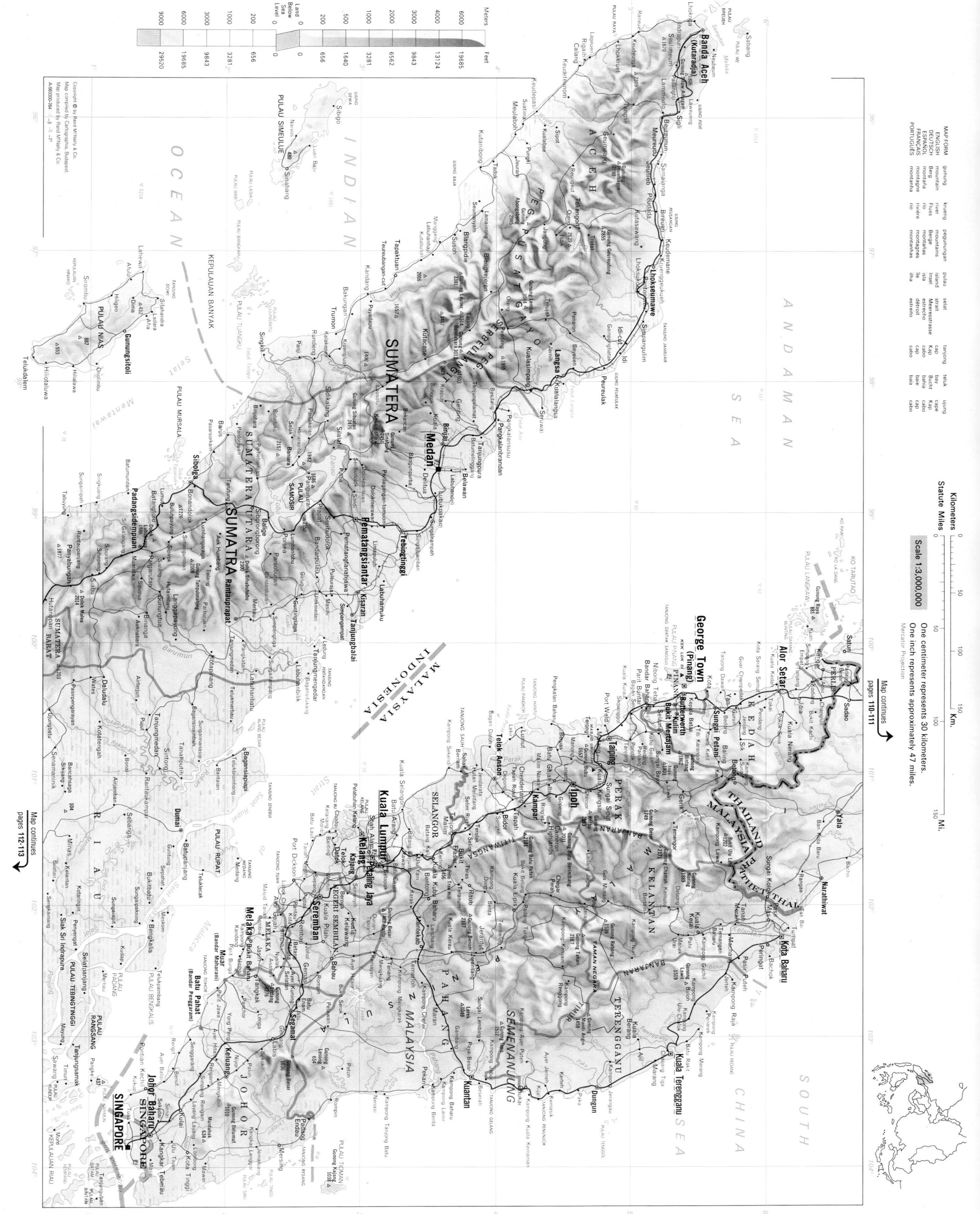

114

Scale 1:3,000,000

One centimeter represents approximately 30 kilometers.
One inch represents approximately 47 miles.

Mercator Projection

Map continues
pages 110-111

Map continues
pages 112-113

MAP FORM	
ENGLISH	
DEUTSCH	
ESPAÑOL	
FRANÇAIS	
PORTUGUÊS	

mountain	gunung
Berg	peguntungan
montaña	montanas
montagne	
montanha	
river	krueng
Fluss	river
rio	Fluss
rivière	rio
rio	rivière
	rio
mountains	peguntungan
Berge	mountains
montañas	Berge
montagnes	montañas
montanhas	montagnes
	montanhas
island	pulau
Insel	island
isla	Insel
île	isla
ilha	île
strait	selat
Meeresstrasse	strait
estrecho	Meeresstrasse
détroit	estrecho
estreito	détroit
cape	tanjung
Kap	ujung
cabo	Kap
cap	cabo
cabo	cap
bay	teluk
Bucht	bay
bahía	Bucht
baie	bahía
baía	baie

Copyright © by Rand McNally & Co.
Map compiled by Cartographia, Budapest.
Map produced by Rand McNally & Co.

INDIAN OCEAN

ANDAMAN SEA

SOUTH CHINA SEA

SUMATERA

SUMATRA

THAILAND

MALAYSIA

INDONESIA

SINGAPORE

Java • Lesser Sunda Islands / Java • Kleine Sundainseln
Java • Islas Menores de la Sonda
Java • Petites Îles de la Sonde / Java • Ilhas Menores da Sonda

115

JAWA
JAVA

LAUT JAWA
JAVA SEA

INDIAN OCEAN

Laut Flores
Flores Sea

Laut Sawu
Savu Sea

Selat Sumba

FLORES

SUMBA

SUMBAWA

LOMBOK

BALI

NUSA TENGGARA BARAT

NUSA TENGGARA TIMUR

NUSA TENGGARA

LESSER SUNDA ISLANDS

JAKARTA
BANDUNG
SURABAYA
SEMARANG
YOGYAKARTA
SURAKARTA
Malang
Denpasar
Mataram

Mi.
Km.

Kilometers
Statute Miles

Scale 1:3,000,000

One centimeter represents 30 kilometers.
One inch represents approximately 47 miles.

Mercator Projection

Copyright © by Rand McNally & Co.

Map compiled by Cartographia, Budapest.
Map produced by Rand McNally GmbH, Stuttgart.

MAP FORM				
ENGLISH	gunung	mountain	tanjung	cape
DEUTSCH	Berg		Kap	
ESPAÑOL	montaña		cabo	
FRANÇAIS	montagne		cap	
PORTUGUÊS	montanha		cabo	

pulau	island	teluk	bay
Insel		Bucht	
isla		bahía	
île		baie	
ilha		baía	

Feet
19685
13124
9843
6562
3281
1640
656
0

Meters
6000
4000
3000
2000
1000
500
200
0

Land Below Sea Level

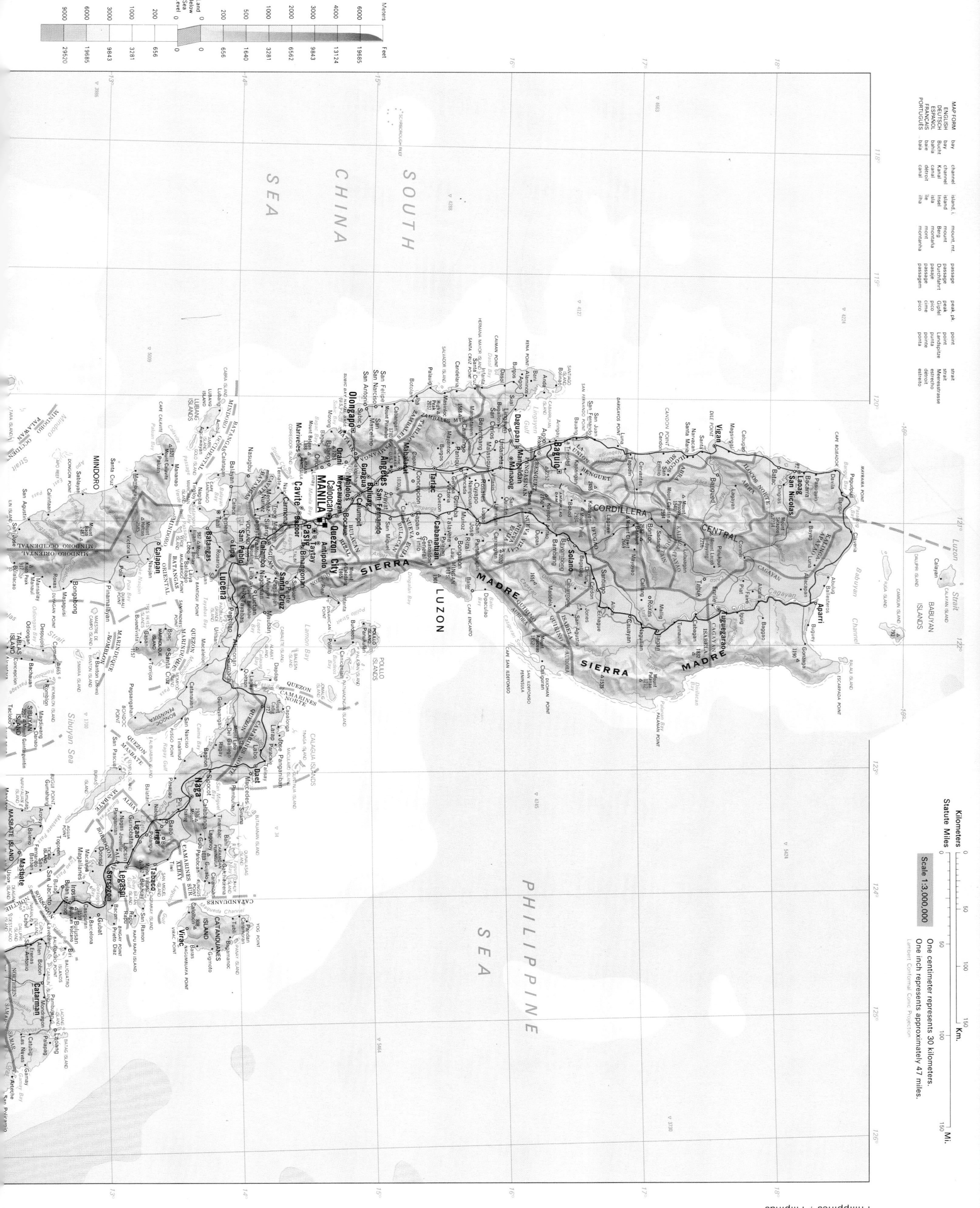

MAP FORM

ENGLISH	DEUTSCH	ESPAÑOL	FRANÇAIS	PORTUGUÊS
bay	Bucht	bahía	baie	baía
channel	Kanal	canal	canal	canal
channel	Durchfahrt	canal	détroit	canal
island, I.	Insel	isla	île	ilha
island	Insel	isla	île	ilha
mount, mt.	Berg	montaña	mont	montanha
mount	Berg	montaña	mont	montanha
passage	Durchfahrt	passage	passage	passagem
peak, pk.	Gipfel	pico	pic	pico
peak	Gipfel	pico	cime	pico
point	Landspitze	punta	pointe	ponta
point	Landspitze	punta	pointe	ponta
strait	Meeresstrasse	estrecho	détroit	estreito
strait	Meeresstrasse	estrecho	détroit	estreito

Scale 1:3,000,000

One centimeter represents approximately 30 kilometers.
One inch represents approximately 47 miles.

Lambert Conformal Conic Projection

SOUTH CHINA SEA

PHILIPPINE SEA

LUZON

SULU SEA
CELEBES SEA
MINDANAO
PALAWAN
NEGROS
PANAY
BOHOL
CEBU
LEYTE
SAMAR
BORNEO
KALIMANTAN
SULU ARCHIPELAGO
CUYO ISLANDS
CAGAYAN ISLANDS
BASILAN ISLAND
JOLO ISLAND
TAWI-TAWI ISLAND
PHILIPPINES PILIPINAS
MALAYSIA
Puerto Princesa
Sandakan
Zamboanga
Iloilo
Bacolod
Cebu
Tacloban
Cagayan de Oro
Davao
Cotabato
Butuan
Surigao
General Santos
Jolo
Moro Gulf
Davao Gulf
Bohol Sea
Visayan Sea
Panay Gulf
Map continues pages 112-113
Copyright © by Rand McNally & Co.
Map prepared by Rand McNally & Co.
A-563100-764 -3 -5 -71

Map continues pages 22-23

Map continues pages 134-135

MAP FORM	gulf	jabal	jazirat	range	ra's	shan
ENGLISH	gulf	mountain	island	range	cape	mountain(s)
DEUTSCH	Golf	Berg	Insel	Gebirge	Kap	Berg(e)
ESPAÑOL	golfo	montaña	isla	sierra	cabo	montaña(s)
FRANÇAIS	golfe	montagne	île	chaîne	cap	montagne(s)
PORTUGUÊS	golfo	montanha	ilha	serra	cabo	montanha(s)

Kilometers 0   200   400   600 Km.
Statute Miles 0   200   400   600 Mi.

Scale 1:12,000,000
One centimeter represents 120 kilometers.
One inch represents approximately 190 miles.
Lambert Conformal Conic Projection

India, Pakistan and Southwest Asia / Indien, Pakistan und Südwestasien / India, Pakistán y Asia Sud-occidental
Inde, Pakistan et Asie du Sud-Ouest / Índia, Paquistão e Ásia do Sudoeste

119

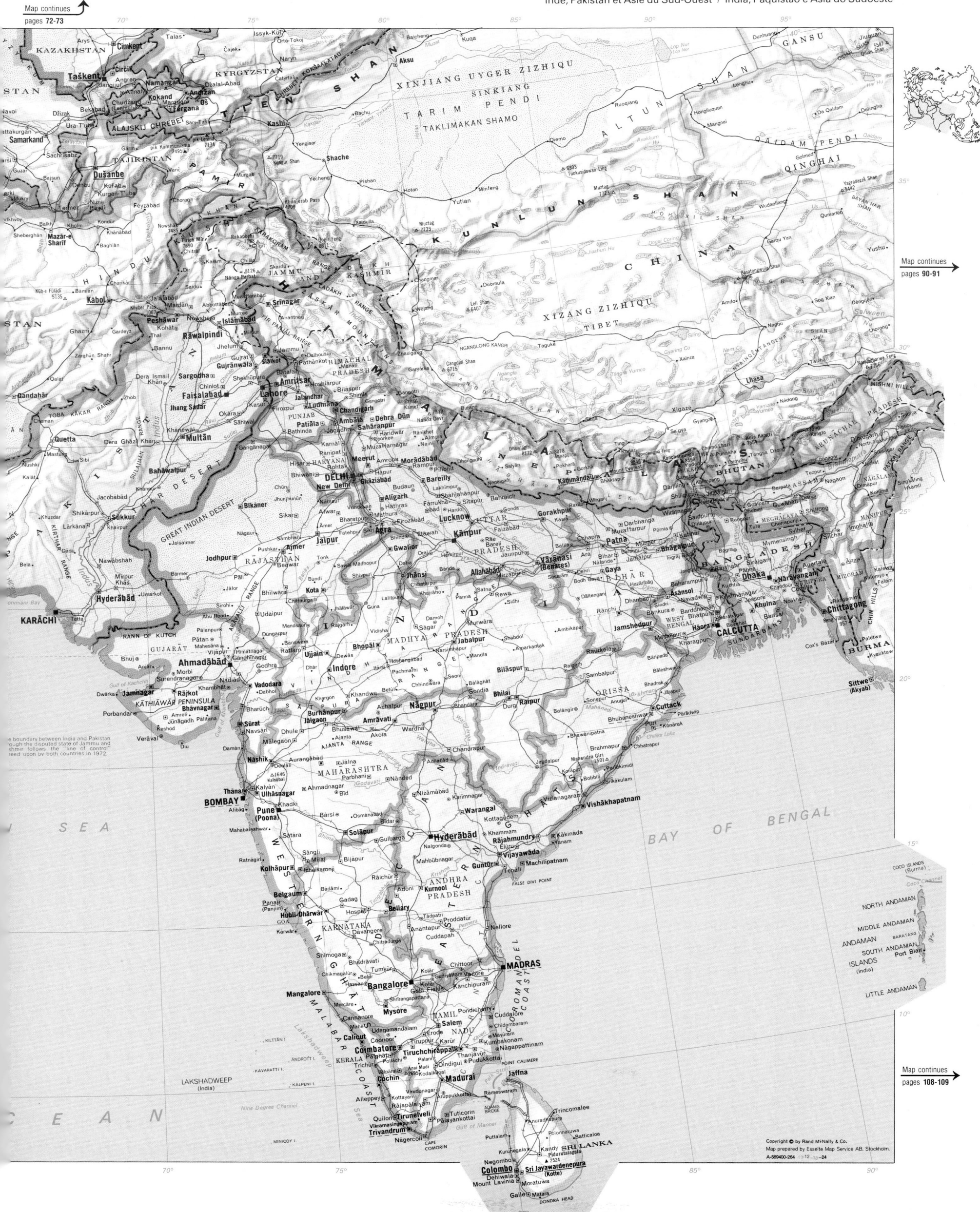

Map continues
pages 72-73

Map continues
pages 90-91

Map continues
pages 108-109

Copyright © by Rand McNally & Co.
Map prepared by Esselte Map Service AB, Stockholm.
A-569400-264   -12 -13 -24

120

Northern India and Pakistan / Nordindien und Pakistan / India Septentrional y Pakistán
Inde Septentrionale et Pakistan / Índia Setentrional e Paquistão

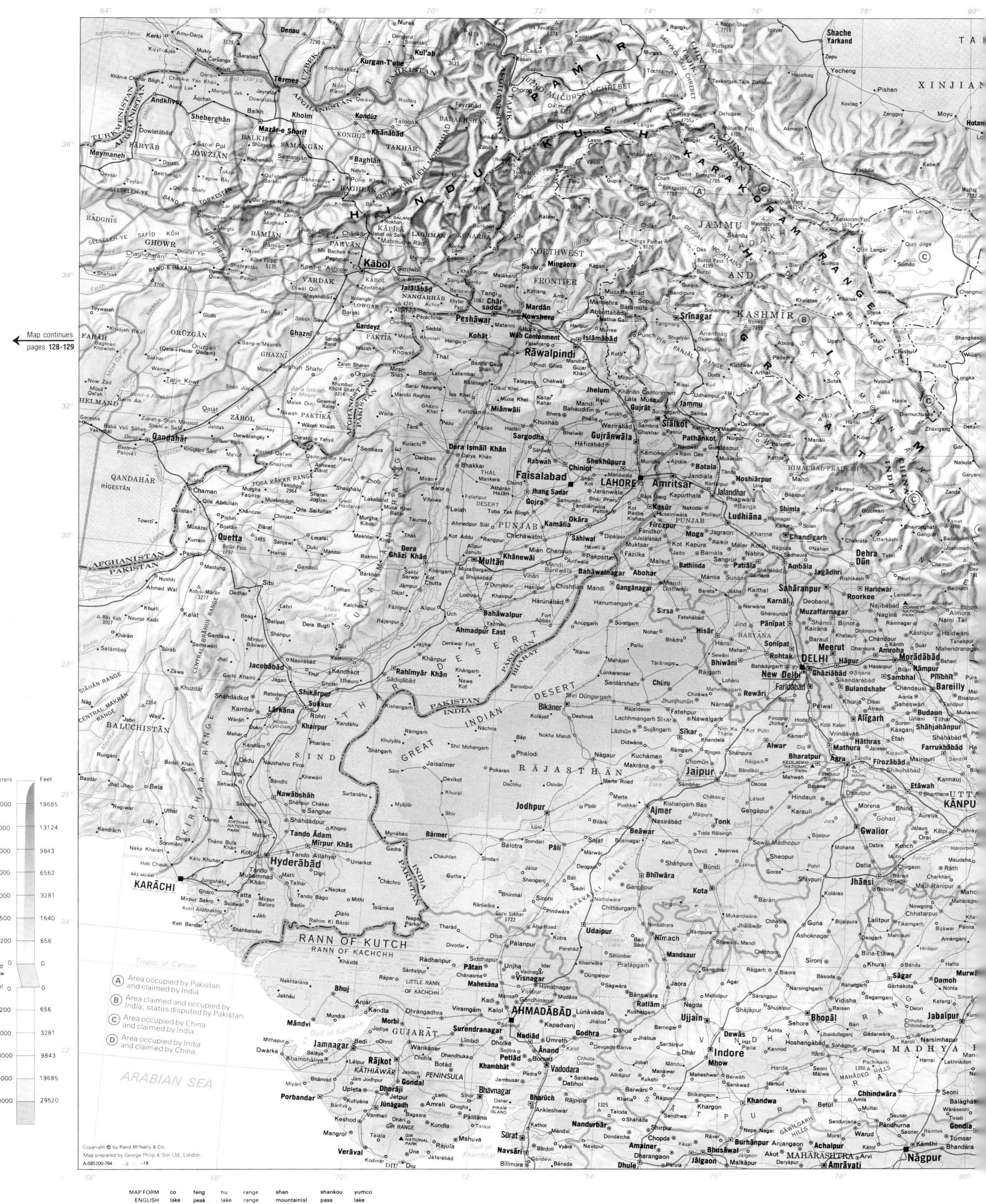

Map continues
pages 128-129

(A) Area occupied by Pakistan
    and claimed by India.

(B) Area claimed and occupied by
    India; status disputed by Pakistan.

(C) Area occupied by China
    and claimed by India.

(D) Area occupied by India
    and claimed by China.

Copyright © by Rand McNally & Co.
Map prepared by George Philip & Son Ltd., London.
A-565200-764   -8   -3   -18

MAP FORM	co	feng	hu	range	shan	shankou	yumco
ENGLISH	lake	peak	lake	range	mountain(s)	pass	lake
DEUTSCH	See	Gipfel	See	Gebirge	Berg(e)	Pass	See
ESPAÑOL	lago	pico	lago	sierra	montaña(s)	paso	lago
FRANCAIS	lac	cime	lac	chaîne	montagne(s)	col	lac
PORTUGUÊS	lago	pico	lago	serra	montanha(s)	passo	lago

Northern India and Pakistan / Nordindien und Pakistan / India Septentrional y Pakistán
Inde Septentrionale et Pakistan / Índia Setentrional e Paquistão

121

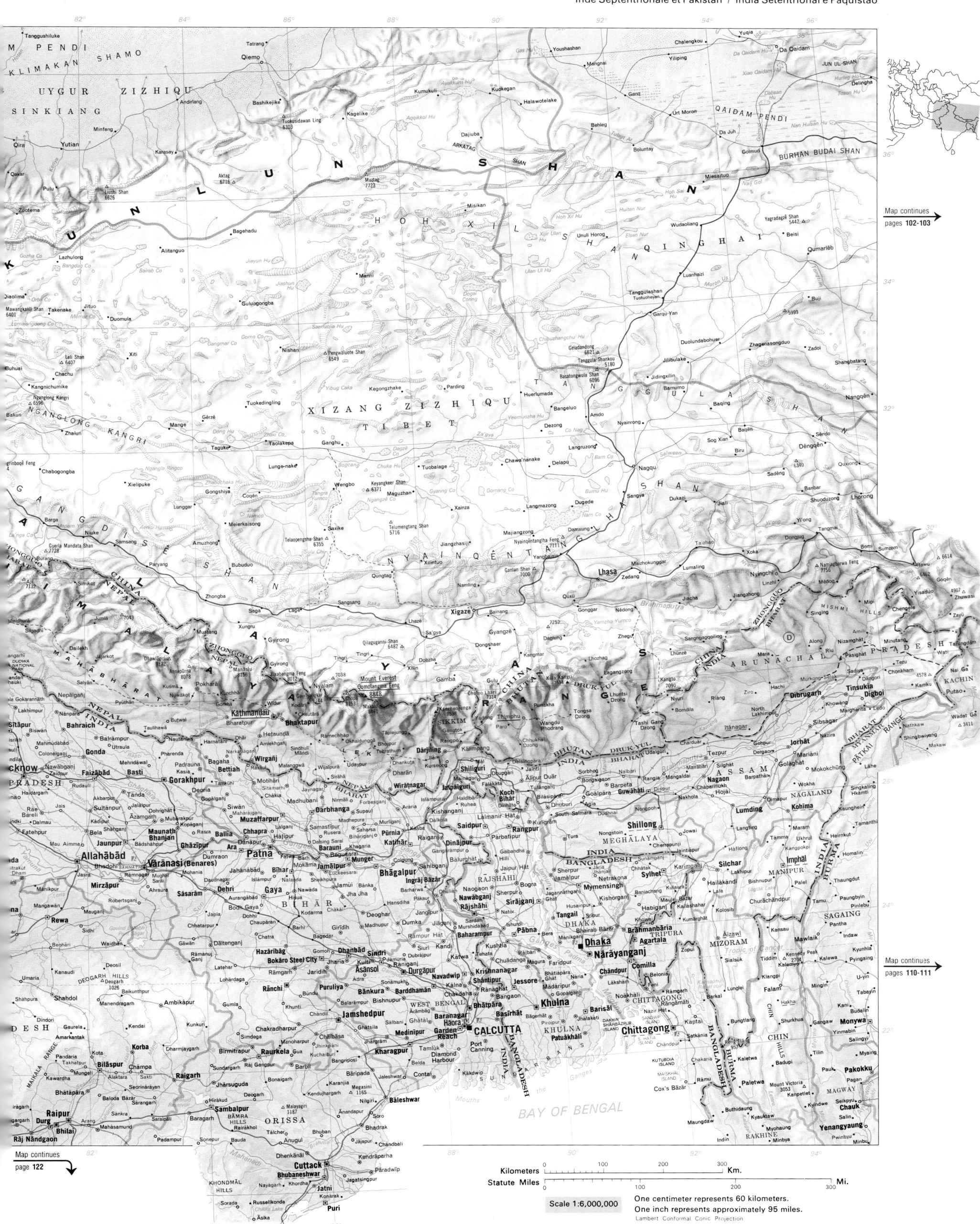

Map continues
pages 102-103

Map continues
pages 110-111

Map continues
page 122

BAY OF BENGAL

Kilometers 0 100 200 300 Km.

Statute Miles 0 100 200 300 Mi.

Scale 1:6,000,000

One centimeter represents 60 kilometers.
One inch represents approximately 95 miles.

Lambert Conformal Conic Projection

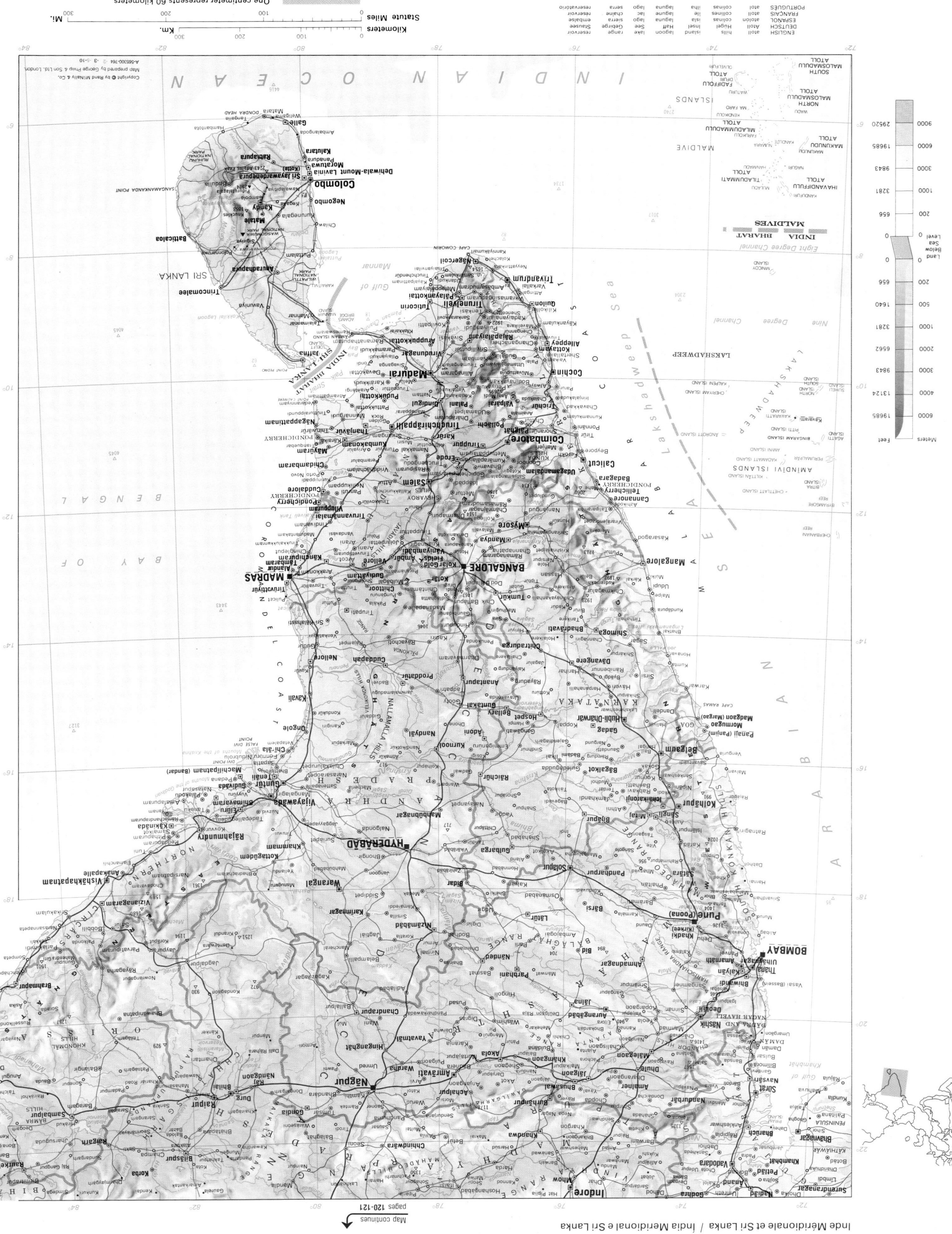

Scale 1:6,000,000
One centimeter represents 60 kilometers.
One inch represents approximately 95 miles.
Lambert Conformal Conic Projection.

122

Southern India and Sri Lanka / Südindien und Sri Lanka / India Meridional y Sri Lanka
Inde Méridionale et Sri Lanka / India Meridionale e Sri Lanka

Map continues
pages 120–121

Inde Méridionale et Sri Lanka / Índia Meridional e Sri Lanka
ENGLISH	atoll	hills	island	lagoon	lake	range	reservoir
DEUTSCH	Atoll	Hugel	Insel	Haff	See	Gebirge	Stausee
ESPAÑOL	atolón	colinas	isla	laguna	lago	sierra	embalse
FRANÇAIS	atoll	collines	île	lagune	lac	chaîne	réservoir
PORTUGUÊS	atol	colinas	ilha	laguna	lago	serra	reservatório
Kilometers 0 100 200 300 Km.
Statute Miles 0 100 200 300 Mi.

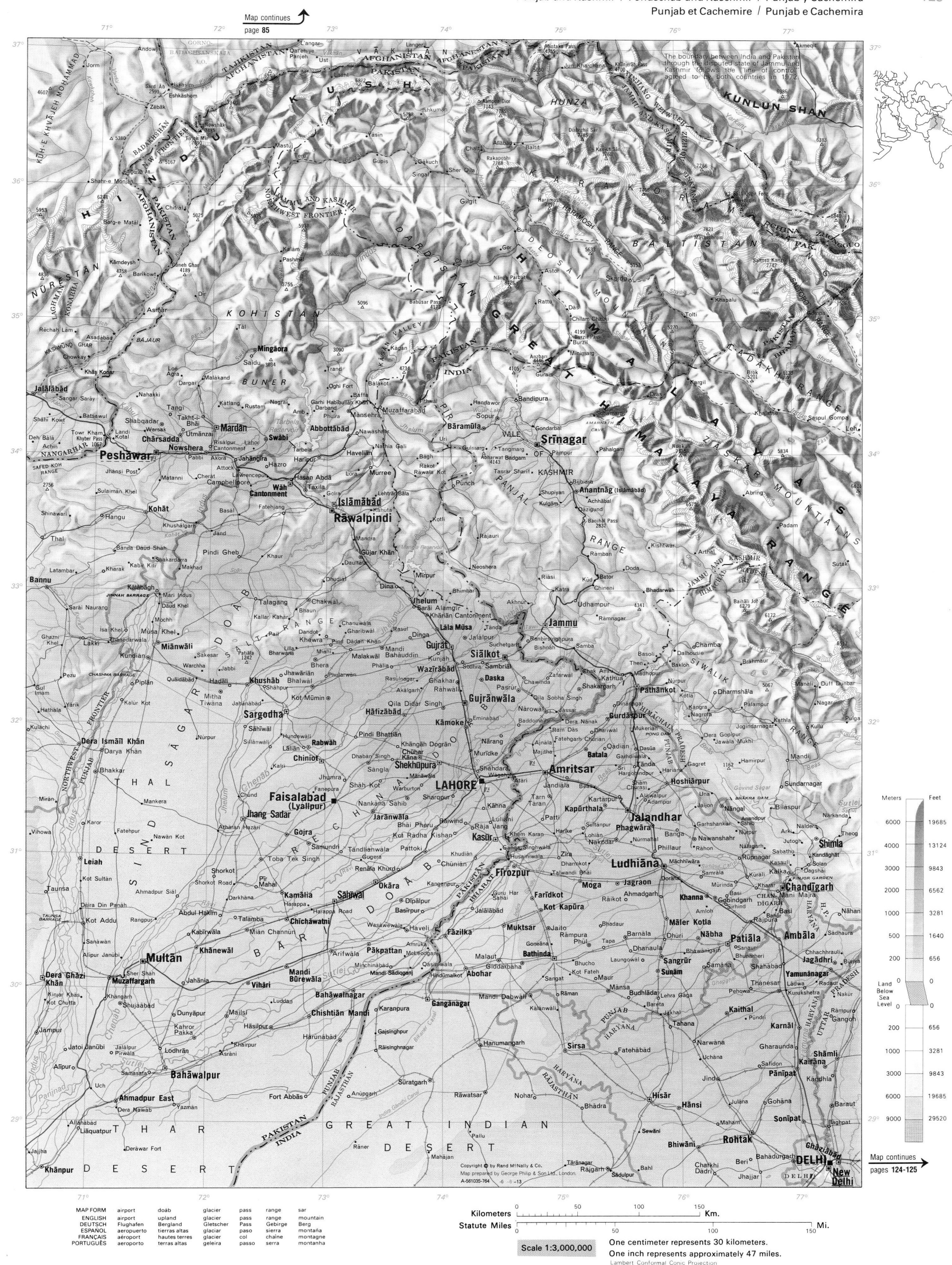

Ganges Lowland and Nepal / Gangestiefland und Nepal / Llanuras del Ganges y Nepal
Plaine du Gange et Népal / Planicie do Ganges e Nepal

Map continues page 123

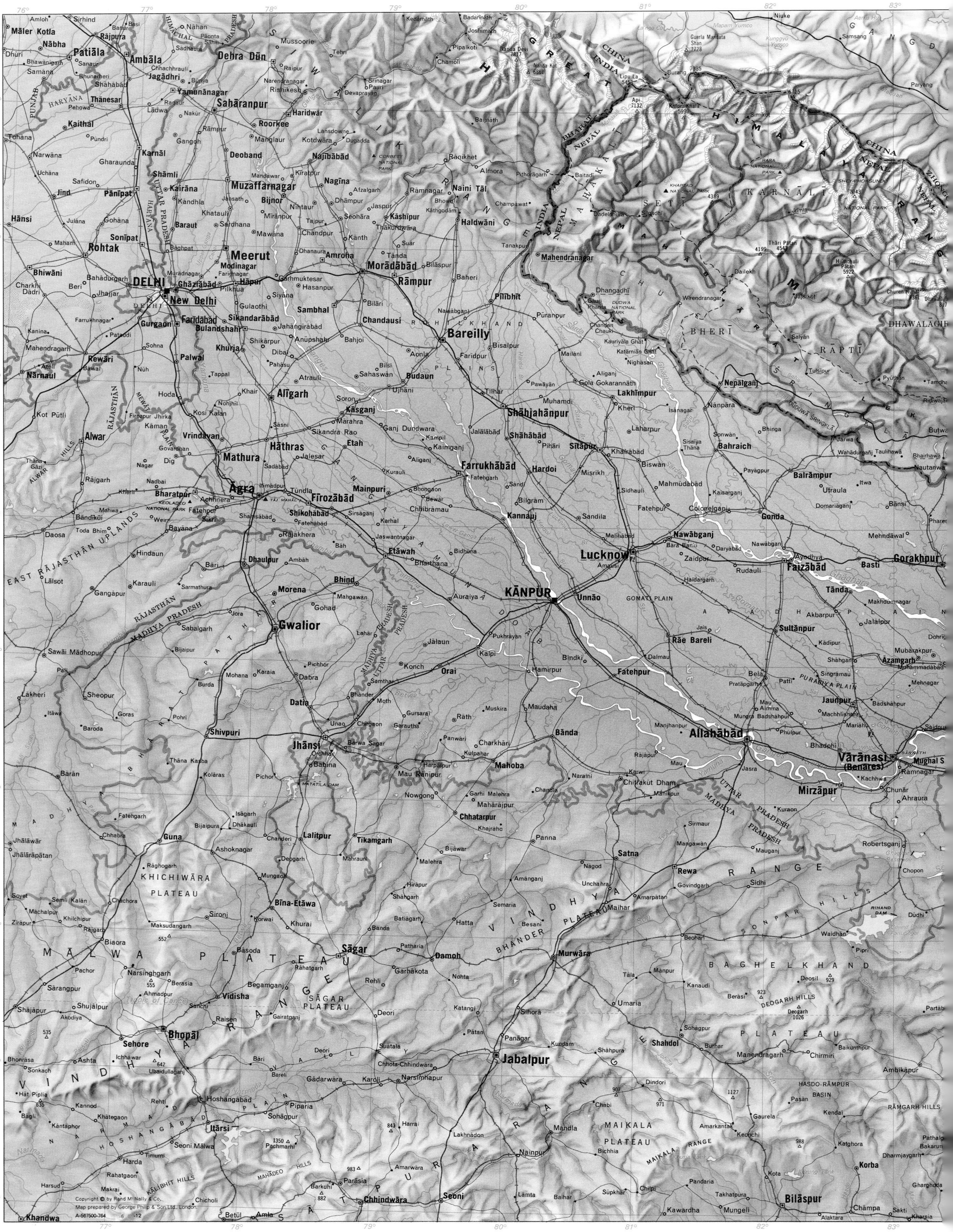

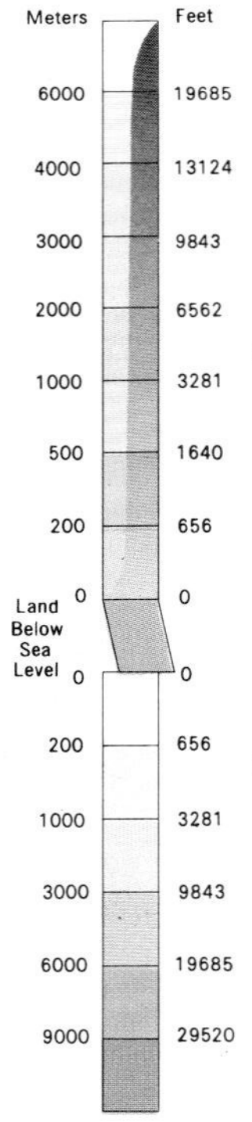

MAP FORM	hills	plains	plateau	range	shan	yumco
ENGLISH	hills	plains	plateau	range	mountains	lake
DEUTSCH	Hügel	Ebenen	Hochebene	Gebirge	Berge	See
ESPAÑOL	colinas	llanos	meseta	sierra	montañas	lago
FRANÇAIS	collines	plaines	plateau	chaîne	montagnes	lac
PORTUGUÊS	colinas	planícies	planalto	serra	montanhas	lago

Kilometers 0 50 100 150 Km.
Statute Miles 0 50 100 150 Mi.

Scale 1:3,000,000

One centimeter represents 30 kilometers.
One inch represents approximately 47 miles.
Lambert Conformal Conic Projection

Ganges Lowland and Nepal / Gangestiefland und Nepal / Llanuras del Ganges y Nepal
Plaine du Gange et Népal / Planície do Ganges e Nepal

125

Kilometers
Statute Miles

Scale 1:1,000,000

One centimeter represents 10 kilometers.
One inch represents approximately 16 miles.
Lambert Conformal Conic Projection

Map continues pages 130-131

Map continues page 84

Map continues pages 144-145

Map continues pages 140-141

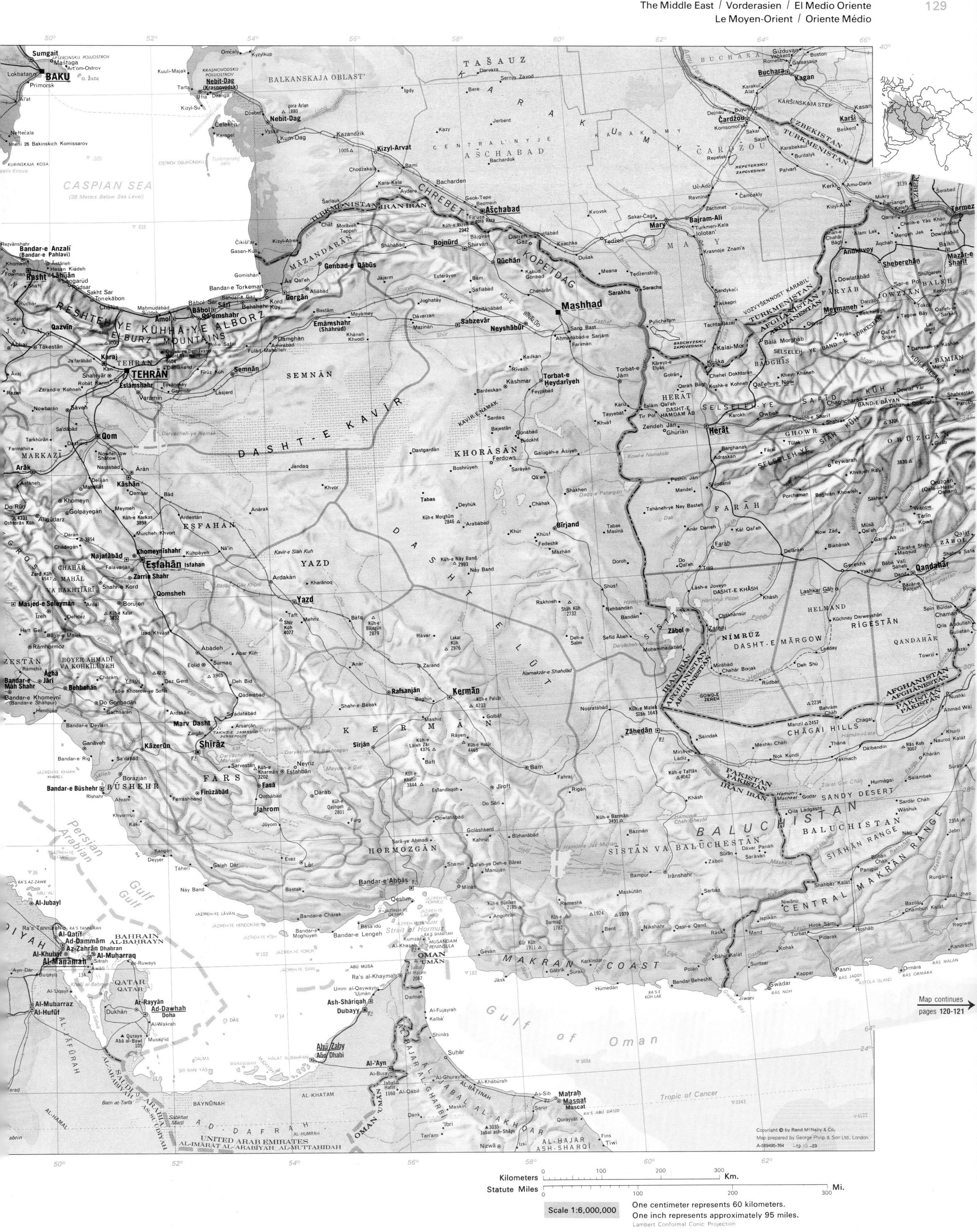

Scale 1:6,000,000

Kilometers
Statute Miles

One centimeter represents 60 kilometers.
One inch represents approximately 95 miles.
Lambert Conformal Conic Projection

Map continues,
pages 120-121

Turkey and Cyprus / Türkei und Zypern / Turquía y Chipre
Turquie et Chypre / Turquia e Chipre

Map continues pages **38-39**

Meters	Feet
6000	19685
4000	13124
3000	9843
2000	6562
1000	3281
500	1640
200	656
Land Below Sea Level	0
0	0
200	656
1000	3281
3000	9843
6000	19685
9000	29520

The Turkish Republic of Northern Cyprus unilaterally declared its independence on November 15, 1983.

MAP FORM	burnu	dag, dağı	dağlar	gölü	jabal	körfezi	sabkhat
ENGLISH	cape	mountain	mountains	lake	mountain	bay, gulf	salt marsh
DEUTSCH	Kap	Berg	Berge	See	Berge	Bucht, Golf	Salzmarsch
ESPAÑOL	cabo	montaña	montañas	lago	montañas	bahía, golfo	pantano salado
FRANÇAIS	cap	montagne	montagnes	lac	montagnes	baie, golfe	marais salé
PORTUGUÊS	cabo	montanha	montanhas	lago	montanhas	baía, golfo	pântano salgado

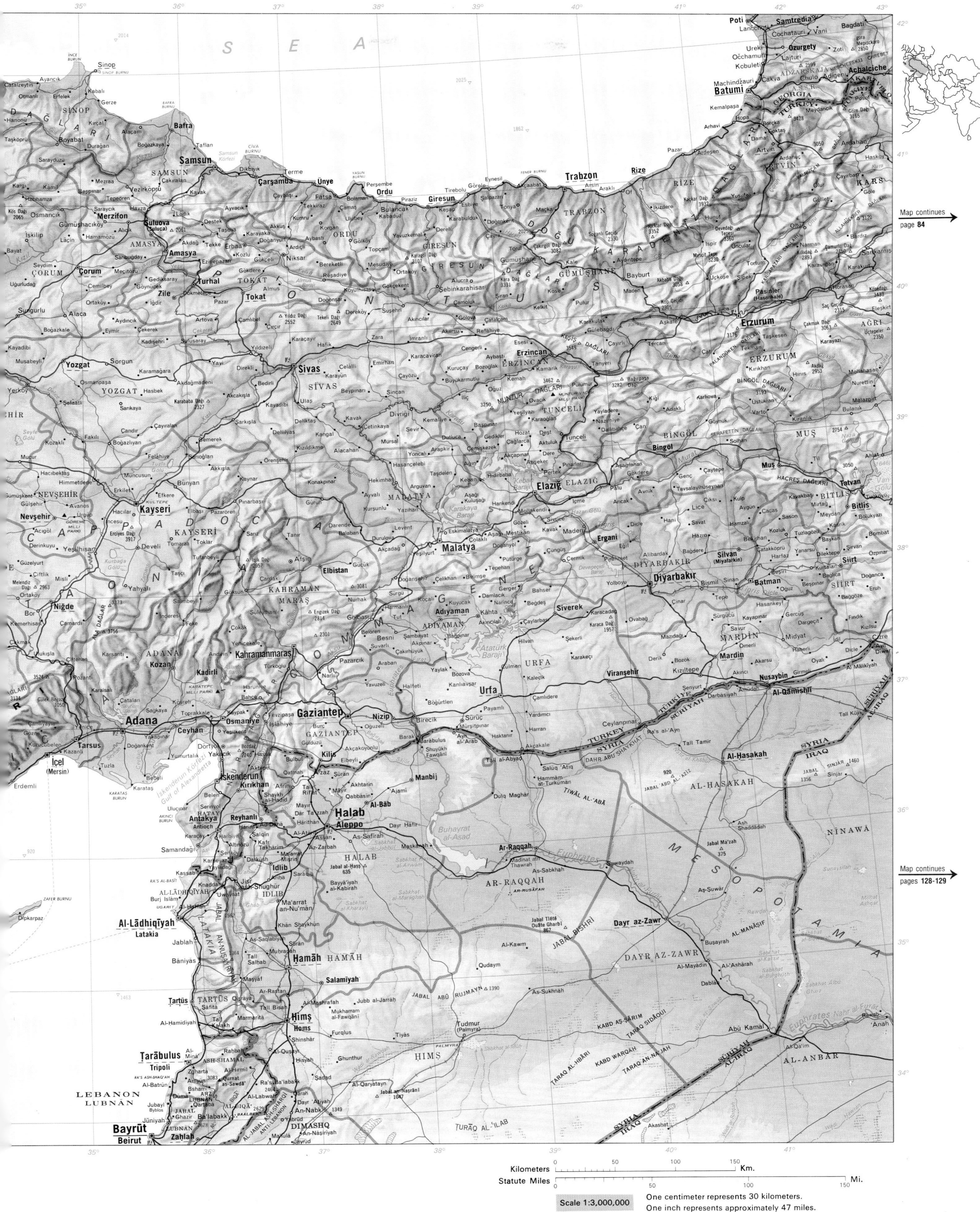

Map continues
page **84**

Map continues
pages **128-129**

Kilometers

Statute Miles

Scale 1:3,000,000

One centimeter represents 30 kilometers.
One inch represents approximately 47 miles.
Conic Projection, Two Standard Parallels

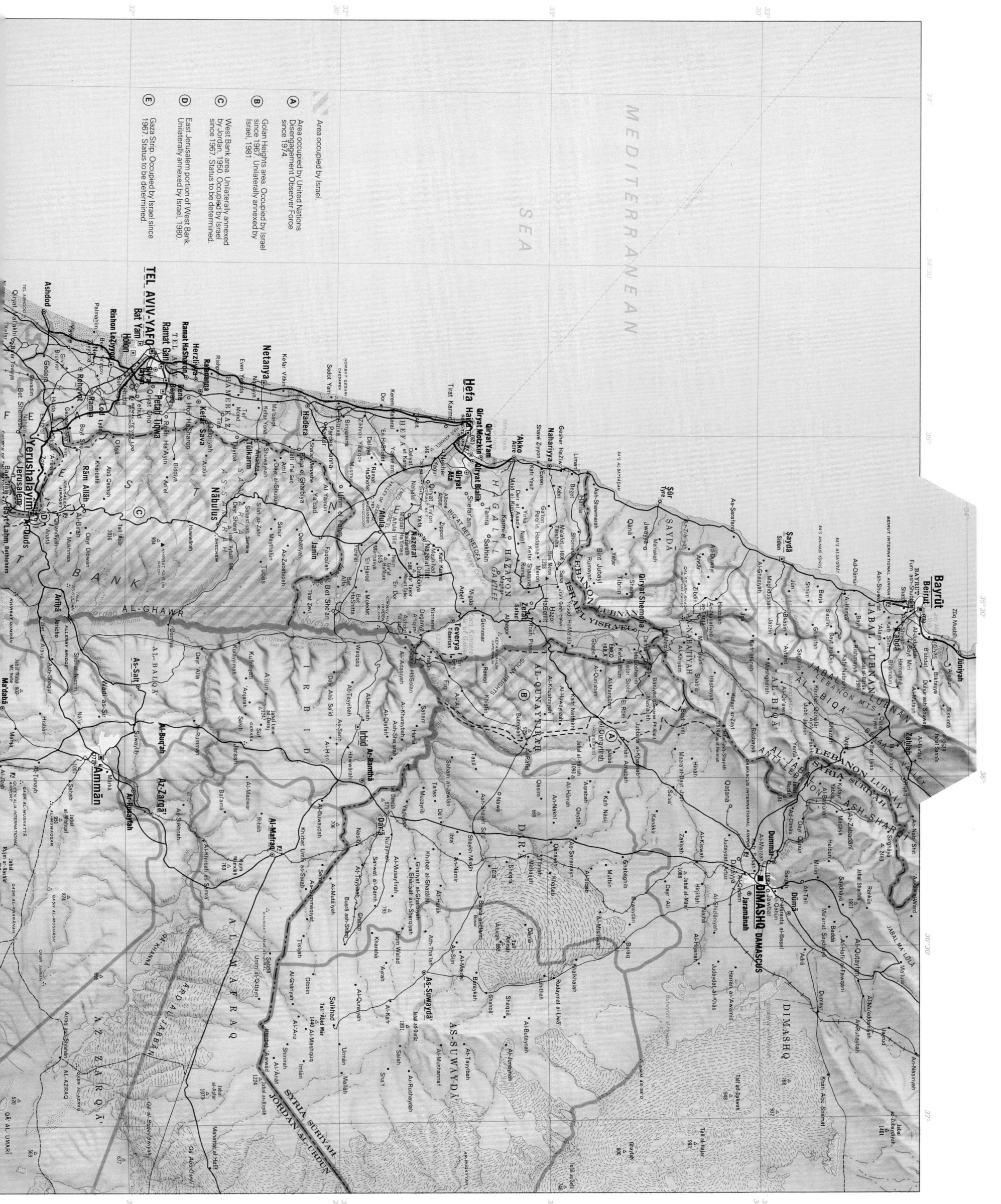

Area occupied by Israel.

Ⓐ Area occupied by United Nations
Disengagement Observer Force
since 1974.

Ⓑ Golan Heights area. Occupied by Israel
since 1967. Unilaterally annexed by
Israel, 1981.

Ⓒ West Bank area. Unilaterally annexed
by Jordan, 1950. Occupied by Israel
since 1967. Status to be determined.

Ⓓ East Jerusalem portion of West Bank.
Unilaterally annexed by Israel, 1980.

Ⓔ Gaza Strip. Occupied by Israel since
1967. Status to be determined.

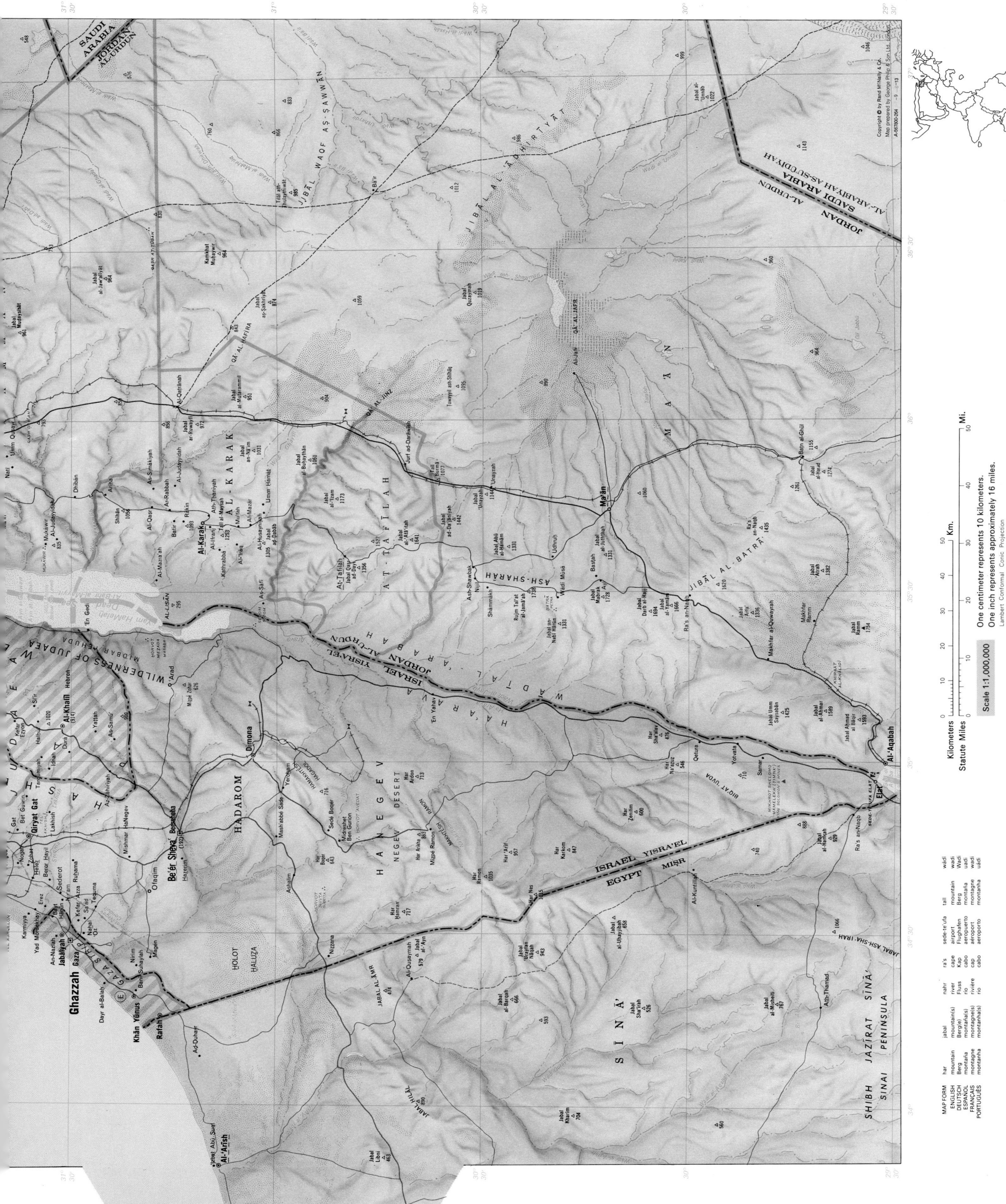

Scale 1:1,000,000

Kilometers

Statute Miles

One centimeter represents 10 kilometers.
One inch represents approximately 16 miles.
Lambert Conformal Conic Projection

MAP FORM				
har	jabal	nahr	ra's	sede-te'ufa
ENGLISH	mountain	river	cape	airport
DEUTSCH	Berg	Fluss	Kap	Flughafen
ESPAÑOL	montaña(s)	rio	cabo	aeropuerto
FRANÇAIS	montagne	riviere	cap	aeroport
PORTUGUÊS	montanha	rio	cabo	aeroporto

tall	wadi
mountain	wadi
Berg	Wadi
montaña	uadi
montagne	oued
montanha	uadi

Copyright © by Rand McNally & Co.
Map prepared by George Philip & Son, Ltd. London.
A-56790-364 -9 -13

Western North Africa / West Nordafrika / Región Occidental de Africa Septentrional
Afrique du Nord Occidentale / África do Norte Ocidental

MAP FORM	bahr, bahr	chott	jabal	lake	mountains	oued	wahât
ENGLISH	river, sea	salt marsh	mountain(s)	lake	mountains	wadi	oasis
DEUTSCH	Fluss, Meer	Salzmarsch	Berg(e)	See	Berge	Wadi	Oase
ESPAÑOL	río, mar	pantano salado	montaña(s)	lago	montañas	uadi	oasis
FRANÇAIS	rivière, mer	marais salé	montagne(s)	lac	montagnes	wadi	oasis
PORTUGUÊS	rio, mar	pântano salgado	montanha(s)	lago	montanhas	uâdi	oásis

Western North Africa / West Nordafrika / Región Occidental de Africa Septentrional
Afrique du Nord Occidentale / África do Norte Ocidental

135

Map continues
pages 22-23

Map continues
pages 136-137

Map continues
pages 138-139

MEDITERRANEAN SEA

ITALY

GREECE

TURKEY

NORTH CYPRUS

CYPRUS

MALTA   Valletta

Ionian Sea

TUNISIA

ALGERIA

LIBYA

EGYPT

S A H A R A

FAZZAN   FEZZAN

TARABULUS
TRIPOLITANIA

BARQAH
CYRENAICA

WESTERN
DESERT

AL-QĀHIRAH   CAIRO

Tripoli   Ṭarābulus

Banghāzī

Al-Iskandarīyah
Alexandria

Tropic of Cancer

NIGER

CHAD

SUDAN

NIGERIA

CAMEROON

CENTRAL AFRICAN
REPUBLIC

ZAIRE

CONGO

GABON

EQUAT. GUINEA

SAHEL

Lake Chad
Lac Tchad

N'Djamena

Lagos

Yaoundé

Bangui

Gulf

of

Guinea

Bight of Benin

Bight of Biafra

SAO TOME AND
PRINCIPE

Kilometers
Statute Miles

Km.

Mi.

Scale 1:12,000,000
One centimeter represents 120 kilometers.
One inch represents approximately 190 miles.
Miller Oblated Stereographic Projection

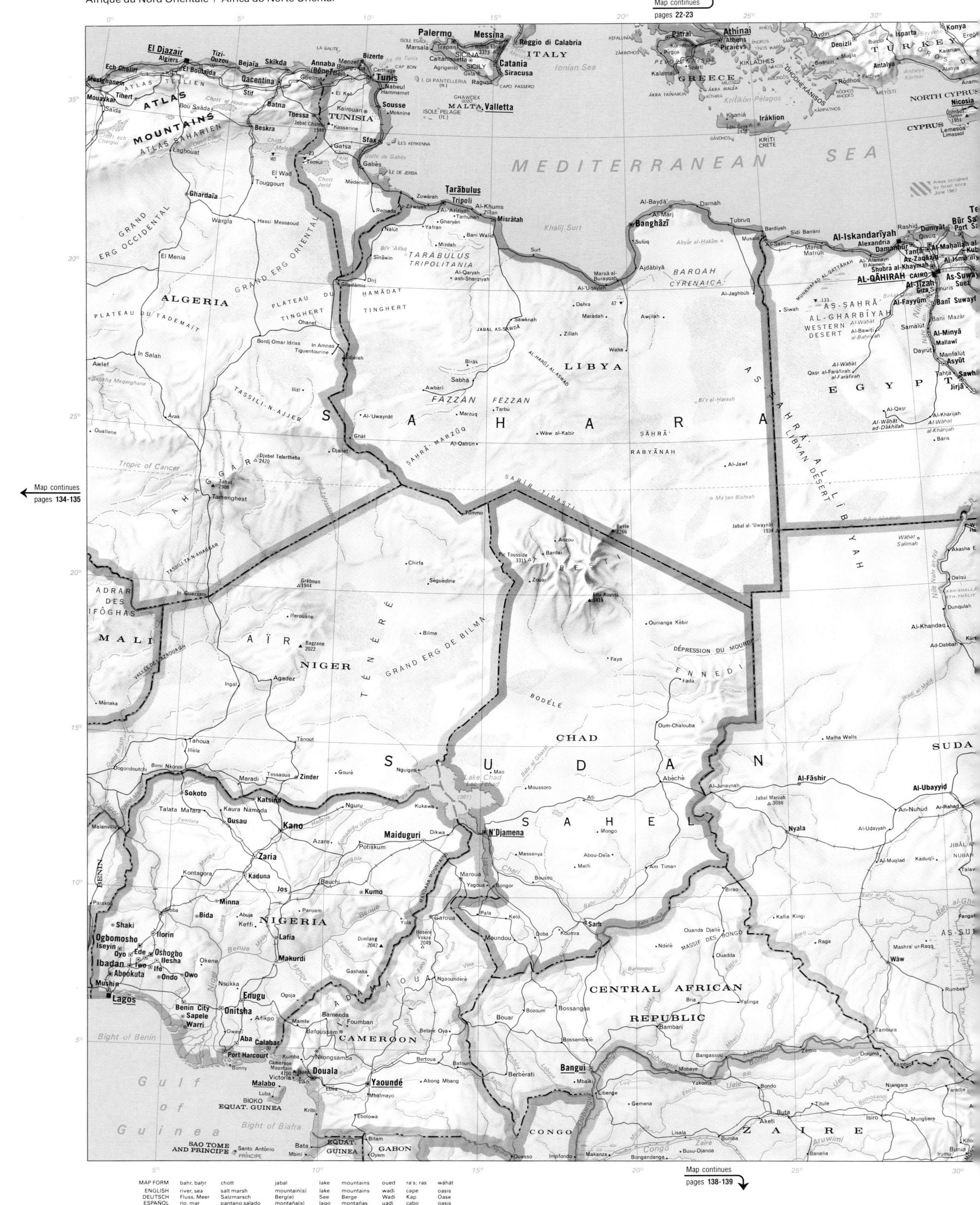

Map continues
pages 22-23

Map continues
pages 134-135

Map continues
pages 138-139

	MAP FORM	bahr, baḥr	chott	jabal	lake	mountains	oued	ra's; ras	wāḥāt
ENGLISH		river, sea	salt marsh	mountain(s)	lake	mountains	wadi	cape	oasis
DEUTSCH		Fluss, Meer	Salzmarsch	Berg(e)	See	Berge	Wadi	Kap	Oase
ESPAÑOL		rio, mar	pantano salado	montaña(s)	lago	montañas	uadi	cabo	oasis
FRANÇAIS		rivière, mer	marais salé	montagne(s)	lac	montagnes	wadi	cap	oasis
PORTUGUÊS		rio, mar	pântano salgado	montanha(s)	lago	montanhas	uádi	cabo	óasis

Eastern North Africa / Ost Nordafrika / Región Oriental de Africa Septentrional
Afrique du Nord Orientale / África do Norte Oriental

137

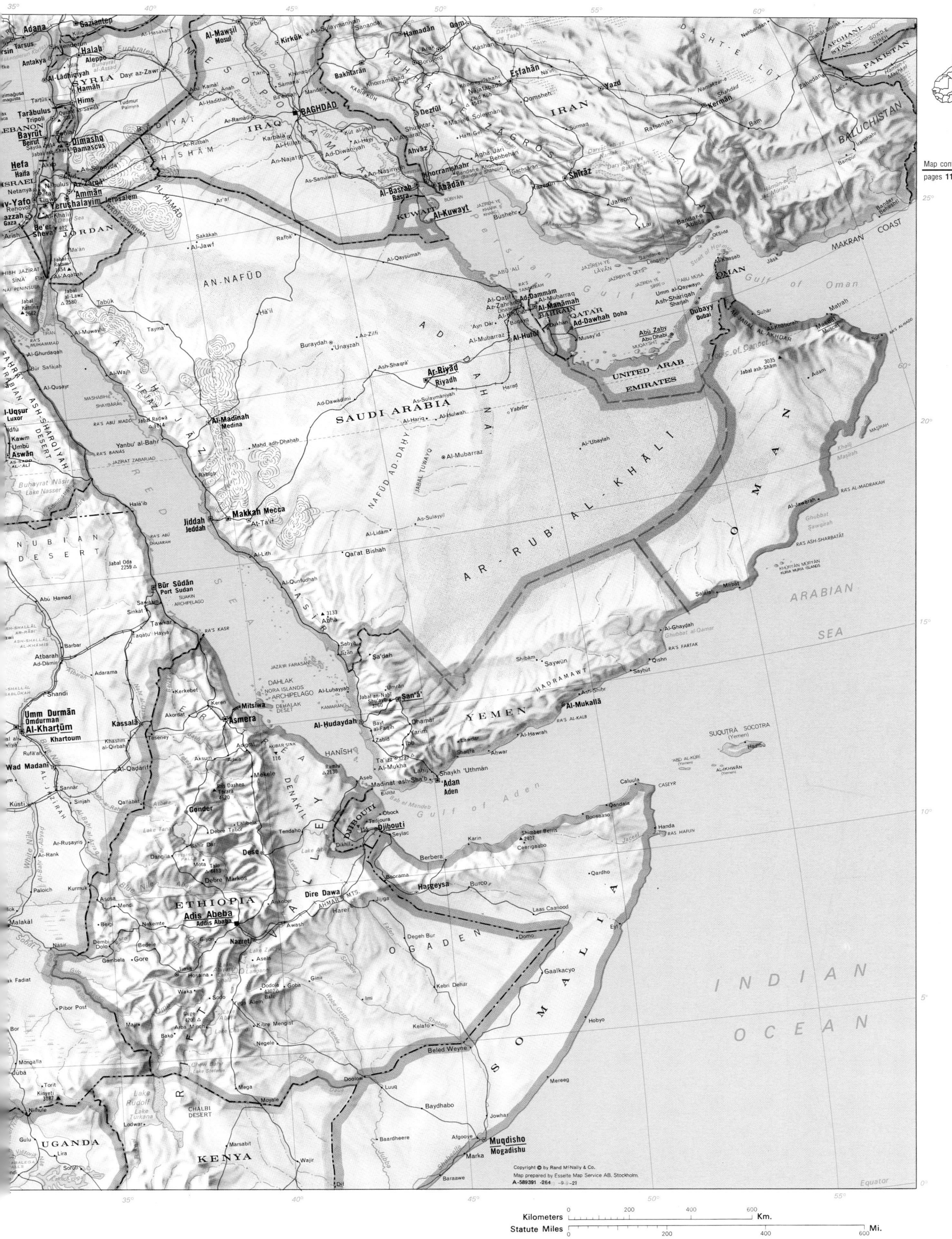

Map continues
pages 118-119

Kilometers 0   200   400   600 Km.
Statute Miles 0   200   400   600 Mi.

Scale 1:12,000,000

One centimeter represents 120 kilometers.
One inch represents approximately 190 miles.
Miller Oblated Stereographic Projection

Copyright © by Rand McNally & Co.
Map prepared by Esselte Map Service AB, Stockholm.
A-589391 -264 -9 - -21

Map continues
pages 136-137

INDIAN OCEAN

SOMALIA

KENYA
Nairobi

Mombasa

TANZANIA

MASAI
STEPPE

Tanga
Zanzibar
Dar es Salaam

SEYCHELLES
Victoria

AMIRANTE ISLANDS
(Sey.)

MALAWI

Nampula
Nacala

COMOROS
Moroni

Antsiranana

MOZAMBIQUE

Mahajanga

MADAGASCAR

Antananarivo

Antsirabe

Fianarantsoa

Beira

Toliara

Port Louis
Curepipe
MAURITIUS
Saint-Denis
RÉUNION
(Fr.)

MASCARENE
ISLANDS

Tropic of Capricorn

Xai-Xai

INDIAN OCEAN

CAP SAINTE-MARIE

Copyright © by Rand McNally & Co.
Map prepared by Esselte Map Service AB, Stockholm.
A-589200-264   -11.10 -21

Kilometers   0   200   400   600   Km.
Statute Miles   0   200   400   600   Mi.

Scale 1:12,000,000

One centimeter represents 120 kilometers.
One inch represents approximately 190 miles.
Miller Oblated Stereographic Projection

Map continues
pages 128-129

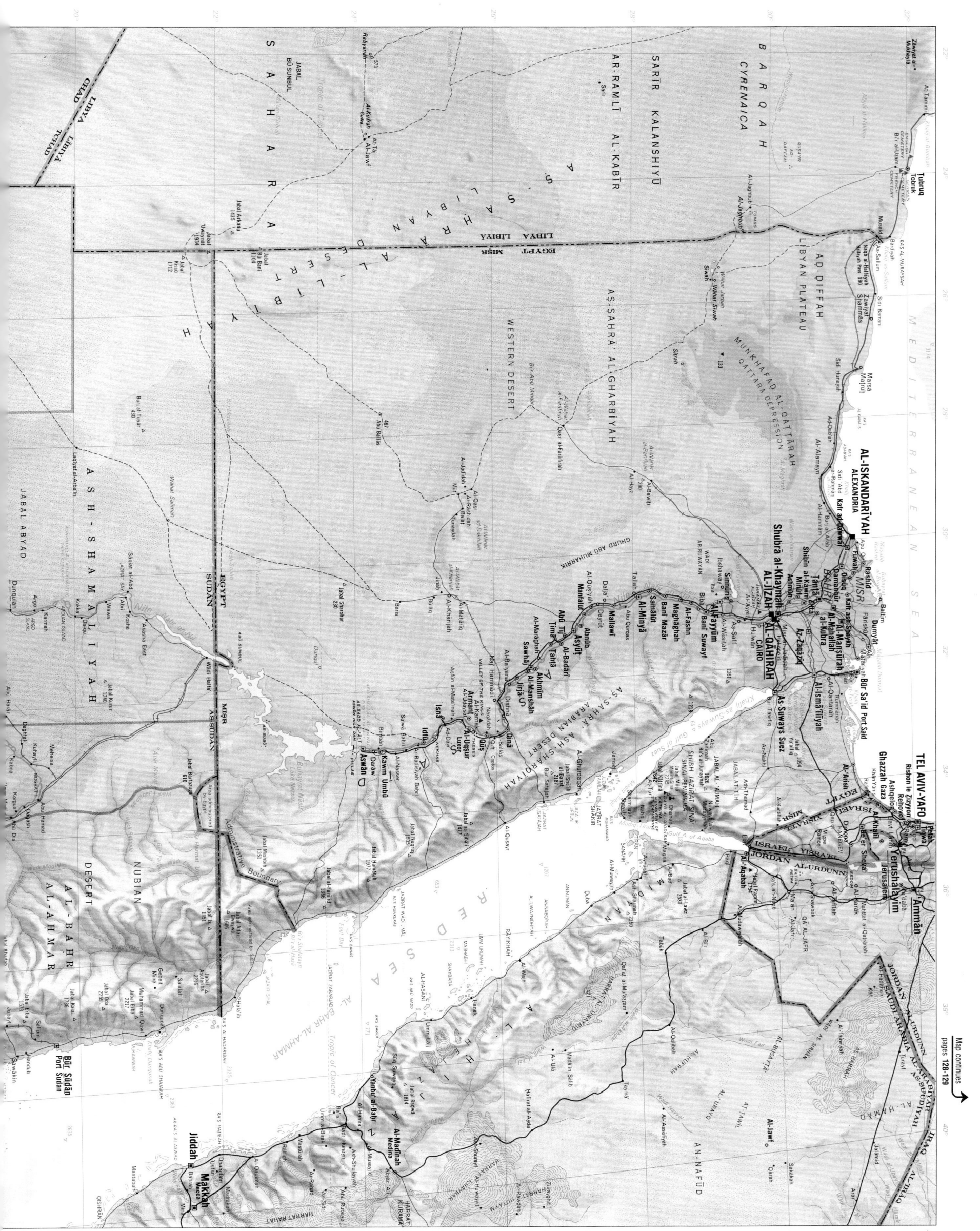
MEDITERRANEAN SEA
AL-ISKANDARĪYAH
ALEXANDRIA
AL-QĀHIRAH
CAIRO
AL-JĪZAH
Shubrā al-Khaymah
TEL AVIV-YAFO
Yerushalayim
Jerusalem
'Ammān
Būr Sa'īd Port Said
As-Suways Suez
Al-Ismā'īlīyah
Az-Zaqāzīq
Ṭanṭā
Al-Manṣūrah
Al-Maḥallah al-Kubrā
Dumyāṭ
Rashīd
Al-Fayyūm
Banī Suwayf
Al-Minyā
Mallawī
Asyūṭ
Sawhāj
Akhmīm
Jirjā
Qinā
Al-Uqṣur
Luxor
Isnā
Idfū
Kawm Umbū
Aswān
Marsā Maṭrūḥ
Sīwah
Tubruq
Tobruk
BARQAH
CYRENAICA
AD-DIFFAH
LIBYAN PLATEAU
MUNKHAFAḌ AL-QAṬṬĀRAH
QATTARA DEPRESSION
AṢ-ṢAḤRĀ' AL-GHARBĪYAH
WESTERN DESERT
AṢ-ṢAḤRĀ' AL-LĪBĪYAH
LIBYAN DESERT
SAHARA
SARĪR KALANSHIYŪ
AR-RAMLĪ AL-KABĪR
JABAL BŪ SUNBUL
AṢ-ṢAḤRĀ' ASH-SHARQĪYAH
ARABIAN DESERT
SHIBH JAZĪRAT SĪNĀ'
SINAI PENINSULA
Gulf of Suez
Gulf of Aqaba
RED SEA
AL-BAḤR AL-AḤMAR
Tropic of Cancer
EGYPT
MIṢR
LIBYA
LĪBIYĀ
SUDAN
AS-SŪDĀN
CHAD
TCHAD
ISRAEL
YISRA'EL
JORDAN
AL-URDUNN
SAUDI ARABIA
AL-'ARABĪYAH AS-SU'ŪDĪYAH
IRAQ
AL-'IRĀQ
AL-ḤIJĀZ
MIDYAN
AN-NAFŪD
AL-ḤAMĀD
Al-Madīnah
Medina
Makkah
Mecca
Jiddah
Yanbu' al-Baḥr
Al-'Aqabah
Tabūk
Būr Sūdān
Port Sudan
Wādī Ḥalfā'
NUBIAN DESERT
AL-BAḤR AL-AḤMAR
ASH-SHAMĀLĪYAH
JABAL ABYAD
Administrative Boundary
Buḥayrat Nāṣir
Lake Nasser
Al-Khārijah
Al-Wāḥāt al-Khārijah
Al-Qaṣr
Mūṭ
Al-Farāfirah
Al-Jaghbūb
As-Sallūm
Al-'Alamayn
Ad-Dab'ah
Ghazzah Gaza
Al-'Arīsh
Be'er Sheva'
Ma'ān
Al-Jawf
Taymā'
Dunqulah
Karmah

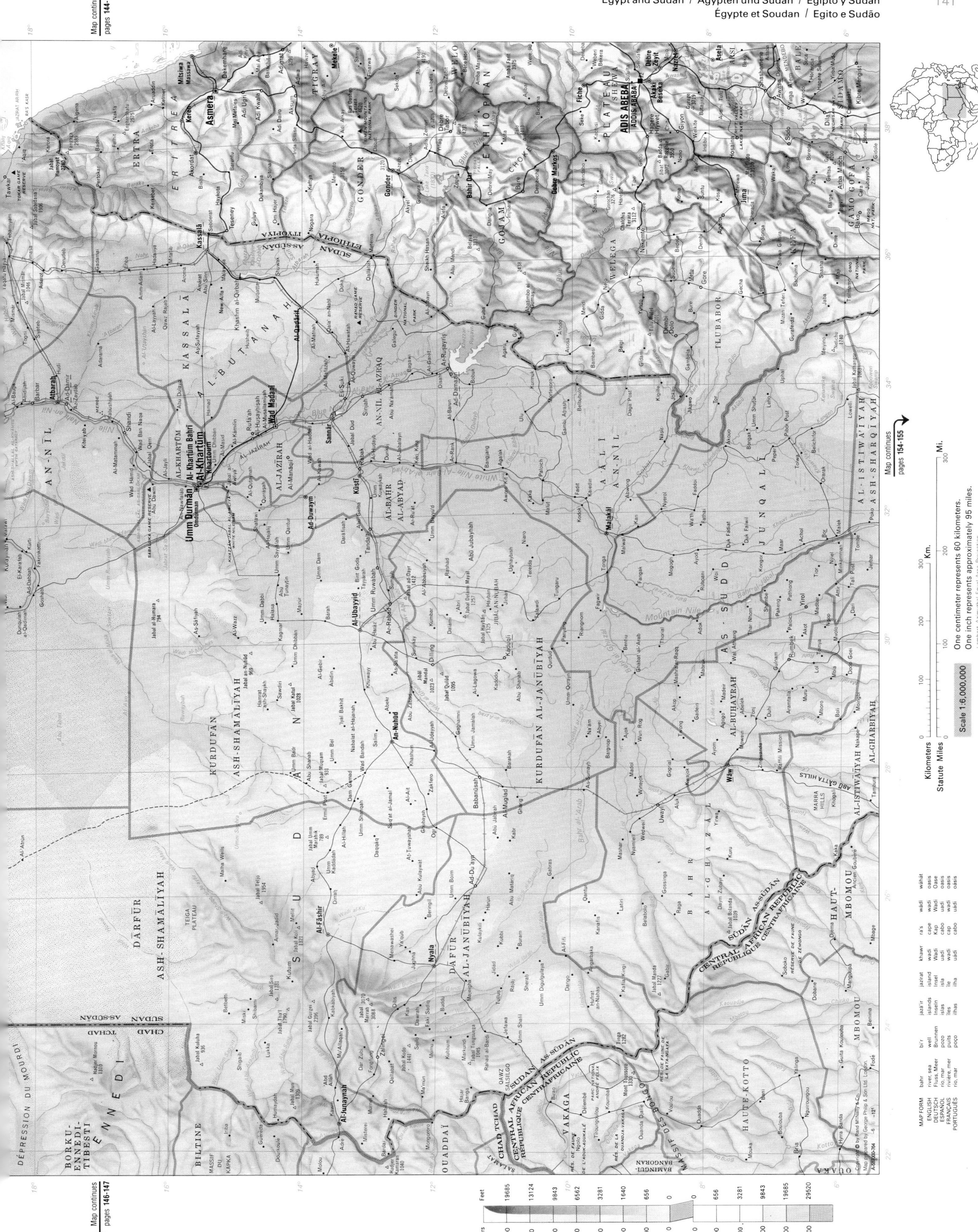

Map continues
pages 144-145

Map continues
pages 154-155

Map continues
pages 146-147

Scale 1:6,000,000

One centimeter represents 60 kilometers.
One inch represents approximately 95 miles.
Lambert Azimuthal Equal-Area Projection

Kilometers

Statute Miles

Km.

Mi.

MAP FORM					
ENGLISH	bahr	bi'r	jaza'ir	jaziral	khawr	ra's	wadi	wahat
DEUTSCH	river, sea	well	islands	island	wadi	cape	wadi	oasis
ESPAÑOL	río, mar	pozo	islas	isla	uadi	cabo	uadi	oasis
FRANÇAIS	rivière, mer	puits	îles	île	uadi	cap	uadi	oasis
PORTUGUÊS	rio, mar	poço	ilhas	ilha	uadi	cabo	uadi	oasis

Feet
19685
13124
9843
6562
3281
1640
656
0
Land
Below
Sea
Level
0
656
3281
9843
19685
29520

Meters
6000
4000
3000
2000
1000
500
200
0
0
200
1000
3000
6000
9000

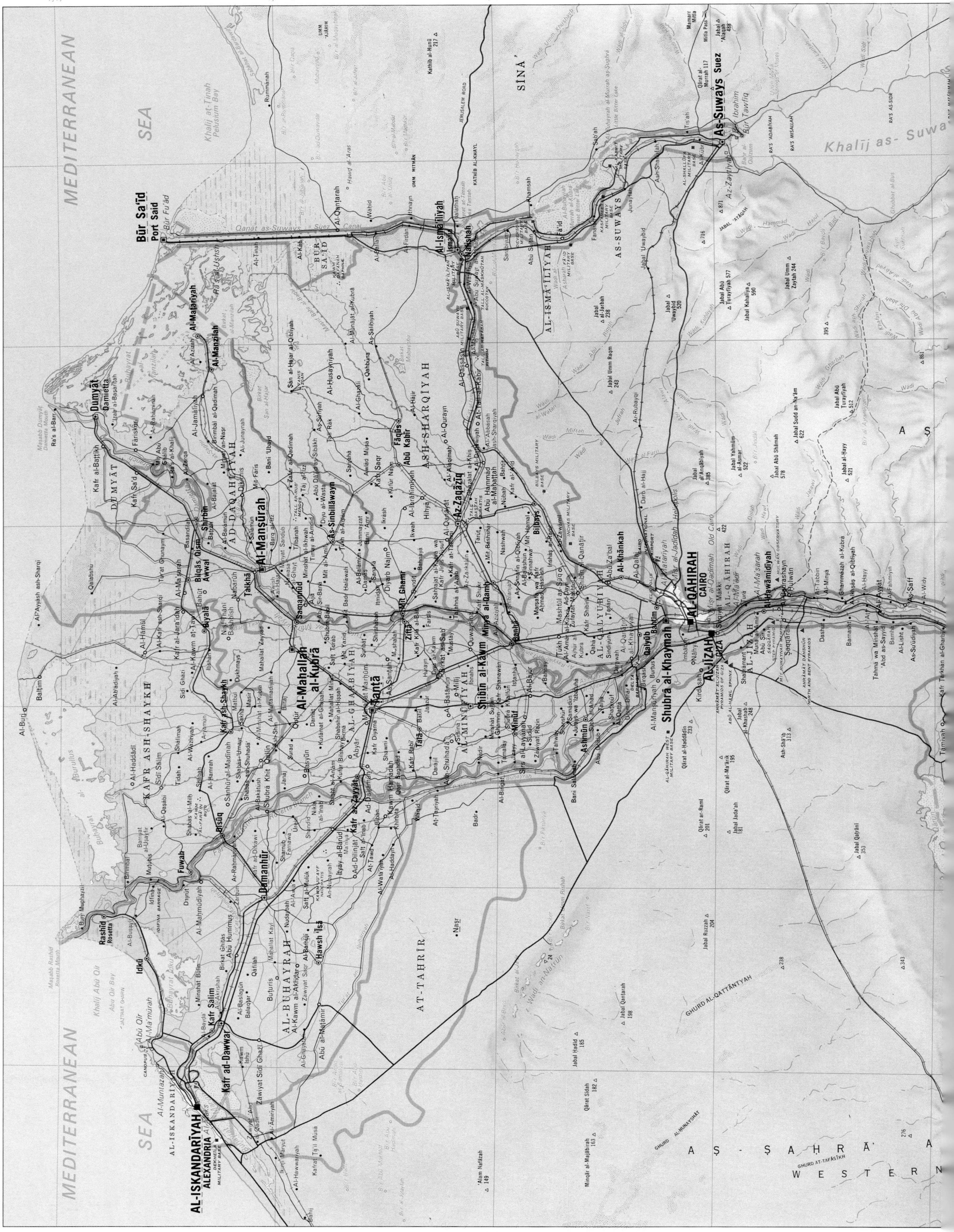
MEDITERRANEAN SEA
AL-ISKANDARĪYAH
ALEXANDRIA
Būr Sa'īd
Port Said
Dumyāṭ
Damietta
Rashīd
Rosetta
Al-Manṣūrah
Al-Maḥallah al-Kubrá
Ṭanṭā
Az-Zaqāzīq
Banhā
Shubrā al-Khaymah
AL-QĀHIRAH
CAIRO
Al-Jīzah
Gīza
Al-Ismā'īlīyah
Ismailia
As-Suways
Suez
Damanhūr
Kafr ad-Dawwār
AT-TAḤRĪR
SĪNĀ'
AṢ-ṢAḤRĀ' AL-GHARBĪYAH
WESTERN
Khalīj as-Suways
Qanāt as-Suways (Suez Canal)
AL-BUḤAYRAH
KAFR ASH-SHAYKH
AD-DAQAHLĪYAH
ASH-SHARQĪYAH
AL-QALYŪBĪYAH
AL-MINŪFĪYAH
AL-GHARBĪYAH
AL-ISMĀ'ĪLĪYAH
AS-SUWAYS
DUMYĀṬ
BŪR SA'ĪD

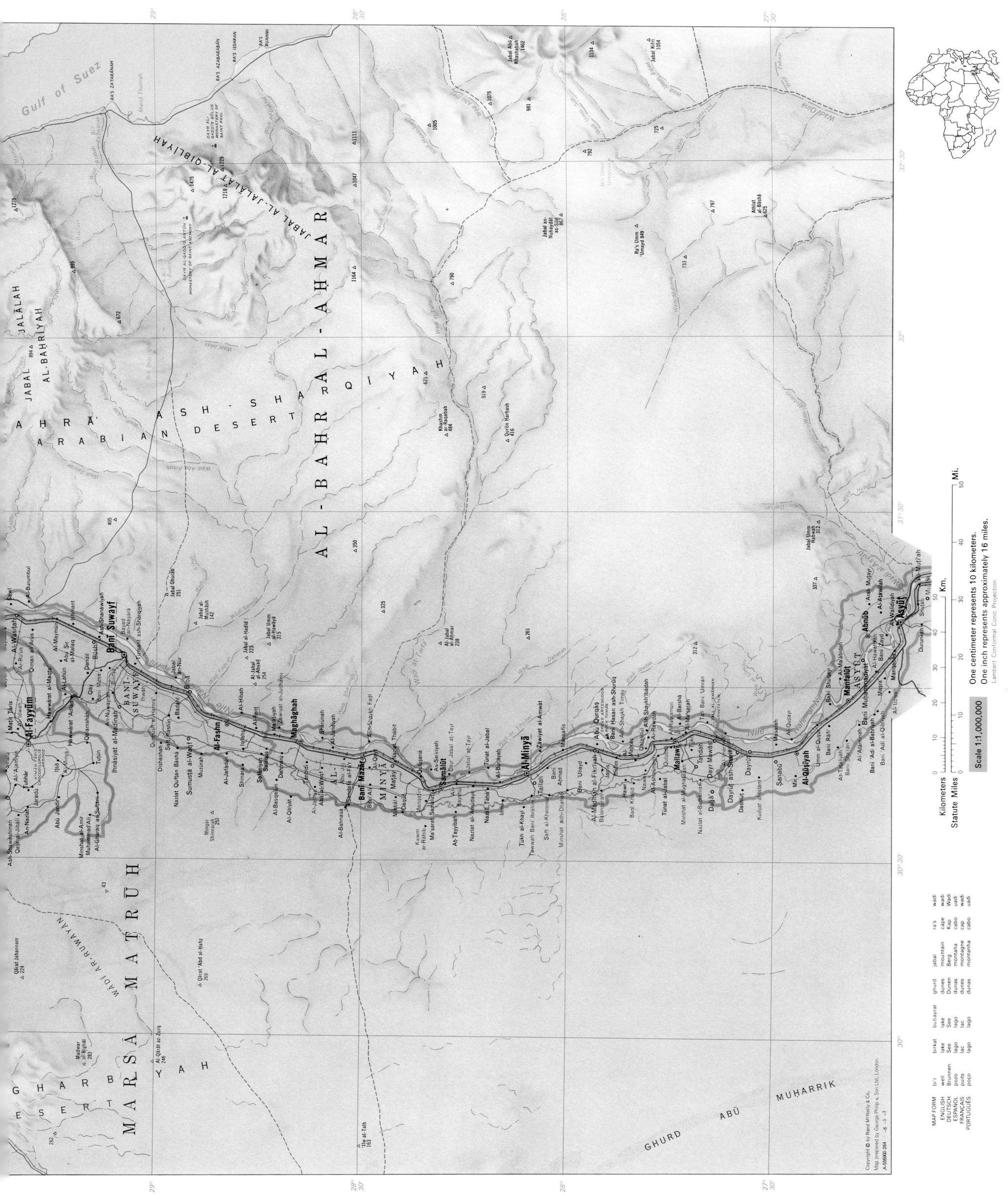

Scale 1:1,000,000

One centimeter represents 10 kilometers.
One inch represents approximately 16 miles.
Lambert Conformal Conic Projection

Kilometers
Statute Miles

MAP FORM	bir	birkat	buhayrat	ghurd	jabal	ra's	wadi
ENGLISH	well	lake	lake	dunes	mountain	cape	wadi
DEUTSCH	Brunnen	See	See	Dünen	Berg	Kap	Wadi
ESPAÑOL	pozo	lago	lago	dunas	montaña	cabo	uadi
FRANÇAIS	puits	lac	lac	dunes	montagne	cap	uadi
PORTUGUÊS	poço	lago	lago	dunas	montanha	cabo	uadi

RED SEA · AL-BAHR AL-AHMAR

EGYPT · MIŞR

SUDAN · AS-SÜDÄN

Area administered by Sudan

Area administered by Egypt

NUBIAN DESERT

AL-BAHR AL-AHMAR

AN-NIL

AN-NIL AL-AZRAQ

AL-JAZÏRAH

AL-KHARTÜM

KHARTÜM

KASSALÄ

ETHIOPIA · ITYOPIYA

ERTRA

Asmera

TIGRAY

GONDER

GOJAM

WELO

ETHIOPIAN

DJIBOUTI

ETHIOPIA · ITYOPIYA

Djibouti

Gulf of Aden

Berbera

SANAAG

SAUDI ARABIA

Makkah

Jiddah

Al-Tä'if

HARRAT RAHAT

'ASÏR

SAUDI ARABIA
YEMEN

AR RUB' AL-KHALI

NAJD

JABAL TUWAYQ

'URÜQ AS-SUBAY'

NAFÜD

AD DAHY

YEMEN · AL-YAMAN

Şan'ä'

Ta'izz

Aden
Adan
Madïnat ash-Sha'b
(Al-Ittihäd)
Shaykh 'Uthmän

Al-Hudaydah

Al-Mukallä

HADRAMAWT

AL-'ARABÏYAH AS-SU'ÜDÏYAH
AL-YAMAN

RAMLAT AS-SAB'ATAYN

Bür Südän
Port Sudan

Keren

Mitsiwa
Massawa

Mekele

DAHLAK ARCHIPELAGO

JAZÂ'IR FARASÄN

Aşab

SUAKIN ARCHIPELAGO

Bahir Dar

Gonder

Wad Madani

Sinjah

Al-Qadärif

Kassalä

Al-Ubayyid

Ethiopia, Somalia and Yemen / Äthiopien, Somalia und Jemen / Etiopía, Somalía y Yemen
Ethiopie, Somalie et Yemen / Etiópia, Somália e Iêmen

145

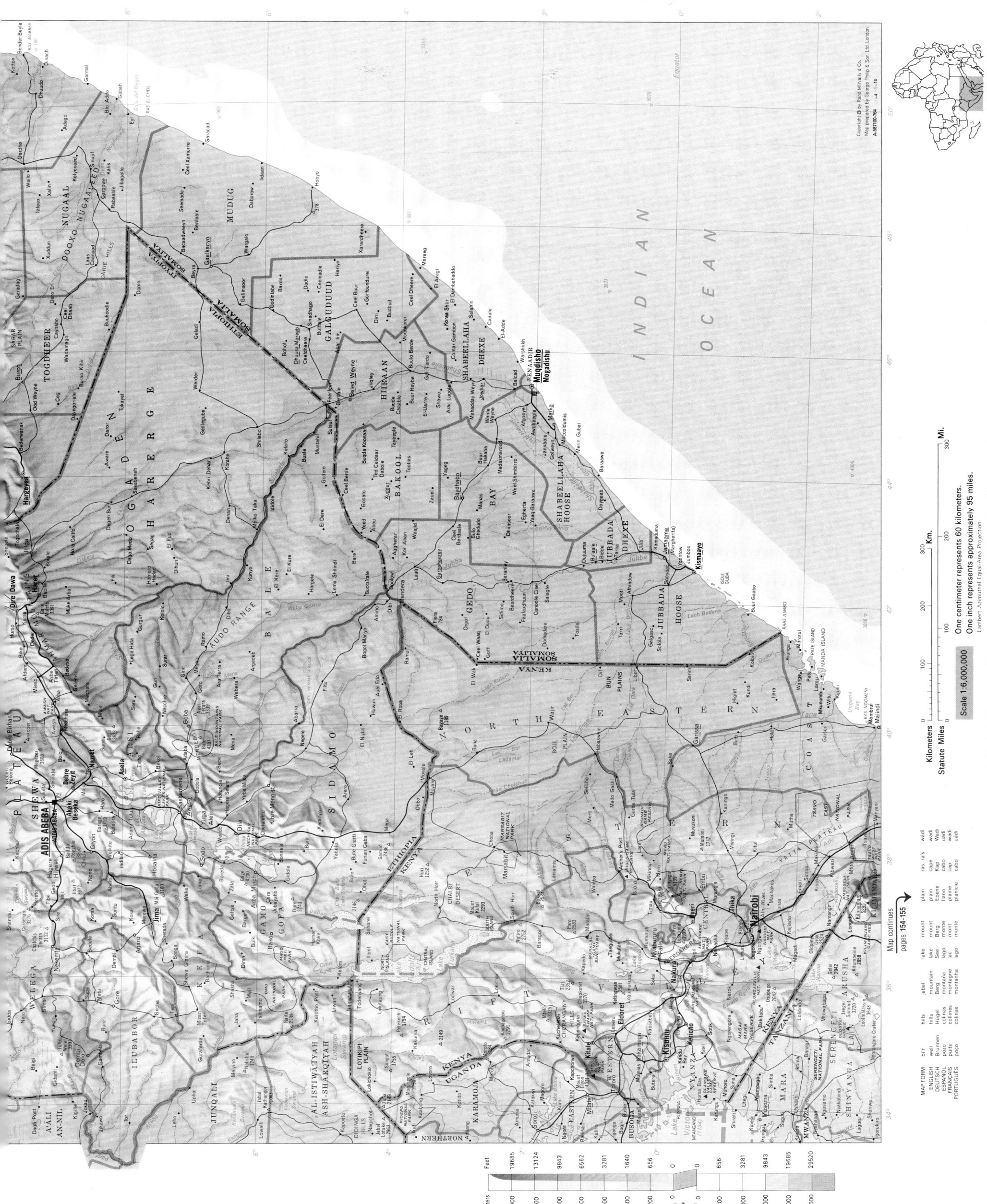

Mi.

One centimeter represents 60 kilometers.
One inch represents approximately 95 miles.

Scale 1:6,000,000

Lambert Azimuthal Equal-Area Projection

MAP FORM						
ENGLISH	b'r	hills	jabal	lake	plain	ras, ra's
DEUTSCH	well	Hügel	mountain	See	plain	cape
ESPAÑOL	Brunnen	Berg	mountain	lago	Ebene	Kap
FRANÇAIS	puits	colinas	montaña	lac	plaine	cap
PORTUGUÊS	poço	colinas	montanha	lago	planície	cabo

mount	wadi	
mount	wadi	
Berg	Wadi	
mont	uadi	
monte	uadi	

Map continues
pages 154-155

Feet
19685
13124
9843
6562
3281
1640
656
0
Land
Below
Sea
Level
0
656
3281
9843
19685
29520

Meters
6000
4000
3000
2000
1000
500
200
0
0
200
1000
3000
6000
9000

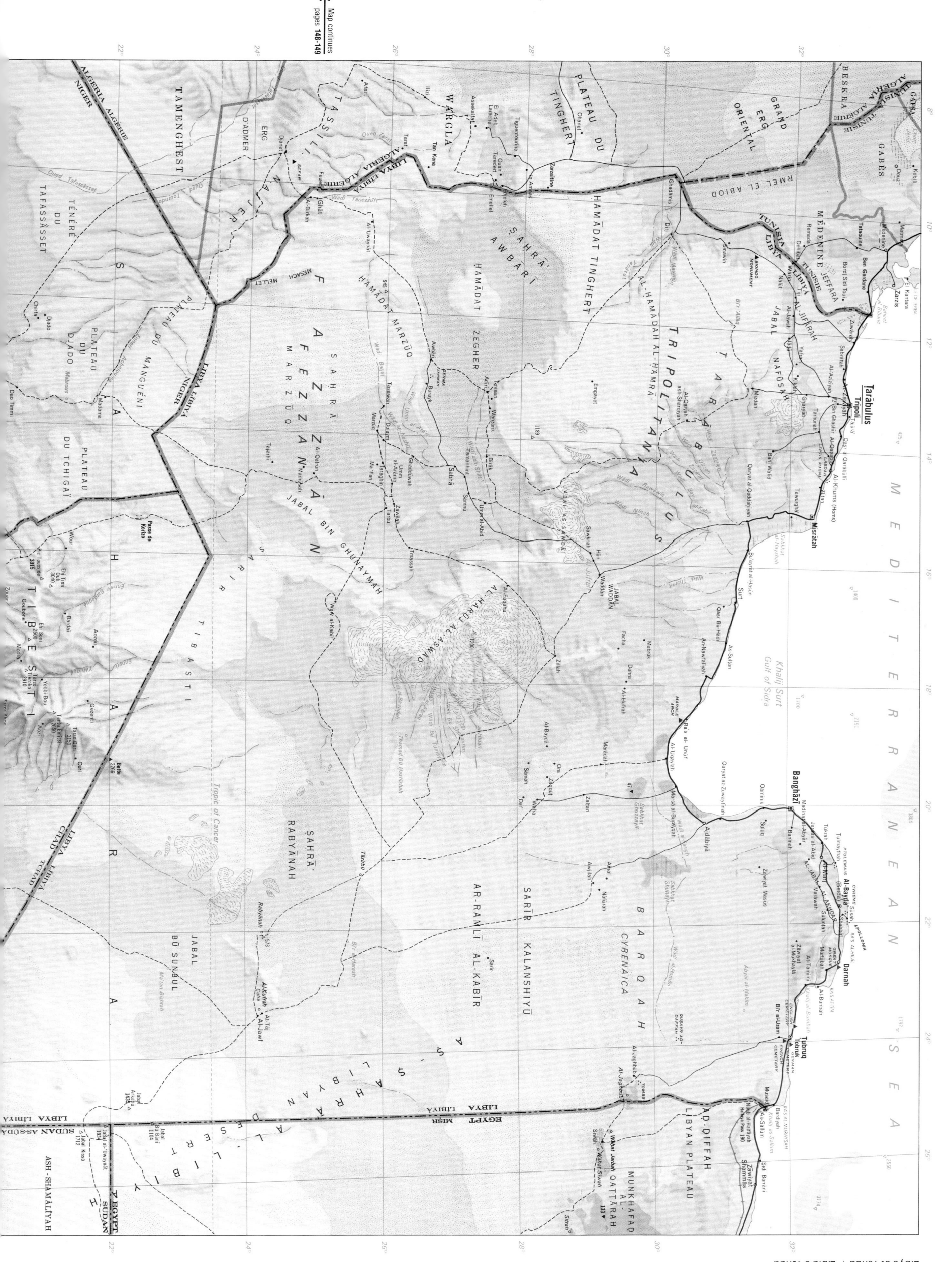

pages **148-149**
Map continues

Libya and Chad / Libyen und Tschad / Libia y el Chad
Libye et Tchad / Libia e Tchad
146

Map continues pages 140-141

Map continues pages 150-151

Meters	Feet
6000	19685
4000	13124
3000	9843
2000	6562
1000	3281
500	1640
200	656
Land 0	0
Below Sea Level 0	0
200	656
1000	3281
3000	9843
6000	19685
9000	29520

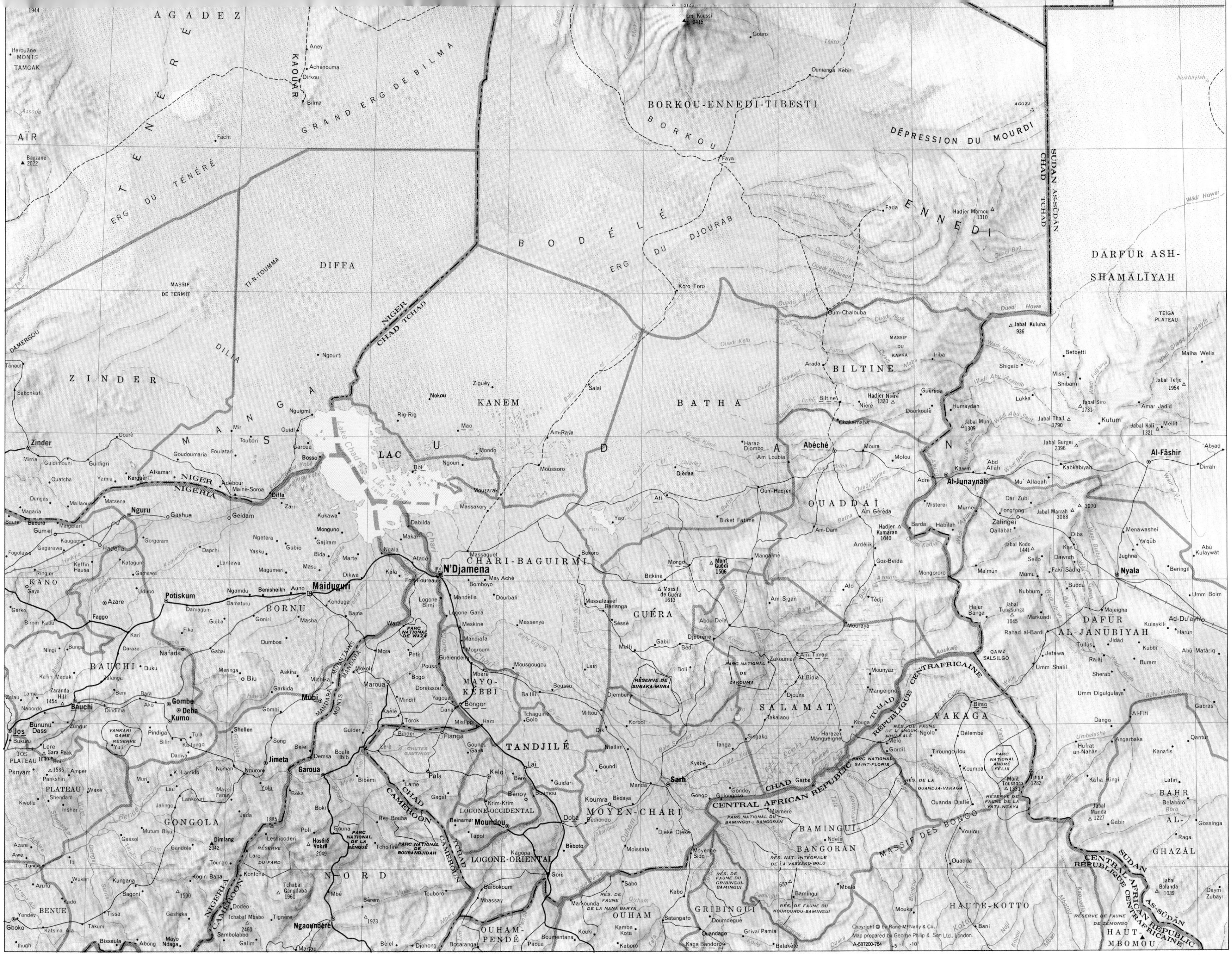

Map continues pages 152-153

MAP FORM	bahr	hadjer	jabal	massif	ouadi	ra's	sarīr	wādī
ENGLISH	river	mountain	mountain	massif	wadi	cape	desert	wadi
DEUTSCH	Fluss	Berg	Berg	Gebirgsmassiv	Wadi	Kap	Wüste	Wadi
ESPAÑOL	río	montaña	montaña	macizo	uadi	cabo	desierto	uadi
FRANÇAIS	rivière	montagne	montagne	massif	wadi	cap	désert	wadi
PORTUGUÊS	rio	montanha	montanha	maciço	uádi	cabo	deserto	uádi

Kilometers 0 100 200 300 Km.
Statute Miles 0 100 200 300 Mi.

Scale 1:6,000,000

One centimeter represents 60 kilometers.
One inch represents approximately 95 miles.
Lambert Azimuthal Equal-Area Projection

Map continues pages 34-35

Scale

Meters	Feet
6000	19685
4000	13124
3000	9843
2000	6562
1000	3281
500	1640
200	656
0	0
Land Below Sea Level	
0	0
200	656
1000	3281
3000	9843
6000	19685
9000	29520

Azores inset (a)

ATLANTIC OCEAN
CORVO
FLORES
Santa Cruz das Flores
GRACIOSA
Santa Cruz da Graciosa
TERCEIRA
Praia da Vitória
Angra do Heroísmo
FAIAL
Horta
Velas — SÃO JORGE
São Mateus
PICO — Ponta do Pico 2351
A Ç O R E S
SÃO MIGUEL
Ribeira Grande
Ponta Delgada
Povoação
(Port.)
SANTA MARIA
Vila do Porto
© R. MIN.

Main map

ATLANTIC OCEAN

ARQUIPÉLAGO DA MADEIRA
MADEIRA ISLANDS (Port)
PORTO SANTO
Pico Ruivo 1862
MADEIRA
Funchal
Machico
ILHAS DESERTAS

ILHAS SELVAGENS (Mad Is)

ISLAS CANARIAS
CANARY ISLANDS (Sp.)
LA PALMA
PARQ. NAC. DE LA CALDERA DE TABURIENTE
Los Llanos
Santa Cruz de la Palma
Pico de la Cruz
La Orotava
TENERIFE
San Cristóbal de la Laguna
Santa Cruz de Tenerife
PARQ. NAC. DEL TEIDE — Pico de Teide 3715
GOMERA
San Sebastián de la Gomera
San Miguel
San Nicolás
Arucas
Las Palmas de Gran Canaria
Telde
GRAN CANARIA
Valverde
HIERRO / FERRO
ISLA ALEGRANZA
ISLA GRACIOSA
LANZAROTE
Arrecife
ISLA DE LOBOS
Puerto del Rosario
FUERTEVENTURA
CAP JUBY
Tarfaya
La'Youn
CAP BOJADOR

OCEAN

Western Sahara has been occupied by Morocco.

MOROCCO AL-MAGREB
WESTERN SAHARA
El Aaiún / La youn
Lemsid
Smara
Hawza
Al Mahbas
CAP BOUJDOUR
Sebkhet Arida

Dakhla
Bir Enzaran
CAP BARBAS
ADRAR
Golfe de Cintra
Khlij Oued edh Dheheb
Ümmil
Tropic of Cancer

ZEMMOUR
Galtat Zemmour
Bir Mogrein (Fort-Trinquet)
Sebkhet Iguetti

TIRIS ZEMMOUR
Fdérik
Zouêrat
Kediet ej Jill
EL HAMMAMI
EL KHATT
Sebkhet Oumm ed Droûs Telli
Sebkhet Oumm ed Droûs Gueblî
Sebkha de Rhallamane

MAQTEÏR
SOUTTOUF
TIRES

WESTERN SAHARA
MAURITANIA / MAURITANIE
Nouâdhibou
La Gouéra / Cansado
RAS AGÂDIR / RAS NOUÂDHIBOU
DAKHLET NOUADHIBOU
INCHIRI
PARC NATIONAL DU BANC D'ARGUIN
Atâr
Techlé
Choûm
Passe de Ouarâne
Sebkhet el Jill
Ouadâne
Chinguetti
ADRAR
OUÂRÂNE
Guelb er Richât
Sebkhet Chemchâm
KÂ GHET
KREB EN NAGA
TIGUESMAT
TOUNASSINE
Oued el Ma

ALGERIA / ALGÉRIE
HAMADA DU DRÂA
ERG IGUIDI
EL EGLAB
EL MCHERRAH
AГТОUT
Tindouf
Sebkha de Tindouf
Chenachane
EL KHNÂCHICH
ERG CHECH
HAMADA EL HARICHA
Taoudenni
Bîr Ounâne

MALI
HODH ECH CHARGUI
TOMBOUCTOU
ADRAR
Foum el Alba

Morocco region (right side)

ESPAÑA / PORTUGAL
Córdoba
Odemira
BEJA
Almodôvar
Sevilla
Écija
Huelva
Morón de la Frontera
Antequera
Faro
Jerez de la Frontera
Arcos de la Frontera
Ronda
Málaga
Marbella
Cádiz
Estepona
CABO TRAFALGAR
Algeciras
La Línea
Gibraltar (U.K.)
Strait of Gibraltar
CAP SPARTEL
Tanger / Tangier
Ceuta
Tétouan
Asilah
Al-Hoceima
Chaouen
Larache
Ksar-el-Kebir
Rab-Taza
Ouezzane
RIF
Souk Larbat Gharb
Kenitra
Salé
Rabat
Mohammedia (Fedala)
CASABLANCA
DAR-EL-BEIDA
El-Jadida (Mazagan)
Azemmour
Berrechid
Settat
Khouribga
Oued-Zem
Boujad
Kasba-Tadla
Beni-Mellal
Safi
Youssoufia
El-Kelâa des-Srarhna
Essaouira (Mogador)
CAP SIM
Marrakech
Demnate
Azilal
Ouarzazate
HAUT ATLAS
Jbel Toubkal 4165
Taroudant
Agadir
Aït-Melloul
Tiznit
MOYEN ATLAS
Fès
Meknès
Sefrou
Khemisset
El-Hajeb
Midelt
El-Rachidia
Erfoud
Rissani
ANTI ATLAS
Ifni
Sidi Ifni
Goulimime
Foum-el-Hisn
Akka
Tata
Zagora
MOROCCO AL-MAGREB
ALGERIA / ALGÉRIE
HAMADA DU DRÂA
Oued Drâa
Tan-Tan

Copyright © by Rand McNally & Co.
Map prepared by George Philip & Son Ltd., London

MAP FORM	cap	chott	djebel	erg	hamada	jbel	oued	sebkha
ENGLISH	cape	intermittent lake	mountain	sand desert	desert	mountain	wadi	salt flat
DEUTSCH	Kap	periodischer See	Berg	Sandwüste	Wüste	Berg	Wadi	Salzebene
ESPAÑOL	cabo	lago intermitente	montaña	desierto arenoso	desierto	montaña	uadi	salar
FRANÇAIS	cap	lac périodique	montagne	désert de sable	désert	montagne	wadi	saline
PORTUGUÊS	cabo	lago intermitente	montanha	deserto arenoso	deserto	montanha	uádi	salina

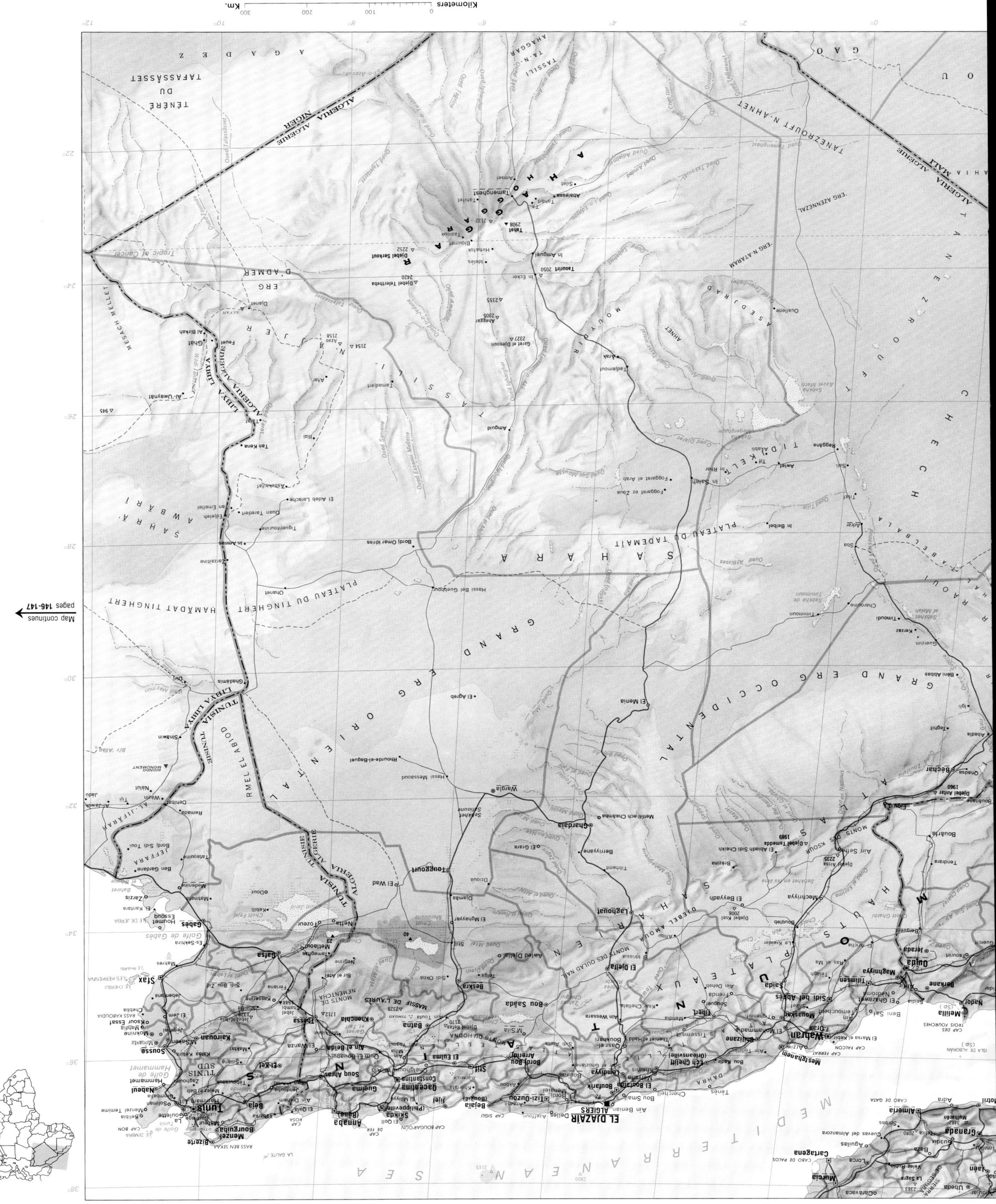

Northwestern Africa / Nordwestafrika / Africa Nor-occidental
Afrique du Nord-Ouest / Africa Nord-occidental

Scale 1:6,000,000
One centimeter represents 60 kilometers.
One inch represents approximately 95 miles.
Lambert Azimuthal Equal-Area Projection

Map continues pages 146-147

MAP FORM	coast	dhar	game reserve	ilha	lac	monts	mountains	vallée
ENGLISH	coast	escarpment	game reserve	island	lake	mountains	mountains	valley
DEUTSCH	Küste	Landstufe	Wildpark	Insel	See	Berge	Berge	Tal
ESPAÑOL	costa	escarpa	vedado de caza	isla	lago	montes	montañas	valle
FRANÇAIS	côte	escarpement	réserve à gibier	île	lac	monts	montagnes	vallée
PORTUGUÊS	costa	escarpa	reserva de caça	ilha	lago	montes	montanhas	vale

Scale 1:6,000,000
One centimeter represents 60 kilometers.
One inch represents approximately 95 miles.
Lambert Azimuthal Equal-Area Projection.

Map continues pages 152-153

Map continues pages 146-147

Map continues pages 148-149

152

Western Congo Basin / Westliches Kongobecken / Cuenca Occidental del Congo
Bassin du Congo, partie Occidentale / Bacia Ocidental do Congo

Map continues
pages 146-147

Map continues
pages 150-151

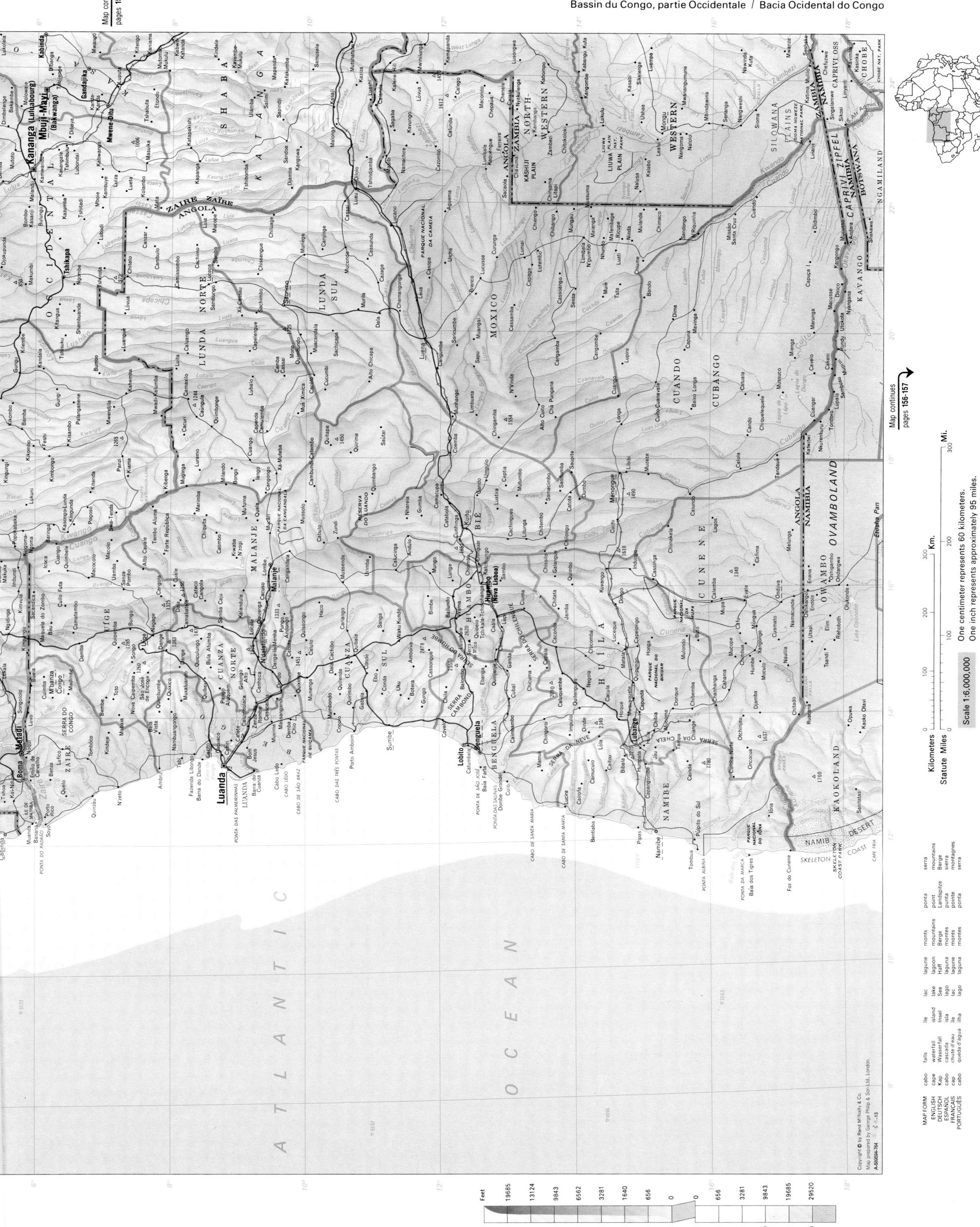

Western Congo Basin / Westliches Kongobecken / Cuenca Occidental del Congo
Bassin du Congo, partie Occidentale / Bacia Ocidental do Congo

153

Map continues
pages 154-155

Map continues
pages 156-157

Scale 1:6,000,000

One centimeter represents 60 kilometers.
One inch represents approximately 95 miles.

Lambert Azimuthal Equal-Area Projection

Kilometers

Statute Miles

MAP FORM						
ENGLISH	cape	falls	island	lac	lagoon	lake
DEUTSCH	Kap	Wasserfall	Insel	See	Haff	See
ESPAÑOL	cabo	cascada	isla	lago	laguna	lago
FRANÇAIS	cap	chute d'eau	île	lac	lagune	lac
PORTUGUÊS	cabo	queda d'água	ilha	lago	laguna	lago

mountains	point	serra
monts	ponta	mountains
Berge	point	Berge
montes	Landspitze	sierra
montagnes	punta	montagnes
montes	pointe	sierra
	ponta	serra

A T L A N T I C   O C E A N

ENGLISH	DEUTSCH	ESPAÑOL	FRANÇAIS	PORTUGUÊS
falls	Wasserfall	cascada	chute d'eau	queda d'agua
game reserve	Wildreservat	vedado de caza	réserve à gibier	reserva de caça
island	Insel	isla	île	ilha
lake	See	lago	lac	lago
mountains	Berge	montañas	montagnes	montanhas
national park	Nationalpark	parque nacional	parc national	parque nacional
plain	Ebene	plano	plaine	planície
swamp	Sumpf	pantano	marais	pântano

Kilometers

Statute Miles

Scale 1:6,000,000

One centimeter represents 60 kilometers.
One inch represents approximately 95 miles.

Lambert Azimuthal Equal-Area Projection

0   100   200   Km.

0   100   200   300   Mi.

Map continues
pages 140-141 →

Map continues
pages 144-145 →

East Africa and Eastern Congo Basin / Ostafrika und Östliches Kongobecken / Africa Oriental y Cuenca Oriental del Congo
Afrique Orientale et Bassin du Congo, partie Orientale / Africa Oriental e Bacia Oriental do Congo

154

East Africa and Eastern Congo Basin / Ostafrika und Östliches Kongobecken / África Oriental y Cuenca Oriental del Congo
Afrique Orientale et Bassin du Congo, partie Orientale / África Oriental e Bacia Oriental do Congo

155

MOZAMBIQUE CHANNEL

Map continues
pages 156-157

Feet
19685
13124
9843
6562
3281
1640
656
0

Meters
6000
4000
3000
2000
1000
500
200
0

Land Below Sea Level

0
200
656
1000
3281
3000
9843
6000
19685
9000
29520

Map continues
pages 152-153

A T L A N T I C

O C E A N

Meters	Feet
6000	19685
4000	13124
3000	9843
2000	6562
1000	3281
500	1640
200	656
0	0
Land Below Sea Level	
0	0
200	656
1000	3281
3000	9843
6000	19685
9000	29520

Copyright © by Rand McNally & Co.
Map prepared by George Philip & Son Ltd. London.
A-589292-764

MAP FORM	bay	cape	game reserve	ilha	lake	national park
ENGLISH	bay	cape	game reserve	island	lake	national park
DEUTSCH	Bucht	Kap	Wildpark	Insel	See	Nationalpark
ESPAÑOL	bahía	cabo	vedado de caza	isla	lago	parque nacional
FRANÇAIS	baie	cap	réserve à gibier	île	lac	parc national
PORTUGUÊS	baía	cabo	reserva de caça	ilha	lago	parque nacional

Kilometers
Statute Miles

Scale 1:6,000,000

One centimeter represents 60 kilometers.
One inch represents approximately 95 miles.
Lambert Azimuthal Equal-Area Projection

Southern Africa and Madagascar / Südafrika und Madagaskar / África Meridional y Madagascar
Afrique Méridionale et Madagascar / África Meridional e Madagascar

157

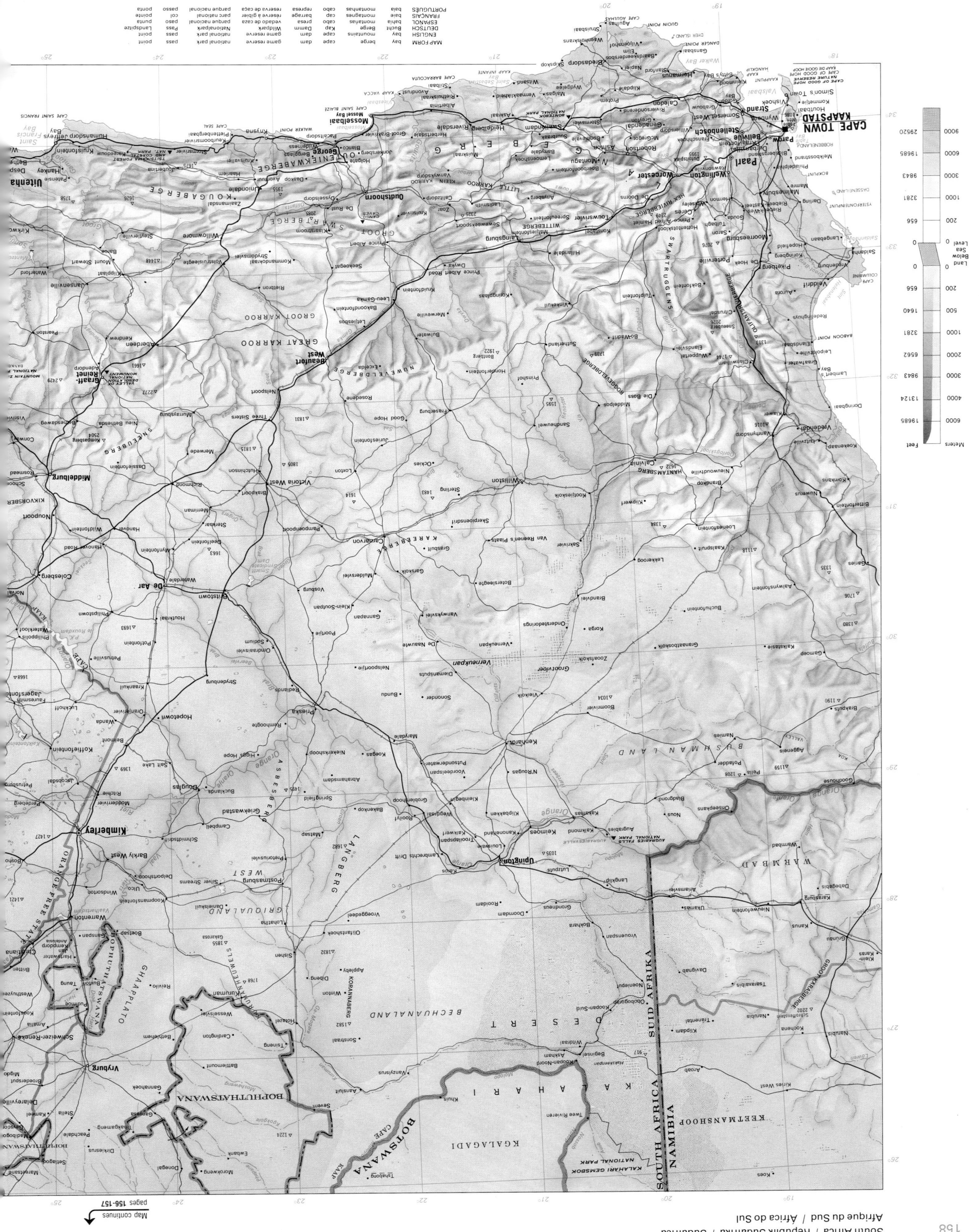

South Africa / Republik Südafrika / Sudáfrica
Afrique du Sud / África do Sul

Map continues
pages 156-157

MAP FORM					
ENGLISH	DEUTSCH	FRANÇAIS	ESPAÑOL	PORTUGUÊS	
bay	Bucht	baie	bahía	baía	
berge	Berge	montagnes	montañas	montanhas	
cape	Kap	cabo	cabo	cabo	
dam	Damm	barrage	represa	presa	
game reserve	Wildpark	réserve à gibier	reserva de caza	reserva de caça	
national park	Nationalpark	parc national	parque nacional	parque nacional	
mountains	Berge	montagnes	montañas	montanhas	
pass	Pass	col	paso	passo	
point	Landspitze	pointe	punta	ponta	
dam	Damm	barrage	presa	represa	
point	Spitze	pointe	punta	ponta	

CAPE TOWN
KAAPSTAD

South Africa / Republik Südafrika / Sudáfrica
Afrique du Sud / África do Sul

Bophuthatswana, Ciskei, Transkei, and Venda
are not internationally recognized.

MOZAMBIQUE

MAPUTO
(Lourenço Marques)

SWAZILAND

LESOTHO

TRANSVAAL

NATAL

ORANGE VRYSTAAT

TRANSKEI

CISKEI

GRIQUALAND

PONDOLAND

DRAKENSBERG

INDIAN OCEAN

Pretoria
Johannesburg
Soweto
Krugersdorp
Randfontein
Roodepoort-Maraisburg
Carletonville
Vanderbijlpark
Vereeniging
Potchefstroom
Klerksdorp
Orkney
Stilfontein
Kroonstad
Welkom
Virginia
Odendaalsrus
Bethlehem
Harrismith
Bloemfontein
Maseru
Ladysmith
Dundee
Newcastle
Vryheid
Pietermaritzburg
Edendale
DURBAN
Stanger
Richard's Bay
Mbabane
Manzini
Piet Retief
Ermelo
Standerton
Queenstown
King William's Town
East London
Oos-Londen
Grahamstown
Port Elizabeth
Umtata
Kokstad
Matatiele
Port Saint Johns
Margate
Port Edward
Barkly East
Aliwal North

Copyright © by Rand McNally & Co.
Map prepared by George Philip & Son Ltd., London
A-584600-764

Kilometers
Statute Miles
Scale 1:3,000,000
One centimeter represents 30 kilometers.
One inch represents approximately 47 miles.
Lambert Conformal Conic Projection

Australia / Australien / Australia
Australie / Austrália

Map continues
pages **108-109**

INDONESIA

G. Slamet 1428
Tasik-
malaya Cilacap Magelang Kediri Malang Jember
Yogyakarta Surakarta Madiun Blitar Banyuwangi BALI Singaraja Mataram
JAWA JAVA Gunung Denpasar Praya SUMBAWA Sumbawa Besar
Semeru 3676 LOMBOK

NUSA TENGGARA
LESSER SUNDA FLORES
Waingapu Ende Soe TIMOR
Waikabubak SUMBA Baing Savu Sea PULAU SEMAU Kupang
Laut Sawu PULAU SAWU PULAU ROTTI

Timor

Sea

Arafu

HIBERNIA REEF

ASHMORE ISLANDS CARTIER ISLANDS (Austl.)

MELVILLE
ISLAND CAPE CROKER
BATHURST CROKER ISL.
ISLAND GOULBU
Beagle PENINSULA
Gulf Van Diemen
CAPE Gulf
LONDONDERRY Darwin Humpty Doo Jabiru
POINT BLAZE Rum Jungle ARNHEM LAN
Pine Creek
Katherine Bird

INDIAN

BROWSE
ISLAND
BONAPARTE
ARCHIPELAGO
SCOTT REEF York Sound

ADÈLE ISLAND Collier KIMBERLEY PLATEAU
BUCCANEER Bay Wyndham Kununurra
ARCHIPELAGO Lake Victoria Daly Waters
CAPE LEVEQUE BEAGLE Argyle River Downs
REEF Derby KING LEOPOLD RANGES DURACK RANGES Wave Hill
ROWLEY SHOALS Mount Ord Fitzroy Crossing Halls Creek Newcastle
937 Waters Lake
Broome Woods

OCEAN CAPE LATOUCHE TREVILLE Fitzroy NORTHERN

La Grange

EIGHTY MILE BEACH TANAMI TERRITOR

Lake Gregory DESERT Lake White Barrow Cre

Goldsworthy GREAT SANDY DESERT
Port Hedland Shay Gap Lake
DAMPIER Roebourne De Grey Wills Lake Mackay
MONTE BELLO ARCHIPELAGO Lake
ISLANDS Dampier Karratha Marble Bar Dora Lake Auld
BARROW ISLAND Nullagine Mount Leister Mount Liebig Mount Zeil
MUIRON ISLANDS HAMERSLEY Fortescue Witteroom 897 1524 1511
NORTH WEST CAPE RANGE Lake
Onslow Pannawonica Mount Bruce Disappointment MACDONNELL
Exmouth Mount Brockman 1235 Lake RANGES
Gulf 1132 Mount Meharry Macdonald Lake Neale
POINT CLOATES Tom Price 1251 Lake Amadeus
Paraburdoo Newman WESTERN Lake
GIBSON DESERT
Mount Olga AUST
1105 906 1069 Ayers Rock
Mount Augustus Mount Essendon Mount Cockburn 867
CAPE CUVIER Lake Macleod 1138
Geographe Channel Robinson Peak Hill Mount Aloysius Mount Woodroffe
BERNIER ISLAND Carnarvon Range 1085 1440
DORRE ISLAND Shark Gascoyne
DIRK HARTOG Bay Wooramel Lake Carnegie GREAT VICTORIA DESERT SOUT
ISLAND Denham Lake Gillen
STEEP POINT Wiluna Lake Mingwal
Tropic of Capricorn Naturaliste Channel Meekatharra AUSTRALIA Lake Maurice
Nannine Agnew Yeo Lake Marafinga
Cue Mount Redcliffe Ooldea
Kalbarri Lake Austin 562 Laverton
Sandstone Leonora Malcolm Lake Carey
Mount Magnet Lake Ballard
Northampton Menzies
Geraldton Yalgoo Lake Barlee
HOUTMAN Mullewa Pindar Mongers
ABROLHOS Dongara Lake Lake Moore Lake Lefroy NULLARBOR PLAIN
Three Kalgoorlie Boulder Zanthus Rawlinna Haig
Springs Dalwallinu Coolgardie Forrest Deakin
GREEN HEAD Bonnie Rock Lake Cowan Eucla
Bencubbin Southern Cross Lake Carey Norseman CAPE ADIEU
Mooria Bullfinch Lake Dundas SAINT PETER ISLAND
Wanneroo Northam Merredin POINT CULVER Eyre
Perth York Kellerberrin Lake Johnston
Fremantle Beverley Hyden
DARLING RANGE Brookton CAPE
Pinjarra Narrogin Newdegate Great Australian Bight INVESTI
Wagin Ravensthorpe
Bunbury Collie Nyabing
Busselton Bridgetown Katanning Esperance CAPE ARID
CAPE NATURALISTE Gnowangerup Hopetoun ARCHIPELAGO
Geographe Manjimup Hood Point OF THE
Bay Augusta Pemberton Bluff Knoll Esperance Bay RECHERCHE
CAPE LEEUWIN 1096
Mount Barker
POINT D'ENTRECASTEAUX Albany
WEST CAPE HOWE CAPE VANCOUVER
George Sound

SOUTHERN OCE

ENGLISH	bay	cape	island	lake	mount	point	range	reef
DEUTSCH	Bucht	Kap	Insel	See	Berg	Landspitze	Gebirge	Riff
ESPAÑOL	bahía	cabo	isla	lago	montaña	punta	cordillera	arrecife
FRANÇAIS	baie	cap	île	lac	mont	pointe	chaîne	récif
PORTUGUÊS	baía	cabo	ilha	lago	monte	ponta	cordilheira	recife

SOLOMON ISLANDS

PAPUA
NEW GUINEA
NEW GUINEA

Port Moresby

Coral Sea

PACIFIC

OCEAN

Tasman

Sea

QUEENSLAND

GREAT ARTESIAN

BASIN

GREAT   DIVIDING   RANGE

SIMPSON

DESERT

AUSTRALIA

NEW SOUTH WALES

Broken Hill

Adelaide

Canberra
A.C.T.

SYDNEY
Campbelltown
Wollongong

Newcastle

VICTORIA

MELBOURNE

Geelong

Ballarat

TASMANIA

Hobart

Launceston

Kilometers   0   200   400   600   Km.

Statute Miles   0   200   400   600   Mi.

Scale 1:12,000,000

One centimeter represents 120 kilometers.
One inch represents approximately 190 miles.
Lambert Conformal Conic Projection

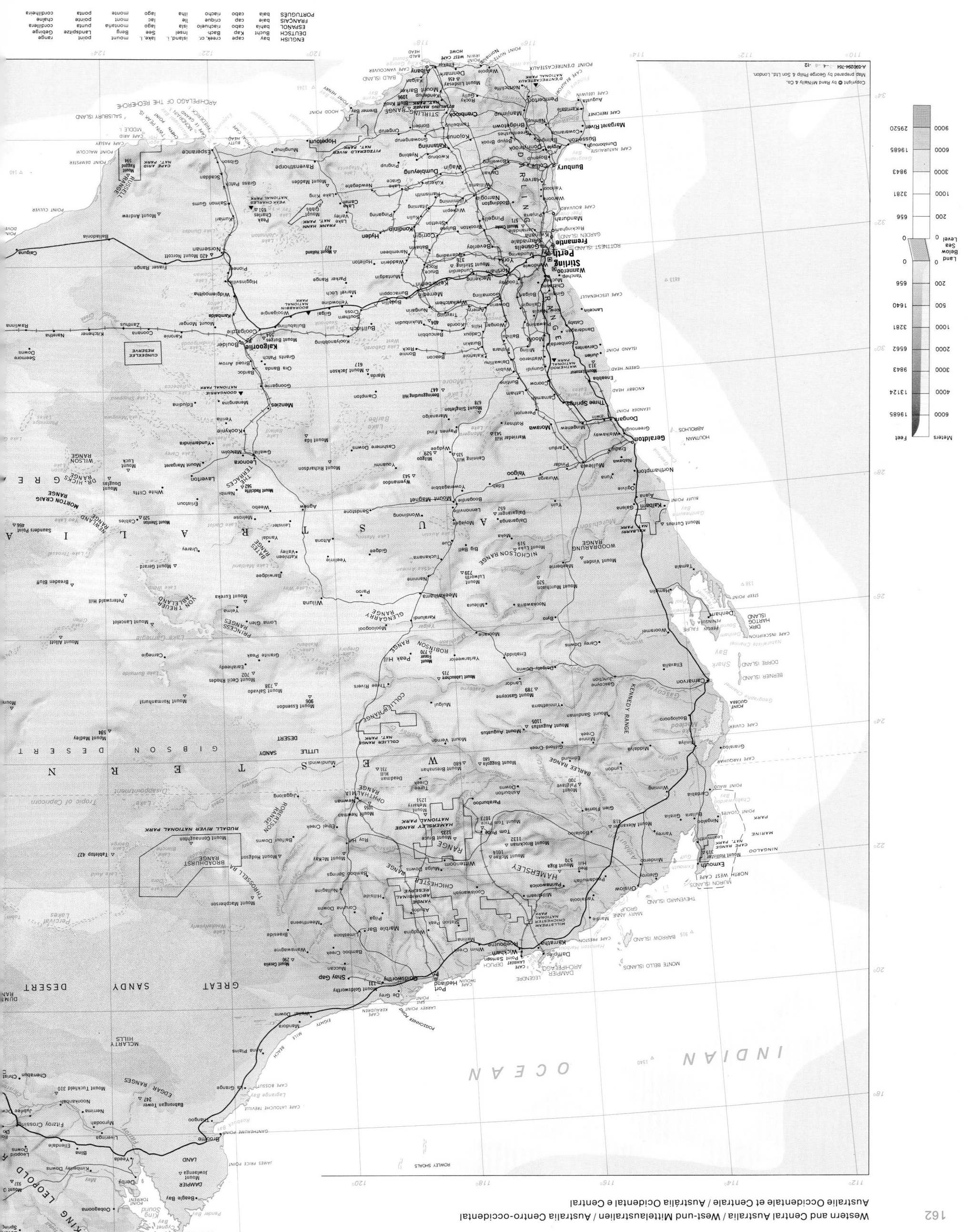

Western and Central Australia / West- und Mittelaustralien / Australia Centro-occidental
Australie Occidentale et Centrale / Australia Occidentale et Centrale

INDIAN OCEAN

GREAT SANDY DESERT

GIBSON DESERT

WESTERN AUSTRALIA

ENGLISH	DEUTSCH	ESPAÑOL	FRANÇAIS	PORTUGUÊS
bay	Bucht	bahía	baie	baía
cape, c.	Kap	cabo	cap	cabo
creek, cr.	Bach	riachuelo	crique	riacho
island, I.	Insel	isla	île	ilha
lake, L.	See	lago	lac	lago
mount	Berg	montaña	monte	monte
point	Landspitze	punta	pointe	ponta
range	Gebirge	cordillera	chaîne	cordilheira

Meters	Feet	
	29520	9000
	19685	6000
	9843	3000
	3281	1000
	656	200
	0	Sea Level
	0	Land Below
0		
200	656	
500	1640	
1000	3281	
2000	6562	
3000	9843	
4000	13124	
6000	19685	

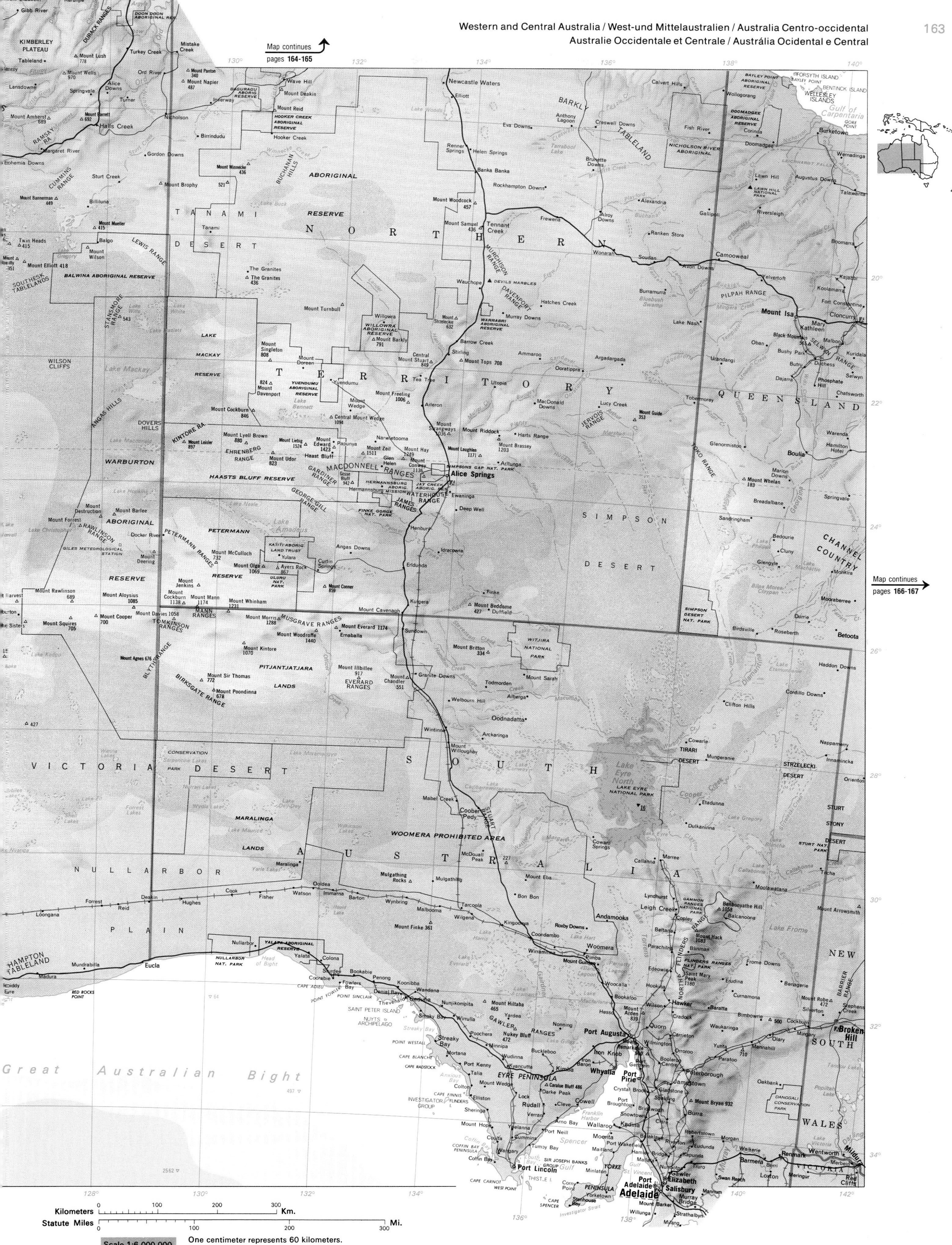

Western and Central Australia / West- und Mittelaustralien / Australia Centro-occidental
Australie Occidentale et Centrale / Austrália Ocidental e Central

163

Map continues
pages 164-165

Map continues
pages 166-167

Kilometers
0   100   200   300
0   Km.
Statute Miles
0   100   200   300
Mi.

Scale 1:6,000,000

One centimeter represents 60 kilometers.
One inch represents approximately 95 miles.

Lambert Conformal Conic Projection

164

Northern Australia and New Guinea / Nordaustralien und Neuguinea / Australia Septentrional y Nueva Guinea
Australie Septentrionale et Nouvelle Guinée / Austrália Setentrional e Nova Guiné

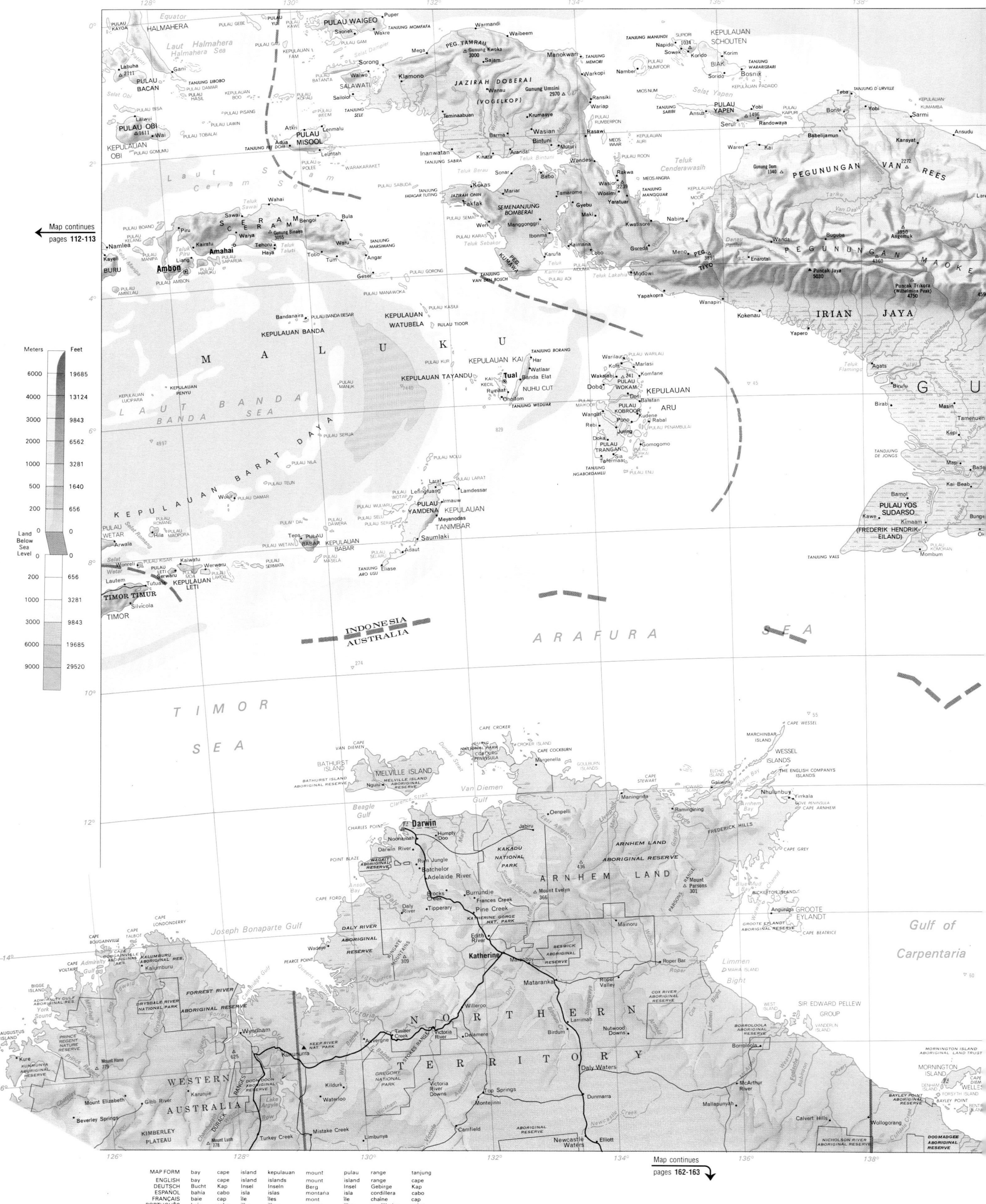

Map continues
pages 112-113

Map continues
pages 162-163

MAP FORM	bay	cape	island	kepulauan	mount	pulau	range	tanjung
ENGLISH	bay	cape	island	islands	mount	island	range	cape
DEUTSCH	Bucht	Kap	Insel	Inseln	Berg	Insel	Gebirge	Kap
ESPAÑOL	bahia	cabo	isla	islas	montaña	isla	cordillera	Kap
FRANÇAIS	baie	cap	île	îles	mont	île	chaîne	cap
PORTUGUÊS	baia	cabo	ilha	ilhas	monte	ilha	cordilheira	cabo

Northern Australia and New Guinea / Nordaustralien und Neuguinea / Australia Septentrional y Nueva Guinea
Australie Septentrionale et Nouvelle Guinée / Austrália Setentrional e Nova Guiné

165

Map continues
pages 166-167

Kilometers 0   100   200   300 Km.

Statute Miles 0   100   200   300 Mi.

Scale 1:6,000,000

One centimeter represents 60 kilometers.
One inch represents approximately 95 miles.
Lambert Conformal Conic Projection

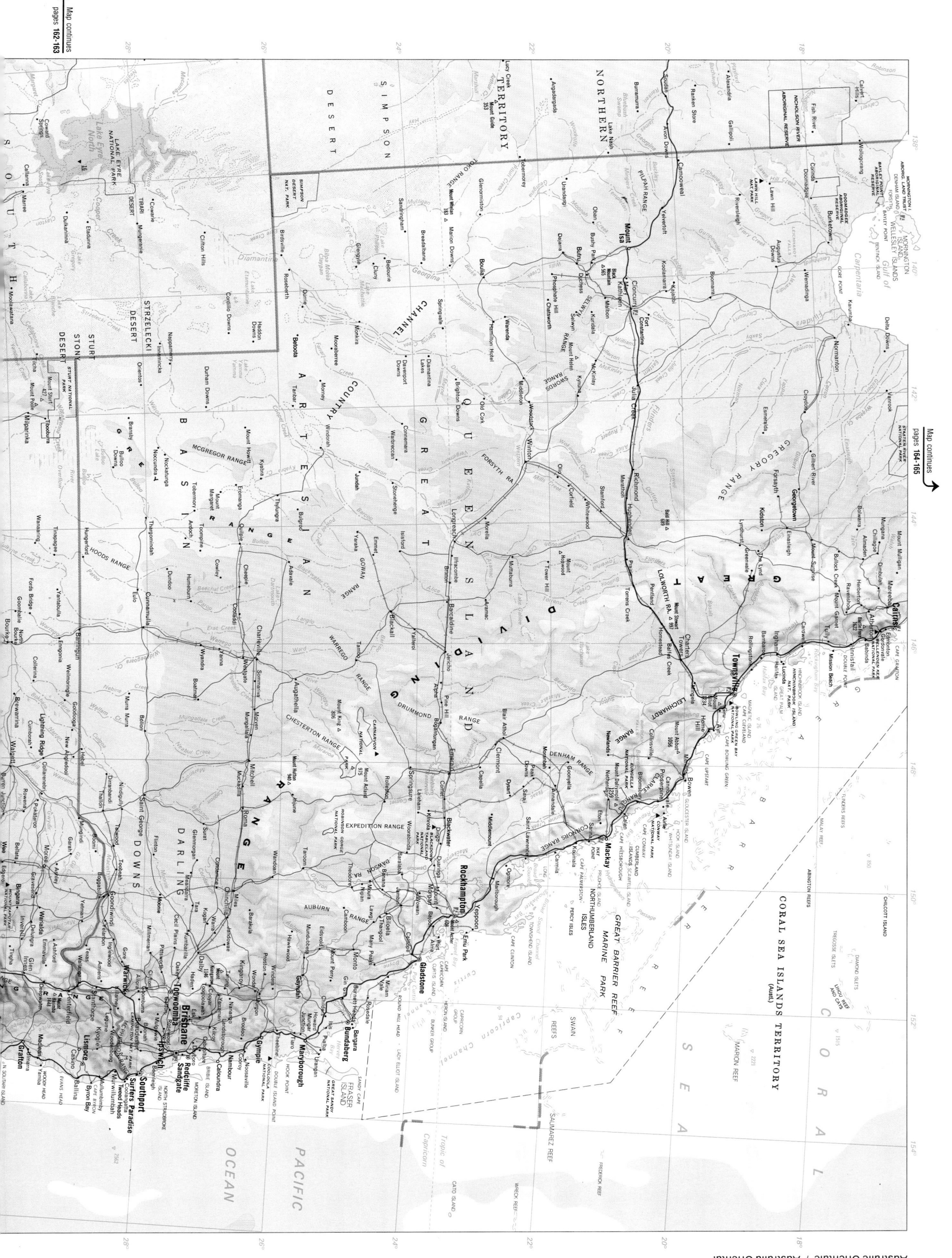

Map continues
pages 164-165

SOUTH

NORTHERN TERRITORY

Gulf of Carpentaria

SIMPSON DESERT

Lake Eyre North

LAKE EYRE NATIONAL PARK

STURT STONY DESERT

STRZELECKI DESERT

STURT NATIONAL PARK

TIBARI DESERT

CHANNEL COUNTRY

QUEENSLAND

CHANNEL

GREAT ARTESIAN BASIN

Mount Isa

Cloncurry

MCGREGOR RANGE

WARREGO RANGE

DARLING DOWNS

GREAT DIVIDING RANGE

LEICHHARDT RANGE

CONNORS RANGE

Cairns

Townsville

Mackay

Rockhampton

Gladstone

Bundaberg

Maryborough

Gympie

Redcliffe
Sandgate
Brisbane
Ipswich
Toowoomba

Southport
Surfers Paradise

Warwick

Lismore

Grafton

GREAT BARRIER REEF MARINE PARK

NORTHUMBERLAND ISLES

FRASER ISLAND

CORAL SEA ISLANDS TERRITORY (Austl.)

CORAL SEA

PACIFIC OCEAN

Tropic of Capricorn

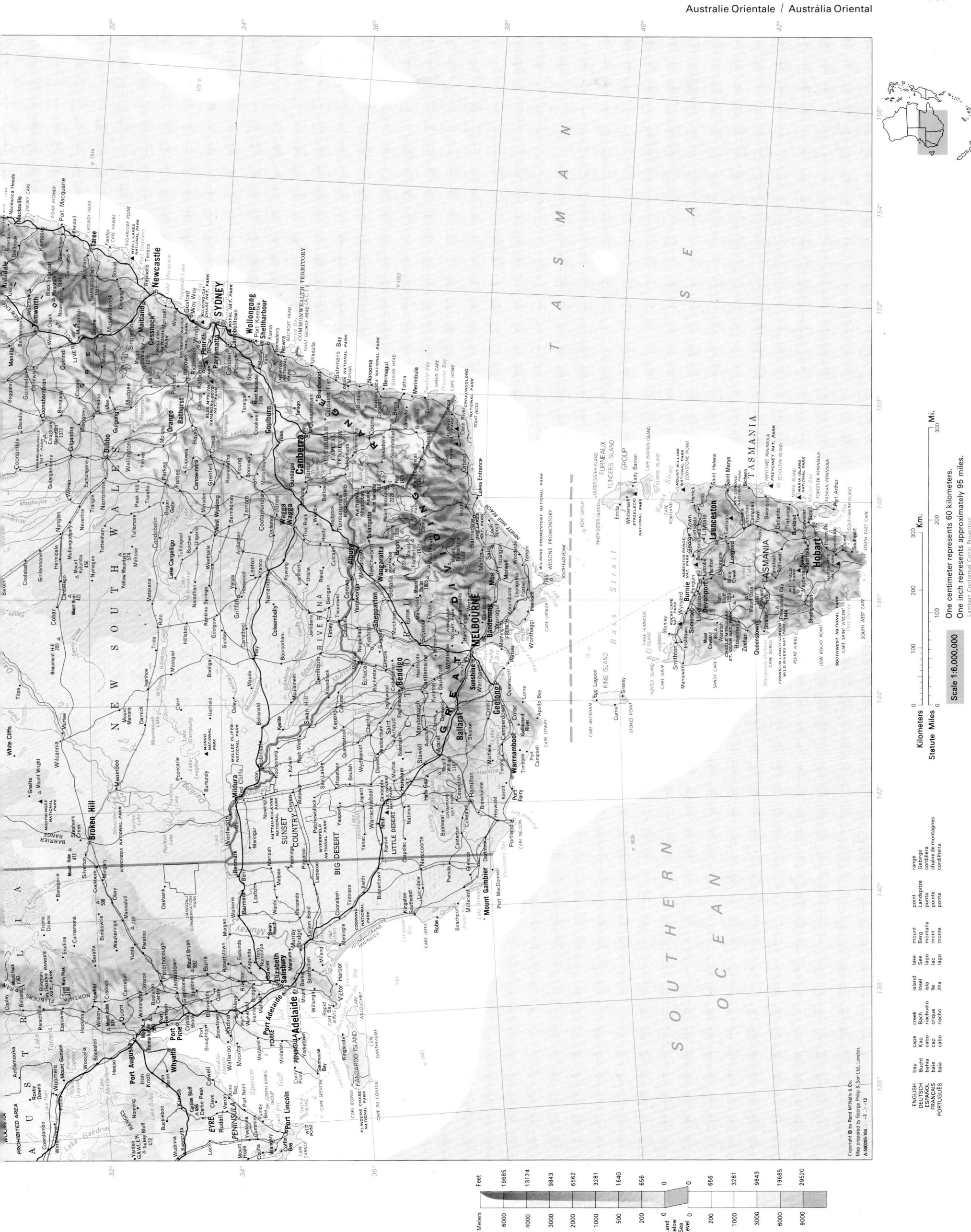

Copyright © by Rand McNally & Co.
Map prepared by George Philip & Son Ltd., London.
A-590056-784   -3 -.? -.?2

Scale 1:6,000,000

One centimeter represents 60 kilometers.
One inch represents approximately 95 miles.

Lambert Conformal Conic Projection

ENGLISH	bay	cape	creek	island	lake	mount	point	range
DEUTSCH	Bucht	Kap	Bach	Insel	See	Berg	Landspitze	Gebirge
ESPAÑOL	bahía	cabo	riachuelo	isla	lago	montaña	punta	cordillera
FRANCAIS	baie	cap	crique	île	lac	mont	pointe	chaîne de montagnes
PORTUGUÊS	baía	cabo	riacho	ilha	lago	monte	ponta	cordilheira

Feet		Meters
19685		6000
13124		4000
9843		3000
6562		2000
3281		1000
1640		500
656		200
0	Land Below Sea Level	0
0		
656		200
3281		1000
9843		3000
19685		6000
29520		9000

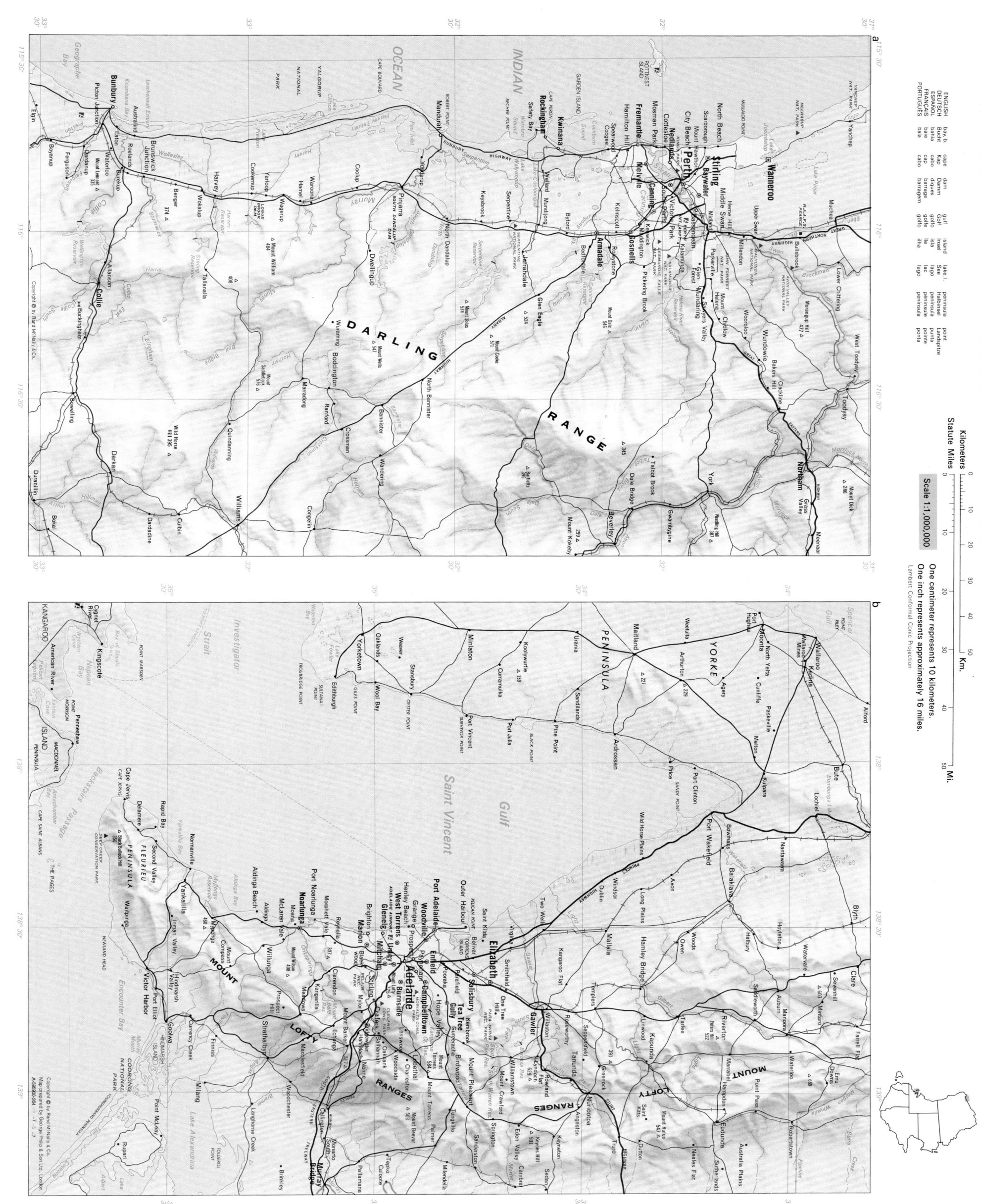

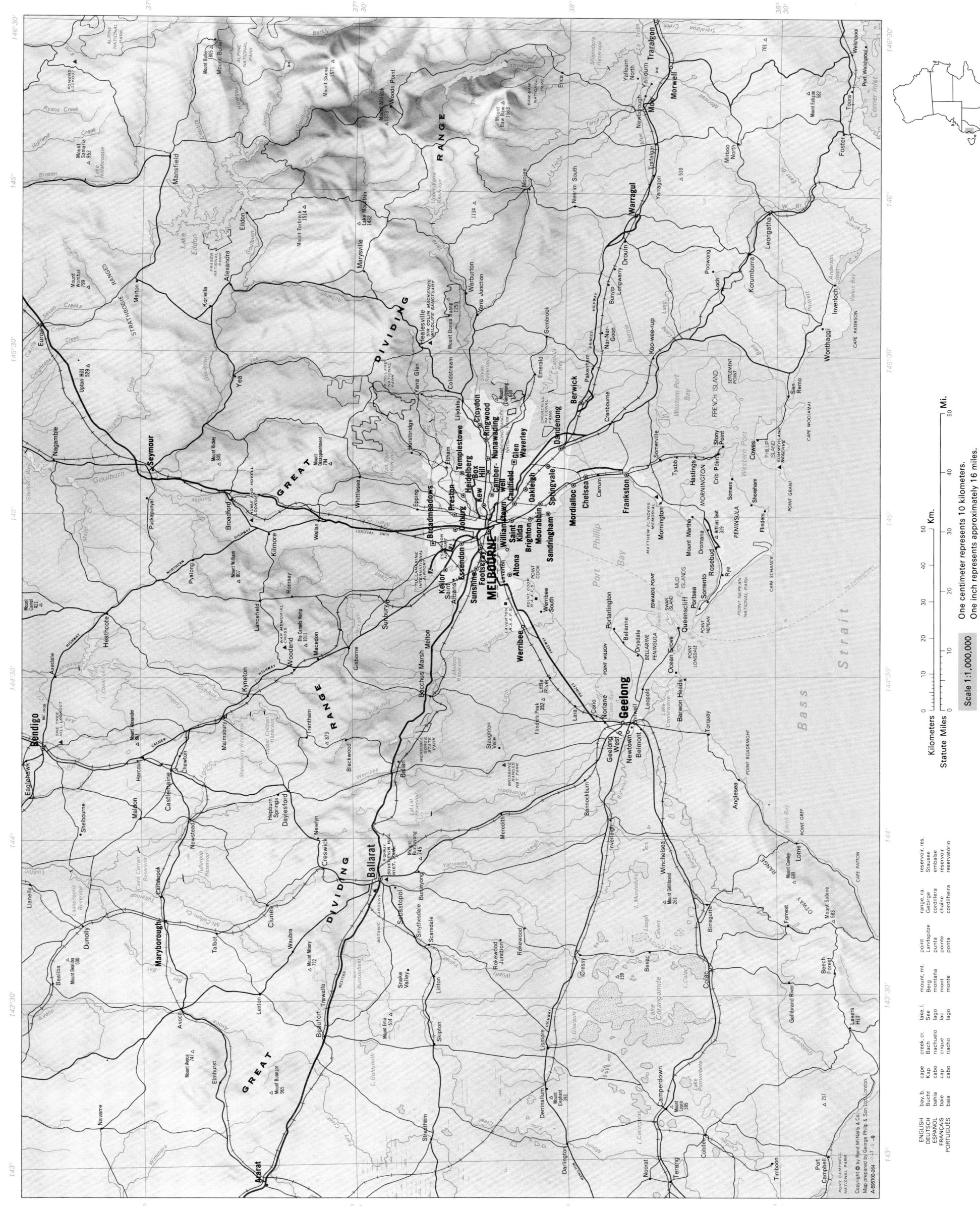

Scale 1:1,000,000

Kilometers

Statute Miles

One centimeter represents 10 kilometers.
One inch represents approximately 16 miles.
Lambert Conformal Conic Projection

ENGLISH	bay, b.	cape	creek, cr.	lake, l.	mount, mt.	point	range, ra.	reservoir, res.
DEUTSCH	Bucht	Kap	Bach	See	Berg	Landspitze	Gebirge	Stausee
ESPAÑOL	bahía	cabo	riachuelo	lago	montaña	punta	cordillera	embalse
FRANÇAIS	baie	cap	ruisseau	lac	mont	pointe	chaîne	réservoir
PORTUGUÊS	baía	cabo	riacho	lago	monte	ponta	cordilheira	reservatório

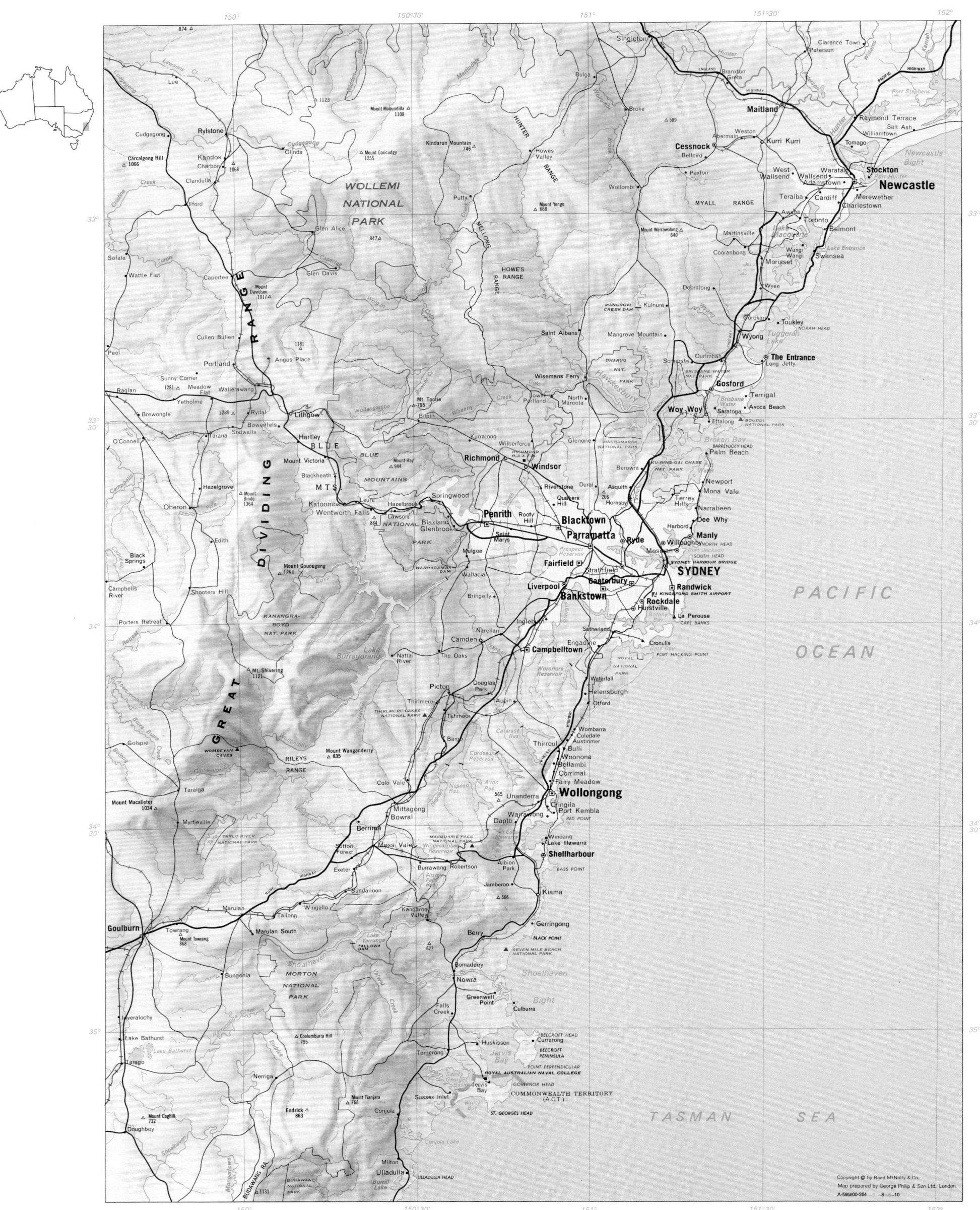

ENGLISH	bight	creek, cr.	head	mount	range	reservoir, res.
DEUTSCH	Bucht	Bach	Vorgebirge	Berg	Gebirge	Stausee
ESPAÑOL	ensenada pequeña	riachuelo	promontorio	montaña	cordillera	estanque
FRANÇAIS	anse	crique	promontoire	mont	chaîne	reservoir
PORTUGUÊS	enseada	riacho	promontório	monte	cordilheira	reservatório

Kilometers   0 10 20 30 40 50
                                    Km.
Statute Miles 0 10 20 30 40 50
                                    Mi.

Scale 1:1,000,000

One centimeter represents 10 kilometers.
One inch represents approximately 16 miles.
Lambert Conformal Conic Projection

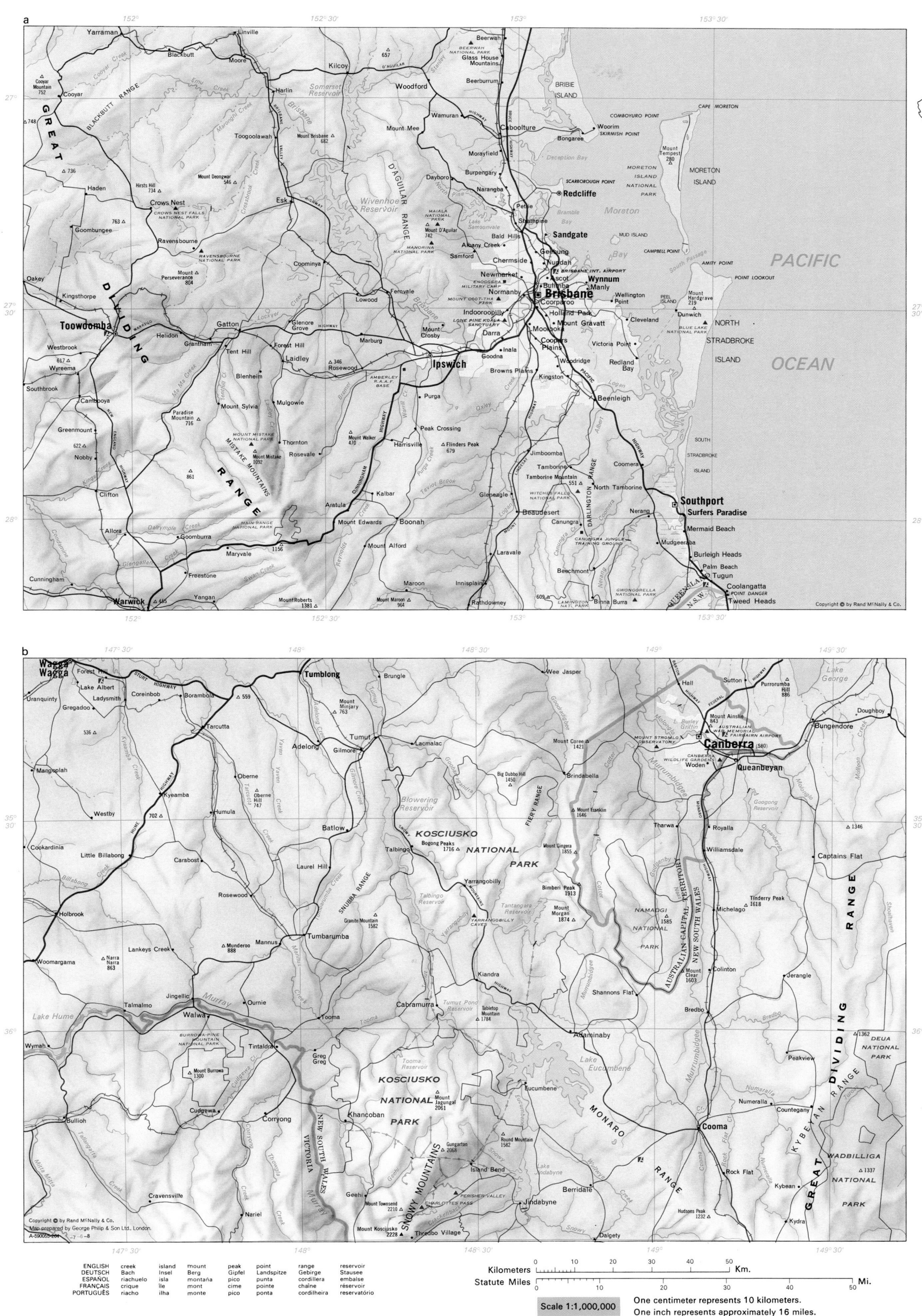

a

GREAT DIVIDING RANGE

Yarraman
Linville
Blackbutt
Moore
Kilcoy
D'AGUILAR
Woodford
Beerwah
BEERWAH NATIONAL PARK
Glass House Mountains
Beerburrum
BRIBIE ISLAND
COMBOYURO POINT
CAPE MORETON

Cooyar
Mountain 752
Cooyar
ERNEST JUNCTION

736
Haden
Hirsts Hill 734
Mount Deongwar 546
Harlin

657

Somerset Reservoir

Caboolture
Woorim
SKIRMISH POINT

Wamuran

Mount Mee

Mount Brisbane 682
Toogoolawah

Crows Nest
CROWS NEST FALLS NATIONAL PARK

763

Goombungee
Ravensbourne
RAVENSBOURNE NATIONAL PARK
Esk
Coominya
MAIALA NATIONAL PARK
Mount D'Aguilar 742
MANORINA NATIONAL PARK

Dayboro
Morayfield
Deception Bay
Mount Tempest 280
MORETON ISLAND NATIONAL PARK
MORETON ISLAND

Burpengary
Narangba
SCARBOROUGH POINT

Oakey
Kingsthorpe
Mount Perseverance 804

Fernvale
Samford
ENOGGERA MILITARY CAMP
Albany Creek
Samsonvale
Geebung
Nudgah
Petrie
Strathpine
Redcliffe

Bald Hills
Sandgate
MUD ISLAND
Moreton
CAMPBELL POINT
Bay
South Passage
AMITY POINT

Westbrook
817
Wyreema
Toowoomba

Helidon
Gatton
Lowood
Glenore Grove

Chermside
Newmarket
Ascot
BRISBANE INT. AIRPORT
Manly
Wynnum
Wellington Point
PEEL ISLAND
PACIFIC
Point Lookout
Mount Hardgrave 219

622
Nobby
Greenmount
Cambooya
Paradise Mountain 716

Grantham
Tent Hill
Forest Hill
Laidley
Marburg

Mount Sylvia
Mulgowie
346
Rosewood

Blenheim

Buttaba
Normanby
MOUNT COOT-THA PARK
Brisbane
Coorparoo
Holland Park
Mount Gravatt
Cleveland
Victoria Point
BLUE LAKE NATIONAL PARK
NORTH STRADBROKE ISLAND
Dunwich

Southbrook

Clifton
861

Thornton
Rosevale

Mount Walker 470
Harrisville
Ipswich
AMBERLEY R.A.A.F. BASE
Purga
Goodna
Darra
Moorooka
Coopers Plains
Inala
Woodridge
Kingston
Browns Plains
Redland Bay

OCEAN

Allora
Goomburra

Maryvale
1156

Mount Edwards
Boonah
Mount Alford

Peak Crossing
Flinders Peak 679

Beenleigh
Jimboomba
Tamborine
Tamborine Mountain 551
North Tamborine
WITCHES FALLS NATIONAL PARK
Coomera
SOUTH STRADBROKE ISLAND

Cunningham
Freestone
Yangan

Warwick
445
Mount Roberts 1381
Mount Maroon 964
Maroon
Rathdowney
609
LAMINGTON NATL. PARK
Binna Burra
QUEENSLAND
N.S.W.

Laravale
Beaudesert
Canungra
CANUNGRA JUNGLE TRAINING GROUND
Beechmont
GWONGORELLA NATIONAL PARK

Gleneagle
Nerang
Southport
Surfers Paradise
Mermaid Beach
Mudgeeraba
Burleigh Heads
Palm Beach
Tugun
Coolangatta
POINT DANGER
Tweed Heads

Copyright © by Rand McNally & Co.

b

Wagga Wagga
Forest Hill
Lake Albert
STURT HIGHWAY
Tumblong
Brungle
Wee Jasper
Hall
Sutton
Purrorumba Hill 886
LAKE GEORGE

Uranquinty
Gregadoo
Coreinbob
Borambola
559
Mount Minjary 763

Mangoplah
536
Tarcutta
Tumut
Adelong
Gilmore
Lacmalac

Bungendore
Mount Coree 1421
CANBERRA
MOUNT STROMLO OBSERVATORY
AUSTRALIAN WAR MEMORIAL
FAIRBAIRN AIRPORT
Mount Ainslie 843
Canberra 580
Queanbeyan
Doughboy

Westby
702
Kyeamba
Humula
Oberne
Oberne Hill 747
Big Dubbo Hill 1450
Brindabella
CANBERRA WILDLIFE GARDENS
Woden

Cookardinia
Little Billabong
Carabost
Batlow
Laurel Hill
KOSCIUSKO NATIONAL PARK
Mount Franklin 1646
Mount Gingera 1855
Tharwa
Royalla
Williamsdale
1346
Captains Flat

Holbrook
Rosewood
SNUBBA RANGE
Talbingo
Bogong Peaks 1716
Yarrangobilly
Bimberi Peak 1913
Mount Morgan 1874
NAMADGI NATIONAL PARK
Tinderry Peak 1618
Michelago

Woomargama
Narra Narra 863
Lankeys Creek
Munderoo 888
Mannus
Tumbarumba
Granite Mountain 1582
Talbingo Reservoir
Tantangara Reservoir
YARRANGOBILLY CAVES
Mount Clear 1603
Colinton
Jerangle

Jingellic
Murray
Ournie
Cabramurra
Tumut Pond Reservoir
Tabletop Mountain 1784
Shannons Flat
Bredbo

Talmalmo
Walwa
BURROWA-PINE MOUNTAIN NATIONAL PARK
Tooma
Adaminaby
1362
DEUA NATIONAL PARK

Wymah
Lake Hume
Tintaldra
Greg Greg
Tooma Reservoir
KOSCIUSKO NATIONAL PARK
Lake Eucumbene
Peakview

Bullioh
Mount Burrowa 1300
Cudgewa
Corryong
Khancoban
Mount Jagungal 2061
Kiandra
Eucumbene
Numeralla
Countegany

Mount Townsend 2210
Mount Kosciusko 2228
NEW SOUTH WALES
VICTORIA
SNOWY MOUNTAINS
Gungartan 2068
Round Mountain 1582
Island Bend
Berridale
Jindabyne
Cooma
MONARO RANGE
Rock Flat
Kybean
WADBILLIGA NATIONAL PARK
1337

Cravensville
Nariel
Geehi
Mount Townsend 2210
PERISHER VALLEY
CHARLOTTES PASS
Thredbo Village
Hudsons Peak 1232
Dalgety
Kydra

Copyright © by Rand McNally & Co.
Map prepared by George Philip & Son Ltd., London.
A-590035-230
J-7-6-8

ENGLISH   creek   island   mount   peak   point   range   reservoir
DEUTSCH   Bach   Insel   Berg   Gipfel   Landspitze   Gebirge   Stausee
ESPAÑOL   riachuelo   isla   montaña   pico   punta   cordillera   embalse
FRANÇAIS   crique   île   mont   cime   pointe   chaîne   réservoir
PORTUGUÊS   riacho   ilha   monte   pico   ponta   cordilheira   reservatório

Kilometers   0 10 20 30 40 50 Km.
Statute Miles   0 10 20 30 40 50 Mi.

Scale 1:1,000,000
One centimeter represents 10 kilometers.
One inch represents approximately 16 miles.
Lambert Conformal Conic Projection

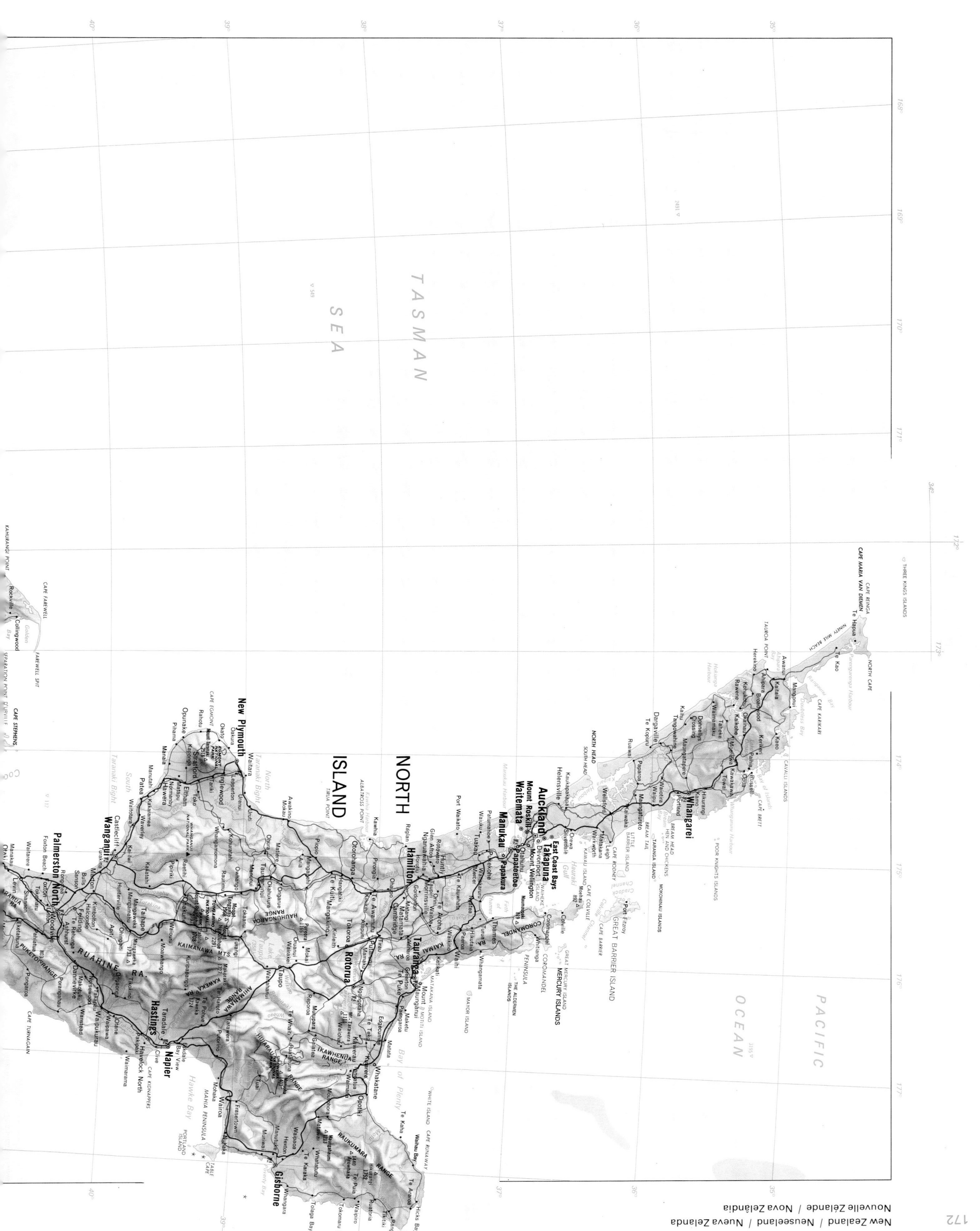

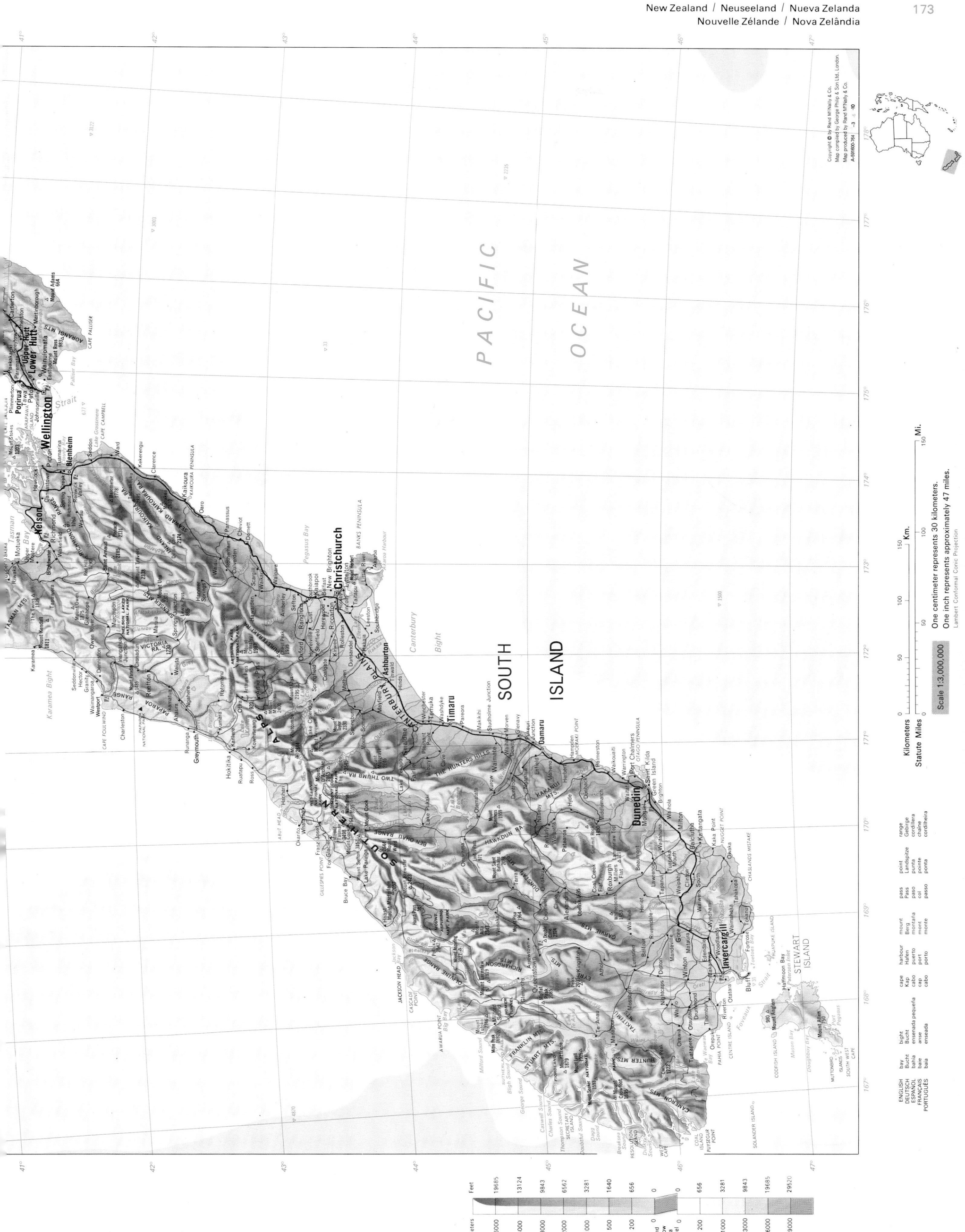

Copyright © by Rand McNally & Co.
Map compiled by George Philip & Son Ltd. London.
Map produced by Rand McNally & Co.
A-591600-764   -3 : -10

PACIFIC

OCEAN

SOUTH

ISLAND

STEWART
ISLAND

Scale 1:3,000,000

One centimeter represents 30 kilometers.
One inch represents approximately 47 miles.
Lambert Conformal Conic Projection

Kilometers

Statute Miles

ENGLISH	bay	bight	cape	harbour	mount	pass	point	range
DEUTSCH	Bucht	Bucht	Kap	Hafen	Berg	Pass	Landspitze	Gebirge
ESPAÑOL	bahía	ensenada pequeña	cabo	puerto	montaña	paso	punta	cordillera
FRANÇAIS	baie	anse	cap	port	monte	col	pointe	chaîne
PORTUGUÊS	baia	enseada	cabo	porto	monte	passo	ponta	cordilheira

Feet	Meters
19685	6000
13124	4000
9843	3000
6552	2000
3281	1000
1640	500
656	200
0	Land Below Sea Level
656	200
3281	1000
9843	3000
19685	6000
29520	9000

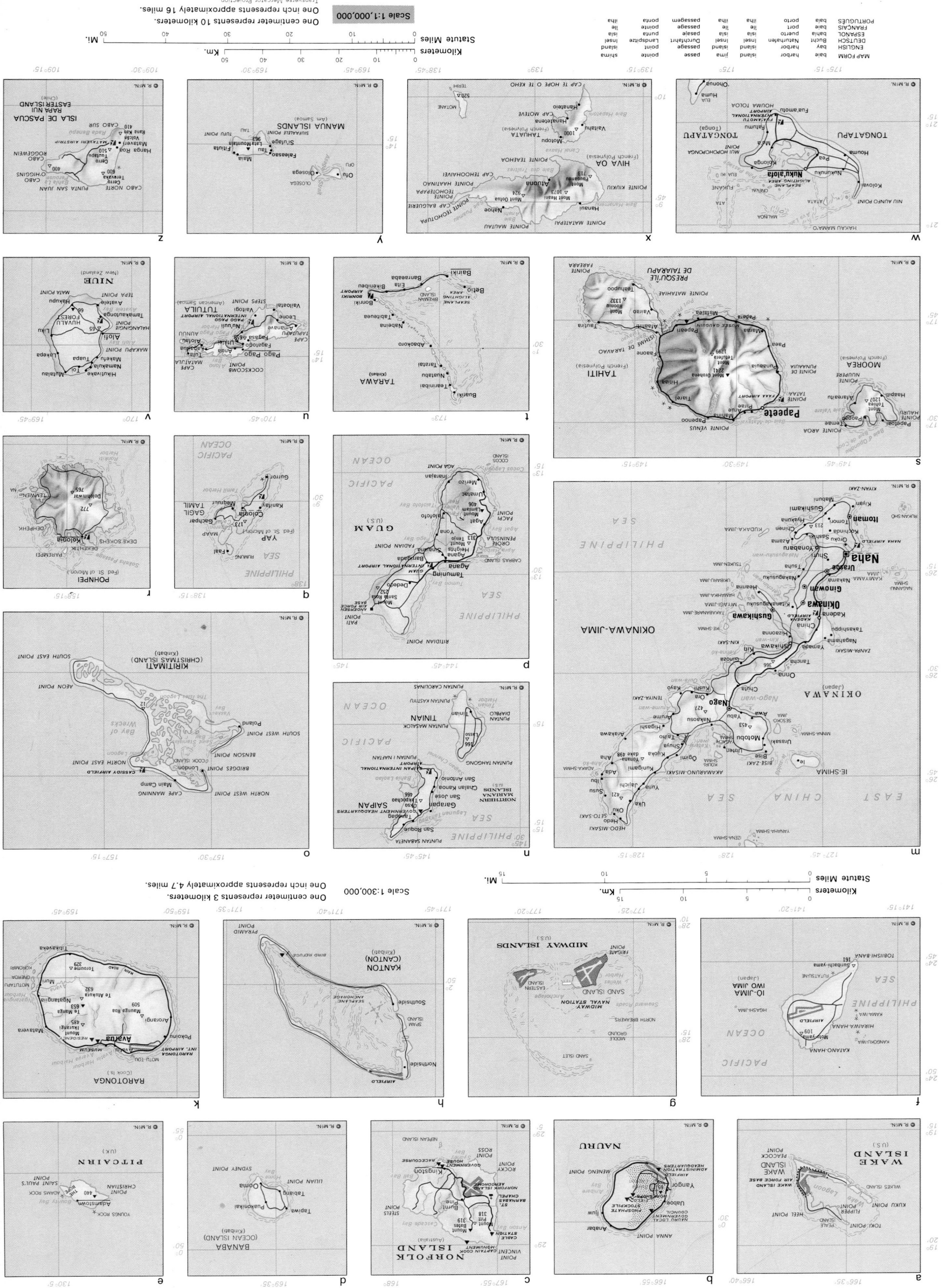

Islands of the Pacific / Pazifische Inseln / Islas del Pacífico
Îles du Pacifique / Ilhas do Pacífico

174

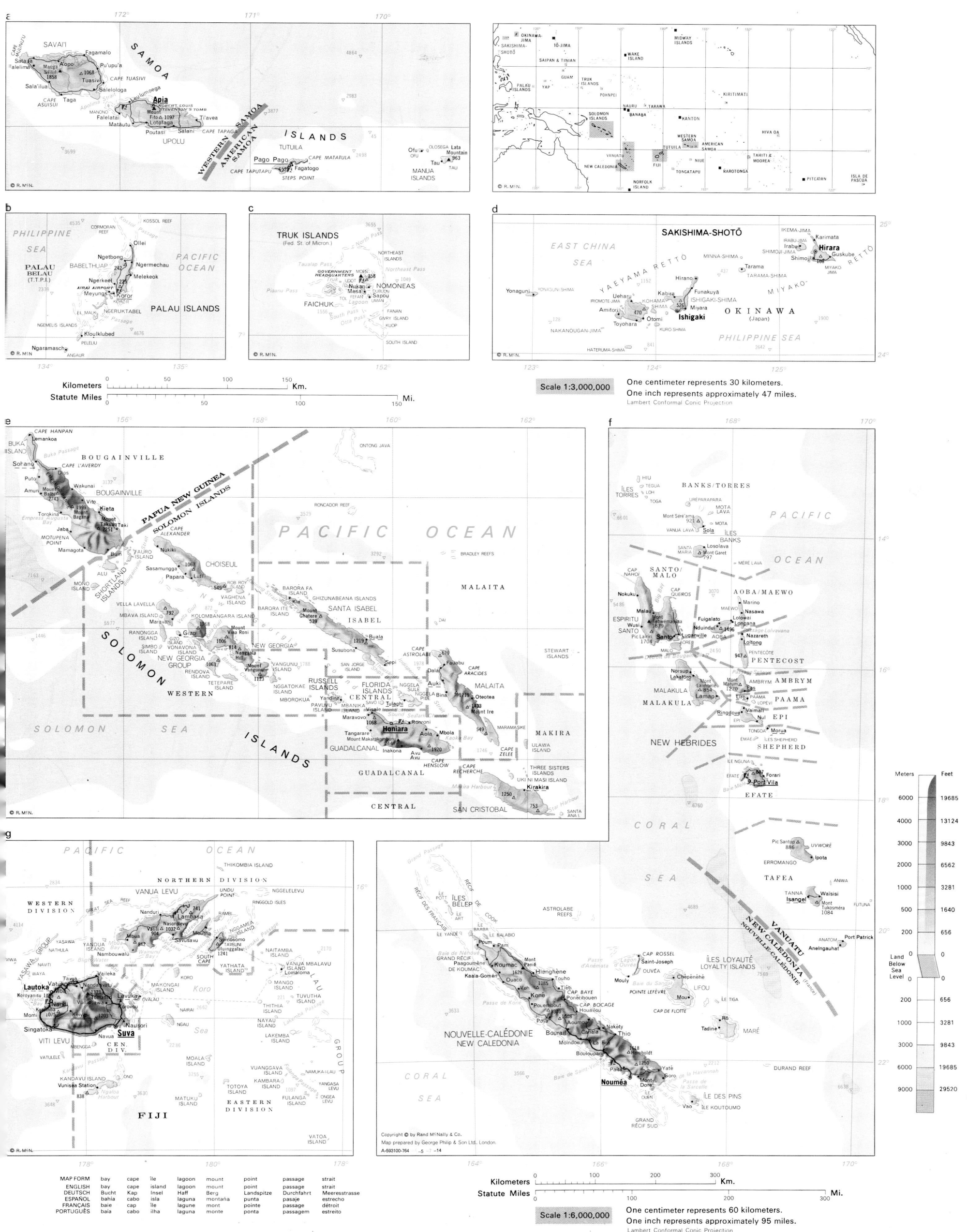

Map continues
pages **178-179**

ENGLISH	bay	cape	island	lake, l.	mountains, mts.	point	range	strait
DEUTSCH	Bucht	Kap	Insel	See	Berge	Landspitze	Gebirge	Meeresstrasse
ESPAÑOL	bahía	cabo	isla	lago	montañas	punta	sierra	estrecho
FRANÇAIS	baie	cap	île	lac	montagnes	pointe	chaîne	détroit
PORTUGUÊS	baía	cabo	ilha	lago	montanhas	ponta	serra	estreito

Kilometers

Km.

Statute Miles

Mi.

Scale 1:12,000,000

One centimeter represents 120 kilometers.
One inch represents approximately 190 miles.

Lambert Conformal Conic Projection

Map continues pages 230-231

ENGLISH	DEUTSCH	ESPAÑOL	FRANÇAIS	PORTUGUÊS
bay	Bucht	bahía	baie	baía
cape	Kap	cabo	cap	cabo
desert	Wüste	desierto	desert	deserto
island	Insel	isla	île	ilha
lake	See	lago	lac	lago
mountains	Berge	montañas	montagnes	montanhas
peak	Gipfel	pico	cime	pico
range	Gebirge	sierra	chaîne	serra

Map continues
pages **176-177**

Kilometers 0 200 400 600 Km.
Statute Miles 0 200 400 600 Mi.

Scale 1:12,000,000
One centimeter represents 120 kilometers.
One inch represents approximately 190 miles.

Albers Conical Equal-Area Projection

Map continues
pages 176-177

Map continues
pages 182-183

Kilometers

Statute Miles

Scale 1:6,000,000

One centimeter represents 60 kilometers.
One inch represents approximately 95 miles.
Lambert Conformal Conic Projection

Southwestern Canada / Südwestkanada / Canadá Sud-occidental
Sud-Ouest du Canada / Canadá: Sudoeste

Map continues
pages **180-181**

ENGLISH	creek	Indian reserve	inlet	island	lake, l.	mountain	peak	provincial park	sound
DEUTSCH	Bach	Indianerreservation	Einfahrt	Insel	See	Berg	Gipfel	Provinz-Park	Sund
ESPAÑOL	riachuelo	reserva de Indios	abra	isla	lago	montaña	pico	parque de provincia	sonda
FRANÇAIS	crique	réserve indienne	bras de mer	île	lac	montagne	cime	parc provincial	détroit
PORTUGUÊS	riacho	reserva indígena	enseada	ilha	lago	montanha	pico	parque provincial	estreito

Copyright © by Rand McNally & Co.
Map prepared by Rand McNally & Co.
A-620020-764   -5 -6   -8¹

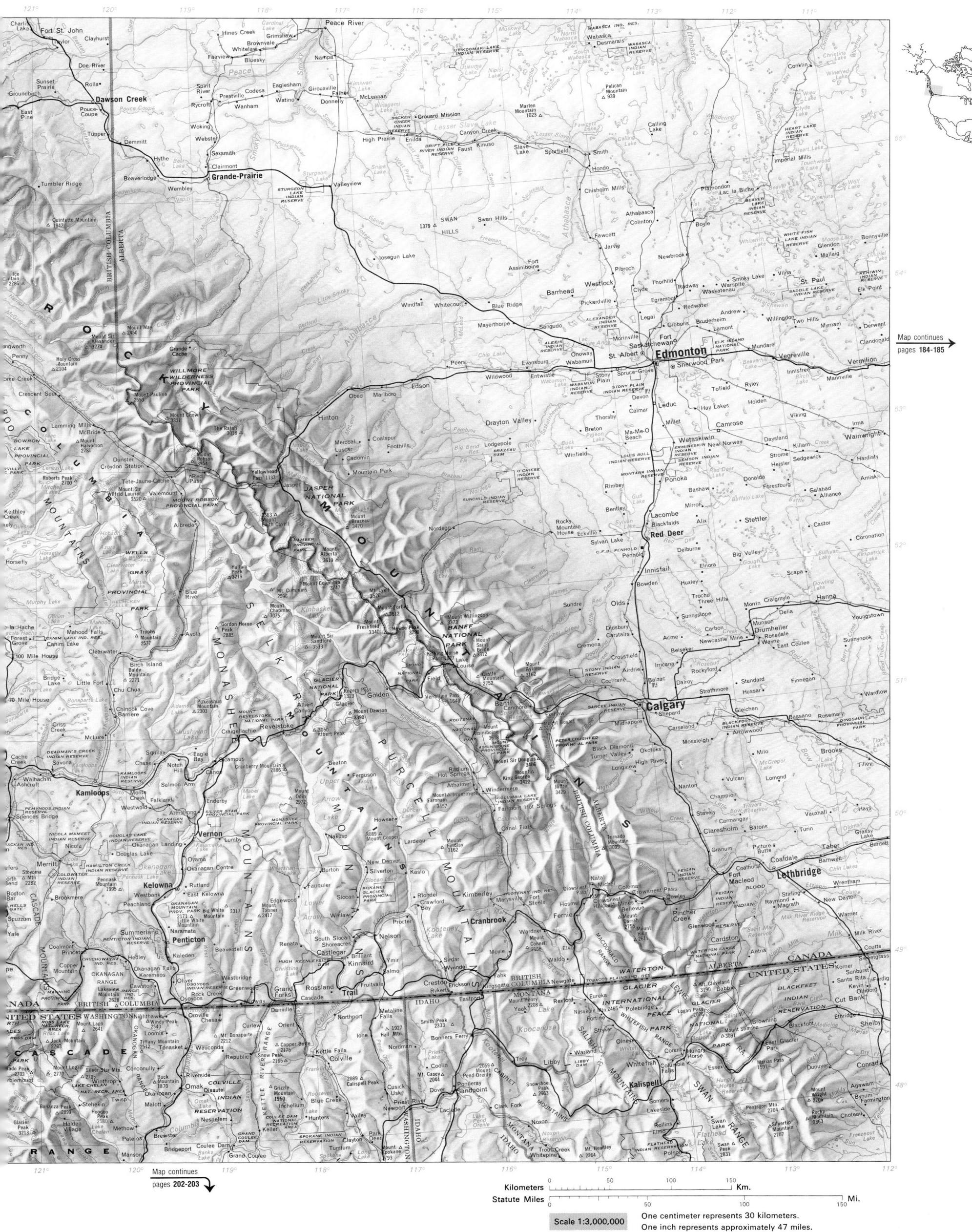

Kilometers |0 50 100 150| Km.
Statute Miles |0 50 100 150| Mi.

Scale 1:3,000,000

One centimeter represents 30 kilometers.
One inch represents approximately 47 miles.
Lambert Conformal Conic Projection

Map continues
pages 184-185 →

Map continues
pages 202-203 ↓

Map continues pages 198-199
Map continues pages 202-203
Map continues pages 182-183

ENGLISH	DEUTSCH	ESPAÑOL	FRANÇAIS	PORTUGUÊS
creek, cr.	Bach	riachuelo	ruisseau	riacho
hills	Hügel	colinas	collines	colinas
Indian reserve	Indianerreservation	reserva de indios	réserve indienne	reserva indígena
island, i.	Insel	isla	île	ilha
lake, l.	See	lago	lac	lago
provincial park	Provinz-Park	parque de provincia	parc provincial	parque provincial

Copyright © by Rand McNally & Co.
Map prepared by Rand McNally & Co.
A-520218-164

184

South-Central Canada / Südliches Mittelkanada / Centro Meridional del Canadá
Canada Central, partie Méridionale / Canadá Central, parte meridional

South-Central Canada / Südliches Mittelkanada / Centro Meridional del Canadá
Canada Central, partie Méridionale / Canadá Central, parte meridional

185

Map continues
pages 190-191

Kilometers

Statute Miles

Scale 1:3,000,000

One centimeter represents 30 kilometers.
One inch represents approximately 47 miles.
Lambert Conformal Conic Projection

pages 188-189
Map continues

ENGLISH	DEUTSCH	ESPAÑOL	FRANÇAIS	PORTUGUÊS
bay	Bucht	bahía	baie	baía
cape	Kap	cabo	cap	cabo
dam	Damm	presa	barrage	represa
island	Insel	isla	île	ilha
lake, l.	See	lago	lac	lago
mountain	Berg	montaña	montagne	montanha
point	Landspitze	punta	pointe	ponta
strait	Meeresstrasse	estrecho	détroit	estreito

Feet	Meters			
29520	9000			
19685	6000			
9843	3000			
3281	1000			
656	200			
0	Land Below Sea Level / Sea Level 0			
656	200			
1640	500			
3281	1000			
6562	2000			
9843	3000			
13124	4000			
19685	6000			

Kilometers

Statute Miles

Scale 1:3,000,000

One centimeter represents 30 kilometers.
One inch represents approximately 47 miles.
Lambert Conformal Conic Projection

Copyright © by Rand McNally & Co.
Map prepared by Rand McNally & Co.
A-520219-764

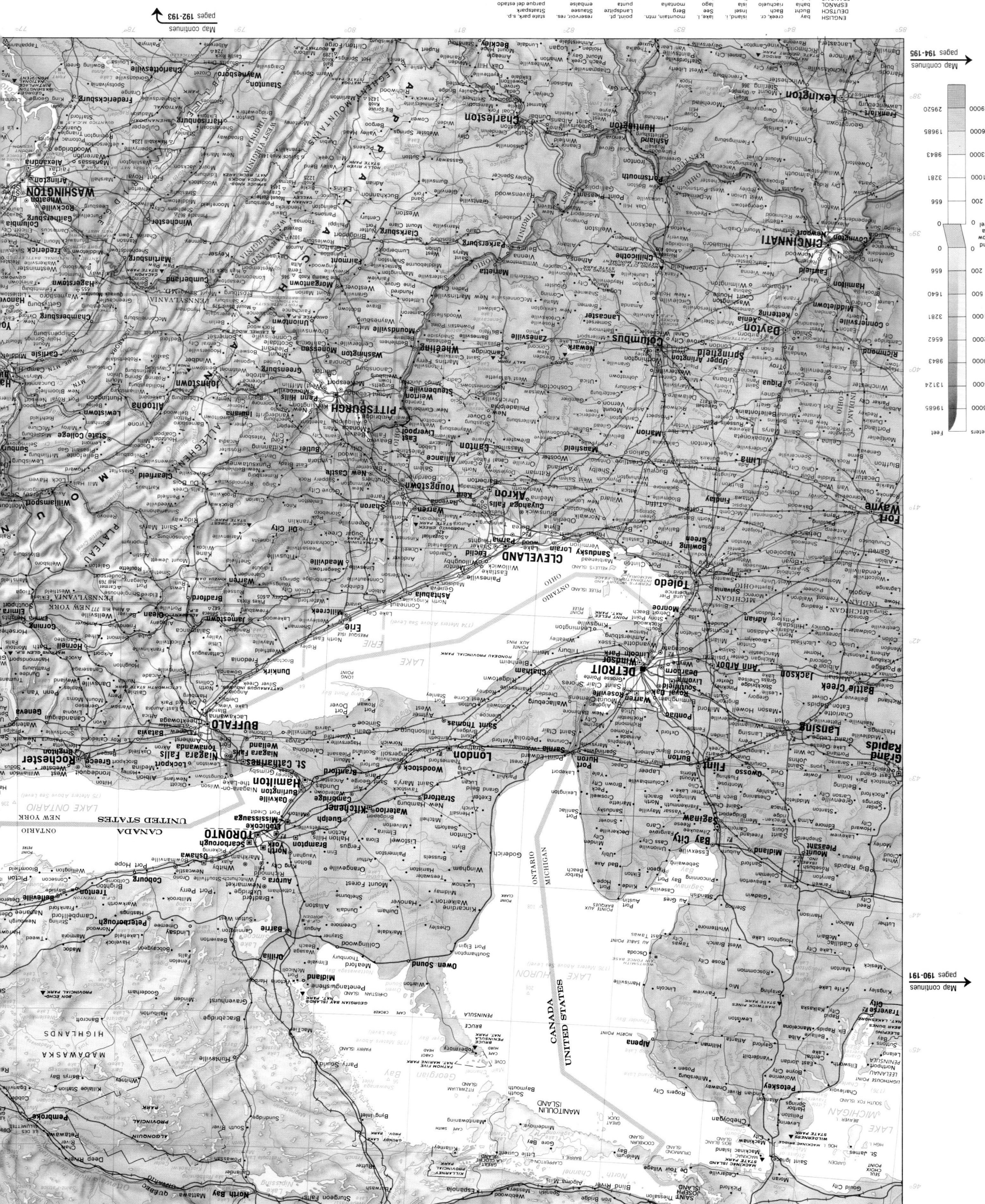

Map continues pages 194-195

Map continues pages 190-191

ENGLISH	DEUTSCH	FRANÇAIS	ESPAÑOL	PORTUGUÊS
bay	Bucht	baie	bahía	baía
creek, cr.	Bach	riacho	riacho	riacho
island, i.	Insel	île	isla	ilha
lake, l.	See	lac	lago	lago
mountain, mtn.	Berg	montagne	montaña	montanha
point, pt.	Landspitze	pointe	punta	ponta
reservoir, res.	Stausee	reservoir	parque regional	parque estadual
state park, s.p.	Staatspark	parc regional	parque del estado	parque estadual

Northeastern United States / Nordöstliche Vereinigte Staaten / Nor-este de los Estados Unidos
Nord-Est des États-Unis / Estados Unidos: Nordeste

Northeastern United States / Nordöstliche Vereinigte Staaten / Nor-este de los Estados Unidos
Nord-Est des États-Unis / Estados Unidos: Nordeste

189

Map continues
pages 186-187

Copyright © by Rand McNally & Co.
Map prepared by Rand McNally & Co.
A-500596-764

Kilometers

Statute Miles

Scale 1:3,000,000

One centimeter represents 30 kilometers.
One inch represents approximately 47 miles.
Albers Conical Equal-Area Projection

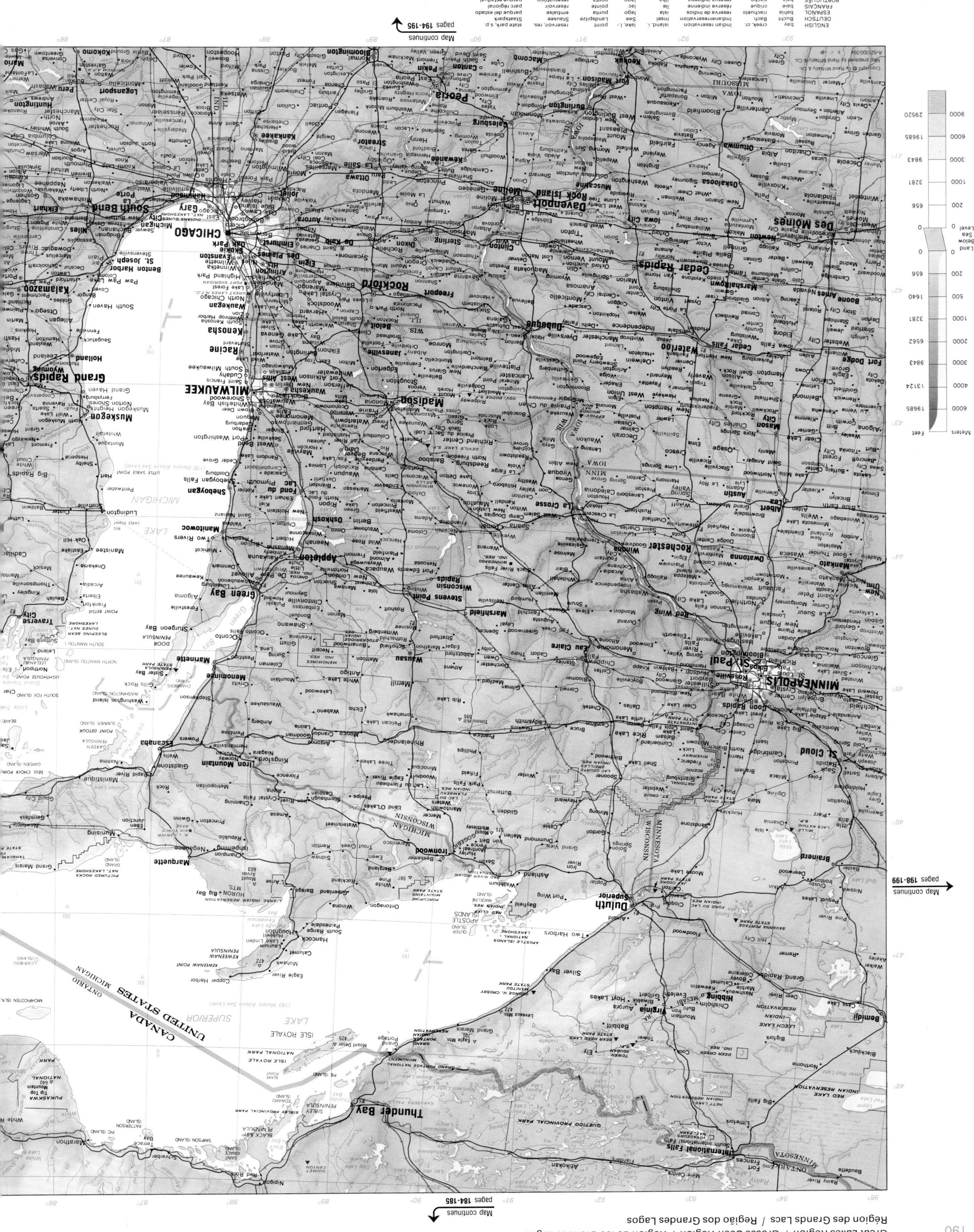

Map continues pages 194-195

Map continues pages 198-199

Map continues pages 184-185

	ENGLISH	DEUTSCH	FRANÇAIS	ESPAÑOL	PORTUGUÊS
	bay	Bucht	baie	bahía	baía
	creek, cr.	Bach	crique	riachuelo	riacho
	Indian reservation	Indianerreservation	réserve indienne	reserva de indios	reserva indígena
	island, I.	Insel	île	isla	ilha
	lake, L.	See	lac	lago	lago
	point	Landspitze	pointe	punta	ponta
	reservoir, res.	Stausee	réservoir	embalse	represa
	state park, s.p.	Staatspark	parc régional	parque del estado	parque estadual

Great Lakes Region / Grosse Seen-Region / Région de los Grandes Lagos
Région des Grands Lacs / Região dos Grandes Lagos

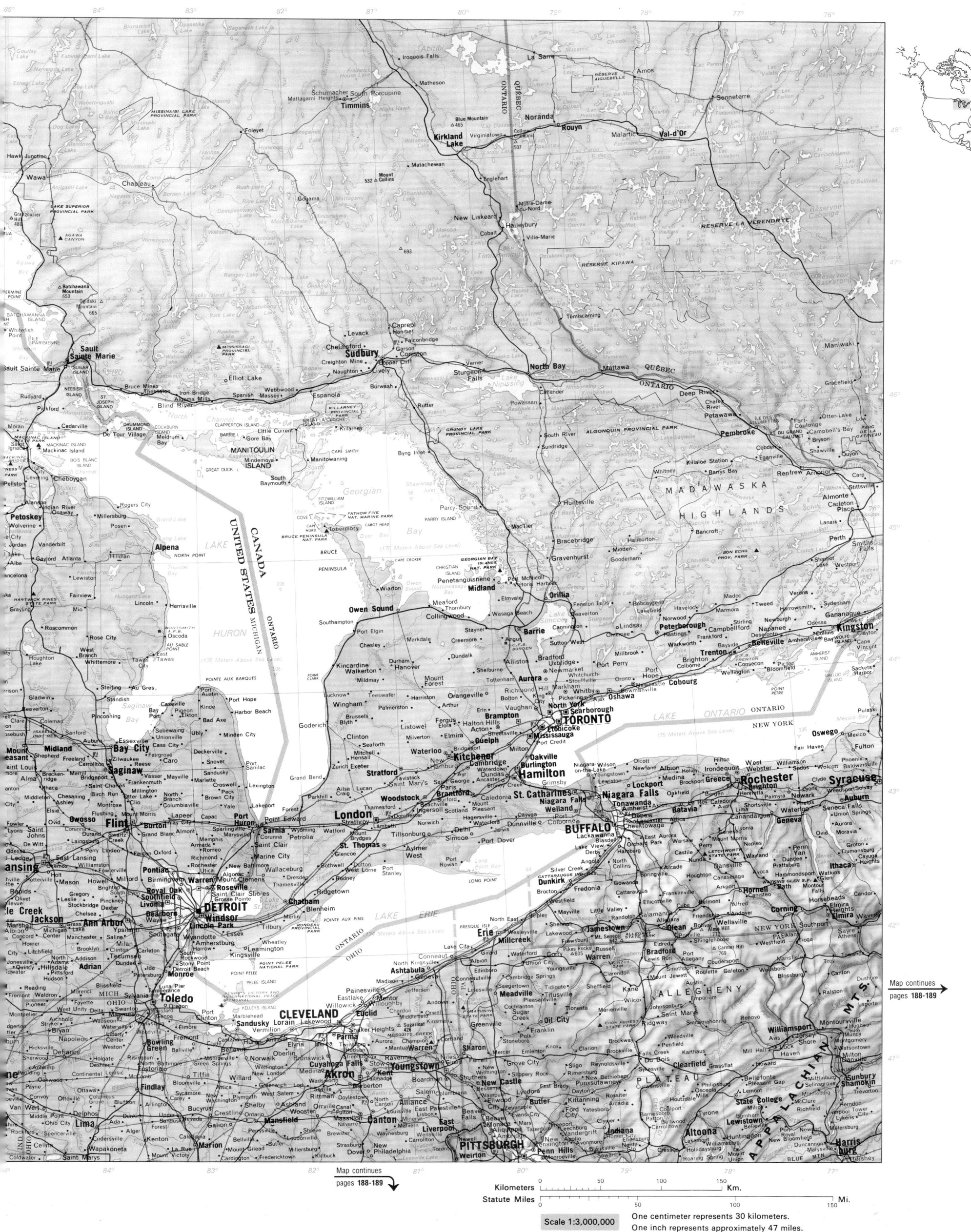

Map continues
pages 188-189 →

Map continues
pages 188-189 ↓

Kilometers
Statute Miles

Scale 1:3,000,000

One centimeter represents 30 kilometers.
One inch represents approximately 47 miles.

Albers Conical Equal-Area Projection

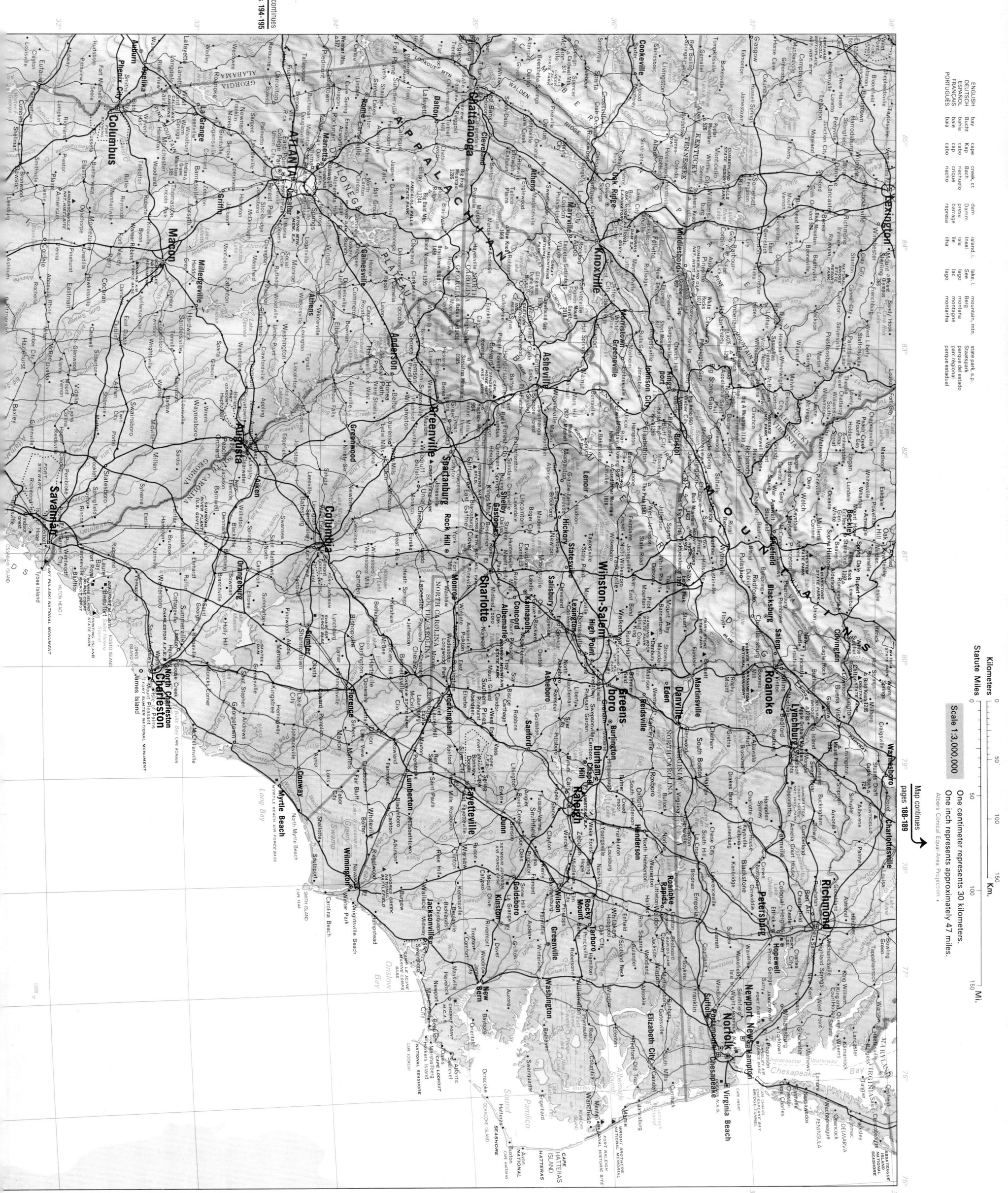

ENGLISH
DEUTSCH
ESPAÑOL
FRANÇAIS
PORTUGUÊS

	bay	cape	creek, cr.	dam	island, I.	lake, l.	mountain, mtn.	state park, s.p.
	Bucht	Kap	Bach	Damm	Insel	See	Berg	Staatspark
	bahía	cabo	riachuelo	presa	isla	lago	montaña	parque del estado
	baie	cap	crique	barrage	île	lac	montagne	parc régional
	baía	cabo	riacho	represa	ilha	lago	montanha	parque estadual

Kilometers

Statute Miles

Scale 1:3,000,000

0   50   100   150   Km.

0   50   100   150   Mi.

One centimeter represents approximately 30 kilometers.
One inch represents approximately 47 miles.

Albers Conical Equal-Area Projection

Map continues
pages 188-189

Southeastern United States / Südöstliche Vereinigte Staaten / Sud-este de los Estados Unidos
Sud-Est des États-Unis / Estados Unidos: Sudeste

193

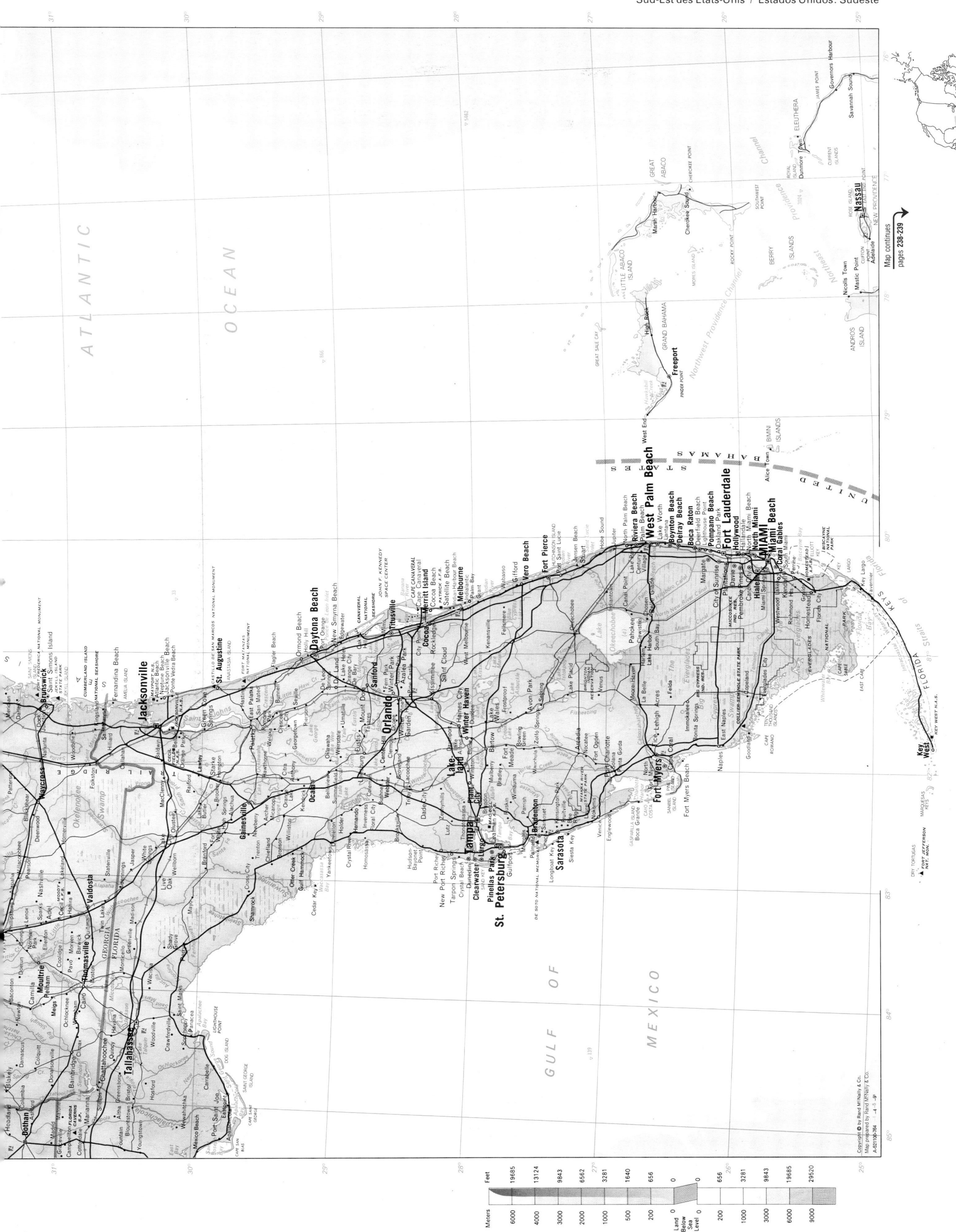

Map continues
pages 238-239

pages 198-199

Map continues
pages 190-191

Map continues
pages 188-189

Mississippi Valley / Mississippi-Tiefland / Valle del Misisipí
Vallée du Mississippi / Vale do Mississipí

Map continues
pages 192-193

Map continues
pages 196-197

Copyright © by Rand McNally & Co.
Map prepared by Rand McNally & Co.
A-491280.764   -4   -9

One centimeter represents 30 kilometers.
One inch represents approximately 47 miles.

Scale 1:3,000,000

Albers Conical Equal-Area Projection

Kilometers

Statute Miles

Km.

Mi.

ENGLISH	bay	bayou, bay	creek, cr.	damm	lake	mountain, mtn.	reservoir, res.	state park, s.p.
DEUTSCH	Bucht	Altwasser	Bach	Damm	See	Berg	Stausee	Staatspark
ESPAÑOL	ensenada	ensenada	riachuelo	presa	lago	montaña	embalse	parque del estado
FRANÇAIS	baie	bayou	crique	barrage	lac	montagne	réservoir	parc
PORTUGUÊS	baía	ensenada	riacho	represa	lago	montanha	reservatório	parque estadual

Feet
19685 6000
13124 4000
9843 3000
6562 2000
3281 1000
1640 500
656 200
0 0
Land
Below
Sea
Level
0 0
656 200
3281 1000
9843 3000
19685 6000
29520 9000
Meters

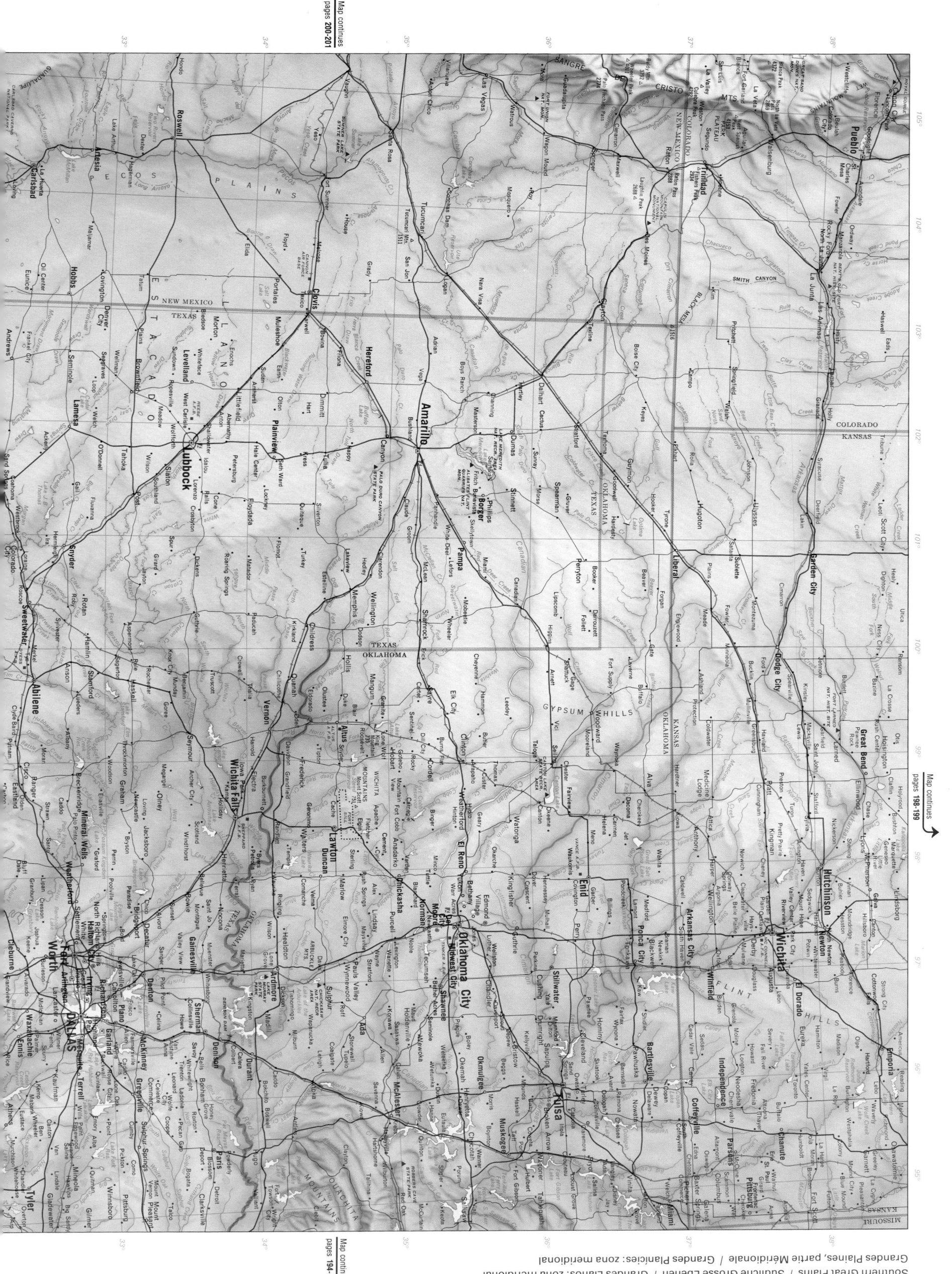

Map continues
pages 200-201

Map continues
pages 198-199

Map continues
pages 194-195

Southern Great Plains / Südliche Grosse Ebenen / Grandes Llanos: zona meridional
Grandes Plaines, partie Méridionale / Grandes Planicies: zona meridional

Southern Great Plains / Südliche Grosse Ebenen / Grandes Llanos: zona meridional
Grandes Plaines, partie Méridionale / Grandes Planícies: zona meridional

197

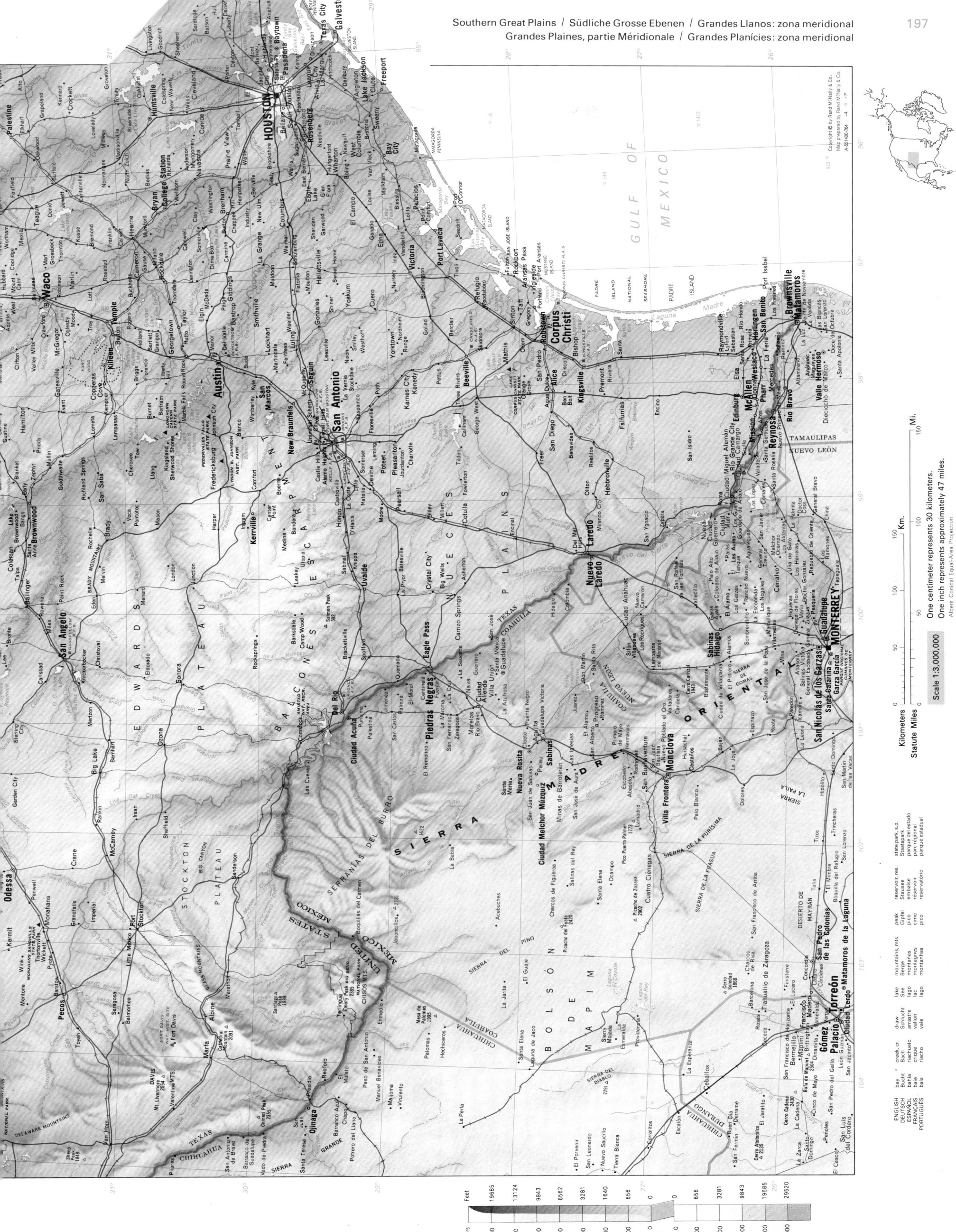

Scale 1:3,000,000

One centimeter represents 30 kilometers.
One inch represents approximately 47 miles.

Albers Conical Equal-Area Projection

ENGLISH	bay	creek, cr.	draw	lake	mountains, mts.	peak	reservoir, res.	state park, s.p.
DEUTSCH	Bucht	Bach	Schlucht	See	Berge	Gipfel	Stausee	Staatspark
ESPAÑOL	bahía	riachuelo	arrastre	lago	montañas	pico	embalse	parque del estado
FRANÇAIS	baie	ruisseau	vallon	lac	montagnes	cime	réservoir	parc régional
PORTUGUÊS	baía	riacho	vale	lago	montanhas	pico	reservatório	parque estadual

Kilometers

Km.

Statute Miles

Mi.

Feet
19685
13124
9843
6562
3281
1640
656
0

Meters
6000
4000
3000
2000
1000
500
200
0

Land
Below
Sea
Level

0
200
656
1000
3281
3000
9843
6000
19685
9000
29520

Northern Great Plains / Nördliche Grosse Ebenen / Grandes Llanos: zona septentrional
Grandes Plaines, partie Septentrionale / Grandes Planícies: zona setentrional

Map continues pages 190-191

Map continues pages 184-185

Map continues pages 202-203

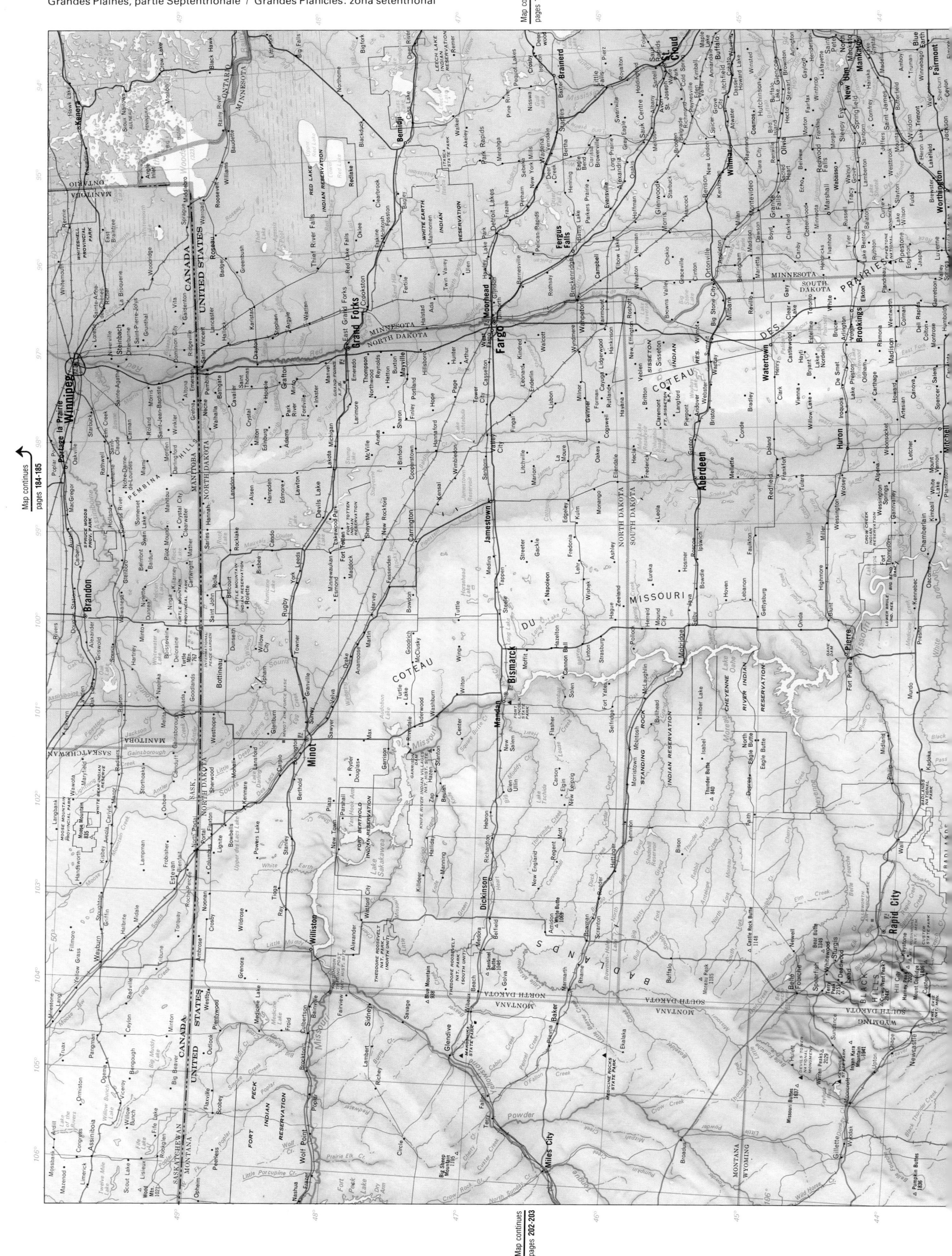

Northern Great Plains / Nördliche Grosse Ebenen / Grandes Llanos: zona septentrional
Grandes Plaines, partie Septentrionale / Grandes Planícies: zona setentrional

199

Map continues pages 194-195

Map continues pages 196-197

Map continues pages 200-201

Scale 1:3,000,000

One centimeter represents 30 kilometers.
One inch represents approximately 47 miles.

Albers Conical Equal-Area Projection

Kilometers
Statute Miles

ENGLISH	creek, cr.	dam	Indian reservation, Ind. res.	lake, l.	mountain, mtn.	peak	reservoir, res.	state park
DEUTSCH	Bach	Damm	Indianerreservation	See	Berg	Gipfel	Stausee	Staatspark
ESPAÑOL	riachuelo	presa	reserva de Indios	lago	montaña	pico	embalse	parque del estado
FRANÇAIS	crique	barrage	reserve indienne	lac	montagne	cime	reservoir	parc regional
PORTUGUÊS	riacho	barragem	reserva indigena	lago	montanha	pico	reservatorio	parque estadual

Copyright © by Rand McNally & Co.
Map prepared by Rand McNally & Co.
A-351300-764

Feet	Meters
19685	6000
13124	4000
9843	3000
6562	2000
3281	1000
1640	500
656	200
0	0
656	200
3281	1000
9843	3000
19685	6000
29520	9000

Land Below Sea Level

200

Southern Rocky Mountains / Südliches Felsengebirge / Montañas Rocosas: zona meridional
Montagnes Rocheuses, partie Méridionale / Montanhas Rochosas: zona meridional

Map continues pages 198-199

Map continues pages 202-203

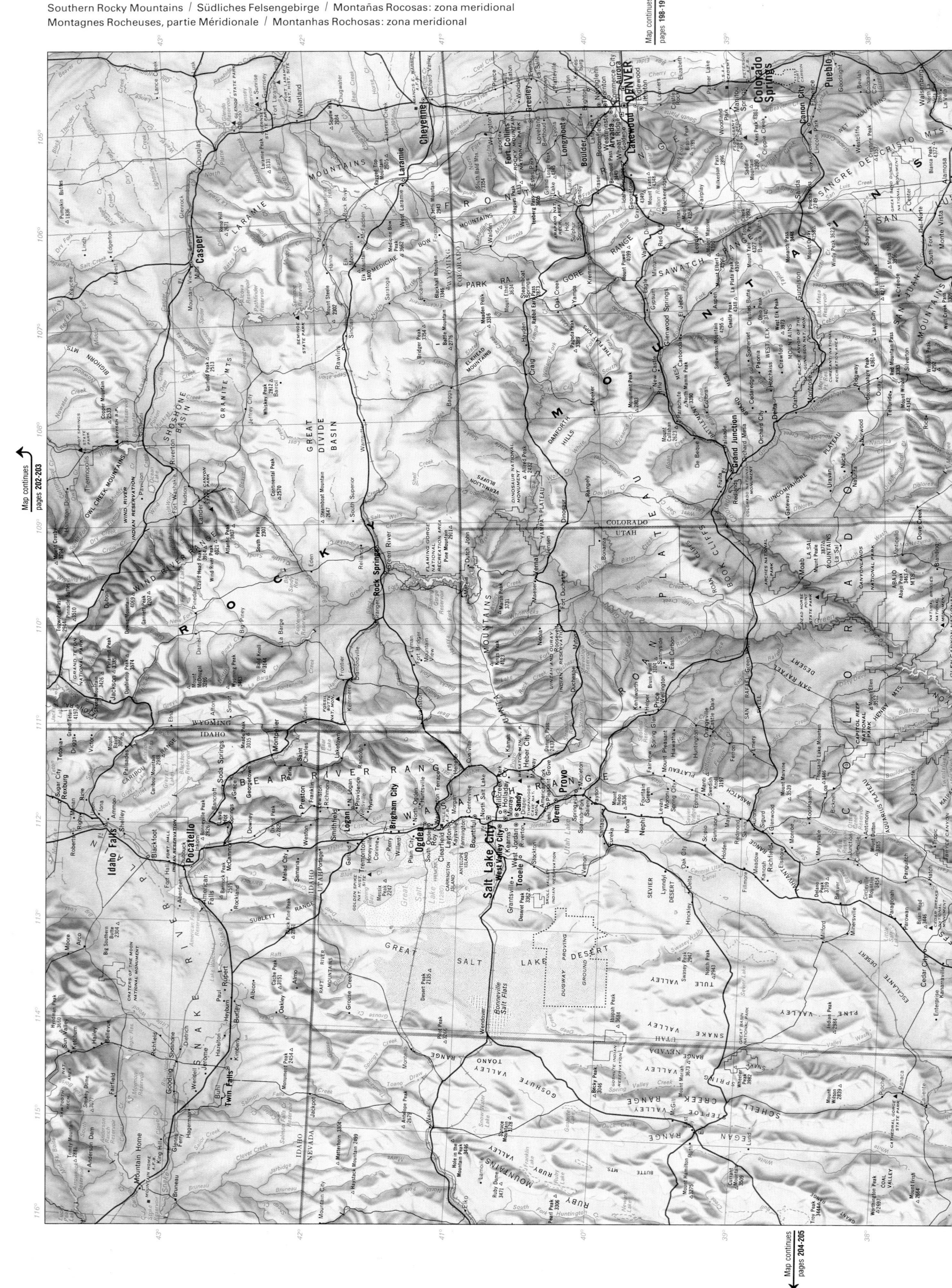

Map continues pages 204-205

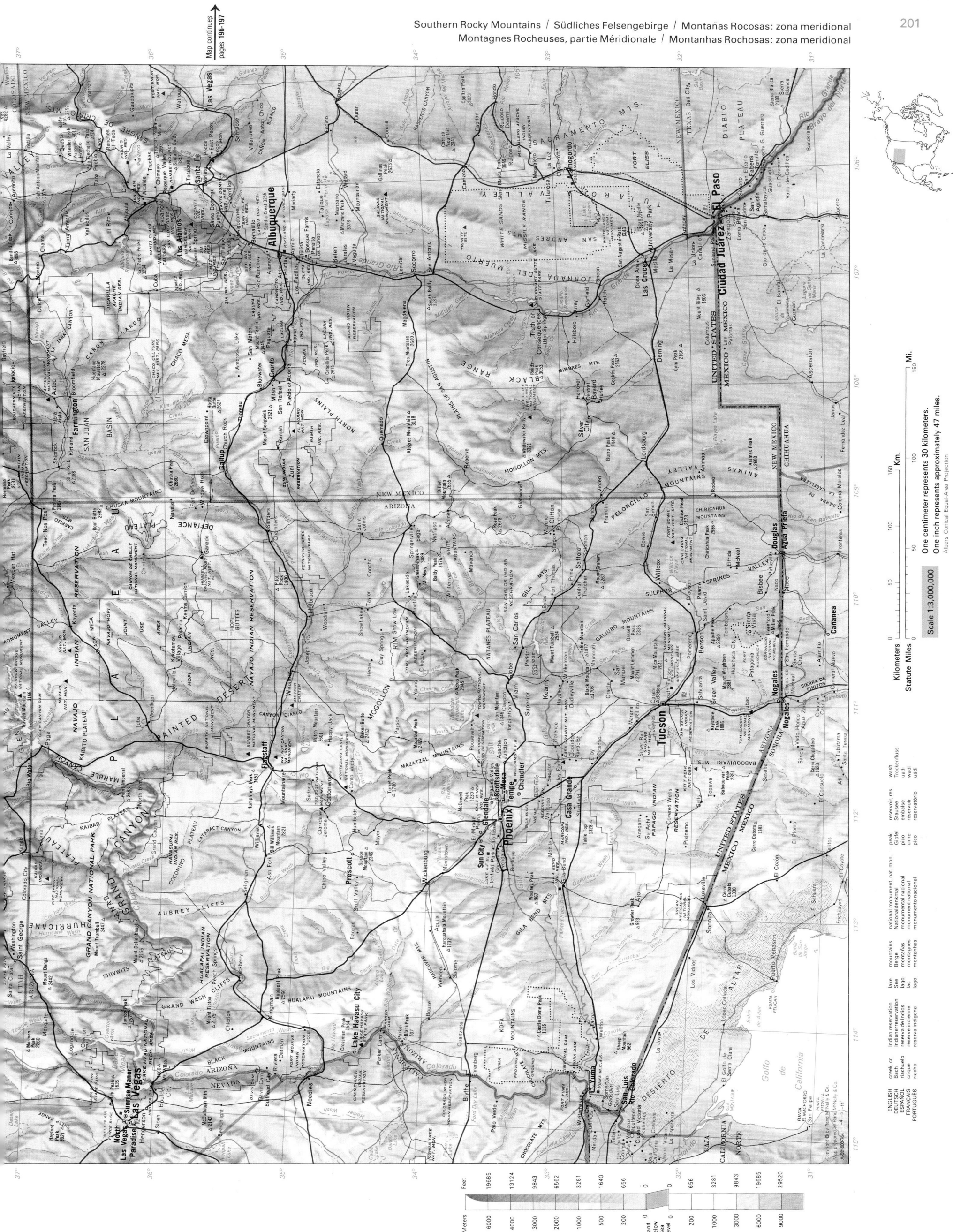

Southern Rocky Mountains / Südliches Felsengebirge / Montañas Rocosas: zona meridional
Montagnes Rocheuses, partie Méridionale / Montanhas Rochosas: zona meridional

201

Map continues
pages 196-197

One centimeter represents 30 kilometers.
One inch represents approximately 47 miles.

Scale 1:3,000,000

Albers Conical Equal-Area Projection

ENGLISH	creek, cr.	Indian reservation	national monument, nat. mon.	peak	reservoir, res.	wash
DEUTSCH	Bach	Indianerreservation	Nationaldenkmal	Gipfel	Stausee	Trockenfluss
ESPAÑOL	riachuelo	reserva de indios	monumento nacional	pico	embalse	uadi
FRANÇAIS	crique	réserve indienne	monument national	cime	reservoir	wadi
PORTUGUÊS	riacho	reserva indígena	monumento nacional	pico	reservatório	uádi

	lake	mountains
	See	Berge
	lago	montañas
	lac	montagnes
	lago	montanhas

202

Northwestern United States / Nordwestliche Vereinigte Staaten / Nor-oeste de los Estados Unidos
Nord-Ouest des États-Unis / Noroeste dos Estados Unidos

Map continues
pages 182-183

Map continues
pages 204-205

	ENGLISH	creek, cr.	Indian reservation	lake, l.	mountain, mtn.	pass	peak	range	reservoir, res.
	DEUTSCH	Bach	Indianerreservation	See	Berg	Pass	Gipfel	Gebirge	Stausee
	ESPAÑOL	riachuelo	reserva de Indios	lago	montaña	paso	pico	sierra	embalse
	FRANÇAIS	crique	réserve indienne	lac	montagne	col	cime	chaîne	réservoir
	PORTUGUÊS	riacho	reserva indígena	lago	montanha	passo	pico	serra	reservatório

Northwestern United States / Nordwestliche Vereinigte Staaten / Nor-oeste de los Estados Unidos
Nord-Ouest des États-Unis / Noroeste dos Estados Unidos

203

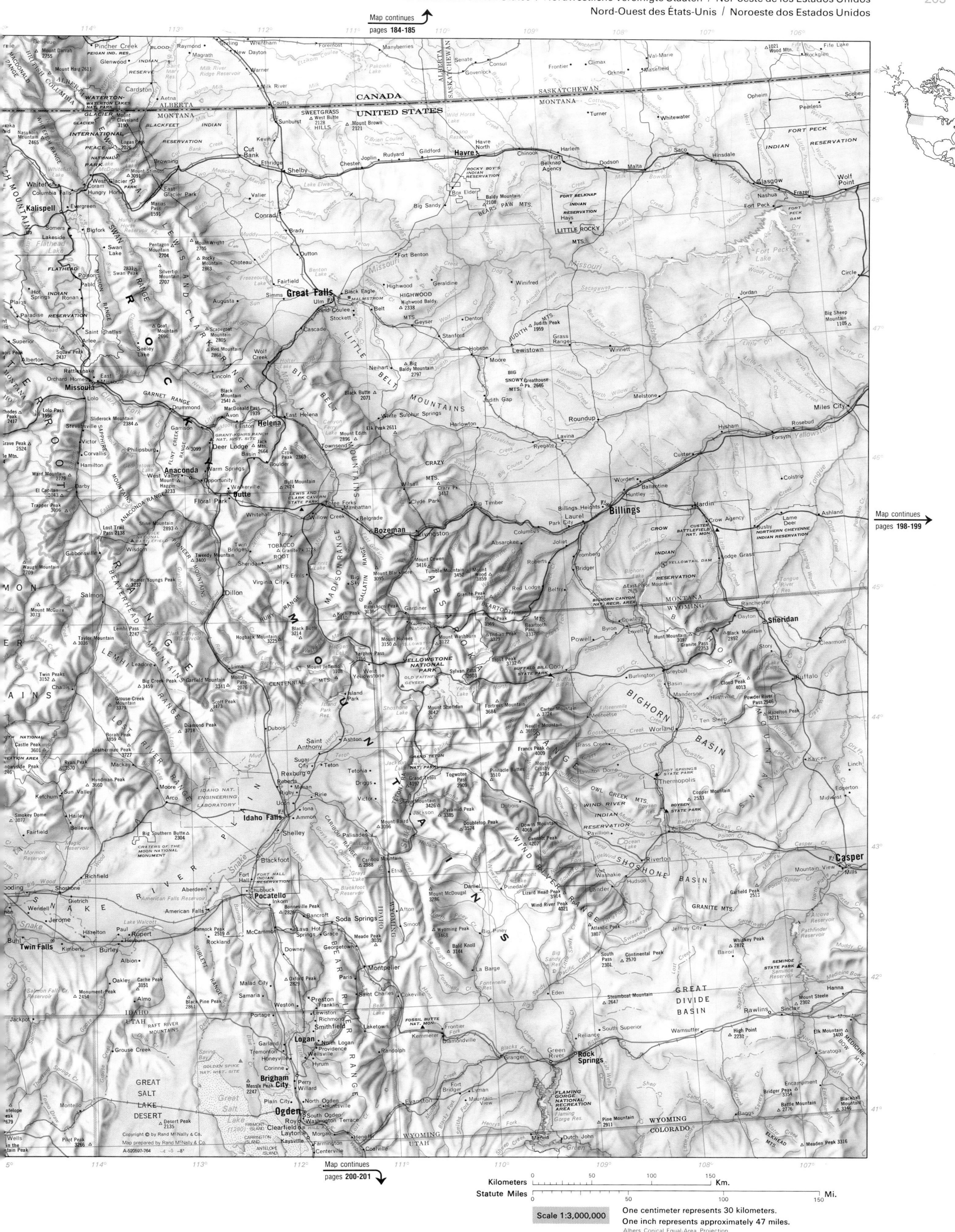

Map continues
pages 184-185

Map continues
pages 198-199

Map continues
pages 200-201

Kilometers

Statute Miles

Scale 1:3,000,000

One centimeter represents 30 kilometers.
One inch represents approximately 47 miles.
Albers Conical Equal-Area Projection

Map continues
pages 200-201

Map continues
pages 202-203

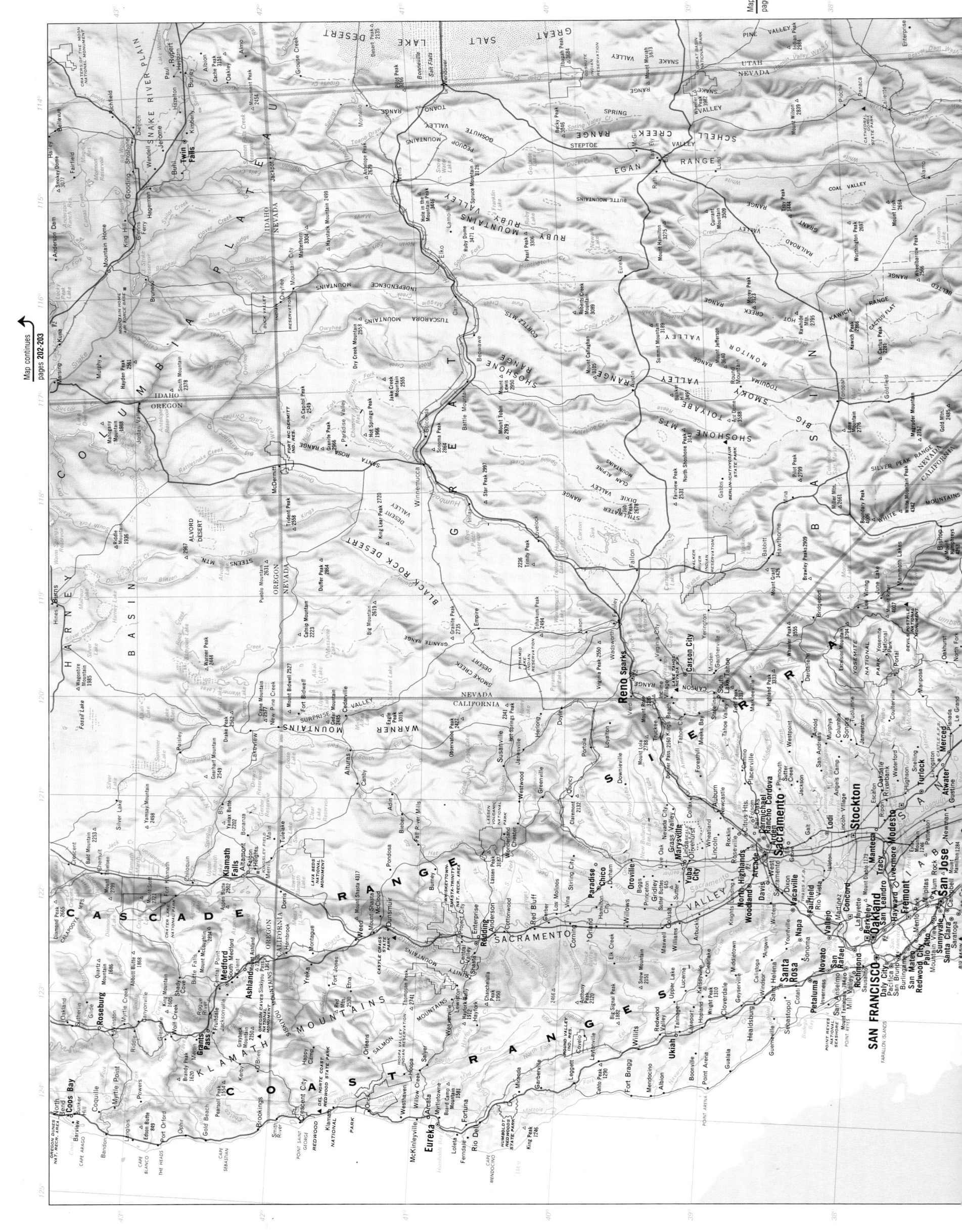

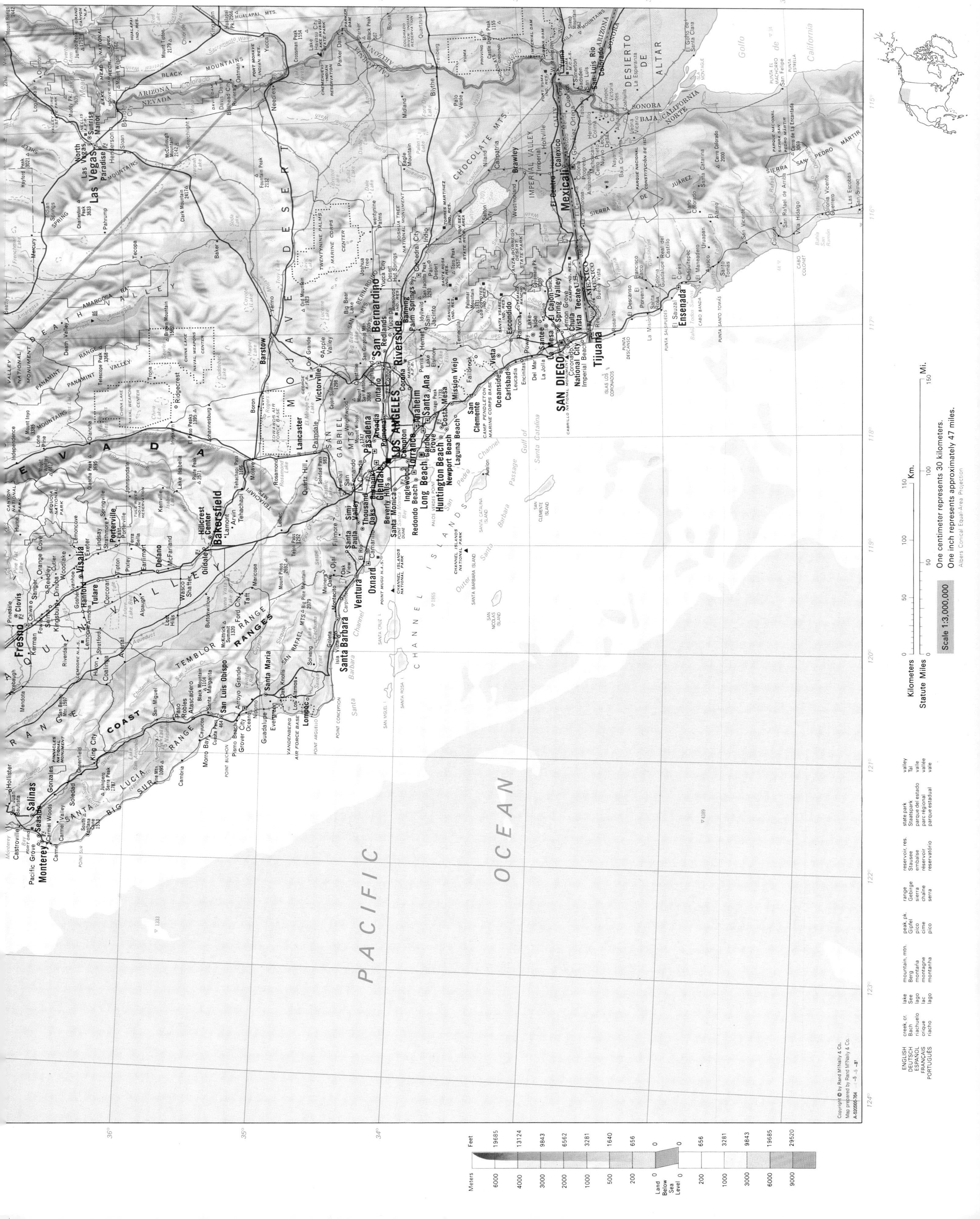
PACIFIC OCEAN
NEVADA
ARIZONA
CALIFORNIA
BAJA CALIFORNIA NORTE
SONORA
MOJAVE DESERT
DEATH VALLEY
SIERRA NEVADA
COAST RANGES
TEMBLOR RANGE
SAN RAFAEL MTS.
SAN GABRIEL MTS.
SAN BERNARDINO MTS.
CHOCOLATE MTS.
IMPERIAL VALLEY
DESIERTO DE ALTAR
CHANNEL ISLANDS
Gulf of Santa Catalina
Santa Barbara Channel
Golfo de California
LOS ANGELES
SAN DIEGO
Las Vegas
Fresno
Bakersfield
San Bernardino
Riverside
Santa Ana
Anaheim
Long Beach
Pasadena
Santa Barbara
Ventura
Oxnard
Salinas
Monterey
Visalia
Tijuana
Mexicali
Ensenada
Yuma
San Luis Obispo
Palm Springs
Lancaster
Barstow
Needles
Kilometers
Statute Miles
Scale 1:3,000,000
One centimeter represents 30 kilometers.
One inch represents approximately 47 miles.
Albers Conical Equal-Area Projection
ENGLISH creek, cr. lake mountain, mtn. peak, pk. range reservoir, res. state park valley
DEUTSCH Bach See Berg Gipfel Gebirge Stausee Staatspark Tal
ESPAÑOL riachuelo lago montaña pico sierra embalse parque del estado valle
FRANÇAIS crique lac montagne cime chaîne réservoir parc régional vallée
PORTUGUÊS riacho lago montanha pico serra reservatório parque estadual vale
Copyright © by Rand McNally & Co.
Map prepared by Rand McNally & Co.
Feet
Meters
Land Below Sea Level

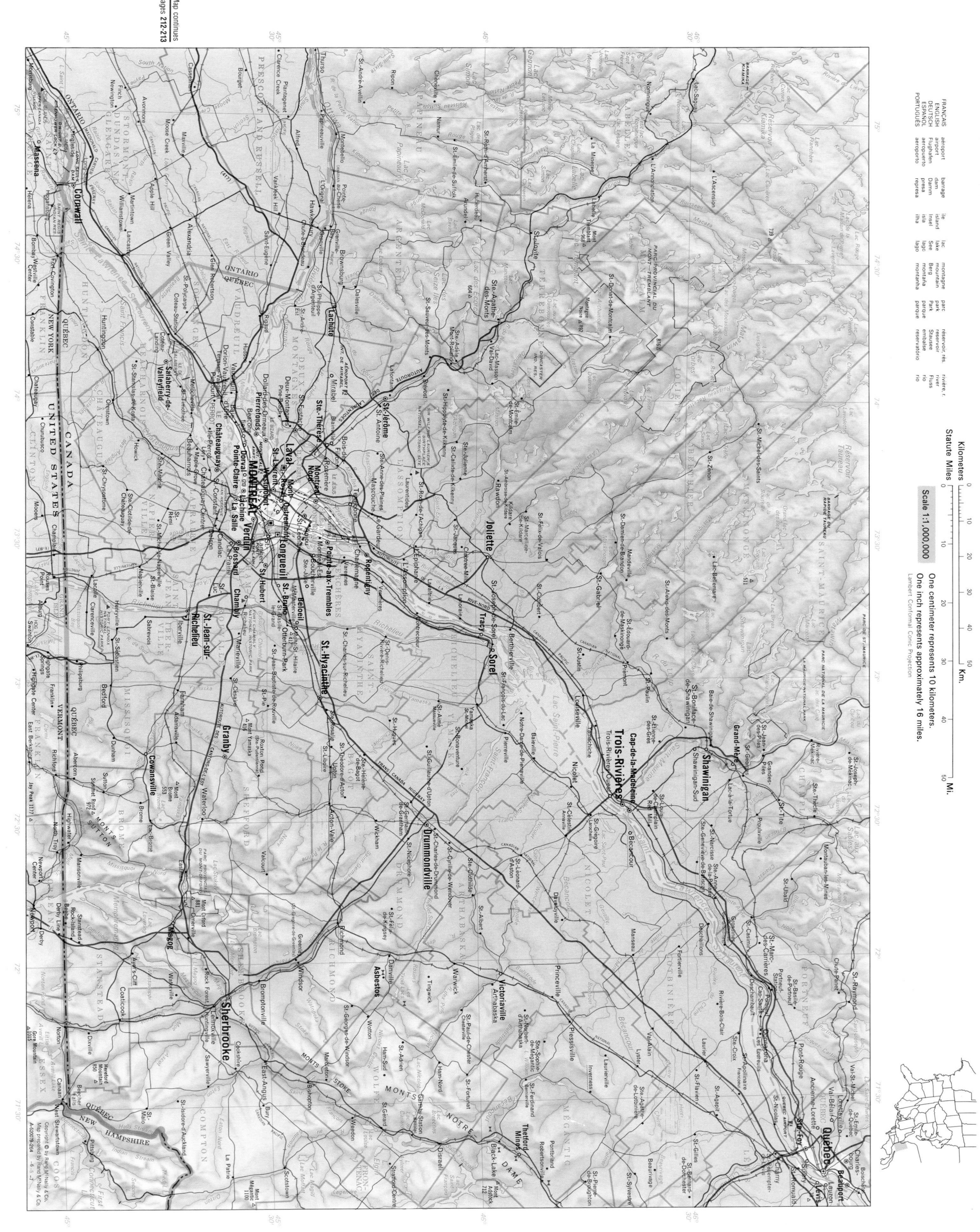

FRANÇAIS	aérogport
ENGLISH	airport
DEUTSCH	Flughafen
ESPAÑOL	aeropuerto
PORTUGUÊS	aeroporto

barrage	dam
Damm	presa
represa	

lac	lake
Insel	lago
isla	lago

île	island
Insel	
isla	
ilha	

montagne	mountain
Berg	montaña
montanha	

parc	park
Park	parque
parque	

réservoir rés.	reservoir
Stausee	embalse
reservatório	

rivière, r.	river
Fluss	río
rio	

Kilometers

Statute Miles

Scale 1:1,000,000

One centimeter represents 10 kilometers.
One inch represents approximately 16 miles.

Lambert Conformal Conic Projection

Copyright © by Rand McNally & Co.
Map prepared by Rand McNally & Co.
A-000-N-264

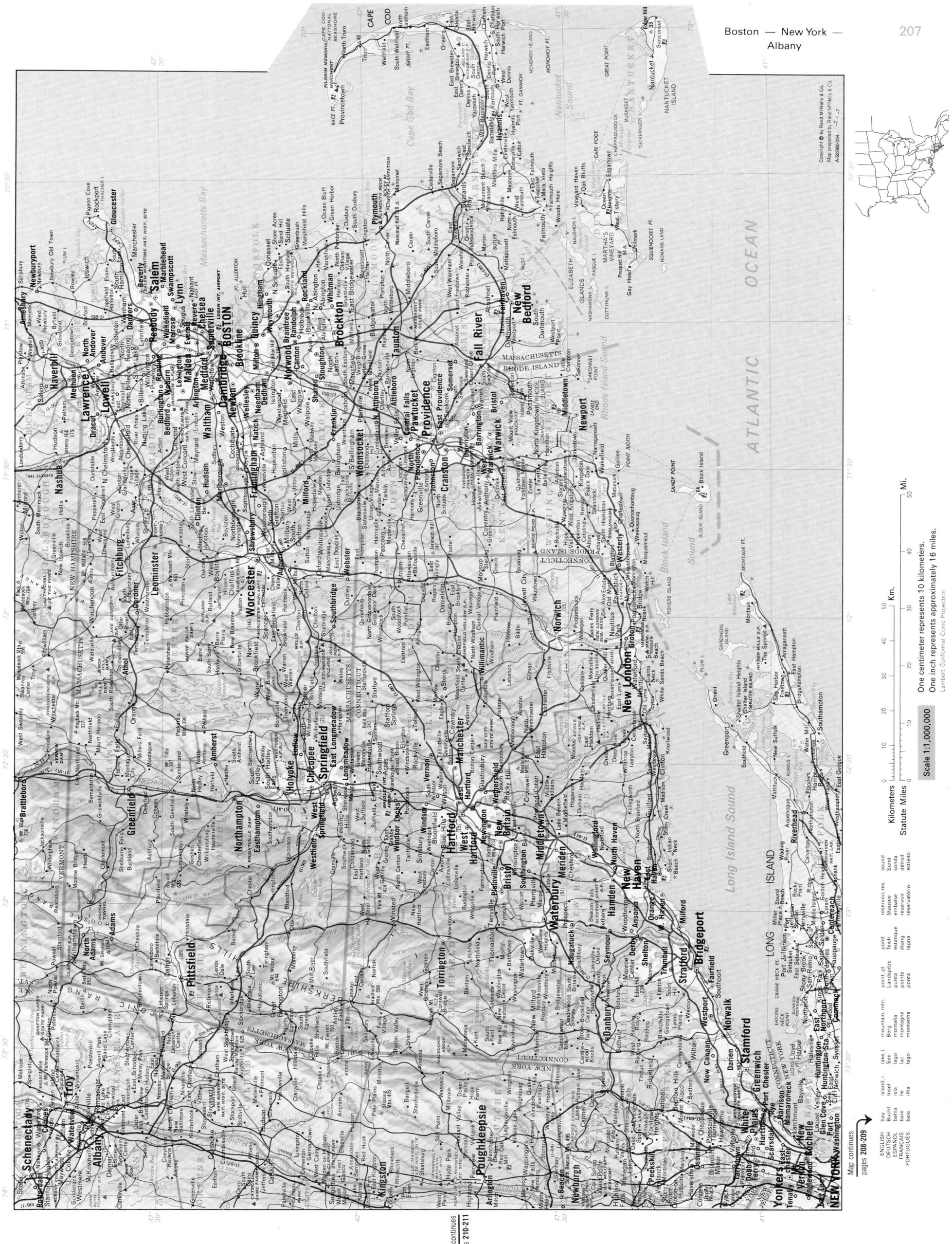

Map continues
pages 210-211

Map continues
pages 208-209

Scale 1:1,000,000

One centimeter represents 10 kilometers.
One inch represents approximately 16 miles.
Lambert Conformal Conic Projection

Kilometers
Statute Miles

ENGLISH	bay	island, i.	lake, l.	mountain, mtn.	point, pt.	pond	reservoir, res.	sound
DEUTSCH	Bucht	Insel	See	Berg	Landspitze	Teich	Stausee	Sund
ESPAÑOL	bahía	isla	lago	montaña	punta	estanque	embalse	sonda
FRANÇAIS	baie	île	lac	montagne	pointe	étang	réservoir	détroit
PORTUGUÊS	baía	ilha	lago	montanha	ponta	lagoa	reservatório	estreito

ATLANTIC OCEAN

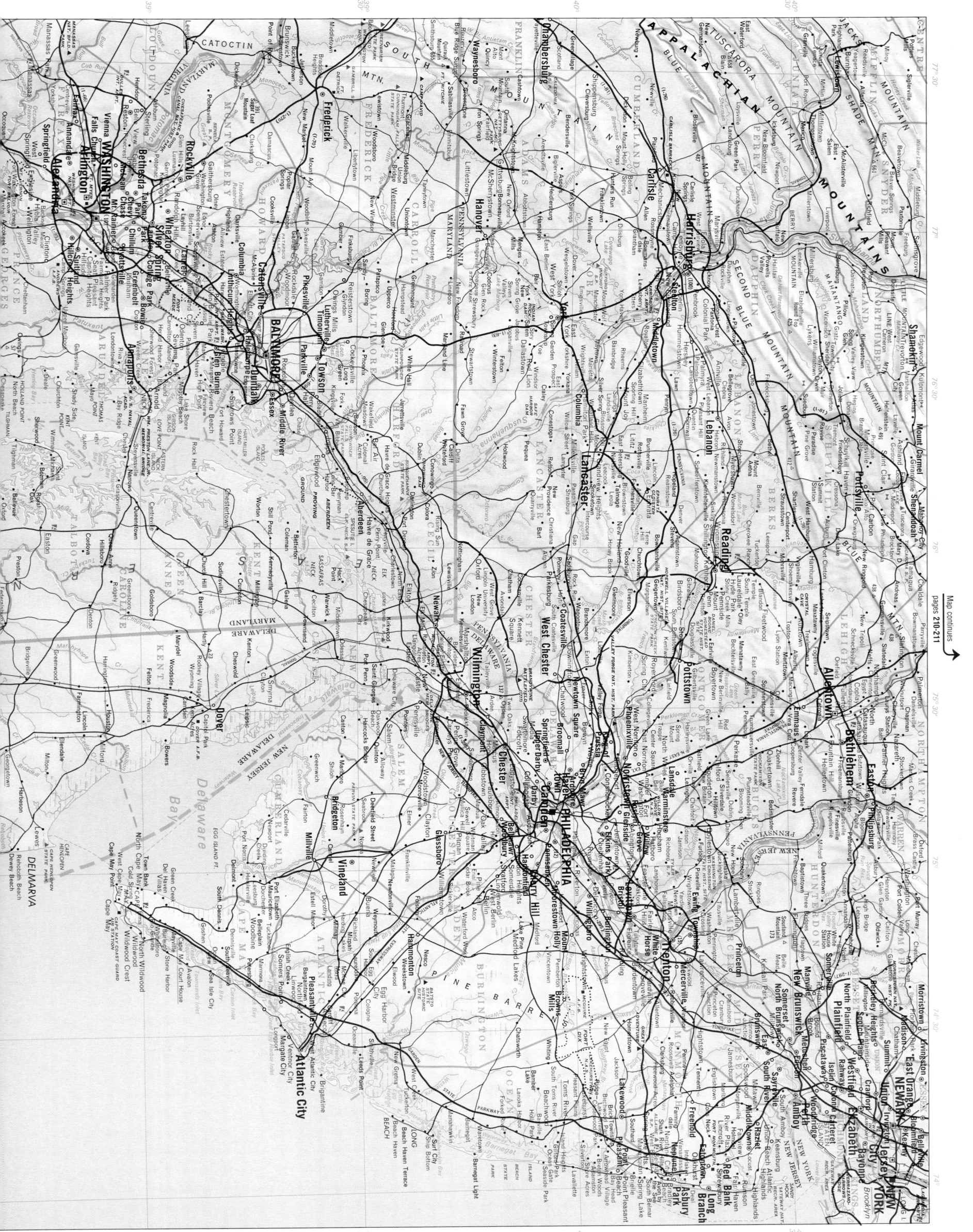

NEW YORK
NEWARK
Elizabeth
Jersey City
Bayonne
Trenton
Princeton
New Brunswick
PHILADELPHIA
Camden
Chester
Wilmington
Atlantic City
Vineland
Allentown
Bethlehem
Easton
Reading
Lancaster
Harrisburg
York
Pottsville
Lebanon
BALTIMORE
Annapolis
WASHINGTON
Arlington
Alexandria
Frederick
Dover
DELMARVA
APPALACHIAN MOUNTAINS
BLUE MOUNTAIN
Delaware Bay
PINE BARRENS

Map continues pages 210-211

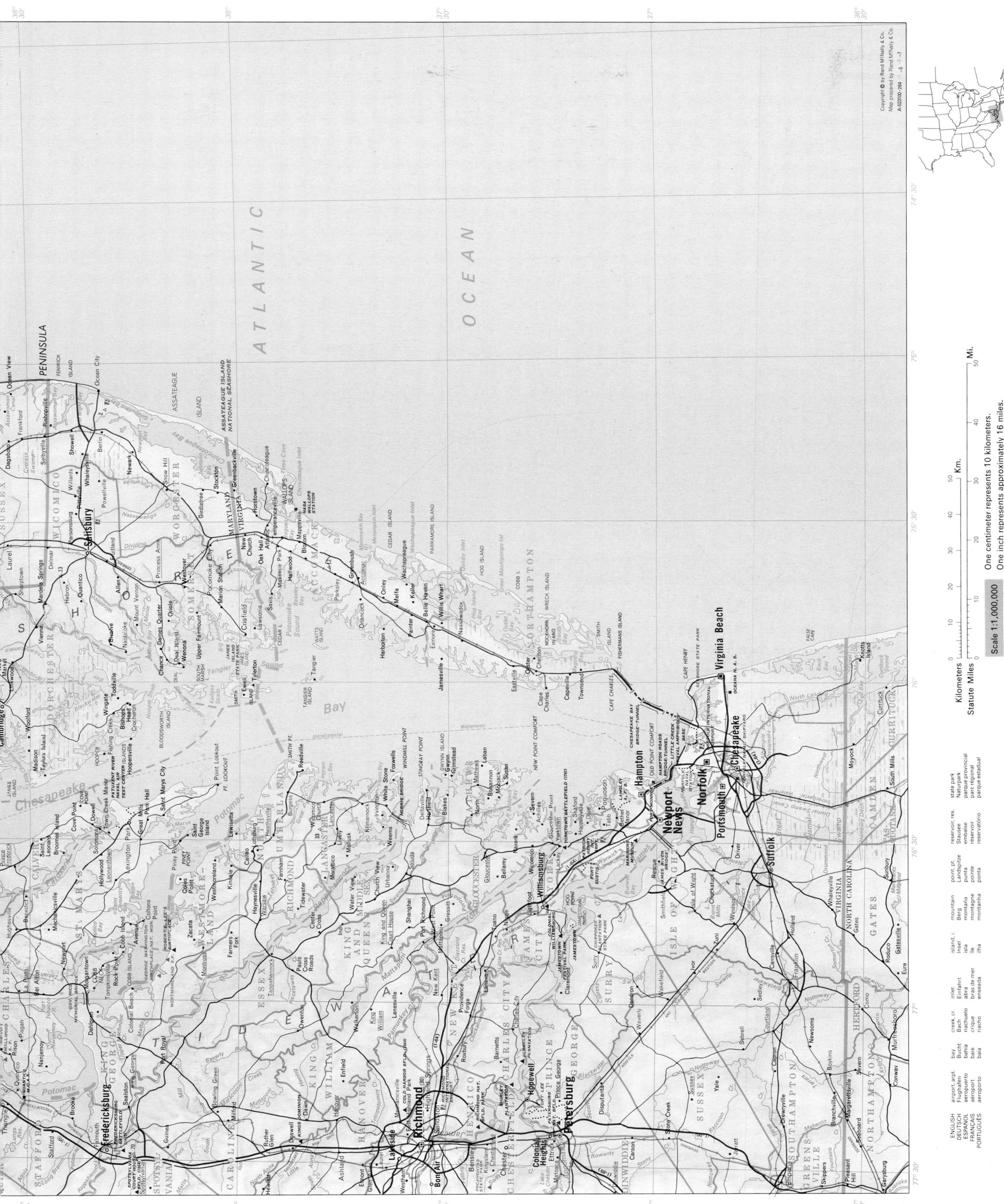

Scale 1:1,000,000

One centimeter represents 10 kilometers.
One inch represents approximately 16 miles.
Lambert Conformal Conic Projection

ENGLISH	bay	creek, cr.	inlet	island, i.	mountain	point, pt.	reservoir, res.	state park
DEUTSCH	Bucht	Bach	Einfahrt	Insel	Berg	Landspitze	Stausee	Naturpark
ESPAÑOL	bahía	riachuelo	abra	isla	montaña	punta	embalse	parque provincial
FRANÇAIS	baie	ruisseau	bras de mer	île	montagne	pointe	réservoir	parc provincial
PORTUGUÊS	baía	riacho	enseada	ilha	montanha	ponta	reservatório	parque estadual

Map continues pages 212-213

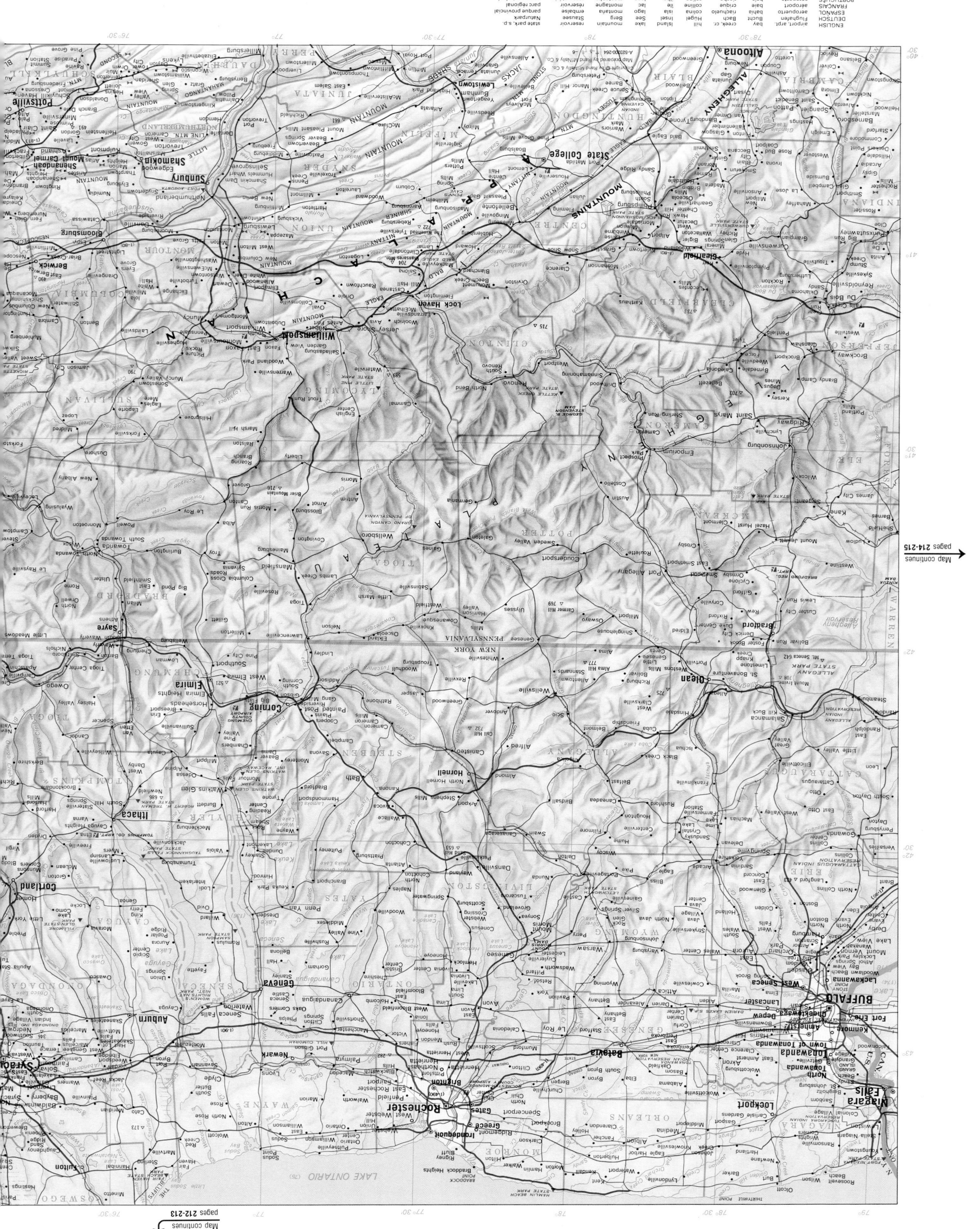
LAKE ONTARIO
Niagara Falls
Lockport
Rochester
Irondequoit
BUFFALO
Batavia
Geneva
Auburn
Cortland
Ithaca
Hornell
Corning
Elmira
Olean
Bradford
Sayre
Williamsport
Lock Haven
State College
Clearfield
Altoona
Lewistown
Sunbury
Shamokin
Pottsville
Bloomsburg
Berwick
NEW YORK
PENNSYLVANIA
ALLEGHENY PLATEAU
APPALACHIAN MOUNTAINS
Copyright © by Rand McNally & Co.
Map prepared by Rand McNally & Co.
A-523300-264

Map continues pages 214-215

ENGLISH	airport, arpt.	bay	creek, cr.	hill	island	lake	mountain	reservoir	state park, s.p.
DEUTSCH	Flughafen	Bucht	Bach	Hügel	Insel	See	Berg	Stausee	Naturpark
ESPAÑOL	aeropuerto	bahia	riachuelo	colina	isla	lago	montaña	embalse	parque provincial
FRANÇAIS	aéroport	baie	crique	colline	île	lac	montagne	réservoir	parc régional
PORTUGUÊS	aeroporto	baía	riacho	colina	ilha	lago	montanha	reservatório	parque estadual

Map continues
page 207 →

Map continues
pages 208-209 ↓

Kilometers

Statute Miles

Scale 1:1,000,000

One centimeter represents 10 kilometers.
One inch represents approximately 16 miles.

Lambert Conformal Conic Projection

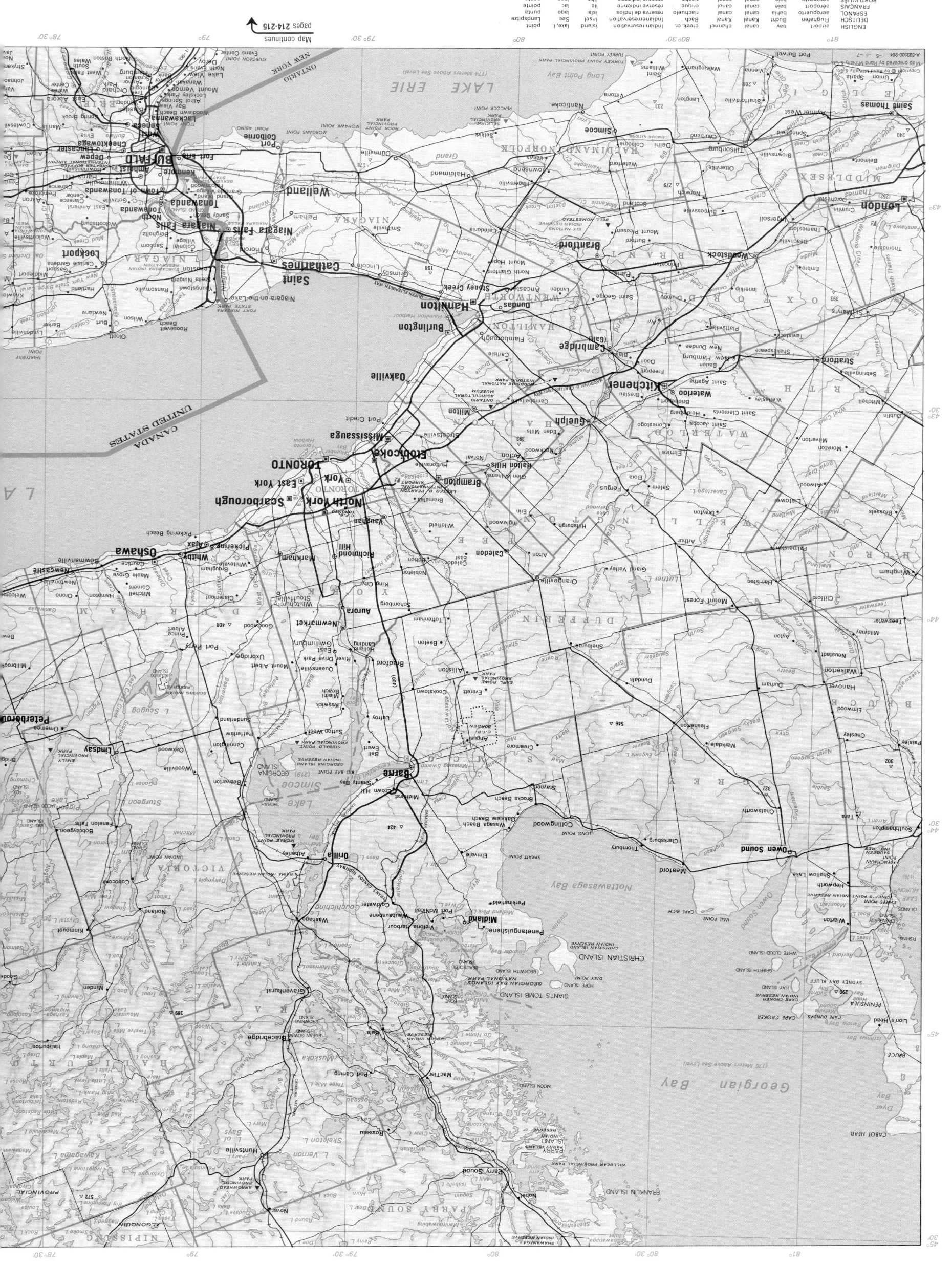

ENGLISH	DEUTSCH	FRANÇAIS	ESPAÑOL	PORTUGUÊS
airport	Flughafen	aéroport	aeropuerto	aeroporto
bay	Bucht	baie	bahía	baía
canal	Kanal	canal	canal	canal
channel	Kanal	canal	canal	canal
creek, cr.		crique		riacho
Indianerreservation	reserva de indios	reserva indígena
Indian reservation	Indianerreservat	réserve indienne	reserva de indios	reserva indígena
island	Insel	île	isla	ilha
lake, l.	See	lac	lago	lago
point	Landspitze	pointe	punta	ponta

LAKE ERIE (174 Meters Above Sea Level)

Georgian Bay (176 Meters Above Sea Level)

Map continues
page 206

Map continues
pages 210-211

Kilometers |⊢⊢⊢⊢⊢⊢⊢⊢⊢⊢⊢⊢ 0   10   20   30   40   50   Km.

Statute Miles ⊢⊢⊢⊢⊢⊢⊢⊢⊢ 0   10   20   30   40   50   Mi.

Scale 1:1,000,000

One centimeter represents 10 kilometers.
One inch represents approximately 16 miles.

Lambert Conformal Conic Projection

Map continues
page 218

ENGLISH	DEUTSCH	FRANÇAIS	ESPAÑOL	PORTUGUÊS
creek, cr.	Fluchgraben		riacho	
airport	Flughafen	aéroport	aeropuerto	aeroporto
hill	Hügel	colline	colina	colina
lake, l.	See	lac	lago	lago
mountain, mtn.	Berg	montagne	montaña	montanha
		pointe	punta	ponta
point, pt.	Landspitze	pointe	punta	ponta
reservoir, res.	Stausee	réservoir	embalse	reservatório
state park	Naturpark	parc provincial	parque provincial	parque estadual
		parc régional	reservatório	

LAKE ERIE

LAKE HURON

UNITED STATES

CANADA

Map continues
pages 216-217

Map continues
pages 212-213

Map continues
pages 210-211

Kilometers

Statute Miles

Scale 1:1,000,000

One centimeter represents 10 kilometers.
One inch represents approximately 16 miles.
Lambert Conformal Conic Projection

LAKE MICHIGAN

(176 Meters Above Sea Level)

MILWAUKEE
CHICAGO
Madison
Racine
Kenosha
Waukegan
Rockford
Gary
Joliet
Aurora
Elgin
Kankakee
Valparaiso
La Porte
Michigan City
East Chicago
Hammond
Merrillville
Lafayette
West Lafayette
Bloomington
Normal
Pontiac
Streator
Kankakee
De Kalb
Janesville
Beloit
Ottawa
La Salle
Peru
Waukesha
Evanston
Skokie
Oak Park
Cicero
Berwyn
Elmhurst
Des Plaines
Schaumburg
Naperville
Bolingbrook
Crystal Lake

Muskegon
Muskegon Heights
Ruddiman Terrace
Roosevelt Park
Norton Shores
Grand Haven
GRAND HAVEN STATE PARK

DODGE   WASHINGTON   OZAUKEE
JEFFERSON   WAUKESHA   MILWAUKEE
WALWORTH   RACINE   KENOSHA
WINNEBAGO   BOONE   McHENRY   LAKE
OGLE   DE KALB   KANE   DU PAGE   COOK
LEE   KENDALL   WILL
LA SALLE   GRUNDY   KANKAKEE
LIVINGSTON   WOODFORD   FORD   IROQUOIS
McLEAN   DE WITT   CHAMPAIGN   VERMILION
WISCONSIN
ILLINOIS
INDIANA
LAKE   PORTER   LA PORTE   BERRIEN
NEWTON   JASPER   PULASKI   STARKE
BENTON   WHITE   CARROLL   CASS
WARREN   TIPPECANOE   CLINTON   FULTON
FOUNTAIN

LAKE MICHIGAN

Map continues page 219

ENGLISH	airport	creek, cr.	ditch	lake, l.	reservoir	state park, s.p.
DEUTSCH	Flughafen	Bach	Graben	See	Stausee	Naturpark
ESPAÑOL	aeropuerto	riachuelo	acequia	lago	embalse	parque provincial
FRANÇAIS	aéroport	crique	fossé	lac	réservoir	parc régional
PORTUGUÊS	aeroporto	riacho	fosso	lago	reservatório	parque estadual

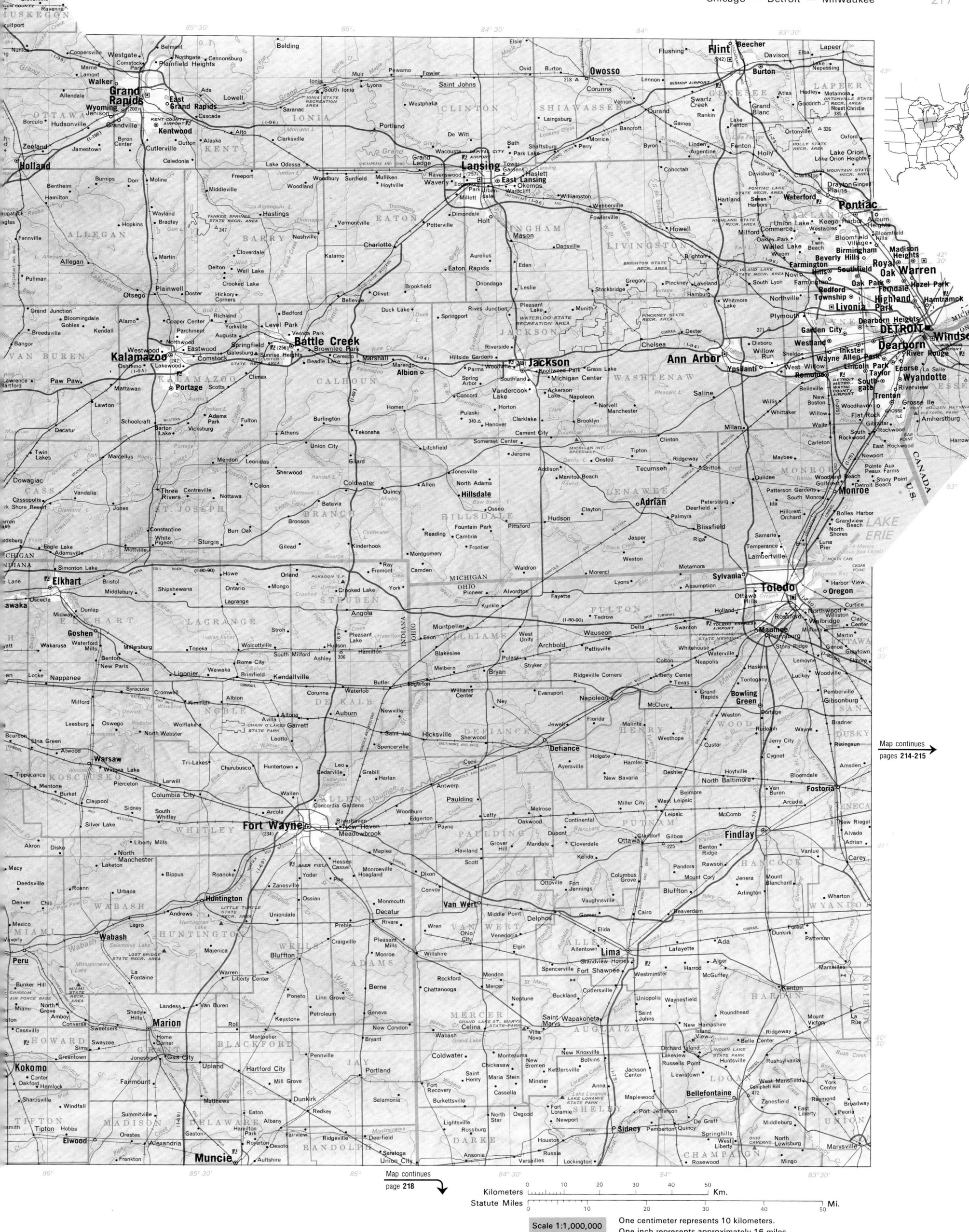

Map continues
pages 214-215 ➜

Map continues
page 218 ➘

Kilometers |0   10   20   30   40   50| Km.

Statute Miles |0   10   20   30   40   50| Mi.

Scale 1:1,000,000

One centimeter represents 10 kilometers.
One inch represents approximately 16 miles.

Lambert Conformal Conic Projection

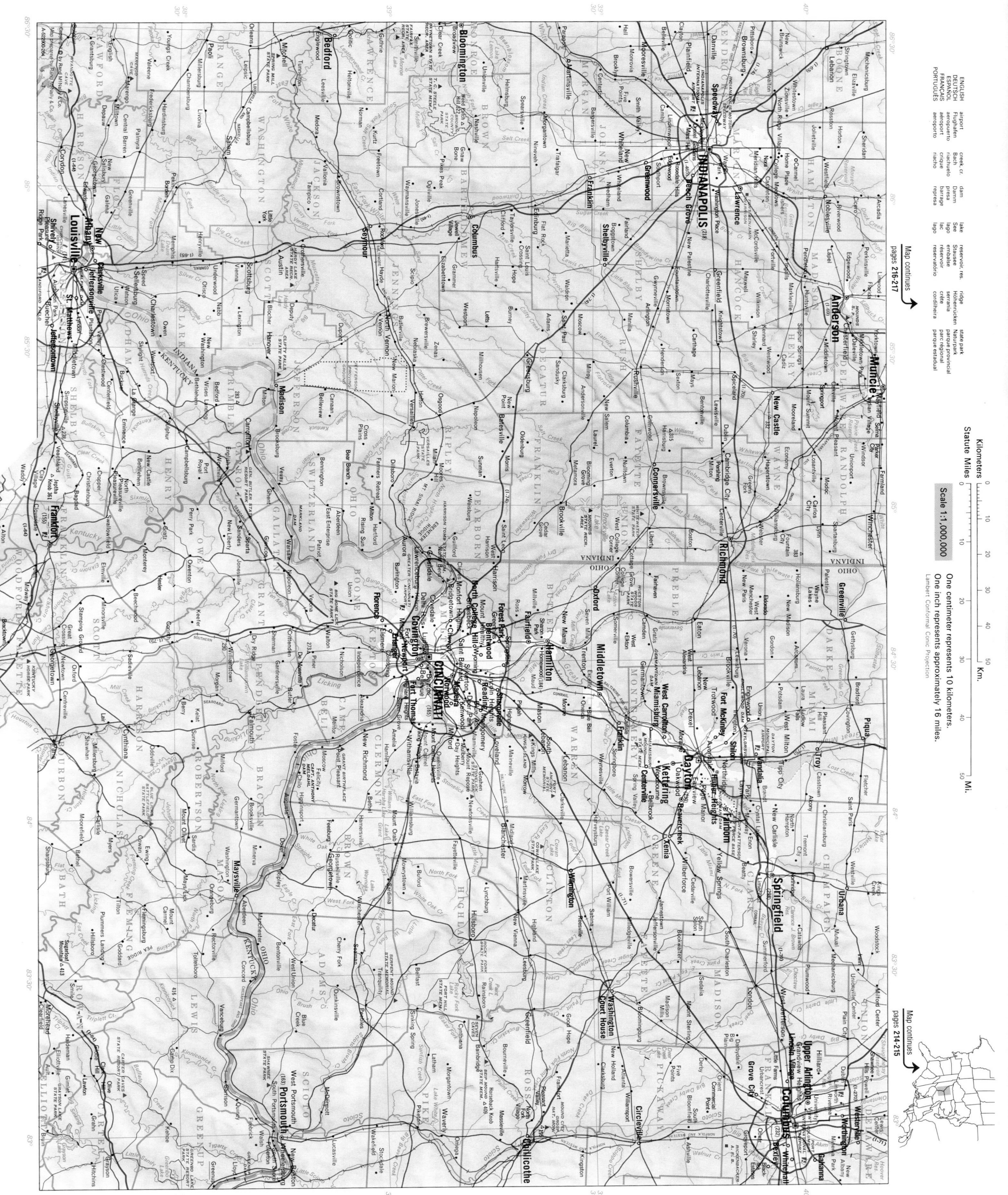
Map continues pages 214-215
Map continues pages 216-217
ENGLISH airport creek, cr. dam lake reservoir, res. ridge state park
DEUTSCH Flughafen Bach Damm See Stausee Höhenrücken Naturpark
ESPAÑOL aeropuerto riachuelo presa lago embalse serranía parque provincial
FRANÇAIS aéroport crique barrage lac réservoir crête parc régional
PORTUGUÊS aeroporto riacho represa lago reservatório cordilheira parque estadual
Kilometers
Statute Miles
Scale 1:1,000,000
One centimeter represents 10 kilometers.
One inch represents approximately 16 miles.
Lambert Conformal Conic Projection
OHIO
INDIANA

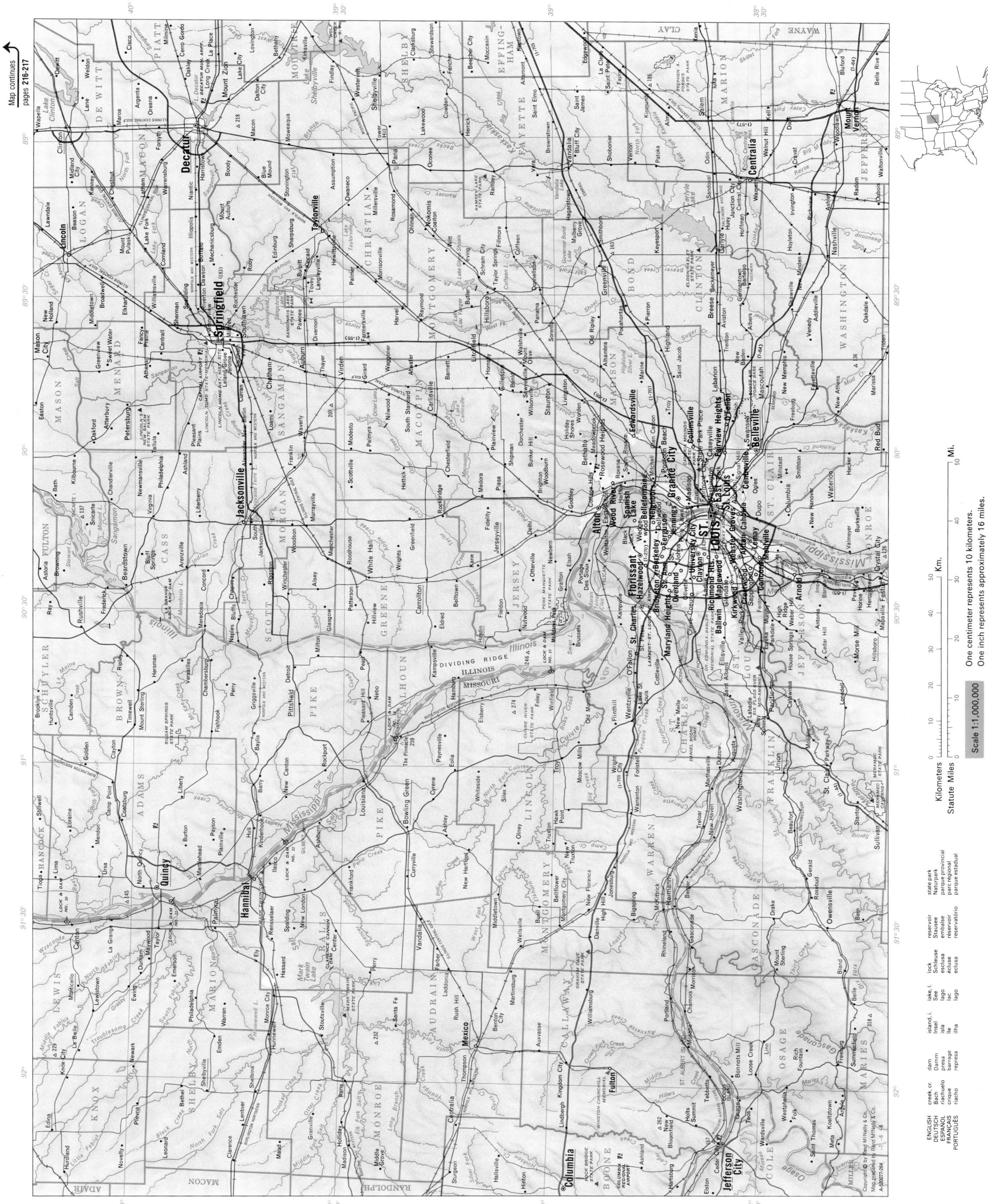

Map continues pages 216-217

Scale 1:1,000,000

Kilometers

Statute Miles

One centimeter represents 10 kilometers.
One inch represents approximately 16 miles.
Lambert Conformal Conic Projection

ENGLISH	creek, cr.	dam	island, i.	lake, l.	lock	reservoir	state park
DEUTSCH	Bach	Damm	Insel	See	Schleuse	Stausee	Naturpark
ESPAÑOL	riachuelo	presa	isla	lago	esclusa	embalse	parque provincial
FRANÇAIS	crique	barrage	île	lac	écluse	réservoir	parc régional
PORTUGUÊS	riacho	represa	ilha	lago	eclusa	reservatório	parque estadual

© Rand McNally & Co.
Map modified by Rand McNally & Co.
A-20007-364

ENGLISH	bay	canal	cape	creek, cr.	inlet	island	key	lake, l.	swamp
DEUTSCH	Bucht	Kanal	Kap	Bach	Einfahrt	Insel	Klippe	See	Sumpf
ESPAÑOL	bahia	canal	cabo	riachuelo	abra	isla	cayo	lago	pantano
FRANÇAIS	baie	canal	cap	crique	bras de mer	île	caye	lac	marais
PORTUGUÊS	baía	canal	cabo	riacho	enseada	ilha	recife	lago	pântano

Kilometers 0 10 20 30 40 50 Km.
Statute Miles 0 10 20 30 40 50 Mi.

Scale 1:1,000,000

One centimeter represents 10 kilometers.
One inch represents approximately 16 miles.
Lambert Conformal Conic Projection

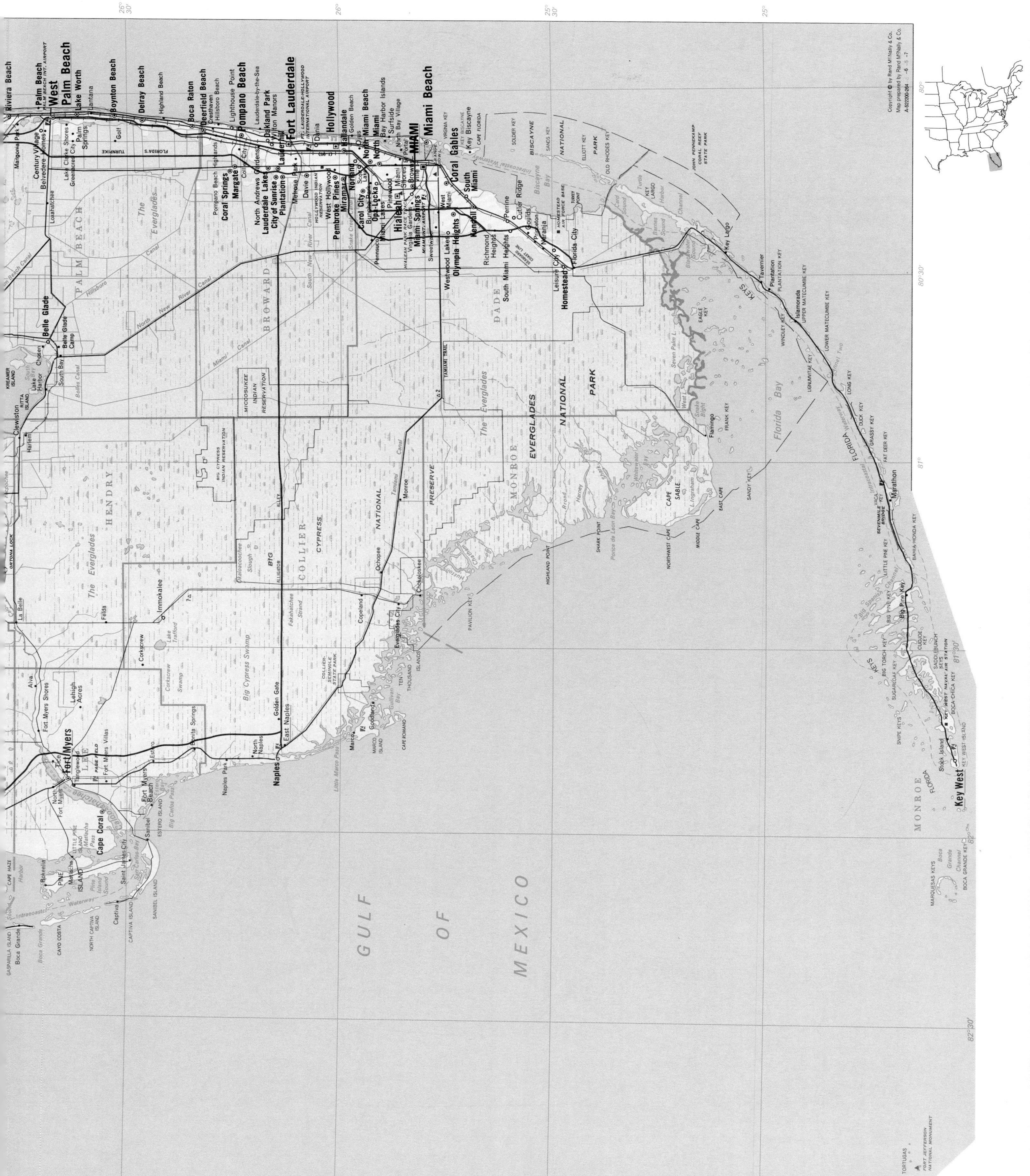
Copyright © by Rand McNally & Co.
Map prepared by Rand McNally & Co.
A-522000-264 -6-5-7
GULF
OF
MEXICO
Riviera Beach
Palm Beach
West Palm Beach
Lake Worth
Lantana
Boynton Beach
Delray Beach
Highland Beach
Boca Raton
Deerfield Beach
Hillsboro Beach
Lighthouse Point
Pompano Beach
Lauderdale-by-the-Sea
Oakland Park
Wilton Manors
Fort Lauderdale
Hollywood
Dania
Hallandale
Golden Beach
North Miami Beach
North Miami
Bay Harbor Islands
Surfside
North Bay Village
Miami Beach
MIAMI
Coral Gables
Key Biscayne
South Miami
Kendall
Perrine
Cutler Ridge
Homestead
Florida City
Leisure City
Naranja
Princeton
Goulds
Richmond Heights
South Miami Heights
Westwood Lakes
Olympia Heights
Sweetwater
Hialeah
Miami Springs
Opa-locka
Carol City
Miramar
Pembroke Pines
West Hollywood
Davie
Plantation
City of Sunrise
Lauderdale Lakes
North Andrews Gardens
Margate
Coral Springs
Pompano Beach Highlands
Century Village
Belvedere Homes
Lake Clarke Shores
Palm Springs
Greenacres City
Belle Glade
Belle Glade Camp
Chosen
South Bay
Lake Harbor
Clewiston
Harlem
La Belle
Felda
Immokalee
Corkscrew
Alva
Fort Myers Shores
Lehigh Acres
Fort Myers
Tice
Tanglewood
North Fort Myers
Cape Coral
Fort Myers Villas
Fort Myers Beach
Estero
Bonita Springs
Naples Park
North Naples
Naples
East Naples
Golden Gate
Marco
Goodland
Everglades City
Chokoloskee
Copeland
Ochopee
Monroe
Sanibel
Captiva
St. James City
Bokeelia
Boca Grande
PALM BEACH
BROWARD
HENDRY
COLLIER
LEE
DADE
MONROE
The Everglades
BIG CYPRESS INDIAN RESERVATION
MICCOSUKEE INDIAN RESERVATION
BIG CYPRESS NATIONAL PRESERVE
EVERGLADES NATIONAL PARK
BISCAYNE NATIONAL PARK
JOHN PENNEKAMP CORAL REEF STATE PARK
TAMIAMI TRAIL
Florida Bay
Flamingo
CAPE SABLE
FLORIDA KEYS
Key Largo
Tavernier
Plantation
Islamorada
Marathon
SEVENMILE BRIDGE
Big Pine Key
Stock Island
Key West
BOCA CHICA KEY
KEY WEST NAVAL AIR STATION
MARQUESAS KEYS
DRY TORTUGAS
FORT JEFFERSON NATIONAL MONUMENT
26° 30'
26°
25° 30'
25°
80° 30'
81°
81° 30'
82°
82° 30'

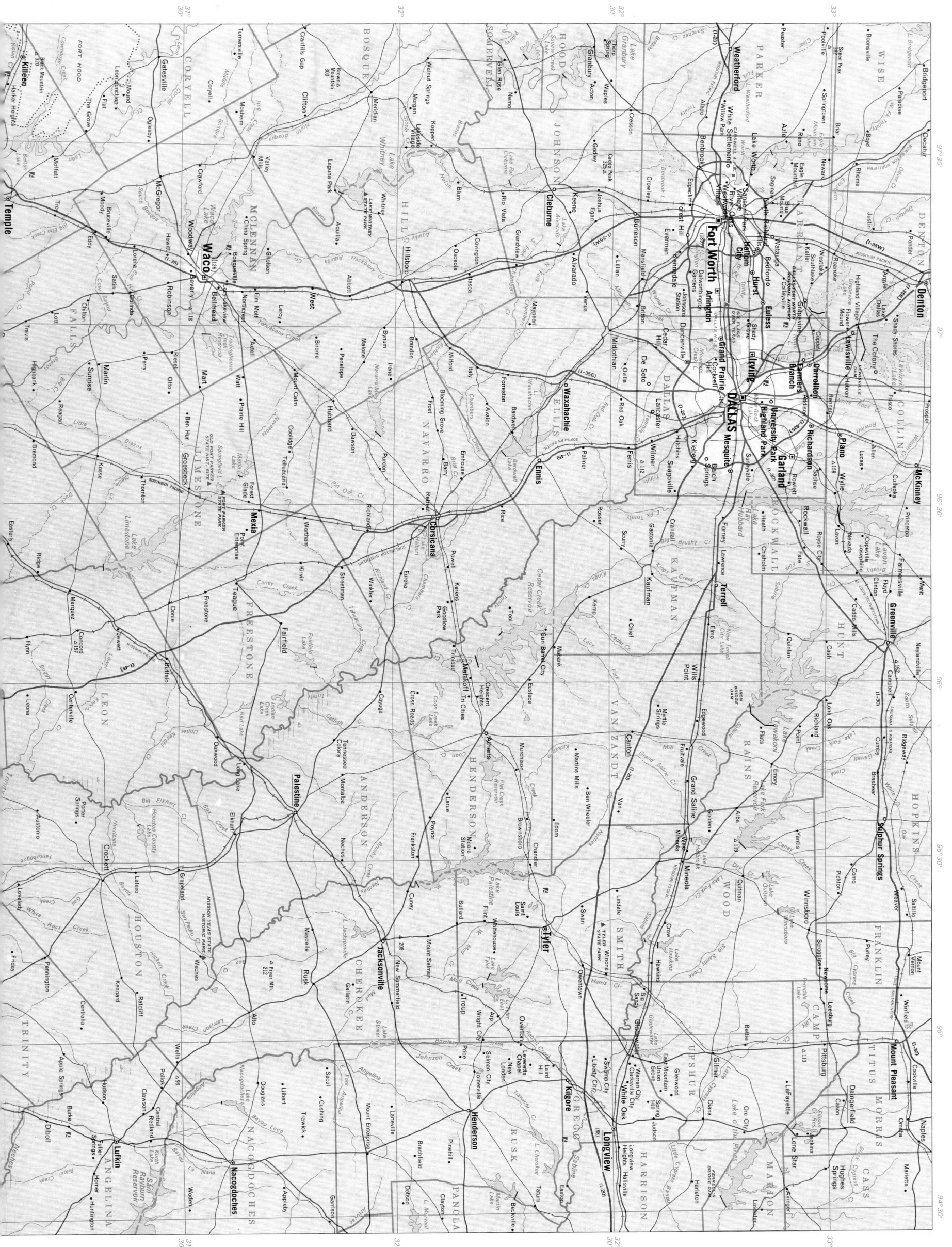
Denton
McKinney
Greenville
Mount Pleasant
Sulphur Springs
Longview
Kilgore
Henderson
Nacogdoches
Lufkin
Tyler
Jacksonville
Palestine
Athens
Terrell
Kaufman
Corsicana
Mexia
Ennis
Waxahachie
DALLAS
Fort Worth
Arlington
Irving
Grand Prairie
Garland
Mesquite
Richardson
Plano
Lewisville
Carrollton
Weatherford
Cleburne
Hillsboro
Waco
Temple
Killeen
Crockett
Fairfield
Canton
Mineola
Gilmer
Pittsburg
Daingerfield
Rusk

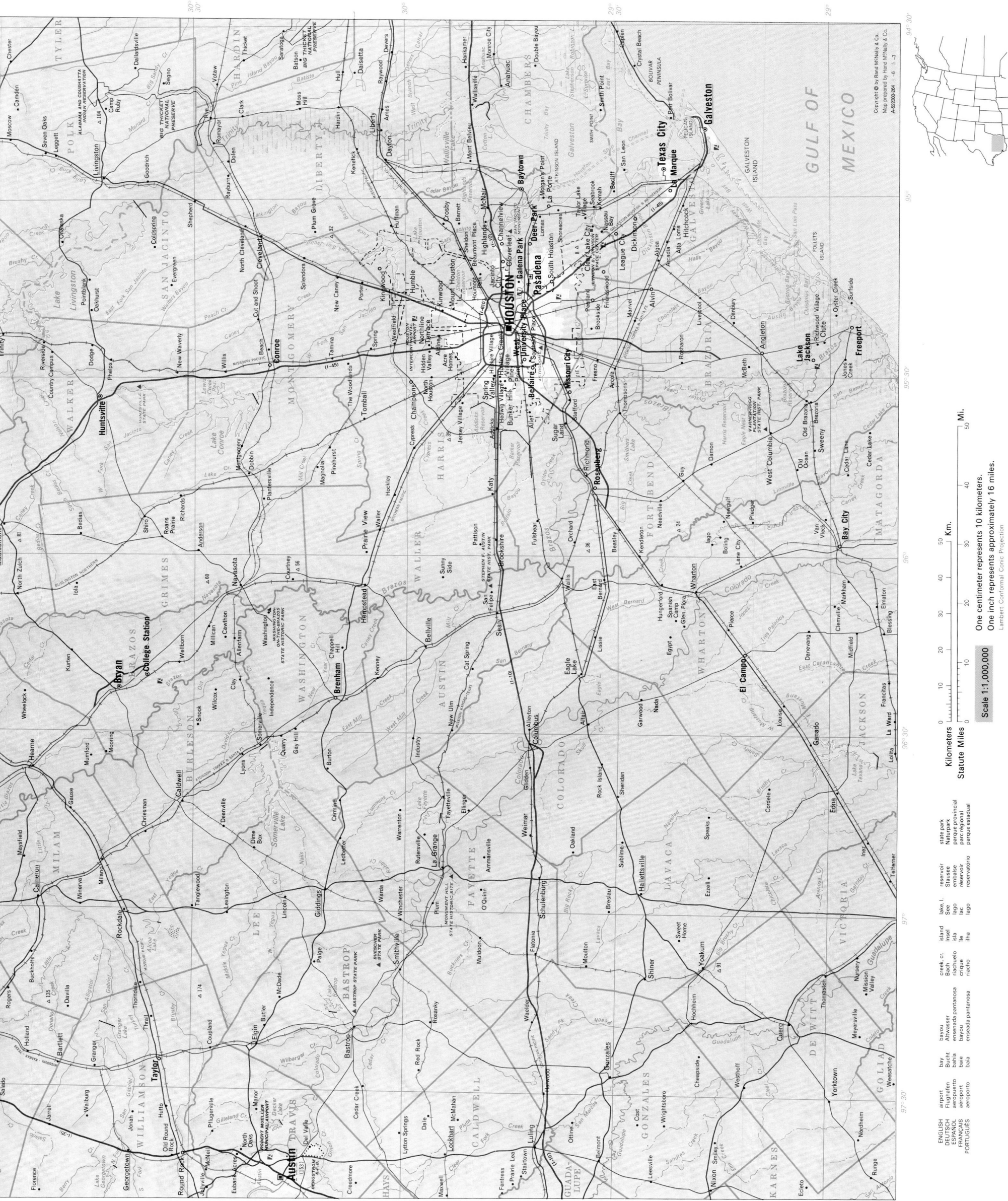

GULF OF MEXICO

Kilometers

Statute Miles

Scale 1:1,000,000

One centimeter represents 10 kilometers.
One inch represents approximately 16 miles.
Lambert Conformal Conic Projection

ENGLISH	airport	bay	bayou	creek, cr.	island	lake, l.	reservoir	state park
DEUTSCH	Flughafen	Bucht	Atwasser	Bach	Insel	See	Stausee	Naturpark
ESPAÑOL	aeropuerto	bahía	ensenada pantanosa	riachuelo	isla	lago	embalse	parque provincial
FRANÇAIS	aéroport	baie	bayou	ruisseau	île	lac	réservoir	parque regional
PORTUGUÊS	aeroporto	baía	ensenada pantanosa	riacho	ilha	lago	reservatório	parque estadual

VANCOUVER
New Westminster
Burnaby
North Vancouver
Richmond
Nanaimo
Victoria
Esquimalt
Oak Bay
Port Alberni
VANCOUVER ISLAND
SEYMOUR RANGE
Strait of Georgia
Strait of Juan de Fuca
Haro Strait
CANADA
UNITED STATES
BRITISH COLUMBIA
WASHINGTON
SAN JUAN ISLANDS
Bellingham
Anacortes
Mount Vernon
Everett
Edmonds
SEATTLE
Bellevue
Renton
Kent
Federal Way
Tacoma
Bremerton
Port Angeles
Port Townsend
WHIDBEY ISLAND
Puget Sound
OLYMPIC MOUNTAINS
OLYMPIC NATIONAL PARK
CASCADE MOUNTAINS
NORTH CASCADES NATIONAL PARK
WENATCHEE MOUNTAINS
Chilliwack
Abbotsford
Cle Elum

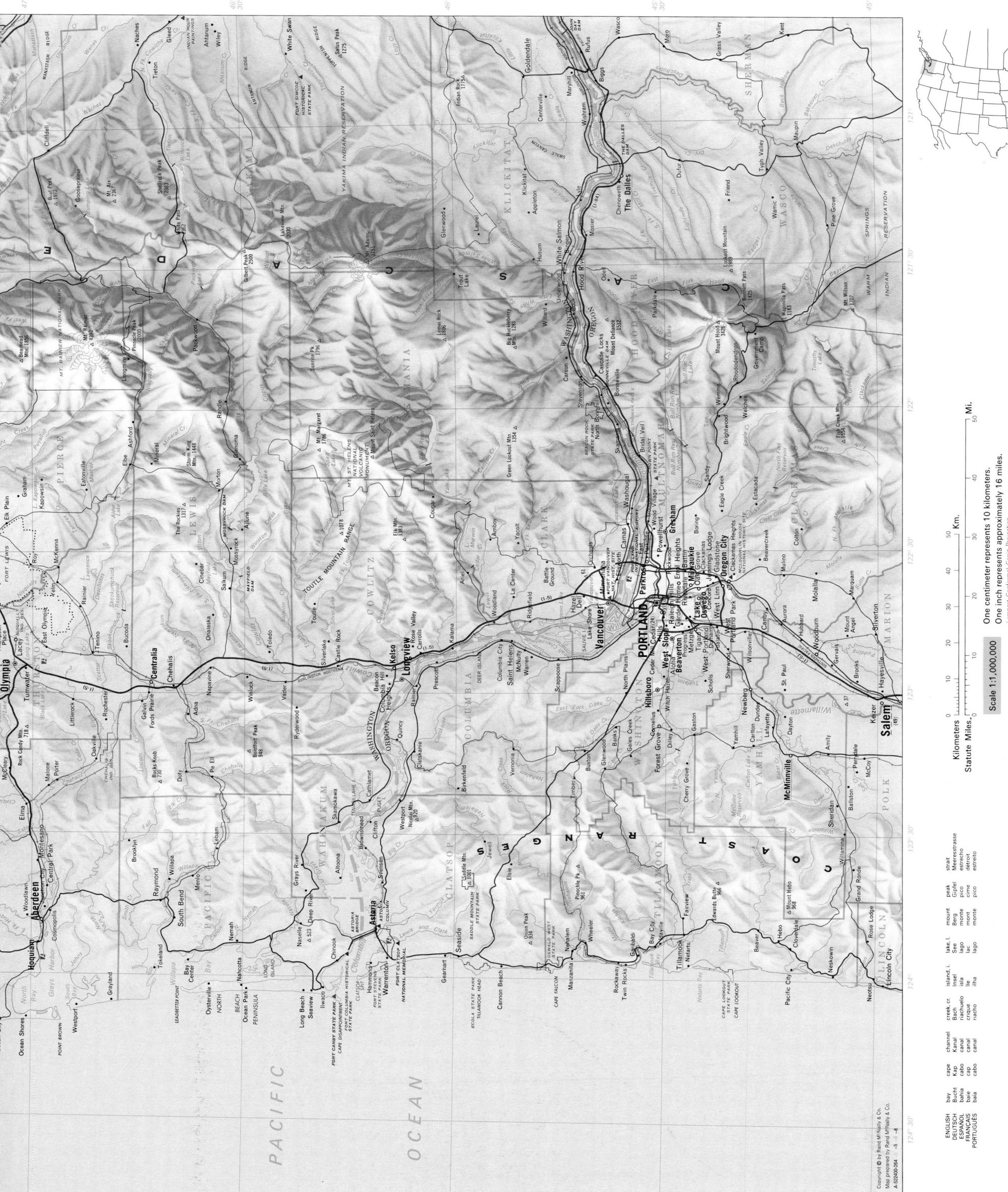

Scale 1:1,000,000

Kilometers

Statute Miles

One centimeter represents 10 kilometers.
One inch represents approximately 16 miles.

Lambert Conformal Conic Projection

ENGLISH	bay	cape	channel	creek, cr.	island, I.	lake, I.	mount	peak	strait
DEUTSCH	Bucht	Kap	Kanal	Bach	Insel	See	Berg	Gipfel	Meeresstrasse
ESPAÑOL	bahía	cabo	canal	riachuelo	isla	lago	monte	pico	estrecho
FRANÇAIS	baie	cap	canal	crique	île	lac	mont	cime	détroit
PORTUGUÊS	baía	cabo	canal	riacho	ilha	lago	monte	pico	estreito

Copyright © by Rand McNally & Co.
Map prepared by Rand McNally & Co.
A-522400-564   —5 - —8

SAN FRANCISCO
Oakland
Sacramento
Stockton
Reno
Sparks
Carson City
South Lake Tahoe
Lake Tahoe
SIERRA NEVADA
SACRAMENTO VALLEY
Modesto
Fremont
Vallejo
Santa Rosa
Marysville
Yuba City
Oroville
Lodi
Davis
Woodland
Fairfield
Vacaville
Napa
Petaluma
Concord
Berkeley
Hayward
Palo Alto
Turlock
Tracy
Manteca
Roseville
Auburn
Placerville
Truckee
Yerington
Bridgeport
Lee Vining
PINE NUT MOUNTAINS
SWEETWATER MTS.
CATHEDRAL RANGE
CARSON RANGE
YOSEMITE NATIONAL PARK
122°30'
122°
121°30'
121°
120°30'
120°
119°30'
39° 30'
39°
38° 30'
38°
37° 30'

Map continues
page 228

One centimeter represents 10 kilometers.
One inch represents approximately 16 miles.

Scale 1:1,000,000
Lambert Conformal Conic Projection

Kilometers

Statute Miles

ENGLISH	bay	canal	creek, cr.	lake, l.	mountain, mtn.	pass	range	reservoir	slough
DEUTSCH	Bucht	Kanal	Bach	See	Berg	Pass	Gebirge	Stausee	verlandete Wasserfläche
ESPAÑOL	bahía	canal	riachuelo	lago	montaña	paso	sierra	embalse	pantano
FRANÇAIS	baie	canal	crique	lac	montagne	col	chaîne	réservoir	fondrière
PORTUGUÊS	baía	canal	riacho	lago	montanha	passo	serra	reservatório	pântano

Copyright © by Rand McNally & Co.
Map prepared by Rand McNally & Co.

PACIFIC OCEAN

Map continues
pages 226-227

PACIFIC OCEAN

Gulf of Santa Catalina

ENGLISH	canyon	creek, cr.	lake, l.	mountain, mtn.	pass	peak	point	reservoir, res.
DEUTSCH	Cañon	Bach	See	Berg	Pass	Gipfel	Landspitze	Stausee
ESPAÑOL	cañón	riachuelo	lago	montaña	paso	pico	punta	embalse
FRANÇAIS	canyon	crique	lac	montagne	col	cime	pointe	réservoir
PORTUGUÊS	canhão	riacho	lago	montanha	passo	pico	ponta	reservatório

Kilometers 0 10 20 30 40 50 Km.

Statute Miles 0 10 20 30 40 50 Mi.

Scale 1:1,000,000
One centimeter represents 10 kilometers.
One inch represents approximately 16 miles.
Lambert Conformal Conic Projection

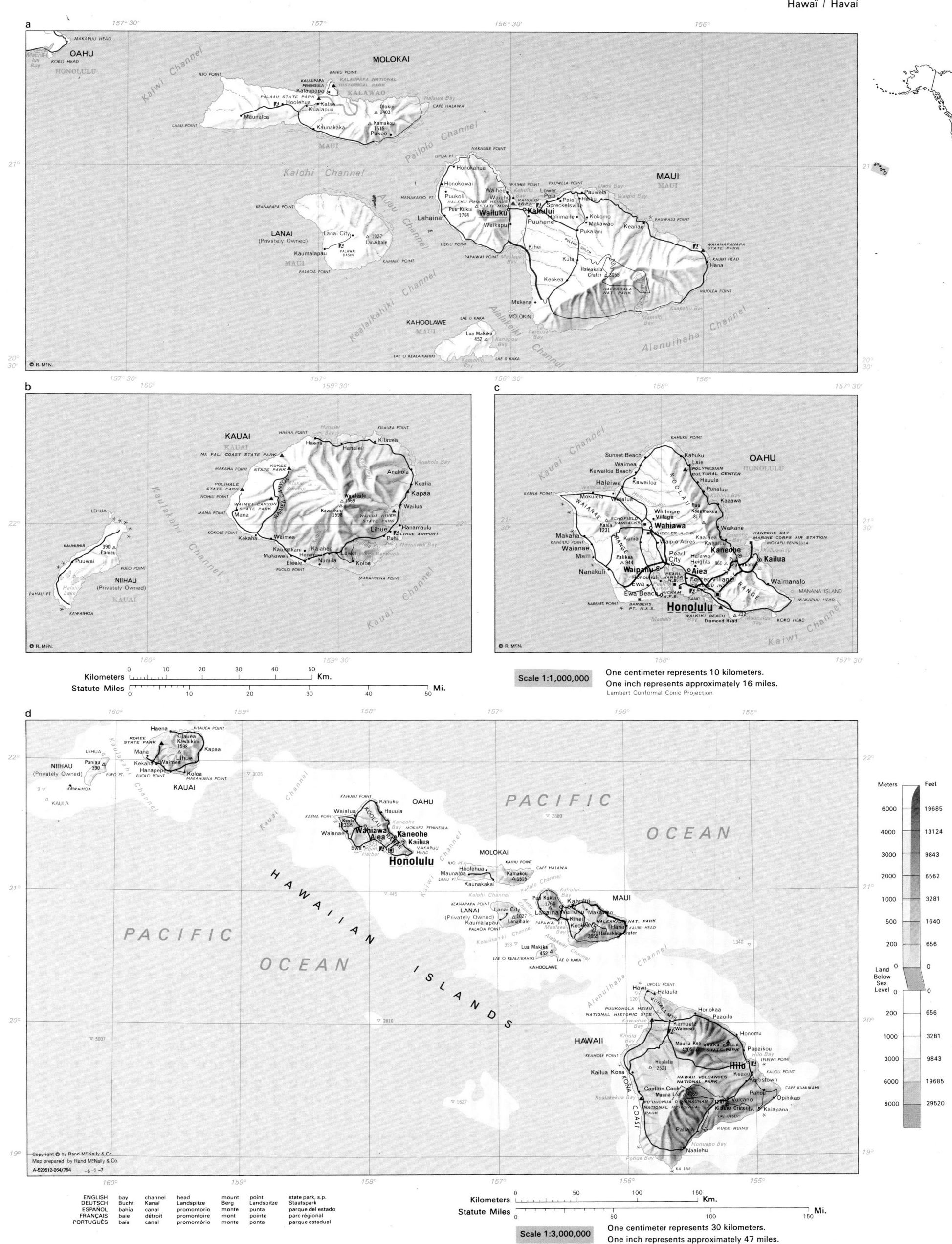

a

OAHU
HONOLULU
MAKAPUU HEAD
KOKO HEAD
Makai Bay

MOLOKAI
KAHIU POINT
KALAUPAPA NATIONAL HISTORICAL PARK
KALAWAO
KALAUPAPA PENINSULA
Kalaupapa
PALAAU STATE PARK
Hoolehua
Kala
Kualapuu
Kaunakakai
Maunaloa
Olokui △ 1403
Kamakou △ 1515
Pukoo
LAAU POINT
IUO POINT
CAPE HALAWA
Halawa Bay
MAUI

Kaiwi Channel
Pailolo Channel
Kalohi Channel
Kalamaki Channel
Auau Channel

Nakalele Point
LIPOA POINT
Honokahua
Honokowai
Puukolii
Waihee
Kahului Lower Paia
Paia
Waihee
Hali'imaile
Spreckelsville
Pauwela
Pauwela Point
Puu Kukui 1764
HALEKII-PIHANA HEIAU STATE MON.
WAILUKU
KAHULUI AIRP.
Kahului
Waikapu
Puunene
Makawao
Kokomo
Keanae
PAUWALU POINT
MAUI
MAUI
Lahaina
Kihei
PAILOLO VALLEY
Pukalani
WAIANAPANAPA STATE PARK
KAUIKI HEAD
Hana
HEKILI POINT
Kula
Keokea
Haleakala Crater △ 3055
HALEAKALA NAT. PARK
MUOLEA POINT
PAPAWAI POINT
Maalaea Bay
Makena
Kaapahu Bay
LANAI
(Privately Owned)
Lanai City
△ 1027
Lanaihale
PALAWAI BASIN
Kaumalapau
KAHOOLAWE
MAUI
LAE O KAKA
Lua Makika △ 452
Kanapou Bay
MOLOKINI
LAE O KEALAIKAHIKI
LAE O KAKA
Mamalu Bay
Honuaula Bay
Alenuihaha Channel

© R. MfN.

b

KAUAI
KAUAI
HAENA POINT
Haena
Hanalei
KILAUEA POINT
Kilauea
NA PALI COAST STATE PARK
Hanalei Bay
Anahola
KOKEE STATE PARK
Kealia
MAKAHA POINT
Waialeale △ 1569
Kapaa
POLIHALE STATE PARK
WAIMEA CANYON STATE PARK
Kawaikini △ 1598
Wailua
WAILUA RIVER STATE PARK
NOHILI POINT
Mana
Anahola Bay
MANA POINT
Lihue
Hanamaulu
LIHUE AIRPORT
KOKOLE POINT
Waimea
Kekaha
Kaumakani
Kalaheo
Puhi
Nawiliwili Bay
Eleele
Koloa
Hanapepe
Numila
PUOLO POINT
MAKAHUENA POINT

LEHUA
KAUNUNUI
390 △ Paniau
Puuwai
PUEO POINT
NIIHAU
(Privately Owned)
KAUAI
PAHAU PT.
Halalii
Kawaihoa

Kaulakahi Channel
Kauai Channel

© R. MfN.

c

KAHUKU POINT
Sunset Beach
Waimea
Kawailoa Beach
Haleiwa
Kawailoa
Mokuleia
Kahuku
Laie
POLYNESIAN CULTURAL CENTER
Hauula
Punaluu
OAHU
HONOLULU
Kaaawa
KAENA POINT
SCHOFIELD BARRACKS
Kaala △ 1231
Wahiawa
Whitmore Village
Puu Kaua △ 817
Kahana Bay
WHEELER A.F.B.
Kaneohe Bay
Waikane
MOKAPU PENINSULA
MARINE CORPS AIR STATION
Makaha
Kunia
Waialua Acres
Kaneohe
Kailua
Kailua Bay
WAIANAE RANGE
Waianae
Maili
Waipio Acres
Palikea △ 944
Halawa Heights
860 △
KOOLAU RANGE
Nanakuli
Waipahu
Pearl City
Aiea
Waimanalo
PEARL HARBOR
Ewa
Foster Village
Ewa Beach
MANANA ISLAND
BARBERS POINT N.A.S.
BARBERS PT.
Honolulu
SAND I.
Diamond Head
△ 232
KOKO HEAD
MAKAPUU HEAD
Waikiki Beach
Mamala Bay
Kaiwi Channel

© R. MfN.

Scale 1:1,000,000
One centimeter represents 10 kilometers.
One inch represents approximately 16 miles.
Lambert Conformal Conic Projection

Kilometers 0 10 20 30 40 50 Km.
Statute Miles 0 10 20 30 40 50 Mi.

d

NIIHAU
(Privately Owned)
LEHUA
Paniau 390
KAULA
KAUAI
KOKEE STATE PARK
Haena
Maha
Kilauea
Kawaikini 1598
Kapaa
Kekaha
Lihue
Hanapepe
Waimea
Koloa
PUEO PT.
PUOLO POINT
MAKAHUENA POINT

Kaneohe
Waialua
Kahuku
Hauula
OAHU
Kaala 1315
Wahiawa
Aiea
Kaneohe
Kailua
KAENA POINT
Waianae
Ewa
Pearl Harbor
Honolulu
MAKAPUU HEAD
MOKAPU PENINSULA
Kaneohe Bay

MOLOKAI
KAHIU POINT
Hoolehua
Kamakou 1515
Maunaloa
Kaunakakai
CAPE HALAWA
LAAU PT.
IUO PT.

LANAI
(Privately Owned)
Lanai City
1027
Lanaihale
Kaumalapau
PALAOA POINT
KEANAPAPA POINT
393 △

Puu Kukui 1764
Wailuku Kahului
Lahaina
Kihei
MAUI
Makawao
Hana
KAUIKI HEAD
HALEAKALA NAT. PARK
Keokea
3055 Haleakala Crater
PAPAWAI POINT

KAHOOLAWE
Lua Makika 452
LAE O KEALAIKAHIKI

PACIFIC OCEAN

PACIFIC OCEAN

HAWAIIAN ISLANDS

Kaulakahi Channel
Kauai Channel
Kaiwi Channel
Kalohi Channel
Pailolo Channel
Alalakeiki Channel
Alenuihaha Channel

UPOLU POINT
Hawi
Halaula
KOHALA MTS.
PUUKOHOLA HEIAU NATIONAL HISTORIC SITE
Kawaihae
Kamuela
Waimea
Honokaa
Paauilo
Honomu
Papaikou
Hilo Bay
LELEIWI POINT
Honomu
Mauna Kea △ 4205
MAUNA KEA STATE PARK
HAWAII
KEAHOLE POINT
Hualalai △ 2521
Kailua Kona
Hilo
Keaau
Kurtistown
KALOLI POINT
CAPE KUMUKAHI
Captain Cook
Mauna Loa △ 4169
HAWAII VOLCANOES NATIONAL PARK
Volcano
Kilauea Crater
Pahoa
Kalapana
KONA COAST
PUUHONUA O HONAUNAU NATIONAL HISTORICAL PARK
KUEE RUINS
Pahala
KAU DESERT
Naalehu
Opihikao
Kealakekua Bay
Honuapo Bay
Pohue Bay
KA LAE

Copyright © by Rand McNally & Co.
Map prepared by Rand McNally & Co.
A-520512-264/764   -6-6-7

ENGLISH	bay	channel	head	mount	point	state park, s.p.
DEUTSCH	Bucht	Kanal	Landspitze	Berg	Landspitze	Staatspark
ESPAÑOL	bahía	canal	promontorio	monte	punta	parque del estado
FRANÇAIS	baie	détroit	promontoire	mont	pointe	parc régional
PORTUGUÊS	baía	canal	promontório	monte	ponta	parque estadual

Kilometers 0 50 100 150 Km.
Statute Miles 0 50 100 150 Mi.

Scale 1:3,000,000
One centimeter represents 30 kilometers.
One inch represents approximately 47 miles.
Lambert Conformal Conic Projection

Meters	Feet
6000	19685
4000	13124
3000	9843
2000	6562
1000	3281
500	1640
200	656
0	0
Land Below Sea Level	
200	656
1000	3281
3000	9843
6000	19685
9000	29520

Middle America / Mittelamerika / México, Centroamérica y Las Antillas
Mexique, Amérique Centrale et Région des Caraïbes / México, América Central e Antilhas

Map continues
pages 178-179

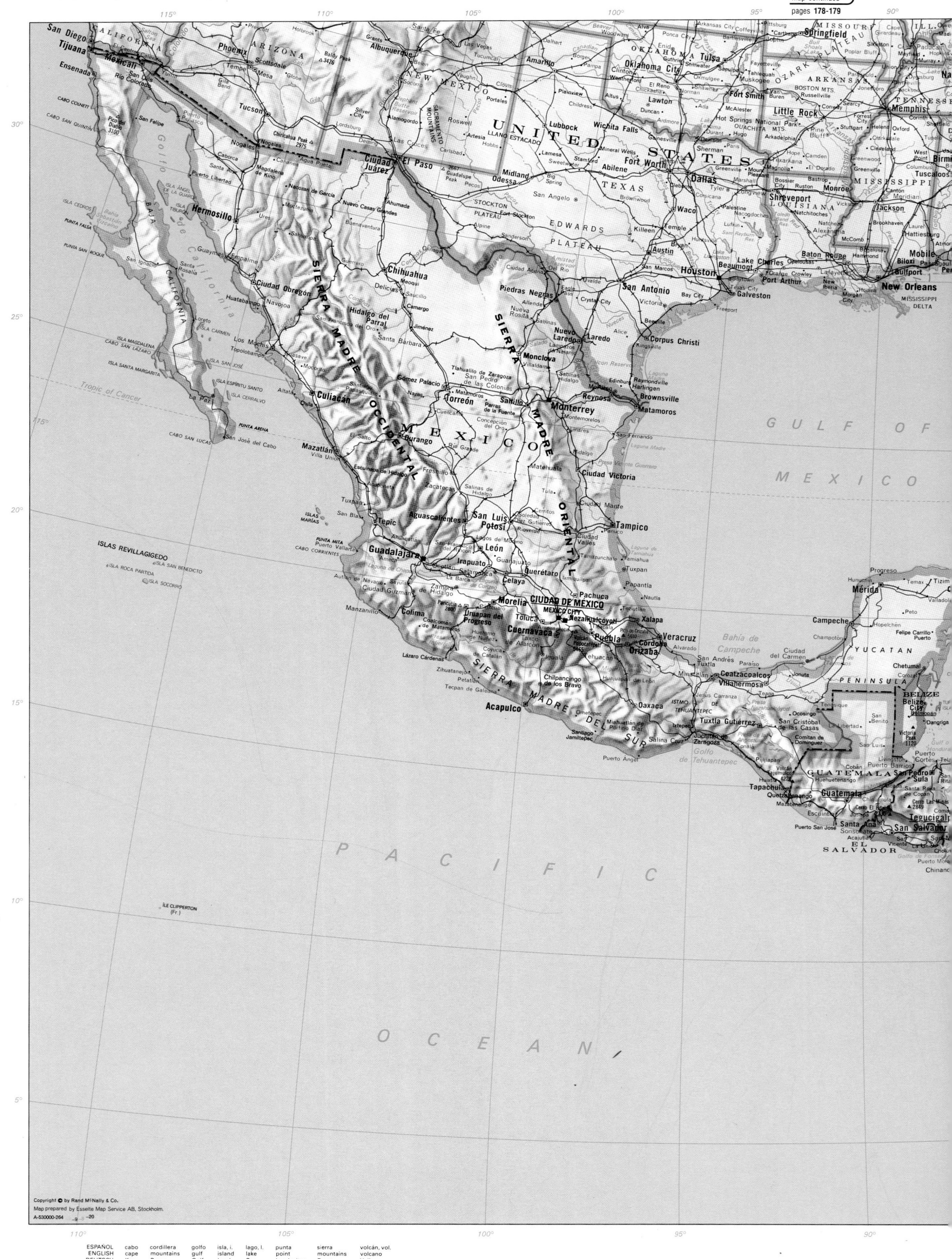

	cabo	cordillera	golfo	isla, i.	lago, l.	punta	sierra	volcán, vol.
ESPAÑOL	cabo	cordillera	golfo	isla, i.	lago, l.	punta	sierra	volcán, vol.
ENGLISH	cape	mountains	gulf	island	lake	point	mountains	volcano
DEUTSCH	Kap	Berge	Golf	Insel	See	Landspitze	Berge	Vulkan
FRANÇAIS	cap	montagnes	golfe	île	lac	pointe	montagnes	volcan
PORTUGUÊS	cabo	cordilheira	golfo	ilha	lago	ponta	serra	vulcão

Middle America / Mittelamerika / México, Centroamérica y Las Antillas
Mexique, Amérique Centrale et Région des Caraïbes / México, América Central e Antilhas

231

Map continues
pages 242-243

Kilometers 0   200   400   600   Km.

Statute Miles 0   200   400   600   Mi.

Scale 1:12,000,000

One centimeter represents 120 kilometers.
One inch represents approximately 190 miles.
Oblique Conic Conformal Projection

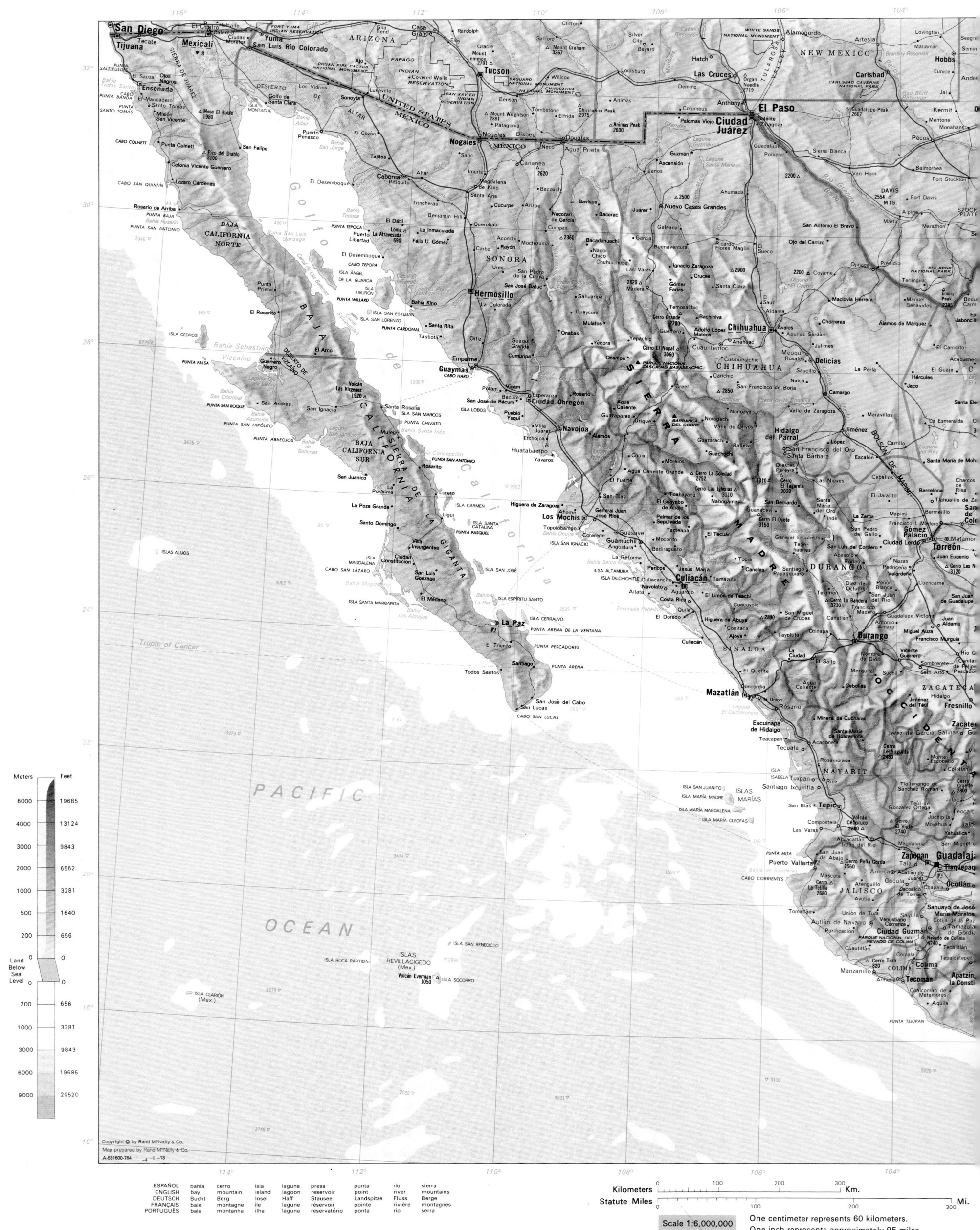

Scale 1:6,000,000
One centimeter represents 60 kilometers.
One inch represents approximately 95 miles.
Lambert Conformal Conic Projection

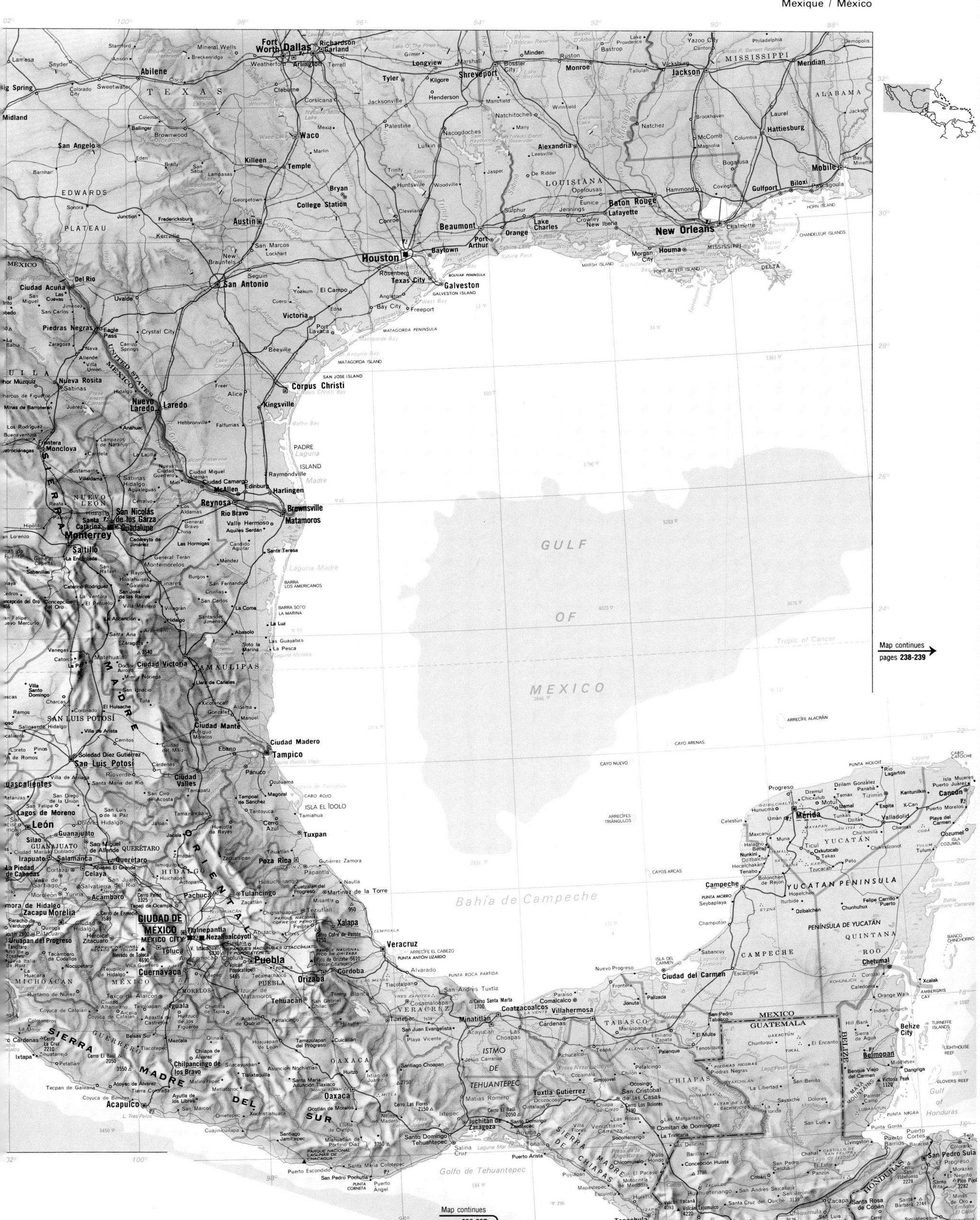

GULF

OF

MEXICO

Bahía de Campeche

Map continues
pages 238-239

Map continues
pages 236-237

Map continues
pages **232-233**

Meters	Feet
6000	19685
4000	13124
3000	9843
2000	6562
1000	3281
500	1640
200	656
0	0
Land Below Sea Level	
0	0
200	656
1000	3281
3000	9843
6000	19685
9000	29520

PACIFIC OCEAN

ESPANOL	arroyo	boca	cerro	lago	laguna	punta	rio	sierra	volcán
ENGLISH	brook	entrance	butte	lake	lagoon	point	river	ranges	volcano
DEUTSCH	Bach	Einfahrt	Restberg	See	Haff	Landspitze	Fluss	Bergketten	Vulkan
FRANÇAIS	ruisseau	entrée	butte	lac	lagune	pointe	rivière	chaîne	volcan
PORTUGUÊS	riacho	entrada	cerro	lago	laguna	ponta	rio	serra	vulcão

Map continues
pages 232-233

Map continues
pages 236-237

Kilometers

Statute Miles

Scale 1:3,000,000

One centimeter represents 30 kilometers.
One inch represents approximately 47 miles.

Lambert Conformal Conic Projection

Central America / Zentralamerika / América Central
Amérique Centrale / América Central

Map continues
pages **232-233**

Map continues
pages **234-235**

Meters	Feet
6000	19685
4000	13124
3000	9843
2000	6562
1000	3281
500	1640
200	656
Land Below Sea Level 0	0
0	0
200	656
1000	3281
3000	9843
6000	19685
9000	29520

ESPAÑOL	bahía	cerro	cordillera	isla	lago	laguna	punta	sierra	volcán
ENGLISH	bay	mountain	mountains	island	lake	lagoon	point	mountains	volcano
DEUTSCH	Bucht	Berg	Berge	Insel	See	Haff	Landspitze	Berge	Vulkan
FRANÇAIS	baie	montagne	montagnes	île	lac	lagune	pointe	montagnes	volcan
PORTUGUÊS	baía	montanha	cordilheira	ilha	lago	laguna	ponta	serra	vulcão

Kilometers
Statute Miles

0   50   100   150 Km.
0   50   100   150 Mi.

Scale 1:3,000,000

One centimeter represents 30 kilometers.
One inch represents approximately 47 miles.

Lambert Conformal Conic Projection

Caribbean Region / Mittelamerikanische Inselwelt / Región del Caribe
Région des Caraïbes / Região do Caribe

GULF OF MEXICO

UNITED STATES
FLORIDA

West Palm Beach
Fort Myers
Belle Glade
Palm Beach
Lake Worth
Delray Beach
Boca Raton
Pompano Beach
Fort Lauderdale
Hollywood
Hialeah
MIAMI
Miami Beach
Coral Gables
Naples
Homestead
Everglades City

Key West

FLORIDA KEYS

Straits of Florida

West End
Freeport
GRAND BAHAMA
ABACO
Marsh Harbour
BAHAM

Nassau
NEW PROVIDENCE
Governor's Harbour
ELEUTHERA
Rock Sound

ANDROS
Andros Town

Arthur's Town
CAT ISLAND
Mount Alvernia
Port Howe
COLUMBUS POINT

EXUMA
Georgetown
Clarence Town
LONG ISLAND
Deadman's Cay

RAGGED ISLAND
W E S T

LA HABANA
HAVANA
San Antonio de los Baños
Matanzas
Cárdenas
Guanajay
Artemisa
San José de las Lajas
Güira de Melena
Güines
Jovellanos
Colón
Sagua la Grande
Caibarién
Camajuaní
CUBA
Santa Clara
Placetas
Cienfuegos
Sancti Spíritus
Trinidad
Ciego de Ávila
Florida
Camagüey
Las Tunas
Holguín
Banes
Bayamo
Manzanillo
Palma Soriano
Santiago de Cuba
Guantánamo

CAYMAN ISLANDS
(U.K.)
George Town
Grand Cayman

G R E A T E R

Montego Bay
Falmouth
Ocho Rios
Port Maria
Port Antonio
JAMAICA
Kingston
Spanish Town
May Pen
Mandeville

ISLAS SANTANILLA
(Hond.)

Gulf of Honduras
ISLAS DE LA BAHÍA
Roatán
Utila

HONDURAS
LA MOSQUITIA

NICARAGUA
Tegucigalpa

CARIBBEA

CAYOS MISKITOS
Puerto Cabezas

San Andrés
SAN ANDRÉS
Y PROVIDENCIA
(Col.)

Managua
Granada

COSTA RICA
San José

PANAMÁ
Colón
Panamá

PACIFIC OCEAN

BARRANQUILLA
Soledad
Cartagena

MAP CONTINUES
pages 232-233

MAP CONTINUES
pages 236-237

Meters	Feet
6000	19685
4000	13124
3000	9843
2000	6562
1000	3281
500	1640
200	656
0	0
Land Below Sea Level	
0	0
200	656
1000	3281
3000	9843
6000	19685
9000	29520

Copyright © by Rand McNally & Co.
Map prepared by Rand McNally & Co.
A-530100-764

MAP FORM	bahía	cabo	cerro	channel	golfo	isla	passage	pico	punta
ENGLISH	bay	cape	mountain	channel	gulf	isle	passage	peak	point
DEUTSCH	Bucht	Kap	Berg	Kanal	Golf	Insel	Durchfahrt	Gipfel	Landspitze
ESPAÑOL	bahía	cabo	cerro	canal	golfo	isla	pasaje	pico	punta
FRANÇAIS	baie	cap	montagne	détroit	golfe	île	passage	cime	pointe
PORTUGUÊS	baía	cabo	montanha	canal	golfo	ilha	passagem	pico	ponta

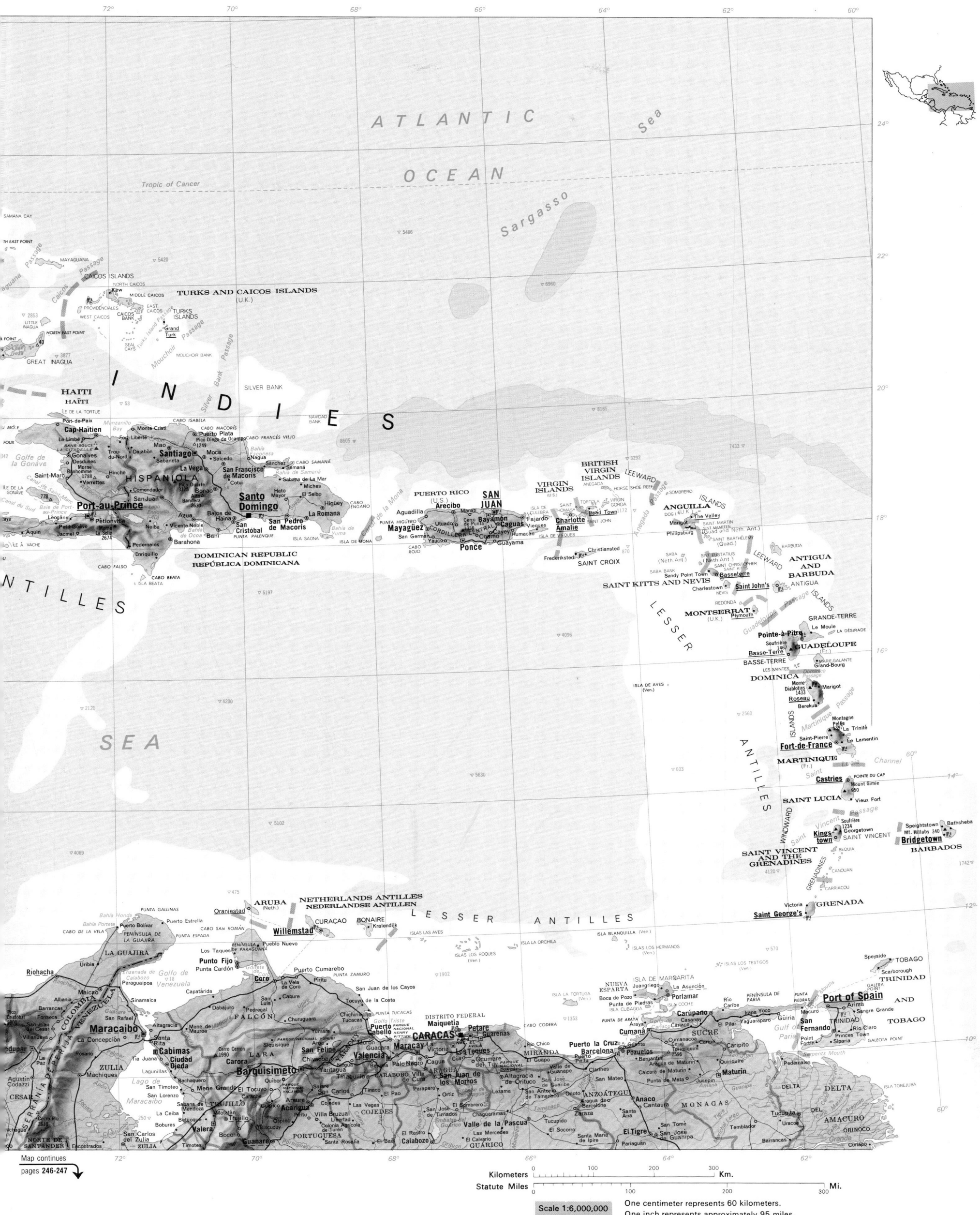

Map continues
pages 246-247

Kilometers
Statute Miles

Scale 1:6,000,000

One centimeter represents 60 kilometers.
One inch represents approximately 95 miles.
Lambert Conformal Conic Projection

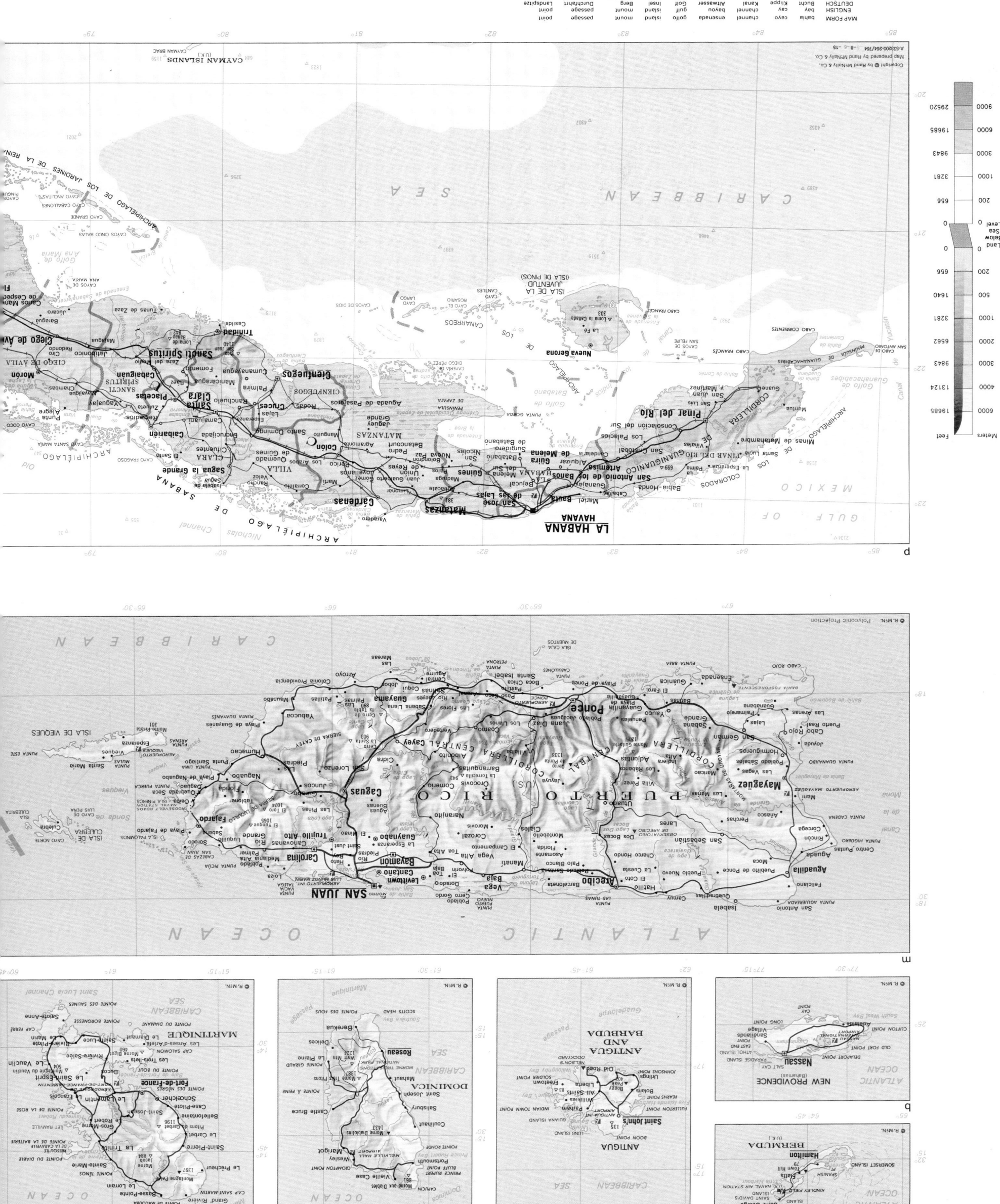

Islands of the West Indies / Westindische Inseln / Islas de las Antillas
Îles des Antilles / Ilhas do Caribe (Indias Occidentais)

240

Islands of the West Indies / Westindische Inseln / Islas de las Antillas
Îles des Antilles / Ilhas do Caribe (Índias Ocidentais)

241

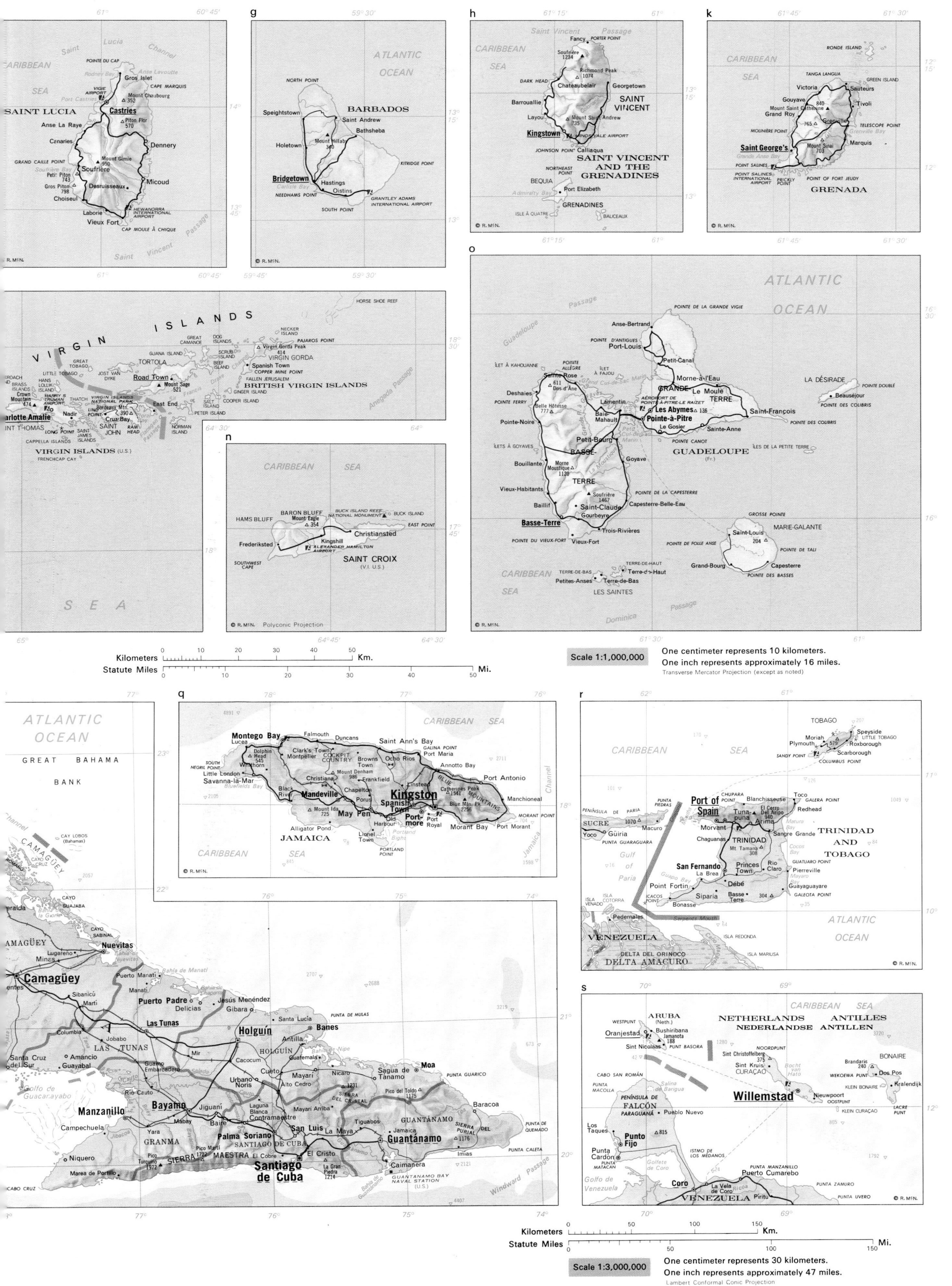

Northern South America / Südamerika, nördlicher Teil / América del Sur: zona septentrional
Amérique du Sud Septentrionale / América do Sul: zona setentrional

Map continues
pages 230-231

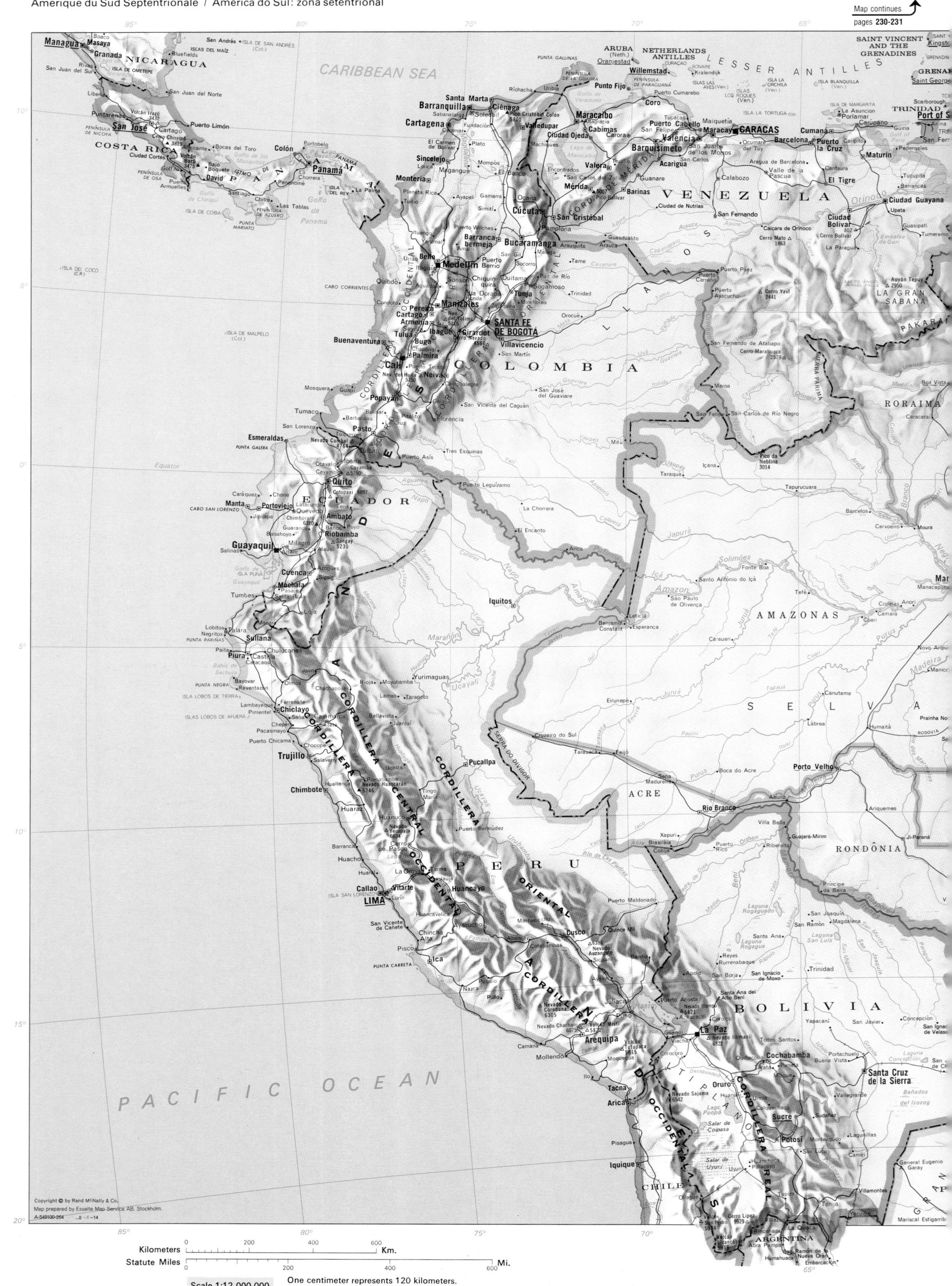

CARIBBEAN SEA

NICARAGUA

COSTA RICA

PANAMA

PACIFIC OCEAN

COLOMBIA

VENEZUELA

ECUADOR

AMAZONAS

SELVA

ACRE

RONDÔNIA

PERU

BOLIVIA

CHILE

ARGENTINA

LESSER ANTILLES

SANTA FE DE BOGOTA

CARACAS

Quito

LIMA

La Paz

Arequipa

Kilometers   200   400   600   Km.
Statute Miles   200   400   600   Mi.

Scale 1:12,000,000   One centimeter represents 120 kilometers.
One inch represents approximately 190 miles.

Oblique Conic Conformal Projection

Copyright © by Rand McNally & Co.
Map prepared by Esselte Map Service AB, Stockholm.
A-549100-054

Northern South America / Südamerika, nördlicher Teil / América del Sur: zona septentrional
Amérique du Sud Septentrionale / América do Sul: zona setentrional

243

ATLANTIC OCEAN

Equator

BARBADOS
Bridgetown

Georgetown
GUYANA

Charity
Garden
Hyde Park
Bartica
Rockstone
Corriverton

Paramaribo
New Amsterdam
Nieuw Nickerie
SURINAME
Wismar
Linden

FRENCH
GUIANA

Cayenne
Saint-Laurent-du-Maroni
Regina
Saint-Georges

Juliana Top
1230

Oiapoque

TUMUC-HUMAC MTS.
ACARAÍ MTS.

AMAPÁ

CABO ORANGE

830

Serra do Navio

Macapá
CABO MAGUARI

ILHA DE MARAJÓ

Belém

Santarém

Amazonas

PARÁ

Represa
de
Tucuruí

Imperatriz
Marabá

SERRA DOS CARAJÁS

SERRA DO CACHIMBO

MARANHÃO

São Luís

Parnaíba

Fortaleza
ATOL DAS ROCAS
ILHA FERNANDO
DE NORONHA
(Brazil)

CABO DE SÃO ROQUE

Teresina

CEARÁ

Natal
Mossoró
RIO GRANDE DO NORTE

PIAUÍ

Juazeiro
do Norte
Campina Grande
João Pessoa
PONTA DO SEIXAS

PARAÍBA
PERNAMBUCO
Caruaru
Recife
Olinda

TOCANTINS

BRAZIL

ILHA
DO
BANANAL

Petrolina
Juazeiro

Paulo
Afonso
ALAGOAS
Arapiraca
Maceió

SERGIPE
Aracaju
São Cristóvão

BAHIA

Feira de Santana

Salvador
Pico das
Almas
1836
ILHA DE TINHARÉ

SERRA DO ESPINHAÇO

Vitória
da Conquista
Ilhéus
Itabuna

MATO GROSSO

PLANALTO DO
MATO GROSSO

Cuiabá

Rondonópolis

SERRA DO CAIAPÓ

GOIÁS

Brasília
Anápolis
Goiânia

PLANALTO
CENTRAL

MINAS GERAIS

Montes
Claros

Governador
Valadares
ESPÍRITO
SANTO

MATO GROSSO
DO SUL

Corumbá

Campo Grande

Presidente Prudente

Uberlândia
Uberaba

Belo
Horizonte

Vitória
Vila Velha

Franca

Ribeirão
Preto

São José
do Rio Preto

SÃO PAULO

Campinas

SÃO PAULO
Santo André
Santos

Juiz de Fora

Volta
Redonda
Niterói
RIO DE
JANEIRO

Tropic of Capricorn

Map continues
pages 244-245

MAP FORM	cerro	cordillera	ilha	lago	nevado	peninsula	serra
ENGLISH	mountain	range	island	lake	mountain	peninsula	mountains
DEUTSCH	Berg	Gebirge	Insel	See	Berg	Halbinsel	Berge
ESPAÑOL	montaña	cordillera	isla	lago	montaña	península	montañas
FRANÇAIS	montagne	chaîne	île	lac	montagne	péninsule	montagnes
PORTUGUÊS	montanha	cordilheira	ilha	lago	montanha	península	montanhas

244

Southern South America / Südamerika, südlicher Teil / América del Sur: zona meridional
Amérique du Sud Méridionale / América do Sul: zona meridional

Map continues
pages **242-243**

20°

Tropic of Capricorn

85°

25°

ISLA SAN FÉLIX
(Chile)

ISLA SAN AMBROSIO
(Chile)

30°

ARCHIPIÉLAGO
JUAN FERNÁNDEZ
(Chile)

ISLA RÓBINSON CRUSOE
(ISLA MÁS A TIERRA)

ISLA ALEJANDRO SELKIRK
ISLA MÁS AFUERA

35°

P A C I F I C

90°

O C E A N

40°

45°

BOLIVIA

PARA

Asunción

Formosa

Resistencia **Corrientes**

CHILE

ARGENTINA

Córdoba

Santa Fe **Concordia**
Paraná

Rosario

San Isidro

BUENOS AIRES **Avellane**

La Pi

**Mar
P**

Bahía Blanca

Comodoro Rivadavia

P A T A G O N I A

**FALKLAN
ISLAND**
(U.K.)

JASON ISLANDS

WEST
FALKLAND

EAST
FALKLA

ISLA GRANDE
DE TIERRA DEL FUEGO

CABO DE HORNOS
CAPE HORN

95°   90°   85°   80°   75°   70°   65°   60°

MAP FORM	cerro, co.	golfo	ilha	isla	lago	lagoa	monte	salar
ENGLISH	butte	gulf	island	isle	lake	lake	mountain	saltflat
DEUTSCH	Restberg	Golf	Insel	Insel	See	See	Berg	Salzebene
ESPAÑOL	cerro	golfo	isla	isla	lago	lago	montaña	salobral
FRANÇAIS	butte	golfe	île	île	lac	lac	montagne	salina
PORTUGUÊS	colina	golfo	ilha	ilha	lago	lago	montanha	salina

Southern South America / Südamerika, südlicher Teil / América del Sur: zona meridional
Amérique du Sud Méridionale / América do Sul: zona meridional

245

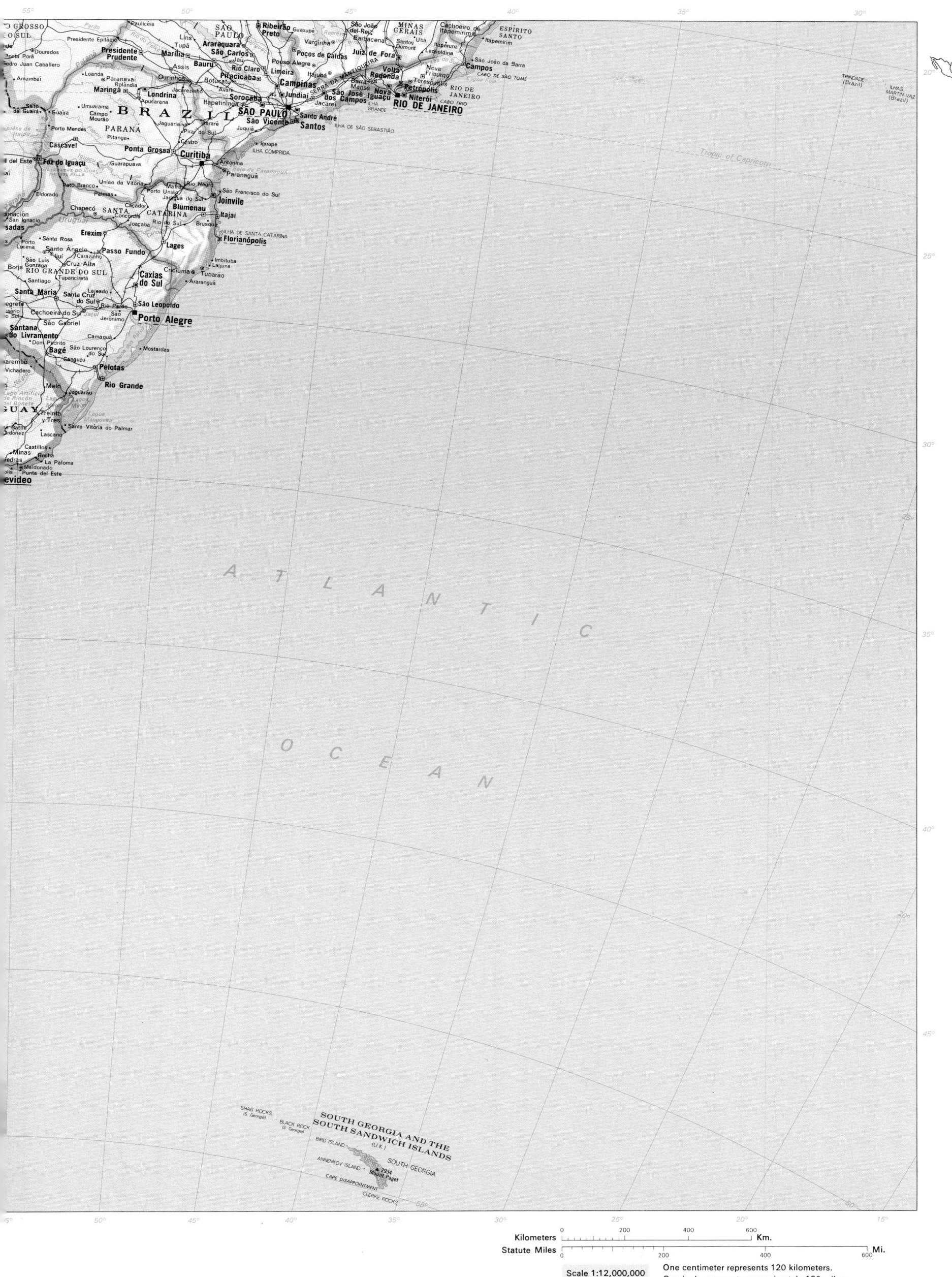

Tropic of Capricorn

A T L A N T I C

O C E A N

SHAG ROCKS
(S. Georgia)

BLACK ROCK
(S. Georgia)

SOUTH GEORGIA AND THE
SOUTH SANDWICH ISLANDS
(U.K.)

BIRD ISLAND

ANNENKOV ISLAND

2934
Mount Paget

SOUTH GEORGIA

CAPE DISAPPOINTMENT

BLAERKE ROCKS

Kilometers |⊢⊢⊢⊢⊢⊢⊢⊢⊢⊢⊢⊢⊢⊢⊢| Km.
                0   200   400   600

Statute Miles |⊢⊢⊢⊢⊢⊢⊢⊢⊢⊢⊢| Mi.
                0   200   400   600

Scale 1:12,000,000

One centimeter represents 120 kilometers.
One inch represents approximately 190 miles.

Oblique Conic Conformal Projection

246

Colombia, Ecuador, Venezuela and Guyana / Kolumbien, Ecuador, Venezuela und Guayana / Colombia, Ecuador, Venezuela y Guyana
Colombie, Équateur, Venezuela et Guyane / Colômbia, Equador, Venezuela e Guiana

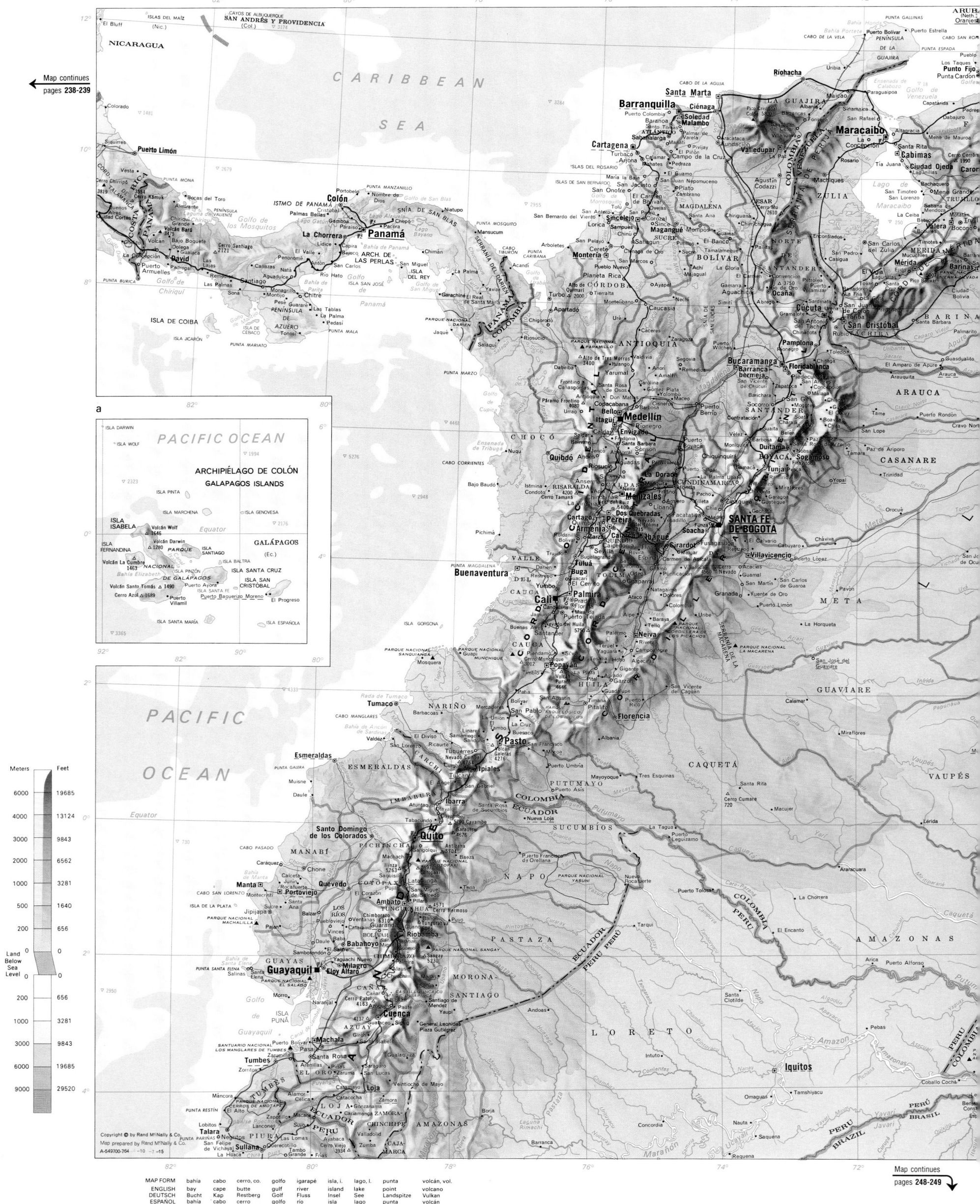

Map continues
pages 238-239

Map continues
pages 248-249

MAP FORM	bahía	cabo	cerro, co.	golfo	igarapé	isla, i.	lago, l.	punta	volcán, vol.
ENGLISH	bay	cape	butte	gulf	river	island	lake	point	volcano
DEUTSCH	Bucht	Kap	Restberg	Golf	Fluss	Insel	See	Landspitze	Vulkan
ESPAÑOL	bahía	cabo	cerro	golfo	río	isla	lago	punta	volcán
FRANÇAIS	baie	cap	butte	golfe	rivière	île	lac	pointe	volcan
PORTUGUÊS	baía	cabo	colina	golfo	rio	ilha	lago	ponta	vulcão

Colombia, Ecuador, Venezuela and Guyana / Kolumbien, Ecuador, Venezuela und Guayana / Colombia, Ecuador, Venezuela y Guyana
Colombie, Équateur, Venezuela et Guyane / Colômbia, Equador, Venezuela e Guiana

247

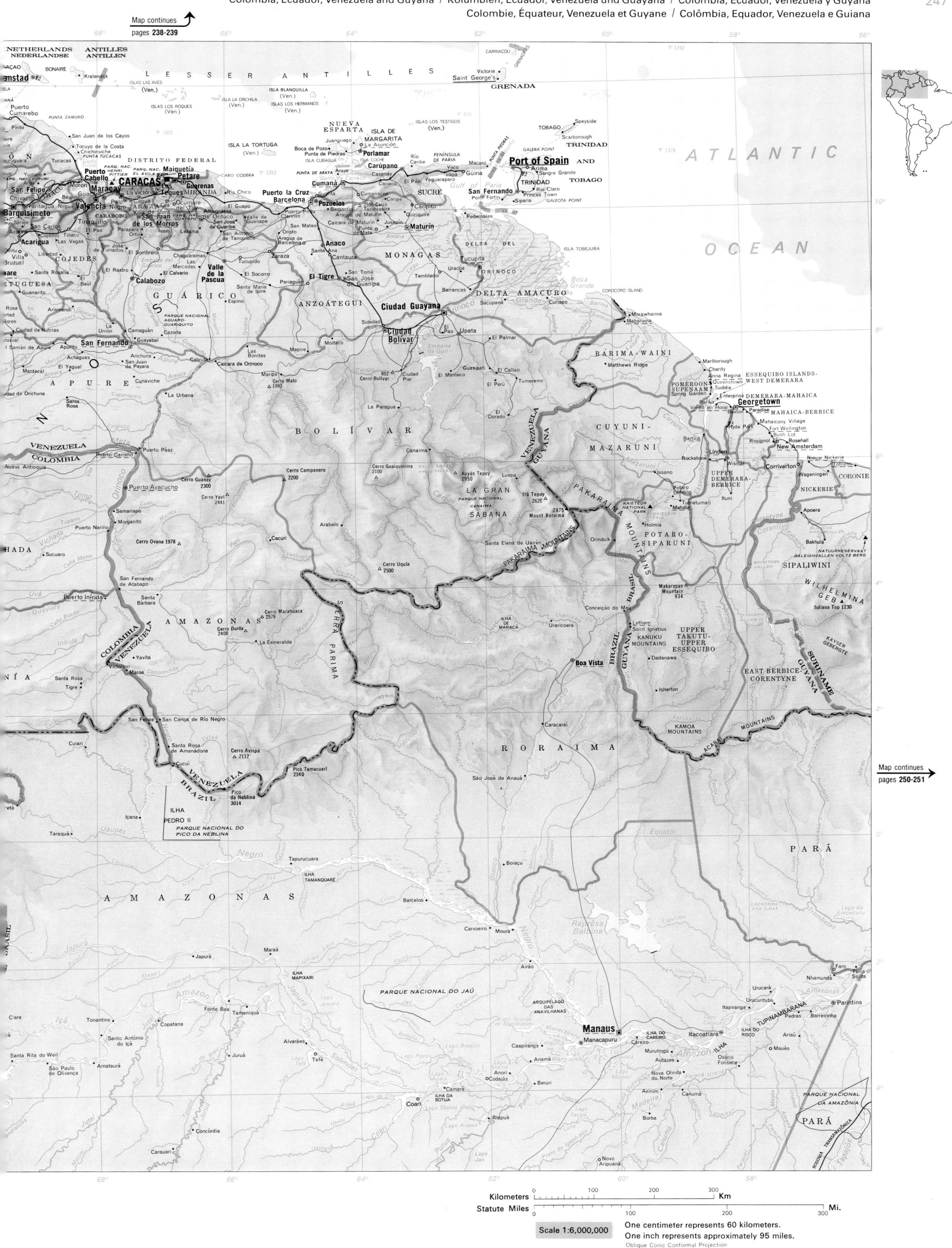

Map continues
pages 238-239

Map continues
pages 250-251

Kilometers
0   100   200   300   Km
Statute Miles
0   100   200   300   Mi.

Scale 1:6,000,000

One centimeter represents 60 kilometers.
One inch represents approximately 95 miles.
Oblique Conic Conformal Projection

248

Peru, Bolivia and Western Brazil / Peru, Bolivien und westliches Brasilien / Perú, Bolivia y Brasil Occidental
Pérou, Bolivie et Brésil Occidental / Peru, Bolívia e Brasil Ocidental

MAP FORM	cerro	cordillera	isla, i.	lago, l.	nevado	punta	rio	serra
ENGLISH	mountain	mountains	island	lake	mountain	point	river	mountains
DEUTSCH	Berg	Berge	Insel	See	Berg	Landspitze	Fluss	Berge
ESPAÑOL	montaña	montañas	isla	lago	nevado	punta	rio	sierra
FRANÇAIS	montagne	montagnes	île	lac	montagne	pointe	rivière	montagnes
PORTUGUÊS	montanha	montanhas	ilha	lago	pico nevado	ponta	rio	serra

Peru, Bolivia and Western Brazil / Peru, Bolivien und westliches Brasilien / Perú, Bolivia y Brasil Occidental
Pérou, Bolivie et Brésil Occidental / Peru, Bolívia e Brasil Ocidental

249

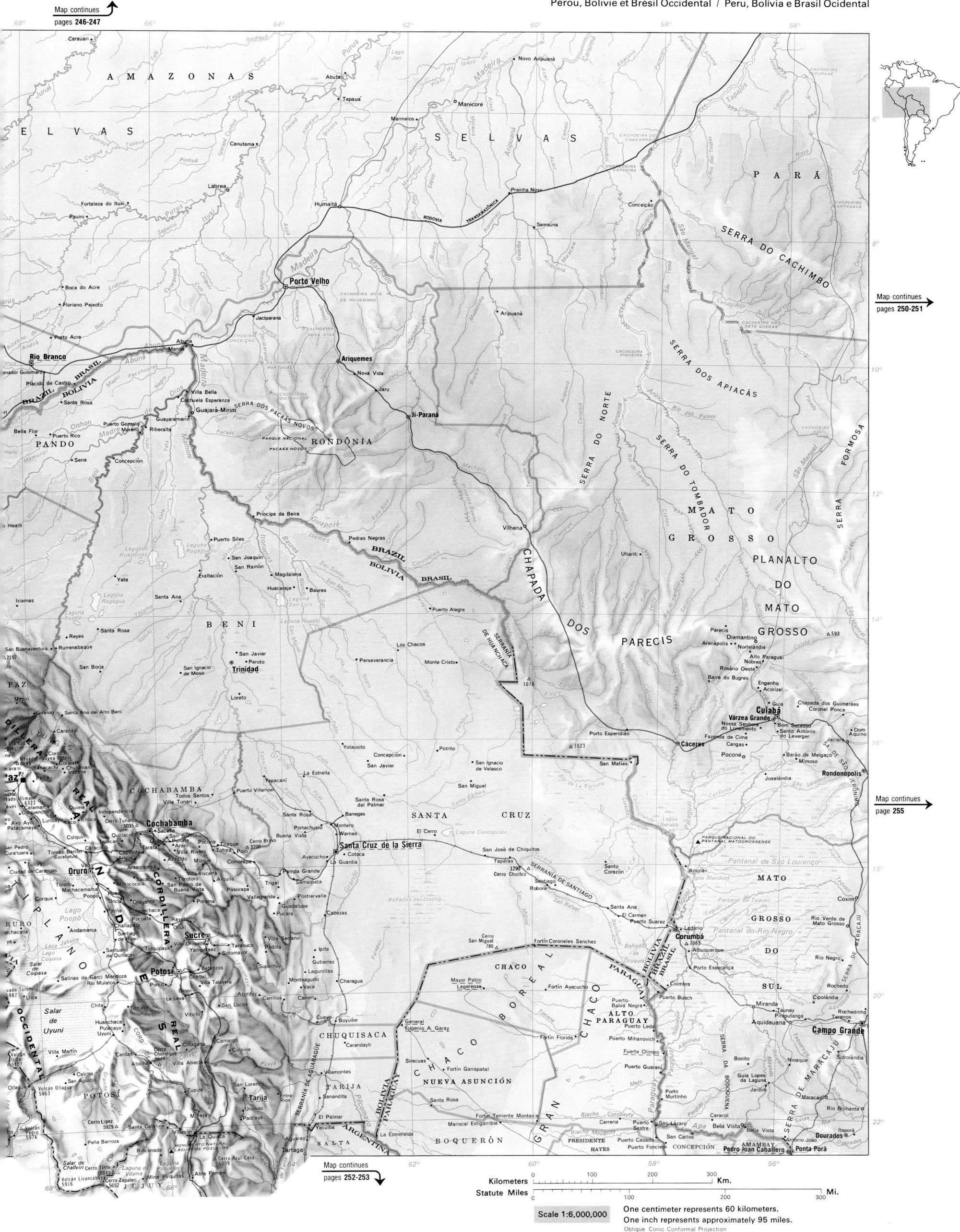

Map continues
pages 246-247

Map continues
pages 250-251

Map continues
page 255

Map continues
pages 252-253

Kilometers

Statute Miles

Scale 1:6,000,000

One centimeter represents 60 kilometers.
One inch represents approximately 95 miles.

Oblique Conic Conformal Projection

ATLANTIC

OCEAN

Equator

Kilometers

Statute Miles

Scale 1:6,000,000

One centimeter represents 60 kilometers.
One inch represents approximately 95 miles.
Oblique Conic Conformal Projection

Copyright © by Rand McNally & Co.
Map prepared by Rand McNally & Co.
A-540396-764   -6-6 -9

Map continues
pages 248-249

Map continues
page 254

MAP FORM	cabo	cerro	cuchilla	ilha	laguna	punta	salar	sierra	volcán
ENGLISH	cape	mountain	hills	island	lagoon; lake	point	saltflat	mountains	volcano
DEUTSCH	Kap	Berg	Hügel	Insel	Haff; See	Landspitze	Salzebene	Berge	Vulkan
ESPAÑOL	cabo	cerro	cuchilla	isla	laguna; lago	punta	salar	sierra	volcán
FRANÇAIS	cap	montagne	collines	île	lagune; lac	pointe	salina	montagnes	volcan
PORTUGUÊS	cabo	montanha	colina	ilha	laguna	ponta	salina	serra	vulcão

Copyright © by Rand McNally & Co.
Map prepared by Rand McNally & Co.
A-540191-764

Central Argentina and Chile / Mittelargentinien und Mittelchile / Argentina y Chile: zonas centrales
Argentine et Chili, parties Centrales / Argentina e Chile: zonas centrais

253

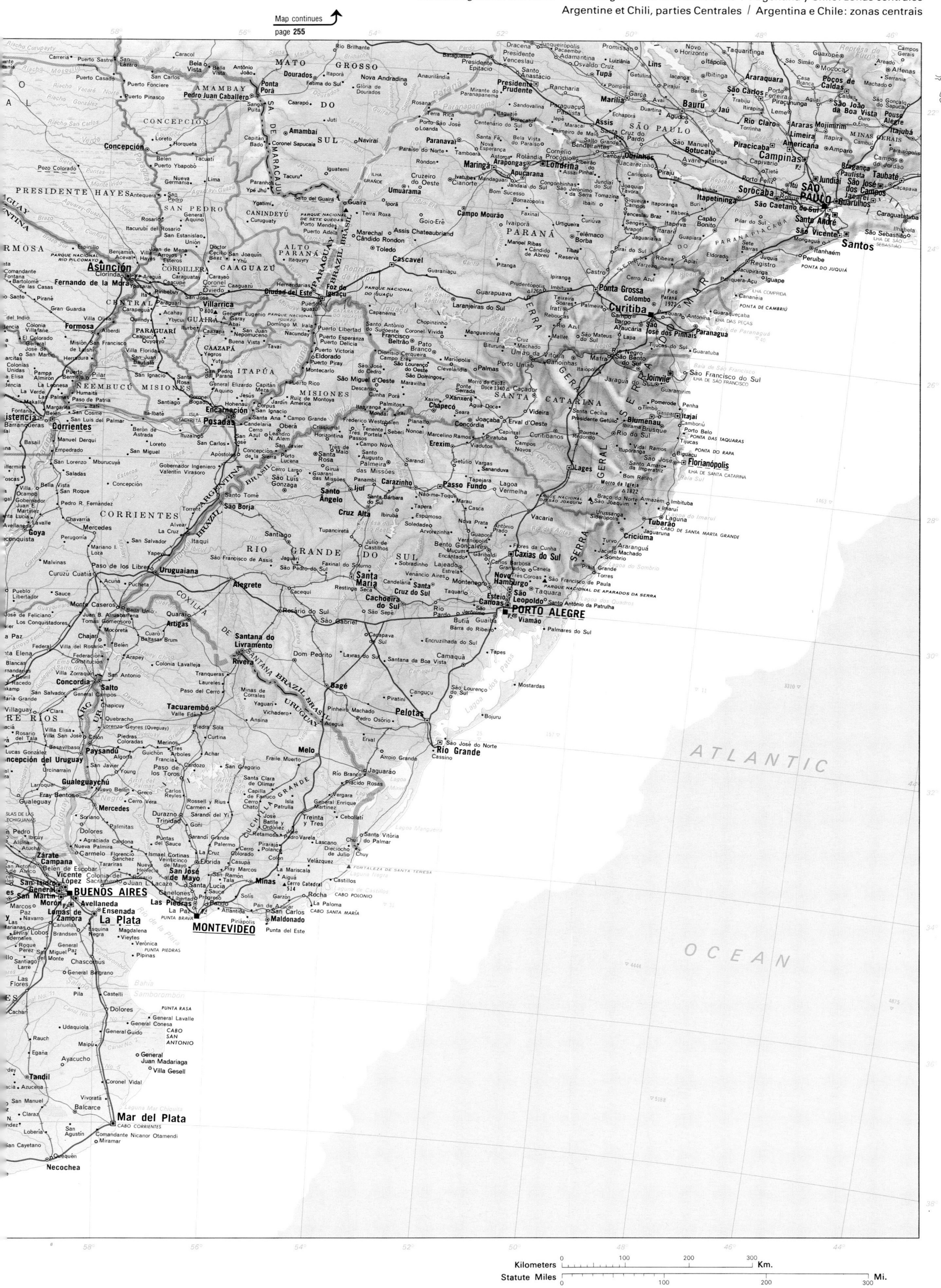

Map continues
page 255

Kilometers

Statute Miles

Km.

Mi.

Scale 1:6,000,000

One centimeter represents 60 kilometers.
One inch represents approximately 95 miles.

Oblique Conic Conformal Projection

Southern Argentina and Chile / Südliches Argentinien und südliches Chile / Argentina y Chile: zonas meridionales
Argentine et Chili, parties Méridionales / Argentina e Chile: zonas meridionais

Map continues
pages 252-253

PACIFIC OCEAN

ATLANTIC OCEAN

FALKLAND ISLANDS (U.K.)

Meters	Feet
6000	19685
4000	13124
3000	9843
2000	6562
1000	3281
500	1640
200	656
0	0
Land Below Sea Level 0	0
200	656
1000	3281
3000	9843
6000	19685
9000	29520

MAP FORM	bahia	cabo	cerro	isla	lago	monte	punta
ENGLISH	bay	cape	mountain, hill	isle	lake	mountain	point
DEUTSCH	Bucht	Kap	Berg, Hügel	Insel	See	Berg	Landspitze
ESPAÑOL	bahia	cabo	cerro	isla	lago	monte	punta
FRANÇAIS	baie	cap	montagne, colline	île	lac	montagne	pointe
PORTUGUÉS	baia	cabo	montanha, colina	ilha	lago	monte	ponta

Kilometers   0   100   200   300 Km.

Statute Miles   0   100   200   300 Mi.

Scale 1:6,000,000

One centimeter represents 60 kilometers.
One inch represents approximately 95 miles.
Oblique Conic Conformal Projection

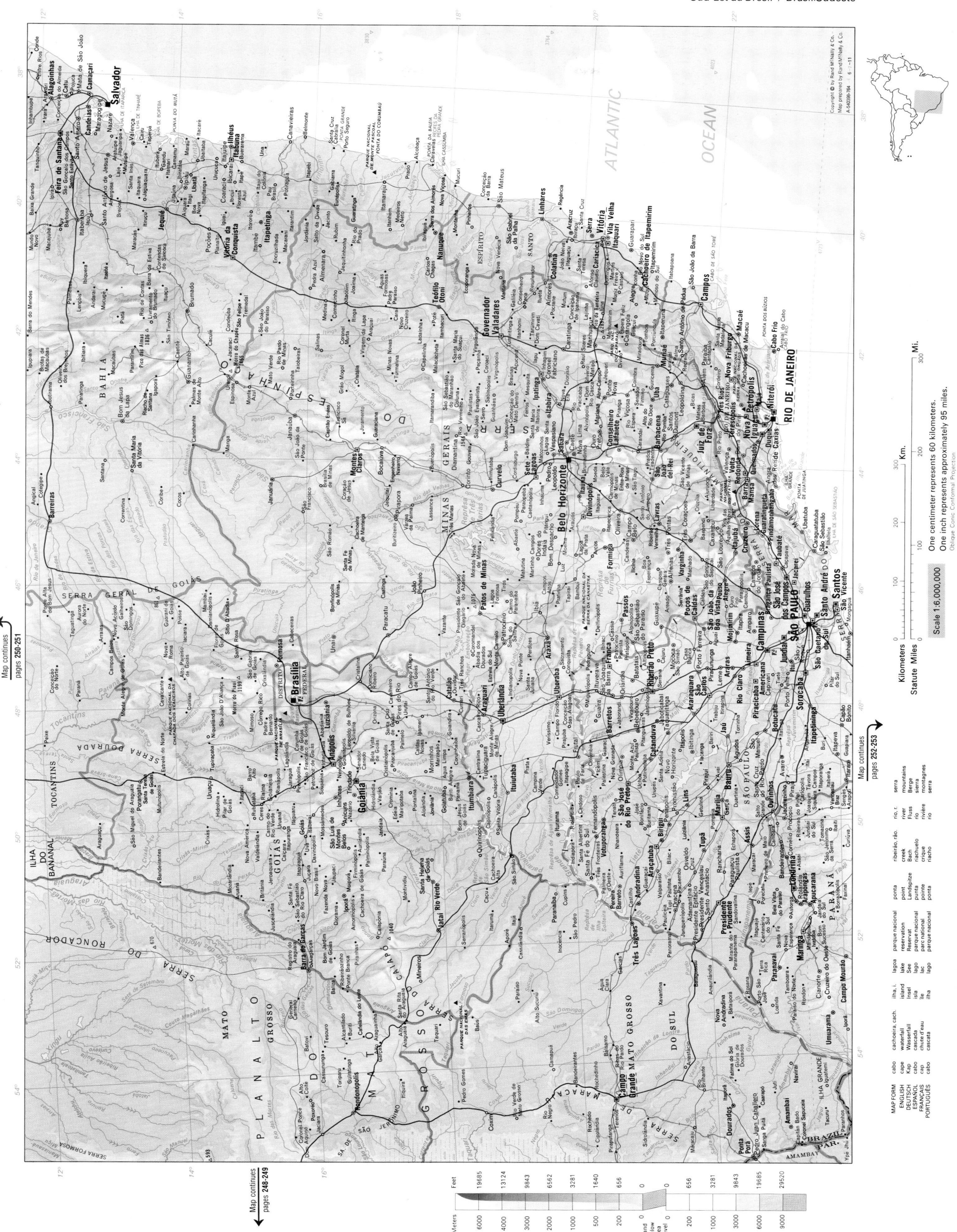

Map continues pages 250-251
Map continues pages 248-249
Map continues pages 252-253

Scale 1:6,000,000
Oblique Conic Conformal Projection

One centimeter represents 60 kilometers.
One inch represents approximately 95 miles.

Kilometers
Statute Miles

MAP FORM						
ENGLISH	cabo	cape	cachoeira, cach.	waterfall	ilha, i.	island	lagoa	lake	ponta	point	parque nacional	reservation	ribeirão, rão.	creek	rio, r.	river	serra	mountains
DEUTSCH	Kap		Wasserfall		Insel		See		Landspitze		Reservat		Bach		Fluss		Berge	
ESPAÑOL	cabo		cascada		isla		lago		punta		parque nacional		riachuelo		río		sierra	
FRANÇAIS	cap		chute d'eau		île		lac		pointe		parc national		crique		rivière		montagnes	
PORTUGUÊS	cabo		cascata		ilha		lago		ponta		parque nacional		riacho		rio		serra	

Feet
19685
13124
9843
6562
3281
1640
656
0

Meters
6000
4000
3000
2000
1000
500
200
0
Land Below Sea Level
0
200
656
1000
3281
3000
9843
6000
19685
9000
29520

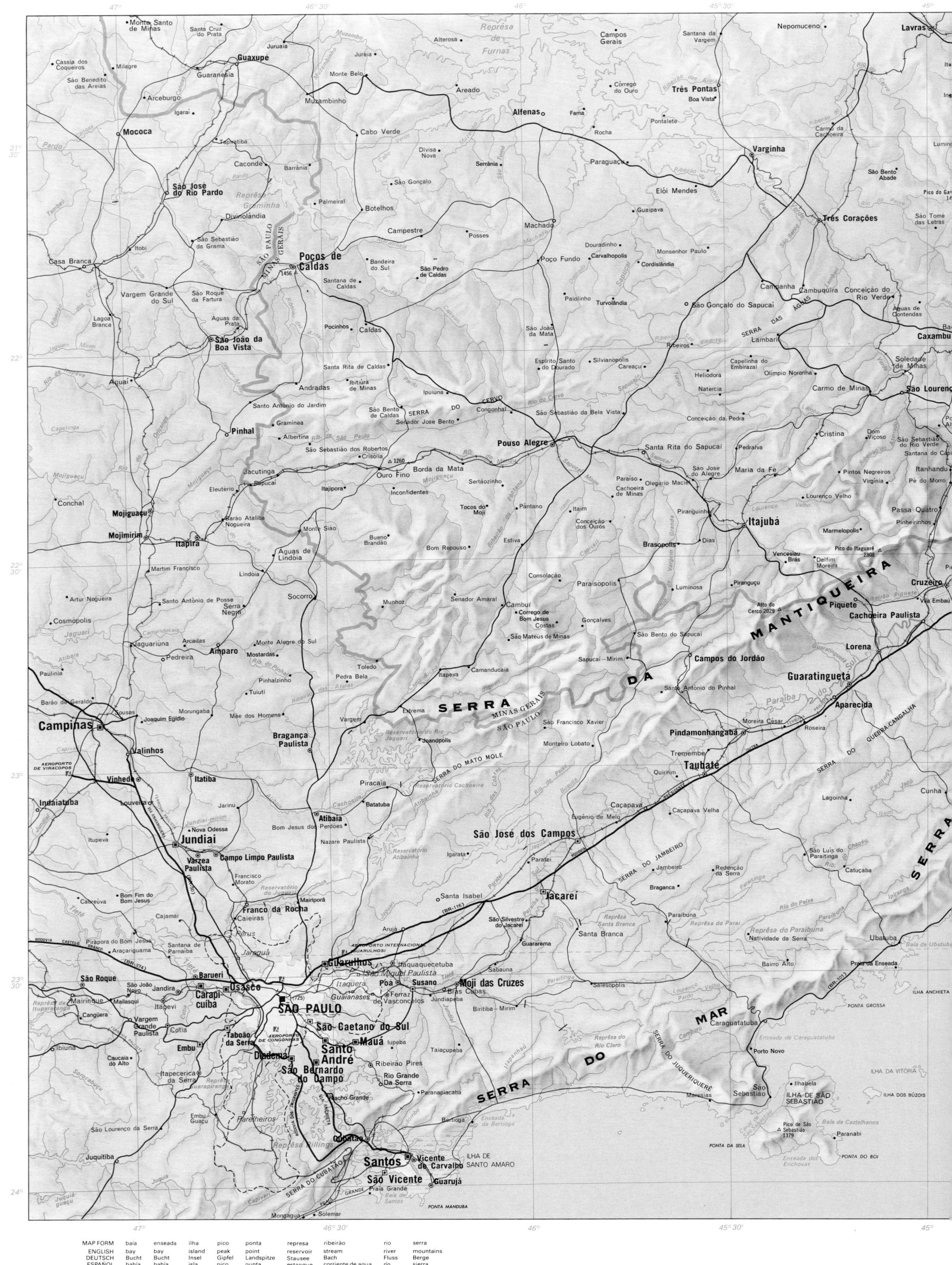

MAP FORM	baía	enseada	ilha	pico	ponta	represa	ribeirão	rio	serra
ENGLISH	bay	bay	island	peak	point	reservoir	stream	river	mountains
DEUTSCH	Bucht	Bucht	Insel	Gipfel	Landspitze	Stausee	Bach	Fluss	Berge
ESPAÑOL	bahía	bahia	isla	pico	punta	estanque	corriente de agua	río	sierra
FRANÇAIS	baie	baie	île	cime	pointe	réservoir	cours d'eau	rivière	montagnes
PORTUGUÊS	baía	enseada	ilha	pico	ponta	represa	ribeirão	rio	serra

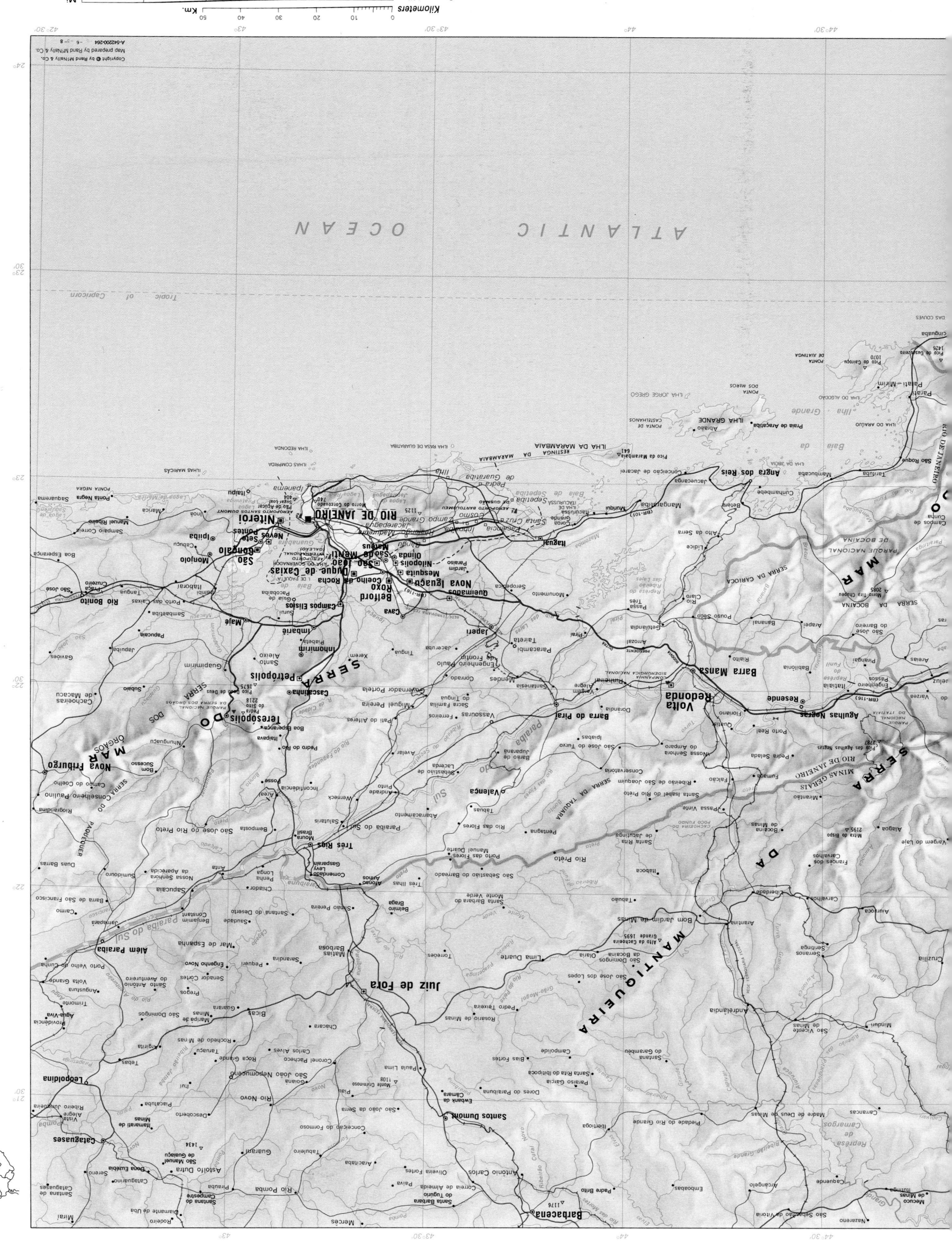

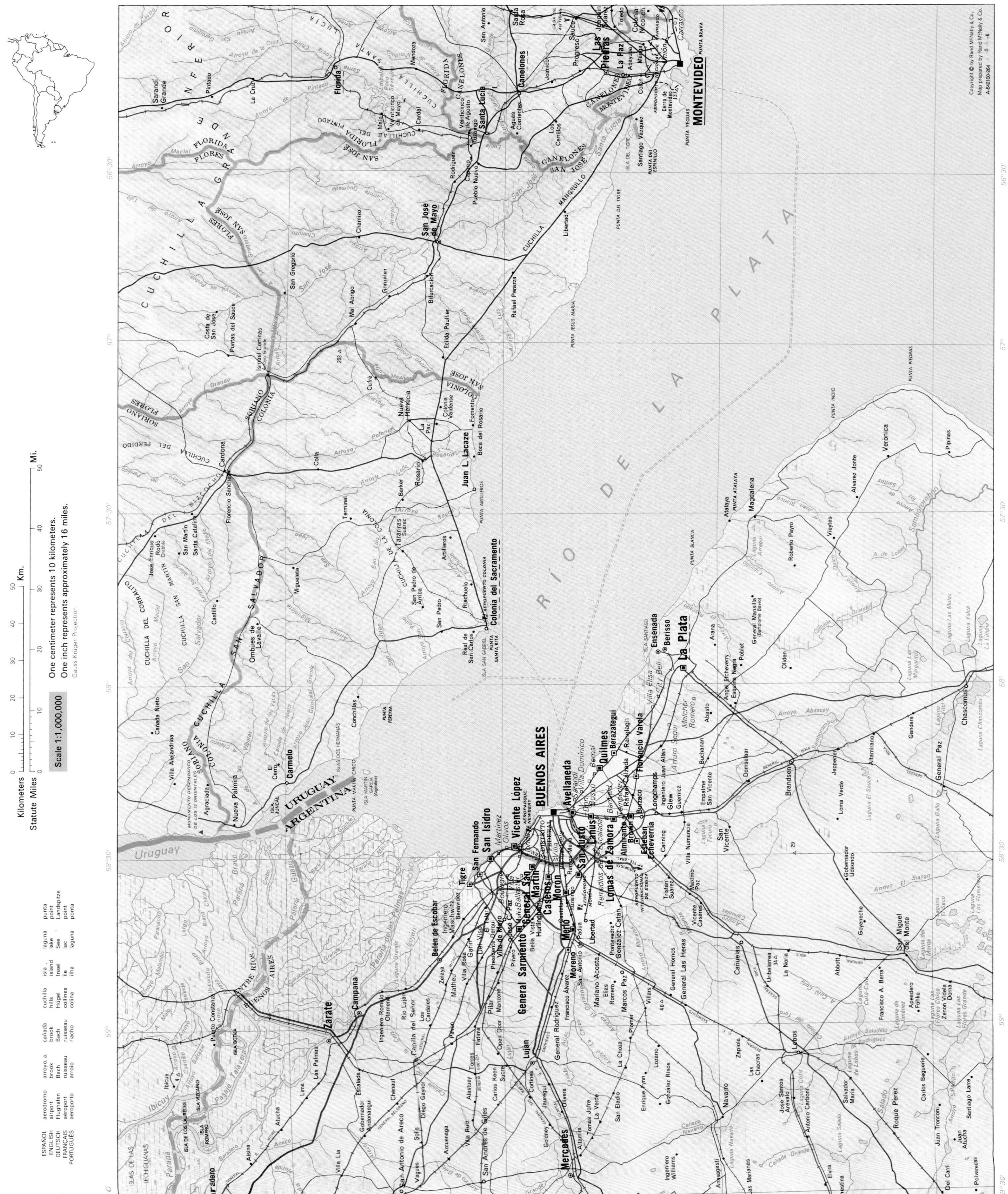
Kilometers
Statute Miles
Scale 1:1,000,000
One centimeter represents 10 kilometers.
One inch represents approximately 16 miles.
Gauss Krüger Projection
ESPAÑOL aerodromo arroyo, a. cañada cuchilla isla laguna punta
ENGLISH airport brook brook hills island lake point
DEUTSCH Flughafen Bach Bach Hügel Insel See Landspitze
FRANÇAIS aéroport ruisseau ruisseau collines île lac point
PORTUGUÊS aeroporto arroio riacho colina ilha laguna ponta
BUENOS AIRES
MONTEVIDEO
RÍO DE LA PLATA
URUGUAY
ARGENTINA
La Plata
Colonia del Sacramento
San José de Mayo
Canelones
Copyright © by Rand McNally & Co.

Metropolitan Area Maps/Karten von Stradtregionen
Mapas de las Areas Metropolitanas/Cartes des Zones Métropolitaines
Mapas das Áreas Metropolitanas

259

THIS SECTION CONSISTS of 60 maps of the world's major metropolitan areas, at the scale of 1:300,000. The maps show the generalized land-use patterns in and around each city—the total urban extent, major industrial areas, parks and preserves, and wooded areas. Airports are shown, as are many details of the highway and rail transportation networks. Selected points of interest appear, such as Fisherman's Wharf and Chinatown in San Francisco, the Welcome monument in Jakarta, the Temple of the Jade Buddha in Shanghai, and the Cristo Redentor statue in Rio de Janeiro.

The maps name and locate a great number of towns, villages, and suburbs, and also sections or neighborhoods within limits of the larger cities. Prominent physical features, including elevations, named and unnamed, have been indicated to give a general impression of the local topography. Shaded relief has been omitted, however, to permit display of such details as streams, parks, airport runways, important public buildings and monuments, and the names of major streets. The corporate limits of major cities are also outlined. For the symbols used on these maps see the Legend to Maps.

Maps of major world cities usually vary widely in scale, and heretofore have not been consistent in design and coverage. For this section, a special effort has been made to portray these varied metropolitan areas in as standard and comparable a fashion as possible. However, for a few cities (notably several in Asia) there has not been adequate source material to include certain information, such as major industrial areas and corporate limits.

The order of presentation is generally regional, with some exceptions where for ease of comparison major capitals or industrial centers or cities located in similar physical surroundings have been juxtaposed. Many American cities and some European cities, with their lower densities and more extensive areas, require larger maps than do Asiatic cities of comparable population. The total land area and population within the confines of each map are stated in the margin as a further aid to comparison.

DIESER KARTENTEIL UMFASST 60 Karten der bedeutendsten Stadtregionen der Erde im Massstab 1:300 000. Die Karten zeigen in generalisierter Form die Landnutzung in und um jede Stadt: die gesamte Ausdehnung des verstädterten Gebietes, wichtige Industriegebiete, Parks, Landflächen in Gemeinbesitz und Wald. Flughäfen werden ebenso dargestellt wie viele Einzelheiten des Strassen- und Eisenbahnnetzes. Bekannte Sehenswürdigkeiten sind eingetragen wie die "Fisherman's Wharf" und "Chinatown" in San Francisco, das Willkomm-Denkmal in Jakarta, der Tempel des Jade-Buddhas in Shanghai und die "Cristo Redentor"-Statue in Rio de Janeiro.

Die Karten verzeichnen Name and Lage einer grossen Zahl von Städten, Dörfern, Vororten ebenso wie eingemeindete Ortsteile bei grösseren Städten. Hervortretende physische Formen wie benannte und unbenannte Erhebungen sind aufgenommen, um eine allgemeine Vorstellung des lokalen Reliefs zu geben. Auf die Schummerung wurde jedoch verzichtet, um klar solche Einzelheiten wie Flüsse, Parks, Start- und Landebahnen der Flughäfen, bedeutende öffentliche Gebäude und Denkmäler sowie die Namen der wichtigsten Strassen herausstellen zu können. Eingetragen sind ferner die Gemeindegrenzen der wichtigsten Städte. Zu den auf diesen Karten verwendeten Signaturen siehe "Zeichenerklärung".

Karten der bedeutendsten Weltstädte differieren normalerweise sehr stark in ihren Massstäben und sind daher uneinheitlich in ihrer Gestaltung und Begrenzung. Deshalb wurde in diesem Kartenteil besonderer Wert darauf gelegt, die verschiedenen städtischen Ballungsgebiete in möglichst einheitlicher und vergleichbarer Form darzustellen. Für einige Städte, vor allem mehrere asiatische, war das Quellenmaterial jedoch nicht ausreichend genug, um gewisse Informationen wie Hauptindustriegebiete oder Stadtgrenzen einzutragen.

Im allgemeinen sind diese Karten nach regionalen Gesichtspunkten geordnet. Um Vergleiche zu erleichtern wurden einige Ausnahmen gemacht, indem wichtige Hauptstädte, Industriezentren oder Städte in vergleichbarer landschaftlicher Lage einander gegenübergestellt wurden. Viele amerikanische und einige europäische Städte mit ihrer geringen Bevölkerungsdichte, aber ausgedehnteren Fläche erfordern eine grössere Kartenfläche als asiatische Städte von vergleichbarer Bevölkerungszahl. Die gesamte Landfläche und die Bevölkerung innerhalb des dargestellten Gebietes ist am Kartenrand verzeichnet als ein weiteres Hilfsmittel für Vergleiche.

INTEGRAN ESTA SECCION 60 mapas de las áreas metropolitanas más importantes del mundo, a la escala de 1:300 000. Los mapas muestran los patrones de uso del suelo dentro de cada ciudad y en sus alrededores—la extensión total del conglomerado urbano, las principales áreas industriales, parques y reservas, y zonas boscosas. Aparecen los aeropuertos, así como muchos otros detalles de las redes de carreteras y ferrocarriles. Se seleccionaron también puntos de interés, como el Muelle de los Pescadores y el Barrio Chino de San Francisco, el monumento de Bienvenida de Jakarta, el Templo del Buda de Jade de Shanghai y la estatua del Cristo Redentor de Rio de Janeiro.

Los mapas incluyen los nombres y la ubicación de gran número de ciudades, poblaciones menores, suburbios, e inclusive barrios y distritos de algunas de las ciudades más importantes. Las características físicas sobresalientes, e incluso algunas elevaciones con o sin nombre, están indicados para dar una impresión general de la topografía local. Se omitió sin embargo el relieve sombreado, lo cual permite mostrar detalles como ríos y arroyos, parques, pistas de aterrizaje, edificios y monumentos públicos notables y los nombres de las calles principales. También están marcados los límites territoriales de las ciudades más grandes. Para la interpretación de los símbolos usados en estos mapas, véanse Leyendas para Mapas.

Los mapas de las ciudades más importantes del mundo varían generalmente en escala, y hasta ahora no han sido consistentes en diseño ni en contenido. En esta sección hemos hecho un esfuerzo de presentar las distintas áreas metropolitanas en la forma más uniforme posible, para facilitar sus comparaciones. Para algunas ciudades (la mayoría de ellas en Asia), no fué posible obtener de las propias fuentes material adecuado para la inclusión de ciertos datos, tales como las mayores áreas industriales y los límites municipales.

Los mapas de áreas metropolitanas se presentan por regiones, a excepción de unos cuantos que aparecen yuxtapuestos para facilitar la comparación entre grandes capitales, o centros comerciales, o ciudades ubicadas en contextos físicos similares. Muchas ciudades de América y algunas ciudades de Europa, por su baja densidad de población y su área extensa, requieren mapas más grandes que los ocupados por ciudades asiáticas con poblaciones comparables. Al margen de cada mapa se anotaron el área total y la población de territorio representado, lo cual facilita también las comparaciones.

CETTE PARTIE COMPREND 60 cartes des principales zones métropolitaines à l'échelle du 1:300 000e. Les cartes représentent les principaux types d'occupation du sol des villes et de leurs environs, c'est-à-dire de toute la zone urbanisée, les principales zones industrielles, les parcs et réserves naturelles, et les régions boisées. Les aéroports sont aussi représentés ainsi que de nombreux éléments des réseaux routier et ferroviaire. Certains lieux particulièrement intéressants sont indiqués, tels que le quai des pêcheurs et la ville chinoise à San Francisco, le monument de la Bienvenue à Jakarta, le temple du Bouddha de Jade à Shanghai et la statue du Christ Rédempteur à Rio de Janeiro.

Les cartes permettent de localiser un grand nombre de villes, villages et banlieues, ainsi que des quartiers de grandes villes. Les caractéristiques topographiques notables, comme les hauteurs sont indiqués même si elles ne portent pas de nom, pour donner une idée du site de l'aire métropolitaine. L'estompage du relief est omis cependant pour permettre de représenter cours d'eau, parcs, pistes d'envol des aéroports, monuments et bâtiments publics importants, noms des principales rues, ainsi que les limites municipales des grandes villes. (Pour la signification des symboles voir légende.)

En général, les échelles des cartes des grandes villes du monde varient considérablement, et jusqu'ici la présentation et le contenu de ces cartes n'étaient pas comparables. Dans cette partie de l'Atlas, un effort spécial a été fait pour représenter les diverses zones métropolitaines de manière aussi homogène que possible. Cependant, dans certains cas (en Asie notamment), les documents de base n'étaient pas assez complets pour qu'il fût possible d'inclure avec précision des données comme les zones industrielles et les limites municipales.

L'ordre de présentation est régional, avec des exceptions quand, pour faciliter les comparaisons, de grandes capitales de grands centres industriels ou encore des villes possédant un même environnement naturel, sont juxtaposés. Beaucoup de villes américaines et quelques villes européennes ont une faible densité de population et une étendue considérable; elles requièrent, par conséquent, des cartes plus grandes que des villes asiatiques de population similaire. La superficie et la population de chaque carte sont indiquées dans la marge.

INTEGRAM ESTA SEÇÃO 60 mapas das áreas metropolitanas mais importantes do mundo, em escala de 1:300 000. Os mapas mostram os principais tipos de uso do solo em cada cidade e seus arredores, seja, a extensão total da zona urbanizada, as principais áreas industriais, os parques e reservas, e as áreas florestais. Mostram os aeroportos, e muitos detalhes das redes rodo e ferroviária. Indicam também pontos de interesse, selecionados, tais como o Cais dos Pescadores e o Bairro Chinês de San Francisco, o monumento de Boasvindas, em Jakarta, o templo do Buda de Jade, em Shanghai, e a Estátua do Cristo Redentor, no Rio de Janeiro.

Os mapas apresentam o nome e a localização de grande número de cidades, vilas e subúrbios, e incluem bairros das cidades mais importantes. Foram indicadas as características físicas principais, inclusive elevações, com ou sem nome, com o objetivo de proporcionar uma idéia geral da topografia local. No entanto, omitiu-se o sombreado do relevo, para permitir a indicação de detalhes tais como cursos d'água, parques, pistas de aeroportos, edifícios públicos e monumentos notáveis, e os nomes das principais ruas, bem como os limites municipais das grandes cidades. Para a interpretação dos símbolos usados nesses mapas, ver as Legendas dos mapas.

Os mapas das cidades mais importantes do mundo variam consideravelmente, de modo geral, quanto à escala, e até o presente não são comparáveis nem na forma de apresentação nem no conteúdo. Nesta seção, fez-se um esforço especial para representar as diversas áreas metropolitanas do modo mais uniforme e comparável possível. No entanto, para algumas cidades, a maioria das quais da Ásia, não foi possível obter fontes fidedignas de informações, tais como áreas industriais principais e limites municipais.

A ordem de apresentação dos mapas das áreas metropolitanas é geralmente regional, exceto em certos casos em que, para facilidade de comparação, capitais ou centros industriais e cidades importantes localizadas em meio físico semelhante foram justapostos. Muitas cidades da América e algumas da Europa, por sua baixa densidade demográfica e áreas mais extensas, exigem mapas maiores que as cidades asiáticas de população comparável. À margem de cada mapa indicam-se a área terrestre e a população total do território representado, também para maior facilidade de comparação.

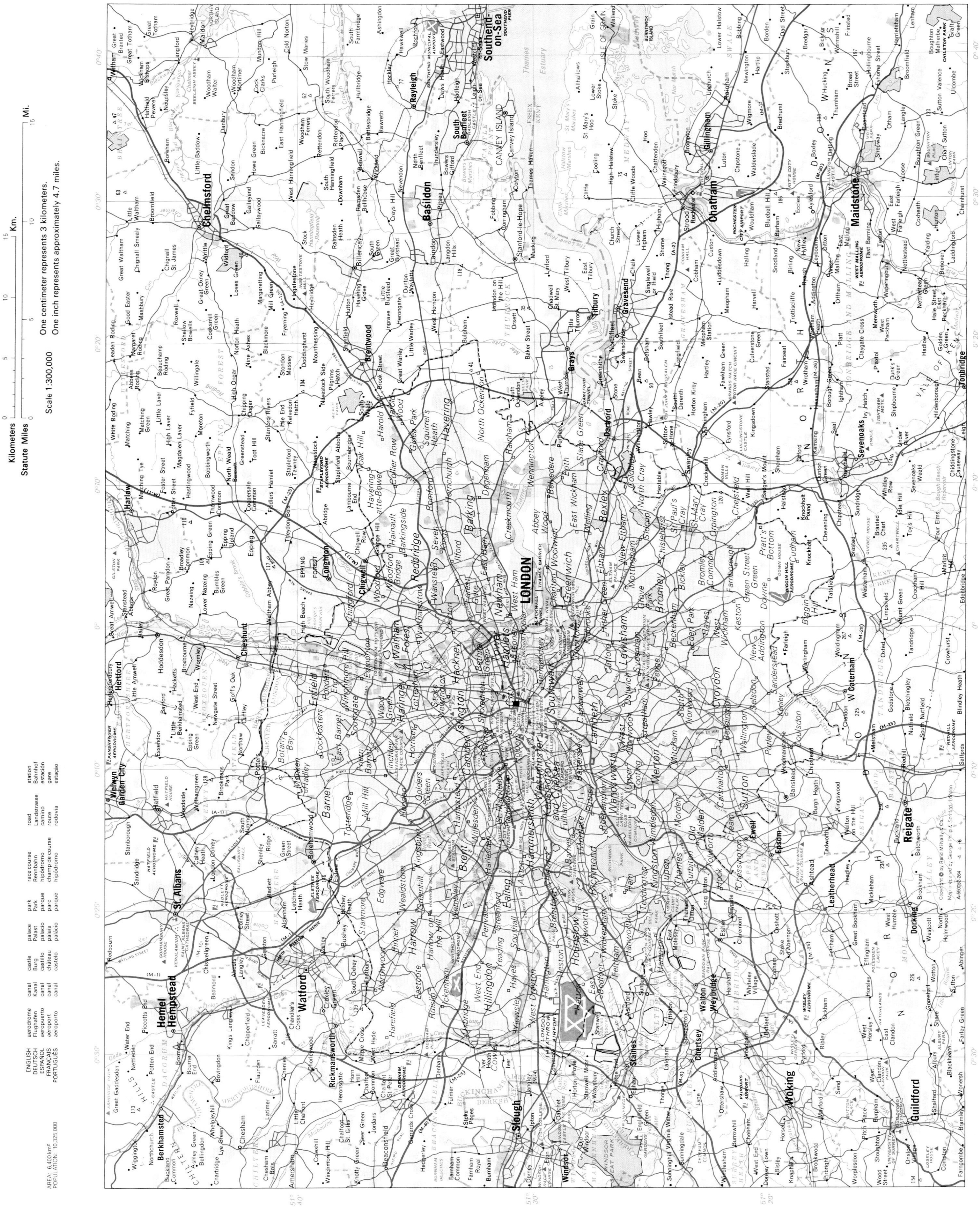
ENGLISH aerodrome canal castle palace park race course road station
DEUTSCH Flughafen Kanal Burg Palast Park Rennbahn Landstrasse Bahnhof
ESPAÑOL aeropuerto canal castillo palacio parque hipódromo camino estación
FRANÇAIS aéroport canal château palais parc champ de course route gare
PORTUGUÊS aeroporto canal castelo palácio parque hipódromo rodovia estação
Kilometers 0 5 10 15 Km.
Statute Miles 0 5 10 15 Mi.
Scale 1:300,000
One centimeter represents 3 kilometers.
One inch represents approximately 4.7 miles.
AREA 6,400 km²
POPULATION 10,325,000
Copyright by Rand McNally & Co.
Map prepared by George Philip & Son Ltd. London
LONDON
Southend-on-Sea
Chelmsford
Basildon
Rayleigh
Canvey Island
Thames Estuary
Isle of Grain
Tilbury
Grays
Gravesend
Dartford
Chatham
Rochester
Gillingham
Maidstone
Sevenoaks
Tonbridge
Reigate
Dorking
Leatherhead
Epsom
Croydon
Guildford
Woking
Weybridge
Chertsey
Staines
Windsor
Slough
Watford
Rickmansworth
Hemel Hempstead
Berkhamsted
St. Albans
Hertford
Welwyn Garden City
Harlow
Cheshunt
Epping
Loughton
Chigwell
Brentwood
Romford

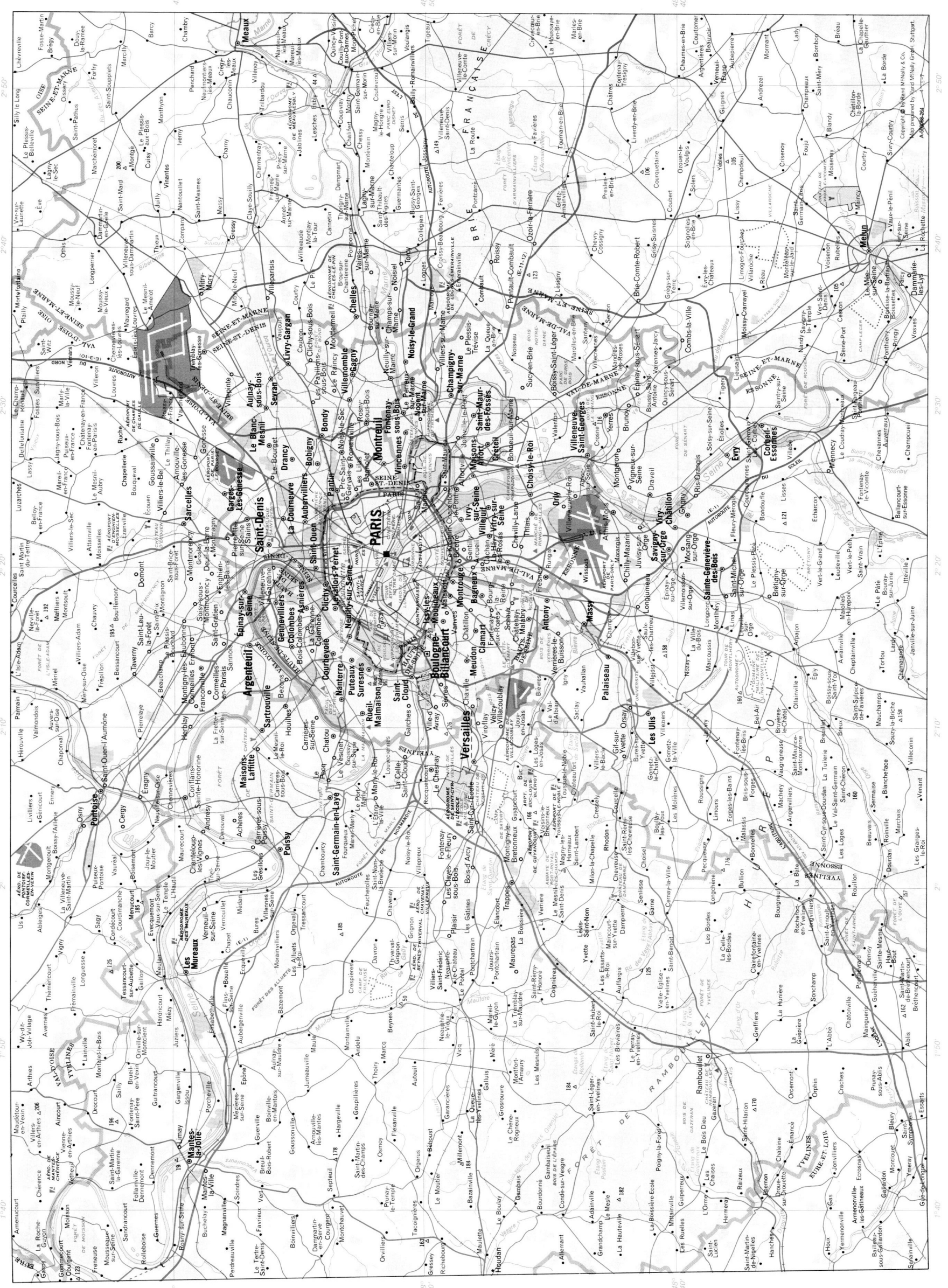

Map prepared by Rand McNally Graph. Gmbft, Stuttgart.
A-0528-291

Mi.

15

Km.

One centimeter represents 3 kilometers.
One inch represents approximately 4.7 miles.

Scale 1:300,000

Kilometers   15   10   5   0   5
Statute Miles   0   5   10   15

FRANCAIS	aerodrome	bois	château	etang	forêt	ruisseau
ENGLISH	aerodrome	woods	castle	pond	forest	brook
DEUTSCH	Flughafen	Gehölz	Burg	Teich	Wald	Bach
ESPAÑOL	aeropuerto	bosques	castillo	charca	bosque	arroyo
PORTUGUÊS	aeroporto	bosques	castelo	lagoa	floresta	arroio

AREA 6,500 km²
POPULATION 9,800,000

AREA: 5,650 km²
POPULATION: 6,275,000

ENGLISH	bank	canal	hill	moor	park	railway station	reservoir	tower
DEUTSCH	Bank	Kanal	Hügel	Ried	Park	Bahnhof	Stausee	Turm
ESPAÑOL	banco	canal	colina	páramo	parque	terminal ferroviaria	estanque	torre
FRANÇAIS	banc	canal	colline	lande	parc	gare	réservoir	tour
PORTUGUÊS	banco	canal	colina	charneca	parque	estação ferroviária	reservatório	torre

Kilometers 0 5 10 15 Km.
Statute Miles 0 5 10 15 Mi.

Scale 1:300,000

One centimeter represents 3 kilometers.
One inch represents approximately 4.7 miles.

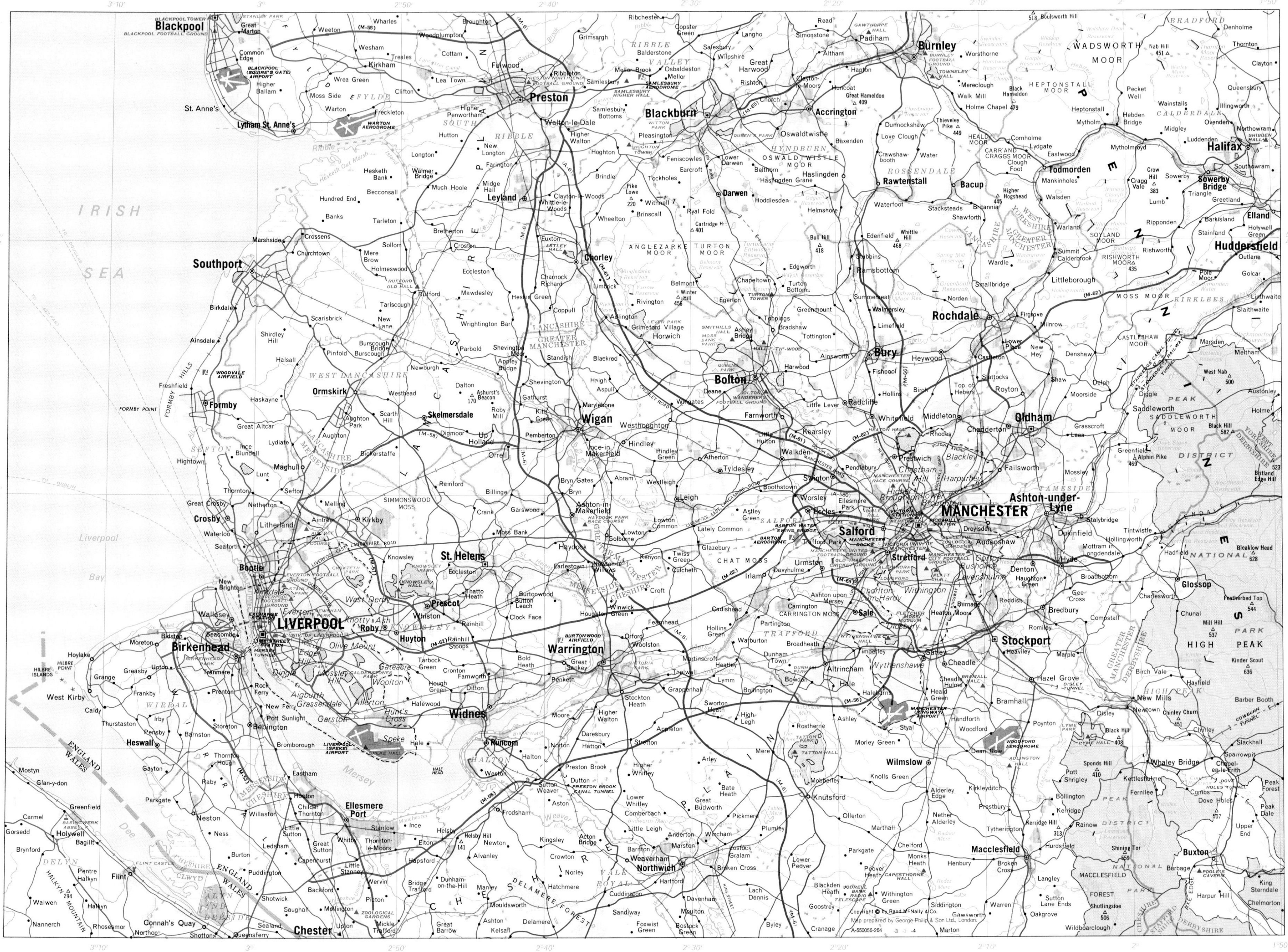

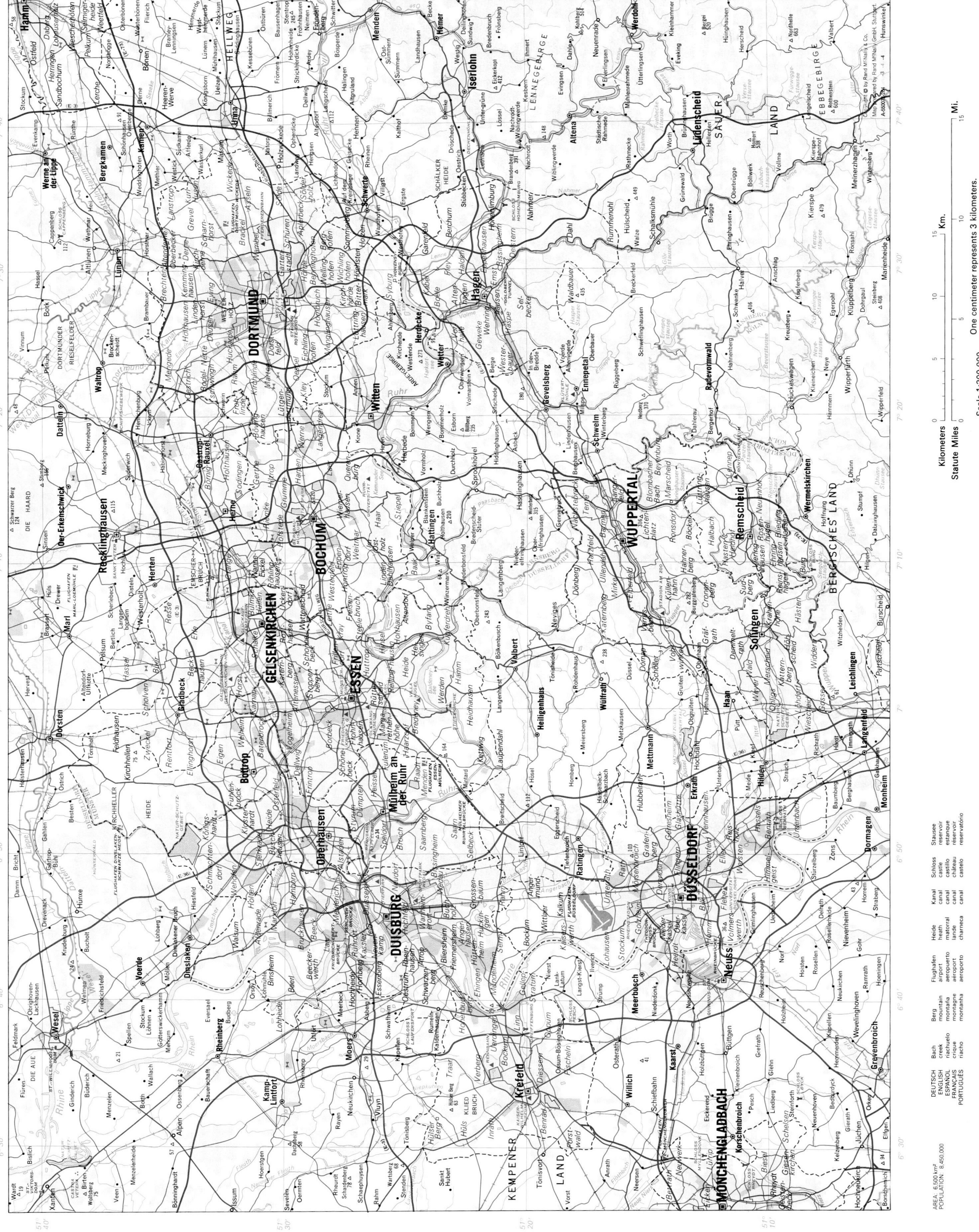

One centimeter represents 3 kilometers.
One inch represents approximately 4.7 miles.

Scale 1:300,000

AREA 6,500 km²
POPULATION 8,450,000

DEUTSCH	Bach	Berg	Flughafen	Heide	Kanal	Schloss	Stausee
ENGLISH	creek	mountain	airport	heath	canal	castle	reservoir
ESPAÑOL	riachuelo	montaña	aeropuerto	matorral	canal	castillo	estanque
FRANÇAIS	crique	montagne	aéroport	lande	canal	château	réservoir
PORTUGUÊS	riacho	montanha	aeroporto	charneca	canal	castelo	reservatório

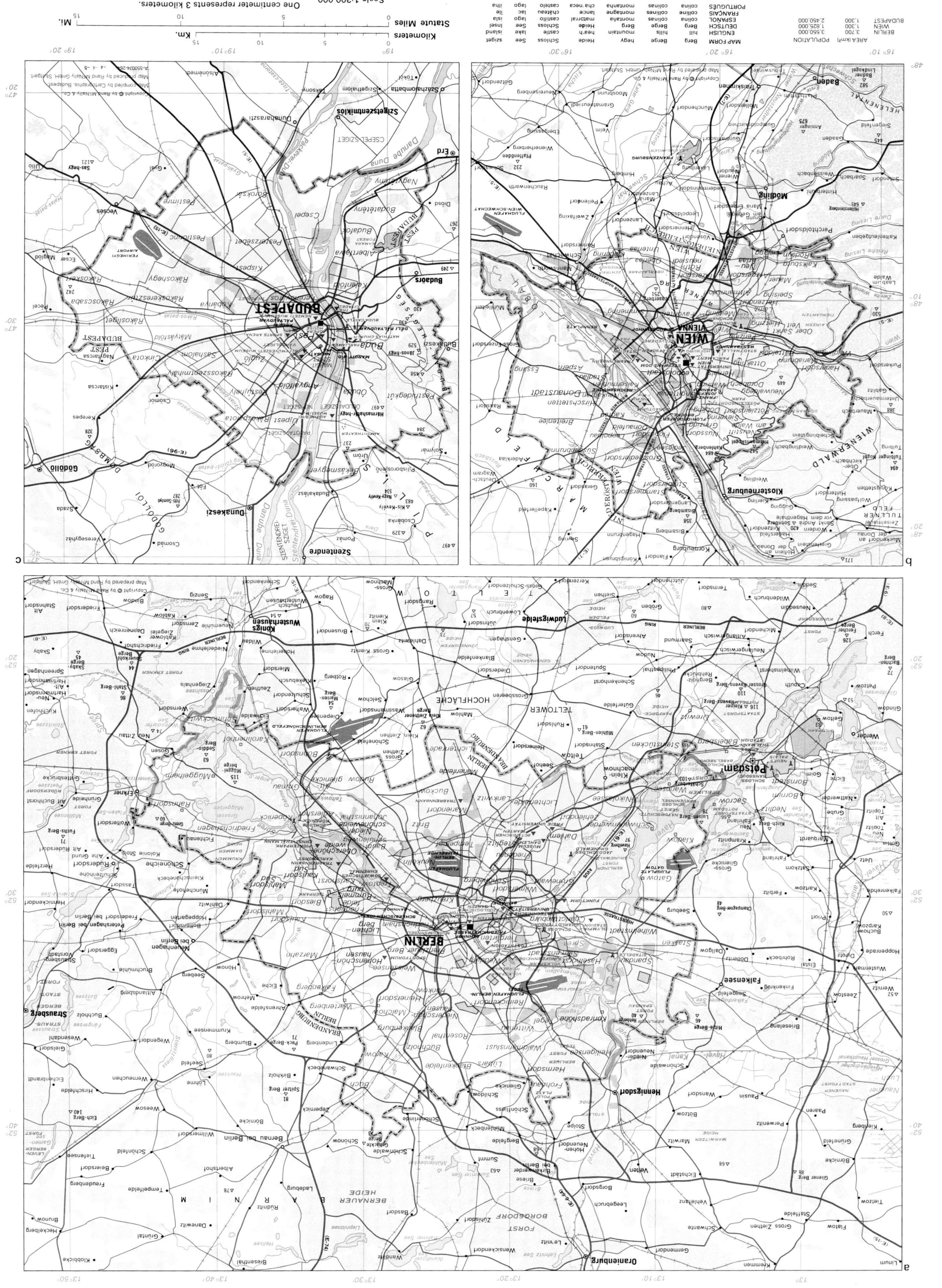

MAP FORM	ENGLISH	DEUTSCH	ESPAÑOL	FRANÇAIS	PORTUGUÊS
hegy	Berge	Berg	montaña	montagne	montanha
Heide	Heide	Heide	landa	lande	charneca
Schloss	castle	Schloss	castillo	château	castelo
See	lake	See	lago	lac	lago
Berg	hill	Berg	colina	colline	colina
hers'h	mountain	Berge	colinas	collines	colinas
island	island	Insel	isla	île	ilha
sziget	island	Insel	isla	île	ilha

	AREA (km²)	POPULATION
BERLIN	3,700	3,660,000
WIEN	1,300	1,825,000
BUDAPEST	1,300	2,450,000

Scale 1:300,000
One centimeter represents 3 kilometers.
One inch represents approximately 4.7 miles.

Kilometers

Statute Miles

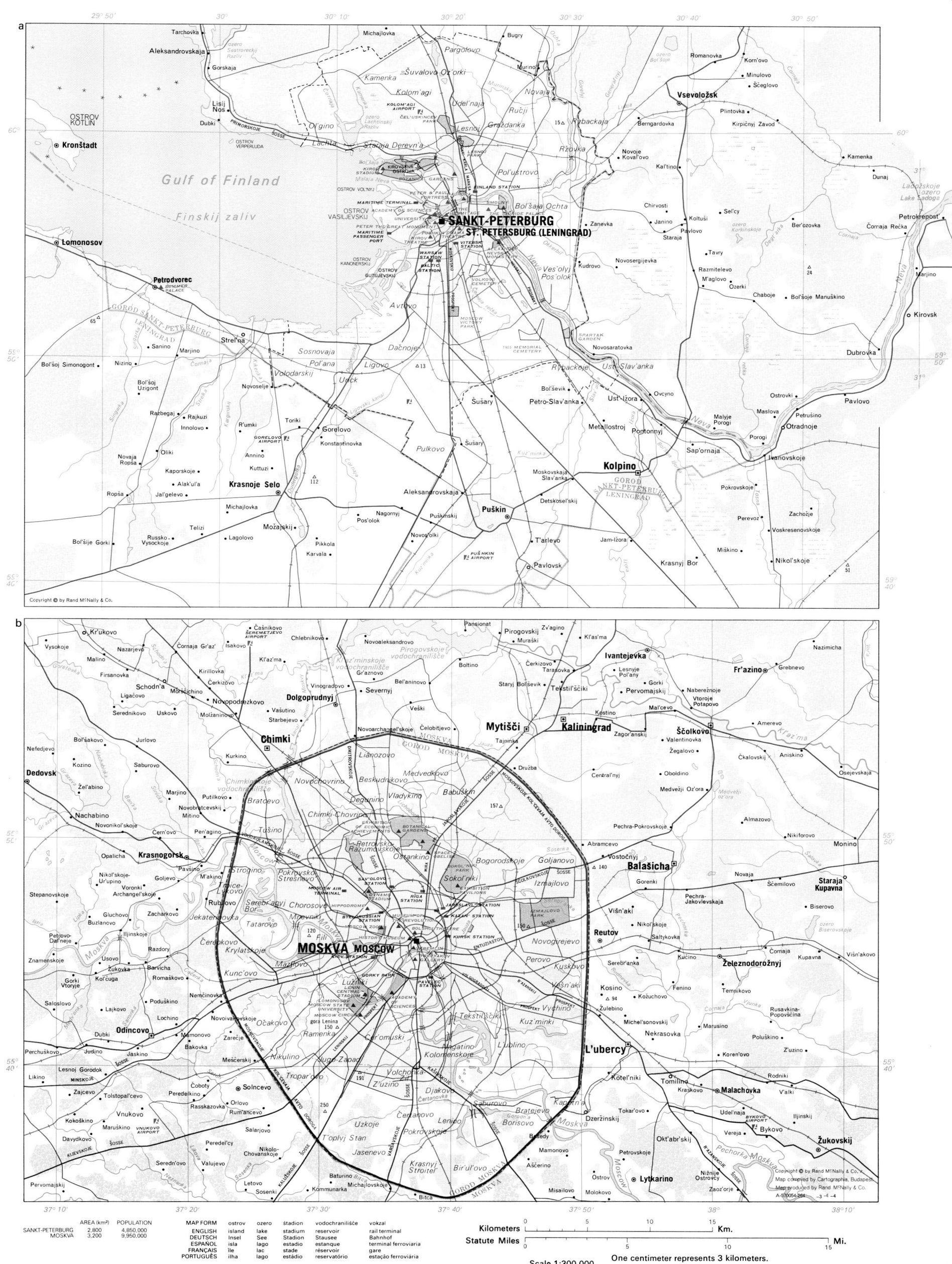

	AREA (km²)	POPULATION
SANKT-PETERBURG	2,800	4,850,000
MOSKVA	3,200	9,950,000

MAP FORM					
ENGLISH	ostrov island	ozero lake	stadion stadium	vodochranilišče reservoir	vokzal rail terminal
DEUTSCH	Insel	See	Stadion	Stausee	Bahnhof
ESPAÑOL	isla	lago	estadio	estanque	terminal ferroviaria
FRANÇAIS	île	lac	stade	réservoir	gare
PORTUGUÊS	ilha	lago	estádio	reservatório	estação ferroviária

Kilometers

Statute Miles

Scale 1:300,000

One centimeter represents 3 kilometers.
One inch represents approximately 4.7 miles.

	AREA (km²)	POPULATION
MADRID	1,250	3,875,000
MILANO	1,900	3,975,000
LISBOA	1,150	2,150,000
BARCELONA	950	3,825,000

MAP FORM	aeroporto	arroyo	estación	ponta	ribeira	riera
ENGLISH	airport	brook	station	point	creek	creek
DEUTSCH	Flughafen	Bach	Bahnhof	Landspitze	Bach	Bach
ESPAÑOL	aeropuerto	arroyo	estación	punta	riachuelo	riera
FRANÇAIS	aéroport	ruisseau	gare	pointe	crique	crique
PORTUGUÊS	aeroporto	arroio	estação	ponta	riacho	riacho

Kilometers 0 5 10 15 Km.

Statute Miles 0 5 10 15 Mi.

Scale 1:300,000

One centimeter represents 3 kilometers.

One inch represents approximately 4.7 miles

a

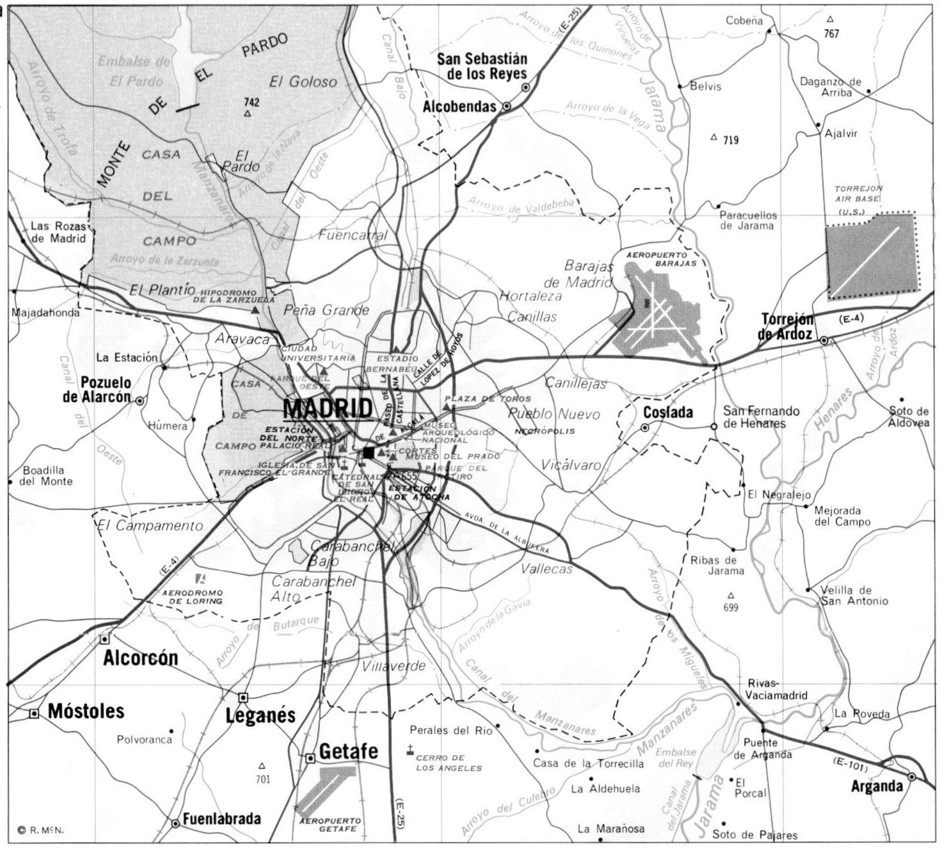

b

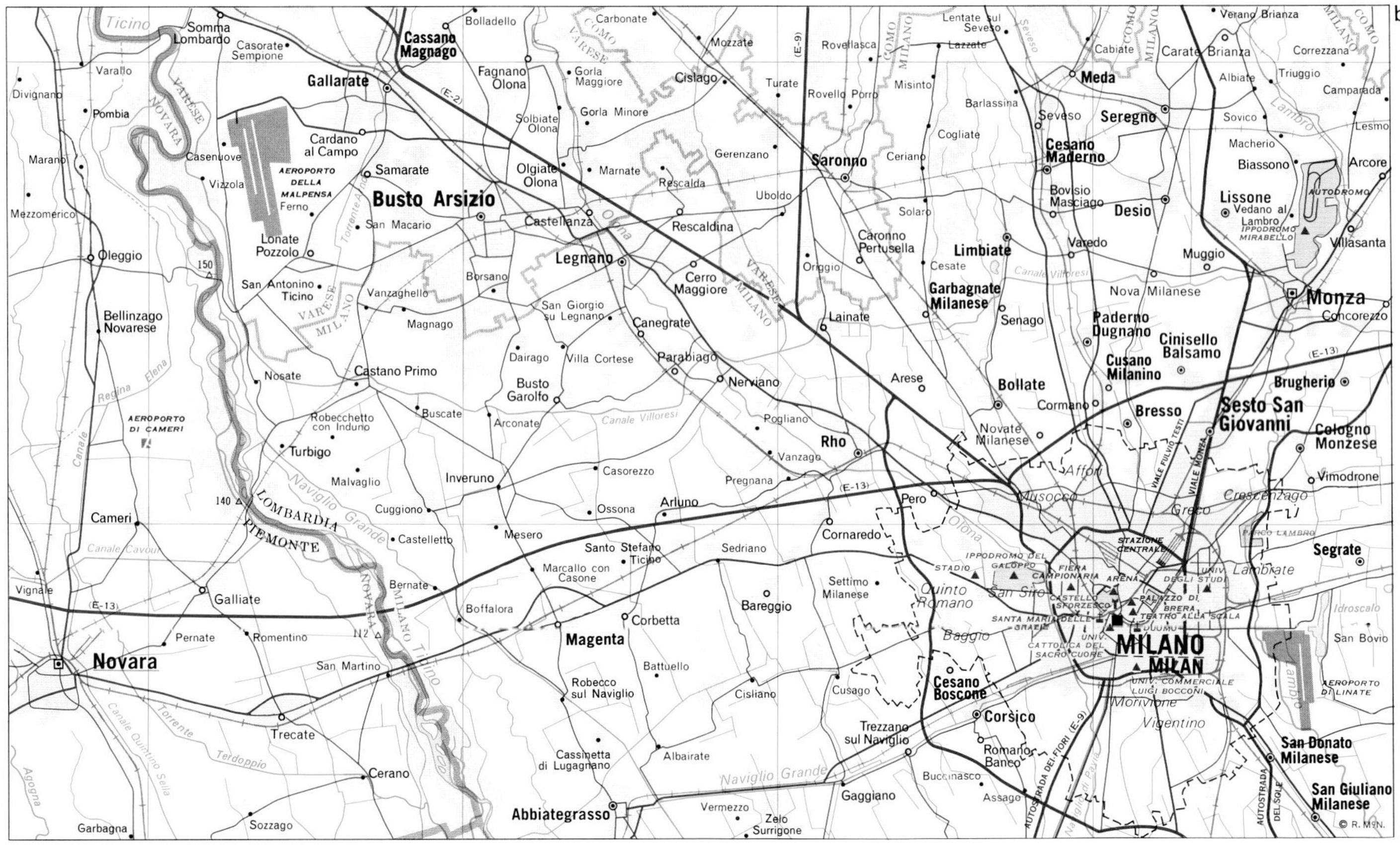

c

d

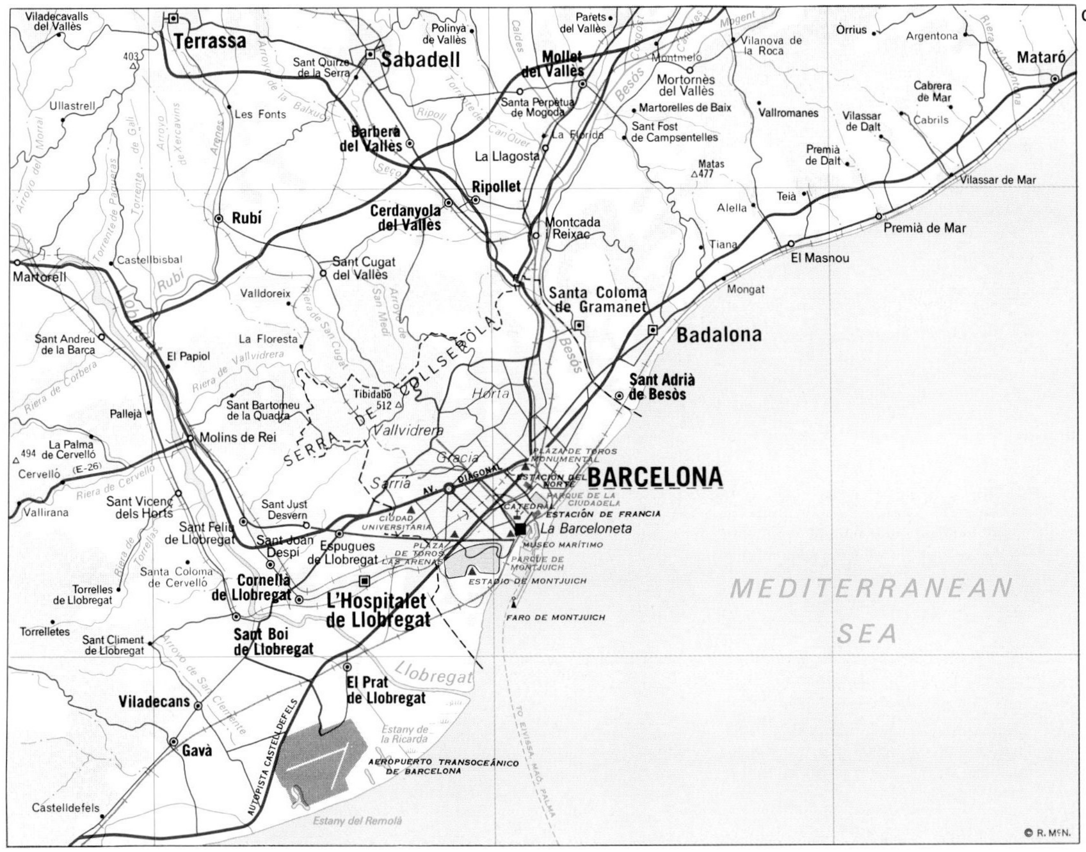

a

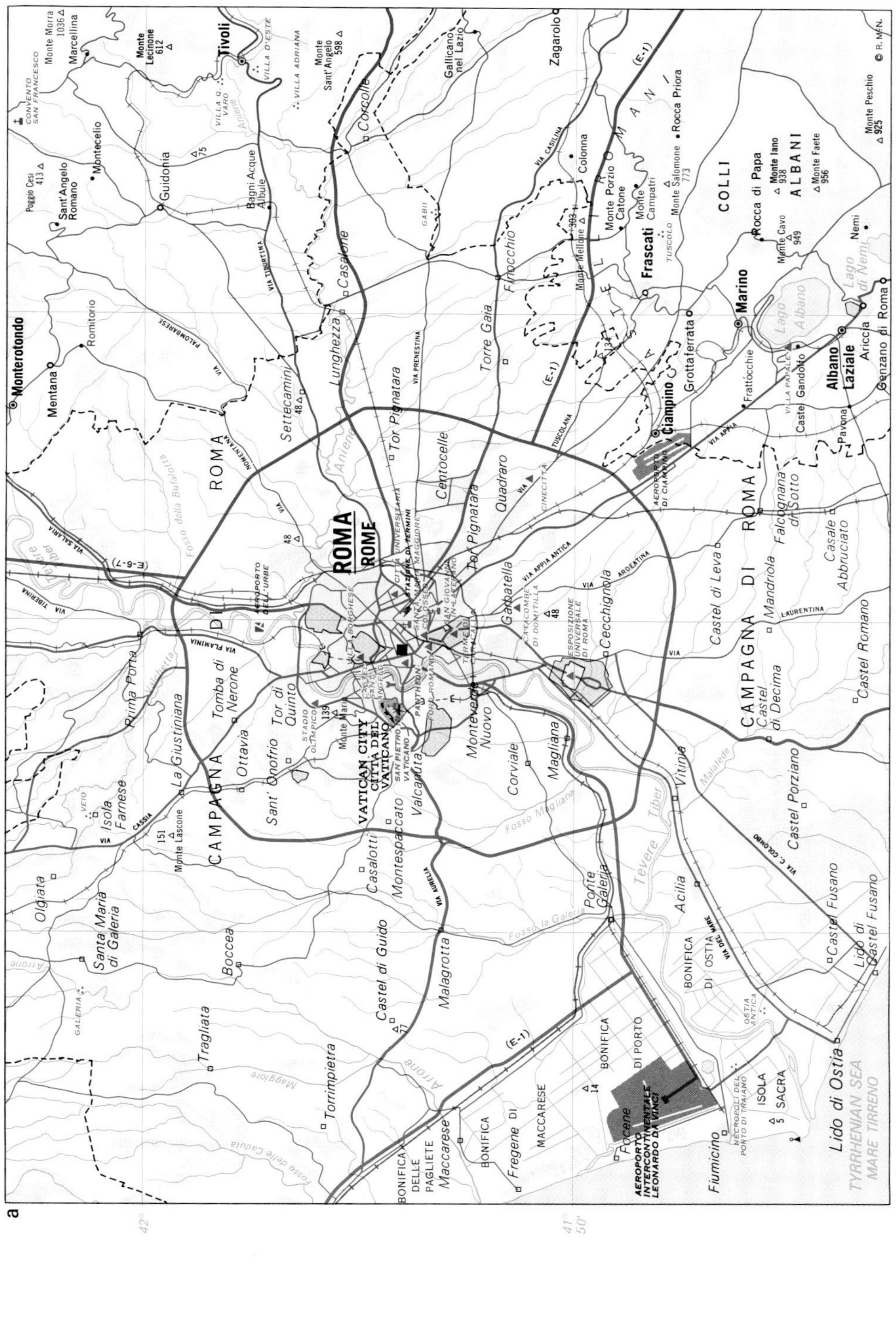

b

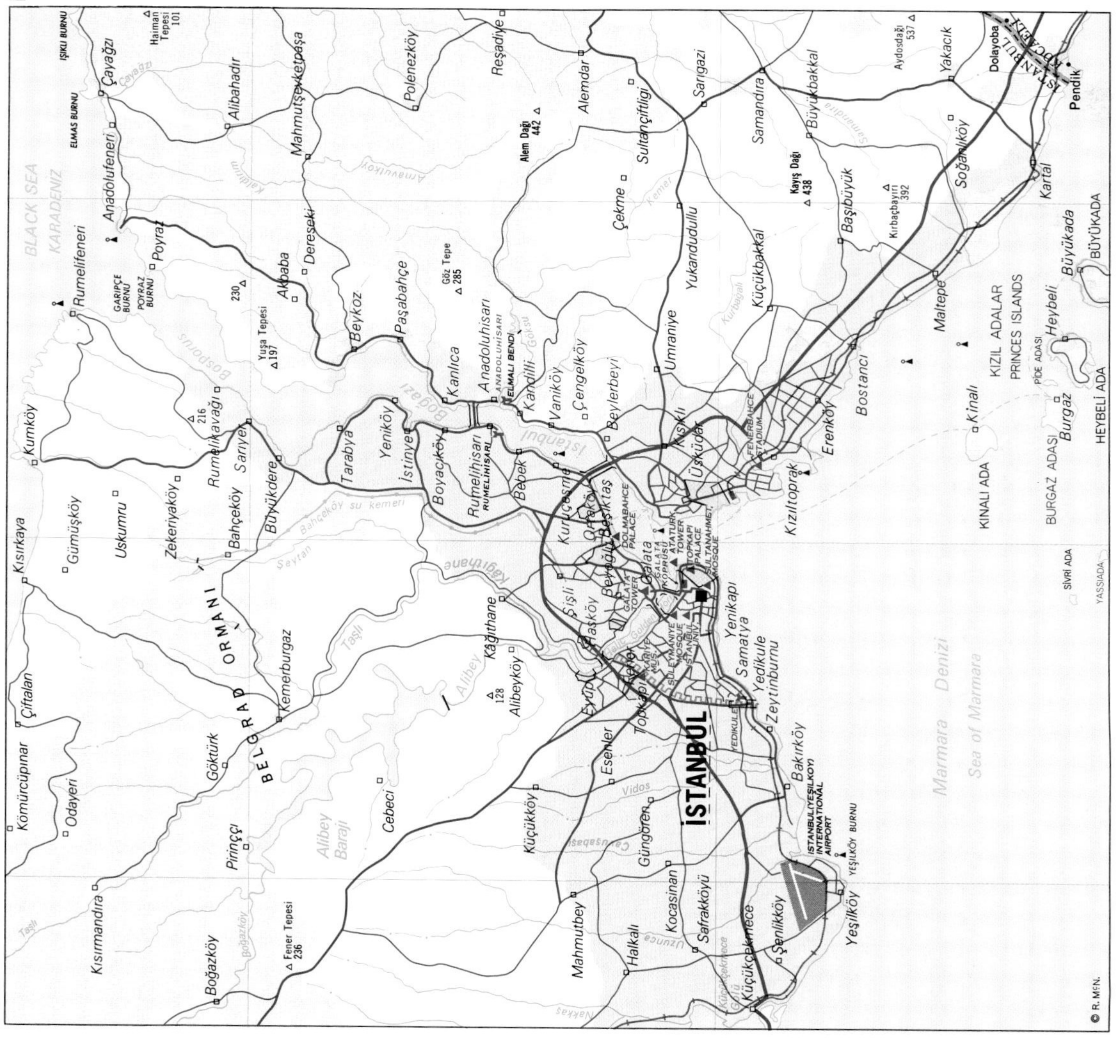

c

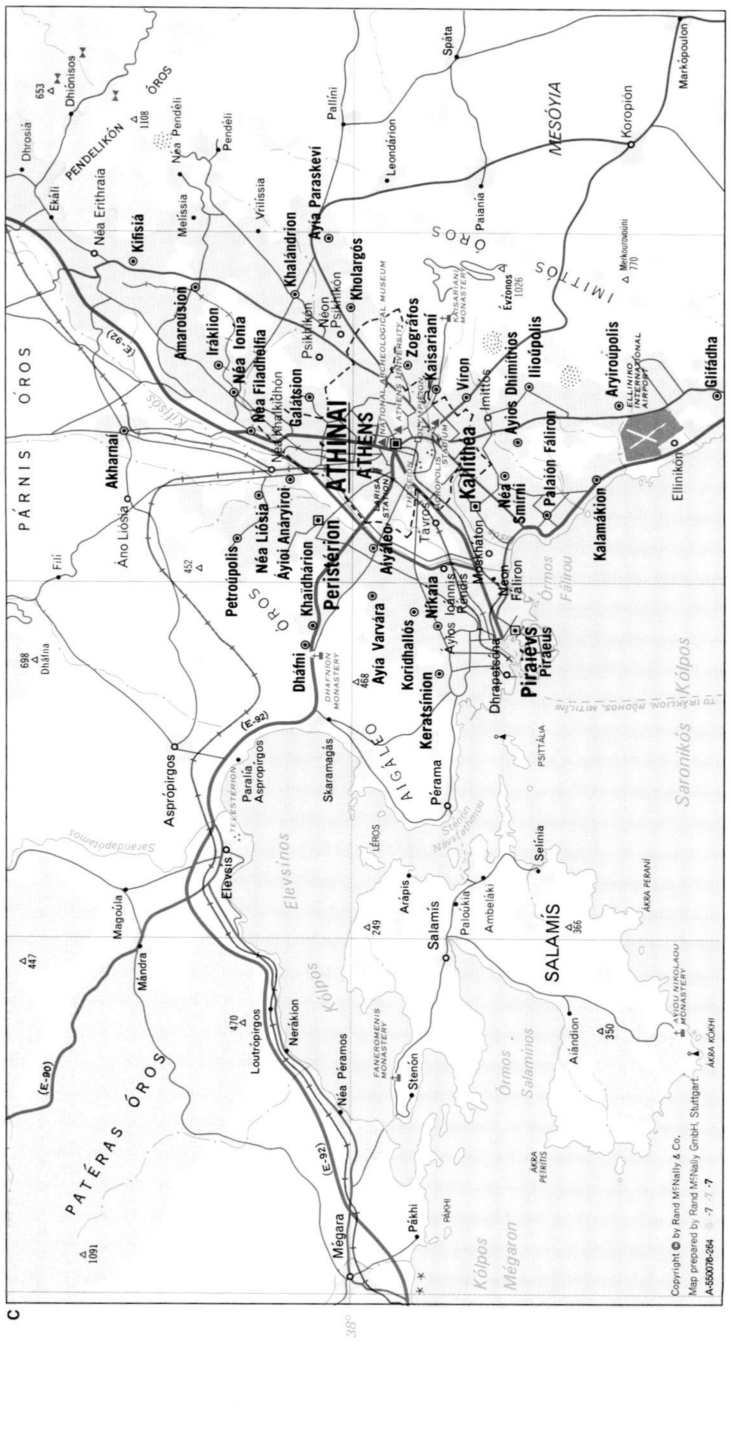

d

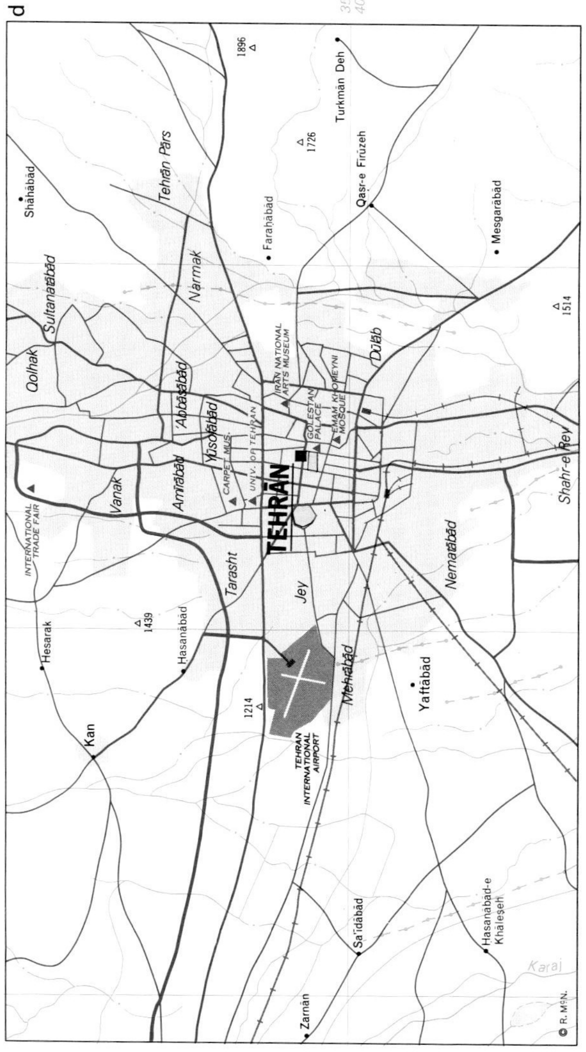

Kilometers 0 5 10 15 Km.
Statute Miles 0 5 10 15 Mi.

Scale 1:300,000

One centimeter represents 3 kilometers.
One inch represents approximately 4.7 miles.

	AREA (km²)	POPULATION
RŌMA	2,000	3,250,000
ATHÍNAI	1,100	3,350,000
İSTANBUL	1,300	4,300,000
TEHRĀN	950	5,200,000

MAP FORM	ada	burnu	camii	deresi	fosso	moní	monte
ENGLISH	island	cape	mosque	river	brook	monastery	mount
DEUTSCH	Insel	Kap	Moschee	Fluss	Bach	Kloster	Berg
ESPAÑOL	isla	cabo	mezquita	río	arroyo	monasterio	monte
FRANÇAIS	île	cap	mosquée	rivière	ruisseau	monastère	mont
PORTUGUÊS	ilha	cabo	mesquita	rio	arroio	mosteiro	monte

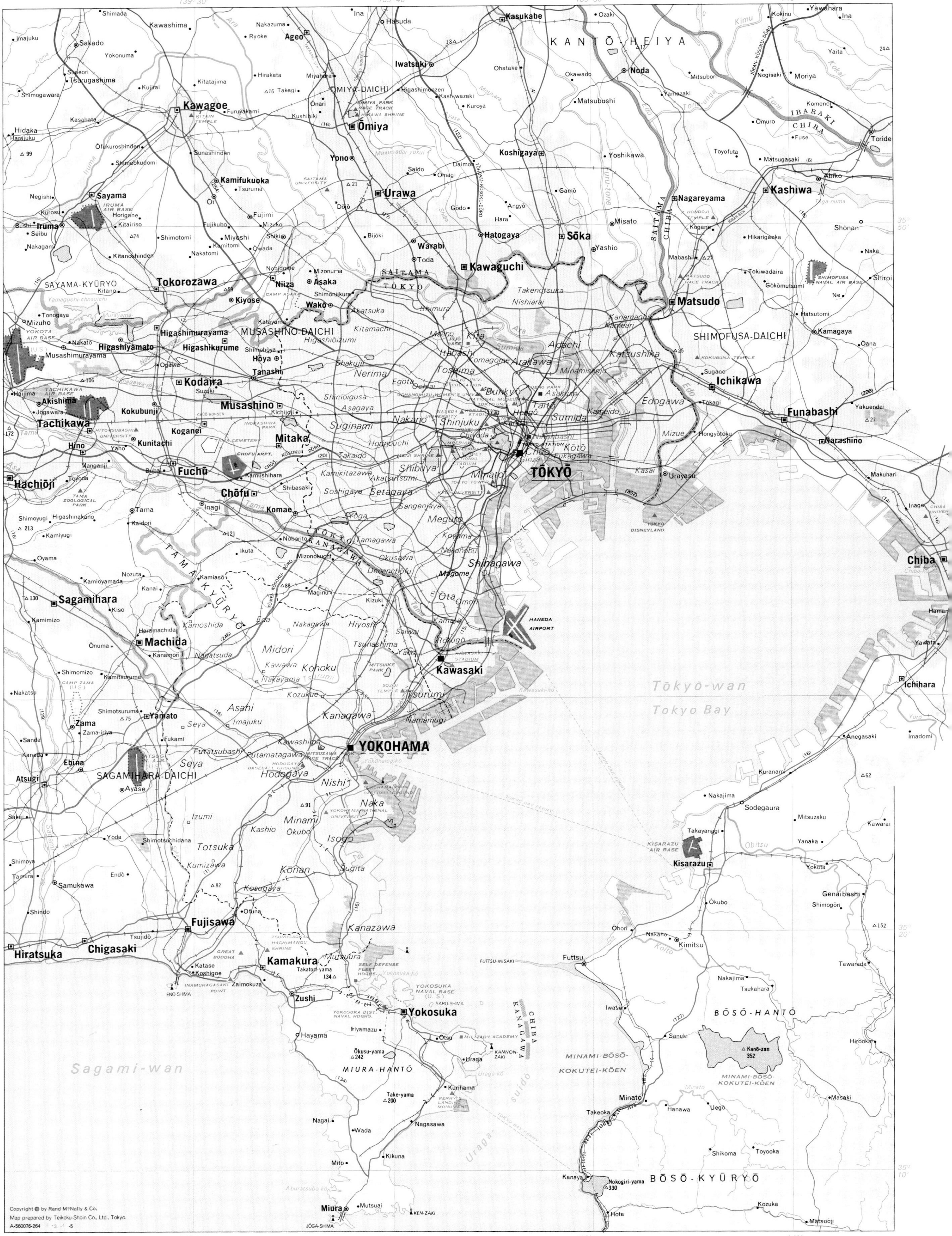

AREA (km²): 5,350
POPULATION: 24,350,000

MAP FORM	air base	camp	-daichi	-kō	-shima	temple	-yama
ENGLISH	air base	camp	plateau	harbor	island	temple	mountain
DEUTSCH	Luftstützpunkt	Lager	Hochebene	Hafen	Insel	Tempel	Berg
ESPAÑOL	base aérea	campo	meseta	puerto	isla	templo	montaña
FRANÇAIS	base aérienne	camp	plateau	port	île	temple	montagne
PORTUGUÊS	base aérea	campo	planalto	porto	ilha	templo	montanha

Kilometers 0 5 10 15 Km.
Statute Miles 0 5 10 15 Mi.

Scale 1:300,000
One centimeter represents 3 kilometers.
One inch represents approximately 4.7 miles.

a

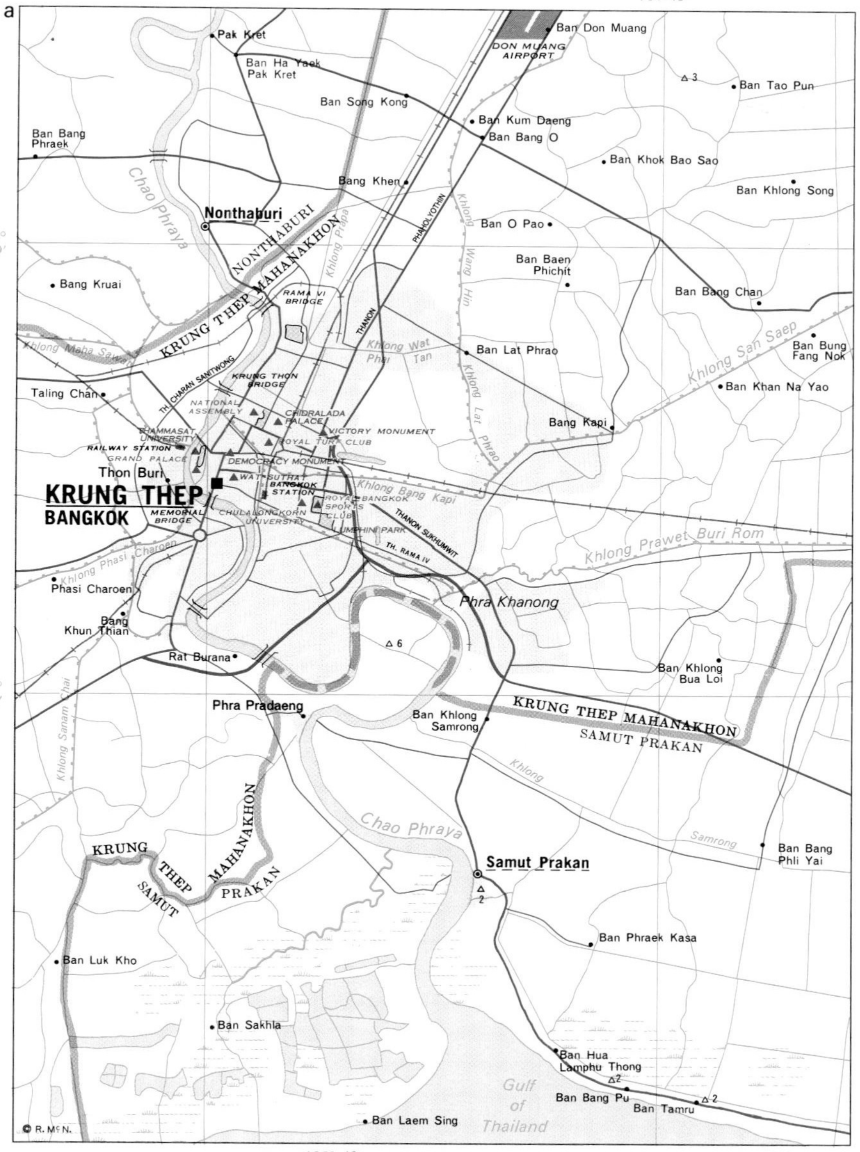

b

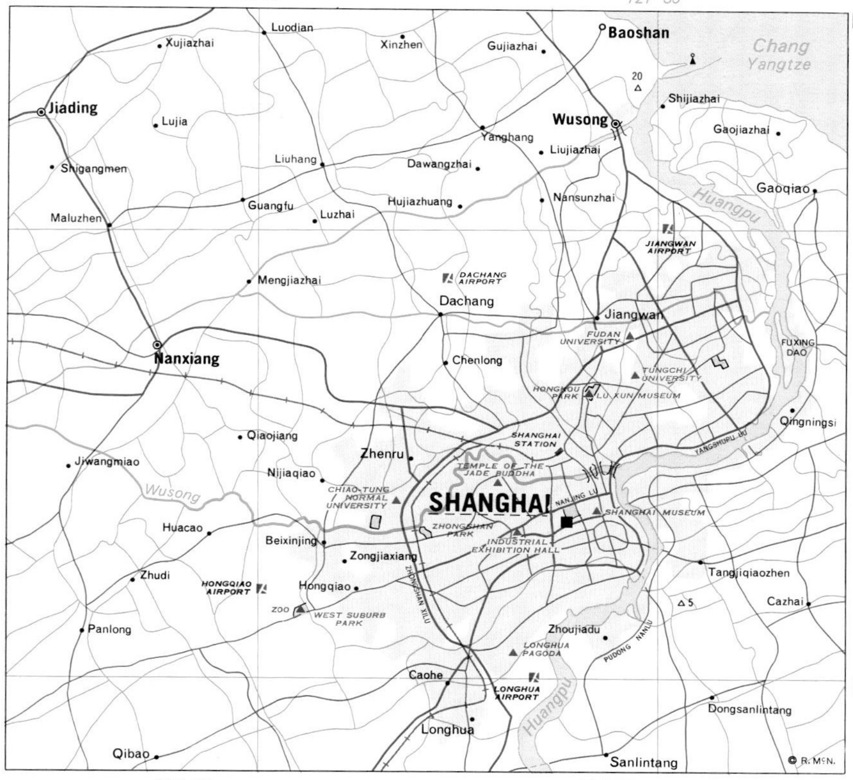

c

d

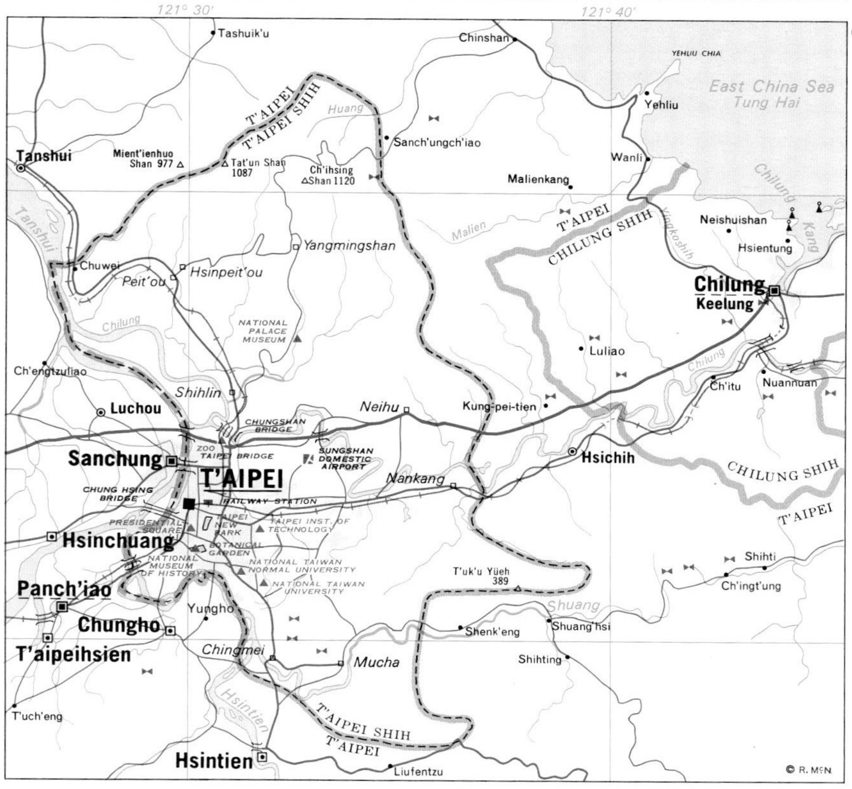

e

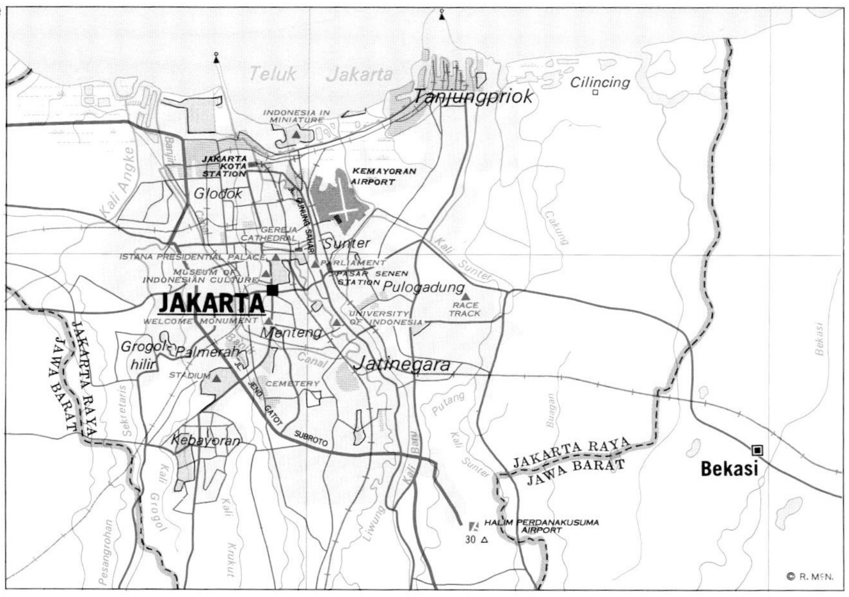

f

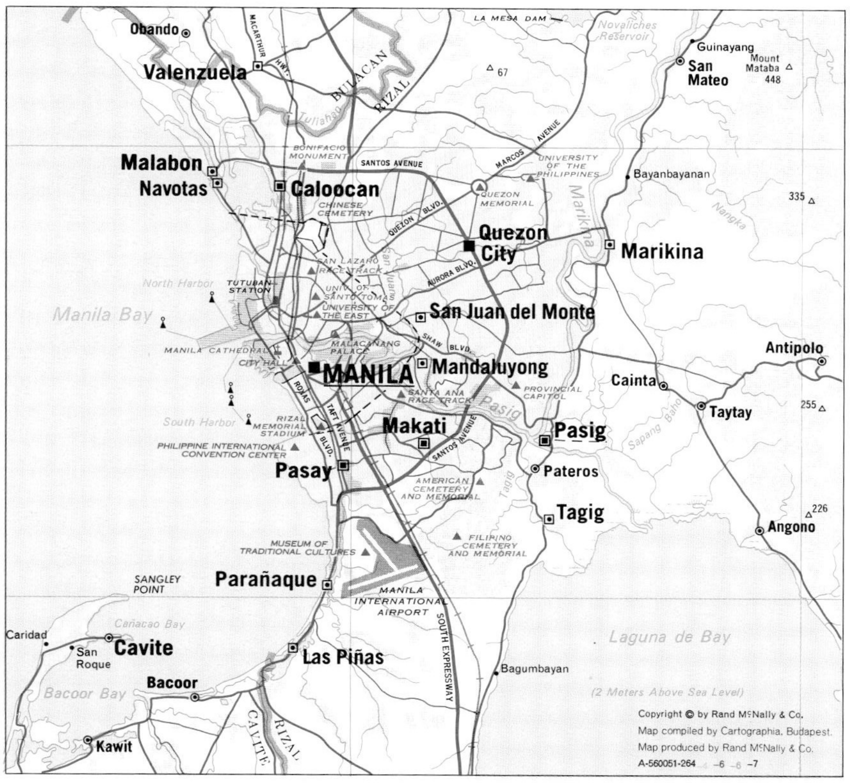

	AREA (km²)	POPULATION
KRUNG THEP (BANGKOK)	1,450	5,300,000
SAI-GON	750	2,400,000
JAKARTA	700	6,450,000
SHANGHAI	1,000	8,400,000
T'AIPEI	950	4,125,000
MANILA	650	5,900,000

MAP FORM	kali	khlong	monument	shan
ENGLISH	stream	stream	monument	mountain
DEUTSCH	Bach	Bach	Denkmal	Berg
ESPAÑOL	corriente de agua	corriente de agua	monumento	montaña
FRANÇAIS	cours d'eau	cours d'eau	monument	montagne
PORTUGUÊS	corrente de água	corrente de água	monumento	montanha

Kilometers 0 5 10 15 Km.

Statute Miles 0 5 10 15 Mi.

Scale 1:300,000

One centimeter represents 3 kilometers.
One inch represents approximately 4.7 miles.

AREA: 5,350 km²
POPULATION: 15,050,000

MAP FORM	-ko	-san	-sanchi	-tōge	-yama	-zan
ENGLISH	lake	mountain	mountains	pass	mountain	mountain
DEUTSCH	See	Berg	Berge	Pass	Berg	Berg
ESPAÑOL	lago	montaña	montañas	paso	montaña	montaña
FRANÇAIS	lac	montagne	montagnes	col	montagne	montagne
PORTUGUÊS	lago	montanha	montanhas	passo	montanha	montanha

Kilometers 0 5 10 15 Km.
Statute Miles 0 5 10 15 Mi.
Scale 1:300,000
One centimeter represents 3 kilometers.
One inch represents approximately 4.7 miles.

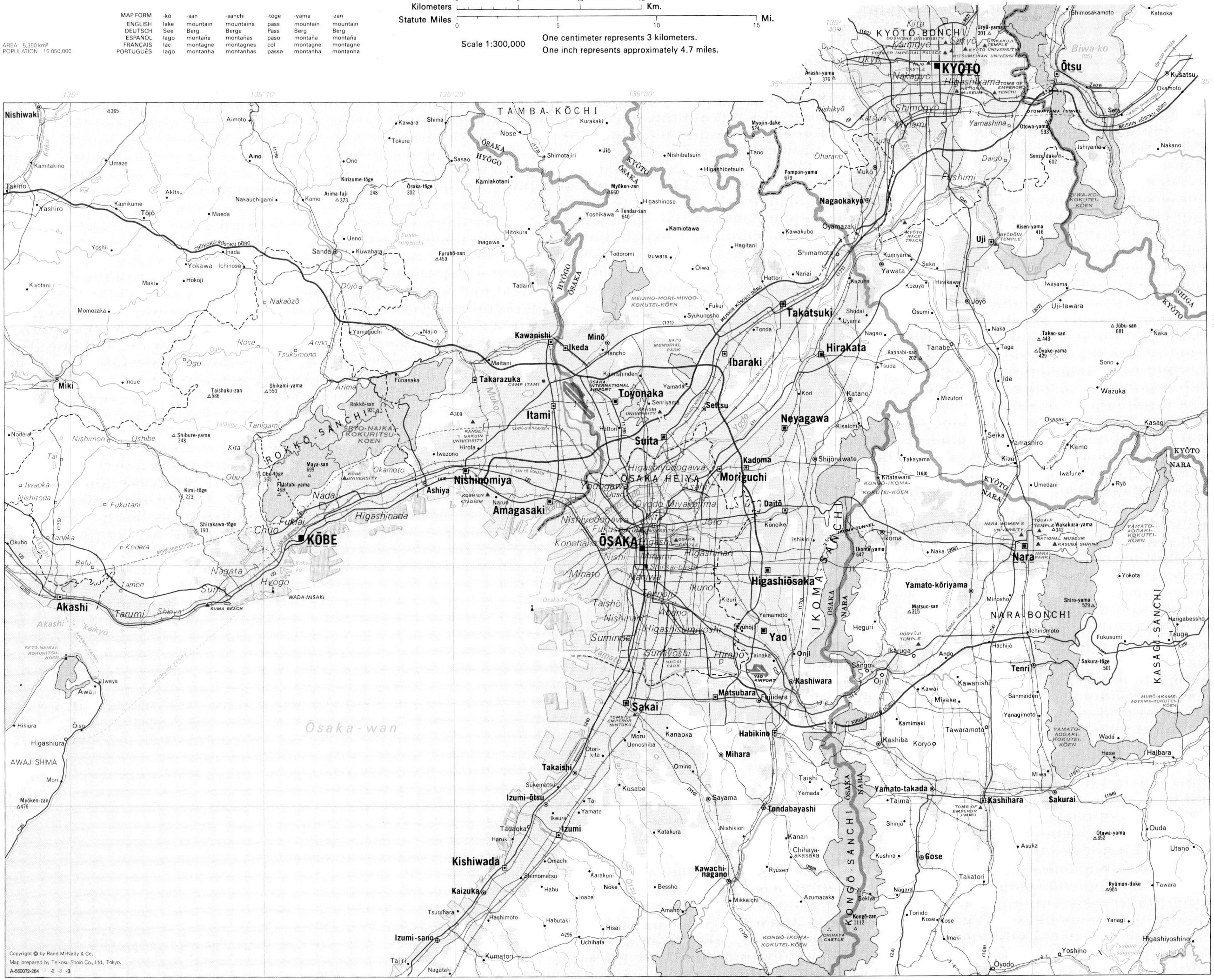

Map prepared by Teikoku-Shoin Co., Ltd., Tokyo.
A-560072-264 -2 -3 -3

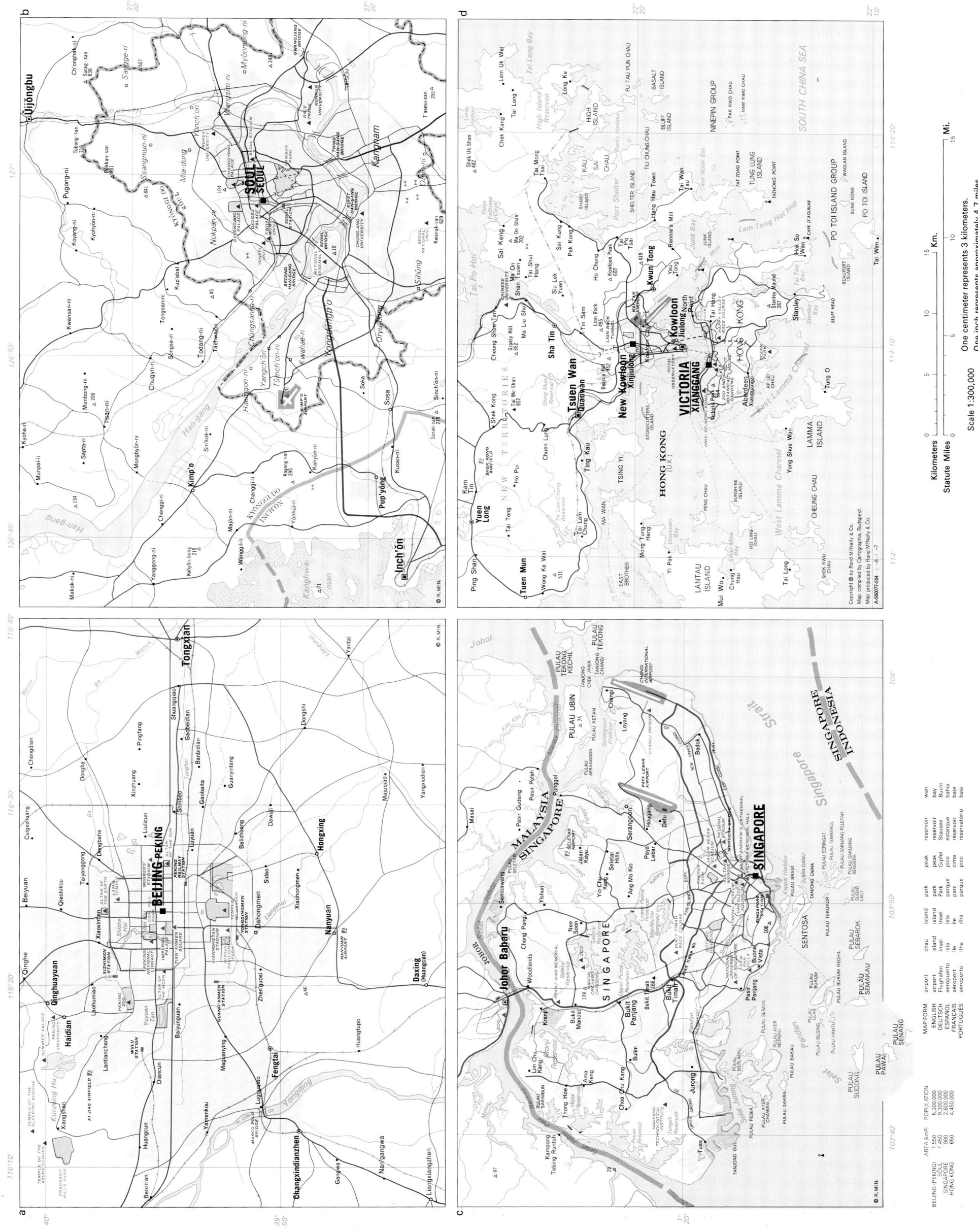

b (Sŏul area map)

Ŭijŏngbu

Ch'ŏngha-ni
Sŏrak 538
Sanggye-ni
△507
△ Sanggok-ni
Myŏnmŏng-ni
GWANGNŬNG
MONASTERY
Tobong-san
Pugong-ni △ 834
△ Pohan-san 651
Kwansan-ni
Koyang-ni
Kyohŭigon-ni
Kwanak-san 629
Kup'abal
△ 45
△ 10
Songsu-ni
Kwangju-ni

SŎUL
△104

Todang-ni
Tongsan-ni

Kyoha-ri
Munbong-ni
△ 209
Songga-ri
Taehwaibo
△ 194
Kimp'o
Kimp'o
AIRPORT
Sosa
Sinch'ŏn-ri
Sorae 138 △
278
Kanghwa Do

Munsan-ni
Hŭngbi-bong 215 △
Mongch'on-ni
Yangdong-ni
Changgi-ri
Changja-ri

KYŎNGGI DO
INCH'ŎN
Kahyŏn-bong 399 △
Kahyŏ-ri
Kusan-ni

Makkol-ni

Wŏnjŏ-ni

Pup'yŏng

Inch'ŏn

a (Beijing/Peking area map)

Changlin
Wenyu
Tongxian

Changgudian
Beiyuan
Dongba
Qieshikou
Cuigezhuang
Liulicun
Shibao
Tuanjiehu
Gaobeidian
Pingfang
Banbidian
Shuangqiao

Qinghuayuan
Xiaodian
Xinzhuang
Dongshi
Guanyintang
Majuqiao
Yangqiao

Haidian
BEIJING • PEKING
Luyuan
Balizhuang
Dawijji

Lihuimiao
Lantianchang
Zhen'guosi
Hongxing

Maquanying
Daxing
(Huangcun)

Fengtai
Huangcun
Zhoukoudian
Changxindianzhen
Luigouqiao
Nangangwa
△71
△46

Taihenkou
Banxin
Gangwa
Luangxiangzhen
Nanjangwa

d (Hong Kong area map)

SOUTH CHINA SEA

Lam Uk Wei
Long Ke
Tai Long
High Island
Tai Mong
Tsai
Chek Kang
Shek Uk Shan
△482
Sai Kung
Ma Yau Tong
HIGH
ISLAND

NINEPIN
GROUP
BASALT
ISLAND
BLUFF
ISLAND
FU TAU PUN CHAU
PAK KWO CHAU
NAM KWO CHAU

Port Shelter
SHELTER ISLAND
KAU SAI CHAU

Sha Tin
Cheung Sha Tin
Grassy Hill △ 652
Kowloon Peak 602
Shatin
Siu Lek Yuen
Ho Chung
Tin Sam
Lin Rock

Kwun Tong

TUNG LUNG ISLAND
FAT TONG POINT

New Kowloon
Xinjiulong
Kowloon
Jiulong
North Point
KOWLOON CITY

Tsuen Wan
Quanwan

VICTORIA
XIANGGANG

HONG KONG

HONG KONG (U.K.)

Yuen Long

NEW TERRITORIES

Ping Shan
Kam Tin

Tuen Mun
△511

Mong Tung Hang

LANTAU ISLAND
Mui Wo

Stanley
△387

LAMMA ISLAND

East Lamma Channel
West Lamma Channel

CHEUNG CHAU

PO TOI ISLAND GROUP

c (Singapore area map)

Johor
PULAU TEKONG KECHIL
PULAU TEKONG
CHANGI
CHANGI INTERNATIONAL AIRPORT

PULAU UBIN
PULAU KETAM

MALAYSIA
SINGAPORE

Masai
Pasir Gudang

Johor Baharu

Woodlands
Kranji
Nee Soon
Chong Pang
Seletar Hills
Pang
Yio Chu Kang
Ang Mo Kio
Paya Lebar
Serangoon
Bedok

SINGAPORE

Bukit Panjang
Bukit Timah
Bukit Batok

SENTOSA

PULAU SEBAROK

Jurong
Pasir Panjang

Strait Singapore

SINGAPORE
INDONESIA

Scale 1:300,000

Kilometers
Statute Miles

One centimeter represents 3 kilometers.
One inch represents approximately 4.7 miles.

	AREA (km²)	POPULATION
BEIJING (PEKING)	1,550	5,300,000
SŎUL	1,450	9,300,000
SINGAPORE	900	2,600,000
HONG KONG	660	4,450,000

MAP FORM						
ENGLISH	airport	island	chau	park	peak	reservoir	wan
DEUTSCH	Flughafen	Insel	Insel	Park	Gipfel	Stausee	Bucht
ESPAÑOL	aeropuerto	isla	isla	parque	pico	embalse	bahía
FRANÇAIS	aéroport	île	île	parc	cime	réservoir	baie
PORTUGUÊS	aeroporto	ilha	ilha	parque	pico	reservatório	baía

© by Rand McNally & Co.
Map compiled by Cartographia, Budapest.
Map produced by Rand McNally & Co.
A-590077-264

	AREA (km²)	POPULATION
DELHI	1,400	5,500,000
BOMBAY	1,050	8,250,000
CALCUTTA	3,100	11,200,000

ENGLISH	airport	dock	island	lake	point	railroad station	road	temple
DEUTSCH	Flughafen	Dock	Insel	See	Punkt	Bahnhof	Landstrasse	Tempel
ESPAÑOL	aeropuerto	muelle	isla	lago	punta	terminal ferroviaria	camino	templo
FRANÇAIS	aéroport	quai	île	lac	pointe	gare	route	temple
PORTUGUÊS	aeroporto	cais	ilha	lago	ponta	estação ferroviária	rodovia	templo

Kilometers 0 5 10 15 Km.
Statute Miles 0 5 10 15 Mi.

Scale 1:300,000

One centimeter represents 3 kilometers.
One inch represents approximately 4.7 miles.

a

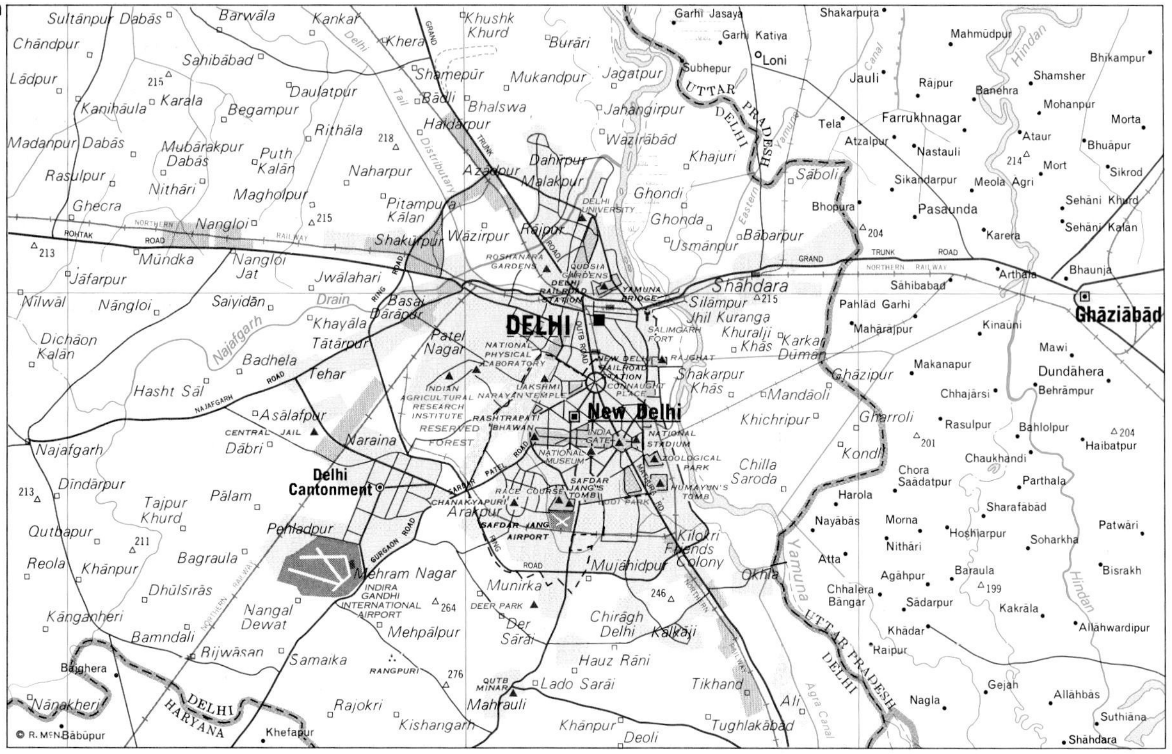

b

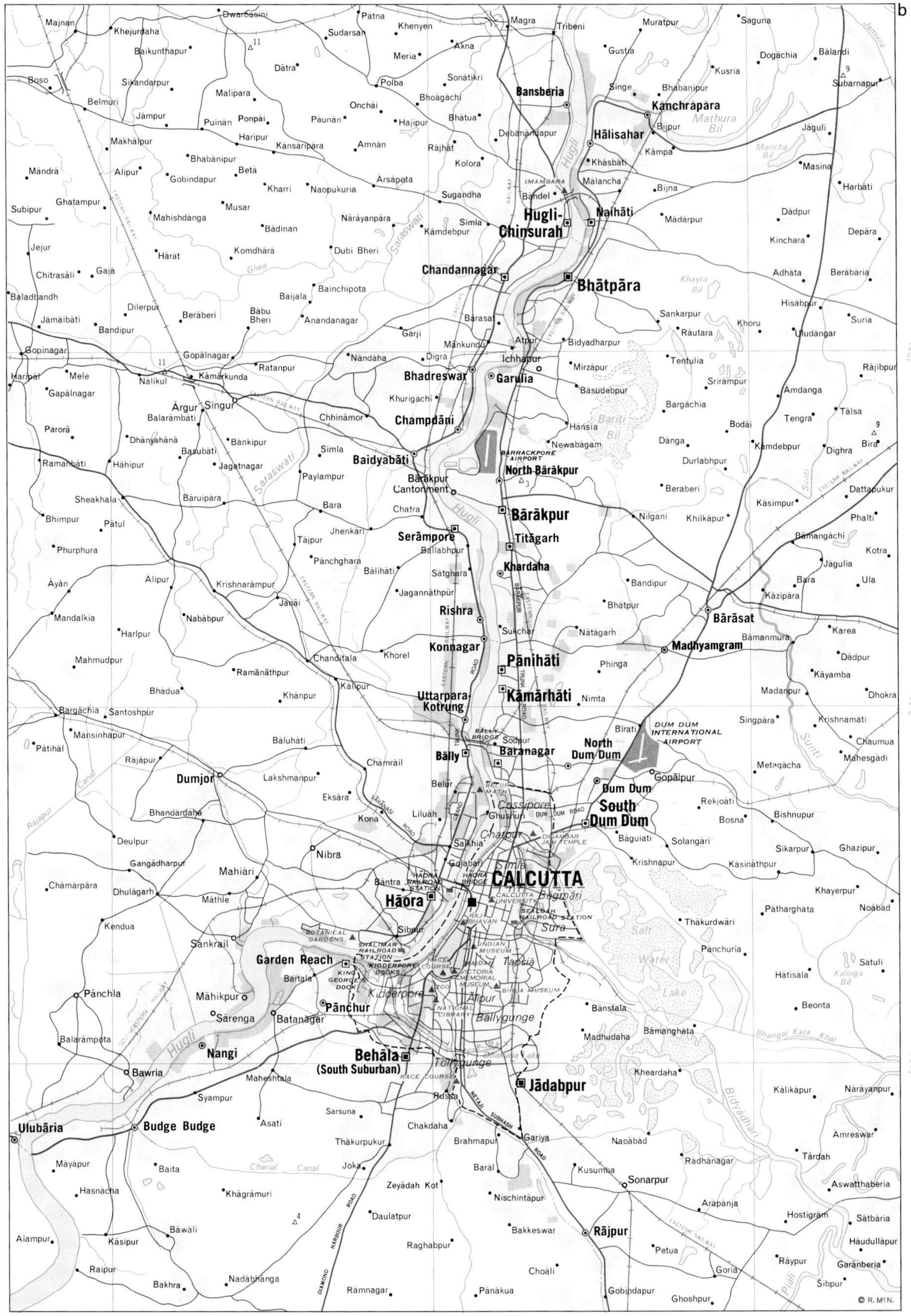

c

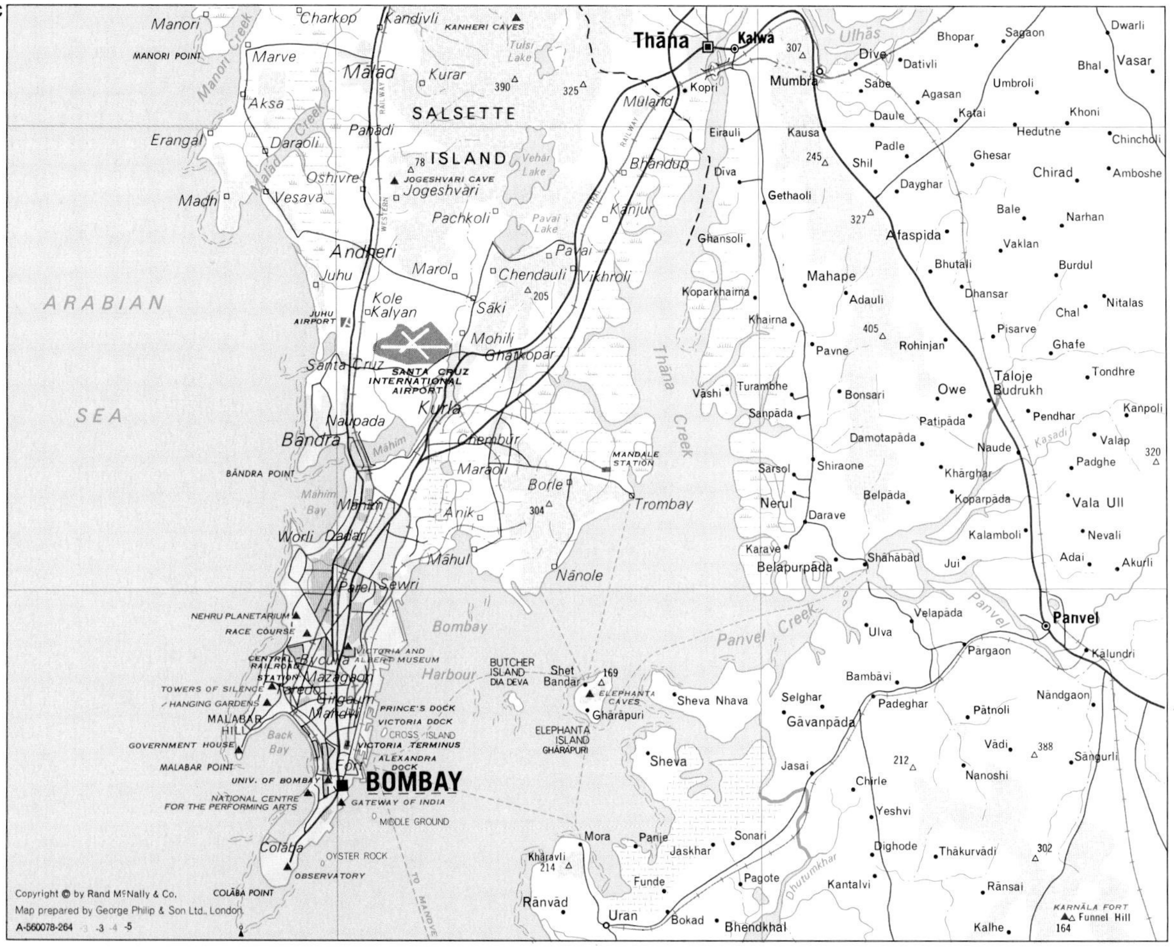

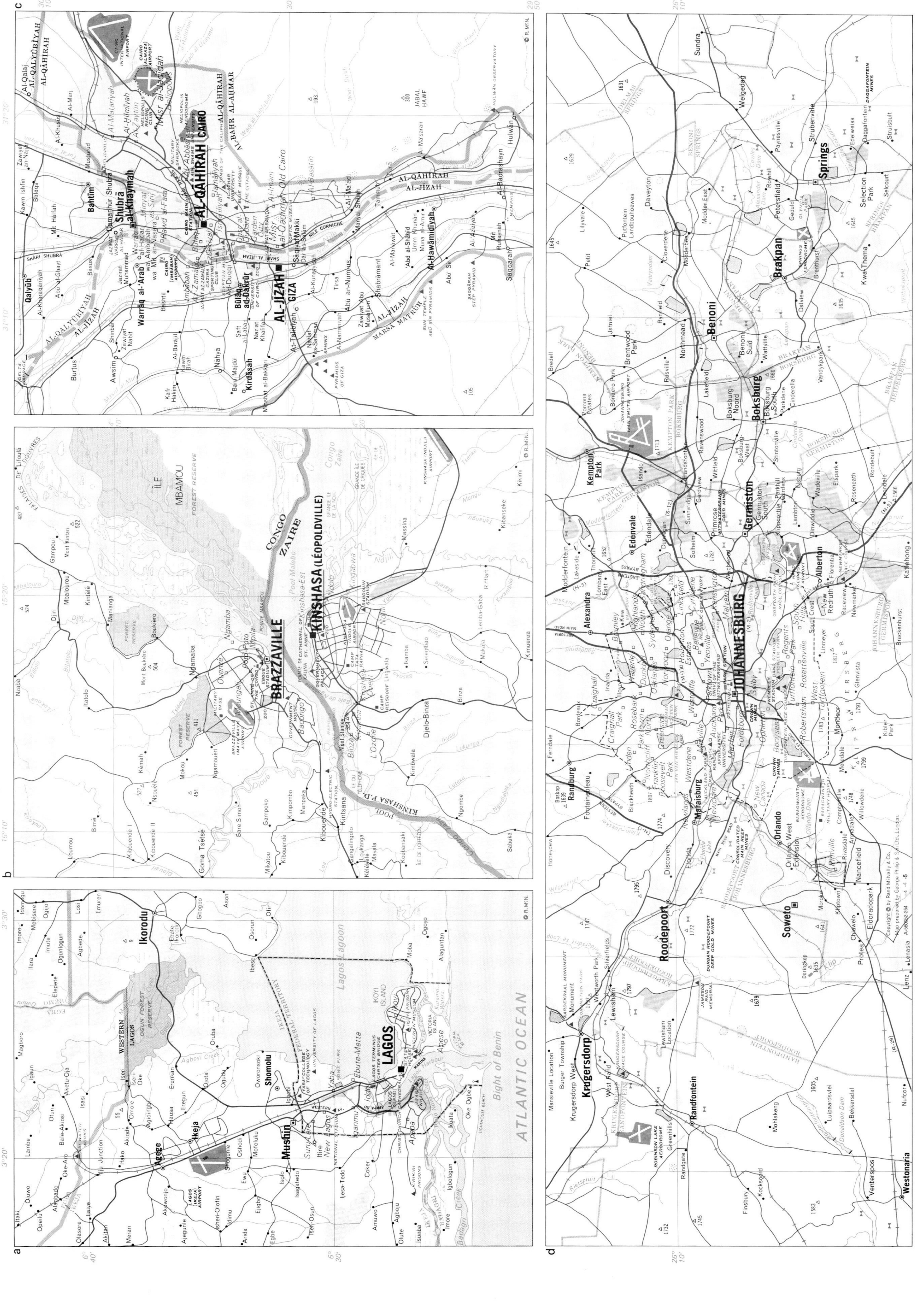

	AREA (km²)	POPULATION
LAGOS	750	2,400,000
KINSHASA–BRAZZAVILLE	1,150	2,750,000
AL-QĀHIRAH (CAIRO)	1,200	8,900,000
JOHANNESBURG	2,650	3,300,000

MAP FORM	airport	creek	dam	île	park	race course	tur'at	wadi
ENGLISH	airport	creek	dam	island	park	race course	canal	wadi
DEUTSCH	Flughafen	Bach	Damm	Insel	Park	Rennbahn	Kanal	Wadi
ESPAÑOL	aeropuerto	riachuelo	presa	isla	parque	hipódromo	canal	uadi
FRANÇAIS	aéroport	crique	barrage	île	parc	champ de course	canal	wadi
PORTUGUÊS	aeroporto	riacho	represa	ilha	parque	hipódromo	canal	uádi

Kilometers 0 5 10 15 Km.
Statute Miles 0 5 10 15 Mi.

Scale 1:300,000

One centimeter represents 3 kilometers.
One inch represents approximately 4.7 miles.

a

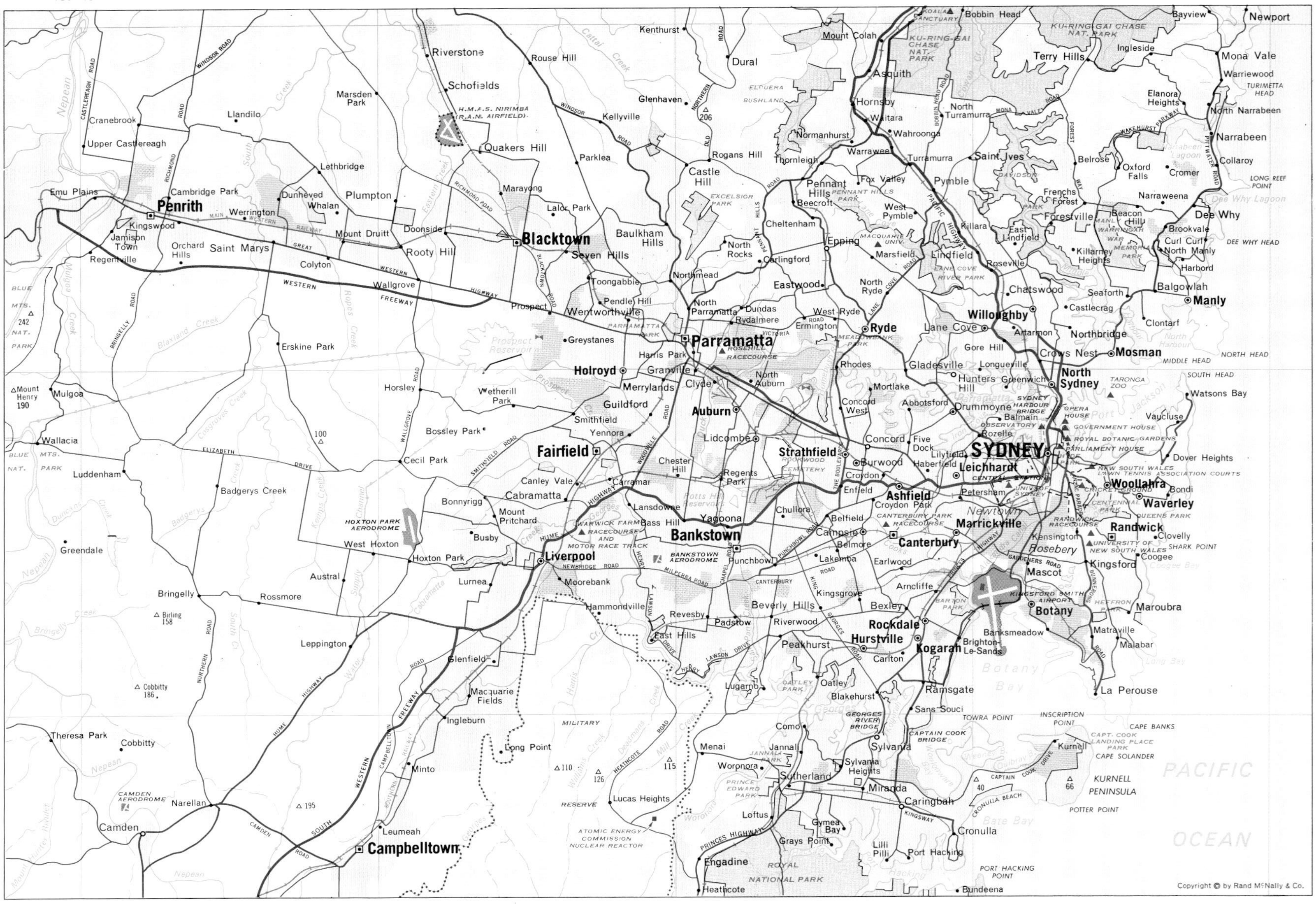

b

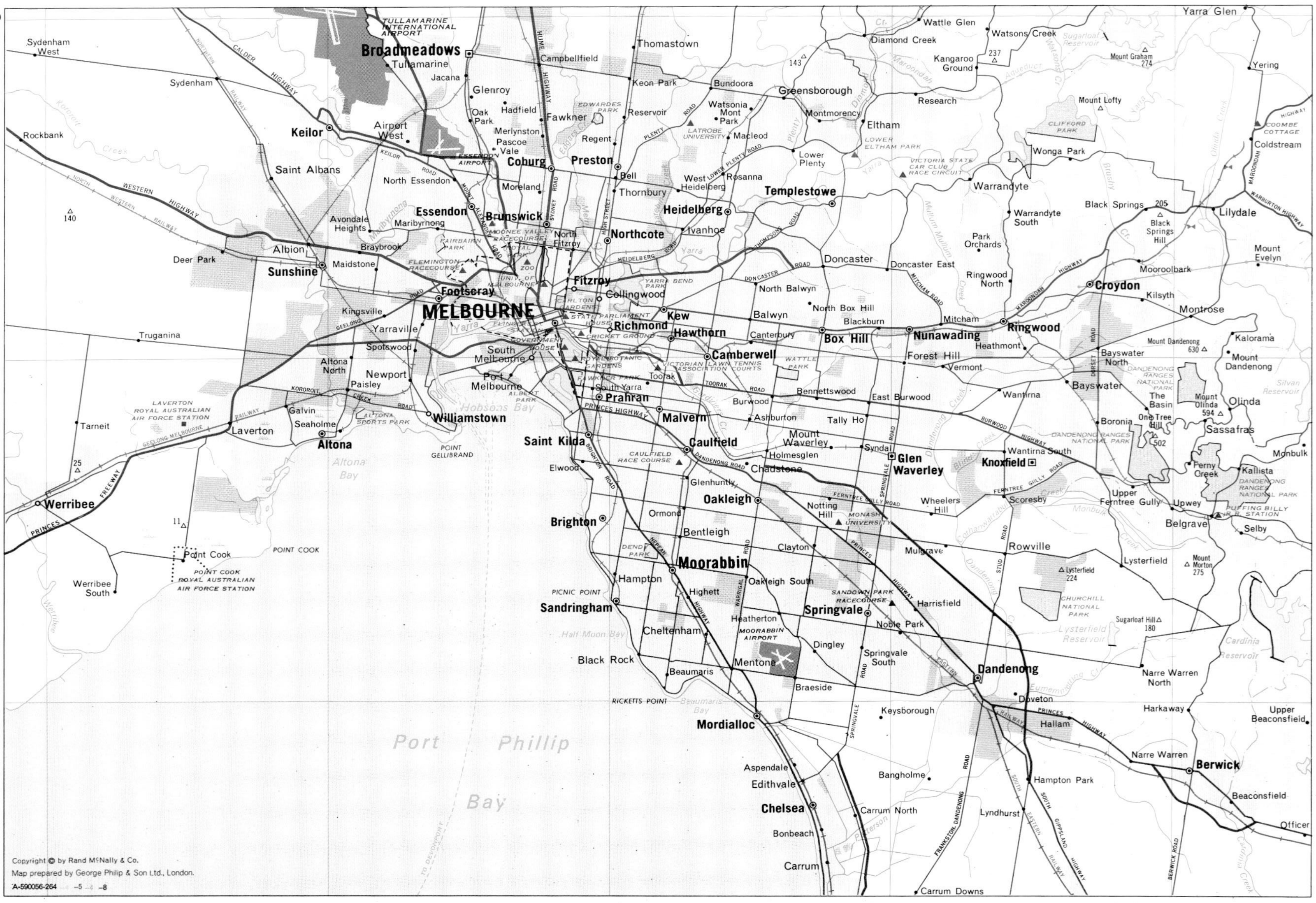

	AREA (km²)	POPULATION
MELBOURNE	2,600	2,425,000
SYDNEY	2,800	2,850,000

ENGLISH	bay, b.	bridge	creek, cr.	highway	point	road
DEUTSCH	Bucht	Brücke	Bach	Landstrasse	Landspitze	Landstrasse
ESPAÑOL	bahía	puente	riachuelo	camino	punta	camino
FRANÇAIS	baie	pont	crique	route	pointe	route
PORTUGUÊS	baía	ponte	riacho	rodovia	ponta	rodovia

Kilometers 0 5 10 15 Km.

Statute Miles 0 5 10 15 Mi.

Scale 1:300,000

One centimeter represents 3 kilometers.
One inch represents approximately 4.7 miles.

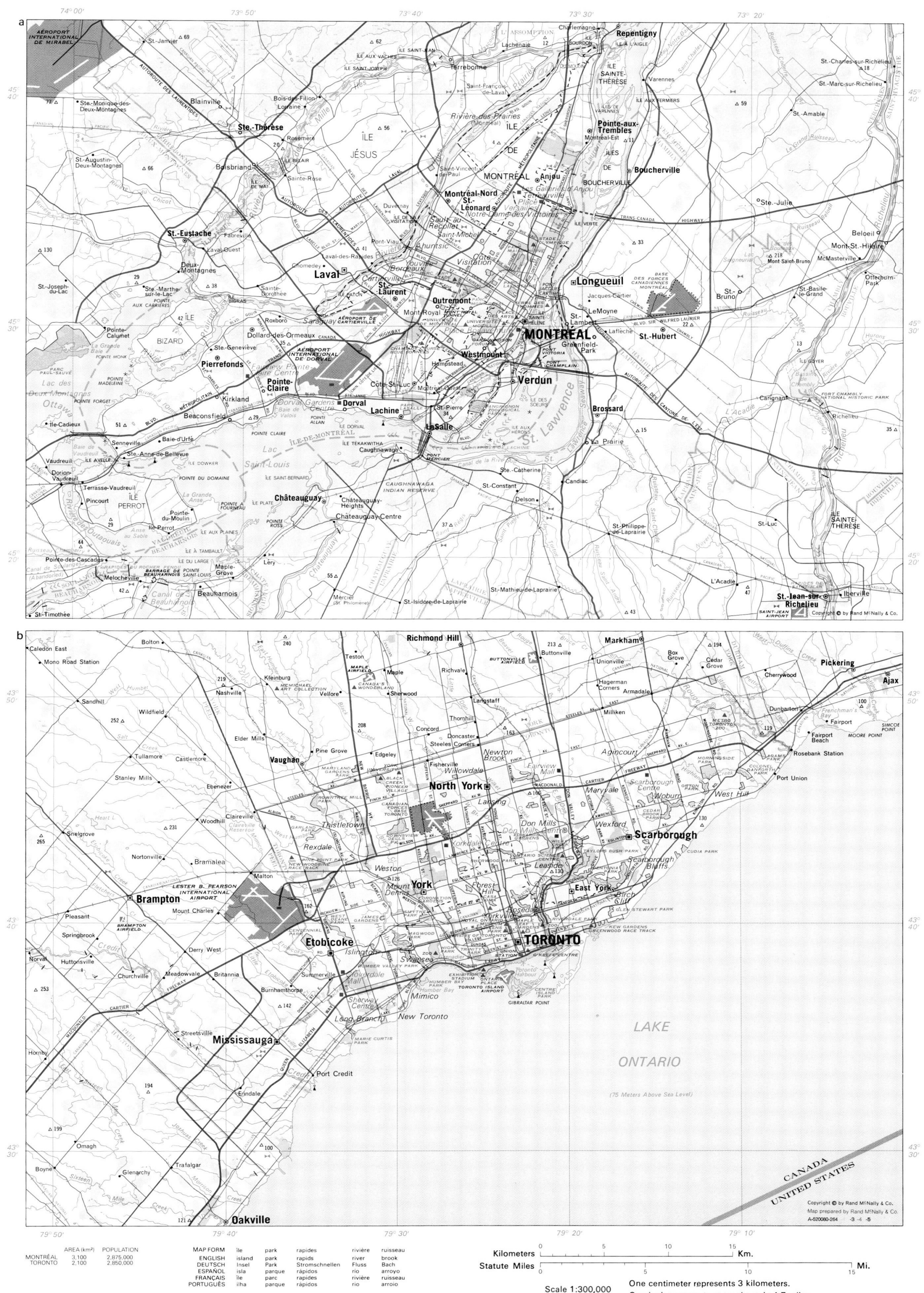

Scale 1:300,000

One centimeter represents 3 kilometers.
One inch represents approximately 4.7 miles.

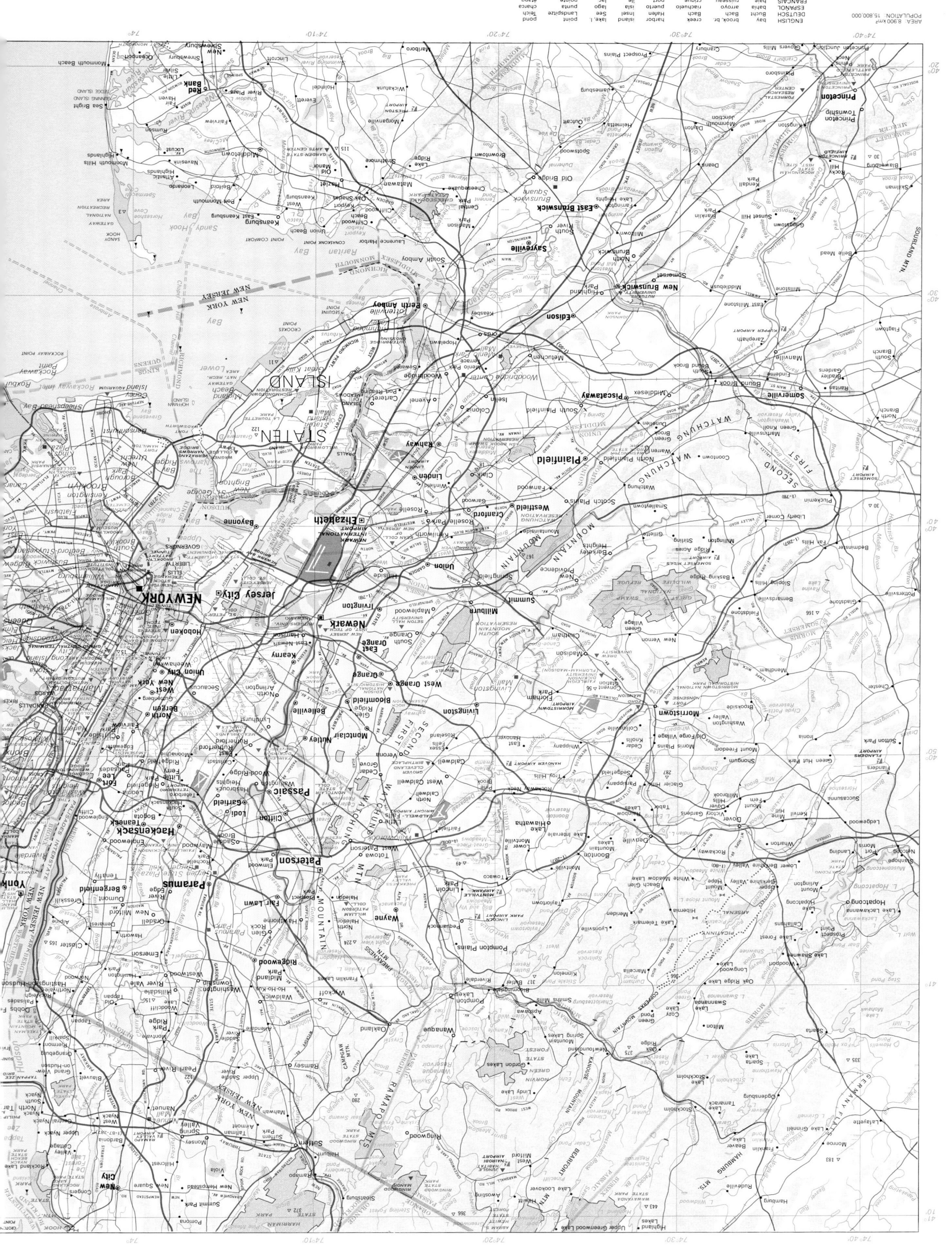

ENGLISH	bay	brook, br.	creek	harbor	point	island	lake, L.	See	Landspitze
DEUTSCH		Bach		Hafen		Insel			
ESPAÑOL	bahía		riachuelo	puerto	punta	isla	lago	lac	punta
FRANÇAIS	baie		ruisseau	port	pointe	île	lac		pointe
PORTUGUÊS	baía	arroio	riacho	porto	ponta	ilha	lago	lago	ponta

AREA: 8.900 km²
POPULATION: 15.800.000

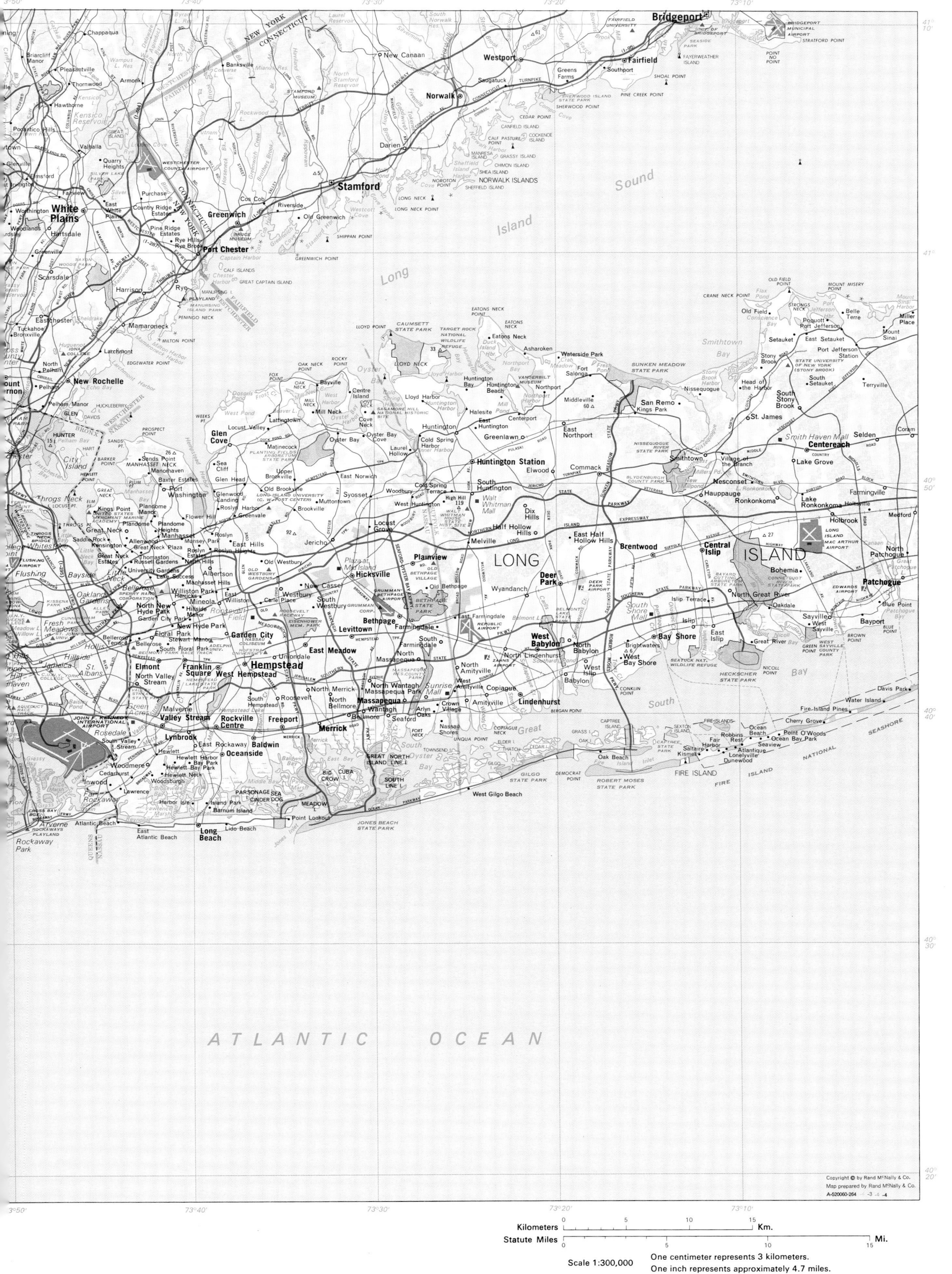

Kilometers |___|___|___|___|___|___|___|___|___|___| Km.
0   5   10   15

Statute Miles |___|___|___|___|___|___| Mi.
0   5   10   15

Scale 1:300,000

One centimeter represents 3 kilometers.
One inch represents approximately 4.7 miles.

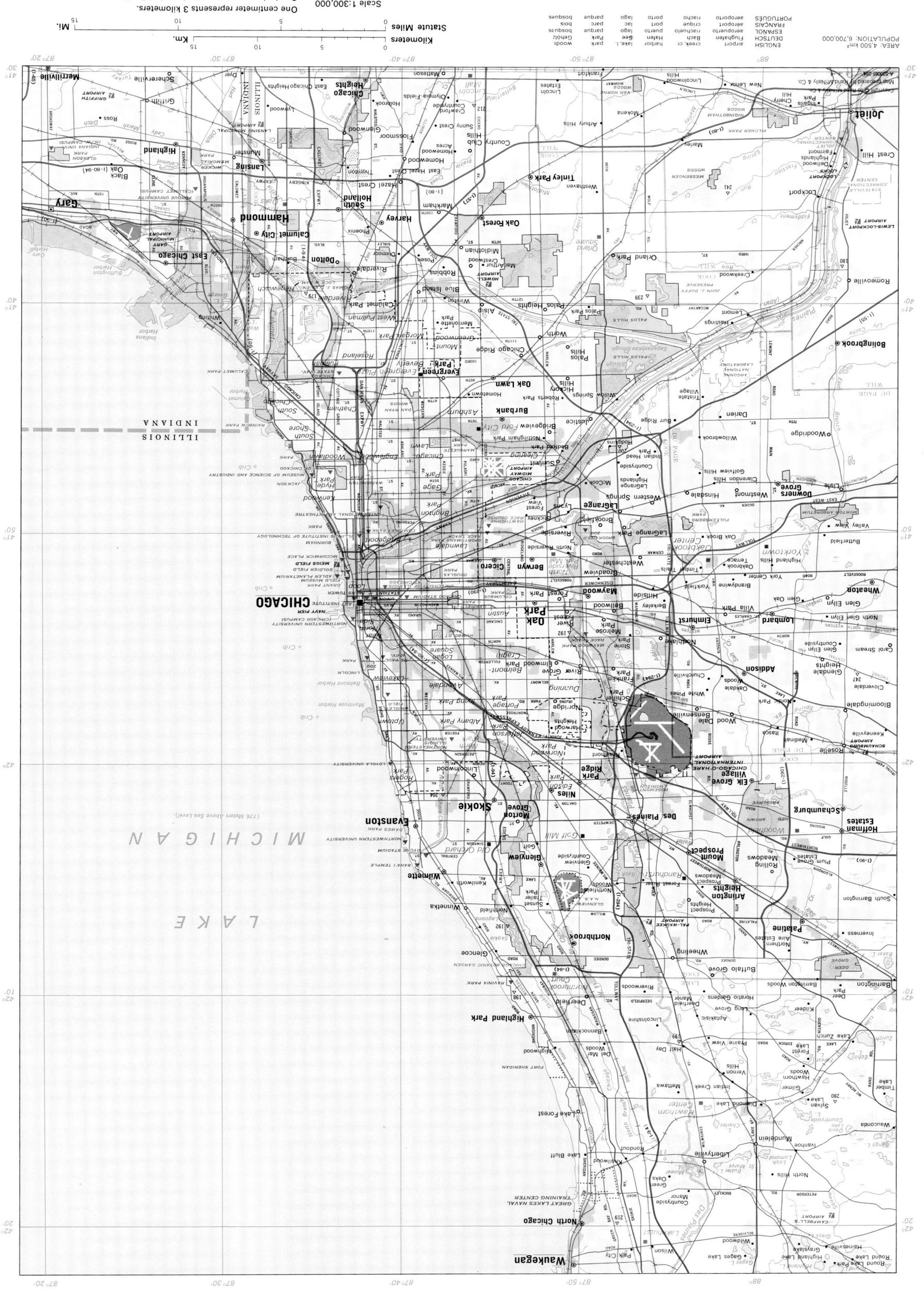

Chicago

AREA: 4,500 km²
POPULATION: 6,700,000
ENGLISH	airport	creek, cr.	harbor	lake, l.	park	woods
DEUTSCH	Flughafen	Bach	Hafen	See	Park	Gehölz
ESPAÑOL	aeropuerto	riachuelo	puerto	lago	parque	bosques
FRANÇAIS	aéroport	crique	port	lac	parc	bois
PORTUGUÊS	aeroporto	riacho	porto	lago	parque	bosques
Kilometers 0 5 10 15 Km.
Statute Miles 0 5 10 15 Mi.
Scale 1:300,000
One centimeter represents 3 kilometers.
One inch represents approximately 4.7 miles.

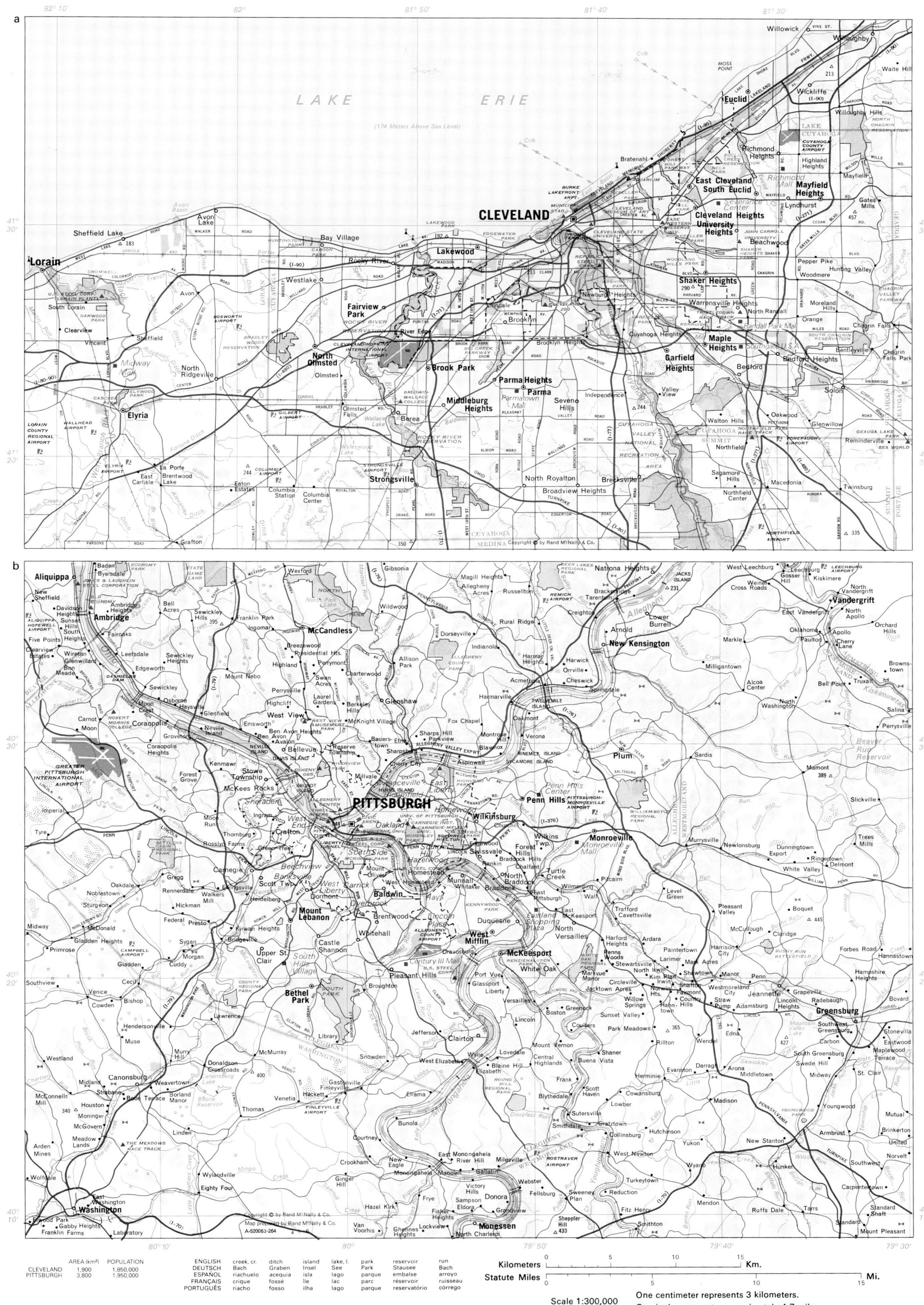

	AREA (km²)	POPULATION
CLEVELAND	1,900	1,850,000
PITTSBURGH	3,800	1,950,000

	ENGLISH	creek, cr.	ditch	island	lake, l.	park	reservoir	run
	DEUTSCH	Bach	Graben	Insel	See	Park	Stausee	Bach
	ESPAÑOL	riachuelo	acequia	isla	lago	parque	embalse	arroyo
	FRANÇAIS	crique	fossé	île	lac	parc	réservoir	ruisseau
	PORTUGUÊS	riacho	fosso	ilha	lago	parque	reservatório	córrego

Kilometers 0   5   10   15   Km.

Statute Miles 0   5   10   15   Mi.

Scale 1:300,000

One centimeter represents 3 kilometers.
One inch represents approximately 4.7 miles.

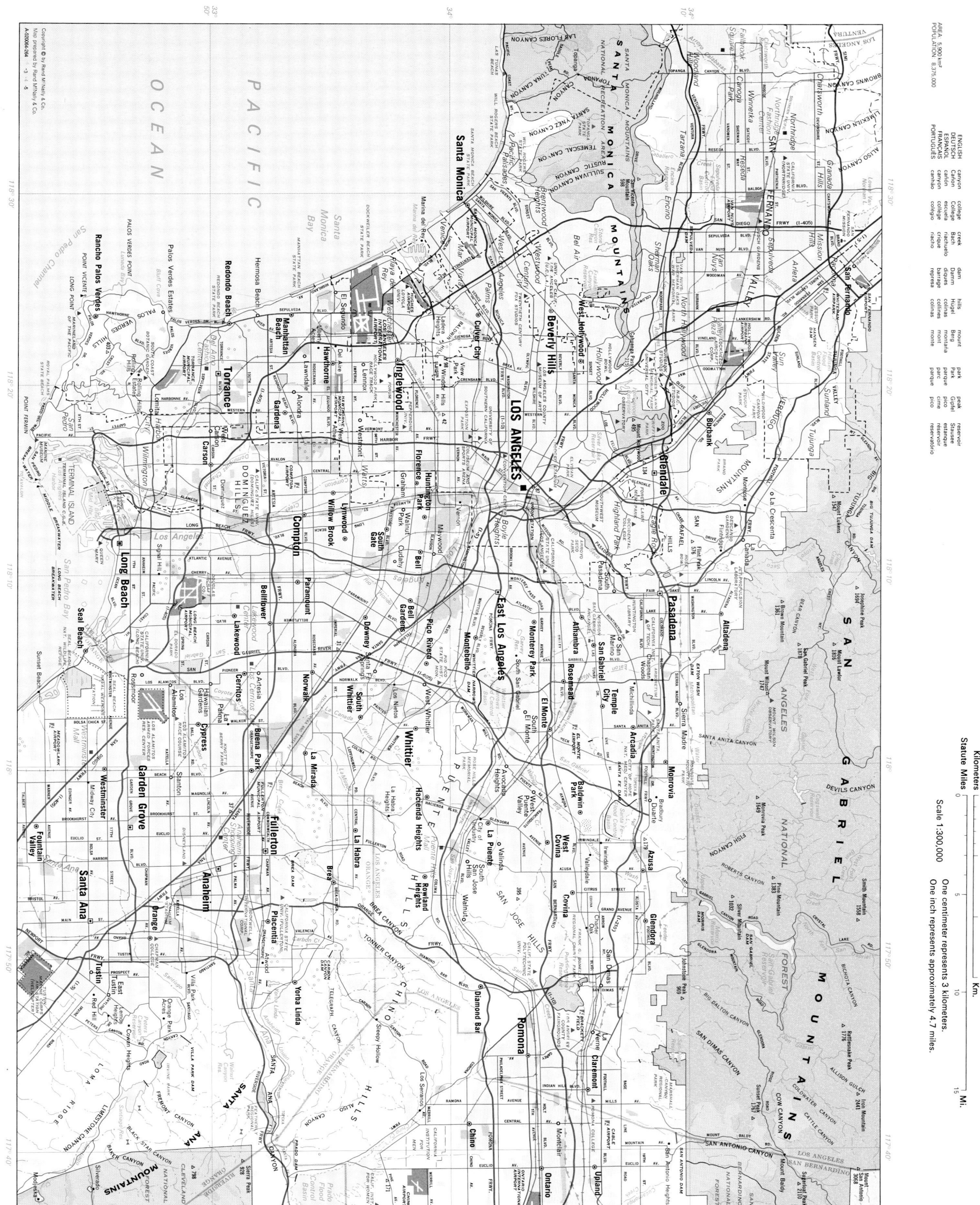

Copyright © by Rand McNally & Co.
Map prepared by Rand McNally & Co.
A-52006-294
-3, -4, -5

AREA 5,500 mi²
POPULATION 8,376,000

ENGLISH	DEUTSCH	ESPAÑOL	FRANÇAIS	PORTUGUÊS
canyon	Cañon	cañon	cañon	canhão
college	College	escuela	rachuelo	college
creek	Bach	riachuelo	crique	crique
dam	Damm	diques	barrage	represa
hills	Hügel	colinas	collines	colinas
mount	Berg	montaña	mont	monte
park	Park	parque	parc	parque
peak	Gipfel	pico	cime	pico
reservoir	Stausee	estanque	reservoir	reservatório

Kilometers
Statue Miles

Scale 1:300,000

One centimeter represents 3 kilometers.
One inch represents approximately 4.7 miles.

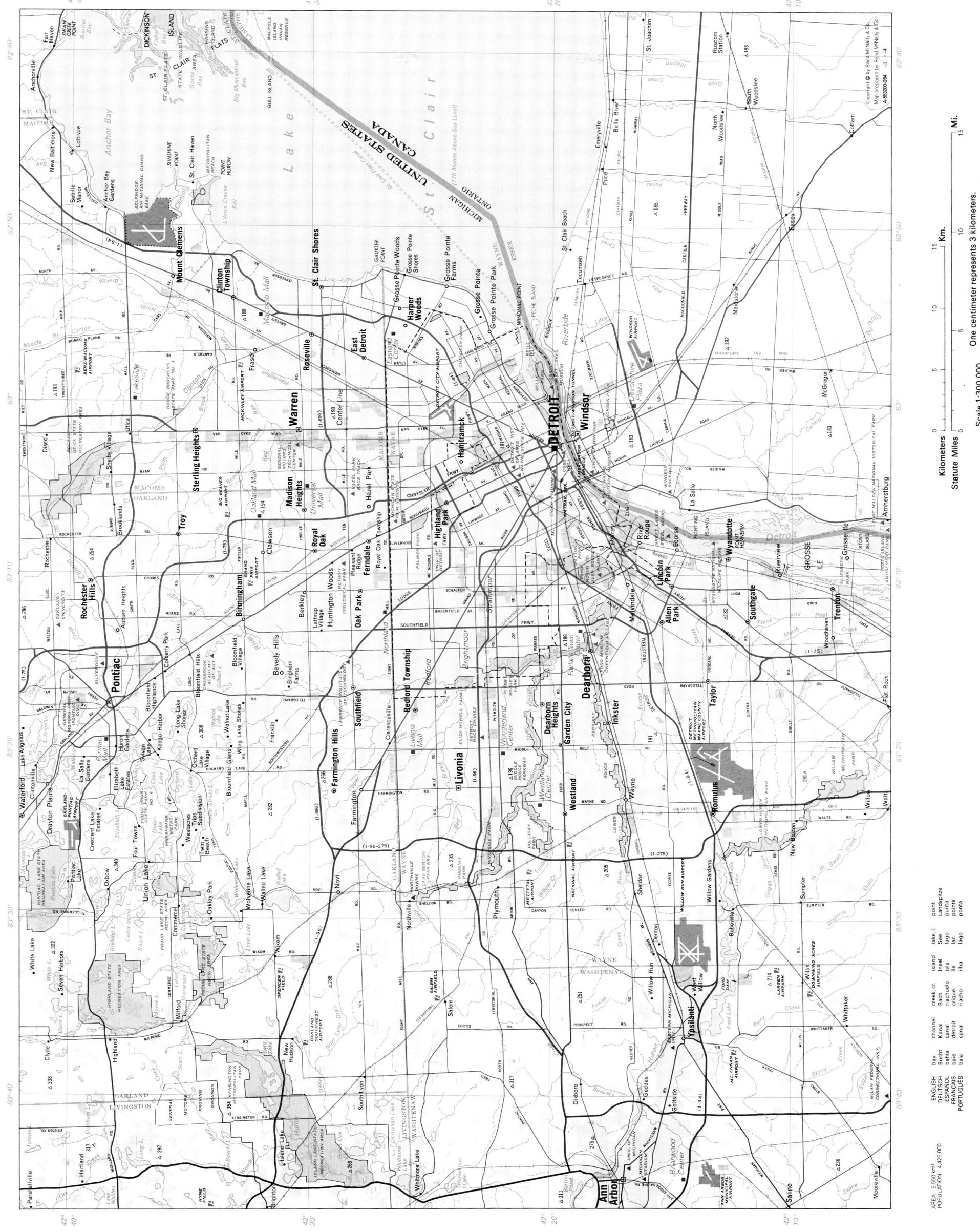

Mi.
15

Km.
15   10   5   0
Kilometers

Statute Miles   15   10   5   0

Scale 1:300,000

One centimeter represents 3 kilometers.
One inch represents approximately 4.7 miles.

ENGLISH	bay	channel	creek, cr.	island	lake, l.	point
DEUTSCH	Bucht	Kanal	Bach	Insel	See	Landspitze
ESPAÑOL	bahía	canal	riachuelo	isla	lago	punta
FRANÇAIS	baie	detroit	crique	île	lac	pointe
PORTUGUÊS	baía	canal	riacho	ilha	lago	ponta

AREA, 5,550 km²
POPULATION, 4,425,000

PACIFIC

OCEAN

San Francisco Bay

San Pablo Bay

SAN FRANCISCO

OAKLAND

Berkeley

Richmond

San Rafael

Novato

Vallejo

Benicia

Martinez

Concord

Pleasant Hill

Walnut Creek

Lafayette

Orinda

Moraga

Danville

San Ramon

Dublin

Pleasanton

Pittsburg

Antioch

Clayton

Alameda

Piedmont

Emeryville

Albany

El Cerrito

Kensington

El Sobrante

Pinole

Hercules

Rodeo

Crockett

San Leandro

Castro Valley

Ashland

San Lorenzo

Cherryland

Hayward

Union City

Fremont

Newark

Milpitas

Daly City

Brisbane

Colma

South San Francisco

Pacifica

San Bruno

Millbrae

Burlingame

Hillsborough

San Mateo

Foster City

Belmont

San Carlos

Redwood City

Atherton

Menlo Park

East Palo Alto

North Fair Oaks

Woodside

Palo Alto

Stanford

Mountain View

Los Altos

Los Altos Hills

Sunnyvale

Santa Clara

SAN JOSE

Cupertino

Campbell

Saratoga

Half Moon Bay

El Granada

Montara

Moss Beach

La Honda

Mount Diablo

Mount Diablo State Park

Eagle Peak 722

Mount Diablo 1173

San Francisco International Airport

Metropolitan Oakland International Airport

Hayward Municipal Airport

Half Moon Bay Airport

San Carlos Airport

Palo Alto Airport

Alameda Naval Air Station

Moffett Field Naval Air Station

Oakland-Alameda County Coliseum

Golden Gate

Golden Gate National Recreation Area

SANTA CRUZ MOUNTAINS

CONTRA COSTA

ALAMEDA

SAN MATEO

SANTA CLARA

MARIN

SONOMA

SOLANO

Angel Island

Alcatraz Island

Treasure Island

Yerba Buena Island

Bair Island

Bay Farm Island

Brooks Island

Red Rock

Montezuma Hills

Suisun Bay

Carquinez Strait

Mare Island

Briones Hills

Las Trampas Ridge

Rocky Ridge

Pleasanton Ridge

Walpert Ridge

Sunol Ridge

San Pablo Ridge

Sobrante Ridge

Pinole Ridge

Mt. Tamalpais 784

Mt. Caroline Livermore 238

Mission Peak 767

Black Mountain 860

Mindego Hill 653

Borel Hill 784

Langley Hill 688

Sierra Morena 737

Mindego Hill

AREA: 4,750 km²
POPULATION: 4,175,000

ENGLISH	bay	beach	creek, cr.	island	lake	point	reservoir
DEUTSCH	Bucht	Strand	Bach	Insel	See	Punkt	Stausee
ESPAÑOL	bahía	playa	riachuelo	isla	lago	punta	estanque
FRANÇAIS	baie	plage	crique	île	lac	pointe	réservoir
PORTUGUÊS	baía	praia	riacho	ilha	lago	ponta	reservatório

Kilometers   0   5   10   15   Km.

Statute Miles   0   5   10   15   Mi.

Scale 1:300,000

One centimeter represents 3 kilometers.
One inch represents approximately 4.7 miles.

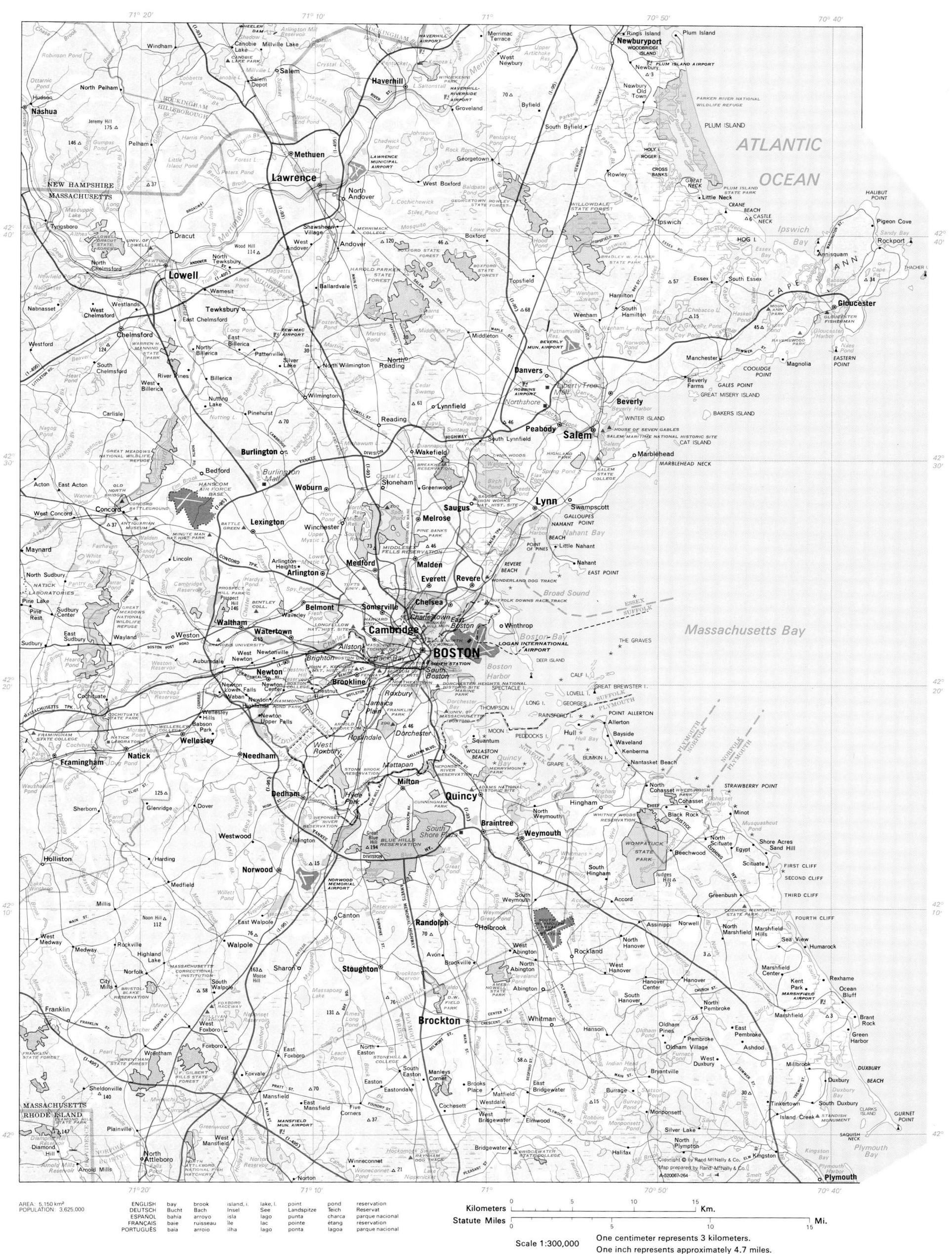

AREA: 5,150 km²
POPULATION: 3,625,000

ENGLISH	bay	brook	island, i.	lake, l.	point	pond	reservation
DEUTSCH	Bucht	Bach	Insel	See	Landspitze	Teich	Reservat
ESPAÑOL	bahía	arroyo	isla	lago	punta	charca	parque nacional
FRANÇAIS	baie	ruisseau	île	lac	pointe	étang	reservation
PORTUGUÊS	baía	arroio	ilha	lago	ponta	lagoa	parque nacional

Kilometers

Statute Miles

Scale 1:300,000

One centimeter represents 3 kilometers.
One inch represents approximately 4.7 miles.

	AREA (km²)	POPULATION
BUFFALO	2,550	1,450,000
BALTIMORE	1,150	1,500,000
WASHINGTON	1,550	2,225,000

ENGLISH	airport	bridge	creek, cr.	island, i.	park	point	run	university
DEUTSCH	Flughafen	Brücke	Bach	Insel	Park	Landspitze	Bach	Universität
ESPAÑOL	aeropuerto	puente	riachuelo	isla	parque	punta	arroyo	universidad
FRANÇAIS	aéroport	pont	crique	île	parc	pointe	ruisseau	université
PORTUGUÊS	aeroporto	ponte	riacho	ilha	parque	ponta	córrego	universidade

Kilometers 0 5 10 15 Km.
Statute Miles 0 5 10 15 Mi.
Scale 1:300,000
One centimeter represents 3 kilometers.
One inch represents approximately 4.7 miles.

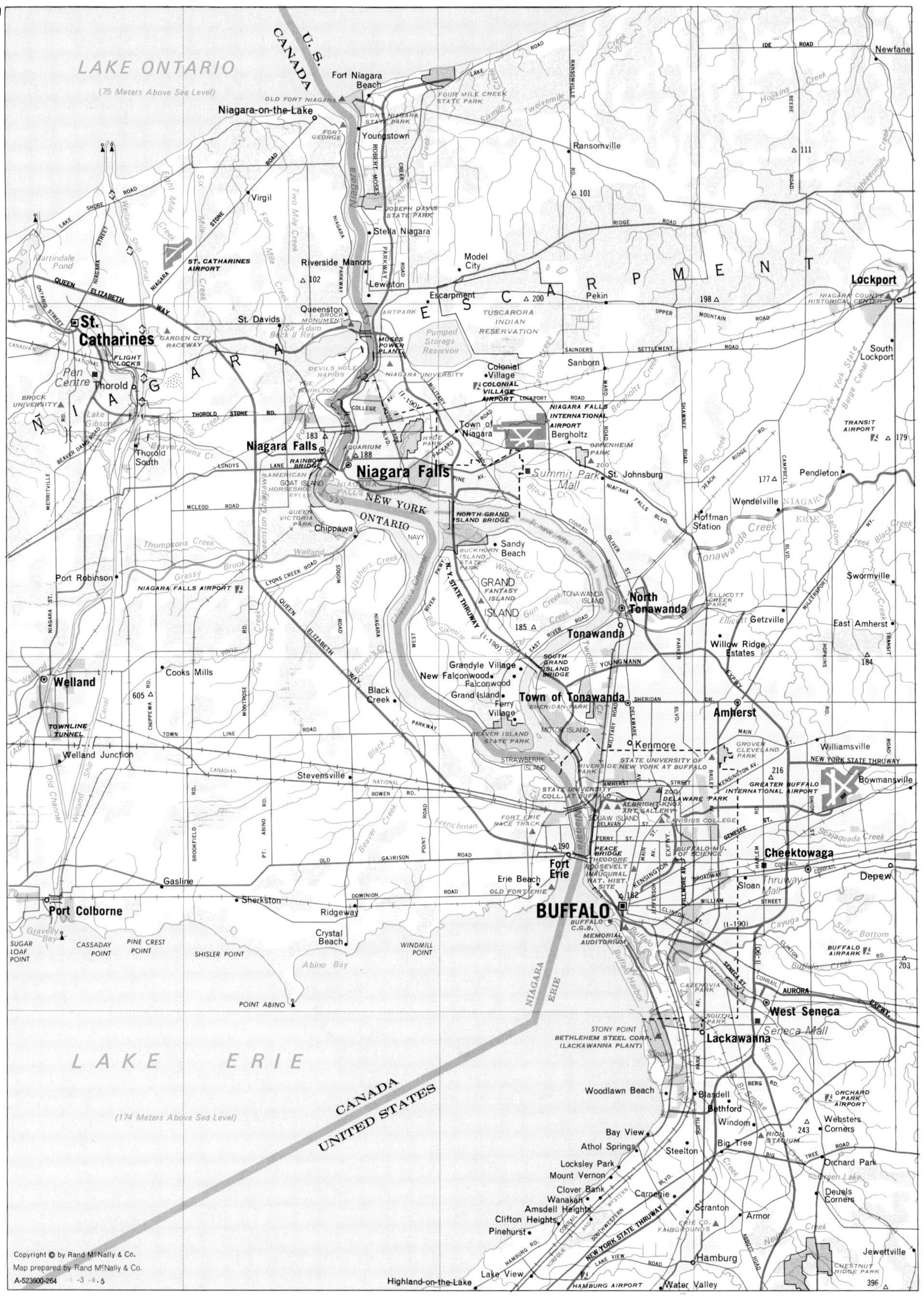

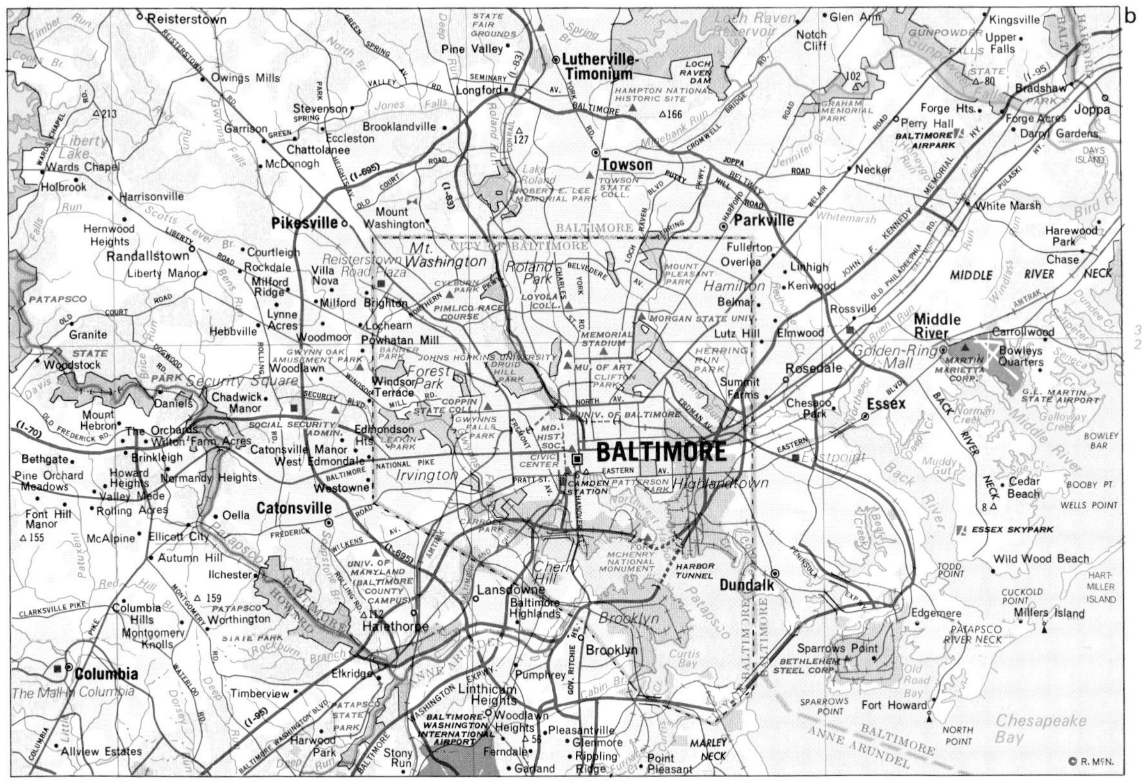

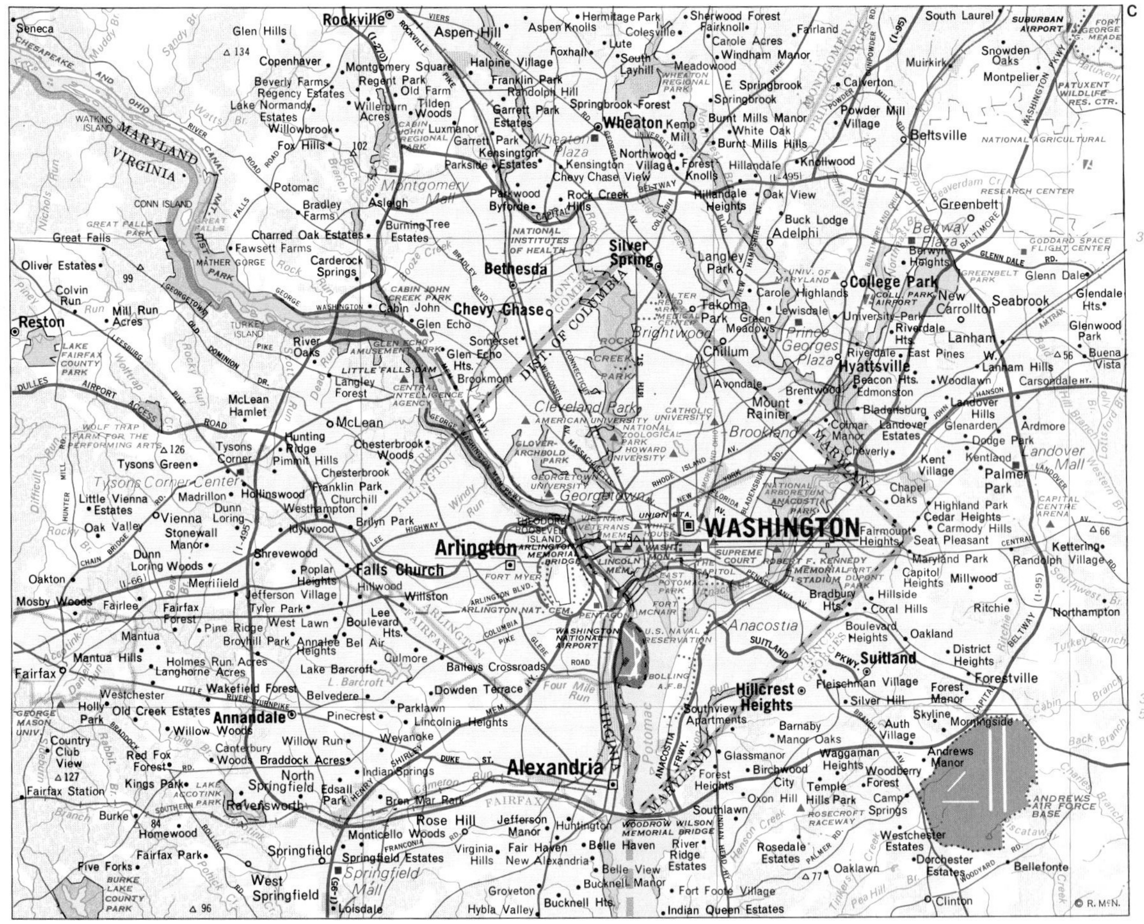

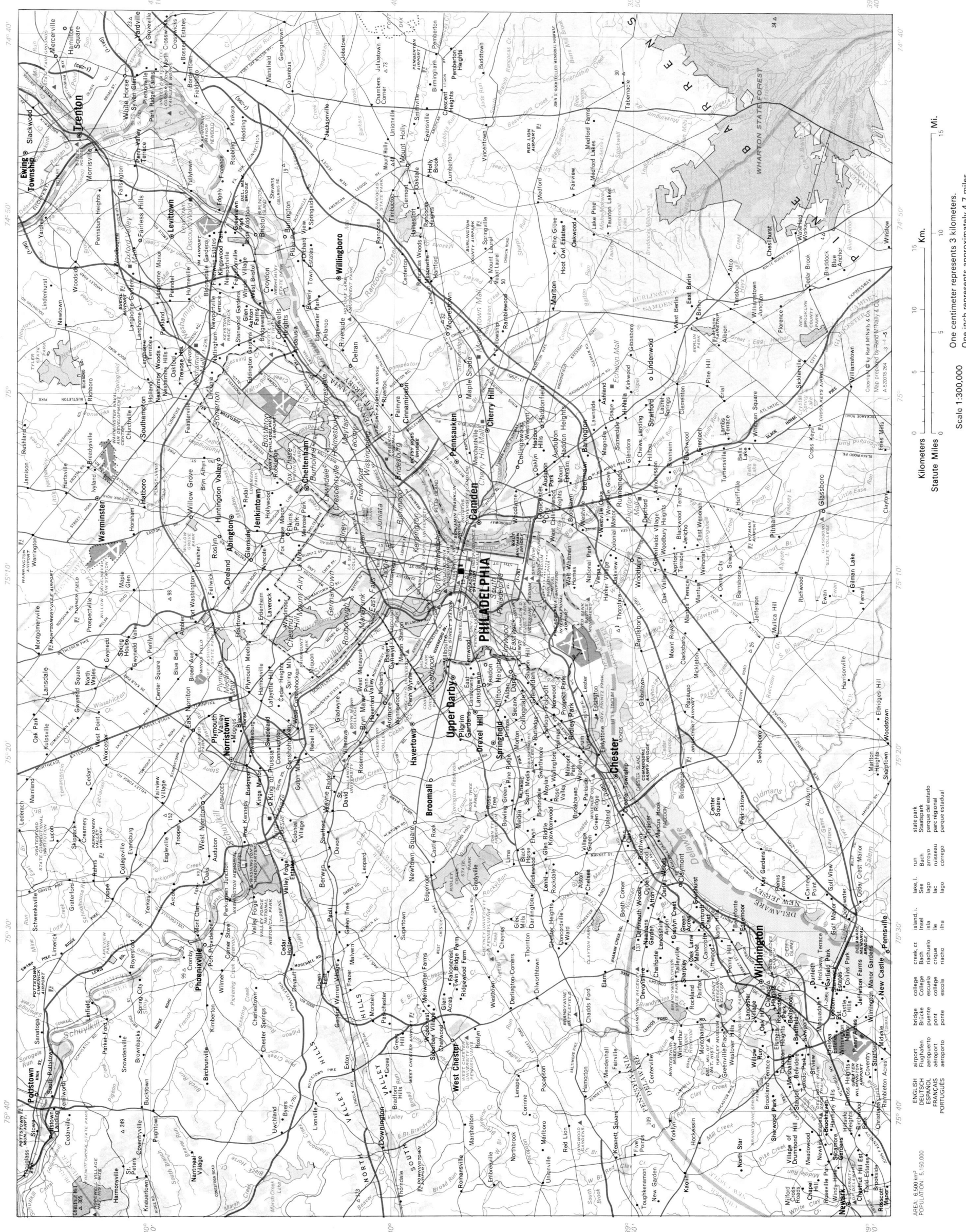

Scale 1:300,000

One centimeter represents 3 kilometers.
One inch represents approximately 4.7 miles.

AREA 6,500 km²
POPULATION 5,150,000

ENGLISH	airport	bridge	college	creek, cr.	island, i.	lake, l.	run	state park
DEUTSCH	Flughafen	Brücke		Bach	Insel	See		Staatspark
ESPAÑOL	aeropuerto	puente	escuela	arroyo	isla	lago	arroyo	parque del estado
FRANÇAIS	aéroport	pont	collège	crique	île	lac	rousseau	parc régional
PORTUGUÊS	aeroporto	ponte	escola	riacho	ilha	lago	córrego	parque estadual

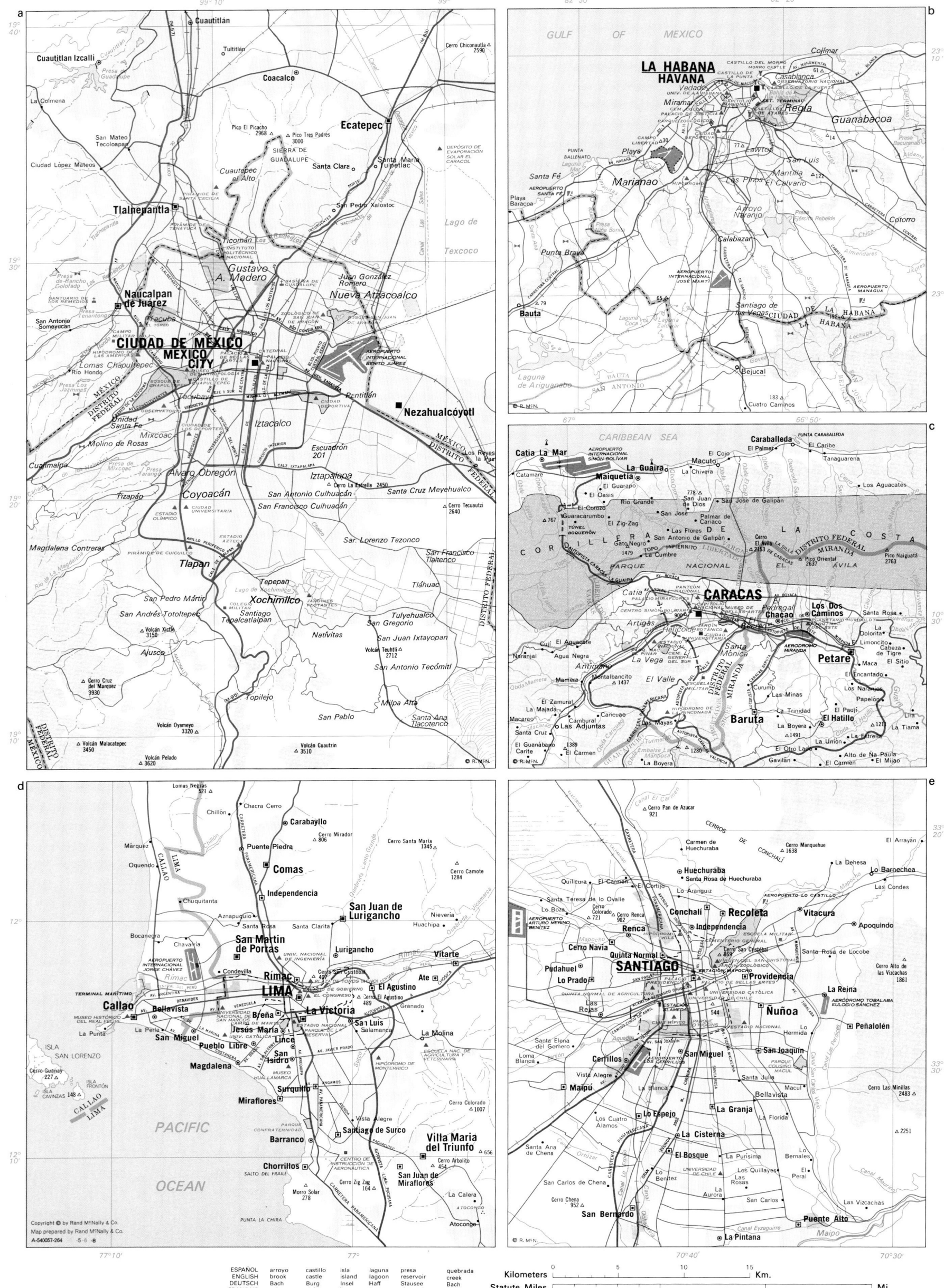

ESPANOL	arroyo	castillo	isla	laguna	presa	quebrada
ENGLISH	brook	castle	island	lagoon	reservoir	creek
DEUTSCH	Bach	Burg	Insel	Lagune	Stausee	Bach
FRANÇAIS	ruiseau	château	île	lagune	réservoir	crique
PORTUGUÊS	arroio	castelo	ilha	laguna	reservatório	riacho

Scale 1:300,000

One centimeter represents 3 kilometers.
One inch represents approximately 4.7 miles.

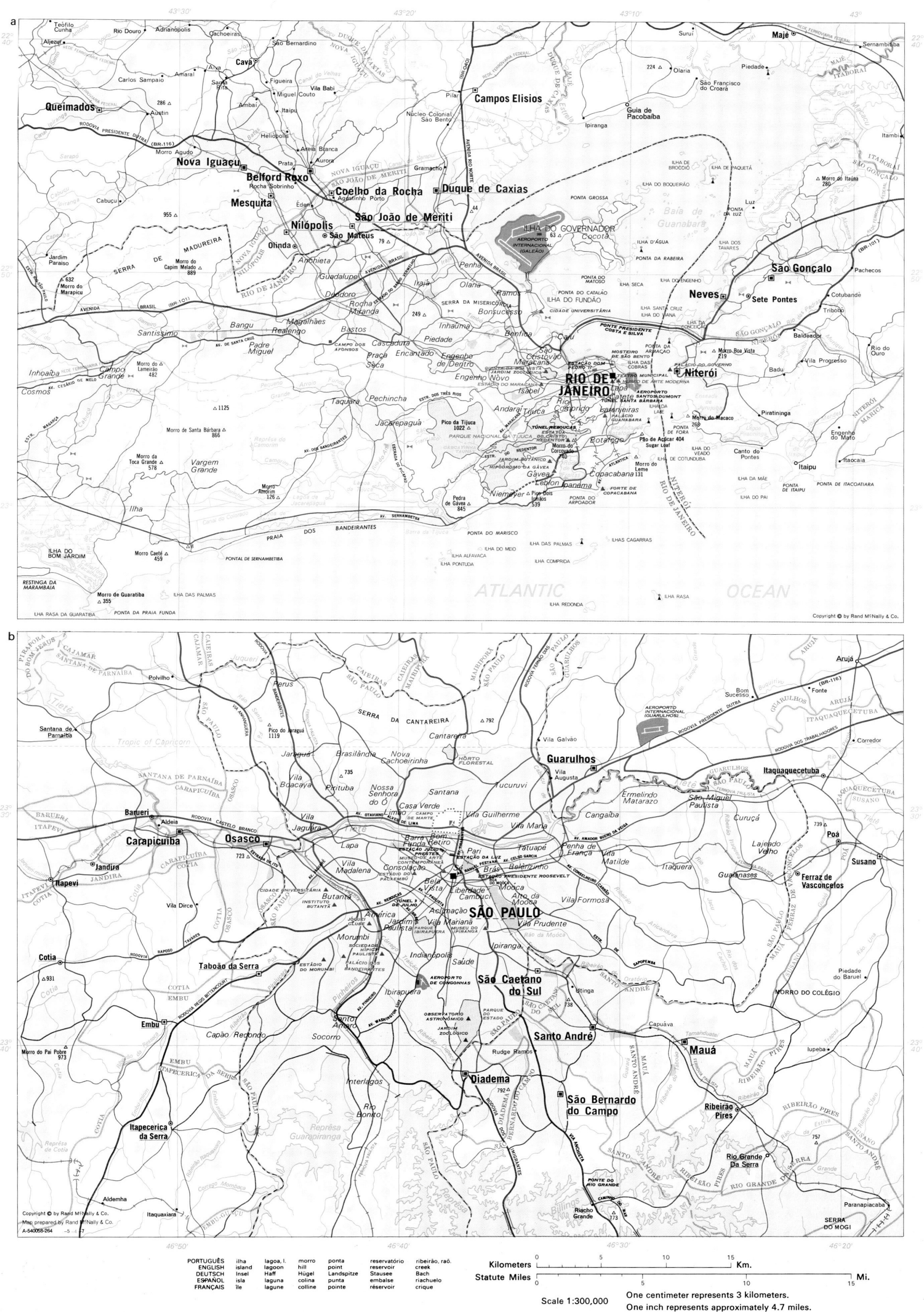

PORTUGUÊS ilha lagoa, l. morro ponta reservatório ribeirão, raó.
ENGLISH island lagoon hill point reservoir creek
DEUTSCH Insel Haff Hügel Landspitze Stausee Bach
ESPAÑOL isla laguna colina punta embalse riachuelo
FRANÇAIS île lagune colline pointe réservoir crique

Kilometers 0 5 10 15 Km.
Statute Miles 0 5 10 15 Mi.

Scale 1:300,000

One centimeter represents 3 kilometers.
One inch represents approximately 4.7 miles.

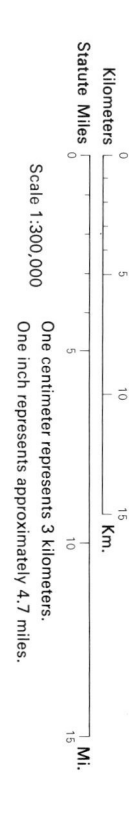

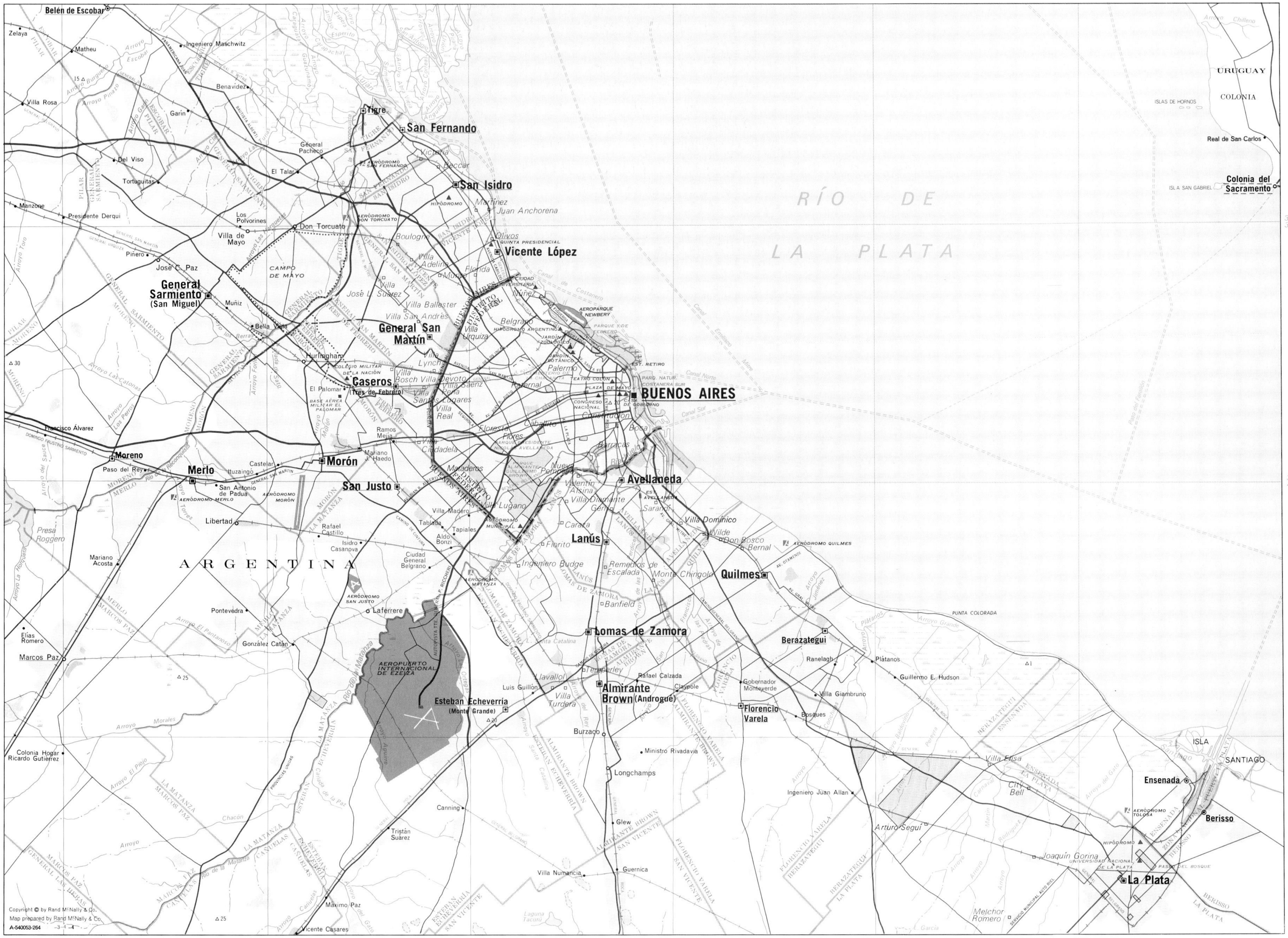

Maps of the United States and Canada

MAP LEGEND

CULTURAL FEATURES

Political Boundaries

International

Secondary (State)

.... County

Populated Places

Cities, towns, and villages

•••••● Symbol size represents population of the place

Chicago
Gary
Racine   Type size represents
Glenview   relative importance of the place
Edgewood

Major Urban Areas
Area of continuous commercial, industrial, and residential development in and around a major city

○ Community within a city

⊛ Capital of major political unit

✪ Capital of U.S. state

○ County Seat

▲ Military Installation

Transportation

——— Major Highway

Railroad

Tunnel

Miscellaneous

National Park

National Monument

Indian Reservation

△ Point of Interest

Dam

Bridge

Pier

LAND FEATURES

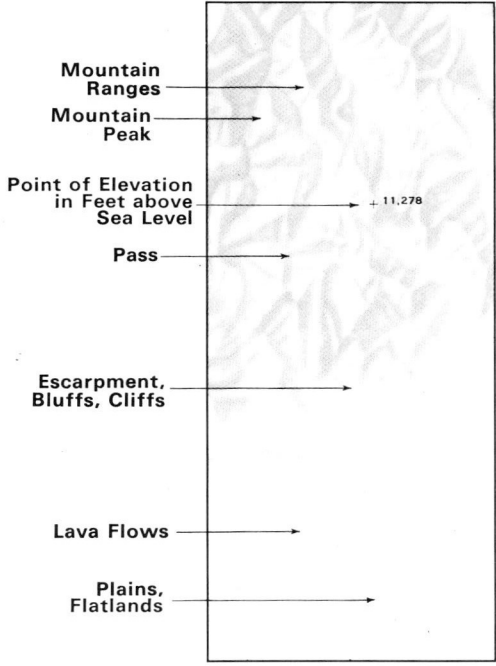

Mountain Ranges

Mountain Peak

Point of Elevation in Feet above Sea Level   + 11,278

Pass

Escarpment, Bluffs, Cliffs

Lava Flows

Plains, Flatlands

WATER FEATURES

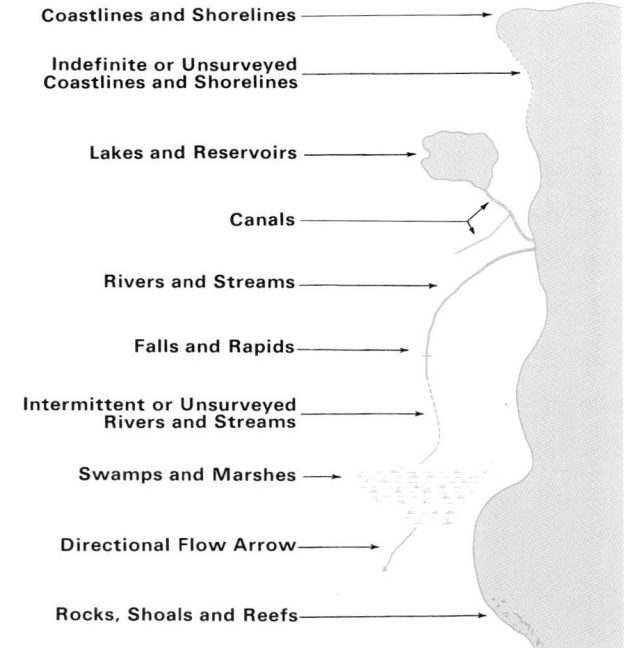

Coastlines and Shorelines

Indefinite or Unsurveyed Coastlines and Shorelines

Lakes and Reservoirs

Canals

Rivers and Streams

Falls and Rapids

Intermittent or Unsurveyed Rivers and Streams

Swamps and Marshes

Directional Flow Arrow

Rocks, Shoals and Reefs

Note: Size of type varies according to importance and available space. Letters for names of major features are spread across the extent of the feature.

TYPE STYLES USED TO NAME FEATURES

CANADA	Country, State, or Province	*UINTA DESERT*	Major Terrain Features
Naval Air Station	Military Installation	MT. MORIAH	Individual Mountain
CROCKETT	County	*MESA VERDE SAN XAVIER*	National Park or Monument, Indian Res.
		NUNIVAK	Island or Coastal Feature
		Ocean Lake River Canal	Hydrographic Features

BRITISH COLUMBIA
ALBERTA
SASKATCHEWAN
MANITOBA
WASHINGTON
OREGON
IDAHO
MONTANA
WYOMING
NORTH DAKOTA
SOUTH DAKOTA
NEBRASKA
KANSAS
OKLAHOMA
TEXAS
NEVADA
UTAH
COLORADO
CALIFORNIA
ARIZONA
NEW MEXICO
GREAT BASIN
BAJA CALIFORNIA NORTE
SONORA
CHIHUAHUA
COAHUILA
NUEVO LEON
TAMAULIPAS
MEXICO
Pacific Ocean
Gulf of California
Seattle
Portland
San Francisco
Los Angeles
San Diego
Sacramento
Salt Lake City
Denver
Phoenix
Albuquerque
El Paso
San Antonio
Oklahoma City
Vancouver
Calgary
Edmonton
ALASKA
RUSSIA
YUKON
NORTHWEST TERR.
Anchorage
Fairbanks
Juneau
Bering Sea
Gulf of Alaska
ALEUTIAN ISLANDS
Same Scale as Main Map
HAWAIIAN ISLANDS
Honolulu
OAHU
HAWAII
Statute Miles
Kilometers
A-520500-71 -8- -12
COSMO SERIES UNITED STATES
Copyright by RAND McNALLY & COMPANY
Made in U. S. A.
© RM&Co.

Cities and Towns

Albertville 14,507 **A3**
Alexander City 14,917 **C4**
Andalusia 9,269 **D3**
Anniston 26,623 **B4**
Arab 6,321 **A3**
Athens 16,901 **A3**
Atmore 8,046 **D2**
Auburn 33,830 **C4**
Bay Minette 7,168 **E2**
Bessemer 33,497 **B3**
Birmingham 265,968 **B3**
Bluff Park 8,000 **g7**
Boaz 6,928 **A3**
Brewton 5,885 **D2**
Center Point 22,000 **f7**
Childersburg 4,579 **B3**
Clanton 7,669 **C3**
Cullman 13,367 **A3**
Decatur 48,761 **A3**
Demopolis 7,512 **C2**
Dothan 53,589 **D4**
Enterprise 20,123 **D4**
Eufaula 13,220 **D4**
Fairfield 12,200 **B3**
Fayette 4,909 **B2**
Florence 36,426 **A2**
Fort Payne 11,838 **A4**
Gadsden 42,523 **A3**
Geneva 4,681 **D4**
Greenville 7,492 **D3**
Guntersville 7,038 **A3**
Haleyville 4,452 **A2**
Hamilton 5,787 **A2**
Hartselle 10,795 **A3**
Homewood 22,922 **g7**
Hueytown 15,280 **g6**
Huntsville 159,789 **A3**
Jackson 5,819 **D2**
Jacksonville 10,283 **B4**
Jasper 13,553 **B2**
Lanett 8,985 **C4**
Leeds 9,946 **B3**
Mobile 196,278 **E1**
Monroeville 6,993 **D2**
Montgomery 187,106 **C3**
Moundville 1,348 **C2**
Mountain Brook 19,810 **g7**
Muscle Shoals 9,611 **A2**
Northport 17,366 **B2**
Opelika 22,122 **C4**
Opp 6,985 **D3**
Ozark 12,922 **D4**
Pell City 8,118 **B3**
Phenix City 25,312 **C4**
Piedmont 5,288 **B4**
Prattville 19,587 **C3**
Prichard 34,311 **E1**
Roanoke 6,362 **B4**
Russellville 7,812 **A2**
Saraland 11,751 **E1**
Scottsboro 13,786 **A3**
Selma 23,755 **C2**
Sheffield 10,380 **A2**
Spanish Fort 3,732 **E2**
Sylacauga 12,520 **B3**
Talladega 18,175 **B3**
Tallassee 5,112 **C4**
Troy 13,051 **D4**
Tuscaloosa 77,759 **B2**
Tuscumbia 8,413 **A2**
Tuskegee 12,257 **C4**
Vestavia Hills 19,749 **g7**
Warrior 3,280 **B3**
Wetumpka 4,670 **C3**

A-520501-71 -8 -13
COSMO SERIES ALABAMA
Copyright by
RAND McNALLY & COMPANY
Made in U.S.A.

Statute Miles
Kilometers

Lambert Conformal Conic Projection
SCALE 1:1,831,000 1 Inch = 29 Statute Miles

Longitude West of Greenwich

Statute Miles 50 25 0   50   100   150   200   250
Kilometers 50 0   100   200   300

Polyconic Projection
SCALE 1:12,000,000 1 Inch = 189 Statute Miles

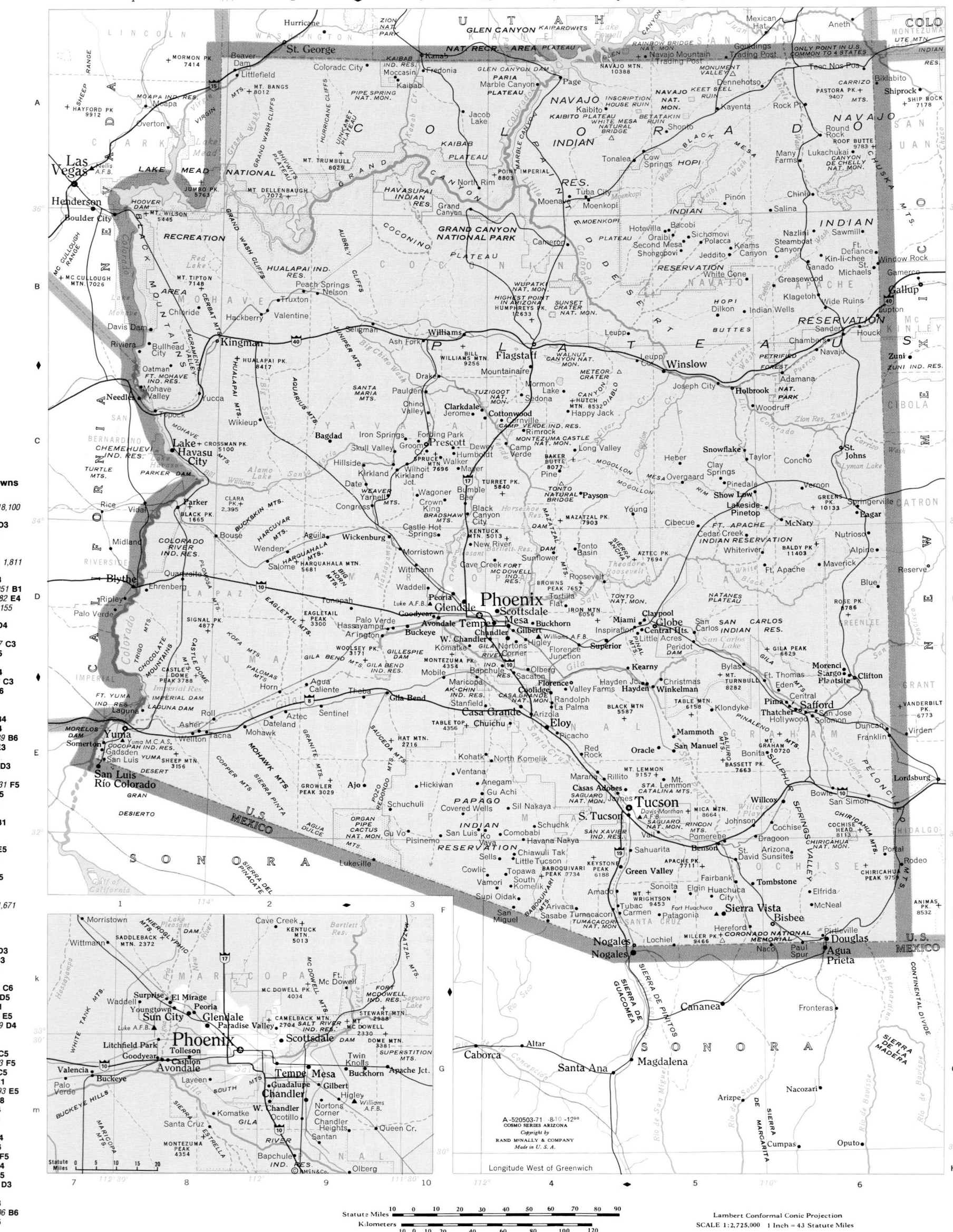

A-520503-71 -8-10 -12⁰⁰
COSMO SERIES ARIZONA
Copyright by
RAND McNALLY & COMPANY
Made in U.S.A.

Longitude West of Greenwich

Statute Miles

Kilometers

Lambert Conformal Conic Projection
SCALE 1:2,725,000   1 Inch = 43 Statute Miles

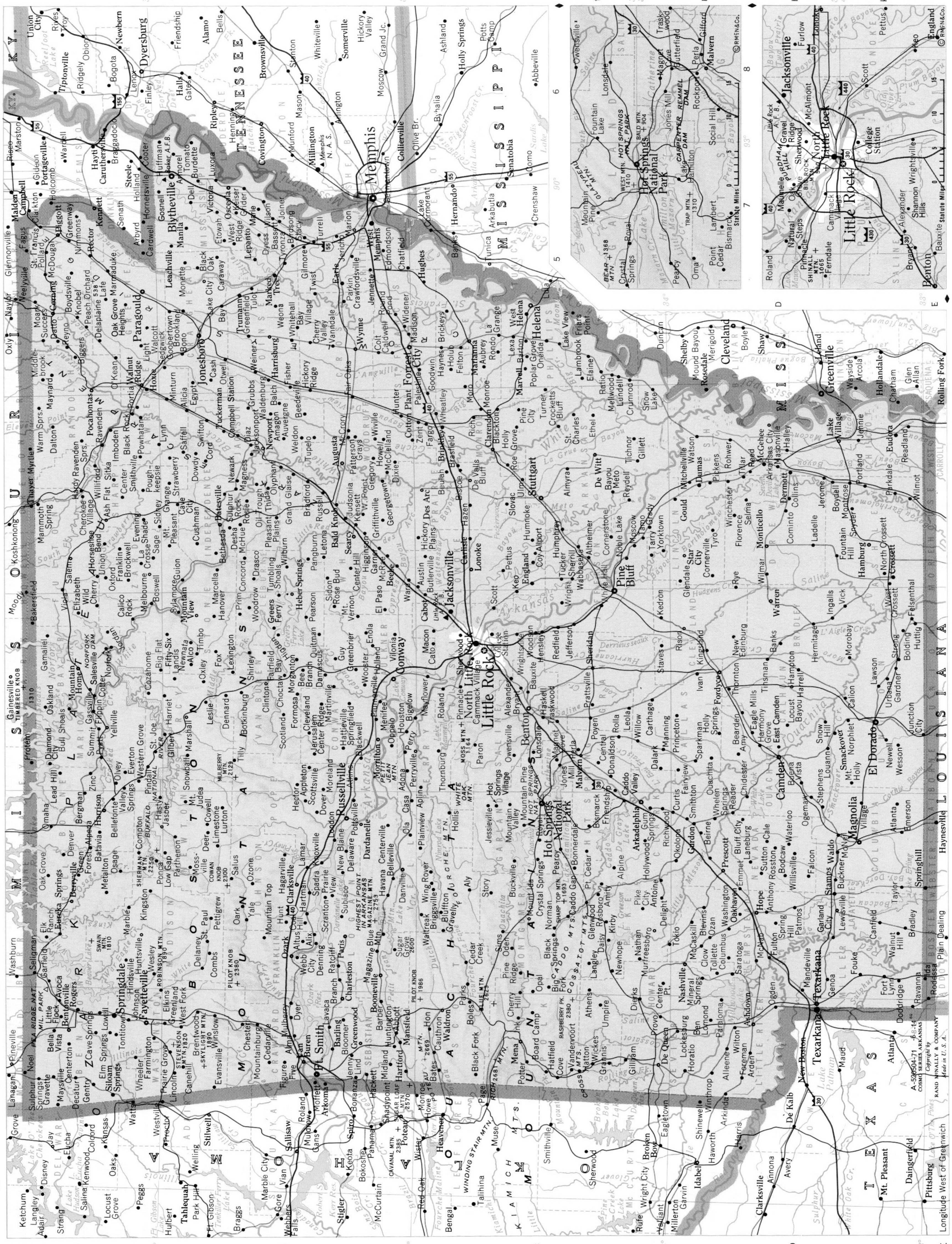

Statute Miles 5 0 5 10 20 30 40
Kilometers 5 0 5 15 25 35 45 55

Lambert Conformal Conic Projection
SCALE 1:1,832,000 1 Inch = 29 Statute Miles

Cities and Towns

Arkadelphia 10,014 C2
Ashdown 5,150 D1
Barling 4,078 B1
Batesville 9,187 B4
Beebe 4,455 B4
Benton 18,177 C3
Bentonville 11,257 A1
Berryville 3,212 A2
Blytheville 22,906 B6
Booneville 3,804 B2
Brinkley 4,234 C4
Cabot 8,319 C3
Camden 14,380 D3
Clarksville 5,833 B2
Conway 26,481 B3
Corning 3,323 A5
Crossett 6,282 D4
Dardanelle 3,722 B2
De Queen 4,633 C1
Dermott 4,715 D4
De Witt 3,553 C4
Dumas 5,520 D4
El Dorado 23,146 D3
Eudora 3,155 D4
Eureka Springs 1,900 A2
Fayetteville 42,099 A1
Fordyce 4,729 D3
Forrest City 13,364 B5
Fort Smith 72,798 B1
Harrison 9,922 A2
Heber Springs 5,628 B3
Helena 7,491 C5
Hope 9,643 D2
Hot Springs National Park 32,462 C2
Jacksonville 29,101 C3
Jonesboro 46,535 B5
Little Rock 175,795 C3
Lonoke 4,022 C4
Magnolia 11,151 D2
Malvern 9,256 C3
Marianna 5,910 C5
McGehee 4,997 D4
Mena 5,475 C1
Monticello 8,116 D4
Morrilton 6,551 B3
Mountain Home 9,027 A3
Mountain View 2,439 B3
Nashville 4,639 D2
Newport 7,459 B4
North Little Rock 61,741 C3
Osceola 8,930 B6
Ozark 3,330 B2
Paragould 18,540 A5
Paris 3,674 B2
Piggott 3,777 A5
Pine Bluff 57,140 C3
Pocahontas 6,151 A5
Prescott 3,673 D2
Rogers 24,692 A1
Russellville 21,260 B2
Searcy 15,180 B4
Sherwood 18,893 C3
Siloam Springs 8,151 A1
Springdale 29,941 A1
Stuttgart 10,420 C4
Texarkana 22,631 D1
Tontitown 460 A1
Trumann 6,304 B5
Van Buren 14,979 B1
Walnut Ridge 4,388 A5
Warren 6,455 D3
West Helena 9,695 C5
West Memphis 28,259 B5
Wynne 8,187 B5

Cities and Towns

Anaheim *266,406* **F5**
Antioch *62,195* **h9**
Bakersfield *174,820* **E4**
Berkeley *102,724* **D2**
Beverly Hills *31,971* **m12**
Burbank *93,643* **E4**
Calexico *18,633* **F6**
Chico *40,079* **C3**
Chula Vista *135,163* **F5**
Concord *111,348* **h8**
Costa Mesa *96,357* **n13**
Davis *46,209* **C3**
East Los Angeles *126,379* **m12**
El Cajon *88,693* **F5**
El Centro *31,384* **F6**
Escondido *108,635* **F5**
Eureka *27,025* **B1**
Fairfield *77,211* **C2**
Fremont *173,339* **D2**
Fresno *354,202* **D4**
Fullerton *114,144* **n13**
Garden Grove *143,050* **n13**
Glendale *180,038* **m12**
Hayward *111,498* **h8**
Huntington Beach *181,519* **F4**
Indio *36,793* **F5**
Lancaster *97,291* **E4**
Lompoc *37,649* **E3**
Long Beach *429,433* **F4**
Los Angeles *3,485,398* **E4**
Marysville *12,324* **C3**
Menlo Park *28,040* **k8**
Merced *56,216* **D3**
Modesto *164,730* **D3**
Monterey *31,954* **D3**
Napa *61,842* **C2**
Newport Beach *66,643* **n13**
Oakland *372,242* **D2**
Oceanside *128,398* **F5**
Ontario *133,179* **E5**
Oxnard *142,216* **E4**
Palm Springs *40,181* **F5**
Palo Alto *55,900* **D2**
Pasadena *131,591* **E4**
Pomona *131,723* **E5**
Redding *66,462* **B2**
Redwood City *66,072* **D2**
Richmond *87,425* **D2**
Riverside *226,505* **F5**
Sacramento *369,365* **C3**
Salinas *108,777* **D3**
San Bernardino *164,164* **E5**
San Clemente *41,100* **F5**
San Diego *1,110,549* **F5**
San Francisco *723,959* **D2**
San Jose *782,248* **D3**
San Juan Capistrano *26,183* **F5**
San Luis Obispo *41,958* **E3**
Santa Ana *293,742* **F5**
Santa Barbara *85,571* **E4**
Santa Cruz *49,040* **D2**
Santa Maria *61,284* **E3**
Santa Monica *86,905* **m12**
Santa Rosa *113,313* **C2**
South Lake Tahoe *21,586* **C4**
Stockton *210,943* **D3**
Sunnyvale *117,229* **k8**
Torrance *133,107* **n12**
Tulare *33,249* **D4**
Turlock *42,198* **D3**
Vallejo *109,199* **C2**
Ventura (San Buenaventura) *92,575* **E4**
Visalia *75,636* **D4**
Yuba City *27,437* **C3**

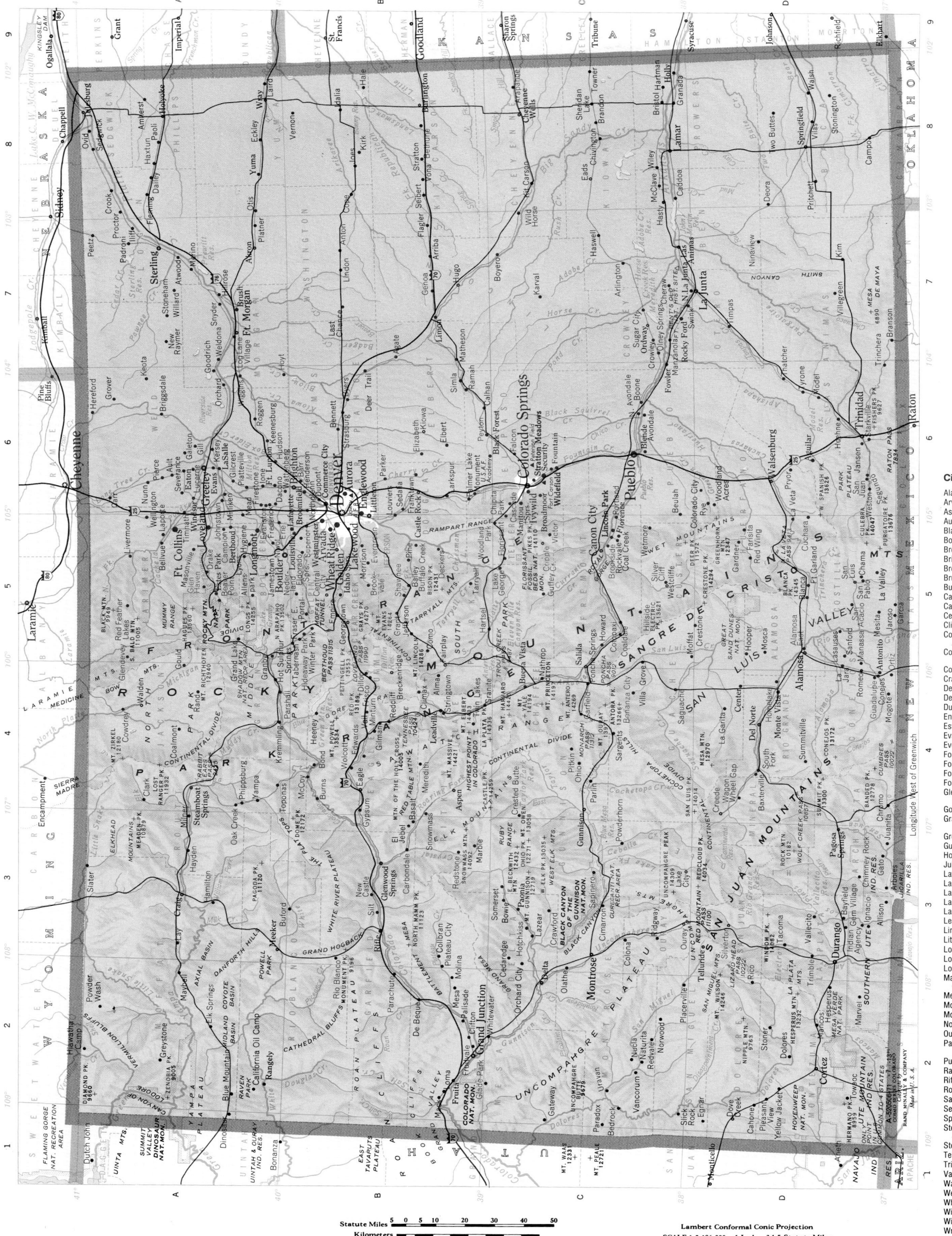

Statute Miles 5 0 5 10   20   30   40   50

Kilometers 5 0 5 15 25   35 45 55 65 75

Lambert Conformal Conic Projection
SCALE 1:2,186,000   1 Inch = 34.5 Statute Miles

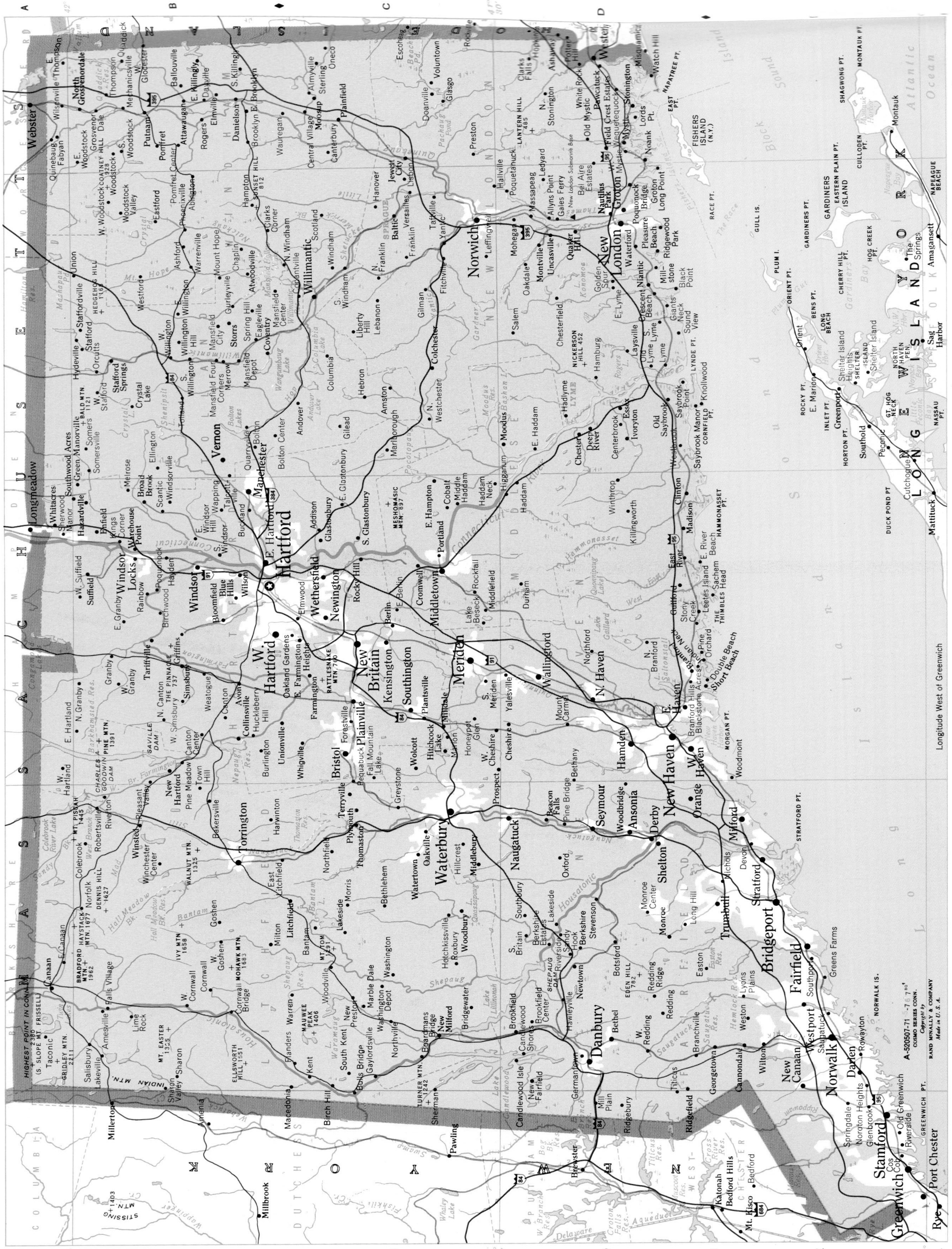

Lambert Conformal Conic Projection
SCALE 1:545,000 1 Inch = 8.6 Statute Miles

Cities and Towns*

Ansonia *18,403* **D3**
Bethel *8,835* **D2**
Bloomfield *7,120* **B5**
Blue Hills *3,206* **B5**
Branford *5,688* **D4**
Bridgeport *141,686* **E3**
Bristol *60,640* **C4**
Cheshire *5,759* **D4**
Clinton *3,439* **D5**
Cromwell *1,100* **C5**
Danbury *65,585* **D2**
Darien *18,130* **E2**
Derby *12,199* **D3**
East Hartford *50,452* **B5**
East Haven *26,144* **D4**
Enfield *8,458* **B5**
Fairfield *53,418* **E2**
Glastonbury *7,082* **C5**
Greenwich *58,441* **E1**
Groton *9,837* **D7**
Hamden *52,434* **D4**
Hartford *139,739* **B5**
Hazardville *5,179* **B5**
Kensington *8,306* **C4**
Manchester *51,618* **B5**
Meriden *59,479* **C4**
Middletown *42,762* **C5**
Milford *48,168* **E3**
Monroe Center *7,900* **D3**
Mystic *2,618* **D8**
Naugatuck *30,625* **D3**
Nautilus Park *6,500* **D7**
New Britain *75,491* **C4**
New Canaan *17,864* **E2**
New Haven *130,474* **D4**
Newington *29,208* **C5**
New London *28,540* **D7**
North Haven *22,249* **D4**
Norwalk *78,331* **E2**
Norwich *37,391* **C7**
Oakville *8,741* **C3**
Orange *12,830* **D3**
Plainville *17,392* **C4**
Plantsville *7,050* **C4**
Portland *5,645* **C5**
Putnam *6,835* **B8**
Ridgefield *6,363* **D2**
Seymour *14,288* **D3**
Shelton *35,418* **D3**
Sherwood Manor *6,357* **A5**
Simsbury *5,577* **B4**
Southington *38,518* **C4**
South Windsor *10,800* **B5**
Southwood Acres *8,963* **A5**
Stamford *108,056* **E1**
Storrs *12,198* **B7**
Stratford *49,389* **E3**
Terryville *5,426* **C3**
Torrington *33,687* **B3**
Trumbull *32,000* **E3**
Wallingford *17,827* **D4**
Waterbury *108,961* **C3**
Watertown *5,920* **C3**
West Hartford *60,110* **B4**
West Haven *54,021* **D4**
Westport *24,407* **E2**
Wethersfield *25,651* **C5**
Willimantic *14,746* **C7**
Wilton *7,200* **E2**
Windsor *27,817* **B5**
Windsor Locks *12,358* **B5**
Winsted *8,254* **B3**
Wolcott *6,070* **C4**
Woodbridge *7,924* **D3**

*Populations are for localities, not incorporated towns.

Cities and Towns

SCALE 1:533,000   1 Inch = 8.5 Statute Miles

Lambert Conformal Conic Projection

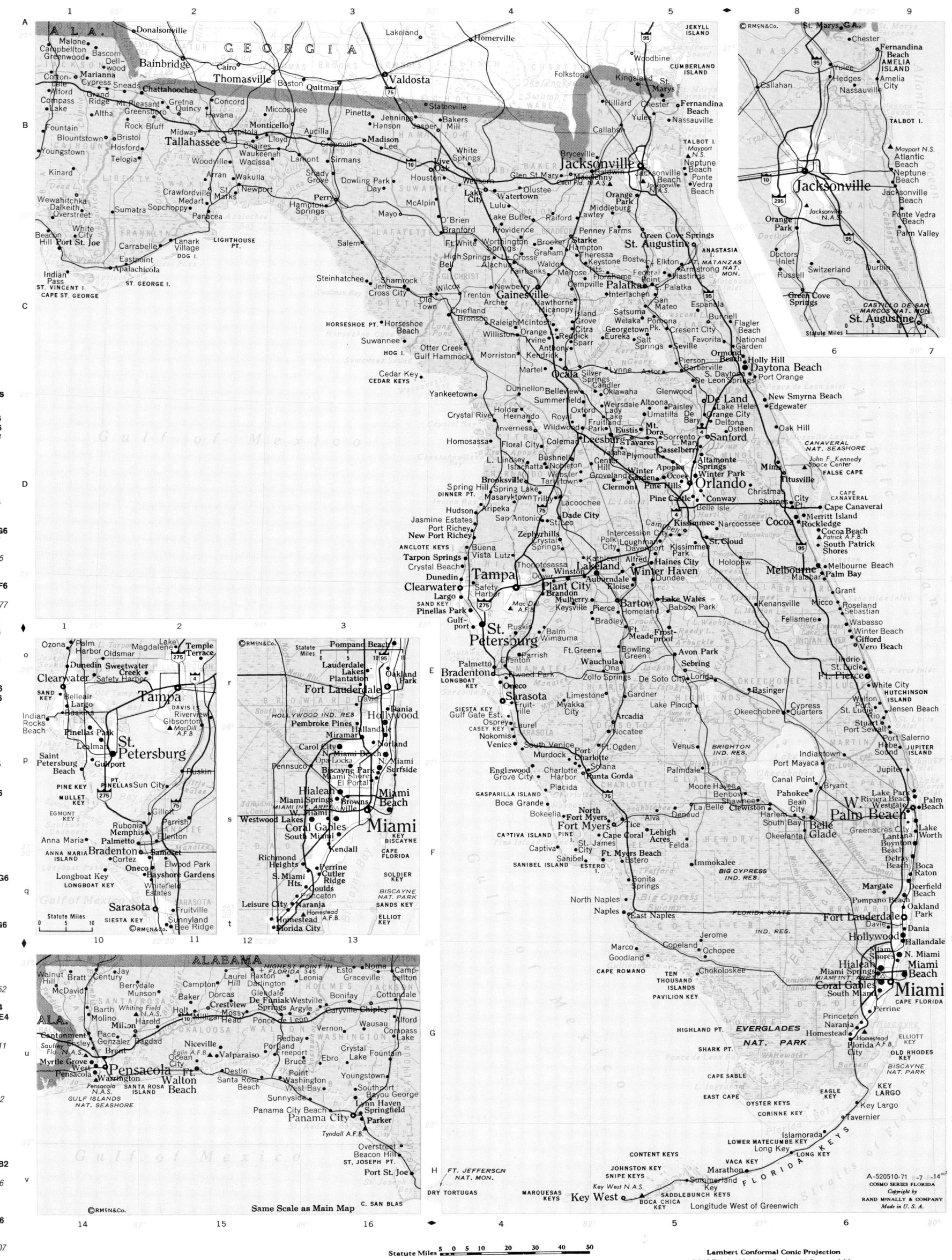

Statute Miles

Kilometers

Lambert Conformal Conic Projection
SCALE 1:2,425,000   1 Inch = 38 Statute Miles

Same Scale as Main Map

A-520510-71
COSMO SERIES FLORIDA
Copyright by
RAND MNALLY & COMPANY
Made in U.S.A.

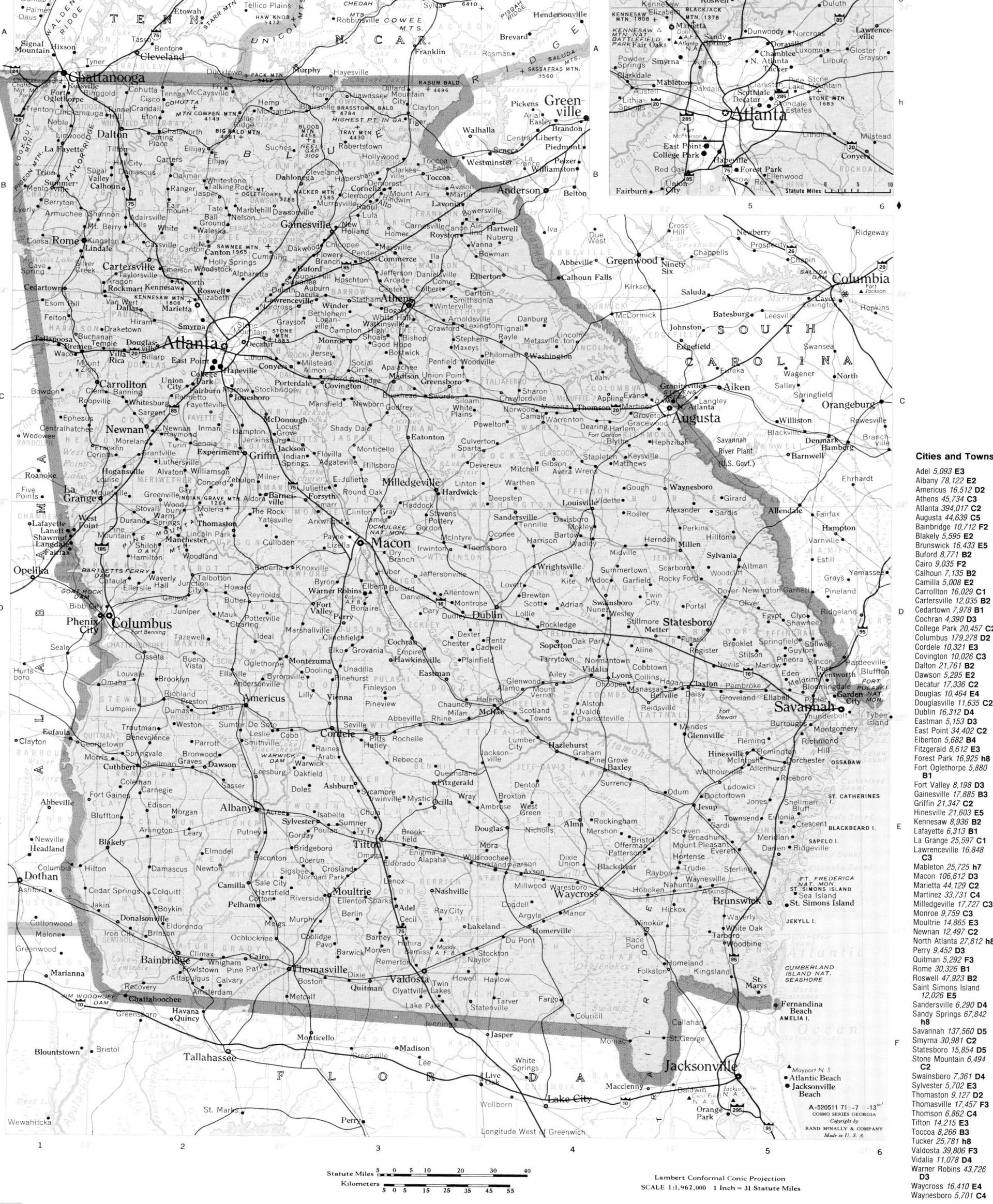

Lambert Conformal Conic Projection
SCALE 1:1,962,000 1 Inch = 31 Statute Miles

A-520511 71 -7 -13^ml
COSMO SERIES GEORGIA
Copyright by
RAND McNALLY & COMPANY
Made in U.S.A.

Cities and Towns

Adel 5,093 **E3**
Albany 78,122 **E2**
Americus 16,512 **D2**
Athens 45,734 **C3**
Atlanta 394,017 **C2**
Augusta 44,639 **C5**
Bainbridge 10,712 **F2**
Blakely 5,595 **E2**
Brunswick 16,433 **E5**
Buford 8,771 **B2**
Cairo 9,035 **F2**
Calhoun 7,135 **B2**
Camilla 5,008 **E2**
Carrollton 16,029 **C1**
Cartersville 12,035 **B2**
Cedartown 7,978 **B1**
Cochran 4,390 **D3**
College Park 20,457 **C2**
Columbus 179,278 **D2**
Cordele 10,321 **E3**
Covington 10,026 **C3**
Dalton 21,761 **B2**
Dawson 5,295 **E2**
Decatur 17,336 **C2**
Douglas 10,464 **E4**
Douglasville 11,635 **C2**
Dublin 16,312 **D4**
Eastman 5,153 **D3**
East Point 34,402 **C2**
Elberton 5,682 **B4**
Fitzgerald 8,612 **E3**
Forest Park 16,925 **h8**
Fort Oglethorpe 5,880
  B1
Fort Valley 8,198 **D3**
Gainesville 17,885 **B3**
Griffin 21,347 **C2**
Hinesville 21,603 **E5**
Kennesaw 8,936 **B2**
Lafayette 6,313 **B1**
La Grange 25,597 **C1**
Lawrenceville 16,848
  C3
Mableton 25,725 **h7**
Macon 106,612 **D3**
Marietta 44,129 **C2**
Martinez 33,731 **C4**
Milledgeville 17,727 **C3**
Monroe 9,759 **C3**
Moultrie 14,865 **E3**
Newnan 12,497 **C2**
North Atlanta 27,812 **h8**
Perry 9,452 **D3**
Quitman 5,292 **F3**
Rome 30,326 **B1**
Roswell 47,923 **B2**
Saint Simons Island
  12,026 **E5**
Sandersville 6,290 **D4**
Sandy Springs 67,842
  h8
Savannah 137,560 **D5**
Smyrna 30,981 **C2**
Statesboro 15,854 **D5**
Stone Mountain 6,494
  C2
Swainsboro 7,361 **D4**
Sylvester 5,702 **E3**
Thomaston 9,127 **D2**
Thomasville 17,457 **F3**
Thomson 6,862 **C4**
Tifton 14,215 **E3**
Toccoa 8,266 **B3**
Tucker 25,781 **h8**
Valdosta 39,806 **F3**
Vidalia 11,078 **D4**
Warner Robins 43,726
  D3
Waycross 16,410 **E4**
Waynesboro 5,701 **C4**

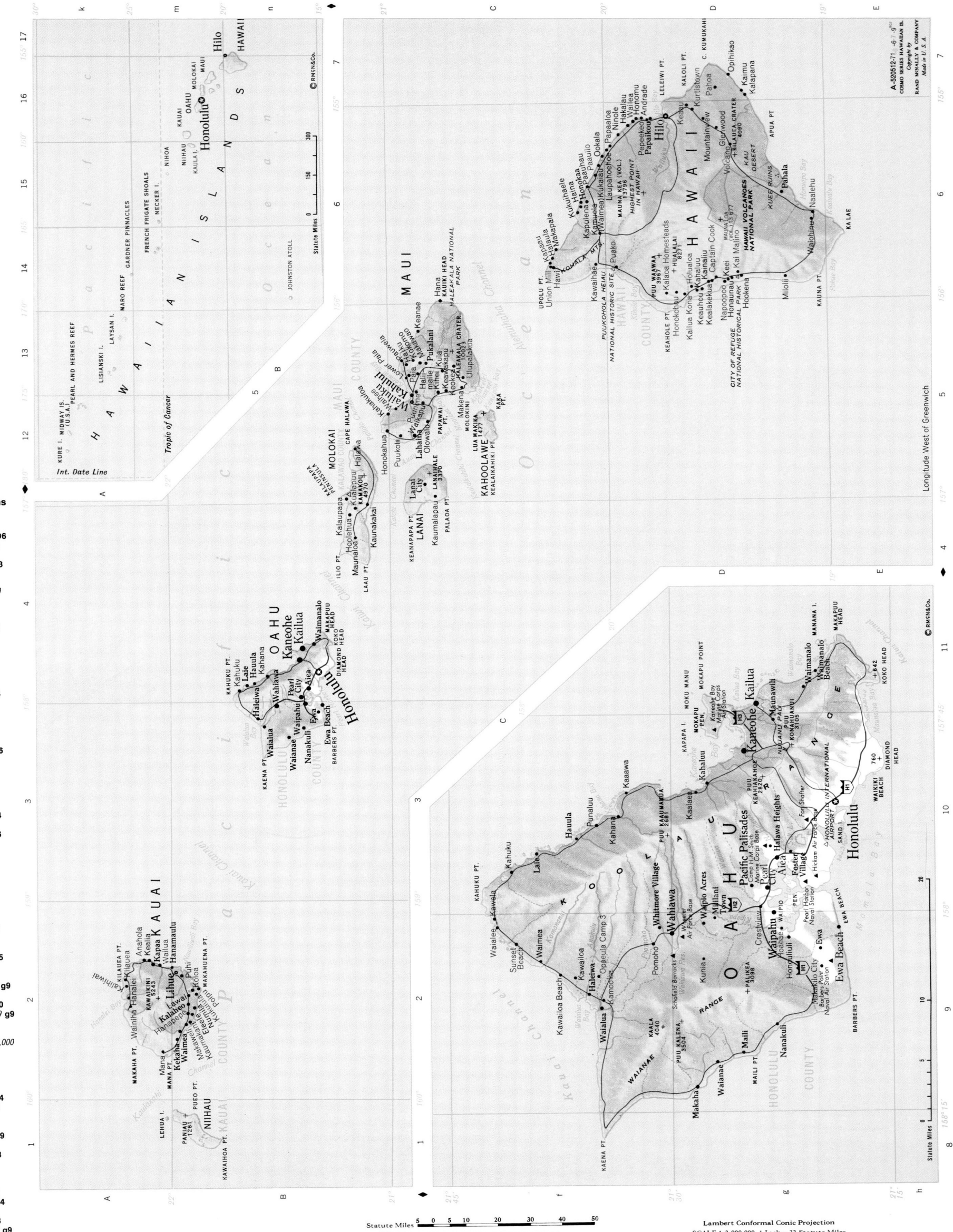

Cities and Towns

Aiea *8,906* **B4**
Anahola *1,181* **A2**
Captain Cook *2,696* **D6**
Crestview *1,000* **g10**
Ewa *3,780* **B3**
Ewa Beach *14,315* **B3**
Foster Village *3,700* **g10**
Halawa Heights *7,000* **g10**
Haleiwa *2,442* **B3**
Haliimaile *841* **C5**
Hanamaulu *3,611* **B2**
Hanapepe *1,395* **B2**
Hauula *3,479* **B4**
Hawi *924* **C6**
Hilo *37,808* **D6**
Holualoa *3,834* **D6**
Honokaa *2,186* **C6**
Honolulu *365,272* **B4**
Kaaawa *1,138* **f10**
Kahaluu *3,068* **g10**
Kahuku *2,063* **B4**
Kahului *16,889* **C5**
Kailua *36,818* **B4**
Kailua Kona *9,126* **D6**
Kalaheo *3,592* **B2**
Kamuela (Waimea) *5,972* **C6**
Kaneohe *35,448* **B4**
Kapaa *8,149* **A2**
Kaumakani *803* **B2**
Kaunakakai *2,658* **B4**
Keaau *1,584* **D6**
Kealakekua *1,453* **D6**
Kekaha *3,506* **B2**
Keokea *900* **C5**
Kihei *11,107* **C5**
Kilauea *1,685* **A2**
Koloa *1,791* **B2**
Kula *1,300* **C5**
Kurtistown *910* **D6**
Lahaina *9,073* **C5**
Laie *5,577* **B4**
Lanai City *2,400* **C5**
Lawai *1,787* **B2**
Lihue *5,536* **B2**
Lower Paia *1,500* **C5**
Maili *6,059* **g9**
Makaha *7,990* **g9**
Makakilo City *9,828* **g9**
Makawao *5,405* **C5**
Maunawili *4,847* **g10**
Mililani Town *29,359* **g9**
Naalehu *1,027* **D6**
Nanakuli *9,575* **B3**
Pacific Palisades *10,000* **g10**
Pahala *1,520* **D6**
Pahoa *1,027* **D7**
Paia *2,091* **C5**
Papaikou *1,634* **D6**
Pearl City *30,993* **B4**
Pepeekeo *1,813* **D6**
Puhi *1,210* **B2**
Pukalani *5,879* **C5**
Sunset Beach *800* **f9**
Volcano *1,516* **D6**
Wahiawa *17,386* **B3**
Waialua *3,943* **B3**
Waianae *8,758* **B3**
Wailua *2,018* **A2**
Wailuku *10,688* **C5**
Waimanalo *3,508* **B4**
Waimea *5,972* **B2**
Waipahu *31,435* **B3**
Waipio Acres *5,307* **g9**
Whitmore Village *3,373* **f9**

Statute Miles
Kilometers

Lambert Conformal Conic Projection
SCALE 1:2,000,000   1 Inch = 32 Statute Miles

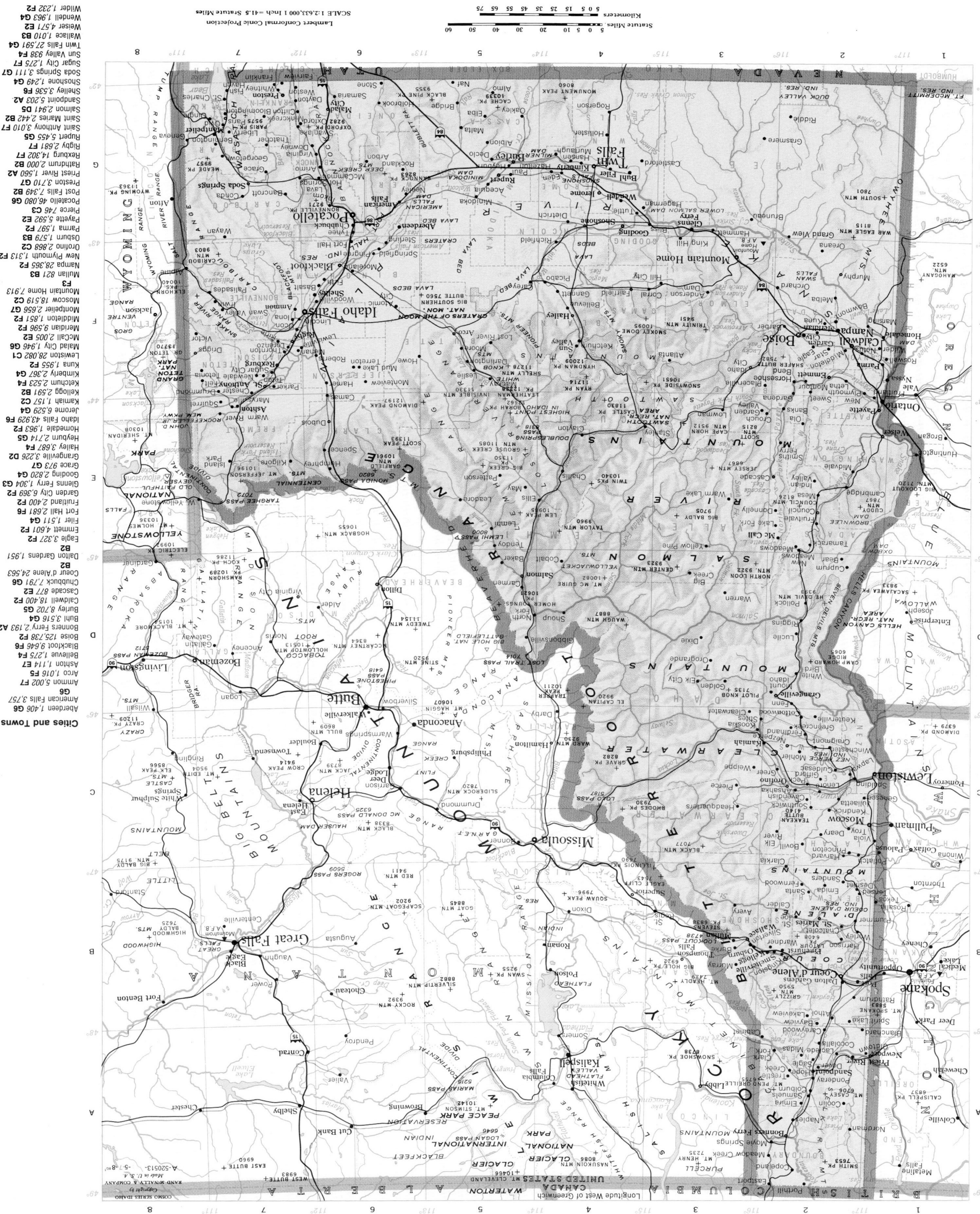

Cities and Towns

Aberdeen 1,406 G6
American Falls 3,757 G6
Ammon 5,002 F7
Arco 1,016 F5
Ashton 1,114 E7
Bellevue 1,275 F4
Blackfoot 9,646 F6
Boise 125,738 E2
Bonners Ferry 2,193 A2
Buhl 3,516 G4
Burley 8,702 G5
Caldwell 18,400 F2
Cascade 877 E2
Chubbuck 7,791 G6
Coeur d'Alene 24,563 B2
Dalton Gardens 1,951 B2
Eagle 3,327 F2
Emmett 4,601 F2
Filer 1,511 G4
Fort Hall 2,681 F6
Fruitland 2,400 F2
Garden City 6,369 F2
Glenns Ferry 1,304 G3
Gooding 2,820 G4
Grace 973 G7
Grangeville 3,226 D2
Hailey 3,687 F4
Hayden 4,929 F6
Heyburn 2,714 G5
Homedale 1,963 F2
Idaho Falls 43,929 F6
Jerome 6,529 G4
Kamiah 1,157 C2
Kellogg 2,591 B2
Ketchum 2,523 F4
Kimberly 2,367 G4
Kuna 1,955 F2
Lewiston 28,082 C1
Mackay 566 F5
Malad City 1,946 G6
McCall 2,005 E2
Meridian 9,596 F2
Middleton 1,851 F2
Montpelier 2,656 G7
Moscow 18,519 C2
Mountain Home 7,913 F3
Mullan 821 B3
Nampa 28,365 F2
New Plymouth 1,313 F2
Orofino 2,868 C2
Osburn 1,597 F2
Parma 1,597 F2
Payette 5,592 E2
Pierce 746 C3
Pocatello 46,080 G6
Post Falls 7,349 B2
Preston 3,710 G7
Priest River 1,560 A2
Rathdrum 2,000 B2
Rexburg 14,302 F7
Rigby 2,681 F7
Rupert 5,455 G5
Saint Anthony 3,010 F7
Saint Maries 2,941 D5
Saint Maries 2,442 B2
Salmon 3,203 A2
Sandpoint 5,203 A2
Shelley 3,536 F6
Shoshone 1,249 G5
Soda Springs 3,111 G7
Sugar City 1,275 F7
Sun Valley 938 F4
Twin Falls 27,591 G4
Wallace 1,010 B3
Weiser 4,571 E2
Wendell 1,963 G4
Wilder 1,232 F2

SCALE 1:2,633,000 1 Inch = 41.5 Statute Miles
Lambert Conformal Conic Projection

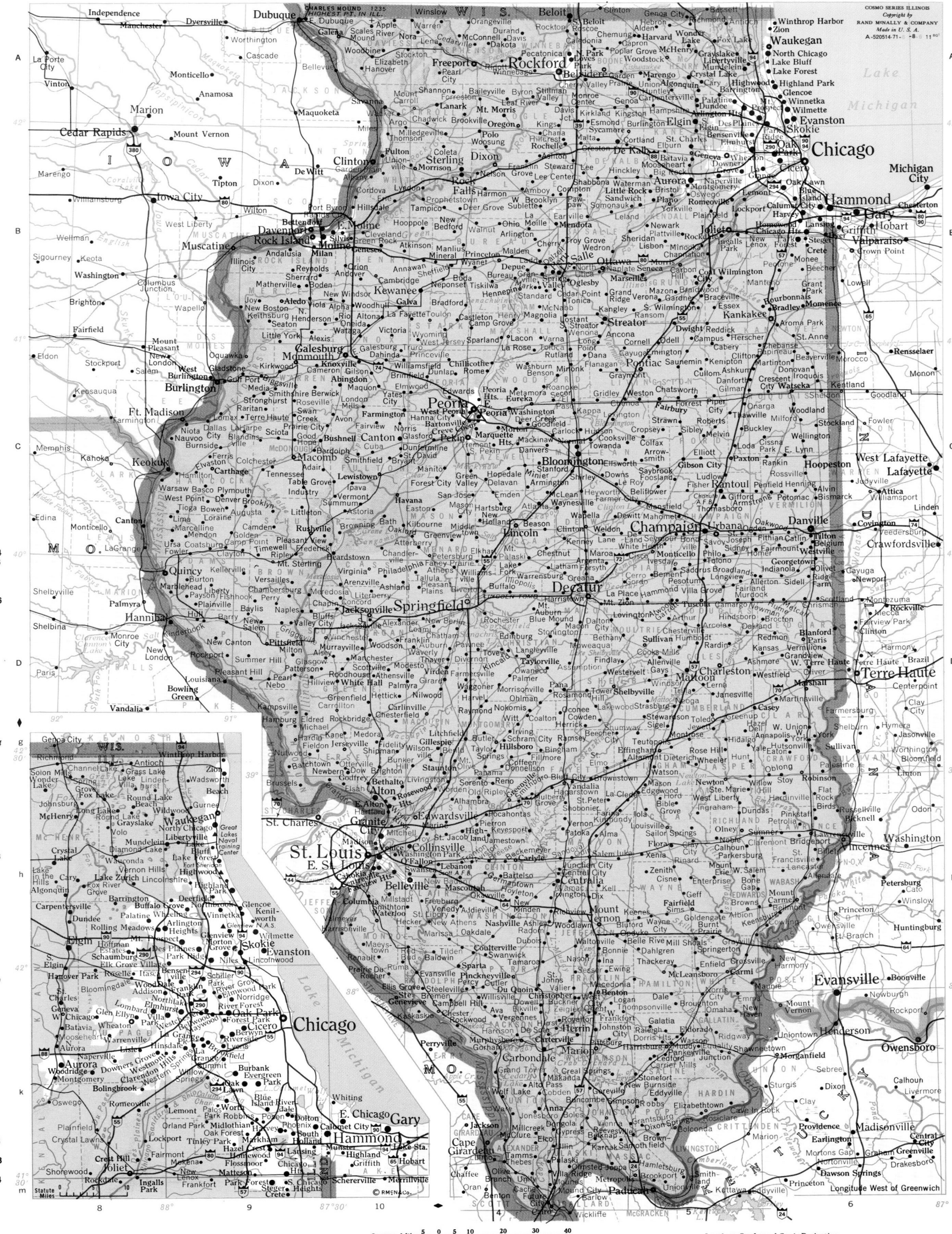

Statute Miles
Kilometers

Lambert Conformal Conic Projection
SCALE 1:1,997,000   1 Inch = 31.5 Statute Miles

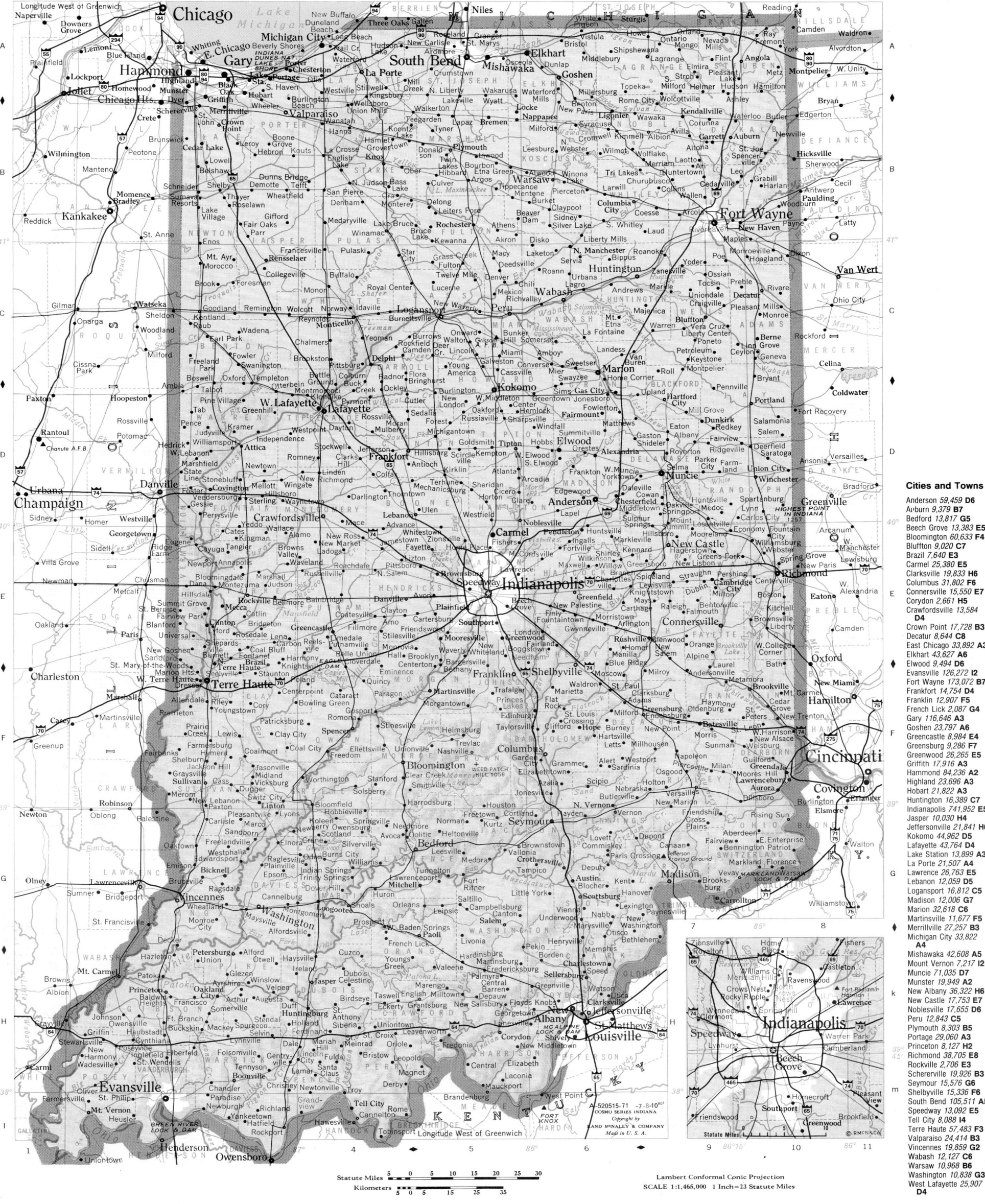

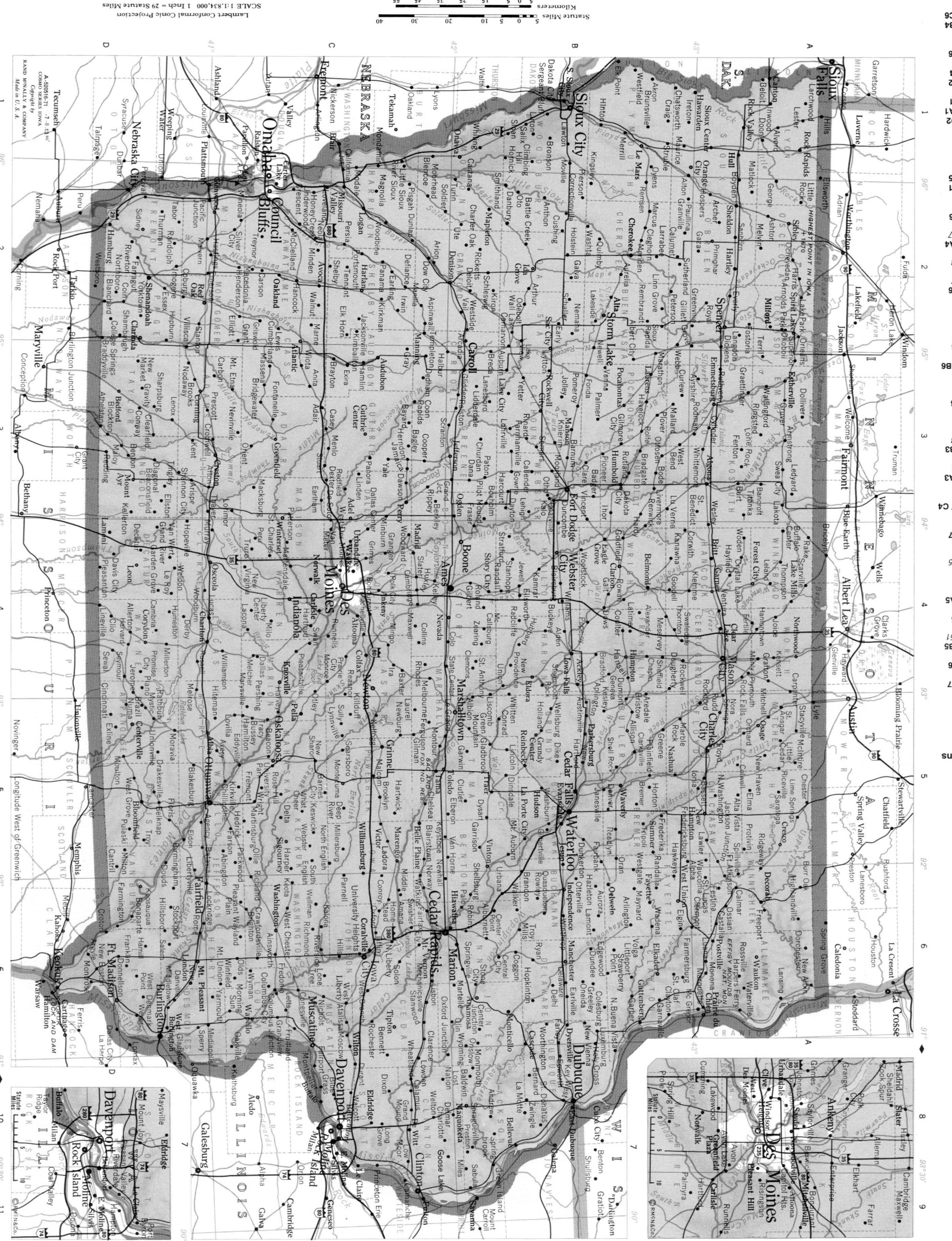

Cities and Towns

Algona 6,015 A3
Ames 47,198 B4
Amana 540 C6
Anamosa 5,100 B6
Ankeny 18,482 C4
Atlantic 7,432 C2
Bettendorf 28,132 C7
Boone 12,392 B4
Burlington 27,208 D6
Carroll 9,579 B3
Cedar Falls 34,298 B5
Cedar Rapids 108,751 C6
Centerville 5,936 D5
Chariton 4,616 C4
Charles City 7,878 A5
Cherokee 6,026 B2
Clarinda 5,104 D2
Clinton 29,201 C7
Council Bluffs 54,315 C2
Creston 7,911 C3
Davenport 95,333 C7
Decorah 8,063 A6
Denison 6,604 B2
Des Moines 193,187 C4
De Witt 4,514 C7
Dubuque 57,546 B7
Emmetsburg 3,940 A3
Estherville 6,720 A3
Fairfield 8,768 C6
Fort Dodge 25,894 B3
Fort Madison 11,618 D6
Glenwood 4,571 C2
Grinnell 8,902 C5
Guthrie Center 2,257 B3
Hampton 4,133 B4
Harlan 5,148 C2
Humboldt 4,438 B3
Independence 5,972 B6
Indianola 11,340 C4
Iowa City 50,508 C6
Iowa Falls 5,424 B4
Jefferson 4,292 B3
Keokuk 14,631 D6
Knoxville 8,232 C4
Le Mars 8,454 B1
Manchester 5,137 B6
Maquoketa 6,111 B7
Marion 20,403 B6
Marshalltown 25,178 B5
Mason City 29,040 A4
Mount Pleasant 8,027 D6
Muscatine 22,881 C6
Newton 14,789 C4
Oelwein 6,493 B6
Orange City 4,940 B1
Oskaloosa 10,632 C5
Ottumwa 24,488 C5
Pella 9,270 C5
Perry 6,652 C3
Red Oak 6,264 D2
Sheldon 4,937 A2
Shenandoah 5,572 D2
Sioux Center 5,074 A1
Sioux City 80,505 B1
Spencer 11,066 A2
Storm Lake 8,769 B2
Urbandale 10,632 C5
Vinton 5,103 B5
Washington 7,074 C6
Waterloo 66,467 B5
Waverly 8,539 B5
Webster City 7,894 B4
West Branch 1,908 C6
West Des Moines 31,702 C4

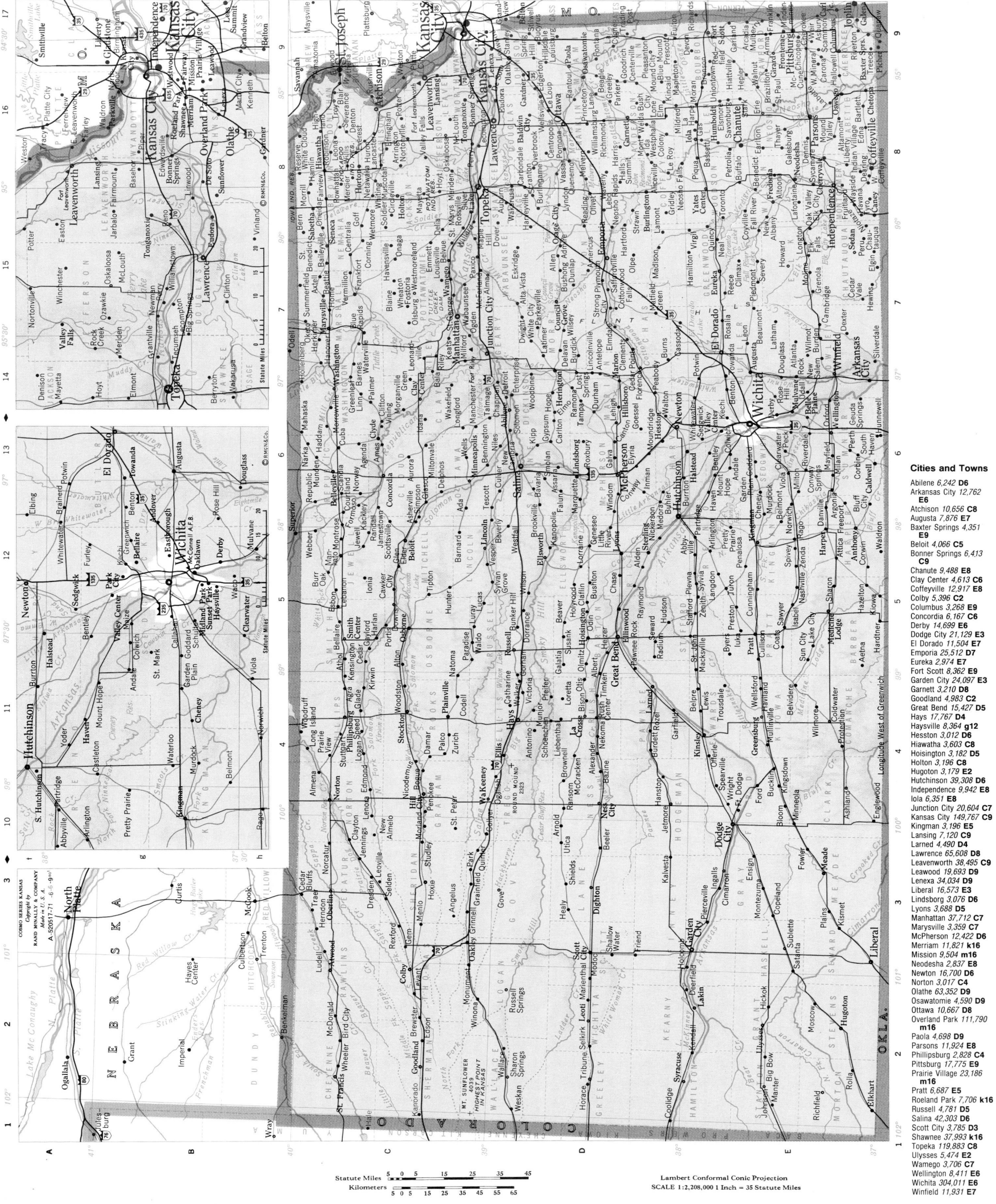

Cities and Towns

Abilene 6,242 **D6**
Arkansas City 12,762 **E6**
Atchison 10,656 **C8**
Augusta 7,876 **E7**
Baxter Springs 4,351 **E9**
Beloit 4,066 **C5**
Bonner Springs 6,413 **C9**
Chanute 9,488 **E8**
Clay Center 4,613 **C6**
Coffeyville 12,917 **E8**
Colby 5,396 **C2**
Concordia 6,167 **C6**
Derby 14,699 **E6**
Dodge City 21,129 **E3**
El Dorado 11,504 **E7**
Emporia 25,512 **D7**
Eureka 2,974 **E7**
Fort Scott 8,362 **E9**
Garden City 24,097 **E3**
Garnett 3,210 **D8**
Goodland 4,983 **C2**
Great Bend 15,427 **D5**
Hays 17,767 **D4**
Haysville 8,364 **g12**
Hesston 3,012 **D6**
Hiawatha 3,603 **C8**
Hoisington 3,182 **D5**
Holton 3,196 **C8**
Hugoton 3,179 **E2**
Hutchinson 39,308 **D6**
Independence 9,942 **E8**
Iola 6,351 **E8**
Junction City 20,604 **C7**
Kansas City 149,767 **C9**
Kingman 3,196 **E5**
Lansing 7,120 **C9**
Larned 4,490 **D4**
Lawrence 65,608 **D8**
Leavenworth 38,495 **C9**
Leawood 19,693 **D9**
Lenexa 34,034 **D9**
Liberal 16,573 **E3**
Lindsborg 3,076 **D6**
Lyons 3,688 **D5**
Manhattan 37,712 **C7**
Marysville 3,359 **C7**
McPherson 12,422 **D6**
Merriam 11,821 **k16**
Mission 9,504 **m16**
Newton 16,700 **D6**
Neodesha 2,837 **E8**
Norton 3,017 **C4**
Olathe 63,352 **D9**
Osawatomie 4,590 **D9**
Ottawa 10,667 **D8**
Overland Park 111,790 **m16**
Paola 4,698 **D9**
Parsons 11,924 **E8**
Phillipsburg 2,828 **C4**
Pittsburg 17,775 **E9**
Prairie Village 23,186 **m16**
Pratt 6,687 **E5**
Roeland Park 7,706 **k16**
Russell 4,781 **D5**
Salina 42,303 **D6**
Scott City 3,785 **D3**
Shawnee 37,993 **k16**
Topeka 119,883 **C8**
Ulysses 5,474 **E2**
Wamego 3,706 **C7**
Wellington 8,411 **E6**
Wichita 304,011 **E6**
Winfield 11,931 **E7**

Cities and Towns

Alexandria *5,592* **B5**
Ashland *23,622* **B7**
Barbourville *3,658* **D6**
Bardstown *6,801* **C4**
Berea *9,126* **C5**
Bowling Green *40,641* **D3**
Campbellsville *9,577* **C4**
Carrollton *3,715* **B4**
Cave City *1,953* **C4**
Central City *4,979* **C2**
Corbin *7,419* **D5**
Covington *43,264* **A5**
Cynthiana *6,497* **B5**
Danville *12,420* **C5**
Edgewood *8,143* **h13**
Elizabethtown *18,167* **C4**
Elsmere *6,847* **B5**
Erlanger *15,979* **A5**
Fairdale *6,563* **B4**
Fern Creek *16,406* **g11**
Flatwoods *7,799* **B7**
Florence *18,624* **A5**
Fort Mitchell *7,438* **h13**
Fort Thomas *16,032* **h14**
Frankfort *25,968* **B5**
Franklin *7,607* **D3**
Georgetown *11,414* **B5**
Glasgow *12,351* **C4**
Greenville *4,689* **C2**
Harrodsburg *7,335* **C5**
Hazard *5,416* **C6**
Henderson *25,945* **C2**
Hopkinsville *29,809* **D2**
Independence *10,444* **B5**
Jeffersontown *23,221* **B4**
Lawrenceburg *5,911* **B5**
Lebanon *5,695* **C4**
Leitchfield *4,965* **C3**
Lexington *225,366* **B5**
London *5,757* **C5**
Louisville *269,063* **B4**
Madisonville *16,200* **C2**
Mayfield *9,935* **f9**
Maysville *7,169* **B6**
Middlesboro *11,328* **D6**
Monticello *5,357* **D5**
Morehead *8,357* **B6**
Mount Sterling *5,362* **B6**
Murray *14,439* **f9**
Newport *18,871* **A5**
Nicholasville *13,603* **C5**
Okolona *18,902* **g11**
Owensboro *53,549* **C2**
Paducah *27,256* **e9**
Paris *8,730* **B5**
Pikeville *6,324* **C7**
Pleasure Ridge Park *25,131* **g11**
Prestonsburg *3,558* **C7**
Providence *4,123* **C2**
Radcliff *19,772* **C4**
Richmond *21,155* **C5**
Russellville *7,454* **D3**
Saint Matthews *15,800* **B4**
Scottsville *4,278* **D3**
Shelbyville *6,238* **B4**
Shepherdsville *4,805* **C4**
Shively *15,535* **B4**
Somerset *10,733* **C5**
Tompkinsville *2,861* **D4**
Valley Station *22,840* **g11**
Versailles *7,269* **B5**
Westwood *5,300* **B7**
Williamsburg *5,493* **D5**
Winchester *15,799* **C5**

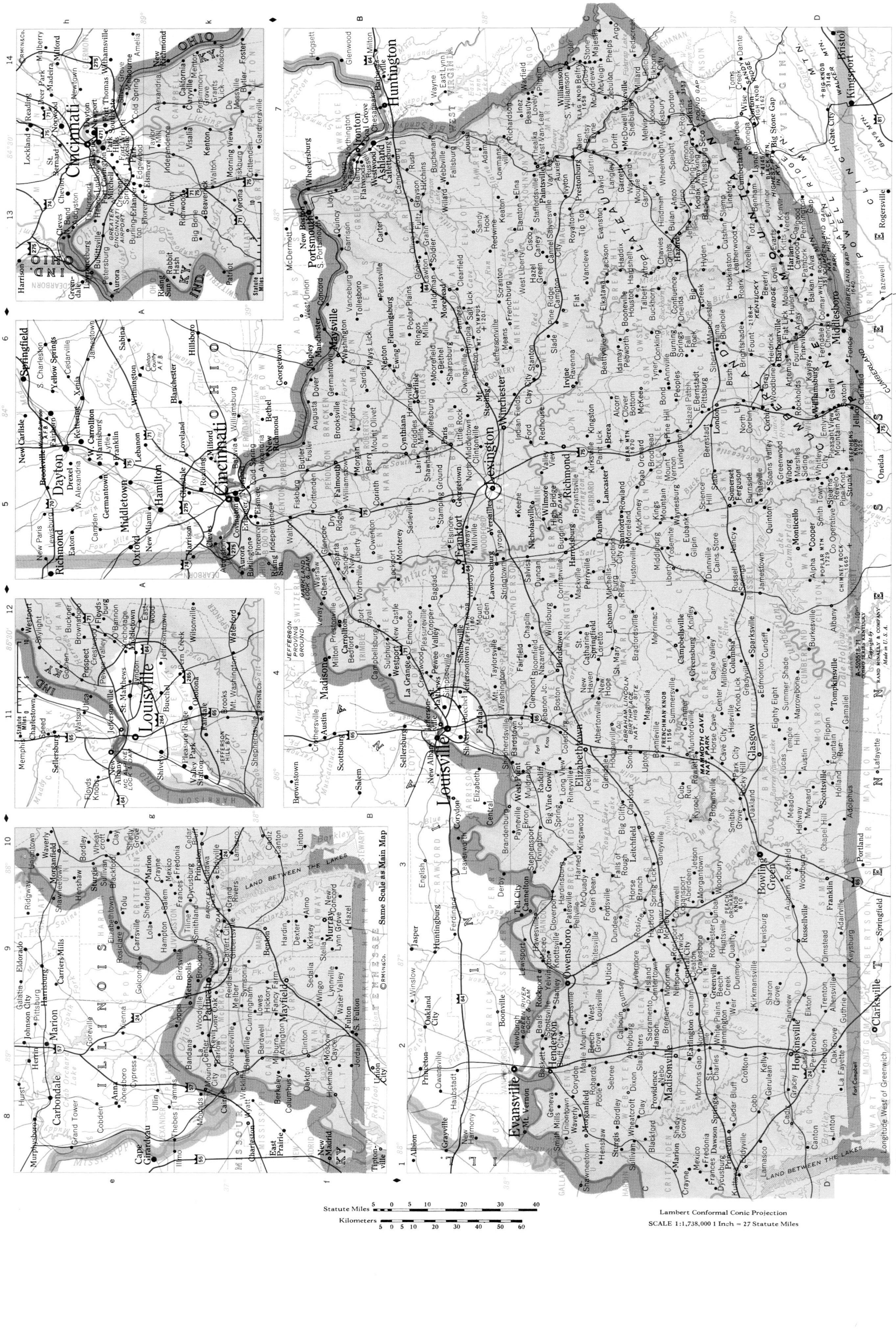

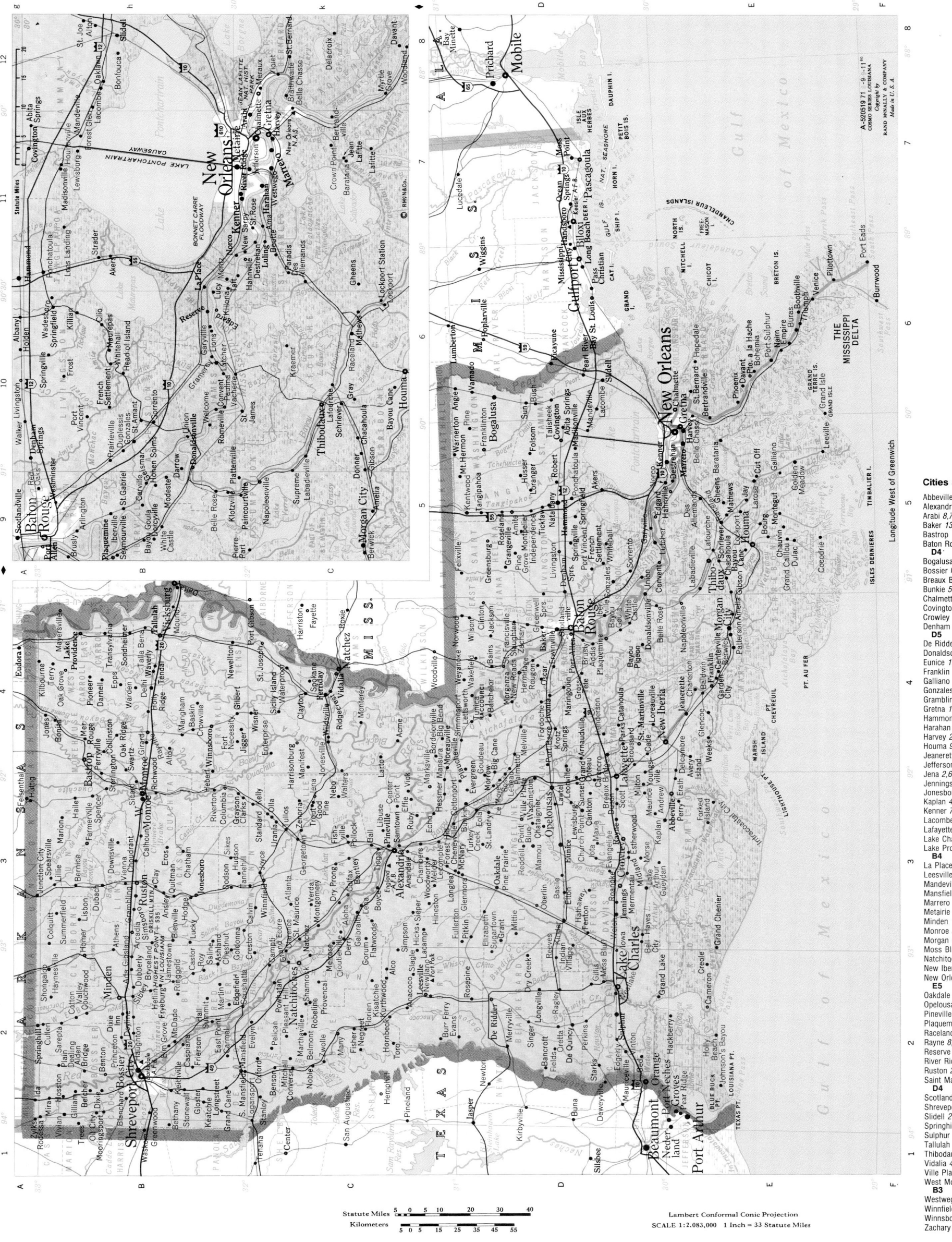

Lambert Conformal Conic Projection

SCALE 1:2,083,000   1 Inch = 33 Statute Miles

Statute Miles 5 0 5 10   20   30   40

Kilometers 5 0 5 15 25 35 45 55

Cities and Towns

Abbeville *11,187* **E3**
Alexandria *49,188* **C3**
Arabi *8,787* **k11**
Baker *13,233* **D4**
Bastrop *13,916* **B4**
Baton Rouge *219,531*
  D4
Bogalusa *14,280* **D6**
Bossier City *52,721* **B2**
Breaux Bridge *6,515* **D4**
Bunkie *5,044* **D3**
Chalmette *31,860* **E6**
Covington *7,691* **D5**
Crowley *13,983* **D3**
Denham Springs *8,381*
  D5
De Ridder *9,868* **D2**
Donaldsonville *7,949* **D4**
Eunice *11,162* **D3**
Franklin *9,004* **E4**
Galliano *4,294* **E5**
Gonzales *7,003* **D5**
Grambling *5,484* **B3**
Gretna *17,208* **E5**
Hammond *15,871* **D5**
Harahan *9,927* **k11**
Harvey *21,222* **E5**
Houma *96,982* **E5**
Jeanerette *6,205* **E4**
Jefferson *14,521* **k11**
Jena *2,626* **C3**
Jennings *11,305* **D3**
Jonesboro *4,305* **B3**
Kaplan *4,535* **D3**
Kenner *72,033* **E5**
Lacombe *6,523* **D6**
Lafayette *94,440* **D3**
Lake Charles *70,580* **D2**
Lake Providence *5,380*
  B4
La Place *24,194* **h11**
Leesville *7,638* **C2**
Mandeville *7,083* **D5**
Mansfield *5,389* **B2**
Marrero *36,671* **E5**
Metairie *149,428* **k11**
Minden *13,661* **B2**
Monroe *54,909* **B3**
Morgan City *14,531* **E4**
Moss Bluff *8,039* **D2**
Natchitoches *16,609* **C2**
New Iberia *31,828* **D4**
New Orleans *496,938*
  E5
Oakdale *6,832* **D3**
Opelousas *18,151* **D3**
Pineville *12,251* **C3**
Plaquemine *7,186* **D4**
Raceland *5,564* **E5**
Rayne *8,502* **D3**
Reserve *8,847* **h10**
River Ridge *14,800* **k11**
Ruston *20,027* **B3**
Saint Martinville *7,137*
Scotlandville *15,113* **D4**
Shreveport *198,525* **B2**
Slidell *24,124* **D6**
Springhill *5,668* **A2**
Sulphur *20,125* **D2**
Tallulah *8,526* **B4**
Thibodaux *14,035* **E5**
Vidalia *4,953* **C4**
Ville Platte *9,037* **D3**
West Monroe *14,096*
  B3
Westwego *11,218* **k11**
Winnfield *6,138* **C3**
Winnsboro *5,755* **B4**
Zachary *9,036* **D4**

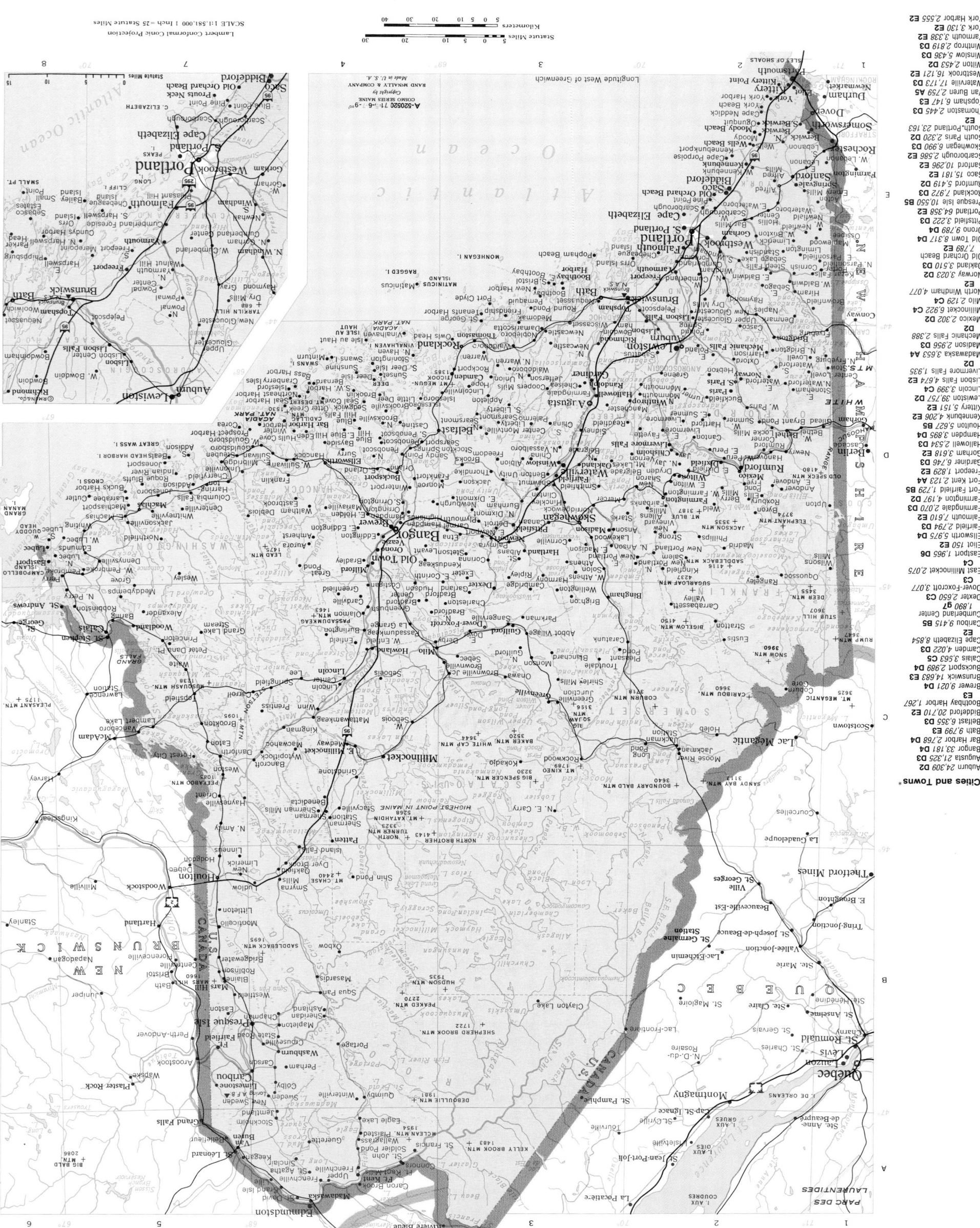

Populations are for localities, not incorporated towns.

SCALE 1:1,581,000 1 Inch = 25 Statute Miles
Lambert Conformal Conic Projection

Copyright by
RAND MCNALLY & COMPANY
Made in U.S.A.
COSMO SERIES MAINE
A-520520 71°-6-'-90'

Longitude West of Greenwich

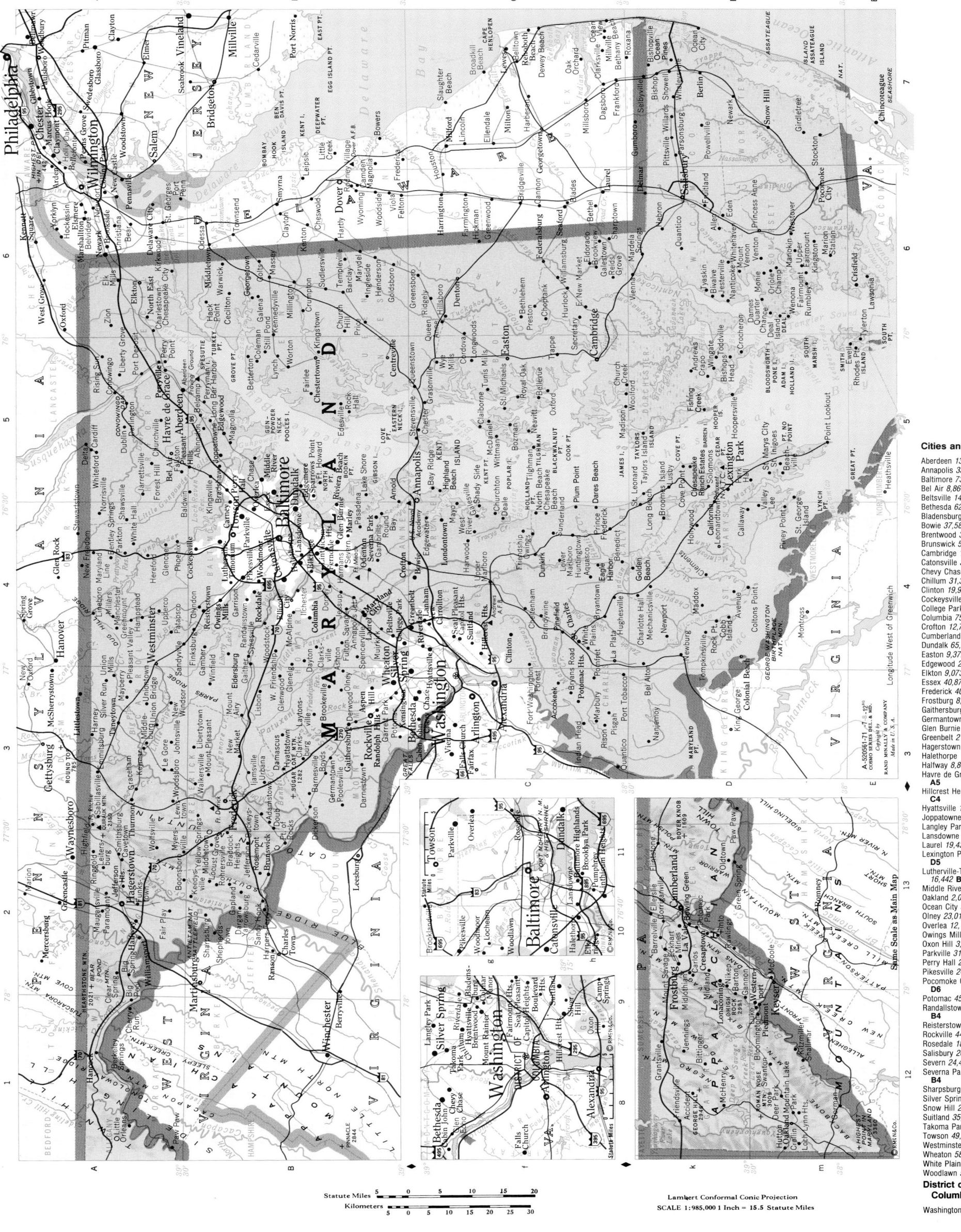

A-520561-71 -7 -8-12^80
COSMO SERIES DEL & MD.
Copyright by
RAND M?NALLY & COMPANY
Made in U. S. A.

Lambert Conformal Conic Projection
SCALE 1:985,000 1 Inch = 15.5 Statute Miles

Statute Miles 5 0 5 10 15 20
Kilometers 5 0 5 10 15 20 25 30

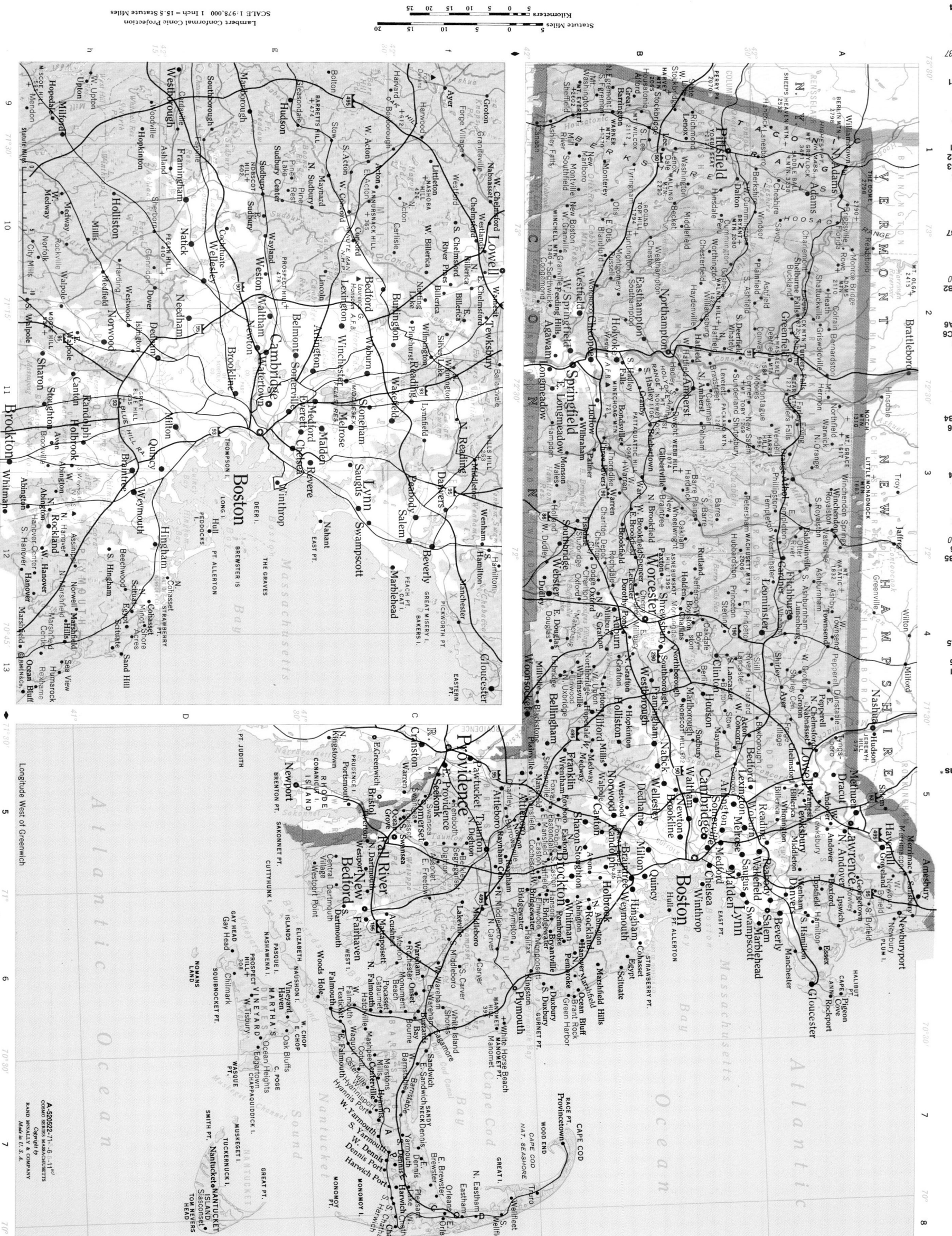

Cities and Towns*

Amherst 17,824 B2
Arlington 54,630 B5
Attleboro 38,383 C5
Beverly 38,195 A6
Belmont 24,720 911
Boston 574,283 B5
Brockton 54,718 B5
Brookline 41,519 B5
Burlington 23,302 911
Cambridge 95,802 B5
Chatham 1,922 C8
Chelmsford 32,383 A5
Chelsea 28,710 B5
Chicopee 56,632 B2
Concord 4,680 B5
Dedham 23,782 B5
Danvers 24,174 A6
Dracut 25,594 A5
Fall River 92,703 C5
Fitchburg 41,194 A4
Framingham 64,994 B5
Great Barrington 2,810 B1
Greenfield 14,016 A2
Haverhill 51,418 A5
Holyoke 43,704 B2
Lawrence 70,207 A5
Leominster 38,145 A4
Lexington 28,974 B5
Lowell 103,439 A5
Lynn 81,245 B6
Malden 53,884 B5
Marblehead 19,971 B6
Marlborough 31,813 B4
Medford 57,407 911
Melrose 28,150 B5
Methuen 35,990 A5
Milford 23,339 B4
Milton 25,725 B5
Natick 30,100 B5
Nantucket 23,557 911
New Bedford 99,922 C6
Newton 82,585 B5
Northampton 29,289 B2
North Attleboro 30,510 C5
Peabody 47,039 A6
Pittsfield 48,622 B1
Plymouth 16,178 C6
Quincy 84,985 B6
Randolph 30,093 B5
Reading 22,539 A5
Revere 42,786 911
Somerville 76,210 B5
Southbridge 13,631 B3
Springfield 156,983 B2
Stoneham 22,203 911
Stoughton 26,777 B5
Taunton 49,832 C5
Vineyard Haven 1,762 D6
Wakefield 2,825 B5
Waltham 57,878 B5
Watertown 33,284 911
Wellesley 26,615 B5
Westfield 36,372 B2
West Springfield 27,537 B2
Woburn 35,943 B5
Winthrop 18,127 B6
Weymouth 54,063 B6
Worcester 169,759 B4

SCALE 1:978,000 · 1 Inch = 15.5 Statute Miles
Lambert Conformal Conic Projection

Statute Miles
0 5 10 15 20 25

Kilometers
0 5 10 15 20 25

Longitude West of Greenwich

A-525522-75--6--11
Copyright by
RAND MCNALLY & COMPANY
Made in U.S.A.

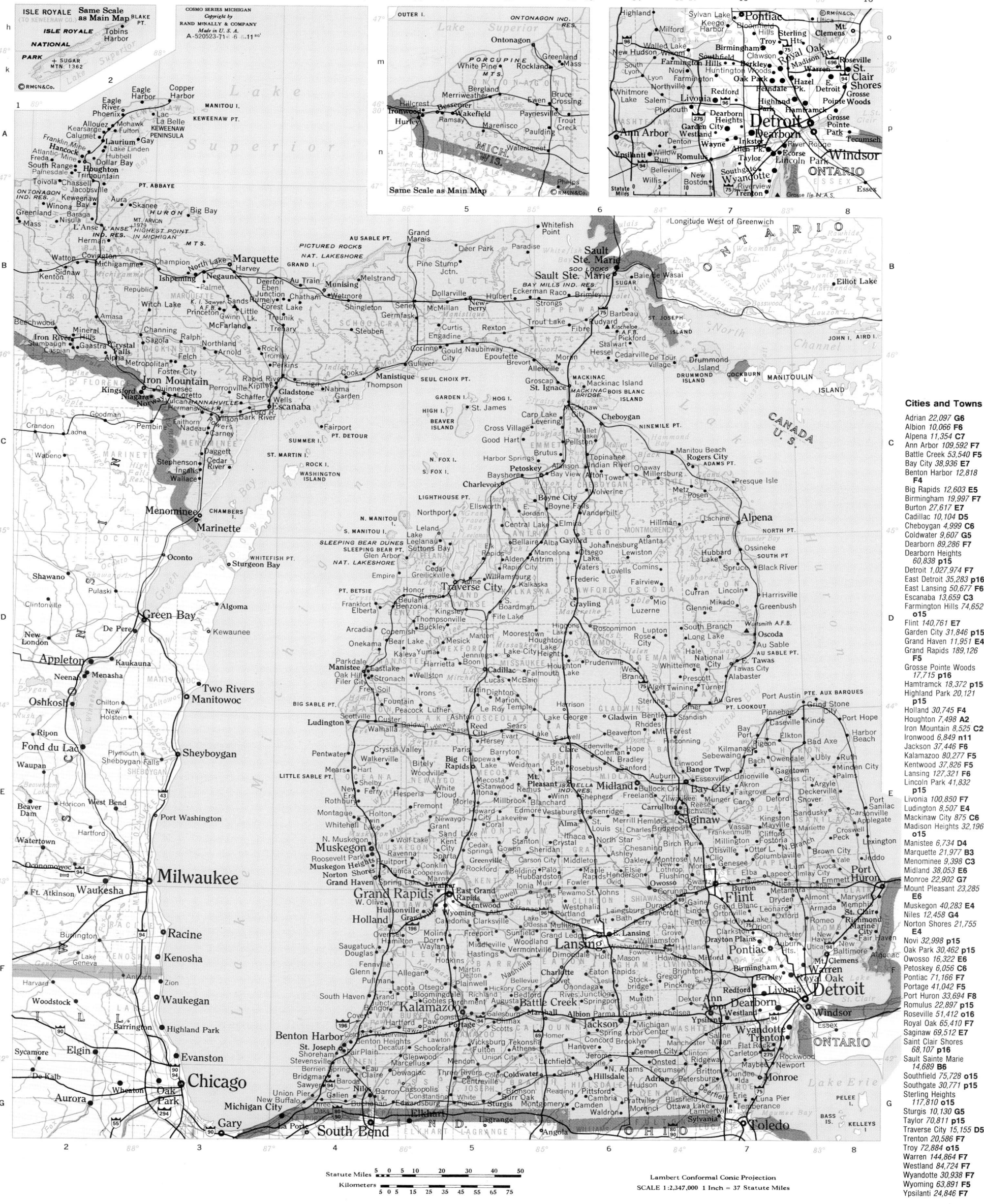

Cities and Towns

Adrian 22,097 **G6**
Albion 10,066 **F6**
Alpena 11,354 **C7**
Ann Arbor 109,592 **F7**
Battle Creek 53,540 **F5**
Bay City 38,936 **E7**
Benton Harbor 12,818 **F4**
Big Rapids 12,603 **E5**
Birmingham 19,997 **F7**
Burton 27,617 **E7**
Cadillac 10,104 **D5**
Cheboygan 4,999 **C6**
Coldwater 9,607 **G5**
Dearborn 89,286 **F7**
Dearborn Heights 60,838 **p15**
Detroit 1,027,974 **F7**
East Detroit 35,283 **p16**
East Lansing 50,677 **F6**
Escanaba 13,659 **C3**
Farmington Hills 74,652 **o15**
Flint 140,761 **E7**
Garden City 31,846 **p15**
Grand Haven 11,951 **E4**
Grand Rapids 189,126 **F5**
Grosse Pointe Woods 17,715 **p16**
Hamtramck 18,372 **p15**
Highland Park 20,121 **p15**
Holland 30,745 **F4**
Houghton 7,498 **A2**
Iron Mountain 8,525 **C2**
Ironwood 6,849 **n11**
Jackson 37,446 **F6**
Kalamazoo 80,277 **F5**
Kentwood 37,826 **F5**
Lansing 127,321 **F6**
Lincoln Park 41,832 **p15**
Livonia 100,850 **F7**
Ludington 8,507 **E4**
Mackinaw City 875 **C6**
Madison Heights 32,196 **o15**
Manistee 6,734 **D4**
Marquette 21,977 **B3**
Menominee 9,398 **C3**
Midland 38,053 **E6**
Monroe 22,902 **G7**
Mount Pleasant 23,285 **E6**
Muskegon 40,283 **E4**
Niles 12,458 **G4**
Norton Shores 21,755 **E4**
Novi 32,998 **p15**
Oak Park 30,462 **p15**
Owosso 16,322 **E6**
Petoskey 6,056 **C6**
Pontiac 71,166 **F7**
Portage 41,042 **F5**
Port Huron 33,694 **F8**
Romulus 22,897 **p15**
Roseville 51,412 **o16**
Royal Oak 65,410 **F7**
Saginaw 69,512 **E7**
Saint Clair Shores 68,107 **F8**
Sault Sainte Marie 14,689 **B6**
Southfield 75,728 **o15**
Southgate 30,771 **p15**
Sterling Heights 117,810 **o15**
Sturgis 10,130 **G5**
Taylor 70,811 **F7**
Traverse City 15,155 **D5**
Trenton 20,586 **F7**
Troy 72,884 **o15**
Warren 144,864 **F7**
Westland 84,724 **F7**
Wyandotte 30,938 **F7**
Wyoming 63,891 **F5**
Ypsilanti 24,846 **F7**

Cities and Towns

Albert Lea *18,310* **G5**
Alexandria *7,838* **E3**
Anoka *17,192* **E5**
Apple Valley *34,598* **n12**
Austin *21,907* **G6**
Bemidji *11,245* **C4**
Blaine *38,975* **m12**
Bloomington *86,335* **F5**
Brainerd *12,353* **D4**
Brooklyn Center *28,887* **E5**
Brooklyn Park *56,381* **m12**
Burnsville *51,288* **F5**
Chisholm *5,290* **C6**
Cloquet *10,885* **D6**
Columbia Heights *18,910* **m12**
Coon Rapids *52,978* **E5**
Cottage Grove *22,935* **n13**
Crookston *8,119* **C2**
Crystal *23,788* **m12**
Detroit Lakes *6,635* **D3**
Duluth *85,493* **D6**
Eagan *47,409* **n12**
East Bethel *8,050* **E5**
East Grand Forks *8,658* **C2**
Eden Prairie *39,311* **n12**
Edina *46,070* **F5**
Ely *3,968* **C7**
Fairmont *11,265* **G4**
Faribault *17,085* **F5**
Fergus Falls *12,362* **D2**
Fridley *28,335* **m12**
Golden Valley *20,971* **n12**
Grand Marais *1,171* **k9**
Grand Rapids *7,976* **C5**
Hibbing *18,046* **C6**
Hutchinson *11,523* **F4**
International Falls *8,325* **B5**
Inver Grove Heights *22,477* **n12**
Lakeville *24,854* **F5**
Litchfield *6,041* **E4**
Little Falls *7,232* **E4**
Mankato *31,477* **F5**
Maple Grove *38,736* **m12**
Maplewood *30,954* **n12**
Marshall *12,023* **F3**
Minneapolis *368,383* **F5**
Minnetonka *48,370* **n12**
Montevideo *5,499* **F3**
Moorhead *32,295* **D2**
Morris *5,613* **E3**
New Brighton *22,207* **m12**
New Hope *21,853* **m12**
New Ulm *13,132* **F4**
Northfield *14,684* **F5**
Owatonna *19,386* **F5**
Pipestone *4,554* **G2**
Plymouth *50,889* **m12**
Red Wing *15,134* **F6**
Redwood Falls *4,859* **F3**
Richfield *35,710* **F5**
Rochester *70,745* **F6**
Roseville *33,485* **m12**
Saint Cloud *48,812* **E4**
Saint Louis Park *43,787* **n12**
Saint Paul *272,235* **F5**
Saint Peter *9,421* **F5**
Shoreview *24,587* **m12**
South Saint Paul *20,197* **n12**
Thief River Falls *8,010* **B2**
Virginia *9,410* **C6**
Waseca *8,385* **F5**
West Saint Paul *19,248* **n12**
White Bear Lake *24,704* **E5**
Willmar *17,531* **E3**
Winona *25,399* **F7**
Worthington *9,977* **G3**

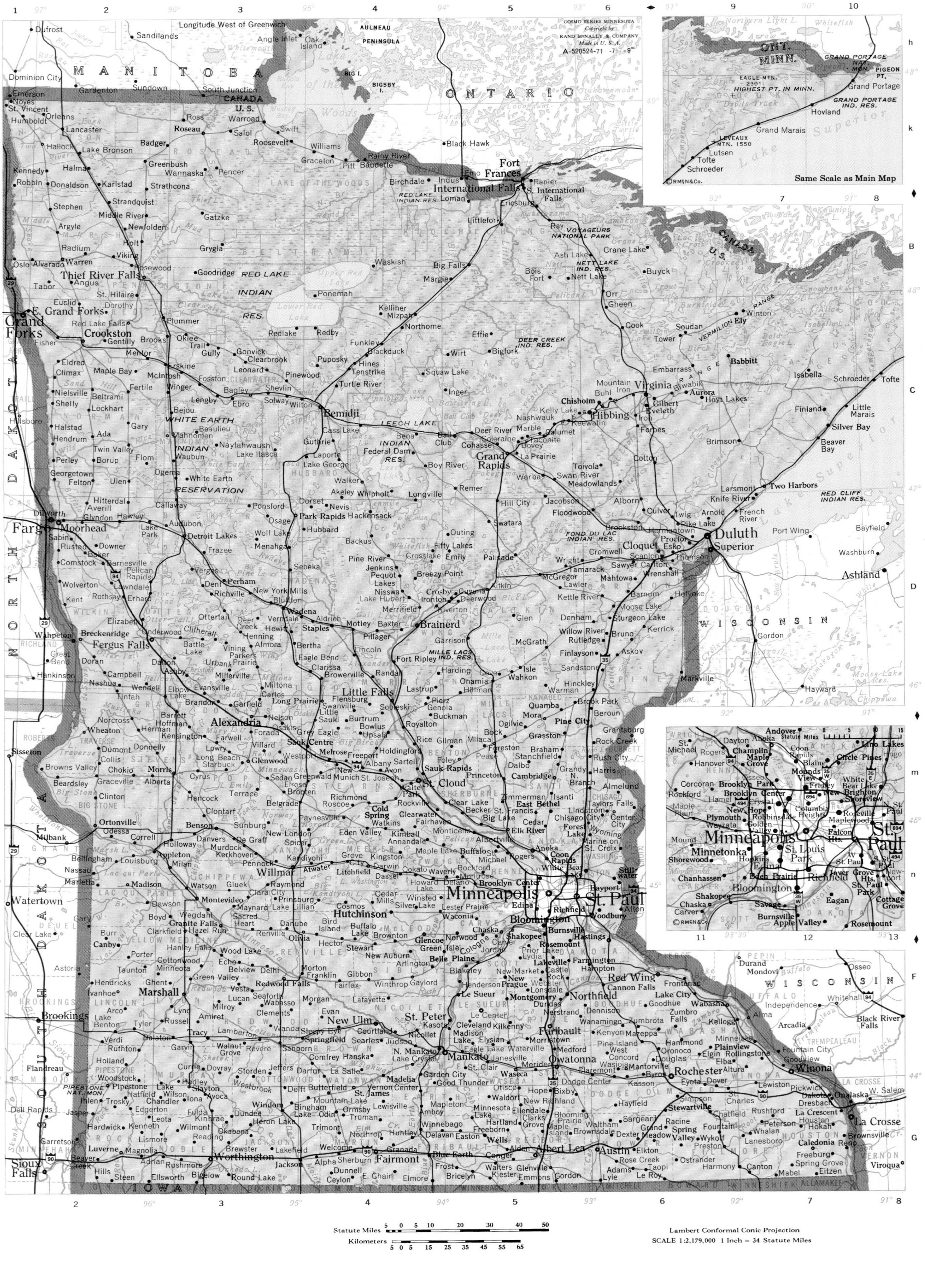

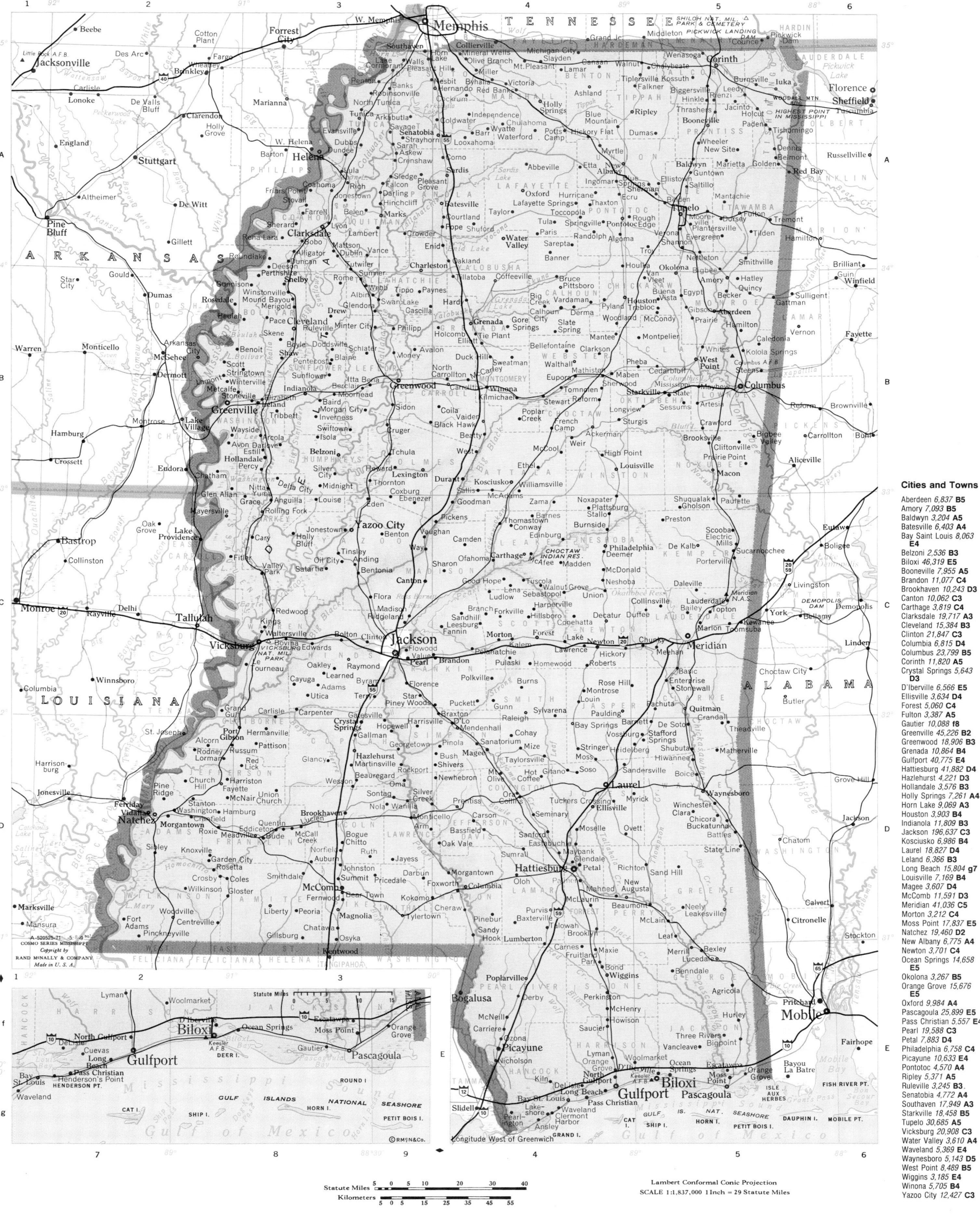

Lambert Conformal Conic Projection
SCALE 1:1,837,000 1 Inch = 29 Statute Miles

Statute Miles
Kilometers

Lambert Conformal Conic Projection
SCALE 1:2,283,000   1 Inch = 36 Statute Miles

Statute Miles
Kilometers

Cities and Towns

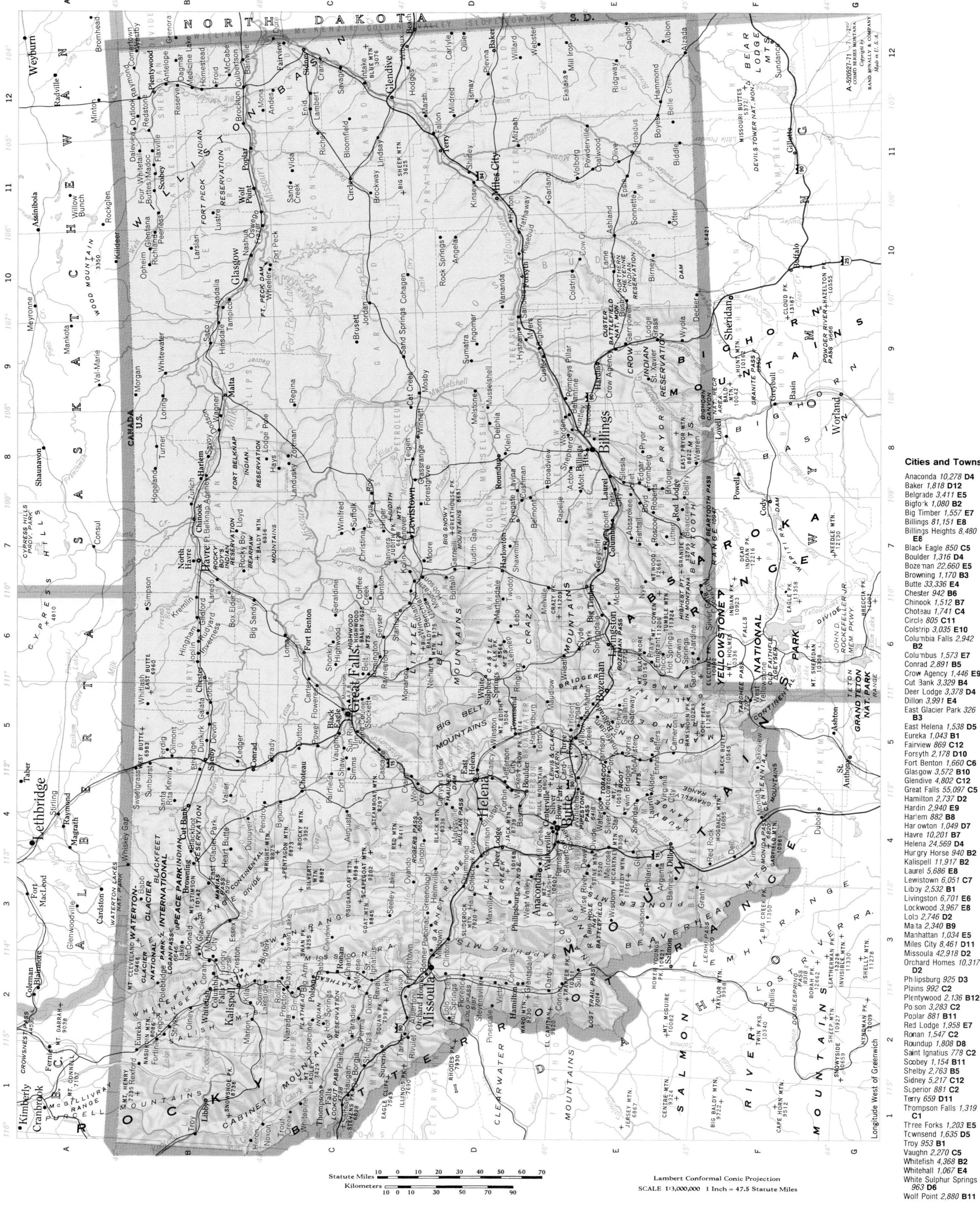

Statute Miles 10 0 10 20 30 40 50 60 70
Kilometers 10 0 10 20 30 40 50 60 70 80 90

Lambert Conformal Conic Projection
SCALE 1:3,000,000   1 Inch = 47.5 Statute Miles

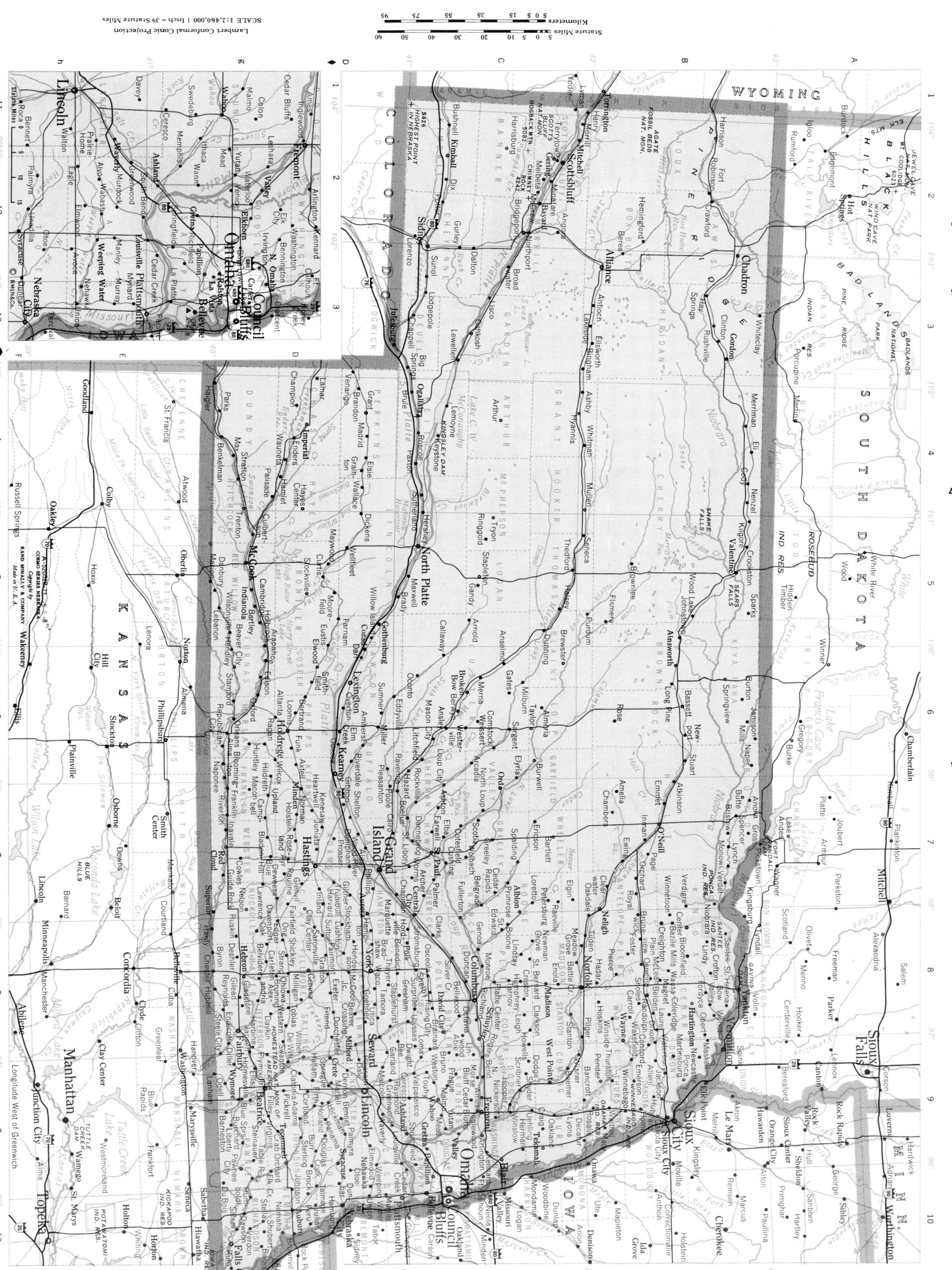

SCALE 1:2,460,000 1 Inch = 39 Statute Miles
Lambert Conformal Conic Projection

Kilometers
Statute Miles

Cities and Towns

Ainsworth 1,870 B6
Albion 1,916 C7
Alliance 9,765 B3
Ashland 2,136 C9
Atkinson 1,380 B7
Auburn 3,443 D10
Aurora 3,810 D7
Beatrice 12,354 D9
Bellevue 30,982 C10
Blair 6,860 C9
Bridgeport 1,581 C2
Broken Bow 3,778 C6
Central City 2,868 C7
Chadron 5,588 B3
Columbus 19,480 C8
Cozad 3,823 D6
Crete 4,841 D9
David City 2,522 C8
Fairbury 4,335 D8
Falls City 4,769 D10
Fremont 23,680 C9
Fullerton 1,452 C8
Geneva 2,310 D8
Gering 7,946 C2
Gibbon 1,525 D7
Gordon 1,803 B3
Gothenburg 3,232 D5
Grand Island 39,386 D7
Gretna 2,249 C9
Hartington 1,583 B8
Hastings 22,837 D7
Hebron 1,765 D8
Hildreth 5,671 D6
Imperial 2,007 D4
Kearney 24,396 D6
Kimball 2,574 C2
La Vista 9,840 g12
Lexington 6,601 D6
Lincoln 191,972 D9
Madison 2,135 C8
McCook 8,112 D5
Milford 1,886 D8
Minden 2,749 D7
Mitchell 1,743 C2
Nebraska City 6,547 D10
Neligh 1,742 B7
Norfolk 21,476 B8
North Platte 22,605 C5
Ogallala 5,095 C4
Omaha 335,795 C10
O'Neill 3,852 B7
Ord 2,481 C7
Papillion 6,399 c9
Pierce 1,615 B8
Plattsmouth 6,412 D10
Ralston 6,236 g12
Saint Paul 2,009 C7
Schuyler 4,052 C8
Scottsbluff 13,711 C2
Seward 5,634 D8
Sidney 5,959 C3
South Sioux City 9,677
.... B9
Stanton 1,549 C8
Superior 2,397 D7
Syracuse 1,646 D9
Tekamah 1,852 C9
Valentine 2,826 B5
Valley 1,775 C9
Wahoo 3,681 C9
Waverly 1,869 D9
Wayne 5,142 B8
West Point 3,250 C9
Wilber 1,527 D9
Wymore 1,611 D9
York 7,884 D8

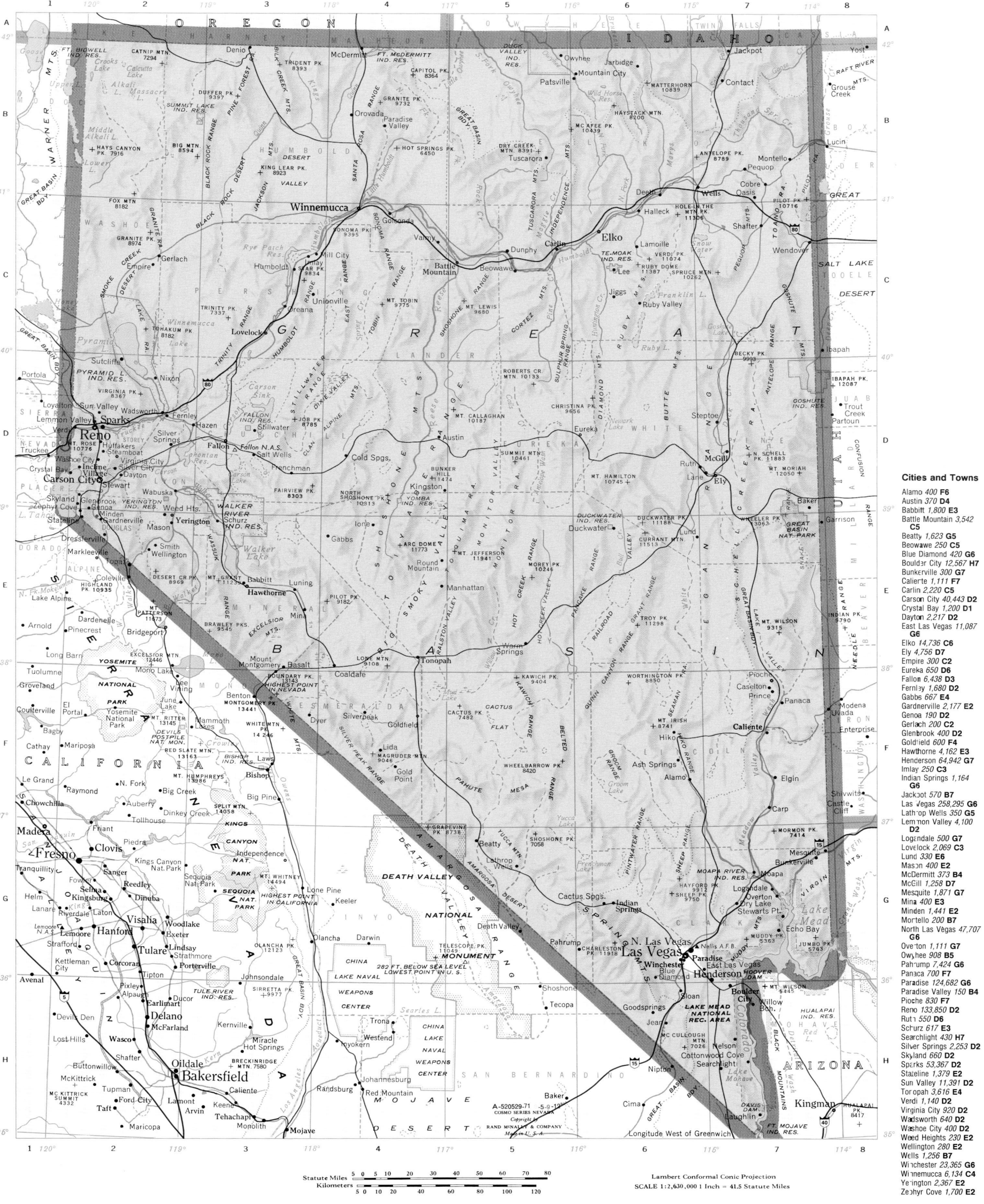

Statute Miles 5 0 5 10 20 30 40 50 60 70 80
Kilometers 5 0 10 20 30 40 60 80 100 120

Lambert Conformal Conic Projection
SCALE 1:2,630,000 1 Inch = 41.5 Statute Miles

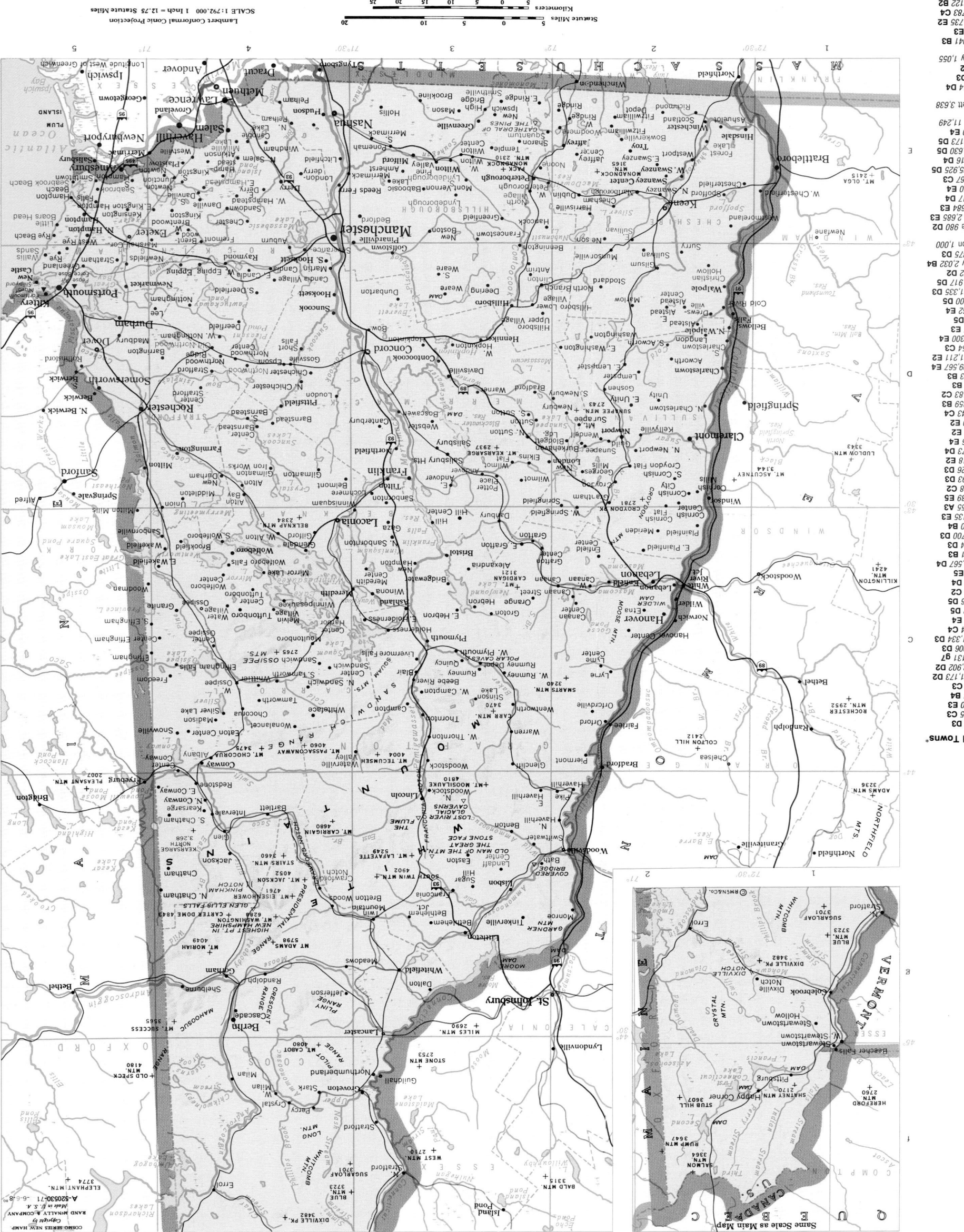

Cities and Towns*

*Populations are for localities, not incorporated towns.

SCALE 1:792,000 1 Inch = 12.75 Statute Miles

Lambert Conformal Conic Projection

Kilometers / Statute Miles

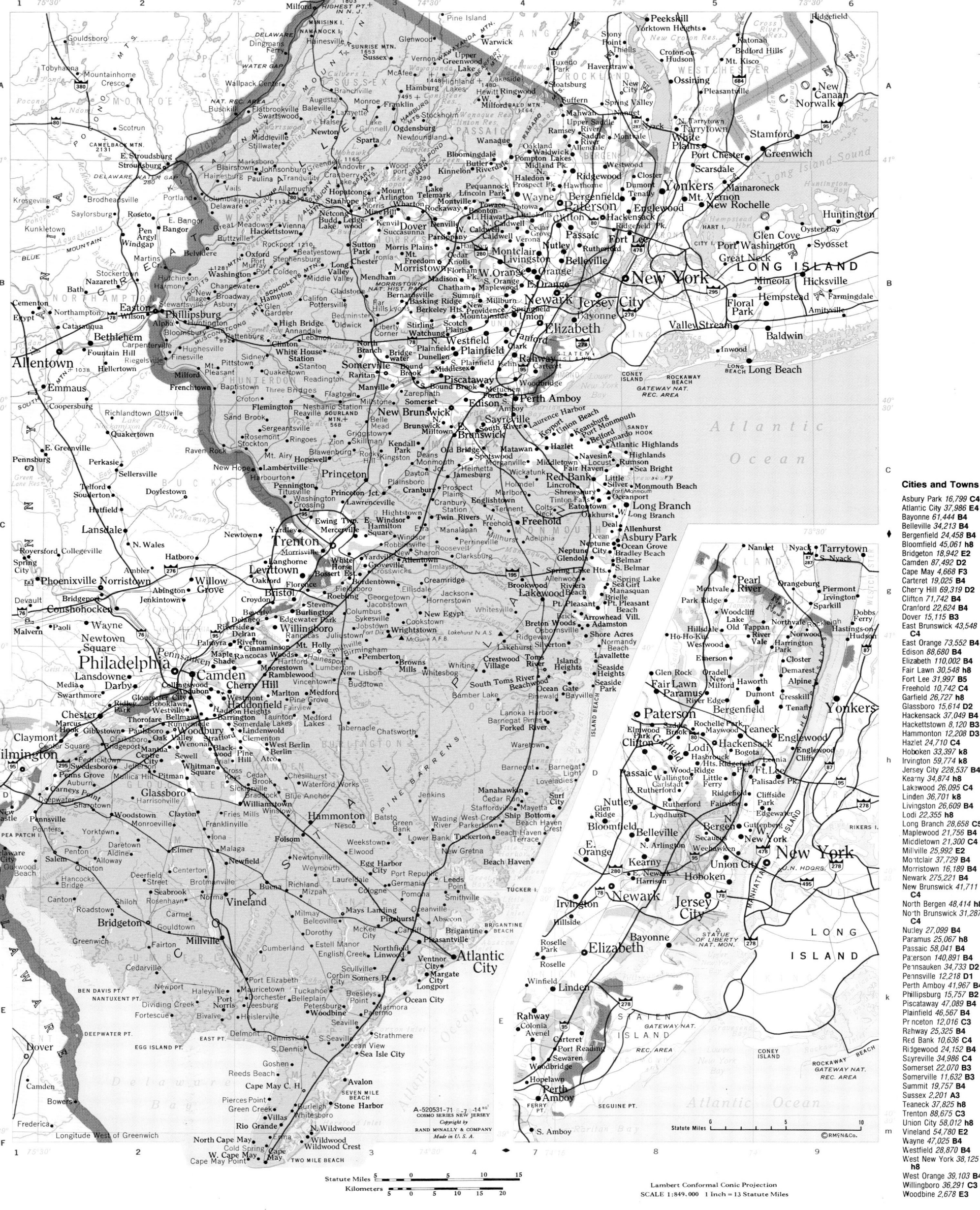

Lambert Conformal Conic Projection
SCALE 1:849,000 1 Inch = 13 Statute Miles

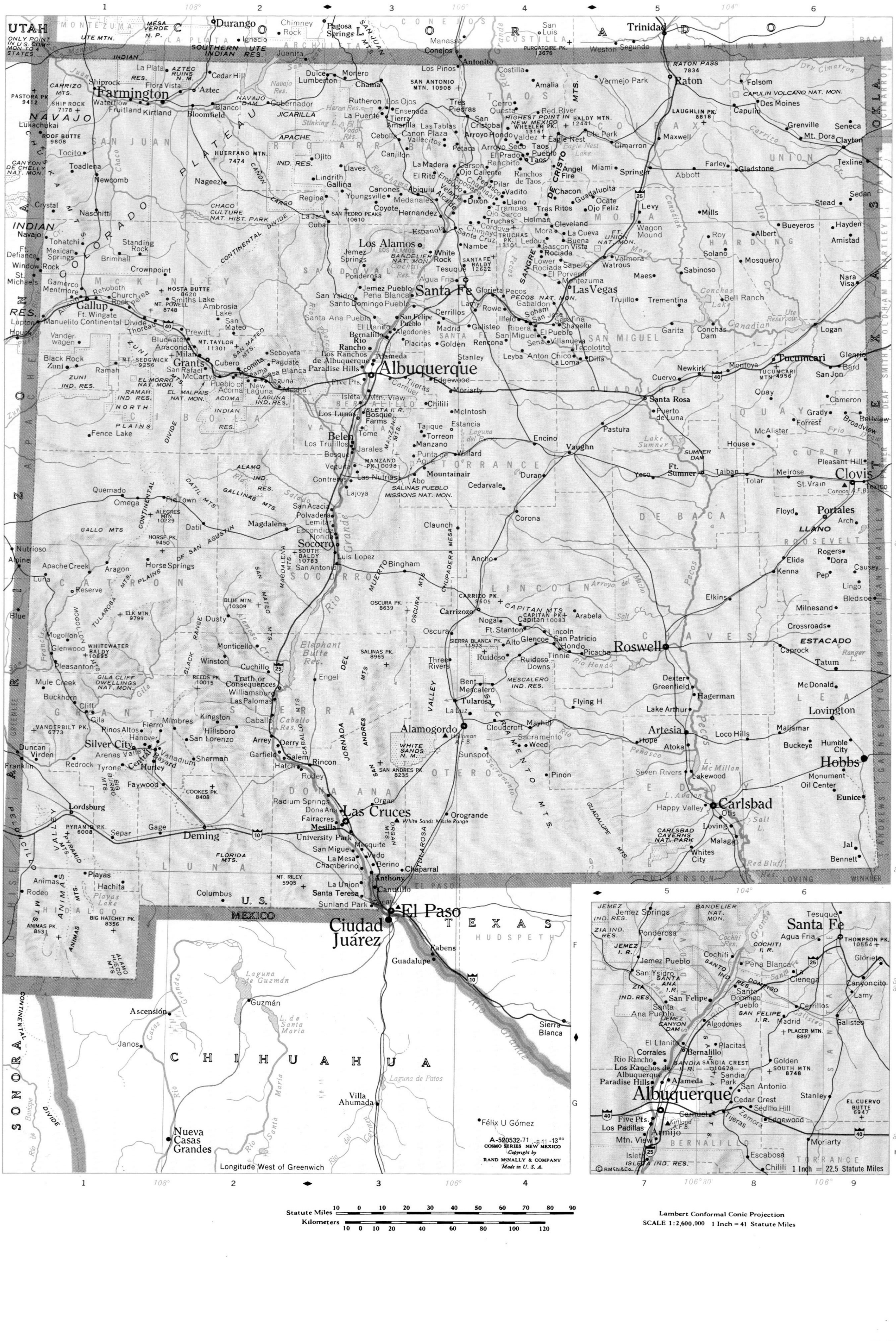

Cities and Towns

Alameda 5,900 **B3**
Alamogordo *27,596* **E4**
Albuquerque *384,736* **B3**
Anthony *5,160* **F3**
Armijo *14,600* **k7**
Artesia *10,610* **E5**
Aztec *5,479* **A2**
Bayard *2,598* **E1**
Belen *6,547* **C3**
Bernalillo *5,960* **B3**
Bloomfield *5,214* **A2**
Carlsbad *24,952* **E5**
Carrizozo *1,075* **D4**
Central *1,835* **E1**
Chama *1,048* **A3**
Chimayo *2,789* **A4**
Clayton *2,484* **A6**
Clovis *30,954* **C6**
Crownpoint *2,108* **B1**
Deming *10,970* **E2**
Dulce *2,438* **A2**
Espanola *8,389* **B3**
Eunice *2,676* **E6**
Farmington *33,997* **A1**
Five Points *4,200* **B3**
Fort Sumner *1,269* **C5**
Gallup *19,154* **B1**
Grants *8,626* **B2**
Hatch *1,136* **E2**
Hobbs *29,115* **E6**
Hurley *1,534* **E1**
Isleta *1,703* **C3**
Jal *2,156* **E6**
Jemez Pueblo *1,301* **B3**
Kirtland *3,552* **A1**
La Luz *1,625* **D4**
Las Cruces *62,126* **E3**
Las Vegas *14,753* **B4**
Lordsburg *2,951* **E1**
Los Alamos *11,455* **B3**
Los Lunas *6,013* **C3**
Los Ranchos de Albuquerque *3,955* **B3**
Loving *1,243* **E5**
Lovington *9,322* **E6**
Magdalena *861* **C2**
Mescalero *1,159* **D4**
Mesilla *1,975* **E3**
Milan *1,911* **B2**
Moriarty *1,399* **C3**
Mountain View *2,300* **C3**
Paradise Hills *5,513* **B3**
Portales *10,690* **C6**
Questa *1,707* **A4**
Ranchos de Taos *1,779* **A4**
Raton *7,372* **A5**
Roswell *44,654* **D5**
Ruidoso *4,600* **D4**
Ruidoso Downs *920* **D4**
Santa Fe *55,859* **B4**
Santa Rosa *2,263* **C5**
Santo Domingo Pueblo *2,866* **B3**
Shiprock *7,687* **A1**
Silver City *10,683* **E1**
Socorro *8,159* **C3**
Springer *1,262* **A5**
Sunland Park *8,179* **F3**
Taos *4,065* **A4**
Tesuque *1,490* **B4**
Thoreau *1,099* **B1**
Truth or Consequences (Hot Springs) *6,221* **D2**
Tucumcari *6,831* **B6**
Tularosa *2,615* **D3**
University Park *4,520* **E3**
Zuni (Zuni Pueblo) *5,857* **B1**

Cities and Towns

Albany *101,082* **C7**
Amherst *45,600* **C2**
Amityville *9,286* **E7**
Amsterdam *20,714* **C6**
Auburn *31,258* **C4**
Batavia *16,310* **C2**
Binghamton *53,008* **C5**
Brentwood *45,218* **E7**
Brighton *34,455* **B3**
Buffalo *328,123* **C2**
Centereach *26,720* **n15**
Central Islip *26,028* **n15**
Cheektowaga *84,387* **C2**
Cooperstown *2,180* **C6**
Corning *11,938* **C3**
Cortland *19,801* **C4**
Deer Park *28,840* **n15**
Dunkirk *13,989* **C1**
Elmira *33,724* **C4**
Elmont *28,612* **k13**
Freeport *39,894* **n15**
Fulton *12,929* **B4**
Geneseo *7,187* **C3**
Geneva *14,143* **C4**
Glens Falls *15,023* **B7**
Gloversville *16,656* **B6**
Greece *15,632* **B3**
Hempstead *49,453* **n15**
Hicksville *40,174* **E7**
Hornell *9,877* **C3**
Hudson *8,034* **C7**
Hyde Park *2,550* **D7**
Irondequoit *52,322* **B3**
Ithaca *29,541* **C4**
Jamestown *34,681* **C1**
Kingston *23,095* **D6**
Lackawanna *20,585* **C2**
Lake Placid *2,485* **A7**
Levittown *53,286* **E7**
Lockport *24,426* **B2**
Long Beach *33,510* **E7**
Massena *11,719* **f10**
Middletown *24,160* **D6**
Mount Vernon *67,153* **h13**
Newburgh *26,454* **D6**
New City *33,673* **D6**
New Rochelle *67,265* **E7**
New York *7,322,564* **E7**
Niagara Falls *61,840* **B1**
North Tonawanda *34,989* **B2**
Ogdensburg *13,521* **f9**
Olean *16,946* **C2**
Oneonta *13,954* **C5**
Ossining *22,582* **D7**
Oswego *19,195* **B4**
Palmyra *3,566* **B3**
Plattsburgh *21,255* **f11**
Port Chester *24,728* **E7**
Poughkeepsie *28,844* **D7**
Rochester *231,636* **B3**
Rome *44,350* **B5**
Rotterdam *21,228* **C6**
Saratoga Springs *25,001* **B7**
Schenectady *65,566* **C7**
Syracuse *163,860* **B4**
Ticonderoga *2,770* **B7**
Troy *54,269* **C7**
Utica *68,637* **B5**
Valley Stream *33,946* **n15**
Watertown *29,429* **B5**
West Point *8,024* **D7**
West Seneca *47,866* **C2**
White Plains *48,718* **D7**
Yonkers *188,082* **E7**

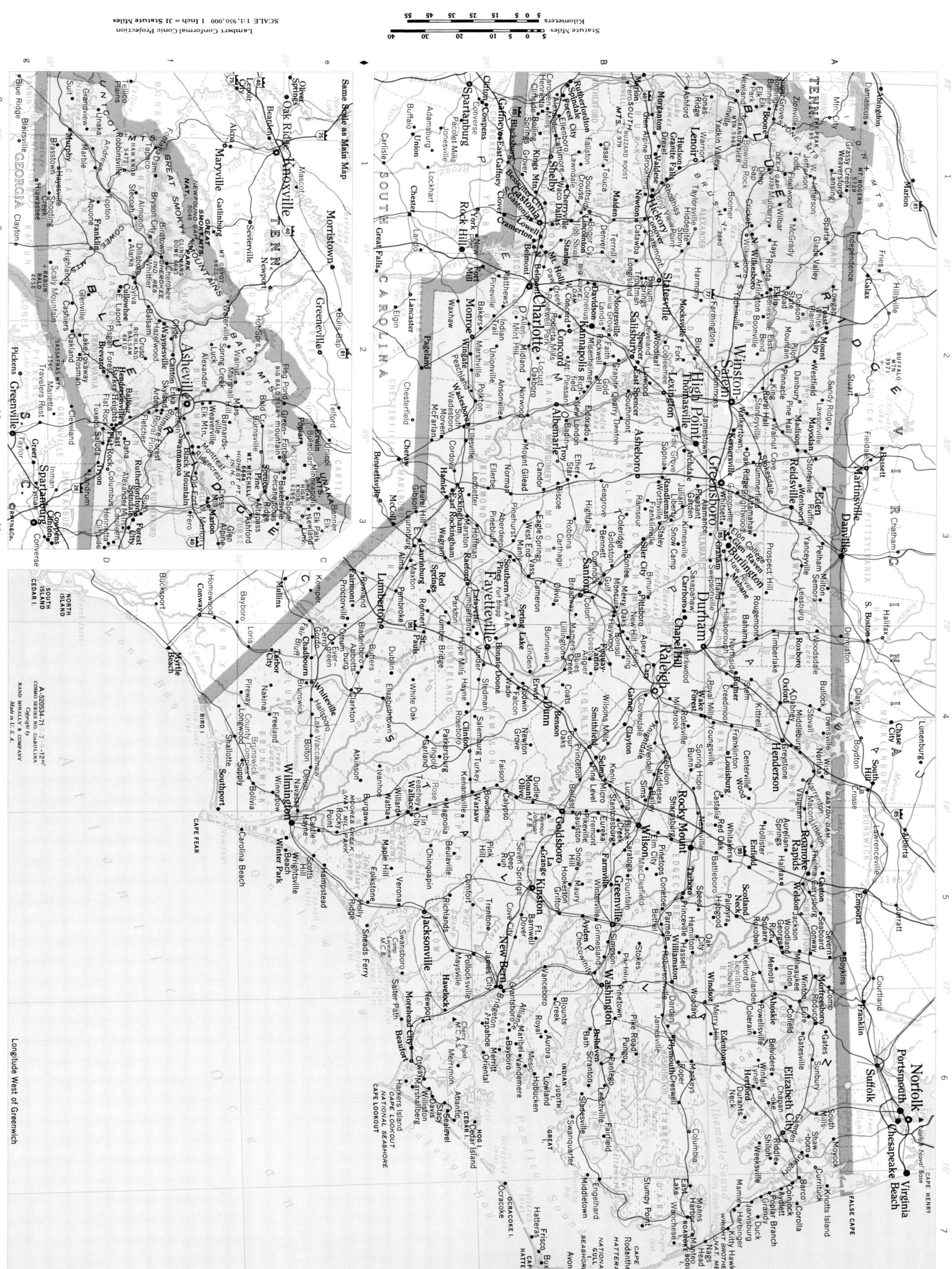

SCALE 1:1,950,000 1 Inch = 31 Statute Miles
Lambert Conformal Conic Projection

Statute Miles
Kilometers

Longitude West of Greenwich

A-500534-71 7-5-12ncl
RAND McNALLY
SERIES MAP, NORTH CAROLINA.
Copyright by
RAND McNALLY & COMPANY
Made in U.S.A.

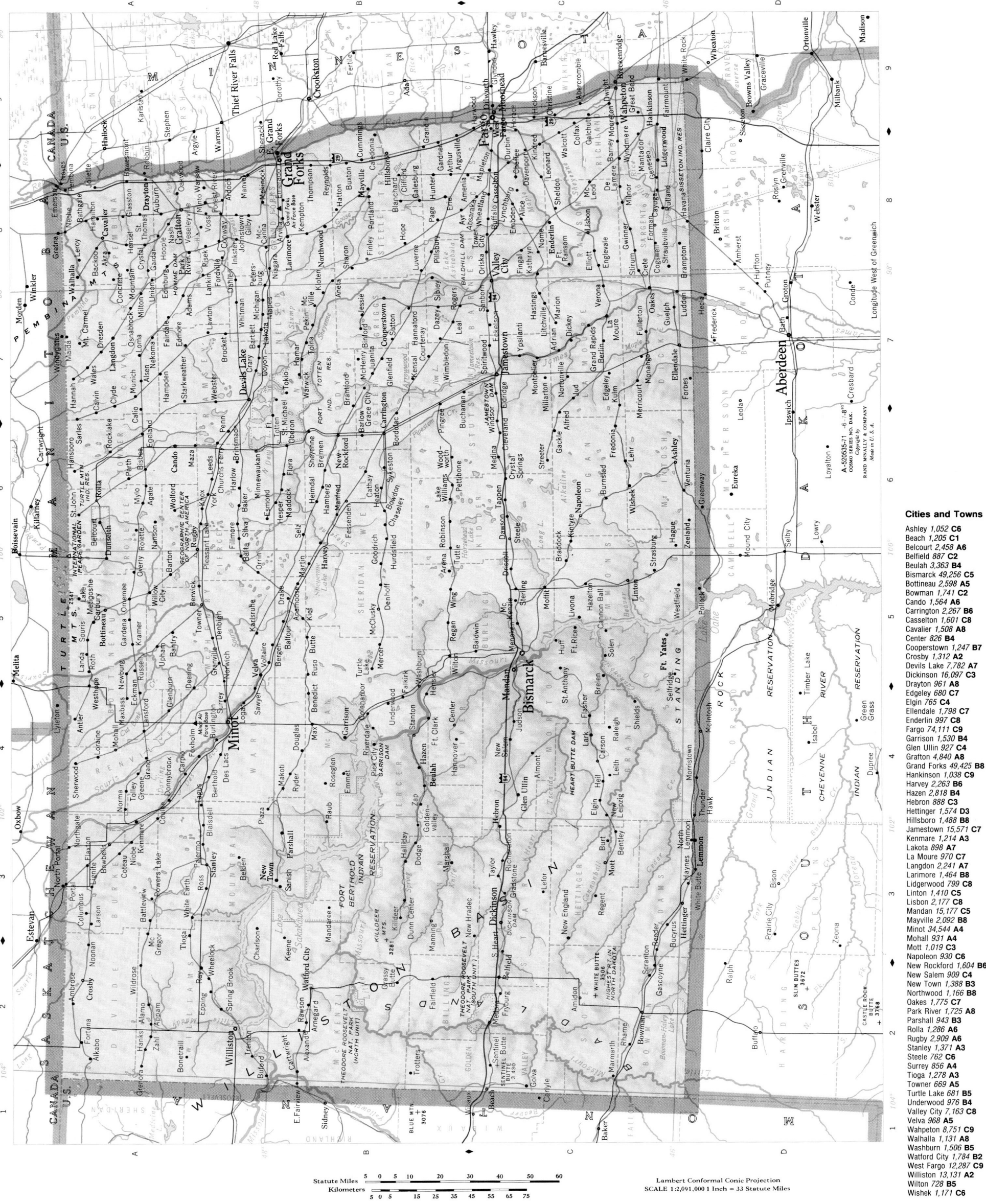

Statute Miles
Kilometers

Lambert Conformal Conic Projection
SCALE 1:2,091,000 1 Inch = 33 Statute Miles

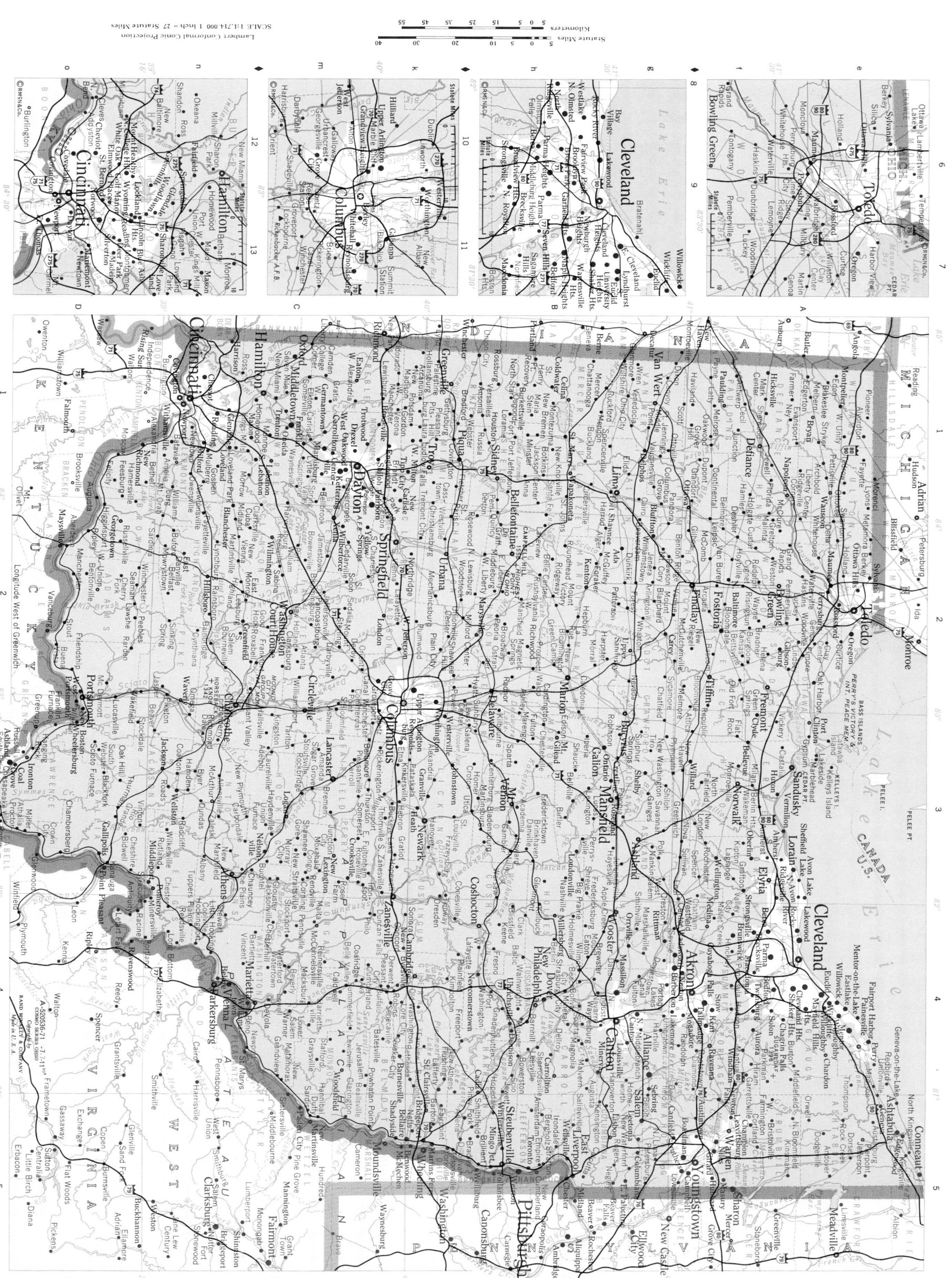

Cities and Towns

SCALE 1:1,774,000   1 Inch = 27 Statute Miles
Lambert Conformal Conic Projection

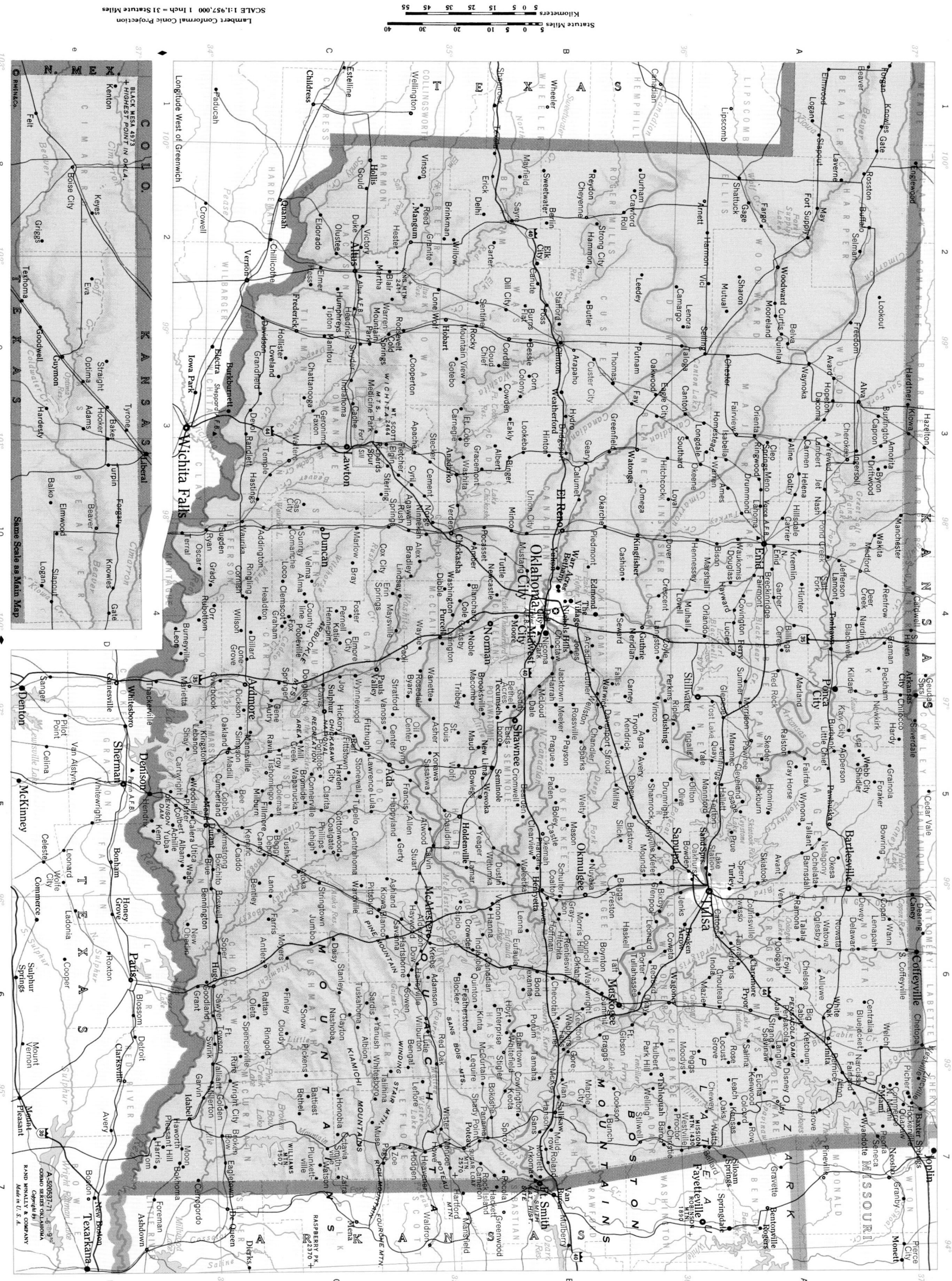

SCALE 1:1,957,000   1 Inch = 31 Statute Miles
Lambert Conformal Conic Projection

Longitude West of Greenwich

Cities and Towns

Ada 15,820 C5
Altus 21,910 C2
Anadarko 6,586 B3
Alva 5,495 A5
Ardmore 23,079 C4
Bartlesville 34,256 A6
Bethany 20,075 B4
Bixby 9,502 B6
Blackwell 7,538 A4
Bristow 4,062 B5
Broken Arrow 58,043 A6
Broken Bow 3,961 C7
Chickasha 14,988 B4
Choctaw 8,545 B3
Claremore 9,298 B3
Clinton 9,298 B3
Coweta 6,159 B6
Cushing 7,218 B5
Duncan 9,823 C4
Durant 21,732 C4
Edmond 52,315 B4
Elk City 10,428 B2
El Reno 15,414 B4
Enid 45,309 A4
Frederick 5,221 C2
Guthrie 10,518 B4
Guymon 7,803 A9
Henryetta 5,872 B6
Hobart 4,305 B2
Holdenville 4,792 B5
Idabel 6,957 D7
Kingfisher 4,091 B4
Lawton 80,561 C3
Madill 3,069 C5
Marlow 4,416 C4
McAlester 16,370 C6
Miami 13,142 A7
Midwest City 52,267 B4
Moore 40,318 B4
Muskogee 37,708 B6
Mustang 10,434 B4
Norman 80,071 B4
Nowata 3,896 A6
Oklahoma City 444,719 B4
Okmulgee 13,441 B6
Owasso 11,151 A6
Pauls Valley 5,150 C4
Pawhuska 3,825 A5
Perry 4,978 A4
Ponca City 26,359 A4
Poteau 7,210 B7
Pryor 8,327 A6
Purcell 4,784 B4
Sallisaw 7,122 B7
Sand Springs 15,346 A5
Sapulpa 18,074 B5
Seminole 7,071 B5
Shawnee 26,017 B5
Stillwater 36,676 A4
Sulphur 4,824 C5
Tahlequah 10,398 B7
Tecumseh 5,750 B5
The Village 10,353 B4
Tulsa 367,302 A6
Vinita 5,804 A6
Wagoner 6,894 B6
Warr Acres 9,288 B4
Watonga 3,408 B3
Weatherford 10,124 B3
Wewoka 4,050 B5
Woodward 12,340 A2
Yukon 20,935 B4

BLACK MESA 4,973
+HIGHEST POINT IN OKLA.

Same Scale as Main Map

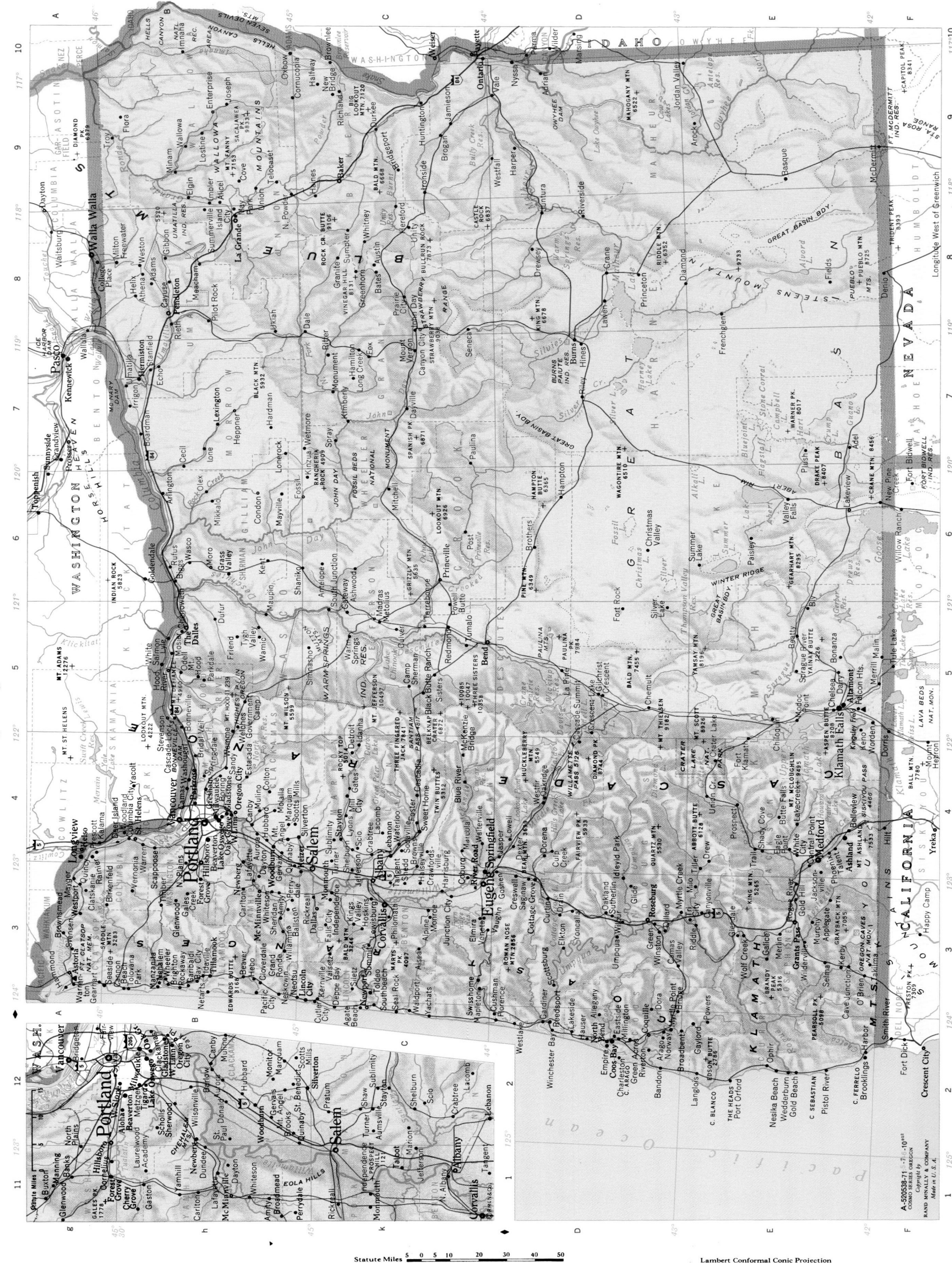

Cities and Towns

Albany 29,462 **C3**
Aloha 34,284 **h12**
Altamont 18,591 **E5**
Ashland 16,234 **E4**
Astoria 10,069 **A3**
Baker 9,140 **C9**
Beaverton 53,310 **B4**
Bend 20,469 **C5**
Burns 2,913 **D7**
Canby 8,983 **B4**
Central Point 7,509 **E4**
Coos Bay 15,076 **D2**
Coquille 4,121 **D2**
Corvallis 44,757 **C3**
Cottage Grove 7,402 **D3**
Crater Lake 25 **E4**
Dallas 9,422 **C3**
Eugene 112,669 **C3**
Florence 5,162 **D2**
Forest Grove 13,559 **B3**
Gladstone 10,152 **B4**
Grants Pass 17,488 **E3**
Gresham 68,235 **B4**
Hermiston 10,040 **B7**
Hillsboro 37,520 **B4**
Hood River 4,632 **B5**
Independence 4,425 **C3**
John Day 1,836 **C8**
Keizer 21,884 **C3**
Klamath Falls 17,737 **E5**
La Grande 11,766 **B8**
Lake Oswego 30,576 **B4**
Lakeview 2,526 **E6**
Lebanon 10,950 **C4**
Lincoln City 5,892 **C3**
McMinnville 17,894 **B3**
Medford 46,951 **E4**
Metzger 3,149 **h12**
Milton-Freewater 5,533 **B8**
Milwaukie 18,692 **B4**
Monmouth 6,288 **C3**
Myrtle Point 2,712 **D2**
Newberg 13,086 **B4**
Newport 8,437 **C2**
North Bend 9,614 **D2**
Oak Grove 12,576 **B4**
Ontario 9,392 **C10**
Oregon City 14,698 **B4**
Parkrose 21,108 **B4**
Pendleton 15,126 **B8**
Portland 437,319 **B4**
Prineville 5,355 **C6**
Redmond 7,163 **C5**
Reedsport 4,796 **D2**
River Road 9,443 **C3**
Roseburg 17,032 **D3**
Saint Helens 7,535 **B4**
Salem 107,786 **C4**
Scappoose 3,529 **B4**
Seaside 5,359 **B3**
Silverton 5,635 **C4**
Springfield 44,683 **C4**
Stayton 5,011 **C4**
Sutherlin 5,020 **D3**
Sweet Home 6,850 **C4**
The Dalles 11,060 **B5**
Tigard 29,344 **h12**
Tillamook 4,001 **B3**
Tri City 3,585 **E3**
Umatilla 3,046 **B7**
West Linn 16,367 **B4**
West Slope 7,959 **g12**
White City 5,891 **E4**
Woodburn 13,404 **B4**

A-520538-71   Rand McNally & Company
Made in U.S.A.

Statute Miles

Kilometers

Lambert Conformal Conic Projection

SCALE 1:2,329,000   1 Inch = 37 Statute Miles

Cities and Towns

Aliquippa 13,374 E1
Allentown 105,090 E11
Altoona 51,881 E5
Baldwin 21,923 K14
Beaver Falls 10,687 E1
Berwick 10,976 D9
Bethel Park 33,823 K14
Bethlehem 71,428 E9
Bloomsburg 12,439 E9
Bradford 9,625 C4
Broomall 10,930 p20
Butler 15,714 E2
Carbondale 10,664 C10
Carlisle 18,419 F7
Chambersburg 16,647 G6
Chester 41,856 G11
Coatesville 11,038 G10
Connellsville 9,229 F2
Du Bois 8,286 D4
Easton 26,276 E11
Ephrata 12,133 F9
Erie 108,718 B1
Gettysburg 7,025 G7
Greensburg 16,318 F2
Hanover 14,399 G8
Harrisburg 52,376 F8
Hazleton 11,860 F8
Hershey 13,174 E3
Indiana 15,174 E3
Jeannette 11,221 F2
Johnstown 28,134 F4
Lancaster 55,551 F9
Lansdale 16,362 F11
Latrobe 9,265 F3
Lebanon 24,800 F9
Lewistown 9,341 E6
Lock Haven 9,230 D7
McCandless 28,781 h13
McKeesport 26,016 F2
Meadville 14,318 C1
Middletown 9,254 F8
Millcreek Township 46,100 B1
Monroeville 29,169 k14
Mount Lebanon 33,362 F1
New Castle 28,334 D1
New Kensington 15,894 E2
Norristown 30,749 F11
Oil City 11,949 D2
Penn Hills 51,430 K14
Philadelphia 1,585,577 G11
Pittsburgh 369,879 F1
Plum 25,609 K14
Pottstown 21,831 F10
Pottsville 16,603 E9
Punxsutawney 6,782 E4
Reading 78,380 F10
Scranton 81,805 D10
Sharon 17,493 D1
Shamokin 9,184 E8
Springfield 24,160 p20
State College 38,923 E6
Sunbury 11,591 E8
Uniontown 12,034 G2
Upper Darby 81,177 G11
Warminster 32,832 F11
Warren 11,122 C3
Washington 15,864 F1
Waynesboro 9,576 G6
West Chester 18,041 G10
West Mifflin 23,644 F2
Wilkes-Barre 47,523 D10
Wilkinsburg 21,080 F2
Williamsport 31,933 D7
York 42,192 G8

SCALE 1:1,593,000 1 Inch = 25 Statute Miles

Lambert Conformal Conic Projection

Statute Miles

Kilometers

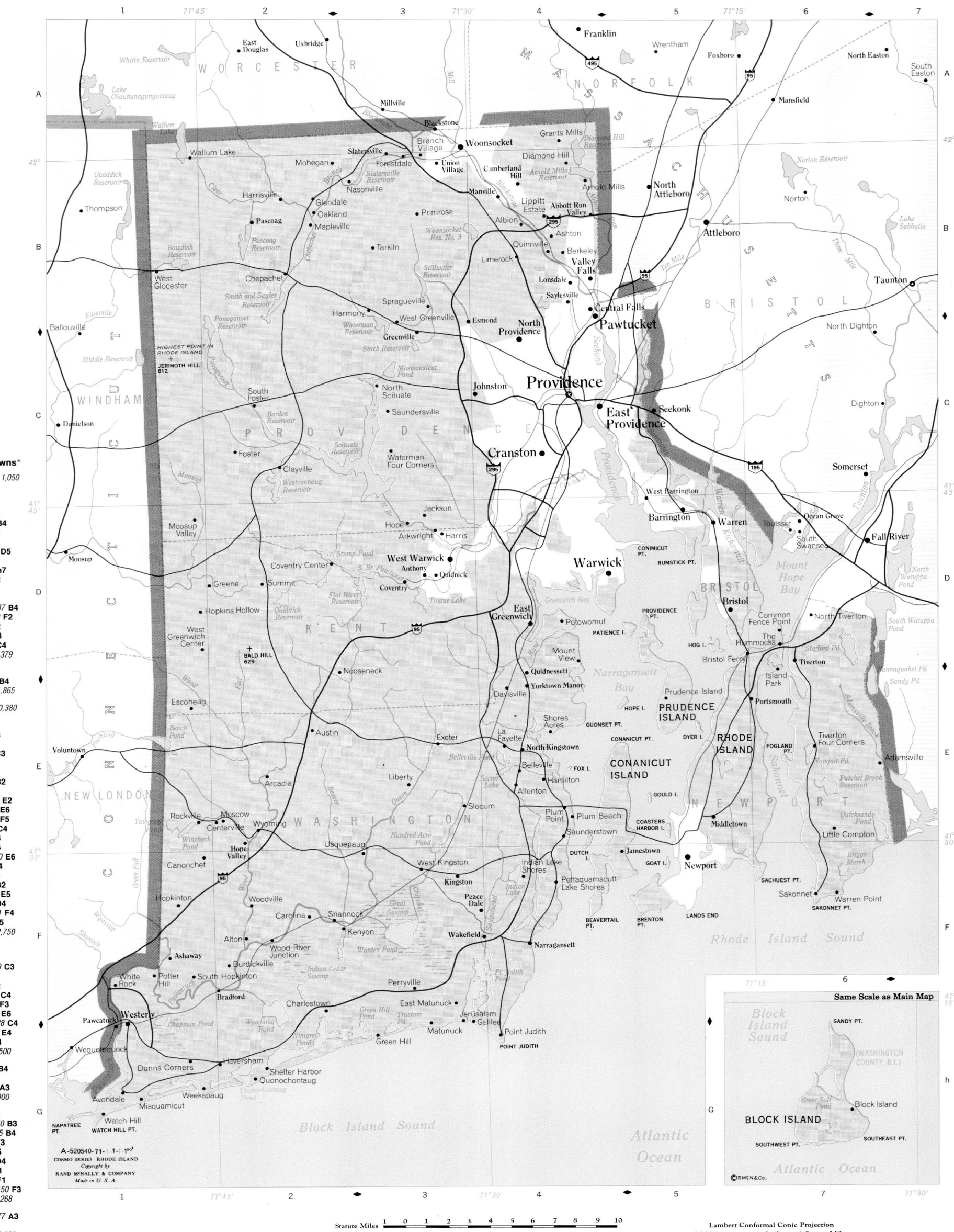

*Populations are for localities, not incorporated towns.

Statute Miles

Kilometers

A-520540-71- -1- -1

COSMO SERIES RHODE ISLAND
Copyright by
RAND M?NALLY & COMPANY
Made in U. S. A.

Lambert Conformal Conic Projection
SCALE 1:304,000   1 Inch = 4.9 Statute Miles

Same Scale as Main Map

BLOCK ISLAND

©RM?N&Co.

A-520541-71 -6 6-'12nd
COSMO SERIES SO. CAROLINA
Copyright by
RAND McNALLY & COMPANY
Made in U.S.A.

Lambert Conformal Conic Projection
SCALE 1:1,566,000   1 Inch = 25 Statute Miles

Statute Miles
Kilometers

Cities and Towns

Abbeville 5,778 C3
Aiken 19,872 D4
Allendale 4,410 E5
Anderson 26,184 B2
Barnwell 5,255 E5
Batesburg 4,082 D4
Beaufort 9,576 G6
Belton 4,646 B3
Belvedere 6,133 D4
Bennettsville 9,345 B8
Berea 13,535 B3
Bishopville 3,560 C7
Camden 6,696 C6
Cayce 11,163 D5
Charleston 80,414 F8
Cheraw 5,505 B8
Chester 7,158 B5
Clemson 11,096 B2
Clinton 7,987 C4
Columbia 98,052 C5
Conway 9,819 D9
Cowpens 2,176 A4
Darlington 7,311 C8
Denmark 3,762 E5
Dillon 6,829 C9
Easley 15,195 B2
Florence 29,813 C8
Fort Mill 4,930 A6
Fountain Inn 4,388 B3
Gaffney 13,145 A4
Georgetown 9,517 E9
Goose Creek 24,692 F7
Greenville 58,282 B3
Greenwood 20,807 C3
Greer 10,322 B3
Hanahan 13,176 F7
Hartsville 8,372 C7
Hilton Head Island 23,694 G6
Honea Path 3,841 C3
James Island 24,124 k12
Kingstree 3,858 D8
Ladson 13,540 F7
Lake City 7,153 D8
Lancaster 8,914 B6
Laurel Bay 4,972 G6
Laurens 9,694 C3
Manning 4,428 D7
Marion 7,658 C9
Mauldin 11,587 B3
Moncks Corner 5,607 E7
Mount Pleasant 30,108 F8
Mullins 5,910 C9
Myrtle Beach 24,848 D10
Newberry 10,542 C4
North Augusta 15,351 D4
North Charleston 70,218 F8
North Myrtle Beach 8,636 D10
Orangeburg 13,739 E6
Rock Hill 41,643 B5
Saint Andrews 9,908 F7
Saint Andrews 25,692 C5
Seneca 7,726 B2
Shannontown 7,900 D7
Simpsonville 11,708 B3
Spartanburg 43,467 B4
Summerville 22,519 E7
Sumter 41,943 D7
Taylors 19,619 B3
Union 9,836 B4
Walhalla 3,755 B1
West Columbia 10,588 D5
Williamston 3,876 B3
Woodruff 4,365 B3
York 6,709 B5

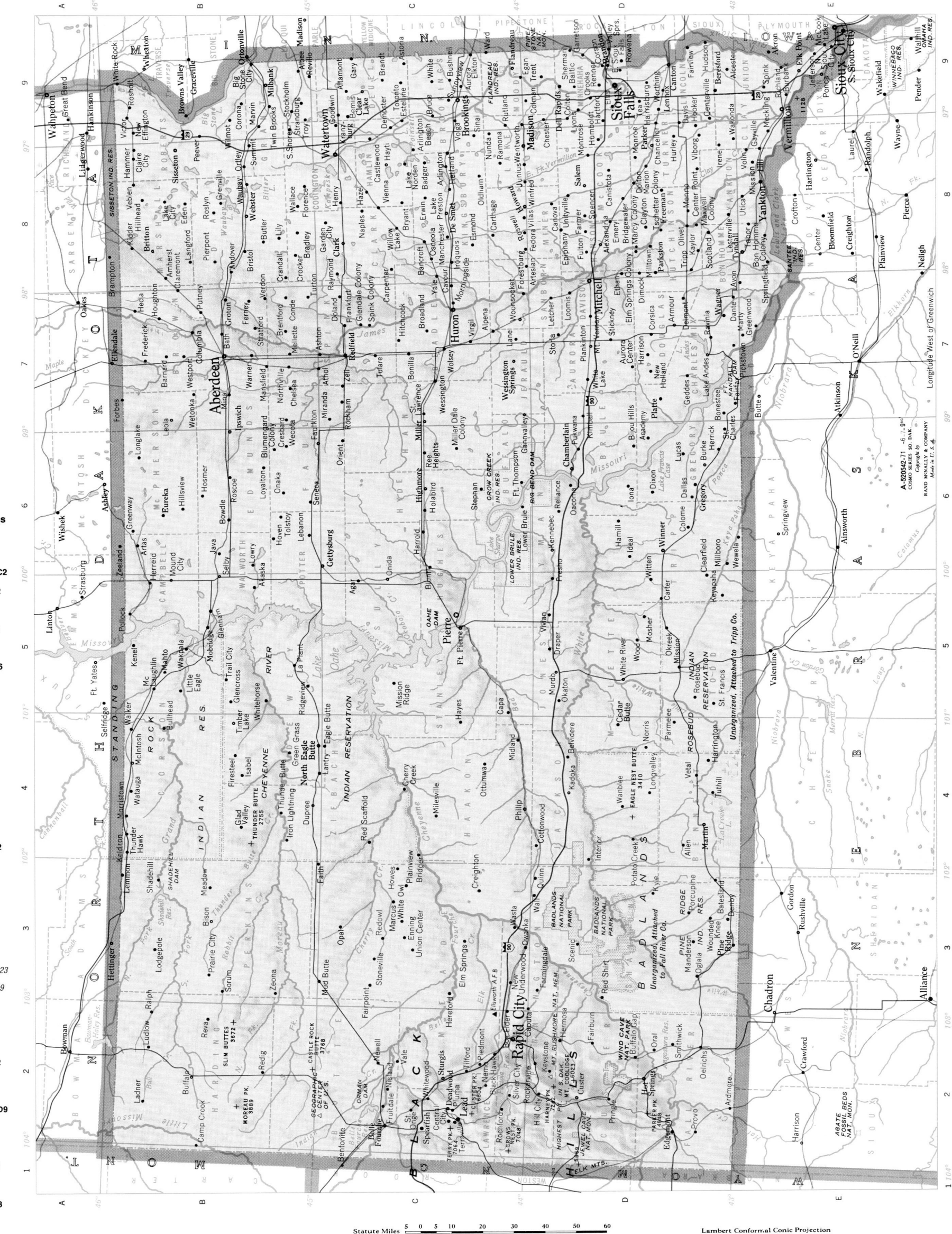

Cities and Towns

Aberdeen 24,927 **B7**
Alcester 843 **D9**
Arlington 908 **C8**
Armour 854 **D7**
Belle Fourche 4,335 **C2**
Beresford 1,849 **D9**
Black Hawk 1,955 **C2**
Box Elder 2,680 **C2**
Brandon 3,543 **D9**
Britton 1,394 **B8**
Brookings 16,270 **C9**
Burke 756 **D6**
Canton 2,787 **D9**
Centerville 887 **D9**
Chamberlain 2,347 **D6**
Clark 1,292 **C8**
Clear Lake 1,247 **C9**
Custer 1,741 **D2**
Deadwood 1,830 **C2**
De Smet 1,172 **C8**
Edgemont 906 **D2**
Elk Point 1,423 **E9**
Eureka 1,197 **B6**
Faulkton 809 **B6**
Flandreau 2,311 **C9**
Fort Pierre 1,854 **C5**
Freeman 1,293 **D8**
Garretson 924 **D9**
Gettysburg 1,510 **C6**
Gregory 1,384 **D6**
Groton 1,196 **B7**
Hartford 1,262 **D9**
Highmore 835 **C6**
Hot Springs 4,325 **D2**
Howard 1,156 **C8**
Huron 12,448 **C7**
Ipswich 965 **B6**
Lake Andes 846 **D7**
Lead 3,632 **C2**
Lemmon 1,614 **B3**
Lennox 1,767 **D9**
Martin 1,151 **D4**
Milbank 3,879 **B9**
Miller 1,678 **C7**
Mitchell 13,798 **D7**
Mobridge 3,768 **B5**
North Eagle Butte 1,423
    B4
North Sioux City 2,019
    E9
Parker 984 **D8**
Parkston 1,572 **D8**
Philip 1,077 **C4**
Pierre 12,906 **C5**
Pine Ridge 2,596 **D3**
Platte 1,311 **D7**
Rapid City 54,523 **C2**
Redfield 2,770 **C7**
Salem 1,289 **D8**
Scotland 968 **D8**
Selby 707 **B5**
Sioux Falls 100,814 **D9**
Sisseton 2,181 **B8**
Spearfish 6,966 **C2**
Springfield 834 **E8**
Sturgis 5,330 **C2**
Tyndall 1,201 **E8**
Vermillion 10,034 **E9**
Volga 1,263 **C9**
Wagner 1,462 **D7**
Wall 834 **D3**
Watertown 17,592 **C8**
Webster 2,017 **B8**
Wessington Springs
    1,083 **C7**
Winner 3,354 **D6**
Yankton 12,703 **E8**

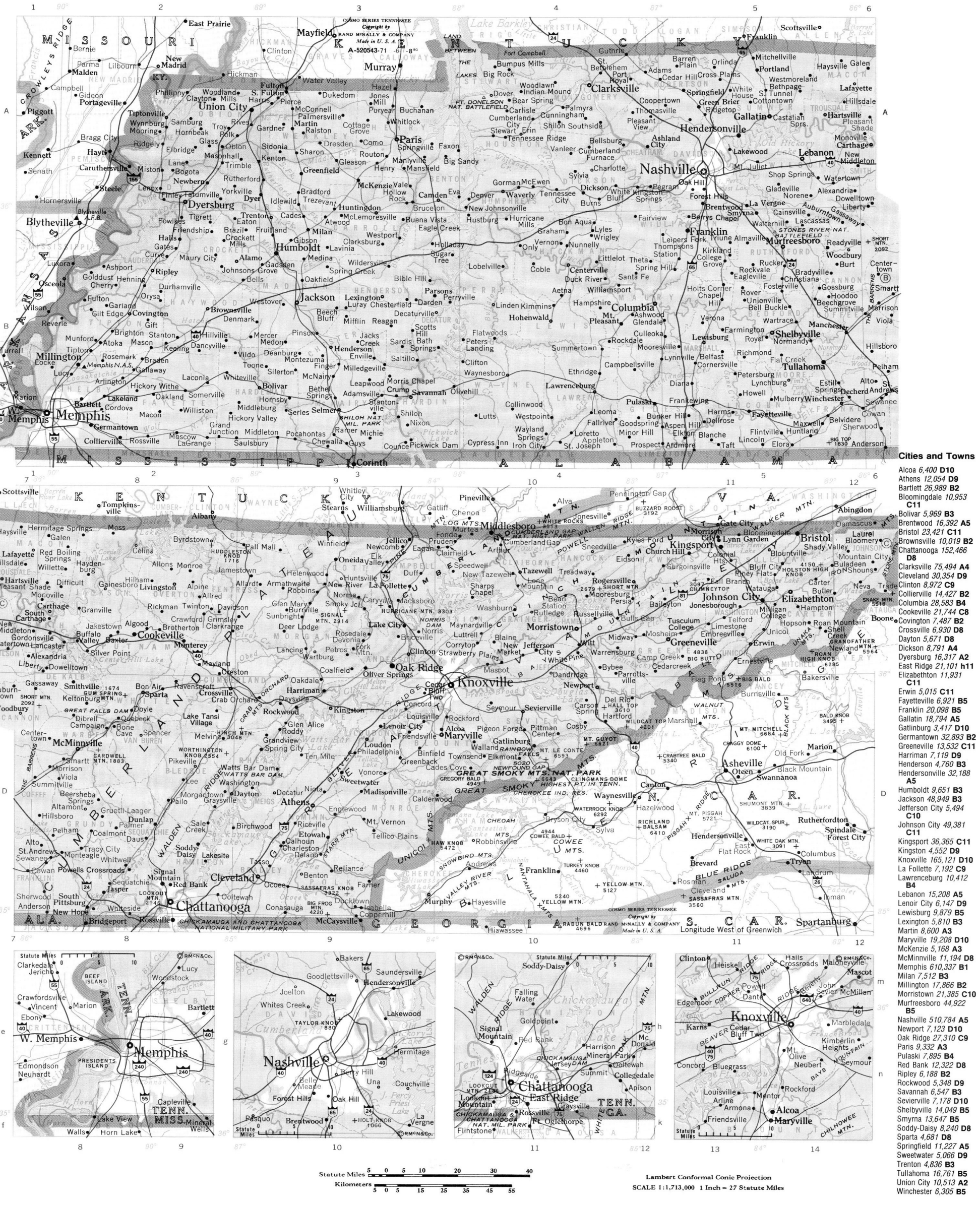

Statute Miles

Kilometers

Lambert Conformal Conic Projection

SCALE 1:1,713,000   1 Inch = 27 Statute Miles

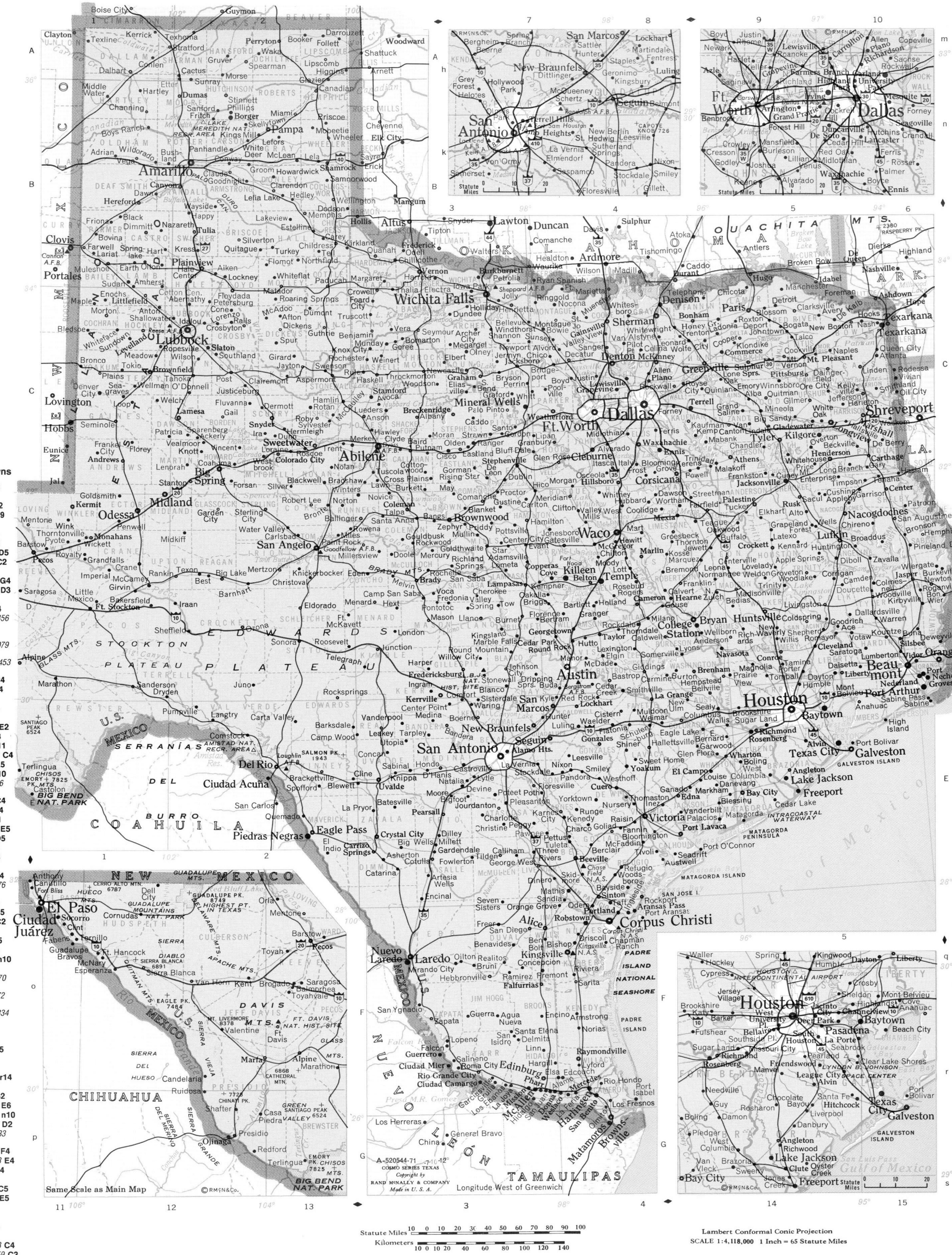

Statute Miles

Kilometers

Lambert Conformal Conic Projection
SCALE 1:4,118,000   1 Inch = 65 Statute Miles

Cities and Towns

SCALE 1:2,100,000 1 Inch = 33 Statute Miles
Lambert Conformal Conic Projection
COSMO SERIES, UTAH
A-520545-71 -8-9-12

Copyright by
RAND McNALLY & COMPANY
Made in U.S.A.

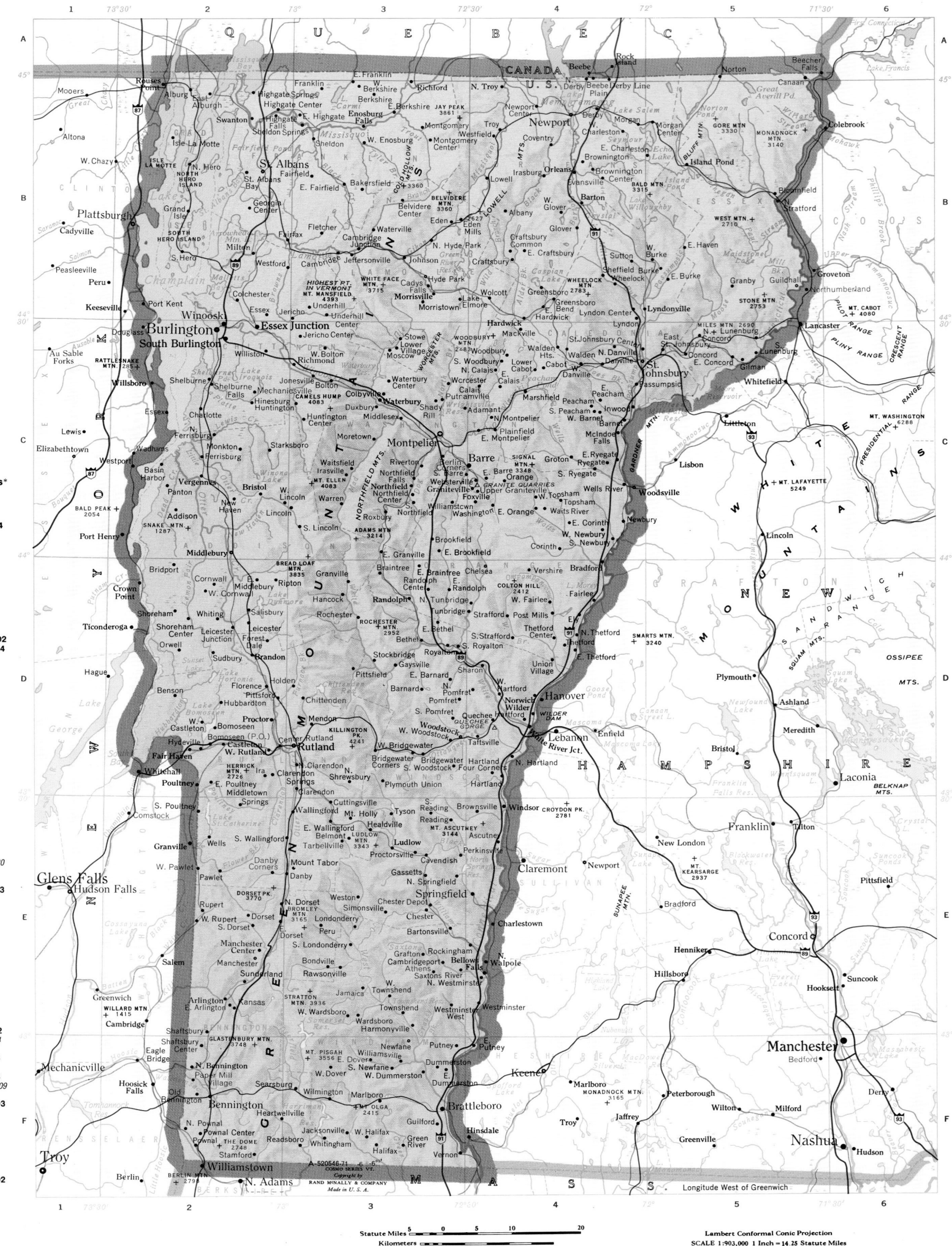

Statute Miles

Kilometers

Lambert Conformal Conic Projection
SCALE 1:903,000 1 Inch = 14.25 Statute Miles

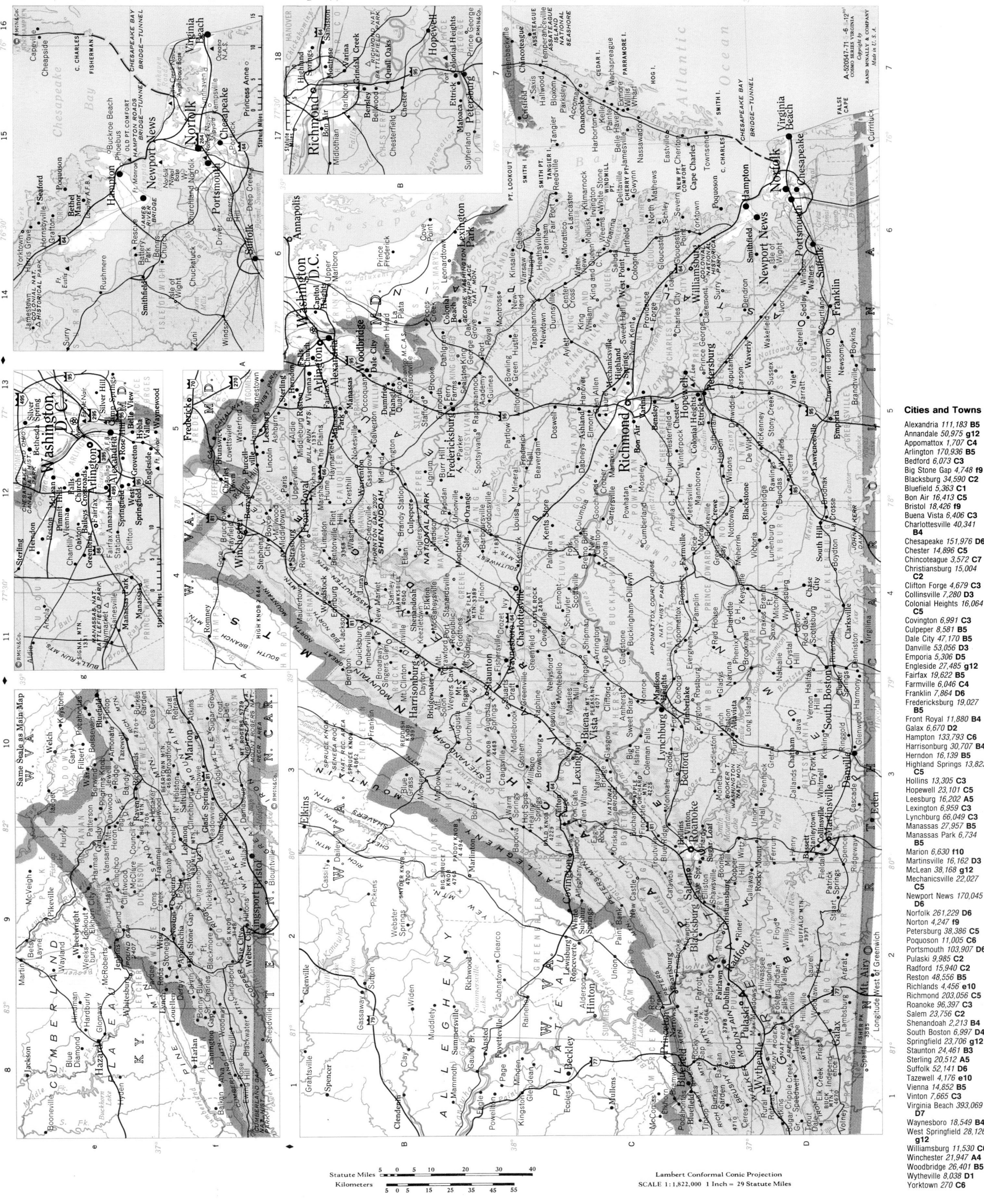

A-520547-71 ─ 6 -12"
COSMO SERIES VIRGINIA
Copyright by
RAND M°NALLY & COMPANY
Made in U. S. A.

Lambert Conformal Conic Projection
SCALE 1:1,822,000   1 Inch = 29 Statute Miles

Statute Miles
Kilometers

Cities and Towns

Alexandria 111,183 **B5**
Annandale 50,975 **g12**
Appomattox 1,707 **C4**
Arlington 170,936 **B5**
Bedford 6,073 **C3**
Big Stone Gap 4,748 **f9**
Blacksburg 34,590 **C2**
Bluefield 5,363 **C1**
Bon Air 16,413 **C5**
Bristol 18,426 **f9**
Buena Vista 5,406 **C3**
Charlottesville 40,341 **B4**
Chesapeake 151,976 **D6**
Chester 14,896 **C5**
Chincoteague 3,572 **C7**
Christiansburg 15,004 **C2**
Clifton Forge 4,679 **C3**
Collinsville 7,280 **D3**
Colonial Heights 16,064 **C5**
Covington 6,991 **C3**
Culpeper 8,581 **B5**
Dale City 47,170 **B5**
Danville 53,056 **D3**
Emporia 5,306 **D5**
Engleside 27,485 **g12**
Fairfax 19,622 **B5**
Farmville 6,046 **C4**
Franklin 7,864 **D6**
Fredericksburg 19,027 **B5**
Front Royal 11,880 **B4**
Galax 6,670 **D2**
Hampton 133,793 **C6**
Harrisonburg 30,707 **B4**
Herndon 16,139 **B5**
Highland Springs 13,823 **C5**
Hollins 13,305 **C3**
Hopewell 23,101 **C5**
Leesburg 16,202 **A5**
Lexington 6,959 **C3**
Lynchburg 66,049 **C3**
Manassas 27,957 **B5**
Manassas Park 6,734 **B5**
Marion 6,630 **f10**
Martinsville 16,162 **D3**
McLean 38,168 **g12**
Mechanicsville 22,027 **C5**
Newport News 170,045 **C6**
Norfolk 261,229 **D6**
Norton 4,247 **f9**
Petersburg 38,386 **C5**
Poquoson 11,005 **C6**
Portsmouth 103,907 **D6**
Pulaski 9,985 **C2**
Radford 15,940 **C2**
Reston 48,556 **B5**
Richlands 4,456 **e10**
Richmond 203,056 **C5**
Roanoke 96,397 **C3**
Salem 23,756 **C2**
Shenandoah 2,213 **B4**
South Boston 6,997 **D4**
Springfield 23,706 **g12**
Staunton 24,461 **B3**
Sterling 20,512 **A5**
Suffolk 52,141 **D6**
Tazewell 4,176 **e10**
Vienna 14,852 **B5**
Vinton 7,665 **C3**
Virginia Beach 393,069 **D7**
Waynesboro 18,549 **B4**
West Springfield 28,126 **g12**
Williamsburg 11,530 **C6**
Winchester 21,947 **A4**
Woodbridge 26,401 **B5**
Wytheville 8,038 **D1**
Yorktown 270 **C6**

Same Scale as Main Map

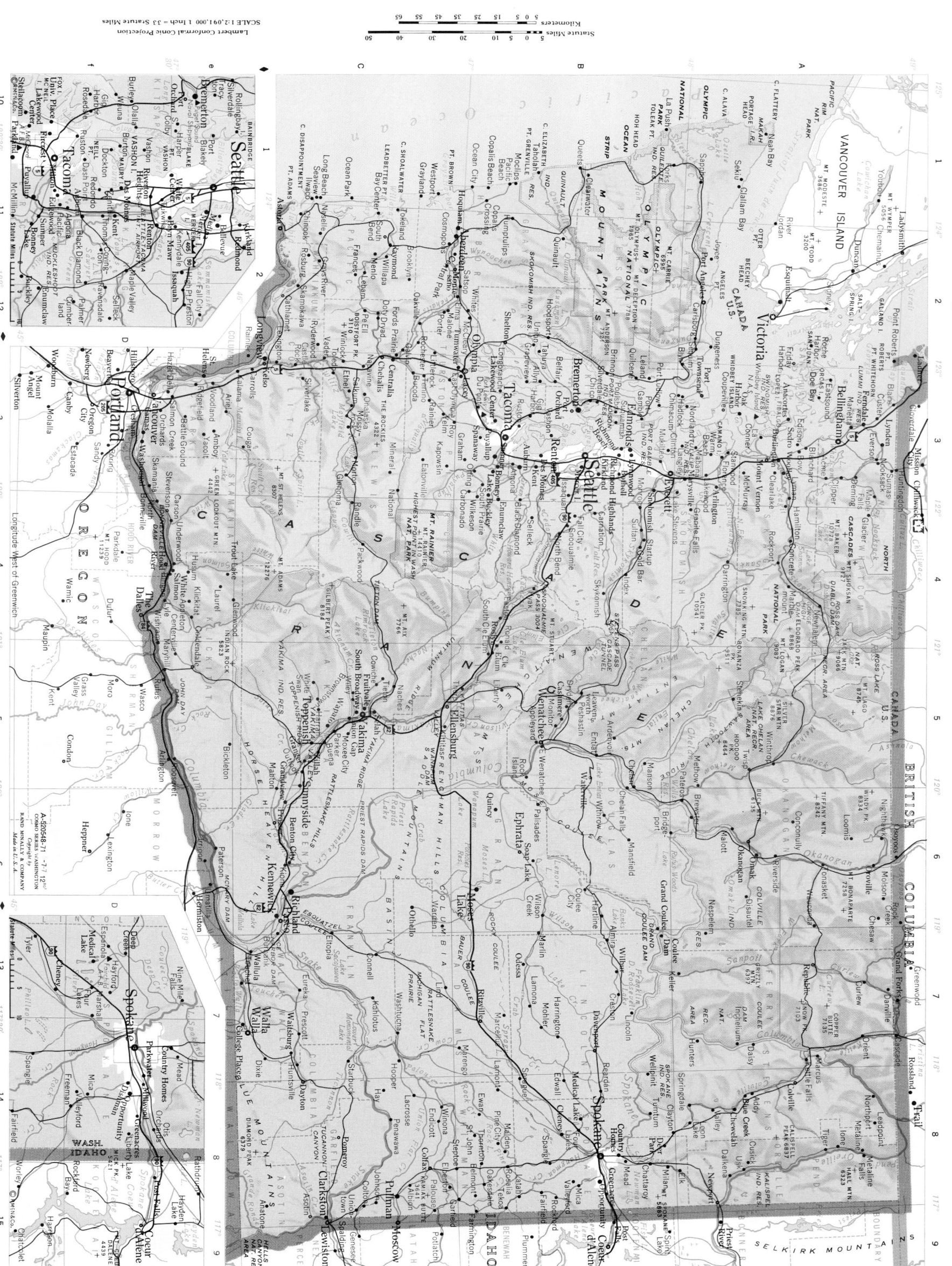

Lambert Conformal Conic Projection
SCALE 1:2,091,000 1 Inch = 33 Statute Miles

A-520548-71 7-7 12½°
COSMO SERIES ½
Made in U.S.A.

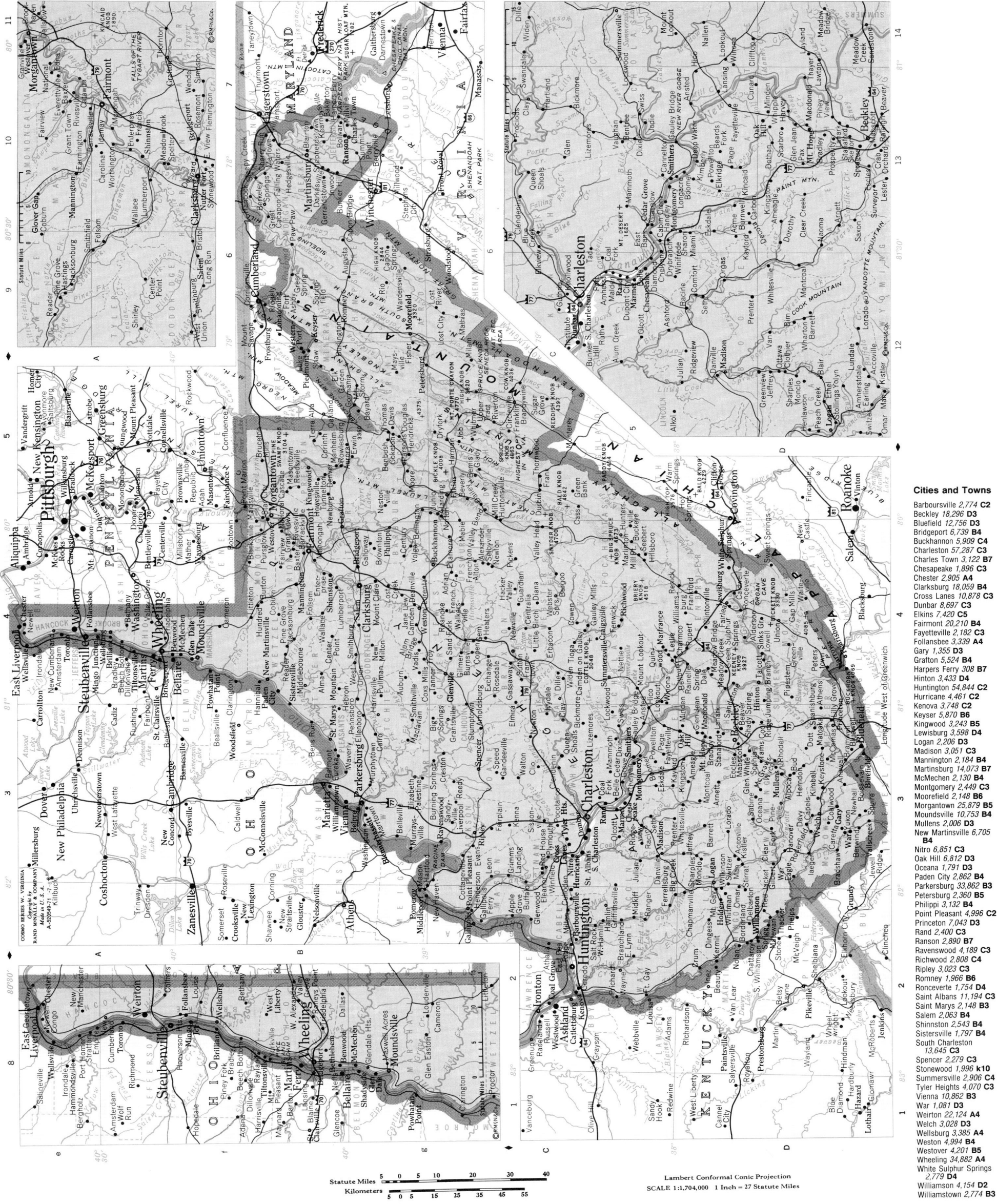

COSMO SERIES W. VIRGINIA
Prepared and printed by
RAND McNALLY & COMPANY
Made in U.S.A.
A-305648

Lambert Conformal Conic Projection
SCALE 1:1,704,000   1 Inch = 27 Statute Miles

Statute Miles 5 0 5 10 20 30 40
Kilometers 5 0 5 10 15 25 35 45 55

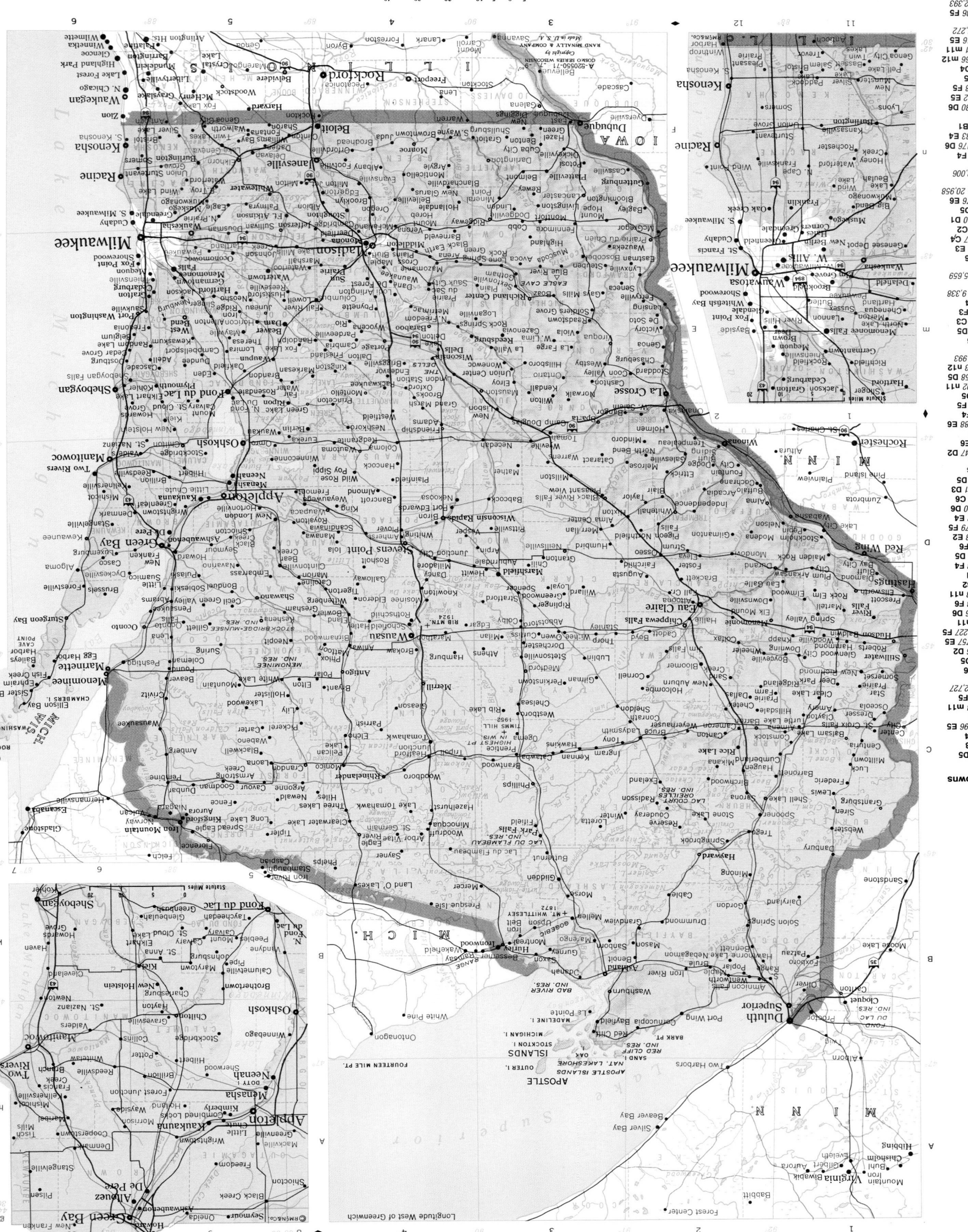

Wisconsin Rapids
18,245 D4
Wisconsin Dells 2,393
E4
Whitewater 12,636 F5
Whitefish Bay 14,272
m12
West Allis 63,221 m11
West Bend 28,916 E5
Wausau 37,060 D4
Waukesha 56,958 F5
Waupun 8,207 E5
Watertown 19,142 E5
Two Rivers 13,030 D6
Tomah 7,570 D3
Superior 27,134 B1
Sun Prairie 15,333 E4
Sturgeon Bay 9,176 D6
Stevens Point 23,006
D4
Stoughton 8,786 F4
South Milwaukee 20,958
F6
Sheboygan 49,676 E6
Shawano 7,598 D5
River Falls 10,610 D1
Rice Lake 7,998 C4
Rhinelander 7,427 C4
Reedsburg 5,834 E3
Racine 84,298 F6
Prairie du Chien 5,659
E2
Port Washington 9,338
E6
Portage 8,640 E3
Platteville 9,708 F3
Park Falls 3,104 C3
North Lake
Oshkosh 55,006 D5
Oconto 4,474 D6
Oconomowoc 10,993
E5
Oak Creek 19,513 n12
New London 6,658 D5
New Berlin 33,592 n11
Neenah 23,219 D5
Muskego 16,813 F5
Monroe 10,241 F4
Milwaukee 628,088 E6
Merrill 9,860 C4
Mequon 18,885 E6
Menomonie 13,547 D2
Menomonee Falls
26,840 E5
Marshfield 18,291 D3
Marinette 11,843 C6
Manitowoc 32,520 D6
Madison 191,262 E4
Lake Geneva 5,979 F5
La Crosse 51,003 E2
Kenosha 80,352 F6
Kaukauna 11,982 D5
Janesville 51,131 F4
Hudson 6,378 D1
Hayward 1,897 B2
Greenfield 33,403 n11
Greendale 15,128 F6
Green Bay 96,466 D6
Franklin 21,855 n11
Fort Atkinson 10,227 F5
Fond du Lac 37,757 E5
Eau Claire 56,856 D2
De Pere 16,569 D5
Cudahy 18,659 F6
Chippewa Falls 12,727
D2
Burlington 8,855 F5
Brookfield 35,184 m11
Beloit 35,573 F4
Beaver Dam 14,196 E5
Baraboo 9,203 E4
Ashland 8,695 B3
Appleton 65,695 D5
Antigo 8,276 C4

Cities and Towns

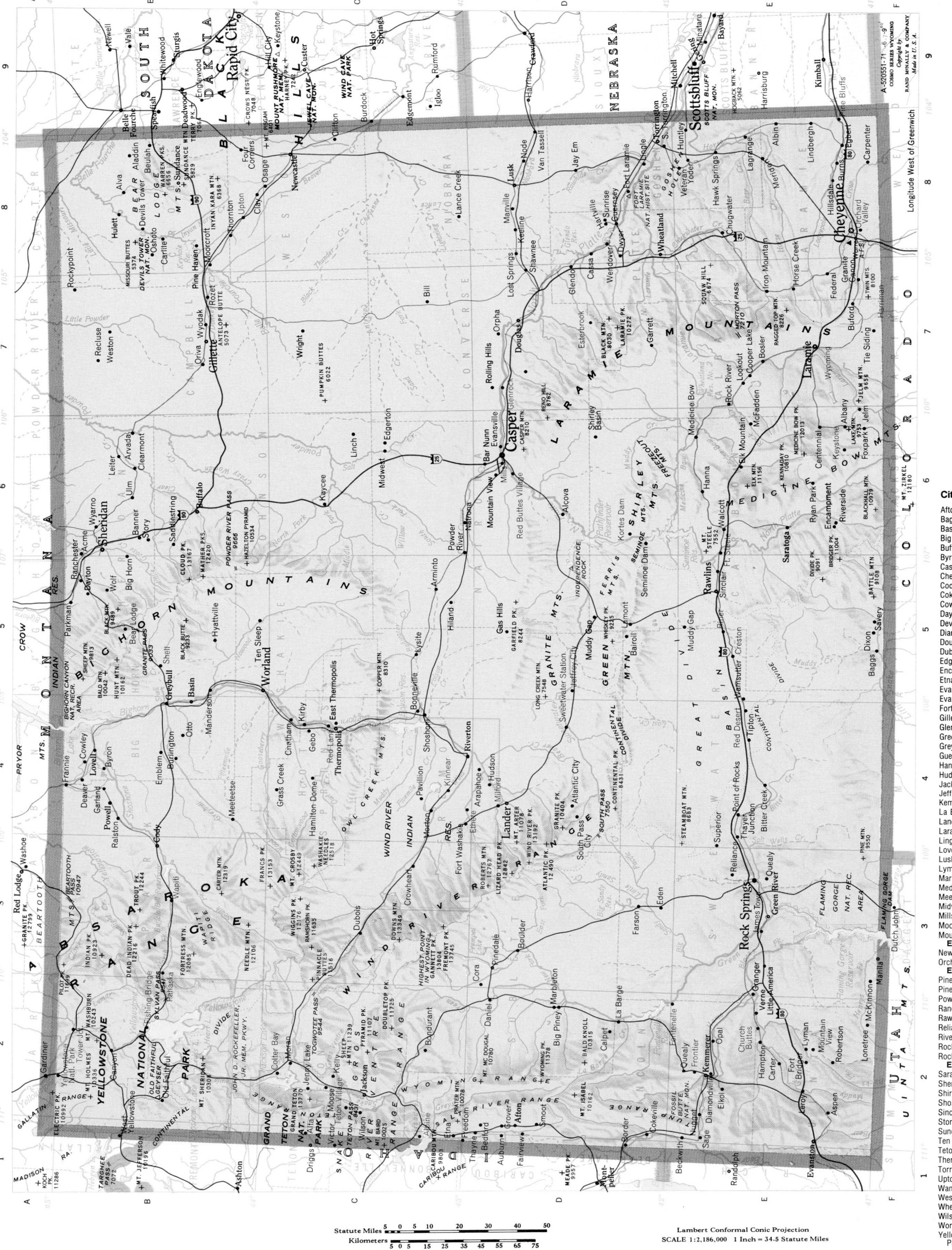

Cities and Towns

Afton 1,394 **D2**
Baggs 272 **E5**
Basin 1,180 **B4**
Big Piney 454 **D2**
Buffalo 3,302 **B6**
Byron 470 **B4**
Casper 46,742 **D6**
Cheyenne 50,008 **E8**
Cody 7,897 **B3**
Cokeville 493 **D2**
Cowley 477 **B4**
Dayton 565 **B5**
Devils Tower 40 **B8**
Diamondville 864 **E2**
Douglas 5,076 **D7**
Dubois 895 **C3**
Edgerton 247 **C6**
Encampment 490 **E6**
Etna 200 **C1**
Evanston 10,903 **E2**
Evansville 1,403 **D6**
Fort Laramie 243 **D8**
Gillette 17,635 **B7**
Glenrock 2,153 **D7**
Green River 12,711 **E3**
Greybull 1,789 **B4**
Guernsey 1,155 **D8**
Hanna 1,076 **E6**
Hudson 392 **D4**
Jackson 4,472 **C2**
Jeffrey City 1,882 **D5**
Kemmerer 3,020 **E2**
La Barge 493 **D2**
Lander 7,023 **D4**
Laramie 26,687 **E7**
Lingle 473 **D8**
Lovell 2,131 **B4**
Lusk 1,504 **D8**
Lyman 1,896 **E2**
Marbleton 634 **D2**
Medicine Bow 389 **E6**
Meeteetse 368 **B4**
Midwest 495 **C6**
Mills 1,574 **D6**
Moorcroft 768 **B8**
Mountain View 1,189 **E2**
Newcastle 3,003 **C8**
Orchard Valley 3,321 **E8**
Pine Bluffs 1,054 **E8**
Pinedale 1,181 **D3**
Powell 5,292 **B4**
Ranchester 676 **B5**
Rawlins 9,380 **E5**
Reliance 500 **E3**
Riverton 9,202 **C4**
Rock River 190 **E7**
Rock Springs 19,050 **E3**
Saratoga 1,969 **E6**
Sheridan 13,900 **B6**
Shirley Basin 100 **D6**
Shoshoni 497 **C4**
Sinclair 500 **E5**
Story 700 **B6**
Sundance 1,139 **B8**
Ten Sleep 311 **B5**
Teton Village 250 **C2**
Thermopolis 3,247 **C4**
Torrington 5,651 **D8**
Upton 980 **B8**
Wamsutter 240 **E5**
West Laramie 2,000 **E7**
Wheatland 3,271 **D8**
Wilson 500 **C2**
Worland 5,742 **B5**
Yellowstone National Park 400 **B2**

Statute Miles   5 0 5 10   20   30   40   50
Kilometers   5 0 5 15 25 35 45 55 65 75

Lambert Conformal Conic Projection
SCALE 1:2,186,000   1 Inch = 34.5 Statute Miles

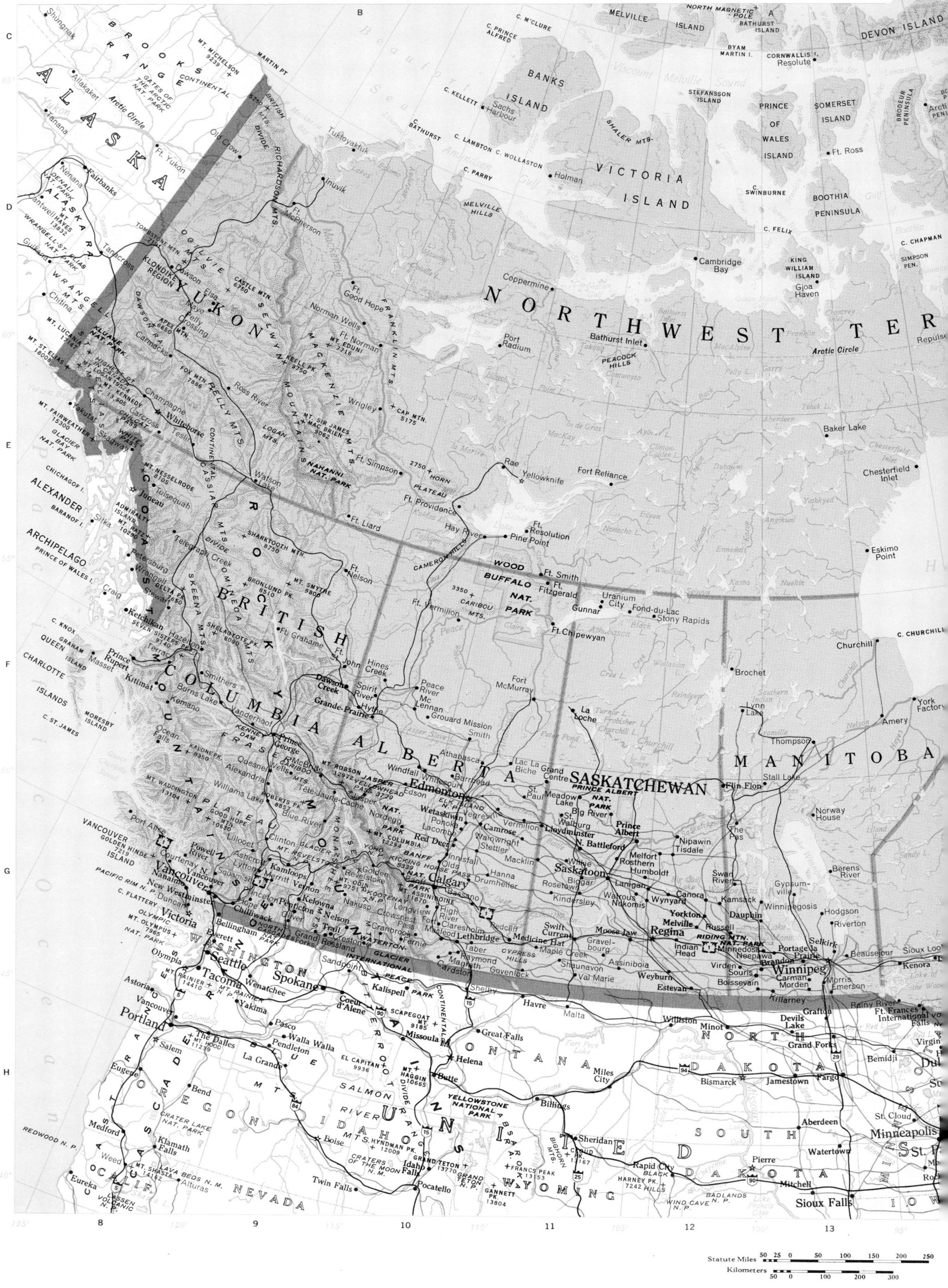

Statute Miles 50 25 0   50   100   150   200   250

Kilometers 50 0   100   200   300

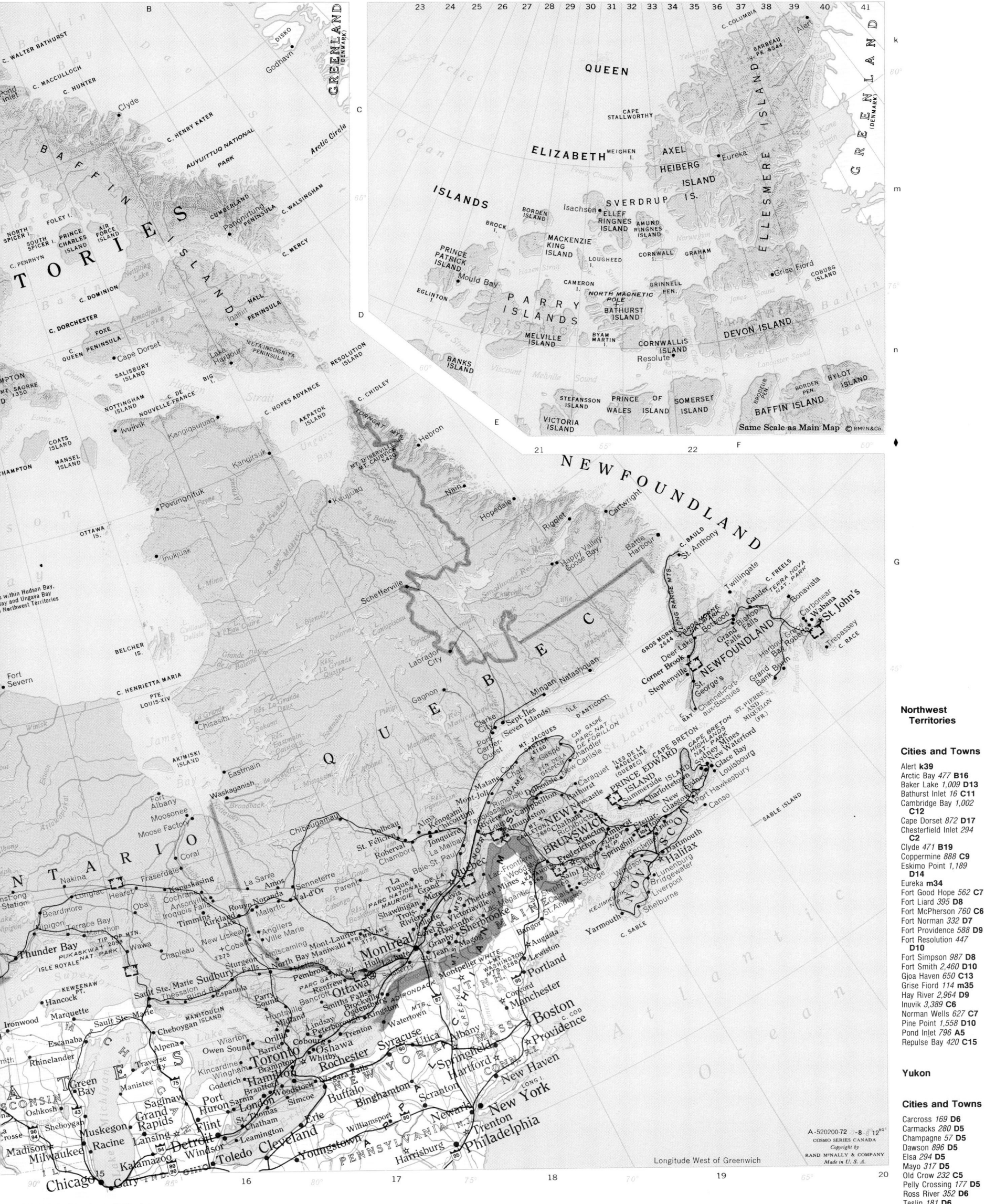

Lambert Conformal Conic Projection
SCALE 1:12,000,000 1 Inch = 189 Statute Miles

Longitude West of Greenwich

A-520200-72 -8 12°
COSMO SERIES CANADA
Copyright by
RAND McNALLY & COMPANY
Made in U.S.A.

Northwest Territories

Cities and Towns

Alert **k39**
Arctic Bay *477* **B16**
Baker Lake *1,009* **D13**
Bathurst Inlet *16* **C11**
Cambridge Bay *1,002*
  C12
Cape Dorset *872* **D17**
Chesterfield Inlet *294*
  C2
Clyde *471* **B19**
Coppermine *888* **C9**
Eskimo Point *1,189*
  D14
Eureka **m34**
Fort Good Hope *562* **C7**
Fort Liard *395* **D8**
Fort McPherson *760* **C6**
Fort Norman *332* **D7**
Fort Providence *588* **D9**
Fort Resolution *447*
  D10
Fort Simpson *987* **D8**
Fort Smith *2,460* **D10**
Gjoa Haven *650* **C13**
Grise Fiord *114* **m35**
Hay River *2,964* **D9**
Inuvik *3,389* **C6**
Norman Wells *627* **C7**
Pine Point *1,558* **D10**
Pond Inlet *796* **A5**
Repulse Bay *420* **C15**

Yukon

Cities and Towns

Carcross *169* **D6**
Carmacks *280* **D5**
Champagne *57* **D5**
Dawson *896* **D5**
Elsa *294* **D5**
Mayo *317* **D5**
Old Crow *232* **C5**
Pelly Crossing *177* **D5**
Ross River *352* **D6**
Teslin *181* **D6**
Watson Lake *826* **D7**
Whitehorse *15,199* **D5**

Cities and Towns

Airdrie 10,390 **D3**
Athabasca 1,970 **B4**
Banff **D3**
Barrhead 3,991 **B3**
Bonnyville 5,470 **B5**
Bow Island 1,650 **E5**
Brooks 9,464 **D5**
Calgary 636,104 **D3**
Camrose 12,968 **C4**
Canmore 4,182 **D3**
Cardston 3,497 **E4**
Claresholm 3,382 **D4**
Coaldale 4,796 **E4**
Cold Lake 3,195 **B5**
Coronation 1,310 **C5**
Crowsnest Pass 6,912 **E3**
Devon 3,691 **C4**
Didsbury 3,184 **D3**
Drayton Valley 5,290 **C3**
Drumheller 6,366 **D4**
Edmonton 573,982 **C4**
Edson 7,323 **C2**
Fairview 2,998 **A1**
Fort Chipewyan 922 **f8**
Fort Macleod 3,123 **E4**
Fort McMurray 34,949 **A5**
Fort Saskatchewan 11,983 **C4**
Gibbons 2,335 **C4**
Grand Centre 3,655 **B5**
Grande Cache 3,646 **C1**
Grande Prairie 26,471 **B1**
Grimshaw 2,579 **A2**
Hanna 3,017 **D5**
High Prairie 2,817 **B2**
High River 5,096 **D4**
Hinton 8,629 **C2**
Innisfail 5,535 **C4**
Jasper **C1**
Lac La Biche 2,553 **B5**
La Crete 689 **f7**
Lake Louise 688 **D2**
Leduc 13,126 **C4**
Lethbridge 58,841 **E4**
Lloydminster 17,356 **C5**
Magrath 1,637 **E4**
Medicine Hat 41,804 **D5**
Morinville 5,364 **C4**
Nordegg 53 **C2**
Okotoks 5,214 **C4**
Olds 4,871 **D3**
Peace River 6,288 **A2**
Pincher Creek 3,800 **E4**
Ponoka 5,473 **C4**
Raymond 2,957 **E4**
Redcliff 3,834 **D5**
Red Deer 54,425 **C4**
Rocky Mountain House 5,182 **C3**
Saint Albert 36,710 **C4**
Saint Paul 5,030 **B5**
Slave Lake 5,429 **B3**
Smith 251 **B3**
Spruce Grove 11,918 **C4**
Stettler 5,147 **C4**
Stony Plain 5,802 **C3**
Strathmore 3,544 **D4**
Swan Hills 2,403 **B3**
Sylvan Lake 3,937 **C3**
Taber 6,382 **E4**
Valleyview 1,987 **B2**
Vegreville 5,276 **C4**
Vermilion 3,879 **C5**
Vulcan 1,420 **D4**
Wainwright 4,665 **C5**
Westlock 4,532 **B4**
Wetaskiwin 10,071 **C4**
Whitecourt 5,737 **B3**

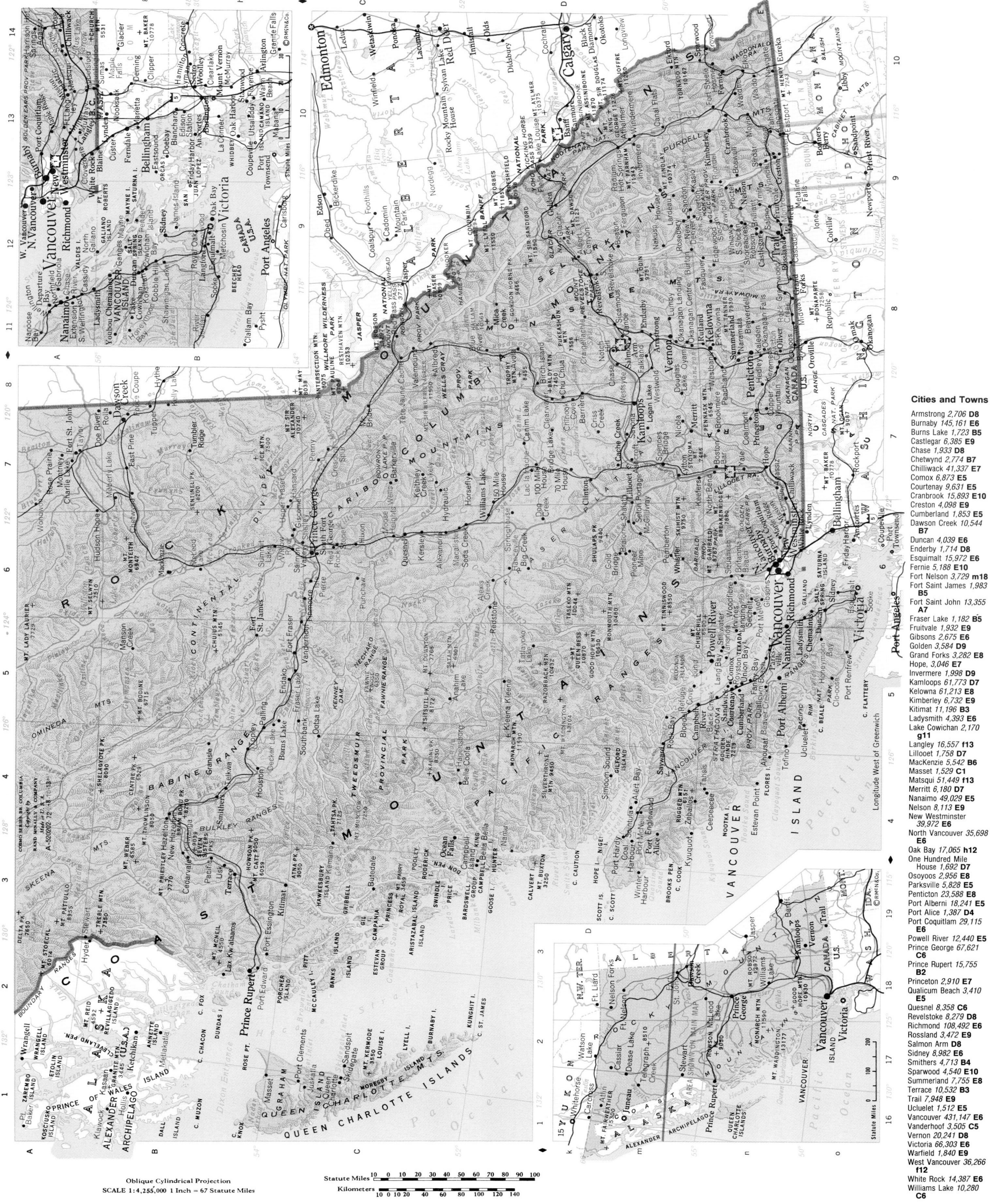

Oblique Cylindrical Projection
SCALE 1:4,255,000 1 Inch = 67 Statute Miles

Statute Miles 10 0 10 20 30 40 50 60 70 80 90 100
Kilometers 10 0 10 20 40 60 80 100 120 140

Cities and Towns

Armstrong 2,706 **D8**
Burnaby 145,161 **E6**
Burns Lake 1,723 **B5**
Castlegar 6,385 **E9**
Chase 1,933 **D8**
Chetwynd 2,774 **B7**
Chilliwack 41,337 **E7**
Comox 6,873 **E5**
Courtenay 9,631 **E5**
Cranbrook 15,893 **E10**
Creston 4,098 **E9**
Cumberland 1,853 **E5**
Dawson Creek 10,544 **B7**
Duncan 4,039 **E6**
Enderby 1,714 **D8**
Esquimalt 15,972 **E6**
Fernie 5,188 **E10**
Fort Nelson 3,729 **m18**
Fort Saint James 1,983 **B5**
Fort Saint John 13,355 **A7**
Fraser Lake 1,182 **B5**
Fruitvale 1,932 **E9**
Gibsons 2,675 **E6**
Golden 3,584 **D9**
Grand Forks 3,282 **E8**
Hope 3,046 **E7**
Invermere 1,998 **D9**
Kamloops 61,773 **D7**
Kelowna 61,213 **E8**
Kimberley 6,732 **E9**
Kitimat 11,196 **B3**
Ladysmith 4,393 **E6**
Lake Cowichan 2,170 **g11**
Langley 16,557 **f13**
Lillooet 1,758 **D7**
MacKenzie 5,542 **B6**
Masset 1,529 **C1**
Matsqui 51,449 **f13**
Merritt 6,180 **D7**
Nanaimo 49,029 **E5**
Nelson 8,113 **E9**
New Westminster 39,972 **E6**
North Vancouver 35,698 **E6**
Oak Bay 17,065 **h12**
One Hundred Mile House 1,692 **D7**
Osoyoos 2,956 **E8**
Parksville 5,828 **E5**
Penticton 23,588 **E8**
Port Alberni 18,241 **E5**
Port Alice 1,387 **D4**
Port Coquitlam 29,115 **E6**
Powell River 12,440 **E5**
Prince George 67,621 **C6**
Prince Rupert 15,755 **B2**
Princeton 2,910 **E7**
Qualicum Beach 3,410 **E5**
Quesnel 8,358 **C6**
Revelstoke 8,279 **D8**
Richmond 108,492 **E6**
Rossland 3,472 **E9**
Salmon Arm **D8**
Sidney 8,982 **E6**
Smithers 4,713 **B4**
Sparwood 4,540 **E10**
Summerland 7,755 **E8**
Terrace 10,532 **B3**
Trail 7,948 **E9**
Ucluelet 1,512 **E5**
Vancouver 431,147 **E6**
Vanderhoof 3,505 **C5**
Vernon 20,241 **D8**
Victoria 66,303 **E6**
Warfield 1,840 **E9**
West Vancouver 36,266 **f12**
White Rock 14,387 **E6**
Williams Lake 10,280 **C6**

Oblique Cylindrical Projection
SCALE 1:3,167,000   1 Inch = 50 Statute Miles

Statute Miles
10 0 10 20 30 40 50 60 70

Kilometers
10 0 10 20 40 60 80 100

A-502203-72   1-7-100°
COSMO SERIES MANITOBA
Copyright
RAND M9NALLY & COMPANY
Made in U.S.A.

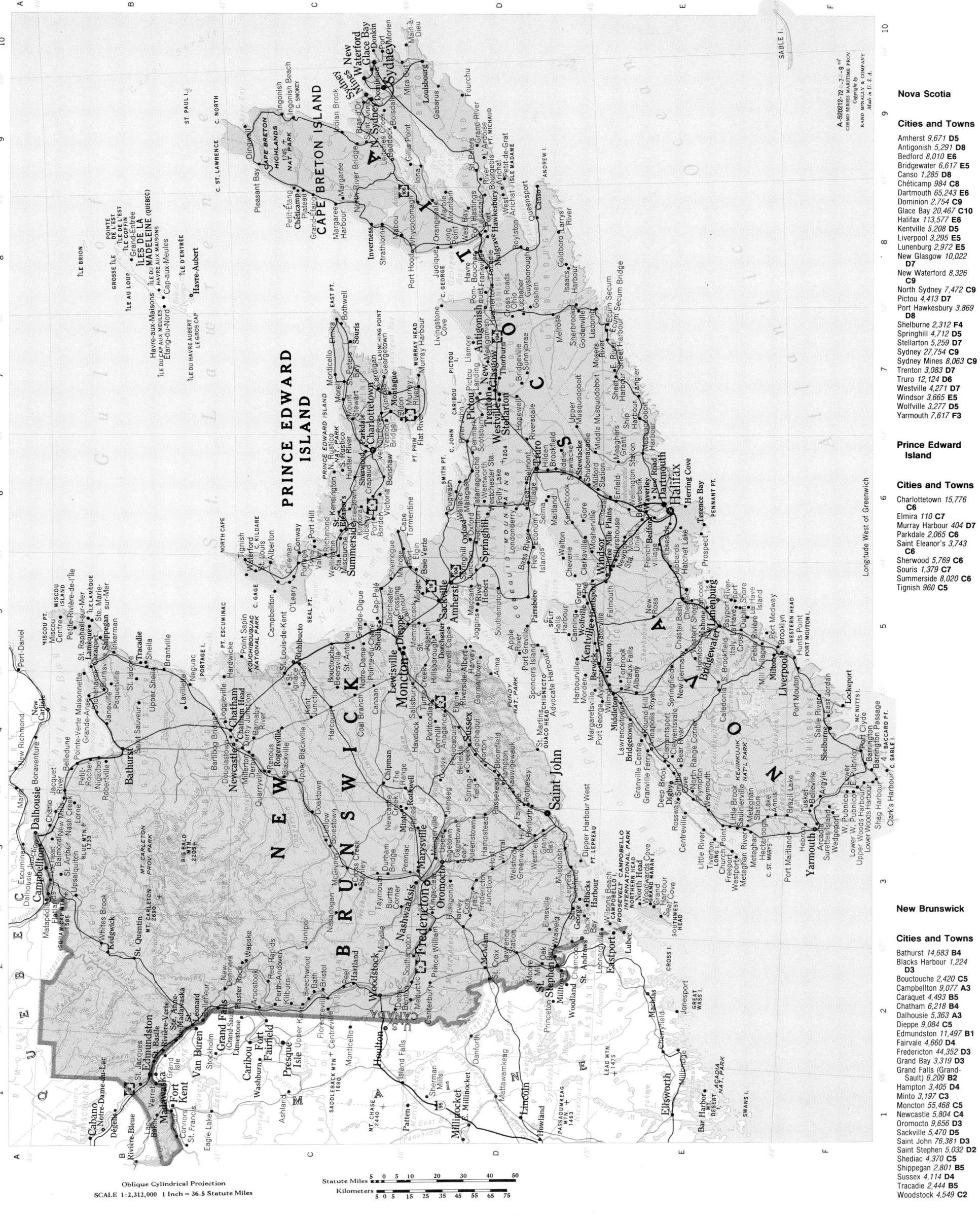

A-500212-72 -7, -9 m²
COSMO SERIES MARITIME PROV
Copyrighted by
RAND M⁹NALLY & COMPANY
Made in U. S. A.

Nova Scotia

Cities and Towns

Amherst 9,671 **D5**
Antigonish 5,291 **D8**
Bedford 8,010 **E6**
Bridgewater 6,617 **E5**
Canso 1,285 **D8**
Chéticamp 984 **C8**
Dartmouth 65,243 **E6**
Dominion 2,754 **C9**
Glace Bay 20,467 **C10**
Halifax 113,577 **E6**
Kentville 5,208 **D5**
Liverpool 3,295 **E5**
Lunenburg 2,972 **E5**
New Glasgow 10,022 **D7**
New Waterford 8,326 **C9**
North Sydney 7,472 **C9**
Pictou 4,413 **D7**
Port Hawkesbury 3,869 **D8**
Shelburne 2,312 **F4**
Springhill 4,712 **D5**
Stellarton 5,259 **D7**
Sydney 27,754 **C9**
Sydney Mines 8,063 **C9**
Trenton 3,083 **D7**
Truro 12,124 **D6**
Westville 4,271 **D7**
Windsor 3,665 **E5**
Wolfville 3,277 **D5**
Yarmouth 7,617 **F3**

Prince Edward Island

Cities and Towns

Charlottetown 15,776 **C6**
Elmira 110 **C7**
Murray Harbour 404 **D7**
Parkdale 2,065 **C6**
Saint Eleanor's 3,743 **C6**
Sherwood 5,769 **C6**
Souris 1,379 **C7**
Summerside 8,020 **C6**
Tignish 960 **C5**

New Brunswick

Cities and Towns

Bathurst 14,683 **B4**
Blacks Harbour 1,224 **D3**
Bouctouche 2,420 **C5**
Campbellton 9,077 **A3**
Caraquet 4,493 **B5**
Chatham 6,218 **B4**
Dalhousie 5,363 **A3**
Dieppe 9,084 **C5**
Edmundston 11,497 **B1**
Fairvale 4,660 **D4**
Fredericton 44,352 **D3**
Grand Bay 3,319 **D3**
Grand Falls (Grand-Sault) 6,209 **B2**
Hampton 3,405 **D4**
Minto 3,197 **C3**
Moncton 55,468 **C5**
Newcastle 5,804 **C4**
Oromocto 9,656 **D3**
Sackville 5,470 **D5**
Saint John 76,381 **D3**
Saint Stephen 5,032 **D2**
Shediac 4,370 **C5**
Shippegan 2,801 **B5**
Sussex 4,114 **D4**
Tracadie 2,444 **B5**
Woodstock 4,549 **C2**

Oblique Cylindrical Projection
SCALE 1:2,312,000 1 Inch = 36.5 Statute Miles

Statute Miles 5 0 10   20   30   40   50
Kilometers 5 0 15 25 35 45 55 65 75

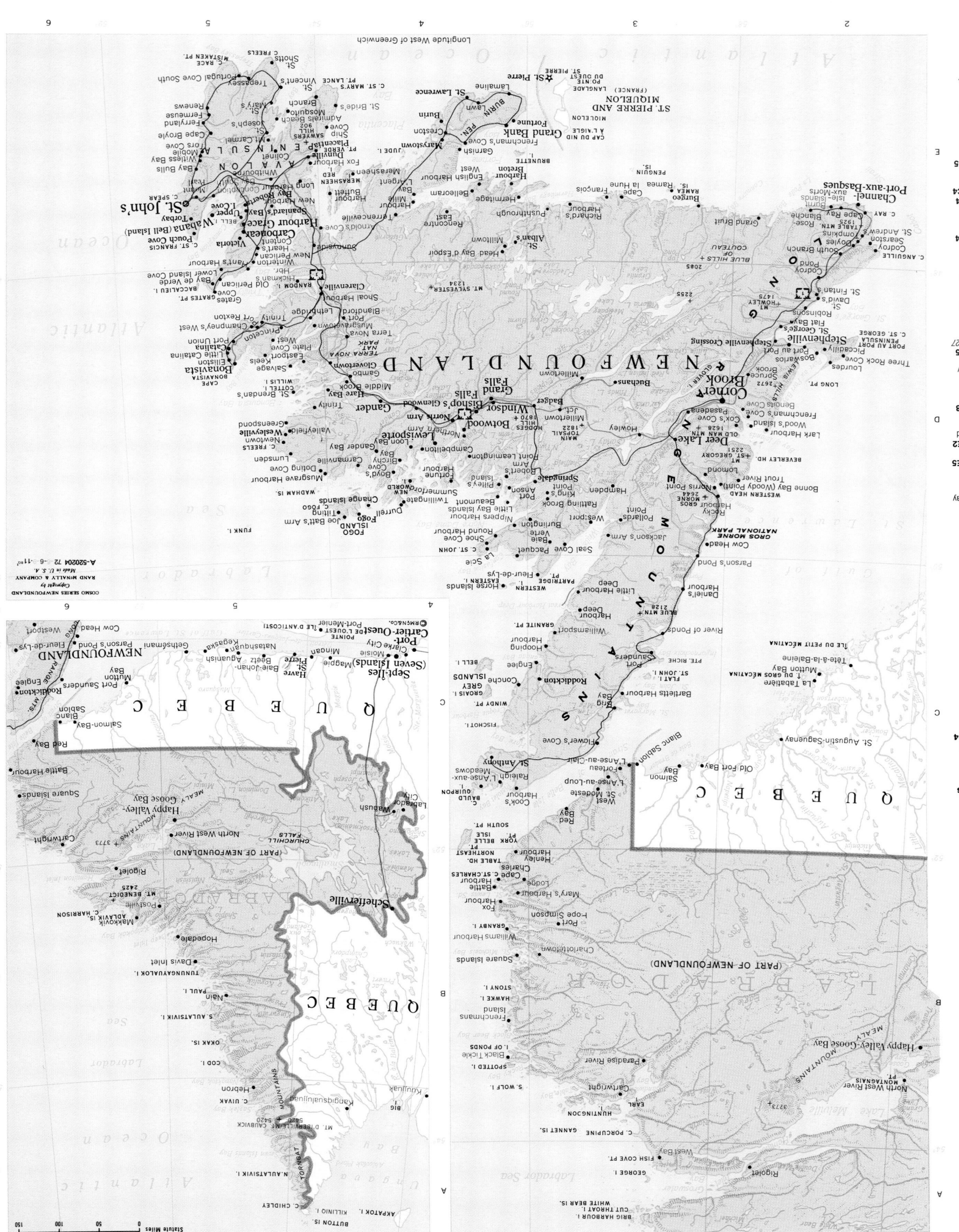

SCALE 1 : 3,000,000   1 Inch = 47 Statute Miles
Lambert Conformal Conic Projection

Cities and Towns

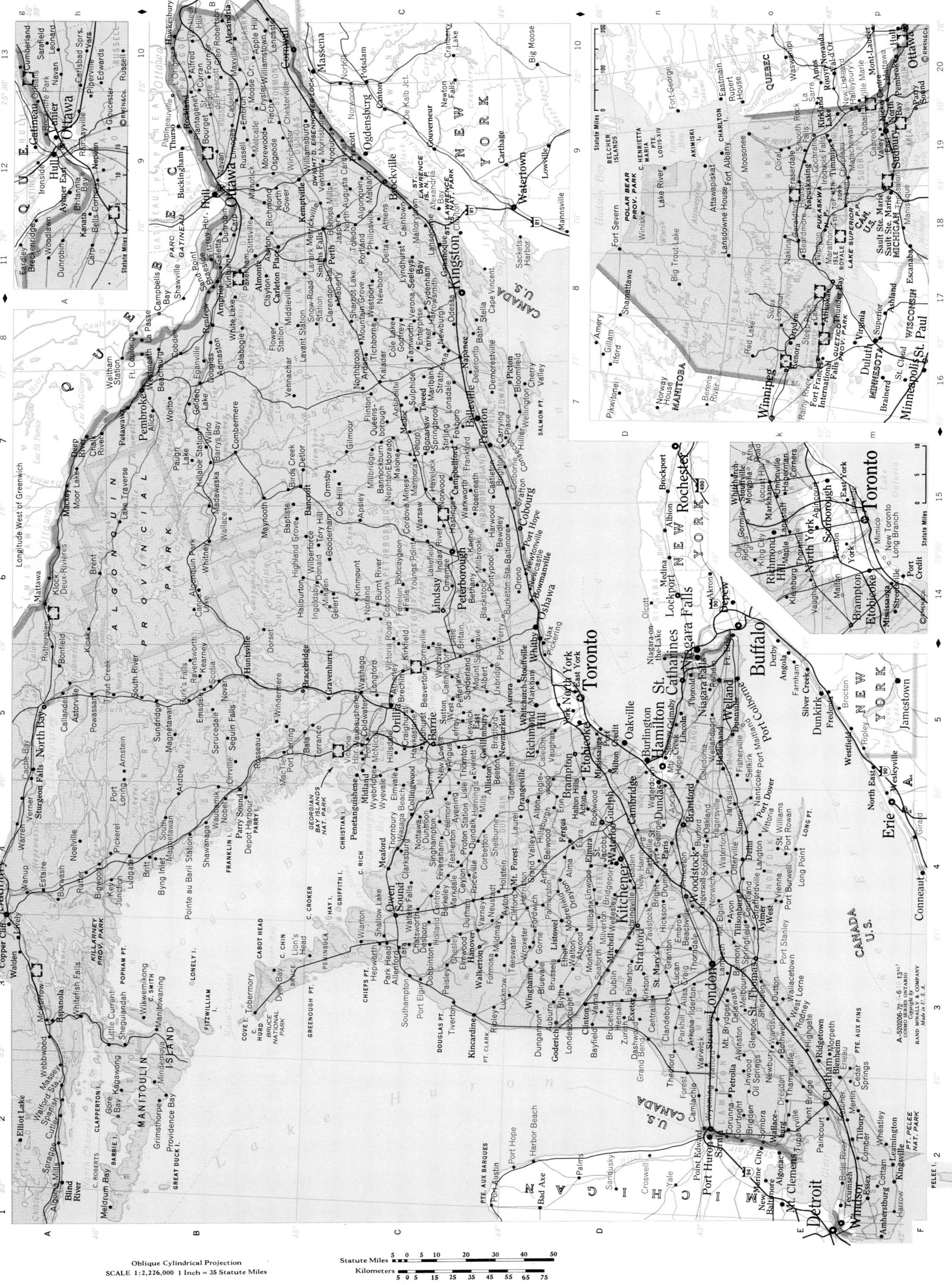

Oblique Cylindrical Projection
SCALE 1:2,226,000 1 Inch = 35 Statute Miles

Statute Miles
Kilometers

Cities and Towns

Ajax 36,550 **D6**
Barrie 48,287 **C5**
Belleville 36,041 **C7**
Brampton 188,498 **D5**
Brantford 76,146 **D4**
Brockville 20,880 **C9**
Burlington 116,675 **D5**
Cambridge 79,920 **D4**
Chatham 42,211 **E2**
Cobourg 13,197 **D6**
Cornwall 46,425 **B10**
Dryden 6,462 **o16**
Dundas 20,118 **D5**
East York 101,085 **D5**
Etobicoke 302,973 **D5**
Fergus 6,372 **D4**
Fort Erie 23,253 **E6**
Gloucester 89,810 **h12**
Guelph 78,235 **D4**
Haileybury 4,820 **p20**
Hamilton 306,728 **D5**
Hawkesbury 9,710 **B10**
Kapuskasing 11,378
  o19
Kenora 9,621 **o16**
Kingston 55,050 **C8**
Kirkland Lake 11,604
  o19
Kitchener 150,604 **D4**
Leamington 12,828 **E2**
Lindsay 14,455 **C6**
London 269,140 **E3**
Markham 114,597 **D5**
Midland 12,092 **C5**
Milton 32,037 **D5**
Mississauga 374,005
  D5
Moosonee 216 **o19**
Nanticoke 20,202 **E4**
Nepean 95,490 **h12**
Newcastle 34,073 **D6**
Newmarket 34,923 **C5**
Niagara Falls 72,107 **D5**
North Bay 50,623 **A5**
North York 556,297 **D5**
Oakville 87,107 **D5**
Orillia 24,077 **C5**
Oshawa 123,651 **D6**
Ottawa 300,763 **B9**
Owen Sound 19,804 **C4**
Pembroke 14,131 **B7**
Petawawa 5,580 **B7**
Peterborough 61,049
  C6
Pickering 48,959 **D5**
Port Colborne 18,281
  E5
Richmond Hill 46,766
  D5
Saint Catharines
  123,455 **D5**
Sarnia 49,033 **E2**
Sault Sainte Marie
  80,905 **p18**
Scarborough 484,676
  m15
Sioux Lookout 3,098
  o17
Smiths Falls 9,163 **C8**
Stratford 26,451 **D3**
Sturgeon Falls 5,895 **A5**
Sudbury 88,717 **A4**
Tecumseh 7,731 **E2**
Thunder Bay 112,272
  o17
Timmins 46,657 **o19**
Toronto 612,289 **D5**

Trenton 15,311 **C7**
Vanier 18,426 **h12**
Vaughan 65,058 **D5**
Waterloo 58,718 **D4**
Welland 45,054 **E5**
Whitby 45,819 **D6**
Windsor 193,111 **E1**
Woodstock 26,386 **D4**
York 135,401 **D5**

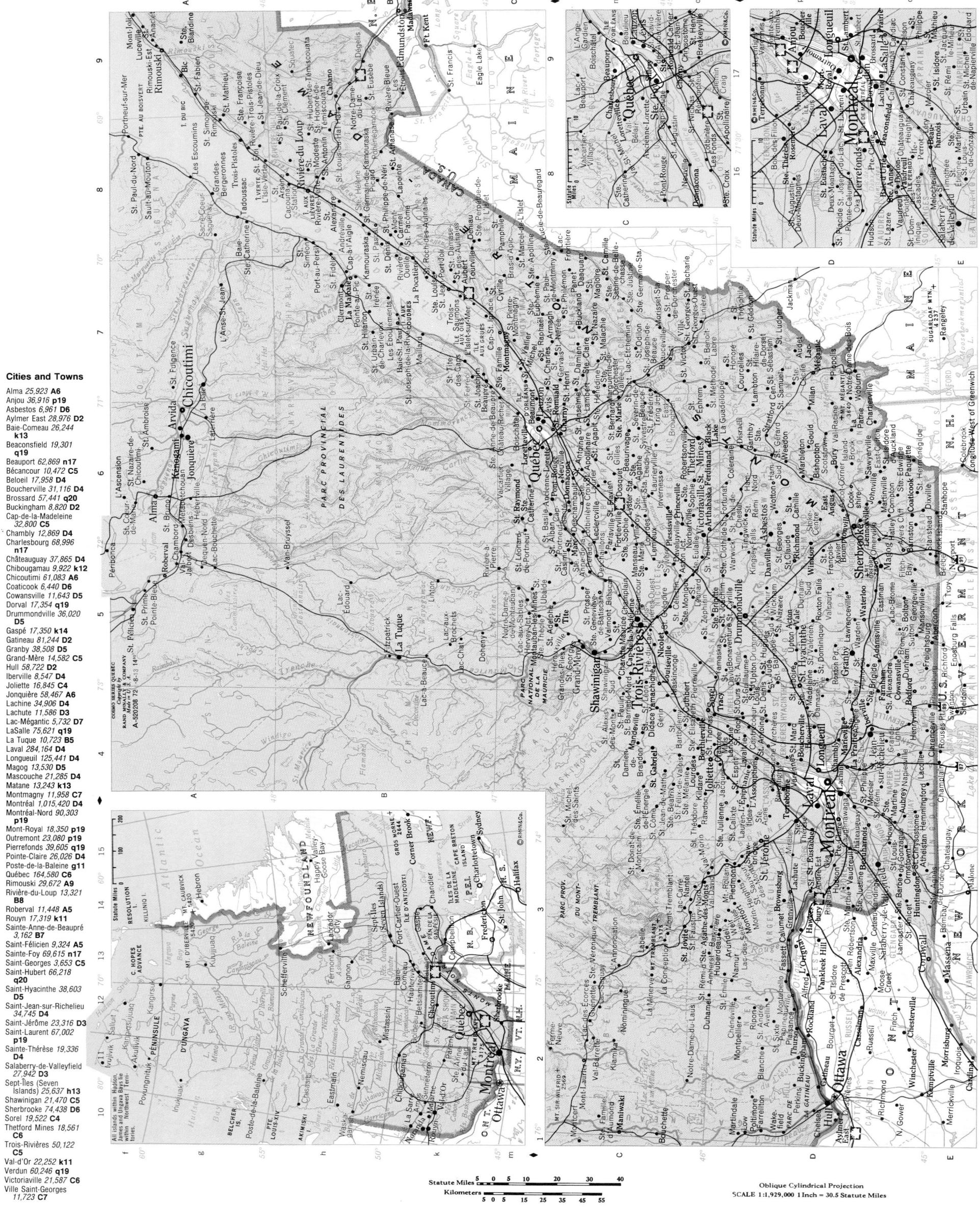

Cities and Towns

Alma 25,923 **A6**
Anjou 36,916 **p19**
Asbestos 6,961 **D6**
Aylmer East 28,976 **D2**
Baie-Comeau 26,244 **k13**
Beaconsfield 19,301 **q19**
Beauport 62,869 **n17**
Bécancour 10,472 **C5**
Beloeil 17,958 **D4**
Boucherville 31,116 **D4**
Brossard 57,441 **q20**
Buckingham 8,820 **D2**
Cap-de-la-Madeleine 32,800 **C5**
Chambly 12,869 **D4**
Charlesbourg 68,996 **n17**
Châteauguay 37,865 **D4**
Chibougamau 9,922 **k12**
Chicoutimi 61,083 **A6**
Coaticook 6,440 **D6**
Cowansville 11,643 **D5**
Dorval 17,354 **q19**
Drummondville 36,020 **D5**
Gaspé 17,350 **k14**
Gatineau 81,244 **D2**
Granby 38,508 **D5**
Grand-Mère 14,582 **C5**
Hull 58,722 **D2**
Iberville 8,547 **D4**
Joliette 16,845 **C4**
Jonquière 58,467 **A6**
Lachine 34,906 **D4**
Lachute 11,586 **D3**
Lac-Mégantic 5,732 **D7**
LaSalle 75,621 **q19**
La Tuque 10,723 **B5**
Laval 284,164 **D4**
Longueuil 125,441 **D4**
Magog 13,530 **D5**
Mascouche 21,285 **D4**
Matane 13,243 **k13**
Montmagny 11,958 **C7**
Montréal 1,015,420 **D4**
Montréal-Nord 90,303 **p19**
Mont-Royal 18,350 **p19**
Outremont 23,080 **p19**
Pierrefonds 39,605 **q19**
Pointe-Claire 26,026 **D4**
Poste-de-la-Baleine **g11**
Québec 164,580 **C6**
Rimouski 29,672 **A9**
Rivière-du-Loup 13,321 **B8**
Roberval 11,448 **A5**
Rouyn 17,319 **k11**
Sainte-Anne-de-Beaupré 3,162 **B7**
Saint-Félicien 9,324 **A5**
Sainte-Foy 69,615 **n17**
Saint-Georges 3,653 **C5**
Saint-Hubert 66,218 **q20**
Saint-Hyacinthe 38,603 **D5**
Saint-Jean-sur-Richelieu 34,745 **D4**
Saint-Jérôme 23,316 **D3**
Saint-Laurent 67,002 **p19**
Sainte-Thérèse 19,336 **D4**
Salaberry-de-Valleyfield 27,942 **D3**
Sept-Îles (Seven Islands) 25,637 **h13**
Shawinigan 21,470 **C5**
Sherbrooke 74,438 **D6**
Sorel 19,522 **C4**
Thetford Mines 18,561 **C6**
Trois-Rivières 50,122 **C5**
Val-d'Or 22,252 **k11**
Verdun 60,246 **q19**
Victoriaville 21,587 **C6**
Ville Saint-Georges 11,723 **C7**

Statute Miles
Kilometers

Oblique Cylindrical Projection
SCALE 1:1,929,000 1 Inch = 30.5 Statute Miles

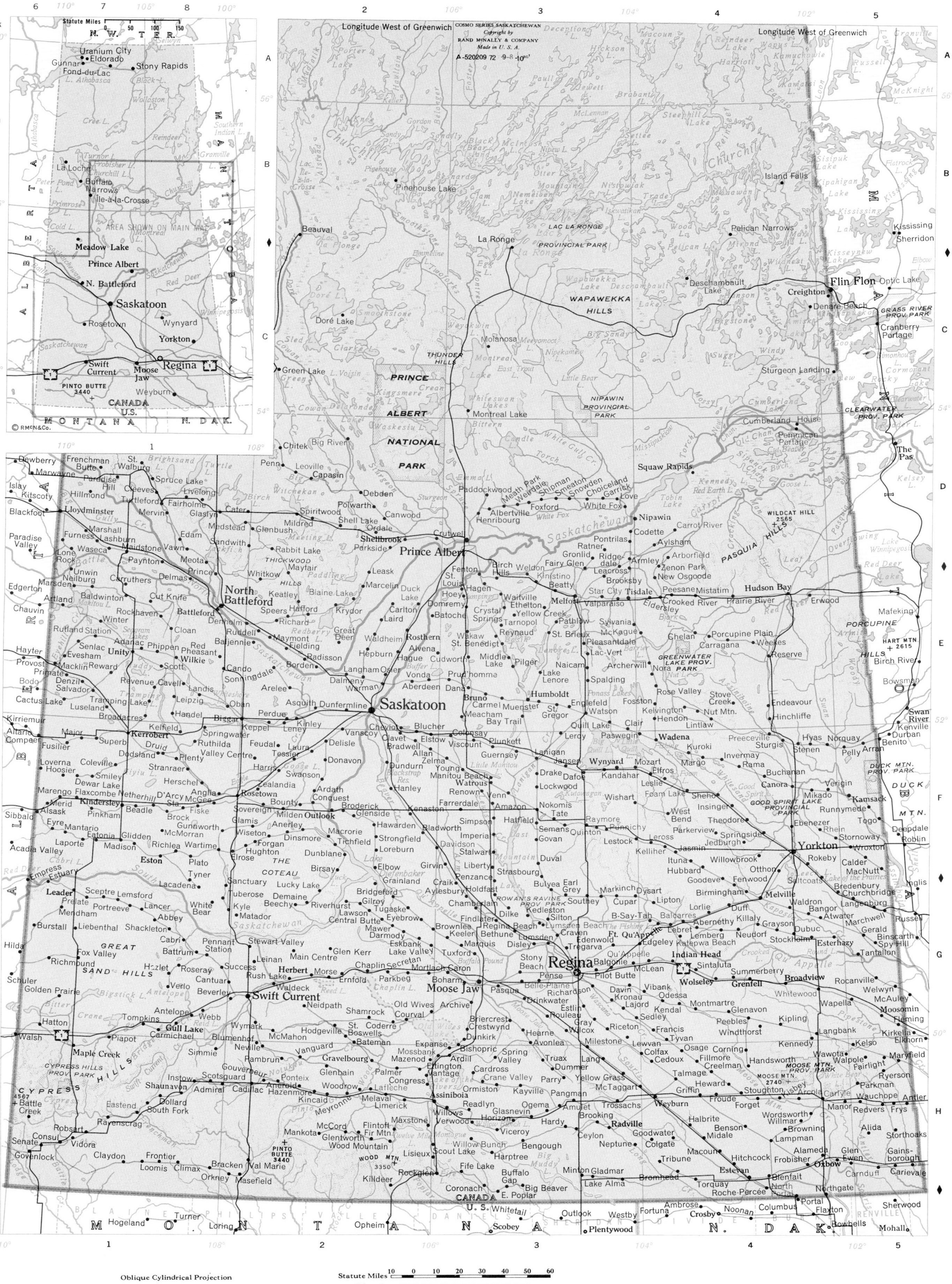

Oblique Cylindrical Projection
SCALE 1:2,827,000 1 Inch = 44 Statute Miles

Statute Miles 10 0 10 20 30 40 50 60
Kilometers 10 0 10 20 40 60 80

Cities and Towns

Assiniboia *3,001* **H2**
Battleford *3,833* **E1**
Biggar *2,626* **E1**
Buffalo Narrows *1,183* **m7**
Canora *2,602* **F4**
Carlyle *1,172* **H4**
Carnduff *1,090* **H5**
Carrot River *1,101* **D4**
Coronach *1,006* **H3**
Creighton *1,620* **C5**
Dalmeny *1,328* **E2**
Davidson *1,183* **F3**
Esterhazy *3,083* **G4**
Estevan *10,161* **H4**
Eston *1,383* **F1**
Foam Lake *1,535* **F4**
Fort Qu'Appelle *1,915* **G4**
Gravelbourg *1,305* **H2**
Grenfell *1,274* **G4**
Gull Lake *1,164* **G1**
Herbert *964* **G2**
Hudson Bay *2,133* **E4**
Humboldt *5,089* **E3**
Île-à-la-Crosse *1,030* **m7**
Indian Head *1,886* **G4**
Kamsack *2,565* **F5**
Kelvington *1,084* **E4**
Kerrobert *1,288* **F1**
Kindersley *4,912* **F1**
Kipling *1,033* **G4**
La Loche *1,623* **m7**
Langenburg *1,371* **G5**
Langham *1,193* **E2**
Lanigan *1,698* **F3**
La Ronge *2,696* **B3**
Leader *1,130* **G1**
Lloydminster *17,356* **D1**
Lumsden *1,369* **G3**
Macklin *1,131* **E1**
Maidstone *1,112* **D1**
Maple Creek *2,452* **H1**
Meadow Lake *3,976* **n7**
Melfort *6,078* **E3**
Melville *5,123* **G4**
Moose Jaw *35,073* **G3**
Moosomin *2,557* **G5**
Nipawin *4,588* **D4**
North Battleford *14,876* **E1**
Outlook *2,137* **F2**
Oxbow *1,229* **H4**
Pilot Butte *1,387* **G3**
Preeceville *1,272* **F4**
Prince Albert *33,686* **D3**
Radville *960* **H3**
Regina *175,064* **G3**
Rosetown *2,663* **F1**
Rosthern *1,594* **E2**
Saskatoon *177,641* **E2**
Shaunavon *2,153* **H1**
Shellbrook *1,238* **D2**
Spiritwood *1,025* **D2**
Swift Current *15,666* **G2**
Tisdale *3,184* **E3**
Unity *2,471* **E1**
Wadena *1,602* **F4**
Wakaw *1,010* **E3**
Warman *2,455* **E2**
Watrous *1,953* **F3**
Weyburn *10,153* **H4**
Whitewood *1,107* **G4**
Wilkie *1,526* **E1**
Wolseley *896* **G4**
Wynyard *2,079* **F3**
Yorkton *15,574* **F4**

The Index includes in a single alphabetical list some 160,000 names appearing on the maps on pages 1-288. This index does not include places shown on the United States and Canada maps on pages 290-351. The indexes for these maps are conveniently located in the margins of each map. Each name is followed by a page reference to one or more maps and by the location of the feature on the map, in coordinates of latitude and longitude. If a page contains several maps, a lowercase letter identifies the particular map. The page reference for two-page maps is always to the left-hand page.

Most map features are indexed to the largest-scale map on which they appear. However, a feature usually is not indexed to a Metropolitan Area map if it is also shown on another map where it can be seen in a broader setting. Countries, mountain ranges, and other extensive features are generally indexed to the largest-scale map that shows them in their entirety.

The features indexed are of three types: point, areal, and linear. For point features (for example, cities, mountain peaks, dams), latitude and longitude coordinates give the location of the point on the map. For areal features (countries, mountain ranges, etc.), the coordinates generally indicate the approximate center of the feature. For linear features (rivers, canals, aqueducts), the coordinates locate a terminating point—for example, the mouth of a river, or the point at which a feature reaches the map margin.

Name Forms Names in the Index, as on the maps, are generally in the local language and insofar as possible are spelled according to official practice. Diacritical marks are included, except that those used to indicate tone, as in Vietnamese, are usually not shown. Most features that extend beyond the boundaries of one country have no single official name, and these are usually named in English. Many English, German, Spanish, French, and Portuguese names, which may not be shown on the maps, appear in the Index as cross references. All cross references are indicated by the symbol→. A name that appears in a shortened version on the map due to space limitations is given in full in the Index, with the portion that is omitted on the map enclosed in brackets, for example, Acapulco [de Juárez].

Transliteration For names in languages not written in the Roman alphabet, the locally official transliteration system has been used where one exists. Thus, names in Russia and Bulgaria have been transliterated according to the systems adopted by the academies of science of these countries. Similarly, the transliteration for mainland Chinese names follows the Pinyin system, which has been officially adopted in mainland China. For languages with no one locally accepted transliteration system, notably Arabic, transliteration in general follows closely a system adopted by the United States Board on Geographic Names.

Alphabetization Names are alphabetized in the order of the letters of the English alphabet. Spanish *ll* and *ch*, for example, are not treated as distinct letters. Furthermore, diacritical marks are disregarded in alphabetization—German or Scandinavian ä or ö are treated as a or o.

The names of physical features may appear inverted, since they are always alphabetized under the proper, not the generic, part of the name, thus: "Gibraltar, Strait of ⊔." Otherwise every entry, whether consisting of one word or more, is alphabetized as a single continuous entity. "Lakeland," for example, appears after "La Crosse" and before "La Salle." Names beginning with articles (Le Havre, Den Helder, Al-Qāhirah, As-Suways) are not inverted. Names beginning "St." and "Sainte" are alphabetized as though spelled "Saint."

In the case of identical names, towns are listed first, then political divisions, then physical features. Entries that are completely identical (including symbols, discussed below) are distinguished by abbreviations of their official country names and are sequenced alphabetically by country name. The many duplicate names in Canada, the United Kingdom, and the United States are further distinguished by abbreviations of the names of their primary subdivisions. (See list of abbreviations).

Abbreviation and Capitalization Abbreviation and styling have been standardized for all languages. A period is used after every abbreviation even when this may not be the local practice. The abbreviation "St." is used only for "Saint." "Sankt" and other forms of the term are spelled out.

All names are written with an initial capital letter except for a few Dutch names, such as 's-Gravenhage. Capitalization of noninitial words in a name generally follows local practice.

Symbol The symbols that appear in the Index represent graphically the broad categories of the features named, for example, ∧ for mountain (Everest, Mount ∧). An abbreviated key to the symbols appears at the foot of each pair of Index pages in five languages. Superior numbers following some symbols in the Index indicate finer distinctions, for example, $\wedge^1$ for volcano (Fuji-san $\wedge^1$). A complete list of the symbols and superior numbers is given on page I·1.

	LOCAL NAME	ENGLISH
Ab., Can.	Alberta	Alberta, Can.
Afg.	Afghānestān	Afghanistan
Afr.	. . .	Africa
Ak., U.S.	Alaska	Alaska, U.S.
Al., U.S.	Alabama	Alabama, U.S.
Alg.	Algérie / Djazaïr	Algeria
Am. Sam.	American Samoa / Amerika Samoa	American Samoa
And.	Andorra	Andorra
Ang.	Angola	Angola
Anguilla	Anguilla	Anguilla
Ant.	. . .	Antarctica
Antig.	Antigua and Barbuda	Antigua and Barbuda
Ar., U.S.	Arkansas	Arkansas, U.S.
Arg.	Argentina	Argentina
Ar. Su.	Al-'Arabīyah as-Su'ūdīyah	Saudi Arabia
Aruba	Aruba	Aruba
Asia	. . .	Asia
Austl.	Australia	Australia
Az., U.S.	Arizona	Arizona, U.S.
Azer.	Azerbaijan	Azerbaijan
Ba.	Bahamas	Bahamas
Baḥr.	Al-Baḥrayn	Bahrain
Barb.	Barbados	Barbados
B.A.T.	British Antarctic Territory	British Antarctic Territory
B.C., Can.	British Columbia / Colombie-Britannique	British Columbia, Can.
Bdi.	Burundi	Burundi
Bel.	Belgique / België	Belgium
Belize	Belize	Belize
Bela.	Belarus	Belarus
Bénin	Bénin	Benin
Ber.	Bermuda	Bermuda
B.I.O.T.	British Indian Ocean Territory	British Indian Ocean Territory
Blg.	Bălgarija	Bulgaria
Bngl.	Bangladesh	Bangladesh
Bol.	Bolivia	Bolivia
Boph.	Bophuthatswana	Bophuthatswana
Bos.	Bosna i Hercegovina	Bosnia and Hercegovina
Bots.	Botswana	Botswana
Bra.	Brasil	Brazil
Bru.	Brunei	Brunei
Br. Vir. Is.	British Virgin Islands	British Virgin Islands
Burkina	Burkina Faso	Burkina Faso
Ca., U.S.	California	California, U.S.
Cam.	Cameroun / Cameroon	Cameroon
Can.	Canada	Canada
Cay. Is.	Cayman Islands	Cayman Islands
Centraf.	République centrafricaine	Central African Republic
Česko.	Československo	Czechoslovakia
Chile	Chile	Chile
Christ. I.	Christmas Island	Christmas Island
Ciskei	Ciskei	Ciskei
C. Iv.	Côte d'Ivoire	Ivory Coast
C.M.I.K.	Chosŏn-minjujuŭi-inmīn-konghwaguk	Korea, North
Co., U.S.	Colorado	Colorado, U.S.
Cocos Is.	Cocos (Keeling) Islands	Cocos (Keeling) Islands
Col.	Colombia	Colombia
Comores	Comores / Al-Qumur	Comoros
Congo	Congo	Congo
Cook Is.	Cook Islands	Cook Islands
C.R.	Costa Rica	Costa Rica
Ct., U.S.	Connecticut	Connecticut, U.S.
Cuba	Cuba	Cuba
C.V.	Cabo Verde	Cape Verde
Dan.	Danmark	Denmark
D.C., U.S.	District of Columbia	District of Columbia, U.S.
De., U.S.	Delaware	Delaware, U.S.
Dji.	Djibouti	Djibouti
Dom.	Dominica	Dominica
Dtsch.	Deutschland	Germany
D.Y.	Druk-Yul	Bhutan
Ec.	Ecuador	Ecuador
Eesti	Eesti	Estonia
Ellás	Ellás	Greece
El Sal.	El Salvador	El Salvador
Eng., U.K.	England	England, U.K.
Esp.	España	Spain
Europe	. . .	Europe
Falk. Is.	Falkland Islands	Falkland Islands
Fiji	Fiji	Fiji
Fl., U.S.	Florida	Florida, U.S.
Før.	Føroyar	Faeroe Islands
Fr.	France	France
Ga., U.S.	Georgia	Georgia, U.S.
Gabon	Gabon	Gabon
Gam.	Gambia	Gambia
Ghana	Ghana	Ghana
Gib.	Gibraltar	Gibraltar
Gren.	Grenada	Grenada
Guad.	Guadeloupe	Guadeloupe
Guam	Guam	Guam
Guat.	Guatemala	Guatemala
Guernsey	Guernsey	Guernsey
Gui.-B.	Guiné-Bissau	Guinea-Bissau
Gui. Ecu.	Guinea Ecuatorial	Equatorial Guinea
Guinée	Guinée	Guinea
Guy.	Guyana	Guyana
Guy. fr.	Guyane française	French Guiana
Haï.	Haïti	Haiti
Haya.	Hayastan	Armenia
Hi., U.S.	Hawaii	Hawaii, U.S.
H.K.	Hong Kong	Hong Kong
Hond.	Honduras	Honduras
Hrv.	Hrvatska	Croatia
Ia., U.S.	Iowa	Iowa, U.S.
I.A.M.	Al-Imārāt al-'Arabīyah al-Muttaḥidah	United Arab Emirates
Id., U.S.	Idaho	Idaho, U.S.
Il., U.S.	Illinois	Illinois, U.S.
In., U.S.	Indiana	Indiana, U.S.
India	India / Bharat	India
Indon.	Indonesia	Indonesia
I. of Man	Isle of Man	Isle of Man
Īrān	Īrān	Iran
'Irāq	Al-'Irāq	Iraq
Ire.	Ireland / Éire	Ireland
Ísland	Ísland	Iceland
Isr. Occ.	. . .	Israeli Occupied Areas
It.	Italia	Italy
Ityo.	Ityopiya	Ethiopia
Jam.	Jamaica	Jamaica
Jersey	Jersey	Jersey
Jugo.	Jugoslavija	Yugoslavia
Kal. Nun.	Kalaallit Nunaat / Grønland	Greenland
Kâm.	Kâmpŭchéa	Cambodia
Kaz.	Kazachstan	Kazakhstan
Kenya	Kenya	Kenya
Kıbrıs	Kuzey Kıbrıs	Cyprus, North
Kípros	Kípros / Kıbrıs	Cyprus
Kiribati	Kiribati	Kiribati
Ks., U.S.	Kansas	Kansas, U.S.
Kuwayt	Al-Kuwayt	Kuwait
Ky., U.S.	Kentucky	Kentucky, U.S.
Kyrg.	Kyrgyzstan	Kyrgyzstan
La., U.S.	Louisiana	Louisiana, U.S.
Lao	Lao	Laos
Lat.	Latvija	Latvia
Leso.	Lesotho	Lesotho
Liber.	Liberia	Liberia
Lībiyā	Lībiyā	Libya
Liech.	Liechtenstein	Liechtenstein
Liet.	Lietuva	Lithuania
Lubnān	Lubnān	Lebanon
Lux.	Luxembourg	Luxembourg
Ma., U.S.	Massachusetts	Massachusetts, U.S.
Macau	Macau	Macao
Madag.	Madagasikara / Madagascar	Madagascar
Magreb	Al-Magreb	Morocco
Magy.	Magyarország	Hungary
Mak.	Makedonija	Macedonia
Malawi	Malawi	Malawi
Malay.	Malaysia	Malaysia
Mald.	Maldives	Maldives
Mali	Mali	Mali
Malta	Malta	Malta
Marsh. Is.	Marshall Islands	Marshall Islands
Mart.	Martinique	Martinique
Maur.	Mauritanie / Mūrītāniyā	Mauritania
Maus.	Mauritius	Mauritius
Mayotte	Mayotte	Mayotte
Mb., Can.	Manitoba	Manitoba, Can.
Md., U.S.	Maryland	Maryland, U.S.
Me., U.S.	Maine	Maine, U.S.
Méx.	México	Mexico
Mi., U.S.	Michigan	Michigan, U.S.
Micron.	Federated States of Micronesia	Federated States of Micronesia
Mid. Is.	Midway Islands	Midway Islands
Mişr	Mişr	Egypt
Mn., U.S.	Minnesota	Minnesota, U.S.
Mo., U.S.	Missouri	Missouri, U.S.
Moç.	Moçambique	Mozambique
Mol.	Moldova	Moldova
Monaco	Monaco	Monaco
Mong.	Mongol Ard Uls	Mongolia
Monts.	Montserrat	Montserrat
Ms., U.S.	Mississippi	Mississippi, U.S.
Mt., U.S.	Montana	Montana, U.S.
Mya.	Myanmar	Burma
N.A.	. . .	North America
Namibia	Namibia	Namibia
Nauru	Nauru / Naoero	Nauru
N.B., Can.	New Brunswick / Nouveau-Brunswick	New Brunswick, Can.
N.C., U.S.	North Carolina	North Carolina, U.S.
N. Cal.	Nouvelle-Calédonie	New Caledonia
N.D., U.S.	North Dakota	North Dakota, U.S.
Ne., U.S.	Nebraska	Nebraska, U.S.
Ned.	Nederland	Netherlands
Ned. Ant.	Nederlandse Antillen	Netherlands Antilles
Nepāl	Nepāl	Nepal
Nf., Can.	Newfoundland / Terre-Neuve	Newfoundland, Can.
N.H., U.S.	New Hampshire	New Hampshire, U.S.
Nic.	Nicaragua	Nicaragua
Nig.	Nigeria	Nigeria
Niger	Niger	Niger
Nihon	Nihon	Japan
N. Ire., U.K.	Northern Ireland	Northern Ireland, U.K.
Niue	Niue	Niue
N.J., U.S.	New Jersey	New Jersey, U.S.
N.M., U.S.	New Mexico	New Mexico, U.S.
N. Mar. Is.	Northern Mariana Islands	Northern Mariana Islands
Nor.	Norge	Norway
Norf. I.	Norfolk Island	Norfolk Island
N.S., Can.	Nova Scotia / Nouvelle-Écosse	Nova Scotia, Can.
N.T., Can.	Northwest Territories / Territoires du Nord-Ouest	Northwest Territories, Can.
Nv., U.S.	Nevada	Nevada, U.S.
N.Y., U.S.	New York	New York, U.S.
N.Z.	New Zealand	New Zealand
Oc.	. . .	Oceania
Oh., U.S.	Ohio	Ohio, U.S.
Ok., U.S.	Oklahoma	Oklahoma, U.S.
On., Can.	Ontario	Ontario, Can.
Or., U.S.	Oregon	Oregon, U.S.
Öst.	Österreich	Austria
Pa., U.S.	Pennsylvania	Pennsylvania, U.S.
Pāk.	Pākistān	Pakistan
Palau	Palau / Belau	Palau
Pan.	Panamá	Panama
Pap. N. Gui.	Papua New Guinea	Papua New Guinea
Para.	Paraguay	Paraguay
P.E., Can.	Prince Edward Island / Île-du-Prince-Édouard	Prince Edward Island, Can.
Perú	Perú	Peru
Pil.	Pilipinas / Philippines	Philippines
Pit.	Pitcairn	Pitcairn
Pol.	Polska	Poland
Poly. fr.	Polynésie française	French Polynesia
Port.	Portugal	Portugal
P.Q., Can.	Québec	Quebec, Can.
P.R.	Puerto Rico	Puerto Rico
P.S.N.Á.	Plazas de Soberanía en el Norte de África	Spanish North Africa
Qaṭar	Qaṭar	Qatar
Rep. Dom.	República Dominicana	Dominican Republic
Réu.	Réunion	Reunion
R.I., U.S.	Rhode Island	Rhode Island, U.S.
Rom.	România	Romania
Ross.	Rossija	Russia
Rw.	Rwanda	Rwanda
S.A.	. . .	South America
S. Afr.	South Africa / Suid-Afrika	South Africa
Sak.	Sakartvelo	Georgia
S.C., U.S.	South Carolina	South Carolina, U.S.
Schw.	Schweiz / Suisse / Svizzera	Switzerland
Scot., U.K.	Scotland	Scotland, U.K.
S.D., U.S.	South Dakota	South Dakota, U.S.
Sén.	Sénégal	Senegal
Sey.	Seychelles	Seychelles
S. Geor.	South Georgia and the South Sandwich Islands	South Georgia and the South Sandwich Islands
Shq.	Shqipëri	Albania
Sing.	Singapore	Singapore
Sk., Can.	Saskatchewan	Saskatchewan, Can.
S.L.	Sierra Leone	Sierra Leone
S. Lan.	Sri Lanka	Sri Lanka
Slo.	Slovenija	Slovenia
S. Mar.	San Marino	San Marino
Sol. Is.	Solomon Islands	Solomon Islands
Som.	Somaliya	Somalia
St. Hel.	St. Helena	St. Helena
St. K./N.	St. Kitts and Nevis	St. Kitts and Nevis
St. Luc.	St. Lucia	St. Lucia
S. Tom./P.	São Tomé e Príncipe	Sao Tome and Principe
St. P./M.	Saint-Pierre-et-Miquelon	St. Pierre and Miquelon
St. Vin.	St. Vincent and the Grenadines	St. Vincent and the Grenadines
Sūd.	As-Sūdān	Sudan
Suomi	Suomi / Finland	Finland
Sur.	Suriname	Suriname
Sūrīy.	Sūrīyah	Syria
Sve.	Sverige	Sweden
Swaz.	Swaziland	Swaziland
T.a.a.f.	Terres australes et antarctiques françaises	French Southern and Antarctic Territories
Taehan	Taehan-min'guk	Korea, South
T'aiwan	T'aiwan	Taiwan
Taj.	Tajikistan	Tajikistan
Tan.	Tanzania	Tanzania
Tchad	Tchad	Chad
T./C. Is.	Turks and Caicos Islands	Turks and Caicos Islands
Thai	Prathet Thai	Thailand
Tn., U.S.	Tennessee	Tennessee, U.S.
Togo	Togo	Togo
Tok.	Tokelau	Tokelau
Tonga	Tonga	Tonga
Transkei	Transkei	Transkei
Trin.	Trinidad and Tobago	Trinidad and Tobago
Tun.	Tunisie / Tunis	Tunisia
Tür.	Türkiye	Turkey
Turk.	Turkmenistan	Turkmenistan
Tuvalu	Tuvalu	Tuvalu
Tx., U.S.	Texas	Texas, U.S.
Ug.	Uganda	Uganda
U.K.	United Kingdom	United Kingdom
Ukr.	Ukraina	Ukraine
'Umān	'Umān	Oman
Ur.	Uruguay	Uruguay
Urd.	Al-Urdun	Jordan
U.S.	United States	United States
Ut., U.S.	Utah	Utah, U.S.
Uzb.	Uzbekistan	Uzbekistan
Va., U.S.	Virginia	Virginia, U.S.
Vanuatu	Vanuatu	Vanuatu
Vat.	Città del Vaticano	Vatican City
Ven.	Venezuela	Venezuela
Venda	Venda	Venda
Viet	Viet Nam	Vietnam
Vir. Is., U.S.	Virgin Islands	Virgin Islands (U.S.)
Vt., U.S.	Vermont	Vermont, U.S.
Wa., U.S.	Washington	Washington, U.S.
Wake I.	Wake Island	Wake Island
Wales, U.K.	Wales	Wales, U.K.
Wal./F.	Wallis et Futuna	Wallis and Futuna
Wi., U.S.	Wisconsin	Wisconsin, U.S.
W. Sah.	. . .	Western Sahara
W. Sam.	Western Samoa / Samoa i Sisifo	Western Samoa
W.V., U.S.	West Virginia	West Virginia, U.S.
Wy., U.S.	Wyoming	Wyoming, U.S.
Yaman	Al-Yaman	Yemen
Yis.	Yisra'el / Isrā'īl	Israel
Yk., Can.	Yukon Territory	Yukon Territory, Can.
Zaïre	Zaïre	Zaire
Zam.	Zambia	Zambia
Zhg.	Zhongguo	China
Zimb.	Zimbabwe	Zimbabwe

Key to Index Symbols

The symbols below represent the categories into which the physical and cultural features are classified in the Index. Broad categories appear in **boldface** type. Symbols with superior numbers identify subcategories.

Schlüssel zu den Symbolen des Registers

Die folgenden Symbole veranschaulichen die Kategorien, nach denen physische und kulturgeographische Objekte im Register geordnet sind. Die Oberbegriffe sind in **Fettdruck** hervorgehoben. Symbole mit hochgestellten Nummern kennzeichnen Unterbegriffe.

Clave de los Símbolos del Índice

Los símbolos abajo representan las categorías dentro de las cuales están clasificados los rasgos físicos y culturales que están incluídos en el Índice. Las grandes categorías aparecen en **negrilla**. Los símbolos que tienen números en su parte superior identifican las subcategorías.

Signification des Symboles de l'Index

Les symboles ci-dessous représentent les catégories sous lesquelles les données physiques et culturelles sont classées dans l'indes. Les symboles en caractèter **gras** correspondent aux catégories principales. Ceux suivis d'un indice désignent les subdivisions d'une même catégorie.

Chave dos Símbolos do Índice

Os símbolos abaixo representam as categorias em que estão classificados os acidentes físicos e culturais no Índice. As grandes categorias aparecem em **negrito**. Os símbolos acompanhados de números altos identificam as subcategorias.

ENGLISH	DEUTSCH	ESPANOL	FRANCAIS	PORTUGUES
∧ **Mountain**	∧ **Berg**	∧ **Montaña**	∧ **Montagne**	∧ **Montanha**
∧[1] Volcano	∧[1] Vulkan	∧[1] Volcán	∧[1] Volcan	∧[1] Vulcão
∧[2] Hill	∧[2] Hügel	∧[2] Colina	∧[2] Colline	∧[2] Colina
⋏ **Mountains**	⋏ **Gebirge**	⋏ **Montañas**	⋏ **Montagnes**	⋏ **Montanhas**
⋏[1] Plateau	⋏[1] Hochebene	⋏[1] Meseta	⋏[1] Plateau	⋏[1] Planalto
⋏[2] Hills	⋏[2] Hügel	⋏[2] Colinas	⋏[2] Collines	⋏[2] Colinas
)(**Pass**	)(**Paß**	)(**Paso**	)(**Col**	)(**Passo**
V **Valley, Canyon**	V **Tal, Cañon**	V **Valle, Cañón**	V **Vallée, Canyon**	V **Vale, Canhão**
≚ **Plain**	≚ **Ebene**	≚ **Llano**	≚ **Plaine**	≚ **Planície**
≚[1] Basin	≚[1] Becken	≚[1] Cuenca	≚[1] Bassin	≚[1] Bacia
≚[2] Delta	≚[2] Delta	≚[2] Delta	≚[2] Delta	≚[2] Delta
› **Cape**	› **Kap**	› **Cabo**	› **Cap**	› **Cabo**
›[1] Peninsula	›[1] Halbinsel	›[1] Península	›[1] Péninsule	›[1] Península
›[2] Spit, Sand Bar	›[2] Landzunge, Sandbarre	›[2] Lengua de Tierra, Bajo	›[2] Flèche, Banc de sable	›[2] Ponta de Terra, Banco de Areia
I **Island**	I **Insel**	I **Isla**	I **Île**	I **Ilha**
I[1] Atoll	I[1] Atoll	I[1] Atolón	I[1] Atoll	I[1] Atol
I[2] Rock	I[2] Fels	I[2] Roca	I[2] Rocher	I[2] Rochedo
II **Islands**	II **Inseln**	II **Islas**	II **Îles**	II **Ilhas**
II[1] Rocks	II[1] Felsen	II[1] Rocas	II[1] Rochers	II[1] Rochedos
± **Other Topographic Features**	± **Andere Topographische Objekte**	± **Otros Elementos Topográficos**	± **Autres données topographiques**	± **Outros Acidentes Topográficos**
±[1] Continent	±[1] Erdteil	±[1] Continente	±[1] Continent	±[1] Continente
±[2] Coast, Beach	±[2] Küste, Strand	±[2] Costa, Playa	±[2] Côte, Plage	±[2] Costa, Praia
±[3] Isthmus	±[3] Landenge	±[3] Istmo	±[3] Isthme	±[3] Istmo
±[4] Cliff	±[4] Kliff	±[4] Risco	±[4] Falaise	±[4] Falésia
±[5] Cave, Caves	±[5] Höhle, Höhlen	±[5] Cueva, Cuevas	±[5] Caverne, Cavernes	±[5] Caverna, Cavernas
±[6] Crater	±[6] Krater	±[6] Cráter	±[6] Cratère	±[6] Cratera
±[7] Depression	±[7] Senke	±[7] Depresión	±[7] Dépression	±[7] Depressão
±[8] Dunes	±[8] Dünen	±[8] Dunas	±[8] Dunes	±[8] Dunas
±[9] Lava Flow	±[9] Lavastrom	±[9] Corriente de Lava	±[9] Coulée de lave	±[9] Corrente de Lava
≏ **River**	≏ **Fluß**	≏ **Río**	≏ **Rivière, Fleuve**	≏ **Rio**
≏[1] River Channel	≏[1] Flussarm	≏[1] Brazo de Río	≏[1] Bras de rivière	≏[1] Canal de Rio
≊ **Canal**	≊ **Kanal**	≊ **Canal**	≊ **Canal**	≊ **Canal**
≊[1] Aqueduct	≊[1] Aquädukt	≊[1] Acueducto	≊[1] Aqueduc	≊[1] Aqueduto
∟ **Waterfall, Rapids**	∟ **Wasserfall, Stromschnellen**	∟ **Cascada, Rápidos**	∟ **Chute d'eau, Rapides**	∟ **Quedas d'água, Rápidos**
ꓵ **Strait**	ꓵ **Meereßtrasse**	ꓵ **Estrecho**	ꓵ **Détroit**	ꓵ **Estreito**
⊂ **Bay, Gulf**	⊂ **Bucht, Golf**	⊂ **Bahía, Golfo**	⊂ **Baie, Golfe**	⊂ **Baía, Golfo**
⊂[1] Estuary	⊂[1] Trichtermündung	⊂[1] Estuario	⊂[1] Estuaire	⊂[1] Estuário
⊂[2] Fjord	⊂[2] Fjord	⊂[2] Fiordo	⊂[2] Fjord	⊂[2] Fiorde
⊂[3] Bight	⊂[3] Bucht	⊂[3] Bahía	⊂[3] Baie	⊂[3] Enseada
⊜ **Lake, Lakes**	⊜ **See, Seen**	⊜ **Lago, Lagos**	⊜ **Lac, Lacs**	⊜ **Lago, Lagos**
⊜[1] Reservoir	⊜[1] Stausee	⊜[1] Embalse	⊜[1] Réservoir, Retenue	⊜[1] Reservatório
⩸ **Swamp**	⩸ **Sumpf**	⩸ **Pantano**	⩸ **Marais**	⩸ **Pântano**
⍓ **Ice Features, Glacier**	⍓ **Eis- und Gletscherformen**	⍓ **Accidentes Glaciales, Glaciar**	⍓ **Formes glaciaires, Glacier**	⍓ **Acidentes Glaciares, Geleira**
⍑ **Other Hydrographic Features**	⍑ **Andere Hydrographische Objekte**	⍑ **Otros Elementos Hidrográficos**	⍑ **Autres données hydrographiques**	⍑ **Outros Acidentes Hidrográficos**
⍑[1] Ocean	⍑[1] Ozean	⍑[1] Océano	⍑[1] Océan	⍑[1] Oceano
⍑[2] Sea	⍑[2] Meer	⍑[2] Mar	⍑[2] Mer	⍑[2] Mar
⍑[3] Anchorage	⍑[3] Ankerplatz	⍑[3] Ancladero	⍑[3] Ancrage	⍑[3] Ancoradouro
⍑[4] Oasis, Well, Spring	⍑[4] Oase, Brunnen, Quelle	⍑[4] Oasis, Pozo, Manantial	⍑[4] Oasis, Puits, Source	⍑[4] Oásis, Poço, Fonte, Manancial

ENGLISH	DEUTSCH	ESPANOL	FRANCAIS	PORTUGUES
✢ **Submarine Features**	✢ **Untermeerische Objekte**	✢ **Accidentes Submarinos**	✢ **Formes de relief sous-marin**	✢ **Acidentes Submarinos**
✢[1] Depression	✢[1] Senke	✢[1] Depresión	✢[1] Dépression	✢[1] Depressão
✢[2] Reef, Shoal	✢[2] Riff, Untiefe	✢[2] Arrecife, Bajo	✢[2] Récif, Haut-fond	✢[2] Recife, Baixio
✢[3] Mountain, Mountains	✢[3] Berg, Gebirge	✢[3] Montaña, Montañas	✢[3] Montagne, Montagnes	✢[3] Montanha, Montanhas
✢[4] Slope, Shelf	✢[4] Abhang, Schelf	✢[4] Talud, Plataforma	✢[4] Talus, Plateau continental	✢[4] Talude, Plataforma
□ **Political Unit**	□ **Politische Einheit**	□ **Unidad Política**	□ **Entité politique**	□ **Unidade Política**
□[1] Independent Nation	□[1] Unabhängiger Staat	□[1] Nación Independiente	□[1] État indépendant	□[1] País Independente
□[2] Dependency	□[2] Abhängiges Gebiet	□[2] Dependencia	□[2] Dépendance	□[2] Dependência
□[3] State, Canton, Republic	□[3] Land, Kanton, Republik	□[3] Estado, Cantón, República	□[3] État, Canton, République	□[3] Estado, Cantão, República
□[4] Province, Region, Oblast	□[4] Provinz, Landschaft, Oblast	□[4] Provincia, Región, Oblast	□[4] Province, Région, Oblast	□[4] Província, Região, Oblast
□[5] Department, District, Prefecture	□[5] Département, Distrikt, Präfektur	□[5] Departamento, Distrito, Prefectura	□[5] Département, District, Préfecture	□[5] Departamento, Distrito, Prefeitura
□[6] County	□[6] Grafschaft	□[6] Condado	□[6] Comté	□[6] Condado
□[7] City, Municipality	□[7] Stadt, Stadtkreis	□[7] Ciudad, Municipalidad	□[7] Ville, Municipalité	□[7] Cidade, Municipalidade
□[8] Miscellaneous	□[8] Verschiedenes	□[8] Misceláneo	□[8] Divers	□[8] Diversos
□[9] Historical	□[9] Historisch	□[9] Histórico	□[9] Historique	□[9] Sítio Histórico
♥ **Cultural Institution**	♥ **Kulturelle Institution**	♥ **Institución Cultural**	♥ **Institution culturelle**	♥ **Instituição Cultural**
♥[1] Religious Institution	♥[1] Religiöse Institution	♥[1] Institución Religiosa	♥[1] Institution religieuse	♥[1] Instituição Religiosa
♥[2] Educational Institution	♥[2] Erziehungsinstitution	♥[2] Institución Educacional	♥[2] Établissement d'éducation	♥[2] Estabelecimento de Ensino
♥[3] Scientific, Industrial Facility	♥[3] Wissenschaftliche, Industrielle Anlage	♥[3] Institución Científica o Industrial	♥[3] Établissement scientifique ou industriel	♥[3] Estabelecimento Científico ou Industrial
⊥ **Historical Site**	⊥ **Historische Stätte**	⊥ **Sitio Histórico**	⊥ **Site historique**	⊥ **Sítio Histórico**
♠ **Recreational Site**	♠ **Erholungs- und Ferienort**	♠ **Sitio de Recreo**	♠ **Centre de loisirs**	♠ **Área de Lazer**
⊠ **Airport**	⊠ **Flughafen**	⊠ **Aeropuerto**	⊠ **Aéroport**	⊠ **Aeroporto**
■ **Military Installation**	■ **Militäranlage**	■ **Instalación Militar**	■ **Installation militaire**	■ **Instalação Militar**
◆ **Miscellaneous**	◆ **Verschiedenes**	◆ **Misceláneo**	◆ **Divers**	◆ **Diversos**
◆[1] Region	◆[1] Region	◆[1] Región	◆[1] Région	◆[1] Região
◆[2] Desert	◆[2] Wüste	◆[2] Desierto	◆[2] Désert	◆[2] Deserto
◆[3] Forest, Moor	◆[3] Wald, Moor	◆[3] Bosque, Páramo	◆[3] Forêt, Lande	◆[3] Floresta, Pântano
◆[4] Reserve, Reservation	◆[4] Reservat	◆[4] Reserva, Reservación	◆[4] Réserve	◆[4] Reserva
◆[5] Transportation	◆[5] Verkehr	◆[5] Transporte	◆[5] Transport	◆[5] Transporte
◆[6] Dam	◆[6] Damm	◆[6] Presa	◆[6] Barrage	◆[6] Represa
◆[7] Mine, Quarry	◆[7] Bergwerk, Steinbruch	◆[7] Mina, Cantera	◆[7] Mine, Carrière	◆[7] Mina, Pedreira
◆[8] Neighborhood	◆[8] Nachbarschaft	◆[8] Barrio	◆[8] Quartier	◆[8] Arredores, Vizinhança
◆[9] Shopping Center	◆[9] Einkaufszentrum	◆[9] Mercado	◆[9] Centre commercial	◆[9] Shopping Center

A

Aa ≏	**50**	51.01 N	2.06 E
Aach	**58**	47.50 N	8.51 E
Aachen	**56**	50.47 N	6.05 E
Aach im Allgäu	**58**	47.31 N	9.58 E
Aach-Linz	**58**	47.54 N	9.11 E
Aadorf	**58**	47.30 N	8.54 E
Aaiun — El Aaiún	**148**	27.09 N	13.12 W
Aalen	**56**	48.50 N	10.05 E
A'ālī an-Nīl □[4]	**140**	9.30 N	31.00 E
Aalsmeer	**52**	52.16 N	4.45 E
Aalst (Alost), Bel.	**50**	50.56 N	4.02 E
Aalst, Ned.	**52**	51.23 N	5.29 E
Aalten	**52**	51.56 N	6.35 E
Aalter	**50**	51.05 N	3.27 E
Aalwynsfontein	**158**	30.27 S	18.38 E
Äänekoski	**26**	62.36 N	25.44 E
Aansluit	**158**	26.44 S	22.28 E
Aar ≏	**56**	50.23 N	8.00 E
Aarau	**58**	47.23 N	8.03 E
Aarberg	**58**	47.03 N	7.16 E
Aarburg	**58**	47.19 N	7.54 E
Aardenburg	**52**	51.16 N	3.27 E
Aare ≏	**58**	47.37 N	8.13 E
Aareschlucht ♠	**58**	46.44 N	8.12 E
Aargau □[3]	**58**	47.30 N	8.10 E
Aarle-Rixtel	**52**	51.31 N	5.38 E
Aaronsburg	**210**	40.54 N	77.27 W
Aarschot	**56**	50.59 N	4.50 E
Aarwangen	**58**	47.15 N	7.46 E
Aazanèn	**34**	35.13 N	3.10 W
Aba, Nig.	**150**	5.06 N	7.21 E
Aba, Zaïre	**154**	3.52 N	30.14 E
Aba, Zhg.	**102**	33.06 N	101.59 E
Abā al-Bawl, Qurayn ∧[2]	**128**	24.56 N	51.13 E
Abā al-Waqf	**142**	28.35 N	30.46 E
Abā as-Su'ūd	**144**	17.29 N	44.08 E
Abacaxis ≏	**242**	3.54 S	58.47 W
Abaco I	**238**	26.28 N	77.05 W
Abacou, Pointe ›	**238**	18.03 N	73.47 W
Abadab, Jabal ∧	**140**	18.53 N	35.59 E
Ābādān	**128**	30.20 N	48.16 E
Ābādeh	**128**	31.10 N	52.37 E
Abadia dos Dourados	**255**	18.28 S	47.24 W
Abadiânia	**255**	16.06 S	48.48 W
Abadla	**148**	31.01 N	2.44 W
Abaeté	**255**	19.09 S	45.27 W
Abaeté ≏	**255**	18.02 S	45.12 W
Abaetetuba	**250**	1.42 S	48.54 W
Abagajtuj	**88**	49.35 N	117.49 E
Abagnar Qi	**102**	43.58 N	116.04 E
Abag Qi	**102**	43.53 N	114.33 E
Abaí	**252**	26.01 S	55.57 W
Abaj, Kaz.	**86**	49.38 N	72.52 E
Abaj, Ross.	**86**	50.27 N	85.05 E
Abaji	**150**	8.28 N	6.57 E
Abajo Mountains ⋏	**200**	37.50 N	109.25 W
Abajo Peak ∧	**200**	37.51 N	109.28 W
Abak	**150**	4.57 N	7.47 E
Abakaliki	**150**	6.21 N	8.06 E
Abakan	**86**	53.43 N	91.26 E
Abakan ≏	**86**	53.43 N	91.30 E
Abakanovo	**76**	59.18 N	37.39 E
Abakanskij chrebet ⋏	**86**	52.20 N	88.50 E
Abala, Congo	**152**	1.21 S	15.30 E
Abala, Niger	**150**	14.56 N	3.26 E
Abalak, Niger	**150**	15.27 N	6.17 E
Abalak, Ross.	**86**	58.08 N	68.36 E
Abalemma, Vallée d' V	**150**	15.34 N	6.23 E
Abalessa	**148**	22.54 N	4.50 E
Aban	**88**	56.41 N	96.04 E
Abancay	**248**	13.35 S	72.55 W
Abanga ≏	**152**	0.20 S	10.30 E
Abano Terme	**64**	45.21 N	11.47 E
Abaokoro	**174t**	1.29 N	173.02 E
Abar Irir	**144**	4.53 N	46.10 E
Abar Kūh	**128**	31.08 N	53.17 E
Abarra	**144**	5.23 N	39.58 E
Abarracamento	**256**	22.12 S	43.30 W
Abaša	**84**	42.12 N	42.13 E
Abascay, Arroyo ≏	**258**	35.17 S	58.07 W
Abashiri	**92a**	44.01 N	144.17 E
Abasolo, Méx.	**196**	25.57 N	100.24 W
Abasolo, Méx.	**196**	27.12 N	101.24 W
Abasolo, Méx.	**204**	32.39 N	115.21 W
Abasolo, Méx.	**232**	25.18 N	104.40 W
Abasolo, Méx.	**232**	24.04 N	98.22 W
Abasolo, Méx.	**234**	20.27 N	101.32 W
Abasolo del Valle	**234**	17.44 N	95.29 W
Abasto	**258**	34.58 S	58.06 W
Abastumani	**84**	41.46 N	42.50 E
Abate	**85**	39.03 N	77.36 E
Abate Alonia, Lago di ⊜	**68**	41.01 N	15.45 E
Abatimbo el Gumas	**144**	10.36 N	35.13 E
Abatskij	**86**	56.18 N	70.28 E
Abau	**164**	10.11 S	148.42 E
Abava ≏	**76**	57.06 N	21.54 E
Abaya, Lake ⊜	**144**	6.20 N	37.55 E
Abay — Blue Nile ≏	**140**	15.38 N	32.31 E
Abayuba	**258**	34.51 S	56.14 W
Abaza	**86**	52.39 N	90.06 E
Abba	**152**	5.20 N	15.11 E
Abbabach ≏	**263**	51.28 N	7.41 E
Abbadia San Salvatore	**66**	42.53 N	11.41 E
'Abbāsābād ◆[8]	**267d**	35.44 N	51.25 E
Abbasanta	**71**	40.08 N	8.49 E
Abbaye, Étang de l' ⊜	**261**	48.41 N	1.56 E
Abbé, Lac (Lake Abe) ⊜	**144**	11.06 N	41.50 E
Abbehausen	**52**	53.29 N	8.26 E
Abbekås	**41**	55.24 N	13.36 E
Abbensen	**52**	52.23 N	10.11 E
Abbert ≏	**48**	53.25 N	8.53 W
Abbess Roding	**260**	51.47 N	0.17 E
Abbeville, Fr.	**50**	50.06 N	1.50 E
Abbeville, Ga., U.S.	**192**	31.59 N	83.18 W
Abbeville, La., U.S.	**194**	29.58 N	92.08 W
Abbeville, Ms., U.S.	**194**	34.30 N	89.30 W
Abbeville, S.C., U.S.	**192**	34.10 N	82.22 W
Abbey	**184**	50.43 N	108.45 W
Abbeydorney	**48**	52.19 N	9.41 W
Abbeyfeale	**48**	52.24 N	9.18 W
Abbey Head ›	**44**	54.46 N	3.58 W
Abbeyleix	**48**	52.55 N	7.20 W
Abbey Peak ∧	**164**	14.18 S	144.29 E
Abbey Wood ◆[8]	**260**	51.29 N	0.08 E
Abbiategrasso	**62**	45.24 N	8.54 E
Abbot, Mount ∧	**166**	20.03 S	147.45 E
Abbots Bromley	**42**	52.48 N	1.52 W
Abbotsbury	**42**	50.40 N	2.36 W
Abbotsford, Austl.	**274a**	33.51 S	151.08 E
Abbotsford, B.C., Can.	**224**	49.03 N	122.17 W
Abbotsford, Wi., U.S.	**190**	44.56 N	90.18 W
Abbots Langley	**260**	51.43 N	0.25 W
Abbott, Arg.	**258**	35.17 S	58.48 W
Abbott, Tx., U.S.	**222**	31.53 N	97.04 W
Abbottābād	**123**	34.09 N	73.13 E
Abbott Butte ∧	**202**	42.57 N	122.33 W
Abbottstown	**208**	39.53 N	76.59 W
Abchazskaja Avtonomnaja Sovetskaja Socialističeskaja Respublika □[3]	**84**	43.10 N	41.00 E
Abcoude	**52**	52.16 N	4.58 E
'Abd al-'Azīz, Jabal ⋏	**130**	36.25 N	40.20 E
'Abd al-Ḥafiẓ, Qārat ∧[2]	**142**	28.53 N	30.08 E
'Abd al-Kūrī I	**118**	12.12 N	52.13 E
'Abd Allāh	**140**	13.30 N	23.02 E
'Abd Allāh, Khawr ꓵ	**128**	29.50 N	48.20 E
'Abd al-Shāhīd	**273c**	29.55 N	31.13 E
Ābdānān	**128**	32.58 N	47.26 E
Ábdēra ⊥	**38**	40.59 N	24.58 E
Abdrachmanovo	**80**	54.46 N	52.30 E
Abdul Hakīm	**123**	30.33 N	72.07 E
Abdulino	**80**	53.42 N	53.40 E
Abdulovo	**80**	54.16 N	53.27 E
Abe ≏	**94**	34.56 N	138.24 E
Abe, Lake (Lac Abbé) ⊜	**144**	11.06 N	41.50 E
Abéché	**146**	13.49 N	20.49 E
Abéjar	**34**	41.48 N	2.47 W
Abejonal, Cerro ∧	**236**	11.39 N	86.10 W
Abejorral	**246**	5.47 N	75.26 W
Abekr	**140**	12.43 N	28.55 E
Abelek	**140**	7.23 N	28.46 E
Abel Tasman National Park ♠	**172**	40.55 S	173.00 E
Abelti	**144**	8.10 N	37.34 E
Abemama I[1]	**14**	0.21 N	173.51 E
Abenberg	**56**	49.14 N	10.57 E
Abengourou	**150**	6.44 N	3.29 W
Abeno ◆[8]	**270**	34.38 N	135.32 E
Abenójar	**34**	38.53 N	4.21 W
Åbenrå	**41**	55.02 N	9.26 E
Åbenrå Fjord ⊂	**41**	55.03 N	9.34 E
Abens ≏	**60**	48.51 N	11.46 E
Abensberg	**60**	48.49 N	11.51 E
Abeokuta	**150**	7.10 N	3.26 E
Aber	**154**	2.12 N	32.21 E
Aberaeron	**42**	52.15 N	4.15 W
Aberaman	**42**	51.42 N	3.25 W
Aberavon — Port Talbot	**42**	51.36 N	3.47 W
Abercarn	**42**	51.39 N	3.08 W
Aberchirder	**46**	57.33 N	2.38 W
Abercorn	**206**	45.02 N	72.40 W
Abercorn — Mbala	**154**	8.50 S	31.22 E
Abercrombie ≏	**170**	34.09 S	149.40 E
Aberdare	**42**	51.43 N	3.27 W
Aberdare National Park ♠	**154**	0.30 S	36.45 E
Aberdare Range ⋏	**154**	0.25 S	36.38 E
Aberdaron	**42**	52.49 N	4.43 W
Aberdeen, Sk., Can.	**184**	52.19 N	106.17 W
Aberdeen (Xianggangzi), H.K.	**271d**	22.15 N	114.09 E
Aberdeen, S. Afr.	**158**	32.29 S	24.05 E
Aberdeen, Scot., U.K.	**46**	57.10 N	2.04 W
Aberdeen, Id., U.S.	**202**	42.56 N	112.50 W
Aberdeen, Md., U.S.	**208**	39.30 N	76.09 W
Aberdeen, Ms., U.S.	**194**	33.49 N	88.32 W
Aberdeen, N.C., U.S.	**192**	35.07 N	79.25 W
Aberdeen, Oh., U.S.	**218**	38.39 N	83.45 W
Aberdeen, S.D., U.S.	**198**	45.27 N	98.29 W
Aberdeen, Wa., U.S.	**224**	46.58 N	123.48 W
Aberdeen Lake ⊜	**176**	64.27 N	99.00 W
Aberdeen Lake ⊜[1]	**194**	33.55 N	88.30 W
Aberdeen Proving Ground ■	**208**	39.25 N	76.10 W
Aberdour	**46**	56.03 N	3.19 W
Aberdulais	**42**	51.41 N	3.48 W
Aberdyfi	**42**	52.33 N	4.02 W
Aberfeldy	**46**	56.37 N	3.54 W
Aberfoyle	**46**	56.11 N	4.23 W
Abergavenny	**42**	51.50 N	3.00 W
Abergele	**44**	53.17 N	3.34 W
Abergwynfi	**42**	51.40 N	3.35 W
Abergynolwyn	**42**	52.40 N	3.58 W
Aberjona ≏	**283**	42.27 N	71.08 W
Abermain	**170**	32.49 S	151.25 E
Abernathy	**196**	33.50 N	101.51 W
Abernethy, Sk., Can.	**184**	50.45 N	103.25 W
Abernethy, Scot., U.K.	**46**	56.20 N	3.19 W
Aberporth	**42**	52.09 N	4.33 W
Abersoch	**42**	52.50 N	4.29 W
Abersychan	**42**	51.44 N	3.04 W
Abert, Lake ⊜	**202**	42.38 N	120.13 W
Abertillery	**42**	51.45 N	3.09 W
Aberuthven	**46**	56.19 N	3.39 W
Aberystwyth	**42**	52.25 N	4.05 W
Abessinien, Hochland von — Ethiopian Plateau ⋏[1]	**144**	9.00 N	38.00 E
Abetone	**66**	44.08 N	10.40 E
Abez'	**24**	66.32 N	61.42 E
Abhā	**144**	18.13 N	42.30 E
Abhar	**128**	36.09 N	49.13 E
Abharwat ∧	**123**	34.02 N	74.25 E
Abhayāpuri	**124**	26.20 N	90.40 E
Abhaynagar	**126**	23.01 N	89.28 E
Abiaca Creek ≏	**194**	33.20 N	90.15 W
Abid, Oued el ≏	**148**	32.18 N	7.03 W
Ābidīn	**140**	13.33 N	29.38 E
'Abīdīyah	**140**	18.14 N	33.57 E
Abidjan	**150**	5.19 N	4.02 W
'Ābid Mār, Tall ∧	**132**	32.26 N	36.42 E
Abiengama	**154**	2.35 N	27.46 E
Abiko	**94**	35.52 N	140.03 E
Abilene, Ks., U.S.	**198**	38.55 N	97.12 W
Abilene, Tx., U.S.	**196**	32.26 N	99.43 W

≏ River	Fluß	Río	Rivière	Rio	
≊ Canal	Kanal	Canal	Canal	Canal	
∟ Waterfall, Rapids	Wasserfall, Stromschnellen	Cascada, Rápidos	Chute d'eau, Rapides	Cascata, Rápidos	
ꓵ Strait	Meeresstraße	Estrecho	Détroit	Estreito	
⊂ Bay, Gulf	Bucht, Golf	Bahía, Golfo	Baie, Golfe	Baía, Golfo	
⊜ Lake, Lakes	See, Seen	Lago, Lagos	Lac, Lacs	Lago, Lagos	
⩸ Swamp	Sumpf	Pantano	Marais	Pântano	
⍓ Ice Features, Glacier	Eis- und Gletscherformen	Accidentes Glaciales	Formes glaciaires	Acidentes glaciares	
⍑ Other Hydrographic Features	Andere Hydrographische Objekte	Otros Elementos Hidrográficos	Autres données hydrographiques	Outros acidentes hidrográficos	

✢ Submarine Features	Untermeerische Objekte	Accidentes Submarinos	Formes de relief sous-marin	Acidentes submarinos
□ Political Unit	Politische Einheit	Unidad Politica	Entité politique	Unidade política
♥ Cultural Institution	Kulturelle Institution	Institución Cultural	Institution culturelle	Institução cultural
⊥ Historical Site	Historische Stätte	Sitio Histórico	Site historique	Sitio histórico
♠ Recreational Site	Erholungs- und Ferienort	Sitio de Recreo	Centre de loisirs	Area de Lazer
⊠ Airport	Flughafen	Aeropuerto	Aéroport	Aeroporto
■ Military Installation	Militäranlage	Instalación Militar	Installation militaire	Instalação militar
◆ Miscellaneous	Verschiedenes	Misceláneo	Divers	Diversos

Symbols in the index entries represent the broad categories identified in the key at the right. Symbols with superior numbers (✷) identify subcategories (see complete key on page 1 · 1).

Les symboles de l'index représentent les catégories indiquées dans la légende à droite. Les symboles suivis d'un indice (✷) représentent des sous-catégories (voir légende complète à la page 1 · 1).

Die Symbole im Register stellen die rechts im Schlüssel erläuterten Kategorien dar. Symbole mit hochgestellten Ziffern (✷) bezeichnen Unterkategorien einer Kategorie (vgl. vollständiger Schlüssel auf Seite 1 · 1).

Os símbolos incluídos no texto do índice representam as grandes categorias identificadas com a chave à direita. Os símbolos com números em sua parte superior (✷) identificam as subcategorias (veja-se a chave completa en la pagina 1 · 1).

Los símbolos incluidos en el texto del índice representan las grandes categorías identificadas con la clave a la derecha. Los símbolos con números en su parte superior (✷) identifican las subcategorías (véase la clave completa a la página 1 · 1).

Features	Other Topographic Features	Islands	Mountains	Mountanhas
⊳ Cape	Other Topographic Objekte	Islands Insel	Mountains	Montaña Montagne Montagnes
V Valley, Canyon	Andere Topographische	II Islands Island	Berg	Montanha
Plain	Outros Elementos	Island Isla	Gebirge	Passo Col
Passo	Topográficos	Ilha Île	Pass	Planicie
Planície	Outras acidentes	Ilhas Islas	Tal, Cañon	
topográficos	topographiques	Ilhas Îles	Valle, Cañón	

ESPAÑOL Nombre	Página	Lat.°′	Long.°′ W = Oeste
Agadyr'	86	48.17 N	72.53 E
Agafonovka	80	50.36 N	47.26 E
Agåhpur	272a	28.34 N	77.22 E
Agaie	150	9.03 N	6.18 E
Ägäisches Meer			
— Aegean Sea ⊤²	38	38.30 N	25.00 E
Agalak	140	11.01 N	32.42 E
Agalega Islands II	138	10.24 S	56.37 E
Agal Terara ∧	144	6.57 N	40.08 E
Agan ≃	72	61.23 N	74.35 E
Agana	174p	13.28 N	144.45 E
Agana Heights	174p	13.28 N	144.45 E
Aganó ≃	92	37.57 N	139.08 E
Agapa	74	71.27 N	89.15 E
Aga Point �People	174p	13.15 N	144.43 E
Agapovka	86	53.18 N	59.28 E
Agar	120	23.42 N	76.01 E
Agara	84	42.03 N	43.49 E

Legend (bottom of page):

Symbol	Español	Flußetc.
≃	River / Río	Fluß
≅	Canal	Kanal
↳	Waterfall, Rapids / Cascada, Rápidos	Wasserfall, Stromschnellen
ᴜ	Strait / Estrecho	Meeresstraße
c	Bay, Gulf / Bahía, Golfo	Bucht, Golf
⊘	Lake, Lakes / Lago, Lagos	See, Seen
≈	Swamp / Pantano	Sumpf
⊤	Ice Features, Glaciar / Otros Elementos	Eis- und Gletscherformen
⊤	Other Hydrographic Features / Otros Elementos Hidrográficos	Andere Hydrographische Objekte

✦ Submarine Features / Accidentes Submarinos	Untermeerische Objekte
◊ Political Unit / Unidad Política	Politische Einheit
◉ Cultural Institution / Institución Cultural	Kulturelle Institution
▴ Historical Site / Sitio histórico	Historische Stätte
● Recreational Site / Sitio de Recreo	Erholungs- und Ferienort
✈ Airport / Aeropuerto	Flughafen
■ Military Installation / Instalación Militar	Militäranlage
⚬ Miscellaneous / Misceláneo	Verschiedenes

Symbols / Les symboles / Symbole / Los símbolos / Os simbolos

Symbols in the index entries represent the broad categories identified in the key at the right. Symbols with superior index numbers (✱) identify subcategories (see complete key on page I·1).

Les symboles de l'index représentent les catégories indiquées dans la légende à droite. Les symboles suivis d'un indice (✱) représentent des sous-catégories (voir légende complète à la page I·1).

Die Symbole im Register stellen die rechts im Schlüssel erklärten Kategorien dar. Symbole mit hochgestellten Ziffern (✱) bezeichnen Unterabteilungen einer Kategorie (vgl. vollständiger Schlüssel auf Seite I·1).

Los símbolos incluidos en el index del índice representan las grandes categorías identificadas con la clave a la derecha. Los símbolos con números en su parte superior (✱) identifican las subcategorías (véase la clave completa en la página I·1).

Os simbolos incluídos no texto do índice representam as grandes categorías identificadas com a chave à direita. Os simbolos com números en sua parte superior (✱) identificam as subcategorias (veja-se a chave completa à página I·1).

Other Topographic Features / Autres Elements Topographiques / Andere Topographische Objekte / Otros Elementos Topográficos / Outros Elementos topográficos

English	Français	Deutsch	Español	Português
▲ Mountain	▲ Montagne	▲ Berg	▲ Montaña	▲ Montanha
⌒ Pass	⌒ Col	⌒ Paß	⌒ Paso	⌒ Passo
Ⅴ Valley, Canyon	Ⅴ Vallée, Canyon	Ⅴ Tal, Cañon	Ⅴ Valle, Cañón	Ⅴ Vale, Canhão
Plain	Plaine	Ebene	Llano	Planície
⊵ Cape	⊳ Cap	Kap	Cabo	Cabo
Ⅰ Island	Ⅰ Ile	Insel	Isla	Ilha
Ⅱ Islands	Ⅱ Iles	Inseln	Islas	Ilhas

ESPAÑOL — Nombre / Página / Lat.°′ / Long.°′ (W = Oeste)
FRANÇAIS — Nom / Page / Lat.°′ / Long.°′ (W = Ouest)
PORTUGUÊS — Nome / Página / Lat.°′ / Long.°′ (W = Oeste)

Nombre	Página	Lat.	Long.
Algeciras, Esp.	34	36.08 N	5.30 W
Algemesí	34	39.11 N	0.26 W
Algena	144	17.19 N	38.31 E
Alger	2*6	40.42 N	83.50 W
Alger, Baie d' c	34	36.50 N	3.15 E
Alger — El Djazaïr	148	36.47 N	3.03 E
Algeria (Algérie) □¹, Áfr.	134	28.00 N	3.00 E
Algeria (Algérie) □¹, Áfr.	148	28.00 N	3.00 E
Algerie — Algeria □¹	148	28.00 N	3.00 E
Algerien — Algeria □¹	148	28.00 N	3.00 E
Algermissen	52	52.15 N	9.58 E
Algès	266c	38.43 N	9.13 W
Al-Ghāb ⌀	130	35.30 N	36.18 E
Al-Gharaq as-Sultānī	142	29.08 N	30.42 E
Al-Gharbīyah □⁴	142	30.45 N	31.00 E
Al-Ghārīyah	142	32.23 N	36.39 E
Al-Ghāt	128	26.00 N	45.03 E
Al-Ghawr √	132	31.50 N	35.3C E
Al-Ghayatah	142	30.57 N	30.0€ E
Al-Ghaydah	118	16.12 N	52.15 E
Al-Ghazālah	128	26.48 N	41.19 E
Al-Ghazālī	142	30.49 N	31.49 E
Al-Ghāzīyah	132	33.31 N	35.22 E
Alghero	71	40.34 N	8.19 E
Al-Ghurayfah	128	24.00 N	56.29 E
Al-Ghurdaqah	140	27.14 N	33.50 E
Algier — El Djazaïr	148	36.47 N	3.03 E
Algiers — El Djazaïr	148	36.47 N	3.03 E
Alginet	34	39.16 N	0.28 W
Algoa	222	29.24 N	95.11 W
Algoabaai c	158	33.50 S	25.50 E
Algodão, Ilha do I	256	23.13 S	44.36 W
Algodón ≃	246	2.23 S	71.56 W
Algodones	200	35.02 N	106.28 W
Algodor ≃	34	39.55 N	3.53 W
Algoma	190	44.36 N	87.25 W
Algoma Mills	190	46.10 N	82.50 W
Algona, Ia., U.S.	190	43.04 N	94.13 W
Algona, Wa., U.S.	224	47.16 N	122.15 W
Algonac	214	42.37 N	82.31 W
Algonquin	216	42.09 N	88.17 W
Algonquin Lake ⌀	216	42.40 N	85.20 W
Algonquin Provincial Park ♦	190	46.11 N	78.26 W
Algood	194	36.11 N	85.26 W
Algorta, Esp.	34	43.22 N	3.01 W
Algorta, Ur.	252	32.25 S	57.23 W
Alguierão-Mem Martins	266c	38.48 N	9.20 W
Al-Haddādī	142	31.20 N	30.47 E
Al-Haddayn	142	30.44 N	30.58 E
Al-Hadīthah	142	34.07 N	42.23 E
Al-Hadr	128	35.35 N	42.44 E
Al-Haffah	128	35.35 N	36.02 E
Al-Hafir Al-Fawqānī	142	34.35 N	36.28 E
Al-Hajāll	140	14.36 N	51.19 E
Al-Hajarah ♦	128	30.00 N	44.00 E
Al-Hajar al-Gharbī ⋏	128	24.00 N	56.15 E
Al-Hajar ash-Sharqī ⋏	128	22.45 N	59.00 E
Al Hajeb	148	33.43 N	5.13 W
Al-Hājir	128	30.41 N	31.49 E
Al-Hallāyah	128	21.49 N	47.26 E
Al-Hamād ≃	128	32.00 N	39.30 E
Alhama de Granada	34	37.00 N	3.59 W
Alhama de Murcia	34	37.51 N	1.25 W
Al-Hamal ♦¹	142	23.30 N	49.45 E
Alhambra, Ca., U.S.	228	34.05 N	118.07 W
Alhambra, Il., U.S.	219	38.53 N	89.44 W
Al-Hamīdīyah	130	34.43 N	35.56 E
Al-Hammām	140	30.50 N	29.23 E
Al-Hamrā', Ar. Su.	128	23.57 N	38.52 E
'Al-Hamrā', Lubnān	132	33.42 N	35.27 E
Al-Hamrah	142	31.10 N	30.52 E
Al-Hamrāt ≃	142	31.19 N	31.10 E
Alhandra	250	7.26 S	34.54 W
Alhandra, Mouchão de I	266c	38.54 N	9.00 W
Al-Harāk	132	32.44 N	36.18 E
Al-Harīq	128	23.37 N	46.31 E
Al-Harrah ≃	132	33.03 N	36.00 E
Al-Harrah ±⁹	128	31.00 N	38.30 E
Al-Harūj al-Aswad ⋏²	146	27.00 N	17.10 E
Al-Hasakah □⁴	128	36.29 N	40.45 E
Al-Hasakah	128	36.30 N	41.00 E
Al-Hasānī I	128	24.58 N	37.05 E
Alhaurín el Grande	34	36.38 N	4.41 W
Al-Hawāmidīyah	273c	29.54 N	31.15 E
Al-Hawātah	140	13.25 N	34.38 E
Al-Hawātikah	142	27.16 N	31.01 E
Al-Hawrah	142	13.49 N	47.37 E
Al-Hawtah	142	14.50 N	48.27 E
Al-Hawwārīyah	142	30.58 N	29.41 E
Al-Hayy, 'Irāq	128	32.10 N	46.03 E
Al-Hayy, Misr	142	29.39 N	31.18 E
Al-Hayyānīyah	142	28.38 N	42.45 E
Al-Hayz	142	28.02 N	28.39 E
Al-Hibah	142	31.33 N	30.55 E
Al-Hijānah	132	33.21 N	36.33 E
Al-Hijāz ♦¹	118	24.30 N	38.30 E
Al-Hillah, 'Irāq	128	32.29 N	44.25 E
Al-Hillah, Süd.	127	21.00 N	27.08 E
Al-Hilmīyah ♦⁸	273c	30.07 N	31.19 E
Al-Hindīyah	128	32.33 N	44.13 E
Al-Hirmil	130	34.23 N	36.23 E
Al-Hisn	132	32.29 N	35.52 E
Al-Hoceïma	148	35.15 N	3.55 W
Al-Hoceïma, Baie d' c	148	35.00 N	4.30 W
Alhos Vedros	266c	38.39 N	9.02 W
Alhucemas, Peñón de I	34	35.13 N	3.53 W
Al-Hudayb	140	13.00 N	32.50 E
Al-Hudaydah	144	14.48 N	42.57 E
Al-Hufrah	128	29.10 N	13.02 E
Al-Hufrah ♦¹	128	28.40 N	30.30 E
Al-Hufūf	128	25.22 N	49.34 E
Al-Hulwah	128	23.27 N	43.47 E
Al-Humayshah	128	13.41 N	45.52 E
Al-Humrah ♦¹	128	23.20 N	54.30 E
Al-Huṣayhiṣah	140	14.44 N	33.18 E
Al-Husaynīyah	140	30.52 N	31.55 E
Al-Husaynīyah ⊓⁴	144	17.48 N	44.27 E
Al-Huwayliẓah	128	28.38 N	45.48 E
Al-Huwaymī	144	14.05 N	47.44 E
Al-Huwaymil	128	25.36 N	40.23 E
Al-Huwayyit	128	25.36 N	40.25 E
Alī	70	38.02 N	15.25 E
Alī ♦⁸	272a	28.31 N	77.18 E
'Alī, As-Sadd al- (Aswan High Dam) ⊓⁶	140	23.58 N	32.52 E
Alía, Esp.	34	39.27 N	5.13 W
Alia, It.	70	37.47 N	13.43 E
Aliabad, Azer.	84	41.29 N	46.37 E
'Alīābād, Īrān	128	36.11 N	54.59 E
Alīābād, Pāk.	123	36.18 N	74.17 E
Aliade	150	7.16 N	8.28 E
Aliaga, Esp.	34	40.40 N	0.42 W
Aliağa, Tür.	30	38.48 N	26.59 E
Aliákmon ≃	30	40.30 N	22.36 E
Aliákmonos, Tekhnití Límni ⌀	38	40.15 N	22.00 E
Alibadir ♦⁸	267b	41.11 N	29.12 E
Al-Bajramīj	84	39.56 N	40.25 E
Alibates Flint Quarries National Monument ♦	196	35.35 N	101.39 W
Alibejil	84	41.23 N	46.49 E
Alibey I	267b	41.03 N	28.56 E

Nombre	Página	Lat.	Long.
Al-Karak □⁸	132	31.11 N	35.42 E
Al-Karak □⁸	132	31.10 N	35.45 E
Al-Karnak	140	25.43 N	32.39 E
Al-Kawah	140	13.44 N	32.30 E
Al-Kawd	144	13.05 N	45.22 E
Al-Kawm	130	35.11 N	38.52 E
Al-Kawm al-Akhdar	142	30.58 N	30.17 E
Al-Kawm At-Tawīl	142	31.12 N	31.05 E
Al-Khabrā'	128	26.04 N	43.33 E
Al-Khābūrah	128	23.59 N	57.08 E
Al-Khabaqān ≃	128	23.24 N	40.24 E
Al-Khalīl (Hebron)	132	31.32 N	35.06 E
Al-Khālis	128	33.49 N	44.32 E
Al-Khandaq	140	18.36 N	30.34 E
Al-Khānkah	142	30.13 N	31.21 E
Al-Kharaqānīyah	273c	30.10 N	31.10 E
Al-Khārijah	140	25.26 N	30.33 E
Al-Khārijah (Khartoum)	140	15.36 N	32.32 E
Al-Khartūm ♦¹	140	15.45 N	32.30 E
Al-Khartūm Bahrī	140	15.38 N	32.33 E
Al-Khasab	128	26.12 N	56.15 E
Al-Khatam ♦¹	128	24.00 N	55.16 E
Al-Khirbah as-Samrā'	132	34.00 N	36.10 E
Al-Khiyām	132	33.19 N	35.36 E
Al-Khubar	128	26.17 N	50.12 E
Al-Khums (Homs)	146	32.39 N	14.16 E
Al-Khuraybah, Urd.	132	32.40 N	35.52 E
Al-Khuraybah, Yaman	144	15.06 N	48.19 E
Al-Khurmah	142	21.54 N	42.03 E
Al-Khushnīyah	132	33.00 N	35.48 E
Al-Khusūs	273c	30.09 N	31.19 E
Al-Kifl	128	32.14 N	44.22 E
Al-Kiswah	132	33.21 N	36.14 E
Alkmaar	52	52.37 N	4.44 E
Alkoven	61	48.17 N	14.06 E
Al-Kūbrī	140	30.02 N	32.33 E
Al-Kūfah	128	32.02 N	44.24 E
Al-Kufrah (Cufra) ⊓⁴	146	24.20 N	23.15 E
Al-Kunayyisah	273c	29.59 N	31.11 E
Al-Kuntillah	140	30.00 N	34.41 E
Al-Kūt	128	32.25 N	45.49 E
Al-Kuwayt	128	29.20 N	47.59 E
Al-Kuwayt — Kuwait ⊓¹	128	29.30 N	47.45 E
Al-Labwah	130	34.12 N	36.21 E
Allacapan	116	18.15 N	121.35 E
Allach-Jun'	74	61.08 N	138.03 E
Alladā	150	6.39 N	2.09 E
Al-Lādhiqīyah (Latakia)	130	35.31 N	35.47 E
Al-Lādhiqīyah □⁸	130	35.30 N	36.00 E
Allagash ≃	186	47.05 N	69.02 W
Allagen	58	51.28 N	8.14 E
Al-Lagowa	140	11.24 N	29.08 E
Allāhābād, India	124	25.27 N	81.51 E
Allāhābād, Pāk.	123	28.57 N	70.53 E
Allāhbās	272a	28.51 N	77.25 E
Allahüekber Dağları ⋏	130	40.35 N	42.32 E
Al-Lāhūn	272a	29.13 N	30.59 E
Allapardipur	272a	28.20 N	77.26 E
Allaines	58	48.12 N	1.50 E
Allaire State Park ♦	208	40.10 N	74.08 W
Allakaket	180	66.34 N	152.41 W
Allaman	50	46.28 N	6.24 E
Allambie	210	40.55 N	74.48 W
Allan	184	51.53 N	106.04 W
Allan, Pointe ⅄	275a	46.10 N	73.45 W
Allanche	32	45.14 N	2.56 E
Allan Island I	224	48.28 N	122.42 W
Allanmyo	110	19.22 N	95.13 E
Allanridge	158	27.55 S	26.44 E
Allanson	168a	3.20 S	116.06 E
Allanton	46	55.47 N	3.51 W
Allan Water ≃	46	56.08 N	3.56 W
Allapattah Flats ≖	220	27.29 N	82.34 W
Allardt	194	36.22 N	84.53 W
Allariz	34	42.11 N	7.48 W
Allatoona Lake ⌀¹	194	34.10 N	84.38 W
Allauch	32	43.20 N	5.29 E
Al-Layyah	140	16.16 N	35.25 E
Alldays	156	22.44 S	29.04 E
Alle, Bel.	56	49.51 N	4.58 E
Alle, Schw.	58	47.26 N	7.08 E
Alleberg ⋏²	58	58.08 N	13.36 E
Allegan	216	42.31 N	85.51 W
Allegan, Lake ⌀	216	42.33 N	85.55 W
Allegany	216	42.06 N	78.29 W
Allegany □⁶	210	42.13 N	78.02 W
Allegany Indian Reservation ♦	210	42.10 N	78.47 W
Allegany State Park ♦	210	42.05 N	78.44 W
Alleghe	64	46.25 N	12.01 E
Alleghany □⁶	194	36.28 N	81.08 W
Allegheny ≃	210	40.27 N	80.01 W
Allegheny Acres	279b	40.37 N	79.53 W
Allegheny Center ♦	279b	40.27 N	80.01 W
Allegheny County Airport ♦	279b	40.21 N	79.56 W
Allegheny County Park ♦	279b	40.34 N	79.56 W
Allegheny Mountains ⋏	188	38.30 N	80.00 W
Allegheny Observatory ♦³	279b	40.29 N	80.01 W
Allegheny Plateau ⋏¹	188	41.30 N	78.00 W
Allegheny Portage Railroad National Historic Site ⌂	208	40.28 N	78.32 W
Allegheny Reservoir ⌀¹	210	42.00 N	78.56 W
Allègre	32	45.12 N	3.42 E
Allègre, Pointe ⅄	241d	16.22 N	61.45 W
Allemagne — Germany ⊓¹	30	51.00 N	10.00 E
Allemands, Lac Des ⌀	287a	29.55 N	90.35 W
Allemanskraaldam ⌀¹	158	28.16 S	27.07 E
Allemont	62	45.07 N	6.02 E
Allen, Arg.	252	38.58 S	67.50 W
Allen, Pil.	116	12.30 N	124.17 E
Allen, Md., U.S.	208	38.17 N	75.41 W
Allen, Ne., U.S.	198	42.24 N	96.50 W
Allen, Ne., U.S.	198	42.27 N	96.50 W
Allen, Ok., U.S.	222	34.53 N	96.25 W
Allen □⁶	216	40.46 N	86.00 W
Allen □⁶, Oh., U.S.	216	40.46 N	84.06 W
Allen, Lough ⌀	48	54.08 N	8.08 W
Allen, Mount ⋏	180	62.14 N	142.13 W
Allen, Mount ⋏, Ak., U.S.	180	61.24 N	142.10 W
Allenby Bridge ♦⁵	132	31.52 N	35.32 E
Allendale, Il., U.S.	194	38.47 N	87.43 W
Allendale, Mi., U.S.	216	42.58 N	85.57 W
Allendale, N.J., U.S.	210	41.02 N	74.08 W
Allendale, S.C., U.S.	194	33.00 N	81.18 W
Allendale Town	44	54.54 N	2.15 W
Allende, Méx.	232	28.20 N	100.51 W
Allende, Méx.	234	20.51 N	100.09 W
Allendorf	56	51.02 N	8.38 E
Allen Park	216	42.15 N	83.12 W
Allenport, Pa., U.S.	210	40.08 N	79.51 W
Allenport, Pa., U.S.	214	40.06 N	79.51 W
Allensbach	58	47.43 N	9.04 E

Nom	Page	Lat.	Long.
Albey Adası I	130	39.20 N	26.38 E
Albey Baraji ⊓¹	267b	41.07 N	28.55 E
Albeyköy ♦⁸	267b	41.04 N	28.56 E
Albijaban Island I	116	13.20 N	122.43 E
Albori	150	11.56 N	3.17 E
Al-Ibrāhīmīyah	142	30.57 N	31.35 E
Alibunar	38	45.05 N	20.58 E
Alicante			
— Alacant	34	38.21 N	0.29 W
Alice, Ciskei	158	32.47 S	26.50 E
Alice, Tx., U.S.	196	27.45 N	98.04 W
Alice ≃, Austl.	164	15.22 S	141.58 E
Alice ≃, Austl.	166	24.02 S	144.50 E
Alice, Punta ⅄	68	55.29 N	129.29 W
Alice Arm	182	55.29 N	129.29 W
Alicedale	158	33.19 S	26.05 E
Alice Downs	162	17.45 S	127.56 E
Alice Springs	162	23.42 S	133.53 E
Alice Superiore	62	45.28 N	7.47 E
Alice Town	238	25.44 N	79.17 W
Aliceville	194	33.07 N	88.09 W
Alicia, Pil.	116	16.45 N	121.42 E
Alicia, Pil.	116	7.30 N	122.55 E
Alick	130	40.49 N	35.21 E
Alick Creek ≃	166	20.25 S	142.00 E
Alicudi, Isola I	70	38.32 N	14.21 E
Alicurá, Embalse de ⌀	254	40.40 S	71.00 W
Alí-'Idwah	142	29.21 N	30.55 E
Alief	222	29.43 N	95.35 W
Al-Ifranj	132	31.11 N	35.41 E
Alīganj, India	124	28.07 N	80.36 E
Alīganj, India	124	27.30 N	79.11 E
Alīganj	124	27.53 N	78.05 E
Alignements de Carnac ⊥	32	47.35 N	3.05 W
Alīgūdarz	128	33.24 N	49.41 E
Alijos, Islas II	232	24.57 N	115.44 W
Alīktūm ⊓⁴	142	33.57 N	69.45 E
Al-khslis al-Qiblīyah	142	29.42 N	31.17 E
Al-Ikhwān II	118	12.08 N	53.10 E
Alikovo	80	55.45 N	46.45 E
Alima ≃	152	1.36 S	16.36 E
Al-Imām ♦⁸	273c	30.01 N	31.10 E
Al-Imārāt al-'Arabīyah al-Muttahidah — United Arab Emirates □¹	128	24.00 N	54.00 E
Al-'Imārīyah	142	27.37 N	30.53 E
Alimena	70	37.42 N	14.07 E
Alimini Grande ⌀	68	40.12 N	18.27 E
Alimini Piccolo ⌀	68	40.10 N	18.27 E
Aliminusa	70	37.52 N	13.47 E
Alim Island I	164	2.55 S	147.05 E
Alimodian	116	10.49 N	122.26 E
Alindao	152	5.02 N	21.13 E
Alingsås	26	57.56 N	12.31 E
Ālipur, India	272b	22.43 N	88.12 E
Ālipur, India	272b	22.55 N	88.11 E
Ālipur, Pāk.	123	29.23 N	70.55 E
Ālipur Duār	124	26.29 N	89.44 E
Ālipur Jarnūbī	123	30.13 N	71.18 E
Aliquippa	214	40.38 N	80.14 W
Aliquippa-Hopewell Airport ♦	279b	40.35 N	80.17 W
Al-'Irāq	120	21.49 N	74.21 E
Al-'Irāq	132	31.05 N	35.39 E
Al-'Irāq — Iraq ⊓¹	128	33.00 N	44.00 E
Al-'Irqah	144	13.30 N	47.22 E
Ali-Sabieh	144	11.09 N	42.42 E
Al-'Ïsāwīyah	128	30.38 N	37.53 E
Aliseda	34	39.26 N	6.41 W
Alise-Sainte-Reine	58	47.32 N	4.29 E
Alīshahr	128	39.02 N	47.15 E
Al-Iskandarīyah (Alexandria)	142	31.12 N	29.54 E
Al-Iskandarīyah ⊓⁴	142	30.35 N	29.53 E
Al-Ismā'īlīyah (Ismailia)	142	30.35 N	32.16 E
Al-Ismā'īlīyah ⊓⁴	142	30.30 N	32.15 E
Al-Ismā'īlīyah Military Base ♦	142	30.35 N	32.14 E
Aliso Canyon Ⅴ, Ca., U.S.	280	34.18 N	118.33 W
Aliso Canyon Ⅴ, Ca., U.S.	280	33.53 N	117.40 W
Aliso Creek ≃	228	33.33 N	117.45 W
Al-Istiwā'īyah ash-Sharqīyah ⊓⁴	154	4.30 N	33.00 E
Alistráti	38	41.04 N	23.57 E
Alitak, Cape ⅄	180	56.51 N	154.21 W
Alitak, Bay c	180	57.00 N	154.05 W
Alitangou	120	35.10 N	83.30 E
Al Terme	108	38.01 N	15.26 E
Alivérion	38	38.25 N	24.02 E
Aliwal North	158	30.45 S	26.45 E
Alix	182	52.24 N	113.11 W
Alizay	58	49.20 N	1.14 E
Al-Jabal al-Abyad ⋏	140	28.46 N	31.00 E
Al-Jabal al-Ahmar ⋏²	140	30.37 N	79.53 W
Al-Jabalayn	140	12.36 N	32.48 E
Al-Jadīdah	128	25.34 N	28.51 E
Al-Jafūn	142	32.28 N	36.13 E
Al-Jafr	132	30.18 N	36.13 E
Al-Jifrah ♦¹	128	29.20 N	50.00 E
Al-Jaghbūb	146	29.45 N	24.31 E
Al-Jaghbūb ⊓⁴	146	29.24 N	24.43 E
Al-Jahrah	128	29.20 N	47.40 E
Al-Jamālīyah	142	31.11 N	31.51 E
Al-Jarrāfī ≃	142	29.50 N	32.43 E
Al-Jawf, Ar. Su.	128	29.50 N	39.52 E
Al-Jawf, Lībyā	146	24.11 N	23.19 E
Al-Jawsh	146	32.00 N	11.40 E
Al-Jayīlī	130	36.01 N	32.36 E
Al-Jazā'ir	148	28.00 N	3.00 E
Al-Jazā'ir — Algeria ⊓¹	148	28.00 N	3.00 E
Al-Jazīrah ♦¹	128	34.30 N	39.00 E
Al-Jazīrah (Giza), Misr	273c	30.01 N	31.13 E
Al-Jīzah, Urd.	132	31.43 N	35.58 E
Al-Jīzah, Urd.	132	31.42 N	35.57 E
Al-Jubayl	128	27.01 N	49.40 E
Al-Jubayt	140	12.07 N	35.10 E
Aljucén ≃	34	38.56 N	6.25 W
Al-Judaydah	130	33.54 N	35.34 E
Al-Judayyidah, Urd.	132	33.54 N	35.34 E
Al-Judayyidah, Urd.	132	31.05 N	36.09 E
Al-Jufrah ♦¹	146	29.10 N	16.00 E
Al-Junaydah ♦¹	142	29.10 N	31.21 E
Al-Junaynah, Misr	142	31.06 N	31.41 E
Al-Junaynah, Süd.	140	13.27 N	22.27 E
Al-Kāb	140	25.08 N	32.48 E
Al-Kabrit Military Base ♦	142	30.15 N	32.29 E

Nome	Página	Lat.	Long.
Al-Ma'sarah ♦⁸	142	29.54 N	31.17 E
Al-Mashqūq	132	32.24 N	36.43 E
Al-Mashrafah	130	34.50 N	36.52 E
Al-Maṣīd	140	15.15 N	32.57 E
Al-Masmā'	130	39.57 N	0.03 W
Al-Matammah	140	16.43 N	33.20 E
Al-Matarīyah, Misr	142	31.11 N	32.02 E
Al-Matarīyah ♦⁸	142	30.07 N	31.19 E
Al-Matnah	140	13.47 N	35.03 E
Al-Mawsil (Mosul)	128	36.20 N	43.08 E
Allenwood, N.J., U.S.	208	40.12 N	74.13 W
Allenwood, N.Y., U.S.	276	40.48 N	73.44 W
Allenwood, Pa., U.S.	210	41.07 N	76.54 W
Alleppey	122	9.29 N	76.19 E
Aller ≃	30	52.57 N	9.11 E
Allerona	66	42.49 N	11.58 E
Allersberg	60	49.15 N	11.15 E
Allershausen	60	48.26 N	11.36 E
Allerslev	41	55.05 N	12.03 E
Allerton, Ia., U.S.	190	40.42 N	93.21 W
Allerton, Ma., U.S.	283	42.18 N	70.53 W
Allerton □⁶	262	53.22 N	2.53 W
Allerton, Point ⅄	283	42.18 N	70.53 W
Allestree	42	52.57 N	1.29 W
Allevard	62	45.24 N	6.04 E
Alley Park ♦	276	40.45 N	73.44 W
Alleyton	222	29.43 N	96.29 W
Allgäu ♦¹	60	47.35 N	10.10 E
Allgäuer Alpen ⋏	58	47.20 N	10.25 E
Allhallows	260	51.28 N	0.39 E
Alli ±	68	38.51 N	16.40 E
Alliance, Ab., Can.	182	52.26 N	111.47 W
Alliance, Mi., U.S.	214	42.55 N	82.57 W
Alliance, R.I., U.S.	207	41.32 N	71.28 W
Alliance, Oh., U.S.	198	42.06 N	102.52 W
Alliance, Oh., U.S.	214	40.55 N	81.06 W
Allibaudieres	50	48.35 N	4.07 E
Al-Lidām	144	20.29 N	44.50 E
Allier ≃⁵	32	46.25 N	3.00 E
Allier ≃, Fr.	32	46.58 N	3.04 E
Allier ≃, Fr.	62	45.05 N	3.35 E
Alligator Creek ≃, Ga., U.S.	192	31.58 N	82.22 W
Alligator Creek ≃, Tx., U.S.	222	30.42 N	97.07 W
Alligator Lake ⌀	220	28.13 N	81.13 W
Alligator Pond	241q	17.52 N	77.34 W
Alligny-en-Morvan	50	47.13 N	4.03 E
Allihies	48	51.38 N	10.03 W
Allinagaram	122	10.02 N	77.30 E
Allinge	26	55.16 N	14.49 E
Allington Castle ⊥	260	51.17 N	0.31 E
Allison	190	42.45 N	92.47 W
Allison, Mount ⋏	282	37.30 N	121.52 W
Allison Gulch Ⅴ	280	34.16 N	117.44 W
Allison Park	214	40.34 N	79.57 W
Alliston	212	44.09 N	79.52 W
Al-Līth	144	20.09 N	40.16 E
Allmendingen	58	48.20 N	9.43 E
Alloa	46	56.07 N	3.49 W
Allocchio, Galleria degli ♦	66	44.03 N	11.30 E
Allogny	50	47.13 N	2.19 E
Allonby	44	54.46 N	3.25 W
Alloné Abba	132	32.44 N	35.10 E
Allones, Dtsch.	58	47.58 N	0.09 E
Allonnes, Fr.	58	48.10 N	1.40 E
Allora	171a	28.02 S	151.59 E
Allos	62	44.14 N	6.38 E
Allott, Mount ⋏²	160	26.06 S	124.46 E
Allouez	190	44.28 N	88.00 W
Alloway	46	39.33 N	75.21 W
Alloway Creek ≃	208	39.27 N	75.30 W
Allport	210	40.53 N	78.12 W
Allred Peak ⋏	200	38.23 N	116.06 W
All Saints	240c	17.03 N	61.48 W
Allschwil	58	47.33 N	7.33 E
Allstedt	54	51.24 N	11.23 E
Allston	283	42.22 N	71.08 W
Alluets, Forêt des ♦	261	48.55 N	1.55 E
Al-Luhayyah	144	15.42 N	42.42 E
Allumette Lake ⌀	210	45.53 N	77.13 W
Allumettes, Île des I	190	45.50 N	77.05 W
Allumiere	66	42.09 N	11.54 E
Allview Estates	208	39.12 N	76.51 W
Allyn	224	47.23 N	122.49 W
Alma, N.B., Can.	186	45.36 N	64.57 W
Alma, P.Q., Can.	180	48.33 N	71.39 W
Alma, Ar., U.S.	194	35.28 N	94.13 W
Alma, Ga., U.S.	192	31.32 N	82.27 W
Alma, Il., U.S.	219	38.43 N	88.55 W
Alma, Ks., U.S.	198	39.01 N	96.17 W
Alma, Ne., U.S.	198	40.06 N	99.21 W
Alma, Wi., U.S.	190	44.19 N	91.55 W
Alma-Ata	85	43.15 N	76.57 E
Alma-Atinskij zapovednik ♦	85	43.10 N	77.25 E
Alma Center	190	44.26 N	90.54 W
Almada	34	38.41 N	9.09 W
Almaden, Austl.	166	17.20 S	144.41 E
Almadén, Esp.	34	38.46 N	4.50 W
Almadén de la Plata	34	37.52 N	6.04 W
Al-Madīnah (Medina)	144	24.28 N	39.36 E
Al-Madīnah al-Fikrīyah	142	27.56 N	30.49 E
Al-Madwar	132	32.17 N	36.00 E
Al-Mafāzah	140	13.36 N	34.54 E
Al-Mafraq ⊓⁸	132	32.15 N	36.30 E
Al-Maghārīm	142	15.01 N	47.53 E
Al-Maghrah ⊤⁴	146	30.17 N	28.56 E
Almagor	132	32.55 N	35.36 E
Almagre, Laguna ⌀	234	23.48 N	97.48 W
Al-Magreb — Morocco ⊓¹	148	32.00 N	5.00 W
Almagro	34	38.53 N	3.43 W
Almagro Island I	116	11.56 N	124.18 E
Al-Mahallah al-Kubrā	142	30.58 N	31.10 E
Al-Mahārīq	140	25.33 N	30.40 E
Al-Mahbas	148	27.13 N	9.44 W
Alma Hill ⋏²	210	42.01 N	78.01 W
Al-Mahmūdīyah	142	31.11 N	30.32 E
Al-Mahras	142	27.49 N	30.48 E
Al-Majd	142	30.34 N	32.01 E
Al-Majma'ah	128	25.54 N	45.20 E
Almajului, Munţii ⋏	38	44.43 N	22.12 E
Al-Maks ♦⁸	142	31.09 N	29.51 E
Al-Mālikīyah	84	40.50 N	69.35 E
Al-Manāmah	128	26.13 N	50.35 E
Al-Manāqil	140	14.15 N	32.59 E
Al-Manṣūrah	142	31.03 N	31.23 E
Al-Manṣūrah, Isr. Occ	132	33.08 N	35.48 E
Al-Manṣūrah	140	14.23 N	31.28 E
Al-Manzilah	142	31.09 N	31.56 E
Al-Marāghah	142	26.42 N	31.36 E
Al-Marj	146	32.30 N	20.54 E
Al-Marj ♦⁸	273c	30.09 N	31.20 E
Almas ≃	250	11.14 S	47.23 W
Almas, Pico das ⋏	255	13.33 S	41.56 W
Al-Ma'sarah, Misr	142	27.47 N	30.52 E

Nome	Página	Lat.	Long.
Alor Star	114	6.07 N	100.22 E
— Alor Setar	114	6.07 N	100.22 E
Alorton	219	38.36 N	90.08 W
Al'oškino	88	58.35 N	100.32 E
Al'ošna ≃, Ross.	76	53.38 N	33.29 E
Al'ošn a, Ross.	82	54.14 N	37.16 E
Alosno	34	37.33 N	7.07 W
Alost			
— Aalst	50	50.56 N	4.02 E
Alotau	164	10.14 S	150.30 E
Alouette ≃	224	49.16 N	122.42 W
Alouette Lake ⌀	224	49.19 N	122.28 W
Alovo	80	54.38 N	46.27 E
Aloxe-Corton	58	47.04 N	4.52 E
Aloysius, Mount ⋏	162	26.01 S	128.34 E
Alpachiri	252	37.22 S	63.46 W
Alpaugh	226	35.53 N	119.29 W
Alpe di Siusi ⋏	52	51.35 N	6.30 E
Alpena, Ar., U.S.	194	36.17 N	93.17 W
Alpena, Mi., U.S.	190	45.03 N	83.25 W
Alpena, S.D., U.S.	198	44.10 N	98.21 W
Alpen			
— Alps ⋏	32	46.25 N	10.00 E
Alpercatas ≃	250	6.02 S	44.19 W
Alpes			
— Alps ⋏	32	46.25 N	10.00 E
Alpes Dinàricos ⋏	36	43.50 N	16.35 E
Alpes Maritimes ≃⁵	64	44.00 N	7.10 E
Alpes Maritimos			
— Maritime Alps ⋏	64	44.15 N	7.10 E
Alpes Transilvanos			
— Carpaţii Meridionali ⋏	38	45.30 N	24.15 E
Alpha, Austl.	166	23.39 S	146.38 E
Alpha, Il., U.S.	190	41.12 N	90.23 W
Alpha, Mi., U.S.	190	46.02 N	88.22 W
Alpha, N.J., U.S.	210	40.40 N	75.09 W
Alpha, N.Y., U.S.	276	40.57 N	73.55 W
Alpha, Tx., U.S.	222	32.19 N	96.44 W
Alphen aan den Rijn	52	52.07 N	4.40 E
Alphington	42	50.42 N	3.31 W
Alphin Pike ⋏²	262	53.31 N	2.00 W
Alphonse Island I	138	7.00 S	52.45 E
Alpi	64	40.07 N	15.59 E
Alpi			
— Alps ⋏	32	46.25 N	10.00 E
Alpiarça	34	39.15 N	8.35 W
Alpi Dinariche			
— Dinara ⋏	36	43.50 N	16.35 E
Alpignano	62	45.06 N	7.31 E
Alpilles, Chaîne des ⋏	62	43.45 N	4.50 E
Alpine, Az., U.S.	200	33.50 N	109.08 W
Alpine, Ca., U.S.	204	32.50 N	116.47 W
Alpine, N.J., U.S.	276	40.57 N	73.55 W
Alpine, N.Y., U.S.	210	42.19 N	76.44 W
Alpine, Tx., U.S.	196	30.21 N	103.39 W
Alpine, Ut., U.S.	226	38.41 N	119.47 W
Alpine ⊓⁴	287	37.19 N	122.17 W
Alpine Creek ≃			
Alpine National Park ♦	166	37.00 S	147.15 E
Alpinópolis	255	20.52 S	46.23 W
Alpi Retiche			
— Rhaetian Alps ⋏	58	46.30 N	10.00 E
Alpirsbach	58	48.21 N	8.23 E
Alplaus Kill ≃	210	42.51 N	73.54 W
Alpnachstad	58	46.57 N	8.17 E
Alps ⋏	32	46.25 N	10.00 E
Alpsee	58	47.34 N	10.17 E
Alpu	130	39.47 N	30.58 E
Al-Qābil	128	23.57 N	55.48 E
Al-Qadam	132	33.33 N	36.20 E
Al-Qadārif	140	14.02 N	35.24 E
Al-Qadīmah	144	22.21 N	39.09 E
Al-Qādisīyah ⊓⁴	128	31.55 N	45.00 E
Al-Qāhirah (Cairo), Misr	142	30.03 N	31.15 E
Al-Qāhirah ⊓⁴, Misr	273c	30.03 N	31.15 E
Al-Qāhirah ⊓⁴	142	30.03 N	31.17 E
Al-Qāhirah West Military Base ♦	142	30.06 N	30.56 E
Al-Qarnah	128	34.21 N	41.07 E
Al-Qaṣabīyah ⊓⁴	142	26.27 N	45.35 E
Al-Qaṣr, Urd.	132	31.19 N	35.45 E
Al-Qaṣr, Misr	140	25.42 N	28.53 E
Al-Qaṣṣāṣīn	142	30.35 N	31.51 E
Al-Qaṣṣāṣīn ♦⁸	142	30.35 N	31.55 E
Al-Qaṭīf	128	26.33 N	50.00 E
Al-Qaṭrānah	132	31.15 N	36.03 E
Al-Qaṭrūn	146	24.56 N	14.38 E
Al-Qaysūmah	128	28.18 N	46.08 E
Al-Qir'an	142	24.21 N	37.43 E
Al-Qūšīyah	140	27.26 N	30.49 E
Al-Qūṣ	140	25.55 N	32.46 E
Al-Qusayr, Misr	144	26.06 N	34.17 E
Al-Qusayr, Sūrīy.	130	34.31 N	36.35 E
Al-Quṭayfah	132	33.44 N	36.36 E
Al-Quwayr	140	13.18 N	35.34 E
Al-Qūwaysī ⊓⁴	142	29.35 N	31.14 E
Aln ≃	44	55.23 N	1.37 W
Alnā	273c	30.14 N	31.08 E
Al-Nasser	140	24.32 N	32.55 E
Alnes	26	62.33 N	6.10 E
Alness	46	57.41 N	4.15 W
Alnmouth	44	55.23 N	1.37 W
Alnö	26	62.25 N	17.26 E
Alnor	41	54.55 N	9.36 E
Alnwick	44	55.25 N	1.42 W
Alnwick Indian Reserve ♦	212	44.10 N	78.06 W
Alo	146	12.13 N	176.10 W
Aloândia	256	17.43 S	49.29 W
Alofi	174v	19.01 S	169.55 W
Alofi Bay c	174v	19.03 S	169.56 W
Aloja	76	57.46 N	24.53 E
Alónnisos I	38	39.10 N	23.55 E
Alonso ≃	246	1.46 N	72.55 W
Alor, Kepulauan II	112	8.15 S	124.35 E
Alor, Pulau I	112	8.15 S	124.45 E
Alor, Selat 보	112	8.13 S	123.48 E
Alor Gajah	114	2.23 N	102.13 E

Nome	Página	Lat.	Long.
Alor Setar	114	6.07 N	100.22 E
Alós	34	42.42 N	0.54 E
Alotau	164	10.14 S	150.30 E
Alpnach	58	46.56 N	8.17 E
Alsónémedi	264c	47.19 N	19.10 E
Alsager	44	53.06 N	2.17 W
Alsasua	34	42.54 N	2.10 W
Alsdorf	52	50.53 N	6.10 E
Alsea	224	44.22 N	123.38 W
Alsea ≃	224	44.25 N	124.04 W
Alsenz	60	49.44 N	7.49 E
Alsfeld	52	50.45 N	9.16 E
Alsh, Loch c	46	57.15 N	5.39 W
Alsip	288	41.40 N	87.44 W
Alsónémedi	264c	47.19 N	19.10 E
Alstätte	52	52.08 N	6.55 E

ENGLISH: Name · Page · Lat.°' · Long.°'
DEUTSCH: Name · Seite · Breite°' · Länge°' E = Ost

Symbols in the index entries represent the broad categories identified in the key at the right. Symbols with superior numbers (⋏[1]) identify subcategories (see complete key on page *I* · *1*).

Symbole im Register stellen die rechts im Schlüssel erklärten Kategorien dar. Symbole mit hochgestellten Ziffern (⋏[1]) bezeichnen Unterabteilungen einer Kategorie (vgl. vollständiger Schlüssel auf Seite *I* · *1*).

Los símbolos incluídos en el texto del índice representan las grandes categorias identificadas con la clave a la derecha. Los símbolos con numeros en su parte superior (⋏[1]) identifican las subcategorías (véase la clave completa en la página *I* · *1*).

Les symboles de l'index représentent les catégories indiquées dans la légende à droite. Les symboles suivis d'un indice (⋏[1]) représentent des sous-catégories (voir légende complète à la page *I* · *1*).

Os símbolos incluídos no texto do índice representam as grandes categorias identificadas com a chave à direita. Os símbolos com números em sua parte superior (⋏[1]) identificam as subcategorias (veja-se a chave completa à página *I* · *1*).

∧ Mountain	Berg	Montaña	Montagne	Montanha
⋏ Mountains	Gebirge	Montañas	Montagnes	Montanhas
)(Pass	Paß	Paso	Col	Passo
V Valley, Canyon	Tal, Cañon	Valle, Cañón	Vallée, Canyon	Vale, Canhão
≚ Plain	Ebene	Llano	Plaine	Planície
> Cape	Kap	Cabo	Cap	Cabo
I Island	Insel	Isla	Île	Ilha
II Islands	Inseln	Islas	Îles	Ilhas
• Other Topographic Features	Andere Topographische Objekte	Otros Elementos Topográficos	Autres données topographiques	Outros acidentes topográficos

ESPAÑOL

Nombre	Página	Lat.°′	Long.°′ W = Oeste
Amsterdam, N.Y., U.S.	210	42.56 N	74.11 W
Amsterdam, Oh., U.S.	214	40.28 N	80.55 W
Amsterdam, Île I	6	37.52 S	77.32 E
Amsterdam-Rijnkanaal ≊	52	51.57 N	5.20 E
Amstetten	61	48.07 N	14.53 E
Amston	207	41.37 N	72.20 W
Āmta	126	22.35 N	88.01 E
Amt'ae-do I	98	34.50 N	126.07 E
Āmtala	126	23.55 N	88.27 E
Amtāli	126	22.08 N	90.14 E
Am Timan	146	11.02 N	20.17 E
Amtrak Station ◆[5]	281	42.19 N	83.04 W
Amubri	236	9.31 N	82.56 W
ʿĀmūdah	130	37.05 N	40.54 E
Amu-Darja	128	37.53 N	65.15 E
Amu Darya (Amudarja) ≃	72	43.40 N	59.01 E
Amudat	154	1.57 N	34.57 E
Amugulang → Xin Barag Zuoqi	88	48.14 N	118.18 E
Amukta Island I	180	52.29 N	171.15 W
Amukta Pass)(	180	52.25 N	172.00 W
Amulree	46	56.30 N	3.47 W
Amun	175e	5.57 S	154.45 E
Amundsen Bay ᑕ	9	66.55 S	50.00 E
Amundsen Gulf ᑕ	176	71.00 N	124.00 W
Amundsen-Scott ᵿ[3]	9	90.00 S	0.00
Amundsen Sea ⫪[2]	9	72.30 S	112.00 W
Amung, Mount ∧	164	7.26 S	146.36 E
Amungen ⊜	26	61.09 N	15.39 E
Amuntai	112	2.26 S	115.15 E
Amur (Heilong) ≃	74	52.56 N	141.10 E
ʿAmūr, Wādī V	140	18.56 N	33.34 E
Amurang	112	1.11 N	124.35 E
Amuria	154	2.01 N	33.38 E
Amursk	89	50.13 N	136.52 E
Amurskaja Oblast' □[8]	89	53.00 N	129.00 E
Amurskij liman ᑕ	89	52.45 N	141.40 E
Amursko-Zejskaja ravnina ⺈[1]	89	52.30 N	128.30 E
Amurzet	89	47.42 N	131.05 E
Amutag	116	12.23 N	123.16 E
Amuwo	273a	6.28 N	3.18 E
Amuyimusu	98	42.25 N	113.21 E
Amuzhong	120	30.33 N	84.28 E
Amvamg	152	1.45 N	10.29 E
Amvrakikós Kólpos ᑕ	38	39.00 N	21.00 E
Amvrosijevka	83	47.47 N	38.29 E
Amwom, Khawr V	140	7.50 N	31.13 E
Amyl ≃	86	53.47 N	92.54 E
Amyūn	130	34.18 N	35.49 E
Amz'a	80	56.13 N	54.23 E
Amzi, Oued ti-n- V	148	20.30 N	4.35 E
An	110	19.47 N	94.02 E
Anaa I[1]	14	17.25 S	145.30 W
Anabanua	112	3.57 S	120.04 E
Anabar	174b	0.30 S	166.57 E
Anabar ≃	74	73.08 N	113.36 E
ʿAnabtā	132	32.19 N	35.07 E
Anabuki	96	34.02 N	134.11 E
Anacapri	68	40.33 N	14.13 E
Anaco	246	9.27 N	64.28 W
Anacoco	194	31.15 N	93.20 W
Anacoco, Bayou ≃	194	30.52 N	93.34 W
Anaconda	202	46.07 N	112.56 W
Anaconda Range ⺈	202	45.55 N	113.30 W
Anacortes	224	48.30 N	122.36 W
Anacostia ◆[8]	284c	38.52 N	76.59 W
Anacostia ≃	284c	38.52 N	77.01 W
Anacostia, Little Paint Branch ≃	284c	39.01 N	76.56 W
Anacostia, Northeast Branch ≃	284c	38.57 N	76.57 W
Anacostia, Paint Branch ≃	284c	38.58 N	76.55 W
Anacostia Park ♠	284c	38.54 N	76.58 W
Anacuao, Mount ∧	116	16.16 N	121.53 E
Anadarko	196	35.04 N	98.14 W
Anadia	250	9.42 S	36.18 W
Anadolufeneri ◆[8]	267b	41.12 N	29.09 E
Anadoluhisarı ⊥	267b	41.04 N	29.03 E
Anadyr'	180	64.45 N	177.29 E
Anadyr' ≃	74	64.55 N	176.05 E
Anadyrskaja nizmennost' ≚	180	65.30 N	176.00 E
Anadyrskij liman ᑕ	180	64.30 N	177.45 E
Anadyrskij zaliv ᑕ	180	64.00 N	179.00 W
Anadyrskoje ploskogorje ⺈[1]	180	67.00 N	174.00 E
Anáfi I	38	36.21 N	25.50 E
Anagni	66	41.44 N	13.09 E
ʿĀnah	128	34.28 N	41.56 E
Anaheim	228	33.50 N	117.54 W
Anaheim Shopping Center ◆[9]	280	33.51 N	117.56 W
Anaheim Stadium ♠	280	33.51 N	117.57 W
Anaheim Union Canal ≊	280	33.54 N	117.52 W
Anahi, Baie ᑕ	174x	9.45 S	138.56 W
Anahim Lake	182	52.28 N	125.18 W
Anahola	229b	22.08 N	159.18 W
Anahola Bay ᑕ	229b	22.09 N	159.18 W
Anáhuac, Méx.	196	25.48 N	97.45 W
Anáhuac, Méx.	232	27.14 N	100.09 W
Anáhuac, Méx.	232	28.25 N	106.40 W
Anahuac, Tx., U.S.	222	29.46 N	94.41 W
Anahuac, Lake ⊜	222	29.48 N	94.41 W
Anaimala	122	10.35 N	76.56 E
Ānai Mudi ∧	122	10.10 N	77.04 E
Anajás	250	0.59 S	49.57 W
Anajás, Ilha I	250	0.20 S	50.30 W
Anajatuba	250	3.16 S	44.37 W
Anakāpalle	122	17.41 N	83.01 E
Anaklia	84	42.24 N	41.34 E
Anaktuvuk ≃	180	69.32 N	151.30 W
Anaktuvuk Pass	180	68.10 N	151.50 W
Analalava	157b	14.38 S	47.45 E
Analapatsy	157b	25.10 S	46.42 E
Analavoka	157b	22.33 S	46.30 E
Analomink	210	41.03 N	75.13 W
Anamã	246	3.35 S	61.22 W
Anamã, Lago ⊜	246	3.32 S	61.35 W
Anama Bay	184	51.56 N	98.05 W
Ana María, Cayos de II	240p	21.29 N	78.46 W
Ana María, Golfo de ᑕ	240p	21.25 N	78.40 W
Anambas, Kepulauan II	112	3.00 N	106.00 E
Anambra □[3]	150	6.30 N	7.20 E
Anambra ≃	150	6.11 N	6.46 E
Anamizu	94	37.14 N	136.54 E
Anamoose	198	47.52 N	100.14 W
Anamosa	190	42.06 N	91.17 W
Anamu ≃	250	0.56 N	57.03 W
Anamur	130	36.06 N	32.50 E
Anamur Burnu ›	130	36.03 N	32.48 E
Anan, Nihon	94	35.19 N	137.49 E
Anan, Nihon	96	33.55 N	134.39 E
Ānand	120	22.34 N	72.56 E
Ananda	150	7.17 N	4.16 W
Anandanagar	272b	22.51 N	88.16 E
Ānandapur, India	120	21.14 N	86.07 E
Anandapur, India	126	22.34 N	87.25 E
Anandpur Sahib	123	31.15 N	76.30 E
Ananea	248	14.42 S	69.33 W
Ananindeua	250	1.22 S	48.23 W
Ananjev	78	47.40 N	29.55 E
Ananjevo	85	42.45 N	77.40 E
Anantapur	122	14.41 N	77.36 E
Anantnāg (Islāmābād)	123	33.44 N	75.09 E
Anao-aon	116	9.47 N	125.25 E
Anapa	78	44.53 N	37.19 E
Anapo ≃	70	47.03 N	15.16 E
Anápolis	255	16.20 S	48.58 W
Anapu ≃	250	1.53 S	50.53 W
Anapurus	250	3.40 S	43.06 W
Anār, Īrān	128	30.53 N	55.18 E
Anar, Kaz.	86	50.38 N	72.27 E
Anāra	126	23.28 N	86.33 E

FRANÇAIS

Nom	Page	Lat.°′	Long.°′ W = Ouest
Anārak	128	33.20 N	53.42 E
Anarchaj	85	44.02 N	75.15 E
Anār Darreh	128	32.46 N	61.39 E
Anaš	86	54.52 N	91.00 E
Anasagasti	258	35.01 S	59.24 W
Añasco	240m	18.17 N	67.08 W
Ånäset	26	64.16 N	21.03 E
Anastácio	255	21.31 S	54.08 W
Anastasia Island I	192	29.48 N	81.16 W
Anastasijevka	83	47.34 N	38.31 E
Anastasijevskaja	78	45.13 N	37.53 E
ʿAnātā	132	31.49 N	35.16 E
Anatahan I	108	16.22 N	145.40 E
Anatoljevka	78	46.48 N	31.13 E
Anatom I	175f	20.12 S	169.45 E
Añatuya	252	28.28 S	62.50 W
Anauá ≃	246	0.58 N	61.21 W
Anaurilândia	255	22.03 S	52.45 W
Anavilhanas, Arquipélago das II	246	2.42 S	60.45 W
Anawalt	192	37.20 N	81.26 W
Anbanjing	102	23.57 N	100.55 E
Anbei, Zhg.	102	40.45 N	96.06 E
Anbei, Zhg.	102	40.49 N	108.56 E
Anbianbu	102	37.39 N	108.11 E
Anbo	98	39.51 N	122.19 E
Anbu	100	23.28 N	116.44 E
Anbyŏn	98	39.03 N	127.32 E
Ancarano	66	42.50 N	13.44 E
Ancash □[5]	248	9.30 S	77.45 W
Ancaster, On., Can.	212	43.12 N	80.00 W
Ancaster, Eng., U.K.	44	52.59 N	0.32 W
Ancasti	252	28.49 S	65.30 W
Ancasti, Sierra de ⺈	252	28.50 S	65.39 W
Ance ≃, Fr.	62	45.17 N	4.08 E
Ance ≃, Fr.	62	44.58 N	3.40 E
Ancenis	32	47.22 N	1.11 W
Ancerville	58	48.38 N	5.02 E
Anchang	100	30.09 N	120.30 E
Anchau	150	10.59 N	8.23 E
Anchieta ◆[8]	287a	22.49 S	43.24 W
Anchieta, Ilha I	256	23.33 S	45.04 W
Anch'ing → Anqing	100	30.31 N	117.02 E
Ancho, Canal)(	254	49.54 S	74.23 W
Ancholme ≃	44	53.41 N	0.32 W
Anchor	216	40.34 N	88.32 W
Anchorage	180	61.13 N	149.54 W
Anchor Bay ᑕ	214	42.38 N	82.45 W
Anchor Bay Gardens	214	42.39 N	82.49 W
Anchorena	252	35.41 S	65.27 W
Anchor Point	180	59.46 N	151.52 W
Anchor Point ›	180	59.47 N	151.52 W
Anchorville	214	42.42 N	82.41 W
Anchuras	34	39.29 N	4.50 W
Anci (Langfang)	105	39.31 N	116.41 E
Ancien Ekalla	152	1.27 S	14.00 E
Ancien Goubéré	140	5.51 N	26.46 E
Ancienne-Lorette	206	46.48 N	71.21 W
Anciferovo, Ross.	76	58.58 N	34.01 E
Anciferovo, Ross.	82	55.33 N	38.49 E
Ancipa, Lago di ⊜	70	37.50 N	14.34 E
Anclitas, Cayo I	240p	20.48 N	78.54 W
Anclote ≃	220	39.59 N	88.49 W
Anclote Keys II	220	28.12 N	82.51 W
Ancón, Méx.	234	22.35 N	101.11 W
Ancón, Perú	248	11.47 S	77.11 W
Ancona, It.	66	43.38 N	13.30 E
Ancona, S. Afr.	158	27.40 S	26.32 E
Ancona □[4]	66	43.33 N	13.10 E
Ancón de Sardinas, Bahía de ᑕ	246	1.30 N	79.00 W
Ancoraimes	248	15.54 S	68.58 W
Ancram	210	42.03 N	73.38 W
Ancre ≃	50	49.54 N	2.28 E
Ancrum	46	55.31 N	2.35 W
Ancuabe	154	12.58 S	39.54 E
Ancud	254	41.52 S	73.50 W
Ancud, Golfo de ᑕ	254	42.05 S	73.00 W
Ancy-le-Franc	50	47.46 N	4.10 E
Ancy-sur-Moselle	56	49.03 N	6.04 E
Anda, Pil.	116	16.17 N	119.57 E
Anda, Zhg.	89	46.24 N	125.19 E
Andacollo, Arg.	252	37.11 S	70.41 W
Andacollo, Chile	252	30.14 S	71.06 W
Andahuaylas	248	13.39 S	73.23 W
Andaingo	157b	18.12 S	48.17 E
Andāl	124	23.36 N	87.12 E
Andalgalá	252	27.36 S	66.19 W
Andalo	64	46.10 N	11.00 E
Åndalsnes	26	62.34 N	7.42 E
Andalucía □[4]	34	37.30 N	4.30 W
Andalucía □[9]	34	37.36 N	4.30 W
Andalusia, Al., U.S.	194	31.19 N	86.29 W
Andalusia, Pa., U.S.	285	40.04 N	74.58 W
Andaman and Nicobar Islands □[8]	110	11.00 N	93.00 E
Andaman Basin ✣[1]	12	10.00 N	94.00 E
Andamanen → Andaman Islands II	110	12.00 N	92.45 E
Andaman Islands II	110	12.00 N	92.45 E
Andaman Sea ⫪[2]	110	10.00 N	95.00 E
Andamarca, Bol.	248	18.49 S	67.31 W
Andamarca, Perú	248	11.46 S	74.44 W
Andamooka	166	30.27 S	137.12 E
Andance	62	45.14 N	4.47 E
Andapa	157b	14.39 S	49.39 E
Andara	152	18.03 S	21.27 E
Andaraí	255	12.48 S	41.20 W
Andaraí ◆[8]	287a	22.56 S	43.15 W
Andarax ≃	34	36.48 N	2.26 W
Andaray	248	15.49 S	72.50 W
Andau	61	47.46 N	17.02 E
Andechs, Kloster ᵿ[1]	64	47.58 N	11.10 E
Andeer	58	46.36 N	9.26 E
Andelfingen	58	47.36 N	8.41 E
Andelle ≃	50	49.19 N	1.44 E
Andelot	58	48.15 N	5.18 E
Andelot-en-Montagne	58	46.51 N	5.56 E
Andelu	261	48.53 N	1.50 E
Anden → Andes ⺈	18	20.00 S	67.00 W
Andenes	24	69.16 N	16.08 E
Andenne	56	50.29 N	5.06 E
Andéranboukane	150	15.26 N	3.02 E
Ånderdalen Nasjonalpark ♠	24	69.14 N	17.17 E
Anderlecht	50	50.50 N	4.18 E
Anderlues	50	50.24 N	4.16 E
Andermatt	58	46.38 N	8.36 E
Andernach	56	50.26 N	7.24 E
Andersen Air Force Base ■	174p	13.35 N	144.56 E
Anderslöv	41	55.26 N	13.22 E
Anderson, Al., U.S.	194	34.55 N	87.15 W
Anderson, Ak., U.S.	180	64.21 N	149.10 W
Anderson, Ca., U.S.	204	40.26 N	122.17 W
Anderson, In., U.S.	218	40.06 N	85.40 W
Anderson, Mo., U.S.	194	36.39 N	94.26 W
Anderson, S.C., U.S.	192	34.30 N	82.39 W
Anderson, Tx., U.S.	222	30.29 N	95.59 W
Anderson □[6], Ky., U.S.	218	38.05 N	84.55 W
Anderson □[6], Tx., U.S.	222	31.47 N	95.40 W
Anderson ≃	180	69.43 N	128.58 W
Anderson, Mount ∧	224	47.43 N	123.20 W
Anderson Creek ≃	194	33.18 N	94.26 W
Anderson Dam	202	43.30 N	115.30 W
Anderson Inlet ᑕ	169	38.39 S	145.48 E
Anderson Island I	224	47.10 N	122.42 W
Anderson Lake ⊜	182	50.41 N	122.07 W
Anderson Lake ⊜[1]	226	37.11 N	121.37 W
Anderson Peak ∧	228	34.08 N	116.53 W
Anderson Ranch Reservoir ⊜[1]	202	43.25 N	115.20 W
Andersonville	218	39.30 N	85.17 W
Andersonville National Historical Site ⊥	192	32.12 N	84.07 W
Anderstorp	26	57.17 N	13.38 E
Anderten	52	52.21 N	9.51 E

PORTUGUÊS

Nome	Página	Lat.°′	Long.°′ W = Oeste
Anderton	262	53.17 N	2.32 W
Andes, Col.	246	5.40 N	75.53 W
Andes, N.Y., U.S.	210	42.12 N	74.47 W
Andes ⺈	18	20.00 S	67.00 W
Andes, Lake ⊜	198	43.11 N	98.27 W
Andeville	50	49.15 N	2.10 E
Andevoranto	157b	18.57 S	49.06 E
Andfjorden)(	24	69.10 N	16.20 E
Andheri ◆[8]	272c	19.07 N	72.51 E
Andhra Lake ⊜	122	18.54 N	73.32 E
Andhra Pradesh □[3]	122	16.00 N	79.00 E
Andijk	52	52.45 N	5.12 E
Andijskoje Kojsu ≃	84	42.47 N	46.48 E
Andikíthira I	38	35.52 N	23.18 E
Andilamena	157b	17.01 S	48.35 E
Andimákhia	38	36.48 N	27.07 E
Andīmeshk	128	32.27 N	48.21 E
Andingpu	102	37.58 N	107.02 E
Anding Zhan	105	39.38 N	116.29 E
Andinkerke	50	51.04 N	2.36 E
Andíparos I	38	37.00 N	25.03 E
Andirá ≃	250	2.45 S	56.49 W
Andirá, Riozinho do ≃	248	9.21 S	67.31 W
Andırın	130	37.34 N	36.20 E
Andirlang	120	37.36 N	83.50 E
Andisleben	54	51.04 N	10.56 E
Ándissa	38	39.14 N	25.59 E
Andižan	85	40.45 N	72.22 E
Andkhvoy	120	36.56 N	65.08 E
Andlau-au-Val	58	48.23 N	7.25 E
Ando	270	34.37 N	135.46 E
Andoam	164	12.40 S	141.55 E
Andoas	246	2.50 S	76.30 W
Andoga ≃	76	59.10 N	37.27 E
Andogskaja gr'ada ∧	76	59.25 N	37.30 E
Andolsheim	58	48.04 N	7.25 E
Andomskij Pogost	24	61.14 N	36.36 E
Andong, Taehan	98	36.35 N	128.44 E
Andong, Zhg.	100	30.16 N	121.13 E
Andong-chŏsuji ⊜[1]	98	36.41 N	128.49 E
Andong-ni	98	39.28 N	127.27 E
Andora	62	43.59 N	8.08 E
Andorf	60	48.23 N	13.35 E
Andorno Micca	62	45.37 N	8.03 E
Andorra	34	42.30 N	1.31 E
Andorra □[1], Europe	22	42.30 N	1.30 E
Andorra □[1], Europe	34	42.30 N	1.30 E
Andorre → Andorra □[1]	34	42.30 N	1.30 E
Andover, Eng., U.K.	42	51.13 N	1.28 W
Andover, Ct., U.S.	207	41.44 N	72.22 W
Andover, Me., U.S.	188	44.38 N	70.45 W
Andover, Ma., U.S.	207	42.39 N	71.08 W
Andover, N.J., U.S.	210	40.59 N	74.44 W
Andover, N.Y., U.S.	210	42.09 N	77.47 W
Andover, Oh., U.S.	214	41.36 N	80.34 W
Andover, S.D., U.S.	198	45.24 N	97.54 W
Andowj	123	37.02 N	71.27 E
Andøya I	24	69.08 N	15.54 E
Andradas	256	22.04 S	46.34 W
Andrade Pinto	256	22.14 S	43.22 W
Andradina	255	20.54 S	51.23 W
Andramasina	157b	19.11 S	47.35 E
Andranopasy	157b	21.17 S	43.44 E
Andranovory	157b	23.08 S	44.10 E
Andrate	62	45.32 N	7.53 E
Andreafsky ≃	180	62.02 N	163.16 W
Andreafsky, East Fork ≃	180	62.03 N	163.07 W
Andreanof Islands II	180	52.00 N	176.00 W
Andreapol'	76	56.39 N	32.15 E
Andreas, I. of Man	44	54.22 N	4.26 W
Andreas, Pa., U.S.	208	40.45 N	75.48 W
André Félix, Parc National ♠	146	9.25 N	23.20 E
Andrejevka, Kaz.	86	52.59 N	67.23 E
Andrejevka, Kaz.	86	45.50 N	80.35 E
Andrejevka, Ross.	80	55.42 N	54.23 E
Andrejevka, Ross.	80	52.19 N	51.55 E
Andrejevka, Ross.	82	55.07 N	38.37 E
Andrejevka, Ross.	82	55.59 N	37.08 E
Andrejevka, Ukr.	78	49.32 N	36.38 E
Andrejevka, Ukr.	78	47.06 N	36.35 E
Andrejevka, Ukr.	83	48.49 N	37.33 E
Andrejevka, Ukr.	83	47.28 N	37.39 E
Andrejevo	80	55.56 N	41.08 E
Andrejevo-Ivanovka	78	47.28 N	30.28 E
Andrejevsk	88	58.06 N	114.08 E
Andrejevskaja	80	47.21 N	43.02 E
Andrejevskoje, Ross.	82	54.23 N	36.12 E
Andrejevskoje, Ross.	82	56.24 N	39.01 E
Andrejevskoje, Ross.	82	55.46 N	36.35 E
Andrejkoviči	76	52.25 N	33.00 E
Andrelândia	256	21.44 S	44.18 W
Andrésy	261	48.59 N	2.04 E
Andretta	68	40.56 N	15.19 E
Andrew	182	53.53 N	112.21 W
Andrew, Mount ∧	162	32.52 S	122.56 E
Andrews, In., U.S.	216	40.51 N	85.36 W
Andrews, Mi., U.S.	216	41.57 N	86.22 W
Andrews, N.C., U.S.	192	35.12 N	83.49 W
Andrews, S.C., U.S.	192	33.18 N	79.17 W
Andrews, Tx., U.S.	196	32.19 N	102.32 W
Andrews Air Force Base ■	208	38.48 N	76.52 W
Andrews Manor	284c	38.49 N	76.54 W
Andrezel	261	48.37 N	2.49 E
Andrézieux Bouthéon	62	45.32 N	4.16 E
Andria	68	41.13 N	16.18 E
Andriamena	157b	17.26 S	47.30 E
Andriandampy	157b	22.45 S	45.41 E
Andriba	157b	17.36 S	46.55 E
Andrija, Otok I	36	43.02 N	15.45 E
Andrijevica	38	42.44 N	19.46 E
Androka	157b	25.02 S	44.05 E
Andronovskoje	76	60.39 N	34.46 E
Andropov → Rybinsk	76	58.03 N	38.52 E
Ándros	38	37.50 N	24.57 E
Andros I, Ba.	238	24.26 N	77.57 W
Ándros I, Ellás	38	37.45 N	24.42 E
Androscoggin ≃	188	43.55 N	69.55 W
Androsovka	80	52.41 N	49.35 E
Andros Town	238	24.43 N	77.47 W
Āndrott Island I	122	10.50 N	73.41 E
Andrupene	76	56.11 N	27.23 E
Andr'ušino	86	59.12 N	62.59 E
Andrušovka	78	50.01 N	29.01 E
Andrychów	30	49.52 N	19.21 E
Andudu	154	2.29 N	28.41 E
Andújar	34	38.03 N	4.04 W
Andulo	152	11.30 S	16.45 E
Anduze	62	44.03 N	3.59 E
Andžijevskij	84	44.14 N	43.05 E
Âne, Dos d' ∧	241o	16.19 N	61.46 W
Aneby	26	57.50 N	14.48 E
Anécho	150	6.14 N	1.36 E
Anecón Grande, Cerro ∧	254	41.25 S	70.16 W
Anefis i-n-Darane	150	18.03 N	0.36 E
Anegada I	238	18.45 N	64.20 W
Anegada, Bahía ᑕ	254	40.15 S	62.15 W
Anegada Passage)(	238	18.30 N	63.40 W
Anegam	200	32.22 N	112.01 W
Anegasaki	268	35.28 N	140.02 E
Anelngauhat	175f	20.14 S	169.44 E
Añelo	252	38.21 S	68.47 W
Anémata, Passe d')(	175f	20.31 S	166.12 E
Anepahan Peak ∧	116	9.40 N	118.25 E
Aneroid	184	49.43 N	107.20 W
Anet	50	48.51 N	1.26 E
Aneta	198	47.40 N	97.59 W
Aneto, Pico de ∧	34	42.38 N	0.40 E
Aney	146	19.24 N	12.56 E
Anfeng, Zhg.	100	32.44 N	120.24 E
Anfeng, Zhg.	100	33.06 N	120.08 E
Anfengqiao	100	26.41 N	118.08 E
Anfo	64	45.46 N	10.29 E
Anfu	100	27.23 N	114.37 E
Anfuzhen, Zhg.	107	28.47 N	104.41 E
Anfuzhen, Zhg.	107	29.21 N	105.28 E
Anga	88	53.58 N	106.12 E

Angamacutiro [de la Unión]	234	20.10 N	101.41 W
Angamos, Punta ›	252	23.01 S	70.32 W
Angangueo	234	19.37 N	100.18 W
Ang'angxi	89	47.09 N	123.48 E
An'ganka	89	52.18 N	126.17 E
Angao	100	33.08 N	112.22 E
Angar	164	3.39 S	130.50 E
Angara ≃	88	58.06 N	93.00 E
Angara-Débou	150	11.19 N	3.03 E
Angarbaka	140	9.44 N	24.44 E
Āngāria	126	22.29 N	90.22 E
Angarsk	88	52.34 N	103.54 E
Angas ≃	168b	35.23 S	138.59 E
Angas Downs	162	24.49 S	132.14 E
Angas Hills ⺈[2]	162	22.55 S	128.00 E
Angastaco	252	25.38 S	66.11 W
Angaston	168b	34.30 S	139.02 E
Angat ≃	116	14.53 N	120.46 E
Angatuba	255	23.29 S	48.25 W
Angaul	88	53.49 N	100.18 E
Angaur I	175b	6.54 N	134.09 E
Angden Pass)(	124	29.43 N	86.17 E
Angduo	102	32.20 N	98.55 E
Ånge	26	62.31 N	15.37 E
Ángel, Salto (Angel Falls) ᒐ	246	5.57 N	62.30 W
Angel Albino Corzo	234	15.55 N	92.43 W
Angel City	220	28.20 N	80.40 W
Ángel de la Guarda, Isla I	232	29.20 N	113.25 W
Angeles	116	15.09 N	120.35 E
Angeles National Forest ♠	280	34.15 N	117.56 W
Angel Etcheverry	258	35.02 S	58.04 W
Angel Falls → Ángel, Salto ᒐ	246	5.57 N	62.30 W
Ängelholm	41	56.15 N	12.51 E
Ängelholm flygplats ⊠	41	56.20 N	12.51 E
Angelica	210	42.18 N	78.00 W
Angelina □[6]	222	31.17 N	94.42 W
Angelina ≃	194	30.53 N	94.12 W
Angelina, East Fork ≃	222	31.50 N	94.56 W
Angel Island I	282	37.52 N	122.26 W
Angellala Creek ≃	166	26.40 S	146.08 E
Angeln ◆[1]	41	54.39 N	9.44 E
Angelo ≃	162	23.43 S	117.45 E
Angel R. Cabada	234	18.35 N	95.26 W
Ängelsberg	40	59.58 N	16.00 E
Angels Camp	226	38.04 N	120.33 W
Angels Creek ≃	226	38.01 N	120.33 W
Angelus, Lake ⊜	281	42.41 N	83.20 W
Angemuk ∧	164	3.30 S	138.34 E
Anger	61	47.16 N	15.42 E
Angera	62	45.46 N	8.35 E
Angerbach ≃	263	51.23 N	6.44 E
Angereb ≃	144	13.51 N	36.08 E
Angeren	52	51.55 N	5.58 E
Angerhausen ◆[8]	263	51.23 N	6.44 E
Ångermanälven ≃	26	62.48 N	17.56 E
Ångermanland □[9]	26	63.30 N	18.05 E
Angermund ◆[8]	263	51.20 N	6.47 E
Angermünde	54	53.01 N	14.00 E
Angern, Dtsch.	54	52.21 N	11.44 E
Angern, Öst.	61	48.22 N	16.50 E
Angers	32	47.28 N	0.33 W
Angerville	50	48.19 N	2.00 E
Angervilliers	261	48.36 N	2.04 E
Ångesön I	26	63.43 N	20.55 E
Angevillers	56	49.23 N	6.02 E
Anggowala, Bukit ∧	112	4.15 S	121.44 E
Anghelu Ruiu, Necropoli ⊥	71	40.38 N	8.20 E
Anghiari	66	43.32 N	12.03 E
Angical	255	12.00 S	44.42 W
Angical do Piauí	250	6.05 S	42.44 W
Angicos	250	5.40 S	36.36 W
Angier	192	35.30 N	78.44 W
Angijak Island I	176	65.40 N	62.15 W
Angikuni Lake ⊜	176	62.13 N	99.50 W
Angke, Kali ≃	269e	6.06 S	106.46 E
Angkor Wat ⊥	110	13.26 N	103.52 E
Ângk Tasaôm	110	11.01 N	104.41 E
Anglais, Baie des ᑕ	186	49.15 N	68.07 W
Anglais, Jardin ♠	261	48.38 N	1.49 E
Anglais, Rivière des (English) ≃	206	45.13 N	73.50 W
Angle	42	51.41 N	5.06 W
Angle Inlet	198	49.21 N	95.04 W
Anglem, Mount ∧	172	46.44 S	167.56 E
Anglesea	169	38.25 S	144.11 E
Anglesey I	44	53.17 N	4.22 W
Anglet	32	43.29 N	1.31 W
Angleterre → England □[8]	28	52.30 N	1.30 W
Angleton	222	29.10 N	95.25 W
Anglezarke Moor ◆[3]	262	53.40 N	2.33 W
Anglezarke Reservoir ⊜[1]	262	53.39 N	2.35 W
Angling ≃	184	56.45 N	93.36 W
Angling Lake ⊜	184	53.55 N	93.52 W
Anglona ◆[1]	71	40.50 N	8.45 E
Anglo-Normandes, Îles → Channel Islands II	28	49.20 N	2.20 W
Anglure	50	48.35 N	3.49 E
Angmagssalik	176	65.36 N	37.41 W
Angmering	42	50.48 N	0.28 W
Ang Mo Kio	271c	1.22 N	103.51 E
Ango	154	4.02 N	25.52 E
Angoche	154	16.15 S	39.54 E
Angoche, Ilha I	154	16.20 S	39.50 E
Angohrān	128	26.35 N	57.54 E
Angol	252	37.48 S	72.43 W
Angola, In., U.S.	216	41.38 N	84.59 W
Angola, N.Y., U.S.	210	42.38 N	79.01 W
Angola □[1], Afr.	138	12.30 S	18.30 E
Angola □[1], Afr.	152	12.30 S	18.30 E
Angola Basin ✣[1]	10	15.00 S	3.00 E
Angola Lake Shore	214	42.37 N	79.05 W
Angono	269f	14.31 N	121.09 E
Angoon	180	57.30 N	134.35 W
Angora → Ankara	130	39.56 N	32.52 E
Angoram	164	4.04 S	144.04 E
Angostura	232	25.22 N	108.11 W
Angostura, Presa de la ⊜[1]	234	16.10 N	92.40 W
Angostura → Ciudad Bolívar	246	8.08 N	63.33 W
Angostura Reservoir ⊜[1]	198	43.18 N	103.27 W
Angoulême	32	45.39 N	0.09 E
Angoumois □[9]	32	45.30 N	0.05 W
Angra, Meos I	164	2.42 S	134.50 E
Angra do Heroísmo	148a	38.39 N	27.13 W
Angra do Heroísmo □[5]	148a	38.50 N	27.30 W
Angra dos Reis	256	23.00 S	44.18 W
Angren	85	41.01 N	70.12 E
Angren ≃	85	40.48 N	68.53 E
Angri	68	40.44 N	14.34 E
Angrignon Zoological Park ♠	275a	45.26 N	73.36 W
Angrogna	62	44.50 N	7.13 E
Ängsö	40	59.32 N	16.51 E
Ängsö Nationalpark ♠	40	59.39 N	18.44 E
Ang Thong	110	14.35 N	100.27 E
Angu	154	3.33 N	24.28 E
Angu ≃	256	21.48 S	42.30 W
Angualasto	252	30.03 S	69.09 W
Anguang	89	45.31 N	123.45 E
Anguchang	107	29.30 N	103.39 E
Anguciana, Cerro ∧	236	8.50 N	83.07 W
Anguilas, Arroyo ≃	288	34.26 S	58.31 W
Anguilla	194	32.58 N	90.49 W
Anguilla □[2], N.A.	230	18.15 N	63.05 W
Anguilla □[2], N.A.	238	18.15 N	63.05 W
Anguilla Cays II	238	23.31 N	79.33 W
Anguillara Sabazia	66	42.05 N	12.16 E
Anguillara Veneta	64	45.08 N	11.53 E

Anguille, Cape ›	186	47.55 N	59.25 W
Anguli Nur ⊜	98	41.13 N	114.32 E
Angumu	154	0.07 S	27.42 E
Anguo	98	38.25 N	115.19 E
Anguozhuang	105	39.44 N	117.59 E
Anguruga	164	14.00 S	136.29 E
Angus	212	44.19 N	79.53 W
Angus Place	170	33.20 S	150.06 E
Angustura	256	21.45 S	42.41 W
Angusville	184	50.44 N	101.01 W
Angwa ≃	154	15.51 S	30.35 E
Angwin	226	38.34 N	122.26 W
Angyalföld ◆[8]	264c	47.33 N	19.05 E
Angyō	268	35.51 N	139.46 E
An Hai, Viet	110	15.13 N	108.56 E
Anhai, Zhg.	100	24.45 N	118.27 E
Anhalt □[9]	54	52.00 N	11.30 E
Anholt	52	51.52 N	6.27 E
Anholt I	26	56.42 N	11.34 E
Anhovo	64	46.03 N	13.37 E
Anhua	102	28.18 N	111.14 E
Anhuai	100	33.04 N	117.50 E
Anhui (Anhwei) □[4]	100	32.00 N	117.00 E
Anhŭng	98	36.41 N	126.10 E
Anhwei → Anhui □[4]	100	32.00 N	117.00 E
Aniak	180	61.35 N	159.33 W
Aniak ≃	180	61.34 N	159.30 W
Aniakchak National Monument ♠	180	56.50 N	157.50 W
Anibare Bay ᑕ	174b	0.32 S	166.57 E
Aniche	50	50.20 N	3.15 E
Anicuns	255	16.28 S	49.58 W
Anié	150	7.45 N	1.12 E
Anié ≃	150	7.40 N	1.18 E
Anie, Pic d' ∧	32	42.57 N	0.43 W
Aniene ≃	66	41.56 N	12.30 E
Anif	64	47.45 N	13.04 E
Anik ◆[8]	272c	19.02 N	72.53 E
Anikino, Ross.	86	56.32 N	73.56 E
Anikino, Ross.	88	53.26 N	120.20 E
Anikovo	76	59.23 N	43.45 E
Anil	250	2.32 S	44.14 W
Anil, Rio do ≃	287a	22.59 S	43.21 W
Animas	200	31.56 N	108.48 W
Animas ≃	200	36.43 N	108.13 W
Animas Peak ∧	200	31.35 N	108.47 W
Animas Valley V	200	31.45 N	108.50 W
Anin	110	15.40 N	97.46 E
Anina	38	45.05 N	21.51 E
Anipemza	84	40.27 N	43.37 E
Aniskino	82	55.54 N	38.06 E
Añisoc	152	1.51 N	10.46 E
Anita, Ia., U.S.	198	41.26 N	94.45 W
Anita, Pa., U.S.	214	41.00 N	78.58 W
Anıtkaya	130	38.57 N	30.18 E
Aniva	89	46.43 N	142.32 E
Aniva, mys ›	89	46.01 N	143.25 E
Aniva, zaliv ᑕ	89	46.16 N	142.48 E
Anivorano	157b	18.44 S	48.58 E
Anivorano Nord	157b	12.44 S	49.13 E
Aniwa I	175f	19.17 S	169.35 E
Anizy-le-Château	50	49.30 N	3.27 E
Anjad	120	22.02 N	75.03 E
Anjan	26	63.41 N	12.49 E
Anjangaon	120	21.10 N	77.18 E
Anjār, India	120	23.08 N	70.01 E
ʿAnjar, Lubnān	132	33.42 N	35.54 E
ʿAnjarah	132	32.18 N	35.45 E
Anjavimihavana	157b	12.32 S	49.16 E
Anji	106	30.43 N	119.41 E
Anjiabe	157b	12.07 S	49.20 E
Anjiang	105	40.45 N	117.38 E
Anjigami Lake ⊜	190	47.51 N	84.34 W
Anjō	94	34.57 N	137.05 E
Anjou	206	45.36 N	73.33 W
Anjou □[9]	32	47.20 N	0.30 W
Anjozorobe	157b	18.24 S	47.52 E
Anju, C.M.I.K.	98	39.36 N	125.40 E
Anju, Zhg.	100	31.45 N	113.11 E
Anju, Zhg.	107	30.21 N	105.27 E
Anjudin	24	62.33 N	58.12 E
Anjuzhen	107	29.59 N	106.02 E
Anka	150	12.07 N	5.55 E
Ankang	102	32.42 N	109.05 E
Ankara	130	39.56 N	32.52 E
Ankara □[4]	130	39.50 N	32.50 E
Ankara ≃	130	39.51 N	31.55 E
Ankaramena	157b	21.57 S	46.39 E
Ankaratra ⺈	157b	19.25 S	47.12 E
Ankarimbelo	157b	22.08 S	47.20 E
Ankaroaka ∧	157b	17.48 S	48.32 E
Ankarsrum	26	57.42 N	16.19 E
Ankasakasa	157b	16.21 S	44.52 E
Ankata	80	50.44 N	51.34 E
Ankavandra	157b	18.46 S	45.18 E
Ankazoabo	157b	22.18 S	44.31 E
Ankazobe	157b	18.21 S	47.07 E
Ankazomiriotra	157b	19.38 S	46.32 E
Ankeny	190	41.43 N	93.36 W
An Khe	110	13.57 N	108.39 E
Ankilimalinika	157b	22.58 S	43.45 E
Ankilizato	157b	20.25 S	45.01 E
Anking → Anqing	100	30.31 N	117.02 E
Ankisabe	157b	19.17 S	46.29 E
Anklam	54	53.51 N	13.41 E
Ankleshwar	120	21.36 N	73.00 E
Ankober	144	9.35 N	39.44 E
Ankoro	154	6.45 S	26.57 E
Ankororoka	157b	25.30 S	45.11 E
Ankou	100	25.03 N	113.24 E
An'kovo	80	56.57 N	39.57 E
Ankpa	150	7.23 N	7.37 E
Ankum	52	52.32 N	7.52 E
Ankwe ≃	150	8.03 N	9.26 E
Anlinnuoer	98	41.11 N	114.31 E
Anliu	100	23.42 N	115.42 E
Anloga	150	5.47 N	0.50 E
Anlong	102	25.02 N	105.31 E
Ânlóng Vêng	110	14.14 N	104.05 E
Anlu	100	31.17 N	113.40 E
Anma-do I	98	35.21 N	126.02 E
Anmyŏn-do I	98	36.30 N	126.22 E
Ånn ⊜	26	63.16 N	12.34 E
Ann, Cape ›, Ant.	9	66.10 S	51.22 E
Ann, Cape ›, Ma., U.S.	283	42.39 N	70.38 W
Anna, Ross.	78	51.29 N	40.25 E
Anna, Il., U.S.	194	37.27 N	89.14 W
Anna, Oh., U.S.	216	40.23 N	84.10 W
Anna, Tx., U.S.	196	33.21 N	96.33 W
Anna, Lake ⊜[1]	188	38.04 N	77.45 W
Annaba (Bône)	148	36.54 N	7.46 E
Annaba □[5]	148	36.50 N	8.00 E
An-Nabaṭīyah □[4]	132	33.20 N	35.30 E
An-Nabaṭīyah at-Taḥtā	132	33.23 N	35.29 E
Annaberg, Öst.	61	47.52 N	15.22 E
Annaberg, Öst.	64	47.31 N	13.26 E
Annaberg-Buchholz	54	50.35 N	13.00 E
An-Nabī Shīt	132	33.52 N	36.07 E
An-Nabk	130	34.01 N	36.44 E
An-Nabqīyah I	128	26.44 N	36.01 E
Annaburg	54	51.44 N	13.03 E
Annaburger Heide ◆[3]	54	51.40 N	13.05 E
An-Nafūd ◆[2]	128	28.30 N	41.00 E
Annagassan	48	53.53 N	6.20 W
Annahütte	54	51.34 N	13.53 E
An-Najaf	128	31.59 N	44.20 E
An-Najaf □[4]	128	31.00 N	44.00 E
Annaka	94	36.19 N	138.54 E
An-Nakhl, Miṣr	140	29.55 N	33.45 E
An-Nakhl, Sūrīy.	132	33.00 N	36.07 E
Annalee ≃	48	54.03 N	7.24 W
Annalee Heights	208	38.51 N	77.10 W
Annalong	48	54.06 N	5.53 W
Anna Maria	220	27.31 N	82.44 W
Anna Maria Island I	220	27.30 N	82.43 W
An-Nāmir	132	32.47 N	36.13 E
Annamitique, Chaîne ⺈	110	17.00 N	106.00 E

Annam → Trung Phan □[9]	110	15.00 N	108.00 E
Annan	44	54.59 N	3.16 W
Annan ≃	44	54.59 N	3.16 W
Annanberg	164	4.55 S	144.40 E
Annandale, Austl.	166	21.57 S	148.22 E
Annandale, Mn., U.S.	190	45.15 N	94.07 W
Annandale, N.J., U.S.	210	40.38 N	74.52 W
Annandale, Va., U.S.	208	38.49 N	77.11 W
Annandale V	44	55.10 N	3.25 W
Annandale-on-Hudson	210	42.01 N	73.54 W
Anna Pink, Bahía ᑕ	254	45.50 S	74.50 W
Anna Plains	162	19.17 S	121.37 E
Anna Point ›	174b	0.30 S	166.56 E
Annapolis	208	38.58 N	76.29 W
Annapolis Basin ᑕ	186	44.39 N	65.42 W
Annapolis Royal	186	44.45 N	65.31 W
Annapūrṇa ∧	124	28.34 N	83.50 E
Annapūrṇapratham ∧	124	28.31 N	84.08 E
An-Naqīrah ⫪[4]	128	27.53 N	48.15 E
Ann Arbor	216	42.16 N	83.43 W
Ann Arbor Municipal Airport ⊠	281	42.14 N	83.45 W
Anna Regina	246	7.16 N	58.30 W
Annaricken Brook ≃	285	40.03 N	74.42 W
An-Nāṣirīyah, ʿIrāq	128	31.02 N	46.16 E
An-Nāṣirīyah, Sūrīy.	130	33.52 N	36.49 E
Annaspan ⊜	158	28.33 S	25.47 E
An-Nawfalāb	140	15.52 N	32.32 E
An-Nawfalīyah	146	30.47 N	17.50 E
An-Nazlah	132	31.32 N	34.29 E
An-Nazlat	142	29.19 N	30.39 E
Annbank	44	55.28 N	4.30 W
Annean, Lake ⊜	162	26.54 S	118.14 E
Anne Arundel □[6]	208	38.59 N	76.30 W
Annebault	50	49.15 N	0.04 E
Annecy	58	45.54 N	6.07 E
Annecy, Lac d' ⊜	58	45.51 N	6.11 E
Annecy-le-Vieux	58	45.55 N	6.09 E
Annemasse	58	46.12 N	6.15 E
Annen	263	51.27 N	7.22 E
Annenkov Island I	244	54.29 S	37.05 W
Annenskij Most	76	60.45 N	37.10 E
Annenskoje	86	53.08 N	60.26 E
Anner ≃	48	52.22 N	7.39 W
Annet I	42a	49.54 N	6.21 W
Annet-sur-Marne	261	48.56 N	2.43 E
Annette	182	55.03 N	131.34 W
Annette Island I	182	55.10 N	131.28 W
Annevoie-Rouillon	56	50.21 N	4.50 E
Annezin	50	50.32 N	2.37 E
Annfield Plain	44	54.51 N	1.45 W
An Nhon	110	13.53 N	109.06 E
Anniangniang	89	51.33 N	125.49 E
Annicco	62	45.14 N	9.52 E
An-Nīl □[4]	140	19.00 N	33.00 E
An-Nīl al-Azraq □[4]	140	12.00 N	34.00 E
Anning	102	24.59 N	102.18 E
Anningdu	102	36.56 N	104.31 E
Anninger ∧	264b	48.03 N	16.15 E
Annino	265a	59.46 N	30.03 E
Anninskije Mineral'nyje Vody	89	52.44 N	140.12 E
Annisquam	283	42.39 N	70.41 W
Annisquam ≃	283	42.39 N	70.41 W
Anniston	194	33.39 N	85.49 W
Annobón I	138	1.25 S	5.36 E
Annonay	62	45.14 N	4.40 E
Annopol	30	50.54 N	21.52 E
Anno-Rebrikovo	83	49.36 N	40.12 E
Annot	62	43.58 N	6.40 E
Annotto Bay	241q	18.16 N	76.46 W
Annsjön ⊜	40	58.48 N	15.26 E
An-Nubayrah	142	30.54 N	30.35 E
An-Nuhūd	140	12.42 N	28.26 E
An-Nuʿmān I	128	27.08 N	35.46 E
An-Nuʿmānīyah	128	32.32 N	45.25 E
An-Nuwayrah	142	29.06 N	30.59 E
Annville, Ky., U.S.	192	37.19 N	83.58 W
Annville, Pa., U.S.	208	40.19 N	76.30 W
Annweiler am Trifels	56	49.12 N	7.58 E
Anō	94	34.46 N	136.27 E
Anoia	68	38.27 N	16.05 E
Anoia ≃	34	41.28 N	1.56 E
Anoka	190	45.11 N	93.23 W
Áno Liósia	267c	38.05 N	23.42 E
Año Nuevo Bay ᑕ	226	37.07 N	122.19 W
Anopino	80	55.42 N	40.40 E
Anori, Bra.	246	3.47 S	61.38 W
Anorí, Col.	246	7.05 N	75.08 W
Anorotsangana	157b	13.56 S	47.55 E
Anosibe	157b	19.26 S	48.13 E
Anosyennes, Chaînes ⺈	157b	24.30 S	46.50 E
Anotaié ≃	250	3.29 N	52.04 W
Anpilogovo	78	51.47 N	36.01 E
Anping, Zhg.	98	38.16 N	115.30 E
Anping, Zhg.	98	34.01 N	115.07 E
Anping, Zhg.	100	26.33 N	113.22 E
Anping, Zhg.	104	41.11 N	123.26 E
Anping, Zhg.	105	39.43 N	116.53 E
Anpu	102	21.27 N	110.00 E
ʿAnqābīyah, Jabal al- ∧[2]	142	30.01 N	31.37 E
Anqing	100	30.31 N	117.02 E
Anqiu	98	36.25 N	119.10 E
Anrath	56	51.17 N	6.28 E
Anren, Zhg.	100	28.04 N	119.20 E
Anren, Zhg.	100	26.42 N	113.16 E
Anrenzhen	107	30.31 N	103.38 E
Anröchte	52	51.33 N	8.19 E
Ans, Bel.	56	50.39 N	5.32 E
Ans, Dan.	41	56.19 N	9.36 E
Ansager	41	55.42 N	8.45 E
Ansai	102	36.54 N	109.10 E
ʿAnṣār	132	33.23 N	35.21 E
Ansbach	56	49.17 N	10.34 E
Anschan → Anshan	104	41.08 N	122.59 E
Anschlag	263	51.10 N	7.29 E
Anse	58	45.56 N	4.43 E
Anseba ≃	144	17.03 N	37.24 E
Anse-Bertrand	241o	16.29 N	61.31 W
Anse-d'Hainault	238	18.30 N	74.27 W
Anse La Raye	241f	13.57 N	61.03 W
Anselmo	198	41.37 N	99.51 W
Anseremme	56	50.15 N	4.54 E
Anserma	246	5.13 N	75.48 W
Ansfelden	61	48.13 N	14.17 E
Anshan	104	41.08 N	122.59 E
Anshun	102	26.15 N	105.56 E
Ansina	252	31.54 S	55.28 W
Ansley	198	41.17 N	99.22 W
Anson	196	32.45 N	99.53 W
Anson Bay ᑕ, Austl.	164	13.20 S	130.06 E
Anson Bay ᑕ, Norf. I.	174c	29.01 S	167.55 E
Anson Creek ≃	212	44.53 N	79.03 W
Ansŏng	98	37.02 N	127.16 E
Ansongo	150	15.40 N	0.30 E
Ansonia, Ct., U.S.	207	41.20 N	73.04 W
Ansonia, Oh., U.S.	216	40.12 N	84.38 W
Ansonville, N.C., U.S.	192	35.06 N	80.06 W
Ansonville, Pa., U.S.	214	40.51 N	78.34 W
Ansouis	62	43.44 N	5.28 E
Ansted	188	38.08 N	81.05 W
Anstey	42	52.40 N	1.11 W
Anstruther	46	56.13 N	2.42 W
Anstruther Lake ⊜	212	44.45 N	78.12 W
Ansudu	164	2.08 S	139.20 E
Ansus	164	1.44 S	135.49 E
Anta, Bra.	256	22.03 S	42.59 W
Anta, Perú	248	13.29 S	72.09 W
Antabamba	248	14.19 S	72.55 W
Antakya (Antioch)	130	36.14 N	36.07 E
Antalaha	157b	14.53 S	50.16 E
Antalieptė	76	55.40 N	25.51 E
Antalovcy	78	48.38 N	22.31 E
Antalya	130	36.53 N	30.42 E
Antalya □[4]	130	37.00 N	31.00 E
Antalya, Gulf of → Antalya Körfezi ᑕ	130	36.30 N	31.00 E

≃	River	Fluß	Río	Rivière	Rio
≊	Canal	Kanal	Canal	Canal	Canal
ᒐ	Waterfall, Rapids	Wasserfall, Stromschnellen	Cascada, Rápidos	Chute d'eau, Rapides	Cascata, Rápidos
)(	Strait	Meeresstraße	Estrecho	Détroit	Estreito
ᑕ	Bay, Gulf	Bucht, Golf	Bahía, Golfo	Baie, Golfe	Baía, Golfo
⊜	Lake, Lakes	See, Seen	Lago, Lagos	Lac, Lacs	Lago, Lagos
≚	Swamp	Sumpf	Pantano	Marais	Pântano
⌂	Ice Features, Glacier	Eis- und Gletscherformen	Accidentes Glaciales	Formes glaciaires	Acidentes glaciares
⫪	Other Hydrographic Features	Andere Hydrographische Objekte	Otros Elementos Hidrográficos	Autres données hydrographiques	Outros acidentes hidrográficos
✣	Submarine Features	Untermeerische Objekte	Accidentes Submarinos	Formes de relief sous-marin	Acidentes submarinos
□	Political Unit	Politische Einheit	Unidad Politica	Entité politique	Unidade política
ᵿ	Cultural Institution	Kulturelle Institution	Institución Cultural	Institution culturelle	Instituição cultural
⊥	Historical Site	Historische Stätte	Sitio Histórico	Site historique	Sitio histórico
♠	Recreational Site	Erholungs- und Ferienort	Sitio de Recreo	Centre de loisirs	Area de Lazer
⊠	Airport	Flughafen	Aeropuerto	Aéroport	Aeroporto
■	Military Installation	Militäranlage	Instalación Militar	Installation militaire	Instalação militar
◆	Miscellaneous	Verschiedenes	Misceláneo	Divers	Diversos

Arch-Arvi I · 9

ESPAÑOL

Nombre	Página	Lat. °′	Long. °′ W = Oeste
Arches	58	48.07 N	6.32 E
Arches National Park ♠	200	38.42 N	109.45 W
Archi	66	42.05 N	14.23 E
Archiac	32	45.31 N	0.18 W
Archidona	34	37.05 N	4.23 W
Archipo-Osipovka	78	44.22 N	38.33 E
Archipovka	80	56.38 N	41.14 E
Archipovo	24	66.26 N	45.52 E
Archonskaja	84	43.07 N	44.30 E
Archshofen	56	49.27 N	10.04 E
Archville	276	41.07 N	73.52 W
Arci, Monte ∧	71	39.47 N	8.44 E
Arcidosso	66	42.52 N	11.33 E
Arcille	66	42.48 N	11.15 E
Arcinazzo Romano	66	41.48 N	13.12 E
Arcisate	62	45.54 N	8.52 E
Arcis-sur-Aube	50	48.32 N	4.08 E
Arciz	78	46.00 N	29.26 E
Arckaringa	162	27.56 S	134.45 E
Arckaringa Creek ≃	162	28.10 S	135.22 E
Arc-les-Gray	58	47.27 N	5.35 E
Arco, It.	64	45.55 N	10.53 E
Arco, Id., U.S.	202	43.38 N	113.17 W
Arco de Baúlhe	34	41.29 N	7.58 W
Arcola, Sk., Can.	184	49.37 N	102.30 W
Arcola, It.	64	44.07 N	9.54 E
Arcola, Il., U.S.	194	39.41 N	88.18 W
Arcola, In., U.S.	216	41.06 N	85.17 W
Arcola, Ms., U.S.	194	33.16 N	90.52 W
Arcola, Pa., U.S.	285	40.09 N	75.27 W
Arcola, Tx., U.S.	222	29.31 N	95.27 W
Arconate	266b	45.32 N	8.51 E
Arcore	266b	45.38 N	9.19 E
Arcos	255	20.17 S	45.32 W
Arcos de la Frontera	34	36.45 N	5.48 W
Arcot	122	12.54 N	79.20 E
Arcoverde	250	8.25 S	37.04 W
Arctic Bay	176	73.02 N	85.11 W
Arctic Ocean ⍑[1]	16	85.00 N	170.00 E
Arctic Red ≃	180	67.27 N	133.46 W
Arctic Red River	180	67.27 N	133.46 W
Arctic Village	180	68.08 N	145.19 W
Arctique, Océan Glacial → Arctic Ocean ⍑[1]	16	85.00 N	170.00 E
Arctowski ⊎[3]	9	62.09 S	58.28 W
Arcturus	154	17.47 S	31.20 E
Arcueil	261	48.48 N	2.20 E
Arcuentu, Monte ∧	71	39.35 N	8.33 E
Arcy-sur-Cure	50	47.36 N	3.45 E
Ard, Loch ⊜	46	56.11 N	4.28 W
Ard, Ra's al- ›	128	29.21 N	48.05 E
Arda ≃, Europe	38	41.39 N	26.29 E
Arda ≃, It.	64	45.02 N	10.02 E
Ardabīl	128	38.15 N	48.18 E
Ardagger	61	48.11 N	14.50 E
Ardagh	48	52.28 N	9.04 W
Ardahan	130	41.07 N	42.41 E
Ardakān, Īrān	128	30.16 N	52.01 E
Ardakān, Īrān	128	32.19 N	53.59 E
Ardal	128	31.59 N	50.39 E
Ardalanish, Rubh' ›	46	56.17 N	6.18 W
Årdalsfjorden ⊂[2]	26	61.12 N	7.30 E
Årdalstangen	26	61.14 N	7.43 E
Ardanuç	130	41.08 N	42.04 E
Ardara, Ire.	48	54.46 N	8.25 W
Árdara, It.	71	40.37 N	8.48 E
Ardara, Pa., U.S.	279b	40.22 N	79.44 W
Ardarroch	46	57.25 N	5.38 W
Ardatov, Ross.	80	55.15 N	43.06 E
Ardatov, Ross.	80	54.51 N	46.13 E
Ardbeg	46	55.39 N	6.05 W
Ardcharnich	46	57.51 N	5.05 W
Ardea	66	41.36 N	12.33 E
Ardèche □[5]	62	44.40 N	4.20 E
Ardèche ≃	62	44.16 N	4.39 E
Ardee	48	53.52 N	6.33 W
Ardélik	146	12.26 N	21.25 E
Arden, Mb., Can.	184	50.17 N	99.14 W
Arden, Ca., U.S.	226	38.36 N	121.23 W
Arden, De., U.S.	208	39.48 N	75.29 W
Arden, Forest of ◆[3]	42	52.23 N	1.42 W
Arden, Mount ∧	166	32.09 S	137.59 E
Ardenay-sur-Mérize	50	48.00 N	0.25 E
Arden Mines	279b	40.12 N	80.17 W
Ardennes □[5]	50	49.40 N	4.40 E
Ardennes ◆[1]	56	50.10 N	5.45 E
Ardennes, Canal des ≅	50	49.26 N	4.02 E
Ardenno	58	46.10 N	9.39 E
Ardentinny	46	56.03 N	4.55 W
Ardenza	66	43.31 N	10.19 E
Arderin ∧[2]	48	53.02 N	7.40 W
Ardersier	46	57.34 N	4.02 W
Ardeşen	130	41.12 N	41.00 E
Ardestān	128	33.22 N	52.23 E
Ardey	263	51.28 N	7.43 E
Ardeygebirge ⋏[2]	263	51.25 N	7.20 E
Ardez	58	46.46 N	10.11 E
Ardfern	46	56.10 N	5.32 W
Ardglass	48	54.16 N	5.37 W
Ardgroom	48	51.42 N	9.52 W
Ardıçlı	130	40.40 N	37.00 E
Ardila ≃	34	38.12 N	7.28 W
Ardill	184	49.53 N	105.49 W
Ardino	38	41.35 N	25.08 E
Ardlethan	166	34.21 S	146.54 E
Ardlui	46	56.18 N	4.43 W
Ardlussa	46	56.02 N	5.47 W
Ardmolich	46	56.49 N	5.41 W
Ardmore, Ire.	48	51.57 N	7.43 W
Ardmore, Al., U.S.	194	34.59 N	86.50 W
Ardmore, In., U.S.	216	41.41 N	86.19 W
Ardmore, Md., U.S.	284c	38.56 N	76.51 W
Ardmore, Ok., U.S.	196	34.10 N	97.08 W
Ardmore, Pa., U.S.	208	40.01 N	75.18 W
Ardmore Point ›, Scot., U.K.	46	55.42 N	6.01 W
Ardmore Point ›, Scot., U.K.	46	56.39 N	6.07 W
Ardnamurchan ›[1]	46	56.43 N	6.00 W
Ardnamurchan, Point of ›	46	56.44 N	6.13 W
Ardnaree	48	54.06 N	9.08 W
Ardnave Point ›	46	55.54 N	6.20 W
Ardoch	166	27.26 S	144.08 E
Ardon, Ross.	84	43.12 N	44.18 E
Ardon, Schw.	58	46.13 N	7.15 E
Ardon ≃	84	43.17 N	44.18 E
Ardon, Har ∧	132	30.38 N	34.57 E
Ardooie	50	50.59 N	3.12 E
Ardore	68	38.11 N	16.10 E
Ardoux ≃	50	47.42 N	1.35 E
Ardoz, Arroyo de ≃	266a	40.26 N	3.27 W
Ardres	50	50.51 N	1.59 E
Ardres ≃	50	49.18 N	3.40 E
Ardrishaig	46	56.01 N	5.27 W
Ardrossan, Austl.	168b	34.25 S	137.55 E
Ardrossan, Scot., U.K.	46	55.39 N	4.49 W
Ardsley, Eng., U.K.	44	53.32 N	1.28 W
Ardsley, N.Y., U.S.	276	41.00 N	73.50 W
Ardtalnaig	46	56.31 N	4.06 W
Arduan Island I	140	19.55 N	30.22 E
Ardusson ≃	50	48.30 N	3.32 E
Ardvasar	46	57.04 N	5.54 W
Åre	26	63.24 N	13.04 E
Areado	256	21.21 S	46.09 W
Areal	256	22.14 S	43.07 W
Arèches	62	45.41 N	6.34 E
Arecibo	240m	18.28 N	66.43 W
Arecibo, Observatorio de ⊎[3]	240m	18.20 N	66.46 W
Areco ≃	258	33.56 S	59.16 W
Areeiro	266c	38.39 N	9.12 W
Arefjevo	86	57.01 N	90.40 E
Areguá	252	25.18 S	57.25 W
Areia, Bra.	250	6.58 S	35.42 W
Areia, Port.	266c	38.43 N	9.08 W
Areia, Ribeirão da ≃	255	16.07 S	45.52 W
Areia Branca, Bra.	250	4.56 S	37.07 W

FRANÇAIS

Nom	Page	Lat. °′	Long. °′ W = Ouest
Areia Branca, Bra.	287a	22.44 S	43.25 W
Areias	256	22.35 S	44.42 W
Arena	68	38.34 N	16.13 E
Arena, Point ›	204	38.57 N	123.44 W
Arena, Punta ›	232	23.33 N	109.28 W
Arena de la Ventana, Punta ›	232	24.04 N	109.52 W
Arena Island I	116	9.14 N	120.46 E
Arenal, C.R.	236	10.29 N	84.53 W
Arenal, P.R.	240m	17.59 N	66.19 W
Arenal, Laguna de ⊜	236	10.32 N	84.56 W
Arenal, Volcán ∧[1]	236	10.28 N	84.44 W
Arenápolis	248	14.26 S	56.49 W
Arenas, Cayo I	232	22.08 N	91.24 W
Arenas, Punta ›	240m	18.07 N	65.35 W
Arenas, Punta de ›	254	53.09 S	68.13 W
Arenas de San Pedro	34	40.12 N	5.05 W
Arendal	26	58.27 N	8.48 E
Arendonk	56	51.19 N	5.05 E
Arendsee	54	52.53 N	11.30 E
Arendsee ⊜	54	52.53 N	11.30 E
Arendtsville	208	39.55 N	77.18 W
Arenes ≃	266d	41.29 N	2.02 E
Arenig Fawr ∧	42	52.55 N	3.45 W
Arenillas	246	3.33 S	80.04 W
Arenosa Creek ≃	196	28.52 N	96.44 W
Arenys de Mar	34	41.35 N	2.33 E
Arenzano	62	44.24 N	8.41 E
Arenzville	219	39.53 N	90.22 W
Arequipa	248	16.24 S	71.33 W
Arequipa □[5]	248	16.00 S	72.15 W
Arequito	252	33.09 S	61.28 W
Arero	144	4.45 N	38.49 E
Arês, Bra.	250	6.11 S	35.09 W
Arès, Fr.	32	44.46 N	1.08 W
Arese	266b	45.33 N	9.05 E
Aresing	60	48.32 N	11.18 E
Åreskutan ∧	26	63.26 N	13.06 E
Areuse ≃	58	46.56 N	6.53 E
Arévalo	34	41.04 N	4.43 W
Arezzo	66	43.25 N	11.53 E
Arezzo □[4]	66	43.32 N	11.50 E
Arfa', Jabal ∧	132	29.51 N	35.27 E
'Arfā', Wādī al- V	132	30.16 N	36.34 E
Arga ≃	34	42.18 N	1.47 W
Argada	88	54.14 N	110.41 E
Argadargada	166	21.40 S	136.40 E
Argajaš	86	55.29 N	60.52 E
Argamasilla de Alba	34	39.07 N	3.06 W
Arganda	34	40.18 N	3.26 W
Argao	116	9.52 N	123.36 E
Arga-Sala ≃	74	68.30 N	112.12 E
Argedeb	144	6.10 N	41.10 E
Argegno	58	45.56 N	9.08 E
Argel → El Djazaïr	148	36.47 N	3.03 E
Argelès-Gazost	32	43.01 N	0.06 E
Argelès-sur-Mer	32	42.33 N	3.01 E
Argelia → Algeria □[1]	148	28.00 N	3.00 E
Argen ≃	58	47.35 N	9.33 E
Argens ≃	62	43.24 N	6.44 E
Argent	158	26.04 S	28.50 E
Argent, Côte d' ⊥[2]	32	43.30 N	1.30 W
Argenta, It.	66	44.37 N	11.50 E
Argenta, Il., U.S.	219	39.58 N	88.49 W
Argentan	32	48.45 N	0.01 W
Argentario, Monte ∧	66	42.24 N	11.09 E
Argentat	32	45.06 N	1.56 E
Argentera	62	44.24 N	6.57 E
Argentera ∧	62	44.10 N	7.18 E
Argenteuil	50	48.57 N	2.15 E
Argenteuil □[6]	206	45.45 N	74.30 W
Argentia	186	47.18 N	53.59 W
Argentiera	71	40.44 N	8.09 E
Argentière	58	45.59 N	6.56 E
Argentières	261	48.39 N	2.52 E
Argentina □[1]	244	34.00 S	64.00 W
Argentina ≃	62	43.50 N	7.51 E
Argentine	216	42.47 N	83.51 W
Argentine → Argentina □[1]	244	34.00 S	64.00 W
Argentine Basin ✦[1]	18	45.00 S	45.00 W
Argentinien → Argentina □[1]	244	34.00 S	64.00 W
Argentino, Hipódromo ♠	283	34.34 S	58.26 W
Argentino, Lago ⊜	254	50.13 S	72.25 W
Argentona	266d	41.33 N	2.24 E
Argentona, Riera d' ≃	266d	41.31 N	2.26 E
Argenton-Château	32	46.59 N	0.27 W
Argenton-sur-Creuse	32	46.35 N	1.31 E
Argent-sur-Sauldre	50	47.33 N	2.27 E
Argeș □[6]	38	45.00 N	24.45 E
Argeș ≃	38	44.04 N	26.37 E
Arghandāb ≃	128	31.27 N	64.23 E
Arghastān ≃	120	31.23 N	65.45 E
Argirita	256	21.37 S	42.50 W
Argıthanı	130	38.17 N	31.43 E
Argo	140	19.31 N	30.25 E
Ārgoal	126	21.58 N	87.38 E
Argo Island I	140	19.25 N	30.27 E
Argolikós Kólpos ⊂	38	37.33 N	22.45 E
Argonia	198	37.15 N	97.45 W
Argonne	190	45.39 N	88.52 W
Argonne ◆[1]	56	49.30 N	5.00 E
Argonne National Laboratory ⊎[3]	216	41.43 N	87.58 W
Argopuro, Gunung ∧	115a	7.57 S	113.33 E
Árgos, Ellás	38	37.39 N	22.44 E
Argos, In., U.S.	216	41.14 N	86.15 W
Árgos Orestikón	38	40.28 N	21.16 E
Argostólion	38	38.10 N	20.30 E
Argoules	50	50.21 N	1.50 E
Argueil	50	49.32 N	1.31 E
Arguello, Point ›	204	34.35 N	120.39 W
Argun	84	43.16 N	45.52 E
Argun ≃	84	43.22 N	45.55 E
Argun' (Ergun) ≃, Asia	74	53.20 N	121.28 E
Argungu	150	12.45 N	4.31 E
Arguni, Teluk ⊂	164	3.06 S	133.42 E
Ārgur	272b	22.48 N	88.13 E
Argut	86	49.51 N	87.03 E
Argut ≃	86	50.16 N	86.43 E
Arguvan	130	38.47 N	38.17 E
Argyle, Austl.	162	33.32 S	115.46 E
Argyle, Mn., U.S.	198	48.19 N	96.49 W
Argyle, Mo., U.S.	219	38.18 N	92.02 W
Argyle, N.Y., U.S.	210	43.14 N	73.30 W
Argyle, Tx., U.S.	222	33.07 N	97.11 W
Argyle, Lake ⊜[1]	164	16.15 S	128.45 E
'Arhāb, Wādī V	142	28.55 N	31.09 E
Arhavi	130	41.22 N	41.16 E
Arhéa Epídavros ⊥	38	37.37 N	23.02 E
Århus	41	56.09 N	10.13 E
Århus □[6]	41	56.15 N	10.05 E
Århus Bugt ⊂	41	56.09 N	10.18 E
Aria	172	38.33 S	174.59 E
Aria ≃	164	5.45 S	149.15 E
Ariadnoje	89	45.08 N	134.25 E
Ariah	126	23.33 N	86.20 E
Ariake-kai ⊂	92	33.00 N	130.20 E
Ariāl Khān ≃	126	23.56 N	90.46 E
Ariamácina, Lago di ⊜[1]	68	39.20 N	16.32 E
Ariamsvlei	156	28.07 S	19.49 E
Ariana	36	36.52 N	10.12 E
Ariano, Isola d' I	64	45.10 N	12.10 E
Ariano Irpino	68	41.09 N	15.05 E
Ariano nel Polesine	64	44.56 N	12.07 E
Ariari ≃	246	2.35 N	72.47 W
Arias	252	33.38 S	62.25 W
Arias, Arroyo de ≃	258	34.17 S	56.06 W
Arias, Cañada ≃	258	34.39 S	58.59 W
Ariaú	250	3.11 S	57.14 W
Aribinda	150	14.14 N	0.52 W
Arica, Chile	248	18.29 S	70.20 W
Arica, Col.	246	2.08 S	71.47 W
Arıcak	130	38.33 N	39.48 E
Aricanduva, Ribeirão ≃	287b	23.32 S	46.33 W

PORTUGUÊS

Nome	Página	Lat. °′	Long. °′ W = Oeste
Ariccia	66	41.43 N	12.40 E
Arichat	186	45.31 N	61.01 W
Arichuna	246	7.42 N	67.08 W
Arid, Cape ›	162	34.00 S	123.09 E
Arida, Nig.	273a	6.34 N	3.16 E
Arida, Nihon	96	34.05 N	135.07 E
Arida ≃	96	34.05 N	135.06 E
Aridal, Sabkhat ⊜	148	26.12 N	14.05 W
Aridhaía	38	40.59 N	22.03 E
Ariège □[5]	32	43.00 N	1.30 E
Ariège ≃	32	43.31 N	1.25 E
Ari'el, Isr. Occ	132	32.06 N	35.06 E
Ariel, Wa., U.S.	224	45.57 N	122.34 W
Arienzo	68	41.01 N	14.30 E
Arieș ≃	38	46.26 N	23.59 E
'Arif, Har ∧	132	30.26 N	34.44 E
Ārifwāla	123	30.17 N	73.04 E
Ariguanabo, Laguna de ⊜	286b	22.56 N	82.33 W
Ariguaní ≃	246	9.35 N	73.46 W
Arīḥā (Jericho), Isr. Occ	132	31.52 N	35.27 E
Arīḥā, Sūrīy.	130	35.48 N	36.36 E
Arīḥā, Urd.	132	31.25 N	35.47 E
Arikaree ≃	198	40.01 N	101.56 W
Arikaree, North Fork ≃	198	39.39 N	102.57 W
Arikawa	92	32.59 N	129.07 E
Arikha, Har ∧[2]	132	30.39 N	34.47 E
Arild	41	56.16 N	12.34 E
Arima	241r	10.38 N	61.17 W
Arima ◆[8]	270	34.48 N	135.15 E
Arima ≃	270	34.52 N	135.15 E
Arima-fuji ∧[2]	270	34.55 N	135.14 E
Arimine-dam ◆[6]	94	36.29 N	137.27 E
Arinagour	46	56.37 N	6.31 W
Aringay	116	16.26 N	120.21 E
Arino ◆[8]	270	34.50 N	135.14 E
Arinos ≃	248	10.25 S	58.20 W
Arinthod	58	46.23 N	5.34 E
Ario de Rosales	234	19.12 N	101.43 W
Ariogala	76	55.16 N	23.30 E
Aripeka	220	28.25 N	82.39 W
Ariporo ≃	246	6.03 N	69.54 W
Aripuanã	248	9.10 S	60.38 W
Aripuanã ≃	248	5.07 S	60.24 W
Ariquemes	248	9.56 S	63.04 W
Arisa ≃	246	7.32 N	64.00 W
Arisaig	46	56.51 N	5.51 W
Arisaig, Sound of ⊂	46	56.51 N	5.51 W
'Arīsh, Wādī al- V	140	31.09 N	33.49 E
Arismendi	246	8.29 N	68.22 W
Aristazabal Island I	182	52.30 N	129.05 W
Aristes	210	40.49 N	76.20 W
Aristizábal, Cabo ›	254	45.13 S	66.31 W
Aristovo	82	54.37 N	36.40 E
Arıt	130	41.41 N	32.39 E
Aritao	116	16.18 N	121.02 E
Ariton	194	31.36 N	85.43 W
Aritzo	71	39.57 N	9.12 E
Arivonimamo	157b	19.01 S	47.15 E
Ariyalūr	122	11.08 N	79.05 E
Arizaro, Salar de ≡	252	24.42 S	67.45 W
Arizgoiti	34	43.13 N	2.54 W
Arizona	252	35.43 S	65.18 W
Arizona □[3], U.S.	178	34.00 N	112.00 W
Arizona □[3], U.S.	200	34.00 N	112.00 W
Arizpe	232	30.20 N	110.10 W
Arja	80	57.30 N	46.00 E
Årjäng	26	59.23 N	12.08 E
Arjasa	112	6.51 S	115.16 E
Arjawinangun	115a	6.39 S	108.24 E
Arjay	192	36.48 N	83.38 W
Arjeplog	24	66.00 N	17.58 E
Arjona, Col.	246	10.15 N	75.21 W
Arjona, Esp.	34	37.56 N	4.03 W
Arka	74	60.03 N	142.12 E
Arkabutla Lake ⊜[1]	194	34.45 N	90.06 W
Arkadak	80	51.58 N	43.28 E
Arkadelphia	194	34.07 N	93.03 W
Arkaig, Loch ⊜	46	56.58 N	5.08 W
Arkalyk	86	50.13 N	66.50 E
Arkansas □[3], U.S.	178	34.50 N	92.30 W
Arkansas □[3], U.S.	194	34.50 N	92.30 W
Arkansas ≃	178	33.48 N	91.04 W
Arkansas, Salt Fork ≃	196	36.36 N	97.03 W
Arkansas City, Ar., U.S.	194	33.36 N	91.12 W
Arkansas City, Ks., U.S.	198	37.03 N	97.02 W
Arkansas Post National Memorial ⊥	194	33.55 N	91.26 W
Arkanū, Jabal ∧	146	22.13 N	24.41 E
Arkatag Shan ⋏	120	36.48 N	89.10 E
Arken-Ahon ∧	146	20.05 N	18.25 E
Arkhangélos	38	36.12 N	28.08 E
Arkhangel'sk → Archangel'sk, Ross.	24	64.34 N	40.32 E
Arki	123	31.09 N	76.58 E
Árki I	38	37.22 N	26.45 E
Arkit	85	41.47 N	71.58 E
Arklow	48	52.48 N	6.09 W
Arkoma	194	35.21 N	94.26 W
Arkona, Kap ›	54	54.41 N	13.26 E
Arkösund	26	58.30 N	16.56 E
Arkport	210	42.23 N	77.41 W
Arktičeskij, mys ›	74	81.15 N	95.45 E
Arktičeskogo Instituta, ostrova II	74	75.20 N	81.55 E
Arkul'	80	57.17 N	50.03 E
Arkville	210	42.08 N	74.37 W
Arkwright	207	41.43 N	71.33 W
Ärla	40	59.17 N	16.40 E
Arlan	80	55.58 N	54.15 E
Arlan, gora ∧	128	39.40 N	54.33 E
Arlanc	62	45.25 N	3.44 E
Arlanda flygplats ⊠	40	59.37 N	17.55 E
Arlanza ≃	34	42.06 N	4.09 W
Arlanzón ≃	34	42.03 N	4.17 W
Arlbergpass)(	64	47.08 N	10.12 E
Arlberg-Tunnel ◆[5]	58	47.08 N	10.12 E
Arlee	202	47.09 N	114.05 W
Arles	62	43.40 N	4.38 E
Arles à Port de Bouc, Canal d' ≅	62	43.40 N	4.37 E
Arlesey	42	52.01 N	0.14 W
Arlesheim	58	47.30 N	7.37 E
Arleta ◆[8]	280	34.15 N	118.26 W
Arleux	50	50.17 N	3.06 E
Arley	262	53.19 N	2.30 W
Arli	150	11.35 N	1.28 E
Arli, Parc National de l' ♠	150	11.35 N	1.30 E
Arlington, S. Afr.	158	28.06 S	27.54 E
Arlington, Ga., U.S.	192	31.26 N	84.43 W
Arlington, In., U.S.	218	39.38 N	85.34 W
Arlington, Ia., U.S.	190	42.44 N	91.40 W
Arlington, Ks., U.S.	198	37.53 N	98.10 W
Arlington, Ky., U.S.	194	36.47 N	89.00 W
Arlington, Ma., U.S.	207	42.24 N	71.09 W
Arlington, Mn., U.S.	190	44.36 N	94.04 W
Arlington, Ne., U.S.	198	41.27 N	96.21 W
Arlington, N.Y., U.S.	210	41.41 N	73.53 W
Arlington, Oh., U.S.	216	40.53 N	83.39 W
Arlington, Or., U.S.	202	45.43 N	120.11 W
Arlington, S.D., U.S.	198	44.21 N	97.07 W
Arlington, Tn., U.S.	194	35.18 N	89.40 W
Arlington, Tx., U.S.	222	32.44 N	97.06 W
Arlington, Vt., U.S.	210	43.04 N	73.09 W
Arlington, Va., U.S.	208	38.52 N	77.06 W
Arlington, Wa., U.S.	224	48.11 N	122.07 W
Arlington □[6]	284c	38.50 N	77.10 W
Arlington, Lake ⊜[1]	222	32.42 N	97.13 W
Arlington Heights, Il., U.S.	216	42.05 N	87.58 W
Arlington Heights, Ma., U.S.	283	42.25 N	71.11 W
Arlington Memorial Bridge ◆[5]	284c	38.53 N	77.03 W

Arlington Mill Reservoir ⊜[1]	283	42.48 N	71.13 W
Arlington National Cemetery ◆	284c	38.53 N	77.04 W
Arlit	150	19.00 N	7.38 E
Arlod	58	46.06 N	5.49 E
Arlon	56	49.41 N	5.49 E
Arlöv	41	55.39 N	13.05 E
Arltunga	162	23.26 S	134.41 E
Arl'uk	86	55.26 N	84.50 E
Arluno	62	45.30 N	8.56 E
Arly ≃	62	45.40 N	6.23 E
Arlyn Oaks	276	40.40 N	73.27 W
Arm ≃	184	50.46 N	105.00 W
Arma	198	37.32 N	94.42 W
Armação, Ponta da ›	287a	22.53 S	43.08 W
Armada	214	42.50 N	82.53 W
Armadale, Austl.	168a	32.09 S	116.00 E
Armadale, On., Can.	275b	43.50 N	79.15 W
Armadale, S. Afr.	273d	26.17 S	27.57 E
Armadale, Scot., U.K.	46	55.54 N	3.42 W
Arma di Taggia	62	43.50 N	7.51 E
Armageddon → Tel Megiddo ⊥	132	32.35 N	35.11 E
Armagh, N. Ire., U.K.	48	54.21 N	6.39 W
Armagh, Pa., U.S.	214	40.27 N	79.02 W
Armagnac □[9]	32	43.45 N	0.10 E
Armah, Wādī V	144	18.12 N	51.02 E
Armainvilliers, Étang d' ⊜	261	48.45 N	2.44 E
Armainvilliers, Forêt d' ♠	261	48.45 N	2.45 E
Armance ≃	50	47.26 N	3.33 E
Armançon ≃, Fr.	50	47.57 N	3.30 E
Armançon ≃, Fr.	58	47.33 N	4.17 E
Arm'ansk	78	46.07 N	33.41 E
Armant	140	25.37 N	32.32 E
Armavir	72	45.00 N	41.08 E
Armazém	252	28.16 S	49.01 W
Armbrust	214	40.13 N	79.33 W
Armells Creek ≃	202	47.37 N	108.40 W
Armenia	246	4.31 N	75.41 W
Armenia □[9]	84	40.30 N	43.30 E
Armenia □[1], Asia	72	40.00 N	45.00 E
Armenia (Hayastan) □[1], Asia	84	40.00 N	45.00 E
Armenija → Armenia □[1]	72	40.00 N	45.00 E
Armeniș	38	45.12 N	22.19 E
Armenistís	38	37.36 N	26.08 E
Armeniya → Armenia □[1]	72	40.00 N	45.00 E
Armeno	62	45.49 N	8.26 E
Armenonville-les-Gâtineaux	261	48.33 N	1.39 E
Armentières	50	50.41 N	2.53 E
Armento	68	40.18 N	16.04 E
Armería	234	18.56 N	103.58 W
Armería ≃	234	18.52 N	103.59 W
Armero	246	4.58 N	74.54 W
Armidale	166	30.31 S	151.39 E
Armijo	200	35.03 N	106.40 W
Armitage	42	52.44 N	1.53 W
Armit Lake ⊜	176	64.10 N	91.32 W
Armizonskoje	86	55.57 N	67.42 E
Armona	226	36.19 N	119.42 W
Armonk	276	41.07 N	73.42 W
Armor	210	42.44 N	78.48 W
Armori	122	20.28 N	79.59 E
Armour	198	43.19 N	98.20 W
Armoy	58	46.21 N	6.31 E
Armstrong, Arg.	252	32.47 S	61.36 W
Armstrong, B.C., Can.	182	50.27 N	119.12 W
Armstrong, Il., U.S.	216	40.18 N	87.53 W
Armstrong, Ia., U.S.	198	43.23 N	94.28 W
Armstrong, Mo., U.S.	194	39.16 N	92.42 W
Armstrong □[6]	214	40.49 N	79.32 W
Armstrong ≃	164	16.46 S	131.12 E
Armstrong, Mount ∧	180	63.12 N	133.16 W
Armstrong Station	176	50.18 N	89.02 W
Armthorpe	44	53.32 N	1.03 W
Ārmūr	122	18.48 N	78.17 E
Armutlu	130	40.31 N	28.50 E
Arnå ≃	41	54.57 N	8.53 E
Arnaccio	66	43.40 N	10.17 E
Arnaía	38	40.29 N	23.35 E
Arnarfjörður ⊂[2]	24a	65.45 N	23.40 W
Arnäs	40	58.41 N	13.35 E
Arnaud ≃	176	59.59 N	69.46 W
Arnaudville	194	30.24 N	91.56 W
Arnavad, gora ∧	85	38.33 N	71.31 E
Arnavutköy ≃	267b	41.13 N	29.12 E
Arnay-le-Duc	58	47.08 N	4.29 E
Arnaz	62	45.38 N	7.43 E
Arnborg	41	56.01 N	8.59 E
Arnbruck	60	49.08 N	13.00 E
Arncliffe	274a	33.56 S	151.09 E
Arneburg	54	52.40 N	12.00 E
Arnedo	34	42.13 N	2.06 W
Arneiro dos Marinheiros	266c	38.51 N	9.25 W
Arneiroz	250	6.20 S	40.08 W
Arnejevo	82	54.58 N	37.35 E
Arnemuiden	52	51.30 N	3.41 E
Årnes	26	60.09 N	11.28 E
Arnett	196	36.08 N	99.46 W
Arney ≃	48	54.16 N	7.37 W
Arnhem	52	51.59 N	5.55 E
Arnhem, Cape ›	164	12.21 S	136.21 E
Arnhem Bay ⊂	164	12.20 S	136.12 E
Arnhem Land ◆[1]	164	13.10 S	134.30 E
Arnhem Land Aboriginal Reserve ◆[4]	164	13.10 S	134.30 E
Arni	64	44.04 N	10.15 E
Arnis	41	54.38 N	9.56 E
Árnissa	38	40.48 N	21.50 E
Arno I[1]	14	7.05 N	171.41 E
Arno ≃	66	43.41 N	10.17 E
Arno, Torrente ≃	266b	45.42 N	8.48 E
Arno Bay	166	33.54 S	136.34 E
Arnold, B.C., Can.	224	49.08 N	122.03 W
Arnold, Eng., U.K.	44	53.00 N	1.08 W
Arnold, Ca., U.S.	204	38.15 N	120.21 W
Arnold, Md., U.S.	208	39.01 N	76.30 W
Arnold, Mn., U.S.	190	46.52 N	92.05 W
Arnold, Mo., U.S.	219	38.25 N	90.22 W
Arnold, Ne., U.S.	198	41.25 N	100.11 W
Arnold, Pa., U.S.	214	40.34 N	79.46 W
Arnold ≃	164	15.19 S	134.06 E
Arnold Arboretum ♠	283	42.18 N	71.08 W
Arnold Mills	283	41.58 N	71.23 W
Arnold Mills Reservoir ⊜[1]	283	41.59 N	71.25 W
Arnolds Park	198	43.22 N	95.08 W
Arnoldstein	64	46.33 N	13.43 E
Arnon ≃	50	48.16 N	0.38 E
Arnos Vale Airport ⊠	241h	13.09 N	61.13 W
Arnot	210	41.39 N	77.07 W
Arnouville-lès-Gonesse	261	49.00 N	2.25 E
Arnouville-lès-Mantes	261	48.55 N	1.44 E
Arnoya ≃	34	42.15 N	8.09 W
Arnprior	212	45.26 N	76.21 W
Arnsberg	56	51.24 N	8.03 E
Arnsberg □[5]	52	51.20 N	8.00 E
Arnschwang	60	49.16 N	12.49 E
Arnsdorf	54	51.05 N	13.59 E
Arnside	44	54.12 N	2.50 W
Arnstadt	54	50.50 N	10.57 E
Arnstein	56	49.58 N	9.58 E
Arnstorf	60	48.34 N	12.49 E
Arnum	41	55.15 N	8.59 E
Ārø I	41	55.15 N	9.45 E
Aro ≃	246	8.01 N	64.11 W
Aroa	246	10.26 N	68.54 W
Aroa ≃	246	10.40 N	68.19 W
Aroa, Pointe ›	174s	17.28 S	149.46 W
Aroab	156	26.47 S	19.40 E
Aroali	126	24.03 N	87.56 E
Arochukwu	150	5.23 N	7.55 E
Aroeiras	250	7.31 S	35.41 W

Ar'ofino	80	58.16 N	39.15 E
Arolla	58	46.02 N	7.29 E
Arolsen	56	51.23 N	9.01 E
Aroma	140	15.49 N	36.08 E
Aroma Park	216	41.04 N	87.48 W
Aromas	226	36.53 N	121.39 W
Aromaševo	86	56.52 N	68.39 E
Aron ≃	50	47.15 N	2.02 E
Arona, It.	62	45.46 N	8.34 E
Arona, Pap. N. Gui.	164	6.20 S	146.00 E
Arona, Pa., U.S.	279b	40.16 N	79.39 W
Aroostook ≃	186	46.48 N	67.45 W
Arop Island I	164	5.20 S	147.05 E
Aropuk Lake ⊜	180	61.12 N	163.50 W
Arorae I	14	2.38 S	176.49 E
Arorangi	174k	21.13 S	159.49 W
Aroroy	116	12.31 N	123.24 E
Aros ≃	232	29.09 N	109.40 W
Arosa	58	46.47 N	9.41 E
Arosa, Ría de ⊂[1]	34	42.28 N	8.57 W
Arosbaya	115a	6.56 S	112.51 E
Årøsund	41	55.16 N	9.45 E
Aro Usu, Tanjung ›	164	8.20 S	130.45 E
Arowhana ∧	172	38.07 S	177.52 E
Arp	222	32.13 N	95.03 W
Arpa ≃	84	39.28 N	44.57 E
Arpaçay	84	40.52 N	43.20 E
Arpaçay (Achur'an) ≃	84	40.06 N	43.39 E
Arpačin	83	47.14 N	40.11 E
Arpaia	68	41.02 N	14.33 E
Arpajon	50	48.35 N	2.15 E
Ārpāra	126	23.23 N	89.23 E
Arpino	66	41.39 N	13.36 E
Arpoador, Ponta do ›	287a	22.59 S	43.12 W
Arquà Petrarca	64	45.16 N	11.43 E
Arquà Polesine	64	45.01 N	11.45 E
Arquata del Tronto	66	42.46 N	13.18 E
Arquata Scrivia	62	44.41 N	8.53 E
Arque	248	17.48 S	66.23 W
Arques	50	50.44 N	2.17 E
Arques-la-Bataille	50	49.53 N	1.08 E
Ar-Rabad	128	23.11 N	39.32 E
Ar-Rabbah	132	31.16 N	35.44 E
Arracourt	58	48.44 N	6.32 E
Ar-Radīsīyah Baḥrī	140	24.57 N	32.53 E
Ar-Rafīd	132	32.57 N	35.53 E
Arraga	252	28.04 S	64.14 W
Arrah	150	6.40 N	3.58 W
Ar-Rahad	140	12.43 N	30.39 E
Ar-Raḥāminah	142	31.18 N	31.45 E
Ar-Raḥmānīyah	142	31.06 N	30.38 E
Arraial do Cabo	255	22.58 S	42.01 W
Arraias	255	12.56 S	46.57 W
Arraias ≃, Bra.	250	11.10 S	53.35 W
Arraias ≃, Bra.	255	12.28 S	47.18 W
'Arrām, Wādī V	132	32.55 N	36.10 E
Ar-Ramādī	128	33.25 N	43.17 E
Ar-Ramthā	132	32.34 N	36.00 E
Arran, Island of I	46	55.35 N	5.15 W
Ar-Rank	140	11.45 N	32.48 E
Arran Lake ⊜	212	44.29 N	81.16 W
Ar-Raqqah	130	35.56 N	39.01 E
Ar-Raqqah □[8]	130	36.00 N	39.00 E
Arras	50	50.17 N	2.47 E
Arras, Nuraghe ⊥	71	39.40 N	9.25 E
Ar-Rāshidah	140	25.35 N	28.56 E
Ar-Rass	128	25.52 N	43.28 E
Ar-Rastan	130	34.55 N	36.44 E
Arrats ≃	32	44.06 N	0.52 E
Ar-Rawḍah, Ar. Su.	128	26.05 N	40.37 E
Ar-Rawḍah, Miṣr	142	27.48 N	30.52 E
Ar-Rawḍah, Miṣr	142	29.27 N	31.00 E
Ar-Rawḍah, Yaman	144	14.28 N	47.17 E
Ar-Rāwuk	144	15.45 N	48.54 E
Ar-Rayramūn	142	27.45 N	30.52 E
Ar-Rayyāḥ ar-Minūfīya ≅	142	30.20 N	31.00 E
Ar-Rayyāḥ at-Tawfīqī ≅	142	30.11 N	31.07 E
Ar-Rayyān	128	25.18 N	51.27 E
Arrecife	148	28.57 N	13.32 W
Arrecifes	252	34.03 S	60.07 W
Arrée, Montagnes d' ⋏	32	48.26 N	3.55 W
Arregui, Laguna ⊜	258	35.05 S	57.33 W
Arrentela	266c	38.38 N	9.06 W
Arresø ⊜	41	55.58 N	12.08 E
Arrey	200	32.50 N	107.19 W
Arriaga	234	16.14 N	93.54 W
Arriba	198	39.17 N	103.16 W
Arrild	41	55.09 N	8.58 E
Ar-Riyāḍ (Riyadh)	128	24.38 N	46.43 E
Arrochar	46	56.12 N	4.44 W
Arroio Grande	252	32.14 S	53.05 W
Arrojado ≃	255	13.24 S	44.20 W
Arronches	34	39.07 N	7.17 W
Arrone ≃, It.	66	41.52 N	12.11 E
Arrone ≃, It.	66	42.18 N	11.38 E
Arros ≃	32	43.40 N	0.02 W
Arroscia ≃	62	44.03 N	8.11 E
Arroux ≃	32	46.29 N	3.58 E
Arrow ≃, Eng., U.K.	42	52.12 N	2.43 W
Arrow ≃, Eng., U.K.	42	52.09 N	1.53 W
Arrow, Lough ⊜	48	54.04 N	8.21 W
Arrow Creek ≃	202	47.43 N	109.50 W
Arrowhead, Lake ⊜[1], Ca., U.S.	228	34.15 N	117.11 W
Arrowhead, Lake ⊜[1], Tx., U.S.	196	33.40 N	98.20 W
Arrowhead Peak ∧	228	34.13 N	117.16 W
Arrowhead Provincial Park ♠	212	45.24 N	79.13 W
Arrowhead Village	208	40.04 N	74.07 W
Arrow Lake ⊜	190	48.08 N	90.18 W
Arrowrock Reservoir ⊜[1]	202	43.36 N	115.51 W
Arrowsmith	216	40.27 N	88.38 W
Arrowsmith, Mount ∧, Austl.	166	30.09 S	141.50 E
Arrowsmith, Mount ∧, B.C., Can.	224	49.13 N	124.36 W
Arrowsmith, Mount ∧, N.Z.	172	43.21 S	170.59 E
Arrowtown	172	44.56 S	168.50 E
Arrowwood	182	50.44 N	113.09 W
Arroyan, Arroyo ≃[1]	288	34.24 S	58.32 W
Arroyito	252	31.25 S	63.03 W
Arroyo	240m	17.58 N	66.04 W
Arroyo de la Luz	34	39.29 N	6.35 W
Arroyo Grande	204	35.07 N	120.35 W
Arroyo Grande → Ismael Cortinas	258	33.58 S	57.06 W
Arroyo Hondo	200	36.32 N	105.40 W
Arroyo Naranjo ◆[8]	286b	23.02 N	82.23 W
Arroyo Seco	252	33.14 S	60.50 W
Arroyo Seco Park ♠	280	34.06 N	118.12 W
Arroyos y Esteros	252	25.04 S	57.06 W
Arrozal	256	22.37 S	44.03 W
Ar-Ru'at	140	12.21 N	32.17 E
Ar-Rub' al-Khālī ◆[2]	118	20.00 N	51.00 E
Ar-Rubayqī	142	30.10 N	31.46 E
Ar-Ruḥaybah	132	33.45 N	36.42 E
Ar-Rukhaymīyah ⍑[4]	128	29.14 N	45.35 E
Ar-Rumaythah	128	31.32 N	45.12 E
Ar-Rummān	132	32.10 N	35.50 E
Ar-Ruqayyah ⊥	132	32.47 N	37.05 E
Ar-Ruṣāfah ⊥	130	35.37 N	38.45 E
Ar-Ruṣayfah	132	32.01 N	36.03 E
Ar-Ruṣayriṣ	140	11.51 N	34.23 E
Ar-Rushaydah	132	32.40 N	36.50 E
Ar-Ruṭbah	128	33.02 N	40.17 E
Ar-Ru'ūs	142	29.21 N	31.04 E
Ar-Ruways	128	26.08 N	51.13 E
Års	26	56.48 N	9.32 E
Aršan, Ross.	88	51.54 N	102.27 E
Aršan, Ross.	88	53.54 N	99.54 E
Arsanjān	128	29.56 N	53.18 E
Aršan'-Zel'men'	80	47.36 N	44.36 E
Ārsāpota	272b	22.55 N	88.18 E
Arsbeck	56	51.08 N	6.12 E
Arsenal de Marinha ■	266c	38.39 N	9.09 W
Arsenal Football Club ♠	260	51.33 N	0.06 W

Arsenault Lake ⊜	184	55.06 N	108.30 W
Arsenjev	89	44.10 N	133.15 E
Arsenjevka ≃	89	44.54 N	133.35 E
Arsenjevo	76	53.44 N	36.40 E
Ars-en-Ré	32	46.12 N	1.31 W
Arsi □[4]	144	8.00 N	39.40 E
Arsiè	64	45.59 N	11.45 E
Arsiero	64	45.48 N	11.21 E
Arsikere	122	13.20 N	76.15 E
Arsin	130	40.58 N	39.56 E
Aršincevo	78	45.17 N	36.25 E
Arsk	80	56.06 N	49.54 E
Arslanbob	85	41.21 N	72.56 E
Årslev	41	55.18 N	10.29 E
Arso	164	2.56 S	140.47 E
Arsoli	66	42.02 N	13.01 E
Ársos	130	34.50 N	32.46 E
Ars-sur-Formans	58	45.59 N	4.49 E
Ars-sur-Moselle	56	49.05 N	6.04 E
Årsta havsbad	40	59.05 N	18.10 E
Arsufhsa ≃	84	39.08 N	46.50 E
Årsunda	40	60.32 N	16.44 E
Art, Île I	175f	19.43 S	163.38 E
Árta, Ellás	38	39.09 N	20.59 E
Artà, Esp.	34	39.42 N	3.21 E
Artarmon	274a	33.49 S	151.11 E
Artašat	84	39.59 N	44.33 E
Arta Terme	64	46.28 N	13.01 E
Arteaga	234	18.28 N	102.25 W
Arteche	116	12.17 N	125.22 E
Arte Contemporânea, Museu de ⊎	287b	23.32 S	46.38 W
Artegna	64	46.14 N	13.09 E
Artemare	62	45.52 N	5.42 E
Artemisa	240p	22.49 N	82.46 W
Artemón	38	36.59 N	24.43 E
Artémou	150	15.31 N	12.16 W
Artemovsk → Art'omovsk	83	48.35 N	38.00 E
Artèn	64	46.00 N	11.50 E
Artenay	50	48.05 N	1.53 E
Artern	54	51.22 N	11.17 E
Artesia, Ca., U.S.	280	33.51 N	118.04 W
Artesia, Ms., U.S.	194	33.24 N	88.38 W
Artesia, N.M., U.S.	196	32.50 N	104.24 W
Artesia Lake ⊜	226	38.57 N	119.22 W
Artesia → Mosomane	156	24.04 S	26.15 E
Artesian	198	44.00 N	97.55 W
Arth	58	47.04 N	8.31 E
Arthabaska	206	46.02 N	71.55 W
Arthabaska □[6]	206	46.05 N	72.00 W
Arthal	123	33.16 N	76.11 E
Arthala	272a	28.40 N	77.24 E
Arthies	261	49.06 N	1.48 E
Arthonnay	50	47.56 N	4.13 E
Arthur, On., Can.	212	43.50 N	80.32 W
Arthur, Il., U.S.	194	39.43 N	88.28 W
Arthur, Ne., U.S.	198	41.34 N	101.41 W
Arthur, N.D., U.S.	198	47.06 N	97.13 W
Arthur, Tn., U.S.	192	36.32 N	83.40 W
Arthur ≃, Austl.	166	41.03 S	144.40 E
Arthur ≃, Austl.	168a	33.31 S	116.50 E
Arthur, Lake ⊜[1]	214	40.57 N	80.05 W
Arthur Creek ≃	162	22.55 S	136.45 E
Arthur Kill ⊔	276	40.30 N	74.15 W
Arthurs Pass	172	42.57 S	171.34 E
Arthurs Pass)(	172	42.54 S	171.34 E
Arthur's Pass National Park ♠	172	42.50 S	171.40 E
Arthurs Seat ∧[2]	169	38.21 S	144.57 E
Arthur's Town	238	24.38 N	75.42 W
Arthurton	168b	34.16 S	137.45 E
Arti	86	56.26 N	58.32 E
Artibonite ≃	238	19.15 N	72.47 W
Artico, Océano → Arctic Ocean ⍑[1]	16	85.00 N	170.00 E
Artigas	252	30.24 S	56.28 W
Artigas ◆[8]	286c	10.30 N	66.56 W
Artigas, Casa de ⊥	258	34.39 S	56.03 W
Artik	84	40.37 N	43.59 E
Artilleros	258	34.22 S	57.34 W
Artilleros, Punta ›	258	34.28 S	57.32 W
Artillery Lake ⊜	176	63.09 N	107.52 W
Artlenburg	52	53.22 N	10.29 E
Artney, Glen V	46	56.20 N	4.04 W
Artois □[9]	50	50.30 N	2.30 E
Artois, Collines de l' ⋏[2]	50	50.25 N	2.10 E
Art'om	89	43.22 N	132.13 E
Art'om-Ostrov	84	40.28 N	50.20 E
Art'omovka, Ukr.	78	49.46 N	35.04 E
Art'omovka, Ukr.	83	48.29 N	37.23 E
Art'omovka, Ukr.	83	47.53 N	38.38 E
Art'omovo	83	48.22 N	37.53 E
Art'omovsk, Ross.	86	54.21 N	93.26 E
Art'omovsk, Ukr.	83	48.27 N	38.42 E
Art'omovsk, Ukr.	83	48.35 N	38.00 E
Art'omovskij, Ross.	86	57.21 N	61.54 E
Art'omovskij, Ross.	88	58.12 N	114.45 E
Art'omovskij, Ross.	89	43.27 N	132.22 E
Artova	130	40.03 N	36.19 E
Artpark ♠	284a	43.10 N	79.03 W
Artrutx, Cap d' ›	34	39.56 N	3.48 E
Artuby ≃	62	43.44 N	6.22 E
Artur Nogueira	256	22.35 S	47.09 W
Arturo Merino Benítez, Aeropuerto ⊠	286e	33.23 S	70.49 W
Arturo Segui ◆[8]	258	34.51 S	58.09 W
Artvin	130	41.11 N	41.49 E
Artvin □[4]	130	41.05 N	42.00 E
Artybaš	86	51.48 N	87.16 E
Artyk	74	64.12 N	145.06 E
Aru, Kepulauan II	164	6.00 S	134.30 E
Aru, Tanjung ›	112	2.10 S	116.34 E
Aru, Teluk ⊂	114	4.09 N	98.12 E
Arua	154	3.01 N	30.55 E
Aruã ≃	250	2.39 S	55.38 W
Aruaddin	144	16.15 N	38.43 E
Aruanã	255	14.54 S	51.05 W
Aruângua (Luangwa) ≃	154	15.36 S	30.25 E
Aruba □[2]	241s	12.30 N	69.58 W
Aru Basin ✦[1]	14	5.00 S	134.00 E
Arucas	148	28.07 N	15.31 W
Arue	174s	17.32 S	149.32 W
Arufu	150	7.50 N	9.14 E
Arujá	256	23.24 S	46.20 W
Arujá □[7]	287b	23.24 S	46.20 W
Arumanduba	250	1.29 S	52.29 W
Arume	174m	26.36 N	128.07 E
Arume-wan ⊂	174m	26.35 N	128.08 E
Arun (Pong) ≃, Asia	124	26.49 N	87.09 E
Arun ≃, Eng., U.K.	42	50.48 N	0.33 W
Arunāchal Pradesh □[3]	120	28.30 N	95.00 E
Arundel, P.Q., Can.	206	45.58 N	74.37 W
Arundel, Eng., U.K.	42	50.51 N	0.34 W
Arun Qi	89	48.07 N	123.28 E
Årup	41	55.23 N	10.04 E
Aruppukkottai	122	9.31 N	78.06 E
Arurandeua ≃	250	3.43 S	48.50 W
Arusha	154	3.22 S	36.41 E
Arusha □[4]	154	4.00 S	36.15 E
Arusha Chini	154	3.35 S	37.20 E
Arusha National Park ♠	154	3.17 S	36.56 E
Arut ≃	112	2.42 S	111.34 E
Aruvi ≃	122	8.49 N	79.55 E
Aruwimi ≃	138	1.13 N	23.36 E
Arvada	200	39.48 N	105.05 W
Arvagh	48	53.55 N	7.34 W
Arvajcheer	90	46.15 N	102.48 E
Arve ≃	58	46.12 N	6.08 E
Arverne ◆[8]	276	40.35 N	73.48 W
Arves, Les Aiguilles d' ∧	62	45.08 N	6.21 E
Arvi	120	20.59 N	78.14 E
Arvida	186	48.25 N	71.11 W
Arvidsjaur	24	65.35 N	19.07 E
Arvier	62	45.42 N	7.11 E

	English	Deutsch	Español	Français	Português
≃	River	Fluß	Río	Rivière	Rio
≅	Canal	Kanal	Canal	Canal	Canal
⌊	Waterfall, Rapids	Wasserfall, Stromschnellen	Cascada, Rápidos	Chute d'eau, Rapides	Cascata, Rápidos
⊔	Strait	Meeresstraße	Estrecho	Détroit	Estreito
⊂	Bay, Gulf	Bucht, Golf	Bahía, Golfo	Baie, Golfe	Baía, Golfo
⊜	Lake, Lakes	See, Seen	Lago, Lagos	Lac, Lacs	Lago, Lagos
≡	Swamp	Sumpf	Pantano	Marais	Pântano
⊓	Ice Features, Glacier	Eis- und Gletscherformen	Accidentes Glaciales	Formes glaciaires	Acidentes glaciares
⍑	Other Hydrographic Features	Andere Hydrographische Objekte	Otros Elementos Hidrográficos	Autres données hydrographiques	Outros acidentes hidrográficos

	English	Deutsch	Español	Français	Português
✦	Submarine Features	Untermeerische Objekte	Accidentes Submarinos	Formes de relief sous-marin	Acidentes submarinos
□	Political Unit	Politische Einheit	Unidad Política	Entité politique	Unidade política
⊎	Cultural Institution	Kulturelle Institution	Institución Cultural	Institution culturelle	Instituição cultural
⊥	Historical Site	Historische Stätte	Sitio Histórico	Site historique	Sitio histórico
♠	Recreational Site	Erholungs- und Ferienort	Sitio de Recreo	Centre de loisirs	Area de Lazer
⊠	Airport	Flughafen	Aeropuerto	Aéroport	Aeroporto
■	Military Installation	Militäranlage	Instalación Militar	Installation militaire	Instalação militar
◆	Miscellaneous	Verschiedenes	Misceláneo	Divers	Diversos

ENGLISH: Name | Page | Lat.°′ | Long.°′ — DEUTSCH: Name | Seite | Breite°′ | Länge°′ E = Ost

Name	Page	Lat.°′	Long.°′
Arvieux	62	44.46 N	6.44 E
Arvika	26	59.39 N	12.36 E
Arvillard	62	45.27 N	6.07 E
Arvin	228	35.12 N	118.49 W
Arvo, Lago ⊜	68	39.14 N	16.29 E
Arvon, Mount ∧	190	46.45 N	88.09 W
Arvonia	192	37.40 N	78.20 W
Arvorezinha	252	28.53 S	52.10 W
Arwal	124	25.15 N	84.41 E
Arwala	112	7.41 S	126.49 E
Arxan	89	47.11 N	119.57 E
Aryamūn	142	31.11 N	30.54 E
Aryiroúpolis	267c	37.54 N	23.45 E
Arys'	85	42.26 N	68.48 E
Arys' ≃	85	42.48 N	68.12 E
Arys, ozero ⊜	86	45.50 N	66.20 E
Arzachena	71	41.05 N	9.23 E
Arzamas	80	55.23 N	43.50 E
Arzana	71	39.55 N	9.31 E
Arzano	68	40.55 N	14.16 E
Arzberg	60	50.04 N	12.12 E
Arzew, Golfe d' ⊂	34	35.50 N	0.10 W
Arzew, Salines d' ⊜	34	35.40 N	0.15 W
Arzfeld	56	50.05 N	6.16 E
Arzignano	64	45.31 N	11.20 E
Arziw	148	35.51 N	0.19 W
Arz Lubnān ◆[3]	130	34.14 N	36.03 E
Arzni	84	40.19 N	44.36 E
Arzon ≃	62	45.11 N	3.54 E
Arzúa	34	42.56 N	8.09 W
As, Bel.	56	51.01 N	5.35 E
Aš, Česko.	54	50.10 N	12.10 E
Ås, Nor.	26	59.40 N	10.48 E
Asa, Nihon	96	34.33 N	132.26 E
Aša, Ross.	86	55.00 N	57.16 E
Asa ≃, Nihon	94	35.39 N	139.26 E
Asa ≃, Nihon	96	34.01 N	131.09 E
Asa ≃, Ven.	246	6.50 N	63.18 W
Asab	156	25.29 S	17.59 E
Asaba, Nig.	150	6.12 N	6.44 E
Asaba, Nihon	94	34.42 N	137.56 E
Asad, Buḥayrat al- ⊜[1]	130	36.00 N	38.10 E
Asadābād, Afg.	120	34.52 N	71.09 E
Asadābād, Īrān	128	34.47 N	48.07 E
Asafo	150	6.11 N	0.28 W
Asaga Strait ʮ	174y	14.11 S	169.40 W
Asagaya ◆[8]	268	35.42 N	139.38 E
Aşağıbostancı	130	35.10 N	33.00 E
Aşağıçiğil	130	38.03 N	31.52 E
Aşağı Dağ ∧	84	40.01 N	43.11 E
Aşağı Kuluşağı	130	38.39 N	38.39 E
Aşağılahan	130	38.50 N	39.59 E
Aşağı Mestikân	130	38.25 N	38.46 E
Ašagy-G'ojn'uk	84	41.18 N	47.00 E
Asahan	114	2.23 N	102.33 E
Asahan ≃	114	3.02 N	99.52 E
Asahi, Nihon	94	35.14 N	137.22 E
Asahi, Nihon	94	35.43 N	140.39 E
Asahi, Nihon	94	36.14 N	140.31 E
Asahi, Nihon	94	35.02 N	136.40 E
Asahi, Nihon	94	36.07 N	137.52 E
Asahi, Nihon	94	36.05 N	137.21 E
Asahi, Nihon	94	35.59 N	136.07 E
Asahi, Nihon	94	36.57 N	137.34 E
Asahi, Nihon	96	34.59 N	133.50 E
Asahi, Nihon	96	34.51 N	132.16 E
Asahi, Nihon	96	34.17 N	131.28 E
Asahi ◆[8], Nihon	268	35.29 N	139.33 E
Asahi ◆[8], Nihon	270	34.44 N	135.34 E
Asahi ≃	96	34.36 N	133.58 E
Asahi-dake ∧, Nihon	92a	43.40 N	142.51 E
Asahi-dake ∧, Nihon	94	37.14 N	139.21 E
Asahigawa → Asahikawa	92a	43.46 N	142.22 E
Asahi-gawa-daiichi-dam ◆[6]	96	34.53 N	133.22 E
Asahikawa	92a	43.46 N	142.22 E
Asahikawa-chūtonchi, Rikujō-Jieitai- ■	92a	43.49 N	142.25 E
Asahi-ko ⊜[1]	96	34.56 N	133.51 E
Asahi-sanchi ⋏	92	38.25 N	139.50 E
Asaka	94	35.48 N	139.36 E
Asaka, Camp ■	268	35.47 N	139.36 E
Asakanskij Golec, gora ∧	88	50.18 N	109.55 E
Asakawa	94	37.05 N	140.25 E
Asake ≃	94	35.00 N	136.41 E
Asako	96	35.14 N	134.48 E
Asakura	96	33.23 N	130.44 E
Asakusa ◆[8]	268	35.43 N	139.49 E
Asālafpur ◆[8]	272a	28.38 N	77.05 E
Asale	144	14.22 N	40.32 E
Asale, Lake ⊜	144	14.19 N	40.18 E
Asamankese	150	5.52 N	0.42 W
Asama-yama ∧	94	36.24 N	138.31 E
Asanbani, India	126	22.43 N	86.20 E
Asanbāni, India	126	24.07 N	87.27 E
Asani	154	4.25 S	29.05 E
Asankrangwa	150	5.48 N	2.26 W
Asan-man ⊂	98	36.56 N	126.51 E
Āsānsol, India	126	24.14 N	87.17 E
Āsānsol, India	126	23.41 N	86.59 E
Ašap	86	57.07 N	56.30 E
Asar	88	47.56 N	117.38 E
Åsarna	26	62.39 N	14.21 E
Asarum	26	56.12 N	14.50 E
Asashina	94	36.16 N	138.25 E
Āsāsuni	126	22.32 N	89.10 E
Asati	272b	22.29 N	88.14 E
Asa-yama ∧	96	34.47 N	132.23 E
Asayita	144	11.33 N	41.30 E
Asbach	56	50.40 N	7.25 E
Asbeck	263	51.21 N	7.18 E
Asberg	263	51.26 N	6.40 E
Asbesberg ⋏	158	28.55 S	23.15 E
Asbest	86	57.00 N	61.30 E
Asbestos	206	45.46 N	71.57 W
Asbestos Range National Park ♠	166	41.08 S	146.39 E
Asbe Teferi	144	9.02 N	40.58 E
Åsbro	40	59.00 N	15.03 E
Asbury	210	40.41 N	75.00 W
Asbury Park	208	40.13 N	74.01 W
Ascea	68	40.08 N	15.11 E
Ascensión	232	31.06 N	107.59 W
Ascension I	10	7.57 S	14.22 W
Ascent	158	27.12 S	29.03 E
Aščerino	265b	55.36 N	37.46 E
Asch	58	47.57 N	10.49 E
Aščhabad	128	37.57 N	58.23 E
Aščhabad □[8]	128	38.30 N	58.25 E
Aschach an der Donau	61	48.22 N	14.02 E
Aschaffenburg	56	49.59 N	9.09 E
Aschbach Markt	61	48.04 N	14.45 E
Ascheberg, Dtsch.	52	51.47 N	7.37 E
Ascheberg, Dtsch.	54	54.08 N	10.20 E
Aschendorf	52	53.04 N	7.22 E
Aschersleben	54	51.45 N	11.27 E
Asciano	66	43.14 N	11.33 E
Aščikol', ozero ⊜	86	45.05 N	67.15 E
Aščiozek ≃	80	49.12 N	48.06 E
Aščitastysor, ozero ⊜	86	49.19 N	63.59 E
Ascoli Piceno	66	42.51 N	13.34 E
Ascoli Piceno □[4]	66	43.01 N	13.34 E
Ascoli Satriano	68	41.12 N	15.34 E
Ascona	58	46.09 N	8.46 E
Ascope	248	7.43 S	79.07 W
Ascot, Austl.	171a	27.26 S	153.04 E
Ascot, Eng., U.K.	42	51.25 N	0.41 W
Ascot ≃	206	45.21 N	71.51 W
Ascotán	252	21.44 S	68.18 W
Ascros	62	43.55 N	7.01 E
Aščykol', ozero ⊜	85	43.32 N	70.35 E
Aščysu ≃	86	49.54 N	78.58 E
Aseb	144	13.00 N	42.45 E
Åseda	26	57.10 N	15.20 E
Asedjrad ⋏[1]	148	24.28 N	1.52 E
Asekejevo	80	53.36 N	52.49 E
Asela	144	7.59 N	39.08 E
Åsele	26	64.10 N	17.20 E
Asem ≃	115a	6.14 S	107.42 E
Asembagus	115a	7.45 S	114.14 E
Asembourg	56	49.43 N	6.02 E
Åsen	26	63.36 N	11.03 E
Asendabo	144	9.50 N	37.33 E
Asendorf	52	52.46 N	9.00 E
Asenovgrad	38	42.01 N	24.52 E
Åsensbruk	26	58.48 N	12.25 E
Aseri	76	59.27 N	26.52 E
Aşfar, Jabal al- ∧	132	32.12 N	36.54 E
Asfordby	42	52.46 N	0.57 W
Aşfūn al-Maṭā'inah	140	25.23 N	32.32 E
Åsgårdstrand	26	59.21 N	10.28 E
Ash, Eng., U.K.	42	51.17 N	1.16 E
Ash, Eng., U.K.	42	51.15 N	0.44 W
Ashalim	132	30.58 N	34.40 E
Åshammar	40	60.39 N	16.32 E
Ashanti □[4]	150	6.45 N	1.30 W
'Asharah, Wādī al- V	142	30.21 N	32.15 E
Asharoken	276	40.56 N	73.22 W
Ashaway	207	41.25 N	71.47 W
Ashbourne, Ire.	48	53.31 N	6.24 W
Ashbourne, Eng., U.K.	44	53.02 N	1.44 W
Ash Brook Swamp Reservation ♠	276	40.37 N	74.21 W
Ashburn, Ga., U.S.	192	31.42 N	83.39 W
Ashburn, Mo., U.S.	219	39.33 N	91.10 W
Ashburn, Va., U.S.	208	39.02 N	77.29 W
Ashburnham	207	42.38 N	71.54 W
Ashburton, Austl.	274b	37.52 S	145.05 E
Ashburton, N.Z.	172	43.55 S	171.45 E
Ashburton, Eng., U.K.	42	50.31 N	3.45 W
Ashburton ≃, Austl.	162	21.40 S	114.56 E
Ashburton ≃, N.Z.	172	44.04 S	171.48 E
Ashburton, North Branch ≃	172	43.54 S	171.44 E
Ashburton, South Branch ≃	172	43.44 S	171.32 E
Ashburton Downs	162	23.24 S	117.04 E
Ashby	207	42.40 N	71.49 W
Ashby, Lake ⊜	220	28.56 N	81.07 W
Ashby-de-la-Zouch	42	52.46 N	1.28 W
Ashchurch	42	52.00 N	2.07 W
Ash Creek ≃, Ca., U.S.	204	41.05 N	121.08 W
Ash Creek ≃, Ct., U.S.	276	41.08 N	73.14 W
Ashcroft	182	50.43 N	121.17 W
Ashdod, Ma., U.S.	283	42.04 N	70.45 W
Ashdod, Yis.	132	31.49 N	34.40 E
Ashdod, Tel ⊥	132	31.45 N	34.40 E
Ashdot Ya'aqov	132	32.40 N	35.35 E
Ashdown	194	33.40 N	94.07 W
Asheboro	192	35.42 N	79.48 W
Ashern	184	51.11 N	98.21 W
Asherton	196	28.26 N	99.45 W
Asheville	192	35.36 N	82.33 W
Ashewat Ziārat	120	31.22 N	68.32 E
Asheweig ≃	176	54.17 N	87.12 W
Ashfield, Austl.	274a	33.53 S	151.08 E
Ashfield, Ma., U.S.	207	42.31 N	72.47 W
Ash Flat	194	36.13 N	91.36 W
Ashford, Austl.	166	29.20 S	151.06 E
Ashford, Eng., U.K.	42	51.08 N	0.53 E
Ashford, Eng., U.K.	260	51.26 N	0.27 W
Ashford, Al., U.S.	194	31.10 N	85.14 W
Ashford, Wa., U.S.	224	46.46 N	122.02 W
Ashford Airport ⊠	42	51.04 N	1.01 E
Ash Fork	200	35.13 N	112.28 W
Ash Grove	194	37.18 N	93.35 W
Ashhurst	172	40.18 S	175.45 E
Ashibe	92	33.48 N	129.46 E
Ashibetsu	92a	43.31 N	142.11 E
Ashida ≃	96	34.26 N	133.25 E
Ashikaga	94	36.20 N	139.27 E
Ashikagga-gakkō ⊥	94	36.22 N	139.30 E
Ashingdon	260	51.36 N	0.42 E
Ashington	44	55.12 N	1.35 W
Ashino-ko ⊜	94	35.13 N	139.00 E
Ashio	94	36.38 N	139.27 E
Ashio-sanchi ⋏	94	36.35 N	139.30 E
Ashippun	216	43.14 N	88.31 W
Ashippun ≃	216	43.10 N	88.33 W
Ashitaka-yama ∧	94	35.12 N	138.49 E
Ashiya, Nihon	96	33.53 N	130.40 E
Ashiya, Nihon	96	34.43 N	135.17 E
Ashiya ≃	270	34.43 N	135.18 E
Ashiyasu	94	35.38 N	138.23 E
Ashiyoro	92a	43.15 N	143.30 E
Ashizuri-misaki ›	92	32.44 N	133.01 E
Ashizuri-Uwakai-kokuritsu-kōen ♠, Nihon	92	32.45 N	132.45 E
Ashizuri-Uwakai-kokuritsu-kōen ♠, Nihon	96	33.07 N	132.27 E
Ashkhabad → Aščhabad	128	37.57 N	58.23 E
Ashkum	216	40.53 N	87.57 W
Ashland, Al., U.S.	194	33.16 N	85.50 W
Ashland, Ca., U.S.	226	37.41 N	122.06 W
Ashland, Il., U.S.	219	39.53 N	90.00 W
Ashland, Ks., U.S.	198	37.11 N	99.45 W
Ashland, Ky., U.S.	188	38.28 N	82.38 W
Ashland, Me., U.S.	186	46.37 N	68.24 W
Ashland, Ma., U.S.	207	42.15 N	71.27 W
Ashland, Ms., U.S.	194	34.49 N	89.10 W
Ashland, Mo., U.S.	219	38.46 N	92.15 W
Ashland, Mt., U.S.	202	45.35 N	106.16 W
Ashland, Ne., U.S.	198	41.02 N	96.22 W
Ashland, N.H., U.S.	188	43.41 N	71.37 W
Ashland, N.J., U.S.	285	39.51 N	75.00 W
Ashland, N.Y., U.S.	210	42.18 N	74.20 W
Ashland, Oh., U.S.	214	40.52 N	82.19 W
Ashland, Or., U.S.	202	42.11 N	122.42 W
Ashland, Pa., U.S.	210	40.46 N	76.20 W
Ashland, Va., U.S.	208	37.45 N	77.28 W
Ashland, Wi., U.S.	190	46.35 N	90.53 W
Ashland □[6]	214	40.52 N	82.19 W
Ashland, Mount ∧	202	42.05 N	122.43 W
Ashland City	194	36.16 N	87.03 W
Ashley, Austl.	166	29.19 S	149.49 E
Ashley, Eng., U.K.	262	53.21 N	2.20 W
Ashley, Il., U.S.	219	38.20 N	89.11 W
Ashley, In., U.S.	216	41.32 N	85.04 W
Ashley, Mi., U.S.	190	43.11 N	84.28 W
Ashley, Mo., U.S.	219	39.15 N	91.14 W
Ashley, N.D., U.S.	198	46.01 N	99.22 W
Ashley, Oh., U.S.	214	40.24 N	82.57 W
Ashley, Pa., U.S.	210	41.12 N	75.53 W
Ashley ≃	172	43.16 S	172.43 E
Ashley Creek ≃	200	40.21 N	109.22 W
Ashley Falls	207	42.03 N	73.20 W
Ashley Green	260	51.44 N	0.35 W
Ashmore	194	39.32 N	88.01 W
Ashmore Islands II	160	12.14 S	123.05 E
Ashmūn	142	30.18 N	30.58 E
Ashokan Reservoir ⊜[1]	210	41.58 N	74.10 W
Ashoknagar	120	24.34 N	77.43 E
Ashqelon	132	31.40 N	34.35 E
Ashridge Park ♠	260	51.48 N	0.34 W
Ash-Shabakah	128	30.49 N	43.39 E
Ash-Shabb ⊤[4]	140	22.19 N	29.46 E
Ash-Shaddādah	130	36.02 N	40.45 E
Ash-Shāgūr	132	31.50 N	35.39 E
Ash-Shā'ib ∧[2]	142	29.50 N	30.56 E
Ash-Shajarah	132	32.39 N	35.56 E
Ash-Shallūfah	142	30.07 N	32.34 E
Ash-Shamāl □[4]	130	34.30 N	36.00 E
Ash-Shamālīyah □[4]	140	19.15 N	29.00 E
Ash-Shāmīyah	128	31.57 N	44.36 E
Ash-Shanāwīyah	142	29.08 N	31.08 E
Ash-Sharāh ◆[1]	132	30.20 N	35.30 E
Ash-Shāriqah	128	25.22 N	55.23 E
Ash-Sharmah	128	28.01 N	35.18 E
Ash-Sharqāṭ	128	35.27 N	43.16 E
Ash-Sharqīyah □[4]	142	30.48 N	31.48 E
Ash-Sharqīyah ◆[1]	128	27.00 N	49.00 E
Ash-Shaṭrah	128	31.25 N	46.10 E
Ash-Shawāshinah	142	29.22 N	30.36 E
Ash-Shawbak	132	30.32 N	35.34 E
Ash-Shawmarah	132	33.07 N	35.08 E
Ash-Shaykh Faḍl	142	28.29 N	30.50 E
Ash-Shaykh 'Ibādah	142	27.48 N	30.52 E
Ash-Shaykh Sa'd	132	32.50 N	36.02 E
Ash-Shaykh Timay	142	27.53 N	30.51 E
Ash-Shiḥr	144	14.44 N	49.35 E
Ash-Shīn	142	31.01 N	30.53 E
Ash-Shināfīyah	128	31.35 N	44.39 E
Ash-Shīyāḥ	132	33.51 N	35.30 E
Ash-Shufayyah	128	23.50 N	39.08 E
Ash-Shuhadā'	142	30.36 N	30.54 E
Ash-Shumlul	128	26.31 N	47.19 E
Ash-Shuqayq	144	17.43 N	42.01 E
Ash-Shurayf	128	25.43 N	39.14 E
Ash-Shurayk	140	18.48 N	33.34 E
Ash-Shuwayfāt	132	33.49 N	35.31 E
Ash Slough ≃	226	37.02 N	120.32 W
Ashta, India	122	16.57 N	74.24 E
Ashta, India	124	23.01 N	76.43 E
Ashtabula	214	41.51 N	80.47 W
Ashtabula □[6]	214	41.44 N	80.46 W
Ashtabula ≃	214	41.55 N	80.47 W
Ashtabula, East Branch ≃	214	41.48 N	80.37 W
Ashtabula, Lake ⊜[1]	198	47.11 N	97.58 W
Ashtabula, West Branch ≃	214	41.48 N	80.37 W
Ashtead	260	51.19 N	0.18 W
Ashton, S. Afr.	158	33.50 S	20.05 E
Ashton, Eng., U.K.	262	53.13 N	2.45 W
Ashton, Id., U.S.	202	44.04 N	111.26 W
Ashton, Il., U.S.	190	41.51 N	89.13 W
Ashton, Ia., U.S.	198	43.18 N	95.47 W
Ashton, Md., U.S.	208	39.08 N	77.00 W
Ashton, Ne., U.S.	198	41.14 N	98.47 W
Ashton, R.I., U.S.	207	41.46 N	71.25 W
Ashton-in-Makerfield	262	53.29 N	2.39 W
Ashton-under-Lyne	262	53.29 N	2.06 W
Ashton upon Mersey	262	53.26 N	2.19 W
Ashuanipi Lake ⊜	176	52.35 N	66.10 W
Ashuelot ≃	188	42.46 N	72.29 W
Ashurst's Beacon ∧[2]	262	53.34 N	2.45 W
Ashville, Al., U.S.	194	33.52 N	86.17 W
Ashville, N.Y., U.S.	214	42.06 N	79.23 W
Ashville, Oh., U.S.	218	39.42 N	82.57 W
Ashville, Pa., U.S.	214	40.34 N	78.33 W
Ashwater	42	50.44 N	4.16 W
Ashwaubenon	190	44.30 N	88.06 W
Ashworth Moor Reservoir ⊜[1]	262	53.38 N	2.16 W
Asi (Nahr al-'Āṣī) ≃	130	36.02 N	35.58 E
Asia ≐[1]	4	50.00 N	100.00 E
Asia ≐[1]	12	50.00 N	100.00 E
Asia, Kepulauan II	108	1.03 N	131.18 E
Asiago	64	45.52 N	11.30 E
Asia Menor → Asia Minor □[9]	22	39.00 N	32.00 E
Asia Minor □[9]	22	39.00 N	32.00 E
Asid Gulf ⊂	116	12.07 N	123.30 E
Asie → Asia ≐[1]	12	50.00 N	100.00 E
Asie Mineure → Asia Minor □[9]	22	39.00 N	32.00 E
Asien → Asia ≐[1]	12	50.00 N	100.00 E
āsika	120	19.36 N	84.39 E
Asikuma	150	5.35 N	1.00 W
Asilah	148	35.32 N	6.00 W
Asinara, Golfo dell' ⊂	71	41.00 N	8.32 E
Asinara, Isola I	71	41.04 N	8.16 E
Asinaro ≃	70	36.53 N	15.08 E
Asino	86	57.00 N	86.09 E
Asipoquobah Lake ⊜	184	53.40 N	91.15 W
'Asīr ◆[1]	144	19.00 N	42.00 E
Ašitkovo	82	55.26 N	38.36 E
Aşkale	130	39.55 N	40.42 E
Askam in Furness	44	54.11 N	3.13 W
Askanija-Nova	78	46.27 N	33.52 E
Askanija-nova zapovednik ♠	78	46.37 N	33.54 E
Askarovo	86	53.21 N	58.30 E
Askeaton	48	52.36 N	8.58 W
Asker	26	59.50 N	10.26 E
Askern	44	53.37 N	1.09 W
Askersund	40	58.53 N	14.54 E
Askham	158	26.59 S	20.47 E
Askim	26	59.35 N	11.10 E
Askino	86	56.05 N	56.34 E
Askira	146	10.39 N	12.55 E
Askival ∧	46	56.59 N	6.17 W
Askiz	86	53.08 N	90.32 E
Askja ∧[1]	24a	65.00 N	16.48 W
Askø I	41	54.54 N	11.30 E
Asköping	40	59.09 N	16.04 E
Askov	41	55.28 N	9.06 E
Askraal	158	34.09 S	20.52 E
Askrigg	44	54.19 N	2.04 W
Askvoll	26	61.21 N	5.04 E
Aslanapa	130	39.13 N	29.52 E
Aslan-Sara	84	39.02 N	48.16 E
Aslantaş Barajı ⊜[1]	130	37.20 N	36.15 E
Asleigh	284c	39.01 N	77.10 W
Åsljunga	41	56.19 N	13.22 E
Ašlyk	86	57.33 N	68.40 E
Ašlyk ≃	86	57.50 N	69.12 E
Asmār	120	35.02 N	71.22 E
Asmara → Asmera	144	15.20 N	38.53 E
Asmera	144	15.20 N	38.53 E
Asmundtorp	41	55.53 N	12.56 E
Asnæs	41	55.49 N	11.31 E
Asnæs ›[1]	41	55.40 N	11.00 E
Asnebumskit Hill ∧[2]	207	42.18 N	71.54 W
Åsnen ⊜	26	56.38 N	14.42 E
Asni	148	31.14 N	7.55 W
Asnières [-sur-Seine]	50	48.55 N	2.17 E
Asō, Nihon	94	35.59 N	140.29 E
Aso, Nihon	96	32.58 N	131.02 E
Aso ≃	66	43.06 N	13.51 E
Asoc	152	1.26 N	11.18 E
Aso-kokuritsu-kōen ♠	92	33.00 N	131.07 E
Asola	64	45.13 N	10.24 E
Asolo	64	45.48 N	11.54 E
Asomante	240m	18.23 N	66.36 W
Ason	273a	6.34 N	3.31 E
Asosa	144	10.03 N	34.32 E
Aso-san ∧	92	32.53 N	131.06 E
Asoteriba, Jabal ∧	140	21.51 N	36.30 E
Asotin	202	46.20 N	117.02 W
Asouf, Oued V	148	25.51 N	1.33 E
Asowsches Meer → Azovskoje more ⊤[2]	78	46.00 N	36.00 E
Asp	34	38.21 N	0.46 W
Aspach	60	48.11 N	13.18 E
Aspach-le-Bas	58	47.46 N	7.09 E
Aspang Markt	61	47.33 N	16.06 E
Aspara ≃	85	43.17 N	73.28 E
Aspatria	44	54.46 N	3.20 W
Aspe, Gave d' ≃	32	43.12 N	0.36 W
Aspen	200	39.11 N	106.49 W
Aspen Butte ∧	202	42.19 N	122.05 W
Aspendale	274b	38.02 S	145.07 E
Aspendos ⊥	130	37.00 N	31.10 E
Aspen Hill	284c	39.04 N	77.04 W
Aspen Knolls	284c	39.05 N	77.05 W
Aspen Lake ⊜	202	42.18 N	122.00 W
Asperg	56	48.54 N	9.07 E
Aspermont	196	33.08 N	100.13 W
Aspern ◆[8]	264b	48.13 N	16.29 E
Aspers	208	39.59 N	77.13 W
Asperup	41	55.29 N	9.55 E
Aspid, Mount ∧	180	53.30 N	167.33 W
Aspindza	84	41.36 N	43.15 E
Aspinwall	279b	40.29 N	79.54 W
Aspinwall → Colón	236	9.22 N	79.54 W
Aspiring, Mount ∧	172	44.23 S	168.44 E
Aspö	40	59.29 N	17.02 E
Aspres-sur-Buëch	62	44.31 N	5.45 E
Aspromonte ⋏	68	38.10 N	15.55 E
Asprópirgos	267c	38.04 N	23.35 E
Aspull	262	53.34 N	2.35 W
Aspy Bay ⊂	186	46.55 N	60.25 W
Asquins	50	47.29 N	3.45 E
Asquith, Austl.	274a	33.41 S	151.06 E
Asquith, Sk., Can.	184	52.08 N	107.13 W
Asralt chajrchan ∧	88	48.29 N	107.24 E
Asrāni	123	29.31 N	72.07 E
Assa, Kaz.	85	43.02 N	71.10 E
Assa, Magreb	148	28.34 N	9.27 W
Assa ≃, Kaz.	85	43.55 N	70.25 E
Assa ≃, Ross.	84	43.13 N	45.25 E
As-Sa'ata	140	13.37 N	29.59 E
Assab → Aseb	144	13.00 N	42.45 E
Assabet ≃	283	42.28 N	71.21 W
As-Sabkhah	130	35.48 N	39.15 E
Aş-Şadārah	144	14.30 N	48.04 E
As-Sa'dīyah	128	34.11 N	45.07 E
Aş-Şaff	140	29.34 N	31.17 E
Aş-Şaffānīyah	128	27.58 N	48.47 E
Aş-Şāfī	132	31.02 N	35.28 E
Aş-Şafīrah	130	36.04 N	37.22 E
Aş-Şāfiyah	140	15.31 N	30.07 E
Assago	266b	45.24 N	9.08 E
Assaí	255	23.22 S	50.49 W
Aş-Şa'īd □[9]	140	26.00 N	32.00 E
Assaikwatamo ≃	184	56.52 N	95.50 W
Assal, Lac ⊜	144	11.41 N	42.25 E
'Assāl al-Ward	132	33.52 N	36.24 E
Aş-Şāliḥīyah	142	30.47 N	31.59 E
As-Salīmah	144	14.02 N	45.46 E
As-Sallūm	140	31.34 N	25.09 E
As-Salmān	128	30.30 N	44.32 E
As-Salṭ	132	32.03 N	35.44 E
Assam □[3]	120	26.00 N	93.00 E
As-Samāwah	128	31.18 N	45.17 E
As-Samū'	132	31.24 N	35.04 E
Assam Valley V	124	26.30 N	90.30 E
'Assān	130	36.05 N	37.14 E
Aş-Şanāfīn Al-Qiblīyah	142	30.27 N	31.18 E
Aş-Şanamayn	132	33.05 N	36.10 E
As-Santah	142	30.45 N	31.08 E
Assaq, Oued V	148	25.41 N	14.40 W
Aş-Şaqlabiyah	130	35.22 N	36.23 E
Aş-Şarafand	132	33.27 N	35.18 E
Assaré	250	6.52 S	39.52 W
Aş-Şarīḥ	132	32.30 N	35.54 E
As-Sarīrīyah	142	28.20 N	30.45 E
Assateague Island I	208	38.05 N	75.10 W
Assateague Island National Seashore ♠	208	38.00 N	75.15 W
Assawoman Bay ⊂	208	38.25 N	75.05 W
Assawoman Canal ≅	208	38.31 N	75.04 W
Assawompset Pond ⊜	207	41.50 N	70.55 W
Asse	50	50.55 N	4.12 E
Asse ≃	62	43.53 N	5.53 E
Assean Lake ⊜	184	56.13 N	96.30 W
Assebroek	50	51.12 N	3.16 E
Assekaifaf	148	27.08 N	8.50 E
Assel	52	53.41 N	9.25 E
Asseln ◆[8]	263	51.32 N	7.35 E
Assembleia Nacional, Palacio da ʊ	266c	38.43 N	9.09 W
Assemini	71	39.17 N	9.00 E
Assen	52	52.59 N	6.34 E
Assendelft	52	52.27 N	4.45 E
Assenede	50	51.14 N	3.45 E
Assens	41	55.16 N	9.55 E
Asserbo	41	56.01 N	12.01 E
Assergi	66	42.25 N	13.30 E
Asseria ⊥	36	44.02 N	15.39 E
As-Sīb	128	23.41 N	58.11 E
As-Sidr	128	23.27 N	39.45 E
As-Sijn	132	32.47 N	36.28 E
As-Simākīyah	132	31.18 N	35.48 E
As-Sinbillāwayn	142	30.53 N	31.27 E
Assíni ⊥	38	37.36 N	22.48 E
Assiniboia	184	49.38 N	105.59 W
Assiniboine ≃	184	49.53 N	97.08 W
Assiniboine, Mount ∧	182	50.52 N	115.39 W
Assiniboine Indian Reserve ◆[4]	184	50.21 N	103.28 W
Assinika ≃	184	52.37 N	96.10 W
Assinippi	283	42.09 N	70.51 W
Assis	255	22.40 S	50.25 W
Assis Chataaubriand	252	24.29 S	53.32 W
Assiscunk Creek ≃	208	40.05 N	74.51 W
Assisi	66	43.04 N	12.37 E
Asslar	56	50.35 N	8.28 E
Assling	60	48.00 N	12.00 E
Asso	62	45.52 N	9.16 E
Assodé ⊤[4]	150	18.26 N	8.28 E
Assomada	150a	15.06 N	23.41 W
Assonet	207	41.47 N	71.04 W
Assoro	70	37.37 N	14.25 E
As-Subū' ⊥	140	22.45 N	32.34 E
As-Sūdān → Sudan □[1]	140	15.00 N	30.00 E
As-Sudd ◆[1]	140	8.00 N	31.00 E
As-Sufāl	144	14.06 N	48.42 E
Aş-Şufayyah	140	15.30 N	34.42 E
Aş-Şūfīyah	142	30.55 N	31.46 E
As-Sukhnah, Sūrīy.	130	34.52 N	38.52 E
As-Sukhnah, Urd.	132	32.08 N	36.04 E
As-Sulaymānīyah, Ar. Su.	128	24.09 N	47.19 E
As-Sulaymānīyah, 'Irāq	128	35.33 N	45.26 E
As-Sulaymānīyah □[4]	128	35.30 N	45.25 E
As-Sulaymī	128	26.17 N	41.21 E
As-Sulayyil	144	20.27 N	45.34 E
As-Sulṭān	146	31.07 N	17.10 E
As-Sumayḥ	140	9.49 N	27.39 E
Aş-Şummān ◆[1]	128	25.00 N	47.00 E
As-Summāqīyāt	132	32.26 N	36.24 E
Assumption, Il., U.S.	219	39.31 N	89.02 W
Assumption, Oh., U.S.	216	41.40 N	83.54 W
Assumption Island I	138	9.45 S	46.30 E
Assunpink Creek ≃	285	40.13 N	74.46 W
As-Su'ūdīyah	142	29.33 N	31.14 E
Aş-Şuwār	130	35.30 N	40.39 E
As-Suwaydā'	132	32.42 N	36.34 E
As-Suwaydā' □[8]	132	32.45 N	36.45 E
As-Suways (Suez)	142	29.58 N	32.33 E
As-Suways □[4]	142	30.12 N	32.30 E
Assynt, Loch ⊜	46	58.11 N	5.06 W
Ašt	85	40.41 N	70.20 E
Asta, Cima d' ∧	64	46.10 N	11.36 E
Astachovo	83	47.52 N	39.37 E
Astaffort	32	44.04 N	0.40 E
Astakós	38	38.32 N	21.05 E
Āstāneh, Īrān	128	37.17 N	49.59 E
Āstāneh, Īrān	128	33.53 N	49.22 E
Astara, Azer.	84	38.28 N	48.52 E
Āstārā, Īrān	128	38.26 N	48.52 E
Aštarak	84	40.18 N	44.22 E
Astaškovo	82	55.32 N	38.38 E
Astatula	220	28.43 N	81.44 W
Asten, Ned.	52	51.24 N	5.45 E
Asten, Öst.	61	48.13 N	14.25 E
Asti	62	44.54 N	8.12 E
Asti □[4]	62	44.55 N	8.10 E
Astica	252	30.56 S	67.23 W
Astico ≃	64	45.37 N	11.37 E
Astillero	34	43.24 N	3.49 W
Astipálaia	38	36.30 N	26.30 E
Astipálaia I	38	36.35 N	26.25 E
Astley Bridge	262	53.36 N	2.26 W
Astley Green	262	53.29 N	2.27 W
Astley Hall ⊥	262	53.39 N	2.38 W
Astola Island I	128	25.07 N	63.51 E
Astolfo Dutra	256	21.19 S	42.52 W
Aston, Eng., U.K.	262	53.18 N	2.40 W
Aston, Pa., U.S.	285	39.52 N	75.26 W
Aston Clinton	42	51.48 N	0.44 W
Aston-on-Trent	42	52.52 N	1.23 W
Astor	123	35.22 N	74.51 E
Astor ≃	123	35.34 N	74.41 E
Astorga, Bra.	255	23.13 S	51.40 W
Astorga, Esp.	34	42.27 N	6.03 W
Astorga, Pil.	116	6.54 N	125.27 E
Astoria, Il., U.S.	219	40.13 N	90.21 W
Astoria, Or., U.S.	224	46.11 N	123.49 W
Astoria ◆[8]	276	40.46 N	73.55 W
Astoria Bridge ◆[5]	224	46.13 N	123.52 W
Astoria Column ⊥	224	46.11 N	123.50 W
Åstorp	41	56.08 N	12.57 E
Astove Island I	138	10.06 S	47.45 E
Astra	254	45.44 S	67.30 W
Astrachan'	80	46.21 N	48.03 E
Astrachanka	86	51.33 N	69.47 E
Astrachanskij	80	46.12 N	47.16 E
Astrachanskij zapovednik ◆[4]	80	46.00 N	48.32 E
Astrakhan → Astrachan'	80	46.21 N	48.03 E
Astrodome ♠	222	29.41 N	95.25 W
Astrolabe, Cape ›	175e	8.20 S	160.34 E
Astrolabe Bay ⊂	164	5.20 S	145.50 E
Astrolabe Reefs ✢[2]	175f	19.48 S	165.37 E
Astudillo	34	42.12 N	4.18 W
Astura, Torre ⊥	66	41.24 N	12.46 E
Asturias	116	10.34 N	123.43 E
Asturias □[4], Esp.	34	43.20 N	6.00 W
Asturias □[4], Esp.	34	43.20 N	6.00 W
Astwood Bank	42	52.15 N	1.56 W
Asubulak	86	49.31 N	83.03 E
Asuisui, Cape ›	175a	13.47 S	172.29 W
Asuka	96	34.28 N	135.50 E
Asuka ʊ[3]	9	71.32 S	24.08 E
Asuke	94	35.08 N	137.19 E
Asunción	252	25.16 S	57.40 W
Asunción, Bahía ⊂	232	27.06 N	114.11 W
Asuncion Island I	108	19.40 N	145.24 E
Asunción Ixtaltepec	234	16.30 N	95.03 W
Asunción Mita	236	14.20 N	89.43 W
Asunción Nochixtlán	234	17.28 N	97.14 W
Åsunden ⊜, Sve.	26	57.58 N	15.50 E
Åsunden ⊜, Sve.	26	57.44 N	13.22 E
Asunga, Wādī V	146	13.21 N	22.17 E
Asuni	71	39.52 N	8.56 E
'Āṣūr, Tall ∧	132	31.59 N	35.17 E
Asuwa	94	36.01 N	136.16 E
Asuwa ≃	94	36.04 N	136.11 E
Aswad, Ar-Ra's al- ›	144	21.22 N	39.08 E
Aswān	140	24.05 N	32.53 E
Aswān High Dam → 'Ālī, As-Sadd al- ◆[6]	140	23.58 N	32.52 E
Aswatthaberia	272b	22.26 N	88.32 E
Asy ≃	85	43.31 N	78.20 E
Asyūṭ	142	27.11 N	31.11 E
Asyūṭ □[4]	142	27.20 N	30.50 E
Asyūṭī, Wādī al- V	142	27.11 N	31.16 E
Aszód	30	47.39 N	19.31 E
'Ata I, Tonga	14	22.20 S	176.12 W
Ata I, Tonga	174w	21.03 S	175.00 W
Atabaj	85	43.30 N	68.20 E
Atabapo ≃	246	4.03 N	67.42 W
Atabasca, Lago → Athabasca, Lake ⊜	176	59.07 N	110.00 W
Atabasca → Athabasca ≃	176	58.40 N	110.50 W
Atabey	130	37.57 N	30.39 E
Atacama □[4]	252	27.30 S	70.00 W
Atacama, Desierto de ◆[2]	18	24.30 S	69.15 W
Atacama, Puna de ⋏[1]	252	24.30 S	67.30 W
Atacama, Salar de ≚	252	23.30 S	68.15 W
Ataco	246	3.35 N	75.23 W
Atacora, Chaîne de l' ⋏	150	10.45 N	1.30 E
Atacuari ≃	246	3.47 S	70.44 W
Atafu I[1]	14	8.33 S	172.30 W
Atagaj	88	55.06 N	99.23 E
Atago-yama ∧, Nihon	94	35.07 N	139.59 E
Atago-yama ∧, Nihon	96	35.03 N	135.37 E
Ātāi ≃[1]	126	22.51 N	89.33 E
'Aṭā'iṭah, Jabal al- ∧	132	30.40 N	35.39 E
Atakakup Indian Reserve ◆[4]	184	53.24 N	106.55 W
Atakano-seki ⊥	94	36.24 N	136.25 E
Ataki	78	48.25 N	27.47 E
Atakora □[5]	150	10.00 N	1.35 E
Atakora, Réserve d' ◆[4]	150	11.30 N	2.10 E
Atakpamé	150	7.32 N	1.08 E
Atalaia, Bra.	250	9.31 S	36.02 W
Atalaia, Port.	266c	38.42 N	8.55 W
Atalándi	38	38.39 N	23.00 E
Atalanka	88	54.50 N	103.05 E
Atalaya, Arg.	258	35.02 S	57.32 W
Atalaya, Pan.	236	8.03 N	80.56 W
Atalaya, Perú	248	10.44 S	73.45 W
Atalaya, Cerro ∧, Chile	254	52.45 S	72.42 W
Atalaya, Cerro ∧, Perú	248	12.38 S	71.56 W
Atalaya, Punta ›	258	35.01 S	57.31 W
Atamanovka	88	51.56 N	113.37 E
Atamanovo	86	56.24 N	93.36 E
Atambua	112	9.07 S	124.54 E
Atami	94	35.05 N	139.04 E
Atapupu	112	9.00 S	124.51 E
'Atāq	144	14.33 N	46.48 E
'Atāqah, Jabal ⋏	142	29.58 N	32.20 E
Atâr	150	20.31 N	13.03 W
Ataram, 'Erg n- ◆[2]	148	23.46 N	1.44 E
Atarés, Castillo de ⊥	286b	23.08 N	82.21 W
Atāri	123	31.36 N	74.35 E
Atary	80	57.32 N	49.18 E
Atascadero	226	35.29 N	120.40 W
Atascosa ≃	196	28.26 N	98.12 W
At'aševo	80	54.36 N	46.06 E
Atasu	86	48.42 N	71.38 E
Atas uul ∧	102	43.18 N	96.36 E
Atata I	174w	21.03 S	175.15 W
Atatürk Barajı ⊜[1]	130	37.30 N	38.30 E
Ataturk Tower ⊥	267b	41.00 N	28.59 E
Ataur	272a	28.43 N	77.24 E
Atauro, Pulau I	112	8.13 S	125.35 E
Atbara ('Aṭbarah) ≃	140	17.40 N	33.56 E
'Aṭbarah	140	17.42 N	33.59 E
'Aṭbarah (Atbara) ≃	140	17.40 N	33.56 E
Atbasar	86	51.48 N	68.20 E
At-Baši	85	41.10 N	75.48 E
Atbaši ≃	85	41.24 N	75.38 E
Atbaši, chrebet ⋏	85	40.55 N	75.40 E
Atchafalaya ≃	194	29.53 N	91.28 W
Atchafalaya Bay ⊂	194	29.25 N	91.20 W
Atchison	198	39.33 N	95.07 W
Atco	208	39.46 N	74.53 W
Ate	286d	12.03 S	76.58 W
Atebubu	150	7.45 N	0.59 W
Ateca	34	41.20 N	1.47 W
Atelchu ≃	255	12.05 S	53.46 W
Ateleta	66	41.51 N	14.12 E
Ateli	124	28.06 N	76.17 E
Atella	68	40.52 N	15.39 E
Atemajac de Brizuela	234	20.11 N	103.42 W
Atemar	80	54.11 N	45.24 E
Atemble	164	5.05 S	144.45 E
Atena Lucana	68	40.27 N	15.33 E
Atenango del Río	234	18.05 N	99.06 W
Atenas → Athínai	38	37.58 N	23.43 E
Atencingo	234	18.30 N	98.36 W
Atengo ≃	234	21.50 N	104.43 W
Atenguillo	234	20.25 N	104.31 W
Atenguillo ≃	234	20.55 N	104.38 W
Atenquique	234	19.31 N	103.30 W
Atepcevo	82	55.20 N	36.46 E
Aterno ≃	66	42.11 N	13.51 E
Aterrado, Ribeirão do ≃	256	22.09 S	45.03 W
Atessa	66	42.04 N	14.27 E
Atfīh	142	29.24 N	31.15 E
Aṭfīhī, Wādī al- V	142	29.23 N	31.16 E
Ātgharia	126	24.06 N	89.14 E
Atglen	208	39.57 N	75.58 W
Ath	50	50.38 N	3.47 E
Athabasca	182	54.43 N	113.17 W
Athabasca ≃	176	58.40 N	110.50 W
Athabasca, Lake ⊜	176	59.07 N	110.00 W
Athalmer	182	50.32 N	116.02 W
Athapapuskow Lake ⊜	184	54.33 N	101.40 W
Athārabānki ≃[1]	126	22.49 N	89.39 E
Athārān Hazāri	123	31.11 N	72.06 E
Athboy	48	53.37 N	6.55 W
Athea	48	52.28 N	9.17 W
Athena	202	45.48 N	118.29 W
Athen → Athínai	38	37.58 N	23.43 E
Athènes → Athínai	38	37.58 N	23.43 E
Athenry	48	53.18 N	8.45 W
Athens, On., Can.	212	44.38 N	75.57 W
Athens, Al., U.S.	194	34.48 N	86.58 W
Athens, Ga., U.S.	192	33.57 N	83.22 W
Athens, Il., U.S.	219	39.57 N	89.43 W
Athens, La., U.S.	194	32.39 N	93.01 W
Athens, Mi., U.S.	216	42.05 N	85.14 W
Athens, N.Y., U.S.	210	42.15 N	73.48 W
Athens, Oh., U.S.	188	39.19 N	82.06 W
Athens, Pa., U.S.	210	41.57 N	76.31 W
Athens, Tn., U.S.	192	35.26 N	84.35 W
Athens, Tx., U.S.	222	32.12 N	95.51 W
Athens, W.V., U.S.	192	37.25 N	81.00 W
Athens, Wi., U.S.	190	45.01 N	90.04 W
Athens → Athínai	38	37.58 N	23.43 E
Athenstedt	54	51.56 N	10.55 E
Athens University ʊ[2]	267c	37.59 N	23.44 E
Atherley	212	44.36 N	79.22 W
Atherstone	42	52.35 N	1.31 W
Atherton, Austl.	166	17.16 S	145.29 E
Atherton, Eng., U.K.	262	53.31 N	2.31 W
Atherton, Ca., U.S.	226	37.27 N	122.11 W
Athi ≃	154	2.59 S	38.31 E
Athiaínou	130	35.04 N	33.32 E
Athiémé	150	6.35 N	1.40 E
Athies-sous-Laon	50	49.34 N	3.41 E
Athínai (Athens), Ellás	38	37.58 N	23.43 E
Athínai (Athens), Ellás	267c	37.58 N	23.43 E
Äthiopien → Ethiopia □[1]	144	9.00 N	39.00 E
Athi River	154	1.27 S	36.59 E
Athis-Mons	261	48.43 N	2.24 E
Athlat al-Bāshā ∧[2]	142	27.31 N	32.20 E
Athleague	48	53.34 N	8.15 W
Athlone	48	53.25 N	7.56 W
Athni	122	16.44 N	75.04 E
Athok	110	17.12 N	95.05 E
Athol, N.Z.	172	45.31 S	168.35 E
Athol, Ma., U.S.	207	42.35 N	72.13 W
Athol Bay ⊂	212	43.53 N	77.15 W
Athol Island I	240b	25.05 N	77.16 W
Atholl, Forest of ◆[3]	46	56.50 N	4.00 W
Athol Springs	210	42.46 N	78.52 W
Áthos ∧	38	40.09 N	24.19 E
Ath-Tha'lah	132	32.42 N	36.26 E
Ath-Thamad	140	29.41 N	34.18 E
Ath-Thanīyah	132	31.10 N	35.43 E
Athus	56	49.34 N	5.50 E
Athy	48	53.00 N	7.00 W
Ati	146	13.13 N	18.20 E
Atiak	154	3.15 N	32.07 E
Atibaia	256	23.07 S	46.33 W
Atibainha ≃	256	22.42 S	47.17 W
Atibainha, Reservatório ⊜[1]	256	23.10 S	46.20 W
Atico	248	16.14 S	73.39 W
Aticonipi, Lac ⊜	186	51.52 N	59.22 W
Atienza	34	41.12 N	2.52 W
Atigun Pass)(	180	68.08 N	149.29 W
Atik Lake ⊜	184	55.16 N	96.00 W
Atikokan	190	48.45 N	91.37 W
Atikonak Lake ⊜	176	52.40 N	64.30 W
Atil	200	30.50 N	111.35 W
Atimari ≃	248	9.04 S	67.23 W
Atimonan	116	14.00 N	121.55 E
Atina	66	41.37 N	13.48 E
Atiparaná ≃[1]	246	1.51 S	65.37 W
Atiquizaya	236	13.58 N	89.46 W
Atirāmpattinam	122	10.21 N	79.24 E
Atitlán, Lago de ⊜	236	14.42 N	91.12 W
Atitlán, Volcán ∧[1]	236	14.35 N	91.11 W
Atiu I	14	20.02 S	158.07 W
Atka, Ross.	74	60.50 N	151.48 E
Atka, Ak., U.S.	180	52.12 N	174.12 W
Atka Island I	180	52.15 N	174.30 W
Atkaracalar	130	40.50 N	33.04 E
Atkarsk	80	51.52 N	45.00 E
Atkins	194	35.14 N	92.56 W
Atkinson, Il., U.S.	190	41.25 N	90.00 W
Atkinson, Ne., U.S.	198	42.31 N	98.58 W
Atkinson, N.H., U.S.	207	42.50 N	71.08 W
Atkinson, N.C., U.S.	192	34.31 N	78.10 W
Atkinson Island I	222	29.40 N	94.58 W
Atkinson Lake ⊜	184	55.59 N	94.48 W
Atkri	164	1.44 S	130.04 E
Atlacomulco	234	19.48 N	99.53 W
Atlanta, Ga., U.S.	192	33.44 N	84.23 W
Atlanta, Il., U.S.	194	40.15 N	89.14 W
Atlanta, Mi., U.S.	190	45.00 N	84.08 W
Atlanta, Mo., U.S.	194	39.53 N	92.28 W
Atlanta, N.Y., U.S.	210	42.33 N	77.28 W
Atlanta, Oh., U.S.	218	39.34 N	83.11 W
Atlanta, Tx., U.S.	194	33.06 N	94.09 W
Atlantic, Ia., U.S.	198	41.24 N	95.00 W
Atlantic, N.C., U.S.	192	34.53 N	76.20 W
Atlantic, Pa., U.S.	214	41.30 N	80.21 W
Atlantic, Va., U.S.	208	37.54 N	75.30 W
Atlantic □[6]	208	39.27 N	74.44 W
Atlantic Beach, Fl., U.S.	192	30.20 N	81.23 W
Atlantic Beach, N.Y., U.S.	276	40.35 N	73.44 W
Atlantic City	208	39.21 N	74.25 W
Atlantic Highlands	208	40.24 N	74.02 W
Atlantic-Indian Basin ✢[1]	6	60.00 S	15.00 E
Atlantic-Indian Ridge ✢[3]	4	53.00 S	15.00 E
Atlántico □[5]	246	10.45 N	75.00 W
Atlántico, Océano → Atlantic Ocean ⊤[1]	8	5.00 S	25.00 W
Atlantic Ocean ⊤[1]	4	5.00 S	25.00 W
Atlantic Ocean ⊤[1]	8	5.00 S	25.00 W
Atlantic Peak ∧	200	42.37 N	109.00 W
Atlántida	252	34.46 S	55.45 W
Atlántida □[5]	236	15.40 N	87.00 W
Atlantique	276	40.39 N	73.10 W
Atlantique □[5]	150	6.35 N	2.15 E
Atlantique, Océan → Atlantic Ocean ⊤[1]	8	5.00 S	25.00 W
Atlantischer Ozean → Atlantic Ocean ⊤[1]	8	5.00 S	25.00 W
Atlas, Mi., U.S.	216	42.56 N	83.32 W
Atlas, Pa., U.S.	208	40.48 N	76.26 W
Atlasburg	214	40.20 N	80.23 W
Atlas Mountains ⋏	148	33.00 N	2.00 W
Atlasova, ostrov I	74	50.53 N	155.27 E
Atlasovo	92a	46.01 N	142.09 E
Atlas Saharien ⋏	148	33.25 N	1.20 E
Atlas Tellien ⋏	148	36.00 N	3.00 E
Atlin	180	59.35 N	133.42 W
Atlin Lake ⊜	180	59.20 N	133.45 W
'Atlit	132	32.41 N	34.56 E
Atlixco	234	18.54 N	98.26 W
Ātmakūr	122	15.53 N	78.35 E
Atmanov Ugol	80	53.07 N	41.23 E
Atmis	80	53.28 N	43.57 E
Atmore	194	31.01 N	87.29 W
Åtna ≃	26	61.44 N	10.49 E
Ätna → Etna, Monte ∧[1]	70	37.46 N	15.00 E
Atna Peak ∧	182	53.57 N	128.03 W
Atnarko ≃	182	52.22 N	126.04 W
Atnis	86	58.48 N	69.38 E
Atnosen	26	61.44 N	10.49 E

Symbols in the index entries represent the broad categories identified in the key at the right. Symbols with superior numbers (⋏[1]) identify subcategories (see complete key on page *I · 1).*

Symbole im Register stellen die rechts im Schlüssel erklärten Kategorien dar. Symbole mit hochgestellten Ziffern (⋏[1]) bezeichnen Unterabteilungen einer Kategorie (vgl. vollständiger Schlüssel auf Seite *I · 1).*

Los símbolos incluídos en el texto del índice representan las grandes categorias identificadas con la clave a la derecha. Los símbolos con numeros en su parte superior (⋏[1]) identifican las subcategorías (véase la clave completa en la página *I · 1).*

Les symboles de l'index représentent les catégories indiquées dans la légende à droite. Les symboles suivis d'un indice (⋏[1]) représentent des sous-catégories (voir légende complète à la page *I · 1).*

Os símbolos incluídos no texto do índice representam as grandes categorias identificadas com a chave à direita. Os símbolos com números em sua parte superior (⋏[1]) identificam as subcategorias (veja-se a chave completa à página *I · 1).*

∧	Mountain	Berg	Montaña	Montagne	Montanha
⋏	Mountains	Gebirge	Montañas	Montagnes	Montanhas
)(	Pass	Paß	Paso	Col	Passo
V	Valley, Canyon	Tal, Cañon	Valle, Cañón	Vallée, Canyon	Vale, Canhão
≚	Plain	Ebene	Llano	Plaine	Planície
›	Cape	Kap	Cabo	Cap	Cabo
I	Island	Insel	Isla	Île	Ilha
II	Islands	Inseln	Islas	Îles	Ilhas
≐	Other Topographic Features	Andere Topographische Objekte	Otros Elementos Topográficos	Autres données topographiques	Outros acidentes topográficos

Nombre / Nom / Nome	Página / Page / Página	Lat.°	Long.° W = Oeste / Ouest / Oeste

ESPAÑOL

Nombre	Página	Lat.°′	Long.°′ W=Oeste
Atō	96	34.24 N	131.43 E
Atocha	248	20.56 S	66.14 W
Atocha, Estación de ⇒⁵	266a	40.24 N	3.41 W
Atocongo	286d	12.08 S	76.56 W
Atocongo ⊥	286d	12.12 S	76.55 W
Atoka	196	34.23 N	96.07 W
Atotonilco	232	24.15 N	102.45 W
Atotonilco, Cerro ⋀	196	26.08 N	104.43 W
Atotonilco, Lago ⊜	234	20.22 N	103.39 W
Atotonilco de Tula	234	20.00 N	99.13 W
Atotonilco El Alto	234	20.33 N	102.31 W
Atoui, Khatt ⋁	150	20.04 N	15.59 W
Atoyac	234	20.01 N	103.32 W
Atoyac ≃, Méx.	234	17.05 N	100.29 W
Atoyac ≃, Méx.	234	19.02 N	96.08 W
Atoyac ≃, Méx.	234	18.10 N	98.31 W
Atoyac ≃, Méx.	234	16.30 N	97.31 W
Atoyac de Álvarez	234	17.12 N	100.26 W
Atoyaquillo □	234	16.37 N	97.41 W
Atpur	272b	22.50 N	88.23 E
Atrā	26	59.59 N	8.45 E
'Atrah, Jabal ⋀	132	29.40 N	35.34 E
Atrai ≃	124	24.29 N	89.03 E
Atrak (Atrek) ≃	128	37.28 N	53.57 E
Ätran ≃	26	56.53 N	12.30 E
Atrato ≃	246	8.17 N	76.58 W
Atrauli	124	28.02 N	78.17 E
Atrek (Atrak) ≃	128	37.28 N	53.57 E
Atri	66	42.35 N	13.58 E
Atripalda	68	40.55 N	14.50 E
Atrisco	200	34.59 N	106.41 W
Atrop ⬥⁻⁸	263	51.24 N	6.43 E
Atsion Lake ⊜	285	39.44 N	74.44 W
Atsugi	94	35.27 N	139.22 E
Atsugi-hikōjō ⊡	94	35.28 N	139.27 E
Atsumi, Ni'hon	92	38.37 N	139.35 E
Atsumi, Ni'hon	94	34.37 N	137.07 E
Atsumi-hantō ⊁¹	94	34.39 N	137.15 E
Atta	272a	28.34 N	77.20 E
At-Tabbīn	142	29.47 N	31.18 E
At-Tafīlah	132	30.50 N	35.36 E
At-Tafīlah □⁸	132	30.45 N	35.45 E
At-Tahrīr □⁴	142	30.40 N	30.15 E
At-Tā'if	144	21.16 N	40.24 E
Attainville	261	49.03 N	2.21 E
At-Tāj	146	24.13 N	23.18 E
At-Talibīyah	273c	30.00 N	31.11 E
At-Tall	132	33.36 N	36.18 E
Attalla	194	34.01 N	86.05 W
At-Tall al-Kabīr	142	30.34 N	31.47 E
At-Ta'mīm □⁴	128	35.25 N	44.20 E
At-Tarmīmī	146	32.20 N	23.04 E
Attapu	110	14.48 N	106.50 E
Attar, Oued el ⋁	148	33.27 N	5.26 E
At-Tatālīyah	142	27.20 N	30.56 E
Attáviros ⋀	38	36.12 N	27.52 E
Attawapiskat	176	52.55 N	82.26 W
Attawapiskat ≃	176	52.57 N	82.18 W
Attawapiskat Lake ⊜	176	52.18 N	87.54 W
Attawaugan	207	41.52 N	71.52 W
At-Tawd	142	30.47 N	30.37 E
At-Tawīl ⋀	132	29.20 N	39.35 E
At-Tayfīyah	142	30.39 N	30.46 E
At-Tayyibah	142	28.01 N	44.00 E
At-Tayyibah, Miṣr	142	28.16 N	30.39 E
At-Tayyibah, Sūrīy.	132	32.33 N	36.14 E
At-Tayyibah, Sūrīy.	132	32.48 N	36.46 E
At-Tayyibah, Urd.	132	32.33 N	35.43 E
Attel ≃	64	48.01 N	12.11 E
Attendorn	58	51.07 N	7.54 E
Attenhausen	58	47.59 N	10.20 E
Attenkirchen	60	48.30 N	11.46 E
Atterbury	219	40.04 N	89.55 W
Attersee ⊜	64	47.52 N	13.33 E
Attersee	64	47.52 N	13.33 E
Attert ≃	58	49.42 N	12.55 E
Attica, In., U.S.	216	40.17 N	87.14 W
Attica, Ks., U.S.	198	37.14 N	98.13 W
Attica, N.Y., U.S.	210	42.52 N	78.16 W
Attica, Oh., U.S.	210	41.03 N	82.53 W
Attigliano	66	42.31 N	12.17 E
Attigny	58	49.29 N	4.35 E
Attiki □⁵	267c	38.00 N	23.40 E
Attíkí □⁹	38	38.00 N	23.30 E
'Attīl	132	32.22 N	35.04 E
At-Tīnah	64	46.11 N	13.16 E
Attingal	122	8.41 N	76.50 E
Attir	140	6.04 N	30.50 E
Attleboro	207	41.56 N	71.17 W
Attleborough	42	52.31 N	1.01 E
Attnang	60	48.01 N	13.43 E
Attock	123	33.54 N	72.15 E
Attoyac ≃	194	31.29 N	94.18 W
Attu	181a	52.56 N	173.14 E
Attu Island	144	12.40 N	43.30 E
Attu Island I	181a	52.55 N	173.00 E
At-Tunayb	132	31.48 N	35.57 E
Āttūr, India	122	11.36 N	78.37 E
At-Tūr, Miṣr	140	28.14 N	33.37 E
At-Tuwayshah	144	12.21 N	26.32 E
At-Tuwayyah	144	23.36 N	41.13 E
Attymon	248	53.19 N	8.36 W
Atucatiquini ≃	248	7.44 S	67.57 W
Atucha	258	33.58 S	59.18 W
Atuel ≃	252	36.17 S	66.50 W
Atuel, Bañados del ≃	252	36.30 S	66.55 W
Atuntaqui	248	0.20 N	78.13 W
Atuona	174x	9.48 S	139.02 W
At'urjevo	54	54.21 N	43.19 E
Ätushi	86	39.43 N	76.08 E
Ätvidaberg	26	58.12 N	16.00 E
Atwater, Sk., Can.	184	50.24 N	103.28 W
Atwater, Ca., U.S.	226	37.20 N	120.36 W
Atwater, Il., U.S.	219	39.20 N	89.44 W
Atwater, Mn., U.S.	198	45.08 N	94.46 W
Atwater, Oh., U.S.	214	41.01 N	81.10 W
Atwood, Can.	210	43.40 N	81.01 W
Atwood, Ca., U.S.	228	33.52 N	117.50 W
Atwood, Il., U.S.	194	39.48 N	88.28 W
Atwood, In., U.S.	216	41.15 N	85.58 W
Atwood, Tn., U.S.	194	35.58 N	88.40 W
Atwood Lake ⊜	214	40.33 N	81.13 W
Atzalpur	272a	28.23 N	77.21 E
Atzendorf	54	51.55 N	11.35 E
Atzgersdorf ⬥⁻⁸	264b	48.09 N	16.18 E
Au	58	47.19 N	9.59 E
Auagrām	126	23.31 N	87.41 E
Auaia-Miçu ≃	250	10.51 S	53.08 W
Aual Island I	146	1.27 S	143.04 E
Aual Edo	144	4.14 N	40.37 E
Auari ≃	246	3.33 N	63.40 W
Auau Channel ⋃	229a	20.51 N	156.45 W
Aub	56	49.33 N	10.04 E
Aubá	112	9.02 S	125.22 E
Aubagne	50	43.17 N	5.34 E
Aubange	58	49.35 N	5.48 E
Aube □⁵	58	48.15 N	4.05 E
Aube ≃	58	48.34 N	3.43 E
Auberas ⬥	62	44.37 N	4.23 E
Aubergenville	261	48.58 N	1.51 E
Auberive	58	47.47 N	5.03 E
Auberry	226	37.04 N	119.29 W
Aubervilliers	261	48.55 N	2.23 E
Aubeterre	60	48.49 N	4.21 E
Aubette ≃	261	49.00 N	1.54 E
Aubigny-en-Artois	50	50.17 N	2.35 E
Aubigny-sur-Nère	58	47.29 N	2.26 E
Aubin	50	44.32 N	2.15 E
Aubinadong ≃	190	46.51 N	83.22 W
Aubonne	58	46.28 N	6.24 E
Aubouè	58	49.13 N	5.59 E
Aubrac ⋀	32	44.40 N	3.00 E
Aubrey Cliffs ⋏ ⁴	200	35.45 N	113.00 W
Aubrey Lake ⊜ ¹	190	46.54 N	83.11 W
Aubrives	58	50.06 N	4.46 E
Aubry Lake ⊜	180	67.23 N	126.30 W
Auburn, Austl.	168b	34.01 S	138.41 E

FRANÇAIS

Nom	Page	Lat.°′	Long.°′ W=Ouest
Auburn, Austl.	274a	33.51 S	151.02 E
Auburn, Al., U.S.	194	32.36 N	85.28 W
Auburn, Ca., U.S.	226	38.53 N	121.04 W
Auburn, Il., U.S.	219	39.35 N	89.44 W
Auburn, In., U.S.	216	41.22 N	85.03 W
Auburn, Ky., U.S.	194	37.02 N	86.54 W
Auburn, Ma., U.S.	188	44.05 N	70.13 W
Auburn, Ma., U.S.	207	42.11 N	71.50 W
Auburn, Ne., U.S.	198	40.23 N	95.50 W
Auburn, N.J., U.S.	285	39.42 N	75.22 W
Auburn, N.Y., U.S.	210	42.55 N	76.33 W
Auburn, Pa., U.S.	208	40.35 N	76.05 W
Auburn, Wa., U.S.	224	47.18 N	122.13 W
Auburn ≃	166	25.38 S	151.12 E
Auburndale, Fl., U.S.	220	28.03 N	81.47 W
Auburndale, Ma., U.S.	283	42.21 N	71.22 W
Auburn Heights	285	42.43 N	83.13 W
Auburn Range ⋏	166	25.10 S	150.30 E
Auburn Ravine ⋁	226	38.51 N	121.31 W
Auburn Southeast	210	42.54 N	76.32 W
Aubusson	32	45.57 N	2.11 E
Auby-sur-Semois	56	49.49 N	5.10 E
Auca Mahuida ⋀	252	37.53 S	68.31 W
Auca Mahuida, Cerro ⋀	252	37.45 S	68.56 W
Aucará	248	14.15 S	74.05 W
Auce	76	56.28 N	22.53 E
Auch	32	43.39 N	0.35 E
Auchel	50	50.30 N	2.28 E
Auchenblae	46	56.54 N	2.26 W
Auchencairn	44	54.51 N	3.53 W
Auchi	150	7.02 N	6.14 E
Auchinleck	46	55.28 N	4.17 W
Auchterarder	46	56.18 N	3.43 W
Auchterderran	46	56.09 N	3.16 W
Auchtermuchty	46	56.17 N	3.15 W
Aucilla ≃	192	30.05 N	83.59 W
Auckland	178	36.52 S	174.46 E
Auckland Islands II	92	50.40 S	166.30 E
Auckland Park ⬥⁻⁸	273d	26.11 S	28.00 E
Auckland Park Race Course ⋁	273d	26.11 S	28.00 E
Aude □⁵	32	43.05 N	2.30 E
Aude ≃	32	43.13 N	3.14 E
Audenge	32	44.41 N	1.00 W
Audenshaw	262	53.28 N	2.08 W
Audenshaw Reservoirs ⊜¹	262	53.28 N	2.08 W
Auderghem	50	50.49 N	4.26 E
Auderville	261	49.43 N	1.56 W
Auderne	32	48.01 N	4.32 W
Audincourt	58	47.29 N	6.50 E
Audley	44	53.03 N	2.18 W
Audobon Park	285	39.54 N	75.05 W
Audo Range ⋏	144	6.30 N	41.30 E
Audrain □⁶	219	39.12 N	91.50 W
Audresselles	50	50.49 N	1.36 E
Audruicq	50	50.53 N	2.05 E
Audubon, Ia., U.S.	198	41.43 N	94.55 W
Audubon, N.J., U.S.	208	39.53 N	75.04 W
Audubon, Pa., U.S.	285	40.07 N	75.27 W
Audubon Park	218	38.12 N	85.43 W
Audun-le-Roman	58	49.22 N	5.53 E
Aue ≃	52	53.05 N	8.04 E
Aue	54	50.35 N	12.42 E
Auer → Ora	64	46.21 N	11.18 E
Auersberg ⋀	54	50.27 N	12.39 E
Auerswalde	54	50.54 N	12.55 E
Auezov	86	49.46 N	81.38 E
Auf dem Kreinberge	263	51.27 N	7.36 E
Auffargis	261	48.42 N	1.53 E
Aufhausen	56	48.33 N	9.26 E
Aufseß	56	49.58 N	11.13 E
Augarten ⬥	264b	48.14 N	16.23 E
Augathella	166	25.48 S	146.35 E
Augher	48	54.26 N	7.09 W
Aughnacloy	48	54.25 N	6.58 W
Aughton, Eng., U.K.	262	53.33 N	3.00 W
Aughton, Eng., U.K.	44	53.22 N	1.18 W
Aughton, Eng., U.K.	262	53.32 N	2.56 W
Aughton Park	262	53.33 N	2.53 W
Aughwick Creek ≃	214	40.22 N	77.50 W
Auglaize □⁶	216	40.34 N	84.12 W
Auglaize ≃	216	41.17 N	84.21 W
Augrabies	158	28.37 S	20.20 E
Augrabies Falls National Park ⋌	158	28.35 S	20.19 E
Augrabiesvalle ⊾	158	28.35 S	20.19 E
Au Gres	190	44.02 N	83.41 W
Au Gres ≃	190	44.02 N	83.40 W
Au Gres, East Branch ≃	190	44.05 N	83.41 W
Augsburg	58	48.23 N	10.53 E
Augusta, Austl.	162	34.19 S	115.10 E
Augusta, It., U.S.	70	37.13 S	15.13 E
Augusta, Ar., U.S.	194	35.16 N	91.21 W
Augusta, Ga., U.S.	192	33.28 N	82.01 W
Augusta, Ks., U.S.	198	37.40 N	96.58 W
Augusta, Me., U.S.	188	44.18 N	69.46 W
Augusta, Me., U.S.	219	38.12 N	81.30 W
Augusta, Mo., U.S.	219	38.34 N	90.53 W
Augusta, Wi., U.S.	198	44.40 N	91.07 W
Augusta, Golfo di ⊂	70	37.12 N	15.13 E
Augustenborg	52	54.57 N	9.53 E
Augustine Island I	180	59.22 N	153.28 W
Augusto Severo	250	5.52 S	37.19 W
Augustów	30	53.51 N	22.59 E
Augustowski, Kanał ⚏	76	53.54 N	23.26 E
Augustus, Mount ⋀	162	24.20 S	116.50 E
Augustus Downs	166	18.33 S	139.52 E
Augustus Island I	164	15.20 S	124.30 E
Auila, Ribeirão ≃	255	12.09 S	53.20 W
Au in der Hallertau	60	48.33 N	11.45 E
Aujon ≃	58	48.09 N	4.48 E
Aulander	192	36.14 N	77.06 W
Aulanko ⬥	26	61.02 N	24.27 E
Auld, Lake ⊜	162	22.32 S	123.44 E
Auldearn	46	57.34 N	3.49 W
Aulendorf	58	47.57 N	9.38 E
Aulestad	26	61.16 N	10.17 E
Aulla	66	44.14 N	9.58 E
Aulnay	32	46.01 N	0.21 W
Aulnay-sous-Bois	32	48.56 N	2.31 E
Aulnay-sur-Mauldre	261	48.56 N	1.51 E
Aulne ≃	32	48.17 N	4.16 W
Aulneau Peninsula ⊁¹	184	49.23 N	94.29 W
Aulnois-sur-Seille	58	48.52 N	6.19 E
Aulnoye-Aymeries	50	50.12 N	3.50 E
Ault, Fr.	50	50.06 N	1.27 E
Ault, Co., U.S.	200	40.35 N	104.43 W
Ault, Ky., U.S.	218	38.11 N	85.55 W
Aultbea	46	57.50 N	5.35 W
Aultman	214	40.46 N	79.16 W
Aultshire ⬥	216	40.13 N	85.19 W
Aumale	50	50.42 N	1.45 E
Aumia Point ⋏	146	1.27 S	149.46 E
Aumont-Aubrac	32	44.43 N	3.17 E
Auna	150	10.12 N	4.45 E
Auneau	58	48.28 N	1.46 E
Auneuil	50	49.22 N	2.00 E
Auning	26	56.26 N	10.23 E

PORTUGUÊS

Nome	Página	Lat.°′	Long.°′ W=Oeste
Auno	146	11.50 N	12.53 E
Aunuu I	174u	14.17 S	170.33 W
Auob ≃	156	26.25 S	20.35 E
Auponhia	112	1.56 S	125.29 E
Aups	62	43.37 N	6.14 E
Aur, Pulau I	112	2.27 N	104.31 E
Aura	26	60.36 N	22.34 E
Aurach	56	49.15 N	10.25 E
Aurach ≃	56	49.34 N	10.59 E
Aurachmat	85	41.34 N	70.07 E
Auraiya	124	26.28 N	79.31 E
Aurangābād, India	122	19.53 N	75.20 E
Aurangābād, India	124	24.45 N	84.22 E
Auray	32	47.40 N	2.59 W
Aurdal	26	60.56 N	9.24 E
Aure	26	63.16 N	8.32 E
Aurei, Kepulauan II	164	1.59 S	134.42 E
Aurich	52	53.28 N	7.29 E
Auriesville Shrine ⬥¹	210	42.54 N	74.19 W
Aurillama	255	20.41 S	50.34 W
Aurillac	32	44.56 N	2.26 E
Aurina, Valle ⋁	64	47.00 N	12.00 E
Aurine, Alpi (Zillertaler Alpen) ⋀	64	47.00 N	11.55 E
Aurino ≃	64	46.48 N	11.55 E
Auriol	62	43.23 N	5.38 E
Aurisina	64	45.45 N	13.41 E
Aurlandsfjorden ⊂²	26	60.55 N	7.02 E
Aurlandsvangen	26	60.54 N	7.11 E
Aurolzmünster	60	48.15 N	13.27 E
Auron ≃	62	44.14 N	6.56 E
Auronzo di Cadore	64	46.33 N	12.26 E
Aurora, Bra.	250	6.57 S	38.58 W
Aurora, Bra.	287a	22.46 S	43.24 W
Aurora, On., Can.	212	44.00 N	79.28 W
Aurora, S. Afr.	158	32.42 S	18.29 E
Aurora, Co., U.S.	200	39.43 N	104.49 W
Aurora, Il., U.S.	216	41.45 N	88.19 W
Aurora, In., U.S.	218	39.03 N	84.54 W
Aurora, Me., U.S.	188	44.51 N	68.19 W
Aurora, Mn., U.S.	190	47.31 N	92.14 W
Aurora, Mo., U.S.	194	36.58 N	93.43 W
Aurora, Ne., U.S.	198	40.52 N	98.00 W
Aurora, N.Y., U.S.	210	42.45 N	76.42 W
Aurora, N.C., U.S.	192	35.18 N	76.47 W
Aurora, Oh., U.S.	214	41.19 N	81.20 W
Aurora, Ut., U.S.	224	45.13 N	122.45 W
Aurora, Ut., U.S.	200	38.55 N	111.56 W
Aurora, W.V., U.S.	188	39.19 N	79.33 W
Aurora ≃	116	16.00 N	121.40 E
Aurora □	265a	59.57 N	30.21 E
Aurora Pond ⊜	279a	41.20 N	81.23 W
Auroux	62	44.45 N	3.44 E
Aurukun Aboriginal Land Trust ⬥⁴	164	13.45 S	141.45 E
Aurunci, Monti ⋀	156	26.40 S	16.15 E
Aus	158	40.34 N	84.23 W
Ausable ≃, On., Can.	190	43.19 N	81.46 W
Au Sable ≃, Mi., U.S.	190	44.25 N	83.20 W
Au Sable, North Branch ≃	190	44.40 N	84.23 W
Au Sable, South Branch ≃	190	44.40 N	84.23 W
Au Sable Forks	188	44.26 N	73.40 W
Au Sable Point ⊁	190	44.20 N	83.20 W

ENGLISH

DEUTSCH

Symbols in the index entries represent the broad categories identified in the key at the right. Symbols with superior numbers (⋏1) identify subcategories (see complete key on page *I · 1)*.

Symbole im Register stellen die rechts im Schlüssel erklärten Kategorien dar. Symbole mit hochgestellten Ziffern (⋏1) bezeichnen Unterabteilungen einer Kategorie (vgl. vollständiger Schlüssel auf Seite *I · 1)*.

Los símbolos incluídos en el texto del índice representan las grandes categorías identificadas con la clave a la derecha. Los símbolos con numeros en su parte superior (⋏1) identifican las subcategorías (véase la clave completa en la página *I · 1)*.

Les symboles de l'index représentent les catégories indiquées dans la légende à droite. Les symboles suivis d'un indice (⋏1) représentent des sous-catégories (voir légende complète à la page *I · 1)*.

Os símbolos incluídos no texto do índice representam as grandes categorias identificadas com a chave à direita. Os símbolos com números em sua parte superior (⋏1) identificam as subcategorias (veja-se a chave completa à página *I · 1)*.

∧ Mountain	Berg	Montaña	Montagne	Montanha
⋏ Mountains	Gebirge	Montañas	Montagnes	Montanhas
)(Pass	Paß	Paso	Col	Passo
V Valley, Canyon	Tal, Cañon	Valle, Cañón	Vallée, Canyon	Vale, Canhão
≚ Plain	Ebene	Llano	Plaine	Planície
> Cape	Kap	Cabo	Cap	Cabo
I Island	Insel	Isla	Île	Ilha
II Islands	Inseln	Islas	Îles	Ilhas
✦ Other Topographic Features	Andere Topographische Objekte	Otros Elementos Topográficos	Autres données topographiques	Outros acidentes topográficos

ESPAÑOL			FRANÇAIS			PORTUGUÊS									

ENGLISH DEUTSCH

Symbols in the index entries represent the broad categories identified in the key at the right. Symbols with superior numbers (*1) identify subcategories (see complete key on page I · 1).

Symbole im Register stellen die rechts im Schlüssel erklärten Kategorien dar. Symbole mit hochgestellten Ziffern (*1) bezeichnen Unterabteilungen einer Kategorie (vgl. vollständiger Schlüssel auf Seite I · 1).

Les symboles de l'index représentent les catégories indiquées dans la légende à droite. Les symboles suivis d'un indice (*1) représentent des sous-catégories (voir légende complète à la page I · 1).

Los símbolos incluidos en el texto del índice representan las grandes categorías identificadas con a clave a la derecha. Los símbolos con números en su parte superior (*1) identifican las subcategorías (véase la clave completa en la página I · 1).

Os símbolos incluídos no texto do índice representam as grandes categorias identificadas com a chave à direita. Os símbolos com números em sua parte superior (*1) identificam as subcategorias (veja-se a chave completa à página I · 1).

Features	Andere Topographische Objekte	Autres données topographiques	Otros Elementos Topográficos	Outros Elementos topográficos
▲ Mountain	Berg	Montagne	Montaña	Montanha
▲ Mountains	Gebirge	Montagnes	Montañas	Montanhas
✕ Pass	Paß	Col	Paso	Passo
≡ Plain	Ebene	Plaine	Llano	Planicie
V Valley, Canyon	Tal, Cañon	Vallée, Canyon	Valle, Cañón	Vale, Canhão
> Cape	Kap	Cap	Cabo	Cabo
I Island	Insel	Île	Isla	Ilha
II Islands	Inseln	Îles	Islas	Ilhas

| ESPAÑOL Nombre | Página | Lat.ᵒʳ | Long.ᵒʳ W=Oeste | FRANÇAIS Nom | Page | Lat.ᵒʳ | Long.ᵒʳ W=Ouest | PORTUGUÊS Nome | Página | Lat.ᵒʳ | Long.ᵒʳ W=Oeste |

≃ River	Fluß	Río	Rivière	Rio
⋍ Canal	Kanal	Canal	Canal	Canal
ᴸ Waterfall, Rapids	Wasserfall, Stromschnellen	Cascada, Rápidos	Chute d'eau, Rapides	Cascata, Rápidos
ʮ Strait	Meeresstraße	Estrecho	Détroit	Estreito
⊂ Bay, Gulf	Bucht, Golf	Bahía, Golfo	Baie, Golfe	Baía, Golfo
⊜ Lake, Lakes	See, Seen	Lago, Lagos	Lac, Lacs	Lago, Lagos
≋ Swamp	Sumpf	Pantano	Marais	Pântano
❄ Ice Features, Glacier	Eis- und Gletscherformen	Accidentes Glaciales	Formes glaciaires	Acidentes glaciares
⊤ Other Hydrographic Features	Andere Hydrographische Objekte	Otros Elementos Hidrográficos	Autres données hydrographiques	Outros acidentes hidrográficos

✛ Submarine Features	Untermeerische Objekte	Accidentes Submarinos	Formes de relief sous-marin	Acidentes submarinos
□ Political Unit	Politische Einheit	Unidad Política	Entité politique	Unidade política
⌂ Cultural Institution	Kulturelle Institution	Institución Cultural	Institution culturelle	Instituição cultural
∴ Historical Site	Historische Stätte	Sitio Histórico	Site historique	Sítio Histórico
♦ Recreational Site	Erholungs- und Ferienort	Sitio de Recreo	Centre de loisirs	Area de Lazer
⊕ Airport	Flughafen	Aeropuerto	Aéroport	Aeroporto
⚔ Military Installation	Militäranlage	Instalación Militar	Installation militaire	Instalação militar
⬩ Miscellaneous	Verschiedenes	Misceláneo	Divers	Diversos

Name	Page	Lat. °′	Long. °′
Battlemount	158	26.57 S	23.46 E
Battle Mountain	204	40.38 N	116.56 W
Battle Mountain ʌ	200	41.02 N	107.16 W
Battlesbridge	260	51.37 N	0.34 E
Battonya	30	46.17 N	21.01 E
Battuello	266b	45.27 N	8.56 E
Batu	115a	7.52 S	112.31 E
Batu ʌ	144	6.55 N	39.46 E
Batu, Bukit ʌ	112	2.16 N	113.43 E
Batu, Kepulauan II	110	0.18 S	98.28 E
Batuan	116	12.25 N	123.47 E
Batu Arang	114	3.19 N	101.28 E
Batuata, Pulau I	112	6.12 S	122.42 E
Batuata, Tanjung ➤	115b	9.37 S	120.29 E
Batu-Batu	112	4.09 S	119.52 E
Batu Berinchang, Gunong ʌ	114	4.30 N	101.24 E
Batubetumpang	112	2.53 S	106.09 E
Batubrok, Bukit ʌ	112	1.10 N	114.36 E
Batu Caves	114	3.14 N	101.40 E
Batudaka, Pulau I	112	0.28 S	121.48 E
Batu Enam	114	2.35 N	102.43 E
Batu Gajah	114	4.28 N	101.03 E
Batui	112	1.17 S	122.33 E
Batui, Pegunungan ⩘	112	1.15 S	122.10 E
Batuidu	112	10.38 S	123.25 E
Batukau, Bukit ʌ	115b	8.20 S	115.05 E
Batukelau	112	0.48 N	115.01 E
Batu Laut	114	2.41 N	101.31 E
Batulicin	112	3.27 S	116.00 E
Batumata Point ➤	164	10.17 S	148.57 E
Batumi	84	41.38 N	41.38 E
Batumundan	114	1.17 N	98.50 E
Batu Pahat (Bandar Penggaram)	114	1.51 N	102.56 E
Batupanjang	114	1.43 N	101.31 E
Batu Puteh, Gunong ʌ	114	4.13 N	101.27 E
Batuputih	112	1.24 N	118.29 E
Baturaja	112	4.08 S	104.10 E
Batu Rakit	114	5.27 N	103.03 E
Baturetno	115a	7.59 S	110.56 E
Baturin	78	51.21 N	32.51 E
Baturino, Ross.	86	57.48 N	85.12 E
Baturino, Ross.	265b	55.35 N	37.31 E
Baturinskaja	78	45.47 N	39.22 E
Baturité	250	4.20 S	38.53 W
Baturotok	115b	8.42 S	117.10 E
Baturusa	112	2.02 S	106.07 E
Batusangkar	112	0.27 S	100.35 E
Batutinggi	112	1.55 S	113.19 E
Bat Yam	132	32.01 N	34.45 E
Batyrevo	80	55.04 N	47.38 E
Batyr-Mala, ozero ⊜	80	47.35 N	44.45 E
Bau	112	1.25 N	110.08 E
Baú ≃	250	7.26 S	54.47 W
Bauang	116	16.31 N	120.20 E
Baubašata, gory ⩘	85	41.20 N	72.45 E
Baubau	112	5.28 S	122.38 E
Bauchi	150	10.19 N	9.50 E
Bauchi □³	146	10.30 N	10.15 E
Baucina	70	37.55 N	13.32 E
Baud	32	47.52 N	3.01 W
Bauda	120	20.50 N	84.19 E
Baudette	190	48.42 N	94.35 W
Baudó ≃	246	4.57 N	77.22 W
Baudouin Stadium ♦	273b	4.20 S	15.20 E
Baudour	50	50.29 N	3.49 E
Bauernschaft	263	51.34 N	6.33 E
Bauerstown	279b	40.30 N	79.59 W
Baugo Creek ≃	216	41.40 N	86.04 W
Baukau	112	8.27 S	126.27 E
Bauld, Cape ➤	186	51.38 N	55.25 W
Baulkham Hills	274a	33.46 S	151.00 E
Baulmes	58	46.48 N	6.32 E
Bauma	58	47.23 N	8.53 E
Baumberg	263	51.07 N	6.54 E
Baume ≃	62	44.26 N	4.20 E
Baume-les-Dames	58	47.21 N	6.22 E
Baumholder	56	49.37 N	7.20 E
Baumschulenweg ◆⁸	264a	52.28 N	13.29 E
Baun	112	10.18 S	123.43 E
Baunach	56	49.59 N	10.50 E
Baunach ≃	56	49.59 N	10.51 E
Baunatal	56	51.16 N	9.25 E
Baunei	71	40.02 N	9.40 E
Baunt	88	55.16 N	113.08 E
Baunt, ozero ⊜	88	55.12 N	113.00 E
Bāuphal	126	22.25 N	90.33 E
Baure	150	12.50 N	8.45 E
Baures	248	13.35 S	63.35 W
Baures ≃	248	12.30 S	64.18 W
Bauru	255	22.19 S	49.04 W
Baús	255	18.19 S	53.10 W
Bausendorf	56	50.01 N	6.59 E
Bausenhagen	263	51.31 N	7.48 E
Bauska	76	56.24 N	24.14 E
Bauta	240p	22.59 N	82.33 W
Bauta □⁷	286b	22.59 N	82.33 W
Bautino	84	44.33 N	50.15 E
Bautzen	54	51.11 N	14.26 E
Bauxite	194	34.33 N	92.31 W
Bauya	150	8.11 N	12.34 W
Bavans	58	47.29 N	6.44 E
Bavari	62	44.26 N	9.01 E
Bavaria — Bayern □³	30	49.00 N	11.30 E
Bavarian Alps — Bayerische Alpen ⩘	64	47.30 N	11.00 E
Bavay	50	50.18 N	3.47 E
Båven ⊜	40	59.01 N	16.56 E
Baveno	58	45.55 N	8.30 E
Bavilliers	58	47.37 N	6.50 E
Bavispe	232	30.24 N	108.50 W
Bavispe ≃	232	29.15 N	109.11 W
Bavleny	80	56.24 N	39.34 E
Bavly	80	54.25 N	53.17 E
Bavnhöj ʌ²	41	55.55 N	10.07 E
Bavtugaj	84	43.11 N	46.49 E
Baw	110	23.19 N	95.50 E
Bāwal	124	28.05 N	76.35 E
Bawal, Pulau I	112	2.44 S	110.06 E
Bāwāli	272b	22.25 N	88.12 E
Bawang	115a	7.06 S	109.55 E
Baw Baw, Mount ʌ	169	37.50 S	146.17 E
Baw Baw National Park ♦	169	37.55 S	146.22 E
Bawbeese Lake ⊜	216	41.54 N	84.36 W
Bawdeswell	42	52.45 N	1.01 E
Bawdwin	110	23.06 N	97.18 E
Bawean, Pulau I	115a	5.46 S	112.40 E
Baweigang	106	31.57 N	120.14 E
Bawku	150	11.05 N	0.14 W
Bawlake	110	19.11 N	97.21 E
Bawmi	110	17.19 N	94.35 E
Bawria	126	22.29 N	88.10 E
Bawtry	44	53.26 N	1.01 W
Baxdo	144	5.46 N	47.15 E
Baxenden	262	53.44 N	2.20 W
Baxian, Zhg.	105	39.06 N	116.23 E
Baxian (Yudongxi), Zhg.	107	29.23 N	106.32 E
Baxley	192	31.46 N	82.20 W
Baxter, Ia., U.S.	190	41.49 N	93.09 W
Baxter, Mn., U.S.	190	46.20 N	94.17 W
Baxter, Tn., U.S.	194	36.09 N	85.38 W
Baxter Estates	276	40.50 N	73.42 W
Baxter Springs	198	37.02 N	94.44 W
Baxter State Park ♦	188	46.00 N	68.58 W
Baxterville	194	31.05 N	89.35 W
Bay	194	35.44 N	90.33 W
Bay □⁴	144	2.30 N	43.30 E
Bay, Laguna de ⊜	116	14.23 N	121.15 E
Baya, Zaïre	152	4.57 N	19.43 E
Baya, Zaïre	154	11.52 S	27.27 E
Bayādah, Wādī al- V	146	26.08 N	18.35 E
Bayāḍ an-Naṣārā	142	29.04 N	31.08 E
Bayag	116	18.16 N	121.02 E
Bayala	158	27.47 S	32.08 E
Bay al-Kabīr, Wādī V	146	31.15 N	15.57 E
Bayambang	116	15.49 N	120.27 E
Bayamo	240p	20.23 N	76.39 W
Bayamo ≃	240p	20.34 N	76.44 W
Bayamón	240m	18.24 N	66.09 W
Bayan, Indon.	115b	8.16 S	116.26 E
Bayan, Zhg.	89	46.05 N	127.24 E
Bāyan, Band-e ⩘	120	34.20 N	65.30 E
Bayāna	124	26.54 N	77.17 E
Bayanbayanan	269f	14.39 N	121.06 E
Bayanchagan	89	47.19 N	124.03 E
Bayang	116	7.48 N	124.12 E
Bayanga	152	2.53 N	16.19 E
Bayange	102	39.19 N	107.31 E
Bayan Har Shan ⩘	102	33.48 N	98.10 E
Bayanheshuomiao	89	48.51 N	119.46 E
Bayanjie	89	49.36 N	124.37 E
Bayanluke	89	50.52 N	119.33 E
Bayannaobao	102	39.44 N	107.40 E
Bayano, Lago ⊜¹	246	9.10 N	78.40 W
Bayan Obo	102	41.58 N	110.02 E
Bayan Tal	89	43.44 N	123.16 E
Bayard, Ia., U.S.	198	41.51 N	94.33 W
Bayard, Ne., U.S.	198	41.45 N	103.19 W
Bayard, N.M., U.S.	200	32.45 N	108.07 W
Bayard, Oh., U.S.	214	40.46 N	81.04 W
Bayard, W.V., U.S.	188	39.16 N	79.21 W
Bayard, Col ⩘	62	44.37 N	6.05 E
Bayard Cutting Arboretum State Park ♦	276	40.45 N	73.10 W
Bayat, Indon.	112	2.06 S	103.38 E
Bayat, Tür.	130	38.59 N	30.56 E
Bayat, Tür.	130	40.39 N	34.15 E
Bayawan	116	9.22 N	122.48 E
Bayawan ≃	116	9.22 N	122.48 E
Baybay	116	10.41 N	124.48 E
Bayberry	210	43.08 N	76.13 W
Bayble	46	58.12 N	6.13 W
Bayboro	192	35.08 N	76.46 W
Bay Bulls	186	47.19 N	52.49 W
Bayburt	130	40.16 N	40.15 E
Bay Center	224	46.37 N	123.57 W
Bay City, Mi., U.S.	190	43.35 N	83.53 W
Bay City, Or., U.S.	224	45.31 N	123.53 W
Bay City, Tx., U.S.	222	28.58 N	95.58 W
Bay Creek ≃, Il., U.S.	194	37.16 N	88.31 W
Bay Creek ≃, Il., U.S.	219	39.20 N	90.46 W
Baydā', Bi'r ≠⁴	142	29.45 N	32.13 E
Bay de Verde	186	48.05 N	52.54 W
Baydhabo	144	3.07 N	43.39 E
Bay du Nord ≃	186	47.44 N	55.25 W
Baye, Cap ➤	175f	20.57 S	165.25 E
Bayel	58	48.12 N	4.47 E
Bayerische Alpen ⩘	64	47.30 N	11.00 E
Bayerisch Eisenstein	60	49.07 N	13.12 E
Bayerischer Wald ⩘	60	49.00 N	12.40 E
Bayerischer Wald, Nationalpark ♦	60	48.56 N	13.28 E
Bayern □³	30	49.00 N	11.30 E
Bayeuen	114	4.36 N	97.53 E
Bayeux, Bra.	250	7.08 S	34.56 W
Bayeux, Fr.	32	49.16 N	0.42 W
Bay Farm Island I	282	37.43 N	122.14 W
Bayfield, Co., U.S.	200	37.13 N	107.35 W
Bayfield, Wi., U.S.	190	46.48 N	90.49 W
Bayfield, Île I	186	51.13 N	58.23 W
Bayford	260	51.46 N	0.06 W
'Bayh	132	33.44 N	35.31 E
Bayḥān al-Qaṣāb	144	14.48 N	45.43 E
Bay Harbor Islands	220	25.53 N	80.08 W
Bayhead, Scot., U.K.	46	57.33 N	7.24 W
Bay Head, N.J., U.S.	208	40.04 N	74.03 W
Bayiji	98	34.18 N	117.41 E
Bayındır	130	38.13 N	27.40 E
Bayingzi	104	41.28 N	120.46 E
Baykan	130	38.09 N	41.47 E
Baykonur — Bajkonyr	86	47.50 N	66.03 E
Bay Kurt	85	39.58 N	75.33 E
Bay L'Argent	186	47.33 N	54.54 W
Bayley Point ➤	164	16.56 S	139.02 E
Bayley Point Aboriginal Reserve ◆⁴	166	16.57 S	138.55 E
Baylis	219	39.44 N	90.54 W
Bay Meadows Race Track ◆	282	37.32 N	122.18 W
Bay Minette	194	30.52 N	87.46 W
Baynūnah ◆¹	128	23.50 N	52.50 E
Bayo	34	43.09 N	8.58 W
Bayombong	116	16.29 N	121.09 E
Bayon	58	48.29 N	6.19 E
Bayona	34	42.07 N	8.51 W
Bayonne, Fr.	32	43.29 N	1.29 W
Bayonne, N.J., U.S.	210	40.40 N	74.06 W
Bayonne ≃	206	46.05 N	73.10 W
Bayonne Bridge ◆⁵	276	40.38 N	74.09 W
Bayons	62	44.20 N	6.10 E
Bayou Bodcau Reservoir ⊜¹	194	32.45 N	93.30 W
Bayou Cane	194	29.37 N	90.45 W
Bayou D'Arbonne Lake ⊜¹	194	32.45 N	92.25 W
Bayou La Batre	194	30.24 N	88.14 W
Bayovar	248	5.50 S	81.03 W
Bay Park	276	40.38 N	73.40 W
Bayport, Fl., U.S.	220	28.33 N	82.39 W
Bay Port, Mi., U.S.	190	43.50 N	83.22 W
Bayport, Mn., U.S.	190	45.01 N	92.46 W
Bayport, N.Y., U.S.	210	40.44 N	73.03 W
Bayramiç	130	39.48 N	26.37 E
Bayramören	130	40.57 N	33.12 E
Bayreuth	60	49.57 N	11.35 E
Bay Ridge	208	38.56 N	76.27 W
Bay Ridge ◆⁸	276	40.37 N	74.02 W
Bay Ridge Channel	276	40.39 N	74.02 W
Bayrischzell	64	47.40 N	12.00 E
Bay Roberts	186	47.36 N	53.16 W
Bayrūt (Beirut)	130	33.53 N	35.30 E
Bayrūt □⁴	132	33.56 N	35.30 E
Bays, Lake of ⊜	212	45.15 N	79.04 W
Bay Saint Louis	194	30.18 N	89.19 W
Bay Shore	210	40.43 N	73.14 W
Bayshore Gardens	220	27.25 N	82.35 W
Bayside, On., Can.	212	44.07 N	77.30 W
Bayside, Ma., U.S.	283	42.18 N	70.53 W
Bayside, Wi., U.S.	216	43.10 N	87.54 W
Bayside ◆⁸	276	40.46 N	73.46 W
Bay Springs	194	31.58 N	89.17 W
Bay Springs Lake ⊜¹	194	34.35 N	88.20 W
Bayston Hill	42	52.40 N	2.45 W
Bayswater	274b	37.51 S	145.16 E
Bayswater North	274b	37.49 S	145.17 E
Bayt ad-Dīn	132	33.42 N	35.35 E
Bayt al-Faqīh	144	14.32 N	43.20 E
Bayt Hānūn	132	31.32 N	34.32 E
Bayt Jālā	132	31.43 N	35.11 E
Bayt Jinn	132	33.19 N	35.53 E
Bayt Laḥm (Bethlehem)	132	31.43 N	35.12 E
Bayt Mirī	132	33.52 N	35.36 E
Baytown	222	29.44 N	94.58 W
Bayt Sāḥūr	132	31.42 N	35.13 E
Bayt Sīrā	132	31.53 N	35.03 E
Bayunglencir	112	2.03 S	103.41 E
Bayview, Austl.	274a	33.40 S	151.18 E
Bay View, N.Z.	172	39.25 S	176.53 E
Bay View, N.Y., U.S.	214	42.47 N	78.51 W
Bay View, Oh., U.S.	214	41.28 N	82.50 W
Bayview ◆⁸	282	37.44 N	122.23 W
Bay Village	214	41.29 N	81.55 W
Bayville, N.J., U.S.	208	39.54 N	74.09 W
Bayville, N.Y., U.S.	210	40.54 N	73.33 W
Baywater	168a	31.55 S	115.56 E
Baywood Park	226	35.20 N	120.50 W
Bayyāḍah, Ra's al- ➤	132	33.10 N	35.10 E
Bayyā'iyah al-Kabīrah	130	35.42 N	37.09 E
Bayyūḍah, Ṣaḥrā' ≠⁴	140	17.32 N	32.07 E
Bayzo	150	13.52 N	4.45 E
Baza	34	37.29 N	2.46 W
Baza, Sierra de ⩘	34	37.15 N	2.45 W
Bazai	100	24.32 N	114.10 E
Bazainville	261	48.48 N	1.40 E
Bazalija	78	49.43 N	26.27 E
Bazar	88	53.58 N	116.05 E
Bazarčaj	84	39.40 N	45.48 E
Bazard'uz'u, gora ʌ	84	41.13 N	47.51 E
Bāzār-e Panjvā'ī	120	31.32 N	65.28 E
Bazargic — Dobrič	38	43.34 N	27.50 E
Bazar-Kurgan	85	41.02 N	72.45 E
Bazarnyje Mataki	80	54.56 N	49.56 E
Bazarnyj Karabulak	80	52.16 N	46.25 E
Bazarnyj Syzgan	80	53.45 N	46.46 E
Bazarovo	82	54.47 N	38.10 E
Bazaršolan	80	49.04 N	51.56 E
Bazartobe	80	49.23 N	51.50 E
Bazaruto, Ilha do I	156	21.40 S	35.28 E
Bazas	32	44.26 N	0.13 W
Bazavluk ≃	78	47.34 N	34.04 E
Bazdār	120	26.21 N	65.03 E
Bazeilles	56	49.40 N	4.59 E
Bazemont	261	48.56 N	1.52 E
Bazetta	214	41.20 N	80.47 W
Bazhong	102	31.51 N	106.39 E
Bazi	100	24.46 N	113.10 E
Baziège	32	43.27 N	1.37 E
Bažigan	84	44.33 N	45.41 E
Bazine	198	38.26 N	99.41 W
Baziqiao	106	32.07 N	119.52 E
Bazkovskaja	80	49.36 N	41.43 E
Bazmān	128	27.49 N	60.12 E
Bazmān, Kūh-e ʌ	128	28.04 N	60.00 E
Bazoches-les-Gallerandes	50	48.10 N	2.03 E
Bazoches-sur-Hoëne	50	48.33 N	0.28 E
Bazoj	86	55.45 N	83.22 E
Bazzano	64	44.30 N	11.05 E
Be ≃	110	11.06 N	106.58 E
Be, Nosy I	157b	13.20 S	48.15 E
Beach, Il., U.S.	216	42.26 N	87.50 W
Beach, N.D., U.S.	198	46.55 N	104.00 W
Beach, Tx., U.S.	222	30.20 N	95.29 W
Beach Channel	276	40.35 N	73.50 W
Beach City	214	40.39 N	81.34 W
Beach City Lake ⊜¹	214	40.41 N	81.36 W
Beach Glen	276	40.56 N	74.29 W
Beach Haven, N.J., U.S.	208	39.33 N	74.14 W
Beach Haven, Pa., U.S.	210	41.04 N	76.11 W
Beach Haven Terrace	208	39.35 N	74.13 W
Beach Lake	210	41.36 N	75.09 W
Beach Lake ⊜	281	42.33 N	83.43 W
Beach Pond State Park ♦	207	41.35 N	71.45 W
Beachport	166	37.30 S	140.01 E
Beachville	212	43.05 N	80.49 W
Beachwood, N.J., U.S.	208	39.56 N	74.11 W
Beachwood, Oh., U.S.	214	41.27 N	81.30 W
Beachy Head ➤	42	50.44 N	0.16 E
Beacon, Austl.	162	30.26 S	117.51 E
Beacon, N.Y., U.S.	210	41.30 N	73.58 W
Beacon Falls	207	41.26 N	73.03 W
Beacon Heights	284c	38.57 N	76.54 W
Beacon Hill, Austl.	274a	33.45 S	151.15 E
Beacon Hill, Wa., U.S.	224	46.08 N	122.57 W
Beacon Hill ʌ², H.K.	271d	22.21 N	114.09 E
Beacon Hill ʌ², Wales, U.K.	42	52.23 N	3.12 W
Beacon Rock State Park ♦	224	45.38 N	122.03 W
Beaconsfield, Austl.	166	41.12 S	146.48 E
Beaconsfield, Austl.	274b	38.03 S	145.22 E
Beaconsfield, P.Q., Can.	206	45.26 N	73.50 W
Beaconsfield, Eng., U.K.	260	51.37 N	0.39 W
Beaconsfield □⁸	260	51.34 N	0.35 W
Beadle Lake	216	42.18 N	85.12 W
Beagh, Slieve ʌ²	48	54.21 N	7.12 W
Beagle, Canal	254	54.53 S	68.10 W
Beagle Bay	162	16.58 S	122.40 E
Beagle Gulf c	164	12.00 S	130.20 E
Beagle Reef ◆²	160	15.20 S	123.29 E
Bealanana	157b	14.33 S	48.44 E
Beale, Cape ➤	182	48.44 N	125.20 W
Beale Air Force Base ■	226	39.08 N	121.20 W
Bealiba	169	36.48 S	143.33 E
Bealiba, Mount ʌ²	169	36.49 S	143.38 E
Beallsville	214	40.04 N	80.01 W
Beals Creek ≃	196	32.10 N	100.51 W
Beaminster	42	50.49 N	2.45 W
Bean	260	51.25 N	0.17 E
Beanblossom Creek ≃	194	39.20 N	86.39 W
Bean Creek ≃	216	41.35 N	84.19 W
Bear ≃, Sk., Can.	184	54.33 N	103.58 W
Bear ≃, U.S.	200	41.30 N	112.08 W
Bear ≃, Ca., U.S.	226	38.57 N	121.35 W
Bear, Mount ʌ	180	61.17 N	141.09 W
Beara	164	7.30 S	144.50 E
Bear Bay c	176	75.47 N	87.00 W
Bear Branch	218	38.55 N	85.05 W
Bear Brook ≃, On., Can.	212	45.25 N	75.10 W
Bear Brook ≃, N.J., U.S.	276	41.02 N	74.03 W
Bear Brook State Park ♦	188	43.05 N	71.26 W
Bear Butte ʌ	198	44.28 N	103.26 W
Bear Canyon V	280	34.14 N	118.07 W
Bear Cove	182	50.44 N	127.27 W
Bear Creek	210	41.11 N	75.45 W
Bear Creek ≃, On., Can.	214	42.44 N	82.23 W
Bear Creek ≃, U.S.	194	34.46 N	88.05 W
Bear Creek ≃, U.S.	196	37.45 N	101.23 W
Bear Creek ≃, U.S.	216	41.17 N	83.57 W
Bear Creek ≃, Al., U.S.	194	33.11 N	88.05 W
Bear Creek ≃, Ca., U.S.	226	38.56 N	122.20 W
Bear Creek ≃, Ca., U.S.	226	38.02 N	121.18 W
Bear Creek ≃, Ca., U.S.	226	37.17 N	120.50 W
Bear Creek ≃, Ca., U.S.	228	34.10 N	117.01 W
Bear Creek ≃, Ca., U.S.	280	34.14 N	117.53 W
Bear Creek ≃, Co., U.S.	200	39.40 N	105.00 W
Bear Creek ≃, Il., U.S.	219	39.33 N	89.23 W
Bear Creek ≃, Il., U.S.	219	40.07 N	91.29 W
Bear Creek ≃, Md., U.S.	284b	39.13 N	76.30 W
Bear Creek ≃, Mo., U.S.	219	39.03 N	91.14 W
Bear Creek ≃, N.D., U.S.	198	46.10 N	98.06 W
Bear Creek ≃, Oh., U.S.	218	39.39 N	84.17 W
Bear Creek ≃, Or., U.S.	202	42.26 N	122.58 W
Bear Creek ≃, Or., U.S.	202	44.06 N	120.46 W
Bear Creek ≃, Pa., U.S.	214	41.23 N	78.50 W
Bear Creek ≃, Wy., U.S.	198	41.41 N	104.13 W
Bear Creek, South Fork ≃	219	40.09 N	91.18 W
Bear Creek, West Fork ≃	280	34.16 N	117.53 W
Bearden	194	33.43 N	92.36 W
Beardmore	176	49.36 N	87.57 W
Beardmore Glacier ⩘	9	83.45 S	171.00 E
Beardsley Lake ⊜¹	226	38.13 N	120.03 W
Beardstown, Il., U.S.	219	40.01 N	90.25 W
Beardstown, In., U.S.	216	41.08 N	86.36 W
Beardy and Okemasis Indian Reserves ◆⁴	184	52.48 N	106.20 W
Bearfort Mountain ʌ	276	41.09 N	74.23 W
Bear Head Creek ≃	194	30.18 N	93.35 W
Bear Head Lake ⊜	184	55.33 N	96.10 W
Bear Head Lake State Park ♦	190	47.49 N	92.04 W
Bearhead Mountain ʌ	224	47.02 N	121.53 W
Bear Hill ʌ², Ct., U.S.	207	41.39 N	73.24 W
Bear Hill ʌ², N.Y., U.S.	210	41.18 N	74.00 W
Bear-in-the-Lodge Creek ≃	198	43.41 N	101.50 W
Bear Island I, Ant.	9	74.30 S	110.45 W
Bear Island I, Mb., Can.	184	54.53 N	98.04 W
Bear Island I, Ire.	48	51.40 N	9.48 W
Bear Island I, Va., U.S.	284c	38.59 N	77.14 W
Bear Island — Bjørnøya I	12	74.25 N	19.00 E
Bear Lake, B.C., Can.	182	56.11 N	126.51 W
Bear Lake, Pa., U.S.	214	42.00 N	79.30 W
Bear Lake ⊜, Ab., Can.	182	55.16 N	119.00 W
Bear Lake ⊜, B.C., Can.	182	56.06 N	126.45 W
Bear Lake ⊜, Mb., Can.	184	55.08 N	96.00 W
Bear Lake ⊜, On., Can.	212	45.26 N	79.35 W
Bear Lake ⊜, U.S.	200	42.00 N	111.20 W
Bear Mountain ʌ, Ca., U.S.	228	35.12 N	118.38 W
Bear Mountain ʌ, Ky., U.S.	192	37.32 N	84.16 W
Bear Mountain ʌ, Or., U.S.	202	43.51 N	122.53 W
Bear Mountain ʌ²	210	41.18 N	74.01 W
Bear Mountain State Park ♦	210	41.17 N	74.00 W
Béarn □⁹	32	43.20 N	0.45 W
Bear Pond ⊜	276	40.58 N	74.40 W
Bear River	186	44.34 N	65.39 W
Bear River Range ⩘	200	41.50 N	111.30 W
Bear Run ≃	279b	40.33 N	80.04 W
Bearsden	46	55.56 N	4.20 W
Bears Paw Mountains ⩘	202	48.15 N	109.30 W
Bearstead	260	51.16 N	0.35 E
Bearsville	210	42.02 N	74.09 W
Bear Swamp ≃	285	39.54 N	74.47 W
Bear Swamp ≡	285	39.53 N	74.45 W
Bear Swamp Brook ≃	276	41.04 N	74.13 W
Bear Swamp Lake ⊜	276	41.06 N	74.13 W
Beartooth Mountains ⩘	202	45.00 N	109.30 W
Beartooth Pass)(	202	44.58 N	109.28 W
Bear Town	194	31.13 N	90.27 W
Beas	123	31.31 N	75.17 E
Beās ≃	123	31.10 N	74.59 E
Beasain	34	43.03 N	2.11 W
Beas de Segura	34	38.15 N	2.53 W
Beasley	222	29.30 N	95.55 W
Beasley Bay c	208	37.51 N	75.44 W
Beason	219	40.09 N	89.12 W
Beata, Cabo ➤	238	17.36 N	71.25 W
Beata, Isla I	238	17.35 N	71.31 W
Beatenberg	58	46.42 N	7.48 E
Beato ◆⁸	266c	38.44 N	9.06 W
Beaton	182	50.44 N	117.44 W
Beatrice, Al., U.S.	194	31.44 N	87.12 W
Beatrice, Ne., U.S.	198	40.16 N	96.44 W
Beatrice, Zimb.	154	18.15 S	30.55 E
Beatrice, Cape ➤	164	14.15 S	136.59 E
Beattie	198	39.51 N	96.25 W
Beattock	44	55.18 N	3.28 W
Beatton ≃	176	56.10 N	120.25 W
Beatty, Nv., U.S.	204	36.54 N	116.45 W
Beatty, Oh., U.S.	218	39.53 N	83.50 W
Beatty Saugeen ≃	212	44.08 N	81.02 W
Beattyville	192	37.34 N	83.42 W
Beaubru	56	49.46 N	5.05 E
Beaucaire	62	43.48 N	4.38 E
Beauce ◆¹	50	48.22 N	1.50 E
Beauceville	188	46.12 N	70.46 W
Beauchamp	261	49.01 N	2.12 E
Beauchamp Roding	260	51.46 N	0.18 E
Beauchêne, Lac ⊜	190	46.39 N	78.55 W
Beauchêne Island I	254	52.55 S	59.12 W
Beaucoup Creek ≃, Il., U.S.	194	37.47 N	89.17 W
Beaucoup Creek ≃, Il., U.S.	219	38.13 N	89.20 W
Beaucourt	58	47.29 N	6.55 E
Beaudesert	171a	27.59 S	153.00 E
Beaudette ≃	206	45.12 N	74.19 W
Beaudry, Lac ⊜	190	47.44 N	78.55 W
Beauduc, Pointe de ➤	62	43.22 N	4.34 E
Beaufays	56	50.34 N	5.38 E
Beaufort, Austl.	169	37.26 S	143.23 E
Beaufort, Fr.	58	46.34 N	5.26 E
Beaufort, Fr.	62	45.43 N	6.35 E
Beaufort, Lux.	56	49.51 N	6.18 E
Beaufort, Malay.	112	5.20 N	115.45 E
Beaufort, Mo., U.S.	219	38.26 N	91.12 W
Beaufort, N.C., U.S.	192	34.43 N	76.39 W
Beaufort, S.C., U.S.	192	32.25 N	80.40 W
Beaufort, Cape ➤	162	34.26 S	115.32 E
Beaufort, Massif de ⩘¹	62	45.44 N	6.35 E
Beaufort Castle — Qal'at ash-Shaqīf ⊥	132	33.19 N	35.32 E
Beaufort Island I	271d	22.11 N	114.15 E
Beaufort Marine Corps Air Station ■	192	32.30 N	80.44 W
Beaufort Sea ▼²	16	73.00 N	140.00 W
Beaufort West	158	32.18 S	22.36 E
Beaugency	50	47.47 N	1.38 E
Beauharnois	206	45.19 N	73.52 W
Beauharnois □⁶	206	45.15 N	74.00 W
Beauharnois, Barrage de ◆⁶	275a	45.19 N	73.55 W
Beauharnois, Canal de ≃	206	45.19 N	73.54 W
Beaujeu	58	46.09 N	4.35 E
Beaujolais □⁹	58	46.05 N	4.10 E
Beaulieu	42	50.49 N	1.27 W
Beaulieu-lès-Loches	50	47.07 N	1.01 E
Beaulieu-sur-Mer	62	43.42 N	7.20 E
Beauly	46	57.29 N	4.29 W
Beauly ≃	46	57.28 N	4.28 W
Beauly Firth c¹	46	57.30 N	4.23 W
Beaumaris, Austl.	274b	37.59 S	145.02 E
Beaumaris, Wales, U.K.	44	53.16 N	4.05 W
Beaumaris Bay c	274b	38.00 S	145.03 E
Beaumes-de-Venise	62	44.07 N	5.02 E
Beaumesnil	50	49.01 N	0.43 E
Beaumetz-lès-Loges	50	50.14 N	2.39 E
Beaumont, Bel.	50	50.14 N	4.14 E
Beaumont, Nf., Can.	186	49.37 N	55.41 W
Beaumont, Fr.	32	49.40 N	1.51 W
Beaumont, N.Z.	172	45.49 S	169.32 E
Beaumont, Ca., U.S.	228	33.55 N	116.58 W
Beaumont, Ms., U.S.	194	31.10 N	88.55 W
Beaumont, Tx., U.S.	194	30.05 N	94.06 W
Beaumont-du-Gâtinais	50	48.08 N	2.29 E
Beaumont-en-Argonne	56	49.32 N	5.03 E
Beaumont Hill ʌ²	166	31.33 S	145.13 E
Beaumont-la-Ronce	50	47.34 N	0.40 E
Beaumont-le-Roger	50	49.05 N	0.47 E
Beaumont Place	222	29.50 N	95.14 W
Beaumont-sur-Oise	50	49.08 N	2.17 E
Beaumont-sur-Sarthe	50	48.13 N	0.08 E
Beaune	58	47.02 N	4.50 E
Beaune-la-Rolande	50	48.04 N	2.26 E
Beauport	206	46.52 N	71.11 W
Beaupré	186	47.03 N	70.54 W
Beaupréau	32	47.12 N	1.00 W
Beaupre Island I	212	44.26 N	76.19 W
Beaupré Lake ⊜	184	54.30 N	107.10 W
Beauraing	56	50.07 N	4.58 E
Beaurepaire	62	45.20 N	5.03 E
Beaurepaire-en-Bresse	58	46.40 N	5.23 E
Beaurières	62	44.35 N	5.33 E
Beaurivage	206	46.25 N	71.14 W
Beaurivage ≃	206	46.42 N	71.16 W
Beauséjour, Mb., Can.	184	50.04 N	96.33 W
Beauséjour, Guad.	241o	16.18 N	61.04 W
Beausoleil	62	43.45 N	7.26 E
Beausoleil Island I	212	44.51 N	79.52 W
Beautor	50	49.39 N	3.20 E
Beauvais, Fr.	50	49.26 N	2.05 E
Beauvais, Fr.	261	48.32 N	2.03 E
Beauvais Creek ≃	202	45.29 N	107.45 W
Beauvais-Tillé, Aéroport ≋	50	49.28 N	2.07 E
Beauval, Sk., Can.	184	55.09 N	107.37 W
Beauval, Fr.	50	50.06 N	2.20 E
Beauvezer	62	44.09 N	6.36 E
Beauville	32	44.17 N	0.52 E
Beauvoir	261	48.39 N	2.52 E
Beauvoir-sur-Mer	32	46.55 N	2.02 W
Beauvoir-sur-Niort	32	46.11 N	0.28 W
Beaux Arts	224	47.35 N	122.11 W
Beaver, Ak., U.S.	180	66.22 N	147.24 W
Beaver, Ok., U.S.	196	36.48 N	100.31 W
Beaver, Or., U.S.	224	45.16 N	123.49 W
Beaver, Pa., U.S.	214	40.41 N	80.18 W
Beaver, Ut., U.S.	200	38.16 N	112.38 W
Beaver, Wa., U.S.	224	48.03 N	124.19 W
Beaver, W.V., U.S.	192	37.44 N	81.08 W
Beaver □⁶	214	40.40 N	80.25 W
Beaver ≃, Can.	176	59.43 N	124.16 W
Beaver ≃, Can.	184	55.25 N	107.45 W
Beaver ≃, On., Can.	212	44.34 N	80.27 W
Beaver ≃, U.S.	196	36.35 N	99.30 W
Beaver ≃, N.Y., U.S.	188	43.54 N	75.30 W
Beaver ≃, Pa., U.S.	214	40.40 N	80.18 W
Beaver ≃, Ut., U.S.	200	39.10 N	112.57 W
Beaver Brook	210	40.55 N	75.59 W
Beaver Brook ≃, U.S.	207	42.40 N	71.19 W
Beaver Brook ≃, Ma., U.S.	283	42.23 N	71.14 W
Beaver Brook ≃, Ma., U.S.	283	42.03 N	70.58 W
Beaver Brook ≃, Ma., U.S.	283	42.36 N	71.21 W
Beaver Brook ≃, N.J., U.S.	276	40.54 N	74.30 W
Beaver Brook ≃, N.J., U.S.	276	40.58 N	74.35 W
Beaver City	198	40.08 N	99.49 W
Beaver Creek, Yk., Can.	180	62.22 N	140.52 W
Beavercreek, Oh., U.S.	218	39.43 N	84.03 W
Beavercreek, Or., U.S.	224	45.17 N	122.32 W
Beaver Creek ≃, On., Can.	212	44.30 N	77.42 W
Beaver Creek ≃, On., Can.	212	44.44 N	76.58 W
Beaver Creek ≃, On., Can.	275b	43.51 N	79.20 W
Beaver Creek ≃, On., Can.	284a	42.58 N	79.01 W
Beaver Creek ≃, U.S.	198	47.20 N	103.39 W
Beaver Creek ≃, U.S.	198	40.04 N	99.20 W
Beaver Creek ≃, U.S.	198	43.25 N	103.59 W
Beaver Creek ≃, U.S.	216	40.58 N	87.49 W
Beaver Creek ≃, Ak., U.S.	180	66.15 N	147.32 W
Beaver Creek ≃, Ca., U.S.	226	38.12 N	120.19 W
Beaver Creek ≃, Co., U.S.	198	40.20 N	103.33 W
Beaver Creek ≃, Co., U.S.	198	38.22 N	104.58 W
Beaver Creek ≃, Il., U.S.	216	42.16 N	88.56 W
Beaver Creek ≃, Il., U.S.	219	38.33 N	89.30 W
Beaver Creek ≃, Ky., U.S.	218	38.31 N	84.11 W
Beaver Creek ≃, Md., U.S.	208	39.32 N	77.42 W
Beaver Creek ≃, Mo., U.S.	194	36.38 N	93.02 W
Beaver Creek ≃, Mt., U.S.	202	48.29 N	107.24 W
Beaver Creek ≃, Ne., U.S.	198	40.42 N	97.20 W
Beaver Creek ≃, Ne., U.S.	198	41.26 N	97.42 W
Beaver Creek ≃, N.J., U.S.	285	39.45 N	75.23 W
Beaver Creek ≃, N.Y., U.S.	212	44.36 N	75.22 W
Beaver Creek ≃, N.D., U.S.	198	46.15 N	100.29 W
Beaver Creek ≃, Oh., U.S.	216	41.25 N	83.51 W
Beaver Creek ≃, Oh., U.S.	218	40.30 N	84.45 W
Beaver Creek ≃, Oh., U.S.	218	39.57 N	83.46 W
Beaver Creek ≃, Ok., U.S.	196	34.00 N	97.57 W
Beaver Creek ≃, Or., U.S.	224	44.56 N	121.22 W
Beaver Creek ≃, Pa., U.S.	285	40.00 N	75.42 W
Beaver Creek ≃, Tx., U.S.	196	33.53 N	98.49 W
Beaver Creek ≃, Wy., U.S.	202	42.58 N	108.26 W
Beaver Creek State Park ♦	214	40.44 N	80.35 W
Beaver Crossing	198	40.46 N	97.16 W
Beaverdale	214	40.19 N	78.41 W
Beaver Dam, Ky., U.S.	194	37.24 N	86.52 W
Beaverdam, Oh., U.S.	216	40.50 N	83.59 W
Beaver Dam, Wi., U.S.	190	43.27 N	88.50 W
Beaverdam Brook ≃	276	40.26 N	74.28 W
Beaverdam Creek ≃, U.S.	284c	38.55 N	76.57 W
Beaverdam Creek ≃, Md., U.S.	284c	39.01 N	76.54 W
Beaverdam Creek ≃, N.J., U.S.	285	39.56 N	74.45 W
Beaver Dams	210	42.17 N	76.58 W
Beaver Dams Creek ≃	284a	43.06 N	79.11 W
Beaver Dam Wash V	200	36.54 N	114.55 W
Beaverdell	182	49.26 N	119.05 W
Beaver Falls, N.Y., U.S.	212	43.53 N	75.25 W
Beaver Falls, Pa., U.S.	214	40.45 N	80.19 W
Beaverhead	202	45.31 N	112.21 W
Beaverhead Mountains ⩘	202	45.00 N	113.20 W
Beaverhill Lake ⊜, Ab., Can.	182	53.27 N	112.32 W
Beaver Hill Lake ⊜, Mb., Can.	184	54.16 N	94.53 W
Beaverhouse Lake ⊜	190	48.32 N	92.05 W
Beaver Island I	190	45.40 N	85.31 W
Beaver Island State Park ♦	210	42.58 N	78.57 W
Beaver Kill ≃	210	41.59 N	75.08 W
Beaver Lake	210	41.07 N	74.33 W
Beaver Lake ⊜, Ab., Can.	182	54.43 N	111.50 W
Beaver Lake ⊜, On., Can.	212	44.30 N	77.02 W
Beaver Lake ⊜, On., Can.	212	44.44 N	78.17 W
Beaver Lake ⊜, N.J., U.S.	276	41.05 N	74.33 W
Beaver Lake ⊜, N.Y., U.S.	276	40.53 N	73.34 W
Beaver Lake ⊜¹	194	36.20 N	93.55 W
Beaver Lake Indian Reserve ◆⁴	182	54.39 N	111.54 W
Beaverlodge	182	55.13 N	119.26 W
Beaver Meadow	210	42.40 N	75.41 W
Beaver Meadows	210	40.55 N	75.54 W
Beaver Mountains ⩘	180	62.54 N	156.58 W
Beaver Run ≃, N.J., U.S.	276	41.11 N	74.36 W
Beaver Run ≃, Pa., U.S.	279b	40.34 N	79.33 W
Beaver Run ≃, Pa., U.S.	285	40.10 N	75.40 W
Beaver Run Reservoir ⊜¹	214	40.29 N	79.33 W
Beavers Bend State Park ♦	194	34.08 N	94.42 W
Beaver Springs	208	40.45 N	77.13 W
Beaver Swamp Brook ≃	276	40.57 N	73.43 W
Beaverton, On., Can.	212	44.26 N	79.09 W
Beaverton, Mi., U.S.	190	43.52 N	84.29 W
Beaverton, Or., U.S.	224	45.29 N	122.48 W
Beaverton ≃	212	44.26 N	79.10 W
Beavertown	210	40.45 N	77.10 W
Beaverville	216	40.57 N	87.39 W
Beāwar	120	26.06 N	74.19 E
Beazley	252	33.45 S	66.39 W
Bebao	157b	17.22 S	44.33 E
Bebar ≃	114	3.07 N	103.27 E
Bebedouro	255	20.56 S	48.28 W
Bebeji	150	11.40 N	8.19 E
Bebek ◆⁸	267b	41.04 N	29.02 E
Bebelevo	82	54.32 N	36.30 E
Bebeli	130	36.41 N	35.27 E
Beberibe	250	4.11 S	38.08 W
Bebertal	54	52.15 N	11.18 E
Bebington	44	53.23 N	3.01 W
Bèboto	146	8.16 N	16.56 E
Bebra	56	50.58 N	9.47 E
Becal	232	20.27 N	90.02 W
Bécancour	206	46.20 N	72.26 W
Bécancour ≃	206	46.22 N	72.27 W
Beccar ◆⁸	288	34.28 S	58.31 W
Beccaria	214	40.46 N	78.27 W
Beccles	42	52.28 N	1.34 E
Becconsall	262	53.42 N	2.50 W
Bečej	38	45.37 N	20.03 E
Beceni	38	45.23 N	26.46 E
Becerra Creek ≃	196	28.05 N	98.55 W
Becerreá	34	42.51 N	7.10 W
Becerro, Cayos II	236	15.57 N	83.17 W
Béchar	148	31.37 N	2.13 W
Béchar □⁵	148	29.00 N	3.00 W
Becharof Lake ⊜	180	58.00 N	156.30 W
Bechater	36	37.18 N	9.45 E
Bechem	150	7.05 N	2.02 W
Becher Bay c	224	48.19 N	123.37 W
Becher Point ➤	168a	32.23 S	115.44 E
Bechet	38	43.46 N	23.58 E
Bechevin Bay c	180	55.00 N	163.27 W
Bechhofen	56	49.09 N	10.33 E
Bechtelsville	208	40.22 N	75.38 W
Bechuanaland ◆¹	158	27.10 S	22.10 E
Bechyně	30	49.18 N	14.29 E
Becke	263	51.24 N	7.47 E
Beckemeyer	219	38.36 N	89.26 W
Beckenham ◆⁸	260	51.24 N	0.02 W
Beckenried	58	46.58 N	8.29 E
Becket	207	42.19 N	73.05 W
Beckhausen ◆⁸	263	51.34 N	7.02 E
Beckingen	56	49.24 N	6.42 E
Beckington	42	51.16 N	2.18 W
Beck Lake ⊜	278	42.04 N	87.52 W
Beckler ≃	224	47.43 N	121.21 W
Beckley	188	37.46 N	81.11 W
Beck Pond ⊜	283	42.36 N	70.49 W
Becks Creek ≃	219	39.08 N	88.56 W
Beckum	52	51.45 N	8.02 E
Beckville	222	32.14 N	94.27 W
Beckwith Island I	212	44.52 N	80.08 W
Becky Peak ʌ	204	39.58 N	114.36 W
Beclean	38	47.11 N	24.10 E
Bečov nad Teplou	54	50.02 N	12.19 E
Becsehely	61	46.27 N	16.48 E
Bedale	44	54.17 N	1.35 W
Bédarieux	32	43.37 N	3.09 E
Bédarrides	62	44.02 N	4.54 E
Bedaya	146	8.55 N	17.52 E
Bedburdyck	56	51.07 N	6.34 E
Bedburg, Dtsch.	56	50.59 N	6.35 E
Bedburg, Dtsch.	56	51.03 N	8.23 E
Bedburg-Hau	52	51.45 N	6.10 E
Beddgelert	44	53.01 N	4.06 W
Beddingestrand	41	55.21 N	13.29 E
Beddington ◆⁸	260	51.22 N	0.08 W
Beddome, Mount ʌ	162	25.50 S	134.22 E
Beddouza, Ras ➤	148	32.34 N	9.19 W
Bedele	144	8.33 N	36.23 E
Beden Brook ≃	276	40.25 N	74.38 W
Bedeque Bay c	186	46.22 N	63.53 W
Beder	41	56.04 N	10.13 E
Bederkesa	52	53.38 N	8.50 E
Bederwanak	144	9.34 N	44.23 E
Bedesa	144	8.54 N	40.47 E
Bedford, P.Q., Can.	206	45.07 N	72.59 W
Bedford, S. Afr.	158	32.41 S	26.05 E
Bedford, Eng., U.K.	42	52.08 N	0.29 W
Bedford, In., U.S.	218	38.51 N	86.29 W
Bedford, Ia., U.S.	198	40.40 N	94.43 W
Bedford, Ky., U.S.	218	38.35 N	85.19 W
Bedford, Ma., U.S.	207	42.29 N	71.16 W
Bedford, Mi., U.S.	216	42.23 N	85.13 W
Bedford, N.Y., U.S.	210	41.12 N	73.39 W
Bedford, Oh., U.S.	214	41.23 N	81.32 W
Bedford, Pa., U.S.	188	40.01 N	78.30 W
Bedford, Tx., U.S.	222	32.50 N	97.08 W
Bedford, Va., U.S.	192	37.20 N	79.31 W
Bedford □⁶	214	40.09 N	78.30 W
Bedford, Cape ➤	164	15.14 S	145.21 E
Bedfordale	168a	32.10 S	116.03 E
Bedford Harbour c	162	33.35 S	120.35 E
Bedford Heights	279a	41.25 N	81.31 W
Bedford Hills	210	41.14 N	73.41 W
Bedford Island I	126	21.51 N	88.05 E
Bedford Level ≡	42	52.27 N	0.02 W
Bedford Park	278	41.46 N	87.49 W
Bedford Park ◆⁸	276	40.52 N	73.53 W
Bedfordshire □⁶	42	52.05 N	0.30 W
Bedford-Stuyvesant ◆⁸	276	40.41 N	73.55 W
Bedi, India	120	22.30 N	70.02 E
Bédi, Tchad	146	11.06 N	18.33 E
Bedias	222	30.46 N	95.57 W
Bedias Creek ≃	222	30.54 N	95.37 W
Bedinggong	112	2.42 S	106.13 E
Bédiondo	146	8.39 N	17.12 E
Bedirli	130	39.35 N	36.38 E
Bedlington	44	55.08 N	1.35 W
Bedminster, N.J., U.S.	276	40.40 N	74.38 W
Bedminster, Pa., U.S.	208	40.26 N	75.11 W
Bedmond	260	51.43 N	0.25 W
Bednodemjanovsk	80	53.56 N	43.10 E
Bedoba	88	58.48 N	97.12 E

Symbols in the index entries represent the broad categories identified in the key at the right. Symbols with superior numbers (⩘¹) identify subcategories (see complete key on page I · 1).

Symbole im Register stellen die rechts im Schlüssel erklärten Kategorien dar. Symbole mit hochgestellten Ziffern (⩘¹) bezeichnen Unterabteilungen einer Kategorie (vgl. vollständiger Schlüssel auf Seite I · 1).

Los símbolos incluidos en el texto del índice representan las grandes categorías identificadas con la clave a la derecha. Los símbolos con numeros en su parte superior (⩘¹) identifican las subcategorías (véase la clave completa en la página I · 1).

Les symboles de l'index représentent les catégories indiquées dans la légende à droite. Les symboles suivis d'un indice (⩘¹) représentent des sous-catégories (voir légende complète à la page I · 1).

Os símbolos incluídos no texto do índice representam as grandes categorias identificadas com a chave à direita. Os símbolos com números em sua parte superior (⩘¹) identificam as subcategorias (veja-se a chave completa à página I · 1).

	English	Deutsch	Español	Français	Português
ʌ	Mountain	Berg	Montaña	Montagne	Montanha
⩘	Mountains	Gebirge	Montañas	Montagnes	Montanhas
)(	Pass	Paß	Paso	Col	Passo
V	Valley, Canyon	Tal, Cañon	Valle, Cañón	Vallée, Canyon	Vale, Canhão
≡	Plain	Ebene	Llano	Plaine	Planície
➤	Cape	Kap	Cabo	Cap	Cabo
I	Island	Insel	Isla	Île	Ilha
II	Islands	Inseln	Islas	Îles	Ilhas
◆	Other Topographic Features	Andere Topographische Objekte	Otros Elementos Topográficos	Autres données topographiques	Outros acidentes topográficos

ESPAÑOL: Nombre | Página | Lat.°' | Long.°' W = Oeste
FRANÇAIS: Nom | Page | Lat.°' | Long.°' W = Ouest
PORTUGUÊS: Nome | Página | Lat.°' | Long.°' W = Oeste

Nombre / Nom / Nome	Página / Page	Lat.°'	Long.°' W = Oeste / Ouest
Bédoin	62	44.07 N	5.10 E
Bedok	271c	1.19 N	103.57 E
Bedong	114	5.44 N	100.31 E
Bedonia	62	44.30 N	9.38 E
Bedourie	166	24.21 S	139.28 E
Bedum	52	53.17 N	6.36 E
Bedwas	42	51.35 N	3.13 W
Bedworth	42	52.28 N	1.29 W
Beeac	169	38.12 S	143.38 E
Beebe, P.Q., Can.	206	45.01 N	72.09 W
Beebe, Ar., U.S.	194	35.04 N	91.52 W
Beech ≃	194	35.37 N	88.10 W
Beechal Creek ≃	166	27.24 S	145.13 E
Beech Bottom	214	40.13 N	80.39 W
Beech Brook ≃	276	41.08 N	74.18 W
Beech Creek	194	37.10 N	87.03 W
Beech Creek ≃	210	41.04 N	77.34 W
Beechcrest	214	41.05 N	81.20 W
Beecher, Il., U.S.	216	41.20 N	87.37 W
Beecher, Mi., U.S.	216	43.05 N	83.42 W
Beecher City	219	39.11 N	88.47 W
Beecher Falls	206	45.00 N	71.30 W
Beechey Head ≻	224	48.19 N	123.39 W
Beech Forest	169	38.38 S	143.34 E
Beech Fork ≃	194	37.46 N	85.41 W
Beech Grove	218	39.43 N	86.05 W
Beechmont	171a	28.07 S	153.11 E
Beechview ◆[8]	279b	40.25 N	80.02 W
Beechwood, Ky., U.S.	218	38.24 N	84.44 W
Beechwood, Ma., U.S.	283	42.12 N	70.49 W
Beechwood, Mi., U.S.	216	46.09 N	88.46 W
Beechworth	166	36.22 S	146.41 E
Beechy	184	50.51 N	107.25 W
Beeck ◆[8]	263	51.29 N	6.44 E
Beeckerwerth ◆[8]	263	51.29 N	6.41 E
Beecroft	274a	33.45 S	151.04 E
Beecroft Head ≻	170	35.01 S	150.51 E
Beecroft Peninsula ≻[1]	170	35.02 S	150.50 E
Beedenbostel	52	52.38 N	10.16 E
Beef Island I	240m	18.27 N	64.31 W
Beek, Ned.	52	51.51 N	5.54 E
Beek, Ned.	52	51.32 N	5.38 E
Beek, Ned.	56	50.56 N	5.49 E
Beela ≃	44	54.13 N	2.47 W
Beeleigh Abbey ʋ[1]	260	51.44 N	0.40 E
Beelen	52	51.55 N	8.07 E
Beelitz	54	52.14 N	12.58 E
Beemer	198	41.55 N	96.48 W
Beemster ◆[1]	52	52.35 N	4.55 E
Beendorf	54	52.14 N	11.05 E
Beenleigh	171a	27.43 S	153.12 E
Beerburrum	171a	26.58 S	152.58 E
Beerfelden	56	49.34 N	8.58 E
Bee Ridge	220	27.17 N	82.28 W
Beeringgnurding Hill ∧[2]	162	29.53 S	117.55 E
Beernem	50	51.09 N	3.20 E
Beerse	56	51.19 N	4.52 E
Beersheba → Be'ér Sheva'	132	31.14 N	34.47 E
Beersheba Springs	194	35.28 N	85.39 W
Be'ér Sheva (Beersheba)	132	31.14 N	34.47 E
Be'er Sheva', Naḥal V	132	31.11 N	34.35 E
Beerta	52	53.10 N	7.05 E
Be'ér Toviyya	132	31.44 N	34.44 E
Beervlei Brak ≃	158	29.58 S	23.12 E
Beerwah	171a	26.51 S	152.58 E
Beerwah National Park ♠	171a	26.54 S	152.53 E
Be'er Ya'agov	132	31.56 N	34.50 E
Beesenlaublingen	54	51.42 N	11.41 E
Beeskow	54	52.10 N	14.14 E
Beestekraal	156	25.23 S	27.38 E
Beesten	52	52.26 N	7.30 E
Beeston	42	52.56 N	1.12 W
Beet ≃	115a	6.16 S	107.15 E
Beethoven Peninsula ≻[1]	9	71.40 S	73.45 W
Beeton	212	44.05 N	79.47 W
Beetsterzwaag	52	53.03 N	6.05 E
Beetz, Lac ⊜	186	50.34 N	62.42 W
Beetzendorf	54	52.42 N	11.05 E
Beeville	196	28.24 N	97.44 W
Beevor, Mount ∧[2]	168b	34.56 S	139.02 E
Befale	152	0.28 N	20.58 E
Befandriana	157b	15.16 S	48.32 E
Befandriana Atsimo	157b	22.06 S	43.54 E
Befasy	157b	20.33 S	44.23 E
Befori	152	0.06 N	22.17 E
Befotaka, Madag.	157b	13.15 S	48.16 E
Befotaka, Madag.	157b	14.32 S	48.01 E
Befotaka, Madag.	157b	23.49 S	46.59 E
Befotaka, Madag.	157b	21.29 S	44.44 E
Befu ◆[8]	270	34.40 N	135.02 E
Beg, Lough ⊜	48	54.47 N	6.28 W
Bega	166	36.40 S	149.50 E
Bega (Begej) ≃	38	45.13 N	20.19 E
Begamganj, Bngl.	124	22.49 N	91.07 E
Begamganj, India	124	23.36 N	78.20 E
Begampur ◆[8]	272a	28.44 N	77.04 E
Beğdeş	130	37.51 N	39.05 E
Begej (Bega) ≃	38	45.13 N	20.19 E
Beger	102	45.42 N	97.10 E
Beggs	196	35.44 N	96.04 W
Begičevskij	76	53.47 N	38.15 E
Beginsel	158	26.57 S	20.39 E
Beglickaja, kosa ≻[2]	83	47.07 N	38.35 E
Begna ≃	26	60.10 N	10.16 E
Begoml'	76	54.44 N	28.04 E
Begonias, Presa ⊜[1]	234	20.55 N	100.50 W
Begoro	150	6.23 N	0.23 W
Begovat → Bekabad	85	40.13 N	69.14 E
Begun'	78	51.24 N	28.17 E
Begunicy	76	59.35 N	29.19 E
Begur, Cap de ≻	34	41.57 N	3.14 E
Begusarai	124	25.25 N	86.08 E
Behāla	126	22.31 N	88.19 E
Behauge, Pointe ≻	250	4.40 N	51.54 W
Behbahān	128	30.35 N	50.14 E
Behleg	120	36.47 N	91.41 E
Behm Canal ʯ	182	55.41 N	131.35 W
Beho	56	50.13 N	6.00 E
Béhoust	261	48.50 N	1.43 E
Behrāmpur	272a	28.38 N	77.24 E
Behren-lès-Forbach	56	49.10 N	6.57 E
Behring, Détroit de → Bering Strait ʯ	180	65.30 N	169.00 W
Behringen, Dtsch.	52	53.07 N	9.58 E
Behringen, Dtsch.	54	51.01 N	10.31 E
Behshahr	128	36.43 N	53.34 E
Beht, Oued ≃	148	34.25 N	6.26 W
Bei ≃	90	23.09 N	112.48 E
Bei'an	89	48.16 N	126.36 E
Beianhe	105	40.04 N	116.06 E
Beibaihua	105	38.57 N	114.51 E
Beibaozhen	106	31.33 N	121.38 E
Beibei	107	29.49 N	106.26 E
Beicai	106	31.12 N	121.34 E
Beicang	105	39.13 N	117.07 E
Beida ≃	102	40.18 N	99.26 E
Beïda, Chott ⊜	34	35.56 N	5.49 E
Beida → Al-Bayḍā'	146	32.46 N	21.43 E
Beidaihe	98	39.54 N	119.29 E
Beidaoqiao	86	44.12 N	89.38 E
Beidouzhen	107	30.02 N	104.26 E
Beidun	100	26.42 N	118.57 E
Beierfeld	54	50.33 N	12.47 E
Beiersdorf	264a	52.42 N	13.47 E
Beifangcun	105	40.20 N	116.42 E
Beifangzi	104	41.22 N	121.03 E
Beigang	100	29.20 N	113.41 E
Beighton	44	53.20 N	1.20 W
Beigi	144	9.20 N	34.29 E
Beiguan Dao I	100	27.10 N	120.32 E
Beiguo	106	31.47 N	120.33 E
Beihai	102	21.29 N	109.05 E
Bei Hai ⊜	271a	39.56 N	116.22 E
Beihedian	105	39.13 N	115.45 E
Beiheishang'gou	105	39.53 N	118.15 E
Beihuaidian	105	39.16 N	117.33 E
Beijialing	104	41.08 N	124.02 E
Beijiao	100	26.22 N	119.58 E
Beijiean	106	32.15 N	121.12 E
Beijijiazhuang	105	40.01 N	114.51 E
Beijing (Peking), Zhg.	105	39.55 N	116.25 E
Beijing (Peking), Zhg.	271a	39.55 N	116.25 E
Beijing Ji Chang (Capitol Airport) ⊠	105	40.03 N	116.35 E
Beijing Shi (Peking Shih) □[7]	98	40.15 N	116.30 E
Beiji Shan I	100	27.38 N	121.12 E
Beijuma ≃	105	39.30 N	115.56 E
Beikan	100	32.23 N	121.21 E
Beilen	52	52.52 N	6.31 E
Beili	110	19.10 N	108.43 E
Beilifang	104	41.59 N	121.57 E
Beiling	100	24.36 N	115.20 E
Beiliu	102	22.42 N	110.22 E
Beiliuwangshui	105	38.57 N	115.03 E
Beilizigu	105	39.30 N	117.28 E
Beilngries	60	49.02 N	11.29 E
Beilong Shan I	100	27.40 N	120.58 E
Beilrode	54	51.35 N	13.03 E
Beilstein, Dtsch.	56	49.02 N	9.18 E
Beilstein, Dtsch.	56	50.36 N	8.14 E
Beilstein, Dtsch.	56	50.06 N	7.14 E
Beimaizhu	105	39.31 N	117.44 E
Beiminjiatun	104	42.38 N	122.43 E
Beimuzhen	107	29.31 N	105.05 E
Beinamar	146	8.40 N	15.23 E
Beine-Nauroy	50	49.15 N	4.13 E
Beinette	62	44.22 N	7.39 E
Beinwil	58	47.22 N	7.35 E
Beinwil am See	58	47.16 N	8.13 E
Beipa	164	8.30 S	146.35 E
Beipan ≃	102	25.05 N	106.00 E
Beipanxiaozhen	106	31.44 N	121.26 E
Beipiao	104	41.49 N	120.46 E
Beipo	102	21.14 N	109.53 E
Beiqi	98	40.27 N	122.20 E
Beiqiao	106	31.03 N	121.24 E
Beira	156	19.49 S	34.52 E
Beira Baixa □[9]	34	39.45 N	7.30 W
Beira Litoral □[9]	34	40.15 N	8.25 W
Beiru ≃	100	33.43 N	113.35 E
Beirut → Bayrūt	130	33.53 N	35.30 E
Beirut International Airport ⊠	132	33.49 N	35.30 E
Beisanjia	98	42.04 N	124.42 E
Beiseker	182	51.23 N	113.32 W
Beishakou	105	39.08 N	116.07 E
Beishan	102	24.28 N	108.35 E
Bei Shan ʎ	102	41.30 N	96.00 E
Beishangcun	105	39.28 N	116.58 E
Beishipian	105	40.43 N	116.55 E
Beishuangdong	105	40.32 N	117.24 E
Beishuiquan	98	40.05 N	114.40 E
Beisi	102	34.59 N	95.07 E
Beisu	98	38.13 N	114.46 E
Beitaitou	98	37.06 N	118.31 E
Beitang	105	39.07 N	117.42 E
Beitanshiqiao	106	31.05 N	121.38 E
Beitbridge	154	22.13 S	30.00 E
Beith	46	55.45 N	4.38 W
Beitstadfjorden ⊂[2]	26	63.53 N	11.00 E
Beiuș	38	46.40 N	22.21 E
Beiwei	106	32.05 N	121.12 E
Beiwenquan	107	29.51 N	106.24 E
Beiwu	105	40.04 N	116.48 E
Beiwudu	100	33.39 N	113.39 E
Beixiadai	106	32.12 N	120.08 E
Beixiejiadang	105	40.30 N	114.50 E
Beixili	89	51.47 N	125.45 E
Beixin'an	271a	39.55 N	116.08 E
Beixindian	105	39.44 N	116.44 E
Beixing	89	48.29 N	125.40 E
Beixinjing	106	31.13 N	121.22 E
Beixinliu	105	39.16 N	116.31 E
Beixinzhen	106	31.49 N	121.31 E
Beiyan	98	36.33 N	118.42 E
Beiyi ≃	105	39.19 N	115.39 E
Beiyin	106	31.07 N	120.47 E
Beiyindai	104	42.35 N	122.22 E
Beiyuan	105	40.01 N	116.24 E
Beizhaijiawopeng	104	41.14 N	122.41 E
Beizhen, Zhg.	98	37.22 N	118.01 E
Beizhen (Gaoshanzi), Zhg.	104	41.36 N	121.47 E
Beizhouzhuang	106	31.52 N	120.24 E
Beizifu	98	42.09 N	120.29 E
Beja, Bra.	250	1.36 S	48.47 W
Beja, Port.	34	38.01 N	7.52 W
Beja, Ross.	86	53.03 N	90.54 E
Béja, Tun.	148	36.44 N	9.11 E
Beja □[5]	34	37.50 N	8.00 W
Béja □[8]	148	36.35 N	9.20 E
Bejaïa (Bougie)	148	36.45 N	5.05 E
Bejaïa □[5]	148	36.50 N	4.40 E
Bejaïa, Golfe de ⊂	34	36.45 N	5.25 E
Béjar	34	40.23 N	5.46 W
Bejhi ≃	120	29.47 N	67.58 E
Bejlagan	84	39.47 N	47.37 E
Bejneu	86	45.15 N	55.07 E
Bejsug ≃	78	45.54 N	38.56 E
Bejsugskij liman ⊂	78	46.07 N	38.25 E
Bejtonovo	89	53.14 N	124.27 E
Bejucal	240p	22.56 N	82.23 W
Bejucal □[7]	286b	22.56 N	82.23 W
Bejuco	236	8.36 N	79.53 W
Bejucos ≃	234	18.36 N	100.40 W
Bejuma	246	10.11 N	68.16 W
Bek ≃	152	2.29 N	15.15 E
Béka	146	9.04 N	12.53 E
Bekaa Valley → Al-Biqā' V	128	33.50 N	36.00 E
Bekabad	85	40.13 N	69.14 E
Bekancan	114	3.18 N	98.24 E
Bekasi	115a	6.14 S	106.59 E
Bekasi ≃	269e	6.10 S	107.02 E
Békásmegyer ◆[8]	264c	47.36 N	19.03 E
Bekasovo	82	55.26 N	36.49 E
Bekdaš	72	41.34 N	52.32 E
Békés	30	46.46 N	21.08 E
Békés □[6]	30	46.46 N	21.08 E
Békéscsaba	30	46.41 N	21.06 E
Beketovo	89	53.13 N	125.01 E
Bekilli	130	38.14 N	29.26 E
Bekily	157b	24.13 S	45.19 E
Bekirhan	130	38.10 N	41.19 E
Bekisopa	157b	21.40 S	45.54 E
Bekitro	157b	24.33 S	45.18 E
Bekkaria	36	35.22 N	8.15 E
Bekkersdal	273d	26.18 S	27.42 E
Bekkevoort	56	50.57 N	4.58 E
Beklemiševo, Ross.	80	53.52 N	47.25 E
Beklemiševo, Ross.	88	52.07 N	112.40 E
Bekodoka	157b	16.58 S	45.07 E
Bekoji	144	7.34 N	39.17 E
Bekok	114	2.18 N	103.08 E
Bekopaka	157b	19.09 S	44.48 E
Bekovo	80	52.28 N	43.43 E
Bektauata, gora ∧	86	47.30 N	74.50 E
Bektyševo	82	56.34 N	39.14 E
Bekwai	150	6.27 N	1.35 W
Bela, India	124	25.56 N	81.59 E
Bela, Pāk.	120	26.14 N	66.19 E
Bela, Zaïre	154	0.38 N	29.14 E
Bélabo	152	5.00 N	13.20 E
Belabolo	140	8.57 N	25.51 E
Bélâbre	32	46.33 N	1.09 E
Bela Crkva	38	44.54 N	21.26 E
Bela Cruz	250	3.03 S	40.11 W
Belaga	108	2.42 N	113.47 E
Bel'agaš	86	50.48 N	80.44 E
Bel-Air, Fr.	261	48.37 N	2.10 E
Bel Air, Md., U.S.	208	39.32 N	76.20 W
Bel Air, Va., U.S.	284c	38.52 N	77.10 W
Bel Air ◆[8]	280	34.05 N	118.27 W
Bélair, Île I	275a	45.37 N	73.48 W
Bel Aire Estates	207	41.23 N	72.00 W
Belair Recreation Park ♠	168b	35.01 S	138.39 E
Belaja, Ross.	78	51.03 N	35.43 E
Belaja, Ross.	80	57.59 N	51.42 E
Belaja ≃, Ross.	78	45.04 N	39.23 E
Belaja ≃, Ross.	84	44.45 N	39.50 E
Belaja ≃, Ross.	86	55.54 N	53.33 E
Belaja ≃, Ross.	180	65.45 N	173.20 E
Belaja ≃, Ukr.	83	49.18 N	38.52 E
Belaja ≃, Ukr.	83	48.35 N	39.10 E
Belaja, gora ∧, Ross.	88	53.10 N	119.50 E
Belaja, gora ∧, Ross.	180	65.50 N	174.40 E
Belaja Ber'ozka	76	52.23 N	33.29 E
Belaja Cerkov'	78	49.49 N	30.07 E
Belaja Cholunica	86	58.50 N	50.48 E
Belaja Gora	76	58.31 N	31.45 E
Belaja Kalitva	78	48.11 N	40.46 E
Belaja Krinica, Ukr.	78	47.21 N	33.10 E
Belaja Krinica, Ukr.	78	50.38 N	29.29 E
Bel'ajevka, Ross.	86	51.24 N	56.26 E
Bel'ajevka, Ross.	86	57.28 N	55.28 E
Bel'ajevka, Ukr.	78	46.29 N	30.12 E
Bel'ajevo	76	55.31 N	31.06 E
Belalcázar	34	38.34 N	5.10 W
Bel Alton	208	38.27 N	76.58 W
Belambanganumpu	112	4.54 S	105.03 E
Belampalli	122	19.02 N	79.30 E
Bělá nad Radbuzou	60	49.36 N	12.44 E
Belang	112	0.57 N	124.47 E
Bélanger ≃	184	53.26 N	97.40 W
Bel'aninovo	265b	55.57 N	37.39 E
Bel'anskij	80	47.45 N	41.33 E
Bela Palanka	38	43.13 N	22.19 E
Bělá pod Bezdězem	54	50.30 N	14.50 E
Belapurpāda	272c	19.01 N	73.02 E
Belarus □[1], Europe	22	53.50 N	28.00 E
Belarus □[1], Europe	76	53.50 N	28.00 E
Belas	266c	38.47 N	9.16 W
Belau → Palau □[2]	14	5.00 N	137.00 E
Belavenona	157b	24.50 S	47.04 E
Bela Vista, Ang.	152	7.50 S	13.40 E
Bela Vista, Bra.	252	22.06 S	56.31 W
Bela Vista, Moç.	156	26.20 S	32.40 E
Bela Vista ◆[8]	287b	23.33 S	46.38 W
Bela Vista de Goiás	255	16.58 S	48.57 W
Bela Vista do Paraíso	255	23.00 S	51.12 W
Belawan	114	3.47 N	98.41 E
Belaya ∧	144	11.25 N	36.12 E
Belayan ≃	112	0.14 S	116.36 E
Belaya Tserkov' → Belaja Cerkov'	78	49.49 N	30.07 E
Belbo ≃	62	44.54 N	8.31 E
Belbubulo	140	9.57 N	34.04 E
Belbunia	126	23.17 N	87.09 E
Bel'c'	78	47.46 N	27.56 E
Belcamp	208	39.28 N	76.14 W
Belcastro	68	39.02 N	16.47 E
Bełchatów	30	51.22 N	19.21 E
Belchen ∧	58	47.49 N	7.50 E
Belcher	194	32.44 N	93.49 W
Belcherāgh	120	35.50 N	65.14 E
Belcher Creek ≃	276	41.08 N	74.23 W
Belcher Islands II	176	56.20 N	79.30 W
Belchertown	207	42.16 N	72.24 W
Belchite	34	41.18 N	0.45 W
Bělčice	60	49.30 N	13.53 E
Belcoo	48	54.17 N	7.52 W
Belcourt	198	48.50 N	99.44 W
Belda	126	22.05 N	87.21 E
Beldānga	126	23.56 N	88.15 E
Bel'd'ažki	76	52.39 N	35.42 E
Belding	216	43.05 N	85.13 W
Bele, ozero ⊜	86	54.39 N	90.12 E
Belebej	80	54.07 N	54.07 E
Belebelka	76	57.34 N	30.56 E
Belecke	52	51.29 N	8.20 E
Beled Weyne	144	4.45 N	45.12 E
Bélel, Cam.	152	7.03 N	14.26 E
Belel, Nig.	146	9.38 N	13.12 E
Belém, Bra.	250	1.27 S	48.29 W
Belém, Moç.	154	14.13 S	35.58 E
Belém ◆[8]	266c	38.42 N	9.12 W
Belém, Torre de ⊥	266c	38.42 N	9.13 W
Belém de São Francisco	250	8.46 S	38.58 W
Belén, Arg.	252	27.39 S	67.02 W
Belén, Bol.	248	19.48 S	65.33 W
Belén, Chile	248	18.29 S	69.31 W
Belén, Col.	246	6.00 N	72.55 W
Belén, Nic.	236	11.30 N	85.53 W
Belén, Para.	252	23.30 S	57.06 W
Belen, Tür.	130	36.32 N	36.10 E
Belen, N.M., U.S.	200	34.39 N	106.46 W
Belén, Ur.	252	30.47 S	57.47 W
Belén ≃	252	28.00 S	66.52 W
Belén de Escobar	258	34.21 S	58.47 W
Belén del Refugio	234	21.31 N	102.25 W
Belene	38	43.39 N	25.07 E
Belenichino	78	50.56 N	36.37 E
Belen'kaja ≃	83	48.53 N	38.29 E
Belen'koje, Ukr.	78	47.37 N	35.03 E
Belen'koje, Ukr.	83	48.46 N	37.38 E
Belènzinho ◆[8]	287b	23.32 S	46.35 W
Bélep, Îles II	175f	19.45 S	163.40 E
Beles ≃	144	11.10 N	36.10 E
Belesar, Embalse de ⊜[1]	34	42.45 N	7.40 W
Belet Uen → Beled Weyne	144	4.45 N	45.12 E
Belews Lake ⊜[1]	192	36.17 N	80.03 W
Belfair	224	47.27 N	122.49 W
Belfast, N.Z.	172	43.27 S	172.38 E
Belfast, S. Afr.	156	25.43 S	30.03 E
Belfast, N. Ire., U.K.	48	54.35 N	5.55 W
Belfast, Me., U.S.	188	44.25 N	69.00 W
Belfast, N.Y., U.S.	210	42.20 N	78.06 W
Belfast, Oh., U.S.	218	39.03 N	83.32 W
Belfast (Aldergrove) Airport ⊠	48	54.38 N	6.12 W
Belfast Lough ⊂	48	54.40 N	5.50 W
Belfeld	52	51.19 N	6.06 E
Belfield, Austl.	274a	33.54 S	151.05 E
Belfield, N.D., U.S.	198	46.53 N	103.11 W
Belfiore	64	45.23 N	11.12 E
Belford, Eng., U.K.	44	55.36 N	1.49 W
Belford, N.J., U.S.	276	40.25 N	74.05 W
Belford Roxo	256	22.46 S	43.24 W
Belfort	58	47.38 N	6.52 E
Belfort □[8]	58	47.38 N	6.55 E
Belforte del Chienti	66	43.10 N	13.14 E
Belfry, Ky., U.S.	192	37.37 N	82.16 W
Belfry, Mt., U.S.	202	45.08 N	109.00 W
Belgaum	122	15.52 N	74.31 E
Belgern	54	51.29 N	13.07 E
Bélgica → Belgium □[1]	30	50.50 N	4.00 E
Belgica Mountains ʎ	9	72.35 S	31.10 E
België → Belgium □[1]	30	50.50 N	4.00 E
Belgien → Belgium □[1]	30	50.50 N	4.00 E
Belgioioso	62	45.10 N	9.19 E
Belgique → Belgium □[1]	30	50.50 N	4.00 E
Belgium □[1], Europe	22	50.50 N	4.00 E
Belgium □[1], Europe	30	50.50 N	4.00 E
Belgodère	36	42.35 N	9.01 E
Belgorod	78	50.36 N	36.35 E
Belgorod-Dnestrovskij	78	46.12 N	30.20 E
Belgrad → Beograd	38	44.50 N	20.30 E
Belgrade, Mn., U.S.	198	45.27 N	95.00 W
Belgrade, Mt., U.S.	202	45.46 N	111.10 W
Belgrade, Ne., U.S.	198	41.28 N	98.04 W
Belgrade → Beograd	38	44.50 N	20.30 E
Belgrado → Beograd	38	44.50 N	20.30 E
Belgrad Ormanı ◆[3]	267b	41.10 N	28.55 E
Belgrano ◆[8]	288	34.34 S	58.28 W
Belgrano ≃	254	48.15 S	71.14 W
Belgrano, Lago ⊜	254	47.50 S	72.09 W
Belgrano II ʋ[3]	9	77.46 S	38.11 W
Belgrave	274b	37.55 S	145.21 E
Belhar	124	24.55 N	86.36 E
Belhaven	192	35.32 N	76.37 W
Belhus Park ♠	260	51.31 N	0.17 E
Beliābera	126	22.17 N	86.57 E
Beliātor	126	23.20 N	87.13 E
Belica, Cro.	61	46.26 N	16.27 E
Belica, Ross.	78	51.07 N	35.34 E
Belice ≃	70	37.35 N	12.52 E
Belice → Belize □[1]	232	17.15 N	88.45 W
Belice → Belize City	232	17.30 N	88.12 W
Belichifor	140	6.33 N	33.16 E
Beliči	78	50.29 N	30.19 E
Belici ≃	70	37.31 N	13.50 E
Beličij, ostrov I	89	54.26 N	137.51 E
Belick	76	52.55 N	30.27 E
Belickoje	83	48.25 N	37.13 E
Beli Drim ≃	38	42.06 N	20.25 E
Beliki	78	49.15 N	34.16 E
Beliling, Gunung ∧	115b	8.37 S	119.59 E
Beli Manastir	38	45.46 N	18.36 E
Belin	32	44.30 N	0.47 W
Belinga	152	1.13 N	13.12 E
Belington	188	39.01 N	79.56 W
Belinskij	80	52.58 N	43.26 E
Belinyu	112	1.38 S	105.46 E
Belitung I	112	2.50 S	107.55 E
Belize □[1], N.A.	230	17.15 N	88.45 W
Belize □[1], N.A.	232	17.15 N	88.45 W
Belize ≃	232	17.32 N	88.14 W
Belize City	232	17.30 N	88.12 W
Belize Inlet ⊂	182	51.08 N	127.15 W
Belka	78	50.49 N	28.11 E
Belknap Crater ⊥[6]	202	44.17 N	121.50 W
Belkofski	180	55.05 N	162.02 W
Bel'kovo	82	56.15 N	38.48 E
Bel'kovskij, Ostrov I	74	75.32 N	135.44 E
Bell, Austl.	274b	37.45 S	145.00 E
Bell, Ciskei	158	33.15 S	27.23 E
Bell, Ca., U.S.	280	33.58 N	118.11 W
Bell □[6]	222	31.03 N	97.27 W
Bell ≃, P.Q., Can.	176	49.48 N	77.38 W
Bell ≃, Yk., Can.	180	67.17 N	137.46 W
Bella	68	40.45 N	15.32 E
Bella Bella	182	52.09 N	128.07 W
Bellac	32	46.07 N	1.02 E
Bella Coola	182	52.22 N	126.46 W
Bella Coola ≃	182	52.22 N	126.43 W
Bell Acres	279b	40.36 N	80.10 W
Bella Flor	248	11.09 S	67.49 W
Bellagio	58	45.59 N	9.15 E
Bellahy	48	53.58 N	8.48 W
Bellair	192	30.10 N	81.44 W
Bellaire, Mi., U.S.	190	44.58 N	85.12 W
Bellaire, Oh., U.S.	188	40.00 N	80.45 W
Bellaire, Tx., U.S.	222	29.42 N	95.27 W
Bella Isla, Estrecho de → Belle Isle, Strait of ʯ	176	51.35 N	56.30 W
Bella Lake ⊜	212	45.27 N	79.02 W
Bellambi	170	34.21 S	150.55 E
Bellamy, Al., U.S.	194	32.26 N	88.08 W
Bellamy, Va., U.S.	208	37.24 N	76.34 W
Bellano	58	46.03 N	9.18 E
Bellaria	66	44.09 N	12.28 E
Bellarine	169	38.08 S	144.37 E
Bellarine Peninsula ≻[1]	169	38.13 S	144.35 E
Bellariva	68	41.55 N	15.58 E
Bellary	122	15.09 N	76.56 E
Bellas Artes, Museo de ʋ	286c	10.30 N	66.53 W
Bellas Artes, Palacio de ʋ	286a	19.26 N	99.08 W
Bellata	166	29.55 S	149.47 E
Bella Tola ∧	58	46.15 N	7.39 E
Bella Unión	252	30.15 S	57.35 W
Bella Vista, Arg.	252	28.30 S	59.03 W
Bella Vista, Arg.	252	27.02 S	65.18 W
Bella Vista, Arg.	258	34.33 S	58.41 W
Bellavista, Chile	286e	33.31 S	70.37 W
Bella Vista, Para.	252	22.08 S	56.31 W
Bellavista, Perú	248	4.54 S	80.42 W
Bellavista, Perú	248	7.04 S	76.35 W
Bellavista, Perú	286d	12.04 S	77.08 W
Bellbird	170	32.51 S	151.21 E
Bellbrook, Austl.	166	30.49 S	152.31 E
Bellbrook, Oh., U.S.	218	39.38 N	84.04 W
Bell Brook ≃	168a	33.01 S	116.15 E
Bell Crags ∧[2]	44	55.03 N	2.22 W
Bell Creek ≃, Ca., U.S.	280	34.12 N	118.36 W
Bell Creek ≃, In., U.S.	218	40.09 N	85.27 W
Bellé, Sén.	150	14.25 N	12.18 W
Belle, Mo., U.S.	219	38.17 N	91.43 W
Belle, W.V., U.S.	188	38.13 N	81.32 W
Belle ≃, On., Can.	214	42.17 N	82.43 W
Belle ≃, Mi., U.S.	214	42.43 N	82.30 W
Belleair	220	27.55 N	82.48 W
Belleau	50	49.06 N	3.18 E
Belle Ayr Mountain ∧	210	42.07 N	74.29 W
Belle Bay ⊂	186	47.36 N	55.18 W
Belle Center	216	40.30 N	83.44 W
Belledonne, Chaîne de ʎ	62	45.18 N	6.08 E
Belle-Église	50	49.12 N	2.13 E
Belleek	48	54.28 N	8.06 W
Belle Farm Estates	208	39.23 N	76.45 W
Bellefontaine, Fr.	58	46.33 N	6.04 E
Bellefontaine, Fr.	261	49.06 N	2.28 E
Bellefontaine, Mart.	240e	14.40 N	61.10 W
Bellefontaine, Oh., U.S.	216	40.21 N	83.45 W
Bellefontaine Neighbors	219	38.44 N	90.13 W
Bellefonte, De., U.S.	208	39.45 N	75.30 W
Bellefonte, Md., U.S.	284c	38.47 N	76.52 W
Bellefonte, Pa., U.S.	214	40.54 N	77.46 W
Belle Fourche	198	44.40 N	103.51 W
Belle Fourche ≃	198	44.26 N	102.19 W
Belle Fourche Reservoir ⊜[1]	198	44.44 N	103.42 W
Bellegarde, Fr.	58	46.06 N	5.49 E
Bellegarde, Fr.	62	43.45 N	4.31 E
Bellegarde-du-Loiret	50	47.59 N	2.26 E
Bellegem	50	50.47 N	3.16 E
Belle Glade	220	26.41 N	80.40 W
Belle Glade Camp	220	26.40 N	80.41 W
Bellegrove	208	40.22 N	76.33 W
Belle Haven, Va., U.S.	208	37.33 N	75.49 W
Belle Haven, Va., U.S.	284c	38.47 N	77.04 W
Belleherbe	58	47.16 N	6.40 E
Belle Hôtesse ∧	241o	16.16 N	61.46 W
Belle-Île I	32	47.20 N	3.10 W
Belle Isle	220	28.27 N	81.21 W
Belle Isle I, Nf., Can.	176	51.55 N	55.20 W
Belle Isle I, Mi., U.S.	281	42.20 N	82.58 W
Belle Isle, Strait of ʯ	176	51.35 N	56.30 W
Belle Isle Park ♠	281	42.20 N	82.59 W
Bellelay	58	47.16 N	7.10 E
Bellême	50	48.22 N	0.34 E
Belle Mead	208	40.28 N	74.39 W
Bellemoor	285	39.43 N	75.35 W
Bellencombre	50	49.42 N	1.14 E
Bellenden Ker National Park ♠	164	17.15 S	145.53 E
Belleoram	186	47.31 N	55.25 W
Belleplain	208	39.16 N	74.52 W
Belle-Plaine, Sk., Can.	184	50.24 N	105.09 W
Belle Plaine, Ia., U.S.	190	41.53 N	92.16 W
Belle Plaine, Ks., U.S.	198	37.23 N	97.16 W
Belle Plaine, Mn., U.S.	190	44.37 N	93.46 W
Belle Rive	219	38.14 N	88.45 W
Belle River	214	42.18 N	82.43 W
Bellerose	276	40.44 N	73.43 W
Bellerose ◆[8]	276	40.45 N	73.43 W
Bellerose Terrace	276	40.43 N	73.43 W
Belle Terre	276	40.58 N	73.04 W
Bellevaux-Ligneuville	56	50.24 N	6.00 E
Belle Vernon	214	40.07 N	79.52 W
Bellevesvre	58	46.50 N	5.22 E
Belleview, Fl., U.S.	192	29.03 N	82.03 W
Belleview, In., U.S.	218	38.53 N	85.23 W
Belle View, Va., U.S.	208	38.46 N	77.03 W
Belleville, On., Can.	212	44.10 N	77.23 W
Belleville, Fr.	56	48.49 N	6.06 E
Belleville, Il., U.S.	219	38.31 N	89.59 W
Belleville, In., U.S.	218	39.41 N	86.29 W
Belleville, Ks., U.S.	198	39.49 N	97.37 W
Belleville, Mi., U.S.	216	42.12 N	83.29 W
Belleville, N.J., U.S.	210	40.47 N	74.09 W
Belleville, N.Y., U.S.	212	43.47 N	76.07 W
Belleville, Pa., U.S.	214	40.36 N	77.43 W
Belleville, R.I., U.S.	207	41.33 N	71.28 W
Belleville, Wi., U.S.	216	42.51 N	89.32 W
Belleville Lake ⊜	281	42.12 N	83.29 W
Belleville-sur-Meuse	56	49.11 N	5.23 E
Belleville-sur-Saône	58	46.06 N	4.45 E
Bellevue, Ab., Can.	182	49.35 N	114.22 W
Bellevue, Fr.	50	49.53 N	4.12 E
Bellevue, Id., U.S.	202	43.27 N	114.15 W
Bellevue, Ia., U.S.	190	42.15 N	90.25 W
Bellevue, Ky., U.S.	218	39.06 N	84.28 W
Bellevue, Md., U.S.	208	38.42 N	76.11 W
Bellevue, Mi., U.S.	216	42.26 N	85.01 W
Bellevue, Ne., U.S.	198	41.08 N	95.53 W
Bellevue, Oh., U.S.	214	41.16 N	82.50 W
Bellevue, Pa., U.S.	214	40.29 N	80.03 W
Bellevue, Tx., U.S.	196	33.38 N	98.01 W
Bellevue, Wa., U.S.	224	47.36 N	122.11 W
Bellevue ◆[8]	273d	26.11 S	28.05 E
Belle Vue Zoological Gardens ♠	262	53.28 N	2.11 W
Bell Ewart	212	44.16 N	79.33 W
Belley	62	45.46 N	5.41 E
Belleydoux	58	46.15 N	5.46 E
Belle Yella	150	7.22 N	10.00 W
Bellflower, Ca., U.S.	228	33.52 N	118.06 W
Bellflower, Il., U.S.	216	40.20 N	88.32 W
Bellflower, Mo., U.S.	219	39.00 N	91.21 W
Bell Gardens	228	33.57 N	118.09 W
Bellheim	56	49.11 N	8.16 E
Bell Hill ∧[2]	210	43.09 N	75.07 W
Bell Homestead ⊥	212	43.04 N	80.18 W
Bellicourt	50	49.57 N	3.14 E
Bellingdon	260	51.44 N	0.38 W
Bellinge	41	55.20 N	10.20 E
Bellingen	166	30.27 S	152.54 E
Bellingham, Eng., U.K.	44	55.09 N	2.16 W
Bellingham, Ma., U.S.	207	42.05 N	71.28 W
Bellingham, Mn., U.S.	198	45.08 N	96.17 W
Bellingham, Wa., U.S.	224	48.45 N	122.29 W
Bellingham Bay ⊂	224	48.45 N	122.35 W
Bellingshausen ʋ[3]	9	62.12 S	58.58 W
Bellingshausen Sea ⊤[2]	9	71.00 S	85.00 W
Bellingwolde	52	53.07 N	7.09 E
Bellinzago Novarese	62	45.34 N	8.38 E
Bellinzona	58	46.11 N	9.02 E
Bell Island I, Nf., Can.	186	47.36 N	52.58 W
Bell Island I, Nf., Can.	186	50.44 N	55.35 W
Bell Island Hot Springs	182	55.56 N	131.34 W
Bellmawr	208	39.52 N	75.05 W
Bellmead	222	31.35 N	97.06 W
Bellmore	276	40.40 N	73.31 W
Bell Mountain	228	34.35 N	117.15 W
Bellnhausen	56	50.42 N	8.43 E
Bello, Col.	246	6.20 N	75.33 W
Bello, Cuba	286b	23.07 N	82.24 W
Bello Horizonte → Belo Horizonte	255	19.55 S	43.56 W
Bellona	210	42.46 N	77.01 W
Bellona, Récifs ✣[2]	160	21.30 S	159.00 E
Bellona Plateau ✣[3]	14	20.30 S	158.30 E
Bellone, Cap ≻	157b	16.14 S	49.51 E
Bellosguardo	68	40.25 N	15.19 E
Bellot Strait ʯ	176	71.58 N	94.45 W
Bellows Falls	188	43.08 N	72.26 W
Belloy-en-France	261	49.05 N	2.22 E
Bellpat	120	28.59 N	68.00 E
Bell Peninsula ≻[1]	176	63.50 N	82.00 W
Bell Point	279b	40.33 N	79.33 W
Bells, Tn., U.S.	194	35.43 N	89.05 W
Bells, Tx., U.S.	196	33.37 N	96.25 W
Bellsbank	44	55.18 N	4.23 W
Bells Bay ⊂	212	45.30 N	77.51 W
Bells Corners	212	45.19 N	75.50 W
Bellshill	46	55.49 N	4.01 W
Bells Lake	285	39.44 N	75.02 W
Bells Lake ⊜	285	39.45 N	75.04 W
Belltown, De., U.S.	208	38.44 N	75.10 W
Belltown, Il., U.S.	219	39.23 N	90.25 W
Belluno	64	46.09 N	12.13 E
Belluno □[4]	64	46.15 N	12.08 E
Bellvale	210	41.15 N	74.18 W
Bell Ville, Arg.	252	32.37 S	62.42 W
Bellville, S. Afr.	158	33.53 S	18.36 E
Bellville, Oh., U.S.	214	40.37 N	82.30 W
Bellville, Tx., U.S.	222	29.57 N	96.15 W
Bellwood, Il., U.S.	278	41.52 N	87.52 W
Bellwood, Ne., U.S.	198	41.20 N	97.14 W
Bellwood, Pa., U.S.	214	40.36 N	78.19 W
Bellwood, Lake ⊜	212	43.46 N	80.20 W
Belly ≃	182	49.46 N	113.02 W
Bellyk	86	54.32 N	91.17 E
Belm	52	52.18 N	8.08 E
Belmar, Md., U.S.	284b	39.21 N	76.32 W
Belmar, N.J., U.S.	208	40.10 N	74.01 W
Bélmez	34	38.16 N	5.12 W
Belmiro Braga	256	21.57 S	43.25 W
Belmond	190	42.50 N	93.36 W
Belmont, Austl.	169	38.10 S	144.21 E
Belmont, Austl.	170	33.02 S	151.40 E
Belmont, Mb., Can.	184	49.24 N	99.27 W
Belmont, N.S., Can.	186	45.25 N	63.23 W
Belmont, On., Can.	212	42.53 N	81.05 W
Belmont, S. Afr.	158	29.28 S	24.22 E
Belmont, Eng., U.K.	262	53.38 N	2.30 W
Belmont, Ca., U.S.	226	37.31 N	122.16 W
Belmont, Ma., U.S.	283	42.23 N	71.10 W
Belmont, Mi., U.S.	216	43.05 N	85.37 W
Belmont, Ms., U.S.	194	34.30 N	88.12 W
Belmont, N.H., U.S.	188	43.26 N	71.28 W
Belmont, N.Y., U.S.	210	42.13 N	78.02 W
Belmont, Pa., U.S.	214	40.17 N	78.53 W
Belmont, S.C., U.S.	192	34.02 N	81.01 W
Belmont, Tx., U.S.	222	29.31 N	97.41 W
Belmont, Wi., U.S.	190	42.44 N	90.20 W
Belmont □[6]	214	40.05 N	80.54 W
Belmonte, Bra.	255	15.51 S	38.54 W
Belmonte, Esp.	34	39.34 N	2.42 W
Belmonte, Esp.	34	43.17 N	6.14 W
Belmonte, Port.	34	40.21 N	7.21 W
Belmonte Calabro	68	39.09 N	16.05 E
Belmonte Mezzagno	70	38.02 N	13.23 E
Belmont Harbor ⊂	278	41.57 N	87.38 W
Belmont Lake ⊜, On., Can.	212	44.30 N	77.50 W
Belmont Lake ⊜, N.Y., U.S.	276	40.44 N	73.20 W
Belmont Lake State Park ♠	276	40.43 N	73.20 W
Belmont Park	214	41.10 N	80.39 W
Belmont Park Race Track ♠	276	40.43 N	73.43 W
Belmont Reservoir ⊜[1]	262	53.39 N	2.30 W
Belmont Slough ≃	282	37.33 N	122.14 W
Belmopan	232	17.15 N	88.46 W
Belmore, Austl.	274a	33.55 S	151.05 E
Belmore, Oh., U.S.	216	41.09 N	83.56 W
Belmullet	48	54.14 N	10.00 W
Belmuri	272b	22.57 N	88.09 E
Belo	157b	19.42 S	44.33 E
Belœil, Bel.	50	50.33 N	3.43 E
Beloeil, P.Q., Can.	206	45.34 N	73.12 W
Belœil, Château de ʋ	50	50.35 N	3.44 E
Beloeil, Ruisseau ≃	275a	45.39 N	73.12 W
Beloglazovo	86	56.05 N	72.40 E
Belogorje, Ross.	78	50.30 N	40.01 E
Belogorje, Ukr.	78	50.01 N	26.25 E
Belogorka	80	50.42 N	53.27 E
Belogornoje	80	52.25 N	47.35 E
Belogorode	82	54.23 N	38.31 E
Belogorodka	78	50.00 N	26.39 E
Belogorovka	83	48.55 N	38.15 E
Belogorsk, Ross.	86	55.05 N	88.28 E
Belogorsk, Ross.	89	50.57 N	128.25 E
Belogorsk, Ukr.	78	45.03 N	34.36 E
Belogorskij	86	49.27 N	83.10 E
Belogorskoje	80	53.35 N	48.12 E
Belogradčik	38	43.38 N	22.41 E
Beloguša	78	51.57 N	26.56 E
Beloha	157b	25.10 S	45.03 E
Belo Horizonte	255	19.55 S	43.56 W
Beloit, Ks., U.S.	198	39.27 N	98.06 W
Beloit, Oh., U.S.	214	40.55 N	80.59 W
Beloit, Wi., U.S.	216	42.30 N	89.01 W
Belo Jardim	250	8.20 S	36.26 W
Belojarsk	86	53.28 N	83.54 E
Beloje, Kaz.	86	48.55 N	82.58 E
Beloje, Ross.	80	58.23 N	39.24 E
Beloje, Ukr.	83	48.31 N	39.04 E
Beloje, ozero ⊜	76	60.11 N	37.37 E
Beloje more (White Sea) ⊤[2]	24	65.30 N	38.00 E
Belokamenskoje ◆[8]	83	48.41 N	38.06 E
Belokany	84	41.43 N	46.26 E
Belokurakino	83	49.33 N	38.44 E
Belokuricha	86	51.59 N	84.59 E
Beloluck	83	49.41 N	39.02 E
Belomestnaja	76	52.24 N	37.37 E
Belomestnaja Dvojn'a	80	52.42 N	41.03 E
Belomorsk	24	64.32 N	34.48 E
Belomorsko-Baltijskij kanal ≍	24	62.48 N	34.48 E
Belondo	152	0.16 S	19.31 E
Belonge	152	2.06 S	19.32 E
Belonia	124	23.15 N	91.27 E
Beloomut	76	54.57 N	39.20 E
Beloozersk	76	52.28 N	25.11 E
Belopolje	78	51.09 N	34.18 E
Belorado	34	42.25 N	3.11 W
Belorečensk	78	44.46 N	39.52 E
Beloreck	86	53.58 N	58.24 E
Belören, Tür.	130	37.12 N	32.33 E
Belören, Tür.	130	40.51 N	33.30 E
Belören, Tür.	130	37.39 N	37.34 E
Belorussia → Belarus □[1]	22	53.35 N	28.00 E
Belorussija → Belarus □[1]	72	53.50 N	28.00 E
Belorussiya → Belarus □[1]	72	53.50 N	28.00 E
Belorusskaja gr'ada ∧	76	53.40 N	27.00 E
Beloščelje	24	64.52 N	46.56 E
Belo-sur-mer	157b	20.44 S	44.00 E
Belot, Lac ⊜	180	66.55 N	126.18 W
Belousovka, Kaz.	86	50.08 N	82.33 E
Belousovka, Ukr.	78	49.57 N	32.20 E
Belousovo	82	55.05 N	36.40 E
Bel'ov	76	53.48 N	36.08 E
Belo Vale	255	20.25 S	44.01 W
Belovežskaja Pušča, zapovednik ♠	76	52.40 N	23.50 E
Belovo, Ross.	86	52.57 N	82.16 E
Belovo, Ross.	86	54.25 N	86.18 E
Belovodsk	83	49.12 N	39.35 E
Belovodskoje	85	42.50 N	74.06 E
Beloz'orje, Ukr.	78	49.29 N	31.35 E
Beloz'orje, Ukr.	78	49.18 N	31.54 E
Beloz'orka	78	46.37 N	32.27 E
Beloz'orsk	76	60.02 N	37.48 E
Beloz'orskoje	78	48.33 N	37.04 E
Belp	58	46.53 N	7.30 E
Belpāda	272c	19.02 N	73.03 E
Belpasso	70	37.35 N	14.58 E
Belper	44	53.01 N	1.29 W
Belpre	188	39.16 N	81.34 W
Belrose	274a	33.44 S	151.13 E
Belsano	214	40.31 N	78.52 W
Belsele	50	51.09 N	4.05 E
Bel'skaja Vol'a	78	51.27 N	25.49 E
Bel'skoje, Ross.	80	54.44 N	40.22 E
Bel'skoje, Ross.	86	57.49 N	92.09 E
Belson Run ≃	279b	40.12 N	79.37 W
Belspring	192	37.11 N	80.36 W
Belt	202	47.23 N	110.55 W
Beltana	166	30.48 S	138.25 E
Belt Creek ≃	202	47.36 N	111.02 W
Belted Range ʎ	204	37.25 N	116.10 W
Belterra	250	2.38 S	54.57 W
Belthorn	262	53.43 N	2.26 W
Beltinci	61	46.36 N	16.15 E
Belton, Eng., U.K.	42	52.34 N	1.41 E
Belton, Eng., U.K.	44	53.33 N	0.49 W
Belton, Mo., U.S.	194	38.48 N	94.31 W
Belton, S.C., U.S.	192	34.31 N	82.29 W
Belton, Tx., U.S.	222	31.03 N	97.27 W
Belton Lake ⊜[1]	222	31.08 N	97.32 W
Beltra	48	54.13 N	8.37 W
Beltrán	252	27.50 S	64.04 W
Beltsville, Md., U.S.	208	39.02 N	76.54 W
Beltsville, Md., U.S.	284c	39.02 N	76.54 W
Bel'tsy → Bel'c'	78	47.46 N	27.56 E
Belturbet	48	54.06 N	7.28 W
Beltway Plaza ◆[9]	284c	39.00 N	76.54 W
Bel'tyrskij	86	53.02 N	90.16 E
Beltzville Lake ⊜[1]	210	40.52 N	75.37 W
Beltzville State Park ♠	210	40.52 N	75.36 W
Belucha, gora ∧	86	49.48 N	86.40 E
Belucha, ozero ⊜	80	49.20 N	46.05 E
Belugino	82	54.47 N	37.54 E
Belumut, Gunong ∧	114	2.02 N	103.34 E
Belūr, India	122	13.10 N	75.52 E
Belur, India	272b	22.38 N	88.18 E
Beluran	112	5.54 N	117.33 E
Belur Math ʋ[1]	272b	22.38 N	88.22 E
Belušje	24	66.54 N	47.31 E
Belvedere, It.	64	45.44 N	13.23 E
Belvedere, Ca., U.S.	226	37.52 N	122.28 W
Belvedere, Va., U.S.	284c	38.50 N	77.10 W
Belvedere ◆[8]	260	51.29 N	0.09 E
Belvedere ʋ	264b	48.11 N	16.23 E
Belvedere di Spinello	68	39.12 N	16.53 E
Belvedere Homes	220	26.43 N	80.06 W
Belvedere Marittimo	68	39.37 N	15.52 E
Belvedere Ostrense	66	43.34 N	13.09 E
Belvès	32	44.47 N	1.00 E
Belvidere, De., U.S.	208	39.43 N	75.37 W
Belvidere, Il., U.S.	216	42.15 N	88.50 W
Belvidere, N.J., U.S.	210	40.49 N	75.04 W
Belview	198	44.36 N	95.19 W
Belvis	266a	40.33 N	3.33 W
Belvís de la Jara	34	39.45 N	4.57 W
Belvoir, Vale of V	42	52.57 N	0.53 W
Belvoir → Kokhav HaYarden ⊥	132	32.36 N	35.31 E
Belyando ≃	166	21.38 S	146.50 E
Belyj	76	55.50 N	32.56 E
Belyj, ostrov I	74	73.10 N	70.45 E
Belyje Berega	76	53.12 N	34.40 E
Belyje Kolodezi	82	54.55 N	38.42 E
Belyje Stolby	82	55.20 N	37.52 E
Belyje Vody	85	42.25 N	69.50 E
Belyj Gorodok	76	56.58 N	37.30 E
Belyj Jar, Ross.	80	53.57 N	48.58 E
Belyj Jar, Ross.	86	53.36 N	91.24 E
Belyj Jar, Ross.	86	58.26 N	85.01 E
Belyj Kalodez'	78	50.02 N	38.40 E

Symbol	English	Deutsch	Español	Français	Português
≃	River	Fluß	Río	Rivière	Rio
≍	Canal	Kanal	Canal	Canal	Canal
ʟ	Waterfall, Rapids	Wasserfall, Stromschnellen	Cascada, Rápidos	Chute d'eau, Rapides	Cascata, Rápidos
ʯ	Strait	Meeresstraße	Estrecho	Détroit	Estreito
⊂	Bay, Gulf	Bucht, Golf	Bahía, Golfo	Baie, Golfe	Baía, Golfo
⊜	Lake, Lakes	See, Seen	Lago, Lagos	Lac, Lacs	Lago, Lagos
⩨	Swamp	Sumpf	Pantano	Marais	Pântano
⌂	Ice Features, Glacier	Eis- und Gletscherformen	Accidentes Glaciales	Formes glaciaires	Acidentes glaciares
⊤	Other Hydrographic Features	Andere Hydrographische Objekte	Otros Elementos Hidrográficos	Autres données hydrographiques	Outros acidentes hidrográficos
✣	Submarine Features	Untermeerische Objekte	Accidentes Submarinos	Formes de relief sous-marin	Acidentes submarinos
□	Political Unit	Politische Einheit	Unidad Politica	Entité politique	Unidade política
ʋ	Cultural Institution	Kulturelle Institution	Institución Cultural	Institution culturelle	Institução cultural
⊥	Historical Site	Historische Stätte	Sitio Histórico	Site historique	Sitio histórico
♠	Recreational Site	Erholungs- und Ferienort	Sitio de Recreo	Centre de loisirs	Area de Lazer
⊠	Airport	Flughafen	Aeropuerto	Aéroport	Aeroporto
■	Military Installation	Militäranlage	Instalación Militar	Installation militaire	Instalação militar
◆	Miscellaneous	Verschiedenes	Misceláneo	Divers	Diversos

Symbols in the index entries represent the broad categories identified in the key at the right. Symbols follow superior numbers (*) at the right. Symbols following superior numbers (*) identify subcategories (see complete key on page I · 1).

Symbole im Register stellen die rechts im Schlüssel erklärten Kategorien dar. Symbole mit hochgestellten Ziffern (*) bezeichnen Unterkategorien einer Kategorie (vgl. vollständiger Schlüssel auf Seite I · 1).

Les symboles de l'index représentent les catégories indiquées dans la légende à droite. Les symboles suivis d'un indice (*) représentent des sous-catégories (voir légende complète à la page I · 1).

Os símbolos incluídos no texto do índice representam as grandes categorias identificadas com a chave à direita. Os símbolos com números de su parte superior (*) identificam as subcategorias (veja-se a chave completa à página I · 1).

Los símbolos incluídos en el texto del índice representan las grandes categorías con a la derecha. Los símbolos con números en su parte superior (*) identifican las subcategorías (véase la clave completa en la página I · 1).

	English	Deutsch	Français	Português	Español
▲	Mountain	Berg	Montagne	Montanha	Montaña
▲	Mountains	Gebirge	Montagnes	Montanhas	Montañas
)	Pass	Paß	Col	Passo	Paso
∨	Valley, Canyon	Tal, Cañon	Vallée, Canyon	Vale, Canhão	Valle, Cañón
≍	Plain	Ebene	Plaine	Planície	Llano
>	Cape	Kap	Cap	Cabo	Cabo
ı	Island	Insel	Île	Ilha	Isla
ıı	Islands	Inseln	Îles	Ilhas	Islas
〓	Other Topographic Features	Andere Topographische Objekte	Autres Éléments Topographiques	Outros Elementos Topográficos	Otros Elementos Topográficos

ESPAÑOL

Nombre	Página	Lat.°′	Long.°′ W = Oeste
Bethlehem, S. Afr.	158	27.10 S	24.00 E
Bethlehem, Ct., U.S.	207	41.38 N	73.12 W
Bethlehem, In., U.S.	218	38.32 N	85.25 W
Bethlehem, Ky., U.S.	218	38.24 N	85.04 W
Bethlehem, Pa., U.S.	210	40.37 N	75.22 W
Bethlehem, W.V., U.S.	188	40.02 N	80.41 W
Bethlehem → Bayt Laḥm	132	31.43 N	35.12 E
Bethlehem Center	210	42.40 N	73.42 W
Bethlehem Steel Corporation ♁[3], Md., U.S.	284b	39.13 N	76.29 W
Bethlehem Steel Corporation (Lackawanna Plant) ♁[3], N.Y., U.S.	284a	42.49 N	78.52 W
Bethnal Green ◆[8]	260	51.32 N	0.03 W
Bethoncourt	58	47.32 N	6.48 E
Bethpage	210	40.44 N	73.28 W
Bethpage State Park ♠	210	40.45 N	73.27 W
Bethulie	158	30.32 S	25.59 E
Bethune, Sk., Can.	184	50.43 N	105.08 W
Béthune, Fr.	50	50.32 N	2.38 E
Bethune, S.C., U.S.	192	34.24 N	80.20 W
Béthune ≏	50	49.53 N	1.09 E
Beticos, Sistemas ⋀	34	37.00 N	4.00 W
Betijoque	246	9.23 N	70.44 W
Betil	126	24.14 N	89.43 E
Betio	174t	1.21 N	172.56 E
Betioky	157b	23.42 S	44.22 E
Betis ≏	114	4.53 N	101.48 E
Betlica	76	54.01 N	33.57 E
Betna ≏	126	22.34 N	89.12 E
Bet Netofa, Biq'at ≚	132	32.49 N	35.19 E
Betnoti	126	21.44 N	86.51 E
Beton-Bazoches	50	48.42 N	3.15 E
Betong, Malay.	112	1.24 N	111.31 E
Betong, Thai	110	5.45 N	101.05 E
Betoota	166	25.42 S	140.44 E
Bétou	152	3.03 N	18.31 E
Betpak-Dala ◆[2]	86	46.00 N	70.00 E
Betroka	157b	23.16 S	46.06 E
Betsham	260	51.25 N	0.19 E
Bet Sh'ean	132	32.30 N	35.30 E
Bet She'arim, Horbat ⊥	132	32.42 N	35.08 E
Bet Shemesh	132	31.45 N	35.00 E
Betsiamites	186	48.56 N	68.38 W
Betsiamites ≏	186	48.56 N	68.38 W
Betsiamites, Barrage ◆[6]	186	49.22 N	69.47 W
Betsiamites, Pointe de ›	186	48.55 N	68.37 W
Betsiamites, Réserve indienne de ◆[4]	186	49.05 N	68.37 W
Betsiboka ≏	157b	16.03 S	46.36 E
Betsie, Point ›	190	44.42 N	86.16 W
Betsioky	157b	21.31 S	44.28 E
Betsukai	92a	43.23 N	145.17 E
Betsy Layne	192	37.33 N	82.38 W
Betsy Ross Bridge ◆[5]	285	39.59 N	75.04 W
Bette ∧	146	22.00 N	19.12 E
Bettembourg	56	49.32 N	6.02 E
Bettendorf	190	41.31 N	90.30 W
Betterton	208	39.21 N	76.03 W
Bettiah	124	26.48 N	84.30 E
Bettie	222	32.48 N	94.58 W
Bettles Field	180	66.55 N	151.30 W
Bettola	62	44.47 N	9.36 E
Bettona	66	43.01 N	12.29 E
Bettrath ◆[8]	263	51.13 N	6.26 E
Bettsville	214	41.14 N	83.14 W
Bettyhill	46	58.32 N	4.14 W
Betty's Bay	158	34.22 S	18.52 E
Betūl	124	21.55 N	77.54 E
Betumbe-Bongo	152	2.11 S	18.46 E
Betung, Indon.	112	1.52 S	103.16 E
Betung, Indon.	112	2.50 S	104.14 E
Betuwe ◆[1]	52	51.55 N	5.30 E
Betwa ≏	124	25.55 N	80.12 E
Betws-y-Coed	44	53.05 N	3.48 W
Betz	50	49.09 N	2.57 E
Betz ≏	50	48.09 N	2.45 E
Betzdorf	56	50.47 N	7.53 E
Betzenstein	60	49.41 N	11.25 E
Béu	152	6.14 S	15.28 E
Beucha	54	51.19 N	12.34 E
Beugneux	50	49.14 N	3.25 E
Beuil	62	44.06 N	6.59 E
Beulah, Austl.	166	35.56 S	142.26 E
Beulah, Co., U.S.	200	38.04 N	104.59 W
Beulah, Mi., U.S.	190	44.37 N	86.05 W
Beulah, Ms., U.S.	194	33.47 N	90.58 W
Beulah, N.D., U.S.	198	47.15 N	101.46 W
Beulah, Lake ⊜	216	42.49 N	88.23 W
Beulah Beach	214	41.25 N	82.22 W
Beulah Reservoir ⊜[1]	202	43.56 N	118.09 W
Beulaville	192	34.55 N	77.46 W
Beult ≏	260	51.14 N	0.25 E
Beure	58	47.12 N	6.00 E
Beureunun	114	5.18 N	95.59 E
Beuron	58	48.03 N	8.58 E
Beuthen → Bytom	30	50.22 N	18.54 E
Beuvron ≏, Fr.	50	47.28 N	3.31 E
Beuvron ≏, Fr.	50	47.29 N	1.15 E
Beuvronne ≏	261	48.56 N	2.44 E
Beuvry	50	50.31 N	2.41 E
Beuzeville	50	49.20 N	0.21 E
Bevagna	66	42.56 N	12.36 E
Bevensen	52	53.05 N	10.34 E
Bever ≏	52	52.01 N	7.46 E
Bevera ≏	62	43.49 N	7.34 E
Beveren	50	51.13 N	4.15 E
B. Everett Jordan Lake ⊜[1]	192	35.45 N	79.00 W
Beverino	62	44.14 N	9.47 E
Beverley, Austl.	168a	32.06 S	116.56 E
Beverley, Eng., U.K.	44	53.52 N	0.26 W
Beverley Minster ♁[1]	44	53.50 N	0.27 W
Beverley Springs	162	16.43 S	125.28 E
Beverlo	56	51.05 N	5.12 E
Beverly, Ma., U.S.	207	42.33 N	70.52 W
Beverly, N.J., U.S.	208	40.03 N	74.55 W
Beverly, Tx., U.S.	222	31.30 N	97.10 W
Beverly ◆[8]	278	41.43 N	87.41 W
Beverly Farms, Md., U.S.	284c	39.04 N	77.11 W
Beverly Farms, Ma., U.S.	283	42.34 N	70.49 W
Beverly Harbor ⊂	283	42.32 N	70.53 W
Beverly Hills, Austl.	274a	33.57 S	151.05 E
Beverly Hills, Ca., U.S.	228	34.04 N	118.23 W
Beverly Hills, Fl., U.S.	220	28.56 N	82.28 W
Beverly Hills, Mi., U.S.	216	42.31 N	83.13 W
Beverly Lake ⊜	176	64.36 N	100.30 W
Beverly Municipal Airport ⊠	283	42.35 N	70.55 W
Beverly Run ≏	208	37.55 N	77.11 W
Beverly Shores	216	41.41 N	86.58 W
Bevern	52	51.51 N	9.29 E
Beverstausee ⊜[1]	263	51.09 N	7.23 E
Beverstedt	52	53.26 N	8.49 E
Beverungen	52	51.39 N	9.22 E
Beverwijk	52	52.28 N	4.40 E
Bevier	194	39.45 N	92.34 W
Bevin, Lac ⊜	206	45.57 N	74.35 W
Bevoalavo	157b	25.13 S	45.26 E
Bewani	164	3.02 S	141.10 E
Bewani Mountains ⋀	164	3.10 S	141.25 E
Bewār	124	27.13 N	79.18 E
Bewdley, On., Can.	212	44.05 N	78.19 W
Bewdley, Eng., U.K.	42	52.22 N	2.19 W
Bewl Water ⊜[1]	42	51.04 N	0.24 E
Bex	58	46.15 N	7.01 E
Bexhill	42	50.50 N	0.29 E
Bexley, Austl.	274a	33.57 S	151.08 E
Bexley, Oh., U.S.	218	39.58 N	82.56 W

FRANÇAIS

Nom	Page	Lat.°′	Long.°′ W = Ouest
Bexley ◆[8]	260	51.26 N	0.10 E
Beyazköy	130	41.21 N	27.42 E
Beybach ≏	56	50.13 N	7.23 E
Beyçayırı	130	40.15 N	26.55 E
Beycuma	130	41.19 N	31.59 E
Bey Dağları ⋀	130	36.40 N	30.15 E
Beydagları Olimpos Milli Parkı ♠	130	36.40 N	30.25 E
Beydili	130	40.10 N	31.01 E
Beyenburg ◆[8]	263	51.15 N	7.18 E
Beykoz ◆[8]	267b	41.08 N	29.05 E
Beyla	150	8.41 N	8.37 W
Beylerbeyi ◆[8]	267b	41.03 N	29.03 E
Beylikahır	130	39.42 N	31.13 E
Beylul	144	13.10 N	42.26 E
Beynes	261	48.51 N	1.53 E
Beynes-Thiverval, Aérodrome de ⊠	261	48.51 N	1.54 E
Beyoğlu ◆[8]	267b	41.02 N	28.59 E
Beypazarı	130	40.10 N	31.56 E
Beypınarı	130	39.31 N	37.44 E
Beypore	122	11.11 N	75.49 E
Beyra	144	6.57 N	47.19 E
Beyrouth → Bayrūt	130	33.53 N	35.30 E
Beyşehir	130	37.41 N	31.43 E
Beyşehir Gölü ⊜	130	37.40 N	31.30 E
Beytüşşebap	128	37.34 N	43.10 E
Bezaha	157b	23.30 S	44.31 E
Bežanickaja vozvyšennost' ⋀[1]	76	56.54 N	29.20 E
Bežanicy	76	56.58 N	29.53 E
Bezau	58	47.23 N	9.54 E
Bezavona ∧	157b	15.02 S	49.52 E
Bezdež	76	52.19 N	25.18 E
Bezděz ∧	54	50.32 N	14.43 E
Bezděz ⊥	54	50.32 N	14.46 E
Bèze	58	47.28 N	5.16 E
Bežeck	76	57.47 N	36.39 E
Bežeckij Verch ⋀[1]	76	57.36 N	36.54 E
Bezenčuk	80	52.59 N	49.26 E
Bezerra ≏	255	13.16 S	47.31 W
Bezerros	250	8.14 S	35.45 W
Bezet	132	33.05 N	35.08 E
Béziers	32	43.21 N	3.15 E
Bezmein	128	38.05 N	58.12 E
Bezmenšur	80	56.29 N	51.17 E
Bezons	261	48.56 N	2.13 E
Bežta	84	42.08 N	46.08 E
Bezwada → Vijayawāda	122	16.31 N	80.37 E
Bezym'anka	80	49.56 N	43.15 E
Bezym'annaja	80	51.20 N	46.26 E
Bezymennoje	83	47.06 N	37.56 E
Bezzecca	64	45.55 N	10.43 E
Bezzubovo	82	55.27 N	38.55 E
Bhabānipur, India	272b	22.57 N	88.27 E
Bhabānipur, India	272b	22.56 N	88.13 E
Bhabhua	124	25.03 N	83.37 E
Bhābta	126	23.59 N	88.15 E
Bhadarwāh	123	32.59 N	75.43 E
Bhadaur	123	30.29 N	75.19 E
Bhādgāon → Bhaktapur	124	27.42 N	85.27 E
Bhadohi	124	25.25 N	82.34 E
Bhādra	123	29.07 N	75.10 E
Bhadra ≏[1]	126	22.19 N	89.31 E
Bhadrāchalam	122	17.40 N	80.53 E
Bhadrak	120	21.03 N	86.30 E
Bhadrapur	124	26.32 N	88.06 E
Bhadra Reservoir ⊜[1]	122	13.40 N	75.35 E
Bhadrāvati	122	13.52 N	75.43 E
Bhadreswar	126	22.50 N	88.21 E
Bhādua	272b	22.41 N	88.12 E
Bhāg	120	29.02 N	67.49 E
Bhagaiya	124	25.12 N	87.29 E
Bhāgalpur	124	25.15 N	87.00 E
Bhāgīrathi ≏, India	124	30.08 N	78.35 E
Bhāgīrathi ≏, India	126	23.25 N	88.23 E
Bhagirathpur	126	24.05 N	88.29 E
Bhagwānpur	126	22.07 N	87.45 E
Bhainsa	122	19.06 N	77.58 E
Bhāi Pheru	123	31.12 N	73.57 E
Bhairab ≏[1]	126	22.51 N	89.34 E
Bhairab Bāzār	120	24.04 N	90.58 E
Bhairhawā	124	27.31 N	83.24 E
Bhaironghāti	120	31.01 N	78.53 E
Bhakkar	123	31.38 N	71.04 E
Bhākra Dam ◆[6]	123	31.24 N	76.30 E
Bhaktapur	124	27.42 N	85.27 E
Bhal	272c	19.11 N	73.08 E
Bhālki	122	18.02 N	77.13 E
Bhalswa ◆[8]	272a	28.44 N	77.10 E
Bhalwāl	123	32.16 N	72.54 E
Bhamdūn	132	33.48 N	35.39 E
Bhamo	110	24.16 N	97.14 E
Bhandāra	120	21.10 N	79.39 E
Bhandārdaha	272b	22.37 N	88.13 E
Bhandāria	126	22.29 N	90.04 E
Bhānder	124	25.44 N	78.45 E
Bhander Plateau ⋀[1]	124	24.10 N	80.20 E
Bhāndup ◆[8]	272c	19.09 N	72.57 E
Bhānga	126	23.22 N	89.59 E
Bhāngar	126	22.31 N	88.37 E
Bhāngar Kāta Khāl ≏	272b	22.31 N	88.33 E
Bhanvad	120	21.56 N	69.47 E
Bhārat → India □[1]	118	20.00 N	77.00 E
Bharatpur, India	124	27.13 N	77.29 E
Bharatpur, India	126	23.53 N	88.05 E
Bharatpur, Nepāl	124	27.14 N	84.21 E
Bharthana	124	26.45 N	79.14 E
Bharūch	120	21.42 N	72.58 E
Bhātai	126	23.36 N	89.11 E
Bhātāpāra	120	21.44 N	81.56 E
Bhātār	126	23.25 N	87.54 E
Bhatgaon → Bhaktapur	124	27.42 N	85.27 E
Bhātghar Lake ⊜[1]	122	18.12 N	73.49 E
Bhātiāpāra Ghāt	124	23.13 N	89.42 E
Bhatkal	122	13.58 N	74.34 E
Bhātpāra	126	22.52 N	88.24 E
Bhātpur	272b	22.43 N	88.25 E
Bhātsāla	126	22.33 N	90.30 E
Bhattapratāp	126	22.45 N	89.48 E
Bhattiprolu	122	16.06 N	80.47 E
Bhātua	272b	22.57 N	88.22 E
Bhaun	123	32.52 N	72.45 E
Bhaunja	272a	28.40 N	77.25 E
Bhavāni	122	11.27 N	77.41 E
Bhāvnagar	122	21.46 N	72.09 E
Bhawānīgarh	124	30.16 N	76.02 E
Bhawani Mandi	120	24.25 N	75.50 E
Bhawānipatna	122	19.54 N	83.10 E
Bhedia	126	23.36 N	87.42 E
Bheigeir, Beinn ∧[2]	46	55.44 N	6.05 W
Bhendkhal	272c	18.53 N	72.59 E
Bhera	123	32.29 N	72.55 E
Bheramara	126	24.02 N	88.58 E
Bherī □[8]	124	28.30 N	81.45 E
Bherī ≏	124	28.44 N	81.16 E
Bheula, Beinn ∧	46	56.08 N	4.58 W
Bhīkampur	272a	28.45 N	77.27 E
Bhīkangaon	120	21.52 N	75.57 E
Bhilai	120	21.13 N	81.26 E
Bhilainagar → Bhilai	120	21.13 N	81.26 E
Bhīlwāra	120	25.21 N	74.38 E
Bhīma ≏	122	16.24 N	77.18 E
Bhīmavaram	122	16.32 N	81.32 E
Bhimbar	123	32.59 N	74.04 E
Bhīmphedī	124	27.32 N	85.07 E
Bhīmpur, India	126	22.37 N	87.08 E
Bhimpur, India	272b	22.46 N	88.08 E
Bhind	124	26.34 N	78.48 E
Bhinga	124	27.43 N	81.56 E
Bhīnmāl	120	25.00 N	72.15 E
Bhiwandi	122	19.18 N	73.04 E
Bhiwāni	124	28.47 N	76.08 E
Bhoāgāchi	272b	22.57 N	88.20 E
Bhojpur	124	27.10 N	87.03 E
Bhojudih	126	23.38 N	86.27 E
Bhokardan	122	20.16 N	75.46 E

PORTUGUÊS

Nome	Página	Lat.°′	Long.°′ W = Oeste
Bhola	124	22.41 N	90.39 E
Bhola ≏[1]	126	22.04 N	89.49 E
Bhongaon	124	27.15 N	79.11 E
Bhongīr	122	17.31 N	78.53 E
Bhonrāsa	124	22.59 N	76.12 E
Bhopāl	124	23.16 N	77.24 E
Bhopar	272c	19.12 N	73.05 E
Bhopura	272a	28.42 N	77.20 E
Bhoutan → Bhutan □[1]	120	27.30 N	90.30 E
Bhowali	124	29.23 N	79.31 E
Bhuāpur	272a	28.43 N	77.26 E
Bhuban	120	20.53 N	85.50 E
Bhubaneshwar	120	20.14 N	85.50 E
Bhucho	123	30.13 N	75.06 E
Bhuj	120	23.16 N	69.40 E
Bhunarheri	124	30.13 N	76.27 E
Bhunya	158	26.32 S	31.01 E
Bhusāwal	120	21.03 N	75.46 E
Bhūshana	126	23.24 N	89.40 E
Bhutali	272c	19.07 N	73.04 E
Bhutan (Druk-Yul) □[1], Asia	118	27.30 N	90.30 E
Bhutan (Druk-Yul) □[1], Asia	120	27.30 N	90.30 E
Bia ≏, Afr.	150	5.21 N	3.11 W
Biá ≏, Bra.	246	3.28 S	67.23 W
Bia, Phou ∧	110	18.59 N	103.09 E
Bībābānak	128	32.11 N	64.11 E
Biabo ≏	248	6.58 S	76.23 W
Biacesa	64	45.56 N	10.47 E
Biache-Saint-Vaast	50	50.18 N	2.57 E
Biadene	64	45.47 N	12.04 E
Biafra, Bight of ⊂[3]	134	4.00 N	8.00 E
Biak I	164	1.00 S	136.00 E
Biała	30	50.23 N	17.40 E
Biała ≏	30	50.03 N	20.55 E
Biała Piska	30	53.37 N	22.04 E
Biała Podlaska	30	52.02 N	23.06 E
Biała Podlaska □[4]	30	52.00 N	23.00 E
Biała Rawska	30	51.49 N	20.29 E
Białobrzegi	30	51.40 N	20.57 E
Białogard	30	54.01 N	16.00 E
Białowieski Park Narodowy ♠	30	52.40 N	23.50 E
Biały Bór	30	53.54 N	16.51 E
Białystok	30	53.09 N	23.09 E
Białystok □[4]	30	53.00 N	23.00 E
Bian ≏	164	8.07 S	139.56 E
Bian, Bidean nam ∧	46	56.38 N	5.02 W
Biancavilla	70	37.38 N	14.52 E
Bianchi	68	39.06 N	16.24 E
Bianco	68	38.05 N	16.09 E
Bianco, Canale ≡	64	45.02 N	11.30 E
Bianco, Capo ›	70	37.23 N	13.16 E
Bianco, Monte (Mont Blanc) ∧	62	45.50 N	6.52 E
Bian'er	102	31.14 N	101.28 E
Bianga	152	4.51 N	20.25 E
Bian'gezhuang	105	39.28 N	115.53 E
Biankouma	150	7.44 N	7.37 W
Bianlinzhen	98	37.26 N	116.32 E
Bianminchang	107	29.41 N	105.04 E
Bianniulupucun	104	41.30 N	123.42 E
Bianquanwopu	104	41.21 N	120.48 E
Bianzè	62	45.18 N	8.07 E
Biaora	124	23.55 N	76.54 E
Biaro, Pulau I	112	2.05 N	125.20 E
Biarritz	32	43.29 N	1.34 W
Biasca	58	46.22 N	8.58 E
Bias Fortes	256	21.36 S	43.46 W
Biassono	62	45.37 N	9.16 E
Biaza	86	56.38 N	78.18 E
Bibā	142	28.55 N	30.59 E
Bibai	92a	43.19 N	141.52 E
Bibala	152	14.46 S	13.21 E
Bībān	142	30.47 N	30.40 E
Bibane, Bahiret el ⊂	148	33.16 N	11.19 E
Bibanga	152	6.15 S	23.56 E
Bibban, Khawr V	140	11.00 N	32.41 E
Bibb City	192	32.30 N	84.59 W
Bibbiano	64	44.40 N	10.28 E
Bibbiena	66	43.42 N	11.49 E
Bibbona	66	43.16 N	10.35 E
Bibémi	146	9.19 N	13.53 E
Biberach	58	48.20 N	8.02 E
Biberach an der Riss	58	48.06 N	9.47 E
Biberbach	56	48.31 N	10.48 E
Biberonne ≏	261	48.59 N	2.41 E
Bibert ≏	56	49.27 N	10.59 E
Bibey ≏	34	42.24 N	7.13 W
Bibiani	150	6.28 N	2.20 W
Bībi Chīni	126	22.28 N	90.12 E
Bibione	64	45.38 N	13.00 E
Bibir'ovo	76	54.28 N	33.08 E
Biblián	246	2.42 S	78.52 W
Biblis	56	49.41 N	8.27 E
Bibo	102	29.02 N	99.20 E
Bic	186	48.22 N	68.42 W
Biča	86	57.53 N	70.37 E
Bicas	256	21.43 S	43.04 W
Bicaz	38	46.54 N	26.05 E
Biccari	68	41.24 N	15.11 E
Bicester	42	51.54 N	1.09 W
Bičevinka	76	59.44 N	37.40 E
Biche, Lac la ⊜	182	54.50 N	112.03 W
Bichena	144	10.27 N	38.12 E
Bicheno	166	41.53 S	148.18 E
Bichhia	124	22.27 N	80.42 E
Bichl	64	47.43 N	11.24 E
Bichlbach	58	47.25 N	10.47 E
Bichota Canyon V	280	34.16 N	117.48 W
Biči ≏	89	52.10 N	139.50 E
Bičigt	88	47.06 N	95.05 E
Bickerstaffe	262	53.32 N	2.50 W
Bickerton, Cape ›	9	66.20 S	136.56 E
Bickerton Island I	164	13.45 S	136.12 E
Bickle Knob ∧	188	38.56 N	79.44 W
Bickley ◆[8]	260	51.24 N	0.03 E
Bicknacre, Eng., U.K.	42	51.41 N	0.35 E
Bicknacre, Eng., U.K.	260	51.42 N	0.35 E
Bicknell, In., U.S.	194	38.46 N	87.18 W
Bicknell, Ut,. U.S.	200	38.20 N	111.32 W
Bicknor	260	51.18 N	0.40 E
Bicol ≏	116	13.44 N	123.07 E
Bicske	30	47.29 N	18.37 E
Bicudo ≏	255	18.04 S	44.33 W
Bičura	88	50.36 N	107.35 E
Bičurina	86	56.51 N	55.25 E
Bīd	122	18.59 N	75.46 E
Bida, Nig.	146	12.20 N	13.25 E
Bida, Nig.	150	9.05 N	6.01 E
Bīdar	122	17.54 N	77.33 E
Bidde	144	0.58 N	42.37 E
Biddeford	188	43.29 N	70.27 W
Biddenden	42	51.07 N	0.39 E
Biddiyā	132	32.07 N	35.05 E
Biddulph	44	53.08 N	2.10 W
Bideford	42	51.01 N	4.13 W
Bidente ≏	66	44.24 N	12.12 E
Bidford-on-Avon	42	52.10 N	1.51 W
Bidhūna	124	26.49 N	79.31 E
Bidian	100	32.38 N	113.03 E
Bīdokht	128	34.21 N	58.46 E
Bidoni	71	40.07 N	8.56 E
Bidor	114	4.07 N	101.17 E
Bidston	262	53.24 N	3.05 W
Bidwell	188	38.55 N	82.17 W
Bidwell, Mount ∧	204	41.58 N	120.10 W
Bidya ≏[1]	126	21.56 N	88.42 E
Bidyādhari ≏	272b	22.23 N	88.35 E
Bidyādharpur	272b	22.50 N	88.24 E
Bidžan	89	47.58 N	131.58 E
Bidžan ≏	89	47.44 N	132.19 E
Bie	40	59.05 N	16.12 E
Bié □[5]	152	12.30 S	17.15 E
Biebelried	56	49.46 N	10.04 E
Bieber, Dtsch.	56	50.09 N	9.19 E
Bieber, Ca., U.S.	204	41.07 N	121.08 W
Biebrza ≏	30	53.13 N	22.25 E
Biecz	30	49.44 N	21.14 E
Biedenkopf	56	50.55 N	8.32 E
Biederitz	54	52.09 N	11.43 E
Biedermannsdorf	264b	48.05 N	16.21 E
Bieguzhuang	105	39.19 N	116.39 E
Biei	92a	43.35 N	142.28 E
Biel (Bienne)	58	47.10 N	7.12 E
Bielawa	30	50.41 N	16.38 E
Bielawski, Mount ∧	226	37.13 N	122.06 W
Bielefeld	52	52.01 N	8.31 E
Bieler Lake ⊜	176	70.20 N	73.00 W
Bielersee ⊜	58	47.05 N	7.10 E
Bielin	54	52.47 N	14.28 E
Biella	62	45.34 N	8.03 E
Bielsk	30	52.40 N	19.49 E
Bielsko-Biała	30	49.49 N	19.02 E
Bielsko-Biała □[4]	30	49.40 N	19.10 E
Bielsk Podlaski	30	52.47 N	23.12 E
Biemenhorst	52	51.49 N	6.36 E
Bienenbüttel	52	53.08 N	10.29 E
Bienfait	184	49.08 N	102.47 W
Bien Hoa	110	10.57 N	106.49 E
Bienne ≏, Fr.	50	48.15 N	0.04 E
Bienne ≏, Fr.	58	46.20 N	5.38 E
Bienne → Biel	58	47.10 N	7.12 E
Bienno	64	45.56 N	10.18 E
Bientina	66	43.42 N	10.37 E
Bienville	194	32.21 N	92.58 W
Bienville, Lac ⊜	176	55.05 N	72.40 W
Biere, Dtsch.	54	51.58 N	11.39 E
Bière, Schw.	58	46.33 N	6.20 E
Bierné	28	47.49 N	0.32 W
Bieruń Stary	30	50.06 N	19.06 E
Bierutów	30	51.08 N	17.32 E
Bierwart	56	50.34 N	5.01 E
Biesbos ◆[1]	52	51.45 N	4.50 E
Biesdorf ◆[8]	264a	52.31 N	13.33 E
Biese ≏	54	52.45 N	11.37 E
Biesel ◆[8]	263	51.10 N	6.29 E
Biesenthal	54	52.46 N	13.37 E
Bieshan	105	39.58 N	117.29 E
Biesiesvlei	158	26.22 S	25.55 E
Biesles	58	48.05 N	5.18 E
Bieszczadzki Park Narodowy ♠	30	49.05 N	22.45 E
Bieteluobaoluosika	89	48.35 N	119.56 E
Bietigheim	56	48.54 N	8.14 E
Bietigheim-Bissingen	56	48.58 N	9.07 E
Bietschhorn ∧	58	46.24 N	7.51 E
Bièvre	56	49.56 N	5.01 E
Bièvre ≏	261	48.47 N	2.20 E
Bièvres	261	48.45 N	2.13 E
Biferno ≏	66	41.59 N	15.02 E
Bifoun	152	0.22 S	10.23 E
Bifuka	92a	44.29 N	142.21 E
Bifurcación	258	34.19 S	56.48 W
Big ≏, Austl.	169	37.18 S	146.02 E
Big ≏, N.T., Can.	176	72.30 N	125.14 W
Big ≏, Sk., Can.	184	53.50 N	107.02 W
Big ≏, Ak., U.S.	180	63.00 N	154.56 W
Big ≏, Mo., U.S.	219	38.28 N	90.37 W
Biga	130	40.13 N	27.14 E
Bigadiç	130	39.23 N	28.08 E
Big A Mountain ∧	192	37.03 N	82.02 W
Big Annemessex River ⊂	208	38.03 N	75.50 W
Big Antelope Creek ≏	202	42.28 N	117.13 W
Big Bald Mountain ∧, N.B., Can.	186	47.12 N	66.25 W
Big Bald Mountain ∧, Ga., U.S.	192	34.45 N	84.19 W
Big Baldy ∧	202	44.47 N	115.13 W
Big Baldy Mountain ∧	202	46.58 N	110.37 W
Big Bar Creek	182	51.12 N	122.06 W
Big Basin Redwoods State Park ♠	226	37.09 N	122.17 W
Big Bay	190	46.49 N	87.44 W
Big Bay ⊂, N.Z.	172	44.18 S	168.05 E
Big Bay ⊂, Vanuatu	175f	15.06 S	166.54 E
Big Bay De Noc ⊂	190	45.46 N	86.43 W
Big Bay Point ›	212	44.24 N	79.31 W
Big Bear City	228	34.15 N	116.50 W
Big Bear Lake	228	34.15 N	116.53 W
Big Bear Lake ⊜	228	34.15 N	116.55 W
Big Beaver, Sk., Can.	184	49.08 N	105.10 W
Big Beaver, Pa., U.S.	214	40.50 N	80.20 W
Big Beaver Airport ⊠	281	42.33 N	83.06 W
Big Beaver Creek ≏, Mi., U.S.	281	42.32 N	83.01 W
Big Beaver Creek ≏, Oh., U.S.	218	39.01 N	83.03 W
Big Beaver Creek ≏, Wa., U.S.	224	48.40 N	121.08 W
Big Bell	162	27.21 S	117.40 E
Big Belt Mountains ⋀	202	46.40 N	111.25 W
Big Bend, Swaz.	158	26.50 S	31.57 E
Big Bend, Wi., U.S.	216	42.52 N	88.12 W
Big Bend National Park ♠	196	29.12 N	103.12 W
Big Bend Reservoir ⊜[1]	182	52.57 N	115.37 W
Big Black ≏	194	32.00 N	91.05 W
Big Blue ≏, U.S.	198	39.11 N	96.32 W
Big Blue ≏, In., U.S.	218	39.20 N	85.59 W
Big Blue, West Fork ≏	198	40.42 N	96.59 W
Big Bone Lick State Park ♠	218	38.53 N	84.45 W
Big Bonito Creek ≏	200	33.34 N	109.56 W
Big Brook ≏	276	40.19 N	74.10 W
Big Brushy Creek ≏, Tx., U.S.	222	32.32 N	96.20 W
Big Brushy Creek ≏, Tx., U.S.	222	29.12 N	96.55 W
Big Bureau Creek ≏	194	41.17 N	89.21 W
Bigbury Bay ⊂	42	50.16 N	3.48 W
Big Cabin Creek ≏	194	36.26 N	95.08 W
Big Canyon V	196	30.05 N	101.55 W
Big Carlos Pass ⊂	220	26.24 N	81.52 W
Big Cedar Lake ⊜	212	44.37 N	78.10 W
Big Chino Wash V	200	34.52 N	112.28 W
Big Clear Lake ⊜	212	44.43 N	76.55 W
Big Clifty	194	37.32 N	86.09 W
Big Coulee Creek ≏	202	46.17 N	108.56 W
Big Cow Creek ≏	194	30.34 N	93.44 W
Big Creek, B.C., Can.	182	51.44 N	123.03 W
Big Creek, Ca., U.S.	226	37.12 N	119.14 W
Big Creek ≏, B.C., Can.	182	51.40 N	122.50 W
Big Creek ≏, On., Can.	214	42.19 N	82.27 W
Big Creek ≏, On., Can.	214	42.36 N	80.27 W
Big Creek ≏, Ar., U.S.	194	34.21 N	91.03 W
Big Creek ≏, Ca., U.S.	226	37.12 N	119.19 W
Big Creek ≏, Ca., U.S.	226	36.53 N	119.15 W
Big Creek ≏, Id., U.S.	202	45.06 N	114.44 W
Big Creek ≏, Il., U.S.	219	39.07 N	88.52 W
Big Creek ≏, In., U.S.	216	40.38 N	86.46 W
Big Creek ≏, In., U.S.	218	38.48 N	85.39 W
Big Creek ≏, Ks., U.S.	198	38.47 N	98.55 W
Big Creek ≏, La., U.S.	194	32.10 N	91.53 W
Big Creek ≏, Mo., U.S.	194	40.02 N	94.07 W
Big Creek ≏, Mo., U.S.	219	38.52 N	90.50 W
Big Creek ≏, Oh., U.S.	279a	41.27 N	81.41 W
Big Creek ≏, Or., U.S.	224	46.11 N	123.35 W
Big Creek ≏, Tx., U.S.	222	29.22 N	95.34 W
Big Creek ≏, Tx., U.S.	222	31.09 N	96.52 W
Big Creek ≏, Wa., U.S.	224	47.15 N	121.10 W
Big Creek, East Fork ≏	194	40.16 N	94.03 W
Big Creek, West Fork ≏	194	40.16 N	94.03 W
Big Creek Parkway ♠	279a	41.24 N	81.45 W
Big Creek Peak ∧	202	44.28 N	113.32 W
Big Crow Island I	276	40.37 N	73.33 W
Big Cypress Creek ≏	222	33.00 N	94.51 W
Big Cypress Indian Reservation ◆[4]	220	26.14 N	80.49 W
Big Cypress National Preserve ♠	220	25.55 N	81.10 W
Big Cypress Swamp ≕	220	26.10 N	81.38 W
Big Dalton Canyon V	280	34.10 N	117.48 W
Big Dalton Wash V	280	34.04 N	117.58 W
Big Darby Creek ≏	218	39.37 N	82.58 W
Big Delta	180	64.09 N	145.50 W
Big Desert ◆[2]	166	35.40 S	141.00 E
Big Diomede Island → Ratmanova, ostrov I	180	65.46 N	169.02 W
Big Ditch ≡	216	40.13 N	88.22 W
Big Dry Creek ≏	202	47.30 N	106.19 W
Big Dubbo Hill ∧	171b	35.25 S	148.36 E
Big Eau Pleine ≏	190	44.48 N	90.00 W
Big Elk Creek ≏	208	39.35 N	75.52 W
Big Elkhart Creek ≏	222	31.22 N	95.41 W
Big Elm Creek ≏	222	30.53 N	96.56 W
Bigelow Bight ⊂[3]	188	43.15 N	70.30 W
Big Escambia Creek ≏	194	30.58 N	87.14 W
Big Falls	190	48.11 N	93.48 W
Big Flat	194	36.00 N	92.24 W
Big Flat Creek ≏	194	31.33 N	87.31 W
Big Flats	210	42.08 N	76.56 W
Bigfork, Mn., U.S.	190	47.44 N	93.39 W
Bigfork, Mt., U.S.	202	48.04 N	114.04 W
Big Fork ≏	190	48.31 N	93.43 W
Big Four Ditch ≡	216	40.27 N	88.10 W
Big Frog Mountain ∧	192	35.00 N	84.32 W
Biggar, Sk., Can.	184	52.04 N	108.00 W
Biggar, Scot., U.K.	46	55.38 N	3.32 W
Biggarsberg ⋀	158	28.12 S	29.48 E
Bigge	56	51.21 N	8.28 E
Bigge Island I	164	14.35 S	125.10 E
Biggers	194	36.19 N	90.48 W
Biggestausee ⊜[1]	56	51.05 N	7.55 E
Biggin Hill ◆[8]	42	51.18 N	0.04 E
Biggin Hill Aerodrome ⊠	260	51.19 N	0.03 E
Biggleswade	42	52.05 N	0.17 W
Biggs, Ca., U.S.	226	39.24 N	121.42 W
Biggs, Or., U.S.	224	45.40 N	120.50 W
Big Gull Lake ⊜	212	44.50 N	76.58 W
Big Gully Creek ≏	184	53.13 N	109.03 W
Bighāi ≏[1]	126	22.10 N	90.13 E
Big Hawk Lake ⊜	212	45.10 N	78.44 W
Bighead ≏	212	44.36 N	80.35 W
Big Hole ≏	202	45.34 N	112.20 W
Big Hole National Battlefield ⊥	202	45.35 N	113.35 W
Bighorn ≏	202	46.09 N	107.28 W
Bighorn Basin ≚[1]	202	44.15 N	108.10 W
Bighorn Canyon National Recreation Area ♠	202	45.00 N	108.15 W
Big Horn Lake ⊜[1]	202	45.06 N	108.08 W
Bighorn Mountains ⋀	202	44.00 N	107.30 W
Bight, Head of ›	162	31.30 S	131.10 E
Big Huckleberry Mountain ∧	224	45.51 N	121.47 W
Big Island	192	37.32 N	79.21 W
Big Island I, N.T., Can.	176	62.43 N	70.43 W
Big Island I, On., Can.	184	49.10 N	94.40 W
Big Island I, On., Can.	212	44.33 N	78.30 W
Big Knob ∧	192	36.40 N	82.31 W
Big Koniuji Island I	180	55.06 N	159.33 W
Big Lake, Ak., U.S.	180	61.33 N	149.52 W
Big Lake, Mn., U.S.	190	45.19 N	93.44 W
Big Lake, Tx., U.S.	196	31.11 N	101.27 W
Big Lake, Wa., U.S.	224	48.24 N	122.14 W
Big Lake ⊜, Me., U.S.	188	45.10 N	67.40 W
Big Lake ⊜, Wa., U.S.	224	48.23 N	122.12 W
Bigler	214	40.59 N	78.19 W
Biglerville	208	39.55 N	77.14 W
Big Lick Creek ≏	216	40.22 N	85.27 W
Big Lookout Mountain ∧	202	44.37 N	117.17 W
Big Lost ≏	202	43.50 N	112.44 W
Big Monon Ditch ≡	216	40.52 N	86.46 W
Big Mossy Point ›	184	53.41 N	97.57 W
Big Mountain ∧, B.C., Can.	180	56.53 N	131.31 W
Big Mountain ∧, Nv., U.S.	204	41.17 N	119.04 W
Big Mountain Creek ≏	182	55.04 N	118.39 W
Big Muddy ≏	194	37.35 N	89.31 W
Big Muddy, Casey Fork ≏	194	38.06 N	88.57 W
Big Muddy Creek ≏, Mt., U.S.	198	48.08 N	104.36 W
Big Muddy Creek ≏, N.D., U.S.	198	46.37 N	101.24 W
Big Muddy Lake ⊜	184	49.08 N	104.54 W
Big Muscamoot Bay ⊂	281	42.33 N	82.40 W
Bignasco	58	46.20 N	8.36 E
Big Nasty Creek ≏	198	45.41 N	102.51 W
Big Nemaha, North Fork ≏	198	40.04 N	95.43 W
Bignona	150	12.49 N	16.14 W
Big Oak Flat	226	37.49 N	120.16 W
Bigosovo	76	55.49 N	27.43 E
Bigot, Morne ∧[2]	240e	14.31 N	61.04 W
Big Otter ≏	192	37.07 N	79.23 W
Big Otter Creek ≏	212	42.38 N	80.48 W
Big Ox Creek ≏	218	38.44 N	85.52 W
Big Pine	204	37.09 N	118.17 W
Big Pine Creek ≏	216	40.18 N	87.15 W
Big Pine Key	220	24.40 N	81.21 W
Big Pine Key I	220	24.42 N	81.23 W
Big Pine Mountain ∧	204	34.42 N	119.39 W
Big Piney	200	42.32 N	110.06 W
Big Piney ≏	194	37.53 N	92.04 W
Big Piney Creek ≏	194	35.20 N	93.20 W
Big Pipe Creek ≏	208	39.36 N	77.17 W
Big Plain	218	39.50 N	83.17 W
Big Pocono State Park ♠	210	41.03 N	75.19 W
Bigpoint	194	30.35 N	88.28 W
Big Pond	210	41.53 N	76.43 W
Big Porcupine Creek ≏	202	46.16 N	106.43 W
Big Porcupine Lake ⊜	212	45.27 N	78.36 W
Big Prairie	214	40.40 N	82.06 W
Big Prairie Creek ≏	194	32.35 N	87.45 W
Big Quilcene ≏	224	47.49 N	122.52 W
Big Quill Lake ⊜	184	51.55 N	104.22 W
Big Raccoon Creek ≏	194	39.46 N	87.22 W
Big Rapids	190	43.41 N	85.29 W
Bigras, Île I	275a	45.31 N	73.51 W
Big Rib ≏	190	44.56 N	89.41 W
Big Rideau Lake ⊜	212	44.45 N	76.14 W
Big River	184	53.50 N	107.01 W
Big River Indian Reserve ◆[4]	184	53.33 N	107.10 W
Big Rock	216	41.46 N	88.33 W
Big Rock Creek ≏	216	41.38 N	88.32 W
Big Rocky Creek ≏	222	29.34 N	96.50 W
Big Run	214	40.58 N	78.52 W
Big Sable ≏	190	44.02 N	86.31 W
Big Sable Point ›	190	44.03 N	86.31 W
Big Salmon ≏	180	61.52 N	134.56 W
Big Salmon Range ⋀	180	61.10 N	133.45 W
Big Sand Lake ⊜	176	57.45 N	99.42 W
Big Sandy, Mt., U.S.	202	48.10 N	110.06 W
Big Sandy, Tn., U.S.	194	36.14 N	88.05 W
Big Sandy, Tx., U.S.	222	32.35 N	95.07 W
Big Sandy ≏, U.S.	188	38.25 N	82.36 W
Big Sandy ≏, Az., U.S.	200	34.19 N	113.31 W
Big Sandy ≏, Tn., U.S.	194	36.15 N	88.06 W
Big Sandy ≏, Wy., U.S.	202	41.51 N	109.47 W
Big Sandy Creek ≏, Ca., U.S.	226	35.47 N	120.43 W
Big Sandy Creek ≏, Co., U.S.	198	38.06 N	102.29 W
Big Sandy Creek ≏, Ga., U.S.	192	32.42 N	82.57 W
Big Sandy Creek ≏, Mt., U.S.	202	48.34 N	109.48 W
Big Sandy Creek ≏, Ne., U.S.	198	40.13 N	97.18 W
Big Sandy Creek ≏, Tx., U.S.	196	33.11 N	97.40 W
Big Sandy Creek ≏, Tx., U.S.	222	32.33 N	95.05 W
Big Sandy Creek ≏, Tx., U.S.	222	30.31 N	94.28 W
Big Sandy Lake ⊜, Sk., Can.	184	54.26 N	104.04 W
Big Sandy Lake ⊜, Mn., U.S.	190	46.45 N	93.17 W
Big Sandy Reservoir ⊜[1]	200	42.16 N	109.26 W
Big Satilla Creek ≏	192	31.27 N	82.03 W
Bigsby Island I	184	49.04 N	94.35 W
Big Sewickley Creek ≏	279b	40.35 N	80.13 W
Big Shawnee Creek ≏	216	40.15 N	87.18 W
Big Sheep Mountain ∧	202	47.03 N	105.43 W
Big Signal Peak ∧	204	39.31 N	123.06 W
Big Sinking Creek ≏	194	37.55 N	86.31 W
Big Sioux ≏	198	42.30 N	96.25 W
Big Sixmile Creek ≏	284a	43.02 N	79.01 W
Big Sky	202	45.17 N	111.17 W
Big Slough ≏	192	30.56 N	84.33 W
Big Smoky Valley V	204	38.30 N	117.15 W
Big Snowy Mountains ⋀	202	46.50 N	109.30 W
Big Southern Butte ∧	202	43.23 N	113.01 W
Big Spanish Channel ʮ	220	24.44 N	81.20 W
Bigspring, Mo., U.S.	219	38.38 N	91.28 W
Big Spring, Tx., U.S.	196	32.15 N	101.28 W
Big Springs	198	41.03 N	102.04 W
Big Spruce Knob ∧	188	38.16 N	80.12 W
Big Squaw Mountain ∧	188	45.30 N	69.45 W
Bigstick Lake ⊜	184	50.16 N	109.20 W
Bigstone ≏	184	55.55 N	94.36 W
Big Stone City	198	45.17 N	96.27 W
Big Stone Gap	192	36.52 N	82.44 W
Bigstone Lake ⊜, Mb., Can.	184	53.42 N	95.44 W
Big Stone Lake ⊜, U.S.	198	45.25 N	96.40 W
Big Sunflower ≏	194	32.40 N	90.40 W
Big Sur	226	36.16 N	121.48 W
Big Sur ≏	226	36.17 N	121.51 W
Big Sur ◆[1]	226	35.45 N	121.20 W
Big Swamp Creek ≏	194	32.19 N	86.49 W
Big Swan Creek ≏	194	35.46 N	87.24 W
Big Thicket National Preserve ♠	222	32.35 N	94.40 W
Big Thompson ≏	200	40.21 N	104.45 W
Big Timber	202	45.50 N	109.57 W
Big Timber Creek ≏	285	39.53 N	75.08 W
Big Timber Creek, North Branch ≏	285	39.50 N	75.05 W
Big Timber Creek, South Branch ≏	285	39.50 N	75.05 W
Big Torch Key I	220	24.43 N	81.26 W
Big Tree	210	42.46 N	78.49 W
Big Trout Lake ⊜, On., Can.	176	53.45 N	90.00 W
Big Trout Lake ⊜, On., Can.	212	44.56 N	78.56 W
Big Tujunga Canyon V	228	34.16 N	118.18 W
Big Tujunga Dam ◆[6]	280	34.18 N	118.12 W
Biguaçu	252	27.30 S	48.40 W
Big Valley	182	52.02 N	112.46 W
Bigwa	154	7.13 S	39.09 E
Big Walnut Creek ≏, In., U.S.	194	39.30 N	86.57 W
Big Walnut Creek ≏, Oh., U.S.	218	39.48 N	83.01 W
Big Warrambool ≏	166	30.05 S	147.33 E
Big Water	200	37.05 N	111.41 W
Big Wells	196	28.34 N	99.34 W
Big White Mountain ∧	182	49.42 N	118.58 W
Big Wills Creek ≏	194	33.59 N	86.00 W
Big Wood ≏	202	42.52 N	114.54 W
Bihać	36	44.49 N	15.52 E
Bīhar	124	25.11 N	85.31 E
Bihār □[3]	124	25.00 N	86.00 E
Biharamulo	154	2.38 S	31.20 E
Bihārīganj	124	25.44 N	86.59 E
Bihor □[6]	38	47.00 N	22.15 E
Bihor, Vîrful ∧	38	46.27 N	22.42 E
Bihoro	92a	43.49 N	144.07 E
Bihu	100	28.21 N	119.48 E
Bija ≏	86	52.25 N	85.05 E
Bijagós, Arquipélago dos II	150	11.25 N	16.20 W
Bijainagar	120	25.56 N	74.38 E
Bijaipur	124	26.03 N	77.22 E
Bijaipura	124	24.46 N	77.48 E
Bijāpur	122	16.50 N	75.42 E
Bījār	128	35.52 N	47.36 E
Bijāwar	124	24.38 N	79.30 E
Bijbān Chāh	128	26.54 N	64.42 E
Bījbiāra	123	33.48 N	75.06 E
Bijeljina	38	44.45 N	19.13 E
Bijelo Polje	38	43.02 N	19.44 E
Bijiang	110	26.30 N	98.55 E
Bijia Shan ∧	105	40.17 N	116.50 E
Bijie	102	27.18 N	105.20 E
Bijlikol', ozero ⊜	85	43.03 N	70.41 E
Bijna	272b	22.55 N	88.27 E
Bijni	124	26.31 N	90.40 E
Bijnor	124	29.22 N	78.08 E
Bijōki	268	35.49 N	139.39 E
Bijou Creek ≏	198	40.17 N	103.52 W
Bijpur	126	22.56 N	88.26 E
Bijsk	86	52.34 N	85.15 E
Bijuk-Karasu ≏	78	45.27 N	34.47 E
Bijwāsan ◆[8]	272a	28.32 N	77.03 E
Bīkāner	120	28.01 N	73.18 E
Bīkaner Canal ≡	123	30.08 N	73.57 E
Bikar I[1]	14	12.15 N	170.06 E
Bikbulovo	80	55.39 N	53.26 E
Bike	144	9.30 N	41.18 E
Bikeman Island I	174t	1.22 N	173.00 E
Bikenibeu	174t	1.21 N	173.07 E
Bikeqi	102	40.45 N	111.17 E
Bikeru	112	5.15 S	120.07 E
Bikfayyā	132	33.55 N	35.41 E
Bikié	152	3.06 S	13.52 E
Bikin	89	46.48 N	134.16 E
Bikin ≏	89	46.51 N	134.02 E
Bikini I[1]	14	11.35 N	165.23 E
Bikita	154	20.06 S	31.41 E
Bikl'an'	80	55.37 N	52.10 E
Bikoro	152	0.45 S	18.07 E
Bikuar, Parque Nacional do ♠	152	15.12 S	14.42 E
Bila ≏	114	2.30 N	100.08 E
Bilaa Point ›	116	9.49 N	125.26 E
Bilac	255	21.24 S	50.28 W
Bilād Zahrān ◆[1]	144	20.16 N	41.14 E
Bílá hora ⊥	54	50.10 N	14.10 E

≏ River	Fluß	Río	Rivière	Rio			
≡ Canal	Kanal	Canal	Canal	Canal			
↳ Waterfall, Rapids	Wasserfall, Stromschnellen	Cascada, Rápidos	Chute d'eau, Rapides	Cascata, Rápidos			
ʮ Strait	Meeresstraße	Estrecho	Détroit	Estreito			
⊂ Bay, Gulf	Bucht, Golf	Bahía, Golfo	Baie, Golfe	Baía, Golfo			
⊜ Lake, Lakes	See, Seen	Lago, Lagos	Lac, Lacs	Lago, Lagos			
≕ Swamp	Sumpf	Pantano	Marais	Pântano			
⊓ Ice Features, Glacier	Eis- und Gletscherformen	Accidentes Glaciales	Formes glaciaires	Acidentes glaciares			
⊤ Other Hydrographic Features	Andere Hydrographische Objekte	Otros Elementos Hidrográficos	Autres données hydrographiques	Outros acidentes hidrográficos			
✢ Submarine Features	Untermeerische Objekte	Accidentes Submarinos	Formes de relief sous-marin	Acidentes submarinos			
□ Political Unit	Politische Einheit	Unidad Politica	Entité politique	Unidade política			
♁ Cultural Institution	Kulturelle Institution	Institución Cultural	Institution culturelle	Instituição cultural			
⊥ Historical Site	Historische Stätte	Sitio Histórico	Site historique	Sitio histórico			
♠ Recreational Site	Erholungs- und Ferienort	Sitio de Recreo	Centre de loisirs	Area de Lazer			
⊠ Airport	Flughafen	Aeropuerto	Aéroport	Aeroporto			
■ Military Installation	Militäranlage	Instalación Militar	Installation militaire	Instalação militar			
◆ Miscellaneous	Verschiedenes	Misceláneo	Divers	Diversos			

ENGLISH   **DEUTSCH**

Name	Page	Lat.°	Long.°		Name	Seite	Breite°	Länge° E=Ost

ESPAÑOL · FRANÇAIS · PORTUGUÊS

Nombre / Nom / Nome	Página / Page / Página	Lat.°′	Long.°′ W = Oeste / W = Ouest / W = Oeste
Blackville	192	33.21 N	81.16 W
Black Volta (Volta Noire) ≏	150	8.41 N	1.33 W
Blackwall Tunnel ◆[5]	260	51.30 N	0.01 E
Blackwalnut Point ›	208	38.40 N	76.20 W
Black Warrior ≏	194	32.32 N	87.51 W
Blackwatch Hills	210	43.05 N	77.27 W
Blackwater, Austl.	166	23.35 S	148.53 E
Blackwater, Ire.	48	52.26 N	6.21 W
Blackwater ≏, Europe	44	54.31 N	6.34 W
Blackwater ≏, Ire.	48	51.51 N	7.50 W
Blackwater ≏, Ire.	48	53.39 N	6.43 W
Blackwater ≏, Eng., U.K.	260	51.45 N	1.00 E
Blackwater ≏, U.S.	194	30.36 N	87.02 W
Blackwater ≏, Md., U.S.	208	38.21 N	76.01 W
Blackwater ≏, Mo., U.S.	194	38.56 N	92.51 W
Blackwater ≏, Va., U.S.	208	36.33 N	76.55 W
Blackwater Creek ≏, Austl.	166	25.56 S	144.20 E
Black Water Creek ≏, Fl., U.S.	220	28.51 N	81.24 W
Blackwater Draw V	196	33.35 N	101.50 W
Blackwaterfoot	46	55.30 N	5.19 W
Blackwater Lake ◎	180	64.00 N	123.05 W
Blackwater Reservoir ◎[1], Scot., U.K.	46	56.41 N	4.46 W
Blackwater Reservoir ◎[1], Scot., U.K.	46	56.44 N	3.14 W
Blackwater Sound Ʉ	220	25.10 N	80.25 W
Blackwell, Ok., U.S.	196	36.48 N	97.16 W
Blackwell, Tx., U.S.	196	32.05 N	100.19 W
Blackwood, Austl.	168b	35.02 S	138.37 E
Blackwood, Austl.	169	37.29 S	144.19 E
Blackwood, N.J., U.S.	285	39.48 N	75.03 W
Blackwood ≏	162	34.19 S	115.11 E
Blackwood, Cape ›	164	7.50 S	144.30 E
Blackwood Terrace	285	39.48 N	75.05 W
Bladel	52	51.23 N	5.13 E
Bladenboro	192	34.32 N	78.47 W
Bladensburg, Md., U.S.	284c	38.56 N	76.56 W
Bladensburg, Oh., U.S.	214	40.17 N	82.17 W
Blades	208	38.38 N	75.36 W
Bladgrond	158	28.52 S	19.57 E
Bladnoch ≏	44	54.51 N	4.25 W
Bladworth	184	51.18 N	106.09 W
Blaenau Ffestiniog	42	52.59 N	3.56 W
Blaenavon	42	51.48 N	3.05 W
Bláfell ∧	24a	64.32 N	19.53 W
Blagaj	36	43.15 N	17.50 E
Blagdon	42	51.20 N	2.43 W
Blagodarnoje	86	47.03 N	82.10 E
Blagodarnyj	72	45.06 N	43.27 E
Blagodatnoje, Kaz.	86	51.18 N	72.49 E
Blagodatnoje, Ross.	78	51.32 N	34.54 E
Blagodatnoje, Ukr.	83	47.42 N	37.25 E
Blagodatnoje, Ukr.	83	47.53 N	38.29 E
Blagodatovka	80	52.14 N	50.27 E
Blagoevgrad	38	42.01 N	23.06 E
Blagoveščenka, Kaz.	86	54.22 N	66.58 E
Blagoveščenka, Ross.	80	51.19 N	44.03 E
Blagoveščenka, Ross.	86	52.50 N	79.52 E
Blagoveščensk, Ross.	86	55.01 N	55.59 E
Blagoveščensk, Ross.	89	50.17 N	127.32 E
Blagoveščenskoje, Kaz.	85	43.18 N	74.12 E
Blagoveščenskoje, Ross.	86	58.08 N	62.58 E
Blåhø ∧	26	62.45 N	9.19 E
Blåhøj	41	55.51 N	9.01 E
Blaichach	58	47.34 N	10.15 E
Blaikfjället ∧	26	64.33 N	16.12 E
Blain, Fr.	32	47.29 N	1.46 W
Blain, Pa., U.S.	208	40.20 N	77.31 W
Blaina	42	51.46 N	3.10 W
Blain City	214	40.45 N	78.34 W
Blaine, Mn., U.S.	190	45.09 N	93.14 W
Blaine, Wa., U.S.	224	48.59 N	122.44 W
Blaine Creek ≏	188	38.11 N	82.37 W
Blaine Hill	279b	40.16 N	79.53 W
Blaine Lake	184	52.50 N	106.54 W
Blaineys	224	48.53 N	123.47 W
Blainville	206	45.40 N	73.52 W
Blainville-sur-l'Eau	58	48.33 N	6.24 E
Blair, On., Can.	212	43.23 N	80.23 W
Blair, Ne., U.S.	198	41.32 N	96.07 W
Blair, Ok., U.S.	196	34.46 N	99.20 W
Blair, Wi., U.S.	190	44.18 N	91.14 W
Blair □[6]	214	40.30 N	78.25 W
Blair Athol	166	22.42 S	147.33 E
Blair Atholl	46	56.46 N	3.51 W
Blairgowrie	46	56.36 N	3.21 W
Blairs Mills	214	40.17 N	77.43 W
Blairstown, Ia., U.S.	190	41.54 N	92.05 W
Blairstown, N.J., U.S.	210	40.59 N	74.57 W
Blairsville, Ga., U.S.	192	34.52 N	83.57 W
Blairsville, Pa., U.S.	214	40.25 N	79.15 W
Blaise ≏, Fr.	50	48.46 N	1.25 E
Blaise ≏, Fr.	58	48.38 N	4.43 E
Blaisy-Bas	58	47.22 N	4.44 E
Blaj	38	46.11 N	23.55 E
Blakehurst	274a	33.59 S	151.07 E
Blakeley Canal ≖	226	36.09 N	119.48 W
Blakely, Ga., U.S.	192	31.22 N	84.56 W
Blakely, Pa., U.S.	210	41.28 N	75.35 W
Blakely Island I	224	48.33 N	122.50 W
Blakeney, Eng., U.K.	42	51.46 N	2.29 W
Blakeney, Eng., U.K.	42	52.58 N	1.00 E
Blake Plateau ✦[4]	16	31.00 N	79.00 W
Blake Point ›	190	48.12 N	88.25 W
Blake Ridge ✦[3]	16	29.00 N	73.30 W
Blakes	208	37.30 N	76.22 W
Blakesburg	190	40.57 N	92.38 W
Blakeslee, Oh., U.S.	216	41.31 N	84.44 W
Blakeslee, Pa., U.S.	210	41.06 N	75.36 W
Blalock Island I	202	45.53 N	119.41 W
Blâmont, Fr.	58	48.35 N	6.51 E
Blamont, Fr.	58	47.23 N	6.51 E
Blanc, Cap ›	36	37.20 N	9.51 E
Blanc, Cap → Nouâdhibou, Râs ›	148	20.46 N	17.03 W
Blanc, Mont ∧, P.Q., Can.	186	48.47 N	66.52 W
Blanc, Mont (Monte Bianco) ∧, Europe	62	45.50 N	6.52 E
Blanca	200	37.27 N	105.31 W
Blanca, Bahía c	252	38.55 S	62.10 W
Blanca, Isla I	248	9.06 S	78.38 W
Blanca, Laguna ◎	254	52.25 S	71.10 W
Blanca, Punta ›, Arg.	258	34.57 S	57.40 W
Blanca, Punta ›, Chile	252	25.06 S	70.30 W
Blanca, Sierra ∧	200	31.15 N	105.26 W
Blanca Lake ◎	224	47.53 N	121.21 W
Blanca Peak ∧	200	37.35 N	105.29 W
Blancas, Peñas ✗	236	13.15 N	85.41 W
Blanc du Cheilon, Mont ∧	58	45.59 N	7.25 E
Blanchard, Ok., U.S.	196	35.08 N	97.39 W
Blanchard, Pa., U.S.	210	41.04 N	77.36 W
Blanchard, Wa., U.S.	224	48.35 N	122.24 W
Blanchard ≏	216	41.02 N	84.18 W
Blanchardville	190	42.48 N	89.51 W
Blanche ≏, On., Can.	190	47.34 N	79.32 W
Blanche ≏, P.Q., Can.	206	46.40 N	72.08 W
Blanche, Cape ›	162	33.01 S	134.09 E
Blanche, Dent ∧	58	46.03 N	7.36 E
Blanche, Lake ◎, Austl.	162	22.25 S	123.17 E
Blanche, Lake ◎, Austl.	166	29.15 S	139.39 E
Blanche, Mer → Beloje more ⫪[2]	24	65.30 N	38.00 E
Blanche Channel Ʉ	175e	8.30 S	157.30 E
Blancheface	261	48.32 N	2.06 E
Blanche Marie Val ⌊	250	4.44 N	56.53 W
Blanchester	218	39.17 N	83.59 W
Blanchisseuse	241r	10.47 N	61.18 W
Blanco, S. Afr.	158	33.57 S	22.24 E
Blanco, Tx., U.S.	196	30.06 N	98.25 W
Blanco ≏, Arg.	252	30.12 S	69.05 W
Blanco ≏, Arg.	254	47.22 S	71.12 W
Blanco ≏, Bol.	248	13.09 S	63.46 W
Blanco ≏, Ec.	246	0.28 N	79.25 W
Blanco ≏, Tx., U.S.	196	29.51 N	97.55 W
Blanco, Cabo ›	236	9.34 N	85.07 W
Blanco, Cabo → Nouâdhibou, Râs ›	148	20.46 N	17.03 W
Blanco, Cañon V	200	35.20 N	105.05 W
Blanco, Cape ›	202	42.50 N	124.34 W
Blanco, Lago ◎	254	54.03 S	69.00 W
Blanco, Mar → Beloje more ⫪[2]	24	65.30 N	38.00 E
Blanco, Monte → Blanc, Mont ∧	62	45.50 N	6.52 E
Blanco, Rio ≏	200	37.07 N	107.03 W
Blanco Creek ≏	196	28.19 N	97.19 W
Blanc-Sablon	186	51.25 N	57.07 W
Bland, Mo., U.S.	219	38.18 N	91.37 W
Bland, Va., U.S.	192	37.06 N	81.06 W
Blanda ≏	24a	65.39 N	20.18 W
Blandburg	214	40.41 N	78.24 W
Blandford	207	42.10 N	72.55 W
Blandford Forum	42	50.52 N	2.11 W
Blanding	200	37.37 N	109.28 W
Blandinsville	190	40.33 N	90.51 W
Blandon	208	40.26 N	75.53 W
Blandy	261	48.34 N	2.47 E
Blanes	34	41.41 N	2.48 E
Blangkejeren	114	3.59 N	97.20 E
Blangpidie	114	3.45 N	96.51 E
Blangy-le-Château	50	49.14 N	0.17 E
Blangy-sur-Bresle	50	49.56 N	1.38 E
Blanice ≏	61	49.05 N	14.03 E
Blankenberg	56	50.45 N	7.22 E
Blankenberge	50	51.19 N	3.08 E
Blankenburg	54	51.48 N	10.58 E
Blankenburg ◆[8]	264a	52.35 N	13.28 E
Blankenese ◆[8]	52	53.33 N	9.48 E
Blankenfelde	54	52.20 N	13.23 E
Blankenfelde ◆[8]	264a	52.37 N	13.23 E
Blankenhain	54	50.51 N	11.21 E
Blankenheim, Dtsch.	54	51.31 N	11.25 E
Blankenheim, Dtsch.	56	50.26 N	6.39 E
Blankensee	54	52.14 N	13.08 E
Blankenstein	263	51.24 N	7.14 E
Blanket	196	31.49 N	98.47 W
Blanquilla, Isla I	246	11.51 N	64.37 W
Blansko	30	49.22 N	16.39 E
Blanský Les ◆[3]	61	48.52 N	14.16 E
Blantyre	154	15.47 S	35.00 E
Blanzac	62	45.07 N	3.51 E
Blanzy	58	46.42 N	4.23 E
Blaricum	52	52.16 N	5.15 E
Blarney	48	51.56 N	8.34 W
Blarney Castle ⊥	48	51.56 N	8.34 W
Blasdell	210	42.47 N	78.49 W
Blasheim	52	52.18 N	8.34 E
Błaszki	30	51.39 N	18.27 E
Blatná	60	49.26 N	13.53 E
Blatnica	38	43.42 N	28.31 E
Blatten	58	46.25 N	7.50 E
Blatzheim	56	50.51 N	6.38 E
Blau ≏	58	48.23 N	9.49 E
Blaubeuren	58	48.24 N	9.47 E
Blauen ∧	58	47.47 N	7.42 E
Blauer Nil → Blue Nile ≏	140	15.38 N	32.31 E
Blaufelden	56	49.18 N	9.58 E
Blaustein	58	48.25 N	9.53 E
Blauvelt	276	41.03 N	73.57 W
Blauvelt State Park ♠	276	41.04 N	73.56 W
Blåvands Huk ›	26	55.33 N	8.05 E
Blawenburg	276	40.24 N	74.42 W
Blawnox	279b	40.29 N	79.51 W
Blaxland	170	33.45 S	150.36 E
Blaxland Creek ≏	274a	33.48 S	150.46 E
Blaydon	44	54.58 N	1.42 W
Blaye-et-Sainte-Luce	32	45.08 N	0.39 W
Blayney	166	33.32 S	149.15 E
Blaze, Point ›	164	12.56 S	130.12 E
Błażowa	30	49.54 N	22.05 E
Bleaker Island I	254	52.13 S	58.53 W
Bleaklow Head ∧	262	53.28 N	1.50 W
Blean	42	51.19 N	1.02 E
Bleckede	54	53.17 N	10.44 E
Bled	36	46.22 N	14.06 E
Bledsoe	196	33.38 N	103.01 W
Bleecker	210	43.07 N	74.22 W
Blefjell ∧	26	59.48 N	9.10 E
Blega	115a	7.08 S	113.03 E
Bleibach	58	48.07 N	8.01 E
Bleiberg ob Villach	64	46.37 N	13.41 E
Bleiburg	61	46.35 N	14.48 E
Bleicherode	54	51.26 N	10.34 E
Blekendorf	54	54.16 N	10.38 E
Blekinge □[9]	26	56.20 N	15.05 E
Blekinge Län □[6]	26	56.20 N	15.20 E
Blendecques	50	50.43 N	2.16 E
Bléneau	50	47.42 N	2.57 E
Blenheim, Austl.	171a	27.39 S	152.20 E
Blenheim, On., Can.	214	42.20 N	82.00 W
Blenheim, N.Z.	172	41.31 S	173.57 E
Blenheim, N.J., U.S.	285	39.48 N	75.05 W
Blenheim Palace ᵿ	42	51.47 N	1.21 W
Blenio, Val V	58	46.27 N	8.58 E
Blénod-lès-Pont-à-Mousson	56	48.53 N	6.03 E
Blénod-lès-Toul	58	48.36 N	5.50 E
Bléone ≏	62	44.03 N	6.00 E
Blérancourt	50	49.31 N	3.09 E
Bléré	50	47.20 N	1.00 E
Blerick	52	51.23 N	6.10 E
Blériot-Plage	50	50.57 N	1.50 E
Blesbokspruit ≏	273d	26.14 S	28.29 E
Blessing	222	28.52 N	96.13 W
Blessington	48	53.10 N	6.32 W
Bletchingley	260	51.14 N	0.06 W
Bletchley	42	52.00 N	0.46 W
Bletterans	58	46.45 N	5.27 E
Bleu → Chang ≏	90	31.48 N	121.10 E
Bleue, Mer ⁝	212	45.24 N	75.30 W
Bleury	261	48.31 N	1.45 E
Bleus, Monts ✗	154	1.30 N	30.30 E
Blevio	62	45.50 N	9.05 E
Blewett Falls Lake ◎[1]	192	35.03 N	79.54 W
Blexen	52	53.32 N	8.32 E
Blidö I	40	59.37 N	18.54 E
Blidworth	44	53.06 N	1.07 W
Bliedinghausen ◆[8]	263	51.09 N	7.12 E
Bliersheim ◆[8]	263	51.23 N	6.43 E
Blies ≏	56	49.07 N	7.04 E
Blieskastel	56	49.14 N	7.16 E
Bligh Sound Ʉ	172	44.50 S	167.32 E
Bligh Water Ʉ	175g	17.00 S	178.00 E
Bligny	50	49.11 N	3.52 E
Bligny-sur-Ouche	58	47.06 N	4.40 E
Blik, Mount ∧	116	6.58 N	124.15 E
Blina	162	17.46 S	124.32 E
Blind ≏	276	40.57 N	73.42 W
Blind Creek ≏	274b	37.54 S	145.12 E
Blindley Heath	260	51.12 N	0.04 W
Blind River	190	46.10 N	82.58 W
Blinman	166	31.06 S	138.41 E
Blinnenhorn ∧	58	46.26 N	8.19 E
Blinovskij	80	49.23 N	42.19 E
Bliss	210	42.34 N	78.15 W
Blissfield, Mi., U.S.	216	41.49 N	83.51 W
Blissfield, Oh., U.S.	214	40.24 N	81.58 W
Blitar	115a	8.06 S	112.09 E
Blithe ≏	42	52.45 N	1.50 W
Blithfield Reservoir ◎[1]	42	52.48 N	1.53 W
Blitta	150	8.19 N	0.59 E
Blizn'uki	78	48.52 N	36.33 E
Blocher	218	38.43 N	85.39 W
Block Dam ◆[6]	212	45.12 N	76.54 W
Block Island	207	41.10 N	71.33 W
Block Island I	207	41.11 N	71.35 W
Block Island Sound Ʉ	207	41.10 N	71.45 W
Blockley	42	52.01 N	1.45 W
Blockton	198	40.36 N	94.28 W
Blodgett Mills	210	42.34 N	76.08 W
Bloed ≏	158	28.15 S	30.30 E
Bloedel	182	50.07 N	125.23 W
Bloedrivier, S. Afr.	158	28.06 S	30.33 E
Bloedrivier, S. Afr.	158	27.53 S	30.30 E
Bloekomspruit	158	26.45 S	28.21 E
Bloemendaal	52	52.24 N	4.37 E
Bloemfontein	158	29.12 S	26.07 E
Bloemhof	158	27.38 S	25.32 E
Bloemhofdam ◎[1]	158	27.40 S	25.40 E
Blois	50	47.35 N	1.20 E
Blokhus	26	57.15 N	9.35 E
Blokzijl	52	52.44 N	5.57 E
Blombacher Bach ◆[8]	263	51.15 N	7.14 E
Blombacka	40	59.37 N	13.47 E
Blomberg	52	51.56 N	9.05 E
Blomstermåla	26	56.59 N	16.20 E
Blonay	58	46.28 N	6.54 E
Blönduós	24a	65.39 N	20.15 W
Blongas	115b	8.53 S	116.02 E
Blonville-sur-Mer	50	49.19 N	0.02 E
Blood Indian Creek ≏	184	50.55 N	111.03 W
Blood Indian Reserve ◆[4]	182	49.30 N	113.10 W
Blood Mountain ∧	192	34.44 N	83.56 W
Blood River ⊥	158	28.20 S	30.35 E
Bloodsworth Island I	208	38.10 N	76.03 W
Bloodvein ≏	184	51.45 N	96.44 W
Bloody Foreland ›	48	55.09 N	8.17 W
Bloomdale	216	41.10 N	83.33 W
Bloomer	190	45.06 N	91.29 W
Bloomfield, On., Can.	212	43.59 N	77.14 W
Bloomfield, Ct., U.S.	207	41.49 N	72.43 W
Bloomfield, In., U.S.	194	39.01 N	86.56 W
Bloomfield, Ia., U.S.	190	40.45 N	92.24 W
Bloomfield, Ky., U.S.	194	37.54 N	85.19 W
Bloomfield, Mo., U.S.	194	36.53 N	89.55 W
Bloomfield, Ne., U.S.	198	42.35 N	97.38 W
Bloomfield, N.J., U.S.	210	40.48 N	74.11 W
Bloomfield, N.M., U.S.	200	36.42 N	107.59 W
Bloomfield, Oh., U.S.	214	40.03 N	81.44 W
Bloomfield ◆[8]	279b	40.27 N	79.56 W
Bloomfield Glens	281	42.33 N	83.20 W
Bloomfield Highlands	281	42.36 N	83.16 W
Bloomfield Hills	216	42.35 N	83.14 W
Bloomfield Village	216	42.33 N	83.15 W
Bloomingburg, N.Y., U.S.	210	41.33 N	74.26 W
Bloomingburg, Oh., U.S.	218	39.36 N	83.23 W
Bloomingdale, Il., U.S.	216	41.57 N	88.04 W
Bloomingdale, Mi., U.S.	216	42.22 N	85.57 W
Bloomingdale, N.J., U.S.	210	41.00 N	74.19 W
Bloomingdale, Oh., U.S.	214	40.21 N	80.49 W
Blooming Glen	208	40.22 N	75.15 W
Blooming Grove, In., U.S.	218	39.30 N	85.04 W
Blooming Grove, N.Y., U.S.	210	41.25 N	74.11 W
Blooming Grove, Pa., U.S.	210	41.21 N	75.09 W
Blooming Grove, Tx., U.S.	222	32.06 N	96.43 W
Blooming Prairie	190	43.52 N	93.03 W
Bloomington, Ca., U.S.	228	34.04 N	117.23 W
Bloomington, Il., U.S.	216	40.29 N	88.59 W
Bloomington, In., U.S.	218	39.09 N	86.31 W
Bloomington, Mn., U.S.	190	44.50 N	93.17 W
Bloomington, N.Y., U.S.	210	41.53 N	74.03 W
Bloomington, Tx., U.S.	196	28.38 N	96.53 W
Bloomington, Wi., U.S.	190	42.53 N	90.55 W
Bloomington, Lake ◎[1]	216	40.37 N	88.55 W
Blooming Valley	214	41.40 N	80.03 W
Bloomsburg	210	41.00 N	76.27 W
Bloomsbury, Austl.	166	20.43 S	148.35 E
Bloomsbury, N.J., U.S.	210	40.39 N	75.05 W
Bloomsdale Gardens	285	40.07 N	74.52 W
Bloomville, N.Y., U.S.	210	42.20 N	74.48 W
Bloomville, Oh., U.S.	214	41.03 N	83.00 W
Blora	115a	6.57 S	111.25 E
Bloserville	208	40.12 N	77.24 W
Blossburg	210	41.40 N	77.03 W
Blossom	196	33.39 N	95.23 W
Blossom Hill	208	40.05 N	76.19 W
Blötberget	40	60.07 N	15.04 E
Blotzheim	58	47.36 N	7.29 E
Blouberg	156	23.08 S	28.56 E
Blouberg ∧	156	23.01 S	28.59 E
Bloubergstrand	158	33.47 S	18.28 E
Blouin, Lac ◎	190	48.10 N	77.44 W
Bloumet	148	23.27 N	6.06 E
Blountstown	192	30.26 N	85.02 W
Blountsville	194	34.04 N	86.35 W
Blountville	192	36.31 N	82.19 W
Blovice	60	49.35 N	13.33 E
Blovstrød	41	55.52 N	12.24 E
Blowering Reservoir ◎[1]	171b	35.30 S	148.15 E
Blowing Rock	192	36.08 N	81.40 W
Bloxham	42	52.02 N	1.22 W
Bloxom	208	37.49 N	75.37 W
Blšanka ≏	54	50.10 N	13.34 E
Blšany	54	50.10 N	13.29 E
Bludenz	58	47.09 N	9.49 E
Bludnaja ≏	88	51.24 N	110.39 E
Blue ≏, Az., U.S.	200	33.13 N	109.11 W
Blue ≏, Co., U.S.	200	40.03 N	106.24 W
Blue ≏, In., U.S.	216	41.07 N	85.30 W
Blue ≏, In., U.S.	218	38.11 N	86.19 W
Blue ≏, Ok., U.S.	196	33.53 N	95.56 W
Blue, Middle Fork ≏	218	38.33 N	86.07 W
Blue, South Fork ≏	218	38.26 N	86.11 W
Blue, West Fork ≏	218	38.33 N	86.07 W
Blue Anchor	285	39.41 N	74.52 W
Blue Anchor Brook ≏	285	39.42 N	74.49 W
Blue Ash	218	39.13 N	84.22 W
Blue Ball	218	39.29 N	84.21 W
Blue Bell	208	40.09 N	75.16 W
Bluebell Hill	260	51.20 N	0.30 E
Blue Bonnets, Champ de Course ♠	275a	45.29 N	73.39 W
Blue Brook ≏	276	40.40 N	74.25 W
Blue Buck Knob ∧[2]	194	36.57 N	92.07 W
Bluebush Swamp ⁝	162	20.30 S	137.25 E
Blue Creek, Oh., U.S.	218	38.47 N	83.20 W
Blue Creek, Wa., U.S.	182	48.19 N	117.49 W
Blue Creek, Wa., U.S.	202	48.19 N	117.49 W
Blue Creek ≏, Ca., U.S.	226	38.28 N	120.22 W
Blue Creek ≏, Id., U.S.	202	42.02 N	116.08 W
Blue Creek ≏, Ne., U.S.	198	41.19 N	102.10 W
Blue Creek ≏, Oh., U.S.	216	41.07 N	84.26 W
Blue Creek ≏, Ut,. U.S.	200	41.31 N	112.24 W
Blue Cypress Lake ◎	220	27.44 N	80.45 W
Blue Earth	190	43.38 N	94.06 W
Blue Earth ≏	190	44.09 N	94.02 W
Bluefield, Va., U.S.	192	37.15 N	81.16 W
Bluefield, W.V., U.S.	192	37.16 N	81.13 W
Bluefields	236	12.00 N	83.45 W
Bluefields, Bahía de c	236	12.02 N	83.44 W
Bluefields Bay c	241q	18.10 N	78.03 W
Blue Grass Airport ⊠	218	38.02 N	84.36 W
Blue Grotto → Azzurra, Grotta ≗[5]	68	40.35 N	14.14 E
Blue Hill, Me., U.S.	188	44.24 N	68.35 W
Blue Hill, Ne., U.S.	198	40.19 N	98.26 W
Blue Hill Bay c	188	44.15 N	68.30 W
Blue Hills	207	41.40 N	72.56 W
Blue Hills of Couteau ✗[2]	186	47.59 N	57.43 W
Blue Hills Reservation ♠	283	42.13 N	71.05 W
Blue Island	216	41.39 N	87.40 W
Blue Jay	228	34.15 N	117.13 W
Bluejoint Lake ◎	202	42.35 N	119.40 W
Blue Knob ∧	214	40.17 N	78.34 W
Blue Knob State Park ♠	214	40.16 N	78.35 W
Blue Lagoon National Park ♠	154	15.30 S	27.25 E
Blue Lake National Park ♠	171a	27.31 S	153.29 E
Blue Licks Battlefield State Park ♠	218	38.26 N	84.00 W
Blue Marsh Lake ◎[1]	208	40.25 N	76.05 W
Blue Mesa Reservoir ◎[1]	200	38.27 N	107.10 W
Blue Mosque ᵿ[1]	273c	30.02 N	31.15 E
Blue Mound, Il., U.S.	219	39.42 N	89.07 W
Blue Mound, Ks., U.S.	198	38.05 N	95.00 W
Blue Mound, Tx., U.S.	222	32.51 N	97.19 W
Blue Mountain, Ms., U.S.	194	34.40 N	89.01 W
Blue Mountain, N.Y., U.S.	210	42.07 N	74.01 W
Blue Mountain ∧, N.B., Can.	186	47.49 N	66.19 W
Blue Mountain ∧, Nf., Can.	186	50.24 N	57.10 W
Blue Mountain ∧, Ar., U.S.	194	34.41 N	94.03 W
Blue Mountain ∧, Mt., U.S.	198	47.16 N	104.10 W
Blue Mountain ∧, N.H., U.S.	188	44.47 N	71.28 W
Blue Mountain ∧, Pa., U.S.	188	40.15 N	77.30 W
Blue Mountain ∧[2], On., Can.	190	48.15 N	80.07 W
Blue Mountain ∧[2], On., Can.	212	44.40 N	77.58 W
Blue Mountain Peak ∧	241q	18.03 N	76.35 W
Blue Mountains ✗, Austl.	170	33.37 S	150.17 E
Blue Mountains ✗, Jam.	241q	18.06 N	76.40 W
Blue Mountains ✗, U.S.	202	45.30 N	118.15 W
Blue Mountains ✗, Me., U.S.	188	44.50 N	70.35 W
Blue Mountains National Park ♠	170	33.40 S	150.25 E
Blue Mud Bay c	164	13.26 S	135.56 E
Blue Nile (Al-Baḥr al-Azraq) (Abay) ≏	140	15.38 N	32.31 E
Bluenose Lake ◎	180	68.25 N	119.45 W
Blue Point	276	40.45 N	73.02 W
Blue Point ›	276	40.44 N	73.02 W
Blue Rapids	198	39.40 N	96.39 W
Blue Ridge, Ab., Can.	182	54.08 N	115.22 W
Blue Ridge, Ga., U.S.	192	34.51 N	84.19 W
Blue Ridge, Il., U.S.	216	40.17 N	88.29 W
Blue Ridge ✗	178	37.00 N	82.00 W
Blue Ridge Summit	208	39.43 N	77.28 W
Blue River	182	52.05 N	119.17 W
Blue Rock Springs Park ♠	282	38.08 N	122.12 W
Bluesky	182	56.04 N	118.14 W
Blue Springs	198	40.08 N	96.39 W
Blue Stack Mountains ✗	48	54.45 N	8.05 W
Bluestone ≏	192	37.34 N	80.59 W
Bluestone Dam ◆[6]	192	37.36 N	80.53 W
Bluestone Lake ◎[1]	192	37.30 N	80.50 W
Bluestone State Park ♠	192	37.37 N	80.56 W
Bluewater	200	35.15 N	107.59 W
Blue Water Bridge ◆[5]	214	43.00 N	82.25 W
Bluff, N.Z.	172	46.36 S	168.20 E
Bluff, Ut,. U.S.	200	37.17 N	109.33 W
Bluff Cape ›	110	18.00 N	94.26 E
Bluff City, Il., U.S.	219	38.57 N	89.02 W
Bluff City, Tn., U.S.	192	36.28 N	82.15 W
Bluff Cove c	280	33.48 N	118.24 W
Bluff Creek ≏, U.S.	196	36.58 N	97.26 W
Bluff Creek ≏, Ks., U.S.	198	37.02 N	99.29 W
Bluff Dale	196	32.21 N	98.01 W
Bluff Head ›	271d	22.11 N	114.12 E
Bluff Island I	271d	22.19 N	114.21 E
Bluff Knoll ∧	162	34.23 S	118.20 E
Bluff Park	194	33.24 N	86.51 W
Bluff Point ›	162	27.50 S	114.06 E
Bluffs	219	39.45 N	90.32 W
Bluff Springs	219	39.59 N	90.21 W
Bluffton, In., U.S.	216	40.44 N	85.10 W
Bluffton, Oh., U.S.	216	40.53 N	83.53 W
Bluffton, S.C., U.S.	192	32.14 N	80.51 W
Bluffy Lake ◎	184	50.47 N	92.55 W
Bluford	219	38.20 N	88.45 W
Blum	222	32.09 N	97.24 W
Blumberg, Dtsch.	54	52.36 N	13.37 E
Blumberg, Dtsch.	58	47.50 N	8.31 E
Blumenau	252	26.56 S	49.03 W
Blumenhof	184	50.01 N	107.41 W
Blümlisalp ∧	58	46.30 N	7.47 E
Blunt	198	44.30 N	99.59 W
Blup Blup Island I	164	3.30 S	144.37 E
Bly	202	42.23 N	121.02 W
Blying Sound Ʉ	180	59.50 N	149.15 W
Blyth, Austl.	168b	33.51 S	138.29 E
Blyth, On., Can.	190	43.44 N	81.26 W
Blyth, Eng., U.K.	44	55.07 N	1.30 W
Blyth ≏, Austl.	164	12.04 S	134.35 E
Blyth ≏, Eng., U.K.	42	52.18 N	1.40 E
Blyth ≏, Eng., U.K.	44	55.08 N	1.31 W
Blyth Bridge	46	55.42 N	3.24 W
Blythe	204	33.36 N	114.35 W
Blythedale	214	40.15 N	79.48 W
Blytheswood	214	42.07 N	82.36 W
Blytheville	194	35.55 N	89.55 W
Blytheville Air Force Base ■	194	35.57 N	89.57 W
Blyth Range ✗	162	26.50 S	129.00 E
Bnei Braq → Bene Beraq	132	32.05 N	34.50 E
Bø, Nor.	24	68.37 N	14.33 E
Bø, Nor.	26	59.25 N	9.04 E
Bo, S.L.	150	7.56 N	11.21 W
Boa	154	10.32 S	28.06 E
Boac	116	13.27 N	121.50 E
Boaco	236	12.28 N	85.40 W
Boaco □[5]	236	12.30 N	85.30 W
Boadilla del Monte	266a	40.24 N	3.53 W
Boa Esperança, Bra.	255	21.05 S	45.34 W
Boa Esperança, Bra.	256	22.48 S	42.34 W
Boa Esperança, Bra.	256	22.24 S	43.05 W
Boa Esperança, Represa ◎[1]	250	6.50 S	44.00 W
Bo'ai	102	35.10 N	113.04 E
Boali	152	4.48 N	18.07 E
Boalia	126	23.35 N	88.57 E
Boalsburg	214	40.46 N	77.48 W
Boane	156	26.06 S	32.19 E
Boano, Pulau I	164	2.56 S	127.56 E
Boa Nova	255	14.22 S	40.10 W
Bo'ao	110	19.14 N	110.34 E
Boara Pisani	64	45.08 N	11.47 E
Boara Polesine	64	45.07 N	11.48 E
Board Camp Mountain ∧	204	40.42 N	123.43 W
Boardman	214	41.01 N	80.39 W
Boardman ≏	190	44.46 N	85.38 W
Boarhills	46	56.19 N	2.42 W
Boario Terme	64	45.54 N	10.10 E
Boat Basin	182	49.29 N	126.25 W
Boat Channel Ʉ	212	44.10 N	76.31 W
Boath	46	57.44 N	4.23 W
Boat Lake ◎	212	44.44 N	81.13 W
Boatman	166	27.16 S	146.55 E
Boat of Garten	46	57.20 N	3.44 W
Boa Viagem	250	5.07 S	39.44 W
Boa Vista, Bra.	246	2.49 N	60.40 W
Boa Vista, Bra.	256	21.25 S	45.35 W
Boa Vista I	150a	16.05 N	22.50 W
Boa Vista, Morro ∧[2]	287a	22.53 S	43.06 W
Boavita	246	6.20 N	72.35 W
Boawai	115b	8.46 S	121.10 E
Boayan Island I	116	10.34 N	119.09 E
Boaz	194	34.12 N	86.09 W
Boba	115b	8.57 S	121.04 E
Bobai	102	22.12 N	109.52 E
Bobbau	54	51.41 N	12.16 E
Bobbili	122	18.34 N	83.22 E
Bobbing	260	51.21 N	0.43 E
Bobbingworth	260	51.44 N	0.13 E
Bobbin Head	274a	33.39 S	151.08 E
Bobbio	62	44.46 N	9.23 E
Bobbio Pellice	62	44.48 N	7.07 E
Bobbys Run ≏	285	39.58 N	74.48 W
Bobcaygeon	212	44.33 N	78.33 W
Bobenheim-Roxheim	56	49.35 N	8.21 E
Bobigny	50	48.54 N	2.27 E
Böbingen, Dtsch.	56	48.49 N	9.54 E
Bobingen, Dtsch.	58	48.16 N	10.50 E
Bobitz	54	53.47 N	11.20 E
Bob Lake ◎	212	44.55 N	78.47 W
Böblingen	56	48.41 N	9.01 E
Boblo Island Amusement Park ♠	281	42.06 N	83.07 W
Bobo Dioulasso	150	11.12 N	4.18 W
Boboiob, gora ∧	85	40.52 N	70.21 E
Bobo Island I	164	9.08 S	143.14 E
Bobolice	30	53.57 N	16.36 E
Bobonaza ≏	246	2.36 S	76.38 W
Bobonong	156	21.58 S	28.17 E
Bobos ≏	234	20.15 N	96.47 W
Bobotsari	115a	7.18 S	109.22 E
Bobr	76	54.20 N	29.16 E
Bobr ≏, Bela.	76	54.03 N	28.51 E
Bóbr ≏, Pol.	30	52.04 N	15.04 E
Bobrik ≏	76	52.08 N	26.46 E
Bobrikovo	83	47.56 N	39.13 E
Bobrinec	78	48.03 N	32.09 E
Bobrka	78	49.38 N	24.18 E
Bobrov	78	51.06 N	40.02 E
Bobrovica	78	50.44 N	31.22 E
Bobrujsk	76	53.09 N	29.14 E
Bobs Creek ≏	219	38.57 N	90.42 W
Bobs Lake ◎	212	44.40 N	76.35 W
Bobtown	188	39.45 N	79.58 W
Bobuk	140	11.30 N	34.05 E
Bobures	246	9.15 N	71.11 W
Boby, Pic ∧	157b	22.12 S	46.55 E
Boca ◆[8]	288	34.38 S	58.21 W
Bôca, Cachoeira da ⌊	250	5.27 S	54.24 W
Boca Brava, Isla I	236	8.13 N	82.16 W
Boca Chica	240m	17.59 N	66.32 W
Boca Chica Key I	220	24.34 N	81.42 W
Bôca da Mata	250	9.41 S	36.11 W
Boca del Monte	236	8.21 N	82.07 W
Boca del Río	234	19.06 N	96.06 W
Boca del Rosario	258	34.26 S	57.17 W
Boca de Pozo	246	11.00 N	64.23 W
Boca de Quadra Ʉ	182	55.08 N	130.50 W
Boca do Acre	248	8.45 S	67.23 W
Bôca do Jari	250	1.07 S	51.58 W
Bocage, Cap ›	175f	21.12 S	165.35 E
Boca Grande	220	26.44 N	82.15 W
Boca Grande Channel Ʉ	220	24.34 N	82.03 W
Boca Grande Key I	220	24.32 N	82.00 W
Bocaina ≏	256	22.40 S	45.00 W
Bocaina, Parque Nacional de ♠	256	23.00 S	44.15 W
Bocaina, Serra da ✗	256	22.43 S	44.40 W
Bocaina de Minas	256	22.10 S	44.24 W
Bocaiúva	255	17.07 S	43.49 W
Bocanda	150	7.04 N	4.30 W
Bocanegra	286d	12.01 S	77.07 W
Bocaranga	152	6.59 N	15.39 E
Boca Raton	220	26.21 N	80.05 W
Boca Reservoir ◎[1]	226	39.24 N	120.06 W
Bocas del Toro	236	9.20 N	82.15 W
Bocas del Toro □[4]	236	8.50 N	82.10 W
Bocas del Toro, Archipiélago de II	236	9.20 N	82.10 W
Bocaue	116	14.48 N	120.55 E
Bocay	236	14.19 N	85.10 W
Bocay ≏	236	14.20 N	85.10 W
Boccaleone	66	44.39 N	11.48 E
Boccea ◆[8]	267a	41.58 N	12.19 E
Bocchigliero	68	39.25 N	16.45 E
Boccon	64	45.19 N	11.39 E
Bocconi	64	44.01 N	11.46 E
Bočejkovo	76	55.01 N	29.09 E
Bochan	88	53.09 N	103.48 E
Bochil	234	16.59 N	92.55 W
Böch Möron	86	49.40 N	90.20 E
Bochnia	30	49.58 N	20.26 E
Bocholt, Bel.	56	51.10 N	5.35 E
Bocholt, Dtsch.	52	51.50 N	6.36 E
Bocholtz	56	50.49 N	6.00 E
Bochov	54	50.06 N	13.02 E
Bochum, Dtsch.	56	51.28 N	7.13 E
Bochum, Dtsch.	263	51.28 N	7.13 E
Bochum, S. Afr.	156	23.17 S	29.07 E
Bockel	52	53.12 N	9.17 E
Böckel ◆[8]	263	51.13 N	7.12 E
Bockenem	52	52.00 N	10.07 E
Bockhorn	52	53.23 N	8.01 E
Böckstein	64	47.05 N	13.07 E
Bockum ◆[8], Dtsch.	263	51.21 N	6.38 E
Bockum ◆[8], Dtsch.	263	51.20 N	6.44 E
Bockum-Hövel	52	51.42 N	7.46 E
Bocognano	36	42.05 N	9.03 E
Bocón, Caño ≏	246	3.42 N	67.53 W
Boconó	246	9.15 N	70.16 W
Bocq ≏	56	50.20 N	4.53 E
Bocșa	38	45.23 N	21.47 E
Boczów	54	52.19 N	14.58 E
Boda, Centraf.	152	4.19 N	17.28 E
Böda, Sve.	26	57.15 N	17.03 E
Boda, Sve.	26	61.01 N	15.13 E
Bodafors	26	57.30 N	14.42 E
Boda Glasbruk	26	56.44 N	15.40 E
Bodāi	272b	22.48 N	88.29 E
Bodajbo	88	57.51 N	114.10 E
Bodalangi	152	3.14 N	22.14 E
Bodalla	166	36.05 S	150.03 E
Bodallin	162	31.22 S	118.52 E
Bodåsgruvan	40	60.25 N	16.26 E
Bodcau Creek ≏	194	33.01 N	93.31 W
Boddam, Scot., U.K.	46	57.28 N	1.47 W
Boddam, Scot., U.K.	46a	59.55 N	1.17 W
Boddington	168a	32.48 S	116.28 E
Bode	198	42.52 N	94.17 W
Bode ≏	54	52.01 N	11.12 E
Bodega Bay c	204	38.15 N	123.00 W
Bodegraven	52	52.05 N	4.45 E
Bodélé ◆[1]	146	16.30 N	16.30 E
Bodelschwingh ◆[8]	263	51.33 N	7.22 E
Boden	26	65.50 N	21.42 E
Bodenburg	52	52.01 N	10.01 E
Bodenfelde	52	51.38 N	9.33 E
Boden → Fleres	64	46.58 N	11.21 E
Bodenheim	56	49.56 N	8.18 E
Bodenmais	60	49.04 N	13.06 E
Bodensee (Lake Constance) ◎	58	47.35 N	9.25 E
Bodenteich	54	52.50 N	10.41 E
Bodenwerder	52	51.59 N	9.31 E
Bodenwies ∧	61	47.45 N	14.34 E
Bodenwöhr	60	49.16 N	12.19 E
Boderg, Lough ◎	48	53.52 N	7.58 W
Bode Sadu	150	9.00 N	4.47 E
Bodhan	122	18.40 N	77.54 E
Bodh Gaya	124	24.42 N	84.59 E
Bodiam	42	51.00 N	0.33 E
Bodināyakkanūr	122	10.01 N	77.21 E
Bodine, Mount ∧	182	55.37 N	125.49 W
Bodjoki	152	2.59 N	22.18 E
Bodjokola	152	3.54 N	20.17 E
Bodmin	42	50.29 N	4.43 W
Bodmin Moor ◆[3]	42	50.33 N	4.33 W
Bodø	24	67.17 N	14.23 E
Bodocó	250	7.47 S	39.55 W
Bodoquena, Serra da ✗[1]	248	21.00 S	56.50 W
Bodoukpa	152	5.43 N	17.36 E
Bodri ≏	115a	6.52 S	110.10 E
Bodrog ≏	38	48.07 N	21.25 E
Bodrum	130	37.02 N	27.26 E
Bodstedt	54	54.22 N	12.37 E
Bo Duc	110	11.58 N	106.48 E
Bodzentyn	30	50.56 N	20.57 E
Boè, Piz ∧	64	46.31 N	11.48 E
Boëge	58	46.13 N	6.25 E
Boekelo	52	52.13 N	6.47 E
Boele ◆[8]	263	51.24 N	7.28 E
Boémbé	152	2.54 S	15.39 E
Boende	152	0.13 S	20.52 E
Bœng Lvea	110	12.36 N	105.34 E
Boeni	157a	12.55 S	45.06 E
Boën-sur-Lignon	62	45.44 N	3.59 E
Boeo, Capo ›	70	37.48 N	12.25 E
Boerboonfontein	158	33.43 S	20.32 E
Boerne	196	29.47 N	98.43 W
Boeslunde	41	55.18 N	11.17 E
Boesmanland □[5]	156	19.30 S	20.00 E
Boesmans ≏, S. Afr.	158	28.46 S	30.09 E
Boesmans ≏, S. Afr.	158	33.42 S	26.39 E
Boesmansriviermond	158	33.42 S	26.39 E
Boetsap	158	27.59 S	24.30 E
Boeuf ≏	194	31.52 N	91.47 W
Boeuf Creek ≏	219	38.36 N	91.09 W
Boffa	150	10.10 N	14.02 W
Boffalora	266b	45.28 N	8.50 E
Boffzen	52	51.45 N	9.23 E
Bofoku	152	0.57 S	20.53 E
Bofors	40	59.20 N	14.32 E
Bofosso	150	8.40 N	9.42 W
Bōfu → Hōfu	96	34.03 N	131.34 E
Boga	154	1.03 N	29.56 E
Bogachiel ≏	224	47.55 N	124.28 W
Bogadjim	164	5.25 S	145.45 E
Bogal, Lagh ≏	154	0.45 N	40.50 E
Bogale	110	16.17 N	95.24 E
Bogalusa	194	30.47 N	89.50 W
Bogan ≏	166	29.57 S	146.21 E
Bogandé	150	12.59 N	0.08 W
Bog and Vly Meadows ⁝	276	40.56 N	74.19 W
Bogan Gate	166	33.07 S	147.48 E
Bogangolo	152	5.34 N	18.15 E
Bogantungan	166	23.39 S	147.18 E
Bogart, Mount ∧	182	50.55 N	115.14 W
Bogastow Brook ≏	283	42.12 N	71.22 W
Bogata	196	33.28 N	95.13 W
Bogataja Černeščina	78	48.59 N	35.35 E
Bogatiščevo-Jepišino	82	54.47 N	38.25 E
Bogatoje	80	53.04 N	51.24 E
Bogatyje Saby	80	56.01 N	50.27 E
Bogatynia	54	50.53 N	15.00 E
Bogatyr'	80	53.25 N	50.02 E
Bogatyrevo	80	50.22 N	48.46 E
Boğazkale	130	40.02 N	34.37 E
Boğazkaya	130	41.27 N	35.54 E
Boğazköy ◆[8]	267b	41.11 N	28.46 E
Boğazköy ≏	267b	41.10 N	28.49 E
Boğazlıyan	130	39.12 N	35.15 E
Bogbonga	152	1.35 N	19.25 E
Bogcang ≏	120	31.56 N	87.24 E
Bogd	102	45.11 N	100.43 E
Bogdanovič	86	56.47 N	62.01 E
Bogdanovka, Ross.	80	52.42 N	50.46 E
Bogdanovka, Ross.	80	52.10 N	52.37 E
Bogdanovka, Sak.	84	41.18 N	43.35 E
Bogda Shan ✗	90	43.30 N	89.45 E
Bogdo Ula ∧	86	43.50 N	88.20 E
Bogel	56	50.11 N	7.48 E
Bogembaj	86	52.29 N	72.20 E
Bogen	60	48.55 N	12.43 E
Bogense	41	55.34 N	10.06 E
Boger City	192	35.29 N	81.12 W
Boges	56	50.11 N	7.48 E
Bogess Creek ≏	282	37.18 N	122.19 W
Boget	80	49.40 N	47.59 E
Boggabilla	166	28.37 S	150.21 E
Boggabri	166	30.42 S	150.02 E
Boggeragh Mountains ✗	48	52.03 N	8.55 W
Boggola, Mount ∧	162	23.48 S	117.40 E
Boggs Run ≏	279b	40.32 N	80.14 W
Boggstown	218	39.34 N	85.55 W
Boggy Creek ≏	222	31.07 N	95.46 W
Boggy Peak ∧	240c	17.03 N	61.51 W
Bogia	164	4.15 S	144.55 E
Bogie Lake ◎	281	42.37 N	83.31 W
Bogilima	152	3.34 N	19.16 E
Bogliasco	62	44.23 N	9.04 E
Bognanco Fonti	58	46.07 N	8.12 E
Bognes	24	68.10 N	16.00 E
Bognor Regis	42	50.47 N	0.41 W
Bogny-sur-Meuse	56	49.51 N	4.46 E
Bogo, Cam.	146	10.44 N	14.36 E
Bogo, Pil.	116	11.03 N	124.00 E
Bogø I	41	54.56 N	12.04 E
Bogo Bay c	116	11.05 N	124.01 E
Bogoduchov	78	50.10 N	35.30 E
Bogol Manyo	144	4.31 N	41.32 E
Bogol'ubovo, Ross.	76	55.32 N	32.57 E
Bogol'ubovo, Ross.	80	56.13 N	40.31 E
Bogomila	38	41.36 N	21.28 E
Bogong, Mount ∧	166	36.45 S	147.18 E
Bogong Peaks ✗	171b	35.34 S	148.28 E
Bogor	115a	6.35 S	106.47 E
Bogoria, Lake ◎	154	0.15 N	36.06 E
Bogoro	154	1.24 N	30.17 E
Bogorodčany	78	48.48 N	24.32 E
Bogorodick	76	53.46 N	38.08 E
Bogorodickoje	80	46.20 N	41.10 E
Bogorodičnoje	83	49.01 N	37.30 E
Bogorodsk, Ross.	24	62.16 N	52.28 E
Bogorodsk, Ross.	80	56.06 N	43.31 E
Bogorodskoje, Ross.	80	57.51 N	50.45 E
Bogorodskoje, Ross.	80	46.20 N	43.53 E
Bogorodskoje, Ross.	82	55.02 N	38.29 E
Bogorodskoje, Ross.	82	55.26 N	36.14 E
Bogorodskoje, Ross.	89	52.22 N	140.30 E
Bogorodskoje ◆[8]	265b	55.49 N	37.44 E
Bogoso	150	5.34 N	2.01 W
Bogosskij chrebet ✗	84	42.15 N	46.05 E
Bogota	276	40.52 N	74.01 W
Bogotá → Santa Fe de Bogotá	246	4.36 N	74.05 W
Bogotol	86	56.12 N	89.33 E
Bogou	150	10.39 N	0.11 E
Bogovarovo	24	58.59 N	47.01 E

≏ River	Fluß	Río	Rivière	Rio	
≖ Canal	Kanal	Canal	Canal	Canal	
⌊ Waterfall, Rapids	Wasserfall, Stromschnellen	Cascada, Rápidos	Chute d'eau, Rapides	Cascata, Rápidos	
Ʉ Strait	Meeresstraße	Estrecho	Détroit	Estreito	
c Bay, Gulf	Bucht, Golf	Bahía, Golfo	Baie, Golfe	Baía, Golfo	
◎ Lake, Lakes	See, Seen	Lago, Lagos	Lac, Lacs	Lago, Lagos	
⁝ Swamp	Sumpf	Pantano	Marais	Pântano	
⊓ Ice Features, Glacier	Eis- und Gletscherformen	Accidentes Glaciales	Formes glaciaires	Acidentes glaciares	
⫪ Other Hydrographic Features	Andere Hydrographische Objekte	Otros Elementos Hidrográficos	Autres données hydrographiques	Outros acidentes hidrográficos	
✦ Submarine Features	Untermeerische Objekte	Accidentes Submarinos	Formes de relief sous-marin	Acidentes submarinos	
□ Political Unit	Politische Einheit	Unidad Politica	Entité politique	Unidade política	
ᵿ Cultural Institution	Kulturelle Institution	Institución Cultural	Institution culturelle	Instituição cultural	
⊥ Historical Site	Historische Stätte	Sitio Histórico	Site historique	Sitio histórico	
♠ Recreational Site	Erholungs- und Ferienort	Sitio de Recreo	Centre de loisirs	Area de Lazer	
⊠ Airport	Flughafen	Aeropuerto	Aéroport	Aeroporto	
■ Military Installation	Militäranlage	Instalación Militar	Installation militaire	Instalação militar	
◆ Miscellaneous	Verschiedenes	Misceláneo	Divers	Diversos	

Symbols in the index entries represent the broad categories identified in the key at the right. Symbols with superior numbers (*') identify subcategories (see complete key on page 1 · 1).

Symbole im Register stellen die rechts im Schlüssel erklärten Kategorien dar. Symbole mit hochgestellten Ziffern (*') bezeichnen Unterabteilungen einer Kategorie (vgl. vollständiger Schlüssel auf Seite 1 · 1).

Les symboles de l'index représentent les catégories indiquées dans la légende à droite. Les symboles suivis d'un indice (*') représentent des sous-catégories (voir légende complète à la page 1 · 1).

Los símbolos del índice representan las categorías identificadas en la clave a la derecha. Los símbolos con números en su parte superior (*') identifican las subcategorías (véase la clave completa en la página 1 · 1).

Os símbolos incluídos no texto do índice representam as grandes categorias identificadas a direita. Os símbolos com números em sua parte superior (*') identificam as subcategorias (veja-se a clave completa a página 1 · 1).

Other Topographic Features	Andere Topographische Objekte	Otros Elementos Topográficos	Autres données topographiques	Outros acidentes topográficos
▲ Mountain	Berg	Montagne	Montaña	Montanha
)(Pass	Paß	Col	Paso	Passo
⋁ Valley, Canyon	Tal, Cañon	Vallée, Canyon	Valle, Cañon	Vale, Canhão
✕ Plain	Ebene	Plaine	Llano	Planície
⋗ Cape	Kap	Cap	Cabo	Cabo
⌐ Island	Insel	Île	Isla	Ilha
II Islands	Inseln	Îles	Islas	Ilhas

ESPAÑOL

Nombre	Página	Lat.°′	Long.°′ W = Oeste
Boquilla, Presa de la ⊜[1]	232	27.30 N	105.30 W
Boquilla del Refugio	196	25.33 N	102.28 W
Boquillas del Carmen	232	29.17 N	102.53 W
Boquim	250	11.09 S	37.37 W
Bor, Česko.	60	49.43 N	12.47 E
Bor, Jugo.	38	44.05 N	22.07 E
Bor, Ross.	24	63.00 N	42.38 E
Bor, Ross.	80	56.22 N	44.05 E
Bor, Sūd.	140	6.12 N	31.33 E
Bor, Tür.	130	37.54 N	34.34 E
Bor, Lak ≃	154	1.18 N	40.40 E
Bora-Bora I	14	16.30 S	151.45 W
Borabu	110	16.02 N	103.07 E
Boracay Island I	116	11.59 N	121.55 E
Boraha, Nosy I	157b	16.50 S	49.55 E
Borah Peak ∧	202	44.08 N	113.48 W
Boraldaj ≃	85	42.33 N	69.07 E
Borale	144	9.10 N	42.35 E
Borambola	171b	35.12 S	147.41 E
Borang, Tanjung >	164	5.16 S	133.07 E
Borås	26	57.43 N	12.55 E
Borāzjān	128	29.16 N	51.12 E
Borba, Bra.	246	4.24 S	59.35 W
Borba, Port.	34	38.48 N	7.27 W
Borbeck ◆[8]	263	51.29 N	6.57 E
Borbera ≃	62	44.42 N	8.52 E
Borca di Cadore	64	46.26 N	12.13 E
Borcea, Brațul ≃	38	44.40 N	27.53 E
Borchen	52	51.39 N	8.44 E
Borçka	130	41.22 N	41.40 E
Borculo, Ned.	52	52.07 N	6.31 E
Borculo, Mi., U.S.	216	42.53 N	86.01 W
Borda, Cape >	166	35.45 S	136.34 E
Borda da Mata	256	22.16 S	46.10 W
Bordeaux, Fr.	32	44.50 N	0.34 W
Bordeaux, S. Afr.	273d	26.06 S	28.01 E
Bordeaux ◆[8]	275a	45.33 N	73.41 W
Bordeaux Mountain ∧[2]	240m	18.20 N	64.44 W
Borden, Austl.	162	34.05 S	118.16 E
Borden, Sk., Can.	184	52.25 N	107.13 W
Borden, Eng., U.K.	260	51.20 N	0.42 E
Borden, In., U.S.	218	38.28 N	85.57 W
Borden, Canadian Forces Base ■	212	44.17 N	79.55 W
Borden Lake ⊜	190	47.50 N	83.18 W
Borden Peninsula >[1]	176	73.00 N	83.00 W
Bordentown	208	40.08 N	74.42 W
Border Mountains ⋏	164	3.40 S	141.05 E
Borders □[4]	46	55.37 N	3.15 W
Bordertown	166	36.19 S	140.47 E
Bordesholm	30	54.11 N	10.01 E
Borđeyri	24a	65.15 N	21.10 W
Bordighera	62	43.46 N	7.39 E
Bording	41	56.12 N	9.17 E
Bording Kirkeby	41	56.10 N	9.15 E
Bordino, Fiume di ≃	70	37.53 N	12.37 E
Bordj Bou Arreridj	148	36.04 N	4.46 E
Bordj Bounaama	34	35.51 N	1.36 E
Bordj Menaïel	148	36.44 N	3.43 E
Bordj Omar Idriss	148	28.09 N	6.43 E
Bordj Sidi Toui	148	32.44 N	11.22 E
Bordunskij	85	42.40 N	75.37 E
Bore, It.	62	44.43 N	9.47 E
Bore, Ityo.	144	4.40 N	37.40 E
Boré, Mali	150	15.08 N	3.29 W
Boreda	144	6.32 N	37.48 E
Boreham	260	51.46 N	0.33 E
Borehamwood	260	51.40 N	0.16 W
Borel Hill ∧	282	37.19 N	122.12 W
Borello, It.	64	41.55 N	14.18 E
Borello, It.	66	44.03 N	12.11 E
Borensberg	26	58.34 N	15.17 E
Boreray I	46	57.42 N	7.18 W
Boretto	64	44.54 N	10.33 E
Borgallo, Galleria del ◆[5]	62	44.25 N	9.53 E
Borgå → Porvoo	26	60.24 N	25.40 E
Borgarnes	24a	64.35 N	21.53 W
Borgata Costiera	70	37.43 N	12.39 E
Børgefjell Nasjonalpark ♠	24	65.10 N	14.00 E
Borgentreich	52	51.34 N	9.14 E
Börger, Dtsch.	52	52.54 N	7.32 E
Borger, Ned.	52	52.55 N	6.46 E
Borger, Tx., U.S.	196	35.40 N	101.23 W
Borgerhout	50	51.13 N	4.26 E
Borgetto	70	38.03 N	13.08 E
Borggård	40	58.44 N	15.32 E
Borghetto	64	45.41 N	10.56 E
Borghetto di Vara	62	44.13 N	9.43 E
Borghetto Lodigiano	62	45.13 N	9.30 E
Borghetto Santo Spirito	62	44.06 N	8.14 E
Borgholm	26	56.53 N	16.39 E
Borghorst	52	52.07 N	7.23 E
Borgia	68	38.49 N	16.30 E
Borgio-Verezzi	62	44.10 N	8.18 E
Borgloon	56	50.48 N	5.20 E
Borg Mountain ∧	9	72.42 S	3.30 W
Borgne, Lake ⊂	194	30.05 N	89.40 W
Borgnesse, Pointe >	240e	14.27 N	60.54 W
Borgo	64	46.03 N	11.27 E
Borgo alla Collina	66	43.45 N	11.43 E
Borgo a Mozzano	66	43.59 N	10.33 E
Borgo Cerreto	66	42.49 N	12.54 E
Borgo d'Ale	62	45.21 N	8.03 E
Borgoforte	64	45.03 N	10.45 E
Borgofranco d'Ivrea	62	45.30 N	7.51 E
Borgolavezzaro	62	45.19 N	8.42 E
Borgomanero	62	45.42 N	8.28 E
Borgomaro	62	43.58 N	7.56 E
Borgonovo Val Tidone	62	45.01 N	9.26 E
Borgo Pace	66	43.39 N	12.17 E
Borgoricco	64	45.32 N	11.58 E
Borgorose	66	42.11 N	13.13 E
Borgo San Dalmazzo	62	44.20 N	7.30 E
Borgo San Giacomo	64	45.21 N	9.58 E
Borgo San Lorenzo	66	43.57 N	11.23 E
Borgosatollo	64	45.28 N	10.14 E
Borgosesia	62	45.43 N	8.16 E
Borgo Ticino	266b	45.41 N	8.36 E
Borgo Tossignano	66	44.16 N	11.35 E
Borgou □[5]	150	10.30 N	2.50 E
Borgo Val di Taro	62	44.29 N	9.46 E
Borgo Vercelli	62	45.21 N	8.28 E
Borgsdorf	54	52.42 N	13.14 E
Borgsdorf, Forst ◆[3]	264a	52.42 N	13.19 E
Borgu Game Reserve ◆[4]	150	10.15 N	4.10 E
Borgund ʊ[1]	26	61.03 N	7.49 E
Bori	150	4.42 N	7.21 E
Borig Delijn els ◆[2]	88	50.00 N	94.00 E
Borikhan	110	18.33 N	103.43 E
Borilovo	76	53.22 N	35.58 E
Borinage □[9]	50	50.30 N	4.00 E
Boring, Md., U.S.	208	39.31 N	76.49 W
Boring, Or., U.S.	224	45.25 N	122.22 W
Borinskoje	76	52.27 N	39.22 E
Borislav	78	49.16 N	23.27 E
Borisoglebsk	80	51.23 N	42.06 E
Borisoglebskij	80	57.16 N	39.09 E
Borisov, Bela.	76	54.15 N	28.30 E
Borisov, Ukr.	78	50.11 N	26.31 E
Borisovka, Ross.	76	52.50 N	39.58 E
Borisovka, Ross.	78	50.36 N	36.01 E
Borisovo	82	55.25 N	36.03 E
Borisovo ◆[8]	265b	55.38 N	37.45 E
Borisovo-Sudskoje	76	59.54 N	36.01 E
Borisovskaja	76	60.12 N	39.48 E
Borispol'	78	50.21 N	30.57 E
Borja, Esp.	34	41.50 N	1.32 W
Borja, Perú	246	4.26 S	77.33 W
Bork	52	51.40 N	7.30 E
Borken, Dtsch.	52	51.51 N	6.51 E
Borken, Dtsch.	56	51.03 N	9.16 E
Borkenwirthe	52	51.53 N	6.50 E
Borki, Ross.	86	59.08 N	82.15 E
Borki, Ukr.	78	49.42 N	36.02 E
Borkoldoj, chrebet ⋏	85	41.25 N	77.50 E

FRANÇAIS

Nom	Page	Lat.°′	Long.°′ W = Ouest
Børkop	41	55.39 N	9.39 E
Borkou ◆[1]	146	18.15 N	18.50 E
Borkou-Ennedi-Tibesti □[5]	146	18.15 N	18.50 E
Borkoviči	76	55.40 N	28.20 E
Borkum	52	53.35 N	6.40 E
Borkum I	52	53.35 N	6.41 E
Borland Manor	279b	40.15 N	80.09 W
Borlänge	40	60.29 N	15.25 E
Borle ◆[8]	272c	19.02 N	72.55 E
Borlu	130	38.44 N	28.27 E
Bormes-les-Mimosas	62	43.09 N	6.20 E
Bormida ≃	62	44.23 N	8.13 E
Bormida di Millesimo ≃	62	44.40 N	8.20 E
Bormida di Spigno ≃	62	44.40 N	8.20 E
Bormio	64	46.28 N	10.22 E
Born, Dtsch.	41	54.23 N	12.31 E
Born, Dtsch.	54	52.22 N	11.28 E
Born, Dtsch.	54	45.22 N	12.31 E
Borna, Dtsch.	54	51.19 N	13.11 E
Borna, Dtsch.	54	51.07 N	12.30 E
Borndiep ⊂	52	53.25 N	5.35 E
Borne	52	52.18 N	6.45 E
Borne ≃	62	45.03 N	3.54 E
Borneo (Kalimantan) I	112	0.30 N	114.00 E
Bornheim	56	50.46 N	6.59 E
Bornholm I	26	55.10 N	15.00 E
Bornholte	52	51.52 N	8.29 E
Bornhöved	54	54.04 N	10.16 E
Börnicke, Dtsch.	54	52.41 N	12.56 E
Börnicke, Dtsch.	264a	52.40 N	13.38 E
Börnig ◆[8]	263	51.33 N	7.16 E
Bornim ◆[8]	264a	52.26 N	13.00 E
Borno	64	45.56 N	10.12 E
Bornos, Embalse de ⊜[1]	34	36.50 N	5.30 W
Bornsdorf	54	51.46 N	13.41 E
Bornstedt ◆[8]	264a	52.25 N	13.02 E
Bornu □[3]	146	12.00 N	12.45 E
Boro ≃	140	8.52 N	26.11 E
Borobudur ⊥	115a	7.36 S	110.12 E
Borod'anka	78	50.39 N	29.56 E
Borodarou	150	10.59 N	2.53 E
Borodino, Ross.	82	55.32 N	35.50 E
Borodino, Ross.	82	56.53 N	37.00 E
Borodino, Ross.	88	55.55 N	94.55 E
Borodino, Ukr.	78	46.18 N	29.13 E
Borodulicha	86	50.43 N	80.55 E
Borodulino	80	57.59 N	54.20 E
Borogoncy	74	62.42 N	131.08 E
Borohoro Shan ⋏	86	44.06 N	83.10 E
Boroko	112	0.55 N	123.16 E
Boroml'a	78	50.37 N	34.59 E
Boromo	150	11.45 N	2.56 W
Boron, Mali	150	14.01 N	7.30 W
Boron, Ca., U.S.	228	34.59 N	117.38 W
Boronga Islands II	110	19.58 N	93.06 E
Borongan	116	11.37 N	125.26 E
Boronia	274b	37.52 S	145.17 E
Boron'ki	76	53.09 N	32.08 E
Borore	71	40.13 N	8.48 E
Borotou	150	8.44 N	7.30 W
Boroughbridge	44	54.06 N	1.23 W
Borough Green	260	51.17 N	0.19 E
Borough Park ◆[8]	276	40.38 N	74.00 W
Borovaja, Ukr.	78	50.12 N	30.07 E
Borovaja, Ukr.	83	49.24 N	37.40 E
Borovaja ≃	83	48.58 N	38.24 E
Borovan	38	43.26 N	23.45 E
Borovany	61	48.54 N	14.39 E
Boroviči	76	58.24 N	33.55 E
Borovik ≃	83	49.11 N	38.33 E
Borovka ≃	80	52.54 N	52.00 E
Borovl'anka	86	52.38 N	84.29 E
Borovoj	24	59.55 N	51.38 E
Borovoje, Kaz.	86	53.04 N	70.19 E
Borovoje, Ukr.	78	51.06 N	27.13 E
Borovsk	82	55.12 N	36.30 E
Borovskaja	24	60.46 N	41.06 E
Borovskij	86	57.03 N	65.44 E
Borovskoj	86	53.48 N	64.12 E
Borovskoje, Ross.	86	52.39 N	82.08 E
Borovskoje, Ukr.	83	48.51 N	38.34 E
Borovucha	76	55.36 N	28.37 E
Borovy	60	49.33 N	13.18 E
Borozdino	82	54.07 N	38.22 E
Borraan	144	10.14 N	48.44 E
Borrachudo ≃	255	18.12 S	45.16 W
Borrazópolis	255	23.56 S	51.36 W
Borrby	26	55.27 N	14.10 E
Borre	41	55.00 N	12.28 E
Borre ⊥	26	59.23 N	10.28 E
Borreby	41	55.14 N	11.19 E
Borriana, Esp.	34	39.53 N	0.05 W
Borriana, It.	62	45.30 N	8.02 E
Borris	48	52.35 N	6.06 W
Borrisokane	48	52.59 N	8.07 W
Borrisoleigh	48	52.45 N	7.57 W
Borroloola	164	16.04 S	136.17 E
Borroloola Aboriginal Reserve ◆[4]	164	16.00 S	136.15 E
Borrowdale	44	54.31 N	3.10 W
Börry	52	52.01 N	9.27 E
Borș	38	47.07 N	21.49 E
Borșa, Rom.	38	46.56 N	23.40 E
Borșa, Rom.	38	47.39 N	24.40 E
Borsad	120	22.25 N	72.54 E
Borsano	266b	45.35 N	8.51 E
Borschemich	263	51.04 N	6.25 E
Borščov	78	48.48 N	26.03 E
Borščovo	82	56.30 N	36.51 E
Borščovočnyj chrebet ⋏	88	52.00 N	117.00 E
Borsdorf	54	51.21 N	12.32 E
Borskoje	80	53.02 N	51.43 E
Borsod-Abaúj-Zemplén □[6]	30	48.15 N	21.00 E
Börssum	54	52.04 N	10.35 E
Borstendorf	54	50.46 N	13.10 E
Bortala ≃	86	44.50 N	82.45 E
Borth, Dtsch.	52	51.36 N	6.33 E
Borth, Wales, U.K.	42	52.29 N	4.03 W
Borthwick Water ≃	44	55.24 N	2.50 W
Bortigali	71	40.17 N	8.50 E
Bortigiadas	71	40.53 N	9.02 E
Bort-les-Orgues, Fr.	32	45.24 N	2.30 E
Bort-les-Orgues, Fr.	32	43.49 N	2.53 E
Bortniči	78	50.22 N	30.41 E
Borto	88	53.35 N	111.53 E
Bortondale	285	39.54 N	79.24 W
Boru	164	10.14 S	148.50 E
Boruca	236	9.00 N	83.20 W
Borūjen	128	31.59 N	51.18 E
Borūjerd	128	33.54 N	48.46 E
Bor Ul Shan ⋏	102	41.20 N	98.55 E
Borve	46	56.58 N	7.32 W
Borz'a	88	50.24 N	116.31 E
Borz'a ≃	88	50.38 N	115.38 E
Borzna	78	51.15 N	32.25 E
Boržomi	84	41.50 N	43.21 E
Boržomskij zapovednik ♠	84	41.50 N	43.10 E
Borzonasca	62	44.25 N	9.23 E
Borzyszkowy	30	54.03 N	17.22 E
Bosa	71	40.18 N	8.30 E
Bosaga	86	47.55 N	72.58 E
Bosambi	152	2.24 N	22.39 E
Bosanska Dubica	36	45.11 N	16.49 E
Bosanska Gradiška	36	45.09 N	17.15 E
Bosanska Krupa	36	44.53 N	16.10 E
Bosanski Novi	36	45.03 N	16.23 E
Bosanski Petrovac	36	44.33 N	16.22 E
Bosanski Šamac	38	45.03 N	18.28 E
Bosansko Grahovo	36	44.11 N	16.22 E
Bősárkány	61	47.41 N	17.14 E
Bosau	54	54.06 N	10.25 E
Bosavi, Mount ∧	164	6.35 S	142.50 E
Boscastle	42	50.41 N	4.42 W
Bosco, It.	66	44.53 N	12.14 E
Bosco, It.	66	43.08 N	12.28 E
Boscobel	190	43.08 N	90.42 W
Bosco Chiesanuova	64	45.37 N	11.02 E

PORTUGUÊS

Nome	Página	Lat.°′	Long.°′ W = Oeste
Bosco Marengo	62	44.49 N	8.41 E
Boscoreale	68	40.46 N	14.28 E
Bose	102	23.54 N	106.37 E
Bösel	52	53.00 N	7.58 E
Bosencheve, Parque Nacional ♠	234	19.36 N	100.15 W
Bosenge	152	1.18 N	22.19 E
Bósforo, Estrecho del → İstanbul Boğazı ʮ	130	41.06 N	29.04 E
Bosham	42	50.49 N	0.52 W
Boshan	98	36.29 N	117.50 E
Boshkung Lake ⊜	212	45.04 N	78.44 W
Boshoek	156	25.30 S	27.09 E
Boshof	158	28.34 S	25.04 E
Boshrūyeh	128	33.53 N	57.26 E
Bosilegrad	38	42.29 N	22.28 E
Bösingen	58	48.14 N	8.34 E
Bosjökloster	41	55.54 N	13.31 E
Boškajnar	85	38.13 N	68.51 E
Boskoop	52	52.04 N	4.35 E
Boskop	158	26.34 S	27.08 E
Boskop ∧	273d	26.05 S	27.57 E
Boskovice	30	49.29 N	16.40 E
Boskuil	158	27.23 S	25.51 E
Bosman	164	4.10 S	144.40 E
Bosna	272b	22.37 N	88.30 E
Bosna ≃	38	45.04 N	18.29 E
Bosna-Hercegovina → Bosnia and Hercegovina □[1]	36	44.15 N	17.30 E
Bošn'akovo	89	49.38 N	142.10 E
Bosnia and Hercegovina (Bosna-Hercegovina) □[1]	36	44.15 N	17.30 E
Bosnik	164	1.10 S	136.14 E
Boso	272b	22.58 N	88.08 E
Bosobolo	152	4.11 N	19.54 E
Boso-Djafo	152	1.06 N	19.14 E
Bosogo	85	41.09 N	76.25 E
Bōsō-hantō >[1]	94	35.18 N	140.10 E
Bōsō-kyūryō ⋏[2]	268	35.08 N	139.56 E
Bososama	152	4.18 N	20.00 E
Bösperde	263	51.28 N	7.46 E
Bosphore, Détroit du → İstanbul Boğazı ʮ	130	41.06 N	29.04 E
Bosporus → İstanbul Boğazı ʮ	130	41.06 N	29.04 E
Bosque □[6]	222	31.55 N	97.35 W
Bosque, Paseo del ♠	288	34.55 S	57.56 W
Bosque Farms	200	34.53 N	106.40 W
Bosques	288	34.49 S	58.14 W
Bosques Petrificados, Monumento Natural ♠	254	47.39 S	68.07 W
Bosqueville	222	31.38 N	97.13 W
Bossangoa	152	6.29 N	17.27 E
Bossdorf	54	51.59 N	12.40 E
Bossé Bangou	150	13.21 N	1.18 E
Bossembélé	152	5.16 N	17.39 E
Bossentele	152	5.41 N	16.38 E
Bossert Estates	285	40.09 N	74.44 W
Bossier City	194	32.30 N	93.43 W
Bossley Park	274a	33.52 S	150.54 E
Bosso	146	13.42 N	13.19 E
Bosso, Dallol V	150	12.25 N	2.50 E
Bossolasco	62	44.32 N	8.02 E
Bossut, Cape >	162	18.43 S	121.38 E
Bostān, Īrān	128	31.43 N	48.00 E
Bostān, Pāk.	120	30.26 N	67.02 E
Bostancı ◆[8]	267b	40.57 N	29.05 E
Bostandyk	80	49.38 N	48.54 E
Bosten Hu ⊜	90	42.00 N	87.00 E
Bostock Green	262	53.13 N	2.30 W
Boston, Pil.	116	7.52 N	126.22 E
Boston, Eng., U.K.	44	52.59 N	0.01 W
Boston, Ga., U.S.	192	30.47 N	83.47 W
Boston, In., U.S.	218	39.44 N	84.51 W
Boston, Ma., U.S.	207	42.21 N	71.03 W
Boston, Ma., U.S.	283	42.21 N	71.03 W
Boston, N.Y., U.S.	210	42.38 N	78.44 W
Boston, Pa., U.S.	279b	40.18 N	79.49 W
Boston Bar	182	49.52 N	121.26 W
Boston Bay ⊂	283	42.22 N	70.54 W
Boston Brook ≃	283	42.37 N	71.00 W
Boston College ʊ[2]	283	42.20 N	71.10 W
Boston Common ♠	283	42.21 N	71.05 W
Boston Corners	210	42.03 N	73.31 W
Boston Creek ≃	212	43.02 N	79.56 W
Boston Harbor	224	47.08 N	122.54 W
Boston Harbor ⊂	283	42.20 N	70.58 W
Boston Heights	214	41.15 N	81.30 W
Boston Mill	214	41.16 N	81.34 W
Boston Mountains ⋏	194	35.50 N	93.20 W
Boston Spa	44	53.54 N	1.21 W
Boston University ʊ[2]	283	42.21 N	71.07 W
Bosumtwi, Lake ⊜	150	6.30 N	1.25 W
Bosut ≃	38	44.57 N	19.22 E
Boswell, In., U.S.	216	40.31 N	87.22 W
Boswell, Ok., U.S.	196	34.01 N	95.52 W
Boswell, Pa., U.S.	214	40.09 N	79.01 W
Boswell Bay	180	60.24 N	146.08 W
Bosworth	194	39.28 N	93.20 W
Bosworth Airport ⊠	279a	41.26 N	82.00 W
Bosworth Field ⊥	42	52.36 N	1.25 W
Botād	120	22.10 N	71.40 E
Botafogo ◆[8]	287a	22.57 S	43.11 W
Botafogo, Enseada de ⊂	287a	22.57 S	43.10 W
Botany	274a	33.57 S	151.12 E
Botany Bay ◆[8]	260	51.41 N	0.07 W
Botany Bay ⊂	170	33.59 S	151.12 E
Botejevo	78	46.41 N	35.52 E
Botelhos	256	21.39 S	46.24 W
Botera	152	11.37 S	14.17 E
Botersleegte	158	30.35 S	21.22 E
Botesdale	42	52.20 N	1.01 E
Boteti ≃	156	20.08 S	23.23 E
Botev ∧	38	42.43 N	24.55 E
Botevgrad	38	42.54 N	23.47 E
Botha's Hill	158	29.45 S	30.45 E
Bothaville	158	27.27 S	26.36 E
Bothell	224	47.45 N	122.12 W
Bothe-Napa Valley State Park ♠	226	38.32 N	122.32 W
Bothnia, Gulf of ⊂	26	63.00 N	20.00 E
Bothwell, Austl.	166	42.23 S	147.00 E
Bothwell, On., Can.	214	42.38 N	81.52 W
Boticas	34	41.41 N	7.40 W
Botija, Ilha da I	246	3.58 S	62.53 W
Botija, Isla I	258	33.52 S	59.02 W
Botkins	216	40.28 N	84.10 W
Botkul', ozero ⊜	80	48.46 N	46.40 E
Botkyrka	40	59.14 N	17.49 E
Botlich	84	42.39 N	46.14 E
Bot Makak	152	4.00 N	10.55 E
Botna ≃	78	46.45 N	29.34 E
Botnia, Golfo de → Bothnia, Gulf of ⊂	26	63.00 N	20.00 E
Botola	152	1.17 S	18.13 E
Botolan	116	15.17 N	120.01 E
Botoșani	38	47.45 N	26.40 E
Botoșani □[6]	38	48.00 N	26.45 E
Botoșanița	38	47.53 N	26.07 E
Botou	150	12.40 N	2.03 E
Botovo	82	56.03 N	38.26 E
Bo Trach	110	17.35 N	106.32 E
Botrange ∧	56	50.30 N	6.08 E
Botricello	68	38.56 N	16.51 E
Botro	150	7.51 N	5.19 W
Botsford	210	41.21 N	73.15 W
Botswana □[1], Afr.	138	22.00 S	24.00 E
Botswana □[1], Afr.	156	22.00 S	24.00 E
Botte Donato, Monte ∧	68	39.17 N	16.26 E
Bottenhavet (Selkämeri) ⊂	26	62.00 N	20.00 E
Bottenviken (Perämeri) ⊂	26	65.00 N	23.00 E

Bottesford	42	52.56 N	0.48 W
Bottineau	198	48.49 N	100.26 W
Bottisham	42	52.13 N	0.16 E
Bottnischer Meerbusen → Bothnia, Gulf of ⊂	26	63.00 N	20.00 E
Bottoms Reservoir ⊜[1]	262	53.28 N	1.58 W
Bottrop	52	51.31 N	6.55 E
Botucatu	255	22.52 S	48.26 W
Botwood	186	49.09 N	55.21 W
Boty	88	52.24 N	118.32 E
Bötzingen	58	48.04 N	7.44 E
Bötzow	54	52.39 N	13.08 E
Bötzsee ⊜	264a	52.34 N	13.50 E
Bouaflé, C. Iv.	150	6.59 N	5.45 W
Bouafle, Fr.	261	48.58 N	1.54 E
Bou Ahmed	148	35.25 N	5.00 W
Bouaké	150	7.41 N	5.02 W
Bou Ali, Oued V	148	31.14 N	4.16 E
Bouânane	148	32.03 N	3.03 W
Bouandougou	150	8.13 N	5.40 W
Bouar	152	5.57 N	15.36 E
Bou Arada	36	36.20 N	9.38 E
Bou Areg, Sebkha ⊂	34	35.10 N	2.45 W
Bouârfa	148	32.30 N	1.59 W
Bouaye	32	47.09 N	1.42 W
Boubandjidah, Parc National de ♠	146	8.45 N	14.45 E
Bou Bernous	148	27.18 N	2.59 W
Boubín ∧	60	48.59 N	13.51 E
Bouca	152	6.30 N	18.17 E
Bouchain	50	50.17 N	3.19 E
Bouchegouf	36	36.28 N	7.44 E
Boucher ≃	186	49.10 N	69.06 W
Boucher, Lac ⊜	186	51.07 N	59.35 W
Boucherville	206	45.36 N	73.27 W
Boucherville, Îles de II	275a	45.37 N	73.28 W
Bouches-du-Rhône □[5]	62	43.30 N	5.00 E
Bouchoir	50	49.45 N	2.41 E
Bouclans	58	47.14 N	6.15 E
Boucle du Baoulé, Parc National de la ♠	150	13.50 N	9.00 W
Bouddi National Park ♠	170	33.31 S	131.24 E
Boudjellil	34	36.20 N	4.21 E
Boudnib	148	31.57 N	4.38 W
Boudouaou	34	36.43 N	3.25 E
Boudry	58	46.57 N	6.50 E
Boué	50	50.01 N	3.42 E
Bouenza □[5]	152	4.00 S	13.45 E
Boufarik	148	36.34 N	2.55 E
Bouffémont	261	49.03 N	2.18 E
Bou Ficha	36	36.18 N	10.29 E
Bougaa	34	36.20 N	5.05 E
Bougainville □[5]	175e	6.00 S	155.00 E
Bougainville I	175e	6.00 S	155.00 E
Bougainville, Cape >	164	13.54 S	126.06 E
Bougainville, Détroit de ʮ	175f	15.50 S	167.10 E
Bougainville Reef ✦[2]	164	15.30 S	147.06 E
Bougainville Strait ʮ	175e	6.40 S	156.10 E
Bougar'oûn, Cap >	34	37.06 N	6.28 E
Bough Beech Reservoir ⊜[1]	260	51.13 N	0.08 E
Boughton	44	53.12 N	1.00 W
Boughton Green	260	51.14 N	0.32 E
Boughton Malherbe	260	51.13 N	0.42 E
Boughton Place ʊ	260	51.13 N	0.32 E
Bougie → Bejaïa	148	36.45 N	5.05 E
Bougou	152	3.45 S	11.12 E
Bougouni	150	11.25 N	7.29 W
Bougouriba ≃	150	10.42 N	2.56 W
Bougzoul	34	35.42 N	2.51 E
Bou Hadjar	36	36.30 N	8.06 E
Bou Hajar	36	35.42 N	10.48 E
Bouillante	241o	16.06 N	61.45 W
Bouillon	56	49.48 N	5.04 E
Bouilly	50	48.12 N	4.00 E
Bouïra	148	36.23 N	3.54 E
Bouïra □[5]	148	36.00 N	4.00 E
Bouisy, Ru de ≃	261	48.34 N	2.45 E
Bou Izakarn	148	29.09 N	9.44 W
Boujad	148	32.48 N	6.26 W
Boujailles	58	46.53 N	6.05 E
Boujdour, Cap >	148	26.08 N	14.30 W
Bouka ≃	150	11.00 N	10.50 W
Bou Kadir	148	36.04 N	1.07 E
Bou Khadra	36	35.45 N	8.02 E
Boukiéro	273b	4.12 S	15.18 E
Boukiéro, Mont ∧[2]	273b	4.11 S	15.17 E
Boukombé	150	10.11 N	1.06 E
Boula Ibib	146	9.34 N	13.46 E
Boulaide	56	49.54 N	5.49 E
Boularderie Island I	186	46.15 N	60.30 W
Boulay-Moselle	56	49.11 N	6.30 E
Boulbon	62	43.52 N	4.41 E
Boulder, Austl.	162	30.47 S	121.29 E
Boulder, Co., U.S.	200	40.00 N	105.16 W
Boulder, Mt., U.S.	202	46.14 N	112.07 W
Boulder ≃	202	45.52 N	111.57 W
Boulder City	204	35.58 N	114.49 W
Boulder Creek	226	37.07 N	122.07 W
Boulder Creek ≃	200	37.47 N	111.22 W
Boulder Hill	216	41.41 N	88.25 W
Bouleaux, Lac des ⊜	275a	45.33 N	73.19 W
Bouli ≃	150	13.15 N	0.03 E
Boulia	166	22.54 S	139.54 E
Bouligny	56	49.17 N	5.45 E
Boullay-les-Troux	261	48.41 N	2.03 E
Boulmane	148	33.22 N	4.45 W
Boulmane □[4]	148	33.00 N	4.00 W
Boulogne ◆[8]	258	34.31 S	58.34 W
Boulogne, Bois de ♠	261	48.50 N	2.15 E
Boulogne-Billancourt	50	48.50 N	2.15 E
Boulogne-sur-Gesse	32	43.18 N	0.39 E
Boulogne-sur-Mer	50	50.43 N	1.37 E
Bouloire	50	47.58 N	0.33 E
Boulouli	150	15.34 N	9.21 W
Bouloupari	175f	21.52 S	166.04 E
Boulouris-sur-Mer	62	43.25 N	6.48 E
Boulsa	150	12.39 N	0.34 W
Boulsworth Hill ∧	262	53.48 N	2.06 W
Bouly	150	15.19 N	11.48 W
Bou Maad, Djebel ∧	34	36.26 N	2.08 E
Boumalne	148	31.32 N	5.27 W
Boumba ≃	152	2.02 N	15.12 E
Boumbé I ≃	152	4.04 N	15.23 E
Boumbé II ≃	152	4.08 N	15.08 E
Boumboum	150	15.01 N	1.42 W
Boûmdeïd	150	17.26 N	9.50 W
Bou Medfaa	34	36.22 N	2.28 E
Boumentana	152	6.59 N	16.56 E
Boumnyebe	152	3.52 N	10.49 E
Boumou	146	9.02 N	16.26 E
Bouna	150	9.16 N	3.00 W
Boundary	180	64.04 N	141.06 W
Boundary Bay ⊂	224	49.00 N	122.58 W
Boundary Peak ∧	204	37.51 N	118.21 W
Boundary Ranges ⋏	180	59.00 N	134.00 W
Bound Brook	210	40.34 N	74.32 W
Bound Brook ≃, Ma., U.S.	283	42.13 N	70.47 W
Bound Brook ≃, N.J., U.S.	276	40.35 N	74.30 W
Boundiali	150	9.31 N	6.29 W
Boun Nua	110	21.38 N	101.54 E
Bountiful	200	40.53 N	111.52 W
Bounty Bay ⊂	174e	25.04 S	130.05 W
Bounty Islands II	14	47.42 S	179.04 E
Bounty Trough ✦[1]	14	46.00 S	178.00 E
Bouqteb	148	34.02 N	0.05 E
Bouquet Reservoir ⊜[1]	228	34.35 N	118.24 W
Bouqueval	261	49.01 N	2.26 E
Boura	150	12.25 N	4.33 W
Bouradière	62	43.58 N	5.19 E
Bourail	175f	21.34 S	165.30 E
Bouray-sur-Juine	261	48.31 N	2.18 E
Bourbeuse ≃	194	38.24 N	90.53 W
Bourbeuse, Dry Fork ≃	194	38.16 N	91.26 W
Bourbon, In., U.S.	216	41.17 N	86.06 W
Bourbon, Mo., U.S.	194	38.09 N	91.14 W
Bourbon □[6]	218	38.14 N	84.14 W
Bourbon ≃	206	46.17 N	71.55 W
Bourbon-Lancy	32	46.38 N	3.46 E
Bourbonnais	216	41.08 N	87.52 W
Bourbonnais □[9]	32	46.20 N	3.00 E
Bourbonne-les-Bains	58	47.57 N	5.45 E
Bourbourg	50	50.57 N	2.12 E
Bourbre ≃	62	45.47 N	5.11 E
Bourdeaux	62	44.35 N	5.08 E
Bourdon, Île I	275a	45.43 N	73.29 W
Bourdon, Réservoir du ⊜[1]	50	47.36 N	3.07 E
Bourdonné	261	48.45 N	1.40 E
Bou Regreg, Oued ≃	148	34.03 N	6.50 W
Bourem	150	16.57 N	0.21 W
Bourg	194	29.33 N	90.36 W
Bourg-Achard	50	49.21 N	0.49 E
Bourganeuf	32	45.57 N	1.46 E
Bourg-Argental	62	45.18 N	4.33 E
Bourg-de-Péage	62	45.02 N	5.03 E
Bourg-en-Bresse	58	46.12 N	5.13 E
Bourges	32	47.05 N	2.24 E
Bourget	206	45.26 N	75.09 W
Bourget, Lac du ⊜	62	45.44 N	5.52 E
Bourg-la-Reine	261	48.47 N	2.19 E
Bourg-Lastic	32	45.39 N	2.33 E
Bourg-lès-Valence	62	44.57 N	4.53 E
Bourgneuf	261	48.36 N	2.00 E
Bourgneuf-en-Retz	32	47.02 N	1.57 W
Bourgogne	50	49.21 N	4.04 E
Bourgogne (Burgundy) □[9]	32	47.00 N	4.30 E
Bourgogne, Canal de ≅	50	47.58 N	3.30 E
Bourgoin-Jallieu	62	45.35 N	5.17 E
Bourg-Saint-Andéol	62	44.22 N	4.39 E
Bourg-Saint-Maurice	62	45.37 N	6.46 E
Bourg-Saint-Pierre	58	45.57 N	7.12 E
Bourgtheroulde	50	49.18 N	0.53 E
Bourgueil	50	47.17 N	0.10 E
Bou Rjeïmât ⊤[4]	150	19.04 N	15.08 W
Bourke	166	30.05 S	145.56 E
Bourmont	58	48.12 N	5.35 E
Bourne	42	52.46 N	0.23 W
Bourne ≃, Fr.	62	45.04 N	5.15 E
Bourne ≃, Eng., U.K.	42	51.02 N	1.47 W
Bournebridge	260	51.38 N	0.11 E
Bourne End	260	51.45 N	0.32 W
Bournemouth	42	50.43 N	1.54 W
Bourneville, Fr.	50	49.23 N	0.37 E
Bourneville, Oh., U.S.	218	39.17 N	83.09 W
Bourn Vincent Memorial Park ♠	48	52.01 N	9.30 W
Bouroum	150	13.37 N	0.39 W
Bourron-Marlotte	50	48.20 N	2.42 E
Bourscheid	56	49.55 N	6.04 E
Bourtange	52	53.00 N	7.11 E
Bourtanger Moor ◆[3]	52	53.00 N	7.15 E
Bourton-on-the-Water	42	51.53 N	1.45 W
Bourzanga	150	13.41 N	1.33 W
Bou Saâda	148	35.12 N	4.11 E
Bou Salem	36	36.36 N	8.59 E
Bousbecque	50	50.46 N	3.05 E
Bouse	200	33.55 N	114.00 W
Bou Sellam, Oued ≃	34	36.26 N	4.34 E
Bouse Wash V	200	34.02 N	114.20 W
Bou Smail	148	36.38 N	2.41 E
Boussac	32	46.21 N	2.13 E
Boussé, Burkina	150	12.39 N	1.53 W
Bousse, Fr.	56	49.17 N	6.12 E
Boussières	58	47.09 N	5.54 E
Bousso	146	10.29 N	16.43 E
Boussois	50	50.17 N	4.03 E
Boussouma	150	12.55 N	1.05 W
Boussu	50	50.26 N	3.48 E
Boussy-Saint-Antoine	261	48.41 N	2.32 E
Bout, Pointe du >	240e	14.34 N	61.03 W
Bouteille, Lac de la ⊜	206	46.42 N	73.41 W
Bouteldja	36	36.47 N	8.12 E
Bou Temezguida ∧	148	29.21 N	9.55 W
Boutilimit	150	17.33 N	14.42 W
Bouttencourt	50	49.56 N	1.38 E
Bouvard, Cape >	168a	32.41 S	115.37 E
Bouvetøya I	9	54.26 S	3.24 E
Bouvier Bay ⊂	281	42.39 N	82.38 W
Bouvières	62	44.30 N	5.13 E
Bouxières-aux-Dames	56	48.45 N	6.10 E
Bouxwiller	56	48.49 N	7.29 E
Bouyon	62	43.50 N	7.07 E
Bouza	150	14.25 N	6.02 E
Bou Zadjar	34	35.35 N	1.09 W
Bouzonville	56	49.18 N	6.32 E
Bov	41	54.50 N	9.23 E
Bova	68	38.00 N	15.56 E
Bøvågen	26	60.40 N	4.58 E
Bovalino Marina	68	38.10 N	16.11 E
Bova Marina	68	37.56 N	15.55 E
Bovard	279b	40.19 N	79.30 W
Bovec	36	46.20 N	13.33 E
Bovegno	64	45.48 N	10.16 E
Bovenden	52	51.35 N	9.55 E
Bovenkarspel	52	52.42 N	5.15 E
Bøverdal	26	61.43 N	8.21 E
Boves, Fr.	50	49.51 N	2.23 E
Boves, It.	62	44.19 N	7.33 E
Bovey	190	47.17 N	93.25 W
Bovey ≃	42	50.34 N	3.37 W
Bovey Tracey	42	50.36 N	3.40 W
Bovill	202	46.51 N	116.23 W
Boville Ernica	66	41.38 N	13.28 E
Bovina	196	34.31 N	102.53 W
Bovina Center	210	42.16 N	74.47 W
Bovingdon	260	51.44 N	0.32 W
Bövinghausen ◆[8]	263	51.31 N	7.19 E
Bovington Camp	42	50.42 N	2.14 W
Bovino	68	41.15 N	15.20 E
Bovisio Masciago	266b	45.37 N	9.09 E
Bovolenta	64	45.16 N	11.56 E
Bovolone	64	45.15 N	11.07 E
Bovril	252	31.21 S	59.26 W
Bovrup	41	54.59 N	9.36 E
Bow	224	48.33 N	122.23 W
Bow ≃, Austl.	162	16.32 S	128.39 E
Bow ≃, Ab., Can.	182	49.56 N	111.42 W
Bow ≃, Sk., Can.	184	54.56 N	105.13 W
Bo-Wadrif	158	32.26 S	20.07 E
Bowang	106	31.34 N	118.50 E
Bowbells	198	48.48 N	102.14 W
Bow Brook ≃	42	52.04 N	2.07 W
Bowburn	44	54.43 N	1.31 W
Bow Creek ≃	198	39.35 N	99.14 W
Bowden	182	51.55 N	114.02 W
Bowdle	198	45.27 N	99.39 W
Bowdoin, Lake ⊜	202	48.24 N	107.41 W
Bowdon, Eng., U.K.	262	53.23 N	2.22 W
Bowdon, Ga., U.S.	192	33.32 N	85.15 W
Bowdon, N.D., U.S.	198	47.28 N	99.42 W
Bowelling	168a	33.25 S	116.29 E
Bowen, Arg.	252	35.00 S	67.31 W
Bowen, Austl.	166	20.01 S	148.15 E
Bowen, Il., U.S.	194	40.14 N	91.04 W
Bowen ≃	166	20.24 S	147.21 E
Bowenfels	170	33.31 S	150.07 E
Bowens Creek ≃	170	33.21 S	150.35 E
Bowers	208	39.15 N	75.36 W
Bowers Gifford	260	51.34 N	0.32 E
Bowers Mansion ⊥	226	39.17 N	119.50 W
Bowers Marshes ☷	260	51.33 N	0.32 E
Bowers Ridge ✦[3]	16	54.00 N	179.00 E
Bowerston	214	40.25 N	81.11 W
Bowersville	218	39.34 N	83.43 W
Bowgreave	44	53.52 N	2.45 W
Bowie, Az., U.S.	200	32.19 N	109.29 W
Bowie, Md., U.S.	208	39.00 N	76.46 W
Bowie, Tx., U.S.	196	33.33 N	97.50 W
Bowie Creek ≃	194	31.26 N	89.24 W
Bow Island	184	49.52 N	111.22 W
Bowland, Forest of ◆[3]	44	53.58 N	2.32 W
Bowles Creek ≃	222	32.02 N	94.59 W
Bowley Bar >[2]	284b	39.18 N	76.23 W
Bowleys Quarters	284b	39.19 N	76.24 W
Bowling Green, Fl., U.S.	220	27.38 N	81.49 W
Bowling Green, Ky., U.S.	194	36.59 N	86.26 W
Bowling Green, Mo., U.S.	219	39.20 N	91.11 W
Bowling Green, Oh., U.S.	216	41.22 N	83.39 W
Bowling Green, Pa., U.S.	285	39.55 N	75.23 W
Bowling Green, Va., U.S.	208	38.02 N	77.20 W
Bowling Green, Cape >	166	19.19 S	147.25 E
Bowling Green Bay National Park ♠	166	19.28 S	147.14 E
Bowman, Ca., U.S.	226	38.57 N	121.03 W
Bowman, Ga., U.S.	192	34.12 N	83.01 W
Bowman, N.D., U.S.	198	46.10 N	103.23 W
Bowman, S.C., U.S.	192	33.20 N	80.40 W
Bowman, Mount ∧	182	51.10 N	121.55 W
Bowman Creek ≃, Pa., U.S.	210	41.31 N	75.58 W
Bowman Creek ≃, Wa., U.S.	224	45.50 N	121.03 W
Bowman-Haley Lake ⊜[1]	198	46.00 N	103.20 W
Bowman Island I	9	65.17 S	103.08 E
Bowman Lake ⊜[1]	226	39.27 N	120.38 W
Bowmans	168b	34.09 S	138.16 E
Bowmansdale	208	40.10 N	76.59 W
Bowmanstown	208	40.48 N	75.40 W
Bowmansville, N.Y., U.S.	212	42.56 N	78.41 W
Bowmansville, Pa., U.S.	208	40.10 N	76.04 W
Bowmanville	212	43.55 N	78.41 W
Bowmanville Creek ≃	212	43.53 N	78.40 W
Bowmont Water ≃	44	55.34 N	2.09 W
Bowmore	46	55.45 N	6.17 W
Bowness-on-Windermere	44	54.22 N	2.55 W
Bowokan, Kepulauan II	112	2.05 S	123.35 E
Bowral	170	34.28 S	150.25 E
Bowraville	166	30.39 S	152.51 E
Bowron ≃	182	54.04 N	121.48 W
Bowron Lake Provincial Park ♠	182	53.10 N	121.06 W
Bowsman	184	52.14 N	101.14 W
Bowwood	154	17.07 S	26.17 E
Box	42	51.26 N	2.15 W
Boxberg	56	49.29 N	9.38 E
Box Butte Creek ≃	198	42.28 N	102.37 W
Box Creek ≃, Tx., U.S.	222	31.33 N	95.43 W
Box Creek ≃, Tx., U.S.	222	31.35 N	95.10 W
Box Elder	202	48.19 N	110.00 W
Boxelder Creek ≃, U.S.	198	45.59 N	103.57 W
Boxelder Creek ≃, Co., U.S.	198	40.33 N	105.00 W
Box Elder Creek ≃, Co., U.S.	198	40.23 N	104.28 W
Box Elder Creek ≃, Mt., U.S.	202	46.57 N	108.04 W
Boxelder Creek ≃, S.D., U.S.	198	44.01 N	102.27 W
Boxey	186	47.25 N	55.34 W
Boxey Point >	186	47.24 N	55.35 W
Boxford	207	42.39 N	70.59 W
Boxford State Forest ♠	283	42.39 N	71.02 W
Box Grove	275b	43.51 N	79.14 W
Box Hill	169	37.49 S	145.08 E
Boxholm	26	58.12 N	15.03 E
Boxian	100	33.53 N	115.45 E
Boxing	98	37.08 N	118.07 E
Boxley	260	51.18 N	0.33 E
Boxmeer	52	51.39 N	5.57 E
Boxmoor	260	51.45 N	0.29 W
Boxodoi	98	42.34 N	115.18 E
Boxtel	52	51.35 N	5.20 E
Boyabat	130	41.28 N	34.47 E
Boyabo	152	3.43 N	18.46 E
Boyacá □[5]	246	5.30 N	73.30 W
Boyacıköy ◆[8]	267b	41.06 N	29.02 E
Boyalı	130	41.02 N	33.19 E
Boyalık	130	41.15 N	28.37 E
Boyang	100	28.59 N	116.40 E
Boyanup	168a	33.29 S	115.44 E
Boyasengese	152	3.29 N	20.33 E
Boyce	194	31.23 N	92.40 W
Boyceville	190	45.02 N	92.02 W
Boyd, Mn., U.S.	198	44.50 N	95.54 W
Boyd, Tx., U.S.	222	33.05 N	97.34 W
Boyd ≃	166	29.51 S	152.35 E
Boyd's Cove	186	49.27 N	54.39 W
Boydton	192	36.40 N	78.23 W
Boyenge	152	0.25 N	18.51 E
Boyer ≃	198	41.28 N	95.55 W
Boyera	152	0.38 S	19.25 E
Boyer Aḥmadī va Kohkīlūyeh □[4]	128	30.40 N	50.40 E
Boyer Run ≃	279b	40.13 N	79.32 W
Boyers	214	41.06 N	79.54 W
Boyer's Creek ≃	284a	43.00 N	79.02 W
Boyertown	208	40.20 N	75.38 W
Boyes Hot Springs	226	38.19 N	122.29 W
Boykins	208	36.34 N	77.12 W
Boyle, Ab., Can.	182	54.35 N	112.49 W
Boyle, Ire.	48	53.58 N	8.18 W
Boyle, Ms., U.S.	194	33.42 N	90.50 W
Boyle Drain ≃	212	43.42 N	81.06 W
Boyle Heights ◆[8]	280	34.02 N	118.13 W
Boylston, Al., U.S.	194	32.26 N	86.17 W
Boylston, Ma., U.S.	207	42.23 N	71.42 W
Boyne	275b	43.29 N	79.50 W
Boyne ≃, Austl.	166	23.56 S	151.21 E
Boyne ≃, Mb., Can.	184	49.34 N	97.52 W
Boyne ≃, On., Can.	212	44.10 N	79.49 W
Boyne ≃, Ire.	48	53.43 N	6.15 W
Boyne Battlesite ⊥	48	53.42 N	6.23 W
Boyne City	190	45.12 N	85.00 W
Boynton	196	35.38 N	95.39 W
Boynton Beach	220	26.31 N	80.04 W
Boyo	152	5.43 N	21.33 E
Boyolali	115a	7.32 S	110.35 E
Boysen Reservoir ⊜[1]	202	43.19 N	108.11 W
Boysen State Park ♠	202	43.23 N	108.07 W
Boys Ranch	196	35.32 N	102.15 W
Boyuibe	248	20.25 S	63.17 W
Boyup Brook	162	33.50 S	116.24 E
Bozburun	130	36.41 N	28.04 E
Boz Burun >	130	40.32 N	28.46 E
Bozburun Yarımadası >[1]	130	36.40 N	28.10 E
Bozcaada	130	39.50 N	26.04 E
Boz Dağ ∧, Tür.	130	37.18 N	29.12 E
Boz Dağ ∧, Tür.	130	38.19 N	28.08 E
Bozdağ ∧, Tür.	130	36.50 N	36.22 E
Boz Dağlar ⋏	130	38.20 N	27.45 E
Bozdoğan	130	37.40 N	28.19 E
Bozel	62	45.27 N	6.39 E
Bozeman	202	45.40 N	111.02 W
Bozen → Bolzano	64	46.31 N	11.22 E
Bozene	152	2.56 N	19.12 E
Bozhen	98	38.07 N	116.32 E
Boží Dar	54	50.24 N	12.55 E
Bozkır	130	37.11 N	32.15 E
Bozkurt, Tür.	130	37.49 N	29.37 E
Bozkurt, Tür.	130	41.57 N	34.01 E
Bozman	208	38.46 N	76.16 W
Bozoğlak	130	39.38 N	38.49 E
Bozok	130	37.18 N	40.22 E
Bozoum	152	6.19 N	16.23 E

Symbol	English	Deutsch	Español	Français	Português
≃	River	Fluß	Río	Rivière	Rio
≅	Canal	Kanal	Canal	Canal	Canal
∟	Waterfall, Rapids	Wasserfall, Stromschnellen	Cascada, Rápidos	Chute d'eau, Rapides	Cascata, Rápidos
ʮ	Strait	Meeresstraße	Estrecho	Détroit	Estreito
⊂	Bay, Gulf	Bucht, Golf	Bahía, Golfo	Baie, Golfe	Baía, Golfo
⊜	Lake, Lakes	See, Seen	Lago, Lagos	Lac, Lacs	Lago, Lagos
☷	Swamp	Sumpf	Pantano	Marais	Pântano
◚	Ice Features, Glacier	Eis- und Gletscherformen	Accidentes Glaciales	Formes glaciaires	Acidentes glaciares
⊤	Other Hydrographic Features	Andere Hydrographische Objekte	Otros Elementos Hidrográficos	Autres données hydrographiques	Outros acidentes hidrográficos
✦	Submarine Features	Untermeerische Objekte	Accidentes Submarinos	Formes de relief sous-marin	Acidentes submarinos
□	Political Unit	Politische Einheit	Unidad Politica	Entité politique	Unidade política
ʊ	Cultural Institution	Kulturelle Institution	Institución Cultural	Institution culturelle	Instituição cultural
⊥	Historical Site	Historische Stätte	Sitio Histórico	Site historique	Sitio histórico
♠	Recreational Site	Erholungs- und Ferienort	Sitio de Recreo	Centre de loisirs	Area de Lazer
⊠	Airport	Flughafen	Aeropuerto	Aéroport	Aeroporto
■	Military Installation	Militäranlage	Instalación Militar	Installation militaire	Instalação militar
◆	Miscellaneous	Verschiedenes	Misceláneo	Divers	Diversos

ENGLISH: Name / Page / Lat.°′ / Long.°′ — DEUTSCH: Name / Seite / Breite°′ / Länge°′ E = Ost

Symbols in the index entries represent the broad categories identified in the key at the right. Symbols with superior numbers (⋏[1]) identify subcategories (see complete key on page *I · 1*).

Symbole im Register stellen die rechts im Schlüssel erklärten Kategorien dar. Symbole mit hochgestellten Ziffern (⋏[1]) bezeichnen Unterabteilungen einer Kategorie (vgl. vollständiger Schlüssel auf Seite *I · 1*).

Los símbolos incluídos en el texto del índice representan las grandes categorias identificadas con la clave a la derecha. Los símbolos con numeros en su parte superior (⋏[1]) identifican las subcategorías (véase la clave completa en la página *I · 1*).

Les symboles de l'index représentent les catégories indiquées dans la légende à droite. Les symboles suivis d'un indice (⋏[1]) représentent des sous-catégories (voir légende complète à la page *I · 1*).

Os símbolos incluídos no texto do índice representam as grandes categorias identificadas com a chave à direita. Os símbolos com números em sua parte superior (⋏[1]) identificam as subcategorias (veja-se a chave completa à página *I · 1*).

∧ Mountain	Berg	Montaña	Montagne	Montanha
⋏ Mountains	Gebirge	Montañas	Montagnes	Montanhas
)(Pass	Paß	Paso	Col	Passo
V Valley, Canyon	Tal, Cañon	Valle, Cañón	Vallée, Canyon	Vale, Canhão
≚ Plain	Ebene	Llano	Plaine	Planície
› Cape	Kap	Cabo	Cap	Cabo
I Island	Insel	Isla	Île	Ilha
II Islands	Inseln	Islas	Îles	Ilhas
⊥ Other Topographic Features	Andere Topographische Objekte	Otros Elementos Topográficos	Autres données topographiques	Outros acidentes topográficos

ESPAÑOL — Nombre | Página | Lat.°′ | Long.°′ W = Oeste
FRANÇAIS — Nom | Page | Lat.°′ | Long.°′ W = Ouest
PORTUGUÊS — Nome | Página | Lat.°′ | Long.°′ W = Oeste

Brimfield, In., U.S. 216 41.27 N 85.24 W
Brimfield, Ma., U.S. 207 42.07 N 72.12 W
Brimfield, Oh., U.S. 214 41.06 N 81.21 W
Brimington 44 53.16 N 1.23 W
Brindabella 171b 35.23 S 148.45 E
Brindisi 68 40.38 N 17.56 E
Brindisi □[4] 68 40.35 N 17.40 E
Brindisi Montagna 68 40.37 N 15.57 E
Brindle 262 53.43 N 2.36 W
Brindley Heath 260 51.12 N 0.03 W
Bringelly 170 33.56 S 150.44 E
Bringelly Creek ≃ 274a 33.58 S 150.38 E
Brinje 36 45.00 N 15.08 E
Brinkerton 279b 40.13 N 79.32 W
Brinkhaven 214 40.28 N 82.12 W
Brinkleigh 284b 39.18 N 76.50 W
Brinkley, Austl. 168b 35.14 S 139.13 E
Brinkley, Ar., U.S. 194 34.53 N 91.11 W
Brinkum 52 53.00 N 8.47 E
Brinkworth 166 33.42 S 138.24 E
Brinnon 224 47.40 N 122.53 W
Brinon-sur-Beuvron 50 47.17 N 3.30 E
Brins, Ābār al- ⩪[4] 142 30.29 N 30.05 E
Brinscall 262 53.41 N 2.34 W
Brinyan 46 59.07 N 2.59 W
Brion, Île I 186 47.48 N 61.28 W
Brione 58 46.18 N 8.47 E
Briones Hills ⩕[2] 282 37.56 N 122.08 W
Briones Regional Park ♠ 282 37.56 N 122.08 W
Briones Reservoir ⊜[1] 282 37.55 N 122.12 W
Brionne 50 49.12 N 0.43 E
Brion-sur-Ource 58 47.55 N 4.39 E
Brioude 32 45.18 N 3.23 E
Briouze 32 48.42 N 0.22 W
Brisbane, Austl. 171a 27.28 S 153.02 E
Brisbane, Ca., U.S. 226 37.41 N 122.24 W
Brisbane ≃ 171a 27.24 S 153.09 E
Brisbane, Mount ∧ 171a 27.05 S 152.32 E
Brisbane International Airport ⊠ 171a 27.27 S 153.11 E
Brisbane Ranges National Park ♠ 169 37.52 S 144.14 E
Brisbane Water ⊂ 170 33.28 S 151.20 E
Brisbane Water National Park ♠ 170 33.30 S 151.15 E
Brisben 210 42.22 N 75.41 W
Brisbin 214 40.50 N 78.21 W
Briseñas 234 20.16 N 102.33 W
Brisighella 66 44.13 N 11.46 E
Brissac 62 43.52 N 3.42 E
Brissago 58 46.07 N 8.43 E
Bristol, Eng., U.K. 42 51.27 N 2.35 W
Bristol, Ct., U.S. 207 41.41 N 72.57 W
Bristol, Fl., U.S. 192 30.25 N 84.58 W
Bristol, Il., U.S. 216 41.39 N 88.27 W
Bristol, In., U.S. 216 41.43 N 85.49 W
Bristol, N.H., U.S. 188 43.35 N 71.44 W
Bristol, Pa., U.S. 208 40.06 N 74.51 W
Bristol, R.I., U.S. 207 41.40 N 71.16 W
Bristol, S.D., U.S. 198 45.20 N 97.44 W
Bristol, Tn., U.S. 192 36.35 N 82.11 W
Bristol, Vt., U.S. 188 44.08 N 73.04 W
Bristol, Va., U.S. 192 36.35 N 82.11 W
Bristol, Wi., U.S. 216 42.33 N 88.02 W
Bristol □[6], Ma., U.S. 207 41.54 N 71.06 W
Bristol □[6], R.I., U.S. 207 41.42 N 71.18 W
Bristol (Lulsgate) Airport ⊠ 42 51.23 N 2.43 W
Bristol Bay ⊂ 180 58.00 N 159.00 W
Bristol-Blake Reservation ♠ 283 42.06 N 71.19 W
Bristol Center 210 42.49 N 77.23 W
Bristol Channel ʮ 42 51.20 N 4.00 W
Bristol Lake ⊜ 204 34.28 N 115.41 W
Bristolville 214 41.23 N 80.52 W
Bristow 196 35.49 N 96.23 W
Britânia 255 15.14 S 51.09 W
Británicas, Islas → British Isles II 4 54.00 N 4.00 W
Britannia 275b 43.37 N 79.41 W
Britannia Beach 182 49.38 N 123.12 W
Britische Jungfern-Inseln → British Virgin Islands □[2] 240m 18.30 N 64.30 W
Britisches Antarktis-Territorium → British Antarctic Territory □[2] 9 60.00 S 45.00 W
British Antarctic Territory □[2] 9 60.00 S 45.00 W
British Columbia □[4], Can. 176 54.00 N 125.00 W
British Columbia □[4], Can. 182 54.00 N 125.00 W
British Honduras → Belize □[1] 232 17.15 N 88.45 W
British Indian Ocean Territory □[2] 12 7.00 S 72.00 E
British Isles II 4 54.00 N 4.00 W
British Mountains ⩕ 180 69.00 N 140.20 W
British Museum ɵ 260 51.31 N 0.08 W
British Solomon Islands → Solomon Islands □[1] 175e 8.00 S 159.00 E
British Virgin Islands □[2], N.A. 230 18.30 N 64.30 W
British Virgin Islands □[2], N.A. 240m 18.30 N 64.30 W
Britland Edge Hill ∧[2] 262 53.31 N 1.50 W
Briton Ferry 42 51.38 N 3.49 W
Brits 158 25.42 S 27.45 E
Britstown 158 30.37 S 23.30 E
Britt 190 43.05 N 93.48 W
Brittany → Bretagne □[9] 32 48.00 N 3.00 W
Brittas 48 53.14 N 6.27 W
Britten 158 27.42 S 25.17 E
Brittingham 196 25.45 N 103.24 W
Britton, Mi., U.S. 216 41.59 N 83.49 W
Britton, S.D., U.S. 198 45.47 N 97.45 W
Britton, Tx., U.S. 222 32.33 N 97.04 W
Britton, Mount ∧[2] 162 26.31 S 134.43 E
Britz 54 52.53 N 13.49 E
Britz ◆[8] 264a 52.27 N 13.26 E
Brive-la-Gaillarde 32 45.10 N 1.32 E
Brives-Charensac 62 45.03 N 3.56 E
Briviesca 34 42.33 N 3.19 W
Brivio 62 45.44 N 9.27 E
Brixen im Thale 64 47.27 N 12.15 E
Brixham 42 50.24 N 3.30 W
Brixlegg 64 47.25 N 11.53 E
Brixton 166 23.32 S 144.57 E
Brixworth 42 52.20 N 0.54 W
Brlik 85 43.40 N 73.49 E
Brloh 61 48.56 N 14.13 E
Brno 30 49.12 N 16.37 E
Bro 40 59.31 N 17.38 E
Broa, Ensenada de la ⊂ 240p 22.35 N 82.00 W
Broad ≃, U.S. 192 34.00 N 81.04 W
Broad ≃, Fl., U.S. 220 25.28 N 81.09 W
Broad ≃, Ga., U.S. 192 33.59 N 82.39 W
Broadalbin 210 43.03 N 74.11 W
Broad Arrow 162 30.20 S 121.27 E
Broad Axe 285 40.10 N 75.15 W
Broadback ≃ 176 51.21 N 78.52 W
Broad Bay ⊂ 46 58.15 N 6.15 W
Broadbottom 262 53.26 N 2.01 W
Broad Brook 207 41.54 N 72.32 W
Broad Chalke 42 51.02 N 1.57 W
Broadclyst 42 50.46 N 3.26 W
Broad Creek ⊂ 208 38.45 N 76.15 W
Broad Creek ≃ 208 39.42 N 76.14 W
Broadford, Austl. 169 37.13 S 145.03 E
Broadford, Scot., U.K. 46 57.14 N 5.54 W
Broad Haven ⊂ 48 54.18 N 9.55 W
Broadheath 262 53.24 N 2.21 W
Broadhurst Range ⩕ 162 22.23 S 122.09 E
Broadkill ≃ 208 38.47 N 75.10 W
Broad Law ∧ 46 55.30 N 3.22 W
Broadley Common 260 51.45 N 0.04 E
Broadmeadows 169 37.40 S 144.54 E
Broadmoor 226 37.41 N 122.29 W
Broad Neck ≻[1] 208 39.03 N 76.27 W
Broad Oak 42 50.57 N 0.36 E
Broad Pass)(180 63.18 N 149.09 W
Broad Run ≃, Pa., U.S. 285 39.56 N 75.41 W
Broad Run ≃, Pa., U.S. 285 39.59 N 75.40 W
Broad Run ≃, Va., U.S. 208 38.41 N 77.29 W
Broad Sound ʮ, Austl. 166 22.10 S 149.45 E
Broad Sound ʮ, Ma., U.S. 283 42.25 N 70.58 W
Broad Sound Channel ʮ 166 22.05 S 150.20 E
Broadstairs 42 51.22 N 1.27 E
Broad Street 260 51.17 N 0.38 E
Broad Top 214 40.12 N 78.08 W
Broadus 198 45.26 N 105.24 W
Broadview, Sk., Can. 184 50.20 N 102.30 W
Broadview, Il., U.S. 216 41.51 N 87.51 W
Broadview, In., U.S. 218 39.10 N 87.33 W
Broadview Heights 214 41.18 N 81.41 W
Broadwater 198 41.35 N 102.51 W
Broadway, Eng., U.K. 42 52.02 N 1.51 W
Broadway, Oh., U.S. 214 40.20 N 83.24 W
Broadway, Va., U.S. 188 38.38 N 78.46 W
Broadwell 219 40.04 N 89.27 W
Broadwindsor 42 50.49 N 2.48 W
Broadwood 172 35.16 S 173.23 E
Broager 41 54.53 N 9.41 E
Brobo 150 7.43 N 4.42 W
Broby 26 56.15 N 14.05 E
Brobyværk 41 55.14 N 10.15 E
Broc 58 46.36 N 7.06 E
Brocēni 76 56.42 N 22.35 E
Brochel 46 57.26 N 6.01 W
Brochet 176 57.53 N 101.40 W
Brochet, Lac au ⊜ 186 49.40 N 69.37 W
Brochterbeck 52 52.13 N 7.44 E
Brock 184 51.27 N 108.42 W
Brock ≃ 44 53.52 N 2.47 W
Brock Creek ≃ 285 40.15 N 74.50 W
Brocken ∧ 54 51.48 N 10.36 E
Brockenhurst 42 50.49 N 1.34 W
Brockenscheidt 263 51.38 N 7.25 E
Brockhagen 52 51.59 N 8.20 E
Brockham 260 51.14 N 0.17 W
Brockman ≃ 168a 31.41 S 116.07 E
Brockman, Mount ∧ 162 22.28 S 117.18 E
Brock Monument ⊥ 284a 43.09 N 79.04 W
Brockport, N.Y., U.S. 210 43.12 N 77.56 W
Brockport, Pa., U.S. 214 41.16 N 78.44 W
Brocks Beach 212 44.27 N 80.06 W
Brocks Creek 164 13.28 S 131.25 E
Brockton, Ma., U.S. 207 42.05 N 71.01 W
Brockton, Mt., U.S. 198 48.09 N 104.54 W
Brockton, Pa., U.S. 208 40.45 N 76.04 W
Brockton Reservoir ⊜[1] 283 42.07 N 71.03 W
Brock University ɵ[2] 284a 43.07 N 79.15 W
Brockville 212 44.35 N 75.41 W
Brockway 214 41.15 N 78.47 W
Brockworth 42 51.51 N 2.09 W
Brocoió, Ilha de I 287a 22.45 S 43.07 W
Brocton 214 42.23 N 79.26 W
Brod, Česko. 60 49.51 N 12.45 E
Brod, Mac. 38 41.31 N 21.12 E
Broddbo 40 59.59 N 16.28 E
Brodenbach 56 50.14 N 7.26 E
Broderick 226 38.35 N 121.30 W
Brodeur Peninsula ≻[1] 176 73.00 N 88.00 W
Brodhead, Ky., U.S. 192 37.24 N 84.24 W
Brodhead, Wi., U.S. 190 42.37 N 89.22 W
Brodhead Creek ≃ 210 40.59 N 75.08 W
Brodheadsville 210 40.55 N 75.24 W
Brodick 46 55.35 N 5.09 W
Brodnax 192 36.42 N 78.01 W
Brodnica 30 53.16 N 19.23 E
Brodokalmak 86 55.35 N 62.06 E
Brody, Pol. 30 51.45 N 14.45 E
Brody, Ukr. 78 50.06 N 25.10 E
Broedersput 158 26.49 S 25.08 E
Broek [op Langendijk] 52 52.40 N 4.48 E
Brogan 202 44.14 N 117.30 W
Broglie 50 49.01 N 0.32 E
Brohlbach ≃ 56 50.29 N 7.20 E
Broich ◆[8] 263 51.25 N 6.51 E
Broichweiden 56 50.49 N 6.09 E
Brok 30 52.43 N 21.52 E
Brok ∧ 123 34.32 N 76.35 E
Brokdorf 52 53.52 N 9.19 E
Broke 170 32.45 S 151.06 E
Broke Inlet ⊂ 162 34.55 S 116.25 E
Broken ≃ 169 36.41 S 146.00 E
Broken Arrow 196 36.03 N 95.47 W
Broken Bay ⊂ 170 33.34 S 151.18 E
Broken Bow, Ne., U.S. 198 41.24 N 99.38 W
Broken Bow, Ok., U.S. 194 34.01 N 94.44 W
Broken Bow Lake ⊜[1] 194 34.10 N 94.40 W
Broken Cross, Eng., U.K. 262 53.15 N 2.29 W
Broken Cross, Eng., U.K. 262 53.15 N 2.10 W
Brokenhead ≃ 184 50.25 N 96.40 W
Broken Hill 166 31.57 S 141.27 E
Broken Hill → Kabwe 154 14.27 S 28.27 E
Broken Ridge ⊹[3] 12 31.30 S 95.00 E
Brokenstraw Creek ≃ 214 41.51 N 79.09 W
Broken Sword Creek ≃ 214 40.46 N 83.11 W
Brokopondo 250 5.04 N 54.58 W
Brokopondo □[5] 250 4.40 N 55.00 W
Brokopondo Stuwmeer ⊜[1] 250 4.45 N 55.00 W
Brölbach ≃ 56 50.47 N 7.18 E
Brolo 70 38.09 N 14.50 E
Bromberg → Bydgoszcz 30 53.08 N 18.00 E
Bromborough 262 53.19 N 2.59 W
Brome, P.Q., Can. 206 45.12 N 72.34 W
Brome, Dtsch. 54 52.36 N 10.56 E
Brome □[6] 206 45.10 N 72.30 W
Brome, Lac ⊜ 206 45.15 N 72.30 W
Brome, Mont ∧ 206 45.17 N 72.38 W
Bromham 42 52.09 N 0.31 W
Bromley ◆[8] 260 51.24 N 0.02 E
Bromley Common ◆[8] 260 51.22 N 0.03 E
Bromley Plateau ⊹[3] 18 32.00 S 35.00 W
Bromma ◆[8] 40 59.21 N 17.55 E
Bromma flygplats ⊠ 40 59.21 N 17.55 E
Brommö I 40 58.50 N 13.41 E
Bromo, Gunung ∧ 115a 7.57 S 112.57 E
Bromölla 26 56.04 N 14.28 E
Brompton, Eng., U.K. 44 54.22 N 1.25 W
Brompton, Eng., U.K. 260 51.23 N 0.33 E
Brompton, Lac ⊜ 206 45.27 N 72.09 W
Bromptonville 206 45.28 N 71.57 W
Bromsgrove 42 52.20 N 2.03 W
Bromyard 42 52.11 N 2.30 W
Bron 62 45.44 N 4.55 E
Bron, Aéroport de ⊠ 62 45.43 N 4.56 E
Brønderslev 26 57.16 N 9.58 E
Bronevskaja 24 61.43 N 39.10 E
Brong-Ahafo □[4] 150 7.45 N 1.30 W
Broni 62 45.04 N 9.16 E
Bronickaja Guta 78 50.56 N 27.19 E
Bronkhorstspruit 158 25.48 S 28.44 E
Bronkhorstspruitdam ⊜[1] 158 25.55 S 28.42 E
Bronkow 54 51.40 N 13.55 E
Bronllys 42 52.01 N 3.16 W
Bronlund Peak ∧ 176 57.26 N 126.38 W
Bronn 60 49.44 N 11.28 E
Bronnicy 82 55.25 N 38.16 E
Bronnikovo 86 58.32 N 68.25 E
Bronnoje 76 52.19 N 30.29 E
Brønnøysund 24 65.30 N 12.10 E
Bronnzell 56 50.31 N 9.41 E
Brøns 41 55.11 N 8.44 E
Bronson, Fl., U.S. 192 29.26 N 82.38 W
Bronson, Ks., U.S. 198 37.54 N 95.04 W
Bronson, Mi., U.S. 216 41.52 N 85.11 W
Bronson, Tx., U.S. 194 31.21 N 94.01 W
Bronson Lake ⊜ 184 53.52 N 109.43 W
Bronte, It. 70 37.47 N 14.50 E
Bronte, Tx., U.S. 196 31.53 N 100.18 W
Bronte Creek ≃ 212 43.23 N 79.43 W
Bronwood 192 31.49 N 84.21 W
Bronx □[6] 210 40.49 N 73.56 W
Bronx ◆[8] 276 40.49 N 73.56 W
Bronx ≃ 276 40.49 N 73.52 W
Bronx Park ♠ 276 40.52 N 73.53 W
Bronxville 276 40.56 N 73.49 W
Bronx-Whitestone Bridge ◆[5] 276 40.48 N 73.50 W
Bronx Zoo ♠ 276 40.51 N 73.53 W
Bronzolo (Branzoll) 64 46.24 N 11.19 E
Brooch, Lac ⊜ 186 50.44 N 67.58 W
Broodsnyersplaas 158 26.03 S 29.29 E
Brook 216 40.51 N 87.21 W
Brookdale 226 37.06 N 122.06 W
Brooke 208 38.23 N 77.22 W
Brooke □[6] 214 40.18 N 80.33 W
Brookeborough 48 54.19 N 7.24 W
Brookeland 194 31.09 N 94.00 W
Brooker 192 29.53 N 82.19 W
Brooke's Point 116 8.47 N 117.50 E
Brookfield, N.S., Can. 186 45.15 N 63.17 W
Brookfield, Ct., U.S. 207 41.28 N 73.24 W
Brookfield, Il., U.S. 216 41.49 N 87.51 W
Brookfield, Ma., U.S. 207 42.12 N 72.06 W
Brookfield, Mi., U.S. 216 42.27 N 84.47 W
Brookfield, Mo., U.S. 194 39.47 N 93.04 W
Brookfield, N.Y., U.S. 210 42.48 N 75.19 W
Brookfield, Oh., U.S. 214 41.14 N 80.34 W
Brookfield, Wi., U.S. 216 43.03 N 88.06 W
Brookfield Center 207 41.27 N 73.23 W
Brookfield Zoo ♠ 278 41.50 N 87.50 W
Brookford 192 35.42 N 81.20 W
Brookhaven, De., U.S. 285 39.42 N 75.41 W
Brookhaven, Ms., U.S. 194 31.34 N 90.26 W
Brookhaven, Pa., U.S. 285 39.52 N 75.22 W
Brookhaven Manor 278 41.44 N 87.58 W
Brookhaven National Laboratory ɵ[3] 207 40.54 N 72.52 W
Brookings, Or., U.S. 202 42.03 N 124.16 W
Brookings, S.D., U.S. 198 44.18 N 96.47 W
Brookland, Eng., U.K. 42 50.59 N 0.50 E
Brookland, Ar., U.S. 194 35.54 N 90.34 W
Brookland ◆[8] 284c 38.56 N 76.59 W
Brooklands 214 42.38 N 83.06 W
Brookland Terrace 285 39.44 N 75.37 W
Brooklandville 284b 39.25 N 76.40 W
Brooklawn 285 39.52 N 75.07 W
Brooklet 192 32.22 N 81.39 W
Brooklin 212 43.57 N 78.57 W
Brookline, Ma., U.S. 207 42.21 N 71.07 W
Brookline, N.H., U.S. 207 42.44 N 71.39 W
Brooklyn, N.S., Can. 186 44.03 N 64.42 W
Brooklyn, Ct., U.S. 207 41.47 N 71.57 W
Brooklyn, Il., U.S. 219 40.14 N 90.46 W
Brooklyn, In., U.S. 218 39.32 N 86.22 W
Brooklyn, Ia., U.S. 190 41.44 N 92.26 W
Brooklyn, Md., U.S. 284b 39.14 N 76.37 W
Brooklyn, Mi., U.S. 216 42.06 N 84.14 W
Brooklyn, Ms., U.S. 194 31.03 N 89.11 W
Brooklyn, Oh., U.S. 214 41.26 N 81.44 W
Brooklyn, Pa., U.S. 210 41.45 N 75.48 W
Brooklyn, Wa., U.S. 224 46.47 N 123.31 W
Brooklyn, Wi., U.S. 216 42.51 N 89.22 W
Brooklyn ◆[8], Md., U.S. 284b 39.14 N 76.36 W
Brooklyn ◆[8], N.Y., U.S. 210 40.42 N 74.00 W
Brooklyn Battery Tunnel ◆[5] 276 40.42 N 74.01 W
Brooklyn Bridge ◆[5] 276 40.42 N 74.00 W
Brooklyn Center 190 45.04 N 93.19 W
Brooklyn Heights 279a 41.24 N 81.40 W
Brooklyn Marine Park ♠ 276 40.35 N 73.55 W
Brooklyn Museum ɵ 276 40.40 N 73.58 W
Brookmans Park 260 51.43 N 0.12 W
Brookmere 182 49.49 N 120.53 W
Brookmont 284c 38.57 N 77.07 W
Brookneal 192 37.03 N 78.56 W
Brook Park 214 41.23 N 81.48 W
Brookport 194 37.07 N 88.37 W
Brooks, Ab., Can. 182 50.35 N 111.53 W
Brooks, Ca., U.S. 226 38.45 N 122.09 W
Brooks, Me., U.S. 188 44.33 N 69.07 W
Brooks, Or., U.S. 224 45.02 N 122.57 W
Brooks, Mount ∧ 180 63.11 N 150.40 W
Brooks Air Force Base ■ 196 29.21 N 98.25 W
Brooks Bay ⊂ 182 50.13 N 127.55 W
Brooksburg 218 38.44 N 85.15 W
Brookshire 222 29.47 N 95.57 W
Brookside, De., U.S. 285 39.40 N 75.43 W
Brookside, N.J., U.S. 276 40.48 N 74.34 W
Brookside, Pa., U.S. 214 42.08 N 80.00 W
Brookside, Tx., U.S. 222 29.35 N 95.18 W
Brookside Park ♠ 279a 41.27 N 81.43 W
Brooks Island I 282 37.54 N 122.21 W
Brooks Mountain ∧ 180 65.33 N 167.09 W
Brooks Place 283 42.02 N 71.01 W
Brooks Range ⩕ 180 68.00 N 154.00 W
Brookston 216 40.36 N 86.52 W
Brook Street 260 51.37 N 0.17 E
Brooksville, Fl., U.S. 220 28.33 N 82.23 W
Brooksville, Ky., U.S. 218 38.40 N 84.03 W
Brooksville, Ms., U.S. 194 33.14 N 88.34 W
Brookton 162 32.22 S 117.01 E
Brooktondale 210 42.23 N 76.24 W
Brookvale 274a 33.46 S 151.17 E
Brookview 210 42.32 N 73.43 W
Brookville, In., U.S. 218 39.25 N 85.00 W
Brookville, Ma., U.S. 207 42.07 N 71.00 W
Brookville, N.Y., U.S. 276 40.48 N 73.34 W
Brookville, Oh., U.S. 218 39.50 N 84.24 W
Brookville, Pa., U.S. 214 41.09 N 79.05 W
Brookville Lake ⊜[1] 218 39.30 N 85.00 W
Brookwood, Eng., U.K. 260 51.18 N 0.38 W
Brookwood, In., U.S. 278 40.30 N 87.22 W
Brooloo 166 26.29 S 152.42 E
Broom, Little Loch ⊂ 46 57.54 N 5.22 W
Broom, Loch ⊂ 46 57.52 N 5.08 W
Broomall 285 39.58 N 75.21 W
Broome 162 17.58 S 122.14 E
Broome □[6] 210 42.08 N 75.54 W
Broome County Airport ⊠ 210 42.13 N 75.59 W
Broomes Island 208 38.25 N 76.32 W
Broomfield, Eng., U.K. 260 51.14 N 0.38 E
Broomfield, Eng., U.K. 260 51.46 N 0.28 E
Broomfield, Co., U.S. 200 39.55 N 105.05 W
Broons 32 48.19 N 2.16 W
Brooten 198 45.30 N 95.07 W
Brophy, Mount ∧[2] 162 19.11 S 128.51 E
Brora 46 58.01 N 3.51 W
Brora ≃ 46 58.01 N 3.52 W
Brørup 41 55.29 N 9.01 E
Broseley 42 52.37 N 2.29 W
Brosewere Bay ⊂ 276 40.37 N 73.42 W
Brosna ≃ 48 53.13 N 7.58 W
Brošnev-Osada 78 49.00 N 24.13 E
Brossac 32 45.20 N 0.03 W
Brossard 206 45.26 N 73.29 W
Brossasco 62 44.34 N 7.21 E
Brosso 62 45.30 N 7.48 E
Brotas de Macaúbas 255 12.00 S 42.38 W
Brothers Brook ≃ 276 41.02 N 73.36 W
Brötjärna 40 60.30 N 15.01 E
Broto 34 42.36 N 0.06 W
Brotterode 54 50.49 N 10.26 E
Brotton 44 54.34 N 0.56 W
Brou 50 48.13 N 1.11 E
Brough, Eng., U.K. 44 54.32 N 2.19 W
Brough, Eng., U.K. 44 53.44 N 0.35 W
Brough, Scot., U.K. 46 58.39 N 3.20 W
Brougham 212 43.55 N 79.06 W
Brough Head ≻ 46 59.08 N 3.17 W
Broughshane 48 54.54 N 6.12 W
Broughton, Eng., U.K. 42 52.23 N 0.46 W
Broughton, Eng., U.K. 44 53.34 N 0.33 W
Broughton, Eng., U.K. 44 53.49 N 2.44 W
Broughton, Eng., U.K. 262 53.49 N 2.43 W
Broughton, Scot., U.K. 46 55.37 N 3.25 W
Broughton, Wales, U.K. 44 53.10 N 2.59 W
Broughton, Pa., U.S. 214 40.21 N 79.59 W
Broughton in Furness 44 54.17 N 3.12 W
Broughton Island I 176 67.35 N 63.50 W
Broughtown 46 59.15 N 2.36 W
Broughty Ferry 46 56.28 N 2.53 W
Broumov 30 50.35 N 16.20 E
Brousseval 58 48.29 N 4.58 E
Brou-sur-Chantereine 261 48.53 N 2.38 E
Brouvelieures 58 48.14 N 6.44 E
Brouwersdam ◆[6] 52 51.46 N 3.51 E
Brouwershaven 52 51.44 N 3.54 E
Brovary 78 50.31 N 30.46 E
Brovst 26 57.06 N 9.32 E
Broward □[6] 220 26.09 N 80.29 W
Browerville 198 46.05 N 94.51 W
Brown □[6], Il., U.S. 219 39.59 N 90.45 W
Brown □[6], In., U.S. 218 39.12 N 86.15 W
Brown □[6], Oh., U.S. 218 38.52 N 83.54 W
Brown, Mount ∧ 202 48.52 N 111.09 W
Brown, Point ≻ 224 46.56 N 124.10 W
Brownbacks 285 40.11 N 75.37 W
Brown City 190 43.12 N 82.59 W
Brown Clee Hill ∧[2] 42 52.28 N 2.35 W
Brown County State Park ♠ 218 39.09 N 86.14 W
Brown Creek ≃ 276 40.43 N 73.04 W
Browndale 210 41.40 N 75.27 W
Brown Deer 216 43.09 N 87.57 W
Browne Bay ⊂ 176 73.08 N 97.30 W
Brownfield 196 33.10 N 102.16 W
Brown Gelly ∧[2] 42 50.32 N 4.32 W
Brownhills 42 52.39 N 1.55 W
Browning, Il., U.S. 219 40.08 N 90.22 W
Browning, Mo., U.S. 194 40.02 N 93.09 W
Browning, Mt., U.S. 202 48.33 N 113.00 W
Browning Entrance ⊂ 182 53.41 N 130.30 W
Browning Island I 212 45.00 N 79.25 W
Brown Lake ⊜ 176 65.55 N 91.15 W
Brownlee Park 216 42.18 N 85.05 W
Brownlee Reservoir ⊜[1] 202 44.40 N 117.05 W
Brown Mountain ∧, Ca., U.S. 204 35.41 N 117.01 W
Brown Mountain ∧, Ca., U.S. 280 34.14 N 118.08 W
Brown Mountain ∧[2] 222 31.51 N 97.39 W
Brown Point ≻ 276 40.43 N 73.04 W
Brownsberg, Natuurpark ♠ 250 4.50 N 55.10 W
Brownsboro 222 32.18 N 95.37 W
Browns Brook ≃ 276 41.09 N 73.17 W
Brownsburg, P.Q., Can. 206 45.41 N 74.25 W
Brownsburg, In., U.S. 218 39.50 N 86.23 W
Browns Canyon V 280 34.18 N 118.35 W
Brownsdale 190 43.44 N 92.52 W
Browns Island I 282 38.02 N 121.52 W
Browns Lake 216 42.42 N 88.14 W
Brownsmead 224 46.13 N 123.32 W
Browns Mills 208 39.58 N 74.35 W
Browns Point 224 47.18 N 122.21 W
Browns Town, Jam. 241q 18.24 N 77.22 W
Brownstown, Il., U.S. 219 38.59 N 88.57 W
Brownstown, In., U.S. 218 38.52 N 86.02 W
Brownstown, Pa., U.S. 208 40.08 N 76.13 W
Brownstown Creek ≃ 281 42.06 N 83.13 W
Browns Valley, Ca., U.S. 226 39.15 N 121.23 W
Browns Valley, Mn., U.S. 198 45.35 N 96.49 W
Brownsville, On., Can. 212 42.52 N 80.50 W
Brownsville, Ca., U.S. 226 39.28 N 121.16 W
Brownsville, Fl., U.S. 220 25.50 N 80.17 W
Brownsville, In., U.S. 218 39.39 N 85.00 W
Brownsville, Ky., U.S. 194 37.11 N 86.16 W
Brownsville, La., U.S. 194 32.30 N 92.10 W
Brownsville, Or., U.S. 202 44.23 N 122.59 W
Brownsville, Pa., U.S. 188 40.01 N 79.53 W
Brownsville, Tn., U.S. 194 35.35 N 89.15 W
Brownsville, Tx., U.S. 196 25.54 N 97.29 W
Brownton 190 44.43 N 94.21 W
Browntown 276 40.24 N 74.19 W
Brownvale 182 56.08 N 117.53 W
Brownville, Al., U.S. 194 33.23 N 87.45 W
Brownville, Me., U.S. 188 45.18 N 69.02 W
Brownville, Ne., U.S. 198 40.23 N 95.39 W
Brownville, N.Y., U.S. 212 44.00 N 75.59 W
Brownville Junction 188 45.21 N 69.03 W
Brown Willy ∧[2] 42 50.35 N 4.36 W
Brownwood 196 31.42 N 98.59 W
Brownwood, Lake ⊜[1] 196 31.51 N 99.02 W
Browse Island I 160 14.07 S 123.33 E
Broxbourne 260 51.45 N 0.01 W
Broxbourne □[8] 260 51.44 N 0.04 W
Broxton 192 31.37 N 82.53 W
Broye ≃ 58 46.55 N 7.02 E
Broyhill Park 284c 38.51 N 77.11 W
Broža 76 52.57 N 29.07 E
Brozas 34 39.37 N 6.46 W
Brozzo 64 45.43 N 10.14 E
Brtonigla 64 45.23 N 13.38 E
Brû 58 48.21 N 6.41 E
Bruay-en-Artois 50 50.29 N 2.33 E
Bruay-sur-l'Escaut 50 50.23 N 3.32 E
Bruce, Ms., U.S. 194 33.59 N 89.20 W
Bruce, S.D., U.S. 198 44.26 N 96.53 W
Bruce, Wi., U.S. 190 45.27 N 91.16 W
Bruce □[6] 212 44.30 N 81.15 W
Bruce, Mount ∧ 162 22.36 S 118.08 E
Bruce Bay 172 43.35 S 169.41 E
Bruce Creek ≃ 275b 43.52 N 79.18 W
Bruce Lake 184 50.48 N 93.24 W
Bruce Lake ⊜ 184 50.49 N 93.20 W
Bruce Mines 190 46.18 N 83.48 W
Bruce Museum ɵ 276 41.01 N 73.37 W
Bruce Peninsula ≻[1] 190 44.50 N 81.20 W
Bruce Peninsula National Park ♠ 190 45.12 N 81.40 W
Bruce Rock 162 31.53 S 118.09 E
Bruceville 222 31.19 N 97.14 W
Bruchberg ∧ 54 51.47 N 10.29 E
Bruchhausen 56 51.26 N 8.01 E
Bruchhausen-Vilsen 52 52.50 N 9.00 E
Bruchmühlbach-Miesau 56 49.24 N 7.26 E
Bruchmühle 264a 52.33 N 13.47 E
Br'uchoveckaja 78 45.48 N 38.59 E
Bruchsal 56 49.07 N 8.35 E
Brück, Dtsch. 54 52.12 N 12.46 E
Bruck, Öst. 64 47.17 N 12.49 E
Bruck an der Leitha 61 47.57 N 16.44 E
Bruck an der Mur 61 47.25 N 15.16 E
Bruckhausen ◆[8] 263 51.29 N 6.44 E
Bruck in der Oberpfalz 60 49.15 N 12.18 E
Brückl 61 46.45 N 14.32 E
Bruckmühl 64 47.53 N 11.54 E
Brucoli ◆[8] 70 37.17 N 15.11 E
Brudager 41 55.07 N 10.41 E
Bruderheim 182 53.47 N 112.56 W
Brue ≃ 42 51.13 N 3.00 W
Brue-Auriac 62 43.32 N 5.57 E
Brueil-en-Vexin 261 49.02 N 1.49 E
Brüel 54 53.44 N 11.43 E
Bruff 48 52.29 N 8.33 W
Bruges → Brugge 50 51.13 N 3.14 E
Brugg 58 47.29 N 8.12 E
Brugge (Bruges), Bel. 50 51.13 N 3.14 E
Brügge, Dtsch. 263 51.13 N 7.34 E
Brüggen 56 51.14 N 6.11 E
Brugherio 62 45.33 N 9.18 E
Brugnato 62 44.14 N 9.43 E
Brühl 56 50.48 N 6.54 E
Bruin, Ky., U.S. 218 38.11 N 83.01 W
Bruin, Pa., U.S. 214 41.04 N 79.44 W
Bruinisse 52 51.40 N 4.06 E
Bruin Point ∧ 200 39.39 N 110.22 W
Bruit, Pulau I 112 2.35 N 111.20 E
Bruja, Cerro ∧ 236 9.29 N 79.34 W
Brule 198 41.05 N 101.53 W
Brule ≃ 190 45.57 N 88.12 W
Brûlé, Lac ⊜, Can. 176 52.17 N 63.52 W
Brûlé, Lac ⊜, P.Q., Can. 190 46.57 N 77.12 W
Brule Lake ⊜ 212 45.03 N 77.04 W
Brûly 50 49.58 N 4.31 E
Brumadinho 255 20.08 S 44.13 W
Brumado 255 14.13 S 41.40 W
Brumath 56 48.44 N 7.43 E
Brumby Creek ≃ 162 24.09 S 118.39 E
Brummen 52 52.05 N 6.09 E
Brumunddal 26 60.53 N 10.56 E
Bruna ≃ 66 42.45 N 10.53 E
Brunate 62 45.49 N 9.06 E
Brunau 54 52.45 N 11.28 E
Brundall 42 52.37 N 1.26 E
Brundby 41 55.49 N 10.37 E
Brundidge 194 31.43 N 85.48 W
Brune ≃ 50 49.45 N 3.47 E
Bruneau 202 42.52 N 115.47 W
Bruneau ≃ 202 42.57 N 115.58 W
Brunei □[1], Asia 108 4.30 N 114.40 E
Brunei □[1], Asia 112 4.30 N 114.40 E
Brunei, Teluk ⊂ 112 5.05 N 115.18 E
Brunei → Bandar Seri Begawan 112 4.56 N 114.55 E
Brünen 52 51.43 N 6.39 E
Brunette Creek ≃ 162 18.47 S 135.41 E
Brunette Downs 162 18.38 S 135.57 E
Brunette Island I 186 47.16 N 55.54 W
Brunflo 26 63.05 N 14.49 E
Brungle 171b 35.10 S 148.14 E
Brunico (Bruneck) 64 46.48 N 11.56 E
Brünigpass)(58 46.46 N 8.09 E
Brüninghausen 263 51.13 N 7.41 E
Brunkeberg 26 59.26 N 8.29 E
Brünn, Dtsch. 54 50.27 N 10.51 E
Brunn, Dtsch. 54 53.40 N 13.22 E
Brunna 40 59.51 N 17.26 E
Brunn am Gebirge 61 48.07 N 16.17 E
Brünn → Brno 30 49.12 N 16.37 E
Brunnen, Dtsch. 60 48.38 N 11.18 E
Brunnen, Schw. 58 47.00 N 8.36 E
Brunner, Lake ⊜ 172 42.37 S 171.27 E
Brunnerville 208 40.11 N 76.17 W
Brunni 58 47.03 N 8.42 E
Brunnsvik 40 60.12 N 15.08 E
Bruno 184 52.15 N 105.30 W
Brunot Island I 279b 40.28 N 80.03 W
Brunow 264a 52.44 N 13.52 E
Brunoy 50 48.42 N 2.30 E
Brunsbüttel 52 53.54 N 9.07 E
Brunsbüttelkoog 52 53.54 N 9.08 E
Brunson 192 32.55 N 81.11 W
Brunssum 56 50.56 N 5.59 E
Brunswick, Austl. 274b 37.46 S 144.58 E
Brunswick, Ga., U.S. 192 31.08 N 81.29 W
Brunswick, Me., U.S. 188 43.54 N 69.57 W
Brunswick, Md., U.S. 208 39.18 N 77.37 W
Brunswick, Mo., U.S. 194 39.25 N 93.07 W
Brunswick, Oh., U.S. 214 41.14 N 81.50 W
Brunswick ≃ 168a 33.15 S 115.45 E
Brunswick, Península ≻[1] 254 53.30 S 71.25 W
Brunswick → Braunschweig 52 52.16 N 10.31 E
Brunswick Junction 168a 33.15 S 115.51 E
Brunswick Lake ⊜ 190 49.00 N 83.23 W
Brunswick Naval Air Station ■ 188 43.54 N 69.56 W
Brunswick Square ◆[9] 276 40.25 N 74.23 W
Bruntál 30 49.59 N 17.28 E
Bruree 48 52.26 N 8.36 W
Brus, Laguna de ⊂ 236 15.50 N 84.35 W
Brus'any 80 53.13 N 49.24 E
Brusasco 62 45.09 N 8.04 E
Bruselas → Bruxelles 50 50.50 N 4.20 E
Brusendorf 264a 52.19 N 13.31 E
Brush 198 40.15 N 103.37 W
Brush Creek ≃, Oh., U.S. 216 41.26 N 84.24 W
Brush Creek ≃, Pa., U.S. 279b 40.23 N 79.46 W
Brush Run ≃, Pa., U.S. 279b 40.18 N 80.07 W
Brush Run ≃, Pa., U.S. 279b 40.16 N 80.10 W
Brush Valley 214 40.32 N 79.04 W
Brushy Creek ≃, Austl. 274b 37.43 S 145.17 E
Brushy Creek ≃, Ok., U.S. 196 34.55 N 95.34 W
Brushy Creek ≃, Tx., U.S. 222 32.59 N 96.12 W
Brushy Creek ≃, Tx., U.S. 222 30.48 N 95.09 W
Brushy Creek ≃, Tx., U.S. 222 31.55 N 95.26 W
Brushy Creek ≃, Tx., U.S. 222 30.43 N 97.03 W
Brushy Creek ≃, Tx., U.S. 222 29.04 N 96.34 W
Brusilov 78 50.17 N 29.32 E
Brusio 58 46.14 N 10.07 E
Brus Laguna 236 15.47 N 84.35 W
Brusovo 76 57.51 N 35.24 E
Brusque 252 27.06 S 48.56 W
Brussel → Bruxelles 50 50.50 N 4.20 E
Brussels, On., Can. 212 43.44 N 81.15 W
Brussels, Il., U.S. 219 38.57 N 90.36 W
Brussels → Bruxelles 50 50.50 N 4.20 E
Brusson 62 45.45 N 7.44 E
Brüssow 54 53.24 N 14.07 E
Brusy 30 53.53 N 17.45 E
Brutelles 50 50.08 N 1.31 E
Bruthen 166 37.43 S 147.48 E
Bruton 42 51.07 N 2.27 W
Bruxelles (Brussels) (Brussel) 56 50.50 N 4.20 E
Bruxelles National, Aéroport ⊠ 50 50.54 N 4.30 E
Brüx → Most 54 50.32 N 13.39 E
Bruyères 58 48.12 N 6.43 E
Bruyères-le-Châtel 261 48.36 N 2.11 E
Bruzual 246 8.03 N 69.19 W
Bruzzano Zeffirio 68 38.02 N 16.05 E
Brwinów 30 52.09 N 20.43 E
Bryan, Oh., U.S. 216 41.28 N 84.33 W
Bryan, Tx., U.S. 222 30.40 N 96.22 W
Bryan, Mount ∧ 166 33.26 S 138.59 E
Bryan Coast ⍓[2] 9 73.45 S 82.00 W
Bryansk → Br'ansk 76 53.15 N 34.22 E
Bryans Road 208 38.37 N 77.04 W
Bryant, Ar., U.S. 194 34.35 N 92.29 W
Bryant, In., U.S. 216 40.32 N 84.58 W
Bryant, S.D., U.S. 198 44.35 N 97.28 W
Bryant Creek ≃ 194 36.36 N 92.17 W
Bryant Mountain ∧ 207 42.28 N 72.58 W
Bryantville 207 42.02 N 70.50 W
Bryas, Lac ⊜ 206 46.44 N 73.05 W
Bryce Canyon National Park ♠ 200 37.29 N 112.12 W
Bryher I 42a 49.57 N 6.20 W
Brykalansk 24 65.30 N 54.12 E
Brykovka 80 52.32 N 48.35 E
Bryli 76 53.54 N 30.33 E
Brymbo 44 53.06 N 3.04 W
Bryn 262 53.30 N 2.39 W
Brynamman 42 51.49 N 3.52 W
Bryn Athyn 285 40.08 N 75.04 W
Bryn Brawd ∧[2] 42 52.09 N 3.54 W
Bryncethin 42 51.33 N 3.34 W
Bryne 26 58.44 N 5.39 E
Brynford 262 53.16 N 3.14 W
Bryn Gates 262 53.30 N 2.37 W
Bryn'kovskaja 78 46.02 N 38.35 E
Brynmawr, Wales, U.K. 42 51.49 N 3.11 W
Bryn Mawr, Ca., U.S. 228 34.03 N 117.14 W
Bryn Mawr, Pa., U.S. 208 40.01 N 75.18 W
Bryn Mawr College ɵ[2] 285 40.02 N 75.19 W
Bryrup 41 56.01 N 9.31 E
Bryson, P.Q., Can. 188 45.41 N 76.37 W
Bryson, Tx., U.S. 196 33.10 N 98.23 W
Bryson City 192 35.25 N 83.26 W
Bryte 226 38.36 N 121.33 W
Brza Palanka 38 44.28 N 22.27 E
Brzeg 30 50.52 N 17.27 E
Brześć Kujawski 30 52.37 N 18.55 E
Brześć nad Bugiem → Brest 76 52.06 N 23.42 E
Brzesko 30 49.59 N 20.36 E
Brzeszcze 30 49.59 N 19.08 E
Brzeziny 30 51.48 N 19.46 E
Brzozów 30 49.42 N 22.02 E
Bsharrī 130 34.15 N 36.01 E
Bua ≃ 154 12.42 S 34.13 E
Bu'aale 144 1.05 N 42.35 E
Buada Lagoon ⊂ 174b 0.31 S 166.55 E
Buad Island I 116 11.40 N 124.51 E
Buagan ≃ 269e 6.17 S 106.55 E
Buala 175e 8.08 S 159.35 E
Bū al-Ḥīdān, Wādī V 146 27.25 N 19.22 E
Buangor, Mount ∧ 169 37.18 S 143.13 E
Buapinang 112 4.46 S 121.34 E
Buariki 174t 1.36 N 172.58 E
Buatan 114 0.44 N 101.51 E
Bua Yai 110 15.35 N 102.25 E
Buayan ≃ 116 6.06 N 125.14 E
Bu'ayrāt al-Ḥasūn 146 31.24 N 15.44 E
Buba 150 11.36 N 14.55 W
Bubai 268 35.40 N 139.29 E
Bū Bānī, Jabal ∧ 140 22.38 N 25.00 E
Bubanza 154 3.06 S 29.23 E
Bubaque 150 11.17 N 15.50 W
Bubendorf 58 47.27 N 7.44 E
Bubia 164 6.40 S 146.55 E
Būbiyān I 128 29.45 N 48.15 E
Bubu ≃ 154 6.03 S 35.19 E
Bubu, Gunong ∧ 114 4.42 N 100.47 E
Bubuan Island I, Pil. 116 6.21 N 121.58 E
Bubuan Island I, Pil. 116 6.11 N 120.58 E
Bubuduo 120 30.06 N 84.38 E
Buburu 152 1.26 N 18.03 E
Bubye ≃ 154 22.20 S 31.07 E
Buc 261 48.46 N 2.08 E
Bučač 78 49.04 N 25.23 E
Bucak 130 37.28 N 30.36 E
Bucakkışla 130 36.57 N 33.02 E
Bucaramanga 246 7.08 N 73.09 W
Bucarest → București 38 44.26 N 26.06 E
Bucas Grande Island I 116 9.40 N 125.57 E
Buccaneer Archipelago II 160 16.17 S 123.20 E
Buccheri 70 37.08 N 14.51 E
Bucchianico 66 42.18 N 14.11 E
Buccinasco 266b 45.24 N 9.07 E
Buccino 68 40.37 N 15.23 E
Buccurale 144 4.31 N 42.01 E
Bucelas 266c 38.54 N 9.07 W
Bucelas ∧[2] 266c 38.53 N 9.07 W
Buch ◆[8] 264a 52.38 N 13.30 E
Buchanan, Arg. 258 34.58 S 58.13 W
Buchanan, Sk., Can. 184 51.43 N 102.45 W
Buchanan, Liber. 150 5.57 N 10.02 W
Buchanan, Ga., U.S. 192 33.48 N 85.11 W
Buchanan, Mi., U.S. 216 41.49 N 86.21 W
Buchanan, N.Y., U.S. 210 41.16 N 73.56 W
Buchanan, Va., U.S. 192 37.31 N 79.40 W
Buchanan, Lake ⊜ 166 21.28 S 145.52 E
Buchanan, Lake ⊜[1] 196 30.48 N 98.25 W
Buchanan Creek ≃ 162 19.11 S 136.16 E
Buchanan Field ⊠ 282 37.59 N 122.03 W
Buchanan Hills ⩕[2] 162 18.53 S 131.02 E
Buchan Ness ≻ 46 57.28 N 1.45 W
Buchans 186 48.49 N 56.52 W
Buchara 128 39.48 N 64.25 E
Buchara □[8] 128 40.00 N 64.00 E
Bucharest → București 38 44.26 N 26.06 E
Buchbach 60 48.19 N 12.17 E
Buchelay 261 48.59 N 1.40 E
Büchen, Dtsch. 52 53.29 N 10.36 E
Buchen, Dtsch. 56 49.32 N 9.17 E
Buchenberg 58 47.42 N 10.14 E
Büchenbeuren 56 49.55 N 7.16 E
Buchenwald-Denkmal ⊥ 54 51.01 N 11.15 E
Buchholz, Dtsch. 54 52.10 N 12.55 E
Buchholz, Dtsch. 56 50.41 N 7.23 E
Buchholz, Dtsch. 263 51.23 N 7.15 E
Buchholz, Dtsch. 264a 52.35 N 13.47 E
Buchholz ◆[8], Dtsch. 263 51.23 N 6.46 E
Buchholz ◆[8], Dtsch. 264a 52.36 N 13.26 E
Buchholz in der Nordheide 52 53.20 N 9.52 E
Büchlberg 60 48.40 N 13.30 E
Buchloe 58 48.02 N 10.44 E
Bucholt 263 51.39 N 6.43 E
Buchon, Point ≻ 226 35.15 N 120.54 W
Buchow-Karpzow 264a 52.31 N 12.57 E
Buchs, Schw. 58 47.23 N 8.04 E
Buchs, Schw. 58 47.10 N 9.28 E
Buchufontein 158 30.18 S 19.36 E
Buchy 50 49.35 N 1.22 E
Bučina 60 48.58 N 13.36 E
Bucine 66 43.29 N 11.37 E
Buck, Lake ⊜ 162 19.38 S 130.21 E
Buckatunna 194 31.32 N 88.31 W
Buckatunna Creek ≃ 194 31.30 N 88.32 W
Buck Branch ≃ 284b 39.01 N 77.10 W
Buck Creek 216 40.29 N 86.46 W
Buck Creek ≃, U.S. 196 34.35 N 99.58 W
Buck Creek ≃, In., U.S. 218 39.37 N 85.56 W
Buck Creek ≃, In., U.S. 218 40.11 N 85.30 W
Buck Creek ≃, Ky., U.S. 192 36.59 N 84.29 W
Buck Creek ≃, Oh., U.S. 218 39.56 N 83.51 W
Buck Creek ≃, Pa., U.S. 285 40.15 N 74.50 W
Buckden, Eng., U.K. 42 52.17 N 0.16 W
Buckden, Eng., U.K. 44 54.12 N 2.05 W
Bückeburg 52 52.16 N 9.02 E
Bücken 52 52.46 N 9.07 E

English	Deutsch	Español	Français	Português
≃ River	Fluß	Río	Rivière	Rio
≊ Canal	Kanal	Canal	Canal	Canal
⌞ Waterfall, Rapids	Wasserfall, Stromschnellen	Cascada, Rápidos	Chute d'eau, Rapides	Cascata, Rápidos
ʮ Strait	Meeresstraße	Estrecho	Détroit	Estreito
⊂ Bay, Gulf	Bucht, Golf	Bahía, Golfo	Baie, Golfe	Baía, Golfo
⊜ Lake, Lakes	See, Seen	Lago, Lagos	Lac, Lacs	Lago, Lagos
⩩ Swamp	Sumpf	Pantano	Marais	Pântano
⍓ Ice Features, Glacier	Eis- und Gletscherformen	Accidentes Glaciales	Formes glaciaires	Acidentes glaciares
⩪ Other Hydrographic Features	Andere Hydrographische Objekte	Otros Elementos Hidrográficos	Autres données hydrographiques	Outros acidentes hidrográficos
⊹ Submarine Features	Untermeerische Objekte	Accidentes Submarinos	Formes de relief sous-marin	Acidentes submarinos
□ Political Unit	Politische Einheit	Unidad Politica	Entité politique	Unidade política
ɵ Cultural Institution	Kulturelle Institution	Institución Cultural	Institution culturelle	Institução cultural
⊥ Historical Site	Historische Stätte	Sitio Histórico	Site historique	Sitio histórico
♠ Recreational Site	Erholungs- und Ferienort	Sitio de Recreo	Centre de loisirs	Area de Lazer
⊠ Airport	Flughafen	Aeropuerto	Aéroport	Aeroporto
■ Military Installation	Militäranlage	Instalación Militar	Installation militaire	Instalação militar
◆ Miscellaneous	Verschiedenes	Misceláneo	Divers	Diversos

ENGLISH — DEUTSCH

Name	Page / Seite	Lat.°′ / Breite°′	Long.°′ / Länge°′ E = Ost
Buckeye	200	33.22 N	112.34 W
Buckeye Creek ≃	226	38.54 N	121.55 W
Buckeye Lake	188	39.56 N	82.28 W
Buckeystown	208	39.20 N	77.25 W
Buckfastleigh	42	50.29 N	3.46 W
Buckhannon	188	38.59 N	80.13 W
Buckhaven	46	56.11 N	3.03 W
Buck Hill Falls	210	41.11 N	75.15 W
Buck Hollow ≃	224	45.10 N	120.50 W
Buckholts	222	30.52 N	97.08 W
Buckhorn ≃	180	66.13 N	161.10 W
Buckhorn Draw V	196	30.39 N	100.52 W
Buckhorn Island State Park ♠	284a	43.03 N	78.59 W
Buckhorn Lake ⊜, On., Can.	212	44.28 N	78.23 W
Buckhorn Lake ⊜, Ca., U.S.	228	34.50 N	117.59 W
Buckie	46	57.40 N	2.58 W
Buckingham, Austl.	168a	33.24 S	116.19 E
Buckingham, P.Q., Can.	188	45.35 N	75.25 W
Buckingham, Eng., U.K.	42	52.00 N	1.00 W
Buckingham, Pa., U.S.	208	40.18 N	75.01 W
Buckingham, Va., U.S.	192	37.32 N	78.37 W
Buckingham Bay c	164	12.10 S	135.46 E
Buckingham Palace ♥	260	51.30 N	0.08 W
Buckinghamshire □[6]	42	51.45 N	0.48 W
Buck Island I	241n	17.48 N	64.37 W
Buck Island Reef National Monument ♠	241n	17.48 N	64.37 W
Buck Lake ⊜, Ab., Can.	182	53.00 N	114.45 W
Buck Lake ⊜, On., Can.	212	45.25 N	79.24 W
Buckland, Austl.	166	42.37 S	147.43 E
Buckland, Eng., U.K.	260	51.15 N	0.15 W
Buckland, Ak., U.S.	180	65.59 N	161.07 W
Buckland, Ma., U.S.	207	42.35 N	72.47 W
Buckland, Oh., U.S.	216	40.37 N	84.16 W
Buckland Brewer	42	50.57 N	4.14 W
Buckland Common	260	51.45 N	0.39 W
Bucklands	158	29.03 S	23.44 E
Buckleboo	166	32.55 S	136.12 E
Buckley, Wales, U.K.	44	53.09 N	3.04 W
Buckley, Il., U.S.	216	40.36 N	88.02 W
Buckley, Wa., U.S.	224	47.09 N	122.01 W
Buckley ≃	166	20.22 S	137.57 E
Buckley Bay c	9	68.16 S	148.12 E
Bucklin, Ks., U.S.	198	37.32 N	99.38 W
Bucklin, Mo., U.S.	194	39.46 N	92.53 W
Buck Lodge	284c	39.01 N	76.58 W
Buck Mountain ∧, Va., U.S.	192	36.40 N	81.15 W
Buck Mountain ∧, Wa., U.S.	202	48.26 N	119.50 W
Bucknell Heights	284c	38.46 N	77.04 W
Bucknell Manor	208	38.46 N	77.04 W
Buckner	218	38.23 N	85.26 W
Buckner Creek ≃	198	38.11 N	99.34 W
Buckners Creek ≃	222	29.53 N	96.53 W
Buckow	54	52.34 N	14.04 E
Buckow ◆[8]	264a	52.25 N	13.26 E
Bucks □[6]	208	40.19 N	75.08 W
Bucksburn	46	57.12 N	2.18 W
Buckshot Lake ⊜	212	45.00 N	77.04 W
Buckskin Creek ≃	218	39.14 N	83.17 W
Buckskin Gulch V	200	37.01 N	111.52 W
Bucks Knob ∧	224	46.41 N	123.20 W
Bucksport	188	44.34 N	68.47 W
Bucktown	285	40.10 N	75.43 W
Bückwitz	54	52.52 N	12.29 E
Buc-Louis-Blériot, Aérodrome de ⊠	261	48.45 N	2.05 E
Bučmany	78	51.04 N	28.04 E
Bucoda	224	46.47 N	122.52 W
Buco Zau	152	4.46 S	12.33 E
Bucquoy	50	50.08 N	2.42 E
Buctouche	186	46.28 N	64.43 W
Bucun	98	36.37 N	117.27 E
București (Bucharest)	38	44.26 N	26.06 E
Bucutua Island I	116	6.09 N	121.49 E
Bucy-lès-Pierrepont	50	49.39 N	3.54 E
Bucyrus	214	40.48 N	82.58 W
Bud	26	62.55 N	6.55 E
Buda, Il., U.S.	190	41.19 N	89.40 W
Buda, Tx., U.S.	196	30.05 N	97.51 W
Buda ◆[8]	264c	47.30 N	19.02 E
Buda Castle ⊥	264c	47.30 N	19.02 E
Budafok ◆[8]	264c	47.26 N	19.02 E
Budagovo	88	54.38 N	100.08 E
Budai-hegység ⋏	264c	47.31 N	18.58 E
Budakalász	264c	47.37 N	19.03 E
Budakeszi	264c	47.31 N	18.56 E
Buda-Kosel'ovo	76	52.43 N	30.34 E
Budalin	110	22.22 N	95.08 E
Budaörs	264c	47.27 N	18.58 E
Budapest, Magy.	30	47.30 N	19.05 E
Budapest, Magy.	264c	47.30 N	19.05 E
Budapest □[7]	264c	47.30 N	19.05 E
Búđardalur	24a	65.10 N	21.42 W
Budarin	80	47.54 N	42.36 E
Budarino	80	50.31 N	51.04 E
Budatétény ◆[8]	264c	47.25 N	19.01 E
Budaun	124	28.03 N	79.07 E
Budawang National Park ♠	170	35.26 S	150.02 E
Budawang Range ⋏	170	35.20 S	150.03 E
Budayuan	98	40.56 N	125.19 E
Budberg	263	51.32 N	6.38 E
Budbud	144	4.11 N	46.28 E
Budd Coast ±[2]	9	66.30 S	113.00 E
Buddh Gaya → Bodh Gaya	124	24.42 N	84.59 E
Budd Inlet c	224	47.06 N	122.54 W
Budd Lake	210	40.52 N	74.44 W
Buddtown	285	39.56 N	74.42 W
Buddu	140	11.54 N	24.08 E
Buddusò	71	40.35 N	9.15 E
Bude, Eng., U.K.	42	50.50 N	4.33 W
Bude, Ms., U.S.	194	31.27 N	90.51 W
Bude Bay c	42	50.50 N	4.37 W
Budel	52	51.17 N	5.35 E
Budelli, Isola I	71	41.17 N	9.21 E
Büdelsdorf	41	54.18 N	9.40 E
Büderich	52	51.37 N	6.34 E
Buderus	263	51.33 N	7.38 E
Budești	38	44.14 N	26.28 E
Budge Budge	126	22.27 N	88.10 E
Buḍhāthum	124	28.04 N	84.50 E
Budhhāta	126	22.36 N	89.10 E
Budhī Gaṇḍakī ≃	124	27.48 N	84.45 E
Budhlāda	123	29.56 N	75.34 E
Budi	152	3.04 S	23.56 E
Büdingen	56	50.17 N	9.07 E
Búđir	24a	64.56 N	13.58 W
Budišov nad Budišovkou	30	49.47 N	17.38 E
Budjala	152	2.39 N	19.42 E
Budkov	61	49.03 N	15.39 E
Budleigh Salterton	42	50.38 N	3.20 W
Budogošč'	76	59.17 N	32.27 E
Budogovišči	76	53.36 N	36.18 E
Budoni	71	40.43 N	9.42 E
Bud'onnovka	80	50.52 N	52.48 E
Bud'onnovsk	84	44.46 N	44.09 E
Bud'onnovskaja	80	46.56 N	41.33 E
Bud'onnyj, Kyrg.	85	42.30 N	72.35 E
Bud'onnyj, Ross.	83	47.27 N	39.46 E
Budrio	64	44.32 N	11.32 E
Budslav	76	54.47 N	27.27 E
Budweis → České Budějovice	30	48.59 N	14.28 E
Budworth Mere ⊜	262	53.17 N	2.31 W
Budy	78	49.53 N	36.02 E
Budylka	78	50.30 N	34.26 E
Budyně nad Ohří	54	50.22 N	14.09 E
Budžak ⋏[1]	78	46.10 N	29.00 E
Buea	152	4.09 N	9.14 E
Buëch ≃	62	44.12 N	5.57 E
Buechel	218	38.11 N	85.39 W
Buehl Airport ⊠	285	40.11 N	74.54 W
Bueil	50	48.56 N	1.27 E
Buela	152	5.55 S	14.33 E
Buell	219	39.02 N	91.27 W
Bue Marino, Grotta del •[5]	71	40.15 N	9.38 E
Buena	208	39.30 N	74.55 W
Buena Esperanza	252	34.45 S	65.15 W
Buena Esperanza, Cabo de → Good Hope, Cape of ›	158	34.24 S	18.30 E
Buena Park, Ca., U.S.	228	33.52 N	117.59 W
Buena Park, Wi., U.S.	216	42.48 N	88.14 W
Buenaventura, Col.	246	3.53 N	77.04 W
Buenaventura, Méx.	232	29.51 N	107.29 W
Buena Vista, Bol.	248	17.27 S	63.40 W
Buena Vista, Méx.	204	32.32 N	116.44 W
Buenavista, Méx.	234	22.36 N	100.09 W
Buena Vista, Para.	252	26.08 S	56.03 W
Buenavista, Pil.	116	8.59 N	125.24 E
Buenavista, Pil.	116	13.15 N	121.57 E
Buenavista, Pil.	116	10.04 N	118.49 E
Buenavista, Pil.	116	7.15 N	122.16 E
Buena Vista, Co., U.S.	200	38.50 N	106.07 W
Buena Vista, Fl., U.S.	220	28.11 N	82.44 W
Buena Vista, Ga., U.S.	192	32.19 N	84.31 W
Buena Vista, Md., U.S.	284c	38.57 N	76.50 W
Buena Vista, Ms., U.S.	194	33.53 N	88.50 W
Buena Vista, Pa., U.S.	279b	40.17 N	79.48 W
Buena Vista, Va., U.S.	192	37.44 N	79.21 W
Buena Vista, Bahía de c	240p	22.30 N	79.08 W
Buena Vista Canal ≍	228	35.21 N	119.06 W
Buenavista de Cuéllar	234	18.27 N	99.25 W
Buena Vista Lake Bed ⊜	204	35.11 N	119.17 W
Buenavista Tomatlán	234	19.12 N	102.36 W
Buen Día	196	26.21 N	104.32 W
Buendia, Embalse de ⊜[1]	34	40.25 N	2.43 W
Buenga ≃	152	6.07 S	15.58 E
Bueno ≃	254	40.13 S	73.43 W
Bueno Brandão	256	22.27 S	46.21 W
Buenópolis	255	17.54 S	44.11 W
Buenos Aires, Arg.	258	34.36 S	58.27 W
Buenos Aires, Arg.	288	34.36 S	58.27 W
Buenos Aires, Col.	246	3.02 N	76.38 W
Buenos Aires, C.R.	236	9.10 N	83.20 W
Buenos Aires □[4]	252	36.00 S	60.00 W
Buenos Aires, Lago (Lago General Carrera) ⊜	254	46.35 S	72.00 W
Buen Pasto	254	45.05 S	69.28 W
Buer ◆[8]	263	51.36 N	7.03 E
Buerarema	255	14.57 S	39.19 W
Buerāt, Bi'r ⊤[4]	142	28.59 N	32.10 E
Buertuokai	85	39.35 N	74.58 E
Buesaco	246	1.23 N	77.09 W
Buescher State Park ♠	222	30.02 N	97.09 W
Buet, Le ∧	58	46.02 N	6.52 E
Buey ≃	240p	20.28 N	77.05 W
Bufalotta, Fosso della ≃	267a	41.59 N	12.30 E
Buffalo, Il., U.S.	219	39.51 N	89.25 W
Buffalo, In., U.S.	216	40.53 N	86.45 W
Buffalo, Ks., U.S.	198	37.42 N	95.41 W
Buffalo, Mn., U.S.	190	45.10 N	93.52 W
Buffalo, Mo., U.S.	194	37.38 N	93.05 W
Buffalo, N.Y., U.S.	210	42.53 N	78.52 W
Buffalo, N.Y., U.S.	284a	42.53 N	78.52 W
Buffalo, Oh., U.S.	188	39.54 N	81.31 W
Buffalo, Ok., U.S.	196	36.50 N	99.37 W
Buffalo, S.C., U.S.	192	34.43 N	81.41 W
Buffalo, S.D., U.S.	198	45.35 N	103.32 W
Buffalo, Tx., U.S.	222	31.28 N	96.04 W
Buffalo, Wy., U.S.	202	44.20 N	106.41 W
Buffalo ≃, Can.	176	60.55 N	115.00 W
Buffalo ≃, S. Afr.	158	28.43 S	30.37 E
Buffalo ≃, Ar., U.S.	194	36.10 N	92.26 W
Buffalo ≃, Mn., U.S.	198	47.06 N	96.49 W
Buffalo ≃, Ms., U.S.	194	31.04 N	91.34 W
Buffalo ≃, N.Y., U.S.	284a	42.53 N	78.53 W
Buffalo ≃, Tn., U.S.	194	36.00 N	87.50 W
Buffalo ≃, Wi., U.S.	190	44.22 N	91.55 W
Buffalo, State University College at ♥[2]	284a	42.56 N	78.53 W
Buffalo Airpark ⊠	284a	42.52 N	78.43 W
Buffalo Bayou ≃	222	29.46 N	95.05 W
Buffalo Bill Ranch State Historical Park ♠	198	41.10 N	100.48 W
Buffalo Bill Reservoir ⊜[1]	202	44.29 N	109.13 W
Buffalo Bill State Park ♠	202	44.30 N	109.14 W
Buffalo Center	190	43.23 N	93.56 W
Buffalo Coast Guard Base ■	284a	42.52 N	78.54 W
Buffalo Creek ≃, U.S.	198	45.57 N	102.56 W
Buffalo Creek ≃, U.S.	214	40.16 N	80.37 W
Buffalo Creek ≃, Il., U.S.	278	42.08 N	87.55 W
Buffalo Creek ≃, Ia., U.S.	190	42.06 N	91.18 W
Buffalo Creek ≃, Ks., U.S.	198	39.35 N	97.43 W
Buffalo Creek ≃, Ky., U.S.	218	38.28 N	83.03 W
Buffalo Creek ≃, Mn., U.S.	198	44.51 N	94.00 W
Buffalo Creek ≃, N.Y., U.S.	210	42.52 N	78.47 W
Buffalo Creek ≃, Ok., U.S.	196	36.47 N	99.15 W
Buffalo Creek ≃, Pa., U.S.	208	40.29 N	77.08 W
Buffalo Creek ≃, Pa., U.S.	210	40.58 N	76.53 W
Buffalo Creek ≃, Pa., U.S.	214	40.40 N	79.41 W
Buffalo Grove	216	42.09 N	87.57 W
Buffalo Harbor c	284a	42.51 N	78.52 W
Buffalo Lake	198	44.44 N	94.37 W
Buffalo Lake ⊜, Ab., Can.	182	52.27 N	112.54 W
Buffalo Lake ⊜, N.T., Can.	176	60.10 N	115.30 W
Buffalo Lake ⊜[1]	196	34.54 N	102.07 W
Buffalo Museum of Science ♥	284a	42.54 N	78.51 W
Buffalo Narrows	184	55.51 N	108.30 W
Buffalo National River ♠	194	35.58 N	92.53 W
Buffalo Pound Lake ⊜	184	50.39 N	105.30 W
Buffalo Pound Provincial Park ♠	184	50.36 N	105.30 W
Buffalo Run ≃	279b	40.12 N	79.37 W
Buffalo Zoo ♠	284a	42.56 N	78.51 W
Buffels ≃, S. Afr.	156	29.41 S	17.03 E
Buffels ≃, S. Afr.	158	33.45 S	21.11 E
Buffington Harbor c	278	41.38 N	87.25 W
Buffum, Lake ⊜	220	27.48 N	81.40 W
Buford, Ga., U.S.	192	34.07 N	84.00 W
Buford, Oh., U.S.	218	39.04 N	83.50 W
Buford Dam ◆[6]	192	34.11 N	84.03 W
Buftea	38	44.34 N	25.57 E
Bug ≃	22	52.31 N	21.05 E
Buga, Col.	246	3.54 N	76.17 W
Buga, Nig.	150	8.30 N	7.21 E
Bugajevka, Ross.	83	49.39 N	39.42 E
Bugajevka, Ukr.	83	48.25 N	38.53 E
Bugajevka, Ukr.	83	49.28 N	37.23 E
Bugalagrande	246	4.11 N	76.09 W
Bugala Island I	154	0.40 S	32.20 E
Bugallon	116	15.57 N	120.13 E
Buganga	154	0.03 S	31.59 E
Bugasong	116	11.03 N	122.04 E
Bugat, Mong.	86	48.59 N	90.10 E
Bugat, Mong.	88	47.55 N	101.16 E
Bugbrooke	42	52.12 N	1.01 W
Bug Catooti	144	10.44 N	50.35 E
Buğdaylı	130	40.13 N	27.46 E
Bugeat	32	45.35 N	1.59 E
Bugel, Ujung ›	115a	6.26 S	111.03 E
Bugene	154	1.35 S	31.08 E
Bugey ◆[1]	58	45.55 N	5.30 E
Buggenhout	50	51.01 N	4.12 E
Buggerru	71	39.24 N	8.24 E
Bugio I	266c	38.39 N	9.18 W
Bugiri	154	0.34 N	33.45 E
Bugle	42	50.24 N	4.47 W
Bug Méridional → Južnyj Bug ≃	78	46.59 N	31.58 E
Bugojno	36	44.03 N	17.27 E
Bugøynes	24	69.58 N	29.39 E
Bugrino	24	68.48 N	49.09 E
Bugry, Ross.	76	58.46 N	35.15 E
Bugry, Ross.	265a	60.04 N	30.24 E
Bugsanga ≃	116	12.26 N	120.59 E
Bugsuk Island I	116	8.15 N	117.18 E
Bugt, Zhg.	89	48.46 N	121.57 E
Bugt, Zhg.	98	42.20 N	120.43 E
Buguba	164	3.41 S	137.30 E
Buguey	116	18.17 N	121.50 E
Bugui Point ›	116	12.36 N	123.14 E
Bugul'dejka	88	52.33 N	106.05 E
Bugul'ma	80	54.33 N	52.48 E
Bugul'minsko-Belebejevskaja vozvyšennost' ⋏[1]	80	54.54 N	52.42 E
Bugun' ≃	85	42.58 N	68.35 E
Bugun'skoje vodochranilišče ⊜[1]	85	42.45 N	69.05 E
Buguruslan	80	53.39 N	52.26 E
Buh ≃	102	36.58 N	99.48 E
Buhanhua	104	42.39 N	122.46 E
Bū Hashīshah, Thamad ⊤[4]	146	26.23 N	18.47 E
Buḥayrah, Rayyāḥ al- ≍	142	30.43 N	30.45 E
Buḥaythān, Jabal al- ∧	132	30.55 N	35.53 E
Buhera	154	19.18 S	31.29 E
Buhi	116	13.26 N	123.31 E
Buhi, Lake ⊜	116	13.26 N	123.31 E
Bühl, Dtsch.	56	48.42 N	8.08 E
Buhl, Fr.	58	47.56 N	7.11 E
Buhl, Id., U.S.	202	42.35 N	114.45 W
Buhl, Mn., U.S.	190	47.29 N	92.46 W
Buhler	198	38.08 N	97.46 W
Bühler ≃	56	49.10 N	9.47 E
Bühlertal	56	48.41 N	8.10 E
Buhuai	120	33.22 N	80.36 E
Buhuși	38	46.43 N	26.41 E
Bui Dam ◆[6]	150	8.22 N	2.10 W
Buie, Loch c	46	56.20 N	5.52 W
Buile Hill Park ♠	262	53.29 N	2.18 W
Builth Wells	42	52.09 N	3.24 W
Buin, Chile	252	33.44 S	70.45 W
Buin, Pap. N. Gui.	175e	6.50 S	155.44 E
Buin, Piz ∧	58	46.50 N	10.08 E
Buinen	52	52.55 N	6.50 E
Buinsk, Ross.	80	55.12 N	47.03 E
Buinsk, Ross.	80	54.57 N	48.17 E
Buíque	250	8.37 S	37.09 W
Buis-les-Baronnies	62	44.16 N	5.16 E
Buitenpost	52	53.15 N	6.09 E
Buj	80	58.30 N	41.30 E
Buj ≃	80	56.13 N	54.12 E
Bujaki	24	59.03 N	48.40 E
Bujalance	34	37.54 N	4.22 W
Bujant, Mong.	86	48.33 N	89.34 E
Bujant, Mong.	86	48.10 N	91.55 E
Bujant ≃	88	47.08 N	97.38 E
Bujant-Ovoo	102	44.58 N	107.05 E
Bujaraloz	34	41.30 N	0.09 W
Buje	36	45.24 N	13.40 E
Buji	102	33.58 N	95.22 E
Bujnaksk	84	42.49 N	47.07 E
Bujnoviči	78	51.52 N	28.33 E
Bujr nuur ⊜	88	47.48 N	117.42 E
Bujukly	89	49.30 N	142.47 E
Bujumbura	154	3.23 S	29.22 E
Bük, Magy.	61	47.23 N	16.45 E
Buk, Pol.	30	52.22 N	16.31 E
Buka	85	40.48 N	69.11 E
Bukačača	88	52.59 N	116.55 E
Bukačevcy	78	49.15 N	24.29 E
Buka Island I	175e	5.15 S	154.35 E
Bukama	154	9.12 S	25.51 E
Būkān, Īrān	128	36.31 N	46.12 E
Bukan', Ross.	76	53.55 N	34.42 E
Bukanovskaja	80	49.42 N	42.18 E
Buka Passage Ʉ	175e	5.25 S	154.41 E
Bukarest → București	38	44.26 N	26.06 E
Bukarevo	82	55.57 N	36.44 E
Bukavu	154	2.30 S	28.52 E
Bukene	154	4.14 S	32.53 E
Bukhara → Buchara	128	39.48 N	64.25 E
Bukhayt, Bi'r ⊤[4]	142	29.13 N	32.17 E
Bukide, Pulau I	112	3.47 N	125.36 E
Bukidnon □[4]	116	8.00 N	125.00 E
Bukima	154	1.48 S	33.25 E
Bukit Baharu	114	2.13 N	102.16 E
Bukitbatu	114	1.27 N	102.00 E
Bukit Betong	114	4.15 N	101.56 E
Bukit Fraser	114	3.43 N	101.45 E
Bukit Kachi	114	6.24 N	100.32 E
Bukit Mandai	271c	1.25 N	103.45 E
Bukit Mertajam	114	5.22 N	100.28 E
Bukit Panjang	271c	1.23 N	103.46 E
Bukit Serok	114	2.55 N	102.50 E
Bukit Timah	271c	1.20 N	103.47 E
Bukit Timah Race Course ♠	271c	1.20 N	103.48 E
Bukittinggi	112	0.19 S	100.22 E
Bükk ⋏	30	48.05 N	20.30 E
Bukoba	154	1.20 S	31.49 E
Bukombe	154	3.31 S	32.03 E
Bukovica ◆[1]	36	44.10 N	15.40 E
Bukovina □[9]	78	48.00 N	25.30 E
Bukrino	82	54.48 N	36.14 E
Bukuka	88	51.11 N	116.39 E
Bukukun	88	49.27 N	111.08 E
Bukum, Pulau I	271c	1.14 N	103.47 E
Bukumbirwa	154	0.46 S	28.44 E
Bukum Kechil, Pulau I	271c	1.14 N	103.46 E
Bukunga	154	7.41 S	25.56 E
Bukuru	150	9.48 N	8.51 E
Bukuya	154	0.41 N	31.50 E
Bula	164	3.06 S	130.30 E
Bula ≃	80	55.12 N	48.23 E
Bula Atumba	152	8.40 S	14.48 E
Bulacan □[4]	116	15.00 N	121.05 E
Bulacaue Point ›	116	11.36 N	123.09 E
Bülach	58	47.31 N	8.32 E
Bulajevo	86	54.54 N	70.26 E
Bulak	88	51.02 N	115.21 E
Bulaka ≃	164	8.06 S	139.12 E
Bulak Gölü ⊜	130	38.32 N	32.55 E
Bulalacao	116	12.20 N	121.20 E
Bulalacao Island I	116	11.45 N	120.10 E
Bulalaqui Point ›	116	11.17 N	124.03 E
Bulan, Pil.	116	12.40 N	123.52 E
Bulan, Pil.	116	6.44 N	124.47 E
Bulan, Ky., U.S.	192	37.18 N	83.09 W
Bulanaš	86	57.16 N	62.00 E
Bulancak	130	40.57 N	38.14 E
Bulandshahr	124	28.24 N	77.51 E
Bulanicha	86	52.48 N	84.57 E
Bulanık	130	39.05 N	42.15 E
Bulan Island I	116	6.08 N	121.50 E
Bulanovo	86	52.27 N	55.10 E
Būlāq	140	25.12 N	30.32 E
Būlāq ◆[8]	273c	30.04 N	31.14 E
Būlāq ad-Dakrūr	273c	30.02 N	31.11 E
Bulava	89	51.55 N	140.25 E
Bulavinovka	83	49.25 N	38.58 E
Bulawa, Gunung ∧	112	0.30 N	123.34 E
Bulawayo	154	20.09 S	28.36 E
Bulbjerg ∧[2]	26	57.09 N	9.02 E
Bulbul	130	36.46 N	36.49 E
Bulbul, Wādī V	140	10.59 N	24.33 E
Bulcherry Island I	126	21.33 N	88.31 E
Buldan	130	38.03 N	28.51 E
Buldāna	122	20.32 N	76.11 E
Buldern	52	51.52 N	7.22 E
Buldibuyo	248	8.07 S	77.22 W
Buldir Island I	181a	52.21 N	175.54 E
Buldon	116	7.33 N	124.25 E
Buldurtinskij	80	50.05 N	53.11 E
Buldyrty ≃	80	49.48 N	52.34 E
Bulembu	158	25.56 S	31.06 E
Bulga	170	32.39 S	151.01 E
Bulgakovka	83	49.11 N	38.33 E
Bulgakovo	76	55.14 N	32.08 E
Bulgan, Mong.	86	46.53 N	91.05 E
Bulgan, Mong.	88	48.45 N	103.34 E
Bulgan, Mong.	102	44.05 N	103.32 E
Bulgan □[4]	88	49.00 N	103.30 E
Bulgar	80	54.57 N	49.05 E
Bulgaria (Bâlgarija) □[1], Europe	22	43.00 N	25.00 E
Bulgaria (Bâlgarija) □[1], Europe	38	43.00 N	25.00 E
Bulgarie → Bulgaria □[1]	38	43.00 N	25.00 E
Bulgarien → Bulgaria □[1]	38	43.00 N	25.00 E
Bulger	214	40.23 N	80.20 W
Bulgnéville	58	48.13 N	5.50 E
Bulgroo	166	25.48 S	143.59 E
Bulhale	144	5.20 N	46.29 E
Buliluyan	116	8.20 N	117.12 E
Buliluyan, Cape ›	116	8.20 N	117.11 E
Bulim	271c	1.22 N	103.43 E
Bulimba	171a	27.25 S	153.04 E
Bulki	144	6.10 N	36.40 E
Bulkington	42	52.29 N	1.25 W
Bulkley ≃	182	55.13 N	127.40 W
Bulkley Ranges ⋏	182	54.30 N	127.30 W
Bull ≃	182	49.28 N	115.26 W
Bullabulling	162	31.01 S	120.32 E
Bullaque ≃	34	38.59 N	4.17 W
Bullara	162	22.40 S	114.03 E
Bullard	222	32.08 N	95.19 W
Bulla Regia ⊥	36	36.34 N	8.46 E
Bullas	34	38.03 N	1.40 W
Bullaxaar	144	10.23 N	44.25 E
Bullay	56	50.03 N	7.08 E
Bull Creek ≃, Nv., U.S.	204	38.43 N	115.34 W
Bull Creek ≃, N.Y., U.S.	284a	43.03 N	78.50 W
Bull Creek ≃, Oh., U.S.	214	40.42 N	80.32 W
Bull Creek ≃, S.D., U.S.	198	43.41 N	99.28 W
Bull Creek ≃, S.D., U.S.	198	45.40 N	103.18 W
Bull Creek ≃, Tx., U.S.	196	32.36 N	101.10 W
Bulldog	164	7.45 S	146.25 E
Bulle	58	46.37 N	7.04 E
Buller ≃	172	41.44 S	171.35 E
Buller, Mount ∧	169	37.09 S	146.26 E
Bullfinch	162	30.59 S	119.06 E
Bullfrog Creek ≃	200	37.19 N	110.44 W
Bull Harbour	182	50.54 N	127.55 W
Bullhead	198	45.45 N	101.04 W
Bullhead City	204	35.08 N	114.34 W
Bull Hide Creek ≃	222	31.23 N	97.01 W
Bull Hill ∧[2]	262	53.40 N	2.21 W
Bulli	170	34.20 S	150.55 E
Bullicame ♠	66	42.22 N	12.04 E
Büllingen	56	50.25 N	6.16 E
Bullioh	171b	36.12 S	147.20 E
Bullion	261	48.37 N	2.00 E
Bull Lake ⊜[1]	202	43.11 N	109.07 W
Bull Lake Creek ≃	202	43.14 N	109.02 W
Bull Mountain ∧	202	46.05 N	112.04 W
Bullock	192	36.30 N	78.33 W
Bullock Creek	166	17.43 S	144.31 E
Bullock Creek ≃	166	21.40 S	145.09 E
Bulloo ≃	166	28.43 S	142.30 E
Bulloo Downs	166	28.31 S	142.57 E
Bulloo Lake ⊜	166	28.43 S	142.25 E
Bulloo River Overflow ≡	166	28.50 S	142.40 E
Bullpound Creek ≃	182	51.05 N	111.58 W
Bull Run ≃, Or., U.S.	224	45.26 N	122.15 W
Bull Run ≃, Va., U.S.	208	38.43 N	77.23 W
Bull Run Lake ⊜	224	45.27 N	121.50 W
Bull Run Reservoir Number 2 ⊜[1], Or., U.S.	224	45.28 N	122.10 W
Bull Run Reservoir Number 1 ⊜[1], Or., U.S.	224	45.30 N	122.04 W
Bullrun Rock ∧	202	44.21 N	118.17 W
Bulls	172	40.10 S	175.23 E
Bulls Bay c	192	32.59 N	79.33 W
Bullsbrook	168a	31.40 S	116.01 E
Bulls Gap	192	36.15 N	83.05 W
Bull Shoals	194	36.23 N	92.34 W
Bull Shoals Lake ⊜[1]	194	36.30 N	92.50 W
Bullskin Creek ≃	218	38.10 N	85.19 W
Bullville	210	41.33 N	74.22 W
Bully Creek ≃	202	43.58 N	117.15 W
Bully Hill	214	41.22 N	79.50 W
Bully-les-Mines	50	50.26 N	2.43 E
Bulmke-Hüllen ◆[8]	263	51.31 N	7.06 E
Bulnaj nuruu ⋏	88	49.05 N	98.30 E
Bulnes	252	36.44 S	72.18 W
Bulo Ghedudo	144	2.52 N	43.01 E
Bulolo	164	7.10 S	146.40 E
Bulpham	260	51.33 N	0.22 E
Bulpitt	219	39.35 N	89.26 W
Bulsār	122	20.38 N	72.56 E
Bulstrode ≃	206	46.02 N	72.15 W
Bultei	71	40.27 N	9.03 E
Bultfontein	158	28.20 S	26.05 E
Buluan	116	6.44 N	124.47 E
Buluan ≃	116	6.47 N	124.47 E
Buluan, Lake ⊜	116	6.40 N	124.49 E
Buluduku	114	2.20 N	98.14 E
Bulugansk	88	52.24 N	110.23 E
Bulukumba	112	5.33 S	120.11 E
Bulukuto	152	0.12 S	21.42 E
Bululawang	115a	8.05 S	112.38 E
Bulungu, Zaïre	152	6.04 S	21.54 E
Bulungu, Zaïre	152	4.33 S	18.36 E
Bulupayung	114	1.38 N	99.11 E
Bulusan	116	12.45 N	124.08 E
Bulusan Volcano ∧	116	12.46 N	124.03 E
Bulwater	158	32.29 S	21.48 E
Bulwer	158	29.46 S	29.47 E
Bulyčevo	82	55.06 N	37.15 E
Bulyee	162	32.22 S	117.31 E
Bumba	152	2.11 N	22.28 E
Bumbah, Khalīj al- c	146	32.20 N	23.10 E
Bumbire Island I	154	1.40 S	31.53 E
Bumbles Green	260	51.44 N	0.02 E
Bumbo	152	6.55 S	19.16 E
Bumbu ≃	273b	4.23 S	15.18 E
Bumbulan	112	0.29 N	122.04 E
Bumbun, Pulau I	112	4.27 N	118.40 E
Bumbuna	150	9.03 N	11.44 W
Bumbunga Lake ⊜	168b	33.54 S	138.11 E
Bumiayu	115a	7.15 S	109.00 E
Bumijawa	115a	7.10 S	109.07 E
Bumkin Island I	283	42.17 N	70.54 W
Bumping ≃	224	46.59 N	121.06 W
Bumping Lake ⊜	224	46.52 N	121.19 W
Bumpus, Mount ∧[2]	176	69.33 N	112.40 W
Bumtang ≃	124	26.56 N	90.51 E
Bumu Hu ⊜	120	31.15 N	91.10 E
Buna, Kenya	154	2.47 N	39.31 E
Buna, Pap. N. Gui.	164	8.40 S	148.25 E
Buna, Tx., U.S.	194	30.26 N	93.58 W
Buna, Zaïre	152	3.15 S	18.59 E
Bunagāti	126	23.19 N	89.25 E
Bunai	164	2.11 S	147.14 E
Bunaj	85	38.26 N	71.32 E
Bun'atino	82	56.24 N	37.15 E
Bunavista	196	35.39 N	101.28 W
Bunawan	116	8.12 N	125.57 E
Bunazi	154	1.13 S	31.24 E
Bunbeg	48	55.03 N	8.18 W
Bunbury	168a	33.19 S	115.38 E
Bunceton	194	38.47 N	92.47 W
Bunclody	48	52.38 N	6.40 W
Buncrana	48	55.08 N	7.27 W
Bundaberg	166	24.52 S	152.21 E
Bundanoon	170	34.39 S	150.18 E
Bundarra	166	30.10 S	151.05 E
Bunde, Dtsch.	52	53.11 N	7.16 E
Bünde, Dtsch.	52	52.12 N	8.35 E
Bunde, Ned.	56	50.54 N	5.45 E
Bundeena	274a	34.05 S	151.09 E
Bundenthal	56	49.06 N	7.48 E
Bundey ≃	162	21.46 S	135.37 E
Bündheim	54	51.53 N	10.32 E
Būndi, India	120	25.27 N	75.39 E
Bundi, Pap. N. Gui.	164	5.40 S	145.15 E
Bundick Creek ≃	194	30.36 N	92.57 W
Bundoora	274b	37.42 S	145.04 E
Bundoran	48	54.28 N	8.17 W
Būndu, India	124	23.11 N	85.35 E
Bundu, S. Afr.	158	29.45 S	22.02 E
Bunduqiyah	154	5.06 N	30.53 E
Bund'ur	86	57.32 N	82.01 E
Buner □[9]	123	34.35 N	72.35 E
Bunessan	46	56.19 N	6.14 W
Bunga	150	11.04 N	9.38 E
Bunga ≃	150	11.23 N	9.56 E
Bungamas	112	3.42 S	102.23 E
Bungay	42	52.28 N	1.26 E
Bungbulang	115a	7.27 S	107.35 E
Bunge	26	57.51 N	19.01 E
Bungegep	164	7.48 S	139.52 E
Bungendore	171b	35.15 S	149.27 E
Bunger Hills ⋏[2]	9	66.17 S	100.47 E
Bung Kan	110	18.23 N	103.37 E
Bungku	112	2.33 S	121.58 E
Bungo	152	7.26 S	15.23 E
Bungoma	154	0.34 N	34.34 E
Bungonia	170	34.51 S	149.57 E
Bungo-suidō Ʉ	92	33.00 N	132.13 E
Bungo-takada	96	33.33 N	131.27 E
Bungsberg ∧[2]	54	54.12 N	10.43 E
Bungtlang	120	22.20 N	92.46 E
Bungu	154	7.38 S	39.03 E
Buni ≃	115a	7.26 S	106.47 E
Bunia	154	1.34 N	30.15 E
Bunianga	152	3.34 S	20.06 E
Būnīken, Kūh-e ∧	128	26.46 N	58.12 E
Buninyong	169	37.39 S	143.53 E
Buninyong, Mount ∧	169	37.39 S	143.56 E
Bunji	123	35.40 N	74.36 E
Bunkeflo strand	41	55.33 N	12.57 E
Bunker	194	37.27 N	91.12 W
Bunker Group II	166	23.48 S	152.20 E
Bunker Hill, Il., U.S.	219	39.02 N	89.57 W
Bunker Hill, In., U.S.	216	40.40 N	86.06 W
Bunker Hill, Or., U.S.	202	43.21 N	124.12 W
Bunker Hill, Tx., U.S.	222	29.46 N	95.32 W
Bunker Hill ∧	204	39.15 N	117.08 W
Bunker Hill Monument ⊥	283	42.22 N	71.04 W
Bunkeya	154	10.07 S	27.17 E
Bunkie	194	30.57 N	92.10 W
Bunkyō ◆[8]	268	35.43 N	139.45 E
Bunnahowen	48	54.11 N	9.54 W
Bunnell	192	29.27 N	81.15 W
Bunnik	52	52.04 N	5.12 E
Bünningstedt	52	53.41 N	10.13 E
Bunola	214	40.14 N	79.56 W
Bun Plains ≡	154	0.44 N	40.42 E
Bunratty Castle ⊥	48	52.42 N	8.48 W
Bunschoten	52	52.14 N	5.22 E
Bunsuru ≃	150	13.21 N	6.23 E
Bunta	112	0.48 S	122.10 E
Buntine	162	29.59 S	116.34 E
Buntingford	42	51.57 N	0.01 W
Buntok	112	1.42 S	114.48 E
Bununu Dass	150	10.00 N	9.31 E
Bunut	112	0.46 N	112.30 E
Bunyambili	154	2.21 S	29.25 E
Bünyan	130	38.51 N	35.52 E
Bunyip	169	38.06 S	145.43 E
Bunyip ≃	169	38.13 S	145.27 E
Bunyolo	34	39.25 N	0.47 W
Bunyrevo	82	54.34 N	37.09 E
Bunyu, Pulau I	112	3.30 N	117.50 E
Bunza	150	12.08 N	4.00 E
Buochs	58	46.58 N	8.22 E
Buol	112	1.10 N	121.26 E
Buolkalach	74	72.56 N	119.50 E
Buonalbergo	68	41.13 N	14.59 E
Buona Vista	271c	1.16 N	103.47 E
Buon Bu N'jang	110	12.06 N	107.40 E
Buonconvento	66	43.08 N	11.29 E
Buon Me Thuot	110	12.40 N	108.03 E
Buon Mrong	110	12.48 N	108.28 E
Buon Ngo	110	12.30 N	108.28 E
Buon Thach Hom	110	12.17 N	108.48 E
Buon Ya Soup	110	13.05 N	107.52 E
Buor-Chaja, guba c	74	71.30 N	131.00 E
Buor-Chaja, mys ›	74	71.56 N	132.40 E
Bupul	164	7.31 S	140.52 E
Buqay'āwīyah, Qā' al- ≡	132	32.03 N	37.07 E
Buqayq	128	25.56 N	49.40 E
Buqda Koosaar	144	4.31 N	44.49 E
Buqde Caqable	144	4.04 N	45.15 E
Buquira ≃	256	23.10 S	45.54 W
Buquirivu ≃	287b	23.28 S	46.28 W
Buqūm, Ḥarrat al- ±[9]	144	20.54 N	42.00 E
Bur	88	58.47 N	107.01 E
Bura, Kenya	154	3.30 S	38.18 E
Bura, Kenya	154	1.06 S	39.57 E
Bura Gaurānga ≃[1]	126	22.00 N	90.33 E
Burakin	162	30.31 S	117.10 E
Buraly	80	55.04 N	52.52 E
Buram	140	10.49 N	25.10 E
Buran	86	48.04 N	85.15 E
Burang	120	30.16 N	81.14 E
Burangulovo	86	53.26 N	58.23 E
Buranhém ≃	255	16.27 S	39.04 W
Burankol'	86	46.14 N	54.12 E
Burannoje	86	50.59 N	54.28 E
Burano ≃	66	43.37 N	12.40 E
Burao Kibir	144	8.42 N	45.29 E
Burāq	132	33.10 N	36.29 E
Burāri ◆[8]	272a	28.46 N	77.12 E
Buras	194	29.21 N	89.31 W
Buraševo	82	56.44 N	35.52 E
Burauen	116	10.58 N	124.53 E
Burayd, Bi'r ⊤[4]	142	29.08 N	32.07 E
Buraydah	128	26.20 N	43.59 E
Burayk	146	26.33 N	13.08 E
Buraykah	132	32.50 N	36.34 E
Burbach	56	50.45 N	8.05 E
Burbage, Eng., U.K.	42	51.20 N	1.40 W
Burbage, Eng., U.K.	262	53.15 N	1.56 W
Burbank, Ca., U.S.	226	37.19 N	121.55 W
Burbank, Ca., U.S.	228	34.10 N	118.18 W
Burbank, Il., U.S.	216	41.45 N	87.45 W
Burbank, Oh., U.S.	214	40.59 N	81.59 W
Burbank, Wa., U.S.	202	46.12 N	119.00 W
Burbank Studios ♥[3]	280	34.09 N	118.21 W
Burbure	50	50.32 N	2.28 E
Burç	130	37.02 N	37.10 E
Burcei	71	39.21 N	9.21 E
Burcevo	82	55.02 N	38.09 E
Burcher	166	33.32 S	147.18 E
Burcin	62	45.26 N	5.26 E
Burco	144	9.31 N	45.34 E
Burda	124	25.50 N	77.35 E
Burdalyk	128	38.25 N	64.20 E
Burdekin ≃	166	19.39 S	147.30 E
Burdekin Falls ⌊	166	20.39 S	147.09 E
Burden	198	37.18 N	96.45 W
Burdeos	116	14.51 N	121.58 E
Burdeos Bay c	116	14.44 N	122.06 E
Burdeos → Bordeaux	32	44.50 N	0.34 W
Burdett, Ab., Can.	182	49.50 N	111.32 W
Burdett, Ks., U.S.	198	38.11 N	99.31 W
Burdett, N.Y., U.S.	210	42.25 N	76.50 W
Burdul	272c	19.07 N	73.07 E
Burdur	130	37.43 N	30.17 E
Burdur □[4]	130	37.30 N	30.00 E
Burdur Gölü ⊜	130	37.44 N	30.12 E
Burdwood Bank ✦[3]	18	54.15 S	59.00 W
Bure, Ityo.	144	8.15 N	35.09 E
Bure, Ityo.	144	10.47 N	37.06 E
Bure ≃	42	52.37 N	1.43 E
Bure, Pic de ∧	62	44.38 N	5.56 E
Bureå	26	64.37 N	21.12 E
Bureälven ≃	26	64.37 N	21.13 E
Bureg Changaj	88	48.14 N	103.57 E
Bureinskij chrebet ⋏	89	50.35 N	133.35 E
Bureja	89	49.52 N	129.48 E
Bureja ≃	89	49.25 N	129.35 E
Burekup	168a	33.19 S	115.49 E
Büren, Dtsch.	52	51.33 N	8.33 E
Büren, Mong.	88	47.13 N	95.54 E
Büren an der Aare	58	47.08 N	7.23 E
Büren Chaan	88	49.29 N	99.14 E
Bürengijn nuruu ⋏	88	49.15 N	104.30 E
Bures	261	48.57 N	1.58 E
Bures-sur-Yvette	261	48.42 N	2.10 E
Burey-en-Vaux	58	48.34 N	5.40 E
Burfjord	24	69.56 N	22.00 E
Burford, On., Can.	212	43.06 N	80.26 W
Burford, Eng., U.K.	42	51.49 N	1.38 W
Būr Fu'ād ◆[8]	142	31.15 N	32.19 E
Burg, Dtsch.	54	51.49 N	14.08 E
Burg, Dtsch.	54	52.16 N	11.51 E
Burg, Dtsch.	56	50.42 N	8.19 E
Burg ◆[8]	263	51.08 N	7.09 E
Burg, Schloss ⊥	263	51.08 N	7.10 E
Burga	76	58.45 N	32.29 E
Burgas	38	42.30 N	27.28 E
Burgas □[4]	130	42.10 N	27.00 E
Burgaski zaliv c	38	42.30 N	27.33 E
Burgau	58	48.26 N	10.25 E
Burg [auf Fehmarn]	54	54.26 N	11.12 E
Burgaw	192	34.33 N	77.55 W
Burgaz ◆[8]	267b	40.53 N	29.03 E
Burgaz Adası I	267b	40.53 N	29.04 E
Burgbernheim	56	49.27 N	10.19 E
Burgdorf, Dtsch.	52	52.27 N	10.00 E
Burgdorf, Schw.	58	47.04 N	7.37 E
Burgebrach	56	49.50 N	10.44 E
Bürgel	54	50.56 N	11.45 E
Burgenland □[3]	61	47.30 N	16.20 E
Burgeo	186	47.37 N	57.37 W
Burgersdorp	158	31.00 S	26.20 E
Burger Township	273d	26.05 S	27.46 E
Burges, Mount ∧[2]	162	30.50 S	121.06 E
Burgess	208	37.53 N	76.21 W
Burgess Hill	42	50.57 N	0.07 W
Burgessville	212	43.01 N	80.39 W
Burgettstown	214	40.22 N	80.23 W
Burggrafenberg ∧[2]	263	51.13 N	7.07 E
Burghausen	60	48.09 N	12.49 E
Burghead	46	57.42 N	3.30 W
Burgheim	60	48.42 N	11.01 E
Burgh Heath	260	51.18 N	0.13 W
Burghill	214	41.22 N	80.34 W
Burgh le Marsh	44	53.09 N	0.15 E
Burghūth, Sabkhat al- ⊜	130	34.58 N	41.06 E
Burgin	194	37.45 N	84.46 W
Burgio	70	37.36 N	13.17 E
Burgjoss	56	50.12 N	9.29 E
Burgkirchen	60	48.12 N	13.06 E
Burgkunstadt	54	50.08 N	11.14 E
Bürglen, Schw.	58	46.53 N	8.40 E
Bürglen, Schw.	58	47.33 N	9.09 E
Burglengenfeld	60	49.13 N	12.03 E
Burgoon	214	41.16 N	83.15 W
Burgos, Esp.	34	42.21 N	3.42 W
Burgos, It.	71	40.23 N	8.59 E
Burgos, Méx.	232	24.57 N	98.47 W
Burgos, Pil.	116	16.04 N	119.52 E
Burgos, Pil.	116	15.30 N	120.24 E
Burgos □[4]	34	42.20 N	3.40 W
Burgsinn	56	50.09 N	9.38 E
Burgstädt	54	50.55 N	12.49 E
Burgstall	54	52.24 N	11.41 E
Burgstall → Postal	64	46.36 N	11.11 E
Burg Stargard	54	53.29 N	13.18 E
Burgsvik	26	57.03 N	18.16 E
Burgueño, Arroyo ≃	288	34.24 S	58.47 W
Burgund → Bourgogne □[9]	32	47.00 N	4.30 E
Burgundy → Bourgogne □[9]	32	47.00 N	4.30 E
Burgusio (Burgeis)	64	46.42 N	10.31 E
Burgwedel	52	52.29 N	9.51 E
Burgwindheim	56	49.49 N	10.35 E
Burhābalang ≃	126	21.28 N	87.04 E
Burham	260	51.20 N	0.29 E
Burhan Budai Shan ⋏	102	36.00 N	96.00 E
Burhaniye, Tür.	130	37.57 N	28.45 E
Burhaniye, Tür.	130	39.30 N	26.58 E
Burhānpur	120	21.18 N	76.14 E
Burhar	124	23.13 N	81.32 E
Burhave	52	53.34 N	8.21 E
Burholme ◆[8]	285	40.03 N	75.05 W
Buri	255	23.48 S	48.35 W
Burias Island I	116	12.57 N	123.08 E
Burias Pass Ʉ	116	13.00 N	123.15 E
Buribaj	86	51.57 N	58.11 E
Būr Ibrāhīm ◆[8]	142	29.57 N	32.34 E
Burica, Punta ›	236	8.03 N	82.53 W
Burien	224	47.28 N	122.20 W
Burigi, Lake ⊜	154	2.05 S	31.15 E
Burila Mare	38	44.27 N	22.34 E
Burin	186	47.02 N	55.10 W
Burin Peninsula ›[1]	186	47.00 N	55.40 W
Buri Ram	110	15.00 N	103.07 E
Buriswar ≃[1]	126	21.58 N	90.02 E
Buritama	255	21.03 S	50.08 W
Buriti, Bra.	250	3.55 S	42.57 W
Buriti, Bra.	255	16.27 S	53.27 W
Buriti ≃	248	12.50 S	58.28 W
Buriti Alegre	255	18.09 S	49.03 W
Buriti Bravo	250	5.50 S	43.50 W
Buriticupu ≃	250	4.13 S	46.33 W
Buriti dos Lopes	250	3.10 S	41.52 W
Buritizeiro	255	17.21 S	44.58 W
Būriya	124	30.09 N	77.21 E
Burj al-'Arab	140	30.55 N	29.32 E
Burjassot	34	39.31 N	0.25 W
Burjatskaja Avtonomnaja Sovetskaja Socialističeskaja Respublika □[3]	88	53.00 N	109.00 E
Burji	144	5.20 N	37.57 E
Burj Islām	130	35.41 N	35.48 E
Burj Mughayzil	142	31.27 N	30.23 E
Burkan ≃	85	41.43 N	76.46 E
Burkau	54	51.10 N	14.10 E
Burkburnett	196	34.05 N	98.34 W
Burke, S.D., U.S.	198	43.10 N	99.17 W
Burke, Tx., U.S.	222	31.14 N	94.46 W
Burke, Va., U.S.	284c	38.47 N	77.16 W
Burke ≃	166	23.12 S	139.33 E

Symbols in the index entries represent the broad categories identified in the key at the right. Symbols with superior numbers (⋏[1]) identify subcategories (see complete key on page I · 1).

Symbole im Register stellen die rechts im Schlüssel erklärten Kategorien dar. Symbole mit hochgestellten Ziffern (⋏[1]) bezeichnen Unterabteilungen einer Kategorie (vgl. vollständiger Schlüssel auf Seite I · 1).

Los símbolos incluídos en el texto del índice representan las grandes categorías identificadas con la clave a la derecha. Los símbolos con numeros en su parte superior (⋏[1]) identifican las subcategorías (véase la clave completa en la página I · 1).

Les symboles de l'index représentent les catégories indiquées dans la légende à droite. Les symboles suivis d'un indice (⋏[1]) représentent des sous-catégories (voir légende complète à la page I · 1).

Os símbolos incluídos no texto do índice representam as grandes categorias identificadas com a chave à direita. Os símbolos com números em sua parte superior (⋏[1]) identificam as subcategorias (veja-se a chave completa à página I · 1).

	English	Deutsch	Español	Français	Português
∧	Mountain	Berg	Montaña	Montagne	Montanha
⋏	Mountains	Gebirge	Montañas	Montagnes	Montanhas
×	Pass	Paß	Paso	Col	Passo
V	Valley, Canyon	Tal, Cañon	Valle, Cañón	Vallée, Canyon	Vale, Canhão
≡	Plain	Ebene	Llano	Plaine	Planície
›	Cape	Kap	Cabo	Cap	Cabo
I	Island	Insel	Isla	Île	Ilha
II	Islands	Inseln	Islas	Îles	Ilhas
±	Other Topographic Features	Andere Topographische Objekte	Otros Elementos Topográficos	Autres données topographiques	Outros acidentes topográficos

ESPAÑOL — Nombre | Página | Lat.°′ | Long.°′ W = Oeste
FRANÇAIS — Nom | Page | Lat.°′ | Long.°′ W = Ouest
PORTUGUÊS — Nome | Página | Lat.°′ | Long.°′ W = Oeste

Burke Channel ʊ 182 52.07 N 127.38 W
Burke Island I 9 73.15 S 104.35 W
Burke Lake County Park ♠ 284c 38.45 N 77.18 W
Burke Lakefront Airport ⊠ 279a 41.31 N 81.41 W
Burkesville 194 36.47 N 85.22 W
Burket 216 41.09 N 85.58 W
Burketown 166 17.43 S 139.34 E
Burkett Gardens 226 37.57 N 121.15 W
Burkettsville 216 40.21 N 84.39 W
Burkhardtsdorf 54 50.44 N 12.55 E
Burkina Faso □[1], Afr. 134 13.00 N 1.30 W
Burkina Faso □[1], Afr. 150 13.00 N 1.30 W
Burkit 80 47.03 N 50.42 E
Burksville 219 38.16 N 90.09 W
Burla 86 53.19 N 78.21 E
Burla ≃ 86 53.20 N 78.02 E
Burladingen 58 48.17 N 9.07 E
Burleigh 208 39.02 N 74.51 W
Burleigh Falls 212 44.34 N 78.13 W
Burleigh Heads 171a 28.06 S 153.27 E
Burleson 222 32.32 N 97.19 W
Burleson □[6] 222 30.30 N 96.43 W
Burley, Id., U.S. 202 42.32 N 113.47 W
Burley, Wa., U.S. 224 47.25 N 122.37 W
Burley Griffin, Lake ⊜ 171b 35.13 S 149.05 E
Burli, Kaz. 80 51.25 N 52.44 E
Burli, Kaz. 86 53.36 N 61.55 E
Burlingame, Ca., U.S. 226 37.35 N 122.21 W
Burlingame, Ks., U.S. 198 38.45 N 95.00 W
Burlingame State Park ♠ 207 41.22 N 71.43 W
Burlington, Nf., Can. 186 49.45 N 56.02 W
Burlington, On., Can. 212 43.19 N 79.47 W
Burlington, Co., U.S. 198 39.18 N 102.16 W
Burlington, Ct., U.S. 207 41.46 N 72.57 W
Burlington, Il., U.S. 216 42.03 N 88.33 W
Burlington, In., U.S. 216 40.29 N 86.24 W
Burlington, Ia., U.S. 190 40.48 N 91.06 W
Burlington, Ks., U.S. 198 38.11 N 95.44 W
Burlington, Ky., U.S. 218 39.01 N 84.43 W
Burlington, Ma., U.S. 207 42.30 N 71.11 W
Burlington, Mi., U.S. 216 42.06 N 85.05 W
Burlington, N.J., U.S. 208 40.04 N 74.51 W
Burlington, N.C., U.S. 192 36.05 N 79.26 W
Burlington, N.D., U.S. 198 48.16 N 101.25 W
Burlington, Pa., U.S. 210 41.47 N 76.37 W
Burlington, Tx., U.S. 222 31.01 N 96.60 W
Burlington, Vt., U.S. 188 44.28 N 73.12 W
Burlington, Wa., U.S. 224 48.28 N 122.19 W
Burlington, Wi., U.S. 216 42.40 N 88.16 W
Burlington, Wy., U.S. 202 44.26 N 108.25 W
Burlington □[6] 208 39.50 N 74.47 W
Burlington Beach 216 41.30 N 87.03 W
Burlington County Airpark ⊠ 285 39.56 N 74.50 W
Burlington Island I 285 40.05 N 74.51 W
Burlington Junction 194 40.26 N 95.03 W
Burlington Mall ◆[9] 283 42.29 N 71.13 W
Burlit 89 46.33 N 134.14 E
Burluk 80 50.34 N 44.33 E
Burma (Myanmar) □[1] 110 22.00 N 98.00 E
Burmā, Tall ∧ 132 30.38 N 35.50 E
Burmakino 80 57.27 N 40.20 E
Burn ≃ 44 54.12 N 1.38 W
Burnaby 224 49.15 N 122.57 W
Burnaby Island I 182 52.24 N 131.20 W
Burnage 262 53.26 N 2.12 W
Burnas, ozero ⊜ 78 45.52 N 30.08 E
Burnet 196 30.45 N 98.13 W
Burnett ≃ 166 24.46 S 152.25 E
Burnett Bay c 176 73.53 N 124.00 W
Burnett Brook ≃ 276 40.46 N 74.38 W
Burnett Heads 166 24.46 S 152.25 E
Burnettsville 216 40.46 N 86.36 W
Burney, Ca., U.S. 204 40.52 N 121.39 W
Burney, In., U.S. 218 39.19 N 85.38 W
Burnham, Eng., U.K. 260 51.33 N 0.39 W
Burnham, Il., U.S. 278 41.39 N 87.34 W
Burnham, Pa., U.S. 208 40.38 N 77.34 W
Burnham Beeches ◆[3] 260 51.34 N 0.38 W
Burnham Market 42 52.57 N 0.44 E
Burnham-on-Crouch 42 51.38 N 0.49 E
Burnham-on-Sea 42 51.15 N 3.00 W
Burnhamthorpe 275b 43.37 N 79.36 W
Burnhaven 46 57.29 N 1.47 W
Burnie 166 41.04 S 145.54 E
Burning Tree Estates 284c 39.01 N 77.12 W
Burnips 216 42.44 N 85.50 W
Burniston 44 54.19 N 0.26 W
Burnley 44 53.48 N 2.14 W
Burnley □[8] 262 53.46 N 2.15 W
Burnley Creek ≃ 212 44.13 N 77.51 W
Burnley Football Ground ♠ 262 53.48 N 2.14 W
Burnmouth 46 55.50 N 2.04 W
Burnoje 85 42.37 N 70.46 E
Burno-Okt'abr'skoje 85 42.42 N 70.49 E
Burnpur 126 23.40 N 86.57 E
Burns, Ks., U.S. 198 38.05 N 96.53 W
Burns, Or., U.S. 202 43.35 N 119.03 W
Burns, Tn., U.S. 194 36.03 N 87.18 W
Burns, Wy., U.S. 198 41.11 N 104.21 W
Burns Creek ≃ 198 47.22 N 104.25 W
Burns Flat 196 35.20 N 99.10 W
Burns Harbor 216 41.37 N 87.10 W
Burnside, Austl. 168b 34.57 S 138.40 E
Burnside, Ky., U.S. 192 36.59 N 84.36 W
Burnside, Pa., U.S. 214 40.49 N 78.47 W
Burnside ≃ 176 66.51 N 108.04 W
Burnside, Lake ⊜ 162 25.33 S 123.02 E
Burns Lake 182 54.14 N 125.46 W
Burnsville, Al., U.S. 194 32.28 N 86.53 W
Burnsville, Ms., U.S. 194 34.50 N 88.18 W
Burnsville, N.C., U.S. 192 35.55 N 82.18 W
Burnsville, W.V., U.S. 188 38.51 N 80.39 W
Burnt ≃, On., Can. 212 44.35 N 78.46 W
Burnt ≃, Or., U.S. 202 44.22 N 117.14 W
Burnt Cabins 214 40.05 N 77.54 W
Burnt Corn Creek ≃ 194 31.06 N 87.04 W
Burnt Hills 210 42.54 N 73.53 W
Burnt Island, Nf., Can. 186 47.36 N 58.53 W
Burntisland, Scot., U.K. 46 56.03 N 3.15 W
Burnt Meadow Brook ≃ 276 41.05 N 74.18 W
Burnt Mills, Lake ⊜ 208 36.50 N 76.38 W
Burnt Mills Hills 284c 39.02 N 77.00 W
Burnt Mills Manor 284c 39.02 N 77.00 W
Burnt Mountain ∧ 228 33.12 N 117.04 W
Burntop 158 26.49 S 30.54 E
Burnt Pine 174c 29.02 S 167.56 E
Burnt Pond ⊜ 186 48.11 N 57.24 W
Burntwick Island I 260 51.25 N 0.41 E
Burntwood 42 52.41 N 1.56 W
Burntwood ≃ 184 56.08 N 96.30 W
Burntwood Lake ⊜ 184 55.29 N 100.07 W
Burnyj, porog ∟ 86 57.43 N 95.18 E
Buro 144 11.28 N 49.41 E
Buron 84 42.48 N 44.03 E
Buronzo 62 45.29 N 8.16 E
Burow 54 53.46 N 13.16 E
Burpengary 171a 27.10 S 152.57 E
Burpham 260 51.15 N 0.33 W
Burqin 86 47.43 N 86.53 E
Burqin ≃ 86 47.40 N 86.55 E
Burra 166 33.40 S 138.56 E
Burra Burra Creek ≃ 170 34.10 S 149.38 E
Burracoppin 162 31.23 S 118.29 E
Burra Creek ≃ 168b 33.51 S 139.18 E
Burrage 283 42.02 N 70.51 W
Burrage Pond ⊜ 283 42.01 N 70.52 W
Burragorang, Lake ⊜[1] 170 33.57 S 150.26 E
Burramurra 166 20.30 S 137.20 E
Burravoe 46a 60.32 N 1.28 W
Burrawang 170 34.36 S 150.31 E
Burray I 46 58.51 N 2.54 W
Burrel, Shq. 38 41.37 N 20.00 E
Burrel, Ca., U.S. 226 36.30 N 119.59 W
Burrendong Reservoir ⊜[1] 166 32.39 S 149.15 E
Burren Junction 166 30.06 S 148.58 E
Burrill Lake c 170 35.23 S 150.27 E
Burrinjuck Reservoir ⊜[1] 166 35.00 S 148.45 E
Burro, Serranías del ⋏ 196 29.10 N 102.05 W
Burr Oak, In., U.S. 216 41.15 N 86.25 W
Burr Oak, Ks., U.S. 198 39.51 N 98.18 W
Burr Oak, Mi., U.S. 216 41.50 N 85.19 W
Burro Burro ≃ 246 4.48 N 58.51 W
Burro Creek ≃ 200 34.32 N 113.35 W
Burro Peak ∧ 200 32.35 N 108.26 W
Burrowa, Mount ∧ 171b 36.05 S 147.42 E
Burrowa-Pine Mountain National Park ♠ 171b 36.06 S 147.44 E
Burrow Head > 44 54.41 N 4.24 W
Burrowhill 260 51.21 N 0.36 W
Burrows 216 40.40 N 86.30 W
Burrows Island I 224 48.29 N 122.42 W
Burr Ridge 278 41.46 N 87.55 W
Burrs Mill Brook ≃ 285 39.53 N 74.42 W
Burrton 198 38.01 N 97.40 W
Burrumbeet, Lake ⊜ 169 37.30 S 143.39 E
Burrundie 164 13.32 S 131.42 E
Burruyacú 252 26.30 S 64.45 W
Burrwood 194 28.58 N 89.22 W
Burry Holms I 42 51.37 N 4.18 W
Burry Port 42 51.42 N 4.15 W
Bürs 58 47.09 N 9.48 E
Bursa 130 40.11 N 29.04 E
Bursa □[4] 130 40.10 N 29.00 E
Būr Safājah 140 26.44 N 33.56 E
Būr Sa'īd (Port Said) 142 31.16 N 32.18 E
Būr Sa'īd □[4] 142 30.36 N 32.15 E
Burscheid 56 51.05 N 7.06 E
Burscough 262 53.35 N 2.51 W
Burscough Bridge, Eng., U.K. 44 53.36 N 2.52 W
Burscough Bridge, Eng., U.K. 262 53.36 N 2.51 W
Bursey, Mount ∧ 9 76.00 S 132.40 W
Bursol' 86 53.11 N 78.27 E
Bürstadt 56 49.38 N 8.27 E
Burstall 184 50.40 N 109.54 W
Burštyn 78 49.17 N 24.37 E
Būr Sūdān (Port Sudan) 140 19.37 N 37.14 E
Burt, Ia., U.S. 190 43.11 N 94.13 W
Burt, N.Y., U.S. 210 43.19 N 78.43 W
Būr Tawfīq ◆[8] 128 29.57 N 32.34 E
Burtenbach 58 48.20 N 10.26 E
Burt Lake ⊜ 190 45.27 N 84.40 W
Burtnieku ezers ⊜ 76 57.45 N 25.16 E
Burton, B.C., Can. 182 49.59 N 117.54 W
Burton, Eng., U.K. 42 50.44 N 1.45 W
Burton, Eng., U.K. 262 53.16 N 3.01 W
Burton, Il., U.S. 219 39.55 N 91.15 W
Burton, Mi., U.S. 216 43.02 N 83.36 W
Burton, Mi., U.S. 216 43.01 N 84.16 W
Burton, Oh., U.S. 214 41.28 N 81.08 W
Burton, Tx., U.S. 222 30.11 N 96.36 W
Burton, Wa., U.S. 224 47.23 N 122.27 W
Burton, Lake ⊜[1] 192 34.50 N 83.33 W
Burton Fleming 44 54.08 N 0.20 W
Burton Latimer 42 52.23 N 0.41 W
Burtons Bridge 216 42.17 N 88.14 W
Burton Seamount ✢[3] 14 32.00 S 171.45 W
Burtonsville 208 39.07 N 76.56 W
Burton upon Stather 44 53.39 N 0.41 W
Burton upon Trent 42 52.49 N 1.36 W
Burtonwood 262 53.26 N 2.39 W
Burtonwood Airfield ⊠ 262 53.24 N 2.39 W
Burträsk 26 64.31 N 20.39 E
Burtundy 166 33.44 S 142.16 E
Burṭus 142 30.09 N 31.08 E
Buru I 108 3.24 S 126.40 E
Buruanga 116 11.51 N 121.53 E
Burukan 89 53.02 N 136.03 E
Buruldaj 85 42.48 N 75.52 E
Burullus, Buḥayrat al- ⊜ 142 31.30 N 30.50 E
Burūm 144 14.22 N 48.57 E
Burundaj 85 43.23 N 76.51 E
Burundi □[1], Afr. 138 3.15 S 30.00 E
Burundi □[1], Afr. 154 3.15 S 30.00 E
Burundučicha 80 58.21 N 46.07 E
Burun-Šibertuj, gora ∧ 88 49.42 N 109.59 E
Bururi 154 3.57 S 29.37 E
Burutu 150 5.21 N 5.31 E
Buruz Bāgān 126 23.03 N 89.00 E
Burwash 190 46.19 N 80.48 W
Burwash Landing 180 61.21 N 139.00 W
Burwell, Eng., U.K. 42 52.16 N 0.19 E
Burwell, Ne., U.S. 198 41.46 N 99.07 W
Burwell Bay c 208 37.04 N 76.38 W
Burwick 46 58.44 N 2.57 W
Burwood, Austl. 274a 33.53 S 151.06 E
Burwood, Austl. 274b 37.51 S 145.06 E
Bury, P.Q., Can. 206 45.28 N 71.30 W
Bury, Eng., U.K. 42 50.54 N 0.34 W
Bury, Eng., U.K. 262 53.36 N 2.17 W
Bury □[8] 262 53.35 N 2.19 W
Buryn' 78 51.13 N 33.49 E
Bury Saint Edmunds 42 52.15 N 0.43 E
Burzaco 258 34.49 S 58.24 W
Burzet 62 44.44 N 4.15 E
Burzil 123 34.52 N 75.07 E
Burzil Pass)(123 34.54 N 75.06 E
Būṣ, Ghubbat al- c 142 29.36 N 32.22 E
Busa, Mount ∧ 116 6.08 N 124.39 E
Busachi 71 40.02 N 8.54 E
Busalla 62 44.34 N 8.57 E
Busambra, Rocca ∧ 70 37.51 N 13.24 E
Busana 64 44.22 N 10.19 E
Busanga 152 0.51 S 22.04 E
Busanga Swamp ≡ 154 14.10 S 25.50 E
Busangu 154 8.32 S 25.31 E
Busan → Pusan 98 35.06 N 129.03 E
Buṣayrah 130 35.09 N 40.26 E
Busby, Austl. 274a 33.54 S 150.53 E
Busby, Mt., U.S. 202 45.32 N 106.57 W
Busca 62 44.31 N 7.29 E
Buscate 266b 45.32 N 8.49 E
Buscbusc ≃ 144 1.08 S 41.49 E
Buschberg ∧[2] 61 48.34 N 16.23 E
Busche 64 46.02 N 11.59 E
Busch Gardens ♠ 280 34.13 N 118.28 W
Buschhausen ◆[8] 263 51.30 N 6.51 E
Busdorf 41 54.29 N 9.32 E
Buseck 56 50.36 N 8.47 E
Buseto Palizzolo 70 38.01 N 12.43 E
Būsh 142 29.09 N 31.08 E
Bush ≃, N. Ire., U.K. 44 55.13 N 6.32 W
Bush ≃, S.C., U.S. 192 34.08 N 81.36 W
Būshehr □[4] 128 28.50 N 51.20 E
Bushenyi 154 0.32 S 30.11 E
Bushey 260 51.39 N 0.22 W
Bushey Heath 260 51.38 N 0.20 W
Bushi 268 35.50 N 139.22 E
Bushimaie ≃ 152 6.02 S 23.45 E
Bushiribana 241s 12.33 N 69.58 W
Bushkill 210 41.06 N 75.00 W
Bush Kill ≃ 210 41.05 N 74.59 W
Bushkill Falls ∟ 210 41.09 N 75.01 W
Bushland 196 35.11 N 102.04 W
Bush Lot 246 6.12 N 57.16 W
Bushman Land □[9] 158 29.15 S 20.00 E
Bushmills 48 55.12 N 6.32 W
Bushnell, Fl., U.S. 220 28.39 N 82.06 W
Bushnell, Il., U.S. 190 40.33 N 90.30 W
Bush River ≃ 208 39.21 N 76.14 W
Bushton 198 38.30 N 98.23 W
Bū Shubayrim, Wādī V 146 27.07 N 19.30 E
Bushwick ◆[8] 276 40.42 N 73.55 W
Bushy Park 166 21.16 S 139.43 E
Bushy Park ♠ 260 51.25 N 0.20 W
Bushy Run ≃ 279b 40.20 N 79.40 W
Bushy Run Battlefield ⊥ 279b 40.21 N 79.38 W
Busia 154 0.28 N 34.05 E
Busigny 50 50.02 N 3.28 E
Busing, Pulau I 271c 1.14 N 103.45 E
Businga 152 3.20 N 20.53 E
Büsingen 58 47.42 N 8.41 E
Busira ≃ 152 0.15 S 18.59 E
Busjön ⊜, Sve. 40 60.06 N 13.28 E
Busjön ⊜, Sve. 40 60.31 N 13.58 E
Busk 78 49.58 N 24.37 E
Buskerud □[6] 26 60.25 N 9.12 E
Buskhyttan 40 58.40 N 16.56 E
Busko Zdrój 30 50.28 N 20.44 E
Buskul' 86 53.45 N 61.12 E
Busle 144 5.28 N 44.25 E
Busoga □[5] 154 0.40 N 33.30 E
Busovača 36 44.06 N 17.53 E
Buṣrā al-Ḥarīrī (Bosor) 132 32.50 N 36.20 E
Buṣrá ash-Shām 132 32.31 N 36.29 E
Bussana 62 43.49 N 7.51 E
Bussang 58 47.53 N 6.51 E
Bussang, Col de)(58 47.54 N 6.54 E
Busselton 162 33.39 S 115.20 E
Busseri ≃ 140 7.41 N 28.03 E
Busseto 64 44.59 N 10.02 E
Bussey 190 41.12 N 92.52 W
Bussières 62 45.50 N 4.16 E
Bussi sul Tirino 66 42.12 N 13.49 E
Busskoje 84 43.50 N 44.37 E
Bussolengo 64 45.28 N 10.51 E
Bussoleno 62 45.08 N 7.09 E
Bussum 52 52.16 N 5.10 E
Bussy-Rabutin, Château de ⊥ 58 47.35 N 4.31 E
Bussy-Saint-Georges 261 48.51 N 2.42 E
Bustamante, Méx. 232 26.33 N 100.30 W
Bustamante, Méx. 234 23.26 N 99.47 W
Bustān, Wādī al- V 142 28.24 N 30.49 E
Buštěhrad 54 50.09 N 14.10 E
Bușteni 38 45.25 N 25.32 E
Busti 214 42.02 N 79.17 W
Bustleton ◆[8] 285 40.05 N 75.02 W
Busto Arsizio 62 45.37 N 8.51 E
Busto Garolfo 62 45.33 N 8.53 E
Buston, Taj. 85 40.31 N 69.19 E
Buston, Uzb. 128 40.04 N 64.49 E
Buštyna 78 48.04 N 23.27 E
Busu-Adula 152 2.05 N 21.40 E
Busuanga 116 12.10 N 119.55 E
Busuanga Island I 116 12.05 N 120.05 E
Busu-Djanoa 152 1.43 N 21.23 E
Bušuicha 76 59.02 N 40.26 E
Bušulej 88 52.45 N 117.13 E
Büsum 30 54.08 N 8.51 E
Busu-Melo 152 1.48 N 20.15 E
Bū Sunbul, Jabal ⋏[2] 146 23.10 N 22.21 E
Buta, Ross. 80 55.02 N 51.57 E
Buta, Zaïre 154 2.48 N 24.44 E
Butag 116 12.38 N 123.56 E
Butajira 144 8.07 N 38.22 E
Butala 164 6.42 S 147.37 E
Butan 38 43.39 N 23.45 E
Bután → Bhutan □[1] 120 27.30 N 90.30 E
Butand State Park ♠ 226 37.13 N 122.20 W
Butantã ◆[8] 287b 23.34 S 46.43 W
Butantã, Instituto ◉[3] 287b 23.34 S 46.43 W
Buta Ranquil 252 37.03 S 69.50 W
Butare 154 2.36 S 29.44 E
Butaritari I[1] 14 3.07 N 172.48 E
Butarque, Arroyo de ≃ 266a 40.19 N 3.39 W
Butauanan Island I 116 14.07 N 123.17 E
Butchart Gardens ♠ 224 48.33 N 123.28 W
Butcher Island (Dia Deva) I 272c 18.58 N 72.54 E
Bute 168b 33.52 S 138.01 E
Bute, Island of I 46 55.50 N 5.06 W
Bute, Kyles of ʊ 46 55.53 N 5.13 W
Bute, Sound of ʊ 46 55.44 N 5.12 W
Büteelijn nuruu ⋏ 88 50.00 N 104.50 E
Bute Giarti 144 4.33 N 37.45 E
Bute Inlet c 182 50.37 N 124.53 W
Butemba 154 1.09 N 31.36 E
Butembo 154 0.09 N 29.17 E
Butendorf ◆[8] 263 51.33 N 6.59 E
Butera 70 37.11 N 14.11 E
Butere 154 0.13 N 34.30 E
Bütgenbach 56 50.26 N 6.12 E
Butha Buthe 158 28.45 S 28.15 E
Butha Qi (Zalantun) 89 48.02 N 122.43 E
Buthidaung 110 20.52 N 92.32 E
Buthier ≃ 62 45.44 N 7.22 E
Buthroton ⊥ 38 39.46 N 20.00 E
Buti 66 43.44 N 10.35 E
Butiá 252 30.07 S 51.58 W
Butiaba 154 1.49 N 31.19 E
Butig Mountains ⋏ 116 7.39 N 124.20 E
Butka 86 56.47 N 63.47 E
Butler, Al., U.S. 194 32.05 N 88.13 W
Butler, Ga., U.S. 192 32.33 N 84.14 W
Butler, Il., U.S. 219 39.12 N 89.32 W
Butler, In., U.S. 216 41.25 N 84.52 W
Butler, Ky., U.S. 218 38.47 N 84.22 W
Butler, Mo., U.S. 194 38.15 N 94.19 W
Butler, N.J., U.S. 210 41.00 N 74.20 W
Butler, Oh., U.S. 214 40.35 N 82.25 W
Butler, Ok., U.S. 196 35.38 N 99.11 W
Butler, Pa., U.S. 214 40.51 N 79.53 W
Butler, Tx., U.S. 222 30.19 N 97.18 W
Butler, Wi., U.S. 216 43.06 N 88.04 W
Butler □[6], Oh., U.S. 218 39.26 N 84.30 W
Butler □[6], Pa., U.S. 214 40.52 N 79.54 W
Butler, Lake ⊜ 220 28.28 N 81.33 W
Butler Lake ⊜ 278 42.17 N 87.58 W
Butler Point > 207 41.40 N 70.43 W
Butler Reservoir ⊜[1] 276 40.59 N 74.23 W
Butlers Bridge 48 54.02 N 7.22 W
Butlerville 218 39.02 N 85.30 W
Butmīyah 132 32.56 N 35.53 E
Butnau Lake ⊜ 184 56.13 N 95.20 W
Butner 192 36.07 N 78.45 W
Buto 152 15.46 S 15.09 E
Buton, Pulau I 112 5.00 S 122.55 E
Butong 112 1.06 S 114.50 E
Butru 166 21.30 S 139.43 E
Butsha 154 0.57 N 29.13 E
Buttapietra 64 45.20 N 11.00 E
Butte, Mt., U.S. 202 46.00 N 112.32 W
Butte, Ne., U.S. 198 42.54 N 98.50 W
Butte □[6] 226 39.27 N 121.30 W
Butte City 226 39.28 N 121.59 W
Butte Creek ≃, Ca., U.S. 204 39.12 N 121.56 W
Butte Creek ≃, Or., U.S. 224 45.09 N 122.46 W
Butte du Lion ♠ 50 50.40 N 4.24 E
Butte Falls 202 42.32 N 122.33 W
Buttelstedt 54 51.05 N 11.20 E
Butte Mountains ⋏ 204 39.50 N 115.05 W
Butten 56 48.58 N 7.13 E
Butter Brook ≃ 283 42.31 N 71.24 W
Butter Creek ≃ 202 45.52 N 119.19 W
Butterfield, Il., U.S. 278 41.50 N 88.02 W
Butterfield, Mn., U.S. 198 43.57 N 94.47 W
Butterfield Creek ≃ 278 41.33 N 87.37 W
Butterfield Lake ⊜ 212 44.19 N 75.46 W
Butterley Reservoir ⊜[1] 262 53.35 N 1.56 W
Buttermere 44 54.33 N 3.17 W
Butternut 190 46.00 N 90.29 W
Butternut Creek ≃, N.Y., U.S. 210 42.25 N 75.22 W
Butternut Creek ≃, N.Y., U.S. 210 43.06 N 76.00 W
Butterwick 44 52.59 N 0.05 E
Butterworth, Malay. 114 5.25 N 100.24 E
Butterworth, Transkei 158 32.23 S 28.04 E
Buttevant 48 52.14 N 8.40 W
Büttgen 56 51.12 N 6.36 E
Buttlar 56 50.45 N 9.57 E
Buttle Lake ⊜ 182 49.46 N 125.36 W
Button Islands II 176 60.35 N 64.45 W
Buttonville 275b 43.52 N 79.22 W
Buttonville Airfield ⊠ 275b 43.52 N 79.23 W
Buttonwillow 226 35.24 N 119.28 W
Buttrio 64 46.01 N 13.20 E
Buttstädt 54 51.07 N 11.25 E
Butty Head > 162 33.54 S 121.38 E
Buttzville 210 40.49 N 75.00 W
Butuan 116 8.57 N 125.33 E
Butuan Bay c 116 9.06 N 125.20 E
Butuj 88 53.27 N 112.22 E
Bū Tumayyim, Wādī V 146 26.56 N 19.13 E
Buṭūris 142 31.00 N 30.15 E
Buturlino, Ross. 80 55.34 N 44.55 E
Buturlino, Ross. 82 54.55 N 37.29 E
Buturlinovka 78 50.50 N 40.36 E
Butwal 124 27.42 N 83.27 E
Butylicy 80 55.32 N 41.31 E
Butzbach 56 50.26 N 8.40 E
Bützfleth 52 53.39 N 9.28 E
Bützow 54 53.50 N 11.59 E
Bützsee ⊜ 54 52.49 N 12.53 E
Butztown 208 40.39 N 75.22 W
Buuhoodle 144 8.15 N 46.20 E
Buulo Berde 144 3.51 N 45.34 E
Buur Gaabo 144 1.12 S 41.51 E
Buurgplaatz ∧ 56 50.10 N 6.01 E
Buur Hakaba 144 2.47 N 44.05 E
Buur Haybe 144 3.57 N 45.07 E
Buwarah, Sabkhat al- ≡ 130 35.09 N 41.12 E
Buwaydān 132 33.12 N 36.26 E
Buxar 124 25.35 N 83.59 E
Buxtehude 52 53.28 N 9.41 E
Buxton, Boph. 158 27.38 S 24.42 E
Buxton, Guy. 246 6.47 N 58.02 W
Buxton, Eng., U.K. 262 53.15 N 1.55 W
Buxton, N.C., U.S. 192 35.16 N 75.32 W
Buxton, N.D., U.S. 198 47.36 N 97.05 W
Buxton, Or., U.S. 224 45.41 N 123.11 W
Buxton, Mount ∧ 182 51.35 N 127.55 W
Buxy 58 46.43 N 4.41 E
Buye 154 4.38 N 27.30 E
Buyiqiao 106 31.47 N 119.48 E
Buyo 150 6.16 N 7.03 W
Buyo, Barrage de ◆[6] 150 6.15 N 7.05 W
Buyuan ≃ 102 21.51 N 101.13 E
Büyükada 130 40.52 N 29.07 E
Büyükada I 267b 40.52 N 29.07 E
Büyükarmutlu 130 39.35 N 38.26 E
Büyükbakkal ◆[8] 267b 40.59 N 29.11 E
Büyükçeçeli 130 39.43 N 33.52 E
Büyükçekmece 130 41.01 N 28.34 E
Büyükdere ◆[8] 267b 41.09 N 29.02 E
Büyükeceli 130 36.11 N 33.40 E
Büyükkale 130 38.01 N 27.34 E
Büyükkarıştıran 130 41.18 N 27.32 E
Büyükkemikli Burnu > 130 40.18 N 26.14 E
Büyükmenderes ≃ 130 37.28 N 27.11 E
Büyükzap → Great Zab ≃ 128 36.00 N 43.21 E
Buyun Shan ∧ 98 40.06 N 122.42 E
Buyun Uzun 128 39.13 N 63.19 E
Buzan ≃ 80 46.18 N 49.06 E
Buzanaj, peski ◆[2] 80 47.30 N 49.50 E
Buzançais 32 46.53 N 1.25 E
Buzancy 56 49.25 N 4.57 E
Bužaninovo 82 56.23 N 38.18 E
Bužarovo 82 55.59 N 36.47 E
Buzău 38 45.09 N 26.49 E
Buzău □[6] 38 45.15 N 26.45 E
Buzău ≃ 38 45.26 N 27.44 E
Buzen 96 33.37 N 131.08 E
Búzi ≃ 156 19.50 S 34.43 E
Buziaș 38 45.39 N 21.36 E
Buziji 100 33.49 N 118.14 E
Buzinovka 80 48.32 N 43.53 E
Búzios, Ilha dos I 256 23.48 S 45.08 W
Búzios, Ponta dos > 255 22.44 S 41.53 W
Buzlanovo 265b 55.46 N 37.13 E
Buzovna 84 40.31 N 50.04 E
Buzuluk, Kaz. 86 51.55 N 66.16 E
Buzuluk, Ross. 80 52.47 N 52.15 E
Buzuluk ≃, Ross. 80 50.13 N 42.12 E
Buzuluk ≃, Ross. 80 52.47 N 52.16 E
Buzzards Bay 207 41.44 N 70.37 W
Buzzards Bay c 207 41.33 N 70.47 W
Bwana Mkubwa 154 13.01 S 28.42 E
Bwasa 152 3.53 S 18.25 E
Bwendi 154 4.01 N 26.41 E
Bwlch 42 51.54 N 3.15 W
By 40 60.12 N 16.28 E
Byādgi 122 14.41 N 75.29 E
Byam Channel ʊ 176 75.20 N 105.20 W
Byam Martin Channel ʊ 176 75.45 N 104.00 W
Byam Martin Island I 176 75.15 N 104.00 W
Byberry Creek ≃ 285 40.04 N 74.59 W
Byblos → Jubayl 130 34.07 N 35.39 E
Byček ≃ 83 48.26 N 37.47 E
Bychawa 30 51.01 N 22.32 E
Bychov 76 53.32 N 30.12 E
Byčicha 76 55.41 N 29.58 E
Byčki, Ross. 76 54.15 N 34.39 E
Byčki, Ross. 80 53.38 N 40.54 E
Byculla ◆[8] 272c 18.58 N 72.49 E
Byczyna 30 51.07 N 18.11 E
Bydalen 26 63.06 N 13.47 E
Bydgoszcz 30 53.08 N 18.00 E
Bydgoszcz □[4] 30 53.15 N 18.00 E
Byelorussia → Belarus □[1], Europe 72 53.50 N 28.00 E
Byelorussian Station ◆[5] 265b 55.47 N 37.35 E
Byers, Pa., U.S. 285 40.05 N 75.41 W
Byers, Tx., U.S. 196 34.04 N 98.11 W
Byersdale 279b 40.37 N 80.13 W
Byers Run ≃ 279b 40.24 N 79.42 W
Byesville 188 39.58 N 81.32 W
Byfang ◆[8] 263 51.24 N 7.06 E
Byfield, Eng., U.K. 42 52.11 N 1.14 W
Byfield, Ma., U.S. 207 42.45 N 70.56 W
Byfleet 260 51.20 N 0.29 W
Byford 168a 32.13 S 116.00 E
Byforde 284c 39.01 N 77.05 W
Bygdeå 26 64.04 N 20.51 E
Bygdeträsket ⊜ 26 64.26 N 20.32 E
Bygdin 26 61.20 N 8.48 E
Bygdin ⊜ 26 61.21 N 8.36 E
Bygi 80 57.13 N 53.44 E
Byglandsfjord 26 58.41 N 7.48 E
Byglandsfjorden ⊜ 26 58.48 N 7.50 E
Byhalia 194 34.52 N 89.41 W
Byk ≃ 78 46.55 N 29.28 E
Bykle 26 59.21 N 7.20 E
Bykov 89 47.21 N 142.32 E
Bykovec 78 47.13 N 28.27 E
Bykovka, Ross. 82 55.29 N 37.40 E
Bykovka, Ukr. 78 50.17 N 27.58 E
Bykovo, Ross. 80 49.47 N 45.22 E
Bykovo, Ross. 82 54.01 N 37.54 E
Bykovo, Ross. 82 55.37 N 38.04 E
Bykovo Airport ⊠ 265b 55.36 N 38.05 E
Bylas 200 33.08 N 110.07 W
Bylbasovka 83 48.51 N 37.30 E
Bylderup 41 54.57 N 9.07 E
Byley 262 53.13 N 2.25 W
Bylkyldak 86 48.38 N 75.16 E
Bylnice 30 49.04 N 18.01 E
Bylot Island I 176 73.13 N 78.34 W
Byng Inlet 190 45.46 N 80.33 W
Bynum, Mt., U.S. 182 47.58 N 112.18 W
Bynum, N.C., U.S. 192 35.46 N 79.08 W
Bynum, Tx., U.S. 222 31.58 N 97.00 W
Byōdōin Temple ◉[1] 270 34.53 N 135.48 E
Byram ≃ 276 40.59 N 73.39 W
Byramgore Reef ✢[2] 122 11.54 N 71.49 E
Byram Lake Reservoir ⊜[1] 276 41.10 N 73.41 W
Byrd, Lac ⊜ 190 47.01 N 76.56 W
Byrdstown 194 36.34 N 85.07 W
Byrka 88 50.39 N 118.31 E
Byrnedale 214 41.17 N 78.30 W
Byro 162 26.05 S 116.09 E
Byrock 166 30.40 S 146.24 E
Byron, Ca., U.S. 226 37.52 N 121.38 W
Byron, Ga., U.S. 192 32.39 N 83.45 W
Byron, Il., U.S. 190 42.07 N 89.15 W
Byron, Mi., U.S. 216 42.49 N 83.57 W
Byron, N.Y., U.S. 210 43.04 N 78.03 W
Byron, Wy., U.S. 202 44.47 N 108.30 W
Byron, Cape > 166 28.39 S 153.38 E
Byron, Isla I 254 47.47 S 75.12 W
Byron Bay 166 28.39 S 153.37 E
Byron Center 216 42.49 N 85.42 W
Byrranga, gory ⋏ 74 75.00 N 104.00 E
Byšice-Liblice 54 50.19 N 14.38 E
Bysjön ⊜ 40 60.23 N 14.30 E
Byske 26 64.57 N 21.12 E
Byskeälven ≃ 26 64.57 N 21.13 E
Bystraja ≃ 80 47.58 N 41.00 E
Bystřany 54 50.38 N 13.51 E
Bystrica ≃ 80 58.38 N 49.05 E
Bystřice 30 49.45 N 14.41 E
Bystřice pod Hostýnem 30 49.24 N 17.40 E
Bystrij Tanyp ≃ 86 55.46 N 54.35 E
Bystrovka 85 42.47 N 75.43 E
Bystryj 86 57.50 N 73.58 E
Bystryj Istok 86 52.23 N 84.24 E
Bystrzyca Kłodzka 30 50.18 N 16.38 E
Bytantaj ≃ 74 68.46 N 134.20 E
Bytča, Bela. 76 54.18 N 28.24 E
Bytča, Česko. 30 49.14 N 18.36 E
Byten' 76 52.54 N 25.29 E
Bytkov 78 48.38 N 24.26 E
Bytom (Beuthen) 30 50.22 N 18.54 E
Bytoš' 76 53.50 N 34.06 E
Bytów 30 54.11 N 17.30 E
Byumba 154 1.35 S 30.04 E
Byvalki 78 51.51 N 30.37 E
Byxelkrok 26 57.20 N 17.00 E
Bzyb' ≃ 84 43.12 N 40.18 E
Bzybskij chrebet ⋏ 84 43.18 N 40.41 E

C

Ca ≃ 110 18.46 N 105.47 E
Čaa-Chol' 86 51.32 N 92.23 E
Caacupé 252 25.23 S 57.09 W
Čaadajevka 80 53.09 N 45.56 E
Čaadajevo 80 55.40 N 42.02 E
Caaguazú 252 25.26 S 56.02 W
Caaguazú □[5] 252 25.00 S 55.45 W
Caála 152 12.51 S 15.33 E
Caamaño Sound ʊ 182 52.49 N 129.28 W
Caapiranga 246 3.18 S 61.13 W
Caapucú 252 26.13 S 57.12 W
Caarapó 255 22.38 S 54.48 W
Caatinga 255 17.10 S 45.53 W
Caazapá 252 26.09 S 56.24 W
Caazapá □[5] 252 26.10 S 56.00 W
Cabaçal ≃ 248 16.00 S 57.42 W
Cabadbaran 116 9.10 N 125.38 E
Cabadiangan Plateau ⋏[1] 116 9.50 N 122.36 E
Cabagan 116 17.26 N 121.46 E
Cabaiguán 240p 22.05 N 79.30 W
Cabalete Island I 116 14.17 N 121.50 E
Cabalian 116 10.16 N 125.10 E
Cabaliana, Lago ⊜ 246 3.20 S 60.50 W
Cabalian Bay c 116 10.13 N 125.10 E
Cabalian Point > 116 12.06 N 122.01 E
Caballero Creek ≃ 280 34.11 N 118.32 W
Caballito ◆[8] 288 34.37 S 58.27 W
Caballones, Cayo I 240p 20.52 N 79.00 W
Caballo Reservoir ⊜[1] 200 32.58 N 107.18 W
Cabana 248 8.24 S 78.02 W
Cabanaconde 248 15.37 S 71.59 W
Cabañas 240p 22.58 N 82.55 W
Cabanatuan 116 15.29 N 120.58 E
Cabangan 116 15.10 N 120.03 E
Çabano 186 47.41 N 68.53 W
Čabanovka 83 49.02 N 38.46 E
Cabarroguis 116 16.33 N 121.32 E
Cabarruyan Island I 116 16.18 N 119.59 E
Cabaun Island I 116 12.34 N 124.30 E
Cabeceiras 255 15.48 S 46.59 W
Cabeço de Montachique 266c 38.54 N 9.11 W
Cabellera, Sierra de la ⋏ 200 30.55 N 109.07 W
Cabery 216 41.00 N 88.12 W
Cabeza del Buey 34 38.43 N 5.13 W
Cabeza de Tigre 286c 10.28 N 66.46 W
Cabezas 248 18.46 S 63.24 W
Cabiao 116 15.15 N 120.51 E
Cabiate 266b 45.40 N 9.10 E
Cabildo, Arg. 252 38.29 S 61.54 W
Cabildo, Chile 252 32.26 S 71.05 W
Cabimas 246 10.23 N 71.28 W
Cabin Branch ≃, Md., U.S. 284b 39.13 N 76.35 W
Cabin Branch ≃, Md., U.S. 284c 38.51 N 76.48 W
Cabin Creek ≃ 198 46.55 N 104.52 W
Cabinda 152 5.33 S 12.12 E
Cabinda □[5] 152 5.00 S 12.30 E
Cabinet Mountains ⋏ 202 48.20 N 116.00 W
Cabingaan Island I 116 5.41 N 121.03 E
Cabin John 208 38.58 N 77.09 W
Cabin John Creek ≃ 284b 38.58 N 77.09 W
Cabin John Creek Park ♠ 284c 38.59 N 77.09 W
Cabin John Regional Park ♠ 284c 39.02 N 77.09 W
Cabiri 152 8.52 S 13.39 E
Cabixi ≃ 248 13.41 S 60.44 W
Cable 190 46.12 N 91.17 W
Cable Airport ⊠ 280 34.08 N 117.41 W
Cables 162 27.59 S 123.23 E
Cabo 250 8.17 S 35.02 W
Cabo Blanco 254 47.12 S 65.45 W
Cabo de Hornos, Parque Nacional ♠ 250 55.45 S 67.25 W
Cabo Delgado □[5] 154 12.35 S 39.00 E
Cabo Frio 255 22.53 S 42.01 W
Cabo Gracias a Dios 236 14.59 N 83.10 W
Cabo Ledo 152 9.39 S 13.17 E
Cabonga, Réservoir ⊜[1] 190 47.20 N 76.35 W
Cabool 194 37.07 N 92.06 W
Caboolture 166 27.05 S 152.57 E
Cabo Orange, Parque Nacional do ♠ 250 3.00 N 51.00 W
Cabora Bassa 154 15.35 S 32.48 E
Cabora Bassa Dam ◆[6] 154 15.35 S 32.42 E
Cabo Raso 254 44.21 S 65.14 W
Caborca 232 30.37 N 112.06 W
Cabo Rojo 240m 18.05 N 67.09 W
Cabot, Ar., U.S. 194 34.58 N 92.00 W
Cabot, Pa., U.S. 214 40.46 N 79.46 W
Cabot, Mount ∧ 188 44.31 N 71.24 W
Cabot Head > 212 45.14 N 81.17 W
Cabot Strait ʊ 186 47.20 N 59.30 W
Cabo Verde 256 21.28 S 46.24 W
Cabo Verde ≃ 256 21.28 S 46.17 W
Cabo Verde → Cape Verde □[1] 150a 16.00 N 24.00 W
Cabra 34 37.28 N 4.27 W
Cabra Corral, Embalse ⊜[1] 252 25.15 S 65.25 W
Cabra Island I 116 13.53 N 120.02 E
Cabramatta 274a 33.54 S 150.56 E
Cabramatta Creek ≃ 274a 33.54 S 150.57 E
Cabramurra 171b 35.58 S 148.23 E
Cabras 71 39.56 N 8.32 E
Cabras, Stagno di ⊜ 71 39.57 N 8.29 E
Cabras Island I 174p 13.27 N 144.40 E
Cabrel 234 20.06 N 105.14 W
Cabrera ≃, Col. 246 3.26 N 75.07 W
Cabrera ≃, Esp. 34 42.25 N 6.49 W
Cabrera, Illa de I 34 39.09 N 2.56 E
Cabrera, Sierra de la ⋏ 34 42.12 N 6.40 W
Cabrera de Mar 266d 41.32 N 2.24 E
Cabreúva 256 23.18 S 47.08 W
Cabri 184 50.37 N 108.28 W
Cabriel ≃ 34 39.14 N 1.03 W
Cabrillo National Monument ♠ 228 32.41 N 117.15 W
Cabrils 266d 41.32 N 2.22 E
Cabrobó 250 8.31 S 39.19 W
Cabruta 246 7.38 N 66.15 W
Cabucgayan 116 11.29 N 124.34 E
Cabuçu 256 22.50 S 42.55 W
Cabuçu ≃, Bra. 287a 22.59 S 43.37 W
Cabuçu ≃, Bra. 287a 22.48 S 43.37 W
Cabuçu de Cima ≃ 287b 23.31 S 46.33 W
Cabugao 116 17.48 N 120.27 E
Cabulauan Island I 116 11.23 N 120.06 E
Cabullónes, Punta > 240m 17.58 N 66.35 W
Cabulo 152 10.15 S 16.40 E
Cabure 246 11.08 N 69.38 W
Cabuta 152 9.50 S 14.48 E
Cabuya 236 9.36 N 85.06 W
Cabuyal 236 10.40 N 85.40 W
Cabuyaro 246 4.18 N 72.49 W
Caca 80 48.11 N 44.40 E
Caçador 252 26.47 S 51.00 W
Čačak 38 43.53 N 20.21 E
Cacaohatán 236 14.59 N 92.10 W
Cacaoui, Lac ⊜ 186 50.53 N 66.58 W
Caçapava 256 23.06 S 45.42 W
Caçapava do Sul 252 30.30 S 53.30 W
Caçapava Velha 256 23.07 S 45.39 W
Cacapon ≃ 188 39.37 N 78.16 W
Cacapon State Park ♠ 188 39.32 N 78.23 W
Cacas 130 38.23 N 41.17 E
Caccamo 70 37.56 N 13.40 E
Caccia, Capo > 71 40.34 N 8.09 E
Çaccuri 68 39.14 N 16.47 E
Čačenka ≃ 265b 55.46 N 37.18 E
Cacequi 252 29.53 S 54.49 W
Cáceres, Bra. 248 16.04 S 57.41 W
Cáceres, Col. 246 7.35 N 75.20 W
Cáceres, Esp. 34 39.29 N 6.22 W
Cáceres □[4] 34 39.40 N 6.05 E
Cachan 261 48.48 N 2.20 E
Cacharí 252 36.24 S 59.32 W
Cache 196 34.37 N 98.37 W
Cache ≃, Ar., U.S. 194 34.42 N 91.20 W
Cache ≃, Il., U.S. 194 37.04 N 89.10 W
Caché, Lac ⊜ 206 46.21 N 74.39 W
Cache Creek 182 50.48 N 121.19 W
Cache Creek ≃, Ca., U.S. 226 38.42 N 121.42 W
Cache Creek ≃, Ca., U.S. 228 35.06 N 117.58 W
Cache Creek, North Fork ≃ 226 38.59 N 122.30 W
Cache la Poudre ≃ 200 40.25 N 104.36 W
Cache la Poudre, North Fork ≃ 198 40.54 N 105.22 W
Cache Mountain ∧ 180 65.31 N 147.20 W
Cache Peak ∧, Ca., U.S. 228 35.13 N 118.15 W
Cache Peak ∧, Id., U.S. 202 42.11 N 113.40 W
Cache Slough ≃ 226 38.11 N 121.40 W
Cacheu 150 12.16 N 16.10 W
Cacheu c[1] 150 12.10 N 16.21 W
Cachí 252 25.06 S 66.11 W
Cachimbo 250 9.24 S 54.56 W
Cachimbo, Serra do ⋏ 250 8.30 S 55.50 W
Cachimo 152 8.21 S 21.20 E
Cachingues 152 13.05 S 16.43 E
Cachir 88 48.06 N 98.52 E
Cachkadzor 84 40.33 N 44.43 E
Cachoeira ≃ 256 23.06 S 46.29 W
Cachoeira, Reservatório ⊜[1] 256 23.03 S 46.15 W
Cachoeira, Rio da ≃ 287a 23.00 S 43.18 W
Cachoeira Alta 255 18.48 S 50.58 W
Cachoeira de Goiás 255 16.44 S 50.38 W
Cachoeira de Manteiga 255 16.39 S 45.16 W
Cachoeira de Minas 256 22.21 S 45.47 W
Cachoeira do Arari 250 1.01 S 48.58 W
Cachoeira do Sul 252 30.02 S 52.54 W
Cachoeira Grande, Alto da ∧ 256 21.54 S 44.06 W
Cachoeira Paulista 256 22.40 S 45.01 W
Cachoeiras 287a 22.39 S 43.28 W
Cachoeiras de Macacu 256 22.28 S 42.39 W
Cachoeirinha 250 8.29 S 36.14 W
Cachoeiro de Itapemirim 255 20.51 S 41.06 W
Cachos, Punta > 252 27.39 S 71.02 W
Çachos, Rio dos ≃ 287b 23.36 S 46.26 W
Čachrov 60 49.16 N 13.18 E
Cachuela Esperanza 248 10.32 S 65.38 W
Cachuma, Lake ⊜[1] 204 34.35 N 119.55 W
Cacilhas 266c 38.41 N 9.09 W
Cacine 150 11.08 N 14.57 W
Caciporé ≃ 250 3.51 N 51.08 W
Caciporé, Cabo > 250 3.55 N 51.07 W
Căciulați 38 44.38 N 26.10 E
Cacnipa Island I 116 10.30 N 119.04 E
Cacocum 240p 20.44 N 76.23 W
Cacólo 152 10.07 S 19.17 E
Caconda 152 13.43 S 15.06 E
Caconde 256 21.33 S 46.38 W
Cacra 248 12.48 S 75.48 W
Cactus 196 36.04 N 102.00 W
Cactus Flat ≡ 204 37.45 N 116.45 W
Cactus Peak ∧ 204 37.47 N 116.53 W
Caçu 255 18.37 S 51.04 W
Cacuaco 152 8.47 S 13.22 E
Cacula 152 14.29 S 14.10 E
Caculé 255 14.30 S 42.13 W
Caculuvar ≃ 152 16.46 S 14.36 E
Cacuri, Ang. 152 8.14 S 18.20 E
Cacuri, Ven. 246 4.48 N 65.21 W
Cacuso 152 9.26 S 15.43 E
Çadale 144 2.45 N 46.19 E
Čadan 86 51.17 N 91.35 E
Cadaqués 34 42.17 N 3.17 E
Çadariri ≃ 248 6.20 S 57.46 W
Čadca 30 49.26 N 18.48 E
Caddington 42 51.51 N 0.27 W
Caddo, Ok., U.S. 196 34.07 N 96.15 W
Caddo, Tx., U.S. 196 32.38 N 98.40 W
Caddo ≃ 194 34.10 N 93.03 W
Caddo Creek ≃ 196 34.14 N 96.59 W
Caddo Lake ⊜[1] 194 32.42 N 94.01 W
Caddo Mills 222 33.04 N 96.14 W
Caddo Peak ∧ 222 32.29 N 97.24 W
Caddy Vista 216 42.50 N 87.54 W
Cadell ≃ 166 22.51 S 141.55 E
Cadena, Arroyo de la ≃ 196 26.17 N 104.00 W
Cadena, Cerro ∧ 196 25.50 N 104.04 W
Cadena, Punta > 240m 18.18 N 67.14 W
Cadenberge 52 53.46 N 9.04 E
Cadenet 62 43.44 N 5.22 E
Cadeo 62 44.58 N 9.48 E
Cader Bronwyn ∧ 42 52.54 N 3.22 W
Cadereyta de Jiménez 232 25.36 N 100.00 W
Cader Idris ∧ 42 52.42 N 3.54 W
Cadibarrawirracanna, Lake ⊜ 162 28.52 S 135.27 E
Cadig, Mount ∧ 116 14.09 N 122.27 E
Cadillac, Sk., Can. 184 49.44 N 107.43 W

≃ River	Fluß	Río	Rivière	Rio
≊ Canal	Kanal	Canal	Canal	Canal
∟ Waterfall, Rapids	Wasserfall, Stromschnellen	Cascada, Rápidos	Chute d'eau, Rapides	Cascata, Rápidos
ʊ Strait	Meeresstraße	Estrecho	Détroit	Estreito
c Bay, Gulf	Bucht, Golf	Bahía, Golfo	Baie, Golfe	Baía, Golfo
⊜ Lake, Lakes	See, Seen	Lago, Lagos	Lac, Lacs	Lago, Lagos
≡ Swamp	Sumpf	Pantano	Marais	Pântano
✗ Ice Features, Glacier	Eis- und Gletscherformen	Accidentes Glaciales	Formes glaciaires	Acidentes glaciares
⊤ Other Hydrographic Features	Andere Hydrographische Objekte	Otros Elementos Hidrográficos	Autres données hydrographiques	Outros acidentes hidrográficos
✢ Submarine Features	Untermeerische Objekte	Accidentes Submarinos	Formes de relief sous-marin	Acidentes submarinos
□ Political Unit	Politische Einheit	Unidad Politica	Entité politique	Unidade política
◉ Cultural Institution	Kulturelle Institution	Institución Cultural	Institution culturelle	Instituição cultural
⊥ Historical Site	Historische Stätte	Sitio Histórico	Site historique	Sitio histórico
♠ Recreational Site	Erholungs- und Ferienort	Sitio de Recreo	Centre de loisirs	Area de Lazer
⊠ Airport	Flughafen	Aeropuerto	Aéroport	Aeroporto
■ Military Installation	Militäranlage	Instalación Militar	Installation militaire	Instalação militar
◆ Miscellaneous	Verschiedenes	Misceláneo	Divers	Diversos

Cadillac, Fr. 32 44.38 N 0.19 W
Cadillac, Mi., U.S. 190 44.15 N 85.24 W
Cadipietra (Steinhaus) 64 46.59 N 11.59 E
Cadishead 262 53.25 N 2.26 W
Cadix
— Cádiz 34 36.32 N 6.18 W
Cádiz, Esp. 34 36.32 N 6.18 W
Cadiz, Pil. 116 10.57 N 123.18 E
Cadiz, In., U.S. 218 39.57 N 85.30 W
Cadiz, Ky., U.S. 194 36.51 N 87.50 W
Cadiz, Oh., U.S. 214 40.16 N 80.59 W
Cádiz □⁴ 34 36.35 N 5.50 W
Cádiz, Bahía de c 34 36.32 N 6.16 W
Cádiz, Golfo de c 34 36.50 N 7.10 W
Cadiz Lake @ 204 34.18 N 115.24 W
Cadlao Island I 116 11.13 N 119.21 E
Çadnam 42 50.55 N 1.35 W
Çadobec 88 58.40 N 98.51 E
Čadobec ≃ 88 58.40 N 98.50 E
Cadogan 214 50.45 N 79.34 W
Cadomin 182 53.02 N 117.20 W
Cadoneghe 64 45.26 N 11.55 E
Cadore ◆¹ 64 46.30 N 12.20 E
Cadosia 210 41.58 N 75.16 W
Cadott 190 44.56 N 91.09 W
Cadoux 162 30.47 S 117.08 E
Caduruan Point ⊁ 116 11.45 N 124.05 E
Caduta, Fosso delle ≃ 267a 41.56 N 12.12 E
Cadwell 192 32.20 N 83.02 W
Cady Marsh Ditch ≃ 84 41.33 N 87.29 W
Cady Mountain ∧² 224 48.33 N 123.07 W
Čadyr-Lunga 78 46.03 N 28.47 E
Cadzand 52 51.22 N 3.25 E
Caen 32 49.11 N 0.21 W
Caengo (Kwenge) ≃ 152 4.50 S 18.42 E
Caerano di San Marco 64 45.47 N 12.00 E
Caere ⊥ 66 42.02 N 12.07 E
Caergwrle 44 53.07 N 3.03 W
Caerleon 42 51.37 N 2.57 W
Caernarfon 42 53.08 N 4.16 W
Caernarfon Bay c 44 53.05 N 4.30 W
Caernarfon Castle ⊥ 44 53.08 N 4.16 W
Caerphilly 42 51.35 N 3.14 W
Caerphilly Castle ⊥ 42 51.34 N 3.14 W
Caersws 42 52.31 N 3.25 W
Caesar Creek ≃ 218 39.29 N 84.06 W
Caesar Creek, Anderson Fork ≃ 218 39.33 N 83.58 W
Caesar Creek Lake @¹ 218 39.30 N 84.00 W
Caesarea — Qesari, Ḥorbat ⊥ 132 32.30 N 34.53 E
Castanópolis 255 19.18 S 44.24 W
Caeté 255 19.54 S 43.40 W
Caeté 248 9.03 S 68.39 W
Caeté, Morro ∧² 287a 23.03 S 43.31 W
Caetité 255 14.04 S 42.29 W
Cafayate 252 26.05 S 65.58 W
Cafelândia do Leste 255 16.40 S 53.25 W
Cafima 152 16.39 S 16.27 E
Cafu 152 16.27 S 15.14 E
Cafuini ≃ 246 1.17 N 57.11 W
Cagaan Chajrchan 86 49.25 N 94.15 E
Cagaan Gol 86 48.52 N 89.07 E
Cagaan Nuur, Mong. 88 49.32 N 89.42 E
Cagaannuur, Mong. 88 50.20 N 105.03 E
Cagaan-Ovoo 102 45.51 N 105.17 E
Cagaan Uul 88 49.28 N 98.30 E
Cagaan-Üür 88 50.30 N 101.31 E
Čagačo ≃ 256 22.02 S 43.09 W
Çagan ≃ 78 50.50 N 51.20 E
Cagan-Aman 80 47.34 N 46.43 E
Cagan-Churtej, chrebet ∧ 88 51.32 N 110.00 E
Cagarras, Ilhas II 287a 23.02 S 43.12 W
Cagayan ≃ 116 18.00 N 121.50 E
Cagayan ≃ 116 18.22 N 121.37 E
Cagayancillo 116 9.34 N 121.12 E
Cagayan de Oro 116 8.29 N 124.39 E
Cagayan de Tawi-Tawi 116 7.01 N 118.30 E
Cagayan Island I 116 9.36 N 121.14 E
Cagayan Islands II 116 9.40 N 121.16 E
Cagayan Sulu Island I 116 7.01 N 118.30 E
Çagda 74 58.45 N 130.37 E
Cageri 64 42.39 N 42.45 E
Caggiano 68 40.34 N 15.29 E
Caggy 130 39.30 N 28.01 E
Cagliarca 130 39.05 N 39.10 E
Cagli 66 43.33 N 12.39 E
Cagliari 71 39.13 N 9.07 E
Cagliari □⁴ 71 39.30 N 8.45 E
Cagliari, Golfo di c 71 39.08 N 9.11 E
Cagliari, Stagno di @ 71 39.13 N 9.02 E
Caglinka 86 53.59 N 69.47 E
Cagnano Varano 68 41.49 N 15.47 E
Cagnes-sur-Mer 62 43.40 N 7.09 E
Çagoda 76 59.05 N 35.18 E
Çagodošča ≃ 76 58.57 N 36.35 E
Cagojan 89 52.08 N 128.15 E
Cagra ≃ 80 52.37 N 48.15 E
Cagraray Island I 116 13.18 N 123.52 E
Cagua 250 10.11 N 67.27 W
Caguán ≃ 248 0.08 S 74.18 W
Caguas 240m 18.14 N 66.02 W
Cagveri 84 41.48 N 43.29 E
Cagwait 116 8.55 N 126.18 E
Cahaba ≃ 194 32.20 N 87.05 W
Cahabón 236 15.34 N 89.36 W
Cahabón ≃ 236 15.25 N 89.36 W
Cahama 152 16.17 S 14.19 E
Caha Mountains ∧ 48 51.45 N 9.45 W
Caher 48 52.21 N 7.56 W
Caherdaniel 48 51.45 N 10.05 W
Caherciveen 48 51.57 N 10.13 W
Cahokia 219 38.34 N 90.11 W
Cahokia Creek ≃ 219 38.47 N 90.01 W
Cahokia Mounds State Park ⊥ 219 38.39 N 90.03 W
Cahoon Creek ≃ 279a 41.29 N 81.55 W
Cahoon Park ◆ 279a 41.29 N 81.56 W
Cahoonzie 210 41.26 N 74.43 W
Cahore Point ⊁ 48 52.34 N 6.11 W
Cahors 32 44.27 N 1.26 E
Cahto Peak ∧ 226 39.45 N 123.33 W
Cahuita Indian Reservation ◆⁴ 204 33.30 N 116.43 W
Cahuinari ≃ 246 1.21 S 70.44 W
Cahuita, Punta ⊁ 236 9.45 N 82.49 W
Cai ≃ 34 36.58 N 5.16 E
Caia ≃ 34 38.50 N 7.05 W
Caianda 152 11.02 S 23.31 E
Caiapó ≃, Bra. 250 8.52 S 49.36 W
Caiapó ≃, Bra. 255 15.49 S 51.53 W
Caiapó, Serra do ∧ 255 17.00 S 52.00 W
Caiapônia 255 16.57 S 51.49 W
Caiari ≃ 142 41.11 N 14.22 E
Caibarién 240p 22.31 N 79.28 W
Cai Bau, Dao I 108 21.10 N 107.27 E
Caibirian 116 11.34 N 124.35 E
Caiçara, Bra. 250 6.36 S 35.29 W
Caiçara, Bra. 255 11.35 S 50.12 W
Caicara de Maturín 246 9.49 N 63.34 W
Caicara de Orinoco 246 7.37 N 66.10 W
Caicedonia 246 4.20 N 75.50 W
Caicó 250 6.27 S 37.06 W
Caicos Bank ◆⁴ 236 21.35 N 71.55 W
Caicos Islands II 236 21.56 N 71.58 W
Caicos Passage ⋃ 236 21.55 N 72.45 W
Caieiras 256 23.22 S 46.44 W
Caieiras □⁷ 287b 23.22 S 46.44 W
Caigou 88 32.17 N 115.25 E
Caihuaping 105 26.54 N 113.23 E
Caijiagang 107 29.44 N 106.29 E
Caijiagang 107 32.55 N 106.21 E
Caijialou 104 41.24 N 121.06 E
Caijiang 100 41.17 N 107.39 E

Caijiazhuang 105 40.48 N 114.44 E
Caille 62 43.46 N 6.44 E
Cailloma 248 15.12 S 71.46 W
Caillou Bay c 194 29.06 N 90.56 W
Caima Bay c 116 13.42 N 122.48 E
Caimán, Islas — Cayman Islands □² 238 19.30 N 80.40 W
Caimanera 240p 19.59 N 75.09 W
Caimanes — Cayman Islands □² 238 19.30 N 80.40 W
Caiman Point ⊁ 116 15.55 N 119.46 E
Caimbambo 152 12.58 S 14.01 E
Cain ≃ 42 52.46 N 3.08 W
Cain Creek ≃ 198 44.17 N 98.10 W
Cainde 152 15.42 S 13.12 E
Caine ≃ 248 18.23 S 65.21 W
Caino 64 45.38 N 10.18 E
Cains ≃ 186 46.40 N 65.47 W
Cainsdorf 50 50.41 N 12.29 E
Cainsville 194 40.28 N 93.59 W
Cai Nuoc 110 8.56 N 105.01 E
Cairano 68 40.54 N 15.22 E
Cairari 250 2.33 S 49.07 W
Caird Coast ✚² 9 76.00 S 24.30 W
Caire, Le — Al-Qāhirah 142 30.03 N 31.15 E
Cairmbrook 214 40.07 N 78.49 W
Cairn Curran Reservoir @¹ 169 37.04 S 143.59 E
Cairndow 44 56.15 N 4.56 W
Cairngorm Mountains ∧ 46 57.04 N 3.50 W
Cairn Mountain ∧ 180 61.10 N 155.20 W
Cairnryan 44 54.58 N 5.02 W
Cairns 166 16.55 S 145.46 E
Cairns Lake @ 184 51.42 N 94.30 W
Cairnsmore of Carsphairn ∧ 44 55.15 N 4.12 W
Cairnsmore of Fleet ∧ 44 54.59 N 4.20 W
Cairn Table ∧ 44 55.29 N 4.02 W
Cairn Water ≃ 44 55.07 N 3.45 W
Cairo, Ga., U.S. 192 30.52 N 84.12 W
Cairo, Il., U.S. 194 37.00 N 89.10 W
Cairo, Ne., U.S. 198 41.00 N 98.36 W
Cairo, N.Y., U.S. 210 42.17 N 73.59 W
Cairo, Oh., U.S. 216 40.49 N 84.05 W
Cairo, W.V., U.S. 188 39.12 N 81.09 W
Cairo (Almaza) Airport ≈, Miṣr 273c 30.06 N 31.22 E
Cairo (Imbābah) Airport ≈, Miṣr 273c 30.04 N 31.12 E
Cairo, University of v² 273c 30.02 N 31.12 E
Cairo — Al-Qāhirah 142 30.03 N 31.15 E
Cairoçu, Pico do ∧ 256 23.18 S 44.36 W
Cairofa 152 14.05 S 12.54 E
Cairo International Airport ≈ 142 30.08 N 31.24 E
Cairo Main Station ≈ 273c 30.04 N 31.15 E
Cairo Montenotte 62 44.24 N 8.16 E
Cairu 255 13.30 S 39.03 W
Caister-on-Sea 42 52.39 N 1.44 E
Caistor 44 53.30 N 0.20 W
Caitingqiao 105 39.54 N 117.39 E
Caitou 152 14.28 S 13.06 E
Caiundo 152 15.46 S 17.28 E
Caivano 68 40.57 N 14.18 E
Caiwan 102 25.50 N 110.50 E
Caixi 100 25.15 N 116.28 E
Caiyu 105 39.39 N 116.37 E
Caizhuang 98 34.17 N 114.08 E
Caizi Hu @ 100 30.48 N 117.05 E
Caja ≃, Ross. 86 58.08 N 82.67 E
Caja ≃, Ross. 88 58.15 N 109.35 E
Cajabamba, Ec. 246 1.42 S 78.45 W
Cajabamba, Perú 248 7.37 S 78.03 W
Cajacay 248 10.10 S 77.26 W
Caja de Muertos, Isla I 240m 17.54 N 66.32 W
Cajamar 256 23.21 S 46.53 W
Cajamarca 248 7.10 S 78.31 W
Cajamarca □⁵ 248 6.15 S 78.50 W
Cajapió 255 2.53 S 44.38 W
Cajari 85 43.02 N 69.23 E
Cajari 250 0.48 S 51.43 W
Cajatambo 248 10.29 S 77.02 W
Cajetyn, chrebet ∧ 89 52.25 N 138.25 E
Caj-Aksŭ ≃ 85 38.34 N 68.34 W
Çajek 81 41.56 N 74.30 E
Çajkovskij 80 56.47 N 54.09 E
Cajniče 38 43.34 N 19.04 E
Cajones ≃ 234 17.45 N 95.55 W
Cajones, Cayos I 234 16.05 N 83.12 W
Cajon Mountain ∧ 228 34.16 N 117.25 W
Cajon Pass ⋍ 228 34.19 N 117.26 W
Cajon Summit ⋍ 228 34.21 N 117.27 W
Caju □⁷ 287a 22.53 S 43.13 W
Caju ≃ 255 21.17 S 47.18 W
Čaka 102 46.58 N 98.02 E
Čakar Yanhu 102 36.40 N 99.20 E
Čakčar, chrebet ∧ 85 38.35 N 67.28 E
Cakenki 152 17.48 S 19.27 E
Çakir 82 57.01 N 103.35 E
Çakırlar 130 40.34 N 35.42 E
Çakırgöl Dağı ∧ 130 40.34 N 39.42 E
Çakırhüyük 130 37.34 N 37.50 E
Çakmak 130 34.19 E
Çakmak Dağı ∧ 130 39.46 N 42.12 E
Cakovec 61 46.23 N 16.26 E
Çakovice □⁸ 269e 50.06 S 106.56 E
Çal 130 38.05 N 29.24 E
Cala, Transkei 158 31.30 S 27.45 E
Cala, Tür. 158 41.05 N 43.21 E
Cala, Embalse de @ 34 37.50 N 6.00 W
Calababdias 234 23.13 N 99.45 W
Calabanga 116 13.42 N 123.12 E
Calabar 150 4.57 N 8.19 E
Calabasas, Arroyo ≃ 280 34.12 N 118.36 W
Calabazas Creek ≃ 282 37.25 N 122.58 W
Calabernardo 70 36.52 N 15.08 E
Calabogie 212 45.18 N 76.43 W
Calabogie Lake @ 212 45.16 N 76.45 W
Calabozo 246 8.56 N 67.26 W
Calabozo, Ensenada de c 246 11.30 N 71.45 W
Calabria □⁴ 38 39.00 N 16.30 E
Calabria, Parco Nazionale di ◆ 68 38.09 N 16.54 E
Calabritto 68 40.45 N 15.13 E
Calacuccia 38 42.19 N 9.01 E
Calafat 38 43.59 N 22.56 E
Calafquén, Lago @ 252 39.31 S 72.10 W
Calagnaan Island I 116 11.23 N 123.13 E
Cala Gonone 71 40.17 N 9.37 E
Calagua Islands II 116 14.27 N 122.58 E
Calahorra 34 42.18 N 1.58 W
Calais, Fr. 32 50.57 N 1.50 E
Calais, Me., U.S. 188 45.11 N 67.16 W
Calais, Pas de (Strait of Dover) ⋃ 50 51.00 N 1.30 E
Calaíla 152 12.59 S 23.30 E
Calalaste, Sierra de ∧ 252 25.30 S 67.30 W
Calalzo di Cadore 64 46.27 N 12.23 E

Calama 252 22.28 S 68.56 W
Calamar, Col. 246 10.15 N 74.55 W
Calamar, Col. 246 1.58 N 72.41 W
Calamarca 248 16.55 S 68.09 W
Calamba, Pil. 116 14.13 N 121.10 E
Calamba, Pil. 116 8.35 N 123.39 E
Calamian Group II 116 12.00 N 120.00 E
Calamity Creek ≃ 196 29.13 N 103.42 W
Calamocha 34 40.55 N 1.18 W
Calamonaci 70 37.31 N 13.17 E
Calamus ≃ 198 41.48 N 99.09 W
Calañas 34 37.39 N 6.53 W
Calanca, Val V 58 46.22 N 9.07 E
Calang 34 40.56 N 0.14 W
Calandagan Island I 116 10.39 N 120.15 E
Calang 114 4.38 N 95.34 E
Calangianus 71 40.56 N 9.11 E
Calanna 68 38.11 N 15.43 E
Calapan 116 13.25 N 121.11 E
Calape 116 9.54 N 123.52 E
Calapooia ≃ 202 44.38 N 123.08 W
Calapooya Mountains ∧ 202 43.30 N 122.50 W
Cǎlǎraşi 38 44.11 N 27.20 E
Cǎlǎraşi □⁶ 38 44.20 N 27.13 E
Calarcá 246 4.31 N 75.38 W
Calascibetta 70 37.35 N 14.16 E
Calasetta 71 39.07 N 8.22 E
Calatabiano 70 37.49 N 15.14 E
Calatafimi 70 37.55 N 12.52 E
Calatagan 116 13.50 N 120.38 E
Calatayud 34 41.21 N 1.38 W
Calau 54 51.45 N 13.56 E
Calauag Bay c 116 14.02 N 122.13 E
Calavà, Capo ⊁ 70 38.11 N 14.56 E
Calaveras ≃ 226 38.12 N 120.41 W
Calaveras ≃ 226 37.58 N 121.22 W
Calaveras, North Fork ≃ 226 38.12 N 120.43 W
Calaveras Big Trees State Park ◆ 226 38.16 N 120.19 W
Calaveras Point ⊁ 282 37.28 N 122.03 W
Calaveras Reservoir @¹ 226 37.28 N 121.49 W
Calavino 64 46.03 N 10.59 E
Calavite, Cape ⊁ 116 13.27 N 120.18 E
Calavite, Mount ∧ 116 13.29 N 120.24 E
Calavon ≃ 62 43.51 N 5.00 E
Calawah, North Fork ≃ 224 47.56 N 124.27 W
Calawah, South Fork ≃ 224 47.58 N 124.20 W
Calayan 116 19.16 N 121.28 E
Calayan Island I 116 19.20 N 121.27 E
Calba 89 52.43 N 131.27 E
Calbayog 116 12.04 N 124.36 E
Calbe 54 51.54 N 11.46 E
Calbiga 116 11.38 N 125.01 E
Calbuco 252 41.46 S 73.08 W
Calca 248 13.20 S 71.57 W
Calçado ≃ 256 22.05 S 43.04 W
Calcasieu ≃ 194 30.05 N 93.20 W
Calcasieu Lake c 194 29.50 N 93.17 W
Calceta 246 0.51 S 80.10 W
Calcha 248 21.06 S 67.31 W
Calchaquí 252 29.54 S 60.18 W
Calchaqui ≃ 252 26.03 S 65.50 W
Calcinaia 68 40.35 N 16.11 E
Calcinato 64 43.41 N 10.27 E
Calcio 64 45.37 N 9.50 E
Calcium 212 44.01 N 75.51 W
Calçoene 250 2.30 N 50.57 W
Calçoene ≃ 250 2.30 N 50.50 W
Calcutta, India 126 22.32 N 88.22 E
Calcutta, Oh., U.S. 214 40.40 N 80.34 W
Calcutta University v² 272b 22.35 N 88.22 E
Caldaro (Kaltern) 64 46.25 N 11.14 E
Caldarola 66 43.08 N 13.13 E
Caldas, Bra. 256 21.56 S 46.23 W
Caldas, Col. 246 6.05 N 75.38 W
Caldas ≃ 246 5.15 N 75.30 W
Caldas da Rainha 34 39.24 N 9.08 W
Caldas de Reyes 34 42.36 N 8.38 W
Caldas Novas 255 17.45 S 48.38 W
Caldé 68 45.57 N 8.38 E
Caldecott Tunnel ≈⁵ 282 37.52 N 122.12 W
Calder ≃, Eng., U.K. 44 53.44 N 1.21 W
Calder ≃, Eng., U.K. 262 53.49 N 2.24 W
Calder, Loch @ 46 58.31 N 3.36 W
Calder 252 27.04 S 70.50 W
Caldera, Parque de Taburiente, Parque Nacional de la ◆ 148 28.48 N 17.52 W
Calder and Hebble Navigation Canal ≋ 262 53.43 N 1.54 W
Calder Bridge 44 54.27 N 3.29 W
Calderbrook 262 53.39 N 2.05 W
Calderdale □⁸ 262 53.44 N 2.00 W
Calderstones Park ◆ 262 53.23 N 2.54 W
Caldes 64 46.23 N 10.56 E
Caldicot 266d 51.35 N 2.45 W
Caldiero 64 45.24 N 11.11 E
Caldwell, Id., U.S. 202 43.39 N 116.41 W
Caldwell, Ks., U.S. 198 37.01 N 97.36 W
Caldwell, N.J., U.S. 210 40.50 N 74.17 W
Caldwell, Oh., U.S. 188 39.44 N 81.31 W
Caldwell, Tx., U.S. 222 30.31 N 96.41 W
Caldwell Creek ≃ 214 41.37 N 79.37 W
Caldwell-Wright Airport ≈ 276 40.53 N 74.17 W
Caldy 262 53.21 N 3.10 W
Calela ≃ 34 4.57 N 8.19 E
Caledon, On., Can. 212 43.52 N 80.00 W
Caledon, S. Afr. 158 34.12 S 19.23 E
Caledon (Mohokare) ≃ 158 30.31 S 26.05 E
Caledon East 212 43.52 N 79.52 W
Caledonia, Belize 232 18.14 N 88.29 W
Caledonia, N.S., Can. 186 44.22 N 65.02 W
Caledonia, On., Can. 212 43.04 N 79.56 W
Caledonia, Mn., U.S. 190 43.38 N 91.30 W
Caledonia, N.Y., U.S. 194 42.58 N 77.51 W
Caledonia, N.Y., U.S. 210 42.58 N 77.51 W
Caledonia □⁶ 194 44.22 N 83.40 W
Caledonian Canal ≋ 46 56.50 N 5.06 W
Caledonia State Park ◆ 208 39.56 N 77.29 W
Calego 152 12.10 S 23.36 E
Calella 34 41.37 N 2.40 E
Calemba 152 16.04 S 15.44 E
Calender 166 20.54 S 148.46 E
Calenzana 38 42.37 N 8.52 E
Calera, Al., U.S. 194 33.06 N 86.45 W
Calera, Ok., U.S. 196 33.56 N 96.25 W
Caleta Buena 248 19.52 S 70.09 W
Caleta Olivia 252 46.26 S 67.32 W

Calf Pasture Point ⊁ 276 41.05 N 73.24 W
Calgary 182 51.03 N 114.05 W
Calhan 198 39.02 N 104.17 W
Calhariz ✚⁸ 266c 38.44 N 9.12 W
Calhoun, Al., U.S. 194 32.03 N 86.32 W
Calhoun, Ga., U.S. 192 34.30 N 84.57 W
Calhoun, Ky., U.S. 194 37.32 N 87.15 W
Calhoun, Mo., U.S. 194 38.27 N 93.37 W
Calhoun, Tn., U.S. 192 35.17 N 84.44 W
Calhoun □⁶, Il., U.S. 219 39.09 N 90.37 W
Calhoun □⁶, Mi., U.S. 216 42.14 N 85.00 W
Calhoun City 194 33.51 N 89.18 W
Calhoun Falls 192 34.05 N 82.35 W
Cali, Col. 246 3.27 N 76.31 W
Cali, Tür. 130 40.10 N 28.54 E
Calian Island I 116 6.07 N 125.42 E
Calian Point ⊁ 116 10.59 N 125.48 E
Calico Ghost Town ⊥ 228 34.57 N 116.52 W
Calico Rock 194 36.07 N 92.08 W
Calicut 122 11.15 N 75.46 E
Caliente, Ca., U.S. 228 35.17 N 118.48 W
Caliente, Nv., U.S. 204 37.36 N 114.30 W
Caliente Creek ≃ 228 35.17 N 118.48 W
Califon 210 40.43 N 74.50 W
California, Mo., U.S. 194 38.37 N 92.33 W
California, Pa., U.S. 214 40.03 N 79.53 W
California □³, U.S. 178 37.30 N 119.30 W
California □⁴, U.S. 178 37.30 N 119.30 W
California, Golfo de c 232 28.00 N 112.00 W
California, University of v² 282 37.52 N 122.15 W
California Aqueduct ≋¹ 204 33.52 N 117.12 W
California City 228 35.08 N 117.58 W
California Creek ≃ 196 33.05 N 99.33 W
California Institute of Technology v² 280 34.08 N 118.08 W
California Institution for Men v² 280 33.59 N 117.40 W
California Institution for Women v² 280 33.57 N 117.38 W
California-Los Angeles, University of (U.C.L.A.) v² 280 34.04 N 118.26 W
California State Polytechnic University v² 280 34.04 N 117.49 W
California State University (Los Angeles) v², Ca., U.S. 280 34.04 N 118.10 W
California State University (Northridge) v², Ca., U.S. 280 34.14 N 118.32 W
California State University (Dominguez Hills) v², Ca., U.S. 280 33.52 N 118.17 W
California State University (Fullerton) v², Ca., U.S. 280 33.53 N 117.53 W
California State University (Long Beach) v², Ca., U.S. 280 33.47 N 118.06 W
California State University (Hayward) v², Ca., U.S. 282 37.39 N 122.04 W
Călimăneşti 38 45.14 N 24.20 E
Cǎlimani, Munţii ∧ 38 47.07 N 25.03 E
Calimera, It. 68 40.15 N 18.17 E
Calimere, Point ⊁ 122 10.18 N 79.52 E
Calimesa 228 34.00 N 117.03 W
Calindó ≃ 255 14.26 S 43.51 W
Calingasta 252 31.19 S 69.25 W
Calingiri 162 31.06 S 116.27 E
Calintaan 116 12.35 N 120.56 E
Calion 194 33.19 N 92.32 W
Calipatria 228 33.07 N 115.30 W
Calispell Peak ∧ 202 48.26 N 117.34 W
Calistoga 226 38.34 N 122.34 W
Calitri 68 40.54 N 15.27 E
Calitzdorp 158 33.33 S 21.42 E
Calizzano 62 44.14 N 8.07 E
Calkinskoje vodochranilišče @¹ 84 41.38 N 44.03 E
Calkojody 85 40.44 N 73.39 E
Callabonna, Lake @ 166 29.45 S 140.04 E
Callabonna Creek ≃ 166 29.38 S 140.08 E
Callac 32 48.24 N 3.26 W
Callaghan, Mount ∧ 204 39.42 N 116.57 W
Callahan 192 30.33 N 81.49 W
Callahan, Mount ∧ 200 39.26 N 108.07 W
Callahans 166 40.58 N 74.37 W
Callan 48 52.33 N 7.23 W
Callander, On., Can. 190 46.13 N 79.23 W
Callander, Scot., U.K. 46 56.15 N 4.14 W
Callang ≃ 116 17.10 N 121.38 E
Callanish ⊥ 46 58.12 N 6.43 W
Callanna 166 29.39 S 140.08 E
Callantsoog 52 52.50 N 4.42 E
Callao, Perú 248 12.04 S 77.09 W
Callao, Va., U.S. 208 37.58 N 76.33 W
Callao □⁶ 286d 12.04 S 77.04 W
Callaquén, Volcán ∧¹ 252 37.54 S 71.26 W
Callas 62 43.30 N 6.28 E
Callaway, Id., U.S. 202 43.39 N 116.41 W
Callaway □⁶ 219 38.50 N 91.52 W
Callaway Gardens ◆ 192 32.51 N 84.52 W
Calle 56 51.20 N 8.13 E
Callensburg 214 40.45 N 80.02 W
Call Hill ∧² 210 42.13 N 77.40 W
Calliano, It. 64 45.56 N 11.05 E
Calliano, It. 62 45.05 N 8.15 E
Callicoon 210 41.46 N 75.03 W
Callicoon Center 210 41.50 N 74.57 W
Callitham 196 28.58 N 98.21 W
Calling Lake @ 182 55.15 N 113.12 W
Calling Lake 182 55.15 N 113.12 W
Callington, Austl. 168b 35.07 S 139.03 E
Callington, Eng., U.K. 42 50.30 N 4.18 W
Calliope 166 24.00 S 151.12 E
Callosa d'En Sarriá 34 38.39 N 0.07 W
Callosa de Segura 34 38.08 N 0.52 W
Calloway Canal ≋ 228 35.24 N 119.01 W
Calmar, Ab., Can. 182 53.16 N 113.49 W
Calmar, Ia., U.S. 190 43.11 N 91.51 W

Caloundra 166 26.48 S 153.09 E
Calouste-Gulbenkian, Museu de ◆ 266c 38.44 N 9.08 W
Caloveto 68 39.30 N 16.45 E
Calp 34 38.39 N 0.03 E
Calpulalpan 234 19.35 N 98.35 W
Čalpy 80 55.05 N 53.06 E
Calshot 42 50.49 N 1.19 W
Calstock 42 50.30 N 4.12 W
Caltabellotta 70 37.34 N 13.13 E
Caltagirone 70 37.14 N 14.31 E
Caltagirone ≃ 70 37.21 N 14.42 E
Caltanissetta 70 37.29 N 14.04 E
Caltanissetta □⁴ 70 37.29 N 14.04 E
Caltavuturo 70 37.49 N 13.53 E
Caltıbük 130 39.57 N 28.36 E
Čaltra 48 53.26 N 8.25 W
Čaltyr' 83 47.17 N 39.30 E
Caluango 152 8.21 S 19.40 E
Calubian 116 11.27 N 124.26 E
Calucinga 152 11.18 S 16.12 E
Cǎlugǎreni 38 44.07 N 26.01 E
Caluire-et-Cuire 62 45.48 N 4.51 E
Calumbolaca 152 9.03 S 13.48 E
Calumet, Mi., U.S. 190 47.14 N 88.27 W
Calumet, Il., U.S. 190 47.19 N 93.16 W
Calumet, Mn., U.S. 190 47.19 N 93.16 W
Calumet, Pa., U.S. 214 40.10 N 79.28 W
Calumet ≃ 278 41.44 N 87.32 W
Calumet, Lake @ 216 41.41 N 87.35 W
Calumet City 216 41.36 N 87.31 W
Calumet Harbor c 278 41.44 N 87.32 W
Calumet Park 216 41.39 N 87.39 W
Calumet Park ◆ 278 41.43 N 87.32 W
Calumet Sag Channel ≋ 278 41.42 N 87.57 W
Calumpit 116 14.55 N 120.46 E
Calunda 152 12.06 S 23.23 E
Caluquembe 152 13.47 S 14.44 E
Calusa Island I 116 9.37 N 121.01 E
Caluula 144 11.58 N 50.45 E
Caluula, Raasiga ⊁ 144 11.59 N 50.47 E
Caluya Island I 116 11.55 N 121.34 E
Calvados □⁵ 32 49.10 N 0.30 W
Calvello 68 40.28 N 15.51 E
Calver 42 53.15 N 1.38 W
Calvert, Al., U.S. 194 31.09 N 88.01 W
Calvert, Tx., U.S. 222 30.58 N 96.40 W
Calvert ≃ 208 38.33 N 76.35 W
Calvert □⁶ 208 38.33 N 76.35 W
Calvert, Lough @ 164 16.17 S 137.44 E
Calvert, Lough @ 169 38.11 S 143.42 E
Calvert City 194 37.02 N 88.21 W
Calvert Hills 166 17.15 S 137.20 E
Calvert Island I 182 51.33 N 128.00 W
Calverton, Eng., U.K. 44 53.02 N 1.05 W
Calverton, Md., U.S. 284c 39.03 N 76.56 W
Calverton, N.Y., U.S. 207 40.55 N 72.45 W
Calvi 32 42.34 N 8.45 E
Calvillo 234 21.51 N 102.43 W
Calvi dell'Umbria 66 42.24 N 12.51 E
Calvia 34 39.34 N 2.31 E
Calvin, Ok., U.S. 196 34.58 N 96.14 W
Calvin, Pa., U.S. 214 40.20 N 78.05 W
Calvinia 158 31.25 S 19.45 E
Calvisano 64 45.20 N 10.20 E
Calvo, Monte ∧ 68 41.44 N 15.46 E
Calvörde 54 52.23 N 11.17 E
Calw 56 48.43 N 8.44 E
Calypso 192 35.09 N 78.06 W
Calzada 248 6.02 S 77.02 W
Cam ≃ 42 52.21 N 0.15 E
Camabatela 152 8.11 S 15.22 E
Çamaça ≃ 248 6.35 S 66.27 W
Camaçari 255 12.42 S 38.19 W
Camachigama, Lac @ 190 47.50 N 76.19 W
Camacupa 152 12.03 S 17.30 E
Camaguán 246 8.06 N 67.36 W
Camagüe ≃ 240p 21.23 N 77.55 W
Camagüey 240p 21.30 N 78.00 W
Camagüey □⁴ 240p 21.30 N 77.50 W
Camaiore 64 43.56 N 10.18 E
Camaiú □² 248 3.20 S 59.42 W
Camajuani 240p 22.28 N 79.44 W
Camaldoli, Eremo di ⊥ 66 43.46 N 11.47 E
Camamu 255 13.57 S 39.07 W
Camaná 248 16.39 S 72.42 W
Camaná ≃ 248 16.39 S 72.46 W
Camanau ≃ 246 1.51 S 61.14 W
Camanche 190 41.47 N 90.15 W
Camanche Reservoir @¹ 226 38.13 N 120.58 W
Camapuã 255 19.32 S 54.05 W
Camapuã ≃ 255 19.30 S 54.05 W
Camaquã 252 30.51 S 51.49 W
Camaquã ≃ 252 31.17 S 51.47 W
Camará ≃ 246 5.45 S 58.50 W
Camarajibe 250 8.01 S 34.58 W
Camararé ≃ 248 13.02 S 58.58 W
Camarat, Cap ⊁ 62 43.12 N 6.41 E
Camarda 66 42.23 N 13.29 E
Camarés 32 43.49 N 2.53 E
Camargo, Bol. 248 20.39 S 65.13 W
Camargo, Méx. 232 27.40 N 105.10 W
Camargo, Represa de @¹ 256 21.25 S 44.30 W
Camargue ✚¹ 62 43.34 N 4.34 E
Camargue, Parc Naturel Regional de ◆ 62 43.30 N 4.28 E
Camarillo 228 34.12 N 119.02 W
Camarillo Heights 228 34.14 N 119.02 W
Camarinas 34 43.07 N 9.10 W
Camarines Norte □⁴ 116 14.10 N 122.45 E
Camarines Sur □⁴ 116 13.35 N 123.20 E
Camarón, Arroyo ≃ 196 27.00 N 100.00 W
Camarón, Cabo ⊁ 236 16.00 N 85.05 W
Camarones 252 44.48 S 65.42 W
Camarones, Bahía c 252 44.48 S 65.42 W
Camas, Esp. 34 37.24 N 6.02 W
Çamaş, Tür. 130 40.55 N 37.32 E
Camas, Wa., U.S. 224 45.35 N 122.24 W
Camas Creek ≃, Id., U.S. 202 43.20 N 114.24 W
Camas Creek ≃, Id., U.S. 202 44.53 N 114.44 W
Camas Creek ≃, Or.. U.S. 202 45.01 N 118.59 W
Camastra 248 2.15 S 49.30 W
Camatagua, Embalse @ 246 9.50 S 15.18 E
Camaxilo 152 8.30 S 18.58 E
Cambados 34 42.30 N 8.48 W
Cambambe ⊥ 152 9.45 S 14.33 E
Cambará 256 23.03 S 50.05 W
Cambarinha 287b 38.42 N 9.08 W
Cambé 256 23.17 S 51.16 W
Cambará 70 37.15 N 13.47 E

Camboundja, Serra ∧ 152 12.06 S 14.00 E
Camboon 166 25.03 S 150.26 E
Cambooya 171a 27.42 S 151.52 E
Camboriú 252 27.01 S 48.38 W
Camborne 42 50.11 N 5.19 W
Cambra 42 41.11 N 76.18 W
Cambrai, Austl. 168b 34.39 S 139.17 E
Cambrai, Fr. 50 50.10 N 3.14 E
Cambremer 50 49.09 N 0.03 E
Cambria, Ca., U.S. 226 35.33 N 121.04 W
Cambria, In., U.S. 216 40.22 N 86.33 W
Cambria, Mi., U.S. 216 41.49 N 84.39 W
Cambria, Wi., U.S. 190 43.32 N 89.06 W
Cambria □⁶ 214 40.29 N 79.16 W
Cambria Ice Field ⊠ 182 55.55 N 129.30 W
Cambrian Mountains ∧ 42 52.35 N 3.35 W
Cambrian Park 226 37.15 N 121.55 W
Cambridge (Galt), On., Can. 212 43.22 N 80.19 W
Cambridge, N.Z. 172 37.53 S 175.28 E
Cambridge, Eng., U.K. 42 52.13 N 0.08 E
Cambridge, Id., U.S. 202 44.34 N 116.41 W
Cambridge, Il., U.S. 190 41.18 N 90.11 W
Cambridge, Ia., U.S. 190 41.53 N 93.31 W
Cambridge, Md., U.S. 208 38.33 N 76.04 W
Cambridge, Ma., U.S. 207 42.22 N 71.06 W
Cambridge, Mn., U.S. 190 45.34 N 93.13 W
Cambridge, Ne., U.S. 198 40.16 N 100.09 W
Cambridge, N.Y., U.S. 210 43.01 N 73.22 W
Cambridge, Oh., U.S. 188 40.02 N 81.35 W
Cambridge, Wi., U.S. 190 43.00 N 89.01 W
Cambridge Bay 176 69.03 N 105.05 W
Cambridge City 218 39.48 N 85.10 W
Cambridge Fiord c² 176 71.20 N 74.44 W
Cambridge Gulf c 164 15.14 S 128.15 E
Cambridge Park 274a 33.45 S 150.43 E
Cambridge Reservoir @¹ 267a 42.24 N 71.16 W
Cambridgeshire □⁶ 42 52.20 N 0.05 E
Cambridge Springs 214 41.48 N 80.03 W
Cambrils 34 41.04 N 1.03 E
Cambriú, Ponta de ⊁ 252 25.10 S 47.55 W
Cambucí ✚⁸ 287b 23.34 S 46.37 W
Cambulo 152 7.48 S 21.14 E
Cambundi-Catembo 152 10.09 S 17.31 E
Cambuquira 256 21.51 S 45.18 W
Cambural 286c 10.26 N 66.59 W
Camburú ≃ 256 23.41 S 45.23 W
Camby 218 39.40 N 86.19 W
Čamčakly 128 37.56 N 63.06 E
Camden, Austl. 170 34.03 S 150.42 E
Camden, S. Afr. 158 26.38 S 30.07 E
Camden, Al., U.S. 194 31.59 N 87.17 W
Camden, Ar., U.S. 194 33.35 N 92.50 W
Camden, De., U.S. 208 39.06 N 75.32 W
Camden, In., U.S. 216 40.09 N 86.32 W
Camden, Me., U.S. 188 44.12 N 69.03 W
Camden, Mi., U.S. 216 41.45 N 84.45 W
Camden, N.J., U.S. 210 39.55 N 75.07 W
Camden, N.Y., U.S. 210 43.20 N 75.44 W
Camden, N.C., U.S. 192 36.19 N 76.10 W
Camden, Oh., U.S. 218 39.37 N 84.38 W
Camden, S.C., U.S. 192 34.14 N 80.36 W
Camden, Tn., U.S. 192 36.03 N 88.05 W
Camden, Tx., U.S. 222 30.55 N 94.44 W
Camden □⁶, N.J. 276 39.57 N 75.00 W
Camden □⁶, N.C. 192 36.28 N 76.21 W
Camden 48 51.33 S 0.10 W
Camden ✚⁸ 260 51.33 N 0.10 W
Camden Aerodrome ≈ 274a 34.03 S 150.41 E
Camden Bay c 274a 34.03 S 150.41 E
Camden Hills State Park ◆ 188 44.17 N 69.05 W
Camden Lake @ 194 44.25 N 76.52 W
Camden Station ≈⁵ 284b 39.17 N 76.37 W
Camdenton 194 38.00 N 92.44 W
Camedo 58 46.09 N 8.37 E
Cameia, Parque Nacional da ◆ 152 11.45 S 21.01 E
Camel ≃ 42 50.33 N 4.55 W
Camel, Mount ∧² 169 36.45 S 144.43 E
Camelback Mountain ∧, Ak., U.S. 210 41.03 N 75.21 W
Camelback Mountain ∧, Pa., U.S. 210 50.37 N 4.41 W
Cameleford 130 37.05 N 29.20 E
Camelî 188 44.19 N 72.53 W
Camels Hump ∧ 188 44.19 N 72.53 W
Cameo Acres 282 37.51 N 121.58 W
Cameri 62 45.30 N 8.39 E
Cameri, Aeroporto di ≈ 266b 45.32 N 8.40 E
Cameron, Ca., U.S. 226 38.39 N 120.56 W
Cameron, La., U.S. 194 29.47 N 93.19 W
Cameron, Mo., U.S. 194 39.44 N 94.14 W
Cameron, N.Y., U.S. 210 42.12 N 77.24 W
Cameron, Tx., U.S. 222 30.51 N 96.58 W
Cameron, W.V., U.S. 188 39.49 N 80.34 W
Cameron, Wi., U.S. 190 45.24 N 91.44 W
Cameron □⁶ 222 26.08 N 97.31 W
Cameron Highlands ◆ 110 4.28 N 101.27 E
Cameron Hills ✚² 176 59.48 N 118.00 W
Cameron Lake @ 224 49.17 N 124.37 W
Cameron Mills 210 42.11 N 77.22 W
Cameron Run ≃ 284c 38.48 N 77.04 W
Cameroon (Cameroun) □¹ 134 6.00 N 12.00 E
Cameroon ∧¹ 152 4.12 N 9.11 E
Cameroun □¹ 134 6.00 N 12.00 E
— Cameroon □¹ 134 6.00 N 12.00 E
Camerino 66 43.08 N 13.04 E
Camfield 164 17.03 S 131.21 E
Camici Gölü @ 130 37.30 N 27.25 E
Camiguin Island I, Pil. 116 9.10 N 124.40 E
Camiguin Island I, Pil. 116 18.56 N 121.55 E
Camin 76 51.27 N 31.17 E
Camin 54 53.32 N 10.38 E
Caminha 34 41.52 N 8.50 W
Camino 226 38.44 N 120.40 W
Camiri 248 20.03 S 63.31 W
Camiroaga 34 38.58 N 15.43 E
Camisano Vicentino 64 45.31 N 11.48 E
Camisea ≃ 248 11.35 S 72.58 W
Camissombo 152 8.07 S 20.41 E
Çamköy 130 37.04 N 28.10 E
Camlica, Tür. 130 37.04 N 28.10 E
Çamlıca, Tür. 130 39.20 N 33.59 E
Çamlıdere, Tür. 130 40.30 N 32.28 E
Çamlıdere, Tür. 130 40.25 N 28.29 E
Çamlık □⁵ 130 38.10 N 30.07 E
Çamlıyayla 130 40.25 N 28.49 E
Cammal 210 41.24 N 77.19 W
Cammarata 70 37.38 N 13.38 E
Cammarata, Monte ∧ 70 37.37 N 13.36 E

ESPAÑOL

Nombre	Página	Lat.°′	Long.°′ W = Oeste
Camoapa	236	12.23 N	85.31 W
Camocim	250	2.54 S	40.50 W
Camogli	62	44.21 N	9.09 E
Çamoluk	130	40.08 N	38.45 E
Camonica, Val V	64	46.00 N	10.20 E
Camooweal	166	19.55 S	138.07 E
Camopi ≃	250	3.11 N	52.20 W
Camorim ≃	287a	22.59 S	43.25 W
Camorim, Représa do ⊜[1]	287a	22.58 S	43.27 W
Camorta Island I	110	8.08 N	93.30 E
Camote, Cerro ∧	286d	11.57 S	77.06 W
Camotes Islands II	116	10.40 N	124.24 E
Camotes Sea ⍑[2]	116	10.30 N	124.15 E
Camotlán ≃	234	22.01 N	104.15 W
Camowen ≃	48	54.36 N	7.18 W
Camp □[6]	222	33.00 N	94.58 W
Campagna	68	40.40 N	15.08 E
Campagna di Roma ◆[1]	66	41.50 N	12.35 E
Campagna Lupia	64	45.21 N	12.06 E
Campagnano di Roma	66	42.08 N	12.23 E
Campagnatico	66	42.53 N	11.16 E
Campagne-lès-Hesdin	50	50.24 N	1.52 E
Campaign	194	35.46 N	85.37 W
Campamento	236	14.33 N	86.42 W
Campana, Arg.	258	34.10 S	58.57 W
Campana, It.	68	39.24 N	16.50 E
Campana, Isla I	254	48.20 S	75.15 W
Campanario	34	38.52 N	5.37 W
Campanario, Cerro de ∧	248	5.57 S	77.31 W
Campanella, Punta ›	68	40.34 N	14.19 E
Campanero, Cerro ∧	246	5.54 N	65.12 W
Campanha	256	21.50 S	45.24 W
Campania □[4]	68	40.55 N	14.50 E
Campania Island I	182	53.05 N	129.30 W
Camparada	266b	45.39 N	9.19 E
Campaspe ≃, Austl.	166	21.00 S	146.24 E
Campaspe ≃, Austl.	169	36.41 S	144.31 E
Campbell, S. Afr.	158	28.48 S	23.44 E
Campbell, Ca., U.S.	226	37.17 N	121.56 W
Campbell, Mn., U.S.	198	46.05 N	96.24 W
Campbell, Mo., U.S.	194	36.29 N	90.04 W
Campbell, Ne., U.S.	198	40.18 N	98.44 W
Campbell, N.Y., U.S.	210	42.13 N	77.11 W
Campbell, Oh., U.S.	214	41.04 N	80.35 W
Campbell, Tx., U.S.	222	33.09 N	95.57 W
Campbell □[6]	218	38.55 N	84.20 W
Campbell, Cape ›	172	41.44 S	174.17 E
Campbell Airport ⊠	279b	40.21 N	80.11 W
Campbellfield	274b	37.41 S	144.57 E
Campbellford	212	44.18 N	77.48 W
Campbell Hall	210	41.27 N	74.16 W
Campbell Hill ∧[2]	216	40.22 N	83.43 W
Campbell Island	182	52.10 N	128.09 W
Campbell Island I	9	52.30 S	169.05 E
Campbell Lake ⊜	182	50.01 N	125.27 W
Campbell Plateau ✢[3]	9	51.00 S	170.00 E
Campbell Point ›	171a	27.22 S	153.55 E
Campbellpore	123	33.46 N	72.22 E
Campbell Range ⩘	180	61.08 N	129.45 W
Campbell River	182	50.01 N	125.15 W
Campbells ≃	170	33.42 S	149.37 E
Campbell's Airport ⊠	278	42.20 N	88.04 W
Campbell's-Bay	188	45.44 N	76.36 W
Campbellsburg, In., U.S.	218	38.39 N	86.15 W
Campbellsburg, Ky., U.S.	218	38.31 N	85.12 W
Campbell Slough ≃	226	39.22 N	121.51 W
Campbellsport	190	43.35 N	88.16 W
Campbells River	170	33.54 S	149.37 E
Campbells Run ≃	279b	40.24 N	80.05 W
Campbellsville	194	37.20 N	85.20 W
Campbellton, N.B., Can.	186	48.00 N	66.40 W
Campbellton, Nf., Can.	186	49.17 N	54.56 W
Campbellton, P.E., Can.	186	46.47 N	64.18 W
Campbellton, Fl., U.S.	192	30.56 N	85.24 W
Campbell Town, Austl.	166	41.56 S	147.29 E
Campbelltown, Austl.	168b	34.53 S	138.40 E
Campbelltown, Austl.	170	34.04 S	150.49 E
Campbelltown, Pa., U.S.	208	40.17 N	76.35 W
Campbellville	212	43.29 N	79.59 W
Campbeltown	44	55.26 N	5.36 W
Camp Creek ≃, Ca., U.S.	226	38.38 N	120.40 W
Camp Creek ≃, Mo., U.S.	219	39.02 N	91.12 W
Camp Creek Lake ⊜[1]	222	31.03 N	96.19 W
Camp David ʋ	208	39.38 N	77.28 W
Camp de Frileuse ■	261	48.52 N	1.55 E
Camp de Satory ■	261	48.47 N	2.06 E
Camp Dix	218	38.29 N	83.17 W
Camp Douglas	190	43.55 N	90.16 W
Campeche	232	19.51 N	90.32 W
Campeche □[3]	232	19.00 N	90.30 W
Campeche, Bahía de ⊂	232	20.00 N	94.00 W
Campeche Bank ✢[4]	16	22.00 N	90.00 W
Campechuela	240p	20.14 N	77.17 W
Campegine	64	44.45 N	10.32 E
Campello Monti	58	45.56 N	8.15 E
Camperdown, Austl.	169	38.14 S	143.09 E
Camperdown, S. Afr.	158	29.42 S	30.33 E
Camperville	184	51.59 N	100.09 W
Campestre	256	21.43 S	46.15 W
Cam Pha	110	21.01 N	107.19 E
Camp Hill, Al., U.S.	194	32.48 N	85.39 W
Camp Hill, Pa., U.S.	208	40.14 N	76.55 W
Campi Bisenzio	66	43.49 N	11.08 E
Campidano ◆[1]	71	39.30 N	8.47 E
Campiglia dei Fosci	66	43.27 N	11.03 E
Campiglia Marittima	66	43.03 N	10.37 E
Campillo de Llerena	34	38.30 N	5.50 W
Campillos	34	37.03 N	4.51 W
Campina ◆[1]	34	37.45 N	4.45 W
Campina Grande	250	7.13 S	35.53 W
Campinas	256	22.54 S	47.05 W
Campina Verde	255	19.31 S	49.28 W
Campinho, Rio do ≃	287a	22.52 S	43.37 W
Campione del Garda	64	45.45 N	10.45 E
Campi Salentina	68	40.24 N	18.01 E
Campitello	64	46.28 N	11.44 E
Camp King	150	4.55 N	7.58 W
Camp Lake	216	42.32 N	88.09 W
Camp Lake ⊜	212	45.27 N	78.54 W
Camp Leger ■	261	48.34 N	2.34 E
Camp Lejeune Marine Corps Base ■	192	34.40 N	77.21 W
Campli	66	42.43 N	13.41 E
Camplong	112	10.02 S	123.55 E
Campo, Cam.	152	2.22 N	9.49 E
Campo, Moç.	156	17.44 S	36.21 E
Campo, Co., U.S.	198	37.06 N	102.34 W
Campo, Réserve de ◆[4]	152	2.35 N	9.57 E
Campoalegre	246	2.41 N	75.20 W
Campo Alegre ≃	250	9.19 S	50.06 W
Campo Alegre de Goiás	255	17.39 S	47.45 W
Campobasso	66	41.34 N	14.39 E
Campobasso □[4]	66	41.38 N	14.35 E
Campobello di Licata	70	37.15 N	13.55 E
Campobello di Mazara	70	37.38 N	12.45 E
Campobello Island I	186	44.53 N	66.55 W
Campo Belo	255	20.53 S	45.16 W
Campo Blenio	58	46.34 N	8.56 E
Campo Catino	66	41.48 N	13.20 E
Campocologno	58	46.13 N	10.08 E
Campodarsego	64	45.30 N	11.54 E
Campo de Criptana	34	39.24 N	3.07 W
Campo de la Cruz	246	10.23 N	74.53 W
Campo de Marte ♠	286d	12.04 S	77.03 W

FRANÇAIS

Nom	Page	Lat.°′	Long.°′ W = Ouest
Campo de Marte ■	287b	23.30 S	46.37 W
Campo de Mayo ■	288	34.32 S	58.38 W
Campo di Giove	66	42.01 N	14.03 E
Campo di Trens (Trens)	64	46.52 N	11.29 E
Campo do Coelho	256	22.15 S	42.39 W
Campodolcino	58	46.24 N	9.21 E
Campo Erê	252	26.23 S	53.03 W
Campofelice di Fitalia	70	37.50 N	13.29 E
Campofelice di Roccella	70	37.59 N	13.53 E
Campofiorito	70	37.45 N	13.16 E
Campo Florido	255	19.47 S	48.35 W
Campoformido	64	46.01 N	13.09 E
Campo Formoso	250	10.31 S	40.20 W
Campofranco	70	37.30 N	13.43 E
Campogalliano	64	44.41 N	10.50 E
Campo Gallo	252	26.35 S	62.51 W
Campo Grande, Arg.	252	27.13 S	54.58 W
Campo Grande, Bra.	255	20.27 S	54.37 W
Campo Grande ◆[8], Bra.	256	22.54 S	43.34 W
Campo Grande ◆[8], Port.	266c	38.45 N	9.09 W
Campo Indian Reservation ◆[4]	204	32.40 N	116.20 W
Campo Largo, Arg.	252	26.48 S	60.50 W
Campo Largo, Bra.	252	25.26 S	49.32 W
Campolaro	64	45.55 N	10.20 E
Campolasta (Astfeld)	64	46.40 N	11.22 E
Campolato, Capo ›	70	37.17 N	15.12 E
Campo Libertad ■	286b	23.05 N	82.26 W
Campolide	256	21.36 S	43.53 W
Campolieto	66	41.38 N	14.46 E
Campo Ligure	62	44.32 N	8.42 E
Campo Limpo Paulista	256	23.12 S	46.48 W
Campo Maior, Bra.	250	4.49 S	42.10 W
Campo Maior, Port.	34	39.01 N	7.04 W
Campomarino	66	41.57 N	15.02 E
Campo Militar Número Uno ■	286a	19.27 N	99.14 W
Campomorone	62	44.30 N	8.53 E
Campo Mourão	255	24.03 S	52.22 W
Campo Novo	252	27.42 S	53.48 W
Campo Pequeno ♠	266c	38.44 N	9.08 W
Campo Quijano	252	24.55 S	65.39 W
Campora	68	40.19 N	15.17 E
Camporeale	70	37.54 N	13.06 E
Camporgiano	64	44.09 N	10.20 E
Camporredondo	248	6.07 S	78.21 W
Campos	255	21.45 S	41.18 W
Campos Altos	255	19.41 S	46.10 W
Camposampiero	64	45.34 N	11.56 E
Campo Santo, Arg.	252	24.40 S	65.06 W
Camposanto, It.	64	44.47 N	11.08 E
Campos Belos	255	13.03 S	46.53 W
Campos de Cunha	256	22.55 S	44.49 W
Campos do Jordão	256	22.44 S	45.35 W
Campos Elisios	256	22.42 S	43.17 W
Campos Gerais	256	21.14 S	45.46 W
Campos Novos	252	27.24 S	51.12 W
Campos Sales	250	7.04 S	40.23 W
Campo Tencia, Pizzo ∧	58	46.26 N	8.43 E
Campotosto	66	42.33 N	13.22 E
Campotosto, Lago di ⊜	66	42.32 N	13.22 E
Campo Tures (Sand in Taufers)	64	46.55 N	11.57 E
Campovalano	66	42.44 N	13.40 E
Camp Parks Communications Annex ■	282	37.44 N	121.54 W
Camp Pendleton Marine Corps Base ■	228	33.19 N	117.18 W
Camp Point	219	40.02 N	91.04 W
Camp Ruby	222	30.42 N	94.45 W
Campsie	274a	33.55 S	151.06 E
Campsie Fells ⩘[2]	46	56.02 N	4.12 W
Camp Springs	208	38.48 N	76.54 W
Campti	194	31.53 N	93.07 W
Campton	192	37.44 N	83.32 W
Camptonville	226	39.27 N	121.03 W
Camptown	210	41.43 N	76.14 W
Campus	216	41.01 N	88.18 W
Campuya ≃	246	1.43 S	73.30 W
Camp Verde	200	34.33 N	111.51 W
Campville	210	42.06 N	76.09 W
Camp Wood	196	29.40 N	100.01 W
Cam Ranh	110	11.54 N	109.09 E
Cam Ranh, Vinh ⊂	110	11.53 N	109.10 E
Camrose, Ab., Can.	182	53.01 N	112.50 W
Camrose, Wales, U.K.	42	51.51 N	5.01 W
Camsell ≃	176	65.40 N	118.07 W
Camu ≃	250	1.15 N	57.09 W
Camucia	66	43.16 N	11.58 E
Camucuio	152	14.12 S	13.20 E
Camurí Chiquito, Quebrada ≃	286c	10.37 N	66.52 W
Çamurlu Dağ ∧	130	40.21 N	42.26 E
Camuy	240m	18.29 N	66.51 W
Çam Xuyen	110	18.15 N	106.00 E
Čamyndy	85	41.37 N	74.20 E
Čamzinka	80	54.24 N	45.47 E
Çan, Tür.	130	40.02 N	27.03 E
Çan, Tür.	130	39.09 N	40.13 E
Çan ≃	260	51.48 N	0.25 E
Čaňa	30	48.37 N	21.18 E
Canaan, Ct., U.S.	207	42.01 N	73.19 W
Canaan, Fl., U.S.	220	28.48 N	81.14 W
Canaan, In., U.S.	218	38.52 N	85.25 W
Canaan, N.Y., U.S.	210	42.25 N	73.27 W
Canaan, Vt., U.S.	206	44.59 N	71.32 W
Canaan ≃	186	45.55 N	65.47 W
Canaan Lake ⊜	276	40.47 N	73.01 W
Canaan Valley State Park ♠	188	39.02 N	79.32 W
Cana-brava ≃, Bra.	255	13.11 S	48.11 W
Cana-brava ≃, Bra.	255	12.12 S	48.40 W
Cañacao Bay ⊂	269f	14.29 N	120.55 E
Canaçarí, Lago ⊜	250	2.57 S	58.15 W
Canada □[1]	176	60.00 N	95.00 W
Cañada, Loma la ∧[2]	240p	21.41 N	82.57 W
Canada Bay ⊂	186	50.43 N	56.10 W
Cañada de Caracheo	234	20.22 N	100.57 W
Cañada de Gómez	252	32.49 S	61.24 W
Cañada Honda	252	31.59 S	68.33 W
Canada Lake ⊜	210	43.10 N	74.32 W
Cañada Nieto	258	33.43 S	58.05 W
Canadarago Lake ⊜	210	42.48 N	75.01 W
Canada's Wonderland ♠	275b	43.51 N	79.33 W
Cañada Verde → Villa Huidobro	252	34.50 S	64.35 W
Canadaway Creek ≃	214	42.28 N	79.22 W
Canadensis	210	41.11 N	75.15 W
Canadian	196	35.54 N	100.22 W
Canadian ≃, U.S.	196	35.27 N	95.03 W
Canadian ≃, Co., U.S.	200	40.53 N	106.20 W
Canadian, Deep Fork ≃	196	35.28 N	95.50 W
Canadian Forces Base Trenton ■	212	44.07 N	77.33 W
Canadice Lake ⊜	210	42.43 N	77.34 W
Cañadón Seco	254	46.33 S	67.35 W
Canaguá ≃	246	7.57 N	69.36 W
Canaima	246	6.14 N	62.52 W
Canaima, Parque Nacional ♠	246	4.27 N	62.00 W
Canajoharie	210	42.54 N	74.34 W
Çanakkale	130	40.09 N	26.24 E
Çanakkale □[4]	130	40.10 N	26.45 E
Çanakkale Boğazı (Dardanelles) ⋓	130	40.15 N	26.25 E
Canal, Islas del → Channel Islands II	28	49.20 N	2.20 W
Canala	175f	21.32 S	165.57 E
Canale	62	44.48 N	8.00 E

PORTUGUÊS

Nome	Página	Lat.°′	Long.°′ W = Oeste
Canale, Val V	64	46.29 N	13.30 E
Canale del Ferro ≃	64	46.21 N	13.07 E
Canalejas	234	19.57 N	99.39 W
Canal Flats	182	50.09 N	115.48 W
Canal Fulton	214	40.53 N	81.35 W
Canal Lake ⊜	212	44.34 N	79.03 W
Canal Lewisville	214	40.18 N	81.50 W
Canal Point	220	26.51 N	80.38 W
Canals	252	33.33 S	62.53 W
Canal Winchester	188	39.51 N	82.48 W
Canamã ≃	248	8.45 S	59.15 W
Canandaigua	210	42.52 N	77.20 W
Canandaigua Lake ⊜	210	42.49 N	77.16 W
Canandaigua Outlet ≃	210	43.04 N	77.00 W
Cananea	232	30.57 N	110.18 W
Cananéia	252	25.01 S	47.57 W
Canan Station	214	40.28 N	78.26 W
Canapine, Forca)(	66	42.45 N	13.12 E
Canápolis	255	18.44 S	49.13 W
Canapville	50	49.19 N	0.08 E
Cañar	246	2.33 S	78.56 W
Cañar □[4]	246	2.30 S	79.00 W
Canard ≃	214	42.09 N	83.06 W
Canard, Lac au ⊜	206	45.48 N	71.31 W
Canarias, Islas (Canary Islands) II	148	28.00 N	15.30 W
Canaries	241f	13.55 N	61.04 W
Canaro	64	44.56 N	11.40 E
Canarreos, Archipiélago de los II	240p	21.50 N	82.30 W
Canarsie ◆[8]	276	40.38 N	73.53 W
Canarsie Park ♠	276	40.38 N	73.53 W
Canarsie Pol I	276	40.37 N	73.52 W
Canary Basin ✢[1]	10	30.00 N	25.00 W
Canary Islands → Canarias, Islas II	148	28.00 N	15.30 W
Cañas	236	10.25 N	85.07 W
Canaseraga	210	42.27 N	77.46 W
Canaseraga Creek ≃	210	42.45 N	77.50 W
Cañasgordas	246	6.45 N	76.01 W
Canastota	210	43.04 N	75.45 W
Canatlán	232	24.31 N	104.47 W
Canaveral, Cape ›	220	28.27 N	80.32 W
Canaveral Bight ⊂[3]	220	28.26 N	80.33 W
Canaveral National Seashore ♠	220	28.45 N	80.45 W
Canaveral Peninsula ›[1]	220	28.28 N	80.34 W
Cañaveras	34	40.22 N	2.24 W
Canavese □[9]	62	45.20 N	7.40 E
Canavieiras	255	15.39 S	38.57 W
Cañazas	236	8.19 N	81.13 W
Canazei	64	46.28 N	11.46 E
Canbelego	166	31.33 S	146.19 E
Canberra	171b	35.17 S	149.08 E
Canberra Wildlife Gardens ♠	171b	35.20 S	149.09 E
Canby, Ca., U.S.	204	41.26 N	120.52 W
Canby, Mn., U.S.	198	44.42 N	96.16 W
Canby, Or., U.S.	224	45.15 N	122.41 W
Cancajanang, Mount ∧	116	11.04 N	124.47 E
Cancale	32	48.41 N	1.51 W
Cancano, Lago di ⊜	64	46.31 N	10.18 E
Cance ≃	62	45.12 N	4.48 E
Cancellara	68	40.44 N	15.56 E
Cancello e Arnone	68	41.04 N	14.03 E
Canchaque	248	5.24 S	79.36 W
Canche ≃	50	50.31 N	1.39 E
Cancon	32	44.32 N	0.38 E
Cancún	232	21.05 N	86.46 W
Čančur	88	53.49 N	106.59 E
Canda	64	45.03 N	11.30 E
Candala → Qandala	144	11.28 N	49.52 E
Candarave	248	17.16 S	70.15 W
Çandarlı	130	38.56 N	26.56 E
Çandarlı Körfezi ⊂	130	38.52 N	26.55 E
Candás	34	43.35 N	5.46 W
Candé	32	47.34 N	1.02 W
Candeias, Bra.	255	12.40 S	38.33 W
Candeias, Bra.	255	20.47 S	45.16 W
Candeias ≃	248	8.39 S	63.31 W
Candela, It.	68	41.08 N	15.31 E
Candela, Méx.	232	26.50 N	100.40 W
Candela, Río de ≃	196	27.16 N	100.18 W
Candelaria, Arg.	252	27.28 S	55.44 W
Candelaria, Arg.	252	32.04 S	65.49 W
Candelária, Bra.	252	29.40 S	52.48 W
Candelaria, Col.	246	3.25 N	76.20 W
Candelaria, Cuba	240p	22.44 N	82.58 W
Candelaria, Pil.	116	15.38 N	119.56 E
Candelaria ≃	232	18.37 N	91.14 W
Candelaria Loxicha	234	15.54 N	96.31 W
Candelaro ≃	68	41.34 N	15.53 E
Candeleda	34	40.09 N	5.14 W
Candelo, Austl.	166	36.46 S	149.42 E
Candelo, It.	62	45.33 N	8.07 E
Candiac	206	45.23 N	73.31 W
Candia Canavese	62	45.20 N	7.53 E
Candia → Iráklion	38	35.20 N	25.09 E
Candia Lomellina	62	45.11 N	8.36 E
Cándido Aguilar	232	25.30 N	98.02 W
Cândido de Abreu	252	24.35 S	51.20 W
Cândido Mendes	250	1.27 S	45.43 W
Candies Creek ≃	192	35.18 N	84.51 W
Candijay	116	9.49 N	124.30 E
Çandır, Tür.	130	40.16 N	33.29 E
Çandır, Tür.	130	39.15 N	35.32 E
Candle	180	65.55 N	161.56 W
Candle Lake ⊜	184	53.50 N	105.18 W
Candlemas Islands II	18	57.03 S	26.40 W
Candlestick	194	32.15 N	90.20 W
Candlestick Park ♠	282	37.43 N	122.23 W
Candlewood, Lake ⊜	207	41.32 N	73.27 W
Candlewood Isle	207	41.28 N	73.27 W
Candlewood Knolls	207	41.28 N	73.27 W
Candlewood Shores	207	41.28 N	73.26 W
Čandman', Mong.	86	50.02 N	92.03 E
Čandman', Mong.	102	45.20 N	97.59 E
Cando, Ang.	152	16.30 S	18.19 E
Cando, Sk., Can.	184	52.23 N	108.14 W
Cando, N.D., U.S.	198	48.29 N	99.12 W
Candombé ≃	152	16.54 S	21.52 E
Candon	116	17.12 N	120.27 E
Candon Point ›	116	17.13 N	120.24 E
Candor, N.Y., U.S.	210	42.13 N	76.20 W
Candor, N.C., U.S.	192	35.17 N	79.44 W
Candover	158	27.28 S	31.57 E
Cane ≃, Austl.	162	21.33 S	115.23 E
Cane ≃, La., U.S.	194	31.31 N	92.43 W
Cane ≃, N.C., U.S.	192	36.00 N	82.16 W
Caneadea	210	42.23 N	78.09 W
Canea → Khaniá	38	35.31 N	24.02 E
Caneças	266c	38.49 N	9.14 W
Cane Creek ≃	194	36.29 N	90.28 W
Canegrate	266b	45.34 N	8.56 E
Canela	252	29.22 S	50.50 W
Canelas	232	25.06 N	106.34 W
Canelles, Embalse de ⊜[1]	34	42.10 N	0.30 E
Canelli	62	44.43 N	8.17 E
Canelones	258	34.32 S	56.17 W
Canelones □[5]	258	34.35 S	56.15 W
Canelón Grande, Arroyo ≃	258	34.30 S	56.24 W
Cane Run ≃	218	38.13 N	84.37 W
Cañete, Chile	252	37.48 S	73.24 W
Cañete, Esp.	34	40.03 N	1.35 W
Caneva	64	45.58 N	12.26 E
Caney	198	37.00 N	95.56 W
Caney ≃	196	36.20 N	95.42 W
Caney Brook ≃	276	41.07 N	73.50 W
Caney Creek ≃, Ar., U.S.	194	33.46 N	93.07 W
Caney Creek ≃, Tx., U.S.	196	28.46 N	95.39 W
Caney Creek ≃, Tx., U.S.	222	32.48 N	95.33 W

Caney Creek ≃, Tx., U.S.	222	30.28 N	95.38 W
Caney Creek ≃, Tx., U.S.	222	30.04 N	96.08 W
Caney Creek ≃, Tx., U.S.	222	31.52 N	96.13 W
Caney Creek ≃, Tx., U.S.	222	31.03 N	94.33 W
Caney Creek ≃, Tx., U.S.	222	30.53 N	95.48 W
Caney Creek ≃, Tx., U.S.	222	30.07 N	95.10 W
Canfield	214	41.01 N	80.45 W
Canfield Island I	276	41.06 N	73.23 W
Canfranc	34	42.43 N	0.31 W
Cangaíba ◆[8]	287b	23.30 S	46.31 W
Cangallo	248	13.33 S	74.12 W
Cangamba	152	13.40 S	19.54 E
Cangandala	152	9.45 S	16.33 E
Cangandala, Parque Nacional da ♠	152	9.45 S	16.50 E
Cangas, Bra.	248	16.05 S	56.33 W
Cangas, Esp.	34	42.16 N	8.47 W
Cangas de Narcea	34	43.11 N	6.33 W
Cangas de Onís	34	43.21 N	5.07 W
Cangbu	100	30.49 N	114.35 E
Can Gioc ≃	269c	10.42 N	106.37 E
Cangkuang, Tanjung ›	115a	6.51 S	105.15 E
Cangniutun	105	39.23 N	115.54 E
Cango Caves ⊥[5]	158	33.23 S	22.14 E
Cangola	152	7.58 S	15.52 E
Cangombe	152	14.24 S	19.59 E
Cangongo	152	9.24 S	17.30 E
Cangqian, Zhg.	106	30.18 N	120.00 E
Cangqian, Zhg.	106	30.17 N	120.25 E
Cangshangtun	105	40.03 N	117.32 E
Canguaretama	250	6.24 S	35.08 W
Canguçu	252	31.24 S	52.41 W
Canguera	256	23.36 S	47.09 W
Cangumbe	152	12.00 S	19.17 E
Cangwu	102	23.22 N	111.13 E
Çangxi	102	31.48 N	105.57 E
Čangyrtas	85	40.53 N	72.50 E
Cangyuan	102	23.12 N	99.16 E
Cangzhou	98	38.19 N	116.51 E
Canhoca	152	9.15 S	14.41 E
Canhotinho	250	8.53 S	36.12 W
Caniapiscau ≃	176	57.40 N	69.30 W
Caniapiscau, Lac ⊜	176	54.10 N	69.55 W
Canicanian	116	14.46 N	122.01 E
Canicattì	70	37.21 N	13.51 E
Canicattini Bagni	70	37.02 N	15.04 E
Canigao Channel ⋓	116	10.15 N	124.42 E
Canigou, Pic du ∧	32	42.31 N	2.27 E
Canillas ◆[8]	266a	40.28 N	3.38 W
Canillejas ◆[8]	266a	40.27 N	3.37 W
Canim Lake	182	51.46 N	120.54 W
Canim Lake ⊜	182	51.52 N	120.45 W
Canim Lake Indian Reserve ◆[4]	182	51.47 N	121.00 W
Canindé	250	4.22 S	39.19 W
Canindé ≃	250	6.15 S	42.52 W
Canindeyú □[5]	252	24.15 S	55.15 W
Canino	66	42.28 N	11.45 E
Canipaan	116	8.35 N	117.16 E
Canipo Island I	116	10.59 N	120.57 E
Canisius College ʋ[2]	284a	42.55 N	78.52 W
Canisp ∧	46	58.07 N	5.03 W
Canistear Reservoir ⊜[1]	276	41.08 N	74.29 W
Canisteo	210	42.16 N	77.36 W
Canisteo ≃	210	42.07 N	77.08 W
Canistota	198	43.35 N	97.17 W
Cañitas de Felipe Pescador	234	23.36 N	102.43 W
Canjáyar	34	37.00 N	2.44 W
Canjinge	152	10.12 S	21.17 E
Cankhor	144	10.46 N	46.13 E
Çankırı	130	40.36 N	33.37 E
Çankırı □[4]	130	40.45 N	33.25 E
Čanlaon	116	10.22 N	123.12 E
Canlaon Volcano ∧[1]	116	10.25 N	123.08 E
Canley Vale	274a	33.53 S	150.57 E
Canmore	182	51.05 N	115.21 W
Canna	68	40.05 N	16.30 E
Canna I	46	57.04 N	6.34 W
Canna, Sound of ⋓	46	57.03 N	6.25 W
Cannanore	122	11.51 N	75.22 E
Cannara	66	43.00 N	12.35 E
Canne ⊥	68	41.18 N	16.09 E
Cannel City	192	37.47 N	83.16 W
Cannelton	194	37.54 N	86.44 W
Canner ≃	56	49.24 N	6.16 E
Cannero-Riviera	58	46.01 N	8.41 E
Cannes	62	43.33 N	7.01 E
Cannes, Bayou des ≃	194	30.12 N	92.35 W
Canneto, It.	66	43.12 N	10.44 E
Canneto, It.	70	38.29 N	14.58 E
Canneto sull'Oglio	64	45.09 N	10.25 E
Cannich	46	57.21 N	4.46 W
Cannich ≃	46	57.21 N	4.44 W
Cannifton	212	44.12 N	77.23 W
Canning, Arg.	288	34.53 S	58.30 W
Canning, Austl.	168a	32.02 S	115.56 E
Canning, N.S., Can.	186	45.09 N	64.25 W
Canning ≃, Austl.	168a	32.01 S	115.51 E
Canning ≃, Ak., U.S.	180	70.05 N	145.30 W
Canning Hill ∧[2]	162	28.50 S	117.49 E
Canning Lake ⊜	212	44.56 N	78.38 W
Canning Reservoir ⊜[1]	168a	32.10 S	116.09 E
Cannington, On., Can.	212	44.21 N	79.02 W
Cannington, Eng., U.K.	42	51.09 N	3.04 W
Cannobio	58	46.04 N	8.42 E
Cannock	42	52.42 N	2.09 W
Cannock Chase ◆[4]	42	52.43 N	2.00 W
Cannon ≃	190	44.35 N	92.33 W
Cannon Air Force Base ■	196	34.23 N	103.18 W
Cannon Ball	198	46.23 N	100.35 W
Cannonball ≃	198	46.26 N	100.38 W
Cannon Beach	224	45.53 N	123.57 W
Cannondale	207	41.12 N	73.25 W
Cannon Falls	190	44.30 N	92.54 W
Cannonsburg	216	43.03 N	85.28 W
Cannonsville Reservoir ⊜[1]	210	42.08 N	75.19 W
Cannonvale	166	20.17 S	148.42 E
Cann River	166	37.34 S	149.10 E
Caño, Isla del I	236	8.44 N	83.53 W
Canoas	252	29.56 S	51.11 W
Canoas ≃, Bra.	252	27.36 S	51.25 W
Canoas ≃, Bra.	256	21.30 S	47.09 W
Canobie Lake	283	42.48 N	71.14 W
Canobie Lake ⊜	283	42.49 N	71.15 W
Canobie Lake Park ♠	283	42.48 N	71.15 W
Canoe	182	50.45 N	119.13 W
Canoe ≃, B.C., Can.	182	52.09 N	118.27 W
Canoe ≃, Ma., U.S.	283	41.58 N	71.08 W
Canoe Brook ≃	276	40.45 N	74.22 W
Canoe Brook Reservoirs ⊜[1]	276	40.45 N	74.21 W
Canoe Creek Indian Reserve ◆[4]	182	51.32 N	122.15 W
Canoe Lake ⊜	184	55.11 N	108.15 W
Canoe Lake Indian Reserve ◆[4]	184	55.08 N	108.12 W
Canoga Park ◆[8]	280	34.12 N	118.35 W
Canoinhas	252	26.10 S	50.24 W
Canol	180	65.14 N	126.56 W
Canon	192	34.21 N	83.07 W
Canon ≃	224	46.36 N	123.53 W
Canonbie	44	55.05 N	2.57 W
Canon City	200	38.24 N	105.13 W
Cañón del Sumidero, Parque Nacional ♠	234	16.45 N	93.05 W
Caño Negro	236	10.54 N	84.44 W
Canonsburg	214	40.15 N	80.11 W
Canonsburg Lake ⊜	279b	40.16 N	80.07 W

Canoochee ≃	192	31.59 N	81.18 W
Canoole Cise	144	2.02 N	42.19 E
Canopus ⊥	142	31.18 N	30.03 E
Canora	184	51.37 N	102.26 W
Canosa di Puglia	68	41.13 N	16.04 E
Canossa ⊥	64	44.35 N	10.27 E
Canot, Pointe ›	241o	16.12 N	61.28 W
Canouan I	238	12.43 N	61.20 W
Canova	198	43.52 N	97.30 W
Canova Beach	220	28.08 N	80.34 W
Cañovanas	240m	18.23 N	65.54 W
Cánoves ≃	266d	41.37 N	2.22 E
Canow	54	53.12 N	12.54 E
Canowindra	166	33.34 S	148.38 E
Can Quer, Torrente de ≃	266d	41.31 N	2.11 E
Cansado	148	20.51 N	17.02 W
Cansanção	250	10.41 S	39.31 W
Canso	186	45.20 N	61.00 W
Canso, Strait of ⋓	186	45.37 N	61.25 W
Canta	248	11.25 S	76.38 W
Cantabria	234	19.50 N	101.44 W
Cantabria (Santander) □[4], Esp.	34	43.15 N	4.00 W
Cantabria □[4], Esp.	34	43.15 N	4.00 W
Cantábrica, Cordillera ⩘	34	43.00 N	5.00 W
Cantabriques → Cantábrica, Cordillera ⩘	34	43.00 N	5.00 W
Cantagalo	255	21.58 S	42.22 W
Cantagalo, Cachoeira ʟ	250	7.18 S	54.52 W
Cantal □[5]	32	45.05 N	2.45 E
Cantalejo	34	41.15 N	3.55 W
Cantalupo in Sabina	66	42.18 N	12.39 E
Cantalupo nel Sannio	66	41.31 N	14.24 E
Čantal'vejergyn ≃	180	67.38 N	179.22 W
Cantanhede, Bra.	250	3.39 S	44.24 W
Cantanhede, Port.	34	40.21 N	8.36 W
Cantareira ◆[8]	287b	23.27 S	46.37 W
Cantareira, Serra da ∧	287b	23.25 S	46.39 W
Cantaura	246	9.19 N	64.21 W
Cant Clough Reservoir ⊜[1]	262	53.46 N	2.09 W
Canteleu	50	49.27 N	1.02 E
Canterbury, Austl.	274a	33.55 S	151.07 E
Canterbury, Austl.	274b	37.49 S	145.05 E
Canterbury, N.B., Can.	186	45.53 N	67.29 W
Canterbury, Eng., U.K.	42	51.17 N	1.05 E
Canterbury Bight ⊂[3]	172	44.15 S	171.38 E
Canterbury Cathedral ʋ[1]	42	51.17 N	1.05 E
Canterbury Park Racecourse ♠	274a	33.54 S	151.07 E
Canterbury Plains ≍	172	44.00 S	171.45 E
Canterbury Woods	284c	38.49 N	77.15 W
Can Tho	110	10.02 N	105.47 E
Cantiano	66	43.28 N	12.38 E
Cantil	228	35.18 N	117.58 W
Cantiles, Cayo I	240p	21.36 N	82.02 W
Cantin Lake ⊜	184	53.27 N	95.10 W
Canto do Buriti	250	8.07 S	42.58 W
Canto do Pontes	287a	22.58 S	43.04 W
Canto Grande, Quebrada V	286d	11.59 S	77.01 W
Cantoira	62	45.21 N	7.23 E
Canton, Ct., U.S.	207	41.49 N	72.53 W
Canton, Ga., U.S.	192	34.14 N	84.29 W
Canton, Il., U.S.	190	40.33 N	90.02 W
Canton, Ks., U.S.	198	38.23 N	97.25 W
Canton, Ma., U.S.	207	42.09 N	71.08 W
Canton, Mn., U.S.	190	43.31 N	91.55 W
Canton, Ms., U.S.	194	32.36 N	90.02 W
Canton, Mo., U.S.	219	40.07 N	91.37 W
Canton, N.J., U.S.	208	39.28 N	75.24 W
Canton, N.Y., U.S.	188	44.35 N	75.10 W
Canton, N.C., U.S.	192	35.31 N	82.50 W
Canton, Oh., U.S.	214	40.47 N	81.22 W
Canton, Ok., U.S.	196	36.03 N	98.35 W
Canton, Pa., U.S.	210	41.39 N	76.51 W
Canton, S.D., U.S.	198	43.18 N	96.35 W
Canton, Tx., U.S.	222	32.33 N	95.51 W
Canton Airport ⊠	174h	2.46 S	171.43 W
Canton → Guangzhou	100	23.06 N	113.16 E
Canton → Kanton I	174h	2.50 S	171.40 W
Canton Lake ⊜[1]	196	36.08 N	98.36 W
Canton Lake State Recreational Area ♠	196	36.08 N	98.39 W
Cantonment	194	30.36 N	87.20 W
Cantorbéry → Canterbury	42	51.17 N	1.05 E
Cantrall	219	39.56 N	89.41 W
Cantribana	266c	38.53 N	9.25 W
Cantù	62	45.44 N	9.08 E
Cantu ≃	252	24.46 S	52.54 W
Cantua Creek	226	36.30 N	120.19 W
Cantua Creek ≃	226	36.28 N	120.17 W
Cantwell	180	63.23 N	148.57 W
Cañuelas	258	35.03 S	58.44 W
Cañuelas □[5]	288	34.56 S	58.41 W
Cañuelas, Arroyo ≃	258	34.55 S	58.38 W
Canumã	246	4.02 S	59.04 W
Canumã ≃	246	3.55 S	59.10 W
Canungra	171a	28.01 S	153.10 E
Canungra Creek ≃	171a	27.55 S	153.06 E
Canungra Jungle Training Ground ■	171a	28.02 S	153.10 E
Canutama	248	6.32 S	64.20 W
Canutillo	200	31.54 N	106.35 W
Canvastown	172	41.18 S	173.40 E
Canvey Island	260	51.32 N	0.36 E
Çanvey Island I	260	51.33 N	0.34 E
Čany	86	55.19 N	76.46 E
Čany, ozero ⊜	86	54.50 N	77.30 E
Cany-Barville	50	49.47 N	0.38 E
Canyon, Yk., Can.	180	60.52 N	137.02 W
Canyon, Ca., U.S.	282	37.49 N	122.09 W
Canyon, Tx., U.S.	196	34.58 N	101.55 W
Canyon City	202	44.23 N	118.56 W
Canyon Country	228	34.25 N	118.28 W
Canyon Creek	182	55.22 N	115.05 W
Canyon Creek ≃, Az., U.S.	200	33.49 N	110.40 W
Canyon Creek ≃, Ca., U.S.	226	39.22 N	120.45 W
Canyon Creek ≃, Id., U.S.	202	42.59 N	115.59 W
Canyon Creek ≃, Wa., U.S.	224	45.57 N	122.22 W
Canyon Creek ≃, Wa., U.S.	224	48.43 N	120.55 W
Canyon de Chelly National Monument ♠	200	36.01 N	109.26 W
Canyon Ferry Lake ⊜[1]	202	46.33 N	111.37 W
Canyon Lake ⊜[1]	196	29.52 N	98.16 W
Canyonlands National Park ♠	200	38.10 N	110.00 W
Canyonville	202	42.55 N	123.16 W
Canzar	152	7.38 S	21.32 E
Canzo	62	45.51 N	9.16 E
Cao ≃, Zhg.	98	40.29 N	124.08 E
Cao ≃, Zhg.	105	38.52 N	115.46 E
Cao Bang	110	22.40 N	106.15 E
Caochi	107	30.19 N	104.24 E
Caocun	106	31.42 N	118.56 E
Caodian, Zhg.	100	28.39 N	120.23 E
Caodian, Zhg.	100	33.21 N	112.39 E
Caodian, Zhg.	102	32.32 N	111.11 E
Cao'e	100	30.01 N	120.52 E
Cao'e ≃	100	30.06 N	120.46 E
Caofang	100	26.04 N	116.35 E
Caogezhai	105	40.09 N	117.50 E
Caohe, Zhg.	105	38.57 N	115.32 E
Caohe, Zhg.	269b	31.09 N	121.25 E

Caohecheng	104	40.46 N	124.02 E
Caohekou	104	40.54 N	123.53 E
Caohezhang	104	41.04 N	124.03 E
Caojian	102	25.38 N	99.07 E
Caojiawopeng	104	42.00 N	122.20 E
Caojiawopu	104	42.37 N	122.19 E
Caojiawu	105	39.24 N	116.31 E
Caojiazhen	106	31.55 N	121.38 E
Caojiezi	107	29.53 N	106.24 E
Caojing	106	30.47 N	121.24 E
Caojun	100	29.41 N	116.17 E
Cao Lanh	110	10.27 N	105.38 E
Caolaoji	100	33.06 N	117.22 E
Caolisport, Loch ⊂	46	55.54 N	5.37 W
Caomaji	98	34.52 N	116.17 E
Caombo	152	8.43 S	16.51 E
Caonao ≃	240p	22.05 N	78.05 W
Caonian	100	32.56 N	120.20 E
Caonillas, Lago ⊜	240m	18.16 N	66.39 W
Caopeng	106	31.44 N	121.17 E
Caoping	100	28.48 N	118.22 E
Caopu	98	34.34 N	118.52 E
Caoqiao	106	31.32 N	119.59 E
Caorle	64	45.36 N	12.53 E
Caorso	62	45.03 N	9.52 E
Caoshi, Zhg.	98	42.17 N	125.16 E
Caoshi, Zhg.	100	33.32 N	116.29 E
Caota	100	29.42 N	120.08 E
Caotang	106	31.16 N	118.59 E
Caoxi	100	28.42 N	117.18 E
Caoxian	98	34.53 N	115.33 E
Caoyangxi	100	26.34 N	118.47 E
Cap, Le → Cape Town	158	33.55 S	18.22 E
Cap, Pointe du ›	241f	14.07 N	60.57 W
Capac	190	43.00 N	82.55 W
Capaccio	68	40.25 N	15.05 E
Capacciotti, Lago di ⊜[1]	68	41.10 N	15.47 E
Capaci	70	38.10 N	13.14 E
Çapage	152	13.21 S	21.05 E
Čapajev	80	50.12 N	51.10 E
Čapajevka, Ross.	82	54.38 N	35.50 E
Čapajevka, Ukr.	78	49.33 N	32.06 E
Čapajevka, Ukr.	78	49.23 N	30.26 E
Čapajevka, Ukr.	78	47.29 N	36.20 E
Čapajevka ≃	80	53.08 N	49.37 E
Čapajevo	78	49.21 N	35.54 E
Čapajevsk	80	52.58 N	49.41 E
Capala	152	13.37 S	14.45 E
Capalbio	66	42.27 N	11.25 E
Capalonga	116	14.20 N	122.30 E
Capanaparo ≃	246	7.01 N	67.07 W
Capanema, Bra.	250	1.12 S	47.11 W
Capanema, Bra.	252	25.40 S	53.48 W
Capangombe	152	15.05 S	13.08 E
Capanne, Monte ∧	66	42.46 N	10.10 E
Capannoli	66	43.35 N	10.41 E
Capannori	66	43.50 N	10.34 E
Capão Bonito	255	24.01 S	48.20 W
Capão Doce, Morro do ∧	252	26.43 S	51.25 W
Capão Redondo ◆[8]	287b	23.40 S	46.46 W
Capaotigamau, Lac ⊜	186	50.18 N	68.14 W
Caparaó, Parque Nacional do ♠	255	20.33 S	41.45 W
Caparica	266c	38.40 N	9.12 W
Caparo Viejo ≃	246	7.46 N	70.23 W
Capas	116	15.20 N	120.35 E
Capatárida	246	11.11 N	70.37 W
Cap-aux-Meules (Grindstone Island)	186	47.23 N	61.52 W
Cap aux Meules, Île du I	186	47.23 N	61.54 W
Capay	226	38.32 N	122.03 W
Cap-Chat	186	49.06 N	66.42 W
Cap-de-la-Madeleine	206	46.22 N	72.31 W
Cape (Kaap) □[4]	156	31.00 S	23.00 E
Cape ≃	166	20.49 S	146.51 E
Cape Arid National Park ♠	162	33.40 S	123.25 E
Cape Barren Island I	166	40.25 S	148.12 E
Cape Basin ✢[1]	8	37.00 S	7.00 E
Cape Bougainville Aboriginal Reserve ◆[4]	164	14.10 S	126.30 E
Cape Breton Highlands National Park ♠	186	46.45 N	60.45 W
Cape Breton Island I	186	46.00 N	60.30 W
Cape Broyle	186	47.06 N	52.57 W
Cape Canaveral	220	28.24 N	80.36 W
Cape Canaveral Air Force Station ■	220	28.29 N	80.35 W
Cape Charles	208	37.16 N	76.01 W
Cape Coast	150	5.05 N	1.15 W
Cape Cod Bay ⊂	207	41.52 N	70.22 W
Cape Cod Canal ≊	207	41.47 N	70.30 W
Cape Cod National Seashore ♠	207	41.56 N	70.00 W
Cape Comorin → Kanniyākumari	122	8.05 N	77.34 E
Cape Coral	220	26.33 N	81.56 W
Cape Croker Indian Reserve ◆[4]	212	44.55 N	81.01 W
Cape Dorset	176	64.14 N	76.32 W
Cape Elizabeth	188	43.33 N	70.12 W
Cape Fear ≃	192	33.53 N	78.00 W
Cape Girardeau	194	37.18 N	89.31 W
Cape Hatteras National Seashore ♠	192	35.30 N	76.35 W
Cape Henlopen State Park ♠	208	38.45 N	75.06 W
Cape Jervis	168b	35.36 S	138.06 E
Cape Johnson Tablemount ✢[3]	14	17.08 N	177.15 W
Cape Krusenstern National Monument ♠	180	67.30 N	163.40 W
Capela	250	10.30 S	37.04 W
Cape LaHave Island I	186	44.12 N	64.22 W
Cape la Hune	186	47.33 N	56.52 W
Capel Curig	44	53.06 N	3.54 W
Capelengue	152	9.12 S	19.43 E
Capelinha	255	17.42 S	42.31 W
Capelinha do Embirazal	256	22.02 S	45.26 W
Cape Lisburne	180	68.52 N	166.05 W
Capel'ka	76	58.03 N	28.59 E
Capella	166	23.05 S	148.02 E
Capella ∧	164	5.00 S	141.05 E
Capelle [aan de IJssel]	52	51.55 N	4.35 E
Capellen	56	49.38 N	5.59 E
Capelongo	152	14.54 S	15.08 E
Cape Lookout National Seashore ♠	192	34.40 N	76.23 W
Cape Lookout State Park ♠	224	45.21 N	123.59 W
Capel Saint Mary	42	52.00 N	1.04 E
Cape May	208	38.56 N	74.54 W
Cape May □[6]	208	38.56 N	74.55 W
Cape May Coast Guard Air Station ■	208	38.57 N	74.53 W
Cape May Court House	208	39.04 N	74.49 W
Cape May Point	208	39.09 N	74.46 W
Capembé ≃	152	16.10 S	21.00 E
Cape Melville National Park ♠	164	14.20 S	144.30 E
Capenda Camulemba	152	9.24 S	18.27 E
Capenga ≃	287a	22.49 S	43.37 W
Capenhurst	262	53.15 N	2.57 W
Cape of Good Hope Nature Reserve ◆[4]	158	34.18 S	18.26 E
Cape Pole	180	55.58 N	133.48 W
Cape Pond ⊜	283	42.38 N	70.38 W
Cape Porpoise	188	43.22 N	70.26 W
Cape Range National Park ♠	162	22.10 S	113.55 E

≃ River	Fluß	Río	Rivière	Rio	✢ Submarine Features	Untermeerische Objekte	Accidentes Submarinos	Formes de relief sous-marin	Acidentes submarinos
≊ Canal	Kanal	Canal	Canal	Canal	□ Political Unit	Politische Einheit	Unidad Politica	Entité politique	Unidade política
ʟ Waterfall, Rapids	Wasserfall, Stromschnellen	Cascada, Rápidos	Chute d'eau, Rapides	Cascata, Rápidos	ʋ Cultural Institution	Kulturelle Institution	Institución Cultural	Institution culturelle	Instituição cultural
⋓ Strait	Meeresstraße	Estrecho	Détroit	Estreito	⊥ Historical Site	Historische Stätte	Sitio Histórico	Site historique	Sitio histórico
⊂ Bay, Gulf	Bucht, Golf	Bahía, Golfo	Baie, Golfe	Baía, Golfo	♠ Recreational Site	Erholungs- und Ferienort	Sitio de Recreo	Centre de loisirs	Area de Lazer
⊜ Lake, Lakes	See, Seen	Lago, Lagos	Lac, Lacs	Lago, Lagos	⊠ Airport	Flughafen	Aeropuerto	Aéroport	Aeroporto
≋ Swamp	Sumpf	Pantano	Marais	Pântano	■ Military Installation	Militäranlage	Instalación Militar	Installation militaire	Instalação militar
⌂ Ice Features, Glacier	Eis- und Gletscherformen	Accidentes Glaciales	Formes glaciaires	Acidentes glaciares	◆ Miscellaneous	Verschiedenes	Misceláneo	Divers	Diversos
⍑ Other Hydrographic Features	Andere Hydrographische Objekte	Otros Elementos Hidrográficos	Autres données hydrographiques	Outros acidentes hidrográficos					

I · 30 Cape-Cart

ENGLISH: Name | Page | Lat.°′ | Long.°′ — DEUTSCH: Name | Seite | Breite°′ | Länge°′ E = Ost

Cape Rise ✢³ 8 42.00 S 15.00 E
Capernaum
— Kefar Naḥum ⊥ 132 32.53 N 35.34 E
Cape Romanzof 180 61.49 N 165.56 W
Capertee 170 33.09 S 149.59 E
Capertee ≏ 170 33.12 S 150.28 E
Cape Sable Island I 186 43.25 N 65.37 W
Cape Scott Provincial Park ♦ 182 50.45 N 128.20 W
Capesterre 241o 15.54 N 61.13 W
Capesterre, Pointe de la ≻ 241o 16.03 N 61.33 W
Capesterre-Belle-Eau 241o 16.03 N 61.34 W
Capesthorne Hall ⊥ 262 53.15 N 2.14 W
Capestrano 66 42.16 N 13.46 E
Capetinga ≏ 256 22.04 S 47.14 W
Cape Tormentine 186 46.08 N 63.47 W
Cape Town (Kaapstad) 158 33.55 S 18.22 E
Cape Verde (Cabo Verde) □¹, Afr. 134 16.00 N 24.00 W
Cape Verde (Cabo Verde) □¹, Afr. 150a 16.00 N 24.00 W
Cape Verde Basin ✢¹ 8 15.00 N 30.00 W
Cape Verde Islands
— Cape Verde □¹ 150a 16.00 N 24.00 W
Cape Verde Terrace ✢³ 10 18.00 N 20.00 W
Capeville 208 37.12 N 75.57 W
Cape Vincent 212 44.07 N 76.19 W
Cape Yakataga 180 60.04 N 142.26 W
Cape York Peninsula ≻¹ 164 14.00 S 142.30 E
Cap-Haïtien 238 19.45 N 72.12 W
Capilla de Farruco 252 32.53 S 55.25 W
Capilla del Monte 252 30.51 S 64.31 W
Capilla del Señor 258 34.18 S 59.06 W
Capim ≏ 250 1.40 S 47.47 W
Capim Melado, Morro do ∧ 287a 22.50 S 43.29 W
Capinas Point ≻ 116 11.05 N 125.14 E
Capinópolis 255 18.41 S 49.35 W
Capinota 248 17.43 S 66.14 W
Capinzal 252 27.20 S 51.36 W
Capira 236 8.45 N 79.53 W
Cap Island I 116 5.57 N 120.06 E
Capistrano, Bra. 250 4.28 S 38.55 W
Capistrano, It. 68 38.41 N 16.17 E
Capistrano Beach 228 33.27 N 117.40 W
Capistrello 66 41.57 N 13.23 E
Capitachouane ≏ 190 47.36 N 76.54 W
Capitachouane, Lac ⊜ 190 48.05 N 75.55 W
Capital Airport ⊠ 219 39.51 N 89.41 W
Capital Centre Arena ♦ 284c 38.54 N 76.51 W
Capital City Airport ⊠ 216 42.47 N 84.35 W
Capitan 200 33.32 N 105.34 W
Capitán Aracena, Isla I 254 54.10 S 71.20 W
Capitán Arturo Prat ♥³ 9 62.30 S 59.41 W
Capitán Bado 255 23.16 S 55.32 W
Capitán Bermúdez 252 32.49 S 60.43 W
Capitán Meza 252 26.55 S 55.15 W
Capitan Peak ∧ 200 33.36 N 105.16 W
Capitán Sarmiento 252 34.10 S 59.48 W
Capitão de Campos 250 4.28 S 41.57 W
Capitão Enéas 255 16.21 S 43.43 W
Capitola 226 36.58 N 121.57 W
Capitol Heights 208 38.53 N 76.54 W
Capitol Park 208 39.08 N 75.30 W
Capitol Peak ∧ 204 41.50 N 117.18 W
Capitol Reef National Park ♦ 200 38.11 N 111.20 W
Capitol View 192 33.57 N 80.56 W
Capivari 255 23.00 S 47.31 W
Capivari ≏, Bra. 248 19.16 S 57.10 W
Capivari ≏, Bra. 255 12.30 S 39.55 W
Capivari ≏, Bra. 256 22.14 S 44.57 W
Capivari ≏, Bra. 256 24.09 S 46.48 W
Capivari ≏, Bra. 256 21.53 S 46.15 W
Capivari ≏, Bra. 256 22.26 S 45.47 W
Capivari ≏, Bra. 256 22.56 S 47.16 W
Capivari ≏, Bra. 256 21.30 S 44.20 W
Capivari ≏, Bra. 256 21.12 S 44.52 W
Capivari, Canal ≅ 287a 22.42 S 43.21 W
Capiz □⁴ 116 11.30 N 122.30 E
Capiz
— Roxas 116 11.35 N 122.45 E
Capizzi 70 37.51 N 14.29 E
Çaplan 186 48.06 N 65.41 W
Čaplejevka 78 51.43 N 33.12 E
Caplen 222 29.29 N 94.33 W
Caples Lake ⊜¹ 226 38.42 N 120.03 W
Çaplina ≏ 248 18.14 S 70.33 W
Čaplinka 78 46.23 N 33.32 E
Čaplino, Ross. 180 64.25 N 172.15 W
Čaplino, Ukr. 78 48.09 N 36.14 E
Čapljina 36 43.07 N 17.42 E
Çaplone, Monte ∧ 64 45.48 N 10.38 E
Čaplygin 76 53.14 N 39.58 E
Cap Mountain ∧ 180 63.25 N 123.29 W
Capnoyan Island I 116 10.44 N 120.54 E
Capoche ≏ 154 15.23 S 32.53 E
Capodichino, Aeroporto di ⊠ 68 40.50 N 14.17 E
Capodimonte 66 42.33 N 11.55 E
Capo di Ponte 64 46.02 N 10.21 E
Capo d'Orlando 70 38.10 N 14.53 E
Capoeira, Corredeira ⌞ 250 6.48 S 58.21 W
Capolago 58 45.55 N 8.59 E
Capoliveri 66 42.45 N 10.22 E
Caporolo ≏ 152 12.56 S 13.00 E
Caposele 68 40.49 N 15.13 E
Capostrada 66 43.57 N 10.54 E
Capot ≏ 240e 14.51 N 61.05 W
Capoterra 71 39.11 N 8.58 E
Capoti-an, Mount ∧ 116 11.45 N 125.15 E
Capotoan, Mount ∧ 116 12.09 N 124.57 E
Cappadocia □⁹ 130 38.30 N 36.00 E
Cappamore 48 52.37 N 8.20 W
Cap-Pelé 186 46.13 N 64.18 W
Cappella Islands II 240m 18.17 N 64.54 W
Cappelle 66 42.03 N 13.22 E
Cappelle sul Tavo 66 42.28 N 14.06 E
Cappeln 52 52.48 N 8.07 E
Cappenberg 263 51.39 N 7.32 E
Cappenberg, Schloss ⊥ 263 51.39 N 7.32 E
Cappercleuch 44 55.29 N 3.12 W
Cappoquin 48 52.08 N 7.50 W
Capracotta 66 41.50 N 14.16 E
Capraia 66 43.03 N 9.50 E
Capraia, Isola I 66 42.08 N 15.31 E
Capraia, Isola di I 66 43.02 N 9.49 E
Capranica 66 42.15 N 12.11 E
Caprara, Punta ≻ 71 41.07 N 8.19 E
Caprarola 66 42.19 N 12.14 E
Capreol 190 46.43 N 80.56 W
Caprera, Isola I 71 41.12 N 9.28 E
Caprese Michelangelo 66 43.39 N 11.59 E
Capri 68 40.33 N 14.14 E
Capri, Isola di I 68 40.33 N 14.13 E
Capriati a Volturno 68 41.28 N 14.08 E
Capricorn, Cape ≻ 166 23.30 S 151.13 E
Capricorn Channel ꝏ 166 23.00 S 152.20 E
Capricorn Group II 166 23.28 S 152.00 E
Capri Leone 70 38.05 N 14.44 E
Caprino Veronese 64 45.36 N 10.47 E
Caprivi Oss □⁵ 156 17.45 S 24.00 E
Caprivi Zipfel (Caprivi Strip) □⁹ 156 17.59 S 23.00 E
Caprolace, Lago di ⊜ 66 41.21 N 12.58 E
Capron, Il., U.S. 216 42.24 N 88.44 W
Capron, Va., U.S. 208 36.42 N 77.12 W
Cap Saint Jacques
— Vung Tau 110 10.21 N 107.04 E
Cap-Santé 206 46.40 N 71.47 W
Capstone 260 51.21 N 0.34 E
Captain Anthony Meldahl Dam ◆⁶ 218 38.48 N 84.11 W
Captain Cook 229d 19.29 N 155.55 W
Captain Cook Bridge ◆⁵ 274a 34.00 S 151.08 E
Captain Cook Landing Place Park ⊥ 274a 34.00 S 151.14 E
Captain Cook Monument ⊥ 174c 29.00 S 167.56 E
Captain Daniel Wright Woods ♦ 278 42.13 N 87.56 W
Captain Harbor ⊂ 276 41.00 N 73.36 W
Captain Pond ⊜ 283 42.48 N 71.10 W
Captains Flat 171b 35.35 S 149.27 E
Captieux 32 44.18 N 0.16 W
Captina Creek ≏ 188 39.52 N 80.48 W
Captiva 220 26.31 N 82.11 W
Captiva Island I 220 26.31 N 82.11 W
Captree Island I 276 40.39 N 73.16 W
Captree State Park ♦ 276 40.39 N 73.16 W
Capua 68 41.06 N 14.12 E
Capual Island I 116 6.02 N 121.24 E
Capuáva 287b 23.39 S 46.29 W
Capuça I 152 17.22 S 21.18 E
Capucapu ≏ 246 1.45 S 58.35 W
Capucin ≻ 240d 15.38 N 61.28 W
Capul 116 12.25 N 124.11 E
Capulín, Río del ≏ 196 27.31 N 101.33 W
Capulin Mountain National Monument ♦ 196 36.48 N 103.55 W
Capul Island I 116 12.26 N 124.10 E
Capuna 152 15.38 S 19.43 E
Capunda 152 14.57 S 14.03 E
Capurro 258 34.25 S 56.28 W
Capurso 68 41.03 N 16.55 E
Caputh 54 52.21 N 13.00 E
Cap-Vert
— Cape Verde □¹ 150a 16.00 N 24.00 W
Caquende 256 21.20 S 44.33 W
Caquetá □⁸ 246 1.00 N 74.00 W
Caquetá (Japurá) ≏ 246 3.08 S 64.46 W
Çaquiaviri 248 17.03 S 68.38 W
Čar ≏ 86 50.22 N 80.55 E
Çara, Ityo. 144 5.52 N 37.12 E
Čara, Ross. 88 56.54 N 118.12 E
Čara ≏ 74 60.22 N 120.50 E
Cará, Ilha do I 250 0.01 S 50.50 W
Caraballeda 286c 10.37 N 66.50 W
Caraballeda, Punta ≻ 286c 10.37 N 66.50 W
Carabanchel Alto ◆⁸ 266a 40.22 N 3.45 W
Carabanchel Bajo ◆⁸ 266a 40.23 N 3.47 W
Carabao Island I 116 12.04 N 121.56 E
Carabaya ≏ 248 14.43 S 70.17 W
Carabaya, Cordillera de ⋏ 248 13.50 S 70.45 W
Carabayllo 286d 11.52 S 77.02 W
Carabelas Grande ≏ 258 34.15 S 58.43 W
Carabinani ≏ 246 1.58 S 61.31 W
Carabobo □³ 246 10.10 N 68.05 W
Carabost 171b 35.36 S 147.44 E
Caracal 38 44.07 N 24.21 E
Caracalla, Terme di ⊥ 267a 41.53 N 12.29 E
Caracaraí 246 1.50 N 61.08 W
Caracas, Ven. 246 10.30 N 66.56 W
Çaracas, Ven. 286c 10.30 N 66.56 W
Čarach 86 59.03 N 62.15 E
Carache 246 9.38 N 70.14 W
Caracol, Bra. 250 9.17 S 43.20 W
Caracol, Bra. 252 22.01 S 57.02 W
Caracollo 248 17.39 S 67.10 W
Caracorum
— Karakoram Range ⋏ 120 35.30 N 77.00 E
Carácuaro de Morelos 234 18.46 N 101.02 W
Caradoc Indian Reserve ◆⁴ 214 42.48 N 81.29 W
Caraffa di Catanzaro 68 38.53 N 16.29 E
Caraga 116 7.20 N 126.34 E
Caraga ≏ 116 7.20 N 126.34 E
Caragh, Lough ⊜ 48 52.03 N 9.52 W
Caraghnan Mountain ∧ 166 31.20 S 149.03 E
Caraglio 62 44.25 N 7.26 E
Caraguata, Arroyo ≏ 288 34.24 S 58.38 W
Caraguatatuba 256 23.37 S 45.25 W
Caraguatatuba, Enseada de ⊂ 256 23.40 S 45.20 W
Caraguatay 252 25.14 S 56.52 W
Caraí 255 17.12 S 41.42 W
Caraibamba 248 14.24 S 73.09 W
Caraïbes, Îles des
— West Indies II 230 19.00 N 70.00 W
Caraïbes, Mer des
— Caribbean Sea ⚲² 230 15.00 N 73.00 W
Caraigres, Cerro ∧ 236 9.43 N 84.05 W
Caraíva ≏ 255 16.48 S 39.08 W
Carajari ≏ 250 4.45 S 54.20 W
Carajás 250 6.06 S 50.23 W
Carajás, Serra dos ⋏ 250 5.50 S 51.20 W
Caralue Bluff ∧² 166 33.26 S 136.16 E
Caramagna-Piemonte 62 44.46 N 7.44 E
Caramanico Terme 66 42.09 N 14.00 E
Caramay 116 10.11 N 119.14 E
Caramoan 116 13.46 N 123.52 E
Caramoan Peninsula ≻¹ 116 13.48 N 123.40 E
Caramoran 116 13.59 N 124.08 E
Caramy ≏ 62 43.26 N 6.12 E
Caranavi 248 15.46 S 67.36 W
Carandaí 255 20.57 S 43.48 W
Carandayti 248 20.45 S 63.04 W
Carangola 255 20.44 S 42.02 W
Carano 64 46.16 N 11.27 E
Caransebeș 38 45.25 N 22.13 E
Carapá ≏ 252 24.30 S 54.20 W
Carapachay ≏¹ 288 34.25 S 58.35 W
Carapajó 250 2.16 S 49.22 W
Cara-Paraná ≏ 246 1.45 S 73.13 W
Carapeguá 252 25.48 S 57.14 W
Carapelle ≏ 68 41.30 N 15.55 E
Carapicuíba 256 23.31 S 46.50 W
Carapicuíba □⁷ 287b 23.31 S 46.53 W
Carapo ≏ 246 7.30 N 64.02 W
Caraquet 186 47.48 N 64.57 W
Caraquez 246 0.36 S 80.25 W
Carare ≏ 246 6.48 N 74.06 W
Carasco 62 44.21 N 9.21 E
Caraș-Severin □⁶ 38 45.00 N 22.00 E
Caratasca, Laguna de ⊂ 236 15.23 N 83.55 W
Carate Brianza 62 45.41 N 9.14 E
Caratinga 255 19.47 S 42.08 W
Carauari 246 4.52 S 66.54 W
Caraúbas 250 5.47 S 37.34 W
Caravaca 34 38.06 N 1.51 W
Caravaggio 62 45.30 N 9.38 E
Caravela, Ilha I 150 11.30 N 16.20 W
Caravelas 255 17.45 S 39.15 W
Caraveli 248 15.46 S 73.22 W
Caravelle, Presqu'île de la ≻¹ 240e 14.45 N 60.55 W
Caravius, Monte ∧ 71 39.09 N 8.49 E
Caraway 194 35.45 N 90.19 W
Carayaó 252 25.10 S 56.26 W
Caraz 248 9.03 S 77.45 W
Caraza ◆⁸ 288 34.42 S 58.26 W
Carazinho 252 28.18 S 52.48 W
Carazo □⁵ 236 11.45 N 86.15 W
Carballiño 34 42.26 N 8.04 W
Carballo 34 43.13 N 8.41 W
Carberry 184 49.52 N 99.20 W
Carbet, Pitons du ∧ 240e 14.42 N 61.07 W
Carbo 232 29.42 N 110.58 W
Carbol ≏ 70 37.32 N 12.59 E
Carbon, Ab., Can. 182 51.29 N 113.09 W
Carbon, Pa., U.S. 279b 40.17 N 79.34 W
Carbon, Tx., U.S. 196 32.16 N 98.50 W
Carbon □⁶ 210 40.52 N 75.45 W
Carbon ≏ 224 47.07 N 122.13 W
Carbon, Cap ≻ 34 36.47 N 5.06 E
Carbonado 224 47.04 N 122.03 W
Carbonara, Capo ≻ 71 39.06 N 9.31 E
Carbonara, Pizzo ∧ 70 37.54 N 14.02 E
Carbonare 64 45.56 N 11.13 E
Carbonate 266b 45.41 N 8.56 E
Carbon-Blanc 32 44.53 N 0.31 W
Carbon Canyon Dam ◆⁶ 280 33.55 N 117.50 W
Carbon Creek ≏ 280 33.49 N 118.04 W
Carbondale, Co., U.S. 200 39.24 N 107.12 W
Carbondale, Il., U.S. 194 37.43 N 89.13 W
Carbondale, Ks., U.S. 198 38.49 N 95.41 W
Carbondale, Pa., U.S. 210 41.34 N 75.30 W
Carbone 68 40.09 N 16.05 E
Carbonear 186 47.45 N 53.13 W
Carboneras de Guadazaon 34 39.53 N 1.48 W
Carbon Hill 194 33.53 N 87.31 W
Carbonia 71 39.10 N 8.31 E
Carbonin 64 46.37 N 12.13 E
Carbost 46 57.18 N 6.22 W
Carcaixent 34 39.08 N 0.27 W
Carcajou ≏ 180 65.37 N 128.43 W
Carcalgong Hill ∧ 170 32.52 S 149.41 E
Carcans, Lac de ⊂ 32 45.08 N 1.08 W
Carcar 116 10.06 N 123.38 E
Carcarañá 252 32.51 S 61.09 W
Carcarañá ≏ 252 32.27 S 60.48 W
Carcare 62 44.21 N 8.18 E
Carcar Point ≻ 116 10.05 N 123.41 E
Carcassonne 32 43.13 N 2.21 E
Carcastillo 34 42.23 N 1.26 W
Carcavelos, Port. 266c 38.41 N 9.20 W
Carcavelos, Port. 266c 38.53 N 9.14 W
Carceri, Eremo delle ♥¹ 66 43.05 N 12.42 E
Carcès 62 43.28 N 6.11 E
Carchi □⁴ 246 0.45 N 78.00 W
Carcroft 44 53.34 N 1.11 W
Carcross 180 60.10 N 134.42 W
Cardabia 162 23.06 S 113.48 E
Çardak, Tür. 130 38.06 N 36.49 E
Čardak, Uzb. 85 41.37 N 69.56 E
Cardal 258 34.18 S 56.24 W
Çardano al Campo 266b 45.39 N 8.47 E
Čardara 85 41.17 N 67.55 E
Čardara, step' ⋏¹ 85 42.00 N 68.00 E
Čardarinskoje vodochranilišče ⊜¹ 85 41.10 N 68.15 E
Cardeña 34 38.13 N 4.19 W
Cárdenas, Cuba 240p 23.02 N 81.12 W
Cárdenas, Méx. 234 22.00 N 99.40 W
Cárdenas, Méx. 234 17.59 N 93.22 W
Cárdenas, Nic. 236 11.12 N 85.31 W
Cárdenas, Bahía de ⊂ 240p 23.05 N 81.10 W
Cardener ≏ 34 41.41 N 1.51 E
Carderock Springs 284c 38.59 N 77.10 W
Cardiel, Lago ⊜ 254 48.55 S 71.15 W
Cardiff, Austl. 170 32.57 S 151.41 E
Cardiff, Wales, U.K. 42 51.29 N 3.13 W
Cardiff, Md., U.S. 208 39.43 N 76.20 W
Cardiff, N.J., U.S. 208 39.24 N 74.35 W
Cardiff by the Sea 228 33.01 N 117.16 W
Cardigan, P.E., Can. 186 46.14 N 62.37 W
Cardigan, Wales, U.K. 42 52.06 N 4.40 W
Cardigan Bay ⊂, P.E., Can. 186 46.10 N 62.30 W
Cardigan Bay ⊂, Wales, U.K. 42 52.30 N 4.20 W
Cardigan Island I 42 52.08 N 4.41 W
Cardigan State Park ♦ 188 43.38 N 71.54 W
Cardinal 212 44.47 N 75.23 W
Cardinale 68 38.38 N 16.23 E
Cardinal Heights 212 45.27 N 75.37 W
Cardinal Lake ⊜ 182 56.14 N 117.44 W
Cardington, Boph. 158 27.11 S 23.30 E
Cardington, Oh., U.S. 214 40.30 N 82.53 W
Cardinia Creek ≏ 274b 38.12 S 145.23 E
Cardinia Reservoir ⊜¹ 169 37.58 S 145.25 E
Cardona 258 33.53 S 57.23 W
Cardonal, Punta ≻ 232 28.28 N 111.45 W
Cardoso 255 20.04 S 49.54 W
Cardozo 252 32.38 S 56.21 W
Card Sound ꝏ 220 25.20 N 80.18 W
Cardston 182 49.12 N 113.18 W
Cardwell, Austl. 166 18.16 S 146.02 E
Cardwell, Mo., U.S. 194 36.02 N 90.17 W
Çardwell Mountain ∧ 194 35.41 N 85.41 W
Čardžou 128 39.06 N 63.34 E
Čardžou □⁸ 128 38.51 N 63.34 E
Careaçu 256 22.02 S 45.42 W
Careen Lake ⊜ 184 57.00 N 108.10 W
Carega, Cima ∧ 64 45.44 N 11.08 E
Carei 38 47.42 N 22.28 E
Careiro 246 3.12 S 59.45 W
Careiro, Ilha do I 246 3.10 S 59.44 W
Çarén 252 30.51 S 70.47 W
Čarencavan 84 40.24 N 44.38 E
Carencro 194 30.19 N 92.02 W
Carentan 32 49.18 N 1.14 W
Careri 68 38.10 N 16.07 E
Cares ≏ 34 43.19 N 4.36 W
Caresana 62 45.13 N 8.30 E
Caretta 192 37.20 N 81.40 W
Careviščina 80 52.27 N 46.43 E
Carey 214 40.57 N 83.22 W
Carey, Lake ⊜ 162 29.05 S 122.15 E
Carey Downs 162 25.38 S 115.27 E
Careysburg 150 6.30 N 10.32 W
Cargados Carajos Shoals II 12 16.38 S 59.38 E
Cargill 46 56.30 N 3.22 W
Carhaix-Plouguer 32 48.17 N 3.35 W
Carhuamayo 248 10.55 S 76.02 W
Carhuanca 248 13.45 S 73.48 W
Carhuaz 248 9.16 S 77.38 W
Carhué 252 37.11 S 62.44 W
Caria □⁹ 130 37.30 N 28.00 E
Cariacica 255 20.16 S 40.25 W
Cariaco 246 10.29 N 63.33 W
Cariaco, Golfo de ⊂ 246 10.30 N 64.00 W
Cariamanga 246 4.20 S 79.35 W
Cariango 152 10.37 S 15.20 E
Caribana, Punta ≻ 246 8.37 N 76.52 W
Caribbean Sea ⚲² 230 15.00 N 73.00 W
Caribe, Mar
— Caribbean Sea ⚲² 230 15.00 N 73.00 W
Cariboo ⋏ 182 52.40 N 121.40 W
Cariboo Mountains ⋏ 182 53.00 N 121.00 W
Caribou, Nb., Can. 186 45.44 N 62.42 W
Caribou, Me., U.S. 186 46.51 N 68.00 W
Caribou ≏ 176 59.20 N 94.44 W
Caribou, Lac du ⊜ 206 46.56 N 72.50 W
Caribou Island I 190 47.22 N 85.49 W
Caribou Mountain ∧, Id., U.S. 202 43.06 N 111.18 W
Caribou Mountain ∧, Me., U.S. 188 45.26 N 70.38 W
Caribou Mountains ⋏ 176 59.12 N 115.40 W
Caribou Range ⋏ 202 43.05 N 111.15 W
Caričanka 78 48.57 N 34.22 E
Carichic 232 27.56 N 107.03 W
Caricuao 286c 10.26 N 66.59 W
Caricuao, Quebrada ≏ 286c 10.26 N 66.59 W
Caricyn
— Volgograd 80 48.44 N 44.25 E
Caridad, Pil. 116 10.50 N 124.45 E
Caridad, Pil. 269f 14.29 N 120.53 E
Caridade 250 4.13 S 39.12 W
Carife 68 41.01 N 15.12 E
Carigara 116 11.18 N 124.41 E
Carigara Bay ⊂ 116 11.24 N 124.40 E
Carignan, P.Q., Can. 275a 45.27 N 73.18 W
Carignan, Fr. 56 49.38 N 5.10 E
Carignano, It. 62 44.55 N 7.40 E
Carignano, It. 66 43.49 N 12.56 E
Cari Laufquen Grande, Lago ⊜ 254 41.07 S 69.30 W
Carinda 166 30.28 S 147.41 E
Cariñena 34 41.20 N 1.13 W
Caringbah 274a 34.03 S 151.08 E
Carinhanha 255 14.18 S 43.47 W
Carinhanha ≏ 255 14.20 S 43.47 W
Carini 70 38.08 N 13.11 E
Carini, Golfo di ⊂ 70 38.12 N 13.22 E
Carinish 46 57.31 N 7.18 W
Carinola 68 41.11 N 13.58 E
Carioca, Serra da ∧ 256 22.47 S 44.18 W
Caripe 246 10.12 N 63.29 W
Caripi ≏ 250 3.56 N 51.27 W
Caripito 246 10.08 N 63.06 W
Carira 250 10.21 S 37.42 W
Cariré 250 3.57 S 40.27 W
Caririaçu 250 7.02 S 39.17 W
Carisbrook 169 37.02 S 143.49 E
Carisbrooke 42 50.41 N 1.19 W
Carisolo 64 46.10 N 10.45 E
Carite 286c 10.24 N 67.01 W
Carite, Lago ⊜ 240m 18.04 N 66.06 W
Çariús 250 6.32 S 39.30 W
Čarkesar 85 41.02 N 70.53 E
Carlentini 70 37.16 N 15.01 E
Carle Place 276 40.45 N 73.36 W
Carles 116 11.34 N 123.08 E
Carlet 34 39.14 N 0.31 W
Carleton, Mi., U.S. 216 42.03 N 83.23 W
Carleton, Ne., U.S. 198 40.18 N 97.40 W
Carleton, Mount ∧ 186 47.23 N 66.53 W
Carleton Place 212 45.08 N 76.09 W
Carletonville 158 26.23 S 27.22 E
Carlin 204 40.42 N 116.06 W
Carling 56 49.10 N 6.43 E
Carlingford 274a 33.47 S 151.03 E
Carlingford Lough ⊂ 44 54.04 N 6.10 W
Carlinville 219 39.16 N 89.52 W
Carlinville, Lake ⊜¹ 219 39.14 N 89.51 W
Carlisle, On., Can. 212 43.23 N 79.59 W
Carlisle, Eng., U.K. 44 54.54 N 2.55 W
Carlisle, Ar., U.S. 194 34.46 N 91.44 W
Carlisle, In., U.S. 194 38.58 N 87.24 W
Carlisle, Ia., U.S. 190 41.30 N 93.29 W
Carlisle, Ky., U.S. 218 38.18 N 84.01 W
Carlisle, Ma., U.S. 283 42.31 N . 0 W
Carlisle, N.Y., U.S. 210 42.45 N 74.27 W
Carlisle, Oh., U.S. 218 39.35 N 84.20 W
Carlisle, Pa., U.S. 208 40.12 N 77.11 W
Carlisle Barracks ■ 208 40.13 N 77.11 W
Carlisle Bay ⊂ 241g 13.05 N 59.37 W
Carlisle Gardens 210 43.11 N 78.39 W
Carlisle Island I 180 52.52 N 170.02 W
Carlisle Springs 208 40.16 N 77.10 W
Carl Junction 194 37.10 N 94.33 W
Carlls ≏ 276 40.41 N 73.20 W
Carloforte 71 39.08 N 8.18 E
Carlopoli 68 39.03 N 16.27 E
Carlópolis 255 23.25 S 49.41 W
Carlos, Isla I 254 54.03 S 73.20 W
Carlos Alves 256 21.37 S 43.07 W
Carlos Barbosa 252 29.18 S 51.30 W
Carlos Beguerie 258 35.29 S 59.06 W
Carlos Casares 252 35.38 S 61.21 W
Carlos Chagas 255 17.43 S 40.45 W
Carlos City 218 40.02 N 85.02 W
Carlos Forseca Amador 236 11.59 N 86.31 W
Carlos Keen 258 34.29 S 59.14 W
Carlos Manuel de Céspedes 240p 21.35 N 78.17 W
Carlos Pellegrini 252 32.03 S 61.48 W
Carlos Reyles 252 33.03 S 56.29 W
Carlos Sampaio 287a 22.42 S 43.31 W
Carlos Tejedor 252 35.23 S 62.25 W
Carlow 48 52.50 N 6.55 W
Carlow □⁶ 48 53.40 N 6.50 W
Carloway 46 58.17 N 6.48 W
Carl Sandburg Home National Historic Site ⊥ 192 35.16 N 82.27 W
Carlsbad, Ca., U.S. 228 33.09 N 117.20 W
Carlsbad, N.M., U.S. 196 32.25 N 104.13 W
Carlsbad, Tx., U.S. 196 31.36 N 100.38 W
Carlsbad Caverns National Park ♦ 196 32.08 N 104.35 W
Carlsbad
— Karlovy Vary 54 50.11 N 12.52 E
Carlsberg Ridge ✢³ 12 6.00 N 61.00 E
Carlsborg 224 48.05 N 123.10 W
Carlsfeld 54 50.26 N 12.35 E
Carlstadt 276 40.50 N 74.05 W
Carlton, Austl. 274a 33.58 S 151.08 E
Carlton, Eng., U.K. 42 52.58 N 1.05 W
Carlton, Eng., U.K. 44 53.42 N 1.01 W
Carlton, Mn., U.S. 190 46.39 N 92.25 W
Carlton, Or., U.S. 224 45.18 N 123.11 W
Carlton, Tx., U.S. 196 31.55 N 98.10 W
Carlton Gardens ♦ 274b 37.48 S 144.59 E
Carlton Lake ⊜ 224 45.18 N 123.11 W
Carluke 46 55.45 N 3.51 W
Carlyle, Sk., Can. 184 49.38 N 102.16 W
Carlyle, Il., U.S. 219 38.36 N 89.22 W
Carlyle Lake ⊜¹ 219 38.40 N 89.18 W
Carmacks 180 62.05 N 136.18 W
Carmagnola 62 44.51 N 7.43 E
Carman 184 49.32 N 98.00 W
Carmanah Creek ≏ 224 48.37 N 124.44 W
Carmangay 182 50.08 N 113.07 W
Carmanville 186 49.24 N 54.17 W
Carmarthen 42 51.52 N 4.19 W
Carmarthen Bay ⊂ 42 51.40 N 4.30 W
Carmaux 32 44.03 N 2.09 E
Carmel, Wales, U.K. 262 53.17 N 3.15 W
Carmel, Ca., U.S. 226 36.33 N 121.55 W
Carmel, In., U.S. 218 39.58 N 86.07 W
Carmel, N.J., U.S. 208 39.26 N 75.07 W
Carmel, N.Y., U.S. 210 41.26 N 73.41 W
Carmel ≏ 226 36.32 N 121.56 W
Carmel, Mount ∧ 226 36.23 N 121.47 W
Carmel, Mount
— Karmel, Har ∧ 132 32.44 N 35.02 E
Carmel Bay ⊂ 226 36.33 N 121.57 W
Carmel Head ≻ 44 53.24 N 4.34 W
Carmel Highlands 226 36.30 N 121.56 W
Carmel Hills 226 36.32 N 121.53 W
Carmel Mountain ∧² 226 32.55 N 117.13 W
Carmelo 258 34.00 S 58.17 W
Carmel Point ≻ 226 36.31 N 121.55 W
Carmel Valley 226 36.29 N 121.43 W
Carmel Woods 226 36.33 N 121.54 W
Carmen, Pil. 116 8.59 N 125.17 E
Carmen, Pil. 116 9.50 N 124.12 E
Carmen, Pil. 116 10.35 N 124.01 E
Carmen, Pil. 116 12.07 N 122.07 E
Carmen, Ok., U.S. 196 36.34 N 98.27 W
Carmen, Ur. 252 33.15 S 56.01 W
Carmen, Isla I 232 25.57 N 111.12 W
Carmen, Isla del I 232 18.42 N 91.40 W
Carmen, Río del ≏ 252 28.45 S 70.30 W
Carmen Alto 252 23.11 S 69.40 W
Carmen
— Ciudad del Carmen 232 18.38 N 91.50 W
Carmen de Apicalá 246 4.09 N 74.44 W
Carmen de Areco 252 34.22 S 59.49 W
Carmen de Huechuraba 286e 33.21 S 70.40 W
Carmen de Patagones 254 40.48 S 62.59 W
Carmer Hill ∧² 214 41.54 N 77.58 W
Carmi 194 38.05 N 88.09 W
Carmi, Lake ⊜ 206 44.58 N 72.53 W
Carmiano 68 40.21 N 18.03 E
Carmichael 226 38.37 N 121.19 W
Carmignano di Brenta 64 45.38 N 11.42 E
Carmila 166 21.55 S 149.25 E
Carmine 222 30.09 N 96.41 W
Carmo 256 21.56 S 42.37 W
Carmo, Monte ∧ 62 44.11 N 8.11 E
Carmo, Ribeirão do ≏ 256 21.20 S 45.10 W
Carmo, Rio do ≏ 250 5.02 S 37.12 W
Carmo da Cachoeira 256 21.28 S 45.13 W
Carmo de Minas 256 22.07 S 45.08 W
Carmo do Paranaíba 255 18.59 S 46.21 W
Carmo do Rio Verde 255 15.21 S 49.42 W
Carmody Hills 284c 38.54 N 76.54 W
Carmona, Esp. 34 37.28 N 5.38 W
Carmona, Pil. 116 14.19 N 121.03 E
Carmópolis de Minas 255 20.33 S 44.38 W
Carmzow 54 53.23 N 14.02 E
Carnaíba 250 7.48 S 37.49 W
Carnamah 162 29.42 S 115.53 E
Carnarvon, Austl. 162 24.53 S 113.40 E
Carnarvon, S. Afr. 158 30.56 S 22.08 E
Carnarvon
— Caernarfon 44 53.08 N 4.16 W
Carnarvon National Park ♦ 166 25.00 S 148.00 E
Carnatic □⁹ 118 12.30 N 78.15 E
Carnation 224 47.38 N 121.54 W
Carnaval, Arroyo ≏ 288 34.52 S 58.02 W
Carnaxide 266c 38.43 N 9.15 W
Carncastle 48 54.54 N 5.53 W
Carndonagh 48 55.15 N 7.15 W
Carnduff 184 49.10 N 101.50 W
Carnedd Llewelyn ∧ 44 53.10 N 3.58 W
Carnedd Wen ∧ 42 52.41 N 3.35 W
Carnegie, Austl. 162 25.43 S 122.59 E
Carnegie, N.Y., U.S. 210 42.45 N 78.51 W
Carnegie, Ok., U.S. 196 35.06 N 98.36 W
Carnegie, Pa., U.S. 214 40.24 N 80.05 W
Carnegie, Lake ⊜ 162 26.10 S 122.30 E
Carnegie Institute ♥² 279b 40.27 N 79.57 W
Carnegie-Mellon University ♥² 279b 40.27 N 79.57 W
Carnegie Ridge ✢³ 18 1.00 S 85.00 W
Carnelian Bay 226 39.14 N 120.05 W
Carnetin 261 48.54 N 2.42 E
Carnew 48 52.43 N 6.30 W
Carneys Point 208 39.42 N 75.28 W
Carnforth 44 54.08 N 2.46 W
Carnia 64 46.22 N 13.08 E
Carnia ◆¹ 64 46.25 N 13.00 E
Carniche, Alpi (Karnische Alpen) ⋏ 64 46.40 N 13.00 E
Car Nicobar Island I 110 9.10 N 92.47 E
Carnide ◆⁸ 266c 38.46 N 9.11 W
Carnières 50 50.10 N 3.21 E
Carniques
— Karnische Alpen ⋏ 64 46.40 N 13.00 E
Carnlough 48 54.59 N 6.00 W
Carno 42 52.33 N 3.31 W
Carnon-Plage 62 43.32 N 3.59 E
Carnot, Centraf. 152 4.56 N 15.52 E
Carnot, Pa., U.S. 214 40.31 N 80.13 W
Carnot, Cape ≻ 166 34.57 S 135.38 E
Carnoules 62 43.18 N 6.11 E
Carnoustie 46 56.30 N 2.44 W
Carnsore Point ≻ 48 52.10 N 6.22 W
Carnwath 46 55.43 N 3.38 W
Carnwath ≏ 180 68.26 N 128.50 W
Caro 190 43.29 N 83.23 W
Caroga Creek ≏ 210 42.58 N 74.38 W
Caroga Lake 210 43.08 N 74.29 W
Carol Beach Estates 216 42.31 N 87.49 W
Carol City 220 25.56 N 80.14 W
Carole Acres 284c 39.04 N 77.00 W
Caroleen 192 35.16 N 81.47 W
Carole Highlands 284c 38.58 N 76.59 W
Carolei 68 39.15 N 16.13 E
Carolina, Bra. 250 7.20 S 47.28 W
Carolina, Col. 246 6.43 N 75.17 W
Carolina, El Sal. 236 13.51 N 88.19 W
Carolina, P.R. 240m 18.23 N 65.57 W
Carolina, S. Afr. 158 26.05 S 30.06 E
Carolina, R.I., U.S. 207 41.27 N 71.39 W
Carolina Beach 192 34.02 N 77.53 W
Carolinas, Puntan ≻ 174n 14.55 N 145.38 E
Caroline □⁶, Md., U.S. 208 38.53 N 75.50 W
Caroline □⁶, Va., U.S. 208 38.00 N 77.20 W
Caroline I¹ 14 9.58 S 150.13 W
Caroline du Nord
— North Carolina □³ 192 35.30 N 80.00 W
Caroline du Sud
— South Carolina □³ 192 34.00 N 81.00 W
Caroline Islands II 14 8.00 N 147.00 E
Caroline Livermore, Mount ∧² 282 37.52 N 122.26 W
Caroline Peak ∧ 172 45.56 S 167.13 E
Carol Stream 278 41.54 N 88.08 W
Caron 184 50.28 N 105.52 W
Caron, Lac ⊜ 190 48.00 N 78.53 W
Çarona 64 46.01 N 9.47 E
Čaronda 76 60.34 N 38.59 E
Caroní ≏ 246 8.21 N 62.43 W
Caronia 70 38.01 N 14.26 E
Caronia ≏ 70 38.03 N 14.26 E
Caronno Pertusella 266b 45.36 N 9.03 E
Carora 246 10.11 N 70.05 W
Carosino 68 40.27 N 17.23 E
Carouge 58 46.11 N 6.09 E
Car'ov 80 48.40 N 45.22 E
Carovigno 68 40.42 N 17.39 E
Carovilli 66 41.43 N 14.17 E
Çar'ovščina 80 53.37 N 44.45 E
Čarozero 76 60.28 N 38.39 E
Carp 212 45.21 N 76.02 W
Carp ≏, On., Can. 212 45.29 N 76.14 W
Carp ≏, Mi., U.S. 190 46.02 N 84.42 W
Carpaneto Piacentino 62 44.55 N 9.47 E
Carpanzano 68 39.09 N 16.18 E
Carpates
— Carpathian Mountains ⋏ 22 48.00 N 24.00 E
Carpathian Mountains ⋏ 22 48.00 N 24.00 E
Carpații Meridionali ⋏ 38 45.30 N 24.15 E
Cárpatos
— Carpathian Mountains ⋏ 22 48.00 N 24.00 E
Carpegna 66 43.47 N 12.20 E
Carpenedolo 64 45.22 N 10.26 E
Carpentaria, Gulf of ⊂ 164 14.00 S 139.00 E
Carpenter 198 41.02 N 104.21 W
Carpenter Creek ≏ 216 40.54 N 87.12 W
Carpenter Lake ⊜ 182 50.50 N 122.30 W
Carpentersville 216 42.07 N 88.15 W
Carpentertown 279b 40.40 N 79.51 W
Carpentras 62 44.03 N 5.03 E
Carpet Museum ♥ 267d 35.43 N 51.24 E
Carpi 64 44.47 N 10.53 E
Carpignano Sesia 62 45.32 N 8.25 E
Carpina 250 7.51 S 35.15 W
Carpineti 64 44.28 N 10.31 E
Carpineto Romano 66 41.36 N 13.05 E
Carpino 68 41.51 N 15.51 E
Carpinone 66 41.35 N 14.19 E
Carpinteria 204 34.23 N 119.31 W
Carpio 198 48.26 N 101.42 W
Carp Lake ⊜ 182 54.45 N 123.20 W
Carpolac 166 36.44 S 141.19 E
Carquefou 32 47.18 N 1.30 W
Carqueiranne 62 43.05 N 6.05 E
Carquinez Bridge ◆⁵ 282 38.04 N 122.14 W
Carquinez Strait ꝏ 282 38.02 N 122.12 W
Carra, Lough ⊜ 48 53.41 N 9.14 W
Carrabelle 192 29.51 N 84.39 W
Carradale 46 55.35 N 5.28 W
Carramar 274a 33.53 S 150.58 E
Carrancas 256 21.30 S 44.39 W
Carr and Craggs Moor ◆³ 262 53.43 N 2.09 W
Carranglan 116 15.58 N 121.04 E
Carranza, Cabo ≻ 252 35.36 S 72.38 W
Carrao ≏ 246 6.17 N 62.51 W
Carrara 64 44.05 N 10.06 E
Carrascal 116 9.22 N 125.56 E
Carrasco ◆⁸ 258 34.54 S 56.05 W
Carrasco, Aeropuerto Nacional de ⊠ 258 34.52 S 56.02 W
Carrathool 166 34.24 S 145.26 E
Carrauntoohil ∧ 48 51.59 N 9.45 W
Carrazedo 250 1.36 S 51.54 W
Carrboro 192 35.54 N 79.04 W
Carr Bridge 46 57.17 N 3.49 W
Carrcroft 285 39.47 N 75.30 W
Carrcroft Crest 285 39.47 N 75.30 W
Carrefour Pompadour ♦ 261 48.46 N 2.26 E
Carregueira, Serra da ⋏² 266c 38.48 N 9.15 W
Carreria 252 21.59 S 58.35 W
Carreta, Punta ≻ 248 14.13 S 76.18 W
Carreta Quemada, Arroyo ≏ 258 34.21 S 56.41 W
Carriacou I 238 12.30 N 61.27 W
Carrick ◆⁸ 279b 40.23 N 79.59 W
Carrick ◆¹ 44 55.12 N 4.38 W
Carrickart 48 55.10 N 7.47 W
Carrickfergus 48 54.43 N 5.49 W
Carrickmacross 48 53.58 N 6.43 W
Carrick on Shannon 48 53.57 N 8.05 W
Carrick on Suir 48 52.21 N 7.25 W
Carrie, Mount ∧ 224 47.53 N 123.39 W
Carriere 194 30.37 N 89.39 W
Carrière, Lac ⊜ 190 47.14 N 77.12 W
Carrières, Pointe aux ≻ 275a 45.31 N 73.54 W
Carrières-sous-Bois 261 48.57 N 2.07 E
Carrières-sous-Poissy 261 48.57 N 2.03 E
Carrières-sur-Seine 261 48.55 N 2.11 E
Carriers Mills 194 37.41 N 88.38 W
Carrieton 166 32.26 S 138.32 E
Carrigahorig 48 53.04 N 8.09 W
Carrigaline 48 51.48 N 8.24 W
Carrigallen 48 53.59 N 7.39 W
Carrillo, C.R. 236 9.52 N 85.30 W
Carrillo, Méx. 232 26.54 N 103.55 W
Carrington, Eng., U.K. 262 53.26 N 2.24 W
Carrington, N.D., U.S. 198 47.26 N 99.07 W
Carrington Island I 202 41.00 N 112.37 W
Carrington Moss ◆³ 262 53.25 N 2.23 W
Carr Inlet ⊂ 224 47.17 N 122.42 W
Carrión ≏ 34 41.53 N 4.32 W
Carrión de los Condes 34 42.20 N 4.36 W
Carrizal ≏ 234 23.03 N 97.46 W
Carrizal, Cerro ∧ 196 26.43 N 100.36 W
Carrizal Bajo 252 28.05 S 71.10 W
Carrizo 34 42.35 N 5.50 W
Carrizo Creek ≏, U.S. 196 36.05 N 102.36 W
Carrizo Creek ≏, N.M., U.S. 196 35.40 N 103.43 W
Carrizo Mountain ∧ 200 33.41 N 105.42 W
Carrizo Mountains ⋏ 200 36.45 N 109.10 W
Carrizo Plain ⩡ 226 35.25 N 120.00 W
Carrizo Springs 196 28.31 N 99.51 W
Carrizo Wash V, U.S. 200 34.36 N 109.26 W
Carrizo Wash V, Ca., U.S. 204 33.05 N 115.56 W
Carrizozo 200 33.38 N 105.52 W
Carro 62 43.20 N 5.02 E
Carrodano 62 44.14 N 9.39 E
Carroll, Ia., U.S. 198 42.03 N 94.52 W
Carroll, Ne., U.S. 198 42.16 N 97.11 W
Carroll □⁶, In., U.S. 216 40.36 N 86.41 W
Carroll □⁶, Ky., U.S. 218 38.39 N 85.06 W
Carroll □⁶, Md., U.S. 208 39.35 N 77.00 W
Carroll □⁶, Oh., U.S. 214 40.34 N 81.05 W
Carroll Lake ⊜ 184 51.07 N 95.05 W
Carroll Park ♦ 284b 39.17 N 76.39 W
Carrolls 224 46.05 N 122.52 W
Carrollton, Al., U.S. 194 33.10 N 88.06 W
Carrollton, Ga., U.S. 192 33.35 N 85.05 W
Carrollton, Il., U.S. 219 39.18 N 90.24 W
Carrollton, Ky., U.S. 218 38.40 N 85.10 W
Carrollton, Mi., U.S. 190 43.27 N 83.55 W
Carrollton, Ms., U.S. 194 33.30 N 89.55 W
Carrollton, Mo., U.S. 194 39.21 N 93.29 W
Carrollton, Oh., U.S. 214 40.34 N 81.05 W
Carrollton, Tx., U.S. 222 32.57 N 96.53 W
Carrollton Manor 208 39.05 N 76.35 W
Carrolltown 214 40.36 N 78.43 W
Carrollwood 284b 39.20 N 76.23 W
Carron ≏, Austl. 166 17.42 S 141.06 E
Carron ≏, Scot., U.K. 46 57.25 N 5.27 W
Carron ≏, Scot., U.K. 46 56.02 N 3.44 W
Carron ≏, Scot., U.K. 46 57.53 N 4.21 W
Carron, Loch ⊂ 46 57.22 N 5.31 W
Carronbridge 44 55.16 N 3.48 W
Carron Valley Reservoir ⊜¹ 46 56.02 N 4.05 W
Carros 62 43.48 N 7.11 E
Carrot ≏ 184 53.50 N 101.17 W
Carrot River 184 53.17 N 103.35 W
Carrouges 28 48.34 N 0.09 W
Carrowmore Lake ⊜ 48 54.12 N 9.47 W
Carrsville 208 36.43 N 76.50 W
Carrù 62 44.29 N 7.52 E
Carrum 169 38.05 S 145.08 E
Carrum Downs 274b 38.06 S 145.11 E
Carrum North 274b 38.03 S 145.09 E
Carrville 194 32.32 N 85.52 W
Carryduff 48 54.31 N 5.53 W
Carry Falls Reservoir ⊜¹ 188 44.25 N 74.45 W
Carry-le-Rouet 62 43.20 N 5.09 E
Carsaig 46 56.17 N 6.00 W
Çarşamba 130 41.12 N 36.44 E
Čaršanga 128 37.30 N 66.01 E
Carseland 182 50.51 N 113.28 W
Çarshalton ◆⁸ 260 51.22 N 0.10 W
Čarsk 86 49.35 N 81.05 E
Carsoli 66 42.06 N 13.05 E
Carson, Ca., U.S. 228 33.49 N 118.16 W
Carson, N.D., U.S. 198 46.25 N 101.33 W
Carson, Va., U.S. 208 37.02 N 77.23 W
Carson, Wa., U.S. 224 45.43 N 121.49 W
Carson ≏ 204 39.45 N 118.40 W
Carson, East Fork ≏ 226 38.59 N 119.49 W
Carson, West Fork ≏ 226 38.59 N 119.49 W
Carson City, Mi., U.S. 190 43.10 N 84.50 W
Carson City, Nv., U.S. 226 39.10 N 119.46 W
Carsondale 284c 38.57 N 76.50 W
Carson Lake ⊜, On., Can. 212 45.31 N 77.46 W
Carson Lake ⊜, Nv., U.S. 204 39.19 N 118.43 W
Carson Range ⋏ 226 39.15 N 119.50 W
Carson Sink ⊜ 204 39.50 N 118.25 W
Carson Valley V 226 39.00 N 119.48 W
Carstairs, Ab., Can. 182 51.34 N 114.06 W
Carstairs, Scot., U.K. 46 55.42 N 3.42 W
Carstensz-Toppen
— Jaya, Puncak ∧ 164 4.05 S 137.11 E
Carswell Air Force Base ■ 222 32.47 N 97.26 W
Cartagena, Chile 252 33.33 S 71.37 W
Cartagena, Col. 246 10.25 N 75.32 W
Cartagena, Esp. 34 37.36 N 0.59 W
Cartago, Col. 246 4.45 N 75.55 W
Cartago, C.R. 236 9.52 N 83.55 W
Cartago □⁴ 236 9.50 N 83.45 W
Cartak 85 41.05 N 71.50 E
Cartaxo 34 39.09 N 8.47 W
Cartaxos ∧² 266c 38.42 N 9.20 W
Cartaya 34 37.17 N 7.09 W
Carter 196 35.13 N 99.30 W
Carter □⁶ 218 38.20 N 83.05 W
Carter Bridge ◆⁵ 273a 6.28 N 3.23 E
Carter Caves State Resort Park ♦ 218 38.22 N 83.10 W
Carteret 210 40.34 N 74.13 W

Symbols in the index entries represent the broad categories identified in the key at the right. Symbols with superior numbers (⋏¹) identify subcategories (see complete key on page I · 1).

Symbole im Register stellen die rechts im Schlüssel erklärten Kategorien dar. Symbole mit hochgestellten Ziffern (⋏¹) bezeichnen Unterabteilungen einer Kategorie (vgl. vollständiger Schlüssel auf Seite I · 1).

Los símbolos incluidos en el texto del índice representan las grandes categorías identificadas con la clave a la derecha. Los símbolos con numeros en su parte superior (⋏¹) identifican las subcategorías (véase la clave completa en la página I · 1).

Les symboles de l'index représentent les catégories indiquées dans la légende à droite. Les symboles suivis d'un indice (⋏¹) représentent des sous-catégories (voir légende complète à la page I · 1).

Os símbolos incluídos no texto do índice representam as grandes categorias identificadas com a chave à direita. Os símbolos com números em sua parte superior (⋏¹) identificam as subcategorias (veja-se a chave completa à página I · 1).

∧ Mountain	Berg	Montaña	Montagne	Montanha
⋏ Mountains	Gebirge	Montañas	Montagnes	Montanhas
✕ Pass	Paß	Paso	Col	Passo
V Valley, Canyon	Tal, Cañon	Valle, Cañón	Vallée, Canyon	Vale, Canhão
⩡ Plain	Ebene	Llano	Plaine	Planície
≻ Cape	Kap	Cabo	Cap	Cabo
I Island	Insel	Isla	Île	Ilha
II Islands	Inseln	Islas	Îles	Ilhas
♦ Other Topographic Features	Andere Topographische Objekte	Otros Elementos Topográficos	Autres données topographiques	Outros acidentes topográficos

Nombre	Página	Lat.° W = Oeste
Carter Lake	198	41.17 N 95.55 W
Carter Mountain ▲	202	44.12 N 109.25 W
Carters Lake ◍ ¹	192	34.35 N 84.35 W
Cartersville	192	34.09 N 84.48 W
Carterton, N.Z.	172	41.02 S 175.31 E
Carterton, Eng., U.K.	42	51.45 N 1.35 W
Carterville	194	37.45 N 89.04 W
Carthage, Tun.	148	36.51 N 10.21 E
Carthage, Ar., U.S.	194	34.04 N 92.33 W
Carthage, Il., U.S.	190	40.24 N 91.08 W
Carthage, In., U.S.	218	39.44 N 85.34 W
Carthage, Ms., U.S.	194	32.43 N 89.32 W
Carthage, Mo., U.S.	194	37.10 N 94.18 W
Carthage, N.Y., U.S.	212	43.58 N 75.36 W
Carthage, N.C., U.S.	192	35.20 N 79.25 W
Carthage, S.D., U.S.	198	44.10 N 97.42 W
Carthage, Tn., U.S.	194	36.15 N 85.57 W
Carthage, Tx., U.S.	194	32.09 N 94.20 W
Carthage ⊥	36	36.52 N 10.20 E
Cartier Islands II	160	12.32 S 123.32 E
Cartierville ⬦ ⁸	275a	45.32 N 73.42 W
Cartierville, Aéroport de ⬦	275a	45.31 N 73.43 W
Cartridge Hill ▲ ²	262	53.41 N 2.30 W
Cartura	66	45.16 N 11.50 E
Cartwright, Mb., Can.	184	49.06 N 99.20 W
Cartwright, Nf., Can.	176	53.42 N 57.01 W
Caruaru	250	8.17 S 35.58 W
Caruban	115a	7.33 S 111.39 E
Carûngol	88	49.14 N 106.29 E
Carupamba ⬌	152	13.57 S 12.25 E
Carupano	246	10.40 N 63.14 W
Caruray	116	10.20 N 119.00 E
Carutapera	250	1.13 S 46.01 W
Caruthers	226	36.32 N 119.50 W
Caruthersville	194	36.11 N 89.39 W
Carutu ⩰	246	5.05 N 63.28 W
Carvahopolis	256	21.47 S 46.51 W
Carvalhos	256	22.00 S 44.28 W
Carver	207	41.53 N 70.45 W
Carversville	208	40.23 N 75.04 W
Carvin	46	50.30 N 2.57 E
Carvoeiro, Cabo ﹥	34	39.21 N 9.24 W
Cary, Il., U.S.	216	42.12 N 88.14 W
Cary, Ms., U.S.	194	32.48 N 90.55 W
Cary, N.C., U.S.	192	35.47 N 78.46 W
Cary ⩰	42	51.09 N 2.59 W
Caryčekskij zapovednik ⬦	85	46.13 N 71.55 E
Caryk, ozero ◉	80	46.13 N 42.43 E
Čarymovo	86	58.31 N 77.42 E
Čaryn ⩰	86	43.46 N 79.24 E
Čaryš ⩰	86	52.22 N 83.45 E
Čaryšskoje	86	51.24 N 83.35 E
Caryville, Fl., U.S.	194	30.46 N 85.48 W
Caryville, Tn., U.S.	194	36.17 N 84.13 W
Casablanca (Dar-el-Beida)	148	33.39 N 7.35 W
Casablanca ◻ ⁴	148	33.35 N 7.30 W
Casablanca ⬦ ⁸	286b	23.09 N 82.20 W
Casabona	68	39.15 N 16.57 E
Casabranca	256	21.46 S 47.04 W
Casacalenda	64	41.44 N 14.51 E
Casa de la Torrecilla	266a	40.19 N 3.37 W
Casa del Campo ⬦	266a	40.32 N 3.47 W
Casa de Piedra, Embalse ◍ ¹	252	38.15 S 67.20 W
Casa Grande	200	32.52 N 111.45 W
Casa Grande National Monument ⬦	200	32.59 N 111.32 W
Casainhos	266c	38.53 N 9.10 W
Casalanguida	66	42.03 N 14.30 E
Casalattico	66	41.37 N 13.43 E
Casalbordino	66	42.09 N 14.35 E
Casalbuono	66	40.13 N 15.41 E
Casalbuttano	66	45.15 N 9.58 E
Casal di Principe	66	41.00 N 14.08 E
Casale Abbruciato ⬦ ⁸	267a	41.44 N 12.33 E
Casalecchio di Reno	66	44.28 N 11.16 E
Casale Monferrato	62	45.08 N 8.27 E
Casale sul Sile	66	45.36 N 12.19 E
Casaletto Spartano	68	40.09 N 15.37 E
Casalmaggiore	64	44.59 N 10.26 E
Casalmorano	62	45.17 N 9.54 E
Casalnuovo Monterotaro	66	41.37 N 15.06 E
Casa Loma ⬦	275b	43.41 N 79.25 W
Casalone ⬦ ⁸	267a	41.56 N 12.41 E
Casalotti ⬦ ⁸	267a	41.55 N 12.22 E
Casalpusterlengo	62	45.11 N 9.39 E
Casal Velino	66	40.11 N 15.06 E
Casalvieri	66	41.38 N 13.43 E
Casamance ⩰	150	12.33 N 16.46 W
Casamari, Abbazia di ⬦ ¹	66	41.41 N 13.29 E
Casamassima	68	40.57 N 16.55 E
Casamicciola Terme	68	40.45 S 13.54 E
Casanare ⬌	246	5.45 N 72.00 W
Casanare ⬌	246	6.02 N 69.30 W
Casanay	246	10.30 N 63.25 W
Casa Nova	250	9.07 S 40.58 W
Casarano	68	40.00 N 18.10 E
Casar de Cáceres	34	39.34 N 6.25 W
Casarsa della Delizia	64	45.57 N 12.51 E
Casas	234	23.44 N 98.45 W
Casas Adobes	200	32.19 N 110.59 W
Casas Grandes ⩰	232	30.21 N 107.31 W
Casas Ibáñez	34	39.17 N 1.28 W
Casasimarro	34	39.22 N 2.02 W
Casaubon ⬌	116	7.16 N 126.17 E
Casavieja	34	40.17 N 4.46 W
Casbas	252	36.45 S 62.30 W
Casca	252	28.34 S 51.59 W
Casca, Rio da ⩰	248	14.52 S 55.52 W
Cascadas Basaseachic, Parque Nacional ⬦	232	28.10 N 108.22 W
Cascade, B.C., Can.	180	49.10 N 118.13 W
Cascade, Id., U.S.	202	44.30 N 116.02 W
Cascade, Ia., U.S.	190	42.17 N 91.00 W
Cascade, Mt., U.S.	216	42.55 N 85.30 W
Cascade, Mt., U.S.	202	47.16 N 111.41 W
Cascade, ⬌, N.Z.	172	43.30 N 88.00 W
Cascade ⬌, Wa., U.S.	224	44.02 S 168.22 E
Cascade Bay ◡	174c	29.01 S 167.58 E
Cascade Locks	224	45.40 N 121.53 W
Cascade Mountains (Cascade Range) ⋌	220	45.00 N 121.30 W
Cascade Park ⬦	279a	41.23 N 82.06 W
Cascade Point ﹥	172	44.00 S 168.22 E
Cascade Range ⋌	178	45.00 N 121.30 W
Cascade Reservoir ◍ ¹	202	44.35 N 116.03 W
Cascade Tunnel ⬦ ⁵	224	47.40 N 121.03 W
Cascadura ⬦ ⁸	287a	32.33 N 42.20 W
Cascais	34	38.42 N 9.25 W
Cascalho Rico	256	18.34 S 47.52 W
Cascapédia ⩰	176	48.11 N 65.54 W
Cascatinha	256	22.29 S 43.09 W
Cascavel, Bra.	250	4.07 S 38.14 W
Cascavel, Bra.	252	24.57 S 53.28 W
Casci	66	43.41 N 11.09 E
Cascina	66	43.41 N 10.33 E
Cascina Terme	66	43.41 N 10.32 E
Casco Bay ◡	188	43.45 N 70.00 W
Cascumpec Bay ◡	186	46.45 N 64.03 W
Cascy	82	55.01 N 8.55 E
Casei Gerola	62	45.01 N 8.56 E
Case Inlet ◡	224	47.19 N 122.53 W
Casekow	62	53.12 N 14.12 E
Casella	62	44.32 N 9.00 E
Caselle, Aeroporto di ⬦	62	45.13 N 7.40 E
Caselle in Pittari	68	40.10 N 15.33 E
Caselle Torinese	62	45.10 N 7.39 E
Cà Selva, Lago di ◍ ¹	64	46.12 N 12.40 E

Nom	Page	Lat.° W = Ouest
Casenove	66	42.58 N 12.50 E
Casentino V	66	43.40 N 11.50 E
Casenuove	266b	45.38 N 8.42 E
Case-Pilote	240e	14.38 N 61.08 W
Caseros	258	34.36 S 58.33 W
Caserta	68	41.04 N 14.20 E
Caserta ◻ ⁴	68	41.14 N 14.10 E
Caseville	190	43.56 N 83.16 W
Case Western Reserve University ⬦ ²	279a	41.30 N 81.36 W
Casey, Il., U.S.	194	39.17 N 87.59 W
Casey, Ia., U.S.	198	41.30 N 94.31 W
Casey, Mount ▲	66	61.17 S 110.32 E
Casey Bay ◡	9	67.20 S 48.00 E
Casey Key ⬌	220	27.10 N 82.29 W
Caseyr ﹥	144	11.49 N 51.15 E
Caseyville	219	38.38 N 90.02 W
Cash	222	32.59 N 96.07 W
Cashel, Ire.	48	53.25 N 9.48 W
Cashel, Ire.	48	52.31 N 7.53 W
Cashie ⩰	192	35.53 N 76.49 W
Cashiers	192	35.06 N 83.05 W
Cashmere	202	47.31 N 120.28 W
Cashmere Downs	162	28.58 S 119.35 E
Cashton	190	43.44 N 90.46 W
Casigua	246	8.46 N 72.30 W
Casiguran, Pil.	116	16.17 N 122.07 E
Casiguran, Pil.	116	12.52 N 124.00 E
Casiguran Sound ⨆	116	16.06 N 121.58 E
Casilda, Arg.	252	33.03 S 61.10 W
Casilda, Cuba	240p	21.46 N 79.59 W
Casimcea	38	44.43 N 28.23 E
Casimiro Castillo	234	19.38 N 104.28 W
Casina	64	44.30 N 10.30 E
Casino	166	28.52 S 153.03 E
Casiquiare ⩰	246	2.01 N 67.07 W
Casita	200	31.00 N 110.53 W
Casitas Springs	228	34.22 N 119.18 W
Casma	248	9.28 S 78.19 W
Čašniki	76	54.52 N 29.08 E
Čašnikovo	285b	55.59 N 37.25 E
Casnočor, gora ▲	24	67.45 N 33.25 E
Casola in Lunigiana	66	44.13 N 10.10 E
Casola Valsenio	66	44.13 N 11.37 E
Casole d'Elsa	66	43.20 N 11.02 E
Casoli	66	42.07 N 14.18 E
Cason	222	33.02 N 94.49 W
Casorate Primo	62	45.19 N 9.01 E
Casorate Sempione	62	45.40 N 8.44 E
Casorezzo	266b	45.31 N 8.54 E
Casoria	68	40.54 N 14.17 E
Casse Jar	83	48.35 N 37.50 E
Casovo	24	62.01 N 50.36 E
Caspe	34	41.14 N 0.02 W
Casper	200	42.52 N 106.18 W
Casper Creek, Middle Fork ⩰	200	43.01 N 106.29 W
Caspian	190	46.03 N 88.37 W
Caspian Sea ⊤ ²	72	42.00 N 50.30 E
Caspien, Mer — Caspian Sea ⊤ ²	72	42.00 N 50.30 E
Caspio, Depresión del — Prikaspijskaja nizmennost' ⩶	80	48.00 N 52.00 E
Caspio, Mar — Caspian Sea ⊤ ²	72	42.00 N 50.30 E
Caspoggio	64	46.16 N 9.52 E
Cass ◯ ⁶, Il., U.S.	219	39.57 N 90.13 W
Cass ◯ ⁶, Mi., U.S.	216	40.45 N 86.01 W
Cass ◯ ⁶, N.D., U.S.	216	41.55 N 86.01 W
Cass ◯ ⁶, Tx., U.S.	222	33.05 N 94.32 W
Cass ⩰	190	43.23 N 83.59 W
Cassadaga	214	42.20 N 79.18 W
Cassadaga Creek ⩰	214	42.05 N 79.08 W
Cassadaga Lakes ◍	214	42.21 N 79.19 W
Cassaday Point ﹥	284a	42.52 N 79.13 W
Cassagnas	46	44.16 N 3.45 E
Cassai	152	10.33 S 21.59 E
Cassai (Kasai) ⩰	152	3.02 S 16.57 E
Cassandra	152	13.06 S 20.18 E
Cassandre ﹥	214	40.04 N 78.38 W
Cassano ⬦ ⁸	248	17.06 S 57.23 W
Cassano allo Ionio	68	39.47 N 16.20 E
Cassano d'Adda	62	45.32 N 9.31 E
Cassano delle Murge	68	40.53 N 16.46 E
Cassano Magnago	62	45.41 N 8.50 E
Cassaro	70	37.07 N 14.56 E
Cass Benton Parkway ♦	281	42.25 N 83.28 W
Cass City	190	43.36 N 83.10 W
Cassel	50	50.48 N 2.29 E
Casselberry	220	28.40 N 81.19 W
Casselman	206	45.19 N 75.05 W
Casselton	198	46.54 N 97.12 W
Cássia, Bra.	255	20.36 S 46.56 W
Cassia, Fl., U.S.	220	28.49 N 81.28 W
Cássia dos Coqueiros	256	21.17 S 47.10 W
Cassiar	180	59.16 N 129.40 W
Cassiar Mountains ⋌	189	59.00 N 129.00 W
Cassibile	70	36.57 N 15.11 E
Cassidy Airfield ⬦	174o	1.57 N 157.18 W
Cassilândia	255	19.09 S 51.45 W
Cassimbazar	126	24.07 N 88.16 E
Cassine	62	44.45 N 8.31 E
Cassinetta di Lugagnano	266b	45.25 N 8.54 E
Cassino, Bra.	252	32.11 S 52.10 W
Cassino, It.	66	41.30 N 13.49 E
Cassio	66	44.35 N 10.02 E
Cassipore ⬦ ⁸	272b	22.37 N 88.22 E
Cass Lake	190	47.22 N 94.36 W
Cass Lake ◉, Mi., U.S.	281	42.36 N 83.22 W
Cass Lake ◉, Mn., U.S.	190	47.25 N 94.32 W
Cassley ⩰	46	57.58 N 4.35 W
Cassolaia	152	9.30 S 14.22 E
Cassoango	152	13.42 S 20.56 E
Cassolnovo	62	45.22 N 8.48 E
Cassone	64	45.44 N 10.46 E
Cassongue	152	11.51 S 15.05 E
Cassopolis	216	41.54 N 86.00 W
Cassumba, Ilha I	255	17.46 S 39.17 W
Cassunga	255	16.03 S 53.38 W
Cassville, In., U.S.	216	40.33 N 86.01 W
Cassville, N.Y., U.S.	210	42.57 N 75.15 W
Cassville, Pa., U.S.	214	40.18 N 78.02 W
Cassville, Wi., U.S.	190	42.42 N 90.59 W
Castac Lake ◉	228	34.50 N 118.51 W
Castagnaro	64	45.07 N 11.24 E
Castagneto Carducci	66	43.10 N 10.36 E
Castaic Creek ⩰	228	34.25 N 118.37 W
Castaic Lake ◍ ¹	228	34.35 N 118.37 W
Castalia	214	41.24 N 82.48 W
Castañ̃ares	258	24.40 S 65.07 W
Castañeda	34	39.50 N 8.13 W
Castanheira de Pêra	34	40.00 N 8.13 W
Castanheiro	246	0.26 N 63.13 W
Castañones, Punta ﹥	236	12.28 N 87.11 W
Castanos Primo	234	26.47 N 101.25 W
Casteggio	62	45.01 N 9.07 E
Castel	43b	49.28 N 2.34 W
Castel Baronia	68	41.03 N 15.11 E
Castel Bolognese	66	44.19 N 11.48 E
Castelbuono	70	37.56 N 14.05 E
Casteldaccia	70	38.03 N 13.32 E
Castel d'Ario	64	45.11 N 10.58 E

Nome	Página	Lat.° W = Oeste
Casteldarne (Ehrenburg)	64	46.48 N 11.50 E
Castel del Monte	66	42.22 N 13.43 E
Castel del Piano	66	42.53 N 11.32 E
Castel del Rio	66	44.12 N 11.30 E
Castel di Decima ⬦ ⁸	267a	41.45 N 12.26 E
Castel di Guido ⬦ ⁸	267a	41.54 N 12.17 E
Castel di Ieri	66	42.06 N 13.44 E
Castel di Iudica	70	37.30 N 14.38 E
Castel di Leva ⬦ ⁸	267a	41.47 N 12.32 E
Castel di Lucio	70	37.53 N 14.19 E
Castel di Sangro	66	41.47 N 14.06 E
Castel di Tora	66	42.13 N 12.58 E
Castelfidardo	66	43.28 N 13.33 E
Castelfiorentino	66	43.36 N 10.58 E
Castelfondo	64	46.27 N 11.07 E
Castelforte	66	41.18 N 13.49 E
Castelfranco Emilia	66	44.37 N 11.03 E
Castelfranco in Miscano	68	41.18 N 15.05 E
Castelfranco Veneto	64	45.40 N 11.55 E
Castel Frentano	66	42.12 N 14.22 E
Castel Fusano ⬦ ⁸	267a	41.44 N 12.19 E
Castel Gandolfo	66	41.45 N 12.39 E
Castel Giorgio	66	42.42 N 11.59 E
Castelgrande	68	40.47 N 15.26 E
Castelhanos, Baía de ◡	256	23.51 S 45.15 W
Castelhanos, Ponta dos ﹥	256	23.10 S 44.06 W
Casteljaloux	46	44.19 N 0.05 E
Castellabate	68	40.17 N 14.57 E
Castell'Alfero	62	44.59 N 8.13 E
Castellalto	66	42.40 N 13.49 E
Castellammare, Golfo di ◡	70	38.08 N 12.54 E
Castellammare del Golfo	70	38.01 N 12.53 E
Castellammare di Stabia	68	40.42 N 14.29 E
Castellamonte	62	45.23 N 7.42 E
Castellana Grotte	68	40.53 N 17.07 E
Castellana Sicula	70	37.47 N 14.02 E
Castellane	46	43.51 N 6.31 E
Castellaneta	68	40.37 N 16.57 E
Castellanza	62	45.37 N 8.54 E
Castell'Arquato	62	44.51 N 9.52 E
Castell'Azzara	66	42.46 N 11.42 E
Castellazzo Bormida	62	44.51 N 8.34 E
Castellbisbal	266d	41.29 N 1.59 E
Castelldefels	266d	41.17 N 1.59 E
Castelletto	266b	45.18 N 9.46 E
Castelletto di Brenzone	64	45.41 N 10.45 E
Castelli, Arg.	252	36.06 S 57.47 W
Castelli, It.	66	42.29 N 13.43 E
Castellina in Chianti	66	43.28 N 11.17 E
Castellina Marittima	66	43.25 N 10.35 E
Castelli Romani ⬦ ¹	267a	41.46 N 12.42 E
Castello ◻ ⁴	34	40.10 N 0.10 W
Castello, Monte ▲	34	43.03 N 9.49 E
Castello d'Annone	62	44.51 N 8.19 E
Castello de la Plana	34	39.59 N 0.02 W
Castello di Fiemme	64	46.17 N 11.26 E
Castello Lavazzo	64	46.17 N 12.18 E
Castellote	34	40.48 N 0.19 W
Castello Tesino	64	46.04 N 11.38 E
Castelluccio	68	40.00 N 15.58 E
Castell'Umberto	70	38.05 N 14.48 E
Castelluzzo	70	38.06 N 12.44 E
Castel Madama	66	41.58 N 12.52 E
Castel Maggiore	64	44.34 N 11.22 E
Castelmassa	64	45.01 N 11.18 E
Castelmauro	66	41.50 N 14.43 E
Castelmezzano	68	40.32 N 16.03 E
Castelmoron-sur-Lot	46	44.24 N 0.30 E
Castelnaudary	46	43.19 N 1.57 E
Castelnau-Montratier	46	44.16 N 1.21 E
Castelnovo di Sotto	64	44.46 N 10.34 E
Castelnovo ne'Monti	66	44.26 N 10.24 E
Castelnuovo Berardenga	66	43.21 N 11.30 E
Castelnuovo dell'Abate	66	43.00 N 11.31 E
Castelnuovo della Daunia	68	41.35 N 15.07 E
Castelnuovo di Garfagnana	66	44.06 N 10.24 E
Castelnuovo di Porto	66	42.07 N 12.30 E
Castelnuovo Don Bosco	62	43.12 N 10.59 E
Castelnuovo Nigra	62	45.26 N 7.41 E
Castelnuovo Rangone	64	44.33 N 10.56 E
Castelnuovo Scrivia	62	44.59 N 8.53 E
Castelo	255	20.36 S 41.12 W
Castelo Branco	34	39.49 N 7.30 W
Castelo do Piauí	250	5.20 S 41.33 W
Castel Pagano	68	41.24 N 14.48 E
Castel Porziano ⬦ ⁸	267a	41.44 N 12.24 E
Castelraimondo	66	43.12 N 13.04 E
Castel Romano ⬦ ⁸	267a	41.44 N 12.27 E
Castel San Gimignano	66	43.24 N 11.00 E
Castel San Giorgio	68	40.47 N 14.42 E
Castel San Giovanni	62	45.04 N 9.26 E
Castel San Lorenzo	68	40.25 N 15.14 E
Castel Sant'Elia	66	42.15 N 12.22 E
Castelsardo	68	40.55 N 8.43 E
Castelsarrasin	38	39.16 N 16.46 E
Castelsilano	68	39.16 N 16.46 E
Casteltermini	70	37.32 N 13.39 E
Castelvecchio Subequo	66	42.08 N 13.44 E
Castelvetere in Val Fortore	68	41.27 N 14.56 E
Castelvetrano	70	37.41 N 12.47 E
Castelvetro di Modena	64	44.23 N 10.57 E
Castelvetro Piacentino	64	45.05 N 9.58 E
Castel Viscardo	66	42.45 N 12.00 E
Castel Volturno	66	41.01 N 13.55 E
Castenaso	64	44.30 N 11.28 E
Castenedolo	64	45.28 N 10.18 E
Casterton	166	37.35 S 141.24 E
Castets	32	43.53 N 1.09 W
Castiglioncello	66	43.24 N 10.24 E
Castiglione d'Adda	62	45.13 N 9.31 E
Castiglione dei Pepoli	66	44.08 N 11.09 E
Castiglione del Lago	66	43.07 N 12.03 E
Castiglione della Pescaia	66	42.46 N 10.53 E
Castiglione delle Stiviere	64	45.23 N 10.29 E
Castiglione di Sicilia	70	37.53 N 15.07 E
Castiglion Fibocchi	66	43.32 N 11.46 E
Castiglion Fiorentino	66	43.20 N 11.55 E
Castilblanco	34	39.17 N 5.05 W
Castilla	248	5.12 S 80.38 W

Nombre		Lat.° W = Oeste
Castilla, Playa de ⌂ ²	34	37.00 N 6.33 W
Castilla-La Mancha ◻ ⁴	34	39.30 N 3.00 W
Castilla la Nueva ◻ ⁹	34	40.00 N 3.45 W
Castilla la Vieja ◻ ⁹	34	41.30 N 4.00 W
Castilla-León ◻ ⁴	34	41.30 N 5.00 W
Castillo	258	33.53 S 57.40 W
Castillo, Cerro ▲	254	43.03 S 71.57 W
Castillo, Pampa del ⩶	254	45.58 S 68.24 W
Castillo de San Marcos National Monument ⬦	192	29.44 N 81.20 W
Castillo Incaico de Ingalirca ⊥	246	2.34 S 78.50 W
Castillon-la-Bataille	32	44.51 N 0.03 W
Castillos	252	34.12 S 53.50 W
Castillos, Laguna de ◉	252	34.20 S 53.54 W
Castine	188	44.23 N 68.48 W
Castione della Presolana	64	45.54 N 10.04 E
Castions di Strada	64	45.54 N 13.11 E
Castle Acre	42	52.42 N 0.41 E
Castle Air Force Base ⬦	226	37.22 N 120.34 W
Castlebar	48	53.52 N 9.17 W
Castlebay	46	56.57 N 7.28 W
Castlebellingham	48	53.54 N 6.23 W
Castleberry	194	31.17 N 87.01 W
Castleblayney	48	54.07 N 6.44 W
Castle Bruce	240d	15.26 N 61.16 W
Castle Cape ﹥	180	56.15 N 158.06 W
Castle Cary	42	51.06 N 2.31 W
Castlecliff	172	39.57 S 174.59 E
Castlecomer	48	52.48 N 7.12 W
Castleconnell	48	52.43 N 8.30 W
Castlecrag ⬦ ⁸	274a	33.48 S 151.13 E
Castle Crags State Park ♦	204	41.10 N 122.20 W
Castle Creek	210	42.14 N 75.55 W
Castle Creek ⩰, Id., U.S.	202	43.06 N 116.16 W
Castle Dale	200	39.23 N 110.27 W
Castledawson	44	54.47 N 6.33 W
Castlederg	44	54.42 N 7.36 W
Castledermot	48	52.55 N 6.50 W
Castle Dome Peak ▲	200	33.05 N 114.08 W
Castle Donington	42	52.51 N 1.19 W
Castle Douglas	44	54.57 N 3.56 W
Castlefinn	48	54.47 N 7.35 W
Castleford	44	53.44 N 1.21 W
Castlegar	182	49.19 N 117.40 W
Castle Harbour ◡	240a	32.21 N 64.40 W
Castle Hill	274a	33.44 S 151.00 E
Castle Hills, De., U.S.	208	39.41 N 75.33 W
Castle Hills, Tx., U.S.	196	29.32 N 98.31 W
Castleisland	48	52.14 N 9.27 W
Castlemaine, Austl.	169	37.04 S 144.13 E
Castlemaine, Ire.	48	52.10 N 9.42 W
Castlemartyr	48	51.55 N 8.03 W
Castlemore	275b	43.47 N 79.41 W
Castle Mountain ▲, Ab., Can.	182	51.18 N 115.55 W
Castle Mountain ▲, Yk., Can.	180	64.32 N 135.25 W
Castle Neck ﹥ ¹	283	42.41 N 70.45 W
Castle Neck ﹥	283	42.40 N 70.44 W
Castle Park	228	32.36 N 117.04 W
Castle Peak ▲, Co., U.S.	200	39.01 N 106.52 W
Castle Peak ▲, Id., U.S.	202	44.02 N 114.35 W
Castle Peak ▲, Wa., U.S.	224	48.58 N 120.51 W
Castlepoint	172	40.54 S 176.13 E
Castle Point ⬦ ⁸	260	51.33 N 0.35 E
Castlepollard	48	53.40 N 7.17 W
Castlerea	48	53.46 N 8.29 W
Castlereagh ⩰	166	30.12 S 147.32 E
Castle Rock, Co., U.S.	200	39.22 N 104.51 W
Castle Rock, Pa., U.S.	285	39.58 N 75.26 W
Castle Rock, Wa., U.S.	224	46.16 N 122.54 W
Castle Rock ▲, Or., U.S.	202	44.02 N 118.11 W
Castle Rock ▲, Va., U.S.	192	37.57 N 78.44 W
Castle Rock Butte ▲	198	45.00 N 103.27 W
Castle Rock Lake ◍	190	43.56 N 89.58 W
Castle Shannon	285	40.21 N 80.01 W
Castleside	44	54.50 N 1.52 W
Castleton, Eng., U.K.	44	53.35 N 1.46 W
Castleton, Eng., U.K.	44	54.28 N 0.56 W
Castleton, In., U.S.	218	39.54 N 86.03 W
Castleton, Vt., U.S.	188	43.36 N 73.10 W
Castleton on Hudson	210	42.32 N 73.45 W
Castletown, I. of Man	44	54.04 N 4.40 W
Castletown, Scot., U.K.	46	58.35 N 3.23 W
Castletown Bearhaven (Castletown Bere) — Castletown Bere	48	51.39 N 9.55 W
Castletown Bere	48	51.39 N 9.55 W
Castletown-Geoghegan	48	53.26 N 7.38 W
Castletownroche	48	52.10 N 8.28 W
Castletownshend	48	51.32 N 9.11 W
Castlewellan	44	54.16 N 5.57 W
Castlewood, Ky., U.S.	218	38.04 N 84.27 W
Castlewood, S.D., U.S.	198	44.43 N 97.01 W
Castlewood, Va., U.S.	192	36.53 N 82.16 W
Castor, On., Can.	212	45.30 N 74.10 W
Castor ⩰, Mo., U.S.	194	36.51 N 89.44 W
Castor Creek ⩰	194	31.53 N 92.22 W
Castorland	212	43.53 N 75.30 W
Castres, Fr.	32	43.36 N 2.15 E
Castries, St. Luc.	240g	14.01 N 61.00 W
Castries, Port ◡	240g	14.00 N 61.00 W
Castro, Bra.	252	24.47 S 50.00 W
Castro, Chile	254	42.29 S 73.46 W
Castro, It.	68	40.00 N 18.26 E
Castro, Arroyo de ⩰	266a	40.22 N 3.52 W
Castro, Punta ﹥	254	43.22 S 65.02 W
Castro Barros	258	29.05 S 67.04 W
Castrocaro Terme	66	44.10 N 11.57 E
Castrocielo	66	41.32 N 13.42 E
Castro dei Volsci	66	41.34 N 13.24 E
Castro del Río	34	37.41 N 4.28 W
Castrojeriz	34	42.17 N 4.08 W
Castro Marim	34	37.13 N 7.26 W
Castronovo di Sicilia	70	37.40 N 13.36 E
Castropol	34	43.32 N 7.02 W
Castrop-Rauxel	52	51.34 N 7.18 E
Castro-Urdiales	34	43.23 N 3.13 W
Castro Verde	34	37.41 N 8.05 W

	Página	Lat.° W = Oeste
Castrovillari	68	39.49 N 16.13 E
Castroville, Ca., U.S.	226	36.45 N 121.45 W
Castroville, Tx., U.S.	196	29.21 N 98.52 W
Castrovirreyna	248	13.16 S 75.19 W
Castuera	34	38.43 N 5.33 W
Çat uul ⩰	86	48.40 N 90.45 E
Catt, Mount ▲	162	54.21 N 128.47 W
Cattai Creek ⩰	274a	33.40 S 150.56 E
Cattaraugus ⬌	214	42.19 N 78.52 W
Cattaraugus ◻ ⁶	214	42.19 N 78.45 W
Cattaraugus Creek ⩰	214	42.35 N 79.10 W
Cattaraugus Creek, South Branch ⩰	214	42.26 N 78.53 W
Cattaraugus Indian Reservation ⬦ ⁴	210	42.33 N 78.56 W
Cattenom	50	49.25 N 6.15 E
Catterick	44	54.22 N 1.38 W
Catterick Garrison	44	54.22 N 1.43 W
Cattle Canyon V	280	34.14 N 117.46 W
Cattolica	66	43.58 N 12.44 E
Cattolica del Sacro Cuore, Università ◻ ²	266b	45.27 N 9.11 E
Cattolica Eraclea	70	37.26 N 13.24 E
Catton	44	54.55 N 2.15 W
Catu	255	12.21 S 38.23 W
Catuala	152	16.29 S 19.03 E
Catuane	156	26.48 S 32.18 E
Catubig	116	12.24 N 125.03 E
Catubig ⩰	116	12.34 N 125.10 E
Catuçaba	256	23.15 S 45.12 W
Catumbela	152	12.25 S 13.34 E
Catumbela ⩰	152	12.27 S 13.29 E
Catur	154	13.45 S 35.30 E
Catus	32	44.34 N 1.20 E
Catwick, Îles II	110	10.00 N 109.00 E
Çatyrk'ol', ozero ◉	85	40.38 N 75.17 E
Çatyrtaš	85	40.55 N 76.26 E
Cau ⩰	110	21.07 N 106.18 E
Cau, Rach ⩰	269c	10.51 N 106.49 E
Cauaburi ⩰	246	0.17 S 65.56 W
Cauayan, Pil.	116	16.56 N 121.46 E
Cauayan, Pil.	116	9.58 N 122.37 E
Caubvick, Mount (Mont d'Iberville) ▲	176	58.53 N 63.43 W
Cauca ◻ ⁵	246	2.30 N 76.50 W
Cauca ⩰	246	8.54 N 74.28 W
Caucaia	250	3.42 S 38.39 W
Caucaia do Alto	256	23.41 S 47.02 W
Caucase, Monts du — Bol'šoj Kavkaz ⋌		42.30 N 45.00 E
Catania	70	37.30 N 15.06 E
Catania ◻ ⁴	70	37.30 N 15.06 E
Catania, Golfo di ◡	70	37.24 N 15.09 E
Catania, Piana di ⩶	70	37.23 N 14.51 E
Cataño	240m	18.27 N 66.07 W
Catanzaro	68	38.54 N 16.36 E
Catanzaro ◻ ⁴	68	38.54 N 16.36 E
Catanzaro Lido	68	38.49 N 16.36 E
Catania ◻ ⁹	30	38.00 N 35.00 E
Catará ⩰	152	13.34 S 12.35 E
Cataract Canyon V	200	38.13 N 110.23 W
Cataract Reservoir ◍	170	34.16 S 150.48 E
Catarama	246	1.35 S 79.28 W
Cataraqui	212	44.14 N 76.32 W
Cataraqui ⩰ ¹	212	44.13 N 76.28 W
Catarina, Pil.	116	6.12 S 39.54 W
Catarman, Pil.	116	9.08 N 124.42 E
Catarman, Pil.	116	12.30 N 124.38 E
Catarroja	34	39.24 N 0.24 W
Catasauqua	208	40.39 N 75.29 W
Catatumbo ⩰	246	9.22 N 71.45 W
Catawba	218	40.06 N 80.54 W
Catawba ◻ ⁶	192	35.40 N 81.10 W
Catawba ⩰	192	34.41 N 80.52 W
Catawba Island	214	41.35 N 82.50 W
Catawissa, Mo., U.S.	219	38.25 N 90.47 W
Catawissa, Pa., U.S.	210	40.57 N 76.27 W
Catawissa Creek ⩰	210	40.57 N 76.28 W
Catba	154	45.00 N 0.16 E
Cat Ba, Dao I	110	20.50 N 107.02 E
Catbalogan	116	11.46 N 124.53 E
Catchabutan, Punta ﹥	236	15.50 N 86.32 W
Catchacoma Lake ◉	212	44.45 N 78.20 W
Cateco Cangola	152	8.27 S 15.48 E
Cateel, Cerro ▲ ²	152	34.23 S 64.40 W
Cateel	116	7.48 N 126.27 E
Cateel Bay ◡	116	7.54 N 126.26 E
Catemaco	234	18.25 N 95.07 W
Catemaco, Laguna ◉	234	18.25 N 95.07 W
Catende	156	26.00 S 32.33 E
Catenanuova	70	37.34 N 14.41 E
Caterham	260	51.17 N 0.04 W
Caterino Rodríguez	232	24.51 N 100.19 W
Catete	152	9.06 S 13.43 E
Catete ⬦ ⁸	287a	22.55 S 43.10 W
Cathair Saidhbhín	250	6.04 S 54.09 W
Cathedral City	228	33.47 N 116.28 W
Cathedral Gorge State Park ♦	204	37.50 N 114.30 W
Cathedral Mountain ▲	196	30.10 N 103.40 W
Cathedral of the Pines ⬦	207	42.47 N 71.58 W
Cathedral Provincial Park ♦	202	49.05 N 120.10 W
Cathedral Range ⋌	226	37.51 N 119.21 W
Catherines Peak ▲	241q	18.04 N 76.42 W
Catheys Valley	226	37.25 N 120.06 W
Cathlamet	224	46.12 N 123.23 W
Catholic University of ⬦ ²	284c	38.56 N 77.00 W
Catia La Mar	286c	10.37 N 67.00 W
Catignano	66	42.29 N 13.57 E
Catio	150	11.17 N 15.15 W
Catira, Punta ﹥	286d	10.40 N 63.57 W
Cat Island I, Ba.	238	24.27 N 75.30 W
Cat Island I, Ms., U.S.	194	30.13 N 89.06 W
Catkal ⩰	86	41.30 N 70.01 E
Catkal'skij chrebet ⋌	85	41.40 N 71.05 E
Catlettsburg	214	38.24 N 82.36 W
Catlin	216	40.04 N 87.42 W
Catlodge	46	56.59 N 4.22 W
Catnip Mountain ▲	204	41.50 N 119.15 W
Cato	210	43.10 N 76.34 W
Catoche, Cabo ﹥	232	21.36 N 87.04 W
Catoctin Creek ⩰	208	39.18 N 77.33 W
Catole do Rocha	250	6.21 S 37.45 W
Catolica, Universidad ◻ ², Chile	286e	33.27 S 70.39 W
Catolica, Universidad ◻ ², Perú	286d	12.05 S 77.05 W
Catoosa	222	36.11 N 95.45 W
Catorce	234	23.42 N 100.52 W
Catorce, Sierra de ⋌	234	23.40 N 100.50 W
Catrimani	246	0.28 N 61.44 W
Catrine	44	55.30 N 4.20 W
Cats, Mont des ▲ ²	50	50.47 N 2.40 E
Catshill	42	52.22 N 2.03 W
Catskill	210	42.13 N 73.51 W

	Página	Lat.° W = Oeste
Catskill Creek ⩰	210	42.12 N 73.51 W
Catskill Game Farm ♦	210	42.15 N 74.01 W
Catskill Mountains ⋌	210	42.10 N 74.30 W
Catskill Park ♦	210	42.00 N 74.30 W
Cat Spring	222	29.51 N 96.20 W
Catt, Mount ▲	182	54.21 N 128.47 W
Cattai Creek ⩰	274a	33.40 S 150.56 E
Cattaraugus ⬌	214	42.19 N 78.52 W
Cattaraugus ◻ ⁶	214	42.19 N 78.45 W
Cattaraugus Creek ⩰	214	42.35 N 79.10 W
Cattaraugus Creek, South Branch ⩰	214	42.26 N 78.53 W
Cattaraugus Indian Reservation ⬦ ⁴	210	42.33 N 78.56 W
Cattenom	50	49.25 N 6.15 E
Catterick	44	54.22 N 1.38 W
Catterick Garrison	44	54.22 N 1.43 W
Cattle Canyon V	280	34.14 N 117.46 W
Cattolica	66	43.58 N 12.44 E
Cattolica del Sacro Cuore, Università ◻ ²	266b	45.27 N 9.11 E
Cattolica Eraclea	70	37.26 N 13.24 E
Catton	44	54.55 N 2.15 W
Catu	255	12.21 S 38.23 W
Catuala	152	16.29 S 19.03 E
Catuane	156	26.48 S 32.18 E
Catubig	116	12.24 N 125.03 E
Catubig ⩰	116	12.34 N 125.10 E
Catuçaba	256	23.15 S 45.12 W
Catumbela	152	12.25 S 13.34 E
Catumbela ⩰	152	12.27 S 13.29 E
Catur	154	13.45 S 35.30 E
Catus	32	44.34 N 1.20 E
Catwick, Îles II	110	10.00 N 109.00 E
Çatyrk'ol', ozero ◉	85	40.38 N 75.17 E
Çatyrtaš	85	40.55 N 76.26 E
Cau ⩰	110	21.07 N 106.18 E
Cau, Rach ⩰	269c	10.51 N 106.49 E
Cauaburi ⩰	246	0.17 S 65.56 W
Cauayan, Pil.	116	16.56 N 121.46 E
Cauayan, Pil.	116	9.58 N 122.37 E
Caubvick, Mount (Mont d'Iberville) ▲	176	58.53 N 63.43 W
Cauca ◻ ⁵	246	2.30 N 76.50 W
Cauca ⩰	246	8.54 N 74.28 W
Caucaia	250	3.42 S 38.39 W
Caucaia do Alto	256	23.41 S 47.02 W
Caucase, Monts du — Bol'šoj Kavkaz ⋌	84	42.30 N 45.00 E
Caucasia	246	8.00 N 75.12 W
Caucaso — Bol'šoj Kavkaz ⋌	84	42.30 N 45.00 E
Caucasus — Bol'šoj Kavkaz ⋌	84	42.30 N 45.00 E
Caucete	252	31.39 S 68.17 W
Cauchari, Salar de ⩰ ²	252	23.50 S 66.50 W
Cauchon Lake ◉	184	55.25 N 96.30 W
Caudebec-en-Caux	50	49.31 N 0.44 E
Caudebec-lès-Elbeuf	50	49.17 N 1.02 E
Caudry	50	50.08 N 3.25 E
Caughdenoy	210	43.16 N 76.12 W
Caughnawaga	275a	45.25 N 73.41 W
Caughnawaga Indian Reserve ⬦ ⁴	206	45.23 N 73.41 W
Cauitan, Mount ▲	116	17.16 N 121.00 E
Cauit Point ﹥, Pil.	116	12.16 N 122.38 E
Cauit Point ﹥, Pil.	116	9.18 N 126.12 E
Cauldcleuch Head ▲	169	37.53 S 145.03 E
Caulfield	169	37.53 S 145.03 E
Caulfield Racecourse ♦	274b	37.53 S 145.02 E
Caulkerbush	44	54.56 N 3.40 W
Caulonia	68	38.23 N 16.25 E
Caumont-sur-Durance	62	43.54 N 4.57 E
Çaumsett State Park ♦	276	40.55 N 73.28 W
Caúngula	152	8.25 S 18.40 E
Caunskaja guba ◡	74	69.20 N 170.00 E
Caura ⩰	246	7.38 N 64.53 W
Caurés ⩰	246	1.21 S 62.20 W
Caurimare ⬦ ⁸	286c	10.28 N 66.48 W
Causapscal	186	67.14 N 90.58 W
Causovo	82	54.49 N 36.55 E
Causside	34	44.10 N 1.22 E
Causy	76	53.48 N 30.58 E
Cautário ⩰	248	12.13 S 64.34 W
Caution, Cape ﹥	182	51.10 N 127.47 W
Cauto ⩰	240p	20.33 N 77.14 W
Cauvery ⩰	50	49.40 N 0.40 E
Cauvar	50	49.40 N 1.02 E
Caux, Pays de ⩶	50	49.40 N 0.40 E
Cava		
Cava de' Tirreni	68	40.42 N 14.42 E
Cávado ⩰	34	41.32 N 8.48 W
Cavaglià	62	45.25 N 8.05 E
Cavaillon	62	43.50 N 5.02 E
Cavalaire-sur-Mer	62	43.10 N 6.32 E
Cavalcante	255	13.48 S 47.30 W
Cavalese	64	46.17 N 11.27 E
Cavaleiro	255	15.15 S 48.02 W
Cavalier	198	48.47 N 97.37 W
Cavalière	62	43.10 N 6.26 E
Cavalla (Cavally) ⩰	150	4.22 N 7.32 W
Cavalleria, Cap de ﹥	34	40.05 N 4.05 E
Cavallermaggiore	62	44.43 N 7.41 E
Cavalli Islands II	172	35.02 S 173.58 E
Cavallino, Litorale di ⩰	64	45.27 N 12.30 E
Cavallo, Île I	71	41.22 N 9.16 E
Cavallo, Monte ▲	66	46.08 N 13.42 E
Cavalos, Ribeirão ⩰	256	21.29 S 44.13 W
Casa Manara	255	25.08 S 9.07 E
Cavan	48	54.00 N 7.21 W
Cavan ◻ ⁶	48	53.55 N 7.15 W
Cavanaugh, Lake ◉	224	48.23 N 122.00 W
Cavan'ga	24	66.06 N 37.47 E
Cave	150	43.12 S 171.10 E
Cave, It.	66	41.49 N 12.56 E
Cave, N.J., U.S.	194	44.19 N 170.57 E
Cave City, Ar., U.S.	194	30.13 N 89.06 W
Cave City, Ky., U.S.	194	37.08 N 85.58 W
Cave del Predil	64	46.26 N 13.34 E
Cave Creek	200	33.50 N 111.57 W
Cave del Predil	64	46.26 N 13.34 E
Cave In Rock	194	37.28 N 88.10 W
Caveiras ⩰	252	27.35 S 50.56 W
Cavendish	152	17.33 S 19.21 E
Cavenagh Range ⋌	164	26.12 S 135.43 E
Cavendish	168	37.32 S 142.02 E
Cave Spring	192	34.06 N 85.20 W
Cavernoso, Serra do ⋌	252	25.40 S 52.20 W
Cavertitz	52	51.28 N 13.08 E
Cavezzo	64	44.50 N 11.03 E
Caviana, Ilha I	250	0.10 N 50.10 W
Cavíglia ⬌	116	9.17 N 120.50 E
Cavillargues	62	44.05 N 4.31 E
Cavite	116	14.29 N 120.54 E
Cavnic	38	47.39 N 23.52 E
Cavo		
Cavo, Monte ▲	267a	41.45 N 12.43 E
Cavour	62	44.47 N 7.22 E
Cavour, Canale ⩰	62	45.11 N 7.54 E
Cavriago	64	44.43 N 10.35 E
Çavu		

Feature				
Montagne	Montaña	Montanha	Berg	Mountain
Montagnes	Montañas	Montanhas		Mountains
Col	Paso	Passo	Pass	Pass
Plaine	Llano	Planície	Ebene	Plain
Vallée, Canyon	Valle, Cañón	Vale, Canhão	Tal, cañon	Valley, Canyon
Cap	Cabo	Cabo	Kap	Cape
Île	Isla	Ilha	Insel	Island
Îles	Islas	Ilhas	Inseln	Islands
Autres données topographiques	Otros Elementos topográficos	Outros Elementos topográficos	Andere Topographische Objekte	Other Topographic Features

Cerv-Chap I · 33

ESPAÑOL — FRANÇAIS — PORTUGUÊS

Nombre / Nom / Nome	Página / Page / Página	Lat.°′	Long.°′ W = Oeste / W = Ouest / W = Oeste
Cervin, Mont → Matterhorn ∧	58	45.59 N	7.43 E
Cervinara	68	41.01 N	14.37 E
Cervino (Matterhorn) ∧	58	45.59 N	7.43 E
Çervione	36	42.20 N	9.31 E
Červl'onnaja	84	43.30 N	45.54 E
Cervo, Esp.	34	43.40 N	7.25 W
Cervo, It.	62	43.55 N	8.07 E
Cervo ≃	62	45.22 N	8.24 E
Cervo, Capo >	62	43.55 N	8.08 E
Cervo, Rio do ≃, Bra.	256	22.07 S	45.49 W
Cervo, Rio do ≃, Bra.	256	21.12 S	45.10 W
Çervo, Serra do ∧	256	22.06 S	46.07 W
Çervonaja Kamenka	78	48.38 N	33.26 E
Çervonoarmejsk, Ukr.	78	50.08 N	25.16 E
Çervonoarmejsk, Ukr.	78	50.28 N	28.14 E
Červonoarmejskoje, Ukr.	78	45.47 N	28.44 E
Červonoarmejskoje, Ukr.	78	47.57 N	35.27 E
Çervonograd	78	50.24 N	24.14 E
Çervonogranitnoje	78	50.34 N	28.33 E
Çervonoje, Ukr.	78	51.46 N	34.04 E
Çervonoje, Ukr.	78	49.57 N	28.53 E
Çervonoje, ozero ⊜	76	52.24 N	27.57 E
Çervonopartizansk	83	48.04 N	39.50 E
Červonyj Donec	78	49.29 N	36.34 E
Cesana Torinese	62	44.57 N	6.47 E
Cesano, It.	66	43.45 N	13.10 E
Cesano, It.	66	42.07 N	12.21 E
Cesano ≃	66	43.45 N	13.10 E
Cesano Boscone	266b	45.27 N	9.06 E
Cesano Maderno	62	45.38 N	9.08 E
Cesar □[5]	246	9.20 N	73.30 W
Cesar ≃	246	9.00 N	73.58 W
Cesaró	70	37.50 N	14.43 E
Cesate	266b	45.36 N	9.05 E
Cesena	66	44.08 N	12.15 E
Cesenatico	66	44.12 N	12.24 E
Cesi, Poggio ∧[2]	267a	42.02 N	12.44 E
Cesiomaggiore	64	46.05 N	11.59 E
Cēsis	76	57.18 N	25.15 E
Česká Kamenice	54	50.47 N	14.26 E
Česká Kublice	60	49.22 N	12.52 E
Česká Lípa	54	50.42 N	14.32 E
Česká Republika □[3]	30	49.40 N	15.10 E
Česká Třebová	30	49.54 N	16.27 E
České Budějovice	61	48.59 N	14.28 E
České středohoří ⋀	54	50.35 N	14.09 E
Českomoravská vrchovina ⋀[1]	30	49.20 N	15.30 E
Československo → Czechoslovakia □[1]	30	49.30 N	17.00 E
Český Brod	54	50.02 N	14.58 E
Český Krumlov	61	48.49 N	14.19 E
Česma	86	53.50 N	60.40 E
Çeşme	130	38.18 N	26.19 E
Çessalto	64	45.42 N	12.36 E
Češskaja guba c	24	67.30 N	46.30 E
Cessnock	170	32.50 S	151.21 E
Cesson	261	48.34 N	2.36 E
Cestos ≃	150	5.40 N	9.10 W
Çesvaine	76	56.58 N	26.19 E
Čet' ≃	86	56.51 N	86.48 E
Cetara	68	40.39 N	14.42 E
Cetate	38	44.06 N	23.03 E
Cetatea Albă → Belgorod-Dnestrovskij	78	46.12 N	30.20 E
Četbulak	85	41.17 N	73.58 E
Cetian	100	25.44 N	116.22 E
Cetina ≃	36	43.26 N	16.42 E
Cetinje	38	42.23 N	18.55 E
Çetinkaya	130	39.15 N	37.38 E
Cetona	66	42.58 N	11.54 E
Cetona, Monte ∧	66	42.56 N	11.52 E
Cetraro	68	39.31 N	15.56 E
Çetronia	208	40.35 N	75.31 W
Četyrboki	78	50.02 N	27.01 E
Céüse, Montagne de ∧	62	44.31 N	5.57 E
Ceuta	34	35.53 N	5.19 W
Ceva	62	44.23 N	8.02 E
Cevedale, Monte (Zufallspitze) ∧	64	46.27 N	10.37 E
Cevennen → Cévennes ◆[1]	32	44.00 N	3.30 E
Cévennes ◆[1]	32	44.00 N	3.30 E
Cévennes, Parc National des ♠	32	44.15 N	3.40 E
Cevins	62	45.35 N	6.28 E
Cevio	58	46.19 N	8.36 E
Cevizli	130	37.12 N	31.45 E
Ceyhan	130	37.04 N	35.47 E
Ceyhan ≃	130	36.45 N	35.41 E
Ceylanpınar	130	36.51 N	40.02 E
Ceylon, Sk., Can.	184	49.28 N	104.36 W
Ceylon, Mn., U.S.	198	43.32 N	94.37 W
Ceylon → Sri Lanka □[1]	122	7.00 N	81.00 E
Ceyzériat	58	46.10 N	5.19 E
Cèze ≃	62	44.06 N	4.42 E
Chaam, Ned.	52	51.31 N	4.52 E
Cha-am, Thai	110	12.48 N	99.58 E
Chaanling	100	29.39 N	113.49 E
Chaatl Island I	182	53.00 N	132.25 W
Chabanais	32	45.52 N	0.43 E
Chabang Tiga	114	5.19 N	103.08 E
Chabaricha	24	65.50 N	52.16 E
Chabařovice	54	50.40 N	13.56 E
Chabarovo	72	69.39 N	60.24 E
Chabarovsk	89	48.27 N	135.06 E
Chabarovsk □[8]	89	54.00 N	136.00 E
Chabarowsk → Chabarovsk	89	48.27 N	135.06 E
Chabary	86	53.37 N	79.33 E
Chabás	252	33.15 S	61.22 W
Chabeuil	62	44.54 N	5.01 E
Chabez	84	44.02 N	41.47 E
Chābi	124	22.49 N	80.41 E
Chabjuwardoo Bay c	162	22.57 S	113.48 E
Chablais ◆[1]	58	46.18 N	6.39 E
Chablis	50	47.49 N	3.48 E
Chabogongba	120	31.47 N	81.14 E
Chaboje	265a	59.53 N	30.46 E
Chabot, Lake ⊜, Ca., U.S.	282	38.08 N	122.14 W
Chabot, Lake ⊜, Ca., U.S.	282	37.43 N	122.07 W
Chabris	50	47.15 N	1.39 E
Chabuchaer	86	43.42 N	81.04 E
Chabu-Rabot, pereval)(	85	38.40 N	70.43 E
Chacabuco	252	34.38 S	60.29 W
Chacaito, Quebrada ≃	286c	10.29 N	66.52 W
Chacaltianguis	234	18.20 N	95.50 W
Chacao	286c	10.30 N	66.51 W
Chácara	256	21.41 S	43.13 W
Chacarita, Cementerio de la ◆	288	34.33 S	58.28 W
Chacarrão, Cachoeira do ⌊	250	6.32 S	58.12 W
Chacayán	248	10.24 S	76.25 W
Chachani, Nevado ∧	248	16.12 S	71.33 W
Chachapoyas, Perú	242	6.13 S	77.51 W
Chachapoyas, Perú	248	6.13 S	77.51 W
Chachas	248	15.30 S	72.16 W
Chachoengsao	110	13.42 N	101.05 E
Chāchora	124	24.10 N	76.59 E
Chāchro	120	25.07 N	70.15 E
Chachu	120	33.16 N	81.41 E
Chačinčaj ≃	84	40.13 N	47.18 E
Chaclacyo	248	11.59 S	76.46 W
Chačmas	84	41.28 N	48.48 E
Chaco □[4]	252	26.25 S	60.30 W
Chaco □[5]	248	20.00 S	60.30 W
Chaco ≃	200	36.46 N	108.39 W
Chaco Austral ◆[1]	252	26.30 S	61.30 W
Chaco Boreal ◆[1]	252	23.00 S	60.00 W
Chaco Central ◆[1]	252	25.00 S	59.45 W
Chaco Culture National Historical Park ♠	200	36.06 N	108.00 W
Chaco Mesa ∧	200	35.47 N	107.35 W
Chacón, Arroyo ≃	288	34.53 S	58.39 W
Chacon, Cape >	182	54.42 N	132.00 W
Chacra Cerro	286d	11.55 S	77.04 W
Chacuaco Creek ≃	196	37.34 N	103.38 W
Chad (Tchad) □[1], Afr.	136	15.00 N	19.00 E
Chad (Tchad) □[1], Afr.	146	15.00 N	19.00 E
Chad, Lake (Lac Tchad) ⊜	146	13.20 N	14.00 E
Chada-Bulak	88	50.38 N	116.18 E
Chadbourn	192	34.19 N	78.49 W
Chadderton	262	53.33 N	2.08 W
Chadds Ford	285	39.52 N	75.35 W
Chādegān	128	32.46 N	50.39 E
Chadian, Zhg.	102	26.48 N	105.48 E
Chadian, Zhg.	105	39.14 N	117.45 E
Chadian, Zhg.	107	30.14 N	105.56 E
Chadianzi	107	30.31 N	104.22 E
Chadiza	154	14.05 S	32.28 E
Chadron	198	42.49 N	103.00 W
Chadstone	274b	37.53 S	145.05 E
Chadwell Saint Mary	260	51.29 N	0.22 E
Chadwick	190	42.01 N	89.53 W
Chadwick Manor	284b	39.19 N	76.46 W
Chadwick Pond ⊜	283	42.44 N	71.05 W
Chadwicks	210	43.01 N	75.16 W
Chadyžensk	78	44.25 N	39.33 E
Chadžalmachi	84	42.26 N	47.13 E
Chadžibejskij liman ⊜	78	46.39 N	30.33 E
Chae Hom	110	18.43 N	99.35 E
Chaem ≃	110	18.11 N	98.38 E
Chaersen	89	46.19 N	121.54 E
Chaeryŏng	98	38.24 N	125.36 E
Chafarinas, Islas II	34	35.11 N	2.26 W
Chafe	150	11.56 N	6.55 E
Chaffee	194	37.10 N	89.39 W
Chaffins	207	42.21 N	71.51 W
Chāgai	128	29.18 N	64.42 E
Chāgai Hills ⋀[2]	128	29.30 N	64.15 E
Chagandianlisu	102	41.47 N	103.29 E
Chagang Do □[4]	98	40.50 N	126.30 E
'Chaghcharān	120	34.32 N	65.15 E
Chagny	58	46.55 N	4.45 E
Chagos Archipelago II	12	6.00 S	72.00 E
Chagos-Laccadive Plateau ✣[3]	12	3.00 N	73.00 E
Chagrin ≃	214	41.40 N	81.27 W
Chagrin, Aurora Branch ≃	279a	41.25 N	81.25 W
Chagrin Falls	214	41.26 N	81.24 W
Chagrin Falls Park	214	41.21 N	81.32 W
Chagrin Valley Parkway ♠	279a	41.26 N	81.25 W
Chaguanas	241r	10.31 N	61.25 W
Chaguaramas	246	9.20 N	66.16 W
Chahaignes	50	47.44 N	0.31 E
Chāhak	128	33.17 N	58.54 E
Chahal	236	15.45 N	89.34 W
Chahancheluo	98	41.39 N	114.22 E
Chahanwusu → Dulan	102	36.16 N	98.28 E
Chahār Borjak	128	30.17 N	62.03 E
Chahār Deh-ye Ghowrband	120	34.59 N	68.44 E
Chahār Maḥāl va Bakhtīārī □[4]	128	32.00 N	51.00 E
Chahayang	89	48.24 N	124.15 E
Chahe, Zhg.	100	33.16 N	119.02 E
Chahe, Zhg.	102	33.48 N	97.22 E
Chahe, Zhg.	105	39.50 N	115.21 E
Chāh Gheybī, Hāmūn-e ⩩	128	28.06 N	60.50 E
Chahuamiao	100	33.00 N	115.56 E
Chahuites	234	16.17 N	94.11 W
Chai ≃	104	42.20 N	123.52 E
Chai Badan	110	15.04 N	101.05 E
Chāībāsa	124	22.34 N	85.49 E
Chaigou	98	36.15 N	119.36 E
Chaihe	89	44.47 N	129.42 E
Chaijiawan	100	29.10 N	113.06 E
Chaillé-les-Marais	32	46.24 N	1.01 W
Chailley	50	48.05 N	3.42 E
Chailly-en-Bière	50	48.28 N	2.35 E
Chai Nat	110	15.11 N	100.08 E
Chainhurst	260	51.12 N	0.29 E
Chain O'Lakes State Park ♠, Il., U.S.	216	42.27 N	88.11 W
Chain O'Lakes State Park ♠, In., U.S.	216	41.20 N	85.26 W
Chainpur	124	23.08 N	84.15 E
Chaipudyrskaja guba c	24	68.30 N	59.30 E
Chaiqiao	100	29.51 N	121.56 E
Chairel, Laguna de c	234	22.17 N	97.57 W
Chaishudian	105	40.46 N	116.30 E
Chaiši	84	42.57 N	42.12 E
Chait	85	39.11 N	70.53 E
Chaital	126	22.31 N	88.47 E
Chaitén	254	42.55 S	72.43 W
Chaiwopu	86	43.33 N	87.59 E
Chaiya	110	9.23 N	99.14 E
Chaiyaphum	110	15.48 N	102.02 E
Chajarí	252	30.46 S	57.59 W
Chajdarken	85	39.57 N	71.21 E
Chajia	107	29.37 N	104.27 E
Chajian	100	32.40 N	118.46 E
Chajianling	98	39.14 N	114.36 E
Chajiaqiao	100	34.00 N	120.07 E
Chajrchan	88	48.35 N	101.56 E
Chajrchandulaan	102	45.57 N	102.03 E
Chajul	236	15.30 N	91.02 W
Chaka	154	4.49 N	31.14 E
Chakachamna Lake ⊜	180	61.13 N	152.35 W
Chakāltor	126	23.14 N	86.22 E
Chak Amru	123	32.22 N	75.11 E
Chakari	154	18.05 S	29.51 E
Chakaria	120	21.45 N	92.05 E
Chakarnaba	146	14.13 N	20.51 E
Chakasskaja Avtonomnaja Sovetskaja Socialističeskaja Respublika □[3]	86	53.00 N	90.00 E
Chākdaha, India	126	23.05 N	88.31 E
Chakdaha, India	272b	22.20 N	88.20 E
Chake Chake	154	5.15 S	39.46 E
Chakhānsūr	128	31.10 N	62.04 E
Chākia	124	26.25 N	85.03 E
Chakkarat	110	15.00 N	102.16 E
Chakou, Zhg.	98	38.03 N	113.36 E
Chakou, Zhg.	105	38.53 N	116.41 E
Chakradharpur	124	22.42 N	85.38 E
Chakrāta	120	30.42 N	77.51 E
Chāksu	120	26.36 N	75.57 E
Chākulia	126	22.29 N	86.43 E
Chakwadām	102	27.29 N	98.31 E
Chakwāl	123	32.56 N	72.52 E
Chal	272c	19.06 N	73.08 E
Chala	248	15.52 S	74.16 W
Chalabesa	154	11.22 S	31.01 E
Chalais	32	45.16 N	0.02 E
Chālakuda	122	10.18 N	76.20 E
Chalamont	58	46.00 N	5.10 E
Chalampé	58	47.49 N	7.33 E
Chalan Kanoa	174n	15.08 N	145.43 E
Chalatenango	236	14.03 N	88.56 W
Chalaua	154	16.06 S	39.11 E
Chalaux ≃	50	47.23 N	3.54 E
Chalaxung	102	34.10 N	97.44 E
Chalbi Desert ◆[2]	154	3.00 N	37.20 E
Chalchgol	88	48.11 N	114.54 E
Chalchihuites	234	23.29 N	103.53 W
Chalchis Terara ∧	144	9.08 N	36.44 E
Chalchuapa	236	13.59 N	89.41 W
Chalchyn ≃	88	47.55 N	117.47 E
Chalcis → Khalkís	38	38.28 N	23.36 E
Chalco ≃	286a	19.19 N	99.08 W
Chaldan	84	40.43 N	47.15 E
Chaldon	260	51.17 N	0.07 W
Chaleine	261	48.36 N	1.43 E
Chalengkou	120	38.02 N	93.54 E
Châlette-sur-Loing	50	48.01 N	2.44 E
Chaleur Bay c	186	48.00 N	65.45 W
Chalfant	279b	40.25 N	79.52 W
Chalfant Run ≃	279b	40.25 N	79.48 W
Chalfont	208	40.17 N	75.13 W
Chalfont Common	260	51.38 N	0.33 W
Chalfonte	285	39.49 N	75.32 W
Chalfont Saint Giles	260	51.38 N	0.34 W
Chalfont Saint Peter	260	51.37 N	0.33 W
Chalford	42	51.45 N	2.09 W
Chalhuanca	248	14.17 S	73.15 W
Chalía ≃	254	49.35 S	69.34 W
Chalifert	261	48.53 N	2.46 E
Chalilovo	86	51.24 N	58.04 E
Chalindrey	58	47.48 N	5.26 E
Chaling	100	26.47 N	113.33 E
Chālisgaon	122	20.28 N	75.01 E
Chalisi	102	32.55 N	102.04 E
Chaliun	88	48.50 N	103.59 E
Chalk	260	51.26 N	0.25 E
Chalkabad	86	42.42 N	59.43 E
Chalk Draw V	196	29.36 N	103.15 W
Chalk River	190	46.01 N	77.27 W
Chalkyitsik	180	66.39 N	143.43 W
Challakere	122	14.19 N	76.39 E
Challans	32	46.51 N	1.53 W
Challapata	248	18.54 S	66.47 W
Challenge	226	39.29 N	121.13 W
Challenger, Mount ∧	224	48.50 N	121.20 W
Challenger Deep ✣[1]	14	11.21 N	142.12 E
Challes-les-Eaux	62	45.33 N	5.59 E
Challis	202	44.30 N	114.13 W
Challviri, Salar de ⩩	248	22.32 S	67.34 W
Chal'mer-Ju	24	67.58 N	64.50 E
Chalmers	216	40.39 N	86.52 W
Chalmette	194	29.56 N	89.57 W
Chalone Creek ≃	226	36.21 N	121.14 W
Chalonnes-sur-Loire	32	47.21 N	0.46 W
Châlons-sur-Marne	50	48.57 N	4.22 E
Chalon-sur-Saône	58	46.47 N	4.51 E
Chalosse ◆[1]	32	43.45 N	0.30 W
Chalt	123	36.15 N	74.20 E
Chaltel, Cerro (Monte Fitzroy) ∧	254	49.17 S	73.05 W
Chalturin	80	58.33 N	48.50 E
Chalturino	78	49.31 N	35.17 E
Chaluhe	89	43.43 N	126.00 E
Châlus, Fr.	32	45.39 N	0.59 E
Chālūs, Īrān	128	36.38 N	51.26 E
Cham, Dtsch.	60	49.13 N	12.41 E
Cham, Schw.	58	47.11 N	8.28 E
Chama	200	36.54 N	106.34 W
Chama ≃	246	9.03 N	71.40 W
Chama, Rio ≃	200	36.03 N	106.05 W
Chamah, Gunong ∧	114	5.13 N	101.33 E
Chamaicó	252	35.03 S	64.58 W
Chamama	154	12.55 S	33.43 E
Chamamat'urt	84	43.36 N	46.30 E
Chaman	120	30.55 N	66.27 E
Chamangonge	152	11.16 S	20.24 E
Chamao, Khao ∧	110	12.57 N	101.45 E
Chamarande	261	48.31 N	2.13 E
Chamar-Daban, chrebet ⋀	88	51.15 N	105.00 E
Chāmārpāra	272b	22.35 N	88.08 E
Chamaya ≃	248	5.44 S	78.39 W
Chamb ≃	60	49.13 N	12.42 E
Chamba, India	123	32.34 N	76.08 E
Chamba, Moç.	154	12.07 S	36.57 E
Chamba, Tan.	154	11.35 S	36.58 E
Chambal ≃	120	26.30 N	79.15 E
Chambaran, Plateau de ⋀[1]	62	45.15 N	5.15 E
Chambas	240p	22.12 N	78.55 W
Chamberlain, Sk., Can.	184	50.50 N	105.34 W
Chamberlain, S.D., U.S.	198	43.48 N	99.19 W
Chamberlain ≃	164	15.08 S	128.06 E
Chamberlain Lake ⊜	186	46.17 N	69.20 W
Chamberlin, Mount ∧	180	69.16 N	144.55 W
Chamberry, Ruisseau ≃	275a	45.20 N	73.58 W
Chambers, Az., U.S.	200	35.11 N	109.25 W
Chambers, Ne., U.S.	198	42.12 N	98.44 W
Chambers, N.Y., U.S.	210	42.16 N	76.57 W
Chambers □[6]	222	29.42 N	94.40 W
Chambers Brook ≃	276	40.35 N	74.41 W
Chambersburg, Il., U.S.	219	39.49 N	90.39 W
Chambersburg, In., U.S.	218	38.31 N	86.24 W
Chambersburg, Pa., U.S.	208	39.56 N	77.39 W
Chambers Corner	285	40.01 N	74.44 W
Chambers Creek ≃	222	31.58 N	96.10 W
Chambers Creek, North Fork ≃	222	32.16 N	96.58 W
Chambers Creek, South Fork ≃	222	32.16 N	96.58 W
Chambers Island I	190	45.11 N	87.21 W
Chambéry	62	45.34 N	5.56 E
Chambeshi ≃	154	11.21 S	30.37 E
Chambi, Jebel ∧	148	35.11 N	8.42 E
Chambira ≃, Perú	246	3.55 S	73.45 W
Chambira ≃, Perú	246	4.28 S	74.50 W
Chamblee	192	33.53 N	84.17 W
Chambley-Bussières	56	49.03 N	5.54 E
Chambly, P.Q., Can.	206	45.27 N	73.17 W
Chambly, Fr.	50	49.10 N	2.15 E
Chambly □[6]	206	45.30 N	73.20 W
Chambly, Bassin de ⊜	206	45.27 N	73.17 W
Chambly, Canal de ≅	275a	45.25 N	73.15 W
Chambois	50	48.48 N	0.07 E
Chambon-sur-Dolore	62	45.30 N	3.37 E
Chambon-sur-Voueize	32	46.11 N	2.25 E
Chambord, Château de ⊥	50	47.37 N	1.31 E
Chambourcy	261	48.54 N	2.03 E
Chambri Lake ⊜	164	4.16 S	143.08 E
Chambry	261	49.00 N	2.54 E
Chamburi Kalāt	128	26.09 N	64.43 E
Chamdo → Qamdo	102	31.11 N	97.15 E
Chāme, Nepāl	124	28.33 N	84.15 E
Chame, Pan.	236	8.35 N	79.53 W
Chame, Punta >	236	8.39 N	79.42 W
Chamela	234	19.32 N	105.05 W
Chamelecón	236	15.24 N	88.01 W
Chamelecón ≃	236	15.51 N	87.49 W
Chamical	252	30.21 S	66.19 W
Chamizo	258	34.10 S	56.41 W
Chamizo, Arroyo ≃	258	34.15 S	56.44 W
Chamkanī	120	33.48 N	69.49 E
Chāmlūjā ≃	124	29.38 N	80.24 E
Chamo, Lake ⊜	144	5.50 N	37.33 E
Chamois, It.	62	45.50 N	7.37 E
Chamois, Mo., U.S.	219	38.40 N	91.46 W
Chamojie	89	49.25 N	124.45 E
Chamoli	124	30.24 N	79.21 E
Chamonix-Mont-Blanc	58	45.55 N	6.52 E
Chamousset	62	45.33 N	6.12 E
Chamoux-sur-Gelon	62	45.32 N	6.13 E
Chāmpa	124	22.03 N	82.39 E
Champagne, Yk., Can.	180	60.47 N	136.29 W
Champagne, Fr.	62	45.16 N	4.48 E
Champagne □[9]	32	49.00 N	4.30 E
Champagne Castle ∧	158	29.06 S	29.20 E
Champagne-en-Valromay	58	45.54 N	5.41 E
Champagner-Berg ∧[2]	264a	52.31 N	13.05 E
Champagne-sur-Seine	50	48.24 N	2.48 E
Champagney	58	47.42 N	6.41 E
Champagnole	58	46.45 N	5.55 E
Champagny	62	45.27 N	6.42 E
Chāmpāhāti	126	22.23 N	88.29 E
Champaign	194	40.06 N	88.14 W
Champaign □[6], Il., U.S.	216	40.07 N	88.12 W
Champaign □[6], Oh., U.S.	218	40.07 N	83.45 W
Champapur	126	24.02 N	86.31 E
Champaquí, Cerro ∧	252	31.59 S	64.56 W
Champasak	110	14.53 N	105.52 E
Champāwat	124	29.20 N	80.06 E
Champcueil	261	48.31 N	2.27 E
Champdāni	126	22.48 N	88.21 E
Champdeniers	32	46.29 N	0.24 W
Champdepraz	62	45.41 N	7.39 E
Champdeuil	261	48.37 N	2.44 E
Champdor	58	46.01 N	5.36 E
Champdoré, Lac ⊜	176	55.55 N	65.49 W
Champeaux	50	48.35 N	2.48 E
Champeix	32	45.36 N	3.08 E
Champerico	236	14.18 N	91.55 W
Champéry	58	46.10 N	6.52 E
Champex	58	46.02 N	7.07 E
Champier	62	45.27 N	5.17 E
Champigneulles	56	48.44 N	6.10 E
Champigny-sur-Marne	261	48.49 N	2.31 E
Champion, Ab., Can.	182	50.14 N	113.09 W
Champion, Mi., U.S.	190	46.30 N	87.57 W
Champion, Oh., U.S.	214	41.17 N	80.51 W
Champion, Pa., U.S.	214	40.05 N	79.21 W
Champions	222	29.59 N	95.31 W
Champlain	206	44.59 N	73.26 W
Champlain □[6]	206	46.45 N	72.35 W
Champlain ≃	206	46.27 N	72.17 W
Champlain, Lake ⊜	188	44.45 N	73.15 W
Champlain, Pont ◆[5]	206	45.28 N	73.32 W
Champlain Canal ≅	210	43.20 N	73.34 W
Champlan	261	48.43 N	2.16 E
Champlin Creek ≃	276	40.43 N	73.12 W
Champlitte-et-le-Prélot	58	47.37 N	5.31 E
Champlon	56	50.07 N	5.28 E
Champoluc	62	45.50 N	7.44 E
Champotón	232	19.21 N	90.43 W
Champrond-en-Gâtine	50	48.24 N	1.05 E
Champs	50	47.44 N	3.36 E
Champs-sur-Marne	261	48.51 N	2.36 E
Chāmpua	124	22.05 N	85.40 E
Champvans	58	47.06 N	5.26 E
Chāmrāil	272b	22.38 N	88.18 E
Chāmrājnagar Rāmasamudram	122	11.55 N	76.57 E
Chamrousse	62	45.08 N	5.52 E
Chamsara ≃	88	52.42 N	95.46 E
Chamusca	34	39.21 N	8.29 W
Chamza Chakimzada	85	40.26 N	71.30 E
Chana	110	6.55 N	100.44 E
Chanabadskij	85	40.49 N	72.58 E
Chanakyapuri □[9]	272a	28.36 N	77.11 E
Chañar	252	30.32 S	65.58 W
Chañaral	252	26.21 S	70.37 W
Chañaral, Isla I	252	29.02 S	71.35 W
Chanas	62	45.18 N	4.49 E
Chānasma	120	23.43 N	72.07 E
Chanbogd	102	43.12 N	107.10 E
Chancay	248	11.35 S	77.16 W
Chancay ≃	248	11.37 S	77.15 W
Chance	208	38.10 N	75.56 W
Chanceaux	58	47.31 N	4.42 E
Chanceaux-sur-Choisille	50	47.28 N	0.42 E
Chanch	88	51.30 N	100.40 E
Chanchelulla Peak ∧	204	40.28 N	122.59 W
Chanchiang → Zhanjiang	102	21.16 N	110.28 E
Chanchöchij uul ⋀	88	49.30 N	94.30 E
Chanchongor	102	43.50 N	104.25 E
Chanco	252	35.44 S	72.32 W
Chancy	58	46.08 N	6.00 E
Chanda	88	55.00 N	107.14 E
Chanda ≃	88	55.00 N	107.14 E
Chāndābila	126	22.05 N	87.00 E
Chanda → Chandrapur	122	19.57 N	79.18 E
Chandagajty	86	50.44 N	92.03 E
Chandalar	180	67.30 N	148.30 W
Chandalar ≃	180	66.36 N	145.48 W
Chandalar, East Fork ≃	180	67.05 N	147.16 W
Chandalar, Middle Fork ≃	180	67.10 N	148.19 W
Chandalar, North Fork ≃	180	67.10 N	148.19 W
Chandan Chauki	124	28.33 N	80.47 E
Chandankiāri	126	23.34 N	86.22 E
Chandannagar	126	22.51 N	88.21 E
Chandanpratāp	126	23.33 N	89.24 E
Chāndar	126	23.54 N	89.58 E
Chandausi	124	28.27 N	78.46 E
Chāndbāli	120	20.47 N	86.46 E
Chandeleur Islands II	194	29.48 N	88.51 W
Chandeleur Sound ɥ	194	29.55 N	89.10 W
Chanderi	124	24.43 N	78.08 E
Chandernagore → Chandannagar	126	22.51 N	88.21 E
Chandīgarh	123	30.44 N	76.55 E
Chandīgarh □[8]	123	30.45 N	76.50 E
Chāndil	124	22.58 N	86.03 E
Chandīpur	126	23.59 N	89.01 E
Chanditala	272b	22.41 N	88.16 E
Chandla	124	25.05 N	80.12 E
Chandler, P.Q., Can.	186	48.21 N	64.41 W
Chandler, Az., U.S.	200	33.18 N	111.50 W
Chandler, In., U.S.	194	38.02 N	87.22 W
Chandler, Ok., U.S.	196	35.42 N	96.52 W
Chandler, Tx., U.S.	222	32.18 N	95.29 W
Chandler ≃	180	69.27 N	151.30 W
Chandler, Mount ∧[2]	162	27.00 S	133.20 E
Chandler Lake ⊜	180	68.15 N	152.43 W
Chandler Park ♠	281	42.24 N	82.58 W
Chandler's Cross	260	51.40 N	0.27 W
Chandler's Ford	42	50.59 N	1.23 W
Chandlers Valley	214	41.56 N	79.18 W
Chandlerville	219	40.02 N	90.09 W
Chandless ≃	248	9.08 S	69.51 W
Chāndor Hills ⋀[2]	122	20.30 N	74.00 E
Chandos Lake ⊜	212	44.49 N	78.00 W
Chāndpara	126	22.58 N	88.47 E
Chāndpur, Bngl.	120	22.08 N	91.55 E
Chāndpur, Bngl.	124	23.13 N	90.39 E
Chāndpur, India	124	29.09 N	78.16 E
Chāndpur ◆[8]	272a	28.45 N	77.01 E
Chāndra	126	22.28 N	87.09 E
Chandrabhāga ≃	123	32.59 N	76.25 E
Chandra Dighalia	126	23.04 N	89.46 E
Chandrakona	126	22.44 N	87.31 E
Chandrakona Road	126	22.44 N	87.21 E
Chandrapur	122	19.57 N	79.18 E
Chāndvad	122	20.20 N	74.15 E
Chandyga	74	62.40 N	135.36 E
Chanfang	105	39.56 N	115.55 E
Chang (Yangtze) ≃, Zhg.	90	31.48 N	121.10 E
Chang ≃, Zhg.	100	26.53 N	119.41 E
Chang ≃, Zhg.	100	28.59 N	116.42 E
Chang, Ko I	110	12.05 N	102.20 E
Changa	84	44.27 N	50.36 E
Changaj	88	47.52 N	99.28 E
Changajn nuruu ⋀	90	47.30 N	100.00 E
Changal	88	49.19 N	104.24 E
Changalane	156	26.17 S	32.11 E
Chang'an	102	26.00 N	109.34 E
Changanācheri	122	9.28 N	76.33 E
Changane ≃	156	24.43 S	33.32 E
Changan → Xi'an	102	34.15 N	108.52 E
Chang'anzhen	106	30.28 N	120.27 E
Changara	154	16.54 S	33.14 E
Changarul'skij chrebet ⋀	88	51.10 N	103.00 E
Changbai	98	41.26 N	128.11 E
Changbai Shan ⋀	98	41.40 N	128.00 E
Changbu	100	23.48 N	115.26 E
Changcaocun	105	39.49 N	115.47 E
Changchaoling	106	31.00 N	119.40 E
Changcheng, Zhg.	100	31.49 N	116.54 E
Changcheng, Zhg.	110	19.24 N	108.42 E
Chang Cheng (Great Wall) ⊥	98	40.30 N	116.30 E
Chang Chenmo ≃	120	34.17 N	78.19 E
Changchiak'ou → Zhangjiakou	105	40.50 N	114.53 E
Ch'angchih → Changzhi	102	36.11 N	113.08 E
Changchou → Zhangzhou	100	24.33 N	117.39 E
Changchow → Changzhou	106	31.47 N	119.57 E
Changchun	89	43.53 N	125.19 E
Changchunling	89	45.22 N	125.28 E
Changdan	98	37.56 N	126.45 E
Changdang Hu ⊜	106	31.35 N	119.35 E
Changdao (Sihou)	98	37.56 N	120.42 E
Changde	102	29.02 N	111.41 E
Changdian	105	40.01 N	116.32 E
Ch'angdo	98	38.30 N	127.40 E
Ch'ang-dong	98	39.03 N	126.34 E
Change Islands	186	49.40 N	54.25 W
Changeon ≃	50	47.16 N	0.05 E
Changfeng	100	32.27 N	117.09 E
Changgang	100	24.38 N	113.05 E
Changgangzi	104	41.26 N	122.41 E
Changge	100	34.15 N	113.50 E
Changgi-ap >	98	36.05 N	129.34 E
Changgi-li	271b	37.35 N	126.44 E
Changgi-ri	271b	37.38 N	126.41 E
Changgou	105	39.34 N	115.53 E
Changgouyu	105	39.44 N	115.52 E
Changguandian	100	32.58 N	115.16 E
Changguowei	100	29.15 N	121.56 E
Changgye-ri	98	34.33 N	126.49 E
Changgyong Palace ʊ	271b	37.36 N	127.00 E
Changhai	98	39.18 N	122.35 E
Chang-hai → Shanghai	106	31.14 N	121.28 E
Changhang	98	36.01 N	126.40 E
Changhe	106	30.11 N	120.11 E
Changhowŏn	98	37.08 N	127.39 E
Chang Hu ⊜	100	30.15 N	112.35 E
Changhua, T'aiwan	100	24.05 N	120.32 E
Changhua, Zhg.	100	30.11 N	119.13 E
Changhŭng	98	34.41 N	126.52 E
Changhŭng-ni	98	40.24 N	128.19 E
Changi	271c	1.23 N	103.59 E
Changi, Tanjong >	271c	1.23 N	104.00 E
Changi International Airport ⊠	271c	1.22 N	103.59 E
Changi Prison ʊ	271c	1.22 N	103.58 E
Changji	86	44.01 N	87.19 E
Changjiang, Zhg.	100	25.19 N	113.56 E
Changjiang, Zhg.	110	19.17 N	109.02 E
Changjiangbu	100	30.52 N	113.43 E
Changjiapuzi	104	40.51 N	123.43 E
Changjiazhuang	105	40.35 N	115.24 E
Changjie	100	29.16 N	121.40 E
Changjing	106	31.45 N	120.29 E
Changjin-gang ≃	98	41.24 N	127.45 E
Changjin-ŭp	98	40.23 N	127.15 E
Changkai	100	28.04 N	116.18 E
Changkalajier	85	40.09 N	76.59 E
Changkeng	106	30.19 N	121.57 E
Changkiakow → Zhangjiakou	105	40.50 N	114.53 E
Changlapod Pass)(	124	30.08 N	87.06 E
Changle, Zhg.	98	36.42 N	118.49 E
Changle, Zhg.	100	29.25 N	120.37 E
Changle, Zhg.	100	26.00 N	119.31 E
Changlejie	100	28.52 N	113.19 E
Changleqiao	106	30.21 N	119.51 E
Changlezhen	106	31.56 N	121.15 E
Changli, Zhg.	98	36.57 N	119.45 E
Changli, Zhg.	98	39.43 N	119.11 E
Changling	89	44.15 N	123.58 E
Changlingfeng	105	40.11 N	118.24 E
Changlingji	100	32.30 N	114.54 E
Changlingzi, Zhg.	98	39.47 N	122.43 E
Changlingzi, Zhg.	98	39.33 N	121.19 E
Changlinhe	100	31.40 N	117.29 E
Changlun	114	6.26 N	100.26 E
Changmar	120	34.15 N	79.45 E
Changmong-ni	98	34.58 N	128.41 E
Changning, Zhg.	102	26.19 N	112.21 E
Changning, Zhg.	102	24.55 N	99.35 E
Changning (Anningqiao), Zhg.	102	28.21 N	104.53 E
Changning, Zhg.	105	39.59 N	114.55 E
Ch'angnyŏng	98	35.33 N	128.29 E
Changnyŏn-ni	98	38.37 N	125.16 E
Changokurt	72	61.58 N	64.18 E
Ch'angpin	100	23.19 N	121.27 E
Changping	105	40.14 N	116.14 E
Changputong	102	28.05 N	98.29 E
Ch'angp'yŏng-dong	98	41.27 N	127.31 E
Changqiao, Zhg.	100	24.15 N	117.39 E
Changqiao, Zhg.	100	26.49 N	118.50 E
Changqing	98	36.34 N	116.43 E
Changsa	102	19.51 N	110.53 E
Changsan-got >	98	38.08 N	124.39 E
Changsha, Zhg.	100	28.12 N	112.58 E
Changsha, Zhg.	100	24.13 N	116.07 E
Changshaba Shuiku ⊜[1]	107	29.42 N	104.40 E
Changshageng	107	30.00 N	104.35 E
Changshan, Zhg.	98	36.54 N	117.50 E
Changshan, Zhg.	100	28.55 N	118.30 E
Changshan, Zhg.	107	29.30 N	104.13 E
Changshan ≃	100	28.57 N	118.50 E
Changshan Qundao II	98	39.00 N	122.45 E
Changsheng	100	26.16 N	116.01 E
Changshengqiao	107	29.31 N	106.39 E
Changshitai	104	42.33 N	120.43 E
Changshitou	102	35.03 N	99.11 E
Changshou	102	29.51 N	107.06 E
Changshoudian	100	31.26 N	112.35 E
Changshoujie	100	28.44 N	113.57 E
Changshu	106	31.39 N	120.45 E
Changshui	102	34.21 N	111.29 E
Changsŏng	98	35.20 N	126.49 E
Changsŏng-ni	98	40.58 N	127.04 E
Changsu	98	35.40 N	127.32 E
Changtai, Zhg.	100	24.40 N	117.46 E
Changtai, Zhg.	100	28.34 N	118.37 E
Changtai, Zhg.	104	41.34 N	122.00 E
Changtancun	104	41.33 N	123.02 E
Ch'angte → Changde	102	29.02 N	111.41 E
Changteh → Anyang	98	36.06 N	114.21 E
Changting, Zhg.	89	44.32 N	128.47 E
Changting, Zhg.	100	25.52 N	116.20 E
Changtumiao	102	43.30 N	114.34 E
Changuinola	236	9.25 N	82.32 W
Changuinola ≃	236	9.28 N	82.27 W
Changwu, Zhg.	89	46.00 N	125.36 E
Changwu, Zhg.	102	35.09 N	107.42 E
Changxindianzhen	105	39.49 N	116.12 E
Changxing	106	31.01 N	119.54 E
Changxing Dao I, Zhg.	98	39.34 N	121.23 E
Changxing Dao I, Zhg.	106	31.24 N	121.42 E
Changxingdian, Zhg.	104	41.27 N	121.44 E
Changxingdian, Zhg.	104	41.33 N	123.23 E
Changxingzhen	104	41.40 N	122.14 E
Changxuanling	100	31.08 N	114.20 E
Changyi	98	36.51 N	119.23 E
Changyŏn	98	38.15 N	125.06 E
Changyuan	98	35.13 N	114.39 E
Changyukou	105	40.46 N	115.08 E
Changzhi	102	36.11 N	113.08 E
Changzhou (Changchow)	106	31.47 N	119.57 E
Chanhanga	152	16.04 S	14.07 E
Chanh Hung	269c	10.44 N	106.41 E
Chani	88	57.05 N	120.58 E
Chani ≃	88	57.02 N	120.59 E
Chanino	76	54.13 N	36.37 E
Chanka, ozero (Xingkai Hu) ⊜	89	45.00 N	132.24 E
Chankiang → Zhanjiang	102	21.16 N	110.28 E
Chankou	102	35.52 N	104.27 E
Chanlar	84	40.34 N	46.20 E
Channagiri	122	14.02 N	75.56 E
Channahon	216	41.26 N	88.14 W
Channapatna	122	12.39 N	77.13 E
Channel Country ◆[1]	166	24.45 S	141.00 E
Channel Islands II, Europe	43b	49.20 N	2.20 W
Channel Islands II, Ca., U.S.	204	33.30 N	119.15 W
Channel Islands National Park ♠	204	33.28 N	119.02 W
Channel Lake	216	42.29 N	88.08 W
Channel-Port-aux-Basques	186	47.34 N	59.09 W
Channelview	222	29.46 N	95.06 W
Channing, Mi., U.S.	190	46.08 N	88.05 W
Channing, Tx., U.S.	196	35.41 N	102.20 W
Chānpādānga	126	22.50 N	87.58 E
Chantada	34	42.37 N	7.46 W
Chantajskoje, ozero ⊜	74	68.20 N	91.00 E
Chantajskoje vodochranilišče ⊜[1]	72	68.00 N	88.00 E
Chantang	100	33.41 N	117.37 E
Chantau	86	44.13 N	73.51 E
Chanteloup	261	48.51 N	2.44 E
Chanteloup-les-Vignes	261	48.59 N	2.02 E
Chanthaburi	110	12.36 N	102.09 E
Chantilly	50	49.12 N	2.28 E
Chantonnay	32	46.41 N	1.03 W
Chantraine	58	48.10 N	6.26 E
Chantrans	58	47.03 N	6.09 E
Chantrey Inlet c	176	67.48 N	96.20 W
Chanty-Mansijsk	74	61.00 N	69.06 E
Chanty-Mansijskij Avtonomnyj Okrug □[8]	86	60.15 N	70.45 E
Chanujn ≃	88	49.22 N	102.22 E
Chanumla	110	8.19 N	93.05 E
Chanute	198	37.40 N	95.27 W
Chanute Air Force Base ■	216	40.18 N	88.09 W
Chanuwāla	123	32.44 N	73.08 E
Chanžonkovo	83	48.06 N	38.06 E
Chao ≃	105	40.36 N	117.08 E
Chao, Isla I	248	8.45 S	78.47 W
Chao'an	100	23.41 N	116.38 E
Chaobai ≃	105	39.48 N	117.08 E
Chaobai Xinhe ≃	105	39.37 N	117.26 E
Chaocheng	98	36.05 N	115.35 E
Ch'aochou	100	22.33 N	120.32 E
Ch'aochou → Chao'an	100	23.41 N	116.38 E
Chao Hu ⊜	100	31.31 N	117.33 E
Chaomidian	105	39.04 N	117.01 E
Chao Phraya ≃	110	13.32 N	100.36 E
Chaor ≃	89	46.48 N	123.37 E
Chaoshui, Zhg.	89	49.44 N	127.21 E
Chaoshui, Zhg.	98	37.42 N	120.55 E
Chaouen	148	35.10 N	5.16 W
Chaouen □[4]	148	35.15 N	5.00 W
Chaource	50	48.04 N	4.08 E
Chaoxian	100	31.36 N	117.52 E
Chaoyang, Zhg.	89	44.34 N	126.20 E
Chaoyang, Zhg.	100	23.17 N	116.37 E
Chaoyang, Zhg.	104	41.35 N	120.28 E
Chaoyangchuan	98	42.54 N	129.21 E
Chaoyangcun	89	50.02 N	124.16 E
Chaoyanggou	104	42.07 N	121.04 E
Chaoyangpo	89	43.37 N	124.42 E
Chaoyangshan	89	43.02 N	125.40 E
Chaozhuang	98	34.18 N	114.56 E
Chapada dos Guimarães	248	15.26 S	55.45 W
Chapada dos Veadeiros, Parque Nacional da ♠	255	13.58 S	47.30 W
Chapadinha	250	3.44 S	43.21 W
Chapala	234	20.18 N	103.12 W
Chapala, Laguna de ⊜	234	20.15 N	103.00 W
Chapare ≃, Bol.	248	15.58 S	64.42 W
Chapare ≃, Bol.	248	16.25 S	64.35 W
Chapareillan	62	45.28 N	5.58 E
Chāparmukh	120	26.12 N	92.32 E
Chaparra, Bahía de c	240p	21.13 N	76.31 W
Chaparral	246	3.43 N	75.28 W
Chapčeranga	88	49.42 N	112.24 E
Chapeauroux	62	44.50 N	3.44 E
Chapecó	252	27.06 S	52.36 W
Chapel-en-le-Frith	262	53.20 N	1.54 W
Chapelfell Top ∧	44	54.41 N	2.13 W
Chapelhall	46	55.50 N	3.56 W
Chapel Hill, De., U.S.	285	39.42 N	75.44 W
Chapel Hill, N.C., U.S.	192	35.54 N	79.03 W
Chapel Hill, Tn., U.S.	194	35.37 N	86.41 W
Chapel Hill Channel ɥ	276	40.32 N	74.02 W
Chapelle Creek ≃	198	44.16 N	99.55 W
Chapellerie	261	49.02 N	2.26 E
Chapel Oaks	284c	38.54 N	76.55 W
Chapel Point >	42	50.16 N	4.46 W
Chapel Saint Leonards	44	53.13 N	0.19 E
Chapelton	241q	18.05 N	77.16 W
Chapeltown, Eng., U.K.	44	53.28 N	1.28 W
Chapeltown, Eng., U.K.	262	53.38 N	2.24 W
Chapet	261	48.58 N	1.56 E
Chapéu, Morro do ∧	255	14.55 S	42.31 W
Chapéu, Ribeirão do ≃	256	23.14 S	45.18 W
Chapicuy	252	31.39 S	57.54 W
Chapimarca	248	13.58 S	73.04 W
Chapin	219	39.46 N	90.24 W
Chapin, Lake ⊜	216	41.56 N	86.21 W
Chaplain, Lake ⊜[1]	224	47.57 N	121.51 W
Chapleau	190	47.50 N	83.24 W
Chapleau ≃	190	48.29 N	82.57 W
Chapleau, Lac ⊜	206	46.14 N	74.57 W
Chaplin, Sk., Can.	184	50.28 N	106.40 W
Chaplin, Ct., U.S.	207	41.47 N	72.07 W
Chaplin ≃	194	37.50 N	85.11 W
Chaplin Lake ⊜	184	50.18 N	106.35 W
Chapman, Ks., U.S.	198	38.58 N	97.01 W
Chapman, Ne., U.S.	198	41.01 N	98.09 W
Chapman, Pa., U.S.	208	40.46 N	75.24 W
Chapman, Cape >	176	69.12 N	88.59 W
Chapman, Mount ∧	182	51.50 N	118.20 W
Chapman College ʊ[2]	280	33.47 N	117.51 W
Chapman Creek ≃	198	38.58 N	97.00 W
Chapman Lake ⊜	184	56.58 N	98.12 W
Chapman's (Okwa) ≃	156	22.30 S	23.00 E
Chapmanville	188	37.58 N	82.01 W
Chapman Woods	280	34.08 N	118.05 W
Chapo	196	29.17 N	104.20 W
Chaponval	261	49.04 N	2.09 E
Chappaqua	210	41.09 N	73.45 W
Chappell	198	41.05 N	102.28 W
Chappell Hill	222	30.09 N	96.16 W
Chāpra	126	23.32 N	88.33 E
Chapry	83	47.14 N	39.31 E
Chaptico Bay c	208	38.21 N	76.49 W
Chapultepec, Méx.	204	31.50 N	116.38 W
Chapultepec, Méx.	204	32.22 N	115.05 W
Chapultepec, Bosque de ♠	286a	19.25 N	99.12 W
Chapultepec, Castillo de ⊥	286a	19.25 N	99.11 W

≃ River	Fluß	Río	Rivière	Rio
≅ Canal	Kanal	Canal	Canal	Canal
⌊ Waterfall, Rapids	Wasserfall, Stromschnellen	Cascada, Rápidos	Chute d'eau, Rapides	Cascata, Rápidos
ɥ Strait	Meeresstraße	Estrecho	Détroit	Estreito
c Bay, Gulf	Bucht, Golf	Bahía, Golfo	Baie, Golfe	Baía, Golfo
⊜ Lake, Lakes	See, Seen	Lago, Lagos	Lac, Lacs	Lago, Lagos
⩩ Swamp	Sumpf	Pantano	Marais	Pântano
Ice Features, Glacier	Eis- und Gletscherformen	Accidentes Glaciales	Formes glaciaires	Acidentes glaciares
Other Hydrographic Features	Andere Hydrographische Objekte	Otros Elementos Hidrográficos	Autres données hydrographiques	Outros acidentes hidrográficos
✣ Submarine Features	Untermeerische Objekte	Accidentes Submarinos	Formes de relief sous-marin	Acidentes submarinos
□ Political Unit	Politische Einheit	Unidad Politica	Entité politique	Unidade política
ʊ Cultural Institution	Kulturelle Institution	Institución Cultural	Institution culturelle	Institução cultural
⊥ Historical Site	Historische Stätte	Sitio Histórico	Site historique	Sitio histórico
♠ Recreational Site	Erholungs- und Ferienort	Sitio de Recreo	Centre de loisirs	Area de Lazer
⊠ Airport	Flughafen	Aeropuerto	Aéroport	Aeroporto
■ Military Installation	Militäranlage	Instalación Militar	Installation militaire	Instalação militar
◆ Miscellaneous	Verschiedenes	Misceláneo	Divers	Diversos

ENGLISH: Name, Page, Lat.°′, Long.°′ — DEUTSCH: Name, Seite, Breite°′, Länge°′ E = Ost

Name	Page	Lat.°′	Long.°′
Chá Pungana	152	13.44 S	18.39 E
Chaqui	248	19.36 S	65.32 W
Chaquiago	252	27.32 S	66.21 W
Char ≃	42	50.44 N	2.53 W
Char ∓[4]	148	21.31 N	12.51 W
Charaa ≃	88	49.38 N	105.49 E
Charabali	80	47.24 N	47.16 E
Chara-Chužar	88	52.30 N	99.39 E
Charadai	252	27.38 S	59.54 W
Charagua	248	19.48 S	63.13 W
Charagun	88	51.36 N	111.05 E
Char-Ajrag	102	45.49 N	109.17 E
Charal	88	51.58 N	96.39 E
Charalá	246	6.17 N	73.10 W
Charām	128	30.45 N	50.44 E
Charaña	248	17.36 S	69.28 W
Charanor	88	50.05 N	116.40 E
Charanpur	126	23.45 N	87.02 E
Charapán	234	19.41 N	102.06 W
Charapucu, Ilha I	250	0.18 S	50.48 W
Charata	252	27.13 S	61.12 W
Charauz	88	52.16 N	106.17 E
Charavines-les-Bains	62	45.26 N	5.31 E
Charazani → Amarete	248	15.14 S	68.58 W
Charazargaj	88	52.57 N	104.41 E
Charbala	74	64.07 N	120.19 E
Char Bansi	126	22.59 N	90.43 E
Charbatovo	88	53.46 N	106.00 E
Charbon	170	32.54 S	149.58 E
Charcana	248	15.15 S	73.04 W
Charcas	234	23.08 N	101.07 W
Charco Azul, Bahía de c	236	8.15 N	82.45 W
Charco Hondo	240m	18.25 N	66.43 W
Charcos de Figueroa	232	27.45 N	102.11 W
Charcos de Risa	232	26.15 N	103.10 W
Charcot Island I	9	69.45 S	75.15 W
Charcyzsk	83	48.02 N	38.09 E
Chard	42	50.53 N	2.58 W
Chardon	214	41.36 N	81.08 W
Charduār	120	26.52 N	92.46 E
Chardzhou → Čardžou	128	39.06 N	63.34 E
Charef, Oued V	148	34.07 N	2.05 W
Charente □[5]	32	45.40 N	0.10 E
Charente ≃	32	45.57 N	1.05 W
Charente-Maritime □[5]	32	45.30 N	0.45 W
Charenton-du-Cher	32	46.44 N	2.38 E
Charenton-le-Pont	261	48.49 N	2.25 E
Charentonne ≃	50	49.07 N	0.44 E
Charest ≃	206	46.36 N	72.14 W
Chārghāt	126	24.17 N	88.45 E
Char Hāim	126	23.04 N	90.38 E
Chari ≃	146	12.58 N	14.31 E
Chariāl Canal ≅	272b	22.28 N	88.11 E
Chari-Baguirmi □[5]	146	11.30 N	16.30 E
Charik	88	54.15 N	101.39 E
Chārīkār	120	35.01 N	69.11 E
Charing	42	51.13 N	0.48 E
Charing Cross	214	42.20 N	82.06 W
Charino, Ross.	76	59.57 N	43.44 E
Charino, Ross.	82	54.33 N	37.52 E
Charistvala	84	42.26 N	43.02 E
Chariton	190	41.00 N	93.18 W
Chariton ≃	194	39.19 N	92.57 W
Chariton, Mussel Fork ≃	194	39.24 N	92.55 W
Charitonovo, Ross.	24	61.27 N	47.28 E
Charitonovo, Ross.	82	56.52 N	36.44 E
Charity	246	7.24 N	58.36 W
Charkhāri	124	25.24 N	79.45 E
Charkhi Dādri	124	28.37 N	76.16 E
Char'kin	80	48.46 N	51.49 E
Charkop ⊸[8]	272c	19.13 N	72.49 E
Char'kov (Kharkov)	78	50.00 N	36.15 E
Char'kov □[8]	83	49.42 N	37.10 E
Charkow → Char'kov	78	50.00 N	36.15 E
Char Lākhpur	126	24.04 N	90.40 E
Charland, Lac ⊜	206	46.52 N	74.11 W
Charlbury	42	51.53 N	1.29 W
Charl Cilliers	158	26.39 S	29.12 E
Charlemagne	206	45.43 N	73.29 W
Charlemont	207	42.37 N	72.52 W
Charleroi, Bel.	50	50.25 N	4.26 E
Charleroi, Pa., U.S.	214	40.08 N	79.53 W
Charleroi à Bruxelles, Canal de ≅	50	50.51 N	4.19 E
Charles □[6]	208	38.32 N	76.59 W
Charles ≃	207	42.22 N	71.03 W
Charles, Cape ›	208	37.08 N	75.58 W
Charles, Lake ⊜	278	42.15 N	87.58 W
Charles, Peak ∧	162	32.52 S	121.11 E
Charlesbourg	206	46.51 N	71.16 W
Charles Branch ≃	284c	38.47 N	76.48 W
Charles City, Ia., U.S.	190	43.03 N	92.40 W
Charles City, Va., U.S.	208	37.20 N	77.04 W
Charles City □[6]	208	37.20 N	77.02 W
Charles de Gaulle, Aéroport ⊠	50	49.01 N	2.33 E
Charles Island I	176	62.40 N	74.15 W
Charles Lee Tilden Regional Park ♠	282	37.54 N	122.15 W
Charles Mill Lake ⊜[1]	214	40.45 N	82.22 W
Charles Mound ∧[2]	190	42.30 N	90.14 W
Charles Point ›	164	12.23 S	130.36 E
Charles Sound ﾛ	172	45.02 S	167.04 E
Charleston, Austl.	168b	34.55 S	138.54 E
Charleston, N.Z.	172	41.54 S	171.26 E
Charleston, Ar., U.S.	194	35.17 N	94.02 W
Charleston, Il., U.S.	194	39.29 N	88.10 W
Charleston, Ms., U.S.	194	34.00 N	90.03 W
Charleston, Mo., U.S.	194	36.55 N	89.21 W
Charleston, S.C., U.S.	192	32.46 N	79.55 W
Charleston, W.V., U.S.	188	38.20 N	81.37 W
Charleston Air Force Base ■	192	32.55 N	80.03 W
Charleston Lake ⊜	212	44.32 N	76.00 W
Charleston Peak ∧	204	36.16 N	115.42 W
Charlestown, Austl.	170	32.58 S	151.42 E
Charlestown, Ire.	48	53.57 N	8.49 W
Charlestown, St. K.-N.	238	17.08 N	62.37 W
Charlestown, S. Afr.	158	27.30 S	29.55 E
Charlestown, In., U.S.	218	38.27 N	85.40 W
Charlestown, Md., U.S.	208	39.34 N	75.58 W
Charlestown, N.H., U.S.	188	43.14 N	72.25 W
Charlestown, Pa., U.S.	285	40.06 N	75.33 W
Charlestown, R.I., U.S.	207	41.22 N	71.38 W
Charles Town, W.V., U.S.	188	39.17 N	77.51 W
Charlestown ⊸[8]	283	42.23 N	71.04 W
Charlestown of Aberlour	46	57.28 N	3.14 W
Charlesworth	262	53.26 N	1.59 W
Charleville	166	26.24 S	146.15 E
Charleville-Mézières	56	49.46 N	4.43 E
Charleville → Ráth Luirc	48	52.21 N	8.41 W
Charlevoix	190	45.19 N	85.15 W
Charlevoix, Lake ⊜	190	45.15 N	85.08 W
Charley ≃	180	65.20 N	142.49 W
Charlie Bluff	216	42.50 N	88.58 W
Charlie Creek ≃	220	27.21 N	81.49 W
Charlie Lake	182	56.16 N	120.57 W
Charlieu	32	46.10 N	4.10 E
Charlotte, Mi., U.S.	216	42.33 N	84.50 W
Charlotte, N.C., U.S.	192	35.13 N	80.50 W
Charlotte, Tn., U.S.	194	36.10 N	87.20 W
Charlotte, Tx., U.S.	196	28.51 N	98.42 W
Charlotte □[6]	220	26.54 N	81.58 W
Charlotte Amalie	240m	18.21 N	64.56 W
Charlotte Court House	192	37.03 N	78.39 W
Charlotte Creek ≃	210	42.27 N	75.01 W
Charlotte Harbor	220	26.57 N	82.04 W
Charlotte Harbor c	220	26.45 N	82.12 W
Charlotte Lake ⊜	182	52.11 N	125.20 W
Charlottenberg	26	59.53 N	12.17 E
Charlottenburg ⊸[8]	264a	52.31 N	13.16 E
Charlottenburg, Schloss ⊥	264a	52.31 N	13.14 E
Charlottesburg Reservoir ⊜[1]	276	41.02 N	74.26 W
Charlottes Pass ♠	171b	36.25 S	145.20 E
Charlottesville, In., U.S.	218	39.47 N	85.36 W
Charlottesville, Va., U.S.	192	38.01 N	78.28 W
Charlottetown	186	46.14 N	63.08 W
Charlotteville	210	42.33 N	74.40 W
Charlovka	24	68.47 N	37.15 E
Charlton, Austl.	166	36.16 S	143.21 E
Charlton, Ma., U.S.	207	42.08 N	71.58 W
Charlton ⊸[8]	260	51.29 N	0.02 E
Charlton City	207	42.08 N	71.59 W
Charlton Island I	176	52.00 N	79.30 W
Charlton Kings	42	51.53 N	2.03 W
Charlu	24	61.48 N	30.52 E
Charly-sur-Marne	50	48.58 N	3.17 E
Charm	214	40.30 N	81.47 W
Charmentray	261	48.57 N	2.47 E
Charmes	58	48.22 N	6.17 E
Charmes-sur-Rhône	62	44.52 N	4.50 E
Charmey	58	46.38 N	7.10 E
Charminster	42	50.43 N	2.28 W
Charmois-l'Orgueilleux	58	48.06 N	6.16 E
Charmont-en-Beauce	50	48.14 N	2.06 E
Charmouth	42	50.45 N	2.55 W
Charnay-lès-Mâcon	58	46.18 N	4.47 E
Charneca	266c	38.44 N	9.27 W
Charneca ⊸[8]	266c	38.47 N	9.08 W
Charnley ≃	164	16.25 S	124.57 E
Charnock Richard	262	53.38 N	2.41 W
Char nuur ⊜, Mong.	88	48.20 N	96.05 E
Char nuur ⊜, Mong.	88	48.06 N	93.12 E
Charnwood Forest ⊸[3]	42	52.43 N	1.15 W
Charny, P.Q., Can.	206	46.43 N	71.16 W
Charny, Fr.	50	47.53 N	3.06 E
Charny, Fr.	261	48.58 N	2.46 E
Charny-sur-Meuse	56	49.12 N	5.22 E
Charo	234	19.45 N	101.03 W
Charolles	32	46.26 N	4.17 E
Charouine	148	29.01 N	0.16 W
Charovsk	76	59.59 N	40.11 E
Charpi ≃	89	49.40 N	136.10 E
Charquemont	58	47.13 N	6.49 E
Charred Oak Estates	284c	39.00 N	77.10 W
Charrette Creek ≃	219	38.37 N	91.03 W
Charron Lake ⊜	184	52.45 N	95.15 W
Charroux	32	46.09 N	0.24 E
Chars	50	49.10 N	1.56 E
Chārsadda	123	34.09 N	71.44 E
Charter Oak, Ca., U.S.	280	34.06 N	117.52 W
Charter Oak, Ia., U.S.	198	42.04 N	95.35 W
Charters Towers	166	20.05 S	146.16 E
Charterwood	279b	40.33 N	80.00 W
Chartiers Creek ≃	214	40.28 N	80.03 W
Chartiers Run ≃, Pa., U.S.	279b	40.36 N	79.43 W
Chartiers Run ≃, Pa., U.S.	279b	40.15 N	80.12 W
Chartley	207	41.56 N	71.13 W
Chartres	50	48.27 N	1.30 E
Chartrettes	50	48.29 N	2.42 E
Chartridge	260	51.44 N	0.39 W
Chart Sutton	260	51.13 N	0.35 E
Chartwell ⊥	260	51.14 N	0.05 E
Char Us nuur ⊜	90	48.00 N	92.10 E
Charutajuvom	24	66.49 N	59.30 E
Chās	126	23.38 N	86.10 E
Chasav'urt	84	43.15 N	46.37 E
Chascomús	258	35.34 S	58.01 W
Chascomús, Laguna ⊜	258	35.36 S	58.01 W
Chašdala	85	39.42 N	67.07 E
Chase, B.C., Can.	182	50.49 N	119.41 W
Chase, Ak., U.S.	180	62.27 N	150.07 W
Chase, Ks., U.S.	198	38.21 N	98.20 W
Chase, Md., U.S.	208	39.21 N	76.22 W
Chase, Mount ∧	188	46.07 N	68.29 W
Chase Brook ≃	283	42.48 N	71.27 W
Chase City	192	36.47 N	78.27 W
Chase Field Naval Air Station ■	196	28.21 N	97.40 W
Chasefu	154	11.55 S	33.08 E
Chase Lake	212	43.46 N	75.19 W
Chase River	224	49.08 N	123.55 W
Chashma Barrage ⊸[6]	123	32.26 N	71.23 E
Chasicó	254	40.18 S	68.58 W
Chasidaba	104	42.19 N	121.19 E
Chaska	190	44.47 N	93.36 W
Chaslands Mistake ›	172	46.38 S	169.22 E
Chasŏng	98	41.27 N	126.37 E
Chasŏngganggu	98	41.34 N	126.36 E
Chassahowitzka	220	28.43 N	82.34 W
Chassahowitzka Bay c	220	28.41 N	82.40 W
Chassahowitzka Swamp ≡	220	28.38 N	82.37 W
Chasseron, Mont ∧	58	46.51 N	6.33 E
Chasse-sur-Rhône	62	45.34 N	4.49 E
Chassezac ≃	62	44.26 N	4.19 E
Chašuri	84	42.00 N	43.36 E
Chasurta	88	52.17 N	108.52 E
Chasuta	248	6.35 S	76.11 W
Chāt	128	37.59 N	55.16 E
Chatanbulag	102	43.09 N	109.08 E
Chatanga	74	71.58 N	102.30 E
Chatanga ≃	74	72.55 N	106.00 E
Chatangskij zaliv c	74	73.30 N	109.00 E
Chatanika	180	65.07 N	147.31 W
Chatanika ≃	180	65.04 N	149.18 W
Château-Arnoux	62	44.06 N	6.00 E
Chateaubelair	241h	13.17 N	61.15 W
Châteaubriant	32	47.43 N	1.23 W
Château-Chinon	32	47.04 N	3.56 E
Château d'Oex	58	46.28 N	7.08 E
Château-du-Loir	50	47.42 N	0.25 E
Châteaudun	50	48.05 N	1.20 E
Châteaufort	261	48.44 N	2.06 E
Chateaugay	206	44.55 N	74.04 W
Château-Gontier	32	47.50 N	0.42 W
Châteauguay	206	45.23 N	73.45 W
Châteauguay □[6]	206	45.15 N	73.45 W
Châteauguay ≃	188	45.24 N	73.45 W
Châteauguay-Centre	206	45.21 N	73.45 W
Châteauguay Heights	275a	45.23 N	73.44 W
Château-Landon	50	48.09 N	2.42 E
Château-la-Vallière	50	47.33 N	0.19 E
Châteaulin	32	48.12 N	4.05 W
Châteaumeillant	32	46.34 N	2.12 E
Châteauneuf	62	43.23 N	5.10 E
Châteauneuf-de-Randon	62	44.39 N	3.40 E
Châteauneuf-du-Pape	62	44.03 N	4.50 E
Châteauneuf-du-Rhône	62	44.29 N	4.43 E
Châteauneuf-en-Thymerais	50	48.35 N	1.15 E
Châteauneuf-sur-Charente	32	45.36 N	0.03 W
Châteauneuf-sur-Loire	50	47.52 N	2.14 E
Châteauneuf-sur-Sarthe	32	47.41 N	0.30 W
Châteauneuf-Val-de-Bargis	50	47.17 N	3.14 E
Château-Porcien	56	49.32 N	4.15 E
Château-Queyras	62	44.45 N	6.47 E
Châteauredon	62	44.01 N	6.13 E
Châteaurenard, Fr.	50	47.56 N	2.56 E
Châteaurenard, Fr.	62	43.53 N	4.51 E
Château-Renault	50	47.35 N	0.55 E
Château-Richer	186	46.58 N	71.01 W
Châteauroux	32	46.49 N	1.42 E
Château-Salins	56	48.49 N	6.30 E
Château-Thierry	50	49.03 N	3.24 E
Châteauvillain	58	48.02 N	4.55 E
Châtel	58	46.17 N	6.50 E
Châtel-Censoir	50	47.31 N	3.38 E
Châtelet	50	50.24 N	4.31 E
Châtelineau	56	50.25 N	4.31 E
Châtellerault	32	46.49 N	0.33 E
Châtel-Saint-Denis	58	46.32 N	6.54 E
Châtel-sur-Moselle	58	48.18 N	6.24 E
Châtelus-Malvaleix	32	46.18 N	2.01 E
Châtenay-en-France	261	49.04 N	2.27 E
Châtenay-Malabry	261	48.46 N	2.17 E
Châtenois, Fr.	58	48.18 N	5.50 E
Châtenois, Fr.	58	48.16 N	7.24 E
Châtenois-les-Forges	58	47.34 N	6.51 E
Chatfield, Mn., U.S.	190	43.50 N	92.11 W
Chatfield, Oh., U.S.	214	40.57 N	82.56 W
Chatgal	88	50.26 N	100.09 E
Chatham, N.B., Can.	186	47.02 N	65.28 W
Chatham, On., Can.	214	42.24 N	82.11 W
Chatham, Eng., U.K.	42	51.23 N	0.32 E
Chatham, Il., U.S.	219	39.40 N	89.42 W
Chatham, La., U.S.	194	32.18 N	92.27 W
Chatham, Ma., U.S.	207	41.40 N	69.57 W
Chatham, N.J., U.S.	210	40.44 N	74.23 W
Chatham, N.Y., U.S.	210	42.21 N	73.35 W
Chatham, Oh., U.S.	214	41.06 N	82.01 W
Chatham, Pa., U.S.	208	39.51 N	75.49 W
Chatham, Va., U.S.	192	36.49 N	79.23 W
Chatham ⊸[8]	278	41.45 N	87.37 W
Chatham ≃	220	25.42 N	81.17 W
Chatham, Isla I	254	50.40 S	74.20 W
Chatham Head	186	47.00 N	65.33 W
Chatham Islands II	14	43.55 S	176.30 W
Chatham Rise ⊹[3]	14	43.30 S	178.00 W
Chatham Sound ﾛ	182	54.32 N	130.35 W
Chatham Strait ﾛ	180	57.30 N	134.45 W
Chatian	100	27.54 N	118.58 E
Châtillon, Fr.	261	48.48 N	2.17 E
Châtillon, It.	62	45.45 N	7.37 E
Châtillon-Coligny	50	47.50 N	2.51 E
Châtillon-en-Bazois	32	47.03 N	3.40 E
Châtillon-en-Diois	62	44.41 N	5.28 E
Châtillon-la-Borde	261	48.33 N	2.49 E
Châtillon-sur-Chalaronne	58	46.07 N	4.58 E
Châtillon-sur-Indre	32	46.59 N	1.11 E
Châtillon-sur-Loire	50	47.35 N	2.45 E
Châtillon-sur-Marne	50	49.06 N	3.45 E
Châtillon-sur-Seine	58	47.51 N	4.33 E
Chating	106	31.21 N	119.25 E
Chātmohar	126	24.13 N	89.15 E
Chat Moss ⊸[3]	262	53.27 N	2.27 W
Chato, Cerro ∧	254	42.29 S	72.01 W
Chatom	194	31.27 N	88.15 W
Chatonville	261	48.33 N	1.52 E
Chatou	261	48.54 N	2.09 E
Chatpur ⊸[8]	272b	22.36 N	88.22 E
Chatra, India	124	24.13 N	84.52 E
Chatra, India	272b	22.46 N	88.20 E
Châtres	261	48.43 N	2.49 E
Chats, Lac des ⊜	212	45.28 N	76.23 W
Chatsquot Mountain ∧	182	53.08 N	127.30 W
Chatswood	274a	33.48 S	151.12 E
Chatsworth, Austl.	166	21.58 S	140.19 E
Chatsworth, On., Can.	212	44.27 N	80.54 W
Chatsworth, Ga., U.S.	192	34.45 N	84.46 W
Chatsworth, Il., U.S.	216	40.45 N	88.17 W
Chatsworth, N.J., U.S.	208	39.49 N	74.32 W
Chatsworth, Zimb.	154	19.38 S	31.13 E
Chatsworth ⊸[8]	280	34.15 N	118.36 W
Chatsworth Reservoir ⊜[1]	228	34.14 N	118.37 W
Chattahoochee	192	30.42 N	84.50 W
Chattahoochee ≃	192	30.52 N	84.57 W
Chattanooga, Oh., U.S.	216	40.38 N	84.47 W
Chattanooga, Tn., U.S.	194	35.02 N	85.18 W
Chattaroy	192	37.42 N	82.16 W
Chattenden	260	51.25 N	0.32 E
Chatteris	42	52.27 N	0.03 E
Châttillon-de-Michaille	58	46.08 N	5.47 E
Chattolanee	284b	39.24 N	76.45 W
Chatton	44	55.33 N	1.55 W
Chatun'	82	55.00 N	37.50 E
Chaturat	110	15.34 N	101.51 E
Chatwood	208	39.58 N	75.35 W
Chatyrka	74	62.03 N	175.15 E
Chaubaria	126	22.59 N	88.40 E
Chaubourg, Mount ∧[2]	241f	14.02 N	60.57 W
Chauconin	261	48.58 N	2.51 E
Chaudes-Aigues	32	44.51 N	3.00 E
Chaudfontaine	56	50.35 N	5.38 E
Chaudière ≃	186	46.45 N	71.17 W
Chau Doc	110	10.42 N	105.07 E
Chauekuktuli, Lake ⊜	180	60.03 N	158.45 W
Chauffayer	62	44.45 N	6.01 E
Chaugācha, Bngl.	126	23.16 N	89.01 E
Chaugācha, Bngl.	126	23.16 N	89.01 E
Chauhtan	120	25.29 N	71.04 E
Chauk	110	20.54 N	94.50 E
Chaukhandi	272a	28.37 N	77.24 E
Chaullay	248	12.57 S	72.39 W
Chaulnes	50	49.49 N	2.48 E
Chaumergy	58	46.51 N	5.29 E
Chaumes-en-Brie	261	48.40 N	2.51 E
Chaumont, Fr.	58	48.07 N	5.08 E
Chaumont, N.Y., U.S.	212	44.04 N	76.07 W
Chaumont ≃	212	44.04 N	76.08 W
Chaumont Bay c	212	44.02 N	76.13 W
Chaumont-en-Vexin	50	49.16 N	1.53 E
Chaumont-Porcien	50	49.39 N	4.15 E
Chaumont-sur-Aire	56	48.56 N	5.15 E
Chaumont-sur-Loire	50	47.29 N	1.11 E
Chaumont-sur-Tharonne	50	47.37 N	1.54 E
Chaumua	272b	22.39 N	88.33 E
Chauncey	188	39.23 N	82.07 W
Chaŭn-do I	98	34.53 N	126.03 E
Chaungwabyin	110	13.41 N	98.22 E
Chaungzon	110	16.22 N	97.32 E
Chauny	50	49.37 N	3.13 E
Chaupāran	124	24.23 N	85.15 E
Chaussin	58	46.58 N	5.25 E
Chausu-yama ∧	94	35.14 N	137.39 E
Chausuyama-kofun ⊥	94	36.25 N	139.50 E
Chautārā	124	27.46 N	85.42 E
Chautauqua	214	42.12 N	79.28 W
Chautauqua □[6]	214	42.15 N	79.30 W
Chautauqua Creek ≃	214	42.20 N	79.36 W
Chautauqua Lake ⊜	214	42.12 N	79.27 W
Chautengo, Laguna c	234	16.37 N	99.07 W
Chauvigny	32	46.34 N	0.39 E
Chauvin, Ab., Can.	184	52.42 N	110.07 W
Chauvin, La., U.S.	194	29.26 N	90.35 W
Chauvirey-le-Châtel	58	47.47 N	5.45 E
Chauvry	261	49.03 N	2.16 E
Chavakkad	122	10.32 N	76.06 E
Chaval	250	3.02 S	41.15 W
Chavanges	58	48.31 N	4.34 E
Chavannes, Lac ⊜	190	46.51 N	77.10 W
Chavarría, Arg.	252	28.57 S	58.35 W
Chavarría, Perú	286d	12.01 S	77.05 W
Chavast	85	40.13 N	68.50 E
Chavenay	261	48.51 N	1.59 E
Chavenay-Villepreux, Aérodrome de ⊠	261	48.51 N	1.58 E
Chavertovo	82	54.17 N	39.12 E
Chaves, Bra.	250	0.10 S	49.55 W
Chaves, Port.	34	41.44 N	7.28 W
Chaville	261	48.48 N	2.10 E
Chaviña	248	14.59 S	73.50 W
Cháviva	246	4.22 N	72.20 W
Chavki	82	54.20 N	38.13 E
Chavornay	58	46.43 N	6.34 E
Chavuma	152	13.05 S	22.40 E
Chawa'nanake	120	31.36 N	89.41 E
Chawang	110	8.25 N	99.30 E
Chawinda	123	32.21 N	74.42 E
Chay ≃	110	21.39 N	105.12 E
Chayanta	248	18.27 S	66.30 W
Chayuan, Zhg.	100	29.20 N	121.34 E
Chayuan, Zhg.	100	27.40 N	112.57 E
Chayue	106	30.49 N	119.21 E
Chazay-d'Azergues	62	45.53 N	4.37 E
Chazelles-sur-Lyon	62	45.38 N	4.23 E
Chazratišoch, chrebet ⋀	85	38.30 N	70.15 E
Chazy	188	44.53 N	73.26 W
Chbar ≃	110	13.19 N	107.05 E
Cheadle, Eng., U.K.	42	52.59 N	1.59 W
Cheadle, Eng., U.K.	262	53.24 N	2.13 W
Cheadle Hulme	262	53.22 N	2.12 W
Cheaha Mountain ∧	194	33.30 N	85.47 W
Cheakamus Indian Reserve ⊸[4]	182	49.48 N	123.11 W
Cheam ⊸[8]	260	51.21 N	0.13 W
Cheam View	224	49.15 N	121.41 W
Cheapside	222	29.17 N	97.24 W
Cheat ≃	188	39.45 N	79.54 W
Cheat, Shavers Fork ≃	188	39.06 N	79.33 W
Cheb	54	50.01 N	12.25 E
Chebacco Lake ⊜	283	42.37 N	70.48 W
Chebanse	216	41.00 N	87.54 W
Chebba	148	35.14 N	10.02 E
Chebeigou	89	43.28 N	127.04 E
Chebogue Point ›	186	43.45 N	66.07 W
Cheboksary → Čeboksary	80	56.09 N	47.15 E
Cheboygan	190	45.38 N	84.28 W
Chech, Erg ⊸[2]	148	25.00 N	2.15 W
Ch'ech'eng	100	22.05 N	120.42 E
Chech'on	98	37.08 N	128.12 E
Chęciny	30	50.48 N	20.28 E
Checleset Bay c	182	50.03 N	127.40 W
Checoslovaquia → Czechoslovakia □[1]	30	49.30 N	17.00 E
Checotah	196	35.28 N	95.31 W
Chedabucto Bay c	186	45.23 N	61.10 W
Chedaoyu	105	40.22 N	117.57 E
Cheddar	42	51.17 N	2.46 W
Cheddleton	44	53.04 N	2.02 W
Cheduba Island I	110	18.48 N	93.38 E
Cheduba Strait ﾛ	110	18.56 N	93.45 E
Chedun	100	24.09 N	117.19 E
Chée ≃	56	48.45 N	4.39 E
Cheektowaga	210	42.55 N	78.46 W
Cheepie	166	26.39 S	145.01 E
Cheesequake	276	40.25 N	74.17 W
Cheesequake Creek ≃	276	40.28 N	74.16 W
Cheesequake State Park ♠	276	40.26 N	74.16 W
Cheetham Hill ⊸[8]	262	53.31 N	2.15 W
Chefang, Zhg.	104	41.35 N	121.26 E
Chefang, Zhg.	106	31.15 N	120.45 E
Chef-Boutonne	32	46.07 N	0.04 W
Chefoo → Yantai	98	37.33 N	121.20 E
Chefornak	180	60.13 N	164.12 W
Chefumage ≃	152	12.15 S	22.19 E
Chefuzwe	156	17.38 S	24.30 E
Chegar Perah	114	4.25 N	101.56 E
Chegga ∓[4]	148	25.30 N	5.46 W
Chegutu	154	18.10 S	30.14 E
Chehalis	224	46.39 N	122.57 W
Chehalis ≃	224	46.57 N	123.50 W
Chehalis, South Fork ≃	224	46.40 N	123.15 W
Chehalis Indian Reservation ⊸[4]	224	46.49 N	123.13 W
Chehe	102	25.00 N	107.38 E
Chehel Dokhtarān	128	35.06 N	62.19 E
Cheheqiao	105	40.21 N	118.16 E
Cheil, Ras el ›	144	7.44 N	49.50 E
Cheine	54	52.52 N	11.04 E
Cheiron, Cime du ∧	62	43.49 N	6.58 E
Chejiatun	104	41.57 N	123.01 E
Chejiawopeng	104	42.29 N	123.07 E
Cheju	90	33.31 N	126.32 E
Cheju-do I	90	33.20 N	126.30 E
Chekiang → Zhejiang □[4]	100	29.00 N	120.00 E
Chek Jawa, Tanjong ›	271c	1.24 N	104.00 E
Chek Kang	271d	22.26 N	114.21 E
Chela, Serra da ∧	152	16.00 S	13.10 E
Chelan	202	47.50 N	120.00 W
Chelan □[6]	224	47.56 N	120.52 W
Chelan, Lake ⊜	202	48.05 N	120.30 W
Chelas ⊸[8]	266c	38.45 N	9.07 W
Cheleiros	266c	38.53 N	9.20 W
Cheleiros, Ribeira de ≃	266c	38.54 N	9.22 W
Chelelektu	144	6.00 N	38.09 E
Chelford	262	53.16 N	2.16 W
Chelforó	252	39.04 S	66.32 W
Chelghoum el Aïd	148	36.10 N	6.10 E
Chéliff, Oued ≃	148	36.01 N	0.07 E
Chelīk-e Yās Khān	120	37.05 N	66.14 E
Chellaston	42	52.53 N	1.27 W
Chelles	50	48.53 N	2.36 E
Chelles-le-Pin, Aérodrome de ⊠	261	48.55 N	2.35 E
Chełm	30	51.10 N	23.28 E
Chełm □[4]	30	51.20 N	23.20 E
Chelmer ≃	260	51.48 N	0.40 E
Chelmer and Blackwater Navigation ≅	260	51.44 N	0.43 E
Chełmno	30	53.22 N	18.26 E
Chelmorton	262	53.13 N	1.50 W
Chelmsford, On., Can.	190	46.35 N	81.12 W
Chelmsford, Eng., U.K.	260	51.44 N	0.28 E
Chelmsford, Ma., U.S.	207	42.35 N	71.21 W
Chelmsford □[8]	260	51.44 N	0.30 E
Chelmsford Dam ⊜[1]	158	28.02 S	29.52 E
Chełmża	30	53.12 N	18.37 E
Chelsea, Austl.	169	38.03 S	145.07 E
Chelsea, Ia., U.S.	190	41.55 N	92.23 W
Chelsea, Ma., U.S.	207	42.23 N	71.02 W
Chelsea, Mi., U.S.	216	42.19 N	84.01 W
Chelsea, Ok., U.S.	196	36.32 N	95.25 W
Chelsea, Pa., U.S.	285	39.52 N	75.28 W
Chelsea, Vt., U.S.	188	43.59 N	72.26 W
Chelsea Estates	208	39.41 N	75.36 W
Chelsea Park	224	47.28 N	122.21 W
Chelsfield ⊸[8]	260	51.21 N	0.08 E
Cheltenham, Austl.	274a	33.46 S	151.05 E
Cheltenham, Austl.	274b	37.58 S	145.03 E
Cheltenham, Eng., U.K.	42	51.54 N	2.04 W
Cheltenham, Md., U.S.	208	38.44 N	76.49 W
Cheltenham, Pa., U.S.	208	40.03 N	75.05 W
Chel'ul'ja	26	61.44 N	30.41 E
Chelvand	128	38.18 N	48.50 E
Chelyabinsk → Čel'abinsk	86	55.10 N	61.24 E
Chelyuskintsy Ice Tongue ⊠	9	66.20 S	82.00 E
Chemaïa	148	32.05 N	8.37 W
Chemainus	224	48.55 N	123.43 W
Chemainus ≃	224	48.55 N	123.43 W
Chemaogang	106	31.33 N	121.52 E
Chemax	232	20.39 N	87.56 W
Chemba	154	17.08 S	34.52 E
Chembür ⊸[8]	272c	19.04 N	72.54 E
Chemchâm, Sebkhet ⊜	148	21.05 N	12.05 W
Chemčik ≃	86	51.47 N	92.00 E
Chemehuevi Indian Reservation ⊸[4]	204	34.30 N	114.23 W
Chemillé	32	47.13 N	0.44 W
Chemin	58	46.59 N	5.19 E
Cheminis, Colline ∧[2]	190	48.08 N	79.31 W
Chemnitz	54	50.50 N	12.55 E
Chemnitz ≃	54	50.59 N	12.47 E
Chemor	114	4.43 N	101.07 E
Chemulpo → Inch'ŏn	98	37.28 N	126.38 E
Chemult	202	43.13 N	121.46 W
Chemung, Il., U.S.	216	42.25 N	88.40 W
Chemung, N.Y., U.S.	210	42.01 N	76.37 W
Chemung □[6]	210	42.06 N	76.49 W
Chemung ≃	210	41.55 N	76.31 W
Chemung County Airport ⊠	210	42.10 N	76.53 W
Chemung Lake ⊜	212	44.25 N	78.22 W
Chena, Cerro ∧	286e	33.36 N	70.45 W
Chenāb ≃	123	29.23 N	71.02 E
Chenachane	148	26.00 N	4.15 W
Chenail Ecarté ≃[1]	214	42.28 N	82.29 W
Chenango □[6]	210	42.32 N	75.31 W
Chenango ≃	210	42.05 N	75.55 W
Chenango Bridge	210	42.10 N	75.51 W
Chenango Forks	210	42.14 N	75.50 W
Chenango Valley State Park ♠	210	42.14 N	75.50 W
Chenārān	128	36.39 N	59.06 E
Chenaut	258	34.15 S	59.13 W
Chen Barag Qi	89	49.21 N	119.31 E
Chenbofang	98	37.27 N	115.18 E
Chencai	100	29.37 N	120.22 E
Chenchiang → Zhenjiang	106	32.13 N	119.26 E
Chencun	100	22.58 N	113.13 E
Chendai	100	23.48 N	117.24 E
Chendauli ⊸[8]	272c	19.07 N	72.54 E
Chenderiang	114	4.16 N	101.14 E
Chenderoh, Tasek ⊜	114	4.58 N	100.57 E
Chêne, Rivière du ≃, P.Q., Can.	206	46.34 N	72.00 W
Chêne, Rivière du ≃, P.Q., Can.	206	45.33 N	73.54 W
Chenele	152	12.54 S	23.54 E
Chenequa	216	43.06 N	88.23 W
Chénéville	206	45.53 N	75.03 W
Cheney, Ks., U.S.	198	37.37 N	97.46 W
Cheney, Wa., U.S.	202	47.29 N	117.34 W
Cheney Reservoir ⊜[1]	198	37.45 N	97.50 W
Cheneys Point	214	42.08 N	79.24 W
Cheneyville	194	31.00 N	92.17 W
Chenfang	100	28.01 N	117.32 E
Cheng'an	98	36.27 N	114.41 E
Chengannūr	122	9.20 N	76.38 E
Chengbu	102	26.18 N	110.13 E
Chengchow → Zhengzhou	102	34.48 N	113.39 E
Chengde, Zhg.	105	40.58 N	117.53 E
Chengde (Xiabancheng), Zhg.	105	40.47 N	118.08 E
Chengdu (Chengtu)	107	30.39 N	104.04 E
Chengele	120	28.47 N	96.16 E
Chenggang	100	26.32 N	115.26 E
Chenggu	102	33.10 N	107.22 E
Chenghai	100	23.30 N	116.46 E
Cheng Hu ⊜	106	31.13 N	120.49 E
Chenghuang	102	22.32 N	109.39 E
Chengjia	100	24.50 N	112.50 E
Chengjiahe	100	32.18 N	112.27 E
Chengjiang	102	24.45 N	102.54 E
Chengjiangzhen	107	29.52 N	106.23 E
Chengjiazhen	107	29.24 N	104.36 E
Chengkou	102	31.54 N	108.41 E
Chenglingji	100	29.26 N	113.09 E
Chenglong	100	24.51 N	114.41 E
Chengmai	110	19.48 N	110.02 E
Chengmao	106	31.10 N	120.53 E
Chengpu	100	25.46 N	118.48 E
Chengqian	98	35.21 N	117.21 E
Chengqianwei	100	28.09 N	116.13 E
Chengshan Jiao ›	98	37.24 N	122.42 E
Chengteh → Chengde	105	40.58 N	117.53 E
Chengtu → Chengdu	107	30.39 N	104.04 E
Ch'engtzuliao	269d	25.06 N	121.27 E
Chengwu	98	34.58 N	115.52 E
Chengxian	102	33.43 N	105.41 E
Chengxi Hu ⊜	100	32.24 N	116.15 E
Chengyang, Zhg.	98	36.18 N	120.22 E
Chengyang, Zhg.	100	29.59 N	119.44 E
Chengzi, Zhg.	98	41.57 N	117.16 E
Chengzi, Zhg.	105	39.58 N	116.02 E
Chengzitan	98	39.30 N	122.30 E
Ch'enhsien → Chenxian	100	25.48 N	112.59 E
Chen Hu ⊜	100	30.29 N	113.22 E
Chenies	260	51.41 N	0.32 W
Chenil, Lac ⊜	186	51.51 N	59.41 W
Cheniménil	58	48.08 N	6.36 E
Chenji	100	33.50 N	119.11 E
Chenjiachang, Zhg.	107	29.35 N	104.52 E
Chenjiachang, Zhg.	107	30.04 N	105.15 E
Chenjiagang	98	34.25 N	119.49 E
Chenjiahe	102	29.28 N	109.59 E
Chenjiaji	100	30.42 N	114.21 E
Chenjiapang	106	31.14 N	119.42 E
Chenjiapu	105	40.31 N	115.37 E
Chenjiaqiao	106	31.27 N	121.16 E
Chenjiatun, Zhg.	104	42.20 N	124.06 E
Chenjiatun, Zhg.	104	40.57 N	121.01 E
Chenjiawan	106	31.02 N	120.35 E
Chenjiaxiang	100	31.29 N	113.45 E
Chenjiazhen	106	31.30 N	121.48 E
Chenjiazui	105	39.17 N	116.59 E
Chenkeng	100	25.06 N	116.15 E
Chenlingjiao	106	30.23 N	118.47 E
Chenliu	98	34.43 N	114.31 E
Chenlong	269b	31.17 N	121.25 E
Chennevières	261	49.00 N	2.07 E
Chennevières-lès-Lovres	261	49.03 N	2.33 E
Chenoa	216	40.44 N	88.43 W
Chenonceaux	50	47.20 N	1.04 E
Chenonceaux, Château de ⊥	50	47.20 N	1.04 E
Chenôve	58	47.17 N	5.00 E
Chenoweth	224	45.37 N	121.13 W
Chenqiao	98	34.58 N	114.32 E
Chenquingqiao	89	49.08 N	127.16 E
Chenshanzhuang	105	39.43 N	117.30 E
Chenshichang	107	29.17 N	106.00 E
Chens-sur-Léman	58	46.20 N	6.16 E
Chentang	102	23.54 N	110.39 E
Chentejn nuruu ⋀	88	48.30 N	108.30 E
Chentij	88	48.05 N	109.45 E
Chentij □[4]	88	48.00 N	110.30 E
Chenxi	102	27.51 N	109.59 E
Chenxian	100	25.48 N	112.59 E
Chenxiangtun	104	41.36 N	123.30 E
Chenyang	100	33.47 N	120.10 E
Chenyang → Shenyang	104	41.48 N	123.27 E
Cheonan → Ch'ŏnan	98	36.48 N	127.09 E
Cheongju → Ch'ŏngju	98	36.39 N	127.31 E
Cheo Reo	110	13.24 N	108.27 E
Chepachet	207	41.54 N	71.40 W
Chepaúa	152	12.58 S	22.43 E
Chepén	248	7.13 S	79.27 W
Chépénéhé	175f	20.47 S	167.09 E
Chepes	252	31.21 S	66.36 W
Chepkotet ∧	154	1.15 N	35.26 E
Chepo	246	9.10 N	79.06 W
Chepstow	42	51.39 N	2.41 W
Cheptainville	261	48.33 N	2.16 E
Cher □[5]	32	47.05 N	2.30 E
Cher ≃	32	47.21 N	0.29 E
Cheradi, Isole II	68	40.27 N	17.10 E
Cherain	56	50.11 N	5.52 E
Cherán	234	19.41 N	101.57 W
Chéran ≃	62	45.53 N	5.56 E
Cheranchi	150	12.40 N	7.42 E
Cherangany Hills ⋀[2]	154	1.15 N	35.27 E
Cherasco	62	44.39 N	7.51 E
Cherāt	123	33.49 N	71.53 E
Cheraw	192	34.41 N	79.53 W
Cheraw State Park ♠	192	34.36 N	79.55 W
Cherbaniani Reef ⊹[2]	122	12.18 N	71.53 E
Cherbourg	32	49.39 N	1.39 W
Cherchell	148	36.36 N	2.12 E
Cheremkhovo → Čeremchovo	88	53.09 N	103.05 E
Chérence	261	49.05 N	1.41 E
Chereponi	150	10.09 N	0.17 E
Cherepovets → Čerepovec	76	59.08 N	37.54 E
Chergui, Chott ech ⊜	148	34.21 N	0.30 E
Chergui, Île I	148	34.44 N	11.14 E
Chergui, Zahrez ⊜	148	35.12 N	3.32 E
Cheribon → Cirebon	115a	6.44 S	108.34 E
Cherio ≃	64	45.46 N	9.55 E
Cherita, Sebkhet ⊜	36	35.21 N	10.19 E
Cheriton	208	37.17 N	75.58 W
Cheriyam Island I	122	10.09 N	73.40 E
Cherkassy → Čerkassy	78	49.26 N	32.04 E
Cherkessk → Čerkessk	84	44.14 N	42.04 E
Cherlen → Kerulen ≃	90	48.48 N	117.00 E
Chermside	171a	27.23 S	153.02 E
Chernigov → Černigov	78	51.30 N	31.18 E
Chernobyl → Černobyl'	78	51.16 N	30.14 E
Chernofski	180	53.24 N	167.33 W
Chernogorsk → Černogorsk	86	53.49 N	91.18 E
Chernovtsy → Černovcy	78	48.18 N	25.56 E
Chero ≃	62	44.58 N	9.51 E
Cherokee, Al., U.S.	194	34.45 N	87.58 W
Cherokee, Ia., U.S.	198	42.44 N	95.33 W
Cherokee, Ks., U.S.	198	37.20 N	94.48 W
Cherokee, Ok., U.S.	196	36.45 N	98.21 W
Cherokee, Tx., U.S.	196	30.59 N	98.43 W
Cherokee □[6]	222	31.48 N	95.10 W
Cherokee, Lake ⊜[1]	222	32.21 N	94.39 W
Cherokee Canal ≅	226	39.18 N	121.55 W
Cherokee Lake ⊜[1]	192	36.16 N	83.20 W
Cherokee Point ›	192	26.16 N	77.03 W
Cherokee Ranch	208	40.25 N	75.55 W
Cherokees, Lake O' The ⊜[1]	194	36.39 N	94.49 W
Cherokee Village	194	36.17 N	91.30 W
Chéroy	50	48.12 N	3.00 E
Cherpuči	89	53.01 N	138.52 E
Cherquenco	252	38.41 S	72.00 W
Cherrabun	162	18.29 S	125.19 E
Cherrapunji	120	25.18 N	91.42 E
Cherry Brook ≃, Ma., U.S.	283	42.23 N	71.17 W
Cherry Brook ≃, N.J., U.S.	276	41.01 N	74.00 W
Cherry City	279b	40.29 N	79.58 W
Cherry Creek, B.C., Can.	224	49.17 N	124.47 W
Cherry Creek, N.Y., U.S.	214	42.17 N	79.06 W
Cherry Creek ≃, Az., U.S.	200	33.41 N	110.49 W
Cherry Creek ≃, Ca., U.S.	226	37.53 N	119.58 W
Cherry Creek ≃, Co., U.S.	198	39.45 N	105.01 W
Cherry Creek ≃, Mt., U.S.	198	46.48 N	105.15 W
Cherry Creek ≃, N.D., U.S.	198	47.41 N	103.02 W
Cherry Creek ≃, S.D., U.S.	198	44.36 N	101.30 W
Cherry Creek ≃, Tx., U.S.	196	31.13 N	103.34 W
Cherry Creek, East Fork ≃	226	38.06 N	119.47 W
Cherry Creek, West Fork ≃	226	38.04 N	119.54 W
Cherry Fork	218	38.53 N	83.37 W
Cherry Grove, N.Y., U.S.	210	40.39 N	73.06 W
Cherry Grove, Or., U.S.	224	45.26 N	123.14 W
Cherry Hill, Il., U.S.	278	41.32 N	88.02 W
Cherry Hill, N.J., U.S.	208	39.56 N	75.01 W
Cherry Hill ⊸[8]	284b	39.15 N	76.38 W
Cherry Hill Mall ⊸[9]	285	39.56 N	75.02 W
Cherry Island I	285	39.43 N	75.31 W
Cherry Lake ⊜[1]	226	38.00 N	119.54 W
Cherryland	226	37.41 N	122.06 W
Cherry Lane	279b	40.34 N	79.33 W
Cherryplain	210	42.38 N	73.22 W
Cherry Point Marine Corps Air Station ■	192	34.54 N	76.54 W
Cherryvale	198	37.16 N	95.33 W
Cherry Valley, Ar., U.S.	194	35.24 N	90.45 W
Cherry Valley, Ca., U.S.	228	33.57 N	116.53 W
Cherry Valley, Il., U.S.	216	42.14 N	88.56 W
Cherry Valley, Ma., U.S.	207	42.14 N	71.52 W
Cherry Valley, N.Y., U.S.	210	42.47 N	74.45 W
Cherry Valley, Pa., U.S.	214	41.10 N	79.48 W
Cherry Valley Creek ≃	210	42.35 N	74.56 W
Cherryville, N.C., U.S.	192	35.22 N	81.22 W
Cherryville, Pa., U.S.	208	40.45 N	75.33 W
Cherrywood	275b	43.52 N	79.08 W
Cherson	78	46.38 N	32.35 E
Chersonesskij, mys ›	78	44.35 N	33.23 E
Chertsey	260	51.24 N	0.30 W
Cherwell ≃	42	51.44 N	1.15 W
Chesaco Park	284b	39.19 N	76.30 W
Chesaning	190	43.11 N	84.06 W
Chesapeake	208	36.49 N	76.16 W
Chesapeake and Delaware Canal ≅	208	39.32 N	75.51 W
Chesapeake and Ohio Canal National Historical Park ♠	208	39.03 N	77.16 W
Chesapeake Bay c	208	38.40 N	76.25 W
Chesapeake Bay Bridge-Tunnel ⊸[5]	208	37.00 N	76.02 W
Chesapeake Beach	208	38.41 N	76.32 W
Chesaw	182	48.56 N	119.03 W
Chesdin, Lake ⊜[1]	208	37.15 N	77.33 W
Cheseaux	58	46.35 N	6.36 E
Chesham	260	51.43 N	0.38 W
Chesham Bois	260	51.41 N	0.37 W
Cheshire, Ct., U.S.	207	41.29 N	72.54 W
Cheshire, Ma., U.S.	207	42.33 N	73.09 W
Cheshire, N.Y., U.S.	210	42.49 N	77.20 W
Cheshire □[6], Eng., U.K.	44	53.23 N	2.30 W
Cheshire □[6], N.H., U.S.	207	42.50 N	72.15 W
Cheshire Plain ≍	44	53.17 N	2.40 W
Cheshire Reservoir ⊜[1]	207	42.27 N	73.11 W
Chesht-e Sharīf	128	34.21 N	63.44 E
Cheshunt	42	51.43 N	0.02 W
Chesil Beach ⊥[2]	42	50.38 N	2.33 W
Chesilhurst	285	39.43 N	74.52 W
Cheslatta Lake ⊜	182	53.44 N	125.18 W

Symbols in the index entries represent the broad categories identified in the key at the right. Symbols with superior numbers (∧[1]) identify subcategories (see complete key on page *I · 1*).

Symbole im Register stellen die rechts im Schlüssel erklärten Kategorien dar. Symbole mit hochgestellten Ziffern (∧[1]) bezeichnen Unterabteilungen einer Kategorie (vgl. vollständiger Schlüssel auf Seite *I · 1*).

Los símbolos incluidos en el texto del índice representan las grandes categorías identificadas con la clave a la derecha. Los símbolos con numeros en su parte superior (∧[1]) identifican las subcategorías (véase la clave completa en la página *I · 1*).

Les symboles de l'index représentent les catégories indiquées dans la légende à droite. Les symboles suivis d'un indice (∧[1]) représentent des sous-catégories (voir légende complète à la page *I · 1*).

Os símbolos incluídos no texto do índice representam as grandes categorias identificadas com a chave à direita. Os símbolos com números em sua parte superior (∧[1]) identificam as subcategorias (veja-se a chave completa à página *I · 1*).

∧ Mountain	Berg	Montaña	Montagne	Montanha
⋀ Mountains	Gebirge	Montañas	Montagnes	Montanhas
✕ Pass	Paß	Paso	Col	Passo
V Valley, Canyon	Tal, Cañon	Valle, Cañón	Vallée, Canyon	Vale, Canhão
≍ Plain	Ebene	Llano	Plaine	Planície
› Cape	Kap	Cabo	Cap	Cabo
I Island	Insel	Isla	Île	Ilha
II Islands	Inseln	Islas	Îles	Ilhas
⊥ Other Topographic Features	Andere Topographische Objekte	Otros Elementos Topográficos	Autres données topographiques	Outros acidentes topográficos

Ches-Chit I · 35

ESPAÑOL: Nombre, Página, Lat. °′, Long. °′ W = Oeste
FRANÇAIS: Nom, Page, Lat. °′, Long. °′ W = Ouest
PORTUGUÊS: Nome, Página, Lat. °′, Long. °′ W = Oeste

Nombre	Página	Lat.°′	Long.°′ W = Oeste
Chesley	212	44.17 N	81.05 W
Chesnee	192	35.08 N	81.51 W
Chess ≃	260	51.38 N	0.27 W
Chessington ◆[8]	260	51.21 N	0.18 W
Chessy	261	48.53 N	2.46 E
Chest Creek ≃	214	40.53 N	78.44 W
Chester, Eng., U.K.	262	53.12 N	2.54 W
Chester, Ca., U.S.	204	40.18 N	121.13 W
Chester, Ct., U.S.	207	41.24 N	72.27 W
Chester, Il., U.S.	194	37.54 N	89.49 W
Chester, Md., U.S.	208	38.58 N	76.17 W
Chester, Ma., U.S.	207	42.16 N	72.58 W
Chester, Mt., U.S.	202	48.30 N	110.58 W
Chester, Ne., U.S.	198	40.00 N	97.37 W
Chester, N.J., U.S.	210	40.47 N	74.41 W
Chester, Ok., U.S.	196	36.12 N	98.55 W
Chester, Pa., U.S.	208	39.50 N	75.21 W
Chester, S.C., U.S.	192	34.42 N	81.12 W
Chester, Tx., U.S.	222	30.55 N	94.36 W
Chester, Vt., U.S.	188	43.15 N	72.35 W
Chester, Va., U.S.	208	37.21 N	77.26 W
Chester, W.V., U.S.	214	40.36 N	80.33 W
Chester □[6]	208	39.58 N	75.36 W
Chester □[8]	262	53.16 N	2.52 W
Chester ≃	208	39.00 N	76.10 W
Chester Basin	186	44.34 N	64.19 W
Chesterbrook	284c	38.55 N	77.09 W
Chester Brook ≃	283	42.23 N	71.14 W
Chesterbrook Woods	284c	38.56 N	77.08 W
Chester Creek ≃	208	39.50 N	75.22 W
Chester Creek, East Branch ≃	285	39.56 N	75.32 W
Chester Creek, West Branch ≃	285	39.54 N	75.27 W
Chesterfield, Eng., U.K.	44	53.15 N	1.25 W
Chesterfield, Ct., U.S.	207	41.24 N	72.11 W
Chesterfield, Il., U.S.	219	39.15 N	90.04 W
Chesterfield, In., U.S.	218	40.06 N	85.35 W
Chesterfield, Ma., U.S.	207	42.23 N	72.50 W
Chesterfield, S.C., U.S.	192	34.44 N	80.05 W
Chesterfield, Va., U.S.	192	37.22 N	77.30 W
Chesterfield □[6]	208	37.20 N	77.25 W
Chesterfield, Île I	157b	16.20 S	43.58 E
Chesterfield, Îles II	160	19.30 S	158.00 E
Chesterfield Inlet	176	63.21 N	90.42 W
Chesterfield Inlet c	176	63.25 N	90.45 W
Chester Heights	285	39.53 N	75.28 W
Chester Hill, Austl.	274a	33.53 S	151.00 E
Chesterhill, Oh., U.S.	188	39.29 N	81.51 W
Chester Hill, Pa., U.S.	214	40.53 N	78.14 W
Chester Island I	285	39.50 N	75.21 W
Chesterland	214	41.31 N	81.21 W
Chester-le-Street	44	54.52 N	1.34 W
Chester Morse Lake ⊜[1]	224	47.23 N	121.42 W
Chesters	44	55.23 N	2.36 W
Chester Springs	285	40.06 N	75.37 W
Chesterton	216	41.36 N	87.03 W
Chesterton Range ⋏	166	25.30 S	147.27 E
Chestertown	208	39.12 N	76.04 W
Chesterville, On., Can.	212	45.06 N	75.14 W
Chesterville, Oh., U.S.	214	40.29 N	82.41 W
Chestnut	219	40.03 N	89.11 W
Chestnut Hill, Ma., U.S.	283	42.20 N	71.10 W
Chestnut Hill, Pa., U.S.	210	40.04 N	75.12 W
Chestnut Hill ◆[8]	285	40.04 N	75.13 W
Chestnut Hill ʌ[2]	285	40.13 N	75.45 W
Chestnut Hill Estates	285	39.41 N	75.42 W
Chestnut Hill Reservoir ⊜[1]	283	42.20 N	71.10 W
Chestnut Ridge ʌ	214	40.09 N	79.24 W
Chestnut Ridge Park ♦	284a	42.43 N	78.46 W
Chest Peak ʌ	172	43.06 S	172.01 E
Chesuncook Lake ⊜	188	46.00 N	69.20 W
Cheswick	214	40.32 N	79.47 W
Cheswold	208	39.13 N	75.35 W
Chet ≃	42	52.33 N	1.32 E
Cheta ≃	74	71.54 N	102.06 E
Chetaibi	36	37.04 N	7.23 E
Chetco ≃	202	42.03 N	124.16 W
Chetek	190	45.18 N	91.39 W
Chéticamp	186	46.38 N	61.01 W
Chet Iter, Oued V	148	21.39 N	2.30 E
Chetopa	198	37.02 N	95.05 W
Chettlatt Island I	122	11.42 N	72.42 E
Chetumal	232	18.30 N	88.18 W
Chetumal, Bahía c	232	18.20 N	88.05 W
Chetwynd	182	55.42 N	121.40 W
Cheung Chau I	271d	22.12 N	114.01 E
Cheung Shue Tan	271d	22.26 N	114.12 E
Chevak	180	61.39 N	165.17 W
Cheval-Blanc, Montagne du ⋏	62	44.07 N	6.26 E
Chevannes	261	48.32 N	2.27 E
Chevelon Creek ≃	200	34.57 N	110.31 W
Chevening	260	51.18 N	0.08 E
Chevenoz	58	46.20 N	6.39 E
Cheverly	284c	38.55 N	76.54 W
Cheverny	50	47.30 N	1.28 E
Chevillon	58	48.32 N	5.08 E
Chevilly-Larue	261	48.46 N	2.21 E
Cheviot, N.Z.	172	42.49 S	173.16 E
Cheviot, Oh., U.S.	218	39.09 N	84.36 W
Cheviot Hills ⋏[2]	44	55.22 N	2.22 W
Chevreuse	50	48.42 N	2.03 E
Chèvreville	261	49.07 N	2.51 E
Chevril, Lac du ⊜	62	45.29 N	6.56 E
Chevry-Cossigny	261	48.43 N	2.40 E
Chevy Chase	284c	38.58 N	77.04 W
Chevy Chase Heights	214	40.36 N	79.08 W
Chevy Chase View	284c	39.01 N	77.05 W
Chewaucan ≃	202	42.30 N	120.18 W
Chew Bahir (Lake Stefanie) ⊜	144	4.40 N	36.50 E
Chewelah	202	48.16 N	117.42 W
Chew Magna	42	51.22 N	2.35 W
Chew Reservoir ⊜[1]	262	53.31 N	1.56 W
Chews Landing	285	39.50 N	75.04 W
Chewton, Austl.	169	37.05 S	144.16 E
Chewton, Pa., U.S.	214	40.53 N	80.20 W
Chexbres	58	46.29 N	6.47 E
Cheyenne, Ok., U.S.	196	35.36 N	99.40 W
Cheyenne, Wy., U.S.	200	41.08 N	104.49 W
Cheyenne ≃	198	44.40 N	101.15 W
Cheyenne, Dry Fork ≃	198	43.25 N	105.23 W
Cheyenne River Indian Reservation ◆[4]	198	45.00 N	100.40 W
Cheyenne Wells	198	38.49 N	102.21 W
Cheyne Bay c	162	34.35 S	118.50 E
Cheyne Point ›	162	33.58 S	122.34 E
Cheyney	285	39.56 N	75.31 W
Cheyney University of Pennsylvania ʋ[2]	285	39.56 N	75.32 W
Chezhen	98	37.54 N	117.37 E
Chhabra	124	24.40 N	76.50 E
Chhachhrauli	124	30.15 N	77.22 E
Chhajārsi	272a	28.38 N	77.23 E
Chhalera Bāngar	272a	28.33 N	77.20 E
Chhanka	126	23.59 N	89.55 E
Chhapra	124	25.46 N	84.45 E
Chhātak	120	25.02 N	91.40 E
Chhatarpur, India	124	24.23 N	84.11 E
Chhatarpur, India	124	24.55 N	79.36 E
Chhātna	126	23.18 N	86.58 E
Chhatrapur	122	19.21 N	84.59 E
Chhattīsgarh ≚	122	21.15 N	82.00 E
Chhay Arêng ≃	110	11.31 N	103.25 E
Chhêb Kândal	110	13.45 N	105.24 E
Chhibrāmau	124	27.09 N	79.31 E
Chhināmor	272b	22.48 N	88.18 E
Chhindwāra	124	22.04 N	78.56 E
Chhiruti	126	24.01 N	88.11 E
Chhitauni	124	27.09 N	83.58 E
Chhlong ≃	110	12.15 N	105.58 E
Chhota Bāisdia	126	22.00 N	90.27 E
Chhota-Chhindwāra	124	23.03 N	79.29 E
Chhota Udepur	120	22.19 N	74.01 E
Chhukha Dzong	124	27.09 N	89.36 E
Chi ≃, Thai	110	15.11 N	104.43 E
Chi ≃, Thai	110	15.18 N	103.31 E
Chi ≃, Zhg.	100	32.51 N	117.59 E
Chía	246	4.52 N	74.04 W
Chia, Laguna ⊜	234	22.10 N	98.02 W
Chiador	256	22.01 S	43.03 W
Chiahsien	100	23.05 N	120.35 E
Chiahsing → Jiaxing	106	30.46 N	120.45 E
Chiai	100	23.29 N	120.27 E
Chialamberto	62	45.22 N	7.21 E
Chiali	100	23.10 N	120.10 E
Chiambala ≃	152	16.22 S	11.49 E
Chiampo	64	45.33 N	11.17 E
Chiampo ≃	64	45.20 N	11.16 E
Chiamussu → Jiamusi	89	46.50 N	130.21 E
Chiana, Val di V	66	43.15 N	11.50 E
Chianciano Terme	66	43.03 N	11.50 E
Chiang Dao	110	19.22 N	98.58 E
Chiange	152	15.45 S	13.48 E
Chiang Kham	110	19.32 N	100.18 E
Chiang Khan	110	17.52 N	101.36 E
Chiang Khian	110	19.37 N	100.00 E
Chiang Mai	110	18.47 N	98.59 E
Chiangmen → Jiangmen	100	22.35 N	113.05 E
Chiang Rai	110	19.54 N	99.50 E
Chiang Saen	110	20.16 N	100.05 E
Chiangtu → Yangzhou	100	32.24 N	119.26 E
Chiangyin → Jiangyin	106	31.55 N	120.16 E
Chiani ≃	66	42.52 N	12.14 E
Chian → Ji'an	100	27.07 N	114.58 E
Chianni	66	43.29 N	10.38 E
Chianti □[4]	66	43.22 N	11.23 E
Chianti ⋏[1]	66	43.25 N	11.20 E
Chianti, Monti del ⋏	66	43.32 N	11.25 E
Chiaohsi	100	24.49 N	121.46 E
Chiaohsien → Jiaoxian	98	36.18 N	119.58 E
Chiaopan	100	24.50 N	121.21 E
Chiaotso → Jiaozuo	102	35.15 N	113.13 E
Chiao-Tung Normal University ʋ[2]	269b	31.14 N	121.24 E
Chiapa	248	19.32 S	69.13 W
Chiapa de Corzo	234	16.42 N	93.00 W
Chiapaot'ai	100	24.11 N	121.00 E
Chiapas □[3]	232	16.30 N	92.30 W
Chiaramonte Gulfi	70	37.02 N	14.42 E
Chiaramonti	71	40.45 N	8.49 E
Chiaravalle	66	43.36 N	13.19 E
Chiaravalle Centrale	68	38.41 N	16.25 E
Chiareggio	64	46.19 N	9.47 E
Chiari	62	45.32 N	9.56 E
Chiaromonte	68	40.07 N	16.13 E
Chiasso	58	45.50 N	9.01 E
Chiautla de Tapia	234	18.17 N	98.36 W
Chiautzingo	234	19.12 N	98.28 W
Chiavari	62	44.19 N	9.19 E
Chiavenna	58	46.19 N	9.24 E
Chiawelo	273d	26.17 S	27.52 E
Chiba	94	35.36 N	140.07 E
Chiba □[5]	94	35.30 N	140.20 E
Chibabava	156	20.19 S	33.39 E
Chiba-kō c	268	35.35 N	140.06 E
Chibakou	100	29.36 N	113.01 E
Chibango	152	13.38 S	21.56 E
Chiba University ʋ[2]	268	35.38 N	140.06 E
Chibemba	152	15.45 S	14.05 E
Chibi	154	20.19 S	30.30 E
Chibia	152	15.11 S	13.41 E
Chibouet ≃	206	45.47 N	72.52 W
Chibougamau	176	49.55 N	74.22 W
Chibuto	156	24.44 S	33.33 E
Chibuzhangchu Hu ⊜	120	33.25 N	90.15 E
Chibwe	154	14.12 S	28.31 E
Chicago, Il., U.S.	216	41.51 N	87.39 W
Chicago, Il., U.S.	278	41.51 N	87.39 W
Chicago, North Branch ≃	216	41.53 N	87.38 W
Chicago, North Branch, West Fork ≃	278	42.03 N	87.54 W
Chicago, South Branch ≃	278	41.53 N	87.38 W
Chicago, University of ʋ[2]	278	41.47 N	87.36 W
Chicago Botanic Garden ♦	278	42.09 N	87.47 W
Chicago Harbor c	278	41.53 N	87.37 W
Chicago Heights	216	41.30 N	87.38 W
Chicago-Hinsdale Airport ⊠	278	41.46 N	87.56 W
Chicago Lawn ◆[8]	278	41.47 N	87.41 W
Chicago-Midway Airport ⊠	216	41.47 N	87.45 W
Chicago-O'Hare International Airport ⊠	278	41.59 N	87.54 W
Chicago Park	226	39.09 N	120.58 W
Chicago Portage National Historic Site ⊥	278	41.48 N	87.49 W
Chicago Ridge	216	41.42 N	87.46 W
Chicago Sanitary and Ship Canal ≚	216	41.32 N	88.05 W
Chicago Stadium ♦	278	41.53 N	87.40 W
Chicama ≃	248	7.56 S	79.17 W
Chicamacomico ≃	208	38.26 N	75.59 W
Chicamba, Barragem de ◆[6]	156	19.08 S	33.00 E
Chicapa ≃	152	6.26 S	20.47 E
Chicayán ≃	234	21.59 N	94.06 W
Chic-Chocs, Monts ⋏	186	48.55 N	66.00 W
Chichagof Island I	180	57.30 N	135.30 W
Chichas, Cordillera de ⋏	248	21.00 S	66.20 W
Chīchāwatni	123	30.32 N	72.42 E
Chiché ≃	250	8.15 S	53.30 W
Chicheng	98	40.54 N	115.46 E
Chichén Itzá ⊥	232	20.40 N	88.35 W
Chichester, Eng., U.K.	42	50.50 N	0.48 W
Chichester, N.Y., U.S.	210	42.06 N	74.19 W
Chichester Range ⋏	162	22.00 S	118.50 E
Chichi	100	23.50 N	120.47 E
Chichibu	94	35.59 N	139.05 E
Chichibu-Tama-kokuritsu-kōen ♦	94	35.52 N	139.00 E
Chichica	236	8.22 N	81.40 W
Chichicastenango	236	14.56 N	91.07 W
Chichigalpa	236	12.34 N	87.02 W
Chichigapa	234	17.47 N	94.25 W
Ch'ich'ihaerh → Qiqihar	89	47.19 N	123.55 E
Chichihualco	234	17.41 N	99.39 W
Chichijima-rettō II	14	27.06 N	142.12 E
Chichimilá	232	20.37 N	88.13 W
Chichiriviche	246	10.56 N	68.16 W
Chicholi	124	22.01 N	77.40 E
Chichra	126	22.19 N	86.53 E
Chickahominy ≃	208	37.14 N	76.53 W
Chickaloon	180	61.48 N	148.28 W
Chickamauga	192	34.52 N	85.17 W
Chickamauga Lake ⊜[1]	192	35.22 N	85.02 W
Chickamin ≃	182	55.47 N	130.58 W
Chickasaw, Al., U.S.	194	30.45 N	88.04 W
Chickasaw, Oh., U.S.	216	40.26 N	84.30 W
Chickasaw Bogue ≃	194	32.17 N	87.55 W
Chickasawhatchie Creek ≃	192	31.19 N	84.29 W
Chickasawhay ≃	194	31.00 N	88.45 W
Chickasaw National Recreation Area ♦	196	34.25 N	96.59 W
Chickasha	196	35.03 N	97.56 W
Chicken	180	64.04 N	141.56 W
Chicken Brook ≃	283	42.08 N	71.25 W
Chickerell	42	50.37 N	2.30 W
Chickies Creek ≃	208	40.03 N	76.32 W
Chiclana de la Frontera	34	36.25 N	6.08 W
Chiclayo	248	6.46 S	79.51 W
Chico, Ca., U.S.	204	39.43 N	121.50 W
Chico, Tx., U.S.	196	33.17 N	97.47 W
Chico, Wa., U.S.	224	47.36 N	122.42 W
Chico ≃, Arg.	254	43.48 S	66.25 W
Chico ≃, Arg.	254	42.25 S	70.30 W
Chico ≃, Arg.	254	49.56 S	68.32 W
Chico ≃, Cuba	286b	23.02 N	82.17 W
Chico ≃, Pan.	236	8.20 N	80.28 W
Chico ≃, Pil.	116	17.58 N	121.36 E
Chico ≃, S.A.	254	51.40 S	69.09 W
Chicoasén, Presa ⊜[1]	234	16.55 N	93.05 W
Chicobi, Lac ⊜	190	48.53 N	78.30 W
Chico Creek ≃	198	38.15 N	104.20 W
Chicolete Creek ≃	222	29.05 N	96.49 W
Chicomba	152	14.09 S	14.57 E
Chicomo	156	24.31 S	34.17 E
Chicomuselo	232	15.46 N	92.16 W
Chiconautla, Cerro ʌ	286a	19.39 N	98.58 W
Chiconono	154	12.56 S	35.43 E
Chicontepec de Tejeda	234	20.58 N	98.10 W
Chicopee, Ga., U.S.	192	34.15 N	83.50 W
Chicopee, Ma., U.S.	207	42.08 N	72.36 W
Chicopee ≃	207	42.09 N	72.37 W
Chicora	214	40.56 N	79.44 W
Chicot, Lake ⊜	194	33.20 N	91.14 W
Chicot, Rivière du ≃	275a	45.35 N	73.51 W
Chicot State Park ♦	194	30.47 N	92.19 W
Chicoutimi	186	48.26 N	71.04 W
Chicoutimi ≃	186	48.26 N	71.05 W
Chicoutimi, Réserve ♦	186	48.30 N	70.15 W
Chicú, Cerro ʌ	236	8.35 N	80.51 W
Chicualoque	234	20.23 N	97.39 W
Chicuma	152	13.23 S	14.51 E
Chicxulub	232	21.08 N	89.31 W
Chidambaram	122	11.24 N	79.42 E
Chiddingfold	42	51.06 N	0.37 W
Chiddingstone Causeway	260	51.12 N	0.10 E
Chidenguele	156	24.54 S	34.13 E
Chidlow	168a	31.52 S	116.14 E
Chi-do I	98	35.04 N	126.13 E
Chidralada Palace ʋ	269a	13.46 N	100.32 E
Chief	222	32.33 N	96.10 W
Chief Justice William Cushing Memorial State Park ♦	283	42.10 N	70.45 W
Chiefland	192	29.28 N	82.51 W
Chiefs Point ›	212	44.42 N	81.18 W
Chief's Point Indian Reserve ◆[4]	212	44.41 N	81.17 W
Chiehyang → Jieyang	100	23.35 N	116.21 E
Chiemgauer Alpen ⋏	64	47.40 N	12.30 E
Chiemsee ⊜	64	47.54 N	12.29 E
Chien, Bayou de ≃	194	36.35 N	89.11 W
Chienes (Kiens)	64	46.48 N	11.50 E
Chiengi	154	8.39 S	29.10 E
Chiengo	152	13.20 S	21.55 E
Chiens, Rivière aux ≃	275a	45.39 N	73.46 W
Chienti ≃	66	43.18 N	13.45 E
Chieo Lan Reservoir ⊜[1]	110	9.00 N	98.45 E
Chieri	62	45.01 N	7.49 E
Chiers ≃	56	49.39 N	5.00 E
Chiesa in Valmalenco	64	46.16 N	9.51 E
Chiese ≃	64	45.08 N	10.25 E
Chieti	66	42.21 N	14.10 E
Chieti □[4]	66	42.07 N	14.21 E
Chietla	234	18.31 N	98.35 W
Chieuti	68	41.51 N	15.10 E
Chieveley	42	51.27 N	1.19 W
Chièvres	50	50.35 N	3.48 E
Chifeng (Ulanhad)	98	42.18 N	119.00 E
Chigasaki	94	35.19 N	139.24 E
Chiginagak, Mount ʌ	180	57.08 N	156.59 W
Chigmit Mountains ⋏	180	60.00 N	153.00 W
Chignahuapan	234	19.50 N	98.02 W
Chignall Saint James	260	51.46 N	0.25 E
Chignall Smealy	260	51.47 N	0.25 E
Chignecto, Cape ›	186	45.20 N	64.57 W
Chignecto Bay c	186	45.35 N	64.45 W
Chignik	180	56.18 N	158.23 W
Chignik Bay c	180	56.22 N	158.15 W
Chignik Lagoon	180	56.21 N	158.31 W
Chignik Lake	180	56.15 N	158.45 W
Chignolo Po	62	45.09 N	9.29 E
Chigombe ≃	156	23.26 S	33.19 E
Chigorodó	246	7.41 N	76.42 W
Chigu	100	27.34 N	114.40 E
Chigubo	156	22.50 S	33.34 E
Chigu Co ⊜	120	28.40 N	91.45 E
Chigwell	260	51.38 N	0.05 E
Chigwell Row	260	51.37 N	0.07 E
Chigyŏng	98	39.51 N	127.26 E
Chihaya-akasaka	270	34.24 N	135.38 E
Chihaya Castle ⊥	270	34.24 N	135.40 E
Chihe	100	32.32 N	117.58 E
Ch'ihfeng → Chifeng	98	42.18 N	119.00 E
Chihli, Gulf of → Bo Hai c	98	38.30 N	120.00 E
Chihpen	100	22.42 N	121.02 E
Ch'ihshang	100	23.07 N	121.12 E
Chihsi → Jixi	89	45.17 N	130.59 E
Ch'ihsing Shan ʌ, T'aiwan	100	25.10 N	121.33 E
Ch'ihsing Shan ʌ, T'aiwan	269d	25.10 N	121.33 E
Ch'ihsing Yen I	100	21.46 N	120.49 E
Chihtungtsun	100	22.44 N	120.14 E
Chihu	100	24.07 N	117.51 E
Chihuahua	232	28.38 N	106.05 W
Chihuahua □[3]	232	28.30 N	106.00 W
Chihuahuan Desert ◆[2]	16	35.00 N	106.00 W
Chii-san ʌ	98	35.20 N	127.44 E
Chii-san Kukrip Kongwŏn ♦	98	35.20 N	127.39 E
Chiitola	26	61.16 N	29.38 E
Chikaskia ≃	196	36.37 N	97.15 W
Chik Ballāpur	122	13.28 N	77.44 E
Chikhli	122	20.21 N	76.15 E
Chikindzonot	232	20.20 N	88.29 W
Chikmagalūr	122	13.19 N	75.47 E
Chiknai ≃	126	24.06 N	89.17 E
Chiknāyakanhalli	122	13.26 N	76.37 E
Chikoa	154	13.24 S	32.07 E
Chikodi	122	16.26 N	74.36 E
Chikou	100	30.44 N	117.32 E
Chikrêng ≃	110	12.51 N	104.14 E
Ch'iku	100	23.08 N	120.07 E
Chikugo	96	33.12 N	130.30 E
Chikugo ≃	92	33.09 N	130.21 E
Chikujō-kichi, Kōkū-jieitai- ■	96	33.41 N	131.03 E
Chikuma ≃	94	36.59 N	138.35 E
Chikuminuk Lake ⊜	180	60.14 N	159.00 W
Chikura	94	34.57 N	139.57 E
Chikusa	96	35.09 N	134.26 E
Chikusa ≃	96	34.44 N	134.24 E
Chikushino	96	33.29 N	130.31 E
Chikwawa	154	16.03 S	34.48 E
Chi-kyaw	110	20.17 N	93.54 E
Chikyu-misaki ›	92a	42.18 N	141.00 E
Chila	152	12.04 S	14.29 E
Chilacachapa	234	18.17 N	99.43 W
Chilakalūrupet	122	16.05 N	80.10 E
Chilako ≃	182	53.54 N	122.59 W
Chilam Chauki	123	35.03 N	75.07 E
Chilanga	154	15.34 S	28.17 E
Chilanko Forks	182	52.06 N	124.10 W
Chilapa de Álvarez	234	17.36 N	99.10 W
Chilās	123	35.26 N	74.05 E
Chilaw	122	7.34 N	79.47 E
Chilca, Perú	248	12.32 S	76.44 W
Chilca, Perú	248	12.09 S	75.11 W
Chilca, Punta ›	248	12.27 S	76.48 W
Chilchota	234	19.51 N	102.08 W
Chilcotin ≃	182	51.45 N	122.24 W
Chilcott Island I	166	16.58 S	149.58 E
Childers	166	25.14 S	152.17 E
Childersburg	194	33.16 N	86.21 W
Childer Thornton	262	53.17 N	2.57 W
Childress	196	34.25 N	100.12 W
Childs	210	41.34 N	75.32 W
Chile □[1]	244	30.00 S	71.00 W
Chile, Hipódromo ♦	286e	33.24 S	70.41 W
Chile, Universidad de ʋ[2]	286e	33.27 S	70.40 W
Chile Basin ✣[1]	18	33.00 S	80.00 W
Chile Chico	254	46.33 S	71.44 W
Chilecito, Arg.	252	29.10 S	67.30 W
Chilecito, Arg.	252	33.53 S	69.03 W
Chilengue, Serra do ⋏	152	13.10 S	15.18 E
Chileno, Arroyo ≃, Ur.	258	33.55 S	58.08 W
Chileno, Arroyo ≃, Ur.	288	34.22 S	57.54 W
Chile Rise ✣[3]	18	40.00 S	90.00 W
Chilete	248	7.14 S	78.51 W
Chilham	42	51.15 N	0.57 E
Chilhowie	192	36.47 N	81.40 W
Chili	216	40.52 N	86.02 W
Chili ≃	248	16.23 S	71.46 W
Chili, Ouadi V	146	16.44 N	20.53 E
Chilia, Brațul ≃[1]	78	45.18 N	29.40 E
Chili Center	210	43.06 N	77.44 W
Chili → Chile □[1]	244	30.00 S	71.00 W
Chilika Lake ⊜	122	19.45 N	85.25 E
Chililabombwe (Bancroft)	154	12.18 S	27.43 E
Chilingchang	107	28.58 N	105.31 E
Chilin → Jilin	89	43.51 N	126.33 E
Chilivani	71	40.36 N	8.56 E
Chilkat Pass)(	180	59.43 N	136.35 W
Chilko ≃	182	52.08 N	123.30 W
Chilko Lake ⊜	182	51.20 N	124.05 W
Chilko Lake Indian Reserve ◆[4]	182	51.25 N	124.07 W
Chillagoe	166	17.09 S	144.32 E
Chillán	252	36.36 S	72.07 W
Chillar	252	37.18 S	59.59 W
Chilla Saroda ◆[8]	272a	28.36 N	77.18 E
Chillicothe, Il., U.S.	190	40.55 N	89.29 W
Chillicothe, Mo., U.S.	194	39.47 N	93.33 W
Chillicothe, Oh., U.S.	218	39.19 N	82.58 W
Chillicothe, Tx., U.S.	196	34.15 N	99.30 W
Chilliwack	224	49.10 N	121.57 W
Chilliwack ≃	224	49.05 N	121.57 W
Chilliwack Lake ⊜	224	49.03 N	121.25 W
Chillón	286d	11.55 S	77.05 W
Chillón ≃	248	11.57 S	77.09 W
Chillon, Château de ⊥	58	46.25 N	6.56 E
Chillum	284c	38.58 N	76.59 W
Chilly	84	39.25 N	49.05 E
Chilly-Mazarin	261	48.42 N	2.19 E
Chilmāri	124	25.33 N	89.43 E
Chilmark	207	41.20 N	70.44 W
Chilo	218	38.48 N	84.08 W
Chiloane, Ilha I	156	20.40 S	34.55 E
Chiloé, Isla Grande de I	254	42.30 S	73.55 W
Chilok	88	51.21 N	110.28 E
Chilok ≃	88	51.19 N	106.59 E
Chilón	232	17.14 N	92.25 W
Chilonga	154	12.03 S	31.21 E
Chilongo	152	13.55 S	16.35 E
Chiloquin	202	42.34 N	121.51 W
Chilovo	76	57.46 N	29.23 E
Chilpancingo de los Bravo	234	17.33 N	99.30 W
Chilpi	124	22.15 N	81.33 E
Chilston Park ♦	260	51.12 N	0.42 E
Chiltern □[8]	260	51.40 N	0.37 W
Chiltern Hills ⋏[2]	42	51.42 N	0.48 W
Chilton, Eng., U.K.	44	54.39 N	1.33 W
Chilton, Tx., U.S.	222	31.16 N	97.03 W
Chilton, Wi., U.S.	190	44.01 N	88.09 W
Chiluage	152	9.30 S	21.47 E
Chilubula Mission	154	10.09 S	31.00 E
Chilumba	154	10.28 S	34.12 E
Chilung	100	25.08 N	121.44 E
Chilung ≃	269d	25.07 N	121.27 E
Chilung Kang c	269d	25.09 N	121.45 E
Chilung Shih □[7]	269d	25.08 N	121.45 E
Chiluvya	154	12.18 S	34.01 E
Chilwa, Lake ⊜	154	15.12 S	35.50 E
Chilwell	169	38.10 S	144.21 E
Chimaco	152	15.12 S	21.56 E
Chimacum	224	48.00 N	122.46 W
Chimacum Creek ≃	224	48.03 N	122.45 W
Chimakela	152	15.24 S	16.58 E
Chimaltenango	236	14.40 N	90.49 W
Chimaltenango □[5]	236	14.40 N	90.55 W
Chimaltitán	234	21.46 N	103.50 W
Chimán	246	8.42 N	78.37 W
Chimanimani National Park ♦	154	19.48 S	33.56 E
Chimay	50	50.03 N	4.19 E
Chimayo	200	36.00 N	105.55 W
Chimbarongo	252	34.42 S	71.03 W
Chimbas	252	31.29 S	68.32 W
Chimborazo □[4]	246	2.00 S	78.40 W
Chimborazo ʌ	236	13.05 N	85.58 W
Chimborazo ʌ[1]	246	1.28 S	78.48 W
Chimbote	248	9.05 S	78.36 W
Chimbu □[5]	164	6.05 S	145.00 E
Chimbua	152	16.32 S	15.08 E
Ch'imei Yü I	100	23.13 N	119.26 E
Chimichagua	246	9.15 N	73.49 W
Chimkent → Čimkent	85	42.18 N	69.36 E
Chimki	82	55.54 N	37.26 E
Chimki-Chovrino ◆[8]	265b	55.51 N	37.30 E
Chimkinskoje vodochranilišče ⊜[1]	265b	55.51 N	37.28 E
Chimney Reservoir ⊜[1]	204	41.25 N	117.10 W
Chimney Rock National Historic Site ♦	198	41.39 N	103.20 W
Chimoio	156	19.08 S	33.29 E
Chimon Island I	276	41.04 N	73.23 W
Chimpay	252	39.10 S	66.09 W
Chimpembe	154	9.31 S	29.33 E
Chimpôro ≃	152	17.20 S	17.17 E
Chin □[8]	110	22.00 N	93.30 E
China, Méx.	232	25.42 N	99.14 W
Chinā, Nihon	174m	26.24 N	127.46 E
China (Zhongguo) □[1]	90	35.00 N	105.00 E
China, Tanjong ›	271c	1.14 N	103.51 E
Chinácota	246	7.37 N	72.36 W
China Grove	192	35.34 N	80.34 W
China Lake ⊜	204	35.46 N	117.39 W
China Lake Naval Weapons Center ■	204	35.35 N	117.10 W
Chinameca	236	13.30 N	88.21 W
China Meridional, Mar de → South China Sea ⍑[2]	108	10.00 N	113.00 E
Chinan	98	35.48 N	127.25 E
Chinandega	236	12.37 N	87.09 W
Chinandega □[5]	236	12.45 N	87.05 W
Chinan → Jinan	98	36.40 N	116.57 E
China Spring	222	31.39 N	97.18 W
Chinati Peak ʌ	196	29.57 N	104.29 W
Chinatown ◆[8]	282	37.48 N	122.26 W
Chincha Alta	248	13.27 S	76.08 W
Chinchaga ≃	176	58.50 N	118.20 W
Chincheros	248	13.27 S	73.44 W
Chinchiang → Quanzhou	100	24.54 N	118.35 E
Chinchilla, Austl.	166	26.45 S	150.38 E
Chinchilla, Pa., U.S.	210	41.28 N	75.41 W
Chinchiná	246	4.58 N	75.36 W
Chincholi	272c	19.10 N	73.08 E
Chinchón, Esp.	34	40.08 N	3.25 W
Chinch'ŏn, Taehan	98	36.52 N	127.26 E
Chinchorro, Banco ✣[4]	232	18.35 N	87.22 W
Chinchou → Jinzhou	104	41.07 N	121.08 E
Chincilla de Monte Aragón	34	38.55 N	1.43 W
Chincolco	252	32.13 S	70.50 W
Chincoteague	208	37.55 N	75.22 W
Chincoteague Bay c	208	38.06 N	75.15 W
Chincoteague Inlet c	208	37.53 N	75.25 W
Chinde	156	18.37 S	36.24 E
Chindo	98	34.28 N	126.15 E
Chin-do I	98	34.25 N	126.15 E
Chindong	98	35.07 N	128.29 E
Chindwinn ≃	110	21.26 N	95.15 E
Chine (la République populaire de) → China □[1], Asia	90	35.00 N	105.00 E
Chine (nationaliste) → Taiwan □[1], Asia	100	23.30 N	121.00 E
Chinen	174m	26.09 N	127.49 E
Chineni	123	33.02 N	75.17 E
Chine Orientale, Mer de → East China Sea ⍑[2]	90	30.00 N	126.00 E
Chinese Camp	226	37.52 N	120.26 W
Chinese Cemetery ◆	269f	14.38 N	120.59 E
Chinese University ʋ[2]	271d	22.26 N	114.12 E
Chingamba	152	12.49 S	18.20 E
Chingansk	89	49.07 N	131.11 E
Chingarora Creek ≃	276	40.27 N	74.12 W
Ch'ingchiang → Qingjiang	100	33.35 N	119.02 E
Chingford ◆[8]	260	51.38 N	0.01 E
Chingleput	122	12.42 N	79.59 E
Chingmei ◆[8]	269d	24.59 N	121.32 E
Chingola	154	12.32 S	27.52 E
Chingoni	157a	12.48 S	45.08 E
Chingoroi	152	13.37 S	14.01 E
Chingshih → Jinshi	102	29.39 N	111.52 E
Ch'ingtao → Qingdao	98	36.06 N	120.19 E
Chingtechen → Jingdezhen	100	29.16 N	117.11 E
Ch'ingt'ung	269d	25.02 N	121.43 E
Chinguar	152	12.36 S	16.20 E
Chinguetti	150	20.27 N	12.22 W
Chingune	156	20.38 S	34.55 E
Chinhae	98	35.09 N	128.40 E
Chinhae-man c	98	35.01 N	128.34 E
Chin Hills ⋏[2]	110	22.30 N	93.30 E
Chinhoyi	154	17.22 S	30.12 E
Chinhsien → Jinxian	98	39.04 N	121.40 E
Chinhua → Jinhua	100	29.07 N	119.39 E
Ch'inhuangtao → Qinhuangdao	98	39.56 N	119.36 E
Chīni	120	31.32 N	78.15 E
Chiniak, Cape ›	180	57.36 N	152.08 W
Chining → Jining, Zhg.	98	35.25 N	116.36 E
Chining → Jining, Zhg.	102	40.57 N	113.02 E
Chiniot	123	31.43 N	72.59 E
Chinit ≃	110	12.55 N	105.35 E
Chinitna Point ›	180	59.43 N	153.02 W
Chinizíua	156	19.00 S	35.09 E
Chinjan	120	30.34 N	67.58 E
Chinju	98	35.11 N	128.05 E
Chinkiang → Zhenjiang	106	32.13 N	119.26 E
Chinko ≃	136	4.50 N	23.53 E
Chinkuashih	100	25.07 N	121.51 E
Chin Lakes ⊜	182	49.37 N	112.13 W
Chinle	200	36.09 N	109.33 W
Chinle Creek ≃	200	37.12 N	109.43 W
Chinle Wash V	200	36.54 N	109.45 W
Chinley	262	53.20 N	1.56 W
Chinley Churn ʌ[2]	262	53.21 N	1.57 W
Chinmen	100	24.27 N	118.21 E
Chinmen Tao I	100	24.27 N	118.23 E
Chinnampo → Namp'o	98	38.45 N	125.23 E
Chinnor	42	51.43 N	0.56 W
Chino, Nihon	94	35.59 N	138.09 E
Chino, Ca., U.S.	228	34.00 N	117.41 W
Chino Airport ⊠	280	33.59 N	117.38 W
Chino Creek ≃	280	33.53 N	117.38 W
Chino Hills ⋏[2]	280	33.56 N	117.45 W
Chinon	50	47.10 N	0.15 E
Chinook, Ab., Can.	184	51.27 N	110.56 W
Chinook, Mt., U.S.	202	48.35 N	109.13 W
Chinook, Wa., U.S.	224	46.16 N	123.56 W
Chinook Cove	182	51.14 N	120.10 W
Chino Valley	200	34.45 N	112.27 W
Chinowths Corner	226	36.20 N	119.19 W
Chinpāi	126	23.50 N	87.28 E
Chinquapin	192	34.49 N	77.49 W
Chinsali	154	10.34 S	32.03 E
Chinshan	100	25.13 N	121.38 E
Chinshui	100	24.36 N	120.53 E
Chintāmani	122	13.24 N	78.04 E
Chintembwe	154	13.25 S	33.59 E
Chintheche	154	11.52 S	34.09 E
Chinú	246	9.06 N	75.24 W
Chinunje	154	11.19 S	37.19 E
Chinwangtao → Qinhuangdao	98	39.56 N	119.36 E
Chiny	56	49.44 N	5.20 E
Chinyama Litapi	152	13.31 S	22.21 E
Chioco	154	16.25 S	32.50 E
Chioggia	64	45.13 N	12.17 E
Chiomonte	62	45.07 N	6.59 E
Chios → Khíos	38	38.22 N	26.08 E
Chios → Khíos I	38	38.22 N	26.00 E
Chipamanu (Xipamanu) ≃	248	10.43 S	67.50 W
Chipao	248	14.15 S	73.57 W
Chipata (Fort Jameson)	154	13.39 S	32.40 E
Chipei Tao I	100	23.45 N	119.37 E
Chipera	154	15.28 S	32.30 E
Chiperone ʌ	154	16.28 S	35.12 E
Chipili	154	10.44 S	29.04 E
Chiping	98	36.37 N	116.16 E
Chipinge	154	20.12 S	32.38 E
Chip Lake ⊜	182	53.40 N	115.20 W
Chipley	194	30.46 N	85.32 W
Chiplūn	122	17.32 N	73.31 E
Chipman	186	46.11 N	65.53 W
Chipogolo	154	6.52 S	36.02 E
Chipoka	154	14.00 S	34.31 E
Chipola ≃	192	30.01 N	85.05 W
Chippawa ◆[8]	284a	43.04 N	79.03 W
Chippawa Channel ≃[1]	284a	43.04 N	79.01 W
Chippego Lake ⊜	212	44.34 N	76.49 W
Chippenham	42	51.28 N	2.07 W
Chipperfield	260	51.42 N	0.29 W
Chippewa ≃, Mi., U.S.	190	43.35 N	84.17 W
Chippewa ≃, Mn., U.S.	198	44.56 N	95.44 W
Chippewa ≃, Wi., U.S.	190	44.25 N	92.10 W
Chippewa, East Branch ≃	198	45.20 N	95.36 W
Chippewa, East Fork ≃	190	45.53 N	91.05 W
Chippewa, Lake ⊜	190	45.56 N	91.13 W
Chippewa Bay c	212	44.27 N	75.47 W
Chippewa Creek ≃	212	44.27 N	75.46 W
Chippewa Falls	190	44.56 N	91.23 W
Chippewa Lake	214	41.04 N	81.54 W
Chippewanuck Creek ≃	216	41.07 N	86.12 W
Chipping Campden	42	52.03 N	1.46 W
Chipping Norton	42	51.56 N	1.32 W
Chipping Ongar	260	51.43 N	0.15 E
Chipping Sodbury	42	51.33 N	2.24 W
Chippis	58	46.17 N	7.33 E
Chippokes Plantation State Park ♦	208	37.08 N	76.44 W
Chipps Island I	282	38.03 N	121.55 W
Chipre → Cyprus □[1]	130	35.00 N	33.00 E
Chipstead, Eng., U.K.	260	51.17 N	0.09 E
Chipstead, Eng., U.K.	260	51.18 N	0.10 W
Chipuriro	154	16.39 S	30.42 E
Chiquelequele	152	16.40 S	19.06 E
Chiquián	248	10.09 S	77.11 W
Chiquihuitlán	234	17.59 N	96.48 W
Chiquimula	236	14.48 N	89.33 W
Chiquimula □[5]	236	14.40 N	89.25 W
Chiquimulilla	236	14.05 N	90.23 W
Chiquinquirá	246	5.37 N	73.50 W
Chiquintirca	248	13.09 S	73.41 W
Chiquita	152	8.38 S	17.05 E
Chiquito ≃	234	18.29 N	101.07 W
Chiquito Creek ≃	226	37.20 N	119.20 W
Chira ≃	246	4.54 S	81.08 W
Chira, Isla I	236	10.06 N	85.09 W
Chirad	272c	19.09 N	73.07 E
Chiradzulu	154	15.42 S	35.10 E
Chirāgh Delhi ◆[8]	272a	28.32 N	77.14 E
Chīrāla	122	15.49 N	80.21 E
Chiramba	154	16.55 S	34.39 E
Chirape	156	21.18 S	33.33 E
Chirāwa	120	28.15 N	75.38 E
Chirchik → Čirčik	85	41.29 N	69.35 E
Chire (Shire) ≃	154	17.42 S	35.19 E
Chiredzi	154	21.03 S	31.45 E
Chireno	194	31.30 N	94.21 W
Chirens	62	45.25 N	5.33 E
Chirfa	146	20.57 N	12.21 E
Chīrgaon	124	25.35 N	78.49 E
Chiriaco ≃	248	5.05 S	78.19 W
Chiricahua Mountains ⋏	200	31.50 N	109.15 W
Chiricahua National Monument ♦	200	32.02 N	109.19 W
Chiricahua Peak ʌ	200	31.52 N	109.20 W
Chiriguaná	246	9.22 N	73.36 W
Chirikof Island I	180	55.50 N	155.35 W
Chirilagua	236	13.13 N	88.08 W
Chirinos	248	5.16 S	78.52 W
Chiriquí	236	8.24 N	82.19 W
Chiriquí □[4]	236	8.30 N	82.00 W
Chiriquí, Golfo de c	246	8.00 N	82.20 W
Chiriquí, Laguna de c	236	9.03 N	82.00 W
Chiriquí Grande	236	8.57 N	82.07 W
Chiriquí Viejo ≃	236	8.20 N	82.41 W
Chirk	42	52.56 N	3.03 W
Chirki	126	24.03 N	86.09 E
Chirle	272c	18.56 N	73.02 E
Chirmiri	124	23.12 N	82.21 E
Chirnside	46	55.48 N	2.13 W
Chiromo	154	16.33 S	35.08 E
Chirovo	76	58.56 N	33.24 E
Chirripó ≃	236	10.41 N	83.41 W
Chirripó, Cerro ʌ	236	9.29 N	83.30 W
Chirripó, Parque Nacional ♦	236	9.30 N	83.30 W
Chirsa	84	41.31 N	46.06 E
Chirundu	154	15.59 S	28.54 E
Chirvosti	265a	59.57 N	30.37 E
Chiryū	94	35.00 N	137.02 E
Chisago City	190	45.22 N	92.53 W
Chisamba	154	14.58 S	28.23 E
Chisana	180	62.09 N	142.10 W
Chisasibi	176	53.50 N	79.00 W
Chiscas	246	6.33 N	72.29 W
Chisec	236	15.49 N	90.17 W
Chiseldon	42	51.31 N	1.44 W
Chisenga	154	9.56 S	33.26 E
Chisep'o	98	34.50 N	128.42 E
Ch'ishan	100	22.53 N	120.28 E
Chishanji	98	36.56 N	122.23 E
Chishi	100	27.42 N	117.58 E
Chishisi	100	25.32 N	113.11 E
Chisholm, Al., U.S.	194	32.25 N	86.15 W
Chisholm, Me., U.S.	188	44.28 N	70.12 W
Chisholm, Mn., U.S.	190	47.29 N	92.53 W
Chisholm, Tx., U.S.	222	32.51 N	96.22 W
Chisholm Mills	182	54.55 N	114.08 W
Chishtiān Mandi	123	29.48 N	72.52 E
Chishui	102	28.29 N	105.38 E
Chishui ≃, Zhg.	102	28.53 N	105.48 E
Chishui ≃, Zhg.	107	28.49 N	105.50 E
Chishuihe	102	27.50 N	105.32 E
Chišig-Öndör	88	48.19 N	103.25 E
Chisimaio → Kismaayo	144	0.22 N	42.32 E
Chișinău → Kišin'ov	78	47.00 N	28.50 E
Chișineu-Criș	38	46.31 N	21.31 E
Chislaviči	76	54.11 N	32.10 E
Chislehurst ◆[8]	260	51.25 N	0.04 E
Chisone ≃	62	44.49 N	7.25 E
Chisone, Valle del V	62	45.01 N	7.07 E
Chisos Mountains ⋏	196	29.15 N	103.20 W
Chisseaux	50	47.20 N	1.05 E
Chissengue	152	9.14 S	20.42 E
Chissilo	152	13.34 S	16.30 E
Chistochina	180	62.34 N	144.40 W
Chistopol → Čistopol'	80	55.21 N	50.37 E
Chiswellgreen	260	51.44 N	0.22 W
Chiswick ◆[8]	260	51.29 N	0.16 W
Chita, Bol.	248	20.06 S	66.57 W
Chita, Col.	246	6.11 N	72.28 W
Chita, Nihon	94	35.00 N	136.51 E
Chita → Čita	88	52.03 N	113.30 E
Chitado	152	17.20 S	13.54 E
Chitagá	246	7.09 N	72.40 W
Chita-hantō ›[1]	94	34.50 N	136.53 E
Chitambo	154	12.55 S	30.39 E
Chitanda ≃	152	16.01 S	15.12 E
Chitarda	126	21.50 N	86.57 E
Chitata	152	13.47 S	15.43 E
Chitato	152	7.20 S	20.47 E
Chita-wan c	94	34.47 N	136.58 E
Chitek ≃	184	54.06 N	108.16 W
Chitek Lake ⊜, Mb., Can.	184	52.26 N	99.25 W
Chitek Lake ⊜, Sk., Can.	184	53.44 N	107.47 W
Chitembo	152	13.34 S	16.40 E
Chitina	180	61.31 N	144.27 W
Chitina ≃	180	61.30 N	144.28 W
Chitipa	154	9.43 S	33.16 E
Chitokoloki	152	13.50 S	23.13 E
Chitose	92a	42.49 N	141.39 E
Chitose-chūtonchi, Rikujō-jieitai- ■	92a	42.46 N	141.40 E
Chitou Shan I	100	27.40 N	120.50 E
Chitra ≃[1]	126	22.53 N	89.40 E
Chitradurga	122	14.14 N	76.24 E
Chitrakūt Dham	124	25.11 N	80.52 E
Chitrāl	123	35.51 N	71.47 E
Chitrasāli	272b	22.52 N	88.09 E
Chitrāvati ≃	122	14.48 N	78.14 E
Chitré	236	7.58 N	80.26 W
Chittagong	120	22.20 N	91.50 E
Chittagong □[5]	120	23.00 N	91.00 E
Chīttāpur	122	17.07 N	77.05 E

Symbol	English	Deutsch	Español	Français	Português
≃	River	Fluß	Río	Rivière	Rio
≚	Canal	Kanal	Canal	Canal	Canal
ʟ	Waterfall, Rapids	Wasserfall, Stromschnellen	Cascada, Rápidos	Chute d'eau, Rapides	Cascata, Rápidos
ʊ	Strait	Meeresstraße	Estrecho	Détroit	Estreito
c	Bay, Gulf	Bucht, Golf	Bahía, Golfo	Baie, Golfe	Baía, Golfo
⊜	Lake, Lakes	See, Seen	Lago, Lagos	Lac, Lacs	Lago, Lagos
⁝⁝	Swamp	Sumpf	Pantano	Marais	Pântano
⍓	Ice Features, Glacier	Eis- und Gletscherformen	Accidentes Glaciales	Formes glaciaires	Acidentes glaciares
⍑	Other Hydrographic Features	Andere Hydrographische Objekte	Otros Elementos Hidrográficos	Autres données hydrographiques	Outros acidentes hidrográficos
✣	Submarine Features	Untermeerische Objekte	Accidentes Submarinos	Formes de relief sous-marin	Acidentes submarinos
□	Political Unit	Politische Einheit	Unidad Politica	Entité politique	Unidade política
ʋ	Cultural Institution	Kulturelle Institution	Institución Cultural	Institution culturelle	Institução cultural
⊥	Historical Site	Historische Stätte	Sitio Histórico	Site historique	Sitio histórico
♦	Recreational Site	Erholungs- und Ferienort	Sitio de Recreo	Centre de loisirs	Area de Lazer
⊠	Airport	Flughafen	Aeropuerto	Aéroport	Aeroporto
■	Military Installation	Militäranlage	Instalación Militar	Installation militaire	Instalação militar
◆	Miscellaneous	Verschiedenes	Misceláneo	Divers	Diversos

Column 1

Name	Page	Lat.	Long.
Chittaranjan	126	23.52 N	86.52 E
Chittaurgarh	120	24.53 N	74.38 E
Chittenango	210	43.02 N	75.52 W
Chittenango Creek ≃	210	43.11 N	76.00 W
Chittenango Falls	210	42.59 N	75.50 W
Chittering	162	31.29 S	116.06 E
Chittoor	122	13.12 N	79.07 E
Chittur	122	10.42 N	76.45 E
Chittu, Ityo.	144	8.36 N	37.59 E
Ch'itu, T'aiwan	269d	25.06 N	121.43 E
Chitungwiza	154	17.45 S	31.16 E
Chiuchiang — Jiujiang	100	29.44 N	115.59 E
Chiuchiu	252	22.21 S	68.39 W
Chiuduno	62	45.40 N	9.51 E
Chiumbe	152	12.29 S	16.08 E
Chiumbe ≃	152	7.00 S	21.12 E
Chiúme	152	15.03 S	21.14 E
Chiuppano	64	45.46 N	11.28 E
Chiuro	64	46.10 N	9.59 E
Chiusa (Klausen)	64	46.38 N	11.34 E
Chiusa di Pesio	62	44.19 N	7.40 E
Chiusa di San Michele	62	45.06 N	7.19 E
Chiusaforte	64	46.24 N	13.18 E
Chiusa Sclafani	62	37.41 N	13.16 E
Chiusella ≃	62	45.24 N	7.55 E
Chiusi	66	43.01 N	11.57 E
Chiusi, Lago di ⊜	66	43.03 N	11.58 E
Chiuta, Lake ⊜	154	14.55 S	35.50 E
Chiv	84	41.46 N	47.54 E
Chiva	72	41.24 N	60.22 E
Chivacoa	248	10.10 N	68.54 W
Chivasso	62	45.11 N	7.53 E
Chivato, Punta ꭥ	232	27.05 N	111.59 W
Chivay	248	15.40 S	71.35 W
Chivhu	154	19.01 S	30.53 E
Chivilcoy	252	34.53 S	60.01 W
Chivirira Falls ᴗ	154	21.14 S	32.20 E
Chiwanda	154	11.22 S	34.54 E
Chiwawa	224	47.47 N	120.40 W
Chixi	100	28.22 N	116.22 E
Chixoy (Salinas) ≃	232	16.28 N	90.33 W
Chixoy, Embalse ⊜¹	236	15.55 N	90.30 W
Chiyoda, Nihon	94	36.12 N	139.26 E
Chiyoda, Nihon	94	36.11 N	140.14 E
Chiyoda, Nihon	96	34.41 N	132.32 E
Chiyoda ⚬⁸	268	35.41 N	139.44 E
Chizarira National Park ♦	154	17.45 S	28.00 E
Chizhen	100	31.55 N	118.12 E
Chizizhen	100	32.22 N	115.11 E
Chizu	96	35.16 N	134.14 E
Chjargas	88	49.30 N	93.48 E
Chjargas nuur ⊜	88	49.12 N	93.24 E
Chkalov — Orenburg	80	51.54 N	55.06 E
Chlebnikovo, Ross.	80	56.38 N	49.56 E
Chlebnikovo, Ross.	265b	55.58 N	37.31 E
Chlebodarnyj	80	46.41 N	40.50 E
Chlebodarovka	83	47.29 N	37.23 E
Chlevnoje	76	52.12 N	39.05 E
Chloride	200	35.24 N	114.11 W
Chlum	82	48.52 N	13.55 E
Chlum ∧	61	48.42 N	14.04 E
Chmelevicy	80	57.45 N	46.22 E
Chmelevoje	82	56.09 N	39.08 E
Chmelevoje	78	48.34 N	31.24 E
Chmelita	76	55.25 N	33.53 E
Chmel'nickij	78	49.25 N	27.00 E
Chmel'nik	78	49.33 N	27.57 E
Chmel'niki, Ross.	82	56.52 N	38.13 E
Chmel'niki, Ross.	82	56.53 N	38.39 E
Chmielnik	30	50.37 N	20.46 E
Chmost' ≃	76	54.34 N	32.34 E
Choa Chu Kang	271c	1.22 N	103.41 E
Choäli	272b	22.24 N	88.24 E
Chôâm Khsant	110	14.13 N	104.56 E
Choba	154	2.26 N	38.03 E
Chobe ⚬⁵	156	18.30 S	25.00 E
Chobe ≃	156	17.50 S	25.05 E
Chobeju	24	64.63 N	60.10 E
Chobe National Park ♦	156	18.45 S	24.15 E
Chobham	260	51.21 N	0.36 W
Chobham Common ♦	260	51.23 N	0.37 W
Chobi ≃	124	21.41 N	41.53 E
Chocamán	234	18.59 N	97.01 W
Choccolocco Creek ≃	194	33.33 N	86.11 W
Choceň	30	50.00 N	16.13 E
Chocenice	78	49.33 N	13.31 E
Chochis, Cerro ∧	248	16.04 S	60.03 W
Choch'iwŏn	98	36.37 N	127.18 E
Chochloma	80	56.58 N	43.54 E
Chöchmor't	98	47.21 N	94.33 E
Chochol'skij	78	51.34 N	38.45 E
Cho Chu	110	21.54 N	105.59 E
Chocianów	30	51.25 N	15.55 E
Chociwel	30	53.29 N	15.19 E
Chocó ⚬⁵	246	6.00 N	77.00 W
Chocolate Bay c	222	29.11 N	95.09 W
Chocolate Bayou ≃	222	29.13 N	95.13 W
Chocolate Mountains ∧	204	33.20 N	115.15 W
Chocontá	246	5.09 N	73.41 W
Chocope	248	7.47 S	79.13 W
Choctawhatchee, East Fork ≃	194	31.21 N	85.33 W
Choctawhatchee, West Fork ≃	194	31.21 N	85.33 W
Choctawhatchee Bay c	194	30.25 N	86.21 W
Choctaw Lake ⊜¹	218	30.58 N	83.29 W
Chocz	30	52.36 N	99.19 E
Chodaváram	122	17.50 N	82.57 E
Chodecz	92	52.24 N	19.01 E
Ch'o-do I, C.M.I.K.	98	38.32 N	124.50 E
Ch'o-do I, Taehan	98	34.14 N	127.15 E
Chodoi	114	22.50 N	103.48 E
Chodorov	24	49.24 N	24.17 E
Chodosy	78	56.34 N	31.29 E
Chodovaja Griva	80	57.08 N	50.16 E
Chodovaricha	46	68.57 N	53.40 E
Chodov	54	50.11 N	12.43 E
Chodžaderra	80	51.15 N	41.48 E
Chodžamet	32	38.38 N	76.13 W
Chodžakala	128	38.43 N	56.20 E
Chodželji	128	42.24 N	59.25 E
Chodzież	30	52.59 N	16.56 E
Choele-Choel	252	39.16 S	65.41 W
Chofombo	154	15.36 S	33.43 E
Chofu	98	34.39 N	139.33 E
Chofu Airport ⊠	268	35.40 N	139.32 E
Chogo Lungma Glacier ⧉	123	36.23 N	75.19 E
Chogot	88	53.15 N	105.52 E
Choiceland	178	53.30 N	104.28 W
Choichuft, Laga ⚬	154	1.34 N	39.24 E
Choire, Loch ⊜	46	58.13 N	4.21 W
Choisel	261	48.41 N	2.17 W
Choiseul I	175e	7.00 S	157.00 E
Choiseul Sound ᴗ	254	52.10 S	59.00 W
Choisy	261	49.05 N	2.55 E
Choisy-le-Roi	261	48.46 N	2.25 E
Choix	232	26.43 N	108.17 W
Chojna	30	52.58 N	14.28 E
Chojnice	30	53.42 N	17.34 E
Chojnów	30	51.17 N	15.56 E
Chōkai-san ∧	92	39.06 N	140.03 E
Choke ꭥ	95	10.58 S	121.33 E
Choke Canyon Lake	196	28.30 N	98.20 W
Chokio	198	45.34 N	96.10 W
Chokoloskee	220	25.48 N	81.21 W
Chokwé	156	24.36 S	33.00 E
Cholame	226	35.43 N	120.17 W
Cholame Creek ≃	226	35.43 N	120.22 W
Cholame Hills ꭥ²	226	35.45 N	120.30 W

Column 2

Name	Page	Lat.	Long.
Choldarkipčak	85	39.51 N	68.52 E
Cholet	32	47.04 N	0.53 W
Cholila	254	42.31 S	71.27 W
Chôlla Namdo ⚬⁴	98	34.45 N	127.00 E
Chôlla Pukdo ⚬⁴	98	35.45 N	127.15 E
Cholm	76	57.09 N	31.11 E
Cholmeč', Bela.	78	52.09 N	30.37 E
Cholmec, Ross.	76	56.34 N	33.21 E
Cholmogorovka	86	44.25 N	78.31 E
Cholmogorskaja	24	63.49 N	40.39 E
Cholmogory	24	64.15 N	41.40 E
Cholmsk	89	47.03 N	142.03 E
Cholmskij	82	44.50 N	38.24 E
Cholmy, Ross.	82	54.56 N	38.33 E
Cholmy, Ukr.	78	51.52 N	32.36 E
Cholm-Žirkovskij	76	55.31 N	33.29 E
Cholodnaja Balka	83	48.02 N	38.04 E
Choloj ≃	88	53.12 N	112.47 E
Choloma	236	15.34 N	87.56 W
Cholónbujr	88	47.55 N	112.57 E
Cholopeniči	76	54.31 N	28.58 E
Ch'ôsan	98	40.46 N	124.40 E
Cholsey	42	51.34 N	1.10 W
Choltobino	82	54.11 N	38.28 E
Choltoson	88	50.20 N	103.20 E
Choloj, Ross.	80	56.34 N	41.53 E
Choloj, Ross.	80	56.04 N	42.08 E
Choluia [de Rivadabia]	234	19.04 N	98.18 W
Choloteca	236	13.18 N	87.12 W
Choluteca ≃⁵	236	13.20 N	87.14 W
Choluteca ⚬⁵	236	13.07 N	87.19 W
Choma	154	16.48 S	26.59 E
Cholmy, Russ.			
Chomätov	78	52.56 N	35.23 E
Chomérac	62	44.42 N	4.39 E
Chomen Swamp ⚬	144	9.25 N	37.20 E
Chomérac	62	44.42 N	4.39 E
Chomiomo ≃	80	48.11 N	45.01 E
Cho Moi, Viet	110	10.33 N	105.24 E
Cho Moi, Viet	110	10.51 N	106.38 E
Chomo Lhāri ∧	124	27.50 N	89.15 E
Chom Thong	110	18.25 N	98.41 E
Chomütom	120	27.10 N	75.44 E
Chomutec	78	50.06 N	33.44 E
Chomutov	54	50.06 N	13.26 E
Chomutovka	78	51.56 N	34.33 E
Chomutovka ≃	54	50.11 N	13.37 E
Chomutovo, Ross.	76	52.51 N	37.27 E
Chomutovo, Ross.	88	52.28 N	104.25 E
Chomutovskaja	83	47.03 N	40.04 E
Chomutovskaja Step', zapovednik			
Chon, Nihon	94	35.24 N	140.14 E
Ch'ônan, Taehan	98	36.48 N	127.09 E
Chon'atino	82	55.11 N	38.07 E
Chon Buri	110	13.22 N	100.59 E
Chonchi	254	42.38 S	73.47 W
Choncholoj	88	51.08 N	108.14 E
Chon Daen	110	16.11 N	100.51 E
Chone	246	0.41 S	80.06 W
Chone ≃	246	0.35 S	80.25 W
Chong'an	100	27.45 N	118.02 E
Ch'ôngdan	98	38.05 N	125.28 E
Ch'ôngdo	98	35.38 N	128.43 E
Chonggu	106	31.12 N	121.10 E
Ch'ôngha	98	36.13 N	129.20 E
Chonghak-ni	271b	37.43 N	127.05 E
Chonghe	98	44.43 N	127.45 E
Ch'ôngjin	98	41.47 N	129.50 E
Chôngju, C.M.I.K.	98	39.41 N	125.13 E
Ch'ôngju, Taehan	98	36.39 N	127.31 E
Chông Kal	110	13.57 N	103.35 E
Chongkanzhen	100	28.00 N	105.37 E
Chôngp'al (Xiwanzi)	98	40.54 N	115.16 E
Chongming	106	31.37 N	121.24 E
Chongming Dao I	106	31.36 N	121.33 E
Chongoene	156	25.00 S	33.47 E
Chongor	102	45.59 N	112.45 E
Chongos Bajo	248	12.07 S	75.16 W
Chongoyape	248	6.39 S	79.24 W
Chong Pang	271c	1.26 N	103.50 E

Column 3

Name	Page	Lat.	Long.
Chorro Creek ≃	226	35.20 N	120.50 W
Chort'ak, gora ∧	88	53.15 N	110.45 E
Ch'ôrwôn	98	38.16 N	127.12 E
Chorzele	30	53.16 N	20.55 E
Ch'osan	98	40.50 N	125.47 E
Chosanch'am	98	42.22 N	126.11 E
Chosedachard	24	67.02 N	59.22 E
Chosen	220	26.42 N	80.41 W
Choshūtovo	80	47.02 N	47.50 E
Chōshi	94	35.44 N	140.50 E
Chōshi-ōhashi ⟶⁵	94	35.44 N	140.50 E
Chōshi-zuka-kofun ꭥ	94	34.42 N	137.50 E
Choshui ≃	100	24.24 N	120.24 E
Chosica	248	11.54 S	76.42 W
Chos Malal	252	37.23 S	70.16 W
Chosôn Minjujuûi In'min Konghwaguk — Korea, North ⚬¹	98	40.00 N	127.00 E
Chosrech	84	41.59 N	47.18 E
Chosta	84	43.33 N	39.53 E
Choszczno	30	53.10 N	15.26 E
Chota	248	6.33 S	78.39 W
Chotanāgpur Plateau ꭥ¹	124	23.30 N	84.30 E
Chotčta ≃	82	56.54 N	37.35 E
Choteau	202	47.48 N	112.10 W
Choteau Creek ≃	198	42.51 N	98.09 W
Chotěboř	30	49.43 N	15.40 E
Choten'	78	51.07 N	34.46 E
Chotěšov, Česko.	60	49.39 N	13.12 E
Chotěšov, Ukr.	78	51.43 N	24.47 E
Chotila	120	22.25 N	71.11 E
Chotilovo	76	57.44 N	34.05 E
Chotimsk	76	53.26 N	32.35 E
Chotin	78	48.29 N	26.30 E
Chotisino	82	54.24 N	36.33 E
Chot'kovo, Ross.	76	52.56 N	35.23 E
Chot'kovo, Ross.	76	53.46 N	35.14 E
Chot'kovo, Ross.	82	56.15 N	38.00 E
Choton'a	76	53.17 N	30.32 E
Chotuš'	82	54.32 N	37.44 E
Chotynec	76	53.08 N	35.24 E
Chotyniči	76	52.38 N	26.18 E
Chouchiak'ou — Shangshui	100	33.33 N	114.34 E
Chouk'ou — Shangshui	100	33.33 N	114.34 E
Choûm	148	21.18 N	13.01 W
Chouteau	196	36.11 N	95.20 W
Chovaling	85	38.21 N	69.58 E
Chovd, Mong.	86	48.16 N	90.55 E
Chovd, Mong.	86	48.08 N	91.23 E
Chovd, Mong.	86	48.01 N	91.38 E
Chovd ≃	102	44.42 N	102.24 E
Chovd ⚬⁴	86	48.00 N	91.30 E
Chövsgöl ⚬⁴	102	43.36 N	109.39 E
Chövsgöl	88	50.00 N	100.00 E
Chövsgöl nuur ⊜	88	51.00 N	100.30 E
Chovu-Aksy	88	51.11 N	93.33 E
Chowan ≃	192	36.00 N	76.40 W
Chowchilla	226	37.07 N	120.15 W
Chowchilla ≃	226	37.07 N	120.32 W
Chowchilla, East Fork ≃	226	37.20 N	119.50 W
Chowchilla, West Fork ≃	226	37.20 N	119.50 W
Chowkay	123	34.41 N	70.36 E
Chowen, Mount ∧	182	53.24 N	119.22 W
Ch'owôn-ni	98	39.40 N	127.17 E
Choya	252	28.30 S	64.52 W
Choyak-to I	98	34.22 N	126.54 E
Chrapun'	78	51.42 N	27.29 E
Chr'aščevka	80	53.48 N	49.36 E
Chrast	60	49.43 N	15.56 E
Chrebtovo	82	56.35 N	38.16 E
Chrenovoje	80	51.07 N	40.17 E
Chreščatij	83	49.37 N	39.42 E
Chřibská	54	50.50 N	14.29 E
Chriesman	222	30.36 N	96.46 W
Chrisman	194	39.48 N	87.40 W
Chrissiesmeer	158	26.16 S	30.13 E
Chrissiesmeer ⊜	158	26.19 S	30.13 E

Column 4

Name	Page	Lat.	Long.
Chuãdanga	124	23.38 N	88.51 E
Chualar	226	36.34 N	121.31 W
Chuanbu	106	31.17 N	119.49 E
Chuanchang ≃	100	33.46 N	119.51 E
Chuanergu	105	39.20 N	117.43 E
Chuan'gang	100	31.57 N	121.04 E
Chuangiapuzi	104	40.50 N	124.06 E
Chuanliao	100	28.17 N	120.13 E
Chuansha	106	31.12 N	121.42 E
Chuanshan	100	29.53 N	121.57 E
Chuanxindian	104	41.25 N	120.30 E
Chuanyao Gang c	106	32.12 N	121.25 E
Chuathbaluk	180	61.40 N	159.15 W
Chubbuck	202	42.55 N	112.27 W
Chūbu-Sangaku- kokuritsu-kōen ♦	94	36.30 N	137.41 E
Chubut ⚬⁴	254	44.00 S	69.00 W
Chubut ≃	254	43.20 S	65.03 W
Ch'üchiang — Shaoguan	100	24.50 N	113.37 E
Chuchi Lake ⊜	182	55.10 N	124.33 W
Chuchou — Zhuzhou	100	27.50 N	113.09 E
Chuchra	78	50.13 N	34.49 E
Chu Chua	182	51.21 N	120.10 W
Chuchuwayha Indian Reserve ⚬⁴	182	49.21 N	120.06 W
Chuckatuck	208	36.52 N	76.35 W
Chučni	84	41.57 N	47.55 E
Chucuito	248	15.53 S	69.53 W
Chucun	100	33.04 N	116.32 E
Chucunaque ≃	238	8.09 N	77.44 W
Chudan ≃	88	52.08 N	109.40 E
Chudanskij chrebet ꭥ	88	52.00 N	110.00 E
Chudat	84	41.38 N	48.42 E
Chudeč	60	49.58 N	13.05 E
Chudleigh	42	50.36 N	3.38 W
Chudopelan'	88	54.42 N	99.37 E
Chudźend (Leninabad)	85	40.17 N	69.37 E
Chudzirt	88	47.05 N	91.10 E
Chuen Lung	271d	22.24 N	114.06 E
Chugach Islands II	180	59.06 N	151.42 W
Chugach Mountains ∧	180	61.00 N	145.00 W
Chuginadak Island I	180	52.49 N	169.50 W
Chūgoku-sanchi ꭥ	96	34.58 N	132.57 E
Chugwater	200	41.45 N	104.49 W
Chugwater Creek ≃	198	42.07 N	104.51 W
Chugyn-ri	271b	37.39 N	126.50 E
Chühe Käna	123	31.45 N	73.48 E
Chühe	100	34.03 N	113.35 E
Chuhuichupa	232	29.38 N	108.22 W
Chuí	252	33.41 S	53.27 W
Chuius Mountain ∧	182	54.51 N	124.54 W
Chukai	114	4.15 N	103.25 E
Chukchi Sea ᵀ²	16	69.00 N	171.00 W
Chuke Hu ⊜	120	31.40 N	88.00 E
Chukou	100	32.04 N	113.22 E
Chulalongkorn University ᵥ²	269a	13.44 N	100.33 E
Chula Vista	226	32.38 N	117.05 W
Chuld	92	44.20 N	61.00 E
Chulilla	64	39.39 N	0.54 W
Chulleigh	42	50.55 N	3.52 W
Chulo	84	41.41 N	42.18 E
Chulucanas	248	5.07 S	80.10 W
Chulumani	248	16.24 S	67.31 W
Chuluota	220	28.38 N	81.10 W
Chuma	248	15.24 S	68.56 W
Chumalag	85	43.14 N	44.28 E
Chumbicha	252	28.52 S	66.14 W
Chumni, ozero ⊜	88	51.08 N	137.17 E
Chum Phae	110	16.32 N	102.06 E
Chumphon	110	10.30 N	99.10 E
Chumphon Buri	110	15.21 N	103.24 E
Chumpi	248	15.06 S	73.46 W
Chum Saeng	110	15.54 N	100.19 E
Chumysh ≃	86	53.53 N	83.29 E
Chun'an	100	29.35 N	118.58 E
Chunār	124	25.08 N	82.54 E
Chuncheon	98	37.52 N	127.43 E
Ci ≃, Zhg.	98	38.19 N	115.23 E
Chunchi, Ec.	246	2.17 S	78.55 W
Chunchi, Zhg.	100	27.22 N	119.20 E
Ch'unch'ŏn	98	37.52 N	127.43 E
Chunchula	194	30.55 N	88.12 W
Chūnd	123	31.26 N	72.16 E
Chung-ang University	271b	37.30 N	126.58 E
Chungari ≃	89	50.04 N	136.55 E
Ch'ungch'ŏng Namdo	98	36.30 N	127.00 E
Ch'ungch'ŏng Pukdo	98	36.30 N	127.00 E
Chunggang	98	36.45 N	128.00 E
Chunggye	98	40.52 N	127.20 E
Chungju	98	36.59 N	127.55 E
Chunggang-do	98	36.30 N	127.00 E
Chung Hau	271d	22.16 N	114.00 E
Chungho	269d	25.00 N	121.29 E
Chung Hsing Bridge ⟶⁸	269d	25.03 N	121.28 E
Chunghwa	98	38.52 N	125.47 E
Chungju	98	36.30 N	127.58 E
Chungking — Chongqing	100	29.34 N	106.35 E
Chungli	269	24.57 N	121.13 E
Ch'ungmu	98	34.51 N	128.25 E
Chungp'u	269	23.25 N	120.31 E
Chungp'yŏng	98	41.11 N	128.03 E
Chungsam-ri	98	40.49 N	126.02 E
Chungsanha-ri ⟶⁸	271	37.35 N	126.54 E
Chungshan Bridge ⟶⁸	269d	25.05 N	121.31 E
Chungshan — Zhongshan	98	22.31 N	113.22 E
Chunguj ≃	88	48.51 N	93.32 E
Chunheji	100	32.12 N	115.22 E
Chunhua, Zhg.	100	34.50 N	108.31 E
Chunhua, Zhg.	100	31.56 N	118.56 E
Chunhux	234	20.58 N	89.33 W
Chunlän	123	36.58 N	73.59 E
Chuntuquí	232	17.04 N	90.00 W
Chunya	154	8.32 S	33.25 E
Ch'unyang, Taehan	98	36.56 N	128.54 E
Chunyang, Zhg.	104	43.23 N	130.40 E
Chūō ≃⁸, Nihon	268	35.40 N	139.47 E
Chūō ⟶⁸, Nihon	268	34.42 N	135.11 E
Chuôr Phnum	110	12.00 N	103.15 E
Chuosijia	102	31.53 N	101.59 E
Chupaca	248	12.04 S	75.19 W
Chupadero ≃	200	33.45 N	106.37 W
Chupadero, Cerro ∧	200	31.01 N	111.37 W
Chupara Point ꭥ	241r	10.48 N	61.23 W
Chuquibamba	248	15.50 S	72.39 W
Chuquibambilla	248	14.07 S	72.43 W
Chuquicamata	252	22.19 S	68.56 W
Chuquisaca ⚬⁵	248	20.00 S	64.20 W
Chuquitanta	248	11.58 S	77.06 W
Churach ≃	84	46.51 N	9.32 E
Churãchāndpur	124	24.20 N	93.40 E
Churcampa	248	12.44 S	74.24 W
Church	262	53.45 N	2.24 W
Churchdown	42	51.53 N	2.10 W
Church Hill	196	36.30 N	82.42 W

Column 5

Name	Page	Lat.	Long.
Churchill, Cape ꭥ	176	58.46 N	93.12 W
Churchill, Mount ∧, B.C., Can.	182	49.58 N	123.51 W
Churchill, Mount ∧, Ak., U.S.	180	61.25 N	141.43 W
Churchill Downs ⚬	218	38.12 N	85.46 W
Churchill Falls ᴗ	176	53.35 N	64.27 W
Churchill Lake	184	55.55 N	108.20 W
Churchill National Park ♦	169	37.58 S	145.17 E
Church Point	194	30.24 N	92.12 W
Church Rock	200	35.32 N	108.35 W
Church Street	260	51.26 N	0.28 E
Church Stretton	42	52.32 N	2.49 W
Churchton	208	38.48 N	76.32 W
Churchtown, Eng., U.K.	262	53.40 N	2.58 W
Churchtown, Pa., U.S.	208	40.08 N	75.58 W
Church View	208	37.41 N	76.41 W
Churchville, On., Can.	275b	43.38 N	79.45 W
Churchville, Md., U.S.	208	39.33 N	76.14 W
Churchville, N.Y., U.S.	210	43.06 N	77.53 W
Churchville, Pa., U.S.	208	40.11 N	75.01 W
Churdan	198	42.09 N	94.28 W
Churen Himāl ∧	124	28.44 N	83.12 E
Chure Śringkĺä ꭥ	124	27.40 N	83.40 E
Churfirsten ꭥ	58	47.08 N	9.17 E
Chürmen	102	43.20 N	104.05 E
Churmuli	89	51.00 N	156.50 E
Churn ≃	42	51.38 N	1.53 W
Churn Creek ≃	182	51.30 N	122.17 W
Churnet ≃	42	52.55 N	1.50 W
Churni ≃¹	126	23.08 N	88.30 E
Chursdorf	54	50.46 N	12.15 E
Chūru	120	28.18 N	74.57 E
Churubusco, In., U.S.	216	41.13 N	85.19 W
Churubusco, N.Y., U.S.	206	44.57 N	73.56 W
Churuguara	246	10.49 N	69.32 W
Churumuco de Morelos	234	18.37 N	101.38 W
Churwalden	58	46.47 N	9.33 E
Chušenga	88	51.27 N	110.55 E
Chushan	100	23.45 N	120.40 E
Chushul	120	33.36 N	78.39 E
Chuska Mountains ∧	200	36.15 N	108.50 W
Chuska Peak ∧	200	35.53 N	108.50 W
Chusovoy	24	58.18 N	57.50 E
Chusovskoj	46	59.43 N	56.35 E
Chust — Čusovoj	86	41.00 N	71.14 E
Chrust	78	48.10 N	23.18 E
Chusuut uul ∧	88	47.45 N	105.45 E
Chūta	174m	26.32 N	127.58 E
Chutag	88	49.23 N	102.43 E
Chutag Uul ∧	88	49.12 N	102.04 E
Chute-à-Blondeau	206	45.35 N	74.29 W
Chute-Panet	206	46.51 N	71.51 W
Chutorskoj	83	46.52 N	42.59 E
Chutung	269	24.44 N	121.05 E
Chuŭl	98	41.33 N	129.34 E
Chuwang	98	36.02 N	114.52 E
Chuwang-san Kukrip Kongwŏn ♦	98	36.20 N	129.10 E
Chuwei	269d	25.08 N	121.27 E
Chuxian	100	32.19 N	118.17 E
Chuxiong	102	25.02 N	101.30 E
Chuzey	252	33.41 S	60.21 W
Chuzeni-ko ⊜	94	36.44 N	139.29 E
Chuzhai	100	33.22 N	113.37 E
Chuzhir	88	53.11 N	107.20 E
Chūzu	94	35.06 N	136.00 E
Chvalynsk	80	52.30 N	48.07 E
Chval'čkara	84	42.34 N	43.01 E
Chvastoviči	76	53.28 N	35.06 E
Chvatovka	80	52.26 N	46.34 E
Chvojnaja	76	58.54 N	34.32 E
Chvorost'anka	80	52.36 N	48.59 E
Chvostovo	92a	46.08 N	132.04 E
Chwefru ≃	42	52.08 N	3.25 W
Chwiiya-ri	98	38.03 N	125.32 E
Chynčešt'	78	46.49 N	28.34 E
Chypre — Cyprus ⚬¹	130	35.00 N	33.00 E
Chyrov	30	49.31 N	22.49 E
Ciacova	62	45.30 N	21.08 E
Ciadîr-Lunga	78	46.03 N	28.50 E

Column 6

Name	Page	Lat.	Long.
Ciénaga de Oro	246	8.53 N	75.37 W
Ciénaga de Flores	196	25.57 N	100.11 W
Cienfuegos	240p	22.09 N	80.27 W
Cienfuegos ⚬⁴	240p	22.10 N	80.25 W
Cienfuegos, Bahía de c	240p	22.07 N	80.29 W
Cíerna [nad Tisou]	30	48.25 N	22.05 E
Cíerny Balog	30	48.45 N	19.40 E
Cies, Islas II	34	42.13 N	8.54 W
Cieszanów	30	50.16 N	23.08 E
Cieszyn	30	49.45 N	18.38 E
Cieza	34	38.14 N	1.25 W
Çiftalan ⟶⁸	267b	41.15 N	28.54 E
Çiftehan	130	37.31 N	34.46 E
Çifteler	130	39.22 N	31.03 E
Çiftlik	130	38.11 N	34.30 E
Cifuentes, Cuba	240p	22.39 N	80.03 W
Cifuentes, Esp.	34	40.47 N	2.37 W
Çiganak, Kaz.	86	45.06 N	73.58 E
Çiganak, Ross.	80	51.47 N	46.11 E
Ciganaki	47	47.57 N	43.05 E
Cigirin	78	49.04 N	32.40 E
Cigliano	62	45.18 N	8.01 E
Cigorak	92	48.13 N	14.23 E
Cigou	100	33.51 N	113.35 E
Cigüela ≃	34	39.08 N	3.44 W
Cihanbeyli	130	38.40 N	32.56 E
Cihara	115a	6.52 S	106.06 E
Çihuatlán	234	19.14 N	104.35 W
Ciili	86	44.10 N	66.45 E
Cijara, Embalse de ⊜¹	34	39.18 N	4.52 W
Cijen	88	43.08 N	75.55 E
Cijiawu	105	39.48 N	115.59 E
Çijirčik, pereval)(	85	40.15 N	73.20 E
Cijli ≃	85	40.17 N	72.38 E
Cijulang	115a	7.44 S	108.27 E
Cikajang	115a	7.22 S	107.47 E
Çikalong-kulon	115a	6.42 S	107.12 E
Çikampek	115a	6.24 S	107.27 E
Cikan	88	54.54 N	105.39 E
Cikarang	115a	6.15 S	107.09 E
Çikatomas	115a	7.37 S	108.15 E
Çikišl'ar	128	37.34 N	53.55 E
Çikoj	88	50.16 N	106.54 E
Çikoj ≃	88	51.02 N	106.39 E
Çikola ≃	84	43.12 N	43.55 E
Çikou	100	29.42 N	114.46 E
Çiksi	130	30.40 N	40.55 E
Cilamaya	115a	6.15 S	107.35 E
Cilavegna	62	45.19 N	8.44 E
Çildir	84	41.08 N	43.07 E
Çildir Gölü ⊜	84	41.04 N	43.15 E
Ciledug	115a	6.54 S	108.44 E
Cilekovo	80	48.17 N	45.06 E
Cilento ꭥ	68	40.17 N	15.19 E
Cilento ꭥ¹	68	40.15 N	15.10 E
Cil'gazi	85	40.35 N	70.39 E
Cili	102	29.11 N	111.10 E
Cijara, Embalse de ⊜⁹	130	36.40 N	34.20 E
Çilik, Kaz.	86	43.36 N	78.15 E
Çilik, Kaz.	85	43.05 N	78.28 E
Cililin	115a	6.56 S	107.26 E
Cilimus	115a	6.52 S	108.29 E
Cimahi	115a	6.53 S	107.32 E
Cimalaka	115a	6.49 S	107.56 E
Cimalotto	58	46.17 N	8.29 E
Cimarron, Ks., U.S.	198	37.48 N	100.21 W
Cimarron, N.M., U.S.	200	36.30 N	104.54 W
Cimarron ≃, U.S.	196	36.10 N	96.17 W
Cimarron, N.M., ≃	200	36.20 N	104.31 W
Cimarron, North Fork ≃	196	37.25 N	101.13 W
Cîmbaj	92	42.57 N	59.47 E
Cimčinej, gora ∧²	180	63.37 N	178.04 E
Cimini, Monti ꭥ	66	42.23 N	12.13 E
Ciminna	70	37.54 N	13.34 E
Cimino, Monte ∧	66	42.24 N	12.13 E
Çîmion	85	40.16 N	71.31 E
Cimišlija	78	46.31 N	28.44 E
Cimitile	68	40.56 N	14.31 E
Çimkent	86	42.18 N	69.36 E
Ciml'ansk	80	47.38 N	42.05 E
Ciml'anskoje vodochranilišče ⊜¹	80	48.00 N	43.00 E
Cimolais	64	46.17 N	12.26 E
Cîmpeni, Monte ∧	64	44.12 N	10.42 E
Cîmpia Turzii	62	46.33 N	23.53 E
Cîmpina	62	45.08 N	25.44 E
Cîmpulung	62	45.16 N	25.03 E
Cîmpulung Moldovenesc	62	47.32 N	25.34 E
Cîmtarga, gora ∧	85	39.12 N	68.10 E
Cina, Tanjung ꭥ	112	5.56 S	104.45 E
Cinaruco ≃	246	6.41 N	67.07 W
Cinca ≃	34	41.26 N	0.21 E
Cincar ∧	62	43.54 N	17.05 E
Cincinnati, Ia., U.S.	190	40.37 N	92.55 W
Cincinnati, Oh., U.S.	218	39.09 N	84.27 W
Cincinnatus	210	42.32 N	75.53 W
Cinco Balas, Cayos II	240p	21.06 N	79.20 W
Cinco de Mayo	234	25.46 N	104.19 W
Cinco Pinos	236	13.14 N	86.52 W
Cinco Saltos	252	38.49 S	68.04 W
Cinco Villas ꭥ	34	42.20 N	1.10 W
Cinderella Dam ⊜¹	273d	26.15 S	28.14 E
Cinder Island I	276	51.50 S	2.29 W
Çine	84	37.37 N	28.04 E
Cinebar	224	46.36 N	122.32 W
Çiçekli, Sgurr na ∧³	46	56.58 N	5.00 W
Çiney	50	50.18 N	5.06 E
Cingala ≃	156	13.14 S	26.00 E
Cingely	80	54.05 N	52.06 E
Cingoli	66	43.23 N	13.13 E
Cinigiano	66	42.54 N	11.24 E
Ciniselo Balsamo	62	45.33 N	9.13 E
Çiniševka	85	40.33 N	71.01 E
Cinisi	70	38.09 N	13.06 E
Cinis-Voryk	24	63.18 N	55.00 E
Cinnaminson	285	40.00 N	74.59 W
Cinque, Lac des ⊜	206	46.51 N	72.59 W
Cinq Doigts, Lac ⊜	206	47.20 N	72.18 W
Cinquefrondi	68	38.25 N	16.06 E
Cinqueterre, Piano ꭥ	66	41.50 N	14.07 E
Cinqueterre ꭥ	66	44.10 N	9.45 E
Cintalapa	234	16.44 N	93.43 W
Cinto, Monte ∧	36	42.23 N	8.56 E
Cinto Euganeo	64	45.16 N	11.40 E

Column 7 (additional left entries)

Name	Page	Lat.	Long.
Christansborg — Cristóbal Colón, Pico ∧	246	10.50 N	73.41 W
Christopher	194	37.58 N	89.03 W
Christopher, Lake ⊜	164	24.49 S	127.42 E
Christoval	196	31.12 N	100.30 W
Chroma ≃	42	51.53 N	2.10 W
Chrudim	86	50.17 N	58.27 E
Chrustal'nyj	83	48.04 N	39.23 E
Chrzanów	30	50.09 N	19.24 E
Chu (Xam) ≃, Asia	110	19.53 N	105.45 E
Chu ≃, Zhg.	100	32.08 N	118.43 E
Chu ≃, Zhg.	100	23.39 N	113.15 E

∧ Mountain	Berg	Montaña	Montagne	Montanha
∧ Mountains	Gebirge	Montañas	Montagnes	Montanhas
)(Pass	Paß	Paso	Col	Passo
V Valley, Canyon	Tal, Cañon	Valle, Cañón	Vallée, Canyon	Vale, Canhão
⊳ Plain	Ebene	Llano	Plaine	Planície
ꭥ Cape	Kap	Cabo	Cap	Cabo
I Island	Insel	Isla	Île	Ilha
II Islands	Inseln	Islas	Îles	Ilhas
⚬ Other Topographic Features	Andere Topographische Objekte	Otros Elementos Topográficos	Autres données topographiques	Outros acidentes topográficos

ESPAÑOL — Nombre | Página | Lat.°′ | Long.°′ W = Oeste
FRANÇAIS — Nom | Page | Lat.°′ | Long.°′ W = Ouest
PORTUGUÊS — Nome | Página | Lat.°′ | Long.°′ W = Oeste

Nombre / Nom / Nome	Página / Page	Lat.°′	Long.°′
Cintra, Golfe de c	148	23.00 N	16.20 W
Cintra → Sintra	34	38.48 N	9.23 W
Ciocănești	38	44.12 N	27.04 E
Ciociaria ◆[1]	66	41.45 N	13.15 E
Ciomas	115a	6.12 S	106.01 E
Čiovo, Otok I	36	43.30 N	16.20 E
Cipa ≃	88	55.23 N	115.55 E
Ciparay	115a	7.03 S	107.43 E
Cipatujah	115a	7.45 S	108.00 E
Cipikan	88	54.55 N	113.21 E
Cipikan ≃	88	55.14 N	113.05 E
Cipó	250	11.06 S	38.31 W
Cipó ≃	255	18.40 S	43.59 W
Cipolândia	255	20.08 S	55.24 W
Cipolletti	252	38.56 S	67.59 W
Ciqikou	107	29.35 N	106.26 E
Čir	80	48.29 N	43.10 E
Čir ≃	80	48.35 N	42.51 E
Çiraadhame	144	10.30 N	49.22 E
Čirachčaj ≃	84	41.40 N	48.11 E
Čiragidzor	84	40.27 N	46.19 E
Ciranjang	115a	6.49 S	107.14 E
Circeo, Monte ʌ	66	41.14 N	13.03 E
Circeo, Parco Nazionale del ♦	66	41.17 N	13.05 E
Čirčik	85	41.29 N	69.35 E
Čirčik ≃	85	40.54 N	68.41 E
Çırçır	130	40.04 N	36.48 E
Circle, Ak., U.S.	180	65.50 N	144.04 W
Circle, Mt., U.S.	202	47.20 N	105.35 W
Circle Hot Springs	180	65.28 N	144.39 W
Circleville, N.Y., U.S.	210	41.31 N	75.23 W
Circleville, Oh., U.S.	218	39.36 N	82.56 W
Circleville, Pa., U.S.	279b	40.20 N	79.44 W
Circleville, Ut,. U.S.	200	38.10 N	112.16 W
Circleville Mountain ʌ	200	38.12 N	112.24 W
Circular Reef ✦[2]	164	3.25 S	147.47 E
Circus World ♦	220	28.14 N	81.38 W
Cirebon	115a	6.44 S	108.34 E
Cireglio	66	43.59 N	10.51 E
Ciremay, Gunung ʌ	115a	6.54 S	108.24 E
Cirencester	42	51.44 N	1.59 W
Cirey-sur-Vezouze	58	48.35 N	6.57 E
Čirgalandy	88	50.36 N	97.20 E
Ciriè	62	45.14 N	7.36 E
Cirigliano	68	40.24 N	16.10 E
Čirikovo	82	55.23 N	37.14 E
Ciriquiri ≃	248	8.05 S	65.18 W
Cirk, gora ʌ	180	64.33 N	175.25 E
Cîrlibaba	38	47.35 N	25.07 E
Ciró	68	39.23 N	17.04 E
Ciró Marina	68	39.22 N	17.08 E
Ciro Redondo	240p	22.01 N	78.43 W
Čirpan	38	42.12 N	25.20 E
Ciruas	115a	6.06 S	106.13 E
Cisa, Passo della)(	64	44.28 N	9.55 E
Cisano	64	45.32 N	10.43 E
Cisarua	115a	6.40 S	106.59 E
Cisco, Il., U.S.	219	40.01 N	88.43 W
Cisco, Tx., U.S.	196	32.23 N	98.58 W
Cishan	98	36.37 N	114.07 E
Cishangang	106	30.55 N	119.31 E
Ciskei □[1], Afr.	138	32.50 S	27.00 E
Ciskei □[1], Afr.	158	32.50 S	27.00 E
Cislago	62	45.39 N	8.58 E
Cisliano	266b	45.27 N	8.59 E
Çismar	54	54.11 N	10.59 E
Čismena	82	56.02 N	36.13 E
Cismon ≃	64	46.55 N	11.43 E
Cismon del Grappa	64	45.55 N	11.44 E
Čišmy	86	54.35 N	55.20 E
Cisnădie	38	45.43 N	24.09 E
Cisne	194	38.31 N	88.26 W
Cisneros	246	6.33 N	75.04 W
Cisnes ≃	254	44.45 S	72.42 W
Cisolok	115a	6.57 S	106.26 E
Cison di Valmarino	64	45.58 N	12.10 E
Cispus ≃	224	46.25 N	122.10 W
Cisse ≃	50	47.25 N	0.47 E
Cissna Park	216	40.33 N	87.53 W
Čistá, Česko.	54	50.06 N	12.44 E
Čistá, Česko.	60	50.02 N	13.35 E
Cisterna di Latina	66	41.35 N	12.49 E
Cisternino	68	40.44 N	17.25 E
Cistern Point ›	238	23.43 N	77.35 W
Cistierna	34	42.48 N	5.07 W
Čistoje	80	56.32 N	43.02 E
Čistooz'ornoje	86	54.43 N	76.33 E
Čistopol'	80	55.21 N	50.37 E
Čistopolje, Kaz.	86	52.34 N	67.15 E
Čistopolje, Ross.	83	47.31 N	39.27 E
Čistovodovka	83	49.24 N	37.20 E
Čita	88	52.03 N	113.30 E
Čita □[8]	88	52.00 N	117.00 E
Čita ≃	88	52.00 N	113.30 E
Citac, Nevado ʌ	248	12.48 S	75.14 W
Citaré ≃	250	1.11 N	54.41 W
Cité Universitaire ♥[2]	261	48.49 N	2.20 E
Citra	192	29.24 N	82.06 W
Citronelle	194	31.05 N	88.13 W
Citrus □[6]	220	28.52 N	82.28 W
Citrusdal	158	32.36 S	19.00 E
Citrus Heights	226	38.42 N	121.16 W
Citrus Springs	220	29.00 N	82.27 W
Citrus Tower ♥	220	28.33 N	81.44 W
Cittadella	64	45.39 N	11.47 E
Città della Pieve	66	42.57 N	12.00 E
Città del Vaticano → Vatican City □[1]	66	41.54 N	12.27 E
Città di Castello	66	43.27 N	12.14 E
Cittaducale	66	42.23 N	12.57 E
Cittanova	68	38.21 N	16.05 E
Cittareale	66	42.37 N	13.10 E
Città Sant'Angelo	66	42.31 N	14.03 E
Città Universitaria ♥[2]	267a	41.55 N	12.31 E
City Beach	168a	31.56 S	115.45 E
City Bell ◆[8]	258	34.52 S	58.05 W
City Island ◆[8]	276	40.51 N	73.47 W
City Mills	283	42.06 N	71.21 W
City of Hope National Medical Center ♥	280	34.08 N	117.58 W
City Of Industry	280	34.01 N	117.57 W
City of London ◆[8]	260	51.31 N	0.05 W
City of Refuge → Pu'uhonua o Honaunau National Historic Site ♦	229d	19.25 N	155.54 W
City of Sunrise	220	26.08 N	80.14 W
City of Westminster ◆[8]	260	51.30 N	0.09 W
City Point	220	28.24 N	80.45 W
City University of New York Brooklyn College ♥[2]	276	40.38 N	73.57 W
City University of New York City College ♥[2]	276	40.49 N	73.57 W
City University of New York Queens College ♥[2]	276	40.44 N	73.49 W
City University of New York York College ♥[2]	276	40.42 N	73.48 W
Ciucaș, Vîrful ʌ	38	45.31 N	25.55 E
Ciudad Acuña	232	29.18 N	100.55 W
Ciudad Altamirano	234	18.20 N	100.40 W
Ciudad Barrios	236	13.46 N	88.16 W
Ciudad Bolívar	246	8.08 N	63.33 W
Ciudad Bolivia	246	8.21 N	70.34 W
Ciudad Camargo	232	26.19 N	98.50 W
Ciudad Constitución	232	24.59 N	111.39 W
Ciudad Cortés	236	8.58 N	83.32 W
Ciudad Cuauhtémoc	234	22.28 N	102.20 W
Ciudad Darío	236	12.43 N	86.08 W
Ciudad de Carangas	248	17.53 S	66.11 W
Ciudad de Guayana → Ciudad Guayana	246	8.22 N	62.40 W
Ciudad de la Habana □[4]	240p	23.08 N	82.22 W
Ciudad del Cabo → Cape Town	158	33.55 S	18.22 E
Ciudad del Carmen	232	18.38 N	91.50 W
Ciudad del Este	252	25.30 S	54.36 W
Ciudad del Maíz	234	22.24 N	99.36 W
Ciudad de los Deportes ♦	286a	19.23 N	99.11 W
Ciudad del Vaticano → Vatican City □[1]	66	41.54 N	12.27 E
Ciudad de México (Mexico City), Méx.	234	19.24 N	99.09 W
Ciudad de México (Mexico City), Méx.	286a	19.24 N	99.09 W
Ciudad de Nutrias	246	8.05 N	69.18 W
Ciudad Deportiva ♦, Cuba	286b	23.07 N	82.22 W
Ciudad Deportiva ♦, Méx.	286a	19.24 N	99.06 W
Ciudadela, Parque de la ♦	266d	41.23 N	2.11 E
Ciudad General Belgrano	288	34.43 S	58.32 W
Ciudad Guayana	246	8.22 N	62.40 W
Ciudad Guzmán	234	19.41 N	103.29 W
Ciudad Hidalgo, Méx.	234	19.41 N	100.34 W
Ciudad Hidalgo, Méx.	236	14.41 N	92.09 W
Ciudad Juárez	232	31.44 N	106.29 W
Ciudad Lerdo	196	25.32 N	103.32 W
Ciudad Lerdo de Tejada	234	18.37 N	95.31 W
Ciudad Lineal ◆[8]	266a	40.27 N	3.40 W
Ciudad López Mateos	286a	19.33 N	99.15 W
Ciudad Madero	234	22.16 N	97.50 W
Ciudad Mante	234	22.44 N	98.57 W
Ciudad Manuel Doblado	234	20.44 N	101.56 W
Ciudad Mendoza	234	18.48 N	97.11 W
Ciudad Miguel Alemán	232	26.23 N	99.01 W
Ciudad Morelos	232	32.38 N	114.52 W
Ciudad Obregón	232	27.29 N	109.56 W
Ciudad Ojeda (Lagunillas)	246	10.12 N	71.19 W
Ciudad Piar	246	7.27 N	63.19 W
Ciudad Real	34	38.59 N	3.56 W
Ciudad Real □[4]	34	38.50 N	3.45 W
Ciudad Rodrigo	34	40.36 N	6.32 W
Ciudad Sahagún	234	19.47 N	98.33 W
Ciudad Sandino	236	13.43 N	86.08 W
Ciudad Serdán	234	18.59 N	97.27 W
Ciudad Tecún Umán	236	14.40 N	92.09 W
Ciudad Trujillo → Santo Domingo	238	18.28 N	69.54 W
Ciudad Universitaria ◆[8]	266a	40.27 N	3.44 W
Ciudad Universitaria ♥[2], Esp.	266a	40.27 N	3.43 W
Ciudad Universitaria ♥[2], Méx.	286a	19.20 N	99.11 W
Ciudad Universitaria ♥[2], Ven.	286c	10.29 N	66.53 W
Ciudad Valles	234	21.59 N	99.01 W
Ciudad Victoria, Méx.	204	32.20 N	115.06 W
Ciudad Victoria, Méx.	234	23.44 N	99.08 W
Ciudad Vieja	236	14.31 N	90.46 W
Ciuma	152	13.14 S	15.40 E
Ciutadella	34	40.02 N	3.50 E
Civa Burnu ›	130	41.22 N	36.35 E
Civate	62	45.50 N	9.21 E
Civenna	58	45.56 N	9.16 E
Civetta, Monte ʌ	64	46.23 N	12.03 E
Civezzano	64	46.05 N	11.11 E
Cividale del Friuli	64	46.06 N	13.25 E
Cividate al Piano	62	45.33 N	9.50 E
Cividate Camuno	64	45.57 N	10.17 E
Civil' ≃	80	56.08 N	47.35 E
Civil'sk	80	55.53 N	47.29 E
Civita	68	39.49 N	16.18 E
Civitacampomarano	66	41.47 N	14.41 E
Civita Castellana	66	42.17 N	12.25 E
Civita di Bagno	66	42.18 N	13.26 E
Civitanova Alta	66	43.19 N	13.40 E
Civitanova del Sannio	66	41.40 N	14.24 E
Civitanova Marche	66	43.18 N	13.44 E
Civitaquana	66	42.19 N	13.54 E
Civitavecchia	66	42.06 N	11.48 E
Civitella del Tronto	66	42.46 N	13.40 E
Civitella di Romagna	66	44.00 N	11.56 E
Civitella in Val di Chiana	66	43.25 N	11.43 E
Civitella Marittima	66	43.00 N	11.17 E
Civitella Roveto	66	41.54 N	13.25 E
Civray	32	46.09 N	0.18 E
Çivril	130	38.18 N	29.45 E
Ciwidey	115a	7.06 S	107.27 E
Cixerri ≃	71	39.17 N	8.59 E
Cixi	100	30.11 N	121.15 E
Cixian	98	36.22 N	114.23 E
Ciyutuo	104	41.31 N	122.53 E
Čiža	24	67.06 N	44.19 E
Čižapka ≃	86	59.01 N	79.36 E
Čiža Vtoraja	80	50.52 N	49.40 E
Cize	58	46.12 N	5.26 E
Cizhuping	107	29.11 N	103.36 E
Čižinskije razlivy ≡	80	50.25 N	49.40 E
Cizre	130	37.20 N	42.12 E
C.J. Strike Reservoir ⊜[1]	202	42.57 N	115.53 W
Čkalovo, Kaz.	86	53.38 N	70.24 E
Čkalovo, Ukr.	78	46.28 N	34.11 E
Čkalov → Orenburg	86	51.54 N	55.06 E
Čkalovsk, Kaz.	85	41.15 N	68.00 E
Čkalovsk, Ross.	80	56.46 N	43.16 E
Čkalovsk, Taj.	85	40.13 N	69.50 E
Čkalovskij	265b	55.54 N	38.04 E
C K Creek ≃	202	47.36 N	108.29 W
Čkyně	60	49.07 N	13.49 E
Čl'a, ozero ⊜	89	53.27 N	140.03 E
Clachan	46	55.45 N	5.34 W
Clackamas	224	45.24 N	122.34 W
Clackamas □[6]	224	45.10 N	122.16 W
Clackamas ≃	224	45.22 N	122.36 W
Clackamas, Oak Grove Fork ≃	224	45.05 N	122.03 W
Clackamas Heights	224	45.23 N	122.34 W
Clackline	168a	31.43 S	116.31 E
Clackmannan	46	56.06 N	3.46 W
Clacton-on-Sea	42	51.48 N	1.09 E
Cladich	46	56.21 N	5.05 W
Claerwen ≃	42	52.16 N	3.35 W
Claerwen Reservoir ⊜[1]	42	52.17 N	3.43 W
Claflin	198	38.31 N	98.32 W
Claiborne	194	31.32 N	87.31 W
Clain ≃	32	46.47 N	0.32 E
Claire, Lake ⊜	176	58.35 N	112.05 W
Claire, Pointe ›	275a	45.25 N	73.50 W
Clairefontaine-en-Yvelines	50	48.37 N	1.55 E
Clair Engle Lake ⊜[1]	204	40.52 N	122.43 W
Claireville	275b	43.45 N	79.38 W
Claireville Reservoir ⊜[1]	275b	43.44 N	79.39 W
Clairis ≃	50	48.07 N	2.45 E
Clairmarais	50	50.46 N	2.18 E
Clairmont	182	55.16 N	118.47 W
Clairton	214	40.17 N	79.52 W
Clairvaux-les-Lacs	58	46.34 N	5.45 E
Claix	62	45.07 N	5.40 E
Clallam □[6]	224	48.10 N	123.49 W
Clallam Bay	224	48.15 N	124.15 W
Clam ≃, Mi., U.S.	190	44.05 N	85.00 W
Clam ≃, Wi., U.S.	190	45.57 N	92.33 W
Clam, North Fork ≃	190	45.46 N	92.18 W
Clamart	261	48.48 N	2.16 E
Clamecy	50	47.27 N	3.31 E
Clam Gulch	180	60.15 N	151.22 W
Clam Lake ⊜	184	55.19 N	105.43 W
Clampton	162	29.56 S	119.06 E
Clan Alpine Mountains ʌʌ	204	39.40 N	117.55 W
Clandonald	182	53.34 N	110.44 W
Clandon Park ♦	260	51.15 N	0.30 W
Clandulla	170	32.55 S	149.57 E
Clane	48	53.18 N	6.41 W
Clans	62	44.00 N	7.09 E
Clanton	194	32.50 N	86.37 W
Clanwilliam	158	32.11 S	18.54 E
Claonaig	46	55.46 N	5.22 W
Clapham	42	52.09 N	0.29 W
Clapier, Mont ʌ	62	44.07 N	7.25 E
Clapperton Island I	190	46.02 N	82.13 W
Clapp Farm	214	41.24 N	79.32 W
Clàr, Loch nan ⊜	46	58.17 N	4.08 W
Clara, Arg.	252	31.50 S	58.49 W
Clara, Ire.	48	53.20 N	7.36 W
Clara, Ms., U.S.	194	31.34 N	88.41 W
Clara ≃	166	18.30 S	141.18 E
Clara City	198	44.57 N	95.21 W
Clara Island I	110	10.54 N	97.55 E
Claraz	252	37.54 S	59.17 W
Clare, Austl.	166	33.25 S	143.55 E
Clare, Austl.	168b	33.50 S	138.36 E
Clare, Eng., U.K.	42	52.25 N	0.35 E
Clare, Mi., U.S.	190	43.49 N	84.46 W
Clare □[6]	48	52.50 N	9.00 W
Clare ≃, On., Can.	212	44.28 N	77.17 W
Clare ≃, Ire.	48	53.20 N	9.03 W
Clarecastle	48	52.49 N	8.57 W
Claregalway	48	53.21 N	8.57 W
Clare Island I	48	53.48 N	10.00 W
Claremont, On., Can.	212	43.58 N	79.07 W
Claremont, Eng., U.K.	260	51.21 N	0.22 W
Claremont, Ca., U.S.	228	34.05 N	117.43 W
Claremont, N.H., U.S.	188	43.22 N	72.20 W
Claremont, S.D., U.S.	198	45.40 N	98.00 W
Claremont, Va., U.S.	208	37.13 N	76.57 W
Claremont ʌ	204	39.53 N	120.57 W
Claremore	196	36.18 N	95.36 W
Claremorris	48	53.44 N	9.00 W
Clarence, N.Z.	172	42.10 S	173.56 E
Clarence, Il., U.S.	216	40.28 N	87.58 W
Clarence, Ia., U.S.	190	41.53 N	91.03 W
Clarence, Mo., U.S.	219	39.44 N	92.15 W
Clarence, N.Y., U.S.	210	42.59 N	78.35 W
Clarence, Pa., U.S.	214	41.03 N	77.56 W
Clarence ≃, Austl.	166	29.25 S	153.22 E
Clarence ≃, N.Z.	172	42.10 S	173.57 E
Clarence, Isla I	254	54.10 S	71.50 W
Clarence, Port c	180	65.15 N	166.40 W
Clarence Cannon Dam ◆[6]	219	39.31 N	91.39 W
Clarence Center	210	43.00 N	78.35 W
Clarence Creek	206	45.30 N	75.13 W
Clarence Fahnestock Memorial State Park ♦	210	41.26 N	73.50 W
Clarence Island I	9	61.09 S	54.06 W
Clarence J. Brown Reservoir ⊜[1]	218	39.58 N	83.44 W
Clarence Strait ʉ, Austl.	164	12.00 S	131.00 E
Clarence Strait ʉ, Ak., U.S.	180	55.25 N	132.00 W
Clarence Town, Austl.	170	32.35 S	151.47 E
Clarence Town, Ba.	238	23.06 N	74.59 W
Clarenceville, P.Q., Can.	206	45.04 N	73.15 W
Clarenceville, Mi., U.S.	281	42.27 N	83.19 W
Clarendon, Austl.	168b	35.07 S	138.38 E
Clarendon, Ar., U.S.	194	34.41 N	91.18 W
Clarendon, N.Y., U.S.	210	43.11 N	78.04 W
Clarendon, Pa., U.S.	214	41.46 N	79.05 W
Clarendon, Tx., U.S.	196	34.56 N	100.53 W
Clarendon Hills	278	41.47 N	87.57 W
Clarens	158	28.30 S	28.29 E
Clarenville	186	48.10 N	53.58 W
Claresholm	182	50.02 N	113.35 W
Claret	62	43.52 N	3.54 E
Clarholz	52	51.54 N	8.11 E
Claridge	214	40.21 N	79.37 W
Clarie Coast ⊥[2]	9	66.30 S	133.00 E
Clarin	116	9.58 N	124.01 E
Clarinda	198	40.44 N	95.02 W
Clarines	246	9.56 N	65.10 W
Clarington	214	41.20 N	79.07 W
Clarion, Ia., U.S.	190	42.43 N	93.43 W
Clarion, Pa., U.S.	214	41.12 N	79.23 W
Clarion □[6]	214	41.13 N	79.24 W
Clarion ≃	214	41.07 N	79.41 W
Clarión, Isla I	232	18.22 N	114.44 W
Clarion, West Branch ≃	214	41.29 N	78.41 W
Clarion Fracture Zone ✦	16	18.00 N	122.00 W
Clarissa	198	46.07 N	94.56 W
Clark, N.J., U.S.	276	40.38 N	74.18 W
Clark, Oh., U.S.	214	40.27 N	81.54 W
Clark, S.D., U.S.	198	44.52 N	97.43 W
Clark, Tx., U.S.	222	30.23 N	94.46 W
Clark □[6], In., U.S.	218	38.17 N	85.44 W
Clark □[6], Oh., U.S.	218	39.56 N	83.49 W
Clark □[6], Wa., U.S.	224	45.48 N	122.31 W
Clark, Lake ⊜	180	60.15 N	154.15 W
Clark, Mount ʌ	180	64.25 N	124.12 W
Clark, Point ›	190	44.04 N	81.45 W
Clark Air Base (U.S.) ■	116	15.11 N	120.32 E
Clark Branch ≃	285	39.43 N	74.45 W
Clark Canyon Reservoir ⊜[1]	202	44.58 N	112.51 W
Clark Creek ≃	208	40.22 N	76.58 W
Clarkdale	200	34.46 N	112.03 W
Clarke ≃	166	19.12 S	145.30 E
Clarke City	186	50.12 N	66.38 W
Clarke Island I	166	40.33 S	148.10 E
Clarke Lake ⊜	184	54.25 N	106.51 W
Clarke Range ʌʌ	166	20.50 S	148.33 E
Clarkesville	192	34.36 N	83.31 W
Clarkfield	198	44.47 N	95.48 W
Clark Fork	202	48.08 N	116.10 W
Clark Fork ≃	202	48.09 N	116.15 W
Clark Hill	218	38.18 N	83.12 W
Clarklake	216	42.04 N	84.21 W
Clark Lake ⊜	216	42.07 N	84.19 W
Clark Mills	210	43.06 N	75.22 W
Clark Mountain ʌ, Ca., U.S.	204	35.32 N	115.35 W
Clark Mountain ʌ, Wa., U.S.	224	48.03 N	120.57 W
Clarks, La., U.S.	194	32.01 N	92.08 W
Clarks, Ne., U.S.	198	41.12 N	97.50 W
Clarks ≃	194	37.03 N	88.33 W
Clarks, West Fork ≃	194	36.59 N	88.31 W
Clarksboro	285	39.47 N	75.13 W
Clarksburg, On., Can.	212	44.43 N	80.27 W
Clarksburg, Ca., U.S.	226	38.25 N	121.32 W
Clarksburg, Il., U.S.	219	39.20 N	88.44 W
Clarksburg, In., U.S.	218	39.26 N	85.20 W
Clarksburg, Md., U.S.	208	39.14 N	77.16 W
Clarksburg, N.J., U.S.	208	40.11 N	74.26 W
Clarksburg, Oh., U.S.	218	39.30 N	83.09 W
Clarksburg, W.V., U.S.	188	39.16 N	80.20 W
Clarksburg State Park ♦	207	42.43 N	73.06 W
Clarks Creek ≃, Ks., U.S.	198	39.05 N	96.42 W
Clarks Creek ≃, Ky., U.S.	218	38.40 N	84.44 W
Clarksdale	194	34.12 N	90.34 W
Clarks Green	210	41.30 N	75.42 W
Clark's Harbour	186	43.26 N	65.38 W
Clarks Hill	216	40.14 N	86.43 W
Clarks Hill Lake ⊜[1]	192	33.50 N	82.20 W
Clarks Island I	283	42.01 N	70.38 W
Clarks Mills	214	41.24 N	80.11 W
Clarkson, On., Can.	275b	43.31 N	79.37 W
Clarkson, Ky., U.S.	194	37.29 N	86.13 W
Clarkson, Ne., U.S.	198	41.43 N	97.07 W
Clarkson, N.Y., U.S.	210	43.14 N	77.56 W
Clarks Point	180	58.51 N	158.30 W
Clarks Summit	210	41.29 N	75.42 W
Clarkston, Mi., U.S.	216	42.44 N	83.25 W
Clarkston, Wa., U.S.	202	46.24 N	117.02 W
Clark's Town	241q	18.25 N	77.34 W
Clarksville, Ar., U.S.	194	35.28 N	93.27 W
Clarksville, De., U.S.	208	38.32 N	75.08 W
Clarksville, In., U.S.	218	38.15 N	85.47 W
Clarksville, Ia., U.S.	190	42.47 N	92.40 W
Clarksville, Md., U.S.	208	39.12 N	76.56 W
Clarksville, Mi., U.S.	216	42.50 N	85.14 W
Clarksville, Mo., U.S.	219	39.22 N	90.54 W
Clarksville, N.Y., U.S.	210	42.35 N	73.58 W
Clarksville, Oh., U.S.	218	39.24 N	83.58 W
Clarksville, Tn., U.S.	194	36.31 N	87.21 W
Clarksville, Tx., U.S.	196	33.36 N	95.03 W
Clarksville, Va., U.S.	192	36.37 N	78.33 W
Clarksville City	222	32.32 N	94.34 W
Clarkton, Mo., U.S.	194	36.27 N	89.58 W
Clarkton, N.C., U.S.	192	34.29 N	78.39 W
Claro ≃, Bra.	248	13.25 S	56.35 W
Claro ≃, Bra.	255	15.28 S	51.43 W
Claro ≃, Bra.	255	19.06 S	47.52 W
Claro ≃, Bra.	255	19.08 S	50.40 W
Claro, Arroyo ≃	288	34.25 S	58.41 W
Claro, Ribeirão ≃	287b	23.40 S	46.17 W
Clary	50	50.05 N	3.24 E
Claryville	210	41.55 N	74.34 W
Clashmore	48	52.00 N	7.48 W
Clatskanie	224	46.06 N	123.12 W
Clatskanie ≃	224	46.08 N	123.14 W
Clatsop □[6]	224	46.01 N	123.41 W
Clatsop Spit ›[2]	224	46.13 N	124.01 W
Clatteringshaws Lake ⊜	44	55.05 N	4.17 W
Claude	196	35.07 N	101.22 W
Claudy	48	54.54 N	7.09 W
Claughton	44	54.06 N	2.40 W
Claussnitz	54	50.56 N	12.53 E
Clausthal-Zellerfeld	52	51.48 N	10.20 E
Claver	116	9.35 N	125.44 E
Claverack	210	42.13 N	73.44 W
Claveria, Pil.	116	18.37 N	121.05 E
Claveria, Pil.	116	8.38 N	124.55 E
Clavet	184	52.00 N	106.23 W
Clavey ≃	226	37.52 N	120.07 W
Clawit, Mount ʌ	116	16.58 N	120.58 E
Clawson, Mi., U.S.	281	42.32 N	83.08 W
Clawson, Tx., U.S.	222	31.24 N	94.47 W
Claxton	192	32.09 N	81.54 W
Clay, Ky., U.S.	194	37.28 N	87.49 W
Clay, Tx., U.S.	222	30.23 N	96.21 W
Clay, W.V., U.S.	188	38.27 N	81.05 W
Clay □[6]	219	38.45 N	88.40 W
Claybank Creek ≃	194	31.10 N	85.44 W
Clay Center, Ks., U.S.	198	39.22 N	97.07 W
Clay Center, Ne., U.S.	198	40.31 N	98.03 W
Clay Center, Oh., U.S.	214	41.33 N	83.21 W
Clay City, Il., U.S.	194	38.41 N	88.21 W
Clay City, In., U.S.	194	39.16 N	87.06 W
Clay City, Ky., U.S.	192	37.51 N	83.55 W
Clay Creek ≃	198	38.06 N	102.31 W
Clay Cross	44	53.10 N	1.24 W
Claydon	42	52.06 N	1.07 E
Claye-Souilly	50	48.57 N	2.42 E
Claygate	260	51.22 N	0.20 W
Claygate Cross	260	51.16 N	0.19 E
Clayhole Wash V	200	36.59 N	113.17 W
Clayhurst	182	56.15 N	120.01 W
Claymont	208	39.48 N	75.27 W
Clayoquot Sound ʉ	182	49.11 N	126.08 W
Claypole	288	34.48 S	58.20 W
Claypool, Az., U.S.	200	33.24 N	110.50 W
Claypool, In., U.S.	216	41.07 N	85.52 W
Claysburg	214	40.17 N	78.27 W
Clay Springs	200	34.21 N	110.17 W
Claysville	214	40.07 N	80.24 W
Clayton, Austl.	274b	37.56 S	145.07 E
Clayton, Eng., U.K.	262	53.47 N	1.52 W
Clayton, Al., U.S.	194	31.52 N	85.26 W
Clayton, Ca., U.S.	282	37.57 N	121.56 W
Clayton, De., U.S.	208	39.17 N	75.38 W
Clayton, Ga., U.S.	192	34.52 N	83.24 W
Clayton, Il., U.S.	219	40.01 N	90.57 W
Clayton, In., U.S.	218	39.41 N	86.31 W
Clayton, La., U.S.	194	31.43 N	91.32 W
Clayton, Mi., U.S.	216	41.52 N	84.14 W
Clayton, Mo., U.S.	219	38.38 N	90.19 W
Clayton, N.J., U.S.	208	39.39 N	75.05 W
Clayton, N.M., U.S.	196	36.27 N	103.11 W
Clayton, N.Y., U.S.	212	44.14 N	76.05 W
Clayton, N.C., U.S.	192	35.39 N	78.27 W
Clayton, Ok., U.S.	196	34.35 N	95.21 W
Clayton, Tx., U.S.	222	32.06 N	94.28 W
Clayton, Wa., U.S.	182	48.00 N	117.33 W
Clayton ≃	166	29.06 S	138.05 E
Claytonia	214	41.00 N	79.58 W
Clayton-le-Moors	262	53.47 N	2.23 W
Clayton-le-Woods	262	53.41 N	2.38 W
Clayton Park ♦	285	39.52 N	75.29 W
Clayton Valley V	282	37.58 N	121.58 W
Claytonville	216	40.34 N	87.49 W
Clay Village	218	38.11 N	85.07 W
Clayville	210	42.59 N	75.15 W
Clear ≃	182	56.11 N	119.42 W
Clear, Cape ›, Ire.	48	51.24 N	9.30 W
Clear, Cape ›, Ak., U.S.	180	59.48 N	147.54 W
Clear, Lake ⊜	212	45.26 N	77.12 W
Clear, Mount ʌ	171b	35.52 S	149.04 E
Clear Boggy Creek ≃	196	34.03 N	95.47 W
Clearbrook, B.C., Can.	224	49.08 N	122.26 W
Clearbrook, Mn., U.S.	198	47.41 N	95.25 W
Clear Creek	218	39.07 N	86.32 W
Clear Creek ≃, Al., U.S.	194	34.00 N	87.19 W
Clear Creek ≃, Az., U.S.	200	34.59 N	110.38 W
Clear Creek ≃, Ca., U.S.	204	40.31 N	122.22 W
Clear Creek ≃, Ca., U.S.	280	34.17 N	118.12 W
Clear Creek ≃, Ca., U.S.	282	37.20 N	122.21 W
Clear Creek ≃, Ky., U.S.	218	38.10 N	85.17 W
Clear Creek ≃, Mo., U.S.	194	38.00 N	93.56 W
Clear Creek ≃, Mt., U.S.	202	48.46 N	109.25 W
Clear Creek ≃, Ne., U.S.	198	41.08 N	99.06 W
Clear Creek ≃, Oh., U.S.	218	39.33 N	84.20 W
Clear Creek ≃, Or., U.S.	224	45.23 N	122.29 W
Clear Creek ≃, Or., U.S.	224	45.09 N	121.31 W
Clear Creek ≃, Tn., U.S.	192	36.05 N	84.42 W
Clear Creek ≃, Tx., U.S.	196	33.16 N	97.03 W
Clear Creek ≃, Tx., U.S.	222	29.33 N	95.05 W
Clear Creek ≃, Tx., U.S.	222	29.09 N	97.23 W
Clear Creek ≃, Wa., U.S.	224	46.07 N	122.00 W
Clear Creek ≃, Wy., U.S.	202	44.53 N	106.04 W
Clear Creek State Park ♦	214	41.20 N	79.05 W
Clearfield, Ia., U.S.	198	40.48 N	94.28 W
Clearfield, Ky., U.S.	218	38.09 N	83.25 W
Clearfield, Pa., U.S.	214	41.01 N	78.26 W
Clearfield, Ut,. U.S.	200	41.06 N	112.01 W
Clearfield □[6]	214	41.02 N	78.27 W
Clearfield Creek ≃	214	41.02 N	78.24 W
Clear Fork Reservoir ⊜[1]	214	40.42 N	82.38 W
Clearing ◆[8]	278	41.47 N	87.47 W
Clear Island I	48	51.26 N	9.30 W
Clearlake, Ca., U.S.	226	38.57 N	122.38 W
Clear Lake, Ia., U.S.	190	43.08 N	93.22 W
Clear Lake, S.D., U.S.	198	44.44 N	96.40 W
Clearlake, Wa., U.S.	224	48.28 N	122.14 W
Clear Lake, Wi., U.S.	190	45.15 N	92.16 W
Clear Lake ⊜, Mb., Can.	184	50.42 N	100.00 W
Clear Lake ⊜, On., Can.	212	44.59 N	79.33 W
Clear Lake ⊜, On., Can.	212	45.14 N	79.57 W
Clear Lake ⊜, On., Can.	212	44.30 N	78.13 W
Clear Lake ⊜, In., U.S.	216	41.44 N	84.50 W
Clear Lake ⊜[1], Ca., U.S.	204	39.02 N	122.50 W
Clear Lake ⊜[1], La., U.S.	194	31.55 N	93.05 W
Clearlake Oaks	226	39.07 N	122.40 W
Clearlake Park	226	38.58 N	122.39 W
Clear Lake Reservoir ⊜[1]	204	41.52 N	121.08 W
Clear Lake Shores	222	29.33 N	95.02 W
Clearmont	202	44.38 N	106.22 W
Clear Run	214	41.08 N	78.45 W
Clear Site	180	64.19 N	149.11 W
Clearview, Oh., U.S.	214	41.25 N	82.10 W
Clearview, Wa., U.S.	224	47.45 N	122.06 W
Clearview, W.V., U.S.	214	40.09 N	80.41 W
Clearview Estates	279b	40.34 N	80.16 W
Clearwater, B.C., Can.	182	51.38 N	120.02 W
Clearwater, Mb., Can.	184	49.08 N	99.01 W
Clearwater, Fl., U.S.	220	27.57 N	82.48 W
Clearwater, Ks., U.S.	198	37.30 N	97.30 W
Clearwater, Ne., U.S.	198	42.10 N	98.11 W
Clearwater, S.C., U.S.	192	33.29 N	81.53 W
Clearwater, Wa., U.S.	224	47.34 N	124.17 W
Clearwater ≃, Can.	184	56.44 N	111.23 W
Clearwater ≃, Ab., Can.	182	52.23 N	114.50 W
Clearwater ≃, B.C., Can.	182	51.42 N	120.00 W
Clearwater ≃, Id., U.S.	202	46.25 N	117.02 W
Clearwater ≃, Mn., U.S.	198	47.54 N	96.16 W
Clearwater ≃, Mt., U.S.	202	46.58 N	113.23 W
Clearwater ≃, Wa., U.S.	224	47.33 N	124.21 W
Clearwater, Middle Fork ≃	202	46.09 N	115.59 W
Clearwater, North Fork ≃	202	46.30 N	116.19 W
Clearwater, South Fork ≃	202	46.09 N	115.59 W
Clear Water Bay c	271d	22.17 N	114.18 E
Clearwater Beach Island I	220	27.59 N	82.49 W
Clearwater Lake ⊜, B.C., Can.	182	52.15 N	120.13 W
Clearwater Lake ⊜, Mb., Can.	184	54.05 N	101.00 W
Clearwater Lake Provincial Park ♦	184	54.03 N	101.10 W
Clearwater Mountains ʌʌ	202	46.00 N	115.30 W
Cleator Moor	44	54.31 N	3.30 W
Clebit	196	34.21 N	94.52 W
Cleburne	222	32.20 N	97.23 W
Cleckheaton	44	53.43 N	1.43 W
Cle Elum	224	47.11 N	120.56 W
Cle Elum ≃	224	47.11 N	121.01 W
Cle Elum Lake ⊜[1]	224	47.18 N	121.06 W
Cleethorpes	44	53.34 N	0.02 W
Cleeve Cloud ʌ[2]	42	51.34 N	2.00 W
Clefmont	58	48.06 N	5.31 E
Cleggan	48	53.33 N	10.09 W
Cleland Conservation Park ♦	168b	34.59 S	138.44 E
Cleland Heights	285	39.44 N	75.34 W
Clelles	62	44.50 N	5.37 E
Clementon	285	39.48 N	74.59 W
Clementsport	186	44.40 N	65.37 W
Clemson	192	34.41 N	82.50 W
Clemville	222	29.00 N	96.08 W
Clendenin	188	38.29 N	81.20 W
Clendening Lake ⊜[1]	214	40.16 N	81.13 W
Clenze	54	52.56 N	10.58 E
Cleobury Mortimer	42	52.23 N	2.29 W
Cleona	208	40.20 N	76.28 W
Cléon-d'Andran	62	44.37 N	4.56 E
Cleopatra Needle ʌ	116	10.07 N	118.58 E
Clères	50	49.36 N	1.07 E
Clerke Rocks II[1]	244	55.01 S	34.41 W
Clermont, Austl.	166	22.49 S	147.39 E
Clermont, P.Q., Can.	186	47.41 N	70.14 W
Clermont, Fr.	50	49.23 N	2.24 E
Clermont, Fl., U.S.	220	28.32 N	81.46 W
Clermont, N.J., U.S.	285	39.59 N	74.48 W
Clermont, Pa., U.S.	214	41.41 N	78.29 W
Clermont □[6]	218	39.05 N	84.11 W
Clermont-en-Argonne	56	49.06 N	5.04 E
Clermont-Ferrand	32	45.47 N	3.05 E
Clermont State Park ♦	210	42.05 N	73.55 W
Clerval	58	47.24 N	6.30 E
Clervaux	56	50.04 N	6.01 E
Cléry-Saint-André	50	47.49 N	1.45 E
Cles	64	46.22 N	11.02 E
Cleve	166	33.42 S	136.30 E
Clevedon	42	51.27 N	2.51 W
Cleveland, Austl.	171a	27.32 S	153.17 E
Cleveland, Al., U.S.	194	33.59 N	86.34 W
Cleveland, Fl., U.S.	220	26.57 N	82.00 W
Cleveland, Ga., U.S.	192	34.35 N	83.45 W
Cleveland, Ms., U.S.	194	33.44 N	90.43 W
Cleveland, N.Y., U.S.	210	43.14 N	75.53 W
Cleveland, N.C., U.S.	192	35.43 N	80.40 W
Cleveland, Oh., U.S.	214	41.29 N	81.41 W
Cleveland, Oh., U.S.	279a	41.29 N	81.41 W
Cleveland, Ok., U.S.	196	36.18 N	96.27 W
Cleveland, Tn., U.S.	194	35.09 N	84.52 W
Cleveland, Tx., U.S.	222	30.20 N	95.05 W
Cleveland, Va., U.S.	192	36.56 N	82.09 W
Cleveland □[6]	44	54.35 N	1.15 W
Cleveland, Cape ›	166	19.11 S	147.01 E
Cleveland, Mount ʌ, Austl.	166	41.25 S	145.23 E
Cleveland, Mount ʌ, Mt., U.S.	202	48.56 N	113.51 W
Cleveland Heights	214	41.31 N	81.33 W
Cleveland Hills ʌʌ[2]	44	54.23 N	1.05 W
Cleveland-Hopkins International Airport ⊠	279a	41.25 N	81.51 W
Clevelândia	252	26.24 S	52.21 W
Clevelândia do Norte	250	3.49 N	51.52 W
Cleveland Museum of Art ♥	279a	41.31 N	81.37 W
Cleveland National Forest ♦	280	33.47 N	117.38 W
Cleveland Park ◆[8]	284c	38.56 N	77.04 W
Cleveland Peninsula ›[1]	182	55.45 N	132.00 W
Cleveland Pond ⊜	283	42.07 N	70.58 W
Cleveland State University ♥[2]	279a	41.30 N	81.40 W
Cleveland Zoo ♦	279a	41.27 N	81.43 W
Cleveleys	44	53.53 N	3.03 W
Cleversburg	208	40.02 N	77.28 W
Cleves	218	39.10 N	84.45 W
Cleves → Kleve	52	51.48 N	6.09 E
Clew Bay c	48	53.50 N	9.50 W
Clewer	158	25.55 S	29.07 E
Clewiston	220	26.45 N	80.56 W
Cley next the Sea	42	52.58 N	1.03 E
Clichy	50	48.54 N	2.18 E
Clichy-sous-Bois	261	48.55 N	2.33 E
Clifden	48	53.29 N	10.01 W
Clifden Bay c	48	53.28 N	10.05 W
Cliffdale Creek ≃	166	16.56 S	138.48 E
Cliffdell	224	46.44 N	120.42 W
Cliffe	260	51.28 N	0.30 E
Cliffe Marshes ≡	260	51.28 N	0.30 E
Cliffe Woods	260	51.26 N	0.30 E
Clifford, On., Can.	212	43.58 N	80.58 W
Clifford, S. Afr.	158	31.04 S	27.28 E
Clifford, In., U.S.	218	39.16 N	85.52 W
Clifford, Pa., U.S.	210	41.39 N	75.36 W
Clifford Park ♦	274b	37.43 S	145.16 E
Cliffside	210	42.31 N	74.59 W
Cliffside Park	276	40.58 N	73.57 W
Cliffwood	276	40.26 N	74.14 W
Cliffwood Beach	276	40.26 N	74.13 W
Clifton, Austl.	171a	27.56 S	151.54 E
Clifton, Eng., U.K.	262	53.46 N	2.49 W
Clifton, Az., U.S.	200	33.03 N	109.17 W
Clifton, Il., U.S.	216	40.56 N	87.56 W
Clifton, Ks., U.S.	198	39.34 N	97.16 W
Clifton, N.J., U.S.	210	40.51 N	74.09 W
Clifton, N.Y., U.S.	210	43.03 N	77.49 W
Clifton, Or., U.S.	224	46.12 N	123.27 W
Clifton, Tn., U.S.	194	35.23 N	87.59 W
Clifton, Tx., U.S.	222	31.46 N	97.34 W
Clifton, Lake ⊜	168a	32.49 S	115.41 E
Clifton Court Forebay ⊜[1]	226	37.50 N	121.35 W
Clifton Forge	192	37.48 N	79.49 W
Clifton Gorge V	42	51.28 N	2.37 W
Clifton Heights, N.Y., U.S.	284a	42.44 N	78.56 W
Clifton Heights, Pa., U.S.	285	39.55 N	75.17 W
Clifton Hills	166	26.52 S	138.50 E
Clifton Knolls	210	42.52 N	73.46 W
Clifton Park ♦	284b	39.19 N	76.35 W
Clifton Point ›	240b	25.01 N	77.34 W
Clifton Springs	210	42.57 N	77.08 W
Clifty, Mount ʌ	224	47.07 N	121.10 W
Clifty Creek ≃	218	39.09 N	85.54 W
Clifty Falls State Park ♦	218	38.45 N	85.26 W
Clignon ≃	50	49.07 N	3.04 E
Climax, Sk., Can.	184	49.13 N	108.23 W
Climax, Co., U.S.	200	39.22 N	106.10 W
Climax, Ga., U.S.	192	30.52 N	84.25 W
Climax, Mi., U.S.	216	42.14 N	85.20 W
Climax, Pa., U.S.	214	40.59 N	79.23 W
Clinch ≃	192	35.53 N	84.29 W
Clinchco	192	37.09 N	82.21 W
Clingen	54	51.14 N	10.55 E
Clingmans Dome ʌ	192	35.35 N	83.30 W
Clinton, B.C., Can.	182	51.05 N	121.35 W
Clinton, On., Can.	190	43.37 N	81.32 W
Clinton, N.Z.	172	46.12 S	169.22 E
Clinton, Al., U.S.	194	32.55 N	88.00 W
Clinton, Ar., U.S.	194	35.35 N	92.27 W
Clinton, Ct., U.S.	207	41.16 N	72.31 W
Clinton, Il., U.S.	219	40.09 N	88.57 W
Clinton, In., U.S.	194	39.39 N	87.23 W
Clinton, Ia., U.S.	190	41.50 N	90.11 W
Clinton, Ky., U.S.	194	36.40 N	88.59 W
Clinton, La., U.S.	194	30.51 N	91.00 W
Clinton, Me., U.S.	188	44.38 N	69.30 W
Clinton, Md., U.S.	208	38.45 N	76.53 W
Clinton, Ma., U.S.	207	42.25 N	71.41 W
Clinton, Mi., U.S.	216	42.04 N	83.58 W
Clinton, Mn., U.S.	198	45.27 N	96.26 W
Clinton, Ms., U.S.	194	32.20 N	90.19 W
Clinton, Mo., U.S.	194	38.22 N	93.46 W
Clinton, N.J., U.S.	210	40.38 N	74.54 W
Clinton, N.Y., U.S.	210	43.02 N	75.22 W
Clinton, N.C., U.S.	192	34.59 N	78.19 W
Clinton, Oh., U.S.	214	40.56 N	81.42 W
Clinton, Ok., U.S.	196	35.30 N	98.58 W
Clinton, Pa., U.S.	214	40.29 N	80.18 W
Clinton, S.C., U.S.	192	34.28 N	81.52 W
Clinton, Tn., U.S.	192	36.06 N	84.07 W
Clinton, Tx., U.S.	222	33.06 N	96.14 W
Clinton, Wa., U.S.	224	47.58 N	122.21 W
Clinton, Wi., U.S.	216	42.33 N	88.51 W
Clinton □[6], Il., U.S.	219	38.37 N	89.22 W
Clinton □[6], In., U.S.	216	40.17 N	86.31 W
Clinton □[6], Mi., U.S.	216	42.56 N	84.36 W
Clinton □[6], N.Y., U.S.	206	44.57 N	73.42 W
Clinton □[6], Oh., U.S.	218	39.27 N	83.50 W
Clinton □[6], Pa., U.S.	210	41.08 N	71.26 W
Clinton ≃	214	42.36 N	82.48 W
Clinton, Cape ›	166	22.32 S	150.47 E
Clinton, Lake ⊜[1]	194	40.10 N	88.50 W
Clinton, Middle Branch ≃	281	42.36 N	82.54 W
Clinton, North Branch ≃	214	42.36 N	82.54 W
Clinton-Colden Lake ⊜	176	63.58 N	107.27 W
Clintondale	210	41.01 N	77.29 W
Clinton Lake ⊜[1]	198	38.55 N	95.25 W
Clinton Park	210	42.36 N	73.43 W
Clinton Reservoir ⊜[1]	276	41.05 N	74.27 W
Clinton Township	214	42.33 N	82.53 W
Clintonville, Mi., U.S.	281	42.43 N	83.22 W
Clintonville, Pa., U.S.	214	41.12 N	79.53 W
Clintonville, Wi., U.S.	190	44.37 N	88.45 W
Clintwood	192	37.09 N	82.27 W
Clio, Al., U.S.	194	31.42 N	85.36 W
Clio, Mi., U.S.	190	43.10 N	83.44 W
Clio, S.C., U.S.	192	34.34 N	79.32 W
Clipperton, Île I[1]	230	10.17 N	109.13 W
Clipperton Fracture Zone ✦	16	10.00 N	115.00 W
Clisham ʌ	46	57.57 N	6.49 W
Clisson	32	47.05 N	1.17 W
Clitheroe	44	53.53 N	2.23 W
Clitunno ≃	66	42.56 N	12.37 E
Clive	172	39.35 S	176.55 E
Cloates, Point ›	162	22.43 S	113.40 E
Clock Face	262	53.25 N	2.43 W
Clocolan	158	29.00 S	27.30 E
Clodomira	252	27.35 S	64.08 W
Cloe	214	40.56 N	78.56 W
Cloete	196	27.55 N	101.10 W
Cloghan, Ire.	48	54.51 N	7.56 W
Cloghan, Ire.	48	53.13 N	7.53 W
Cloghane	48	52.13 N	10.12 W
Clogheen	48	52.16 N	8.00 W
Clogher	48	54.25 N	7.12 W
Clogher Head ›	48	53.48 N	6.12 W
Cloghjordan	48	52.57 N	8.02 W
Clonakilty	48	51.37 N	8.54 W
Clonakilty Bay c	48	51.35 N	8.50 W
Cloncurry	166	20.42 S	140.30 E
Cloncurry ≃	166	18.37 S	140.40 E
Clondalkin	48	53.19 N	6.24 W
Clonee	48	53.25 N	6.26 W
Clones	48	54.11 N	7.15 W
Clonfert	48	53.14 N	8.05 W
Clonmacnois ⊥	48	53.20 N	7.59 W
Clonmany	48	55.14 N	7.25 W
Clonmel	48	52.21 N	7.42 W
Clonroche	48	52.27 N	6.43 W
Clontarf	274a	33.48 S	151.16 E
Cloone	48	53.57 N	7.46 W
Clo-oose	224	48.40 N	124.49 W
Cloppenburg	52	52.50 N	8.02 E
Cloquallum Creek ≃	224	46.58 N	123.24 W
Cloquet	190	46.43 N	92.27 W
Cloquet ≃	190	46.52 N	92.35 W
Clorinda	252	25.17 S	57.43 W
Closter	276	40.58 N	73.57 W
Cloudcroft	200	32.57 N	105.44 W
Cloud Peak ʌ, Ak., U.S.	180	68.24 N	148.26 W
Cloud Peak ʌ, Wy., U.S.	202	44.25 N	107.10 W
Cloudy Bay c	172	41.27 S	174.10 E
Cloudy Mountain ʌ	180	63.11 N	156.05 W
Clough	48	54.18 N	5.50 W
Clough Foot	262	53.43 N	2.08 W

Symbol	English	Deutsch	Español	Français	Português
≃	River	Fluß	Río	Rivière	Rio
≍	Canal	Kanal	Canal	Canal	Canal
⌊	Waterfall, Rapids	Wasserfall, Stromschnellen	Cascada, Rápidos	Chute d'eau, Rapides	Cascata, Rápidos
ʉ	Strait	Meeresstraße	Estrecho	Détroit	Estreito
c	Bay, Gulf	Bucht, Golf	Bahía, Golfo	Baie, Golfe	Baía, Golfo
⊜	Lake, Lakes	See, Seen	Lago, Lagos	Lac, Lacs	Lago, Lagos
≡	Swamp	Sumpf	Pantano	Marais	Pântano
⊓	Ice Features, Glacier	Eis- und Gletscherformen	Accidentes Glaciales	Formes glaciaires	Acidentes glaciares
⊤	Other Hydrographic Features	Andere Hydrographische Objekte	Otros Elementos Hidrográficos	Autres données hydrographiques	Outros acidentes hidrográficos
✦	Submarine Features	Untermeerische Objekte	Accidentes Submarinos	Formes de relief sous-marin	Acidentes submarinos
□	Political Unit	Politische Einheit	Unidad Politica	Entité politique	Unidade política
♥	Cultural Institution	Kulturelle Institution	Institución Cultural	Institution culturelle	Institução cultural
⊥	Historical Site	Historische Stätte	Sitio Histórico	Site historique	Sitio histórico
♦	Recreational Site	Erholungs- und Ferienort	Sitio de Recreo	Centre de loisirs	Area de Lazer
⊠	Airport	Flughafen	Aeropuerto	Aéroport	Aeroporto
■	Military Installation	Militäranlage	Instalación Militar	Installation militaire	Instalação militar
◆	Miscellaneous	Verschiedenes	Misceláneo	Divers	Diversos

ENGLISH / DEUTSCH

Name	Page (Seite)	Lat.°′ (Breite°′)	Long.°′ (Länge°′ E = Ost)
Clova	46	56.50 N	3.06 W
Clova, Glen V	46	56.49 N	3.04 W
Clove Lakes Park ♣	276	40.37 N	74.07 W
Clovelly, Austl.	274a	33.55 S	151.16 E
Clovelly, Eng., U.K.	42	51.00 N	4.24 W
Clover	192	35.06 N	81.13 W
Clover Bank	210	42.45 N	78.53 W
Clover Creek ≏, Id., U.S.	202	42.34 N	115.38 W
Clover Creek ≏, Id., U.S.	202	43.00 N	115.11 W
Cloverdale, B.C., Can.	224	49.06 N	122.44 W
Cloverdale, Al., U.S.	194	34.56 N	87.46 W
Cloverdale, Ca., U.S.	204	38.48 N	123.00 W
Cloverdale, Il., U.S.	278	41.56 N	88.07 W
Cloverdale, In., U.S.	194	39.30 N	86.47 W
Cloverdale, Ky., U.S.	218	38.10 N	84.53 W
Cloverdale, Mi., U.S.	216	42.32 N	85.23 W
Cloverdale, Oh., U.S.	216	41.01 N	84.18 W
Cloverdale, Or., U.S.	224	45.12 N	123.53 W
Cloverdale Mall ◆[9]	275b	43.38 N	79.34 W
Cloverdene	273d	26.09 S	28.22 E
Cloverleaf	222	29.46 N	95.10 W
Clover Pass	182	55.28 N	131.47 W
Cloverport	194	37.50 N	86.37 W
Cloverville	216	43.11 N	86.10 W
Clovis, Ca., U.S.	226	36.49 N	119.42 W
Clovis, N.M., U.S.	196	34.24 N	103.12 W
Clowbridge Reservoir ⊜[1]	262	53.45 N	2.16 W
Clowne	44	53.18 N	1.16 W
Cloyes-sur-le-Loir	50	48.00 N	1.14 E
Cloyne	48	51.51 N	8.08 W
Cluain Meala → Clonmel	48	52.21 N	7.42 W
Cluanie, Loch ⊜	46	57.07 N	5.05 W
Cluj-Napoca	38	46.47 N	23.36 E
Cluj-Napoca □[6]	38	46.45 N	23.45 E
Clun	42	52.26 N	3.00 W
Clun ≏	42	52.22 N	2.53 W
Clune	214	40.34 N	79.18 W
Clunes	169	37.18 S	143.47 E
Clun Forest ◆[3]	42	52.28 N	3.07 W
Clunie Water ≏	46	57.00 N	3.24 W
Cluny, Austl.	166	24.31 S	139.35 E
Cluny, Fr.	58	46.26 N	4.39 E
Cluses	58	46.04 N	6.36 E
Clusone	64	45.53 N	9.57 E
Clute	222	29.01 N	95.23 W
Clutha ≏	172	46.21 S	169.48 E
Clwyd □[6]	44	53.05 N	3.20 W
Clwyd ≏	44	53.20 N	3.30 W
Clwyd, Vale of V	44	53.12 N	3.24 W
Clwydian Range ⋏	44	53.10 N	3.20 W
Clydach	42	51.43 N	3.50 W
Clyde, Austl.	274a	33.50 S	151.00 E
Clyde, Ab., Can.	182	54.09 N	113.39 W
Clyde, N.Z.	172	45.11 S	169.19 E
Clyde, Ca., U.S.	226	38.02 N	122.02 W
Clyde, Ks., U.S.	198	39.35 N	97.23 W
Clyde, Mi., U.S.	281	42.41 N	83.37 W
Clyde, N.Y., U.S.	210	43.05 N	76.52 W
Clyde, N.C., U.S.	192	35.32 N	82.54 W
Clyde, Oh., U.S.	214	41.18 N	82.58 W
Clyde, Tx., U.S.	196	32.24 N	99.30 W
Clyde ≏, Austl.	170	35.23 S	150.15 E
Clyde ≏, N.S., Can.	186	43.35 N	65.25 W
Clyde ≏, On., Can.	212	44.58 N	76.22 W
Clyde ≏, Scot., U.K.	46	55.56 N	4.29 W
Clyde ≏, N.Y., U.S.	210	43.04 N	77.00 W
Clyde ≏, Vt., U.S.	188	44.56 N	72.12 W
Clyde, Firth of ⊂[1]	46	55.42 N	5.00 W
Clydebank	46	55.54 N	4.24 W
Clydegale Lake ⊜	212	45.25 N	78.23 W
Clyde Lake ⊜	182	55.18 N	111.28 W
Clyde No.03	214	39.59 N	80.03 W
Clyde Park	202	45.53 N	110.36 W
Clyde Potts Reservoir ⊜[1]	276	40.48 N	74.35 W
Clyde River	176	70.25 N	68.30 W
Clydesdale	158	26.54 S	27.55 E
Clydesdale V	46	55.42 N	3.50 W
Clymer, N.Y., U.S.	214	42.01 N	79.37 W
Clymer, Pa., U.S.	214	40.40 N	79.00 W
Clynnog-fawr	44	53.01 N	4.23 W
Clywedog ≏	42	52.27 N	3.32 W
Ćmielów	30	50.53 N	21.31 E
Cna ≏, Bela.	76	52.10 N	27.03 E
Cna ≏, Ross.	76	57.33 N	34.36 E
Cna ≏, Ross.	80	54.32 N	42.05 E
Cna ≏, Ross.	82	55.03 N	39.09 E
Côa ≏	34	41.05 N	7.06 W
Coacalco	286a	19.37 N	9.05 W
Coachella	204	33.40 N	116.10 W
Coachella Canal ≡	204	33.34 N	116.00 W
Coachford	48	51.53 N	8.48 W
Coacoyole	232	24.31 N	106.34 W
Coacuilco	234	21.07 N	98.35 W
Coahoma	196	32.18 N	101.18 W
Coahuayana	234	18.44 N	103.41 W
Coahuayutla de Guerrero	234	18.19 N	101.49 W
Coahuila	200	32.12 N	114.59 W
Coahuila □[3]	232	27.20 N	102.00 W
Coal ≏	180	59.39 N	126.57 W
Coalbrook	158	26.51 S	27.53 E
Coalbrookdale	42	52.38 N	2.30 W
Coalburg	214	41.11 N	80.36 W
Coalburn	46	55.36 N	3.54 W
Coal City	216	41.17 N	88.17 W
Coalcomán ≏	234	18.11 N	103.08 W
Coalcomán de Matamoros	234	18.47 N	103.09 W
Coal Creek	180	65.22 N	143.10 W
Coal Creek ≏, Co., U.S.	198	40.30 N	104.26 W
Coal Creek ≏, In., U.S.	194	39.57 N	87.25 W
Coal Creek ≏, Wa., U.S.	202	47.19 N	118.36 W
Coal Creek Flat	172	45.29 S	169.18 E
Coaldale, Ab., Can.	182	49.43 N	112.37 W
Coaldale, Pa., U.S.	210	40.49 N	75.54 W
Coal Fire Creek ≏	194	33.15 N	88.18 W
Coal Fork	188	38.19 N	81.32 W
Coalgate, N.Z.	172	43.29 S	171.58 E
Coalgate, Ok., U.S.	196	34.32 N	96.13 W
Coal Grove	188	38.30 N	82.38 W
Coal Harbour	182	50.36 N	127.35 W
Coal Hill	194	35.26 N	93.40 W
Coal Hill Park ♣	271a	39.56 N	116.23 E
Coalhurst	182	49.45 N	112.56 W
Coalinga	226	36.08 N	120.21 W
Coalisland	48	54.33 N	6.42 W
Coal Island I	172	46.07 S	166.38 E
Coalmont	182	49.31 N	120.41 W
Coalpit Heath	42	51.32 N	2.28 W
Coalport	214	40.44 N	78.32 W
Coal River	180	59.45 N	126.55 W
Coal Run ≏	279b	40.21 N	80.07 W
Coalspur	182	53.11 N	117.01 W
Coalton	219	39.17 N	89.19 W
Coaltown	214	41.02 N	80.20 W
Coal Valley V	204	38.00 N	115.05 W
Coalville, S. Afr.	158	26.01 S	29.10 E
Coalville, Eng., U.K.	42	52.44 N	1.20 W
Coalville, Ut,. U.S.	200	40.55 N	111.23 W
Coamo	240m	18.05 N	66.22 W
Coamo, Lago ⊜[1]	240m	18.01 N	66.23 W
Coapilla	234	17.08 N	93.10 W
Coaraci	255	14.38 S	39.32 W
Coari	246	4.05 S	63.08 W
Coari ≏	246	4.30 S	63.33 W
Coari, Lago de ⊜	246	4.15 S	63.22 W
Coarsegold	226	37.16 N	119.42 W
Coast □[4]	154	3.00 S	39.30 E
Coast Mountains ⋏	176	55.00 N	129.00 W
Coast Ranges ⋏	178	41.00 N	123.30 W
Coatán ≏	236	14.48 N	92.31 W
Coatbridge	46	55.52 N	4.01 W
Coatepec	234	19.27 N	96.58 W
Coatepec Harinas	234	18.54 N	99.43 W
Coatepeque	236	14.42 N	91.52 W
Coatepeque, Lago de ⊜	236	13.52 N	89.33 W
Coates Creek ≏	212	44.24 N	79.54 W
Coatesville	208	39.58 N	75.49 W
Coaticook	206	45.08 N	71.48 W
Coaticook ≏	206	45.20 N	71.53 W
Coatsburg	219	40.02 N	91.10 W
Coats Island I	176	62.30 N	83.00 W
Coats Land ◆[1]	9	77.00 S	28.00 W
Coatzacoalcos	234	18.09 N	94.25 W
Coatzacoalcos ≏	234	18.10 N	94.27 W
Coatzintla	234	20.29 N	97.27 W
Coayllo	248	12.44 S	76.28 W
Coazze	62	45.03 N	7.18 E
Cobá ⊥	232	20.36 N	87.35 W
Cobadin	38	44.04 N	28.13 E
Coballo Cocha	246	3.54 S	70.32 W
Cobalt, On., Can.	190	47.24 N	79.41 W
Cobalt, Ct., U.S.	207	41.33 N	72.33 W
Cobán	236	15.29 N	90.19 W
Çobanlar	130	38.41 N	30.47 E
Cobar	166	31.30 S	145.49 E
Cobargo	166	36.23 S	149.53 E
Cobb	226	38.49 N	122.43 W
Cobb Creek ≏	196	35.05 N	98.25 W
Cobberas, Mount ∧	166	36.52 S	148.10 E
Cobbetts Pond ⊜	283	42.48 N	71.17 W
Cobbin's Brook ≏	260	51.41 N	0.01 W
Cobb Island	208	38.16 N	76.51 W
Cobb Island I, Md., U.S.	208	38.16 N	76.51 W
Cobb Island I, Va., U.S.	208	37.20 N	75.44 W
Cobbitty	274a	34.01 S	150.41 E
Cobbitty ∧[2]	274a	33.59 S	150.42 E
Cobble Hill	224	48.41 N	123.36 W
Cobble Mountain Reservoir ⊜[1]	207	42.08 N	72.55 W
Cobblestone Mountain ∧	228	34.37 N	118.52 W
Cobb Neck >[1]	208	38.20 N	76.55 W
Cobbs Creek ≏	285	39.54 N	75.15 W
Cobbs Creek Park ♣	285	39.58 N	75.16 W
Cobb Seamount ✧[3]	16	46.46 N	130.49 W
Cobden, Austl.	169	38.20 S	143.05 E
Cobden, On., Can.	190	45.38 N	76.53 W
Cobden, Il., U.S.	194	37.31 N	89.15 W
Cobeña	266a	40.34 N	3.30 W
Cobequid Bay ⊂	186	45.21 N	63.45 W
Cobequid Mountains ⋏	186	45.31 N	64.05 W
Cobh	48	51.51 N	8.17 W
Cobham, Eng., U.K.	260	51.23 N	0.24 E
Cobham, Eng., U.K.	260	51.20 N	0.25 W
Cobham ≏	184	53.15 N	93.58 W
Cobham Hall ⊥	260	51.23 N	0.25 E
Cobija, Bol.	248	11.02 S	68.44 W
Cobija, Chile	252	22.33 S	70.16 W
Coblenz → Koblenz	56	50.21 N	7.35 E
Cobleskill	210	42.40 N	74.29 W
Cobleskill Creek ≏	210	42.43 N	74.20 W
Coboconk	212	44.39 N	78.48 W
Cobo Hall ⊥	281	42.19 N	83.03 W
Cobolgo, gora ∧	84	42.50 N	46.23 E
Çoboto, Cerro ∧	200	31.29 N	112.05 W
Čoboty	265b	55.39 N	37.21 E
Cobourg	212	43.58 N	78.10 W
Cobourg Peninsula >[1]	164	11.20 S	132.15 E
Cobquecura	252	36.08 S	72.47 W
Cobram	166	35.55 S	145.39 E
Cobras, Ilha das I	287a	22.54 S	43.10 W
Cobras, Ribeirão das ≏	256	23.08 S	46.05 W
Cobre ≏	236	8.01 N	81.18 W
Cobre, Barranca del V	232	27.28 N	107.50 W
Cóbuè	154	12.04 S	34.50 E
Coburg, Austl.	169	37.45 S	144.58 E
Coburg, Dtsch.	56	50.15 N	10.58 E
Coburg Island I	176	76.00 N	79.25 W
Coburn	210	40.52 N	77.28 W
Coburn Mountain ∧	188	45.28 N	70.06 W
Coca ≏	246	0.29 S	76.58 W
Coca, Laguna ⊜	286b	22.57 N	82.27 W
Coca, Pizzo di ∧	64	46.04 N	10.01 E
Cocachacra	248	17.06 S	71.46 W
Cocais, Ribeirão dos ≏	256	21.59 S	47.15 W
Cocal	250	3.28 S	41.34 W
Cocalico Creek ≏	208	40.07 N	76.14 W
Coccaglio	64	45.34 N	9.58 E
Cocconato	62	45.05 N	8.02 E
Cocentaina	34	38.45 N	0.26 W
Cochabamba	248	17.24 S	66.09 W
Çochabamba □[5]	248	17.30 S	65.40 W
Čochatauri	84	42.01 N	42.15 E
Cochato ≏	283	42.10 N	71.01 W
Coche, Isla I	246	10.45 N	63.55 W
Cochem	56	50.11 N	7.09 E
Cochesett	283	42.01 N	71.02 W
Cochetopa Creek ≏	200	38.31 N	106.47 W
Cochichewick, Lake ⊜	283	42.42 N	71.06 W
Cochin	122	9.58 N	76.14 E
Cochin China → Nam Phan □[9]	110	11.00 N	107.00 E
Cochinos, Bahía de (Bay of Pigs) ⊂	240p	22.07 N	81.10 W
Cochinos, Cayos II	236	15.57 N	86.33 W
Cochise Head ∧	200	32.03 N	109.18 W
Cochiti Indian Reservation ◆[4]	200	35.37 N	106.20 W
Cochituate	207	42.19 N	71.21 W
Cochituate, Lake ⊜	283	42.17 N	71.22 W
Cochituate State Park ♣	207	42.20 N	71.22 W
Cochran	192	32.23 N	83.21 W
Cochrane, Ab., Can.	182	51.11 N	114.28 W
Cochrane, On., Can.	176	49.04 N	81.01 W
Cochrane, Chile	254	47.16 S	72.33 W
Cochrane, Wi., U.S.	190	44.13 N	91.50 W
Cochrane ≏	176	57.52 N	101.38 W
Cochrane, Cerro (Monte San Lorenzo) ∧	254	47.37 S	72.19 W
Cochrane, Lago (Lago Pueyrredón) ⊜	254	47.20 S	72.00 W
Cochranton	214	41.31 N	80.02 W
Cochranville	208	39.53 N	75.55 W
Cochstedt	54	51.53 N	11.24 E
Cockatoo-Inseln → Buccaneer Archipelago II	160	16.17 S	123.20 E
Cock Bridge	46	57.09 N	3.14 W
Cockburn	166	32.05 S	141.00 E
Cockburn, Canal ʯ	254	54.20 S	71.30 W
Cockburn, Cape >	164	11.20 S	132.52 E
Cockburn, Mount ∧	162	22.46 S	130.36 E
Cockburn Island I	190	45.55 N	83.22 W
Cockburn Sound ʯ	168a	32.12 S	115.42 E
Cockburnspath	46	55.56 N	2.21 W
Cock Clarks	260	51.42 N	0.37 E
Cockenoe Island I	276	41.05 N	73.21 W
Cockenzie	46	55.58 N	2.58 W
Cocker ≏	44	54.39 N	3.22 W
Cockerham	44	53.59 N	2.50 W
Cockermouth	44	54.40 N	3.21 W
Cockeysville	208	39.28 N	76.38 W
Cockfield	44	54.37 N	1.48 W
Cockfosters ◆[8]	260	51.39 N	0.09 W
Cocklebiddy	162	32.02 S	126.06 E
Cockpit Country ◆[1]	241q	18.18 N	77.43 W
Cockrell Hill	222	32.44 N	96.53 W
Cockroach Island I	240m	18.24 N	65.04 W
Cockscomb Point >	174u	14.14 S	170.40 W
Coclé □[4]	236	8.30 N	80.15 W
Coclé del Norte ≏	236	9.05 N	80.35 W
Coclois	50	48.28 N	4.20 E
Coco ≏	236	15.00 N	83.10 W
Coco, Cayo I	240p	22.30 N	78.28 W
Coco, Isla del I	230	5.32 N	87.04 W
Côco, Rio do ≏	250	9.27 S	50.02 W
Cocoa	220	28.23 N	80.44 W
Cocoa Beach	220	28.19 N	80.36 W
Cocobeach	152	0.59 N	9.36 E
Coco Channel ʯ	110	13.45 N	93.00 E
Cococi	250	6.25 S	40.30 W
Cocodrie Lake ⊜[1]	194	30.58 N	92.25 W
Coco Islands II	110	14.05 N	93.18 E
Coconino Plateau ⋏[1]	200	35.50 N	112.30 W
Cocorocuma, Cayos ✧[2]	236	15.45 N	83.00 W
Cocos	255	14.10 S	44.33 W
Cocos (Keeling) Islands □[2]	14	12.10 S	96.55 E
Cocos Bay ⊂	241r	10.27 N	61.00 W
Cocos Island I	174p	13.14 N	144.39 E
Cocos Lagoon ⊂	174p	13.14 N	144.38 E
Cocos Ridge ✧[3]	16	5.30 N	86.00 W
Cocotá ◆[8]	287a	22.49 S	43.11 W
Cocuiza ≏	246	10.59 N	71.17 W
Cocula, Méx.	234	18.14 N	99.40 W
Cocula, Méx.	234	20.23 N	103.50 W
Cod ≏	44	54.10 N	1.22 W
Cod, Cape >[1]	207	41.42 N	70.15 W
Codăești	38	46.52 N	27.46 E
Codajás	246	3.50 S	62.05 W
Codaruina	71	40.56 N	8.49 E
Coddenham	42	52.09 N	1.07 E
Codera, Cabo >	246	10.35 N	66.05 W
Coderre	184	50.10 N	106.23 W
Coderre, Ruisseau ≏	275a	45.43 N	73.19 W
Codesa	182	55.45 N	118.04 W
Codfish Island I	172	46.47 S	167.38 E
Codigoro	66	44.49 N	12.08 E
Cod Island I	176	57.45 N	61.50 W
Codlea	38	45.42 N	25.27 E
Codnor	44	53.03 N	1.23 W
Codó	250	4.29 S	43.53 W
Codogno	62	45.09 N	9.42 E
Codorus	208	39.48 N	76.52 W
Codorus Creek ≏	208	40.03 N	76.38 W
Codorus State Park ♣	208	39.48 N	76.54 W
Codòzinho	250	4.46 S	44.10 W
Çodpa	248	18.50 S	69.44 W
Čodro	86	50.50 N	88.34 E
Codroipo	64	45.58 N	12.59 E
Codrongianos	71	40.39 N	8.41 E
Codroy	186	47.53 N	59.24 W
Codroy Pond	186	48.04 N	58.52 W
Codru-Moma, Munții ⋏	38	46.30 N	22.20 E
Codsall	42	52.38 N	2.12 W
Cody, Ne., U.S.	198	42.56 N	101.14 W
Cody, Wy., U.S.	202	44.31 N	109.03 W
Coeburn	192	36.56 N	82.27 W
Coelemu	252	36.29 S	72.42 W
Coelho da Rocha	256	22.47 S	43.23 W
Coelho Neto	250	4.15 S	43.00 W
Coemba	152	12.08 S	18.05 E
Coen	164	13.56 S	143.12 E
Coen ≏, Austl.	164	13.56 S	142.02 E
Coén ≏, C.R.	236	9.34 N	82.58 W
Coeneo [de la Libertad]	234	19.49 N	101.35 W
Coeroeni ≏	250	3.21 N	57.31 W
Coesfeld	52	51.56 N	7.10 E
Coetivy Island I	138	7.08 S	56.16 E
Coeur d'Alene	202	47.40 N	116.46 W
Coeur d'Alene ≏	202	47.28 N	116.48 W
Coeur d'Alene Indian Reservation ◆[4]	202	47.18 N	116.45 W
Coeur d'Alene Lake ⊜	202	47.32 N	116.48 W
Coeur d'Alene Mountains ⋏	202	47.50 N	116.05 W
Coevorden	52	52.40 N	6.45 E
Coeymans	210	42.28 N	73.48 W
Coffeen	219	39.05 N	89.24 W
Coffeen Lake ⊜[1]	219	39.03 N	89.20 W
Coffeeville	194	33.58 N	89.40 W
Coffeyville	198	37.02 N	95.36 W
Coffin Bay	162	34.37 S	135.29 E
Coffin Bay ⊂	162	34.27 S	135.19 E
Coffin Bay Peninsula >[1]	162	34.32 S	135.15 E
Coffs Harbour	166	30.18 S	153.08 E
Cofimvaba	158	32.00 S	27.35 E
Cofradía	236	15.24 N	88.09 W
Cofre de Perote, Cerro ∧	234	19.29 N	97.08 W
Cofre de Perote, Parque Nacional ♣	234	19.32 N	97.10 W
Cofrents	34	39.14 N	1.04 W
Coggeshall	42	51.52 N	0.41 E
Coggiola	62	45.41 N	8.11 E
Coggon	190	42.16 N	91.31 W
Coghill, Mount ∧	170	35.10 S	149.44 E
Coghinas ≏	71	40.56 N	8.48 E
Coghinas, Lago del ⊜	71	40.45 N	9.02 E
Coglians, Monte (Hohe Warte) ∧	64	46.37 N	12.53 E
Cogliate	266b	45.39 N	9.05 E
Cognac	32	45.42 N	0.20 W
Cogne	62	45.37 N	7.21 E
Cognin	62	45.34 N	5.54 E
Cogo	152	1.05 N	9.42 E
Cogoleto	62	44.23 N	8.39 E
Cogolin	62	43.15 N	6.32 E
Cogollo del Cengio	64	45.47 N	11.25 E
Cogolludo	34	40.57 N	3.05 W
Cogolo	64	46.21 N	10.41 E
Çogoon ≏	166	27.19 S	148.50 E
Čograjuskoje vodochranilišče ⊜[1]	80	45.30 N	44.25 E
Cogswell	198	46.06 N	97.46 W
Cogswell Reservoir ⊜[1]	280	34.14 N	117.58 W
Cogt	102	45.20 N	96.38 E
Cogtoandman'	102	45.50 N	104.28 E
Cogton Bay ⊂	116	9.51 N	124.33 E
Cogt-Ovoo	102	44.25 N	105.20 E
Çoğun	130	39.20 N	34.08 E
Čohansey ≏	208	39.21 N	75.22 W
Cohasset	207	42.14 N	70.48 W
Cohasset Harbor ⊂	283	42.15 N	70.47 W
Cohengu ≏	248	10.17 S	73.57 W
Cohoctah	216	42.46 N	83.57 W
Cohocton	210	42.30 N	77.30 W
Cohocton ≏	210	42.09 N	77.05 W
Cohoe	180	60.23 N	151.18 W
Cohoes	210	42.46 N	73.42 W
Cohoon, Lake ⊜[1]	208	36.45 N	76.38 W
Cohuna	166	35.49 S	144.13 E
Coiba, Isla de I	246	7.27 N	81.45 W
Coig ≏	254	50.58 S	69.11 W
Coigeach, Rubha >	46	58.06 N	5.26 W
Coignières	261	48.45 N	1.55 E
Coihaique	254	45.34 S	72.04 W
Coils Creek ≏	204	39.32 N	116.16 W
Coimbatore	122	11.00 N	76.58 E
Coimbra, Bra.	248	19.55 S	57.47 W
Coimbra, Bra.	255	20.52 S	42.48 W
Coimbra, Port.	34	40.12 N	8.25 W
Coín, Esp.	34	36.40 N	4.45 W
Coin, Ia., U.S.	198	40.39 N	95.13 W
Coina ≏	266c	38.38 N	9.03 W
Coipasa, Lago ⊜	248	19.12 S	68.07 W
Coipasa, Salar de ≚	248	19.26 S	68.09 W
Coire → Chur	58	46.51 N	9.32 E
Čojbalsan, Mong.	88	48.25 N	114.52 E
Čojbalsan, Mong.	88	48.04 N	114.30 E
Čojbalsan uul ∧	88	47.49 N	107.00 E
Cojedes	246	9.37 N	68.55 W
Cojedes □[3]	246	9.20 N	68.20 W
Cojímar ◆[8]	286b	23.10 N	82.18 W
Cojímar ≏	286b	23.10 N	82.17 W
Cojudo Blanco, Cerro ∧	254	47.05 S	69.20 W
Cojumatlán de Régules	234	20.07 N	102.50 W
Cojutepeque	236	13.43 N	88.56 W
Çokak	130	37.45 N	36.19 E
Čokato	190	45.04 N	94.11 W
Cokeburg	214	40.06 N	80.04 W
Coker	273a	6.29 N	3.20 E
Çokeville	200	42.04 N	110.57 W
Čoktal	85	42.36 N	76.44 E
Čokurdach	74	70.38 N	147.55 E
Colāba ◆[8]	272c	18.54 N	72.48 E
Colāba Point >	272c	18.53 N	72.48 E
Colac	169	38.20 S	143.35 E
Colac, Lake ⊜	169	38.18 S	143.35 E
Çolaklı	130	38.22 N	38.33 E
Colalao del Valle	252	26.22 S	65.57 W
Colapsin Point >	116	6.38 N	125.25 E
Colares, Bra.	250	0.56 S	48.17 W
Colares, Port.	266c	38.48 N	9.27 W
Colares, Ribeira de ≏	266c	38.49 N	9.28 W
Colatina	255	19.32 S	40.37 W
Cölbe	56	50.51 N	8.48 E
Colbeck, Cape >	9	77.06 S	157.48 W
Colberry Park	281	42.36 N	83.16 W
Colbert	196	33.51 N	96.30 W
Colbinabbin	166	36.35 S	144.49 E
Colbitz	54	52.19 N	11.36 E
Colbitz-Letzlinger Heide ◆[3]	54	52.27 N	11.35 E
Colborne, On., Can.	212	42.51 N	80.19 W
Colborne, On., Can.	212	44.00 N	77.53 W
Colbún	252	35.42 S	71.25 W
Colbún, Embalse ⊜[1]	252	35.40 S	71.20 W
Colburn, Eng., U.K.	44	54.23 N	1.41 W
Colburn, In., U.S.	216	40.31 N	86.42 W
Colby, Ks., U.S.	198	39.23 N	101.03 W
Colby, Wi., U.S.	190	44.54 N	90.18 W
Colca	248	12.18 S	75.13 W
Colca ≏	248	15.51 S	72.26 W
Colcamar	248	6.16 S	77.55 W
Colchester, On., Can.	214	41.59 N	82.56 W
Colchester, Eng., U.K.	42	51.54 N	0.54 E
Colchester, Ct., U.S.	207	41.34 N	72.19 W
Colchester, Il., U.S.	190	40.25 N	90.47 W
Coldbackie	46	58.31 N	4.23 W
Cold Bay	180	55.11 N	162.30 W
Cold Bay ⊂	180	55.13 N	162.33 W
Coldblow ◆[8]	260	51.26 N	0.10 E
Cold Brook	210	43.15 N	75.03 W
Cold Creek ≏	212	44.12 N	77.36 W
Colden	210	42.39 N	78.41 W
Cold Fell ∧	44	54.54 N	2.36 W
Cold Harbor Battlefield ⊥	208	37.36 N	77.20 W
Coldingham	46	55.53 N	2.10 W
Colditz	54	51.07 N	12.48 E
Cold Lake	184	54.27 N	110.10 W
Cold Lake ⊜	184	54.33 N	110.05 W
Cold Lake, Canadian Forces Base ■	184	54.25 N	110.17 W
Cold Lake Indian Reserve ◆[4]	184	54.33 N	110.10 W
Cold Norton	260	51.40 N	0.40 E
Coldrano	64	46.38 N	10.50 E
Cold Spring, Ky., U.S.	218	39.01 N	84.26 W
Cold Spring, Mn., U.S.	190	45.27 N	94.25 W
Cold Spring, N.J., U.S.	208	38.58 N	74.55 W
Cold Spring, N.Y., U.S.	210	41.25 N	73.57 W
Coldspring, Tx., U.S.	222	30.36 N	95.08 W
Cold Spring Harbor	276	40.52 N	73.27 W
Cold Spring Harbor ⊂	276	40.53 N	73.28 W
Coldsprings, On., Can.	212	44.17 N	78.18 W
Cold Springs, N.Y., U.S.	210	43.08 N	76.15 W
Cold Spring Terrace	276	40.50 N	73.26 W
Coldstream, Austl.	169	37.44 S	145.23 E
Coldstream, Scot., U.K.	46	55.39 N	2.15 W
Cold Stream ≏	226	39.35 N	120.22 W
Coldwater, On., Can.	212	44.42 N	79.40 W
Coldwater, Ks., U.S.	198	37.16 N	99.19 W
Coldwater, Mi., U.S.	216	41.56 N	85.00 W
Coldwater, Ms., U.S.	194	34.41 N	89.58 W
Coldwater, Oh., U.S.	216	40.28 N	84.37 W
Coldwater ≏, On., Can.	212	44.44 N	79.39 W
Coldwater ≏, Mi., U.S.	216	42.04 N	85.08 W
Coldwater ≏, Ms., U.S.	194	34.11 N	90.13 W
Coldwater Canyon V	280	34.14 N	117.44 W
Coldwater Creek ≏	196	36.40 N	101.08 W
Coldwater Indian Reserve ◆[4]	182	50.04 N	120.48 W
Coldwater Lake ⊜	216	41.49 N	84.58 W
Cole □[6]	219	38.30 N	92.13 W
Cole ≏, Ang.	152	9.07 S	15.50 E
Cole ≏, Eng., U.K.	42	51.42 N	1.42 W
Coleambally	166	34.49 S	145.52 E
Colebrook, N.H., U.S.	188	44.53 N	71.29 W
Colebrook, Oh., U.S.	214	41.32 N	80.46 W
Colebrook River Lake ⊜[1]	207	42.03 N	73.04 W
Cole Camp	194	38.27 N	93.12 W
Coledale	170	34.17 S	150.57 E
Coleen ≏	180	67.05 N	142.31 W
Coleford, Eng., U.K.	42	51.14 N	2.27 W
Coleford, Eng., U.K.	42	51.48 N	2.36 W
Colégio, Morro do ∧	287b	23.38 S	46.21 W
Coleman, Ab., Can.	182	49.38 N	114.30 W
Coleman, Fl., U.S.	220	28.47 N	82.04 W
Coleman, Md., U.S.	208	39.20 N	76.04 W
Coleman, Mi., U.S.	190	43.45 N	84.35 W
Coleman, Tx., U.S.	196	31.49 N	99.25 W
Coleman, Wi., U.S.	190	45.03 N	88.02 W
Coleman ≏	164	15.06 S	141.38 E
Coleman, Lake ⊜[1]	196	32.02 N	99.30 W
Colembert	50	50.45 N	1.50 E
Colen Lakes ⊜	184	54.33 N	95.25 W
Colenso	158	28.50 S	29.44 E
Colerain	214	40.07 N	80.49 W
Coleraine, Austl.	166	37.36 S	141.42 E
Coleraine, N. Ire., U.K.	48	55.08 N	6.40 W
Coleraine, Mn., U.S.	190	47.17 N	93.25 W
Coleridge	198	42.30 N	97.12 W
Coleridge, Lake ⊜	172	43.17 S	171.30 E
Coles	194	31.16 N	91.01 W
Coles, Punta >	248	17.42 S	71.23 W
Colesberg	158	30.45 S	25.05 E
Coles Brook ≏	276	40.55 N	74.02 W
Coleshill, Eng., U.K.	42	52.30 N	1.42 W
Coleshill, Eng., U.K.	260	51.39 N	0.38 W
Coles Point	208	38.09 N	76.38 W
Colesville, Md., U.S.	284c	39.05 N	77.00 W
Colesville, N.J., U.S.	210	41.15 N	74.39 W
Coleto Creek ≏	196	28.41 N	97.01 W
Coleville, Sk., Can.	184	51.43 N	109.16 W
Coleville, Ca., U.S.	226	38.33 N	119.30 W
Colfax, Ca., U.S.	226	39.06 N	120.57 W
Colfax, Il., U.S.	216	40.34 N	88.36 W
Colfax, In., U.S.	194	40.11 N	86.40 W
Colfax, Ia., U.S.	190	41.40 N	93.14 W
Colfax, La., U.S.	194	31.31 N	92.42 W
Colfax, Wa., U.S.	202	46.52 N	117.21 W
Colfax, Wi., U.S.	190	44.59 N	91.43 W
Colfiorito	66	43.02 N	12.55 E
Colgate	216	43.12 N	88.12 W
Colgate Creek ≏	284b	39.15 N	76.32 W
Colgong	124	25.16 N	87.13 E
Colgrave Sound ʯ	46a	60.37 N	0.58 W
Colhué Huapi, Lago ⊜	254	45.30 S	68.48 W
Coliban ≏	169	36.56 S	144.33 E
Colibris, Pointe des >, Guad.	241o	16.15 N	61.11 W
Colibris, Pointe des >, Guad.	241o	16.17 N	61.06 W
Colico	58	46.08 N	9.22 E
Coligny, Fr.	58	46.23 N	5.21 E
Coligny, S. Afr.	158	26.17 S	26.15 E
Colijnsplaat	52	51.46 N	3.51 E
Colima, Méx.	200	32.25 N	115.05 W
Colima, Méx.	234	19.14 N	103.43 W
Colima □[3]	234	19.10 N	104.00 W
Colima, Nevado de ∧	234	19.33 N	103.38 W
Colimes ≏	246	1.32 S	80.00 W
Colin ≏	50	47.08 N	2.32 E
Colina	252	33.12 S	70.41 W
Colinas, Bra.	250	6.02 S	44.14 W
Colinas, Bra.	255	14.12 S	48.03 W
Colinet	186	47.13 N	53.33 W
Colinton, Austl.	171b	35.51 S	149.09 E
Colinton, Ab., Can.	182	54.37 N	113.15 W
Coll I	46	56.38 N	6.34 W
Colla	258	34.04 S	57.21 W
Colla, Arroyo ≏	258	34.19 S	57.20 W
Collagna	64	44.21 N	10.16 E
Collalbo (Klobenstein)	64	46.32 N	11.28 E
Collalto Sabino	66	42.08 N	13.02 E
Collamer	210	43.06 N	76.04 W
Collarenebri	166	29.33 S	148.35 E
Collarmele	66	42.03 N	13.38 E
Collaroy	274a	33.44 S	151.18 E
Collazzone	66	42.54 N	12.26 E
Collbran	200	39.14 N	107.57 W
Collecchio	64	44.45 N	10.13 E
Collecorvino	66	42.27 N	14.01 E
Colle di Tora	66	42.13 N	12.57 E
Colle di Val d'Elsa	66	43.25 N	11.07 E
Colleen Bawn	154	21.00 S	29.13 E
Colleferro	66	41.44 N	12.59 E
College	180	64.51 N	147.47 W
College City	226	39.00 N	122.00 W
College Corner	218	39.30 N	84.36 W
Collegedale	194	35.04 N	85.03 W
College Meadows	218	39.56 N	86.07 W
College Park, Ga., U.S.	192	33.39 N	84.26 W
College Park, Md., U.S.	208	38.58 N	76.56 W
College Park Airport ⊠	284c	38.58 N	76.55 W
College Place	202	46.02 N	118.23 W
College Point ◆[8]	276	40.47 N	73.51 W
College Station, Ar., U.S.	194	34.43 N	92.13 W
College Station, Tx., U.S.	222	30.37 N	96.20 W
Collegeville, In., U.S.	216	40.54 N	87.09 W
Collegeville, Pa., U.S.	208	40.11 N	75.27 W
Collégien	261	48.50 N	2.40 E
Collegno	62	45.05 N	7.34 E
Colle Isarco (Gossensass)	64	46.56 N	11.26 E
Collepardo	66	41.46 N	13.22 E
Collepasso	68	40.04 N	18.10 E
Collepietro	66	42.13 N	13.46 E
Collerina	166	29.41 S	146.38 E
Collesalvetti	66	43.35 N	10.28 E
Colle Sannita	68	41.22 N	14.50 E
Collesano	70	37.55 N	13.56 E
Colletorto	66	41.40 N	14.58 E
Colleymount	182	54.01 N	126.09 W
Colleyville	222	32.52 N	97.09 W
Colliano	68	40.43 N	15.17 E
Colli a Volturno	66	41.36 N	14.06 E
Colli del Tronto	66	42.52 N	13.44 E
Colli di Monte Bove	66	42.06 N	13.09 E
Collie	168a	33.21 S	116.09 E
Collie ≏	168a	33.18 S	115.44 E
Collie East ≏	168a	33.18 S	116.10 E
Collier □[6]	220	26.10 N	81.22 W
Collier Bay ⊂	160	16.10 S	124.15 E
Collier Bridge ◆[5]	220	26.57 N	82.04 W
Collier City	220	26.14 N	80.09 W
Collier Law ∧[2]	44	54.46 N	1.58 W
Collier Range ⋏	162	24.43 S	119.12 E
Collier Range National Park ♣	162	24.40 S	119.15 E
Collier Row ◆[8]	260	51.36 N	0.10 E
Colliers	214	40.22 N	80.32 W
Collier-Seminole State Park ♣	220	25.59 N	81.36 W
Colliersville	210	42.29 N	74.59 W
Collierville	194	35.02 N	89.39 W
Collie South ≏	168a	33.18 S	116.10 E
Collieston	46	57.21 N	1.56 W
Colliford Lake Reservoir ⊜[1]	42	50.32 N	4.33 W
Colligan ≏	48	52.06 N	7.38 W
Collin □[6]	222	33.07 N	96.35 W
Collina, Passo della)(	66	44.01 N	10.56 E
Collingbourne Kingston	42	51.18 N	1.13 W
Collingdale	208	39.54 N	75.16 W
Collingham	44	53.54 N	1.24 W
Collingswood	285	39.55 N	75.04 W
Collingwood, Austl.	274b	37.48 S	145.00 E
Collingwood, On., Can.	212	44.29 N	80.13 W
Collingwood, N.Z.	172	40.40 S	172.41 E
Collingwood Bay ⊂	164	9.20 S	149.30 E
Collins, Ga., U.S.	192	32.10 N	82.06 W
Collins, Ia., U.S.	190	41.54 N	93.18 W
Collins, Ms., U.S.	194	31.38 N	89.33 W
Collins, N.Y., U.S.	210	42.30 N	78.55 W
Collins, Oh., U.S.	214	41.16 N	82.30 W
Collins ≏	194	35.48 N	85.37 W
Collins, Mount ∧[2]	190	47.51 N	80.59 W
Collins Bay	212	44.15 N	76.36 W
Collinsburg	214	40.13 N	79.46 W
Collins Center	210	42.30 N	78.51 W
Collins Lake ⊜	212	44.22 N	76.27 W
Collins Park	208	39.41 N	75.33 W
Collinston	194	32.41 N	91.52 W
Collinsville, Austl.	166	20.34 S	147.51 E
Collinsville, Al., U.S.	194	34.15 N	85.51 W
Collinsville, Ca., U.S.	282	38.05 N	121.51 W
Collinsville, Ct., U.S.	207	41.48 N	72.55 W
Collinsville, Il., U.S.	219	38.40 N	89.59 W
Collinsville, Ms., U.S.	194	32.29 N	88.50 W
Collinsville, N.J., U.S.	276	40.49 N	74.28 W
Collinsville, Ok., U.S.	196	36.21 N	95.50 W
Collinsville, Tx., U.S.	196	33.32 N	96.54 W
Collinwood	194	35.10 N	87.44 W
Collio	64	45.48 N	10.20 E
Collipulli	252	37.57 S	72.26 W
Collister	202	43.38 N	116.15 W
Collobrières	62	43.14 N	6.18 E
Collombey	58	46.16 N	6.57 E
Collomsville	210	41.09 N	77.09 W
Collon	48	53.47 N	6.29 W
Collonges	58	46.08 N	5.54 E
Collooney	48	54.11 N	8.29 W
Collserola, Serra de ⋏	266d	41.26 N	2.07 E
Colma	226	37.41 N	122.28 W
Colma Creek ≏	282	37.38 N	122.23 W
Colman	198	43.58 N	96.48 W
Colmar	58	48.05 N	7.22 E
Colmar Manor	284c	38.55 N	76.56 W
Colmars	62	44.11 N	6.38 E
Colmenar	34	36.54 N	4.20 W
Colmenar de Oreja	34	40.06 N	3.23 W
Colmenar Viejo	34	40.40 N	3.46 W
Colmeneros	234	18.06 N	101.40 W
Colmesneil	194	30.54 N	94.25 W
Colmnitz	54	50.54 N	13.31 E
Colmonell	44	55.08 N	4.55 W
Coln ≏	42	51.42 N	1.42 W
Colnbrook	260	51.29 N	0.31 W
Colne	44	53.52 N	2.09 W
Colne ≏, Eng., U.K.	42	51.48 N	1.01 E
Colne ≏, Eng., U.K.	260	51.26 N	0.30 W
Colney Heath	260	51.44 N	0.15 W
Colney Street	260	51.42 N	0.20 W
Colo	190	42.01 N	93.18 W
Colo ≏	170	33.26 S	150.53 E
Colobraro	68	40.11 N	16.25 E
Cologna Veneta	64	45.18 N	11.23 E
Cologne, Mn., U.S.	190	44.46 N	93.46 W
Cologne, N.J., U.S.	208	39.30 N	74.36 W
Cologne → Köln	56	50.56 N	6.59 E
Cologno al Serio	62	45.37 N	9.42 E
Cologno Monzese	266b	45.32 N	9.17 E
Cololo, Nevado ∧	248	14.53 S	69.06 W
Coloma, Ca., U.S.	226	38.48 N	120.53 W
Coloma, Mi., U.S.	216	42.11 N	86.18 W
Coloma, Wi., U.S.	190	44.02 N	89.31 W
Colomb-Béchar → Béchar	148	31.37 N	2.13 W
Colombes	50	48.55 N	2.15 E
Colombey-les-Belles	58	48.32 N	5.54 E
Colombey-les-Deux-Eglises	58	48.13 N	4.53 E
Colômbia, Bra.	255	20.30 S	48.37 W
Colombia, Col.	246	3.24 N	74.49 W
Colombia, Cuba	240p	20.59 N	77.25 W
Colombia, Méx.	196	27.42 N	99.45 W
Colombia □[1], S.A.	242	4.00 N	72.00 W
Colombia □[1], S.A.	246	4.00 N	72.00 W
Colombian Basin ✧[1]	16	13.00 N	76.00 W
Colombie-Britannique → British Columbia □[4]	182	54.00 N	125.00 W
Colombie → Colombia □[1]	246	4.00 N	72.00 W
Colombier	58	46.58 N	6.52 E
Colombo, Bra.	252	25.17 S	49.14 W
Colombo, S. Lan.	122	6.56 N	79.51 E
Colome	198	43.15 N	99.42 W
Colomiers	32	43.37 N	1.20 E
Colón, Arg.	252	33.53 S	61.07 W
Colón, Arg.	252	32.13 S	58.08 W
Colón, Cuba	240p	22.43 N	80.54 W
Colón, Méx.	234	20.48 N	100.03 W
Colón, Pan.	236	9.22 N	79.54 W
Colon, Mi., U.S.	216	41.57 N	85.19 W
Colón, Ur.	252	33.53 S	54.43 W
Colón, Ur.	258	34.48 S	56.14 W
Colón □[4]	236	9.00 N	80.20 W
Colón □[5]	236	15.40 N	85.30 W
Colón, Archipiélago de (Galapagos Islands) II	246a	0.30 S	90.30 W
Colón, Cementerio ◆	286b	23.08 N	82.23 W
Colón, Isla I	236	9.24 N	82.17 W
Colón, Montañas de ⋏	236	14.55 N	84.45 W
Colón, Teatro ♣	288	34.36 S	58.23 W
Colona	162	31.38 S	132.05 E
Colonard-Corubert	50	48.25 N	0.39 E
Colonarie ≏	241h	13.14 N	61.06 W
Colonel Danforth Park ♣	275b	43.47 N	79.10 W
Colonelganj	124	27.08 N	81.42 E
Colonești	38	46.34 N	27.18 E
Colonet	204	31.05 N	116.10 W
Colonet, Cabo >	204	30.58 N	116.19 W
Colongulac, Lake ⊜	169	38.10 S	143.11 E
Colonia, Micron.	174q	9.31 N	138.08 E
Colonia, N.J., U.S.	210	40.34 N	74.18 W
Colonia □[5]	258	34.10 S	57.30 W
Colônia ≏	255	15.11 S	39.45 W
Colonia, Aeropuerto ⊠	258	34.28 S	57.49 W
Colonia, Cuchilla de la ⋏[2]	258	34.15 S	57.35 W
Colonia Alvear	252	35.00 S	67.40 W
Colonia Caroya	252	31.02 S	64.05 W
Colonia del Sacramento	258	34.28 S	57.51 W
Colonia Dora	252	28.36 S	62.57 W
Colonia Elisa	252	26.56 S	59.32 W
Colonia Guadalupe	204	32.04 N	116.37 W
Colonia Hogar Ricardo Gutiérrez	288	34.51 S	58.51 W
Colonia José Mármol	252	26.59 S	60.44 W
Colonia → Köln	56	50.56 N	6.59 E
Colonial Acres	208	39.31 N	76.20 W
Colonia Lavalleja	252	31.06 S	57.01 W
Colonial Beach	208	38.15 N	76.57 W
Colonial Crest	208	40.20 N	76.50 W
Colônia Leopoldina	250	8.57 S	35.39 W
Colonial Heights, Il., U.S.	278	41.05 N	88.01 W
Colonial Heights, Va., U.S.	208	37.14 N	77.24 W
Colonial Manor	285	39.51 N	75.09 W
Colonial National Historical Park ♣	208	37.12 N	76.45 W
Colonial Park	208	40.18 N	76.48 W
Colonial Village, N.Y., U.S.	210	43.08 N	78.58 W
Colonial Village, Pa., U.S.	285	40.04 N	75.24 W
Colonial Village Airport ⊠	284a	43.08 N	78.58 W
Colonial Williamsburg ⊥	208	37.16 N	76.42 W
Colonia Morelos	200	30.50 N	109.10 W
Colonia Nicolich	258	34.50 S	56.02 W
Colonia Progreso	204	32.35 N	115.37 W
Colonia Providencia	240m	17.59 N	66.00 W
Colonias Unidas	252	26.42 S	59.38 W
Colonia Valdense	258	34.20 S	57.14 W
Colonia Vicente Guerrero	232	30.45 N	116.00 W
Colonia Villafañe	252	26.12 S	59.05 W
Colonie	210	42.43 N	73.50 W
Colon Koret	152	0.34 N	23.28 E
Colonna	267a	41.50 N	12.45 E
Colonna, Capo >	68	39.02 N	17.11 E
Colonnata	64	44.05 N	10.10 E
Colón Ridge ✧[3]	18	2.00 N	96.00 W
Colonsay	184	51.59 N	105.53 W
Colonsay I	46	56.04 N	6.13 W
Colony	198	38.04 N	95.21 W
Colora	208	39.40 N	76.06 W
Colorada, Laguna ≡	254	44.50 S	68.15 W
Colorada, Punta >	288	34.45 S	58.06 W
Coloradas, Lomas ⋏[2]	254	43.24 S	67.24 W
Colorado, C.R.	236	10.46 N	83.35 W
Colorado, Hond.	236	15.47 N	87.19 W
Colorado, Ak., U.S.	180	63.09 N	149.26 W
Colorado □[6]	222	29.40 N	96.30 W
Colorado □[3]	178	39.00 N	105.30 W
Colorado ≏, Arg.	244	39.50 S	62.08 W
Colorado ≏, Bra.	248	13.03 S	62.20 W
Colorado ≏, Méx.	234	16.30 N	97.31 W
Colorado ≏, N.A.	200	31.54 N	114.57 W
Colorado ≏, Tx., U.S.	196	28.36 N	95.58 W
Colorado, Canal do ≡	287a	23.00 S	43.25 W
Colorado, Cerro ∧, Arg.	254	45.02 S	69.38 W
Colorado, Cerro ∧, Chile	286e	33.24 S	70.45 W
Colorado, Cerro ∧, Perú	286d	12.07 S	76.55 W
Colorado, Williams Fork ≏	200	40.03 N	106.11 W
Colorado City, Az., U.S.	200	36.59 N	112.58 W
Colorado City, Co., U.S.	200	37.56 N	104.50 W
Colorado City, Tx., U.S.	196	32.23 N	100.51 W
Colorado de Abajo	196	26.28 N	99.54 W
Colorado Grande, Salina ≚	252	38.15 S	63.47 W
Colorado National Monument ♣	200	39.04 N	108.25 W
Colorado Plateau ⋏[1]	200	36.30 N	108.00 W
Colorado River Aqueduct ≡[1]	204	33.50 N	117.23 W
Colorado River Indian Reservation ◆[4]	200	34.00 N	114.25 W
Colorados, Archipiélago de los II	240p	22.36 N	84.20 W
Colorado Springs	200	38.50 N	104.49 W
Colorines	234	19.07 N	100.12 W
Colorno	64	44.56 N	10.23 E

Symbols in the index entries represent the broad categories identified in the key at the right. Symbols with superior numbers (⋏[1]) identify subcategories (see complete key on page *I · 1).*

Symbole im Register stellen die rechts im Schlüssel erklärten Kategorien dar. Symbole mit hochgestellten Ziffern (⋏[1]) bezeichnen Unterabteilungen einer Kategorie (vgl. vollständiger Schlüssel auf Seite *I · 1).*

Los símbolos incluídos en el texto del índice representan las grandes categorias identificadas con la clave a la derecha. Los símbolos con numeros en su parte superior (⋏[1]) identifican las subcategorías (véase la clave completa en la página *I · 1).*

Les symboles de l'index représentent les catégories indiquées dans la légende à droite. Les symboles suivis d'un indice (⋏[1]) représentent des sous-catégories (voir légende complète à la page *I · 1).*

Os símbolos incluídos no texto do índice representam as grandes categorias identificadas com a chave à direita. Os símbolos com números em sua parte superior (⋏[1]) identificam as subcategorias (veja-se a chave completa à página *I · 1).*

English	Deutsch	Español	Français	Português
∧ Mountain	Berg	Montaña	Montagne	Montanha
⋏ Mountains	Gebirge	Montañas	Montagnes	Montanhas
)(Pass	Paß	Paso	Col	Passo
V Valley, Canyon	Tal, Cañon	Valle, Cañón	Vallée, Canyon	Vale, Canhão
≚ Plain	Ebene	Llano	Plaine	Planície
> Cape	Kap	Cabo	Cap	Cabo
I Island	Insel	Isla	Île	Ilha
II Islands	Inseln	Islas	Îles	Ilhas
± Other Topographic Features	Andere Topographische Objekte	Otros Elementos Topográficos	Autres données topographiques	Outros acidentes topográficos

ESPAÑOL

Nombre	Página	Lat.°′	Long.°′ W = Oeste
Colosimi	68	39.07 N	16.24 E
Colosseo ⊥	267a	41.54 N	12.29 E
Colotepec ≃	234	15.47 N	97.03 W
Colotlán	234	22.06 N	103.16 W
Colotlán ≃	234	22.06 N	103.42 W
Colotlipa	234	17.25 N	99.09 W
Colo Vale	170	34.24 S	150.29 E
Čolpon	85	42.12 N	75.28 E
Čolpon-Ata	85	42.40 N	77.06 E
Colpoys Bay ⊂	212	44.47 N	81.05 W
Colquechaca	248	18.40 S	66.01 W
Colquencha	248	17.00 S	68.17 W
Colquiri	248	17.25 S	67.08 W
Colquitt	192	31.10 N	84.44 W
Colsterworth	42	52.48 N	0.37 W
Colstrip	202	45.53 N	106.37 W
Colt	194	35.07 N	90.48 W
Colta	248	15.10 S	73.18 W
Coltauco	252	34.18 S	71.06 W
Coltishall	42	52.44 N	1.22 E
Colton, Austl.	162	33.29 S	134.56 E
Colton, Ca., U.S.	228	34.04 N	117.18 W
Colton, Oh., U.S.	216	41.28 N	83.57 W
Colton, Or., U.S.	224	45.10 N	122.26 W
Colton, S.D., U.S.	198	43.47 N	96.55 W
Coltons Point	208	38.13 N	76.45 W
Colts Neck	208	40.17 N	74.10 W
Coltsville Center	214	41.05 N	80.34 W
Columbia, Al., U.S.	192	31.17 N	85.06 W
Columbia, Ca., U.S.	226	38.02 N	120.24 W
Columbia, Ct., U.S.	207	41.42 N	72.18 W
Columbia, Il., U.S.	219	38.26 N	90.12 W
Columbia, In., U.S.	218	39.35 N	85.12 W
Columbia, Ky., U.S.	194	37.06 N	85.18 W
Columbia, La., U.S.	194	32.06 N	92.04 W
Columbia, Md., U.S.	208	39.14 N	76.50 W
Columbia, Ms., U.S.	194	31.15 N	89.50 W
Columbia, Mo., U.S.	219	38.57 N	92.20 W
Columbia, N.J., U.S.	210	40.55 N	75.05 W
Columbia, N.C., U.S.	192	35.55 N	76.15 W
Columbia, Pa., U.S.	208	40.02 N	76.30 W
Columbia, S.C., U.S.	192	34.00 N	81.02 W
Columbia, Tn., U.S.	194	35.36 N	87.02 W
Columbia □[6], N.Y., U.S.	210	42.15 N	73.47 W
Columbia □[6], Or., U.S.	224	45.57 N	123.03 W
Columbia □[6], Pa., U.S.	210	41.00 N	76.28 W
Columbia ≃	176	46.15 N	124.05 W
Columbia, Cape ›	16	83.08 N	70.35 W
Columbia, Lake ⊜[1]	216	42.05 N	84.18 W
Columbia, Mount ∧	182	52.09 N	117.25 W
Columbia Airport ⊠	279a	41.19 N	81.58 W
Columbia Basin ≚[1]	202	46.45 N	119.05 W
Columbia Center	279a	41.19 N	81.56 W
Columbia City, In., U.S.	216	41.09 N	85.29 W
Columbia City, Or., U.S.	224	45.53 N	122.48 W
Columbia Cross Roads	210	41.50 N	76.48 W
Columbia Falls, Me., U.S.	188	44.39 N	67.43 W
Columbia Falls, Mt., U.S.	202	48.22 N	114.10 W
Columbia Heights	224	46.09 N	122.58 W
Columbia Hills	284b	39.15 N	76.50 W
Columbia Icefield ⩍	182	52.10 N	117.30 W
Columbia Lake ⊜	182	50.15 N	115.57 W
Columbia Lake Indian Reserve ◆[4]	182	50.25 N	115.57 W
Columbia Mountains ⩕	182	52.00 N	119.00 W
Columbiana, Al., U.S.	194	33.10 N	86.36 W
Columbiana, Oh., U.S.	214	40.53 N	80.41 W
Columbiana □[6]	214	40.47 N	80.46 W
Columbia Plateau ⩕[1]	202	44.00 N	117.30 W
Columbia Regional Airport ⊠	219	38.50 N	92.13 W
Columbia Road Reservoir ⊜[1]	198	45.45 N	98.15 W
Columbia State Historical Park ♠	226	38.02 N	120.25 W
Columbia Station	214	41.20 N	81.57 W
Columbia University ☗[2]	276	40.48 N	73.58 W
Columbiaville, Mi., U.S.	190	43.09 N	83.24 W
Columbiaville, N.Y., U.S.	210	42.19 N	73.45 W
Columbine, Cape ›	158	32.47 S	17.52 E
Columbrets, Illes II	34	39.52 N	0.40 E
Columbus, Ga., U.S.	192	32.29 N	84.59 W
Columbus, In., U.S.	218	39.12 N	85.55 W
Columbus, Ks., U.S.	198	37.10 N	94.50 W
Columbus, Ms., U.S.	194	33.29 N	88.25 W
Columbus, Mt., U.S.	202	45.38 N	109.15 W
Columbus, Ne., U.S.	198	41.25 N	97.22 W
Columbus, N.J., U.S.	208	40.04 N	74.43 W
Columbus, N.M., U.S.	200	31.49 N	107.38 W
Columbus, N.C., U.S.	192	35.15 N	82.11 W
Columbus, N.D., U.S.	198	48.54 N	102.46 W
Columbus, Oh., U.S.	214	39.57 N	82.59 W
Columbus, Pa., U.S.	214	41.56 N	79.35 W
Columbus, Tx., U.S.	222	29.42 N	96.32 W
Columbus, Wi., U.S.	190	43.20 N	89.00 W
Columbus Air Force Base ■	194	33.38 N	88.26 W
Columbus Grove	216	40.55 N	84.03 W
Columbus Junction	190	41.16 N	91.21 W
Columbus Lake ⊜[1]	194	33.35 N	88.30 W
Columbus Park ♠	278	41.53 N	87.47 W
Columbus Point ›, Ba.	238	24.08 N	75.16 W
Columbus Point ›, Trin.	241r	11.08 N	60.48 W
Columbus Salt Marsh ≡	204	38.04 N	117.58 W
Coluna	255	18.14 S	42.50 W
Colusa	226	39.12 N	122.00 W
Colusa □[6]	226	39.13 N	122.01 W
Colusa Trough ≊	226	39.02 N	121.59 W
Colver	214	40.32 N	78.47 W
Colville, N.Z.	172	36.38 S	175.28 E
Colville, Wa., U.S.	202	48.32 N	117.54 W
Colville ≃, Ak., U.S.	180	70.25 N	150.30 W
Colville ≃, Wa., U.S.	202	48.37 N	118.05 W
Colville, Cape ›	172	36.28 S	175.21 E
Colville Channel ⊔	172	36.23 S	175.24 E
Colville Indian Reservation ◆[4]	202	48.15 N	119.00 W
Colville Lake ⊜	180	67.10 N	126.00 W
Colvin Run	284c	38.58 N	77.18 W
Colwell	44	55.04 N	2.04 W
Colwood	224	48.26 N	123.29 W
Colwyn	285	39.55 N	75.15 W
Colwyn Bay	44	53.18 N	3.43 W
Colyton, Austl.	274a	33.47 S	150.48 E
Colyton, Eng., U.K.	42	50.44 N	3.04 W
Comacchio	66	44.42 N	12.11 E
Comacchio, Valli di ⊂	66	44.38 N	12.06 E
Comal	115a	6.55 S	109.31 E
Comala	234	19.19 N	103.45 W
Comalapa, Guat.	236	14.44 N	90.53 W
Comalapa, Nic.	236	12.17 N	85.31 W
Comalcalco	234	18.16 N	93.13 W
Comallo, Arroyo ≃	254	40.29 S	70.12 W
Coman, Mount ∧	9	74.02 S	65.04 W
Comana	38	43.54 N	28.19 E
Comanche, Ok., U.S.	196	34.22 N	97.57 W
Comanche, Tx., U.S.	196	31.53 N	98.36 W
Comanche Creek ≃, Co., U.S.	198	39.53 N	104.19 W
Comanche Creek ≃, Tx., U.S.	196	31.06 N	102.24 W
Comandante Ferraz ☗[3]	9	62.05 S	58.23 W
Comandante Fontana	252	25.20 S	59.41 W
Comandante Leal	252	30.53 S	65.47 W
Comandante Luis Piedrabuena	254	49.59 S	68.54 W

FRANÇAIS

Nom	Page	Lat.°′	Long.°′ W = Ouest
Comandante Nicanor Otamendi	252	38.07 S	57.51 W
Comănești	38	46.25 N	26.26 E
Comanjá de Corona	234	21.19 N	101.42 W
Comarapa	248	17.54 S	64.29 W
Comar Gambon	144	3.10 N	45.47 E
Comas, Perú	248	11.46 S	75.02 W
Comas, Perú	286d	11.57 S	77.04 W
Comayagua	236	14.25 N	87.37 W
Comayagua □[5]	236	14.30 N	87.40 W
Comayagua, Montañas de ⩕	236	14.23 N	87.26 W
Combahee ≃	192	32.30 N	80.31 W
Combarbalá	252	31.11 S	71.02 W
Combeaufontaine	58	47.43 N	5.53 E
Combe Martin	42	51.13 N	4.02 W
Comber, On., Can.	214	42.14 N	82.33 W
Comber, N. Ire., U.K.	48	54.33 N	5.45 W
Comberbach	262	53.17 N	2.32 W
Combermere Bay ⊂	110	19.37 N	93.34 E
Comberton	42	52.11 N	0.02 E
Combe Seamount ⊹[3]	14	12.32 S	177.35 W
Combie, Lake ⊜[1]	226	39.01 N	121.02 W
Comblain-au-Pont	56	50.28 N	5.35 E
Combles	50	50.01 N	2.52 E
Combloux	62	45.54 N	6.39 E
Combourg	32	48.25 N	1.45 W
Comboyne	166	31.36 S	152.29 E
Comboyuro Point ›	171a	27.04 S	153.24 E
Combres	50	48.19 N	1.04 E
Combronde	32	45.59 N	3.05 E
Combs	262	53.18 N	1.57 W
Combs-la-Ville	50	48.40 N	2.34 E
Combs Reservoir ⊜[1]	262	53.19 N	1.57 W
Comburg ☗[1]	56	49.06 N	9.44 E
Comb Wash V	200	37.13 N	109.42 W
Come by Chance	186	47.51 N	53.58 W
Comeglians	64	46.31 N	12.52 E
Comelico Superiore	64	46.35 N	12.30 E
Comendado Levy Gasparain	256	22.01 S	43.12 W
Comendador	238	18.53 N	71.42 W
Comendador Gomes	255	19.41 S	49.05 W
Comer	192	34.03 N	83.07 W
Comercinho	255	16.19 S	41.47 W
Comerío	240m	18.13 N	66.14 W
Comet	166	23.37 S	148.33 E
Comet ≃	166	23.34 S	148.32 E
Cometela	156	21.51 S	34.29 E
Comfort, N.C., U.S.	192	35.00 N	77.30 W
Comfort, Tx., U.S.	196	29.58 N	98.54 W
Comfort, Cape ›	176	65.08 N	83.21 W
Comfort, Point ›	276	40.27 N	74.08 W
Comfrey	198	44.06 N	94.54 W
Comilla	124	23.27 N	91.12 E
Comines	50	50.46 N	3.01 E
Comino, Capo ›	71	40.32 N	9.49 E
Comino → Kemmuna I	36	36.00 N	14.20 E
Comiskey Park ♠	278	41.50 N	87.38 W
Comiso	70	36.56 N	14.36 E
Comitan de Dominguez	232	16.15 N	92.08 W
Comitini	70	37.24 N	13.39 E
Comloșu Mare	38	45.54 N	20.38 E
Commack	210	40.50 N	73.17 W
Commagene □[9]	130	37.50 N	38.00 E
Commencement Bay ⊂	224	47.17 N	122.28 W
Commentry	32	46.17 N	2.44 E
Commerce, Ga., U.S.	192	34.12 N	83.27 W
Commerce, Mi., U.S.	216	42.34 N	83.30 W
Commerce, Ok., U.S.	196	36.56 N	94.52 W
Commerce, Tx., U.S.	196	33.14 N	95.53 W
Commerce City	198	39.49 N	104.56 W
Commerciale Luigi Bocconi, Università ☗[2]	266b	45.26 N	9.11 E
Commercial Point	218	39.46 N	83.04 W
Commercy	56	48.45 N	5.35 E
Commewijne □[5]	250	5.50 N	55.00 W
Comminges ◆[1]	32	43.15 N	0.45 E
Committee Bay ⊂	176	68.30 N	86.30 W
Commodore	214	40.43 N	78.57 W
Commodore Barry Bridge ◆[5]	285	39.49 N	75.22 W
Commondale	158	27.20 S	30.56 E
Common Edge	262	53.47 N	3.02 W
Commonwealth Bay ⊂	9	66.54 S	142.40 E
Commonwealth Range ⩕	9	84.15 S	172.20 E
Commoron Creek ≃	166	28.22 S	150.08 E
Community Center	228	34.16 N	118.44 W
Como, Austl.	274a	34.00 S	151.04 E
Como, It.	62	45.47 N	9.05 E
Como, Ms., U.S.	194	34.30 N	89.56 W
Como, N.C., U.S.	208	36.30 N	77.00 W
Como, Tx., U.S.	222	33.03 N	95.28 W
Como, Wi., U.S.	216	42.37 N	88.28 W
Como □[4]	58	45.59 N	9.13 E
Como, Lago di ⊜	58	46.00 N	9.20 E
Como, Lake ⊜	216	42.36 N	88.29 W
Como, Mount ∧	226	39.02 N	119.28 W
Comodoro Rivadavia	254	45.52 S	67.30 W
Como Lake ⊜	190	47.55 N	83.30 W
Comologno	58	46.12 N	8.34 E
Comonfort	234	20.43 N	100.46 W
Comoras → Comoros □[1]	157a	12.10 S	44.15 E
Comores, Archipel des II	157a	12.10 S	44.15 E
Comores → Comoros □[1]	157a	12.10 S	44.15 E
Comorin, Cape ›	122	8.06 N	77.33 E
Comoros (Comores) □[1], Afr.	138	12.10 S	44.15 E
Comoros (Comores) □[1], Afr.	157a	12.10 S	44.15 E
Comox	182	49.40 N	124.55 W
Comox, Canadian Forces Base ■	182	49.43 N	124.54 W
Companhia Siderúrgica Nacional ☗[3]	256	22.31 S	44.07 W
Compans	261	49.00 N	2.40 E
Compatsch	58	46.58 N	10.25 E
Compiègne	50	49.25 N	2.50 E
Compo Cove ⊂	276	41.07 N	73.21 W
Compostela, Méx.	234	21.15 N	104.53 W
Compostela, Pil.	116	7.40 N	126.02 E
Comprida, Ilha I, Bra.	252	24.50 S	47.42 W
Comprida, Ilha I, Bra.	287a	23.02 S	43.12 W
Comps-sur-Artuby	62	43.43 N	6.30 E
Compstall	262	53.25 N	2.03 W
Compton, Eng., U.K.	260	51.13 N	0.38 W
Compton, Ca., U.S.	228	33.53 N	118.13 W
Compton, Il., U.S.	216	41.42 N	89.05 W
Compton □[6]	206	45.20 N	71.25 W
Compton Airport ⊠	280	33.53 N	118.15 W
Compton Creek ≃, Ca., U.S.	280	33.50 N	118.12 W
Compton Creek ≃, N.J., U.S.	276	40.26 N	74.05 W
Comptonville	273d	26.17 S	27.58 E
Comrie	46	56.22 N	4.00 W
Comstock, Mi., U.S.	216	42.17 N	85.30 W
Comstock, Ne., U.S.	198	41.33 N	99.15 W
Comstock, Tx., U.S.	196	29.41 N	101.11 W
Comstock Park	216	43.02 N	85.40 W
Comunanza	66	42.57 N	13.25 E
Con ≃, Ross.	76	52.54 N	36.00 E
Çon ≃, Viet	110	19.02 N	104.58 E
Čona ≃, Ross.	74	62.54 N	111.06 E
Cona ≃, Scot., U.K.	46	56.46 N	5.14 W
Co Nag ⊜	120	32.00 N	91.15 E
Conakry	150	9.31 N	13.43 W
Conambo ≃	246	2.07 S	76.03 W
Conanicut Island I	207	41.32 N	71.21 W
Cona Niyeo	254	41.53 S	67.00 W
Conara Junction	166	41.50 S	147.26 E
Conasauga ≃	192	34.33 N	84.55 W

PORTUGUÊS

Nome	Página	Lat.°′	Long.°′ W = Oeste
Conaskonk Point ›	276	40.27 N	74.11 W
Conca ≃	66	43.58 N	12.43 E
Concarán	252	32.34 S	65.15 W
Concarneau	32	47.52 N	3.55 W
Conceição, Bra.	248	7.24 S	58.05 W
Conceição, Bra.	250	7.33 S	38.31 W
Conceição, Moç.	156	18.45 S	36.10 E
Conceição, Cachoeira ∟	248	9.34 S	64.22 W
Conceição, Ilha da I	287a	22.52 S	43.07 W
Conceição da Barra	255	18.35 S	39.45 W
Conceição da Pedra	256	22.09 S	45.27 W
Conceição das Alagoas	255	19.55 S	48.23 W
Conceição de Ipanema	255	19.55 S	41.41 W
Conceição de Jacareí	256	23.02 S	44.09 W
Conceição do Almeida	255	12.48 S	39.12 W
Conceição do Araguaia	250	8.15 S	49.17 W
Conceição do Canindé	250	7.54 S	41.34 W
Conceição do Coité	250	11.33 S	39.16 W
Conceição do Formoso	256	21.25 S	43.21 W
Conceição do Mato Dentro	255	19.01 S	43.25 W
Conceição do Maú	246	3.35 N	59.53 W
Conceição do Norte	255	12.13 S	47.18 W
Conceição do Rio Verde	256	21.53 S	45.05 W
Conceição dos Ouros	256	22.25 S	45.47 W
Concepción, Arg.	252	28.23 S	57.53 W
Concepción, Arg.	252	27.20 S	65.35 W
Concepción, Bol.	248	11.29 S	66.31 W
Concepción, Bol.	248	16.15 S	62.04 W
Concepción, Chile	252	36.50 S	73.03 W
Concepción, Col.	246	6.46 N	72.42 W
Concepción, Para.	252	23.25 S	57.17 W
Concepción, Perú	248	11.55 S	75.17 W
Concepcion, Pil.	116	11.13 N	123.06 E
Concepcion, Pil.	116	10.42 N	123.03 E
Concepcion, Pil.	116	12.24 N	122.06 E
Concepcion, Pil.	116	15.19 N	120.39 E
Concepción □[5]	252	23.00 S	57.00 W
Concepción, Bahía ⊂	232	26.39 N	111.48 W
Concepción, Canal ⊔	254	50.30 S	74.55 W
Concepción, Laguna ⊜	248	17.29 S	61.25 W
Concepción, Volcán ∧[1]	236	11.34 N	85.37 W
Concepcion Bay ⊂	116	11.15 N	123.07 E
Concepción de Ataco	236	13.52 N	89.51 W
Concepción de Buenos Aires	234	19.58 N	103.16 W
Concepción de la Sierra	252	27.59 S	55.31 W
Concepcíon del Oro	232	24.38 N	101.25 W
Concepción del Uruguay	252	32.29 S	58.14 W
Concepción Huista	236	15.37 N	91.41 W
Concepción Quezaltepeque	236	14.06 N	88.58 W
Conception, Point ›	204	34.27 N	120.27 W
Conception Bay ⊂, Nf., Can.	186	47.45 N	53.00 W
Conception Bay ⊂, Namibia	156	23.53 S	14.28 E
Concession	154	17.22 S	30.57 E
Conchagua	236	13.19 N	87.52 W
Conchagua, Volcán ∧[1]	236	13.14 N	87.46 W
Conchal	256	22.20 S	47.10 W
Conchalí	286e	33.24 S	70.39 W
Conchalí, Cerros de ⩕	286e	33.20 S	70.38 W
Conchas ≃	196	35.23 N	104.18 W
Conchas Dam	196	35.22 N	104.11 W
Conchas Lake ⊜[1]	196	35.25 N	104.14 W
Conche	186	50.53 N	55.54 W
Conches-en-Ouche	50	48.58 N	0.56 E
Conchi	252	22.02 S	68.38 W
Conchillas	258	34.15 S	58.04 W
Conchitas, Arroyo ≃	288	34.45 S	58.09 W
Concho	200	34.28 N	109.36 W
Concho ≃	196	31.34 N	99.43 W
Conchos ≃, Méx.	232	29.35 N	104.25 W
Conchos ≃, Méx.	232	24.55 N	97.40 W
Concise	58	46.51 N	6.43 E
Conco	64	45.48 N	11.36 E
Concón	252	32.55 S	71.31 W
Concononongon Point ›	116	12.14 N	120.13 E
Conconully	182	48.33 N	119.44 W
Concord, Austl.	274a	33.52 S	151.06 E
Concord, On., Can.	275b	43.48 N	79.29 W
Concord, Ca., U.S.	226	37.58 N	122.01 W
Concord, Ga., U.S.	192	33.05 N	84.26 W
Concord, Il., U.S.	219	39.49 N	90.22 W
Concord, Ky., U.S.	218	38.41 N	83.29 W
Concord, Ma., U.S.	207	42.27 N	71.20 W
Concord, Mi., U.S.	216	42.10 N	84.38 W
Concord, Mo., U.S.	219	38.31 N	90.23 W
Concord, N.H., U.S.	188	43.12 N	71.32 W
Concord, N.C., U.S.	192	35.24 N	80.34 W
Concord, Pa., U.S.	214	40.15 N	77.42 W
Concord, Tx., U.S.	222	31.16 N	96.09 W
Concord ≃	283	42.39 N	71.18 W
Concord Battleground ⊥	283	42.28 N	71.21 W
Concordia, Arg.	252	31.24 S	58.02 W
Concórdia, Bra.	246	4.35 S	66.35 W
Concórdia, Bra.	252	27.14 S	52.01 W
Concordia, Méx.	234	23.17 N	106.04 W
Concordia, Perú	246	4.30 S	74.55 W
Concordia, Ks., U.S.	198	39.34 N	97.39 W
Concordia, Mo., U.S.	194	38.59 N	93.34 W
Concordia Gardens	216	41.09 N	85.08 W
Concordia Sagittaria ⊥	64	45.45 N	12.51 E
Concordia sulla Secchia	64	44.55 N	10.59 E
Concord Naval Weapons Station ■	282	38.03 N	122.02 W
Concordville	285	39.53 N	75.31 W
Concord West	274a	33.51 S	151.05 E
Concorezzo	62	45.35 N	9.20 E
Concrete	224	48.32 N	121.44 W
Con Cuong	110	19.02 N	104.54 E
Conda	152	11.06 S	14.20 E
Condamine	166	26.56 S	150.08 E
Condamine ≃	166	27.07 S	149.48 E
Condat-en-Féniers	32	45.21 N	2.46 E
Condé, Ang.	152	10.50 S	14.37 E
Conde, Bra.	255	11.49 S	37.37 W
Condé, Fr.	32	48.51 N	0.33 W
Conde, S.D., U.S.	198	45.09 N	98.05 W
Condécourt	261	49.02 N	1.57 E
Condé-en-Brie	50	49.00 N	3.33 E
Condega	236	13.21 N	86.24 W
Condeixa	250	0.54 S	48.36 W
Condé-sur-l'Escaut	50	50.27 N	3.35 E
Condè-sur-Vesgre	261	48.45 N	1.40 E
Condeúba	255	14.53 S	41.59 W
Condevilla	286d	12.02 S	77.05 W
Condino	64	45.53 N	10.36 E
Condobolin	166	33.05 S	147.09 E
Condom	32	43.58 N	0.22 E
Condon	202	45.14 N	120.11 W
Condoto	246	5.06 N	76.37 W
Condove	62	45.07 N	7.18 E
Condrieu	62	45.27 N	4.46 E
Condroz □[9]	56	50.25 N	5.00 E
Cone	196	33.48 N	101.23 W
Conecuh ≃	194	30.58 N	87.14 W
Conegliano	64	45.53 N	12.18 E
Conejos	200	37.05 N	106.01 W
Conejos ≃	200	37.18 N	105.44 W
Conemaugh	214	40.24 N	78.52 W
Conemaugh ≃	214	40.28 N	79.27 W
Conemaugh River Lake ⊜[1]	214	40.28 N	79.17 W
Conembaro, Cerro ∧	234	18.40 N	102.06 W
Cone Mountain ∧	180	66.12 N	156.03 W
Conero, Monte ∧	66	43.33 N	13.36 E
Conestoga	208	39.57 N	76.21 W
Conestoga Creek ≃	208	39.56 N	76.23 W
Conestogo	212	43.32 N	80.30 W
Conestogo ≃	212	43.32 N	80.29 W
Conestogo Lake ⊜	212	43.44 N	80.44 W
Conesus	210	42.43 N	77.41 W
Conesus Lake ⊜	210	42.47 N	77.43 W
Conesville	214	40.11 N	81.53 W
Conewago Creek ≃	208	40.07 N	76.42 W
Conewago Lake ⊜	208	40.06 N	76.52 W
Conewango Creek ≃	214	41.50 N	79.09 W
Coney Island ◆[8]	276	40.34 N	74.00 W
Confederation Lake ⊜	184	51.05 N	92.44 W
Configni	66	42.25 N	12.38 E
Conflans-en-Jarnisy	56	49.10 N	5.51 E
Conflans-Sainte-Honorine	50	48.59 N	2.06 E
Conflenti	68	39.04 N	16.17 E
Conflict Group II	164	10.45 S	151.45 E
Confluence	188	39.48 N	79.21 W
Confolens	32	46.01 N	0.41 E
Confraternidad, Parque ♠	286d	12.09 S	77.02 W
Confusion Bay ⊂	186	49.58 N	55.47 W
Confuso ≃	252	25.09 S	57.34 W
Cong	48	53.32 N	9.19 W
Congamond	207	42.01 N	72.46 W
Congaree ≃	192	33.45 N	80.37 W
Congelin	168a	32.50 S	116.54 E
Congers	210	41.09 N	73.56 W
Congers Lake ⊜	276	41.09 N	73.57 W
Cong Hoa Stadium ♠	269c	10.45 N	106.40 E
Conghua	100	23.32 N	113.32 E
Congjiang	102	25.41 N	108.47 E
Congleton	44	53.10 N	2.13 W
Congo □[1], Afr.	138	1.00 S	15.00 E
Congo □[1], Afr.	152	1.00 S	15.00 E
Congo (Zaire) (Zaïre) ≃	138	6.04 S	12.24 E
Congo, Democratic Republic of the → Zaire □[1]	138	4.00 S	25.00 E
Congo, République démocratique du → Zaire □[1]	138	4.00 S	25.00 E
Congo, république du → Congo □[1]	152	1.00 S	15.00 E
Congo, Serra do ⩕	152	6.30 S	13.43 E
Congo Basin ≚[1]	10	0.00	20.00 E
Congonhal	256	22.09 S	46.02 W
Congonhas, Aeroporto de ⊠	256	23.38 S	46.38 W
Congost ≃	266d	41.33 N	2.15 E
Congresbury	42	51.23 N	2.48 W
Congress, Sk., Can.	184	49.46 N	106.00 W
Congress, Oh., U.S.	214	40.55 N	82.03 W
Conie ≃	50	48.06 N	1.30 E
Conigli, Isola dei I	70a	35.30 N	12.33 E
Coningsby	44	53.07 N	0.10 W
Conisbrough	44	53.29 N	1.13 W
Coniston, On., Can.	190	46.29 N	80.51 W
Coniston, Eng., U.K.	44	54.22 N	3.05 W
Coniston Water ⊜	44	54.20 N	3.04 W
Conitaca	232	24.10 N	106.43 W
Conjeeveram → Kānchipuram	122	12.50 N	79.43 E
Conjola	170	35.13 S	150.27 E
Conjola Lake ⊂	170	35.16 S	150.27 E
Čon-Kemin ≃	85	42.42 N	75.54 E
Conklin, Ab., Can.	182	55.38 N	111.05 W
Conklin, N.Y., U.S.	210	42.02 N	75.48 W
Conklingville Dam ◆[6]	210	43.17 N	74.02 W
Conklin Point ›	276	40.41 N	73.17 W
Conkouati	152	4.00 S	11.13 E
Conliège	58	46.39 N	5.36 E
Conlin, Lake ⊜	220	28.14 N	81.07 W
Conn, Lough ⊜	48	54.04 N	9.20 W
Connah's Quay	44	53.13 N	3.03 W
Connaught □[9]	48	53.45 N	9.00 W
Connaughton	285	40.05 N	75.19 W
Connaughton, Mount ∧[2]	162	22.42 S	122.40 E
Connaught Place ♠	272a	28.38 N	77.12 E
Connaux	62	44.05 N	4.36 E
Conneaut	214	41.56 N	80.33 W
Conneaut Creek ≃	214	41.58 N	80.33 W
Conneaut Lake	214	41.36 N	80.19 W
Conneaut Lake ⊜	214	41.37 N	80.18 W
Conneaut Outlet ≃	214	41.33 N	80.06 W
Conneautville	214	41.45 N	80.22 W
Connecticut □[3], U.S.	178	41.45 N	72.45 W
Connecticut □[3], U.S.	207	41.45 N	72.45 W
Connecticut ≃	188	41.17 N	72.21 W
Connell	202	46.39 N	118.51 W
Connell, Mount ∧	182	49.18 N	115.38 W
Connellsville	188	40.01 N	79.35 W
Connelly	210	41.55 N	73.59 W
Connel Park	44	55.23 N	4.12 W
Connemara	166	24.13 S	142.17 E
Connemara ◆[1]	48	53.25 N	9.45 W
Conner	116	17.48 N	121.19 E
Conner, Mount ∧	162	25.23 S	131.54 E
Connerré	50	48.03 N	0.30 E
Connersville, Fl., U.S.	220	27.54 N	81.47 W
Connersville, In., U.S.	218	39.38 N	85.08 W
Connetquot ≃	276	40.43 N	73.08 W
Connetquot Brook ≃	276	40.45 N	73.09 W
Connetquot River State Park ♠	210	40.46 N	73.09 W
Connewarre, Lake ⊜	169	38.14 S	144.27 E
Conn Island I	284c	39.00 N	77.16 W
Conn Lake ⊜	176	70.34 N	73.30 W
Connoquenessing	214	40.49 N	80.59 W
Connoquenessing Creek ≃	214	40.51 N	80.19 W
Connors Range ⩕	166	21.40 S	149.10 E
Conodoguinet Creek ≃	208	40.17 N	76.55 W
Conon ≃	46	57.34 N	4.26 W
Cononaco ≃	246	1.32 S	75.35 W
Cononbridge	46	57.34 N	4.26 W
Conorochite ≃	246	2.41 N	67.29 W
Conotton Creek ≃	214	40.34 N	81.23 W
Conover	192	35.42 N	81.13 W
Conowingo	208	39.40 N	76.09 W
Conowingo ◆[6]	208	39.33 N	76.04 W
Conowingo Creek ≃	208	39.41 N	76.12 W
Conowingo Dam ◆[6]	208	39.39 N	76.10 W
Conquest	184	51.32 N	107.17 W
Conquista	255	19.56 S	47.33 W
Conrad, Ia., U.S.	190	42.13 N	92.52 W
Conrad, Mt., U.S.	202	48.10 N	111.56 W
Conrado	256	22.32 S	43.33 W
Conroe	222	30.18 N	95.27 W
Conroe, Lake ⊜[1]	222	30.25 N	95.37 W
Çonsandolo	66	44.39 N	11.46 E
Čon-Saryoj	85	42.37 N	76.53 E
Conscience Bay ⊂	276	40.57 N	73.07 W
Consdorf	56	49.46 N	6.20 E
Consecon	212	44.00 N	77.31 W
Conselheiro Lafaiete	255	20.40 S	43.48 W
Conselheiro Paulino	256	22.13 S	42.31 W
Conselheiro Pena	255	19.10 S	41.30 W
Conselice	66	44.31 N	11.49 E
Conselve	64	45.14 N	11.52 E
Conservatória	256	22.18 S	43.57 W
Consett	44	54.51 N	1.49 W
Conshohocken	208	40.04 N	75.18 W
Consolação	256	22.33 S	45.55 W
Consolação ◆[8]	287b	23.33 S	46.39 W
Consolación del Sur	240p	22.30 N	83.31 W
Consolidated Main Reef Mines ◆[7]	273d	26.11 S	27.56 E
Con Son II	110	8.43 N	106.36 E
Consort	184	52.01 N	110.46 W
Constable	206	44.56 N	74.18 W
Constableville	212	43.34 N	75.25 W
Constance, Lake → Bodensee ⊜	58	47.35 N	9.25 E
Constance → Konstanz	58	47.40 N	9.10 E
Constance Lake ⊜	212	45.25 N	75.58 W
Constância	34	39.28 N	8.20 W
Constanța	38	44.11 N	28.39 E
Constanța □[6]	38	44.20 N	28.20 E
Constant Creek ≃	212	45.17 N	76.46 W
Constantia	210	43.14 N	76.00 W
Constantina	34	37.52 N	5.37 W
Constantine	216	41.50 N	85.40 W
Constantine, Cape ›	180	58.25 N	158.50 W
Constantine → Qacentina	148	36.22 N	6.37 E
Constantinople → İstanbul	130	41.01 N	28.58 E
Constant Lake ⊜	212	45.24 N	77.00 W
Constitución, Chile	252	35.20 S	72.25 W
Constitución, Ur.	252	31.05 S	57.50 W
Constitución ◆[8]	288	34.37 S	58.23 W
Constitución de 01080507, Parque Nacional ♠	204	32.05 N	115.55 W
Constitution, Mount ∧	224	48.40 N	122.50 W
Consuegra	34	39.28 N	3.36 W
Consul	184	49.21 N	109.30 W
Consuma	66	43.47 N	11.35 E
Consuma, Passo della)(	66	43.47 N	11.36 E
Contai	126	21.47 N	87.45 E
Contamana	248	7.15 S	74.54 W
Contarina	64	45.00 N	12.13 E
Contas, Rio de ≃	255	14.17 S	39.01 W
Contee	208	39.05 N	76.52 W
Contendas do Sincorá	255	13.45 S	41.02 W
Contentnea Creek ≃	192	35.21 N	77.23 W
Contes	62	43.49 N	7.19 E
Contessa Entellina	70	37.44 N	13.11 E
Contigliano	66	42.24 N	12.46 E
Continental	216	41.06 N	84.15 W
Continental Peak ∧	200	42.16 N	108.43 W
Contoocook Lake ⊜	207	42.47 N	72.01 W
Contraalmirante Cordero	252	38.44 S	68.10 W
Contra Costa □[6]	226	37.55 N	121.55 W
Contra Costa Canal ≊	282	38.02 N	121.58 W
Contra Loma Reservoir ⊜[1]	282	37.58 N	121.49 W
Contramaestre	240p	20.18 N	76.15 W
Contramaestre ≃	240p	20.31 N	76.18 W
Contratación	246	6.18 N	73.29 W
Contrecoeur	206	45.51 N	73.14 W
Contre Island ›[1]	276	40.54 N	73.32 W
Contreras, Embalse de ⊜[1]	34	39.32 N	1.30 W
Contreras, Isla I	254	51.55 S	74.55 W
Contres	50	47.25 N	1.26 E
Contrexéville	58	48.11 N	5.54 E
Contrisson	56	48.48 N	4.57 E
Controller Bay ⊂	180	60.07 N	144.15 W
Contumazá	248	7.22 S	78.49 W
Contursi	68	40.39 N	15.14 E
Contwoyto Lake ⊜	176	65.42 N	110.50 W
Conty	50	49.44 N	2.09 E
Contz-les-Bains	56	49.27 N	6.21 E
Convención	246	8.28 N	73.21 W
Convent	194	30.01 N	90.49 W
Convento	236	9.21 N	83.30 W
Convent Station	276	40.47 N	74.26 W
Conversano	68	40.58 N	17.08 E
Converse	216	40.34 N	85.52 W
Converse Lake ⊜	276	41.08 N	73.39 W
Converse Pond Brook ≃	276	41.03 N	73.40 W
Convoy	216	40.55 N	84.42 W
Conway, P.E., Can.	186	46.40 N	63.59 W
Conway, S. Afr.	158	31.43 S	25.16 E
Conway, Ar., U.S.	194	35.05 N	92.26 W
Conway, Fl., U.S.	220	28.30 N	81.19 W
Conway, Ma., U.S.	207	42.30 N	72.42 W
Conway, Mo., U.S.	194	37.30 N	92.49 W
Conway, N.H., U.S.	188	43.58 N	71.07 W
Conway, N.C., U.S.	192	36.26 N	77.13 W
Conway, Pa., U.S.	214	40.39 N	80.14 W
Conway, S.C., U.S.	192	33.50 N	79.02 W
Conway, Wa., U.S.	224	48.21 N	122.21 W
Conway, Cape ›	166	20.32 S	148.56 E
Conway, Lake ⊜	162	28.17 S	135.35 E
Conway, Lake ⊜[1]	194	35.00 N	92.25 W
Conway, Mount ∧	162	23.45 S	133.25 E
Conway National Park ♠	166	20.22 S	148.51 E
Conway Springs	198	37.23 N	97.38 W
Conwy	44	53.17 N	3.50 W
Conwy ≃	44	53.17 N	3.50 W
Conwy, Vale of V	44	53.12 N	3.48 W
Conwy Bay ⊂	44	53.18 N	3.55 W
Conyers	192	33.40 N	84.01 W
Conyngham	210	40.59 N	76.03 W
Coo	56	50.24 N	5.52 E
Coober Pedy	162	29.01 S	134.43 E
Coogee, Austl.	168a	32.07 S	115.46 E
Coogee, Austl.	274a	33.55 S	151.16 E
Coogee Bay ⊂	274a	33.55 S	151.16 E
Cook, Austl.	162	30.37 S	130.25 E
Cook, In., U.S.	216	41.22 N	87.26 W
Cook, Mn., U.S.	190	47.51 N	92.41 W
Cook, Ne., U.S.	198	40.30 N	96.09 W
Cook, Wa., U.S.	224	45.43 N	121.40 W
Cook □[6]	216	41.53 N	87.45 W
Cook, Bahía ⊂	254	55.10 S	70.10 W
Cook, Baie de ⊂	174s	17.29 S	149.49 W
Cook, Cape ›	182	50.08 N	127.55 W
Cook, Mount ∧	172	43.36 S	170.10 E
Cook, Point ›	274b	37.55 S	144.48 E
Cook, Récif de ⊹[2]	175f	19.25 S	163.50 E
Cookardinia	171b	35.34 S	147.14 E
Cook Bay ⊂	212	44.15 N	79.30 W
Cook Creek ≃	224	47.17 N	124.05 W
Cooke, Mount ∧	168a	32.25 S	116.18 E
Cookernup	168a	33.00 S	115.54 E
Cookes Peak ∧	200	32.32 N	107.44 W
Cookeville	194	36.09 N	85.30 W
Cook Forest State Park ♠	214	41.22 N	79.12 W
Cookham	42	51.34 N	0.43 W
Cookhouse	158	32.45 S	25.49 E
Cook Ice Shelf ⩍	9	68.40 S	152.30 E
Cooking Lake ⊜	182	53.25 N	113.02 W
Cook Inlet ⊂	180	60.30 N	152.00 W
Cook-Inseln → Cook Islands □[2]	14	20.00 S	158.00 W
Cook Island I	174o	1.57 N	157.28 W
Cook Islands □[2]	14	20.00 S	158.00 W
Cooks ≃	274a	33.56 S	151.10 E
Cooksburg	214	41.20 N	79.12 W
Cooks Falls	210	41.57 N	74.59 W
Cook's Harbour	186	51.36 N	55.52 W
Cookshire	206	45.25 N	71.38 W
Cooksmill Green	260	51.44 N	0.22 E
Cooks Mills	284a	43.00 N	79.11 W
Cookstown, On., Can.	212	44.11 N	79.42 W
Cookstown, N. Ire., U.K.	48	54.39 N	6.45 W
Cook Strait ⊔	172	41.15 S	174.30 E
Cooksville, Il., U.S.	216	40.33 N	88.43 W
Cooksville, Md., U.S.	208	39.19 N	77.01 W
Cooksville, Wi., U.S.	216	42.50 N	89.14 W
Cooksville Creek ≃	275b	43.34 N	79.34 W
Cooktown	164	15.28 S	145.15 E
Cookville	222	33.11 N	94.51 W
Coolabah	166	31.02 S	146.43 E
Cooladdi	166	26.39 S	145.28 E
Coolah	166	31.50 S	149.42 E
Coolamon	166	34.49 S	147.12 E
Coolaney	48	54.11 N	8.29 W
Coolangatta	171a	28.10 S	153.32 E
Coolawanyah	162	21.47 S	117.48 E
Coole ≃	50	48.56 N	4.21 E
Cooleemee	192	35.48 N	80.33 W
Cooley Lake ⊜	281	42.37 N	83.27 W
Coolgardie	162	30.57 S	121.10 E
Coolidge, Az., U.S.	200	32.58 N	111.31 W
Coolidge, Ga., U.S.	192	31.00 N	83.51 W
Coolidge, Tx., U.S.	222	31.45 N	96.38 W
Coolidge, Mount ∧	198	43.44 N	103.29 W
Coolidge Dam ◆[6]	200	33.00 N	110.20 W
Coolidge Point ›	283	42.34 N	70.44 W
Coolin	202	48.28 N	116.50 W
Cooling	260	51.27 N	0.32 E
Cooloola National Park ♠	166	26.05 S	153.00 E
Cooloongup, Lake ⊜	168a	32.18 S	115.47 E
Coolspring	214	41.02 N	79.05 W
Coolumburra Hill ∧	170	35.01 S	150.10 E
Coolup	168a	32.44 S	115.53 E
Cooma	171b	36.14 S	149.08 E
Cooma Creek ≃	171b	36.07 S	149.11 E
Coombe Cottage ⊥	274b	37.43 S	145.23 E
Coomberdale	162	30.28 S	116.02 E
Coomera	171a	27.52 S	153.19 E
Coomera ≃	171a	27.53 S	153.24 E
Coominya	171a	27.23 S	152.30 E
Coonabarabran	166	31.16 S	149.17 E
Coonalpyn	166	35.42 S	139.51 E
Coonamble	166	30.57 S	148.23 E
Coonana	162	31.01 S	123.07 E
Coon Creek ≃, Ca., U.S.	226	38.51 N	121.34 W
Coon Creek ≃, Il., U.S.	216	42.15 N	88.48 W
Coon Creek ≃, Tx., U.S.	222	31.59 N	95.52 W
Coon Creek Lake ⊜[1]	222	32.04 N	95.52 W
Coondambo	166	31.04 S	135.52 E
Coongan ≃	162	20.53 S	119.47 E
Coonoor	122	11.21 N	76.49 E
Coon Rapids, Ia., U.S.	198	41.52 N	94.41 W
Coon Rapids, Mn., U.S.	190	45.10 N	93.19 W
Coontown	276	40.37 N	74.31 W
Coon Valley	190	43.42 N	91.00 W
Cooper	196	33.22 N	95.41 W
Cooper ≃, N.J., U.S.	285	39.57 N	75.07 W
Cooper ≃, Wa., U.S.	224	47.23 N	121.23 W
Cooper, Mount ∧, Austl.	162	26.11 S	127.56 E
Cooper, Mount ∧, B.C., Can.	182	50.11 N	117.12 W
Cooper, North Branch ≃	285	39.55 N	75.02 W
Cooper Center	216	42.23 N	85.37 W
Cooper Creek ≃	166	28.29 S	137.46 E
Cooper Island I	240m	18.22 N	64.30 W
Cooper Landing	180	60.29 N	149.51 W
Cooper Mountain ∧	180	60.23 N	149.51 W
Cooper River Parkway ♠	285	39.55 N	75.03 W
Cooper Road	194	32.26 N	93.48 W
Coopers	194	32.46 N	86.33 W
Coopersale Common	260	51.42 N	0.08 E
Coopersburg	208	40.30 N	75.23 W
Coopers Plains, Austl.	171a	27.34 S	153.02 E
Coopers Plains, N.Y., U.S.	210	42.11 N	77.08 W
Cooperstown, N.Y., U.S.	210	42.42 N	74.55 W
Cooperstown, N.D., U.S.	198	47.26 N	98.07 W
Cooperstown, Pa., U.S.	214	41.30 N	79.52 W
Cooperstown, Pa., U.S.	214	40.43 N	79.57 W
Coopersville	216	43.03 N	85.56 W
Coorabie	162	31.54 S	132.18 E
Cooranbong	170	33.04 S	151.27 E
Coorong National Park ♠	166	36.01 S	139.32 E
Coorow	162	29.53 S	116.01 E
Cooroy	166	26.25 S	152.55 E
Coorparoo	171a	27.30 S	153.03 E
Coos □[6]	206	45.04 N	71.20 W
Coosa ≃	194	32.30 N	86.16 W
Coosawhatchie ≃	192	32.32 N	80.52 W
Coos Bay	202	43.22 N	124.12 W
Coos Bay ⊂	202	43.23 N	124.16 W
Cootamundra	166	34.39 S	148.02 E
Cootehill	48	54.04 N	7.05 W
Cooyar	171a	26.59 S	151.50 E
Cooyar Creek ≃	171a	26.50 S	152.04 E
Çooyar Mountain ∧	171a	26.57 S	151.47 E
Čop	78	48.26 N	22.10 E
Copacabana, Arg.	252	28.12 S	67.29 W
Copacabana, Bol.	248	16.10 S	69.05 W
Copacabana, Col.	246	6.20 N	75.30 W
Copacabana ◆[8]	287a	22.58 S	43.11 W
Copacabana, Forte de ⊥	287a	22.59 S	43.11 W
Copainalá	234	17.05 N	93.12 W
Copake	210	42.06 N	73.33 W
Copake Falls	210	42.07 N	73.31 W
Copala	234	16.37 N	98.58 W
Copalillo	234	18.02 N	99.07 W
Copalis ≃	224	47.07 N	124.13 W
Copalis Beach	224	47.06 N	124.10 W
Copalita ≃	234	15.46 N	96.03 W
Copán, Hond.	236	14.50 N	89.09 W
Copan, Ok., U.S.	196	36.53 N	95.55 W
Copán □[5]	236	14.50 N	89.00 W
Copán ⊥	236	14.50 N	89.09 W
Copanatoyac	234	17.15 N	98.45 W
Copándaro	234	19.53 N	101.13 W
Copan Lake ⊜[1]	196	36.55 N	95.56 W
Copano Bay ⊂	196	28.05 N	97.05 W
Copatana	246	2.48 S	67.04 W
Cope	198	39.39 N	102.51 W
Copeá, Paraná ≃[1]	246	3.52 S	63.20 W
Copeau ≃	184	52.45 N	103.00 W
Copeland	220	25.57 N	81.21 W
Copeland Island I	48	54.41 N	5.32 W
Copenhagen	212	43.53 N	75.40 W
Copenhagen → København	41	55.40 N	12.35 E
Copenhague → København	41	55.40 N	12.35 E
Copenhaver	284c	39.04 N	77.11 W
Copertino	68	40.16 N	18.03 E
Copetonas	252	38.43 S	60.27 W
Copeville	222	33.05 N	96.25 W
Copiague	210	40.40 N	73.24 W
Copiague Neck ›[1]	276	40.40 N	73.22 W
Copiapó	252	27.22 S	70.20 W
Copiapó ≃	252	27.19 S	70.56 W
Copinsay I	46	58.54 N	2.40 W
Coplay	208	40.40 N	75.29 W
Copley, Austl.	166	30.32 S	138.25 E
Copley, Oh., U.S.	214	41.06 N	81.39 W
Copmanthorpe	44	53.55 N	1.08 W
Copoas, Mount ∧	116	10.48 N	119.17 E
Çopolo	152	10.22 S	14.07 E
Čopoviči	78	50.49 N	27.58 E
Copparo	64	44.54 N	11.49 E
Coppell	222	32.57 N	97.01 W
Coppename ≃	250	5.48 N	55.55 W
Coppenbrügge	52	52.07 N	9.32 E
Copper ≃	180	60.30 N	144.50 W
Copperas Cove	196	31.07 N	97.54 W
Copperas Mountain ∧	276	41.02 N	74.28 W
Copperbelt □[4]	154	13.00 S	28.00 E
Copper Butte ∧	202	48.42 N	118.28 W
Copper Canyon → Cobre, Barranca del V	232	27.28 N	107.50 W
Copper Center	180	61.58 N	145.19 W
Copper Cliff	190	46.28 N	81.04 W
Copper Creek ≃	192	36.40 N	82.45 W
Copper Harbor	190	47.27 N	87.53 W
Coppermine	176	67.50 N	115.05 W
Coppermine ≃	176	67.49 N	115.04 W
Copper Mine Point ›, Br. Vir. Is.	240m	18.26 N	64.25 W

Symbol	English	Deutsch	Español	Français	Português
≃	River	Fluß	Río	Rivière	Rio
≊	Canal	Kanal	Canal	Canal	Canal
∟	Waterfall, Rapids	Wasserfall, Stromschnellen	Cascada, Rápidos	Chute d'eau, Rapides	Cascata, Rápidos
⊔	Strait	Meeresstraße	Estrecho	Détroit	Estreito
⊂	Bay, Gulf	Bucht, Golf	Bahía, Golfo	Baie, Golfe	Baía, Golfo
⊜	Lake, Lakes	See, Seen	Lago, Lagos	Lac, Lacs	Lago, Lagos
≡	Swamp	Sumpf	Pantano	Marais	Pântano
⩍	Ice Features, Glacier	Eis- und Gletscherformen	Accidentes Glaciales	Formes glaciaires	Acidentes glaciares
⊤	Other Hydrographic Features	Andere Hydrographische Objekte	Otros Elementos Hidrográficos	Autres données hydrographiques	Outros acidentes hidrográficos
⊹	Submarine Features	Untermeerische Objekte	Accidentes Submarinos	Formes de relief sous-marin	Acidentes submarinos
□	Political Unit	Politische Einheit	Unidad Politica	Entité politique	Unidade política
☗	Cultural Institution	Kulturelle Institution	Institución Cultural	Institution culturelle	Instituição cultural
⊥	Historical Site	Historische Stätte	Sitio Histórico	Site historique	Sitio histórico
♠	Recreational Site	Erholungs- und Ferienort	Sitio de Recreo	Centre de loisirs	Area de Lazer
⊠	Airport	Flughafen	Aeropuerto	Aéroport	Aeroporto
■	Military Installation	Militäranlage	Instalación Militar	Installation militaire	Instalação militar
◆	Miscellaneous	Verschiedenes	Misceláneo	Divers	Diversos

Name	Page	Lat.°′	Long.°′
Coppermine Point ≻, On., Can.	190	46.59 N	84.47 W
Copper Mountain	182	49.20 N	120.33 W
Copper Mountain ʌ, Ak., U.S.	182	55.14 N	132.36 W
Copper Mountain ʌ, Wy., U.S.	200	43.27 N	107.57 W
Copperopolis	226	37.59 N	120.38 W
Coppet	58	46.19 N	6.12 E
Coppin State College ʊ[2]	284b	39.19 N	76.40 W
Copplestone	42	50.49 N	3.45 W
Coppull	262	53.37 N	2.40 W
Copster Green	262	53.48 N	2.30 W
Coptic Museum ʊ	273c	30.00 N	31.13 E
Copton Creek ≃	182	54.16 N	119.15 W
Copton Point ≻	116	10.00 N	123.22 E
Coqên	120	31.20 N	85.25 E
Coquet ≃	44	55.22 N	1.37 W
Coquet Dale V	44	55.16 N	1.50 W
Coquí	240m	17.59 N	66.14 W
Coquilhatville → Mbandaka	152	0.04 N	18.16 E
Coquille	202	43.10 N	124.11 W
Coquille ≃	202	43.07 N	124.26 W
Coquille, East Fork ≃	202	43.06 N	124.04 W
Coquille, Middle Fork ≃	202	43.05 N	124.09 W
Coquille, South Fork ≃	202	43.02 N	124.07 W
Coquimatlán	234	19.12 N	103.48 W
Coquimbo	252	29.58 S	71.21 W
Coquimbo □[4]	252	30.45 S	71.00 W
Coquina Key I	220	27.44 N	82.38 W
Corabia	38	43.46 N	24.30 E
Coração de Jesus	255	16.42 S	44.22 W
Coração de Maria	255	12.14 S	38.45 W
Corace ≃	68	38.49 N	16.37 E
Coracora	248	15.02 S	73.47 W
Corail, Mer de → Coral Sea ⊤[2]	14	20.00 S	158.00 E
Coral	214	40.29 N	79.10 W
Coral Bay c, Pil.	116	8.25 N	117.20 E
Coral Bay c, Vir. Is., U.S.	240m	18.20 N	64.41 W
Coral Gables	220	25.43 N	80.16 W
Coral Harbour	176	64.08 N	83.10 W
Coral Hills	284c	38.52 N	76.55 W
Coralque ≃	248	16.26 S	70.45 W
Coral Sea ⊤[2]	14	20.00 S	158.00 E
Coral Sea Basin ✢[1]	14	14.00 S	152.00 E
Coral Sea Islands Territory □[8]	166	18.30 S	152.00 E
Coral Springs	220	26.16 N	80.13 W
Coralville	190	41.40 N	91.34 W
Coralville Lake ⊜[1]	190	41.47 N	91.48 W
Coram, Mt., U.S.	202	48.25 N	114.02 W
Coram, N.Y., U.S.	210	40.52 N	73.00 W
Corangamite, Lake ⊜	169	38.10 S	143.25 E
Corantijn (Corentyne) ≃	250	5.55 N	57.05 W
Coraopolis	214	40.31 N	80.10 W
Coraopolis Heights	279b	40.29 N	80.10 W
Corato	68	41.09 N	16.25 E
Corbara, Lago di ⊜[1]	66	42.43 N	12.15 E
Corbeil-Essonnes	50	48.36 N	2.29 E
Corbenay	58	47.54 N	6.20 E
Corbeny	50	49.28 N	3.49 E
Corbeolona	62	45.10 N	9.22 E
Corbera, Riera de ≃	266d	41.27 N	1.59 E
Corberon	58	47.01 N	4.59 E
Corbett	210	42.03 N	75.02 W
Corbetta	62	45.28 N	8.55 E
Corbett National Park ♦	124	29.40 N	78.45 E
Corbettsville	210	42.01 N	75.48 W
Corbie	50	49.55 N	2.30 E
Corbière Point ≻	43b	49.11 N	2.15 W
Corbières ⋏	32	42.55 N	2.38 E
Corbigny	50	47.15 N	3.40 E
Corbin	192	36.56 N	84.05 W
Corbion	56	49.48 N	5.00 E
Corbola	64	45.00 N	12.05 E
Corbones ≃	34	37.36 N	5.39 W
Corbridge	44	54.58 N	2.01 W
Corbu	38	44.29 N	24.43 E
Corby	42	52.29 N	0.40 W
Corcaigh → Cork	48	51.54 N	8.28 W
Córcega	240m	18.19 N	67.15 W
Córcega, Isla de → Corse I	36	42.00 N	9.00 E
Corciano	66	43.08 N	12.17 E
Corcieux	58	48.10 N	6.53 E
Corcolle ◆[8]	267a	41.55 N	12.46 E
Corcoran	226	36.05 N	119.33 W
Corcovado, Golfo c	254	43.30 S	73.30 W
Corcovado, Morro do ʌ	287a	22.57 S	43.13 W
Corcovado, Parque Nacional ♦	236	8.35 N	83.40 W
Corcovado, Volcán ʌ[1]	254	43.12 S	72.48 W
Corcubión	34	42.57 N	9.11 W
Cordeaux Reservoir ⊜[1]	170	34.22 S	150.45 E
Cordeiro	255	22.02 S	42.22 W
Cordele, Ga., U.S.	192	31.57 N	83.46 W
Cordele, Tx., U.S.	222	29.08 N	96.38 W
Cordell	196	35.17 N	98.59 W
Cordell Hull Reservoir ⊜[1]	194	36.25 N	85.40 W
Cordenons	64	45.59 N	12.42 E
Corder	194	39.05 N	93.38 W
Cordes	32	44.04 N	1.57 E
Cordignano	64	45.57 N	12.25 E
Cordillera □[5]	252	25.15 S	57.00 W
Cordillera de los Picachos, Parque Nacional ♦	246	3.00 N	74.30 W
Cordillo Downs	166	26.43 S	140.38 E
Cordisburgo	255	19.07 S	44.21 W
Cordislândia	256	21.48 S	45.43 W
Córdoba, Arg.	252	31.24 S	64.11 W
Córdoba, Esp.	34	37.53 N	4.46 W
Córdoba, Méx.	234	18.53 N	96.56 W
Córdoba □[4], Arg.	252	32.00 S	64.00 W
Córdoba □[4], Esp.	34	38.00 N	4.50 W
Córdoba □[5]	246	8.20 N	75.40 W
Córdoba, Península ≻[1]	254	53.20 S	72.50 W
Cordon	116	16.40 N	121.28 E
Córdova, Perú	248	14.04 S	75.03 W
Cordova, Al., U.S.	194	33.45 N	87.11 W
Cordova, Ak., U.S.	180	60.33 N	145.46 W
Cordova, Il., U.S.	190	41.41 N	90.19 W
Cordova, Md., U.S.	208	38.52 N	75.59 W
Cordova Bay c	182	54.55 N	132.35 W
Cordova → Córdoba	34	37.53 N	4.46 W
Cordova Lake ⊜	212	44.35 N	77.49 W
Cordova Peak ʌ	180	60.51 N	145.16 W
Corea, Estrecho de → Korea Strait ⋓	90	34.00 N	129.00 E
Corea del Norte → Korea, North □[1]	98	40.00 N	127.00 E
Corea del Sur → Korea, South □[1]	98	36.30 N	128.00 E
Coreaú	250	3.33 S	40.39 W
Coreaú ≃	250	2.54 S	40.50 W
Core Creek ≃	285	40.11 N	74.55 W
Corée, Détroit de → Korea Strait ⋓	90	34.00 N	129.00 E
Coree, Mount ʌ	171b	35.18 S	148.48 E
Corée du Nord → Korea, North □[1]	98	40.00 N	127.00 E
Corée du Sud → Korea, South □[1]	98	36.30 N	128.00 E
Coreglia Antelminelli	64	44.04 N	10.31 E
Coreinbob	171b	35.13 S	147.38 E
Coremas	250	7.01 S	37.58 W
Corentyne (Corantijn) ≃	250	5.55 N	57.05 W
Corerepe	232	25.40 N	108.40 W
Corese Terra	66	42.10 N	12.42 E
Corey Lake ⊜	216	41.55 N	85.45 W
Corfe Castle	42	50.38 N	2.04 W
Corfield	166	21.43 S	143.22 E
Corfu	210	42.57 N	78.24 W
Corfu → Kérkira	38	39.36 N	19.56 E
Corfu → Kérkira I	38	39.40 N	19.42 E
Corhanwarrabul Creek ≃	274b	37.55 S	145.12 E
Cori	66	41.39 N	12.55 E
Coria	34	39.59 N	6.32 W
Coria del Río	34	37.16 N	6.03 W
Coribe	255	13.50 S	44.28 W
Coricudgy, Mount ʌ	170	32.50 S	150.22 E
Corigliano Calabro	68	39.36 N	16.31 E
Corigliano d'Otranto	68	40.09 N	18.15 E
Corinaldo	66	43.39 N	13.03 E
Corinda	166	17.53 S	138.35 E
Corinne, Pa., U.S.	285	39.54 N	75.40 W
Corinne, Ut,. U.S.	200	41.33 N	112.06 W
Corinne, W.V., U.S.	192	37.34 N	81.21 W
Corinth, Ky., U.S.	218	38.29 N	84.33 W
Corinth, Ms., U.S.	194	34.56 N	88.31 W
Corinth, N.Y., U.S.	210	43.14 N	73.49 W
Corinth, Gulf of → Korinthiakós Kólpos c	38	38.19 N	22.04 E
Corinth Canal → Korínthou, Dhiórix ≍	38	37.57 N	22.56 E
Corinth → Kórinthos	38	37.56 N	22.56 E
Corinto, Bra.	255	18.21 S	44.27 W
Corinto, El Sal.	236	13.49 N	87.58 W
Corinto, Nic.	236	12.29 N	87.10 W
Corio	169	38.04 S	144.23 E
Corio Bay c	169	38.07 S	144.24 E
Coripata	248	16.18 S	67.36 W
Corire	248	16.14 S	72.28 W
Coris	248	9.50 S	77.45 W
Corisco, Isla de I	152	0.53 N	9.20 E
Corixo Grande (Curiche Grande) ≃	248	17.43 S	57.43 W
Cork (Corcaigh)	48	51.54 N	8.28 W
Cork □[6]	48	51.58 N	8.35 W
Cork Airport ⊠	48	51.51 N	8.29 W
Cork Harbour c	48	51.45 N	8.15 W
Corkscrew	220	26.28 N	81.33 W
Corkscrew Swamp ≡	220	26.25 N	81.34 W
Čorku	85	39.58 N	70.33 E
Corlay	32	48.19 N	3.03 W
Corleone	70	37.49 N	13.18 E
Corleto Perticara	68	40.23 N	16.03 E
Çorlu	130	41.09 N	27.48 E
Cormainville	50	48.08 N	1.36 E
Cormano	266b	45.33 N	9.10 E
Cormatin	58	46.33 N	4.41 E
Cormeilles	50	49.15 N	0.23 E
Cormeilles-en-Parisis	50	48.59 N	2.12 E
Cormery	50	47.16 N	0.51 E
Cormons	64	45.58 N	13.28 E
Cormoran Reef ✦[2]	175b	7.50 N	134.32 E
Cormorant	184	54.14 N	100.35 W
Cormorant Lake ⊜	184	54.13 N	100.47 W
Corna	64	45.53 N	10.10 E
Čornaja, Ross.	24	68.35 N	56.30 E
Čornaja, Ross.	82	55.45 N	38.04 E
Čornaja, Ukr.	78	47.37 N	29.20 E
Čornaja ≃, Ross.	265a	59.47 N	30.10 E
Čornaja ≃, Ross.	265a	59.50 N	30.00 E
Čornaja ≃, Ross.	265a	60.01 N	30.10 E
Čornaja ≃, Ross.	265a	59.55 N	30.59 E
Čornaja ≃, Ross.	265b	55.41 N	37.58 E
Čornaja Cholunica	86	58.51 N	51.42 E
Čornaja Gr'az', Ross.	82	54.31 N	35.52 E
Čornaja Gr'az', Ross.	82	54.58 N	36.48 E
Čornaja Gr'az', Ross.	265b	55.58 N	37.19 E
Čornaja Rečka	265a	59.56 N	30.58 E
Čornaja rečka ≃, Ross.	265a	59.46 N	30.45 E
Čornaja rečka ≃, Ross.	265a	59.55 N	30.22 E
Čornaja Sloboda	24	60.48 N	37.46 E
Cornaredo	266b	45.30 N	9.02 E
Cornas	62	44.58 N	4.51 E
Cornedo Vicentino	64	45.37 N	11.20 E
Cornelia, S. Afr.	158	27.13 S	28.52 E
Cornelia, Ga., U.S.	192	34.30 N	83.31 W
Cornélio Procópio	255	23.08 S	50.39 W
Cornelius, N.C., U.S.	192	35.29 N	80.51 W
Cornelius, Or., U.S.	224	45.31 N	123.03 W
Cornelius Grinnell Bay c	176	63.20 N	64.50 W
Cornell, Il., U.S.	216	41.00 N	88.44 W
Cornell, Wi., U.S.	190	45.10 N	91.08 W
Cornellà de Llobregat	266d	41.21 N	2.05 E
Corner Brook	186	48.57 N	57.57 W
Corner Inlet c	169	38.43 S	146.20 E
Corner Store	285	40.07 N	75.30 W
Cornersville	194	35.21 N	86.50 W
Cornes, Lac des ⊜	206	46.43 N	75.09 W
Corneta, Punta ≻	234	15.39 N	96.34 W
Cornforth	44	54.42 N	1.31 W
Cornhill	46	57.36 N	2.42 W
Cornholme	262	53.44 N	2.08 W
Cornia ≃	66	42.57 N	10.33 E
Corniglia	62	44.07 N	9.42 E
Corniglio	64	44.28 N	10.05 E
Corning, Ar., U.S.	194	36.24 N	90.34 W
Corning, Ca., U.S.	204	39.55 N	122.10 W
Corning, Ia., U.S.	198	40.59 N	94.44 W
Corning, Ks., U.S.	198	39.39 N	96.01 W
Corning, N.Y., U.S.	210	42.08 N	77.03 W
Corning, Oh., U.S.	188	39.36 N	82.05 W
Cornish	188	43.48 N	70.48 W
Cornish, Mount ʌ	162	20.13 S	126.28 E
Cornland	219	39.56 N	89.24 W
Çorno ≃	66	42.49 N	12.55 E
Čornobajevka	78	46.42 N	32.32 E
Çorno Grande ʌ	66	42.28 N	13.34 E
Čornoje, Kaz.	86	51.44 N	77.34 E
Čornoje, Ross.	80	57.32 N	46.25 E
Čornolesskoje	84	44.42 N	43.42 E
Čornomorskij	78	44.51 N	38.29 E
Čornomorskoje, Ukr.	78	45.03 N	35.58 E
Čornomorskoje, Ukr.	78	45.30 N	32.42 E
Čornoreck	86	52.45 N	76.40 E
Cornuda	64	45.50 N	12.00 E
Cornwall, On., Can.	206	45.02 N	74.44 W
Cornwall, N.Y., U.S.	210	41.26 N	74.01 W
Cornwall, Pa., U.S.	208	40.16 N	76.24 W
Cornwall □[6]	42	50.30 N	4.40 W
Cornwall Bridge	207	41.49 N	73.22 W
Cornwallis Island I	176	75.15 N	94.30 W
Cornwall on Hudson	210	41.27 N	74.00 W
Cornwell	220	27.23 N	81.05 W
Cornwells Heights	285	40.04 N	74.56 W
Čornyj Jar	80	48.04 N	46.08 E
Čornyj Mys, Ross.	24	68.20 N	38.37 E
Čornyj Mys, Ross.	86	55.33 N	80.04 E
Čornyj Ostrov	78	49.32 N	26.46 E
Čornyj Otrog	86	51.55 N	55.59 E
Čornyj Tašlyk ≃	78	48.11 N	30.51 E
Corny Point	166	34.55 S	137.03 E
Coro	246	11.25 N	69.41 W
Coro, Golfete de c	241s	11.30 N	69.55 W
Coroaci	255	18.35 S	42.17 W
Coroa Grande	256	22.54 S	43.52 W
Coroatá	250	4.08 S	44.08 W
Çoroca ≃	152	15.43 S	11.55 E
Čoroch (Çoruh) ≃	130	41.36 N	41.35 E
Corocoro	248	17.12 S	68.29 W
Corocoro Island I	246	8.30 N	60.10 W
Coroico	248	16.10 S	67.44 W
Coroico ≃	248	15.27 S	67.50 W
Coromandel, Bra.	255	18.28 S	47.13 W
Coromandel, N.Z.	172	36.46 S	175.30 E
Coromandel Coast ≛[2]	122	13.30 N	80.30 E
Coromandel Peninsula ≻[1]	172	36.50 S	175.35 E
Coromandel Range ⋏	172	37.00 S	175.40 E
Coron	116	12.00 N	120.12 E
Corona, Ca., U.S.	228	33.52 N	117.33 W
Corona, N.M., U.S.	200	34.15 N	105.36 W
Corona ◆[8]	276	40.45 N	73.52 W
Coronación, Golfo de la → Coronation Gulf c	176	68.25 N	110.00 W
Coronación, Isla de la → Coronation Island I	9	60.37 S	45.30 W
Corona del Mar ◆[8]	228	33.36 N	117.52 W
Coronado, Méx.	234	22.55 N	100.56 W
Coronado, Ca., U.S.	228	32.41 N	117.10 W
Coronado, Bahía de c	236	9.00 N	83.50 W
Coronado National Memorial ♦	200	31.10 N	110.29 W
Coronado Naval Amphibious Base ■	228	32.40 N	117.10 W
Coronados, Golfo c	254	41.40 S	74.00 W
Coronation	182	52.05 N	111.27 W
Coronation Gardens ♦	275b	43.41 N	79.29 W
Coronation Gulf c	176	68.25 N	110.00 W
Coronation Island I, B.A.T.	9	60.37 S	45.30 W
Coronation Island I, Ak., U.S.	180	55.52 N	134.15 W
Coronation Park ♦	273d	26.06 S	27.47 E
Coron Bay c	116	11.54 N	120.08 E
Coronda	252	31.58 S	60.55 W
Coronel	252	37.01 S	73.08 W
Coronel Bogado	252	27.11 S	56.18 W
Coronel Dorrego	252	38.42 S	61.17 W
Coronel Du Graty	252	27.40 S	60.56 W
Coronel Eugenio del Busto	252	38.57 S	64.15 W
Coronel Fabriciano	255	19.31 S	42.38 W
Coronel Moldes, Arg.	252	25.16 S	65.29 W
Coronel Moldes, Arg.	252	33.38 S	64.36 W
Coronel Murta	255	16.37 S	42.11 W
Coronel Oviedo	252	25.25 S	56.27 W
Coronel Pacheco	256	21.35 S	43.16 W
Coronel Ponce	255	15.34 S	55.01 W
Coronel Pringles	252	37.58 S	61.22 W
Coronel Sapucaia	255	23.15 S	55.31 W
Coronel Suárez	252	37.28 S	61.55 W
Coronel Vidal	252	37.27 S	57.43 W
Coronel Vivida	252	25.58 S	52.34 W
Corongo	248	8.35 S	77.55 W
Corongoros	234	19.17 N	102.48 W
Coronie □[5]	250	5.50 N	56.20 W
Coron Island I	116	11.55 N	120.14 E
Coronita	228	33.52 N	117.36 W
Coropuna, Nevado ʌ	248	15.31 S	72.42 W
Çorovodë	38	40.30 N	20.13 E
Corowa	166	36.02 S	146.23 E
Corozal, Belize	232	18.24 N	88.24 W
Corozal, Col.	246	9.19 N	75.18 W
Corozal, Hond.	236	15.48 N	86.43 W
Corozal, P.R.	240m	18.21 N	66.17 W
Corps	62	44.49 N	5.57 E
Corpus	252	27.07 S	55.31 W
Corpus Christi	196	27.48 N	97.23 W
Corpus Christi, Lake ⊜[1]	196	28.10 N	97.53 W
Corpus Christi Bay c	196	27.48 N	97.20 W
Corpus Christi Naval Air Station ■	196	27.42 N	97.16 W
Corque	248	18.21 S	67.42 W
Corquín	236	14.34 N	88.52 W
Corral	254	39.52 S	73.26 W
Corral de Almaguer	34	39.46 N	3.11 W
Corral de Bustos	252	33.17 S	62.12 W
Corralero, Laguna c	234	16.12 N	98.07 W
Corralillo	240p	22.59 N	80.35 W
Corralito	252	32.03 S	64.12 W
Corralito, Arroyo del ≃	258	33.39 S	58.03 W
Corralito, Cuchilla del ⋏[2]	258	33.40 S	57.44 W
Corralitos, Méx.	196	26.57 N	104.39 W
Corralitos, Ca., U.S.	226	36.59 N	121.48 W
Corran	46	56.43 N	5.14 W
Corraun Peninsula ≻[1]	48	53.54 N	9.53 W
Correas, Arroyo ≃	288	34.24 S	58.32 W
Correboi, Arcu)(	71	40.05 N	9.21 E
Correctionville	198	42.28 N	95.47 W
Corredor	287b	23.27 S	46.19 W
Correggio	64	44.46 N	10.47 E
Corregidor Island I	116	14.23 N	120.35 E
Corrego do Bom Jesus	256	22.38 S	46.02 W
Córrego do Ouro	256	21.22 S	45.47 W
Córrego Rico	255	15.14 S	47.48 W
Correia de Almeida	256	21.17 S	43.38 W
Corrente	250	10.27 S	45.10 W
Corrente ≃, Bra.	255	19.19 S	50.50 W
Corrente ≃, Bra.	255	13.08 S	43.28 W
Correntes	250	9.08 S	36.19 W
Correntes ≃	248	17.21 S	55.37 W
Correntes, Cabo das ≻	156	24.11 S	35.34 E
Correnti, Isola delle I	70	36.38 N	15.05 E
Correntina	255	13.20 S	44.39 W
Corrèze □[5]	32	45.20 N	1.50 E
Correzzana	266b	45.40 N	9.18 E
Corrib, Lough ⊜	48	53.26 N	9.14 W
Corridonia	66	43.15 N	13.30 E
Corrientes	252	27.28 S	58.50 W
Corrientes □[4]	252	29.00 S	58.00 W
Corrientes ≃, Arg.	252	30.21 S	59.33 W
Corrientes ≃, S.A.	246	3.43 S	74.35 W
Corrientes, Bahía de c	240p	21.51 N	84.36 W
Corrientes, Cabo ≻, Arg.	252	38.01 S	57.32 W
Corrientes, Cabo ≻, Col.	246	5.30 N	77.34 W
Corrientes, Cabo ≻, Cuba	240p	21.45 N	84.31 W
Corrientes, Cabo ≻, Méx.	234	20.25 N	105.42 W
Corrigan	222	30.59 N	94.49 W
Corrigin	162	32.21 S	117.52 E
Corrimal	170	34.22 S	150.54 E
Corringham	260	51.31 N	0.28 E
Corriverton	246	5.53 N	57.08 W
Corrofin	48	52.56 N	9.03 W
Corroios	266c	38.38 N	9.09 W
Corropoli	66	42.49 N	13.50 E
Corrumpa Creek ≃	196	36.36 N	102.52 W
Corry	214	41.55 N	79.38 W
Corryong	171b	36.12 S	147.54 E
Corryong Creek ≃	171b	36.06 S	147.59 E
Corryvreckan, Gulf of ⋓	46	56.09 N	5.44 W
Corsano	68	39.53 N	18.22 E
Corse (Corsica) I	36	42.00 N	9.00 E
Corse, Cap ≻	62	43.00 N	9.25 E
Corse-du-Sud □[5]	36	41.50 N	9.00 E
Corserine ʌ	44	55.09 N	4.22 W
Corsham	42	51.26 N	2.11 W
Corsica, Pa., U.S.	214	41.10 N	79.12 W
Corsica, S.D., U.S.	198	43.25 N	98.24 W
Corsica → Corse I	36	42.00 N	9.00 E
Corsicana	222	32.05 N	96.28 W
Corsica River c	208	39.05 N	76.08 W
Corsico	62	45.26 N	9.07 E
Corsock	44	55.04 N	3.57 W
Corson Inlet c	208	39.12 N	74.39 W
Cortaccia (Kurtatsch)	64	46.19 N	11.13 E
Cortachy	46	56.43 N	2.58 W
Cort Adelaer, Kap ≻	176	62.00 N	42.00 W
Cortale	68	38.50 N	16.25 E
Cortazar	234	20.29 N	100.56 W
Corte	36	42.18 N	9.08 E
Corte Alto	254	40.57 S	73.10 W
Cortegana	34	37.55 N	6.49 W
Corte Madera	226	37.55 N	122.31 W
Corte Madera Creek ≃	282	37.23 N	122.14 W
Cortemaggiore	64	44.59 N	9.56 E
Cortemilia	62	44.35 N	8.12 E
Corteno Golgi	64	46.10 N	10.15 E
Cortes	116	9.17 N	126.11 E
Cortés □[5]	236	15.30 N	88.00 W
Cortes ʊ	266a	40.25 N	3.41 W
Cortés, Bahía de c	240p	22.05 N	83.52 W
Cortez, Co., U.S.	200	37.20 N	108.35 W
Cortez, Fl., U.S.	220	27.28 N	82.41 W
Cortez, Sea of → California, Golfo de c	232	28.00 N	112.00 W
Cortez Mountains ⋏	204	40.20 N	116.20 W
Cortina Creek ≃	226	39.06 N	122.02 W
Cortina d'Ampezzo	64	46.32 N	12.08 E
Cortines	258	34.34 S	59.13 W
Čortkov	78	49.01 N	25.48 E
Cortland, Il., U.S.	216	41.55 N	88.41 W
Cortland, In., U.S.	218	38.58 N	85.58 W
Cortland, Ne., U.S.	198	40.30 N	96.42 W
Cortland, N.Y., U.S.	210	42.36 N	76.10 W
Cortland, Oh., U.S.	214	41.19 N	80.43 W
Cortland □[6]	210	42.36 N	76.11 W
Corton	42	52.32 N	1.44 E
Cortona	66	43.16 N	11.59 E
Corubal (Koliba) ≃	150	11.57 N	15.06 W
Čoruch-Dajron	85	40.24 N	69.40 E
Coruche	34	38.57 N	8.31 W
Çoruh (Čoroch) ≃	130	41.36 N	41.35 E
Çorum, Tür.	130	39.14 N	28.27 E
Çorum, Tür.	130	40.33 N	34.58 E
Çorum □[4]	130	40.30 N	34.40 E
Corumbá	248	19.01 S	57.39 W
Corumbá ≃	255	18.19 S	48.55 W
Corumbá de Goiás	255	15.55 S	48.48 W
Corumbaíba	255	18.09 S	48.34 W
Corumbataí ≃	252	23.55 S	51.57 W
Corumbaú, Ponta do ≻	255	16.53 S	39.06 W
Corumbiara ≃	248	13.13 S	62.06 W
Corumo ≃	246	6.49 N	60.52 W
Corund	38	46.28 N	25.11 E
Corunna, On., Can.	214	42.53 N	82.26 W
Corunna, In., U.S.	216	41.26 N	85.08 W
Corunna, Mi., U.S.	216	42.58 N	84.07 W
Corunna Downs	162	21.28 S	119.51 E
Corunna → La Coruña	34	43.22 N	8.23 W
Coruripe	250	10.08 S	36.10 W
Corvallis, Mt., U.S.	202	46.18 N	114.06 W
Corvallis, Or., U.S.	202	44.33 N	123.15 W
Corvara in Badia	64	46.33 N	11.52 E
Corve Dale V	42	52.30 N	2.40 W
Corvey, Kloster ʊ[1]	52	51.46 N	9.25 E
Corviale ◆[8]	267a	41.52 N	12.25 E
Corvo I	148a	39.42 N	31.06 W
Corwen	42	52.59 N	3.22 W
Corwin, Cape ≻	180	59.54 N	165.41 W
Corwith	190	42.59 N	93.57 W
Corydon, In., U.S.	218	38.12 N	86.07 W
Corydon, Ia., U.S.	190	40.45 N	93.19 W
Corydon, Ky., U.S.	194	37.44 N	87.42 W
Coryell	222	31.33 N	97.37 W
Coryell □[6]	222	31.25 N	97.40 W
Coryell Creek ≃	222	31.23 N	97.35 W
Coryton	260	51.31 N	0.31 E
Coryville	214	41.53 N	78.24 W
Corzu	38	44.28 N	23.10 E
Corzuela	252	26.57 S	60.58 W
Cosa (Ansedonia) ⊥	66	42.25 N	11.18 E
Cosamaloapan [de Carpio]	232	18.22 N	95.48 W
Cosapa	248	18.11 S	68.40 W
Coscile ≃	68	39.42 N	16.28 E
Cos Cob	276	41.02 N	73.36 W
Cos Cob Harbor c	276	41.01 N	73.36 W
Coscomatepec [de Bravo]	234	19.04 N	97.02 W
Coseley	42	52.33 N	2.06 W
Cosenza	68	39.17 N	16.15 E
Cosenza □[4]	68	39.28 N	16.25 E
Cosgroves Creek ≃	274a	33.50 S	150.46 E
Coshocton	214	40.16 N	81.51 W
Coshocton □[6]	214	40.16 N	81.51 W
Cosigüina, Punta ≻	236	12.54 N	87.41 W
Cosigüina, Volcán ʌ[1]	236	12.59 N	87.34 W
Cos → Kos I	38	36.50 N	27.10 E
Coslada	266a	40.26 N	3.34 W
Cosmo ◆[8]	256	22.54 S	43.37 W
Cosmoledo Island I	138	9.43 S	47.35 E
Cosmópolis, Bra.	256	22.38 S	47.12 W
Cosmopolis, Wa., U.S.	224	46.57 N	123.46 W
Cosmos	198	44.56 N	94.41 W
Cosmos ◆[8]	287a	22.55 S	44.37 W
Cosne-Cours-sur-Loire	50	47.24 N	2.55 E
Cosoleacaque	234	18.00 N	94.37 W
Cospán	248	7.26 S	78.33 W
Cosquín	252	31.15 S	64.29 W
Cossato	62	45.34 N	8.10 E
Cossatot ≃	194	33.48 N	94.09 W
Cossayuna	210	43.11 N	73.26 W
Cossayuna Lake ⊜	210	43.12 N	73.25 W
Cossebaude	54	51.05 N	13.38 E
Cossé-le-Vivien	28	47.57 N	0.55 W
Cossoine	71	40.27 N	8.43 E
Cosson ≃	50	47.30 N	1.15 E
Cossonay	58	46.37 N	6.31 E
Cost	222	29.26 N	97.32 W
Costa, Cayo I	220	26.41 N	82.15 W
Costa, Cordillera de la ⋏	286c	10.33 N	66.52 W
Costa, Sierra de la → Coast Ranges ⋏	178	41.00 N	123.30 W
Costacciaro	66	43.21 N	12.42 E
Costa de Caparica	266c	38.38 N	9.14 W
Costa del Marfil → Ivory Coast □[1]	150	8.00 N	5.00 W
Costa de San José	258	33.51 S	56.53 W
Costa di Rovigo	64	45.03 N	11.42 E
Costa Mesa	228	33.38 N	117.55 W
Costanera, Cadena → Coast Mountains ⋏	176	55.00 N	129.00 W
Costanera Sur, Parque Natural ♦	288	34.37 S	58.21 W
Costanero, Canal de ≍	288	34.28 S	58.28 W
Costa Rica	232	24.32 N	107.18 W
Costa Rica □[1], N.A.	230	10.00 N	84.00 W
Costa Rica □[1], N.A.	236	10.00 N	84.00 W
Costaros	62	44.54 N	3.50 E
Costas	256	22.39 S	45.56 W
Costello	214	41.36 N	78.03 W
Costelloe	48	53.17 N	9.32 W
Costermansville → Bukavu	154	2.30 S	28.52 E
Costessey	42	52.40 N	1.11 E
Costești	38	44.40 N	24.53 E
Costiera, Catena ⋏	68	39.20 N	16.05 E
Costigan Lake ⊜	184	56.56 N	105.55 W
Costigliole d'Asti	62	44.47 N	8.11 E
Costigliole Saluzzo	62	44.34 N	7.29 E
Costilla	200	36.58 N	105.31 W
Costilla Creek ≃	200	36.59 N	105.43 W
Cosumnes ≃	226	38.16 N	121.26 W
Cosumnes, Middle Fork ≃	226	38.33 N	120.51 W
Cosumnes, North Fork ≃	226	38.33 N	120.51 W
Cosumnes, South Fork ≃	226	38.33 N	120.49 W
Coswig, Dtsch.	54	51.07 N	13.34 E
Coswig, Dtsch.	54	51.53 N	12.26 E
Cotabambas	248	13.45 S	72.21 W
Cotabato	116	7.13 N	124.15 E
Cotacajes ≃	248	16.00 S	67.01 W
Cotagaita	248	20.50 S	65.41 W
Cotagaita ≃	248	21.01 S	65.23 W
Cotahuasi	248	15.12 S	72.56 W
Cotão ʌ[2]	266c	38.45 N	9.18 W
Cotati	226	38.20 N	122.42 W
Coteau-Landing	206	45.15 N	74.13 W
Coteau-Station	206	45.17 N	74.14 W
Coteaux	238	18.12 N	74.02 W
Côte d'Ivoire → Ivory Coast □[1]	150	8.00 N	5.00 W
Côte-d'Or □[5]	50	47.30 N	4.50 E
Cotegipe	255	12.02 S	44.15 W
Cote Indian Reserve ◆[4]	184	51.38 N	101.53 W
Cotentin ≻[1]	32	49.30 N	1.30 W
Côte-Saint-Luc	275a	45.28 N	73.40 W
Côtes-d'Armor □[5]	32	48.25 N	2.40 W
Côte Visitation ◆[8]	275a	45.33 N	73.36 W
Cothi ≃	42	51.52 N	4.10 W
Coti ≃	248	8.36 S	65.33 W
Cotia	256	23.37 S	46.56 W
Cotia □[7]	287b	23.38 S	46.56 W
Cotia ≃	256	23.31 S	46.51 W
Cotia, Reprêsa de ⊜[1]	287b	23.44 S	46.57 W
Cotignac	62	43.32 N	6.09 E
Cotignola	66	44.23 N	11.56 E
Cotija de la Paz	234	19.49 N	102.43 W
Cotingo ≃	246	3.55 N	60.30 W
Cotis, Laguna ⊜	258	35.11 S	59.16 W
Cotmeana ≃	38	44.24 N	24.45 E
Cotoca	248	17.49 S	63.03 W
Cotonou	150	6.21 N	2.26 E
Cotopaxi □[4]	246	0.55 S	78.55 W
Cotopaxi ʌ[1]	246	0.40 S	78.26 W
Cotopaxi, Parque Nacional ♦	246	0.15 S	78.25 W
Cotorra, Isla I	241r	10.02 N	62.16 W
Cotorro ◆[8]	286b	23.03 N	82.16 W
Cotronei	68	39.09 N	16.47 E
Cotswold Hills ⋏[2]	42	51.45 N	2.10 W
Cottage Grove, In., U.S.	218	39.36 N	84.52 W
Cottage Grove, Or., U.S.	202	43.47 N	123.03 W
Cottage Grove, Wi., U.S.	216	43.05 N	89.12 W
Cottage Hills	219	38.55 N	90.04 W
Cottageville	192	32.56 N	80.28 W
Cottam, On., Can.	214	42.08 N	82.45 W
Cottam, Eng., U.K.	262	53.47 N	2.46 W
Cottanello	66	42.24 N	12.41 E
Cottbus	54	51.45 N	14.19 E
Cottekill	210	41.51 N	74.06 W
Cottel Island I	186	48.51 N	53.42 W
Cottenham	42	52.18 N	0.09 E
Cotter	194	36.16 N	92.32 W
Cotter ≃	171b	35.19 S	148.57 E
Cottesloe	168a	31.59 S	115.45 E
Cottiennes, Alpes (Alpi Cozie) ⋏	62	44.45 N	7.00 E
Cottingham	44	53.47 N	0.24 W
Cottleville	219	38.44 N	90.39 W
Cottondale, Al., U.S.	194	33.11 N	87.27 W
Cottondale, Fl., U.S.	192	30.47 N	85.22 W
Cotton Lake ⊜, Mb., Can.	184	55.05 N	96.50 W
Cotton Lake ⊜, Tx., U.S.	222	29.48 N	94.48 W
Cotton Plant	194	35.00 N	91.15 W
Cottonport	194	30.59 N	92.03 W
Cotton Valley	194	32.49 N	93.25 W
Cottonwood, Az., U.S.	200	34.44 N	112.00 W
Cottonwood, Ca., U.S.	204	40.23 N	122.16 W
Cottonwood, Id., U.S.	202	46.02 N	116.20 W
Cottonwood, Mn., U.S.	198	44.36 N	95.40 W
Cottonwood ≃, Ks., U.S.	198	38.23 N	96.03 W
Cottonwood ≃, Mn., U.S.	198	44.17 N	94.25 W
Cottonwood Creek ≃, Ca., U.S.	226	36.52 N	120.12 W
Cottonwood Creek ≃, Ca., U.S.	226	36.27 N	119.20 W
Cottonwood Creek ≃, Mt., U.S.	202	48.33 N	107.45 W
Cottonwood Creek ≃, N.D., U.S.	198	46.16 N	98.15 W
Cottonwood Creek ≃, Ok., U.S.	196	35.54 N	97.27 W
Cottonwood Creek ≃, Or., U.S.	202	43.53 N	117.43 W
Cottonwood Creek ≃, Tx., U.S.	196	31.23 N	103.46 W
Cottonwood Creek ≃, Tx., U.S.	196	32.48 N	100.21 W
Cottonwood Creek ≃, Ut,. U.S.	200	39.09 N	110.55 W
Cottonwood Creek ≃, Wy., U.S.	202	43.51 N	108.09 W
Cottonwood Creek, Middle Fork ≃	204	40.23 N	122.20 W
Cottonwood Creek, South Fork ≃	204	40.23 N	122.20 W
Cottonwood Falls	198	38.22 N	96.32 W
Cottonwood Wash V, Az., U.S.	200	35.00 N	110.39 W
Cottonwood Wash V, Az., U.S.	200	36.19 N	113.59 W
Cotubandê	287a	22.51 S	43.01 W
Cotuhé ≃	246	2.53 S	69.44 W
Cotui	238	19.03 N	70.09 W
Cotuit	207	41.37 N	70.26 W
Cotulla	196	28.26 N	99.14 W
Cotunduba, Ilha de I	287a	22.58 S	43.09 W
Coubert	261	48.40 N	2.42 E
Coubre, Pointe de la ≻	32	45.41 N	1.13 W
Coubron	261	48.55 N	2.35 E
Couches-les-Mines	58	46.52 N	4.34 E
Couchiching, Lake ⊜	212	44.40 N	79.23 W
Coucouron	62	44.48 N	3.58 E
Coucy-le-Château-Auffrique	50	49.31 N	3.19 E
Coudekerque-Branche	50	51.02 N	2.24 E
Coudersport	214	41.46 N	78.01 W
Coudres, Île aux I	186	47.24 N	70.23 W
Couesnon ≃	32	48.37 N	1.31 W
Cougar	224	46.03 N	122.17 W
Cougar Reservoir ⊜[1]	202	44.06 N	122.12 W
Couhé	32	46.18 N	0.11 E
Couillet	50	50.23 N	4.27 E
Couilly-Pont-aux-Dames	261	48.53 N	2.52 E
Coulanges-la-Vineuse	50	47.42 N	3.35 E
Coulanges-sur-Yonne	50	47.31 N	3.32 E
Coulee City	202	47.36 N	119.17 W
Coulee Dam	202	47.57 N	118.58 W
Coulee Dam National Recreation Area ♦	202	48.10 N	118.15 W
Coulihaut	240d	15.30 N	61.29 W
Coulman Island I	9	73.27 S	169.40 E
Coulmier-le-Sec	58	47.45 N	4.29 E
Coulogne	50	50.55 N	1.53 E
Coulomby	50	50.42 N	2.00 E
Coulommiers	50	48.49 N	3.05 E
Coulon ≃	62	43.51 N	5.00 E
Coulonge ≃	190	45.51 N	76.46 W
Coulonge Est ≃	190	46.06 N	76.44 W
Coulsdon ◆[8]	260	51.19 N	0.08 W
Coulta	166	34.23 S	135.29 E
Coulters	279b	40.18 N	79.48 W
Coulterville, Ca., U.S.	226	37.42 N	120.11 W
Coulterville, Il., U.S.	194	38.11 N	89.36 W
Counce	194	35.02 N	88.16 W
Council	202	44.44 N	116.26 W
Council Bluffs	198	41.15 N	95.51 W
Council Grove	198	38.39 N	96.29 W
Council Grove Lake ⊜[1]	198	38.42 N	96.31 W
Coundon	44	54.40 N	1.39 W
Countegany	171b	36.11 S	149.27 E
Countesthorpe	42	52.33 N	1.08 W
Country Campus	222	30.49 N	95.26 W
Country Club Estates	220	28.03 N	81.57 W
Country Club Hills	278	41.34 N	87.43 W
Country Club View	284c	38.49 N	77.19 W
Country Hills	279b	40.19 N	79.42 W
Country Homes	202	47.44 N	117.24 W
Country Ridge Estates	276	41.02 N	73.41 W
Countryside	278	41.46 N	87.52 W
Countryside Lake ⊜	278	42.15 N	88.03 W
Countryside Manor	278	42.18 N	87.56 W
Coupar Angus	46	56.33 N	3.17 W
Coupeville	224	48.13 N	122.41 W
Coupland	222	30.28 N	97.24 W
Coupon	214	40.32 N	78.31 W
Coupvray	261	48.54 N	2.48 E
Courbevoie	50	48.54 N	2.15 E
Courbons	62	44.06 N	6.12 E
Courçay	50	47.15 N	0.52 E
Courcelle	261	48.42 N	2.06 E
Courcelles, Bel.	50	50.28 N	4.22 E
Courcelles, Fr.	261	49.07 N	2.18 E
Courcelles-Chaussy	56	49.07 N	6.24 E
Courcelles-sur-Nied	56	49.04 N	6.18 E
Courchevel	62	45.25 N	6.38 E
Cour-Cheverny	50	47.30 N	1.27 E
Courcibo ≃	250	4.53 N	53.00 W
Courçon	32	46.15 N	0.49 W
Courcouronnes	261	48.37 N	2.24 E
Courdimanche	261	49.02 N	2.00 E
Cour-et-Buis	62	45.26 N	5.00 E
Courgent	261	48.54 N	1.40 E
Courland → Kurzeme □[9]	76	56.50 N	22.30 E
Courmayeur	62	45.47 N	6.58 E
Couronne, Cap ≻	62	43.19 N	5.03 E
Couronnement, Île du → Coronation Island I	9	60.37 S	45.30 W
Courpière	62	45.45 N	3.33 E
Courquetaine	261	48.41 N	2.45 E
Course Brook ≃	283	42.17 N	71.22 W
Courseulles	28	49.20 N	0.27 W
Courson-les-Carrières	50	47.36 N	3.30 E
Court	58	47.14 N	7.20 E
Courtacon	50	48.42 N	3.17 E
Courtalain	50	48.05 N	1.09 E
Courtenay, B.C., Can.	182	49.41 N	125.00 W
Courtenay, Fr.	50	48.02 N	3.03 E
Courthézon	62	44.05 N	4.53 E
Courtice	212	43.55 N	78.46 W
Courtisols	56	48.59 N	4.31 E
Courtland, On., Can.	212	42.51 N	80.38 W
Courtland, Al., U.S.	194	34.40 N	87.18 W
Courtland, Ca., U.S.	226	38.20 N	121.34 W
Courtland, Va., U.S.	208	36.42 N	77.04 W
Courtleigh	284b	39.22 N	76.46 W
Courtmacsherry	48	51.38 N	8.43 W
Courtmacsherry Bay c	48	51.35 N	8.40 W
Courtney, Pa., U.S.	279b	40.13 N	79.58 W
Courtney, Tx., U.S.	222	30.16 N	96.04 W
Courtney Creek ≃	196	31.16 N	102.50 W
Courtomer, Fr.	50	48.38 N	0.22 E
Courtomer, Fr.	261	48.39 N	2.54 E
Courtown	48	52.38 N	6.13 W
Courtrai → Kortrijk	50	50.50 N	3.16 E
Courtright	214	42.49 N	82.28 W
Courtry, Fr.	261	48.33 N	2.46 E
Courtry, Fr.	261	48.55 N	2.36 E
Court-Saint-Étienne	50	50.39 N	4.34 E
Courville-sur-Eure	50	48.27 N	1.15 E
Coushatta	194	32.00 N	93.20 W
Cousin ≃	50	47.15 N	4.04 E
Cousiño Macul, Parque ♦	286e	33.30 S	70.35 W
Cousolre	50	50.15 N	4.09 E
Coussegrey	50	47.57 N	4.01 E
Coussey	58	48.25 N	5.41 E
Coustellet	62	43.53 N	5.11 E
Coutances	32	49.03 N	1.26 W
Coutevroult	261	48.52 N	2.51 E
Couto do Magalhães	250	8.17 S	49.16 W
Couto Magalhães ≃	255	13.37 S	53.09 W
Coutras	32	45.02 N	0.08 W
Coutts	182	49.00 N	111.57 W
Couture, Lac ⊜	176	60.07 N	75.20 W
Couture-sur-Loir	50	47.45 N	0.41 E
Couves, Ilha das I	256	23.25 S	44.52 W
Couvet	58	46.56 N	6.38 E
Couvin	50	50.03 N	4.29 E
Cova da Piedade	266c	38.40 N	9.10 W
Covane	156	21.22 S	33.56 E
Covasna	38	45.51 N	26.11 E
Covasna □[6]	38	46.00 N	26.00 E
Cove, Scot., U.K.	46	57.51 N	5.42 W
Cove, Or., U.S.	202	45.17 N	117.48 W
Cove Bay	46	57.06 N	2.04 W
Covedale	218	39.07 N	84.36 W
Cove Harbor c	276	41.03 N	73.30 W
Cove Island I	190	45.17 N	81.44 W
Covelo, Ang.	152	12.06 S	13.55 E
Covelo, Ca., U.S.	204	39.47 N	123.14 W
Cove Neck	276	40.53 N	73.31 W
Cove Neck ≻[1]	276	40.53 N	73.30 W
Coventry, Eng., U.K.	42	52.25 N	1.30 W
Coventry, Ct., U.S.	207	41.46 N	72.18 W
Coventry, De., U.S.	285	39.40 N	75.38 W
Coventry, R.I., U.S.	207	41.41 N	71.34 W
Coventry Cathedral ʊ[1]	42	52.25 N	1.30 W
Coventryville	285	40.10 N	75.41 W
Cove Palisades State Park ♦	202	44.34 N	121.15 W
Cove Point	208	38.22 N	76.23 W
Cove Point ≻	208	38.23 N	76.23 W
Cover ≃	44	54.17 N	1.46 W
Covered Wells	200	31.48 N	111.59 W
Covert	216	42.17 N	86.15 W
Covigliaio	66	44.08 N	11.18 E
Covilhã	34	40.17 N	7.30 W
Covina	228	34.05 N	117.53 W
Covington, Ga., U.S.	192	33.35 N	83.51 W
Covington, In., U.S.	194	40.08 N	87.23 W
Covington, Ky., U.S.	218	39.05 N	84.30 W
Covington, La., U.S.	194	30.28 N	90.06 W
Covington, Oh., U.S.	218	40.07 N	84.21 W
Covington, Ok., U.S.	196	36.18 N	97.35 W
Covington, Pa., U.S.	210	41.45 N	77.05 W
Covington, Tn., U.S.	194	35.33 N	89.38 W
Covington, Tx., U.S.	222	32.11 N	97.16 W
Covington, Va., U.S.	192	37.47 N	79.59 W
Covões	266c	38.50 N	9.20 W
Covunco, Arroyo ≃	252	38.29 S	69.32 W
Cow ≃	190	47.23 N	83.59 W
Cowal ≻[1]	46	56.05 N	5.08 W
Cowal, Lake ⊜	166	33.35 S	147.25 E
Cowan, Ky., U.S.	218	38.24 N	83.54 W
Cowan, Tn., U.S.	194	35.09 N	86.00 W
Cowan, Lake ⊜	162	31.50 S	121.50 E
Cowan Creek ≃	274a	33.40 S	151.10 E
Cowanesque	210	41.56 N	77.30 W
Cowanesque ≃	210	42.00 N	77.07 W
Cowan Heights	280	33.47 N	117.47 W
Cowan Lake ⊜, Sk., Can.	184	54.00 N	107.15 W
Cowan Lake ⊜, Oh., U.S.	218	39.23 N	83.54 W
Cowan Lake State Park ♦	218	39.23 N	83.53 W
Cowansburg	279b	40.15 N	79.46 W
Cowanshannock Creek ≃	214	40.51 N	79.30 W
Cowansville, P.Q., Can.	206	45.12 N	72.45 W
Cowansville, Pa., U.S.	214	40.53 N	79.36 W
Cowaramup	162	33.52 S	115.05 E

Symbols in the index entries represent the broad categories identified in the key at the right. Symbols with superior numbers (⋏[1]) identify subcategories (see complete key on page *I · 1*).

Symbole im Register stellen die rechts im Schlüssel erklärten Kategorien dar. Symbole mit hochgestellten Ziffern (⋏[1]) bezeichnen Unterabteilungen einer Kategorie (vgl. vollständiger Schlüssel auf Seite *I · 1*).

Los símbolos incluídos en el texto del índice representan las grandes categorias identificadas con la clave a la derecha. Los símbolos con numeros en su parte superior (⋏[1]) identifican las subcategorías (véase la clave completa en la página *I · 1*).

Les symboles de l'index représentent les catégories indiquées dans la légende à droite. Les symboles suivis d'un indice (⋏[1]) représentent des sous-catégories (voir légende complète à la page *I · 1*).

Os símbolos incluídos no texto do índice representam as grandes categorias identificadas com a chave à direita. Os símbolos com números em sua parte superior (⋏[1]) identificam as subcategorias (veja-se a chave completa à página *I · 1*).

ʌ Mountain	Berg	Montaña	Montagne	Montanha
⋏ Mountains	Gebirge	Montañas	Montagnes	Montanhas
)(Pass	Paß	Paso	Col	Passo
V Valley, Canyon	Tal, Cañon	Valle, Cañón	Vallée, Canyon	Vale, Canhão
≚ Plain	Ebene	Llano	Plaine	Planície
≻ Cape	Kap	Cabo	Cap	Cabo
I Island	Insel	Isla	Île	Ilha
II Islands	Inseln	Islas	Îles	Ilhas
≛ Other Topographic Features	Andere Topographische Objekte	Otros Elementos Topográficos	Autres données topographiques	Outros acidentes topográficos

ESPAÑOL — Nombre | Página | Lat.°′ | Long.°′ W = Oeste
FRANÇAIS — Nom | Page | Lat.°′ | Long.°′ W = Ouest
PORTUGUÊS — Nome | Página | Lat.°′ | Long.°′ W = Oeste
Cowa-Cuan I · 41

Coward 192 33.58 N 79.44 W
Coward Springs 166 29.24 S 136.49 E
Cowarie 166 27.43 S 138.20 E
Cow Bayou ≃ 222 31.19 N 97.00 W
Cowbridge 42 51.28 N 3.27 W
Cowburn Tunnel •[5] 262 53.21 N 1.52 W
Cow Canyon ∨ 280 34.01 N 120.06 W
Cowcowing Lakes ⊜ 162 31.01 S 117.18 E
Cow Creek ≃, Ks., U.S. 198 38.02 N 97.56 W
Cow Creek ≃, Mt., U.S. 202 47.47 N 108.56 W
Cow Creek ≃, Ok., U.S. 196 34.10 N 98.00 W
Cow Creek ≃, Or., U.S. 202 42.57 N 123.20 W
Cow Creek ≃, Wa., U.S. 202 46.45 N 118.09 W
Cowden, Il., U.S. 219 39.15 N 88.52 W
Cowden, Pa., U.S. 279b 40.19 N 80.13 W
Cowdenbeath 46 56.07 N 3.21 W
Coweeman ≃ 224 46.06 N 122.52 W
Cowell 166 33.41 S 136.55 E
Cowen 188 38.24 N 80.33 W
Cowen, Mount ∧ 202 45.23 N 110.29 W
Cowes, Austl. 169 38.27 S 145.14 E
Cowes, Eng., U.K. 42 50.45 N 1.18 W
Cowessess Indian Reserve •[4] 184 50.31 N 102.42 W
Coweta 196 35.57 N 95.39 W
Cow Green Reservoir ⊜[1] 44 54.40 N 2.18 W
Cow Gulch ≃ 202 46.02 N 107.52 W
Cow Head 186 49.55 N 57.48 W
Cowhouse Creek ≃ 222 31.10 N 97.35 W
Cowichan ≃ 224 48.46 N 123.38 W
Cowichan Bay 224 48.44 N 123.40 W
Cowichan Lake ⊜ 224 48.54 N 124.20 W
Cowiche Creek, North Fork ≃ 224 46.38 N 120.41 W
Cowiche Creek, South Fork ≃ 224 46.38 N 120.41 W
Cowie Water ≃ 46 56.58 N 2.12 W
Cowles Dam ⊜[1] 273d 26.13 S 28.28 E
Cowlesville 210 42.51 N 78.28 W
Cowley, Austl. 166 26.54 S 144.49 E
Cowley, Ab., Can. 182 49.34 N 114.05 W
Cowley, Eng., U.K. 42 51.43 N 1.12 W
Cowley, Wy., U.S. 202 44.53 N 108.28 W
Cowley •[8] 260 51.32 N 0.29 W
Cowley, Mount ∧ 169 38.33 S 143.52 E
Cowlitz □[6] 224 46.07 N 122.43 W
Cowlitz ≃ 224 46.05 N 122.53 W
Cowm Reservoir ⊜[1] 262 53.40 N 2.11 W
Cow Palace ⊕ 282 37.42 N 122.25 W
Cowpasture ≃ 188 37.48 N 79.45 W
Cowpens 192 35.01 N 81.48 W
Cowpens National Battlefield ♠ 192 35.06 N 81.46 W
Cowra 166 33.50 S 148.41 E
Cox ≃ 164 15.19 S 135.25 E
Cox, Mount ∧[2] 162 24.55 S 125.36 E
Coxá ≃ 255 14.16 S 44.11 W
Cox Creek ≃ 212 43.35 N 80.29 W
Coxheath 42 51.14 N 0.29 E
Coxim 255 18.30 S 54.45 W
Coxim ≃ 255 18.34 S 54.46 W
Coxipi, Lac ⊜ 186 51.33 N 58.25 W
Coxquihui 234 20.11 N 97.35 W
Cox River Aboriginal Reserve •[4] 164 15.40 S 134.45 E
Coxs ≃ 170 33.57 S 150.25 E
Coxsackie 210 42.21 N 73.48 W
Cox's Bāzār 120 21.26 N 91.59 E
Cox's Cove 186 49.07 N 58.05 W
Coyaguaima, Cerro ∧ 252 22.55 S 66.35 W
Coyah 150 9.43 N 13.23 W
Coyame 232 29.28 N 105.06 W
Coyanosa Draw ∨ 196 31.18 N 103.06 W
Coya Sur 252 22.25 S 69.38 W
Coyle, Water of ≃ 44 55.28 N 4.32 W
Coyoacán •[8] 286a 19.20 N 99.10 W
Coyote 226 37.13 N 121.44 W
Coyote Creek ≃, Ca., U.S. 204 33.13 N 116.13 W
Coyote Creek ≃, Ca., U.S. 226 37.28 N 122.03 W
Coyote Creek ≃, Ca., U.S. 280 33.47 N 118.05 W
Coyote Creek, East Fork ≃ 226 37.10 N 121.30 W
Coyote Creek, Middle Fork ≃ 226 37.10 N 121.30 W
Coyote Hills ⩘[2] 282 37.33 N 122.05 W
Coyote Hills Regional Park ♠ 282 37.33 N 122.06 W
Coyote Lake ⊜ 204 35.04 N 116.45 W
Coyote Lake ⊜[1] 226 37.06 N 121.32 W
Coyotepec 234 19.46 N 99.12 W
Coyote Point › 282 37.35 N 122.19 W
Coyote Wash ∨, Az., U.S. 200 32.40 N 114.08 W
Coyote Wash ∨, N.M., U.S. 200 36.11 N 108.33 W
Coy Pond ⊜ 283 42.36 N 70.49 W
Coyuca de Benítez 234 17.02 N 100.04 W
Coyuca de Catalán 234 18.20 N 100.39 W
Coyutla 234 20.15 N 97.39 W
Cozad 198 40.51 N 99.59 W
Cozes 32 45.35 N 0.50 W
Cozie, Alpi (Alpes Cottiennes) ⩘ 62 44.45 N 7.00 E
Cozoyoapan 234 16.46 N 98.15 W
Cozumel 232 20.31 N 86.55 W
Cozumel, Isla I 232 20.25 N 86.55 W
Cozy Lake 276 41.01 N 74.30 W
Crab Alley Bay ⊂ 208 38.55 N 76.17 W
Crab Creek ≃ 202 46.49 N 119.55 W
Crab Meadow ⩸ 276 40.55 N 73.20 W
Crab Orchard, Ky., U.S. 192 37.27 N 84.30 W
Crab Orchard, Tn., U.S. 192 35.54 N 84.52 W
Crab Orchard Lake ⊜[1] 194 37.43 N 89.05 W
Crabtree 214 40.21 N 79.28 W
Crabtree Creek ≃ 279b 40.21 N 79.30 W
Crabtree Mills 206 45.58 N 73.28 W
Craches 261 48.34 N 1.49 E
Crackenback ≃ 171b 36.21 S 148.36 E
Craco 68 40.23 N 16.26 E
Cracovie → Kraków 30 50.03 N 19.58 E
Cradle Mountain-Lake Saint Clair National Park ♠ 166 42.00 S 146.00 E
Cradock, Austl. 166 32.04 S 138.30 E
Cradock, S. Afr. 158 32.08 S 25.36 E
Cradock Channel ⊔ 172 36.11 S 175.15 E
Crafers 168b 35.01 S 138.47 E
Crafton 214 40.26 N 80.03 W
Crafts Creek ≃ 285 40.07 N 74.46 W
Cragg Vale 262 53.42 N 2.00 W
Cragsmoor 210 41.40 N 74.23 W
Crai 42 51.55 N 3.36 W
Craig, B.C., Can. 224 49.18 N 124.15 W
Craig, Ak., U.S. 182 55.29 N 133.09 W
Craig, Co., U.S. 200 40.30 N 107.32 W
Craig, Mo., U.S. 194 40.11 N 95.22 W
Craig, Ne., U.S. 198 41.47 N 96.21 W
Craig, Point ∧ 162 26.51 S 126.19 E
Craigavon 48 54.27 N 6.24 W
Craig Beach 214 41.07 N 81.01 W
Craig Creek ≃ 192 37.39 N 79.49 W
Craigellachie 182 50.59 N 118.43 W
Craighall •[8] 273d 26.07 S 28.02 E
Craighall Park •[8] 273d 26.08 S 28.01 E
Craighouse 46 55.51 N 5.57 W
Craigmont 202 46.14 N 116.27 W
Craigmyle 182 51.40 N 112.15 W
Craignish Point › 46 56.07 N 5.37 W
Craignure 46 56.28 N 5.42 W
Craigsville, Pa., U.S. 214 40.51 N 79.39 W
Craigsville, Va., U.S. 192 38.04 N 79.23 W
Craigville 216 40.47 N 85.06 W
Craik 184 51.03 N 105.49 W
Crail 46 56.16 N 2.38 W
Crailsheim 56 49.08 N 10.04 E
Craiova 38 44.19 N 23.48 E
Crake ≃ 44 54.14 N 3.03 W
Craley 208 39.57 N 76.31 W
Cramant 50 48.59 N 3.59 E
Cramlington 44 55.05 N 1.36 W
Cranage 262 53.12 N 2.22 W
Cranberry 214 41.21 N 79.43 W
Cranberry Brook ≃ 283 42.11 N 71.01 W
Cranberry Creek 210 43.09 N 74.14 W
Cranberry Island I 212 44.44 N 81.18 W
Cranberry Lake 210 40.57 N 74.44 W
Cranberry Lake ⊜, On., Can. 212 44.26 N 76.19 W
Cranberry Lake ⊜, On., Can. 212 44.47 N 75.50 W
Cranberry Lake ⊜, N.Y., U.S. 188 44.10 N 74.50 W
Cranberry Lake ⊜, Wa., U.S. 224 47.17 N 123.05 W
Cranberry Mountain ∧ 182 50.42 N 118.12 W
Cranberry Pond ⊜ 276 41.08 N 74.12 W
Cranberry Portage 184 54.35 N 101.23 W
Cranborne Chase •[3] 42 50.55 N 2.05 W
Cranbourne 169 38.06 S 145.17 E
Cranbrook, Austl. 162 34.18 S 117.32 E
Cranbrook, B.C., Can. 182 49.31 N 115.46 W
Cranbrook, Eng., U.K. 42 51.06 N 0.33 E
Cranbrook Academy of Art ⊕ 281 42.34 N 83.14 W
Cranbury 276 40.18 N 74.30 W
Cranbury Brook ≃ 276 40.19 N 74.37 W
Crandall 222 32.37 N 96.27 W
Crandon 190 45.34 N 88.54 W
Crandon Lakes 210 41.07 N 74.50 W
Crane, Az., U.S. 204 32.42 N 114.40 W
Crane, In., U.S. 194 38.53 N 86.54 W
Crane, Mo., U.S. 194 36.54 N 93.34 W
Crane, Tx., U.S. 196 31.23 N 102.20 W
Crane Beach ⩲[2] 283 42.41 N 70.46 W
Cranebrook 274a 33.43 S 150.42 E
Crane Creek ≃ 190 43.01 N 91.58 W
Crane Lake ⊜, On., Can. 212 45.13 N 79.57 W
Crane Lake ⊜, Sk., Can. 184 50.06 N 109.06 W
Crane Mountain ∧ 202 42.04 N 120.13 W
Crane Neck Point › 210 40.58 N 73.10 W
Crane River Indian Reserve •[4] 184 51.30 N 99.14 W
Cranesville 214 41.54 N 80.21 W
Cranfield 42 52.05 N 0.35 W
Cranfills Gap 222 31.46 N 97.50 W
Cranford 210 40.39 N 74.19 W
Crange •[8] 263 51.32 N 7.11 E
Cran-Gévrier 58 45.54 N 6.06 E
Crank 262 53.29 N 2.45 W
Cranleigh 42 51.09 N 0.30 W
Crans 58 46.19 N 7.28 E
Cranston 207 41.46 N 71.26 W
Cranston Heights 285 39.38 N 75.38 W
Craon 32 47.51 N 0.57 W
Craonne 50 49.26 N 3.47 E
Craponne, Fr. 62 45.44 N 4.43 E
Craponne, Fr. 62 45.20 N 3.51 E
Craponne, Canal de ≊ 62 43.40 N 4.39 E
Craryville 210 42.11 N 73.35 W
Crasna, Rom. 38 45.36 N 26.08 E
Crasna, Rom. 38 46.31 N 27.51 E
Crasna (Kraszna) ≃ 38 48.09 N 22.20 E
Crassier 58 46.22 N 6.11 E
Crater Lake ⊜ 202 42.56 N 122.06 W
Crater Lake National Park ♠ 202 42.49 N 122.08 W
Crater Mount ∧ 164 6.30 S 145.10 E
Crater Point › 164 5.22 S 152.09 E
Craters of the Moon National Monument ♠ 202 43.20 N 113.35 W
Crateús 250 5.10 S 40.40 W
Crathie 46 57.02 N 3.12 W
Crati ≃ 68 39.43 N 16.31 E
Crato 250 7.14 S 39.23 W
Crau •[1] 62 43.36 N 4.50 E
Crauford, Cape › 176 73.43 N 84.50 W
Craughwell 48 53.13 N 8.43 W
Cravant 50 47.41 N 3.41 E
Cravari ≃ 248 12.06 S 58.03 W
Cravat 219 38.25 N 89.06 W
Craven 184 50.39 N 104.50 W
Craven Arms 42 52.26 N 2.50 W
Cravensville 171b 36.24 S 147.34 E
Cravo Norte 246 6.18 N 70.12 W
Cravo Norte ≃ 246 6.18 N 70.12 W
Cravo Sur ≃ 246 4.42 N 71.36 W
Crawfish ≃ 216 43.00 N 88.49 W
Crawford, Scot., U.K. 44 55.28 N 3.40 W
Crawford, Co., U.S. 200 38.42 N 107.36 W
Crawford, Ms., U.S. 194 33.18 N 88.36 W
Crawford, Ne., U.S. 198 42.40 N 103.24 W
Crawford, Tx., U.S. 222 31.32 N 97.27 W
Crawford □[6], In., U.S. 218 38.20 N 86.28 W
Crawford □[6], Oh., U.S. 214 40.48 N 82.58 W
Crawford □[6], Pa., U.S. 214 41.39 N 80.10 W
Crawford Bay 182 49.42 N 116.48 W
Crawford Countryside 278 41.32 N 87.43 W
Crawford Notch State Park ♠ 188 44.13 N 71.25 W
Crawfordsville, Ar., U.S. 194 35.13 N 90.19 W
Crawfordsville, In., U.S. 194 40.02 N 86.52 W
Crawfordville, Fl., U.S. 192 30.10 N 84.22 W
Crawfordville, Ga., U.S. 192 33.33 N 82.53 W
Crawinkel 54 50.47 N 10.47 E
Crawley 42 51.07 N 0.12 W
Crawshawbooth 262 53.43 N 2.17 W
Crayford •[8] 260 51.27 N 0.11 E
Crays Hill 260 51.36 N 0.28 E
Crazy Mountains ⩘ 202 46.08 N 110.20 W
Crazy Peak ∧ 202 46.01 N 110.16 W
Crazy Woman Creek ≃ 202 44.29 N 106.08 W
Creagan 46 56.33 N 5.17 W
Creagorry 46 57.26 N 7.19 W
Creal Springs 194 37.37 N 88.50 W
Creamery 285 40.13 N 75.25 W
Crean Lake ⊜ 184 54.05 N 106.10 W
Crêches-sur-Saône 58 46.15 N 4.47 E
Crécy, Forêt de ♠ 261 48.48 N 2.53 E
Crécy-en-Brie 50 48.51 N 2.55 E
Crécy-en-Ponthieu 50 50.15 N 1.53 E
Crécy-sur-Serre 50 49.42 N 3.37 E
Credenhill 42 52.06 N 2.48 W
Credit ≃ 212 43.33 N 79.35 W
Crediton 42 50.47 N 3.39 W
Cree ≃, Sk., Can. 176 59.00 N 105.47 W
Cree ≃, Scot., U.K. 44 54.52 N 4.20 W
Creede 200 37.50 N 106.55 W
Creedmoor 192 36.07 N 78.41 W
Creedmore 222 30.12 N 97.43 W
Creegh 48 52.44 N 9.26 W
Creek Brook ≃ 283 42.47 N 71.08 W
Creek Locks 210 41.52 N 74.03 W
Creekmouth •[8] 260 51.31 N 0.06 E
Creekside 214 40.40 N 79.11 W
Creekwood 278 41.39 N 87.59 W
Creel 232 27.45 N 107.38 W
Cree Lake ⊜ 176 57.30 N 106.30 W
Creemore 212 44.19 N 80.06 W
Creetown 44 54.54 N 4.23 W
Cregganbaun 48 53.42 N 9.51 W
Creglingen 56 49.28 N 10.01 E
Crégy-lès-Meaux 261 48.58 N 2.52 E
Créhange 56 49.03 N 6.35 E
Creighton, Sk., Can. 184 54.45 N 101.54 W
Creighton, S. Afr. 158 30.01 S 29.51 E
Creighton, Ne., U.S. 198 42.28 N 97.54 W
Creighton, Pa., U.S. 214 40.35 N 79.46 W
Creighton Mine 190 46.28 N 81.11 W
Creightons Creek ≃ 169 36.43 S 145.22 E
Creil, Fr. 50 49.16 N 2.29 E
Creil, Ned. 52 52.45 N 5.40 E
Crema 62 45.22 N 9.41 E
Cremia 58 46.05 N 9.16 E
Crémieu 62 45.43 N 5.15 E
Cremlingen 54 52.15 N 10.39 E
Cremona, Ab., Can. 182 51.33 N 114.29 W
Cremona, It. 64 45.07 N 10.02 E
Cremona □[4] 64 45.12 N 10.00 E
Crenshaw, Ms., U.S. 194 34.30 N 90.12 W
Crenshaw, Pa., U.S. 214 41.15 N 78.46 W
Crep Nudo ∧ 64 46.13 N 12.24 E
Crepori ≃ 250 5.42 S 57.08 W
Crépy-en-Laonnois 50 49.36 N 3.31 E
Crépy-en-Valois 50 49.14 N 2.54 E
Créquy 50 50.29 N 2.03 E
Creran, Loch ⊜ 46 56.31 N 5.20 W
Cres 36 44.58 N 14.25 E
Cres, Otok I 36 44.50 N 14.25 E
Cresaptown 188 39.35 N 78.50 W
Crescent, N.Y., U.S. 210 42.49 N 73.43 W
Crescent, Ok., U.S. 196 35.57 N 97.35 W
Crescent, Or., U.S. 202 43.27 N 121.41 W
Crescent, Lake ⊜ 224 48.05 N 123.50 W
Crescent Beach, B.C., Can. 224 49.04 N 122.53 W
Crescent Beach, Fl., U.S. 220 27.15 N 82.32 W
Crescent City, Ca., U.S. 204 41.45 N 124.12 W
Crescent City, Fl., U.S. 192 29.25 N 81.30 W
Crescent City, Il., U.S. 216 40.46 N 87.51 W
Crescent Ditch ≊ 226 36.29 N 120.07 W
Crescent Heights, N.J., U.S. 285 39.58 N 74.43 W
Crescent Heights, Tx., U.S. 222 32.11 N 95.56 W
Crescentino 62 45.11 N 8.06 E
Crescent Lake ⊜, Fl., U.S. 192 29.28 N 81.30 W
Crescent Lake ⊜, Or., U.S. 202 43.29 N 121.59 W
Crescent Lake Estates 281 42.38 N 83.25 W
Crescent Spur 182 53.35 N 120.41 W
Crescentville •[8] 285 40.02 N 75.05 W
Crescenzago •[8] 266b 45.30 N 9.15 E
Cresco, Ia., U.S. 190 43.22 N 92.06 W
Cresco, Pa., U.S. 210 41.09 N 75.17 W
Crespano del Grappa 64 45.49 N 11.50 E
Crespian 62 43.53 N 4.06 E
Crespières 261 48.53 N 1.55 E
Crespin 50 50.25 N 3.39 E
Crespino 64 44.59 N 11.53 E
Crespo 252 32.02 S 60.19 W
Cressbrook Creek ≃ 171a 27.05 S 152.27 E
Cressely 261 48.43 N 2.05 E
Cressey 226 37.25 N 120.40 W
Cresskill 276 40.56 N 73.57 W
Cresskill Brook ≃ 276 40.57 N 73.58 W
Cresson, Pa., U.S. 214 40.27 N 78.35 W
Cresson, Tx., U.S. 222 32.32 N 97.37 W
Cressona 208 40.37 N 76.11 W
Cressy 169 38.02 S 143.38 E
Crest 62 44.44 N 5.02 E
Cresta 58 46.28 N 9.31 E
Crested Butte 200 38.52 N 106.59 W
Cresthaven 220 26.03 N 80.08 W
Crest Hill 216 41.33 N 88.05 W
Crestline, Ca., U.S. 228 34.14 N 117.17 W
Crestline, Oh., U.S. 214 40.47 N 82.44 W
Creston, B.C., Can. 182 49.06 N 116.31 W
Creston, Nf., Can. 186 47.09 N 55.11 W
Creston, Ca., U.S. 226 35.31 N 120.31 W
Creston, Il., U.S. 216 41.56 N 88.58 W
Creston, Ia., U.S. 198 41.03 N 94.21 W
Creston, Oh., U.S. 214 40.59 N 81.53 W
Crestone Peak ∧ 200 37.58 N 105.36 W
Crestview, Fl., U.S. 194 30.45 N 86.34 W
Crestview, Wi., U.S. 216 42.49 N 87.49 W
Crestview Heights 210 42.05 N 76.07 W
Crestwood, Il., U.S. 278 41.39 N 87.45 W
Crestwood, Ky., U.S. 218 38.19 N 85.28 W
Crestwood, Mo., U.S. 219 38.33 N 90.22 W
Crestwood Hills 192 35.56 N 84.05 W
Creswell, Eng., U.K. 44 53.16 N 1.12 W
Creswell, Or., U.S. 202 43.55 N 123.01 W
Creswell Bay ⊂ 176 72.35 N 93.25 W
Creswell Creek ≃ 162 18.10 S 135.11 E
Creswell Downs 162 17.57 S 135.55 E
Creswick 169 37.26 S 143.54 E
Creta → Kríti I 38 35.29 N 24.42 E
Crete, Il., U.S. 216 41.27 N 87.38 W
Crete, Ne., U.S. 198 40.37 N 96.57 W
Crete, Sea of → Kritikón Pélagos ⍑[2] 38 35.46 N 23.54 E
Créteil 50 48.48 N 2.28 E
Crete → Kríti I 38 35.29 N 24.42 E
Crétéville 36 36.40 N 10.20 E
Cretin, Cape › 164 6.40 S 147.52 E
Creus, Cap de › 34 42.19 N 3.19 E
Creuse □[5] 32 46.05 N 2.00 E
Creuse ≃ 32 47.00 N 0.34 E
Creussen 60 49.51 N 11.37 E
Creutzwald 56 49.12 N 6.41 E
Creuzburg 56 51.03 N 10.15 E
Crevacuore 62 45.41 N 8.15 E
Crevalcore 64 44.43 N 11.09 E
Creve Coeur, Il., U.S. 190 40.38 N 89.35 W
Creve Coeur, Mo., U.S. 219 38.39 N 90.25 W
Crèvecœur-en-Auge 50 49.07 N 0.01 E
Crèvecœur-en-Brie 261 48.45 N 2.55 E
Crèvecœur-le-Grand 50 49.36 N 2.05 E
Crevillent 34 38.15 N 0.48 W
Crevoladossola 58 46.09 N 8.18 E
Crewe, Eng., U.K. 44 53.05 N 2.27 W
Crewe, Va., U.S. 192 37.10 N 78.07 W
Crewkerne 42 50.53 N 2.48 W
Crews Lake ⊜ 220 28.23 N 82.31 W
Crewsville 220 27.16 N 81.36 W
Crianlarich 46 56.23 N 4.36 W
Crib Point 169 38.22 S 145.12 E
Cricamola ≃ 236 8.59 N 81.54 W
Cricaré ≃ 255 18.37 S 40.05 W
Criccieth 42 52.55 N 4.14 W
Crichi 68 38.57 N 16.38 E
Criciúma 252 28.40 S 49.23 W
Crick 42 52.21 N 1.07 W
Cricket 192 36.10 N 81.11 W
Crickhowell 42 51.53 N 3.07 W
Cricklade 42 51.39 N 1.51 W
Cridersville 216 40.39 N 84.09 W
Crieff 46 56.23 N 3.52 W
Criel-sur-Mer 50 50.01 N 1.19 E
Criffell ∧ 44 54.57 N 3.38 W
Crikvenica 36 45.11 N 14.42 E
Crillon, Mount ∧ 180 58.40 N 137.10 W
Crimea → Krymskij poluostrov ›[1] 78 45.00 N 34.00 E
Crimmitschau 54 50.49 N 12.23 E
Crimond 46 57.36 N 1.54 W
Crinan 46 56.05 N 5.34 W
Crîngeni 38 44.01 N 24.47 E
Cringila 170 34.28 S 150.53 E
Cripple Creek 200 38.44 N 105.10 W
Criquetot l'Esneval 50 49.39 N 0.16 E
Crirninoso, Monte ∧ 256 21.32 S 43.25 W
Crisenoy 261 48.36 N 2.45 E
Crisfield 208 37.59 N 75.51 W
Crisólia 256 22.15 S 46.25 W
Crisóstomo, Ribeirão ≃ 250 10.19 S 50.26 W
Crispiano 68 40.36 N 17.14 E
Criss Creek 182 51.03 N 120.44 W
Crissiumal 252 27.30 S 54.07 W
Cristal, Monts de ⩘ 152 0.30 N 10.30 E
Cristal, Sierra del ⩘ 240p 20.33 N 75.31 W
Cristalândia 250 10.36 S 49.11 W
Cristália 255 16.43 S 42.52 W
Cristalina 255 16.45 S 47.36 W
Cristalino ≃ 255 12.38 S 50.40 W
Cristallo ∧ 64 46.34 N 12.12 E
Cristianópolis 255 17.13 S 48.45 W
Cristina 256 22.13 S 45.16 W
Cristinápolis 250 11.29 S 37.46 W
Cristino Castro 250 8.49 S 44.13 W
Cristóbal 236 9.21 N 79.55 W
Cristóbal Colón, Pico ∧ 246 10.50 N 73.41 W
Cristóbal Obregón 234 16.20 N 93.30 W
Cristoforo Colombo, Aeroporto di ⊠ 62 44.25 N 8.49 E
Cristo Redentor ⊥ 252 32.50 S 70.05 W
Cristo Redentor, Estatua do ⊕[1] 287a 22.57 S 43.13 W
Cristuru-Secuiesc 38 46.17 N 25.02 E
Crişul Alb ≃ 38 46.42 N 21.17 E
Crişul Negru ≃ 38 46.42 N 21.16 E
Crişul Repede (Sebes Körös) ≃ 38 46.55 N 20.59 E
Crittenden 218 38.46 N 84.36 W
Crivitz, Dtsch. 54 53.35 N 11.38 E
Crivitz, Wi., U.S. 190 45.13 N 88.00 W
Crixalândia 255 15.18 S 47.15 W
Crixás 255 14.27 S 49.58 W
Crixás ≃ 250 11.02 S 48.34 W
Crixás-Açu ≃ 255 13.19 S 50.36 W
Crixás-Mirim ≃ 255 13.30 S 50.30 W
Črna 61 46.28 N 14.51 E
Crna ≃ 38 41.35 N 21.59 E
Crna Gora □[3] 38 42.30 N 19.18 E
Črni vrh ∧ 61 46.29 N 15.14 E
Črnomelj 36 45.34 N 15.11 E
Croachy 46 57.19 N 4.14 W
Croagh Patrick ∧ 48 53.46 N 9.40 W
Croajingolong National Park ♠ 166 37.40 S 149.30 E
Croal ≃ 262 53.33 N 2.23 W
Croatia (Hrvatska) □[1] 36 45.10 N 15.30 E
Croce dello Scrivano, Passo)(68 40.34 N 15.50 E
Croce Domini, Passo di)(64 45.54 N 10.24 E
Crocefieschi 62 44.35 N 9.01 E
Crocetta del Montello 64 45.50 N 12.02 E
Crocheron 208 38.14 N 76.03 W
Crockenhill 260 51.23 N 0.10 E
Crocker 194 37.56 N 92.15 W
Crocker, Banjaran ⩘ 112 5.40 N 116.14 E
Crockery Creek ≃ 216 43.02 N 86.05 W
Crocketford 44 55.02 N 3.50 W
Crockett, Ca., U.S. 226 38.03 N 122.12 W
Crockett, Tx., U.S. 222 31.19 N 95.27 W
Crockham Hill 260 51.14 N 0.04 E
Crocus Hill → The Valley 238 18.13 N 63.04 W
Croft 262 53.26 N 2.33 W
Crofton, B.C., Can. 224 48.52 N 123.38 W
Crofton, Ky., U.S. 194 37.02 N 87.29 W
Crofton, Md., U.S. 208 39.00 N 76.41 W
Crofton, Ne., U.S. 198 42.43 N 97.29 W
Croft State Park ♠ 192 34.49 N 81.52 W
Croggan 46 56.22 N 5.42 W
Croghan 212 43.53 N 75.23 W
Croglin 44 54.49 N 2.39 W
Croick 46 57.53 N 4.35 W
Croil Islands II 206 44.58 N 74.58 W
Croisette, Cap › 62 43.13 N 5.20 E
Croisilles 50 50.12 N 2.53 E
Croissy-Beaubourg 261 48.50 N 2.40 E
Croissy-sur-Seine 261 48.53 N 2.09 E
Croix 50 50.40 N 3.09 E
Croix, Lac à la ⊜ 186 51.16 N 70.13 W
Croix, Lac la ⊜ 190 48.21 N 92.05 W
Croker, Cape ›, Austl. 164 10.58 S 132.35 E
Croker, Cape ›, On., Can. 212 44.58 N 80.59 W
Croker Island I 164 11.12 S 132.32 E
Crolles 62 45.17 N 5.53 E
Cromarty 46 57.40 N 4.02 W
Cromarty Firth ⊂[1] 46 57.41 N 4.07 W
Cromby 285 40.09 N 75.32 W
Cromer, Austl. 274a 33.44 S 151.17 E
Cromer, Eng., U.K. 42 52.56 N 1.18 E
Cromford 44 53.06 N 1.34 W
Cromínia 255 17.17 S 49.21 W
Cromore 46 58.09 N 6.29 W
Crompton Point › 240d 15.35 N 61.19 W
Cromwell, N.Z. 172 45.03 S 169.12 E
Cromwell, Al., U.S. 194 32.13 N 88.16 W
Cromwell, Ct., U.S. 207 41.35 N 72.38 W
Cromwell, In., U.S. 216 41.24 N 85.36 W
Cromwell Park ♠ 279a 41.28 N 82.08 W
Cronadun 172 42.02 S 171.52 E
Cronenberg •[8] 263 51.12 N 7.08 E
Cronin, Mount ∧ 182 54.54 N 126.52 W
Cronton 262 53.23 N 2.46 W
Cronulla 170 34.03 S 151.09 E
Cronulla Beach ⩲[2] 274a 34.02 S 151.11 E
Croob, Slieve ∧[2] 48 54.20 N 5.58 W
Crook, Eng., U.K. 44 54.43 N 1.44 W
Crook, Co., U.S. 198 40.51 N 102.48 W
Crooked ≃, B.C., Can. 182 54.50 N 122.54 W
Crooked ≃, Mo., U.S. 194 39.13 N 93.49 W
Crooked ≃, Or., U.S. 202 44.34 N 121.16 W
Crooked Creek 180 61.52 N 158.08 W
Crooked Creek ≃, U.S. 196 36.57 N 100.06 W
Crooked Creek ≃, Ar., U.S. 194 36.14 N 92.29 W
Crooked Creek ≃, Il., U.S. 219 38.30 N 89.25 W
Crooked Creek ≃, In., U.S. 216 40.45 N 86.30 W
Crooked Creek ≃, Mo., U.S. 219 39.34 N 91.55 W
Crooked Creek ≃, Pa., U.S. 210 41.55 N 77.08 W
Crooked Creek ≃, Pa., U.S. 214 40.45 N 79.33 W
Crooked Creek Lake ⊜[1] 214 40.42 N 79.30 W
Crooked Island I 238 22.45 N 74.13 W
Crooked Island Passage ⊔ 238 22.55 N 74.35 W
Crooked Lake, In., U.S. 216 41.41 N 85.02 W
Crooked Lake, Mi., U.S. 216 42.29 N 85.25 W
Crooked Lake ⊜, Nf., Can. 186 48.24 N 56.17 W
Crooked Lake ⊜, Sk., Can. 184 50.36 N 102.45 W
Crooked Lake ⊜, N.A. 190 48.13 N 91.50 W
Crooked Lake ⊜, Fl., U.S. 220 27.48 N 81.35 W
Crooked Lake ⊜, In., U.S. 216 41.40 N 85.03 W
Crooked River 184 52.51 N 103.44 W
Crookes Point › 276 40.32 N 74.08 W
Crookham 279b 40.12 N 79.59 W
Crookston 198 47.46 N 96.36 W
Crookstown 48 51.50 N 8.50 W
Crooksville 188 39.46 N 82.05 W
Crookwell 166 34.28 S 149.28 E
Croom 48 52.31 N 8.42 W
Cropalati 68 39.31 N 16.43 E
Cropani 68 38.58 N 16.47 E
Cropper 218 38.18 N 85.06 W
Crosby, Eng., U.K. 262 53.30 N 3.02 W
Crosby, Mn., U.S. 190 46.28 N 93.57 W
Crosby, Ms., U.S. 194 31.17 N 91.03 W
Crosby, N.D., U.S. 198 48.54 N 103.17 W
Crosby, Pa., U.S. 214 41.45 N 78.24 W
Crosby, Tx., U.S. 222 29.55 N 95.04 W
Crosby, Mount ∧ 202 43.53 N 109.20 W
Crosby Lake ⊜ 212 44.45 N 76.26 W
Crosbyton 196 33.39 N 101.14 W
Crosia 68 39.34 N 16.46 E
Crosne 261 48.43 N 2.28 E
Cross ≃ 152 4.42 N 8.21 E
Cross Banks II 283 42.43 N 70.49 W
Cross Bay ⊂ 184 53.15 N 99.25 W
Cross Bay Bridge •[5] 276 40.35 N 73.49 W
Crossbost 46 58.08 N 6.23 W
Cross City 192 29.38 N 83.07 W
Cross County Center •[9] 276 40.56 N 73.51 W
Cross Creek ≃, Ca., U.S. 226 36.08 N 119.38 W
Cross Creek ≃, Oh., U.S. 214 40.18 N 80.36 W
Crossen 54 50.45 N 12.29 E
Crossens 262 53.41 N 2.57 W
Crossett 194 33.07 N 91.57 W
Cross Fell ∧ 44 54.42 N 2.29 W
Crossfield 182 51.26 N 114.02 W
Crossgar 48 54.24 N 5.45 W
Cross Hands 42 51.48 N 4.04 W
Crosshaven 48 51.48 N 8.17 W
Crosshill 44 55.19 N 4.39 W
Crossinsee ⊜ 264a 52.22 N 13.41 E
Cross Island I 272c 18.57 N 72.51 E
Cross Keys 285 39.42 N 75.01 W
Cross Keys Airfield ⊠ 285 39.42 N 75.02 W
Cross Lake 184 54.37 N 97.47 W
Cross Lake ⊜, Mb., Can. 184 54.45 N 97.30 W
Cross Lake ⊜, On., Can. 190 46.53 N 79.57 W
Cross Lake ⊜, N.Y., U.S. 210 43.08 N 76.29 W
Crossley, Mount ∧ 172 42.50 S 172.04 E
Crossmaglen 48 54.05 N 6.37 W
Crossman 168a 32.47 S 116.36 E
Crossman ≃ 168a 32.47 S 116.32 E
Crossman Peak ∧ 200 34.32 N 114.07 W
Crossmolina 48 54.06 N 9.20 W
Cross Plains, In., U.S. 218 38.57 N 85.12 W
Cross Plains, Tx., U.S. 196 32.08 N 99.11 W
Cross Plains, Wi., U.S. 190 43.06 N 89.39 W
Cross River □[3] 150 5.50 N 8.30 E
Cross Roads 222 32.03 N 95.58 W
Cross Sound ⊔ 180 58.10 N 136.30 W
Crossville, Il., U.S. 194 38.09 N 88.03 W
Crossville, Tn., U.S. 194 35.56 N 85.01 W
Crosswicks 285 40.09 N 74.38 W
Crosswicks Creek ≃ 208 40.09 N 74.43 W
Crostolo ≃ 64 44.55 N 10.38 E
Croston, Eng., U.K. 44 53.39 N 2.46 W
Croston, Eng., U.K. 262 53.40 N 2.46 W
Croswell 190 43.16 N 82.37 W
Crotch Lake ⊜ 212 44.55 N 76.48 W
Crotenay 58 46.45 N 5.49 E
Crothersville 218 38.48 N 85.50 W
Croton 214 40.14 N 82.41 W
Crotona Park ♠ 276 40.50 N 73.54 W
Croton Creek ≃ 196 33.18 N 100.25 W
Crotone 68 39.05 N 17.07 E
Croton Falls 210 41.21 N 73.40 W
Croton-on-Hudson 210 41.12 N 73.53 W
Croton Point › 276 41.10 N 73.54 W
Crottendorf 54 50.30 N 12.56 E
Crouch ≃ 42 51.37 N 0.57 E
Crouse Run ≃ 279b 40.35 N 79.58 W
Crouy 50 49.24 N 3.22 E
Crow ≃ 190 45.15 N 93.31 W
Crow, North Fork ≃ 190 45.05 N 93.45 W
Crow, South Fork ≃ 190 45.05 N 93.45 W
Crow Agency 202 45.36 N 107.27 W
Crowborough 42 51.03 N 0.09 E
Crow Creek ≃, U.S. 198 40.23 N 104.29 W
Crow Creek ≃, Ca., U.S. 282 37.42 N 122.03 W
Crow Creek ≃, Il., U.S. 194 40.56 N 89.27 W
Crow Creek ≃, Mt., U.S. 198 45.45 N 105.06 W
Crow Creek ≃, Mt., U.S. 202 46.11 N 111.29 W
Crow Creek ≃, S.D., U.S. 198 43.57 N 99.15 W
Crow Creek ≃, Wy., U.S. 202 43.19 N 109.09 W
Crow Creek Indian Reservation •[4] 198 44.11 N 99.30 W
Crowder, Ms., U.S. 194 34.10 N 90.08 W
Crowder, Ok., U.S. 196 35.07 N 95.40 W
Crowduck Lake ⊜ 184 50.08 N 95.15 W
Crowdy Head › 166 31.50 S 152.45 E
Crowe ≃ 212 44.22 N 77.46 W
Crowe Lake ⊜ 212 44.29 N 77.46 W
Crowell 196 33.59 N 99.43 W
Crowfoot, Mount ∧ 172 45.33 S 167.03 E
Crow Hill ∧[2] 262 53.42 N 1.58 W
Crowhurst 260 51.12 N 0.01 W
Crow Indian Reservation •[4] 202 45.27 N 108.00 W
Crow Lake 184 49.12 N 93.57 W
Crow Lake ⊜ 212 44.43 N 76.37 W
Crowland 42 52.41 N 0.11 W
Crowle 44 53.37 N 0.49 W
Crowley, Ca., U.S. 226 36.21 N 119.17 W
Crowley, La., U.S. 194 30.12 N 92.22 W
Crowley, Tx., U.S. 222 32.34 N 97.21 W
Crowley, Lake ⊜[1] 204 37.37 N 118.44 W
Crowleys Ridge ∧ 194 35.45 N 90.45 W
Crowlin Islands II 46 57.20 N 5.44 W
Crown 214 41.23 N 79.16 W
Crown Hill 212 44.26 N 79.39 W
Crown Island I 164 5.05 S 146.55 E
Crown Memorial Beach ♠ 282 37.46 N 122.16 W
Crown Mines •[7] 273d 26.13 S 28.00 E
Crown Mountain ∧ 240m 18.21 N 64.58 W
Crown Point, In., U.S. 216 41.25 N 87.21 W
Crownpoint, N.M., U.S. 200 35.40 N 108.09 W
Crown Point, N.Y., U.S. 188 43.57 N 73.26 W
Crown Point State Park ♠ 224 45.32 N 122.15 W
Crown Prince Frederik Island I 176 70.02 N 86.50 W
Crown Village 276 40.40 N 73.27 W
Crow Peak ∧ 202 46.18 N 111.54 W
Crow Rock Creek ≃ 202 47.06 N 106.15 W
Crows Fork Creek ≃ 219 38.47 N 91.52 W
Crows Landing 226 37.24 N 121.04 W
Crows Nest, Austl. 171a 27.16 S 152.03 E
Crows Nest, Austl. 274a 33.50 S 151.12 E
Crowsnest, Ab., Can. 182 49.38 N 114.41 W
Crows Nest Falls National Park ♠ 171a 27.16 S 152.08 E
Crowsnest Pass 182 49.36 N 114.26 W
Crowsnest Pass)(182 49.39 N 114.45 W
Crows Nest Peak ∧ 198 44.03 N 103.58 W
Crowthorne 42 51.23 N 0.49 W
Crowton 262 53.16 N 2.38 W
Crow Wing ≃ 198 46.19 N 94.20 W
Croxley Green 260 51.39 N 0.27 W
Croxteth Park ♠ 262 53.26 N 2.53 W
Croy 46 57.31 N 4.02 W
Croyde 42 51.07 N 4.13 W
Croydon, Austl. 166 18.12 S 142.14 E
Croydon, Austl. 169 37.48 S 145.17 E
Croydon, Austl. 274a 33.53 S 151.07 E
Croydon, Pa., U.S. 208 40.05 N 74.54 W
Croydon •[8] 260 51.23 N 0.06 W
Croydon Park 274a 33.54 S 151.07 E
Croydon Peak ∧ 188 43.28 N 72.13 W
Croydon Station 182 53.05 N 119.44 W
Crozet 192 38.04 N 78.42 W
Crozet, Îles II 6 46.00 S 52.00 E
Crozet Basin ⊸[1] 6 39.00 S 60.00 E
Crozon 32 48.15 N 4.29 W
Cruachan, Ben ∧ 46 56.25 N 5.08 W
Cruas 62 44.39 N 4.46 E
Crucea 38 44.32 N 28.14 E
Crucero 248 14.21 S 70.00 W
Cruces, Cuba 240p 22.21 N 80.16 W
Cruces, Méx. 232 29.26 N 107.24 W
Crucoli 68 39.25 N 17.00 E
Cruden Bay 46 57.25 N 1.50 W
Crudgington 42 52.46 N 2.33 W
Crudine Creek ≃ 170 33.05 S 149.40 E
Cruger 194 33.19 N 90.13 W
Cruillas 232 24.45 N 98.31 W
Crum Creek ≃ 285 39.51 N 75.19 W
Crumhorn Mountain ∧ 210 42.33 N 74.55 W
Crumlin, On., Can. 212 43.01 N 81.09 W
Crumlin, N. Ire., U.K. 48 54.37 N 6.14 W
Crum Lynne 285 39.52 N 75.20 W
Crummock Water ⊜ 44 54.34 N 3.18 W
Crump Lake ⊜ 202 42.17 N 119.50 W
Crumpton 208 39.14 N 75.55 W
Crumstown 216 41.38 N 86.25 W
Crupet 56 50.21 N 4.48 E
Cruseilles 58 46.02 N 6.07 E
Cruser Brook ≃ 276 40.27 N 74.39 W
Crusheen 48 52.58 N 8.53 W
Crusnes 56 49.26 N 5.55 E
Crusnes ≃ 56 49.27 N 5.36 E
Crustepec, Cerro ∧ 234 21.15 N 97.53 W
Cruz, Arroyo de la ≃, Ca., U.S. 226 35.42 N 121.09 W
Cruz, Arroyo de la ≃, Ur. 258 34.00 S 56.08 W
Cruz, Cabo › 240p 19.51 N 77.44 W
Cruz, Cañada de la ≃ 258 34.09 S 58.58 W
Cruz, Cayo I 240p 22.15 N 77.49 W
Cruz, Pico de la ∧ 148 28.44 N 17.52 W
Cruz Alta, Arg. 252 33.01 S 61.49 W
Cruz Alta, Bra. 252 28.39 S 53.36 W
Cruz Bay 240m 18.20 N 64.48 W
Cruz de Elorza 234 23.49 N 100.29 W
Cruz del Eje 252 30.44 S 64.48 W
Cruz del Marquez, Cerro ∧ 286a 19.12 N 99.15 W
Cruzeiro 256 22.34 S 44.58 W
Cruzeiro do Oeste 255 23.46 S 53.04 W
Cruzeiro do Sul 248 7.38 S 72.36 W
Cruzeta 250 6.25 S 36.47 W
Cruz Grande, Chile 252 29.25 S 71.18 W
Cruz Grande, Méx. 234 16.44 N 99.08 W
Cruzília 256 21.50 S 44.48 W
Cruz Machado 252 26.01 S 51.21 W
Cruzy-le-Châtel 50 47.51 N 4.12 E
Crvenka 38 45.39 N 19.28 E
Crymych 42 51.59 N 4.40 W
Crynant 42 51.43 N 3.45 W
Crysler 188 45.13 N 75.09 W
Crystal, Mn., U.S. 190 45.01 N 93.21 W
Crystal, N.D., U.S. 198 48.35 N 97.40 W
Crystal ≃ 200 39.25 N 107.14 W
Crystal Bay 226 39.13 N 120.00 W
Crystal Bay ⊂ 220 28.55 N 82.43 W
Crystal Beach, On., Can. 284a 42.52 N 79.04 W
Crystal Beach, Fl., U.S. 220 28.05 N 82.46 W
Crystal Beach, Tx., U.S. 222 29.27 N 94.38 W
Crystal Brook 166 33.21 S 138.13 E
Crystal Cave ⩲[5] 208 40.32 N 75.51 W
Crystal City, Mb., Can. 184 49.09 N 98.56 W
Crystal City, Mo., U.S. 219 38.13 N 90.22 W
Crystal City, Tx., U.S. 196 28.40 N 99.49 W
Crystal Creek ≃ 278 41.58 N 87.51 W
Crystal Falls 190 46.05 N 88.20 W
Crystal Gardens 216 42.14 N 88.23 W
Crystal Lake, Il., U.S. 216 42.14 N 88.18 W
Crystal Lake, N.Y., U.S. 210 42.31 N 74.12 W
Crystal Lake, N.Y., U.S. 210 42.28 N 78.20 W
Crystal Lake ⊜, On., Can. 212 44.45 N 78.30 W
Crystal Lake ⊜, Ma., U.S. 283 42.29 N 71.05 W
Crystal Lake ⊜, Ma., U.S. 283 42.48 N 71.09 W
Crystal Lake ⊜, Mi., U.S. 190 44.40 N 86.10 W
Crystal Lake ⊜, N.J., U.S. 276 41.02 N 74.15 W
Crystal Lakes 218 39.52 N 84.04 W
Crystal Lawns 216 41.34 N 88.09 W
Crystal Manor 216 42.14 N 88.17 W
Crystal Palace Stadium and Motor Race Track ♠ 260 51.25 N 0.04 W
Crystal River 192 28.54 N 82.35 W
Crystal Spring Lake ⊜ 285 39.43 N 75.01 W
Crystal Springs, Fl., U.S. 220 28.10 N 82.09 W
Crystal Springs, Ms., U.S. 194 31.59 N 90.21 W
Crystal Springs Dam •[6] 282 37.32 N 122.22 W
Crystal Vista 216 42.14 N 88.24 W
Csepel •[8] 264c 47.24 N 19.14 E
Csepel-sziget I 30 47.15 N 18.57 E
Csepreg 61 47.24 N 16.43 E
Cserhát ⩘ 30 47.55 N 19.30 E
Cserta ≃ 61 46.35 N 16.36 E
Csesznek ⊥ 30 47.16 N 17.53 E
Csesztreg 61 46.43 N 16.31 E
Csobánka 264c 47.38 N 18.58 E
Csomád 264c 47.40 N 19.15 E
Csömodér 61 46.37 N 16.39 E
Csömör 264c 47.33 N 19.14 E
Csömöri-patak ≃ 264c 47.36 N 19.07 E
Csongrád 30 46.43 N 20.09 E
Csongrád □[6] 30 46.25 N 20.15 E
Csorna 30 47.37 N 17.16 E
Csurgó 30 46.16 N 17.06 E
Ču 85 43.36 N 73.45 E
Ču ≃ 86 45.00 N 67.44 E
Cúa 246 10.10 N 66.54 W
Cuacnopalan 234 18.49 N 97.30 W
Cuácua ≃ 154 17.54 S 36.48 E
Cuajimalpa •[8] 286a 19.21 N 99.18 W
Cuajinicuilapa 234 16.28 N 98.25 W
Cuajone 248 17.00 S 70.43 W
Cuále 152 8.06 S 16.03 E
Cua Lo 110 18.49 N 105.43 E
Cuamato 152 17.05 S 15.09 E
Cuamba 154 14.49 S 36.33 E
Cuambog 116 7.20 N 125.52 E
Cuanavale ≃ 152 15.07 S 19.14 E
Cuando 152 16.32 S 22.07 E
Cuando (Kwando) ≃ 152 18.27 S 23.32 E
Cuando Cubango □[5] 152 16.00 S 20.00 E
Cuangar 152 17.36 S 18.39 E
Cuango, Ang. 152 14.30 S 18.59 E
Cuango, Ang. 152 9.10 S 17.58 E
Cuango, Ang. 152 6.17 S 16.41 E

Symbol	English	Deutsch	Español	Français	Português
≃	River	Fluß	Río	Rivière	Rio
≊	Canal	Kanal	Canal	Canal	Canal
⌊	Waterfall, Rapids	Wasserfall, Stromschnellen	Cascada, Rápidos	Chute d'eau, Rapides	Cascata, Rápidos
⊔	Strait	Meeresstraße	Estrecho	Détroit	Estreito
⊂	Bay, Gulf	Bucht, Golf	Bahía, Golfo	Baie, Golfe	Baía, Golfo
⊜	Lake, Lakes	See, Seen	Lago, Lagos	Lac, Lacs	Lago, Lagos
⩸	Swamp	Sumpf	Pantano	Marais	Pântano
⛆	Ice Features, Glacier	Eis- und Gletscherformen	Accidentes Glaciales	Formes glaciaires	Acidentes glaciares
⍑	Other Hydrographic Features	Andere Hydrographische Objekte	Otros Elementos Hidrográficos	Autres données hydrographiques	Outros acidentes hidrográficos
⊸	Submarine Features	Untermeerische Objekte	Accidentes Submarinos	Formes de relief sous-marin	Acidentes submarinos
□	Political Unit	Politische Einheit	Unidad Política	Entité politique	Unidade política
⊕	Cultural Institution	Kulturelle Institution	Institución Cultural	Institution culturelle	Institução cultural
⊥	Historical Site	Historische Stätte	Sitio Histórico	Site historique	Sitio histórico
♠	Recreational Site	Erholungs- und Ferienort	Sitio de Recreo	Centre de loisirs	Area de Lazer
⊠	Airport	Flughafen	Aeropuerto	Aéroport	Aeroporto
■	Military Installation	Militäranlage	Instalación Militar	Installation militaire	Instalação militar
•	Miscellaneous	Verschiedenes	Misceláneo	Divers	Diversos

ENGLISH / DEUTSCH

Name	Page	Lat.°′	Long.°′
Cuango (Kwango) ≃	152	3.14 S	17.23 E
Cuanza ≃	152	9.19 S	13.08 E
Cuanza Norte ▫[5]	152	8.50 S	14.30 E
Cuanza Sul ▫[5]	152	10.50 S	14.50 E
Cuao ≃	246	4.55 N	67.40 W
Cuapiaxtla	234	19.18 N	97.46 W
Cuareim (Quaraí) ≃	252	30.12 S	57.36 W
Cuaró	252	30.37 S	56.54 W
Cuartillo, Arroyo ≃	258	33.45 S	59.06 W
Cuarto ≃	252	33.25 S	62.56 W
Cuatir ≃	152	17.01 S	18.09 E
Cuatro Caminos	286b	22.54 N	82.23 W
Cuatro Ciénegas [de Carranza]	196	26.59 N	102.05 W
Cuatro Islands II	116	10.31 N	124.39 E
Cuauhtémoc, Méx.	232	28.25 N	106.52 W
Cuauhtémoc, Méx.	234	19.20 N	103.36 W
Cuauhtémoc, Méx.	234	22.38 N	98.08 W
Cuautepec el Alto ◆[8]	286a	19.34 N	99.08 W
Cuautitlán	234	19.26 N	104.23 W
Cuautitlán ≃	286a	19.41 N	99.13 W
Cuautitlán [de Romero Rubio]	234	19.40 N	99.11 W
Cuautitlán Izcalli	286a	19.39 N	99.13 W
Cuautla, Méx.	234	20.11 N	104.21 W
Cuautla, Méx.	234	18.48 N	98.57 W
Cuautzin, Volcán ∧[1]	286a	19.09 N	99.06 W
Cuba, Port.	34	38.10 N	7.53 W
Cuba, Al., U.S.	194	32.25 N	88.22 W
Cuba, Il., U.S.	190	40.29 N	90.11 W
Cuba, Ks., U.S.	198	39.48 N	97.27 W
Cuba, Mo., U.S.	194	38.03 N	91.24 W
Cuba, N.M., U.S.	200	36.01 N	106.57 W
Cuba, N.Y., U.S.	210	42.13 N	78.16 W
Cuba ▫[1], N.A.	230	21.30 N	80.00 W
Cuba ▫[1], N.A.	240p	21.30 N	80.00 W
Cubabi, Cerro ∧	200	31.42 N	112.46 W
Cubadak	112	0.19 N	100.00 E
Cubagua, Isla I	246	10.48 N	64.10 W
Cuba Island I	276	40.38 N	73.32 W
Cubal	152	13.02 S	14.19 E
Cubal ≃, Ang.	152	15.22 S	12.39 E
Cubal ≃, Ang.	152	12.42 S	13.56 E
Cubal ≃, Ang.	152	11.19 S	13.48 E
Cuba Lake ⊜	210	42.15 N	78.18 W
Cubanea	254	41.02 S	70.16 W
Cubango (Okavango) ≃	138	18.50 S	22.25 E
Cubangui ≃	152	14.22 S	19.58 E
Čubaricha	86	57.37 N	68.22 E
Čubarovo	82	55.12 N	36.56 E
Cubatão	256	23.53 S	46.25 W
Cubatão, Serra do ≐[4]	256	23.52 S	46.28 W
Cubati	250	6.51 S	36.21 W
Cub Hills ∧∧[2]	184	54.20 N	104.30 W
Cubia ≃	152	16.01 S	21.50 E
Čublas	24	64.44 N	45.00 E
Cub Run ≃	208	38.48 N	77.28 W
Çubuk	130	40.15 N	33.02 E
Cuc ≃	250	1.22 N	53.33 W
Cucamonga	228	34.06 N	117.35 W
Cucamonga Creek ≃	280	33.57 N	117.37 W
Cucamonga Peak ∧	228	34.14 N	117.36 W
Cuccaro Vetere	68	40.09 N	15.18 E
Cucco, Monte ∧	66	43.22 N	12.45 E
Čučeviči	76	52.35 N	26.52 E
Cucharas ≃	198	37.55 N	104.32 W
Cucharas, Sierra ∧∧	234	22.20 N	98.55 W
Cuchi	152	14.36 S	16.58 E
Cuchi ≃	152	15.28 S	17.21 E
Cuchibi ≃	152	15.00 S	20.45 E
Cuchilla Alta, Cerro ∧	236	15.10 N	88.12 W
Cuchillo-Có	252	38.20 S	64.37 W
Cuchillo Negro Creek ≃	200	33.08 N	107.14 W
Cuchivero ≃	246	7.40 N	65.57 W
Čuchloma	76	58.45 N	42.41 E
Čuchlomskoje, ozero ⊜	76	58.46 N	42.35 E
Cuchumatanes, Sierra los ∧∧	236	15.35 N	91.25 W
Cuckels Brook ≃	276	40.33 N	74.33 W
Cuckfield	42	51.00 N	0.09 W
Cuckney	44	53.15 N	1.08 W
Cuckold Point >	284b	39.14 N	76.24 W
Čučkovo, Ross.	76	59.36 N	41.14 E
Čučkovo, Ross.	80	54.17 N	41.26 E
Cucuí	246	1.12 N	66.50 W
Čučuleny	78	47.02 N	28.22 E
Cucumbi	152	10.17 S	19.05 E
Cucuron	62	43.47 N	5.26 E
Cucurpe	232	30.20 N	110.43 W
Cúcuta	246	7.54 N	72.31 W
Cudachar	84	42.21 N	47.11 E
Cudahy, Ca., U.S.	280	33.57 N	118.11 W
Cudahy, Wi., U.S.	216	42.57 N	87.51 W
Cuddalore	122	11.45 N	79.45 E
Cuddapah	122	14.28 N	78.49 E
Cuddeback Lake ⊜	228	35.18 N	117.28 W
Cuddebackville	210	41.28 N	74.36 W
Cuddia ≃	70	37.53 N	12.37 E
Cuddington, Eng., U.K.	44	53.14 N	2.36 W
Cuddington, Eng., U.K.	262	53.14 N	2.36 W
Cuddle Lake ⊜	184	55.25 N	95.47 W
Cuddy	279b	40.21 N	80.09 W
Cuddy Mountain ∧	202	44.46 N	116.47 W
Cudgegong	170	32.48 S	149.49 E
Cudgegong ≃	170	32.37 S	149.43 E
Cudgewa	171b	36.12 S	147.46 E
Cudgewa Creek ≃	171b	36.03 S	147.55 E
Cudham ◆[8]	260	51.19 N	0.05 E
Cudia Park ♦	275b	43.43 N	79.13 W
Čudin	76	52.44 N	26.59 E
Cudjoe Key I	220	24.40 N	81.30 W
Čudnov	78	50.04 N	28.06 E
Čudovo	76	59.07 N	31.41 E
Čudskoje ozero (Peipsi järv) ⊜	76	58.45 N	27.30 E
Cudworth, Sk., Can.	184	52.30 N	105.45 W
Cudworth, Eng., U.K.	44	53.35 N	1.25 W
Cue	162	27.25 S	117.54 E
Cuebe ≃	152	15.48 S	17.30 E
Cueio ≃, Ang.	152	15.27 S	21.21 E
Cueio ≃, Ang.	152	16.17 S	17.46 E
Cuelei ≃	152	15.33 S	17.21 E
Cuéllar	34	41.24 N	4.19 W
Cuenca, Ec.	246	2.53 S	78.59 W
Cuenca, Esp.	34	40.04 N	2.08 W
Cuenca ▫[4]	34	39.55 N	2.10 W
Cuencamé [de Ceniceros]	232	24.53 N	103.42 W
Cuerámaro	234	20.37 N	101.43 W
Cuernavaca	234	18.55 N	99.15 W
Cuero	222	29.05 N	97.17 W
Cuers	62	43.14 N	6.04 E
Cuervos	204	32.38 N	114.52 W
Cuesmes	50	50.26 N	3.55 E
Cuesta Pass)(	226	35.21 N	120.38 W
Cueto	240p	20.39 N	75.56 W
Cuetzala del Progreso	234	18.07 N	99.50 W
Cuetzalan del Progreso	234	20.02 N	97.31 W
Cuevas del Almanzora	34	37.18 N	1.53 W
Çuevo	248	20.27 S	63.32 W
Čufarovo	80	54.06 N	47.19 E
Cuffley	260	51.42 N	0.07 W
Cufra → Al-Kufrah ⊤[4]	146	24.20 N	23.15 E
Cufré	258	34.12 S	57.06 W
Cufré, Arroyo ≃	258	34.27 S	57.09 W
Cuggiono	62	45.31 N	8.49 E
Cugir	38	45.50 N	23.22 E
Cuglieri	71	40.11 N	8.34 E
Cugo ≃	152	7.18 S	16.39 E
Čugujev	78	49.50 N	36.41 E
Čugujevka	89	44.08 N	133.53 E
Čugunaš	86	52.52 N	87.46 E
Čuguš, gora ∧	84	43.47 N	40.16 E
Cuiabá	248	15.35 S	56.05 W
Cuiabá ≃	248	17.53 S	57.27 W
Cuiari	246	1.30 N	68.11 W
Cuiari ≃	246	1.30 N	68.11 W
Cuicatlán	234	17.48 N	96.58 W
Cuichapa	234	17.59 N	94.15 W
Cuieiras ≃	246	2.50 S	60.31 W
Cuigezhuang, Zhg.	105	40.01 N	116.28 E
Cuigezhuang, Zhg.	105	40.02 N	117.54 E
Cuihuangkou	105	39.32 N	117.11 E
Cuijiatun	104	40.57 N	121.09 E
Cuijiazhuang	104	40.57 N	122.44 E
Cuilapa	236	14.17 N	90.18 W
Cuilcagh ∧	48	54.10 N	7.48 W
Cuilco	236	15.24 N	91.58 W
Ču-Ilijskije gory ∧∧	85	43.52 N	75.00 E
Cuillin Hills ∧∧[2]	46	57.15 N	6.15 W
Cuilo (Kwilu) ≃, Afr.	152	3.22 S	17.22 E
Cuilo ≃, Afr.	152	5.52 S	16.35 E
Cuilo Futa	152	6.25 S	15.44 E
Cuimba	152	6.08 S	14.38 E
Cuio	152	12.58 S	12.58 E
Cuiqiao	98	34.12 N	114.36 E
Cuiseaux	58	46.30 N	5.24 E
Cuisery	58	46.33 N	5.00 E
Cuisy	261	49.01 N	2.46 E
Cuité	250	6.29 S	36.09 W
Cuitláhuac	234	18.49 N	96.43 W
Cuíto ≃	152	18.01 S	20.48 E
Cuíto-Cuanavale	152	15.10 S	19.10 E
Cuitzeo, Laguna de ⊜	234	19.55 N	101.05 W
Cuitzeo del Porvenir	234	19.59 N	101.09 W
Cuiuni ≃	246	0.45 S	63.07 W
Cuivre ≃	219	38.56 N	90.42 W
Cuivre, North Fork ≃	219	39.02 N	90.59 W
Cuivre, West Fork ≃	219	39.02 N	90.59 W
Cuivre River State Park ♦	219	39.02 N	90.57 W
Čuja	88	59.12 N	112.25 E
Čuja ≃, Ross.	86	50.24 N	86.39 E
Čuja ≃, Ross.	88	59.17 N	112.24 E
Cují	286c	10.28 N	67.02 W
Çukas	112	0.25 S	104.18 E
Čukčagirskoje ozero ⊜	89	52.00 N	136.36 E
Čukotskaja Avtonomnaja Oblast' ▫[8]	180	66.00 N	178.00 E
Čukotskij, mys >	180	64.14 N	173.10 W
Čukotskij poluostrov >[1]	180	66.00 N	175.00 W
Çukurca	128	37.15 N	43.37 E
Čukurčak	85	41.47 N	71.07 E
Cukurino	83	48.05 N	37.18 E
Culaba	116	11.40 N	124.32 E
Čulak-Kurgan	85	43.46 N	69.12 E
Culaman	116	5.58 N	125.40 E
Culari ≃	250	1.27 N	53.42 W
Culasi, Pil.	116	11.26 N	122.03 E
Culasi, Pil.	116	10.43 N	125.43 E
Culasian	116	8.51 N	117.29 E
Culasi Point >	116	11.37 N	122.42 E
Culbertson, Mt., U.S.	198	48.08 N	104.30 W
Culbertson, Ne., U.S.	198	40.13 N	100.50 W
Culbertson Run ≃	285	40.03 N	75.45 W
Culbin	168a	33.10 S	116.50 E
Culburra	170	34.57 S	150.47 E
Culcairn	166	35.40 S	147.03 E
Culcheth	262	53.27 N	2.32 W
Culdaff	48	55.18 N	7.11 W
Culdaff Bay ⊂	48	55.17 N	7.10 W
Culebra	240m	18.18 N	65.18 W
Culebra, Isla de I	240m	18.19 N	65.17 W
Culebra, Sierra de la ∧∧	34	41.54 N	6.20 W
Culebra Peak ∧	200	37.07 N	105.11 W
Culebrinas ≃	240m	18.24 N	67.11 W
Culebrita, Isla I	240m	18.19 N	65.14 W
Culebro, Arroyo del ≃	266a	40.19 N	3.34 W
Culemborg	52	51.56 N	5.13 E
Culgoa ≃	166	29.56 S	146.20 E
Culham Inlet ⊂	162	33.55 S	120.04 E
Culiacán, Méx.	232	24.48 N	107.24 W
Culiacán, Méx.	232	24.04 N	107.05 W
Culiacán, Cerro ∧	234	20.20 N	100.58 W
Culiacancito	232	24.50 N	107.32 W
Culijón, Nevado ∧	248	14.38 S	69.14 W
Culion	116	11.53 N	120.01 E
Culion Island I	116	11.50 N	119.55 E
Cúllar de Baza	34	37.35 N	2.34 W
Cull Creek ≃	282	37.42 N	122.03 W
Cullen, Scot., U.K.	46	57.41 N	2.49 W
Cullen, La., U.S.	194	32.58 N	93.27 W
Cullen Bullen	170	33.18 S	150.01 E
Cullen Point >	164	11.57 S	141.54 E
Culleoka, Tn., U.S.	194	35.28 N	86.58 W
Culleoka, Tx., U.S.	222	33.08 N	96.29 W
Cullera	34	39.10 N	0.15 W
Cullicudden	46	57.39 N	4.13 W
Cullin, Lough ⊜	48	53.57 N	9.12 W
Cullinan	158	25.40 S	28.31 E
Cullman	194	34.10 N	86.50 W
Culloden Battlesite ⊥	46	57.28 N	4.05 W
Cullom	216	40.53 N	88.16 W
Cullompton	42	50.52 N	3.24 W
Cullowhee	192	35.18 N	83.10 W
Cully	58	46.29 N	6.44 E
Cullybackey	48	54.53 N	6.21 W
Çulm ≃	42	50.46 N	3.31 W
Čul'man	74	56.52 N	124.52 E
Cülmen	130	37.19 N	38.48 E
Culmore	284c	38.51 N	77.08 W
Culoz	62	45.51 N	5.47 E
Culpeper	188	38.28 N	77.59 W
Culpina	248	20.50 S	64.58 W
Culrain	46	57.55 N	4.24 W
Cults	46	57.07 N	2.10 W
Cultus Lake	224	49.04 N	121.58 W
Cultus Lake ⊜	224	49.03 N	121.58 W
Cultus Lake Provincial Park ♦	224	49.03 N	121.58 W
Culú-Culú, Arroyo ≃	258	35.19 S	58.57 W
Culú-Culú, Laguna ⊜	258	35.20 S	58.59 W
Çuluene ≃	255	12.56 S	52.51 W
Çuluunchoroot	88	49.41 N	114.15 E
Çuluut	102	45.48 N	107.05 E
Čuluutyn ≃	88	49.11 N	100.41 E
Culvain ∧	46	56.56 N	5.17 W
Culver, In., U.S.	216	41.13 N	86.25 W
Culver, Or., U.S.	202	44.31 N	121.12 W
Culver, Point >	162	32.54 S	124.43 E
Culver City	228	34.01 N	118.23 W
Culverden	172	42.46 S	172.51 E
Culvers Lake	210	41.10 N	74.48 W
Çulverstone Green	260	51.20 N	0.21 E
Čulym	86	55.06 N	80.58 E
Čulym ≃, Ross.	86	54.38 N	78.16 E
Čulym ≃, Ross.	86	57.43 N	83.51 E
Čulyšman ≃	86	51.20 N	87.45 E
Čum	24	67.06 N	63.07 E
Cuma	152	12.52 S	15.05 E
Çuma (Cumae) ⊥	68	40.50 N	14.06 E
Čumakovo	86	55.41 N	79.02 E
Cumalı	130	36.42 N	27.27 E
Cuman'	78	50.49 N	25.53 E
Cumaná	246	10.28 N	64.10 W
Cumanacoa	246	10.15 N	63.55 W
Cumanayagua	240p	22.09 N	80.12 W
Cumaovası	130	38.15 N	27.09 E
Cumare, Cerro ∧[2]	246	0.28 N	73.52 W
Cumari	255	18.16 S	48.11 W
Cumbal	246	0.54 N	77.47 W
Cumbal, Nevado ∧	246	0.57 N	77.52 W
Cumbe	250	10.21 S	37.14 W
Cumbee	220	28.04 N	81.55 W
Cumberland, B.C., Can.	182	49.37 N	125.01 W
Cumberland, Ia., U.S.	198	41.16 N	94.52 W
Cumberland, Ky., U.S.	192	36.58 N	82.59 W
Cumberland, Md., U.S.	188	39.39 N	78.45 W
Cumberland, Va., U.S.	192	37.29 N	78.14 W
Cumberland, Wa., U.S.	224	47.16 N	121.55 W
Cumberland, Wi., U.S.	190	45.31 N	92.01 W
Cumberland ▫[6], N.J., U.S.	208	39.26 N	75.14 W
Cumberland ▫[6], Pa., U.S.	208	40.12 N	77.12 W
Cumberland ≃	178	37.09 N	88.25 W
Cumberland, Lake ⊜[1]	194	36.57 N	84.55 W
Cumberland, South Fork ≃	192	36.58 N	84.36 W
Cumberland City	194	36.23 N	87.38 W
Cumberland Falls State Resort Park ♦	192	36.50 N	84.20 W
Cumberland Gap)(	192	36.36 N	83.41 W
Cumberland Gap National Historical Park ♦	192	36.36 N	83.40 W
Cumberland Hill	207	41.58 N	71.27 W
Cumberland House	184	53.58 N	102.16 W
Cumberland Indian Reserve ◆[4]	184	53.04 N	104.50 W
Cumberland Island National Seashore ♦	192	30.50 N	81.27 W
Cumberland Islands II	166	20.40 S	149.09 E
Cumberland Lake ⊜	184	54.02 N	102.17 W
Cumberland Peninsula >[1]	176	66.50 N	64.00 W
Cumberland Plateau ∧∧[1]	192	36.20 N	84.30 W
Cumberland Sound ʮ	176	65.10 N	65.30 W
Cumbernauld	46	55.58 N	3.59 W
Cumborah	166	29.44 S	147.46 E
Cumbria ▫[6]	44	54.30 N	3.00 W
Cumbrian Mountains ∧∧	44	54.30 N	3.05 W
Čumbur-Kosa	83	46.57 N	38.53 E
Cumby	222	33.08 N	95.50 W
Cumeral Nuevo	200	30.54 N	110.51 W
Çumiana	62	44.59 N	7.22 E
Čumikan	89	54.42 N	135.19 E
Cuminapanema ≃	250	1.09 S	54.54 W
Cuminá → Paru de Oeste ≃	250	1.30 S	56.00 W
Cuminestown	46	57.32 N	2.20 W
Cumming	192	34.12 N	84.08 W
Cummings Mountain ∧	228	35.03 N	118.34 W
Cummington	207	42.27 N	72.53 W
Cummins	166	34.16 S	135.44 E
Cummins, Mount ∧	182	52.03 N	118.15 W
Cummins Creek ≃	222	29.43 N	96.31 W
Cummins Range ∧∧	162	19.05 S	127.10 E
Cumnock	44	55.27 N	4.16 W
Cumnor	42	51.44 N	1.20 W
Cumpas	232	30.02 N	109.48 W
Çumra	130	37.34 N	32.48 E
Čumshewa Inlet ⊂	182	53.03 N	131.45 W
Cumuripa	232	28.08 N	109.53 W
Çumwhinton	44	54.52 N	2.51 W
Čumyš ≃	86	53.31 N	83.10 E
Čun'a ≃, Ross.	74	61.36 N	96.30 E
Čuna ≃, Ross.	88	57.47 N	95.26 E
Cunani	250	2.52 N	51.06 W
Cunauaru ≃	246	3.10 S	63.01 W
Cunaviche	246	7.22 N	67.25 W
Cunco	252	38.55 S	72.02 W
Cuncumén	252	31.53 S	70.38 W
Cundeelee Reserve ◆[4]	162	30.30 S	123.25 E
Cunderdin	162	31.39 S	117.15 E
Cundinamarca ▫[5]	246	5.00 N	74.00 W
Çunduacán	234	18.04 N	93.10 W
Čundža	86	43.32 N	79.28 E
Cunene ▫[5]	152	16.30 S	15.30 E
Cunene (Kunene) ≃	152	17.20 S	11.50 E
Cuneo	62	44.23 N	7.32 E
Cuneo ▫[4]	62	44.31 N	7.34 E
Cunewalde	54	51.06 N	14.30 E
Cuney	222	32.02 N	95.25 W
Cung Hau, Cua ≃[1]	110	9.46 N	106.34 E
Cung Son	110	13.02 N	108.58 E
Çüngüş	130	38.13 N	39.17 E
Čunha	256	23.05 S	44.58 W
Cunhambebe	256	23.00 S	44.20 W
Cunha Porã	252	26.54 S	53.09 W
Cunhinga	152	12.11 S	16.47 E
Cunhinga ≃	152	10.38 S	16.48 E
Cunhuã, Igarapé ≃	248	5.46 S	64.36 W
Cunlhat	62	45.38 N	3.35 E
Cunliffe	168b	34.05 S	137.45 E
Cunnamulla	166	28.04 S	145.41 E
Cunningham, Austl.	171a	28.09 S	151.51 E
Cunningham, Ks., U.S.	198	37.38 N	98.25 W
Cunningham, Lake ⊜	240b	25.04 N	77.26 W
Cunninghame ▫[9]	46	55.40 N	4.30 W
Cunningham Falls State Park ♦	208	39.35 N	77.27 W
Cunningham Park ♦, Ma., U.S.	283	42.15 N	71.03 W
Cunningham Park ♦, N.Y., U.S.	276	40.44 N	73.46 W
Čunojar	88	57.27 N	97.18 E
Çunqian	100	28.30 N	115.10 E
Čunskij, Ross.	88	56.05 N	99.41 E
Čunskij, Ross.	88	57.26 N	97.31 E
Cuntan	107	29.37 N	106.36 E
Çunucunuma ≃	246	3.13 N	65.58 W
Čuny	76	59.39 N	36.04 E
Čuokkaraš'ša ∧	24	69.57 N	24.32 E
Çuorgnè	62	45.23 N	7.39 E
Čupa	24	66.16 N	33.00 E
Čupachovka	78	50.23 N	34.36 E
Čupalejka	80	55.11 N	42.33 E
Cupar, Sk., Can.	184	50.57 N	104.12 W
Cupar, Scot., U.K.	46	56.19 N	3.01 W
Cupecê, Ribeirão ≃	287b	23.37 S	46.42 W
Cupello	66	42.04 N	14.40 E
Cuperly	50	49.04 N	4.26 E
Cupertino	226	37.19 N	122.01 W
Cupica, Golfo de ⊂	246	6.35 N	77.25 W
Cupins	255	19.51 S	51.03 W
Cupra Marittima	66	43.01 N	13.51 E
Cupramontana	66	43.27 N	13.07 E
Ćuprija	38	43.56 N	21.23 E
Čuprovo	24	64.14 N	46.36 E
Cupsaw Lake ⊜	276	41.07 N	74.15 W
Cuqiao	107	30.36 N	103.59 E
Cuquema ≃	152	12.03 S	17.40 E
Cuquenán ≃	246	4.45 N	61.30 W
Çuquío	234	20.55 N	103.02 W
Čur	80	57.07 N	52.58 E
Curaçá	250	8.59 S	39.54 W
Curaçao I	241s	12.11 N	69.00 W
Curacautín	252	38.26 S	71.53 W
Çuracaví	252	33.24 S	71.09 W
Čuračiki	80	55.44 N	47.26 E
Curaglia	58	46.41 N	8.51 E
Cural Novo, Ribeirão ≃	256	21.17 S	43.51 W
Curanilahue	252	37.28 S	73.21 W
Curanipe	252	35.50 S	72.38 W
Çuranja ≃	248	9.58 S	70.58 W
Čurapča	74	62.00 N	132.24 E
Curapi ≃	250	1.25 N	53.49 W
Çuraray ≃	246	2.20 S	74.05 W
Čurbek	85	39.59 N	69.56 E
Curcani	38	44.12 N	26.35 E
Curdies ≃	169	38.30 S	142.55 E
Cure ≃	50	47.40 N	3.41 E
Curecanti National Recreation Area ♦	200	38.24 N	107.25 W
Curepipe	157c	20.19 S	57.31 E
Curepto	252	35.05 S	72.01 W
Çurequetê ≃	248	8.20 S	65.40 W
Čureški prohod)(	38	42.47 N	23.49 E
Curiapo	246	8.33 N	61.00 W
Curib	84	42.14 N	46.49 E
Curiche Grande (Corixo Grande) ≃	248	17.43 S	57.43 W
Curicó	252	34.59 S	71.14 W
Curicuriari ≃	246	0.14 S	66.48 W
Curières, Lac ⊜	206	46.41 N	74.51 W
Curimatá	250	10.02 S	44.17 W
Curimeo	234	20.01 N	101.42 W
Curinga	68	38.49 N	16.19 E
Curious, Mount ∧	162	27.28 S	114.20 E
Curisevo ≃	255	12.14 S	53.17 W
Curitiba	252	25.25 S	49.15 W
Curitibanos	252	27.18 S	50.36 W
Curiuaú ≃	246	1.51 S	61.14 W
Curiúva	255	24.02 S	50.27 W
Curl Curl	274a	33.46 S	151.18 E
Curlew	182	48.53 N	118.35 W
Curlewis	166	31.07 S	150.16 E
Curnamona	166	31.39 S	139.32 E
Curoca Norte	152	16.18 S	12.58 E
Curone ≃	62	45.03 N	8.54 E
Curon Venosta (Graun)	64	46.49 N	10.32 E
Čurovići	78	52.10 N	32.01 E
Currais Novos	250	6.15 S	36.31 W
Curralinho	250	1.48 S	49.47 W
Curramulka	168b	34.42 S	137.42 E
Curran	219	39.44 N	89.46 W
Currant Creek ≃, Co., U.S.	200	38.29 N	105.24 W
Currant Creek ≃, Mt., U.S.	202	46.22 N	108.39 W
Currant Mountain ∧	204	38.55 N	115.25 W
Currarong	170	35.01 S	150.49 E
Currency Creek	168b	35.28 S	138.46 E
Current ≃, On., Can.	190	48.27 N	89.11 W
Current ≃, U.S.	194	36.16 N	90.57 W
Current Islands II	192	25.22 N	76.49 W
Currie, Austl.	166	39.56 S	143.52 E
Currie, Scot., U.K.	46	55.54 N	3.20 W
Currie, Mn., U.S.	198	44.04 N	95.39 W
Currituck	192	36.26 N	76.00 W
Currituck ▫[6]	208	36.28 N	76.03 W
Currituck Seamount ✦[3]	14	30.00 S	173.30 W
Currituck Sound ʮ	192	36.20 N	75.52 W
Curry	180	62.37 N	150.01 W
Curry, Lake ⊜[1]	226	38.22 N	122.08 W
Curry Rivel	42	51.02 N	2.52 W
Curryville, Mo., U.S.	219	39.20 N	91.20 W
Curryville, Pa., U.S.	214	40.17 N	78.20 W
Cursi	68	40.09 N	18.18 E
Curslack ◆[8]	52	53.27 N	10.13 E
Curtarolo	64	45.31 N	11.50 E
Curtea de Argeș	38	45.08 N	24.41 E
Curtice	214	41.29 N	82.49 W
Curtina	252	32.09 S	56.07 W
Curtin Springs	162	25.20 S	131.45 E
Curtis, Esp.	34	43.07 N	8.03 W
Curtis, Ar., U.S.	194	33.59 N	93.06 W
Curtis, Ne., U.S.	198	40.37 N	100.30 W
Curtis, Port ⊤[3]	166	24.00 S	151.30 E
Curtis Bay ⊂	284b	39.13 N	76.35 W
Curtis Channel ʮ	166	23.30 S	151.45 E
Curtis Creek ⊂	284b	39.12 N	76.35 W
Curtis Island I, Austl.	166	23.38 S	151.09 E
Curtis Island I, N.Z.	14	30.30 S	178.34 W
Curtis Lake ⊜	176	66.38 N	89.02 W
Curtisville	214	40.38 N	79.51 W
Curu ≃	250	3.22 S	39.04 W
Curuá ≃, Bra.	250	5.23 S	54.22 W
Curuá ≃, Bra.	250	1.55 S	55.07 W
Curuá ≃, Bra.	255	13.51 S	51.38 W
Curuá, Ilha do I	250	0.48 N	50.10 W
Curuaés ≃	250	7.30 S	54.45 W
Curuan	116	7.13 N	122.14 E
Curuá-Una ≃	250	2.24 S	54.05 W
Curubandé	236	10.43 N	85.26 W
Curuçá	250	0.43 S	47.50 W
Curuçá ◆[8]	287b	23.30 S	46.25 W
Curuçá ≃	246	4.27 S	71.23 W
Curuçambaba	250	2.08 S	49.18 W
Çurug, Indon.	115a	6.15 S	106.33 E
Čurug, Jugo.	38	45.29 N	20.04 E
Curuguaty	252	24.31 S	55.42 W
Curumo	286c	10.27 N	66.52 W
Curumu	250	1.01 S	51.03 W
Curunga	152	12.51 S	21.12 E
Curup	112	3.28 S	102.32 E
Curupá	250	9.54 S	45.54 W
Curupayty, Riacho ≃	248	22.03 S	58.00 W
C'urupinsk	78	46.37 N	32.43 E
Cururu ≃, Bra.	248	7.12 S	58.03 W
Cururu ≃, Bra.	250	0.39 S	50.11 W
Cururu-Açu ≃	250	8.58 S	57.13 W
Cururupu	250	1.50 S	44.52 W
Curuzú Cuatiá	252	29.47 S	58.03 W
Curva Grande	250	2.37 S	45.27 W
Curvelo	255	18.45 S	44.25 W
Curwensville	214	40.58 N	78.31 W
Curwensville Lake ⊜[1]	214	40.55 N	78.37 W
Curwensville State Park ♦	214	40.55 N	78.34 W
Cusago	266b	45.27 N	9.02 E
Cusano Milanino	62	45.33 N	9.11 E
Cusano Mutri	68	41.20 N	14.30 E
Cusco	248	13.31 S	71.59 W
Cusco ▫[5]	248	12.30 S	72.30 W
Cuscuzeiro, Pico do ∧	256	23.18 S	44.47 W
Cushabatay ≃	248	7.09 S	75.08 W
Cushendall	48	55.06 N	6.04 W
Cushendun	48	55.07 N	6.03 W
Cushina ≃	48	53.11 N	7.05 W
Cushing, Ok., U.S.	196	35.59 N	96.46 W
Cushing, Tx., U.S.	222	31.43 N	94.50 W
Cushing Memorial State Park ♦	283	42.10 N	70.45 W
Cushman	194	35.52 N	91.45 W
Cushman, Lake ⊜[1]	224	47.28 N	123.14 W
Cusiana ≃	246	4.33 N	71.51 W
Cusick	202	48.20 N	117.17 W
Cusihuiriáchic	232	28.14 N	106.50 W
Çusna, Monte ∧	64	44.17 N	10.23 E
Čusovaja ≃	86	58.13 N	56.22 E
Čusovoj	86	58.17 N	57.49 E
Cusset	32	46.08 N	3.28 E
Cusseta	192	32.18 N	84.46 W
Cussewago Creek ≃	214	41.38 N	80.11 W
Cussey-sur-l'Ognon	58	47.20 N	5.56 E
Cusso ≃	152	14.16 S	15.36 E
Çust, N.Z.	172	43.19 S	172.22 E
Čust, Uzb.	85	41.00 N	71.15 E
Custar	216	41.17 N	83.51 W
Custer, Mi., U.S.	190	43.57 N	86.13 W
Custer, Mt., U.S.	202	46.07 N	107.33 W
Custer, Ok., U.S.	196	35.40 N	98.53 W
Custer, S.D., U.S.	198	43.46 N	103.35 W
Custer, Wa., U.S.	224	48.55 N	122.38 W
Custer Battlefield National Monument ♦	202	45.32 N	107.20 W
Custer City	214	41.54 N	78.39 W
Custer Creek ≃	198	46.42 N	105.29 W
Custer State Park ♦	198	43.43 N	103.23 W
Custines	56	48.48 N	6.09 E
Custódia	250	8.07 S	37.39 W
Custonaci	70	38.04 N	12.41 E
Cut, Nuhu I	164	5.35 S	133.00 E
Cut and Shoot	222	30.19 N	95.25 W
Cutato ≃	152	10.33 S	16.48 E
Cut Bank	202	48.37 N	112.19 W
Cutbank ≃	182	54.44 N	118.31 W
Cut Bank Creek ≃, N.A.	198	48.35 N	100.52 W
Cut Bank Creek ≃, Mt., U.S.	202	48.29 N	112.14 W
Çut Beaver Lake ⊜	184	53.47 N	102.38 W
Čutejevo	80	55.16 N	47.47 E
Cutervo	248	6.22 S	78.51 W
Cutervo, Parque Nacional ♦	248	6.10 S	78.45 W
Cuthand Creek ≃	194	33.23 N	94.57 W
Cuthbert	192	31.46 N	84.47 W
Cut Knife	184	52.44 N	109.01 W
Cutler, Ca., U.S.	226	36.31 N	119.17 W
Cutler, Me., U.S.	188	44.39 N	67.12 W
Cutler Ridge	220	25.34 N	80.20 W
Çutlerville	216	42.50 N	85.39 W
Čutovo	78	49.43 N	35.10 E
Cutral-Có	252	38.56 S	69.14 W
Cutro	68	39.02 N	16.59 E
Cutrofiano	68	40.07 N	18.12 E
Cuttack	120	20.30 N	85.50 E
Çuttyhunk Island I	207	41.25 N	70.56 W
Čutyr'	80	57.24 N	53.17 E
Cutzamala ≃	234	18.22 N	100.39 W
Cutzamala de Pinzón	234	18.28 N	100.34 W
Çutzio	234	18.39 N	100.54 W
Čuvašskaja Avtonomnaja Sovetskaja Socialističeskaja Respublika ▫[3]	80	55.30 N	47.00 E
Cuvette ▫[5]	152	0.30 S	16.00 E
Cuvier, Cape >	162	24.05 S	113.22 E
Cuvilly	50	49.33 N	2.42 E
Cuvo ≃	152	10.50 S	13.47 E
Cuxhaven	52	53.52 N	8.42 E
Cuxton	260	51.22 N	0.27 E
Cuyabá → Cuiabá	248	15.35 S	56.05 W
Cuyaguateje ≃	240p	22.05 N	83.58 W
Cuyahoga ▫[6]	214	41.30 N	81.41 W
Cuyahoga ≃	214	41.30 N	81.42 W
Cuyahoga County Airport ⊠	279a	41.34 N	81.29 W
Cuyahoga Falls	214	41.08 N	81.29 W
Cuyahoga Heights	279a	41.26 N	81.39 W
Cuyahoga Valley National Recreation Area ♦	214	41.20 N	81.35 W
Cuyama ≃	204	34.54 N	120.18 W
Cuyamaca Peak ∧	204	32.57 N	116.36 W
Cuyamaca Rancho State Park ♦	204	32.58 N	116.32 W
Cuyamel	236	15.38 N	88.12 W
Cuyapo	116	15.46 N	120.40 E
Cuyk	52	51.44 N	5.52 E
Cuyler	210	42.44 N	75.57 W
Cuylerville	210	42.47 N	77.52 W
Cuyo	116	10.51 N	121.00 E
Cuyo East Pass ʮ	116	11.00 N	121.28 E
Cuyo Island I	116	10.51 N	121.02 E
Cuyo Islands II	116	11.04 N	120.57 E
Cuyo West Pass ʮ	116	11.00 N	120.30 E
Cuyubini ≃	246	8.20 N	60.20 W
Cuyuni ≃	246	6.23 N	58.41 W
Cuyuni-Mazaruni ▫[4]	246	6.00 N	60.00 W
Cuyutlán, Laguna ⊂	234	19.00 N	104.10 W
Cuzco → Cusco	248	13.31 S	71.59 W
Čuzik ≃	86	58.03 N	80.37 E
Cuzna ≃	34	38.04 N	4.41 W
Cuzzago	58	46.00 N	8.22 E
Cvetkovo	78	49.11 N	31.33 E
Cvetnogorsk	86	54.14 N	90.27 E
Cvetnoje	78	48.57 N	32.29 E
Cvikov	54	50.48 N	14.40 E
Cwmbran	42	51.39 N	3.00 W
Cyangugu	154	2.29 S	28.54 E
Cybinka	30	52.12 N	14.48 E
Cybulev	78	49.06 N	29.50 E
Cyclades → Kikládhes II	38	37.30 N	25.00 E
Cyclone	214	41.50 N	78.35 W
Cygnet	216	41.14 N	83.38 W
Cygnet Bay ⊂	162	16.35 S	123.05 E
Cygnet Lake ⊜	184	56.47 N	94.54 W
Cygnet River	168b	35.42 S	137.31 E
Cylburn Park ♦	284b	39.21 N	76.39 W
Cynin ≃	42	51.48 N	4.29 W
Cynthiana, Ky., U.S.	218	38.23 N	84.17 W
Cynthiana, Oh., U.S.	218	39.10 N	83.21 W
Cynwyl Elfed	42	51.55 N	4.22 W
Cypern → Cyprus ▫[1]	130	35.00 N	33.00 E
Cypress, Ca., U.S.	280	33.49 N	118.02 W
Cypress, La., U.S.	194	31.36 N	93.02 W
Cypress, Tx., U.S.	222	29.58 N	95.42 W
Cypress Bayou ≃	194	35.03 N	91.42 W
Cypress Creek ≃, Fl., U.S.	220	28.05 N	82.24 W
Cypress Creek ≃, Tx., U.S.	194	30.19 N	93.45 W
Cypress Creek ≃, Tx., U.S.	222	30.02 N	95.19 W
Cypress Gardens ♦	220	28.00 N	81.42 W
Cypress Hills ∧∧[2]	184	49.40 N	109.30 W
Cypress Hills Provincial Park ♦, Ab., Can.	184	49.39 N	110.10 W
Cypress Hills Provincial Park ♦, Sk., Can.	184	49.39 N	109.30 W
Cypress Island I	224	48.35 N	122.42 W
Cypress Lake ⊜, Sk., Can.	184	49.28 N	109.29 W
Cypress Lake ⊜, Fl., U.S.	220	28.05 N	81.19 W
Cypress Point >	226	36.35 N	121.59 W
Cypress Quarters	220	27.15 N	80.48 W
Cypress River	184	49.34 N	99.05 W
Cypress Swamp ≃	208	37.02 N	76.53 W
Cypress Swamp ≡	208	38.30 N	75.17 W
Cyprus ▫[1], Asia	22	35.00 N	33.00 E
Cyprus ▫[1], Asia	130	35.00 N	33.00 E
Cyprus, North ▫[1], Asia	22	35.15 N	33.40 E
Cyprus, North (Kuzey Kıbrıs) ▫[1], Asia	130	35.15 N	33.40 E
Cyrenaica → Barqah ▫[9]	146	31.00 N	22.30 E
Cyrene	219	39.17 N	91.06 W
Cyrene ⊥	146	32.49 N	21.52 E
Cyril	196	34.53 N	98.12 W
Cyrildene ◆[8]	273d	26.11 S	28.06 E
Cyrus Field Bay ⊂	176	62.50 N	64.55 W
Cysoing	50	50.34 N	3.13 E
Cythera → Kíthira I	38	36.20 N	22.58 E
Czaplinek	30	53.34 N	16.14 E
Czarna Białostocka	30	53.19 N	23.16 E
Czarna Woda	30	53.51 N	18.06 E
Czarne	30	53.42 N	16.57 E
Czarnków	30	52.55 N	16.34 E
Czechoslovakia (Československo) ▫[1], Europe	22	49.30 N	17.00 E
Czechoslovakia (Československo) ▫[1], Europe	30	49.30 N	17.00 E
Czempiń	30	52.10 N	16.47 E
Czerniejewo	30	52.26 N	17.30 E
Czernowitz → Černovcy	78	48.18 N	25.56 E
Czersk	30	53.48 N	18.00 E
Czerwieńsk	30	52.01 N	15.25 E
Częstochowa	30	50.49 N	19.06 E
Częstochowa ▫[4]	30	50.40 N	19.15 E
Człopa	30	53.06 N	16.08 E
Człuchów	30	53.41 N	17.21 E
Czudec	30	49.57 N	21.50 E

D

Name	Page	Lat.°′	Long.°′
Da ≃	100	28.10 N	120.14 E
Daaden	56	50.44 N	7.58 E
Da'an, Zhg.	89	45.28 N	124.18 E
Da'an, Zhg.	100	23.05 N	115.37 E
Da'an, Zhg.	107	29.23 N	106.01 E
Da'an, Zhg.	110	23.19 N	110.34 E
Daanbantayan	116	11.14 N	124.00 E
Daba	104	42.06 N	122.00 E
Ḍabāb, Jabal aḍ- ∧	132	31.02 N	35.38 E
Dabagou	104	42.27 N	122.00 E
Ḍab'ah, Ra's aḍ- >	140	31.05 N	28.26 E
Dabai	150	11.31 N	5.11 E
Dabaizhuang	105	39.27 N	117.23 E
Dabajuro	246	11.02 N	70.40 W
Dabakala	150	8.22 N	4.26 W
Dabali	104	41.51 N	120.37 E
Daba Ling ∧	100	24.28 N	113.17 E
Dabancheng	86	43.21 N	88.19 E
Dabangdian	100	31.37 N	113.41 E
Dabaojiagangzi	104	42.09 N	123.33 E
Dabaozhuang	105	40.18 N	116.58 E
Dabaozi	105	40.11 N	115.10 E
Daba Shan ∧∧	102	31.55 N	109.05 E
Dabasi	107	28.55 N	105.09 E
Dabat	144	12.58 N	37.48 E
Dabayingzi	104	42.11 N	121.35 E
Dabbāgh, Jabal ∧	128	27.52 N	35.45 E
Dabbūriya	132	32.41 N	35.22 E
Dabegabis	158	28.07 S	18.36 E
Dabeiba	246	7.01 N	76.16 W
Dabeiwa	105	40.48 N	117.31 E
Dabeiyingzi	104	42.05 N	122.08 E
Dabendorf	54	52.14 N	13.26 E
Daberas	156	25.38 S	18.29 E
Daberg ◆[8]	263	51.40 N	7.47 E
Dabhoi	120	22.11 N	73.26 E
Dābhol	122	17.36 N	73.10 E
Ḍab'ī, Wādī aḍ- V	132	31.42 N	36.42 E
Dąbie	30	52.06 N	18.49 E
Dąbie ◆[8]	54	53.24 N	14.40 E
Dąbie, Jezioro ⊜	54	53.27 N	14.40 E
Dabie Shan ∧∧	100	31.00 N	115.40 E
Dabilda	146	12.46 N	14.34 E
Da → Black ≃	110	21.15 N	105.20 E
Ḍablān	130	34.52 N	40.34 E
Ďáblice ◆[8]	54	50.08 N	14.29 E
Dabnou	150	14.09 N	5.22 E
Dabo	58	48.39 N	7.14 E
Dabob Bay ⊂	224	47.47 N	122.50 W
Dabobeizhuang	105	39.18 N	117.59 E
Dabola	150	10.45 N	11.07 W
Dabong	114	5.23 N	102.01 E
Daborow	144	6.21 N	48.43 E
Dabou	150	5.19 N	4.23 W
Daboya	150	9.32 N	1.23 W
Dabra	124	25.54 N	78.20 E
Dābri ◆[8]	272a	28.37 N	77.05 E
Dąbrowa Białostocka	30	53.39 N	23.20 E
Dąbrowa Tarnowska	30	50.11 N	21.00 E
Dabsan Hu ⊜	102	36.58 N	94.55 E
Dabu, Zhg.	100	24.19 N	116.43 E
Dabu, Zhg.	100	23.52 N	116.54 E
Dabu, Zhg.	100	24.20 N	114.35 E
Dabus ≃	144	10.48 N	35.10 E
Dabusutu-Ula, gora ∧	86	50.44 N	92.40 E
Dacaitun	104	41.38 N	121.18 E
Dacangzigou	104	40.59 N	121.01 E
Dacaocun	105	40.34 N	117.07 E
Dacca → Dhaka	126	23.43 N	90.25 E
Dachakou	100	29.38 N	118.18 E
Dachang, Zhg.	105	39.53 N	116.59 E
Dachang, Zhg.	106	32.12 N	118.45 E
Dachang, Zhg.	106	31.18 N	121.25 E
Dachang Airport ⊠	269b	31.18 N	121.25 E
Dachangshan Dao I	98	39.10 N	122.34 E
Dachau	60	48.15 N	11.27 E
Dachauer Moos ≡	60	48.12 N	11.25 E
Dacheng	100	28.34 N	115.31 E
Dachengji	100	33.52 N	119.26 E
Dachenjiabao	106	32.11 N	120.22 E
Dachen Shan I	106	30.21 N	121.52 E
Dachixu	100	25.10 N	116.46 E
Dachongyu	105	40.23 N	117.41 E
Dachsberg ∧[2]	263	51.30 N	6.30 E
Dachsteinhöhlen ≐[5]	64	47.32 N	13.43 E
Dačice	61	49.05 N	15.26 E
Dac Lac, Cao Nguyen ∧∧[1]	110	12.50 N	108.05 E
Dačnoje ◆[8]	265a	59.50 N	30.16 E
Dacoma	196	36.39 N	98.33 W
Dacorum ▫[8]	260	51.45 N	0.30 W
Dac To	110	14.42 N	107.51 E
Dacun, Zhg.	102	27.55 N	101.08 E
Dacun, Zhg.	106	31.12 N	119.40 E
Dadal	88	49.01 N	111.37 E
Dadanawa	246	2.50 N	59.30 W
Dadaolizhuang	105	39.59 N	116.59 E
Dadaotun	104	41.46 N	122.13 E
Dadar ◆[8]	272c	19.01 N	72.50 E
Daday	130	41.28 N	33.28 E
Dadayungou	104	41.23 N	123.25 E
Daddys Creek ≃	192	36.05 N	84.47 W
Dade ▫[6]	220	25.33 N	80.32 W
Dade Battlefield Historic Memorial ⊥	220	28.38 N	82.09 W
Dade City	220	28.21 N	82.11 W
Ḍaḍeldhurā	124	29.18 N	80.35 E
Dadès, Oued ≃	148	30.55 N	6.47 W
Dadeville	194	32.49 N	85.45 W
Dādhar	120	29.28 N	67.39 E
Dadian	100	33.36 N	117.16 E
Dadiangas → General Santos	116	6.07 N	125.11 E
Dadianzi	104	42.11 N	124.02 E
Dadingjiawopu	104	41.13 N	122.16 E
D'adino	88	55.44 N	105.45 E
Dadiya	146	9.37 N	11.26 E
Dadle	144	5.20 N	46.58 E
Ḍadnah	128	25.33 N	56.21 E
Dadonggejiang	105	39.51 N	116.48 E
Dadongzhou	104	41.44 N	124.00 E
Dadou ≃	32	43.44 N	1.49 E
Dādpur, India	272b	22.42 N	88.33 E
Dādpur, India	272b	22.54 N	88.31 E
Dādra and Nagar Haveli ▫[8]	122	20.05 N	73.00 E
Dādu	120	26.44 N	67.47 E
Dadu ≃	102	29.33 N	103.45 E
Dadugang	102	22.23 N	100.55 E
Dadukou, Zhg.	100	25.44 N	119.05 E
Dadukou, Zhg.	107	28.45 N	105.13 E
Dadukou, Zhg.	107	29.28 N	106.29 E
Daegu → Taegu	98	35.52 N	128.35 E
Daejeon → Taejŏn	98	36.20 N	127.26 E
Daerhanwangfu	89	44.19 N	122.15 E
Da'erhao	98	41.45 N	116.01 E
Daet	116	14.05 N	122.55 E
Daf'	146	28.03 N	19.57 E
Dafan, Zhg.	100	29.41 N	114.40 E
Dafan, Zhg.	104	42.38 N	122.11 E
Dafang	102	27.04 N	105.31 E
Dafangshen, Zhg.	104	42.25 N	123.14 E
Dafangshen, Zhg.	104	42.34 N	123.28 E
Dafangshen, Zhg.	104	42.36 N	123.04 E
Dafanhe	104	42.13 N	123.43 E
Dafanpuzi	104	41.37 N	122.50 E
Dafeng	100	33.12 N	120.30 E
Dafna	132	33.14 N	35.38 E
Dafoe	184	51.46 N	104.32 W
Dafoe ≃	184	55.55 N	94.48 W
Dafoe Lake ⊜	184	55.43 N	96.15 W
Da Fo Si (Great Buddha Temple) ♥[1]	106	30.16 N	120.09 E
Dafoutuo	105	40.24 N	115.58 E
Dafu	100	29.55 N	118.35 E
Dafu ≃	100	30.52 N	113.32 E
Dāfūr al-Janūbīyah ▫[4]	140	11.45 N	25.25 E
Dagā ≃	110	16.56 N	94.45 E
Daga Medo	144	7.59 N	43.01 E
Dagana	150	16.31 N	15.30 W
Dagang, Zhg.	100	33.12 N	120.07 E
Dagang, Zhg.	100	22.49 N	113.23 E
Dagang, Zhg.	106	32.12 N	119.39 E
Dagangtou	100	28.18 N	119.44 E

Symbols in the index entries represent the broad categories identified in the key at the right. Symbols with superior numbers (∧∧[1]) identify subcategories (see complete key on page *I* · *1*).

Symbole im Register stellen die rechts im Schlüssel erklärten Kategorien dar. Symbole mit hochgestellten Ziffern (∧∧[1]) bezeichnen Unterabteilungen einer Kategorie (vgl. vollständiger Schlüssel auf Seite *I* · *1*).

Los símbolos incluídos en el texto del índice representan las grandes categorias identificadas con la clave a la derecha. Los símbolos con numeros en su parte superior (∧∧[1]) identifican las subcategorías (véase la clave completa en la página *I* · *1*).

Les symboles de l'index représentent les catégories indiquées dans la légende à droite. Les symboles suivis d'un indice (∧∧[1]) représentent des sous-catégories (voir légende complète à la page *I* · *1*).

Os símbolos incluídos no texto do índice representam as grandes categorias identificadas com a chave à direita. Os símbolos com números em sua parte superior (∧∧[1]) identificam as subcategorias (veja-se a chave completa à página *I* · *1*).

	English	Deutsch	Español	Français	Português
∧	Mountain	Berg	Montaña	Montagne	Montanha
∧∧	Mountains	Gebirge	Montañas	Montagnes	Montanhas
)(	Pass	Paß	Paso	Col	Passo
V	Valley, Canyon	Tal, Cañon	Valle, Cañón	Vallée, Canyon	Vale, Canhão
≚	Plain	Ebene	Llano	Plaine	Planície
>	Cape	Kap	Cabo	Cap	Cabo
I	Island	Insel	Isla	Île	Ilha
II	Islands	Inseln	Islas	Îles	Ilhas
≐	Other Topographic Features	Andere Topographische Objekte	Otros Elementos Topográficos	Autres données topographiques	Outros acidentes topográficos

ESPAÑOL

Nombre	Página	Lat.°′	Long.°′ W = Oeste
Daganwangzhai	104	40.49 N	122.33 E
Daganzo de Arriba	266a	40.33 N	3.27 W
Dagaokan	104	40.46 N	122.22 E
Dagaolifangcun	104	41.10 N	122.28 E
Dagaolitun	104	42.26 N	123.53 E
Dagaoyang	106	30.35 N	120.26 E
Daga Post	140	9.12 N	33.58 E
Dağardı	130	39.26 N	29.00 E
Dagash	140	19.22 N	33.24 E
Dağbeli	130	37.12 N	30.31 E
Dagcanglhamo	102	34.02 N	102.30 E
Dagda	76	56.06 N	27.32 E
Dageløkke	41	55.04 N	10.53 E
Dagenham ◆[8]	260	51.32 N	0.10 E
Dagestanskaja Avtonomnaja Sovetskaja Socialističeskaja Respublika □[3]	84	43.00 N	47.00 E
Dagestanskije Ogni	84	42.07 N	48.12 E
Daggafontein	273d	26.18 S	28.28 E
Daggafontein Mines ◆[7]	273d	26.18 S	28.29 E
Daggett	228	34.51 N	116.53 W
Dagg Sound ʮ	172	45.23 S	166.46 E
Daghfalī	140	19.17 N	32.30 E
Dağkızılca	130	38.18 N	27.24 E
Daglung	120	28.54 N	90.33 E
Dagmersellen	58	47.13 N	7.59 E
Dagö → Hiiumaa I	76	58.52 N	22.40 E
Dagomys	84	43.40 N	39.41 E
Dagongtun	89	42.48 N	121.58 E
Dagoretti	154	1.18 S	36.46 E
Dagsboro	208	38.32 N	75.14 W
Dagshai	123	30.53 N	77.03 E
Dagu	105	38.59 N	117.41 E
Dagu ≏	98	36.15 N	120.06 E
Dagua	164	3.25 S	143.20 E
Daguan, Zhg.	100	31.14 N	117.01 E
Daguan, Zhg.	102	27.44 N	104.16 E
Daguan Hu ⊜	100	30.00 N	116.24 E
Daguao	240m	18.14 N	65.41 W
Dagufen'gou	105	40.41 N	116.20 E
D'Aguilar, Cape ≻	271d	22.14 N	114.15 E
D'Aguilar, Mount ∧	171a	27.19 S	152.47 E
D'Aguilar Range ⋌	171a	27.10 S	152.45 E
Dagujia	98	42.22 N	124.52 E
Dagujiazi	104	42.20 N	123.20 E
Da Guokui Shan ∧	89	45.17 N	129.30 E
Dagupan	116	16.03 N	120.20 E
Daguragu Aboriginal Reserve ◆[4]	162	17.35 S	130.30 E
Dagushan	104	41.03 N	123.02 E
Dagus Mines	214	41.21 N	78.36 W
Dagutang	100	29.38 N	116.06 E
Dagwin	110	18.04 N	97.41 E
Dagzê Co ⊜	120	31.55 N	87.35 E
Dahabān	144	21.55 N	39.04 E
Dahalac National Park ♠	144	15.40 N	40.05 E
Dahanchang	105	39.29 N	117.05 E
Dahaneh-ye Ghowrī	120	35.54 N	68.30 E
Dahaneh-ye Kāshār	120	35.09 N	66.14 E
Dahan-e Qowmghī	120	34.28 N	66.31 E
Dahantun	104	42.10 N	122.41 E
Dahasah, Wādī V	142	28.08 N	31.00 E
Dahḍāḥ, Tall ∧[2]	132	32.36 N	36.03 E
Dahe	106	31.42 N	120.37 E
Dahebei	105	39.10 N	117.39 E
Dahei	120	21.42 N	72.35 E
Daheiding Shan ∧	89	47.58 N	129.07 E
Daheiyugou	104	41.21 N	121.55 E
Dahekou	106	32.16 N	119.05 E
Dahengdu	100	29.03 N	121.30 E
Dahenqin Dao I	100	22.06 N	113.30 E
Daheqiao	100	29.25 N	115.16 E
Dahijuri	126	22.31 N	86.59 E
Da Hinggan Ling ⋌	90	49.00 N	122.00 E
Dahīrpur ◆[8]	272a	28.43 N	77.12 E
Dahl	56	51.18 N	7.31 E
Dahl ◆[8]	263	51.11 N	6.26 E
Dahlak Archipelago II	144	15.45 N	40.30 E
Dahle	263	51.18 N	7.45 E
Dahlem	56	50.23 N	6.33 E
Dahlem ◆[8]	264a	52.28 N	13.17 E
Dahlem, Museum ʊ	264a	52.27 N	13.18 E
Dahlen	54	51.22 N	12.59 E
Dahlenburg	54	53.11 N	10.44 E
Dahlerau	263	51.13 N	7.19 E
Dahlewitz	54	52.19 N	13.26 E
Dahlgren, Il., U.S.	194	38.12 N	88.41 W
Dahlgren, Va., U.S.	208	38.19 N	77.03 W
Dahlhausen	54	53.03 N	12.20 E
Dahlia	154	18.35 S	27.08 E
Dahlonega	192	34.31 N	83.59 W
Dahlonega Plateau ⋌[1]	192	34.10 N	84.20 W
Dahlwitz	264a	52.30 N	13.38 E
Dahlwitz-Hoppegarten	54	52.30 N	13.38 E
Dahmani	36	35.57 N	8.50 E
Dahmarū	142	28.41 N	30.49 E
Dahme, Dtsch.	54	51.52 N	13.25 E
Dahme, Dtsch.	54	54.13 N	11.04 E
Dahme ≏	54	52.25 N	13.35 E
Dahn	56	49.09 N	7.47 E
Dāhod	120	22.50 N	74.16 E
Dahomey → Benin □[1]	150	9.30 N	2.15 E
Dahong	106	31.53 N	121.17 E
Dahongmen	105	39.50 N	116.25 E
Dahongqi	104	41.52 N	122.36 E
Dahong Shan ⋌	100	31.30 N	113.00 E
Dahongtaizi	104	41.41 N	121.23 E
Dahoucun	105	38.51 N	115.37 E
Dahra	146	29.34 N	17.50 E
Dahra ⋌	34	36.25 N	1.00 E
Dähre	54	52.48 N	10.54 E
Dahsah, Wādī ad- V	142	27.19 N	31.26 E
Dahshūr	142	29.45 N	31.14 E
Dahu, Zhg.	100	26.22 N	119.06 E
Dahu, Zhg.	100	26.04 N	117.19 E
Dahua	102	23.44 N	107.59 E
Dahuan	100	22.33 N	113.29 E
Dahuangdi	104	42.08 N	122.27 E
Dahuangji	98	35.06 N	115.15 E
Dahuangpu	105	39.26 N	117.16 E
Dahuangshanpu	104	41.16 N	121.23 E
Dahuashan	105	40.17 N	117.04 E
Dahuasi	107	30.05 N	104.08 E
Dahujiang	100	26.10 N	114.57 E
Dahūk	128	36.52 N	43.00 E
Dahūk □[4]	128	37.00 N	43.00 E
Dahuni	164	10.31 S	149.55 E
Dahuofang Shuiku ⊜[1]	98	41.55 N	124.15 E
Dahushan	104	41.37 N	122.09 E
Dahy, Nafūd ad- ◆[2]	118	22.20 N	45.35 E
Dai I	175e	7.57 S	160.37 E
Dai ≏	100	26.14 N	119.40 E
Dai, Pulau I	164	7.33 S	129.41 E
Daia	38	44.00 N	25.59 E
Daian	94	35.05 N	136.33 E
Daibosatsu-rei ∧	94	35.45 N	138.51 E
Daibu, Zhg.	100	32.19 N	117.12 E
Daibu, Zhg.	106	31.18 N	119.30 E
Daibutsu ʊ[1]	94	35.19 N	139.32 E
Daiei	96	35.29 N	133.45 E
Daifang	100	27.32 N	115.41 E
Daigo	94	36.46 N	140.21 E
Daigo ◆[8]	270	34.57 N	135.50 E
Daiguantun	105	39.57 N	117.50 E
Dai Hai ⊜	102	40.31 N	112.43 E
Daihaiyingzi	104	42.30 N	121.26 E
Daiji	100	33.48 N	115.03 E
Daijiagou	107	30.00 N	106.33 E
Daijiayao	100	32.56 N	120.19 E
Daikanbō ∧	96	33.00 N	131.04 E
Daik-u	110	17.47 N	96.40 E
Dā'il	132	32.45 N	36.08 E
Dailekh	124	28.50 N	81.44 E
Dailing	89	47.01 N	129.02 E

FRANÇAIS

Nom	Page	Lat.°′	Long.°′ W = Ouest
Dailly	44	55.16 N	4.43 W
Daimanji-san ∧	92	36.15 N	133.19 E
Daimiel	34	39.04 N	3.37 W
Daimon, Nihon	94	36.44 N	137.03 E
Daimon, Nihon	268	35.53 N	139.44 E
Daimuken-zan ∧	94	35.15 N	138.10 E
Dainan	100	32.43 N	120.06 E
Daingean	48	53.18 N	7.17 W
Daingerfield	222	33.01 N	94.43 W
Dainhāt	126	23.37 N	88.04 E
Dainichiga-take ∧	94	36.00 N	136.50 E
Dainkog	102	32.31 N	97.59 E
Daintree	164	16.15 S	145.19 E
Daintree National Park ♠	164	16.15 S	145.10 E
Daiō-zaki ≻	92	34.17 N	136.54 E
Dāira Dīn Panāh	123	30.34 N	70.56 E
Dairago	266b	45.34 N	8.52 E
Daireaux	252	36.36 S	61.45 W
Dairen → Dalian	98	38.53 N	121.35 E
Dairsie	46	56.20 N	2.56 W
Dairy	46	55.43 N	4.43 W
Dairy City → Cypress	280	33.50 N	118.01 W
Dairy Creek, East Fork ≏	224	45.34 N	123.09 W
Dairy Creek, West Fork ≏	224	45.34 N	123.09 W
Dairyland	210	41.45 N	74.33 W
Dairyland → La Palma	280	33.51 N	118.02 W
Dairyland Reservoir ⊜[1]	190	45.30 N	91.00 W
Dairy Valley → Cerritos	280	33.51 N	118.05 W
Dai-sen ∧	96	35.22 N	133.33 E
Daisen-oki-kokuritsu-kōen ♠	96	35.20 N	133.35 E
Daisen-zan ∧	96	34.07 N	133.56 E
Daisetsu-zan-kokuritsu-kōen ♠	92a	43.30 N	142.57 E
Daisetta	222	30.06 N	94.38 W
Daishan	100	30.14 N	122.12 E
Daishin	94	37.12 N	140.15 E
Daishōji ≏	94	36.18 N	136.15 E
Daisizhen	107	29.14 N	105.09 E
Daitō, Nihon	96	35.19 N	132.58 E
Daitō, Nihon	96	34.42 N	135.38 E
Daiwa, Nihon	96	34.32 N	132.57 E
Daiwa, Nihon	96	34.57 N	132.39 E
Daixi	106	30.40 N	120.01 E
Daixian	102	39.08 N	113.01 E
Daixiqiao	106	31.36 N	120.04 E
Daiya ≏	94	36.45 N	139.46 E
Daiyun Shan ⋌	100	25.46 N	118.16 E
Dajabón	238	19.33 N	71.42 W
Dājal	120	29.33 N	70.23 E
Da'jānīyah, Jabal ad- ∧	132	30.34 N	35.43 E
Dajarra	166	21.41 S	139.31 E
Dajian Shan ∧	102	26.42 N	103.34 E
Dajidian	105	38.50 N	115.26 E
Dajindian	100	34.24 N	112.58 E
Dajing, Zhg.	100	28.24 N	121.07 E
Dajing, Zhg.	100	28.59 N	113.19 E
Dajin Shan II	106	30.41 N	121.26 E
Dajishan	100	24.38 N	114.26 E
Dajitai	104	42.20 N	121.11 E
Dajiuba	120	36.50 N	89.35 E
Daji Yang ʮ	100	30.54 N	122.18 E
Daju	105	39.12 N	115.31 E
Da Juh	102	36.36 N	94.04 E
Dak ⊜	128	32.48 N	61.14 E
Daka ≏	150	8.19 N	0.13 W
Dakangpu	104	41.32 N	121.06 E
Dakanzi	104	40.52 N	122.53 E
Dakar	150	14.40 N	17.26 W
Dakar □[4]	150	14.45 N	17.25 W
Dākātia ≏[1]	126	22.57 N	90.42 E
Dakeng	100	26.18 N	115.32 E
Dakengkou	100	24.33 N	113.37 E
Daketa ≏	144	7.16 N	42.13 E
Dak Gle	110	15.11 N	107.48 E
Dakhal, Bi'r ad- ⊤[4]	142	28.40 N	32.24 E
Dakhal, Wādī ad- V	142	28.49 N	32.45 E
Dākhilah, Al-Wāḥāt ad- ⊤[4]	140	25.30 N	29.05 E
Dakhin Shāhbāzpur Island I	126	22.30 N	90.45 E
Dakhla	148	23.43 N	15.57 W
Dakhlet Nouâdhibou □[4]	148	20.40 N	16.00 W
Dakingari	150	11.37 N	4.01 E
Dakka → Dhaka	124	23.43 N	90.25 E
Dākoānk	110	7.02 N	93.43 E
Dakongcheng	105	39.30 N	117.09 E
Dakongwan	104	40.51 N	122.19 E
Dakoro	150	14.31 N	6.46 E
Dakota City, Ia., U.S.	190	42.43 N	94.12 W
Dakota City, Ne., U.S.	198	42.24 N	96.25 W
Dakou	100	34.27 N	112.44 E
Dakoutun	105	39.35 N	117.14 E
Đakovica	38	42.23 N	20.25 E
Đakovo	38	45.19 N	18.25 E
Dakshin Gangotri ʊ[3]	9	70.05 S	12.00 E
Dakshingram	126	24.03 N	87.48 E
Dakumu	89	48.51 N	124.18 E
Dakunlun	98	36.34 N	117.52 E
Dakwa	154	4.00 N	26.26 E
Dakwah, Tall ad- ∧[2]	132	33.25 N	36.56 E
Dala, Ang.	152	11.03 S	20.17 E
Dala, Ang.	152	8.05 S	15.50 E
Dala, Sol.Is.	175e	8.35 S	160.40 E
Dalaas	58	47.07 N	10.00 E
Dalaba	150	10.42 N	12.15 W
Dalabani	150	10.28 N	9.27 W
Dala Cachibo	152	10.28 S	14.39 E
Dalad Qi	102	40.28 N	110.02 E
Dala-Floda	40	60.31 N	14.47 E
Dalaguete	116	9.46 N	123.32 E
Dalahan (Shiqizhan)	89	52.06 N	125.46 E
Dala-Husby	40	60.21 N	16.00 E
Dala-Järna	26	60.33 N	14.21 E
Dalajchöl	86	47.59 N	90.47 E
Dalaji	89	51.38 N	120.06 E
Dalälven ≏	40	60.38 N	17.27 E
Dalama	130	37.47 N	28.04 E
Dalaman ≏	130	36.40 N	28.45 E
Dalāmī	140	11.52 N	30.28 E
Dalan	100	23.19 N	114.47 E
Dalan Dzadgad	102	43.37 N	104.29 E
Dalandžargalan	102	45.55 N	109.05 E
Dalane ◆[1]	26	58.35 N	6.20 E
Dalang	100	22.57 N	113.56 E
Dalantuozi	104	41.28 N	122.47 E
Dalao	150	11.29 N	13.40 W
Dalarna □[9]	26	61.01 N	14.04 E
Dalarö	40	59.08 N	18.24 E
Dalat, Malay.	112	2.44 N	111.56 E
Da Lat, Viet	110	11.56 N	108.25 E
Dalayaozi	105	40.49 N	117.41 E
Dālbandin	128	28.53 N	64.25 E
Dalbeattie	44	54.56 N	3.49 W
D'Albertis Dome ∧	164	5.00 S	142.05 E
Dalbosjön ⊂	26	58.45 N	12.48 E
Dalby, Austl.	166	27.11 S	151.16 E
Dalby, Sve.	41	55.40 N	13.20 E
Dalby Söderskogs Nationalpark ♠	41	55.43 N	13.17 E
Dalcahue	254	42.23 S	73.40 W
Dalch ≏	42	50.52 N	3.47 W
Dale, Nor.	26	60.35 N	5.49 E
Dale, Nor.	26	61.22 N	5.25 E
Dale, Wales, U.K.	42	51.43 N	5.11 W
Dale, In., U.S.	194	38.10 N	86.59 W
Dale, Pa., U.S.	214	40.18 N	78.54 W
Dale, Tx., U.S.	222	29.56 N	97.34 W
Dale ≏	168a	32.10 S	116.49 E
Dale, Mount ∧	168a	32.08 S	116.18 E
Dale Bridge	168a	32.05 S	116.49 E

PORTUGUÊS

Nome	Página	Lat.°′	Long.°′ W = Oeste
Dalecarlia → Dalarna □[9]	26	61.01 N	14.04 E
Dale City	208	38.38 N	77.18 W
Dale Hollow Lake ⊜[1]	192	36.36 N	85.19 W
Dale Lake ⊜	204	34.08 N	115.42 W
Dalen	26	59.27 N	8.00 E
Dalengtu	98	41.11 N	113.45 E
Dalešice, údolní nádrž ⊜[1]	61	49.09 N	16.05 E
Daleside	158	26.30 S	28.04 E
Dale South ≏	168a	32.16 S	116.47 E
Dalesville	206	45.42 N	74.24 W
Dalesville ≏	206	45.40 N	74.24 W
Daleszyce	30	50.48 N	20.48 E
Dalet	110	19.59 N	93.51 E
Daleville, Al., U.S.	194	31.18 N	85.42 W
Daleville, In., U.S.	218	40.07 N	85.33 W
Daleville, Pa., U.S.	210	41.18 N	75.31 W
Dalfsen	52	52.30 N	6.16 E
Dalgaranga	162	27.46 S	117.02 E
Dalgaranger ∧	162	27.51 S	117.06 E
Dalgety	171b	36.30 S	148.50 E
Dalgety Bay	46	56.02 N	3.20 W
Dalgety Brook ≏	162	25.07 S	115.47 E
Dalgety Downs	162	25.17 S	116.15 E
Dalgomai	124	26.06 N	90.47 E
Dalhalvaig	46	58.28 N	3.54 W
Dalhart	196	36.03 N	102.30 W
Dalhausen	52	51.37 N	9.17 E
Dalhousie, N.B., Can.	186	48.04 N	66.23 W
Dalhousie, India	123	32.32 N	75.59 E
Dalhousie, Cape ≻	180	70.14 N	129.42 W
Dalhousie Island I	126	21.35 N	88.45 E
Dalhousie Lake ⊜	212	44.58 N	76.35 W
Dalhousie Square ♠	272b	22.33 N	88.22 E
Dali, Zhg.	102	34.47 N	109.57 E
Dali, Zhg.	102	25.38 N	100.09 E
Dalian (Dairen)	98	38.53 N	121.35 E
Dalian Dao I	100	25.40 N	119.42 E
Daliangdi	98	41.54 N	115.45 E
Daliang Shan ⋌	102	28.00 N	103.00 E
Dalianhe	104	40.57 N	123.15 E
Daliankeng	105	40.54 N	117.45 E
Dalian Wan ⊂	98	38.57 N	121.45 E
Dalianwukou	106	30.17 N	119.00 E
Daliao ≏	104	40.42 N	122.08 E
Dalías	34	36.49 N	2.52 W
Dalikou	100	26.52 N	118.00 E
Dalin, Zhg.	89	43.43 N	122.45 E
Dalin, Zhg.	107	30.17 N	104.07 E
Daling	104	41.27 N	121.15 E
Daling ≏	98	40.56 N	121.43 E
Dalingbeigou	104	40.42 N	123.08 E
Dalipe Point ≻	116	10.46 N	121.55 E
Daliushugou	104	40.46 N	122.14 E
Daliutai	104	41.25 N	121.55 E
Daliutun	104	42.14 N	122.46 E
Daliuzhen	105	38.51 N	116.19 E
Daliuzhuang	100	33.04 N	114.03 E
Daliyat et Karmil	132	32.42 N	35.03 E
Daliyya	132	32.35 N	35.04 E
Dalizi	98	41.45 N	126.49 E
Dalj	38	45.29 N	18.59 E
Daljā'	142	27.39 N	30.42 E
Dalkarlsberg	40	59.26 N	14.51 E
Dalkeith	46	55.54 N	3.04 W
Dālkola	124	25.52 N	87.51 E
Dall, Mount ∧	180	62.35 N	152.18 W
Dāllah, 'Ayn ⊤[4]	140	27.19 N	27.20 E
Dallardsville	222	30.38 N	94.38 W
Dallas, Scot., U.K.	46	57.33 N	3.28 W
Dallas, Al., U.S.	194	33.50 N	86.39 W
Dallas, Ga., U.S.	192	33.55 N	84.50 W
Dallas, N.C., U.S.	192	35.18 N	81.10 W
Dallas, Or., U.S.	202	44.55 N	123.18 W
Dallas, Pa., U.S.	210	41.20 N	75.57 W
Dallas, Tx., U.S.	222	32.46 N	96.47 W
Dallas, Wi., U.S.	190	45.15 N	91.48 W
Dallas □[6]	222	32.17 N	96.47 W
Dallas Center	190	41.41 N	93.57 W
Dallas City	190	40.38 N	91.10 W
Dallas-Fort Worth Regional Airport ⊠	222	32.54 N	97.01 W
Dallas Naval Air Station ■	222	32.44 N	96.59 W
Dallastown	208	39.53 N	76.38 W
Dallgow	54	52.32 N	13.05 E
Dallıbahçe	130	39.09 N	39.53 E
Dalli Rājhara	122	20.35 N	81.04 E
Dall Island I	182	54.50 N	132.55 W
Dall Lake ⊜	180	60.18 N	163.35 W
Dalmā I	128	24.30 N	52.20 E
Dalmacija □[9]	36	43.00 N	17.00 E
Dalmacio Vélez Sarsfield	252	32.36 S	63.35 W
Dalmally	46	56.24 N	4.58 W
Dal'mamedli	84	40.42 N	46.34 E
Dalmatia	208	40.39 N	76.54 W
Dalmatia → Dalmacija □[9]	36	43.00 N	17.00 E
Dalmatovo	86	56.16 N	62.56 E
Dalmau	124	26.04 N	81.02 E
Dalmellington	44	55.19 N	4.24 W
Dalmeny	184	52.20 N	106.46 W
Dalmine	62	45.39 N	9.36 E
Dalmose	41	55.18 N	11.26 E
Dal'n'aja	89	45.56 N	142.04 E
Dal'n'aja Muja	88	54.21 N	103.37 E
Dalnaspidal	46	56.50 N	4.14 W
Dal'negorsk	89	44.35 N	135.35 E
Dal'neje-Konstantinovo	80	55.49 N	44.06 E
Dal'nerečensk	89	45.55 N	133.43 E
Dal'ne-Rusanovo	82	54.15 N	36.45 E
Dal'nik	78	46.28 N	30.34 E
Daloa	150	6.53 N	6.27 W
Dalongchang	105	39.50 N	116.06 E
Dalonghua	105	39.18 N	115.18 E
Dalongtian	100	24.14 N	115.44 E
Dalovice	54	50.11 N	12.55 E
Dalqū	140	20.07 N	30.37 E
Dalroy	182	51.07 N	113.39 W
Dalry, Scot., U.K.	44	55.07 N	4.10 W
Dalry, Scot., U.K.	46	55.43 N	4.44 W
Dalrymple	44	55.23 N	4.35 W
Dalrymple, Mount ∧	166	21.02 S	148.38 E
Dalrymple Creek ≏	171a	27.59 S	151.46 E
Dalrymple Lake ⊜	212	44.38 N	79.07 W
Dalsbruk (Taalintehdas)	26	60.02 N	22.31 E
Dalsingpara	124	26.47 N	89.22 E
Dalsing Sarai	124	25.40 N	85.50 E
Dalsjöfors	26	57.43 N	13.05 E
Dalsland □[9]	26	58.30 N	12.50 E
Dals-Långed	26	58.55 N	12.18 E
Dal'stroja	180	68.19 N	177.39 W
Dāltenganj	124	24.02 N	84.04 E
Dalton, S. Afr.	158	29.20 S	30.40 E
Dalton, Eng., U.K.	262	53.34 N	2.46 W
Dalton, Ga., U.S.	192	34.47 N	84.58 W
Dalton, Ma., U.S.	207	42.28 N	73.10 W
Dalton, Ne., U.S.	198	41.24 N	102.58 W
Dalton, N.Y., U.S.	210	42.32 N	77.57 W
Dalton, Oh., U.S.	214	40.47 N	81.41 W
Dalton, Pa., U.S.	210	41.32 N	75.44 W
Dalton City	219	39.43 N	88.48 W
Dalton Gardens	202	47.43 N	116.46 W
Dalton Iceberg Tongue ⍓	9	66.15 S	121.30 E
Dalton-in-Furness	44	54.09 N	3.11 W
Dalu	104	41.27 N	123.19 E
Dalubeikou	105	38.59 N	117.12 E
Daludalu	114	1.05 N	100.15 E
Dalu Dao I	98	39.44 N	123.45 E
Daluis, Gorges de V	62	44.04 N	6.49 E
Dalum, Dan.	41	55.22 N	10.22 E
Dalum, Dtsch.	52	52.35 N	7.14 E
Daluojiazhuang	106	32.09 N	120.08 E
Daluotaozi	104	41.17 N	122.52 E
Daluoxi	100	25.14 N	118.36 E
Daluping	100	26.11 N	114.30 E
Dalupiri Island I, Pil.	116	19.05 N	121.14 E
Dalupiri Island I, Pil.	116	12.25 N	124.16 E

Daluxi	100	24.28 N	117.01 E
Dalview	273d	26.15 S	28.21 E
Dalvík	24a	65.59 N	18.32 W
Dalwallinu	162	30.17 S	116.40 E
Dalwhinnie	46	56.56 N	4.14 W
Dalworthington Gardens	222	32.42 N	97.10 W
Daly ≏	164	13.20 S	130.19 E
Daly Bay ⊂	176	64.00 N	89.40 W
Daly City	226	37.43 N	122.31 W
Daly Lake ⊜	184	56.33 N	105.40 W
Daly Point ≻	212	44.53 N	80.14 W
Daly River	164	13.45 S	130.50 E
Daly River Aboriginal Reserve ◆[4]	164	14.20 S	130.00 E
Daly Waters	164	16.15 S	133.22 E
Dam ≏	120	33.56 N	92.41 E
Dāmā, Sūrīy.	132	32.57 N	36.25 E
Dama, Zhg.	100	32.03 N	118.02 E
Damagum	146	11.41 N	11.20 E
Damān	122	20.25 N	72.51 E
Damān □[8]	122	20.10 N	73.00 E
Damanhār Shubra	273c	30.07 N	31.14 E
Damanhūr	142	31.02 N	30.28 E
Damanling	105	40.36 N	115.08 E
Damaopu	104	41.16 N	121.07 E
Damar	130	41.15 N	41.34 E
Damar, Pulau I, Indon.	164	1.00 S	128.24 E
Damar, Pulau I, Indon.	164	7.09 S	128.40 E
Damara	152	4.58 N	18.42 E
Damaraland □[5]	156	21.00 S	14.20 E
Damaraland □[9]	156	22.34 S	17.06 E
Damāṣ	142	30.48 N	31.20 E
Damasco → Dimashq	132	33.30 N	36.18 E
Damascus, Ar., U.S.	194	35.22 N	92.24 W
Damascus, Ga., U.S.	192	34.33 N	84.56 W
Damascus, Md., U.S.	208	39.17 N	77.12 W
Damascus, Oh., U.S.	214	40.54 N	80.58 W
Damascus, Pa., U.S.	210	41.42 N	75.04 W
Damascus, Va., U.S.	192	36.38 N	81.47 W
Damascus → Dimashq	132	33.30 N	36.18 E
Damascus International Airport ⊠	132	33.29 N	36.13 E
Damas → Dimashq	132	33.30 N	36.18 E
Damaskus → Dimashq	132	33.30 N	36.18 E
Damāṭ	142	30.57 N	30.57 E
Damaturu	146	11.45 N	11.58 E
Damāvand	128	35.43 N	52.04 E
Damāvand, Qolleh-ye ∧	128	35.56 N	52.08 E
Damba	152	6.41 S	15.08 E
Dambach-la-Ville	58	48.20 N	7.26 E
Dambarta	150	12.26 N	8.31 E
Dambeck	54	52.48 N	11.09 E
Dambuki	89	54.21 N	127.38 E
Dam Doi	110	8.50 N	105.15 E
Damelevières	58	48.33 N	6.23 E
Damen Dao I	100	27.58 N	121.06 E
Damengjialazi	104	41.04 N	120.53 E
Damengzhuang	105	39.32 N	116.59 E
Damergou ◆[1]	150	15.00 N	8.55 E
Damerham	42	50.57 N	1.52 W
Dämeritzsee ⊜	264a	52.25 N	13.45 E
Damery	50	49.04 N	3.53 E
Dames Quarter	208	38.11 N	75.53 W
Dam Gamad	140	13.17 N	27.28 E
Dāmghān	128	36.09 N	54.22 E
Damianópolis	255	14.33 S	46.10 W
Damianzhen	107	30.36 N	104.10 E
Damiao, Zhg.	98	42.26 N	118.22 E
Damiao, Zhg.	98	34.20 N	117.23 E
Damiao, Zhg.	102	37.18 N	104.39 E
Damiao, Zhg.	104	42.33 N	122.18 E
Damiaochang	107	29.39 N	106.05 E
Damiaogou	104	41.06 N	123.52 E
Damiaojiang	106	31.00 N	120.28 E
Damiaoshang	105	39.56 N	115.12 E
Dămienești	38	46.44 N	26.59 E
Damietta Branch → Dumyāṭ, Far' ≏	142	31.32 N	31.51 E
Damietta → Dumyāṭ	142	31.25 N	31.48 E
Damietta Mouth → Dumyāṭ, Maṣabb ≏[1]	142	31.32 N	31.51 E
Damin	100	28.56 N	120.29 E
Daming	98	36.19 N	115.06 E
Damingzhen	104	42.34 N	123.36 E
Damintun	104	41.52 N	122.56 E
Dāmiyā	132	32.06 N	35.33 E
Damlacık	130	37.56 N	38.39 E
Damm	263	51.40 N	6.48 E
Dammai Island I	116	5.47 N	120.25 E
Dammarie	50	48.21 N	1.30 E
Dammarie-lès-Lys	50	48.31 N	2.39 E
Dammartin-en-Goële	50	49.03 N	2.41 E
Dammartin-en-Serve	50	48.54 N	1.37 E
Dammastock ∧	58	46.39 N	8.25 E
Damme, Bel.	50	51.15 N	3.17 E
Damme, Dtsch.	52	52.30 N	8.08 E
Damme, Dtsch.	54	53.17 N	14.01 E
Dammer Berge ⋌[2]	52	52.32 N	8.10 E
Dāmodar ≏	124	22.17 N	88.05 E
Dāmodar Main Canal ≋	126	23.01 N	87.53 E
Damoh, India	118	23.50 N	79.27 E
Damoh, India	124	23.50 N	79.27 E
Damon	222	29.17 N	95.45 W
Damongo	150	9.05 N	1.49 W
Damotapāda	272c	19.03 N	73.04 E
Damous	34	36.33 N	1.42 E
Damozhuang	105	39.53 N	115.40 E
Dampar, Tasek ⊜	114	3.02 N	102.43 E
Dampelas → Sabang	112	0.11 N	119.51 E
Dampier	162	20.39 S	116.45 E
Dampier, Cape ≻	164	6.02 S	151.02 E
Dampier, Selat ʮ	164	0.40 S	130.40 E
Dampier Archipelago II	162	20.35 S	116.35 E
Dampier Land ≻[1]	162	17.30 S	122.55 E
Dampierre, Fr.	50	48.42 N	1.59 E
Dampierre, Fr.	58	47.09 N	5.45 E
Dampierre, Château de ⊥	261	48.42 N	1.59 E
Dampierre-en-Burly	50	47.46 N	2.31 E
Dampierre-sur-Linotte	58	47.31 N	6.14 E
Dampierre-sur-Salon	58	47.33 N	5.41 E
Dampier Strait ʮ	164	5.36 S	148.12 E
Dampit	115a	8.13 S	112.45 E
Dampmart	261	48.53 N	2.44 E
Damprichard	58	47.15 N	6.53 E
Dâmrei, Chuŏr Phnum ⋌	110	11.00 N	104.05 E
Damují ≏	240p	22.11 N	80.33 W
Damüls	58	47.17 N	9.53 E
Dāmurhuda	126	23.36 N	88.47 E
Damutougou	98	42.28 N	118.56 E
Damville	50	48.52 N	1.04 E
Damvillers	56	49.20 N	5.24 E
Damxung	120	30.31 N	91.08 E
Dan	132	33.14 N	35.39 E
Dan ≏, U.S.	192	36.42 N	78.45 W
Dan ≏, Zhg.	102	33.02 N	111.20 E
Dana, Cam.	146	10.14 N	15.18 E
Dana, In., U.S.	194	39.48 N	87.29 W
Dana, Mount ∧	226	37.54 N	119.13 W
Dana, Pulau I	112	10.50 S	121.16 E
Danahu	102	42.28 N	93.32 E
Danai	112	0.29 N	103.26 E
Danajon Bank ✣[4]	116	10.16 N	124.17 E
Danakil → Denakil ◆[1]	144	13.00 N	41.00 E
Danakil National Park ♠	144	10.50 N	40.45 E
Danané	150	7.16 N	8.09 W

Da Nang	110	16.04 N	108.13 E
Danan'gou	105	40.32 N	117.49 E
Danao, Pil.	116	10.32 N	124.02 E
Danao, Pil.	116	12.29 N	122.39 E
Dana Point	228	33.29 N	117.44 W
Dana Point ≻	228	33.28 N	117.43 W
Dānāpur	124	25.38 N	85.03 E
Danba	102	31.00 N	101.50 E
Danboro	208	40.21 N	75.08 W
Danbury, Eng., U.K.	260	51.44 N	0.33 E
Danbury, Ct., U.S.	207	41.23 N	73.27 W
Danbury, Ia., U.S.	198	42.14 N	95.43 W
Danbury, Ne., U.S.	198	40.02 N	100.24 W
Danbury, N.C., U.S.	192	36.24 N	80.12 W
Danbury, Tx., U.S.	222	29.14 N	95.21 W
Danby Lake ⊜	204	34.14 N	115.07 W
Dancheng	100	33.39 N	115.11 E
Danchengji	100	33.47 N	116.17 E
Dancug	144	10.58 N	49.04 E
Dand	120	31.37 N	65.41 E
Dandaragan	162	30.40 S	115.42 E
Dande ≏	152	8.28 S	13.21 E
Dandeli	122	15.15 N	74.37 E
Dandenong	169	37.59 S	145.12 E
Dandenong, Mount ∧	274b	37.50 S	145.21 E
Dandenong Creek ≏	274b	38.01 S	145.05 E
Dandenong Ranges National Park ♠	169	37.53 S	145.20 E
Danderyd	40	59.25 N	18.01 E
Dandīl	142	29.10 N	31.02 E
Dandong	98	40.08 N	124.20 E
Dandot	123	32.39 N	72.58 E
Dandridge	192	36.00 N	83.24 W
Dan Dume	150	11.27 N	7.10 E
Dane □[6]	216	43.04 N	89.15 W
Dane ≏	44	53.15 N	2.31 W
Dane County Regional Airport-Truax Field ⊠	216	43.08 N	89.20 W
Dänemark → Denmark □[1]	26	56.00 N	10.00 E
Dänemark-Strasse → Denmark Strait ʮ	10	67.00 N	25.00 W
Danevang	222	29.03 N	96.13 W
Danewitz	264a	52.44 N	13.40 E
Danfeng	102	33.40 N	110.17 E
Danfengzhen	102	24.50 N	103.56 E
Danforth, Il., U.S.	216	40.49 N	87.59 W
Danforth, Me., U.S.	188	45.39 N	67.52 W
Danforth Hills ⋌	200	40.15 N	108.00 W
Dang ≏	102	40.30 N	94.42 E
Dānga, Bngl.	126	23.54 N	90.36 E
Dānga, India	272b	22.47 N	88.28 E
Danga ≏	271c	1.27 N	103.43 E
Dangādiha	126	21.30 N	86.19 E
Dangan Liedao II	100	22.00 N	114.14 E
Dangara, Taj.	85	38.06 N	69.22 E
Dangara, Uzb.	85	40.35 N	70.54 E
Dangba	98	40.46 N	118.32 E
Dangchang	102	34.03 N	104.23 E
Dangcheng	98	38.46 N	114.34 E
Dange, Ang.	152	8.09 S	14.46 E
Dange, Ang.	152	7.56 S	15.02 E
Dange, Nig.	150	12.52 N	5.21 E
Dange-lá-Menha	152	9.32 S	14.39 E
Danger, Point ≻	171a	28.10 S	153.33 E
Danger Point ≻	158	34.40 S	19.17 E
Danggali Conservation Park ♠	166	33.20 S	140.40 E
Danghe Nanshan ⋌	102	38.53 N	96.11 E
Danghui	105	40.03 N	117.04 E
Dangila	144	11.16 N	36.50 E
Dangkou	106	31.32 N	120.34 E
Dango	140	10.00 N	24.45 E
Dan Gora	150	11.30 N	8.09 E
Dāngori	120	27.40 N	95.32 E
Dangriga	232	16.58 N	88.13 W
Dangshan	98	34.26 N	116.21 E
Dangtu	100	31.34 N	118.30 E
Dan Gulbi	150	11.38 N	6.16 E
Dangyang	102	30.50 N	111.38 E
Dangyu	105	40.00 N	118.01 E
Dani	150	13.43 N	0.10 W
Dania	220	26.03 N	80.08 W
Daniel	200	42.51 N	110.04 W
Daniel, Mount ∧	224	47.34 N	121.11 W
Daniel Boone Home ⊥	219	38.39 N	90.52 W
Daniel Boone Homestead State Historic Site ⊥	208	40.21 N	75.49 W
Daniel-Johnson, Barrage ◆[6]	186	50.39 N	68.44 W
Daniels	284b	39.26 N	77.03 W
Daniel's Harbour	186	50.14 N	57.35 W
Danielskuil	158	28.11 S	23.33 E
Danielson	207	41.48 N	71.53 W
Daniels Pass)(	200	40.18 N	111.15 W
Daniels Run ≏	284c	38.51 N	77.17 W
Danielsville, Ga., U.S.	192	34.07 N	83.13 W
Danielsville, Pa., U.S.	208	40.48 N	75.32 W
Danilov	80	58.12 N	40.12 E
Danilovka, Kaz.	86	52.23 N	70.39 E
Danilovka, Ross.	80	52.33 N	45.23 E
Danilovka, Ross.	80	50.21 N	44.06 E
Danilovo	82	55.40 N	38.46 E
Danilovskaja vozvyšennost' ⋌[1]	80	58.12 N	40.16 E
Danilovskoje	82	56.48 N	35.45 E
Daning, Zhg.	102	24.39 N	111.51 E
Daning, Zhg.	102	36.33 N	110.38 E
Daningbashi	85	38.45 N	75.04 E
Dänisch Nienhof	54	54.28 N	10.07 E
Daniupucun	104	41.23 N	122.37 E
Danja	150	11.21 N	7.31 E
Danjiangkou Shuiku ⊜[1]	102	32.37 N	111.30 E
Danjo-guntō II	92	32.02 N	128.23 E
Danjoutin	58	47.37 N	6.52 E
Ḍank	128	23.33 N	56.17 E
Dankama	150	13.20 N	7.44 E
Dankersen	52	52.17 N	8.58 E
Danki	82	54.55 N	37.34 E
Dankov	76	53.15 N	39.08 E
Dankova, Pik ∧	85	41.05 N	77.38 E
Danleng, Zhg.	102	29.58 N	103.31 E
Danleng, Zhg.	102	29.18 N	103.10 E
Danleng, Zhg.	107	30.01 N	103.30 E
Danlí	236	14.00 N	86.35 W
Danmark → Denmark □[1]	26	56.00 N	10.00 E
Dannebrog	198	41.07 N	98.32 W
Dannemare	41	54.45 N	11.12 E
Dannemarie	58	47.38 N	7.08 E
Dannemora, Sve.	40	60.11 N	17.49 E
Dannemora, N.Y., U.S.	188	44.43 N	73.43 W
Dannenberg	54	53.06 N	11.05 E
Dannenreich	264a	52.19 N	13.45 E
Dannenwalde	54	53.04 N	13.11 E
Dannevirke	172	40.12 S	176.07 E
Dannewerk	41	54.29 N	9.31 E
Dannhauser	158	28.04 S	30.04 E
Dano	150	11.09 N	3.04 W
Danompari	112	0.09 N	115.02 E
Dañoso, Cabo ≻	254	48.50 S	67.13 W
Dan Ryan Woods ♠	278	41.45 N	87.39 W
Dan Sai	110	17.17 N	101.09 E
Danshan	107	30.06 N	104.54 E
Danshui	100	22.49 N	114.27 E
Dansville, Mi., U.S.	216	42.34 N	84.18 W
Dansville, N.Y., U.S.	210	42.33 N	77.41 W
Dāntan	126	21.57 N	87.16 E
Dante	192	36.58 N	82.17 W
Dantewāra	122	18.54 N	81.21 E
Dantuzhen	106	32.12 N	119.31 E
Danube ≏	22	45.20 N	29.40 E
Danube, Mouths of the ≏[1]	38	45.10 N	29.50 E
Danubio → Danube ≏	22	45.20 N	29.40 E

Danubyu	110	17.15 N	95.35 E
Danvers, Il., U.S.	190	40.31 N	89.10 W
Danvers, Ma., U.S.	207	42.34 N	70.55 W
Danvers ≏	283	42.32 N	70.53 W
Danville, P.Q., Can.	206	45.47 N	72.01 W
Danville, Ar., U.S.	194	35.03 N	93.23 W
Danville, Ca., U.S.	226	37.49 N	121.59 W
Danville, Ga., U.S.	192	32.36 N	83.14 W
Danville, Il., U.S.	194	40.07 N	87.37 W
Danville, In., U.S.	218	39.45 N	86.31 W
Danville, Ky., U.S.	194	37.42 N	84.46 W
Danville, Mo., U.S.	219	38.54 N	91.32 W
Danville, Oh., U.S.	214	40.26 N	82.15 W
Danville, Pa., U.S.	210	40.57 N	76.36 W
Danville, Vt., U.S.	188	44.25 N	72.07 W
Danville, Va., U.S.	192	36.35 N	79.23 W
Danville, Wa., U.S.	182	48.59 N	118.30 W
Danxian (Nada)	110	19.35 N	109.17 E
Danyang, Zhg.	100	26.22 N	119.30 E
Danyang, Zhg.	106	32.00 N	119.35 E
Danzig → Gdańsk	30	54.23 N	18.40 E
Dao	116	10.31 N	121.57 E
Dâo ≏, Port.	34	40.20 N	8.11 W
Dao ≏, Zhg.	100	30.44 N	114.39 E
Daocheng	102	29.06 N	100.38 E
Daodemiao	89	43.41 N	120.19 E
Daodi	105	39.32 N	118.11 E
Daoguanhe	100	30.54 N	114.57 E
Daohu	100	29.42 N	117.29 E
Daolazui	105	40.06 N	115.06 E
Daoliban	104	41.52 N	121.37 E
Daolin	100	27.59 N	112.42 E
Daolinggang	98	34.02 N	114.34 E
Daoliupu	107	30.12 N	105.09 E
Daomaguan	98	39.07 N	114.38 E
Daosa	124	26.53 N	76.20 E
Daoshiwu	106	30.18 N	118.57 E
Daoshuqiao	106	31.51 N	119.41 E
Daotiandi	89	48.53 N	130.03 E
Dao Timmi	146	20.32 N	13.33 E
Daotou	98	37.14 N	120.20 E
Daoukro	150	7.03 N	3.58 W
Daoulas	32	48.22 N	4.15 W
Daoura, Oued V	148	28.15 N	3.30 W
Daoxian	102	25.35 N	111.27 E
Daozhen	102	28.42 N	107.56 E
Daozi	89	45.00 N	123.43 E
Dapa	116	9.46 N	126.03 E
Dapango	150	10.52 N	0.12 E
Dapanzhuang	98	37.20 N	115.28 E
Dapaozi	89	45.27 N	122.07 E
Dapchi	146	12.28 N	11.32 E
Dapdap	116	14.14 N	122.15 E
Dapeng	100	22.34 N	114.29 E
Daphne	194	30.36 N	87.54 W
Dapiak, Mount ∧	116	8.15 N	123.28 E
Daping, Zhg.	100	23.11 N	115.49 E
Daping, Zhg.	100	24.24 N	115.58 E
Dapingshan	102	25.30 N	109.39 E
Dapishi	100	26.30 N	112.54 E
Dapitan	116	8.39 N	123.25 E
Dapitan ≏	116	8.38 N	123.25 E
Dapitan Bay ⊂	116	8.40 N	123.23 E
Dapto	170	34.30 S	150.47 E
Dapu, Zhg.	98	40.34 N	124.12 E
Dapu, Zhg.	100	23.16 N	113.32 E
Dapu, Zhg.	106	31.19 N	119.56 E
Dapujie	100	27.01 N	112.46 E
Da Qaidam	102	37.53 N	95.07 E
Da Qaidam Hu ⊜	102	37.50 N	95.00 E
Daqian	106	30.55 N	120.11 E
Daqiangmen	106	31.29 N	120.27 E
Daqiangzi	104	42.21 N	120.29 E
Daqiao, Zhg.	100	29.39 N	121.26 E
Daqiao, Zhg.	100	24.56 N	113.09 E
Daqiao, Zhg.	100	32.21 N	119.41 E
Daqiao, Zhg.	100	26.38 N	118.54 E
Daqiao, Zhg.	100	28.11 N	114.16 E
Daqiao, Zhg.	106	30.59 N	121.14 E
Daqiao, Zhg.	107	28.52 N	105.40 E
Daqiaojie	106	30.46 N	119.14 E
Daqiaokou	100	27.06 N	113.38 E
Daqiaotou	106	30.47 N	120.52 E
Daqiaozhai	102	25.21 N	106.15 E
Daqing	98	39.13 N	118.51 E
Daqing ≏	105	39.04 N	116.55 E
Daqinggou, Zhg.	98	41.16 N	114.10 E
Daqinggou, Zhg.	98	41.12 N	125.07 E
Daqing Shan ∧, Zhg.	89	45.35 N	127.51 E
Daqing Shan ∧, Zhg.	104	42.03 N	123.45 E
Daqing Shan ∧, Zhg.	104	41.47 N	121.15 E
Daqiu	100	25.24 N	119.39 E
Daqqāq	140	12.56 N	26.58 E
Daquan	102	41.21 N	95.17 E
Daquanshan	98	40.14 N	113.47 E
Daquantou	105	39.31 N	114.46 E
Daquanyan	104	42.37 N	123.32 E
Dāqūf	142	28.24 N	30.38 E
Daqu Shan I	100	30.27 N	122.20 E
Dara, Sén.	150	15.21 N	15.29 W
Dar'ā, Sūrīy.	132	32.37 N	36.06 E
Dar'ā □[8]	132	33.00 N	36.10 E
Dārāb	128	28.45 N	54.34 E
Darāban	120	31.44 N	70.20 E
Darabani	38	48.11 N	26.35 E
Darāfisah	140	13.23 N	31.59 E
Daraga	116	11.54 N	123.52 E
Daragodleh	144	10.10 N	44.51 E
Daraina	157b	13.12 S	49.40 E
Darājīl	142	30.39 N	30.52 E
Daram Island I	116	11.38 N	124.47 E
Dārān	128	32.59 N	50.24 E
Daraoli ◆[8]	272c	19.11 N	72.48 E
Darap	112	1.13 S	112.03 E
Dār as-Salām	273c	29.59 N	31.13 E
Darasun	88	51.40 N	114.00 E
Daraut-Kurgan	85	39.33 N	72.13 E
Darave	272c	19.02 N	73.01 E
Darāw	140	24.25 N	32.56 E
Darawah	142	30.13 N	31.06 E
Dārayyā	132	33.27 N	36.15 E
Darazo	146	11.00 N	10.24 E
Darb Al-Ḥājj	142	30.10 N	31.33 E
Darb al-Ḥajj, Jabal ∧	132	30.05 N	35.26 E
Darband	123	34.20 N	72.52 E
Darbāsīyah	130	37.04 N	40.39 E
Darbaza	85	41.35 N	69.02 E
Darbėnai	76	56.01 N	21.15 E
Dar-Beni-Kriche-Bahri	34	35.30 N	5.20 W
Darbhanga	124	26.10 N	85.54 E
Darbod (Taikang)	89	46.52 N	124.27 E
D'Arbonne, Bayou ≏	194	32.34 N	92.09 W
Darburruk	144	9.44 N	44.31 E
Darby, Mt., U.S.	202	46.01 N	114.10 W
Darby, Pa., U.S.	208	39.55 N	75.15 W
Darby, Cape ≻	180	64.20 N	162.22 W
Darby Creek ≏	285	39.52 N	75.18 W
Darbydale	218	39.51 N	83.11 W
Darčeli	84	42.27 N	41.42 E
Darchan	88	49.29 N	105.55 E
D'Archiac, Mount ∧	172	43.28 S	170.35 E
D'Arcy	182	50.33 N	122.29 W
D'Arcy Island I	224	48.34 N	123.17 W
Darda	38	45.37 N	18.41 E
Dardadine	168a	33.14 S	116.50 E
Dardanelle, Ar., U.S.	194	35.13 N	93.09 W
Dardanelle, Ca., U.S.	226	38.20 N	119.50 W
Dardanelle Lake ⊜[1]	194	35.25 N	93.20 W
Dardanelles → Çanakkale Boğazı ʮ	130	40.15 N	26.25 E
Dardanup	168a	33.24 S	115.45 E
Dardara	34	35.08 N	5.15 W
Dardenelles Cone ∧	226	38.25 N	119.53 W
Dardenne Creek ≏	219	38.52 N	90.32 W
Dardesheim	54	51.59 N	10.49 E
Dardistān □[9]	123	35.30 N	74.00 E
Dare	208	37.10 N	76.26 W
Darebin Creek ≏	274b	37.47 S	145.02 E
Dareda	154	4.13 S	35.33 E
Dar-el-Beida → Casablanca	148	33.39 N	7.35 W

≏ River	Fluß	Río	Rivière	Rio
≋ Canal	Kanal	Canal	Canal	Canal
ᒪ Waterfall, Rapids	Wasserfall, Stromschnellen	Cascada, Rápidos	Chute d'eau, Rapides	Cascata, Rápidos
ʮ Strait	Meeresstraße	Estrecho	Détroit	Estreito
⊂ Bay, Gulf	Bucht, Golf	Bahía, Golfo	Baie, Golfe	Baía, Golfo
⊜ Lake, Lakes	See, Seen	Lago, Lagos	Lac, Lacs	Lago, Lagos
≡ Swamp	Sumpf	Pantano	Marais	Pântano
⍓ Ice Features, Glacier	Eis- und Gletscherformen	Accidentes Glaciales	Formes glaciaires	Acidentes glaciares
⊤ Other Hydrographic Features	Andere Hydrographische Objekte	Otros Elementos Hidrográficos	Autres données hydrographiques	Outros acidentes hidrográficos

✣ Submarine Features	Untermeerische Objekte	Accidentes Submarinos	Formes de relief sous-marin	Acidentes submarinos
□ Political Unit	Politische Einheit	Unidad Politica	Entité politique	Unidade política
ʊ Cultural Institution	Kulturelle Institution	Institución Cultural	Institution culturelle	Institução cultural
⊥ Historical Site	Historische Stätte	Sitio Histórico	Site historique	Sitio histórico
♠ Recreational Site	Erholungs- und Ferienort	Sitio de Recreo	Centre de loisirs	Area de Lazer
⊠ Airport	Flughafen	Aeropuerto	Aéroport	Aeroporto
■ Military Installation	Militäranlage	Instalación Militar	Installation militaire	Instalação militar
◆ Miscellaneous	Verschiedenes	Misceláneo	Divers	Diversos

ENGLISH — Name / Page / Lat.°′ / Long.°′ · **DEUTSCH** — Name / Seite / Breite°′ / Länge°′ E = Ost

Symbols in the index entries represent the broad categories identified in the key at the right. Symbols with superior numbers (⋏1) identify subcategories (see complete key on page I · 1).

Symbole im Register stellen die rechts im Schlüssel erklärten Kategorien dar. Symbole mit hochgestellten Ziffern (⋏1) bezeichnen Unterabteilungen einer Kategorie (vgl. vollständiger Schlüssel auf Seite I · 1).

Los símbolos incluídos en el texto del índice representan las grandes categorías identificadas con la clave a la derecha. Los símbolos con numeros en su parte superior (⋏1) identifican las subcategorías (véase la clave completa en la página I · 1).

Les symboles de l'index représentent les catégories indiquées dans la légende à droite. Les symboles suivis d'un indice (⋏1) représentent des sous-catégories (voir légende complète à la page I · 1).

Os símbolos incluídos no texto do índice representam as grandes categorias identificadas com a chave à direita. Os símbolos com números em sua parte superior (⋏1) identificam as subcategorias (veja-se a chave completa à página I · 1).

∧ Mountain	Berg	Montaña	Montagne	Montanha
⋏ Mountains	Gebirge	Montañas	Montagnes	Montanhas
⋈ Pass	Paß	Paso	Col	Passo
V Valley, Canyon	Tal, Cañon	Valle, Cañón	Vallée, Canyon	Vale, Canhão
≚ Plain	Ebene	Llano	Plaine	Planície
> Cape	Kap	Cabo	Cap	Cabo
I Island	Insel	Isla	Île	Ilha
II Islands	Inseln	Islas	Îles	Ilhas
⊥ Other Topographic Features	Andere Topographische Objekte	Otros Elementos Topográficos	Autres données topographiques	Outros acidentes topográficos

ESPAÑOL — Nombre · Página · Lat.°' · Long.°' W = Oeste
FRANÇAIS — Nom · Page · Lat.°' · Long.°' W = Ouest
PORTUGUÊS — Nome · Página · Lat.°' · Long.°' W = Oeste

De Grey ≃	162	20.12 S	119.11 E
Degt'ari	78	50.35 N	32.45 E
Degt'arka ≃	265a	59.57 N	30.52 E
Degunino ◆8	265b	55.52 N	37.33 E
De Haan	50	51.16 N	3.02 E
Dehak ≃	128	32.01 N	58.35 E
Dehalak Deset I	144	15.40 N	40.05 E
Deharda	126	21.40 N	87.25 E
De Hart Reservoir ⊜1	208	40.28 N	76.45 W
Deh Bālā	123	34.04 N	70.29 E
Deh Bīd	128	30.38 N	53.13 E
Dehdez	128	31.43 N	50.17 E
Deh-e Salm	128	31.12 N	59.19 E
Dehgolān	128	35.17 N	47.25 E
Dehibat	148	32.01 N	10.42 E
Dehiwala-Mount Lavinia	122	6.51 N	79.52 E
Deh Kord	128	33.49 N	48.53 E
Dehlorān	128	32.41 N	47.16 E
De Hoek	158	32.57 S	18.46 E
Dehpehk I	174r	6.57 N	158.18 E
Dehra Dūn	124	30.19 N	78.02 E
Dehri	124	24.52 N	84.11 E
Dehrn	56	50.25 N	8.05 E
Dehu	122	18.35 N	73.51 E
Dehua	100	25.32 N	118.15 E
Dehuang	98	35.12 N	114.25 E
Dehui	89	44.34 N	125.43 E
Deidesheim	56	49.24 N	8.11 E
Deilbach ≃	263	51.23 N	7.05 E
Deilinghofen	56	51.22 N	7.47 E
Deining	60	49.13 N	11.32 E
Deinze	50	50.59 N	3.32 E
Deir el Asad	132	32.56 N	35.16 E
Deister ʎ	52	52.15 N	9.30 E
Deiva Marina	62	44.13 N	9.30 E
Dej	38	47.09 N	23.52 E
Deje	40	59.36 N	13.28 E
Dejima	94	36.05 N	140.20 E
Dejnau	128	39.15 N	63.11 E
De Jongs, Tanjong ›	164	6.56 S	138.32 E
Deka ≃	154	18.04 S	26.42 E
De Kalb, Il., U.S.	216	41.55 N	88.45 W
De Kalb, Ms., U.S.	194	32.46 N	88.39 W
De Kalb, Tx., U.S.	194	33.30 N	94.36 W
De Kalb □6, Il., U.S.	216	41.59 N	88.41 W
De Kalb □6, In., U.S.	216	41.22 N	85.04 W
De Kalb Junction	212	44.30 N	75.16 W
Dekan, Hochland von → Deccan ʎ1	122	17.00 N	78.00 E
De-Kastri	89	51.28 N	140.47 E
Dekehtik I	174r	7.00 N	158.12 E
Dekemhare	144	15.05 N	39.02 E
Dekese	152	3.27 S	21.24 E
Deke Sokehs I	174r	6.59 N	158.11 E
Dekhgila Military Base ■	142	31.08 N	29.48 E
Dekina	150	7.39 N	7.02 E
Dékoa	152	6.19 N	19.04 E
De Koog	52	53.05 N	4.45 E
De Krim	52	52.38 N	6.38 E
De La Blanche, Lac ⊜	186	50.05 N	69.29 W
Delabole	42	50.37 N	4.42 W
Delafield	216	43.03 N	88.24 W
Del Aire	280	33.55 N	118.21 W
Delamere, Austl.	164	15.45 S	131.33 E
Delamere, Austl.	168b	35.35 S	138.11 E
Delamere, Eng., U.K.	262	53.13 N	2.39 W
Delamere Forest ◆3	44	53.14 N	2.38 W
Delami Mayal, Jabal ∧	140	11.38 N	30.23 E
Del Amo Fashion Center ◆9	280	33.50 N	118.21 W
De Lancey, N.Y., U.S.	210	42.12 N	74.58 W
De Lancey, Pa., U.S.	214	40.59 N	78.58 W
Delanco	208	40.03 N	74.57 W
De Land	220	29.01 N	81.18 W
Delanggu	115a	7.37 S	110.41 E
Delano, Ca., U.S.	226	35.46 N	119.14 W
Delano, Mn., U.S.	190	45.02 N	93.47 W
Delano, Pa., U.S.	210	40.50 N	76.04 W
Delano Peak ∧	200	38.22 N	112.23 W
Delanson	210	42.44 N	74.11 W
Delaport Point ›	240b	25.05 N	77.27 W
Delapu	120	31.35 N	90.35 E
Delārām	128	32.11 N	63.25 E
Delareyville	158	26.44 S	25.29 E
Delarof Islands II	181a	51.30 N	178.45 W
Delaronde Lake ⊜	184	54.05 N	107.05 W
Del'atiči	76	53.47 N	25.59 E
Del'atin	78	48.32 N	24.37 E
Delatite ≃	169	37.10 S	146.00 E
Delavan, Il., U.S.	194	40.22 N	89.32 W
Delavan, Wi., U.S.	216	42.37 N	88.38 W
Delavan Lake	216	42.35 N	88.37 W
Delavan Lake ⊜	216	42.37 N	88.38 W
Delaware, On., Can.	214	42.55 N	81.25 W
Delaware, N.J., U.S.	210	40.53 N	75.03 W
Delaware, Oh., U.S.	214	40.17 N	83.04 W
Delaware, Ok., U.S.	196	36.46 N	95.38 W
Delaware □6, In., U.S.	216	40.18 N	85.23 W
Delaware □6, N.Y., U.S.	210	42.17 N	74.55 W
Delaware □6, Oh., U.S.	214	40.18 N	83.04 W
Delaware □6, Pa., U.S.	208	39.55 N	75.23 W
Delaware □3, U.S.	178	39.10 N	75.30 W
Delaware □3, U.S.	208	39.10 N	75.30 W
Delaware ≃, U.S.	188	39.20 N	75.25 W
Delaware ≃, U.S.	196	32.02 N	104.01 W
Delaware ≃, Ks., U.S.	198	39.03 N	95.24 W
Delaware, East Branch ≃	210	41.55 N	75.17 W
Delaware, University of ʊ2	285	39.41 N	75.45 W
Delaware, West Branch ≃	210	41.56 N	75.17 W
Delaware and Raritan Canal ≍	208	40.29 N	74.26 W
Delaware Aqueduct ≍1	210	42.05 N	74.54 W
Delaware Bay c	208	39.05 N	75.15 W
Delaware City	208	39.34 N	75.35 W
Delaware Lake ⊜1	214	40.20 N	83.00 W
Delaware Memorial Bridge ◆5	285	40.07 N	74.50 W
Delaware Memorial Bridges ◆5	208	39.41 N	75.31 W
Delaware Mountains ʎ	196	31.35 N	104.40 W
Delaware Museum of Natural History ʊ	285	39.47 N	75.36 W
Delaware Park	210	40.43 N	75.11 W
Delaware Park ♠	284a	42.56 N	78.52 W
Delaware Park Race Track ♠	285	39.42 N	75.40 W
Delaware Seashore State Park ♠	208	38.38 N	75.04 W
Delaware State Park ♠	214	40.23 N	83.04 W
Delaware Water Gap	210	40.59 N	75.09 W
Delaware Water Gap National Recreation Area ♠	210	41.08 N	74.55 W
Delbrück	52	51.46 N	8.33 E
Delburne	182	52.12 N	113.14 W
Delcambre	194	29.57 N	91.59 W
Del Campillo	252	34.22 S	64.29 W
Del Carril	258	35.31 S	59.30 W
Del City	196	35.26 N	97.26 W
Delcommune, Lac ⊜1	154	10.45 S	25.45 E
Del Dios	228	33.04 N	117.08 W
Delegate	166	37.03 S	148.58 E
Délembé	146	9.53 N	22.37 E
Delémont	58	47.22 N	7.21 E
De Leon	196	32.06 N	98.32 W
De Leon Springs	192	29.07 N	81.21 W
Delet ʯ	26	60.15 N	20.35 E
Delevan	210	42.29 N	78.28 W
Delfim Moreira	256	22.30 S	45.17 W
Delfinópolis	255	20.20 S	46.51 W
Delft	52	52.00 N	4.21 E
Delft Island I	122	9.30 N	79.42 E
Delfzijl	52	53.19 N	6.46 E
Delgada, Punta ›	254	42.46 S	63.38 W
Delgado	236	13.43 N	89.10 W
Delgado, Cabo ›	154	10.40 S	40.35 E
Del Gallego	116	13.56 N	122.36 E
Delgany	48	53.08 N	6.05 W
Delger ≃	88	49.17 N	100.40 E
Delger chaan uul ∧	88	50.00 N	106.22 E
Delgerchangaj	102	45.15 N	104.50 E
Delgerchet	102	45.52 N	110.26 E
Delgercogt	102	46.08 N	106.23 E
Delgerech	102	45.48 N	111.12 E
Del Haven	208	39.03 N	74.56 W
Delhi, On., Can.	212	42.51 N	80.30 W
Delhi, India	124	28.40 N	77.13 E
Delhi, India	272a	28.40 N	77.13 E
Delhi, Ca., U.S.	226	37.26 N	120.46 W
Delhi, Il., U.S.	219	39.03 N	90.15 W
Delhi, Ia., U.S.	190	42.25 N	91.19 W
Delhi, La., U.S.	194	32.27 N	91.29 W
Delhi, N.Y., U.S.	210	42.16 N	74.54 W
Delhi □8	124	28.37 N	77.10 E
Delhi Cantonment	272a	28.36 N	77.08 E
Delhi Hills	218	39.05 N	84.36 W
Delhi Railroad Station ◆5	272a	28.40 N	77.13 E
Delhi Tail Distributary ≍	272a	28.41 N	77.10 E
Delhi University ʊ2	272a	28.42 N	77.13 E
Deli, Pulau I	115a	7.00 S	105.32 E
Delia, Ab., Can.	182	51.38 N	112.23 W
Delia, It.	70	37.21 N	13.55 E
Delia ≃	70	37.19 N	13.58 E
Delianuova	68	38.14 N	15.55 E
Deliblato	38	44.50 N	21.03 E
Delice	130	39.58 N	34.02 E
Delice ≃	130	40.28 N	34.10 E
Delices	240d	15.17 N	61.16 W
Deliceto	68	41.13 N	15.23 E
Delicias, Cuba	240p	21.11 N	76.34 W
Delicias, Méx.	232	28.13 N	105.28 W
De Lier	52	51.57 N	4.15 E
Delight	194	34.01 N	93.30 W
Delightful	214	41.18 N	80.57 W
Deliilyas	130	39.20 N	36.48 E
Delījān	128	33.59 N	50.40 E
Deliktaş	130	39.21 N	37.13 E
Delingde	74	70.08 N	114.00 E
Delingha	102	37.14 N	97.11 E
Dēliņkalns ∧2	76	57.30 N	26.58 E
Déli Pályaudvar ◆5	264c	47.30 N	19.01 E
Delisle	184	51.55 N	107.08 W
Delisle ≃	206	45.17 N	74.11 W
Delitua	114	3.30 N	98.41 E
Delitzsch	54	51.31 N	12.20 E
Delkern	228	35.21 N	119.01 W
Dell	46	58.30 N	6.20 W
Dellach	64	46.40 N	13.05 E
Dell City	200	31.56 N	105.12 W
Delle	58	47.30 N	7.00 E
Dellenbaugh, Mount ∧	200	36.07 N	113.32 W
Dellensjöarna ⊜	26	61.54 N	16.41 E
Delles	148	36.55 N	3.55 E
Delligsen	52	51.57 N	9.48 E
Dello	64	45.25 N	10.04 E
Dell Rapids	198	43.50 N	96.43 W
Dellroy	214	40.33 N	81.11 W
Dellwig	263	51.29 N	7.41 E
Dellwig ◆8	263	51.29 N	6.56 E
Dellwood	219	38.44 N	90.17 W
Dellwood Highlands	278	41.34 N	88.03 W
Del Mar, Ca., U.S.	228	32.57 N	117.15 W
Delmar, De., U.S.	208	38.27 N	75.34 W
Delmar, Ia., U.S.	190	42.00 N	90.36 W
Delmar, Md., U.S.	208	38.27 N	75.34 W
Delmar, N.Y., U.S.	210	42.37 N	73.49 W
Del Mar Hills	196	27.37 N	99.26 W
Delmarva Peninsula ›1	208	38.30 N	75.30 W
Del Mar Woods	278	42.12 N	87.51 W
Delmas, Sk., Can.	184	52.55 N	108.36 W
Delmas, S. Afr.	158	26.08 S	28.43 E
Delmas □5	273d	26.10 S	28.33 E
Delme	56	48.53 N	6.24 E
Delme ≃	52	53.05 N	8.40 E
Delmenhorst	52	53.03 N	8.38 E
Delmiro Gouveia	250	9.23 S	37.59 W
Delmont, N.J., U.S.	208	39.12 N	74.57 W
Delmont, Pa., U.S.	214	40.25 N	79.34 W
Delmont, S.D., U.S.	198	43.16 N	98.09 W
Del Monte Heights	226	36.36 N	121.50 W
Del Monte Park	226	36.36 N	121.56 W
Delnice	36	45.24 N	14.48 E
Del Norte	200	37.40 N	106.21 W
Del Norte Coast Redwood State Park ♠	204	41.38 N	124.05 W
De-Longa, ostrova II	74	76.30 N	153.00 E
De Long Mountains ʎ	180	68.20 N	162.00 W
De-Long-Strasse → Longa, proliv ʯ	74	70.20 N	178.00 E
Deloraine, Austl.	166	41.31 S	146.39 E
Deloraine, Mb., Can.	184	49.12 N	100.29 W
Delorme, Lac ⊜	176	54.31 N	69.52 W
Deloro	212	44.31 N	77.37 W
Delos → Dhílos ⊥	38	37.26 N	25.16 E
Delph, Eng., U.K.	44	53.34 N	2.01 W
Delph, Eng., U.K.	262	53.34 N	2.01 W
Delphi	216	40.35 N	86.40 W
Delphi → Dhelfoí ⊥	38	38.30 N	22.29 E
Delphi Falls	210	42.53 N	75.55 W
Delphos, Ks., U.S.	198	39.16 N	97.46 W
Delphos, Oh., U.S.	216	40.50 N	84.20 W
Delph Reservoir ⊜1	262	53.38 N	2.27 W
Delportshoop	158	28.22 S	24.20 E
Del Puerto Creek ≃	226	37.32 N	121.07 W
Delran	285	40.01 N	74.57 W
Delrath	263	51.08 N	6.47 E
Delray ◆8	281	42.18 N	83.08 W
Delray Beach	220	26.27 N	80.04 W
Del Rey	226	36.40 N	119.36 W
Del Rey Oaks	226	36.36 N	121.50 W
Del Rio, Fl., U.S.	220	28.03 N	82.26 W
Del Rio, Tx., U.S.	196	29.21 N	100.53 W
Del Rosa	228	34.08 N	117.15 W
Delsbo	26	61.48 N	16.35 E
Delson	206	45.22 N	73.33 W
Delstern ◆8	263	51.20 N	7.31 E
Delta, On., Can.	212	44.37 N	76.08 W
Delta, Méx.	200	32.22 N	115.12 W
Delta, Co., U.S.	200	38.44 N	108.04 W
Delta, Mo., U.S.	194	37.11 N	89.44 W
Delta, Oh., U.S.	216	41.34 N	84.00 W
Delta, Pa., U.S.	208	39.43 N	76.19 W
Delta, Ut,. U.S.	200	39.21 N	112.34 W
Delta □9	194	33.30 N	90.45 W
Delta ≃	180	64.09 N	146.18 W
Delta Amacuro □8	246	8.30 N	61.30 W
Delta Barrage ◆6	142	30.11 N	31.07 E
Delta Beach	184	50.11 N	98.19 W
Delta City	194	33.04 N	90.47 W
Delta Downs	166	17.00 S	141.18 E
Delta Junction	180	64.02 N	145.41 W
Delta Mendota Canal ≍	226	37.49 N	121.34 W
Delta Peak ∧	180	56.39 N	129.34 W
Delta Reservoir ⊜1	210	43.17 N	75.26 W
Deltaville	208	37.33 N	76.20 W
Delton	216	42.29 N	85.24 W
Deltona	220	28.54 N	81.15 W
Delungra	166	29.39 S	150.50 E
Del'un-Uranskij chrebet ʎ	88	56.30 N	114.00 E
Delüün	86	47.42 N	90.59 E
De Luz Creek ≃	228	33.22 N	117.19 W
Del Valle	222	30.12 N	97.40 W
Del Valle, Lake ⊜1	226	37.35 N	121.43 W
Del Verme Falls ∟	144	5.27 N	40.17 E
Delvin	48	53.36 N	7.05 W
Delvinë	38	39.57 N	20.06 E
Del Viso	258	34.27 S	58.48 W
Delyn □8	262	53.16 N	3.11 W
Demak	115a	6.53 S	110.38 E
Demaki	80	58.26 N	51.43 E
Dem'ansk	76	57.38 N	32.28 E
Demarcation Point ›	180	69.40 N	141.15 W
Demarest	276	40.57 N	73.57 W
Demarest Brook ≃	276	40.57 N	73.58 W
Demavend, Mount → Damāvand, Qolleh-ye ∧	128	35.56 N	52.08 E
Demba	152	5.30 S	22.16 E
Demba Chio	152	9.41 S	13.41 E
Dembecha	144	10.35 N	37.30 E
Dembéni	157a	11.50 S	43.24 E
Dembi	144	8.05 N	36.27 E
Dembia, Centraf.	154	5.07 N	24.25 E
Dembia, Zaïre	154	3.31 N	25.50 E
Dembi Dolo	144	8.32 N	34.48 E
Dembo	152	3.56 S	12.35 E
Dême ≃	50	47.43 N	0.29 E
Demer ≃	56	50.58 N	4.42 E
Demerara ≃	246	6.48 N	58.10 W
Demerara-Mahaica □4	246	6.40 N	58.00 W
Demerthin	54	52.58 N	12.17 E
Demidov	76	55.16 N	31.31 E
Demidovka	78	50.25 N	25.20 E
Demidovo	76	59.17 N	38.17 E
Deming, N.M., U.S.	200	32.16 N	107.45 W
Deming, Wa., U.S.	224	48.49 N	122.12 W
Demini ≃	246	0.46 S	62.56 W
Demirci	130	39.03 N	28.40 E
Demir Kapija V	38	41.24 N	22.15 E
Demirköprü Barajı ⊜1	130	38.40 N	28.20 E
Demirköy	130	41.49 N	27.45 E
Demirtaş	130	40.16 N	29.06 E
Demitz-Thumitz	54	51.09 N	14.14 E
Demjanka ≃	86	59.34 N	69.20 E
Demjanovo	24	60.22 N	47.03 E
Demjanskoje	86	59.36 N	69.18 E
Demjas	80	51.13 N	49.08 E
Demmeltrath ◆8	263	51.11 N	7.03 E
Demmin	54	53.54 N	13.02 E
Demmitt	182	55.26 N	119.54 W
Demnate	148	31.44 N	6.59 W
Democracy Monument ⊥	269a	13.45 N	100.30 E
Democrat Point ›	276	40.37 N	73.18 W
Demoiselles, Grotte des ≛5	62	43.55 N	3.45 E
Demone, Val ◆1	70	37.58 N	14.35 E
Demonte	62	44.19 N	7.17 E
De Montigny, Lac ⊜	190	48.08 N	77.54 W
Demopolis	194	32.31 N	87.50 W
Demorest	192	34.33 N	83.32 W
De Mossville	218	38.48 N	84.25 W
Demotte	216	41.12 N	87.12 W
Dempo, Gunung ∧	112	4.02 S	103.09 E
Dempster, Point ›	162	33.39 S	123.52 E
Demsa	146	9.32 N	13.14 E
Demta	164	2.20 S	140.08 E
Demurino	78	48.10 N	36.29 E
De Naauwte	158	30.08 S	21.42 E
Denain	50	50.20 N	3.23 E
Denair	226	37.32 N	120.47 W
Denakil ◆1	144	13.00 N	41.00 E
Denali	180	63.11 N	147.28 W
Denali National Park	180	63.44 N	148.54 W
Denali National Park ♠	180	63.15 N	150.30 W
Denan	144	6.30 N	43.30 E
Denare Beach	184	54.40 N	102.05 W
Denau	85	38.16 N	67.54 E
Denbigh, On., Can.	212	45.08 N	77.16 W
Denbigh, Wales, U.K.	44	53.11 N	3.25 W
Denbigh, Cape ›	180	64.23 N	161.31 W
Den Burg	52	53.03 N	4.48 E
Denby Dale	44	53.35 N	1.38 W
Den Chai	110	17.59 N	100.04 E
Dendang	112	3.05 S	107.54 E
Dender (Dendre) ≃	50	51.02 N	4.06 E
Denderleeuw	50	50.53 N	4.04 E
Dendermonde	50	51.02 N	4.07 E
Dendre (Dender) ≃	50	51.02 N	4.06 E
Dendron, S. Afr.	156	23.25 S	29.11 E
Dendron, Va., U.S.	208	37.02 N	76.56 W
Dendy Park ♠	274b	37.56 S	145.00 E
Deneba	144	9.50 N	39.09 E
Denekamp	52	52.23 N	7.00 E
Denenchōfu ◆8	268	35.35 N	139.41 E
Deneysville	158	26.53 S	28.06 E
Denežnikovo, Ross.	82	55.26 N	38.07 E
Denežnikovo, Ukr.	83	49.02 N	38.57 E
Dengcheng	100	33.41 N	114.27 E
Deng Deng	152	5.12 N	13.31 E
Denge	154	3.34 N	28.14 E
Denge Marsh ≡	42	50.57 N	0.55 E
Dengfeng	100	34.29 N	113.04 E
Denggongchang	107	30.24 N	103.49 E
Dengguanzhen	107	29.10 N	104.56 E
Dengkou	102	40.20 N	106.59 E
Denglongshu	98	41.20 N	115.15 E
Dengmingsi	98	37.53 N	116.42 E
Dêngqên	102	31.32 N	95.27 E
Dengshahe	98	39.13 N	122.04 E
Dengta	100	24.01 N	114.49 E
Denguiro	152	5.38 N	23.02 E
Dengxian	102	32.42 N	112.01 E
Dengyoufang	98	41.34 N	114.32 E
Den Haag → 's-Gravenhage	52	52.06 N	4.18 E
Denham, Austl.	162	25.55 S	113.32 E
Denham, Eng., U.K.	260	51.34 N	0.30 W
Denham, In., U.S.	216	41.09 N	86.43 W
Denham, Mount ∧	241q	18.13 N	77.32 W
Denham Aerodrome ⊠	260	51.36 N	0.31 W
Denham Island I	166	16.43 S	139.09 E
Denham Place ʊ	260	51.34 N	0.30 W
Denham Range ʎ	166	21.55 S	147.46 E
Denham Sound ʯ	162	25.40 S	113.15 E
Denham Springs	194	30.29 N	90.57 W
Den Helder	52	52.54 N	4.45 E
Denholme	262	53.48 N	1.54 W
Dénia	34	38.51 N	0.07 E
Denial Bay	162	32.06 S	133.32 E
Dénié	150	11.14 N	7.29 W
Deniliquin	166	35.32 S	144.58 E
Deniskoviči, Bela.	76	52.44 N	26.41 E
Deniskoviči, Ross.	76	52.19 N	31.43 E
Denison, Ia., U.S.	198	42.01 N	95.21 W
Denison, Tx., U.S.	196	33.45 N	96.32 W
Denison, Mount ∧	180	58.25 N	154.27 W
Denison Dam ◆6	196	33.50 N	96.34 W
Denisovka	24	66.14 N	55.20 E
Denisōvo	82	54.28 N	37.51 E
Denisy	261	48.33 N	1.56 E
Denizli	130	37.46 N	29.06 E
Denizli □4	130	37.40 N	29.15 E
Denkanikota	122	12.32 N	77.48 E
Denkendorf	60	48.56 N	11.27 E
Denkingen	58	47.53 N	9.19 E
Denklingen, Dtsch.	56	50.55 N	7.39 E
Denklingen, Dtsch.	58	47.55 N	10.51 E
Den'kovo	82	56.01 N	36.21 E
Denmark, Austl.	162	34.57 S	117.21 E
Denmark, S.C., U.S.	192	33.19 N	81.08 W
Denmark, Wi., U.S.	190	44.20 N	87.49 W
Denmark (Danmark) □1, Europe	22	56.00 N	10.00 E
Denmark (Danmark) □1, Europe	26	56.00 N	10.00 E
Denmark, Lake ⊜	276	40.58 N	74.31 W
Denmark Bay c	172	70.33 N	103.20 W
Denmark Strait ʯ	10	67.00 N	25.00 W
Denmead	42	50.54 N	1.04 W
Dennemont	261	49.01 N	1.42 E
Dennery	241f	13.55 N	60.54 W
Dennis	207	41.44 N	70.11 W
Dennis Head ›	46	59.23 N	2.23 W
Dennison	214	40.23 N	81.20 W
Dennis Port	207	41.39 N	70.07 W
Denniston	172	41.44 S	171.48 E
Denniston Creek ≃	282	37.30 N	122.28 W
Dennisville	208	39.11 N	74.49 W
Denny	46	56.02 N	3.55 W
Den Oever	52	52.56 N	5.02 E
Denouval	261	48.58 N	2.03 E
Denpasar	115b	8.39 S	115.13 E
Denshaw	262	53.35 N	2.02 W
Dent Ditch ≍	279a	41.18 N	82.08 W
Denton, Eng., U.K.	262	53.27 N	2.07 W
Denton, Md., U.S.	208	38.53 N	75.49 W
Denton, Mi., U.S.	281	42.20 N	83.03 W
Denton, Mt., U.S.	202	47.19 N	109.56 W
Denton, N.C., U.S.	192	35.38 N	80.06 W
Denton, Tx., U.S.	222	33.12 N	97.07 W
Denton □6	222	33.07 N	97.10 W
Denton Creek ≃	196	32.58 N	96.57 W
Dentonia Park ♠	275b	43.42 N	79.17 W
D'Entrecasteaux, Point ›	162	34.50 S	116.00 E
D'Entrecasteaux Islands II	164	9.30 S	150.40 E
D'Entrecasteaux National Park ♠	162	34.41 S	115.58 E
Dents du Midi ʎ	58	46.10 N	6.56 E
Denver, Co., U.S.	200	39.44 N	104.59 W
Denver, In., U.S.	216	40.51 N	86.04 W
Denver, Ia., U.S.	190	42.40 N	92.20 W
Denver, Pa., U.S.	208	40.13 N	76.08 W
Denver City	196	32.57 N	102.49 W
Denville	210	40.53 N	74.28 W
Denzlingen	58	48.04 N	7.52 E
Deoband	124	29.42 N	77.41 E
Deocha	126	24.03 N	87.35 E
Deodoro ◆8	287a	22.51 S	43.23 W
Deogarh, India	120	25.32 N	73.54 E
Deogarh, India	122	21.32 N	84.44 E
Deogarh, India	124	24.33 N	78.15 E
Deogarh ∧	124	23.32 N	82.16 E
Deogarh Hills ʎ2	124	23.35 N	82.30 E
Deoghar	124	24.29 N	86.42 E
Deogsu Palace ʊ	271b	37.35 N	126.58 E
Deolāli	122	19.57 N	73.50 E
Deoli	126	22.03 N	86.49 E
Deoli ◆8	272a	28.30 N	77.14 E
Deongwar, Mount ∧	171a	27.12 S	152.16 E
Deopāra	126	22.55 N	90.15 E
Deori, India	124	23.08 N	78.41 E
Deori, India	124	23.24 N	79.01 E
Deoria	124	26.31 N	83.47 E
Deosai Mountains ʎ	123	35.20 N	75.12 E
Deosil	124	23.42 N	82.15 E
Dep ≃	89	52.54 N	127.45 E
Depāl	126	21.44 N	87.33 E
De Panne	50	51.06 N	2.35 E
Depāra	272b	22.53 N	88.34 E
Departure Bay	224	49.12 N	123.58 W
DePaul University ʊ2	278	41.56 N	87.39 W
Depauville	212	44.08 N	76.04 W
Depauw	218	38.20 N	86.13 W
De Peel ≡	52	51.25 N	6.00 E
De Pere	190	44.26 N	88.03 W
Depew, N.Y., U.S.	210	42.54 N	78.41 W
Depew, Ok., U.S.	196	35.48 N	96.30 W
Deping	98	37.28 N	116.57 E
De Pinte	50	51.00 N	3.39 E
Depoe Bay	202	44.48 N	124.03 W
Depok	115a	6.24 S	106.50 E
Deport	196	33.32 N	95.19 W
Deposit	210	42.03 N	75.25 W
Deptford	285	39.50 N	75.07 W
Deptford ◆8	260	51.28 N	0.02 W
Deptford Mall ◆9	285	39.50 N	75.06 W
Deptford Terrace	285	39.48 N	75.09 W
Depuch Island I	162	20.38 S	117.43 E
Depue	190	41.19 N	89.18 W
Deputy	218	38.48 N	85.39 W
Dêqên	102	28.38 N	98.52 E
Deqing, Zhg.	102	23.09 N	111.45 E
Deqing, Zhg.	106	30.33 N	120.05 E
De Queen	194	34.02 N	94.20 W
De Quincy	194	30.27 N	93.25 W
Dera ≃	264c	47.39 N	19.05 E
Dera, Lach (Lak Dera) V	144	0.35 N	41.50 E
Dera Bugti	120	29.02 N	69.09 E
Dera Ghāzi Khān	123	30.03 N	70.38 E
Dera Gopipur	123	31.54 N	76.13 E
Dera Ismāīl Khān	123	31.50 N	70.54 E
Derakht-e Yaḥyá	120	31.50 N	68.08 E
Dera Nānak	123	32.02 N	75.01 E
Dera Nawāb	123	29.06 N	71.16 E
Derāwar Fort	123	28.46 N	71.20 E
Deražn'a	78	49.16 N	27.26 E
Derbent	84	42.03 N	48.18 E
Derbeškinskij	80	55.52 N	53.30 E
Derbetovka	80	45.48 N	43.05 E
Der Bodden ʯ	54	54.16 N	13.12 E
Derby, Austl.	162	17.18 S	123.38 E
Derby, Austl.	166	41.09 S	147.47 E
Derby, S. Afr.	158	25.55 S	27.02 E
Derby, Eng., U.K.	42	52.55 N	1.29 W
Derby, Ct., U.S.	207	41.19 N	73.05 W
Derby, Ks., U.S.	198	37.32 N	97.16 W
Derby, Me., U.S.	188	45.14 N	68.58 W
Derby, N.Y., U.S.	210	42.40 N	78.58 W
Derby, Oh., U.S.	218	39.46 N	83.12 W
Derby, Vt., U.S.	206	44.57 N	72.08 W
Derby Acres	226	35.15 N	119.35 W
Derby Line	206	45.00 N	72.05 W
Derbyshire □6	44	53.00 N	1.33 W
Der-Chantecoq, Lac du ⊜1	58	48.35 N	4.46 E
Derdepoort	156	24.42 S	26.20 E
Dere	130	39.00 N	39.18 E
Derečin	76	53.15 N	24.55 E
Derecske	30	47.21 N	21.34 E
Dereköy, Tür.	130	41.56 N	27.21 E
Dereköy, Tür.	130	39.16 N	27.19 E
Dereköy, Tür.	130	40.08 N	37.47 E
Dereli	130	40.45 N	38.27 E
Derenburg	54	51.52 N	10.54 E
Derendorf ◆8	263	51.15 N	6.48 E
Derenwu	105	39.40 N	116.46 E
Dereseki ◆8	267b	41.08 N	29.08 E
Derev'anka	24	61.34 N	34.27 E
Derg ≃	48	54.44 N	7.25 W
Derg, Lough ⊜, Ire.	48	54.36 N	7.53 W
Derg, Lough ⊜, Ire.	48	52.57 N	8.19 W
Dergači, Ross.	80	51.14 N	48.46 E
Dergači, Ukr.	78	50.07 N	36.07 E
Dergaon	120	26.42 N	93.58 E
Der Grabow c	54	54.23 N	12.50 E
De Ridder	194	30.50 N	93.17 W
De Rijp	52	52.34 N	4.50 E
Derik	130	37.22 N	40.17 E
Derinkuyu	130	38.23 N	34.45 E
Der Kanal → English Channel ʯ	28	50.20 N	1.00 W
Derkul	80	51.16 N	51.18 E
Derkul ≃	83	48.35 N	39.41 E
Dermbach	56	50.43 N	10.06 E
Dermott	194	33.31 N	91.26 W
Dermulo	64	46.20 N	11.04 E
Derne	263	51.35 N	7.41 E
Derne ◆8	263	51.34 N	7.31 E
Dernieres, Isles II	194	29.02 N	90.47 W
Dernoviči	78	51.36 N	29.43 E
Deroche	224	49.11 N	122.04 W
Dero Eri	144	9.01 N	46.43 E
Dêrong	102	28.47 N	99.14 E
Déroute, Passage de la ʯ	32	49.25 N	2.00 W
Derrame	196	26.19 N	104.23 W
Derravaragh, Lough ⊜	48	53.40 N	7.24 W
Derre	154	16.56 S	36.11 E
Derrick City	214	41.78 N	78.34 W
Derrinallum	169	37.57 S	143.13 E
Derry, N.H., U.S.	188	42.52 N	71.19 W
Derry, Pa., U.S.	214	40.20 N	79.18 W
Derrybrien	48	53.04 N	8.36 W
Derrykeighan	48	55.08 N	6.29 W
Derry → Londonderry	48	54.59 N	7.20 W
Derryveagh Mountains ʎ	48	55.00 N	8.05 W
Derry West	275b	43.39 N	79.42 W
Der Sārāi ◆8	272a	28.33 N	77.11 E
Dersau	54	54.07 N	10.20 E
Dersingham	42	52.51 N	0.30 E
Derudeb	140	17.32 N	36.06 E
De Rust	158	33.30 S	22.32 E
Deruta	66	42.59 N	12.25 E
De Ruyter	210	42.45 N	75.53 W
DeRuyter Reservoir ⊜1	210	42.49 N	75.53 W
Der'uzino	82	56.18 N	38.16 E
Derval	32	47.40 N	1.40 W
Derventa	38	44.58 N	17.55 E
Derwent	182	53.39 N	110.58 W
Derwent ≃, Austl.	166	43.03 S	147.22 E
Derwent ≃, Eng., U.K.	44	53.45 N	0.57 W
Derwent ≃, Eng., U.K.	44	54.57 N	1.41 W
Derwent ≃, Eng., U.K.	44	54.38 N	3.34 W
Derwent ≃, Eng., U.K.	44	52.53 N	1.17 W
Derwent Bridge	166	42.08 S	146.13 E
Derwent Reservoir ⊜1	44	54.50 N	2.00 W
Derwent Water ⊜	44	54.34 N	3.08 W
Deržavino	80	53.13 N	52.22 E
Deržavinsk	86	51.03 N	66.19 E
Desaguadero ≃, Arg.	252	34.13 S	66.47 W
Desaguadero ≃, Bol.	248	18.24 S	67.05 W
Desagüe, Canal de ≍	286a	19.29 N	99.05 W
Des Allemands	194	29.49 N	90.28 W
Desamparados	236	9.54 N	84.04 W
Désappointement, Îles du II	14	14.10 S	141.20 W
Des Arc	194	34.58 N	91.29 W
Desborough	42	52.27 N	0.49 W
Descabezado Grande, Volcán ∧1	252	35.36 S	70.45 W
Descanso, Bra.	252	26.50 S	53.35 W
Descanso, Ca., U.S.	204	32.51 N	116.37 W
Descanso, Punta ›	204	32.16 N	117.03 W
Descanso Gardens ♠	280	34.12 N	118.13 W
Descartes	32	46.58 N	0.42 E
Deschaillons	206	46.32 N	72.07 W
Deschambault	206	46.39 N	71.56 W
Deschambault Lake	184	54.55 N	103.22 W
Deschambault Lake ⊜	184	54.40 N	103.35 W
Descharme Lake ⊜	184	57.05 N	109.13 W
Deschênes	212	45.23 N	75.48 W
Deschênes, Lac ⊜	212	45.22 N	75.51 W
Deschutes ≃, Or., U.S.	202	45.38 N	120.54 W
Deschutes ≃, Wa., U.S.	224	47.02 N	122.54 W
Descoberto	256	21.27 S	42.58 W
Desdunes	238	19.17 N	72.39 W
Dese	144	11.05 N	39.41 E
Deseado ≃	254	47.45 S	65.54 W
Deseado, Cabo ›	254	52.44 S	74.44 W
Desembarco de los 0303 Orientales, Monumento ⊥	258	33.48 S	58.25 W
Desengaño, Punta ›	254	49.15 S	67.37 W
Desenzano del Garda	64	45.28 N	10.32 E
Deseret Peak ∧	200	40.28 N	112.38 W
Deseronto	212	44.12 N	77.03 W
Désert ≃	190	46.23 N	75.58 W
Désert, Lac ⊜	190	46.35 N	76.19 W
Desertas, Ilhas II	148	32.30 N	16.30 W
Desert Creek ≃	226	38.48 N	119.19 W
Desert Hot Springs	204	33.57 N	116.30 W
Desert Lake ⊜, On., Can.	212	44.32 N	76.35 W
Desert Lake ⊜, Nv., U.S.	204	36.58 N	115.05 W
Desert Mountains ʎ	226	39.16 N	119.00 W
Desert Peak ∧	200	41.11 N	113.22 W
Desert Valley V	204	41.15 N	118.20 W
Desert View Highlands	228	34.37 N	118.13 W
Desford	42	52.39 N	1.17 W
Desha	194	35.44 N	91.40 W
Deshaies	241o	16.18 N	61.48 W
Desheng	102	24.45 N	108.28 E
Deshengchang	107	29.06 N	105.25 E
Deshengpo	102	26.58 N	103.59 E
Deshengtai	104	42.14 N	123.45 E
Deshengyingzi	104	41.44 N	123.14 E
Deshler, Ne., U.S.	198	40.08 N	97.43 W
Deshler, Oh., U.S.	216	41.12 N	83.53 W
Deshnok	120	27.48 N	73.21 E
Deshon Manor	214	40.52 N	79.57 W
Deshu	128	30.26 N	63.19 E
Deshun	106	31.58 N	120.29 E
Desiderio Tello	252	31.13 S	66.19 W
Desio	62	45.37 N	9.13 E
Des Lacs ≃	198	48.17 N	101.25 W
Deslinde, Arroyo ≃	258	33.44 S	58.52 W
Desloge	194	37.52 N	90.31 W
Desmarais	182	55.56 N	113.49 W
De Smet	198	44.23 N	97.33 W
De Smet, Lake ⊜1	202	44.29 N	106.45 W
Des Moines, Ia., U.S.	190	41.36 N	93.36 W
Des Moines, N.M., U.S.	196	36.45 N	103.50 W
Des Moines, Wa., U.S.	224	47.24 N	122.19 W
Des Moines ≃	178	40.22 N	91.26 W
Des Moines, East Fork ≃	198	42.41 N	94.12 W
Dešná, Česko.	61	48.58 N	15.33 E
Desna, Ukr.	78	50.56 N	30.46 E
Desna ≃, Europe	78	50.33 N	30.32 E
Desna ≃, Ross.	82	55.26 N	37.30 E
Desolación, Isla I	254	53.00 S	74.10 W
Désolation, Cap de la → Disappointment, Cape ›	244	54.53 S	36.07 W
Desolation Point ›	116	10.28 N	125.39 E
Desor, Mount ∧2	190	47.58 N	89.01 W
De Soto, Il., U.S.	194	37.49 N	89.13 W
De Soto, In., U.S.	216	40.15 N	85.17 W
De Soto, Mo., U.S.	194	38.08 N	90.33 W
De Soto, Tx., U.S.	222	32.35 N	96.51 W
De Soto □6	220	27.11 N	81.48 W
De Soto City	220	27.26 N	81.24 W
De Soto National Memorial ⊥	220	27.31 N	82.40 W
De Soto State Park ♠	194	34.28 N	85.36 W
Despatch	158	33.46 S	25.30 E
Despeñaperros, Desfiladero de)(	34	38.24 N	3.30 W
Des Plaines	216	42.02 N	87.53 W
Des Plaines ≃	216	41.24 N	88.16 W
Despotovac	38	44.05 N	21.33 E
Despujols	116	12.31 N	122.01 E
Desroches, Île I	138	5.41 S	53.41 E
Desruisseaux	241f	13.47 N	60.56 W
Dessau	54	51.50 N	12.14 E
Dessel	56	51.14 N	5.07 E
Deşt	130	39.10 N	39.22 E
Destacado Island I	116	12.16 N	124.06 E
Destelbergen	50	51.03 N	3.48 E
Desterro	250	7.17 S	37.06 W
Destin	194	30.23 N	86.29 W
Destruction, Mount ∧2	162	24.35 S	127.59 E
Destruction Bay	180	61.15 N	138.48 W
Destruction Island I	224	47.40 N	124.30 W
Desulo	71	40.01 N	9.14 E
Desvres	50	50.40 N	1.50 E
Deta	38	45.24 N	21.13 E
Detčino	82	54.49 N	36.19 E
Dete	154	18.38 S	26.50 E
Dethlingen	52	52.57 N	10.07 E
Detling	260	51.18 N	0.34 E
Detmold	52	51.56 N	8.52 E
Detmold □6	52	51.48 N	8.00 E
Detour, Point ›	190	45.36 N	86.37 W
De Tour Village	190	46.00 N	83.54 W
Detrital Wash V	200	36.02 N	114.28 W
Detroit, Il., U.S.	219	39.37 N	90.40 W
Detroit, Mi., U.S.	216	42.20 N	83.03 W
Detroit, Mi., U.S.	281	42.20 N	83.03 W
Detroit, Or., U.S.	202	44.44 N	122.08 W
Detroit, Tx., U.S.	196	33.40 N	95.16 W
Detroit ≃	214	42.06 N	83.08 W
Detroit, University of ʊ2	281	42.25 N	83.08 W
Detroit Beach	216	41.55 N	83.20 W
Detroit City Airport ⊠	281	42.25 N	83.01 W
Detroit Institute of Arts ʊ	281	42.22 N	83.04 W
Detroit Lake ⊜1	202	44.42 N	122.10 W
Detroit Lakes	198	46.48 N	95.50 W
Detroit Metropolitan-Wayne County Airport ⊠	281	42.13 N	83.22 W
Detroit Race Course ♠	281	42.23 N	83.19 W
Detroit-Windsor Tunnel ◆5	281	42.20 N	83.02 W
Detroit Zoological Park ♠	281	42.29 N	83.09 W
Detskosel'skij	265a	59.44 N	30.28 E
Dettelbach	56	49.48 N	10.09 E
Dettifoss ∟	24a	65.50 N	16.20 W
Dettingen an der Erms	56	48.32 N	9.20 E
Dettwiller	56	48.45 N	7.28 E
Det Udom	110	14.54 N	105.05 E
Detva	30	48.31 N	19.28 E
Deua National Park ♠	166	36.00 S	149.45 E
Deuben	54	51.06 N	12.04 E
Deuels Corners	284a	42.45 N	78.45 W
Deuil-la-Barre	261	48.59 N	2.20 E
Deūlgaon Rāja	122	20.01 N	76.02 E
Deulpur	272b	22.36 N	88.10 E
Deulti	126	22.26 N	87.56 E
Deurne, Bel.	50	51.13 N	4.28 E
Deurne, Ned.	52	51.28 N	5.47 E
Deusen ◆8	263	51.33 N	7.26 E
Deutsche Bucht c	30	54.30 N	7.30 E
Deutsch Eylau → Iława	30	53.37 N	19.33 E
Deutschfeistritz	61	47.11 N	15.20 E
Deutschkreutz	61	47.36 N	16.38 E
Deutsch Krone → Wałcz	30	53.17 N	16.28 E
Deutschland → Germany □1	30	51.00 N	10.00 E
Deutschlandsberg	61	46.49 N	15.13 E
Deutsch-Neudorf	54	50.38 N	13.27 E
Deutsch Wagram	61	48.18 N	16.34 E
Deutsch Wusterhausen	264a	52.18 N	13.35 E
Deutzen	54	51.06 N	12.26 E
Deux-Montagnes	206	45.32 N	73.53 W
Deux-Montagnes □6	206	45.35 N	74.05 W
Deux Montagnes, Lac des ⊜	206	45.28 N	73.59 W
Deux-Sèvres □5	32	46.30 N	0.20 W
Deva	38	45.53 N	22.55 E
Devakottai	122	9.57 N	78.49 E
De Valls Bluff	194	34.47 N	91.27 W
Devaprayāg	124	30.09 N	78.37 E
Dev'atern'a	80	56.12 N	53.24 E
Dev'atiny	24	60.56 N	36.46 E
Devault	285	40.05 N	75.32 W
Dévaványa	30	47.02 N	20.58 E
Devecikonağı	130	39.55 N	28.34 E
Devecser	30	47.06 N	17.26 E
Devedağı Tepesi ∧	130	40.34 N	41.21 E
Devegeçidi Barajı ⊜1	130	38.05 N	39.55 E
Develi	130	38.23 N	35.30 E
Deventer	52	52.15 N	6.10 E
Deveron ≃	46	57.40 N	2.31 W
Devers	222	30.02 N	94.36 W
Devers Canal, West Branch ≍	222	29.57 N	94.46 W
Deversoir Military Base ■	142	30.25 N	32.20 E
Devès, Monts du ʎ	32	45.00 N	3.45 E
Devgadh Bāriva	120	22.42 N	73.54 E
De View, Bayou ≃	194	34.48 N	91.18 W
Devīkot	120	26.42 N	71.12 E
Devil Lake ⊜	212	44.35 N	76.27 W
Deville	56	49.53 N	4.42 E
Déville-lès-Rouen	50	49.28 N	1.02 E
Devil Peak ∧	226	37.32 N	119.44 W
Devil River Peak ∧	172	40.58 S	172.39 E
Devils ≃	196	29.39 N	100.58 W
Devil's Bridge	42	52.23 N	3.51 W
Devils Brook ≃	276	40.20 N	74.37 W
Devils Canyon V	280	34.16 N	117.58 W
Devil's Den State Park ♠	194	35.46 N	94.16 W
Devils Hole Rapids ∟	284a	43.08 N	79.03 W
Devils Hopyard State Park ♠	207	41.28 N	72.22 W
Devils Island → Diable, Île du I	250	5.17 N	52.35 W
Devils Lake	198	48.06 N	98.51 W
Devils Lake ⊜, Mi., U.S.	216	41.58 N	84.17 W
Devils Lake ⊜, N.D., U.S.	198	48.01 N	98.52 W
Devils Lake State Park ♠	190	43.24 N	89.44 W
Devils Marbles ♠	162	20.30 S	134.14 E
Devils Paw ∧	180	58.44 N	133.50 W
Devils Postpile National Monument ♠	226	37.37 N	119.05 W
Devils Tower ∧	198	44.31 N	104.57 W
Devils Tower National Monument ♠	198	44.31 N	104.57 W
Devil's Water ≃	44	54.58 N	2.02 W
Devin	38	41.45 N	24.24 E
Devine, B.C., Can.	182	50.32 N	122.30 W
Devine, Tx., U.S.	196	29.08 N	98.54 W
Devizes	42	51.22 N	1.59 W
Devladovo	78	48.07 N	33.45 E
Devli	120	25.45 N	75.23 E
De Voe Lake ⊜	276	40.23 N	74.23 W
Devoll ≃	38	40.49 N	19.51 E
Dévoluy ʎ	62	44.39 N	5.53 E
Devon, Ab., Can.	182	53.22 N	113.44 W
Devon, S. Afr.	158	26.21 S	28.48 E
Devon, Pa., U.S.	285	40.02 N	75.25 W
Devon □6	42	50.45 N	3.50 W
Devon ≃, Eng., U.K.	42	53.04 N	0.43 W
Devon ≃, Scot., U.K.	46	56.07 N	3.51 W
Devon Island I	16	75.00 N	87.00 W
Devonport, Austl.	166	41.11 S	146.21 E
Devonport, N.Z.	172	36.49 S	174.48 E
Devonport, Eng., U.K.	42	50.22 N	4.10 W
Devonshire	285	39.49 N	75.32 W
Devonshire Plaza ◆9	281	42.17 N	83.00 W
Devore	228	34.13 N	117.25 W
Devoto	252	31.24 S	62.19 W
Devrek	130	41.13 N	31.57 E
Devrekâni	130	41.36 N	33.51 E
Devrez ≃	130	41.06 N	34.25 E
Dewa, Ujung ›	114	2.55 N	95.48 E
Dewakang-lompo, Pulau I	112	5.24 S	118.25 E
Dewar	196	35.27 N	95.56 W
Dewart	210	41.07 N	76.53 W
Dewart Lake ⊜	216	41.22 N	85.47 W

≃ River	Fluß	Río	Rivière	Rio
≍ Canal	Kanal	Canal	Canal	Canal
∟ Waterfall, Rapids	Wasserfall, Stromschnellen	Cascada, Rápidos	Chute d'eau, Rapides	Cascata, Rápidos
ʯ Strait	Meeresstraße	Estrecho	Détroit	Estreito
c Bay, Gulf	Bucht, Golf	Bahía, Golfo	Baie, Golfe	Baía, Golfo
⊜ Lake, Lakes	See, Seen	Lago, Lagos	Lac, Lacs	Lago, Lagos
≡ Swamp	Sumpf	Pantano	Marais	Pântano
Ice Features, Glacier	Eis- und Gletscherformen	Accidentes Glaciales	Formes glaciaires	Acidentes glaciares
Other Hydrographic Features	Andere Hydrographische Objekte	Otros Elementos Hidrográficos	Autres données hydrographiques	Outros acidentes hidrográficos
Submarine Features	Untermeerische Objekte	Accidentes Submarinos	Formes de relief sous-marin	Acidentes submarinos
□ Political Unit	Politische Einheit	Unidad Politica	Entité politique	Unidade política
ʊ Cultural Institution	Kulturelle Institution	Institución Cultural	Institution culturelle	Instituição cultural
⊥ Historical Site	Historische Stätte	Sitio Histórico	Site historique	Sítio histórico
♠ Recreational Site	Erholungs- und Ferienort	Sitio de Recreo	Centre de loisirs	Área de Lazer
⊠ Airport	Flughafen	Aeropuerto	Aéroport	Aeroporto
■ Military Installation	Militäranlage	Instalación Militar	Installation militaire	Instalação militar
◆ Miscellaneous	Verschiedenes	Misceláneo	Divers	Diversos

Name	Page	Lat.°′	Long.°′
Dewās	120	22.58 N	76.04 E
Dewa-sanchi ⋏[2]	92	39.05 N	140.10 E
Dewdney	224	49.10 N	122.12 W
Dewetsdorp	158	29.33 S	26.34 E
Dewey, Il., U.S.	216	40.19 N	88.17 W
Dewey, Ok., U.S.	196	36.47 N	95.56 W
Dewey, Wa., U.S.	224	48.25 N	122.37 W
Dewey Beach	208	38.41 N	75.04 W
Deweyville	194	30.18 N	93.45 W
De Witt, Ar., U.S.	194	34.17 N	91.20 W
Dewitt, Il., U.S.	219	40.11 N	88.47 W
De Witt, Ia., U.S.	190	41.49 N	90.32 W
De Witt, Mi., U.S.	216	42.50 N	84.34 W
De Witt, Ne., U.S.	198	40.23 N	96.55 W
De Witt, N.Y., U.S.	210	43.02 N	76.03 W
De Witt □[6], Il., U.S.	216	40.12 N	88.55 W
De Witt □[6], Tx., U.S.	222	29.07 N	97.20 W
Dewittville	214	42.14 N	79.27 W
Dewsbury	44	53.42 N	1.37 W
Dexing	100	28.54 N	117.36 E
Dexingjie	98	39.54 N	122.50 E
Dexter, Me., U.S.	188	45.01 N	69.17 W
Dexter, Mi., U.S.	216	42.20 N	83.53 W
Dexter, Mo., U.S.	194	36.47 N	89.57 W
Dexter, N.M., U.S.	196	33.11 N	104.22 W
Dexter, N.Y., U.S.	212	44.00 N	76.02 W
Dexterity Fiord c[2]	176	71.11 N	73.03 W
Deyang	102	31.14 N	104.22 E
Dey-Dey, Lake ⊜	162	29.12 S	131.04 E
Deyhūk	128	33.17 N	57.30 E
Deyyer	128	27.50 N	51.55 E
Dez ≃	128	31.39 N	48.52 E
Dezfūl	128	32.23 N	48.24 E
Dez Gerd	128	30.45 N	51.57 E
Dezhou	98	37.27 N	116.18 E
Dežneva, mys ›	180	66.06 N	169.45 W
Dezong	120	32.09 N	90.20 E
Dezzo di Scalve	64	45.59 N	10.05 E
Dgâmcha, Sebkhet te-n- ⊜	150	18.45 N	15.48 W
Dhabān Singh	123	31.44 N	73.34 E
Dhāding	124	27.52 N	84.55 E
Dhādkā	126	22.47 N	86.30 E
Dháfna ∧	267c	38.07 N	23.38 E
Dháfni	38	37.48 N	22.01 E
Dhafnion Monastery ⊎[1]	267c	38.01 N	23.38 E
Dhahab	140	28.29 N	34.32 E
Dhahab, Wādī adh- V	132	32.44 N	35.54 E
Dhahran → Aẓ-Ẓahrān	128	26.18 N	50.08 E
Dhaka (Dacca), Bngl.	126	23.43 N	90.25 E
Dhāka, India	124	26.41 N	85.10 E
Dhaka □[5]	120	24.15 N	90.15 E
Dhākauli	124	24.45 N	77.51 E
Dhakuria Lake ⊜	272b	22.31 N	88.22 E
Dhaleswari ≃	126	23.32 N	90.34 E
Dháli	130	35.01 N	33.25 E
Dhamār	144	14.46 N	44.23 E
Dhāmpur	124	29.19 N	78.31 E
Dhāmrai	126	23.55 N	90.13 E
Dhamtari	122	20.41 N	81.34 E
Dhāmura	126	22.53 N	90.12 E
Dhanaula	123	30.17 N	75.35 E
Dhanaura	124	28.58 N	78.15 E
Dhanbād	126	23.48 N	86.27 E
Dhandhuka	120	22.22 N	71.59 E
Dhanera	126	23.25 N	86.39 E
Dhaneswargāti	126	23.25 N	89.20 E
Dhangaḍhī	124	28.41 N	80.36 E
Dhaniakhāli	126	22.58 N	88.06 E
D'Hanis	196	29.20 N	99.17 W
Dhankuṭa	124	26.59 N	87.20 E
Dhansar	272c	19.07 N	73.05 E
Dhānyahānā	272b	22.48 N	88.11 E
Dhār	120	22.36 N	75.18 E
Dharampur	122	20.32 N	73.11 E
Dharān	124	26.49 N	87.17 E
Dharangaon	120	21.01 N	75.16 E
Dhārāpuram	122	10.44 N	77.31 E
Dhāri	120	21.20 N	71.01 E
Dhārīwāl	123	31.57 N	75.19 E
Dharmābād	122	18.54 N	77.51 E
Dharmapuri	122	12.08 N	78.10 E
Dharmavaram	122	14.26 N	77.43 E
Dharmjaygarh	124	22.28 N	83.13 E
Dharmkot	123	30.57 N	75.14 E
Dharmshāla	123	32.13 N	76.19 E
Dharoor, Tog V	144	10.20 N	50.30 E
Dharug National Park ♠	170	33.25 S	151.05 E
Dhasān ≃	124	25.48 N	79.24 E
Dhātrigrām	126	23.15 N	88.20 E
Dhaulpur	124	26.42 N	77.54 E
Dhawalāgiri □[8]	124	28.30 N	83.30 E
Dhawalāgiri ∧	124	28.42 N	83.30 E
Dhebar Lake ⊜	120	24.16 N	74.00 E
Dhelfoí ⊥	38	38.30 N	22.29 E
Dhenkānāl	120	20.40 N	85.36 E
Dherínia	130	35.03 N	33.57 E
Dhërmiu ⊎[1]	38	40.08 N	19.42 E
Dherue, Loch an ⊜	46	58.25 N	4.27 W
Dheskáti	38	39.55 N	21.49 E
Dheune ≃	58	46.54 N	5.00 E
Dhiavolítsion	38	37.18 N	21.58 E
Dhībān	132	31.30 N	35.47 E
Dhidhimótikhon	38	41.21 N	26.30 E
Dhiinsoor	144	2.24 N	42.59 E
Dhíkti ∧	38	35.08 N	25.22 E
Dhílos ⊥	38	37.26 N	25.16 E
Dhimitsána	38	37.37 N	22.03 E
Dhiónisos	267c	38.06 N	23.53 E
Dhī Qār □[4]	128	31.00 N	46.15 E
Dhirāsrām	126	23.57 N	90.25 E
Dhirwah, Wādī adh- V	132	31.18 N	36.56 E
Dhodhekánisos (Dodecanese) II	38	36.30 N	27.00 E
Dhodhóni ⊥	38	39.34 N	20.47 E
Dhofar → Ẓufār ◆[1]	118	17.00 N	54.10 E
Dhokra	272b	22.40 N	88.34 E
Dholka	120	22.43 N	72.28 E
Dhomhnuill, Sgurr ∧	46	56.45 N	5.27 W
Dhone	122	15.25 N	77.53 E
Dhopākhola	126	23.08 N	89.10 E
Dhorāji	120	21.44 N	70.27 E
Dhosha	126	22.15 N	88.33 E
Dhowa	126	24.03 N	86.54 E
Dhoxáton	38	41.05 N	24.14 E
Dhrāngadhra	120	22.59 N	71.28 E
Dhrapetsóna	267c	37.57 N	23.37 E
Dhrol	120	22.34 N	70.25 E
Dhron ≃	56	49.52 N	6.54 E
Dhubāb	144	12.56 N	43.25 E
Dhuburi	124	26.01 N	89.59 E
Dhudiāl	123	33.04 N	72.58 E
Dhulāgarh	272b	22.35 N	88.11 E
Dhule	120	20.54 N	74.47 E
Dhulia → Dhule	120	20.54 N	74.47 E
Dhuliān	124	24.41 N	87.58 E
Dhulikhel	124	27.37 N	85.33 E
Dhūlsīrās ◆[8]	272a	28.33 N	77.02 E
Dhünn	56	51.06 N	7.16 E
Dhünn-Stausee ⊜[1]	263	51.05 N	7.16 E
Dhupgāri	124	26.36 N	89.01 E
Dhurbo	144	11.37 N	50.20 E
Dhūri	124	30.22 N	75.52 E
Dhutumkhar ≃	272c	18.54 N	73.00 E
Dhuudo	144	9.20 N	50.12 E
Dhuudo V	144	9.14 N	50.39 E
Dhuusa Mareeb	144	5.31 N	46.24 E
Día I	38	35.27 N	25.13 E
Diabaig	46	57.34 N	5.40 W
Diabakania	150	10.38 N	10.58 W
Diable, Île du (Devils Island) I	250	5.17 N	52.35 W
Diable, Lac du ⊜	206	46.31 N	74.20 W
Diable, Pointe du ›	240e	14.47 N	60.54 W
Diable, Rivière du ≃	206	46.03 N	74.38 W
Diables, Morne aux ∧	240d	15.37 N	61.27 W
Diablo, Ca., U.S.	226	37.50 N	121.58 W
Diablo, Wa., U.S.	224	48.43 N	121.09 W
Diablo, Canyon V	200	35.18 N	110.59 W
Diablo, Isla del → Diable, Île du I	250	5.17 N	52.35 W
Diablo, Mount ∧	226	37.53 N	121.55 W
Diablo, Pico del ∧	232	30.59 N	115.45 W
Diablo, Sierra del ⋏	196	27.20 N	104.05 W
Diablo Lake ⊜[1]	224	48.43 N	121.08 W
Diablo Plateau ⋏[1]	200	31.30 N	105.30 W
Diablo Range ⋏	226	37.00 N	121.20 W
Diablotins, Morne ∧	240d	15.30 N	61.24 W
Diabo	150	7.47 N	5.11 W
Diaca	154	11.30 S	39.59 E
Diadema	256	23.42 S	46.37 W
Diadema □[7]	287b	23.42 S	46.36 W
Diafarabé	150	14.09 N	5.01 W
Diagonal	198	40.48 N	94.20 W
Diaka ≃[1]	150	15.13 N	4.14 W
Dialakoto	150	13.19 N	13.18 W
Dialassagou	150	13.45 N	3.37 W
Diamant, Pointe du ›	240e	14.27 N	61.03 W
Diamante, Arg.	252	32.04 S	60.39 W
Diamante, It.	68	39.41 N	15.49 E
Diamante ≃	252	34.31 S	66.56 W
Diamante, Punta ›	234	16.47 N	99.52 W
Diamante de Ubá	256	21.12 S	42.55 W
Diamantina	255	18.15 S	43.36 W
Diamantina ≃	166	26.45 S	139.10 E
Diamantina Fracture Zone ✧	14	36.00 S	105.00 E
Diamantina Lakes	166	23.46 S	141.09 E
Diamantino	248	14.25 S	56.27 W
Diamantino ≃	255	16.08 S	52.28 W
Diamond, Il., U.S.	216	41.17 N	88.15 W
Diamond, Mo., U.S.	194	37.00 N	94.19 W
Diamond, Oh., U.S.	214	41.06 N	81.01 W
Diamond Bar	228	34.01 N	117.48 W
Diamond Brook ≃	276	40.56 N	74.08 W
Diamond Creek	274b	37.41 S	145.09 E
Diamond Creek ≃	169	37.44 S	145.09 E
Diamond Harbour	126	22.12 N	88.12 E
Diamond Head ≗[6]	229c	21.16 N	157.49 W
Diamond Hill	207	41.59 N	71.24 W
Diamond Hill Reservoir ⊜[1]	283	42.00 N	71.24 W
Diamond Hill State Park ♠	283	42.00 N	71.26 W
Diamond Islets II	166	17.25 S	150.58 E
Diamond Lake	216	42.15 N	88.00 W
Diamond Lake ⊜, On., Can.	212	45.04 N	78.02 W
Diamond Lake ⊜, Il., U.S.	278	42.15 N	88.00 W
Diamond Lake ⊜, Mi., U.S.	216	41.54 N	85.59 W
Diamond Lake ⊜, Or., U.S.	202	43.10 N	122.09 W
Diamond Peak ∧, Id., U.S.	202	44.09 N	113.05 W
Diamond Peak ∧, Or., U.S.	202	43.33 N	122.09 W
Diamond Peak ∧, Wa., U.S.	202	46.07 N	117.32 W
Diamond Springs	226	38.41 N	120.48 W
Diamondville	200	41.46 N	110.32 W
Diana	222	32.43 N	94.45 W
Diana Bay c	176	60.50 N	69.50 W
Dianalund	41	55.32 N	11.30 E
Dianbai	102	21.30 N	111.01 E
Dian Chi ⊜	102	24.50 N	102.42 E
Diancun	105	39.55 N	116.14 E
Dianfangba	102	32.54 N	103.35 E
Diangounté Kamara	150	14.33 N	9.31 W
Dianhu	100	33.58 N	119.38 E
Dianji	98	36.32 N	120.27 E
Dianjiang	102	30.21 N	107.23 E
Diano, Vallo di V	68	40.21 N	15.36 E
Diano Marina	62	43.54 N	8.05 E
Dianópolis	250	11.38 S	46.50 W
Dianqianhe	100	30.44 N	116.02 E
Dianra	150	8.45 N	6.14 W
Dianshang	106	31.10 N	118.51 E
Dianshan Hu ⊜	106	31.08 N	120.55 E
Diantou	100	27.18 N	120.11 E
Dianzi	104	41.37 N	122.05 E
Diaobingshan	104	42.28 N	123.33 E
Diao'ecun	105	40.43 N	115.49 E
Diaohetou	105	39.17 N	116.41 E
Diaopu	100	32.22 N	119.54 E
Diaoshuilouzi	104	40.59 N	122.22 E
Diaotai	100	29.40 N	119.39 E
Diaowo	105	39.30 N	116.04 E
Diapaga	150	12.04 N	1.47 E
Diapangou	150	12.07 N	0.11 E
Diapblo, Puntan ›	174n	15.00 N	145.35 E
Dias	256	22.28 S	45.34 W
Diascund Creek Reservoir ⊜[1]	208	37.27 N	76.54 W
Diawala	150	10.07 N	5.28 W
Diaz	194	35.38 N	91.15 W
Diaz Point ›	156	26.38 S	15.05 E
Dibai	124	28.13 N	78.15 E
Dibāng ≃	120	27.50 N	95.32 E
Dibaya	152	6.30 S	22.57 E
Dibay → Dubayy	128	25.18 N	55.18 E
Dibbīn	132	32.26 N	36.34 E
Dibble Iceberg Tongue ⍓	9	65.40 S	135.10 E
Dibeng	158	27.35 S	22.54 E
D'Iberville	194	30.25 N	88.53 W
Dibete	156	23.45 S	26.26 E
Dibi	144	4.13 N	41.56 E
Dibo	144	6.31 N	41.52 E
Diboll	222	31.11 N	94.46 W
Dibrugarh	120	27.29 N	94.54 E
Dibs	140	12.34 N	24.14 E
Dibs, Bi'r ⊤[4]	140	22.12 N	29.32 E
Dichāon Kalān ◆[8]	272a	28.39 N	76.59 E
Dick, Mount ∧[2]	168a	31.35 S	116.42 E
Dickelsbach ≃	263	51.24 N	6.45 E
Dickens	196	33.37 N	100.50 W
Dickerson	208	39.13 N	77.25 W
Dickey ≃	224	47.55 N	124.37 W
Dickey Lake ⊜, On., Can.	212	44.47 N	77.44 W
Dickey Lake ⊜, Wa., U.S.	224	48.06 N	124.31 W
Dickinson, N.D., U.S.	198	46.52 N	102.47 W
Dickinson, Pa., U.S.	208	40.07 N	77.20 W
Dickinson, Tx., U.S.	222	29.27 N	95.03 W
Dickinson Bayou ≃	222	29.28 N	94.58 W
Dickinson Island I	281	42.37 N	82.38 W
Dickins Seamount ✧[3]	16	54.30 N	137.00 W
Dicks	158	27.43 S	30.10 E
Dickson, Ok., U.S.	196	34.11 N	96.59 W
Dickson, Tn., U.S.	194	36.04 N	87.23 W
Dickson City	210	41.28 N	75.36 W
Dicle, Tür.	130	37.18 N	42.04 E
Dicle, Tür.	130	38.22 N	40.04 E
Dicle → Tigris ≃	128	31.00 N	47.25 E
Dicomano	66	43.53 N	11.31 E
Diculom	116	7.54 N	122.14 E
Dicun	100	33.46 N	117.32 E
Didam	52	51.56 N	6.08 E
Didao	89	45.22 N	130.51 E
Didbiran	89	51.58 N	139.20 E
Didcot	42	51.37 N	1.15 W
Didesa ≃	144	9.56 N	35.45 E
Didiéni	150	13.53 N	8.06 W
Didimbo	152	17.30 S	21.45 E
Didinga Hills ⋏	154	4.20 N	33.35 E
Didsbury	182	51.40 N	114.08 W
Didsbury ◆[8]	262	53.25 N	2.14 W
Diduyon ≃	116	16.36 N	121.42 E
Dīdwāna	120	27.24 N	74.34 E
Didy	157b	18.07 S	48.32 E
Die	62	44.45 N	5.22 E
Die Aue ◆[1]	263	51.40 N	6.35 E
Die Berg ∧	156	25.12 S	30.09 E
Die Boss	158	31.59 S	19.44 E
Diébougou	150	10.58 N	3.15 W
Dieburg	56	49.54 N	8.50 E
Dieciocho de Julio	252	33.41 S	53.33 W
Diecke	150	7.21 N	8.58 W
Diedenhofen → Thionville	56	49.22 N	6.10 E
Diedersdorf	264a	52.20 N	13.21 E
Die Erpe ≃	264a	52.27 N	13.38 E
Diefenbaker, Lake ⊜[1]	184	51.00 N	106.55 W
Diego de Almagro	252	26.23 S	70.03 W
Diego de Almagro, Isla I	254	51.25 S	75.10 W
Diego de Ocampo, Pico ∧	238	19.35 N	70.45 W
Diego Garcia I	12	7.20 S	72.25 E
Diego Gaynor	258	34.17 S	59.14 W
Diego Pérez, Cayería de II	240p	22.05 N	81.40 W
Diego Ramírez, Islas II	244	56.30 S	68.44 W
Die Haard ◆[1]	263	51.41 N	7.15 E
Diekirch	56	49.53 N	6.10 E
Dieksee ⊜	54	54.10 N	10.30 E
Dieleemu	86	46.22 N	88.43 E
Dielingen	52	52.26 N	8.20 E
Dielsdorf	58	47.29 N	8.27 E
Diéma	150	14.32 N	9.12 W
Diemansputs	158	29.54 S	21.33 E
Diembéring	150	12.28 N	16.47 W
Diemel ≃	52	51.39 N	9.27 E
Diemel-Talsperre ◆[6]	56	51.22 N	8.43 E
Diemen	52	52.20 N	4.58 E
Diemuchuoke	120	32.42 N	79.29 E
Dien Bien Phu	110	21.23 N	103.01 E
Dien Khanh	110	12.15 N	109.06 E
Diepenau	52	52.25 N	8.44 E
Diepenbeek	56	50.54 N	5.24 E
Diepenheim	52	52.12 N	6.33 E
Diepensee	264a	52.22 N	13.31 E
Diepenveen	52	52.18 N	6.08 E
Diepholz	52	52.35 N	8.21 E
Diepoldsau	58	47.23 N	9.38 E
Dieppe, N.B., Can.	186	46.06 N	64.45 W
Dieppe, Fr.	50	49.56 N	1.05 E
Dierbao	98	40.20 N	114.32 E
Dierdorf	56	50.33 N	7.39 E
Dieren	52	52.03 N	6.06 E
Dierhagen	54	45.18 N	12.21 E
Dierks	194	34.07 N	94.00 W
Diersbach	60	48.25 N	13.34 E
Diersfordt	263	51.42 N	6.33 E
Di'er Songhua ≃	89	45.26 N	124.39 E
Diesdorf	54	52.45 N	10.52 E
Dieskau	54	51.26 N	12.02 E
Diessem ◆[8]	263	51.20 N	6.35 E
Diessen	64	47.56 N	11.06 E
Diessenhofen	58	47.41 N	8.45 E
Diest	56	50.59 N	5.03 E
Dietenheim	58	48.12 N	10.04 E
Dietersburg	60	48.30 N	12.55 E
Dietersdorf	56	50.13 N	10.49 E
Dietfurt	56	48.57 N	10.56 E
Dietfurt an der Altmühl	60	49.02 N	11.35 E
Dietikon	58	47.24 N	8.24 E
Dietmannsried	58	47.49 N	10.17 E
Dietrich	202	42.54 N	114.15 W
Dietzenbach	56	50.01 N	8.47 E
Dietzhölztal	56	50.50 N	8.19 E
Dieue-sur-Meuse	56	49.04 N	5.25 E
Dieulefit	62	44.31 N	5.04 E
Dieulouard	56	48.51 N	6.04 E
Dieuze	56	48.49 N	6.43 E
Dieveniškės	76	54.12 N	25.37 E
Diever	52	52.52 N	6.19 E
Die Ville ⋏[2]	56	50.40 N	6.55 E
Die Wurzen (Koren))(	64	46.31 N	13.45 E
Diez	56	50.22 N	8.01 E
Diez de Octubre	232	24.44 N	104.39 W
Dif	144	0.59 N	40.57 E
Difang	98	35.23 N	117.52 E
Diffa	146	13.19 N	12.37 E
Diffa □[5]	146	16.00 N	13.30 E
Differdange	56	49.32 N	5.52 E
Difficult Run ≃	284c	38.58 N	77.14 W
Diffun	116	16.34 N	121.33 E
Difuri I	122	5.24 N	73.38 E
Digambar Jain Temple ⊎[1]	272b	22.36 N	88.23 E
Digambarpur	126	21.57 N	88.22 E
Digba	154	4.24 N	25.47 E
Digboi	120	27.23 N	95.38 E
Digby	186	44.37 N	65.46 W
Digby Neck ›[1]	186	44.30 N	66.10 W
Dige	98	34.22 N	114.28 E
Digerberget ∧[2]	40	60.35 N	13.25 E
Digges Islands II	176	62.35 N	77.50 W
Diggle	262	53.34 N	1.59 W
Dighalia	126	23.07 N	89.39 E
Dighipāra	126	21.58 N	88.17 E
Dighode	272c	18.54 N	73.02 E
Dighra	272b	22.47 N	88.32 E
Dighton, Ks., U.S.	198	38.28 N	100.28 W
Dighton, Ma., U.S.	207	41.48 N	71.07 W
Di Giorgio	228	35.15 N	118.51 W
Dīglūr	122	18.33 N	77.36 E
Digmoor	262	53.32 N	2.45 W
Dīgnagar	126	23.27 N	87.41 E
Dignano	64	46.05 N	12.56 E
Digne	62	44.06 N	6.14 E
Digoin	32	46.29 N	3.59 E
Digomi	84	41.47 N	44.44 E
Digong	104	42.11 N	122.03 E
Digor	84	40.23 N	43.24 E
Digora	84	43.10 N	44.09 E
Digos	116	6.45 N	125.20 E
Digra	272b	22.50 N	88.20 E
Digras	122	20.07 N	77.43 E
Digri	120	25.10 N	69.07 E
Digui	152	5.28 N	20.50 E
Digul ≃	164	7.07 S	138.42 E
Dihaer	86	42.35 N	89.49 E
Dihun	144	7.18 N	42.42 E
Diirmentobe	86	45.44 N	63.37 E
Dijag	24	65.48 N	57.39 E
Dijlah, Wādī V	142	29.58 N	31.18 E
Dijlah → Tigris ≃	128	31.00 N	47.25 E
Dijle (Dyle) ≃	56	50.53 N	4.42 E
Dijohan Point ›	116	16.19 N	122.14 E
Dijon	58	47.19 N	5.01 E
Dik	146	9.58 N	17.31 E
Dikaja	76	59.15 N	39.30 E
Dikala	154	4.41 N	31.23 E
Dikan'ka	78	49.49 N	34.32 E
Dikbıyık	130	41.13 N	36.38 E
Dike	190	42.27 N	92.37 W
Dikhil	144	11.06 N	42.22 E
Dikili	130	39.04 N	26.53 E
Dikirnis	142	31.05 N	31.35 E
Dikli	76	57.35 N	25.06 E
Diklosmta, gora ∧	84	42.29 N	45.47 E
Dikmen	130	39.53 N	32.50 E
Dikodougou	150	9.04 N	5.46 W
Diksmuide (Dixmude)	50	51.02 N	2.52 E
Dikson	74	73.30 N	80.35 E
Dikwa	146	12.02 N	13.56 E
Dila	144	6.21 N	38.17 E
Dilbeek	50	50.51 N	4.16 E
Dilektepe	130	38.04 N	41.49 E
Dile Point ›	116	17.34 N	120.20 E
Dilerpur	272b	22.51 N	88.10 E
Dili	112	8.33 S	125.35 E
Dilia V	146	16.53 N	11.00 E
Diligent Strait ʯ	110	12.11 N	92.57 E
Di Linh	110	11.35 N	108.04 E
Diližan	84	40.45 N	44.52 E
Diližanskij zapovednik ♠	84	40.40 N	45.00 E
Dill ≃	56	50.33 N	8.29 E
Dill City	196	35.16 N	99.08 W
Dillenburg	56	50.44 N	8.17 E
Diller	198	40.06 N	96.56 W
Dilley, Or., U.S.	224	45.29 N	123.07 W
Dilley, Tx., U.S.	196	28.40 N	99.10 W
Dilling	140	12.03 N	29.39 E
Dillingen	56	49.21 N	6.44 E
Dillingen an der Donau	56	48.34 N	10.29 E
Dillingham	180	59.02 N	158.29 W
Dillon, Co., U.S.	200	39.37 N	106.02 W
Dillon, Mt., U.S.	202	45.12 N	112.38 W
Dillon, S.C., U.S.	192	34.24 N	79.22 W
Dillon ≃	184	55.56 N	108.57 W
Dillon Cone ∧	172	42.16 S	173.13 E
Dillon Lake ⊜	184	55.45 N	109.30 W
Dillon Lake ⊜[1]	188	40.02 N	82.10 W
Dillon Mountain ∧	200	33.51 N	108.48 W
Dillon Reservoir ⊜[1]	200	39.35 N	106.02 W
Dillon State Park ♠	188	40.03 N	82.08 W
Dillonvale	214	40.11 N	80.46 W
Dillsboro	218	39.01 N	85.03 W
Dillsburg	208	40.06 N	77.02 W
Dilltown	214	40.29 N	79.00 W
Dillwyn	192	37.32 N	78.27 W
Dilly	150	15.01 N	7.40 W
Dilolo	152	10.42 S	22.20 E
Dilsen	56	51.02 N	5.44 E
Dilworth	198	46.52 N	96.42 W
Dilworthtown	285	39.54 N	75.34 W
Dima, Ang.	152	15.27 S	20.10 E
Dima, Indon.	114	1.20 N	97.20 E
Dimāpur	120	25.54 N	93.44 E
Dimaro	64	46.20 N	10.52 E
Dimasalang	116	12.12 N	123.51 E
Dimashq (Damascus)	132	33.30 N	36.18 E
Dimashq □[8]	132	33.30 N	37.00 E
Dimass, Rass ›	36	35.37 N	11.03 E
Dimataling	116	7.32 N	123.22 E
Dimbelenge	152	5.33 S	23.07 E
Dimbokro	150	6.39 N	4.42 W
Dimboola	166	36.27 S	142.02 E
Dîmbovița □[6]	38	45.00 N	25.30 E
Dîmbovița ≃	38	44.14 N	26.27 E
Dimbulah	166	17.09 S	145.07 E
Dime	144	6.16 N	36.20 E
Dime Box	222	30.21 N	96.50 W
Dimitrov	83	48.15 N	37.18 E
Dimitrovgrad, Blg.	38	42.03 N	25.36 E
Dimitrovgrad, Jugo.	38	43.01 N	22.47 E
Dimitrovgrad, Ross.	80	54.14 N	49.39 E
Dimitrovo	78	48.36 N	33.01 E
Dimitrovo → Pernik	38	42.36 N	23.02 E
Dimitrovskoje	85	40.16 N	69.03 E
Dimlang ∧	146	8.24 N	11.47 E
Dimmitt	196	34.33 N	102.18 W
Dimo	154	5.19 N	29.10 E
Dimock	210	41.45 N	75.32 W
Dimona	132	31.04 N	35.02 E
Dimondale	216	42.38 N	84.38 W
Dina	123	33.02 N	73.36 E
Dinach	144	9.15 N	50.37 E
Dinagat	116	9.59 N	125.35 E
Dinagat Island I	116	10.12 N	125.35 E
Dinagat Sound ʯ	116	9.59 N	125.50 E
Dinahican Point ›	116	14.42 N	121.44 E
Dinājpur	124	25.38 N	88.38 E
Dinalupihan	116	14.52 N	120.28 E
Dinamarca, Estrecho de → Denmark Strait ʯ	10	67.00 N	25.00 W
Dinamarca → Denmark □[1]	26	56.00 N	10.00 E
Dinami	68	38.31 N	16.09 E
Dinamita	196	25.43 N	103.38 W
Dinamo	80	50.15 N	41.38 E
Dinan	32	48.27 N	2.02 W
Dīnānagar	123	32.09 N	75.28 E
Dinant	56	50.16 N	4.55 E
Dinar	130	38.04 N	30.10 E
Dinara ⋏	36	43.50 N	16.35 E
Dinard	32	48.38 N	2.04 W
Dinaric Alps → Dinara ⋏	36	43.50 N	16.35 E
Dinarische Alpen → Dinara ⋏	36	43.50 N	16.35 E
Dinas, Pil.	116	7.38 N	123.20 E
Dinas, Wales, U.K.	42	52.00 N	4.54 W
Dinas Head ›	42	52.02 N	4.55 W
Dinas Powys	42	51.26 N	3.14 W
Dindanko	150	14.08 N	9.30 W
Dindar, Nahr ad- (Dinder) ≃	140	14.06 N	33.40 E
Dīndārpur ◆[8]	272a	28.36 N	76.59 E
Dinde	152	14.12 S	13.44 E
Dinder (Nahr ad-Dindar) ≃	140	14.06 N	33.40 E
Dinder National Park ♠	140	12.40 N	35.20 E
Dindi ≃	122	16.21 N	79.13 E
Dindigul	122	10.21 N	77.57 E
Dindima	150	10.18 N	10.12 E
Dindori	124	22.57 N	81.05 E
Dineksaray	130	37.23 N	32.37 E
Dinga, Pāk.	120	25.26 N	67.10 E
Dinga, Pāk.	123	32.38 N	73.43 E
Dinga, Zaïre	152	5.19 S	16.34 E
Dingalan Bay c	116	15.18 N	121.25 E
Ding'an	110	19.44 N	110.21 E
Dingba	154	3.24 N	27.55 E
Dingbian	102	37.40 N	107.41 E
Dingbianji	102	36.37 N	108.41 E
Dingbu	106	31.18 N	119.10 E
Dingden	52	51.46 N	6.37 E
Dinge	152	4.58 S	12.22 E
Dingelsdorf	58	47.44 N	9.09 E
Dingelstädt	54	51.18 N	10.19 E
Dingelstedt	54	51.58 N	10.58 E
Dingeryu	105	39.37 N	114.55 E
Dingfeng	106	31.20 N	121.45 E
Dinggou	100	32.34 N	119.39 E
Dinggyê	124	28.29 N	88.06 E
Dinghai	100	30.02 N	122.06 E
Dingila	154	3.39 N	26.22 E
Dingjia	107	29.24 N	106.09 E
Dingjiagou	104	40.40 N	122.35 E
Dingjiandian	106	32.06 N	120.52 E
Dingjiasuo	100	32.32 N	120.40 E
Dingjiazhuang	106	32.11 N	120.16 E
Dingkouzhen	102	39.55 N	106.40 E
Dingle	48	52.08 N	10.15 W
Dingle ◆[8]	262	53.23 N	2.57 W
Dingle Bay c	48	52.05 N	10.15 W
Dingley	274b	37.58 S	145.07 E
Dinglingen	58	48.20 N	7.50 E
Dingman Creek ≃	212	42.55 N	81.25 W
Dingmans Ferry	210	41.14 N	74.53 W
Dingnan	100	24.48 N	114.59 E
Dingnan ≃	100	24.28 N	115.26 E
Dingo	166	23.39 S	149.20 E
Dingolfing	60	48.38 N	12.31 E
Dingras	116	18.06 N	120.42 E
Dingshuzhen	106	31.17 N	119.50 E
Dingtao	98	35.04 N	115.34 E
Dingtuna	40	59.34 N	16.22 E
Dinguira	150	14.11 N	11.16 W
Dinguiraye	150	11.18 N	10.43 W
Dingwall, N.S., Can.	186	46.54 N	60.28 W
Dingwall, Scot., U.K.	46	57.35 N	4.29 W
Dingxi	102	35.33 N	104.32 E
Dingxian	98	38.32 N	114.59 E
Dingxiang	102	38.30 N	113.00 E
Dingxiao	102	25.13 N	105.07 E
Dingxing	105	39.17 N	115.46 E
Dingyan	100	32.23 N	120.45 E
Dingyuan	100	32.32 N	117.40 E
Dingzhouying	105	40.20 N	115.43 E
Dingzichang	107	28.54 N	106.08 E
Dingzi Gang c	98	36.37 N	120.50 E
Dinh, Mui ›	110	11.22 N	109.01 E
Dinhāta	124	26.08 N	89.28 E
Dinh Ca	110	21.45 N	106.03 E
Dinh Lap	110	21.33 N	107.06 E
Dinin ≃	48	52.43 N	7.18 W
Dinkel ≃	52	52.30 N	6.58 E
Dinkelsbühl	56	49.04 N	10.19 E
Dinkelscherben	58	48.21 N	10.35 E
Dinkey Creek ≃	226	36.54 N	119.07 W
Dinklage	52	52.40 N	8.07 E
Dinnebito Wash V	200	35.29 N	111.14 W
Dinner Point ›	220	28.28 N	82.41 W
Dinnet	46	57.03 N	2.54 W
Dinnington	44	53.22 N	1.12 W
Dinokwe	156	23.24 S	26.40 E
Dinorwic	184	49.41 N	92.30 W
Dinorwic Lake ⊜	184	49.37 N	92.33 W
Dinosaur	200	40.14 N	109.00 W
Dinosaur Lake ⊜[1]	182	55.57 N	122.07 W
Dinosaur National Monument ♠	200	40.32 N	108.58 W
Dinosaur Provincial Park ♠	182	50.45 N	111.30 W
Dinskaja	78	45.13 N	39.14 E
Dinslaken	52	51.34 N	6.44 E
Dinslakener Bruch	263	51.35 N	6.43 E
Dinslaken-Schwarze Heide, Flughafen ⊠	263	51.37 N	6.51 E
Dinsmore	184	51.20 N	107.26 W
Dintel ≃	52	51.39 N	4.22 E
Dinteloord	52	51.37 N	4.22 E
Dinuba	226	36.32 N	119.23 W
Dinwiddie, S. Afr.	273d	26.16 S	28.10 E
Dinwiddie, Va., U.S.	208	37.04 N	77.35 W
Dinwiddie □[6]	208	37.10 N	77.20 W
Dinxperlo	52	51.52 N	6.29 E
Diö	26	56.38 N	14.13 E
Diobo	152	2.16 N	20.29 E
Dioïla	150	12.29 N	6.48 W
Diois □[9]	62	44.40 N	5.20 E
Diomede	180	65.47 N	169.00 W
Dion ≃	150	10.12 N	8.39 W
Dionísio	255	19.49 S	42.45 W
Dionísio Cerqueira	252	26.15 S	53.38 W
Dionne, Lac ⊜	186	49.26 N	67.55 W
Dions	62	43.56 N	4.19 E
Diorama	255	16.21 S	51.14 W
Dios	175e	5.33 S	154.58 E
Dios, Cayos de II	240p	21.39 N	81.09 W
Diósd	264c	47.25 N	18.57 E
Diouloulou	150	13.03 N	16.36 W
Dioumanténé	150	10.32 N	5.55 W
Dioundiou	150	12.37 N	3.33 E
Dioungani	150	14.19 N	2.44 W
Dioura	150	14.50 N	5.15 W
Diourbel	150	14.40 N	16.15 W
Diourbel □[4]	150	14.45 N	16.30 W
Dipaculao	116	15.51 N	121.32 E
Dipai	100	23.50 N	114.06 E
Dīpālpur	123	30.40 N	73.39 E
Dipignano	68	39.15 N	16.15 E
Dipilo, Pizzo ∧	70	37.57 N	13.59 E
Dipkarpaz	130	35.36 N	34.23 E
Diplo	120	24.28 N	69.35 E
Dipolog	116	8.35 N	123.20 E
Dippoldiswalde	54	50.54 N	13.40 E
Dipton	172	45.54 S	168.22 E
Dipu	106	30.38 N	119.41 E
Diqiyingzi	104	42.11 N	121.29 E
Dique Florentino Ameghino	254	43.40 S	66.25 W
Dīr	123	35.12 N	71.53 E
Dira, Djebel ∧	34	36.05 N	3.38 E
Diré	150	16.16 N	3.24 W
Direction, Cape ›	164	12.51 S	143.32 E
Dire Dawa	144	9.37 N	41.52 E
Direkli	130	39.43 N	36.40 E
Diriamba	236	11.51 N	86.14 W
Dirico	152	17.58 S	20.47 E
Dirillo, Lago ⊜	70	37.08 N	14.42 E
Diriomo	236	11.52 N	86.03 W
Dirj	146	30.09 N	10.26 E
Dirk Hartog Island I	162	25.48 S	113.00 E
Dirkiesdorp	158	27.10 S	30.25 E
Dirkou	146	19.01 N	12.53 E
Dirkshorn	52	52.45 N	4.45 E
Dirksland	52	51.44 N	4.06 E
Dirnaich	60	48.27 N	12.30 E
Dirrah	140	13.37 N	26.06 E
Dirranbandi	166	28.35 S	148.14 E
Dirri	144	4.20 N	46.37 E
Dirs	144	18.32 N	42.05 E
Dirschau → Tczew	30	54.06 N	18.47 E
Dirty Devil ≃	200	37.53 N	110.24 W
Dīsa	120	24.15 N	72.10 E
Dīsah	140	12.02 N	34.19 E
Disappointment, Cape ›, S. Geor.	244	54.53 S	36.07 W
Disappointment, Cape ›, Wa., U.S.	224	46.18 N	124.03 W
Disappointment, Lake ⊜	162	23.30 S	122.50 E
Disappointment, Mount ∧	169	37.25 S	145.18 E
Disappointment Creek ≃	200	38.01 N	108.51 W
Disaster Bay c	166	37.17 S	150.00 E
Disautel	182	48.22 N	119.14 W
Disbrow Drain ≋	281	42.06 N	83.27 W
Disco	214	42.41 N	83.02 W
Discovery	273d	26.10 S	27.54 E
Discovery Bay c, Austl.	166	38.12 S	141.07 E
Discovery Bay c, H.K.	271d	22.18 N	114.01 E
Discovery Bay c, Wa., U.S.	224	48.05 N	122.52 W
Discovery Island I	224	48.25 N	123.15 W
Discovery Passage ʯ	182	50.00 N	125.15 W
Discovery Tablemount ✧[3]	8	42.00 S	0.10 E
Disentis	58	46.43 N	8.51 E
Dishāshah	142	28.59 N	30.51 E
Dishergarh	126	23.41 N	86.50 E
Dishman	202	47.39 N	117.16 W
Dishnā	140	26.07 N	32.28 E
Dishna ≃	180	63.37 N	157.18 W
Disihao	89	50.28 N	124.35 E
Disko	216	41.00 N	85.57 W
Disko I	176	69.50 N	53.30 W
Disko Bugt c	176	69.15 N	52.00 W
Disley	262	53.21 N	2.02 W
Disley Tunnel ◆[5]	262	53.22 N	2.03 W
Dismal ≃	198	41.50 N	100.05 W
Dismal Lakes ⊜	176	67.26 N	117.07 W
Dismal Swamp Canal ≋	208	36.45 N	76.20 W
Disna	76	55.33 N	28.10 E
Disna ≃	76	55.34 N	28.12 E
Disney	196	36.28 N	95.00 W
Disneyland ♠	228	33.48 N	117.55 W
Disneyworld ♠	220	28.27 N	81.28 W
Diso	68	40.00 N	18.23 E
Dispur	120	26.08 N	91.47 E
Disputanta	208	37.07 N	77.13 W
Disraeli	206	45.54 N	71.21 W
Diss	42	52.23 N	1.07 E
Dissen	52	52.07 N	8.12 E
Dissimieux, Lac ⊜	186	49.51 N	69.48 W
Distant	214	40.58 N	79.21 W
Disteghil Sār ∧	123	36.19 N	75.12 E
Disteln	263	51.36 N	7.09 E
Distington	44	54.36 N	3.32 W
District Heights	284c	38.51 N	76.53 W
District of Columbia □[3]	208	38.54 N	77.01 W
Distrito Especial □[5]	246	4.15 N	74.15 W
Distrito Federal □[5], Arg.	258	34.36 S	58.26 W
Distrito Federal □[5], Bra.	255	15.45 S	47.45 W
Distrito Federal □[5], Méx.	234	19.15 N	99.10 W
Distrito Federal □[5], Ven.	246	10.30 N	66.55 W
Distroff	56	49.20 N	6.16 E

DEUTSCH

Name	Seite	Breite°′	Länge°′ E = Ost
Disūq	142	31.08 N	30.39 E
Ditfurt	54	51.50 N	11.11 E
Dithmarschen ◆[1]	30	54.05 N	9.00 E
Dit Island I	116	11.15 N	120.56 E
Dittáino ≃	70	37.25 N	15.00 E
Ditton, Eng., U.K.	260	51.18 N	0.27 E
Ditton, Eng., U.K.	262	53.22 N	2.45 W
Ditton ≃	206	45.23 N	71.12 W
Ditton Priors	42	52.30 N	2.35 W
Ditzingen	56	48.49 N	9.03 E
Ditzum	52	53.18 N	7.16 E
Diu	120	20.42 N	70.59 E
Diu □[8]	120	20.42 N	70.59 E
Diuata Mountains ⋏	116	9.10 N	125.47 E
Diuata Point ›	116	9.05 N	125.12 E
Dīva	272c	19.09 N	72.59 E
Divalá	236	8.25 N	82.43 W
Dīvāndarreh	128	35.55 N	47.02 E
Dívčice	61	49.06 N	14.19 E
Dive	272c	19.11 N	73.02 E
Divejevo	80	55.03 N	43.15 E
Divenié	152	2.41 S	12.05 E
Divenskaja	76	59.12 N	30.01 E
Diveria ≃	58	46.09 N	8.19 E
Divernon	219	39.33 N	89.39 W
Dives ≃	32	49.19 N	0.05 W
Diviči	84	41.12 N	48.59 E
Dividing Creek	208	39.16 N	75.06 W
Dividing Creek ≃	208	38.05 N	75.32 W
Dividing Ridge ∧	219	39.07 N	90.39 W
Divignano	266b	45.40 N	8.36 E
Divilacan Bay c	116	17.25 N	122.19 E
Divin	78	51.58 N	24.35 E
Divine Corners	210	41.48 N	74.40 W
Divinhe	156	20.40 S	34.49 E
Divino	255	20.37 S	42.09 W
Divinolândia	256	21.40 S	46.45 W
Divinópolis	255	20.09 S	44.54 W
Divion	50	50.28 N	2.30 E
Divi Point ›	122	15.58 N	81.09 E
Divis ∧[2]	48	54.37 N	6.01 W
Divisa Nova	256	21.31 S	46.12 W
Divisor, Serra do (Cordillera Ultraoriental) ⋏[1]	248	8.20 S	73.30 W
Divizija	78	45.57 N	29.59 E
Divnogorsk	86	55.58 N	92.22 E
Divnoje	80	45.55 N	43.22 E
Divo	150	5.50 N	5.22 W
Divodar	120	24.06 N	71.47 E
Divonne-les-Bains	58	46.22 N	6.08 E
Divriği	130	39.23 N	38.07 E
Dīwāl Qol	120	34.19 N	67.54 E
Dix, Il., U.S.	219	38.27 N	88.56 W
Dix, Ne., U.S.	198	41.14 N	103.29 W
Dix ≃	192	37.49 N	84.43 W
Dix, Lac des ⊜	58	46.03 N	7.24 E
Dixboro	216	42.19 N	83.39 W
Dixfield	188	44.32 N	70.27 W
Dix Hills	276	40.49 N	73.22 W
Dixie	275b	43.36 N	79.36 W
Dixie Valley V	204	39.50 N	117.55 W
Dix Milles, Lac ⊜	190	46.46 N	77.45 W
Dixmoor	278	41.38 N	87.40 W
Dixmude → Diksmuide	50	51.02 N	2.52 E
Dixon, Ca., U.S.	226	38.19 N	121.49 W
Dixon, Il., U.S.	190	41.50 N	89.28 W
Dixon, Ky., U.S.	194	37.31 N	87.41 W
Dixon, Mo., U.S.	194	37.59 N	92.05 W
Dixon, N.M., U.S.	200	36.11 N	105.53 W
Dixon, Oh., U.S.	216	40.57 N	84.48 W
Dixon Entrance ʯ	182	54.25 N	132.30 W
Dixons Mills	194	32.04 N	87.47 W
Dixons Pond ⊜	276	40.56 N	74.27 W
Dixonville	214	40.42 N	79.00 W
Dixville	206	45.04 N	71.46 W
Diyā al-Kawm	142	30.38 N	31.05 E
Diyadin	84	39.33 N	43.41 E
Diyālā □[4]	128	34.00 N	45.00 E
Diyālā (Sīrvān) ≃	128	33.14 N	44.31 E
Diyanga	152	1.29 S	11.52 E
Diyarbakır	130	37.55 N	40.14 E
Diyarbakır □[4]	130	38.05 N	40.15 E
Diyarb Najm	142	30.45 N	31.26 E
Diyu al-Wasta	142	30.54 N	31.30 E
Dizangsi	104	41.26 N	120.57 E
Dizhou	102	23.00 N	106.20 E
Dizy	50	49.04 N	3.58 E
Dizzard Point ›	42	50.45 N	4.38 W
Dja ≃	152	2.02 N	15.12 E
Dja, Réserve du ◆[4]	152	3.05 N	13.00 E
Djabalpur → Jabalpur	124	23.10 N	79.57 E
Djabir	152	0.32 N	24.05 E
Djadié ≃	152	0.46 N	12.58 E
Djado	146	21.01 N	12.18 E
Djado, Plateau du ⋏[1]	146	21.45 N	12.50 E
Djaipur → Jaipur	120	26.55 N	75.49 E
Djakarta → Jakarta	269e	6.10 S	106.48 E
Djakonovo	82	54.34 N	38.20 E
Djakovka	80	50.43 N	46.46 E
Djakovo	83	47.57 N	39.09 E
Djakovo ◆[8]	265b	55.39 N	37.40 E
Djamâa	148	33.32 N	6.00 E
Djamba, Ang.	152	16.46 S	13.59 E
Djamba, Zaïre	152	9.49 S	22.07 E
Djambala	152	2.33 S	14.45 E
Djamschedpur → Jamshedpur	126	22.48 N	86.11 E
Djanet	148	24.34 N	9.29 E
Djaouro Mbali	152	5.52 N	13.29 E
Djaret, Oued V	148	26.32 N	1.30 E
Djebobo ∧	150	8.20 N	0.35 E
Djébrène	146	11.14 N	19.01 E
Djédaa	146	13.31 N	18.34 E
Djedda → Jiddah	144	21.30 N	39.12 E
Djedi, Oued V	148	34.28 N	6.05 E
Djéké Djéké	146	8.25 N	18.12 E
Djelo-Binza	273b	4.23 S	15.16 E
Djema	140	6.03 N	25.19 E
Djember	146	10.25 N	17.50 E
Djember → Jember	115a	8.10 S	113.42 E
Djemila ⊥	34	36.25 N	5.44 E
Djénné	150	13.54 N	4.33 W
Djenoun, Garet el ∧	148	25.05 N	5.25 E
Djérem ≃	152	5.20 N	13.24 E
Djibasso	150	13.07 N	4.10 W
Djibo	150	14.06 N	1.38 W
Djibouti	144	11.36 N	43.09 E
Djibouti □[1], Afr.	136	11.30 N	43.00 E
Djibouti □[1], Afr.	144	11.30 N	43.00 E
Djibrouïa	150	13.13 N	11.14 W
Djiri	273b	4.08 S	15.19 E
Djiri ≃	273b	4.11 S	15.20 E
Djohong	152	6.50 N	14.42 E
Djokjakarta → Yogyakarta	115a	7.48 S	110.22 E
Djokoumatombi	152	0.47 N	15.22 E
Djokupunda	152	5.27 S	20.58 E
Djolu	152	0.37 N	22.21 E
Djombo	152	1.21 N	20.22 E
Djoua ≃	152	1.13 N	13.12 E
Djouari ≃	273b	4.13 S	15.08 E
Djoubissi	152	6.12 N	20.45 E
Djoué ≃	273b	4.19 S	15.14 E
Djougou	150	9.42 N	1.40 E
Djoum	152	2.40 N	12.40 E
Djouna	146	10.27 N	20.04 E
Djourab, Erg du ≗[8]	146	16.40 N	18.50 E
Djugu	154	1.55 N	30.30 E
Djúpivogur	24a	64.40 N	14.10 W
Djura	40	60.37 N	15.00 E
Djurås	40	60.33 N	15.08 E
Djurmo	40	60.33 N	15.10 E
Djurö	40	59.19 N	18.41 E
Djurö I	26	58.52 N	13.28 E
Djursholm	40	59.24 N	18.05 E
Dlouhá Ves	60	49.12 N	13.31 E

Symbols in the index entries represent the broad categories identified in the key at the right. Symbols with superior numbers (⋏[1]) identify subcategories (see complete key on page *I · 1).*

Symbole im Register stellen die rechts im Schlüssel erklärten Kategorien dar. Symbole mit hochgestellten Ziffern (⋏[1]) bezeichnen Unterabteilungen einer Kategorie (vgl. vollständiger Schlüssel auf Seite *I · 1).*

Los símbolos incluídos en el texto del índice representan las grandes categorias identificadas con la clave a la derecha. Los símbolos con numeros en su parte superior (⋏[1]) identifican las subcategorías (véase la clave completa en la página *I · 1).*

Les symboles de l'index représentent les catégories indiquées dans la légende à droite. Les symboles suivis d'un indice (⋏[1]) représentent des sous-catégories (voir légende complète à la page *I · 1).*

Os símbolos incluídos no texto do índice representam as grandes categorias identificadas com a chave à direita. Os símbolos com números em sua parte superior (⋏[1]) identificam as subcategorias (veja-se a chave completa à página *I · 1).*

∧ Mountain	Berg	Montaña	Montagne	Montanha
⋏ Mountains	Gebirge	Montañas	Montagnes	Montanhas
)(Pass	Paß	Paso	Col	Passo
V Valley, Canyon	Tal, Cañon	Valle, Cañón	Vallée, Canyon	Vale, Canhão
≚ Plain	Ebene	Llano	Plaine	Planície
› Cape	Kap	Cabo	Cap	Cabo
I Island	Insel	Isla	Île	Ilha
II Islands	Inseln	Islas	Îles	Ilhas
≗ Other Topographic Features	Andere Topographische Objekte	Otros Elementos Topográficos	Autres données topographiques	Outros acidentes topográficos

ESPAÑOL Nombre	Página	Lat.° '	Long.° ' W=Oeste
Dmanisi	84	41.22 N	44.12 E
Dmitr'ašovka	76	52.09 N	39.04 E
Dmitrija Lapteva, proliv ≈	74	73.00 N	142.00 E
Dmitrijevka, Kaz.	85	43.30 N	77.02 E
Dmitrijevka, Ross.	76	52.53 N	40.47 E
Dmitrijevka, Ross.	86	55.10 N	75.36 E
Dmitrijevka, Ukr.	78	50.56 N	32.58 E
Dmitrijevka, Ukr.	83	48.55 N	39.10 E
Dmitrijevka, Ukr.	83	47.56 N	38.56 E
Dmitrijev-L'govskij	78	52.08 N	35.05 E
Dmitrijevskij	86	49.08 N	57.50 E
Dmitrijevskoje, Ross.	85	45.48 N	41.54 E
Dmitrijevskoje, Ross.	82	54.40 N	37.38 E
Dmitriev Usad, Ross.	76	54.08 N	43.08 E
Dmitriev Usad, Ross.	80	54.14 N	43.18 E
Dmitrijevy Gory	80	55.12 N	41.47 E
Dmitrov	82	56.21 N	37.31 E
Dmitrovcy	82	55.16 N	38.55 E
Dmitroviči	78	53.59 N	29.06 E
Dmitrovka, Ukr.	78	48.48 N	32.44 E
Dmitrovka, Ukr.	78	45.29 N	35.04 E
Dmitrovka, Ukr.	78	46.51 N	36.35 E
Dmitrovskij Pogost	76	55.19 N	39.49 E
Dmitrovsk-Orlovskij	78	52.30 N	35.09 E
Dmuchajlovka	78	49.03 N	34.46 E
Dnepr ≈	78	46.30 N	32.18 E
Dnepr'any	78	46.44 N	33.16 E
Dneprodzeržinsk	78	48.30 N	34.37 E
Dneprodzeržinskoje vodochranilišče �container	78	48.45 N	34.00 E
Dnepropetrovsk	78	48.27 N	34.59 E
Dneprovka	78	47.26 N	34.38 E
Dneprovskij liman c	78	46.35 N	31.55 E
Dneprovsko-Bugskij kanal ≈	78	52.03 N	25.35 E
Dneprovskoje	76	55.40 N	33.55 E
Dnestr ≈	78	46.18 N	30.17 E
Dnestrovskij liman c	78	46.15 N	30.17 E
Dnieper — Dnepr ≈	78	46.30 N	32.18 E
Dniepropetrovsk — Dnepropetrovsk	78	48.27 N	34.59 E
Dniester — Dnestr ≈	78	46.18 N	30.17 E
Dno	76	57.50 N	29.59 E
Do, Lac ⌷	150	15.54 N	2.45 W
Doa	154	16.44 S	34.32 E
Do Ãb-e Mīkh-e Zarrīn	120	35.16 N	68.00 E
Doaktown	186	46.33 N	66.08 W
Doangdoangan-Besar, Pulau I	112	5.24 S	117.55 E
Doany	157b	14.22 S	49.31 E
Doba	146	8.39 N	16.51 E
Dobane	140	6.24 N	24.42 E
Dobbertin	54	53.37 N	12.04 E
Dobbiaco (Toblach)	64	46.44 N	12.14 E
Dobbins	222	30.22 N	95.46 W
Dobbins Air Force Base ⥼	192	33.54 N	84.31 W
Dobbs Ferry	210	41.00 N	73.52 W
Dobczyce	30	49.54 N	20.06 E
Dobel	56	48.48 N	8.29 E
Döbeln	54	51.07 N	13.07 E
Doberai, Jazirah (Vogelkop) ⥼	164	1.30 S	132.30 E
Döbritz	264a	32.33 N	13.03 E
Doberlug-Kirchhain	54	51.38 N	13.34 E
Döbern	54	51.37 N	14.36 E
Dobiegniew	30	52.59 N	15.47 E
Döbling ⥼ᵇ	264b	48.15 N	16.22 E
Dobo	164	5.45 S	134.13 E
Doboj	38	44.44 N	18.06 E
Dobra, Pol.	30	51.54 N	18.37 E
Dobra, Pol.	30	53.35 N	15.18 E
Dobra ≈	36	43.53 N	15.18 E
Dobr'anka, Ross.	86	58.27 N	56.24 E
Dobr'anka, Ukr.	78	52.04 N	31.11 E
Dobr'ankka	78	48.21 N	30.54 E
Dobra Stausee ⌷ ¹	61	48.35 N	15.20 E
Dobre Miasto	30	53.59 N	20.25 E
Döbriach	64	46.47 N	13.39 E
Dobrič — Dobrich	38	43.34 N	27.50 E
Dobrich	38	43.34 N	27.50 E
Dobrinka, Ross.	82	52.09 N	40.29 E
Dobrinka, Ross.	80	48.49 N	42.58 E
Dobrinka, Ross.	80	50.49 N	41.51 E
Dobříš	30	49.47 N	14.11 E
Dobritz	54	52.01 N	12.13 E
Dobrodzień	30	50.44 N	18.27 E
Dobroje, Ross.	76	52.52 N	39.48 E
Dobroje, Ross.	76	57.06 N	32.02 E
Dobroslav	78	46.50 N	30.50 E
Dobromil'	78	49.34 N	22.47 E
Dobropolje	78	48.28 N	37.05 E
Dobroslavka ⌷	76	52.24 N	26.15 E
Dobroteasa	38	44.47 N	24.23 E
Dobroveličkovka	78	48.23 N	31.11 E
Dobrovolje	78	48.41 N	36.37 E
Dobrovol'sk	76	54.46 N	22.31 E
Dobrudžansko plato ⌳	38	43.32 N	27.50 E
Dobruja ⥼ ¹	38	44.00 N	28.00 E
Dobruš	76	52.25 N	31.19 E
Dobryn'	78	51.46 N	29.12 E
Dobrzany	30	53.22 N	15.25 E
Dobrzyń nad Wisłą	30	52.38 N	19.20 E
Dobšiná	30	48.49 N	20.23 E
Dobson	192	36.23 N	80.43 W
Dobzha	120	28.28 N	88.14 E
Doce ≈, Bra.	255	19.37 S	39.49 W
Doce ≈, Bra.	255	18.28 S	51.05 W
Doce de Octubre	246	23.28 S	97.47 W
Dochart ≈	44	56.28 N	4.20 W
Dočin ≈	88	49.39 N	114.48 E
Docker River	162	24.52 S	129.05 E
Docking	42	52.55 N	0.38 E
Dock Junction	192	31.11 N	81.31 W
Dockton	224	47.22 N	122.27 W
Dockweiler	56	50.15 N	6.50 E
Dockweiler Beach State Park ♦	280	33.55 N	118.26 W
Doctor Arroyo	234	23.40 N	100.11 W
Doctor Cecilio Báez	252	25.03 S	56.19 W
Doctor Coss	196	25.55 N	99.11 W
Doctor Edmund A. Babler Memorial State Park ♦	219	38.36 N	90.43 W
Doctor Hicks Range ⌳			
Doctor Pedro P. Peña	252	22.26 S	62.22 W
Doctors Creek ≈	208	40.11 N	74.41 W
Doda	123	33.08 N	75.34 E
Dod Ballāpur	122	13.18 N	77.32 E
Doddinghurst, Eng., U.K.	43	51.40 N	0.18 E
Doddinghurst, Eng., U.K.	260	51.40 N	0.18 E
Doddridge	194	33.05 N	93.54 W
Dodds Island I	219	38.35 N	91.59 W
Doddsville	194	33.39 N	90.31 W
Dodecaneso — Dhodhekánisos ⥼	38	36.30 N	27.00 E
Dodéo	152	7.29 N	12.04 E
Dodge, Ne., U.S.	198	41.43 N	96.52 W
Dodge, Tx., U.S.	222	30.45 N	95.24 W
Dodge Center	216	43.14 N	88.40 W
Dodge Brothers State Park Number 4 ♦, Mi., U.S.	281	42.37 N	83.22 W
Dodge Brothers State Park Number 8 ♦, Mi., U.S.	281	42.36 N	83.01 W
Dodge Center	190	44.01 N	92.51 W

FRANÇAIS Nom	Page	Lat.° '	Long.° ' W=Ouest
Dodge City	198	37.45 N	100.01 W
Dodge Park	284c	38.56 N	76.53 W
Dodger Stadium ♦	280	34.04 N	118.14 W
Dodgeville	190	42.57 N	90.07 W
Dodman Point ⥼	42	50.13 N	4.48 W
Dodo Goei	140	5.57 N	29.26 E
Dodola	144	7.02 N	39.07 E
Dodoma	154	6.11 S	35.45 E
Dodoma □⁴	154	6.00 S	36.00 E
Dodori ≈	154	1.52 S	41.02 E
Dodsland	184	51.49 N	108.49 W
Dodson, La., U.S.	194	32.04 N	92.39 W
Dodson, Mt., U.S.	202	48.23 N	108.14 W
Dodson, Tx., U.S.	196	34.46 N	100.02 W
Dodson Peninsula ⥼ ¹	9	75.46 S	62.50 W
Dodurga	130	39.48 N	29.55 E
Doe Lake ⌷	212	45.32 N	79.25 W
Doe River	182	56.00 N	120.05 W
Doerun	192	31.19 N	83.55 W
Doesburg	52	52.01 N	6.09 E
Doetinchem	52	51.58 N	6.17 E
Dog ≈	190	48.51 N	89.37 W
Dogáchia	272b	22.58 N	88.31 E
Dogai Coring ⌷	120	34.30 N	89.15 E
Dōga-mori ⌳	96	33.09 N	132.53 E
Doğanbey, Tür.	130	37.37 N	27.11 E
Doğanbey, Tür.	130	38.04 N	26.53 E
Doğanbey, Tür.	130	37.48 N	31.54 E
Doğanca	130	37.49 N	42.20 E
Doğançay	130	40.37 N	30.20 E
Doğanela	66	41.34 N	12.56 E
Doğanhisar	130	38.09 N	31.41 E
Doğankent, Tür.	130	36.52 N	35.18 E
Doğankent, Tür.	130	40.48 N	38.56 E
Doğanşehir	130	38.06 N	37.53 E
Doğanyol	130	38.19 N	39.03 E
Doğanyurt, Tür.	130	42.00 N	33.27 E
Doğanyurt, Tür.	130	40.41 N	36.43 E
Dog Creek ≈	182	51.35 N	122.15 W
Dog Creek ≈, B.C., Can.	182	51.35 N	122.17 W
Dog Creek ≈, Mt., U.S.	202	47.44 N	109.36 W
Dog Creek ≈, Oh., U.S.	216	41.03 N	84.23 W
Dog Ear Creek ≈	198	43.42 N	99.59 W
Dog Island I, Anguilla	238	18.17 N	63.16 W
Dog Island I, Fl., U.S.	192	29.48 N	84.35 W
Dog Islands II	240m	18.29 N	64.28 W
Dog Lake ⌷, Mb., Can.	184	51.02 N	98.30 W
Dog Lake ⌷, On., Can.	190	48.46 N	89.32 W
Dog Lake ⌷, On., Can.	190	48.18 N	84.10 W
Dogliani	62	44.32 N	7.56 E
Dogna	64	46.27 N	13.19 E
Dōgo I	92	36.15 N	133.16 E
Do Gonbadān	128	30.21 N	50.48 E
Dogondoutchi	150	13.38 N	4.02 E
Dogonyaro ≈	130	40.14 N	37.33 E
Dōgo-yama ⌳	96	35.04 N	133.14 E
Dogpound Creek ≈	182	51.50 N	114.24 W
Dogs, Isle of I	260	51.29 N	0.01 W
D'ogtevo, Ross.	78	49.10 N	40.39 E
D'ogtevo, Ross.	80	49.11 N	40.39 E
Doğubayazıt	42	39.32 N	44.08 E
Doğukaroua	150	13.58 N	5.35 E
Doğu Karadeniz Dağları ⌳	130	40.30 N	40.30 E
Dogura	160	10.05 S	150.05 E
Doha — Ad-Dawḥah	128	25.17 N	51.32 E
Dohhi	126	23.35 N	90.09 E
Dohār	124	23.42 N	84.54 E
Dohna	54	50.57 N	13.51 E
Dohrgaul	263	51.06 N	7.27 E
Dohrighāt	124	26.16 N	83.31 E
Doi	96	33.57 N	133.26 E
Doi, Indon. I	269c	10.43 N	106.37 E
Doilungdêqên	124	29.48 N	90.47 E
Doiran, Lake ⌷	38	41.13 N	22.44 E
Doiras, Embalse de ⌷	34	43.10 N	6.45 W
Dois de Novembro, Cachoeira ⌵	248	8.52 S	62.16 W
Dois Irmãos, Pico ⌳	287a	22.59 S	43.14 W
Dois Irmãos de Goiás	250	9.16 S	49.05 W
Doi Suthep-Pui National Park ♦	110	18.50 N	98.50 E
Dōjō ⌷	268	35.51 N	139.37 E
Dōjō ⌷	270	34.51 N	135.14 E
Doka, Indon.	164	6.39 S	134.15 E
Doka, Süd.	140	13.31 N	35.46 E
Doki ≈	96	34.18 N	133.48 E
Dokka	28	60.50 N	10.05 E
Dokkum	52	53.19 N	6.00 E
Dôkmetepe	130	40.19 N	36.18 E
Dokri	123	27.23 N	68.06 E
Dokšicy	76	54.54 N	27.46 E
Dokská pahorkatina ⌳			
Doksy	54	50.30 N	14.45 E
Dokučajevsk	83	47.44 N	37.40 E
Dôle	54	47.06 N	5.30 E
Dolgellau	42	52.44 N	3.51 W
Dolgellen	54	52.29 N	14.24 E
Dolginovo	54	49.01 N	37.19 E
Dolgoville	210	43.06 N	74.46 W
Dolgij, ostrov I	24	69.15 N	59.04 E
Dolgij Most	88	56.45 N	96.48 E
Dolginovo	54	54.39 N	27.29 E
Dolgoje ⌷	82	53.08 N	38.04 E
Dolgorukovo	82	52.34 N	37.31 E
Dolgoščelje	24	66.03 N	43.24 E
Dolianova	71	39.22 N	9.10 E
Dolina, Ukr.	78	48.58 N	24.01 E
Dolina, Ukr.	83	48.59 N	37.37 E
Dolinnyj	82	51.33 N	52.11 E
Dolinovskoje	83	48.36 N	38.33 E
Dolinsk	89	47.21 N	142.48 E
Dolinskaja	78	48.07 N	32.44 E
Dolisie ≈	43	4.12 S	12.41 E
Dolj □⁶	38	44.15 N	23.50 E
Dollach	64	46.58 N	12.54 E
Dollar	44	56.09 N	3.40 W
Dollard ≈	52	53.17 N	7.10 E
Dollard-des-Ormeaux	206	45.29 N	73.49 W
Dollar Law ⌳	44	55.31 N	3.18 W
Döllbach ≈	56	50.26 N	9.44 E
Dolle	54	52.25 N	11.37 E
Dollern	263	53.32 N	9.32 E
Döllnitz	54	51.24 N	12.01 E
Dollnstein	56	48.52 N	11.05 E
Dolmabahçe Palace ◆	267b	41.02 N	29.00 E
Dolmatovskij	78	50.30 N	32.16 E
Dolni Dăbnik	38	43.24 N	24.27 E
Dolní Dvořiště	61	48.39 N	14.27 E
Dolní Jiřetín	54	50.35 N	13.38 E

PORTUGUÊS Nome	Página	Lat.° '	Long.° ' W=Ouest
Dolni Lom	38	43.31 N	22.47 E
Dolni Žandov	60	50.02 N	12.34 E
Dolný Kubín	30	49.12 N	19.17 E
Doly	64	45.25 N	12.05 E
Dolohmwar ⌳	174r	6.52 N	158.14 E
Dolokmerawan	114	3.10 N	99.08 E
Dolokparibuan	114	3.01 N	98.39 E
Dolomites — Dolomiti ⌳	64	46.25 N	11.50 E
Dolomiti (Dolomiten) ⌳	64	46.25 N	11.50 E
Dolon'	86	50.40 N	79.18 E
Dolon ≈	62	45.18 N	4.46 E
Dolon, pereval ⵠ	85	41.52 N	75.45 E
Dolores, Arg.	252	36.20 S	57.40 W
Dolores, Col.	246	3.33 N	74.54 W
Dolores, Guat.	232	16.31 N	89.25 W
Dolores, Méx.	196	26.20 N	101.29 W
Dolores, Co., U.S.	200	37.28 N	108.30 W
Dolores, Ven.	246	8.18 N	69.34 W
Dolores ≈, Pil.	116	12.02 N	125.29 E
Dolores ≈, U.S.	200	38.49 N	109.17 W
Dolores, Mission ◆	282	37.46 N	122.26 W
Dolores Hidalgo	234	21.10 N	100.56 W
Dolphin, Cape ⥼	254	51.15 S	58.57 W
Dolphin and Union Strait ⵠ	176	69.05 N	114.45 W
Dolphin Head ⌳	241q	18.22 N	78.10 W
Dölsach	64	46.49 N	12.51 E
Dolsk	52	52.00 N	17.03 E
Dol'skoje	82	54.47 N	36.26 E
Dolton, Eng., U.K.	42	50.53 N	4.01 W
Dolton, Il., U.S.	216	41.38 N	87.36 W
Dolwyddelan	44	53.03 N	3.53 W
Dolžik	78	48.21 N	36.12 E
Dolžanskaja, Ross.	78	46.37 N	37.48 E
Dolžanskaja, Ukr.	83	48.03 N	39.39 E
Dolžicy, Ross.	76	58.00 N	29.51 E
Dolžicy, Ross.	76	56.31 N	29.08 E
Dolžik	78	50.13 N	35.55 E
Dom ⌳	58	46.06 N	7.50 E
D'oma, Gunung ⌳	164	2.40 S	136.53 E
Domachia	78	52.09 N	34.58 E
Domačovo	78	51.44 N	23.37 E
Domadare	144	1.50 N	41.13 E
Domaine, Pointe du ⥼	275a	46.23 N	73.54 W
Domanevka	78	47.37 N	30.58 E
Domaniči	76	53.02 N	33.25 E
Dom Aquino	255	15.48 S	54.53 W
Domar, Enneri ⵠ	146	18.11 N	18.04 E
Domariãganj	124	27.13 N	82.40 E
Domart-en-Ponthieu	50	50.04 N	2.07 E
Domasi	154	15.18 S	35.20 E
Domashnev	80	53.00 N	50.47 E
Domaso	58	46.09 N	9.19 E
Domat/Ems	58	46.50 N	9.28 E
Domažlice	60	49.27 N	12.56 E
Dombaj	84	43.17 N	41.37 E
Dombaj-Ul'gen, gora ⌳			
Dombarovskij	86	50.46 N	59.32 E
Dombås	26	62.05 N	9.08 E
Dombasle-sur-Meurthe	58	48.38 N	6.21 E
Dombe Grande	152	12.58 S	13.11 E
Dombes ≈ ¹	58	46.00 N	5.03 E
Dombóvár	30	46.23 N	18.08 E
Dombrád	30	48.14 N	21.56 E
Dombresson	58	47.04 N	6.58 E
Dom Cavati	255	19.23 S	42.06 W
Dôme, Puy de ⌳	32	45.47 N	2.58 E
Dome Creek	182	53.44 N	121.01 W
Domegge di Cadore	64	46.26 N	12.25 E
Domène	58	45.12 N	5.50 E
Dome Peak ⌳, Pil.	116	5.37 N	125.20 E
Dome Peak ⌳, Wa., U.S.	182	48.18 N	121.02 W
Domett	172	42.51 S	173.13 E
Domèvre-en-Haye	58	48.49 N	5.55 E
Domeyko	252	28.57 S	70.54 W
Domeyko, Cordillera ⌳	252	24.30 S	69.00 W
Domfront	32	48.36 N	0.39 W
Domiciano Ribeiro	250	16.56 S	47.46 W
Dominal, Parc ♦	248	44.52 N	6.32 E
Domingo M. Irala	252	25.54 S	54.43 W
Domingos Martins	255	20.22 S	40.40 W
Dominguez Channel ⵠ	280	33.50 N	118.13 W
Dominguez Hills ⌳	280	38.47 N	118.15 W
Dominica □¹, N.A.	230	15.30 N	61.20 W
Dominica □¹, N.A.	240d	15.30 N	61.20 W
Dominican (république) — Dominican Republic □¹	238	19.00 N	70.40 W
Dominical	230	9.13 N	83.51 W
Dominicana, República — Dominican Republic □¹	238	19.00 N	70.40 W
Dominican Republic (República Dominicana) □¹	238	19.00 N	70.40 W
Dominican Republic (República Dominicana) □¹, N.A.	238	19.00 N	70.40 W
Dominican Astrophysical Observatory ◆³	224	48.31 N	123.25 W
Dominion City	184	49.08 N	97.09 W
Dominica □¹	240d	15.30 N	61.20 W
Dominion, Cape ⥼	176	66.13 N	74.28 W
Dominion Astrophysical Observatory ◆³			
Domiongo	152	4.37 S	21.15 E
Domitilla, Catacombe di ◆	267a	41.52 N	12.31 E
Dom Joaquim	255	18.57 S	43.16 W
Domleschg ⵠ	58	46.44 N	9.28 E
Dommartin-lès-Toul	58	48.40 N	5.57 E
Dommartin-Varimont	50	48.58 N	4.46 E
Dommel ≈	52	51.44 N	5.42 E
Dommitzsch	54	51.38 N	12.53 E
Domnau ≈	54	54.32 N	11.26 E
Domneşti	38	44.25 N	25.56 E
Domno ≈	30	54.10 N	38.11 E
Domo Noi ≈	110	16.17 N	105.28 E
Domont	144	7.54 N	46.52 E
Domodedovo	82	55.26 N	37.51 E
Domodossola	58	46.07 N	8.17 E
Domoni	157a	12.15 S	44.32 E
Domont	260	49.02 N	2.20 E
Dom Pedrito	252	30.59 S	54.40 W
Dom Pedro	250	4.29 S	44.27 W
Dom Pedro II, Estação ❊	287a	22.54 S	43.11 W
Dompu	115b	8.32 S	118.28 E
Domrémy	58	48.26 N	5.40 E
Domrémy-la-Pucelle	58	48.27 N	5.40 E
Domsjö	26	63.15 N	18.43 E
Domul ≈	88	51.07 N	114.47 E
Domus de Maria	71	38.56 N	8.51 E
Domusnovas	71	39.19 N	8.39 E
Domuyo, Volcán ⌳ ¹	252	36.38 S	70.26 W

	Página	Lat.° '	Long.° ' W=Oeste
Domvast	50	50.12 N	1.55 E
Dom Viçoso	256	22.13 S	45.09 W
Dom Yaï ≈	110	15.18 N	105.10 E
Donzäle	36	46.08 N	14.36 E
Don ≈, On., Can.	212	43.39 N	79.21 W
Don ≈, India	122	16.17 N	76.27 E
Don ≈, Lao	110	15.07 N	105.48 E
Don ≈, Ross.	72	47.04 N	39.18 E
Don ≈, Eng., U.K.	44	53.39 N	0.59 W
Don ≈, Eng., U.K.	262	53.47 N	2.14 W
Don ≈, Scot., U.K.	46	57.08 N	2.05 W
Don, East Branch ≈, On., Can.	212	43.42 N	79.20 W
Don, East Branch ≈, On., Can.	275b	43.43 N	79.20 W
Dona Ana, Moç.	154	17.25 S	35.07 E
Dona Ana, N.M., U.S.	200	32.23 N	106.48 W
Donada	64	45.02 N	12.12 E
Donadeu	252	26.43 S	62.44 W
Dona Euzébia	256	21.18 S	42.48 W
Donaghadee	48	54.39 N	5.33 W
Donaghmore	48	54.20 N	6.49 W
Donahoe Creek ≈	222	30.49 N	97.12 W
Donald	166	36.22 S	143.00 E
Donalda	182	52.35 N	112.34 W
Donaldson, Ar., U.S.	194	34.14 N	92.55 W
Donaldson, Pa., U.S.	216	41.22 N	86.27 W
Donaldson, Pa., U.S.	208	40.38 N	76.24 W
Donaldson Crossroads	279b	40.16 N	80.07 W
Donaldson Dam ◆ ¹	273d	26.17 S	27.41 E
Donaldsonville	194	30.06 N	90.59 W
Donalsonville	192	31.02 N	84.52 W
Doñana, Parque Nacional de ♦	34	37.00 N	6.30 W
Donau — Danube ≈	22	45.20 N	29.40 E
Donaueschingen	58	47.57 N	8.29 E
Donaueufeld ≈ ᵇ	264b	48.15 N	16.25 E
Donaukanal ≈	264b	48.10 N	16.30 E
Donaumoos ≈, Dtsch.	56	48.30 N	10.15 E
Donaumoos ≈, Dtsch.	60	48.40 N	11.15 E
Donaustadt ⥼ ᵇ	264b	48.13 N	16.30 E
Donaustauf	60	49.02 N	12.13 E
Donauturm ≈	264b	48.14 N	16.25 E
Donauwörth	56	48.43 N	10.46 E
Don Benito	34	38.57 N	5.52 W
Dönberg ⥼ ᵇ	263	51.18 N	7.10 E
Don Bosco ⥼ ᵇ	258	34.42 S	58.18 W
Doncaster, Austl.	274b	37.47 S	145.08 E
Doncaster, On., Can.	275b	43.48 N	79.25 W
Doncaster, Eng., U.K.	44	53.32 N	1.07 W
Doncaster East	274b	37.47 S	145.10 E
Doncaster Indian Reserve ⥼ ⁴	206	46.09 N	74.07 W
Donchéry	56	49.42 N	4.52 E
Doncova	83	49.35 N	39.16 E
Dondaicha	120	21.20 N	74.34 E
Dondo, Ang.	152	9.38 S	14.25 E
Dondo, Moç.	156	19.36 S	34.44 E
Dondo, Teluk c	112	0.55 N	120.30 E
Dondra Head ⥼	122	5.55 N	80.35 E
Dond'ušany	78	48.15 N	27.37 E
Doneck ≈	83	48.00 N	37.48 E
Doneck, Ukr.	83	48.00 N	37.48 E
Doneck ≈	83	48.00 N	37.30 E
Doneckij kr'až ⌳	83	48.15 N	38.45 E
Donegal, Ire.	48	54.39 N	8.07 W
Donegal □⁶, Ire.	48	54.50 N	8.00 W
Donegal, Pa., U.S.	214	40.07 N	79.23 W
Donegal Bay c	48	54.30 N	8.30 W
Doneraile, Ire.	48	52.13 N	8.35 W
Doneraile, S.C., U.S.	192	34.19 N	79.53 W
Donetsk — Doneck	83	48.00 N	37.48 E
Dong ≈, Zhg.	100	25.00 N	118.27 E
Dong ≈, Zhg.	100	23.06 N	114.00 E
Dong ≈, Zhg.	102	23.42 N	117.13 E
Dong ≈, Zhg.	102	42.10 N	101.00 E
Dong'an	100	26.19 N	111.17 E
Dong'an ≈	100	47.20 N	134.10 E
Dongara	162	29.15 S	114.56 E
Dongargarh	124	21.12 N	80.44 E
Dongbei ⥼ ¹	100	45.00 N	125.00 E
Dong Dian ≈	105	39.03 N	116.35 E
Dong'e (Tongcheng)	98	36.14 N	116.16 E
Dongfang (Basuo)	110	19.05 N	108.39 E
Dongfeng, Zhg.	100	42.40 N	125.28 E
Dongfeng, Zhg.	100	36.36 N	118.53 E
Donggala	112	0.40 S	119.44 E
Donggang	100	39.52 N	124.09 E
Donggi Cona ⌷	120	35.15 N	98.30 E
Donggou	100	39.53 N	124.07 E
Donggu	100	26.17 N	115.27 E
Dongguan	100	23.02 N	113.45 E
Dongguang	105	37.53 N	116.32 E
Donghai (Niushan)	100	34.30 N	118.47 E
Donghai Dao I	102	21.02 N	110.25 E
Dong Hai — East China Sea ⵠ²	90	30.00 N	126.00 E
Donghe	105	34.09 N	112.50 E
Donghezhen	100	31.54 N	120.17 E
Dong Hoi	110	17.29 N	106.36 E
Dong Hu ⌷	100	30.33 N	114.25 E
Dongjiang ⌷	100	26.25 N	113.14 E
Dongjiao	110	19.35 N	110.58 E
Dongjing	98	34.09 N	113.21 E
Dongjingcheng	100	44.07 N	129.01 E
Dongjug	102	2.02 S	121.28 E
Dongkou	100	27.05 N	110.33 E
Dongjiangkou	104	32.07 N	121.12 E
Dongla ≈	100	36.00 N	116.00 E
Dongmen	100	28.29 N	114.02 E
Dongming	98	35.18 N	115.08 E
Dong Nai ≈	110	10.45 N	106.46 E
Dongning	89	44.04 N	131.07 E
Dongou	152	2.04 N	18.04 E
Dongping	98	35.55 N	116.18 E
Dongping, Zhg.	100	27.24 N	118.39 E
Dongping, Zhg.	100	28.41 N	89.09 E
Dongping, Zhg.	100	30.19 N	122.09 E
Dongping Hu ⌷	98	36.00 N	116.12 E
Dongpu	100	30.03 N	120.34 E
Dongqian ⌷	104	30.52 N	120.23 E
Dongqing ≈	100	31.49 N	120.03 E
Dongqingduizi	104	41.02 N	122.08 E
Dongsanjiazi	100	41.54 N	122.48 E
Dongsanlintang	105	31.09 N	121.31 E
Dongsha ≈	100	33.38 N	117.09 E
Dongshajiao	100	30.19 N	122.09 E
Dongshan, Zhg.	100	23.42 N	117.24 E
Dongshan, Zhg.	102	19.50 N	110.14 E
Dongshan Dao I	100	31.04 N	120.24 E
Dongshanqiao	104	23.40 N	117.25 E
Dongsheng	100	39.49 N	109.59 E
Dongsheshanzi	104	42.15 N	123.09 E
Dongshi, Zhg.	100	24.42 N	118.27 E
Dongshi, Zhg.	100	24.42 N	118.27 E
Dongshuiyan	105	39.15 N	115.23 E
Dongtai	100	32.51 N	120.20 E
Dongtai Hu ⌷	100	31.05 N	120.30 E
Dongtaipingzhen	89	45.18 N	122.05 E
Dongtangou	105	39.23 N	118.22 E
Dongtianmu Shan ⌳	100	30.24 N	119.31 E
Dongting	100	30.51 N	120.06 E
Dongtinghu ⌷	100	29.20 N	112.54 E
Dongtinghu ⌷	100	29.20 N	112.54 E
Dongtingxi	102	28.34 N	110.36 E
Dongtou	100	27.50 N	121.08 E
Dongtuo Shan I	100	27.05 N	120.46 E
Dongtuoshanzi	104	42.10 N	123.08 E
Dongtuozi	104	41.17 N	121.53 E
Dong Van	110	23.16 N	105.22 E
Dongwan	100	25.00 N	118.27 E
Dongwangzhuang	105	32.16 N	120.32 E
Dongwe ≈	152	13.58 S	23.53 E
Dongwuquan	105	39.20 N	115.43 E
Dongxi ≈, Zhg.	102	28.35 N	122.02 E
Dongxia, Zhg.	100	24.38 N	115.32 E
Dongxia	100	31.11 N	119.05 E
Dongxiagaogao	104	39.39 N	118.24 E
Dongxiang	100	28.13 N	116.35 E
Dongxiang Dao I	100	25.36 N	119.48 E
Dongxin	100	46.23 N	127.52 E
Dongxingchang, Zhg.	107	29.16 N	103.55 E
Dongxingtong	104	39.46 N	124.33 E
Dongxinpu	104	41.58 N	123.32 E
Dongyang	100	29.17 N	120.13 E
Dongyangqiao	104	39.20 N	115.43 E
Dongyian	100	41.43 N	127.23 E
Dongyin	100	36.06 N	117.08 E
Dongyou	100	30.16 N	114.40 E
Dongyou, Zhg.	100	27.10 N	118.53 E
Dongyuemiao	105	32.04 N	119.18 E
Dongyuezhen	107	30.07 N	105.18 E
Dongzhang	100	35.21 N	116.55 E
Dongzhi	100	30.06 N	117.02 E

	Página	Lat.° '	Long.° ' W=Oeste
Dongkalang	112	0.10 N	120.06 E
Dongkeng, Zhg.	100	27.48 N	119.42 E
Dongkeng, Zhg.	100	24.59 N	114.54 E
Dong Khe	110	22.26 N	106.27 E
Dongkou	98	35.29 N	115.20 E
Donglan	102	24.40 N	107.18 E
Donglaohuyu	104	42.28 N	124.17 E
Donglaojunpu	104	41.24 N	121.22 E
Dongli	102	20.50 N	110.20 E
Dongliang	104	41.10 N	121.25 E
Dongliangjia	105	40.52 N	118.17 E
Dongliban	98	36.02 N	118.23 E
Donglinchang	107	29.39 N	104.07 E
Dongling	100	41.50 N	123.35 E
Dongliu, Zhg.	100	30.14 N	116.53 E
Dongliu, Zhg.	100	32.06 N	118.58 E
Dongliujiazi	104	42.21 N	122.44 E
Donglizhuang	105	39.21 N	116.47 E
Donglong	100	23.36 N	116.50 E
Donglucun	89	49.28 N	128.50 E
Dongmen	100	28.29 N	114.02 E
Dong Nhien, Rach ≈	269c	10.49 N	106.46 E
Dongning	89	44.04 N	131.07 E
Dongo, Ang.	152	14.36 S	15.48 E
Dongo, It.	58	46.07 N	9.17 E
Dongo, Zaïre	152	2.43 N	18.24 E
Dongobesh	154	4.04 S	35.23 E
Dongola — Dunqulah	146	19.10 N	30.29 E
Dongon Point ⥼	116	12.44 N	120.48 E
Dongping, Zhg.	100	27.24 N	118.39 E
Dongping Hu ⌷	98	36.00 N	116.12 E
Dongpu	100	30.03 N	120.34 E
Dongqiao	100	30.52 N	120.23 E
Dongqing	100	31.49 N	120.03 E
Dongrang ≈	104	41.02 N	122.08 E
Dongshan	100	31.04 N	120.24 E
Dongsheng	100	39.49 N	109.59 E
Dongtai	100	32.51 N	120.20 E
Dongting	100	30.51 N	120.06 E
Dongyang	100	29.17 N	120.13 E
Dongzhang	100	35.21 N	116.55 E
Dongzhi	100	30.06 N	117.02 E
Donna, Punta sa ⥼	196	26.10 N	98.03 W
Donnacona	206	46.40 N	71.47 W
Donnacona	70	40.45 N	7.46 E
Donnamana	208	40.45 N	76.47 W
Donnellan	219	39.00 N	89.56 W
Donnersberg ⌳	56	49.38 N	7.54 E
Donner Lake ⌷	226	39.19 N	120.15 W
Donner Pass ⵠ	226	39.18 N	120.18 W
Donner und Blitzen ≈	202	43.17 N	118.49 W
Donnersdorf	56	50.00 N	10.24 E
Donnybrook, Austl.	162	33.34 N	115.49 E
Donnybrook, S. Afr.	156	30.00 N	29.48 E
Donora	214	40.10 N	79.51 W
Donostia (San Sebastián)	34	43.19 N	1.59 W
Donoughmore	48	51.57 N	8.44 W

	Página	Lat.° '	Long.° ' W=Oeste
Don Pedro Reservoir ⌷ ¹	226	37.43 N	120.23 W
Don Peninsula ⥼ ¹	182	52.30 N	128.10 W
Donsol	152	15.28 S	14.06 E
Donskaja gr'ada ⥼ ²	80	49.30 N	42.00 E
Donskoj, Ross.	76	53.58 N	38.20 E
Donskoj, Ross.	83	48.49 N	40.06 E
Donskoj, Ross.	83	47.25 N	40.14 E
Donskoje, Ross.	76	52.57 N	39.00 E
Donskoje, Ross.	80	45.21 N	41.59 E
Donskoje belogorje ⌳	78	50.30 N	39.45 E
Donsol	116	12.54 N	123.36 E
Don Torcuato	288	34.30 S	58.38 W
Don Torcuato, Aeródromo ❊	288	34.30 S	58.36 W
Donuzlav, ozero ⌷	78	45.23 N	33.05 E
Donyztau ≈	86	46.25 N	57.00 E
Donzdorf	56	48.41 N	9.48 E
Donzère	62	44.27 N	4.43 E
Donzy	50	47.22 N	3.08 E
Dooagh	48	53.59 N	10.09 W
Dood nuur ⌷	88	53.20 N	99.20 E
Doogort	48	54.01 N	10.01 W
Doolow	144	4.10 N	42.05 E
Doomadgee	166	17.56 S	138.49 E
Doomadgee Aboriginal Reserve ⥼ ⁴	166	17.43 S	138.36 E
Doon ≈, On., Can.	212	43.23 N	80.26 W
Doon, I., U.S.	198	43.16 N	96.13 W
Doon ≈	44	55.26 N	4.38 W
Doon, Loch ⌷	44	55.15 N	4.22 W
Doonbeg ≈	48	52.44 N	9.32 W
Doonbeg	48	52.44 N	9.34 W
Doon Doon Aboriginal Reserve ⥼ ⁴	164	16.15 S	128.15 E
Doonerak, Mount ⌳	180	67.56 N	150.37 W
Doonside	274a	33.46 S	150.52 E
Dooralong	170	33.12 S	151.22 E
Doorn	52	52.03 N	5.21 E
Doorndam	158	28.03 S	21.03 E
Doornik — Tournai	50	50.36 N	3.23 E
Door Peninsula ⥼ ¹	190	44.55 N	87.20 W
Dopping Brook ≈	283	42.12 N	71.23 W
Do Qal'eh	128	32.18 N	61.31 E
Dor	132	32.37 N	34.55 E
Dora	194	33.43 N	87.05 W
Dora, Lake ⌷, Austl.	162	22.05 S	122.55 E
Dora, Lake ⌷, Fl., U.S.	220	29.00 N	81.37 W
Dora Baltea ≈	62	45.11 N	8.05 E
Dorah ≈	62	45.42 N	7.11 E
Dorāh ≈	240m	18.28 N	76.01 E
Dorāha	123	30.49 N	76.01 E
Dorāhān ⌳	123	30.07 N	71.15 E
Dorain, Ben ⌳	46	56.30 N	4.42 W
Dorândia	256	22.27 S	43.57 W
Dora Riparia ≈	62	45.05 N	7.44 E
Dorback ≈	192	33.53 N	84.17 W
Dorback Burn ≈	46	57.31 N	3.40 W
Dorcheat, Bayou ≈	194	32.30 N	93.21 W
Dorchester, N.B., Can.	186	45.54 N	64.31 W
Dorchester, On., Can.	212	42.59 N	81.04 W
Dorchester, Eng., U.K.	42	50.43 N	2.26 W
Dorchester, Eng., U.K.	42	51.39 N	1.10 W
Dorchester, Il., U.S.	219	39.05 N	89.53 W
Dorchester, Ne., U.S.	198	40.38 N	97.06 W
Dorchester, Wi., U.S.	190	45.00 N	90.20 W
Dorchester □⁶	208	38.34 N	76.04 W
Dorchester ⥼ ᵇ	283	42.17 N	71.04 W
Dorchester, Cape ⥼	176	65.29 N	77.30 W
Dorchester Bay c	283	42.19 N	71.02 W
Dorchester Crossing	186	46.10 N	64.34 W
Dorchester Estates	284c	38.47 N	76.55 W
Dorchester Heights National Historic Site ◆	283	42.20 N	71.03 W
Dorchheim	56	50.30 N	8.04 E
Dordabis	156	22.52 S	17.38 E
Dordives	50	48.09 N	2.46 E
Dordogne □⁵	32	45.10 N	0.45 E
Dordogne ≈	32	45.02 N	0.35 W
Dordon	42	52.36 N	1.37 W
Dordrecht, Ned.	52	51.49 N	4.40 E
Dordrecht, S. Afr.	156	31.20 S	27.03 E
Doré ≈, Sk., Can.	184	54.56 N	107.45 W
Doré ≈, Fr.	62	45.50 N	3.35 E
Doré, Monts ⌳	62	45.30 N	2.49 E
Doreissou	146	10.33 N	15.08 E
Doré Lake	184	54.38 N	107.24 W
Doré Lake ⌷	184	54.46 N	107.17 W
Dörentrup	52	52.02 N	8.59 E
Dores de Indaiá	255	19.27 S	45.36 W
Dores do Turvo	256	21.31 S	43.39 W
Dorfgastein	64	47.15 N	13.06 E
Dorfmark	54	52.55 N	9.44 E
Dorgali	71	40.17 N	9.35 E
Dörgön nuur ⌷	93	47.40 N	93.30 E
Dörig ≈	158	31.54 S	18.39 E
Dorikanpo ≈	2734	27.42 N	23.26 E
Dorinkop	156	24.56 S	28.58 E
Dorion-Vaudreuil	206	45.23 N	74.01 W
Dorje Läpka ⌳	124	28.11 N	85.47 E
Dormaa Ahenkro	150	7.17 N	2.52 W
Dormagen	54	51.06 N	6.50 E
Dormans	50	49.04 N	3.38 E
Dormettingen	58	48.16 N	8.48 E
Dormidontovka	89	47.45 N	134.57 E
Dormont	279b	40.23 N	80.02 W
Dornach	58	47.29 N	7.37 E
Dornap ⥼ ᵇ	263	51.15 N	7.06 E
Dornbirn	58	47.25 N	9.44 E
Dornburg	54	51.00 N	11.40 E
Dorndorf, Dtsch.	56	50.50 N	8.07 E
Dorndorf, Dtsch.	56	50.47 N	10.09 E
Dorney	260	51.30 N	0.40 W
Dornhan	58	48.21 N	8.30 E
Dornie	46	57.17 N	5.31 W
Dornoch	46	57.52 N	4.02 W
Dornoch Firth c ¹	46	57.50 N	4.04 W
Dornogov' □⁴	100	44.30 N	110.00 E
Dornsife	208	40.45 N	76.47 W
Dornstadt	56	48.32 N	9.56 E
Dornstetten	58	48.28 N	8.29 E
Dorohoi	38	47.57 N	26.24 E
Dorohusk	30	51.10 N	23.50 E
Dorokempo	115b	8.33 S	118.15 E
Doromata	160	9.25 S	159.17 E
Doroshivtsi	78	48.35 N	25.55 E
Doro, Mali	150	16.09 N	0.51 W
Doro, Indon.	164	7.02 S	109.41 E
Doroh	128	33.28 N	57.55 E
Dorohoi	38	47.56 N	26.24 E
Dorokempo	115b	8.33 S	118.15 E
Dorohedhoo	122	2.48 N	72.55 E
Dorothy, Lake ⌷	180	58.23 N	133.40 W
Dorotkoykeys Run ≈	276	40.59 N	73.58 W
Dorpat — Tartu	76	58.23 N	26.43 E

ENGLISH		DEUTSCH			
Name	Page Lat.° Long.°	Name	Seite Breite° Länge° N E = Ost		

Symbols in the index entries represent the broad categories identified in the key at the right. Symbols with superior numbers (¹) identify subcategories (see complete key on page 1·1).

Los símbolos incluidos en el texto del índice representan las grandes categorías identificadas con la clave a la derecha. Los símbolos con números en su parte superior (¹) identifican las subcategorías (véase la clave completa en la página 1·1).

Os símbolos incluídos no texto do índice representam as grandes categorias identificadas com a chave à direita. Os símbolos com números em sua parte superior (¹) identificam subcategorias (veja-se a chave completa a página 2·1).

Les symboles de l'index représentent les catégories indiquées dans la légende à droite. Les symboles suivis d'un indice (¹) représentent des sous-catégories (voir légende complète à la page 1·1).

Die Symbole im Register stellen die rechts im Schlüssel erklärten Kategorien dar. Symbole mit hochgestellten Ziffern (¹) bezeichnen Unterabteilungen einer Kategorie (vgl. vollständiger Schlüssel auf Seite 1·1).

Features		Objekte		Otros Elementos		Outros topográficos		Autres données topographiques
➤ Other Topographic	Andere Topographische		Otros		Outros Elementos	topográficos		
II Islands	Inseln		Islas		Ilhas		Iles	
I Island	Insel		Isla		Ilha		Ile	
⌐ Cape	Kap		Cabo		Cabo		Cap	
V Valley, Canyon	Tal, Cañon		Valle, Cañón		Vale, Canhão		Vallée, Canyon	
⌐ Plain	Ebene		Llano		Planície		Plaine	
✕ Pass	Paß		Paso		Passo		Col	
⌂ Mountains	Gebirge		Montañas		Montanhas		Montagnes	
⌂ Mountain	Berg		Montaña		Montanha		Montagne	

ESPAÑOL

Nombre	Página	Lat.°'	Long.°' W = Oeste
Dumboa	146	11.10 N	12.45 E
Dumbrăveni	38	46.14 N	24.35 E
Dum Dum	126	22.35 N	88.24 E
Dum Dum International Airport ✈	126	22.38 N	88.25 E
Dume, Point ➤	228	34.00 N	118.48 W
Dumei	100	24.47 N	117.21 E
Dumfries, Scot., U.K.	44	55.04 N	3.37 W
Dumfries, Va., U.S.	208	38.34 N	77.19 W
Dumfries and Galloway □⁴	44	55.00 N	4.00 W
Duminiči	76	53.55 N	35.06 E
Dumjor	272b	22.38 N	88.13 E
Dumka	126	24.16 N	87.15 E
Dumlupinar	130	38.52 N	30.00 E
Dummar	132	33.32 N	36.14 E
Dümmer ∅	52	52.31 N	8.19 E
Dummer Range ⩘	162	20.11 S	125.59 E
Dumoga-Bone National Park ⯑	112	0.30 N	123.25 E
Dumoga Kecil	112	0.31 N	123.55 E
Dumoine ≃	190	46.13 N	77.51 W
Dumoine, Lac ∅	190	46.53 N	77.54 W
Dumont, Ia., U.S.	190	42.45 N	92.58 W
Dumont, Ia., U.S.	210	40.56 N	73.59 W
Dumont, Lac ∅	190	46.04 N	76.27 W
Dumont d'Urville ⬩³	9	66.35 S	140.00 E
Dümpelfeld	56	50.27 N	6.56 E
Dümpten ➤⁸	263	51.27 N	6.54 E
Dumpu	164	5.50 S	145.45 E
Dumra	124	26.34 N	85.31 E
Dumraon	124	25.33 N	84.09 E
Dumuria, Bngl.	126	22.47 N	89.26 E
Dumurã, India	126	22.11 N	86.20 E
Dumyāṭ (Damietta)	142	31.25 N	31.48 E
Dumyāṭ □⁴	142	31.20 N	31.45 E
Dumyāṭ, Far' (Damietta Branch) ≃	142	31.32 N	31.51 E
Dumyāṭ, Masabb (Damietta Mouth) ≃¹	142	31.32 N	31.51 E
Dūn ⩘	54	51.21 N	10.30 E
Dünaburg — Daugavpils	76	55.53 N	26.32 E
Duna — Danube ≃	22	45.20 N	29.40 E
Dunaff Head ➤	48	55.17 N	7.33 W
Dunaföldvár	30	46.48 N	18.55 E
Dunaharaszti	30	47.21 N	19.05 E
Dunaj, Ross.	265a	59.58 N	30.56 E
Dunaj, ostrova II	74	73.52 N	124.29 E
Dunaj — Danube ≃	22	45.20 N	29.40 E
Dunajec ≃	30	50.14 N	20.44 E
Dunajevcy	78	48.54 N	26.51 E
Dunajevo	30	52.05 N	117.02 E
Dunajská Streda	30	48.01 N	17.35 E
Dunakeszi	30	47.38 N	19.08 E
Dunany Point ➤	48	53.52 N	6.14 W
Dunărea — Danube ≃	22	45.20 N	29.40 E
Dunărea Veche, Bratul ≃	38	45.17 N	28.02 E
Duna-Tisza-csatorna ☰	264c	47.21 N	19.05 E
Dunaújváros	30	46.58 N	18.57 E
Dunăvățu-de-Sus	38	44.59 N	29.13 E
Dunav — Danube ≃	22	45.20 N	29.40 E
Duna-Völgyi-fócsatorna ☰	30	46.12 N	18.56 E
Dunback	172	45.23 S	170.38 E
Dunbar, Scot., U.K.	46	56.00 N	2.31 W
Dunbar, W.V., U.S.	188	38.21 N	81.44 W
Dunbarton	275b	43.49 N	79.06 W
Dunbeath	46	58.15 N	3.25 W
Dunblane, Sk., Can.	184	51.11 N	106.52 W
Dunblane, Scot., U.K.	46	56.12 N	3.58 W
Dunboyne	48	53.24 N	6.28 W
Duncan, B.C., Can.	224	48.47 N	123.42 W
Duncan, Az., U.S.	200	32.43 N	109.06 W
Duncan, Ms., U.S.	194	34.02 N	90.44 W
Duncan, Ok., U.S.	196	34.30 N	97.57 W
Duncan ≃	182	50.11 N	116.57 W
Duncan Lake ∅¹	182	50.15 N	116.57 W
Duncannon	208	40.23 N	77.01 W
Duncan Passage ⋓	110	11.00 N	92.30 E
Duncans	241q	18.28 N	77.32 W
Duncansby Head ➤	46	58.39 N	3.02 W
Duncans Creek ≃	274a	33.53 S	150.39 E
Duncansville	214	40.25 N	78.26 W
Duncanville	196	32.39 N	96.54 W
Dunchurch	48	52.14 N	6.39 W
Duncormick	48	52.14 N	6.39 W
Dundaga	76	57.31 N	22.21 E
Dundáhera	272a	28.38 N	77.26 E
Dundalk, On., Can.	212	44.10 N	80.24 W
Dundalk (Dún Dealgan), Ire.	48	54.01 N	6.25 W
Dundalk, Md., U.S.	208	39.15 N	76.31 W
Dundalk Bay c	48	53.57 N	6.17 W
Dundas, Austl.	274a	33.48 S	151.02 E
Dundas, On., Can.	212	43.16 N	79.57 W
Dundas, Mn., U.S.	190	44.25 N	93.12 W
Dundas, Cape ➤	212	44.57 N	81.07 W
Dundas, Lake ∅	162	32.35 S	121.50 E
Dundas Island I	184	54.33 N	130.55 W
Dundas Peninsula ➤¹	176	74.50 N	111.30 W
Dundas Strait ⋓	164	11.20 S	131.35 E
Dún Dealgan — Dundalk	48	54.01 N	6.25 W
Dundee, S. Afr.	148	28.12 S	30.16 E
Dundee, Scot., U.K.	46	56.28 N	2.58 W
Dundee, Fl., U.S.	220	28.01 N	81.37 W
Dundee, Ia., U.S.	216	42.06 N	88.17 W
Dundee, Mi., U.S.	218	41.57 N	83.39 W
Dundee, Ms., U.S.	194	34.01 N	90.27 W
Dundee, Oh., U.S.	214	40.35 N	81.37 W
Dundee, N.Y., U.S.	210	42.31 N	76.58 W
Dundee, Or., U.S.	224	45.16 N	123.01 W
Dundee Creek ≃	284b	39.21 N	76.22 W
Dundgovĭ □⁴	102	45.30 N	106.30 E
Dundlt	142	30.41 N	31.18 E
Dundonald	46	54.36 N	5.48 W
Dundoo	166	27.39 S	144.39 E
Dundrum, N. Ire., U.K.	48	52.33 N	8.03 W
Dundrum Bay c	48	54.16 N	5.51 W
Dundurn	184	54.13 N	106.30 W
Duneaton Water ≃	46	55.49 N	3.45 W
Dunedin, N.Z.	172	45.52 S	170.30 E
Dunedin, Fl., U.S.	220	28.01 N	82.46 W
Dunedoo	166	32.01 S	149.24 E
Duneland Beach	216	41.35 N	86.50 W
Dunellen	276	40.35 N	74.28 W
Dunewood	276	40.38 N	73.11 W
Dunfermline	46	56.04 N	3.29 W
Du Ngae, Khao ⩘	110	15.10 N	98.47 E
Dungannon, N. Ire., U.K.	48	54.31 N	6.46 W
Dungannon, Va., U.S.	192	36.49 N	82.28 W
Dungarpur	124	23.50 N	73.43 E
Dungarvan	48	52.05 N	7.37 W
Dungarvan Harbour c	48	52.05 N	7.35 W
Dungas	150	13.04 N	9.20 E
Dungau ➤¹	60	48.40 N	12.40 E
Dungeness ➤	224	48.08 N	123.06 W
Dungeness, Punta ➤	250	52.24 S	68.25 W
Dungeness Bay c	224	48.10 N	123.07 W
Dungeness Spit ➤²	224	48.10 N	123.00 W
Dungiven	48	54.55 N	6.55 W
Dungog	166	32.24 S	151.46 E
Dungu, Lagoa do ∅	154	11.00 S	18.00 E
Dungun	154	3.37 N	28.34 E
Dungu	154	3.37 N	28.34 E
Dungun	114	4.47 N	103.26 E

FRANÇAIS

Nom	Page	Lat.°'	Long.°' W = Ouest
Dungun	114	4.47 N	103.23 E
Dunham	206	45.08 N	72.48 W
Dunham Lake ∅	281	42.39 N	83.41 W
Dunham-on-the-Hill	262	53.15 N	2.47 W
Dunham Park ⬩	262	53.23 N	2.24 W
Dunham Town	262	53.23 N	2.24 W
Dunheved	274a	33.45 S	150.47 E
— Launceston	42	50.38 N	4.21 W
Dunholme	44	53.18 N	0.28 W
Dunhou	100	27.02 N	114.58 E
Dunhua	89	43.21 N	128.13 E
Dunhuang	102	40.12 N	94.41 E
Dunières	45	45.13 N	4.20 E
Dunilovo, Ross.	76	57.46 N	38.55 E
Dunilovo, Ross.	80	57.00 N	41.27 E
Dunkeld	46	56.34 N	3.35 W
Dunkeld ➤⁸	273d	26.09 S	28.03 E
Dunkellin ≃	48	53.17 N	8.54 W
Dunkelsteinerwald ➤³	61	48.15 N	15.29 E
Dunkern ∅	53	50.09 N	16.52 E
Dunker Pond ∅	276	41.05 N	74.28 W
Dunkerque	50	51.03 N	2.22 E
Dunkerrin	48	52.55 N	7.55 W
Dunkery Hill ⩘²	42	51.11 N	3.35 W
Dunkineely	48	54.38 N	8.23 W
Dunkinsville	218	38.51 N	83.30 W
Dunkirk, Eng., U.K.	42	51.17 N	0.59 E
Dunkirk, In., U.S.	216	40.22 N	85.12 W
Dunkirk, N.Y., U.S.	214	42.28 N	79.20 W
Dunkirk, Oh., U.S.	216	40.47 N	83.38 W
Dunkirk — Dunkerque	50	51.03 N	2.22 E
Dunk's Green	260	51.15 N	0.19 E
Dunku	140	12.50 N	32.49 E
Dunkwa, Ghana	150	5.58 N	1.46 W
Dunkwa, Ghana	150	5.22 N	1.12 W
Dún Laoghaire	48	53.17 N	6.08 W
Dunlap, Ia., U.S.	190	41.38 N	95.55 W
Dunlap, In., U.S.	198	41.51 N	95.36 W
Dunlap, Tn., U.S.	194	35.22 N	85.23 W
Dunlap Acres	228	34.03 N	117.06 W
Dunleary — Dún Laoghaire	48	53.17 N	6.08 W
Dunleer	48	53.50 N	6.24 W
Dunleith	285	39.42 N	75.33 W
Dun-le-Palestel	32	46.18 N	1.40 E
Dunlo	214	40.17 N	78.43 W
Dunlop	46	55.43 N	4.32 W
Dunlop ≃	48	55.01 N	6.25 W
Dunmanus Bay c	48	51.35 N	9.45 W
Dunmanway	48	51.43 N	9.06 W
Dunmarra	164	16.42 S	133.25 E
Dunmore, Ire.	48	53.36 N	8.46 W
Dunmore, Pa., U.S.	210	41.25 N	75.37 W
Dunmore Cave ⬩⁵	48	52.09 N	7.15 W
Dunmore East	48	52.09 N	7.00 W
Dunmore Town	238	25.30 N	76.39 W
Dunmurry	48	54.33 N	6.01 W
Dunn	192	35.18 N	78.36 W
Dunnamanagh	48	54.52 N	7.18 W
Dünnbach ≃	56	50.10 N	8.28 E
Dunnellon	220	29.02 N	82.27 W
Dunnet	46	58.31 N	3.20 W
Dunnet Head ➤	46	58.40 N	3.24 W
Dunnigan	226	38.53 N	121.58 W
Dunning	198	41.49 N	100.06 W
Dunning Creek ≃	214	40.02 N	78.28 W
Dunnington	44	53.57 N	0.59 W
Dunningtown	279b	40.25 N	79.35 W
Dunn Loring	284c	38.53 N	77.14 W
Dunn Loring Woods	284c	38.52 N	77.14 W
Dunnockshaw	262	53.45 N	2.17 W
Dunnottar Castle ⌂	46	56.57 N	2.11 W
Dunns Bridge	216	41.13 N	86.59 W
Dunnville	212	42.54 N	79.36 W
Dunolly	169	36.52 S	143.44 E
Dunoon	46	55.57 N	4.56 W
Dunqul ➤⁴	140	23.26 N	31.37 E
Dunqulah	140	19.10 N	30.29 E
Dunqulah al-Qadīmah	140	18.13 N	30.45 E
Dunqunāb	140	21.06 N	37.05 E
Dunqunāb, Khalij c	140	21.05 N	37.08 E
Dunrea	184	49.25 N	99.44 W
Dun Rig ⩘	46	55.34 N	3.10 W
Duns	46	55.47 N	2.20 W
Dunsandel	172	43.40 S	172.11 E
Dunsborough	162	33.36 S	115.06 E
Dunsford	50	50.41 N	3.40 W
Dunsmuir	204	41.13 N	122.16 W
Dunstable, Eng., U.K.	42	51.53 N	0.32 W
Dunstable, Eng., U.K.	42	51.12 N	0.37 W
Dun-sur-Auron	32	46.53 N	2.34 E
Dun-sur-Meuse	50	49.23 N	5.11 E
Duntelchaig, Loch ∅	46	57.20 N	4.18 W
Dunton Green	260	51.18 N	0.11 E
Dunton Wayletts	260	51.35 N	0.24 E
Duntou	98	29.21 N	119.46 E
Duntroon	172	44.52 S	170.41 E
Dunvant	262	51.37 N	4.04 W
Dunvegan, S. Afr.	273d	26.09 S	28.09 E
Dunvegan, Scot., U.K.	46	57.26 N	6.35 W
Dunvegan, Loch c	46	57.28 N	6.40 W
Dunvegan Head ➤	46	57.31 N	6.43 W
Dunville	186	47.16 N	53.54 W
Dunwich	171a	27.31 S	153.23 E
Duobei ≃	102	29.48 N	71.44 E
Duobukur ≃	89	49.56 N	125.12 E
Duogu nao ∅	102	31.32 N	103.16 E
Duojiandian	98	39.22 N	117.31 E
Duoludabohuer	120	45.50 N	84.41 E
Duoyun ➤	266b	45.27 N	9.11 E
Duoyuanbao ➤	279b	40.25 N	79.36 W
Duoyuichen	120	30.11 N	102.30 E
Duozhu	102	22.59 N	114.43 E
Duozhuang	98	35.35 N	118.02 E
Du Page ≃	216	41.35 N	88.06 W
Du Page, East Branch ≃	278	41.42 N	88.09 W
Dupang Ling ⩘	102	25.32 N	111.11 E
Duparquet, Lac ∅	190	48.28 N	79.16 W
Dupax	116	16.17 N	121.05 E
Dupi	102	27.11 N	108.20 E
Dupl'atka ≃	102	50.10 N	42.20 E
Dupli	82	54.21 N	36.54 E
Dupo	219	38.31 N	90.13 W
Dupont, In., U.S.	216	38.53 N	85.31 W
Dupont, Pa., U.S.	210	41.03 N	84.18 W
Dupont, Wa., U.S.	224	47.05 N	122.37 W
Dupont Research Center ⬩³	285	39.46 N	75.34 W
Düppel, Berliner Forst ⬩³	264a	52.26 N	13.08 E
Dupree	198	45.02 N	101.36 W
Duque Bacelar	250	4.09 S	42.57 W
Duque de Caxias	287a	22.45 S	43.16 W
Duque de Caxias ⬩⁷	287a	22.45 S	43.19 W
Duque de York, Isla I	214	40.22 N	79.51 W
Duquesne	279a	40.26 N	79.59 W
Duquesne University ⬩	279b	40.26 N	79.59 W
Dürä	132	31.30 N	35.02 E
Durack Ranges ⩘	164	15.33 S	127.52 E
Durak Dağı ⩘	130	39.47 N	43.42 E
Dural	274a	33.41 S	151.02 E
Duran	200	34.28 N	105.23 W

PORTUGUÊS

Nome	Página	Lat.°'	Long.°' W = Oeste
Durance ≃	62	43.55 N	4.44 E
Durand, Il., U.S.	190	42.26 N	89.19 W
Durand, Mi., U.S.	218	42.54 N	83.59 W
Durand, Wi., U.S.	190	44.37 N	91.57 W
Durand Reef ⬩²	175f	22.03 S	168.39 E
Duran Durat I	271c	1.15 N	103.51 E
Durango, Esp.	34	43.10 N	2.37 W
Durango, Méx.	234	24.02 N	104.40 W
Durango, Co., U.S.	200	37.16 N	107.52 W
Durango □³	232	24.50 N	104.50 W
Duranillin	168a	33.31 S	116.48 E
Durant, Ia., U.S.	190	41.35 N	90.54 W
Durant, Ms., U.S.	194	33.04 N	89.51 W
Durant, Ok., U.S.	196	33.59 N	96.22 W
Duras	32	44.41 N	0.11 E
Duratón ≃	34	41.37 N	4.07 W
Duraur V	144	10.33 N	49.07 E
Durazno	252	33.22 S	56.31 W
Durazzo — Durrës	38	41.19 N	19.26 E
Durbädänga	126	22.57 N	89.15 E
Durban	158	29.55 S	30.56 E
Durban Occidental — Zapadnaja Dvina ≃	76	57.04 N	24.03 E
Durban Septentrional — Severnaja Dvina ≃	24	64.32 N	40.30 E
Durbanville	158	33.50 S	18.39 E
Durbe	76	56.35 N	21.21 E
D'urbel'dżin	83	41.16 N	74.57 E
Durbin	188	38.32 N	79.49 W
Durbuy	56	50.21 N	5.28 E
Durchholz	263	51.23 N	7.17 E
Durdent ≃	50	49.51 N	0.36 E
Durdevac	36	46.03 N	17.04 E
Durdur V	144	10.34 N	43.58 E
Dureji	120	25.53 N	67.18 E
Düren	56	50.48 N	6.28 E
Durg	124	21.11 N	81.17 E
Durgāpur	126	23.29 N	87.20 E
Durham, On., Can.	212	44.10 N	80.49 W
Durham, Eng., U.K.	44	54.47 N	1.34 W
Durham, Ca., U.S.	204	39.38 N	121.47 W
Durham, Ct., U.S.	207	41.28 N	72.40 W
Durham, Mo., U.S.	219	39.58 N	91.40 W
Durham, N.H., U.S.	188	43.08 N	70.55 W
Durham, N.C., U.S.	192	35.59 N	78.53 W
Durham, Or., U.S.	224	45.25 N	122.46 W
Durham □⁶, On., Can.	212	43.56 N	78.53 W
Durham Cathedral ⬩¹	44	54.45 N	1.45 W
Durham Downs	166	27.05 S	141.54 E
Durham Heights ⩘	176	71.08 N	122.56 W
Durham Pond ∅	276	41.00 N	74.27 W
Durhamville	210	43.08 N	75.40 W
Durian ≃	115a	0.15 N	106.24 E
Durian, Selat ⋓	114	0.42 N	103.42 E
Duriansebatang ≃	114	0.47 S	109.56 E
Durian Tipus ≃	114	3.07 N	102.13 E
D'urinskije razlivy ≈	80	50.25 N	50.20 E
Durlabhpur	272b	22.47 N	88.29 E
Durlach ➤⁸	54	49.00 N	8.28 E
Durlești	78	47.02 N	28.45 E
Durmersheim	54	48.56 N	8.16 E
Durmitor ⩘	38	43.08 N	19.01 E
Durness	46	58.33 N	4.45 W
Durness, Kyle of c	46	58.34 N	4.49 W
Durneva, ostrova II	74	71.50 N	128.00 E
Dürnkrut	61	48.28 N	16.51 E
Dürnstein ⌂	61	48.24 N	15.32 E
Duro ≃	34	5.31 N	37.12 E
Durón	34	40.38 N	2.43 W
Duros Heights	262	39.40 N	75.37 W
Dürre Liesing ≃	264b	48.08 N	16.16 E
Durrell	186	49.40 N	54.44 W
Dürrenboden	58	46.57 N	8.50 E
Durrës	38	41.19 N	19.26 E
Durrie	166	25.38 S	140.16 E
Dursey Air Force Base ⬩	196	32.25 N	99.51 W
Dyfed □⁶	42	52.00 N	4.30 W
Dursley	42	51.41 N	2.21 W
Dursey Head ➤	48	51.35 N	10.14 W
Dursey Island I	48	51.36 N	10.12 W
Dursunbey	130	39.35 N	28.38 E
D'urt'uli	86	55.29 N	54.52 E
Duru	154	4.14 N	28.45 E
Duru Gölü ∅	130	41.20 N	28.35 E
Durulova	130	38.17 N	38.01 E
Durunkah	142	27.08 N	31.10 E
Durūz, Jabal ad- ⩘	132	32.40 N	36.44 E
D'Urville, Tanjung ➤	116	1.28 S	137.54 E
D'Urville Island I	172	40.50 S	173.52 E
Duruma ≃	147	4.11 N	75.44 W
Dury Voe c	46a	60.20 N	1.08 W
Dušak	85	37.13 N	60.02 E
Dušan, Zhg.	102	31.36 N	116.14 E
Dušan, Zhg.	102	25.53 N	107.30 E
Du Shan ⩘	98	39.10 N	70.01 E
Dushanbe	104	38.35 N	68.48 E
Dushanhu	98	30.36 N	116.52 E
Dushantou	106	44.20 N	84.51 E
Dushanzi	98	38.23 N	116.33 E
Dushichang	107	29.10 N	106.31 E
Dushikou	98	41.17 N	115.38 E
Dushore	210	41.31 N	76.24 W
Dushu	100	33.21 N	113.09 E
Dushu Hu ∅	106	31.17 N	120.42 E
Dusios ežeras ∅	76	54.18 N	23.42 E
Dusky Sound ⋓	172	45.47 S	166.28 E
Düsseldorf, Dtsch.	56	51.13 N	6.47 E
Düsseldorf, Dtsch.	263	51.13 N	6.47 E
Düsseldorf □⁶	56	51.15 N	7.00 E
Düsseldorf, Flughafen ✈	56	51.17 N	6.47 E

Dumb-East (ENGLISH)

Name	Page	Lat.°'	Long.°' W = Oeste
Dutun	105	39.46 N	117.02 E
Dutzow	219	38.37 N	90.59 W
Duval	86	47.30 N	91.40 E
Duval, Lac ∅	190	46.19 N	76.55 W
Duvall	224	47.44 N	121.59 W
Duvan	86	55.42 N	57.54 E
Duvanka ≃	83	49.35 N	38.10 E
Duved	26	63.24 N	12.52 E
Duvernay ➤⁸	275a	45.35 N	73.40 W
Duvno	36	43.43 N	17.14 E
Duwamish ≃	224	47.32 N	122.19 W
Duwaydar, Bi'r ad- ▼⁴	142	30.55 N	32.31 E
Duxbury	207	42.02 N	70.40 W
Duxbury Bay c	207	42.02 N	70.39 W
Duxbury Beach ⬩²	283	42.03 N	70.38 W
Duxun	100	23.55 N	117.37 E
Duyagan Point ➤	116	12.36 N	121.33 E
Duyun	102	26.12 N	107.31 E
Düzce	130	40.50 N	31.10 E
Dve Mogili	38	43.36 N	25.52 E
Dzaanhošuu	102	47.03 N	97.15 E
Dzaudžikau — Vladikavkaz	84	43.03 N	44.40 E
Dzamin Üüd	102	43.43 N	111.53 E
Dzamin Üüd	102	43.43 N	111.53 E
Dženiš-Dobo	83	42.10 N	73.15 E
Dzeržinsk	80	56.15 N	43.24 E
— Dzeržinsk	80	56.15 N	43.24 E
Dzeržinsk, Bela.	76	53.41 N	27.08 E
Dzeržinsk, Ross.	80	56.15 N	43.24 E
Dzeržinsk, Ukr.	78	50.09 N	37.56 E
Dzeržinsk, Ukr.	83	48.26 N	37.50 E
Dzeržinskaja, gora ⩘²	76	53.51 N	27.03 E
Dzeržinskij, Ross.	82	55.38 N	37.50 E
Dzeržinskij, Ukr.	78	48.02 N	39.26 E
Dzeržinskij ➤⁸	83	48.02 N	39.26 E
Dzeržinskoje, Kaz.	86	50.40 N	81.07 E
Dzeržinskoje, Ross.	86	56.49 N	95.18 E
Dzetim, chrebet ⩘	85	41.35 N	77.05 E
Dzetygara	86	52.11 N	61.12 E
Dzetyoguz	85	42.27 N	78.14 E
Dzetyoguzskij zapovednik ⬩	85	42.15 N	78.20 E
Dzetysaj	85	40.47 N	68.16 E
Dzezdy	86	48.04 N	67.05 E
Dzezkazgan, Kaz.	86	47.53 N	67.27 E
Dzezkazgan, Kaz.	86	47.47 N	67.46 E
Dzhallabad	84	39.14 N	48.31 E
Dzhambul — Džambul	85	42.54 N	71.22 E
Działdowo	30	53.15 N	20.10 E
Działoszyce	30	50.22 N	20.21 E
Dzibalchén	232	19.31 N	89.45 W
Dzibilchaltun ⌂	232	21.05 N	89.36 W
Džida	88	50.37 N	106.14 E
Džida ≃	88	50.10 N	102.00 E
Dzierzgoń	30	53.56 N	19.21 E
Dzierzoniów (Reichenbach)	30	50.44 N	16.39 E
Dżīlām González	232	21.17 N	88.56 W
Džilav	85	39.19 N	67.45 E
Džilga	85	41.43 N	69.01 E
Džinst	102	45.24 N	104.05 E
Dzioua	148	33.14 N	5.14 E
Džirgatal'	85	39.13 N	71.12 E
Dzitás	232	20.51 N	88.31 W
Dzitbalché	232	20.19 N	90.03 W
Dziwna ≃¹	54	54.01 N	14.44 E
Dziwnów	30	54.03 N	14.45 E
Džizak	85	40.06 N	67.50 E
Dzodze	150	6.14 N	1.00 E
Džubga	78	44.20 N	38.43 E
Džugdžur, chrebet ⩘	74	58.00 N	136.00 E
Džükste	76	56.47 N	23.15 E
Džul'fa	84	38.58 N	45.38 E
Džumabazar	85	39.31 N	67.13 E
Džumgoltau, chrebet ⩘	85	42.18 N	74.32 E
Dzungarian Basin — Junggar Pendi ≃¹	86	45.00 N	88.00 E
Dzungarian Gate — Dzungarskije vorota) ⋋	86	45.25 N	82.25 E
Džungarskij Alatau, chrebet ⩘	86	45.00 N	81.00 E
Dzungarskije vorota — Dzungarian Gate ⋋	86	45.25 N	82.25 E
Džūrak-Sal ≃	84	47.18 N	43.36 E
Dżürch	88	48.55 N	100.10 E
Džurin	78	48.41 N	28.18 E
Dzúsaly	86	45.35 N	64.05 E
Dzüün Changaj	88	49.17 N	95.14 E
Dzüün Charaa	88	48.52 N	106.28 E
Dzüün Gov	88	46.55 N	93.47 E
Dzuunmod	88	47.45 N	106.55 E
Džvari	84	42.43 N	42.04 E
Dzygovka	78	48.22 N	28.19 E

Name	Page	Lat.°'	Long.°'
E			
Eads	198	38.28 N	102.46 W
Eagar	200	34.06 N	109.17 W
Eagle, Ak., U.S.	180	64.46 N	141.16 W
Eagle, Co., U.S.	200	39.39 N	106.49 W
Eagle, N.Y., U.S.	210	42.33 N	78.18 W
Eagle, Wi., U.S.	216	42.52 N	88.28 W
Eagle ≃, Nf., Can.	164	9.00 S	148.45 E
Eagle ≃, Yk., Can.	180	67.20 N	137.10 W
Eagle ≃, Co., U.S.	200	39.39 N	107.04 W
Eagle, Mount ⩘	241n	17.46 N	64.49 W
Eagle Bay	180	46.09 N	95.02 W
Eagle Bend	190	46.09 N	95.02 W
Eagle Bridge	210	42.57 N	73.24 W
Eagle Butte	198	45.00 N	101.14 W
Eagle Creek ≃, Sk., Can.	184	52.22 N	107.24 W
Eagle Creek ≃, Az., U.S.	200	33.16 N	109.25 W
Eagle Creek ≃, Or., U.S.	224	45.21 N	122.23 W
Eagle Creek, East Fork ≃	218	38.47 N	83.43 W
Eagle Creek, West Fork ≃	218	38.47 N	83.43 W
Eagle Creek Reservoir ∅¹	216	39.50 N	86.18 W
Eagledale	224	47.37 N	122.32 W
Eagle Grove	190	42.39 N	93.54 W
Eagle Harbor	282	43.15 N	78.15 W
Eaglehawk	169	36.43 S	144.15 E
Eagle Hill ⩘	210	42.22 N	74.09 W
Eagle Lake, Fl., U.S.	220	27.59 N	81.45 W
Eagle Lake, Me.	188	47.02 N	68.36 W
Eagle Lake, Mi., U.S.	216	41.48 N	86.02 W
Eagle Lake, Tx., U.S.	196	29.35 N	96.20 W
Eagle Lake ∅, On., Can.	182	49.42 N	93.13 W
Eagle Lake ∅, B.C., Can.			
Eagle Lake ∅, Ca., U.S.	204	40.39 N	120.44 W
Eagle Lake ∅, Me., U.S.	188	46.20 N	69.20 W
Eagle Mountain, Ca., U.S.	228	33.49 N	115.27 W
Eagle Mountain ⩘, Mn., U.S.	190	47.54 N	90.33 W
Eagle Mountain Lake ∅¹	222	32.55 N	97.30 W
Eagle Mountain Lake	222	32.52 N	97.30 W
Eagle Nest Butte ⩘	198	43.17 N	101.43 W

Name	Page	Lat.°'	Long.°'
Eagle Nest Lake ∅	222	29.13 N	95.37 W
Eagle Pass	196	28.42 N	100.29 W
Eagle Peak ⩘, Ca., U.S.	204	41.17 N	120.12 W
Eagle Peak ⩘, Ca., U.S.	228	35.15 N	118.28 W
Eagle River, Mi., U.S.	190	47.24 N	88.18 W
Eagle River, Wi., U.S.	190	45.55 N	89.14 W
Eagle Rock	192	37.39 N	79.48 W
Eagle Rock ➤⁸	280	34.09 N	118.12 W
Eagle Rock Reservation ⬩	276	40.49 N	74.14 W
Eaglesfield	44	55.03 N	3.12 W
Eaglesham, Ab., Can.	182	55.47 N	117.53 W
Eaglesham, Scot., U.K.	46	55.44 N	4.18 W
Eagles Mere	210	41.25 N	76.35 W
Earaheedy	162	25.34 S	121.39 E
Eagle Village	184	64.47 N	141.07 W
Eagleville, Ct., U.S.	207	41.47 N	72.16 W
Eagleville, Pa., U.S.	285	40.10 N	75.24 W
Eagleville, Wi., U.S.	216	42.52 N	88.26 W
Ealing ➤⁸	260	51.31 N	0.20 W
Eamont ≃	44	54.40 N	2.39 W
Earby	44	53.56 N	2.08 W
Earcroft	262	53.43 N	2.29 W
Eardisley	42	52.08 N	2.59 W
Eardley Lake ∅	184	52.32 N	96.05 W
Ear Falls	184	50.38 N	93.13 W
Earlestown	262	53.27 N	2.39 W
Earl Grey	184	50.56 N	104.45 W
Earlham	194	41.29 N	94.07 W
Earlimart	226	35.53 N	119.16 W
Earlington	46	57.34 N	6.23 W
Earl Park	216	40.40 N	87.24 W
Earl Rowe Provincial Park ⬩	281	44.10 N	79.54 W
Earls Barton	42	52.15 N	0.45 W
Earls Colne	42	51.56 N	0.42 E
Earl Shilton	42	52.35 N	1.20 W
Earl Soham	42	52.14 N	1.16 E
Earlston	46	55.39 N	2.40 W
Earlton	210	42.21 N	73.54 W
Earlville, Il., U.S.	216	41.35 N	88.55 W
Earlville, N.Y., U.S.	210	42.44 N	75.33 W
Earlville, Pa., U.S.	285	40.04 N	75.21 W
Earlwood	274a	33.56 S	151.08 E
Early, Ia., U.S.	198	42.27 N	95.09 W
Early, Tx., U.S.	196	31.45 N	98.54 W
Early Winters Creek ≃	224	48.35 N	120.35 W
Earn ≃	46	56.23 N	3.19 W
Earn, Loch ∅	46	56.23 N	4.14 W
Earnslaw, Mount ⩘	172	44.37 S	168.24 E
Earth	196	34.14 N	102.24 W
Eas	175f	16.22 S	168.12 E
Easington, Eng., U.K.	44	53.40 N	0.07 E
Easington, Eng., U.K.	44	54.47 N	1.11 W
Easingwold	44	54.07 N	1.11 W
Easky	48	54.18 N	8.58 W
Easley	192	34.49 N	82.36 W
East ≃, On., Can.	190	52.20 N	79.17 W
East Allen ≃	44	54.55 N	2.19 W
East Alliance	214	40.55 N	81.04 W
East Alligator ≃	164	12.08 S	132.42 E
East Alton	219	38.52 N	90.06 W
East Amherst	210	43.01 N	78.42 W
East Angus	206	45.29 N	71.40 W
East Arlington	210	43.05 N	73.43 W
East Atlantic Beach	276	40.35 N	73.43 W
East Aurora	210	42.46 N	78.36 W
East Avon	210	42.55 N	77.42 W
East Baines ≃	164	15.38 S	129.58 E
East Bangor	210	40.53 N	75.11 W
East Barming	260	51.16 N	0.28 E
East Barnet ➤⁸	260	51.39 N	0.09 W
East Bay c	194	29.30 N	89.30 W
East Bay c, Tx., U.S.	222	29.30 N	94.35 W
East Bay c, Fl., U.S.	194	30.05 N	85.32 W
East Bay c, N.Y., U.S.			
U.S.	210	40.38 N	73.32 W
East Bedfont ➤⁸	260	51.27 N	0.26 W
East Bend	192	36.12 N	80.30 W
East Berbice-Corentyne □⁴	246	4.00 N	58.15 W
East Berkshire	206	44.56 N	72.42 W
East Berlin, Pa., U.S.	285	39.48 N	74.55 W
East Berlin, N.J., U.S.	285	39.56 N	76.58 W
East Bernard	222	37.11 N	84.07 W
East Bernstadt	192	37.11 N	84.07 W
East Berwick	210	41.04 N	76.07 W
East Bethany	210	42.54 N	78.08 W
East Bhāgīrath Plain ≃	126	23.30 N	88.30 E
East Bijou Creek ≃	198	39.51 N	104.08 W
East Billerica	283	42.34 N	71.14 W
East Blackstone	207	42.02 N	71.31 W
East Bloomfield	210	42.53 N	77.26 W
East Boston ➤⁸	283	42.23 N	71.02 W
Eastbourne, N.Z.	172	41.18 S	174.54 E
Eastbourne, Eng., U.K.	42	50.46 N	0.17 E
East Brady	214	40.59 N	79.36 W
East Braintree	184	49.37 N	95.38 W
East Branch Lake ∅	214	41.39 N	78.35 W
East Brewster	194	41.46 N	70.03 W
East Bridgewater	207	42.02 N	70.57 W
East Brimfield Lake ∅¹	207	42.06 N	72.10 W
East Brooklyn	207	41.47 N	71.53 W
East Brother I	271d	22.20 N	113.58 E
East Brunswick	210	40.25 N	74.25 W
East Bucas Island I	116	9.43 N	126.02 E
East Burwood	274b	37.51 S	145.09 E
Eastbury	260	51.37 N	0.25 W
East Cache Creek ≃	196	34.08 N	98.16 W
East Caicos I	238	21.40 N	71.35 W
East Calder	45	55.54 N	3.27 W
East Canaan	207	42.02 N	73.17 W
East Canada Creek ≃	210	43.00 N	74.45 W
East Canton	214	40.47 N	81.17 W
East Cape ➤, N.Z.	172	37.41 S	178.33 E
East Cape ➤, Ru.	181a	51.21 N	179.29 E
East Cape ➤, Fl., U.S.	220	25.07 N	81.05 W
East Caranchahua ≃	222	28.51 N	96.19 W
East Carbon	200	39.32 N	110.24 W
East Carillon Basin ≃	14	4.00 N	146.45 E
East Carondelet	279	38.33 N	90.14 W
East Carver	207	41.51 N	70.45 W
East Castor ≃	156	45.16 N	75.17 W
East Catfish Creek ≃	180	68.20 N	133.50 W
East Chatham	210	42.26 N	73.34 W
East Chelmsford	283	42.36 N	71.20 W
Eastchester ➤⁸	276	40.57 N	73.49 W
Eastchester Bay c	276	40.49 N	73.48 W
East Chezzetcook	187	44.44 N	63.13 W
East Chicago	278	41.38 N	87.27 W
East Chicago Heights	278	41.30 N	87.35 W
East China Sea ▼²	92	30.00 N	126.00 E
East Claridon	214	41.32 N	81.07 W
East Cleddau ≃	42	51.46 N	4.52 W

Símbolos / Symbols Legend

≃ River	Fluß	Río	Rivière	Rio	
☰ Canal	Kanal	Canal	Canal	Canal	
⌄ Waterfall, Rapids	Wasserfall, Stromschnellen	Cascada, Rápidos	Cascade, Rapides	Cascata, Rápidos	
⋓ Strait	Meeresstraße	Estrecho	Détroit	Estreito	
c Bay, Gulf	Bucht, Golf	Bahía, Golfo	Baie, Golfe	Baía, Golfo	
∅ Lake, Lakes	See, Seen	Lago, Lagos	Lac, Lacs	Lago, Lagos	
≈ Swamp	Sumpf	Pantano	Marais	Pântano	
⧈ Ice Features, Glacier	Eis- und Gletscherformen	Accidentes Glaciares	Formes glaciaires	Acidentes glaciares	
⬩ Other Hydrographic Features	Andere Hydrographische Objekte	Otros Elementos Hidrográficos	Autres données hydrographiques	Outros acidentes hidrográficos	
➤ Submarine Features	Untermeerische Objekte	Accidentes Submarinos	Formes de relief sous-marin	Acidentes submarinos	
□ Political Unit	Politische Einheit	Unidad Política	Entité politique	Unidade política	
⧈ Cultural Institution	Kulturelle Institution	Institución Cultural	Institution culturelle	Instituição cultural	
⌂ Historical Site	Historische Stätte	Sitio Histórico	Site historique	Sítio histórico	
⬩ Recreational Site	Erholungs- und Ferienort	Sitio de Recreo	Centre de loisirs	Sítio de Lazer	
✈ Airport	Flughafen	Aeropuerto	Aéroport	Aeroporto	
⬥ Military Installation	Militäranlage	Instalación Militar	Installation militaire	Instalação militar	
⬩ Miscellaneous	Verschiedenes	Misceláneo	Divers	Diversos	

Symbols in the index entries represent the broad categories identified in the key at the right. Symbols with superior numbers (✦¹) identify subcategories (see complete key on page 1 : 1).

Los símbolos incluidos en el texto del índice representan las grandes categorías identificadas con a clave a la derecha. Los símbolos con números en su parte superior (✦¹) identifican las subcategorías (véase la clave completa en la página 1 : 1).

Les symboles dans l'index représentent les catégories indiquées dans la légende à droite. Les symboles suivis d'un indice (✦¹) représentent des sous-catégories (voir légende complète à la page 1 : 1).

Os símbolos incluídos no texto do índice representam as grandes categorias identificadas com a clave a direita. Os símbolos com números em sua parte superior (✦¹) identificam as subcategorias (veja a chave completa à pagina 1 : 1).

Symbole im Register stellen die rechts im Schlüssel erklärten Kategorien dar. Symbole mit hochgestellten Ziffern (✦¹) bezeichnen Unterabteilungen einer Kategorie (vgl. vollständiger Schlüssel auf Seite 1 : 1).

Other Topographic Features	Andere Topographische Objekte	Otros Elementos Topográficos	Autres données topographiques	Outros acidentes topográficos
▲ Mountain	Berg	Montaña	Montagne	Montanha
x Pass	Paß	Paso	Col	Passo
≖ Plain	Ebene	Llano	Plaine	Planície
⊐ Valley, Canyon	Tal, Cañon	Valle, Cañón	Vallée, Canyon	Vale, Canhão
ıı Islands	Inseln	Islas	Îles	Ilhas
ı Island	Insel	Isla	Île	Ilha
➤ Cape	Kap	Cabo	Cap	Cabo

ENGLISH

Name	Page	Lat.°	Long.°

DEUTSCH

Name	Seite	Breite°	Länge° E = Ost

ESPAÑOL Nombre	Página	Lat.° '	Long.° ' W=Oeste
Eging	60	48.43 N	13.16 E
Egipto — Egypt □¹	140	27.00 N	30.00 E
Égletons	32	45.24 N	2.03 E
Eglin Air Force Base ▪	194	30.29 N	86.30 W
Eglinton	48	55.22 N	7.11 W
Eglisau	58	47.34 N	8.32 E
Egoskerry	42	50.39 N	4.27 W
Égly	261	48.35 N	2.13 E
Egmond aan Zee	52	52.36 N	4.37 E
Egmond-Binnen	52	52.35 N	4.39 E
Egmont, Cape ▸	172	39.17 S	173.45 E
Egmont, Mount — Taranaki, Mount ∧	172	39.18 S	174.04 E
Egmont Bay c	186	46.35 N	64.12 W
Egmont Channel ṵ	220	27.36 N	82.45 W
Egmont Key	220	27.35 N	82.46 W
Egmont National Park ♦	172	39.15 S	174.05 E
Egna (Neumarkt)	64	46.19 N	11.16 E
Egnach	58	47.33 N	9.23 E
Egnazia ı	68	40.53 N	17.24 E
Egoryevsk — Jegorjevsk	82	55.23 N	39.02 E
Egota ♦⁸	268	35.43 N	139.40 E
Egra	126	21.54 N	87.32 E
Egremont, Ab., Can.	182	54.02 N	113.08 W
Egremont, Eng., U.K.	44	54.29 N	3.33 W
Égreville	32	48.10 N	2.52 E
Eğridir	130	37.52 N	30.51 E
Eğridir Gölü ⊘	130	38.02 N	30.53 E
Eğriköy	130	38.44 N	27.21 E
Egrisskij chrebet ∧	84	42.49 N	42.24 E
Egton	44	54.26 N	0.45 W
Egtved	41	55.37 N	9.18 E
Éguas, Rio das ≃	255	13.26 S	44.14 W
Éguilles	62	43.34 N	5.22 E
Eguisheim	58	48.03 N	7.18 E
Egum Atoll ı¹	164	9.25 S	151.55 E
Egvekinot	180	66.19 N	179.10 W
Egyházasrádóc	61	47.05 N	16.37 E
Egypt, Ma., U.S.	207	42.12 N	70.45 W
Egypt, Pa., U.S.	208	40.41 N	75.32 W
Egypt, Tx., U.S.	222	29.24 N	96.14 W
Egypt (Misr) □¹, Afr.	136	27.00 N	30.00 E
Egypt (Misr) □¹, Afr.	136	27.00 N	30.00 E
Egypte — Egypt □¹	140	27.00 N	30.00 E
Egyptian Museum	273c	30.03 N	31.14 E
Eha-Amufu	150	6.40 N	7.46 E
Ehekirchen	60	48.38 N	11.06 E
Ehen ≃	44	54.25 N	3.30 W
Ehime ᵒ⁵	96	33.40 N	132.50 E
Ehingen	58	48.17 N	9.43 E
Ehingen ▪³	263	51.22 N	6.42 E
Ehle ≃	54	52.12 N	11.44 E
Ehmen	54	52.24 N	10.41 E
Ehra-Lessien	54	52.34 N	10.46 E
Ehrang	54	49.49 N	6.41 E
Ehrenberg	200	33.36 N	114.31 W
Ehrenberg Range ∧	162	23.18 S	130.20 E
Ehrenbreitstein, Feste ∴	56	50.21 N	7.37 E
Ehrenburg ²	56	50.12 N	7.27 E
Ehrenfeld	214	40.22 N	78.46 W
Ehrenfriedersdorf	54	50.38 N	12.58 E
Ehrenhausen	61	46.43 N	15.35 E
Ehreshoven	56	50.58 N	7.20 E
Ehrhardt	192	33.05 N	81.00 W
Ehrhorn	52	53.10 N	9.53 E
Ehringhausen	56	51.11 N	7.33 E
Ehringhausen ▪⁸	263	51.09 N	7.11 E
Ehrwald	58	47.24 N	10.55 E
Ehwa Women's University ¹	271b	37.34 N	126.56 E
Ei	92	31.12 N	130.30 E
Eibar	34	43.11 N	2.28 W
Eibau	54	50.58 N	14.40 E
Eibelstadt	56	49.43 N	10.00 E
Eibenstock	54	50.29 N	12.35 E
Eibergen	52	52.06 N	6.39 E
Eibiswald	61	46.41 N	15.15 E
Eibsee ⊘	58	47.27 N	10.58 E
Eicha	52	50.11 N	10.34 E
Eich-Berg ∧²	264a	52.39 N	13.50 E
Eiche, Dtsch.	264a	52.25 N	12.58 E
Eiche, Dtsch.	264a	52.34 N	13.36 E
Eichenbarleben	54	52.10 N	11.24 E
Eichenbrandt	264a	52.38 N	13.51 E
Eichendorf	60	48.38 N	12.51 E
Eichgraben	61	48.10 N	15.59 E
Eichlinghofen ▪⁸	263	51.29 N	7.24 E
Eichsfeld ▪¹	54	51.25 N	10.20 E
Eichstädt	264a	52.42 N	13.07 E
Eichstätt	60	48.54 N	11.12 E
Eichstetten	58	48.05 N	7.44 E
Eichtersheim	58	49.14 N	8.46 E
Eichwalde	54	52.22 N	13.37 E
Eickelborn	56	51.39 N	8.13 E
Eicken ▪⁸	263	51.13 N	6.26 E
Eickerend	263	51.13 N	6.34 E
Eickerkopf ∧²	263	51.21 N	7.42 E
Eicklingen	52	52.33 N	10.10 E
Eide	26	62.55 N	7.26 E
Eidelstedt ▪⁸	52	53.36 N	9.53 E
Eider ≃	54	54.19 N	8.58 E
Eiderstedt ▸¹	41	54.22 N	8.50 E
Eidfjord	26	60.28 N	7.05 E
Eidsvåg, Nor.	26	60.27 N	5.21 E
Eidsvåg, Nor.	26	62.47 N	8.03 E
Eidsvold	166	25.22 S	151.07 E
Eidsvoll	26	60.19 N	11.14 E
Eifel ∧¹	56	50.10 N	6.45 E
Eiffel, Tour ⊥	261	48.51 N	2.18 E
Eiffel Flats	166	18.15 S	29.58 E
Eigenbach ∧²	263	51.05 N	7.09 E
Eiger, Cam ∧	263	51.17 N	5.07 W
Eigen ∧²	263	51.33 N	6.57 E
Eigenji	94	35.04 N	136.18 E
Eigenrieden	54	51.11 N	10.22 E
Eiger ∧	58	46.35 N	8.00 E
Eigg ı	46	56.54 N	6.10 W
Eigg, Sound of ṵ	46	56.51 N	6.13 W
Eight Degree Channel ṵ	122	8.00 N	73.00 E
Eighteenmile Creek ≃, N.Y., U.S.	210	42.43 N	78.58 W
Eighteenmile Creek ≃, N.Y., U.S.	210	43.21 N	78.43 W
Eight Mile Creek ≃, On., Can.	284a	43.14 N	79.11 W
Eightmile Creek ≃, In., U.S.	216	40.57 N	85.22 W
Eightmile Creek ≃, Or., U.S.	224	45.36 N	121.05 W
Eights Coast ∡²	329	73.30 S	93.00 W
Eighty Four	279b	40.11 N	80.08 W
Eighty Mile Beach ²	162	19.45 S	121.00 E
Eiheiji	94	36.06 N	136.20 E
Eijerlandsche Gat c	52	53.19 N	4.54 E
Eijsden	56	50.47 N	5.43 E
Eikeren ⊘	26	59.53 N	9.58 E
Eikisdalsvatnet ⊘	26	62.36 N	8.11 E
Eildon	169	37.14 S	145.56 E
Eildon, Lake ⊘	169	37.14 S	146.00 E
Eilean Gowan Island ı	212	64.03 N	79.25 W
Eileen	236	41.17 N	88.15 W
Eili Malk ı	175b	7.09 N	134.22 E
Eilpe ▪⁸	263	51.21 N	7.29 E
Eilsleben	54	52.09 N	11.13 E
Eime	52	52.14 N	9.25 E
Eimke	52	52.58 N	10.19 E
Eina	26	60.38 N	10.36 E
Einasleigh	166	18.31 S	144.05 E
Einasleigh ≃	166	17.30 S	142.17 E
Einbeck	52	51.26 N	9.28 E
Eindhoven	56	51.26 N	5.28 E
Eine	50	50.52 N	3.37 E

FRANÇAIS Nom	Page	Lat.° '	Long.° ' W=Ouest
Einme	110	16.54 N	95.11 E
Einöd	56	49.16 N	7.19 E
Einödriegel ∧	60	48.56 N	13.02 E
Einruhr	56	50.35 N	6.22 E
Einsiedel	54	50.46 N	12.58 E
Einsiedeln	58	47.08 N	8.45 E
Einville-au-Jard	58	48.39 N	6.30 E
Eirauli	272c	19.10 N	72.59 E
Éire — Ireland □¹	48	53.00 N	8.00 W
Eiru ≃	248	6.42 S	69.52 W
Eirunepé	248	6.40 S	69.52 W
Eisbach ≃	56	49.38 N	8.22 E
Eisch ≃	56	49.45 N	6.07 E
Eiseb ≃	156	20.33 S	20.59 E
Eisenach	54	50.59 N	10.19 E
Eisenkappel	61	46.29 N	14.35 E
Eisenschmitt	56	50.03 N	6.43 E
Eisenstadt	61	47.51 N	16.32 E
Eisfeld	54	50.26 N	10.54 E
Eisgarn	61	48.54 N	15.06 E
Eishken	46	58.01 N	6.32 W
Eishort, Loch c	46	57.10 N	5.59 W
Eiškiškes	54	54.10 N	25.00 E
Eisk — Jejsk	78	46.42 N	38.16 E
Eisleben	54	51.31 N	11.32 E
Eislingen	56	48.42 N	9.42 E
Eisriesenwelt ± ⁵	61	47.32 N	13.10 E
Eitaf	174t	1.21 N	173.05 E
Eitorf	56	50.46 N	7.26 E
Eivissa	34	38.54 N	1.26 E
Eivissa (Ibiza) ı	34	39.00 N	1.25 E
Ejasi — Eyasi, Lake ⊘	154	3.40 S	35.05 E
Ejby, Dan.	41	55.30 N	12.07 E
Ejby, Dan.	41	55.26 N	9.57 E
Ejea de los Caballeros	34	42.08 N	1.08 W
Ejeda	157b	24.20 S	44.31 E
Ejército Rebelde, Presa ⊘¹	286b	23.01 N	82.20 W
Ejido	246	8.33 N	71.14 W
Ejido Jaboncillos	232	28.57 N	102.39 W
Ejigbo	273a	6.33 N	3.18 E
Ejin Horo Qi	102	39.27 N	109.45 E
Ejin	102	41.50 N	100.50 E
Ejstrup	41	55.59 N	9.17 E
Ejura	150	7.23 N	1.22 W
Ejutla de Crespo	234	16.34 N	96.44 W
Ekalaka	198	45.53 N	104.33 W
Ekáli	267c	38.07 N	23.50 E
Ekanga	152	2.23 S	23.14 E
Ekas	115b	8.53 S	116.27 E
Ekaterinburg — Jekaterinburg	86	56.51 N	60.36 E
Ekaterinodar — Krasnodar	78	45.02 N	39.00 E
Ekaterinoslav — Dnepropetrovsk	78	48.27 N	34.59 E
Ekeby	46	56.00 N	12.58 E
Ekenäs (Taamisaari)	26	59.58 N	23.26 E
Ekenässjön	26	57.30 N	15.00 E
Ekerö ı	46	59.18 N	17.43 E
Eket, Nig.	150	4.39 N	7.56 E
Eket, Nig.	41	56.15 N	13.11 E
Eketahuna	172	40.39 S	175.42 E
Ekhinos	38	41.17 N	24.59 E
Ekiatapskij chrebet ∧	74	68.30 N	179.00 E
Ekibastuz	86	51.42 N	75.22 E
Ekimčan	89	53.04 N	132.58 E
Ekityksskij chrebet ∧	180	67.45 N	179.00 E
Eko — Lagos	150	6.27 N	3.24 E
Ekoli	152	0.23 S	24.16 E
Ekolsund	40	59.45 N	17.37 E
Ekolsund	40	59.35 N	17.24 E
Ekolsundsviken c	152	1.16 N	21.36 E
Ekonda	74	65.47 N	105.17 E
Ekoungounou	152	3.03 S	15.38 E
Ekovamou	152	0.07 N	16.31 E
Ekpoma	150	6.46 N	6.08 E
Eksära	272b	22.38 N	88.17 E
Eksel	56	51.09 N	5.23 E
Eksjö	26	57.40 N	14.57 E
Ekuk	180	58.49 N	158.34 W
Ekuku	152	0.42 S	21.38 E
Ekuta	176	53.14 N	22.13 W
Ekwan ≃	176	53.14 N	82.13 W
Ekwata	152	0.13 S	9.18 E
Ekwendeni	154	11.23 S	33.52 E
Ekwok	180	59.22 N	157.30 W
Ela	110	59.22 N	96.13 E
El Aaiún (La'youn)	148	27.09 N	13.12 W
El Abiadh Sidi Cheikh	148	32.56 N	0.42 E
El 'Açâba ± ²	148	16.10 N	11.30 W
El 'Açâba ± ²	150	16.00 N	12.00 W
El- — Ad-, Al-, An-, Ar-, As-, Ash-, At-, Az-			
El-Adde	144	2.35 N	46.00 E
El Adeb Larache	148	27.22 N	8.62 E
El Adelanto	236	14.10 N	89.50 W
El Affroun	34	36.30 N	2.38 E
El Agreb	148	30.48 N	5.30 E
El Aguacate	286c	10.28 N	66.59 W
El Aguacate	234	18.16 N	100.40 W
El Aguilar	252	23.12 S	65.42 W
El Agustino	252	12.03 S	76.59 W
El Agustino, Cerro ∧²	286d	12.04 S	77.00 W
Elaia	38	39.35 N	20.20 E
Elaine	194	34.18 N	90.51 W
El Alamein — Al-'Alamayn	144	30.49 N	28.57 E
El Álamo, Méx.	196	27.32 N	100.52 W
El Álamo, Méx.	234	26.29 N	99.46 W
El Álamo, Méx.	204	31.34 N	116.02 W
El Alia	36	37.10 N	10.03 E
El Alto, Arg.	252	28.18 S	65.42 W
El Alto, Perú	246	4.18 S	81.07 W
Elamanchili	122	17.33 N	82.52 E
El Amparo de Apure	246	7.06 N	70.45 W
Elan ≃	38	46.07 N	28.04 E
Élancourt	261	48.47 N	1.58 E
Élands ≃, S. Afr.	156	25.10 S	28.10 E
Élands ≃, S. Afr.	156	24.35 S	29.39 E
Elandsbaai	158	32.19 S	18.21 E
Elandsfontein	273d	26.10 S	28.12 E
Elandsvlei	158	32.19 S	19.31 E
El Angel	246	0.37 N	77.56 W
Elanora Heights	274a	33.42 S	151.17 E
El Aouinet	36	35.52 N	7.54 E
El Arahal	34	37.16 N	5.33 W
El Arba	234	28.00 N	113.25 W
El Arenal	232	20.47 N	103.42 W
El Arenal ≃	148	32.45 N	5.02 E
El Aricha	148	34.14 N	1.16 W
Elassón	38	39.54 N	22.11 E
Elat, Gulf of — Aqaba, Gulf of c	128	29.00 N	34.40 E
El Avagi	144	3.36 N	46.57 E
El Ávila, Cerro ∧²	286c	10.32 N	66.52 W
El Ávila, Parque Nacional ♦	246	10.35 N	66.48 W
Elazig	130	38.41 N	39.14 E

PORTUGUÊS Nome	Página	Lat.° '	Long.° ' W=Oeste
Elazig □⁴	130	38.35 N	39.30 E
El Azúcar, Presa de ⊘¹	196	26.10 N	99.00 W
El Azul, Sierra ∢	234	23.25 N	100.30 W
Elba, Al., U.S.	194	31.24 N	86.04 W
Elba, Mi., U.S.	216	43.02 N	83.26 W
Elba, Isola d' ı	66	42.46 N	10.17 E
Elba — Elbe ≃	30	53.50 N	9.00 E
El'ban	89	50.06 N	136.31 E
El Banco	246	9.00 N	73.58 W
El Barco de Ávila	34	40.21 N	5.31 W
El Barco de Valdeorras	34	42.25 N	6.59 W
El Barreal	200	31.17 N	107.10 W
Elbe, Dtsch.	234	23.02 N	102.08 W
Elbe, Dtsch.	54	54.05 N	13.26 E
Elbasan	38	41.06 N	20.05 E
Elbaşı	130	38.41 N	35.59 E
El Baúl	246	8.57 N	68.17 W
El Baúl, Cerro ∧, Méx.	234	17.38 N	100.19 W
Elbe (Labe) ≃	30	53.50 N	9.00 E
Elbe, Île d' — Elba, Isola di ı	66	42.46 N	10.17 E
Elbe-Havel-Kanal ≋	54	52.24 N	12.23 E
El Beïd (Ebeji) ≃	146	12.32 N	14.11 E
El-Beïda — Al-Baydā'	146	32.46 N	21.43 E
Elbe-Lübeck-Kanal ≋	54	53.50 N	10.36 E
Elberfeld ▪⁸	263	51.16 N	7.08 E
Elbert	198	39.13 N	104.32 W
Elbert, Mount ∧	200	39.07 N	106.27 W
Elberta	190	44.37 N	86.13 W
Elberton	192	34.06 N	82.52 W
Elbeuf	32	49.17 N	1.00 E
Elbeyli	130	36.41 N	37.26 E
El Beyyadh	148	33.40 N	1.01 E
Elbing — Elbląg	30	54.10 N	19.25 E
Elbingerode	54	51.45 N	10.46 E
Elbistan	130	38.13 N	37.12 E
Elbląg (Elbing)	30	54.10 N	19.25 E
Elbląg ≃¹	30	54.00 N	19.30 E
El Bluff	236	11.59 N	83.40 W
El Bolsón	254	41.58 S	71.31 W
El Bonillo	34	38.57 N	2.32 W
El-Borj	34	35.43 N	5.40 W
El-Boroui	148	32.30 N	7.10 W
El Bosque, Chile	286e	33.34 S	70.41 W
El Bosque, Méx.	234	17.04 N	92.44 W
El Boulaïda	148	36.28 N	2.50 E
El Boulaïda □⁵	148	36.20 N	2.20 E
Elbow	184	51.07 N	106.35 W
Elbow ≃	182	51.03 N	114.02 W
Elbow Cay ı	238	23.57 N	80.29 W
Elbow Lake	188	45.59 N	95.58 W
Elbow Lake ⊘	184	54.50 N	100.53 W
El'brus, gora (Mount Elbrus) ∧	84	43.21 N	42.26 E
Elbrus, Mount — El'brus, gora ∧	84	43.21 N	42.26 E
El'brusskij	84	43.38 N	42.10 E
Elbsandsteingebirge ∧	54	50.50 N	14.20 E
Elburg	52	52.26 N	5.50 E
El Burgo de Osma	34	41.35 N	3.04 W
Elburn	216	41.53 N	88.28 W
Elburz Mountains — Alborz, Reshteh-ye Kūhhā-ye ∧	128	36.00 N	53.00 E
El'buzd	83	46.53 N	39.41 E
El'buzd ≃	83	46.53 N	39.43 E
El Cabezo, Arrecife ∢⁴	234	19.04 N	95.51 W
El Caburé	252	26.01 S	62.27 W
El Caimanero, Laguna c	234	23.00 N	106.07 W
El Cajon	228	32.47 N	116.57 W
El Cajón, Embalse ⊘¹	236	15.00 N	87.35 W
El Calafate	254	50.20 S	72.18 W
El Callao	246	7.21 N	61.49 W
El Calvario, Col.	246	3.59 N	73.40 W
El Calvario, Ven.	246	8.59 N	67.00 W
El Campamento	286b	23.05 N	82.20 W
El Campamento ▪⁸	266a	40.24 N	3.46 W
El Campo	222	29.11 N	96.16 W
El Capitan ∧, Ca., U.S.	226	37.43 N	119.38 W
El Capitan ∧, Mt., U.S.	202	46.01 N	114.23 W
El Caribe	286a	10.37 N	66.50 W
El Carmen, Arg.	252	24.23 S	65.16 W
El Carmen, Bol.	248	18.49 S	58.33 W
El Carmen, Chile	286e	33.21 S	70.43 W
El Carmen, Méx.	234	15.35 N	93.05 W
El Carmen, Perú	246	13.06 N	76.04 W
El Carmen, Ven.	286c	10.24 N	67.01 W
El Carmen, Ven.	286c	10.24 N	66.50 W
El Carmen ≃	232	30.42 N	106.29 W
El Carmen, Canal ≋	286e	33.18 S	70.41 W
El Carmen, Laguna c	234	9.13 N	93.48 W
El Carmen de Bolívar	248	9.43 N	75.08 W
El Carrizo	232	28.24 N	103.23 W
El Carril	252	25.05 S	65.28 W
El Casco	196	25.34 N	104.35 W
El Castillo de La Concepción ∴	236	11.01 N	84.24 W
El Centinela, Cerro ∧	204	32.38 N	115.40 W
El Centro	204	32.47 N	115.33 W
El Cerrito, Col.	246	3.42 N	76.19 W
El Cerrito, Ca., U.S.	228	37.54 N	122.18 W
El Cerro, Bol.	248	18.00 S	63.35 W
El Cerro, Ur.	286b	34.00 S	58.15 W
El Cerro Del Aripo ∧	241	10.44 N	61.16 W
El Chamal	234	23.56 N	97.54 W
El Chante	232	19.41 N	104.10 W
Elche de la Sierra	34	38.27 N	2.03 W
Elche — Elx	34	38.15 N	0.42 W
El Chichonal, Volcán ∢¹	234	17.22 N	93.14 W
El Chile, Montaña ∧	236	14.22 N	86.51 W
El'chkavvun ≃	180	68.42 N	171.00 E
Elcho	196	45.26 N	89.11 W
Elcho Island ı	164	11.55 S	135.45 E
El Chorrillo	286c	10.43 N	66.50 W
El Ciprés	204	31.48 N	116.34 W
El Cobre	240p	20.03 N	75.57 W
El Cocuy	246	6.25 N	72.27 W
El Cojo, Quebrada ≃	286c	10.37 N	66.53 W
El Colorado	252	26.20 S	59.23 W
El Cóndor, Cerro ∧	252	26.35 S	68.22 W
El Congo	236	13.54 N	89.30 W
El Corazón	246	1.12 S	79.06 W
El Corcovado	254	43.31 S	71.36 W
El Corozo	236	13.12 N	87.03 W
El Corte ≃	204	17.30 N	94.54 W
El Corte de Madera Creek ≃	286	37.19 N	122.20 W
El Cortijo	286e	33.25 S	70.42 W
El Coto	200	18.26 N	66.44 W
El Coyote	196	10.35 N	112.40 W
El Coyote ≃	232	30.32 N	113.02 W

Nombre	Página	Lat.° '	Long.° '
El Coyote, Laguna ⊘	196	27.14 N	103.18 W
El Cozón	232	31.18 N	112.29 W
El Cristo	240p	20.07 N	75.45 W
El Cubo — Casigua	246	8.46 N	72.30 W
El Cuco	236	13.10 N	88.07 W
El Cuervo, Laguna ⊘	232	29.17 N	105.57 W
El Cuidado	234	22.20 N	103.07 W
El Cuy	254	39.56 S	68.20 W
Elda	34	38.29 N	0.47 W
Eldagsen	52	52.10 N	9.40 E
El Dambahaddo	144	3.17 N	46.40 E
El Dátil	232	30.07 N	112.15 W
Elde ≃	54	53.14 N	11.27 E
Eldekanal ≋	54	53.24 N	11.36 E
Eldena, Dtsch.	54	53.13 N	11.25 E
Eldena, Dtsch.	54	54.05 N	13.26 E
El Der ∨	144	8.49 N	47.28 E
El Dere	144	5.07 N	43.10 E
El Descanso	204	32.12 N	116.55 W
El Desemboque, Méx.	232	29.30 N	112.27 W
El Desemboque, Méx.	232	30.30 N	112.59 W
Eldforsen	40	60.36 N	14.13 E
El Inlet c	224	60.48 N	135.11 E
Eldingen	52	52.41 N	10.21 E
El Diamante	234	24.17 N	123.01 W
Eldivan	130	40.32 N	33.31 E
El Diviso	246	1.22 N	78.14 W
El Djazaïr (Algiers)	148	36.47 N	3.03 E
El Djazaïr □⁵	148	36.50 N	3.00 E
El Djelfa	148	34.40 N	3.15 E
El Djelfa □⁵	148	34.35 N	3.45 E
El Doce	234	17.13 N	94.03 W
Eldon, Ia., U.S.	190	40.55 N	92.13 W
Eldon, Mo., U.S.	194	38.20 N	92.34 W
Eldon Hazlet State Park ♦	219	38.39 N	89.22 W
Eldora, Ia., U.S.	190	42.21 N	93.05 W
Eldora, Pa., U.S.	279b	40.10 N	79.53 W
Eldorado, Arg.	252	26.24 S	54.38 W
Eldorado, Bra.	252	24.32 S	48.06 W
El Dorado, Méx.	232	23.12 N	92.39 W
Eldorado, Ar., U.S.	194	33.12 N	92.39 W
Eldorado, Il., U.S.	194	37.49 N	96.51 W
Eldorado, Ks., U.S.	198	39.54 N	84.40 W
Eldorado, Oh., U.S.	216	34.28 N	99.38 W
El Dorado, Ok., U.S.	218	30.51 N	100.36 W
El Dorado, Tx., U.S.	196	30.51 N	100.36 W
El Dorado, Ven.	246	6.44 N	61.38 W
El Dorado ≃	226	38.43 N	120.48 W
Eldorado Hills	226	38.37 N	120.27 W
Eldorado Park ♦	280	33.49 N	118.05 W
El Dorado Peak ∧	224	48.32 N	121.08 W
El Dorado Springs	194	37.52 N	94.01 W
Eldoret	154	0.31 N	35.17 E
Eldred, Il., U.S.	219	39.17 N	90.33 W
Eldred, N.Y., U.S.	210	41.32 N	74.53 W
Eldred, Pa., U.S.	214	41.57 N	78.23 W
Eldridge	180	63.19 N	150.35 W
Eldridge, Mount ∧	180	60.46 N	141.48 W
Eldridges Hill	285	39.40 N	75.18 W
El Dudu	144	2.37 N	41.46 E
El Durazno, Arroyo ≃	258	34.41 S	58.52 W
Eleanor	188	38.32 N	81.55 W
Eleanor, Lake ⊘¹	226	37.59 N	119.51 W
Electra	196	34.02 N	98.55 W
Electric City	202	47.56 N	119.02 W
Elefante, Isla del — Elephant Island ı	329	61.10 S	55.14 W
Elefantes, Estero c²	254	46.10 S	73.41 W
Elefantes, Rio dos (Olifants) ≃	156	24.10 S	32.40 E
Elegest ≃	88	51.32 N	94.05 E
Eleia	146	26.25 N	5.00 W
Elei, Wâdî ∨	144	23.04 N	34.27 E
Elektrénai	26	54.48 N	24.39 E
Elektrogorsk	82	55.53 N	38.47 E
Elektrostal'	82	55.47 N	38.28 E
Elektrougli	82	55.43 N	38.13 E
Elektrozavod	82	52.34 N	54.01 E
Elena	66	42.56 N	24.53 E
El Encantado	286c	10.27 N	66.47 W
El Encanto, Col.	246	1.37 S	73.14 W
El Encanto, Guat.	236	17.17 N	89.34 W
Elend	54	51.38 N	10.41 E
Elephant, Mount ∧²	169	37.58 S	143.12 E
Elephanta Caves ± ⁵	272c	18.58 N	72.56 E
Elephanta Island (Ghārāpurī) ı	272c	18.57 N	72.55 E
Elephant Butte Lake ⊘¹	200	33.11 N	107.10 W
Elephant Butte Reservoir ⊘¹	200	33.19 N	107.10 W
Elephant Lake ⊘	212	58.07 N	94.15 W
Elephant Mountain ∧	188	44.46 N	70.39 W
Eleşkirt	130	39.48 N	42.42 E
Eleonora Veloso	250	28.34 S	51.46 W
Elets — Jelec	72	52.37 N	38.30 E
Eleuthera ı	238	25.10 N	76.14 W
Eleuthera Point ▸	238	24.37 N	76.09 W
Eleva	190	44.34 N	91.28 W
Eleven Point ≃	194	36.09 N	91.05 W
Elevsinós, Kólpos c	267c	38.02 N	23.34 E
Elevsís	38	38.02 N	23.32 E
Elevtheroúpolis	38	40.55 N	24.16 E
El Fahs	36	36.22 N	9.55 E
El Faro, Fl., U.S.	192	34.00 N	80.91 W
El Faro, P.R.	240m	18.00 N	66.47 W
Elfenbeinküste — Ivory Coast □¹	150	8.00 N	5.00 W
El Ferrol del Caudillo	34	43.29 N	8.14 W
Elfers	192	28.13 N	82.43 W
Elfin Cove	180	58.12 N	136.20 W
Elfrida	200	31.41 N	109.41 W
El Fud	144	7.20 N	42.52 E
El Fuerte	196	26.25 N	108.39 W
Elgå	26	62.10 N	11.56 E
El Galpón	252	25.23 S	64.38 W
Elgersburg	54	50.51 N	10.52 E
Elgeyo Escarpment ∧	154	0.45 N	35.30 E
El Ghazawet	148	35.06 N	1.51 W
Elgin, Austl.	169	33.31 S	115.37 E
Elgin, On., Can.	210	44.36 N	76.13 W
Elgin, Scot., U.K.	46	57.39 N	3.20 W
Elgin, Il., U.S.	216	42.02 N	88.16 W
Elgin, N.D., U.S.	198	46.23 N	101.50 W
Elgin, Or., U.S.	202	45.34 N	117.55 W
Elgin, Tx., U.S.	222	30.21 N	97.22 W
Elgin ▪⁸	266a	40.23 N	3.40 W
El Ghoura	36	36.18 N	8.53 E
Elgin City	216	42.02 N	88.18 W
El Goléa	148	30.35 N	2.53 E
El Goloso ▪⁸	266a	40.33 N	3.42 W
Elgon, Mount ∧	154	1.08 N	34.33 E
Elgoras, gora ∧	84	68.03 N	31.35 E

Nombre	Página	Lat.° '	Long.° '
El Grara	148	32.46 N	4.34 E
El Grove	34	42.30 N	8.52 W
El Grullo	234	19.48 N	104.13 W
El Guaje	232	27.52 N	103.18 W
El Guaje, Laguna ⊘	232	28.00 N	103.13 W
El Guarno	246	10.02 N	74.59 W
El Guanábano	286c	10.24 N	67.01 W
El Guapo	286c	10.09 N	65.58 W
El Guayabo	286c	10.56 N	69.22 W
El Guayabo de Abajo	232	26.00 N	107.26 W
El Guayaneco, Parque Nacional ♦	254	48.15 S	75.30 W
El'gygytgyn, ozero ⊘	180	67.30 N	172.00 E
El Hadjar	36	36.48 N	7.45 E
El Hammâmi ▸¹	148	23.00 N	11.30 W
El Hank ± ⁴	148	24.30 N	7.00 W
El Haouaria	36	37.03 N	11.02 E
El Hatillo	286c	10.26 N	66.49 W
El Hatillo, Quebrada ≃	286c	10.21 N	66.47 W
El Huecú	252	37.37 S	70.36 W
El Huisache	234	22.55 N	100.25 W
Elías	164	8.21 S	130.47 E
Elías Romero	258	34.46 S	58.52 W
Eliasville	196	32.57 N	98.46 W
Elida, N.M., U.S.	196	33.56 N	103.39 W
Elida, Oh., U.S.	216	40.47 N	84.12 W
El Idolo, Isla ı	234	21.25 N	97.27 W
El Idrissia	148	34.30 N	2.37 E
Elila ≃	154	2.43 S	25.53 E
Elila	154	2.43 S	25.53 E
Elim, Namibia	156	17.48 S	15.31 E
Elim, S. Afr.	158	34.35 S	19.45 E
Elim, Ak., U.S.	180	64.37 N	162.15 W
Elimsport	214	41.10 N	77.02 W
El Infiernillo, Canal ṵ	232	29.09 N	112.15 W
Elingamppang	152	2.03 S	24.02 E
Elin Pelin	38	42.40 N	23.36 E
Eliot	188	43.09 N	70.48 W
Elipa	152	0.53 S	24.34 E
Élisabeth-Sophien-Koog	41	54.30 N	8.53 E
Élisabethville — Lubumbashi	154	11.40 S	27.28 E
Elisenvaara	24	61.25 N	29.46 E
Eliseu Martins	250	8.13 S	43.42 W
Elista	80	46.16 N	44.14 E
Elizabeth, Austl.	168b	34.43 S	138.40 E
Elizabeth, Co., U.S.	200	39.21 N	104.35 W
Elizabeth, Il., U.S.	190	42.19 N	90.13 W
Elizabeth, La., U.S.	194	30.52 N	92.47 W
Elizabeth, N.J., U.S.	210	40.39 N	74.12 W
Elizabeth, Pa., U.S.	214	40.16 N	79.53 W
Elizabeth, W.V., U.S.	188	39.03 N	81.23 W
Elizabeth ≃, Va., U.S.	276	40.00 N	74.12 W
Elizabeth, Bahía c	246a	0.38 S	91.27 W
Elizabeth, Cape ▸	224	47.22 N	124.22 W
Elizabeth, Cape ▸	282	37.33 N	121.58 W
Elizabeth, West Branch ≃	276	40.42 N	74.14 W
Elizabeth Bay c	156	27.04 S	15.11 E
Elizabeth City	192	36.17 N	76.13 W
Elizabeth Creek ≃	222	33.02 N	97.14 W
Elizabeth Islands ıı	207	41.27 N	70.47 W
Elizabeth Lake ⊘	281	42.38 N	83.23 W
Elizabeth Lake Estates	229b	21.55 S	159.35 W
Elizabeth Park ♦	281	42.07 N	83.11 W
Elizabeth Reef ıı	160	29.56 S	159.04 E
Elizabethton	192	36.20 N	82.12 W
Elizabethtown, Il., U.S.	194	37.26 N	88.18 W
Elizabethtown, Ky., U.S.	194	37.41 N	85.51 W
Elizabethtown, N.Y., U.S.	188	44.12 N	73.35 W
Elizabethtown, N.C., U.S.	192	34.37 N	78.36 W
Elizabethtown, Pa., U.S.	214	40.09 N	76.36 W
Elizabethville	208	40.33 N	76.48 W
Eliza Howell Park ♦	281	42.24 N	83.16 W
Elizaville, In., U.S.	216	40.08 N	86.24 W
Elizaville, N.Y., U.S.	210	42.03 N	73.48 W
Eljas ≃	34	40.00 N	6.50 W
El-Jadida (Mazagan)	148	33.00 N	8.30 W
El Jaralito	232	27.00 N	105.05 W
El Jebel	200	39.23 N	107.05 W
El-Jebha	148	35.13 N	4.40 W
El Jem	148	35.18 N	10.43 E
El Jícaro	236	13.31 N	86.02 W
El Jobean	220	26.58 N	82.13 W
El Julie	232	17.45 N	94.59 W
Elk	30	53.50 N	22.22 E
Elk ≃, Ab., Can.	182	54.26 N	112.52 W
Elk ≃, B.C., Can.	182	53.31 N	118.50 W
Elk ≃, Md., U.S.	208	39.25 N	75.51 W
Elk ≃, Mo., U.S.	194	36.44 N	94.35 W
Elk ≃, Ok., U.S.	218	36.30 N	98.30 W
Elk ≃, Wi., U.S.	196	45.42 N	90.37 W
Elkader	190	42.51 N	91.24 W
El Kantara	148	34.54 N	5.42 E
El-Karafab	144	10.16 N	34.36 E
El Kef	148	36.11 N	8.43 E
El Kere	144	5.51 N	42.06 E
El Kerma	34	35.39 N	0.37 W
Elk Grove	228	38.25 N	121.22 W
El Kerma Village	280	34.32 N	83.58 W
Elkhart, In., U.S.	216	41.41 N	85.58 W
Elkhart, Ks., U.S.	196	37.00 N	101.54 W
Elkhart, Tx., U.S.	222	31.37 N	95.35 W
Elkhart ≃	216	41.43 N	85.58 W
Elkhart Lake	196	43.50 N	88.01 W
El Khatt ± ⁴	148	20.00 N	13.00 W
El Khnàchîch ± ⁴	146	21.40 N	3.50 W
Elkhorn, Mb., Can.	184	49.59 N	101.14 W
Elkhorn, Wi., U.S.	196	42.40 N	88.32 W
Elkhorn ≃	198	41.07 N	96.19 W
Elkhorn City	194	37.18 N	82.21 W
Elkhorn Creek ≃, Ky., U.S.	208	38.29 N	84.52 W

Nombre	Página	Lat.° '	Long.° '
Elkhorn Creek ≃, Mo., U.S.	219	39.05 N	91.20 W
Elkhorn Mountain ∧	182	49.48 N	125.50 W
Elkin	192	36.14 N	80.50 W
Elkins	188	38.55 N	79.50 W
Elkins Park	208	40.04 N	75.07 W
Elk Island ı	184	50.45 N	96.32 W
Elk Island National Park ♦	182	53.37 N	112.45 W
Elkland	210	41.59 N	77.18 W
Elk Mills	188	39.39 N	75.49 W
Elk Mountain ∧	200	41.41 N	106.24 W
Elk Mountain ∧, Wa., U.S.	224	46.08 N	122.28 W
Elk Mountain ∧, Wy., U.S.	200	41.38 N	106.32 W
Elk Neck ▸¹	208	39.35 N	75.55 W
Elk Neck State Park ♦	208	39.30 N	75.58 W
Elko, B.C., Can.	182	49.18 N	115.07 W
Elko, Nv., U.S.	200	40.49 N	115.45 W
El Kouif	36	35.29 N	8.16 E
Elk Peak ∧	202	46.27 N	110.46 W
Elk Plain	224	47.04 N	122.24 W
Elk Point, Ab., Can.	182	53.54 N	110.54 W
Elk Point, S.D., U.S.	198	42.41 N	96.41 W
Elk Rapids	190	44.53 N	85.24 W
El Krib	36	36.19 N	9.09 E
Elkridge	284b	39.12 N	76.42 W
Elk River, Id., U.S.	202	46.47 N	116.10 W
Elk River, Mn., U.S.	196	45.18 N	93.35 W
Elk River ≃	208	39.31 N	75.55 W
Elk State Park ♦	214	46.36 N	4.49 E
Elkton, Ky., U.S.	194	36.48 N	87.09 W
Elkton, Md., U.S.	208	39.36 N	75.50 W
Elkton, Mi., U.S.	190	43.49 N	83.10 W
Elkton, Oh., U.S.	214	40.46 N	80.42 W
Elkton, S.D., U.S.	198	44.14 N	96.28 W
Elkton, Va., U.S.	188	38.24 N	78.37 W
El Kure	144	5.41 N	42.21 E
Elkville	194	37.54 N	89.14 W
Ell, Lake ⊘	162	29.13 S	127.46 E
Ellamar	180	60.54 N	146.42 W
Ellard Lake ⊘	184	54.33 N	91.55 W
Ellás — Greece □¹	38	39.00 N	22.00 E
Ellavalla	162	25.05 S	114.22 E
Ellaville	192	32.14 N	84.18 W
Ellefeld	54	50.29 N	12.23 E
Ellef Ringnes Island ı	16	78.30 N	104.00 W
El Leh	144	3.48 N	39.48 E
Elleker	162	35.00 S	117.43 E
Ellemandsbjerg ∧²	41	56.00 N	10.32 E
Ellen ≃	44	54.43 N	3.30 W
Ellen, Mount ∧	200	38.07 N	110.49 W
Ellen Brook ≃	168a	31.48 S	116.00 E
Ellendale, Austl.	162	17.56 S	124.48 E
Ellendale, De., U.S.	208	38.48 N	75.25 W
Ellendale, Mn., U.S.	190	43.52 N	93.18 W
Ellendale, N.D., U.S.	198	46.00 N	98.31 W
Ellensburg	202	46.59 N	120.32 W
Ellenton, Fl., U.S.	220	27.31 N	82.31 W
Ellenton, Ga., U.S.	192	31.10 N	83.35 W
Ellenville	210	41.43 N	74.23 W
Ellewoutsdijk	52	51.24 N	3.49 E
Ellezelles	50	50.44 N	3.41 E
Ellice ≃	176	68.02 N	103.25 W
Ellice Islands — Tuvalu □¹	14	8.00 S	178.00 E
Ellichpur — Achalpur	120	21.16 N	77.31 E
Elliott City	208	39.16 N	76.47 W
Ellicott Creek ≃	284a	43.01 N	78.50 W
Ellicottville	210	42.16 N	78.40 W
Ellijay	192	34.41 N	84.28 W
El Limón, Méx.	196	23.45 N	101.59 W
El Limón, Méx.	234	19.49 N	105.11 W
El Limoncito	286c	10.29 N	66.47 W
El Limón de Teachi	286c	10.23 N	66.54 W
Ellingen	56	49.04 N	10.58 E
Ellinger	222	29.50 N	96.44 W
Ellinghorst ▪⁸	263	51.34 N	6.57 E
Ellington, Eng., U.K.	44	55.14 N	1.34 W
Ellington, Mo., U.S.	207	41.54 N	72.28 W
Ellington, Mo., U.S.	194	37.14 N	90.58 W
Elliniko International	267c	37.54 N	23.44 E
Elkins	188	44.08 N	103.05 W
Elliot, S. Afr.	156	31.19 S	27.50 E
Elliot, N.T., Austl.	164	17.33 S	133.32 E
Elliot, Mount ∧	166	19.31 S	146.58 E
Elliot Key ı	220	25.27 N	80.11 W
Elliot Lake	190	46.23 N	82.39 W
Elliott, Austl.	164	17.33 S	133.32 E
Elliott, N.D., U.S.	198	46.23 N	97.47 W
Elliott, S.C., U.S.	192	34.05 N	80.11 W
Elliott, Mount ∧	162	20.29 S	126.37 E
Elliott Key ı	220	25.27 N	80.11 W
Elliottville	214	38.11 N	83.16 W
Ellis, Ks., U.S.	198	38.56 N	99.33 W
Ellisras	156	23.40 S	27.46 E
Elliston, Austl.	168	33.39 S	134.55 E
Elliston, Mt., U.S.	184	46.34 N	112.25 W
Ellisville, Mi., U.S.	216	40.46 N	90.35 W
Ellisville, Mo., U.S.	194	38.35 N	90.35 W
Ellmau	60	47.31 N	12.18 E
Ellon	46	57.22 N	2.06 W
Ellore — Elūru	122	16.42 N	81.06 E
Ellport	214	40.51 N	80.15 W
Ellsworth, Il., U.S.	216	40.33 N	88.46 W
Ellsworth, Ks., U.S.	198	38.44 N	98.13 W
Ellsworth, Me., U.S.	188	44.32 N	68.25 W
Ellsworth, Mn., U.S.	198	43.31 N	96.01 W
Ellsworth, Wi., U.S.	190	44.43 N	92.29 W
Ellsworth Air Force Base ▪	198	44.08 N	103.05 W
Ellsworth Land ∀¹	329	75.30 S	80.00 W
El Lucero	196	25.53 N	103.25 W
Ellwangen	56	48.57 N	10.07 E
Ellwanger Berge ∧²	214	49.00 N	10.15 E
Ellwood City	214	40.51 N	80.17 W
Elm, Dtsch.	56	50.13 N	9.12 E
Elm, Schw.	58	46.55 N	9.11 E

ENGLISH — Name | Page | Lat.°′ | Long.°′
DEUTSCH — Name | Seite | Breite°′ | Länge°′ E = Ost

Symbols in the index entries represent the broad categories identified in the key at the right. Symbols with superior numbers (⌃¹) identify subcategories (see complete key on page *I · 1).*

Symbole im Register stellen die rechts im Schlüssel erklärten Kategorien dar. Symbole mit hochgestellten Ziffern (⌃¹) bezeichnen Unterabteilungen einer Kategorie (vgl. vollständiger Schlüssel auf Seite *I · 1).*

Los símbolos incluídos en el texto del índice representan las grandes categorías identificadas con la clave a la derecha. Los símbolos con numeros en su parte superior (⌃¹) identifican las subcategorías (véase la clave completa en la página *I · 1).*

Les symboles de l'index représentent les catégories indiquées dans la légende à droite. Les symboles suivis d'un indice (⌃¹) représentent des sous-catégories (voir légende complète à la page *I · 1).*

Os símbolos incluídos no texto do índice representam as grandes categorias identificadas com a chave à direita. Os símbolos com números em sua parte superior (⌃¹) identificam as subcategorias (veja-se a chave completa à página *I · 1).*

	English	Deutsch	Español	Français	Português
∧	Mountain	Berg	Montaña	Montagne	Montanha
⌃	Mountains	Gebirge	Montañas	Montagnes	Montanhas
)(	Pass	Paß	Paso	Col	Passo
V	Valley, Canyon	Tal, Cañon	Valle, Cañón	Vallée, Canyon	Vale, Canhão
≚	Plain	Ebene	Llano	Plaine	Planície
>	Cape	Kap	Cabo	Cap	Cabo
I	Island	Insel	Isla	Île	Ilha
II	Islands	Inseln	Islas	Îles	Ilhas
♠	Other Topographic Features	Andere Topographische Objekte	Otros Elementos Topográficos	Autres données topographiques	Outros acidentes topográficos

ESPAÑOL — Nombre | Página | Lat.°′ | Long.°′ W = Oeste
FRANÇAIS — Nom | Page | Lat.°′ | Long.°′ W = Ouest
PORTUGUÊS — Nome | Página | Lat.°′ | Long.°′ W = Oeste

Nombre / Nom / Nome	Página / Page	Lat.°′	Long.°′ W = Oeste
Épila	34	41.36 N	1.17 W
Épinac-Les-Mines	58	46.59 N	4.31 E
Épinal	58	48.11 N	6.27 E
Épinay-sous-Sénart	261	48.42 N	2.31 E
Épinay-sur-Orge	261	48.40 N	2.20 E
Épinay-sur-Seine	261	48.57 N	2.19 E
Epirus → Ípeiros □[9]	38	39.40 N	20.50 E
Episcopia	68	40.04 N	16.06 E
Episkopí	130	34.40 N	32.54 E
Époisses	50	47.30 N	4.10 E
Epokiro	156	21.41 S	19.08 E
Epomeo, Monte ∧	68	40.44 N	13.54 E
Épône	261	48.57 N	1.49 E
Eport, Loch c	46	57.33 N	7.11 W
Eppalock, Lake ⊜[1]	169	36.52 S	144.31 E
Eppelborn	56	49.24 N	6.58 E
Eppendorf ✦[8]	263	51.27 N	7.11 E
Eppenhausen ✦[8]	263	51.21 N	7.31 E
Eppeville	50	49.44 N	3.03 E
Epping, Austl.	169	37.39 S	145.02 E
Epping, Austl.	274a	33.46 S	151.05 E
Epping, Eng., U.K.	260	51.43 N	0.07 E
Epping, N.H., U.S.	188	43.02 N	71.04 W
Eppingen	56	49.08 N	8.54 E
Epping Forest □[8]	260	51.43 N	0.10 E
Epping Forest ✦[3]	260	51.40 N	0.03 E
Epping Green, Eng., U.K.	260	51.44 N	0.05 E
Epping Green, Eng., U.K.	260	51.45 N	0.07 W
Epping Upland	260	51.43 N	0.06 E
Epsom	260	51.20 N	0.16 W
Epsom and Ewell □[8]	260	51.20 N	0.16 W
Epsom Downs Race Course ♦	260	51.19 N	0.15 W
Epte ≃	50	49.04 N	1.37 E
Épuisay	50	47.54 N	0.56 E
Epukiro ≃	156	20.45 S	21.05 E
Epupa Falls ↳	152	16.55 S	13.10 E
Epuyén	254	42.14 S	71.21 W
Epworth	44	53.32 N	0.49 W
Eqlīd	128	30.55 N	52.39 E
Equality	194	37.44 N	88.20 W
Équateur □[4]	152	1.00 N	20.30 E
Équateur → Ecuador □[1]	246	2.00 S	77.30 W
Equatorial Guinea (Guinea Ecuatorial) □[1]	152	2.00 N	9.00 E
Équihen-Plage	50	50.41 N	1.34 E
Equimina ≃	152	13.11 S	12.47 E
Equinox Mountain ∧	210	43.10 N	73.08 W
Equinunk	210	41.51 N	75.14 W
Equi Terme	64	44.09 N	10.10 E
Era ≃, It.	66	43.40 N	10.38 E
Era ≃, Pap. N. Gui.	164	7.35 S	144.41 E
Erac Creek ≃	166	26.56 S	145.48 E
Eraclea	64	45.35 N	12.40 E
Eraclea ⊥	68	40.13 N	16.40 E
Eraclea Minoa ⊥	70	37.23 N	13.17 E
Eradu	162	28.41 S	115.02 E
Éragny	261	49.01 N	2.06 E
Eramosa ≃	212	43.32 N	80.14 W
Eran Bay c	116	9.06 N	117.43 E
Eranga	152	1.52 S	18.56 E
Erangal ✦[8]	272c	19.10 N	72.47 E
Erap	164	6.35 S	146.40 E
Erath	194	29.57 N	92.02 W
Erave	164	6.40 S	143.50 E
Erave ≃	164	6.40 S	143.55 E
Erba	62	45.48 N	9.15 E
Erba, Jabal ∧, Sūd.	140	19.04 N	36.46 E
Erba, Jabal ∧, Sūd.	140	20.45 N	36.50 E
Erbaa	130	40.42 N	36.36 E
Erbach, Dtsch.	56	49.40 N	8.59 E
Erbach, Dtsch.	58	48.20 N	9.53 E
Erbendorf	60	49.50 N	12.03 E
Erbeskopf ∧	56	49.44 N	7.05 E
Erchie	68	40.26 N	17.44 E
Erciş	84	39.02 N	43.22 E
Erciyes Dağı ∧	130	38.32 N	35.28 E
Ercolano	68	40.48 N	14.21 E
Ercolano (Herculaneum) ⊥	68	40.46 N	14.20 E
Érd	30	47.23 N	18.56 E
Erdao ≃, Zhg.	98	42.39 N	127.35 E
Erdao ≃, Zhg.	104	42.16 N	122.20 E
Erdao Bai ≃	98	42.34 N	128.08 E
Erdaobaihe	98	42.22 N	128.07 E
Erdaofang, Zhg.	104	41.54 N	123.57 E
Erdaofang, Zhg.	104	41.37 N	122.34 E
Erdaofangshen	104	42.09 N	123.17 E
Erdaogangzi, Zhg.	104	41.57 N	122.09 E
Erdaogangzi, Zhg.	104	42.04 N	123.06 E
Erdaohe	89	43.37 N	127.35 E
Erdaohezi, Zhg.	89	45.07 N	127.16 E
Erdaohezi, Zhg.	89	45.08 N	129.39 E
Erdaojingzi	104	41.49 N	122.20 E
Erdaoliangzi, Zhg.	98	40.50 N	119.04 E
Erdaoliangzi, Zhg.	105	40.31 N	118.03 E
Erdaowan	89	47.58 N	124.33 E
Erdek	130	40.24 N	27.48 E
Erdemli	130	36.37 N	34.18 E
Erdene, Mong.	88	47.48 N	107.55 E
Erdene, Mong.	102	44.15 N	111.14 E
Erdene, Mong.	102	45.08 N	97.45 E
Erdene Bulgan	88	50.07 N	101.35 E
Erdene-Büren	86	48.26 N	91.27 E
Erdenedalaj	102	46.02 N	104.55 E
Erdene Mandal	88	48.30 N	101.21 E
Erdenheim	285	40.05 N	75.12 W
Erdevik	38	45.07 N	19.25 E
Erdiao	106	32.12 N	121.12 E
Erding	60	48.18 N	11.54 E
Erdinger Moos ≡	60	48.22 N	11.52 E
Erdnijevskij	80	46.52 N	46.17 E
Erebato ≃	246	5.54 N	64.16 W
Erebus, Mount ∧	9	77.32 S	167.09 E
Ereğli, Tür.	130	37.31 N	34.04 E
Ereğli, Tür.	130	41.17 N	31.25 E
Eregun	273a	6.36 N	3.22 E
Erei, Monti ⋀	70	37.27 N	14.19 E
Erenas	116	12.25 N	124.19 E
Erenhot	102	43.46 N	112.05 E
Erenköy ✦[8]	267b	40.58 N	29.04 E
Erepecuru, Lago do ⊜	250	1.20 S	56.35 W
Eresma ≃	34	41.26 N	4.45 W
Eressós	38	39.18 N	25.51 E
Erétria	38	38.24 N	23.48 E
Erexim	252	27.38 S	52.17 W
Erez	132	31.34 N	34.34 E
Érezée	56	50.18 N	5.33 E
Erfa ≃	56	49.40 N	9.23 E
Erfde	41	54.19 N	9.19 E
Erfelek	130	41.53 N	34.55 E
Erfenisdam ⊜[1]	158	28.33 S	26.50 E
Erfoud	148	31.28 N	4.10 W
Erft ≃	56	51.11 N	6.44 E
Erftstadt	56	50.48 N	6.46 E
Erfurt	54	50.58 N	11.01 E
Ergak-Targak-Tajga, chrebet ⋀	88	53.25 N	95.30 E
Ergani	130	38.17 N	39.46 E
Ergene ≃	130	41.01 N	26.22 E
Ergenzingen	58	48.29 N	8.48 E
Erges (Erjas) ≃	34	39.40 N	7.01 W
Ērgļi	76	56.54 N	25.38 E
Ergolding	60	48.35 N	12.10 E
Ergoldsbach	60	48.41 N	12.12 E
Ergste	56	51.25 N	7.34 E
Erguig, Bahr ≃	146	11.22 N	15.24 E
Ergun (Argun') ≃	74	53.20 N	121.28 E
Ergun Youqi	89	50.14 N	120.10 E
Ergun Zuoqi	89	50.47 N	121.31 E
Erguvejem ≃	180	65.20 N	176.00 W
Er Hai ⊜	102	25.48 N	100.11 E
Erhlin	100	23.54 N	120.22 E
Erhshui	100	23.49 N	120.36 E
Erhulai	98	41.23 N	125.08 E
Eria ≃	34	42.03 N	5.44 W
Erial	208	39.46 N	75.00 W
Eriba	140	16.37 N	36.04 E
Eriboll	46	58.28 N	4.41 W
Eriboll, Loch c	46	58.31 N	4.41 W
Erica, Austl.	169	37.59 S	146.22 E
Erica, Ned.	52	52.43 N	6.55 E
Erice	70	38.02 N	12.35 E
Ericeira	34	38.59 N	9.25 W
Erichsen Lake ⊜	176	70.38 N	80.21 W
Erichshagen	52	52.40 N	9.14 E
Ericht, Loch ⊜	46	56.48 N	4.24 W
Erick	196	35.12 N	99.51 W
Erickson, B.C., Can.	182	49.05 N	116.28 W
Erickson, Mb., Can.	184	50.30 N	99.55 W
Ericson	198	41.46 N	98.40 W
Erie, Co., U.S.	200	40.03 N	105.03 W
Erie, Il., U.S.	190	41.39 N	90.04 W
Erie, Ks., U.S.	198	37.34 N	95.14 W
Erie, Mi., U.S.	216	41.47 N	83.29 W
Erie, Pa., U.S.	214	42.07 N	80.05 W
Erie □[6], N.Y., U.S.	210	42.54 N	78.53 W
Erie □[6], Oh., U.S.	214	41.27 N	82.42 W
Erie □[6], Pa., U.S.	214	42.08 N	80.04 W
Erie, Lake ⊜	214	42.15 N	81.00 W
Erieau	214	42.16 N	81.56 W
Erie Basin c	276	40.40 N	74.01 W
Erie Beach, On., Can.	214	42.16 N	82.00 W
Erie Beach, On., Can.	284a	42.53 N	78.57 W
Erie Canal → New York State Barge Canal ≍	210	43.05 N	78.43 W
Erie County Fairgrounds ♦	284a	42.45 N	78.49 W
Erie International Airport ⊠	214	42.05 N	80.11 W
Eriksberg ⊥	40	58.56 N	16.22 E
Eriksdale	184	50.52 N	98.06 W
Erímanthos ∧	38	37.59 N	21.51 E
Erimo	92a	42.01 N	143.09 E
Erimo-misaki ›	92a	41.55 N	143.15 E
Erin, On., Can.	212	43.45 N	80.07 W
Erin, N.Y., U.S.	210	42.11 N	76.40 W
Erin, Tn., U.S.	194	36.19 N	87.41 W
Erindale	275b	43.32 N	79.39 W
Ering	60	48.18 N	13.09 E
Eriskay I	46	57.04 N	7.18 W
Erisort, Loch c	46	58.07 N	6.24 W
Eriswil	58	47.05 N	7.51 E
Erith ✦[8]	260	51.29 N	0.10 E
Erithraí	38	38.13 N	23.19 E
Eritrea □[9]	144	15.20 N	39.00 E
Erivan → Jerevan	84	40.11 N	44.30 E
Erjas (Erges) ≃	34	39.40 N	7.01 W
Erjiazhen	106	32.02 N	121.13 E
Erkelenz	56	51.05 N	6.19 E
Erken ⊜	40	59.51 N	18.34 E
Erken-Jurt	84	44.27 N	41.54 E
Erkheim	58	48.02 N	10.20 E
Erkilet	130	38.49 N	35.27 E
Erkina ≃	48	52.51 N	7.23 W
Erkner	54	52.25 N	13.45 E
Erkner, Forst ✦[3]	264a	52.22 N	13.47 E
Erkowit	140	18.46 N	37.07 E
Erkrath	56	51.13 N	6.55 E
Erl	64	47.41 N	12.11 E
Erlach, Öst.	61	47.43 N	16.13 E
Erlach, Schw.	58	47.03 N	7.06 E
Erlands Point	224	47.36 N	122.42 W
Erlangen	60	49.36 N	11.01 E
Erlanger	218	39.01 N	84.36 W
Erlanghe	100	30.19 N	116.04 E
Erlangmiao	100	33.46 N	112.23 E
Erlau ≃	60	48.34 N	13.36 E
Erlauf ≃	61	48.12 N	15.11 E
Erlbach	54	50.18 N	12.22 E
Erldunda	162	25.14 S	133.12 E
Erle ✦[8]	263	51.33 N	7.05 E
Erli	62	44.08 N	8.06 E
Erling	106	31.53 N	119.36 E
Erling, Lake ⊜[1]	194	33.05 N	93.35 W
Erlistoun	162	28.20 S	122.08 E
Erlongshan, Zhg.	89	47.20 N	132.28 E
Erlongshan, Zhg.	89	50.04 N	126.47 E
Erlongshantun	89	48.28 N	126.31 E
Erlsbach	64	46.55 N	12.15 E
Erma	208	38.58 N	74.54 W
Ermana, chrebet ⋀	88	50.00 N	113.30 E
Ermatingen	58	47.41 N	9.06 E
Erme ≃	42	50.18 N	3.56 W
Ermelindo Matarazo ✦[8]	287b	23.29 S	46.29 W
Ermelo, Ned.	52	52.17 N	5.37 E
Ermelo, S. Afr.	158	26.34 S	29.58 E
Ermendegou	104	42.02 N	121.56 E
Ermenek	130	36.38 N	32.54 E
Ermenek ≃	130	36.35 N	33.23 E
Ermenonville	50	49.08 N	2.42 E
Ermidas	34	38.00 N	8.23 W
Ermil Post	140	13.37 N	27.36 E
Ermineskin Indian Reserve ✦[4]	182	52.52 N	113.30 W
Ermington	274a	33.48 S	151.04 E
Ermita de Guadalupe	234	22.36 N	103.03 W
Ermita de los Correas	234	22.54 N	103.01 W
Ermont	50	48.59 N	2.16 E
Ermoúpolis	38	37.26 N	24.56 E
Ermsleben	54	51.44 N	11.21 E
Ernaballa	162	26.17 S	132.07 E
Erndtebrück	56	50.59 N	8.15 E
Erne ≃	48	54.30 N	8.16 W
Erne, Lower Lough ⊜	48	54.26 N	7.46 W
Erne, Upper Lough ⊜	48	54.14 N	7.32 W
Ernée	32	48.18 N	0.56 W
Ernest	214	40.41 N	79.10 W
Ernestina	258	35.16 S	59.34 W
Ernest Sound ⊍	182	55.52 N	132.10 W
Ernici, Monti ⋀	66	41.48 N	13.22 E
Ernstbrunn	61	48.32 N	16.22 E
Ernst Thälmann, Pioneerpark ♦	264a	52.28 N	13.33 E
Ernst-Thälmann-Stadion ♦	264a	52.23 N	13.05 E
Erode	122	11.21 N	77.44 E
Eromanga	166	26.40 S	143.16 E
Erongo	156	21.44 S	15.53 E
Erongo ⋀	156	21.45 S	15.37 E
Erota	144	16.14 N	37.55 E
Erp	56	50.46 N	6.43 E
Erpuzi	105	40.29 N	115.33 E
Erquelinnes	50	50.18 N	4.07 E
Err, Piz d' ∧	58	46.33 N	9.41 E
Errabiddy	162	25.28 S	117.07 E
Er-Rachidia	148	31.58 N	4.25 W
Er-Rachidia □[4]	148	31.15 N	4.05 W
Errego	154	16.02 S	37.14 E
Errer ≃	144	7.32 N	42.05 E
Er-Riad → Ar-Riyāḍ	128	24.38 N	46.43 E
Errigal Mountain ∧	48	55.02 N	8.07 W
Errington	224	49.17 N	124.22 W
Erris Head ›	48	54.19 N	10.00 W
Errochty, Loch ⊜	46	56.45 N	4.12 W
Errogie	46	57.16 N	4.22 W
Errol Heights	224	45.28 N	122.36 W
Erromango I	175f	18.45 S	169.05 E
Ersekë	38	40.20 N	20.41 E
Ershijiazi	104	41.17 N	120.32 E
Ershilipu	105	40.07 N	117.24 E
Ershiqizhan	89	53.23 N	123.16 E
Ershiwuzhan	89	53.22 N	123.55 E
Erskine	198	47.40 N	96.00 W
Erskine, Lake ⊜	276	41.06 N	74.15 W
Erskine Inlet c	176	76.15 N	102.20 W
Erskine Park	274a	33.49 S	150.47 E
Erstein	58	48.26 N	7.40 E
Erste Wiener Hochquellenleitung ≍[1]	61	48.10 N	16.17 E
Erstfeld	58	46.49 N	8.39 E
Ertai, Zhg.	86	46.07 N	90.06 E
Ertai, Zhg.	86	44.14 N	80.52 E
Ertaizi, Zhg.	104	41.52 N	121.56 E
Ertaizi, Zhg.	104	42.05 N	123.35 E
Ertaizi, Zhg.	104	42.35 N	124.00 E
Ertaizi, Zhg.	104	40.47 N	120.54 E
Ertil'	78	51.51 N	40.49 E
Ertingen	58	48.06 N	9.28 E
Ertix (Irtyš) ≃	74	61.04 N	68.52 E
Erto	64	46.16 N	12.22 E
Ertra □[4]	144	15.20 N	39.00 E
Ertuğrul	130	39.34 N	27.43 E
Ertvelde	50	51.11 N	3.45 E
Eruar	126	23.28 N	87.52 E
Erudina	166	31.28 S	139.23 E
Eruh	130	37.46 N	42.11 E
Erundu	156	20.36 S	16.25 E
Erunkan	273a	6.37 N	3.24 E
Erva, Ponta da ›	266c	38.50 N	8.58 W
Erval	252	32.02 S	53.24 W
Erval d'Oeste	252	27.13 S	51.34 W
Ervalla	40	59.22 N	15.15 E
Erving	207	42.36 N	72.23 W
Ervy-le-Châtel	50	48.02 N	3.55 E
Erwin, N.C., U.S.	192	35.19 N	78.40 W
Erwin, Tn., U.S.	192	36.08 N	82.25 W
Erwitte	52	51.37 N	8.20 E
Erwood	184	52.50 N	102.10 W
Erxleben	54	52.13 N	11.14 E
Érythrée → Eritrea □[9]	144	15.20 N	39.00 E
Eryuan	102	26.06 N	99.55 E
Erzaohang	106	31.05 N	121.49 E
Erzberg ✦[7]	61	47.32 N	14.54 E
Erzgebirge (Krušné hory) ⋀	54	50.30 N	13.10 E
Erzhan	89	43.58 N	128.44 E
Erzhuang	105	39.24 N	117.22 E
Erzin	88	50.15 N	95.10 E
Erzincan	130	39.44 N	39.29 E
Erzincan □[4]	130	39.40 N	39.30 E
Erzingen	58	47.39 N	8.25 E
Erzurum	130	39.55 N	41.17 E
Erzurum □[4]	130	40.00 N	41.30 E
Esa'ala	164	9.44 S	150.49 E
Esambo	152	3.40 S	23.24 E
Esan-misaki ›	92a	41.49 N	141.11 E
Esashi, Nihon	92	39.12 N	141.09 E
Esashi, Nihon	92	41.52 N	140.07 E
Esashi, Nihon	92a	44.56 N	142.35 E
Esbiye	130	40.57 N	38.44 E
Esbjerg	26	55.28 N	8.27 E
Esbly	261	48.54 N	2.49 E
Esbo → Espoo	26	60.13 N	24.40 E
Esborn	263	51.23 N	7.20 E
Esca ≃	34	42.37 N	1.03 W
Escada	250	8.22 S	35.14 W
Escalada	258	34.10 S	59.07 W
Escalante, Pil.	116	10.50 N	123.33 E
Escalante, Ut,. U.S.	200	37.46 N	111.36 W
Escalante ≃, Ut,. U.S.	200	37.17 N	110.53 W
Escalante ≃, Ven.	246	9.15 N	71.50 W
Escalante Desert ✦[2]	200	37.50 N	113.30 W
Escalaplano	71	39.37 N	9.21 E
Escalón, Méx.	232	26.45 N	104.20 W
Escalon, Ca., U.S.	226	37.47 N	120.59 W
Escalona	34	40.10 N	4.24 W
Escambia ≃	194	30.32 N	87.11 W
Escanaba	190	45.44 N	87.04 W
Escanaba ≃	190	45.47 N	87.04 W
Escandón, Puerto)(	34	40.17 N	1.00 W
Escárcega	232	18.37 N	90.43 W
Escarpada Point ›	116	18.31 N	122.13 E
Escarpado Peak ∧	116	8.36 N	117.22 E
Escarpment	284a	43.10 N	79.00 W
Escatawpa ≃	194	30.25 N	88.35 W
Escaudain	50	50.20 N	3.21 E
Escaut (Schelde) ≃	50	51.22 N	4.15 E
Esch ≃	56	48.54 N	6.04 E
Eschach	58	47.44 N	9.36 E
Eschau	58	48.29 N	7.43 E
Eschebrügge	52	52.37 N	6.46 E
Eschede	52	52.44 N	10.14 E
Eschen	58	47.13 N	9.31 E
Eschenau	60	49.34 N	11.12 E
Eschenbach	60	49.45 N	11.49 E
Eschenburg	56	50.49 N	8.20 E
Eschenlohe	64	47.36 N	11.11 E
Eschershausen	52	51.56 N	9.38 E
Eschlkam	60	49.18 N	12.55 E
Escholzmatt	58	46.55 N	7.56 E
Eschscholtz Bay c	180	66.18 N	161.25 W
Esch-sur-Alzette	56	49.30 N	5.59 E
Esch-sur-Sûre	56	49.55 N	5.55 E
Eschwege	56	51.11 N	10.04 E
Eschweiler	56	50.49 N	6.16 E
Esclave, Grand Lac de l' → Great Slave Lake ⊜	176	61.30 N	114.00 W
Esclavo, Gran Lago del → Great Slave Lake ⊜	176	61.30 N	114.00 W
Escobal	236	9.09 N	79.58 W
Escobar □[5]	288	34.23 S	58.46 W
Escobar, Arroyo ≃	288	34.21 S	58.44 W
Escobedo, Méx.	196	27.13 N	101.21 W
Escobedo, Méx.	232	29.05 N	102.19 W
Escocesa, Bahía c	238	19.25 N	69.45 W
Escoheag	207	41.36 N	71.45 W
Escondido	228	33.07 N	117.05 W
Escondido ≃, Méx.	196	28.39 N	100.34 W
Escondido ≃, Nic.	236	12.04 N	83.45 W
Escondido Creek ≃	228	33.01 N	117.15 W
Escorial → San Lorenzo de El Escorial	34	40.35 N	4.09 W
Escoutay ≃	62	44.29 N	4.42 E
Escravos ≃[1]	150	5.35 N	5.10 E
Escrick	44	53.53 N	1.02 W
Escuadrón 201 ✦[8]	286a	19.22 N	99.06 W
Escudero, Arroyo ≃	258	34.20 S	57.05 W
Escudo de Veraguas, Isla I	236	9.06 N	81.33 W
Escuinapa de Hidalgo	234	22.51 N	105.48 W
Escuintla, Guat.	236	14.18 N	90.47 W
Escuintla, Méx.	232	15.20 N	92.38 W
Escuintla □[5]	236	14.10 N	91.00 W
Escuminac, Point ›	186	47.04 N	64.46 W
Esebi	154	2.57 N	30.39 E
Eséka	152	3.39 N	10.46 E
Eşen	130	36.27 N	29.16 E
Eşen ≃	130	36.16 N	29.15 E
Esenler ✦[8]	267b	41.02 N	28.51 E
Esens	52	53.39 N	7.37 E
Esera ≃	34	42.06 N	0.15 E
Esesi	130	39.49 N	39.19 E
Eşfahān (Isfahan)	128	32.40 N	51.38 E
Eşfahān □[4]	128	33.00 N	52.00 E
Esfandaqeh	128	28.38 N	57.12 E
Esfarāyen	128	37.02 N	57.27 E
Esgueva ≃	34	41.40 N	4.43 W
Eshan	102	24.11 N	102.22 E
Esher ✦[8]	260	51.23 N	0.22 W
Eshkāshem	123	36.42 N	71.34 E
Eshowe	158	28.58 S	31.29 E
Esh-Sham → Dimashq	132	33.30 N	36.18 E
Eshta'ol	132	31.47 N	35.00 E
Esh Winning	44	54.47 N	1.43 W
Esiama	150	4.56 N	2.21 W
Esigodini	154	20.18 S	28.56 E
Esine	64	45.55 N	10.15 E
Esino ≃	66	43.39 N	13.22 E
Esira	157b	24.20 S	46.42 E
Esk	171a	27.15 S	152.25 E
Esk ≃, N.Z.	172	43.06 S	171.57 E
Esk ≃, U.K.	44	54.58 N	3.04 W
Esk ≃, Eng., U.K.	44	54.29 N	0.37 W
Esk ≃, Eng., U.K.	44	54.21 N	3.23 W
Esk ≃, Scot., U.K.	46	55.57 N	3.03 W
Eskdale, N.Z.	172	39.24 S	176.50 E
Eskdale, W.V., U.S.	188	38.05 N	81.26 W
Eskdale ∨	44	55.10 N	3.00 W
Eske, Lough ⊜	48	54.41 N	8.03 W
Eski Dzhumaya → Târgovište	38	43.15 N	26.34 E
Eskifjörður	24a	65.04 N	13.59 W
Eskiikan	85	43.12 N	68.31 E
Eskilstrup	41	54.51 N	11.54 E
Eskilstuna	40	59.22 N	16.30 E
Eskimalatya	130	38.26 N	38.23 E
Eskimo Lakes ⊜	180	69.15 N	132.17 W
Eskimo Point	176	61.07 N	94.03 W
Eskipazar	130	40.58 N	32.33 E
Eskişehir	130	39.46 N	30.32 E
Eskişehir □[4]	130	39.35 N	31.10 E
Eskridge	198	38.51 N	96.06 W
Esla ≃	34	41.29 N	6.03 W
Eslāmābād	128	34.06 N	46.31 E
Eslām Qal'eh	128	34.40 N	61.04 E
Eslāmshahr	128	35.40 N	51.10 E
Eslarn	60	49.35 N	12.32 E
Eslohe	56	51.15 N	8.09 E
Eslöv	41	55.50 N	13.20 E
Eşme	130	38.24 N	28.59 E
Esmeralda, Austl.	166	18.50 S	142.34 E
Esmeralda, Cuba	240p	21.51 N	78.07 W
Esmeralda, Méx.	196	25.40 N	103.30 W
Esmeralda, Isla I	254	48.57 S	75.25 W
Esmeraldas	246	0.59 N	79.42 W
Esmeraldas □[4]	246	0.40 N	79.30 W
Esmeraldas ≃	246	0.58 N	79.38 W
Esmirna → İzmir	130	38.25 N	27.09 E
Esmond, N.D., U.S.	198	48.02 N	99.45 W
Esmond, R.I., U.S.	207	41.52 N	71.29 W
Esnagi Lake ⊜	190	48.38 N	84.32 W
Esneux	56	50.32 N	5.34 E
Esong	152	2.09 N	10.58 E
Esopus Creek ≃	210	42.04 N	73.56 W
Espada, Punta ›	246	12.05 N	71.07 W
Espagne → Spain □[1]	34	40.00 N	4.00 W
Espalion	32	44.31 N	2.46 E
Espaly-Saint-Marcel	62	45.03 N	3.52 E
España → Spain □[1]	34	40.00 N	4.00 W
Espanola, On., Can.	190	46.15 N	81.46 W
Espanola, N.M., U.S.	200	35.59 N	106.04 W
Española, Isla I	246a	1.25 S	89.42 W
Esparto	226	38.41 N	122.00 W
Esparza	236	9.59 N	84.40 W
Espasingen	58	47.49 N	9.00 E
Espe, Dan.	41	55.12 N	10.25 E
Espe, Kaz.	85	43.52 N	74.10 E
Espejo	34	37.41 N	4.33 W
Espelkamp	52	52.25 N	8.36 E
Espenberg, Cape ›	180	66.33 N	163.36 W
Espenhain	54	51.11 N	12.29 E
Espera, Arroyo ≃[1]	288	34.24 S	58.36 W
Espera Feliz	255	20.39 S	41.55 W
Esperança, Bra.	246	4.24 S	69.52 W
Esperança, Bra.	250	7.01 S	35.51 W
Esperance, Austl.	162	33.51 S	121.53 E
Esperance, N.Y., U.S.	210	42.46 N	74.15 W
Esperance Bay c	162	33.51 S	121.53 E
Esperantina	250	3.54 S	42.14 W
Esperantinópolis	250	4.53 S	44.53 W
Esperanza, Arg.	252	31.27 S	60.56 W
Esperanza, Cuba	240p	22.27 N	80.06 W
Esperanza, Méx.	232	27.35 N	109.56 W
Esperanza, Méx.	234	18.52 N	97.24 W
Esperanza, Pil.	116	8.43 N	125.36 E
Esperanza, Pil.	116	11.44 N	124.03 E
Esperanza, P.R.	240m	18.06 N	65.28 W
Esperanza, S. Afr.	158	30.21 S	30.40 E
Esperanza ⊡[3]	9	63.24 S	56.59 W
Esperanza Inlet c	182	49.48 N	126.50 W
Espergærde	41	56.00 N	12.34 E
Esperia	66	41.23 N	13.41 E
Esperito, Arroyo ≃[1]	288	34.23 S	58.36 W
Espevær	26	59.36 N	5.10 E
Espichel, Cabo ›	34	38.25 N	9.13 W
Espinal	246	4.09 N	74.53 W
Espinazo	196	26.16 N	101.06 W
Espinazo, Sierra del → Espinhaço, Serra do ⋀	255	17.30 S	43.30 W
Espingarda ≃	250	10.03 S	47.13 W
Espinhaço, Serra do ⋀	255	17.30 S	43.30 W
Espinho	34	41.00 N	8.39 W
Espinillo	252	24.58 S	58.34 W
Espinillo, Arroyo ≃	258	34.59 S	57.36 W
Espinillo, Punta del ›	258	34.50 S	56.26 W
Espino	246	8.34 N	66.01 W
Espinosa	255	14.56 S	42.50 W
Espírito Santo □[3]	255	19.30 S	40.30 W
Espírito Santo do Dourado	256	22.03 S	45.58 W
Espírito Santo → Vila Velha	250	3.13 N	51.13 W
Espiritu Santo I	175f	15.15 S	166.50 E
Espíritu Santo, Isla I	232	24.30 N	110.22 W
Espita	232	21.01 N	88.19 W
Espoir, Bay d' c	186	47.50 N	55.51 W
Espoo (Esbo)	26	60.13 N	24.40 E
Esposende	34	41.32 N	8.47 W
Esposizione Universale di Roma ♦	267a	41.50 N	12.28 E
Espugues de Llobregat	266d	41.22 N	2.05 E
Espumoso	252	28.44 S	52.51 W
Espungabera	156	20.29 S	32.48 E
Espy	210	41.00 N	76.24 W
Espyville Station	214	41.36 N	80.29 W
Esquatzel Coulee ∨	202	46.17 N	119.07 W
Esquel	254	42.54 S	71.19 W
Esquimalt	224	48.26 N	123.24 W
Esquina	252	30.01 S	59.32 W
Esquina Negra	258	35.02 S	58.03 W
Esquipulas, Guat.	236	14.34 N	89.21 W
Esquipulas, Nic.	236	12.40 N	85.47 W
Esquiú	252	29.23 S	65.17 W
Esrum Sø ⊜	41	56.00 N	12.24 E
Essa ≃	76	54.53 N	28.40 E
Essaoui Mellene, Oued ∨	148	27.26 N	6.40 E
Essaouira (Mogador)	148	31.30 N	9.47 W
Essaouira □[4]	148	31.25 N	9.30 W
Essarts	261	48.30 N	1.46 E
Essé	152	4.05 N	11.53 E
Esse ≃	66	43.16 N	11.54 E
Esseg → Osijek	38	45.33 N	18.41 E
Es-Sekhira	148	34.17 N	10.06 E
Essen, Bel.	50	51.28 N	4.28 E
Essen, Dtsch.	52	52.43 N	7.57 E
Essen, Dtsch.	56	51.28 N	7.01 E
Essen, Dtsch.	263	51.28 N	7.01 E
Essenbach	60	48.37 N	12.13 E
Essenberg ✦[8]	263	51.26 N	6.42 E
Essendon, Austl.	169	37.46 S	144.55 E
Essendon, Eng., U.K.	260	51.46 N	0.09 W
Essendon, Mount ∧	162	24.59 S	120.28 E
Essendon Airport ⊠	169	37.43 S	144.53 E
Essen-Mülheim, Flughafen ⊠	263	51.24 N	6.58 E
Essentuki → Jessentuki	84	44.03 N	42.51 E
Essequibo ≃	246	6.59 N	58.23 W
Essequibo Islands-West Demerara □[4]	246	6.40 N	58.30 W
Es Sers	36	36.04 N	9.02 E
Essex, On., Can.	214	42.10 N	82.49 W
Essex, Ct., U.S.	207	41.21 N	72.23 W
Essex, Il., U.S.	216	41.11 N	88.11 W
Essex, Ia., U.S.	198	40.50 N	95.18 W
Essex, Md., U.S.	208	39.18 N	76.28 W
Essex, Ma., U.S.	207	42.37 N	70.47 W
Essex, Mo., U.S.	194	36.48 N	89.51 W
Essex, Mt., U.S.	182	48.16 N	113.36 W
Essex □[6], On., Can.	214	42.10 N	82.50 W
Essex □[6], Eng., U.K.	42	51.48 N	0.40 E
Essex □[6], Ma., U.S.	207	42.40 N	70.55 W
Essex □[6], N.J., U.S.	210	40.48 N	74.12 W
Essex □[6], Vt., U.S.	206	44.57 N	71.43 W
Essex □[6], Va., U.S.	208	37.55 N	76.55 W
Essex ≃	283	42.39 N	70.46 W
Essex Bay c	283	42.39 N	70.44 W
Essex Fells	276	40.49 N	74.17 W
Essex Junction	188	44.29 N	73.06 W
Essex Skypark ⊠	284b	39.18 N	76.28 W
Essexville	190	43.36 N	83.50 W
Essing	60	48.56 N	11.47 E
Essington	285	39.52 N	75.18 W
Essling ✦[8]	264b	48.13 N	16.32 E
Esslingen	56	48.45 N	9.16 E
Es Smala es Souassi	36	35.21 N	10.33 E
Esson Lake ⊜	212	45.02 N	78.16 W
Essonne □[5]	50	48.36 N	2.20 E
Essonne ≃	50	48.37 N	2.29 E
Essoyes	58	48.04 N	4.32 E
Es-Suki	140	13.20 N	33.54 E
Essvik	26	62.19 N	17.24 E
Est □[4]	152	4.00 N	14.00 E
Est, Canal de l' ≍	58	48.45 N	5.35 E
Est, Cap ›	157b	15.16 S	50.29 E
Est, Gare ✦[5]	261	48.53 N	2.22 E
Est, Île de l' I	186	47.37 N	61.26 W
Est, Pointe de l' ›	186	49.08 N	61.41 W
Estacada	224	45.17 N	122.19 W
Estaca de Bares, Punta de la ›	34	43.46 N	7.42 W
Estacado, Llano ≚	196	33.30 N	102.40 W
Estación La Colorado	234	23.52 N	102.26 W
Estado, Parque do ♦	287b	23.39 S	46.37 W
Estados, Isla de los (Staten Island) I	254	54.47 S	64.15 W
Estados Unidos → United States □[1]	178	38.00 N	97.00 W
Eşţahbān	128	29.08 N	54.04 E
Estaires	50	50.38 N	2.43 E
Estambul → İstanbul	130	41.01 N	28.58 E
Estância, Bra.	250	11.16 S	37.26 W
Estancia, Pil.	116	11.28 N	123.09 E
Estancia, S. Afr.	158	26.17 S	29.52 E
Estancia, N.M., U.S.	200	34.45 N	106.03 W
Estancia Los López	234	20.53 N	104.31 W
Estanislao del Campo	252	25.03 S	60.06 W
Estanzuelas	236	13.38 N	88.30 W
Estarreja	34	40.45 N	8.34 W
Estats, Pique d' ∧	34	42.40 N	1.24 E
Estavayer-le-Lac	58	46.51 N	6.50 E
Estcourt	158	29.01 S	29.52 E
Este	64	45.14 N	11.39 E
Este ≃	52	53.32 N	9.47 E
Este, Parque Nacional del ♦	286c	10.30 N	66.50 W
Este, Punta ›	240m	18.08 N	65.16 W
Esteban Echeverría	258	34.50 S	58.28 W
Esteban Echeverría □[5]	288	34.51 S	58.32 W
Estefanía, Lago → Stefanie, Lake ⊜	144	4.40 N	36.50 E
Esteio	252	29.51 S	51.10 W
Estelí	236	13.05 N	86.23 W
Estelí □[5]	236	13.10 N	86.20 W
Estella	34	42.40 N	2.02 W
Estelline, S.D., U.S.	198	44.34 N	96.54 W
Estelline, Tx., U.S.	196	34.33 N	100.26 W
Estell Manor	208	39.24 N	74.44 W
Estèng	62	44.14 N	6.45 E
Estepa	34	37.18 N	4.54 W
Estepas de Kirguises → Kirgizskij chrebet ⋀	85	42.30 N	74.00 E
Estepona	34	36.26 N	5.08 W
Ester	180	64.51 N	148.01 W
Esterel ⋀	62	43.30 N	6.50 E
Esterhazy	184	50.40 N	102.08 W
Esterhazy, Schloss ⊥	61	47.51 N	16.32 E
Estérias, Cap ›	152	0.37 N	9.20 E
Esternay	50	48.44 N	3.34 E
Estero	220	26.26 N	81.49 W
Estero Bay c, Ca., U.S.	226	35.24 N	120.53 W
Estero Bay c, Fl., U.S.	220	26.25 N	81.52 W
Estero Island I	220	26.26 N	81.56 W
Estéron ≃	62	43.49 N	7.11 E
Esteros	252	26.37 S	63.39 W
Esterwegen	52	52.59 N	7.38 E
Estes Park	200	40.22 N	105.31 W
Este Sudeste, Cayos del II	236	12.26 N	81.27 W
Estevan	184	49.08 N	102.59 W
Estevan Group II	182	53.05 N	129.40 W
Estevan Point	182	49.23 N	126.33 W
Esther Island I	180	60.50 N	148.05 W
Estherville	198	43.24 N	94.49 W
Estill	192	32.45 N	81.14 W
Estissac	50	48.16 N	3.49 E
Estiva	256	22.28 S	46.02 W
Estiva, Ribeirão da ≃	287b	23.44 S	46.23 W
Estiva, Rio da ≃	255	12.23 S	45.05 W
Estling, Lake ⊜	276	40.53 N	74.30 W
Estocolmo → Stockholm	40	59.20 N	18.03 E
Eston, Sk., Can.	184	51.10 N	108.46 W
Eston, Eng., U.K.	44	54.34 N	1.07 W
Estonia (Eesti) □[1], Europe	22	59.00 N	26.00 E
Estonia (Eesti) □[1], Europe	76	59.00 N	26.00 E
Estoril	34	38.42 N	9.23 W
Estrasburgo → Strasbourg	58	48.35 N	7.45 E
Estrées-Saint-Denis	50	49.26 N	2.39 E
Estrela	252	29.29 S	51.58 W
Estrela ∧	34	40.19 N	7.37 W
Estrela ≃	287a	22.43 S	43.13 W
Estrela, Serra da ⋀	34	40.20 N	7.38 W
Estrela do Norte	255	13.49 S	49.04 W
Estrela do Sul	255	18.46 S	47.42 W
Estrella ≃	226	35.45 N	120.41 W
Estremadura □[9]	34	39.15 N	9.10 W
Estremoz	34	38.51 N	7.35 W
Estribo	234	22.26 N	99.17 W
Estrondo, Serra do ⋀[1]	250	9.00 S	48.45 W
Estuaire □[4]	152	0.15 N	10.00 E
Estuary	184	50.56 N	109.46 W
Esumba, Île I	152	2.00 N	21.12 E
Eszék → Osijek	38	45.33 N	18.41 E
Esztergom	30	47.48 N	18.45 E
Étables	32	48.38 N	2.50 W
Etadunna	166	28.43 S	138.38 E
Etah, India	124	27.38 N	78.40 E
Etah, Kal. Nun.	16	78.19 N	72.38 W
Étain	56	49.13 N	5.38 E
Etajima	96	34.15 N	132.30 E
Eta-jima I	96	34.15 N	132.28 E
Étalle	56	49.41 N	5.36 E
Étamaniou ≃	186	50.17 N	59.58 W
Étampes	50	48.26 N	2.09 E
Etamunbanie, Lake ⊜	166	26.15 S	139.44 E
Étaples	50	50.31 N	1.39 E
États-Unis → United States □[1]	178	38.00 N	97.00 W
Etāwah	124	26.46 N	79.02 E
Etchemin ≃	186	46.46 N	71.14 W
Etchojoa	232	26.55 N	109.38 W
Etéké	152	1.29 S	11.35 E
Etembue	152	1.17 N	9.25 E
Etendard, Pic de l' ∧	62	45.09 N	6.09 E
Ethan	198	43.32 N	97.59 W
Ethel	194	33.07 N	89.27 W
Ethel ≃	162	24.09 S	118.26 E
Ethel, Mount ∧	200	40.39 N	106.41 W
Ethelbert	184	51.31 N	100.22 W
Ethel Creek	162	22.54 S	120.09 E
Ethel Lake ⊜	180	63.21 N	136.00 W
Etherow ≃	262	53.24 N	2.03 W
Ethiopia (Ityopiya) □[1], Afr.	136	9.00 N	39.00 E
Ethiopia (Ityopiya) □[1], Afr.	144	9.00 N	39.00 E
Ethiopian Plateau ⋀[1]	144	9.00 N	38.00 E
Ethiopie → Ethiopia □[1]	144	9.00 N	39.00 E
Ethridge, Mt., U.S.	202	48.33 N	112.07 W
Ethridge, Tn., U.S.	194	35.19 N	87.18 W
Eticoga	150	11.09 N	16.08 W
Eticuera Creek ≃	226	38.41 N	122.16 W
Etigo-heiya ≚	92	37.45 N	139.00 E
Etili	130	39.59 N	26.54 E
Étiolles	261	48.38 N	2.29 E
Etiopía → Ethiopia □[1]	144	9.00 N	39.00 E
Etive, Loch ⊜	46	56.29 N	5.09 W
Etiwanda	228	34.08 N	117.31 W
Etjo ∧	156	21.09 S	16.30 E
Etna, Ca., U.S.	204	41.27 N	122.53 W
Etna, N.Y., U.S.	210	42.29 N	76.23 W
Etna, Pa., U.S.	214	40.30 N	79.56 W
Etna, Wy., U.S.	200	43.02 N	111.00 W
Etna, Monte (Mongibello) ∧[1]	70	37.46 N	15.00 E
Etna Green	216	41.17 N	86.03 W
Etne	26	59.40 N	5.56 E
Etobicoke	212	43.42 N	79.32 W
Etobicoke Creek ≃	212	43.35 N	79.32 W
Etoile	154	11.38 S	27.34 E
Étoile, Chaîne de l' ⋀	62	43.22 N	5.30 E
Etoka	152	0.10 N	23.23 E
Etolin Island I	180	56.08 N	132.26 W
Etolin Strait ⊍	180	60.20 N	165.15 W
Etomami ≃	184	52.48 N	102.33 W
Eton, Austl.	166	21.16 S	148.58 E
Eton, Eng., U.K.	260	51.31 N	0.37 W
Eton College ⊡[2]	260	51.30 N	0.36 W
Etondo	152	7.46 S	23.36 E
Etorofu-tō → Iturup, ostrov I	92a	44.54 N	147.30 E
Etosha National Park ♦	156	19.00 S	15.50 E
Etosha Pan ≚	156	18.45 S	16.15 E
Etoumbi	152	0.01 S	14.57 E
Etowah	192	35.19 N	84.31 W
Etowah ≃	192	34.15 N	85.11 W
Étréchy	50	48.30 N	2.12 E
Étrépagny	50	49.18 N	1.37 E
Étretat	50	49.42 N	0.12 E
Etrotroka	157b	22.53 S	47.36 E
Etroubles	62	45.49 N	7.14 E
Etrusca, Necropoli ⊥	66	42.15 N	11.47 E
Etsch → Adige ≃	64	45.10 N	12.20 E
Ettal	64	47.34 N	11.05 E
Ettalong	170	33.31 S	151.21 E
Ettelbruck	56	49.52 N	6.05 E
Ettenheim	58	48.15 N	7.49 E
Etten-Leur	52	51.34 N	4.38 E
Etterbeek	56	50.50 N	4.23 E
Etters	208	40.09 N	76.45 W
Et Tîdra I	150	19.44 N	16.24 W
Ettington	42	52.09 N	1.36 W
Ettlingen	56	48.56 N	8.24 E
Ettrema Creek ≃	170	34.50 S	150.22 E
Ettrick	208	37.14 N	77.25 W
Ettrick Forest ✦[3]	46	55.30 N	3.00 W
Ettrick Pen ∧	44	55.22 N	3.16 W
Ettrick Water ≃	46	55.31 N	2.55 W
Ettringen, Dtsch.	56	50.21 N	7.13 E
Ettringen, Dtsch.	58	48.06 N	10.39 E
Etuku	154	3.43 S	25.44 E
Etyka	88	51.00 N	116.50 E
Etzatlán	234	20.46 N	104.05 W
Etzikom Coulee ≃	184	49.25 N	111.10 W
Etzná ⊥	232	19.35 N	90.15 W
Eu	50	50.03 N	1.25 E
Eua I	14	21.22 S	174.56 W
Eua Iki I	174w	21.07 S	174.59 W
Eubank Acres	222	30.23 N	97.42 W
Euboea → Évvoia I	38	38.34 N	23.50 E
Eucalyptus Hills	228	32.56 N	116.56 W
Euchiniko ≃	182	53.14 N	123.30 W
Eucla	162	31.43 S	128.52 E
Euclid, Oh., U.S.	214	41.35 N	81.31 W
Euclid, Pa., U.S.	214	41.00 N	79.56 W
Euclid Center	216	42.08 N	86.24 W
Euclid Creek ≃	279a	41.35 N	81.35 W
Euclid Creek Reservation ♦	279a	41.33 N	81.32 W
Euclides da Cunha	250	10.31 S	39.01 W
Eucumbene	171b	36.07 S	148.38 E
Eucumbene ≃	171b	36.21 S	148.38 E
Eucumbene, Lake ⊜[1]	171b	36.05 S	148.45 E
Eudistes, Lac des ⊜	186	50.30 N	65.15 W
Eudora, Ar., U.S.	194	33.06 N	91.15 W
Eudora, Ks., U.S.	198	38.56 N	95.05 W
Eudunda	168b	34.11 S	139.04 E
Eufaula, Al., U.S.	194	31.53 N	85.08 W
Eufaula, Ok., U.S.	196	35.17 N	95.34 W
Eufaula Lake ⊜[1]	196	35.17 N	95.31 W
Eufrates → Euphrates ≃	128	31.00 N	47.25 E
Euganei, Colli ⋀[2]	64	45.19 N	11.40 E
Eugendorf	64	47.52 N	13.07 E
Eugene	202	44.03 N	123.05 W
Eugenia, Punta ›	232	27.50 N	115.05 W
Eugenia Lake ⊜	212	44.20 N	80.30 W
Eugenio Bustos	252	33.46 S	69.04 W
Eugênio de Melo	256	23.09 S	45.47 W
Eugmo I	26	63.49 N	22.45 E
Eugowra	166	33.26 S	148.23 E
Euijeongbu → Ŭijŏngbu	98	37.44 N	127.03 E
Euless	222	32.50 N	97.04 W
Eulo	166	28.10 S	145.03 E
Eume ≃	34	43.25 N	8.08 W
Eumemmerring Creek ≃	274b	38.03 S	145.10 E
Eumungerie	166	31.57 S	148.37 E
Eunápolis	255	16.22 S	39.35 W
Eungella National Park ♦	166	21.00 S	148.30 E
Eunice, La., U.S.	194	30.29 N	92.25 W
Eunice, N.M., U.S.	196	32.26 N	103.09 W
Eupen	56	50.38 N	6.02 E
Euphrates (Fırat) (Nahr al-Furāt) ≃	128	31.00 N	47.25 E
Euphrat → Euphrates ≃	128	31.00 N	47.25 E
Eupora	194	33.32 N	89.16 W
Eure	208	36.25 N	76.51 W
Eure □[5]	50	49.10 N	1.00 E
Eure ≃	50	49.18 N	1.12 E
Eure-et-Loir □[5]	50	48.30 N	1.30 E
Eureka, Ak., U.S.	180	61.56 N	147.10 W
Eureka, Ca., U.S.	204	40.48 N	124.09 W
Eureka, Il., U.S.	190	40.43 N	89.16 W
Eureka, Ks., U.S.	198	37.49 N	96.17 W
Eureka, Mo., U.S.	219	38.30 N	90.37 W
Eureka, Mt., U.S.	202	48.52 N	115.03 W
Eureka, Nv., U.S.	204	39.30 N	115.57 W
Eureka, Pa., U.S.	214	40.15 N	78.46 W
Eureka, S.C., U.S.	192	34.42 N	81.11 W
Eureka, S.D., U.S.	198	45.46 N	99.37 W
Eureka, Tx., U.S.	222	32.01 N	96.18 W
Eureka, Ut,. U.S.	200	39.57 N	112.07 W
Eureka, Mount ∧	162	26.34 S	121.32 E
Eureka Springs	194	36.24 N	93.44 W
Eurialo, Castello ⊥	70	37.06 N	15.14 E
Eurinilla Creek ≃	166	30.50 S	140.01 E
Euroa	169	36.45 S	145.35 E
Euro Disney, Parc ♦	261	48.51 N	2.47 E
Europa, Île I	138	22.20 S	40.22 E
Europa, Picos de ⋀	34	43.12 N	4.48 W
Europabrücke ✦[5]	64	47.11 N	11.23 E
Europa Point ›	34	36.10 N	5.22 W
Europe ⊥[1]	4	50.00 N	28.00 E

Symbol	English	Deutsch	Español	Français	Português
≃	River	Fluß	Río	Rivière	Rio
≍	Canal	Kanal	Canal	Canal	Canal
↳	Waterfall, Rapids	Wasserfall, Stromschnellen	Cascada, Rápidos	Chute d'eau, Rapides	Cascata, Rápidos
⊍	Strait	Meeresstraße	Estrecho	Détroit	Estreito
c	Bay, Gulf	Bucht, Golf	Bahía, Golfo	Baie, Golfe	Baía, Golfo
⊜	Lake, Lakes	See, Seen	Lago, Lagos	Lac, Lacs	Lago, Lagos
≡	Swamp	Sumpf	Pantano	Marais	Pântano
⊓	Ice Features, Glacier	Eis- und Gletscherformen	Accidentes Glaciales	Formes glaciaires	Acidentes glaciares
⊤	Other Hydrographic Features	Andere Hydrographische Objekte	Otros Elementos Hidrográficos	Autres données hydrographiques	Outros acidentes hidrográficos
✧	Submarine Features	Untermeerische Objekte	Accidentes Submarinos	Formes de relief sous-marin	Acidentes submarinos
□	Political Unit	Politische Einheit	Unidad Politica	Entité politique	Unidade política
⊡	Cultural Institution	Kulturelle Institution	Institución Cultural	Institution culturelle	Instituição cultural
⊥	Historical Site	Historische Stätte	Sitio Histórico	Site historique	Sitio histórico
♦	Recreational Site	Erholungs- und Ferienort	Sitio de Recreo	Centre de loisirs	Area de Lazer
⊠	Airport	Flughafen	Aeropuerto	Aéroport	Aeroporto
■	Military Installation	Militäranlage	Instalación Militar	Installation militaire	Instalação militar
✦	Miscellaneous	Verschiedenes	Misceláneo	Divers	Diversos

Name	Page	Lat.°	Long.°	Name	Seite	Breite°	Länge° E = Ost

ENGLISH   DEUTSCH

Symbols in the index entries represent the broad categories identified in the key at the right. Symbols with superior numbers (*¹) identify subcategories (see complete key on page I · 1).

Los símbolos incluidos en el texto del índice representan las grandes categorías identificadas en la clave a la derecha. Los símbolos con números en su parte superior (*¹) identifican las subcategorías (véase la clave completa en la página I · 1).

Os símbolos incluídos no texto do índice representam as grandes categorias identificadas com a chave à direita. Os símbolos com números em sua parte superior (*¹) identificam as subcategorias (veja-se a chave completa à página I · 1).

Les symboles de l'index représentent les catégories indiquées dans la légende à droite. Les symboles suivis d'un indice (*¹) représentent des sous-catégories (voir légende complète à la page I · 1).

Symbole im Register stellen die rechts im Schlüssel erklärten Kategorien dar. Symbole mit hochgestellten Ziffern (*¹) bezeichnen Unterabteilungen einer Kategorie (vgl. vollständiger Schlüssel auf Seite I · 1).

∧ Mountains	∧ Montaña	∧ Montanhas	∧ Montagnes	∧ Berg Gebirge	∧ Montanha Montanhas
Υ Pass	γ Paso	γ Passo	γ Col	γ Paß	γ Passo
Valley, Canyon	Valle, Cañón	Vale, Cânho	Val, Cañon	Tal, Cañon	Vale, Canhão
⌐ Plain	Llano	Ebene	Plaine	Planície
I Islands	islas	ilhas	îles	Inseln	Ilhas
⸗ Island	isla	ilha	île	Insel	Ilha
⌐ Cape	Cabo	Cabo	Cap	Kap	Cabo, Cabeço
Other Topographic Features	Otros Elementos Topográficos	Andere Topographische Objekte	Autres données topographiques	Outras acidentes topográficos

ESPAÑOL

Nombre	Página	Lat.°′	Long.°′ W = Oeste
Far Mountain ∧	182	52.46 N	125.17 W
Farm Pond ⊜, Ma., U.S.	283	42.17 N	71.26 W
Farm Pond ⊜, Ma., U.S.	283	42.14 N	71.21 W
Farmville, N.C., U.S.	192	35.35 N	77.35 W
Farmville, Va., U.S.	192	37.18 N	78.23 W
Färna	40	59.47 N	15.51 E
Farnam	198	40.42 N	100.12 W
Farnawā	142	30.59 N	30.39 E
Farnborough	42	51.17 N	0.46 W
Farnborough ✦[8]	260	51.21 N	0.04 E
Farncombe	260	51.12 N	0.36 W
Farndon	44	53.05 N	0.51 W
Färnebofjärden ⊜	40	60.14 N	16.47 E
Farne Islands II	44	55.38 N	1.38 W
Farnham, P.Q., Can.	206	45.17 N	72.59 W
Farnham, Eng., U.K.	42	51.13 N	0.49 W
Farnham, N.Y., U.S.	214	42.36 N	79.05 W
Farnham, Va., U.S.	208	37.53 N	76.37 W
Farnham, Mount ∧	182	50.29 N	116.30 W
Farnham Common	260	51.33 N	0.37 W
Farnham Royal	260	51.32 N	0.37 W
Farnhamville	198	42.16 N	94.24 W
Farningham	260	51.23 N	0.13 E
Farnroda	54	50.56 N	10.23 E
Farnworth	262	53.33 N	2.24 W
Faro, Bra.	250	2.11 S	56.44 W
Faro, Port.	34	37.01 N	7.56 W
Faro □[5]	34	37.15 N	8.00 W
Faro ≃	146	9.21 N	12.55 E
Faro, Punta del ≻	70	38.16 N	15.39 E
Faro, Réserve du ✦[4]	146	8.10 N	12.35 E
Färöer → Faeroe Islands □[2]	22	62.00 N	7.00 W
Fårön I	26	57.56 N	19.08 E
Fårösund	26	57.52 N	19.03 E
Farquhar, Cape ≻	162	23.37 S	113.37 E
Farquhar Group II	138	10.10 S	51.10 E
Farr	46	57.21 N	4.12 W
Farra d'Isonzo	64	45.56 N	12.31 E
Farragut	198	40.43 N	95.28 W
Farragut State Recreation Area ♠	202	47.55 N	116.35 W
Farrandsville	210	41.10 N	77.31 W
Farrar ≃	46	57.24 N	4.50 W
Farrar Pond ⊜	283	42.25 N	71.21 W
Farrars Creek ≃	166	25.35 S	140.43 E
Farrāshband	128	28.53 N	52.06 E
Farrell	214	41.12 N	80.29 W
Farrell Flat	168b	33.50 S	138.47 E
Farrer Park ♠	271c	1.19 N	103.51 E
Farrington Lake ⊜	276	40.26 N	74.28 W
Farrington Lake Heights	276	40.26 N	74.27 W
Far Rockaway ✦[8]	276	40.36 N	73.45 W
Farrukhābād	124	27.24 N	79.34 E
Farrukhnagar, India	124	28.27 N	76.49 E
Farrukhnagar, India	272a	28.43 N	77.23 E
Fārs □[4]	128	29.00 N	53.00 E
Fársala	38	39.18 N	22.23 E
Farschviller	56	49.06 N	6.54 E
Fārsī	128	33.47 N	63.15 E
Fārsī, Jazīreh-ye I	128	27.58 N	50.11 E
Farsīs	142	30.40 N	31.14 E
Farsø	26	56.47 N	9.21 E
Farsta	40	59.14 N	18.04 E
Farsund	26	58.05 N	6.48 E
Fartak, Ra's ≻	118	15.38 N	52.15 E
Farukolu I	122	6.12 N	73.16 E
Farum	41	55.48 N	12.22 E
Fårvang	41	56.16 N	9.44 E
Farvel, Kap ≻	176	59.45 N	44.00 W
Farwell, Mi., U.S.	190	43.50 N	84.52 W
Farwell, Tx., U.S.	196	30.15 N	103.15 W
Fāryāb □[4]	128	36.00 N	65.00 E
Fasā	128	28.56 N	53.42 E
Fasano	68	40.50 N	17.22 E
Faščovka	83	48.16 N	38.37 E
Fashkhah, 'Ayn ⊤[4]	132	31.43 N	35.27 E
Fåsjön ⊜	40	59.36 N	14.58 E
Fasmund ≻[1]	41	54.32 N	13.35 E
Fassa	150	13.26 N	8.15 W
Fassberg	52	52.54 N	10.10 E
Fasterholt	41	56.01 N	9.07 E
Fastnet Rock I[2]	48	51.24 N	9.35 W
Fastov	78	50.06 N	29.55 E
Fastoveckaja	78	45.56 N	40.09 E
Fatagar Tuting, Tanjung ≻	164	2.46 S	131.57 E
Fataki	154	4.46 S	28.11 E
Fatala ≃	150	10.13 N	14.00 W
Fat Deer Key I	220	24.44 N	81.00 W
Fate	222	32.56 N	96.23 W
Fatehābād, India	123	29.31 N	75.27 E
Fatehābād, India	124	27.01 N	78.19 E
Fatehgarh, India	124	27.22 N	79.38 E
Fatehgarh, India	124	24.48 N	76.58 E
Fatehgarh Chūriān	123	31.52 N	74.58 E
Fatehjang	123	33.34 N	72.39 E
Fatehpur, India	120	27.59 N	74.57 E
Fatehpur, India	124	27.10 N	81.13 E
Fatehpur, India	124	25.56 N	80.48 E
Fatehpur, India	126	22.17 N	88.14 E
Fatehpur, India	126	24.05 N	87.44 E
Fatehpur, Pāk.	123	31.09 N	71.13 E
Fatehpur Sīkri	124	27.06 N	77.40 E
Fathai	140	8.05 N	31.48 E
Fathom Five National Marine Park ♠	190	45.15 N	81.40 W
Fatick	150	14.20 N	16.25 W
Fatick □[4]	150	14.00 N	16.30 W
Fatigue, Mount ∧	169	38.34 S	146.18 E
Fatima, Arg.	258	34.26 S	59.00 W
Fátima, Port.	34	39.37 N	8.39 W
Fatima do Sol	255	22.16 S	54.25 W
Fatima do Sul	252	22.16 S	54.22 W
Fāṭimah, Wādī V	144	21.27 N	39.09 E
Fatoto	150	13.26 N	13.52 W
Fat'ož	78	52.07 N	35.52 E
Fatsa	130	41.02 N	37.31 E
Fatshan → Foshan	100	23.03 N	113.09 E
Fat Tong Point ≻	271d	22.16 N	114.15 E
Fatu-Berlio	112	8.56 S	125.52 E
Fatulla	126	23.38 N	90.29 E
Fatumu	174w	21.13 S	175.07 W
Fatunda	152	4.08 S	17.13 E
Fatwā	124	25.31 N	85.19 E
Fauabu	175e	8.34 S	160.43 E
Faucigny	58	46.07 N	6.22 E
Faucille, Col de la)(	58	46.22 N	6.02 E
Faucilles, Monts ⋀	58	48.07 N	6.16 E
Faucogney	58	47.51 N	6.34 E
Faucon-de-Barcelonnette	62	44.24 N	6.41 E
Fauglia	66	43.34 N	10.31 E
Fauldhouse	46	55.50 N	3.37 W
Faulkton	198	45.02 N	99.07 W
Faulquemont	56	49.03 N	6.36 E
Fauquembergues	50	50.36 N	2.05 E
Fauquier	182	49.53 N	118.05 W
Fauquier □[6]	208	38.35 N	77.35 W
Făurei	38	45.06 N	27.14 E
Faure Island I	162	25.51 S	113.52 E
Fauresmith	158	29.42 S	25.21 E
Fauro Island I	175e	6.55 S	156.04 E
Fauske	24	67.15 N	15.24 E
Faust	182	55.19 N	115.38 W
Faustovo	82	55.26 N	38.29 E
Fauville-en-Caux	50	49.39 N	0.35 E
Fauvillers	56	49.51 N	5.40 E
Faux-Cap	157b	25.33 S	45.32 E
Fåvang	26	61.27 N	10.11 E
Favara	70	37.19 N	13.39 E
Faverges	62	45.45 N	6.18 E
Faverney	58	47.46 N	6.06 E
Faversham	42	51.20 N	0.53 E
Favières	261	48.46 N	2.47 E
Favignana	70	37.56 N	12.20 E
Favignana, Isola I	70	37.56 N	12.19 E
Favoriten ✦[8]	264b	48.11 N	16.23 E

FRANÇAIS

Nom	Page	Lat.°′	Long.°′ W = Ouest
Favourable Lake ⊜	184	52.53 N	93.56 W
Favrieux	261	48.57 N	1.39 E
Fawcett	182	54.32 N	114.05 W
Fawcett Lake ⊜	182	55.19 N	113.57 W
Fawkham Green	260	51.22 N	0.17 E
Fawkner	274b	37.43 S	144.58 E
Fawkner Park ♠	274b	37.50 S	144.59 E
Fawley	42	50.49 N	1.20 W
Fawn ≃, On., Can.	176	55.22 N	88.20 W
Fawn ≃, U.S.	216	41.51 N	85.40 W
Fawn Grove	208	39.44 N	76.27 W
Fawnie Nose ∧	182	53.16 N	125.08 W
Fawnie Range ⋀	182	53.10 N	125.00 W
Fawsett Farms	284c	38.59 N	77.14 W
Faxaflói C	24a	64.25 N	23.00 W
Faxälven ≃	26	63.13 N	17.13 E
Faxinal	255	23.59 S	51.22 W
Faxinal do Soturno	252	29.37 S	53.26 W
Faxon	210	41.15 N	76.58 W
Faya	146	17.55 N	19.07 E
Fayd	128	27.07 N	42.27 E
Fayence	62	43.37 N	6.41 E
Fayerweather Island I	276	41.08 N	73.13 W
Fayette, Al., U.S.	194	33.41 N	87.49 W
Fayette, Ia., U.S.	190	42.50 N	91.48 W
Fayette, Ms., U.S.	194	31.42 N	91.03 W
Fayette, Mo., U.S.	194	39.08 N	92.41 W
Fayette, N.Y., U.S.	210	42.49 N	76.49 W
Fayette, Oh., U.S.	216	41.40 N	84.19 W
Fayette □[6], Il., U.S.	219	38.58 N	89.06 W
Fayette □[6], In., U.S.	218	39.39 N	85.08 W
Fayette □[6], Ky., U.S.	218	38.07 N	84.30 W
Fayette □[6], Oh., U.S.	218	39.32 N	83.26 W
Fayette □[6], Pa., U.S.	214	40.05 N	79.39 W
Fayette □[6], Tx., U.S.	222	29.50 N	96.57 W
Fayette, Lake ⊜[1]	222	29.56 N	96.44 W
Fayette City	214	40.06 N	79.50 W
Fayetteville, Ar., U.S.	194	36.03 N	94.09 W
Fayetteville, Ga., U.S.	192	33.26 N	84.27 W
Fayetteville, Il., U.S.	219	38.22 N	89.48 W
Fayetteville, N.Y., U.S.	210	43.02 N	76.00 W
Fayetteville, N.C., U.S.	192	35.03 N	78.52 W
Fayetteville, Oh., U.S.	218	39.11 N	83.55 W
Fayetteville, Pa., U.S.	208	39.54 N	77.33 W
Fayetteville, Tn., U.S.	194	35.09 N	86.34 W
Fayetteville, Tx., U.S.	222	29.54 N	96.41 W
Fayetteville, W.V., U.S.	188	38.03 N	81.06 W
Faylakah I	128	29.27 N	48.20 E
Fayl-Billot	58	47.47 N	5.36 E
Fayrā	144	13.17 N	43.25 E
Fay-sur-Lignon	62	44.59 N	4.14 E
Fayville	207	42.17 N	71.30 W
Fayyum → Al-Fayyūm	142	29.19 N	30.50 E
Fažana	64	44.55 N	13.49 E
Fazao	150	8.42 N	0.46 E
Fazao, Parc National du ♠	150	8.40 N	0.42 E
Fazeley	42	52.37 N	1.42 W
Fazenda de Cima	248	15.56 S	56.37 W
Fazenda Libongo	152	8.24 S	13.24 E
Fazenda Nova	255	16.11 S	50.48 W
Fāzilka	123	30.24 N	74.02 E
Fāzilpur	120	29.18 N	70.27 E
Fazzān (Fezzan) □[9]	146	26.00 N	14.00 E
Fdérik	148	22.41 N	12.43 W
Feale ≃	48	52.28 N	9.40 W
Fear, Cape ≻	192	33.50 N	77.58 W
Fearnhead	262	53.25 N	2.33 W
Feasterville	208	40.08 N	75.00 W
Feather ≃	204	38.47 N	121.36 W
Feather, Middle Fork ≃	204	39.34 N	121.26 W
Feather, North Fork ≃	204	39.34 N	121.28 W
Feather, North Fork, East Branch ≃	204	40.01 N	121.13 W
Feather, South Fork ≃	204	39.33 N	121.28 W
Featherbed Top ∧	262	53.26 N	1.52 W
Featherly Regional Park ♠	280	33.52 N	117.42 W
Featherston	172	41.07 S	175.20 E
Featherstone, Eng., U.K.	44	53.41 N	1.21 W
Featherstone, Zimb.	154	18.42 S	30.49 E
Feathertop, Mount ∧	166	36.54 S	147.08 E
Fécamp	50	49.45 N	0.22 E
Fedala → Mohammedia	148	33.44 N	7.24 W
Fedderwardergroden	52	53.35 N	8.05 E
Feddet ≻[1]	41	55.09 N	12.07 E
Federación	252	31.00 S	57.54 W
Federal, Arg.	252	30.57 S	58.48 W
Federal, Pa., U.S.	279b	40.23 N	80.09 W
Federal Capital Territory □[3]	150	9.00 N	7.15 E
Federalsburg	208	38.41 N	75.46 W
Federal Territory □[8]	273a	6.29 N	3.25 E
Federal Way	224	47.19 N	122.18 W
Federation Forest State Park ♠	224	47.09 N	121.40 W
Federsee ⊜	58	48.05 N	9.38 E
Fedeshk	128	32.45 N	58.50 E
Fedje	26	60.47 N	4.42 E
Fedorino	82	55.08 N	36.06 E
Fedosejevka	80	46.53 N	44.00 E
Fedosejevskaja	24	62.07 N	40.42 E
Fedosicha	86	54.47 N	81.54 E
Fedosjino	82	55.08 N	38.30 E
Fedotovo	82	55.41 N	39.12 E
Feeagh, Lough ⊜	48	53.55 N	9.36 W
Feeding Hills	207	42.04 N	72.40 W
Feehanville	278	42.05 N	87.54 W
Feerfeer	144	8.30 N	47.55 E
Feesburg	218	38.52 N	83.58 W
Fefan I	175c	7.21 N	151.51 E
Fehérgyarmat	30	47.58 N	22.32 E
Fehmarn I	54	54.28 N	11.08 E
Fehmarnbelt (Femer Bælt) ʉ	41	54.35 N	11.15 E
Fehmarnsund ʉ	54	54.24 N	11.07 E
Fehrbellin	54	52.49 N	12.46 E
Fehring	61	46.56 N	16.01 E
Feia, Lagoa C	255	22.00 S	41.20 W
Feicheng	98	36.15 N	116.46 E
Feichten	58	47.02 N	10.44 E
Feidong	100	31.52 N	117.29 E
Feignies	50	50.18 N	3.55 E
Feigumfossen ᒪ	26	61.23 N	7.26 E
Feiheji	100	33.36 N	115.36 E
Fei Huang ≃	100	33.35 N	119.02 E
Feijó	248	8.09 S	70.21 W
Feiketu	89	45.46 N	127.09 E
Feilding	172	40.13 S	175.34 E
Feiler ∧	58	47.07 N	10.52 E
Feiliqiao	106	31.05 N	119.05 E
Feilitzsch	54	50.22 N	11.56 E
Feilong, Zhg.	107	30.25 N	106.20 E
Feilong, Zhg.	107	30.36 N	105.54 E
Feilongguan	107	28.57 N	105.05 E
Feiluan	100	26.35 N	119.35 E
Feira	154	15.37 S	30.25 E
Feira de Santana	255	12.15 S	38.57 W
Feistritz ≃	61	47.01 N	16.08 E
Feistritz an der Gail	64	46.34 N	13.36 E
Feistritzer Spitze ∧	61	46.31 N	14.45 E
Feixi	100	31.42 N	117.10 E
Feixian	98	35.18 N	117.57 E
Feixiang	98	36.34 N	114.49 E
Feiyun ≃	100	27.48 N	120.36 E
Fejaj, Chott ≋	148	33.55 N	9.10 E
Fejér □[6]	30	47.10 N	18.35 E
Fejø I	41	54.57 N	11.26 E
Feke	130	37.53 N	35.58 E
Feklistova, ostrov I	89	55.02 N	136.55 E
Felâhiye	130	39.06 N	35.35 E
Felanitx	34	39.28 N	3.08 E
Felbertauren-Tunnel ✦[5]	64	47.08 N	12.31 E

PORTUGUÊS

Nome	Página	Lat.°′	Long.°′ W = Oeste
Felda	220	26.33 N	81.26 W
Felda ≃, Dtsch.	56	50.51 N	10.05 E
Felda ≃, Dtsch.	56	50.42 N	9.03 E
Feldafing	64	47.57 N	11.17 E
Feldaist ≃	61	48.19 N	14.34 E
Feld am See	64	46.47 N	13.45 E
Feldbach	61	46.57 N	15.54 E
Feldberg, Dtsch.	54	53.20 N	13.26 E
Feldberg, Dtsch.	58	47.51 N	8.02 E
Feldberg ∧	58	47.52 N	8.00 E
Felderbach ≃	263	51.22 N	7.08 E
Feldhausen ✦[8]	263	51.37 N	6.59 E
Feldis	58	46.48 N	9.26 E
Feldkirch	58	47.14 N	9.36 E
Feldkirchen an der Donau	61	48.21 N	14.03 E
Feldkirchen bei Graz	61	47.01 N	15.27 E
Feldkirchen in Kärnten	61	46.43 N	14.05 E
Feldmark	263	51.41 N	6.38 E
Feldstetten	58	48.28 N	9.37 E
Felhit	144	16.43 N	38.02 E
Feliciano, Méx.	234	18.01 N	101.58 W
Feliciano, P.R.	240m	18.28 N	67.08 W
Feliciano, Arroyo ≃	252	31.06 S	59.54 W
Felicity	218	38.50 N	84.05 W
Felino	64	44.42 N	10.15 E
Felipe Carrillo Puerto, Méx.	234	21.09 N	104.52 W
Felipe Carrillo Puerto, Méx.	234	19.08 N	102.42 W
Felix, Cape ≻	176	69.54 N	97.50 W
Felix, Rio ≃	196	33.08 N	104.19 W
Felixburg	154	19.29 S	30.51 E
Felixdorf	61	47.53 N	16.15 E
Felixlândia	255	18.47 S	44.55 W
Felixstowe	42	51.58 N	1.20 E
Felixton	158	28.50 S	31.53 E
Félix U. Gómez	232	29.50 N	111.30 W
Felizzano	62	44.54 N	8.26 E
Fella ≃	64	46.21 N	13.07 E
Fellbach	56	48.48 N	9.15 E
Felletin	32	45.53 N	2.10 E
Felling	44	54.57 N	1.33 W
Fellingsbro	40	59.26 N	15.35 E
Fellows	226	35.11 N	119.32 W
Fellows Creek ≃	281	42.17 N	83.26 W
Fellowship	285	39.55 N	74.58 W
Fellsburg	214	40.11 N	79.49 W
Fellsmere	220	27.46 N	80.36 W
Fellwick	285	40.08 N	75.11 W
Felpham	42	50.47 N	0.39 W
Felsberg	56	51.08 N	9.25 E
Felső-Válicka ≃	61	46.52 N	16.53 E
Feltham ✦[8]	260	51.27 N	0.24 W
Felt Lake ⊜	282	37.23 N	122.11 W
Felton, Ca., U.S.	226	37.03 N	122.04 W
Felton, De., U.S.	208	39.00 N	75.34 W
Felton, Pa., U.S.	208	39.51 N	76.34 W
Feltre	64	46.01 N	11.54 E
Felts Mills	212	44.01 N	75.46 W
Feltwell	42	52.29 N	0.32 E
Femer Bælt (Fehmarnbelt) ʉ	41	54.35 N	11.15 E
Femme Osage Creek ≃	219	38.39 N	90.44 W
Femmøller	41	56.14 N	10.35 E
Femø I	41	54.58 N	11.33 E
Femund ⊜	26	62.12 N	11.52 E
Femundsenden	26	61.55 N	11.55 E
Femundsmarka Nasjonalpark ♠	26	62.20 N	12.07 E
Fen ≃	102	35.36 N	110.42 E
Fena Valley Reservoir ⊜[1]	174p	13.21 N	144.42 E
Fendaozi	104	41.35 N	120.51 E
Fenelon Falls	212	44.32 N	78.45 W
Fenelton	214	40.52 N	79.44 W
Fener ✦[8]	267b	41.02 N	28.56 E
Fenerbahce Stadium ♠	267b	40.59 N	29.02 E
Fener Burnu ≻	130	41.07 N	39.25 E
Fener Tepesi ∧[2]	267b	41.09 N	28.47 E
Fenestrelle	62	45.02 N	7.03 E
Fénétrange	56	48.51 N	7.01 E
Feng ≃	105	39.25 N	116.57 E
Fengcheng, Zhg.	98	40.27 N	124.02 E
Fengcheng, Zhg.	100	28.10 N	115.46 E
Fengcheng, Zhg.	102	38.32 N	101.50 E
Fengcheng, Zhg.	106	30.55 N	121.38 E
Fengdengwu	105	39.42 N	117.55 E
Fengdian	107	30.41 N	104.51 E
Fengdu	102	29.58 N	107.41 E
Fengfeng	98	36.28 N	114.14 E
Fenggang, Zhg.	100	28.34 N	116.34 E
Fenggang, Zhg.	102	27.58 N	107.47 E
Fenggaopu	107	29.24 N	105.41 E
Fenghua	100	29.40 N	121.24 E
Fenghuang, Zhg.	100	23.58 N	116.44 E
Fenghuang, Zhg.	102	24.25 N	107.17 E
Fenghuang, Zhg.	102	27.58 N	109.19 E
Fenghuang, Zhg.	106	31.21 N	121.44 E
Fenghuangchang	107	29.44 N	106.19 E
Fenghuang Shan ∧	107	28.54 N	106.35 E
Fenghuanjing	100	31.11 N	117.49 E
Fenghui	100	29.56 N	120.58 E
Fengjia, Zhg.	98	37.03 N	121.42 E
Fengjia, Zhg.	104	42.35 N	122.30 E
Fengjiabao	102	36.12 N	104.49 E
Fengjiakou	98	38.11 N	116.44 E
Fengjianjiao	106	30.41 N	120.51 E
Fengjiatun	104	41.14 N	122.00 E
Fengjiawopeng	104	42.19 N	123.40 E
Fengjiaxiang	106	30.56 N	121.06 E
Fengjie	102	31.03 N	109.31 E
Fengjing	106	30.53 N	121.01 E
Fengkou	100	30.05 N	113.18 E
Fengle, Zhg.	89	45.47 N	125.26 E
Fengle, Zhg.	100	27.13 N	118.11 E
Fenglezhen	98	36.14 N	114.18 E
Fengliang	100	23.59 N	116.14 E
Fenglin, T'aiwan	100	23.45 N	121.26 E
Fenglin, Zhg.	100	28.19 N	120.46 E
Fengling Guan)(	100	28.14 N	118.29 E
Fenglingtou	100	28.26 N	117.50 E
Fengman	89	43.46 N	126.41 E
Fengnan (Xugezhuang)	105	39.34 N	118.06 E
Fengning (Dagezhen)	98	41.12 N	116.32 E
Fengpin	100	23.36 N	121.31 E
Fengpingzi	102	32.46 N	105.12 E
Fengqiao, Zhg.	100	29.46 N	120.26 E
Fengqiao, Zhg.	106	31.19 N	120.33 E
Fengqing	102	24.46 N	99.52 E
Fengqiu	98	35.05 N	114.25 E
Fengrun	105	39.50 N	118.07 E
Fengshan, Zhg.	89	46.22 N	128.30 E
Fengshan, Zhg.	98	41.14 N	117.05 E
Fengshan, Zhg.	102	22.01 N	109.59 E
Fengshi	100	24.42 N	116.34 E
Fengshun	100	23.48 N	116.11 E
Fengtai, Zhg.	100	32.44 N	116.43 E
Fengtai, Zhg.	105	39.51 N	116.16 E
Fengtian, Zhg.	100	27.24 N	114.43 E
Fengtian, Zhg.	100	25.46 N	115.30 E
Fengtien → Shenyang	104	41.48 N	123.27 E
Fengting	100	25.16 N	118.54 E
Fengwan	100	24.48 N	113.50 E
Fengxi	102	31.48 N	109.50 E
Fengxian, Zhg.	98	34.42 N	116.34 E
Fengxian, Zhg.	102	33.57 N	106.44 E
Fengxian, Zhg.	106	30.55 N	121.27 E
Fengxiang	102	34.29 N	107.29 E
Fengxin	100	28.43 N	115.23 E
Fengyang, Zhg.	100	32.52 N	117.34 E
Fengyang, Zhg.	100	24.49 N	117.53 E
Fengyi	102	31.44 N	103.53 E
Fengyu	100	26.31 N	119.18 E
Fengyüan	100	24.15 N	120.43 E
Fengzhen	102	40.24 N	113.09 E
Fengzhou	100	25.41 N	113.52 E
Fengzhuangtou	106	31.00 N	118.39 E

Fenholloway ≃	192	29.59 N	83.47 W
Fen Hu ⊜	106	31.00 N	120.47 E
Feni	124	23.00 N	91.24 E
Fenicia Moncata ⊥	70	37.33 N	14.57 E
Feni Islands II	14	4.05 S	153.42 E
Fenimore Pass ʉ	180	52.00 N	175.35 W
Fenino	265b	55.44 N	37.57 E
Fenis	62	45.44 N	7.29 E
Feniscowles	262	53.43 N	2.32 W
Fenjie	106	32.17 N	120.20 E
Fennimore	190	42.59 N	90.39 W
Fennville	216	42.35 N	86.06 W
Fenny Compton	42	52.09 N	1.20 W
Fenny Stratford	42	52.00 N	0.43 W
Feno, Capo di ≻, Fr.	36	41.57 N	8.36 E
Feno, Capo di ≻, Fr.	71	41.23 N	9.06 E
Fenoarivo, Madag.	157b	18.26 S	46.34 E
Fenoarivo, Madag.	157b	21.43 S	46.24 E
Fenoarivo, Madag.	157b	20.52 S	46.53 E
Fenoarivo Atsinanana	157b	17.22 S	49.25 E
Fensfjorden C[2]	26	60.51 N	4.50 E
Fenshui	104	40.41 N	122.32 E
Fenshui ≃	100	29.49 N	119.41 E
Fenshui'ao	100	25.20 N	114.43 E
Fenshuidunshen	106	31.30 N	120.01 E
Fenshuiling, Zhg.	107	28.51 N	105.35 E
Fenshuiling, Zhg.	107	30.20 N	105.15 E
Fenshuipu	107	30.05 N	104.05 E
Fenshuizhen	107	29.44 N	103.55 E
Fenshuizui	100	30.35 N	113.38 E
Fensmark	41	55.17 N	11.49 E
Fenstanton	42	52.18 N	0.04 W
Fenton, Mi., U.S.	216	42.47 N	83.42 W
Fenton, Mo., U.S.	219	38.32 N	90.22 W
Fenton, Lake ⊜	216	42.50 N	83.43 W
Fentou	105	38.53 N	116.32 E
Fentress	222	29.45 N	97.47 W
Fenway Park ♠	283	42.21 N	71.06 W
Fenwick	188	38.13 N	80.34 W
Fenwick Island ≻[1]	208	38.25 N	75.03 W
Fenyang	102	37.17 N	111.48 E
Fenyi	100	27.47 N	114.42 E
Feodosija	78	45.02 N	35.23 E
Feodosijskij zaliv C	78	45.05 N	35.35 E
Fépin	56	50.01 N	4.44 E
Fer, Cap de ≻	148	37.05 N	7.10 E
Ferbane	48	53.15 N	7.49 W
Ferbitz	264a	52.30 N	13.01 E
Ferch	264a	52.19 N	12.56 E
Fercher Berge ∧[2]	264a	52.19 N	12.57 E
Ferchland	54	52.26 N	12.00 E
Ferdig	182	48.45 N	111.46 W
Ferdinand	194	38.13 N	86.51 W
Ferdinandshof	54	53.39 N	13.53 E
Ferdows	128	34.00 N	58.09 E
Fère-Champenoise	50	48.45 N	3.59 E
Fère-en-Tardenois	50	49.12 N	3.31 E
Ferencváros ✦[8]	264c	47.28 N	19.06 E
Ferentillo	66	42.37 N	12.47 E
Ferentino	66	41.42 N	13.15 E
Fergana	85	40.23 N	71.46 E
Ferganskaja dolina V	85	40.50 N	71.30 E
Ferganskij chrebet ⋀	85	41.00 N	74.00 E
Fergus	212	43.42 N	80.22 W
Fergus Falls	198	46.16 N	96.04 W
Ferguson, Austl.	168a	33.26 S	115.51 E
Ferguson, B.C., Can.	182	50.41 N	117.28 W
Ferguson, Ky., U.S.	192	37.04 N	84.36 W
Ferguson, Mo., U.S.	219	38.44 N	90.18 W
Ferguson ≃	168a	33.21 S	115.40 E
Fergusonville	285	40.07 N	74.54 W
Fergusson Island I	164	9.30 S	150.40 E
Fériana	148	34.57 N	8.34 E
Ferihegyi Airport ⊠	264c	47.26 N	19.15 E
Ferkéssédougou	150	9.36 N	5.12 W
Ferla	70	37.07 N	14.56 E
Ferlach	61	46.31 N	14.18 E
Ferleiten	64	47.10 N	12.49 E
Ferlo ✦[1]	150	0.15 N	0.14 W
Ferlo, Vallée du V	150	15.42 N	15.30 W
Fermiers, Île aux I	275a	45.40 N	73.27 W
Fermignano	66	43.40 N	12.39 E
Fermin, Point ≻	228	33.42 N	118.18 W
Fermi National Accelerator Laboratory Ʊ[3]	216	41.50 N	88.15 W
Fermo	66	43.09 N	13.43 E
Fermont	176	52.47 N	67.05 W
Fermoselle	34	41.19 N	6.23 W
Fermoy	48	52.08 N	8.16 W
Fernández	252	27.55 S	63.54 W
Fernández Leal	200	30.51 N	108.17 W
Fernandina, Isla I	246a	0.25 S	91.30 W
Fernandina Beach	192	30.40 N	81.27 W
Fernando de la Mora	252	25.19 S	57.36 W
Fernando de Noronha, Ilha I	250	3.51 S	32.25 W
Fernandópolis	255	20.16 S	50.14 W
Fernando Póo → Bioko I	152	3.30 N	8.40 E
Fernán-Núñez	34	37.40 N	4.43 W
Fernão Veloso, Baía de C	154	14.20 S	40.45 E
Ferndale, S. Afr.	273d	26.05 S	27.59 E
Ferndale, Ca., U.S.	204	40.34 N	124.15 W
Ferndale, Fl., U.S.	220	28.37 N	81.42 W
Ferndale, Md., U.S.	208	39.10 N	76.38 W
Ferndale, Mi., U.S.	216	42.27 N	83.08 W
Ferndale, N.Y., U.S.	210	41.46 N	74.44 W
Ferndale, Pa., U.S.	214	40.17 N	78.54 W
Ferndale, Wa., U.S.	202	48.50 N	122.35 W
Ferndale Lake ⊜	222	32.57 N	95.05 W
Ferndown	42	50.48 N	1.55 W
Ferney-Voltaire	58	46.15 N	6.07 E
Fern Glen	210	40.57 N	76.10 W
Fernhatten ⋀[2]	41	56.15 N	10.48 E
Fernhill Heath	42	52.14 N	2.12 W
Fernie	182	49.30 N	115.03 W
Fernilee	262	53.18 N	1.58 W
Fernilee Reservoir ⊜[1]	262	53.17 N	1.59 W
Fernley	204	39.36 N	119.15 W
Ferno	62	45.37 N	8.45 E
Fernow, Mount ∧	224	47.45 N	121.14 W
Fern Park	220	28.41 N	81.20 W
Fernpass)(	58	47.22 N	10.50 E
Fern Ridge Lake ⊜[1]	202	44.05 N	123.18 W
Ferns	48	52.35 N	6.31 W
Fernvale	171a	27.27 S	152.39 E
Fernway, Il., U.S.	278	41.36 N	87.50 W
Fernway, Pa., U.S.	214	40.41 N	80.07 W
Fernwood, Id., U.S.	202	47.06 N	116.23 W
Fernwood, N.Y., U.S.	210	43.16 N	73.40 W
Fernwood, Pa., U.S.	285	39.57 N	75.15 W
Ferny Creek	274b	37.53 S	145.21 E
Feroé, Islas → Faeroe Islands □[2]	22	62.00 N	7.00 W
Feroës → Faeroe Islands □[2]	22	62.00 N	7.00 W
Ferokh	122	11.11 N	75.51 E
Feroleto Antico	68	38.58 N	16.23 E
Feroleto della Chiesa	68	38.28 N	16.04 E
Ferolle Point ≻	186	51.05 N	57.07 W
Ferozepore → Fīrozpur	123	30.55 N	74.36 E
Ferrandina	68	40.29 N	16.28 E
Ferrara	64	44.50 N	11.35 E
Ferrara □[4]	64	44.48 N	11.50 E
Ferrat, Cap ≻	34	35.54 N	0.23 W
Ferrato, Capo ≻	71	39.18 N	9.38 E
Ferraz de Vasconcelos	256	23.32 S	46.22 W
Ferraz de Vasconcelos □[7]	287b	23.33 S	46.21 W
Ferrazzano	66	41.32 N	14.40 E
Ferré, Cap ≻	240e	14.28 N	60.49 W
Ferreira, Ang.	152	12.53 S	22.48 E
Ferreira, S. Afr.	158	29.13 S	26.10 E
Ferreira do Alentejo	34	38.03 N	8.07 W
Ferreira Gomes	250	0.48 N	51.08 W
Ferreiros	256	22.25 S	43.34 W
Ferrell	285	39.41 N	75.12 W
Ferrell's Bridge Dam ✦[6]	222	32.45 N	94.30 W
Ferreñafe	248	6.38 S	79.45 W
Ferrera Erbognone	62	45.07 N	8.52 E
Ferret	58	45.55 N	7.06 E
Ferret, Cap ≻	32	44.37 N	1.15 W
Ferreyra	252	31.28 S	64.08 W
Ferriday	194	31.37 N	91.33 W
Ferriere	62	44.38 N	9.30 E
Ferrière-la-Grande	50	50.15 N	4.00 E
Ferrières	50	48.05 N	2.47 E
Ferrières-en-Brie	50	48.49 N	2.43 E
Ferris	222	32.32 N	96.39 W
Ferritslev	41	55.18 N	10.36 E
Ferro ≃	255	12.27 S	54.31 W
Ferrol, Península de ≻[1]	248	9.10 S	78.37 W
Ferrol → El Ferrol del Caudillo	34	43.29 N	8.14 W
Ferron	200	39.05 N	111.08 W
Ferron Creek ≃	200	39.09 N	110.55 W
Ferros	255	19.14 S	43.02 W
Ferru, Monte ∧	71	39.44 N	9.38 E
Ferruzzano	68	38.02 N	16.05 E
Ferry, Pointe ≻	241o	16.17 N	61.49 W
Ferryhill	44	54.41 N	1.33 W
Ferryland	186	47.02 N	52.53 W
Ferry Point Park ♠	276	40.49 N	73.50 W
Ferrysburg	216	43.05 N	86.13 W
Ferry Village	284a	43.58 N	78.57 W
Ferryville → Menzel Bourguiba	148	37.10 N	9.48 E
Feršampenuaz	86	53.32 N	59.51 E
Fertile	198	47.32 N	96.16 W
Fertilia, Aeroporto di ⊠	71	40.37 N	8.15 E
Fertő (Neusiedler See) ⊜	61	47.50 N	16.45 E
Fertőd ⊥	61	47.37 N	16.53 E
Fertőrákos	61	47.43 N	16.39 E
Fertőújlak	61	47.40 N	16.51 E
Ferulargiu, Monte ∧	71	40.31 N	9.34 E
Ferzikovo	82	54.32 N	36.45 E
Fès	148	34.05 N	4.57 W
Fès □[4]	148	33.55 N	4.57 W
Feshi	152	6.07 S	18.10 E
Feshie ≃	46	57.08 N	3.55 W
Fessenden	198	47.38 N	99.37 W
Festus	219	38.13 N	90.23 W
Fetcham	260	51.17 N	0.22 W
Fet Dom, Tanjung ≻	164	1.53 S	129.43 E
Fété Bowé	150	14.56 N	13.30 W
Fetești	38	44.23 N	27.50 E
Fethaland, Point of ≻	46a	60.38 N	1.18 W
Fethard	48	52.27 N	7.41 W
Fethiye	130	36.37 N	29.07 E
Fethiye Körfezi C	130	36.40 N	29.00 E
Fetisovo	72	42.46 N	52.38 E
Fetlar I	46a	60.37 N	0.52 W
Fetsund	26	59.56 N	11.10 E
Fetterangus	46	57.33 N	2.01 W
Fettercairn	46	56.51 N	2.34 W
Feucherolles	261	48.52 N	1.58 E
Feucht	60	49.22 N	11.13 E
Feuchtwangen	56	49.10 N	10.20 E
Feudingen	56	50.56 N	8.19 E
Feuerland → Tierra del Fuego, Isla Grande de I	254	54.00 S	69.00 W
Feuet	146	24.57 N	10.04 E
Feuilles, Baie aux C	176	58.55 N	69.20 W
Feuilles, Rivière aux ≃	176	58.47 N	70.04 W
Feuquières-en-Vimeu	50	50.04 N	1.36 E
Feura Bush	210	42.35 N	73.53 W
Feurs	62	45.45 N	4.14 E
Fevik	26	58.23 N	8.42 E
Fevzipaşa	130	37.07 N	36.37 E
Féy	56	49.02 N	6.06 E
Feyẕābād, Afg.	120	37.06 N	70.34 E
Feyẕābād, Īrān	128	35.01 N	58.46 E
Feyzin	62	45.40 N	4.51 E
Fez → Fès	148	34.05 N	4.57 W
Fezzan → Fazzān □[9]	146	26.00 N	14.00 E
Ffestiniog	42	52.58 N	3.55 W
Fforest Fawr ✦[1]	42	51.52 N	3.36 W
F. Gilbert Hills State Forest ♠	283	42.03 N	71.17 W
Fhada, Beinn ∧	46	57.13 N	5.18 W
Fiambalá	252	27.41 S	67.38 W
Fiamignano	66	42.16 N	13.07 E
Fian	150	10.23 N	2.29 W
Fianarantsoa	157b	21.26 S	47.05 E
Fianarantsoa □[4]	157b	22.00 S	47.00 E
Fianga	146	9.55 N	15.09 E
Fiano	62	45.13 N	7.31 E
Fiantsonana	157b	19.09 S	46.12 E
Fiastra, Abbazia di Ʊ[1]	66	43.13 N	13.25 E
Fiavè	64	46.00 N	10.50 E
Ficarazzi	70	38.05 N	13.28 E
Ficarolo	64	44.57 N	11.26 E
Ficarra	70	38.06 N	14.50 E
Fiche	144	9.52 N	38.46 E
Fichtelberg	60	50.01 N	11.51 E
Fichtelberg ∧	54	50.26 N	12.57 E
Fichtelgebirge ⋀	30	50.00 N	11.55 E
Fichtenau	264a	52.27 N	13.42 E
Ficksburg	158	28.57 S	27.50 E
Ficulle	66	42.50 N	12.04 E
Ficuzza ≃	70	37.00 N	14.20 E
Fidalgo ≃	250	7.28 S	42.32 W
Fidalgo Island I	224	48.25 N	122.35 W
Fidān, Wādī al- V	132	30.46 N	35.18 E
Fiddlers Hamlet	260	51.41 N	0.08 E
Fiddletown	226	38.30 N	120.46 W
Fiddyment Creek ≃	278	41.36 N	88.03 W
Fidelity	219	39.09 N	90.10 W
Fidenza	64	44.52 N	10.03 E
Fidīmīn	142	29.23 N	30.46 E
Fiditi	150	7.45 N	3.53 E
Fidji → Fiji □[1]	175g	18.00 S	178.00 E
Fidler Lake ⊜	184	57.11 N	96.57 W
Fidschi → Fiji □[1]	175g	18.00 S	178.00 E
Fiè (Völs)	64	46.31 N	11.30 E
Fieberbrunn	64	47.29 N	12.33 E
Field	182	51.24 N	116.29 W
Fieldale	192	36.42 N	79.56 W
Field Museum Ʊ	278	41.53 N	87.37 W
Fieldon	219	39.07 N	90.30 W
Fieldsboro	285	40.08 N	74.43 W
Fieldstone	276	40.44 N	74.33 W
Fiemme, Val di V	64	46.24 N	11.25 E
Fiener Bruch ≋	54	52.19 N	12.10 E
Fienvillers	50	50.07 N	2.14 E
Fier	38	40.43 N	19.34 E
Fier ≃	58	45.56 N	5.50 E
Fiéra Campionaria ♠	266b	45.28 N	9.09 E
Fiera di Primiero	64	46.10 N	11.49 E
Fierenana	157b	18.29 S	48.24 E
Fiery Creek ≃, Austl.	166	18.23 S	139.52 E
Fiery Creek ≃, Austl.	169	37.44 S	142.56 E
Fiery Range ⋀	171b	35.30 S	148.40 E
Fierzës, Liqeni i ⊜[1]	38	42.10 N	20.15 E
Fiesch	58	46.20 N	8.10 E
Fiesole	66	43.48 N	11.17 E
Fiesso d'Artico	64	45.24 N	12.02 E
Fiesso Umbertiano	64	44.56 N	11.36 E
Fife	224	47.14 N	122.22 W
Fife □[4]	46	56.13 N	3.02 W
Fife Lake, Sk., Can.	184	49.12 N	105.43 W
Fife Lake, Mi., U.S.	190	44.34 N	85.21 W
Fife Lake ⊜	184	49.14 N	105.53 W
Fife Ness ≻	46	56.17 N	2.36 W
Fifield	190	45.52 N	90.25 W
Fifteenmile Creek ≃, Or., U.S.	224	45.37 N	121.07 W
Fifteenmile Creek ≃, Wy., U.S.	202	44.01 N	108.01 W
Fifth Cataract → Khāmis, Ash-Shallāl al- ᒪ	140	18.23 N	33.47 E
Fifth Depot Lake ⊜	212	44.36 N	76.52 W
Figeac	32	44.37 N	2.02 E
Figeholm	26	57.22 N	16.33 E
Fig Garden	226	36.48 N	119.47 W
Fighting Island I	281	42.13 N	83.07 W
Figline Valdarno	66	43.37 N	11.28 E
Figtree	154	20.24 S	28.21 E
Figueira	287a	22.42 S	43.27 W
Figueira, Cachoeira ᒪ	250	9.49 S	58.13 W
Figueira da Foz	34	40.09 N	8.52 W
Figueira → Governador Valadares	255	18.51 S	41.56 W
Figueres	34	42.16 N	2.58 E
Figuig	148	32.10 N	1.15 W
Figuig □[4]	148	32.40 N	2.15 W
Fihaonana	157b	18.36 S	47.12 E
Fiherenana ≃	157b	23.19 S	43.37 E
Fiji □[1], Oc.	14	18.00 S	178.00 E
Fiji □[1], Oc.	175g	18.00 S	178.00 E
Fiji Islands II	14	18.00 S	178.00 E
Fijnaart	52	51.37 N	4.31 E
Fik	144	8.10 N	42.18 E
Fika	146	11.17 N	11.18 E
Fiktūriyā, Bi'r ⊤[4]	142	30.24 N	30.36 E
Filabusi	154	20.34 S	29.20 E
Filadélfia, Bra.	250	7.21 S	47.30 W
Filadelfia, C.R.	236	10.26 N	85.34 W
Filadelfia, It.	68	38.48 N	16.18 E
Filadelfia → Philadelphia	208	39.57 N	75.07 W
Fil'akovo	30	48.17 N	19.51 E
Filandari	68	38.37 N	16.02 E
Filatova Gora	76	57.40 N	28.10 E
Filchner Ice Shelf ⊓	9	79.00 S	40.00 W
Filderstadt	56	48.41 N	9.13 E
File Lake ⊜	184	54.53 N	100.20 W
Filettino	66	41.53 N	13.19 E
Filey	44	54.12 N	0.17 W
Filey Bay C	44	54.12 N	0.16 W
Fili ✦[8]	265b	55.45 N	37.31 E
Filí ⊥	38	38.10 N	23.40 E
Filiano	68	40.49 N	15.42 E
Filiași	38	44.33 N	23.31 E
Filiatrá	38	37.10 N	21.35 E
Filicudi, Isola I	70	38.34 N	14.34 E
Filimonovo	86	56.12 N	95.28 E
Filingué	150	14.21 N	3.19 E
Filipinas, Mar de → Philippine Sea ⊤[2]	14	20.00 N	135.00 E
Filipinas → Philippines □[1]	116	13.00 N	122.00 E
Filipino Cemetery and Memorial ✦	269f	14.31 N	121.02 E
Fílippoi ⊥	38	41.00 N	24.16 E
Filippovka	80	53.59 N	49.46 E
Filippovo	80	58.18 N	50.30 E
Filippovskoje, Ross.	82	56.06 N	38.37 E
Filippovskoje, Ross.	82	56.48 N	39.07 E
Filipstad	40	59.43 N	14.10 E
Filisola	234	17.50 N	94.19 W
Fillmore, Sk., Can.	184	49.50 N	103.25 W
Fillmore, Ca., U.S.	228	34.23 N	118.55 W
Fillmore, Il., U.S.	219	39.07 N	89.17 W
Fillmore, N.Y., U.S.	210	42.27 N	78.06 W
Fillmore, Ut,. U.S.	200	38.58 N	112.19 W
Fillmore Glen State Park ♠	210	42.42 N	76.20 W
Filogaso	68	38.41 N	16.14 E
Filomeno Mata	234	20.12 N	97.42 W
Filonovskaja	80	50.34 N	42.46 E
Filottrano	66	43.26 N	13.21 E
Fils ≃	56	48.42 N	9.25 E
Filskov	41	55.48 N	9.02 E
Filton	42	51.31 N	2.35 W
Filtu	144	5.07 N	40.39 E
Filzbach	58	47.07 N	9.08 E
Fimi ≃	152	3.01 S	16.58 E
Fina, Réserve de ✦[4]	150	12.50 N	8.30 W
Finale Emilia	64	44.50 N	11.17 E
Finale Ligure	62	44.10 N	8.20 E
Finarwa	144	13.06 N	39.01 E
Fincastle	192	37.29 N	79.52 W
Finch	206	45.11 N	75.07 W
Fincham	42	52.37 N	0.30 E
Finchley ✦[8]	260	51.36 N	0.10 W
Finderne	276	40.34 N	74.35 W
Findhorn	46	57.39 N	3.36 W
Findhorn ≃	46	57.38 N	3.38 W
Fındık	130	37.31 N	41.58 E
Findlay, Il., U.S.	219	39.31 N	88.45 W
Findlay, Oh., U.S.	216	41.02 N	83.39 W
Findlay, Mount ∧	182	50.04 N	116.28 W
Findley Lake	214	42.07 N	79.44 W
Findley Lake ⊜	214	42.06 N	79.43 W
Findochty	46	57.41 N	2.54 W
Fine Arts, Museum of Ʊ	283	42.20 N	71.06 W
Finedon	42	52.20 N	0.39 W
Finejevo	82	56.02 N	38.53 E
Finesville	210	40.36 N	75.10 W
Fingal, On., Can.	214	42.43 N	81.19 W
Fingal, N.D., U.S.	198	46.45 N	97.47 W
Finger Lake ⊜	184	53.09 N	93.30 W
Fíngoè	154	15.12 S	31.50 E
Finike	130	36.18 N	30.09 E
Finike Körfezi C	130	36.17 N	30.16 E
Finisk ≃	48	52.07 N	7.50 W
Finistère □[5]	32	48.20 N	4.00 W
Finisterre	196	25.59 N	103.15 W
Finisterre, Cabo de ≻	34	42.53 N	9.16 W
Finisterre → Land's End ≻	42	50.03 N	5.44 W
Finisterre Range ⋀	164	5.50 S	146.05 E
Finja	41	56.10 N	13.41 E
Finjasjön ⊜	41	56.08 N	13.42 E
Finke	162	25.34 S	134.35 E
Finke ≃	162	26.20 S	136.00 E
Finke, Mount ∧[2]	162	30.55 S	134.02 E
Finke Gorge National Park ♠	162	24.15 S	132.50 E
Finkenkrug	264a	52.34 N	13.03 E
Finkenwerder ✦[8]	52	53.31 N	9.52 E
Finksburg	208	39.29 N	76.53 W
Finland (Suomi) □[1], Europe	22	64.00 N	26.00 E
Finland (Suomi) □[1], Europe	24	64.00 N	26.00 E
Finland, Gulf of (Suomenlahti) (Finskij zaliv) C	26	60.00 N	27.00 E
Finlande → Finland □[1]	24	64.00 N	26.00 E
Finlandia, Golfo de → Finland, Gulf of C	26	60.00 N	27.00 E
Finlandia → Finland □[1]	24	64.00 N	26.00 E
Finland Station ✦[5]	265a	59.57 N	30.22 E
Finlas, Loch ⊜	44	55.15 N	4.25 W
Finlay ≃	176	56.54 N	124.57 W
Finley, Austl.	166	35.39 S	145.35 E
Finley, N.D., U.S.	198	47.30 N	97.50 W
Finley Creek ≃	194	36.58 N	93.22 W
Finleyville, Pa., U.S.	214	40.09 N	78.11 W
Finleyville, Pa., U.S.	214	40.15 N	80.00 W
Finleyville Airport ⊠	279b	40.15 N	80.01 W
Finmoore	182	53.59 N	123.37 W
Finn ≃	48	54.50 N	7.29 W
Finne ✦[1]	54	51.13 N	11.19 E
Finnegan	182	51.07 N	112.04 W
Finnentrop	56	51.09 N	7.58 E
Finnerödja	40	58.56 N	14.26 E
Finney Creek ≃	224	48.31 N	121.51 W
Finnhamn	40	59.28 N	18.50 E

≃	River	Fluß	Río	Rivière	Rio
≡	Canal	Kanal	Canal	Canal	Canal
ᒪ	Waterfall, Rapids	Wasserfall, Stromschnellen	Cascada, Rápidos	Chute d'eau, Rapides	Cascata, Rápidos
ʉ	Strait	Meeresstraße	Estrecho	Détroit	Estreito
C	Bay, Gulf	Bucht, Golf	Bahía, Golfo	Baie, Golfe	Baía, Golfo
⊜	Lake, Lakes	See, Seen	Lago, Lagos	Lac, Lacs	Lago, Lagos
≋	Swamp	Sumpf	Pantano	Marais	Pântano
⊓	Ice Features, Glacier	Eis- und Gletscherformen	Accidentes Glaciales	Formes glaciaires	Acidentes glaciares
⊤	Other Hydrographic Features	Andere Hydrographische Objekte	Otros Elementos Hidrográficos	Autres données hydrographiques	Outros acidentes hidrográficos

✢	Submarine Features	Untermeerische Objekte	Accidentes Submarinos	Formes de relief sous-marin	Acidentes submarinos
□	Political Unit	Politische Einheit	Unidad Politica	Entité politique	Unidade política
Ʊ	Cultural Institution	Kulturelle Institution	Institución Cultural	Institution culturelle	Instituição cultural
⊥	Historical Site	Historische Stätte	Sitio Histórico	Site historique	Sitio histórico
♠	Recreational Site	Erholungs- und Ferienort	Sitio de Recreo	Centre de loisirs	Area de Lazer
⊠	Airport	Flughafen	Aeropuerto	Aéroport	Aeroporto
■	Military Installation	Militäranlage	Instalación Militar	Installation militaire	Instalação militar
✦	Miscellaneous	Verschiedenes	Misceláneo	Divers	Diversos

ENGLISH / DEUTSCH

Symbols in the index entries represent the broad categories identified in the key at the right. Symbols with superior numbers (⋏[1]) identify subcategories (see complete key on page I · 1).

Symbole im Register stellen die rechts im Schlüssel erklärten Kategorien dar. Symbole mit hochgestellten Ziffern (⋏[1]) bezeichnen Unterabteilungen einer Kategorie (vgl. vollständiger Schlüssel auf Seite I · 1).

Los símbolos incluídos en el texto del índice representan las grandes categorias identificadas con la clave a la derecha. Los símbolos con numeros en su parte superior (⋏[1]) identifican las subcategorías (véase la clave completa en la página I · 1).

Les symboles de l'index représentent les catégories indiquées dans la légende à droite. Les symboles suivis d'un indice (⋏[1]) représentent des sous-catégories (voir légende complète à la page I · 1).

Os símbolos incluídos no texto do índice representam as grandes categorias identificadas com a chave à direita. Os símbolos com números em sua parte superior (⋏[1]) identificam as subcategorias (veja-se a chave completa à página I · 1).

∧ Mountain	Berg	Montaña	Montagne	Montanha
⋏ Mountains	Gebirge	Montañas	Montagnes	Montanhas
)(Pass	Paß	Paso	Col	Passo
V Valley, Canyon	Tal, Cañon	Valle, Cañón	Vallée, Canyon	Vale, Canhão
≚ Plain	Ebene	Llano	Plaine	Planície
› Cape	Kap	Cabo	Cap	Cabo
I Island	Insel	Isla	Île	Ilha
II Islands	Inseln	Islas	Îles	Ilhas
≗ Other Topographic Features	Andere Topographische Objekte	Otros Elementos Topográficos	Autres données topographiques	Outros acidentes topográficos

ESPAÑOL — Nombre | Página | Lat.°′ | Long.°′ W = Oeste
FRANÇAIS — Nom | Page | Lat.°′ | Long.°′ W = Ouest
PORTUGUÊS — Nome | Página | Lat.°′ | Long.°′ W = Oeste

Fordsburg ⇸ [8] 273d 26.13 S 28.02 E
Fords Prairie 224 46.44 N 122.59 W
Fordsville 194 37.38 N 86.43 W
Fordville 198 48.13 N 97.47 W
Fordyce 194 33.48 N 92.24 W
Fordyce Lake ⊜ [1] 226 39.23 N 120.28 W
Foré 150 13.08 N 10.42 W
Forécariah 150 9.26 N 13.06 W
Forel, Mont ᴧ 176 67.00 N 37.00 W
Foreland Point ⟩ 42 51.16 N 3.47 W
Foreman 194 33.43 N 94.23 W
Foremost 184 49.29 N 111.25 W
Forenza 68 40.51 N 15.51 E
Forepaugh Airport ⊠ 279a 41.21 N 81.30 W
Foresman 216 40.52 N 87.18 W
Forest, Bel. 50 50.48 N 4.19 E
Forest, On., Can. 190 43.06 N 82.00 W
Forest, In., U.S. 216 40.22 N 86.19 W
Forest, Ms., U.S. 194 32.21 N 89.28 W
Forest, Oh., U.S. 216 40.48 N 83.30 W
Forest □ [6] 214 41.29 N 79.27 W
Forest, Middle Branch ≃ 198 48.13 N 97.48 W
Forest Acres 192 34.01 N 80.59 W
Forestburg 182 52.35 N 112.04 W
Forest City, Ia., U.S. 190 43.15 N 93.38 W
Forest City, N.C., U.S. 192 35.20 N 81.51 W
Forest City, Pa., U.S. 210 41.39 N 75.28 W
Forest Creek ≃ 226 38.23 N 120.28 W
Forest Gate ⇸ [8] 260 51.33 N 0.02 E
Forest Glade 222 31.39 N 96.31 W
Forest Grove, B.C., Can. 182 51.46 N 121.06 W
Forest Grove, Or., U.S. 224 45.31 N 123.06 W
Forest Grove, Pa., U.S. 279b 40.18 N 75.04 W
Forest Heights 284c 38.49 N 77.00 W
Forest Hill, Austl. 171a 27.35 S 152.22 E
Forest Hill, Austl. 171b 35.09 S 147.27 E
Forest Hill, Austl. 274b 37.50 S 145.11 E
Foresthill, Ca., U.S. 226 39.01 N 120.49 W
Forest Hill, Md., U.S. 208 39.35 N 76.23 W
Forest Hill, Tx., U.S. 222 32.40 N 97.16 W
Forest Hill ⇸ [8] 275b 43.42 N 79.24 W
Forest Hill Park ♦ 279a 41.31 N 81.35 W
Forest Hill Parkway ♦ 279a 41.33 N 81.36 W
Forest Hills 279b 40.25 N 79.51 W
Forest Hills ⇸ [8] 276 40.42 N 73.51 W
Forest Home 194 31.52 N 86.50 W
Forestier Peninsula ⟩ [1] 166 42.57 S 147.55 E
Forest Knolls 284c 39.02 N 77.01 W
Forest Lake, Il., U.S. 216 42.13 N 88.03 W
Forest Lake, Mn., U.S. 190 45.16 N 92.59 W
Forest Lake ⊜, Il., U.S. 278 42.13 N 88.03 W
Forest Lake ⊜, Ma., U.S. 283 42.43 N 71.15 W
Forest Lawn Memorial Park ⇸ 280 34.09 N 118.19 W
Forest Manor 284c 38.50 N 76.53 W
Forest Park, Ga., U.S. 192 33.37 N 84.22 W
Forest Park, Il., U.S. 278 41.52 N 87.48 W
Forest Park, Oh., U.S. 218 39.16 N 84.34 W
Forest Park ⇸ [8] 284b 39.19 N 76.41 W
Forest Park ♦ 276 40.42 N 73.51 W
Forest River 278 42.05 N 87.54 W
Forest Row 42 51.06 N 0.02 E
Forest View 278 41.49 N 87.47 W
Forestville, Austl. 274a 33.46 S 151.13 E
Forestville, P.Q., Can. 186 48.45 N 69.06 W
Forestville, Md., U.S. 284c 38.50 N 76.52 W
Forestville, N.Y., U.S. 214 42.28 N 79.10 W
Forestville, Pa., U.S. 214 41.06 N 80.00 W
Forestville, Wi., U.S. 190 44.41 N 87.28 W
Forêt l'Orient, Lac de la ⊜ [1] 50 48.17 N 4.20 E
Forêt-Noire — Schwarzwald ⩘ 58 48.00 N 8.15 E
Forez, Monts du ⩘ 32 45.35 N 3.48 E
Forfar 46 56.38 N 2.54 W
Forfry 261 49.03 N 2.51 E
Forgan 196 36.54 N 100.32 W
Forgaria 64 46.13 N 12.58 E
Forge Acres 284b 39.25 N 76.27 W
Forge Heights 284b 39.25 N 76.25 W
Forges-les-Bains 261 48.38 N 2.06 E
Forges-les-Eaux 50 49.37 N 1.33 E
Forget, Pointe ⟩ 275a 45.27 N 73.58 W
Forge Village 207 42.34 N 71.29 W
Forggensee ⊜ 58 47.36 N 10.44 E
Forillon, Parc National de ♦ 186 48.55 N 64.12 W
Forino 68 40.52 N 14.44 E
Foristell 219 38.49 N 90.57 W
Fork 208 39.28 N 76.27 W
Forked Creek ≃ 216 41.19 N 88.09 W
Forked Deer ≃ 194 35.56 N 89.35 W
Forked Deer, Middle Fork ≃ 194 36.01 N 89.13 W
Forked Deer, North Fork ≃ 194 36.00 N 89.26 W
Forked Deer, South Fork ≃ 194 36.00 N 89.26 W
Forked River 208 39.50 N 74.11 W
Forks 224 47.57 N 124.23 W
Forkston 210 41.31 N 76.07 W
Forksville 210 41.29 N 76.36 W
Forleti, Arroyo ≃ 288 34.35 S 58.41 W
Forli 66 44.13 N 12.03 E
Forlì □ [4] 64 44.05 N 12.02 E
Forlimpopoli 66 44.11 N 12.07 E
Forman 198 46.06 N 97.38 W
Formazza 58 46.22 N 8.26 E
Formby 262 53.34 N 3.05 W
Formby Hills ⩘ [2] 262 53.34 N 3.06 W
Formby Point ⟩ 262 53.33 N 3.06 W
Formentera I 34 38.42 N 1.28 E
Formentor, Cap de ⟩ 34 39.58 N 3.12 E
Formerie 50 49.39 N 1.44 E
Formia 66 41.15 N 13.37 E
Formiga 255 20.27 S 45.25 W
Formiga ≃ 250 11.15 S 48.27 W
Formigine 64 44.34 N 10.51 E
Formignana 64 44.50 N 11.51 E
Formosa, Arg. 252 26.11 S 58.11 W
Formosa, Bra. 255 15.32 S 47.20 W
Formosa □ [4] 252 25.00 S 60.00 W
Formosa, Ilha I 150 11.29 N 15.58 W
Formosa, Serra ⩘ [1] 250 12.00 S 55.00 W
Formosa Strait — Taiwan Strait ʮ 100 24.00 N 119.00 E
Formosa — Taiwan □ [1] 100 23.30 N 121.00 E
Formoso ≃, Bra. 250 10.34 S 49.59 W
Formoso ≃, Bra. 255 13.26 S 44.14 W
Formoso ≃, Bra. 255 18.25 S 52.28 W
Formoso ≃, Bra. 256 21.20 S 43.10 W
Forncelle 66 43.55 N 11.06 E
Fornelli 71 41.00 N 8.14 E
Forney 222 32.44 N 96.28 W
Forni Avoltri 64 46.35 N 12.46 E
Forni di sopra 64 46.25 N 12.35 E
Forni di sotto 64 46.23 N 12.40 E
Forni di Val d'Astico 64 45.51 N 11.22 E
Forno 64 46.21 N 11.37 E
Forno Alpi Graie 62 45.22 N 7.13 E
Forno di Zoldo 64 46.21 N 12.11 E
Fornosovo 76 59.35 N 30.35 E
Fornovo di Taro 64 44.42 N 10.06 E
Foro Romano I 267a 41.54 N 12.29 E
Føroyar — Faeroe Islands □ [2] 22 62.00 N 7.00 W
Forport 86 56.47 N 72.10 E
Forres, Arg. 252 27.53 S 63.58 W
Forres, Scot., U.K. 46 57.37 N 3.38 W
Forrest, Austl. 162 30.51 S 128.06 E
Forrest, Austl. 169 38.31 S 143.43 E
Forrest, Il., U.S. 216 40.45 N 88.24 W
Forrest ≃ 164 15.18 S 128.04 E
Forrest, Mount ᴧ 162 24.48 S 127.45 E
Forrestal Research Center ᵾ [3] 276 40.21 N 74.37 W
Forrest City 194 35.00 N 90.47 W
Forrester Island I 182 54.48 N 133.32 W
Forrest Lakes ⊜ 162 29.12 S 128.46 E
Forreston, Il., U.S. 190 42.07 N 89.34 W
Forreston, Tx., U.S. 222 32.16 N 96.52 W
Forrest River Aboriginal Reserve ⇸ [4] 164 15.00 S 127.40 E
Fors 40 60.13 N 16.18 E
Forsan 196 32.07 N 101.22 W
Forsayth 166 18.35 S 143.36 E
Forsbacka 40 60.37 N 16.53 E
Forsby 26 60.30 N 25.56 E
Forserum 26 57.42 N 14.28 E
Forshaga 40 59.32 N 13.28 E
Forsmark 40 60.22 N 18.09 E
Forssa 26 60.49 N 23.38 E
Forst 54 51.44 N 14.39 E
Förste 52 51.44 N 10.10 E
Forster 166 32.11 S 152.31 E
Forstwald ⇸ [8] 263 51.18 N 6.30 E
Forsyth, Ga., U.S. 192 33.02 N 83.56 W
Forsyth, Il., U.S. 219 39.56 N 88.57 W
Forsyth, Mo., U.S. 194 36.41 N 93.07 W
Forsyth, Mt., U.S. 202 46.15 N 106.40 W
Forsyth Island I 164 16.50 S 139.06 E
Forsyth Range ⩘ 166 22.45 S 143.15 E
Fort ⇸ [8] 272c 18.56 N 72.50 E
Fort Abbās 123 29.12 N 72.52 E
Fort Adams 194 31.05 N 91.32 W
Fort Albany 176 52.15 N 81.37 W
Fort Alexander Indian Reserve ⇸ [4] 184 50.27 N 96.15 W
Fortaleza 250 3.43 S 38.30 W
Fortaleza ≃ 248 10.40 S 77.52 W
Fortaleza de Santa Teresa ♦ 252 33.59 S 53.32 W
Fortaleza do Ituxi 248 7.29 S 66.20 W
Fortaleza dos Nogueiras 250 6.54 S 46.09 W
Fort Amherst National Historic Park ♦ 186 46.12 N 63.09 W
Fort Ancient State Memorial ⊥ 218 39.24 N 84.06 W
Fort Anne National Historic Park ♦ 186 44.44 N 65.26 W
Fort Apache Indian Reservation ⇸ [4] 200 34.01 N 110.28 W
Fort-Archambault — Sarh 146 9.09 N 18.23 E
Fort Assiniboine 182 54.20 N 114.46 W
Fort Atkinson 216 42.55 N 88.50 W
Fort Augusta ⊥ 210 40.53 N 76.46 W
Fort Augustus 46 57.09 N 4.41 W
Fort Baker ■ 282 37.50 N 122.29 W
Fort Battleford National Historic Park ♦ 184 52.42 N 108.15 W
Fort Bayard — Zhanjiang 102 21.16 N 110.28 E
Fort Beaufort 158 32.46 S 26.40 E
Fort Beauséjour National Historic Park ♦ 186 45.51 N 64.18 W
Fort Belknap Agency 202 48.28 N 108.45 W
Fort Belknap Indian Reservation ⇸ [4] 202 48.16 N 108.38 W
Fort Belvoir ■ 208 38.44 N 77.10 W
Fort Bend □ [6] 222 29.32 N 95.47 W
Fort Benjamin Harrison ■ 218 39.52 N 86.01 W
Fort Benning ■ 192 32.22 N 84.50 W
Fort Benton 202 47.49 N 110.40 W
Fort Berthold Indian Reservation ⇸ [4] 198 47.40 N 102.25 W
Fort Bidwell 204 41.51 N 120.09 W
Fort Bliss ■ 200 32.15 N 106.00 W
Fort Bowie National Historic Site ⊥ 200 32.09 N 109.24 W
Fort Bragg 204 39.26 N 123.48 W
Fort Bragg ■ 192 35.09 N 79.59 W
Fort Branch 194 38.15 N 87.34 W
Fort Bridger 200 41.19 N 110.23 W
Fort Calhoun 198 41.27 N 96.01 W
Fort Campbell ■ 194 36.39 N 87.29 W
Fort Canby State Park ♦ 224 46.17 N 124.04 W
Fort-Carnot 157b 21.53 S 47.28 E
Fort Caroline National Memorial ⊥ 192 30.20 N 81.30 W
Fort Carson ■ 200 38.44 N 104.48 W
Fort Casey Historical State Park ♦ 224 48.10 N 122.40 W
Fort Chambly National Historic Park ♦ 206 45.27 N 73.17 W
Fort Chipewyan 176 58.42 N 111.08 W
Fort Churchill Historic State Monument ⊥ 226 39.18 N 119.17 W
Fort Clatsop National Memorial ⊥ 224 46.08 N 123.54 W
Fort Cobb 196 35.05 N 98.26 W
Fort Cobb Reservoir ⊜ [1] 196 35.12 N 98.29 W
Fort Collins 200 40.35 N 105.05 W
Fort Columbia Historical State Park ♦ 224 46.15 N 123.56 W
Fort Constantine 166 20.28 S 140.27 E
Fort-Coulonge 188 45.51 N 76.44 W
Fort Covington 206 44.59 N 74.29 W
Fort Custer State Recreation Area ♦ 216 42.18 N 85.20 W
Fort Davis, Al., U.S. 194 32.14 N 85.42 W
Fort Davis, Tx., U.S. 196 30.35 N 103.53 W
Fort Davis National Historic Site ⊥ 196 30.33 N 103.53 W
Fort de Douaumont ⊥ 56 49.13 N 5.25 E
Fort Defiance 200 35.44 N 109.04 W
Fort-de-France 240e 14.36 N 61.05 W
Fort-de-France, Baie de ⊂ 240e 14.34 N 61.04 W
Fort-de-France-Lamentin, Aérodrome de ⊠ 240e 14.35 N 61.00 W
Fort Deposit 194 31.59 N 86.34 W
Fort Detrick ■ 208 39.27 N 77.26 W
Fort de Vaux ⊥ 56 49.12 N 5.28 E
Fort Devens ■ 207 42.32 N 71.37 W
Fort Dix ■ 208 40.00 N 74.33 W
Fort Dodge 190 42.29 N 94.10 W
Fort Donelson National Military Park ♦ 194 36.26 N 87.49 W
Fort Duchesne 200 40.17 N 109.51 W
Fort Dupont Park ♦ 284c 38.53 N 76.57 W
Forte, Monte ᴧ 71 40.43 N 8.15 E
Forteau 186 51.28 N 56.58 W
Forte dei Marmi 64 43.57 N 10.10 E
Forte de Magoito 266c 38.52 N 9.27 W
Fort Edward 210 43.16 N 73.35 W
Forte República 152 7.45 S 16.23 E
Fort Erie 212 42.54 N 78.56 W
Fort Erie Race Track ♦ 284a 42.55 N 78.56 W
Fortescue ≃ 162 21.00 S 116.06 E
Fort Eustis ■ 208 37.09 N 76.35 W
Fortevoit 46 56.20 N 3.32 W
Fortezza (Franzensfeste) 64 46.47 N 11.37 E
Fort Fairfield 186 46.46 N 67.50 W
Fort Fitzgerald 176 59.53 N 111.37 W
Fort Foote Village 284c 38.46 N 77.01 W
Fort-Foureau 146 12.05 N 15.02 E
Fort Frances 190 48.36 N 93.24 W
Fort Franklin 180 65.11 N 123.46 W
Fort Fraser 182 54.04 N 124.33 W
Fort Frederica National Monument ♦ 192 31.12 N 81.26 W
Fort Gaines 192 31.36 N 85.02 W
Fort Garland 200 37.25 N 105.26 W
Fort Gay 188 38.06 N 82.35 W
Fort George ⊥ 284a 43.15 N 79.04 W
Fort George G. Meade ■ 208 39.05 N 76.50 W
Fort Gibson 196 35.47 N 95.15 W
Fort Gibson Lake ⊜ [1] 196 36.00 N 95.18 W
Fort Good Hope 180 66.15 N 128.38 W
Fort Gordon ■ 192 33.25 N 82.11 W
Fort-Gouraud — Fdérik 148 22.41 N 12.43 W
Fort Green 220 27.36 N 81.56 W
Forth 46 55.47 N 3.41 W
Forth ≃ 46 56.03 N 3.44 W
Forth, Carse of ∨ 46 56.08 N 4.05 W
Forth, Firth of ⊂ 46 56.10 N 2.45 W
Förtha 56 50.56 N 10.14 E
Fort Hall 202 43.02 N 112.26 W
Fort Hall Indian Reservation ⇸ [4] 202 43.10 N 112.10 W
Fort Hamilton ■ 276 40.37 N 74.02 W
Forth Bridge ⇸ [5] 46 56.00 N 3.25 W
Fort Hertz — Putao 102 27.21 N 97.24 E
Fort Hill ■ 188 38.04 N 77.19 W
Fort Hill — Chitipa 154 9.43 S 33.16 E
Fort Hill State Memorial ⊥ 218 39.07 N 83.25 W
Fort Hood ■ 222 31.08 N 97.46 W
Fort Howard 208 39.12 N 76.27 W
Fort Huachuca ■ 200 31.33 N 110.20 W
Fort Hunter 210 42.57 N 74.17 W
Fort Hunter Liggett ■ 226 35.55 N 121.15 W
Fortierville 206 46.29 N 72.02 W
Fortín 234 18.54 N 97.00 W
Fortin, Lac ⊜ 186 50.50 N 67.46 W
Fortín Ayacucho 248 19.58 S 59.47 W
Fortín Coroneles Sanchez 248 19.20 S 59.58 W
Fortine 182 48.45 N 114.54 W
Fortín Florida 248 20.45 S 59.17 W
Fortín Garrapatal 248 21.27 S 61.30 W
Fortín Teniente Montania 252 22.04 S 59.57 W
Fortín Uno 252 38.51 S 65.17 W
Fort Jackson ■ 192 34.01 N 80.57 W
Fort Jameson — Chipata 154 13.39 S 32.40 E
Fort Jefferson National Monument ♦ 220 24.37 N 82.54 W
Fort Jennings 216 40.54 N 84.17 W
Fort Jeudy, Point of ⟩ 241k 12.00 N 61.42 W
Fort Johnson 210 42.57 N 74.14 W
Fort Johnston — Mangochi 154 14.28 S 35.16 E
Fort Jones 204 41.36 N 122.50 W
Fort Kent 186 47.15 N 68.35 W
Fort Klamath 202 42.42 N 121.59 W
Fort Knox ■ 194 37.54 N 85.57 W
Fort-Lamy — N'Djamena 146 12.07 N 15.03 E
Fort Langley 224 49.10 N 122.35 W
Fort Langley National Historic Park ♦ 224 49.10 N 122.35 W
Fort Laramie 200 42.12 N 104.31 W
Fort Laramie National Historic Site ⊥ 198 42.09 N 104.41 W
Fort Larned National Historic Site ⊥ 198 38.10 N 99.12 W
Fort Lauderdale 220 26.07 N 80.08 W
Fort Lauderdale-Hollywood International Airport ⊠ 220 26.04 N 80.09 W
Fort Laurens State Memorial ⊥ 214 40.38 N 81.27 W
Fort Leavenworth ■ 198 39.21 N 94.55 W
Fort Le Boeuf ⊥ 214 41.56 N 79.59 W
Fort Lee 210 40.51 N 73.58 W
Fort Lee ■ 208 37.14 N 77.20 W
Fort Lennox National Historic Park ♦ 206 45.06 N 73.16 W
Fort Leonard Wood ■ 194 37.45 N 92.07 W
Fort Lewis ■ 224 47.05 N 122.37 W
Fort Liard 176 60.15 N 123.28 W
Fort-Liberté 238 19.39 N 71.49 W
Fort Lincoln State Park ♦ 198 46.45 N 100.52 W
Fort Littleton 214 40.04 N 77.58 W
Fort Loramie 216 40.21 N 84.22 W
Fort Loudoun Lake ⊜ [1] 192 35.45 N 84.10 W
Fort Lupton 200 40.05 N 104.48 W
Fort Lyon Canal ≅ 198 38.11 N 102.31 W
Fort Macleod 182 49.43 N 113.25 W
Fort Madison 190 40.37 N 91.18 W
Fort-Mahon-Plage 50 50.21 N 1.34 E
Fort Malden National Historic Park ♦ 281 42.06 N 83.07 W
Fort Matanzas National Monument ♦ 192 29.40 N 81.18 W
Fort McClellan ■ 194 33.43 N 85.47 W
Fort McDermitt Indian Reservation ⇸ [4] 202 42.00 N 117.32 W
Fort McDowell Indian Reservation ⇸ [4] 200 33.38 N 111.41 W
Fort McHenry National Monument and Historic Shrine ♦ 208 39.16 N 76.35 W
Fort Mckinley 218 39.47 N 84.15 W
Fort McMurray 184 56.44 N 111.23 W
Fort McNair ■ 284c 38.52 N 77.04 W
Fort McPherson 180 67.27 N 134.53 W
Fort Meade 220 27.45 N 81.48 W
Fort Mill 192 35.00 N 80.56 W
Fort Miller 210 43.10 N 73.35 W
Fort Mitchell, Al., U.S. 192 32.21 N 85.01 W
Fort Mitchell, Ky., U.S. 218 39.03 N 84.32 W
Fort Mojave Indian Reservation ⇸ [4] 200 34.55 N 114.35 W
Fort Monmouth ■ 208 40.19 N 74.02 W
Fort Monroe ■ 208 37.00 N 76.18 W
Fort Montgomery 210 41.20 N 73.59 W
Fort Morgan 198 40.15 N 103.47 W
Fort Myer ■ 284c 38.53 N 77.05 W
Fort Myers 220 26.38 N 81.52 W
Fort Myers Beach 220 26.27 N 81.56 W
Fort Myers Shores 220 26.43 N 81.45 W
Fort Myers Villas 220 26.34 N 81.52 W
Fort Necessity National Battlefield ⊥ 188 39.47 N 79.39 W
Fort Neck ⟩ [1] 276 40.39 N 73.28 W
Fort Nelson 176 58.49 N 122.43 W
Fort Nelson ≃ 176 59.30 N 124.00 W
Fort Niagara Beach 284a 43.15 N 79.03 W
Fort Niagara State Park ♦, N.Y., U.S. 212 43.16 N 79.03 W
Fort Niagara State Park ♦, N.Y., U.S. 284a 43.16 N 79.03 W
Fort Nonsense ⊥ 276 40.48 N 74.29 W
Fort Norman 180 64.54 N 125.34 W
Fort Nottingham 158 29.25 S 29.55 E
Fort Ogden 220 27.05 N 81.57 W
Fort Ord ■ 226 36.40 N 121.48 W
Fortore ≃ 68 41.55 N 15.17 E
Fort Parker State Park ♦ 222 31.36 N 96.33 W
Fort Payne 194 34.26 N 85.43 W
Fort Peck 202 48.00 N 106.26 W
Fort Peck Dam ⇸ [6] 202 47.52 N 106.38 W
Fort Peck Indian Reservation ⇸ [4] 202 48.22 N 105.40 W
Fort Peck Lake ⊜ [1] 202 47.45 N 106.50 W
Fort Pierce 220 27.26 N 80.19 W
Fort Pierce Inlet ⊂ 220 27.28 N 80.18 W
Fort Pierre 198 44.21 N 100.22 W
Fort Pitt Tunnels ⇸ [5] 279b 40.25 N 80.00 W
Fort Plain 210 42.55 N 74.37 W
Fort Point National Historical Site ⊥ 282 37.48 N 122.28 W
Fort Polk ■ 194 31.04 N 93.11 W
Fort Portal 154 0.40 N 30.17 E
Fort Providence 176 61.21 N 117.39 W
Fort Pulaski National Monument ♦ 192 32.01 N 80.59 W
Fort Qu'Appelle 184 50.46 N 103.48 W
Fort Raleigh National Historic Site ⊥ 192 35.55 N 75.40 W
Fort Randall Dam ⇸ [6] 198 42.48 N 98.35 W
Fort Recovery 216 40.24 N 84.46 W
Fort Resolution 176 61.10 N 113.40 W
Fortress Mountain ᴧ 202 44.20 N 109.47 W
Fortress of Louisbourg National Historic Park ♦ 186 45.56 N 59.57 W
Fort Riley ■ 198 39.04 N 96.47 W
Fort Ritchie ■ 208 39.43 N 77.30 W
Fort Rixon 154 20.01 S 29.18 E
Fort Robinson State Park ♦ 198 42.41 N 103.30 W
Fort Rodd Hill National Historic Park ♦ 224 48.26 N 123.28 W
Fortrose, N.Z. 172 46.34 S 168.48 E
Fortrose, Scot., U.K. 46 57.34 N 4.09 W
Fort Rosebery — Mansa 154 11.12 S 28.53 E
Fort Rucker ■ 194 31.20 N 85.42 W
Fort Saint James 182 54.26 N 124.15 W
Fort Saint John 182 56.15 N 120.51 W
Fort Salonga 276 40.55 N 73.18 W
Fort Sam Houston ■ 196 29.27 N 98.27 W
Fort Saskatchewan 182 53.43 N 113.13 W
Fort Scott 198 37.50 N 94.42 W
Fort Seneca 214 41.13 N 83.10 W
Fort-Ševčenko 84 44.31 N 50.16 E
Fort Severn 176 56.00 N 87.38 W
Fort Shawnee 216 40.41 N 84.08 W
Fort Sheridan ■ 216 42.13 N 87.48 W
Fort Sill ■ 196 34.40 N 98.25 W
Fort Simcoe Historical State Park ♦ 224 46.21 N 120.50 W
Fort Simpson 176 61.52 N 121.23 W
Fort Sisseton State Park ♦ 198 45.39 N 97.32 W
Fort Smith, N.T., Can. 176 60.00 N 111.53 W
Fort Smith, Ar., U.S. 194 35.23 N 94.23 W
Fort Steele 182 49.37 N 115.38 W
Fort Stevens State Park ♦ 224 46.10 N 124.00 W
Fort Stewart ■ 192 31.52 N 81.37 W
Fort Stockton 196 30.53 N 102.52 W
Fort Sumner 196 34.28 N 104.14 W
Fort Sumter National Monument ♦ 192 32.44 N 79.46 W
Fort Supply 196 36.34 N 99.34 W
Fort Tejon State Historical Park ♦ 228 34.52 N 118.53 W
Fort Thomas, Az., U.S. 200 33.02 N 109.57 W
Fort Thomas, Ky., U.S. 218 39.04 N 84.26 W
Fort Thompson 198 44.04 N 99.24 W
Fort Tilden ■ 276 40.33 N 73.53 W
Fort Totten 198 47.58 N 98.59 W
Fort Totten Indian Reservation ⇸ [4] 198 47.53 N 98.50 W
Fort Totten Park ♦ 284c 38.57 N 77.00 W
Fort Towson 196 34.01 N 95.15 W
Fort-Trinquet — Bîr Mogreïn 148 25.14 N 11.35 W
Fortuna, Arg. 252 35.07 S 65.23 W
Fortuna, C.R. 236 10.30 N 84.35 W
Fortuna, Ca., U.S. 204 40.35 N 124.09 W
Fortuna, Río de la ≃ 248 16.36 S 58.46 W
Fortuna Ledge (Marshall) 180 61.53 N 162.05 W
Fortune 186 47.04 N 55.50 W
Fortune Bay ⊂ 186 47.25 N 55.25 W
Fortune Ditch ≅ 279a 41.20 N 82.03 W
Fortune Harbour 186 49.31 N 55.15 W
Fortuneswell 42 50.34 N 2.27 W
Fort Union National Monument ♦ 200 35.55 N 105.01 W
Fort Union Trading Post National Historical Site ⊥ 198 48.00 N 104.03 W
Fort Valley 192 32.33 N 83.53 W
Fort Vancouver National Historic Site ⊥ 224 45.38 N 122.37 W
Fort Vermilion 176 58.24 N 116.00 W
Fortville 218 39.55 N 85.50 W
Fort Wadsworth ■ 276 40.36 N 74.04 W
Fort Walton Beach 194 30.24 N 86.37 W
Fort Washakie 200 43.00 N 108.52 W
Fort Washington 208 40.08 N 75.12 W
Fort Washington Forest 208 38.43 N 76.59 W
Fort Washington State Park ♦ 285 40.07 N 75.14 W
Fort Wayne 216 41.07 N 85.07 W
Fort Wayne Military Museum ᵾ 281 42.18 N 83.06 W
Fort Wellington 246 6.24 N 57.36 W
Fort Wellington National Historic Park ♦ 212 44.44 N 75.31 W
Fort White 192 29.55 N 82.42 W
Fort William 46 56.49 N 5.07 W
Fort William — Thunder Bay 190 48.23 N 89.15 W
Fort Worth 222 32.43 N 97.19 W
Fort Yates 198 46.05 N 100.37 W
Forty Foot Drain ≅ 42 52.28 N 0.05 W
Forty Fort 210 41.16 N 75.52 W
Fortymile ≃ 180 64.26 N 140.32 W
Fort Yukon 180 66.34 N 145.17 W
Fort Yuma Indian Reservation ⇸ [4] 204 32.48 N 114.34 W
Forum ♦, P.Q., Can. 275a 45.29 N 73.35 W
Forum ♦, Ca., U.S. 280 33.57 N 118.20 W
Forūr, Jazīreh-ye I 128 26.17 N 54.32 E
Forza d'Agrò 70 37.55 N 15.20 E
Foscagno, Passo di)(64 46.30 N 10.08 E
Fosdinovo 64 44.08 N 10.01 E
Fosforescente, Bahía ⊂ 240m 17.59 N 67.01 W
Fosforitnyj 82 55.19 N 38.54 E
Foshan 100 23.03 N 113.09 E
Fosna ⟩ [1] 24 64.00 N 10.30 E
Fosnavåg 26 62.21 N 5.39 E
Foso 150 5.42 N 1.17 W
Foss 46 56.41 N 3.58 W
Foss ≃, Eng., U.K. 44 53.57 N 1.06 W
Foss ≃, Wa., U.S. 224 47.43 N 121.18 W
Fossacesia 66 42.15 N 14.29 E
Fossacesia Marina 66 42.15 N 14.30 E
Fossa Eugeniana ≅ 263 51.33 N 6.36 E
Fossano 62 44.33 N 7.43 E
Fossanova, Abbazia di ᵾ [1] 66 41.29 N 13.13 E
Fossato, Colle di)(66 43.19 N 12.47 E
Fossato di Vico 66 43.18 N 12.46 E
Fossé 50 49.27 N 5.00 E
Fosse-Martin 261 49.05 N 2.54 E
Fosses 261 49.06 N 2.29 E
Fosses-la-Ville 56 50.24 N 4.42 E
Fossil 202 44.59 N 120.12 W
Fossil Butte National Monument ♦ 202 41.50 N 110.40 W
Fossil Downs 162 18.08 S 125.38 E
Fossil Lake ⊜ 202 43.18 N 120.15 W
Fossombrone 66 43.41 N 12.48 E
Fosston 198 47.34 N 95.45 W
Fos-sur-Mer 62 43.26 N 4.57 E
Foster, Austl. 169 38.39 S 146.12 E
Foster, Ky., U.S. 218 38.47 N 84.12 W
Foster, R.I., U.S. 207 41.51 N 71.45 W
Foster ≃ 184 55.47 N 105.49 W
Foster, Mount ᴧ 180 59.48 N 135.29 W
Foster Brook 214 41.59 N 78.37 W
Foster City 226 37.33 N 122.16 W
Foster Creek ≃ 198 44.34 N 98.12 W
Fosterdale 210 41.42 N 74.58 W
Foster Joseph Sayers Reservoir ⊜ [1] 214 41.02 N 77.40 W
Foster Park 228 34.21 N 119.18 W
Fosters 194 33.05 N 87.41 W
Fosters Pond ⊜ 283 42.37 N 71.08 W
Foster Street 260 51.46 N 0.09 E
Foster Village 229c 21.21 N 157.55 W
Fostoria 214 41.09 N 83.25 W
Fót 264c 47.37 N 19.12 E
Fotadrevo 157b 24.03 S 45.01 E
Fotan 100 24.12 N 117.53 E
Fóti-Somlyó ᴧ [2] 264c 47.38 N 19.13 E
Foucarmont 50 49.51 N 1.34 E
Fou-Chouen — Fushun 104 41.52 N 123.53 E
Fouesnant 32 47.54 N 4.01 W
Foug 56 48.41 N 5.47 E
Fougamou 152 1.13 S 10.36 E
Fougères 32 48.21 N 1.12 W
Fougères-sur-Bièvre 50 47.27 N 1.21 E
Fougerolles 58 47.53 N 6.24 E
Fouhsin — Fuxin 104 42.03 N 121.46 E
Fouju 261 48.35 N 2.47 E
Fouke 194 33.16 N 93.53 W
Foula I 46a 60.08 N 2.05 W
Foulain 58 48.02 N 5.13 E
Foulalaba 150 10.41 N 7.22 W
Foula Mori 150 12.10 N 13.51 W
Foulatari 146 13.41 N 12.03 E
Foul Bay ⊂ 140 23.30 N 35.39 E
Fouling — Fuling 102 29.42 N 107.21 E
Foulness ≃ 44 53.47 N 0.43 W
Foulness Island I 42 51.36 N 0.55 E
Foulness Point ⟩ 42 51.38 N 0.57 E
Foulpointe 157b 17.41 S 49.31 E
Foulsham 42 52.48 N 1.01 E
Foulwind, Cape ⟩ 172 41.45 S 171.28 E
Foumban 152 5.43 N 10.55 E
Foumbot 152 5.30 N 10.38 E
Foumbouni 157a 11.50 S 43.30 E
Foum-el-Hisn 148 28.59 N 8.55 W
Foum-Zguid 148 30.04 N 6.54 W
Foundiougne 150 14.08 N 16.28 W
Fountain, Co., U.S. 198 38.40 N 104.42 W
Fountain, Fl., U.S. 192 30.09 N 85.38 W
Fountain □ [6] 216 40.17 N 87.13 W
Fountain City, In., U.S. 218 39.57 N 84.55 W
Fountain City, Wi., U.S. 190 44.07 N 91.43 W
Fountain Creek ≃, Co., U.S. 198 38.15 N 104.35 W
Fountain Creek ≃, Il., U.S. 219 38.20 N 90.22 W
Fountain Green 200 39.37 N 111.38 W
Fountain Hill 208 40.36 N 75.23 W
Fountain Inn 192 34.41 N 82.11 W
Fountain Park 216 41.50 N 84.32 W
Fountain Peak ᴧ 204 34.57 N 115.32 W
Fountain Place 194 30.31 N 91.09 W
Fountains Abbey ᵾ [1] 44 54.07 N 1.34 W
Fountains Corner 208 36.33 N 77.21 W
Fountaintown 218 39.41 N 85.46 W
Fountain Valley 228 33.42 N 117.57 W
Fourche LaFave ≃ 194 34.58 N 92.35 W
Fourche Maline ≃ 194 34.55 N 94.55 W
Fourchu 186 45.43 N 60.15 W
Four Corners 202 44.55 N 122.58 W
Four Elms 260 51.13 N 0.06 E
Four Hole Swamp ≋ 192 33.03 N 80.24 W
Fouriesburg 158 28.38 S 28.14 E
Fourmies 50 50.00 N 4.03 E
Four Mile Creek ≃, On., Can. 284a 43.15 N 79.08 W
Four Mile Creek ≃, N.Y., U.S. 284a 43.17 N 79.00 W
Four Mile Creek ≃, Oh., U.S. 218 39.26 N 84.32 W
Four Mile Creek State Park ♦ 284a 43.16 N 79.00 W
Fourmile Draw ∨ 196 32.40 N 104.18 W
Four Mile Lake ⊜ 212 44.40 N 78.44 W
Four Mile Run ≃ 284c 38.50 N 77.02 W
Four Mountains, Islands of II 180 52.50 N 170.00 W
Fournaise, Piton de la ᴧ 157c 21.14 S 55.43 E
Fourneau, Pointe à ⟩ 275a 45.22 N 73.51 W
Fourneaux, Fr. 32 47.50 N 1.48 E
Fourneaux, Fr. 62 45.11 N 6.39 E
Fournier, Lac ⊜ 186 51.33 N 65.25 W
Fournière, Lac ⊜ 190 48.04 N 78.03 W
Fournoi I 38 37.34 N 26.30 E
Four Oaks 192 35.26 N 78.25 W
Fourqueux 261 48.53 N 2.04 E
Fours 32 46.49 N 3.43 E
Fourteenmile Creek ≃ 218 38.26 N 85.37 W
Fourth Cataract — Rābi', Ash-Shallāl ar- ↳ 140 18.47 N 32.03 E
Fourth Cliff ⩘ [4] 283 42.09 N 70.42 W
Four Towns 281 42.37 N 83.25 W
Fous, Pointe des ⟩ 240d 15.12 N 61.20 W
Foussard ≃ 50 48.16 N 1.17 E
Fouta Djalon ⩘ [1] 150 11.30 N 12.30 W
Fou-Tcheou — Fuzhou 100 26.06 N 119.17 E
Foux, Cap à ⟩ 238 19.41 N 73.27 W
Fouyang — Fuyang 100 32.54 N 115.49 E
Fouzon ≃ 50 47.16 N 1.27 E
Foveaux Strait ʮ 172 46.35 S 168.00 E
Foveran 46 57.18 N 2.02 W
Fowey 42 50.20 N 4.38 W
Fowler, Ca., U.S. 226 36.37 N 119.40 W
Fowler, Co., U.S. 198 38.07 N 104.01 W
Fowler, In., U.S. 216 40.37 N 87.19 W
Fowler, Ks., U.S. 198 37.23 N 100.11 W
Fowler, Mi., U.S. 216 43.00 N 84.44 W
Fowler, Oh., U.S. 214 41.19 N 80.40 W
Fowler, Lake ⊜ 168b 35.06 S 137.37 E
Fowler, Point ⟩ 162 32.02 S 132.29 E
Fowler Creek ≃ 281 42.17 N 83.30 W
Fowlers Bay 162 31.59 S 132.27 E
Fowlerton 196 28.28 N 98.48 W
Fowlerville 216 42.39 N 84.04 W
Fowliang — Jingdezhen 100 29.16 N 117.11 E
Fowman 128 37.13 N 49.19 E
Fox 180 64.51 N 147.46 W
Fox ≃, Mb., Can. 184 56.03 N 93.18 W
Fox ≃, U.S. 194 40.18 N 91.30 W
Fox ≃, U.S. 216 41.21 N 88.50 W
Fox ≃, Il., U.S. 194 38.32 N 88.08 W
Fox ≃, Wi., U.S. 190 44.32 N 88.01 W
Fox, Cape ⟩ 182 54.47 N 130.51 W
Foxboro, On., Can. 212 44.15 N 77.26 W
Foxboro, Ma., U.S. 207 42.03 N 71.15 W
Foxboro Raceway ♦ 283 42.06 N 71.16 W
Fox Brook ⇸ [8] 276 41.03 N 74.13 W
Foxburg 214 41.09 N 79.41 W
Fox Chapel 279b 40.30 N 79.55 W
Fox Chase ⇸ [8] 285 40.04 N 75.05 W
Fox Chase Manor 285 40.05 N 75.06 W
Fox Creek ≃, Ky., U.S. 218 38.16 N 83.41 W
Fox Creek ≃, N.Y., U.S. 210 42.41 N 74.18 W
Foxe Basin ⊂ 176 68.25 N 77.00 W
Foxe-Becken — Foxe Basin ⊂ 176 68.25 N 77.00 W
Foxe Channel ʮ 176 64.30 N 80.00 W
Foxen ⊜ 26 59.23 N 11.52 E
Foxe Peninsula ⟩ [1] 176 65.00 N 76.00 W
Foxford 48 53.58 N 9.08 W
Fox Glacier 172 43.28 S 170.00 E
Foxhall 284c 39.04 N 77.03 W
Fox Harbour 186 47.19 N 53.55 W
Fox Hills 284c 39.02 N 77.11 W
Foxhole 42 50.21 N 4.52 W
Foxholes 44 54.08 N 0.28 W
Fox Hollow Lake ⊜ 276 41.02 N 74.40 W
Fox Island I, On., Can. 212 44.28 N 78.24 W
Fox Island I, Wa., U.S. 224 47.16 N 122.37 W
Fox Islands II 180 53.30 N 168.00 W
Fox Lake, Il., U.S. 216 42.23 N 88.11 W
Fox Lake, Wi., U.S. 190 43.33 N 88.54 W
Fox Lake ⊜ 216 42.25 N 88.09 W
Fox Mountain ᴧ 180 61.55 N 133.22 W
Foxpark 200 41.05 N 106.09 W
Fox Point 216 43.09 N 87.54 W
Fox Point ⟩ 276 40.54 N 73.35 W
Fox River Estates 216 41.58 N 88.20 W
Fox River Grove 216 42.12 N 88.12 W
Foxton 172 40.28 S 175.18 E
Foxton Beach 172 40.28 S 175.13 E
Foxvale 283 42.02 N 71.14 W
Fox Valley, Austl. 274a 33.45 S 151.06 E
Fox Valley, Sk., Can. 184 50.29 N 109.28 W
Foxwells 208 37.38 N 76.18 W
Foxwist Green 262 53.12 N 2.34 W
Foxworth 194 31.14 N 89.52 W
Foyedong 98 40.41 N 119.12 E
Foyers 46 57.14 N 4.29 W
Foyle ≃ 48 54.59 N 7.18 W
Foyle, Lough ⊂ 48 55.06 N 7.08 W
Foynes 48 52.37 N 9.06 W
Foza 64 45.54 N 11.38 E
Foz do Areia, Represa de ⊜ [1] 252 26.00 S 51.35 W
Foz do Cunene 152 17.16 S 11.50 E
Foz do Iguaçu 252 25.33 S 54.35 W
Foz do Jordão 248 9.23 S 71.56 W
Foz Giraldo 34 40.00 N 7.43 W
Fozilíng 100 31.20 N 116.17 E
Frabosa Soprana 62 44.17 N 7.48 E
Frackville 208 40.47 N 76.13 W
Fraction Run ≃ 278 41.34 N 88.04 W
Fraga, Arg. 252 33.30 S 65.48 W
Fraga, Esp. 34 41.31 N 0.21 E
Fragagnano 68 40.26 N 17.28 E
Fragneto Monforte 68 41.15 N 14.46 E
Fragoso, Cayo I 240p 22.44 N 79.30 W
Fragrant Hills Park ♦ 271a 39.59 N 116.11 E
Fragua, Sierra de la ⩘ 196 26.41 N 102.13 W
Fraile Muerto 252 32.31 S 54.32 W
Fraïn, Chott el ⊜ 34 35.57 N 5.38 E
Fraire 50 50.16 N 4.30 E
Fraisans 58 47.09 N 5.46 E
Fraisse 62 45.23 N 4.15 E
Fraize 58 48.11 N 7.00 E
Fram 61 46.27 N 15.38 E
Frameries 50 50.24 N 3.54 E
Framingham 207 42.16 N 71.25 W
Framingham State College ᵾ [2] 283 42.18 N 71.26 W
Framlingham 42 52.13 N 1.21 E
Frammersbach 56 50.04 N 9.28 E
Framnes Mountains ⩘ 9 67.50 S 62.35 E
Frampol 30 50.41 N 22.40 E
Frampton Cotterell 42 51.32 N 2.29 W
Frampton on Severn 42 51.46 N 2.22 W
França, Bra. 250 11.54 S 40.36 W
Franca, Bra. 255 20.32 S 47.24 W
Franca-Iosifa, Zeml'a (Franz Josef Land) II 12 81.00 N 55.00 E
Français, Récif des ⟩ [2] 175f 19.40 S 163.20 E
Francavilla al Mare 66 42.25 N 14.17 E
Francavilla Angitola 68 38.46 N 16.16 E
Francavilla d'Ete 66 43.11 N 13.32 E
Francavilla di Sicilia 70 37.54 N 15.08 E
Francavilla Fontana 68 40.31 N 17.35 E
Francavilla in Sinni 68 40.05 N 16.12 E
Francavilla Marittima 68 39.49 N 16.23 E
France □ [1], Europe 22 46.00 N 2.00 E
France □ [1], Europe 32 46.00 N 2.00 E
Frances ≃ 180 60.12 N 129.02 W
Francés, Cabo ⟩, Cuba 240p 21.38 N 83.12 W
Francés, Cabo ⟩, Cuba 240p 21.54 N 84.02 W
Frances Creek 164 13.35 S 131.52 E
Francês dos Carvalhos 256 22.05 S 44.29 W
Frances Lake ⊜ 180 61.25 N 129.30 W
Francés Viejo, Cabo ⟩ 238 19.39 N 69.55 W
Francesville 216 40.59 N 86.52 W
Franceville 152 1.38 S 13.35 E
Francfort-sur-Main — Frankfurt am Main 56 50.07 N 8.40 E
Franche-Comté □ [9] 58 47.00 N 6.00 E
Franchère, Lac ⊜ 206 46.47 N 74.58 W
Franches-Montagnes ⩘ 58 47.12 N 7.00 E
Francia 252 32.33 S 56.37 W
Francia, Estación de ⇸ [5] 266d 41.23 N 2.11 E
Francia, Peña de ᴧ 34 42.35 N 8.02 W
Francia — France □ [1] 32 46.00 N 2.00 E
Francis 184 50.00 N 103.55 W
Francis, Lake ⊜ 206 45.02 N 71.20 W
Francis Case, Lake ⊜ [1] 198 43.15 N 99.00 W
Francisco A. Berra 258 35.23 S 58.51 W
Francisco Álvarez 258 34.38 S 58.52 W
Francisco Beltrão 252 26.05 S 53.04 W
Francisco I. Madero, Méx. 232 25.45 N 103.21 W
Francisco I. Madero, Méx. 232 24.32 N 104.22 W
Francisco I. Madero, Méx. 234 21.36 N 104.49 W
Francisco José, Tierra — Franca-Iosifa, Zeml'a II 12 81.00 N 55.00 E
Francisco Morato 256 23.16 S 46.45 W
Francisco Morazán □ [5] 236 14.15 N 87.15 W
Francisco Murguía 234 24.00 N 103.01 W
Francisco Perito Moreno, Parque Nacional ♦ 254 47.50 S 72.08 W
Francisco Sá 255 16.28 S 43.30 W
Francisco Zarco 204 32.06 N 116.30 W
Francis E. Warren Air Force Base ■ 198 41.09 N 104.52 W
Francistown 156 21.11 S 27.32 E
Francitas 222 28.52 N 96.20 W
Franco da Rocha 256 23.20 S 46.43 W
Francofonte 70 37.14 N 14.53 E
François 186 47.35 N 56.45 W
François, Lacs à ⊜ 186 51.40 N 65.49 W
François-Joseph, Îles du — Franca-Iosifa, Zeml'a II 12 81.00 N 55.00 E
François Lake 182 54.04 N 125.44 W

Symbol	English	Deutsch	Español	Français	Português
≃	River	Fluß	Río	Rivière	Rio
≅	Canal	Kanal	Canal	Canal	Canal
↳	Waterfall, Rapids	Wasserfall, Stromschnellen	Cascada, Rápidos	Chute d'eau, Rapides	Cascata, Rápidos
ʮ	Strait	Meeresstraße	Estrecho	Détroit	Estreito
⊂	Bay, Gulf	Bucht, Golf	Bahía, Golfo	Baie, Golfe	Baía, Golfo
⊜	Lake, Lakes	See, Seen	Lago, Lagos	Lac, Lacs	Lago, Lagos
≋	Swamp	Sumpf	Pantano	Marais	Pântano
⌘	Ice Features, Glacier	Eis- und Gletscherformen	Accidentes Glaciales	Formes glaciaires	Acidentes glaciares
⇣	Other Hydrographic Features	Andere Hydrographische Objekte	Otros Elementos Hidrográficos	Autres données hydrographiques	Outros acidentes hidrográficos
⇸	Submarine Features	Untermeerische Objekte	Accidentes Submarinos	Formes de relief sous-marin	Acidentes submarinos
□	Political Unit	Politische Einheit	Unidad Política	Entité politique	Unidade política
ᵾ	Cultural Institution	Kulturelle Institution	Institución Cultural	Institution culturelle	Instituição cultural
⊥	Historical Site	Historische Stätte	Sitio Histórico	Site historique	Sitio histórico
♦	Recreational Site	Erholungs- und Ferienort	Sitio de Recreo	Centre de loisirs	Area de Lazer
⊠	Airport	Flughafen	Aeropuerto	Aéroport	Aeroporto
■	Military Installation	Militäranlage	Instalación Militar	Installation militaire	Instalação militar
✦	Miscellaneous	Verschiedenes	Misceláneo	Divers	Diversos

ENGLISH: Name | Page | Lat.°′ | Long.°′ — DEUTSCH: Name | Seite | Breite°′ | Länge°′ E = Ost

Symbols in the index entries represent the broad categories identified in the key at the right. Symbols with superior numbers (⋏[1]) identify subcategories (see complete key on page *I · 1)*.

Symbole im Register stellen die rechts im Schlüssel erklärten Kategorien dar. Symbole mit hochgestellten Ziffern (⋏[1]) bezeichnen Unterabteilungen einer Kategorie (vgl. vollständiger Schlüssel auf Seite *I · 1)*.

Los símbolos incluídos en el texto del índice representan las grandes categorias identificadas con la clave a la derecha. Los símbolos con numeros en su parte superior (⋏[1]) identifican las subcategorías (véase la clave completa en la página *I · 1)*.

Les symboles de l'index représentent les catégories indiquées dans la légende à droite. Les symboles suivis d'un indice (⋏[1]) représentent des sous-catégories (voir légende complète à la page *I · 1)*.

Os símbolos incluídos no texto do índice representam as grandes categorias identificadas com a chave à direita. Os símbolos com números em sua parte superior (⋏[1]) identificam as subcategorias (veja-se a chave completa à página *I · 1)*.

∧ Mountain	Berg	Montaña	Montagne	Montanha
⋏ Mountains	Gebirge	Montañas	Montagnes	Montanhas
)(Pass	Paß	Paso	Col	Passo
V Valley, Canyon	Tal, Cañon	Valle, Cañón	Vallée, Canyon	Vale, Canhão
≚ Plain	Ebene	Llano	Plaine	Planície
› Cape	Kap	Cabo	Cap	Cabo
I Island	Insel	Isla	Île	Ilha
II Islands	Inseln	Islas	Îles	Ilhas
⊥ Other Topographic Features	Andere Topographische Objekte	Otros Elementos Topográficos	Autres données topographiques	Outros acidentes topográficos

ESPAÑOL — Nombre | Página | Lat.°′ | Long.°′ W = Oeste
FRANÇAIS — Nom | Page | Lat.°′ | Long.°′ W = Ouest
PORTUGUÊS — Nome | Página | Lat.°′ | Long.°′ W = Oeste

Nombre	Página	Lat.°′	Long.°′ W = Oeste
Fuluzhen	**107**	29.18 N	103.40 E
Fulwood	**262**	53.47 N	2.41 W
Fumaça	**256**	22.17 S	44.19 W
Fumahashi	**94**	36.42 N	137.19 E
Fumane	**156**	24.29 S	33.58 E
Fumay	**56**	49.59 N	4.42 E
Fumel	**32**	44.29 N	0.57 E
Fumin, Zhg.	**102**	25.16 N	102.26 E
Fumin, Zhg.	**106**	31.54 N	121.10 E
Fumintun	**98**	42.29 N	126.22 E
Fuminzhen	**106**	31.37 N	121.39 E
Funa ≃	**273b**	4.23 S	15.19 E
Funabashi	**94**	35.42 N	139.59 E
Funafuti I	**14**	8.31 S	179.13 E
Funagawa → Oga	**92**	39.53 N	139.51 E
Funakuyā	**175d**	24.30 N	124.17 E
Funan	**100**	32.39 N	115.32 E
Funan Gaba	**144**	4.25 N	37.57 E
Funaoka	**96**	35.23 N	134.14 E
Funasaka	**270**	34.48 N	135.17 E
Funäsdalen	**26**	62.32 N	12.33 E
Funchal	**148**	32.38 N	16.54 W
Funchal □ [5]	**148**	32.40 N	16.55 W
Fundación	**246**	10.31 N	74.11 W
Fundão	**34**	40.08 N	7.30 W
Fundão, Ilha do I	**287a**	22.51 S	43.14 W
Funde	**272c**	18.54 N	72.58 E
Fundo ≃	**250**	10.12 S	44.39 W
Fundo, Arroio ≃	**287a**	22.58 S	43.22 W
Fundy, Bay of c	**186**	45.00 N	66.00 W
Fundy National Park ♦	**186**	45.38 N	65.00 W
Fünfkirchen → Pécs	**30**	46.05 N	18.13 E
Funhalouro	**156**	23.03 S	34.25 E
Funil, Represa do ⊜ [1]	**256**	22.33 S	44.35 W
Funil, Ribeirão do ≃	**256**	22.02 S	43.46 W
Funil, Rio do ≃	**256**	22.58 S	44.34 W
Funing, Zhg.	**98**	39.54 N	119.14 E
Funing, Zhg.	**100**	33.47 N	119.48 E
Funing, Zhg.	**102**	23.33 N	105.35 E
Funiuchang	**107**	29.03 N	106.33 E
Funiu Shan ⋏	**100**	33.40 N	112.30 E
Funk Island I	**186**	49.46 N	53.10 W
Funks Creek ≃	**226**	39.19 N	122.11 W
Funkturm ⊛	**264a**	52.31 N	13.16 E
Funne ≃	**263**	51.42 N	7.36 E
Funnel Creek ≃	**166**	22.18 S	148.57 E
Funnel Hill ∧ [2]	**272c**	18.54 N	73.07 E
Funo	**96**	34.53 N	132.47 E
Funshinagh, Lough ⊜	**48**	53.31 N	8.07 W
Funsi	**150**	10.17 N	1.58 W
Funtana Coberta ⊥	**71**	39.34 N	9.21 E
Funtua	**150**	11.31 N	7.17 E
Funza	**246**	4.40 N	74.09 W
Fuorn, Pass dal (Ofenpass))(	**58**	46.37 N	10.15 E
Fuping	**102**	34.47 N	109.07 E
Fuqiao	**106**	31.36 N	121.12 E
Fuqikou	**100**	29.44 N	117.48 E
Fuqing	**100**	25.44 N	119.22 E
Fuquay-Varina	**192**	35.35 N	78.48 W
Füramoos	**58**	48.00 N	9.53 E
Furancungo	**154**	14.55 S	33.35 E
Furano	**92a**	43.21 N	142.24 E
Furāt, Nahr al- → Euphrates ≃	**128**	31.00 N	47.25 E
Furci Siculo	**70**	37.57 N	15.23 E
Furculeşti	**38**	43.52 N	25.09 E
Fures	**62**	45.19 N	5.30 E
Fūrg	**128**	28.18 N	55.13 E
Furkapass)(	**58**	46.34 N	8.25 E
Furka-Tunnel ➛ [5]	**58**	46.33 N	8.26 E
Furlong	**208**	40.18 N	75.05 W
Furmanov	**80**	57.15 N	41.07 E
Furmanovka	**86**	44.17 N	72.57 E
Furmanovo	**80**	49.42 N	49.28 E
Furn, Wādī al- V	**142**	30.13 N	31.40 E
Furnace	**46**	56.09 N	5.10 W
Furnace Brook ≃	**283**	42.06 N	70.43 W
Furnace Creek ≃	**284b**	39.11 N	76.35 W
Furnace Pond ⊜	**283**	42.03 N	70.49 W
Furnari	**70**	38.07 N	15.08 E
Furnas, Represa de ⊜ [1]	**255**	20.45 S	46.00 W
Furn ash-Shubbāk	**132**	33.52 N	35.31 E
Furneaux Group II	**166**	40.10 S	148.05 E
Furness Abbey ⊛ [1]	**44**	54.07 N	3.12 W
Furness Fells ⋏ [2]	**44**	54.18 N	3.07 W
Furnes → Veurne	**50**	51.04 N	2.40 E
Furong Shan ∧	**100**	27.30 N	115.52 E
Furqlus	**130**	34.36 N	37.05 E
Fürstenau, Dtsch.	**52**	51.50 N	9.19 E
Fürstenau, Dtsch.	**52**	52.31 N	7.40 E
Fürstenberg, Dtsch.	**52**	51.44 N	9.24 E
Fürstenberg, Dtsch.	**54**	52.09 N	14.40 E
Fürstenberg/Havel	**54**	53.11 N	13.08 E
Fürstenfeld	**61**	47.03 N	16.05 E
Fürstenfeldbruck	**60**	48.10 N	11.15 E
Fürstenhagen	**56**	51.12 N	9.41 E
Fürstenstein	**60**	48.43 N	13.20 E
Fürstenwalde	**54**	52.21 N	14.04 E
Fürstenwerder	**54**	53.24 N	13.34 E
Fürstenzell	**60**	48.32 N	13.19 E
Furtei	**71**	39.34 N	8.57 E
Fürth, Dtsch.	**56**	49.28 N	10.59 E
Fürth, Dtsch.	**56**	49.39 N	8.47 E
Furth im Wald	**60**	49.18 N	12.51 E
Furtwangen	**58**	48.03 N	8.12 E
Furuba ≃	**256**	23.21 S	44.57 W
Furubō-san ∧ [2]	**270**	34.53 N	135.19 E
Furudal	**26**	61.10 N	15.08 E
Furudono	**94**	37.05 N	140.34 E
Furukawa, Nihon	**92**	38.34 N	140.58 E
Furukawa, Nihon	**94**	36.14 N	137.11 E
Furulund	**41**	55.46 N	13.04 E
Furusund	**40**	59.40 N	18.55 E
Furu-tone ≃	**94**	35.48 N	139.51 E
Furuvik	**40**	60.39 N	17.20 E
Furuyakami	**268**	35.55 N	139.32 E
Fürwiggestausee ⊜ [1]	**263**	51.09 N	7.41 E
Fury and Hecla Strait Ա	**176**	69.56 N	84.00 W
Fusagasugá	**246**	4.21 N	74.22 W
Fusain ≃	**50**	48.09 N	2.45 E
Fusan → Pusan	**98**	35.06 N	129.03 E
Fuscaldo	**68**	39.25 N	16.02 E
Fusch	**64**	47.13 N	12.49 E
Fuschl am See	**64**	47.48 N	13.18 E
Fuschun → Fushun	**104**	41.52 N	123.53 E
Fuse	**268**	35.53 N	140.00 E
Fuse → Higashiōsaka	**96**	34.39 N	135.35 E
Fushan, Zhg.	**98**	37.29 N	121.16 E
Fushan, Zhg.	**102**	35.58 N	111.51 E
Fushan, Zhg.	**106**	31.49 N	120.46 E
Fushimi ➛ [8]	**270**	34.55 N	135.46 E
Fushino ≃	**96**	34.03 N	131.24 E
Fushuigang	**100**	31.21 N	113.40 E
Fushun (Funan), Zhg.	**104**	41.52 N	123.53 E
Fushun, Zhg.	**107**	29.11 N	105.00 E
Fushuncheng	**104**	41.53 N	123.51 E
Fusignano	**66**	44.28 N	11.57 E
Fusilier	**184**	51.51 N	109.46 W
Fusine in Valromana	**64**	46.30 N	13.39 E
Fusin → Fuxin	**104**	42.03 N	121.46 E
Fusio	**58**	46.27 N	8.40 E
Fusō	**94**	35.21 N	136.55 E
Fusong	**98**	42.18 N	127.20 E
Fussa	**94**	35.45 N	139.20 E
Füssen	**64**	47.34 N	10.42 E
Fuste, Picacho del ∧	**196**	27.35 N	102.47 W
Fusui	**102**	22.32 N	107.56 E
Futa, Passo della)(	**66**	44.05 N	11.17 E
Futaba	**94**	35.41 N	138.30 E
Futago-san ∧	**96**	33.35 N	131.36 E
Futamatagawa ➛ [8]	**268**	35.28 N	139.33 E
Futamata → Tenryū	**94**	34.52 N	137.49 E
Futami, Nihon	**94**	34.30 N	136.47 E
Futami, Nihon	**96**	33.41 N	132.38 E
Futang, Zhg.	**102**	24.26 N	112.09 E
Futang, Zhg.	**106**	30.40 N	119.35 E
Futaoi-jima I	**96**	34.06 N	130.47 E
Futatabi-yama ∧	**270**	34.43 N	135.11 E
Futatsubashi ➛ [8]	**268**	35.28 N	139.30 E
Futatsu-ne I [2]	**174f**	24.46 N	141.18 E
Fu Tau Pun Chau I	**271d**	22.21 N	114.22 E
Futian	**100**	27.26 N	114.56 E
Futianhe	**100**	31.30 N	115.05 E
Futianpu	**100**	27.22 N	112.47 E
Futjāni ≃	**126**	24.06 N	90.09 E
Futschou → Fuzhou	**100**	26.06 N	119.17 E
Futtsu, Nihon	**94**	35.19 N	139.49 E
Futtsu, Nihon	**94**	35.13 N	139.52 E
Futtsu-misaki ›	**268**	35.19 N	139.46 E
Futun ≃	**100**	26.51 N	117.46 E
Futuna I	**175f**	19.32 S	170.14 E
Futuna, Île I	**14**	14.15 S	178.09 W
Futuyu	**105**	39.18 N	114.50 E
Fuveau	**62**	43.27 N	5.34 E
Fuwah	**142**	31.12 N	30.33 E
Fuwen	**86**	47.13 N	89.39 E
Fuxi, Zhg.	**100**	27.14 N	119.50 E
Fuxi, Zhg.	**100**	25.14 N	113.52 E
Fuxi ≃	**107**	29.09 N	104.57 E
Fuxian (Wafangdian), Zhg.	**98**	39.37 N	122.01 E
Fuxian, Zhg.	**102**	36.02 N	109.13 E
Fuxian Hu ⊜	**102**	24.30 N	102.55 E
Fuxin, Zhg.	**104**	42.08 N	121.45 E
Fuxin, Zhg.	**104**	42.03 N	121.46 E
Fuxing, Zhg.	**107**	30.24 N	104.53 E
Fuxing, Zhg.	**107**	29.54 N	105.43 E
Fuxing, Zhg.	**107**	30.27 N	106.04 E
Fuxingchang	**107**	29.40 N	105.13 E
Fuxing Dao I	**269b**	31.17 N	121.23 E
Fuxinghao	**104**	42.35 N	120.32 E
Fuyang, Zhg.	**100**	32.54 N	115.49 E
Fuyang, Zhg.	**100**	30.03 N	119.57 E
Fuyang, Zhg.	**100**	23.36 N	116.37 E
Fuyang ≃	**98**	38.14 N	116.05 E
Fuyouertuo Shan ∧	**89**	45.52 N	119.48 E
Fuyu, Zhg.	**89**	47.49 N	124.27 E
Fuyu, Zhg.	**89**	45.10 N	124.50 E
Fuyuan, Zhg.	**89**	48.21 N	134.18 E
Fuyuan, Zhg.	**102**	25.39 N	104.12 E
Fuzhai	**100**	29.32 N	120.02 E
Fuzhong	**102**	24.28 N	111.22 E
Fuzhou, Zhg.	**100**	28.01 N	116.20 E
Fuzhou (Foochow), Zhg.	**100**	26.06 N	119.17 E
Fuzhoucheng	**98**	39.45 N	121.47 E
Fuzhuang	**98**	34.57 N	118.17 E
Fuzhuangyi	**98**	38.02 N	116.08 E
Fyfield	**260**	51.45 N	0.16 E
Fylde □ [8]	**262**	53.46 N	2.53 W
Fylde › [1]	**262**	53.47 N	2.56 W
Fylland › [1]	**41**	56.00 N	9.15 E
Fyn □ [6]	**41**	55.20 N	10.25 E
Fyn I	**41**	55.20 N	10.30 E
Fyne, Loch c	**46**	56.00 N	5.24 W
Fyns Hoved ›	**41**	55.37 N	10.36 E
Fyresvatn ⊜	**26**	59.06 N	8.12 E
Fyrisån ≃	**40**	59.47 N	17.39 E
Fysingen ⊜	**40**	59.34 N	17.55 E
Fyvie	**46**	57.25 N	2.23 W
Fzâra, Gara'et ⊜	**36**	36.47 N	7.30 E
G			
Ga	**150**	9.47 N	2.30 W
Gaaden	**264b**	48.03 N	16.12 E
Gaalkacyo	**144**	6.47 N	47.26 E
Gaanderen	**52**	51.56 N	6.21 E
Gabah	**144**	8.08 N	50.02 E
Gabai	**146**	11.05 N	11.39 E
Gabaldon	**116**	15.28 N	121.19 E
Gabare	**38**	43.19 N	23.55 E
Gabarus	**186**	45.50 N	60.09 W
Gabarus Bay c	**186**	45.51 N	60.07 W
Gabas ≃	**32**	43.46 N	0.42 W
Gabbs	**204**	38.52 N	117.55 W
Gabby Heights	**214**	40.09 N	80.15 W
Gabela	**152**	10.48 S	14.20 E
Gaberones → Gaborone	**156**	24.45 S	25.55 E
Gabès	**148**	33.53 N	10.07 E
Gabès □ [8]	**148**	33.15 N	9.00 E
Gabès, Golfe de c	**148**	34.00 N	10.25 E
Gabia	**152**	4.34 S	17.07 E
Gabiarra	**255**	16.15 S	39.41 W
Gabicce Mare	**66**	43.58 N	12.46 E
Gabii ⊥	**267a**	41.54 N	12.43 E
Gabil	**146**	11.09 N	18.12 E
Gabilan Creek ≃	**226**	36.41 N	121.38 W
Gabilan Range ⋏	**226**	36.30 N	121.15 W
Gąbin	**30**	52.25 N	19.44 E
Gabir	**140**	8.35 N	24.40 E
Gable Mountain ∧	**182**	54.30 N	121.40 W
Gablenz	**54**	51.41 N	14.31 E
Gablingen	**58**	48.27 N	10.49 E
Gablitz	**61**	48.14 N	16.09 E
Gablonz → Jablonec nad Nisou	**30**	50.44 N	15.10 E
Gabon □ [1], Afr.	**138**	1.00 S	11.45 E
Gabon □ [1], Afr.	**152**	1.00 S	11.45 E
Gabon, Estuaire du c [1]	**152**	0.25 N	9.20 E
Gaborone	**156**	24.45 S	25.55 E
Gabras	**140**	10.16 N	26.14 E
Gabria	**64**	45.52 N	13.34 E
Gabriel	**250**	11.14 S	41.53 W
Gabriel Strait Ա	**176**	61.45 N	65.30 W
Gabriel y Galan, Embalse de ⊜ [1]	**34**	40.15 N	6.15 W
Gabriel Zamora	**234**	19.05 N	102.05 W
Gābrīk	**128**	25.44 N	58.28 E
Gabriola	**224**	49.12 N	123.50 W
Gabriola Island I	**224**	49.10 N	123.47 W
Gabrovo	**38**	42.52 N	25.19 E
Gabun → Gabon □ [1]	**152**	1.00 S	11.45 E
Gaby	**62**	45.43 N	7.53 E
Gacé	**50**	48.48 N	0.18 E
Gachetá	**246**	4.49 N	73.36 W
Gachpar	**174q**	9.33 N	138.10 E
Gachsārān	**128**	30.12 N	50.47 E
Gackle	**198**	46.37 N	99.08 W
Gacko	**38**	43.10 N	18.32 E
Gad'ač	**78**	50.22 N	34.00 E
Gadag	**122**	15.25 N	75.37 E
Gadamai	**140**	17.09 N	36.06 E
Gādarwāra	**124**	22.55 N	78.47 E
Gadbjerg	**41**	55.46 N	9.20 E
Gäddede	**26**	64.30 N	14.09 E
Gadderbaum	**52**	52.00 N	8.31 E
Gade ≃	**260**	51.38 N	0.28 W
Gadebusch	**54**	53.42 N	11.07 E
Gadein	**140**	8.11 N	28.44 E
Gadera ≃	**64**	46.47 N	11.54 E
Gadevang	**41**	55.58 N	12.18 E
Gadilovići	**76**	53.05 N	30.16 E
Gadis ≃	**114**	1.03 N	98.55 E
Gadmen	**58**	46.44 N	8.21 E
Gado Bravo, Ilha do I	**250**	10.54 S	42.52 W
Gádor	**34**	36.57 N	2.29 W
Gadra	**120**	25.40 N	70.37 E
Gadrut	**84**	39.32 N	47.02 E
Gadsden, Al., U.S.	**194**	34.00 N	86.00 W
Gadsden, Az., U.S.	**200**	32.33 N	114.47 W
Gadwāl	**122**	16.14 N	77.48 E
Gadzi	**152**	4.47 N	16.42 E
Gaerwen	**44**	53.13 N	4.16 W
Găeşti	**38**	44.43 N	25.19 E
Gaeta	**66**	41.12 N	13.35 E
Gaeta, Golfo di c	**66**	41.06 N	13.30 E
Gaferut I	**108**	9.14 N	145.23 E
Gaffney	**192**	35.04 N	81.39 W
Gafour	**36**	36.18 N	9.19 E
Gafsa	**148**	34.25 N	8.48 E
Gafsa □ [8]	**148**	34.15 N	8.25 E
Gafurov	**85**	40.14 N	69.44 E
Gag, Pulau I	**164**	0.27 S	129.52 E
Gagal	**146**	9.01 N	15.08 E
Gagarawa	**150**	12.25 N	9.32 E
Gagarin	**76**	55.33 N	35.00 E
Gage	**196**	36.18 N	99.45 W
Gagere ≃	**150**	13.21 N	6.23 E
Gages Lake	**278**	42.21 N	87.59 W
Gages Lake ⊜	**278**	42.21 N	88.00 W
Gagetown	**186**	45.47 N	66.09 W
Gagetown, Canadian Forces Base ■	**186**	45.43 N	66.15 W
Gaggenau	**56**	48.48 N	8.19 E
Gaggi	**70**	37.51 N	15.13 E
Gaggiano	**62**	45.24 N	9.02 E
Gaghamni	**140**	11.41 N	28.19 E
Gagil Tamil I	**174q**	9.32 N	138.10 E
Gagino	**80**	55.14 N	45.02 E
Gagliano Castelferrato	**70**	37.43 N	14.32 E
Gagliano del Capo	**68**	39.50 N	18.22 E
Gagnef	**40**	60.35 N	15.04 E
Gagnia	**152**	1.28 S	16.02 E
Gagnoa	**150**	6.08 N	5.56 W
Gagnon	**176**	51.53 N	68.10 W
Gagnon, Lac ⊜	**206**	46.07 N	75.07 W
Gagny	**261**	48.53 N	2.32 E
Gagra	**84**	43.20 N	40.15 E
Gagret	**123**	31.40 N	76.04 E
Gahanna	**218**	40.01 N	82.52 W
Gahlen	**52**	51.40 N	6.52 E
Gaiarine	**64**	45.52 N	12.29 E
Gaibandha	**124**	25.19 N	89.33 E
Gaichtpass)(	**58**	47.27 N	10.37 E
Gaigalava	**76**	56.40 N	27.18 E
Gaighāta	**126**	22.56 N	88.44 E
Gaijiatun	**104**	40.50 N	122.37 E
Gail	**196**	32.46 N	101.27 W
Gail ≃	**64**	46.36 N	13.53 E
Gailberg Sattel)(	**64**	46.43 N	12.58 E
Gail Creek ≃	**222**	31.07 N	95.23 W
Gaildorf	**56**	49.00 N	9.46 E
Gaillac	**32**	43.54 N	1.55 E
Gaillard, Château ⊥	**50**	48.09 N	1.54 E
Gaillard, Lac ⊜	**186**	50.06 N	68.47 W
Gaillard, Lake ⊜	**207**	41.21 N	72.46 W
Gaillefontaine	**50**	49.39 N	1.37 E
Gaillimh → Galway	**48**	53.16 N	9.03 W
Gaillon, Fr.	**50**	49.10 N	1.20 E
Gaillon, Fr.	**261**	49.02 N	1.54 E
Gailtaler Alpen ⋏	**64**	46.42 N	13.00 E
Gaima	**164**	8.20 S	142.55 E
Gaimán	**254**	43.17 S	65.29 W
Gaimersheim	**60**	48.49 N	11.22 E
Gaines, Mi., U.S.	**216**	42.52 N	83.54 W
Gaines, Pa., U.S.	**210**	41.45 N	77.34 W
Gainesboro	**194**	36.21 N	85.39 W
Gainesville, Fl., U.S.	**192**	29.39 N	82.19 W
Gainesville, Ga., U.S.	**192**	34.17 N	83.49 W
Gainesville, Mo., U.S.	**194**	36.36 N	92.25 W
Gainesville, N.Y., U.S.	**210**	42.38 N	78.08 W
Gainesville, Tx., U.S.	**196**	33.37 N	97.07 W
Gainford	**44**	54.32 N	1.44 W
Gainsborough, Sk., Can.	**184**	49.10 N	101.26 W
Gainsborough, Eng., U.K.	**44**	53.24 N	0.46 W
Gainsborough Creek ≃	**184**	49.10 N	101.02 W
Gaiole in Chianti	**66**	43.28 N	11.26 E
Gairatganj	**124**	23.24 N	78.13 E
Gairdner ≃	**162**	34.17 S	119.28 E
Gairdner, Lake ⊜	**162**	31.35 S	136.00 E
Gairloch	**46**	57.42 N	5.40 W
Gairloch, Loch c	**46**	57.44 N	5.44 W
Gairn ≃	**46**	57.03 N	3.05 W
Gais, It.	**64**	46.50 N	11.57 E
Gais, Schw.	**58**	47.22 N	9.27 E
Gaisberg ∧	**64**	47.48 N	13.07 E
Gaisbeuren	**58**	47.54 N	9.43 E
Gaital, Cerro ∧	**236**	8.37 N	80.07 W
Gaither	**208**	39.21 N	76.59 W
Gaithersburg	**208**	39.08 N	77.12 W
Gaixian	**98**	40.24 N	122.22 E
Gaizina Kalns ∧ [2]	**76**	56.52 N	25.57 E
Gaj, Cro.	**36**	45.29 N	17.02 E
Gaj, Ross.	**86**	51.27 N	58.27 E
Gajā	**272b**	22.52 N	88.10 E
Gajahmungkur, Waduk ⊜ [1]	**115a**	7.55 S	110.55 E
Gajčur ≃	**78**	47.57 N	36.11 E
Gajendragarh	**122**	15.44 N	75.59 E
Gajiram	**146**	12.30 N	13.12 E
Gajny	**24**	60.15 N	54.15 E
Gājol	**124**	25.13 N	88.12 E
Gajsin	**78**	48.48 N	29.24 E
Gajsinghpur	**123**	29.40 N	73.27 E
Gajuapara ≃	**250**	4.17 S	47.25 W
Gajutino	**76**	58.42 N	38.32 E
Gajvoron	**78**	48.22 N	29.52 E
Gakarosa ∧	**158**	27.54 S	23.33 E
Gakona	**180**	62.18 N	145.18 W
Gākuch	**123**	36.10 N	73.45 E
Gakugsa	**24**	61.34 N	36.26 E
Gāla, Bngl.	**126**	24.18 N	89.54 E
Gala, Zhg.	**124**	28.16 N	89.23 E
Galaassija	**128**	39.52 N	64.27 E
Galāchipa	**126**	22.10 N	90.25 E
Galahad	**182**	52.31 N	111.56 W
Galamares	**266c**	38.48 N	9.25 W
Galán, Cerro ∧	**252**	25.55 S	66.52 W
Galana ≃	**154**	3.09 S	40.08 E
Galangue	**152**	13.48 S	16.09 E
Galanovo	**80**	56.09 N	54.07 E
Galanta	**30**	48.12 N	17.43 E
Galápagos □ [4]	**246a**	0.30 S	90.30 W
Galápagos, Parque Nacional de ♦	**246a**	0.15 S	90.15 W
Galapagos Islands → Colón, Archipiélago de II	**246a**	0.30 S	90.30 W
Galaroza	**34**	37.55 N	6.42 W
Galas ≃	**114**	5.31 N	102.12 E
Galashiels	**46**	55.37 N	2.49 W
Galata ➛ [8]	**267b**	41.01 N	28.58 E
Galata Köprüsü ➛ [5]	**267b**	41.00 N	28.57 E
Galata Tower ⊛	**267b**	41.01 N	28.58 E
Galatea	**172**	38.25 S	176.45 E
Galaţi	**38**	45.26 N	28.03 E
Galaţi □ [6]	**38**	45.45 N	27.45 E
Galatia	**194**	37.50 N	88.36 W
Galatia □ [9]	**130**	39.30 N	32.40 E
Galatina	**68**	40.10 N	18.10 E
Galatone	**68**	40.09 N	18.04 E
Galatro	**68**	38.28 N	16.06 E
Galátsion	**267c**	38.01 N	23.45 E
Galatz → Galaţi	**38**	45.26 N	28.03 E
Galaure ≃	**62**	45.11 N	4.49 E
Gala Water ≃	**46**	55.37 N	2.48 W
Galax	**192**	36.39 N	80.55 W
Galaxídhion	**38**	38.22 N	22.23 E
Galbyn gov' ➛ [2]	**102**	42.30 N	107.00 E
Galdhøpiggen ∧	**26**	61.37 N	8.17 E
Gale, Lac ⊜	**190**	46.46 N	76.51 W
Galeairy Lake ⊜	**212**	45.29 N	78.17 W
Galeana, Méx.	**232**	30.07 N	107.38 W
Galeana, Méx.	**232**	24.50 N	100.04 W
Galeão, Aeroporto do ⊠	**256**	22.50 S	43.15 W
Galeata	**66**	44.00 N	11.55 E
Galegu	**140**	12.36 N	35.02 E
Galeh Dār	**128**	27.38 N	52.42 E
Galela	**108**	1.50 N	127.50 E
Galena, Austl.	**162**	27.50 S	114.41 E
Galena, Ak., U.S.	**180**	64.44 N	156.57 W
Galena, Il., U.S.	**190**	42.25 N	90.25 W
Galena, In., U.S.	**218**	38.21 N	85.56 W
Galena, Ks., U.S.	**198**	37.04 N	94.38 W
Galena, Md., U.S.	**208**	39.20 N	75.52 W
Galena, Mo., U.S.	**194**	36.48 N	93.27 W
Galena, Oh., U.S.	**214**	40.12 N	82.52 W
Galena Park	**222**	29.43 N	95.13 W
Galenbecker See ⊜	**54**	53.38 N	13.43 E
Galeota Point ›	**241r**	10.08 N	60.59 W
Galera ≃	**248**	14.25 S	60.07 W
Galera, Punta ›, Chile	**254**	39.59 S	73.43 W
Galera, Punta ›, Ec.	**246**	0.49 N	80.03 W
Galera, Punta de ›	**34**	39.10 N	1.05 E
Galera Point ›	**241r**	10.49 N	60.55 W
Galeras, Volcán ∧ [1]	**246**	1.13 N	77.22 W
Galeria ⊥	**267a**	42.02 N	12.18 E
Galeria, Fosso la ≃	**267a**	41.48 N	12.21 E
Galesburg, Il., U.S.	**190**	40.56 N	90.22 W
Galesburg, Mi., U.S.	**216**	42.17 N	85.25 W
Gales Creek	**224**	45.35 N	123.12 W
Gales Creek ≃	**224**	45.29 N	123.06 W
Gales Ferry	**207**	41.25 N	72.04 W
Gales Point ›	**283**	42.33 N	70.47 W
Galesville, Md., U.S.	**208**	38.50 N	76.32 W
Galesville, Wi., U.S.	**190**	44.04 N	91.20 W
Galeton	**214**	41.43 N	77.38 W
Galeville	**210**	43.05 N	76.10 W
Galgasc	**144**	0.11 N	41.38 E
Galgate	**44**	54.00 N	2.47 W
Galguduud □ [4]	**144**	5.00 N	46.30 E
Galheiros	**255**	13.18 S	46.25 W
Gali	**84**	42.38 N	41.44 E
Gali, Torrente de ≃	**266d**	41.28 N	2.00 E
Galiano	**224**	48.52 N	123.21 W
Galiano Island I	**224**	48.56 N	123.29 W
Galibier, Col du)(	**62**	45.04 N	6.24 E
Galič, Ross.	**80**	58.23 N	42.21 E
Galič, Ukr.	**78**	49.08 N	24.43 E
Galicia □ [4]	**34**	42.45 N	8.00 W
Galicia □ [9]	**22**	49.00 N	22.00 E
Galičskaja vozvyšennost' ⋏ [2]	**24**	58.25 N	42.20 E
Galičskoje, ozero ⊜	**80**	58.24 N	42.18 E
Galien	**216**	41.47 N	86.29 W
Galien ≃	**216**	41.48 N	86.45 W
Galilee	**207**	41.22 N	71.30 W
Galilee, Lake ⊜	**166**	22.21 S	145.48 E
Galilee, Sea of → Kinneret, Yam ⊜	**132**	32.48 N	35.35 E
Galilee → HaGalil □ [9]	**132**	32.54 N	35.20 E
Galiléia	**255**	19.00 S	41.33 W
Galim	**152**	7.06 N	12.29 E
Galina Point ›	**241q**	18.24 N	76.53 W
Galindo Creek ≃	**282**	37.58 N	122.02 W
Galion	**214**	40.44 N	82.47 W
Galion, Baie du c	**240e**	14.44 N	60.57 W
Galis	**115a**	7.08 S	113.33 E
Galisteo Creek ≃	**200**	35.31 N	106.22 W
Galite, Canal de la Ա	**36**	37.20 N	9.00 E
Galiuro Mountains ⋏	**200**	32.40 N	110.20 W
Galiwinku	**164**	12.02 S	135.34 E
Galižana	**64**	44.56 N	13.52 E
Galka'yo	**144**	6.47 N	47.26 E
Galkhausen	**263**	51.05 N	6.58 E
Galkino, Kaz.	**86**	52.14 N	78.20 E
Galkino, Ross.	**82**	54.46 N	35.49 E
Galkino, Ross.	**86**	55.36 N	62.55 E
Gall'aaral	**85**	40.02 N	67.35 E
Gallan Head ›	**46**	58.14 N	7.03 W
Gallarate	**62**	45.40 N	8.47 E
Gallardon	**50**	48.32 N	1.42 E
Gallatin, Mo., U.S.	**194**	39.54 N	93.57 W
Gallatin, Pa., U.S.	**279b**	40.12 N	79.53 W
Gallatin, Tn., U.S.	**194**	36.23 N	86.26 W
Gallatin, Tx., U.S.	**222**	31.54 N	95.09 W
Gallatin □ [6]	**218**	38.45 N	84.51 W
Gallatin ≃	**202**	45.56 N	111.29 W
Gallatin Range ⋏	**202**	45.15 N	111.05 W
Galle	**122**	6.02 N	80.13 E
Gállego ≃	**34**	41.39 N	0.51 W
Gallegos ≃	**254**	51.36 S	68.59 W
Galles → Wales □ [8]	**28**	52.30 N	3.30 W
Galleyend	**260**	51.42 N	0.29 E
Galley Head ›	**48**	51.30 N	8.57 W
Galleywood	**260**	51.42 N	0.28 E
Galliano	**194**	29.26 N	90.17 W
Galliate	**62**	45.29 N	8.42 E
Gallicano	**64**	44.04 N	10.26 E
Gallicano nel Lazio	**267a**	41.52 N	12.49 E
Gallicchio	**68**	40.17 N	16.08 E
Gallico	**68**	38.10 N	15.41 E
Galliera Veneta	**64**	45.39 N	11.49 E
Gallinara I	**62**	44.02 N	8.14 E
Gallinas ≃	**196**	35.10 N	104.55 W
Gallinas, Punta ›	**246**	12.28 N	71.40 W
Gallinas Creek ≃	**282**	38.01 N	122.30 W
Gallinas Peak ∧	**200**	34.13 N	105.45 W
Gallio	**64**	45.53 N	11.33 E
Gallipoli, Austl.	**166**	19.10 S	137.55 E
Gallipoli, It.	**68**	40.03 N	17.58 E
Gallipoli → Gelibolu	**130**	40.24 N	26.40 E
Gallipoli Peninsula → Gelibolu Yarımadası › [1]	**130**	40.20 N	26.30 E
Gallipolis	**188**	38.48 N	82.12 W
Gallitzin	**214**	40.28 N	78.33 W
Gallivaggio	**58**	46.21 N	9.21 E
Gällivare	**24**	67.07 N	20.45 E
Gallneukirchen	**61**	48.21 N	14.25 E
Gällö	**26**	62.55 N	15.14 E
Gallo, Capo ›	**70**	38.13 N	13.19 E
Gallo, Lago del ⊜ [1]	**64**	46.07 N	10.10 E
Gallo, Lago di ⊜ [1]	**58**	46.37 N	10.10 E
Gallo, Laguna ⊜	**258**	35.30 S	58.28 W
Gallo Arroyo V	**200**	33.55 N	105.00 W
Galloo Island I	**212**	43.54 N	76.25 W
Galloupes Point ›	**283**	42.28 N	70.53 W
Galloway □ [9]	**44**	55.00 N	4.25 W
Galloway, Mull of ›	**44**	54.38 N	4.50 W
Galloway Creek ≃, Md., U.S.	**284b**	39.18 N	76.23 W
Galloway Creek ≃, Mi., U.S.	**281**	42.39 N	83.12 W
Galluis	**261**	48.48 N	1.48 E
Gallup	**200**	35.31 N	108.44 W
Gallupville	**210**	42.40 N	74.14 W
Gallur	**34**	41.52 N	1.19 W
Gallura ➛ [1]	**71**	41.00 N	9.13 E
Gally, Ru de ≃	**261**	48.53 N	1.53 E
Gälnan Ա	**40**	59.31 N	18.45 E
Gålö I	**40**	59.05 N	18.17 E
Galop Island I	**212**	44.46 N	75.24 W
Galoppo, Ippodromo del ♦	**266b**	45.28 N	9.07 E
Galougo	**150**	13.50 N	11.04 W
Galsi	**126**	23.20 N	87.42 E
Galston	**46**	55.36 N	4.24 W
Galt, Mong.	**88**	48.46 N	99.53 E
Galt, Ca., U.S.	**226**	38.15 N	121.17 W
Gal Tardo	**144**	3.34 N	45.58 E
Galtat Zemmour	**148**	25.15 N	12.20 W
Galtelli	**71**	40.23 N	9.37 E
Galten	**41**	56.09 N	9.55 E
Galten c	**40**	59.27 N	16.09 E
Galtür	**58**	46.58 N	10.11 E
Galtymore Mountain ∧	**48**	52.22 N	8.10 W
Galty Mountains ⋏	**48**	52.25 N	8.10 W
Galūgāh-e Āsīyeh	**128**	34.01 N	59.55 E
Galugur	**114**	2.34 N	99.39 E
Galula	**154**	8.36 S	33.02 E
Galunggung, Gunung ∧	**115a**	7.15 S	108.03 E
Galuut	**88**	48.33 N	113.12 E
Galva, Il., U.S.	**190**	41.10 N	90.02 W
Galva, Ia., U.S.	**198**	42.30 N	95.25 W
Galva, Ks., U.S.	**198**	38.22 N	97.32 W
Galvarino	**252**	38.24 S	72.47 W
Galveston, In., U.S.	**216**	40.34 N	86.11 W
Galveston, Tx., U.S.	**222**	29.17 N	94.47 W
Galveston □ [6]	**222**	29.20 N	94.53 W
Galveston Bay c	**222**	29.36 N	94.57 W
Galveston Island I	**222**	29.13 N	94.55 W
Gálvez	**252**	32.02 S	61.13 W
Gálvez ≃	**248**	5.12 S	72.53 W
Galvin, Austl.	**274b**	37.51 S	144.49 E
Galvin, Wa., U.S.	**224**	46.44 N	123.01 W
Galway (Gaillimh), Ire.	**48**	53.16 N	9.03 W
Galway, N.Y., U.S.	**210**	43.01 N	74.02 W
Galway □ [6]	**48**	53.20 N	9.00 W
Galway Bay c	**48**	53.10 N	9.15 W
Gam (Jin) ≃	**110**	21.55 N	105.12 E
Gam, Pulau I	**164**	0.27 S	130.36 E
Gama, Isla I	**254**	40.29 S	62.12 W
Gamaches	**50**	49.59 N	1.33 E
Gamagōri	**94**	34.50 N	137.14 E
Gamalejevka	**80**	52.16 N	53.26 E
Gamaliel	**194**	36.38 N	85.47 W
Ga-Mankoeng	**156**	23.57 S	29.42 E
Gamare, Lake ⊜	**144**	11.30 N	41.40 E
Gamarra	**246**	8.20 N	73.45 W
Gamawa	**146**	12.08 N	10.32 E
Gamay	**116**	12.23 N	125.18 E
Gamay Bay c	**116**	12.21 N	125.21 E
Gamba	**120**	28.17 N	88.32 E
Gambach	**56**	50.28 N	8.44 E
Gambaga	**150**	10.32 N	0.26 W
Gambais	**261**	48.46 N	1.40 E
Gambaiseuil	**261**	48.45 N	1.44 E
Gambang	**114**	3.43 N	103.06 E
Gambara, It.	**64**	45.15 N	10.18 E
Gámbara, Méx.	**234**	18.55 N	102.05 W
Gambarie	**68**	38.10 N	15.50 E
Gambassi	**66**	43.32 N	10.57 E
Gambatesa	**66**	41.30 N	14.54 E
Gambela	**144**	8.18 N	34.37 E
Gambell	**180**	63.46 N	171.46 W
Gambellara	**64**	45.28 N	11.20 E
Gamber	**208**	39.27 N	76.56 W
Gambia □ [1], Afr.	**134**	13.30 N	15.30 W
Gambia □ [1], Afr.	**150**	13.30 N	15.30 W
Gambia (Gambie) ≃	**150**	13.28 N	16.34 W
Gambi Atrash	**140**	10.03 N	33.47 E
Gambie (Gambia) ≃	**150**	13.28 N	16.34 W
Gambie → Gambia □ [1]	**150**	13.30 N	15.30 W
Gambier	**214**	40.22 N	82.23 W
Gambier, Îles II	**6**	21.20 S	136.30 W
Gamble Mansion State Historic Site ⊥	**220**	27.32 N	82.32 W
Gambo, Nf., Can.	**186**	48.46 N	54.14 W
Gambo, Centraf.	**152**	4.39 N	22.16 E
Gamboa	**236**	9.07 N	79.42 W
Gamboli	**120**	29.50 N	68.26 E
Gambolò	**62**	45.15 N	8.51 E
Gamboma	**152**	1.53 S	15.51 E
Gamboula	**152**	4.08 N	15.09 E
Gambrill State Park ♦	**208**	39.30 N	77.30 W
Gamchab ≃	**156**	28.15 S	17.26 E
Gamé	**150**	6.44 N	1.11 E
Game Creek ≃	**285**	39.41 N	75.28 W
Gamen-See ⊜	**264a**	52.40 N	13.51 E
Gaming	**61**	47.56 N	15.06 E
Gamka ≃	**158**	33.18 S	21.39 E
Gamlakarleby → Kokkola	**26**	63.50 N	23.07 E
Gamla Uppsala	**40**	59.54 N	17.38 E
Gamleby	**26**	57.54 N	16.24 E
Gamlitz	**61**	46.43 N	15.33 E
Gammel Estrup ⊥	**26**	56.26 N	10.21 E
Gammelstad ⊛ [1]	**26**	65.38 N	22.01 E
Gammertingen	**58**	48.15 N	9.13 E
Gammon ≃	**184**	51.07 N	95.09 W
Gammon, Point ›	**207**	41.36 N	70.16 W
Gammon Ranges National Park ♦	**166**	30.29 S	139.10 E
Gamō, Nihon	**94**	35.03 N	136.11 E
Gamō, Nihon	**268**	35.52 N	139.48 E
Gamoep	**158**	29.55 S	18.25 E
Ga-Mogara ≃	**158**	27.07 S	22.57 E
Gamo Gofa □ [4]	**144**	5.45 N	37.00 E
Gamon	**150**	13.20 N	12.55 W
Gamova, mys ›	**89**	42.35 N	131.12 E
Gamph, Slieve ⋏	**48**	54.05 N	9.00 W
Gampoko	**273b**	4.16 S	15.10 E
Gampola	**122**	7.10 N	80.34 E
Gampongbatak	**114**	4.48 N	97.39 E
Gampoui	**273b**	4.08 S	15.22 E
Gams	**58**	47.12 N	9.28 E
Gamsfeld ∧	**64**	47.37 N	13.29 E
Gamtoos ≃	**158**	33.58 S	25.01 E
Gamud ∧	**144**	4.05 N	38.03 E
G'amyš, gora ∧	**84**	40.18 N	46.23 E
Gan ≃, Zhg.	**89**	49.12 N	125.14 E
Gan ≃, Zhg.	**100**	29.12 N	116.00 E
Ganado, Az., U.S.	**200**	35.42 N	109.32 W
Ganado, Tx., U.S.	**222**	29.02 N	96.31 W
Ganano ≃	**116**	16.45 N	121.44 E
Gananoque	**212**	44.20 N	76.10 W
Gananoque ≃	**212**	44.19 N	76.09 W
Gananoque Lake ⊜	**212**	44.27 N	76.09 W
Ganaraska ≃	**212**	43.57 N	78.18 W
Ganargua Creek ≃	**210**	43.04 N	77.00 W
Ganassi	**116**	7.49 N	124.06 E
Ganāveh	**128**	29.34 N	50.31 E
Gancevići	**76**	52.45 N	26.26 E
Ganchangba	**107**	28.52 N	103.41 E
Ganči	**85**	39.58 N	69.08 E
Ganda, Ang.	**152**	13.02 S	14.40 E
Ganda, Zaïre	**152**	4.05 N	23.32 E
Gandadiwata, Bulu ∧	**112**	2.42 S	119.27 E
Gandajika	**152**	6.45 S	23.57 E
Gandak (Nārāyaṇi) ≃	**124**	25.39 N	85.13 E
Gaṇḍakī □ [8]	**124**	28.15 N	84.15 E
Gandara	**258**	35.26 S	58.06 W
Ganda Singhwāla	**123**	31.02 N	74.31 E
Gandāva	**120**	28.37 N	67.29 E
Gandavaroyi Falls ᒪ	**154**	17.17 S	29.07 E
Gānde	**126**	24.10 N	86.26 E
Gander	**186**	48.57 N	54.37 W
Gander ≃	**186**	49.15 N	54.30 W
Gander Bay	**186**	49.18 N	54.29 W
Gander Bay c	**186**	49.25 N	54.28 W
Ganderkesee	**52**	53.02 N	8.32 E
Gander Lake ⊜	**186**	48.55 N	54.40 W
Gandesa	**34**	41.03 N	0.26 E
Gandevi	**120**	20.49 N	72.59 E
Gand → Gent	**50**	51.03 N	3.43 E
Gāndhinagar	**120**	23.12 N	72.40 E
Gāndhi Sāgar ⊜ [1]	**120**	24.18 N	75.21 E
Gandi	**150**	12.55 N	5.49 E
Gandi, Wādī V	**140**	11.23 N	24.31 E
Gandia	**34**	38.58 N	0.11 W
Gandino	**62**	45.49 N	9.54 E
Gando	**152**	12.30 S	17.25 E
Gandole	**146**	8.26 N	11.34 E
Gandou	**152**	2.24 N	17.27 E
Gandrange	**56**	49.16 N	6.08 E
Gandria	**58**	46.01 N	9.00 E
Gandu	**255**	13.45 S	39.30 W
Gandy Bridge ➛ [5]	**220**	27.53 N	82.34 W
G'andžačaj ≃	**84**	40.54 N	46.28 E
Ganfang	**100**	28.40 N	114.51 E
Ganfosi	**107**	29.36 N	104.03 E
Gangādharpur	**272b**	22.36 N	88.11 E
Gangafani	**150**	14.23 N	2.24 W
Ganga → Ganges ≃	**124**	23.22 N	90.32 E
Gangājalghāti	**126**	23.25 N	87.07 E
Gangala-Na-Bodio	**154**	3.41 N	29.08 E
Gangalingolo	**273b**	4.20 S	15.09 E
Gan Gan	**254**	42.30 S	68.16 W
Gangānagar	**123**	29.55 N	73.53 E
Gangāpur, India	**120**	25.13 N	74.16 E
Gangāpur, India	**122**	19.41 N	75.01 E
Gangāpur, India	**124**	26.29 N	76.43 E
Gangara, Niger	**150**	14.36 N	8.30 E
Gangara, Niger	**150**	13.33 N	7.14 E
Gāngārāmpur	**124**	25.24 N	88.31 E
Ganga Sāgar	**126**	21.38 N	88.05 E
Gangaw	**110**	22.11 N	94.07 E
Gangāwati	**122**	15.26 N	76.32 E
Gangaw Range ⋏	**110**	24.50 N	96.40 E
Ganga-Yamuna Doāb ⋏ [1]	**124**	26.40 N	79.30 E
Gangcheng	**98**	35.52 N	116.52 E
Gangdaba, Tchabal ∧	**152**	7.44 N	12.45 E
Gangdhār	**120**	23.57 N	75.37 E
Gangdisê Shan ⋏	**120**	31.00 N	82.00 E
Gangelt	**56**	50.59 N	5.59 E
Ganges, B.C., Can.	**224**	48.51 N	123.30 W
Ganges, Fr.	**62**	43.56 N	3.42 E
Ganges (Ganga) (Padma) ≃	**124**	23.22 N	90.32 E
Ganges, Mouths of the ≃ [1]	**120**	22.00 N	89.00 E
Ganges Delta ≅ [2]	**124**	23.00 N	89.00 E
Ganghu	**120**	32.05 N	86.45 E
Gangi	**70**	37.49 N	14.13 E
Gangkofen	**60**	48.26 N	12.34 E
Gangkou, Zhg.	**100**	29.45 N	115.44 E
Gangkou, Zhg.	**100**	29.21 N	117.58 E
Gangkou, Zhg.	**100**	22.38 N	113.22 E
Gangkou, Zhg.	**100**	22.36 N	114.54 E
Gangkou, Zhg.	**100**	29.12 N	113.19 E
Gangkou, Zhg.	**106**	30.44 N	118.54 E
Gangkouzhen	**106**	31.45 N	120.40 E
Gangmar Co ⊜	**120**	33.46 N	84.15 E
Gang Mills	**210**	42.08 N	77.06 W
Gāngnāpur	**126**	23.09 N	88.38 E
Gangneung → Kangnŭng	**98**	37.45 N	128.54 E
Gango ≃	**152**	9.48 S	15.40 E
Gangoa	**102**	37.15 N	100.28 E
Gangoh	**124**	29.46 N	77.15 E
Gangotri, India	**120**	30.56 N	79.02 E
Gangotri, India	**120**	31.01 N	78.27 E
Gangou	**98**	40.30 N	119.27 E
Gangoumen	**98**	41.40 N	116.35 E
Gangouyi	**102**	36.01 N	105.03 E
Gangqiao	**107**	30.13 N	105.22 E
Gang Ranch	**182**	51.33 N	122.20 W
Gangshangji	**100**	28.06 N	116.30 E
Gangtok	**124**	27.20 N	88.37 E
Gangtou	**98**	38.04 N	113.56 E
Gangtouli	**106**	31.42 N	119.02 E
Gangu	**102**	34.45 N	105.20 E
Gangwa, Zaïre	**152**	3.30 S	20.55 E
Gangwa, Zhg.	**105**	39.48 N	116.10 E
Gangwei	**100**	24.20 N	118.01 E
Ganhezi	**86**	44.08 N	88.32 E
Ganhu	**102**	44.33 N	94.09 E
Gani	**164**	0.47 S	128.13 E
Ganišob	**85**	39.03 N	70.47 E
Ganj Dundwara	**124**	27.44 N	78.57 E
Ganjiang	**107**	29.42 N	103.38 E
Ganlan Shan ∧	**124**	29.54 N	90.02 E
Ganlu	**106**	31.32 N	120.35 E
Ganluchang	**107**	29.54 N	104.47 E
Ganluo	**102**	29.03 N	102.59 E
Gannahoek	**158**	26.44 S	24.08 E
Gannan	**89**	47.54 N	123.30 E
Gannano, Lago di ⊜	**68**	40.19 N	16.26 E
Gannapan	**158**	30.23 S	22.12 E
Gannat	**32**	46.06 N	3.12 E
Gannett Peak ∧	**200**	43.11 N	109.39 W
Gannovka	**83**	48.33 N	38.35 E
Gannvalley	**198**	44.02 N	98.59 W
Ganpingsi	**102**	35.13 N	102.30 E
Ganpu	**106**	30.24 N	120.53 E
Ganq	**120**	37.25 N	92.15 E
Ganquan	**102**	36.25 N	109.16 E
Gansbaai	**158**	34.35 S	19.22 E
Gänsbrunnen	**58**	47.16 N	7.28 E
Gänserndorf	**61**	48.20 N	16.43 E
Gansevoort	**210**	43.12 N	73.39 W
Ganspan	**158**	27.57 S	24.47 E
Gansu (Kansu) □ [4]	**102**	37.00 N	103.00 E
Ganta	**150**	7.15 N	8.59 W
Gantan	**100**	29.37 N	119.34 E
Gantang, Zhg.	**100**	26.56 N	119.40 E
Gantang, Zhg.	**102**	22.58 N	109.00 E
Gantao ≃	**98**	38.01 N	114.07 E
Gante → Gent	**50**	51.03 N	3.43 E
Gantheaume, Cape ›	**166**	36.05 S	137.27 E
Gantheaume Bay c	**162**	27.44 S	114.07 E
Gantheaume Point ›	**162**	17.59 S	122.10 E
Gantiadi	**84**	43.24 N	40.06 E
Gantian	**100**	27.30 N	113.10 E
Gantt	**194**	31.24 N	86.29 W
Gantung	**112**	2.58 S	108.09 E
Gantung, Mount ∧	**116**	8.57 N	117.48 E
Gan'uškino	**80**	46.36 N	49.16 E
Ganwo	**150**	11.13 N	4.42 E
Ganxi, Zhg.	**100**	28.08 N	118.06 E
Ganxi, Zhg.	**102**	29.02 N	109.32 E
Ganyanchi	**102**	36.39 N	105.18 E
Ganyesa	**158**	26.35 S	24.10 E
Ganyu (Qing Kou)	**98**	34.52 N	119.10 E
Ganzê	**102**	31.40 N	100.01 E
Ganzhenyi	**100**	30.33 N	113.21 E
Ganzhou, Zhg.	**100**	25.54 N	114.55 E
Ganzhou, Zhg.	**100**	28.49 N	115.25 E
Ganzhou → Zhangye	**102**	38.56 N	100.27 E
Ganzhuermiao	**88**	48.24 N	118.08 E
Ganzlin	**54**	53.23 N	12.15 E
Ganzo Azul	**248**	8.51 S	74.44 W
Gao	**150**	16.16 N	0.03 W
Gao □ [4]	**150**	18.00 N	1.30 E
Gao'an	**100**	28.25 N	115.22 E
Gaobaita	**271a**	39.53 N	116.30 E
Gaobei	**100**	26.37 N	114.38 E
Gaobeidian	**271a**	39.54 N	116.33 E
Gaobu	**100**	27.48 N	117.01 E
Gaochang	**107**	28.49 N	104.24 E
Gaocheng, Zhg.	**98**	38.04 N	114.49 E
Gaocheng, Zhg.	**100**	31.57 N	113.25 E
Gaocheng, Zhg.	**106**	31.28 N	119.48 E
Gaochengzhai	**104**	41.24 N	123.43 E
Gaochun	**106**	31.20 N	118.52 E
Gaocun	**98**	37.05 N	122.12 E
Gaodianzi	**102**	30.40 N	110.01 E
Gao Feng ∧	**106**	30.34 N	118.40 E
Gaogongmiao	**100**	33.25 N	115.53 E
Gaogou	**100**	34.03 N	119.15 E
Gaohe	**100**	22.47 N	112.57 E
Gaohebu	**100**	30.44 N	116.50 E
Gaoil, Sliabh ∧	**46**	55.55 N	5.28 W
Gaojiabu	**102**	38.30 N	110.11 E
Gaojiadi	**98**	41.33 N	114.58 E
Gaojiadian	**98**	42.40 N	124.28 E
Gaojian	**100**	29.04 N	121.14 E
Gaojiapuzi	**104**	41.22 N	123.36 E
Gaojiaqiao	**106**	30.43 N	120.38 E
Gaojiatun	**104**	41.06 N	121.19 E
Gaojiawopeng	**104**	41.28 N	122.10 E
Gaojiawopu	**104**	41.50 N	122.47 E
Gaojiazhai	**269b**	31.23 N	121.33 E
Gaojiazhen	**102**	30.05 N	107.51 E
Gaokan	**104**	40.46 N	122.23 E
Gaokeng	**100**	27.40 N	113.58 E
Gaolan	**102**	36.25 N	103.56 E
Gaolan Dao I	**100**	21.55 N	113.15 E
Gaolao	**104**	41.54 N	120.59 E
Gaoli	**105**	39.17 N	115.38 E
Gaoliang	**107**	29.45 N	105.15 E
Gaoliban	**104**	41.39 N	121.58 E

	English	Deutsch	Español	Français	Português
≃	River	Fluß	Río	Rivière	Rio
≍	Canal	Kanal	Canal	Canal	Canal
ᒪ	Waterfall, Rapids	Wasserfall, Stromschnellen	Cascada, Rápidos	Chute d'eau, Rapides	Cascata, Rápidos
Ա	Strait	Meeresstraße	Estrecho	Détroit	Estreito
c	Bay, Gulf	Bucht, Golf	Bahía, Golfo	Baie, Golfe	Baía, Golfo
⊜	Lake, Lakes	See, Seen	Lago, Lagos	Lac, Lacs	Lago, Lagos
≅	Swamp	Sumpf	Pantano	Marais	Pântano
⩍	Ice Features, Glacier	Eis- und Gletscherformen	Accidentes Glaciales	Formes glaciaires	Acidentes glaciares
⊤	Other Hydrographic Features	Andere Hydrographische Objekte	Otros Elementos Hidrográficos	Autres données hydrographiques	Outros acidentes hidrográficos

	English	Deutsch	Español	Français	Português
✦	Submarine Features	Untermeerische Objekte	Accidentes Submarinos	Formes de relief sous-marin	Acidentes submarinos
□	Political Unit	Politische Einheit	Unidad Politica	Entité politique	Unidade política
⊛	Cultural Institution	Kulturelle Institution	Institución Cultural	Institution culturelle	Institução cultural
⊥	Historical Site	Historische Stätte	Sitio Histórico	Site historique	Sitio histórico
♦	Recreational Site	Erholungs- und Ferienort	Sitio de Recreo	Centre de loisirs	Area de Lazer
⊠	Airport	Flughafen	Aeropuerto	Aéroport	Aeroporto
■	Military Installation	Militäranlage	Instalación Militar	Installation militaire	Instalação militar
➛	Miscellaneous	Verschiedenes	Misceláneo	Divers	Diversos

ENGLISH

Name	Page	Lat.°′	Long.°′
Gaolifangshen	104	42.27 N	123.21 E
Gaolimen	98	40.22 N	124.02 E
Gaoling	105	40.32 N	117.01 E
Gaolinying	105	39.06 N	115.38 E
Gaoliying	105	40.10 N	116.29 E
Gaoliyingzi	104	41.56 N	124.17 E
Gaolong	100	26.56 N	113.45 E
Gaolou	105	39.59 N	116.50 E
Gaolouchang, Zhg.	107	29.51 N	104.41 E
Gaolouchang, Zhg.	107	30.03 N	105.58 E
Gaoluo	98	37.27 N	113.55 E
Gaomi	98	36.23 N	119.44 E
Gaona	252	25.12 S	64.05 W
Gaopi	100	24.14 N	116.39 E
Gaoping, Zhg.	102	35.48 N	112.52 E
Gaoping, Zhg.	107	30.28 N	105.45 E
Gaopingba	107	30.47 N	106.06 E
Gaoqiao, Zhg.	100	30.08 N	119.56 E
Gaoqiao, Zhg.	100	26.36 N	117.46 E
Gaoqiao, Zhg.	102	28.06 N	106.36 E
Gaoqiao, Zhg.	106	32.14 N	119.38 E
Gaoqiao, Zhg.	106	31.21 N	121.34 E
Gaoqiaomen	106	32.01 N	118.51 E
Gaoqiaozhen	104	40.55 N	121.00 E
Gaoqing (Tianzhen)	98	37.11 N	117.47 E
Gaoqipu	104	41.32 N	121.40 E
Gaosha	100	26.27 N	117.56 E
Gaoshaling	105	38.51 N	117.36 E
Gaoshan, Zhg.	100	25.29 N	119.34 E
Gaoshan, Zhg.	107	29.26 N	104.28 E
Gaoshanbao	105	40.40 N	117.29 E
Gaoshangbao	98	39.11 N	118.30 E
Gaoshanpu	102	27.10 N	105.14 E
Gaoshantai	104	42.22 N	122.28 E
Gaoshanzi	104	41.34 N	122.02 E
Gaoshengchang	107	29.59 N	105.31 E
Gaoshengzhen	104	41.20 N	122.12 E
Gaoshi	107	29.36 N	104.44 E
Gaoshikan	107	29.12 N	105.04 E
Gaosichang	107	30.17 N	104.52 E
Gaotai	102	39.20 N	99.58 E
Gaotaishan	104	42.02 N	122.52 E
Gaotan, Zhg.	100	30.23 N	117.23 E
Gaotan, Zhg.	100	23.12 N	115.22 E
Gaotan, Zhg.	102	32.22 N	108.36 E
Gaotang	98	36.54 N	116.14 E
Gaotangji	100	32.24 N	116.01 E
Gaotingsi	100	26.05 N	112.53 E
Gaotuozi	104	41.08 N	122.40 E
Gaoua	150	10.20 N	3.11 W
Gaoual	150	11.45 N	13.12 W
Gaoxian	102	28.20 N	104.38 E
Gaoxingru	100	26.28 N	115.14 E
Gaoxinji	98	34.11 N	115.33 E
Gaoya	98	36.22 N	118.49 E
Gaoyang	98	34.30 N	114.40 E
Gaoyapu	107	29.14 N	106.19 E
Gaoyi	98	37.36 N	114.36 E
Gaoyou, Zhg.	100	32.47 N	119.27 E
Gaoyou, Zhg.	100	28.25 N	115.31 E
Gaoyou Hu ⊜	100	32.50 N	119.20 E
Gaozhangjia	102	36.06 N	107.18 E
Gaozhou	102	21.55 N	110.50 E
Gaozi	106	32.11 N	119.18 E
Gaoziba	107	29.01 N	106.00 E
Gaozuo	100	33.57 N	118.03 E
Gap, Fr.	62	44.34 N	6.05 E
Gap, Pa., U.S.	208	39.59 N	76.01 W
Gapālnagar	272b	22.49 N	88.08 E
Gapan	116	15.19 N	120.57 E
Gapeau ≃	62	43.07 N	6.11 E
Gapern ⊜	40	59.31 N	13.40 E
Gar	120	32.11 N	79.59 E
Gar ≃	120	32.28 N	79.44 E
Gara, Lough ⊜	48	53.55 N	8.25 W
Garacad	144	6.57 N	49.19 E
Garachiné	246	8.04 N	78.22 W
Garadag	144	9.26 N	46.52 E
Gārādāha	126	24.14 N	89.34 E
Garagoa	246	5.05 N	73.21 W
Garaguso	68	40.33 N	16.14 E
Garah	166	29.04 S	149.38 E
Garai ≃ [1]	126	23.32 N	89.31 E
Garaina	164	7.50 S	147.10 E
Gārākhola Madhukhāli	126	23.33 N	89.38 E
Garamba ≃	154	3.53 N	29.12 E
Garamba, Parc National de la ♠	154	4.10 N	29.30 E
Gara Muleta ∧	144	9.17 N	41.47 E
Garānberia	272b	22.24 N	88.34 E
Garancières	261	48.49 N	1.46 E
Garango	150	11.48 N	0.34 W
Garanhuns	250	8.54 S	36.29 W
Garapan	174n	15.12 N	145.43 E
Garara	164	8.37 S	148.17 E
Garautha	124	25.34 N	79.18 E
Garba	146	9.12 N	20.30 E
Garbagna	266b	45.23 N	8.39 E
Garbagnate Milanese	266b	45.35 N	9.05 E
Garbahaarey	144	3.19 N	42.13 E
Garbatella ➜ [8]	267a	41.52 N	12.29 E
Garba Tula	154	0.32 N	38.31 E
Garber	196	36.26 N	97.35 W
Garberville	204	40.06 N	123.47 W
Garbokaraj	88	54.09 N	99.52 E
Garboldisham	42	52.24 N	0.56 E
Garbsen	52	52.25 N	9.34 E
Garça	255	22.14 S	49.37 W
Garças, Rio das ≃	255	15.54 S	52.16 W
Garcevo	76	52.45 N	32.59 E
Garches	261	48.51 N	2.11 E
Garching	60	48.15 N	11.39 E
Garching an der Alz	60	48.08 N	12.34 E
Garchitorena	116	13.52 N	123.40 E
García	232	29.59 N	108.20 W
García, Laguna ⊜	288	34.58 S	58.09 W
García de la Cadena	234	21.09 N	103.28 W
García de Sola, Embalse de ⊜ [1]	34	39.15 N	5.05 W
Garcia Hernandez	116	9.37 N	124.18 E
Garcias	255	20.34 S	52.13 W
Garcitas Creek ≃	222	28.51 N	96.46 W
Gard □ [5]	62	44.00 N	4.00 E
Gard ≃	62	43.51 N	4.37 E
Gard, Pont du ➜ [5]	62	43.56 N	4.36 E
Garda	64	45.34 N	10.42 E
Garda, Lago di ⊜	64	45.40 N	10.41 E
Gardabani	84	41.28 N	45.06 E
Gardanne	62	43.27 N	5.28 E
Garde, Lac la ⊜	190	46.46 N	78.14 W
Gardelegen	54	52.31 N	11.23 E
Garden ≃	190	46.32 N	84.09 W
Gardena	228	33.53 N	118.18 W
Gardena, Val V	64	46.35 N	11.35 E
Garden Acres	226	37.58 N	121.13 W
Garden City, Ga., U.S.	192	32.06 N	81.09 W
Garden City, Ks., U.S.	198	37.58 N	100.52 W
Garden City, Mi., U.S.	216	42.19 N	83.19 W
Garden City, Mo., U.S.	194	38.33 N	94.11 W
Garden City, N.Y., U.S.	210	40.43 N	73.38 W
Garden City, Tx., U.S.	196	31.52 N	101.29 W
Garden City Park	276	40.44 N	73.39 W
Garden City → Qasr al-Dubārā ➜ [8]	273c	30.02 N	31.14 E
Garden City Raceway ♠	284a	43.09 N	79.11 W
Gardendale	194	33.39 N	86.48 W
Garden Farms	226	35.24 N	120.07 W
Garden Gate Village	282	37.20 N	122.02 W
Garden Grove, Ca., U.S.	228	33.46 N	117.56 W
Garden Grove, Ia., U.S.	190	40.50 N	93.36 W
Garden Home	224	45.27 N	122.45 W
Garden Island I, Austl.	168a	32.13 S	115.41 E
Garden Island I, Mi., U.S.	190	45.49 N	85.30 W
Garden Lakes	192	34.17 N	85.16 W
Garden Peninsula › [1]	190	45.45 N	86.35 W
Garden Plain	198	37.39 N	97.41 W
Garden Prairie	216	42.15 N	88.44 W
Garden Reach	126	22.33 N	88.17 E
Gardenside	218	38.03 N	84.33 W
Garden State Arts Center ⊍	276	40.24 N	74.11 W
Garden State Plaza ➜ [9]	276	40.55 N	74.05 W
Gardenton	184	49.05 N	96.40 W
Garden Valley	226	38.51 N	120.51 W
Garden View	210	41.16 N	77.03 W
Gardenville	208	40.22 N	75.07 W
Gardermoen	26	60.13 N	11.06 E
Gardey	252	37.17 S	59.21 W
Gardeyz	120	33.37 N	69.07 E
Gardinas → Grodno	76	53.41 N	23.50 E
Gardiner, Me., U.S.	188	44.13 N	69.46 W
Gardiner, Mt., U.S.	202	45.01 N	110.42 W
Gardiner, N.Y., U.S.	210	41.41 N	74.09 W
Gardiner, Or., U.S.	202	43.43 N	124.06 W
Gardiner, Wa., U.S.	224	48.03 N	122.55 W
Gardiner Dam ➜ [6]	184	51.17 N	106.51 W
Gardiner Range ⋏	162	23.50 S	131.46 E
Gardiners Bay c	207	41.08 N	72.10 W
Gardiners Creek ≃	274b	37.50 S	145.02 E
Gardiners Island I	207	41.05 N	72.07 W
Garding	41	54.20 N	8.46 E
Gardner, Il., U.S.	216	41.11 N	88.18 W
Gardner, Ks., U.S.	198	38.48 N	94.55 W
Gardner, Ma., U.S.	207	42.34 N	71.59 W
Gardner Canal c	182	53.28 N	128.15 W
Gardner Lake ⊜	207	41.31 N	72.13 W
Gardner Pinnacles II [1]	14	25.00 N	167.55 W
Gardnersville	218	38.46 N	84.30 W
Gardnertown	210	41.32 N	74.04 W
Gardnerville	226	38.56 N	119.44 W
Gardno	54	53.15 N	14.38 E
Gardolo	64	46.07 N	11.05 E
Gardon d'Alès ≃	62	44.02 N	4.08 E
Gardon d'Anduze ≃	62	44.02 N	4.08 E
Gardone Riviera	64	45.37 N	10.34 E
Gardone Val Trompia	64	45.41 N	10.11 E
Gårdsjö	40	58.52 N	14.19 E
Gårdskär	40	60.37 N	17.35 E
Gare Loch c	46	56.01 N	4.48 W
Garelochhead	46	56.05 N	4.50 W
Gareloi Island I	181a	51.47 N	178.48 W
Garenfeld ➜ [8]	263	51.24 N	7.31 E
Garenin	46	58.21 N	6.50 W
Gare Simon	273b	4.15 S	15.11 E
Garešnica	36	45.35 N	16.56 E
Garessio	62	44.12 N	8.02 E
Garet, Mont ∧ [1]	175f	14.16 S	167.30 E
Garfield, Ks., U.S.	198	38.04 N	99.14 W
Garfield, N.J., U.S.	210	40.52 N	74.06 W
Garfield, N.M., U.S.	200	32.45 N	107.15 W
Garfield, Wa., U.S.	202	47.00 N	117.08 W
Garfield Heights	214	41.25 N	81.36 W
Garfield Mountain ∧	202	44.31 N	112.37 W
Garfield Park	285	39.42 N	75.33 W
Garfield Park ♠, Il., U.S.	278	41.53 N	87.43 W
Garfield Park ♠, Oh., U.S.	279a	41.26 N	81.36 W
Garfield Peak ∧	200	42.47 N	107.18 W
Garforth	44	53.48 N	1.22 W
Garga	88	54.26 N	110.33 E
Gargaliánoi	38	37.04 N	21.39 E
Gargano, Promontorio del ›	68	41.50 N	16.00 E
Gargano, Testa del ›	68	41.49 N	16.12 E
Gargantua, Cape ›	190	47.36 N	85.02 W
Garga Sarali	152	5.11 N	14.00 E
Gargazzone (Gargazon)	64	46.35 N	11.12 E
Gargellen	58	46.58 N	9.56 E
Gargenville	261	49.00 N	1.49 E
Garges-lès-Gonesse	261	48.58 N	2.25 E
Gargnano	64	45.41 N	10.40 E
Gargouna	150	15.56 N	0.13 E
Gargrave	44	53.59 N	2.06 W
Gargždai	76	55.43 N	21.24 E
Garhākota	124	23.46 N	79.09 E
Garhbeta	126	22.51 N	87.19 E
Garhdīwāla	123	31.44 N	75.45 E
Garhi Habībullāh Khān	123	34.24 N	73.23 E
Garhi Jasaya	272a	28.46 N	77.16 E
Garhi Katiya	272a	28.45 N	77.16 E
Garhi Khairo	120	28.04 N	67.59 E
Garhi Malehra	124	25.02 N	79.40 E
Garhjāt Hills ⋏ [2]	126	21.47 N	86.20 E
Garhmuktesar	124	28.48 N	78.06 E
Garhshankar	123	31.13 N	76.08 E
Garhwa	124	24.11 N	83.49 E
Gari	86	59.26 N	62.21 E
Garibaldi, Bra.	252	29.15 S	51.32 W
Garibaldi, B.C., Can.	182	49.58 N	123.09 W
Garibaldi, Or., U.S.	224	45.34 N	123.55 W
Garibaldi, Casa di ⊥	71	41.13 N	9.27 E
Garibaldi, Mount ∧	182	49.51 N	123.01 W
Garibaldi Provincial Park ♠	182	50.00 N	122.50 W
Garies	158	30.30 S	18.00 E
Garigliano ≃	68	41.13 N	13.45 E
Gariglione, Monte ∧	68	39.09 N	16.41 E
Garín	258	34.26 S	58.44 W
Garín, Arroyo ≃	288	34.23 S	58.43 W
Garin Regional Park ♠	282	37.38 N	122.03 W
Garipçe Burnu ›	267b	41.13 N	29.07 E
Garissa	154	0.28 S	39.38 E
Garita Palmera	236	13.44 N	90.05 W
Gariya	272b	22.28 N	88.23 E
Gārji	272b	22.51 N	88.19 E
Garkida	146	10.25 N	12.36 E
Garko	150	11.38 N	8.48 E
Garland, Al., U.S.	194	31.33 N	86.49 W
Garland, Md., U.S.	284b	39.11 N	76.39 W
Garland, Pa., U.S.	214	41.49 N	79.27 W
Garland, Tx., U.S.	222	32.54 N	96.38 W
Garland, Ut,. U.S.	200	41.44 N	112.09 W
Garland Park ♠	275b	43.44 N	79.35 W
Garland Peak ∧	224	48.01 N	120.43 W
Garlasco	62	45.12 N	8.55 E
Garlate	62	45.49 N	9.23 E
Garlate, Lago di ⊜	58	45.49 N	9.24 E
Garliava	76	54.49 N	23.52 E
Garlieston	44	54.48 N	4.22 W
Garlin	32	43.34 N	0.15 W
Garm	85	39.02 N	70.22 E
Garm Āb	120	32.14 N	65.01 E
Garmal	144	8.35 N	50.19 E
Gärmersdorf	60	49.26 N	11.54 E
Garmī	128	39.01 N	48.03 E
Garmisch-Partenkirchen	64	47.29 N	11.05 E
Garmouth	46	57.40 N	3.07 W
Garmsār	128	35.20 N	52.13 E
Garnavillo	190	42.52 N	91.14 W
Garne	261	48.41 N	1.58 E
Garner, Ia., U.S.	190	43.06 N	93.36 W
Garner, N.C., U.S.	192	35.42 N	78.36 W
Garnet Range ⋏	202	46.45 N	113.15 W
Garnett	198	38.16 N	95.14 W
Garnijskij zapovednik ♠	84	40.00 N	44.55 E
Garnish	186	47.14 N	55.22 W
Garnock ≃	46	55.38 N	4.42 W
Garnpung, Lake ⊜	166	33.30 S	143.12 E
Gāro Hills ⋏ [2]	124	25.30 N	90.30 E
Garona → Garonne ≃	32	45.02 N	0.36 W
Garonne ≃	32	45.02 N	0.36 W
Garoowe	144	8.24 N	48.29 E
Garou, Lac ⊜	150	16.04 N	2.45 W
Garoua, Cam.	146	9.18 N	13.24 E
Garoua, Niger	146	13.53 N	13.11 E
Garoua Boulaï	152	5.53 N	14.33 E
Garove Island I	164	4.40 S	149.30 E
Garpenberg	40	60.19 N	16.12 E
Garphyttan	40	59.19 N	14.56 E
Garphyttans Nationalpark ♠	40	59.17 N	14.51 E
Garqu Yan, Zhg.	118	34.29 N	92.35 E
Garqu Yan, Zhg.	120	33.50 N	92.28 E
Garraf, Costa de ⊥ [2]	266d	41.16 N	2.02 E
Garrattsville	210	42.39 N	75.10 W
Garrel	52	52.57 N	8.01 E
Garret Mountain Reservation ♠	276	40.54 N	74.11 W
Garretson	198	43.43 N	96.30 W
Garrett, In., U.S.	216	41.20 N	85.08 W
Garrett, Ky., U.S.	192	37.28 N	82.49 W
Garrett Creek ≃	222	32.57 N	95.44 W
Garrett Park	208	39.02 N	77.05 W
Garrett Park Estates	284c	39.02 N	77.06 W
Garrettsville	214	41.17 N	81.06 W
Garrison, N. Ire., U.K.	48	54.25 N	8.05 W
Garrison, Ky., U.S.	218	38.36 N	83.10 W
Garrison, Md., U.S.	208	39.24 N	76.45 W
Garrison, Mt., U.S.	202	46.31 N	112.48 W
Garrison, N.Y., U.S.	210	41.23 N	73.56 W
Garrison, N.D., U.S.	198	47.39 N	101.24 W
Garrison, Tx., U.S.	222	31.49 N	94.30 W
Garrison Dam ➜ [6]	198	47.22 N	101.25 W
Garron Point ›	48	55.03 N	5.57 W
Garros	46	57.37 N	6.11 W
Garrovillas	34	39.43 N	6.33 W
Garry ≃	46	56.43 N	3.47 W
Garry, Loch ⊜	206	45.15 N	74.43 W
Garry Bay c	176	68.55 N	85.05 W
Garry Lake ⊜	176	66.00 N	100.00 W
Gars am Kamp	61	48.36 N	15.40 E
Garsdale Head	44	54.19 N	2.20 W
Garsen	154	2.16 S	40.07 E
Garskolk	158	30.41 S	22.02 E
Gårslev	41	55.38 N	9.43 E
Garson	190	46.34 N	80.52 W
Garson Lake ⊜	184	56.19 N	110.02 W
Garstang	44	53.55 N	2.47 W
Garstedt	52	53.41 N	9.58 E
Garsten	61	48.01 N	14.24 E
Garston	260	51.41 N	0.23 W
Garston ➜ [8]	262	53.21 N	2.53 W
Garswood	262	53.29 N	2.40 W
Gartempe ≃	32	46.48 N	0.50 E
Gartenstadt ➜ [8]	263	51.30 N	7.26 E
Garthby Station (Beaulac)	206	45.50 N	71.23 W
Gartow	54	53.02 N	11.29 E
Gartrop-Bühl	263	51.40 N	6.49 E
Gartz	54	53.12 N	14.23 E
Garu	150	10.51 N	0.11 W
Garub	156	26.33 S	16.00 E
Garubhāsa	124	26.33 N	90.22 E
Gārulia	126	22.49 N	88.22 E
Garut	115a	7.13 S	107.54 E
Garve	46	57.37 N	4.42 W
Garvellachs II	46	56.14 N	5.47 W
Garvey Reservoir ⊜ [1]	280	34.13 N	118.07 W
Garvie Mountains ⋏	172	45.30 S	168.50 E
Garwin	190	42.05 N	92.40 W
Garwolin	30	51.54 N	21.37 E
Garwood, N.J., U.S.	276	40.39 N	74.19 W
Garwood, Tx., U.S.	222	29.27 N	96.24 W
Gary, In., U.S.	216	41.35 N	87.20 W
Gary, S.D., U.S.	198	44.47 N	96.27 W
Gary, Tx., U.S.	194	32.07 N	94.22 W
Gary, W.V., U.S.	192	37.21 N	81.33 W
Garyarsa	120	31.44 N	80.21 E
Gary Harbor c	278	41.38 N	87.20 W
Garyi	102	30.54 N	98.56 E
Gary Municipal Airport ⊠	278	41.37 N	87.25 W
Garysburg	208	36.27 N	77.33 W
Garz	54	54.19 N	13.20 E
Garza	252	28.09 S	63.32 W
Garza Ayala	196	26.29 N	100.02 W
Garza García	196	25.40 N	100.24 W
Garzas Creek ≃	226	37.13 N	120.57 W
Garzeno	58	46.08 N	9.15 E
Garzón, Col.	246	2.12 N	75.38 W
Garzón, Ur.	252	34.36 S	54.33 W
Gas	261	48.34 N	1.40 E
Gasan	116	13.19 N	121.51 E
Gasan-Kuli	128	37.27 N	53.59 E
Gas City	216	40.29 N	85.36 W
Gascogne □ [9]	32	44.00 N	0.05 E
Gascogne, Golfe de → Biscay, Bay of c	32	44.00 N	4.00 W
Gasconade	219	38.40 N	91.33 W
Gasconade □ [6]	219	38.27 N	91.30 W
Gasconade ≃	194	38.40 N	91.33 W
Gasconade, Osage Fork ≃	194	37.45 N	92.25 W
Gascoyne ≃	162	24.52 S	113.37 E
Gascoyne, Mount ∧	162	24.58 S	116.33 E
Gascoyne Junction	162	25.03 S	115.12 E
Gash (Nahr al-Qāsh) ≃	140	16.48 N	35.51 E
Gashaka	146	7.21 N	11.27 E
Gasherbrum I ∧	123	35.43 N	76.43 E
Gas Hu ⊜	120	38.10 N	90.42 E
Gashua	146	12.54 N	11.00 E
Gasline	284a	42.53 N	79.11 W
Gasny	50	49.05 N	1.36 E
Gaspar	252	26.56 S	48.58 W
Gaspard Creek ≃	182	51.34 N	122.17 W
Gasparilla Island I	220	26.46 N	82.16 W
Gasparilla Sound ⋓	220	26.48 N	82.15 W
Gaspé	186	48.50 N	64.29 W
Gaspé, Baie de c	186	48.46 N	64.17 W
Gaspé, Cap ›	186	48.45 N	64.10 W
Gaspé Peninsula → Gaspésie, Péninsule de la › [1]	186	48.30 N	65.00 W
Gaspereau Lake ⊜	186	44.57 N	64.34 W
Gasperina	68	38.44 N	16.30 E
Gaspésie, Parc Provincial de la ♠	186	48.55 N	66.00 W
Gaspésie, Péninsule de la › [1]	186	48.30 N	65.00 W
Gaspoltshofen	60	48.08 N	13.46 E
Gasport	210	43.11 N	78.34 W
Gaspra	78	44.27 N	34.07 E
Gassan	150	12.49 N	3.12 W
Gas-san ∧	92	38.32 N	140.01 E
Gassaway	188	38.40 N	80.46 W
Gasse	64	47.23 N	11.09 E
Gasselte	52	52.57 N	6.46 E
Gassin	62	43.13 N	6.35 E
Gassino Torinese	62	45.08 N	7.49 E
Gassol	146	8.32 N	10.28 E
Gastein → Badgastein	64	47.07 N	13.08 E
Gasteiner Tal V	64	47.11 N	13.06 E
Gasteiz → Vitoria	34	42.51 N	2.40 W
Gastello	89	49.07 N	142.58 E
Gaston, In., U.S.	216	40.18 N	85.30 W
Gaston, N.C., U.S.	192	36.30 N	77.38 W
Gaston, Or., U.S.	224	45.26 N	123.08 W
Gaston, Lake ⊜ [1]	192	36.35 N	78.00 W
Gastonia, N.C., U.S.	192	35.15 N	81.11 W
Gastonia, Tx., U.S.	222	32.37 N	96.24 W
Gastonville	279b	40.15 N	79.59 W
Gastoúni	38	37.51 N	21.16 E
Gastre	254	42.17 S	69.14 W
Gästrikland □ [9]	40	60.30 N	16.27 E
Gat	132	31.37 N	34.47 E
Gata, Cabo de ›	34	36.43 N	2.12 W
Gata, Sierra de ⋏	34	40.14 N	6.45 W
Gătaia	38	45.26 N	21.26 E
Gátas, Akrotírion ›	130	34.34 N	33.02 E
Gatčina	76	59.34 N	30.08 E
Gate	196	36.51 N	100.03 W
Gateacre ➜ [8]	262	53.23 N	2.51 W
Gate City	192	36.38 N	82.34 W
Gatehouse of Fleet	44	54.53 N	4.11 W
Gatersleben	54	51.49 N	11.17 E
Gates, N.Y., U.S.	210	43.09 N	77.41 W
Gates, N.C., U.S.	208	36.30 N	76.46 W
Gates □ [6]	208	36.28 N	76.43 W
Gateshead	44	54.58 N	1.37 W
Gateshead Island I	176	70.22 N	100.27 W
Gates Mills	279a	41.31 N	81.24 W
Gates of the Arctic National Park ♠	180	67.45 N	153.30 W
Gatesville, N.C., U.S.	192	36.24 N	76.45 W
Gatesville, Tx., U.S.	222	31.26 N	97.44 W
Gateway	200	38.40 N	108.58 W
Gateway Arch ⊍	219	38.37 N	90.12 W
Gateway National Recreation Area ♠	276	40.34 N	74.06 W
Gateway of India ⊥	272c	18.55 N	72.50 E
Gaths Mine	154	20.00 S	30.31 E
Gathurst	262	53.34 N	2.42 W
Gatié Loumo	150	15.28 N	4.37 W
Gâtine, Hauteurs de ⋏ [2]	32	46.40 N	0.50 W
Gatineau	212	45.29 N	75.38 W
Gatineau □ [6]	212	45.25 N	75.45 W
Gatineau ≃	176	45.27 N	75.40 W
Gatineau, Parc de la ♠	188	45.30 N	76.05 W
Gatley	262	53.23 N	2.14 W
Gatlinburg	192	35.42 N	83.30 W
Gato, Arroyo del ≃, Arg.	288	34.51 S	57.56 W
Gato, Arroyo del ≃, Arg.	288	34.55 S	58.37 W
Ga'ton	132	33.00 N	35.13 E
Gato Negro	286c	10.33 N	66.57 W
Gatow ➜ [8]	264a	52.29 N	13.11 E
Gatow, Flugplatz ⊠	264a	52.28 N	13.08 E
Gattendorf	61	48.01 N	16.59 E
Gattières	62	43.46 N	7.11 E
Gattinara	62	45.37 N	8.22 E
Gatton	171a	27.33 S	152.17 E
Gattorna	62	44.26 N	9.11 E
Gatún, Esclusas de ➜ [5]	236	9.16 N	79.55 W
Gatún, Lago ⊜ [1]	236	9.12 N	79.55 W
Gatvand	128	32.15 N	48.50 E
Gau-Algesheim	56	49.57 N	8.01 E
Gauchy	50	49.49 N	3.16 E
Gaucín	34	36.31 N	5.19 W
Gauer Lake ⊜	184	57.00 N	97.50 W
Gauguin, Musée ⊍	174s	17.45 S	149.23 W
Gauja ≃	76	57.09 N	24.16 E
Gaujiena	76	57.30 N	26.40 E
Gaukler Point ›	281	42.27 N	82.52 W
Gaula ≃	26	63.21 N	10.14 E
Gauley ≃	188	38.10 N	81.12 W
Gauley Bridge	188	38.10 N	81.11 W
Gaultois	186	47.36 N	55.54 W
Gaunless ≃	44	54.40 N	1.41 W
Gau-Odernheim	56	49.47 N	8.11 E
Gaur	124	26.46 N	85.17 E
Gaurain-Ramecroix	50	50.35 N	3.29 E
Gaurambha	126	22.39 N	89.34 E
Gaurela	124	22.45 N	81.54 E
Gaurhāti	126	22.46 N	87.48 E
Gauribaradia	126	23.45 N	89.52 E
Gauribidanūr	122	13.37 N	77.31 E
Gauri Phānta	124	28.41 N	80.33 E
Gauripur	124	26.05 N	89.58 E
Gaurīśaṅgkar ∧	124	27.57 N	86.21 E
Gaurnadi	126	22.58 N	90.14 E
Gause	222	30.47 N	96.43 W
Gausta ∧	26	59.50 N	8.35 E
Gauthiot, Chutes ∟	146	9.43 N	14.34 E
Gauting	60	48.04 N	11.23 E
Gavà	34	41.18 N	2.01 E
Gāvanpāda	272c	18.57 N	73.01 E
Gavardo	64	45.35 N	10.26 E
Gávdhos I	38	34.50 N	24.06 E
Gávea ➜ [8]	287a	22.58 S	43.14 W
Gávea, Hipódromo da ♠	287a	22.58 S	43.13 W
Gávea, Pedra da ∧	287a	23.00 S	43.17 W
Gavel-Långsjön ⊜	40	59.50 N	18.18 E
Gavello	64	45.01 N	11.55 E
Gavet	62	45.04 N	5.52 E
Gavi	62	44.41 N	8.49 E
Gavia, Arroyo de la ≃	266a	40.21 N	3.40 W
Gavião ≃	255	14.06 S	41.01 W
Gavião, Pico do ∧	256	21.37 S	44.50 W
Gavien	164	3.54 S	144.07 E
Gavilán	286c	10.24 N	66.51 W
Gavinana	66	44.05 N	10.45 E
Gavins Point Dam ➜ [6]	198	42.48 N	97.40 W
Gaviões	256	22.34 S	42.33 W
Gavirate	62	45.50 N	8.43 E
Gavja ≃	76	53.49 N	25.35 E
Gāv Khūnī, Bātlāq-e ≡	128	32.10 N	52.50 E
Gävle	40	60.40 N	17.10 E
Gävleborgs Län □ [6]	26	61.30 N	16.15 E
Gävlebukten c	40	60.42 N	17.20 E
Gavnø	41	55.11 N	11.44 E
Gavoi	71	40.10 N	9.12 E
Gavorrano	66	42.55 N	10.54 E
Gavrilov-Jam	80	57.18 N	39.51 E
Gavrilovka	83	48.37 N	37.31 E
Gavrilovka Vtoraja	80	52.53 N	42.46 E
Gavrilov Posad	80	56.33 N	40.07 E
Gávrion	38	37.52 N	24.46 E
Gavry	76	56.55 N	27.53 E
Gawachab	156	27.03 S	17.50 E
Gāwān	124	24.37 N	85.55 E
Gaweinstal	61	48.28 N	16.35 E
Gāwīlgarh Hills ⋏ [2]	122	21.20 N	77.00 E
Gawler	168b	34.37 S	138.44 E
Gawler ≃	168b	34.41 S	138.27 E
Gawler Ranges ⋏	162	32.30 S	136.00 E
Gawso	150	6.48 N	2.31 W
Gawsworth	262	53.13 N	2.10 W
Gawthorpe Hall ⊥	262	53.48 N	2.18 W
Gaxun Nur (Juyanhai) ⊜	102	42.22 N	100.34 E
Gaya, India	124	24.47 N	85.00 E
Gaya, Niger	150	11.53 N	3.27 E
Gaya, Nig.	150	11.53 N	9.02 E
Gay City State Park ♠	207	41.42 N	72.28 W
Gayéri	150	12.39 N	0.29 E
Gay Head	207	41.20 N	70.48 W
Gay Hill	222	30.16 N	96.30 W
Gaylord, Mi., U.S.	190	45.01 N	84.40 W
Gaylord, Mn., U.S.	190	44.33 N	94.13 W
Gaylordsville	207	41.38 N	73.29 W
Gayndah	166	25.37 S	151.36 E
Gays Mills	190	43.19 N	90.50 W
Gayton, Eng., U.K.	42	52.45 N	0.34 E
Gayton, Eng., U.K.	262	53.19 N	3.06 W
Gayt on Sands ✢ [4]	262	53.17 N	3.07 W
Gaza □ [5]	156	23.30 S	32.45 E
Gaza → Ghazzah	128	31.30 N	34.28 E
Gazalkent	85	41.33 N	69.47 E
Gazaoua	150	13.32 N	7.55 E
Gaza Strip □ [9]	132	31.25 N	34.20 E
Gazelle Channel ⋓	164	2.50 S	150.55 E
Gazelle Peninsula › [1]	164	4.40 S	152.00 E
Gazeran	261	48.38 N	1.46 E
Gazeran, Bois de ♠	261	48.40 N	1.45 E
Gazi, Kenya	154	4.25 S	39.30 E
Gazi, Zaïre	154	1.04 N	24.31 E
Gaziantep	130	37.05 N	37.22 E
Gaziantep □ [4]	130	37.00 N	37.20 E
Gazimağusa (Famagusta)	130	35.07 N	33.57 E
Gazimağusa Körfezi c	130	35.15 N	34.10 E
Gazimur ≃	88	52.57 N	120.22 E
Gazimurskij Zavod	88	51.33 N	118.22 E
Gazipaşa	130	36.17 N	32.20 E
Gazira Sporting Club ♠	273c	30.04 N	31.13 E
Gazivoda Jezero ⊜ [1]	38	42.55 N	20.40 E
Gaznau	85	40.10 N	71.02 E
Gazoldo degli Ippoliti	64	45.12 N	10.35 E
Gazos Creek ≃	226	37.10 N	122.22 W
Gazzada	62	45.47 N	8.51 E
Gazzaniga	62	45.48 N	9.50 E
Gazzuolo	64	45.04 N	10.35 E
Gbangbatok	150	7.48 N	12.23 W
Gbanhala ≃	150	10.14 N	8.38 W
Gbaoui Bodanga	152	5.33 N	16.45 E
Gbarnga	150	7.00 N	9.29 W
Gbogbo	273a	6.36 N	3.31 E
Gboko	150	7.20 N	8.57 E
Gbon	150	9.50 N	6.27 W
Gbwado	152	3.54 N	20.46 E
Gcoverega	156	19.08 S	24.15 E
Gdańsk (Danzig)	30	54.23 N	18.40 E
Gdańsk □ [4]	30	54.15 N	18.25 E
Gdansk, Gulf of c	30	54.40 N	19.15 E
Gden'	78	51.20 N	30.25 E
Gdov	76	58.44 N	27.48 E
Gdyel	34	35.48 N	0.26 W
Gdynia	30	54.32 N	18.33 E
Gearhart	224	46.01 N	123.54 W
Gearhart Mountain ∧	202	42.30 N	120.53 W
Gearhartville	214	40.53 N	78.15 W
Geary, N.B., Can.	186	45.46 N	66.29 W
Geary, Ok., U.S.	196	35.43 N	98.22 W
Geauga □ [6]	214	41.35 N	81.12 W
Geauga Lake Park ♠	279a	41.21 N	81.23 W
Geba ≃	150	11.46 N	15.36 W
Gebaberg ∧	56	50.36 N	10.16 E
Gebe, Pulau I	164	0.05 S	129.20 E
Gebeit Mine	140	21.03 N	36.19 E
Gebenbach	60	49.32 N	11.53 E
Gebesee	54	51.07 N	10.56 E
Gebi	84	42.46 N	43.30 E
Gebilu	144	10.35 N	41.28 E
Gebiz	130	37.06 N	30.56 E
Gebra	54	51.24 N	10.35 E
Gebweiler → Guebwiller	58	47.55 N	7.12 E
Gebze	130	40.48 N	29.25 E
Gecha	144	7.31 N	35.22 E
Gechang	106	31.05 N	119.27 E
Geçitkale	130	35.15 N	33.45 E
Gecun	106	32.10 N	119.37 E
Geddes, Mi., U.S.	281	42.16 N	83.40 W
Geddes, S.D., U.S.	198	43.15 N	98.41 W
Gede, Gunung ∧	115a	6.47 S	106.59 E
Gedera	132	31.49 N	34.46 E
Gedern	56	50.25 N	9.12 E
Gedian	100	30.32 N	114.38 E
Gedikler	130	39.06 N	38.49 E
Gediksaray	130	40.27 N	35.38 E
Gedi National Monument ♠	154	3.19 S	40.03 E
Gedinne	56	49.59 N	4.56 E
Gediz	130	39.02 N	29.25 E
Gediz ≃	130	38.35 N	26.48 E
Gedlegube	144	6.52 N	45.02 E
Gedo	144	8.58 N	37.27 E
Gedo □ [4]	144	3.00 N	42.00 E
Gedongdalem	112	5.04 S	105.25 E
Gedongtataan	115a	5.23 S	105.05 E
Gedser	41	54.35 N	11.57 E
Gedser Odde ›	41	54.34 N	11.59 E
Geduld	273d	26.15 S	28.25 E
Gedun	100	27.39 N	118.26 E
Geebung	171a	27.22 S	153.03 E
Gee Cross	262	53.26 N	2.04 W
Geehi	171b	36.24 S	148.11 E
Geehi ≃	171b	36.11 S	148.02 E
Geel	56	51.10 N	5.00 E
Geelong	169	38.08 S	144.21 E
Geelong West	169	38.08 S	144.20 E
Geelvink Channel ⋓	162	28.30 S	114.10 E
Geer ≃	56	50.51 N	5.42 E
Geeste ≃	52	53.32 N	8.35 E
Geesthacht	52	53.26 N	10.22 E
Geeveston	166	43.10 S	146.55 E
Gefell	54	50.26 N	11.52 E
Gefle → Gävle	40	60.40 N	17.10 E
Gefrees	54	50.06 N	11.44 E
Gegang	100	30.04 N	117.38 E
Gegenmiao	89	45.58 N	122.15 E
Gegong	100	30.05 N	117.11 E
Gegou	98	35.24 N	118.32 E
Gegu	105	38.59 N	117.30 E
Gehackte Berge ⋏ [2]	264a	52.41 N	13.30 E
Gehrden	52	52.18 N	9.36 E
Gehren	54	50.39 N	10.59 E
Gehu	100	27.46 N	119.16 E
Ge Hu ⊜	106	31.36 N	119.51 E
Gehua	164	10.20 S	150.25 E
Geidam	146	12.57 N	11.57 E
Geiger	194	32.52 N	88.18 W
Geigertown	208	40.13 N	75.50 W
Geihoku	96	34.44 N	132.17 E
Geikie ≃	176	57.45 N	103.52 W
Geilenkirchen	56	50.57 N	6.07 E
Geilo	26	60.31 N	8.12 E
Geinō	94	34.48 N	136.25 E
Geiranger	26	62.06 N	7.12 E
Geisa	56	50.43 N	9.57 E
Geisberg ∧	60	49.53 N	11.03 E
Geisecke	263	51.27 N	7.37 E
Geisei	96	33.31 N	133.49 E
Geiselhöring	60	48.50 N	12.23 E
Geisenfeld	60	48.41 N	11.37 E
Geisenhausen	60	48.28 N	12.15 E
Geisenheim	56	49.59 N	7.58 E
Geisingen	58	47.55 N	8.38 E
Geislingen an der Steige	56	48.36 N	9.50 E
Geismar	52	51.31 N	9.57 E
Geispolsheim	58	48.31 N	7.39 E
Geisstein ∧	64	47.20 N	12.30 E
Geistenbeck ➜ [8]	263	51.09 N	6.27 E
Geistown	214	40.17 N	78.52 W
Geist Reservoir ⊜ [1], In., U.S.	218	39.56 N	85.56 W
Geist Reservoir ⊜ [1], Pa., U.S.	285	39.57 N	75.24 W
Geisweid	56	50.55 N	8.01 E
Geita	154	2.52 S	32.10 E
Geithain	54	51.03 N	12.41 E
Geiyō-shotō II	96	34.10 N	132.45 E
Gejah	272a	28.31 N	77.23 E
Gejiatun	98	40.27 N	119.55 E
Gejiu (Kokiu)	102	23.22 N	103.06 E
Geka, mys ›	180	64.26 N	178.10 E
Gela	70	37.04 N	14.15 E
Gela ≃	70	37.03 N	14.15 E
Gela, Golfo di c	70	37.03 N	14.10 E
Geladandong ∧	120	33.16 N	91.27 E
Geladi	144	6.57 N	46.25 E
Gelai ∧ [1]	154	2.33 S	36.05 E
Gelan	102	30.03 N	107.04 E
Gelang, Tanjong ›	114	3.58 N	103.26 E
Gelaochang	107	29.36 N	103.39 E
Gelasa, Selat ⋓	112	2.40 S	107.15 E
Gelber Fluss → Huang ≃	90	37.32 N	118.19 E
Gelbes Meer → Yellow Sea ⊤ [2]	90	36.00 N	123.00 E
Gelderland □ [4]	52	52.10 N	5.50 E
Geldermalsen	52	51.53 N	5.17 E
Geldern	52	51.31 N	6.20 E
Geldrop	52	51.25 N	5.33 E
Geleen	56	50.58 N	5.52 E

DEUTSCH

Name	Seite	Breite°′	Länge°′ E = Ost
Gelembe	130	39.10 N	27.50 E
Gelemso	144	8.48 N	40.35 E
Gelenau	54	50.42 N	12.58 E
Gelendost	130	38.07 N	31.01 E
Gelendžik	78	44.33 N	38.06 E
Gelfingen	58	47.13 N	8.16 E
Gelgaudiškis	76	55.05 N	23.00 E
Gelib → Jilib	144	0.29 N	42.46 E
Gelibolu	130	40.24 N	26.40 E
Gelibolu Yarımadası (Gallipoli Peninsula) › [1]	130	40.20 N	26.30 E
Gelibolu Yarımadası Milli Parkı ♠	130	40.05 N	26.10 E
Gelinden	56	50.46 N	5.15 E
Gélise ≃	32	44.11 N	0.17 E
Geliting	115b	8.39 S	122.18 E
Geliting, Teluk c	115b	8.36 S	122.17 E
Gellénháza	61	46.46 N	16.47 E
Gellenstrom ⋓	54	54.28 N	13.03 E
Gellep-Stratum ➜ [8]	263	51.20 N	6.41 E
Gellibrand ≃	169	38.41 S	143.09 E
Gellibrand, Mount ∧ [2]	169	38.14 S	143.48 E
Gellibrand, Point ›	274b	37.52 S	144.54 E
Gellibrand River	169	38.32 S	143.32 E
Gellingen → Ghislenghien	50	50.39 N	3.52 E
Gellinsoor	144	6.26 N	46.42 E
Gel'm'azov	78	49.49 N	31.49 E
Gelnhausen	56	50.11 N	9.11 E
Gelså ≃	41	55.19 N	8.54 E
Gelsdorf	56	50.35 N	7.02 E
Gelsenkirchen	52	51.31 N	7.07 E
Gelsenkirchen-Horst, Galopprennbahn ♠	263	51.32 N	7.02 E
Gelsted	41	55.24 N	9.59 E
Gelt ≃	44	54.56 N	2.47 W
Geltendorf	60	48.07 N	11.01 E
Gelterkinden	58	47.28 N	7.51 E
Gelting	41	54.45 N	9.53 E
Geltow	54	52.22 N	12.58 E
Geltsa	144	6.14 N	37.05 E
Geluji	98	37.08 N	121.50 E
Geluksburg	158	28.30 S	29.33 E
Geluwe	50	50.48 N	3.04 E
Gemas	114	2.35 N	102.37 E
Gembloux	56	50.34 N	4.41 E
Gembrook	169	37.57 S	145.33 E
Gemen	52	51.51 N	6.52 E
Gemena	152	3.15 N	19.46 E
Gémenos	62	43.18 N	5.38 E
Gemerek	130	39.11 N	36.05 E
Gemert	52	51.34 N	5.40 E
Gemla	26	56.52 N	14.38 E
Gemlik	130	40.26 N	29.09 E
Gemlik Körfezi c	130	40.25 N	28.55 E
Gemolong	115a	7.24 S	110.50 E
Gemona del Friuli	64	46.16 N	13.09 E
Gemonio	62	45.53 N	8.40 E
Gemsbok National Park ♠	156	25.15 S	21.10 E
Gemünd	56	50.34 N	6.30 E
Gemünden, Dtsch.	56	50.03 N	9.41 E
Gemünden, Dtsch.	56	50.58 N	8.58 E
Gemünden, Dtsch.	56	49.54 N	7.28 E
Gen ≃	89	50.16 N	119.22 E
Genadendal	158	34.02 S	19.33 E
Genaibashi	268	35.21 N	140.04 E
Genale (Jubba) ≃	144	0.15 S	42.38 E
Genappe	50	50.36 N	4.27 E
Genarp	41	55.36 N	13.23 E
Genazzano	66	41.50 N	12.58 E
Genç	130	38.46 N	40.35 E
Gençay	32	46.23 N	0.24 E
Gencek	130	37.27 N	31.33 E
Gencsapáti	61	47.17 N	16.36 E
Gending	115a	7.48 S	113.18 E
Gendrey	58	47.12 N	5.41 E
Gendringen	52	51.52 N	6.22 E
Gendt	52	51.53 N	5.59 E
Genegantslet Creek ≃	210	42.18 N	75.48 W
Genemuiden	52	52.37 N	6.07 E
General ≃	236	8.59 N	83.11 W
General Acha	252	37.23 S	64.36 W
General Alvear, Arg.	252	36.03 S	60.01 W
General Alvear, Arg.	252	34.58 S	67.42 W
General Aquino	252	24.26 S	56.42 W
General Arenales	252	34.18 S	61.18 W
General Belgrano	252	35.46 S	58.30 W
General Bernardo O'Higgins ⊍ [3]	9	63.19 S	57.54 W
General Bravo	232	25.48 N	99.10 W
General Butler State Resort Park ♠	218	38.40 N	85.10 W
General Cabrera	252	32.48 S	63.52 W
General Campos	252	31.32 S	58.24 W
General Carneiro	255	15.42 S	52.45 W
General Carrera, Lago (Lago Buenos Aires) ⊜	254	46.35 S	72.00 W
General Cepeda	232	25.23 N	101.27 W
General Conesa, Arg.	252	36.30 S	57.20 W
General Conesa, Arg.	254	40.06 S	64.26 W
General Daniel Cerri	252	38.42 S	62.24 W
General del Sur, Cementerio ➜	286c	10.28 N	66.55 W
General Elizardo Aquino	252	26.53 S	56.17 W
General Enrique Martínez	252	33.12 S	53.48 W
General Enrique Mosconi	252	22.36 S	63.49 W
General Escobedo, Méx.	196	25.49 N	100.20 W
General Escobedo, Méx.	232	25.30 N	105.15 W
General Eugenio A. Garay, Para.	248	20.31 S	62.08 W
General Eugenio A. Garay, Para.	252	25.55 S	56.11 W
General Galarza	252	32.43 S	59.24 W
General Güemes	252	24.40 S	65.03 W
General Guido	252	36.40 S	57.46 W
General Hornos	258	34.53 S	58.56 W
General Island I	116	9.25 N	126.00 E
General José de San Martín	252	26.33 S	59.21 W
General Juan José Ríos	232	25.40 N	108.40 W
General Juan Madariaga	252	37.00 S	57.09 W
General La Madrid	252	37.16 S	61.17 W
General Las Heras	258	34.56 S	58.57 W
General Las Heras □ [5]	288	34.56 S	58.51 W
General Lavalle	252	36.24 S	56.58 W
General Leonidas Plaza Gutiérrez	246	2.58 S	78.25 W
General Levalle	252	34.01 S	63.56 W
General Lorenzo Vintter	254	40.44 S	64.29 W
General Luna	116	9.47 N	126.09 E
General MacArthur (Pambuhan Sur)	116	11.15 N	125.32 E
General Mansilla (Bartolomé Bavio)	258	35.05 S	57.45 W
General Manuel Belgrano, Cerro ∧	252	29.01 S	67.49 W
General Mitchell Field ⊠	216	42.57 N	87.54 W
General Motors Corporation (Pontiac Division) ⊍ [3]	281	42.49 N	83.17 W
General Motors Proving Grounds ⊍ [3]	281	42.35 N	83.41 W
General Motors Technical Center ⊍ [3]	281	42.31 N	83.02 W

Symbols in the index entries represent the broad categories identified in the key at the right. Symbols with superior numbers (⋏[1]) identify subcategories (see complete key on page *I · 1*).

Symbole im Register stellen die rechts im Schlüssel erklärten Kategorien dar. Symbole mit hochgestellten Ziffern (⋏[1]) bezeichnen Unterabteilungen einer Kategorie (vgl. vollständiger Schlüssel auf Seite *I · 1*).

Los símbolos incluidos en el texto del índice representan las grandes categorías identificadas con la clave a la derecha. Los símbolos con números en su parte superior (⋏[1]) identifican las subcategorías (véase la clave completa en la página *I · 1*).

Les symboles de l'index représentent les catégories indiquées dans la légende à droite. Les symboles suivis d'un indice (⋏[1]) représentent des sous-catégories (voir légende complète à la page *I · 1*).

Os símbolos incluídos no texto do índice representam as grandes categorias identificadas com a chave à direita. Os símbolos com números em sua parte superior (⋏[1]) identificam as subcategorias (veja-se a chave completa à página *I · 1*).

∧ Mountain	Berg	Montaña	Montagne	Montanha
⋏ Mountains	Gebirge	Montañas	Montagnes	Montanhas
)(Pass	Paß	Paso	Col	Passo
V Valley, Canyon	Tal, Cañon	Valle, Cañón	Vallée, Canyon	Vale, Canhão
≍ Plain	Ebene	Llano	Plaine	Planície
› Cape	Kap	Cabo	Cap	Cabo
I Island	Insel	Isla	Île	Ilha
II Islands	Inseln	Islas	Îles	Ilhas
⊥ Other Topographic Features	Andere Topographische Objekte	Otros Elementos Topográficos	Autres données topographiques	Outros acidentes topográficos

Gene-Girg I · 61

ESPAÑOL | **FRANÇAIS** | **PORTUGUÊS**

Nombre / Nom / Nome	Página / Page / Página	Lat.°′	Long.°′ W = Oeste / W = Ouest / W = Oeste
General'nyj ≃	265a	60.00 N	30.32 E
General O'Brien	252	34.54 S	60.45 W
General Pacheco	288	34.28 S	58.38 W
General Pánfilo Natera	234	22.40 N	102.06 W
General Paz	258	35.31 S	58.19 W
General Pico	252	35.40 S	63.44 W
General Pinedo	252	27.19 S	61.17 W
General Pinto	252	34.46 S	61.53 W
General Pizarro	252	24.13 S	64.01 W
General Roca	252	39.02 S	67.35 W
General Rodríguez	258	34.36 S	58.57 W
General San Martín, Arg.	252	37.59 S	63.34 W
General San Martín, Arg.	258	34.34 S	58.32 W
General San Martín □[5]	288	34.34 S	58.34 W
General Santos (Dadiangas)	116	6.07 N	125.11 E
General Sarmiento	258	34.33 S	58.43 W
General Sarmiento □[5]	288	34.32 S	58.43 W
General'skoje	83	47.28 N	39.35 E
General Terán	232	25.16 N	99.41 W
General Tinio	116	15.21 N	121.03 E
General Toševo	38	43.42 N	28.02 E
General Treviño	196	26.14 N	99.29 W
General Viamonte (Los Toldos)	252	35.01 S	61.01 W
General Villegas	252	35.02 S	63.01 W
General Vintter, Lago (Lago Palena) ⊜	254	43.55 S	71.40 W
General Warren Village	285	40.02 N	75.32 W
General Zuazua	196	25.54 N	100.07 W
Genesee, Id., U.S.	202	46.33 N	116.55 W
Genesee, Pa., U.S.	214	41.59 N	77.52 W
Genesee, Wi., U.S.	216	42.58 N	88.21 W
Genesee □[6], Mi., U.S.	216	42.56 N	83.41 W
Genesee □[6], N.Y., U.S.	210	43.00 N	78.11 W
Genesee ≃	210	43.16 N	77.36 W
Geneseo, Il., U.S.	190	41.26 N	90.09 W
Geneseo, Ks., U.S.	198	38.30 N	98.09 W
Geneseo, N.Y., U.S.	210	42.47 N	77.49 W
Gênes → Genova	62	44.25 N	8.57 E
Geneva, S. Afr.	158	27.50 S	27.08 E
Geneva, Al., U.S.	194	31.01 N	85.51 W
Geneva, Fl., U.S.	220	28.44 N	81.07 W
Geneva, Il., U.S.	216	41.53 N	88.18 W
Geneva, In., U.S.	216	40.35 N	84.57 W
Geneva, Ne., U.S.	198	40.31 N	97.35 W
Geneva, N.Y., U.S.	210	42.52 N	77.00 W
Geneva, Oh., U.S.	214	41.48 N	80.56 W
Geneva, Pa., U.S.	214	41.35 N	80.14 W
Geneva, Wa., U.S.	224	48.45 N	122.24 W
Geneva, Lake (Lac Léman) (Lac de Gèneve) ⊜, Europe	58	46.25 N	6.30 E
Geneva, Lake ⊜, Wi., U.S.	216	42.34 N	88.30 W
Geneva → Genève	58	46.12 N	6.09 E
Geneva-on-the-Lake	214	41.52 N	80.57 W
Genève (Geneva)	58	46.12 N	6.09 E
Genève □[3]	58	46.15 N	6.10 E
Genève, Lac de → Geneva, Lake ⊜	58	46.25 N	6.30 E
Genève-Cointrin, Aéroport ⊠	58	46.14 N	6.06 E
Genevois ◂[1]	58	46.03 N	6.14 E
Genévriers, Île des I	186	51.15 N	58.26 W
Genf → Genève	58	46.12 N	6.09 E
Genga	66	43.26 N	12.56 E
Gengenbach	58	48.24 N	8.01 E
Genghis Khan, Wall of ⊥, Asia	88	49.00 N	115.00 E
Genghis Khan, Wall of ⊥, Mong.	88	49.00 N	116.00 E
Gengji	100	33.47 N	112.47 E
Gengma	102	23.34 N	99.06 E
Gengputou	106	31.12 N	119.55 E
Gengzhuang	104	40.59 N	122.42 E
Geničesk	78	46.11 N	34.48 E
Génicourt	261	49.05 N	2.04 E
Génicourt-sur-Meuse	56	49.02 N	5.26 E
Genil ≃	34	37.42 N	5.19 W
Génissiat	58	46.03 N	5.47 E
Genk	56	50.58 N	5.30 E
Genkai	96	33.51 N	130.30 E
Genkai-kokutei-kōen ♠	96	33.54 N	130.31 E
Genkai-nada ⊤[2]	92	34.00 N	130.00 E
Genkanyj, chrebet ⩕	180	66.15 N	172.20 W
Genlis	58	47.14 N	5.13 E
Gennach ≃	58	48.10 N	10.43 E
Gennargentu, Monti del ⩕	71	40.01 N	9.19 E
Gennebreck	263	51.19 N	7.12 E
Gennep	52	51.42 N	5.58 E
Genner	41	55.07 N	9.26 E
Gennes	32	47.20 N	0.14 W
Gennevilliers	261	48.56 N	2.18 E
Genoa, Austl.	166	37.29 S	149.35 E
Genoa, Il., U.S.	216	42.05 N	88.41 W
Genoa, Ne., U.S.	198	41.26 N	97.43 W
Genoa, Nv., U.S.	226	39.00 N	119.50 W
Genoa, N.Y., U.S.	210	42.40 N	76.32 W
Genoa, Oh., U.S.	214	41.31 N	83.21 W
Genoa, Wi., U.S.	190	43.34 N	91.13 W
Genoa, Arroyo ≃	254	44.58 S	70.06 W
Genoa City	216	42.29 N	88.19 W
Genoa → Genova	62	44.25 N	8.57 E
Genoa Peak ʌ	226	39.03 N	119.53 W
Genola	62	44.35 N	7.39 E
Génolhac	62	44.21 N	3.57 E
Genova (Genoa)	62	44.25 N	8.57 E
Genova □[4]	62	44.30 N	9.04 E
Genova, Golfo di ᑕ	62	44.10 N	8.55 E
Genova, Val V	64	46.11 N	10.40 E
Genovesa, Isla I	246a	0.20 N	89.58 W
Genrijetty, ostrov I	74	77.06 N	156.30 E
Gensan → Wŏnsan	98	39.09 N	127.25 E
Gens de Terre ≃	190	46.53 N	76.00 W
Genshagen	264a	52.19 N	13.19 E
Genshagener Heide ◂[3]	264a	52.20 N	13.18 E
Genshiryoku-kenkyūsho ʊ[3]	94	36.27 N	140.36 E
Gensingen	56	49.53 N	7.55 E
Gensungen	56	51.08 N	9.26 E
Gent (Gand)	50	51.03 N	3.43 E
Gentbrugge	50	51.03 N	3.45 E
Gent-Brugge, Kanaal ≅	50	51.03 N	3.43 E
Genteng	115a	8.22 S	114.09 E
Genteng, Gili I	115a	7.12 S	113.54 E
Genteng, Tanjung ›	115a	7.23 S	106.24 E
Genthin	54	52.24 N	12.09 E
Gentilly	261	48.49 N	2.21 E
Gentilly ≃	206	46.24 N	72.21 W
Genting	114	3.42 N	98.10 E
Gentio do Ouro	250	11.25 S	42.30 W
Gentioux	32	45.47 N	1.59 E
Gentofte	41	55.45 N	12.33 E
Gentry	194	36.16 N	94.29 W
Gentry, Lake ⊜	220	28.08 N	81.15 W
Genua → Genova	62	44.25 N	8.57 E
Genuang	114	2.29 N	102.53 E
Genval	50	50.43 N	4.29 E
Genyem	164	2.46 S	140.12 E
Genzano di Lucania	68	40.51 N	16.02 E
Genzano di Roma	66	41.42 N	12.41 E
Geographe Bay ᑕ	162	33.35 S	115.15 E
Geographe Channel ʯ	162	24.40 S	113.20 E
Geokčaj	84	40.39 N	47.44 E
Geokčaj ≃	84	40.39 N	47.45 E
Geok-Tepe	128	38.09 N	57.58 E
Geonkhāli	126	22.12 N	88.03 E
George, S. Afr.	158	33.58 S	22.24 E
George, Ia., U.S.	198	43.20 N	96.00 W
George, Tx., U.S.	222	30.59 N	96.07 W
George ≃, Austl.	162	20.50 S	117.28 E
George ≃, P.Q., Can.	176	58.49 N	66.10 W
George, Cape ›	186	45.53 N	61.53 W
George, Lake ⊜, Austl.	162	22.37 S	123.38 E
George, Lake ⊜, Austl.	166	35.05 S	149.25 E
George, Lake ⊜, N.A.	190	46.28 N	84.10 W
George, Lake ⊜, Ug.	154	0.02 N	30.12 E
George, Lake ⊜, U.S.	216	41.45 N	85.00 W
George, Lake ⊜, Fl., U.S.	192	29.17 N	81.36 W
George, Lake ⊜, In., U.S.	216	41.40 N	87.30 W
George, Lake ⊜, N.Y., U.S.	188	43.35 N	73.35 W
George Air Force Base ■	228	34.35 N	117.22 W
George B. Stevenson Dam ◂[6]	214	41.25 N	78.01 W
George Gill Range ⩕	162	24.15 S	131.36 E
George H. Crosby Manitou State Park ♠	190	47.29 N	91.10 W
George Island I	254	52.19 S	59.45 W
George Mason University ʊ[2]	284c	38.50 N	77.17 W
Georgensgmünd	56	49.11 N	11.00 E
Georgenthal	54	50.49 N	10.40 E
Georges ≃	170	33.57 S	150.58 E
Georges Bank ⊹[4]	16	41.15 N	67.30 W
Georges Island I	283	42.19 N	70.56 W
George Sound ʯ	172	44.50 S	167.23 E
Georges River Bridge ◂[5]	274a	34.00 S	151.07 E
Georges Run	214	40.21 N	80.37 W
Georges Run ≃	279b	40.23 N	80.06 W
Georgetown, Austl.	166	18.18 S	143.33 E
George Town, Austl.	166	41.06 S	146.50 E
Georgetown, P.E., Can.	186	46.11 N	62.32 W
George Town, Cay. Is.	238	19.18 N	81.23 W
Georgetown, Gam.	150	13.30 N	14.47 W
Georgetown, Guy.	246	6.48 N	58.10 W
George Town (Pinang), Malay.	114	5.25 N	100.20 E
Georgetown, St. Vin.	241h	13.16 N	61.08 W
Georgetown, Ca., U.S.	226	38.54 N	120.50 W
Georgetown, Co., U.S.	200	39.42 N	105.41 W
Georgetown, Ct., U.S.	207	41.15 N	73.26 W
Georgetown, De., U.S.	208	38.41 N	75.23 W
Georgetown, Fl., U.S.	192	29.23 N	81.38 W
Georgetown, Ga., U.S.	192	31.53 N	85.06 W
Georgetown, Id., U.S.	202	42.29 N	111.22 W
Georgetown, Il., U.S.	194	39.58 N	87.38 W
Georgetown, In., U.S.	218	38.17 N	85.58 W
Georgetown, Ky., U.S.	218	38.12 N	84.33 W
Georgetown, Ma., U.S.	207	42.43 N	70.59 W
Georgetown, Ms., U.S.	194	31.52 N	90.09 W
Georgetown, N.J., U.S.	285	40.04 N	74.39 W
Georgetown, N.Y., U.S.	210	42.46 N	75.44 W
Georgetown, Oh., U.S.	218	38.51 N	83.54 W
Georgetown, Pa., U.S.	214	40.39 N	80.30 W
Georgetown, S.C., U.S.	192	33.22 N	79.17 W
Georgetown, Tx., U.S.	222	30.37 N	97.40 W
Georgetown ◂[8]	284c	38.54 N	77.03 W
Georgetown, Lake ⊜[1]	222	30.40 N	97.45 W
Georgetown → Halton Hills	190	43.37 N	79.56 W
Georgetown Lake ⊜	202	46.11 N	113.17 W
Georgetown Rowley State Forest ♠	283	42.42 N	70.58 W
Georgetown University ʊ[2]	284c	38.54 N	77.04 W
George V Coast ±[2]	9	68.30 S	147.30 E
George VI Sound ʯ	9	71.00 S	68.00 W
George Washington Birthplace National Monument ♠	208	38.11 N	76.56 W
George Washington Bridge ◂[5]	276	40.51 N	73.57 W
George Washington Carver National Monument ♠	194	37.00 N	94.19 W
George West	196	28.19 N	98.07 W
Georg Forster ʊ[3]	9	70.47 S	11.51 E
Georgia □[1], Asia	72	42.00 N	44.00 E
Georgia □[1], Asia	84	42.00 N	44.00 E
Georgia □[3], U.S.	178	32.50 N	83.15 W
Georgia □[3], U.S.	192	32.50 N	83.15 W
Georgia, Strait of ʯ	182	49.20 N	124.00 W
Georgia del Sur, Isla de → South Georgia I	244	54.15 S	36.45 W
Georgia Heights	278	41.32 N	87.20 W
Georgiana	194	31.38 N	86.44 W
Georgian Bay ᑕ	190	45.15 N	80.50 W
Georgian Bay Islands National Park ♠	190	44.54 N	79.52 W
Géorgie du Sud → South Georgia I	244	54.15 S	36.45 W
Georgijevka, Kaz.	85	42.11 N	70.00 E
Georgijevka, Kaz.	85	43.03 N	74.43 E
Georgijevka, Kaz.	86	49.19 N	81.35 E
Georgijevka, Ross.	80	53.18 N	51.01 E
Georgijevka, Ukr.	83	48.26 N	39.17 E
Georgijevsk	84	44.09 N	43.28 E
Georgina ≃	166	23.30 S	139.47 E
Georgina Island I	212	44.23 N	79.17 W
Georgina Island Indian Reserve ◂[4]	212	44.22 N	79.19 W
Georgsmarienhütte	52	52.12 N	8.02 E
Georg von Neumayer ʊ[3]	9	70.37 S	8.22 W
Gera	54	50.52 N	12.04 E
Gera ≃	54	51.08 N	10.56 E
Geraardsbergen	50	50.46 N	3.52 E
Geraberg	54	50.43 N	10.50 E
Gerabronn	56	49.15 N	9.55 E
Gerace	68	38.16 N	16.13 E
Geraci Siculo	70	37.51 N	14.09 E
Geral, Serra ±[4], Bra.	250	11.15 S	46.30 W
Geral, Serra ±[4], Bra.	252	26.30 S	50.30 W
Gerald	219	38.23 N	91.19 W
Geral de Goiás, Serra ±[4]	242	13.00 S	46.15 W
Geraldine, N.Z.	172	44.05 S	171.14 E
Geraldine, Mt., U.S.	202	47.36 N	110.15 W
Geraldton, Austl.	162	28.46 S	114.36 E
Geraldton, On., Can.	176	49.44 N	86.57 W
Gerar, Naḥal V	132	31.24 N	34.26 E
Gerard, Lake ⊜	276	41.06 N	74.33 W
Gerard, Mount ʌ	162	27.13 S	122.41 E
Gérardmer	58	48.04 N	6.53 E
Geras	61	48.48 N	15.40 E
Gerasa ⊥	132	32.17 N	35.53 E
Gerasdorf	61	48.18 N	16.28 E
Gerasimovka	86	58.37 N	71.53 E
Gerber	204	40.03 N	122.08 W
Gerber Reservoir ⊜[1]	202	42.12 N	121.06 W
Gerbéviller	58	48.30 N	6.31 E
Gerblingerode	52	51.29 N	10.15 E
Gerbstedt	54	51.38 N	11.37 E
Gerca	78	48.09 N	26.16 E
Gerchsheim	56	49.42 N	9.47 E
Gercüş	130	37.34 N	41.23 E
Gerdau	158	26.28 S	26.06 E
Gerdine, Mount ʌ	180	61.35 N	152.26 W
Gerdview	273d	26.10 S	28.11 E
Gère ≃	62	45.32 N	4.54 E
Gerede	130	40.48 N	32.12 E
Gereja Cathedral ʊ[1]	269e	6.10 S	106.49 E
Gerenzano	266b	45.38 N	9.00 E
Gereshk	120	31.48 N	64.34 E
Geretsried	64	47.51 N	11.28 E
Gérgal	34	37.07 N	2.33 W
Gerge'bil	84	42.31 N	47.05 E
Gerger	130	37.57 N	39.01 E
Geria Nij	126	23.56 N	86.55 E
Gerik	114	5.25 N	101.08 E
Gering	198	41.49 N	103.39 W
Geringswalde	54	51.04 N	12.54 E
Geriş	130	36.58 N	31.44 E
Gerlachovský štít ʌ	30	49.12 N	20.08 E
Gerlafingen	58	47.10 N	7.34 E
Gerli ◂[8]	288	34.41 S	58.23 W
Gerlingen	56	48.48 N	9.03 E
Gerlos	64	47.14 N	12.02 E
Gerlospass)(	64	47.14 N	12.08 E
Gerlova Hut'	60	49.10 N	13.17 E
Germa (Jarmah) ⊥	146	26.33 N	13.04 E
Germagnano	62	45.15 N	7.28 E
Germain, Grand lac ⊜	186	51.12 N	66.41 W
Germania	214	41.39 N	77.40 W
Germano	214	40.25 N	80.57 W
Germanoviči	76	55.25 N	27.44 E
Germansen, Mount ʌ	182	55.37 N	124.50 W
Germansen Lake ⊜	182	55.41 N	124.53 W
Germansen Landing	182	55.47 N	124.43 W
Germansville	208	40.42 N	75.42 W
Germantown, Il., U.S.	219	38.33 N	89.32 W
Germantown, Ky., U.S.	218	38.39 N	83.57 W
Germantown, N.Y., U.S.	210	42.08 N	73.54 W
Germantown, Oh., U.S.	218	39.37 N	84.22 W
Germantown, Tn., U.S.	194	35.05 N	89.48 W
Germantown, Wi., U.S.	216	43.13 N	88.06 W
Germantown ◂[8]	285	40.03 N	75.11 W
Germantown Dam ◂[6]	218	39.38 N	84.24 W
Germany □[1], Europe	22	51.00 N	10.00 E
Germany (Deutschland) □[1], Europe	30	51.00 N	10.00 E
Germany Flats ⁝	276	41.05 N	74.39 W
Germay	58	48.25 N	5.21 E
Germencik	130	37.51 N	27.37 E
Germendorf	54	52.45 N	13.10 E
Germering	60	48.08 N	11.22 E
Germersheim	56	49.13 N	8.22 E
Germfask	190	46.14 N	85.55 W
Germiston	158	26.13 S	28.11 E
Germiston □[5]	273d	26.15 S	28.10 E
Germiston South	273d	26.15 S	28.10 E
Gernika-Lumo (Guernica y Luno)	34	43.19 N	2.41 W
Gernrode	54	51.43 N	11.08 E
Gernsbach	56	48.46 N	8.19 E
Gernsheim	56	49.44 N	8.29 E
Gero	94	35.48 N	137.14 E
Geroda	56	50.17 N	9.53 E
Gerola Alta	58	46.03 N	9.32 E
Geroldsgrün	54	50.20 N	11.35 E
Geroldstein	56	50.06 N	7.56 E
Gerolsbach	60	48.30 N	11.22 E
Gerolstein	56	50.13 N	6.40 E
Gerolzhofen	56	49.54 N	10.21 E
Gerona	116	15.36 N	120.36 E
Gerona → Girona	34	41.59 N	2.49 E
Geronimo	196	34.28 N	98.22 W
Gerpinnes	50	50.20 N	4.31 E
Gerrards Cross	260	51.35 N	0.34 W
Gerrei ◂[1]	71	39.28 N	9.17 E
Gerresheim ◂[8]	263	51.14 N	6.52 E
Gerringong	170	34.45 S	150.50 E
Gerry	214	42.12 N	79.15 W
Gers □[5]	32	43.40 N	0.30 E
Gers ≃	32	44.09 N	0.39 E
Gersau	58	47.00 N	8.32 E
Gersdorf	54	50.45 N	12.42 E
Gersfeld	56	50.27 N	9.55 E
Gershøj	41	55.43 N	11.59 E
Gersprenz ≃	56	49.59 N	9.04 E
Gerstetten	56	48.37 N	10.01 E
Gersthofen	58	48.25 N	10.53 E
Gerstungen	56	50.58 N	10.04 E
Gertak Sanggul, Tanjong ›	114	5.15 N	100.11 E
Gerthe ◂[8]	263	51.31 N	7.17 E
Gerufa	156	19.17 S	26.02 E
Gervais	224	45.06 N	122.53 W
Gerwisch	54	52.10 N	11.44 E
Gerza	142	29.26 N	31.11 E
Gerze, Tür.	130	41.48 N	35.12 E
Gêrzê, Zhg.	120	32.16 N	84.12 E
Gerzen	60	48.31 N	12.25 E
Gerzensee	58	46.51 N	7.33 E
Gescher	52	51.57 N	6.59 E
Geschriebenstein (Írottkő) ʌ	61	47.21 N	16.26 E
Geschwenda	54	50.44 N	10.49 E
Gesees	60	49.54 N	11.32 E
Geseke	52	51.38 N	8.31 E
Geser	164	3.53 S	130.54 E
Gesher HaZiw	132	33.02 N	35.06 E
Gesi	115a	7.20 S	111.01 E
Gesoa	164	8.25 S	143.35 E
Gespunsart	56	49.49 N	4.50 E
Gessertshausen	58	48.20 N	10.44 E
Gesso ≃	62	44.24 N	7.33 E
Gessopalena	66	42.03 N	14.16 E
Gesten	41	55.31 N	9.12 E
Gesualdo	68	41.00 N	15.04 E
Geta	26	60.23 N	19.50 E
Getafe	34	40.18 N	3.43 W
Getafe, Aeropuerto ⊠	266a	40.18 N	3.43 W
Gete ≃	56	50.57 N	5.07 E
Gethaoli	272c	19.08 N	73.01 E
Geti	154	1.13 N	30.12 E
Getinge	26	56.49 N	12.44 E
Gettorf	41	54.24 N	9.58 E
Gettysburg, Oh., U.S.	218	40.06 N	84.29 W
Gettysburg, Pa., U.S.	208	39.49 N	77.13 W
Gettysburg, S.D., U.S.	198	45.00 N	99.57 W
Gettysburg National Military Park ♠	208	39.49 N	77.15 W
Getulândia	256	22.40 S	44.06 W
Getulina	255	21.49 S	49.55 W
Getulio	116	10.45 N	122.40 E
Getúlio Vargas	252	27.50 S	52.16 W
Getz Ice Shelf ⊓	9	75.00 S	129.00 W
Getzville	210	43.01 N	78.46 W
Geumpang	114	4.48 N	96.09 E
Geureudong, Gunung ʌ	114	4.48 N	96.48 E
Gevān	128	26.03 N	57.17 E
Gevaş	128	38.16 N	43.07 E
Gevelsberg	56	51.19 N	7.20 E
Gevgelija	38	41.08 N	22.30 E
Gévora ≃	34	38.53 N	6.57 W
Gevrey-Chambertin	58	47.14 N	4.57 E
Gewane	144	10.10 N	40.39 E
Geweke ◂[8]	263	51.22 N	7.25 E
Gex	58	46.20 N	6.04 E
Geyer	54	50.37 N	12.55 E
Geyer Ditch ≅	216	41.36 N	86.25 W
Geyikli	130	39.48 N	26.12 E
Geysdorp	158	26.32 S	25.18 E
Geyser	202	47.15 N	110.29 W
Geyserville	204	38.42 N	122.54 W
Geyshtasar, Kūh-e ʌ	84	38.51 N	47.14 E
Geyuan	100	28.31 N	117.44 E
Geyve	130	40.30 N	30.18 E
Gézenti	146	21.41 N	18.18 E
Gezer	132	31.52 N	34.55 E
Gföhl	61	48.31 N	15.30 E
Ghaapplato ⩕[1]	158	27.30 S	24.00 E
Ghabāghib	132	33.10 N	36.13 E
Ghābat al-ʿArab	140	9.02 N	29.29 E
Ghadaf, Wādī al- V	132	31.46 N	36.50 E
Ghadāmis	146	30.08 N	9.30 E
Ghaddūwah	146	26.26 N	14.18 E
Ghafe	272c	19.05 N	73.07 E
Ghagghar ≃	123	29.30 N	74.53 E
Ghāghara ≃	124	25.47 N	84.37 E
Ghaghar Reservoir ⊜[1]	124	24.38 N	83.11 E
Ghāghra	124	23.17 N	84.33 E
Ghakhar	123	32.18 N	74.09 E
Ghallah, Wādī al- V	140	10.25 N	27.32 E
Ghammāzah al-Kubrā	142	29.43 N	31.18 E
Ghamrīn	142	30.30 N	30.55 E
Ghana □[1], Afr.	134	8.00 N	1.00 W
Ghana □[1], Afr.	150	8.00 N	1.00 W
Ghansoli	272c	19.08 N	72.59 E
Ghanzi	156	21.38 S	21.45 E
Ghanzi □[5]	156	22.00 S	23.00 E
Ghārāpuri	272c	18.54 N	72.56 E
Gharaunda	124	29.33 N	76.58 E
Gharbah, Wādī V	142	29.40 N	31.58 E
Gharbi, Chott ⊜	148	33.50 N	1.30 W
Gharbi, Oued el V	148	31.50 N	0.51 E
Gharbīyah, Aṣ-Ṣaḥrā' al- (Western Desert) ◂[2]	140	27.00 N	27.00 E
Ghardaïa	148	32.31 N	3.37 E
Ghardimaou	36	36.26 N	8.27 E
Gharghoda	124	22.10 N	83.21 E
Gharībwāl	123	32.41 N	73.10 E
Gharīfah	132	33.38 N	35.33 E
Gharig	140	10.47 N	27.33 E
Ghārīyat al-Gharbīyah	132	32.41 N	36.13 E
Ghārīyat ash-Sharqīyah	132	32.40 N	36.16 E
Gharo	120	24.44 N	67.35 E
Gharrāf, Shaṭṭ al- ≃	128	32.30 N	45.48 E
Gharroli ◂[8]	272a	28.37 N	77.20 E
Gharsa, Chott el ⊜	148	34.06 N	7.50 E
Gharw, Jazīrat I	142	31.21 N	30.06 E
Gharyān	146	32.10 N	13.01 E
Ghaṣm	132	32.33 N	36.22 E
Ghāt	146	24.58 N	10.11 E
Ghātāl	126	22.40 N	87.43 E
Ghatampur	272b	22.54 N	88.10 E
Ghatere, Mount ʌ	175e	7.49 S	158.54 E
Ghates Occidentales → Western Ghāts ⩕	122	14.00 N	75.00 E
Ghates Orientales → Eastern Ghāts ⩕	122	14.00 N	78.50 E
Ghātkopar ◂[8]	272c	19.05 N	72.54 E
Ghātprabha ≃	122	16.20 N	75.48 E
Ghātsīla	126	22.36 N	86.29 E
Għawdex (Gozo) I	36	36.03 N	14.15 E
Ghawr ash-Sharqīyah, Qanāt al- (East Ghor Canal) ≅	132	32.41 N	35.38 E
Ghaylah ʌ[1]	132	33.11 N	37.05 E
Ghayl Bā Wazīr	144	14.48 N	49.21 E
Ghayl Bin Yumayn ⊤[4]	144	15.33 N	49.23 E
Ghayth, Wādī V	132	30.59 N	36.00 E
Ghazāl, Baḥr al- ≃	140	9.31 N	30.25 E
Ghazal, Bahr el V	146	13.01 N	15.28 E
Ghazālat al-Khīs	142	30.34 N	31.34 E
Ghāziābād	123	28.40 N	77.26 E
Ghāzīpur, India	124	25.35 N	83.34 E
Ghazipur, India	272b	22.36 N	88.34 E
Ghāzīpur ◂[8]	272a	28.38 N	77.19 E
Ghazīr	130	34.01 N	35.40 E
Ghazlūna	120	31.24 N	67.49 E
Ghaznī	120	33.33 N	68.26 E
Ghaznī □[4]	120	33.15 N	67.45 E
Ghaznī ≃	120	32.35 N	67.58 E
Ghazni Khel	123	32.33 N	70.44 E
Ghazzah (Gaza), Isr. Occ	132	31.30 N	34.28 E
Ghazzah, Lubnān	132	33.40 N	35.49 E
Gheā ≃	272b	22.52 N	88.19 E
Ghedi	64	45.24 N	10.16 E
Ghemme	62	45.37 N	8.25 E
Ghennes Heights	279b	40.09 N	79.56 W
Ghent, Ky., U.S.	218	38.44 N	85.03 W
Ghent, N.Y., U.S.	210	42.19 N	73.36 W
Ghent, Oh., U.S.	214	41.09 N	81.38 W
Ghent → Gent	50	51.03 N	3.43 E
Gheora ◂[8]	272a	28.42 N	77.01 E
Gheorghe Gheorghiu-Dej	38	46.14 N	26.44 E
Gheorgheni	38	46.43 N	25.36 E
Gherla	38	47.02 N	23.55 E
Ghesar	272c	19.09 N	73.05 E
Ghigo	62	44.53 N	7.03 E
Ghilarza	71	40.07 N	8.50 E
Ghilizane	148	35.44 N	0.30 E
Ghīn, Tall ʌ	132	32.39 N	36.43 E
Ghior	126	23.54 N	89.53 E
Ghislenghien, Bel.	50	50.39 N	3.52 E
Ghislenghien (Gellingen), Bel.	50	50.39 N	3.52 E
Ghisonaccia	36	42.00 N	9.25 E
Ghizar ≃	123	36.15 N	73.25 E
Ghizunabeana Islands II	175e	7.31 S	158.42 E
Ghlin	50	50.28 N	3.53 E
Ghlò, Beinn a' ʌ	46	56.50 N	3.43 W
Ghogha	120	21.41 N	72.17 E
Gholson	222	31.43 N	97.12 W
Ghonda ◂[8]	272a	28.41 N	77.16 E
Ghondi ◂[8]	272a	28.42 N	77.16 E
Ghorāsahan	124	26.50 N	85.08 E
Ghoshpur, Bngl.	126	23.27 N	89.39 E
Ghoshpur, India	272b	22.23 N	88.29 E
Ghotki	120	28.01 N	69.19 E
Ghowr □[4]	128	34.00 N	65.00 E
Ghubaysh	140	12.09 N	27.21 E
Ghudāf, Wādī al- V	128	32.56 N	43.30 E
Ghulayfiqah	144	14.27 N	43.02 E
Ghunthur	130	34.23 N	37.09 E
Ghurāb, Jabal ʌ[2]	142	28.58 N	31.16 E
Ghurayrah	144	18.37 N	42.41 E
Ghūrīān	128	34.21 N	61.30 E
Ghushuri	272b	22.37 N	88.22 E
Ghuwaybah, Wādī V	142	29.36 N	32.20 E
Ghuwayr, ʿAyn al- ⊤[4]	132	31.37 N	35.25 E
Ghuzzayil, Sabkhat ⊜	146	29.50 N	19.35 E
Giaginskaja	78	44.53 N	40.05 E
Gianh ≃	110	17.40 N	106.30 E
Giannutri, Isola di I	66	42.15 N	11.06 E
Giano, Monte ʌ	66	42.25 N	13.06 E
Giano dell'Umbria	66	42.50 N	12.35 E
Giant City State Park ♠	194	37.39 N	89.12 W
Giant Mountain ʌ	188	44.10 N	73.44 W
Giant's Castle ʌ	158	29.21 S	29.27 E
Giant's Castle Game Reserve ◂[4]	158	29.16 S	29.30 E
Giant's Causeway ♠	48	55.14 N	6.30 W
Giants Neck	207	41.18 N	72.13 W
Giants Tomb Island I	212	44.55 N	80.00 W
Gianyar	115b	8.32 S	115.20 E
Gia Rai	110	9.14 N	105.28 E
Giardinello	70	38.05 N	13.09 E
Giardinetto	68	41.19 N	15.24 E
Giardini	70	37.50 N	15.17 E
Giarratana	70	37.03 N	14.48 E
Giarre	70	37.43 N	15.11 E
Giaveno	62	45.02 N	7.21 E
Giazza	64	45.39 N	11.07 E
Giba	71	39.04 N	8.38 E
Gibara	240p	21.07 N	76.08 W
Gibbon, Mn., U.S.	190	44.32 N	94.31 W
Gibbon, Ne., U.S.	198	40.44 N	98.50 W
Gibbons	182	53.50 N	113.20 W
Gibbonsville	202	45.33 N	113.55 W
Gibb River	164	16.25 S	126.22 E
Gibbs, Mount ʌ	162	32.55 S	120.00 E
Gibbsboro	285	39.50 N	74.58 W
Gibbstown	208	39.49 N	75.17 W
Gibellina	70	37.47 N	12.58 E
Gibeon	156	25.09 S	17.43 E
Gibilmanna, Santuario di ʊ[1]	70	37.59 N	14.02 E
Gibraleón	34	37.23 N	6.58 W
Gibraltar, Gib.	34	36.08 N	5.21 W
Gibraltar, Mi., U.S.	216	42.06 N	83.12 W
Gibraltar, Pa., U.S.	208	40.17 N	75.52 W
Gibraltar □[2], Europe	22	36.08 N	5.21 W
Gibraltar □[2], Europe	34	36.08 N	5.21 W
Gibraltar, Strait of (Estrecho de Gibraltar) ʯ	34	35.57 N	5.36 W
Gibraltar Point ›, On., Can.	275b	43.36 N	79.23 W
Gibraltar Point ›, Eng., U.K.	44	53.05 N	0.19 E
Gibsland	194	32.32 N	93.03 W
Gibson, Austl.	162	33.39 S	121.48 E
Gibson, Ga., U.S.	192	33.14 N	82.35 W
Gibson, N.Y., U.S.	210	42.08 N	76.59 W
Gibson, Pa., U.S.	210	41.44 N	75.38 W
Gibson ≃	212	44.58 N	79.51 W
Gibson, Lake ⊜[1]	284a	43.06 N	79.14 W
Gibsonburg	214	41.23 N	83.19 W
Gibson City	216	40.27 N	88.22 W
Gibson Desert ◂[2]	162	24.30 S	126.00 E
Gibson Hill ʌ[2]	214	41.51 N	80.10 W
Gibsonia, Fl., U.S.	220	28.06 N	81.58 W
Gibsonia, Pa., U.S.	214	40.38 N	79.59 W
Gibson Indian Reserve ◂[4]	212	45.01 N	79.44 W
Gibson Island I	208	39.05 N	76.26 W
Gibsons	182	49.24 N	123.30 W
Gibsonton	220	27.51 N	82.22 W
Gidajevo	24	59.57 N	52.22 E
Gidami	144	9.58 N	34.37 E
Gidda	144	9.34 N	35.23 E
Giddalūr	122	15.21 N	78.55 E
Giddarbāha	123	30.12 N	74.40 E
Giddings	222	30.10 N	96.56 W
Gideälven ≃	26	63.20 N	19.08 E
Gidea Park ◂[8]	260	51.35 N	0.12 E
Gideåvallen	26	63.29 N	18.58 E
Gideon	194	36.27 N	89.55 W
Gidgee	162	27.16 S	119.22 E
Gidgi, Lake ⊜	162	29.16 S	126.03 E
Gidhni	126	22.29 N	86.51 E
Gidole	144	5.38 N	37.30 E
Gidrotorf	80	56.28 N	43.33 E
Gidžaki, gora ʌ	84	40.25 N	49.01 E
Giebelstadt	56	49.39 N	9.56 E
Gieboldehausen	52	51.36 N	10.13 E
Giedraičiai	76	55.05 N	25.15 E
Gielow	54	53.42 N	12.44 E
Gielsdorf	264a	52.36 N	13.52 E
Gien	50	47.42 N	2.38 E
Giengen	56	48.37 N	10.14 E
Giens	62	43.02 N	6.08 E
Gier ≃	62	45.35 N	4.46 E
Gierath	263	51.07 N	6.33 E
Gierle	56	51.16 N	4.51 E
Gieselwerder	52	51.36 N	9.33 E
Giesenkirchen ◂[8]	263	51.09 N	6.30 E
Giesing ◂[8]	64	48.06 N	11.35 E
Giessbachfälle ʟ	58	46.42 N	8.03 E
Giessen	56	50.35 N	8.40 E
Giessen □[5]	56	50.40 N	8.40 E
Gieten	52	53.00 N	6.46 E
Giethoorn	52	52.43 N	6.05 E
Gièvres	50	47.16 N	1.40 E
Giez	62	45.45 N	6.15 E
Giffone	68	38.27 N	16.10 E
Giffoni Valle Piana	68	40.44 N	14.56 E
Gifford, Scot., U.K.	46	55.54 N	2.45 W
Gifford, Fl., U.S.	220	27.40 N	80.24 W
Gifford, Il., U.S.	216	40.18 N	88.01 W
Gifford, In., U.S.	216	41.06 N	87.01 W
Gifford, Pa., U.S.	214	41.51 N	78.36 W
Gifford ≃	176	70.21 N	83.05 W
Gifford Creek	162	24.05 S	116.11 E
Gifford Pinchot State Park ♠	208	40.04 N	76.53 W
Giffre ≃	58	46.05 N	6.30 E
Gifhorn	52	52.29 N	10.33 E
Giflitz	56	51.09 N	9.07 E
Gif-sur-Yvette	261	48.42 N	2.08 E
Gifu	94	35.25 N	136.45 E
Gifu □[5]	94	35.45 N	137.00 E
Gigant	80	46.30 N	41.20 E
Giganta, Sierra de la ⩕	232	26.00 N	111.30 W
Gigante	246	2.23 N	75.33 W
Gigante Islands II	116	11.36 N	123.20 E
Gigen	38	43.42 N	24.29 E
Gigena → Alcira	252	32.45 S	64.20 W
Giggleswick	44	54.04 N	2.17 W
Gigha, Sound of ʯ	46	55.41 N	5.42 W
Gigha Island I	46	55.41 N	5.46 W
Gig Harbor	224	47.19 N	122.34 W
Giglio, Isola del I	66	42.21 N	10.54 E
Giglio Castello	66	42.22 N	10.54 E
Gigliola	66	44.51 N	12.14 E
Giglio Porto	66	42.22 N	10.55 E
Gigmoto	116	13.47 N	124.23 E
Gignod	62	45.46 N	7.17 E
Gihu → Gifu	94	35.25 N	136.45 E
Gijón	34	43.32 N	5.40 W
Gikongoro	154	2.29 S	29.34 E
Gila ≃	200	32.43 N	114.33 W
Gila, Middle Fork ≃	200	33.14 N	108.14 W
Gila Bend	200	32.56 N	112.42 W
Gila Bend Indian Reservation ◂[4]	200	33.00 N	112.46 W
Gila Bend Mountains ⩕	200	33.10 N	113.10 W
Gila Cliff Dwellings National Monument ♠	200	33.02 N	108.16 W
Gila Mountains ⩕	200	33.05 N	109.50 W
Gīlān □[4]	128	37.15 N	49.30 E
Gīlān-e Gharb	128	34.08 N	45.55 E
Gila River Indian Reservation ◂[4]	200	33.12 N	112.00 W
Gilātala	126	22.36 N	89.41 E
Gilberdyke	44	53.45 N	0.44 W
Gilbert, La., U.S.	194	32.02 N	91.39 W
Gilbert, Mn., U.S.	190	47.29 N	92.27 W
Gilbert ≃, Austl.	166	16.35 S	141.15 E
Gilbert ≃, Austl.	168b	34.22 S	138.40 E
Gilbert, Mount ʌ	182	50.51 N	124.20 W
Gilbert Airport ⊠	279a	41.22 N	81.58 W
Gilbert Island I	219	39.35 N	91.11 W
Gilbert Islands → Kiribati □[1]	14	5.00 S	170.00 W
Gilbert Lake ⊜	281	42.34 N	83.17 W
Gilbert Lake State Park ♠	210	42.36 N	75.08 W
Gilberton	210	40.48 N	76.13 W
Gilbertown	194	31.52 N	88.19 W
Gilbert Peak ʌ	224	46.30 N	121.25 W
Gilbert Plains	184	51.09 N	100.29 W
Gilbert River	166	18.09 S	142.52 E
Gilberts	216	42.06 N	88.23 W
Gilbert Seamount ⊹[3]	16	52.50 N	150.10 W
Gilbertsville, N.Y., U.S.	210	42.28 N	75.19 W
Gilbertsville, Pa., U.S.	208	40.19 N	75.37 W
Gilbertville	207	42.18 N	72.12 W
Gilbjerg Hoved ›	41	56.08 N	12.17 E
Gilboa	216	41.01 N	83.55 W
Gilboaʿ, Haré ⩕[2]	132	32.30 N	35.23 E
Gilbués	250	9.50 S	45.21 W
Gilching	60	48.07 N	11.17 E
Gildehaus	52	52.18 N	7.06 E
Gildford	202	48.34 N	110.17 W
Gilead	216	41.48 N	85.09 W
Giles, Arroyo de ≃	258	34.20 S	59.23 W
Giles Meteorological Station ʊ[3]	162	25.02 S	128.18 E
Giles Point ›	168b	35.03 S	137.45 E
Gilette	62	43.51 N	7.10 E
Gilford	48	54.23 N	6.22 W
Gilford Island I	182	50.45 N	126.25 W
Gilford Park	208	39.58 N	74.08 W
Gilgai	162	31.15 S	119.56 E
Gilgandra	166	31.42 S	148.39 E
Gilgil	154	0.30 S	36.19 E
Gil Gil Creek ≃	166	29.10 S	148.51 E
Gilgit	123	35.55 N	74.18 E
Gilgit ≃	123	35.44 N	74.38 E
Gilgo Island I	276	40.38 N	73.25 W
Gilgo State Park ♠	276	40.38 N	73.22 W
Gilima	154	3.55 N	28.22 E
Gilimanuk	115a	8.10 S	114.26 E
Gilirang	112	3.55 S	120.09 E
Gil Island I	182	53.13 N	129.15 W
Gill, Lough ⊜	48	54.16 N	8.24 W
Gillam	184	56.21 N	94.43 W
Gilleland Creek ≃	222	30.13 N	97.32 W
Gilleleje	41	56.07 N	12.19 E
Gillen, Lake ⊜	162	26.11 S	124.38 E
Gilles, Lake ⊜	166	32.50 S	136.45 E
Gillespie	219	39.07 N	89.49 W
Gillespies Point ›	172	43.24 S	169.50 E
Gillett, Ar., U.S.	194	34.07 N	91.22 W
Gillett, Pa., U.S.	210	41.57 N	76.48 W
Gillett, Wi., U.S.	190	44.53 N	88.18 W
Gillette, N.J., U.S.	276	40.41 N	74.28 W
Gillette, Wy., U.S.	198	44.17 N	105.30 W
Gillette Castle State Park ♠	207	41.26 N	72.25 W
Gillian, Lake ⊜	176	69.32 N	75.23 W
Gillingham, Eng., U.K.	42	51.02 N	2.17 W
Gillingham, Eng., U.K.	260	51.24 N	0.33 E
Gillingham □[8]	260	51.22 N	0.35 E
Gills Rock	190	45.17 N	87.01 W
Gilman, Ct., U.S.	207	41.34 N	72.11 W
Gilman, Il., U.S.	216	40.46 N	87.59 W
Gilman, Ia., U.S.	190	41.52 N	92.47 W
Gilman, Wi., U.S.	190	45.10 N	90.48 W
Gilman Hot Springs	228	33.50 N	116.59 W
Gilman Lake	285	39.41 N	75.11 W
Gilmer, Il., U.S.	278	42.14 N	88.02 W
Gilmer, Tx., U.S.	222	32.43 N	94.56 W
Gilmer Park	216	41.36 N	86.15 W
Gilmore	171b	35.20 S	148.11 E
Gilmore City	198	42.44 N	94.27 W
Gilmore Creek ≃	171b	35.18 S	148.13 E
Gilo ≃	144	8.10 N	33.15 E
Gilroy	226	37.00 N	121.34 W
Gilserberg	56	50.57 N	9.04 E
Gilsizer Slough ≃	226	38.58 N	121.44 W
Gilston Park ♠	260	51.48 N	0.04 E
Giltner	198	40.46 N	98.09 W
Gil'uj ≃	89	53.58 N	127.30 E
Giluwe, Mount ʌ	164	6.05 S	143.50 E
Gilwern	42	51.51 N	3.06 W
Gilze	52	51.33 N	4.57 E
Gimån ≃	26	62.28 N	16.20 E
Gimbi	144	9.10 N	35.42 E
Gimcheon → Kimch'ŏn	98	36.07 N	128.05 E
Gimie, Mount ʌ	241f	13.52 N	61.01 W
Gimigliano	68	38.58 N	16.32 E
Gimlet	218	38.13 N	83.09 W
Gimli	184	50.38 N	96.59 W
Gimo	40	60.11 N	18.11 E
Gimoly	24	63.03 N	32.19 E
Gimone ≃	32	44.00 N	1.06 E
Gimont	32	43.38 N	0.53 E
Gimpu	112	1.36 S	120.02 E
Ginderich	263	51.39 N	6.32 E
Ginebra → Genève	58	46.12 N	6.09 E
Gineste, Col de la)(	62	43.15 N	5.27 E
Gingell	216	42.43 N	83.17 W
Gingera, Mount ʌ	171b	35.35 S	148.47 E
Ginger Hill	279b	40.12 N	80.00 W
Ginger Island I	240m	18.24 N	64.28 W
Gingin, Austl.	162	31.21 S	115.42 E
Gin Gin, Austl.	166	25.00 S	151.58 E
Gingindlovu	158	29.02 S	31.30 E
Gingoog	116	8.50 N	125.07 E
Gingoog Bay ᑕ	116	8.59 N	125.05 E
Gingst	54	54.27 N	13.16 E
Ginir	144	7.07 N	40.46 E
Ginkakuji Temple ʊ[1]	270	35.03 N	135.47 E
Ginkgo State Park ♠	202	46.59 N	120.01 W
Ginnosar	132	32.51 N	35.31 E
Ginosa	68	40.35 N	16.46 E
Ginostra	70	38.47 N	15.11 E
Ginowan	174m	26.17 N	127.46 E
Ginoza	174m	26.28 N	127.57 E
Ginter	214	40.46 N	78.23 W
Ginza ◂[8]	268	35.40 N	139.47 E
Gioi	68	40.17 N	15.13 E
Gioia, Golfo di ᑕ	68	38.30 N	15.45 E
Gioia dei Marsi	66	41.57 N	13.42 E
Gioia del Colle	68	40.48 N	16.56 E
Gioia Tauro	68	38.26 N	15.54 E
Gioia Vecchio	66	41.54 N	13.44 E
Gioiosa Ionica	68	38.20 N	16.18 E
Gioiosa Marea	70	38.10 N	14.54 E
Giong Rieng	110	9.55 N	105.19 E
Giornico	58	46.24 N	8.52 E
Giovi, Passo dei)(	62	44.33 N	8.57 E
Giovinazzo	68	41.11 N	16.40 E
Giporlos	116	11.07 N	125.27 E
Gipping ≃	42	52.04 N	1.10 E
Gipsy	214	40.48 N	78.53 W
Gipuzkoako □[4]	34	43.10 N	2.10 W
Giraglia, Île de la I	62	43.02 N	9.24 E
Giralia	162	22.41 S	114.21 E
Giraltovce	30	49.07 N	21.31 E
Girard, Il., U.S.	219	39.26 N	89.46 W
Girard, Ks., U.S.	198	37.30 N	94.50 W
Girard, Mi., U.S.	216	42.02 N	85.00 W
Girard, Oh., U.S.	214	41.09 N	80.42 W
Girard, Pa., U.S.	214	42.00 N	80.19 W
Girard, Tx., U.S.	196	33.22 N	100.40 W
Girardot	246	4.18 N	74.48 W
Girardville	208	40.47 N	76.17 W
Giraud, Pointe ›	240d	15.19 N	61.15 W
Giraul ≃	152	15.04 S	12.08 E
Giraumont	56	49.10 N	5.55 E
Girbovu	38	44.44 N	23.21 E
Girdletree	208	38.05 N	75.23 W
Giresun	130	40.55 N	38.24 E
Giresun □[4]	130	40.30 N	38.30 E
Giresun Dağları ⩕	130	40.30 N	39.00 E
Girgarre	166	36.24 S	144.59 E
Girgaum ◂[8]	272c	18.57 N	72.48 E

≃ River	Fluß	Río	Rivière	Rio
≅ Canal	Kanal	Canal	Canal	Canal
ʟ Waterfall, Rapids	Wasserfall, Stromschnellen	Cascada, Rápidos	Chute d'eau, Rapides	Cascata, Rápidos
ʯ Strait	Meeresstraße	Estrecho	Détroit	Estreito
ᑕ Bay, Gulf	Bucht, Golf	Bahía, Golfo	Baie, Golfe	Baía, Golfo
⊜ Lake, Lakes	See, Seen	Lago, Lagos	Lac, Lacs	Lago, Lagos
⁝ Swamp	Sumpf	Pantano	Marais	Pântano
⊓ Ice Features, Glacier	Eis- und Gletscherformen	Accidentes Glaciales	Formes glaciaires	Acidentes glaciares
⊤ Other Hydrographic Features	Andere Hydrographische Objekte	Otros Elementos Hidrográficos	Autres données hydrographiques	Outros acidentes hidrográficos

⊹ Submarine Features	Untermeerische Objekte	Accidentes Submarinos	Formes de relief sous-marin	Acidentes submarinos
□ Political Unit	Politische Einheit	Unidad Politica	Entité politique	Unidade política
ʊ Cultural Institution	Kulturelle Institution	Institución Cultural	Institution culturelle	Institução cultural
⊥ Historical Site	Historische Stätte	Sitio Histórico	Site historique	Sitio histórico
♠ Recreational Site	Erholungs- und Ferienort	Sitio de Recreo	Centre de loisirs	Area de Lazer
⊠ Airport	Flughafen	Aeropuerto	Aéroport	Aeroporto
■ Military Installation	Militäranlage	Instalación Militar	Installation militaire	Instalação militar
◂ Miscellaneous	Verschiedenes	Misceláneo	Divers	Diversos

Symbols in the index entries represent the broad categories identified in the key at the right. Symbols with superior numbers (⋏ 1) identify subcategories (see complete key on page I · 1).

Symbole im Register stellen die rechts im Schlüssel erklärten Kategorien dar. Symbole mit hochgestellten Ziffern (⋏ 1) bezeichnen Unterabteilungen einer Kategorie (vgl. vollständiger Schlüssel auf Seite I · 1).

Los símbolos incluidos en el texto del índice representan las grandes categorías identificadas con la clave a la derecha. Los símbolos con numeros en su parte superior (⋏ 1) identifican las subcategorías (véase la clave completa en la página I · 1).

Les symboles de l'index représentent les catégories indiquées dans la légende à droite. Les symboles suivis d'un indice (⋏ 1) représentent des sous-catégories (voir légende complète à la page I · 1).

Os símbolos incluídos no texto do índice representam as grandes categorias identificadas com a chave à direita. Os símbolos com números em sua parte superior (⋏ 1) identificam as subcategorias (veja-se a chave completa à página I · 1).

∧ Mountain	Berg	Montaña	Montagne	Montanha
⋏ Mountains	Gebirge	Montañas	Montagnes	Montanhas
)(Pass	Paß	Paso	Col	Passo
V Valley, Canyon	Tal, Cañon	Valle, Cañón	Vallée, Canyon	Vale, Canhão
≍ Plain	Ebene	Llano	Plaine	Planície
> Cape	Kap	Cabo	Cap	Cabo
I Island	Insel	Isla	Île	Ilha
II Islands	Inseln	Islas	Îles	Ilhas
♦ Other Topographic Features	Andere Topographische Objekte	Otros Elementos Topográficos	Autres données topographiques	Outros acidentes topográficos

ESPAÑOL — Nombre / Página / Lat.°′ / Long.°′ W = Oeste

Golovino, Ross. 76 55.58 N 40.26 E
Golovino, Ross. 82 56.01 N 39.11 E
Golovinščino 80 53.18 N 43.59 E
Golovinskaja 88 53.26 N 102.43 E
Golovnino 82 54.23 N 36.10 E
Golovno 78 51.21 N 24.04 E
Golovskoje 88 55.30 N 105.32 E
Golpāyegān 128 33.27 N 50.18 E
Gölpazarı 130 40.15 N 30.19 E
Golra 123 33.42 N 72.58 E
Golrān 128 35.06 N 61.41 E
Gols 61 47.54 N 16.55 E
Gol'šany 76 54.15 N 26.01 E
Gölsdorf 54 51.59 N 12.39 E
Golspie, Austl. 170 34.17 S 149.40 E
Golspie, Scot., U.K. 46 57.58 N 3.58 W
Golssen 54 51.58 N 13.36 E
Gol't'ajevo 82 55.13 N 36.02 E
Gol't'avino 88 58.26 N 98.27 E
Golub-Dobrzyń 30 53.08 N 19.02 E
Golubi 76 59.28 N 41.39 E
Golubinskij 80 48.52 N 43.34 E
Golubovka, Kaz. 86 53.09 N 74.12 E
Golubovka, Ukr. 78 48.53 N 35.19 E
Golubovka ◆[8] 83 48.38 N 38.39 E
Golumet' 88 53.03 N 102.21 E
Golungo Alto 152 9.08 S 14.46 E
Golva 198 46.44 N 103.59 W
Golweyn 144 1.40 N 44.35 E
Gölyaka 130 40.47 N 30.59 E
Golynki 76 54.52 N 31.23 E
Golyšmanovo, Ross. 86 56.28 N 68.38 E
Golyšmanovo, Ross. 86 56.23 N 68.23 E
Golzheim ◆[8] 263 51.15 N 6.46 E
Golzow, Dtsch. 54 52.34 N 14.29 E
Golzow, Dtsch. 54 52.16 N 12.36 E
Goma 154 1.41 S 29.14 E
Gomadan-zan ∧ 96 34.03 N 135.34 E
Gomagoi 64 46.35 N 10.32 E
Gomang Co ⊜ 120 31.15 N 89.15 E
Gomaringen 58 48.27 N 9.05 E
Gomas, Sierra de ⋏ 196 26.23 N 100.32 W
Gomati ≃ 124 25.32 N 83.10 E
Gomati Plain ≚ 124 26.30 N 81.10 E
Goma Tsétsé 273b 4.14 S 15.08 E
Gombari 154 2.43 N 29.04 E
Gombe, Nig. 146 10.19 N 11.02 E
Gombe, Zaïre 152 0.42 S 17.35 E
Gombe Stream National Park ♠ 154 4.30 S 29.42 E
Gombi 146 10.10 N 12.45 E
Gomboro 150 13.29 N 2.46 W
Gomel' 76 52.25 N 31.00 E
Gomel' □[8] 78 52.00 N 29.00 E
Gomer 216 40.51 N 84.11 W
Gomera I 148 28.06 N 17.08 W
Gometra I 46 56.29 N 6.17 W
Gometz-la-Ville 261 48.40 N 2.08 E
Gometz-le-Châtel 261 48.41 N 2.08 E
Gomez 220 27.06 N 80.09 W
Gómez Farías, Méx. 232 29.18 N 107.40 W
Gómez Farías, Méx. 234 19.47 N 103.29 W
Gómez Palacio 232 25.34 N 103.30 W
Gómez Plata 246 6.41 N 75.12 W
Gomīshān 128 37.04 N 54.06 E
Gommécourt 261 49.05 N 1.36 E
Gommern 54 52.04 N 11.50 E
Gomo Co ⊜ 120 33.47 N 85.30 E
Gomogomo 164 6.40 S 134.43 E
Gomoh 126 23.52 N 86.10 E
Gompa 123 35.02 N 77.20 E
Goms V 58 46.27 N 8.15 E
Gomshall 260 51.13 N 0.27 W
Gomumu, Pulau I 164 1.49 S 127.38 E
Gonābād 128 34.20 N 58.42 E
Gonaïves 238 19.27 N 72.41 W
Gonaka 152 2.56 S 13.14 E
Gonam 74 57.21 N 131.12 E
Gonam ≃ 74 57.21 N 131.14 E
Gonarezhou National Park ♠ 154 21.30 S 32.00 E
Gonars 64 45.53 N 13.13 E
Gonäs 40 60.09 N 15.06 E
Gonâve, Golfe de la ⊂ 238 19.00 N 73.30 W
Gonâve, Île de la I 238 18.51 N 73.03 W
Gonbad-e Qābūs 128 37.17 N 55.17 E
Gonçalves 256 22.40 S 45.51 W
Gonçalves Dias 250 4.57 S 44.14 W
Gončarovka 78 50.32 N 39.28 E
Goncelin 62 45.20 N 5.59 E
Gonda 124 27.08 N 81.56 E
Gondal 120 21.58 N 70.48 E
Gondang 115a 7.24 S 111.06 E
Gondarbal 123 34.14 N 74.47 E
Gondar → Gonder 144 12.40 N 37.30 E
Gonder 144 12.40 N 37.30 E
Gonder □[4] 144 13.10 N 37.00 E
Gondey 146 9.09 N 19.19 E
Gondia 120 21.27 N 80.12 E
Gondola 156 19.10 S 33.40 E
Gondomar 34 41.09 N 8.32 W
Gondrecourt-le-Château 58 48.31 N 5.30 E
Gondreville 58 48.42 N 5.58 E
Gondrexange, Étang de ⊜ 58 48.42 N 6.54 E
Goneāna 123 30.19 N 74.54 E
Gönen, Tür. 130 40.06 N 27.39 E
Gonén, Yis. 132 33.08 N 35.39 E
Gonesse 50 48.59 N 2.27 E
Gonfaron 62 43.19 N 6.17 E
Gong ≃ 100 26.00 N 115.22 E
Gong'an 102 30.02 N 112.04 E
Gonganbao 86 44.59 N 86.18 E
Gonganpucun 104 41.19 N 123.27 E
Gongbuchang 105 40.17 N 116.15 E
Gongchangling 104 41.06 N 123.30 E
Gongcheng 102 24.49 N 110.46 E
Gongchenqiao 106 30.20 N 120.08 E
Gongchuan, Zhg. 100 26.06 N 117.24 E
Gongchuan, Zhg. 102 23.40 N 107.50 E
Gongcun 105 39.28 N 116.10 E
Gongdaoqiao 100 32.36 N 119.22 E
Gongdian 100 28.06 N 116.56 E
Gongen-yama ∧ 94 35.40 N 139.01 E
Gongfang 100 27.36 N 115.34 E
Gonggar 120 29.17 N 90.46 E
Gongga Shan (Minya Konka) ∧ 102 29.35 N 101.51 E
Gonghe 102 36.20 N 100.48 E
Gonghui 98 41.12 N 114.37 E
Gongjialu 106 31.17 N 121.40 E
Gongjiatun 104 40.55 N 120.37 E
Gongjiazhai 104 41.57 N 124.01 E
Gongjing 107 29.21 N 104.43 E
Gongjingying 105 39.12 N 116.11 E
Gongkou 98 35.38 N 119.47 E
Gongli 98 35.55 N 117.24 E
Gongling 100 26.18 N 119.40 E
Gongliu 86 43.30 N 82.15 E
Gonglu Shan ∧ 106 30.39 N 119.18 E
Gongo 146 9.00 N 18.56 E
Gongola □[3] 146 9.00 N 11.40 E
Gongola ≃ 146 9.30 N 12.04 E
Gongoué 152 0.32 S 9.12 E
Gongo-Yembe 152 1.58 S 18.40 E
Gongpengzi 89 45.09 N 125.39 E
Gongping 100 23.05 N 115.24 E
Gongpingxu 100 26.12 N 112.51 E
Gongshan 102 25.50 N 103.13 E
Gongshiya 120 31.25 N 84.37 E
Gongsizhen 106 31.41 N 121.48 E
Gongtangtou 106 31.48 N 118.42 E
Gongxi 100 27.38 N 115.52 E
Gongxian 102 34.48 N 113.03 E
Gongyefu 98 42.16 N 118.32 E
Gongyemiao 89 43.40 N 121.06 E
Gongyingzi 98 40.54 N 119.41 E

FRANÇAIS — Nom / Page / Lat.°′ / Long.°′ W = Ouest

Gongzhutun 104 42.10 N 123.00 E
Gongzui 107 29.19 N 103.28 E
Goni, It. 71 39.34 N 9.17 E
Goñi, Ur. 252 33.31 S 56.24 W
Goniądz 30 53.30 N 22.45 E
Gonini ≃ 250 4.10 N 54.24 W
Goniri 146 11.30 N 12.20 E
Gonjo 102 30.43 N 98.19 E
Gonnesa 71 39.16 N 8.28 E
Gonnesa, Golfo di ⊂ 71 39.17 N 8.23 E
Gonnosfanadiga 71 39.29 N 8.39 E
Gonnostramatza 71 39.41 N 8.50 E
Gonochovo 86 52.57 N 81.20 E
Gōnoura 92 33.45 N 129.41 E
Gonubie Mouth 158 32.57 S 28.01 E
Gonža 89 53.36 N 125.19 E
Gonzaga, It. 64 44.57 N 10.49 E
Gonzaga, Pil. 116 18.16 N 122.00 E
Gonzales, Ca., U.S. 226 36.30 N 121.26 W
Gonzales, La., U.S. 194 30.14 N 90.55 W
Gonzales, Tx., U.S. 222 29.30 N 97.27 W
Gonzales □[6] 222 29.28 N 97.30 W
González, Méx. 234 22.50 N 98.27 W
González, Ur. 258 34.14 S 56.52 W
González, Riacho ≃ 252 22.48 S 57.54 W
González Catán 258 34.46 S 58.39 W
González Chaves 252 38.02 S 60.06 W
González Moreno 252 35.33 S 63.22 W
González Ortega, Méx. 204 32.40 N 115.23 W
González Ortega, Méx. 234 23.11 N 102.29 W
González Ortega, Méx. 234 23.59 N 103.27 W
González Risos 258 34.52 S 59.13 W
Gonzanamá 246 4.15 S 79.27 W
Goobarragandra ≃ 171b 35.20 S 148.15 E
Goochland 192 37.41 N 77.53 W
Good Easter 260 51.47 N 0.21 E
Goodells 214 42.59 N 82.40 W
Goode Mountain ∧ 224 48.29 N 120.55 W
Goodenough, Mount ∧ 180 67.56 N 135.31 W
Goodenough Bay ⊂ 164 9.55 S 150.00 E
Goodenough Island I 164 9.20 S 150.15 E
Gooderham 212 44.54 N 78.23 W
Goodeve 184 51.04 N 103.10 W
Goodfellow Air Force Base ■ 196 31.26 N 100.25 W
Good Hope, S. Afr. 158 31.51 S 21.55 E
Good Hope, Oh., U.S. 218 39.26 N 83.21 W
Good Hope, Cape of (Kaap die Gooie Hoop) ≻ 158 34.24 S 18.30 E
Goodhope Bay ⊂ 180 66.10 N 163.45 W
Good Hope Mountain ∧ 182 51.09 N 124.10 W
Goodhouse 158 28.57 S 18.13 E
Goodhue 190 44.24 N 92.37 W
Gooding 202 42.56 N 114.42 W
Goodison 214 42.44 N 83.10 W
Goodland, Fl., U.S. 220 25.55 N 81.38 W
Goodland, In., U.S. 216 40.45 N 87.17 W
Goodland, Ks., U.S. 198 39.21 N 101.42 W
Goodlands 184 49.05 N 100.35 W
Goodlow Park 222 32.07 N 96.14 W
Goodman, Ms., U.S. 194 32.58 N 89.54 W
Goodman, Wi., U.S. 190 45.37 N 88.21 W
Goodna 171a 27.37 S 152.54 E
Goodnews Bay 180 59.07 N 161.35 W
Goodnight 200 38.14 N 104.43 W
Goodooga 166 29.07 S 147.27 E
Goodradigbee ≃ 171b 35.08 S 148.41 E
Goodrich, Mi., U.S. 216 42.55 N 83.30 W
Goodrich, N.D., U.S. 198 47.28 N 100.07 W
Goodrich, Tx., U.S. 222 30.36 N 94.57 W
Good Spirit Lake ⊜ 184 51.34 N 102.40 W
Good Spirit Lake Provincial Park ♠ 184 51.36 N 102.45 W
Good Thunder 190 44.00 N 94.03 W
Goodview 190 44.03 N 91.41 W
Goodville 208 40.08 N 76.00 W
Goodwater 194 33.03 N 86.03 W
Goodwell 196 36.35 N 101.38 W
Goodwick 42 52.00 N 5.00 W
Goodwin, Lake ⊜ 224 48.08 N 122.18 W
Goodwives ≃ 276 41.04 N 73.28 W
Goodwood 212 44.02 N 79.12 W
Goodyear 200 33.26 N 112.21 W
Goof, Webi ≃ 144 1.10 N 43.43 E
Googong Reservoir ⊜[1] 171b 35.27 S 149.16 E
Gooie Hoop, Kaap die → Good Hope, Cape of ≻ 158 34.24 S 18.30 E
Goole 44 53.42 N 0.52 W
Goolgowi 166 33.59 S 145.42 E
Goolwa 168b 35.31 S 138.47 E
Goomalling 162 31.19 S 116.49 E
Goombalie 166 29.59 S 145.23 E
Goombungee 171a 27.18 S 151.51 E
Goomburra 171a 28.03 S 152.07 E
Goonda 156 19.51 S 34.00 E
Goondiwindi 166 28.32 S 150.19 E
Goongarrie 162 30.03 S 121.09 E
Goongarrie National Park ♠ 162 29.58 S 121.34 E
Goonyella 166 21.45 S 147.55 E
Goor 52 52.14 N 6.35 E
Goose ≃, Ab., Can. 182 54.58 N 117.11 W
Goose ≃, N.D., U.S. 198 47.28 N 96.52 W
Goose Bay ⊂ 281 42.35 N 82.41 W
Goose Bay → Happy Valley-Goose Bay 176 53.20 N 60.25 W
Gooseberry Creek ≃ 202 43.55 N 108.04 W
Goose Creek 192 32.58 N 80.01 W
Goose Creek ≃, U.S. 202 42.33 N 113.46 W
Goose Creek ≃, Ne., U.S. 198 42.02 N 100.03 W
Goose Creek ≃, N.Y., U.S. 214 42.06 N 79.22 W
Goose Creek ≃, Va., U.S. 208 39.06 N 77.29 W
Goose Island I 182 51.55 N 128.25 W
Goose Lake ⊜, Mb., Can. 184 54.26 N 101.30 W
Goose Lake ⊜, On., Can. 184 51.46 N 93.00 W
Goose Lake ⊜, On., Can. 212 44.25 N 78.52 W
Goose Lake ⊜, On., Can. 214 42.31 N 82.31 W
Goose Lake ⊜, Sk., Can. 184 51.45 N 107.23 W
Goose Lake ⊜, U.S. 204 41.57 N 120.25 W
Goose Lake Canal ≊ 226 35.50 N 119.37 W
Goose Lake Prairie State Park ♠ 216 41.21 N 88.18 W
Gooseprairie 224 46.54 N 121.15 W
Goostrey 262 53.13 N 2.20 W
Gooty 122 15.07 N 77.38 E
Gopālganj, Bngl. 124 23.01 N 89.50 E
Gopālganj, India 124 26.28 N 84.26 E
Gopālnagar, India 126 23.03 N 88.45 E
Gopālnagar, India 272b 22.50 N 88.14 E
Gopālpur, Bngl. 124 24.33 N 89.56 E
Gopālpur, India 272b 22.38 N 88.27 E
Gopeng 114 4.28 N 101.10 E
Göpfritz an der Wild 61 48.43 N 15.24 E
Gopiballabhpur 126 22.13 N 86.54 E
Gopichettipālaiyam 122 11.28 N 77.27 E
Gopinagar 272b 22.50 N 88.07 E
Goppenstein 58 46.22 N 7.45 E
Göppingen 56 48.42 N 9.40 E
Goqên 102 29.15 N 96.59 E
Go Quao 110 9.43 N 105.17 E
Gor 123 35.32 N 74.31 E

PORTUGUÊS — Nome / Página / Lat.°′ / Long.°′ W = Oeste

Góra, Pol. 30 51.40 N 16.33 E
Gora, Ross. 76 60.02 N 41.43 E
Gor'ačegorsk 86 55.24 N 88.55 E
Gor'ačij Kl'uč 84 44.37 N 39.07 E
Gor'ačinsk 88 52.59 N 108.18 E
Goradit 144 11.25 N 38.25 E
Goradiz 84 39.27 N 47.20 E
Góra Kalwaria 30 51.59 N 21.12 E
Gorakhpur 124 26.45 N 83.22 E
Gor'any 76 55.25 N 29.02 E
Goras 124 25.32 N 76.56 E
Goražde 38 43.40 N 18.56 E
Gorbačevo Michajlovka 83 47.50 N 38.00 E
Gorbatov 80 56.08 N 43.04 E
Gorbatovka 80 56.15 N 43.45 E
Gorbica 88 53.06 N 119.13 E
Gorboviči 76 53.49 N 30.41 E
Gorčucha 80 57.43 N 43.43 E
Gorda, Punta ≻, Chile 248 19.18 S 70.18 W
Gorda, Punta ≻, Cuba 240p 22.24 N 82.10 W
Gorda, Punta ≻, Nic. 236 11.26 N 83.48 W
Gorda, Punta ≻, Nic. 236 14.21 N 83.12 W
Gordejevka 76 52.59 N 31.58 E
Gordes, Fr. 62 43.54 N 5.12 E
Gördes, Tür. 130 38.54 N 28.18 E
Gordil 146 9.44 N 21.35 E
Gørding 41 55.29 N 8.48 E
Gordion ⊥ 130 39.41 N 32.01 E
Gordo 194 33.19 N 87.54 W
Gordo, Cerro ∧ 234 20.46 N 102.35 W
Gordola 58 46.11 N 8.52 E
Gordon, Scot., U.K. 46 55.41 N 2.34 W
Gordon, Ga., U.S. 192 32.52 N 83.19 W
Gordon, Ne., U.S. 198 42.48 N 102.12 W
Gordon, Oh., U.S. 218 39.56 N 84.31 W
Gordon, Pa., U.S. 208 40.45 N 76.21 W
Gordon, Wi., U.S. 190 46.14 N 91.47 W
Gordon ≃ 224 48.35 N 124.24 W
Gordon, Isla I 254 54.58 S 69.35 W
Gordon, Lake ⊜[1] 166 42.42 S 146.12 E
Gordon Creek ≃ 198 42.49 N 100.40 W
Gordon Downs 162 18.44 S 128.35 E
Gordon Heights 207 40.51 N 72.58 W
Gordon Horne Peak ∧ 182 51.46 N 118.50 W
Gordon Indian Reserve ◆[4] 184 51.16 N 104.16 W
Gordon Lake ⊜, Ab., Can. 184 56.30 N 110.25 W
Gordon Lake ⊜, Sk., Can. 184 55.50 N 106.26 W
Gordon Lakes 276 41.03 N 74.22 W
Gordon Pass ⊂ 220 26.06 N 81.48 W
Gordon River 224 48.47 N 124.21 W
Gordon's Bay 158 34.10 S 18.52 E
Gordonsville 188 38.08 N 78.11 W
Gordonton 172 37.40 S 175.18 E
Gordonvale 166 17.05 S 145.47 E
Gordonville 220 27.57 N 81.49 W
Gore, Austl. 166 28.17 S 151.29 E
Gore, N.S., Can. 186 45.07 N 63.43 W
Gore, Ityo. 144 8.08 N 35.33 E
Gore, N.Z. 172 46.06 S 168.58 E
Goré, Tchad 146 7.53 N 16.40 E
Gore Bay 190 45.55 N 82.28 W
Gorebridge 46 55.51 N 3.02 W
Goreda 164 3.39 S 134.58 E
Goree 196 33.28 N 99.31 W
Gore Hill 274a 33.49 S 151.11 E
Görele 130 41.02 N 39.00 E
Gorelki 82 54.15 N 37.37 E
Goreloje 80 52.57 N 41.28 E
Gorelovo 265a 59.47 N 30.08 E
Gorelovo Airport ⊠ 265a 59.47 N 30.05 E
Gorelyj ≃ 265a 59.58 N 30.28 E
Göreme Milli Parkı ♠ 130 38.26 N 34.54 E
Gore Mountain ∧ 188 44.55 N 71.48 W
Gorenki 265b 55.48 N 37.55 E
Gore Point ≻, Austl. 166 17.38 S 139.56 E
Gore Point ≻, Ak., U.S. 180 59.12 N 151.00 W
Gore Range ⋏ 200 40.00 N 106.30 W
Goretovka ≃ 265b 55.56 N 37.20 E
Goreville 194 37.33 N 88.58 W
Gorey, Ire. 48 52.40 N 6.18 W
Gorey, Jersey 43b 49.12 N 2.02 W
Gorfoundurei 144 4.30 N 46.41 E
Gorgān 128 36.50 N 54.29 E
Gorgān ≃ 128 36.59 N 54.00 E
Gorgany ⋏ 78 48.30 N 24.00 E
Gorge Lake ⊜[1] 224 48.42 N 121.13 W
Görgeshausen 56 50.24 N 7.56 E
Gorgoglione 68 40.23 N 16.09 E
Gorgol □[4] 150 16.00 N 13.00 W
Gorgol el Abiod ≃ 150 16.14 N 12.58 W
Gorgol el Akhdar ≃ 150 16.13 N 12.58 W
Gorgona, Isla I 246 2.59 N 78.12 W
Gorgonzola 62 45.32 N 9.24 E
Gorgor 248 10.35 S 77.02 W
Gorgora 144 12.13 N 37.16 E
Gorgoram 146 12.38 N 10.43 E
Gorgota 38 44.47 N 26.05 E
Gorgova 38 45.11 N 29.10 E
Gorham, Me., U.S. 188 43.40 N 70.26 W
Gorham, N.H., U.S. 188 44.23 N 71.10 W
Gorham, N.Y., U.S. 210 42.47 N 77.07 W
Gorhambury House ⊥ 260 51.47 N 0.24 W
Gori 84 41.58 N 44.07 E
Goria 272b 22.24 N 88.29 E
Gorica → Gorizia 64 45.57 N 13.38 E
Goričan 61 46.23 N 16.41 E
Goricy 76 57.09 N 36.44 E
Gorinchem 52 51.50 N 5.00 E
Goring 42 51.32 N 1.09 W
Goring-by-Sea 42 50.49 N 0.25 W
Goring Gap V 42 51.32 N 1.08 W
Goris 84 39.31 N 46.23 E
Göritz 54 53.24 N 13.54 E
Göritzhain 54 50.58 N 12.47 E
Gorizia 64 45.57 N 13.38 E
Gorizia □[4] 64 45.55 N 13.30 E
Gorj □[6] 38 45.00 N 23.20 E
Gorjani 38 45.24 N 18.21 E
Gor'kaja Balka 84 44.17 N 43.59 E
Gor'kaja balka ≃ 84 44.38 N 45.00 E
Görke 54 53.51 N 13.38 E
Gorkhā 124 28.00 N 84.37 E
Gorki, Bela. 76 54.17 N 30.59 E
Gorki, Ross. 80 57.38 N 45.05 E
Gorki, Ross. 82 54.18 N 36.08 E
Gorki, Ross. 82 55.32 N 37.45 E
Gorki, Ross. 82 56.54 N 38.51 E
Gorki, Ross. 265b 55.57 N 37.55 E
Gor'kij → Nižnij Novgorod 80 56.20 N 44.00 E
Gorki → Nižnij Novgorod 80 56.20 N 44.00 E
Gorki Vtoryje 265b 55.44 N 37.11 E
Gor'koje, ozero ⊜ 86 52.30 N 81.20 E
Gor'kovskoje 86 55.22 N 74.24 E
Gor'kovskoje vodochranilišče ⊜[1] 80 57.00 N 43.10 E
Gorky → Nižnij Novgorod 80 56.20 N 44.00 E
Gorky Park ♠ 265b 55.44 N 37.36 E
Gorlago 62 45.40 N 9.49 E
Gorla Maggiore 266b 45.40 N 8.53 E
Gorla Minore 266b 45.39 N 8.54 E
Gorleston on Sea 42 52.36 N 1.43 E
Gørlev 41 55.32 N 11.14 E
Gorlice 30 49.40 N 21.10 E
Görlitz 54 51.09 N 14.59 E
Gorlosen 54 53.11 N 11.27 E
Gorlovka, Sak. 84 41.14 N 43.42 E
Gorlovka, Ukr. 83 48.18 N 38.03 E
Gorlovo 76 53.50 N 39.02 E
Gorm, Loch ⊜ 46 55.48 N 6.25 W
Gorman, Ca., U.S. 228 34.48 N 118.51 W
Gorman, Tx., U.S. 196 32.12 N 98.40 W
Gorman Creek ≃ 228 34.38 N 118.45 W
Görmin 54 53.59 N 13.16 E
Gorn'ackij, Ross. 24 67.32 N 64.03 E
Gorn'ackij, Ross. 78 48.17 N 40.55 E
Gorn'ackoje 78 47.42 N 34.08 E
Gorna Dzhumaya → Blagoevgrad 38 42.01 N 23.06 E
Gornaja Prolejka 80 49.24 N 44.59 E
Gorn'ak, Ross. 76 53.36 N 39.29 E
Gorn'ak, Ross. 86 51.00 N 81.29 E
Gorn'ak, Ukr. 78 50.20 N 24.10 E
Gorn'ak, Ukr. 83 48.04 N 37.24 E
Gornalunga ≃ 70 37.24 N 15.03 E
Gorna Orjahovica 38 43.07 N 25.41 E
Gornergrat ♠ 58 45.59 N 7.47 E
Gornja Radgona 61 46.41 N 16.00 E
Gornji Grad 36 46.18 N 14.49 E
Gornji Milanovac 38 44.01 N 20.27 E
Gornji Vakuf 36 43.56 N 17.35 E
Gorno-Altajsk 86 51.58 N 85.58 E
Gorno-Altajskaja Avtonomnaja Sovetskaja Socialističeskaja Respublika □[3] 86 51.00 N 86.00 E
Gorno-Badachšanskaja Avtonomnaja Oblast' □[8] 85 38.30 N 73.00 E
Gornoje 86 48.29 N 85.00 E
Gorno-Lesnoj zapovednik ♠ 85 41.10 N 69.55 E
Gornopravdinsk 86 60.07 N 69.54 E
Gornostajevka 78 47.01 N 33.44 E
Gorno-Vod'anoje 80 49.16 N 44.56 E
Gornovodnoje 89 43.42 N 134.44 E
Gornozavodsk, Ross. 86 58.20 N 58.32 E
Gornozavodsk, Ross. 89 46.34 N 141.49 E
Gornyj, Ross. 80 51.46 N 48.34 E
Gornyj, Ross. 89 50.48 N 136.29 E
Gornyj, Ross. 89 44.57 N 133.59 E
Gornyj Balyklej 80 49.34 N 45.04 E
Gornyje Kl'uči 89 45.12 N 133.31 E
Gornyj Tikič ≃ 78 48.47 N 30.53 E
Goro, Ityo. 144 6.56 N 40.32 E
Goro, N. Cal. 175f 22.16 S 167.02 E
Gorochan ∧ 144 9.22 N 37.04 E
Gorochov 78 50.30 N 24.45 E
Gorochovatka 83 49.21 N 37.31 E
Gorochovec 80 56.12 N 42.40 E
Gorochovje 76 56.31 N 30.29 E
Gorodec, Bela. 76 52.12 N 24.40 E
Gorodec, Bela. 76 52.58 N 30.21 E
Gorodec, Bela. 76 53.33 N 30.02 E
Gorodec, Ross. 76 58.32 N 29.47 E
Gorodec, Ross. 80 56.38 N 43.30 E
Gorodec, Ukr. 78 51.17 N 26.19 E
Gorodeja 76 53.19 N 26.32 E
Gorodenka 38 48.41 N 25.29 E
Gorodišče, Bela. 76 53.44 N 29.48 E
Gorodišče, Bela. 76 53.19 N 26.00 E
Gorodišče, Ross. 76 59.38 N 32.08 E
Gorodišče, Ross. 78 51.09 N 38.04 E
Gorodišče, Ross. 80 53.17 N 45.42 E
Gorodišče, Ross. 80 48.48 N 44.29 E
Gorodišče, Ross. 82 54.53 N 38.13 E
Gorodišče, Ross. 82 56.47 N 38.52 E
Gorodišče, Ukr. 78 49.17 N 31.27 E
Gorodišče, Ukr. 83 48.19 N 38.39 E
Gorodišče, Ukr. 83 49.03 N 39.38 E
Gorodišči 82 55.52 N 39.05 E
Gorodkovka 78 48.23 N 28.42 E
Gorodn'a, Ross. 82 54.57 N 38.49 E
Gorodn'a, Ross. 82 56.43 N 36.19 E
Gorodn'a, Ukr. 78 51.53 N 31.36 E
Gorodn'a ≃ 265b 55.38 N 37.48 E
Gorodnica 78 50.48 N 27.20 E
Gorodno 76 57.32 N 29.35 E
Gorodok, Bela. 76 55.28 N 29.59 E
Gorodok, Ukr. 78 49.10 N 26.34 E
Gorodok, Ukr. 78 49.47 N 23.39 E
Gorod'onka 78 48.41 N 25.29 E
Goroka 164 6.05 S 145.25 E
Gorokan 170 33.16 S 151.30 E
Gorom-Gorom 150 14.26 N 0.14 W
Gorong, Pulau I 164 3.59 S 131.25 E
Gorongosa, Parque Nacional da ♠ 156 18.45 S 34.15 E
Gorongosa, Serra da ∧ 154 18.30 S 34.03 E
Gorongose ≃ 156 20.30 S 34.40 E
Gorontalo 112 0.33 N 123.03 E
Goronyo 150 13.29 N 5.39 E
Goroubi ≃ 150 12.54 N 2.23 E
Gorouol ≃ 150 14.42 N 0.53 E
Górowo Iławeckie 30 54.17 N 20.30 E
Gorple Reservoirs ⊜[1] 262 53.47 N 2.06 W
Gorran ⊜ 40 59.43 N 17.32 E
Gorredijk 52 53.00 N 6.05 E
Gorron 28 48.25 N 0.49 W
Görsdorf 54 51.54 N 13.29 E
Goršečnoje 78 51.32 N 38.02 E
Gorsedd 262 53.17 N 3.16 W
Gorseinon 42 51.40 N 4.02 W
Gorskaja 265a 60.03 N 29.59 E
Gorskoje 83 48.46 N 38.30 E
Gorškovo 82 54.26 N 37.59 E
Gorst 224 47.32 N 122.42 W
Gort 48 53.04 N 8.50 W
Gortahork 48 55.08 N 8.09 W
Gorton ◆[8] 262 53.27 N 2.10 W
Görtschitz ≃ 61 46.45 N 14.32 E
Goru, Vîrful ∧ 38 45.48 N 26.25 E
Görükle 130 40.14 N 28.50 E
Gorumna Island I 48 53.14 N 9.40 W
Gor'un ≃ 89 50.45 N 137.50 E
Gorutuba ≃ 255 14.57 S 43.33 W
Görwihl 58 47.39 N 8.04 E
Gory, Bela. 76 54.16 N 31.13 E
Gory, Kaz. 80 48.38 N 51.46 E
Goryn' ≃ 78 52.08 N 27.17 E
Gorzano, Monte ∧ 66 42.37 N 13.24 E
Gorze 56 49.03 N 6.00 E
Görz → Gorizia 64 45.57 N 13.38 E
Görzig 54 51.40 N 12.00 E
Görzke 54 52.10 N 12.22 E
Górzno 30 53.13 N 19.38 E
Gorzów Śląski 30 51.02 N 18.24 E
Gorzów Wielkopolski (Landsberg an der Warthe) 30 52.44 N 15.15 E
Gorzów Wielkopolski □[4] 30 52.45 N 15.20 E
Górzyca 54 52.29 N 14.40 E
Gosāba 126 22.10 N 88.48 E
Gosairhāt 126 23.05 N 90.26 E
Gosaldo 64 46.13 N 11.58 E
Gosau 64 47.34 N 13.31 E
Gosauseen ⊜ 64 47.32 N 13.31 E
Gosberton 42 52.51 N 0.09 W
Gošča 78 50.36 N 26.41 E
Göschenen 58 46.40 N 8.35 E
Goschen Strait ꓵ 164 10.09 S 150.56 E
Gose 96 34.27 N 135.44 E
Gosen, Dtsch. 264a 52.24 N 13.43 E
Gosen, Nihon 92 37.44 N 139.11 E
Gosford 170 33.26 S 151.21 E
Gosforth, Eng., U.K. 44 55.01 N 1.37 W
Gosforth, Eng., U.K. 44 54.26 N 3.27 W
Gosforth Park ♠ 273d 26.14 S 28.10 E
Gosforth Park Race Course ♠ 273d 26.14 S 28.08 E
Goshabi 140 17.58 N 31.06 E
Goshen, N.S., Can. 186 45.23 N 61.59 W
Goshen, Ca., U.S. 226 36.21 N 119.25 W
Goshen, Ct., U.S. 207 41.49 N 73.13 W
Goshen, In., U.S. 216 41.34 N 85.50 W
Goshen, Ma., U.S. 207 42.26 N 72.48 W
Goshen, N.J., U.S. 208 39.08 N 74.51 W
Goshen, N.Y., U.S. 210 41.24 N 74.19 W
Goshen, Oh., U.S. 218 39.14 N 84.10 W
Goshiki 96 34.24 N 134.47 E
Goshogawara 92 40.48 N 140.27 E
Goshute Indian Reservation ◆[4] 200 39.53 N 114.08 W
Goshute Lake ⊜ 204 40.08 N 114.38 W
Goshute Valley V 204 40.40 N 114.30 W
Goslar 52 51.54 N 10.25 E
Gosnells 168a 32.04 S 116.00 E
Gospić 36 44.33 N 15.23 E
Gosport, Eng., U.K. 42 50.48 N 1.08 W
Gosport, In., U.S. 194 39.21 N 86.40 W
Gossa 54 51.40 N 12.26 E
Gossas 150 14.30 N 16.04 W
Gossau 58 47.25 N 9.15 E
Gosse ◆[8] 263 51.08 N 7.01 E
Gosse Bluff ∧ 162 23.49 S 132.19 E
Gosselies 56 50.28 N 4.25 E
Gössenheim 56 50.01 N 9.46 E
Gossensass → Colle Isarco 64 46.56 N 11.26 E
Gosser Hill 279b 40.37 N 79.37 W
Gossi 150 15.49 N 1.17 W
Gossinga 140 8.39 N 25.59 E
Gössnitz 54 50.53 N 12.26 E
Gossolengo 62 44.59 N 9.37 E
Gössweinstein 60 49.46 N 11.20 E
Gostagajevskaja 78 45.01 N 37.30 E
Gostilovo 82 55.18 N 38.36 E
Gostiščevo 78 50.47 N 36.39 E
Gostivar 38 41.47 N 20.54 E
Göstling an der Ybbs 61 47.48 N 14.55 E
Gostyń 30 51.53 N 17.00 E
Gostynin 30 52.26 N 19.29 E
Gosudarev Bajrak 83 48.21 N 38.08 E
Göta älv ≃ 26 57.42 N 11.52 E
Göta kanal ≊ 40 58.50 N 13.58 E
Gotchen Creek ≃ 224 46.00 N 121.30 W
Got Creek ≃ 284a 43.03 N 78.42 W
Gotebo 196 35.04 N 98.52 W
Göteborg (Gothenburg) 26 57.43 N 11.58 E
Göteborgs Och Bohus län □[6] 26 58.30 N 11.30 E
Gotel Mountains ⋏ 152 6.55 N 11.15 E
Gotemba 94 35.18 N 138.56 E
Götene 26 58.32 N 13.29 E
Goteşty 78 46.09 N 28.10 E
Gotha, Dtsch. 54 50.57 N 10.41 E
Gotha, Fl., U.S. 220 28.32 N 81.31 W
Gothem 26 57.35 N 18.43 E
Gothenburg 198 40.55 N 100.09 W
Gothenburg → Göteborg 26 57.43 N 11.58 E
Gothèye 150 13.52 N 1.34 E
Gotland I 26 57.30 N 18.33 E
Gotlands Län □[6] 26 57.30 N 18.30 E
Gotoputovo 86 56.46 N 70.10 E
Gotō-rettō II 92 32.50 N 129.00 E
Gotska Sandön I 26 58.23 N 19.16 E
Gōtsu 96 35.00 N 132.14 E
Gottenheim 58 48.03 N 7.44 E
Götterswickerhamm 263 51.35 N 6.40 E
Gottesbrücke 264a 52.25 N 13.49 E
Gotthard Tunnel ◆[5] 58 46.35 N 8.35 E
Göttin 264a 52.27 N 12.54 E
Göttingen, Dtsch. 52 51.32 N 9.55 E
Göttingen, Dtsch. 56 50.52 N 8.46 E
Göttin See ⊜ 264a 52.28 N 12.54 E
Gottmadingen 58 47.44 N 8.47 E
Gottolengo 64 45.17 N 10.16 E
Gottorf, Schloss ⊥ 41 54.30 N 9.32 E
Gottsbüren 52 51.35 N 9.30 E
Gottvaterkapelle ʊ[1] 60 49.42 N 11.41 E
Götzendorf 264b 48.01 N 16.35 E
Gőtzis 58 47.20 N 9.38 E
Gouarec 32 48.13 N 3.11 W
Goubangzi 104 41.22 N 121.46 E
Goubone 146 20.43 N 17.08 E
Gouda, Ned. 52 52.01 N 4.43 E
Gouda, S. Afr. 158 33.19 S 19.04 E
Goudet 62 44.53 N 3.55 E
Goudge 252 34.40 S 68.08 W
Goudhurst 42 51.07 N 0.28 E
Goudiry 150 14.11 N 12.43 W
Goudoumaria 146 13.42 N 11.10 E
Goudswaard 52 51.47 N 4.16 E
Gouéké 150 8.02 N 8.43 W
Goûfi, Djebel el ∧ 34 36.57 N 6.27 E
Gougezhuang 105 38.53 N 116.11 E
Gough Island I 10 40.20 S 10.00 W
Gough Lake ⊜ 182 52.02 N 112.28 W
Gouin, Réservoir ⊜[1] 176 48.38 N 74.54 W
Goujiaozhen 107 30.36 N 106.33 E
Goukou 89 48.39 N 122.06 E
Goulais ≃ 190 46.43 N 84.27 W
Goulburn 170 34.45 S 149.43 E
Goulburn ≃ 169 36.41 S 145.12 E
Goulburn Islands II 164 11.33 S 133.26 E
Goulburn Weir ⊜[1] 169 36.45 S 145.08 E
Gould 194 33.59 N 91.33 W
Gould City 190 46.05 N 85.41 W
Gould Park 214 40.04 N 82.53 W
Goulds 220 25.33 N 80.22 W
Gouldsboro 210 41.44 N 75.28 W
Gouldsboro State Park ♠ 210 41.13 N 75.28 W
Goulet Lake ⊜ 184 55.23 N 96.18 W
Goulia 150 10.01 N 7.11 W
Goulicun 106 31.40 N 120.00 E
Goulimime 148 28.56 N 10.04 W
Goulimine □[4] 148 28.30 N 9.45 W
Goulmima 148 31.02 N 5.00 W
Goumbati ∧[2] 150 13.08 N 12.06 W
Goumbou 150 14.59 N 7.27 W
Gouménissa 38 40.57 N 22.27 E
Goumois 58 47.16 N 6.57 E
Gouna 146 8.32 N 13.34 E
Gounda ≃ 146 9.25 N 20.57 E
Goundam 150 16.25 N 3.40 W
Goundi 146 9.22 N 17.22 E
Gounou-Gaya 146 9.38 N 15.31 E
Gouougang, Mount ∧ 170 33.53 S 150.07 E
Goupillières 261 48.53 N 1.46 E
Gouraya 34 36.34 N 1.55 E
Gourbassi 150 13.24 N 11.38 W
Gourbeyre 241o 16.00 N 61.42 W
Gourcy 150 13.13 N 2.21 W
Gourdhead Run ≃ 279b 40.33 N 79.57 W
Gourdon, Fr. 32 44.44 N 1.23 E
Gourdon, Fr. 62 43.43 N 6.59 E
Gouré 150 13.58 N 10.18 E
Gouri ⊥ 124 24.53 N 88.07 E
Gourin 32 48.08 N 3.36 W
Gouripur 124 24.46 N 90.34 E
Gourits ≃ 158 34.21 S 21.52 E
Gourlay Lake ⊜ 190 48.52 N 84.54 W
Gourma Rharous 150 16.53 N 1.55 W
Gournay-en-Bray 50 49.29 N 1.44 E
Gournay-sur-Marne 261 48.52 N 2.34 E
Gouro 146 19.33 N 19.33 E
Gourock 46 55.58 N 4.49 W
Goussainville 50 49.01 N 2.28 E
Goussonville 261 48.55 N 1.46 E
Goutou 105 39.49 N 117.11 E
Gouveia, Bra. 255 18.27 S 43.44 W
Gouveia, Port. 266c 38.50 N 9.26 W
Gouverneur 212 44.20 N 75.27 W
Gouyadong 100 25.10 N 112.55 E
Gouyave 241k 12.10 N 61.44 W
Gov'altaj □[4] 102 45.30 N 96.00 E
Govan 184 51.18 N 105.00 W
Go Vap 269c 10.49 N 106.41 E
Govardhan 124 27.30 N 77.28 E
Gove 198 38.57 N 100.29 W
Govea ≃ 286b 22.56 N 82.30 W
Govena, mys ≻ 74 59.48 N 166.06 E
Govenlock 184 49.15 N 109.48 W
Gove Peninsula ≻[1] 164 12.20 S 136.50 E
Goverla, gora ∧ 78 48.10 N 24.32 E
Governador Portela 256 22.29 S 43.30 W
Governador Valadares 255 18.51 S 41.56 W
Government Camp 224 45.18 N 121.45 W
Governor Bond Lake ⊜[1] 219 38.56 N 89.23 W
Governor Dodge State Park ♠ 190 43.00 N 90.07 W
Governor Generoso 116 6.39 N 126.05 E
Governor Head ≻ 170 35.07 S 150.46 E
Governor Nice Memorial Bridge ◆[5] 208 38.22 N 77.00 W
Governor Printz Park ♠ 285 39.52 N 75.18 W
Governor's Harbour 238 25.10 N 76.14 W
Governors Island I 276 40.41 N 74.01 W
Govind Ballabh Pant Sāgar ⊜[1] 124 24.05 N 82.50 E
Govindgarh 124 24.23 N 81.18 E
Govind Sāgar ⊜[1] 123 31.20 N 76.45 E
Gov'-Ugtaal 102 46.04 N 107.30 E
Gowan ≃ 184 55.49 N 94.08 W
Gowanda 210 42.27 N 78.56 W
Gowan Range ⋏ 166 25.00 S 145.00 E
Gowen City 208 40.45 N 76.32 W
Gower 194 39.36 N 94.35 W
Gower ≻[1] 42 51.36 N 4.10 W
Gowerton 42 51.39 N 4.01 W
Gowienica ≃ 54 53.40 N 14.38 E
Gowmal (Gumal) ≃ 120 31.56 N 70.22 E
Gowmal Kalay 120 32.29 N 68.55 E
Gowna, Lough ⊜ 48 53.51 N 7.34 W
Gowrie 198 42.16 N 94.17 W
Gowy ≃ 262 53.17 N 2.51 W
Goya 252 29.08 S 59.16 W
Goyania → Goiânia 255 16.40 S 49.16 W
Goyatz 54 52.01 N 14.09 E
Goyave 241o 16.08 N 61.34 W
Goyaves, Grande Rivière à ≃ 241o 16.18 N 61.37 W
Goyaves, Îlets à II 241o 16.10 N 61.48 W
Goyder ≃ 164 12.38 S 135.11 E
Goyder Creek ≃ 162 25.39 S 134.47 E
Goyelle, Lac ⊜ 186 50.47 N 60.45 W
Goyeneche 258 35.20 S 58.43 W
Goyer, Île I 275a 45.29 N 73.17 W
Goyerkāta 124 26.42 N 89.02 E
Göynücek 130 40.24 N 35.32 E
Göynük, Tür. 130 40.24 N 30.47 E
Göynük, Tür. 130 39.08 N 40.53 E
Göynük ≃, Tür. 130 38.53 N 40.34 E
Göynük ≃, Tür. 130 40.20 N 30.05 E
Goyt ≃ 262 53.24 N 2.09 W
Goz-Beïda 146 12.13 N 21.25 E
Gozdnica 30 51.26 N 15.06 E
Gozdowice 54 52.45 N 14.18 E
Göze Dağı ∧ 130 41.24 N 42.30 E
Gözeli 130 38.25 N 39.04 E
Gozen-yama 94 36.32 N 140.20 E
Gozha Co ⊜ 120 34.59 N 81.06 E
Gözne 130 36.59 N 34.34 E
Gozo → Għawdex I 36 36.03 N 14.15 E
Göz Tepe ∧[2] 267b 41.06 N 29.06 E
Gozzano 62 45.45 N 8.26 E
Graaff-Reinet 158 32.14 S 24.32 E
Graafwater 158 32.00 S 18.37 E
Graauw 52 51.20 N 4.05 E
Grabc'ovo 82 54.34 N 36.22 E
Graben-Neudorf 56 49.09 N 8.29 E
Grabenstätt 64 47.51 N 12.32 E
Grabill 216 41.12 N 84.58 W
Grabo 150 4.55 N 7.30 W
Grabouw 158 34.09 S 19.02 E
Grabovaja Balka, les ♠ 83 48.09 N 38.37 E
Grabovo 86 53.07 N 74.52 E
Grabow 54 53.16 N 11.34 E
Grabowiec 30 50.50 N 23.33 E
Grabów nad Prosną 30 51.31 N 18.06 E
Gračac 36 44.18 N 15.51 E
Gračanica 38 44.42 N 18.19 E
Gračanica, Manastir ʊ[1] 38 42.36 N 21.09 E
Graçay 50 47.08 N 1.51 E
Grace 202 42.34 N 111.43 W
Gracefield 188 46.06 N 76.03 W
Graceham 208 39.36 N 77.22 W
Graceton 214 40.30 N 79.10 W
Graceville, Fl., U.S. 192 30.57 N 85.31 W
Graceville, Mn., U.S. 198 45.34 N 96.26 W
Gračevka 82 55.06 N 36.49 E
Grächen 58 46.12 N 7.50 E
Grachovo 80 56.04 N 51.58 E
Grači 80 49.49 N 43.33 E
Gracia ◆[8] 266d 41.23 N 2.09 E
Gracias 236 14.35 N 88.35 W
Gracias a Dios □[5] 236 15.10 N 84.20 W
Gracias a Dios, Cabo ≻ 236 15.00 N 83.10 W
Gračiki ≃ 83 48.30 N 39.52 E
Graciosa I 148a 39.04 N 28.00 W
Graciosa, Isla I 148 29.15 N 13.30 W
Gračov 80 49.26 N 41.32 E
Gračovka, Ross. 80 52.07 N 40.01 E
Gračovka, Ross. 80 52.57 N 52.52 E
Gračov Kust 80 51.59 N 49.50 E
Gradačac 38 44.53 N 18.26 E
Gradara 66 43.57 N 12.46 E
Gradaús 250 7.43 S 51.11 W
Gr'adcy 76 56.24 N 31.55 E
Gräddö 40 59.46 N 19.02 E
Gradisca d'Isonzo 64 45.53 N 13.30 E
Gradižsk 78 49.13 N 33.07 E
Grado, Esp. 34 43.23 N 6.04 W
Grado, It. 64 45.40 N 13.23 E
Grado, Laguna di ⊂ 64 45.43 N 13.20 E
Gradoli 66 42.39 N 11.51 E
Grady, Ar., U.S. 194 34.04 N 91.42 W
Grady, N.M., U.S. 196 34.49 N 103.19 W
Gradyville 285 39.57 N 75.28 W
Graemsay I 46 58.56 N 3.17 W
Græsted 41 56.04 N 12.17 E
Graettinger 198 43.14 N 94.45 W
Gräfelfing 60 48.07 N 11.25 E
Grafenau 60 48.52 N 13.25 E
Gräfenberg 60 49.39 N 11.15 E
Grafenberg ◆[8] 263 51.14 N 6.50 E
Gräfenhainichen 54 51.44 N 12.27 E
Gräfenroda 54 50.45 N 10.48 E
Gräfenthal 54 50.31 N 11.18 E
Gräfentonna 54 51.05 N 10.44 E
Grafenwöhr 60 49.43 N 11.54 E
Graffignano 66 42.34 N 12.12 E
Grafham Water ⊜ 42 52.17 N 0.20 W
Gräfinau-Angstedt 54 50.42 N 11.01 E
Grafing bei München 60 48.02 N 11.59 E
Gråfjell ∧ 26 60.16 N 9.29 E
Graford 196 32.56 N 98.14 W
Gräfrath ◆[8] 263 51.13 N 7.04 E
Grafschaft Bentheim □[9] 52 52.30 N 7.00 E
Grafton, Austl. 166 29.41 S 152.56 E
Grafton, On., Can. 212 44.00 N 78.01 W
Grafton, Il., U.S. 219 38.58 N 90.25 W
Grafton, Ma., U.S. 207 42.12 N 71.41 W
Grafton, N.Y., U.S. 210 42.46 N 73.27 W
Grafton, N.D., U.S. 198 48.24 N 97.24 W
Grafton, Oh., U.S. 214 41.16 N 82.03 W
Grafton, W.V., U.S. 188 39.20 N 80.01 W
Grafton, Wi., U.S. 190 43.19 N 87.57 W
Grafton, Cape ≻ 164 16.52 S 145.55 E
Grafton Lakes State Park ♠ 210 42.48 N 73.28 W
Grafty Green 260 51.12 N 0.41 E
Graglia 62 45.33 N 7.59 E

≃	River	Fluß	Río	Rivière	Rio
≊	Canal	Kanal	Canal	Canal	Canal
⌊	Waterfall, Rapids	Wasserfall, Stromschnellen	Cascada, Rápidos	Chute d'eau, Rapides	Cascata, Rápidos
ꓵ	Strait	Meeresstraße	Estrecho	Détroit	Estreito
⊂	Bay, Gulf	Bucht, Golf	Bahía, Golfo	Baie, Golfe	Baía, Golfo
⊜	Lake, Lakes	See, Seen	Lago, Lagos	Lac, Lacs	Lago, Lagos
⩸	Swamp	Sumpf	Pantano	Marais	Pântano
⍓	Ice Features, Glacier	Eis- und Gletscherformen	Accidentes Glaciales	Formes glaciaires	Acidentes glaciares
⍑	Other Hydrographic Features	Andere Hydrographische Objekte	Otros Elementos Hidrográficos	Autres données hydrographiques	Outros acidentes hidrográficos

◆	Submarine Features	Untermeerische Objekte	Accidentes Submarinos	Formes de relief sous-marin	Acidentes submarinos
□	Political Unit	Politische Einheit	Unidad Política	Entité politique	Unidade política
ʊ	Cultural Institution	Kulturelle Institution	Institución Cultural	Institution culturelle	Instituição cultural
⊥	Historical Site	Historische Stätte	Sitio Histórico	Site historique	Sitio histórico
♠	Recreational Site	Erholungs- und Ferienort	Sitio de Recreo	Centre de loisirs	Area de Lazer
⊠	Airport	Flughafen	Aeropuerto	Aéroport	Aeroporto
■	Military Installation	Militäranlage	Instalación Militar	Installation militaire	Instalação militar
◆	Miscellaneous	Verschiedenes	Misceláneo	Divers	Diversos

Symbols in the index entries represent the broad categories identified in the key at the right. Symbols with superior numbers (∧¹) identify subcategories (see complete key on page I · 1).

Symbole im Register stellen die rechts im Schlüssel erklärten Kategorien dar. Symbole mit hochgestellten Ziffern (∧¹) bezeichnen Unterabteilungen einer Kategorie (vgl. vollständiger Schlüssel auf Seite I · 1).

Los símbolos incluídos en el texto del índice representan las grandes categorías identificadas con la clave a la derecha. Los símbolos con numeros en su parte superior (∧¹) identifican las subcategorías (véase la clave completa en la página I · 1).

Les symboles de l'index représentent les catégories indiquées dans la légende à droite. Les symboles suivis d'un indice (∧¹) représentent des sous-catégories (voir légende complète à la page I · 1).

Os símbolos incluídos no texto do índice representam as grandes categorias identificadas com a chave à direita. Os símbolos com números em sua parte superior (∧¹) identificam as subcategorias (veja-se a chave completa à página I · 1).

∧ Mountain	Berg	Montaña	Montagne	Montanha
∧ Mountains	Gebirge	Montañas	Montagnes	Montanhas
x Pass	Paß	Paso	Col	Passo
V Valley, Canyon	Tal, Cañon	Valle, Cañón	Vallée, Canyon	Vale, Canhão
≡ Plain	Ebene	Llano	Plaine	Planície
> Cape	Kap	Cabo	Cap	Cabo
I Island	Insel	Isla	Île	Ilha
II Islands	Inseln	Islas	Îles	Ilhas
≐ Other Topographic Features	Andere Topographische Objekte	Otros Elementos Topográficos	Autres données topographiques	Outros acidentes topográficos

| ESPAÑOL | | | | FRANÇAIS | | | | PORTUGUÊS | | | | Grea-Gros I · 65 |

Nombre — Página — Lat.⁰ʳ — Long.⁰ʳ W = Oeste · Nom — Page — Lat.⁰ʳ — Long.⁰ʳ W = Ouest · Nome — Página — Lat.⁰ʳ — Long.⁰ʳ W = Oeste

Name	Page	Lat.	Long.
Great Kills Park ♦	276	40.33 N	74.08 W
Great La Cloche Island I	190	46.01 N	81.52 W
Great Lake ▲	166	41.52 S	146.45 E
Great Lakes Naval Training Center ■	216	42.18 N	87.50 W
Great Lakes Steel Works	281	42.15 N	83.08 W
Great Machipongo Inlet ⌒	208	37.22 N	75.43 W
Great Malvern	42	52.07 N	2.19 W
Great Marsh ⌑	208	36.32 N	75.57 W
Great Marton	262	53.48 N	3.02 W
Great Massingham	42	52.46 N	0.40 E
Great Meadows	210	40.52 N	74.54 W
Great Meadows National Wildlife Refuge	283	42.29 N	71.20 W
Great Mercury Island	172	36.37 S	175.48 E
Great Meteor Tablemount	18	30.00 N	28.30 W
Great Miami ≃	188	39.06 N	84.49 W
Great Mills	208	38.14 N	76.30 W
Great Misery Island I	283	42.33 N	70.48 W
Great Missenden	42	51.43 N	0.43 W
Great Mis Tor ▲	42	50.34 N	4.01 W
Great Mosque	146	32.46 N	22.40 E
Great Namaqualand □⁹	156	25.00 S	17.00 E
Great Neck ▸¹, Ma., U.S.	276	40.48 N	73.43 W
Great Neck ▸¹, N.Y., U.S.	283	42.42 N	70.48 W
Great Neck Estates	276	40.47 N	73.44 W
Great Nicobar I	110	7.00 N	93.50 E
Great North East Channel ᴗ	164	9.30 S	143.25 E
Great Notch Reservoir ⍟¹	276	40.53 N	74.12 W
Great Ormes Head ▸	44	53.21 N	3.52 W
Great Ouse ≃	42	52.47 N	0.22 E
Great Oxney Green	260	51.44 N	0.28 E
Great Palm Island I	166	18.43 S	146.37 E
Great Parndon	260	51.45 N	0.05 E
Great Patchogue Lake ⍟	276	40.46 N	73.01 W
Great Peconic Bay ⌒	207	40.56 N	72.30 W
Great Pee Dee ≃	192	33.21 N	79.16 W
Great Piece Meadows ⍑	276	40.54 N	74.19 W
Great Plain of the Koukdjuak ⌑	176	66.00 N	73.00 W
Great Plains ⌑	16	42.00 N	100.00 W
Great Point ▸	207	41.23 N	70.03 W
Great Pubnico Lake ⍟	186	43.42 N	65.43 W
Great Quittacas Pond ⍟	207	41.48 N	70.54 W
Great River	276	40.45 N	73.10 W
Great Ruaha ≃	154	7.56 S	37.52 E
Great Sacandaga Lake ⍟	210	43.08 N	74.10 W
Great Saint Bernard Pass — Grand-Saint-Bernard, Col du ⍈	58	45.50 N	7.10 E
Great Sale Cay I	192	27.00 N	78.12 W
Great Salt Lake ⍟	200	41.10 N	112.30 W
Great Salt Lake Desert ⌑	200	40.40 N	113.30 W
Great Salt Plains Lake ⍟¹	196	36.44 N	98.12 W
Great Sand Dunes National Monument ⌑	200	37.43 N	105.36 W
Great Sand Hills ✗²	184	50.35 N	109.05 W
Great Sandy Desert ✦²	162	21.30 S	125.00 E
Great Sandy National Park ✦	166	24.59 S	153.17 E
Great Sankey	44	53.23 N	2.37 W
Great Santa Cruz Island I	116	6.52 N	122.03 E
Great Scarcies (Kolenté) ≃	150	8.55 N	13.08 W
Great Sea Reef ✗	175g	16.15 S	179.00 E
Great Seneca Creek ≃	208	39.08 N	77.20 W
Great Shelford	42	52.09 N	0.09 E
Great Sitkin Island I	180	52.03 N	176.07 W
Great Slave Lake ⍟	176	61.30 N	114.00 W
Great Smoky Mountains ▲	192	35.35 N	83.30 W
Great Smoky Mountains National Park ✦	192	35.39 N	83.30 W
Great Sound ≈, Ber.	240a	32.17 N	64.51 W
Great Sound ≈, N.J., U.S.	208	39.06 N	74.47 W
Great South Bay ⌒	210	40.40 N	73.17 W
Great Stour ≃	42	51.19 N	1.15 E
Great Sutton	262	53.17 N	2.56 W
Great Swamp National Wildlife Refuge	276	40.43 N	74.28 W
Great Tenasserim ≃	110	12.24 N	98.37 E
Great Tobago I	240m	18.27 N	64.48 W
Great Torrington	42	50.57 N	4.08 W
Great Totham	260	51.47 N	0.43 E
Great Usutu (Maputo) (Lusutfu) ≃	158	26.11 S	32.42 E
Great Valley ⌑	210	42.13 N	78.38 W
Great Victoria Desert ✦²	162	28.30 S	127.45 E
Great Wall ✗¹	9	62.13 S	58.58 W
Great Wall — Chang Cheng ⍐	98	40.30 N	116.30 E
Great Waltham	260	51.48 N	0.28 E
Great Warley	260	51.35 N	0.17 E
Great Whernside ▲	44	54.09 N	1.59 W
Great Wicomico ≃	208	37.48 N	76.18 W
Great Wyrley	42	52.41 N	2.01 W
Great Yarmouth	42	52.37 N	1.44 E
Great Zab (Büyükzap) (Az-Zāb al-Kabīr) ≃	128	36.00 N	43.21 E
Great Zimbabwe Ruins National Park ✦	154	20.17 S	30.57 E
Grebbestad	26	58.42 N	11.15 E
Grebenhain	56	50.29 N	9.19 E
Grebenka	78	50.07 N	32.26 E
Grebenstein	56	51.26 N	9.24 E
Grebnevo	265b	55.58 N	38.05 E
Grëb'onki	78	49.57 N	30.12 E
Grëboun ▲	150	20.00 N	8.35 E
Grèce — Greece □¹	38	39.00 N	22.00 E
Grecia	236	10.05 N	84.18 W
Grecia — Greece □¹	38	39.00 N	22.00 E
Grečiškino	78	49.04 N	38.54 E
Grecken □	40	59.35 N	14.44 E
Greco ≃	264b	41.49 N	14.14 E
Greco ▸	58	43.22 N	57.03 W
Greco ▲	266b	45.30 N	9.13 E
Greco, Monte ▲	64	41.48 N	14.00 E
Greco Island I	282	37.31 N	122.11 W
Greding	60	49.03 N	11.21 E
Gredos, Sierra de ▲	34	40.18 N	5.05 W
Gredstedbro	45	55.24 N	8.45 E
Greece	210	43.12 N	77.41 W
Greece (Ellás) □¹, Europe	22	39.00 N	22.00 E
Greece (Ellás) □¹, Europe	38	39.00 N	22.00 E
Greeley, Co., U.S.	200	40.25 N	104.42 W
Greeley, Ks., U.S.	208	38.19 N	95.26 W
Greeley, Ne., U.S.	198	41.33 N	98.32 W

Name	Page	Lat.	Long.
Greeley, Pa., U.S.	210	41.25 N	75.00 W
Greeleyville	192	33.34 N	79.59 W
Green □⁶	216	42.48 N	89.25 W
Green ≃, N.B., Can.	186	47.18 N	68.09 W
Green ≃, U.S.	200	38.11 N	109.53 W
Green ≃, U.S.	207	43.25 N	72.36 W
Green ≃, U.S.	207	42.10 N	73.22 W
Green ≃, Il., U.S.	190	41.28 N	90.23 W
Green ≃, Il., U.S.	216	41.46 N	89.10 W
Green ≃, Ky., U.S.	194	37.55 N	87.30 W
Green ≃, N.D., U.S.	198	46.52 N	102.35 W
Green ≃, Vt., U.S.	210	43.06 N	73.13 W
Green ≃, Wa., U.S.	224	47.33 N	122.20 W
Green ≃, Wa., U.S.	224	46.20 N	122.34 W
Green Acres, Ca., U.S.	226	35.23 N	119.07 W
Green Acres, De., U.S.	285	39.47 N	75.36 W
Green Acres, Wa., U.S.	202	47.39 N	117.06 W
Green Acres ≃⁹	276	40.40 N	73.43 W
Green Acres City	220	26.37 N	80.07 W
Greenbackville	208	38.00 N	75.23 W
Greenbank	224	48.06 N	122.34 W
Green Bay	190	44.31 N	88.01 W
Green Bay ⌒, Nf., Can.	186	49.45 N	55.58 W
Green Bay ⌒, On., Can.	212	44.38 N	76.36 W
Green Bay ⌒, U.S.	190	45.00 N	87.30 W
Greenbelt	284c	39.00 N	76.52 W
Greenbelt Park ✦	284c	38.59 N	76.54 W
Greenbo Lake ⍟	218	38.29 N	82.54 W
Greenbo Lake State Resort Park ✦	218	38.29 N	82.54 W
Greenbooth Reservoir ⍟¹	262	53.38 N	2.13 W
Greenbrae	226	37.57 N	122.31 W
Green Brier, Ar., U.S.	194	35.14 N	92.23 W
Green Brier, Tn., U.S.	194	36.25 N	86.48 W
Greenbrier ≃	192	37.39 N	80.53 W
Greenbrier State Park ✦	208	39.33 N	77.38 W
Green Brook	276	40.36 N	74.27 W
Green Brook ≃	276	40.33 N	74.32 W
Greenburg	194	30.51 N	90.40 W
Greenbush, Ma., U.S.	207	42.11 N	70.45 W
Greenbush, Mn., U.S.	198	48.42 N	96.10 W
Greenbush, Va., U.S.	208	37.45 N	75.41 W
Greenbushes	162	33.51 S	116.03 E
Green Camp	214	40.31 N	83.12 W
Green Cape ▸	166	37.15 S	150.03 E
Greencastle, Ire.	48	55.12 N	6.59 W
Greencastle, In., U.S.	194	39.38 N	86.51 W
Greencastle, Pa., U.S.	208	39.47 N	77.43 W
Green City	194	40.16 N	92.57 W
Green Cove Springs	192	29.59 N	81.40 W
Green Creek	208	39.02 N	74.54 W
Green Creek ≃, Oh., U.S.	214	41.26 N	83.01 W
Green Creek ≃, Pa., U.S.	285	39.50 N	75.28 W
Greencrest Park	214	41.23 N	80.24 W
Greendale, Austl.	274a	33.55 S	150.39 E
Greendale, In., U.S.	218	39.06 N	84.51 W
Greendale, Wi., U.S.	216	42.56 N	87.59 W
Greene, Dtsch.	52	51.52 N	9.56 E
Greene, Ia., U.S.	198	42.53 N	92.48 W
Greene, N.Y., U.S.	210	42.19 N	75.46 W
Greene, R.I., U.S.	207	41.44 N	71.44 W
Greene ≃¹, Il., U.S.	190	39.18 N	90.24 W
Greene ≃³, Il., U.S.	210	42.13 N	73.52 W
Greene ≃⁶, Oh., U.S.	218	39.41 N	83.56 W
Greeneville	192	36.10 N	82.42 W
Greenfield, Eng., U.K.	262	53.32 N	2.01 W
Greenfield, Wales, U.K.	44	53.18 N	3.13 W
Greenfield, Ca., U.S.	226	36.19 N	121.14 W
Greenfield, Il., U.S.	219	39.20 N	90.12 W
Greenfield, In., U.S.	218	39.47 N	85.46 W
Greenfield, Ia., U.S.	198	41.18 N	94.27 W
Greenfield, Ma., U.S.	207	42.35 N	72.36 W
Greenfield, Mo., U.S.	194	37.24 N	93.50 W
Greenfield, Oh., U.S.	218	39.21 N	83.22 W
Greenfield, Tn., U.S.	194	36.09 N	88.48 W
Greenfield, Wi., U.S.	216	42.58 N	88.02 W
Greenfield Park, P.Q., Can.	275a	45.29 N	73.29 W
Greenfield Park, N.Y., U.S.	211	41.44 N	74.29 W
Greenfields	285	75.10 N	39.49 W
Greenfield Village ⍐	281	42.18 N	83.14 W
Greenford □⁸	260	51.32 N	0.21 W
Green Forest	194	36.20 N	93.26 W
Green Harbor	207	42.04 N	70.39 W
Green Harbor ⌒	285	33.24 N	84.19 W
Green Head ▸	162	30.05 S	114.58 E
Green Hill	285	51.35 N	75.36 W
Greenhills, S. Afr.	273d	26.10 S	27.47 E
Greenhills, U.S.	218	39.16 N	84.31 W
Greenhithe	260	51.27 N	0.17 E
Greenhorn Creek ≃	198	38.06 N	104.38 W
Greenhurst	214	42.07 N	79.19 W
Green Hut Park	276	40.50 N	73.19 W
Green Island, N.Z.	172	45.54 S	170.26 E
Greenisland, N. Ire.	48	54.42 N	5.52 W
Green Island, N.Y., U.S.	211	42.45 N	73.41 W
Green Island I	241k	12.14 N	61.35 W
Green Island Bay ⌒	116	10.12 N	119.22 E
Green Islands II	14	4.30 S	154.10 E
Green Knoll	276	40.36 N	74.36 W
Green Lake, Sk., Can.	184	54.17 N	107.47 W
Green Lake, Wi., U.S.	190	43.50 N	88.57 W
Green Lake ⍟, B.C., Can.	182	51.24 N	121.15 W
Green Lake ⍟, Wi., U.S.	190	43.48 N	88.57 W
Green Lakes State Park ✦	212	43.03 N	75.58 W
Greenland (Saint-Grégoire-de-Greenlay)	206	45.34 N	72.01 W
Greenland, Ar., U.S.	194	35.59 N	94.10 W
Greenland, Mi., U.S.	190	46.46 N	89.06 W
Greenland (Kalaallit Nunaat) □	16	70.00 N	40.00 W
Greenland Basin ✦¹	16	73.30 N	5.00 W
Greenland-Iceland Rise ✦	10	67.00 N	27.00 W
Greenlands	158	27.07 S	31.48 E
Greenlaw	46	55.43 N	2.28 W
Green Lane	214	40.20 N	75.28 W
Green Lane ⍟¹	260	51.35 N	0.20 W
Greenleaf	198	39.43 N	96.58 W
Green Lookout Mountain ▲	224	45.52 N	122.08 W
Green Manorville	207	42.00 N	72.32 W
Green Meadows	284c	38.58 N	76.57 W
Greenmount, Austl.	171a	27.47 S	151.54 E
Greenmount, Eng., U.K.	262	53.37 N	2.20 W
Greenmount, Md., U.S.	208	39.37 N	76.51 W
Green Mountains ▲	188	43.45 N	72.45 W

Name	Page	Lat.	Long.
Green Oak Lake ⍟	281	42.27 N	83.43 W
Green Oaks	278	42.19 N	87.55 W
Greenock, Austl.	168b	34.27 S	138.55 E
Greenock, Scot., U.K.	46	55.57 N	4.45 W
Greenock, Pa., U.S.	279b	40.19 N	79.48 W
Greenodd	44	54.14 N	3.04 W
Greenore Point ▸	48	52.15 N	6.18 W
Greenough	162	28.57 S	114.44 E
Greenough ≃	162	28.51 S	114.38 E
Greenough, Mount ▲	180	69.10 N	141.35 W
Green Park	208	40.23 N	77.19 W
Green Peter Lake ⍟¹	202	44.28 N	122.30 W
Green Pond ▸	276	40.43 N	73.06 W
Green Pond, Al., U.S.	194	33.13 N	87.07 W
Green Pond, N.J., U.S.	276	41.01 N	74.29 W
Green Pond Brook ≃	276	41.00 N	74.30 W
Green Ridge	285	39.51 N	75.25 W
Green River, Pap. N. Gui.	164	3.55 S	141.10 E
Green River, Ut., U.S.	200	38.59 N	110.09 W
Green River, Wy., U.S.	200	41.31 N	109.27 W
Green River Lake ⍟¹	194	37.15 N	85.15 W
Greensboro, Al., U.S.	194	32.42 N	87.35 W
Greensboro, Fl., U.S.	192	30.34 N	84.44 W
Greensboro, Ga., U.S.	192	33.34 N	83.10 W
Greensboro, Md., U.S.	208	38.58 N	75.48 W
Greensboro, N.C., U.S.	192	36.04 N	79.47 W
Greensborough	274b	37.42 S	145.06 E
Greensburg, In., U.S.	218	39.20 N	85.29 W
Greensburg, Ks., U.S.	198	37.36 N	99.17 W
Greensburg, Ky., U.S.	194	37.15 N	85.29 W
Greensburg, Pa., U.S.	214	40.18 N	79.32 W
Greens Farms	276	41.07 N	73.19 W
Greens Fork	218	39.53 N	85.02 W
Greenside ✦⁸	273d	26.09 S	28.01 E
Greens Lake ⍟	222	29.16 N	94.59 W
Greens Peak ▲	200	34.07 N	109.35 W
Greenspond	186	49.04 N	53.34 W
Green Springs	214	41.15 N	83.03 W
Greenstead	260	51.42 N	0.14 E
Greenstone	208	39.45 N	77.27 W
Greenstone Point ▸	46	57.55 N	5.38 W
Green Street	260	51.40 N	0.16 W
Green Street Green	260	51.21 N	0.04 E
Greensville □⁶	208	36.40 N	77.30 W
Green Swamp ⌑, Fl., U.S.	220	28.20 N	81.48 W
Green Swamp ⌑, N.C., U.S.	192	34.10 N	78.20 W
Greentown, In., U.S.	216	40.28 N	85.58 W
Greentown, Oh., U.S.	214	40.56 N	81.28 W
Greentown, Pa., U.S.	210	41.19 N	75.18 W
Green Tree	279b	40.24 N	80.02 W
Greenup, Il., U.S.	194	39.14 N	88.09 W
Greenup, Ky., U.S.	218	38.34 N	82.50 W
Greenup Dam ✦⁶	218	38.39 N	82.52 W
Greenvale, Austl.	166	18.59 S	145.07 E
Greenvale, N.Y., U.S.	276	40.49 N	73.38 W
Green Valley, On., Can.	206	45.16 N	74.36 W
Green Valley, Az., U.S.	200	31.52 N	110.59 W
Green Valley, Il., U.S.	190	40.24 N	89.38 W
Green Valley Creek ≃	226	38.13 N	122.08 W
Greenview	219	40.04 N	89.44 W
Green Village, N.J., U.S.	276	40.44 N	74.27 W
Greenvillage, Pa., U.S.	208	40.00 N	77.36 W
Greenville, Liber.	150	5.01 N	9.03 W
Greenville, Al., U.S.	194	31.49 N	86.37 W
Greenville, Ca., U.S.	204	40.08 N	120.57 W
Greenville, Fl., U.S.	192	30.28 N	83.38 W
Greenville, Ga., U.S.	192	33.01 N	84.42 W
Greenville, Il., U.S.	219	38.53 N	89.24 W
Greenville, In., U.S.	218	38.22 N	85.59 W
Greenville, Ky., U.S.	194	37.12 N	87.10 W
Greenville, Me., U.S.	188	45.28 N	69.35 W
Greenville, Mi., U.S.	190	43.10 N	85.15 W
Greenville, Ms., U.S.	194	33.24 N	91.03 W
Greenville, Mo., U.S.	194	37.08 N	90.27 W
Greenville, N.Y., U.S.	210	40.59 N	73.49 W
Greenville, N.C., U.S.	192	35.36 N	77.22 W
Greenville, Oh., U.S.	214	40.06 N	84.37 W
Greenville, Pa., U.S.	214	41.24 N	80.23 W
Greenville, R.I., U.S.	207	41.52 N	71.33 W
Greenville, S.C., U.S.	192	34.51 N	82.23 W
Greenville, Tx., U.S.	222	33.08 N	96.06 W
Greenville Place	285	39.46 N	75.36 W
Greenwater ≃	224	47.09 N	121.39 W
Greenwater Lake Provincial Park ✦	184	52.33 N	103.33 W
Greenwell Point	170	34.55 S	150.44 E
Greenwich, Austl.	274a	33.50 S	151.11 E
Greenwich, Ct., U.S.	207	41.01 N	73.37 W
Greenwich, N.J., U.S.	208	39.23 N	75.20 W
Greenwich, N.Y., U.S.	210	43.05 N	73.30 W
Greenwich, Oh., U.S.	214	41.01 N	82.30 W
Greenwich □⁸	260	51.28 N	0.02 E
Greenwich Cove ⌒	276	41.01 N	73.35 W
Greenwich Creek ≃	276	41.01 N	73.37 W
Greenwich Observatory ⍐	260	51.28 N	0.00
Greenwich Point ▸	276	41.00 N	73.34 W
Greenwich Village ⍐	276	40.44 N	74.00 W
Greenwood, B.C., Can.	182	49.05 N	118.41 W
Greenwood, De., U.S.	208	38.48 N	75.35 W
Greenwood, In., U.S.	218	39.36 N	86.06 W
Greenwood, Ms., U.S.	194	33.30 N	90.10 W
Greenwood, S.C., U.S.	192	34.11 N	82.09 W
Greenwood ≃	184	49.45 N	100.02 W
Greenwood, Lake ⍟	192	34.11 N	81.55 W
Greenwood Cemetery ⍐	276	40.39 N	73.59 W
Greenwood Lake	210	41.13 N	74.17 W
Greenwood Lake ⍟, Ma., U.S.	283	42.00 N	71.17 W
Greenwood Lake ⍟, Ne., U.S.	276	41.11 N	74.19 W
Greenwood Race Track ✦	275b	43.40 N	79.19 W
Greer, Oh., U.S.	214	40.31 N	82.13 W
Greer, S.C., U.S.	192	34.56 N	82.13 W

Name	Page	Lat.	Long.
Greers Ferry Lake ⍟	194	35.30 N	92.10 W
Greerton	172	37.43 S	176.08 E
Grées, Alpi (Alpi Graie) ▲	62	45.30 N	7.10 E
Grez-Doiceau	56	50.44 N	4.42 E
Grez-sur-Loing	52	48.19 N	2.42 E
Greetland	262	53.41 N	1.52 W
Greetsiel	52	53.30 N	7.05 E
Greffers	261	48.37 N	1.51 E
Grefrath, Dtsch.	56	51.20 N	6.20 E
Grefrath, Dtsch.	263	51.10 N	6.38 E
Gregadoo	171b	35.13 S	147.27 E
Gregbe	150	6.48 N	6.43 W
Gregg ≃	279b	40.24 N	80.10 W
Gregg ▸⁶	222	32.30 N	94.50 W
Greggio	62	45.27 N	8.23 E
Greg Greg	171b	36.03 S	148.02 E
Gregório ≃	248	6.50 S	70.46 W
Gregory, Mi., U.S.	216	42.27 N	84.05 W
Gregory, S.D., U.S.	198	43.13 N	99.25 W
Gregory, Tx., U.S.	196	27.55 N	97.17 W
Gregory ≃	166	17.53 S	139.17 E
Gregory, Lake ⍟, Austl.	162	25.38 S	119.58 E
Gregory, Lake ⍟, Austl.	162	20.10 S	127.20 E
Gregory, Lake ⍟, Austl.	166	28.55 S	139.00 E
Gregory National Park ✦	164	16.30 S	130.30 E
Gregory Range ▲	166	19.00 S	143.05 E
Grégy-sur-Yerre	261	48.40 N	2.37 E
Greifenburg	61	46.42 N	14.44 E
Greifendorf	54	49.40 N	103.26 E
Greifenstein	54	51.01 N	13.06 E
Greifensee	58	47.22 N	8.41 E
Greifensee ⍟	58	47.22 N	8.41 E
Greifenstein	264b	48.21 N	16.25 E
Greifswald	54	54.05 N	13.23 E
Greifswalder Bodden ⌒	54	54.15 N	13.35 E
Greifswalder Oie I	54	54.14 N	13.55 E
Greim ▲	61	47.15 N	14.09 E
Greiz	54	50.39 N	12.12 E
Grejdernoje	80	60.43 N	45.01 E
Grejsdal	41	55.45 N	9.32 E
Grekov	80	47.24 N	43.41 E
Grekovo	83	48.54 N	40.14 E
Grem'ačevo	82	54.14 N	36.15 E
Grem'ači	88	57.01 N	108.12 E
Grem'ačinsk, Ross.	88	58.34 N	57.51 E
Grem'ačinsk, Ross.	86	52.48 N	107.57 E
Grem'ačje	78	51.29 N	39.00 E
Gremersdorf	54	54.20 N	10.55 E
Gremicha	24	68.03 N	39.27 E
Grenå	26	56.25 N	10.53 E
Grenada ≃	194	33.46 N	89.48 W
Grenada □¹, N.A.	230	12.07 N	61.40 W
Grenada □¹, N.A.	241k	12.07 N	61.40 W
Grenada Lake ⍟	194	33.50 N	89.40 W
Grenada — Grenada □¹	241k	12.07 N	61.40 W
Grenadier Island I	212	44.03 N	76.22 W
Grenadier Pond ⍟	275b	43.39 N	79.28 W
Grenadines II	238	12.40 N	61.15 W
Grenagh	48	52.00 N	8.37 W
Grenay	50	50.27 N	2.44 E
Grenchen	58	47.11 N	7.24 E
Grenen ▸¹, Dan.	26	57.44 N	10.40 E
Grenen ▸², Dan.	26	57.44 N	10.40 E
Grenfell, Austl.	166	33.54 S	148.10 E
Grenfell, Sk., Can.	285	39.47 N	75.03 W
Grenloch	285	45.10 N	5.43 E
Grenoble	198	37.20 N	96.27 W
Grenora	198	48.37 N	103.56 W
Grenville, P.Q., Can.	274a	33.55 S	74.36 W
Grenville, Cape ▸	164	11.58 S	143.14 E
Grenville Bay ⌒	206	45.38 N	74.36 W
Grenville Channel ᴗ	182	53.40 N	129.40 W
Grenville Bay ⌒	241k	12.07 N	61.36 W
Grenzaa ≃	52	52.39 N	6.45 E
Grenz-Berge ▲²	264a	52.27 N	13.44 E
Grenzlandring ⍐	54	51.11 N	6.17 E
Greoux-les-Bains	62	43.45 N	5.53 E
Greppin	54	51.39 N	12.18 E
Grennitzsee ⍟	54	52.58 N	13.47 E
Gresford	262	53.04 N	12.26 E
Gresham	224	45.29 N	122.25 W
Gresham Park	287	33.42 N	84.19 W
Gresik, Indon.	112	2.18 S	103.57 E
Gresik, Indon.	113	7.09 S	112.38 E
Gressåmoen Nasjonalpark ✦	26	64.15 N	13.08 E
Gresse-en-Vercors	62	44.54 N	5.34 E
Gressey	261	48.54 N	1.37 E
Gressier	240a	18.32 N	72.36 W
Gressoney, Val di ⍱	62	45.47 N	7.49 E
Gressoney-la-Trinité	62	45.50 N	7.49 E
Gressoney-Saint-Jean	62	45.47 N	7.49 E
Gresten	61	48.00 N	15.02 E
Greta ≃, Eng., U.K.	44	54.32 N	1.53 W
Greta ≃, Eng., U.K.	44	54.36 N	3.10 W
Gretna, Mb., Can.	184	49.02 N	97.35 W
Gretna, Scot., U.K.	44	54.59 N	3.04 W
Gretna, La., U.S.	194	29.54 N	90.03 W
Gretna, Va., U.S.	192	36.57 N	79.21 W
Gretz-Armainvilliers	50	48.44 N	2.44 E
Greussen	54	51.14 N	10.57 E
Greve, Dan.	41	55.34 N	12.18 E
Greve, It.	66	43.35 N	11.19 E
Greve ≃	66	43.46 N	11.13 E
Grevel	263	51.34 N	7.33 E
Grevelingen ᴗ	52	51.44 N	4.00 E
Grevelingendam ✗⁵	52	51.41 N	4.10 E
Greven	52	52.05 N	7.36 E
Grevenbroich	56	51.05 N	6.35 E
Greven-Granzin	54	53.26 N	10.48 E
Grevenmacher	56	49.42 N	6.20 E
Grevesmühlen	54	53.51 N	11.10 E
Grevie Strand	41	55.35 N	12.14 E
Grevie Bay ⌒	190	45.48 N	86.08 W
Grevié	78	50.20 N	38.15 E
Grey ≃	172	42.27 S	171.12 E
Grey, Cape ▸	164	13.00 S	136.40 E
Grey, Point ▸, Austl.	163	38.34 S	143.59 E
Grey, Point ▸, B.C., Can.	224	49.16 N	123.16 W
Greyabbey	48	54.32 N	5.33 W
Grey Eagle	198	45.49 N	94.44 W
Grey Islands II	186	50.50 N	55.37 W
Greylock, Mount ▲	207	42.38 N	73.10 W
Greymouth	172	42.27 S	171.12 E
Grey Range ▲	166	27.00 S	143.35 E
Grey River ≃	186	47.34 N	57.05 W
Greys ≃	274a	33.45 S	150.55 E
Greystones	48	53.09 N	6.04 W
Greytown, N.Z.	172	41.05 S	175.27 E
Greytown, S. Afr.	158	29.07 S	30.30 E

Name	Page	Lat.	Long.
Greytown — San Juan del Norte	236	10.55 N	83.42 W
Grez-Doiceau	56	50.44 N	4.42 E
Grez-sur-Loing	52	48.19 N	2.42 E
Grezzana	64	45.31 N	11.01 E
Gribanovskij	80	51.27 N	41.58 E
Gribbel Island I	182	53.25 N	129.00 W
Gribbin Head ▸	42	50.19 N	4.40 W
Gribingui ≃⁵	152	7.00 N	19.15 E
Gribingui ≃	146	8.33 N	19.05 E
Gribingui-Bamingui, Réserve de Faune du ✦⁴	146	8.00 N	19.10 E
Gribovka	82	54.19 N	38.27 E
Gricev	78	49.59 N	27.14 E
Gridley, Ca., U.S.	226	39.21 N	121.41 W
Gridley, Il., U.S.	216	40.44 N	88.52 W
Griebnitz See ⍟	264a	52.24 N	13.06 E
Griechenland — Greece □¹	38	39.00 N	22.00 E
Griekwastad	158	28.49 S	23.15 E
Grier City	210	40.50 N	76.04 W
Gries am Brenner	64	47.03 N	11.29 E
Griesbach im Rottal	60	48.28 N	13.11 E
Griesen	60	47.29 N	10.56 E
Griesheim	56	49.50 N	8.34 E
Gries im Sellrain	64	47.12 N	11.09 E
Grieskirchen	60	48.14 N	13.50 E
Griessem	52	52.00 N	9.12 E
Griesspitzen ▲	64	47.22 N	10.58 E
Griffen	61	46.42 N	14.44 E
Griffin, Sk., Can.	184	49.40 N	103.26 W
Griffin, Ga., U.S.	192	33.14 N	84.15 W
Griffin, Lake ⍟	220	28.52 N	81.51 W
Griffin Bay ⌒	224	48.30 N	122.58 W
Griffiss Air Force Base ■	210	43.14 N	75.26 W
Griffith, Austl.	166	34.17 S	146.03 E
Griffith, In., U.S.	216	41.31 N	87.25 W
Griffith Airport ⍉	278	41.31 N	87.23 W
Griffith Island I, N.T., Can.	176	74.35 N	95.30 W
Griffith Island I, On., Can.	212	44.51 N	80.54 W
Griffith Park ✦	280	34.09 N	118.17 W
Grifton	192	35.22 N	77.26 W
Griggs Drain ≃	281	42.11 N	83.26 W
Griggs Reservoir ⍟	214	40.03 N	83.06 W
Griggstown	276	40.26 N	74.36 W
Grignan	219	39.42 N	90.43 W
Grignasco	62	44.25 N	4.54 E
Grigno	62	45.41 N	8.20 E
Grignols	64	46.01 N	11.38 E
Grigny, Fr.	32	44.23 N	0.03 W
Grigny, Fr.	261	48.51 N	1.57 E
Grigoriopol'	78	47.10 N	29.18 E
Grigorjevka, Kyrg.	85	42.43 N	77.30 E
Grigorjevka, Ross.	83	47.27 N	38.23 E
Grigorjevka, Ukr.	78	46.17 N	30.44 E
Grigorjevskoje, Ross.	82	54.49 N	37.59 E
Grigorjevskoje, Ross.	82	54.38 N	36.20 E
Grigorovka, Ukr.	78	50.05 N	30.39 E
Grigorovo	80	56.42 N	37.35 E
Grigoropolisskaja	83	45.20 N	41.05 E
Grijalva (Cuilco) ≃, Méx.	232	18.36 N	92.39 W
Grijalva ≃, N.A.	232	17.01 N	93.22 W
Grijpskerk	52	53.15 N	6.18 E
Grillby	40	59.37 N	17.15 E
Grillenburg	54	50.57 N	13.31 E
Grim, Cape ▸	166	40.45 S	144.41 E
Grima	152	3.59 N	17.06 E
Grimaïlov	78	49.20 N	26.01 E
Grimaldi	68	39.08 N	16.14 E
Grimari	152	5.44 N	20.03 E
Grimaud	62	43.16 N	6.31 E
Grimbergen	56	50.56 N	4.23 E
Grimeford Village	262	53.36 N	2.34 W
Grimes	226	39.04 N	121.54 W
Grimes ≃	222	30.35 N	96.00 W
Grimlinghausen	56	51.10 N	6.44 E
Grimma	54	51.14 N	12.43 E
Grimmen	54	54.07 N	13.02 E
Grimmenstein	61	47.33 N	16.07 E
Grimmialp	58	46.37 N	7.29 E
Grimnitzsee ⍟	54	52.58 N	13.47 E
Grimsargh	262	53.48 N	2.38 W
Grimsby, On., Can.	214	43.12 N	79.34 W
Grimsby, Eng., U.K.	44	53.35 N	0.05 W
Grimselpass ⍈	58	46.34 N	8.18 E
Grimselsee ⍟	58	46.34 N	8.19 E
Grimsey I	24a	66.33 N	18.00 W
Grimshaw	182	56.11 N	117.36 W
Grimstad	26	58.20 N	8.36 E
Grímsvötn ▲¹	24	64.25 N	17.20 W
Grin'ava	78	47.59 N	24.49 E
Grindavík	24a	63.50 N	22.26 W
Grindelwald	58	46.37 N	8.02 E
Grindsted	41	55.45 N	8.56 E
Grindstone Island I	212	44.16 N	76.07 W
Grindstone Island — Cap-aux-Meules	188	47.23 N	61.52 W
Grinzing ✦⁸	264b	48.15 N	16.21 E
Gripsholm slott ⍐	40	59.15 N	17.13 E
Griqualand East □⁹	158	30.30 S	29.00 E
Griqualand West □⁹	158	28.20 S	23.30 E
Grisdale	224	47.22 N	123.30 W
Grisee	261	48.41 N	2.40 E
— Gresik	115a	7.09 S	112.38 E
Grišino	84	53.10 N	97.37 E
Gris-Nez, Cap ▸	50	50.52 N	1.35 E
Grisolles	32	43.49 N	1.17 E
Grisons — Graubünden □³	58	46.45 N	9.30 E
Grisslehamn	40	60.06 N	18.50 E
Grissom Air Force Base ■	216	40.40 N	86.08 W
Griswold, Mb., Can.	184	49.45 N	100.25 W
Griswold, Ia., U.S.	198	41.14 N	95.08 W
Griswold Creek ≃	279a	41.27 N	81.23 W
Griswoldville	207	42.27 N	71.12 W
Grisy-Suisnes	261	48.41 N	2.40 E
Grival Pamia	78	47.38 N	34.59 E
Grizzana	64	44.16 N	11.09 E
Grizzly Bear Mountain ▲	176	65.22 N	121.00 W
Grizzly Bear's Head and Lead Man Indian Reserve ✦⁴	184	52.33 N	108.16 W
Grizzly Creek ≃	287	37.52 N	122.06 W
Grizzly Flats	226	38.38 N	120.31 W
Grizzly Island I	282	38.08 N	121.55 W
Grizzly Mountain ▲, Id., U.S.	202	47.43 N	116.06 W
Grizzly Mountain ▲, Or., U.S.	202	44.26 N	120.57 W
Grizzly Slough ≃	282	38.06 N	121.53 W
Grmec ▲	66	44.40 N	16.30 E

Name	Page	Lat.	Long.
Groaíras	250	3.53 S	40.23 W
Groais Island I	186	50.57 N	55.35 W
Grobbendonk	56	51.12 N	4.43 E
Gröben	264a	52.17 N	13.10 E
Gröbenzell	60	48.11 N	11.22 E
Gröbener-See ⍟	264a	52.17 N	13.11 E
Grobina	76	56.33 N	21.10 E
Gröbersdal	156	25.15 S	29.25 E
Groblershoop	158	28.55 S	20.59 E
Gröbming	64	47.26 N	13.54 E
Grobogan	115a	7.01 S	110.55 E
Gröbzig	54	51.41 N	11.52 E
Grodekovo	85	42.49 N	71.29 E
Grödig	64	47.44 N	13.02 E
Gröditsch	54	52.03 N	13.59 E
Gröditz	54	51.24 N	13.27 E
Grodków	30	50.43 N	17.22 E
Grodno	76	53.41 N	23.50 E
Grodovka	83	48.15 N	37.23 E
Grodz'anka	83	53.28 N	28.45 E
Grodzisk Mazowiecki	30	52.07 N	20.37 E
Grodzisk [Wielkopolski]	30	52.14 N	16.22 E
Groede	52	51.23 N	3.30 E
Groen ≃, S. Afr.	158	30.43 S	17.33 E
Groen ≃, S. Afr.	158	29.00 S	22.10 E
Grönland □ — Greenland □²	16	70.00 N	40.00 W
Groenlandia — Greenland □²	16	70.00 N	40.00 W
Groenlo	52	52.03 N	6.38 E
Groenvlei	159	27.27 S	30.13 E
Groesbeck, Oh., U.S.	218	39.13 N	84.35 W
Groesbeck, Tx., U.S.	222	31.31 N	96.32 W
Groesbeek	52	51.47 N	5.55 E
Grofa, gora ▲	78	48.37 N	23.56 E
Grogol, Kal. ≃	269e	6.10 S	106.47 E
Grogol-hilir ✦⁸	269e	6.13 S	106.47 E
Grohnde	52	52.01 N	9.25 E
Groitzsch	54	51.09 N	12.16 E
Groix	32	47.38 N	3.28 W
Groix, Île de I	32	47.38 N	3.27 W
Grójec	30	51.52 N	20.52 E
Grolley	58	46.50 N	7.05 E
Grombalia	148	36.36 N	10.58 E
Grömitz	54	54.09 N	10.58 E
Gromo	64	45.58 N	9.56 E
Gromokleja ≃	78	47.21 N	32.14 E
Gromoslavka	80	48.12 N	43.37 E
Gromovka	78	45.19 N	34.06 E
Gronau, Dtsch.	52	52.13 N	7.00 E
Gronau, Dtsch.	52	52.05 N	9.46 E
Grondines (Saint-Charles-des-Grondines)	206	46.36 N	72.03 W
Grondneus	158	28.06 S	20.48 E
Grone	52	51.32 N	9.53 E
Grönenbach	60	47.52 N	10.13 E
Gröningen, Dtsch.	54	51.56 N	11.13 E
Groningen, Ned.	52	53.13 N	6.33 E
Groningen, Sur.	250	5.48 N	55.28 W
Groningen □⁴	52	53.15 N	6.45 E
Grønland □ — Greenland □²	16	70.00 N	40.00 W
Grönlid	184	53.06 N	104.28 W
Grønsund ᴗ	41	54.53 N	12.08 E
Grönwohld	52	53.39 N	10.25 E
Groom	196	35.12 N	101.06 W
Groom Lake ⍟	204	37.15 N	115.48 W
Groot ≃, S. Afr.	158	33.45 S	24.36 E
Groot ≃, S. Afr.	158	33.45 S	24.36 E
Groot-Berg ≃	158	32.47 S	18.08 E
Groot-Brakrivier	158	34.03 S	22.14 E
Grootdraaidam ⍟¹	158	26.56 S	29.20 E
Grootebroek	52	52.43 N	5.13 E
Groote Eylandt I	164	14.00 S	136.40 E
Groote Eylandt Aboriginal Reserve ✦⁴	164	14.00 S	136.40 E
Grootfontein	156	19.32 S	18.05 E
Groot Karasberge ▲	156	27.20 S	18.40 E
Groot Karroo — Great Karroo ✗¹	158	32.35 S	22.40 E
Groot-Kei ≃	158	32.41 S	28.22 E
Groot Laagte ≃	156	20.37 S	21.37 E
Groot-Letaba ≃	158	23.58 S	31.50 E
Groot-Marico	156	25.37 S	26.26 E
Grootpan	156	25.58 S	26.33 E
Groot-Swartberge ▲	158	33.20 S	22.20 E
Groot-Vis ≃	158	33.30 S	27.08 E
Grootvlei	156	26.44 S	28.32 E
Grootvloer ≃	158	30.00 S	20.40 E
Gröpelingen ✦⁸	53	53.07 N	8.46 E
Gropello Cairoli	62	45.15 N	9.00 E
Gropeni	72	45.01 N	27.54 E
Grosbliederstroff	58	49.09 N	7.01 E
Gros Bois, Parc de ✦	261	48.44 N	2.32 E
Groscavallo	62	45.22 N	7.15 E
Grose ≃	170	33.36 S	150.41 E
Grosio	64	46.18 N	10.16 E
Gros Islet	241f	14.05 N	60.58 W
Groslay	261	48.59 N	2.21 E
Gros Mécatina, Cap du ▸	186	50.45 N	59.00 W
Gros-Morne	240e	14.43 N	61.01 W
Gros Morne National Park ✦	186	49.40 N	57.45 W
Grosne ≃	62	46.29 N	4.56 E
Grosnez Point ▸	43b	49.16 N	2.15 W
Grosotto	64	46.20 N	10.15 E
Gros Piton ▲	241f	13.49 N	61.04 W
Grossa, Ponta ▸, Bra.	256	23.35 S	45.13 W
Grossa, Ponta ▸, Bra.	287a	22.57 S	43.11 W
Grossache (Tiroler Ache) ≃	60	47.51 N	12.30 E
Grossalmerode	54	51.16 N	9.46 E
Grossbeeren	54	52.21 N	13.18 E
Gross Berkel	52	52.04 N	9.18 E
Grossbodungen	54	51.29 N	10.32 E
Gross Bönecke ✗	54	53.49 N	13.04 W
Grossbottwar	56	49.00 N	9.25 E
Grossbreitenbach	54	50.35 N	11.02 E
Grossburgwedel	52	52.28 N	9.53 E
Grossdubrau	54	51.15 N	14.28 E
Grosse Dünger ≃	52	52.06 N	10.01 E
Grosse Antillen — Greater Antilles II	238	20.00 N	74.00 W
Grosse Aue ≃	52	52.34 N	9.10 E
Grosse Australische Bicht — Great Australian Bight ⌒	162	35.00 S	135.00 E
Grossefehn	52	53.24 N	7.36 E
Grosse Herrenwiese ▲	264a	52.17 N	13.20 E

Symbol Key

Symbol	English	Deutsch	Español	Français	Português
≃	River	Fluß	Río	Rivière	Rio
≈	Canal	Kanal	Canal	Canal	Canal
ᴗ	Waterfall, Rapids	Wasserfall, Stromschnellen	Cascada, Rápidos	Chute d'eau, Rapides	Cascata, Rápidos
ᴗ	Strait	Meeresstraße	Estrecho	Détroit	Estreito
⌒	Bay, Gulf	Bucht, Golf	Bahía, Golfo	Baie, Golfe	Baía, Golfo
⍟	Lake, Lakes	See, Seen	Lago, Lagos	Lac, Lacs	Lago, Lagos
⍑	Swamp	Sumpf	Pantano	Marais	Pântano
⌻	Ice Features, Glacier	Eis- und Gletscherformen	Accidentes Glaciales	Formes glaciaires	Acidentes glaciares
⍨	Other Hydrographic Features	Andere Hydrographische Objekte	Otros Elementos Hidrográficos	Autres données hydrographiques	Outros acidentes hidrográficos
✦	Submarine Features	Untermeerische Objekte	Accidentes Submarinos	Formes de relief sous-marin	Acidentes submarinos
□	Political Unit	Politische Einheit	Unidad Política	Entité politique	Unidade política
⍐	Cultural Institution	Kulturelle Institution	Institución Cultural	Institution culturelle	Instituição cultural
⍏	Historical Site	Historische Stätte	Sitio Histórico	Site historique	Sítio histórico
■	Recreational Site	Erholungs- und Ferienort	Centro de Recreo	Centre de loisirs	Area de Lazer
⍉	Airport	Flughafen	Aeropuerto	Aéroport	Aeroporto
■	Military Installation	Militäranlage	Instalación Militar	Installation militaire	Instalação militar
⍨	Miscellaneous	Verschiedenes	Misceláneo	Divers	Diversos

Name	Page	Lat.°′	Long.°′
Grossen-Linden	56	50.31 N	8.39 E
Grossenlüder	56	50.35 N	9.32 E
Grossenritte	56	51.15 N	9.23 E
Grossenwiehe	41	54.43 N	9.15 E
Gross-Enzersdorf	61	48.12 N	16.33 E
Grosse Pointe	214	42.23 N	82.54 W
Grosse Pointe ›	241o	16.01 N	61.16 W
Grosse Pointe Farms	214	42.25 N	82.53 W
Grosse Pointe Park	214	42.22 N	82.56 W
Grosse Pointe Shores	214	42.26 N	82.53 W
Grosse Pointe Woods	214	42.26 N	82.54 W
Grosser Arber ∧	60	49.07 N	13.07 E
Grosser Bären-See → Great Bear Lake ⊜	176	66.00 N	120.00 W
Grosser Beerberg ∧	54	50.37 N	10.44 E
Grosser Bösenstein ∧	61	47.26 N	14.24 E
Grosser Buchstein ∧	61	47.36 N	14.35 E
Grosser Chingan → Da Hinggan Ling ⋏	90	49.00 N	122.00 E
Grosser Feldberg ∧	56	50.14 N	8.26 E
Grosser Galtenberg ∧	64	47.20 N	11.58 E
Grosser Gleichberg ∧	54	50.23 N	10.35 E
Grosser Heuberg ⋏[1]	58	48.06 N	8.55 E
Grosser Inselsberg ∧	54	50.52 N	10.28 E
Grosser Jasmunder Bodden c	54	54.31 N	13.29 E
Grosser Knallstein ∧	61	47.19 N	13.58 E
Grosser Königstuhl ∧	64	46.57 N	13.47 E
Grosser Müggelsee ⊜	54	52.26 N	13.39 E
Grosse Röder ≃	54	51.30 N	13.25 E
Grosser oder Kaiser-Kanal → Da Yunhe ≍	90	32.12 N	119.31 E
Grosse Rodl ≃	61	48.20 N	14.09 E
Grosser Peilstein ∧	61	48.18 N	15.06 E
Grosser Plessower See ⊜	264a	52.23 N	12.54 E
Grosser Plöner See ⊜	54	54.06 N	10.25 E
Grosser Priel ∧	61	47.43 N	14.04 E
Grosser Rachel ∧	60	48.59 N	13.24 E
Grosser Ravens-Berg ∧[2]	264a	52.21 N	13.04 E
Grosser Riedelstein ∧	60	49.10 N	12.59 E
Grosser Salz-See → Great Salt Lake ⊜	200	41.10 N	112.30 W
Grosser Seddiner See ⊜	264a	52.17 N	13.02 E
Grosser Selchower See ⊜	54	52.14 N	13.53 E
Grosser Sklaven-See → Great Slave Lake ⊜	176	61.30 N	114.00 W
Grosser Speikkogel ∧	61	46.47 N	14.58 E
Grosser Walfisch-Fluss → Baleine, Grande rivière de la ≃	176	55.16 N	77.47 W
Grosser Wannsee ⊜	264a	52.26 N	13.11 E
Grosser Winterberg ∧[2]	54	50.54 N	14.16 E
Grosser Zern-See ⊜	264a	52.24 N	12.56 E
Grosse Sandspitze ∧	64	46.46 N	12.49 E
Grosse Sandwüste → Great Sandy Desert ◆[2]	162	21.30 S	125.00 E
Grosses Barrier-Riff → Great Barrier Reef ✦[2]	160	18.00 S	145.50 E
Grosses Meer ⊜	52	53.25 N	7.17 E
Grosses Moor ◆[3], Dtsch.	52	52.35 N	8.45 E
Grosses Moor ◆[3], Dtsch.	52	52.40 N	8.20 E
Grosses Schulerloch ♦	60	48.55 N	11.48 E
Grosse Sundainseln → Greater Sunda Islands II	108	2.00 S	110.00 E
Grosses Walsertal V	58	47.14 N	9.56 E
Grosse Syrte → Surt, Khalīj c	146	31.30 N	18.00 E
Grosseto	66	42.46 N	11.08 E
Grosseto □[4]	66	42.50 N	11.15 E
Grosse Tulln ≃	61	48.20 N	16.02 E
Grossevići	89	47.59 N	139.30 E
Gross-Gerau	56	49.55 N	8.29 E
Gross-Gerungs	61	48.34 N	14.57 E
Gross Gleidingen	54	52.14 N	10.25 E
Gross Glienicke	264a	52.28 N	13.07 E
Gross-Glienicker See ⊜	264a	52.28 N	13.06 E
Grossglockner ∧	64	47.04 N	12.42 E
Grossgmain	64	47.43 N	12.55 E
Grossgörschen	54	51.13 N	12.11 E
Gross Grönau	54	53.46 N	10.44 E
Grosshansdorf	52	53.40 N	10.17 E
Grosshartmannsdorf	54	50.48 N	13.19 E
Gross-Hehlen	52	52.39 N	10.03 E
Grossheide	52	53.35 N	7.20 E
Grosshennersdorf	54	50.59 N	14.47 E
Grosshöchstetten	58	46.55 N	7.38 E
Grossholzleute	58	47.41 N	10.05 E
Grossjedlersdorf ◆[8]	264b	48.17 N	16.25 E
Grosskayna	54	51.17 N	11.56 E
Gross Kienitz	264a	52.19 N	13.28 E
Gross-Kollmar	52	53.44 N	9.30 E
Grosskorbetha	54	51.16 N	12.01 E
Gross Kreutz	54	52.24 N	12.46 E
Grosskrut	61	48.38 N	16.43 E
Grosslehna	54	51.18 N	12.10 E
Gross Leine	54	52.00 N	14.03 E
Grosslittgen	56	50.02 N	6.47 E
Grossmachnow	54	52.16 N	13.28 E
Grossmehring	60	48.46 N	11.32 E
Grossmont	228	32.47 N	116.59 W
Gross Muckrow	54	52.04 N	14.26 E
Grössnöbach	60	48.21 N	11.35 E
Gross Oesingen	52	52.38 N	10.29 E
Grossörner	54	51.37 N	11.29 E
Grossos	250	4.59 S	37.09 W
Grossostheim	56	49.55 N	9.04 E
Grosspetersdorf	61	47.14 N	16.19 E
Grosspostwitz	54	51.07 N	14.26 E
Grossquenstedt	54	51.56 N	11.07 E
Grossraming	61	47.53 N	14.33 E
Grossräschen	54	51.35 N	14.00 E
Gross Rhüden	52	51.56 N	10.07 E
Grossrinderfeld	56	49.39 N	9.44 E
Gross Rodensleben	54	52.08 N	11.25 E
Grossröhrsdorf	54	51.08 N	14.01 E
Gross Rosenburg	54	51.55 N	11.53 E
Grossrückerswalde	54	50.38 N	13.07 E
Grossrudestedt	54	51.05 N	11.06 E
Gross Sankt Florian	61	46.49 N	15.19 E
Gross-Sarau	54	53.45 N	10.44 E
Grossschirma	54	50.58 N	13.17 E
Grossschönau	54	50.54 N	14.40 E
Gross Schönebeck	54	52.54 N	13.32 E
Gross-Schulzendorf	264a	52.16 N	13.21 E
Gross-Siegharts	61	48.48 N	15.24 E
Grosssölk	64	47.25 N	13.58 E
Grosstimmern	56	49.52 N	8.50 E
Gross-Umstadt	56	49.52 N	8.55 E
Grossvenediger ∧	64	47.06 N	12.21 E
Grosswardein → Oradea	38	47.03 N	21.57 E
Grossweil	64	47.41 N	11.18 E
Grossweissenbach	61	48.33 N	15.10 E
Gross Windgällen ∧	58	46.49 N	8.44 E
Gross Wittensee	41	54.24 N	9.46 E
Gross Ziethen, Dtsch.	264a	52.24 N	13.27 E
Gross Ziethen, Dtsch.	264a	52.44 N	13.01 E
Gross-Zimmern	56	49.52 N	8.50 E
Grostenquin	56	48.59 N	6.44 E
Grosvenor, Lake ⊜	180	58.40 N	155.15 W
Grosvenor Dale	207	41.58 N	71.53 W
Gros Ventre ≃	202	43.33 N	110.46 W
Groswater Bay c	176	54.20 N	57.30 W
Grote Nete ≃	56	51.07 N	4.34 E
Groton, Ct., U.S.	207	41.21 N	72.04 W
Groton, Ma., U.S.	207	42.36 N	71.34 W
Groton, N.Y., U.S.	210	42.35 N	76.22 W
Groton, S.D., U.S.	198	45.26 N	98.05 W
Grottaferrata	66	41.47 N	12.40 E
Grottaglie	68	40.32 N	17.26 E
Grottaminarda	68	41.04 N	15.02 E
Grottammare	66	42.59 N	13.52 E
Grotte	70	37.24 N	13.42 E
Grotte di Castro	66	42.40 N	11.52 E
Grotteria	68	38.22 N	16.17 E
Grottoes	188	38.16 N	78.49 W
Grottole	68	40.36 N	16.23 E
Grou, Oued V	148	33.56 N	6.45 W
Grouard Mission	182	55.31 N	116.09 W
Groundbirch	182	55.47 N	120.55 W
Groundhog ≃	176	49.43 N	81.58 W
Grouse Creek ≃, Ks., U.S.	198	37.00 N	96.55 W
Grouse Creek ≃, Ut,. U.S.	200	41.22 N	113.55 W
Grouse Creek Mountain ∧	202	44.22 N	113.54 W
Grouw	52	53.05 N	5.45 E
Grove, Eng., U.K.	42	51.36 N	1.25 W
Grove, Ok., U.S.	196	36.35 N	94.46 W
Grove, Pa., U.S.	285	40.01 N	75.38 W
Grove City, Fl., U.S.	220	26.54 N	82.19 W
Grove City, Mn., U.S.	198	45.09 N	94.40 W
Grove City, Oh., U.S.	218	39.52 N	83.05 W
Grove City, Pa., U.S.	214	41.09 N	80.05 W
Grove Hill	194	31.42 N	87.46 W
Groveland, Ca., U.S.	226	37.50 N	120.13 W
Groveland, Fl., U.S.	220	28.33 N	81.51 W
Groveland, Ma., U.S.	207	42.45 N	71.01 W
Groveland, N.Y., U.S.	210	42.39 N	77.46 W
Grovely Ridge ∧	42	51.08 N	2.04 W
Grove Mountains ⋏	9	72.53 S	74.53 E
Grove Park ◆[8]	260	51.26 N	0.01 E
Groveport	218	39.52 N	82.53 W
Grover	210	41.37 N	76.52 W
Grover City	204	35.07 N	120.37 W
Grover Cleveland Birthplace ⊥	276	40.50 N	74.16 W
Grover Cleveland Park ♦	284a	42.57 N	78.49 W
Grover Hill	216	41.01 N	84.28 W
Grovers Mills	276	40.19 N	74.37 W
Groves	194	29.56 N	93.55 W
Groveton, N.H., U.S.	188	44.35 N	71.30 W
Groveton, Pa., U.S.	279b	40.30 N	80.06 W
Groveton, Tx., U.S.	222	31.03 N	95.07 W
Groveton, Va., U.S.	284c	38.46 N	77.05 W
Grovetown	192	33.27 N	82.11 W
Groveville	208	40.10 N	74.40 W
Growa Point ›	150	4.21 N	7.37 W
Growler Peak ∧	200	32.24 N	113.07 W
Growler Wash V	200	32.35 N	113.30 W
Groznoje	85	42.36 N	71.12 E
Groznyj	84	43.20 N	45.42 E
Groznyy → Groznyj	84	43.20 N	45.42 E
Grube, Dtsch.	54	54.14 N	11.01 E
Grube, Dtsch.	264a	52.26 N	12.57 E
Grubišno Polje	36	45.42 N	17.10 E
Grubweg	60	48.35 N	13.29 E
Grudovo	38	42.21 N	27.10 E
Grudziądz	30	53.29 N	18.45 E
Gruesa, Punta ›	248	20.22 S	70.11 W
Gruetli-Laager	194	35.22 N	85.40 W
Grugapark ♦	263	51.26 N	7.00 E
Grugliasco	62	45.04 N	7.35 E
Gruia	38	44.16 N	22.42 E
Gruinard Bay c	46	57.53 N	5.31 W
Gruinart, Loch c	46	55.52 N	6.20 W
Gruiten	56	51.14 N	7.01 E
Gruitrode	56	51.05 N	5.35 E
Grulla	196	26.16 N	98.39 W
Grumello del Monte	62	45.38 N	9.52 E
Grumento Nova	68	40.17 N	15.53 E
Grumentum ⊥	68	40.17 N	15.55 E
Grumman-Bethpage Airport ⊠	276	40.45 N	73.29 W
Grumman Corporation ⊍[3]	276	40.45 N	73.30 W
Grumme ◆[8]	263	51.30 N	7.14 E
Grumo Appula	68	41.01 N	16.42 E
Grums	26	59.21 N	13.06 E
Grun'	78	50.16 N	34.36 E
Grüna	54	50.49 N	12.47 E
Grünau	156	27.44 S	18.23 E
Grünau ◆[8]	264a	52.25 N	13.34 E
Grünau im Almtal	64	47.51 N	13.57 E
Grunavat, Loch ⊜	46	58.10 N	6.55 W
Grünbach	54	50.26 N	12.22 E
Grünberg	56	50.35 N	8.58 E
Grünberg → Zielona Góra	30	51.56 N	15.31 E
Grünburg	61	47.57 N	14.15 E
Grundlsee ⊜	64	47.38 N	13.52 E
Grundy	192	37.16 N	82.05 W
Grundy □[6]	216	41.22 N	88.26 W
Grundy Center	190	42.21 N	92.46 W
Grundy Lake Provincial Park ♦	190	45.48 N	80.34 W
Grünefeld	264a	52.41 N	12.58 E
Grünenplan	52	51.57 N	9.44 E
Grünewald, Dtsch.	54	51.24 N	14.00 E
Grünewald, Dtsch.	263	51.13 N	7.37 E
Grunewald ◆[8]	264a	52.30 N	13.17 E
Grunewald, Berliner Forst ◆[3]	264a	52.28 N	13.13 E
Grunewald, Jagdschloss ⊥	264a	52.28 N	13.16 E
Grünhain	54	50.35 N	12.48 E
Grünhainichen	54	50.46 N	13.08 E
Grünheide	54	52.25 N	13.49 E
Grünsfeld	56	49.36 N	9.44 E
Grünstadt	56	49.34 N	8.10 E
Grüntal	264a	52.45 N	13.44 E
Grunthal	184	49.25 N	96.52 W
Grünwald	60	48.02 N	11.31 E
Gruševka	78	47.55 N	40.40 E
Gruševka ≃	83	47.26 N	40.00 E
Gruševskaja	83	47.26 N	39.57 E
Grušino	76	59.27 N	44.09 E
Gruting	46a	60.14 N	1.30 W
Gruver	196	36.16 N	101.24 W
Gruyère, Lac de la ⊜	58	46.38 N	7.06 E
Gruyères	58	46.35 N	7.05 E
Gruzdžiai	76	56.06 N	23.16 E
Gruzija → Georgia □[1]	72	42.00 N	44.00 E
Gruziya → Georgia □[1]	72	42.00 N	44.00 E
Gruznovka	88	55.09 N	105.12 E
Gruzskaja Balka	78	46.25 N	40.19 E
Gruzskij Jelančik ≃	83	47.07 N	38.04 E
Gruzskoje	83	48.33 N	37.18 E
Gruzsko-Zor'anskoje	83	47.56 N	38.06 E
Grybów	30	49.38 N	20.56 E
Grycken ⊜	40	60.27 N	16.13 E
Gryfice	30	53.56 N	15.12 E
Gryfino	30	53.12 N	14.30 E
Grytgöl	40	58.48 N	15.33 E
Grythyttan	40	59.42 N	14.32 E
Gschnitz	64	47.03 N	11.22 E
Gschütt, Pass)(	64	47.35 N	13.30 E
Gschwend	56	48.56 N	9.44 E
Gstaad	58	46.28 N	7.17 E
Gsteig	58	46.23 N	7.16 E
Gu ≃	100	27.02 N	115.03 E
Gua	124	22.12 N	85.23 E
Guabaria ≃[1]	126	22.10 N	90.30 E
Guabito	236	9.30 N	82.37 W
Guabu	106	32.16 N	118.53 E
Guacanayabo, Golfo de c	240p	20.28 N	77.30 W
Guacara	246	10.14 N	67.53 W
Guacarí	246	3.46 N	76.20 W
Gu Achi	200	32.19 N	112.02 W
Guachinango	234	20.32 N	104.24 W
Guachiría ≃	246	5.27 N	70.36 W
Guachochi	232	26.51 N	107.05 W
Guaçuí	255	20.46 S	41.41 W
Guadajira ≃	34	38.52 N	6.41 W
Guadajoz ≃	34	37.50 N	4.51 W
Guadalajara, Esp.	34	40.38 N	3.10 W
Guadalajara, Méx.	234	20.40 N	103.20 W
Guadalajara □[4]	34	40.50 N	2.30 W
Guadalaviar ≃	34	40.21 N	1.08 W
Guadalcanal	34	38.06 N	5.49 W
Guadalcanal □[4]	175e	9.50 S	160.00 E
Guadalcanal I	175e	9.32 S	160.12 E
Guadalcázar	234	22.37 N	100.24 W
Guadalén ≃	34	38.05 N	3.32 W
Guadalén, Embalse de ⊜[1]	34	38.25 N	3.15 W
Guadalentín ≃	34	37.59 N	1.04 W
Guadalete ≃	34	36.35 N	6.13 W
Guadalhorce ≃	34	36.41 N	4.27 W
Guadalimar ≃	34	38.05 N	3.06 W
Guadalmena ≃	34	38.19 N	2.56 W
Guadalmez ≃	34	38.46 N	5.04 W
Guadalope ≃	34	41.15 N	0.03 W
Guadalquivir ≃	34	36.47 N	6.22 W
Guadalupe, Bol.	248	18.33 S	64.05 W
Guadalupe, Col.	246	2.01 N	75.45 W
Guadalupe, C.R.	236	9.57 N	84.03 W
Guadalupe, Méx.	196	28.09 N	100.36 W
Guadalupe, Méx.	232	25.41 N	100.15 W
Guadalupe, Méx.	234	22.45 N	102.31 W
Guadalupe, Perú	248	7.15 S	79.29 W
Guadalupe, Ca., U.S.	204	34.58 N	120.34 W
Guadalupe □[6]	222	29.37 N	97.45 W
Guadalupe ◆[8]	287a	22.50 S	43.23 W
Guadalupe ≃, Méx.	204	32.05 N	116.53 W
Guadalupe ≃, Ca., U.S.	282	37.25 N	121.58 W
Guadalupe ≃, Tx., U.S.	196	28.30 N	96.53 W
Guadalupe, Basílica de ⊍[1]	286a	19.29 N	99.07 W
Guadalupe, Isla I	178	29.00 N	118.16 W
Guadalupe, Presa de ⊜[1]	286a	19.37 N	99.16 W
Guadalupe, Sierra de ⋏, Esp.	34	39.26 N	5.25 W
Guadalupe, Sierra de ⋏, Méx.	286a	19.35 N	99.08 W
Guadalupe [Bravos]	232	31.23 N	106.07 W
Guadalupe del Norte ≍	286a	19.34 N	99.01 W
Guadalupe de Ramírez	234	17.45 N	98.10 W
Guadalupe → Guadeloupe □[2]	241o	16.15 N	61.35 W
Guadalupe Mountains ⋏	196	32.20 N	105.00 W
Guadalupe Mountains National Park ♦	196	31.55 N	104.55 W
Guadalupe Peak ∧	196	31.50 N	104.52 W
Guadalupe Seamount ✦[3]	14	27.50 N	168.45 E
Guadalupe Slough ≃	282	37.27 N	122.02 W
Guadalupe Victoria, Méx.	196	27.47 N	101.04 W
Guadalupe Victoria, Méx.	232	24.27 N	104.07 W
Guadalupe Victoria, Méx.	234	19.17 N	97.21 W
Guadalupe Victoria, Presa ⊜[1]	234	23.50 N	104.46 W
Guadalupita	200	36.08 N	105.14 W
Guadarrama, Puerto de)(	34	40.43 N	4.10 W
Guadarrama, Sierra de ⋏	34	40.55 N	4.00 W
Guadazaón ≃	34	39.42 N	1.36 W
Guadeloupe □[2], N.A.	230	16.15 N	61.35 W
Guadeloupe □[2], N.A.	241o	16.15 N	61.35 W
Guadeloupe Passage ⊔	238	16.45 N	61.30 W
Guadiana ≃	34	37.14 N	7.22 W
Guadiana, Bahía de c	240p	22.05 N	84.24 W
Guadiana Menor ≃	34	37.56 N	3.15 W
Guadiaro ≃	34	36.17 N	5.17 W
Guadiato ≃	34	38.20 N	5.22 W
Guadiela ≃	34	40.22 N	2.49 W
Guadix	34	37.18 N	3.08 W
Guafo, Isla I	254	43.36 S	74.43 W
Guagnano	68	40.24 N	17.57 E
Guagua	116	14.58 N	120.38 E
Guahe	105	39.12 N	115.00 E
Guaianases ◆[8]	287b	23.33 S	46.25 W
Guaíba	252	30.06 S	51.19 W
Guaíba c[1]	252	30.15 S	51.12 W
Guaicaipuro □[5]	286c	10.25 N	65.57 W
Guaihe	100	33.28 N	112.59 E
Guaimaca	236	14.32 N	86.51 W
Guáimaro	240p	21.03 N	77.21 W
Guaimoreto, Laguna de c	236	15.58 N	85.55 W
Guaimozi	98	41.31 N	125.26 E
Guainía □[5]	246	2.30 N	69.00 W
Guainía ≃	246	2.01 N	67.07 W
Guaió ≃	287b	23.31 S	46.19 W
Guaipava	256	21.40 S	45.43 W
Guaiquinima, Cerro ∧	246	5.49 N	63.40 W
Guaíra, Bra.	252	24.04 S	54.15 W
Guaíra, Bra.	255	20.19 S	48.18 W
Guairá □[5]	252	25.45 S	56.30 W
Guaire ≃	286c	10.25 N	66.46 W
Guáitara ≃	246	1.34 N	77.27 W
Guaitecas, Archipiélago de las II	254	43.57 S	73.50 W
Guajaba, Cayo I	240p	21.50 N	77.30 W
Guajará ≃	250	1.48 S	53.02 W
Guajará-Açu	250	1.38 S	48.07 W
Guajará-Miri	250	1.29 S	48.17 W
Guajará-Mirim	248	10.48 S	65.22 W
Guajataca ≃	240m	18.29 N	66.57 W
Guajataca, Lago de ⊜[1]	240m	18.23 N	66.55 W
Guajiasi	104	41.15 N	120.54 E
Gualaca	236	8.32 N	82.18 W
Gualaceo	246	2.54 S	78.47 W
Gualala	204	38.45 N	123.31 W
Gualán	236	15.08 N	89.22 W
Gualaquiza	246	3.24 S	78.33 W
Gualdo Tadino	66	43.14 N	12.47 E
Gualeguay	252	33.09 S	59.20 W
Gualeguay ≃	252	33.19 S	59.39 W
Gualeguaychú	252	33.01 S	58.31 W
Gualicho, Salina del ≃	254	40.24 S	65.15 W
Gualjaina	254	42.42 S	70.30 W
Gualtieri	64	44.54 N	10.38 E
Guam □[2], Oc.	14	13.28 N	144.47 E
Guam □[2], Oc.	174p	13.28 N	144.47 E
Guamá ≃, Bra.	250	1.29 S	48.30 W
Guamá ≃, Cuba	240p	22.11 N	83.41 W
Guamal, Col.	246	9.09 N	74.14 W
Guamal, Col.	246	3.52 N	73.44 W
Guamal, Quebrada ≃	286c	10.31 N	66.59 W
Guamblín, Isla I	254	44.51 S	75.05 W
Guaminí	252	37.02 S	62.25 W
Guam International Airport ⊠	174p	13.29 N	144.48 E
Guamo	246	4.02 N	74.58 W
Guamo Embarcadero	240p	20.37 N	76.58 W
Guamote	246	1.56 S	78.43 W
Guamúchil, Méx.	232	25.28 N	108.06 W
Guamúchil, Méx.	234	23.55 N	106.05 W
Guamués ≃	246	0.32 N	76.33 W
Gua Musang	114	4.53 N	101.58 E
Gu'an	105	39.26 N	116.18 E
Guan ≃, Zhg.	100	32.16 N	115.42 E
Guan ≃, Zhg.	100	34.29 N	119.49 E
Guanábana	240m	18.01 N	67.07 W
Guanabara, Baía de c	287a	22.50 S	43.10 W
Guanabara, Palácio ⊍	287a	22.56 S	43.11 W
Guanacaste □[4]	236	10.30 N	85.15 W
Guanacaste, Cordillera de ⋏	236	10.45 N	85.05 W
Guanacaste, Parque Nacional ♦	236	10.50 N	85.30 W
Guanacaure, Cerro ∧	236	13.14 N	87.07 W
Guanaceví	232	25.56 N	105.57 W
Guanache ≃	248	5.53 S	74.21 W
Guanahacabibes, Golfo de c	240p	22.08 N	84.35 W
Guanahacabibes, Península de ›[1]	240p	21.57 N	84.35 W
Guana Island I	240m	18.29 N	64.34 W
Guanaja	236	16.27 N	85.54 W
Guanaja, Isla de I	236	16.30 N	85.55 W
Guanajay	240p	22.55 N	82.42 W
Guanajibo ≃	240m	18.10 N	67.11 W
Guanajibo, Punta ›	240m	18.10 N	67.11 W
Guanajuato	234	21.01 N	101.15 W
Guanajuato □[3]	234	21.00 N	101.00 W
Guanambi	255	14.13 S	42.47 W
Guanaparo, Caño ≃	246	8.19 N	68.10 W
Guañape, Islas II	248	8.33 S	78.57 W
Guanare	246	9.03 N	69.45 W
Guanare ≃	246	8.13 N	67.46 W
Guanarito	246	8.42 N	69.12 W
Guanay	248	15.28 S	67.52 W
Guanay, Cerro ∧	246	5.51 N	66.18 W
Guanay, Cerro ∧[2]	286d	12.07 S	77.13 W
Guanbuqiao	100	29.56 N	114.21 E
Guanchao	100	26.41 N	114.58 E
Guancheng, Zhg.	100	30.11 N	121.25 E
Guancheng, Zhg.	107	30.01 N	103.54 E
Guancun	106	31.30 N	119.43 E
Guandacol	252	29.31 S	68.32 W
Guandanghu	100	30.06 N	113.37 E
Guandi, Zhg.	98	41.48 N	116.52 E
Guandi, Zhg.	98	42.37 N	118.27 E
Guandian	100	32.40 N	118.04 E
Guandu, Zhg.	100	24.17 N	113.53 E
Guandu, Zhg.	107	30.04 N	106.25 E
Guane	240p	22.12 N	84.05 W
Guang'an	107	30.28 N	106.39 E
Guang'anmen Station ◆[5]	271a	39.53 N	116.20 E
Guangchang	100	26.50 N	116.14 E
Guangde	106	30.54 N	119.26 E
Guangdong (Kwangtung) □[4]	90	23.00 N	113.00 E
Guangfeng	100	28.25 N	118.11 E
Guangfu, Zhg.	106	31.18 N	120.23 E
Guangfu, Zhg.	107	30.13 N	104.41 E
Guangfu, Zhg.	269b	31.21 N	121.19 E
Guangfuyingzi	104	42.14 N	120.58 E
Guanghua	102	32.25 N	111.36 E
Guangji	100	29.52 N	115.34 E
Guangling, Zhg.	98	39.47 N	114.17 E
Guangling, Zhg.	106	32.06 N	120.13 E
Guanglu Dao I	98	39.09 N	122.21 E
Guangmao Shan ∧	102	27.02 N	100.58 E
Guangming Ding ∧	100	30.07 N	118.10 E
Guangnan	102	24.10 N	105.06 E
Guangningsi, Zhg.	98	39.08 N	121.46 E
Guangningsi, Zhg.	98	40.27 N	118.31 E
Guangping	98	36.30 N	114.57 E
Guangrao	98	37.02 N	118.25 E
Guangsbunchang	107	29.22 N	105.31 E
Guangshan	100	32.02 N	114.52 E
Guangshui	100	31.40 N	114.00 E
Guangxing	107	29.04 N	106.33 E
Guangxi Zhuangzu Zizhiqu (Kwangsi Chuang) □[4]	102	24.00 N	109.00 E
Guangyuan	102	32.26 N	105.52 E
Guangyuanzhen	107	30.37 N	104.47 E
Guangze	100	27.32 N	117.20 E
Guangzhen	106	30.45 N	121.07 E
Guangzhou (Canton)	100	23.06 N	113.16 E
Guangzong	98	37.06 N	115.08 E
Guanhães	255	18.46 S	42.53 W
Guanhu	98	34.26 N	117.59 E
Guánica	240m	17.58 N	66.55 W
Guánica, Laguna de ⊜	240m	18.00 N	66.56 W
Guaniguanico, Cordillera de ⋏	240p	22.35 N	83.45 W
Guanipa ≃	246	9.56 N	62.26 W
Guanjian	107	29.59 N	105.59 E
Guanjian ≃	107	30.00 N	106.01 E
Guankou, Zhg.	100	30.35 N	115.20 E
Guankou, Zhg.	107	30.39 N	103.26 E
Guanlin	106	31.32 N	119.42 E
Guanling	102	25.57 N	105.29 E
Guanlipu	104	41.37 N	123.18 E
Guanmenshan	89	47.23 N	122.20 E
Guannan (Xin'anzhen)	98	34.07 N	119.23 E
Guano	246	1.35 S	78.38 W
Guano Creek ≃	202	42.12 N	119.31 W
Guanputou	105	38.58 N	117.04 E
Guanqian, Zhg.	100	30.42 N	117.39 E
Guanqian, Zhg.	100	27.48 N	118.31 E
Guanqian, Zhg.	100	25.57 N	116.33 E
Guanqian, Zhg.	100	26.12 N	117.57 E
Guanqiao, Zhg.	98	34.58 N	117.14 E
Guanqiao, Zhg.	100	25.03 N	118.06 E
Guanqiaopu	100	31.08 N	112.54 E
Guanshanchang	107	28.46 N	103.42 E
Guanshi	100	26.43 N	112.53 E
Guanshui	98	40.55 N	124.33 E
Guanta	246	10.14 N	64.36 W
Guantánamo	240p	20.08 N	75.12 W
Guantánamo □[4]	240p	20.20 N	75.00 W
Guantánamo ≃	240p	19.55 N	75.12 W
Guantánamo, Bahía de c	240p	20.00 N	75.08 W
Guantanamo Bay Naval Station ■	240p	19.55 N	75.10 W
Guantang	106	31.37 N	119.06 E
Guantangqiao	106	32.09 N	119.27 E
Guantao (Nanguantao)	98	36.35 N	115.19 E
Guanting, Zhg.	100	34.19 N	113.47 E
Guanting, Zhg.	105	40.13 N	115.37 E
Guanting Shuiku ⊜[1]	105	40.20 N	115.38 E
Guantou, Zhg.	100	28.03 N	120.41 E
Guantou, Zhg.	100	26.08 N	119.33 E
Guantunpu	98	40.28 N	113.24 E
Guanxian, Zhg.	98	36.30 N	115.27 E
Guanxian, Zhg.	102	31.00 N	103.40 E
Guanxun	100	24.19 N	117.45 E
Guanyin	107	30.16 N	103.51 E
Guanyinchang, Zhg.	107	29.15 N	104.02 E
Guanyinchang, Zhg.	107	30.28 N	105.16 E
Guanyingzicun	104	41.52 N	121.53 E
Guanyinpu	107	28.58 N	104.53 E
Guanyinqiao, Zhg.	107	29.05 N	104.46 E
Guanyinqiao, Zhg.	107	29.46 N	104.12 E
Guanyinshan	106	32.01 N	120.58 E
Guanyinsi	106	31.48 N	118.57 E
Guanyintan	107	29.35 N	105.14 E
Guanyintang, Zhg.	100	31.01 N	112.35 E
Guanyintang, Zhg.	105	39.52 N	116.31 E
Guanyintang, Zhg.	106	32.09 N	121.09 E
Guanyinzhen	107	29.06 N	104.24 E
Guanyinzhou	100	29.30 N	113.09 E
Guanyun (Dayishan)	98	34.20 N	119.17 E
Guanzhuang, Zhg.	98	37.12 N	114.30 E
Guanzhuang, Zhg.	100	32.49 N	114.16 E
Guanzhuang, Zhg.	100	28.58 N	117.24 E
Guapí	246	2.36 N	77.54 W
Guapiaçu ≃	256	22.40 S	42.55 W
Guapiara	255	24.10 S	48.32 W
Guápiles	236	10.13 N	83.46 W
Guapimirim	256	22.32 S	42.59 W
Guapimirim ≃	256	22.40 S	42.58 W
Guapo Bay c	241r	10.12 N	61.40 W
Guaporé	252	28.51 S	51.54 W
Guaporé (Itenes) ≃	248	11.54 S	65.01 W
Guaqui	248	16.35 S	68.51 W
Guará ≃	255	12.59 S	44.49 W
Guara, Sierra de ⋏	34	42.17 N	0.10 W
Guarabira	250	6.51 S	35.29 W
Guaraçaí	255	21.02 S	51.11 W
Guaracarumbo	286c	10.34 N	66.59 W
Guaraci	255	20.29 S	48.57 W
Guaraciaba do Norte	250	4.10 S	40.46 W
Guaraciana	255	17.03 S	43.41 W
Guaraguara, Punta ›	241r	10.31 N	62.19 W
Guaraí ≃	287a	22.42 S	43.02 W
Guaramirim	252	26.27 S	49.00 W
Guaranda	246	1.36 S	79.00 W
Guaranésia	256	21.18 S	46.48 W
Guarani	256	21.22 S	43.03 W
Guaraniaçu	252	25.06 S	52.52 W
Guarani das Missões	252	28.08 S	54.34 W
Guarani de Goiás	255	13.59 S	46.31 W
Guarapari	255	20.40 S	40.30 W
Guarapiranga, Represa ⊜[1]	256	23.44 S	46.44 W
Guarapuava	252	25.23 S	51.27 W
Guaraqueçaba	252	25.17 S	48.21 W
Guarará	256	21.43 S	43.02 W
Guarará ≃	287b	23.39 S	46.30 W
Guararé	246	7.49 N	80.17 W
Guararema	256	23.25 S	46.02 W
Guaratiba, Morro de ∧	287a	23.04 S	43.33 W
Guaratinga	255	16.34 S	39.34 W
Guaratinguetá	256	22.49 S	45.13 W
Guaratinguetá ≃	256	22.49 S	45.13 W
Guaratuba	252	25.54 S	48.34 W
Guar Chempedak	114	5.52 N	100.28 E
Guarcino	66	41.48 N	13.19 E
Guarda	34	40.32 N	7.16 W
Guardado de Abajo	196	26.22 N	98.57 W
Guardafui, Cape → Caseyr ›	144	11.49 N	51.15 E
Guardavalle	68	38.30 N	16.30 E
Guardea	66	42.37 N	12.18 E
Guardia Escolta	252	28.59 S	62.08 W
Guardiagrele	66	42.11 N	14.13 E
Guardia Lombardi	68	40.57 N	15.12 E
Guardia Mitre	254	40.26 S	63.41 W
Guardia Sanframondi	68	41.15 N	14.36 E
Guardo	34	42.47 N	4.50 W
Guareña	34	38.51 N	6.06 W
Guareña ≃	34	41.29 N	5.23 W
Guarenas	246	10.28 N	66.37 W
Guarenas ≃	286c	10.30 N	66.45 W
Guariba ≃	248	7.41 S	60.18 W
Guarico	246	9.32 N	69.48 W
Guárico □[3]	246	8.40 N	66.35 W
Guárico ≃	246	7.55 N	67.23 W
Guárico, Embalse del ⊜[1]	246	9.05 N	67.25 W
Guarico, Punta ›	240p	20.37 N	74.44 W
Guariquito ≃	246	7.40 N	66.18 W
Guarizama	236	14.55 N	86.20 W
Guarujá	256	24.00 S	46.16 W
Guarulhos	256	23.28 S	46.32 W
Guarulhos □[7]	287b	23.26 S	46.29 W
Guasare ≃	246	11.03 N	72.02 W
Guasave	232	25.34 N	108.27 W
Guasdualito	246	7.15 N	70.44 W
Guasila	71	39.34 N	9.03 E
Guasipati	246	7.28 N	61.54 W
Guastalla	64	44.55 N	10.39 E
Guastatoya	236	14.51 N	90.04 W
Guāsuba ≃[1]	126	21.38 N	88.53 E
Guatajiagua	236	13.40 N	88.13 W
Guatemala, Cuba	240p	20.46 N	75.39 W
Guatemala, Guat.	236	14.38 N	90.31 W
Guatemala □[5]	236	14.40 N	90.30 W
Guatemala □[1], N.A.	230	15.30 N	90.15 W
Guatemala □[1], N.A.	236	15.30 N	90.15 W
Guatemala Basin ✦[1]	16	11.00 N	95.00 W
Guateque	246	5.00 N	73.28 W
Guatimozín	252	33.27 S	62.27 W
Guatopo, Parque Nacional ♦	246	10.05 N	66.25 W
Guatraché	252	37.40 S	63.32 W
Guatuaro Point ›	241r	10.20 N	60.59 W
Guaugurina	164	10.37 S	150.28 E
Guavi ≃	164	7.49 S	143.15 E
Guaviare □[8]	246	2.00 N	72.00 W
Guaviare ≃	246	4.03 N	67.44 W
Guaxindiba ≃	287a	22.44 S	43.02 W
Guaxupé	256	21.18 S	46.42 W
Guayabal, Cuba	240p	20.42 N	77.36 W
Guayabal, Ven.	246	8.00 N	67.24 W
Guayabal, Lago ⊜[1]	240m	18.06 N	66.30 W
Guayabero ≃	246	2.36 N	72.47 W
Guayacán	252	29.58 S	71.22 W
Guayaguayare	241r	10.08 N	61.02 W
Guayalejo ≃	234	22.27 N	98.29 W
Guayama	240m	17.59 N	66.07 W
Guayambre ≃	236	14.26 N	86.02 W
Guayameo	234	18.12 N	101.19 W
Guayana → Ciudad Guayana	246	8.22 N	62.40 W
Guayana → Guyana □[1]	246	5.00 N	59.00 W
Guayaneco, Archipiélago II	254	47.45 S	75.10 W
Guayanés, Punta ›	240m	18.04 N	65.48 W
Guayanilla	240m	18.01 N	66.47 W
Guayanilla, Bahía de c	240m	18.00 N	66.46 W
Guayape	236	14.45 N	86.52 W
Guayape ≃	236	14.26 N	85.58 W
Guayapo ≃	246	4.30 N	67.35 W
Guayaquil	6	2.10 S	79.50 W
Guayaquil, Golfo de c	246	3.00 S	80.30 W
Guayaramerín	248	10.48 S	65.23 W
Guayas □[4]	246	2.00 S	80.00 W
Guayas ≃, Col.	246	1.23 N	74.50 W
Guayas ≃, Ec.	246	2.36 S	79.52 W
Guayatayoc, Laguna de ⊜	252	23.25 S	65.51 W
Guaycora	232	28.50 N	109.21 W
Guaycurú, Arroyo ≃	258	34.00 S	56.50 W
Guaymas	232	27.56 N	110.54 W
Guaynabo	240m	18.22 N	66.07 W
Guayquiraró ≃	252	30.10 S	58.34 W
Guayuriba ≃	246	3.55 N	73.05 W
Guazacapán	236	14.04 N	90.25 W
Guazapares	232	27.22 N	108.15 W
Guazárachi	232	26.57 N	106.43 W
Guazhou	106	32.15 N	119.23 E
Guazunamby, Arroyo ≃	288	34.24 S	58.38 W
Guba, Ityo.	144	10.16 N	35.17 E
Guba, Zaïre	154	10.40 S	26.26 E
Gubacha	86	58.52 N	57.36 E
Gubam	164	8.40 S	141.55 E
Gubany	76	56.37 N	30.40 E
Gubari	80	51.32 N	42.33 E
Gubat	116	12.55 N	124.07 E
Gubavica ∟	36	43.26 N	16.54 E
Gubbi	122	13.19 N	76.56 E
Gubbio	66	43.21 N	12.35 E
Gubeikou	105	40.42 N	117.09 E
Guben	54	51.57 N	14.43 E
Gubentaoligai	104	42.16 N	122.13 E
Gubin	30	51.56 N	14.45 E
Gubinicha	78	48.48 N	35.15 E
Gubino, Ross.	80	53.19 N	48.44 E
Gubino, Ross.	82	55.42 N	39.07 E
Gubio	146	12.29 N	12.48 E
Gubkin	78	51.18 N	37.32 E
Gubug	115a	7.03 S	110.40 E
Gucheng (Zhengjiakou), Zhg.	98	37.22 N	115.56 E
Gucheng, Zhg.	100	33.59 N	117.29 E
Gucheng, Zhg.	100	25.53 N	116.11 E
Gucheng, Zhg.	100	32.46 N	118.32 E
Gucheng, Zhg.	102	32.18 N	111.35 E
Gucheng, Zhg.	105	40.32 N	116.02 E
Gucheng, Zhg.	105	39.08 N	115.42 E
Gucheng, Zhg.	106	30.29 N	119.46 E
Guchengcang	100	32.34 N	115.20 E
Gucheng Hu ⊜	106	31.17 N	118.54 E
Guchengzi, Zhg.	104	42.33 N	123.45 E
Guchengzi, Zhg.	104	40.58 N	122.36 E
Guchengzi, Zhg.	104	40.40 N	120.31 E
Guchengzi, Zhg.	104	41.44 N	123.35 E
Gučin-Us	102	45.27 N	102.25 E
Gücük	130	38.12 N	37.29 E
Güdalūr	122	9.41 N	77.16 E
Gúdar, Sierra de ⋏	34	40.27 N	0.42 W
Gudauta	84	43.06 N	40.37 E
Gudbrandsdalen V	26	61.30 N	10.00 E
Gudenå ≃	26	56.29 N	10.13 E
Gudensberg	56	51.10 N	9.22 E
Gudermes	84	43.20 N	46.08 E
Guderup	41	54.59 N	9.53 E
Gudgenby ≃	171b	35.39 S	149.04 E
Gudhjem	26	55.13 N	14.59 E
Gudianzi	100	31.49 N	116.05 E
Gudivāda	122	16.27 N	80.59 E
Gudiyāttam	122	12.57 N	78.52 E
Gudme	41	55.09 N	10.43 E
Gudow	54	53.33 N	10.46 E
Güdül	130	40.13 N	32.15 E
Güdūr	122	14.08 N	79.51 E
Gudvangen	26	60.52 N	6.50 E
Guebwiller (Gebweiler)	58	47.55 N	7.12 E
Guéckédou	150	8.33 N	10.09 W
Gué-de-Longroi	261	48.30 N	1.43 E
Gué-d'Hossus	50	49.57 N	4.32 E
Guédi, Mont ∧	146	12.14 N	18.58 E
Guéguen, Lac ⊜	190	48.06 N	77.13 W
Guéherville	261	48.32 N	1.53 E
Güéjar ≃	246	2.55 N	73.14 W
Guélendeng	146	10.56 N	15.32 E
Guelma	148	36.28 N	7.26 E
Guelma □[5]	148	36.10 N	7.50 E
Guelph	212	43.33 N	80.15 W
Guéméné-sur-Scorff	32	48.04 N	3.12 W
Güemes	234	23.56 N	99.00 W
Guemes Island I	224	48.33 N	122.37 W
Guené	150	11.44 N	3.13 E
Guenguel ≃	254	45.41 S	70.20 W
Guer	32	47.54 N	2.07 W
Guéra □[5]	146	11.30 N	18.30 E
Guéra, Massif de ∧	146	11.55 N	18.12 E
Guérande	32	47.20 N	2.26 W
Guercif	148	34.15 N	3.21 W
Guerdjoumane, Djebel ∧	34	36.25 N	2.51 E
Güere ≃	246	9.50 N	65.08 W
Guéréda	146	14.31 N	22.05 E
Guéret	32	46.10 N	1.52 E
Guérin Kouka	150	9.41 N	0.37 E
Guerla Mandata Shan ∧	120	30.26 N	81.20 E
Guermantes	261	48.51 N	2.42 E
Guerne	214	40.46 N	81.54 W
Guernes	261	49.01 N	1.38 E
Guerneville	204	38.30 N	123.00 W
Guernica	258	34.56 S	58.25 W
Guernica → Gernika-Lumo	34	43.19 N	2.41 W
Guernsey	200	42.16 N	104.44 W
Guernsey □[6]	214	40.08 N	81.30 W
Guernsey □[2], Europe	22	49.28 N	2.35 W
Guernsey □[2], Europe	43b	49.28 N	2.35 W
Guernsey Reservoir ⊜[1]	198	42.19 N	104.48 W
Guernsey State Park ♦	198	42.20 N	104.50 W
Guerrero, Méx.	196	28.20 N	100.23 W
Guerrero, Méx.	232	28.33 N	107.30 W
Guerrero □[3]	234	17.40 N	100.00 W
Guerrero Negro	232	27.56 N	114.08 W
Guerville	261	48.57 N	1.44 E
Guerzim	148	29.45 N	1.47 W
Guesle ≃	261	48.36 N	1.40 E
Guessou-Sud	150	10.03 N	2.38 E
Guest Peninsula ›[1]	9	76.18 S	148.00 W
Gueydan	194	30.01 N	92.30 W
Guéyo	150	5.49 N	6.36 W
Gufang	100	29.04 N	119.32 E
Guffin Bay c	212	44.01 N	76.09 W
Guga	89	52.43 N	137.35 E
Gugang	100	28.17 N	113.46 E
Guge ∧	144	6.10 N	37.26 E
Gugera	123	30.58 N	73.19 E
Gugging	264b	48.19 N	16.15 E
Güglia, Pass dal)(	58	46.28 N	9.44 E
Güglingen	56	49.04 N	9.00 E
Guglionesi	66	41.55 N	14.55 E
Gugu ∧	144	8.12 N	39.58 E
Guguan	102	40.27 N	99.13 E
Guguan I	108	17.19 N	145.51 E
Guhe	100	31.54 N	117.58 E
Gui ≃	102	23.28 N	111.18 E
Guia	248	15.22 S	56.14 W
Guia de Pacobaíba	256	22.43 S	43.10 W
Guia Lopes da Laguna	248	21.26 S	56.07 W
Guiana Basin ✦[1]	18	11.00 N	52.00 W
Guiana Island I	240c	17.07 N	61.44 W
Guibéroua	150	6.14 N	6.10 W
Guibes	156	26.41 S	16.42 E
Güicán	246	6.28 N	72.25 W
Guichen	32	47.58 N	1.48 W
Guichi	100	30.40 N	117.28 E
Guichón	252	32.21 S	57.12 W
Guicun	100	33.37 N	114.11 E
Guidan Roumji	150	13.40 N	6.42 E
Guidari	146	9.17 N	16.40 E
Guide	102	36.03 N	101.28 E
Guide, Mount ∧[2]	162	22.36 S	136.54 E
Guide Post	44	55.10 N	1.35 W
Guider	146	9.56 N	13.57 E
Guide Rock	198	40.04 N	98.19 W
Guidexiang	107	29.51 N	104.47 E
Guidigri	146	13.40 N	9.51 E
Guidimaka □[4]	150	15.30 N	12.10 W
Guidimouni	150	13.42 N	9.30 E
Guiding	102	26.34 N	107.14 E
Guidizzolo	64	45.19 N	10.35 E
Guidong	100	26.05 N	113.57 E
Guidonia	66	42.01 N	12.45 E
Guidouma	152	1.37 S	10.41 E
Guiers ≃	62	45.37 N	5.37 E
Guiers, Lac de ⊜	150	16.12 N	15.50 W
Guifujie	100	27.20 N	120.01 E
Guiglia	64	44.26 N	10.58 E
Guiglo	150	6.33 N	7.29 W
Guignes-Rabutin	50	48.38 N	2.48 E
Guihuayuan	107	30.37 N	105.25 E
Guihulngan	116	10.07 N	123.16 E
Güija, Lago de ⊜	236	14.17 N	89.31 W
Guijalo	116	13.44 N	123.52 E
Guiji	100	32.51 N	116.33 E
Guijingqiao	106	31.21 N	119.40 E
Guijuelo	34	40.33 N	5.40 W
Guil ≃	62	44.40 N	6.36 E
Guilarte, Monte ∧	240m	18.09 N	66.46 W
Guilderland	210	42.42 N	73.54 W
Guildford, Austl.	274a	33.51 S	150.59 E
Guildford, Eng., U.K.	260	51.14 N	0.35 W
Guildford □[8]	260	51.16 N	0.32 W
Guildford Cathedral ⊍[1]	260	51.14 N	0.35 W
Guildhall	188	44.33 N	71.33 W
Guildtown	46	56.28 N	3.24 W
Guiler	89	46.11 N	121.45 E
Guilford, Ct., U.S.	207	41.17 N	72.40 W
Guilford, In., U.S.	218	39.10 N	84.55 W
Guilford, Me., U.S.	188	45.10 N	69.23 W

Symbols in the index entries represent the broad categories identified in the key at the right. Symbols with superior numbers (⋏[1]) identify subcategories (see complete key on page *I · 1*).

Symbole im Register stellen die rechts im Schlüssel erklärten Kategorien dar. Symbole mit hochgestellten Ziffern (⋏[1]) bezeichnen Unterabteilungen einer Kategorie (vgl. vollständiger Schlüssel auf Seite *I · 1*).

Los símbolos incluídos en el texto del índice representan las grandes categorias identificadas con la clave a la derecha. Los símbolos con numeros en su parte superior (⋏[1]) identifican las subcategorías (véase la clave completa en la página *I · 1*).

Les symboles de l'index représentent les catégories indiquées dans la légende à droite. Les symboles suivis d'un indice (⋏[1]) représentent des sous-catégories (voir légende complète à la page *I · 1*).

Os símbolos incluídos no texto do índice representam as grandes categorias identificadas com a chave à direita. Os símbolos com números em sua parte superior (⋏[1]) identificam as subcategorias (veja-se a chave completa à página *I · 1*).

English	Deutsch	Español	Français	Português
∧ Mountain	Berg	Montaña	Montagne	Montanha
⋏ Mountains	Gebirge	Montañas	Montagnes	Montanhas
)(Pass	Paß	Paso	Col	Passo
V Valley, Canyon	Tal, Cañon	Valle, Cañón	Vallée, Canyon	Vale, Canhão
≚ Plain	Ebene	Llano	Plaine	Planície
› Cape	Kap	Cabo	Cap	Cabo
I Island	Insel	Isla	Île	Ilha
II Islands	Inseln	Islas	Îles	Ilhas
⊥ Other Topographic Features	Andere Topographische Objekte	Otros Elementos Topográficos	Autres données topographiques	Outros acidentes topográficos

ESPAÑOL	FRANÇAIS	PORTUGUÊS			

Column headers: **Nombre / Página / Lat.° / Long.° W=Oeste** · **Nom / Page / Lat.° / Long.° W=Ouest** · **Nome / Página / Lat.° / Long.° W=Oeste**

Column 1 (ESPAÑOL)

Nombre	Página	Lat.°	Long.° W=Oeste
Guilford, N.Y., U.S.	210	42.24 N	75.29 W
Guilford Courthouse National Military Park ♦	192	36.01 N	79.45 W
Guilherand	62	44.56 N	4.52 E
Guilin (Kweilin)	102	25.17 N	110.17 E
Guilinchang	107	30.13 N	105.50 E
Guilinzhen	107	30.15 N	104.53 E
Guillaume-Delisle, Lac ⊜	176	56.15 N	76.17 W
Guillaumes	62	44.05 N	6.51 E
Guillermo E. Hudson	288	34.47 S	58.10 W
Guillestre	62	44.40 N	6.39 E
Guillon	50	47.31 N	4.06 E
Guilsfield	42	52.42 N	3.09 W
Guilvinec	32	47.47 N	4.17 W
Guimarães, Bra.	250	2.08 S	44.36 W
Guimarães, Port.	34	41.27 N	8.18 W
Guimaras Island I	116	10.35 N	122.37 E
Guimaras Strait ⨆	116	10.30 N	122.44 E
Guimba	116	15.40 N	120.46 E
Guimbal	116	10.40 N	122.19 E
Guimeishan	100	24.44 N	114.52 E
Guimu Zhang ⋀	100	24.40 N	116.48 E
Guin	194	33.57 N	87.54 W
Guinan	102	35.24 N	100.57 E
Guinayangan	116	13.54 N	122.27 E
Guinda	226	38.50 N	122.12 W
Guindulman	116	9.46 N	124.29 E
Guindulman Bay c	116	9.44 N	124.29 E
Guinea	208	38.08 N	77.26 W
Guinea (Guinée) □¹, Afr.	134	11.00 N	10.00 W
Guinea (Guinée) □¹, Afr.	150	11.00 N	10.00 W
Guinea, Gulf of c	10	2.00 N	2.30 E
Guinea Basin ♣¹	10	0.00	5.00 W
Guinea-Bissau (Guiné-Bissau) □¹, Afr.	134	12.00 N	15.00 W
Guinea-Bissau (Guiné-Bissau) □¹, Afr.	150	12.00 N	15.00 W
Guineacorr Creek ≃	170	34.21 S	150.05 E
Guinea Ecuatorial — Equatorial Guinea □¹	152	2.00 N	9.00 E
Guinea Rise ♣³	10	8.00 S	0.00
Guinea-Bissau — Guinea-Bissau □¹	134	12.00 N	15.00 W
Guinecourt, Lac ⊜	186	50.55 N	69.16 W
Guinée-Bissau — Guinea-Bissau	150	12.00 N	15.00 W
Guinée équatoriale — Equatorial Guinea □¹	152	2.00 N	9.00 E
Guinée — Guinea □¹	150	11.00 N	10.00 W
Guiné — Guinea-Bissau	150	12.00 N	15.00 W
Güines, Cuba	240p	22.50 N	82.02 W
Guînes, Fr.	50	50.52 N	1.52 E
Guingamp	32	48.33 N	3.11 W
Guinguinéo	150	14.16 N	15.57 W
Guinobatan	116	13.11 N	123.36 E
Guintacan Island I	236	13.51 N	86.55 W
Guintinguintin, Mount ⋀	116	11.19 N	123.54 E
Guintina Island I	116	14.26 N	122.51 E
Guiones, Punta �succ	236	9.54 N	85.41 W
Guiong	116	6.25 N	120.21 E
Guiperreux	261	48.40 N	1.42 E
Guiperreux, Étang de ⊜	261	48.40 N	1.43 E
Guiping	102	23.20 N	110.09 E
Guir, Hammada du ⬩²	148	30.45 N	3.15 W
Guir, Oued V	148	30.29 N	2.17 W
Güira de Melena	240p	22.48 N	82.30 W
Guiraí ≃	255	22.40 S	53.34 W
Guiratinga	255	16.21 S	53.45 W
Guiren	100	33.42 N	118.12 E
Guiria	106	10.34 N	62.18 W
Guiricema	255	21.00 S	42.43 W
Guisachan Forest ♣³	46	57.17 N	4.55 W
Guisanbourg	250	4.25 N	51.56 W
Guisborough	44	54.32 N	1.04 W
Guiscard	50	49.39 N	3.03 E
Guise	50	49.54 N	3.38 E
Guiseley	44	53.53 N	1.42 W
Guisijan	116	11.05 N	122.03 E
Güisisil ⋀	236	12.37 N	86.13 W
Guist Creek ≃	218	38.09 N	85.13 W
Guitiriz	34	43.11 N	7.54 W
Guitou	100	24.58 N	113.25 E
Guitrancourt	261	49.01 N	1.47 E
Guîtres	62	45.03 N	0.11 W
Guitry	150	5.31 N	5.14 W
Guiuan	116	11.02 N	125.43 E
Guixian	102	23.06 N	109.39 E
Guiyang, Zhg.	100	25.46 N	112.43 E
Guiyang (Kweiyang), Zhg.	100	26.35 N	106.43 E
Güiza ≃	246	1.22 N	78.36 W
Guizhou (Kweichow) □⁴	102	27.00 N	107.00 E
Gujar □³	118	22.00 N	72.00 E
Gujar Khân	123	33.16 N	73.19 E
Gujba	146	11.30 N	11.55 E
Gujiabeng	106	30.45 N	120.59 E
Gujiang	100	27.11 N	114.49 E
Gujiatun	107	40.39 N	124.08 E
Gujiathai	269b	31.22 N	121.28 E
Gujiazi, Zhg.	104	42.02 N	123.01 E
Gujiazi, Zhg.	104	41.44 N	124.11 E
Gujrânwâla	123	32.09 N	74.11 E
Gujrât	123	32.34 N	74.05 E
Gukas'an	84	41.03 N	43.52 E
Gukovo	56	48.03 N	39.56 E
Gul, Tanjong ⊁	271c	1.17 N	103.39 E
Gul'a	88	54.41 N	121.01 E
Gul'aj-Borisovka	56	46.38 N	40.13 E
Gul'ajevskije Koški, ostrova II	24	68.55 N	55.10 E
Gül'aipole	78	47.38 N	36.16 E
Gulang	102	37.30 N	102.58 E
Gulaothri	124	28.36 N	77.47 E
Gulargambone	166	31.20 S	148.28 E
Gulbarga	122	17.20 N	76.50 E
Gulbene	76	57.11 N	26.45 E
Gul'ča	85	40.20 N	73.26 E
Guldasteh	285d	35.36 N	51.16 E
Guldborg	41	54.52 N	11.48 E
Guldborg Sund ⨆	41	54.48 N	11.48 E
Guldsmedshyttan	40	59.42 N	15.06 E
Güldüzü	130	36.52 N	37.07 E
Guledagudda	122	16.03 N	75.48 E
Guleitou	100	23.47 N	117.36 E
Gülek Boğazi ⤫	130	37.16 N	34.48 E
Gulf □³	164	7.00 S	145.00 E
Gulf Gate Estates	220	27.15 N	82.31 W
Gulf Hammock	192	29.15 N	82.43 W
Gulf Harbors	220	28.12 N	82.45 W
Gulf Islands National Seashore ♦	194	30.14 N	88.42 W
Gulf of Alaska Seamount Province ♣⁴	16	56.00 N	147.00 W
Gulfport, Fl., U.S.	220	27.45 N	82.40 W
Gulfport, Ms., U.S.	194	30.22 N	89.05 W

Column 2 (FRANÇAIS)

Nom	Page	Lat.°	Long.° W=Ouest
Gulf Shores	194	30.14 N	87.42 W
Gulf State Park ♦	194	30.16 N	87.40 W
Gulf Stream ≃	212	43.51 N	75.56 W
Gulgong	166	32.22 S	149.32 E
Guli	104	31.38 N	120.50 E
Gulian	89	52.55 N	122.19 E
Gulicun	106	31.52 N	118.41 E
Gul Imâm	123	32.16 N	70.32 E
Gülistan, Pâk.	120	30.36 N	66.35 E
Gulistan, Uzb.	85	40.30 N	68.46 E
Guliya Shan ⋀	89	49.48 N	122.25 E
Guljanci	38	43.38 N	24.42 E
Gulkana	180	62.16 N	145.23 W
Gull ≃	212	44.37 N	78.49 W
Gulland Rock I¹	42	50.34 N	4.59 W
Gullane	46	56.02 N	2.50 W
Gullfoss ⌁	24a	64.24 N	20.08 W
Gullholmen	26	58.11 N	11.24 E
Gullion, Slieve ⋀²	48	54.08 N	6.27 W
Gull Island I	281	42.32 N	82.41 W
Gullivan Bay c	220	25.52 N	81.38 W
Gull Lake, Ab.	184	50.08 N	108.27 W
Gull Lake ⊜, Ab., Can.	184	52.35 N	114.00 W
Gull Lake ⊜, On., Can.	281	51.18 N	91.58 W
Gull Lake ⊜, On., Can.	212	44.51 N	78.40 W
Gull Lake ⊜, Mi., U.S.	216	42.24 N	85.25 W
Gull Lake ⊜, Mn., U.S.		46.25 N	94.20 W
Gullrock Lake ⊜	184	50.58 N	93.40 W
Gullspång	40	58.59 N	14.06 E
Güllük	130	37.14 N	27.36 E
Güllük Körfezi c	130	37.12 N	27.20 E
Gulmarg	123	34.03 N	74.23 E
Gulnam	140	6.55 N	29.30 E
Gülnar	130	36.20 N	33.25 E
Gulong	89	45.51 N	124.14 E
Gulpen	56	50.48 N	5.54 E
Gülper See ⊜	54	52.44 N	12.14 E
Gulph Mills	285	40.04 N	75.21 W
Gülpinar	130	39.32 N	26.07 E
Gul ripš ⌁	84	42.57 N	41.06 E
Gul'šad	86	46.39 N	74.24 E
Gülşehir	130	38.45 N	34.38 E
Gulshan	126	23.49 N	90.27 E
Gulsvik	26	60.23 N	9.35 E
Gulu, Ug.	154	2.47 N	32.18 E
Gulu, Zhg.	120	28.06 N	89.17 E
Gulukuluk	115a	7.04 S	113.40 E
Guluogongba	120	34.20 N	84.50 E
Guluy	144	14.44 N	36.43 E
Gulwe	154	6.30 S	36.29 E
Gumaca	116	13.55 N	122.06 E
Gumaharang	116	12.35 N	123.16 E
Gumal (Gowmal) ≃	120	31.56 N	70.22 E
Gumare	156	19.21 S	22.12 E
Gumba, Ang.	152	11.40 S	16.34 E
Gumba, Zaïre	152	2.57 N	21.26 E
Gumbinnen — Gusev	76	54.36 N	22.12 E
Gumbiro	154	10.16 S	35.39 E
Gumiao	100	32.26 N	113.16 E
Gumiénice ♣⁸	54	53.51 N	14.30 E
Gumistskij zapovednik ♦	84	43.15 N	41.05 E
Gumla	124	23.03 N	84.33 E
Gumma □⁵	94	36.30 N	139.00 E
Gummersbach	56	51.02 N	7.34 E
Gummi	150	12.09 N	5.09 E
Gumpas Pond ⊜	283	42.44 N	71.22 W
Gumpas Pond Brook ≃			
Gumpoldskirchen	264b	48.03 N	16.17 E
Gum Swamp Creek ≃	192	32.08 N	82.55 W
Gumti ≃	126	23.32 N	90.43 E
Gümüşçay	130	40.16 N	27.17 E
Gümüşhaciköy	130	40.53 N	35.14 E
Gümüşhane	130	40.27 N	39.28 E
Gümüşhane □⁴	130	40.15 N	39.45 E
Gümüşkent	130	38.50 N	34.32 E
Gümüşköy ♣⁸	267b	41.14 N	28.58 E
Gümüşova	130	40.51 N	30.57 E
Gümüşsu	130	38.13 N	30.01 E
Gun ≃	216	42.28 N	85.40 W
Guna, India	124	24.39 N	77.19 E
Guna, Ityo.	144	8.19 N	39.51 E
Guna ⋀	144	11.43 N	38.12 E
Gunbar	166	34.01 S	145.25 E
Gun Barrel City	222	32.20 N	96.10 W
Gun Creek ≃	284a	43.03 N	78.55 W
Gunda	88	52.47 N	111.44 E
Gundagai	166	35.04 S	148.07 E
Gundelfingen, Dtsch.	58	48.33 N	10.22 E
Gundelfingen, Dtsch.	58	48.03 N	7.52 E
Gundelsheim	56	49.17 N	9.09 E
Gundii	152	7.12 S	110.54 E
Gundji	152	2.05 N	21.27 E
Gundlakamma ≃	122	15.32 N	80.14 E
Gundlupet	122	11.48 N	76.41 E
Gündoğdu ⋀	130	40.15 N	27.07 E
Gündoğmuş	130	36.48 N	32.01 E
Guneh Ghar ⋀	123	35.19 N	71.47 E
Güney	130	38.09 N	29.05 E
Gungan ≃	171b	36.18 S	148.24 E
Güney	152	6.21 S	19.15 E
Güney	152	11.48 S	14.08 E
Güngören ♣⁸	267b	41.01 N	28.53 E
Gun Lake ⊜	216	42.39 N	85.32 W
Gunnar	176	59.23 N	108.53 W
Gunnarn	26	65.01 N	17.40 E
Gunnbjørn Fjeld ⋀	16	68.55 N	29.53 W
Gunnebo	26	57.43 N	16.32 E
Gunnedah	166	30.59 S	150.15 E
Gunning Island I	276	40.03 N	73.59 W
Gunnislake	42	50.31 N	4.12 W
Gunnison, Co., U.S.	200	38.32 N	106.55 W
Gunnison, Ut., U.S.	200	39.09 N	111.49 W
Gunnison ≃	200	39.03 N	108.35 W
Gunnison, Lake Fork ≃	200	38.28 N	107.19 W
Gunnison, North Fork ≃	200	38.47 N	107.50 W
Gunn Peak ⋀	224	47.49 N	121.27 W
Gunong Mulu National Park ♦	112	4.10 N	114.55 E
Gunpowder Creek ≃, Austl.	166	19.14 S	139.58 E
Gunpowder Creek ≃, Ky., U.S.	218	38.53 N	84.47 W
Gunpowder Falls ≃	208	39.24 N	76.20 W
Gunpowder Falls State Park ♦	208	39.22 N	76.40 W
Gunpowder River c	208	39.22 N	76.22 W
— Kunsan	98	35.58 N	126.41 E
Gunskirchen	60	48.08 N	13.54 E
Gunston Cove c	208	38.40 N	77.08 W
Guntakal	122	15.10 N	77.23 E
Gunter	222	33.27 N	96.44 W
Güntersberge	54	51.38 N	11.01 E
Güntersblum	56	49.48 N	8.21 E
Guntersville, Al., U.S.	194	34.21 N	86.18 W
Guntersville Dam ♣⁶	194	34.13 N	86.23 W
Guntersville Lake ⊜	194	34.45 N	86.03 W
Guntingsaga	114	1.32 N	99.39 E
Guntramsdorf	60	48.03 N	16.19 E
Guntung	114	1.38 N	101.34 E
Guntür	122	16.18 N	80.27 E

Column 3 (PORTUGUÊS)

Nome	Página	Lat.°	Long.° W=Oeste
Gunungkencana	115a	6.34 S	106.04 E
Gunungmegang	112	3.27 S	103.52 E
Gunungsahan	112	0.06 N	101.18 E
Gunungsitoli	114	1.17 N	97.37 E
Gunungtua	114	1.30 N	99.37 E
Gunupur	122	19.05 N	83.49 E
Günyidi	162	30.08 S	116.04 E
Günyüzü	130	39.24 N	31.50 E
Gunza ≃	58	48.27 N	10.16 E
Gunza ≃	152	11.10 S	13.50 E
Günzburg	58	48.27 N	10.16 E
Gunzenhausen	56	49.07 N	10.45 E
Gunzigou	104	41.31 N	123.58 E
Guo ≃	100	32.57 N	117.14 E
Guobei	107	29.33 N	105.08 E
Guobie	46	56.02 N	2.50 W
Guoji	100	32.59 N	113.06 E
Guojiadian	104	41.51 N	121.30 E
Guojiajiang	106	32.17 N	120.50 E
Guojiatun, Zhg.	104	41.31 N	117.02 E
Guojiatun, Zhg.	104	42.00 N	122.51 E
Guojiatun, Zhg.	104	40.52 N	122.04 E
Guojiawopeng	104	42.03 N	122.46 E
Guojiayao	105	40.37 N	115.39 E
Guojiayuan	106	32.10 N	120.35 E
Guojiqja	86	43.47 N	80.48 E
Guoleizhuang	100	40.44 N	114.36 E
Guolutan	100	38.24 N	115.40 E
Guosu	98	38.24 N	114.00 E
Guoyang	100	33.32 N	116.12 E
Guoyangzhen	102	38.54 N	112.50 E
Guozhuang	98	35.25 N	117.10 E
Guozhuangmiao	106	31.49 N	119.01 E
Gupei	98	34.09 N	117.54 E
Gupis	123	36.14 N	73.26 E
Gura	80	57.18 N	51.25 E
Gura, Wâdï V	140	17.28 N	35.10 E
Gurabo	240m	18.16 N	65.58 W
Guraferda	144	6.51 N	35.04 E
Gura-Galbena	78	46.43 N	28.42 E
Gurage ⋀	144	8.24 N	38.24 E
Gurahonţ	38	46.16 N	22.21 E
Gura Humorului	38	47.33 N	25.54 E
Gurais	123	34.38 N	74.50 E
Guran	88	54.46 N	100.38 E
Gurara ≃	150	8.12 N	6.41 E
Gurban Anggir	102	37.45 N	97.30 E
Gurban Obo	102	43.14 N	112.28 E
Gurdāspur	123	32.02 N	75.31 E
Gurdon	194	33.55 N	93.09 W
Gurdžaani	84	41.43 N	45.48 E
Güre	130	38.39 N	29.10 E
Gurejev	84	47.21 N	43.16 E
G'urg'an	84	40.23 N	50.19 E
Gurgaon	124	28.28 N	77.02 E
Gurgei, Jabal ⋀	140	12.35 N	23.36 E
Gurghiului, Munţii ⋀	38	46.41 N	25.12 E
Gurgô ≃²	61	46.31 N	16.50 E
Gurgueia ≃	250	6.50 S	43.24 W
Gurgur ≃	144	7.48 N	41.32 E
Guri	144	25.11 N	71.40 E
Guri, Embalse de ⊜¹	246	7.30 N	62.50 W
Gurig National Park ♦	164	11.25 S	132.15 E
Gurjev	84	47.07 N	51.56 E
Gurjev □⁴	86	47.10 N	54.00 E
Gurjevsk, Ross.	76	54.44 N	36.28 E
Gurjevsk, Ross.	86	54.17 N	85.56 E
Gurk ≃	61	46.34 N	14.31 E
Gurk ⋀¹	61	46.36 N	14.15 E
Gürkütaler Alpen ⋀	64	46.55 N	10.40 E
Gür Küh ⋀	128	26.06 N	58.28 E
Gurla Mandhata — Guerla Mandata Shan ⋀	120	30.26 N	81.20 E
Gurlevoo	76	59.28 N	28.54 E
Gurnee	216	42.22 N	87.54 W
Gurnet Point ⊁	283	42.01 N	70.34 W
Gurnley Football Ground ♦	262	53.47 N	2.14 W
Gürpınar	130	38.13 N	43.25 E
Gurror	174q	9.27 N	138.04 E
Gursarai	124	25.37 N	79.11 E
Gurskoje	90	50.21 N	138.12 E
Gurskøy I	26	62.15 N	5.41 E
Guru ≃	154	15.25 S	36.58 E
Guru Har Sahāi	123	30.43 N	74.25 E
Gurumeti ≃	154	2.05 S	33.57 E
Gurun, Malay.	110	5.49 N	100.29 E
Gürün, Tür.	130	38.43 N	37.17 E
Gurupá	250	1.25 S	51.39 W
Gurupi	250	11.43 S	49.04 W
Gurupi ≃	250	1.13 S	46.06 W
Guru Sikhar ⋀	120	24.39 N	72.46 E
Gurvanbulag	102	47.03 N	98.44 E
Gurvansajhan uul ⋀	102	43.30 N	104.00 E
Gurzuf	78	44.33 N	34.17 E
Gus ≃	80	55.00 N	41.11 E
Guşari	85	39.38 N	67.50 E
Gusarka	78	47.23 N	36.31 E
Gus'atin	78	49.05 N	26.11 E
Gusau	150	12.12 N	6.40 E
Gusev, Ross.	76	54.35 N	22.12 E
Gusev, Ross.	98	48.27 N	40.32 E
Gusevo	76	56.06 N	33.21 E
Gusevskij	80	55.40 N	40.34 E
Gushan, Zhg.	98	36.30 N	116.53 E
Gushan, Zhg.	104	39.51 N	123.36 E
Gu Shan ⋀, Zhg.	106	26.05 N	119.22 E
Gu Shan ⋀, Zhg.	104	45.38 N	120.35 E
Gushanbeizifu	104	42.10 N	120.30 E
Gushankou	98	38.38 N	115.49 E
Gushantun	89	43.11 N	125.47 E
Gushanzi, Zhg.	100	40.26 N	120.03 E
Gushanzi, Zhg.	104	41.03 N	123.03 E
Gushi	100	32.12 N	115.41 E
Gushi, Zhg.	98	38.34 N	114.00 E
Gushiago	150	9.55 N	0.12 W
Gushikawa	174m	26.21 N	127.52 E
Gushu	105	39.51 N	116.43 E
Gusi	112	6.07 N	117.14 E
Gusino	76	54.44 N	31.22 E
Gusinoje, ozero ⊜	88	51.12 N	106.24 E
Gusinoje Ozero	88	51.17 N	106.32 E
Gusinozersk	88	51.17 N	106.30 E
Guskef	85	39.02 N	69.20 E
Gushara	124	21.23 N	76.54 E
Gus'-Khrustal'nyj — Gus'-Christal'nyj	80	55.37 N	40.40 E
Guskube	175d	24.45 S	125.26 E
Guspini	64	39.33 N	8.38 E
Gussago	64	45.35 N	10.13 E
Güssing	61	47.04 N	16.20 E
Gusta	272b	22.59 N	88.26 E

Column 4

	Página	Lat.°	Long.° W=Oeste
Gustine, Ca., U.S.	226	37.15 N	120.59 W
Gustine, Tx., U.S.	196	31.51 N	98.24 W
Gustorf	56	51.04 N	6.34 E
Güstrow	54	53.48 N	12.10 E
Gus'-Železnyj	80	55.03 N	41.10 E
Gutach	58	48.15 N	8.13 E
Gutaj	88	49.59 N	108.12 E
Gutanggou	104	42.02 N	124.10 E
Gutara ≃	88	54.30 N	97.23 E
Gutarskij chrebet ⋀	88	54.30 N	97.40 E
Gutau	61	48.25 N	14.37 E
Gutcher	46a	60.40 N	1.00 W
Gutenfels, Burg 1	56	50.07 N	7.46 E
Guten Hoffnung, Kap der — Good Hope, Cape of ⊁	158	34.24 S	18.30 E
Güterfelde	264a	52.22 N	13.12 E
Gütersloh	52	51.54 N	8.23 E
Guthrie, In., U.S.	218	38.59 N	86.31 W
Guthrie, Ky., U.S.	194	36.38 N	87.09 W
Guthrie, Ok., U.S.	196	35.52 N	97.25 W
Guthrie, Tx., U.S.	196	33.37 N	100.19 W
Guthrie Center	198	41.40 N	94.30 W
Guthrie Lake ⊜	184	55.17 N	100.38 W
Gutian, Zhg.	100	26.36 N	118.46 E
Gutian, Zhg.	100	25.15 N	116.46 E
Gutian, Zhg.	100	25.43 N	116.57 E
Gutian, Zhg.	100	24.50 N	116.27 E
Gutierrez	248	19.25 S	63.34 W
Gutiérrez Zamora	234	20.27 N	97.05 W
Gutland □⁹	56	49.40 N	6.10 E
Gutob Bay c	116	12.09 N	119.54 E
Guton, gora ⋀	84	41.51 N	46.45 E
Gutorföle	61	46.39 N	16.44 E
Guttannen	58	46.39 N	8.18 E
Guttau	54	51.15 N	14.34 E
Guttenberg, Ia., U.S.	190	42.47 N	91.05 W
Guttenberg, N.J., U.S.	276	40.47 N	74.00 W
Gutu	154	19.38 S	31.10 E
Gutujevskij, ostrov I	265a	59.54 N	30.14 E
Gulia Nasjonalpark ♦			
Guty	78	50.08 N	35.21 E
Gützkow	54	53.56 N	13.24 E
Güvem	130	40.36 N	32.40 E
Güwähâti	120	26.11 N	91.45 E
Guxhagen	56	51.12 N	9.28 E
Guxi	107	30.18 N	105.52 E
Guxian, Zhg.	98	37.35 N	121.09 E
Guxian, Zhg.	100	32.26 N	113.37 E
Guxian, Zhg.	100	27.09 N	115.31 E
Guxiandu	100	29.06 N	116.50 E
Guxikou	100	32.01 N	116.20 E
Guxiong	106	31.53 N	118.38 E
Guy	222	29.21 N	95.47 W
Guyana □¹, S.A.	242	5.00 N	59.00 W
Guyana □¹, S.A.	246	5.00 N	59.00 W
Guyancourt	261	48.46 N	2.04 E
Guyancourt, Aéroport de ⥬	261	48.45 N	2.05 E
Guyandotte ≃	188	38.26 N	82.23 W
Guyane française — French Guiana □²	250	4.00 N	53.00 W
Guyane — Guyana □¹	246	5.00 N	59.00 W
Guyang, Zhg.	98	34.58 N	114.58 E
Guyang, Zhg.	102	41.03 N	110.03 E
Guye	105	39.44 N	118.25 E
Guy Fawkes River National Park ♦	166	30.02 S	152.18 E
Guyi, Zhg.	100	25.38 N	119.47 E
Guyi, Zhg.	107	30.22 N	103.33 E
Guyin	102	23.58 N	105.47 E
Guymon	196	36.40 N	101.28 W
Guyonne, Ruisseau ≃	261	48.49 N	1.52 E
Guyra	166	30.14 S	151.40 E
Guysborough	186	45.23 N	61.30 W
Guys Mills	214	41.38 N	79.59 W
Guyton	192	32.20 N	81.23 W
Guyuan (Pingdingbu), Zhg.	102	41.40 N	115.41 E
Guyuan, Zhg.	102	36.01 N	106.17 E
Guzar	72	38.36 N	66.15 E
Güzel ⋀	84	39.44 N	43.01 E
Güzelbahçe	130	38.21 N	26.54 E
Güzeloluk	130	36.54 N	31.53 E
Güzelyurt, Tür.	130	35.12 N	32.59 E
Güzelyurt Körfezi c	130	35.12 N	32.59 E
Guzhang	100	28.31 N	109.57 E
Guzhen, Zhg.	100	33.19 N	117.21 E
Guzhen, Zhg.	100	22.37 N	113.11 E
Guzhu	106	26.58 N	116.16 E
Guzmán	200	31.13 N	107.27 W
Guzmán, Laguna de ⊜	200	31.20 N	107.30 W
Guzmán — Ciudad Guzmán	234	19.41 N	103.29 W
Gvardeec	78	54.39 N	21.05 E
Gvardejskoje, Ukr.	78	48.44 N	35.19 E
Gvardejskoje, Ukr.	78	45.07 N	34.01 E
Gvazda	38	43.08 N	24.00 E
Gvozdec	78	48.34 N	25.17 E
Gwa	110	17.36 N	94.35 E
Gwabegar	166	30.36 S	148.58 E
Gwadabawa	150	13.18 N	5.15 E
Gwadar	128	25.07 N	62.19 E
Gwagwada	150	10.14 N	7.14 E
Gwai	154	17.59 S	26.52 E
Gwalagwala	152	2.19 N	18.11 E
Gwal Haidarzai	120	30.44 N	68.48 E
Gwalia	162	28.55 S	121.20 E
Gwalior	124	26.13 N	78.10 E
Gwambygine	168a	31.59 S	116.48 E
Gwanda	156	20.57 S	29.01 E
Gwandu	150	12.30 N	4.41 E
Gwangju — Kwangju	98	35.09 N	126.54 E
Gwarzo	150	11.56 N	7.56 E
Gwasero	150	9.30 N	8.20 W
Gwätar Bay c	128	25.04 N	61.36 E
Gwaun ≃	42	52.00 N	4.58 W
Gwda ≃	54	52.00 N	16.44 E
Gweebarra Bay c	48	54.52 N	8.20 W
Gweedore	48	55.03 N	8.14 W
Gweesalia	48	54.07 N	9.53 W
Gwelo	156	18.45 S	28.36 E
Gwembe	154	16.30 S	27.38 E
Gwendraeth Fäch ≃	42	51.43 N	4.19 W
Gwendraeth Fawr ≃	42	51.43 N	4.18 W
Gwent □⁶	42	51.43 N	3.00 W
Gweru	156	19.27 S	29.49 E
Gweta	156	20.07 S	25.14 E
Gwinhurst	285	39.46 N	75.29 W
Gwinn	190	46.16 N	87.26 W
Gwinner	198	46.11 N	97.39 W
Gwobu	152	2.37 N	26.13 E
Gwoongooralla National ♦	171a	36.15 S	153.17 E
Gwydir ≃	166	29.27 S	149.48 E
Gwynedd	285	40.30 N	75.15 W
Gwynedd □⁶	42	53.00 N	4.00 W
Gwynedd Squäre	285	40.13 N	75.18 W
Gwynedd Valley	285	40.11 N	75.15 W
Gwynne	184	52.44 N	113.14 W

Column 5

	Página	Lat.°	Long.° W=Oeste
Gwynneville	218	39.39 N	85.38 W
Gwynn Island I	208	37.30 N	76.17 W
Gwynn Oak Amusement Park ♦	284b	39.20 N	76.43 W
Gwynns Falls ≃	284b	39.16 N	76.37 W
Gwynns Falls Park ♦	284b	39.18 N	76.41 W
Gy	58	47.24 N	5.49 E
Gyál	264c	47.23 N	19.14 E
Gya La ⤫	124	28.44 N	84.40 E
Gyäi-patak ≃	264c	47.24 N	19.07 E
Gyangtse — Gyangzê	120	28.57 N	89.35 E
Gyangzê	120	28.57 N	89.35 E
Gyaring Co ⊜	120	31.10 N	88.15 E
Gyaring Hu ⊜	102	34.53 N	97.58 E
Gydan	80	56.33 N	51.39 E
Gyda	74	70.52 N	78.30 E
Gydanskaja guba c	74	71.20 N	76.30 E
Gydanskij poluostrov ⊁¹	74	70.50 N	79.00 E
Gyebu	164	3.03 S	133.51 E
Gyemo Chen ⋀	124	27.20 N	88.52 E
Gyeongbog Palace ⌂	271b	37.36 N	126.57 E
Gyeongju — Kyŏngju	98	35.51 N	129.14 E
Gyirong, Zhg.	120	28.29 N	85.20 E
Gyirong, Zhg.	120	28.57 N	85.15 E
Gyldenloves Fjord c²	176	64.30 N	41.30 W
Gyldenlovesho ⋀²	45	55.33 N	11.52 E
Gylling	41	55.53 N	10.11 E
Gymea Bay	274a	34.02 S	151.05 E
Gym Peak ⋀	200	32.04 N	107.35 W
Gympie	166	26.11 S	152.40 E
Gyobingauk	110	18.13 N	95.39 E
Gyomaendröd	30	46.56 N	20.50 E
Gyöngyös	30	47.47 N	19.56 E
Gyöngyös ≃	61	47.14 N	16.55 E
Győr	30	47.42 N	17.38 E
Győr-Sopron □⁶	30	47.40 N	17.15 E
Gypsy Race ≃	44	54.05 N	0.12 W
Gypsum, Co., U.S.	200	39.38 N	106.57 W
Gypsum, Ks., U.S.	198	38.42 N	97.25 W
Gypsum, Oh., U.S.	214	41.29 N	82.52 W
Gypsum Creek ≃, U.S.	200	37.09 N	109.52 W
Gypsum Creek ≃, Ks., U.S.	198	38.51 N	97.25 W
Gypsum Hills ⋀²	196	36.25 N	99.20 W
Gypsum Point ⊁	176	61.53 N	114.35 W
Gypsumville	184	51.45 N	98.35 W
Gyrbovec	78	46.50 N	29.21 E
Gysinge	40	60.17 N	16.53 E
Gyttorp	40	59.31 N	14.58 E
Gyula	30	46.39 N	21.17 E
Gyulafehérvár — Alba-Iulia	38	46.04 N	23.35 E
Gžat ≃	76	55.56 N	34.33 E
Gžatsk	86	55.42 N	78.11 E
Gžel'	82	55.36 N	38.24 E
Gžatsk — Gagarin	76	55.33 N	35.00 E

H

	Página	Lat.°	Long.° W=Oeste
Haag	61	48.07 N	14.34 E
Haag am Hausruck	60	48.11 N	13.38 E
Haagen	58	47.38 N	7.40 E
Haag in Oberbayern	60	48.10 N	12.11 E
Haag — 's-Gravenhage			
Haaksbergen	52	52.09 N	6.44 E
Haalenberg	156	26.52 S	15.30 E
Haamstede	50	51.42 N	3.45 E
Haan	56	51.11 N	7.00 E
Haapajärvi	26	63.45 N	25.20 E
Haapamäki	26	62.15 N	24.28 E
Haapavesi	26	64.08 N	25.22 E
Haapiti	174s	17.34 S	149.52 W
Haapsalu	76	58.56 N	23.33 E
Haar	60	48.06 N	11.44 E
Haar ≃	263	51.26 N	7.13 E
Ha'Arava (Wädï al-'Arabah) V, Asia	132	30.10 N	35.10 E
Ha'Arava (Wädï al-Jayb) V, Asia	132	30.58 N	35.24 E
Haardt ⋀	56	49.15 N	8.00 E
Haaren, Dtsch.	52	51.36 N	5.12 E
Haaren, Ned.	52	51.36 N	5.12 E
Haarlem, Ned.	52	52.23 N	4.38 E
Haarlem, S. Afr.	158	33.46 S	23.20 E
Haarlemmermeer ♣¹	52	52.15 N	4.38 E
Haarstrang ≃	263	51.25 N	8.00 E
Haarzopf ♣⁸	263	51.25 N	6.58 E
Haast	172	43.50 S	169.02 E
Haast ≃	172	43.50 S	169.02 E
Haast Bluff	164	23.26 S	131.50 E
Haast Bluff Reserve ♦⁴	162	23.30 S	130.30 E
Haatinao, Pointe ⊁	174x	9.47 S	138.51 W
Haava, Canal ⨆	174x	9.53 S	139.04 W
Habahe	86	48.03 N	86.24 E
Habana, Bahía de la c	286b	23.08 N	82.20 W
Habaqi, Zhg.	104	42.36 N	122.02 E
Habaqi, Zhg.	104	42.36 N	122.42 E
Habartov	60	50.11 N	12.33 E
Habartsum	128	25.07 N	62.19 E
Habashïyah, Jabal ⋀	144	16.43 N	49.40 E
Habaswein	154	1.01 N	39.29 E
Habay-la-Neuve	52	49.43 N	5.38 E
Habbān	144	14.21 N	47.05 E
Habbānïyah, Hawr al- ⊜	128	33.17 N	43.29 E
Hab Chauki	123	24.53 N	66.42 E
Habère-Poche	58	46.15 N	6.29 E
Haberfield	274a	33.53 S	151.08 E
Habermehl Peak ⋀	167a	72.00 S	74.00 W
Habïb, Wädï V	132	33.17 N	35.29 E
Habiganj	120	24.23 N	91.25 E
Habikino	288	34.33 N	135.37 E
Habilah	140	13.04 N	22.49 E
Habinghorst	263	51.35 N	7.18 E
Habo	40	57.55 N	14.04 E
Habob, Wädï V	140	17.07 N	35.03 E
Haboro	90a	44.22 N	141.42 E
Habra	270	22.49 N	88.39 E
Habrough	44	53.34 N	0.14 W
Habsburg ⌂	58	47.28 N	8.11 E
Habshan	132	23.50 N	53.37 E
Habur (Nahr al-Khäbür) ≃	130	35.07 N	40.26 E
Hache, Lac la ⊜	184	51.56 N	121.32 W
Hachenburg	56	50.39 N	7.49 E
Hachijō	94	33.07 N	139.47 E
Hachijō-jima I	94	33.07 N	139.48 E
Hachiman	94	35.45 N	136.57 E
Hachiōji	94	35.40 N	139.20 E
Hachita	200	31.55 N	108.19 W
Hachiya	94	35.26 N	136.56 E
Hachō	288	34.57 N	136.58 E
Hachōbori ♣⁸	269b	35.40 N	139.46 E
Hachō-misaki ⊁	94	35.45 N	135.12 E

Column 6 (HAGO)

	Página	Lat.°	Long.° W=Oeste
Hacienda Miravalles	236	10.41 N	85.14 W
Hacienda Murciélago	236	10.55 N	85.44 W
Hachamza	41	41.05 N	34.28 E
Haciar	130	38.39 N	35.27 E
Hack, Mount ⋀	166	30.46 S	138.48 E
Hackäs	26	62.55 N	14.31 E
Hackberry, Az., U.S.	200	35.22 N	113.43 W
Hackberry, La., U.S.	194	29.59 N	93.20 W
Hackberry Creek ≃, Ks., U.S.	198	38.48 N	100.03 W
Hackberry Creek ≃, Tx., U.S.	222	31.53 N	97.12 W
Hackensack	210	40.53 N	74.02 W
Hackensack ≃	276	40.43 N	74.06 W
Hackettstown	48	52.52 N	6.33 W
Hackett, Ar., U.S.	194	35.11 N	94.24 W
Hackett, Pa., U.S.	279b	40.15 N	80.01 W
Hacketts	260	51.45 N	0.25 E
Hackettstown	210	40.52 N	74.48 W
Hacking ≃	274a	34.04 S	151.06 E
Hacking, Port c	274a	34.05 S	151.09 E
Hackleburg	194	34.16 N	87.49 W
Hackney ♣⁸	260	51.33 N	0.03 W
Hack Point	208	39.27 N	75.52 W
Häckren ⊜	26	63.11 N	13.35 E
Haco	152	10.12 S	15.44 E
Hacreş Dağlari ⋀	130	38.38 N	41.37 E
Hadäli	123	32.18 N	72.12 E
Hadalïya	140	16.10 N	36.06 E
Hadan, Harrat ⋀⁹	144	21.30 N	41.23 E
Hadano	94	35.22 N	139.14 E
Hadärïbah, Ra's al- ⊁	140	22.04 N	36.54 E
HaDarom □⁵	132	30.40 N	34.50 E
Hadat	89	49.40 N	119.40 E
Hadayingzi	104	42.22 N	121.40 E
Hadd, Ra's al- ⊁	128	22.32 N	59.48 E
Haddad, Ouadi V	146	14.40 N	18.46 E
Haddädïn, Qärät al- ⋀	144		
Haddam	222	30.04 N	30.58 E
Haddam, Ct., U.S.	207	41.28 N	72.30 W
Haddam, Ks., U.S.	198	39.51 N	97.18 W
Haddenham, Eng., U.K.	42	51.46 N	0.56 W
Haddenham, Eng., U.K.	42	52.22 N	0.09 E
Haddington	46	55.58 N	2.47 W
Haddock	192	33.01 N	83.25 W
Haddon Downs	166	26.21 S	140.50 E
Haddonfield	208	39.53 N	75.02 W
Haddon Heights	208	39.53 N	75.03 W
Haddon Hills	285	39.54 N	75.03 W
Hadejia	150	12.30 N	9.59 E
Hadejia ≃	134	12.50 N	10.51 E
Hadeln, Land □⁹	52	53.45 N	8.45 E
Haden	171a	27.14 S	151.53 E
Hadera	132	32.26 N	34.55 E
Hadera ≃	132	32.27 N	34.53 E
Hadersdorf ♣⁸	264b	48.20 N	16.15 E
Hadersdorf	264b	48.23 N	15.43 E
Haderslev	41	55.15 N	9.30 E
Haderslev Fjord c	41	55.17 N	9.40 E
Hadfield, Eng., U.K.	274b	37.42 S	144.56 E
Hadfield, Eng., U.K.	262	53.28 N	1.58 W
Hadlbü	118	12.38 N	54.02 E
Hadïd, Jabal ⋀²	142	30.20 N	30.06 E
Hadïd, Jabal al- ⋀²	128	28.47 N	31.04 E
Hadim	130	36.59 N	32.28 E
Hadjout	34	36.31 N	2.25 E
Hadleigh, Eng., U.K.	42	52.03 N	0.58 E
Hadleigh, Eng., U.K.	260	51.33 N	0.37 E
Hadleigh Castle 1	260	51.33 N	0.36 E
Hadley, Eng., U.K.	42	52.42 N	2.29 W
Hadley, Ma., U.S.	207	42.20 N	72.35 W
Hadley, Mi., U.S.	216	42.57 N	83.24 W
Hadley, N.Y., U.S.	210	43.19 N	73.50 W
Hadley, Pa., U.S.	214	41.25 N	80.13 W
Hadley Bay c	176	72.30 N	107.45 W
Hadley Creek ≃	219	39.37 N	91.12 W
Hadlock	224	48.01 N	122.45 W
Hadlow	260	51.14 N	0.20 E
Hadlyme	207	41.25 N	72.24 W
Hadong, S. Kor.	98	35.04 N	127.45 E
Hadong, Taehan	98	35.05 N	127.44 E
Ha Dong, Viet.	110	20.58 N	105.46 E
Hadramawt ⬩¹	144	15.00 N	50.00 E
Hadrian's Wall 1	44	54.59 N	2.26 W
Hadsund	41	56.20 N	10.04 E
Hadyai	104	35.26 N	116.07 E
— Hat Yai	110	7.01 N	100.28 E
Haeju	98	38.02 N	125.42 E
Haemi	98	36.43 N	126.29 E
Haenam	98	34.34 N	126.35 E
Haena	271m	22.13 N	159.34 W
Haena Point ⊁	271m	22.15 N	159.36 W
Haengyŏng-ni	271b	37.35 N	126.49 E
Haengyŏng-ni	98	41.46 N	129.50 E
Hafeïra, Oued el V	148	33.06 N	1.45 W
Hafelekarspitze ⋀	58	47.18 N	11.23 E
Hafen-Mehr ≃	52	54.44 N	6.28 E
Hafford	184	52.43 N	107.21 W
Haffouz	144	35.38 N	9.41 E
Hafik	130	39.52 N	37.25 E
Hafira, Qâ' al- ≃	132	31.06 N	36.14 E
Hafir el 'Auja	132	30.26 N	39.10 E
Hafit, Jabal ⋀	132	24.03 N	55.47 E
Hafïz, Bi'r ♣⁴	142	30.51 N	29.42 E
Häfïzäbäd	123	32.04 N	73.41 E
Häflong	120	25.10 N	93.01 E
Hafnarfjördur	24a	64.03 N	21.56 W
Haft Gel	128	31.27 N	49.27 E
Hafun, Ras ⊁	144	10.27 N	51.24 E
Haga, Nihon	94	36.32 N	140.04 E
Haga ≃, Nihon	288	34.34 N	135.33 E
HaGädōl, ⬩¹	132	30.56 N	34.59 E
HaMakhtésh ⬩⁷	132	30.56 N	34.59 E
Haga-Haga	158	32.46 S	28.14 E
Hagåtña	40	40.23 N	127.15 E
Hagari ≃	122	15.48 N	76.36 E
Hag Abdullah	140	13.59 N	33.38 E
Hagemeister Island I	180	58.40 N	161.00 W
Hagen, Dtsch.	56	51.22 N	7.28 E
Hagen, Dtsch.	264	53.22 N	9.51 E
Hagen-Gebirge ⋀	60	47.32 N	12.57 E
Hagenbrunn	264b	48.20 N	16.25 E
Hagenau — Haguenau	50	48.49 N	7.47 E
Hagerman	200	33.06 N	104.19 W
Hagerman, N.M., U.S.	196	33.06 N	104.19 W
Hagerman Corners	279b	43.50 N	79.18 E
Hagerstown, In., U.S.	218	39.54 N	85.09 W
Hagersville	212	42.58 N	80.03 W
Hagetmau	62	43.39 N	0.36 W
Hagfors	40	60.02 N	13.42 E
Haggenås	26	63.24 N	14.49 E
Haggett's Pond ⊜	283	42.40 N	71.11 W
Hagi	94	34.24 N	131.24 E
Hä Giang	110	22.50 N	104.59 E
Hagiwara	94	35.52 N	137.12 E
Hägley Museum ⌂	285	39.46 N	75.35 W
Hagondange	62	49.15 N	6.10 E

The body of this page is a multi-column gazetteer index containing several thousand place-name entries with page numbers and latitude/longitude coordinates. Representative entries from the first column:

Name	Page	Lat.	Long.
HaGosherim	132	33.13 N	35.37 E
Hags Head	48	52.57 N	9.30 W
Hague, Sk., Can.	184	52.30 N	106.25 W
Hague, N.D., U.S.	198	46.01 N	99.59 W
Hague, Cap de la	32	49.43 N	1.57 W
Hagueneau	56	48.49 N	7.47 E
Hagues Peak	200	40.29 N	105.38 W
Hahaïa	157a	11.33 S	43.17 E
Hahajima-rettō II	14	26.37 N	142.10 E

ESPAÑOL · FRANÇAIS · PORTUGUÊS

Nombre / Nom / Nome	Página / Page / Página	Lat.°′	Long.°′ W = Oeste / W = Ouest / W = Oeste
Hanover, Mi., U.S.	216	42.06 N	84.33 W
Hanover, N.H., U.S.	188	43.42 N	72.17 W
Hanover, N.M., U.S.	200	32.48 N	108.05 W
Hanover, Oh., U.S.	214	40.04 N	82.15 W
Hanover, Pa., U.S.	208	39.48 N	76.59 W
Hanover, Va., U.S.	208	37.45 N	77.22 W
Hanover, Wi., U.S.	216	42.38 N	89.10 W
Hanover □[6]	208	37.42 N	77.20 W
Hanover, Isla I	254	51.00 S	74.40 W
Hanover Airport ⊠	276	40.50 N	74.21 W
Hanover Center	283	42.07 N	70.50 W
Hanover → Hannover	52	52.24 N	9.44 E
Hanover Park	216	42.00 N	88.09 W
Hanover Road	158	30.58 S	24.33 E
Hanoverton	214	40.45 N	80.56 W
Hanovre → Hannover	52	52.24 N	9.44 E
Hanpan, Cape ›	175e	5.01 S	154.37 E
Hanryeosudo Kukrip Kongwŏn ♠	98	34.46 N	128.30 E
Hansanjiazi	104	41.44 N	122.57 E
Hansard	182	54.05 N	121.52 W
Hanscom Air Force Base ■	207	42.28 N	71.17 W
Hans Creek ≃	210	43.06 N	74.08 W
Hansdiha	124	24.36 N	87.05 E
Hansen Dam ◆[6]	280	34.16 N	118.23 W
Hansen Flood Control Basin ☷[1]	228	34.16 N	118.23 W
Hanshan	100	31.44 N	118.08 E
Hansharo ⊥	94	35.02 N	138.56 E
Hansi, India	120	32.27 N	77.50 E
Hānsi, India	123	29.06 N	75.58 E
Hansia	272b	22.48 N	88.24 E
Hanska	198	44.08 N	94.29 W
Hānskhāli	126	23.21 N	88.37 E
Hans Lollik Island I	240m	18.24 N	64.55 W
Hanslope	42	52.06 N	0.49 W
Hans Meyer Range ⋏	164	4.20 S	152.55 E
Hanson	207	42.04 N	70.52 W
Hanson ≃	162	20.15 S	133.25 E
Hanson Lake ⊜	184	54.42 N	102.49 W
Hanstholm	26	57.07 N	8.38 E
Han-sur-Lesse	56	50.08 N	5.11 E
Han-sur-Nied	56	48.59 N	6.26 E
Hansville	224	47.55 N	122.33 W
Hansweert	52	51.26 N	4.00 E
Hantaj	88	49.31 N	103.13 E
Hāntālbunia	126	22.44 N	89.31 E
Hantamsberg ⋏	158	31.22 S	19.45 E
Hantan → Handan	98	36.37 N	114.29 E
Hantes ≃	50	50.19 N	4.11 E
Hant's Harbour	186	48.01 N	53.16 W
Hantsport	186	45.04 N	64.11 W
Hantu, Pulau I	271c	1.14 N	103.45 E
Hantu, Tanjong ›	114	4.18 N	100.34 E
Hantzsch ≃	176	67.32 N	72.25 W
Hanumangarh	123	29.35 N	74.19 E
Hanumān Nagar	124	26.30 N	86.51 E
Hanušovce nad Topl'ou	30	49.02 N	21.30 E
Hanušovice	30	50.05 N	16.55 E
Hanveden ⋏[2]	40	59.07 N	18.00 E
Hanwood	166	34.20 S	146.03 E
Hanworth ◆[8]	260	51.26 N	0.23 W
Hanxinzhuang	105	40.16 N	116.44 E
Hanyang	107	29.44 N	103.44 E
Hanyangping	102	32.41 N	108.34 E
Hanyin	102	32.42 N	108.50 E
Hanyū	94	36.10 N	139.32 E
Hanyuan	102	29.22 N	102.38 E
Hanyuangai	102	29.30 N	102.31 E
Hanzan	96	34.16 N	133.51 E
Hanzhong	102	33.08 N	107.02 E
Hanzhuang	98	34.38 N	117.24 E
Hao I[1]	14	18.15 S	140.54 W
Hao ≃	100	28.27 N	119.56 E
Haohekou	100	28.38 N	112.49 E
Haojiadian	100	31.47 N	113.44 E
Haoli → Hegang	89	47.24 N	130.17 E
Haoluqi	106	30.38 N	119.34 E
HaOn	132	32.43 N	35.38 E
Hāora	126	22.35 N	88.20 E
Hāora Bridge ◆[5]	272b	22.35 N	88.21 E
Hāora Railroad Station ◆[5]	272b	22.35 N	88.21 E
Haouach, Ouadi V	146	16.45 N	19.35 E
Haoxue	102	30.00 N	112.20 E
Haozhikou	107	29.36 N	105.02 E
Haparanda	26	65.50 N	24.10 E
Hapatoni, Baie ⊂	174x	9.58 S	139.07 W
Hapert	52	51.23 N	5.15 E
Hapeville	192	33.39 N	84.24 W
Happ'o-ri	98	40.40 N	127.49 E
Happy	196	34.45 N	101.52 W
Happy Camp	204	41.47 N	123.22 W
Happy Jack	200	34.45 N	111.11 W
Happy Valley-Goose Bay	176	53.20 N	60.25 W
Happy Valley Race Course ♠	271d	22.16 N	114.10 E
Hapsford	262	53.16 N	2.48 W
Hapsu	98	41.13 N	128.51 E
Hapton	262	53.47 N	2.19 W
Hāpur	124	28.43 N	77.47 E
Ḥaql	128	29.18 N	34.57 E
Haquira	248	14.13 S	72.11 W
Har	164	5.20 S	133.10 E
Har, Laga ≃	154	1.40 N	39.36 E
Hara, Nihon	94	35.58 N	138.14 E
Hara, Nihon	268	35.50 N	139.46 E
Ḥaraḍ, Ar. Su.	128	24.08 N	49.05 E
Härad, Sve.	40	59.23 N	16.55 E
Ḥaraḍ, Yaman	144	16.28 N	43.04 E
Ḥarad, Jabal al- ∧	132	29.40 N	35.49 E
Haraiki I[1]	14	17.28 S	143.27 W
Harajuku	268	35.54 N	139.21 E
Haraldsted	41	55.30 N	11.47 E
Haramachi	92	37.38 N	140.58 E
Haramachida	268	35.33 N	139.27 E
Haramosh ∧	123	35.50 N	74.54 E
Haramosh Range ⋏	123	35.40 N	75.22 E
Harappa	123	30.38 N	72.52 E
Harappa Road	123	30.36 N	72.55 E
Harare (Salisbury)	154	17.50 S	31.03 E
Harar → Harer	144	9.18 N	42.08 E
Ḥarash, Bi'r al- ⊤[4]	146	25.30 N	22.12 E
Ḥarastā al-Baṣal	132	33.34 N	36.22 E
Hārāt	272b	22.53 N	88.11 E
Haraz-Djombo	146	13.57 N	19.26 E
Haraze-Mangueigne	146	9.55 N	20.48 E
Harbāti	272b	22.55 N	88.33 E
Harbert	216	41.52 N	86.38 W
Harbeson	208	38.43 N	75.17 W
Harbin	89	45.45 N	126.41 E
Harbiye	130	36.11 N	36.05 E
Harbke	54	52.12 N	11.03 E
Harbo	40	60.06 N	17.12 E
Harbonnières	50	49.51 N	2.40 E
Harboør	26	56.37 N	8.12 E
Harbor	202	42.03 N	124.15 W
Harbor Beach	190	43.50 N	82.39 W
Harbor City ◆[8]	280	33.48 N	118.17 W
Harborcreek	214	42.10 N	79.57 W
Harbord	170	33.47 S	151.17 E
Harbor Isle	276	40.36 N	73.40 W
Harbor Side	228	32.37 N	117.05 W
Harbor Springs	190	45.25 N	84.59 W
Harborton	208	37.39 N	75.49 W
Harbor Tunnel ◆[5]	284b	39.15 N	76.34 W
Harbor View	214	41.42 N	83.27 W
Harbour Breton	186	47.29 N	55.48 W
Harbour Buffett	186	47.31 N	54.05 W
Harbour Deep	186	50.22 N	56.31 W
Harbour Grace	186	47.42 N	53.13 W
Harbours, Bay of ⊂	254	52.15 S	59.15 W
Harbourville	186	45.09 N	64.49 W
Harburg	56	48.47 N	10.41 E
Harburg ◆[8]	52	53.28 N	9.59 E
Hårby	41	55.13 N	10.07 E
Harchies	50	50.29 N	3.41 E
Harcourt, Austl.	169	37.00 S	144.15 E
Harcourt, Fr.	50	49.10 N	0.48 E
Harcuvar Mountains ⋏	200	34.00 N	113.30 W
Hard	58	47.29 N	9.41 E
Harda	124	22.20 N	77.06 E
Hardangerfjorden ⊂[2]	26	60.10 N	6.00 E
Hardangerjøkulen ⊓	26	60.33 N	7.26 E
Hardangervidda ⋏[1]	26	60.20 N	7.30 E
Hardangervidda Nasjonalpark ♠	26	60.15 N	7.05 E
Hardapdam ⊜[1]	156	24.28 S	17.48 E
Hardee □[6]	220	27.29 N	81.48 W
Hardeeville	192	32.17 N	81.04 W
Hardegarijp	52	53.13 N	5.56 E
Hardegsen	52	51.39 N	9.49 E
Hardelot-Plage	50	50.38 N	1.35 E
Hardenberg	52	52.34 N	6.37 E
Harderwijk	52	52.21 N	5.36 E
Hardesty	196	36.36 N	101.11 W
Hardey ≃	162	22.45 S	116.07 E
Hardgrave, Mount ∧[2]	171a	27.30 S	153.29 E
Hardheim	56	49.36 N	9.28 E
Hardin, Il., U.S.	219	39.09 N	90.37 W
Hardin, Mt., U.S.	202	45.43 N	107.36 W
Hardin, Tx., U.S.	222	30.09 N	94.44 W
Hardin □[6], Oh., U.S.	216	40.39 N	83.36 W
Hardin □[6], Tx., U.S.	222	30.20 N	94.35 W
Harding, S. Afr.	158	30.34 S	29.58 E
Harding, Il., U.S.	216	41.31 N	88.51 W
Harding, Ma., U.S.	283	42.12 N	71.27 W
Harding, Lake ⊜[1]	192	32.40 N	85.06 W
Harding Lake ⊜	184	56.13 N	98.23 W
Harding Lakes	208	39.27 N	74.45 W
Hardinsburg, In., U.S.	218	38.27 N	86.16 W
Hardinsburg, Ky., U.S.	194	37.46 N	86.27 W
Hardisty	182	52.40 N	111.18 W
Hardisty Lake ⊜	176	64.30 N	117.45 W
Hardoi	124	27.25 N	80.07 E
Hardoi Branch ≊	124	28.41 N	80.08 E
Hardricourt	261	49.01 N	1.54 E
Hardscrabble Wash V	200	34.39 N	109.28 W
Hardt	263	51.07 N	6.58 E
Hardtner	198	37.00 N	98.38 W
Hardwick, Ga., U.S.	192	33.04 N	83.13 W
Hardwick, Ma., U.S.	207	42.21 N	72.12 W
Hardwick, Vt., U.S.	188	44.30 N	72.22 W
Hardwood	194	30.49 N	91.23 W
Hardwood Ridge ∧	210	41.15 N	75.23 W
Hardy, Ar., U.S.	194	36.18 N	91.28 W
Hardy, Ne., U.S.	198	40.00 N	97.55 W
Hardy, Península ›[1]	254	55.25 S	68.30 W
Hardy Bay ⊂	176	75.02 N	115.16 W
Hardy Creek ≃	214	42.52 N	81.52 W
Hardy Lake ⊜[1]	218	38.47 N	85.42 W
Hardy Lake State Recreation Area ♠	218	38.44 N	86.26 W
Hardys Pond ⊜	283	42.25 N	71.15 W
Hare, Mount ∧	180	66.38 N	136.12 W
Hare Bay	186	48.51 N	54.01 W
Hare Bay ⊂	186	51.18 N	55.50 W
Harefield ◆[8]	260	51.36 N	0.29 W
Hareid	26	62.22 N	6.02 E
Hare Indian ≃	180	66.18 N	128.38 W
Harelbeke	50	50.51 N	3.18 E
Haren, Dtsch.	52	52.47 N	7.14 E
Haren, Ned.	52	53.10 N	6.35 E
Hareøen I	176	70.25 N	54.50 W
Harer	144	9.18 N	42.08 E
Harerge □[4]	144	8.00 N	43.00 E
Hareskov	41	55.46 N	12.25 E
Hareto	144	9.20 N	37.06 E
Harewa	144	9.55 N	41.59 E
Harewood	172	43.29 S	172.35 E
Harewood Park	284b	39.23 N	76.22 W
Harfaz	130	38.01 N	41.19 E
Harfleur	50	49.30 N	0.12 E
Harford, N.Y., U.S.	210	42.26 N	76.14 W
Harford, Pa., U.S.	210	41.47 N	75.42 W
Harford □[6]	208	39.32 N	76.21 W
Harford Heights	279b	40.22 N	79.46 W
Harford Mills	210	42.25 N	76.12 W
Harg, Sve.	40	59.49 N	18.57 E
Harg, Sve.	40	60.11 N	18.24 E
Hargele	144	5.20 N	42.05 E
Hargeville	261	48.53 N	1.45 E
Hargeysa	144	9.35 N	44.04 E
Harghita □[6]	38	46.35 N	25.30 E
Harghita, Munții ⋏	38	46.15 N	25.45 E
Hargrave ≃	184	54.24 N	98.48 W
Hargrave Lake ⊜	184	54.29 N	99.40 W
Hargshamn	40	60.10 N	18.28 E
Har Hu (Heihai) ⊜	102	38.15 N	97.40 E
Hāriabhānga ≃[1]	126	21.43 N	89.05 E
Hariāna	123	31.38 N	75.51 E
Hariarapitu	114	2.33 N	98.35 E
Ḥarīb	144	14.57 N	45.30 E
Haribes	156	24.20 S	17.40 E
Ḥaricha, Ḥamâda el ◆[2]	148	22.36 N	3.31 W
Haridwār	124	29.58 N	78.10 E
Harigabessho	270	34.37 N	135.58 E
Harihar	122	14.31 N	75.48 E
Harihari	172	43.09 S	170.33 E
Hariharpāra	126	24.02 N	88.27 E
Harīke	123	31.10 N	74.57 E
Ḥārim	130	36.12 N	36.31 E
Ḥarim, Jabal al- ∧	128	25.58 N	56.14 E
Harima	96	34.42 N	134.53 E
Harima-nada ⊤[2]	96	34.29 N	134.35 E
Harinagar	124	27.09 N	84.19 E
Harinākunda	126	23.39 N	89.03 E
Haringey ◆[8]	260	51.35 N	0.07 W
Hāringhāta ≃[1]	126	21.54 N	89.57 E
Haringvliet ɰ	52	51.47 N	4.10 E
Haringvlietbrug ◆[5]	52	51.43 N	4.20 E
Haringvlietdam ◆[5]	52	51.50 N	4.03 E
Haripāl	272b	22.49 N	88.07 E
Haripur, India	126	24.18 N	87.05 E
Haripur, India	272b	22.56 N	88.14 E
Harīpur, Pāk.	123	33.59 N	72.56 E
Harirāmpur	126	23.42 N	89.57 E
Harīrūd (Tedžen) ≃	128	37.24 N	60.38 E
Harischandra Range ⋏	122	19.15 N	74.05 E
Ḥārithān	130	36.16 N	37.05 E
Hariyo	144	5.00 N	47.23 E
Harjavalta	26	61.19 N	22.08 E
Härjedalen □[9]	26	62.20 N	13.00 E
Harkaway	274b	38.00 S	145.21 E
Härkeberga	40	59.42 N	17.11 E
Harkema-Opeinde	52	53.11 N	6.08 E
Harker Heights	222	31.05 N	97.40 W
Harkers Island	192	34.41 N	76.33 W
Harker Village	285	39.51 N	75.09 W
Harkness Memorial State Park ♠	207	41.18 N	72.07 W
Harkortsee ⊜	263	51.24 N	7.25 E
Harlaching ◆[8]	60	48.06 N	11.33 E
Harlan, In., U.S.	216	41.11 N	84.55 W
Harlan, Ia., U.S.	198	41.39 N	95.19 W
Harlan, Ky., U.S.	192	36.50 N	83.19 W
Harlan County Lake ⊜[1]	198	40.04 N	99.16 W
Harlech	42	52.52 N	4.07 W
Harlem, Fl., U.S.	220	26.44 N	80.57 W
Harlem, Ga., U.S.	192	33.24 N	82.18 W
Harlem, Mt., U.S.	202	48.32 N	108.47 W
Harlem ◆[8]	276	40.49 N	73.56 W
Harlem River ɰ	276	40.48 N	73.54 W
Harlem Springs	214	40.31 N	81.02 W
Harlesden ◆[8]	260	51.32 N	0.15 W
Harlesiel	52	53.43 N	7.49 E
Harleston	42	52.24 N	1.18 E
Harleton	222	32.41 N	94.35 W
Hårlev	41	55.21 N	12.15 E
Harleysville	208	40.17 N	75.23 W
Harlin	171a	26.59 S	152.22 E
Harlingen, Ned.	52	53.10 N	5.24 E
Harlingen, Tx., U.S.	196	26.11 N	97.41 W
Harlinger Land ◆[1]	52	53.40 N	7.30 E
Harlingerode	54	51.54 N	10.31 E
Harlington ◆[8]	260	51.29 N	0.26 W
Harlösa	41	55.43 N	13.32 E
Harlow	260	51.47 N	0.08 E
Harlow □[8]	260	51.44 N	0.07 E
Harlowton	202	46.26 N	109.50 W
Harlpur	272b	22.42 N	88.10 E
Harman	188	38.55 N	79.31 W
Harmancık	130	39.41 N	29.10 E
Harmånger	26	61.56 N	17.13 E
Harmanli, Blg.	38	41.56 N	25.54 E
Harmanlı, Tür.	130	37.51 N	37.45 E
Harmanschlag	61	48.39 N	14.47 E
Harmar Heights	279b	40.33 N	79.49 W
Harmarville	279b	40.32 N	79.51 W
Hármashatár-hegy ∧	264c	47.33 N	19.00 E
Harmelen	52	52.05 N	4.58 E
Harmil I	144	16.31 N	40.09 E
Harmonsburg	214	41.40 N	80.19 W
Harmonville	285	40.06 N	75.17 W
Harmony, Ca., U.S.	226	35.35 N	121.01 W
Harmony, In., U.S.	194	39.32 N	87.06 W
Harmony, Mn., U.S.	190	43.33 N	92.00 W
Harmony, N.J., U.S.	210	40.44 N	75.08 W
Harmony, Pa., U.S.	214	40.48 N	80.07 W
Harmony, R.I., U.S.	207	41.53 N	71.35 W
Harmony Brook ≃	276	40.48 N	74.34 W
Harmony Heights	220	27.29 N	80.21 W
Harmony Hills	285	39.42 N	75.41 W
Harmonyville	285	40.11 N	75.43 W
Harnai, India	122	17.48 N	73.06 E
Harnai, Pāk.	120	30.06 N	67.56 E
Harnäs	40	60.39 N	17.22 E
Harnātānr	124	27.19 N	84.01 E
Harndrup	41	55.28 N	10.02 E
Harnes	50	50.27 N	2.54 E
Härnevi	40	59.44 N	17.05 E
Harney ≃	220	25.25 N	81.10 W
Harney, Lake ⊜	220	28.45 N	81.03 W
Harney Basin ☷[1]	202	43.15 N	119.00 W
Harney Lake ⊜	202	43.14 N	119.07 W
Harney Peak ∧	198	43.51 N	103.31 W
Harney Pond Canal ≊	220	27.00 N	81.04 W
Härnösand	26	62.38 N	17.56 E
Haro, Esp.	34	42.35 N	2.51 W
Haro, Ityo.	144	8.28 N	38.37 E
Haro, Cabo ›	232	27.52 N	110.54 W
Ḥarod ≃	132	32.31 N	35.33 E
Harola	272a	28.36 N	77.19 E
Harold Hill ◆[8]	260	51.36 N	0.13 E
Harold Parker State Forest ♠	283	42.37 N	71.05 W
Haroldswick	46a	60.41 N	0.50 W
Harold Wood ◆[8]	260	51.36 N	0.14 E
Haro Strait ɰ	224	48.30 N	123.15 W
Haroué	58	48.28 N	6.11 E
Harpālpur	124	25.17 N	79.20 E
Harpanahalli	122	14.48 N	75.59 E
Harpen ◆[8]	263	51.29 N	7.16 E
Harpenden	42	51.49 N	0.22 W
Harper, Liber.	150	4.25 N	7.43 W
Harper, Ks., U.S.	198	37.17 N	98.01 W
Harper, Tx., U.S.	196	30.18 N	99.15 W
Harper, Wa., U.S.	224	47.31 N	122.31 W
Harper, Mount ∧	180	64.14 N	143.50 W
Harper Lake ⊜	228	35.02 N	117.17 W
Harpers Ferry National Historical Park ♠	188	39.13 N	77.45 W
Harpersfield	210	42.26 N	74.41 W
Harper Town	44	54.55 N	2.31 W
Harper Woods	214	42.25 N	82.55 W
Harpille ∧	62	43.50 N	6.48 E
Harpstedt	52	52.54 N	8.35 E
Harpster	214	40.44 N	83.15 W
Harpsund ᴥ	40	59.06 N	16.29 E
Harpurhey ◆[8]	262	53.31 N	2.13 W
Harpur Hill	262	53.14 N	1.54 W
Harpursville	210	42.11 N	75.38 W
Harqin	98	41.08 N	119.38 E
Harqin Qi (Jinshan)	98	41.56 N	118.36 E
Harquahala Mountain ∧	200	33.49 N	113.21 W
Ḥarrah	144	14.57 N	50.19 E
Ḥārrah, Jabal al- ∧	132	33.04 N	35.59 E
Harrai	124	22.37 N	79.13 E
Harran	130	36.51 N	39.00 E
Ḥarrān al-ʿAwāmīd	132	33.27 N	36.34 E
Harray, Loch of ⊜	46	59.01 N	3.13 W
Harrell	194	33.30 N	92.23 W
Harricana ≃	176	51.15 N	79.45 W
Harrietfield	46	56.25 N	3.39 W
Harrietsham	260	51.15 N	0.41 E
Harriman, N.Y., U.S.	210	41.18 N	74.09 W
Harriman, Tn., U.S.	192	35.56 N	84.33 W
Harriman Reservoir ⊜[1]	207	42.50 N	72.53 W
Harriman State Park ♠	210	41.14 N	74.09 W
Harrington, Eng., U.K.	44	54.37 N	3.34 W
Harrington, De., U.S.	208	38.55 N	75.34 W
Harrington, Me., U.S.	188	44.37 N	67.48 W
Harrington, Wa., U.S.	202	47.28 N	118.15 W
Harrington Creek ≃	282	37.19 N	122.18 W
Harrington Drain ≊	281	42.36 N	82.54 W
Harrington Park	276	40.59 N	73.58 W
Harris, Sk., Can.	184	51.44 N	107.35 W
Harris, Scot., U.K.	46	56.59 N	6.20 W
Harris, Mn., U.S.	190	45.35 N	92.58 W
Harris, N.Y., U.S.	210	41.43 N	74.44 W
Harris, R.I., U.S.	207	41.43 N	71.31 W
Harris □[6]	222	29.50 N	95.22 W
Harris ≃	168a	33.18 S	116.09 E
Harris ◆[1]	46	57.55 N	6.50 W
Harris, Lake ⊜, Austl.	162	31.08 S	135.14 E
Harris, Lake ⊜, Fl., U.S.	220	28.46 N	81.49 W
Harris, Sound of ɰ	46	57.45 N	7.10 W
Harris Bay ⊂	212	45.23 N	77.50 W
Harris Brook ≃	283	42.44 N	71.13 W
Harrisburg, Ar., U.S.	194	35.33 N	90.43 W
Harrisburg, Il., U.S.	194	37.44 N	88.32 W
Harrisburg, In., U.S.	218	39.41 N	85.11 W
Harrisburg, Ne., U.S.	198	41.33 N	103.44 W
Harrisburg, Oh., U.S.	214	40.53 N	81.13 W
Harrisburg, Or., U.S.	202	44.16 N	123.10 W
Harrisburg, Pa., U.S.	208	40.16 N	76.53 W
Harrisburg International Airport ⊠	208	40.12 N	76.45 W
Harris Creek ⊂	208	38.45 N	76.18 W
Harris Creek ≃, Austl.	274a	33.57 S	150.57 E
Harris Creek ≃, Tx., U.S.	222	32.33 N	95.08 W
Harrisfield	274b	37.57 S	145.11 E
Harris Hill	210	42.58 N	78.40 W
Harrislee	41	54.48 N	9.22 E
Harrismith, Austl.	162	32.56 S	117.52 E
Harrismith, S. Afr.	158	28.18 S	29.03 E
Harrison, Ar., U.S.	194	36.13 N	93.06 W
Harrison, Id., U.S.	202	47.27 N	116.47 W
Harrison, Il., U.S.	216	42.25 N	89.11 W
Harrison, Mi., U.S.	190	44.01 N	84.47 W
Harrison, Ne., U.S.	198	42.41 N	103.53 W
Harrison, N.J., U.S.	276	40.44 N	74.09 W
Harrison, N.Y., U.S.	210	40.58 N	73.43 W
Harrison, Oh., U.S.	218	39.15 N	84.49 W
Harrison □[6], In., U.S.	218	38.17 N	86.07 W
Harrison □[6], Ky., U.S.	218	38.25 N	84.19 W
Harrison □[6], Oh., U.S.	214	40.16 N	81.05 W
Harrison □[6], Tx., U.S.	222	32.35 N	94.35 W
Harrison ≃	224	49.14 N	121.57 W
Harrison, Cape ›	176	54.55 N	57.55 W
Harrison Bay ⊂	180	70.30 N	151.30 W
Harrisonburg, La., U.S.	194	31.46 N	91.49 W
Harrisonburg, Va., U.S.	188	38.26 N	78.52 W
Harrison City	279b	40.21 N	79.39 W
Harrison Hot Springs	224	49.18 N	121.47 W
Harrison Islands II	176	69.13 N	90.30 W
Harrison Lake ⊜	182	49.30 N	121.50 W
Harrison Mills	224	49.14 N	121.57 W
Harrisons Brook ≃	276	40.38 N	74.34 W
Harrison Tomb State Memorial ⊥	218	39.09 N	84.46 W
Harrison Valley	214	41.57 N	77.39 W
Harrisonville, Md., U.S.	284b	39.23 N	77.50 W
Harrisonville, Mo., U.S.	194	38.39 N	94.20 W
Harrisonville, N.J., U.S.	285	39.41 N	75.15 W
Harris Park	274a	33.49 S	151.01 E
Harris Pond ⊜	283	42.45 N	71.16 W
Harris Reservoir ⊜[1]	222	29.14 N	95.33 W
Harriston, On., Can.	212	43.54 N	80.53 W
Harriston, Ms., U.S.	194	31.43 N	91.01 W
Harristown	219	39.51 N	89.05 W
Harrisville, Austl.	171a	27.49 S	152.40 E
Harrisville, Mi., U.S.	190	44.39 N	83.17 W
Harrisville, N.Y., U.S.	212	44.09 N	75.19 W
Harrisville, Oh., U.S.	214	40.11 N	80.53 W
Harrisville, Pa., U.S.	214	41.08 N	80.00 W
Harrisville, R.I., U.S.	207	41.57 N	71.40 W
Harrisville, W.V., U.S.	188	39.12 N	81.03 W
Harrod	216	40.42 N	83.55 W
Harrodsburg	194	37.45 N	84.50 W
Harrods Creek ≃	218	38.20 N	85.38 W
Harrogate	44	54.00 N	1.33 W
Harrold	196	34.05 N	99.02 W
Harrop Lake ⊜	184	52.38 N	95.58 W
Harrow	214	42.02 N	82.55 W
Harrow ◆[8]	260	51.35 N	0.21 W
Harrow on the Hill ◆[8]	260	51.34 N	0.20 W
Harrow School ᴥ[2]	260	51.34 N	0.20 W
Harrowsmith	212	44.24 N	76.40 W
Harry S. Truman Airport ⊠	240m	18.21 N	64.59 W
Harry S. Truman Reservoir ⊜[1]	194	38.10 N	93.45 W
Har Sai Shan ∧	102	35.28 N	97.55 E
Harsefeld	52	53.27 N	9.30 E
Harsens Island	214	42.34 N	82.34 W
Harsens Island I	281	42.35 N	82.38 W
Harsewinkel	52	51.58 N	8.13 E
Harsīn	128	34.16 N	47.35 E
Harşit ≃	130	41.01 N	38.52 E
Harskamp	52	52.07 N	5.45 E
Harsleben	54	51.52 N	11.05 E
Harstad	24	68.46 N	16.30 E
Harstena	26	58.16 N	17.01 E
Har Su	89	48.09 N	122.25 E
Harsūd	124	22.06 N	76.44 E
Harsum	52	52.12 N	9.57 E
Hart, Mi., U.S.	190	43.41 N	86.21 W
Hart, Tx., U.S.	196	34.23 N	102.07 W
Hart ≃	180	65.51 N	136.22 W
Hart, Lake ⊜, Austl.	166	31.08 S	136.24 E
Hart, Lake ⊜, Fl., U.S.	220	28.22 N	81.13 W
Ḥartā	132	32.42 N	35.51 E
Hartbees ≃	158	28.45 S	20.32 E
Hartbeesfontein	158	26.42 S	26.26 E
Hartbeespoort	158	25.44 S	27.52 E
Hartberg	61	47.17 N	15.59 E
Hartenholm	52	53.54 N	10.03 E
Hartenstein	54	50.39 N	12.40 E
Hart Fell ∧	44	55.25 N	3.25 W
Hartfield	208	37.34 N	76.30 W
Hartford, Eng., U.K.	262	53.15 N	2.33 W
Hartford, Al., U.S.	194	31.06 N	85.41 W
Hartford, Ar., U.S.	194	35.01 N	94.22 W
Hartford, Ct., U.S.	207	41.46 N	72.41 W
Hartford, Il., U.S.	219	38.50 N	90.05 W
Hartford, In., U.S.	218	38.59 N	84.57 W
Hartford, Ks., U.S.	198	38.18 N	95.57 W
Hartford, Ky., U.S.	194	37.27 N	86.54 W
Hartford, Mi., U.S.	216	42.12 N	86.10 W
Hartford, N.J., U.S.	285	39.58 N	74.53 W
Hartford, N.Y., U.S.	210	43.21 N	73.22 W
Hartford, Oh., U.S.	214	41.19 N	80.34 W
Hartford, S.D., U.S.	198	43.37 N	96.56 W
Hartford, Wi., U.S.	190	43.19 N	88.22 W
Hartford □[6]	207	41.46 N	72.41 W
Hartford City	216	40.27 N	85.22 W
Hartha	54	51.05 N	12.58 E
Hartington	198	42.37 N	97.15 W
Hart Island I	276	40.51 N	73.46 W
Hart Lake ⊜	202	42.24 N	119.51 W
Hartland, N.B., Can.	186	46.18 N	67.32 W
Hartland, Eng., U.K.	42	50.59 N	4.29 W
Hartland, Il., U.S.	216	42.22 N	88.31 W
Hartland, Me., U.S.	188	44.53 N	69.26 W
Hartland, Mi., U.S.	216	42.39 N	83.45 W
Hartland, N.Y., U.S.	210	43.14 N	78.35 W
Hartland, Wi., U.S.	216	43.06 N	88.20 W
Hartland Point ›	42	51.02 N	4.31 W
Hartlepool	44	54.42 N	1.11 W
Hartleton	210	40.54 N	77.10 W
Hartley, Austl.	170	33.33 S	150.11 E
Hartley, Eng., U.K.	260	51.23 N	0.19 E
Hartley, Ia., U.S.	198	43.10 N	95.28 W
Hartley, Tx., U.S.	196	35.53 N	102.24 W
Hartley Bay	182	53.25 N	129.15 W
Hartlip	260	51.21 N	0.39 E
Hart Lot	210	43.01 N	76.28 W
Hartly	208	39.10 N	75.42 W
Hartmannsdorf	54	50.53 N	12.48 E
Hartmannshain	56	50.28 N	9.16 E
Hart-Miller Island I	208	39.15 N	76.23 W
Hart Mountain ∧	184	52.29 N	101.25 W
Hartney	184	49.28 N	100.30 W
Hartola	26	61.35 N	26.01 E
Harts ≃	158	28.24 S	24.17 E
Hartsburg	219	38.41 N	92.18 W
Hartsdale	210	41.01 N	73.47 W
Hartselle	194	34.26 N	86.56 W
Härtsfeld ◆[1]	56	48.50 N	10.15 E
Hartshill	42	52.37 N	1.32 W
Hartshorne	196	34.50 N	95.33 W
Harts Range	162	23.00 S	134.55 E
Hartstene Island I	224	47.14 N	122.53 W
Hartstown	214	41.33 N	80.23 W
Hartsville, In., U.S.	218	39.16 N	85.41 W
Hartsville, Pa., U.S.	285	40.14 N	75.05 W
Hartsville, S.C., U.S.	192	34.22 N	80.04 W
Hartsville, Tn., U.S.	194	36.23 N	86.10 W
Hartswater	158	27.34 S	24.43 E
Hartville, Mo., U.S.	194	37.15 N	92.30 W
Hartville, Oh., U.S.	214	40.57 N	81.19 W
Hartwell	192	34.21 N	82.55 W
Hartwell Lake ⊜[1]	192	34.30 N	82.55 W
Hartwick	210	42.39 N	75.02 W
Hartwick Pines State Park ♠	190	44.47 N	84.41 W
Hartz Mountains National Park ♠	166	43.15 S	146.50 E
Harue	94	36.08 N	136.14 E
Haruki	270	34.29 N	135.23 E
Haruku, Pulau I	164	3.34 S	128.29 E
Hārūn	140	11.20 N	25.43 E
Haruna	94	36.23 N	138.53 E
Hārūnābād	123	29.37 N	73.08 E
Haruna-san ∧	94	36.28 N	138.52 E
Haruniye	130	37.17 N	36.27 E
Haruno, Nihon	94	34.57 N	137.53 E
Haruno, Nihon	96	33.30 N	133.30 E
Harūr	122	12.04 N	78.30 E
Hārūt ≃	128	31.35 N	61.18 E
Harvard, Il., U.S.	216	42.25 N	88.36 W
Harvard, Ma., U.S.	207	42.30 N	71.35 W
Harvard, Ne., U.S.	198	40.37 N	98.05 W
Harvard University ᴥ[2]	283	42.22 N	71.07 W
Harvel, Eng., U.K.	260	51.21 N	0.22 E
Harvel, Il., U.S.	219	39.21 N	89.32 W
Harvest, Mount ∧[2]	162	25.54 S	126.28 E
Harvey, Austl.	168a	33.05 S	115.54 E
Harvey, N.B., Can.	186	45.43 N	64.43 W
Harvey, Il., U.S.	216	41.36 N	87.38 W
Harvey, N.D., U.S.	198	47.46 N	99.56 W
Harvey ≃	168a	32.46 S	115.43 E
Harvey Estuary ⊂[1]	168a	32.43 S	115.42 E
Harvey Mountain ∧	207	42.18 N	73.25 W
Harvey Reservoir ⊜[1]	168a	33.05 S	115.58 E
Harveysburg	218	39.30 N	84.00 W
Harveys Lake	210	41.23 N	76.02 W
Harwell	42	51.37 N	1.18 W
Harwich, Eng., U.K.	42	51.57 N	1.17 E
Harwich, Ma., U.S.	207	41.41 N	70.04 W
Harwich Port	207	41.40 N	70.04 W
Harwick	279b	40.34 N	79.48 W
Harwinton	207	41.46 N	73.03 W
Harwood, Eng., U.K.	262	53.35 N	2.23 W
Harwood, Tx., U.S.	222	29.40 N	97.30 W
Harwood Heights	278	41.58 N	87.48 W
Harwood Mines	210	40.57 N	76.01 W
Harwood Park	284b	39.12 N	76.44 W
Haryāna □[3]	120	29.20 N	76.20 E
Harz ⋏	54	51.45 N	10.30 E
Harzgerode	54	51.38 N	11.08 E
Ḥasā, Bi'r al- ⊤[4]	140	22.58 N	35.40 E
Ḥasā, Wādī al- V	132	31.05 N	35.27 E
Hasafen	86	45.14 N	90.20 E
Ḥaṣāh, Wādī al- V	132	30.38 N	37.09 E
Hasaki	94	35.44 N	140.50 E
Hasalbag	120	37.54 N	76.44 E
Ḥasanābād	267d	35.44 N	51.19 E
Ḥasanābād-e Khāleṣeh	267d	35.37 N	51.12 E
Hasan Abdāl	123	33.49 N	72.41 E
Hasançelebi	130	38.58 N	37.54 E
Hasan Dağı ∧	130	38.08 N	34.12 E
Hasankale → Pasinler	130	39.59 N	41.41 E
Hasankeyf	130	37.43 N	41.25 E
Ḥasan Kīādeh	128	37.24 N	49.58 E
Hasanpur	124	28.43 N	78.17 E
Hasayaz	130	40.15 N	33.20 E
Ḥāṣbānī, Nahr al- ≃	132	33.11 N	35.37 E
Ḥāṣbayyā	132	33.24 N	35.41 E
Hasbek	130	39.33 N	35.33 E
Hasbergen, Dtsch.	52	52.14 N	7.57 E
Hasbergen, Dtsch.	52	53.05 N	8.40 E
Hasbrouck Heights	276	40.51 N	74.04 W
Hascosay I	46a	60.37 N	0.59 W
Hasdo ≃	120	21.44 N	82.44 E
Hasdo-Rāmpur Basin ☷[1]	124	22.50 N	82.35 E
Hase, Nihon	94	35.47 N	138.06 E
Hase, Nihon	270	34.32 N	135.54 E
Hase ≃, Dtsch.	52	52.41 N	7.18 E
Hase ≃, Nihon	270	34.34 N	135.38 E
Hasel ≃	54	50.32 N	10.27 E
Häselgehr	58	47.19 N	10.30 E
Haselhorst ◆[8]	264a	52.33 N	13.15 E
Haselünne	52	52.40 N	7.29 E
Hasenkamp	252	31.31 S	59.51 W
Ḥashā', Jabal al- ∧	144	13.45 N	44.30 E
HaShefela ◆[1]	132	31.40 N	34.55 E
Hashima	94	35.19 N	136.42 E
Hashimoto, Nihon	96	34.19 N	135.37 E
Hashimoto, Nihon	270	34.26 N	135.23 E
Hashira-jima I	96	34.01 N	132.25 E
Hashiri-jima I	96	34.21 N	133.27 E
Hashitai	89	49.24 N	125.18 E
Hasht Sāl ◆[8]	272a	28.38 N	77.03 E
Hasil, Pulau I	164	1.06 S	128.24 E
Hāsilpur	123	29.43 N	72.33 E
Ḥāsīn-e Bozorg	84	39.23 N	44.42 E
Haskayne	262	53.34 N	2.58 W
Haskeir Islands II	46	57.42 N	7.41 W
Haskell, Ok., U.S.	196	35.49 N	95.40 W
Haskell, Tx., U.S.	196	33.09 N	99.44 W
Haskell Pond ⊜	283	42.37 N	70.44 W
Hasketh Bank	262	53.43 N	2.51 W
Haskins	216	41.27 N	83.42 W
Haskovo	38	41.56 N	25.33 E
Haskovo □[4]	130	41.50 N	25.50 E
Hasköy, Tür.	130	41.38 N	26.41 E
Hasköy, Tür.	130	40.59 N	42.52 E
Hasköy ◆[8]	267b	41.02 N	28.58 E
Haslach im Kinzigtal	58	48.16 N	8.06 E
Hasle, Dan.	41	55.11 N	14.43 E
Hasle, Schw.	58	47.01 N	7.39 E
Haslemere	42	51.06 N	0.43 W
Haslett	216	42.44 N	84.24 W
Haslev	41	55.20 N	11.58 E
Haslingden	262	53.43 N	2.18 W
Haslingden Grane	262	53.42 N	2.21 W
Haslington	44	53.06 N	2.24 W
Haslital V	58	46.42 N	8.10 E
Haslum	26	59.50 N	10.22 E
Hasmark	41	55.33 N	10.28 E
Ḥasmat ʿUmar, Bi'r ⊤[4]	140	21.46 N	34.00 E
Hāsnābād	126	22.35 N	88.55 E
Hasnācha	272b	22.26 N	88.09 E
Haspe ◆[8]	263	51.21 N	7.26 E
Hasperos Canyon V	200	33.50 N	105.02 W
Hasper-Stausee ⊜[1]	263	51.18 N	7.25 E
Haspres	50	50.15 N	3.25 E
Ḥaṣṣ, Jabal al- ∧[2]	130	35.52 N	37.22 E
Hassa	130	36.50 N	36.29 E
Hassan	122	13.00 N	76.05 E
Hassard	219	39.39 N	91.40 W
Hassayampa ≃	200	33.20 N	112.43 W
Hassberge ⋏[2]	56	50.12 N	10.29 E
Hassbergen	52	52.44 N	9.13 E
Hassel, Dtsch.	52	52.48 N	9.11 E
Hassel, Dtsch.	263	51.39 N	7.30 E
Hassel ◆[8]	263	51.36 N	7.03 E
Hasselbeck-Schwarzbach	263	51.16 N	6.53 E
Hasselfelde	54	51.41 N	10.51 E
Hasselfors	40	59.05 N	14.39 E
Hassels ◆[8]	263	51.10 N	6.53 E
Hasselt, Bel.	56	50.56 N	5.20 E
Hasselt, Ned.	52	52.35 N	6.05 E
Hassfurt	56	50.02 N	10.31 E
Hassi Bel Guebbour	148	28.46 N	6.27 E
Hassi el Ghella	34	35.28 N	1.03 W
Hassi Mameche	34	35.52 N	0.04 E
Hassi Messaoud	148	31.43 N	5.59 E
Hassi Zehana	34	35.01 N	0.53 W
Hassleben	54	53.13 N	13.41 E
Hässleholm	41	56.09 N	13.46 E
Hasslinghausen	56	51.20 N	7.17 E
Hassloch	56	49.22 N	8.16 E
Hasson Heights	214	41.26 N	79.41 W
Hästbo	40	60.27 N	16.27 E
Hasten ◆[8], Dtsch.	263	51.12 N	7.09 E
Hästen ◆[8], Dtsch.	263	51.09 N	7.06 E
Hastière-Lavaux	56	50.13 N	4.50 E
Hastings, Austl.	169	38.18 S	145.11 E
Hastings, Barb.	241g	13.04 N	59.35 W
Hastings, On., Can.	212	44.18 N	77.57 W
Hastings, N.Z.	172	39.38 S	176.51 E
Hastings, Eng., U.K.	42	50.51 N	0.36 E
Hastings, Fl., U.S.	192	29.43 N	81.30 W
Hastings, Il., U.S.	278	41.41 N	87.58 W
Hastings, Mi., U.S.	216	42.39 N	85.17 W
Hastings, Mn., U.S.	190	44.44 N	92.51 W
Hastings, Ne., U.S.	198	40.35 N	98.23 W
Hastings, N.Y., U.S.	210	43.22 N	76.09 W
Hastings, Pa., U.S.	214	40.39 N	78.42 W
Hastings □[6]	212	44.45 N	77.40 W
Hastings Battlesite ⊥	42	50.53 N	0.31 E
Hastings-on-Hudson	276	40.59 N	73.52 W
Hastingwood	260	51.45 N	0.09 E
Hastrup	41	55.26 N	12.11 E
Hasty	198	38.06 N	102.57 W
Hasuda	94	35.59 N	139.40 E
Hasumi	96	34.52 N	132.37 E
Haswell	198	38.27 N	103.09 W
Hata	94	36.11 N	137.51 E
Hat'ae-do I	98	34.32 N	126.03 E
Ha Tan	110	18.30 N	105.20 E
Hatanagi-dam ◆[6]	94	35.18 N	138.12 E
Hatashō	94	35.10 N	136.15 E
Hatay □[4]	130	36.30 N	36.15 E
Hatboro	208	40.10 N	75.06 W
Hatch, N.M., U.S.	200	32.39 N	107.09 W
Hatch, Ut,. U.S.	200	37.38 N	112.26 W
Hat Chao Mai National Park ♠	110	7.40 N	99.35 E
Hatches Creek	162	20.56 S	135.12 E
Hatchet Creek ≃	194	32.52 N	86.20 W
Hatchet Lake	186	44.35 N	63.40 W
Hatchie ≃	194	35.35 N	89.53 W
Hatchineha, Lake ⊜	220	28.02 N	81.25 W
Hatchlands ⊥	260	51.15 N	0.28 W
Hatchmere	262	53.15 N	2.40 W
Hatchville	207	41.37 N	70.33 W
Hatch Wash V	200	38.32 N	109.36 W
Hat Creek ≃, U.S.	198	43.16 N	103.36 W
Hat Creek ≃, Ca., U.S.	204	40.59 N	121.33 W
Hațeg	38	45.37 N	22.57 E
Hateruma-shima I	175d	24.03 N	123.47 E
Hatfield, Austl.	166	33.52 S	143.45 E
Hatfield, Eng., U.K.	44	53.34 N	1.00 W
Hatfield, Eng., U.K.	260	51.46 N	0.13 W
Hatfield, Ar., U.S.	194	34.29 N	94.22 W
Hatfield, Ma., U.S.	207	42.22 N	72.35 W
Hatfield Aerodrome ⊠	260	51.46 N	0.16 W
Hatfield House ⊥	260	51.46 N	0.13 W
Hatfield Peverel	260	51.47 N	0.35 E
Hatfield Swamp ☷	276	40.50 N	74.20 W
Hathāla	123	32.03 N	70.34 E
Hathaway Pines	226	38.07 N	120.28 W
Hatherleigh	42	50.49 N	4.04 W
Hathersage	44	53.19 N	1.38 W
Hāthras	124	27.36 N	78.03 E
Hātia ɰ	124	22.30 N	91.15 E
Ḥāṭibah, Ra's ›	144	21.55 N	38.58 E
Ha Tien	110	10.23 N	104.29 E
Hatillo	240m	18.29 N	66.49 W
Ha Tinh	110	18.20 N	105.54 E
Hatinoe → Hachinohe	92	40.30 N	141.29 E
Hatiozi → Hachiōji	94	35.39 N	139.20 E
Hatip	130	37.46 N	32.25 E
Hātisāla	272b	22.33 N	88.32 E
Hato, Bocht van ⊂	241s	12.13 N	68.58 W
Hatogaya	94	35.50 N	139.44 E
Hato Mayor [del Rey]	238	18.46 N	69.15 W
Hato Rey	240m	18.25 N	66.03 W
Hatoyama	94	35.59 N	139.20 E
Hāt Pīplia	124	22.46 N	76.18 E
Hatsukaichi	96	34.21 N	132.20 E
Hatsu-shima I	94	35.02 N	139.10 E
Hatsutomi	268	35.46 N	140.01 E
Hatta	124	24.07 N	79.36 E
Hattab, Oued el V	36	35.23 N	9.32 E
Hattah-Kulkyne National Park ♠	166	34.40 S	142.30 E
Hattem	52	52.28 N	6.04 E
Hatten, Dtsch.	52	53.02 N	8.22 E
Hatten, Fr.	56	48.54 N	7.59 E
Hattenhofen	60	48.13 N	11.07 E
Hatteras	192	35.13 N	75.41 W
Hatteras, Cape ›	192	35.13 N	75.32 W
Hatteras Island I	192	35.25 N	75.30 W
Hattiesburg	194	31.19 N	89.17 W
Hatting	41	55.51 N	9.46 E
Hattingen	56	51.23 N	7.10 E
Hattingspruit	158	28.09 S	30.11 E
Hatton, Eng., U.K.	262	53.20 N	2.36 W
Hatton, Scot., U.K.	46	57.25 N	1.54 W
Hatton, Al., U.S.	194	34.33 N	87.24 W
Hatton, N.D., U.S.	198	47.38 N	97.27 W
Hatton ◆[8]	260	51.28 N	0.25 W
Hatton Fields	226	36.33 N	121.54 W
Hattorf [am Harz]	52	51.39 N	10.14 E
Hattori, Nihon	270	34.46 N	135.27 E
Hattori, Nihon	270	34.52 N	135.36 E
Hattstatt	58	48.01 N	7.17 E
Hattstedt	41	54.31 N	9.01 E
Hatunsaray	130	37.35 N	32.21 E
Hatvan	30	47.40 N	19.41 E
Hat Yai	110	7.01 N	100.28 E
Hatzfeld ◆[8]	263	51.17 N	7.11 E
Hatzic	224	49.09 N	122.15 W
Hatzic Lake ⊜	224	49.10 N	122.14 W
Haubourdin	50	50.36 N	2.59 E
Haubstadt	194	38.12 N	87.34 W
Hāudullāpur	272b	22.25 N	88.33 E
Hauge	26	58.18 N	6.15 E
Haugesund	26	59.25 N	5.18 E
Haugh of Urr	44	54.58 N	3.52 W
Haughton Green	262	53.27 N	2.06 W
Haugsdorf	61	48.42 N	16.05 E
Hau Hoi Wan ⊂	100	22.28 N	113.56 E
Hauhungaroa Range ⋏	172	38.50 S	175.34 E
Haukeligrend	26	59.45 N	7.31 E
Haukipudas	26	65.11 N	25.21 E
Haukivesi ⊜	26	62.06 N	28.28 E
Haukivuori	26	62.01 N	27.13 E
Hauldres, Ru des ≃	261	48.37 N	2.28 E
Haulerwijk	52	53.04 N	6.20 E
Haultain ≃	184	55.51 N	106.46 W
Haune ≃	56	50.52 N	9.43 E
Haunersdorf	60	48.36 N	12.43 E
Haunstetten	58	48.18 N	10.54 E
Haunts Creek ɰ	276	40.37 N	73.31 W
Hauppauge	210	40.49 N	73.12 W
Hauptsrus	158	26.33 S	26.18 E
Hauraki Gulf ⊂	172	36.20 S	175.05 E
Hauroko, Lake ⊜	172	46.00 S	167.20 E
Hauru, Pointe ›	174s	17.29 S	149.55 W
Haus	64	47.25 N	13.49 E
Hausa	273a	6.37 N	3.21 E
Hausach	58	48.17 N	8.10 E
Hausham	64	47.45 N	11.50 E
Hausruck ⋏	60	48.07 N	13.35 E
Haussee ⊜	264a	52.38 N	13.41 E
Haussömmern	54	51.11 N	10.49 E
Haut, Isle au I	188	44.03 N	68.38 W
Haut Atlas ⋏	148	31.30 N	6.00 W
Haut-Bout	261	48.32 N	1.55 E
Haute Colme, Canal de la ≊	50	50.50 N	2.12 E
Hautecombe, Abbaye de ᴥ[1]	62	45.45 N	5.50 E
Haute-Corse □[5]	36	42.30 N	9.00 E
Haute-Garonne □[5]	32	43.25 N	1.30 E
Haute-Kotto □[5]	152	7.00 N	23.00 E
Haute-Loire □[5]	32	45.05 N	3.50 E
Hauteluce	62	45.45 N	6.35 E
Haute-Marne □[5]	58	48.05 N	5.10 E
Hauterive	186	49.12 N	68.16 W
Hauterives	62	45.15 N	5.02 E
Hautes-Alpes □[5]	62	44.40 N	6.30 E
Haute-Sangha □[5]	152	4.30 N	16.00 E
Haute-Saône □[5]	58	47.40 N	6.10 E
Haute-Savoie □[5]	32	46.00 N	6.20 E
Haute Seine, Canal de la ≊	50	48.34 N	3.43 E
Hautes Fagnes ⋏	56	50.30 N	6.05 E
Hautes-Pyrénées □[5]	32	43.00 N	0.10 E
Haute Sûre, Lac de la ⊜[1]	56	49.52 N	5.52 E
Haute-Vienne □[5]	32	45.50 N	1.15 E
Hauteville-Lompnes	58	45.58 N	5.36 E

Symbol	English	Deutsch	Español	Français	Português
≃	River	Fluß	Río	Rivière	Rio
≊	Canal	Kanal	Canal	Canal	Canal
∟	Waterfall, Rapids	Wasserfall, Stromschnellen	Cascada, Rápidos	Chute d'eau, Rapides	Cascata, Rápidos
ɰ	Strait	Meeresstraße	Estrecho	Détroit	Estreito
⊂	Bay, Gulf	Bucht, Golf	Bahía, Golfo	Baie, Golfe	Baía, Golfo
⊜	Lake, Lakes	See, Seen	Lago, Lagos	Lac, Lacs	Lago, Lagos
☷	Swamp	Sumpf	Pantano	Marais	Pântano
⊓	Ice Features, Glacier	Eis- und Gletscherformen	Accidentes Glaciales	Formes glaciaires	Acidentes glaciares
⊤	Other Hydrographic Features	Andere Hydrographische Objekte	Otros Elementos Hidrográficos	Autres données hydrographiques	Outros acidentes hidrográficos
✢	Submarine Features	Untermeerische Objekte	Accidentes Submarinos	Formes de relief sous-marin	Acidentes submarinos
□	Political Unit	Politische Einheit	Unidad Politica	Entité politique	Unidade política
ᴥ	Cultural Institution	Kulturelle Institution	Institución Cultural	Institution culturelle	Instituição cultural
⊥	Historical Site	Historische Stätte	Sitio Histórico	Site historique	Sitio histórico
♠	Recreational Site	Erholungs- und Ferienort	Sitio de Recreo	Centre de loisirs	Area de Lazer
⊠	Airport	Flughafen	Aeropuerto	Aéroport	Aeroporto
■	Military Installation	Militäranlage	Instalación Militar	Installation militaire	Instalação militar
◆	Miscellaneous	Verschiedenes	Misceláneo	Divers	Diversos

Name	Page	Lat.°′	Long.°′
Haute Volta → Burkina Faso □1	150	13.00 N	1.30 W
Haut-Folin ∧	32	47.00 N	4.02 E
Haut-Kœnigsbourg, Château du ⊥	58	48.14 N	7.22 E
Haut-Mbomou □5	140	6.00 N	26.00 E
Hautmont	50	50.15 N	3.56 E
Haut-Ogooué □4	152	1.00 S	13.50 E
Haut-Rhin □5	58	47.53 N	7.13 E
Hauts-de-Seine □5	261	48.50 N	2.11 E
Hautvillers	50	49.05 N	3.57 E
Haut-Zaïre □4	154	2.20 N	27.00 E
Hauula	229c	21.36 N	157.54 W
Hauzenberg	60	48.39 N	13.38 E
Hauz Rāni ●8	272a	28.32 N	77.13 E
Havana, Ar., U.S.	194	35.06 N	93.31 W
Havana, Fl., U.S.	192	30.37 N	84.24 W
Havana, Il., U.S.	194	40.18 N	90.03 W
Havana, N.D., U.S.	198	45.57 N	97.37 W
Havana → La Habana	240p	23.08 N	82.22 W
Havane, La → La Habana	240p	23.08 N	82.22 W
Havannah, Canal de la ⌣	175f	22.22 S	167.01 E
Havant	42	50.51 N	0.59 W
Havasu, Lake ⊜1	200	34.30 N	114.20 W
Havasu Creek ≃	200	36.19 N	112.46 W
Havasupai Indian Reservation ●4	200	36.13 N	112.40 W
Havdrup	41	55.32 N	12.08 E
Havel ≃	54	52.53 N	11.58 E
Havelange	56	50.23 N	5.14 E
Havelberg	54	52.50 N	12.04 E
Havelberg ∧2	264a	52.28 N	13.12 E
Haveli	123	30.27 N	73.42 E
Haveliān	123	34.03 N	73.10 E
Havel-Kanal ≆	264a	52.36 N	13.12 E
Havelland ●1	54	52.25 N	12.45 E
Havelländischer Grosser Hauptkanal ≆	264a	52.37 N	13.03 E
Havelländisches Luch ⩸	54	52.40 N	12.40 E
Havelock, On., Can.	212	44.26 N	77.53 W
Havelock, N.Z.	172	41.17 S	173.46 E
Havelock, N.C., U.S.	192	34.52 N	76.54 W
Havelock Island I	110	11.58 N	93.00 E
Havelock North	172	39.40 S	176.53 E
Haven	198	37.53 N	97.46 W
Haverford	285	40.00 N	75.17 W
Haverford College ⊍2	285	40.00 N	75.18 W
Haverfordwest	42	51.49 N	4.58 W
Haverhill, Eng., U.K.	42	52.05 N	0.26 E
Haverhill, Ma., U.S.	207	42.46 N	71.04 W
Haverhill Airport ⊠	283	42.48 N	71.04 W
Haverhill-Riverside Airport ⊠	283	42.46 N	71.02 W
Hāveri	122	14.48 N	75.24 E
Haverigg	44	54.11 N	3.17 W
Havering ●8	260	51.34 N	0.14 E
Havering-atte-Bower ●8	260	51.37 N	0.11 E
Havering's Grove	260	51.38 N	0.23 E
Havern ⊜	26	62.17 N	15.07 E
Haverö	26	62.24 N	15.05 E
Haverstraw	210	41.11 N	73.57 W
Havertown	208	39.58 N	75.18 W
Haviland, Ks., U.S.	198	37.37 N	99.06 W
Haviland, Oh., U.S.	216	41.01 N	84.35 W
Haviland Brook ≃	276	41.07 N	73.33 W
Havīq	128	38.10 N	48.54 E
Havířov	30	49.47 N	18.27 E
Havixbeck	52	51.58 N	7.25 E
Hävla	40	58.55 N	15.52 E
Havlíčkův Brod	30	49.36 N	15.35 E
Havnbjerg	41	55.02 N	9.48 E
Havnsø	41	55.45 N	11.20 E
Havran	130	39.33 N	27.06 E
Havré, Bel.	50	50.28 N	4.02 E
Havre, Mt., U.S.	202	48.32 N	109.40 W
Havre-Aubert	186	47.14 N	61.51 W
Havre Aubert, Île du I	186	47.14 N	61.57 W
Havre aux Maisons, Île du I	186	47.25 N	61.47 W
Havre de Grace	208	39.32 N	76.05 W
Havre de Grace Heights	208	39.35 N	76.07 W
Havre → Le Havre	50	49.30 N	0.08 E
Havre North	202	48.36 N	109.41 W
Havre-Saint-Pierre	186	50.14 N	63.36 W
Havsa	130	41.33 N	26.49 E
Havza	130	40.58 N	35.41 E
Haw ≃	192	35.36 N	79.03 W
Hawaii □3	229d	20.00 N	157.45 W
Hawaii I	229d	19.30 N	155.30 W
Hawaiian Gardens	280	33.49 N	118.04 W
Hawaiian Islands II	229d	20.30 N	157.30 W
Hawaiian Ridge ✣3	14	24.00 N	165.00 W
Hawaii Volcanoes National Park ♦	229d	19.23 N	155.17 W
Hawal ≃	146	10.00 N	12.05 E
Hawarden, Sk., Can.	184	51.23 N	106.36 W
Hawarden, N.Z.	172	42.56 S	172.38 E
Hawarden, Wales, U.K.	44	53.11 N	3.02 W
Hawarden, Ia., U.S.	198	42.59 N	96.29 W
Hawashīyah, Wādī V	140	28.31 N	32.58 E
Haw Creek ≃	218	39.11 N	85.55 W
Hawea, Lake ⊜	172	44.30 S	169.17 E
Hawera	172	39.35 S	174.17 E
Hawes	44	54.18 N	2.12 W
Hawesville	194	37.54 N	86.45 W
Haweswater Reservoir ⊜	44	54.32 N	2.48 W
Hawf, Jabal ⋏2	273c	29.55 N	31.21 E
Hawf, Wādī V	142	29.53 N	31.18 E
Hawi	229d	20.14 N	155.50 W
Hawick	44	55.25 N	2.47 W
Hawk Creek ≃	198	44.44 N	95.25 W
Hawkdun Range ⋏	172	44.46 S	170.00 E
Hawke, Cape ›	166	32.13 S	152.34 E
Hawke Bay c	172	39.20 S	177.30 E
Hawker	166	31.53 S	138.25 E
Hawkes, Mount ∧	9	83.56 S	55.45 W
Hawkes Brook ≃	283	42.45 N	71.08 W
Hawkesbury	206	45.36 N	74.37 W
Hawkesbury ≃	170	33.30 S	151.10 E
Hawkesbury Island I	182	53.38 N	129.00 W
Hawkes Pond ⊜	283	42.30 N	71.02 W
Hawkeye	190	42.56 N	91.57 W
Hawkhurst	42	51.02 N	0.30 E
Hawking	42	51.06 N	1.10 E
Hawkins, Tx., U.S.	222	32.35 N	95.12 W
Hawkins, Wi., U.S.	190	45.30 N	90.43 W
Hawkins, Lake ⊜1	222	32.38 N	95.15 W
Hawkins Island I	180	60.30 N	146.00 W
Hawkinsville	192	32.17 N	83.28 W
Hawk Junction	190	48.05 N	84.34 W
Hawk Lake	184	49.48 N	93.59 W
Haw Knob ∧	192	35.19 N	84.02 W
Hawk Point	219	38.58 N	91.07 W
Hawk Run	214	40.55 N	78.12 W
Hawksbill ∧	188	38.33 N	78.23 W
Hawksbill Creek c	192	26.32 N	78.43 W
Hawks Nest Point ›	238	24.09 N	75.32 W
Hawkwell	260	51.36 N	0.40 E
Hawkwood	166	25.47 S	150.50 E
Hawley, Eng., U.K.	260	51.25 N	0.14 E
Hawley, Mn., U.S.	198	46.52 N	96.18 W
Hawley, Pa., U.S.	210	41.28 N	75.10 W
Hawleyton	210	42.01 N	75.55 W
Hawleyville	207	41.25 N	73.21 W
Haworth	276	40.57 N	73.59 W
Haw Par Villa ⊍	271c	1.16 N	103.47 E
Hawr	142	27.52 N	30.44 E
Hawrān, Wādī V	128	33.58 N	42.34 E
Hawsh ʿĪsā	142	30.55 N	30.17 E
Hawthorn, Austl.	274b	37.49 S	145.02 E
Hawthorn, Pa., U.S.	214	41.01 N	79.17 W
Hawthorne, Ca., U.S.	228	33.54 N	118.21 W
Hawthorne, Fl., U.S.	192	29.35 N	82.05 W
Hawthorne, Nv., U.S.	204	38.31 N	118.37 W
Hawthorne, N.J., U.S.	210	40.56 N	74.09 W
Hawthorne, N.Y., U.S.	210	41.06 N	73.47 W
Hawthorne Lake ⊜	276	41.03 N	74.35 W
Hawthorne Municipal Airport ⊠	280	33.55 N	118.20 W
Hawthorne Race Course ♦	278	41.50 N	87.45 W
Hawthorn Woods	278	42.13 N	88.03 W
Hawwārah	132	32.32 N	35.54 E
Hawwārat ʿAdlān	142	29.12 N	30.58 E
Hawwārat al-Maqṭaʿ	142	29.15 N	30.54 E
Hawza	148	27.06 N	10.55 W
Hawzen	144	13.56 N	39.28 E
Haxby	44	54.01 N	1.04 W
Haxey	44	53.29 N	0.50 W
Haxtun	198	40.38 N	102.37 W
Hay	166	34.30 S	144.51 E
Hay ≃, Austl.	166	25.14 S	138.00 E
Hay ≃, Can.	176	60.52 N	115.44 W
Hay ≃, Wi., U.S.	190	44.59 N	91.51 W
Hay, Cape ›	176	74.25 N	113.00 W
Hay, Mount ∧, Austl.	162	23.28 S	133.05 E
Hay, Mount ∧, Austl.	170	33.37 S	150.26 E
Hay, Mount ∧, N.A.	180	59.15 N	137.37 W
Hay, South Fork ≃	190	45.03 N	91.57 W
Haya	164	3.27 S	129.33 E
Haya ≃, Nihon	94	35.14 N	139.09 E
Haya ≃, Nihon	94	35.25 N	138.27 E
Hayachine-san ∧	92	39.34 N	141.29 E
Hayakawa	94	35.25 N	138.22 E
Hayama, Nihon	94	35.16 N	139.35 E
Hayama, Nihon	96	33.26 N	133.13 E
Hayang	98	35.55 N	128.47 E
Hayange	56	49.20 N	6.03 E
HaYarden → Jordan ≃	132	31.46 N	35.33 E
Hayashima	96	34.36 N	133.50 E
Hayastan → Armenia □1	22	40.00 N	45.00 E
Hayasui-seto ⌣	96	33.18 N	131.59 E
Haybān	140	11.13 N	30.31 E
Haybān, Jabal ∧	140	11.15 N	30.31 E
Hay Bay c	212	44.10 N	76.55 W
Haybes	56	50.00 N	4.43 E
Haydān, Wādī al- V	132	31.27 N	35.36 E
Haydarlı	130	38.16 N	30.23 E
Hayden, Az., U.S.	200	33.00 N	110.47 W
Hayden, Co., U.S.	200	40.29 N	107.15 W
Hayden, In., U.S.	218	38.58 N	85.44 W
Hayden Peak ∧	202	42.59 N	116.39 W
Haydenville, Ma., U.S.	207	42.22 N	72.42 W
Haydenville, Oh., U.S.	188	39.28 N	82.19 W
Haydock	262	53.28 N	2.39 W
Haydock Park Race Course ♦	262	53.29 N	2.37 W
Haydon Bridge	44	54.58 N	2.14 W
Haye, La → 's-Gravenhage	52	52.06 N	4.18 E
Hayes	194	30.06 N	92.55 W
Hayes ●8, Eng., U.K.	260	51.31 N	0.25 W
Hayes ●8, Eng., U.K.	260	51.23 N	0.01 E
Hayes ≃, Mb., Can.	184	57.03 N	92.09 W
Hayes ≃, N.T., Can.	176	67.18 N	95.02 W
Hayes, Mount ∧	180	63.37 N	146.43 W
Hayes Center	198	40.30 N	101.01 W
Hayes State Memorial ⊥	214	41.21 N	83.08 W
Hayesville, N.C., U.S.	192	35.02 N	83.49 W
Hayesville, Oh., U.S.	214	40.46 N	82.15 W
Hayesville, Or., U.S.	224	44.59 N	122.58 W
Hayfield, Eng., U.K.	262	53.23 N	1.57 W
Hayfield, Mn., U.S.	190	43.53 N	92.50 W
Hayford Peak ∧	204	36.40 N	115.11 W
Hayfork	204	40.33 N	123.10 W
Hayfork Bally ∧	204	40.39 N	123.13 W
Hayfork Creek ≃	204	40.37 N	123.26 W
Hay Island I	212	44.53 N	80.58 W
Hayk, Lake ⊜	144	11.21 N	39.43 E
Haykota	144	15.10 N	37.03 E
Hay Lake ⊜	212	45.23 N	78.11 W
Hay Lakes	182	53.13 N	113.03 W
Hayle	42	50.11 N	5.23 W
Haymakers Run ≃	279b	40.25 N	79.43 W
Haymana	130	39.27 N	32.30 E
Haynes	194	34.53 N	90.47 W
Haynes Creek ≃	285	39.53 N	74.50 W
Haynesville, La., U.S.	194	32.57 N	93.08 W
Haynesville, Va., U.S.	208	37.57 N	76.40 W
Hayneville	194	32.11 N	86.34 W
Haynin	144	15.50 N	48.19 E
Hay-on-Wye	42	52.04 N	3.07 W
Hay Point ›	166	21.17 S	149.18 E
Hayrabolu	130	41.12 N	27.06 E
Hay River	176	60.51 N	115.40 W
Hays, Ab., Can.	182	50.06 N	111.48 W
Hays, Ks., U.S.	198	38.52 N	99.19 W
Hays, Mt., U.S.	202	47.59 N	108.41 W
Hays □6	222	30.02 N	97.45 W
Hays ●8	279b	40.23 N	79.56 W
Hayshah, Sabkhat al- ⩸	146	31.45 N	15.20 E
Hays Mill Creek ≃	285	39.44 N	74.50 W
Hay Springs	198	42.41 N	102.41 W
Haystack Mountain ∧	204	41.39 N	115.38 W
Haysville, Ks., U.S.	198	37.33 N	97.21 W
Haysville, Pa., U.S.	279b	40.32 N	80.09 W
Hayti, Mo., U.S.	194	36.14 N	89.44 W
Hayti, Pa., U.S.	208	39.59 N	75.51 W
Hayti, S.D., U.S.	198	44.39 N	97.12 W
Hayward, Ca., U.S.	226	37.40 N	122.04 W
Hayward, Wi., U.S.	190	46.00 N	91.29 W
Hayward Brook ≃	283	42.22 N	71.20 W
Hayward Municipal Airport ⊠	282	37.40 N	122.08 W
Haywards Heath	42	51.00 N	0.06 W
Haywood	184	49.40 N	98.12 W
Ḥayy, Jabal al- ∧	142	29.43 N	31.35 E
HaẒafon □5	132	32.50 N	35.20 E
Hazār, Kūh-e ∧	128	29.30 N	57.18 E
Hazard	192	37.14 N	83.11 W
Hazardville	207	41.59 N	72.32 W
Hazar Gölü ⊜	130	38.30 N	39.25 E
Hazārībāg	124	23.59 N	85.21 E
Hazārībāg Plateau ⋏1	124	24.00 N	85.10 E
Haze, Cape ›	220	26.46 N	82.10 W
Hazebrouck	50	50.43 N	2.32 E
Hazel ≃	188	38.33 N	77.51 W
Hazelbrook	170	33.44 S	150.27 E
Hazel Crest	278	41.34 N	87.41 W
Hazel Dell	224	45.40 N	122.39 W
Hazel Green, Il., U.S.	278	41.41 N	87.45 W
Hazel Green, Wi., U.S.	190	42.31 N	90.26 W
Hazelgrove, Austl.	170	33.40 S	149.52 E
Hazel Grove, Eng., U.K.	262	53.23 N	2.08 W
Hazel Hurst	214	41.42 N	78.35 W
Hazel Kirk	279b	40.11 N	79.57 W
Hazel Park	216	42.27 N	83.06 W
Hazel Park Race Track ♦	281	42.29 N	83.05 W
Hazelton, B.C., Can.	182	55.15 N	127.40 W
Hazelton, Id., U.S.	202	42.35 N	114.08 W
Hazelton, N.D., U.S.	198	46.29 N	100.16 W
Hazelton Mountains ⋏	182	54.30 N	128.20 W
Hazelton Peak ∧	202	44.06 N	107.03 W
Hazelwood, Mo., U.S.	219	38.46 N	90.22 W
Hazelwood, N.C., U.S.	192	35.28 N	83.00 W
Hazelwood ●8	279b	40.25 N	79.56 W
Hazen, Ar., U.S.	194	34.46 N	91.34 W
Hazen, Nv., U.S.	226	39.33 N	119.02 W
Hazen, N.D., U.S.	198	47.17 N	101.37 W
Hazen, Pa., U.S.	214	41.12 N	78.53 W
Hazen Bay c	180	61.00 N	165.10 W
Ḥaẓerim	132	31.14 N	34.43 E
Hazlehurst, Ga., U.S.	192	31.52 N	82.35 W
Hazlehurst, Ms., U.S.	194	31.51 N	90.23 W
Hazlet, Sk., Can.	184	50.25 N	108.36 W
Hazlet, N.J., U.S.	208	40.26 N	74.13 W
Hazleton, Ia., U.S.	190	42.37 N	91.54 W
Hazleton, Pa., U.S.	210	40.57 N	75.58 W
Hazlett, Lake ⊜	162	21.30 S	128.48 E
Ḥaẓor HaGelilit	132	32.59 N	35.33 E
Hazro, Pāk.	123	33.54 N	72.29 E
Hazro, Tür.	130	38.15 N	40.47 E
Hazu	94	34.47 N	137.08 E
He ≃, Zhg.	100	27.05 N	114.59 E
He ≃, Zhg.	102	23.26 N	111.30 E
Heacham	42	52.55 N	0.30 E
Head ≃	212	44.44 N	79.15 W
Head Bay d'Espoir	186	47.56 N	55.45 W
Headcorn	42	51.11 N	0.37 E
Headford	48	53.28 N	9.05 W
Head Lake ⊜	212	44.45 N	78.55 W
Headland	194	31.21 N	85.20 W
Headlands	154	18.14 S	32.03 E
Headley, Eng., U.K.	42	51.07 N	0.50 W
Headley, Eng., U.K.	260	51.17 N	0.16 W
Headley, Mount ∧	202	47.44 N	115.15 W
Head of the Harbor	276	40.54 N	73.10 W
Heald Green	262	53.22 N	2.14 W
Heald Moor ●3	262	53.44 N	2.10 W
Healdsburg	204	38.36 N	122.52 W
Healdton	196	34.13 N	97.29 W
Healesville	169	37.40 S	145.31 E
Healing	44	53.34 N	0.10 W
Healy, Ak., U.S.	180	63.52 N	148.58 W
Healy, Ks., U.S.	198	38.36 N	100.37 W
Healy, Mount ∧	180	63.46 N	149.01 W
Healy Lake ⊜	212	45.10 N	79.55 W
Heani, Mont ∧	174x	9.47 S	139.04 W
Heanna	174m	26.19 N	127.54 E
Heanor	44	53.01 N	1.22 W
Heany Junction	154	20.06 S	28.54 E
Heard Island I	6	53.06 S	73.30 E
Heard Pond ⊜	283	42.21 N	71.22 W
Hearne	222	30.52 N	96.35 W
Hearst	176	49.41 N	83.40 W
Hearst Island I	9	69.25 S	62.10 W
Hearst San Simeon State Historical Park ♦	226	35.42 N	121.10 W
Heart ≃, Ab., Can.	182	56.14 N	117.17 W
Heart ≃, N.D., U.S.	198	46.47 N	100.51 W
Heart Lake ⊜, Ab., Can.	182	55.02 N	111.30 W
Heart Lake ⊜, On., Can.	275b	43.44 N	79.48 W
Heart Lake Indian Reserve ●4	182	55.02 N	111.30 W
Heart Pond ⊜	283	42.34 N	71.23 W
Heart's Content	186	47.53 N	53.22 W
Heath, Ma., U.S.	207	42.40 N	72.49 W
Heath, Oh., U.S.	214	40.02 N	82.28 W
Heath, Tx., U.S.	222	32.50 N	96.29 W
Heath ≃	248	12.31 S	68.38 W
Heath, Pointe ›	186	49.05 N	61.42 W
Heathcote, Austl.	169	36.55 S	144.42 E
Heathcote, Austl.	274a	34.05 S	151.01 E
Heathcote Brook ≃	276	40.23 N	74.37 W
Heath End	42	51.22 N	1.09 W
Heatherton	274b	37.58 S	145.06 E
Heathfield	42	50.59 N	0.17 E
Heathmont	274b	37.49 S	145.15 E
Heath Springs	192	34.35 N	80.40 W
Heathsville	208	37.55 N	76.28 W
Heatley	262	53.24 N	2.27 W
Heaton Hall ⊥	262	53.32 N	2.15 W
Heaton Moor	262	53.25 N	2.11 W
Heaven, Temple of ⊍1	271a	39.53 N	116.25 E
Heavener	194	34.53 N	94.36 W
Heaverham	260	51.18 N	0.15 E
Heaviley	262	53.24 N	2.09 W
Hebaochang	107	29.33 N	105.32 E
Hebao Dao I	100	21.52 N	113.09 E
Hebbronville	196	27.18 N	98.40 W
Hebburn	44	54.59 N	1.30 W
Hebbville	284b	39.20 N	77.46 W
Hebden Bridge	262	53.45 N	2.00 W
Hebden Water ≃	262	53.44 N	2.00 W
Hebei, Zhg.	104	40.43 N	122.12 E
Hebei, Zhg.	104	41.01 N	123.51 E
Hebei (Hopeh) □4	98	38.00 N	116.00 E
Hebeitun	105	39.35 N	117.07 E
Hebel	166	28.59 S	147.48 E
Heber, Az., U.S.	200	34.25 N	110.35 W
Heber, Ca., U.S.	204	32.44 N	115.32 W
Heber City	200	40.30 N	111.24 W
Heber Springs	194	35.29 N	92.01 W
Hebgen Lake ⊜1	202	44.47 N	111.14 W
Hebi	98	35.59 N	114.11 E
Hebian	107	30.29 N	105.08 E
Hebo, Or., U.S.	224	45.13 N	123.51 W
Hebo, Zhg.	102	31.29 N	98.58 E
Hebo, Mount ∧	224	45.12 N	123.45 W
Hébridas, Islas → Hebrides II	46	57.00 N	6.30 W
Hebrides II	46	57.00 N	6.30 W
Hebrides, Sea of the ⩶2	46	57.07 N	6.55 W
Hebron, Nf., Can.	176	58.12 N	62.38 W
Hebron, Ct., U.S.	207	41.39 N	72.21 W
Hebron, Il., U.S.	216	42.28 N	88.25 W
Hebron, In., U.S.	216	41.19 N	87.12 W
Hebron, Ky., U.S.	218	39.03 N	84.42 W
Hebron, Md., U.S.	208	38.25 N	75.41 W
Hebron, Ne., U.S.	198	40.09 N	97.35 W
Hebron, N.D., U.S.	198	46.54 N	102.02 W
Hebron, Pa., U.S.	208	40.21 N	76.24 W
Hebron, Tx., U.S.	222	33.01 N	96.52 W
Hebron, Wi., U.S.	216	42.56 N	88.42 W
Hebron → Al-Khalīl	132	31.32 N	35.06 E
Hebu	100	27.50 N	115.22 E
Hebutu	104	42.19 N	122.20 E
Heby	40	59.56 N	16.53 E
Hecao	105	40.21 N	116.47 E
Hecate Strait ⌣	182	53.00 N	131.00 W
Hecelchakán	232	20.10 N	90.08 W
Heceta Island I	180	55.45 N	133.35 W
Hechi	102	24.42 N	108.02 E
Hechiceros	196	28.33 N	103.38 W
Hechingen	58	48.21 N	8.58 E
Hechtel	56	51.08 N	5.21 E
Hechthausen	52	53.38 N	9.14 E
Hechuan	107	30.00 N	106.16 E
Heckelberg	54	52.44 N	13.50 E
Hecker	219	38.18 N	90.00 W
Heckington	42	52.59 N	0.18 W
Hecklingen	54	51.51 N	11.32 E
Heckscher State Park ♦	210	40.43 N	73.10 W
Hecla, Mb., Can.	184	51.08 N	96.40 W
Hecla, S.D., U.S.	198	45.52 N	98.09 W
Hecla Island I	184	51.08 N	96.45 W
Hecla Provincial Park ♦	184	51.12 N	96.35 W
Hectanooga	186	44.06 N	66.02 W
Hector, N.Z.	172	41.36 S	171.53 E
Hector, Mn., U.S.	198	44.44 N	94.42 W
Hector, Mount ∧	172	40.57 S	175.17 E
Heda	94	34.58 N	138.46 E
Hedal	26	60.37 N	9.42 E
Hedaru	154	4.30 S	37.54 E
Heddal ⊍1	26	59.35 N	9.11 E
Hedding	285	40.06 N	74.44 W
Hédé, Fr.	32	48.18 N	1.48 W
Hede, Sve.	26	62.25 N	13.30 E
Hedehusene	41	55.39 N	12.12 E
Hedel	52	51.45 N	5.15 E
Hedemora	40	60.17 N	15.59 E
Hedemünden	56	51.23 N	9.46 E
Hedensted	41	55.46 N	9.42 E
Hedersleben	54	51.51 N	11.15 E
Hedesunda	40	60.24 N	16.59 E
Hedesundafjärdarna ⊜	40	60.20 N	17.00 E
He Devil ∧	202	45.21 N	116.33 W
Hedge End	42	50.54 N	1.18 W
Hedgerley	260	51.35 N	0.36 W
Hedian	100	32.45 N	114.18 E
Hedley, B.C., Can.	182	49.21 N	120.04 W
Hedley, Tx., U.S.	196	34.52 N	100.39 W
Hedmark □6	26	61.30 N	11.45 E
Hednesford	42	52.43 N	2.00 W
Hedo	174m	26.51 N	128.16 E
Hedo-misaki ›	174m	26.52 N	128.16 E
Hedon	44	53.44 N	0.12 W
Hedrick	190	41.10 N	92.18 W
Hedströmmen ≃	40	59.28 N	16.04 E
Hedutne	272c	19.10 N	73.06 E
Hedwig Village	222	29.47 N	95.27 W
Heek	52	52.07 N	7.06 E
Heel	52	51.11 N	5.53 E
Heel Point ›	174a	19.19 N	166.37 E
Heemskerk	52	52.31 N	4.40 E
Heemstede	52	52.21 N	4.37 E
Heepen	52	52.01 N	8.35 E
Heer, Bel.	56	50.10 N	4.50 E
Heer, Ned.	56	50.50 N	5.44 E
Heerde	52	52.23 N	6.03 E
Heerdt ●8	263	51.13 N	6.43 E
Heerenveen	52	52.57 N	5.55 E
Heeren-Werve	52	51.35 N	7.43 E
Heerhugowaard	52	52.40 N	4.50 E
Heerkan	107	29.32 N	103.56 E
Heerlen	56	50.54 N	5.59 E
Heesch	52	51.44 N	5.32 E
Heeslingen	52	53.19 N	9.20 E
Heessen	52	51.42 N	7.50 E
Heeze	52	51.24 N	5.35 E
Ḥefa (Haifa)	132	32.50 N	35.00 E
Ḥefa □5	132	32.35 N	35.00 E
Ḥefa, Mifraẓ c	132	32.52 N	35.03 E
Ḥefa, Sede-Teʿufa ⊠	132	32.49 N	35.02 E
Hefei	100	31.51 N	117.17 E
Hefengchang	107	30.26 N	104.43 E
Heffron Park ♦	274a	33.57 S	151.15 E
Heflin	194	33.38 N	85.35 W
Hegang	89	47.24 N	130.22 E
Hegau ●1	58	47.50 N	8.45 E
Hégenheim	58	47.34 N	7.32 E
Hegewisch ●8	278	41.40 N	87.33 W
Hegins	208	40.39 N	76.29 W
Hegra	26	63.28 N	11.07 E
Hegura-jima I	92	37.51 N	136.55 E
Heguri	270	34.38 N	135.42 E
Hegyeshalom	61	47.55 N	17.10 E
Hehlen	52	51.59 N	9.28 E
Heho	110	20.43 N	96.49 E
Hehou	100	28.40 N	114.28 E
Hei ≃, Zhg.	102	40.18 N	99.26 E
Hei ≃, Zhg.	105	40.44 N	116.27 E
Heicheng (Karakhoto) ⊥	102	41.47 N	101.03 E
Heichengzhen	102	36.16 N	106.06 E
Heichengzi	104	42.10 N	121.01 E
Heidayingzi	98	40.52 N	116.12 E
Heidberg ∧2	263	51.15 N	7.21 E
Heide	30	54.12 N	9.06 E
Heide ●8, Dtsch.	263	51.26 N	7.01 E
Heide ●8, Dtsch.	263	51.31 N	6.52 E
Heideck	60	49.08 N	11.07 E
Heidelberg, Austl.	169	37.45 S	145.04 E
Heidelberg, On., Can.	212	43.31 N	80.37 W
Heidelberg, Dtsch.	56	49.25 N	8.43 E
Heidelberg, S. Afr.	158	34.06 S	20.59 E
Heidelberg, S. Afr.	158	26.32 S	28.18 E
Heidelberg, Ms., U.S.	194	31.53 N	88.59 W
Heidelberg, Pa., U.S.	279b	40.23 N	80.05 W
Heidelberg □5	273d	26.19 S	28.16 E
Heidelberg, Schloss ⊥	56	49.24 N	8.42 E
Heidelsheim	56	49.06 N	8.38 E
Heiden, Dtsch.	52	51.59 N	8.50 E
Heiden, Schw.	58	47.27 N	9.33 E
Heiden, Port c	180	56.55 N	158.45 W
Heidenau, Dtsch.	52	53.19 N	9.39 E
Heidenau, Dtsch.	54	50.59 N	13.52 E
Heidenheim	56	49.01 N	10.44 E
Heidenheim an der Brenz	56	48.40 N	10.08 E
Heidenheimer	222	31.01 N	97.18 W
Heidenoldendorf	52	51.57 N	8.50 E
Heidenreichstein	61	48.52 N	15.07 E
Heider Ditch ≆	279a	41.31 N	82.01 W
Heiderscheid	56	49.53 N	5.54 E
Heidhausen ●8	263	51.23 N	7.01 E
Heidhof ●8	263	51.11 N	7.11 E
Heidlersburg	208	39.57 N	77.09 W
Heidouwo	105	39.42 N	117.15 E
Heigenbrücken	56	50.02 N	9.23 E
Heigoutaicun	104	41.30 N	123.01 E
Heigun-tō I	96	33.47 N	132.14 E
Heihai → Har Hu ⊜	102	38.15 N	97.40 E
Heihe → Aihui	89	50.16 N	127.28 E
Heijō → P'yŏngyang	98	39.01 N	125.45 E
Heikega-dake ∧	96	34.19 N	131.54 E
Heikendorf	54	54.22 N	10.12 E
Heil	263	51.38 N	7.35 E
Heilangkou	105	39.37 N	117.24 E
Heilbron	158	27.21 S	27.58 E
Heilbronn	56	49.08 N	9.13 E
Heilenbecker-Stausee ⊜1	263	51.15 N	7.22 E
Heiligenberg	58	47.49 N	9.19 E
Heiligenblut	64	47.02 N	12.50 E
Heiligendamm	54	54.08 N	11.50 E
Heiligenhafen	54	54.22 N	10.58 E
Heiligenhaus	56	51.19 N	6.59 E
Heiligensee ●8	264a	52.36 N	13.13 E
Heiligenstadt, Dtsch.	56	51.23 N	10.09 E
Heiligenstadt, Dtsch.	60	49.51 N	11.10 E
Heilin	98	35.01 N	118.58 E
Hei Ling Chau I	271d	22.15 N	114.02 E
Heilong (Amur) ≃	89	52.56 N	141.10 E
Heilongguan	102	36.19 N	111.11 E
Heilongjiang □4	89	48.00 N	128.00 E
Heilongtan, Zhg.	105	40.44 N	116.31 E
Heilongtan, Zhg.	105	40.02 N	116.11 E
Heilongtan Shuiku ⊜1	107	30.03 N	104.02 E
Heiloo	52	52.36 N	4.43 E
Heilsbronn	56	49.20 N	10.47 E
Heiltz-le-Maurupt	56	48.48 N	4.49 E
Heilungkiang → Heilongjiang □4	89	48.00 N	128.00 E
Heilwood	214	40.37 N	78.54 W
Heimaey I	24a	63.26 N	20.17 W
Heimbach	56	50.38 N	6.28 E
Heimbuchenthal	56	49.53 N	9.17 E
Heimburg	54	51.49 N	10.54 E
Heimdal	26	63.21 N	10.22 E
Heimenkirch	58	47.37 N	9.53 E
Heimsheim	56	48.48 N	8.51 E
Heinävesi	26	62.26 N	28.36 E
Heinersdorf, Dtsch.	54	52.27 N	14.13 E
Heinersdorf, Dtsch.	264a	52.23 N	13.20 E
Heinersdorf ●8	264a	52.34 N	13.27 E
Heiniuyingzi	98	41.07 N	120.19 E
Heino	52	52.26 N	6.14 E
Heinola	26	61.13 N	26.02 E
Heinrichshorst	54	52.20 N	11.42 E
Heinsberg	56	51.03 N	6.05 E
Heiquan	102	39.32 N	99.42 E
Heirnkut	110	25.14 N	94.45 E
Heisfelde	52	53.15 N	7.26 E
Heishan	104	41.41 N	122.07 E
Heishanguan	98	38.33 N	113.41 E
Heishantou, Zhg.	89	50.13 N	119.28 E
Heishantou, Zhg.	98	42.28 N	125.33 E
Heishui	98	42.09 N	119.28 E
Heishuisi	102	36.08 N	108.42 E
Heisingen ●8	263	51.25 N	7.04 E
Heisler	182	52.41 N	112.13 W
Heislerville	208	39.13 N	74.59 W
Heissen ●8	263	51.26 N	6.56 E
Heist-aan-Zee	50	51.21 N	3.15 E
Heist-op-den-Berg	56	51.05 N	4.43 E
Heitang	102	26.29 N	105.09 E
Heitersheim	58	47.53 N	7.40 E
Heiwa	94	35.12 N	136.44 E
Heiyanghebao	105	39.07 N	118.15 E
Heiyantang	102	27.28 N	101.11 E
Heiyanzi	105	39.13 N	118.08 E
Hejaz → Al-Ḥijāz ●1	118	24.30 N	38.30 E
Hejiachang	107	29.24 N	104.56 E
Hejian, Zhg.	98	38.26 N	116.05 E
Hejian, Zhg.	105	39.25 N	116.25 E
Hejiang	107	28.49 N	105.50 E
Hejiangzhen	107	29.16 N	104.16 E
Hejiaqiao	100	27.24 N	113.21 E
Hejiawopeng	104	41.32 N	122.07 E
Hejiaying	105	39.55 N	118.19 E
Hejiazhen	107	29.52 N	104.26 E
Hejin	102	35.39 N	110.40 E
Hejlsminde	41	55.22 N	9.37 E
Hejnsvig	41	55.41 N	8.59 E
Hekelgem	50	50.54 N	4.06 E
Hekili Point ›	229a	20.48 N	156.37 W
Hekimhan	130	38.49 N	37.56 E
Hekinan	94	34.51 N	136.58 E
Hekla ∧1	24a	64.00 N	19.39 W
Hekou, Zhg.	100	31.22 N	114.26 E
Hekou, Zhg.	102	36.09 N	103.22 E
Hekou, Zhg.	102	28.22 N	108.14 E
Hekou, Zhg.	102	29.57 N	111.04 E
Hekou, Zhg.	102	22.38 N	103.56 E
Hekouchang	107	29.21 N	104.21 E
Hekouji	100	32.09 N	116.04 E
Hekoujie	102	26.31 N	100.39 E
Hekpoort	158	25.55 S	27.38 E
Hel	30	54.37 N	18.48 E
Helagsfjället ∧	26	62.55 N	12.27 E
Helaluo	102	33.56 N	102.10 E
Helangou	104	41.00 N	123.25 E
Helan Shan ⋏	102	38.40 N	105.57 E
Helbe ≃	54	51.13 N	11.06 E
Helbra	54	51.33 N	11.29 E
Helchteren	56	51.03 N	5.22 E
Heldburg	54	50.17 N	10.44 E
Helden	56	51.07 N	7.56 E
Heldra	56	51.07 N	10.11 E
Heldrungen	54	51.18 N	11.13 E
Helechos, Cañada de los ≃	286a	19.22 N	99.12 W
Helemano Stream ≃	229c	21.35 N	158.06 W
Helen, Mount ∧	166	21.34 S	141.13 E
Helena, Ar., U.S.	194	34.31 N	90.35 W
Helena, Mt., U.S.	202	46.35 N	112.02 W
Helena, N.Y., U.S.	206	44.55 N	74.44 W
Helena, Oh., U.S.	214	41.21 N	83.18 W
Helena, Ok., U.S.	196	36.32 N	98.16 W
Helena ≃	168a	31.54 S	116.00 E
Helena River Reservoir ⊜1	168a	31.59 S	116.13 E
Helendale	228	34.45 N	117.18 W
Helenenberg	56	49.51 N	6.32 E
Helenental ●1	264b	48.01 N	16.11 E
Helen Island I	108	2.58 N	131.49 E
Helensburgh, Austl.	170	34.11 S	150.59 E
Helensburgh, Scot., U.K.	46	56.01 N	4.44 W
Helen Springs	162	18.26 S	133.52 E
Helensville	172	36.40 S	174.28 E
Helenville	216	43.01 N	88.41 W
Helenwood	192	36.25 N	84.32 W
Ḥeleẓ	132	31.35 N	34.40 E
Helfenberg	61	48.32 N	14.08 E
Helfenstein	208	40.45 N	76.27 W
Helfta	54	51.30 N	11.34 E
Helgaå ≃	26	55.53 N	14.08 E
Helgenæs I	41	56.08 N	10.32 E
Helgoland I	30	54.12 N	7.53 E
Helgoländer Bucht c	30	54.10 N	8.04 E
Heli	89	47.05 N	130.16 E
Helicoide ●9	286c	10.29 N	66.55 W
Helidon	171a	27.33 S	152.08 E
Heliodora	256	22.04 S	45.32 W
Heliópolis	287a	22.45 S	43.25 W
Heliopolis ⊥	142	30.08 N	31.17 E
Heliopolis Aerodrome ⊠	273c	30.04 N	31.19 E
Heliopolis → Miṣr al-Jadīdah ●8	273c	30.06 N	31.20 E
Heliopolis Racing Club ♦	273c	30.06 N	31.19 E
Heliuji	100	33.02 N	116.57 E
Helixi	106	30.40 N	118.59 E
Hell	26	63.26 N	10.54 E
Hellam	208	40.00 N	76.36 W
Hellberge ⋏2	54	52.34 N	11.17 E
Hellbrunn, Schloss ⊥	64	47.46 N	13.04 E
Hellebæk	41	56.04 N	12.34 E
Ḥelleh ≃	128	29.10 N	50.40 E
Hellen Blazes, Lake ⊜	220	28.01 N	80.47 W
Hellendoorn	52	52.24 N	6.26 E
Hellenthal	56	50.29 N	6.26 E
Hellerau ●8	54	51.07 N	13.44 E
Hellern	52	52.15 N	7.58 E
Hellersen	263	51.12 N	7.39 E
Hellertown	208	40.34 N	75.20 W
Hellesylt	26	62.05 N	6.54 E
Hellevad	41	55.05 N	9.13 E
Hellevoetsluis	52	51.49 N	4.08 E
Hell Gate ⌣	276	40.47 N	73.56 W
Hell Hole Reservoir ⊜1	226	39.04 N	120.22 W
Hellifield	44	54.01 N	2.12 W
Hellín	34	38.31 N	1.41 W
Helli Ness ›	46a	60.02 N	1.10 W
Hellmonsödt	61	48.26 N	14.18 E
Hell Point ›	186	44.16 N	64.15 W
Hells Canyon V	202	45.20 N	116.45 W
Hellsee ⊜	264a	52.45 N	13.35 E
Hells Gate V	182	49.47 N	121.27 W
Hell-Ville	157b	13.25 S	48.16 E
Hellweg ●1	52	51.32 N	7.47 E
Helm	226	36.31 N	120.05 W
Helmand □4	128	31.00 N	64.00 E
Helmand ≃	128	31.12 N	61.34 E
Helmbrechts	54	50.14 N	11.43 E
Helmcken Falls ⌞	182	51.57 N	120.11 W
Helme ≃	54	51.20 N	11.20 E
Helmeringhausen	156	25.54 S	16.57 E
Helmetta	276	40.22 N	74.25 W
Helmetta Pond ⊜	276	40.23 N	74.26 W
Helmond	52	51.29 N	5.40 E
Helmsburg	218	39.16 N	86.18 W
Helmsdale	46	58.07 N	3.40 W
Helmsdale ≃	46	58.07 N	3.40 W
Helmshore	262	53.41 N	2.20 W
Helmsley	44	54.14 N	1.04 W
Helmstedt	54	52.13 N	11.00 E
Helnæs I	41	55.08 N	10.02 E
Helong	98	42.32 N	128.59 E
Helper	200	39.41 N	110.51 W
Helpmekaar	158	28.29 S	30.29 E
Helpter Berg ∧2	54	53.30 N	13.36 E
Helsby	262	53.16 N	2.46 W
Helsby Hill ∧2	262	53.16 N	2.46 W
Helsingborg	41	56.03 N	12.42 E
Helsinge	41	56.01 N	12.12 E
Helsingfors → Helsinki	26	60.10 N	24.58 E
Helsingør (Elsinore)	41	56.02 N	12.37 E
Helsinki (Helsingfors)	26	60.10 N	24.58 E
Helska, Mierzeja ›2	30	54.45 N	18.39 E

Name	Seite	Breite°′	Länge°′ E = Ost
Helston	42	50.05 N	5.16 W
Heltonville	218	38.55 N	86.22 W
Helvecia	252	31.06 S	60.05 W
Helvellyn ∧	44	54.31 N	3.01 W
Helvick Head ›	48	52.03 N	7.33 W
Helvoirt	52	51.38 N	5.13 E
Hem ≃	50	50.51 N	2.06 E
Ḥemar, Naḥal V	132	31.08 N	35.22 E
Hemau	60	49.03 N	11.47 E
Hemāvati ≃	122	12.31 N	76.27 E
Hembe	152	1.54 N	22.42 E
Hemel Hempstead	260	51.46 N	0.28 W
Hemelingen ●8	52	53.03 N	8.53 E
Hemeln	52	51.30 N	9.36 E
Hemer	56	51.23 N	7.46 E
Hemet	228	33.44 N	116.58 W
Hemfjärden c	40	59.17 N	15.20 E
Hemford	186	44.30 N	64.47 W
Hemfurth-Edersee	56	51.10 N	9.02 E
Hemiksem	50	51.09 N	4.21 E
Héming	58	48.42 N	6.57 E
Hemingford	198	42.19 N	103.04 W
Hemingway	192	33.45 N	79.26 W
Hemlock, In., U.S.	216	40.25 N	86.03 W
Hemlock, N.Y., U.S.	210	42.47 N	77.36 W
Hemlock Lake ⊜	210	42.43 N	77.37 W
Hemmerde	52	51.33 N	7.48 E
Hemmerden	263	51.07 N	6.36 E
Hemmingen-Westerfeld	52	52.19 N	9.45 E
Hemmoor	52	53.41 N	9.08 E
Hemphill	194	31.20 N	93.50 W
Hempnall	42	52.30 N	1.19 E
Hempstead, N.Y., U.S.	210	40.42 N	73.37 W
Hempstead, Tx., U.S.	222	30.05 N	96.04 W
Hempstead Harbor c	276	40.50 N	73.39 W
Hempstead Lake ⊜	276	40.41 N	73.38 W
Hempstead Lake State Park ♦	276	40.41 N	73.38 W
Hemsby	42	52.41 N	1.42 E
Hemse	26	57.14 N	18.22 E
Hemsedal	26	60.52 N	8.34 E
Hemsön I	26	62.43 N	18.05 E
Hemstreet Park	210	42.54 N	73.41 W
Hemsworth	44	53.38 N	1.21 W
Hemujing	98	37.54 N	115.22 E
Henan	102	34.35 N	101.34 E
Henan (Honan) □4	90	34.00 N	114.00 E
Hen and Chickens II	172	35.55 S	174.45 E
Henares ≃	34	40.24 N	3.30 W
Henbury, Austl.	162	24.35 S	133.15 E
Henbury, Eng., U.K.	262	53.15 N	2.11 W
Hendek	130	40.48 N	30.45 E
Henderson, Arg.	252	36.18 S	61.43 W
Henderson, In., U.S.	218	39.40 N	85.31 W
Henderson, Ky., U.S.	194	37.50 N	87.35 W
Henderson, Mn., U.S.	190	44.31 N	93.54 W
Henderson, Ne., U.S.	198	40.46 N	97.48 W
Henderson, Nv., U.S.	204	36.02 N	114.58 W
Henderson, N.Y., U.S.	212	43.51 N	76.11 W
Henderson, N.C., U.S.	192	36.19 N	78.23 W
Henderson, Tn., U.S.	194	35.26 N	88.38 W
Henderson, Tx., U.S.	222	32.09 N	94.47 W
Henderson □6	222	32.13 N	95.50 W
Henderson Bay c, N.Y., U.S.	212	43.54 N	76.10 W
Henderson Bay c, Wa., U.S.	224	47.18 N	122.42 W
Henderson Creek ≃	190	40.52 N	91.02 W
Henderson Island I	6	24.22 S	128.19 W
Hendersonville, N.C., U.S.	192	35.19 N	82.27 W
Hendersonville, Pa., U.S.	214	40.18 N	80.09 W
Hendersonville, Tn., U.S.	194	36.18 N	86.37 W
Hendījān	128	30.14 N	49.43 E
Hendon ●8	260	51.35 N	0.14 W
Hendorābī, Jazīreh-ye I	128	26.40 N	53.37 E
Hendricks, Mn., U.S.	198	44.30 N	96.25 W
Hendricks, W.V., U.S.	188	39.04 N	79.37 W
Hendricks □6	218	39.46 N	86.26 W
Hendrik Verwoerddam ⊜1	158	30.40 S	25.40 E
Hendrina	158	26.11 S	29.45 E
Hendry □6	220	26.36 N	81.13 W
Hendrysburg	214	40.04 N	81.10 W
Hendy	42	51.43 N	4.04 W
Henefer	200	41.01 N	111.29 W
Henfield	42	50.56 N	0.17 W
Heng ≃, Zhg.	102	28.40 N	104.25 E
Heng ≃, Zhg.	107	28.57 N	105.22 E
Hengām, Jazīreh-ye I	128	26.39 N	55.53 E
Henganofi	164	6.15 S	145.35 E
Hengchow → Hengyang	102	26.54 N	112.36 E
Hengdaochuan	98	41.15 N	125.31 E
Hengdaohe	104	42.02 N	123.51 E
Hengdaohezi	89	43.13 N	126.44 E
Hengdaozi	89	43.18 N	127.18 E
Hengdong	100	27.03 N	112.57 E
Hengelo	52	52.15 N	6.45 E
Hengersberg	60	48.47 N	13.03 E
Hengfan	106	30.20 N	119.45 E
Hengfeng	100	28.24 N	117.34 E
Henggang	100	29.32 N	115.27 E
Henggouzi	89	43.12 N	124.47 E
Henghutou	104	42.05 N	124.00 E
Hengjie	106	31.13 N	119.30 E
Hengjing	106	31.11 N	120.32 E
Hengjinghong	106	30.34 N	120.59 E
Hengli	100	23.12 N	114.37 E
Henglin	106	31.42 N	120.06 E
Henglu	98	41.26 N	126.04 E
Henglutou	106	30.19 N	119.19 E
Hengmian	106	31.09 N	121.38 E
Hengoed	42	51.39 N	3.10 W
Hengsen	263	51.29 N	7.38 E
Heng Sha I	106	31.20 N	121.50 E
Hengshan, Zhg.	100	27.15 N	112.51 E
Hengshan, Zhg.	102	37.56 N	108.53 E
Hengshan, Zhg.	106	31.01 N	120.32 E
Heng Shan ∧	100	27.16 N	112.35 E
Heng Shan ⋏	102	39.30 N	113.45 E
Hengshanchang	107	30.33 N	105.24 E
Hengshanqiao	106	31.46 N	120.07 E
Hengshanxia	106	30.18 N	118.44 E
Hengshi, Zhg.	100	26.05 N	114.38 E
Hengshi, Zhg.	100	23.52 N	113.15 E
Hengshi, Zhg.	100	29.32 N	114.41 E
Hengshui	98	37.43 N	115.40 E
Hengsteysee ⊜1	263	51.25 N	7.28 E
Hengtangshi	106	31.41 N	121.02 E
Hengtianchi	107	29.07 N	105.01 E
Hengtianxi	107	29.05 N	105.03 E
Hengxi, Zhg.	100	29.42 N	121.35 E
Hengxi, Zhg.	100	28.46 N	120.29 E
Hengxi, Zhg.	106	31.43 N	118.46 E
Hengxian	102	22.42 N	109.13 E
Hengxiang	106	32.12 N	120.15 E
Hengxikou	100	29.26 N	121.26 E
Hengyang	102	26.54 N	112.36 E
Hénin-Beaumont	50	50.25 N	2.56 E
Henley Beach	168b	34.55 S	138.30 E
Henley-in-Arden	42	52.17 N	1.46 W
Henley-on-Thames	42	51.32 N	0.56 W
Henlopen, Cape ›	208	38.48 N	75.05 W
Henlow	42	52.02 N	0.18 W
Hennan ⊜	26	62.06 N	15.46 E
Hennaya	34	34.58 N	1.22 W
Henneberg	54	50.29 N	10.21 E
Hennebont	32	47.48 N	3.17 W
Hennef	56	50.46 N	7.16 E
Hennen	56	51.27 N	7.39 E
Hennenman	158	27.59 S	27.01 E
Hennepin	190	41.15 N	89.21 W
Hennepin, Point ›	281	42.12 N	83.09 W

Symbols in the index entries represent the broad categories identified in the key at the right. Symbols with superior numbers (⋏1) identify subcategories (see complete key on page I · 1).

Symbole im Register stellen die rechts im Schlüssel erklärten Kategorien dar. Symbole mit hochgestellten Ziffern (⋏1) bezeichnen Unterabteilungen einer Kategorie (vgl. vollständiger Schlüssel auf Seite I · 1).

Los símbolos incluidos en el texto del índice representan las grandes categorías identificadas con la clave a la derecha. Los símbolos con numeros en su parte superior (⋏1) identifican las subcategorías (véase la clave completa en la página I · 1).

Les symboles de l'index représentent les catégories indiquées dans la légende à droite. Les symboles suivis d'un indice (⋏1) représentent des sous-catégories (voir légende complète à la page I · 1).

Os símbolos incluídos no texto do índice representam as grandes categorias identificadas com a chave à direita. Os símbolos com números em sua parte superior (⋏1) identificam as subcategorias (veja-se a chave completa à página I · 1).

∧ Mountain	Berg	Montaña	Montagne	Montanha
⋏ Mountains	Gebirge	Montañas	Montagnes	Montanhas
× Pass	Paß	Paso	Col	Passo
V Valley, Canyon	Tal, Cañon	Valle, Cañón	Vallée, Canyon	Vale, Canhão
≃ Plain	Ebene	Llano	Plaine	Planície
› Cape	Kap	Cabo	Cap	Cabo
I Island	Insel	Isla	Île	Ilha
II Islands	Inseln	Islas	Îles	Ilhas
⊥ Other Topographic Features	Andere Topographische Objekte	Otros Elementos Topográficos	Autres données topographiques	Outros acidentes topográficos

Henn-Hima *I* · *71*

ESPAÑOL Nombre	Página	Lat.°′	Long.°′ W = Oeste
Hennersdorf	264b	48.07 N	16.22 E
Hennessey	196	36.06 N	97.53 W
Hennessey, Lake ⊜[1]	226	38.29 N	122.22 W
Hennickendorf	54	52.30 N	13.51 E
Henniez	58	46.44 N	6.54 E
Hennigsdorf	54	52.38 N	13.12 E
Henniker	188	43.10 N	71.49 W
Henning, Il., U.S.	216	40.18 N	87.42 W
Henning, Mn., U.S.	198	46.19 N	95.26 W
Henning, Tn., U.S.	194	35.40 N	89.34 W
Henri ≃	206	46.30 N	71.47 W
Henri, Cap ›	186	49.48 N	64.23 W
Henri-Chapelle	56	50.40 N	5.56 E
Henrichemont	50	47.18 N	2.32 E
Henrichenburg	263	51.35 N	7.19 E
Henrico □[6]	208	37.30 N	77.20 W
Henrietta, N.Y., U.S.	210	43.03 N	77.36 W
Henrietta, N.C., U.S.	192	35.15 N	81.47 W
Henrietta, Tx., U.S.	196	33.49 N	98.11 W
Henrietta Maria, Cape ›	176	55.09 N	82.20 W
Henri Pittier, Parque Nacional ♦	246	10.25 N	67.43 W
Henry, Il., U.S.	190	41.06 N	89.21 W
Henry, S.D., U.S.	198	44.52 N	97.27 W
Henry □[6], In., U.S.	218	39.55 N	85.22 W
Henry □[6], Ky., U.S.	218	38.26 N	85.09 W
Henry □[6], Oh., U.S.	216	41.20 N	84.04 W
Henry ≃	162	22.40 S	115.40 E
Henry, Cape ›	208	36.55 N	76.01 W
Henry, Mount ∧	202	48.53 N	115.31 W
Henry, Mount ∧[2]	274a	33.50 S	150.38 E
Henry, Point ›	162	34.29 S	119.23 E
Henry Cowell Redwoods State Park ♦	226	37.02 N	122.03 W
Henryetta	196	35.26 N	95.58 W
Henry Island I	224	48.35 N	123.11 W
Henry Kater, Cape ›	176	69.05 N	66.44 W
Henry Mountains ⋏	200	38.00 N	110.50 W
Henrys Bend	214	41.28 N	79.37 W
Henrys Fork ≃, U.S.	200	41.00 N	109.39 W
Henrys Fork ≃, Id., U.S.	202	43.45 N	111.56 W
Henryville, P.Q., Can.	206	45.08 N	73.11 W
Henryville, In., U.S.	218	38.32 N	85.46 W
Henry W. Coe State Park ♦	226	37.12 N	121.30 W
Hensall	190	43.26 N	81.30 W
Henshaw, Lake ⊜[1]	204	33.15 N	116.45 W
Hensley	194	34.30 N	92.12 W
Hensley Lake ⊜[1]	226	37.07 N	119.53 W
Henslow, Cape ›	175e	9.56 S	160.38 E
Henson Creek ≃	284b	38.46 N	77.00 W
Hensonville	210	42.17 N	74.13 W
Henstedt-Ulzburg	52	53.47 N	9.58 E
Henstridge	42	50.59 N	2.24 W
Hentiesbaai	156	22.08 S	14.18 E
Henty	166	35.31 S	147.02 E
Henzada	110	17.38 N	95.28 E
Hepburn	184	52.31 N	106.43 W
Hepburn Springs	169	37.19 S	144.09 E
Hephzibah	192	33.18 N	82.05 W
Heping, Zhg.	100	27.10 N	117.18 E
Heping, Zhg.	100	22.01 N	112.59 E
Heping, Zhg.	100	23.17 N	116.29 E
Heping, Zhg.	100	24.28 N	114.58 E
Heping, Zhg.	106	30.50 N	119.54 E
Heppenheim	56	49.39 N	8.38 E
Heppner	202	45.21 N	119.33 W
Heptonstall	262	53.45 N	2.01 W
Heptonstall Moor ≃	262	53.46 N	2.05 W
Hepu (Lianzhou)	102	21.39 N	109.11 E
Hepworth	212	44.37 N	81.09 W
Heqiao, Zhg.	100	32.55 N	118.22 E
Heqiao, Zhg.	106	31.30 N	119.53 E
Heqing	102	26.34 N	100.12 E
Hequ	102	39.26 N	111.08 E
Héraðsflói ⊂	24a	65.45 N	14.10 W
Hera Lacinia, Tempio di ⊥	68	39.01 N	17.13 E
Herāt	128	34.20 N	62.12 E
Herāt □[4]	128	34.30 N	62.00 E
Hérault □[5]	32	43.40 N	3.30 E
Hérault ≃	32	43.17 N	3.26 E
Herbasse ≃	62	45.02 N	4.57 E
Herbault	50	47.36 N	1.08 E
Herbede	56	51.25 N	7.16 E
Herbern	52	51.44 N	7.39 E
Herbert, Sk., Can.	184	50.26 N	107.12 W
Herbert, N.Z.	172	45.14 S	170.47 E
Herbert ≃	166	18.32 S	146.17 E
Herbert, Mount ∧	172	43.41 S	172.44 E
Herbertabad	110	11.43 N	92.37 E
Herbert Hoover National Historic Site ⊥	190	41.38 N	91.23 W
Herbertingen	58	48.04 N	9.26 E
Herbert Island I	180	52.45 N	170.10 W
Herberton	166	17.23 S	145.23 E
Herbertsdale	158	34.01 S	21.46 E
Herbeumont	56	49.47 N	5.14 E
Herbignac	32	47.27 N	2.19 W
Herb Lake	184	54.47 N	99.47 W
Herblay	50	49.00 N	2.10 E
Herblet Lake ⊜	184	54.56 N	99.54 W
Herbolzheim	58	48.13 N	7.47 E
Herborn	56	50.40 N	8.17 E
Herbrechtingen	56	48.37 N	10.10 E
Herbringhauser-Stausee ⊜[1]	263	51.14 N	7.16 E
Herbsleben	54	51.07 N	10.50 E
Herbstein	56	50.34 N	9.20 E
Herceg-Novi	38	42.27 N	18.32 E
Herculaneum	219	38.16 N	90.22 W
Hércules, Méx.	232	28.02 N	103.48 W
Hercules, Ca., U.S.	282	38.01 N	122.17 W
Herdecke	56	51.24 N	7.26 E
Herdorf	56	50.46 N	7.56 E
Herðubreið ∧	24a	65.13 N	16.18 W
Heredia	236	10.00 N	84.07 W
Heredia □[4]	236	10.30 N	84.00 W
Hereford, Eng., U.K.	42	52.04 N	2.43 W
Hereford, Az., U.S.	200	31.26 N	110.05 W
Hereford, Md., U.S.	208	39.35 N	76.39 W
Hereford, Tx., U.S.	196	34.48 N	102.23 W
Hereford and Worcester □[6]	42	52.10 N	2.30 W
Hereford Cathedral ♁[1]	42	52.04 N	2.43 W
Hereford Mountain ∧	206	45.05 N	71.36 W
Hereke	130	40.48 N	29.39 E
Herekino	172	35.15 S	173.13 E
Herencia	34	39.21 N	3.22 W
Herent	56	50.54 N	4.40 E
Herentals	56	51.11 N	4.50 E
Hereroland Oos □[5]	156	21.00 S	20.00 E
Hereroland Wes □[5]	156	20.30 S	18.15 E
Herfølge	41	55.25 N	12.10 E
Herford	52	52.06 N	8.40 E
Hergatz	58	47.39 N	9.50 E
Hergisdorf	54	51.32 N	11.28 E
Hergla	36	36.02 N	10.31 E
Herhahn	56	50.33 N	6.26 E
Héricourt	58	47.35 N	6.45 E
Hérimoncourt	58	47.26 N	6.53 E
Heringen	54	51.27 N	10.52 E
Heringsdorf	54	54.18 N	11.00 E
Herington	198	38.40 N	96.56 W
Heriot	172	45.50 S	169.16 E
Herisau	58	47.23 N	9.17 E
Heritage Range ⋏	9	79.30 S	84.00 W
Herk ≃	56	50.58 N	5.07 E
Herk-de-Stad	56	50.56 N	5.10 E
Herkimer	210	43.01 N	74.59 W
Herkimer □[6]	210	43.02 N	74.59 W
Herlen → Kerulen ≃	90	48.48 N	117.00 E
Herleshausen	56	51.00 N	10.09 E
Herlev	41	55.43 N	12.27 E

FRANÇAIS Nom	Page	Lat.°′	Long.°′ W = Ouest
Herlong	204	40.09 N	120.08 W
Herlufmagle	41	55.19 N	11.46 E
Herlufsholm	41	55.15 N	11.46 E
Hermagor	64	46.37 N	13.22 E
Herman, Mn., U.S.	198	45.48 N	96.08 W
Herman, Ne., U.S.	198	41.40 N	96.12 W
Herman, Pa., U.S.	214	40.50 N	79.49 W
Herman, Lake ⊜	282	38.05 N	122.09 W
Hermana Mayor Island I	116	15.48 N	119.48 E
Hermanas	196	27.13 N	101.14 W
Herman Eksteen Park ♦	273d	26.10 S	28.02 E
Herma Ness ›	46a	60.50 N	0.55 W
Hermann	219	38.42 N	91.26 W
Hermannsburg, Austl.	162	23.57 S	132.45 E
Hermannsburg, Dtsch.	52	52.50 N	10.05 E
Hermannsburg Aboriginal Reserve ◆[4]	162	24.00 S	132.45 E
Hermanns-Denkmal ⊥	52	51.55 N	8.50 E
Hermannskogel ∧	264b	48.16 N	16.18 E
Hermannstadt → Sibiu	38	45.48 N	24.09 E
Hermano Peak ∧	200	37.13 N	108.48 W
Hermansverk	26	61.11 N	6.51 E
Hermansville	190	45.42 N	87.36 W
Hermanus	158	34.25 S	19.16 E
Hermanville	194	31.57 N	90.50 W
Hermeray	261	48.38 N	1.41 E
Hermes	50	49.22 N	2.15 E
Hermeskeil	56	49.39 N	6.56 E
Hermidale	166	31.33 S	146.43 E
Hermies	50	50.07 N	3.02 E
Herminie	214	40.15 N	79.43 W
Hermiston	202	45.50 N	119.17 W
Hermitage, Nf., Can.	186	47.33 N	55.56 W
Hermitage, Eng., U.K.	42	51.27 N	1.16 W
Hermitage, Ar., U.S.	194	33.26 N	92.10 W
Hermitage, Mo., U.S.	194	37.56 N	93.18 W
Hermitage Bay ⊂	186	47.35 N	56.05 W
Hermitage Park	284c	39.05 N	77.04 W
Hermite, Isla I	254	55.52 S	67.20 W
Hermit Islands II	164	1.30 S	145.05 E
Hermleigh	196	32.38 N	100.46 W
Hermon, S. Afr.	158	33.27 S	18.59 E
Hermon, N.Y., U.S.	212	44.28 N	75.13 W
Hermon, Mount → Shaykh, Jabal ash- ∧	132	33.26 N	35.51 E
Hermosa Beach	280	33.51 N	118.23 W
Hermosillo, Méx.	200	32.30 N	114.59 W
Hermosillo, Méx.	232	29.04 N	110.58 W
Hermoso, Cerro ∧	246	1.10 S	78.12 W
Hermsdorf	54	50.54 N	11.52 E
Hermsdorf ◆[8]	264a	52.37 N	13.18 E
Hermyingyi	110	14.15 N	98.21 E
Hernád ≃	30	47.56 N	21.08 E
Hernals ◆[8]	264b	48.13 N	16.20 E
Hernandarias	252	25.22 S	54.45 W
Hernández	234	23.01 N	102.01 W
Hernandez Reservoir ⊜[1]	226	36.22 N	120.49 W
Hernando, Arg.	252	32.25 S	63.44 W
Hernando, Fl., U.S.	220	28.54 N	82.22 W
Hernando, Ms., U.S.	194	34.49 N	89.59 W
Hernando □[6]	220	28.34 N	82.22 W
Hernando de Magallanes, Parque Nacional ♦	254	54.15 S	72.00 W
Hernani	116	11.20 N	125.37 E
Herndon, Ca., U.S.	226	36.49 N	119.54 W
Herndon, Ks., U.S.	198	39.54 N	100.47 W
Herndon, Pa., U.S.	210	40.42 N	76.50 W
Herndon, Va., U.S.	208	38.58 N	77.23 W
Herndon Canal ≅	226	36.46 N	119.46 W
Herne	52	51.32 N	7.13 E
Herne Bay	42	51.23 N	1.08 E
Herne Hill	168a	31.50 S	116.01 E
Herning	41	56.08 N	8.59 E
Hernwood Heights	284b	39.22 N	77.50 W
Heroica Zitácuaro	234	19.24 N	100.22 W
Herongate	260	51.36 N	0.21 E
Herongen	56	51.24 N	6.15 E
Heron Island I	166	23.26 S	151.55 E
Heron Lake	198	43.47 N	95.19 W
Hérons, Île aux I	275a	45.25 N	73.35 W
Heronsgate	260	51.38 N	0.31 W
Hérouville	261	49.06 N	2.08 E
Hérouville-Saint-Clair	32	49.12 N	0.21 W
Herpf	54	50.34 N	10.20 E
Herradura	252	26.29 S	58.18 W
Herräng	40	60.08 N	18.39 E
Herreid	198	45.50 N	100.04 W
Herrenalb	56	48.48 N	8.26 E
Herrenberg	56	48.35 N	8.52 E
Herrenchiemsee, Schloss ⊥	64	47.52 N	12.23 E
Herrera	252	28.29 S	63.04 W
Herrera □[4]	236	7.54 N	80.38 W
Herrera del Duque	34	39.10 N	5.03 W
Herrera de Pisuerga	34	42.36 N	4.20 W
Herrick, Austl.	166	41.06 S	147.52 E
Herrick, Il., U.S.	219	39.13 N	88.59 W
Herrick Creek ≃	182	54.20 N	121.30 W
Herrick Grove	212	44.04 N	76.12 W
Herricks	276	40.45 N	73.40 W
Herrieden	56	49.14 N	10.30 E
Herrin	194	37.48 N	89.01 W
Herring Bay ⊂	208	38.44 N	76.33 W
Herring Brook ≃	283	42.10 N	70.44 W
Herring Cove, N.S., Can.	186	44.34 N	63.34 W
Herring Cove, Ak., U.S.	182	55.21 N	131.41 W
Herring Creek ≃	208	37.49 N	77.07 W
Herringen	52	51.40 N	7.44 E
Herring Run ≃	284b	39.18 N	76.31 W
Herring Run Park ♦	284b	39.19 N	76.33 W
Herritslev	41	54.42 N	11.41 E
Herrljunga	26	58.05 N	13.02 E
Herrnburg	54	53.47 N	10.45 E
Herrnhut	54	51.01 N	14.44 E
Herrsching am Ammersee	60	48.00 N	11.10 E
Herrs Island I	279b	40.28 N	79.58 W
Herrskogen	40	59.32 N	16.15 E
Herry	50	47.13 N	2.57 E
Hersbruck	60	49.30 N	11.26 E
Herschbach	56	50.34 N	7.44 E
Herscheid	56	51.10 N	7.44 E
Herschel, Sk., Can.	184	51.38 N	108.21 W
Herschel, Transkei	158	30.37 S	27.12 E
Herschel Island I	180	69.35 N	139.05 W
Herscher	216	41.03 N	88.06 W
Herselt	56	51.03 N	4.53 E
Herserange	56	49.31 N	5.47 E
Hersham	260	51.22 N	0.23 W
Hershey, Ne., U.S.	198	41.09 N	101.00 W
Hershey, Pa., U.S.	208	40.17 N	76.39 W
Hersman	219	39.57 N	90.44 W
Herstadberg	40	58.38 N	16.10 E
Herstal	56	50.40 N	5.38 E
Herstmonceux	42	50.53 N	0.20 E
Herten	52	51.35 N	7.07 E
Hertford, Eng., U.K.	260	51.48 N	0.05 W
Hertford, N.C., U.S.	192	36.11 N	76.27 W
Hertford □[6]	208	36.28 N	77.01 W
Hertfordshire □[6]	42	51.50 N	0.10 W
Hertingfordbury	260	51.48 N	0.06 W
Hertsmere □[8]	260	51.41 N	0.17 W
Hertzogville	158	28.08 S	25.33 E
Heruncun	104	40.58 N	123.27 E
Hervás	34	40.16 N	5.51 W
Herve	56	50.38 N	5.48 E
Hervest	263	51.40 N	7.01 E
Hervey Bay ⊂	166	25.00 S	153.00 E
Herxheim	56	49.09 N	8.13 E
Héry, Fr.	50	47.54 N	3.38 E

PORTUGUÊS Nome	Página	Lat.°′	Long.°′ W = Oeste
Héry, Fr.	62	45.46 N	6.28 E
Herzberg, Dtsch.	54	52.54 N	12.58 E
Herzberg, Dtsch.	54	51.41 N	13.14 E
Herzberg am Harz	52	51.39 N	10.20 E
Herzebrock	52	51.53 N	8.14 E
Herzfelde	54	52.29 N	13.50 E
Herzhausen	56	51.11 N	8.53 E
Herzliyya	132	32.10 N	34.51 E
Herznach	58	47.28 N	8.03 E
Herzogenaurach	56	49.34 N	10.53 E
Herzogenbuchsee	58	47.12 N	7.41 E
Herzogenburg	61	48.17 N	15.42 E
Herzogenrath	56	50.52 N	6.06 E
Herzsprung	54	53.04 N	12.28 E
Heṣār, Kūh-e ⋏	120	34.50 N	66.30 E
Hesarak	267d	35.47 N	51.19 E
Hesdin	50	50.22 N	2.02 E
Hesel	52	53.18 N	7.35 E
Hesepe	52	52.26 N	7.58 E
Heshachang	107	30.37 N	105.40 E
Heshan	110	23.52 N	108.52 E
Heshangqiao	100	34.15 N	113.47 E
Heshengqiao	100	30.00 N	114.22 E
Heshi, Zhg.	100	25.04 N	118.37 E
Heshi, Zhg.	107	29.10 N	104.22 E
Heshui, Zhg.	100	24.24 N	114.56 E
Heshui, Zhg.	102	22.48 N	112.29 E
Heshuijian	100	30.33 N	116.05 E
Heshun, Zhg.	100	27.30 N	117.24 E
Heshun, Zhg.	102	37.21 N	113.35 E
Heshuo	86	42.15 N	86.53 E
Hesketh Bank	262	53.42 N	2.51 W
Hesketh Out Marsh ≋	262	53.43 N	2.55 W
Heskin Green	262	53.38 N	2.42 W
Hesler	218	38.28 N	84.47 W
Hesperange	56	49.34 N	6.09 E
Hesperia, Ca., U.S.	228	34.25 N	117.18 W
Hesperia, Mi., U.S.	190	43.34 N	86.02 W
Hesperus Mountain ∧	200	37.27 N	108.05 W
Hess ≃	180	63.34 N	133.57 W
Hesselager	41	55.10 N	10.45 E
Hesselberg ∧	56	49.04 N	10.32 E
Hesselø I	41	56.12 N	11.43 E
Hesselte	52	52.25 N	7.22 E
Hessen	54	52.02 N	10.15 E
Hessen □[3]	30	50.30 N	9.15 E
Hessen Cassal	216	41.00 N	85.05 W
Hessenthal	56	49.55 N	9.17 E
Hessisch Lichtenau	56	51.12 N	9.43 E
Hessisch Oldendorf	52	52.10 N	9.15 E
Hessle	44	53.44 N	0.26 W
Hesso	166	32.08 S	137.27 E
Hess Tablemount ✢[3]	14	17.50 N	174.15 W
Hesston, Ks., U.S.	198	38.08 N	97.25 W
Hesston, Pa., U.S.	214	40.26 N	78.07 W
Heston ◆[8]	260	51.29 N	0.22 W
Heswall	262	53.20 N	3.06 W
Het ≃	110	20.49 N	104.01 E
Hetai	102	23.22 N	112.19 E
Hetanbu	100	28.21 N	117.11 E
Hetang, Zhg.	100	26.40 N	119.09 E
Hetang, Zhg.	106	31.43 N	120.27 E
Hetang, Zhg.	107	28.58 N	106.03 E
Hetaundā	124	85.02 N	27.26 E
Hetch Hetchy Aqueduct ≅[1]	226	37.29 N	122.19 W
Hetch Hetchy Reservoir ⊜[1]	226	37.57 N	119.43 W
Hethersett	42	52.36 N	1.11 E
Hetian, Zhg.	100	25.41 N	116.26 E
Hetian, Zhg.	100	23.19 N	115.38 E
Het Loo, Paleis ♁	52	52.14 N	5.56 E
Hetou	100	24.18 N	113.29 E
Hetoudian	98	37.02 N	120.35 E
Hettange-Grande	56	49.24 N	6.09 E
Hettenleidelheim	56	49.32 N	8.04 E
Hettick	219	39.21 N	90.02 W
Hettingen	58	48.13 N	9.14 E
Hettinger	198	46.00 N	102.38 W
Hetton-le-Hole	44	54.50 N	1.27 W
Hettstedt	54	51.38 N	11.30 E
Hetupu	100	30.50 N	116.03 E
Hetzendorf ◆[8]	264b	48.10 N	16.18 E
Hetzerath	56	49.52 N	6.49 E
Het Zoute	50	51.21 N	3.18 E
Heuchin	50	50.28 N	2.16 E
Heudeber	54	51.54 N	10.50 E
Heule	50	50.50 N	3.14 E
Heuningspruit	158	27.26 S	27.28 E
Heusden	50	51.02 N	5.16 E
Heustreu	56	50.21 N	10.15 E
Heusweiler	56	49.20 N	6.55 E
Heuvelton	212	44.37 N	75.24 W
Hève, Cap de la ›	50	49.31 N	0.04 E
Heven	263	51.26 N	7.17 E
Heverlee	56	50.52 N	4.42 E
Heves	30	47.36 N	20.17 E
Heves □[6]	30	47.50 N	20.15 E
Hevlín	61	48.45 N	16.23 E
Ḥevron, Naḥal V	132	31.15 N	34.50 E
Hewanorra International Airport ⊠	241f	13.45 N	60.56 W
Hewitt, N.J., U.S.	210	41.08 N	74.18 W
Hewitt, Tx., U.S.	222	31.27 N	97.11 W
Hewittsville	219	39.32 N	89.19 W
Hewlett, N.Y., U.S.	276	40.38 N	73.41 W
Hewlett, Va., U.S.	208	37.55 N	77.35 W
Hewlett Bay Park	276	40.38 N	73.42 W
Hewlett Harbor	276	40.38 N	73.41 W
Hewlett Neck	276	40.37 N	73.42 W
Hewlett Point ›	276	40.50 N	73.45 W
Hewopu	104	41.14 N	122.24 E
Hewu	100	26.41 N	113.40 E
Hexen Kopf ∧	58	47.01 N	10.28 E
Hexham	44	54.58 N	2.06 W
Hexi, Zhg.	100	24.52 N	117.15 E
Hexi, Zhg.	102	24.09 N	102.39 E
Hexi, Zhg.	106	31.03 N	119.49 E
Hexian, Zhg.	100	31.43 N	118.22 E
Hexian, Zhg.	102	24.15 N	111.43 E
Hexibao	102	38.34 N	102.11 E
Hexingchang	107	30.05 N	104.35 E
Hexingjie	106	31.55 N	120.36 E
Hexiwu	105	39.38 N	116.58 E
Hex Rivierberge ⋏	158	33.25 S	19.37 E
Hextable	260	51.25 N	0.11 E
Hexton	172	38.37 S	177.58 E
Heyan	104	42.30 N	120.29 E
Heyang, Zhg.	98	35.27 N	118.33 E
Heyang, Zhg.	102	35.15 N	110.06 E
Heybeli ◆[8]	267b	40.53 N	29.05 E
Heybeli Ada I	267b	40.53 N	29.05 E
Heybridge	260	51.44 N	0.41 E
Heyburn	202	42.33 N	113.45 W
Heyerode	54	51.10 N	10.25 E
Heyrieux	62	45.38 N	5.03 E
Heysham	44	54.02 N	2.54 W
Heyuan	100	23.44 N	114.41 E
Heywood, Austl.	166	38.08 S	141.38 E
Heywood, Eng., U.K.	262	53.36 N	2.13 W
Heyworth	216	40.18 N	88.58 W
Heze (Caozhou)	98	35.17 N	115.27 E
Hezhang	102	27.00 N	104.37 E
Hezhao	98	37.08 N	115.17 E
Hezhen	100	29.56 N	120.10 E
Hezheng	102	35.25 N	103.10 E
Hezijian	105	40.13 N	116.03 E
Hezixu	100	24.54 N	115.14 E
Hezuo	102	34.58 N	102.57 E
Hiale	110	15.55 N	107.34 E
Hialeah	220	25.51 N	80.16 W
Hialeah Park Race Track ♦	220	25.51 N	80.17 W
Hiaohexi	100	31.21 N	114.02 E
Hiawassee	192	34.56 N	83.45 W
Hiawatha, Ks., U.S.	198	39.51 N	95.32 W
Hiawatha, Ut,. U.S.	200	39.29 N	111.00 W
Hiba-Dōgo-Taishaku-kokutei-kōen ♦	96	35.07 N	133.08 E

Hibaldstow	44	53.31 N	0.32 W
Hibbing	190	47.25 N	92.56 W
Hibbs, Point ›	166	42.38 S	145.15 E
Hibernia	276	40.57 N	74.30 W
Hibernia Reef ✢[2]	160	12.00 S	123.23 E
Hibiki-nada ⊤[2]	96	34.00 N	130.30 E
Hiburi-shima I	96	33.10 N	132.17 E
Hibuson Island I	116	10.27 N	125.29 E
Hickam Air Force Base ■	229c	21.20 N	157.57 W
Hickey, Mount ∧	169	37.22 S	145.19 E
Hickman, Ca., U.S.	226	37.37 N	120.45 W
Hickman, Ky., U.S.	194	36.34 N	89.11 W
Hickman, Ne., U.S.	198	40.37 N	96.37 W
Hickman, Pa., U.S.	279b	40.23 N	80.09 W
Hickman's Harbour	186	48.06 N	53.44 W
Hickory, Ms., U.S.	194	32.19 N	89.01 W
Hickory, N.C., U.S.	192	35.43 N	81.20 W
Hickory, Pa., U.S.	214	40.18 N	80.18 W
Hickory Corners	216	42.26 N	85.22 W
Hickory Creek ≃, Il., U.S.	278	41.30 N	88.06 W
Hickory Creek ≃, Mi., U.S.	216	42.05 N	86.29 W
Hickory Creek ≃, Tx., U.S.	222	31.29 N	95.07 W
Hickory Flat	194	34.36 N	89.11 W
Hickory Hills	216	41.43 N	87.49 W
Hickory Run State Park ♦	210	41.02 N	75.41 W
Hickory Township	214	41.15 N	80.27 W
Hicks, Point ›	166	37.48 S	149.17 E
Hicks Bay	172	37.36 S	178.18 E
Hickson Lake ⊜	184	56.17 N	104.25 W
Hicksville, N.Y., U.S.	210	40.46 N	73.31 W
Hicksville, Oh., U.S.	216	41.17 N	84.45 W
Hico	196	31.58 N	98.02 W
Hicpochee, Lake ⊜	220	26.50 N	81.10 W
Hida ≃	94	35.26 N	137.03 E
Hida → Hita	96	33.19 N	130.56 E
Hidaka, Nihon	94	35.54 N	139.21 E
Hidaka, Nihon	96	35.28 N	134.47 E
Hidaka, Nihon	96	33.55 N	135.09 E
Hidaka ≃	96	33.52 N	135.09 E
Hidaka-sammyaku ⋏	92a	42.35 N	142.45 E
Hida-Kiso-gawa-kokutei-kōen ♦	94	35.37 N	137.15 E
Hida-kōchi ⋏[1]	94	36.16 N	137.05 E
Hidalgo, Méx.	232	27.47 N	99.52 W
Hidalgo, Méx.	232	25.59 N	100.27 W
Hidalgo, Méx.	232	24.15 N	99.26 W
Hidalgo □[3]	234	20.30 N	99.00 W
Hidalgo del Parral	232	26.56 N	105.40 W
Hida-sammyaku ⋏	94	36.25 N	137.40 E
Hiddenhausen	52	52.08 N	8.38 E
Hidden Hills	228	34.09 N	118.43 W
Hiddensee I	54	54.33 N	13.07 E
Hidden Valley, Ca., U.S.	226	38.46 N	121.09 W
Hidden Valley, Tx., U.S.	222	29.54 N	95.25 W
Hiddesen	52	51.55 N	8.50 E
Hiddinghausen	263	51.22 N	7.17 E
Hıdırbaba	130	38.47 N	39.00 E
Hidrolândia	255	16.58 S	49.14 W
Hidrolina	255	14.37 S	49.25 W
Hieflau	61	47.36 N	14.44 E
Hienghène	175f	20.41 S	164.56 E
Hierapolis → Pamukkale ⊥	130	37.58 N	29.19 E
Hierges	56	50.06 N	4.44 E
Hierro (Ferro) I	148	27.45 N	18.00 W
Hiesfeld	263	51.33 N	6.46 E
Hietzing ◆[8]	264b	48.11 N	16.18 E
Higashi	174m	26.38 N	128.09 E
Higashi ◆[8]	270	34.41 N	135.31 E
Higashibetsuin	270	34.56 N	135.34 E
Higashifuji-enshūjō ■	94	35.17 N	138.51 E
Higashihiroshima	96	34.26 N	132.42 E
Higashiichiki	92	31.40 N	130.20 E
Higashiiyayama	96	33.52 N	133.54 E
Higashiizu	94	34.48 N	139.04 E
Higashi-jima I	174f	24.47 N	141.23 E
Higashikurume	268	35.45 N	139.32 E
Higashimatsuyama	94	36.02 N	139.24 E
Higashimonzen	268	35.56 N	139.40 E
Higashimurayama	94	35.46 N	139.29 E
Higashinada ◆[8]	270	34.43 N	135.16 E
Higashinakano	268	35.38 N	139.25 E
Higashinari ◆[8]	270	34.40 N	135.33 E
Higashine	92	38.26 N	140.24 E
Higashinose	270	34.55 N	135.30 E
Higashiōizumi ◆[8]	268	35.45 N	139.36 E
Higashiōsaka	96	34.39 N	135.35 E
Higashishirakawa	94	35.39 N	137.19 E
Higashisumiyoshi ◆[8]	270	34.37 N	135.32 E
Higashitokonoo-san ∧	96	35.25 N	134.55 E
Higashitsuno	96	33.23 N	133.02 E
Higashiura, Nihon	94	34.59 N	136.58 E
Higashiura, Nihon	270	34.33 N	135.00 E
Higashiyama ◆[8]	270	35.00 N	135.48 E
Higashiyamato	268	35.44 N	139.26 E
Higashiyodogawa ◆[8]	270	34.44 N	135.31 E
Higashiyoshino	94	34.24 N	135.58 E
Higbee	194	39.18 N	92.30 W
Higganum	207	41.29 N	72.33 W
Higgins	196	36.07 N	100.02 W
Higgins, Mount ∧	224	48.19 N	121.45 W
Higgins Lake ⊜	190	44.30 N	84.45 W
Higginsport	218	38.47 N	83.58 W
Higginsville, Austl.	162	31.45 S	121.43 E
Higginsville, Mo., U.S.	194	39.04 N	93.43 W
Higgs' Hope	158	29.19 S	23.16 E
Higham Ferrers	42	52.18 N	0.36 W
Higham Upshire	260	51.26 N	0.28 E
Highbank	222	31.10 N	96.50 W
High Bank Creek ≃	216	42.37 N	85.11 W
High Bar Indian Reserve ◆[4]	182	51.06 N	122.00 W
High Beach	260	51.39 N	0.02 E
High Bentham	44	54.08 N	2.30 W
High Bluff Island I	212	43.58 N	77.45 W
Highbridge, Eng., U.K.	42	51.13 N	2.49 W
High Bridge, N.J., U.S.	210	40.40 N	74.53 W
Highbury	164	16.25 S	143.09 E
Highcliff	279b	40.32 N	80.03 W
Higher Ballam	262	53.46 N	2.59 W
Higher Broughton ◆[8]	262	53.30 N	2.15 W
Higher Hogshead ∧[2]	262	53.42 N	2.09 W
Higher Penwortham	262	53.45 N	2.44 W
Higher Walton, Eng., U.K.	44	53.44 N	2.39 W
Higher Walton, Eng., U.K.	262	53.22 N	2.37 W
Higher Walton, Eng., U.K.	262	53.45 N	2.38 W
Higher Whitley	262	53.19 N	2.35 W
Highett	274b	37.57 S	145.03 E
High Falls	210	41.50 N	74.08 W
High Falls ⌊	212	43.56 N	75.23 W
High Force ⌊	44	54.38 N	2.13 W
Highgate	214	42.30 N	81.49 W
Highgate Center	206	44.56 N	73.02 W
Highgate Springs	206	44.58 N	73.06 W
Highgrove	228	34.01 N	117.20 W
High Halstow	260	51.27 N	0.34 E
High Hesket	44	54.48 N	2.48 W
High Hill	219	38.52 N	91.23 W
High Hill ∧[2]	276	40.49 N	73.25 W
High Hill ≃, Can.	184	56.45 N	110.30 W
High Hill ≃, Mb., Can.	184	55.52 N	94.42 W
High Hill Lake ⊜	184	55.34 N	95.40 W
High Island I, H.K.	271d	22.22 N	114.21 E

High Island I, Mi., U.S.	190	45.42 N	85.40 W
High Island Creek ≃	190	44.35 N	93.54 W
High Island Reservoir ⊜[1]	271d	22.23 N	114.21 W
Highland, Ca., U.S.	228	34.07 N	117.12 W
Highland, Il., U.S.	219	38.44 N	89.40 W
Highland, In., U.S.	216	41.33 N	87.27 W
Highland, Ks., U.S.	198	39.51 N	95.16 W
Highland, Md., U.S.	208	39.11 N	76.57 W
Highland, Mi., U.S.	281	42.38 N	83.37 W
Highland, N.Y., U.S.	210	41.43 N	73.57 W
Highland, Oh., U.S.	218	39.21 N	83.36 W
Highland, Pa., U.S.	279b	40.33 N	80.04 W
Highland □[4]	46	57.40 N	5.00 W
Highland □[6]	218	39.12 N	83.37 W
Highland Beach	220	26.25 N	80.04 W
Highland City	220	27.58 N	81.53 W
Highland Creek ≃, On., Can.	275b	43.46 N	79.08 W
Highland Creek ≃, Ca., U.S.	226	38.24 N	121.14 W
Highland Falls	210	41.22 N	73.58 W
Highland Heights, Ky., U.S.	218	39.04 N	84.27 W
Highland Heights, Oh., U.S.	214	41.33 N	81.28 W
Highland Hills	278	41.52 N	88.01 W
Highland Home	194	31.57 N	86.18 W
Highland Lake, Il., U.S.	278	42.21 N	88.04 W
Highland Lake, Ma., U.S.	283	42.41 N	72.37 W
Highland Lake, N.Y., U.S.	210	41.32 N	74.51 W
Highland Lake ⊜, Ct., U.S.	207	41.54 N	73.06 W
Highland Lake ⊜, Il., U.S.	278	42.22 N	88.04 W
Highland Lake ⊜, N.J., U.S.	276	41.10 N	74.28 W
Highland Lakes	210	41.10 N	74.28 W
Highland-on-the-Lake	284a	42.42 N	79.59 W
Highland Park, Il., U.S.	216	42.10 N	87.48 W
Highland Park, Md., U.S.	284c	38.54 N	76.54 W
Highland Park, Mi., U.S.	216	42.24 N	83.05 W
Highland Park, N.J., U.S.	210	40.29 N	74.25 W
Highland Park, Pa., U.S.	210	40.38 N	77.35 W
Highland Park, Tx., U.S.	222	32.50 N	96.48 W
Highland Park ◆[8]	280	34.07 N	118.13 W
Highland Park ♦, Ma., U.S.	283	42.30 N	70.55 W
Highland Park ♦, Pa., U.S.	279b	40.29 N	79.55 W
Highland Peak ∧	226	38.33 N	119.45 W
Highland Point ›	220	25.30 N	81.12 W
Highlands, N.J., U.S.	208	40.24 N	73.59 W
Highlands, N.C., U.S.	192	35.03 N	83.11 W
Highlands, Tx., U.S.	222	29.49 N	95.03 W
Highlands □[6]	220	27.20 N	81.16 W
Highlands Hammock State Park ♦	220	27.28 N	81.33 W
Highland Silver Lake ⊜[1]	219	38.47 N	89.39 W
Highlands North ◆[8]	273d	26.09 S	28.05 E
Highland Springs	208	37.32 N	77.19 W
Highlands Reservoir ⊜[1]	222	29.50 N	95.02 W
Highland State Recreation Area ♦	216	42.39 N	83.33 W
Highlandtown ◆[8]	284b	39.17 N	76.33 W
High Laver	260	51.45 N	0.13 E
High Legh	262	53.21 N	2.27 W
Highley	42	52.27 N	2.23 W
Highmore	198	44.31 N	99.26 W
High Ongar	260	51.43 N	0.16 E
High Park ♦	275b	43.39 N	79.28 W
High Peak □[8]	262	53.23 N	1.55 W
High Peak ∧, Pil.	116	15.29 N	120.07 E
High Peak ∧, N.Y., U.S.	210	42.09 N	74.05 W
High Peak ◆[1]	44	53.22 N	1.50 W
High Point, Fl., U.S.	220	27.55 N	82.42 W
High Point, N.C., U.S.	192	35.57 N	80.00 W
Highpoint, Oh., U.S.	218	39.14 N	84.24 W
High Point ∧, N.J., U.S.	210	41.19 N	74.40 W
High Point ∧, Wy., U.S.	202	41.37 N	107.47 W
High Point State Park ♦	210	41.18 N	74.41 W
High Prairie	182	55.26 N	116.29 W
High Ridge	219	38.27 N	90.32 W
High River	182	50.35 N	113.52 W
High Rock	192	26.36 N	76.18 W
High Rock ∧	188	39.33 N	79.06 W
Highrock Indian Reserve ◆[4]	184	55.54 N	100.30 W
Highrock Lake ⊜, Mb., Can.	184	55.45 N	100.30 W
Highrock Lake ⊜, Sk., Can.	184	57.04 N	105.30 W
High Rock Lake ⊜[1]	192	35.40 N	80.17 W
High Seat ∧	44	54.24 N	2.18 W
High Spire	208	40.12 N	76.47 W
High Springs	192	29.49 N	82.35 W
High Street ∧	44	54.29 N	2.52 W
Hightown, Eng., U.K.	44	53.31 N	3.03 W
Hightown, Eng., U.K.	262	53.32 N	3.04 W
Hightstown	208	40.16 N	74.31 W
High View	210	41.33 N	74.27 W
Highwater	206	45.01 N	72.26 W
Highway City	226	36.49 N	119.54 W
High Willhays ∧	42	50.41 N	3.59 W
Highwood, Il., U.S.	216	42.11 N	87.48 W
Highwood, Mt., U.S.	202	47.35 N	110.47 W
Highwood ≃	182	50.49 N	113.47 W
Highwood Baldy ∧	202	47.27 N	110.37 W
Highwood Creek ≃	202	47.40 N	111.00 W
Highwood Mountains ⋏	202	47.25 N	110.30 W
Highworth	42	51.38 N	1.43 W
High Wycombe	42	51.38 N	0.46 W
Higlet	154	1.04 S	40.19 E
Higuera Blanca	234	19.42 N	105.10 W
Higuera de Abuya	232	24.16 N	107.04 W
Higuera de Zaragoza	232	25.59 N	109.16 W
Higueras	196	25.58 N	100.01 W
Higüero, Punta ›	240m	18.22 N	67.16 W
Higüey	238	18.37 N	68.42 W
Higuito ≃	236	14.43 N	88.40 W
Hihétro	150	7.32 N	1.06 E
Hihyā	142	30.40 N	31.36 E
Hii ≃	96	35.26 N	132.54 E
Hiidenportin kansallispuisto ♦	26	63.50 N	28.59 E
Hiiraan □[4]	144	4.00 N	45.30 E
Hiiumaa I	76	58.52 N	22.40 E
Hījānah, Buḥayrat al- ⊜	132	33.18 N	36.36 E
Híjar	34	41.10 N	0.27 W
Hiji	96	33.22 N	131.32 E
Hiji ≃	96	33.36 N	132.29 E
Hijikawa	96	33.27 N	132.41 E
Hijiri-dake ∧	94	35.26 N	138.10 E
Hikami	96	35.10 N	135.02 E
Hikari, Nihon	94	35.39 N	140.30 E
Hikari, Nihon	96	33.58 N	131.56 E
Hikarigaoka	268	35.50 N	139.58 E
Hikawa	96	35.25 N	132.50 E
Hikawa Shrine ♁[1]	268	35.54 N	139.38 E
Hiketa	96	34.13 N	134.24 E
Hiki ≃	96	33.33 N	135.27 E
Hikigawa	96	33.34 N	135.27 E

Hikimi	96	34.34 N	132.01 E
Hikimi ≃	96	34.37 N	131.48 E
Hikiura	270	34.33 N	134.58 E
Hikone	94	35.15 N	136.15 E
Hikone-jō ⊥	94	35.15 N	136.14 E
Hiko-san ∧	96	33.27 N	130.54 E
Hikueru I[1]	14	17.36 S	142.37 W
Hikurangi	172	35.36 S	174.18 E
Hikurangi ∧	172	37.55 S	178.04 E
Hikutaia	172	37.17 S	175.39 E
Hikutivake	174v	18.56 S	169.53 W
Hila	112	7.35 S	127.24 E
Hilaban Island I	116	12.03 N	125.34 E
Hilāl, Jabal ⋏	132	30.40 N	34.00 E
Hilāl, Ra's al- ›	146	32.57 N	22.10 E
Hilbersdorf	54	50.55 N	13.23 E
Hilbert	190	44.08 N	88.09 W
Hilbre Islands II	262	53.23 N	3.13 W
Hilbre Point ›	262	53.23 N	3.12 W
Hilchenbach	56	51.00 N	8.06 E
Hilda	184	50.28 N	110.03 W
Hildburghausen	54	50.25 N	10.44 E
Hilden	56	51.10 N	6.56 E
Hildenborough	260	51.13 N	0.15 E
Hilders	56	50.34 N	10.00 E
Hildesheim	52	52.09 N	9.57 E
Hildreth	198	40.20 N	99.02 W
Hilgen	263	51.06 N	7.09 E
Hilialawa	114	0.41 N	97.53 E
Hiligeo	114	1.22 N	97.10 E
Hiliotaluwa	114	0.44 N	97.53 E
Hill □[6]	222	32.02 N	97.10 W
Hillaby, Mount ∧	241g	13.12 N	59.35 W
Hill Air Force Base ■	202	41.05 N	111.58 W
Hillandale, S. Afr.	158	33.06 S	20.36 E
Hillandale, Md., U.S.	284c	39.01 N	76.58 W
Hillandale Heights	284c	39.01 N	76.59 W
Hill Bank	232	17.35 N	88.42 W
Hillburn	210	41.08 N	74.10 W
Hill City, Ks., U.S.	198	39.21 N	99.50 W
Hill City, Mn., U.S.	190	46.59 N	93.35 W
Hill City, S.D., U.S.	198	43.55 N	103.34 W
Hill Creek ≃	200	39.55 N	109.40 W
Hillcrest, Il., U.S.	216	41.57 N	89.04 W
Hillcrest, N.Y., U.S.	210	41.07 N	74.02 W
Hillcrest, N.Y., U.S.	210	42.09 N	75.53 W
Hillcrest Center	228	35.23 N	118.57 W
Hillcrest Heights	284c	38.49 N	76.57 W
Hillcrest Mines	182	49.34 N	114.23 W
Hillcrest Orchard	216	41.51 N	83.29 W
Hillcrest Park	226	38.07 N	122.16 W
Hill Cumorah ⊥	210	43.01 N	77.15 W
Hille, Dtsch.	52	52.20 N	8.44 E
Hille, Sve.	40	60.44 N	17.11 E
Hillegom	52	52.18 N	4.35 E
Hillegossen	52	51.59 N	8.37 E
Hillerød	41	55.56 N	12.19 E
Hillers Creek ≃	219	38.38 N	91.54 W
Hillesheim	56	50.18 N	6.38 E
Hilli	124	25.17 N	89.01 E
Hilliard, Fl., U.S.	192	30.41 N	81.55 W
Hilliard, Oh., U.S.	218	40.02 N	83.09 W
Hilliards	214	41.05 N	79.50 W
Hillingdon ◆[8]	260	51.32 N	0.27 W
Hillisburg	216	40.17 N	86.20 W
Hill Island Lake ⊜	176	60.29 N	109.50 W
Hillister	194	30.40 N	94.23 W
Hillman	190	45.03 N	83.54 W
Hillman ≃	168a	33.26 S	116.48 E
Hillmersdorf	54	51.42 N	13.29 E
Hill of Fearn	46	57.45 N	3.56 W
Hills	198	43.31 N	96.21 W
Hills and Dales	214	39.42 N	84.13 W
Hillsboro, Il., U.S.	219	39.09 N	89.29 W
Hillsboro, Ks., U.S.	198	38.21 N	97.12 W
Hillsboro, Ky., U.S.	218	38.18 N	83.40 W
Hillsboro, Md., U.S.	208	38.55 N	75.56 W
Hillsboro, Mo., U.S.	219	38.13 N	90.33 W
Hillsboro, N.H., U.S.	188	43.06 N	71.53 W
Hillsboro, N.M., U.S.	200	32.55 N	107.33 W
Hillsboro, N.D., U.S.	198	47.24 N	97.03 W
Hillsboro, Oh., U.S.	218	39.12 N	83.36 W
Hillsboro, Or., U.S.	224	45.31 N	122.59 W
Hillsboro, Tx., U.S.	222	32.00 N	97.07 W
Hillsboro, Wi., U.S.	190	43.39 N	90.20 W
Hillsboro Beach	220	26.18 N	80.05 W
Hillsboro Canal ≅	220	26.19 N	80.05 W
Hillsborough, N.B., Can.	186	45.56 N	64.39 W
Hillsborough, N. Ire., U.K.	48	54.28 N	6.05 W
Hillsborough, Ca., U.S.	226	37.34 N	122.22 W
Hillsborough, N.C., U.S.	192	36.04 N	79.06 W
Hillsborough □[6], Fl., U.S.	220	27.55 N	82.15 W
Hillsborough □[6], N.H., U.S.	207	42.49 N	71.41 W
Hillsborough ≃	220	27.56 N	82.27 W
Hillsborough, Cape ›	166	20.54 S	149.03 E
Hillsborough Bay ⊂, P.E., Can.	186	46.10 N	63.05 W
Hillsborough Bay ⊂, Fl., U.S.	220	27.52 N	82.27 W
Hillsborough River State Park ♦	220	28.09 N	82.14 W
Hillsburgh	212	43.47 N	80.09 W
Hills Creek Lake ⊜[1]	202	43.40 N	122.26 W
Hillsdale, Mi., U.S.	216	41.55 N	84.37 W
Hillsdale, N.J., U.S.	276	41.00 N	74.02 W
Hillsdale, N.Y., U.S.	210	42.10 N	73.31 W
Hillsdale, Pa., U.S.	214	40.45 N	78.53 W
Hillsdale □[6]	216	41.53 N	84.36 W
Hillsdale ◆[9]	282	37.32 N	122.18 W
Hillsdale Lake ⊜[1]	198	38.40 N	94.55 W
Hills Flat	226	39.14 N	121.03 W
Hillsgrove	210	41.27 N	76.42 W
Hillside, Austl.	162	21.44 S	119.23 E
Hillside, Scot., U.K.	46	56.44 N	2.29 W
Hillside, Il., U.S.	278	41.52 N	87.54 W
Hillside, Md., U.S.	284c	38.52 N	76.55 W
Hillside, N.J., U.S.	276	40.42 N	74.13 W
Hillside ◆[8]	276	40.42 N	73.47 W
Hillside Gardens	216	42.16 N	84.27 W
Hillside Heights	285	39.41 N	75.41 W
Hillside Lake	210	41.36 N	73.50 W
Hillston	166	33.29 S	145.32 E
Hillsville, Pa., U.S.	214	41.00 N	80.29 W
Hillsville, Va., U.S.	192	36.45 N	80.44 W
Hillswick	46a	60.28 N	1.30 W
Hilltop	208	39.49 N	75.04 W
Hilltop Center ◆[9]	282	37.59 N	122.19 W
Hilltown, N. Ire., U.K.	48	54.12 N	6.09 W
Hilltown, Pa., U.S.	208	40.20 N	75.14 W
Hillview	219	39.27 N	90.33 W
Hillview Reservoir ⊜[1]	276	40.55 N	73.52 W
Hillwood	284c	38.52 N	77.10 W
Hilmar	226	37.25 N	120.51 W
Hilo	229d	19.43 N	155.05 W
Hilo Bay ⊂	229d	19.44 N	155.05 W
Hilonghilong, Mount ∧	116	9.06 N	125.44 E
Hilongos	116	10.23 N	124.45 E
Hilpotstein	60	49.12 N	11.12 E
Hilpsford Point ›	44	54.03 N	3.12 W
Hils ∧	52	51.55 N	9.40 E
Hilshire Village	222	29.49 N	95.26 W
Hiltaba, Mount ∧	162	32.09 S	135.03 E
Hilter	52	52.08 N	8.08 E
Hilton, N.Y., U.S.	210	43.17 N	77.47 W
Hilton, Pa., U.S.	208	40.00 N	76.49 W
Hilton Head Island I	192	32.12 N	80.45 W
Hiltpoltstein	60	49.40 N	11.19 E
Hiltrop ◆[8]	263	51.30 N	7.15 E
Hiltrup	52	51.54 N	7.38 E
Hilvan	130	37.35 N	38.57 E
Hilvarenbeek	52	51.29 N	5.09 E
Hilversum	52	52.14 N	5.10 E
Hima	192	37.07 N	83.46 W

≃	River	Fluß	Río	Rivière	Rio
≅	Canal	Kanal	Canal	Canal	Canal
⌊	Waterfall, Rapids	Wasserfall, Stromschnellen	Cascada, Rápidos	Chute d'eau, Rapides	Cascata, Rápidos
⊔	Strait	Meeresstraße	Estrecho	Détroit	Estreito
⊂	Bay, Gulf	Bucht, Golf	Bahía, Golfo	Baie, Golfe	Baía, Golfo
⊜	Lake, Lakes	See, Seen	Lago, Lagos	Lac, Lacs	Lago, Lagos
≋	Swamp	Sumpf	Pantano	Marais	Pântano
⊠	Ice Features, Glacier	Eis- und Gletscherformen	Accidentes Glaciales	Formes glaciaires	Acidentes glaciares
⊤	Other Hydrographic Features	Andere Hydrographische Objekte	Otros Elementos Hidrográficos	Autres données hydrographiques	Outros acidentes hidrográficos
✢	Submarine Features	Untermeerische Objekte	Accidentes Submarinos	Formes de relief sous-marin	Acidentes submarinos
□	Political Unit	Politische Einheit	Unidad Politica	Entité politique	Unidade política
♁	Cultural Institution	Kulturelle Institution	Institución Cultural	Institution culturelle	Instituição cultural
⊥	Historical Site	Historische Stätte	Sitio Histórico	Site historique	Sitio histórico
♦	Recreational Site	Erholungs- und Ferienort	Sitio de Recreo	Centre de loisirs	Area de Lazer
⊠	Airport	Flughafen	Aeropuerto	Aéroport	Aeroporto
■	Military Installation	Militäranlage	Instalación Militar	Installation militaire	Instalação militar
◆	Miscellaneous	Verschiedenes	Misceláneo	Divers	Diversos

ENGLISH: Name · Page · Lat.°' · Long.°'
DEUTSCH: Name · Seite · Breite°' · Länge°' E = Ost

Symbols in the index entries represent the broad categories identified in the key at the right. Symbols with superior numbers (⋏[1]) identify subcategories (see complete key on page *I · 1).*

Symbole im Register stellen die rechts im Schlüssel erklärten Kategorien dar. Symbole mit hochgestellten Ziffern (⋏[1]) bezeichnen Unterabteilungen einer Kategorie (vgl. vollständiger Schlüssel auf Seite *I · 1).*

Los símbolos incluídos en el texto del índice representan las grandes categorias identificadas con la clave a la derecha. Los símbolos con numeros en su parte superior (⋏[1]) identifican las subcategorías (véase la clave completa en la página *I · 1).*

Les symboles de l'index représentent les catégories indiquées dans la légende à droite. Les symboles suivis d'un indice (⋏[1]) représentent des sous-catégories (voir légende complète à la page *I · 1).*

Os símbolos incluídos no texto do índice representam as grandes categorias identificadas com a chave à direita. Os símbolos com números em sua parte superior (⋏[1]) identificam as subcategorias (veja-se a chave completa à página *I · 1).*

	English	Deutsch	Español	Français	Português
∧	Mountain	Berg	Montaña	Montagne	Montanha
⋏	Mountains	Gebirge	Montañas	Montagnes	Montanhas
)(	Pass	Paß	Paso	Col	Passo
V	Valley, Canyon	Tal, Cañon	Valle, Cañón	Vallée, Canyon	Vale, Canhão
≚	Plain	Ebene	Llano	Plaine	Planície
≻	Cape	Kap	Cabo	Cap	Cabo
I	Island	Insel	Isla	Île	Ilha
II	Islands	Inseln	Islas	Îles	Ilhas
≗	Other Topographic Features	Andere Topographische Objekte	Otros Elementos Topográficos	Autres données topographiques	Outros acidentes topográficos

Home-Hsic *I* · 73

ESPAÑOL — FRANÇAIS — PORTUGUÊS

Nombre / Nom / Nome	Página / Page	Lat.°′	Long.°′ W = Oeste / W = Ouest
Home Gardens	228	33.52 N	117.31 W
Home Hill	166	19.40 S	147.25 E
Homeland, Ca., U.S.	228	33.44 N	117.07 W
Homeland, Fl., U.S.	220	27.49 N	81.49 W
Homeland Canal ≊	226	35.57 N	119.27 W
Homeland Park	192	34.27 N	82.41 W
Home Place	218	39.56 N	86.08 W
Homer, Ak., U.S.	180	59.39 N	151.33 W
Homer, Ga., U.S.	192	34.20 N	83.29 W
Homer, La., U.S.	194	32.47 N	93.03 W
Homer, Mi., U.S.	216	42.08 N	84.48 W
Homer, Ne., U.S.	198	42.19 N	96.29 W
Homer, N.Y., U.S.	210	42.38 N	76.10 W
Homer, Oh., U.S.	214	40.15 N	82.31 W
Homer, Tx., U.S.	222	31.18 N	94.36 W
Homer City	214	40.32 N	79.09 W
Homert ∧[2]	263	51.11 N	7.39 E
Homer Tunnel ◆[5]	172	44.45 S	168.00 E
Homerville, Ga., U.S.	192	31.02 N	82.44 W
Homerville, Oh., U.S.	214	41.02 N	82.08 W
Homer Wash ∨	204	34.20 N	115.02 W
Homer Youngs Peak ∧	202	45.19 N	113.41 W
Home Seamount ✣[3]	14	12.55 S	175.37 W
Homestead, Austl.	166	20.22 S	145.39 E
Homestead, Fl., U.S.	220	25.28 N	80.28 W
Homestead, Pa., U.S.	279b	40.24 N	79.54 W
Homestead Air Force Base ■	220	25.29 N	80.23 W
Homestead National Monument of America ♠	198	40.14 N	96.54 W
Homestead Valley	282	37.54 N	122.32 W
Hometown, Il., U.S.	278	41.44 N	87.43 W
Hometown, Pa., U.S.	210	40.49 N	75.59 W
Homewood, Al., U.S.	194	33.28 N	86.48 W
Homewood, Ca., U.S.	226	39.05 N	120.09 W
Homewood, Il., U.S.	216	41.33 N	87.39 W
Homewood, Oh., U.S.	218	39.23 N	84.33 W
Homewood ◆[8]	279b	40.27 N	79.54 W
Homewood Acres	278	41.34 N	87.43 W
Homeworth	214	40.50 N	81.03 W
Hominy	196	36.24 N	96.23 W
Hominy Creek ≃	196	36.20 N	96.00 W
Hommersåk	26	58.58 N	5.42 E
Hommura	92	34.22 N	139.15 E
Homnābād	122	17.46 N	77.08 E
Homochitto ≃	194	31.09 N	91.31 W
Homoíne	156	23.52 S	35.09 E
Homonhon Island I	116	10.44 N	125.43 E
Homosassa	220	28.46 N	82.36 W
Homosassa Bay c	220	28.45 N	82.43 W
Homosassa Springs	220	28.48 N	82.35 W
Homs → Al-Khums	146	32.39 N	14.16 E
Homs → Ḥimṣ	130	34.44 N	36.43 E
Honai	96	33.30 N	132.25 E
Honaker	192	37.00 N	81.58 W
Honami	96	33.36 N	130.42 E
Honan → Henan □[4]	90	34.00 N	114.00 E
Honan → Luoyang	102	34.41 N	112.28 E
Honāvar	122	14.17 N	74.27 E
Honaz	130	37.45 N	29.17 E
Honbetsu	92a	43.07 N	143.37 E
Hon Chong	110	10.10 N	104.37 E
Honda	246	5.12 N	74.45 W
Honda, Bahía c, Col.	246	12.21 N	71.47 W
Honda, Bahía c, Cuba	240p	22.57 N	83.10 W
Honda, Cañada ≃	258	33.57 S	59.21 W
Honda Bay c	116	9.53 N	118.49 E
Honddu ≃, U.K.	42	51.54 N	2.58 W
Honddu ≃, Wales, U.K.	42	51.57 N	3.23 W
Hondeklipbaai	156	30.20 S	17.18 E
Honderfontein	158	32.12 S	21.22 E
Hon Dien, Nui ∧	110	11.33 N	108.38 E
Hondo, Ab., Can.	182	55.04 N	114.02 W
Hondo, Nihon	92	32.27 N	130.12 E
Hondo, N.M., U.S.	200	33.23 N	105.16 W
Hondo, Tx., U.S.	196	29.20 N	99.08 W
Hondo ≃, Méx.	286a	19.26 N	99.15 W
Hondo ≃, N.A.	232	18.29 N	88.19 W
Hondo, Arroyo ≃	226	37.28 N	121.47 W
Hondo, Rio ≃, Ca., U.S.	280	33.55 N	118.10 W
Hondo, Rio ≃, N.M., U.S.	196	33.22 N	104.24 W
Hondo Creek ≃	196	28.45 N	99.11 W
Hondoji Temple ʋ[1]	268	35.51 N	139.56 E
Hondschoote	50	50.59 N	2.35 E
Hondsrug ⋏[2]	52	52.55 N	6.50 E
Honduras □[1], N.A.	230	15.00 N	86.30 W
Honduras □[1], N.A.	236	15.00 N	86.30 W
Honduras, Cabo de ›	236	16.01 N	86.02 W
Honduras, Gulf of c	230	16.10 N	87.50 W
Honduras, Port c	236	16.13 N	88.41 W
Honea Path	192	34.26 N	82.23 W
Hönebach	56	50.56 N	9.56 E
Hønefoss	26	60.10 N	10.18 E
Honeoye	210	42.47 N	77.31 W
Honeoye Creek ≃	210	42.58 N	77.43 W
Honeoye Falls	210	42.57 N	77.35 W
Honeoye Lake ⊜	210	42.45 N	77.31 W
Honesdale	210	41.34 N	75.15 W
Honey Brook	208	40.05 N	75.54 W
Honey Creek	216	42.44 N	88.18 W
Honey Creek ≃, Ia., U.S.	190	42.09 N	93.03 W
Honey Creek ≃, Mo., U.S.	194	39.53 N	93.34 W
Honey Creek ≃, Oh., U.S.	214	41.05 N	83.12 W
Honey Creek ≃, Pa., U.S.	208	40.36 N	77.35 W
Honey Creek ≃, Wi., U.S.	216	42.41 N	88.17 W
Honeydew	273d	26.05 S	27.55 E
Honeygo Run ≃	284b	39.22 N	76.25 W
Honey Grove	196	33.35 N	95.54 W
Honey Lake ⊜	204	40.16 N	120.19 W
Honeymoon Bay	224	48.49 N	124.10 W
Honeyville	200	41.38 N	112.04 W
Honfleur	50	49.25 N	0.14 E
Høng	41	55.31 N	11.18 E
Hong ≃	100	32.25 N	115.35 E
Honga	152	15.09 S	15.12 E
Hon Gai	110	20.57 N	107.05 E
Hong'an	100	31.18 N	114.37 E
Honga River c	208	38.19 N	76.10 W
Hongawa	96	33.43 N	133.19 E
Hongchang	100	34.05 N	113.20 E
Hongch'ŏn	98	37.42 N	127.52 E
Hongchoudai	100	29.03 N	121.11 E
Hongcun, Zhg.	100	27.10 N	116.48 E
Hongcun, Zhg.	106	31.01 N	119.15 E
Höngen	56	51.02 N	5.56 E
Honggun	98	40.46 N	128.27 E
Honghai Wan c	100	22.40 N	115.10 E
Honghe	102	23.23 N	102.35 E
Honghu	100	29.48 N	113.27 E
Hong Hu ⊜	100	29.52 N	113.23 E
Honghuaerji	89	48.15 N	120.01 E
Honghuaji	100	33.52 N	114.26 E
Honghualiangzi	89	48.06 N	123.12 E
Honghuamu	89	48.33 N	125.39 E
Hongjiang, Zhg.	100	26.49 N	120.03 E
Hongjiang, Zhg.	102	27.07 N	109.56 E
Hong Kong □[2], Asia	90	22.15 N	114.10 E
Hong Kong □[2], Asia	100	22.15 N	114.10 E
Hong Kong I	271d	22.15 N	114.11 E
Hong Kong, University of ʋ[2]	271d	22.17 N	114.08 E
Hong Kong → Victoria	271d	22.17 N	114.09 E
Hongkou Park ♠	269b	31.16 N	121.28 E
Honglai	100	25.08 N	118.32 E
Honglanbu	106	31.37 N	118.57 E
Honglinqiao	106	30.59 N	118.59 E
Hongliutai	85	39.48 N	77.26 E
Hongliuyuan	102	41.04 N	95.26 E
Honglongdian	106	30.30 N	119.00 E
Honglongtang	105	40.41 N	117.37 E
Honglu	100	25.44 N	119.20 E
Hongluan	100	28.31 N	117.01 E
Hongluo Shan ∧	104	40.56 N	120.42 E
Hongluoxian	104	41.01 N	120.53 E
Hongmeichang	105	39.50 N	115.51 E
Hongmendu	102	26.10 N	102.37 E
Hongmenkou	102	27.22 N	100.30 E
Hongmenpu	107	30.37 N	104.08 E
Hongmiaozi	107	28.47 N	104.02 E
Hong Ngu	110	10.48 N	105.21 E
Hongō, Nihon	96	34.24 N	132.59 E
Hongō, Nihon	96	34.17 N	132.02 E
Hongō ◆[8]	268	35.42 N	139.47 E
Hongpailou	107	30.38 N	104.01 E
Hongqi	89	44.23 N	126.32 E
Hongqiao, Zhg.	100	28.14 N	121.01 E
Hongqiao, Zhg.	105	39.50 N	117.44 E
Hongqiao, Zhg.	106	31.29 N	121.49 E
Hongqiao, Zhg.	269b	31.12 N	121.22 E
Hongqiao Ji Chang ⊠	106	31.12 N	121.20 E
Hong → Red ≃	110	20.17 N	106.34 E
Hongrie → Hungary □[1]	30	47.00 N	20.00 E
Hongshan, Zhg.	89	48.02 N	129.00 E
Hongshan, Zhg.	98	36.37 N	118.00 E
Hongshanzi	98	42.34 N	117.14 E
Hongshi, Zhg.	89	43.00 N	127.04 E
Hongshi, Zhg.	98	41.21 N	119.32 E
Hongshidou	104	41.52 N	122.11 E
Hongshili	98	40.41 N	125.03 E
Hongshui	102	37.24 N	104.00 E
Hongshui ≃	102	23.45 N	109.30 E
Hongshuichuan	105	40.06 N	117.55 E
Hongshuyangzi	105	40.36 N	116.36 E
Hongsŏng	98	36.36 N	126.39 E
Hongtang	100	26.06 N	119.14 E
Hongtian	100	25.52 N	117.15 E
Hongtong	102	36.19 N	111.39 E
Hongtuwan	98	41.03 N	113.39 E
Hongtu Zhang ∧	100	23.46 N	115.56 E
Honguedo, Détroit d' ⊔	186	49.15 N	64.00 W
Hongwŏn	98	40.02 N	127.57 E
Hongxin	100	32.43 N	117.47 E
Hongxing	105	39.48 N	116.27 E
Hongxingqiao	106	30.55 N	119.52 E
Hongyang, Zhg.	100	26.32 N	119.27 E
Hongyang, Zhg.	100	23.28 N	116.13 E
Hongyanzi	104	40.38 N	120.31 E
Hongyōtoku	268	35.41 N	139.55 E
Hongze	100	33.19 N	118.53 E
Hongze Hu ⊜	100	33.16 N	118.34 E
Honiara	175e	9.26 S	159.57 E
Honiton	42	50.48 N	3.13 W
Hon-jima I	96	34.23 N	133.47 E
Honjō, Nihon	92	39.23 N	140.03 E
Honjō, Nihon	94	36.24 N	138.01 E
Honjō, Nihon	94	36.14 N	139.11 E
Honkamäki ∧[2]	26	62.58 N	27.05 E
Hon-kawane	94	35.07 N	138.09 E
Honker Bay c	282	38.04 N	121.56 W
Hönne ≃	263	51.28 N	7.46 E
Honnecourt-sur-Escaut	50	50.02 N	3.12 E
Honningsvåg	24	70.59 N	25.59 E
Hönö	26	57.42 N	11.39 E
Honokaa	229d	20.04 N	155.28 W
Honokahua	229a	21.00 N	156.39 W
Honokawai	229a	20.57 N	156.41 W
Honolulu	229c	21.18 N	157.51 W
Honolulu □[6]	229c	21.19 N	157.52 W
Honolulu International Airport ⊠	229c	21.20 N	157.55 W
Honomu	229d	19.52 N	155.07 W
Honouliuli	229c	21.22 N	158.02 W
Hönow	54	52.32 N	13.38 E
Hon Quan	110	11.39 N	106.36 E
Honshū I	92	36.00 N	138.00 E
Hontoon Island State Park ♠	220	28.59 N	81.22 W
Höntrop ◆[8]	263	51.27 N	7.08 E
Honuapo Bay c	229d	19.05 N	155.33 W
Hoo	260	51.25 N	0.34 E
Hood	226	38.22 N	121.31 W
Hood □[6]	222	32.25 N	97.45 W
Hood ≃, N.T., Can.	176	67.26 N	108.53 W
Hood ≃, Or., U.S.	224	45.42 N	121.30 W
Hood, East Fork ≃	224	45.36 N	121.38 W
Hood, Mount ∧	224	45.23 N	121.41 W
Hood, West Fork ≃	224	45.36 N	121.38 W
Hood Canal c	224	47.35 N	123.00 W
Hood Canal Floating Bridge ◆[5]	224	47.52 N	122.38 W
Hoodoo Peak ∧	202	48.15 N	120.19 W
Hood Point ›, Austl.	162	34.23 S	119.34 E
Hood Point ›, Pap. N. Gui.	164	10.05 S	147.45 E
Hood Pond ⊜	283	42.40 N	70.57 W
Hood River	224	45.42 N	121.31 W
Hoodsport	224	47.24 N	123.08 W
Hoods Range ⋏	166	28.35 S	144.30 E
Hoof	56	51.17 N	9.20 E
Hoogerheide	52	51.25 N	4.20 E
Hoogeveen	52	52.43 N	6.29 E
Hoogeveense Vaart ≃	52	52.42 N	6.11 E
Hoogezand-Sappemeer	52	53.09 N	6.47 E
Hoogkerk	52	53.13 N	6.30 E
Hooglede	50	50.59 N	3.05 E
Hoogstede	52	52.34 N	6.56 E
Hoogstraten	56	51.24 N	4.46 E
Hoogte	158	27.28 S	28.03 E
Hoogvliet	52	51.52 N	4.21 E
Hook	42	51.17 N	0.58 W
Hook ◆[8]	260	51.22 N	0.18 W
Hooker	196	36.51 N	101.12 W
Hooker, Bi'r ⍑[4]	142	30.23 N	30.20 E
Hooker Creek	162	18.20 S	130.40 E
Hooker Creek Aboriginal Reserve ◆[4]	162	18.10 S	130.25 E
Hook Head ›	48	52.07 N	6.55 W
Hookina	166	31.45 S	138.20 E
Hook Island I	166	20.08 S	148.55 E
Hook Mountain State Park ♠	276	41.09 N	73.55 W
Hook Norton	42	51.59 N	1.29 W
Hook Point ›	166	25.48 S	153.05 E
Hooks	194	33.28 N	94.15 W
Hooksiel	52	53.38 N	8.01 E
Hoolehua	229a	21.10 N	157.04 W
Hoonah	180	58.07 N	135.26 W
Hoopa	204	41.03 N	123.40 W
Hoopa Valley Indian Reservation ◆[4]	204	41.08 N	123.40 W
Hooper	198	41.36 N	96.32 W
Hooper Bay	180	61.31 N	166.06 W
Hooper Islands II	208	38.20 N	76.13 W
Hooper Strait ⊔	208	38.12 N	76.03 W
Hoopersville	208	38.15 N	76.10 W
Hoopes Reservoir ⊜[1]	285	39.47 N	75.37 W
Hoopeston	216	40.28 N	87.40 W
Hooping Harbour	186	50.37 N	56.17 W
Hoople	198	48.32 N	97.38 W
Hoopstad	158	27.54 S	25.58 E
Hoopstick Brook ≃	276	40.39 N	74.41 W
Höör	41	55.56 N	13.32 E
Hoorn	52	52.38 N	5.04 E
Hoorn, Kap → Hornos, Cabo de ›	254	55.59 S	67.16 W
Hoosac Range ⋏	207	42.45 N	73.02 W
Hoosac Tunnel ◆[5]	207	42.41 N	73.03 W
Hoosic ≃	210	42.54 N	73.39 W
Hoosick	210	42.52 N	73.20 W
Hoosick Falls	210	42.54 N	73.21 W
Hooton	262	53.18 N	2.57 W
Hoot Owl Estates	285	39.53 N	74.50 W
Hoover Dam ◆[6]	200	36.00 N	114.27 W
Hoover Reservoir ⊜[1]	214	40.08 N	82.53 W
Hooversville	214	40.08 N	78.54 W
Hopa	130	41.25 N	41.24 E
Hopatcong	210	40.55 N	74.39 W
Hopatcong, Lake ⊜	210	40.57 N	74.38 W
Hopatcong State Park ♠	276	40.55 N	74.40 W
Hop Bottom	210	41.42 N	75.46 W
Hop Brook ≃	276	40.19 N	74.08 W
Hope, B.C., Can.	182	49.23 N	121.26 W
Hope, Ak., U.S.	180	60.55 N	149.38 W
Hope, Ar., U.S.	194	33.40 N	93.35 W
Hope, In., U.S.	218	39.18 N	85.46 W
Hope, N.J., U.S.	210	40.54 N	74.58 W
Hope, N.D., U.S.	198	47.19 N	97.43 W
Hope, R.I., U.S.	207	41.44 N	71.33 W
Hope, Ben ∧	46	58.24 N	4.37 W
Hope, Loch ⊜	46	58.27 N	4.39 W
Hope, Point ›	180	68.21 N	166.50 W
Hope Bay c	212	44.55 N	81.08 W
Hopedale, Nf., Can.	176	55.28 N	60.13 W
Hopedale, Il., U.S.	194	40.25 N	89.24 W
Hopedale, La., U.S.	194	29.49 N	89.39 W
Hopedale, Ma., U.S.	207	42.07 N	71.32 W
Hopedale, Oh., U.S.	214	40.19 N	80.54 W
Hope Farm	210	41.44 N	73.40 W
Hopefield	158	33.04 S	18.22 E
Hopeh → Hebei □[4]	98	38.00 N	116.00 E
Hope Island I, B.C., Can.	182	50.55 N	127.53 W
Hope Island I, On., Can.	212	44.55 N	80.12 W
Hopeland	208	40.14 N	76.16 W
Hopelawn	276	40.31 N	74.17 W
Hopelchén	232	19.46 N	89.51 W
Hopeman	46	57.42 N	3.25 W
Hope Mills	192	34.58 N	78.56 W
Hopes Advance, Cap ›	176	61.04 N	69.34 W
Hopetoun, Austl.	162	33.57 S	120.07 E
Hopetoun, Austl.	166	35.44 S	142.22 E
Hopetown	158	29.34 S	24.03 E
Hope Vale Aboriginal Reserve ◆[4]	164	15.10 S	145.15 E
Hope Valley, Austl.	168b	34.50 S	138.44 E
Hope Valley, R.I., U.S.	207	41.30 N	71.43 W
Hopewell, N.J., U.S.	208	40.23 N	74.45 W
Hopewell, Pa., U.S.	214	40.08 N	78.16 W
Hopewell, Va., U.S.	208	37.18 N	77.17 W
Hopewell Islands II	176	58.25 N	78.00 W
Hopewell Junction	210	41.35 N	73.48 W
Hopewell Village National Historic Site ⊥	208	40.12 N	75.46 W
Hopfgarten	64	47.27 N	12.10 E
Hopfgarten in Defereggen	64	46.55 N	12.31 E
Hopi Buttes ∧	200	35.20 N	110.15 W
Hopi → Hebi	98	35.59 N	114.11 E
Hopi Indian Reservation ◆[4]	200	35.45 N	110.35 W
Hopkins, Mi., U.S.	216	42.37 N	85.45 W
Hopkins, Mo., U.S.	194	40.33 N	94.49 W
Hopkins □[6]	222	33.07 N	95.35 W
Hopkins ≃	166	38.24 S	142.31 E
Hopkins, Lake ⊜	162	24.15 S	128.50 E
Hopkins Creek ≃	284a	43.17 N	78.46 W
Hopkinsville	194	36.51 N	87.29 W
Hopkinton, Ia., U.S.	190	42.20 N	91.14 W
Hopkinton, Ma., U.S.	207	42.13 N	71.31 W
Hopkinton, R.I., U.S.	207	41.27 N	71.46 W
Hopland	204	38.58 N	123.06 W
Hopólito Bouchard	252	34.43 S	63.31 W
Hoppegarten	264a	52.31 N	13.40 E
Hoppenrade	264a	52.32 N	12.56 E
Hoppo → Hepu	102	21.39 N	109.11 E
Hopsten	52	52.23 N	7.36 E
Hoptrup	41	55.11 N	9.28 E
Ho Pui	271d	22.25 N	114.03 E
Hopwood, Mount ∧	166	21.49 S	144.26 E
Hoque	152	14.39 S	13.54 E
Hoquiam	224	46.58 N	123.53 W
Hoquiam, East Fork ≃	224	46.58 N	123.54 W
Hora Califo	144	8.49 N	43.07 E
Horace Mountain ∧	180	67.40 N	149.06 W
Horado	94	35.36 N	136.50 E
Hōrai	94	34.56 N	137.34 E
Horancia	144	6.31 N	38.44 E
Horasan	130	40.03 N	42.11 E
Horatio	194	33.56 N	94.21 W
Horatio Gardens	278	42.10 N	87.57 W
Horažd'ovice	60	49.20 N	13.43 E
Horb am Neckar	58	48.26 N	8.41 E
Horbelev	41	54.49 N	12.04 E
Horbourg	58	48.05 N	7.23 E
Hörby	41	55.51 N	13.39 E
Horconcitos	236	8.19 N	82.10 W
Hordaland □[6]	26	60.15 N	6.30 E
Hörde ◆[8]	263	51.29 N	7.30 E
Horden	44	54.46 N	1.18 W
Horden ≃	164	3.50 S	141.25 E
Horezu	38	45.08 N	23.59 E
Horgen	58	47.15 N	8.36 E
Hořice	30	50.22 N	15.38 E
Horicon	190	43.27 N	88.37 W
Horigane	268	35.50 N	139.27 E
Horine	219	38.16 N	90.25 W
Horinger	102	40.23 N	111.53 E
Horinouchi	94	37.14 N	138.56 E
Horinouchi ◆[8]	268	35.41 N	139.40 E
Horizon Tablemount ✣[3]	14	19.40 N	168.30 W
Horizontina	252	27.37 S	54.19 W
Horka	54	51.16 N	14.56 E
Hörken	40	60.02 N	14.56 E
Horley	42	51.11 N	0.11 W
Horlick Mountains ⋏	9	85.23 S	121.00 W
Horloff ≃	56	50.20 N	8.52 E
Hormigueros	240m	18.09 N	67.08 W
Hormoz, Jazīreh-ye I	128	27.04 N	56.28 E
Hormozgān □[4]	128	27.50 N	56.00 E
Hormuz, Strait of ⊔	128	26.34 N	56.15 E
Horn, Dtsch.	52	51.52 N	8.56 E
Horn, Öst.	61	48.40 N	15.40 E
Horn ◆[8]	52	53.38 N	10.05 E
Horn ›	24a	66.28 N	22.28 W
Horn ≃, N.T., Can.	176	61.30 N	118.01 W
Horn ≃, Europe	56	49.15 N	7.20 E
Horn, Ben ∧[2]	46	58.01 N	4.02 W
Horn, Cape → Hornos, Cabo de ›	254	55.59 S	67.16 W
Hornaday ≃	180	69.22 N	123.50 W
Hornafjördur c	24a	64.17 N	15.16 W
Hornavan ⊜	24	66.10 N	17.30 E
Hornbach	56	49.11 N	7.22 E
Hornbæk	41	56.05 N	12.28 E
Hornbeak	194	36.19 N	89.17 W
Hornbeck	194	31.19 N	93.23 W
Hornberg	58	48.13 N	8.13 E
Hornbrook	204	41.55 N	122.33 W
Hornburg	54	52.01 N	10.36 E
Hornby, On., Can.	275b	43.34 N	79.50 W
Hornby, N.Z.	172	43.33 S	172.32 E
Hornby Bay c	176	66.35 N	117.50 W
Horncastle	44	53.13 N	0.07 W
Hornchurch ◆[8]	260	51.34 N	0.12 E
Horndal	40	60.18 N	16.25 E
Horndean	42	50.55 N	1.00 W
Horndon on the Hill	260	51.31 N	0.25 E
Horne	41	55.06 N	10.11 E
Horne, Îles de II	14	14.16 S	178.05 W
Hornebach ≃	263	51.39 N	7.38 E
Horneburg, Dtsch.	52	53.30 N	9.34 E
Horneburg, Dtsch.	263	51.38 N	7.18 E
Hörnefors	26	63.38 N	19.54 E
Hornell	210	42.19 N	77.39 W
Hornepayne	176	49.13 N	84.47 W
Hornerstown	208	40.06 N	74.30 W
Hornhausen	54	52.02 N	11.10 E
Horn Head ›	48	55.14 N	7.59 W
Horn Hill	260	51.37 N	0.32 W
Horní Jiřetín	54	50.35 N	13.32 E
Hornindal	26	61.58 N	6.31 E
Hornindalsvatnet ⊜	26	61.56 N	6.22 E
Hørning	41	56.05 N	10.03 E
Hörningsholm	40	59.03 N	17.40 E
Horní Počernice	54	50.06 N	14.38 E
Hornisgrinde ∧	56	48.36 N	8.12 E
Horn Island I, Austl.	164	10.37 S	142.17 E
Horn Island I, Ms., U.S.	194	30.13 N	88.38 W
Horní Slavkov	54	50.07 N	12.46 E
Horní Stropnice	61	48.46 N	14.44 E
Hornito, Cerro ∧	236	8.39 N	82.09 W
Hornitos	226	37.30 N	120.14 W
Horní Vltavice	60	48.57 N	13.46 E
Horn Lake	194	34.58 N	90.02 W
Horn Lake ⊜	212	45.24 N	79.36 W
Hornos, Cabo de (Cape Horn) ›	254	55.59 S	67.16 W
Hornos, Isla I	254	55.57 S	67.17 W
Hornos, Islas de II	288	34.25 S	57.55 W
Hornow	54	51.38 N	14.31 E
Hornoy	50	49.51 N	1.54 E
Horn Plateau ⋏[1]	176	62.15 N	119.15 W
Horn Pond ⊜	283	42.28 N	71.09 W
Hornsby, Austl.	170	33.42 S	151.06 E
Hornsby, Il., U.S.	219	39.10 N	89.45 W
Hornsbyville	208	37.11 N	76.28 W
Hornsea	44	53.55 N	0.10 W
Hornsey ◆[8]	260	51.35 N	0.07 W
Hornslet	41	56.19 N	10.20 E
Hornstorf	54	53.54 N	11.32 E
Hornsyld	41	55.45 N	9.51 E
Horntown	208	37.58 N	75.28 W
Hornu	50	50.26 N	3.49 E
Horoshiri-dake ∧	92a	42.43 N	142.41 E
Horotiu	172	37.43 S	175.12 E
Hořovice	60	49.50 N	13.54 E
Horqin Youyi Qianqi (Ulan Hot)	89	46.05 N	122.05 E
Horqin Youyi Zhongqi	89	45.09 N	121.24 E
Horqin Zuoyi Houqi	89	42.58 N	122.20 E
Horqin Zuoyi Zhongqi	89	44.07 N	123.18 E
Horqueta	252	23.24 S	56.53 W
Horrabridge	42	50.31 N	4.05 W
Horrelville	172	43.20 S	172.20 E
Horrem	263	51.06 N	6.48 E
Hörsching	61	48.14 N	14.11 E
Horse ≃	184	56.43 N	111.23 W
Horseback Knob ∧[2]	218	39.14 N	83.06 W
Horse Cave	194	37.10 N	85.54 W
Horse Creek	200	41.25 N	105.11 W
Horse Creek ≃, U.S.	198	41.57 N	103.58 W
Horse Creek ≃, Co., U.S.	198	38.05 N	103.19 W
Horse Creek ≃, Fl., U.S.	220	27.06 N	81.58 W
Horse Creek ≃, Il., U.S.	219	39.45 N	89.34 W
Horse Creek ≃, Mo., U.S.	194	37.46 N	93.53 W
Horsefly	182	52.20 N	121.24 W
Horsefly Lake ⊜	182	52.25 N	121.00 W
Horsehead Creek ≃	198	43.17 N	103.22 W
Horsehead Lake ⊜	198	47.02 N	99.47 W
Horseheads	210	42.10 N	76.49 W
Horse Islands II	186	50.13 N	55.45 W
Horsell	260	51.19 N	0.34 W
Horseneck Brook ≃	276	41.01 N	73.38 W
Horsens	41	55.52 N	9.52 E
Horsens Fjord c	41	55.50 N	10.05 E
Horseshoe Bend, Ar., U.S.	194	36.15 N	91.43 W
Horseshoe Bend, Id., U.S.	202	43.55 N	116.12 W
Horseshoe Bend National Military Park ♠	194	33.00 N	85.46 W
Horseshoe Cove c	276	40.27 N	74.00 W
Horseshoe Creek ≃	198	42.27 N	104.58 W
Horseshoe Falls ʟ	284a	43.05 N	79.04 W
Horseshoe Lake ⊜, Mb., Can.	184	52.12 N	95.50 W
Horseshoe Lake ⊜, Mi., U.S.	281	42.24 N	83.45 W
Horseshoe Lake ⊜, N.J., U.S.	276	40.52 N	74.38 W
Horse Shoe Reef ✣[2]	240m	18.40 N	64.12 W
Horsfjärden c	40	59.04 N	18.09 E
Horsford	42	52.41 N	1.15 E
Horsforth	44	53.51 N	1.39 W
Horsham, Austl.	166	36.43 S	142.13 E
Horsham, Eng., U.K.	42	51.04 N	0.21 W
Horsham, Pa., U.S.	208	40.10 N	75.07 W
Hørsholm	41	55.53 N	12.30 E
Hörsingen	54	52.16 N	11.09 E
Horsley, Austl.	274a	33.51 S	150.51 E
Horsley, Eng., U.K.	260	51.16 N	0.26 W
Horslunde	41	54.54 N	11.14 E
Horšovský Týn	60	49.32 N	12.56 E
Horst, Dtsch.	52	53.48 N	9.37 E
Horst, Dtsch.	54	53.22 N	10.37 E
Horst, Ned.	52	51.27 N	6.04 E
Horst ◆[8]	263	51.32 N	7.02 E
Horsted Keynes	42	51.02 N	0.01 W
Hörstel	52	52.18 N	7.35 E
Horstmar, Dtsch.	52	52.05 N	7.17 E
Horstmar, Dtsch.	263	51.36 N	7.33 E
Horsunlu	130	37.55 N	28.36 E
Horta	148a	38.32 N	28.38 W
Horta □[5]	148a	38.30 N	29.00 W
Horta ◆[8]	266d	41.26 N	2.00 E
Hortaleza ◆[8]	266a	40.28 N	3.39 W
Horten	26	59.25 N	10.30 E
Hortobágy ◆[1]	30	47.35 N	21.00 E
Hortobágyi Nemzeti Park ♠	30	47.30 N	21.10 E
Horton, Eng., U.K.	260	51.28 N	0.32 W
Horton, In., U.S.	218	40.05 N	86.09 W
Horton, Ks., U.S.	198	39.39 N	95.31 W
Horton, Mi., U.S.	216	42.09 N	84.31 W
Horton ≃	180	70.00 N	126.53 W
Horton in Ribblesdale	44	54.09 N	2.17 W
Horton Kirby	260	51.23 N	0.15 E
Horton Lake ⊜	180	67.29 N	122.31 W
Hortonville, N.Y., U.S.	210	41.46 N	75.02 W
Hortonville, Wi., U.S.	190	44.20 N	88.38 W
Horumersiel	52	53.41 N	8.00 E
Hørup	41	54.56 N	9.55 E
Hørve	41	55.45 N	11.28 E
Horw	58	47.01 N	8.18 E
Horwich	262	53.37 N	2.33 W
Horwood Lake ⊜	190	48.03 N	82.20 W
Hory Matky Boží	60	49.16 N	13.27 E
Hōryūji Temple ʋ[1]	270	34.36 N	135.44 E
Hosaina	144	7.38 N	37.52 E
Hösbach	56	50.00 N	9.12 E
Hosei University ʋ[2]	268	35.42 N	139.44 E
Hösel	56	51.19 N	6.54 E
Hosena	54	51.27 N	14.01 E
Hoséré Vokré ∧	146	8.20 N	13.15 E
Hoseynābād	128	35.33 N	47.08 E
Hoseynīyeh-ye Khodā-Dād	128	32.42 N	48.14 E
Hosford	192	30.23 N	84.47 W
Hoshāb	128	26.01 N	63.56 E
Hoshangābād	124	22.45 N	77.43 E
Hoshangābād Plain ≚	124	22.35 N	77.25 E
Hoshiārpur, India	123	31.32 N	75.54 E
Hoshiarpur, India	272a	28.35 N	77.22 E
Hoshigajō ∧	96	34.31 N	134.19 E
Hosingen	56	50.01 N	6.05 E
Hosjö	40	60.35 N	15.46 E
Hoskins	164	5.27 S	150.30 E
Hosmer, B.C., Can.	182	49.35 N	114.57 W
Hosmer, S.D., U.S.	198	45.34 N	99.28 W
Hosoe	94	34.49 N	137.39 E
Hospental	58	46.37 N	8.34 E
Hospers	198	43.04 N	95.54 W
Hospet	122	15.16 N	76.24 E
Hospital	48	52.29 N	8.25 W
Hospital de Orbigo	34	42.28 N	5.53 W
Hossegor	32	43.40 N	1.27 W
Hosston	194	32.53 N	93.52 W
Hosta Butte ∧	200	35.35 N	108.12 W
Hoste, Isla I	254	55.15 S	69.00 W
Hostěradice	61	48.57 N	16.15 E
Hostetter	214	40.16 N	79.24 W
Hostigrām	272b	22.26 N	88.31 E
Hostivař ◆[8]	54	50.01 N	14.32 E
Hostivice	54	50.04 N	14.15 E
Hošt'ka	54	50.30 N	14.20 E
Hostomice	54	50.35 N	13.46 E
Hostotipaquillo	234	21.04 N	104.04 W
Hostouň	60	49.34 N	12.46 E
Hosūr	122	12.43 N	77.49 E
Hot	110	18.06 N	98.36 E
Hota	268	35.08 N	139.51 E
Hotagen	26	63.59 N	14.15 E
Hotagen ⊜	26	63.53 N	14.29 E
Hotagsfjällen ∧	26	64.20 N	14.30 E
Hotaka	94	36.20 N	137.53 E
Hotaka-dake ∧	94	36.17 N	137.39 E
Hotamış	130	37.36 N	33.13 E
Hotan	120	37.08 N	79.54 E
Hotan ≃	90	40.30 N	80.45 E
Hotarele	38	44.10 N	26.22 E
Hotazel	158	27.15 S	23.00 E
Hotchkiss	200	38.47 N	107.43 W
Hotchkissville	207	41.34 N	73.13 W
Hot Creek Range ⋏	204	38.30 N	116.25 W
Hötensleben	54	52.08 N	11.01 E
Hotevilla	200	35.55 N	110.40 W
Hotham ≃	168a	32.58 S	116.22 E
Hotham Inlet c	180	66.45 N	162.00 W
Hotham Peak ∧	180	66.48 N	160.42 W
Hoting	26	64.07 N	16.10 E
Hot Springs, Mt., U.S.	202	47.36 N	114.40 W
Hot Springs, N.C., U.S.	192	35.53 N	82.49 W
Hot Springs, S.D., U.S.	198	43.25 N	103.28 W
Hot Springs, Va., U.S.	192	37.59 N	79.49 W
Hot Springs National Park	194	34.30 N	93.04 W
Hot Springs Peak ∧, Ca., U.S.	204	40.22 N	120.07 W
Hot Springs Peak ∧, Nv., U.S.	204	41.22 N	117.26 W
Hot Springs State Park ♠	202	43.40 N	108.10 W
Hot Springs → Truth or Consequences	200	33.08 N	107.15 W
Hot Sulphur Springs	200	40.04 N	106.06 W
Hottah Lake ⊜	176	65.04 N	118.29 W
Hottentotbaai c	156	26.05 S	14.58 E
Hottentotskloof	158	33.15 S	19.40 E
Hotton	56	50.16 N	5.27 E
Hötzum	54	52.13 N	10.37 E
Houaïlou	175f	21.17 S	165.38 E
Houamuang	110	20.09 N	103.38 E
Houbaishu	106	31.49 N	119.10 E
Houbao	98	41.54 N	125.14 E
Houcheng	106	31.55 N	120.26 E
Houdahepao	104	41.49 N	123.01 E
Houdain	50	50.27 N	2.32 E
Houdan	50	48.47 N	1.36 E
Houdelaincourt	58	48.33 N	5.28 E
Houdeng-Aimeries	50	50.29 N	4.08 E
Houeillès	32	44.12 N	0.02 E
Houffalize	56	50.08 N	5.47 E
Hougang	271c	1.22 N	103.54 E
Hough Green	262	53.23 N	2.47 W
Houghton, Mi., U.S.	190	47.07 N	88.34 W
Houghton, N.Y., U.S.	210	42.25 N	78.09 W
Houghton, Wa., U.S.	224	47.40 N	122.12 W
Houghton Estates ◆[8]	273d	26.10 S	28.04 E
Houghton Green	262	53.25 N	2.34 W
Houghton Lake	190	44.18 N	84.45 W
Houghton Lake ⊜, Sk., Can.	184	52.23 N	105.08 W
Houghton Lake ⊜, Mi., U.S.	190	44.20 N	84.45 W
Houghton-le-Spring	44	54.51 N	1.28 W
Houghton Regis	42	51.55 N	0.31 W
Houguangzhengtai	104	41.13 N	122.07 E
Hougujiazi	104	42.21 N	123.22 E
Houhuangtukan	104	41.02 N	122.29 E
Houille ≃	56	50.08 N	4.49 E
Houillères de la Sarre, Canal des ≊	56	48.42 N	6.55 E
Houilles	261	48.56 N	2.11 E
Houjiangfushan	105	40.03 N	117.09 E
Houjiaping	107	30.02 N	104.38 E
Houjiaying	105	39.51 N	117.15 E
Houjie	100	22.58 N	113.39 E
Houjiumen	104	42.38 N	123.18 E
Houkou	98	37.34 N	115.09 E
Houliujia	104	40.47 N	122.19 E
Houlka	194	34.02 N	89.01 W
Houlton	188	46.07 N	67.50 W
Houluan	105	39.13 N	116.32 E
Houma, Tonga	174w	21.09 S	175.19 W
Houma, La., U.S.	194	29.35 N	90.43 W
Houma, Zhg.	102	35.36 N	111.21 E
Houmanzhoutun	104	42.29 N	123.14 E
Houmen	100	22.51 N	115.09 E
Houmet Essouq	148	33.59 N	10.51 E
Houmont Park	222	29.50 N	95.13 W
Hound Creek ≃	202	47.13 N	111.23 W
Houndé	150	11.30 N	3.31 W
Hounslow ◆[8]	260	51.29 N	0.22 W
Houplines	50	50.42 N	2.55 E
Houqianjiayu	104	40.50 N	120.41 E
Houqiao	105	40.04 N	116.39 E
Hourn, Loch c	46	57.08 N	5.36 W
Housatonic	207	42.15 N	73.22 W
Housatonic ≃	207	41.10 N	73.07 W
House	196	34.38 N	103.54 W
House ≃	184	56.13 N	112.31 W
House of Seven Gables ⊥	283	42.32 N	70.53 W
Houserville	214	40.50 N	77.50 W
House Springs	219	38.24 N	90.34 W
Houshan	106	31.03 N	120.21 E
Houston, B.C., Can.	182	54.24 N	126.38 W
Houston, De., U.S.	208	38.55 N	75.30 W
Houston, Mn., U.S.	190	43.45 N	91.34 W
Houston, Ms., U.S.	194	33.53 N	88.59 W
Houston, Mo., U.S.	194	37.19 N	91.57 W
Houston, Oh., U.S.	216	40.15 N	84.20 W
Houston, Pa., U.S.	214	40.14 N	80.12 W
Houston, Tx., U.S.	222	29.45 N	95.21 W
Houston □[6]	222	31.20 N	95.20 W
Houston ≃	194	30.16 N	93.13 W
Houston, Lake ⊜[1]	222	29.58 N	95.07 W
Houston County Lake ⊜[1]	222	31.25 N	95.35 W
Houston Creek ≃	218	38.13 N	84.15 W
Houston Intercontinental Airport ⊠	222	29.59 N	95.27 W
Houston Ship Channel ≊	222	29.21 N	94.47 W
Hout ≃	156	23.04 S	29.36 E
Houtbaai	158	34.03 S	18.21 E
Houthalen	56	51.02 N	5.22 E
Houthulst	50	50.59 N	2.57 E
Houtkop	158	26.36 S	27.52 E
Houtkraal	158	30.23 S	24.05 E
Houtman Abrolhos II	162	28.43 S	113.48 E
Houtskär I	26	60.12 N	21.22 E
Houtzdale	214	40.49 N	78.21 W
Houwuliangdian	104	41.31 N	121.55 E
Houwutaigou	104	41.46 N	121.42 E
Houx	261	48.34 N	1.37 E
Houxijie	100	28.46 N	118.49 E
Houxinlitun	104	41.05 N	122.33 E
Houxinqiu	104	42.34 N	122.43 E
Houyatai	104	41.26 N	121.49 E
Houying	105	39.42 N	118.18 E
Houyingzi	98	40.24 N	123.50 E
Houzhangcun	105	40.08 N	116.11 E
Houzhou	106	31.35 N	119.22 E
Houzitun	104	41.04 N	121.18 E
Hov	41	55.55 N	10.16 E
Hova	40	58.52 N	14.13 E
Hovborg	41	55.36 N	8.57 E
Høve, Dan.	41	55.50 N	11.30 E
Hove, Eng., U.K.	42	50.49 N	0.10 W
Hovedgård	41	55.57 N	9.58 E
Hövelhof	52	51.49 N	8.40 E
Hoven, Dan.	41	55.51 N	8.46 E
Hoven, S.D., U.S.	198	45.14 N	99.46 W
Hovenweep National Monument ♠	200	37.25 N	109.04 W
Hovmantorp	26	56.47 N	15.08 E
Hovran ⊜	40	60.16 N	16.03 E
Hovsta	40	59.21 N	15.13 E
Howa, Ouadi (Wādī Howar) ∨	140	17.30 N	27.08 E
Howakil I	144	15.10 N	40.16 E
Howar, Wādī (Ouadi Howa) ∨	140	17.30 N	27.08 E
Howard, Austl.	166	25.19 S	152.34 E
Howard, Ks., U.S.	198	37.28 N	96.15 W
Howard, Oh., U.S.	214	40.24 N	82.19 W
Howard, Pa., U.S.	214	41.00 N	77.39 W
Howard, S.D., U.S.	198	44.00 N	97.31 W
Howard, Wi., U.S.	190	44.32 N	88.05 W
Howard □[6], In., U.S.	216	40.29 N	86.08 W
Howard □[6], Md., U.S.	208	39.16 N	76.48 W
Howard Beach ◆[8]	276	40.40 N	73.51 W
Howard City	190	43.23 N	85.28 W
Howard Draw ∨	196	30.08 N	101.35 W
Howard Hanson Reservoir ⊜[1]	224	47.15 N	121.45 W
Howard Heights	284b	39.17 N	76.50 W
Howardian Hills ⋏[2]	44	54.07 N	1.00 W
Howard Island I	164	12.10 S	135.24 E
Howard Lake	190	45.03 N	94.04 W
Howard Prairie Lake ⊜[1]	202	42.15 N	122.20 W
Howard University ʋ[2]	284c	38.55 N	77.01 W
Howden	44	53.45 N	0.52 W
Howe, In., U.S.	216	41.43 N	85.25 W
Howe, Tx., U.S.	196	33.30 N	96.37 W
Howe, Cape ›	166	37.31 S	149.59 E
Howe Caverns ⏏[5]	210	42.42 N	74.25 W
Howe Green	260	51.42 N	0.32 E
Howe Island I	212	44.17 N	76.15 W
Howeke	150	4.50 N	7.45 W
Howell	216	42.36 N	83.55 W
Howell Airport ⊠	278	41.39 N	87.45 W
Howell Island I	219	38.40 N	90.42 W
Howells	198	41.43 N	97.00 W
Howells Pond ⊜	276	41.03 N	74.42 W
Howes Cave	210	42.41 N	74.23 W
Howe Sound ⊔	182	49.22 N	123.18 W
Howe's Range ⋏	170	33.08 S	150.47 E
Howes Valley	170	32.50 S	150.51 E
Howey In The Hills	220	28.43 N	81.47 W
Howick, P.Q., Can.	206	45.11 N	73.51 W
Howick, S. Afr.	158	29.28 S	30.14 E
Howitt, Mount ∧	166	37.10 S	146.40 E
Howland	188	45.14 N	68.39 W
Howland Island I	14	0.48 N	176.38 W
Howley	186	49.10 N	57.07 W
Howley, Mount ∧	186	48.17 N	58.26 W
Howmore	46	57.18 N	7.23 W
Howqua ≃	169	37.14 S	146.08 E
Howrah → Hāora	126	22.35 N	88.20 E
Howse Peak ∧	182	51.49 N	116.41 W
Howser	182	50.18 N	116.57 W
Howson Peak ∧	182	54.25 N	127.44 W
Howth	48	53.23 N	6.04 W
Howth Head ›	48	53.22 N	6.03 W
Ho Xa	110	17.04 N	107.02 E
Hoxie, Ar., U.S.	194	36.03 N	90.58 W
Hoxie, Ks., U.S.	198	39.21 N	100.26 W
Höxter	52	51.46 N	9.23 E
Hoxtolgay	86	46.35 N	86.01 E
Hoxton Park	274a	33.55 S	150.51 E
Hoxton Park Aerodrome ⊠	274a	33.54 S	150.50 E
Hoy I	46	58.51 N	3.18 W
Hoya, Dtsch.	52	52.48 N	9.08 E
Hōya, Nihon	94	35.43 N	139.34 E
Høyanger	26	61.13 N	6.05 E
Hoyerswerda	54	51.26 N	14.14 E
Hoylake	262	53.23 N	3.11 W
Hoyleton, Austl.	168b	34.01 S	138.33 E
Hoyleton, Il., U.S.	219	38.27 N	89.16 W
Hoym	54	51.47 N	11.19 E
Hoyos	34	40.10 N	6.43 W
Hōyo-shotō II	96	33.52 N	132.18 E
Höytiäinen ⊜	26	62.48 N	29.39 E
Hoyt Lakes	190	47.31 N	92.08 W
Hoytville, Mi., U.S.	216	42.45 N	84.53 W
Hoytville, Oh., U.S.	216	41.11 N	83.47 W
Hozain ≃	50	48.16 N	4.06 E
Hozat	130	39.07 N	39.14 E
Hozumi	94	35.24 N	136.41 E
Hpru-so	110	19.25 N	97.08 E
Hracholusky, údolní nádrž ⊜[1]	60	49.47 N	13.07 E
Hradec Králové	30	50.12 N	15.50 E
Hrádek	61	48.46 N	16.16 E
Hrádek nad Nisou	54	50.48 N	14.51 E
Hradiště ∧	54	50.13 N	13.08 E
Hranice, Česko.	30	49.33 N	17.44 E
Hranice, Česko.	54	50.15 N	12.10 E
Hrdlovka	54	50.36 N	13.40 E
Hřensko	54	50.50 N	14.14 E
Hriňová	30	48.36 N	19.31 E
Hrob	54	50.39 N	13.44 E
Hron ≃	30	47.49 N	18.45 E
Hronov	30	50.29 N	16.12 E
Hrotovice	61	49.06 N	16.07 E
Hrubieszów	30	50.49 N	23.55 E
Hrubý Jeseník ⋏	30	50.00 N	17.20 E
Hrušovany	61	48.50 N	16.23 E
Hrvatska → Croatia □[1]	36	45.10 N	15.30 E
Hsenwi	110	23.18 N	97.58 E
Hsiakuan → Xiaguan	102	25.34 N	100.14 E
Hsiamen → Xiamen	100	24.28 N	118.07 E
Hsiangt'an → Xiangtan	100	27.51 N	112.54 E
Hsiangyang → Xiangfan	102	32.03 N	112.01 E
Hsian → Xi'an	102	34.15 N	108.52 E
Hsiaohungt'ou Yü I	100	21.57 N	121.36 E
Hsichih	269d	25.04 N	121.39 E

English	Deutsch	Español	Français	Português
≃ River	Fluß	Río	Rivière	Rio
≊ Canal	Kanal	Canal	Canal	Canal
ʟ Waterfall, Rapids	Wasserfall, Stromschnellen	Cascada, Rápidos	Chute d'eau, Rapides	Cascata, Rápidos
⊔ Strait	Meeresstraße	Estrecho	Détroit	Estreito
c Bay, Gulf	Bucht, Golf	Bahía, Golfo	Baie, Golfe	Baía, Golfo
⊜ Lake, Lakes	See, Seen	Lago, Lagos	Lac, Lacs	Lago, Lagos
⁝⁝ Swamp	Sumpf	Pantano	Marais	Pântano
⍓ Ice Features, Glacier	Eis- und Gletscherformen	Accidentes Glaciales	Formes glaciaires	Acidentes glaciares
⍑ Other Hydrographic Features	Andere Hydrographische Objekte	Otros Elementos Hidrográficos	Autres données hydrographiques	Outros acidentes hidrográficos
✣ Submarine Features	Untermeerische Objekte	Accidentes Submarinos	Formes de relief sous-marin	Acidentes submarinos
□ Political Unit	Politische Einheit	Unidad Politica	Entité politique	Unidade política
ʋ Cultural Institution	Kulturelle Institution	Institución Cultural	Institution culturelle	Instituição cultural
⊥ Historical Site	Historische Stätte	Sitio Histórico	Site historique	Sitio histórico
♠ Recreational Site	Erholungs- und Ferienort	Sitio de Recreo	Centre de loisirs	Area de Lazer
⊠ Airport	Flughafen	Aeropuerto	Aéroport	Aeroporto
■ Military Installation	Militäranlage	Instalación Militar	Installation militaire	Instalação militar
◆ Miscellaneous	Verschiedenes	Misceláneo	Divers	Diversos

Symbols in the index entries represent the broad categories identified in the key at the right. Symbols with superior numbers (*) identify subcategories (see complete key on page 1·1).

Symbole im Register stellen die rechts im Schlüssel erklärten Kategorien dar. Symbole mit hochgestellten Ziffern (*) bezeichnen Unterkategorie einer Kategorie (vgl. vollständiger Schlüssel auf Seite 1·1).

Los símbolos incluidos en el texto del índice representan las grandes categorías identificadas con la clave a la derecha. Los símbolos con números en su parte superior (*) identifican las subcategorías (véase la clave completa a página 1·1).

Les symboles de l'index représentent les catégories indiquées dans la légende à droite. Les symboles suivis d'un indice (*) représentent des sous-catégories (voir légende complète à la page 1·1).

Os símbolos incluídos no texto no representam as grandes categorias identificadas com a chave à direita. Os símbolos com números em sua parte superior (*) identificam as subcategorias (veja-se a chave completa à página 1·1).

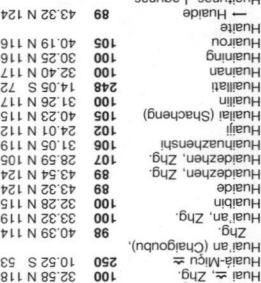

ENGLISH				DEUTSCH				
Name	Page	Lat.°	Long.°	Name	Seite	Breite	Länge°	E=Ost

ESPAÑOL			
Nombre	Página	Lat.	Long. W = Oeste

≈	River	Fluß	Río	Rivière	Rio
≈	Canal	Kanal	Canal	Canal	Canal
ᴸ	Waterfall, Rapids	Wasserfall, Stromschnellen	Cascada, Rápidos	Chute d'eau, Rapides	Cascata, Rápidos
⨆	Strait	Meeresstraße	Estrecho	Détroit	Estreito
c	Bay, Gulf	Bucht, Golf	Bahía, Golfo	Baie, Golfe	Baía, Golfo
⊜	Lake, Lakes	See, Seen	Lago, Lagos	Lac, Lacs	Lago, Lagos
⊠	Swamp	Sumpf	Pantano	Marais	Pântano
⊞	Ice Features, Glacier	Eis- und Gletscherformen	Formas Glaciares	Formes glaciaires	Formas glaciares
	Other Hydrographic Features	Andere Hydrographische Objekte	Otros Elementos Hidrográficos	Autres données hydrographiques	Outros acidentes hidrográficos

◆	Submarine Features	Untermeerische Objekte	Accidentes Submarinos	Formes de relief sous-marin	Acidentes submarinos
□	Political Unit	Politische Einheit	Unidad Política	Entité politique	Unidade política
⨯	Cultural Institution	Kulturelle Institution	Institución Cultural	Institution culturelle	Instituição Cultural
⨁	Historical Site	Historische Stätte	Sitio Histórico	Site historique	Sitio histórico
⨯	Recreational Site	Erholungs- und Ferienort	Sitio de Recreo	Centre de loisirs	Area de Lazer
⨯	Airport	Flughafen	Aeropuerto	Aéroport	Aeroporto
◆	Military Installation	Militäranlage	Instalación Militar	Installation militaire	Instalação militar
◆	Miscellaneous	Verschiedenes	Misceláneo	Divers	Diversos

ENGLISH / DEUTSCH

Name	Page / Seite	Lat.°′ / Breite°′	Long.°′ / Länge°′ E = Ost
Ilek	80	51.30 N	53.22 E
Ilek ≃	72	51.30 N	53.20 E
Ilen ≃	48	51.33 N	9.19 W
Île-Perrot	206	45.23 N	73.57 W
Ileret	154	4.19 N	36.13 E
Îles, Grand lac des ⊜	206	46.43 N	73.30 W
Îles, Lac des ⊜, P.Q., Can.	206	46.06 N	74.02 W
Îles, Lac des ⊜, Sk., Can.	184	54.26 N	109.25 W
Ilesha	150	7.38 N	4.45 E
Ilesha Ibarida	150	8.56 N	3.25 E
Ilet' ≃	80	55.56 N	48.14 E
Ilevskij Pogost	24	60.41 N	43.46 E
Ileza	24	60.43 N	43.54 E
Ilfeld	54	51.34 N	10.47 E
Ilford, Austl.	170	32.58 S	149.51 E
Ilford, Mb., Can.	184	56.04 N	95.35 W
Ilford ◆ 8	260	51.33 N	0.05 E
Ilfov □ 6	38	44.30 N	26.15 E
Ilfracombe, Austl.	166	23.30 S	144.30 E
Ilfracombe, Eng., U.K.	42	51.13 N	4.08 W
Il Fuorn	58	46.40 N	10.12 E
Ilga ≃	88	55.00 N	105.04 E
Ilgaz	130	40.56 N	33.38 E
Ilgaz Dağları ⩘	130	41.00 N	33.35 E
Ilgın	130	38.17 N	31.55 E
Ilha ◆ 8	256	23.00 S	43.33 W
Ilhabela	256	23.47 S	45.21 W
Ilha das Flores	250	10.27 S	36.33 W
Ilha Grande, Baía da c	256	23.09 S	44.30 W
Ilhas, Cachoeira das ㄴ	250	1.03 S	57.33 W
Ilha Solteira, Represa de ⊜ 1	255	20.20 S	51.20 W
Ilhavo	34	40.36 N	8.40 W
Ilhea Point ⟩	156	23.25 S	14.27 E
Ilhéos → Ilhéus	255	14.49 S	39.02 W
Ilhéus	255	14.49 S	39.02 W
Ili ≃	86	45.24 N	74.02 E
Ilia	38	45.56 N	22.39 E
Iliamna	180	59.45 N	154.54 W
Iliamna Lake ⊜	180	59.30 N	155.00 W
Ilian, Mount ʌ	116	10.26 N	119.33 E
Iliatenco	234	16.58 N	98.40 W
İliç	130	39.28 N	38.34 E
Ilıca, Tür.	130	39.52 N	27.46 E
Ilıca, Tür.	130	39.57 N	41.07 E
Ilicínia	255	20.56 S	45.50 W
Iliff	198	40.45 N	103.03 W
Iliff, Lake ⊜	276	41.02 N	74.43 W
Iligan	116	8.14 N	124.14 E
Iligan Bay c	116	8.25 N	124.05 E
Ilijan	116	13.38 N	121.04 E
Ilijsk	85	43.53 N	77.10 E
Ilim ≃	88	57.38 N	102.34 E
Ilimsk	88	56.46 N	103.52 E
Ilin	116	12.15 N	121.02 E
Ilinge	158	31.59 S	27.02 E
Ilin Island I	116	12.14 N	121.05 E
Ilinka	82	54.04 N	38.12 E
Ilinza ʌ	246	0.40 S	78.42 W
Ilion	210	43.00 N	75.02 W
Ilio Point ⟩	229a	21.13 N	157.15 W
Ilioúpolis	267c	37.56 N	23.45 E
Ilir	88	55.13 N	100.40 E
Ilirska Bistrica	36	45.34 N	14.15 E
Ilisós ≃	267c	37.57 N	23.41 E
Ilizi	148	26.29 N	8.28 E
Ilja	76	54.25 N	27.18 E
Iljak	86	60.11 N	77.59 E
Iljič	85	40.50 N	68.27 E
Iljičevsk	84	39.33 N	44.58 E
Iljičovsk	78	46.18 N	30.39 E
Iljincy	78	49.07 N	29.12 E
Iljinka	80	48.32 N	41.05 E
Iljino	76	55.57 N	31.40 E
Iljinskij, Ross.	24	61.02 N	32.41 E
Iljinskij, Ross.	86	58.35 N	55.41 E
Iljinskij, Ross.	88	52.05 N	114.10 E
Iljinskij, Ross.	89	47.58 N	142.12 E
Iljinskij, Ross.	265b	55.37 N	38.06 E
Iljinskij Pogost	82	55.28 N	38.54 E
Iljinskoje, Ross.	76	56.58 N	37.11 E
Iljinskoje, Ross.	76	58.47 N	44.36 E
Iljinskoje, Ross.	76	53.14 N	35.26 E
Iljinskoje, Ross.	76	57.19 N	38.32 E
Iljinskoje, Ross.	80	56.29 N	52.49 E
Iljinskoje, Ross.	82	54.59 N	36.11 E
Iljinskoje, Ross.	82	56.34 N	35.57 E
Iljinskoje, Ross.	265b	55.46 N	37.15 E
Iljinskoje-Chovanskoje	80	56.58 N	39.46 E
Iljinsko-Podomskoje	24	61.08 N	47.56 E
Iljinsko-Zaborskoje	80	57.16 N	44.23 E
Iljiny gory ⩘ 2	76	56.34 N	34.12 E
Il'ka	88	51.43 N	108.32 E
Ilkal	122	15.58 N	76.08 E
Ilkeston	42	52.59 N	1.18 W
Il'kino	80	55.13 N	41.36 E
Ilkley	44	53.55 N	1.50 W
Ill ≃, Fr.	58	48.40 N	7.53 E
Ill ≃, Öst.	58	47.17 N	9.33 E
Illabot Creek ≃	224	48.29 N	121.30 W
Illampu, Nevado ʌ	248	15.50 S	68.34 W
Illana Bay c	116	7.25 N	123.45 E
Illapel	252	31.38 S	71.10 W
Illarionovo	78	48.25 N	35.16 E
Illasi	64	45.28 N	11.10 E
Illawarra, Lake c	170	34.32 S	150.50 E
Illbillee, Mount ʌ	162	27.02 S	132.30 E
Ille-et-Vilaine □ 5	32	48.10 N	1.30 W
Illéla	150	14.28 N	5.15 E
Iller ≃	58	48.23 N	9.58 E
Illertissen	58	48.13 N	10.06 E
Illescas, Esp.	34	40.07 N	3.50 W
Illescas, Méx.	234	23.13 N	102.07 W
Illfurth	58	47.40 N	7.16 E
Illhaeusern	58	48.11 N	7.26 E
Illi, Ba ≃	146	10.44 N	15.21 E
Illiers	50	48.18 N	1.15 E
Illimani, Nevado ʌ	248	16.50 S	67.54 W
Illimo	248	6.28 S	79.51 W
Illingen	56	48.57 N	8.55 E
Illingworth	262	53.45 N	1.54 W
Illinois □ 3, U.S.	178	40.00 N	89.00 W
Illinois □ 3, U.S.	194	40.00 N	89.00 W
Illinois ≃, U.S.	194	35.30 N	95.06 W
Illinois ≃, Co., U.S.	200	40.45 N	106.18 W
Illinois ≃, Il., U.S.	194	38.58 N	90.27 W
Illinois ≃, Or., U.S.	202	42.33 N	124.03 W
Illinois and Michigan Canal ≅	278	41.32 N	88.05 W
Illinois at Chicago, University of ᵾ 2	278	41.52 N	87.39 W
Illinois Beach State Park ♦	216	42.26 N	87.48 W
Illinois Institute of Technology ᵾ 2	278	41.50 N	87.38 W
Illinois Peak ʌ	202	47.02 N	115.04 W
Illiopolis	219	39.51 N	89.14 W
Illkirch-Graffenstaden	58	48.32 N	7.43 E
Illminster	42	50.56 N	2.55 W
Illo	150	11.33 N	3.42 E
Illovo, S. Afr.	158	30.05 S	30.50 E
Illovo, S. Afr.	273d	26.08 S	28.03 E
Illzach	58	47.47 N	7.20 E
Ilm ≃, Dtsch.	54	51.07 N	11.40 E
Ilm ≃, Dtsch.	60	48.49 N	11.45 E
Ilmajoki	26	62.44 N	22.34 E
Il'men', ozero ⊜	76	58.17 N	31.20 E
Ilmenau	54	50.41 N	10.55 E
Ilmenau ≃	54	53.23 N	10.10 E
Il'menskij zapovednik ♦	86	55.16 N	60.17 E
Il'mino	80	53.47 N	45.40 E
Ilo	248	17.38 S	71.20 W
Ilobasco	236	13.51 N	88.51 W
Ilobu	150	7.51 N	4.30 E
Iloc Island I	116	11.18 N	119.41 E
Ilocos Norte □ 4	116	18.10 N	120.45 E
Ilocos Sur □ 4	116	17.05 N	120.35 E
Iloilo	116	10.42 N	122.34 E
Iloilo □ 4	116	11.00 N	122.35 E
Iloilo Strait ꞵ	116	10.43 N	122.36 E
Ilomantsi	26	62.40 N	30.55 E
Ilondola Mission	154	10.42 S	31.47 E
Ilongero	154	4.40 S	34.52 E
Ilop	164	2.54 S	141.13 E
Ilopango, Lago de ⊜	236	13.40 N	89.03 W
Ilora	150	7.45 N	3.50 E
Ilorin	150	8.30 N	4.32 E
Ilovajsk	83	47.56 N	38.13 E
Ilovatka	80	50.31 N	45.55 E
Ilovka	78	50.43 N	38.38 E
Ilovl'a	80	49.18 N	43.59 E
Ilovl'a ≃	80	49.14 N	43.54 E
Iłowa	30	51.30 N	15.12 E
Il Palone ʌ	64	46.02 N	11.04 E
Il'pyrskij	74	59.56 N	164.10 E
Ilsan-ni	271b	37.41 N	126.46 E
Ilse ≃	54	52.06 N	10.35 E
Ilshofen	56	49.10 N	9.55 E
Il'skij	78	44.51 N	38.35 E
Ilskov	41	56.14 N	9.06 E
Il Telegrafo ʌ	66	42.22 N	11.10 E
Ilten	52	52.21 N	9.55 E
Ilu	152	4.12 N	23.02 E
Ilubabor □ 4	144	7.50 N	35.00 E
Iluhār	126	22.48 N	90.06 E
Ilūkste	76	55.58 N	26.18 E
Ilverich	263	51.17 N	6.42 E
Ilwaco	224	46.19 N	124.03 W
Ilwaki	112	7.56 S	126.26 E
Ilwŏl-san ʌ	98	36.50 N	129.06 E
İlyasbey	130	40.13 N	29.52 E
Ilz	61	47.05 N	15.55 E
Ilz ≃	60	48.35 N	13.29 E
Iłża	30	51.11 N	21.14 E
Ima	88	55.13 N	115.55 E
Ima ≃	96	33.45 N	131.01 E
Imabari	96	34.03 N	133.00 E
Imabu ≃	250	0.44 S	57.22 W
Imadomi	268	35.28 N	140.06 E
Imaichi	94	36.43 N	139.41 E
Imajō	94	35.46 N	136.12 E
Imajuku	268	35.58 N	139.21 E
Imajuku ◆ 8	268	35.29 N	139.32 E
Imaki	270	34.24 N	135.46 E
Imaloto ≃	157b	23.27 S	45.13 E
Imambara ᵾ 1	272b	22.54 N	88.25 E
Imanbaj ⊥	86	43.13 N	60.25 E
Imandan-Makit, gora ʌ, Ross.	88	54.15 N	117.38 E
Imandan-Makit, gora ʌ, Ross.	89	54.06 N	117.50 E
Imandra, ozero ⊜	24	67.30 N	33.00 E
Imanombo	157b	24.26 S	45.49 E
Imantau	86	52.58 N	68.22 E
Imari	92	33.16 N	129.53 E
Imaruí	252	28.21 S	48.49 W
Imaruí, Lagoa do c	252	28.21 S	48.52 W
Imasa	140	18.01 N	36.12 E
Imatra	26	61.10 N	28.46 E
Imavere	76	58.44 N	25.48 E
Imazu	94	35.24 N	136.02 E
Imbābah ◆ 8	142	30.04 N	31.13 E
Imbabura □ 4	246	0.22 N	78.25 W
Imba-numa ⊜	94	35.45 N	140.12 E
Imbariê	256	22.39 S	43.13 W
Imbituba	252	28.14 S	48.40 W
Imbituva	252	25.12 S	50.35 W
Imboaçu, Canal ≅	287a	22.48 S	43.04 W
Imboden	194	36.12 N	91.10 W
Imbonga	152	0.43 S	19.46 E
Imbundi	152	5.44 S	16.16 E
Ime, Beinn ʌ	46	56.14 N	4.49 W
Imeni Abaja	86	50.44 N	69.30 E
Imeni Babuškina	76	59.45 N	43.07 E
Imeni 0206 Bakinskich Komissarov	84	39.19 N	49.12 E
Imeni Čapajeva	85	43.28 N	76.50 E
Imeni C'urupy	82	55.30 N	38.39 E
Imeni Džambula, Kaz.	86	45.26 N	74.24 E
Imeni Džambula, Kaz.	86	47.43 N	74.09 E
Imeni Frunze	86	46.23 N	77.20 E
Imeni Il-Go Okt'abr'a	88	55.54 N	119.36 E
Imeni Kalinina, Kaz.	85	43.16 N	74.03 E
Imeni Kalinina, Kyrg.	85	41.28 N	76.22 E
Imeni Kalinina, Ross.	80	51.51 N	52.43 E
Imeni Kalinina, Uzb.	86	43.40 N	59.07 E
Imeni Karla Libknechta	78	51.37 N	35.27 E
Imeni Kirova, Kaz.	86	46.27 N	77.13 E
Imeni Kirova, Ross.	74	59.42 N	128.12 E
Imeni Leninskogo Komsomola	86	50.45 N	66.44 E
Imeni Marta	86	46.57 N	58.58 E
Imeni Michajla Ivanoviča Kalinina	80	57.59 N	45.07 E
Imeni Molodogvardejcev	86	54.03 N	70.44 E
Imeni Panfilova	85	43.23 N	77.07 E
Imeni Poliny Osipenko	89	52.25 N	136.28 E
Imeni Sardarova Karachana	85	38.26 N	68.46 E
Imeni Šeredy	83	46.52 N	40.03 E
Imeni Ševčenko	86	45.58 N	61.04 E
Imeni Stepana Razina	80	54.54 N	44.18 E
Imeni Tel'mana	89	48.36 N	134.59 E
Imeni Timir'azeva	86	53.39 N	65.31 E
Imeni Vladimira Iljiča Lenina	80	53.36 N	46.58 E
Imeni Vorovskogo, Ross.	80	55.43 N	41.06 E
Imeni Vorovskogo, Ross.	82	55.43 N	38.20 E
Imeni XXI Partsjezda	86	50.43 N	67.50 E
Imeni Žel'abova	76	58.57 N	36.36 E
Imera [illegible]	[illegible]	[illegible]	[illegible]
Imerimandroso	157b	17.23 S	48.38 E
Imese	152	2.07 N	18.06 E
Imgenbroich	56	50.34 N	6.16 E
Imi	144	6.28 N	42.18 E
Imias	240p	20.04 N	74.38 W
Imilac	252	24.14 S	68.53 W
Imilili ₸ 4	148	23.18 N	15.54 W
Imi-n'Tanout	148	31.10 N	8.50 W
Imišli	84	39.52 N	48.04 E
Imittós	267c	37.57 N	23.45 E
Imittós Óros ʌ	267c	37.55 N	23.47 E
Imja-do I	98	35.05 N	126.05 E
Imjin-gang ≃	98	37.47 N	126.40 E
Imlay	204	40.39 N	118.08 W
Imlay City	190	43.01 N	83.04 W
Imlaystown	208	40.10 N	74.31 W
Imler	214	40.12 N	78.31 W
Immarna	162	30.30 S	132.09 E
Immendingen	58	47.56 N	8.44 E
Immenhausen	56	51.25 N	9.28 E
Immensen	52	52.23 N	10.04 E
Immenstaad	58	47.40 N	9.22 E
Immenstadt	58	47.33 N	10.13 E
Immigrath	263	51.06 N	6.57 E
Immingham	44	53.36 N	0.13 W
Immokalee	220	26.25 N	81.25 W
Imnaha ≃	202	45.49 N	116.46 W
Imo □ 3	150	5.30 N	7.20 E
Imo ≃	150	4.36 N	7.35 E
Imogiri	115a	7.55 S	110.23 E
Imokt'an	98	38.50 N	126.41 E
Imola	66	44.21 N	11.42 E
Imonda	164	2.51 S	141.10 E
Imore	273a	6.26 N	3.17 E
Imoro	273a	6.43 N	3.30 E
Im Ostholz ◆ 8	263	51.26 N	7.12 E
Imotski	36	43.27 N	17.13 E
Imp'a	98	35.59 N	126.49 E
Impasugong	116	8.19 N	125.00 E
Impe	152	2.44 S	15.17 E
Impendle	158	29.37 S	29.55 E
Imperatore, Campo ⊻	66	42.25 N	13.40 E
Imperatriz	250	5.32 S	47.29 W
Imperia	62	43.53 N	8.03 E
Imperia □ 4	62	43.58 N	7.47 E
Imperial, Sk., Can.	184	51.22 N	105.27 W
Imperial, Perú	248	13.04 S	76.21 W
Imperial, Ca., U.S.	204	32.50 N	115.34 W
Imperial, Mo., U.S.	219	38.22 N	90.22 W
Imperial, Ne., U.S.	198	40.31 N	101.38 W
Imperial, Pa., U.S.	214	40.26 N	80.14 W
Imperial, Tx., U.S.	196	31.16 N	102.41 W
Imperial ≃	254	38.48 S	73.24 W
Imperial Beach	228	32.35 N	117.06 W
Imperial Dam ◆ 6	204	32.55 N	114.30 W
Imperial de Aragón, Canal ≅	34	42.02 N	1.33 W
Imperiale	68	40.07 N	16.35 E
Imperial Mills	182	55.00 N	111.44 W
Imperial Palace ᵾ	268	35.41 N	139.45 E
Imperial Valley V	204	32.50 N	115.30 W
Impflingen	56	49.10 N	8.07 E
Impfondo	152	1.37 N	18.04 E
Imphāl	120	24.49 N	93.57 E
Impilachti	24	61.40 N	31.04 E
Impruneta	66	43.41 N	11.15 E
Impulo	152	13.53 S	13.39 E
İmralı Adası I	130	40.32 N	28.32 E
İmranlı	130	39.54 N	38.07 E
Imroz	130	40.11 N	25.55 E
Imsil	98	35.37 N	127.15 E
Imst	58	47.14 N	10.44 E
Imtān	132	32.24 N	36.49 E
Imuris	232	30.47 N	110.52 W
Imuruan Bay c	116	10.40 N	119.16 E
Imuruk Basin ⊜	180	65.06 N	165.36 W
Imuruk Lake ⊜	180	65.36 N	163.10 W
Imute	273a	6.42 N	3.29 E
Imwŏn-ni	98	37.15 N	129.20 E
Ina, Nihon	94	37.10 N	139.32 E
Ina, Nihon	94	35.59 N	140.03 E
Ina, Nihon	94	35.50 N	137.57 E
Ina, Nihon	268	35.59 N	139.38 E
In'a, Ross.	74	59.24 N	144.48 E
In'a, Ross.	86	53.31 N	82.40 E
In'a, Ross.	86	50.48 N	86.37 E
Ina, Il., U.S.	194	38.09 N	88.54 W
Ina ≃, Nihon	94	37.16 N	139.33 E
Ina ≃, Nihon	96	34.43 N	135.28 E
Ina ≃, Pol.	54	53.32 N	14.38 E
In'a ≃, Ross.	74	59.23 N	144.54 E
In'a ≃, Ross.	86	54.59 N	82.59 E
Inaba	270	34.26 N	135.27 E
Inabe	94	35.07 N	136.33 E
Ina-bonchi ⊻ 1	94	35.45 N	137.57 E
Inabu	94	35.13 N	137.30 E
Inaccessible Island I	10	37.17 S	12.45 W
Inada	270	34.54 N	135.08 E
Inagawa	96	34.53 N	135.22 E
Inagawan	116	9.33 N	118.39 E
Inage	268	35.38 N	140.05 E
Inagi	94	35.38 N	139.30 E
Inajá	250	8.54 S	37.49 W
Inajá ≃	250	8.53 S	49.44 W
In'akino	80	54.26 N	41.07 E
Inakona	175e	9.49 S	160.02 E
Inala	171a	27.35 S	152.58 E
Inamangando ≃	152	14.03 S	12.23 E
Inambari ≃	248	12.41 S	69.44 W
In Amguel	148	23.40 N	5.10 E
Inami, Nihon	94	36.33 N	136.58 E
Inami, Nihon	96	34.45 N	134.54 E
Inami, Nihon	96	33.48 N	135.13 E
In Amnas	148	28.05 N	9.30 E
Inampulugan Island I	116	10.28 N	122.42 E
Inamuragasaki Point ⊥	268	35.18 N	139.32 E
Inanda	273d	26.07 S	28.03 E
Inangahua Junction	172	41.51 S	171.57 E
Inanwatan	164	2.08 S	132.10 E
Iñapari	248	10.57 S	69.35 W
Inaporok	164	8.15 S	141.55 E
In'aptuk, gora ʌ	88	56.22 N	110.11 E
Inari	24	68.54 N	27.01 E
Inarigda	74	63.14 N	107.27 E
Inarijärvi ⊜	24	69.00 N	28.00 E
Inas, Gunong ʌ	114	5.15 N	100.56 E
Inasa	94	34.50 N	137.40 E
Inatsuki	96	33.36 N	130.43 E
Inauini ≃	248	8.30 S	67.24 W
Inawaia	164	8.40 S	146.35 E
Inawashiro-ko ⊜	92	37.29 N	140.06 E
I-n-Azaoua ₸ 4	148	20.49 N	7.30 E
Inazawa	94	35.15 N	136.47 E
Inba	94	35.46 N	140.14 E
Inba-numa ⊜	94	35.46 N	140.12 E
In Belbel	148	27.54 N	1.10 E
Inca	34	39.43 N	2.54 E
Inca de Oro	252	26.45 S	69.54 W
Incaguasi	252	29.13 S	71.03 W
Incahuasi, Nevado de ʌ	252	27.02 S	68.18 W
Ince	262	53.17 N	2.49 W
Ince Blundell	262	53.31 N	3.02 W
İnce Burun ⟩	130	42.06 N	34.56 E
Ince-in-Makerfield	262	53.32 N	2.37 W
İncekum Burnu ⟩	130	36.13 N	33.58 E
İncesu	130	38.38 N	35.11 E
Inch	48	52.08 N	9.59 W
I-n-Chaouag ≃	150	16.23 N	0.10 E
Inchard, Loch c	46	58.27 N	5.04 W
Inchas Military Base ■	142	30.20 N	31.27 E
Inchbare	46	56.47 N	2.38 W
Inchcape I 2	46	56.26 N	2.23 W
Inchelium	182	48.17 N	118.11 W
Inchiri □ 4	150	19.50 N	15.00 W
Inchmarnock I	46	55.47 N	5.09 W
Inchnadamph	46	58.09 N	4.59 W
Inch'ŏn	98	37.28 N	126.38 E
Inch'ŏn □ 4	98	37.30 N	126.38 E
Inchture	46	56.26 N	3.10 W
Inchwagh Lake ⊜	281	42.27 N	83.41 W
İncirliova	130	37.50 N	27.43 E
Incisa in Val d'Arno	66	43.40 N	11.27 E
Incline Village	226	39.16 N	119.56 W
Inconfidência	256	22.16 S	43.13 W
Inconfidentes	256	22.20 S	46.20 W
Inčoun	180	66.18 N	170.17 W
Incudine	64	46.14 N	10.22 E
Incudine, Monte ʌ	36	41.51 N	9.12 E
Incy	24	65.48 N	46.30 E
Indaal, Loch c	46	55.45 N	6.21 W
Indaiá ≃	255	18.27 S	45.22 W
Indaiatuba	256	23.05 S	47.14 W
Indalsälven ≃	26	62.31 N	17.27 E
Indanan	116	5.58 N	120.59 E
Indaparapeo	234	19.47 N	100.58 W
Inda Silase	144	14.05 N	38.20 E
Indaw	110	23.40 N	94.46 E
Indawgyi Lake ⊜	110	25.10 N	96.19 E
Indé	232	25.54 N	105.13 W
Inde ≃	56	50.54 N	6.21 E
Inde → India □ 1	118	20.00 N	77.00 E
Indemini	58	46.06 N	8.50 E
Independence, Ca., U.S.	204	36.48 N	118.11 W
Independence, In., U.S.	216	40.20 N	87.10 W
Independence, Ia., U.S.	190	42.28 N	91.53 W
Independence, Ks., U.S.	198	37.13 N	95.42 W
Independence, Ky., U.S.	218	38.56 N	84.32 W
Independence, La., U.S.	194	30.38 N	90.30 W
Independence, Mo., U.S.	194	39.05 N	94.24 W
Independence, Oh., U.S.	279a	41.23 N	81.38 W
Independence, Or., U.S.	202	44.51 N	123.11 W
Independence, Pa., U.S.	214	40.15 N	80.31 W
Independence, Tx., U.S.	222	30.19 N	96.21 W
Independence, Va., U.S.	192	36.37 N	81.09 W
Independence, Wi., U.S.	190	44.21 N	91.25 W
Independence ≃	188	43.45 N	75.20 W
Independence Creek ≃	196	30.27 N	101.44 W
Independence Hall ⊥	285	39.57 N	75.09 W
Independence Lake ⊜ 1	226	39.26 N	120.18 W
Independence Mountains ⩘	204	41.15 N	115.55 W
Independencia, Bol.	248	17.07 S	66.53 W
Independência, Bra.	250	5.23 S	40.19 W
Independencia, Chile	286e	33.23 S	70.40 W
Independencia, Perú	286d	11.59 S	77.02 W
Independencia, Isla I	248	14.15 S	76.12 W
Independența	38	43.58 N	28.05 E
Inder, ozero ⊜	80	48.27 N	51.54 E
Inderborskij	80	48.33 N	51.44 E
In der Bredde	263	51.20 N	7.23 E
İnderesi	130	37.50 N	35.40 E
Index	224	47.49 N	121.33 W
Index, Mount ʌ	224	47.46 N	121.35 W
Indi	122	17.10 N	75.58 E
India (Bhārat) □ 1	118	20.00 N	77.00 E
India Brook ≃	276	40.47 N	74.37 W
India Gate ⊥	272a	28.37 N	77.18 E
Indialantic	220	28.05 N	80.34 W
Indian ≃, On., Can.	212	45.16 N	76.14 W
Indian ≃, On., Can.	212	44.13 N	78.08 W
Indian ≃, De., U.S.	208	38.36 N	75.10 W
Indian ≃, Ma., U.S.	283	42.47 N	70.58 W
Indian ≃, Mi., U.S.	190	45.59 N	86.15 W
Indian ≃, N.Y., U.S.	212	44.24 N	75.39 W
Indiana	214	40.37 N	79.09 W
Indiana □ 6	214	40.37 N	79.09 W
Indiana □ 3, U.S.	178	40.00 N	86.15 W
Indiana □ 3, U.S.	194	40.00 N	86.15 W
Indiana Dunes National Lakeshore ♦	216	41.40 N	87.00 W
Indiana Dunes State Park ♦	216	41.40 N	87.02 W
Indian Agricultural Research Institute ᵾ 3	272a	28.38 N	77.10 E
Indiana Harbor c	278	41.40 N	87.27 W
Indiana Harbor Canal ≅	278	41.40 N	87.27 W
Indianapolis	218	39.46 N	86.09 W
Indianapolis International Airport ⊠	218	39.43 N	86.16 W
Indianapolis Motor Speedway ♦	218	39.48 N	86.14 W
Indian Bayou ≃	194	34.14 N	91.52 W
Indian Brook	186	46.23 N	60.32 W
Indian Caverns ⩇ 5	214	40.38 N	78.05 W
Indian Church	232	17.45 N	88.40 W
Indian Creek	278	42.14 N	87.59 W
Indian Creek ≃, U.S.	218	39.19 N	84.38 W
Indian Creek ≃, Ca., U.S.	228	35.18 N	118.26 W
Indian Creek ≃, Il., U.S.	216	41.26 N	88.46 W
Indian Creek ≃, Il., U.S.	219	39.56 N	90.32 W
Indian Creek ≃, Il., U.S.	278	42.11 N	87.55 W
Indian Creek ≃, In., U.S.	216	40.55 N	86.42 W
Indian Creek ≃, In., U.S.	218	38.43 N	85.06 W
Indian Creek ≃, In., U.S.	218	38.10 N	86.14 W
Indian Creek ≃, In., U.S.	218	39.23 N	86.29 W
Indian Creek ≃, Md., U.S.	284c	38.59 N	76.55 W
Indian Creek ≃, Mo., U.S.	194	36.33 N	94.29 W
Indian Creek ≃, Mo., U.S.	219	39.10 N	91.11 W
Indian Creek ≃, N.M., U.S.	200	36.11 N	108.23 W
Indian Creek ≃, N.Y., U.S.	276	40.43 N	73.06 W
Indian Creek ≃, Oh., U.S.	218	39.19 N	84.38 W
Indian Creek ≃, Oh., U.S.	279a	41.17 N	81.31 W
Indian Creek ≃, S.D., U.S.	198	44.39 N	103.19 W
Indian Creek ≃, Tn., U.S.	194	35.13 N	88.08 W
Indian Creek Lake ⊜ 1	222	31.44 N	95.58 W
Indianford	216	42.49 N	88.35 W
Indian Grave Mountain ʌ 2	192	32.59 N	84.21 W
Indian Harbor Beach	220	28.08 N	80.35 W
Indian Head, Sk., Can.	184	50.32 N	103.40 W
Indian Head, Md., U.S.	208	38.36 N	77.09 W
Indian Head ≃	283	42.04 N	70.52 W
Indian Head Park	278	41.47 N	87.54 W
Indian Head Pond ⊜	283	42.03 N	70.51 W
Indian Heights	216	40.25 N	86.07 W
Indian Island I	224	48.04 N	122.43 W
Indian Kentuck Creek ≃	218	38.43 N	85.17 W
Indian Lake, Mi., U.S.	216	41.59 N	86.12 W
Indian Lake, N.Y., U.S.	188	43.46 N	74.16 W
Indian Lake ⊜, On., Can.	190	47.08 N	82.08 W
Indian Lake ⊜, Mi., U.S.	190	45.59 N	86.20 W
Indian Lake ⊜, Mi., U.S.	216	42.09 N	85.29 W
Indian Lake ⊜, Mi., U.S.	216	42.00 N	86.13 W
Indian Lake ⊜, N.J., U.S.	276	40.53 N	74.29 W
Indian Lake ⊜, Oh., U.S.	216	40.29 N	83.53 W
Indian Lake Estates	220	27.48 N	81.19 W
Indian Lakes ⊜	216	41.33 N	85.25 W
Indian Lake State Park ♦	216	40.29 N	83.52 W
Indian Mills Brook ≃	285	39.47 N	74.44 W
Indian Mills Lake ⊜	285	39.48 N	74.44 W
Indian Neck	207	41.15 N	72.48 W
Indian Ocean ₸ 1	4	10.00 S	70.00 E
Indian Ocean ₸ 1	6	10.00 S	70.00 E
Indianola, Ia., U.S.	190	41.21 N	93.33 W
Indianola, Ms., U.S.	194	33.27 N	90.39 W
Indianola, Ne., U.S.	198	40.14 N	100.25 W
Indianola, Pa., U.S.	279b	40.34 N	79.51 W
Indianola, Wa., U.S.	224	47.45 N	122.31 W
Indianópolis	255	19.02 S	47.55 W
Indianópolis ◆ 8	287b	23.36 S	46.38 W
Indian Peak ʌ, Ut., U.S.	200	38.16 N	113.53 W
Indian Peak ʌ, Wy., U.S.	202	44.47 N	109.51 W
Indian Point ⟩	212	44.37 N	78.49 W
Indian Prairie Canal ≅	220	27.02 N	80.57 W
Indian Queen Estates	284c	38.46 N	77.02 W
Indian River	190	45.24 N	84.36 W
Indian River □ 6	220	27.43 N	80.36 W
Indian River c	220	28.00 N	80.30 W
Indian River Bay c	208	38.36 N	75.05 W
Indian River Inlet c	208	38.37 N	75.03 W
Indian Rock ʌ	224	45.59 N	120.49 W
Indian Rock Dam ◆ 6	208	39.57 N	76.45 W
Indian Rock Paintings ⊥	224	46.38 N	120.31 W
Indian Rocks Beach	220	27.52 N	82.51 W
Indian Springs, Nv., U.S.	204	36.34 N	115.40 W
Indian Springs, Va., U.S.	284c	38.49 N	77.10 W
Indian Stream ≃	206	45.03 N	71.26 W
Indiantown	220	27.01 N	80.29 W
Indian Town Point ⟩	240c	17.06 N	61.40 W
Indian Valley Reservoir ⊜ 1	226	39.07 N	122.32 W
Indian Village, In., U.S.	218	40.10 N	85.22 W
Indian Village, N.Y., U.S.	210	42.57 N	76.10 W
Indiaporã	255	19.57 S	50.17 W
Indiaroba	250	11.32 S	37.31 W
Indibir	144	8.05 N	37.58 E
Indico, Océano → Indian Ocean ₸ 1	6	10.00 S	70.00 E
Indien, Océan → Indian Ocean ₸ 1	6	10.00 S	70.00 E
Indien, territoires britanniques de l'Ocean → British Indian Ocean Territory □ 2	12	7.00 S	72.00 E
Indien → India □ 1	118	20.00 N	77.00 E
Indiera Alta	240m	18.09 N	66.53 W
Indiga	24	67.41 N	49.00 E
Indigirka ≃	74	70.48 N	148.54 E
Inđija	38	45.03 N	20.05 E
Indin	120	20.16 N	92.57 E
Indio	204	33.43 N	116.12 W
Indio ≃, Nic.	236	10.57 N	83.44 W
Indio ≃, Pan.	236	9.12 N	80.11 W
Indio, Punta ⟩	258	35.16 S	57.13 W
Indios, Canal de los ꞵ	240p	21.56 N	83.16 W
Indira Gandhi Canal ≅	120	31.10 N	75.00 E
Indira Gandhi International Airport ⊠	272a	28.35 N	77.07 E
Indischer Ozean → Indian Ocean ₸ 1	6	10.00 S	70.00 E
Indispensable Reefs ✢ 2	160	12.40 S	160.25 E
Indispensable Strait ꞵ	175e	9.00 S	160.30 E
Indochina ◆ 1	12	16.00 N	107.00 E
Indo → Indus ≃	120	24.20 N	67.47 E
Indom	24	64.36 N	55.22 E
Indonesia □ 1	108	5.00 S	120.00 E
Indonesia, University of ᵾ 2	269e	6.12 S	106.51 E
Indonesia in Miniature ♦	269e	6.08 S	106.49 E
Indonesian Culture, Museum of ᵾ 3	269e	6.09 N	106.49 E
Indonésie → Indonesia □ 1	108	5.00 S	120.00 E
Indonesien → Indonesia □ 1	108	5.00 S	120.00 E
Indooroopilly	171a	27.30 S	152.58 E
Indore	120	22.43 N	75.50 E
Indpur	126	23.10 N	86.56 E
Indragiri ≃	112	0.22 S	103.26 E
Indramayu	115a	6.20 S	108.19 E
Indramayu, Ujung ⟩	115a	6.14 S	108.17 E
Indrapuri	114	5.26 N	95.27 E
Indrāvati ≃	122	18.44 N	80.16 E
Indre □ 5	32	46.45 N	1.30 E
Indre ≃	32	47.16 N	0.19 E
Indre-et-Loire □ 5	32	47.15 N	0.45 E
Indrois ≃	50	47.13 N	0.56 E
Indungo	152	14.48 S	16.17 E
Induno Olona	62	45.52 N	8.51 E
Indura	76	53.27 N	23.53 E
Indur → Indore	120	22.43 N	75.50 E
Indus ≃	120	24.20 N	67.47 E
Industry, Il., U.S.	194	40.20 N	90.36 W
Industry, Pa., U.S.	214	40.39 N	80.25 W
Industry, Tx., U.S.	222	29.58 N	96.30 W
Indwe	158	31.27 S	27.23 E
Indwe ≃	158	32.01 S	27.21 E
Ine	96	35.39 N	135.17 E
İnebolu	130	41.58 N	33.46 E
İnece	130	41.41 N	27.04 E
İnecik	130	40.56 N	27.16 E
In Ecker	148	24.09 N	5.03 E
İnegöl	130	40.05 N	29.31 E
Inerie, Gunung ʌ	115b	8.52 S	120.56 E
Inés, Monte ʌ	254	48.29 S	69.40 W
Ineu	38	46.26 N	21.49 E
Inez, Ky., U.S.	192	37.51 N	82.32 W
Inez, Tx., U.S.	222	28.54 N	96.47 W
Inez, Lake ⊜	276	41.01 N	74.17 W
Infanta, Pil.	116	15.50 N	119.55 E
Infanta, Pil.	116	14.45 N	121.39 E
Infante, Kaap ⟩	158	34.29 S	20.51 E
Inferior, Laguna c	234	16.20 N	94.40 W
Inferno, Cachoeira do ㄴ	250	1.00 S	56.04 W
Infiernillo, Presa del ⊜ 1	234	18.35 N	101.45 W
Infiesto	34	43.21 N	5.22 W
Infreschi, Ponta degli ⟩	68	39.59 N	15.25 E
Ing ≃	110	20.13 N	100.27 E
Ingá	250	7.17 S	35.36 W
Ingabu	110	17.49 N	95.16 E
Ingaí	256	21.24 S	44.55 W
Ingaí ≃	256	21.23 S	44.52 W
Ingal	150	16.47 N	6.56 E
Ingalls	218	39.57 N	85.48 W
Ingalls Creek ≃	224	47.28 N	120.39 W
Ingalls Park	216	41.32 N	88.03 W
Inganda	152	0.05 S	20.57 E
Inganno ≃	70	38.04 N	14.37 E
Ingarö I	40	59.16 N	18.28 E
Ingatestone	42	51.41 N	0.22 E
Ingatestone Hall ⊥	260	51.39 N	0.23 E
Ingelfingen	56	49.18 N	9.39 E
Ingelheim	56	49.59 N	8.05 E
Ingelmunster	50	50.55 N	3.15 E
Ingelstad	26	56.45 N	14.55 E
Ingende	152	0.15 S	18.57 E
Ingeniería, Universidad Nacional de ᵾ 2	286d	12.02 S	77.02 W
Ingeniero Budge ◆ 8	288	34.43 S	58.28 W
Ingeniero Jacobacci	254	41.18 S	69.35 W
Ingeniero Juan Allan	258	34.53 S	58.11 W
Ingeniero Luiggi	252	35.25 S	64.29 W
Ingeniero Luis A. Huergo	252	39.05 S	67.14 W
Ingeniero Maschwitz	258	34.23 S	58.44 W
Ingeniero Romulo Otamendi	258	34.13 S	58.54 W
Ingeniero White	252	38.47 S	62.16 W
Ingeniero Williams	258	34.54 S	59.22 W
Ingenio La Esperanza	252	24.13 S	64.51 W
Ingenio Santa Ana	252	27.28 S	65.41 W
Ingeringbach ≃	61	47.12 N	14.49 E
Ingersheim	58	48.06 N	7.18 E
Ingersoll	212	43.02 N	80.53 W
Ingham	166	18.39 S	146.10 E
Ingham □ 6	216	42.37 N	84.22 W
Ingička	85	39.52 N	67.20 E
Ingleborough ʌ	44	54.11 N	2.23 W
Ingleburn	170	34.00 S	150.52 E
Inglesa, Costa → English Coast ⩇ 2	9	73.45 S	73.00 W
Ingleside, Austl.	274a	33.41 S	151.13 E
Ingleside, On., Can.	206	45.00 N	75.00 W
Ingleside, Il., U.S.	216	42.23 N	88.09 W
Ingleside, Tx., U.S.	196	27.52 N	97.12 W
Ingleside ◆ 8	282	37.43 N	122.28 W
Ingleton	44	54.10 N	2.27 W
Inglewood, Austl.	166	28.25 S	151.05 E
Inglewood, Austl.	166	36.34 S	143.52 E
Inglewood, On., Can.	212	43.47 N	79.56 W
Inglewood, N.Z.	172	39.09 S	174.12 E
Inglewood, Ca., U.S.	228	33.57 N	118.21 W
Inglewood, Wa., U.S.	224	47.44 N	122.15 W
Inglewood Forest ◆ 3	44	54.45 N	2.50 W
Inglis, Mb., Can.	184	50.57 N	101.15 W
Inglis, Fl., U.S.	220	29.02 N	82.40 W
Inglis Lock ◆ 5	220	29.02 N	82.37 W
Ingoda ≃	88	51.42 N	115.48 E
Ingogo	158	27.32 S	29.56 E
Ingoldmells	44	53.11 N	0.20 E
Ingolstadt	60	48.46 N	11.27 E
Ingomar	279b	40.35 N	80.05 W
Ingonish	186	46.42 N	60.22 W
Ingornachoix Bay c	186	50.38 N	57.20 W
Ingraham, Lake ⊜	220	25.09 N	81.08 W
Ingrāj Bāzār	124	25.00 N	88.09 E
Ingram, Pa., U.S.	279b	40.26 N	80.04 W
Ingram, Tx., U.S.	196	30.04 N	99.14 W
Ingram Bay c	208	37.48 N	76.17 W
Ingrave	260	51.36 N	0.21 E
Ingrid Christensen Coast ⩇ 2	9	69.30 S	76.00 E
In Guezzam	150	19.32 N	5.42 E
Ingul ≃	78	47.00 N	31.59 E
Ingulec	78	47.43 N	33.14 E
Ingulec ≃	78	46.41 N	32.48 E
Ingulo-Kamenka	78	48.17 N	32.30 E
Inguri ≃	84	42.24 N	41.33 E
Inguzet	86	58.50 N	83.52 E
Ingvallsbenning	40	60.15 N	15.53 E
Ingwavuma	158	27.09 S	32.00 E
Ingwe	154	13.02 S	26.25 E
Ingwiller	56	48.52 N	7.29 E
Inhaca, Ilha da I	158	26.03 S	32.57 E
Inhafenga	156	20.35 S	33.53 E
Inhambane	156	23.51 S	35.29 E
Inhambane □ 5	156	23.00 S	34.30 E
Inhambane, Baía de c	156	23.58 S	35.51 E
Inhambupe	255	11.47 S	38.21 W
Inhaminga	156	18.24 S	35.00 E
Inhanduí ≃	255	21.37 S	52.59 W
Inhapim	255	19.33 S	42.07 W
Inharrime	156	24.29 S	35.01 E
Inharrime ≃	156	24.29 S	35.01 E
Inhassoro	156	21.33 S	35.11 E
Inhaúma	255	19.29 S	44.22 W
Inhaúma ◆ 8	287a	22.52 S	43.17 W
İnhisar	130	40.03 N	30.23 E
Inhoaíba ◆ 8	256	22.54 S	43.36 W
Inhomirim	256	22.35 S	43.10 W
Inhomirim ≃	287a	22.41 S	43.13 W
Inhuma	250	6.40 S	41.42 W
Inhumas	255	16.22 S	49.30 W
Ini ≃	146	9.30 N	12.20 E
Iniesta	34	39.26 N	1.45 W
Inimutaba	255	18.45 S	44.22 W
Ining → Yining	86	43.54 N	81.21 E
Inírida ≃	246	3.55 N	67.52 W
Inisa	150	7.52 N	4.20 E
Inishbofin I, Ire.	48	55.09 N	8.11 W
Inishbofin I, Ire.	48	53.37 N	10.15 W
Inishcrone	48	54.12 N	9.06 W
Inisheer I	48	53.02 N	9.26 W
Inishkea North I	48	54.08 N	10.12 W
Inishkea South I	48	54.07 N	10.13 W
Inishmaan I	48	53.05 N	9.32 W
Inishmore I	48	53.07 N	9.45 W
Inishmurray I	48	54.26 N	8.40 W
Inishowen ⟩ 1	48	55.12 N	7.20 W
Inishowen Head ⟩	48	55.14 N	6.56 W
Inishshark I	48	53.37 N	10.18 W
Inishtrahull I	48	55.26 N	7.14 W
Inishturk I	48	53.43 N	10.08 W
Inistioge	48	52.29 N	7.04 W
Initao	116	8.30 N	124.18 E
Inje	98	38.05 N	128.09 E
Injibara	144	11.00 N	36.59 E
Injune	166	25.51 S	148.34 E
Inkeroinen	26	60.42 N	26.51 E
Inketete	152	2.37 S	21.53 E
Inkisi (Zadi) ≃	152	4.46 S	14.52 E
Inkom	202	42.47 N	112.15 W
Inkster, Mi., U.S.	216	42.17 N	83.18 W
Inkster, N.D., U.S.	198	48.09 N	97.38 W
Inland Kaikoura Range ⩘	172	42.00 S	173.40 E
Inland Lake ⊜, Mb., Can.	184	52.17 N	99.42 W
Inland Lake ⊜, Ak., U.S.	180	66.27 N	159.47 W
Inland Sea → Seto-naikai ₸ 2	96	34.20 N	133.30 E
Inle Lake ⊜	110	20.32 N	96.55 E
Inman, Ks., U.S.	198	38.13 N	97.46 W
Inman, S.C., U.S.	192	35.02 N	82.05 W
Inman Mills	192	35.02 N	82.06 W
Inman Valley	168b	35.30 S	138.28 E
Inn (En) ≃	32	48.35 N	13.28 E
Innamincka	166	27.45 S	140.44 E
Innbach ≃	61	48.18 N	14.07 E
Innellan	46	55.54 N	4.57 W
Inner Bay c	214	42.37 N	80.24 W
Innerbraz	58	47.09 N	9.55 E
Inner Channel ꞵ	232	16.35 N	88.17 W
Innerferrera	58	46.31 N	9.26 E
Innerfragant	64	46.58 N	13.04 E
Inner Harbor c	276	40.52 N	73.28 W
Inner Hebrides II	46	56.30 N	6.00 W
Innerkip	212	43.13 N	80.42 W
Innerleithen	46	55.38 N	3.05 W
Inner Mongolia → Nei Monggol Zizhiqu □ 4	90	43.00 N	115.00 E
Inner Sister Island I	166	39.42 S	147.55 E
Inner Sound ꞵ	46	57.25 N	5.56 W
Innerste ≃	52	52.15 N	9.50 E
Innerstetalsperre ◆ 6	52	51.55 N	10.17 E
Innerthal	58	47.06 N	8.56 E
Innertkirchen	58	46.42 N	8.14 E
Innervillgraten	64	46.48 N	12.23 E
Innicher → San Candido	64	46.44 N	12.17 E
Inning	60	48.05 N	11.09 E
Innisfail, Austl.	166	17.32 S	146.02 E
Innisfail, Ab., Can.	182	52.02 N	113.57 W
Innisfil Creek ≃	212	44.08 N	79.49 W
Innisfree	182	53.22 N	111.32 W
Innisplain	171a	28.10 S	152.55 E
Innokentjevka	89	49.42 N	136.57 E
Innokentjevskij	89	48.37 N	140.10 E
Innoko ≃	180	62.14 N	159.45 W
Innolovo	265a	59.47 N	29.59 E
Innoshima	96	34.17 N	133.10 E
Inno-shima I	96	34.19 N	133.10 E
Innsbruck	64	47.16 N	11.24 E
Innviertel ◆ 1	60	48.10 N	13.15 E
Inny ≃, Ire.	48	53.33 N	7.48 W
Inny ≃, Eng., U.K.	42	50.35 N	4.17 W
Ino, Nihon	96	33.33 N	133.26 E
Ino, Va., U.S.	208	37.46 N	76.48 W
Inoã	256	22.55 S	42.57 W
Inobonto	112	0.52 N	123.57 E

Symbols in the index entries represent the broad categories identified in the key at the right. Symbols with superior numbers (⩘ 1) identify subcategories (see complete key on page I · 1).

Symbole im Register stellen die rechts im Schlüssel erklärten Kategorien dar. Symbole mit hochgestellten Ziffern (⩘ 1) bezeichnen Unterabteilungen einer Kategorie (vgl. vollständiger Schlüssel auf Seite I · 1).

Los símbolos incluídos en el texto del índice representan las grandes categorías identificadas con la clave a la derecha. Los símbolos con numeros en su parte superior (⩘ 1) identifican las subcategorías (véase la clave completa en la página I · 1).

Les symboles de l'index représentent les catégories indiquées dans la légende à droite. Les symboles suivis d'un indice (⩘ 1) représentent des sous-catégories (voir légende complète à la page I · 1).

Os símbolos incluídos no texto do índice representam as grandes categorias identificadas com a chave à direita. Os símbolos com números em sua parte superior (⩘ 1) identificam as subcategorias (veja-se a chave completa à página I · 1).

Symbol	English	Deutsch	Español	Français	Português
ʌ	Mountain	Berg	Montaña	Montagne	Montanha
⩘	Mountains	Gebirge	Montañas	Montagnes	Montanhas
)(	Pass	Paß	Paso	Col	Passo
V	Valley, Canyon	Tal, Cañon	Valle, Cañón	Vallée, Canyon	Vale, Canhão
⊻	Plain	Ebene	Llano	Plaine	Planície
⟩	Cape	Kap	Cabo	Cap	Cabo
I	Island	Insel	Isla	Île	Ilha
II	Islands	Inseln	Islas	Îles	Ilhas
⩇	Other Topographic Features	Andere Topographische Objekte	Otros Elementos Topográficos	Autres données topographiques	Outros acidentes topográficos

ESPAÑOL Nombre / FRANÇAIS Nom / PORTUGUÊS Nome	Página/Page	Lat.°′	Long.°′ W = Oeste
Inocência	255	19.47 S	147.50 E
Inokashira Park ♦	268	35.42 N	139.34 E
Inokovka	80	52.33 N	42.34 E
Inola	196	36.09 N	95.30 W
Ino-misaki ➤	96	33.01 N	133.06 E
Inoni	152	3.04 S	15.39 E
İnönü	130	39.48 N	30.09 E
Inoue	270	34.48 N	135.03 E
Inowrocław	30	52.48 N	18.15 E
Inozemcevo	84	44.06 N	43.06 E
İnp'ung-dong	98	41.25 N	126.34 E
Inrath ➤•⁸	263	51.21 N	6.32 E
In Rhar	148	27.10 N	1.59 E
Ins	58	47.00 N	7.06 E
In Salah	148	27.12 N	2.28 E
Insar-ni	98	41.01 N	127.21 E
Insar	80	53.52 N	44.21 E
Insar ➤	46	54.33 N	45.18 E
Insch	46	57.21 N	2.37 W
Inscription, Cape ➤	162	25.29 S	112.59 E
Inscription Point ➤	274a	34.00 S	151.13 E
Insel Man — Isle of Man □²	44	54.15 N	4.30 W
Inshar	150	8.49 N	9.40 E
Inshās ar-Raml	142	30.23 N	31.27 E
Insjön	26	60.41 N	15.05 E
İnsko	30	53.27 N	15.33 E
In Sokki, Oued √	148	29.37 N	4.13 E
Inspiration	200	33.24 N	110.52 W
Insterburg — Čern'achovsk	76	54.38 N	21.49 E
Instow	184	49.44 N	108.16 W
Insurgente José María Morelos, Parque Nacional ♦	244	19.35 N	100.55 W
Inta	24	66.02 N	60.08 E
Intendente Alvear	252	35.14 S	63.35 W
Intepe	130	40.00 N	26.20 E
Intercession City	220	28.15 N	81.30 W
Intercourse	208	40.02 N	76.06 W
Interlagos ➤⁸	287b	23.42 S	46.42 W
Interlaken, Schw.	58	46.41 N	7.51 E
Interlaken, Ma., U.S.	210	42.18 N	73.19 W
Interlaken, N.J., U.S.	208	40.14 N	74.01 W
Interlaken, N.Y., U.S.	210	42.37 N	76.43 W
Interlândia	255	16.12 S	49.02 W
Internacional (Guarulhos), Aeroporto ⊠	287b	23.29 S	46.28 W
International Amphitheatre ♦	278	41.49 N	87.39 W
International Falls	190	48.36 N	93.24 W
International Peace Garden ♦	198	49.00 N	100.04 W
International Trade Fair ♦	267d	35.47 N	51.24 E
Interstate State Park ♦	190	45.23 N	92.40 W
Inthanon, Doi ⋀	110	18.35 N	98.29 E
Intibucá	236	14.16 N	88.10 W
Intibucá □⁵	236	14.20 N	88.15 W
Intipucá	236	13.12 N	88.04 W
Intiyaco	252	28.39 S	60.05 W
Intracoastal Waterway ≊, U.S.	192	24.33 N	81.46 W
Intracoastal Waterway ≊, U.S.	196	26.04 N	97.12 W
Intragna	58	46.11 N	8.42 E
Intränget	58	60.20 N	16.09 E
Introbio	58	45.57 N	9.27 E
Introdacqua	66	42.00 N	13.54 E
Intschon — Inch'ŏn	98	37.28 N	126.38 E
Intu	112	0.15 S	115.21 E
Intuto	246	3.39 S	74.44 W
Inubō-saki ➤	94	35.42 N	140.53 E
Inukai	96	33.01 N	131.38 E
Inukjuak	176	58.27 N	78.06 W
Inútil, Bahía c	254	53.30 S	69.50 W
Inuvik	180	68.25 N	133.30 W
Inuya ≊	248	10.41 S	73.30 W
Inuyama	94	35.23 N	136.56 E
In'va ≊	58	58.59 N	55.40 E
Inver	46	57.49 N	3.55 W
Inverallochy	46	57.40 N	1.55 W
Inveralochy	170	34.57 S	149.39 E
Inveraray	46	56.13 N	5.05 W
Inverarish	46	57.21 N	6.04 W
Inverarity	46	56.36 N	2.53 W
Inverbervie	46	56.51 N	2.17 W
Invercargill	172	46.24 S	168.21 E
Invercoe	46	56.40 N	5.07 W
Inverdruie	46	57.10 N	3.48 W
Inverell	166	29.47 S	151.07 E
Invergarry	46	57.02 N	4.47 W
Invergordon	46	57.42 N	4.10 W
Inverkeilor	46	56.38 N	2.32 W
Inverkeithing	46	56.02 N	3.25 W
Inverkeithny	46	57.30 N	2.37 W
Inverleigh	38	38.06 S	144.03 E
Inverloch	166	38.38 S	145.43 E
Invermere	184	51.48 N	103.09 W
Inverness, N.S., Can.	186	46.14 N	61.18 W
Inverness, P.Q., Can.	186	46.15 N	71.31 W
Inverness, Scot., U.K.	46	57.27 N	4.15 W
Inverness, Ca., U.S.	204	38.06 N	122.51 W
Inverness, Fl., U.S.	220	28.50 N	82.19 W
Inverness, Il., U.S.	216	42.07 N	88.05 W
Inverness, Ms., U.S.	194	33.21 N	90.35 W
Inveruglas	46	56.15 N	4.43 W
Inverurie	46	57.17 N	2.23 W
Inverway	162	17.50 S	129.38 E
Investigator Group II	162	33.45 S	134.30 E
Investigator Shoal ➤	108	8.09 N	114.44 E
Investigator Strait ⋃	166	35.25 S	137.10 E
Inwood, Mb., Can.	184	50.30 N	97.30 W
Inwood, On., Can.	214	42.49 N	81.59 W
Inwood, Fl., U.S.	220	28.02 N	81.45 W
Inwood, Ia., U.S.	216	41.19 N	86.12 W
Inwood, Ia., U.S.	198	43.18 N	96.25 W
Inwood, N.Y., U.S.	276	40.37 N	73.44 W
Inwood Hill Park ♦	285	40.52 N	73.55 W
Inyanga	154	18.13 S	32.46 E
Inyanga Mountains ⋀	154	18.00 S	33.00 E
Inyangani ⋀	154	18.20 S	32.50 E
Inyan Kara Mountain ⋀	198	44.13 N	104.21 W
Inyantue	154	18.32 S	26.41 E
Inyati	154	19.39 S	28.54 E
Inyo, Mount ⋀	204	36.44 N	117.59 W
Inyokern	204	35.38 N	117.48 W
Inyo Mountains ⋀	204	36.40 N	118.10 W
Inyonga	154	6.43 S	32.04 E
Inywa	110	23.56 N	96.17 E
Inza	80	53.51 N	46.22 E
Inza ≊	80	53.32 N	45.44 E
Inzago	64	45.32 N	9.29 E
Inzai	94	35.50 N	140.09 E
Inzana Lake @	182	54.58 N	124.40 W
Inžavino	80	52.19 N	42.30 E
Inzell	60	47.46 N	12.44 E
Inzer	86	54.14 N	57.34 E
Inzer ≊	80	54.30 N	56.28 E
Inzersdorf ➤•⁸	264b	48.09 N	16.21 E
Ioánna, gora ⋀	152	64.50 N	178.08 E
Ioco	180	49.18 N	122.52 W
Iō-jima (Iwo Jima) I	174f	24.47 N	141.20 E
Iokanga ≊	24	68.00 N	39.43 E
Iola, Ks., U.S.	198	37.55 N	95.23 W
Iola, Tx., U.S.	210	43.08 N	76.32 W
Iola, Tx., U.S.	222	30.46 N	96.05 W
Iolgo, chrebet ⋀	86	51.30 N	86.25 E
Iolotan'	72	37.18 N	62.21 E
Ioma	164	8.20 S	147.50 E
Iôna, Ang.	152	16.50 S	12.20 E
Iona, N.S., Can.	186	45.58 N	60.48 W
Iona, Id., U.S.	202	43.31 N	111.55 W
Iona I	46	56.19 N	6.25 W
Iôna, Parque Nacional do ♦	152	16.30 S	12.00 E
Iona College √²	276	40.56 N	73.47 W
Ione, Ca., U.S.	226	38.21 N	120.55 W
Ione, Or., U.S.	202	45.30 N	119.50 W
Ione, Wa., U.S.	202	48.44 N	117.24 W
Ionia, Mi., U.S.	216	42.59 N	85.04 W
Ionia, N.Y., U.S.	210	42.56 N	77.30 W
Ionia □⁶	216	42.56 N	85.00 W
Ionian Sea ⊤²	22	39.00 N	19.00 E
Ionia State Recreation Area ♦	216	42.58 N	85.36 W
Ionico, Mer — Ionian Sea ⊤²	22	39.00 N	19.00 E
Ionienne, Mer — Ionian Sea ⊤²	22	39.00 N	19.00 E
Iónioi Nísoi II	38	38.30 N	20.30 E
Ionisches Meer — Ionian Sea ⊤²	22	39.00 N	19.00 E
Ioniveejem ≊	180	66.12 N	174.00 W
Iony, ostrov I	74	56.26 N	143.25 E
Ioppolo	68	38.35 N	15.53 E
Ioppolo Giancaxio	70	37.23 N	13.33 E
Ior ≊	84	41.33 N	46.17 E
Iori ≊	84	41.03 N	46.17 E
Iorskoje ploskogorje ⌒¹	84	41.20 N	46.00 E
Íos	38	36.44 N	25.17 E
Íos I	38	36.42 N	25.24 E
Ioscoe, Lake @	276	44.22 N	74.19 W
Iosegun ≊	182	54.44 N	117.11 W
Iosegun Lake @	182	54.29 N	116.50 W
Iō-shima I	93b	30.48 N	130.18 E
Iota	194	30.19 N	92.29 W
Iovlevo	82	56.10 N	38.20 E
Iowa	194	30.14 N	93.00 W
Iowa □³	178	42.15 N	93.15 W
Iowa ≊	190	41.10 N	91.02 W
Iowa, South Fork ≊	190	42.18 N	93.04 W
Iowa City	190	41.39 N	91.31 W
Iowa Falls	190	42.31 N	93.15 W
Iowa Park	190	33.57 N	98.40 W
Iō-zen ⋀	94	36.31 N	136.48 E
Ipala	154	4.30 S	32.53 E
Ipameri	255	17.43 S	48.09 W
Ipanema ≊	256	22.59 S	43.12 W
Ipanema ≊	250	9.53 S	37.15 W
Ipanguaçu	250	5.30 S	36.52 W
Ipat	24	66.14 N	56.33 E
Ipatinga	255	19.30 S	42.32 W
Ipatovo	80	45.43 N	42.53 E
Ipaumirim	250	6.47 S	38.43 W
Ipava	194	40.21 N	90.19 W
Ipeiros □⁹	38	39.40 N	20.50 E
Iperó (Ipoly) ≊	38	47.49 N	18.52 E
Iperu	154	6.52 N	3.38 E
Iphigenia Bay c	180	55.40 N	133.55 W
Iphofen	56	49.42 N	10.15 E
Ipiabas	256	22.23 S	43.53 W
Ipiales	250	0.50 N	77.37 W
Ipiaú	255	14.08 S	39.44 W
Ipiguá	255	20.50 S	42.57 W
Ipil	116	7.47 N	122.35 E
Ipin — Yibin	107	28.47 N	104.38 E
Ipirá	255	12.10 S	39.44 W
Ipiranga, Bra.	255	25.01 S	50.35 W
Ipiranga ≊, Bra.	287a	22.43 S	43.12 W
Ipiranga ➤•⁸	287b	23.36 S	46.35 W
Ipiranga ≊, Bra.	255	23.21 S	45.10 W
Ipiranga ≊, Bra.	287a	22.48 S	43.37 W
Ipiranga, Canal ≊	287a	22.46 S	43.37 W
Ipiranga, Museu do ♦	287b	23.35 S	46.36 W
Ipitinga ≊	250	0.00 N	53.01 W
Ipixuna	250	4.22 S	44.34 W
Ipixuna ≊, Bra.	248	7.11 S	71.51 W
Ipixuna ≊, Bra.	248	5.45 S	63.02 W
Ipixuna ≊, Bra.	248	6.16 S	61.52 W
Ipixuna, Igarapé ≊	250	3.52 S	52.40 W
Ipoh	114	4.35 N	101.05 E
Ipojuca ≊	250	8.25 S	34.58 W
Ipokera	154	8.03 S	35.41 E
Ipole	154	5.47 S	32.44 E
Ipoly (Ipel') ≊	30	47.49 N	18.52 E
Iporá, Bra.	255	16.28 S	51.07 W
Iporá, Bra.	255	23.59 S	53.07 W
Iporanga	175f	24.35 S	48.36 W
Ipota	73	19.23 S	169.16 E
Ippari ≊	70	36.52 N	14.32 E
Ippesheim	56	49.35 N	10.15 E
Ippy	148	6.15 N	21.12 E
Ipsala	130	40.55 N	26.23 E
Ipswich, Austl.	171a	27.36 S	152.46 E
Ipswich, Eng., U.K.	42	52.04 N	1.10 E
Ipswich, Ma., U.S.	210	42.40 N	70.50 W
Ipswich, S.D., U.S.	198	45.26 N	99.01 W
Ipswich, N.Y., U.S.	207	42.41 N	70.48 W
Ipswich Bay c	210	42.41 N	70.42 W
Ipu	250	4.20 S	40.42 W
Ipubi	250	7.39 S	40.07 W
Ipueiras	250	4.33 S	40.43 W
Ipuh	112	3.00 S	101.30 E
Ipuiúna	256	22.06 S	46.11 W
Ipupiara	250	11.49 S	42.37 W
Iput, Isla I	255	44.37 S	74.46 W
Iput ≊	76	52.28 N	31.02 E
Iqaluit	176	63.44 N	68.28 W
Iqe	102	38.14 N	94.18 E
Iguaçu, Parque Nacional da ♦	252	25.30 S	53.50 W
Iquique	248	20.13 S	70.10 W
Iquitos	246	3.46 S	73.15 W
Ira	196	32.35 N	101.00 W
Iraan	196	30.55 N	101.53 W
Ira Banda	148	5.57 N	22.04 E
Irabu-jima I	175d	24.50 N	125.10 E
Iracema	250	10.29 S	64.05 W
Iracoubo	250	5.48 S	53.18 W
Irago-misaki ➤	94	34.35 N	137.01 E
Irago-suidō ⋃	94	34.35 N	137.00 E
Irai	252	27.11 S	53.15 W
Irajá ➤⁸	287a	22.51 S	43.19 W
Irajá ≊	287a	22.49 S	43.19 W
Irajol	24	64.27 N	55.08 E
Irak — Iraq □¹	128	33.00 N	44.00 E
Iráklion, Ellás	38	35.20 N	25.09 E
Iráklion □⁹	38	35.04 N	25.16 E
Iran (Īrān) □¹, Asia	128	32.00 N	53.00 E
Iran, Pegunungan ⋀	112	2.05 N	114.55 E
Iran National Arts Museum ♦	267	35.41 N	51.27 E
Iränshähr	128	27.13 N	60.41 E
Irapa	250	10.34 N	62.35 W
Irapuato	234	20.41 N	101.21 W
Iraq (Al-'Irāq) □¹, Asia	118	33.00 N	44.00 E
Irba	88	58.07 N	99.00 E
Irbejskoje	88	55.39 N	95.28 E
Irbeni väin (Irves šaurums) ⋃	76	57.48 N	22.05 E
Irbid	132	32.33 N	35.51 E
Irbid □⁸	132	32.30 N	35.45 E
Irbil	128	36.11 N	44.01 E
Irbil □⁴	128	36.10 N	44.00 E
Irbit	86	57.41 N	63.03 E
Irby	262	53.21 N	3.07 W
Irchester	42	52.16 N	0.38 W
Irdning	61	47.33 N	14.01 E
Irdyn'	78	49.23 N	31.44 E
Ire, Mount ⋀	175e	9.10 S	161.05 E
Irebu	152	0.37 S	17.45 E
Irecê	250	11.18 S	41.52 W
Iregua ≊	34	42.27 N	2.24 W
Ireland (Eire) □¹, Europe	22	53.00 N	8.00 W
Ireland (Eire) □¹, Europe	48	53.00 N	8.00 W
Ireland Brook ≊	276	40.25 N	74.29 W
Irene, Ab., Can.	184	49.57 N	110.16 W
Irene, S. Afr.	158	25.53 S	28.13 E
Irene, S.D., U.S.	198	43.05 N	97.10 W
Irene, Tx., U.S.	222	31.59 N	96.52 W
Irene, Mount ⋀	172	45.10 S	167.22 E
Ireng (Maú) ≊	246	3.33 N	59.51 W
Iresick Brook ≊	276	40.24 N	74.22 W
Ireton	42	52.58 N	71.46 E
Irfon ≊	42	52.09 N	3.24 W
Irgakly	84	44.22 N	44.45 E
Irgiz	86	48.37 N	61.16 E
Irgiz ≊	86	48.13 N	62.08 E
Iri	98	35.56 N	126.57 E
Irian Jaya □⁴	164	5.00 S	138.00 E
Iriba	148	15.07 N	22.15 E
Irié	150	8.17 N	9.11 W
Iriga	116	13.25 N	123.25 E
Irigny	62	45.40 N	4.49 E
Irígui ➤¹	150	16.43 N	5.30 W
Iriklinskij	86	51.39 N	58.38 E
Iringa	154	7.46 S	35.42 E
Iringa □⁵	154	9.00 S	35.00 E
Irinjālakuda	122	10.20 N	76.14 E
Iriomote-jima I	175d	24.20 N	123.50 E
Iriona	236	15.57 N	85.11 W
Iriri ≊, Bra.	250	3.52 S	52.37 W
Iriri ≊, Bra.	287a	22.41 S	43.05 W
Iriri Novo ≊	250	8.46 S	53.22 W
Irische See — Irish Sea ⊤²	28	53.30 N	5.20 W
Irish, Mount ⋀	204	37.38 N	115.24 W
Irish Sea ⊤²	28	53.30 N	5.20 W
Irishtown	166	40.55 S	145.30 E
Irituia	250	1.46 S	47.26 W
Iriyamazu	268	35.16 N	139.39 E
Irkăs, Wādī ✔	142	28.57 N	32.00 E
Irkeštam	85	39.41 N	73.55 E
Irkinejeva ≊	88	58.30 N	96.48 E
Irkinejevo	88	58.30 N	96.49 E
Irkliev	78	49.32 N	32.18 E
Irklijevskaja ≊	78	45.51 N	39.39 E
Irkutsk — Irkutsk	88	52.16 N	104.20 E
Irkut ≊	88	52.16 N	104.15 E
Irkutsk	88	52.16 N	104.20 E
Irkutsk □⁸	88	56.00 N	106.00 E
Irlam	44	53.28 N	2.25 W
Irlanda, Mar de — Irish Sea ⊤²	28	53.30 N	5.20 W
Irlande, Mer d' — Irish Sea ⊤²	28	53.30 N	5.20 W
Irlande — Ireland □¹	48	53.00 N	8.00 W
Irland — Ireland □¹	48	53.00 N	8.00 W
Irma	182	52.55 N	111.14 W
Irmauw	164	7.25 S	131.42 E
Irminger Basin ➤¹	70	61.00 N	35.00 W
Irmino ≊	70	36.46 N	14.36 E
Irmino ➤•⁸	83	48.36 N	38.36 E
Irnijärvi ≊	26	65.36 N	29.05 E
Irnsum	52	53.05 N	5.47 E
Iro, Lac ≊	146	10.06 N	19.25 E
Iroise c	62	48.15 N	4.46 W
Iron Baron	168	32.59 S	137.09 E
Iron Belt	190	46.24 N	90.19 W
Iron Bottom Sound ⋃	175e	9.15 S	160.00 E
Iron Bridge, On., Can.	210	46.17 N	83.14 W
Iron Bridge, Eng., U.K.	42	52.38 N	2.29 W
Iron Bridge Dam ➤⁶	222	32.50 N	95.54 W
Iron City	194	35.01 N	87.34 W
Iron Creek c	274a	53.57 N	166.30 W
Irondale, Al., U.S.	194	33.32 N	86.42 W
Irondale, Mo., U.S.	214	37.49 N	90.40 W
Irondale, Oh., U.S.	214	40.34 N	80.37 W
Irondequoit	210	43.12 N	77.36 W
Irondequoit Bay c	210	43.13 N	77.32 W
Iron Gate √	38	44.41 N	22.31 E
Iron Gate Reservoir @	38	44.30 N	22.00 E
Ironia	276	40.49 N	74.37 W
Iron Knob	166	32.44 S	137.08 E
Iron Mountain	190	45.49 N	88.03 W
Iron Mountain ⋀, Az., U.S.	200	33.27 N	111.10 W
Iron Mountain ⋀, Ca., U.S.	204	34.17 N	117.43 W
Iron Mountains ⋀	192	36.30 N	81.50 W
Iron Range	168	12.42 S	143.18 E
Iron Range National Park ♦	164	12.44 S	143.16 E
Iron River, Mi., U.S.	190	46.05 N	88.38 W
Iron River, Wi., U.S.	190	46.33 N	91.24 W
Iron Springs	208	39.46 N	77.25 W
Ironton, Mn., U.S.	190	46.28 N	93.58 W
Ironton, Mo., U.S.	214	37.35 N	90.37 W
Ironton, Oh., U.S.	188	38.32 N	82.40 W
Ironwood	190	46.27 N	90.10 W
Ironworks Creek ≊	285	40.10 N	74.59 W
Iroquois ≊, On., Can.	214	44.51 N	75.19 W
Iroquois, Il., U.S.	216	40.50 N	87.34 W
Iroquois, S.D., U.S.	198	44.22 N	97.51 W
Iroquois ≊	216	40.47 N	87.44 W
Iroquois Falls	190	48.46 N	80.41 W
Iroquois Lock and Dam ➤⁶	212	44.45 N	75.23 W
Irosin	116	12.42 N	124.02 E
Irottko (Geschriebenstein) ⋀	61	47.21 N	16.26 E
Irō-zaki ➤	94	34.36 N	138.51 E
Irpen'	78	50.31 N	30.15 E
Irpen' ≊	78	50.34 N	30.16 E
Irrawaddy, Mouths of the ≊	110	15.45 N	94.50 E
Irrawaddy — Ayeyarwady ≊	110	20.32 N	96.55 E
Irregully Creek ≊	162	23.06 S	116.21 E
Irrel	54	49.51 N	6.28 E
Irricana	182	51.19 N	113.37 W
Irrsee ≊	61	47.54 N	13.18 E
Irsina	67	40.45 N	16.14 E
Irta	44	54.22 N	3.26 W
Irthing ≊	44	54.55 N	52.39 E
Irthlingborough	42	52.20 N	0.37 W
Irtyš ≊	74	61.04 N	68.52 E
Irtysch — Irtyš ≊	72	61.04 N	68.52 E
Irtysh — Irtyš ≊	72	61.04 N	68.52 E
Irtyšsk	86	53.21 N	75.27 E
Irubaj	80	50.11 N	51.21 E
Iruma	94	35.50 N	139.24 E
Iruma Air Base ⬥	268	35.50 N	139.24 E
Iruma-kichi, Kaijō-jieitai- ■	94	35.50 N	139.24 E
Irumu	154	1.27 N	29.52 E
Irún	34	43.21 N	1.47 W
Irupana	248	16.28 S	67.28 W
Irurzun	34	42.55 N	1.50 W
Irú Tepuy ⋀	246	5.25 N	61.02 W
Irves šaurums (Irbeni väin) ⋃	76	57.48 N	22.05 E
Irvine, Ab., Can.	184	49.57 N	110.16 W
Irvine, Scot., U.K.	46	55.37 N	4.40 W
Irvine, Ca., U.S.	228	33.40 N	117.49 W
Irvine, Ky., U.S.	192	37.42 N	83.58 W
Irvine, Ky., U.S.	214	41.50 N	79.17 W
Irvine ≊	46	55.37 N	4.41 W
Irvine, Mount ⋀	210	42.03 N	78.40 W
Irvine Creek ≊	212	43.41 N	80.25 W
Irvine Park ⋍	280	33.48 N	117.45 W
Irvines Landing	182	49.38 N	124.03 W
Irvinestown	48	54.28 N	7.38 W
Irving, Il., U.S.	219	39.12 N	89.24 W
Irving, N.Y., U.S.	214	42.34 N	79.07 W
Irving, Tx., U.S.	222	32.48 N	96.56 W
Irving Park ➤⁸	278	41.57 N	87.43 W
Irvington, Ky., U.S.	192	37.52 N	86.17 W
Irvington, Al., U.S.	194	30.31 N	88.14 W
Irvington, N.J., U.S.	210	40.43 N	73.51 W
Irvington, N.J., U.S.	276	40.43 N	74.14 W
Irvington, N.Y., U.S.	285	40.52 N	73.52 W
Irvington, Oh., U.S.	218	39.51 N	84.15 W
Irvington, Va., U.S.	208	37.39 N	76.25 W
Irvington ➤⁸	284b	39.17 N	76.41 W
Irwell ≊	44	53.27 N	2.17 W
Irwin, Austl.	162	29.12 S	115.04 E
Irwin, Id., U.S.	218	43.20 N	111.17 W
Irwin, Pa., U.S.	208	40.19 N	79.42 W
Irwin, Pa., U.S.	216	40.27 N	84.51 W
Irwin ≊	162	29.15 S	114.56 E
Irwin, Point ➤	162	35.04 S	116.56 E
Irwindale	280	34.06 N	117.56 W
Irwindale	280	34.06 N	117.56 W
Irwinton	192	32.48 N	83.10 W
Irwinville	192	31.40 N	83.26 W
Isa ≊	140	21.49 N	35.39 E
Is, Jabal ⋀	140	21.49 N	35.39 E
Isa	150	13.14 N	6.24 E
'Īsā, Ra's ➤	144	15.11 N	42.39 E
Isaac Lake @, B.C., Can.	182	53.10 N	120.50 W
Isaac Lake @, On., Can.	212	44.47 N	81.14 W
Isabel, Pil.	116	10.56 N	124.26 E
Isabel, S.D., U.S.	198	45.23 N	101.25 W
Isabel □⁴	175e	7.55 S	159.10 E
Isabela, Pil.	116	12.00 N	122.59 E
Isabela, Zaïre	152	2.17 N	24.14 E
Isabela, P.R.	240m	18.30 N	67.01 W
Isabela, Cabo ➤	238	19.56 N	71.01 W
Isabela, Isla I, Ec.	248a	0.30 S	91.06 W
Isabela, Isla I, Méx.	234	21.51 N	105.55 W
Isabela de Sagua	240p	22.57 N	80.01 W
Isabelia, Cordillera ⋀	236	13.45 N	85.15 W
Isabella Indian Reservation ➤⁴	190	43.24 N	84.48 W
Isabella Lake @	212	45.24 N	79.49 W
Isabella Lake @	204	35.40 N	118.26 W
Isabelle ➤	190	47.50 N	91.41 W
Isábena ≊	34	42.11 N	0.21 E
Isaccea	38	45.16 N	28.28 E
Isafjardardjúp c²	24a	66.10 N	23.00 W
Isafjördur	24a	66.04 N	23.09 W
Isagarko	124	24.50 N	77.53 E
Isahaya	92	32.50 N	130.03 E
Isaka, Tan.	154	3.54 S	32.56 E
Isaka-Buku	152	3.55 S	22.03 E
Isa Khel	123	32.41 N	71.17 E
Isakly	80	54.55 N	51.32 E
Isakovka, Ross.	76	60.30 N	41.13 E
Isakovo, Ross.	76	55.11 N	34.40 E
Isakovo, Ross.	76	54.28 N	38.23 E
Isakovo, Ross.	265b	55.59 N	37.23 E
Isajlnta	80	46.24 N	23.44 E
Isala, Massif de l'	157b	22.45 S	45.15 E
Isala, Parc National de l' ♦	157b	22.45 S	45.15 E
Isana (Içana) ≊	246	0.26 N	67.19 W
Isanagel	158	28.21 S	30.39 E
Isandja Etat	152	2.59 S	22.00 E
Isanghi	152	1.26 S	22.18 E
Isangano National Park ♦	154	11.10 S	30.40 E
Isangel	159	19.32 S	169.16 E
Isangi	152	0.46 N	24.15 E
Is'anguolovo	58	54.23 N	56.36 E
Isanu Makutu	152	5.20 S	16.25 E
Isan-ni	98	45.29 N	129.55 E
Isar ≊	56	48.49 N	12.58 E
Isara	150	6.59 N	3.41 E
Isarco, Valle √	64	46.45 N	11.37 E
Isarog, Mount ⋀	116	13.40 N	123.22 E
Isawa	94	39.09 N	141.08 E
Isbergues	54	50.37 N	2.27 E
Isbister	46a	60.36 N	1.19 W
Íscar	34	41.22 N	4.32 W
Íscehisar	130	38.51 N	30.45 E
Ischchi	152	2.57 N	23.11 E
Ischia	66	40.44 N	13.57 E
Ischia, Isola d' I	66	40.43 N	13.54 E
Ischia di Castro	66	42.33 N	11.45 E
Ischim — Išim	86	57.45 N	71.12 E
Ischma — Ižma	24	65.19 N	52.54 E
Ischodnaja, gora ⋀	180	64.50 N	173.26 W
Ischua	210	42.15 N	78.24 W
Ischua Creek ≊	210	42.08 N	78.23 W
Iscuandé	250	2.28 N	77.59 W
Isdell ≊	162	16.27 S	124.51 E
Ise	94	34.29 N	136.42 E
Ise (Uji-yamada)	94	34.29 N	136.42 E
Isefjord c	41	55.52 N	11.49 E
Isehara	94	35.24 N	139.18 E
Isejevka	154	6.18 S	37.46 E
Ise-jima I	84	6.25 S	39.01 E
Iselin, N.J., U.S.	210	40.34 N	74.19 W
Iselin, Pa., U.S.	208	40.33 N	79.23 W
Iselle	58	46.13 N	8.12 E
Iseltwald	58	46.43 N	7.58 E
Isenbüttel	52	52.26 N	10.34 E
Isenyela	154	3.08 S	33.30 E
Iseo	64	45.40 N	10.03 E
Iseo, Lago d' @	58	45.43 N	10.04 E
Iseramagazi	154	4.37 S	32.09 E
Iseran, Col de l' √	62	45.25 N	7.02 E
Isère □⁵	62	45.10 N	5.50 E
Isère ≊	62	44.59 N	4.51 E
Iseri	273a	6.39 N	3.23 E
Iseri-Oke	273a	6.38 N	3.23 E
Iseri-Osun	273a	6.31 N	3.17 E
Iserlohn	56	51.22 N	7.41 E
Isernhagen	52	52.26 N	9.51 E
Isernia	66	41.36 N	14.14 E
Ise-Shima-kokuritsu- ⦶	94	34.23 N	136.48 E
Iset' ≊	86	56.36 N	66.24 E
Isetskoje	86	56.29 N	65.21 E
Ise-wan c	94	34.43 N	136.43 E
Iseyin	150	7.58 N	3.36 E
Isezaki	92	36.19 N	139.12 E
Isfahan — Eşfahān	128	32.40 N	51.38 E
Isfana	85	39.50 N	69.31 E
Isfara	85	40.13 N	69.26 E
Isfjord ≊	24	78.00 N	15.00 E
Isfjorden ⋍	24	78.15 N	13.50 E
Isherton	246	2.19 N	59.22 W
Ishi ⋍	270	34.35 N	135.38 E
Ishibashi	94	36.26 N	139.52 E
Ishigaki	175d	24.20 N	124.09 E
Ishigaki-shima I	175d	24.24 N	124.12 E
Ishige	94	36.07 N	139.58 E
Ishii	96	34.04 N	134.26 E
Ishikari ≊	92a	43.15 N	141.23 E
Ishikari-dake ⋀	92a	43.33 N	143.02 E
Ishikari-heiya ⌐	92a	43.15 N	141.23 E
Ishikari-sanchi ⋀	92a	43.30 N	143.00 E
Ishikari-wan c	92a	43.25 N	141.01 E
Ishikawa, Nihon	94	37.29 N	140.27 E
Ishikawa, Nihon	94m	26.25 N	127.50 E
Ishikawa □⁵	94	36.45 N	136.45 E
Ishiki	96	34.48 N	137.01 E
Ishikiri	270	34.41 N	135.39 E
I-shima I	96	33.51 N	134.49 E
Ishinomaki	94	38.25 N	141.18 E
Ishinomaki-wan c	92	38.18 N	141.18 E
Ishioka	94	36.11 N	140.16 E
Ishiyama	270	34.58 N	135.55 E
Ishizuchi-san ⋀	96	33.46 N	133.07 E
Ishkumān	123	36.32 N	73.49 E
Ishmant	142	29.12 N	31.11 E
Ishpeming	190	46.29 N	87.40 W
Ishuiza	270	34.33 N	135.27 E
Ishurdi	123	24.08 N	89.05 E
Isidro Casanova	288	34.42 S	58.35 W
Isigny	62	49.19 N	1.06 W
Işık Dağı ⋀	130	38.21 N	36.32 E
Işıklı Burnu ➤	267b	41.14 N	29.15 E
Isil'kul'	86	54.54 N	71.16 E
Isili	71	39.44 N	9.06 E
Isingiro	154	1.00 S	30.50 E
Isiolo	154	0.21 N	37.35 E
Isipingo	157b	29.59 S	30.56 E
Isipingo Beach	159	30.00 S	30.56 E
Isiro	154	2.47 N	27.37 E
Isisford	166	24.16 S	144.26 E
Iskandar	85	41.36 N	69.43 E
Iskår ≊	38	43.44 N	24.27 E
Iskår, jazovir @	38	42.28 N	23.35 E
Iskatel'	24	67.54 N	53.10 E
Iskateley, chrebet ⋀	88	66.30 N	179.00 W
Iskenderun	130	36.37 N	36.07 E
İskenderun Körfezi c	130	36.30 N	35.40 E
İskilip	130	40.45 N	34.29 E
Iski-Naukat	85	40.16 N	72.36 E
Iskininskij	80	47.13 N	52.41 E
Iskitim	88	54.38 N	83.18 E
Iskushuban	144	10.18 N	50.14 E
Iskut ≊	180	56.45 N	131.45 W
Isla ≊	46	57.30 N	3.23 W
Isla, Massif de l'	157b	22.45 S	45.15 E
Isla, Salar de la @	252	25.49 S	68.53 W
Isla Cristina	34	37.12 N	7.19 W
Isla de Maipo	252	33.45 S	70.54 W
Islāhīye	130	37.01 N	36.38 E
Islāmābād	123	33.42 N	73.10 E
Islāmābād — Anantnāg	123	33.44 N	75.09 E
Islamkot	124	24.42 N	70.11 E
Islamorada	220	24.55 N	80.37 W
Islāmpur, India	124	17.03 N	74.16 E
Islāmpur, India	124	25.09 N	85.12 E
Islāmpur, India	124	26.16 N	88.11 E
Islāmpur, India	124	21.24 N	87.39 E
Isla Mujeres	232	21.15 N	86.44 W
Island	194	37.26 N	87.08 W
Island ≊	204	40.33 N	122.36 W
Island Bay c	228	33.45 N	118.10 W
Island Beach State Park ♦	208	39.50 N	74.06 W
Island Bend	171b	36.16 S	148.29 E
Island Creek	283	42.00 N	70.43 W
Island Falls, Sk., Can.	184	55.32 N	102.21 W
Island Falls, Me., U.S.	188	46.00 N	68.16 W
Island Heights	208	39.56 N	74.09 W
Islandia — Iceland □¹	24a	65.00 N	18.00 W
Islandia — Iceland □¹	24	65.00 N	18.00 W
Island Lagoon ≊	166	31.30 S	136.40 E
Island Lake ≊, On., Can.	184	54.53 N	94.47 W
Island Lake ≊, Mn., U.S.	184	53.47 N	94.25 W
Island Lake, Il., U.S.	216	42.17 N	88.12 W
Island Lake, Mn., U.S.	184	46.58 N	92.06 W
Island Lake State Recreation Area ♦	216	42.30 N	83.43 W
Island Park, Id., U.S.	202	44.25 N	111.19 W
Island Park, N.Y., U.S.	276	40.36 N	73.39 W
Island Park Reservoir @	202	44.19 N	111.24 W
Island Pond	208	44.49 N	71.53 W
Island Pond @	285	40.58 N	74.18 W
Islands, Bay of c, Nf., Can.	188	49.10 N	58.15 W
Islands, Bay of c, N.Z.	172	35.12 S	174.10 E
Island View	184	53.54 N	94.25 W
Isla Patrulla	252	32.45 S	54.30 W
Islas de la Bahía □⁵	236	16.20 N	86.30 W
Islas Malvinas — Falkland Islands	254	51.45 S	59.00 W
Islay, Punta ➤	248	17.01 S	72.07 W
Islay, Rhinns of ➤¹	46	55.45 N	6.25 W
Islay, Sound of ⋃	46	55.50 N	6.01 W
Isle	190	46.08 N	93.28 W
Isle ≊, Fr.	62	44.55 N	0.15 W
Isle ≊, Eng., U.K.	42	50.59 N	2.53 W
Isle-Adam, Forêt de l' ⋍	261	49.05 N	2.15 E
Isle-aux-Morts	186	47.35 N	58.59 W
Isle of Hope	192	31.58 N	81.05 W
Isle of Man □², Europe	22	54.15 N	4.30 W
Isle of Man □², Europe	44	54.15 N	4.30 W
Isle of Man Airport ⊠	44	54.06 N	4.36 W
Isle of Palms	192	32.47 N	79.48 W
Isle of Wight	208	36.54 N	76.42 W
Isle of Wight □⁶, Eng., U.K.	42	50.40 N	1.20 W
Isle of Wight □⁶, Va., U.S.	208	36.50 N	76.42 W
Isle of Wight Bay c	208	38.22 N	75.06 W
Isle Royale National Park ♦	190	48.00 N	89.00 W
Isles, Lake of the @	212	44.19 N	75.59 W
Isle Saint George	214	41.43 N	82.49 W
Islesboro Island I	188	44.20 N	68.53 W
Isleta	226	34.54 N	106.41 W
Isleta Indian Reservation ➤⁴	200	34.55 N	106.45 W
Isleton	226	38.09 N	121.36 W
Islets-Caribou	186	49.30 N	67.14 W
Isleworth ➤⁸	262	51.28 N	0.20 W
Islington ➤⁸	207	42.13 N	71.11 W
Islington ➤⁸, On., Can.	275b	43.39 N	79.32 W
Islington ➤⁸, Eng., U.K.	42	51.34 N	0.06 W
Islip, Eng., U.K.	42	51.50 N	1.14 W
Islip, N.Y., U.S.	276	40.43 N	73.12 W
Islip Terrace	276	40.44 N	73.11 W
Islivig	46	58.05 N	7.11 W
Isloč ≊	76	53.55 N	26.13 E
Islón	252	29.54 S	71.12 W
Isluga, Volcán ⋀¹	248	19.10 S	68.51 W
Ismael Cortinas (Arroyo Grande)	258	33.58 S	57.06 W
Ismailia — Al-Ismā'īlīyah	142	30.35 N	32.16 E
Ismā'īlīyah ➤⁸	273c	30.03 N	31.14 E
Ismā'īlīyah, Turʻat al- ≊	142	30.04 N	31.16 E
Ismailli	130	38.56 N	27.13 E
Ismailli	130	40.47 N	48.09 E
Ismailovo ➤⁸	265a	55.47 N	37.47 E
Ismaning	60	48.14 N	11.41 E
Isna	140	25.18 N	32.33 E
Isny	58	47.41 N	10.02 E
Isoanala	157b	23.50 S	45.44 E
Isogo ➤⁸	94	35.23 N	139.37 E
Isoka	154	10.10 S	32.35 E
Isokyrö	26	63.00 N	22.19 E
Isola, Fr.	62	44.11 N	7.03 E
Isola del Cantone	64	44.40 N	8.57 E
Isola del Gran Sasso d'Italia	66	42.30 N	13.40 E
Isola della Scala	64	45.16 N	11.00 E
Isola di Capo Rizzuto	68	38.58 N	17.06 E
Isola Dovarese	64	45.10 N	10.18 E
Isola Farnese ➤⁸	64	42.01 N	12.23 E
Isola Vicentina	64	45.43 N	11.25 E
Isoletta	66	41.30 N	13.34 E
Isollōck Peak ⋀	224	49.18 N	121.27 W
Isone	58	46.08 N	8.59 E
Isonzo (Soča) ≊	64	45.43 N	13.32 E
Isosyöte ⋀²	26	65.37 N	27.35 E
Iso-zaki ➤	94	36.23 N	140.38 E
Ispani	130	41.56 N	41.05 E
Isparta	130	37.46 N	30.33 E
Isparta □⁴	130	38.00 N	31.00 E
Isperih	38	43.43 N	26.50 E
Ispica	70	36.47 N	14.54 E
Ispica, Cava d' ⋍	70	36.51 N	14.54 E
Ispra	58	45.49 N	8.37 E
Ispringen	56	48.55 N	8.41 E
Israel (Yisra'el) □¹, Asia	118	31.30 N	35.00 E
Israel (Yisra'el) □¹, Asia	132	31.30 N	35.00 E
Issa	188	53.52 N	44.51 E
Issa ≊	80	53.59 N	45.00 E
Issano	246	5.49 N	59.25 W
Issaquah	272	47.31 N	122.01 W
Issaran, Ra's ➤	142	28.01 N	33.20 E
Issel (Oude IJssel) ≊	52	52.00 N	6.10 E
Isselburg	54	51.50 N	6.28 E
Isselhorst	56	52.00 N	8.24 E
Isser, Oued ≊, Alg.	34	36.48 N	3.30 E
Isser, Oued ≊, Alg.	34	35.58 N	6.35 W
Issia	150	6.29 N	6.35 W
Issigeac	62	44.44 N	0.36 E
Issime	58	45.39 N	7.51 E
Issoire	62	45.33 N	3.15 E
Issoudun	62	46.57 N	1.59 E
Issuna	154	5.23 S	34.46 E
Is-sur-Tille	62	47.31 N	5.06 E
Issy-les-Moulineaux	261	48.49 N	2.17 E
Issyk-Kul' (Rybač'e)	85	42.26 N	76.12 E
Issyk-Kul', ozero @	85	42.25 N	77.15 E
Ïstädeh-ye Moqor, Äb-e @	120	32.32 N	67.57 E
Istana Presidential Palace ♦	269e	6.10 S	106.49 E
Istanbul, Tür.	130	41.01 N	28.58 E
Istanbul, Tür.	267b	41.01 N	28.58 E
Istanbul □⁴	130	41.10 N	28.45 E
Istanbul (Yeşilköy) International Airport ⊠	267b	40.58 N	28.49 E
Istanbul Boğazı (Bosporus) ⋃	267b	41.06 N	29.04 E
Istanbul University ⍓²	267b	41.00 N	28.58 E
Istead Rise	260	51.24 N	0.22 E
Istiaía	38	38.57 N	23.09 E
Istibanja	38	41.52 N	22.39 E
Istinye ➤⁸	267b	41.08 N	29.04 E
Istisu	84	39.57 N	45.59 E
Istmina	250	5.10 N	76.39 W
Isto, Mount ⋀	180	69.12 N	143.48 W
Istok	38	42.47 N	20.29 E
Istokpoga, Lake @	220	27.22 N	81.17 W
Istra ⋍	265a	55.55 N	36.50 E
Istres	62	43.31 N	4.59 E

Legend

	River / Fluß / Río / Rivière / Rio
⧄	Canal / Kanal / Canal / Canal / Canal
⌄	Waterfall, Rapids / Wasserfall, Stromschnellen / Cascada, Rápidos / Chute d'eau, Rapides / Cascata, Rápidos
⋃	Strait / Meeresstraße / Estrecho / Détroit / Estreito
c	Bay, Gulf / Bucht, Golf / Bahía, Golfo / Baie, Golfe / Baía, Golfo
@	Lake, Lakes / See, Seen / Lago, Lagos / Lac, Lacs / Lago, Lagos
≊	Swamp / Sumpf / Pantano / Marais / Pântano
⋈	Ice Features, Glacier / Eis- und Gletscherformen / Formas glaciares / Formes glaciaires / Formas glaciares
⌒	Other Hydrographic Features / Andere Hydrographische Objekte / Otros Elementos Hidrográficos / Autres données hydrographiques / Outros acidentes hidrográficos
➤	Submarine Features / Untermeerische Objekte / Accidentes Submarinos / Formes de relief sous-marin / Acidentes submarinos
□	Political Unit / Politische Einheit / Unidad Política / Entité politique / Unidade política
⍓	Cultural Institution / Kulturelle Institution / Institución Cultural / Institution culturelle / Instituição Cultural
⌂	Historical Site / Historische Stätte / Sitio Histórico / Site historique / Sítio Histórico
♦	Recreational Site / Erholungs- und Ferienort / Sitio de Recreo / Site de loisirs / Sítio de Recreio
⊠	Airport / Flughafen / Aeropuerto / Aéroport / Aeroporto
■	Military Installation / Militäranlage / Instalación Militar / Installation militaire / Instalação militar
•	Miscellaneous / Verschiedenes / Misceláneo / Divers / Diversos

Topographische Objekte			Other Topographic Features		Autres Elementos / Otros Topográficos
Berg	▲ Mountain	✖ Mountain	Montanha / Montagne / Montañas		
Paß	✕ Pass	Passo / Col / Paso			
Tal, Cañon	Ʌ Valley, Canyon	Vale, Canyon / Vallée, Canyon / Valle, Cañón			
Ebene	⌐ Plain	Llano / Plaine / Llano			
Kap	➤ Cape	Cabo / Cap / Cabo			
Insel	I Island	Ilha / Ile / Isla			
Inseln	II Islands	Ilhas / Iles / Islas			
Andere Topographische	● Other Topographic Features	Outros Elementos / Autres données / Otros topográficos			

ENGLISH				DEUTSCH			
Name	Page	Lat.°	Long.°	Name	Seite	Breite	Länge° E=Ost

ESPAÑOL Nombre	Página	Lat.°'	Long.°' W = Oeste	FRANÇAIS Nom	Page	Lat.°'	Long.°' W = Ouest	PORTUGUÊS Nome	Página	Lat.°'	Long.°' W = Oeste

ENGLISH — Name, Page, Lat.°′, Long.°′
DEUTSCH — Name, Seite, Breite°′, Länge°′ E = Ost

Symbols in the index entries represent the broad categories identified in the key at the right. Symbols with superior numbers (⋏[1]) identify subcategories (see complete key on page *I · 1)*.

Symbole im Register stellen die rechts im Schlüssel erklärten Kategorien dar. Symbole mit hochgestellten Ziffern (⋏[1]) bezeichnen Unterabteilungen einer Kategorie (vgl. vollständiger Schlüssel auf Seite *I · 1)*.

Los símbolos incluídos en el texto del índice representan las grandes categorias identificadas con la clave a la derecha. Los símbolos con numeros en su parte superior (⋏[1]) identifican las subcategorías (véase la clave completa en la página *I · 1)*.

Les symboles de l'index représentent les catégories indiquées dans la légende à droite. Les symboles suivis d'un indice (⋏[1]) représentent des sous-catégories (voir légende complète à la page *I · 1)*.

Os símbolos incluídos no texto do índice representam as grandes categorias identificadas com a chave à direita. Os símbolos com números em sua parte superior (⋏[1]) identificam as subcategorias (veja-se a chave completa à página *I · 1)*.

∧ Mountain	Berg	Montaña	Montagne	Montanha
⋏ Mountains	Gebirge	Montañas	Montagnes	Montanhas
)(Pass	Paß	Paso	Col	Passo
V Valley, Canyon	Tal, Cañon	Valle, Cañón	Vallée, Canyon	Vale, Canhão
≚ Plain	Ebene	Llano	Plaine	Planície
› Cape	Kap	Cabo	Cap	Cabo
I Island	Insel	Isla	Île	Ilha
II Islands	Inseln	Islas	Îles	Ilhas
⊥ Other Topographic Features	Andere Topographische Objekte	Otros Elementos Topográficos	Autres données topographiques	Outros acidentes topográficos

ESPAÑOL: Nombre, Página, Lat.°′, Long.°′ W = Oeste — FRANÇAIS: Nom, Page, Lat.°′, Long.°′ W = Ouest — PORTUGUÊS: Nome, Página, Lat.°′, Long.°′ W = Oeste

Nombre / Nom / Nome	Página / Page	Lat.°′	Long.°′
Jobos	240m	17.58 N	66.10 W
Jobos, Bahía de ⊂	240m	17.56 N	66.13 W
Job Peak ∧	204	39.35 N	118.14 W
Jobstown	285	40.02 N	74.41 W
Jochberg	64	47.23 N	12.24 E
Jock ≃	212	45.16 N	75.43 W
Jocketa	54	50.33 N	12.10 E
Jockgrim	56	49.06 N	8.17 E
Jocko ≃	202	47.20 N	114.17 W
Jocolí	252	32.35 S	68.41 W
Jo Co Marsh ⁞	276	40.37 N	73.47 W
Jocón	236	15.17 N	86.58 W
Jocoro	236	13.37 N	88.01 W
Jocotán	236	14.49 N	89.23 W
Jocotepec	234	20.18 N	103.26 W
Jocotitlán	234	19.42 N	99.48 W
Jódar	34	37.50 N	3.21 W
Jodhpur	120	26.17 N	73.02 E
Jodiya	120	22.42 N	70.18 E
Jodoigne	56	50.43 N	4.52 E
Jodrell Bank Radio Telescope ʊ[3]	262	53.14 N	2.18 W
Joe ≃	220	25.17 N	81.05 W
Joe Batt's Arm	186	49.44 N	54.10 W
Joel	158	28.42 S	28.21 E
Joensuu	26	62.36 N	29.46 E
Joetsu	94	37.06 N	138.15 E
Jœuf	56	49.14 N	6.01 E
Jofane	156	21.17 S	34.16 E
Joffre, Mount ∧	182	50.32 N	115.13 W
Jōganzi ≃	94	36.46 N	137.18 E
Jōga-shima I	94	35.08 N	139.37 E
Jōgawara	268	35.42 N	139.22 E
Jōge	96	34.42 N	133.07 E
Jogeshvari ◆[8]	272c	19.08 N	72.51 E
Jogeshvari Cave •[5]	272c	19.08 N	72.51 E
Jõgeva	76	58.45 N	26.24 E
Jog Falls ∟	122	14.13 N	74.45 E
Joggins	186	45.42 N	64.27 W
Joghatāy	128	36.36 N	57.01 E
Jogindarnagar	123	31.59 N	76.46 E
Jogjakarta → Yogyakarta	115a	7.48 S	110.22 E
Jogui ≃	255	23.45 S	54.40 W
Jōhana	94	36.31 N	136.54 E
Johannesburg, S. Afr.	158	26.12 S	28.05 E
Johannesburg, S. Afr.	273d	26.12 S	28.05 E
Johannesburg, Ca., U.S.	228	35.22 N	117.38 W
Johannesburg □[5]	273d	26.13 S	28.02 E
Johannesburg (Jan Smuts) Airport ⊠	273d	26.08 S	28.14 E
Johanngeorgenstadt	54	50.26 N	12.43 E
Johanniskreuz	56	49.20 N	7.49 E
Johannisthal ◆[8]	264a	52.26 N	13.30 E
Jōhen	92	32.57 N	132.35 E
Johi	120	26.41 N	67.37 E
Johilla ≃	124	23.37 N	81.14 E
John ≃	180	66.55 N	151.35 W
John Boyd Thacher State Park ♠	210	42.38 N	74.01 W
John Carroll University ʊ[2]	279a	41.29 N	81.32 W
John Day	202	44.24 N	118.57 W
John Day ≃	202	45.44 N	120.39 W
John Day, Middle Fork ≃	202	44.55 N	119.18 W
John Day, North Fork ≃	202	44.45 N	119.38 W
John Day, South Fork ≃	202	44.28 N	119.31 W
John Day Dam ◆[6]	224	45.43 N	120.41 W
John Day Fossil Beds National Monument ♠	202	44.34 N	119.39 W
John Fitzgerald Kennedy Stadium ♠	285	39.54 N	75.10 W
John F. Kennedy International Airport ⊠	210	40.38 N	73.47 W
John F. Kennedy National Historical Site ⊥	283	42.21 N	71.08 W
John F. Kennedy Space Center ʊ[3]	220	28.40 N	80.40 W
John Forrest National Park ♠	168a	31.53 S	116.06 E
John Hancock Center ʊ	278	41.55 N	87.37 W
John H. Kerr Reservoir ⊜[1]	192	36.35 N	78.35 W
John J. Duffy Preserve ♠	278	41.39 N	87.55 W
John Martin Reservoir ⊜[1]	198	38.05 N	103.02 W
John McLaren Park ♠	282	37.43 N	122.25 W
John Muir National Historical Site ⊥	282	37.59 N	122.08 W
Johnny Run ≃	216	41.17 N	88.21 W
John o'Groats	46	58.38 N	3.05 W
John Pennekamp Coral Reef State Park ♠	220	25.11 N	80.15 W
John Redmond Reservoir ⊜[1]	198	38.18 N	95.55 W
Johns ≃	224	46.54 N	124.01 W
Johns Creek ≃	192	37.30 N	80.06 W
Johnshaven	46	56.47 N	2.20 W
Johns Hopkins University ʊ[2]	284b	39.20 N	76.37 W
Johns Island I	192	32.40 N	80.05 W
Johnson, Ar., U.S.	194	36.07 N	94.09 W
Johnson, Ks., U.S.	198	37.34 N	101.45 W
Johnson, Ne., U.S.	198	40.24 N	95.59 W
Johnson, N.Y., U.S.	210	41.22 N	74.30 W
Johnson, Vt., U.S.	188	44.38 N	72.40 W
Johnson □[6], In., U.S.	218	39.29 N	86.03 W
Johnson □[6], Tx., U.S.	222	32.20 N	97.20 W
Johnson, Mount ∧	226	36.37 N	121.19 W
Johnson Bay ⊂	208	38.03 N	75.20 W
Johnsonburg, N.J., U.S.	210	40.58 N	74.53 W
Johnsonburg, N.Y., U.S.	210	42.44 N	78.18 W
Johnsonburg, Pa., U.S.	214	41.29 N	78.40 W
Johnson City, N.Y., U.S.	210	42.06 N	75.57 W
Johnson City, Tn., U.S.	192	36.18 N	82.21 W
Johnson City, Tx., U.S.	196	30.16 N	98.24 W
Johnson Creek, N.Y., U.S.	210	43.15 N	78.31 W
Johnson Creek, Wi., U.S.	216	43.04 N	88.46 W
Johnson Creek ≃, Id., U.S.	202	44.58 N	115.30 W
Johnson Creek ≃, Ky., U.S.	218	38.27 N	84.04 W
Johnson Creek ≃, N.Y., U.S.	210	43.22 N	78.16 W
Johnson Creek ≃, Tx., U.S.	222	32.02 N	94.59 W
Johnson Creek ≃, Wa., U.S.	224	46.35 N	121.42 W
Johnsondale	204	35.58 N	118.32 W
Johnson Drain ≅	281	42.26 N	83.28 W
Johnson Draw V, Tx., U.S.	196	31.58 N	101.41 W
Johnson Draw V, Tx., U.S.	196	30.08 N	101.07 W
Johnson Hall State Historic Site ⊥	210	43.01 N	74.23 W
Johnson Park ♠	276	40.30 N	74.27 W
Johnson Point ≻	241h	13.07 N	61.12 W
Johnsons Crossing	180	60.29 N	133.16 W
Johnsons Point ≻	240c	17.02 N	61.53 W
Johnsons Pond ⊜	283	42.44 N	71.03 W
Johnsons Station	222	32.42 N	97.08 W
Johnsonville, N.Z.	172	41.14 S	174.47 E
Johnsonville, N.Y., U.S.	210	42.55 N	73.31 W
Johnsonville, S.C., U.S.	192	33.49 N	79.26 W
Johnston, Wales, U.K.	42	51.46 N	5.00 W
Johnston, Ia., U.S.	190	41.40 N	93.41 W
Johnston, R.I., U.S.	207	41.46 N	71.21 W
Johnston, S.C., U.S.	192	33.49 N	81.48 W
Johnston, Lake ⊜	162	32.25 S	120.30 E
Johnston Atoll I[1]	14	16.45 N	169.32 W
Johnston City	194	37.49 N	88.55 W
Johnstone	46	55.50 N	4.31 W
Johnstone Peak ∧	280	34.10 N	117.48 W
Johnstone Strait ⊔	182	50.25 N	126.00 W
Johnston Falls ∟	154	10.35 S	28.40 E
Johnstown, Co., U.S.	200	40.20 N	104.54 W
Johnstown, N.Y., U.S.	210	43.00 N	74.22 W
Johnstown, Oh., U.S.	214	40.09 N	82.41 W
Johnstown, Pa., U.S.	214	40.19 N	78.55 W
Johnstown Center	216	42.42 N	88.50 W
Johnstown Flood National Memorial ⊥	214	40.21 N	78.47 W
John Tyler Arboretum ♠	285	39.56 N	75.26 W
Jōhoku	94	36.28 N	140.22 E
Johol	114	2.36 N	102.16 E
Johor □[3]	114	2.00 N	103.30 E
Johor ≃	114	1.27 N	104.02 E
Johor, Selat ⊔	271c	1.28 N	103.48 E
Johor Baharu	114	1.28 N	103.45 E
Jöhstadt	54	50.30 N	13.05 E
Joice Island I	282	38.08 N	122.02 W
Joigny	50	47.59 N	3.24 E
Joiner	194	35.30 N	90.08 W
Joinerville	222	32.11 N	94.55 W
Joinvile	252	26.18 S	48.50 W
Joinville	58	48.27 N	5.08 E
Joinville, Lac ⊜	206	46.18 N	75.12 W
Joinville Island I	9	63.15 S	55.45 W
Joinville-le-Pont	261	48.49 N	2.28 E
Jōjima	96	33.15 N	130.26 E
Jojogan	115a	6.58 S	111.46 E
Jojutla	234	18.37 N	99.11 W
Joka	272b	22.27 N	88.18 E
Jokau	140	8.24 N	33.49 E
Jokioinen	26	60.49 N	23.28 E
Jokkmokk	24	66.37 N	19.50 E
Jökulsá á Brú ≃	24a	65.41 N	14.13 W
Jökulsárgljúfur National Park ♠	24a	66.00 N	16.20 W
Jolārpettai	122	12.34 N	78.35 E
Jolfā	128	38.57 N	45.38 E
Joliet, Il., U.S.	216	41.31 N	88.04 W
Joliet, Mt., U.S.	202	45.29 N	108.58 W
Joliet Correctional Center ʊ	278	41.33 N	88.04 W
Joliett	208	40.37 N	76.27 W
Joliette	206	46.01 N	73.27 W
Joliette □[6]	206	46.25 N	74.00 W
Jolietville	218	40.03 N	86.15 W
Jöllenbeck	52	52.11 N	8.45 E
Jollyville	222	30.27 N	97.47 W
Jolo	116	6.03 N	121.00 E
Jolo Group II	116	6.00 N	121.09 E
Jolo Island I	116	5.58 N	121.06 E
Jølstravatnet ⊜	26	61.32 N	6.13 E
Jomalig Island I	116	14.42 N	122.22 E
Jomba	102	31.27 N	98.15 E
Jombang	115a	7.33 S	112.14 E
Jombo ≃	152	10.36 S	17.32 E
Jona	58	47.14 N	8.52 E
Jonacatepec	234	18.41 N	98.48 W
Jonah	222	30.38 N	97.32 W
Jönåker	40	58.44 N	16.40 E
Jonathan Dickinson State Park ♠	220	27.01 N	80.08 W
Jonava	76	55.05 N	24.17 E
Jones, Pil.	116	16.33 N	121.42 E
Jones, Mi., U.S.	216	41.54 N	85.48 W
Jones, Ok., U.S.	196	35.33 N	97.17 W
Jones ≃	283	42.00 N	70.42 W
Jones and Laughlin Steel Corporation ʊ[3], Pa., U.S.	279b	40.26 N	79.58 W
Jones and Laughlin Steel Corporation ʊ[3], Pa., U.S.	279b	40.37 N	80.14 W
Jones Beach State Park ♠	210	40.35 N	73.31 W
Jonesboro, Ar., U.S.	194	35.50 N	90.42 W
Jonesboro, Ga., U.S.	192	33.31 N	84.21 W
Jonesboro, Il., U.S.	194	37.27 N	89.16 W
Jonesboro, In., U.S.	216	40.28 N	85.37 W
Jonesboro, La., U.S.	194	32.14 N	92.42 W
Jonesboro, Tn., U.S.	192	36.17 N	82.28 W
Jonesburg	219	38.51 N	91.18 W
Jones Creek	222	28.58 N	95.27 W
Jones Creek ≃, On., Can.	212	44.30 N	75.49 W
Jones Creek ≃, Tx., U.S.	222	29.08 N	96.03 W
Jones Falls ≃	284b	39.18 N	76.37 W
Jones Falls, North Branch ≃	284b	39.25 N	76.42 W
Jones Inlet ⊂	210	40.35 N	73.34 W
Jones Mill	194	34.27 N	92.50 W
Jones Mountains ⋏	9	73.32 S	94.00 W
Jonesport	188	44.31 N	67.35 W
Jones Sound ⊔	176	76.00 N	85.00 W
Jonestown	194	34.19 N	90.27 W
Jonesville, In., U.S.	218	39.04 N	85.53 W
Jonesville, La., U.S.	194	31.37 N	91.49 W
Jonesville, Mi., U.S.	216	41.59 N	84.40 W
Jonesville, N.Y., U.S.	210	42.55 N	73.49 W
Jonesville, N.C., U.S.	192	36.14 N	80.50 W
Jonesville, S.C., U.S.	192	34.50 N	81.40 W
Jonesville, Va., U.S.	192	36.41 N	83.06 W
Jong ≃	150	7.32 N	12.23 W
Jonglei Canal ≅	136	9.21 N	31.32 E
Jongunjärvi ⊜	26	65.17 N	27.15 E
Jónicas, Islas → Iónioi Nísoi II	38	38.30 N	20.30 E
Jónico, Mar → Ionian Sea ⫧[2]	22	39.00 N	19.00 E
Joniškėlis	76	56.02 N	24.10 E
Joniškis	76	56.14 N	23.37 E
Jonkersberg	158	33.55 S	22.15 E
Jönköping	26	57.47 N	14.11 E
Jönköpings Län □[6]	26	57.30 N	14.30 E
Jonquière	186	48.24 N	71.15 W
Jonquières	62	44.07 N	4.54 E
Jonsdorf	54	50.51 N	14.43 E
Jonstorp	41	56.14 N	12.40 E
Jonuta	232	18.05 N	92.08 W
Jonvilliers	261	48.34 N	1.42 E
Jonzac	32	45.27 N	0.26 W
Joondalup, Lake ⊜	168a	31.45 S	115.47 E
Joplin, Mo., U.S.	194	37.05 N	94.30 W
Joplin, Mt., U.S.	202	48.33 N	110.46 W
Joppa, Il., U.S.	194	37.12 N	88.50 W
Joppa, Md., U.S.	208	39.26 N	76.21 W
Jóquei Clube ♠	287b	23.35 S	46.41 W
Joquicingo	234	19.03 N	99.33 W
Jora	124	26.20 N	77.49 E
Jordan, Pil.	116	10.40 N	122.35 E
Jordan, Mn., U.S.	190	44.40 N	93.37 W
Jordan, Mt., U.S.	202	47.19 N	106.54 W
Jordan, N.Y., U.S.	210	43.03 N	76.28 W
Jordan (Al-Urdun) □[1], Asia	118	31.00 N	36.00 E
Jordan (Al-Urdun) □[1], Asia	128	31.00 N	36.00 E
Jordan (Nahr al-Urdunn) (HaYarden) ≃, Asia	132	31.46 N	35.33 E
Jordan ≃, B.C., Can.	224	48.26 N	124.08 W
Jordan ≃, Ut,. U.S.	200	40.49 N	112.08 W
Jordan Creek ≃	202	42.52 N	117.38 W
Jordânia	255	15.54 S	40.11 W
Jordania → Jordan □[1]	128	31.00 N	36.00 E
Jordanie → Jordan □[1]	128	31.00 N	36.00 E
Jordanien → Jordan □[1]	128	31.00 N	36.00 E
Jordan Lake ⊜	216	42.46 N	85.09 W
Jordanów	30	49.40 N	19.50 E
Jordans	260	51.37 N	0.36 W
Jordan Valley	202	42.58 N	117.03 W
Jordanville	210	42.55 N	74.57 W
Jordão ≃	252	25.46 S	52.07 W
Jordbro	40	59.09 N	18.07 E
Jördenstorf	54	53.52 N	12.37 E
Jordet	26	61.25 N	12.09 E
Jorge Chávez, Aeropuerto Internacional ⊠	286d	12.02 S	77.07 W
Jorge Grego, Ilha I	256	23.13 S	44.09 W
Jorge Montt, Isla I	254	51.20 S	74.45 W
Jorge V, Costade → George V Coast •[2]	9	68.30 S	147.30 E
Jorge VI, Estrecho de → George VI Sound ⊔	9	71.00 S	68.00 W
Jorhāt	120	26.46 N	94.13 E
Jork	52	53.32 N	9.41 E
Jörlfeld	41	54.38 N	9.15 E
Jorm	120	36.52 N	70.51 E
Jörn	26	65.04 N	20.02 E
Jornado del Muerto ◆[2]	200	33.20 N	106.50 W
Joroinen	26	62.11 N	27.50 E
Jorong	112	3.58 S	114.56 E
Jørpeland	26	59.01 N	6.03 E
J'orzovka	80	48.56 N	44.38 E
Jos	150	9.55 N	8.53 E
Jose Abad Santos	116	5.38 N	125.27 E
José Batlle y Ordóñez	252	33.28 S	55.07 W
José Bonifácio	255	21.03 S	49.41 W
José Cardel	234	19.22 N	96.22 W
José C. Paz	258	34.30 S	58.45 W
José de Freitas	250	4.45 S	42.35 W
José de San Martín	254	44.02 S	70.29 W
José Enrique Rodó (Drabble)	258	33.41 S	57.34 W
José Francisco Vergara	252	22.28 S	69.38 W
Joselândia	248	16.32 S	56.12 W
José Martí, Aeropuerto Internacional ⊠	286b	23.00 N	82.24 W
Jose Panganiban	116	14.17 N	122.41 E
José Pedro Varela	252	33.27 S	54.32 W
Joseph	202	45.21 N	117.13 W
Joseph, Lac ⊜	176	52.45 N	65.15 W
Joseph, Lake ⊜	212	45.10 N	79.44 W
Joseph Bonaparte Gulf ⊂	164	14.15 S	128.30 E
Joseph City	200	34.57 N	110.20 W
Joseph Creek ≃	202	46.03 N	117.01 W
Joseph Davis State Park ♠	284a	43.13 N	79.03 W
Josephine, Pa., U.S.	214	40.29 N	79.11 W
Josephine, Tx., U.S.	222	33.04 N	96.19 W
Josephine, Lake ⊜	220	27.24 N	81.26 W
Josephine Peak ∧	280	34.17 N	118.09 W
Josephstaal	164	4.44 S	145.01 E
José Santos Arévalo	258	35.10 S	59.14 W
Joshīmath	120	30.34 N	79.34 E
Jōshin-Etsu-kōgen-kokuritsu-kōen ♠	94	36.46 N	138.40 E
Joshua	222	32.28 N	97.23 W
Joshuas Creek ≃	275b	43.29 N	79.37 W
Joshua Tree	204	34.08 N	116.18 W
Joshua Tree National Monument ♠	204	33.55 N	116.00 W
Joshua Trees State Park ♠	228	34.41 N	117.47 W
Joškar-Ola	80	56.38 N	47.52 E
Jos Plateau ⋏[1]	150	9.30 N	9.00 E
Jossa	56	50.14 N	9.35 E
Josselin	32	47.57 N	2.33 W
Jossigny	50	48.50 N	2.45 E
Jostedalsbreen ⊓	26	61.40 N	7.00 E
Jost Van Dyke I	240m	18.28 N	64.45 W
Jōtō ◆[8]	270	34.42 N	135.34 E
Jotunheimen ⋏	26	61.38 N	8.18 E
Jotunheimen Nasjonalpark ♠	26	61.35 N	8.30 E
Jouarre	50	48.56 N	3.08 E
Jouars-Pontchartrain	261	48.47 N	1.54 E
Joubertina	158	33.50 S	23.51 E
Joué-lès-Tours	50	47.21 N	0.40 E
Jougne	58	46.46 N	6.24 E
Jouques	62	43.38 N	5.38 E
Jourdanton	196	28.55 N	98.32 W
Joure	52	52.57 N	5.47 E
Joutsa	26	61.44 N	26.07 E
Joutseno	26	61.06 N	28.30 E
Joutsijärvi	24	66.40 N	28.00 E
Joux, Lac de ⊜	58	46.38 N	6.18 E
Joux, Vallée de V	58	46.35 N	6.15 E
Jouy	50	48.31 N	1.33 E
Jouy-en-Josas	261	48.46 N	2.10 E
Jouy-le-Moutier	261	49.01 N	2.03 E
Jouy-le-Potier	50	47.45 N	1.49 E
Jovellanos	240p	22.48 N	81.12 W
Jovellar	116	13.04 N	123.36 E
Jovet, Mont ∧	62	45.30 N	6.39 E
Joveyn ≃	128	36.48 N	56.28 E
Joviânia	255	17.49 S	49.30 W
Jowai	120	25.27 N	92.12 E
Jowhar	144	2.46 N	45.31 E
Jowlaenga, Mount ∧	162	17.21 S	122.56 E
Jowzjān □[4]	120	36.30 N	66.00 E
Joy	190	41.12 N	90.55 W
Joy, Mount ∧	180	63.46 N	132.55 W
Joyce	194	31.56 N	92.35 W
Joyeuse	62	44.29 N	4.14 E
Jōyō	96	34.51 N	135.47 E
Joyous Pavilion Park ♠	271a	39.52 N	116.22 E
Joyuda	240m	18.07 N	67.11 W
Józefów	30	52.09 N	21.12 E
J. Percy Priest Lake ⊜[1]	194	36.05 N	86.30 W
Ju ≃, Zhg.	100	30.38 N	114.51 E
Ju ≃, Zhg.	105	39.45 N	117.35 E
Juaba	250	2.23 S	49.33 W
Juagdan	116	10.00 N	124.35 E
Juami ≃	246	1.45 S	67.30 W
Juanacatlán	234	20.31 N	103.10 W
Juana Díaz	240m	18.03 N	66.31 W
Juan Aldama	232	24.19 N	103.21 W
Juan Anchorena ◆[8]	288	34.29 S	58.30 W
Juan Atucha	258	35.32 S	59.21 W
Juan B. Arruabarrena	252	30.20 S	58.19 W
Juan Bautista Alberdi	252	27.35 S	65.37 W
Juan Blanco, Arroyo ≃	258	35.05 S	57.26 W
Juancheng	98	35.35 N	115.29 E
Juan de Fuca, Strait of ⊔	224	48.18 N	124.00 W
Juan de Garay	254	38.52 S	64.34 W
Juan de Mena	252	24.55 S	56.44 W
Juan de Nova, Île I	138	17.03 S	42.45 E
Juan Díaz Covarrubias	234	18.07 N	95.09 W
Juan E. Barra	252	37.48 S	60.29 W
Juan Eugenio	232	25.10 N	103.20 W
Juan Fernández, Archipiélago II	244	33.00 S	80.00 W
Juan González Grande, Arroyo ≃	258	34.00 S	58.14 W
Juan González Romero ◆[8]	286a	19.30 N	99.04 W
Juangriego	246	11.05 N	63.57 W
Juan Gualberto Gómez	240p	22.52 N	81.33 W
Juan Guerra	248	6.35 S	76.21 W
Juanita	224	47.42 N	122.13 W
Juan Jorba	252	33.37 S	65.16 W
Juan José Castelli	252	25.57 S	60.37 W
Juán José Perez	248	15.14 S	68.58 W
Juanjuí	248	7.11 S	76.45 W
Juankoski	26	63.04 N	28.21 E
Juan-les-Pins	62	43.34 N	7.06 E
Juan L. Lacaze	258	34.26 S	57.27 W
Juan N. Fernández	252	38.00 S	59.16 W
Juan Perez Sound ⊔	182	52.30 N	131.18 W
Juan Ramírez, Isla I	234	21.50 N	97.40 W
Juan Rodríguez Clara	234	18.00 N	95.25 W
Juan Tronconi	258	35.30 S	59.15 W
Juan Viñas	236	9.54 N	83.45 W
Juárez, Méx.	232	27.37 N	100.44 W
Juárez, Méx.	232	30.19 N	108.05 W
Juárez, Méx.	234	17.39 N	93.10 W
Juárez, Cerro ∧	234	20.37 N	99.17 W
Juárez, Sierra ⋏	234	17.30 N	96.30 W
Juárez, Sierra de ⋏	232	32.00 N	115.50 W
Juárez → Ciudad Juárez	232	31.44 N	106.29 W
Juarzon	150	5.20 N	8.52 W
Juatinga, Ponta de ≻	256	23.17 S	44.30 W
Juazeirinho	250	7.04 S	36.35 W
Juàzeiro	250	9.25 S	40.30 W
Juazeiro do Norte	250	7.12 S	39.20 W
Jūbā	154	4.51 N	31.37 E
Juba ≃	248	14.59 S	57.44 W
Jubachstausee ⊜[1]	263	51.10 N	7.37 E
Jūbāl, Maḍīq ⊔	140	27.40 N	33.55 E
Jubal, Strait of → Jūbāl, Maḍīq ⊔	140	27.40 N	33.55 E
Jubayl (Byblos)	130	34.07 N	35.39 E
Jubaysho	144	5.48 N	37.22 E
Jubayt	140	18.57 N	36.50 E
Jubba (Genale) ≃	144	0.15 S	42.38 E
Jubbada Dhexe □[4]	144	1.00 N	43.00 E
Jubbada Hoose □[4]	144	0.00	42.00 E
Jubbah	128	28.02 N	40.56 E
Jubb al-Jarrāḥ	130	34.49 N	37.19 E
Jubbātā al-Khashab	132	33.13 N	35.49 E
Jubb Jannīn	132	33.37 N	35.47 E
Jubbulpore → Jabalpur	124	23.10 N	79.57 E
Jubilee Downs	162	18.22 S	125.17 E
Jubilee Lake ⊜, Austl.	162	29.12 S	126.38 E
Jubilee Lake ⊜, Nf., Can.	186	48.04 N	55.11 W
Jubones ≃	246	3.13 S	79.57 W
Jūbu-san ∧	270	34.50 N	135.55 E
Juby, Cap ≻	148	27.58 N	12.55 W
Júcar (Xúquer) ≃	34	39.09 N	0.14 W
Juçara	255	15.53 S	50.51 W
Júcaro	240p	21.37 N	78.51 W
Jucás	250	6.32 S	39.32 W
Jüchen	56	51.06 N	6.30 E
Juchhöh	54	50.24 N	11.52 E
Juchipila	234	21.25 N	103.07 W
Juchipila ≃	234	21.03 N	103.25 W
Juchitán de Zaragoza	234	16.26 N	95.01 W
Juchitepec	234	19.06 N	98.53 W
Juchitlán	234	20.05 N	104.07 W
Juchnov	76	54.45 N	35.14 E
Juchoviči	76	56.02 N	28.39 E
Jucuapa	236	13.31 N	88.24 W
Jucurucu ≃	255	17.21 S	39.13 W
Jucurutu	250	6.02 S	37.01 W
Judaea □[9]	132	31.35 N	35.00 E
Judas, Punta ≻	236	9.31 N	84.32 W
Judaydat al-Khās	132	33.24 N	36.33 E
Judaydat ʿArṭūz	132	33.26 N	36.10 E
Juddah → Jiddah	144	21.30 N	39.12 E
Jude Island I	186	47.15 N	54.49 W
Judenau	61	48.17 N	16.00 E
Judenburg	61	47.10 N	14.40 E
Judges Hill ∧[2]	283	42.12 N	70.49 W
Judian	102	27.20 N	99.36 E
Judinki, Ross.	82	54.37 N	37.17 E
Judinki, Ross.	82	55.27 N	35.48 E
Judino, Ross.	76	58.43 N	39.17 E
Judino, Ross.	80	55.51 N	48.55 E
Judino, Ross.	82	54.09 N	38.19 E
Judino, Ross.	265b	55.40 N	37.12 E
Judío, Rambla del ≃	34	38.15 N	1.27 W
Judique	186	45.52 N	61.30 W
Judith ≃	202	47.44 N	109.38 W
Judith, Point ≻	207	41.22 N	71.29 W
Judith Gap	202	46.40 N	109.45 W
Judith Mountains ⋏	202	47.12 N	109.15 W
Judith Peak ∧	202	47.13 N	109.13 W
Judoma ≃	74	59.08 N	135.06 E
Judson, S.C., U.S.	192	34.50 N	82.27 W
Judson, Tx., U.S.	222	32.35 N	94.45 W
Judsonia	194	35.16 N	91.38 W
Jue ≃	100	31.42 N	113.20 E
Juehedian	105	39.26 N	117.06 E
Juelsminde	41	55.43 N	10.01 E
Juexi	100	29.27 N	121.57 E
Juexizhen	107	28.55 N	104.16 E
Jufari ≃	246	1.13 S	62.00 W
Jufayr, Bi'r al- ⫧[4]	142	30.49 N	32.40 E
Jufrah, Wādī al- V	142	30.24 N	31.35 E
Jug	86	57.43 N	56.10 E
Jug ≃	24	60.45 N	46.20 E
Jughna	140	12.24 N	25.06 E
Jugo-Kamskij	86	57.42 N	55.35 E
Jugon	32	48.25 N	2.20 W
Jugo-Osetinskaja Avtonomnaja Oblast' □[8]	84	42.20 N	44.00 E
Jugoslavija → Yugoslavia □[1]	22	44.00 N	19.00 E
Jugoslawien → Yugoslavia □[1]	22	44.00 N	19.00 E
Jugo-Zapad ◆[8]	265b	55.40 N	37.32 E
Juhā	144	16.41 N	42.54 E
Jühnsdorf	264a	52.18 N	13.23 E
Jühnsdorfer Heide ◆[3]	264a	52.19 N	13.24 E
Juhu ◆[8]	272c	19.07 N	72.49 E
Juhua Dao I	98	40.29 N	120.47 E
Juhu Airport ⊠	272c	19.06 N	72.50 E
Jui	272c	19.01 N	73.05 E
Juidongshan	100	23.46 N	117.31 E
Juigalpa	236	12.05 N	85.24 W
Juillac	32	45.19 N	1.19 E
Juilly	261	49.01 N	2.42 E
Juína ≃	248	12.36 S	58.57 W
Juine ≃	50	48.32 N	2.23 E
Juist	52	53.40 N	6.59 E
Juist I	52	53.40 N	7.00 E
Juisui	100	23.30 N	121.21 E
Juiz de Fora	256	21.45 S	43.20 W
Jūjō Base ■	268	35.45 N	139.43 E
Jujurieux	58	46.02 N	5.25 E
Jujuy □[4]	252	23.00 S	66.00 W
Jujuy → San Salvador de Jujuy	252	24.11 S	65.18 W
Jukagirskoje ploskogorje ⋏[1]	74	66.00 N	155.00 E
Jukamenskoje	80	57.53 N	52.15 E
Jukonda ≃	86	59.38 N	67.26 E
Juksa	86	56.55 N	85.10 E
Juksejevo	24	59.52 N	54.19 E
Jukskei ≃	273d	26.06 S	28.06 E
Jukta	74	63.23 N	105.41 E
Jula ≃	24	63.49 N	44.44 E
Julāna	124	29.08 N	76.25 E
Julayfah, Bi'r al- ⫧[4]	142	30.43 N	29.35 E
Julbach	60	48.40 N	13.52 E
Juldybajevo	86	52.20 N	57.52 E
Julebu	98	40.09 N	113.36 E
Julesburg	198	40.59 N	102.15 W
Juli	248	16.13 S	69.27 W
Juliaca	248	15.30 S	70.08 W
Julia Creek	166	20.39 S	141.45 E
Julia Creek ≃	166	20.00 S	141.11 E
Julian	214	40.52 N	77.56 W
Juliana, Lake ⊜	220	28.07 N	81.48 W
Julianakanaal ≅	56	51.05 N	5.50 E
Julian Alps ⋏	36	46.00 N	14.00 E
Juliana Top ∧	250	3.41 N	56.32 W
Julianehåb (Qaqortoq)	176	60.43 N	46.01 W
Julia Pfeiffer Burns State Park ♠	226	36.10 N	120.40 W
Jülich	56	50.55 N	6.21 E
Juliénas	58	46.14 N	4.43 E
Juliette, Lake ⊜[1]	192	33.05 N	83.50 W
Julijske Alpe → Julian Alps ⋏	36	46.00 N	14.00 E
Julimes	232	28.25 N	105.27 W
Júlio de Castilhos	252	29.14 S	53.41 W
Julio Prestes, Estação ◆[5]	287b	23.32 S	46.38 W
Julita ʊ	40	59.09 N	16.02 E
Juliuhe	104	42.03 N	122.55 E
Juliustown	285	40.00 N	74.40 W
Julu	98	37.13 N	115.01 E
Juma	24	65.07 N	33.16 E
Juma ≃	98	39.34 N	115.42 E
Jumaguzino	86	52.54 N	56.23 E
Jumapolo	115a	7.42 S	111.00 E
Jumaševo	80	54.59 N	54.25 E
Jumay, Volcán ∧[1]	236	14.41 N	89.59 W
Jumbilla	248	5.54 S	77.45 W
Jumbo	154	17.28 S	30.55 E
Jumbo, Raas ≻	144	1.39 S	41.36 E
Jumboo	144	0.15 S	42.38 E
Jumbo Peak ∧	204	36.12 N	114.11 W
Jumeauville	261	48.55 N	1.47 E
Jumentos Cays II	238	22.42 N	75.55 W
Jumet	50	50.26 N	4.25 E
Jumièges	50	49.26 N	0.49 E
Jumilla	34	38.29 N	1.17 W
Jumlā	124	29.17 N	82.10 E
Jummayzat Banī ʿAmr	142	30.48 N	31.32 E
Jump ≃	190	45.17 N	91.05 W
Jump, North Fork ≃	190	45.25 N	90.40 W
Jump, South Fork ≃	190	45.25 N	90.40 W
Jumt uul ∧	102	44.29 N	97.10 E
Jūn	132	33.35 N	35.27 E
Jun ≃	100	25.57 N	118.03 E
Jūnāgadh	120	21.31 N	70.28 E
Junan (Shizilu)	98	35.11 N	118.51 E
Junayfah	142	30.12 N	32.25 E
Junaynah, Ra's al- ∧	140	29.01 N	33.58 E
Juncal, Isla I	258	33.58 S	58.24 W
Juncal do Norte ⁞	266c	38.52 N	8.59 W
Juncal do Sul ⁞	266c	38.51 N	8.58 W
Juncheng	98	38.57 N	114.41 E
Juncos	240m	18.14 N	65.55 W
Junction, Tx., U.S.	196	30.29 N	99.46 W
Junction, Ut,. U.S.	200	38.14 N	112.13 W
Junction City, Ar., U.S.	194	33.00 N	92.43 W
Junction City, Il., U.S.	219	38.34 N	89.07 W
Junction City, Ks., U.S.	198	39.01 N	96.49 W
Junction City, Ky., U.S.	194	37.35 N	84.47 W
Junction City, Or., U.S.	202	44.13 N	123.12 W
Junction City, Wa., U.S.	224	46.58 N	123.46 W
Jundah	166	24.50 S	143.04 E
Jundiaí	256	23.11 S	46.52 W
Jundiaí ≃, Bra.	256	23.32 S	46.15 W
Jundiaí ≃, Bra.	256	23.11 S	47.16 W
Jundiaí do Sul	255	23.27 S	50.17 W
Jundiaí-mirim ≃	256	23.10 S	46.56 W
Jundiapeba	256	23.33 S	46.15 W
Jundu Shan ⋏	105	40.30 N	116.05 E
Juneau, Ak., U.S.	180	58.20 N	134.27 W
Juneau, Wi., U.S.	190	43.24 N	88.42 W
Junee	166	34.52 S	147.35 E
June in Winter, Lake ⊜	220	27.18 N	81.24 W
June Lake	226	37.46 N	119.04 W
June Park	220	28.04 N	80.41 W
Jungapeo de Juárez	234	19.27 N	100.29 W
Jungar Qi	102	39.49 N	111.10 E
Jungbluth Ditch ≅	279a	41.27 N	82.07 W
Jungfernheide ◆[3]	264a	52.34 N	13.17 E
Jungfern-Inseln → Virgin Islands □[2]	240m	18.20 N	64.50 W
Jungfern-See ⊜	264a	52.25 N	13.05 E
Jungfrau ∧	58	46.32 N	7.58 E
Jungfraujoch ◆[5]	58	46.33 N	7.58 E
Junggar Pendi (Dzungarian Basin) ⊻[1]	86	45.00 N	88.00 E
Jungle Habitat ♠	276	41.08 N	74.21 W
Junglinster	56	49.43 N	6.15 E
Jungshāhi	120	24.51 N	67.46 E
Juniata	198	40.35 N	98.30 W
Juniata □[6]	208	40.34 N	77.24 W
Juniata ◆[8]	285	40.01 N	75.07 W
Juniata ≃	188	40.24 N	77.01 W
Juniata, Frankstown Branch ≃	214	40.34 N	78.03 W
Juniata, Raystown Branch ≃	214	40.25 N	77.58 W
Juniata Gap	214	40.33 N	78.26 W
Juniata Terrace	208	40.35 N	77.34 W
Junín, Arg.	252	34.35 S	60.57 W
Junín, Ec.	246	0.56 S	80.13 W
Junín, Perú	248	11.10 S	76.00 W
Junín □[5]	248	11.30 S	75.00 W
Junín, Lago de ⊜	248	11.02 S	76.06 W
Junín de los Andes	254	39.56 S	71.05 W
Junior	188	38.59 N	79.57 W
Juniper	186	46.33 N	67.13 W
Junipero Serra Peak ∧	226	36.08 N	121.25 W
Juniville	50	49.24 N	4.23 E
Jūniyah	130	33.59 N	35.38 E
Junk Bay ⊂	271d	22.17 N	114.15 E
Jun Kharchanai	123	36.52 N	75.01 E
Junk Island I	271d	22.17 N	114.16 E
Junkou	100	26.42 N	116.49 E
Junlian	102	28.08 N	104.35 E
Junliangcheng	105	39.04 N	117.27 E
Junling	100	28.17 N	116.28 E
Junnar	122	19.12 N	73.53 E
Juno Beach	220	26.52 N	80.04 W
Junokommunarskoje ◆[8]	83	48.13 N	38.18 E
Junqalī □[4]	140	7.30 N	32.20 E
Junqueiro	250	9.56 S	36.29 W
Junqueirópolis	255	21.32 S	51.26 W
Junsele	26	63.41 N	16.54 E
Juntas	236	10.16 N	85.00 W
Jun Ul Shan ⋏	102	37.30 N	97.00 E
Junxian	102	32.31 N	111.30 E
Jūō	94	36.40 N	140.41 E
Juodkrantė	76	55.33 N	21.08 E
Juodupė	76	56.05 N	25.37 E
Juojärvi ⊜	26	62.43 N	28.33 E
Juparanã, Lagoa ⊜	255	19.35 S	40.18 W
Jupilingo ≃	236	14.48 N	89.14 W
Jupille	56	50.39 N	5.38 E
Jupiter	220	26.56 N	80.05 W
Jupiter ≃	186	49.29 N	63.37 W
Jupiter Inlet ⊂	220	26.57 N	80.04 W
Jupiter Island I	220	27.04 N	80.07 W
Juqueri ≃	256	23.24 S	46.52 W
Juqueri, Reservatório do ⊜[1]	256	23.20 S	46.38 W
Juqueriquerê, Serra do ⋏	256	23.43 S	45.37 W
Juquiá	252	24.19 S	47.38 W
Juquiá ≃	256	23.56 S	47.09 W
Juquiá, Ponta do ≻	252	24.25 S	47.00 W
Juquiá-guaçu ≃	256	24.00 S	47.16 W
Juquitiba	256	23.57 S	47.03 W
Jur, Česko.	30	48.15 N	17.13 E
Jur, Ross.	74	59.52 N	137.39 E
Jur ≃	140	8.39 N	29.18 E
Jura □[3]	58	47.20 N	7.15 E
Jura □[5]	58	46.50 N	5.50 E
Jura ⋏	58	46.45 N	6.30 E
Jura I	46	56.00 N	5.50 W
Jūra ≃	76	55.03 N	22.09 E
Jura, Sound of ⊔	46	55.57 N	5.48 W
Juramento	255	16.50 S	43.35 W
Juratiški	76	54.02 N	25.54 E
Jurayrah, Jabal al- ∧	128	24.06 N	39.16 E
Jurays wa ʿIzbatuhā	142	30.19 N	30.55 E
Jurbarkas	76	55.05 N	22.48 E
Jurcevo	76	60.02 N	32.36 E
Juréia	256	21.17 S	46.22 W
Jurenino	76	59.24 N	42.47 E
Jurevìči	78	51.57 N	29.32 E
Jurf ad-Darāwīsh	132	30.42 N	35.52 E
Jurga	86	55.42 N	84.51 E
Jurgamyš	86	55.21 N	64.28 E
Jurgenson Woods ♠	278	41.34 N	87.36 W
Jurien	162	30.19 S	115.02 E
Juriesfontein	158	31.40 S	22.08 E
Juring	164	6.26 S	134.20 E
Jurino	80	56.18 N	46.18 E
Jurja	24	59.03 N	49.14 E
Jurjevec	80	57.18 N	43.06 E
Jurjevka, Ukr.	78	48.44 N	36.02 E
Jurjevka, Ukr.	83	48.30 N	39.00 E
Jurjev-Pol'skij	80	56.30 N	39.41 E
Jurjevskoje	82	55.05 N	36.13 E
Jurjev → Tartu	76	58.23 N	26.43 E
Jurla	86	59.17 N	54.19 E
Jurlovo, Ross.	82	55.54 N	37.16 E
Jurlovo, Ross.	82	55.19 N	35.52 E
Jūrmala	76	56.58 N	23.42 E
Jurong, Sing.	271c	1.19 N	103.43 E
Jurong, Zhg.	106	31.57 N	119.10 E
Jurong ≃	271c	1.18 N	103.44 E
Jurong, Selat ⊔	271c	1.18 N	103.42 E
Jurovo, Ross.	80	57.30 N	43.50 E
Jurovo, Ross.	82	55.30 N	38.22 E
Jurovo, Ukr.	78	51.22 N	27.50 E
Jurovskoje	86	59.29 N	69.02 E
Jursla	40	58.40 N	16.11 E
Jurty	88	56.03 N	97.37 E
Juruá	246	3.27 S	66.03 W
Juruá ≃	242	2.37 S	65.44 W
Juruaia	256	21.15 S	46.35 W
Juruá-mirim ≃	248	8.08 S	72.48 W
Juruena ≃	248	7.20 S	58.03 W
Jurujuba, Enseada de ⊂	287a	22.56 S	43.07 W
Jurumirim, Represa ⊜[1]	255	23.20 S	49.15 W
Jurumkuvejem ≃	180	66.14 N	173.35 E
Jurupari ≃	248	7.45 S	70.10 W
Jurupari, Arquipélago II	250	0.07 N	50.30 W
Jurupari, Ilha de I	250	0.20 N	50.07 W
Juruti	250	2.09 S	56.04 W
Jur'uzan'	86	54.52 N	58.26 E
Jur'uzan' ≃	86	55.42 N	57.00 E
Jurva	26	62.41 N	21.59 E
Jušala	86	57.04 N	64.17 E
Juscelândia	255	15.20 S	51.19 W
Jusepín	246	9.45 N	63.31 W
Jushiguan	102	24.47 N	97.38 E
Jūshiyama	94	35.06 N	136.46 E
Juskatla	182	53.37 N	132.18 W
Jus'ki	80	56.39 N	53.05 E
Juškovo	76	59.46 N	45.11 E
Juškozero	24	64.44 N	32.06 E
Jūsō ◆[8]	270	34.43 N	135.28 E
Jussey	58	47.49 N	5.54 E
Justa	80	47.07 N	46.18 E
Justice	278	41.44 N	87.50 W
Justin	222	33.05 N	97.18 W
Justineberg ∧[2]	40	58.43 N	15.04 E
Justiniano Posse	252	32.53 S	62.40 W
Justo Daract	252	33.52 S	65.11 W
Justus	214	40.42 N	81.35 W
Jušut ≃	80	56.12 N	48.23 E
Jus'va	24	58.56 N	54.57 E
Jutaí	248	5.11 S	68.54 W
Jutaí ≃	242	2.43 S	66.57 W
Jutaza	80	54.35 N	53.16 E
Jütchendorf	264a	52.16 N	13.10 E
Jüterbog	54	51.59 N	13.04 E
Juththah, Jabal al- ∧	132	30.12 N	35.36 E
Juti	255	22.52 S	54.37 W
Jutiapa	236	14.17 N	89.54 W
Jutiapa □[5]	236	14.10 N	89.50 W
Juticalpa	236	14.42 N	86.15 W
Jutiquile	236	14.45 N	86.08 W
Jutland → Jylland ◆[1]	26	56.00 N	9.15 E
Jutogh	123	31.06 N	77.07 E
Jutrosin	30	51.40 N	17.10 E
Juupajoki	26	61.47 N	24.27 E
Juuru	76	59.04 N	24.59 E
Juva	26	61.54 N	27.51 E
Juventud, Isla de la (Isla de Pinos) I	240p	21.40 N	82.50 W
Juvisy-sur-Orge	50	48.41 N	2.23 E
Juvuln ⊜	26	63.43 N	13.09 E
Juwana	115a	6.42 S	111.09 E
Juwangi	115a	7.10 S	110.45 E
Juxi	100	27.30 N	119.08 E
Juxian	98	35.37 N	118.54 E
Juxing	106	31.56 N	121.33 E
Juyanhai → Gaxun Nur ⊜	102	42.22 N	100.34 E
Juye	98	35.23 N	116.06 E
Jūyom	128	28.34 N	53.56 E
Juyongguan	105	40.18 N	116.04 E
Juža	80	56.35 N	42.01 E
Juzennecourt	58	48.11 N	4.59 E
Juzi ≃	98	40.18 N	123.35 E
Juziers	261	49.00 N	1.51 E
Južna Morava ≃	38	43.41 N	21.24 E
Južno-Aleksandrovka	88	55.51 N	96.10 E
Južno-Aličurskij chrebet ⋏	120	37.30 N	73.20 E
Južno-Golodnostepskij kanal ≅	85	40.15 N	69.08 E
Južno-Jenisejskij	86	58.48 N	94.39 E
Južno-Mujskij chrebet ⋏	88	55.40 N	114.00 E
Južno-Sachalinsk	89	46.58 N	142.42 E
Južno-Suchokumsk	84	44.37 N	45.34 E
Južno-Ural'sk	86	54.26 N	61.15 E
Južnyj, Kaz.	86	49.21 N	73.01 E
Južnyj, Ross.	80	56.08 N	44.09 E
Južnyj, Ross.	80	47.20 N	41.51 E
Južnyj, Ross.	86	53.14 N	83.42 E
Južnyj, Ross.	86	53.33 N	60.02 E
Južnyj, mys ≻	74	57.45 N	156.45 E
Južnyj-Alamyšik	85	40.46 N	72.38 E
Južnyj Bug ≃	78	46.59 N	31.58 E
Južnyj Prijut	84	43.12 N	41.55 E
Južnyj Ural ⋏	86	54.00 N	58.30 E
Juzovka → Doneck	83	48.00 N	37.48 E
Jwālahari ◆[8]	272a	28.40 N	77.06 E

Symbol	English	Deutsch	Español	Français	Português
≃	River	Fluß	Río	Rivière	Rio
≅	Canal	Kanal	Canal	Canal	Canal
∟	Waterfall, Rapids	Wasserfall, Stromschnellen	Cascada, Rápidos	Chute d'eau, Rapides	Cascata, Rápidos
⊔	Strait	Meeresstraße	Estrecho	Détroit	Estreito
⊂	Bay, Gulf	Bucht, Golf	Bahía, Golfo	Baie, Golfe	Baía, Golfo
⊜	Lake, Lakes	See, Seen	Lago, Lagos	Lac, Lacs	Lago, Lagos
⁞	Swamp	Sumpf	Pantano	Marais	Pântano
⊓	Ice Features, Glacier	Eis- und Gletscherformen	Accidentes Glaciales	Formes glaciaires	Acidentes glaciares
⫧	Other Hydrographic Features	Andere Hydrographische Objekte	Otros Elementos Hidrográficos	Autres données hydrographiques	Outros acidentes hidrográficos
✤	Submarine Features	Untermeerische Objekte	Accidentes Submarinos	Formes de relief sous-marin	Acidentes submarinos
□	Political Unit	Politische Einheit	Unidad Politica	Entité politique	Unidade política
ʊ	Cultural Institution	Kulturelle Institution	Institución Cultural	Institution culturelle	Institução cultural
⊥	Historical Site	Historische Stätte	Sitio Histórico	Site historique	Sitio histórico
♠	Recreational Site	Erholungs- und Ferienort	Sitio de Recreo	Centre de loisirs	Area de Lazer
⊠	Airport	Flughafen	Aeropuerto	Aéroport	Aeroporto
■	Military Installation	Militäranlage	Instalación Militar	Installation militaire	Instalação militar
◆	Miscellaneous	Verschiedenes	Misceláneo	Divers	Diversos

Name	Page	Lat.	Long.
Jwayyā	132	33.14 N	35.19 E
Jyderup	41	55.40 N	11.26 E
Jylland (Jutland) ◆[1]	26	56.00 N	9.15 E
Jyllinge	41	55.45 N	12.07 E
Jyväskylä	26	62.14 N	25.44 E

K

Name	Page	Lat.	Long.
K2 (Qogir Feng) ∧	123	35.53 N	76.30 E
Ka ≃	150	11.40 N	4.10 E
Kaaawa	229c	21.33 N	157.51 W
Kaabong	154	3.31 N	34.08 E
Kaachka	128	37.21 N	59.36 E
Kaala ∧	229c	21.31 N	158.09 W
Kaalaea	229c	21.28 N	157.51 W
Kaala-Gomén	175f	20.40 S	164.25 E
Kaalspruit	158	29.15 S	26.10 E
Kaapahu Bay ⊂	229a	20.39 N	156.05 W
Kaapmuiden	156	25.33 S	31.20 E
Kaappunt ≻	158	34.21 S	18.30 E
Kaapstad → Cape Town	158	33.55 S	18.22 E
Kaarli	76	59.24 N	26.27 E
Kaarssen	54	53.12 N	11.02 E
Kaarst	56	51.14 N	6.37 E
Kaaterskill Creek ≃	210	42.13 N	73.53 W
Kaatoan, Mount ∧	116	8.07 N	124.55 E
Kaatsheuvel	52	51.40 N	5.02 E
Kaavi	26	62.59 N	28.30 E
Kaba	150	10.09 N	11.40 W
Kaba ≃	86	47.53 N	86.12 E
Kaba, Goulbin V	150	13.42 N	6.19 E
Kabacan	116	7.08 N	124.49 E
Kabacan ≃	116	7.08 N	124.50 E
Kabadak	126	22.13 N	89.19 E
Kabadak ≃[1]	126	22.13 N	89.18 E
Kabadüz	130	40.53 N	37.56 E
Kabaena, Pulau I	112	5.15 S	121.55 E
Kabaena, Selat Ս	112	5.00 S	122.00 E
Kabah ⊥	232	20.07 N	89.29 W
Kabala	150	9.35 N	11.33 W
Kabale	154	1.15 S	29.59 E
Kabalebo ≃	250	5.02 N	57.21 W
Kabalega Falls ʟ	154	2.17 N	31.41 E
Kabalega Falls National Park ♦	154	2.15 N	31.50 E
Kabali, Indon.	112	1.42 S	121.54 E
Kabalı, Tür.	130	41.52 N	35.05 E
Kabalo	154	6.03 S	26.55 E
Kabambare	154	4.42 S	27.43 E
Kaban'	86	54.39 N	66.28 E
Kabangu Kuta	154	14.00 S	24.03 E
Kabanjahe	114	3.06 N	98.30 E
Kabanje	83	49.13 N	38.12 E
Kabankalan	116	9.59 N	122.49 E
Kabanovka	80	53.39 N	51.18 E
Kabanovo	86	55.20 N	70.52 E
Kabansk	88	52.03 N	106.39 E
Kabardinka	78	44.39 N	37.57 E
Kabardino-Balkarskaja Avtonomnaja Sovetskaja Socialističeskaja Respublika □[3]	84	43.30 N	43.30 E
Kabasalan	116	7.48 N	122.45 E
Kabayan	116	16.37 N	120.51 E
Kabba	150	7.50 N	6.03 E
Kabbani ≃	122	12.13 N	76.54 E
Kåbdalis	24	66.10 N	20.00 E
Kabd aṣ-Ṣārim ◆[1]	130	34.34 N	39.33 E
Kabd Warqah ◆[1]	130	34.20 N	39.37 E
Kabel ◆[8]	263	51.24 N	7.29 E
Kabenung Lake ⊜	190	48.16 N	85.00 W
Kabetogama Lake ⊜	190	48.28 N	92.59 W
Kabeya	154	5.40 S	27.58 E
Kab-hegy ∧	30	47.03 N	17.39 E
Kabia ≃	146	9.54 N	15.10 E
Kabid, Wādī V	132	30.08 N	36.31 E
Kabinakagami Lake ⊜	190	48.54 N	84.25 W
Kabin Buri	110	13.59 N	101.43 E
Kabinda	152	6.08 S	24.29 E
Kabinu	112	4.00 N	116.05 E
Kabir	112	8.17 S	124.13 E
Kabira	175d	24.27 N	124.08 E
Kabīr Kili	123	33.11 N	71.19 E
Kabīr Kūh ⋏	128	33.25 N	46.45 E
Kabīrwāla	123	30.24 N	71.52 E
Kabkābīyah	140	13.39 N	24.05 E
Kablow	264a	52.18 N	13.44 E
Kablower Ziegelei	264a	52.19 N	13.43 E
Kablukovo, Ross.	82	56.50 N	36.12 E
Kablukovo, Ross.	82	56.02 N	38.10 E
Kablumgu, Cape ≻	164	6.20 S	150.00 E
Kabna	140	19.10 N	32.41 E
Kabo	152	7.39 N	18.37 E
Kabobo	154	5.07 S	29.03 E
Kaboe ≃	158	28.55 S	19.17 E
Kābol	120	34.31 N	69.12 E
Kābol □[4]	120	34.30 N	69.15 E
Kābol ≃	120	33.55 N	72.14 E
Kabompo	154	13.36 S	24.12 E
Kabompo ≃	138	14.10 S	23.11 E
Kabondo-Dianda	154	8.53 S	25.40 E
Kabongo, Zaïre	154	7.19 S	25.35 E
Kabongo, Zaïre	154	8.43 S	28.11 E
Kabongo-Lunda, Chutes ʟ	152	7.34 S	17.17 E
Kaboro	152	6.59 N	17.33 E
Kabot	150	10.48 N	14.57 W
Kabotshome	154	3.46 S	26.54 E
Kabou, Centraf.	152	5.20 N	21.43 E
Kabou, Togo	150	9.27 N	0.49 E
Kaboudia, Rass ≻	148	35.14 N	11.10 E
Kaboul → Kābol	120	34.31 N	69.12 E
Kabr	140	10.54 N	26.50 E
Kabri	132	33.01 N	35.09 E
Kabūdarāhang	128	35.12 N	48.44 E
Kabūd Gonbad	128	37.00 N	59.45 E
Kābul → Kābol	120	34.30 N	69.11 E
Kabunda	154	12.25 S	29.22 E
Kabunga	154	1.42 S	28.08 E
Kabura ≃	94	36.17 N	139.04 E
Kaburuang, Pulau I	108	3.48 N	126.48 E
Kabūshīyah	140	16.53 N	33.42 E
Kabwanga	152	7.01 S	22.37 E
Kabwe (Broken Hill)	154	14.27 S	28.27 E
Kabwe-Katanda	152	7.59 S	24.29 E
Kabyčovka	83	49.28 N	39.45 E
Kabylie ◆[1]	34	36.30 N	4.30 E
Kača	78	44.47 N	33.32 E
Kačalinskaja	80	49.07 N	44.03 E
Kačanik	38	42.13 N	21.14 E
Kačanovo	76	57.28 N	27.46 E
Kacbachskij	86	52.58 N	59.40 E
Kačerginė	76	54.56 N	23.44 E
Kacha ≃[1]	126	22.23 N	89.54 E
Kachagalau ∧	154	2.19 N	35.03 E
Kach'ang-ni	98	38.24 N	126.11 E
Kachati	84	42.30 N	41.46 E
Kachchh, Gulf of ⊂	120	22.36 N	69.30 E
Kachemak Bay ⊂	180	59.35 N	151.30 W
Kachess Lake ⊜[1]	224	47.20 N	121.14 W
Kachhwa	124	25.13 N	82.43 E
Kachi	84	41.26 N	46.56 E
Kachia	150	9.53 N	7.58 E
Kachib	84	42.25 N	46.36 E
Kachin □[3]	102	26.00 N	97.30 E
Kach'i-ri	98	34.27 N	126.08 E
Kachisi	144	9.39 N	37.50 E
Kachovka	78	46.47 N	33.30 E
Kachovskoje vodochranilišče ⊜[1]	78	47.25 N	34.10 E
Kachowka-Stausee → Kachovskoje vodochranilišče ⊜[1]	78	47.25 N	34.10 E
K'achta	88	50.26 N	106.25 E
Kachua, Bngl.	126	22.39 N	89.53 E
Kachua, Bngl.	126	23.21 N	90.54 E
Kachul	78	45.54 N	28.11 E
Kačiry	86	53.05 N	76.07 E
Kačkanar	86	58.42 N	59.38 E
Kačkanar, gora ∧	86	58.47 N	59.23 E
Kaçkar Dağı ∧	130	40.50 N	41.10 E
Kačkarovka	78	47.06 N	33.44 E
Kačug	88	53.58 N	105.52 E
Kada ≃	88	55.03 N	102.04 E
Kadada ≃	80	53.09 N	46.01 E
Kadaingti	110	17.37 N	97.32 E
Kadaiyanallūr	122	9.05 N	77.21 E
Kadamatt Island I	122	11.14 N	72.47 E
Kadaň	54	50.20 N	13.15 E
Kadanai (Kadaney) ≃	120	31.02 N	66.09 E
Kadaney (Kadanai) ≃	120	31.02 N	66.09 E
Kadan Kyun I	110	12.30 N	98.22 E
Kadapongan, Pulau I	112	4.43 S	115.44 E
Kadassa ≃	115b	9.24 S	120.02 E
Kaddam ⊜[1]	122	19.07 N	78.46 E
Kade	150	6.05 N	0.50 W
Kadéï ≃	152	3.31 N	16.05 E
Kadena	174m	26.22 N	127.45 E
Kadena Airfield ⊠	174m	26.22 N	127.45 E
Kadeshiki	80	58.08 N	49.11 E
Kadetrenden (Kadet Rinne) Ս	41	54.30 N	12.15 E
Kadgo, Lake ⊜	162	26.42 S	127.18 E
Kadi	120	23.18 N	72.20 E
Kadiana	150	10.45 N	6.30 W
Kadıköy	130	40.46 N	26.46 E
Kadina	168b	33.58 S	137.43 E
Kading ≃	110	18.19 N	104.00 E
Kadınhanı	130	38.15 N	32.14 E
Kadiolo	150	10.33 N	5.46 W
Kadipaten	115a	6.46 S	108.10 E
Kādīpur	124	26.10 N	82.23 E
Kadiri	122	14.07 N	78.10 E
Kadirli	130	37.23 N	36.05 E
Kadışehri	130	40.00 N	35.49 E
Kadiyevka → Stachanov	83	48.34 N	38.40 E
Kadja, Ouadi (Wādī Kaja) V	146	12.02 N	22.28 E
Kadkan	128	35.35 N	58.50 E
Kadnikov	76	59.30 N	40.20 E
Kadnikovskij	76	60.19 N	40.15 E
Kado	150	7.39 N	9.44 E
Ka-do I	98	39.33 N	124.40 E
Kadodo	140	11.04 N	29.31 E
Kadogawa	92	32.28 N	131.39 E
Kadoka	198	43.50 N	101.30 W
Kadom	80	54.34 N	42.30 E
Kadoma, Nihon	270	34.44 N	135.35 E
Kadoma, Zimb.	154	18.21 S	29.55 E
Kadoškino	80	54.01 N	44.25 E
Kadov	60	49.24 N	13.47 E
Kaduj	76	59.12 N	37.09 E
Kadumbul ≃	115b	9.42 S	120.32 E
Kaduna	150	10.33 N	7.27 E
Kaduna □[3]	150	10.30 N	7.45 E
Kaduna ≃	150	8.45 N	5.45 E
Kāduqlī	140	11.01 N	29.43 E
Kadūr	122	13.34 N	76.01 E
Kadyj	80	57.47 N	43.11 E
Kadykčan	74	63.02 N	146.50 E
Kadyšovo	80	54.20 N	46.45 E
Kadžerom	24	64.41 N	55.54 E
Kadži-Saj	85	42.08 N	77.10 E
Kaech'ŏn	98	39.42 N	125.53 E
Kaédi	150	16.09 N	13.30 W
Kaedo-ri	98	34.35 N	127.39 E
Kaegudeck Lake ⊜	186	48.07 N	55.11 W
Kaélé	146	10.07 N	14.27 E
Kaena Point ≻	229c	21.35 N	158.17 W
Kaeo	172	35.06 S	173.47 E
Kaesŏng	98	37.59 N	126.33 E
Kāf	128	31.24 N	37.24 E
Kafakumba	152	9.41 S	23.44 E
Kafan, Haya.	84	39.13 N	46.24 E
Kafan, Haya.	84	39.11 N	46.08 E
Kafanchan	150	9.36 N	8.17 E
Kaffraria □[9]	158	31.30 S	28.30 E
Kaffrine	150	14.06 N	15.33 W
Kafia Kingi	140	9.16 N	24.25 E
Kafin	150	9.30 N	7.04 E
Kafinda	154	12.39 S	30.20 E
Kafin Madaki	150	10.41 N	9.46 E
Kafirévs, Ákra ≻	38	38.09 N	24.36 E
Kafirnigan ≃	120	36.58 N	68.02 E
Kafo ≃	154	1.08 N	31.05 E
Kafr ad-Dawwār	142	31.08 N	30.07 E
Kafr ad-Difrāwī	142	31.03 N	30.40 E
Kafr al-ʿĀ'id	142	30.27 N	31.35 E
Kafr al-Baṭṭīkh	142	31.24 N	31.44 E
Kafr al-Jarā'idah	142	31.13 N	31.16 E
Kafr ash-Shaykh	142	31.07 N	30.56 E
Kafr ash-Shaykh □[4]	142	31.15 N	30.50 E
Kafrat Ṭā'il Mūsā	142	30.53 N	29.44 E
Kafr at-Tamīmī	142	30.37 N	31.21 E
Kafr az-Zayyāt	142	30.49 N	30.49 E
Kafr Diyamā	142	30.48 N	30.52 E
Kafr el-Zaiyat → Kafr az-Zayyāt	142	30.49 N	30.49 E
Kafr Ḥakīm	273c	30.05 N	31.07 E
Kafr Ḥūnah	132	33.29 N	35.35 E
Kafr Kanna	132	32.45 N	35.20 E
Kafr Kilā al-Bāb	142	30.41 N	31.09 E
Kafr Nabrakh	132	33.42 N	35.38 E
Kafr Naffākh	132	33.04 N	35.44 E
Kafr Nāsij	132	33.09 N	36.03 E
Kafr Rabīʿ	142	30.42 N	30.50 E
Kafr Saʿd	142	31.19 N	31.39 E
Kafr Salīm	142	31.09 N	30.06 E
Kafr Ṣaqr	142	30.48 N	31.37 E
Kafr Shanawān	142	30.30 N	31.01 E
Kafr Shibīn	142	30.18 N	31.18 E
Kafr Shīmā	132	33.49 N	35.32 E
Kafr Shukr	142	30.33 N	31.16 E
Kafr Sūsah	132	33.29 N	36.16 E
Kafr Takhārīm	130	36.07 N	36.31 E
Kafr Ṭarkhān al-Gharbī	142	29.29 N	31.13 E
Kafr Yasif	132	32.57 N	35.10 E
Kafue	154	15.47 S	28.11 E
Kafue ≃	154	15.56 S	28.55 E
Kafue Flats ≚	154	15.40 S	27.25 E
Kafue Gorge V	154	15.54 S	28.34 E
Kafue National Park ♦	154	15.00 S	25.45 E
Kafulwe Mission	154	9.00 S	29.02 E
Kafumba	152	5.23 S	18.55 E
Kafwira	154	12.10 S	27.33 E
Kaga	94	36.18 N	136.18 E
Kaga Bandoro	152	6.59 N	19.11 E
Kagalaska Island I	180	51.47 N	176.23 W
Kagal'nickaja	83	46.53 N	40.09 E
Kagal'nik	83	47.05 N	39.19 E
Kagal'nik ≃	83	47.04 N	39.18 E
Kagami	96	33.37 N	133.26 E
Kagamigahara	94	35.24 N	136.54 E
Kagamil Island I	180	53.00 N	169.43 W
Kagamino	96	35.05 N	133.56 E
Kāgān, Pāk.	123	34.47 N	73.32 E
Kagan, Uzb.	128	39.43 N	64.33 E
Kagan Valley V	123	34.25 N	73.17 E
Kagarko	150	9.29 N	7.41 E
Kagarlyk	78	49.51 N	30.50 E
Kagawa	96	34.15 N	134.02 E
Kagawa □[5]	96	34.15 N	134.00 E
Kagawong, Lake ⊜	190	45.49 N	82.18 W
Kagaznagar	122	19.18 N	79.50 E
Kåge	26	64.50 N	20.59 E
Kagelike	120	37.20 N	87.02 E
Kagera (Akagera) ≃	154	0.57 S	31.47 E
Kågeröd	41	56.01 N	13.06 E
Kâgheṭ ◆[1]	148	24.00 N	7.30 W
Kâğıthane ◆[8]	267b	41.04 N	28.58 E
Kagitumba	154	1.04 S	30.27 E
Kağızman	84	40.09 N	43.08 E
Käglan ⋏[2]	40	59.23 N	15.31 E
Kagmar	140	14.24 N	30.25 E
Kagopal	146	8.17 N	16.27 E
Kagoshima	92	31.36 N	130.33 E
Kagoshima □[5]	93b	29.00 N	129.30 E
Kagoshima-wan ⊂	92	31.25 N	130.38 E
Kagran ◆[8]	264b	48.15 N	16.27 E
Kagulu	154	1.15 N	33.18 E
Kagyo-ri	98	34.25 N	126.48 E
Kahalīya, Jabal ∧	142	29.55 N	32.09 E
Kahaluu	229c	21.27 N	157.50 W
Kahama	154	3.50 S	32.36 E
Kahana Bay ⊂	229c	21.34 N	157.52 W
Kahayan ≃	112	3.20 S	114.04 E
Kahe	154	3.30 S	37.26 E
Kahemba	152	7.17 S	19.00 E
Kahia	154	6.21 S	28.24 E
Kahiu Point ≻	229a	21.13 N	156.58 W
Kahk	142	29.25 N	30.38 E
Kahl ≃	56	50.04 N	9.00 E
Kahla	54	50.48 N	11.35 E
Kahl am Main	56	50.04 N	9.00 E
Kahlenberg ∧	264b	48.16 N	16.21 E
Kahler Asten ∧	56	51.11 N	8.29 E
Kahlersberg ∧	64	47.32 N	13.02 E
Kāhna	123	31.22 N	74.22 E
Kahnūj	128	27.58 N	57.45 E
Kahoka	194	40.25 N	91.43 W
Kahoku, Nihon	96	33.39 N	133.47 E
Kahoku, Nihon	96	33.06 N	130.41 E
Kahoku-gata ⊜	94	36.40 N	136.41 E
Kahoolawe I	229a	20.33 N	156.37 W
Kahouanne, Îlet à I	241o	16.22 N	61.47 W
Kahoué, Mont ∧	150	7.06 N	7.15 W
Kahramanmaraş	130	37.36 N	36.55 E
Kahraman Maraş □[4]	130	38.00 N	37.05 E
Kahror Pakka	123	29.37 N	71.55 E
Kahshe Lake ⊜	212	44.52 N	79.16 W
Kâhta	130	37.46 N	38.36 E
Kahuku	229c	21.40 N	157.57 W
Kahuku Point ≻	229c	21.43 N	157.59 W
Kahului	229a	20.54 N	156.28 W
Kahului Airport ⊠	229a	20.54 N	156.26 W
Kahului Bay ⊂	229a	20.54 N	156.28 W
Kahurangi Point ≻	172	40.47 S	172.13 E
Kahūta	123	33.35 N	73.23 E
Kahuzi-Biega, Parc National de ♦	154	1.50 S	28.40 E
Kahyŏn-bong ∧	271b	37.38 N	126.39 E
Kahyŏn-ni	271b	37.32 N	126.44 E
Kai	164	2.15 S	136.32 E
Kai, Kepulauan II	164	5.35 S	132.45 E
Kai, Tanjung ≻	112	2.52 S	118.45 E
Kaia, Wādī V	140	11.31 N	24.15 E
Kaiai, Jabal ∧	140	19.54 N	36.43 E
Kaiama	150	9.37 N	3.58 E
Kaiapit	164	6.15 S	146.15 E
Kaiapoi	172	43.23 S	172.40 E
Kaibab Indian Reservation ◆[4]	200	36.55 N	112.40 W
Kaibab Plateau ⋏[1]	200	36.30 N	112.15 W
Kaibara	96	35.08 N	135.05 E
Kai Beab	164	7.29 S	139.40 E
Kaibing	61	47.12 N	15.50 E
Kaibito Plateau ⋏[1]	200	36.40 N	111.20 W
Kaichengqiao	100	31.18 N	117.44 E
Kaida	94	35.56 N	137.36 E
Kaidori	268	35.37 N	139.27 E
Kaidu ≃	90	41.55 N	86.38 E
Kaiedin	140	9.45 N	32.11 E
Kaieteur Fall ʟ	246	5.10 N	59.28 W
Kaieteur National Park ♦	246	5.10 N	59.45 W
Kaifeng	98	34.51 N	114.21 E
Kaifu	96	33.35 N	134.21 E
Kaifu ≃	96	33.35 N	134.22 E
Kaihe	98	35.42 N	116.20 E
Kaihu	172	35.46 S	173.42 E
Kaihua	100	29.09 N	118.23 E
Kai Iwi	172	39.51 S	174.56 E
Kaijian	102	23.42 N	111.48 E
Kaijiang	102	31.05 N	107.55 E
Kaijo → Kaesŏng	98	37.59 N	126.33 E
Kai Kecil I	164	5.45 S	132.40 E
Kaikohe	172	35.25 S	173.48 E
Kaikoura	172	42.25 S	173.41 E
Kaikoura Peninsula ≻[1]	172	42.26 S	173.42 E
Kaikukang	89	53.07 N	124.46 E
Kailahun	150	8.17 N	10.34 W
Kailāshahar	120	24.20 N	92.01 E
Kailas → Kangrinboqê Feng ∧	120	31.04 N	81.18 E
Kaili	102	26.35 N	107.55 E
Kailu	89	43.36 N	121.14 E
Kailua	229c	21.24 N	157.44 W
Kailua Bay ⊂	229c	21.25 N	157.44 W
Kailua Kona	229d	19.22 N	155.59 W
Kaim ≃	164	6.40 S	141.45 E
Kaimai Range ⋏	172	37.45 S	175.55 E
Kaïmaktsalán ∧	38	40.58 N	21.48 E
Kaimana	164	3.39 S	133.45 E
Kaimanawa Mountains ⋏	172	39.15 S	175.54 E
Kaiman-Inseln → Cayman Islands □[2]	238	19.30 N	80.40 W
Kaimenshan	104	41.03 N	123.08 E
Kaimganj	124	27.34 N	79.21 E
Kaimon-dake ∧	92	31.11 N	130.32 E
Kain	50	50.38 N	3.22 E
Käina	76	58.50 N	22.45 E
Kainab ≃	158	28.31 S	19.35 E
Kainach ≃	61	46.54 N	15.31 E
Kainan, Nihon	96	33.36 N	134.22 E
Kainan, Nihon	96	34.09 N	135.12 E
Kainantu	164	6.15 S	145.55 E
Kainda	85	42.50 N	73.41 E
Kai-Ndunda	152	5.42 S	12.42 E
Kaingan ≃	115a	7.44 S	107.54 E
Kainji Lake ⊜[1]	150	10.30 N	4.35 E
Kaioba	112	5.20 S	122.37 E
Kaipara Harbour ⊂	172	36.25 S	174.13 E
Kaiparowits Plateau ⋏[1]	200	37.20 N	111.15 W
Kaiping, Zhg.	102	22.23 N	112.35 E
Kaiping, Zhg.	105	39.41 N	118.16 E
Kaipuri, Pulau I	164	1.51 S	137.01 E
Kairābani	126	24.08 N	87.02 E
Kairaku-en ♦	94	36.22 N	140.27 E
Kairāna	124	29.24 N	77.12 E
Kairatu	164	3.21 S	128.22 E
Kairiru Island I	164	3.20 S	143.35 E
Kairo → Al-Qāhirah	142	30.03 N	31.15 E
Kairouan	148	35.41 N	10.07 E
Kairouan □[8]	148	35.30 N	9.55 E
Kairuku	164	8.50 S	146.35 E
Kairy	78	46.57 N	33.43 E
Kaisarganj	124	27.15 N	81.33 E
Kaisarianí	267c	37.58 N	23.47 E
Kaisariani Monastery ʋ[1]	267c	37.58 N	23.47 E
Kaisergebirge ⋏	64	47.36 N	12.20 E
Kaisermühlen ◆[8]	264b	48.14 N	16.26 E
Kaiser Pass)(	226	37.17 N	119.06 W
Kaisersesch	56	50.14 N	7.08 E
Kaiserslautern	56	49.26 N	7.46 E
Kaiserstuhl ⋏[2]	58	48.06 N	7.40 E
Kaiserswerth ◆[8]	263	51.18 N	6.44 E
Kaiser-Wilhelm-Museum ʋ	263	51.20 N	6.34 E
Kaishantun	98	42.43 N	129.43 E
Kaisheim	56	48.46 N	10.48 E
Kaišiadorys	76	54.52 N	24.27 E
Kait, Tanjung ≻	112	3.14 S	106.05 E
Kaita	96	34.20 N	132.32 E
Kaitaia	172	35.07 S	173.16 E
Kaitaichi-chūtonchi, Rikujō-jieitai- ▪	96	34.21 N	132.32 E
Kai Tak Airport ⊠	271d	22.20 N	114.12 E
Kaitangata	172	46.18 S	169.51 E
Kaitersberg ⋏	60	49.11 N	12.57 E
Kaithal	124	29.48 N	76.23 E
Kaituma ≃	246	8.11 N	59.41 W
Kaiwaka	172	36.10 S	174.27 E
Kaiwatu	164	8.07 S	127.49 E
Kaiwi Channel Ս	229b	21.15 N	157.30 W
Kaixian	102	31.13 N	108.25 E
Kaiyang	102	26.58 N	106.40 E
Kaiyuan, Zhg.	102	23.44 N	103.11 E
Kaiyuan, Zhg.	104	42.32 N	124.01 E
Kaiyuancheng	98	42.37 N	124.04 E
Kaiyuh Mountains ⋏	180	64.00 N	158.00 W
Kaizhou	104	41.22 N	121.19 E
Kaizu	94	35.13 N	136.38 E
Kaizuka	96	34.27 N	135.21 E
Kaja, Wādī (Ouadi Kadja) V	146	12.02 N	22.28 E
Kajaani	26	64.14 N	27.41 E
Kajabbi	166	20.02 S	140.02 E
Kajakī, Band-e ⊜[1]	128	32.22 N	65.16 E
Kajang, Indon.	112	5.20 S	120.21 E
Kajang, Malay.	114	2.59 N	101.47 E
Kajang, Gunong ∧	114	2.46 N	104.09 E
Kajasan	86	55.12 N	62.16 E
Kajasula	84	44.19 N	44.59 E
Kajen	115a	7.02 S	109.34 E
Kajgy	86	50.55 N	64.43 E
Kajiado	154	1.51 S	36.47 E
Kajikazawa	94	35.33 N	138.27 E
Kajiki	92	31.44 N	130.40 E
Kājlāgarh	126	22.02 N	87.47 E
Kajmanačicha	86	53.32 N	75.11 E
Kajmonovo	88	56.50 N	104.54 E
Kajmysovy	86	59.48 N	76.31 E
Kajnar	86	49.12 N	77.25 E
Kajo Kaji	154	3.53 N	31.40 E
Kajrakkum	85	40.16 N	69.49 E
Kajrakkumskoje vodochranilišce ⊜[1]	85	40.20 N	70.10 E
Kajrakty	86	48.31 N	73.14 E
Kajsackoje	80	49.44 N	46.51 E
Kājū ≃	128	25.34 N	61.13 E
Kājulia	126	23.01 N	89.57 E
Kajuru	150	10.21 N	7.40 E
Kaka, Centraf.	140	6.01 N	26.30 E
Kākā, Sūd.	140	10.36 N	32.11 E
Kaka, Lae o ≻	229a	20.31 N	156.33 W
Kakabeka Falls ʟ	190	48.24 N	89.37 W
Kakabia, Pulau I	112	6.54 S	122.13 E
Kakadu National Park ♦	164	13.00 S	132.45 E
Kakagi Lake ⊜	184	49.13 N	93.52 W
Kakamas	158	28.45 S	20.33 E
Kakamega	154	0.17 N	34.45 E
Kakamigahara	94	35.24 N	136.54 E
Kakana	110	9.07 N	92.49 E
Kakanui Mountains ⋏	172	45.09 S	170.26 E
Kaka Point	172	46.23 S	169.47 E
Kakaramea	172	39.43 S	174.27 E
Kakasa	164	9.20 S	148.45 E
Kakata	150	6.35 N	10.19 W
Kakatahi	172	39.41 S	175.20 E
Kākdwīp	126	21.53 N	88.11 E
Kake, Nihon	96	34.36 N	132.19 E
Kake, Ak., U.S.	180	56.58 N	133.56 W
Kakegawa	94	34.46 N	138.01 E
Kakehashi ≃	94	36.25 N	136.25 E
Kakelwe	154	4.49 S	29.00 E
Kakenge	152	4.51 S	21.55 E
Kakeya	96	35.11 N	132.49 E
Kakhonak	180	59.26 N	154.51 W
Kakhra	126	21.38 N	87.27 E
Kākī	128	28.19 N	51.34 E
Kākināda	122	16.56 N	82.13 E
Kakino	80	55.12 N	44.53 E
Kakinoki	96	34.26 N	131.52 E
Kakisa Lake ⊜	176	60.55 N	117.40 W
Kakizaki	92	37.15 N	138.25 E
Kako ≃, Guy.	246	5.46 N	60.35 W
Kako ≃, Nihon	96	34.44 N	134.49 E
Kakoaka	156	18.40 S	24.22 E
Kakogawa	96	34.46 N	134.51 E
Kakrāla	272a	28.33 N	77.25 E
Kāksa	126	23.28 N	87.28 E
Kaktovik	180	70.08 N	143.37 W
Kakuda	92	37.58 N	140.47 E
Kakui-shima I	96	34.43 N	134.19 E
Kakuma	154	3.43 N	34.52 E
Kakunodate	92	39.35 N	140.34 E
Kakus ≃	112	2.46 N	113.01 E
Kakwa ≃	182	54.36 N	118.28 W
Kala	146	12.05 N	14.27 E
Kala ≃	122	8.18 N	79.50 E
Kalaa Kebira	148	35.52 N	10.32 E
Kalaallit Nunaat → Greenland □[2]	16	70.00 N	40.00 W
Kalaa Sghira	36	35.49 N	10.33 E
Kālābāgh	123	32.58 N	71.34 E
Kalabahi	112	8.13 S	124.31 E
Kalabáka	38	39.42 N	21.43 E
Kalabakan	112	4.25 N	117.29 E
Kalabo	152	14.57 S	22.40 E
Kalabula	86	43.24 N	83.06 E
Kalač	78	50.25 N	41.01 E
Kalačinsk	86	55.03 N	74.34 E
Kalač-Kurtlak	80	49.00 N	42.26 E
Kalač-na-Donu	80	48.43 N	43.31 E
Kalačskaja vozvyšennost' ⋏[1]	80	50.30 N	41.30 E
Kaladan ≃	110	20.09 N	92.57 E
Kaladar	212	44.39 N	77.07 W
Kalae	229a	21.10 N	157.00 W
Ka Lae ≻	229d	18.55 N	155.41 W
Kalaena ≃	112	2.40 S	120.53 E
Kalagan	89	50.30 N	119.55 E
Kalagwe	110	22.31 N	96.31 E
Kalahari Desert ◆[2]	156	24.00 S	21.30 E
Kalahari Gemsbok National Park ♦	156	25.30 S	20.30 E
Kalaheo	229b	21.55 N	159.31 W
Kālaia	126	22.23 N	90.36 E
Kalai-Chumb	85	38.28 N	70.46 E
Kalai-Mor	128	35.39 N	62.33 E
Kalais	80	52.38 N	42.38 E
Kalaiyā	124	27.02 N	85.00 E
Kalajka	88	58.28 N	111.46 E
Kalajoki	26	64.15 N	23.57 E
Kalajoki ≃	26	64.17 N	23.55 E
Kalakamate	156	20.39 S	27.21 E
Kalakan	88	55.08 N	116.45 E
Kalakan ≃	88	55.07 N	116.46 E
Kalakepen	114	2.45 N	97.50 E
Kalām	123	35.32 N	72.35 E
Kalama, Wa., U.S.	224	46.00 N	122.50 W
Kalama, Zaïre	154	2.55 S	28.33 E
Kalama ≃	224	46.02 N	122.52 W
Kalama, Pulau I	112	3.15 N	125.28 E
Kalámai	38	37.04 N	22.07 E
Kalamákion	267c	37.55 N	23.43 E
Kalamalka Lake ⊜	182	50.09 N	119.22 W
Kalamariá	38	40.35 N	22.58 E
Kalamazoo	216	42.17 N	85.35 W
Kalamazoo □[6]	216	42.14 N	85.32 W
Kalamazoo ≃	216	42.40 N	86.10 W
Kalamazoo, North Branch ≃	216	42.14 N	84.44 W
Kalamazoo, South Branch ≃	216	42.14 N	84.44 W
Kalamazoo Lake ⊂	216	42.39 N	86.13 W
Kalamb	122	19.03 N	73.57 E
Kalamba	152	0.26 S	18.17 E
Kalambau, Pulau I	112	4.55 S	115.39 E
Kalambo Falls ʟ	154	8.36 S	31.14 E
Kalamboli	272c	19.01 N	73.06 E
Kalamitskij zaliv ⊂	78	45.05 N	33.23 E
Kalamo	216	42.32 N	85.01 W
Kalampáka	38	39.42 N	21.39 E

ENGLISH Name	Page	Lat.°′	Long.°′

Name	Page	Lat.	Long.
Kalampising	112	3.44 N	116.42 E
Kalamunda	168a	31.57 S	116.03 E
Kalamunda National Park ♦	168a	31.59 S	116.04 E
Kalana	150	10.47 N	8.12 W
Kalančak	78	46.16 N	33.17 E
Kalandula	152	9.06 S	15.57 E
Kalange-Bushimaie ≃	152	7.55 S	23.11 E
Kalanguj	88	51.01 N	116.31 E
Kalankalan	150	10.07 N	8.54 W
Kalannie	162	30.21 S	117.04 E
Kalanshiyū ar-Ramlī al-Kabīr, Sarīr ≗[8]	146	28.00 N	23.00 E
Kālānwāli	123	29.51 N	74.57 E
Kalao, Pulau I	112	7.18 S	120.58 E
Kalaong	116	6.04 N	124.28 E
Kalaotoa, Pulau I	112	7.22 S	121.47 E
Kalapana	229d	19.21 N	154.58 W
Kalāpāra	126	21.59 N	90.14 E
Kalar ≃	88	55.23 N	116.18 E
Kalar, Kūh-e ∧	128	31.50 N	50.53 E
Kalaraš	78	47.16 N	28.19 E
Kälarne	26	62.59 N	16.05 E
Kālāroa	126	22.52 N	89.02 E
Kalasarv	84	39.11 N	48.03 E
Kalasi	86	48.43 N	86.59 E
Kalasin, Indon.	112	0.12 N	114.16 E
Kalasin, Thai	110	16.29 N	103.30 E
Kalašnikovo	76	57.17 N	35.13 E
Kalāt	120	29.02 N	66.35 E
Kalatungan Mountain ∧	116	7.58 N	124.47 E
Kalaupapa	229a	21.11 N	156.59 W
Kalaupapa National Historical Park ♦	229a	21.12 N	156.58 W
Kalaupapa Peninsula ≻[1]	229a	21.13 N	156.58 W
Kalauri	84	41.49 N	45.42 E
Kalaus ≃	80	45.43 N	44.07 E
Kalaus-Kr'akovka	83	48.46 N	38.52 E
Kalavárdha	38	36.20 N	27.57 E
Kalávrita	38	38.01 N	22.06 E
Kalaw	110	20.38 N	96.34 E
Kalawao □[6]	229a	21.12 N	156.58 W
Kal'azin	76	57.15 N	37.52 E
Kalb, Nahr al- ≃	132	33.57 N	35.35 E
Kalb, Ra's al- ≻	144	14.02 N	48.41 E
Kalbā'	128	25.03 N	56.21 E
Kalbar	171a	27.56 S	152.37 E
Kalbarri	162	27.42 S	114.09 E
Kalbarri National Park ♦	162	27.45 S	114.25 E
Kalbe	54	52.40 N	11.25 E
Kalbinskij chrebet ⋏	86	49.10 N	83.00 E
Kalchās	120	29.21 N	69.42 E
Kal'čik ≃	83	47.07 N	37.36 E
Kaldırım ≃	267b	41.10 N	29.12 E
Kaldygajty ≃	80	49.20 N	52.38 E
Kale, Tür.	130	36.14 N	29.59 E
Kale, Tür.	130	40.23 N	39.39 E
Kale, Tür.	130	37.26 N	28.51 E
Kalecik, Tür.	130	40.06 N	33.25 E
Kalecik, Tür.	130	37.17 N	39.02 E
Kaleden	182	49.23 N	119.35 W
Kaledupa, Pulau I	112	5.32 S	123.47 E
Kalegauk Island I	110	15.32 N	97.40 E
Kalehe	154	2.06 S	28.55 E
Kaleindaung ≃	110	18.50 N	94.00 E
Kalema, Tan.	154	1.12 S	31.50 E
Kalema, Zaïre	152	4.08 S	24.15 E
Kalemie (Albertville)	154	5.56 S	29.12 E
Kalemyo	120	23.12 N	94.10 E
Kalene Hill	152	11.11 S	24.10 E
Kaleščatovka	83	49.35 N	39.55 E
Kaletwa	110	21.45 N	92.48 E
Kalety	30	50.34 N	18.54 E
Kalevala	24	65.13 N	31.08 E
Kalewa	110	23.12 N	94.17 E
Kale Water ≃	46	55.32 N	2.28 W
Kaleybar	128	38.47 N	47.02 E
Kálfafell	24a	63.58 N	17.40 W
Kalga	88	50.57 N	118.48 E
Kalgačicha	24	63.20 N	36.44 E
Kalgan	162	34.53 S	118.01 E
Kalgan → Zhangjiakou	105	40.50 N	114.53 E
Kalgin Island I	180	60.28 N	151.55 W
Kalgoorlie	162	30.45 S	121.28 E
Kalhe	272c	18.52 N	73.06 E
Kali	150	12.10 N	11.29 W
Kāli ≃[1]	126	23.40 N	89.12 E
Kālia	126	23.03 N	89.38 E
Kāliāganj	124	25.38 N	88.19 E
Kāliāghaj ≃	126	22.10 N	87.50 E
Kāliākair	126	24.05 N	90.14 E
Kaliakra, nos ≻	38	43.21 N	28.27 E
Kalianda	115a	5.45 S	105.38 E
Kalianget	115a	7.03 S	113.56 E
Kalibek, ozero ⊜	86	53.52 N	70.40 E
Kālībhīt Hills ⋏[2]	124	22.10 N	77.30 E
Kalibo	116	11.43 N	122.22 E
Kalida	216	40.59 N	84.12 W
Kalifornien, Golf von → California, Golfo de ⊂	232	28.00 N	112.00 W
Kālī Gaṇḍakī ≃	124	27.42 N	84.25 E
Kāliganga ≃	126	23.43 N	90.15 E
Kālīganj, Bngl.	126	23.25 N	89.08 E
Kālīganj, Bngl.	126	23.55 N	90.34 E
Kālīganj, Bngl.	126	22.28 N	89.02 E
Kāliganj, India	126	23.44 N	88.14 E
Kalihiwai ≃	229b	22.13 N	159.26 W
Kalijati	115a	6.32 S	107.40 E
Kālikāpur, Bngl.	126	22.43 N	89.26 E
Kālikāpur, Bngl.	126	23.46 N	89.55 E
Kālikāpur, India	126	22.37 N	86.17 E
Kālikāpur, India	272b	22.29 N	88.32 E
Kalikino, Ross.	76	52.57 N	39.50 E
Kalikino, Ross.	80	52.55 N	54.05 E
Kalima, Zaïre	154	2.34 S	26.37 E
Kalima, Zhg.	104	41.32 N	122.40 E
Kalimantan Barat □[4]	112	0.30 N	110.00 E
Kalimantan → Borneo I	112	0.30 N	114.00 E
Kalimantan Selatan □[4]	112	2.30 S	115.30 E
Kalimantan Tengah □[4]	112	2.00 S	113.30 E
Kalimantan Timur □[4]	112	1.30 N	116.30 E
Kálimnos	38	36.57 N	26.59 E
Kálimnos I	38	37.00 N	27.00 E
Kālimpang	124	27.04 N	88.29 E
Kalina, Pointe de ≻	273b	4.18 S	15.16 E
Kālīnadi ≃	122	14.50 N	74.08 E
Kālinagar	126	22.26 N	88.51 E
Kalinga-Apayao □[4]	116	17.50 N	121.10 E
Kalinga Bil ⊜	272b	22.33 N	88.33 E
Kalinin	80	47.11 N	42.10 E
Kalininabad	85	39.45 N	69.08 E
Kaliningrad (Königsberg), Ross.	76	54.43 N	20.30 E
Kaliningrad, Ross.	82	55.55 N	37.49 E
Kalinino, Haya.	84	41.07 N	44.17 E
Kalinino, Ross.	78	45.07 N	39.00 E
Kalinino, Ross.	80	46.21 N	48.53 E
Kalinino, Ross.	86	57.20 N	56.20 E
Kalinino, Ross.	89	49.24 N	129.20 E
Kalinino, Ukr.	83	47.27 N	37.28 E
Kalininsk, Kyrg.	85	42.29 N	72.06 E
Kalininsk, Ross.	80	51.30 N	44.28 E
Kalininskaja, Ross.	78	45.29 N	38.40 E
Kalininskaja, Ross.	80	47.52 N	42.15 E
Kalininskij	83	48.01 N	39.36 E
Kalininskoje, Kyrg.	85	42.50 N	73.49 E
Kalininskoje, Ukr.	78	47.07 N	32.59 E
Kalinin → Tver'	82	56.52 N	35.55 E
Kalinkoviči	78	52.08 N	29.21 E
Kalinku	154	11.12 S	33.12 E
Kalinovik	38	43.31 N	18.26 E
Kalinovka, Kaz.	86	49.58 N	55.22 E

DEUTSCH Name	Seite	Breite°′	Länge°′ E = Ost

Name	Seite	Breite	Länge
Kalinovka, Ross.	78	51.54 N	34.28 E
Kalinovka, Ukr.	78	50.14 N	30.14 E
Kalinovka, Ukr.	78	49.27 N	28.32 E
Kalinovo, Ross.	82	54.54 N	37.17 E
Kalinovo, Ukr.	83	48.34 N	38.31 E
Kālipur	272b	22.41 N	88.17 E
Kaliro	154	0.54 N	33.30 E
Kalis	144	8.23 N	49.05 E
Kalisat	115a	8.08 S	113.48 E
Kalisch → Kalisz	30	51.46 N	18.06 E
Kāli Sindh ≃	124	25.32 N	76.17 E
Kalispell	202	48.11 N	114.18 W
Kalistratcha	86	52.59 N	83.35 E
Kalisz	30	51.46 N	18.06 E
Kalisz □[4]	30	51.40 N	17.45 E
Kalisz Pomorski	30	53.19 N	15.54 E
Kalitva ≃	78	48.10 N	40.46 E
Kaliua	154	5.04 S	31.48 E
Kaliveli Tank ⊜[1]	122	12.05 N	79.50 E
Kaliwiro	115a	7.27 S	109.51 E
Kaliwungu	115a	6.57 S	110.14 E
Kalix	26	65.51 N	23.08 E
Kalixälven ≃	24	65.50 N	23.11 E
Kālka	123	30.50 N	76.56 E
Kālkāji ◆[8]	272a	28.33 N	77.16 E
Kalkaman	86	51.58 N	76.02 E
Kalkan	130	36.15 N	29.24 E
Kalkar	52	50.36 N	6.46 E
Kalkaska	190	44.44 N	85.10 W
Kalkfeld	156	20.53 S	16.11 E
Kalkfontein	156	22.08 S	20.53 E
Kalkfonteindam ⊜[1]	158	29.30 S	25.15 E
Kalkhorst	54	53.58 N	11.02 E
Kalkım	130	39.48 N	27.13 E
Kālkini	126	23.06 N	90.16 E
Kalkmond	158	28.40 S	20.26 E
Kalkrand	156	24.03 S	17.33 E
Kalksburg ◆[8]	264b	48.08 N	16.15 E
Kalk-See ⊜	264a	52.26 N	13.46 E
Kalkstasie	158	30.00 S	18.55 E
Kalkum ◆[8]	263	51.18 N	6.46 E
Kalkutta → Calcutta	126	22.32 N	88.22 E
Kalkwerf	158	28.39 S	21.43 E
Kall	56	50.32 N	6.32 E
Kallakkurichchi	122	11.44 N	78.58 E
Kallakoopah Creek ≃	166	27.29 S	138.15 E
Kållandsö I	26	58.40 N	13.09 E
Kallang ≃	271c	1.19 N	103.52 E
Kallar Kahār	123	32.47 N	72.42 E
Kallaste	76	58.39 N	27.09 E
Kallavesi ⊜	26	62.50 N	27.45 E
Kalletal	52	52.06 N	8.56 E
Källfallet	40	59.50 N	15.31 E
Kallhäll	40	59.27 N	17.48 E
Kalliecahoolie Lake ⊜	184	54.14 N	95.29 W
Kallinge	26	56.14 N	15.17 E
Kallista	274b	37.53 S	145.22 E
Kallithéa	267c	37.57 N	23.42 E
Kallmünz	60	49.09 N	11.58 E
Kallnach	58	47.01 N	7.14 E
Kallsjön ⊜	26	63.37 N	13.00 E
Kalmakkora	86	44.03 N	78.44 E
Kalmakkyrgan ≃	86	46.58 N	64.30 E
Kalmar	26	56.40 N	16.22 E
Kalmar Län □[6]	26	57.20 N	16.00 E
Kalmarsund Ս	26	56.40 N	16.25 E
Kalmit ∧	56	49.19 N	8.05 E
Kal'mius ≃	83	47.05 N	37.34 E
Kalmthout	50	51.23 N	4.28 E
Kalmyckaja Avtonomnaja Sovetskaja Socialističeskaja Respublika □[3]	80	46.30 N	45.30 E
Kalmyckije Mysy	86	51.53 N	82.16 E
Kalmykov	80	49.01 N	42.49 E
Kalmykovka, Ukr.	83	49.17 N	38.39 E
Kalmykovka, Ukr.	83	49.17 N	39.52 E
Kalmykovo	80	49.03 N	51.47 E
Kālna	126	23.13 N	88.22 E
Kalnciems	76	56.50 N	23.37 E
Kal'niboloto	78	48.44 N	31.00 E
Kalnibolotskaja	78	46.01 N	40.28 E
Kalničko Gorje ⋏	36	46.10 N	16.30 E
Kalo	164	10.00 S	147.45 E
Kálócfa	61	46.45 N	16.34 E
Kalocsa	30	46.32 N	18.59 E
Kalofer	38	42.37 N	24.59 E
Kalohi Channel Ս	229a	21.00 N	156.56 W
Kaloko	154	6.47 S	25.48 E
Kalol, India	120	22.36 N	73.27 E
Kālol, India	120	23.15 N	72.29 E
Kalole	154	3.42 S	27.22 E
Kalolio	112	0.11 S	121.38 E
Kaloli Point ≻	229d	19.38 N	154.57 W
Kalomo	154	17.02 S	26.30 E
Kalomo ≃	154	17.57 S	26.24 E
Kalona	190	41.28 N	91.42 W
Kalonda	152	4.48 S	17.33 E
Kalone Peak ∧	182	52.38 N	126.37 W
Kalonga	154	9.10 S	27.25 E
Kalorama	274b	37.49 S	145.22 E
Kaloran	115a	7.15 S	110.15 E
Kalø Vig ⊂	41	56.15 N	10.25 E
Kalpák	38	39.55 N	20.20 E
Kalpeni Island I	122	10.05 N	73.38 E
Kālpi	124	26.07 N	79.44 E
Kāl Qaʿeh	128	32.38 N	62.32 E
Kalri	123	31.39 N	72.33 E
Kalsdorf bei Graz	61	46.57 N	15.28 E
Kalskag	180	61.30 N	160.23 W
Kalsūbai ∧	122	19.36 N	73.43 E
Kaltag	180	64.20 N	158.44 W
Kaltan	86	53.30 N	87.17 E
Kaltbrunn	58	47.12 N	9.02 E
Kalte Herberge ∧	56	50.03 N	7.59 E
Kalteneber	56	51.19 N	10.08 E
Kaltenhouse	56	48.48 N	7.50 E
Kaltenkirchen	52	53.50 N	9.58 E
Kaltenleutgeben	264b	48.07 N	16.12 E
Kaltennordheim	56	50.38 N	10.10 E
Kaltensundheim	56	50.36 N	10.10 E
Kalter Gang ≃	264b	48.02 N	16.25 E
Kalthof	263	51.26 N	7.40 E
Kal'tino	265a	59.58 N	30.40 E
Kaltungo	146	9.50 N	11.19 E
Kaluga	82	54.31 N	36.16 E
Kaluga □[8]	82	54.45 N	36.30 E
Kalugino, Kaz.	80	48.22 N	51.33 E
Kalugino, Ross.	82	54.59 N	37.11 E
Kalukalukuang, Pulau I	112	5.14 S	117.38 E
Kālu Khuhar	120	25.08 N	67.46 E
Kalulushi	154	12.50 S	28.03 E
Kalumba, Mount ∧	166	31.49 S	146.22 E
Kalumburu	164	14.18 S	126.39 E
Kalumburu Aboriginal Reserve ◆[4]	164	14.15 S	126.50 E
Kalundborg	41	55.41 N	11.06 E
Kalundborg Fjord ⊂	41	55.41 N	11.00 E
Kālundri	272c	18.59 N	73.08 E
Kalundu, Zaïre	154	3.26 S	29.08 E
Kalundu, Zam.	154	10.16 S	29.24 E
Kalungwishi ≃	154	9.01 S	28.57 E
Kalūr Kot	123	32.09 N	71.16 E
Kaluš	78	49.03 N	24.23 E
Kałuszyn	30	52.13 N	21.49 E
Kalutara	122	6.35 N	79.58 E
Kalvåg	26	61.46 N	4.53 E
Kalvarija	76	54.21 N	23.14 E
K'alvaz	84	38.39 N	48.18 E
Kalvehave	41	55.00 N	12.10 E
Kälviä	26	63.52 N	23.26 E
Kalwa	272c	19.12 N	72.59 E
Kalwang	61	47.26 N	14.46 E
Kalwaria Zebrzydowska	30	49.52 N	19.41 E
Kalyān	122	19.15 N	73.09 E
Kalyāndurg	122	14.33 N	77.06 E

Symbols in the index entries represent the broad categories identified in the key at the right. Symbols with superior numbers (⋏[1]) identify subcategories (see complete key on page *I · 1)*.

Symbole im Register stellen die rechts im Schlüssel erklärten Kategorien dar. Symbole mit hochgestellten Ziffern (⋏[1]) bezeichnen Unterabteilungen einer Kategorie (vgl. vollständiger Schlüssel auf Seite *I · 1)*.

Los símbolos incluídos en el texto del índice representan las grandes categorias identificadas con la clave a la derecha. Los símbolos con numeros en su parte superior (⋏[1]) identifican las subcategorías (véase la clave completa en la página *I · 1)*.

Les symboles de l'index représentent les catégories indiquées dans la légende à droite. Les symboles suivis d'un indice (⋏[1]) représentent des sous-catégories (voir légende complète à la page *I · 1)*.

Os símbolos incluídos no texto do índice representam as grandes categorias identificadas com a chave à direita. Os símbolos com números em sua parte superior (⋏[1]) identificam as subcategorias (veja-se a chave completa à página *I · 1)*.

	English	Deutsch	Español	Français	Português
∧	Mountain	Berg	Montaña	Montagne	Montanha
⋏	Mountains	Gebirge	Montañas	Montagnes	Montanhas
)(	Pass	Paß	Paso	Col	Passo
V	Valley, Canyon	Tal, Cañon	Valle, Cañón	Vallée, Canyon	Vale, Canhão
≚	Plain	Ebene	Llano	Plaine	Planície
≻	Cape	Kap	Cabo	Cap	Cabo
I	Island	Insel	Isla	Île	Ilha
II	Islands	Inseln	Islas	Îles	Ilhas
♦	Other Topographic Features	Andere Topographische Objekte	Otros Elementos Topográficos	Autres données topographiques	Outros acidentes topográficos

ESPAÑOL / FRANÇAIS / PORTUGUÊS

Nombre / Nom / Nome	Página / Page	Lat.°′	Long.°′ W = Oeste / Ouest
Kam ≃	146	8.15 N	11.00 E
Kama, Mya.	110	19.02 N	95.06 E
Kama, Ross.	80	56.19 N	54.06 E
Kama, Ross.	86	60.08 N	62.10 E
Kama, Zaïre	154	3.32 S	27.07 E
Kama ≃, Ross.	72	55.45 N	52.00 E
Kama ≃, Ross.	86	55.35 N	76.54 E
Kamachumu	154	1.35 S	31.37 E
Kamado-zaki ›	96	33.04 N	132.02 E
Kamae	92	32.48 N	131.56 E
Kamagaya	94	35.45 N	140.01 E
Kamaiki Point ›	229a	20.46 N	156.50 W
Kamaishi	92	39.16 N	141.53 E
Kama-iwa I	174f	24.47 N	141.17 E
Kamajai	76	55.49 N	25.30 E
Kamajri	84	40.48 N	43.50 E
Kamakou ʌ	229a	21.07 N	156.52 W
Kamakura	94	35.19 N	139.33 E
Kamakwie	150	9.30 N	12.14 W
Kamal	115a	7.10 S	112.42 E
Kamālia	123	30.44 N	72.39 E
Kamamaung	110	17.21 N	97.40 E
Kāman, India	124	27.39 N	77.16 E
Kaman, Tür.	130	39.22 N	33.44 E
Kaman ≃	110	14.48 N	106.51 E
Kamana	154	5.59 S	24.56 E
Kamanashi ≃	94	35.33 N	138.28 E
Kamango	154	0.39 N	29.53 E
Kamaniskeg Lake ⊜	212	45.25 N	77.42 W
Kamanjab	156	19.35 S	14.51 E
Kamapanda	152	12.00 S	24.10 E
Kamara Forest ♦	264c	47.26 N	19.00 E
Kamarān I	144	15.21 N	42.35 E
Kamaran, Hadjer ʌ	146	12.41 N	21.46 E
Kamarang ≃	246	5.53 N	60.35 W
Kāmāreddi	122	18.19 N	78.21 E
Kāmārhāti	272b	22.40 N	88.22 E
Kamarik	130	39.37 N	39.18 E
Kāmārkhāli Ghāt	126	23.32 N	89.33 E
Kāmārkunda	272b	22.49 N	88.13 E
Kamas	200	40.38 N	111.16 W
Kamata ◆[8]	268	35.33 N	139.43 E
Kamatsi Lake ⊜	184	56.10 N	102.15 W
Kamay	196	33.51 N	98.48 W
Kamba	150	11.53 N	3.36 E
Kamba Kota	152	7.10 N	17.54 E
Kambalda	162	31.12 S	121.40 E
Kambam	122	9.44 N	77.18 E
Kambang	112	1.42 S	100.42 E
Kambanga	152	13.23 S	23.03 E
Kambar	120	27.36 N	68.00 E
Kambara	94	35.07 N	138.36 E
Kambara Island I	175g	18.57 S	178.57 W
Kambara-tunnel ◆[5]	94	35.02 N	138.31 E
Kambarka	80	56.17 N	54.12 E
Kambia	150	9.07 N	12.55 W
Kambja	76	58.14 N	26.42 E
Kambolé	150	8.45 N	1.36 E
Kambole Mission	154	8.46 S	30.46 E
Kambove	154	10.52 S	26.38 E
Kambu	115b	8.23 S	118.20 E
Kambuye	152	7.18 S	22.50 E
Kamčatka ≃	74	56.15 N	162.30 E
Kamčatka, poluostrov (Kamchatka) ›[1]	74	56.00 N	160.00 E
Kamčatskij poluostrov ›[1]	74	56.15 N	163.00 E
Kamčatskij zaliv c	74	55.35 N	162.21 E
Kamchatka → Kamčatka, poluostrov ›[1]	74	56.00 N	160.00 E
Kâmchay Méa	110	11.35 N	105.40 E
Kamčija ≃	38	43.02 N	27.53 E
Kāmdebpur, India	272b	22.47 N	88.30 E
Kāmdebpur, India	272b	22.54 N	88.20 E
Kāmdeysh	123	35.24 N	71.20 E
Kameari ◆[8]	268	35.46 N	139.51 E
Kameda	92	37.52 N	139.07 E
Kameel	158	26.38 S	24.58 E
Kamegamori ʌ	96	33.47 N	133.12 E
Kameido ◆[8]	268	35.42 N	139.50 E
Kamelik ≃	80	52.06 N	49.30 E
Kamen', Bela.	76	55.01 N	28.53 E
Kamen, Dtsch.	52	51.35 N	7.40 E
Kamen', gora ʌ	74	69.06 N	94.48 E
Kamenda	154	6.28 S	24.33 E
Kamenec	76	52.24 N	23.49 E
Kamenec-Podol'skij	78	48.41 N	26.36 E
Kameng ≃	120	26.38 N	92.54 E
Kamenický Šenov	54	50.45 N	14.29 E
Kamenjak, Rt ›	36	44.46 N	13.55 E
Kamenka, Kaz.	80	51.07 N	50.19 E
Kamenka, Kaz.	85	42.55 N	72.50 E
Kamenka, Kaz.	86	52.22 N	69.04 E
Kamenka, Mol.	78	48.03 N	28.42 E
Kamenka, Ross.	24	65.54 N	44.05 E
Kamenka, Ross.	78	50.43 N	39.25 E
Kamenka, Ross.	80	56.11 N	45.35 E
Kamenka, Ross.	80	57.23 N	41.49 E
Kamenka, Ross.	80	53.13 N	44.03 E
Kamenka, Ross.	80	52.04 N	41.49 E
Kamenka, Ross.	82	54.43 N	38.19 E
Kamenka, Ross.	82	56.11 N	37.18 E
Kamenka, Ross.	82	55.13 N	36.59 E
Kamenka, Ross.	86	58.33 N	95.51 E
Kamenka, Ross.	89	44.28 N	136.01 E
Kamenka, Ross.	265a	59.59 N	30.53 E
Kamenka, Ukr.	78	49.02 N	32.06 E
Kamenka, Ukr.	83	49.38 N	39.22 E
Kamenka, Ukr.	83	49.07 N	37.18 E
Kamenka, Ukr.	83	47.25 N	37.42 E
Kamenka ◆[8]	265a	60.03 N	30.11 E
Kamenka ≃, Ross.	83	47.30 N	38.54 E
Kamenka ≃, Ross.	88	58.33 N	95.51 E
Kamenka ≃, Ross.	265a	60.01 N	30.12 E
Kamenka ≃, Ukr.	78	49.47 N	30.01 E
Kamenka ≃, Ukr.	78	47.39 N	34.02 E
Kamenka ≃, Ukr.	83	49.35 N	39.05 E
Kamenka-Bugskaja	78	50.07 N	24.20 E
Kamenka-Dneprovskaja	78	47.29 N	34.25 E
Kamen'-Kaširskij	78	51.38 N	24.58 E
Kamen'-na-Obi	86	53.47 N	81.20 E
Kamennogorsk	24	60.58 N	29.07 E
Kamennoje, Ukr.	78	51.31 N	27.38 E
Kamennoje, Ukr.	78	47.53 N	35.25 E
Kamennomostskij	84	44.18 N	40.12 E
Kamennye Mogily, zapovednik ♦	78	47.18 N	37.04 E
Kamennyj Brod, Ross.	83	47.26 N	39.51 E
Kamennyj Brod, Ukr.	78	50.25 N	27.49 E
Kamennyj Jar	80	48.27 N	45.34 E
Kamenolomni	83	47.40 N	40.13 E
Kamen'-Rybolov	89	44.46 N	132.02 E
Kamensk	88	51.58 N	106.36 E
Kamenskij	80	50.53 N	45.29 E
Kamenskoje, Ross.	74	62.30 N	166.12 E
Kamenskoje, Ross.	82	55.16 N	36.50 E
Kamenskoje, Ukr.	78	45.49 N	29.16 E
Kamensk-Šachtinskij	83	48.21 N	40.19 E
Kamensk-Ural'skij	86	56.28 N	61.54 E
Kamenz	54	51.16 N	14.06 E
Kameoka	96	35.00 N	135.35 E
Kamerik	52	52.06 N	4.54 E
Kamerunberg → Cameroon Mountain ʌ	152	4.12 N	9.11 E
Kamerun → Cameroon □[1]	134	6.00 N	12.00 E
Kames	46	55.54 N	5.15 W
Kameškovo	80	56.21 N	41.00 E
Kāmet ʌ	120	30.54 N	79.37 E
Kameur, Bahr ≃	146	9.26 N	20.50 E
Kameyama	94	34.51 N	136.27 E
Kami, Nihon	94	34.41 N	137.42 E
Kami, Nihon	96	35.05 N	134.53 E
Kamiah	202	46.13 N	116.01 W
Kamiak Butte ʌ	202	46.52 N	117.10 W
Kamiakotani	270	34.56 N	135.23 E
Kamiasō	268	35.35 N	139.30 E
Kamień Krajeński	30	53.33 N	17.32 E
Kamienna ≃	30	51.06 N	21.47 E
Kamienna Góra	30	50.47 N	16.01 E
Kamień Pomorski	30	53.58 N	14.46 E
Kamieńsk	30	51.12 N	19.30 E
Kamieskroon	156	30.09 S	17.56 E
Kamifukuoka	94	35.52 N	139.32 E
Kamigōri	96	34.52 N	134.22 E
Kamigyō ◆[8]	270	35.02 N	135.45 E
Kamiichi	94	36.42 N	137.22 E
Kamiishihara	268	35.39 N	139.32 E
Kamiiso	92a	41.49 N	140.39 E
Kamiita	96	34.07 N	134.24 E
Kami-jima I	94	34.33 N	136.59 E
Kamikamagari-jima I	96	34.11 N	132.44 E
Kamikatsu	96	33.53 N	134.24 E
Kamikawa, Nihon	92a	43.51 N	142.46 E
Kamikawa, Nihon	94	36.13 N	139.07 E
Kamikitazawa ◆[8]	268	35.40 N	139.38 E
Kamikume	270	34.55 N	135.03 E
Kâmil	130	41.07 N	34.47 E
Kamilukuak Lake ⊜	176	62.22 N	101.40 W
Kamimaki	270	34.34 N	135.43 E
Kamimizo	268	35.33 N	139.22 E
Kamina	154	8.44 S	25.00 E
Kaminaka, Nihon	94	35.28 N	135.51 E
Kaminaka, Nihon	96	33.48 N	134.22 E
Kaminak Lake ⊜	176	62.10 N	95.00 W
Kaminaljuyú ⊥	236	14.38 N	90.33 W
Kaminoho	94	35.37 N	137.03 E
Kaminokawa	94	36.26 N	139.55 E
Kaminokuni	92a	41.48 N	140.06 E
Kaminoseki	96	33.49 N	132.07 E
Kaminoyama	92	38.09 N	140.17 E
Kaminskij	80	57.10 N	41.28 E
Kaminuriak Lake ⊜	176	63.00 N	95.40 W
Kamioka	94	36.16 N	137.18 E
Kamiotawa	270	34.54 N	135.31 E
Kamioyamada	268	35.35 N	139.24 E
Kámiros ⊥	38	36.19 N	27.57 E
Kamisato	94	36.15 N	139.09 E
Kamishak Bay c	180	59.15 N	153.45 W
Kamishii	94	36.04 N	136.24 E
Kamishinden	270	34.49 N	135.30 E
Kamisunagawa	92a	43.30 N	142.00 E
Kamitaira	94	36.24 N	136.54 E
Kamitakara	94	36.17 N	137.22 E
Kamitakino	270	34.57 N	134.59 E
Kamitomi	268	35.49 N	139.31 E
Kamitonda	96	33.43 N	135.27 E
Kamitsuruma	268	35.31 N	139.25 E
Kamitsushima	92	34.50 N	129.28 E
Kamituga	154	3.04 S	28.11 E
Kamiura	96	33.03 N	131.55 E
Kamiyahagi	94	35.18 N	137.29 E
Kamiyama	96	33.58 N	134.23 E
Kamiyamada	94	36.28 N	138.09 E
Kamiyama-jima I	174m	26.15 N	127.35 E
Kamiyugi	268	35.37 N	139.23 E
Kamīzgān	84	38.58 N	47.44 E
Kamkhat Muḥaywir ʌ[2]	132	31.08 N	36.30 E
Kamku	120	27.30 N	96.30 E
Kamla (Kamlā) ≃	124	25.37 N	86.40 E
Kamlach ≃	58	48.30 N	10.22 E
Kamloops	182	50.40 N	120.20 W
Kamloops Indian Reserve ◆[4]	182	50.42 N	120.20 W
Kamloops Lake ⊜	182	50.43 N	120.33 W
Kammon-kaikyō ⊔	96	33.56 N	130.56 E
Kammon-kyō ◆[5]	96	33.56 N	130.55 E
Kammuri-yama ʌ	96	34.28 N	132.05 E
Kamnik	36	46.13 N	14.37 E
Kamniokan	88	56.17 N	111.57 E
Kamo, Haya.	84	40.22 N	45.08 E
Kamo, N.Z.	172	35.41 S	174.19 E
Kamo, Nihon	92	37.39 N	139.03 E
Kamo, Nihon	94	34.50 N	138.46 E
Kamo, Nihon	96	34.45 N	135.52 E
Kamo, Nihon	96	35.10 N	134.04 E
Kamo, Nihon	96	35.20 N	132.55 E
Kamo, Nihon	270	34.55 N	135.13 E
Kamo ≃, Nihon	94	35.06 N	140.06 E
Kamo ≃, Nihon	96	33.56 N	133.09 E
Kamo ≃, Nihon	270	34.56 N	135.44 E
Kamoa Mountains ⋀	246	1.37 N	59.00 W
Kamoda-misaki ›	96	33.50 N	134.45 E
Kamogata	96	34.32 N	133.35 E
Kamogawa, Nihon	94	35.06 N	140.06 E
Kamogawa, Nihon	96	34.51 N	133.49 E
Kamohio Bay c	229a	20.31 N	156.36 W
Kamojima	96	34.04 N	134.21 E
Kāmoke	123	31.58 N	74.13 E
Kamoshida ◆[8]	268	35.34 N	139.30 E
Kamoto	96	33.00 N	130.45 E
Kamp	56	50.14 N	7.37 E
Kamp ≃	61	48.23 N	15.48 E
Kāmpa	272b	22.56 N	88.28 E
Kampala	154	0.19 N	32.25 E
Kampar	114	4.18 N	101.09 E
Kampar ≃	112	0.32 N	103.08 E
Kamparkalns ʌ[2]	76	57.18 N	22.47 E
Kampar Kanan ≃	112	0.16 N	101.41 E
Kampen	52	52.33 N	5.54 E
Kampene	154	3.36 S	26.40 E
Kampfe, Lake ⊜	276	41.02 N	74.21 W
Kamphaeng, Khao ʌ	110	14.37 N	99.18 E
Kamphaeng Phet	110	16.28 N	99.30 E
Kampil	124	27.37 N	79.17 E
Kampinoski Park Narodowy ♦	30	52.20 N	20.35 E
Kampire Dior ʌ	123	36.38 N	74.23 E
Kamp-Lintfort	52	51.30 N	6.31 E
Kamp'o	98	35.48 N	129.29 E
Kampolombo, Lake ⊜	154	11.37 S	29.42 E
Kampong Ayer Puteh	114	4.16 N	103.12 E
Kampong Baharu	114	3.43 N	103.17 E
Kampong Benta	114	3.32 N	103.22 E
Kampong Buloh	114	5.32 N	102.45 E
Kâmpóng Cham	110	12.00 N	105.27 E
Kampong Chenor	114	3.29 N	102.36 E
Kâmpóng Chhnăng	110	12.15 N	104.40 E
Kampong Dong	114	3.54 N	101.54 E
Kampong Guchil	114	5.33 N	102.14 E
Kampong Jabor	114	3.57 N	103.20 E
Kampong Jerangau	114	4.51 N	103.12 E
Kampong Kandang	114	2.11 N	102.18 E
Kâmpóng Kântuŏt	110	11.26 N	104.49 E
Kampong Kenyam	114	4.31 N	102.28 E
Kampong Kuala Kemaman	114	4.14 N	103.27 E
Kampong Lamir	114	3.36 N	103.21 E
Kampong Lawa	114	5.40 N	101.42 E
Kampong Mengkarak	114	3.19 N	102.27 E
Kampong Merang	114	5.32 N	102.57 E
Kampong Nuri	114	5.02 N	102.23 E
Kampong Penarek	114	5.37 N	102.48 E
Kampong Raja	114	5.48 N	102.35 E
Kampong Renggong	114	4.33 N	102.35 E
Kâmpóng Saôm	110	10.38 N	103.30 E
Kâmpóng Saôm, Chhâk c	110	10.50 N	103.32 E
Kampong Sebuyau	112	1.31 N	110.56 E
Kampong Sekendi	114	3.43 N	100.56 E
Kampong Surau	114	5.49 N	100.54 E
Kampong Tanjong Batu	114	3.12 N	103.27 E
Kampong Tebing Runtoh	271c	1.26 N	103.40 E
Kâmpóng Thum	110	12.42 N	104.54 E
Kâmpóng Trâlach	110	11.54 N	104.47 E
Kampong Ulu	110	10.03 N	98.33 E
Kampong Ulu Chalok	114	5.26 N	102.50 E
Kâmpôt	110	10.37 N	104.11 E
Kampsville	194	39.18 N	90.37 W
Kampti	150	10.08 N	3.27 W
Kâmpŭchéa → Cambodia □[1]	110	13.00 N	105.00 E
Kampung ≃	164	5.44 S	138.24 E
Kampungbaru	112	1.12 S	102.57 E
Kampville	219	38.51 N	90.33 W
Kāmrānga	126	23.14 N	90.47 E
Kamrau, Teluk c	164	3.32 S	133.37 E
Kamsack	184	51.34 N	101.54 W
Kamsdorf	54	50.38 N	11.28 E
Kamskij	24	60.04 N	53.13 E
Kamskoje Ustje	80	55.13 N	49.16 E
Kamskoje vodochranilišče ⊜[1]	86	58.52 N	56.15 E
Kamslybas, ozero ⊜	86	46.12 N	61.48 E
Kamsu-ri	98	38.03 N	125.54 E
Kamsuuma	144	0.15 N	42.47 E
Kāmthi	120	21.14 N	79.12 E
Kam Tin	271d	22.27 N	114.03 E
Kamuchawie Lake ⊜	184	56.18 N	101.59 W
Kamudilo	154	7.42 S	27.18 E
Kamuela (Waimea)	229d	20.01 N	155.48 W
Kamui-misaki ›	92a	43.20 N	140.21 E
Kámuk, Cerro ʌ	236	9.17 N	83.04 W
Kamuli	154	0.57 N	33.07 E
Kamundan ≃	164	2.17 S	132.39 E
Kamutambaie ≃	152	7.17 S	23.41 E
Kamwandu	152	6.04 S	22.42 E
Kamyšet	88	55.12 N	98.42 E
Kamyšev, Ross.	80	46.39 N	42.38 E
Kamyšev, Ross.	80	46.53 N	42.31 E
Kamyševacha, Ukr.	78	47.43 N	35.32 E
Kamyševacha, Ukr.	83	48.42 N	38.23 E
Kamyševatskaja	78	46.25 N	37.57 E
Kamyševskaja	80	47.37 N	41.49 E
Kamyšin	80	50.06 N	45.24 E
Kamyškurgon	85	40.34 N	70.24 E
Kamyšla	80	54.07 N	52.10 E
Kamyšlov	86	56.52 N	62.43 E
Kamyslybas	86	46.11 N	61.57 E
Kamyšnaja ≃	83	48.55 N	39.55 E
Kamyšnoje	86	51.58 N	61.47 E
Kamyšovyj	80	46.26 N	45.12 E
Kamyš-Samarskich Ozer, razlivy ☷	80	48.50 N	50.50 E
Kamyz'ak	80	46.07 N	48.05 E
Kamyz'ak ≃	80	46.00 N	48.06 E
Kan, Īrān	128	35.45 N	51.16 E
Kan, Sūd.	140	9.01 N	31.47 E
Kan ≃	86	56.31 N	93.47 E
Kana ≃	154	18.30 S	27.22 E
Kanaaupscow ≃	176	53.39 N	77.09 W
Kanab	200	37.02 N	112.31 W
Kanab Creek ≃	200	36.24 N	112.38 W
Kanab Plateau ⋀[1]	200	36.40 N	112.45 W
Kanada	96	33.41 N	130.47 E
Kanada → Canada □[1]	176	60.00 N	95.00 W
Kanadej	80	53.10 N	47.30 E
Kanae	94	35.30 N	137.49 E
Kanafis	140	9.48 N	25.40 E
Kanaga Island I	180	51.45 N	177.10 W
Kanaga Volcano ʌ[1]	180	51.50 N	177.09 W
Kanagawa □[5]	94	35.30 N	139.30 E
Kanagawa ◆[8]	268	35.28 N	139.38 E
Kanagi	96	34.53 N	132.11 E
Kanai	268	35.35 N	139.28 E
Kānāipur	126	23.33 N	89.47 E
Kanairiktok ≃	176	55.05 N	60.20 W
Kanā'is, Ra's al- ›	140	31.15 N	27.51 E
Kanajevka, Ross.	80	53.07 N	45.35 E
Kanajevka, Ross.	80	52.12 N	49.40 E
Kanaka Creek ≃	226	39.25 N	120.57 W
Kanakapura	122	12.33 N	77.25 E
Kanakeswar	126	23.09 N	90.25 E
Kanákia I	267c	37.55 N	23.24 E
Kanākir	132	33.15 N	36.05 E
Kanal	64	46.05 N	13.38 E
Kanal-Inseln → Channel Islands II	28	49.20 N	2.20 W
Kanam	164	3.25 S	152.10 E
Kanamachi ◆[8]	268	35.46 N	139.53 E
Kanamori	268	35.32 N	139.28 E
Kanan	270	34.29 N	135.38 E
Kananaskis ≃	182	51.05 N	115.03 W
Kananga (Luluabourg)	152	5.54 S	22.25 E
Kananggar	115b	10.03 S	120.22 E
Kanangra-Boyd National Park ♦	170	34.00 S	150.06 E
Kananikol'skoje	86	52.47 N	57.29 E
Kanaoka	270	34.33 N	135.32 E
Kanapou Bay c	229a	20.33 N	156.33 W
Kanarase-yama ʌ	96	33.26 N	131.15 E
Kanarraville	200	37.32 N	113.10 W
Kanaš	80	55.31 N	47.30 E
Kanasagō	94	36.33 N	140.28 E
Kanata	212	45.19 N	75.54 W
Kanaudi	124	23.36 N	81.23 E
Kanava, Ross.	24	61.07 N	54.58 E
Kanava, Ross.	80	47.13 N	45.24 E
Kanavka	80	50.19 N	48.33 E
Kanawha	190	42.56 N	93.47 W
Kanawha ≃	188	38.50 N	82.08 W
Kanaya, Nihon	94	34.49 N	138.08 E
Kanaya, Nihon	96	34.04 N	135.15 E
Kanaya, Nihon	268	35.10 N	139.50 E
Kanayama	94	35.39 N	137.09 E
Kanazawa	94	36.34 N	136.39 E
Kanazawa ◆[8]	268	35.20 N	139.38 E
Kanazu	94	36.13 N	136.14 E
Kanbalu	110	23.12 N	95.31 E
Kanbauk	110	14.36 N	98.02 E
Kančalan ≃	180	65.08 N	176.25 E
Kanchanaburi	110	14.01 N	99.32 E
Kanchanadit	110	9.10 N	99.28 E
Kānchenjunga (Kañchanjanggā) ʌ	124	27.42 N	88.08 E
Kānchipuram	122	12.50 N	79.43 E
Kanchow → Ganzhou	100	25.54 N	114.55 E
Kānchrāpāra	126	22.57 N	88.28 E
Kańczuga	30	49.59 N	22.24 E
Kanda	96	33.47 N	130.59 E
Kanda ◆[8]	268	35.42 N	139.46 E
Kandabulak	80	53.58 N	50.44 E
Kandāghāt	123	30.59 N	77.07 E
Kandahar	184	51.46 N	104.21 W
Kandāhu	120	27.33 N	69.24 E
Kanda-Kanda	152	6.56 S	23.36 E
Kandala	152	6.02 S	19.24 E
Kandalakša	24	67.09 N	32.21 E
Kandalakšskaja guba c	24	66.55 N	32.45 E
Kandalakšskij zapovednik ♦	24	68.50 N	37.30 E
Kandang	114	3.03 N	97.20 E
Kandangan	112	2.47 S	115.16 E
Kandanghaur	115a	6.21 S	108.06 E
Kandat	86	57.08 N	89.02 E
Kandava	76	57.05 N	22.49 E
Kandavu Island I	175g	19.03 S	178.13 E
Kandavu Passage ⊔	175g	18.45 S	178.00 E
Kandé	150	9.57 N	1.03 E
Kandel	56	49.05 N	8.11 E
Kandel ʌ	58	48.04 N	8.01 E
Kander ≃	58	46.43 N	7.38 E
Kandern	58	47.43 N	7.40 E
Kandersteg	58	46.30 N	7.40 E
Kandhkot	120	28.14 N	69.11 E
Kāndhla	124	29.19 N	77.16 E
Kandi, Bénin	150	11.08 N	2.56 E
Kandi, India	126	23.57 N	88.02 E
Kandi, Tanjung ›	112	1.19 N	121.28 E
Kandia ≃	123	35.28 N	73.18 E
Kandiāro	120	27.04 N	68.13 E
Kandik ≃	180	65.24 N	142.34 W
Kandilli ◆[8]	267b	41.04 N	29.03 E
Kandıra	130	41.04 N	30.09 E
Kandivli ◆[8]	272c	19.12 N	72.51 E
Kandla	120	23.02 N	70.14 E
Kando ≃	96	35.22 N	132.40 E
Kandor, Ouadi V	146	17.13 N	20.52 E
Kandos	170	32.52 S	149.58 E
Kāndra	126	23.44 N	87.58 E
Kandrāch	120	25.29 N	65.29 E
Kandreho	157b	17.29 S	46.06 E
Kandrian	164	6.15 S	149.35 E
Kandry	80	54.34 N	54.07 E
Kandufuri I	122	7.05 N	72.48 E
Kandute I	122	6.20 N	72.57 E
Kandy	122	7.18 N	80.38 E
Kane, Il., U.S.	219	39.11 N	90.21 W
Kane, Pa., U.S.	214	41.39 N	78.48 W
Kane □[6]	216	41.53 N	88.18 W
Kaneda	268	35.28 N	139.22 E
Kaneilio Point ›	229c	21.27 N	158.12 W
Kanektok ≃	180	59.45 N	161.55 W
Kanem □[5]	146	15.00 N	16.00 E
Kanemi	116	6.55 N	123.58 E
Kaneohe	229c	21.25 N	157.48 W
Kaneohe Bay c	229c	21.28 N	157.49 W
Kaneohe Bay Marine Corps Air Station ■	229c	21.27 N	157.46 W
Kaneville	216	41.50 N	88.31 W
Kanevskaja	78	46.05 N	38.57 E
Kaneyama	94	35.28 N	137.06 E
Kanfanar	64	45.07 N	13.51 E
Kang	156	23.41 S	22.50 E
Kangaba	150	11.56 N	8.25 W
Kangal	130	39.15 N	37.24 E
Kangalassy	74	62.23 N	129.59 E
Kangān	128	27.50 N	52.03 E
Kānganheri ◆[8]	272a	28.33 N	76.59 E
Kanganpur	123	30.46 N	74.08 E
Kangar	114	6.26 N	100.12 E
Kangaré	150	11.35 N	8.10 W
Kangarilla	168b	35.09 S	138.40 E
Kangaroo ≃	170	34.46 S	150.18 E
Kangaroo Creek Reservoir ⊜[1]	168b	34.52 S	138.46 E
Kangaroo Flat	168b	34.33 S	138.40 E
Kangaroo Ground	274b	37.41 S	145.13 E
Kangaroo Island I	166	35.50 S	137.06 E
Kangaroo Valley	170	34.44 S	150.32 E
Kangasala	26	61.28 N	24.05 E
Kangasniemi	26	61.59 N	26.38 E
Kangāvar	128	34.30 N	47.58 E
Kangaz	78	46.07 N	28.33 E
Kangbao	98	41.53 N	114.40 E
Kangding	102	30.03 N	102.02 E
Kangdong	98	39.09 N	126.05 E
Kangdu	100	27.00 N	116.36 E
Kangean, Kepulauan II	112	6.55 S	115.30 E
Kangean, Pulau I	112	6.54 S	115.20 E
Kangen ≃	140	6.47 N	33.09 E
Kanggezhuang	105	40.26 N	116.44 E
Kanggup'o	98	41.07 N	127.31 E
Kanggye	98	40.58 N	126.34 E
Kanggyŏng	98	36.10 N	127.00 E
Kanghwa	98	37.45 N	126.30 E
Kanghwa-do I	98	37.40 N	126.27 E
Kanghwa-man c	98	37.20 N	126.35 E
Kangil	88	52.15 N	116.20 E
Kangiqsualujjuaq	176	58.41 N	65.57 W
Kangiqsujuaq	176	61.36 N	71.58 W
Kangirsuk	176	60.01 N	70.01 W
Kangjin	98	34.39 N	126.45 E
Kangjinjing	89	46.12 N	126.48 E
Kangkar Lenggor	114	2.16 N	103.44 E
Kangkar Teberau	114	1.32 N	103.45 E
Kangley	216	41.09 N	88.53 W
Kangly	85	40.07 N	67.54 E
Kangmaer	124	30.45 N	85.34 E
Kangmar	120	28.34 N	89.51 E
Kangnam ◆[8]	271b	37.30 N	127.01 E
Kangnam-sanmaek ⋀	98	40.30 N	125.30 E
Kangnichumike	120	33.10 N	80.59 E
Kangnŭng	98	37.45 N	128.54 E
Kango	152	0.09 N	10.08 E
Kangoku-iwa I	174f	24.48 N	141.17 E
Kangombe	152	14.03 S	23.40 E
Kangongo	152	17.57 S	21.02 E
Kangowa	152	9.55 S	22.48 E
Kangping	98	42.44 N	123.21 E
Kāngpokpi	120	25.08 N	93.58 E
Kangpu	102	27.43 N	99.00 E
Kāngra	123	32.06 N	76.16 E
Kangrinboqê Feng ʌ	120	31.29 N	80.45 E
Kangshan	100	22.48 N	120.17 E
Kangsŏ	98	38.58 N	125.26 E
Kangsŏ-ri	98	38.06 N	126.58 E
Kangto ʌ	120	27.52 N	92.30 E
Kangtuyingzi	104	41.47 N	121.31 E
Känguruh-Insel → Kangaroo Island I	166	35.50 S	137.06 E
Kangwŏn Do □[4], C.M.I.K.	98	38.45 N	127.35 E
Kangwŏn Do □[4], Taehan	98	37.45 N	128.15 E
Kangxianzhuang	105	39.06 N	116.27 E
Kangyidaung	110	16.56 N	94.54 E
Kangzhuang	105	40.23 N	115.53 E
Kanhar ≃	124	24.28 N	83.08 E
Kanheri Caves ⩍[5]	272c	19.13 N	72.52 E
Kanholmsfjärden ⊔	40	59.20 N	18.47 E
Kanhsien → Ganzhou	100	25.54 N	114.55 E
Kani, C. Iv.	150	8.29 N	6.36 W
Kani, Mya.	110	22.26 N	94.50 E
Kani, Nihon	94	35.22 N	137.04 E
Kaniama	152	7.31 S	24.11 E
Kaniamba	154	7.27 S	26.57 E
Kanibadam	85	40.17 N	70.25 E
Kanie	94	35.08 N	136.48 E
Kaniepa	154	9.00 S	27.21 E
Kaniere	172	42.45 S	171.00 E
Kaniere, Lake ⊜	172	42.50 S	171.09 E
Kaniet Islands II	164	0.53 S	145.30 E
Kanifay	174q	9.32 N	138.06 E
Kanigiri	122	15.24 N	79.31 E
Kanihāula ◆[8]	272a	28.44 N	77.01 E
Kanin	54	52.17 N	12.50 E
Kanin, poluostrov ›[1]	24	68.00 N	45.00 E
Kanina	124	28.20 N	76.19 E
Kaningo	154	0.49 S	38.32 E
Kanin-Kamen' ʌ	24	68.18 N	45.00 E
Kanin Nos	24	68.39 N	43.14 E
Kanin Nos, mys ›	24	68.39 N	43.16 E
Kaniva	166	36.23 S	141.15 E
Kanjiža	38	46.04 N	20.04 E
Kānjur ◆[8]	272c	19.08 N	72.56 E
Kanjut Sār ʌ	123	36.14 N	75.22 E
Kankaanpää	26	61.48 N	22.25 E
Kankakee	216	41.07 N	87.51 W
Kankakee □[6]	216	41.07 N	87.52 W
Kankakee ≃	216	41.23 N	88.16 W
Kankakee River State Park ♦	216	41.12 N	87.59 W
Kankan	150	10.23 N	9.18 W
Kankar ◆[8]	272a	28.46 N	77.06 E
Kankéla	150	10.50 N	6.40 W
Kānker	122	20.17 N	81.29 E
Kankō → Hamhŭng	98	39.54 N	127.32 E
Kankossa	150	15.56 N	11.31 W
Kankunskij	74	57.37 N	126.08 E
Kanlıavşar	130	37.13 N	38.16 E
Kanlıca ◆[8]	267b	41.06 N	29.04 E
Kanmaw Kyun I	110	11.40 N	98.28 E
Kanmen	100	28.06 N	121.16 E
Kanmuri-jima I	96	35.41 N	135.25 E
Kanmuri-yama ʌ	92	34.28 N	132.05 E
Kanna ≃	94	36.17 N	139.09 E
Kannabe	96	34.32 N	133.23 E
Kannabi-san ʌ[2]	270	34.48 N	135.44 E
Kannack	110	14.07 N	108.37 E
Kannad	122	20.16 N	75.08 E
Kanna-kō c	174m	26.28 N	127.58 E
Kannami	94	35.05 N	138.57 E
Kannapolis	192	35.29 N	80.37 W
Kannauj	124	27.04 N	79.55 E
Kanniyākumari	122	8.05 N	77.34 E
Kannod	124	22.40 N	76.44 E
Kannonkoski	26	62.58 N	25.15 E
Kannon-zaki ›	268	35.15 N	139.45 E
Kannose ≃	96	34.54 N	132.49 E
Kannus	26	63.54 N	23.54 E
Kano, Nig.	150	12.00 N	8.30 E
Kano, Nihon	96	34.14 N	131.49 E
Kano □[3]	150	11.45 N	9.00 E
Kano ≃, Nig.	150	11.50 N	8.31 E
Kano ≃, Nihon	94	35.05 N	138.52 E
Kanona	210	42.22 N	77.22 W
Kanoneiland	158	28.39 S	21.05 E
Kanonerskij, ostrov I	265a	59.54 N	30.13 E
Kanonji	96	34.07 N	133.39 E
Kanopolis	198	38.42 N	98.09 W
Kanopolis Lake ⊜[1]	198	38.38 N	98.00 W
Kanorado	198	39.19 N	102.02 W
Kanosh	200	38.48 N	112.26 W
Kanouse Brook ≃	276	41.02 N	74.26 W
Kanouse Mountain ʌ	276	41.04 N	74.25 W
Kan'ov	78	49.44 N	31.28 E
Kan'ovka	24	67.08 N	39.40 E
Kanovlei	156	19.10 S	19.23 E
Kan'ovskoje vodochranilišče ⊜[1]	78	50.00 N	31.20 E
Kanowit	112	2.06 N	112.09 E
Kanoya	92	31.23 N	130.51 E
Kanō-zan ʌ[2]	268	35.15 N	139.57 E
Kanpetlet	110	21.12 N	94.02 E
Kanpoli	272c	19.04 N	73.09 E
Kānpur	124	26.28 N	80.21 E
Kanra	94	36.13 N	138.55 E
Kansa ≃	94	34.55 N	137.34 E
Kansaj	85	40.30 N	69.41 E
Kansanshi	154	12.05 S	26.26 E
Kānsāripāra	272b	22.56 N	88.14 E
Kansas, Il., U.S.	194	39.33 N	87.56 W
Kansas, Oh., U.S.	214	41.14 N	83.17 W
Kansas □[3], U.S.	178	38.45 N	98.15 W
Kansas □[3], U.S.	198	38.45 N	98.15 W
Kansas ≃	198	39.07 N	94.36 W
Kansas City, Ks., U.S.	198	39.06 N	94.37 W
Kansas City, Mo., U.S.	194	39.05 N	94.34 W
Kansau	110	23.50 N	93.35 E
Kansei Gakuin University ʊ[2]	270	34.46 N	135.21 E
Kansei University ʊ[2]	270	34.46 N	135.31 E
Kansenia	154	10.19 S	26.02 E
Kanshan	106	30.12 N	120.25 E
Kanshi	100	24.56 N	116.54 E
Kansk	86	56.13 N	95.41 E
Kansŏng	98	38.22 N	128.29 E
Kansu	85	39.45 N	75.02 E
Kansu → Gansu □[4]	102	37.00 N	103.00 E
Kansyat	164	2.15 S	138.51 E
Kant	85	42.55 N	74.55 E
Kantabrisches Gebirge → Cantábrica, Cordillera ⋀	34	43.00 N	5.00 W
Kantalvi	272c	18.54 N	73.03 E
Kantang	110	7.25 N	99.31 E
Kāntāphor	124	22.35 N	76.34 E
Kantchari	150	12.29 N	1.31 E
Kantché	150	13.33 N	8.28 E
Kantemirovka, Kaz.	85	42.51 N	70.20 E
Kantemirovka, Ross.	83	49.41 N	39.51 E
Kānth	124	29.04 N	78.38 E
Kantharalak	110	14.39 N	104.39 E
Kānthi Coastal Plain ≚	126	21.45 N	87.45 E
Kantishna ≃	180	64.45 N	149.58 W
Kantner	214	40.06 N	78.56 W
Kantō-heiya ≚	94	36.00 N	139.30 E
Kanton (Canton) I	174h	2.50 S	171.40 W
Kanton → Guangzhou	100	23.06 N	113.16 E
Kantorp	40	59.01 N	16.28 E
Kantō-sanchi ⋀, Nihon	92	35.50 N	138.50 E
Kantō-sanchi ⋀, Nihon	94	35.59 N	138.43 E
Kantuanji	100	32.59 N	116.19 E
Kantubek	86	45.07 N	59.16 E
Kantu-long	110	19.57 N	97.36 E
Kantunilkin	232	21.06 N	87.29 W
Kanturk	48	52.10 N	8.55 W
Kanuku Mountains ⋀	246	3.12 N	59.30 W
Kanuma	94	36.33 N	139.44 E
Kanus	156	27.54 S	18.40 E
Kanuti ≃	180	66.26 N	153.02 W
Kan'utino	76	55.33 N	33.14 E
Kanye	156	24.59 S	25.19 E
Kanygtokynmangkyn, laguna c	180	69.20 N	178.45 E
Kanyu	156	20.05 S	24.39 E
Kanyutkwin	110	18.21 N	96.30 E
Kanzaki ≃	270	34.42 N	135.25 E
Kanzanavolok	24	62.23 N	36.58 E
Kanzenze	154	10.31 S	25.12 E
Kanzi	98	39.34 N	122.39 E
Kaohiung → Kaohsiung	100	22.38 N	120.17 E
Kaohsiung	100	22.38 N	120.17 E
Kaohsiunghsien	100	22.38 N	120.21 E
Kaoje	150	11.14 N	4.07 E
Kaoka Bay c	175e	9.42 S	160.40 E
Kaokoland □[5]	156	18.15 S	13.00 E
Kaoko Otavi	156	18.14 S	13.40 E
Kaoko Veld ⋀[1]	156	20.00 S	14.00 E
Kaolack	150	14.09 N	16.04 W
Kaolack □[4]	150	14.00 N	15.30 W
Kaolin	285	39.48 N	75.43 W
Kaolun → Kowloon	271d	22.18 N	114.10 E
Kaoma	154	14.47 S	24.48 E
Kaongweshi ≃	152	7.53 S	22.20 E
Kaoping → Changzhi	102	36.11 N	113.08 E
Kaoshanji	105	40.11 N	117.17 E
Kaoshanpu	100	30.54 N	114.32 E
Kaouadja ≃	140	6.45 N	24.15 E
Kaouar ◆[1]	146	19.00 N	12.40 E
Kao Valley V	158	28.54 S	18.06 E
Kapaa	229b	22.04 N	159.19 W
Kapadvanj	120	23.01 N	73.04 E
Kapahiang	112	3.39 S	102.34 E
Kapal	86	45.08 N	79.03 E
Kapalong	116	7.35 N	125.42 E
Kapan	112	9.44 S	124.17 E
Kapanga, Zaïre	152	8.21 S	22.35 E
Kapanga, Zaïre	152	5.04 S	16.58 E
Kapangan	116	16.35 N	120.35 E
Kapaonik ⋀	38	43.20 N	20.50 E
Kāpāsia	126	24.07 N	90.32 E
Kapatagan	116	7.52 N	123.44 E
Kapatu	154	9.43 S	30.42 E
Kapčagaj	85	43.53 N	77.12 E
Kapčagajskoje vodochranilišče ⊜[1]	86	43.50 N	78.00 E
Kapchorwa	154	1.24 N	34.27 E
Kapedo	154	1.10 N	36.06 E
Kapelle	52	51.28 N	3.58 E
Kapellen, Bel.	50	51.19 N	4.26 E
Kapellen, Dtsch.	56	51.25 N	6.35 E
Kapellen, Dtsch.	263	51.08 N	6.38 E
Kapellen, Öst.	61	47.38 N	15.37 E
Kapelle-op-den-Bos	50	51.01 N	4.22 E
Kapellerfeld	264b	48.19 N	16.30 E
Kapelln	61	48.15 N	15.45 E
Kapellskär	40	59.43 N	19.04 E
Kapema	154	10.42 S	28.24 E
Kapenguria	154	1.04 N	35.07 E
Kapfenberg	61	47.26 N	15.18 E
Kapia	152	4.17 S	19.46 E
Kapıdağ Yarımadası ›[1]	130	40.28 N	27.50 E
Kapikik Lake ⊜	184	51.32 N	91.57 W
Kapikog Lake ⊜	212	45.09 N	79.53 W
Kapilmuni	126	22.42 N	89.20 E
Kapingamarangi I[1]	14	1.04 N	154.46 E
Kapiri Mposhi	154	13.58 S	28.41 E
Kāpīsā □[4]	120	34.45 N	69.30 E
Kapiskau ≃	176	52.47 N	81.55 W
Kapit	112	2.01 N	112.56 E
Kapitanovka	78	48.54 N	31.42 E
Kapiti Island I	172	40.52 S	174.54 E
Kapiura ≃	164	5.45 S	150.35 E
Kapka, Massif du ⋀	146	15.07 N	21.45 E
Kapkataš	85	40.23 N	74.20 E
Kapkatas, chrebet ⋀	85	41.50 N	76.10 E
Kapkinka	80	48.08 N	43.51 E
Kaplan	194	29.59 N	92.17 W
Kaplice	61	48.45 N	14.30 E
Kapoe	110	9.35 N	98.40 E
Kapoeta	154	4.47 N	33.35 E
Kapona	154	7.11 S	29.09 E
Kaponga	172	39.26 S	174.09 E
Kaporskoje	265a	59.45 N	29.58 E
Kapos ≃	30	46.44 N	18.30 E
Kaposvár	30	46.22 N	17.47 E
Kaposvar Creek ≃	184	50.31 N	101.55 W
Kapotn'a ◆[8]	265b	55.38 N	37.48 E
Kapowsin	224	46.59 N	122.13 W
Kapowsin, Lake ⊜	224	46.58 N	122.13 W
Kapp	26	60.42 N	10.52 E
Kappar	128	25.19 N	62.42 E
Kappel	56	50.00 N	7.21 E
Kappeln	41	54.40 N	9.56 E
Kappelshamn	26	57.51 N	18.47 E
Kapps	156	22.22 S	17.52 E
Kapralicha	86	56.11 N	67.15 E
Kaprijke	50	51.13 N	3.36 E
Kaprun	64	47.16 N	12.46 E
Kapsabet	154	0.12 N	35.06 E
Kapsan	98	41.04 N	128.19 E
Kapstadt → Cape Town	158	33.55 S	18.22 E
Kaptai	120	22.21 N	92.17 E
Kaptipada	126	21.31 N	86.32 E
Kaptol	38	45.26 N	17.44 E
Kapuas ≃, Indon.	112	0.25 S	109.40 E
Kapuas ≃, Indon.	112	3.01 S	114.20 E
Kapuas Hulu, Pegunungan ⋀	112	1.15 N	113.30 E
Kapulo	154	8.18 S	29.15 E
Kapunda	168b	34.21 S	138.54 E
Kapūrthala	123	31.23 N	75.23 E
Kapur Utara, Pegunungan ⋀	115a	6.52 S	111.30 E
Kapuskasing	176	49.25 N	82.26 W
Kapuskasing ≃	176	49.49 N	82.00 W
Kapuskasing Lake ⊜	190	48.30 N	82.55 W
Kapustin Jar	80	48.36 N	45.45 E
Kapustino	78	48.57 N	31.14 E
Kapuvár	30	47.36 N	17.02 E
Kap Verde → Cape Verde □[1]	150a	16.00 N	24.00 W
Kapyrevščina	76	55.15 N	32.53 E
Kapytdžuch, gora ʌ	84	39.13 N	46.00 E
Kara	74	69.14 N	65.00 E
Kara ≃	150	10.01 N	0.25 E
Karaali	130	39.40 N	32.57 E
Karaaul	86	48.57 N	79.15 E
Karababa Dağı ʌ	130	39.31 N	36.10 E
Karabachskij chrebet ⋀	84	39.42 N	46.36 E
Karabagl'ar	84	39.26 N	45.12 E
Kara-Balta	85	42.50 N	73.52 E
Karabanovo	82	56.19 N	38.42 E
Karabaš, Ross.	80	54.42 N	52.36 E
Karabaš, Ross.	86	55.29 N	60.14 E
Karabau	80	48.26 N	52.54 E
Karabekaul	128	38.30 N	64.08 E
Karabiğa	130	40.24 N	27.18 E
Karabil', vozvyšennost' ⋀[1]	128	36.25 N	64.00 E
Kara-Bogaz-Gol, zaliv c	72	41.00 N	53.15 E
Karabudachkent	84	42.41 N	47.34 E
Karabük	130	41.12 N	32.37 E
Karabula	88	58.08 N	97.23 E
Karabula ≃	88	58.22 N	97.02 E
Karabulak, Kaz.	85	42.32 N	69.46 E
Karabulak, Kaz.	86	44.54 N	78.30 E
Karabulak, Kaz.	86	47.34 N	84.41 E
Karabulak, Kyrg.	85	39.51 N	69.38 E
Karabulduk	130	40.50 N	38.34 E
Karaburun	130	38.37 N	26.31 E
Karabutak	86	49.59 N	60.10 E
Karacabey	130	40.13 N	28.21 E
Karacadağ, Tür.	130	37.43 N	39.37 E
Karacadağ, Tür.	130	41.57 N	27.40 E
Karaca Dağ ʌ	130	37.40 N	39.50 E
Karačaj ≃	84	41.28 N	49.00 E
Karačajevo-Čerkesskaja Avtonomnaja Sovetskaja Socialističeskaja Respublika □[3]	84	44.00 N	42.00 E
Karačajevsk	84	43.45 N	41.54 E
Karacaköy	130	41.24 N	28.22 E
Karačala	84	39.48 N	48.57 E
Karacaoğlan	130	41.31 N	27.07 E
Karacasu	130	37.43 N	28.37 E
Karacaviran	130	39.44 N	38.08 E
Karaçay	130	36.10 N	36.02 E
Karaçayır	130	39.55 N	37.01 E
Karačev	76	53.07 N	35.00 E
Karāchi	120	24.52 N	67.03 E
Karachtaj	85	40.55 N	69.46 E
Karači	80	57.59 N	50.28 E
Karād	122	17.17 N	74.12 E
Kara Dağ ʌ	130	40.22 N	39.05 E
Karadarja ≃	85	40.54 N	71.45 E
Karadeniz → Black Sea ⊤[2]	22	43.00 N	35.00 E
Karadere	130	40.40 N	30.50 E
Karadirek	130	38.34 N	30.11 E
Karaftit	88	54.12 N	111.54 E
Karagaj, Kaz.	80	48.39 N	47.38 E
Karagaj, Ross.	80	58.16 N	54.56 E
Karagajly	86	49.20 N	75.48 E
Karaganda	86	49.50 N	73.10 E
Karagel	128	39.23 N	53.11 E
Karagičevskij	80	50.11 N	42.55 E
Karaginskij, ostrov I	74	58.50 N	164.00 E
Karaginskij zaliv c	74	58.50 N	164.00 E
Karagola Road	124	25.29 N	87.23 E
Karagöl Dağı ʌ	130	40.32 N	38.10 E
Kara Gölü ⊜	130	36.42 N	29.50 E
Karagoš, gora ʌ	86	51.44 N	89.24 E
Karagužicha	86	50.47 N	83.00 E
Karahallı	130	38.20 N	29.32 E
Karaia	124	25.54 N	78.01 E
Karaičev	80	48.37 N	42.13 E
Karaidel'	86	55.50 N	56.53 E
Karaidel'skij	86	55.49 N	57.05 E
Kāraikāl	122	10.55 N	79.50 E
Kāraikkudi	122	10.04 N	78.47 E
Karaisalı	130	37.16 N	35.03 E
Karaitivu I	122	8.23 N	79.47 E
Karaj	128	35.48 N	50.59 E
Karaj ≃	267d	35.35 N	51.11 E
Karajantak	85	40.03 N	67.54 E
Karak	114	3.24 N	102.02 E
Karakabak	86	50.33 N	75.09 E
Karakain	85	41.26 N	74.19 E
Kara-Kala	128	38.26 N	56.18 E
Karakalpakskaja Avtonomnaja Sovetskaja Socialističeskaja Respublika □[3]	86	43.00 N	59.00 E

Symbol	English	Deutsch	Español	Français	Português
≃	River	Fluß	Río	Rivière	Rio
≊	Canal	Kanal	Canal	Canal	Canal
⌊	Waterfall, Rapids	Wasserfall, Stromschnellen	Cascada, Rápidos	Chute d'eau, Rapides	Cascata, Rápidos
⊔	Strait	Meeresstraße	Estrecho	Détroit	Estreito
c	Bay, Gulf	Bucht, Golf	Bahía, Golfo	Baie, Golfe	Baía, Golfo
⊜	Lake, Lakes	See, Seen	Lago, Lagos	Lac, Lacs	Lago, Lagos
☷	Swamp	Sumpf	Pantano	Marais	Pântano
⊓	Ice Features, Glacier	Eis- und Gletscherformen	Accidentes Glaciales	Formes glaciaires	Acidentes glaciares
⊤	Other Hydrographic Features	Andere Hydrographische Objekte	Otros Elementos Hidrográficos	Autres données hydrographiques	Outros acidentes hidrográficos
✧	Submarine Features	Untermeerische Objekte	Accidentes Submarinos	Formes de relief sous-marin	Acidentes submarinos
□	Political Unit	Politische Einheit	Unidad Politica	Entité politique	Unidade política
ʊ	Cultural Institution	Kulturelle Institution	Institución Cultural	Institution culturelle	Instituição cultural
⊥	Historical Site	Historische Stätte	Sitio Histórico	Site historique	Sitio histórico
♦	Recreational Site	Erholungs- und Ferienort	Sitio de Recreo	Centre de loisirs	Area de Lazer
⊠	Airport	Flughafen	Aeropuerto	Aéroport	Aeroporto
■	Military Installation	Militäranlage	Instalación Militar	Installation militaire	Instalação militar
◆	Miscellaneous	Verschiedenes	Misceláneo	Divers	Diversos

Name	Page	Lat.°′	Long.°′
Karakaralong, Pulau II	112	4.30 N	125.30 E
Karakastek	85	43.08 N	76.06 E
Karakavak	85	39.41 N	72.43 E
Karakax ≃	120	37.00 N	79.45 E
Karakaya Barajı ⊜[1]	130	38.25 N	38.45 E
Karakeçı	130	37.26 N	39.26 E
Karakeçili	130	39.36 N	33.23 E
Karakelong, Pulau I	108	4.15 N	126.48 E
Karakemer	85	42.55 N	75.20 E
Karakendža	85	39.14 N	71.31 E
Karakitang, Pulau I	112	3.11 N	125.32 E
Karakoin, ozero ⊜	86	46.10 N	68.45 E
Karakojsu ≃	84	42.33 N	46.58 E
Karakojun ≃	85	41.10 N	75.45 E
Karakol (Prževal'sk)	85	42.29 N	78.24 E
Karakolka	85	41.32 N	77.23 E
Karakoram Pass)(	120	35.30 N	77.50 E
Karakoram Range ⋏	120	35.30 N	77.00 E
Karakoro ≃	150	14.43 N	12.03 W
Karaksar	88	51.16 N	115.58 E
Karakudžur ≃	85	41.59 N	75.42 E
Karakul', Ross.	86	57.26 N	70.51 E
Karakul', Taj.	85	39.02 N	73.33 E
Karakul', Uzb.	128	39.32 N	63.50 E
Karakul', ozero ⊜	85	39.05 N	73.25 E
Karakulak	130	39.59 N	40.01 E
Kara-Kul'dža	85	40.37 N	73.35 E
Karakul'dža ≃	85	40.39 N	73.26 E
Karakulino	80	56.01 N	53.43 E
Karakul'skoje	86	54.04 N	62.26 E
Karakum	86	46.49 N	79.33 E
Karakumskij kanal ≊	128	37.35 N	61.50 E
Karakumy ◆[2]	72	39.00 N	60.00 E
Karakuni	270	34.28 N	135.28 E
Karakurt	130	40.10 N	42.36 E
Karala ◆[8]	272a	28.44 N	77.02 E
Karalat	80	45.55 N	48.18 E
Karalon	88	57.02 N	115.52 E
Karalundi	162	26.07 S	118.41 E
Karam	88	55.09 N	107.37 E
Karama ≃	112	2.18 S	119.06 E
Karamağara	130	39.42 N	35.31 E
Karamai → Karamay	86	45.30 N	84.55 E
Karaman	130	37.11 N	33.14 E
Karamanlı	130	37.22 N	29.49 E
Karamay	86	45.30 N	84.55 E
Karambu	112	3.51 S	116.04 E
Karamea	172	41.15 S	172.07 E
Karamea ≃	172	41.16 S	172.06 E
Karamea Bight c[3]	172	41.30 S	171.40 E
Karamıkbataklığı ≡	130	38.25 N	30.50 E
Karamnisa Nāla ⊜[1]	124	25.42 N	83.25 E
Karamoja □[5]	154	2.50 N	34.15 E
Karamola, gora ∧	86	47.58 N	66.35 E
Karamürsel	130	40.42 N	29.36 E
Karamurt	85	42.19 N	69.58 E
Karamyš ≃	80	51.20 N	45.00 E
Karamyševo, Ross.	76	57.45 N	28.45 E
Karamyševo, Ross.	82	54.46 N	36.07 E
Karamyševo, Ross.	88	57.34 N	100.55 E
Karamzino	76	56.00 N	34.33 E
Karang, Gunung ∧	115a	6.16 S	106.03 E
Karang, Tanjung ≻	112	0.38 S	119.44 E
Karangagung	112	2.22 S	104.27 E
Karangampel	115a	6.28 S	108.27 E
Karangana	150	12.13 N	5.02 W
Karangasem	115b	8.27 S	115.37 E
Karangbinangun	115a	7.01 S	112.30 E
Karangbolang, Ujung ≻	115a	7.46 S	109.02 E
Karangbolong	115a	7.45 S	109.28 E
Karanggede	115a	7.22 S	110.37 E
Karangkates, Waduk ⊜[1]	115a	8.11 S	112.34 E
Karangkobar	115a	7.16 S	109.44 E
Karangnunggal	115a	7.38 S	108.06 E
Karangpandan	115a	7.37 S	111.04 E
Karangsembung	115a	6.51 S	108.39 E
Kāranja	122	20.29 N	77.29 E
Karanjia	120	21.47 N	85.58 E
Karanpura	123	29.50 N	73.27 E
Karaoba, Kaz.	86	53.17 N	65.06 E
Karaoba, Kaz.	86	47.03 N	56.20 E
Karaoğlan	130	39.14 N	39.13 E
Karaoj	86	45.54 N	74.45 E
Karaozek, Kaz.	85	43.43 N	77.23 E
Karaozek, Kaz.	86	45.03 N	65.18 E
Karaozek, Uzb.	86	43.16 N	58.40 E
Karapınar, Tür.	130	37.43 N	33.33 E
Karapınar, Tür.	130	41.30 N	32.12 E
Karapyši	78	49.38 N	30.47 E
Karaš	80	56.54 N	39.24 E
Karas, Pulau I	164	3.27 S	132.40 E
Karasaj	85	41.34 N	77.49 E
Kara-Sal ≃	80	47.22 N	43.38 E
Karaşar	130	40.20 N	32.00 E
Karasay	120	36.47 N	83.48 E
Karasburg	156	28.00 S	18.43 E
Karasburg □[5]	156	28.00 S	18.45 E
Kara Sea → Karskoje more ∓[2]	72	76.00 N	80.00 E
Karašengel'	86	47.29 N	75.35 E
Karašjåkka ≃	24	69.26 N	25.49 E
Karasjok	24	69.27 N	25.30 E
Karaskan	85	41.03 N	71.49 E
Karasor, ozero ⊜, Kaz.	86	51.57 N	75.45 E
Karasor, ozero ⊜, Kaz.	86	49.54 N	75.32 E
Karasu, Azer.	84	40.11 N	48.41 E
Karasu, Kaz.	86	52.40 N	65.28 E
Karasu, Kaz.	86	51.20 N	62.21 E
Karasu, Kyrg.	85	43.03 N	73.57 E
Kara-Su, Kyrg.	85	40.44 N	72.53 E
Karasu, Nihon	94	34.39 N	136.32 E
Karasu, Tür.	130	41.06 N	30.41 E
Karasu ≃, Nihon	94	36.15 N	139.17 E
Karasu ≃, Tür.	130	39.07 N	38.44 E
Karasuk	86	53.44 N	78.02 E
Karasuk ≃	86	53.35 N	77.30 E
Karasuyama	94	36.39 N	140.09 E
Karata	84	42.35 N	46.21 E
Karatal, Kaz.	86	45.07 N	77.54 E
Karatal, Kaz.	86	47.36 N	85.12 E
Karatal ≃	86	46.26 N	77.10 E
Karataş, Tür.	130	36.36 N	35.21 E
Karataş, Tür.	130	38.34 N	28.17 E
Karataş Burun ≻	130	36.35 N	35.22 E
Karatau	85	43.10 N	70.28 E
Karatau, chrebet ⋏, Kaz.	72	43.50 N	68.30 E
Karatau, chrebet ⋏, Taj.	85	38.10 N	69.00 E
Karateginskij chrebet ⋏	85	38.50 N	69.40 E
Karatepe Milli Parkı ♠	130	37.17 N	36.13 E
Karatia	126	24.14 N	89.58 E
Karatobe	80	49.41 N	53.31 E
Karatogaj	86	48.42 N	59.40 E
Karaton	86	46.25 N	53.30 E
Karatoya ≃	124	24.13 N	89.36 E
Karatschi → Karāchi	120	24.52 N	67.03 E
Karatsu	92	33.26 N	129.58 E
Karaturuk	85	43.33 N	77.59 E
Karatuzskoje	86	53.36 N	92.53 E
Karau	164	3.45 S	144.20 E
Karaul	74	70.06 N	83.08 E
Karauli	124	26.30 N	77.01 E
Karault'ob'o	85	40.33 N	75.57 E
Karaunk'ur ≃	85	40.54 N	72.20 E
Karaurğan	130	40.15 N	42.17 E
Karauzak	86	42.59 N	60.02 E
Karauzek	80	47.15 N	48.25 E
Karavan	85	41.30 N	71.45 E
Karavannoje, Ross.	80	45.59 N	47.08 E
Karavannoje, Ross.	80	57.47 N	47.41 E
Karavás	38	36.21 N	22.57 E
Karave	272c	19.01 N	73.01 E
Karawa	152	3.20 N	20.18 E
Karawang	115a	6.19 S	107.17 E
Karawang, Tanjung ≻	115a	5.56 S	107.00 E
Karawanken ⋏	36	46.30 N	14.25 E
Karayaka	130	40.45 N	36.37 E
Karayazı	130	39.41 N	42.08 E
Karaye	150	11.48 N	8.02 E
Karayün	130	39.41 N	37.19 E
Karažal	86	48.02 N	70.49 E
Karbalā'	128	32.36 N	44.02 E
Karbalā' □[4]	128	32.00 N	42.15 E
Karbenning	40	60.02 N	16.04 E
Kårberg	40	58.58 N	14.57 E
Karbeyaz	130	36.02 N	36.12 E
Kårböle	26	61.59 N	15.19 E
Karby	40	59.34 N	18.13 E
Karcag	30	47.19 N	20.56 E
Karczew	30	52.06 N	21.15 E
Kardail ≃	80	50.43 N	42.54 E
Kardašova Řečice	61	49.11 N	14.53 E
Karden	56	50.11 N	7.17 E
Kardhámaina	38	36.47 N	27.09 E
Kardhámila	38	38.32 N	26.05 E
Kardhítsa	38	39.21 N	21.55 E
Kärdla	76	59.00 N	22.45 E
Kardymovo	76	54.54 N	32.26 E
Kârdžali	38	41.39 N	25.22 E
Kardžin	84	43.16 N	44.16 E
Karea	272b	22.42 N	88.33 E
Kareeberge ⋏	158	30.53 S	21.57 E
Kareedouw	158	33.57 S	24.18 E
Kareli	84	42.01 N	43.54 E
Karelia □[9]	24	63.00 N	32.00 E
Karelskaja Avtonomnaja Sovetskaja Socialističeskaja Respublika □[3]	24	64.00 N	32.30 E
Karel'skij Gorodok	76	58.04 N	36.30 E
Karema, Pap. N. Gui.	164	9.12 S	147.14 E
Karema, Tan.	154	6.49 S	30.26 E
Karen	110	12.51 N	92.53 E
Karenga ≃	88	54.28 N	116.32 E
Karepino	24	61.02 N	57.02 E
Karera	272a	28.41 N	77.23 E
Karesuando	24	68.25 N	22.30 E
Kärevere	76	58.26 N	26.29 E
Kāreyz-e Elyās	128	35.25 N	61.20 E
Kargali	80	55.12 N	50.54 E
Kargalinskaja	84	43.44 N	46.30 E
Karganaj	180	65.21 N	175.25 E
Kargapazarı Dağları ⋏	130	40.07 N	41.35 E
Kargapolje	86	55.57 N	64.27 E
Kargasok	86	59.07 N	80.53 E
Kargat	86	55.10 N	80.17 E
Kargat ≃	86	54.37 N	78.12 E
Kargı	130	41.08 N	34.30 E
Kargil	123	34.34 N	76.06 E
Karginskaja	80	49.21 N	41.38 E
Karginskij ≃	265a	59.50 N	30.01 E
Kargopol'	24	61.30 N	38.58 E
Karguéri	146	13.27 N	10.25 E
Karhal	124	27.01 N	78.57 E
Karhijärvi ⊜	26	61.35 N	22.30 E
Karhula	26	60.31 N	26.57 E
Kari	146	11.14 N	10.34 E
Karia-Ba-Mohammed	148	34.19 N	5.10 W
Kariaí	38	40.16 N	24.15 E
Karianga	157b	22.22 S	47.26 E
Kariba	154	16.30 S	28.45 E
Kariba, Lake ⊜[1]	154	17.00 S	28.00 E
Karibib	156	21.58 S	15.51 E
Karibib □[5]	156	22.20 S	16.00 E
Karibisches Meer → Caribbean Sea ∓[2]	230	15.00 N	73.00 W
Karibumba	154	0.22 N	29.22 E
Kariega ≃	158	33.03 S	23.28 E
Karigasniemi	24	69.24 N	25.50 E
Karikari, Cape ≻	172	34.47 S	173.24 E
Karimata	175d	24.54 N	125.17 E
Karimata, Kepulauan II	112	1.25 S	109.05 E
Karimata, Pulau I	112	1.36 S	108.55 E
Karimata, Selat (Karimata Strait) ꭒ	112	2.05 S	108.40 E
Karīmganj	120	24.52 N	92.21 E
Karīmnagar	122	18.26 N	79.09 E
Karīmpur	126	23.58 N	88.37 E
Karimun, Pulau I	114	1.03 N	103.22 E
Karimunjawa, Kepulauan II	115a	5.50 S	110.25 E
Karimunjawa, Pulau I	115a	5.51 S	110.27 E
Karin, Som.	144	10.59 N	49.13 E
Karin, Som.	144	10.51 N	45.47 E
Karino	82	54.42 N	38.56 E
Karin Seamount ◆[3]	14	17.55 N	168.58 W
Karinskoje	82	55.42 N	36.41 E
Karintorf	80	58.33 N	50.11 E
Karis (Karjaa)	26	60.05 N	23.40 E
Karise	41	55.18 N	12.13 E
Karisimbi, Volcan ∧[1]	154	1.30 S	29.27 E
Káristos	38	38.00 N	24.24 E
Kariya	94	34.59 N	136.59 E
Kariye Museum ʋ[1]	267b	41.01 N	28.55 E
Kārīz	128	34.49 N	60.47 E
Karjaa → Karis	26	60.05 N	23.40 E
Karjala ◆[1]	26	64.00 N	32.00 E
Karjepolje	24	65.34 N	43.40 E
Kārkal	122	13.12 N	74.59 E
Karkalaj	80	57.00 N	52.24 E
Karkaralinsk	86	49.23 N	75.21 E
Karkar Dūmān ◆[8]	272a	28.39 N	77.18 E
Karkar Island I	164	4.40 S	146.00 E
Karkas, Kūh-e ∧	128	33.29 N	51.50 E
Karkheh ≃	128	31.46 N	47.55 E
Karkīndar	128	25.47 N	59.15 E
Karkinitskij zaliv c	78	45.55 N	33.00 E
Karkkila	26	60.32 N	24.11 E
Karkku	26	61.25 N	23.01 E
Karkom, Har ∧	132	30.17 N	34.44 E
Karkonoski Park Narodowy ♠	30	50.45 N	15.35 E
Kärla	76	58.20 N	22.15 E
Karlholmsbruk	40	60.31 N	17.35 E
Karlik Shan ∧	102	43.08 N	94.20 E
Karlino	30	54.03 N	15.51 E
Karlıova	130	39.18 N	41.01 E
Karlobag	36	44.32 N	15.05 E
Karlo-Libknechtovsk	83	48.42 N	38.04 E
Karlo-Marksovo	83	48.16 N	38.09 E
Karloske ≃	184	55.41 N	93.56 W
Karlovac	36	45.29 N	15.34 E
Karlovka	78	49.27 N	35.08 E
Karlovo	38	42.38 N	24.48 E
Karlovy Vary (Carlsbad)	54	50.11 N	12.52 E
Karlsbad → Karlovy Vary	54	50.11 N	12.52 E
Karlsborg, Sve.	26	58.32 N	14.31 E
Karlsborg, Sve.	26	65.48 N	23.17 E
Karlsburg → Alba Iulia	38	46.04 N	23.35 E
Karlsby	40	58.38 N	15.08 E
Karlsfeld	60	48.13 N	11.28 E
Karlshafen	52	51.38 N	9.27 E
Karlshamn	26	56.10 N	14.51 E
Karlshorst ◆[8]	264a	52.29 N	13.32 E
Karlshorst, Trabrennbahn ♠	264a	52.29 N	13.31 E
Karlshuld	60	48.41 N	11.18 E
Karlskoga	40	59.20 N	14.31 E
Karlskrona	26	56.10 N	15.35 E
Karlslunde Strand	41	55.34 N	12.14 E
Karlsöarna II	26	57.17 N	17.58 E
Karlsruhe	56	49.03 N	8.24 E
Karlsruhe □[5], Dtsch.	56	49.20 N	8.45 E
Karlsruhe □[5], Dtsch.	58	48.30 N	8.30 E
Karlstad, Sve.	40	59.22 N	13.30 E
Karlstad, Mn., U.S.	198	48.34 N	96.31 W
Karlstadt	56	49.57 N	9.45 E
Karlstift	61	48.35 N	14.45 E
Karluk, Ross.	88	53.27 N	105.58 E
Karluk, Ak., U.S.	180	57.34 N	154.28 W
Karl'uk, Uzb.	85	38.12 N	67.42 E
Karma	150	13.40 N	1.49 E
Karma, Ouadi V	146	15.38 N	20.01 E
Karmah	140	19.38 N	30.25 E
Karmāla	122	18.25 N	75.12 E
Karmanovka	80	49.24 N	50.22 E
Karmanovo	76	55.52 N	34.52 E
Karmansbo	40	59.42 N	15.44 E
Karmatānr	126	24.05 N	86.42 E
Karmel, Har (Mount Carmel) ∧	132	32.44 N	35.02 E
Karmi'el	132	32.55 N	35.18 E
Karmiyya	132	31.36 N	34.33 E
Karmøy I	26	59.15 N	5.15 E
Karnack	194	32.40 N	94.10 W
Karnak	194	37.17 N	88.58 W
Karnak → Al-Karnak	140	25.43 N	32.39 E
Karnāl	124	29.41 N	76.59 E
Karnāla Fort ⊥	272c	18.53 N	73.07 E
Karṇālī □[8]	124	29.30 N	82.30 E
Karṇālī ≃	124	28.15 N	81.05 E
Karnap ◆[8]	263	51.31 N	7.01 E
Karnaphuli Reservoir ⊜[1]	120	22.42 N	92.12 E
Karnātaka □[3]	122	14.00 N	76.00 E
Karnauchovka	78	48.28 N	34.44 E
Karnes □[6]	222	29.00 N	97.47 W
Karnes City	196	28.53 N	97.54 W
Karni	150	10.40 N	2.37 W
Karniki	82	54.12 N	38.05 E
Karnische Alpen (Alpi Carniche) ⋏	64	46.40 N	13.00 E
Karnobat	38	42.39 N	26.59 E
Karns City	214	41.00 N	79.44 W
Kärnten □[3]	30	46.50 N	13.50 E
Karnzow	54	52.59 N	12.26 E
Karoi	154	16.50 S	29.40 E
Karokh	128	34.28 N	62.35 E
Karoli	124	22.55 N	79.04 E
Karolinenhof ◆[8]	264a	52.23 N	13.38 E
Karomatan	116	7.46 N	123.44 E
Karompa Lompo, Pulau I	112	7.15 S	121.45 E
Karon	126	24.07 N	86.44 E
Karonga	154	9.56 S	33.56 E
Karonie	162	30.58 S	122.32 E
Karoonda	166	35.06 S	139.54 E
Karor	123	31.13 N	70.57 E
Karora	140	17.42 N	38.22 E
Karos	158	28.24 S	21.35 E
Karosa	112	1.48 S	119.20 E
Karoso, Tanjung ≻	115b	9.33 S	118.50 E
Karotho Post	154	5.11 N	35.50 E
Karou	150	15.07 N	0.39 E
Karow, Dtsch.	54	52.20 N	12.15 E
Karow, Dtsch.	54	53.32 N	12.15 E
Karow ◆[8]	264a	52.37 N	13.29 E
Karpathen → Carpathian Mountains ⋏	22	48.00 N	24.00 E
Kárpathos, Ellás	38	35.30 N	27.14 E
Kárpathos, Ellás	130	35.31 N	27.12 E
Kárpathos I	38	35.40 N	27.10 E
Karpenísion	38	38.55 N	21.40 E
Karpinsk	86	59.45 N	60.01 E
Karpogory	24	64.00 N	44.24 E
Karpovka, Ukr.	83	49.10 N	37.43 E
Karpovka, Ukr.	83	47.57 N	39.36 E
Karpovo, Ross.	76	60.02 N	36.43 E
Karpovo, Ross.	82	55.35 N	38.34 E
Karpunicha	80	57.42 N	45.20 E
Karpuninskij	86	58.43 N	61.50 E
Karpuzlu	130	37.33 N	27.50 E
Karratha	162	20.44 S	116.51 E
Karrats Fjord c[2]	176	71.20 N	54.00 W
Karrebæksminde	41	55.11 N	11.40 E
Karres	58	47.13 N	10.47 E
Kärrgruvan	40	60.05 N	15.56 E
Karridale	162	34.13 S	115.05 E
Kars	84	40.36 N	43.05 E
Kars □[4]	84	40.35 N	43.00 E
Kars ≃	84	40.37 N	43.41 E
Karša	80	49.48 N	51.27 E
Karsakpaj	86	47.49 N	66.41 E
Karsakuwigamak Lake ⊜	184	56.22 N	99.30 W
Kärsämäki	26	63.58 N	25.46 E
Karsantı	130	37.33 N	35.24 E
Kārsava	76	56.47 N	27.40 E
Karsdorf	54	51.17 N	11.39 E
Karši	128	38.53 N	65.48 E
Karsin	30	53.54 N	17.56 E
Karšinskaja step' ≚	128	39.10 N	65.00 E
Karskije Vorota, proliv ꭒ	72	70.30 N	58.00 E
Karskoje more (Kara Sea) ∓[2]	72	76.00 N	80.00 E
Karsovaj	80	58.14 N	53.11 E
Kårsta, Sve.	40	59.39 N	18.14 E
Kärsta, Sve.	40	59.40 N	16.49 E
Karstädt	54	53.09 N	11.44 E
Karst → Kras ⋏[1]	64	45.48 N	14.00 E
Karstula	26	62.52 N	24.47 E
Karsun	80	54.11 N	46.59 E
Kartajol'	24	64.32 N	53.14 E
Kartala ∧	157a	11.45 S	43.22 E
Kartaly	86	53.03 N	60.40 E
Kartārpur	123	31.27 N	75.30 E
Karthaus	214	41.07 N	78.07 W
Kartlijskij chrebet ⋏	84	42.10 N	44.55 E
Kartosuro	115a	7.33 S	110.44 E
Karttula	26	62.53 N	26.58 E
Kartuzy	30	54.20 N	18.12 E
Kartzow	54	52.29 N	12.58 E
Käru	76	58.50 N	25.11 E
Karuah ≃	170	32.39 S	151.58 E
Karufa	164	3.50 S	133.27 E
Karuizawa	94	36.21 N	138.38 E
Karukuwisa	156	18.56 S	19.40 E
Karumai	92	40.19 N	141.28 E
Karumba	166	17.29 S	140.50 E
Kārūn ≃	128	30.26 N	48.10 E
Karungi	26	66.03 N	23.57 E
Karungu	154	0.51 S	34.09 E
Karuni	115b	9.26 S	119.19 E
Karunjie	164	16.18 S	127.12 E
Karunki	26	66.02 N	24.01 E
Karup	41	56.18 N	9.10 E
Karup Å ≃	41	56.18 N	9.10 E
Karūr	122	10.57 N	78.05 E
Karuscia, Punta ≻	70	36.49 N	11.59 E
Karvala	265a	59.41 N	30.09 E
Karviná	30	49.50 N	18.30 E
Kārwār	122	14.48 N	74.08 E
Karwendel ⋏	64	47.27 N	11.20 E
Karwi	124	25.12 N	80.54 E
Karym	86	60.07 N	66.41 E
Karymskoje, Ross.	88	51.37 N	114.21 E
Karymskoje, Ross.	88	54.07 N	101.49 E
Karza	86	58.35 N	80.50 E
Karzachi	84	41.15 N	43.16 E
Kas, Sūd.	140	12.30 N	24.17 E
Kaş, Tür.	130	36.12 N	29.38 E
Kas ≃	86	59.40 N	90.00 E
Kasaan	182	55.32 N	132.24 W
Kasabi	152	14.48 S	23.42 E
Kasach ≃	84	40.03 N	43.52 E
Kasadi ≃	272c	19.01 N	73.03 E
Kasa-do I	98	34.28 N	126.03 E
Kasado-shima I	96	33.57 N	131.51 E
Kasagi	94	34.45 N	135.56 E
Kasagi-sanchi ⋏	270	34.37 N	135.56 E
Kasagi-yama ∧	94	35.31 N	137.21 E
Kasahara	94	35.17 N	137.09 E
Kasahata	268	35.54 N	139.25 E
Kasai	96	34.56 N	134.50 E
Kasai ◆[8]	268	35.39 N	139.53 E
Kasai (Cassai) ≃, Afr.	152	3.02 S	16.57 E
Kāsai ≃, India	124	22.09 N	87.50 E
Kasai-Occidental □[4]	152	5.30 S	21.40 E
Kasai-Oriental □[4]	152	4.00 S	23.30 E
Kasaji	152	10.22 S	23.27 E
Kasakake	94	36.23 N	139.17 E
Kasama, Nihon	94	36.23 N	140.16 E
Kasama, Zam.	154	10.13 S	31.12 E
Kasamatsu	94	35.22 N	136.46 E
Kasan	128	39.02 N	65.35 E
Kasan-dong	98	41.18 N	126.55 E
Kasane	156	17.50 S	25.05 E
Kasanga	154	8.28 S	31.09 E
Kasangale	152	6.20 S	22.42 E
Kasangeshi ≃	152	8.24 S	21.56 E
Kasangulu	152	4.36 S	15.10 E
Kasanka National Park ♠	154	12.35 S	30.12 E
Kasan → Kazan'	80	55.49 N	49.08 E
Kasano-misaki ≻	94	36.21 N	136.18 E
Kasansaj	85	41.15 N	71.32 E
Kasansaj ≃	85	40.57 N	71.30 E
Kasaoka	96	34.30 N	133.30 E
Kāsaragod	122	12.30 N	75.00 E
Kasari ≃	76	58.45 N	23.49 E
Kašary	78	49.03 N	41.00 E
Kasatori-yama ∧, Nihon	94	34.44 N	136.18 E
Kasatori-yama ∧, Nihon	96	33.33 N	132.55 E
Kasauli	123	30.55 N	76.57 E
Kasba	124	25.51 N	87.33 E
Kasbagoas	126	24.11 N	88.30 E
Kasba Kamarda	126	21.46 N	87.21 E
Kasba Lake ⊜	176	60.18 N	102.07 W
Kasba Mirgoda	126	21.42 N	87.28 E
Kasba Nārāyangarh	126	22.10 N	87.23 E
Kasba Patāspur	126	22.02 N	87.32 E
Kasba-Tadla	148	32.34 N	6.18 W
Kaschau → Košice	30	48.43 N	21.15 E
Kåseberga	26	55.23 N	14.04 E
Kaseda	92	31.25 N	130.19 E
Kasempa	154	13.27 S	25.50 E
Kasenga	154	10.22 S	28.38 E
Kasenyi	154	1.24 N	30.26 E
Kasese, Ug.	154	0.10 N	30.05 E
Kasese, Zaïre	154	1.38 S	27.07 E
Kaset Sombun	110	16.17 N	101.57 E
Kasfareet Military Base ■	142	30.15 N	32.24 E
Kāsganj	124	27.49 N	78.39 E
Kashabowie Lake ⊜	190	48.42 N	90.25 W
Kashaf ≃	128	35.58 N	61.07 E
Kashagawigamog Lake ⊜	212	44.59 N	78.37 W
Kāshān	128	33.59 N	51.29 E
Kashasha	154	1.44 S	31.37 E
Kashegelok	180	60.50 N	157.50 W
Kashgar → Kashi	85	39.29 N	75.59 E
Kashi	85	39.29 N	75.59 E
Kashiba	96	34.33 N	135.42 E
Kashihara	96	34.30 N	135.46 E
Kashiji Plain ≚	152	13.20 S	22.30 E
Kashileshi ≃	152	9.46 S	23.05 E
Kashima, Nihon	92	33.07 N	130.06 E
Kashima, Nihon	94	35.58 N	140.38 E
Kashima, Nihon	94	36.58 N	136.55 E
Kashima, Nihon	96	35.30 N	133.01 E
Kashima-jingū ʋ[1]	94	35.59 N	140.40 E
Kashima-nada ∓[2]	94	36.15 N	140.45 E
Kashima-Yariga-take ∧	94	36.37 N	137.45 E
Kashimo	94	35.43 N	137.23 E
Kāshināthpur	126	23.58 N	89.37 E
Kashing → Jiaxing	106	30.46 N	120.45 E
Kashio ◆[8]	268	35.25 N	139.33 E
Kāshīpur, India	124	29.13 N	78.57 E
Kāshipur, India	126	23.26 N	86.40 E
Kashitu	154	13.42 S	28.40 E
Kashiwa	94	35.52 N	139.59 E
Kashiwara	96	34.35 N	135.37 E
Kashiwazaki, Nihon	92	37.22 N	138.33 E
Kashiwazaki, Nihon	268	35.56 N	139.42 E
Kāshmar	128	35.12 N	58.27 E
Kashmir, Vale of V	123	34.00 N	75.00 E
Kashmir → Jammu and Kashmīr □[2]	120	34.00 N	76.00 E
Kashmor	120	28.26 N	69.35 E
Kashmūnd Ghar ⋏	123	34.42 N	70.31 E
Kashunuk ≃	180	61.18 N	165.36 W
Kashwakamak Lake ⊜	212	44.50 N	77.04 W
Kasia	124	26.45 N	83.55 E
Kāsiāni	126	23.14 N	89.45 E
Kasiāri	126	22.08 N	87.14 E
Kasidiji ≃	152	7.57 S	23.12 E
Kasigau ∧	154	3.50 S	38.40 E
Kasigluk	180	60.52 N	162.32 W
Kasilof	180	60.24 N	151.18 W
Kasilovo	78	50.38 N	35.37 E
Kasimbar	112	0.09 S	120.00 E
Kasimov	80	54.56 N	41.24 E
Kāsimpur, Bngl.	126	23.59 N	90.19 E
Kāsimpur, India	272b	22.46 N	88.31 E
Kašin	76	57.21 N	37.37 E
Kāsināthpur	272b	22.35 N	88.31 E
Kasinge	154	6.20 S	26.59 E
Kasinka	156	18.13 S	24.22 E
Kāsipur	272b	22.25 N	88.10 E
Kašira	82	54.51 N	38.10 E
Kaširka ≃	82	54.52 N	38.13 E
Kasiruta, Pulau I	108	0.25 S	127.12 E
Kasiui, Pulau I	164	4.30 S	131.40 E
Kasiwa → Kashiwa	94	35.52 N	139.59 E
Kaskabulak	86	49.34 N	79.52 E
Kaškadarjinskaja Oblast' □[8]	85	39.00 N	67.00 E
Kaskaden-Kette → Cascade Range ⋏	202	45.00 N	121.30 W
Kaskana	85	40.45 N	69.36 E
Kaskaskia ≃	194	37.59 N	89.56 W
Kaskaskia, East Fork ≃	219	38.43 N	89.09 W
Kaskaskia, North Fork ≃	219	38.46 N	89.09 W
Kaskattama ≃	176	57.03 N	90.07 W
Kaskelen	85	43.12 N	76.37 E
Kaskelen ≃	85	43.53 N	77.08 E
Kaskinen → Kaskö	26	62.23 N	21.13 E
Kaskö (Kaskinen)	26	62.23 N	21.13 E
Kašlagač ≃	83	47.45 N	37.16 E
Kaslātu ∧	124	23.58 N	84.54 E
Kasli	86	55.53 N	60.46 E
Kaslo	182	49.55 N	116.55 W
Kasn'a	76	55.24 N	34.20 E
Kasn'a ≃	76	55.51 N	34.25 E
Kaso ≃	115a	7.25 S	106.40 E
Kasongo	154	4.27 S	26.40 E
Kasongo-Lunda	152	6.28 S	16.49 E
Kásos I	38	35.22 N	26.56 E
Kasota	190	44.18 N	93.57 W
Kašperovka	78	49.26 N	29.41 E
Kaspi	84	41.57 N	44.25 E
Kaspijsk	84	42.52 N	47.38 E
Kaspijskij	22	45.22 N	47.24 E
Kaspijskoje more → Caspian Sea ∓[2]	72	42.00 N	50.30 E
Kaspische Senke → Prikaspijskaja nizmennost' ≚	80	48.00 N	52.00 E

ENGLISH

Name	Page	Lat.°′	Long.°′
Kaspisches Meer → Caspian Sea ∓[2]	72	42.00 N	50.30 E
Kaspl'a	76	55.00 N	31.38 E
Kaspl'a ≃	76	55.24 N	30.43 E
Kasr, Ra's ≻	140	18.02 N	38.35 E
Kasrik	130	38.13 N	41.54 E
Kassab	130	35.56 N	35.59 E
Kassai → Cassai (Kasai) ≃	152	3.02 S	16.57 E
Kassa → Košice	30	48.43 N	21.15 E
Kassalā	140	15.28 N	36.24 E
Kassalā □[4]	140	15.00 N	35.00 E
Kassándra ≻[1]	38	40.06 N	23.22 E
Kassándras, Kólpos c	38	40.06 N	23.30 E
Kassel	56	51.19 N	9.29 E
Kassel □[5]	56	51.10 N	9.20 E
Kasserine	148	35.11 N	8.48 E
Kasserine □[8]	148	35.00 N	8.45 E
Kasshabog Lake ⊜	212	44.38 N	77.58 W
Kassikaityu ≃	246	1.49 N	58.32 W
Kassinger	140	18.45 N	31.54 E
Kassîr, Sabkhat al- ⊜	130	35.03 N	41.07 E
Kasslerfeld ◆[8]	263	51.26 N	6.45 E
Kasson	190	44.01 N	92.45 W
Kassou	150	11.35 N	2.03 W
Kassoum	150	13.05 N	3.18 W
Kastamonu	130	41.22 N	33.47 E
Kastamonu □[4]	130	41.40 N	33.45 E
Kastanéai	38	41.38 N	26.28 E
Kastelholm	26	60.14 N	20.04 E
Kastellaun	56	50.04 N	7.26 E
Kastellórizon I	130	36.08 N	29.34 E
Kasterlee	56	51.15 N	4.57 E
Kastiyu, Puntan ≻	174n	14.57 N	145.40 E
Kastl, Dtsch.	60	49.22 N	11.42 E
Kastl, Dtsch.	60	49.50 N	11.54 E
Kastorf	52	53.44 N	10.34 E
Kastoría	38	40.31 N	21.15 E
Kastorías, Límni ⊜	38	40.30 N	21.17 E
Kastornoje	78	51.50 N	38.06 E
Kastrávion, Tekhnití Límni ⊜[1]	38	38.50 N	21.20 E
Kastrup Lufthavn ⊠	41	55.38 N	12.39 E
Kasuga, Nihon	94	35.28 N	136.29 E
Kasuga, Nihon	96	33.32 N	130.27 E
Kasuga, Nihon	96	35.10 N	135.06 E
Kasugai, Nihon	94	35.14 N	136.58 E
Kasugai, Nihon	94	35.39 N	138.39 E
Kasuga-kōkūkichi, Kaijō-jieitai- ■	96	33.31 N	130.28 E
Kasuga Shrine ʋ[1]	270	34.41 N	135.51 E
Kasuka	158	33.40 S	26.41 E
Kasukabe	94	35.58 N	139.45 E
Kasukawa	94	36.24 N	139.13 E
Kasulu	154	4.34 S	30.06 E
Kasumi	96	35.38 N	134.38 E
Kasumiga-ura ⊜	94	36.00 N	140.25 E
Kasum-Ismailov	84	40.36 N	46.47 E
Kasumkent	84	41.41 N	48.07 E
Kasungan	112	1.58 S	113.24 E
Kasungu	154	13.01 S	33.30 E
Kasungu National Park ♠	154	12.55 S	33.15 E
Kasupe	154	15.10 S	35.15 E
Kasūr	123	31.07 N	74.27 E
Kaszuby ◆[1]	30	54.10 N	18.15 E
Kata	88	58.46 N	102.40 E
Kataba	154	16.05 S	25.10 E
Kataeregi	150	9.22 N	6.17 E
Katagum	146	12.17 N	10.21 E
Katahdin, Mount ∧	188	45.55 N	68.55 W
Katai	272c	19.10 N	73.05 E
Katajevo	88	50.57 N	108.41 E
Katajsk	86	56.18 N	62.35 E
Katako-Kombe	152	3.24 S	24.25 E
Katakura	270	34.29 N	135.31 E
Katakwi	154	1.55 N	33.57 E
Katale	154	4.59 S	31.03 E
Katalla	180	60.12 N	144.31 W
Katanda	154	0.50 S	29.22 E
Katanga □[9]	138	10.00 S	26.00 E
Katanga ≃	74	60.08 N	102.13 E
Katangi	124	23.27 N	79.47 E
Katanglad Mountains ⋏	116	8.06 N	124.54 E
Katangli	89	51.42 N	143.14 E
Katanimara	126	22.17 N	87.11 E
Katanning	162	33.42 S	117.33 E
Katano	270	34.47 N	135.40 E
Katano-hana ≻	174f	24.49 N	141.20 E
Katanti	154	2.18 S	27.08 E
Kataoka	270	35.03 N	135.58 E
Katapakishi	152	8.15 S	22.49 E
Katara, Depresión de → Qaṭṭārah, Munkhafaḍ al- ±[7]	140	30.00 N	27.30 E
Katârniān Ghāt	124	28.20 N	81.09 E
Katar → Qatar □[1]	128	25.00 N	51.10 E
Katase	268	35.19 N	139.29 E
Katashina	94	36.46 N	139.14 E
Katašin	76	52.36 N	32.10 E
Katav-Ivanovsk	86	54.45 N	58.12 E
Katayama	268	35.46 N	139.34 E
Katchall Island I	110	7.57 N	93.22 E
Katchewanooka Lake ⊜	212	44.27 N	78.16 W
Katchin-wan c	174m	26.18 N	127.53 E
Katchirga	150	14.03 N	0.06 E
Katchiungo	152	12.35 S	16.13 E
Katech	84	41.39 N	46.34 E
Kateel ≃	180	65.28 N	157.35 W
Katélé	150	10.38 N	5.37 W
Katena-wan c	174m	26.50 N	128.05 E
Katepwa Beach	184	50.42 N	103.38 W
Katerbow	54	52.59 N	12.39 E
Kateríni	38	40.16 N	22.30 E
Katerinopol'	78	48.56 N	30.59 E
Katerloch ±[5]	61	47.16 N	15.32 E
Katernberg ◆[8], Dtsch.	263	51.16 N	7.06 E
Katernberg ◆[8], Dtsch.	263	51.29 N	7.04 E
Katesbridge	48	54.18 N	6.08 W
Kates Needle ∧	180	57.03 N	132.03 W
Katešovo	82	54.08 N	37.00 E
Katete, Malaŵi	154	12.17 S	33.39 E
Katete, Zam.	154	14.05 S	32.07 E
Katghora	124	22.30 N	82.33 E
Katha	110	24.11 N	96.21 E
Kathangor, Jabal ∧	140	5.45 N	33.59 E
Katherine	164	14.28 S	132.16 E
Katherine ≃	164	14.39 S	131.42 E
Katherine Creek ≃	166	23.48 S	143.42 E
Katherine Gorge National Park ♠	164	14.10 S	132.30 E
Kāthgodām	124	29.16 N	79.32 E
Kathiār	120	25.32 N	87.35 E
Kāthiāwār Peninsula ≻[1]	120	22.00 N	71.00 E
Kathīb, Ra's ≻	144	14.55 N	42.53 E
Kathla	123	31.59 N	76.47 E
Kathleen	220	28.07 N	82.01 W
Kathleen Valley	162	27.23 S	120.38 E
Kathlow	54	51.43 N	14.29 E
Kāṭhmāṇḍau	124	27.43 N	85.19 E
Kathmandu → Kāṭhmāṇḍau	124	27.43 N	85.19 E
Kathor	120	21.18 N	72.56 E
Kathrabbā	132	31.08 N	35.37 E
Kathua	123	32.22 N	75.31 E
Kāthuli	126	23.52 N	88.40 E
Kati	150	12.44 N	8.04 W
Kātiādi	126	24.15 N	90.48 E
Katibas ≃	112	2.01 N	112.33 E
Katihār	124	25.32 N	87.35 E
Katikati	172	37.33 S	175.55 E
Katima Mulilo	152	17.27 S	24.14 E

DEUTSCH

Name	Seite	Breite°′	Länge°′ E = Ost
Katimik Lake ⊜	184	52.54 N	99.22 W
Katiola	150	8.08 N	5.06 W
Katipunan	116	8.31 N	123.17 E
Katiti Aboriginal Land Reserve ◆[4]	162	25.10 S	131.15 E
Kātlang	123	34.22 N	72.05 E
Katlehong	273d	26.19 S	28.09 E
Katlenburg-Duhm	52	51.41 N	10.06 E
Katmai, Mount ∧	180	58.17 N	154.56 W
Katmai National Park ♠	180	58.30 N	155.00 W
Kātmāndu → Kāṭhmāṇḍau	124	27.43 N	85.19 E
Katni	80	57.59 N	47.46 E
Katni → Murwāra	124	23.51 N	80.24 E
Káto Akhaïa	38	38.09 N	21.32 E
Kātol	120	21.16 N	78.35 E
Katompi	154	6.11 S	26.20 E
Katonah	210	41.16 N	73.41 W
Katonga ≃	154	0.34 N	31.50 E
Katon-Karagaj	86	49.11 N	85.37 E
Katoomba	170	33.42 S	150.18 E
Katopa	154	2.45 S	25.06 E
Katori-jingū ʋ[1]	94	35.52 N	140.30 E
Katoúna	38	38.47 N	21.07 E
Katovice	60	49.16 N	13.49 E
Katowice	30	50.16 N	19.00 E
Katowice □[4]	30	50.15 N	19.00 E
Katra	123	32.59 N	74.57 E
Kātrās	126	23.48 N	86.17 E
Katričev	80	49.23 N	45.33 E
Kātrīnā, Jabal ∧	140	28.31 N	33.57 E
Katrine, Loch ⊜	46	56.15 N	4.31 W
Katrineholm	40	59.00 N	16.12 E
Katsch, Golf von → Kutch, Gulf of c	120	22.36 N	69.30 E
Katschbach ≃	61	47.08 N	14.17 E
Katschberg)(	64	47.03 N	13.37 E
Katsepe	157b	15.45 S	46.15 E
Katshungu	154	2.27 S	27.23 E
Katsina	150	13.00 N	7.32 E
Katsina □[3]	150	12.20 N	7.45 E
Katsina Ala	150	7.10 N	9.17 E
Katsina Ala ≃	152	7.48 N	8.52 E
Katsunuma	94	35.39 N	138.44 E
Katsura ◆[8]	270	34.59 N	135.42 E
Katsura ≃, Nihon	94	35.36 N	139.15 E
Katsura ≃, Nihon	94	34.53 N	135.42 E
Katsura ≃, Nihon	96	34.02 N	134.35 E
Katsura ≃, Nihon	270	34.53 N	135.42 E
Katsuragi	96	34.15 N	135.30 E
Katsuragi-san ∧	96	34.20 N	135.27 E
Katsushika ◆[8]	268	35.43 N	139.51 E
Katsuta, Nihon	94	36.24 N	140.30 E
Katsuta, Nihon	96	35.04 N	134.11 E
Katsuura, Nihon	94	35.08 N	140.18 E
Katsuura, Nihon	96	33.56 N	134.30 E
Katsuyama, Nihon	94	36.03 N	136.30 E
Katsuyama, Nihon	96	35.05 N	133.41 E
Kattakurgan	72	39.55 N	66.15 E
Kattara-Senke → Qaṭṭārah, Munkhafaḍ al- ±[7]	140	30.00 N	27.30 E
Kattarp	41	56.09 N	12.46 E
Katta-Taldyk	85	40.19 N	73.12 E
Kattaviá	38	35.57 N	27.46 E
Kattegat ꭒ	26	57.00 N	11.00 E
Katternberg ◆[8]	263	51.09 N	7.02 E
Katthammarsvik	26	57.26 N	18.50 E
Kattowitz → Katowice	30	50.16 N	19.00 E
Kattrup	41	55.57 N	9.56 E
Kāttuputtūr	122	10.59 N	78.14 E
Katul, Jabal ∧	140	14.16 N	29.23 E
Katuma	154	6.10 S	30.34 E
Katumba	154	7.45 S	25.18 E
Katun' ≃	86	52.25 N	85.05 E
Katunino	80	58.01 N	45.39 E
Katunki	80	56.50 N	43.14 E
Kātūria	124	24.44 N	86.43 E
Katu Shan ∧	86	45.40 N	82.55 E
Katusice	54	50.26 N	14.50 E
Kātwa	126	23.39 N	88.08 E
Katwijk aan de Rijn	52	52.11 N	4.26 E
Katwijk aan Zee	52	52.13 N	4.24 E
Katy	222	29.47 N	95.49 W
Katyn	76	54.47 N	31.44 E
Kąty Wrocławskie	30	51.02 N	16.46 E
Katzenbuckel ∧	56	49.28 N	9.02 E
Katzenelnbogen	56	50.17 N	7.59 E
Katzenfurt	56	50.37 N	8.21 E
Katzhütte	54	50.33 N	11.03 E
Kaua ≃	156	19.24 S	22.03 E
Kauai □[6]	229b	21.59 N	159.22 W
Kauai I	229b	22.00 N	159.30 W
Kauai Channel ꭒ	229b	21.45 N	158.50 W
Kaub	56	50.05 N	7.46 E
Kau Desert ◆[2]	229d	19.21 N	155.19 W
Kaufbeuren	58	47.53 N	10.37 E
Kaufering	58	48.05 N	10.52 E
Kaufman	222	32.35 N	96.18 W
Kaufman □[6]	222	32.38 N	96.18 W
Kaufungen, Dtsch.	52	51.17 N	9.38 E
Kaufungen, Dtsch.	56	51.17 N	9.38 E
Kaugama	150	12.28 N	9.44 E
Kauhajoki	26	62.26 N	22.11 E
Kauhanevan-Pohjankankaan kansallispuisto ♠	26	63.08 N	22.25 E
Kauhava	26	63.06 N	23.05 E
Kauiki Head ≻	229a	20.45 N	155.59 W
Kaukapakapa	172	36.37 S	174.30 E
Kaukasus → Bol'šoj Kavkaz ⋏	84	42.30 N	45.00 E
Kaukauna	190	44.16 N	88.16 W
Kaukau Veld ⋏[1]	156	19.30 S	20.30 E
Kaukhāli	126	22.38 N	90.04 E
Kaukura I[1]	14	15.45 S	146.42 W
Kaula I	229d	21.45 N	160.30 W
Kaulakahi Channel ꭒ	229b	22.00 N	159.53 W
Kaulille	56	51.11 N	5.31 E
Kauliranta	24	66.27 N	23.41 E
Kaŭl-li	98	37.58 N	124.37 E
Kaulsdorf	54	50.37 N	11.26 E
Kaulsdorf ◆[8]	264a	52.31 N	13.33 E
Kaulsdorf-Süd ◆[8]	264a	52.29 N	13.34 E
Kaumakani	229b	21.55 N	159.37 W
Kaumalapau	229a	20.47 N	156.59 W
Kaunakakai	229a	21.05 N	157.01 W
Kaunas	76	54.54 N	23.54 E
Kauneonga Lake	210	41.41 N	74.50 W
Kauner Tal V	58	47.01 N	10.44 E
Kaunghein	110	25.40 N	95.26 E
Kauniainen → Grankulla	26	60.13 N	24.45 E
Kaununui ≻	229b	21.56 N	160.10 W
Kaup	164	3.50 S	144.00 E
Kaupanger	26	61.11 N	7.14 E
Kaura Namoda	150	12.35 N	6.35 E
Kauriyāla Ghāt	124	28.23 N	81.02 E
Kauru	150	10.33 N	8.12 E
Kausa	272c	19.10 N	73.02 E
Kau Sai Chau I	271d	22.22 N	114.18 E
Kausala	26	60.54 N	26.22 E
Kaušany	78	46.38 N	29.25 E
Kaustinen	26	63.32 N	23.42 E
Kauswagan	116	8.11 N	124.05 E
Kautokeino	24	69.00 N	23.02 E
Kauttua	26	61.06 N	22.10 E
Kau-ye Kyun I	110	11.01 N	98.32 E
Kavača	74	60.16 N	169.51 E
Kavacık	130	39.40 N	28.30 E
Kavadarci	38	41.26 N	22.00 E
Kavajë	38	41.11 N	19.33 E
Kavak, Tür.	130	38.24 N	39.26 E
Kavak, Tür.	130	41.05 N	36.03 E
Kavak, Tür.	130	39.18 N	37.30 E
Kavakbaşı	130	38.29 N	41.49 E
Kavaklıdere	130	37.26 N	28.22 E

Symbols in the index entries represent the broad categories identified in the key at the right. Symbols with superior numbers (⋏[1]) identify subcategories (see complete key on page *I · 1).*

Symbole im Register stellen die rechts im Schlüssel erklärten Kategorien dar. Symbole mit hochgestellten Ziffern (⋏[1]) bezeichnen Unterabteilungen einer Kategorie (vgl. vollständiger Schlüssel auf Seite *I · 1).*

Los símbolos incluídos en el texto del índice representan las grandes categorias identificadas con la clave a la derecha. Los símbolos con numeros en su parte superior (⋏[1]) identifican las subcategorías (véase la clave completa en la página *I · 1).*

Les symboles de l'index représentent les catégories indiquées dans la légende à droite. Les symboles suivis d'un indice (⋏[1]) représentent des sous-catégories (voir légende complète à la page *I · 1).*

Os símbolos incluídos no texto do índice representam as grandes categorias identificadas com a chave à direita. Os símbolos com números em sua parte superior (⋏[1]) identificam as subcategorias (veja-se a chave completa à página *I · 1).*

∧ Mountain	Berg	Montaña	Montagne	Montanha
⋏ Mountains	Gebirge	Montañas	Montagnes	Montanhas
)(Pass	Paß	Paso	Col	Passo
V Valley, Canyon	Tal, Cañon	Valle, Cañón	Vallée, Canyon	Vale, Canhão
≚ Plain	Ebene	Llano	Plaine	Planície
≻ Cape	Kap	Cabo	Cap	Cabo
I Island	Insel	Isla	Île	Ilha
II Islands	Inseln	Islas	Îles	Ilhas
± Other Topographic Features	Andere Topographische Objekte	Otros Elementos Topográficos	Autres données topographiques	Outros acidentes topográficos

ESPAÑOL — Nombre | Página | Lat.°′ | Long.°′ W = Oeste
FRANÇAIS — Nom | Page | Lat.°′ | Long.°′ W = Ouest
PORTUGUÊS — Nome | Página | Lat.°′ | Long.°′ W = Oeste

Nombre / Nom / Nome	Página / Page	Lat.°′	Long.°′
Kavála	38	40.56 N	24.25 E
Kavalerovo	89	44.15 N	135.04 E
Kāvali	122	14.55 N	79.59 E
Kavango □[5]	156	18.30 S	20.15 E
Kavaratti	122	10.34 N	72.39 E
Kavaratti Island I	122	10.33 N	72.38 E
Kavarna	38	43.25 N	28.20 E
Kavendou, Mont ∧	150	10.41 N	12.12 W
Kāveri ≃	122	11.09 N	79.52 E
Kāveri Falls ʟ	122	12.18 N	77.17 E
Kaverino, Ross.	80	54.10 N	41.47 E
Kaverino, Ross.	82	56.11 N	36.15 E
Kavieng	164	2.35 S	150.50 E
Kavimba	156	18.02 S	24.38 E
Kavīr, Dasht-e ◆[2]	128	34.40 N	54.30 E
Kavkazskij zapovednik ♠	84	43.55 N	40.30 E
Kävlinge	41	55.48 N	13.06 E
Kävlingeån ≃	41	55.47 N	13.06 E
Kavungo	152	11.31 S	23.03 E
Kavuu ≃	154	7.40 S	31.46 E
Kavykuči-Gazimurskije	88	51.22 N	118.10 E
Kaw, Guy. fr.	250	4.29 N	52.02 W
Kaw, Ok., U.S.	196	36.46 N	96.50 W
Kawa	110	17.05 N	96.28 E
Kawaba	94	36.41 N	139.07 E
Kawabe, Nihon	94	35.29 N	137.04 E
Kawabe, Nihon	96	33.55 N	135.11 E
Kawachi, Nihon	94	36.24 N	136.38 E
Kawachi, Nihon	94	36.37 N	139.56 E
Kawachi, Nihon	94	35.53 N	140.15 E
Kawachi-nagano	96	34.27 N	135.34 E
Kawagama Lake ⊜	212	45.18 N	78.45 W
Kawage	94	34.47 N	136.33 E
Kawagoe	94	35.55 N	139.29 E
Kawaguchi	94	35.48 N	139.43 E
Kawaguchiko	94	35.30 N	138.46 E
Kawaguchi-ko ⊜	94	35.31 N	138.45 E
Kawahara	96	35.24 N	134.12 E
Kawai, Nihon	94	36.18 N	137.07 E
Kawai, Nihon	270	34.35 N	135.45 E
Kawaihae Bay c	229d	20.02 N	155.50 W
Kawaihoa ›	229b	21.47 N	160.12 W
Kawaikini ∧	229b	22.05 N	159.29 W
Kawailoa	229c	21.36 N	158.05 W
Kawailoa Beach	229c	21.37 N	158.04 W
Kawajiri	96	34.14 N	132.42 E
Kawakami, Nihon	94	35.58 N	138.35 E
Kawakami, Nihon	96	34.44 N	133.29 E
Kawakami, Nihon	96	35.17 N	133.39 E
Kawakawa	172	35.23 S	174.04 E
Kawakubo	270	34.54 N	135.38 E
Kawali	115a	7.11 S	108.22 E
Kawama Mission	154	10.04 S	28.37 E
Kawamata	92	37.39 N	140.36 E
Kawambwa	154	9.47 S	29.05 E
Kawamoto, Nihon	94	36.09 N	139.17 E
Kawamoto, Nihon	96	34.59 N	132.30 E
Kawane	94	34.57 N	138.05 E
Kawanishi, Nihon	94	37.09 N	138.45 E
Kawanishi, Nihon	96	34.49 N	135.24 E
Kawanishi, Nihon	270	34.35 N	135.47 E
Kawanoe	96	34.01 N	133.34 E
Kawara, Nihon	96	33.40 N	130.51 E
Kawara, Nihon	270	34.59 N	135.18 E
Kawara Débé	150	12.20 N	3.26 E
Kawarai	268	35.25 N	140.05 E
Kawardha	124	22.01 N	81.15 E
Kawartha Park	212	44.32 N	78.12 W
Kawasaki, Nihon	94	35.32 N	139.43 E
Kawasaki, Nihon	96	33.35 N	130.49 E
Kawasaki-kō c	268	35.30 N	139.47 E
Kawasaki Stadium ♠	268	35.32 N	139.43 E
Kawashima, Nihon	94	35.21 N	136.50 E
Kawashima, Nihon	94	35.59 N	139.30 E
Kawashima, Nihon	96	34.04 N	134.19 E
Kawashima ◆[8]	268	35.28 N	139.35 E
Kawashiri-misaki ›	96	34.26 N	130.58 E
Kawatana	92	33.04 N	129.52 E
Kawauchi	96	33.48 N	132.55 E
Kawau Island I	172	36.25 S	174.51 E
Kawawa ◆[8]	268	35.31 N	139.33 E
Kawayan	116	11.41 N	124.21 E
Kawazu	94	34.44 N	138.59 E
Kawbein	110	16.33 N	97.52 E
Kawdut	110	15.31 N	97.47 E
Kawe	164	7.50 S	138.14 E
Kawe, Pulau I	164	0.03 S	130.07 E
Kaweenakumik Lake ⊜	184	52.52 N	99.30 W
Kaweka ∧	172	39.17 S	176.23 E
Kaweka Range ϰ	172	39.15 S	176.20 E
Kawerau	172	38.03 S	176.43 E
Kawhia	172	38.04 S	174.49 E
Kawhia Harbour c	172	38.05 S	174.50 E
Kawich Peak ∧	204	37.58 N	116.27 W
Kawich Range ϰ	204	37.40 N	116.30 W
Kawin	164	2.45 S	150.45 E
Kawinda	115b	8.07 S	118.04 E
Kawit	269f	14.27 N	120.54 E
Kawkabān	144	15.40 N	43.52 E
Kawkareik	110	16.33 N	98.14 E
Kaw Lake ⊜[1]	196	36.55 N	96.57 W
Kawludo	110	18.29 N	97.19 E
Kawm	140	13.31 N	22.50 E
Kawm al-Farā'in (Buto) ⊥	142	31.11 N	30.45 E
Kawm ar-Rāhib	142	28.20 N	30.37 E
Kawm Birah	273c	30.05 N	31.08 E
Kawm Dafanah (Daphnæ) ⊥	142	30.52 N	32.11 E
Kawm Ḥamādah	142	30.46 N	30.42 E
Kawm Ishfīn	273c	30.11 N	31.15 E
Kawm Ishū	142	31.07 N	30.00 E
Kawm Ju'ayf (Naucratis) ⊥	142	30.54 N	30.36 E
Kawm Umbū	140	24.28 N	32.57 E
Kawnglanghpu	102	27.04 N	98.21 E
Kawnipi Lake ⊜	190	48.24 N	91.14 W
Kawthaung	110	9.59 N	98.33 E
Kax ≃	86	43.40 N	81.45 E
Kaxgar ≃	85	39.40 N	78.00 E
Kaya, Burkina	150	13.05 N	1.05 W
Kaya, Nihon	96	35.30 N	135.06 E
Kayaapu	112	5.26 S	102.24 E
Kayadibi, Tür.	130	39.29 N	36.43 E
Kayadibi, Tür.	130	39.55 N	34.15 E
Kayah □[3]	110	19.15 N	97.30 E
Kayak Island I	180	59.52 N	144.30 W
Kāyalpattinam	122	8.34 N	78.07 E
Kāyamba	272b	22.41 N	88.32 E
Kayambi	154	9.27 S	31.58 E
Kayan	110	16.54 N	96.34 E
Kayan ≃	112	2.55 N	117.35 E
Kayangel Islands II	108	8.04 N	134.43 E
Kayang-san ∧[2]	271b	37.33 N	126.43 E
Kāyankulam	122	9.11 N	76.30 E
Kayapa	116	16.22 N	120.53 E
Kayapınar	130	37.34 N	41.10 E
Kayaş	130	39.56 N	32.58 E
Kaya-san ∧	98	35.49 N	128.07 E
Kaya-san Kukrip Kongwŏn ♠	98	35.47 N	128.06 E
Kaycee	200	43.42 N	106.38 W
Kayeli	164	3.23 S	127.06 E
Kayembe-Mukulu	152	9.03 S	23.57 E
Kayen	115a	6.54 S	110.59 E
Kayenta	200	36.43 N	110.15 W
Kayes, Congo	152	4.25 S	11.41 E
Kayes, Mali	150	14.27 N	11.26 W
Kayes □[4]	150	14.00 N	11.00 W
Kay Gardens	285	39.45 N	75.25 W
Kayima	150	8.53 N	11.10 W
Kayin □[3]	110	17.30 N	97.45 E
Kayış Dağı ∧	267b	40.59 N	29.10 E
Kaymakçı	130	38.10 N	28.08 E
Kaymaz, Tür.	130	39.31 N	31.11 E
Kaymaz, Tür.	130	40.55 N	30.18 E
Kayna	54	50.59 N	12.14 E
Kaynar	130	38.55 N	36.28 E
Kayō, Nihon	96	34.51 N	133.42 E
Kayō, Nihon	174m	26.33 N	128.07 E
Kayoa, Pulau I	164	0.05 S	127.25 E
Kayombo	154	9.36 S	25.37 E
Kaypak	130	37.08 N	36.27 E
Kay Point ›	180	69.18 N	138.22 W
Kayser Gebergte ϰ	250	3.03 N	56.35 W
Kayseri	130	38.43 N	35.30 E
Kayseri □[4]	130	38.30 N	35.55 E
Kaysersberg	58	48.08 N	7.15 E
Kaysville	200	41.02 N	111.56 W
Kayuadi, Pulau I	112	6.49 S	120.47 E
Kayuagung	112	3.24 S	104.50 E
Kayumas	115a	7.50 S	114.08 E
Kayuta Lake ⊜	210	43.25 N	75.12 W
Kayuyu	154	3.39 S	26.21 E
Kazach	84	41.06 N	45.22 E
Kazachskij melkosopočnik ϰ[2]	86	49.00 N	72.00 E
Kazachstan → Kazakhstan □[1]	72	48.00 N	68.00 E
Kazačij	83	46.58 N	40.03 E
Kazačinskoje, Ross.	86	57.49 N	93.17 E
Kazačinskoje, Ross.	88	56.16 N	107.36 E
Kazačja Lopan'	78	50.21 N	36.11 E
Kazačje	74	70.44 N	136.13 E
Kazačji Lageri	78	46.42 N	32.59 E
Kazačka	80	51.28 N	43.56 E
Kazackij	86	49.20 N	58.31 E
Kazackoje	78	51.18 N	33.29 E
Kazakdarja	86	43.27 N	59.46 E
Kazakevičevo	89	48.17 N	134.46 E
Kazakhstan □[1], Asia	72	48.00 N	68.00 E
Kazakhstan □[1], Asia	86	47.00 N	76.00 E
Kazaki	76	52.38 N	38.16 E
Kazaklija	78	46.00 N	28.37 E
Kazakstan → Kazakhstan □[1]	72	48.00 N	68.00 E
Kazal'cevo	86	59.18 N	80.30 E
Kazalinsk	86	45.46 N	62.07 E
Kazan'	80	55.49 N	49.08 E
Kazan ≃	176	64.02 N	95.30 W
Kazanbulak	84	40.38 N	46.41 E
Kazancı	130	36.30 N	32.53 E
Kazandžik	128	39.16 N	55.32 E
Kazanka, Kaz.	86	53.20 N	67.27 E
Kazanka, Ukr.	78	47.50 N	32.49 E
Kazanka ≃	80	55.48 N	49.01 E
Kazanlâk	38	42.38 N	25.21 E
Kazan Lake ⊜	184	55.33 N	108.21 W
Kazanlı	130	36.50 N	34.45 E
Kazanovka	76	53.46 N	38.34 E
Kazan-rettō (Volcano Islands) II	14	25.00 N	141.00 E
Kazanskaja	78	49.48 N	41.09 E
Kazanskoje, Ross.	82	54.59 N	37.39 E
Kazanskoje, Ross.	86	55.38 N	69.14 E
Kazan' Station ◆[5]	265b	55.46 N	37.40 E
Kazantip, mys ›	78	45.28 N	35.51 E
Kazarman	85	41.24 N	74.03 E
Kazatin	78	49.43 N	28.50 E
Kazatkul'	86	55.02 N	76.03 E
Kazbegi	84	42.39 N	44.39 E
Kazbek, gora ∧	84	42.42 N	44.31 E
Kaz Dağı ∧	130	39.42 N	26.50 E
Kazembe	154	12.11 S	32.37 E
Kāzerūn	128	29.37 N	51.38 E
Kazgorodok, Kaz.	86	52.53 N	70.42 E
Kazgorodok, Kaz.	86	49.56 N	71.36 E
Kažim	24	60.20 N	51.30 E
Kazi-Magomed	84	40.03 N	48.56 E
Kazimierza Wielka	30	50.16 N	20.30 E
Kazimierz Dolny	30	51.20 N	21.58 E
Kazincbarcika	30	48.16 N	20.37 E
Kazinka, Ross.	76	52.32 N	39.42 E
Kazinka, Ross.	78	50.14 N	37.50 E
Kāzipāra	272b	22.43 N	88.31 E
Kāzīr Char	126	22.46 N	90.33 E
Kaziza	152	10.42 S	23.52 E
Kazlų Rūda	76	54.46 N	23.30 E
Kaz'minskoje	84	44.35 N	41.41 E
Kaznačejevo	82	54.31 N	37.16 E
Kazo	94	36.07 N	139.36 E
Kaz'onnyj Torec ≃	83	48.54 N	37.46 E
Kaztalovka	80	49.46 N	48.42 E
Kazuma Pan National Park ♠	154	18.15 S	25.33 E
Kazumba	152	6.25 S	22.02 E
Kazungula	154	17.45 S	25.20 E
Kazuno	92	40.11 N	140.47 E
Kazvin → Qazvīn	128	36.16 N	50.00 E
Kazy	128	39.13 N	57.30 E
Kazym	74	63.40 N	67.14 E
Kazym ≃	74	63.54 N	65.50 E
Kazyr ≃	86	53.47 N	92.53 E
Kbal Dâmrei	110	14.07 N	105.21 E
Kbelnice	60	49.18 N	13.59 E
Kbely ◆[8]	54	50.07 N	14.32 E
Kcynia	30	53.00 N	17.30 E
Kdyně	60	49.23 N	13.02 E
Kéa	38	37.38 N	24.21 E
Kéa I	38	37.34 N	24.22 E
Keaau	229d	19.37 N	155.02 W
Keady	48	54.15 N	6.42 W
Keahole Point ›	229d	19.44 N	156.03 W
Keal, Loch na c	46	56.28 N	6.04 W
Kealaikahiki, Lae o ›	229a	20.32 N	156.42 W
Kealaikahiki Channel ʯ	229a	20.37 N	156.50 W
Kealakekua Bay c	229d	19.28 N	155.56 W
Kealia	229b	22.06 N	159.18 W
Keams Canyon	200	35.48 N	110.11 W
Keanae	229a	20.51 N	156.09 W
Keanapapa Point ›	229a	20.54 N	157.04 W
Kean College of New Jersey ʊ[2]	276	40.41 N	74.14 W
Keansburg	208	40.25 N	74.12 W
Kearney, Mo., U.S.	194	39.22 N	94.21 W
Kearney, Ne., U.S.	198	40.41 N	99.04 W
Kearney, Pa., U.S.	214	40.08 N	78.12 W
Kearns	200	40.39 N	111.59 W
Kearny, Az., U.S.	200	33.03 N	110.54 W
Kearny, N.J., U.S.	210	40.46 N	74.08 W
Kearsley	262	53.32 N	2.23 W
Kearsley Creek ≃	216	43.04 N	83.40 W
Keasbey	276	40.31 N	74.19 W
Keb' ≃	76	57.44 N	28.28 E
Kebajoran ◆[8]	269e	6.13 S	106.46 E
Keban	130	38.48 N	38.45 E
Keban Barajı ⊜[1]	130	38.50 N	39.20 E
Kebanyartimur	115a	7.09 S	112.52 E
Kébara	152	2.27 S	14.25 E
Kebbi	150	12.08 N	4.44 E
Kebeiti	120	36.47 N	79.29 E
Kébémer	150	15.22 N	16.27 W
Kébi, Mayo ≃	146	9.18 N	13.33 E
Kebili	148	33.42 N	8.58 E
Kebîr, Oued el ≃	34	36.50 N	6.07 E
Kebnekaise ∧	24	67.53 N	18.33 E
Kebock Head ›	46	58.01 N	6.20 W
Kebri Dehar	144	6.47 N	44.17 E
Kebumen	115a	7.40 S	109.39 E
Keb'uty	80	45.50 N	44.14 E
Keče	85	43.14 N	71.22 E
Kecel	30	46.32 N	19.16 E
Kech ≃	128	26.00 N	62.44 E
Kechika ≃	176	59.36 N	127.05 W
Keçiborlu	130	37.57 N	30.18 E
Kecksburg	214	40.11 N	79.28 W
Kecskemét	30	46.54 N	19.42 E
Kedabek	84	40.34 N	45.49 E
Kedah □[3]	114	6.00 N	100.40 E
Kėdainiai	76	55.17 N	24.00 E
Kédange-sur-Canner	56	49.19 N	6.20 E
Kedārnāth	124	30.44 N	79.04 E
Kedārpur	126	23.18 N	90.27 E
Kedges Straits ʯ	208	38.03 N	76.02 W
Kedgwick	186	47.39 N	67.21 W
Kedgwick ≃	186	47.40 N	67.29 W
Kédhron	38	39.13 N	22.03 E
Kedian	100	31.23 N	112.51 E
Kediri	115a	7.49 S	112.01 E
Kedjebi	150	8.12 N	0.25 E
Kedon	74	64.08 N	159.14 E
Kedong	89	48.02 N	126.15 E
Kédougou	150	12.33 N	12.11 W
Kedrasju	24	64.36 N	60.24 E
Kedrovka	86	55.32 N	86.03 E
Kedu	102	26.33 N	104.21 E
Kedungdung	115a	7.06 S	113.15 E
Kedungjati	115a	7.10 S	110.37 E
Kedungwuni	115a	6.58 S	109.39 E
Kedvavom	24	64.15 N	53.27 E
Kędzierzyn Kozle	30	50.20 N	18.12 E
Keecheus Lake ⊜	224	47.22 N	121.22 W
Keefer	218	38.32 N	84.38 W
Keefers	182	50.02 N	121.33 W
Keego Harbor	216	42.36 N	83.20 W
Keelby	44	53.34 N	0.15 W
Keele	42	53.00 N	2.17 W
Keele ≃	180	64.24 N	124.50 W
Keele Peak ∧	180	63.26 N	130.19 W
Keeley Lake ⊜	184	54.54 N	108.08 W
Keeling Islands → Cocos Islands □[2]	12	12.10 S	96.55 E
Keels	186	48.36 N	53.24 W
Keelung → Chilung	100	25.08 N	121.44 E
Keen, Mount ∧	46	56.58 N	2.54 W
Keene, On., Can.	212	44.15 N	78.10 W
Keene, Ca., U.S.	228	35.13 N	118.33 W
Keene, Ky., U.S.	192	37.56 N	84.38 W
Keene, N.H., U.S.	188	42.56 N	72.16 W
Keene, Oh., U.S.	214	40.21 N	81.52 W
Keene, Tx., U.S.	222	32.23 N	97.19 W
Keenesburg	200	40.06 N	104.31 W
Keeney Knob ∧	192	37.47 N	80.42 W
Keeneyville	278	41.59 N	88.07 W
Keep River National Park ♠	164	15.48 S	129.03 E
Keerbergen	56	51.00 N	4.37 E
Keer-Weer, Cape ›	164	13.58 S	141.30 E
Keeseg ∧	64	46.58 N	12.14 E
Keeseville	188	44.30 N	73.28 W
Keesler Air Force Base ■	194	30.26 N	88.55 W
Keetmanshoop	156	26.36 S	18.08 E
Keetmanshoop □[5]	156	26.30 S	19.00 E
Keewatin, On., Can.	184	49.46 N	94.34 W
Keewatin, Mn., U.S.	190	47.23 N	93.04 W
Kefa □[4]	144	6.50 N	36.00 E
Kefallinía I	38	38.15 N	20.35 E
Kéfalos	38	36.45 N	27.00 E
Kefamenanu	112	9.27 S	124.29 E
Kefar 'Azza	132	31.29 N	34.32 E
Kefar Blum	132	33.10 N	35.36 E
Kefar 'Eẕyon	132	31.39 N	35.08 E
Kefar Naḥum (Capernaum) ⊥	132	32.53 N	35.34 E
Kefar Sava	132	32.10 N	34.54 E
Kefar Shammay	132	32.57 N	35.27 E
Kefar Szold	132	33.11 N	35.39 E
Kefar Vitkin	132	32.23 N	34.53 E
Kefar Warburg	132	31.43 N	34.44 E
Kefar Yona	132	32.19 N	34.55 E
Kefermarkt	61	48.26 N	14.32 E
Keffi	150	8.51 N	7.52 E
Keffin Hausa	150	12.15 N	9.58 E
Keflavík	24a	64.02 N	22.36 W
Keftya	144	13.54 N	37.07 E
Kega	24	65.10 N	36.54 E
Ke Ga, Mui ›, Viet	110	12.53 N	109.28 E
Ke Ga, Mui ›, Viet	110	10.42 N	107.58 E
Kegalla	122	7.15 N	80.21 E
Kégashka	186	50.12 N	61.17 W
Kégashka, Lac ⊜	186	50.20 N	61.25 W
Kegejli	86	42.45 N	59.35 E
Kegičovka	78	49.17 N	35.46 E
Kegnæs ›[1]	41	54.52 N	9.59 E
Kegon-no-taki ʟ	94	36.44 N	139.31 E
Kegonsa, Lake ⊜	216	42.58 N	89.15 W
Kegonzhake	120	33.00 N	87.53 E
Keg River	176	57.48 N	117.52 W
Kegums	76	56.46 N	24.45 E
Kegworth	42	52.50 N	1.16 W
Kehdingen, Land ◆[1]	52	53.45 N	9.15 E
Kehiwin Indian Reserve ◆[4]	182	54.07 N	110.48 W
Kehl	56	48.35 N	7.50 E
Kehlen	58	47.41 N	9.33 E
Kehoe	218	38.28 N	83.03 W
Kehra	76	59.20 N	25.20 E
Kehrigk	54	52.09 N	13.55 E
Ke-hsi Mānsām	110	21.56 N	97.50 E
Keig	46	57.15 N	2.39 W
Keighley	44	53.52 N	1.54 W
Keihoku	96	35.09 N	135.38 E
Keijō → Sŏul	98	37.33 N	126.58 E
Keila	76	59.18 N	24.25 E
Keilor	169	37.43 S	144.50 E
Keimoes	158	28.41 S	21.00 E
Kei Mouth	158	32.41 S	28.22 E
Keio University ʊ[2]	268	35.38 N	139.45 E
Kei Road	158	32.42 S	27.32 E
Keiser	194	35.40 N	90.05 W
Keiskammahoek	158	32.41 S	27.09 E
Keiskammapunt ›	158	32.40 S	27.10 E
Keïta	150	14.46 N	5.46 E
Kéita, Bahr ≃	146	9.14 N	18.21 E
Keitele	26	63.11 N	26.22 E
Keitele ⊜	26	62.55 N	26.00 E
Keith, Austl.	166	36.06 S	140.21 E
Keith, Scot., U.K.	46	57.32 N	2.57 W
Keith Arm c	176	65.20 N	122.15 W
Keithley Creek	182	52.45 N	121.24 W
Keithsburg	190	41.05 N	90.56 W
Keiyasi	175g	17.54 S	177.45 E
Keizer	224	44.59 N	123.01 W
Kejaman	112	2.39 N	113.45 E
Kejimkujik National Park ♠	186	44.21 N	65.18 W
Kejngypil'gyn, laguna c	180	63.30 N	178.50 E
Kejni, gora ∧	180	64.30 N	174.54 W
Kejvy ϰ	24	67.35 N	38.00 E
Kekaha	229b	21.58 N	159.42 W
Kekek ≃	190	48.24 N	75.48 W
Kekerengu	172	42.00 S	174.01 E
Kékes ∧	30	47.55 N	20.02 E
Kekeyaer	85	38.02 N	75.05 E
Kek Lok Si ʊ[1]	114	5.23 N	100.14 E
Kekpāra	126	22.27 N	86.35 E
Kekri	120	25.58 N	75.09 E
Kekurnoi, Cape ›	180	57.44 N	155.15 W
Kelafo	144	5.40 N	44.20 E
Kelai ≃	112	2.10 N	117.29 E
Kelan	102	38.43 N	111.32 E
Kelanang	114	2.48 N	101.26 E
Kelang	114	3.02 N	101.27 E
Kelang, Pulau I, Indon.	164	3.12 S	127.44 E
Kelang, Pulau I, Malay.	114	3.00 N	101.18 E
Kelani ≃	122	6.58 N	79.52 E
Kelantan	114	0.51 N	101.40 E
Kelantan □[3]	114	5.20 N	102.00 E
Kelantan ≃	114	6.11 N	102.15 E
Kelapa	112	1.52 S	105.42 E
Kelasuri	84	43.08 N	41.13 E
Kelat	218	38.32 N	84.19 W
Kelayres	210	40.54 N	76.00 W
Kelb, Ouadi V	146	15.19 N	18.51 E
Kel'badžar	84	40.07 N	46.02 E
Kelberg	56	50.17 N	6.55 E
Kelbia, Sebkhet ⊜	36	35.51 N	10.16 E
Kelbra	54	51.26 N	11.02 E
Keld Ula ∧	86	43.20 N	85.25 E
Kel'd'ušovo	80	55.01 N	44.59 E
Keleft	128	37.21 N	66.15 E
Kelegou	98	41.57 N	118.11 E
Kélékélé	273b	4.20 S	15.08 E
Kelem	144	4.48 N	35.58 E
Kelenföld ◆[8]	264c	47.28 N	19.03 E
Kelenken, gora ∧	180	66.07 N	170.52 W
Keles, Tür.	130	39.55 N	29.14 E
Keles, Uzb.	85	41.24 N	69.12 E
Keles ≃	85	41.02 N	68.37 E
Keleti-főcsatorna ≊	30	48.01 N	21.20 E
Keleti Pályaudvar ◆[5]	264c	47.30 N	19.06 E
Kelheim	60	48.55 N	11.52 E
Kelibia	148	36.51 N	11.06 E
Kelkheim	56	50.08 N	8.26 E
Kelkit	130	40.08 N	39.27 E
Kelkit ≃	130	40.46 N	36.32 E
Kell	219	38.30 N	88.54 W
Kellé	152	0.06 S	14.33 E
Kellen	52	51.48 N	6.10 E
Kellenhusen	54	54.11 N	11.03 E
Keller, Tx., U.S.	222	32.56 N	97.15 W
Keller, Va., U.S.	208	37.37 N	75.45 W
Keller, Wa., U.S.	182	48.04 N	118.41 W
Kellerberg	64	46.40 N	13.42 E
Kellerberrin	162	31.38 S	117.43 E
Kellerjoch ∧	64	47.19 N	11.46 E
Keller Lake ⊜, N.T., Can.	176	64.00 N	121.30 W
Keller Lake ⊜, Sk., Can.	184	56.04 N	106.46 W
Kellerovka	86	53.50 N	69.17 E
Keller Peak ∧	228	34.12 N	117.03 W
Kellett, Cape ›	176	71.59 N	125.34 W
Kellettville	214	41.33 N	79.16 W
Kelleys Island	214	41.36 N	82.42 W
Kelleys Island I	214	41.36 N	82.42 W
Kelliher	184	51.15 N	103.44 W
Kellinghusen	52	53.57 N	9.43 E
Kellmünz	58	48.07 N	10.08 E
Kelloe	44	54.43 N	1.28 W
Kellogg, Id., U.S.	202	47.32 N	116.07 W
Kellogg, Ia., U.S.	190	41.43 N	92.54 W
Kellogg, Mn., U.S.	190	44.18 N	91.59 W
Kellogg Marsh	224	48.05 N	122.07 W
Kelloggsville	214	41.52 N	80.36 W
Kellojärvi ⊜	26	64.16 N	29.03 E
Kelloselkä	24	66.56 N	28.50 E
Kells, N. Ire., U.K.	44	54.48 N	6.13 E
Kells, N. Ire., U.K.	48	54.48 N	6.13 E
Kells → Ceanannus Mór	48	53.44 N	6.53 W
Kelly Air Force Base ■	196	29.24 N	98.35 W
Kelly Lake ⊜	180	65.30 N	126.10 W
Kelly Run ≃, Pa., U.S.	279b	40.15 N	79.55 W
Kelly Run ≃, Pa., U.S.	279b	40.13 N	79.45 W
Kellyville, Austl.	274a	33.43 S	150.57 E
Kellyville, Ok., U.S.	196	35.56 N	96.12 W
Kelmė	76	55.38 N	22.56 E
Kel'mency	78	48.27 N	26.50 E
Kelmet	144	16.04 N	38.55 E
Kelmscott	168a	32.07 S	116.01 E
Kelo	146	9.19 N	15.48 E
Kelolokan	112	1.08 N	117.54 E
Kelottijärvi	24	68.31 N	22.04 E
Kelowna	182	49.53 N	119.29 W
Kelsall	44	53.13 N	2.43 W
Kelsey Bay	182	50.24 N	125.57 W
Kelsey Head ›	42	50.24 N	5.08 W
Kelsey Lake ⊜	184	53.37 N	101.02 W
Kelseyville	204	38.58 N	122.50 W
Kelso, Scot., U.K.	46	55.36 N	2.25 W
Kelso, Wa., U.S.	224	46.08 N	122.54 W
Kelsterbach	56	50.04 N	8.32 E
Kel'temašat	85	42.30 N	70.17 E
Kelty	46	56.08 N	3.23 W
Keluang	114	2.02 N	103.19 E
Keluang, Tanjung ›	112	3.02 S	110.39 E
Kelud, Gunung ∧	115a	7.56 S	112.18 E
Keluo ≃	89	49.22 N	125.15 E
Keluotun	89	49.16 N	125.44 E
Kelvedon	42	51.51 N	0.42 E
Kelvedon Hatch	260	51.40 N	0.16 E
Kelvington	184	52.10 N	103.30 W
Kelvin Seamount ✦[3]	16	38.50 N	64.00 W
Kelyexeed	144	8.46 N	49.12 E
Kelzenberg	263	51.07 N	6.30 E
Kem'	24	64.57 N	34.36 E
Kem' ≃, Ross.	24	64.57 N	34.41 E
Kem' ≃, Ross.	86	58.31 N	92.04 E
Kema	112	1.23 N	125.04 E
Kema ≃, Ross.	76	60.16 N	37.20 E
Kema ≃, Ross.	76	59.21 N	44.29 E
Ké Macina	150	13.58 N	5.22 W
Kémah, Congo	273b	4.11 S	15.13 E
Kemah, Tür.	130	39.36 N	39.02 E
Kemah, Tx., U.S.	222	29.32 N	95.01 W
Kemaliye	130	39.16 N	38.29 E
Kemalpaşa, Tür.	130	41.30 N	41.30 E
Kemalpaşa, Tür.	130	38.25 N	27.26 E
Kemano	182	53.34 N	127.56 W
Kemasik	114	4.25 N	103.27 E
Kemayan	114	3.08 N	102.22 E
Kemayoran Airport ⊠	269e	6.09 S	106.51 E
Kembani	112	1.34 S	122.54 E
Kembé	152	4.36 N	21.54 E
Kemberg	54	51.46 N	12.38 E
Kemblesville	208	39.45 N	75.50 W
Kembolcha	144	11.02 N	39.43 E
Kembs	58	47.41 N	7.30 E
Kembul	164	5.55 S	150.40 E
Kemčug ≃	86	57.14 N	90.31 E
Kemena ≃	112	3.10 N	113.03 E
Kemeneshát ϰ[2]	61	46.58 N	16.40 E
Kemer, Tür.	130	36.38 N	29.21 E
Kemer, Tür.	130	36.36 N	30.34 E
Kemer, Tür.	130	37.21 N	30.04 E
Kemer ≃	267b	41.04 N	29.07 E
Kemer Barajı ⊜[1]	130	37.34 N	28.31 E
Kemerburgaz ◆[8]	267b	41.09 N	28.54 E
Kemerhisar	130	37.49 N	34.36 E
Kemerovo	86	55.20 N	86.05 E
Kemi	24	65.49 N	24.32 E
Kemie	26	62.14 N	30.20 E
Kemijärvi	24	66.40 N	27.25 E
Kemijärvi ⊜	24	66.36 N	27.24 E
Kemijoki ≃	26	65.47 N	24.30 E
Kemiö → Kimito	26	60.10 N	22.45 E
Keml'a	80	54.42 N	45.15 E
Kemmel	50	50.47 N	2.49 E
Kemmelberg ∧[2]	50	50.47 N	2.50 E
Kemmerer	200	41.47 N	110.32 W
Kemminghausen ◆[8]	263	51.34 N	7.29 E
Kemmuna (Comino) I	36	36.00 N	14.20 E
Kemnader See ⊜	263	51.25 N	7.15 E
Kemnath	60	49.52 N	11.54 E
Kemnay	46	57.14 N	2.27 W
Kemnitz	54	54.04 N	13.31 E
Kémo-Gribingui □[5]	152	6.00 N	19.00 E
Kemp	222	32.26 N	96.13 W
Kemp, Lake ⊜[1]	196	33.45 N	99.13 W
Kemparana	150	12.50 N	4.56 W
Kemp Coast ⊥[2]	9	67.10 S	58.00 E
Kempele	26	64.55 N	25.30 E
Kempen	56	51.22 N	6.25 E
Kempen □[9]	56	51.10 N	5.20 E
Kempener Land ◆[1]	263	51.19 N	6.29 E
Kempenfelt Bay c	212	44.23 N	79.36 W
Kempenich	56	50.25 N	7.07 E
Kemper → Quimper	32	48.00 N	4.06 W
Kempisch Kanaal ≊	56	51.10 N	4.49 E
Kemp Mill	284c	39.02 N	77.01 W
Kempner	196	31.05 N	98.00 W
Kemp Peninsula ›[1]	9	73.08 S	60.15 W
Kemps Bay	238	24.02 N	77.33 W
Kemps Creek ≃	274a	33.51 S	150.46 E
Kempsey, Austl.	166	31.05 S	152.50 E
Kempsey, Eng., U.K.	42	52.08 N	2.12 W
Kempston	42	52.07 N	0.30 W
Kempt, Lac ⊜	176	47.25 N	74.22 W
Kempten (Allgäu)	58	47.43 N	10.19 E
Kempton, Il., U.S.	216	40.56 N	88.14 W
Kempton, In., U.S.	216	40.17 N	86.13 W
Kempton Park	158	26.06 S	28.14 E
Kempton Park □[5]	273d	26.06 S	28.14 E
Kempton Park Race Course ♠	260	51.25 N	0.23 W
Kemptville	212	45.01 N	75.38 W
Kemptville Creek ≃	212	45.03 N	75.39 W
Kemsing	260	51.18 N	0.14 E
Kemubu	114	5.18 N	102.01 E
Kemujan, Pulau I	115a	5.48 S	110.28 E
Kemul, Kong ∧	112	1.52 N	116.11 E
Ken ≃	124	25.46 N	80.31 E
Ken, Loch ⊜	44	55.02 N	4.02 W
Ken, Water of ≃	44	55.04 N	4.08 W
Kena ≃	24	62.05 N	39.06 E
Kenai	180	60.33 N	151.15 W
Kenai Fjords National Park ♠	180	59.45 N	150.00 W
Kenai Mountains ϰ	180	60.00 N	150.00 W
Kenai Peninsula ›[1]	180	60.10 N	150.00 W
Kenamuke Swamp ≡	140	6.15 N	33.48 E
Kenansville, Fl., U.S.	220	27.52 N	80.59 W
Kenansville, N.C., U.S.	192	34.57 N	77.57 W
Kenaral	85	42.32 N	72.08 E
Kenašči	80	50.32 N	53.20 E
Kenashiga-sen ∧	96	35.14 N	133.31 E
Kenaston	184	51.30 N	106.18 W
Kenberma	283	42.17 N	70.52 W
Kenbridge	192	36.57 N	78.07 W
Kenda	126	23.12 N	86.32 E
Kendai	124	22.45 N	82.37 E
Kendal, Sk., Can.	184	50.15 N	103.37 W
Kendal, Indon.	115a	6.55 S	110.12 E
Kendal, S. Afr.	158	26.04 S	28.58 E
Kendal, Eng., U.K.	44	54.20 N	2.45 W
Kendall, Austl.	166	31.38 S	152.43 E
Kendall, Fl., U.S.	220	25.40 N	80.19 W
Kendall, Mi., U.S.	216	42.22 N	85.49 W
Kendall, N.Y., U.S.	210	43.20 N	78.02 W
Kendall, Wi., U.S.	190	43.47 N	90.22 W
Kendall □[6]	216	41.38 N	88.27 W
Kendall, Cape ›	176	63.36 N	87.09 W
Kendall, Mount ∧	172	41.22 S	172.24 E
Kendall Park	208	40.31 N	74.24 W
Kendallville	216	41.26 N	85.15 W
Kendari	112	3.57 S	122.35 E
Kendari, Teluk c	112	3.57 S	122.38 E
Kendawangan	112	2.32 S	110.12 E
Kende	150	11.30 N	4.12 E
Kendenup	162	34.29 S	117.39 E
Kendghāta	126	24.05 N	87.10 E
Kendikolu I	122	5.57 N	73.24 E
Kendiktas ϰ	85	43.35 N	74.45 E
Kendleton	222	29.27 N	96.00 W
Kendrāparha	120	20.30 N	86.25 E
Kendrew	158	32.31 S	24.30 E
Kendrick, Fl., U.S.	192	29.22 N	82.12 W
Kendrick, Id., U.S.	202	46.36 N	116.38 W
Kendrick Creek ≃	226	38.00 N	119.50 W
Kendua	272b	22.34 N	88.10 E
Kendu Bay	154	0.22 S	34.39 E
Kendujhargarh	120	21.38 N	85.35 E
Kendyrlik	86	47.30 N	85.12 E
Kenedy	196	28.49 N	97.50 W
Kenefick	222	30.07 N	94.51 W
Kenema	150	7.52 N	11.12 W
Kenes, Kaz.	85	43.41 N	67.49 E
Kenes, Kaz.	85	43.59 N	73.35 E
Kenesaw	198	40.37 N	98.39 W
Kenga	86	57.27 N	80.57 E
Kenga ≃	86	58.05 N	80.37 E
Kenge	152	4.52 S	16.59 E
Kengeja	154	5.25 S	39.44 E
Kēng Hkam, Mya.	110	21.01 N	98.29 E
Keng Hkam, Mya.	110	21.27 N	97.03 E
Kengkou, Zhg.	100	29.48 N	117.22 E
Kengkou, Zhg.	100	28.27 N	120.26 E
Kengtian	100	25.54 N	119.26 E
Kēng Tung	110	21.17 N	99.36 E
Kengun-chūtonchi, Rikujō-jieitai- ■	92	32.46 N	130.45 E
Kenhardt	158	29.19 S	21.12 E
Kenhorst	208	40.18 N	75.57 W
Kenia	152	2.43 S	17.04 E
Kenia → Kenya □[1]	154	1.00 N	38.00 E
Kenia → Kirinyaga ∧	154	0.10 S	37.20 E
Kéniéba	150	12.50 N	11.14 W
Kenilworth, Eng., U.K.	42	52.21 N	1.34 W
Kenilworth, Il., U.S.	278	42.05 N	87.43 W
Kenilworth, N.J., U.S.	276	40.40 N	74.17 W
Kenilworth, Pa., U.S.	208	40.14 N	75.38 W
Kenilworth, Ut,. U.S.	200	39.41 N	110.48 W
Kenilworth Castle ⊥	42	52.21 N	1.34 W
Keningau	112	5.20 N	116.10 E
Kenitra	148	34.16 N	6.40 W
Kenitra □[4]	148	34.30 N	6.00 W
Kenley ◆[8]	260	51.19 N	0.06 W
Kenli (Xishuanghe)	98	37.40 N	118.35 E
Kenly	192	35.35 N	78.07 W
Kenmare, Ire.	48	51.53 N	9.35 W
Kenmare, N.D., U.S.	198	48.40 N	102.04 W
Kenmare River ≃	48	51.45 N	10.00 W
Kenmawr	279b	40.28 N	80.06 W
Kenmore, Scot., U.K.	46	56.34 N	3.59 W
Kenmore, N.Y., U.S.	210	42.57 N	78.52 W
Kenmore, Wa., U.S.	224	47.45 N	122.14 W
Kennard, In., U.S.	218	39.54 N	85.31 W
Kennard, Pa., U.S.	214	41.28 N	80.20 W
Kennard, Tx., U.S.	222	31.22 N	95.11 W
Kennebec	198	43.54 N	99.51 W
Kennebec ≃	188	44.00 N	69.50 W
Kennebecasis Bay c	186	45.25 N	66.00 W
Kennebec Lake ⊜	212	44.43 N	77.00 W
Kennebunk	188	43.23 N	70.32 W
Kennedale	222	32.38 N	97.13 W
Kennedy, Al., U.S.	194	33.35 N	87.59 W
Kennedy, N.Y., U.S.	214	42.09 N	79.06 W
Kennedy, Zimb.	154	18.52 S	27.10 E
Kennedy, Cape → Canaveral, Cape ›	220	28.27 N	80.32 W
Kennedy, Mount ∧, B.C., Can.	182	50.49 N	125.33 W
Kennedy, Mount ∧, Yk., Can.	180	60.30 N	139.00 W
Kennedy Entrance ʯ	180	59.00 N	152.00 W
Kennedy Lake ⊜	182	49.05 N	125.40 W
Kennedy Peak ∧	110	23.19 N	93.45 E
Kennedy Range ϰ	162	24.30 S	115.00 E
Kennedyville	208	39.18 N	75.59 W
Kennemerduinen, Nationale Park de ♠	52	52.25 N	4.35 E
Kenner	194	29.59 N	90.14 W
Kennerdell	214	41.16 N	79.51 W
Kennet ≃, Eng., U.K.	42	52.26 N	0.28 E
Kennet ≃, Eng., U.K.	42	51.28 N	0.57 W
Kennetcook	186	45.11 N	63.44 W
Kenneth City	220	27.49 N	82.44 W
Kennett	194	36.14 N	90.03 W
Kennett Square	208	39.50 N	75.42 W
Kennewick	202	46.12 N	119.08 W
Kenney	219	40.06 N	89.05 W
Kenney Dam ◆[6]	182	53.37 N	124.58 W
Kennington, Eng., U.K.	42	51.43 N	1.15 W
Kennington, Eng., U.K.	42	51.10 N	0.54 E
Kennisis Lake ⊜	212	45.13 N	78.39 W
Kenn Reef ✦[2]	160	21.12 S	155.46 E
Kenny	222	30.03 N	96.20 W
Kennydale	224	47.31 N	122.12 W
Kennywood Park ♠	279b	40.23 N	79.52 W
Kénogami	186	48.26 N	71.14 W
Kenogami ≃	176	51.06 N	84.28 W
Kénogami, Lac ⊜	186	48.20 N	71.23 W
Kenogamissi Lake ⊜	190	48.15 N	81.31 W
Keno Hill	180	63.55 N	135.18 W
Kenora	184	49.47 N	94.29 W
Kenosha	216	42.35 N	87.49 W
Kenosha □[6]	216	42.35 N	88.03 W
Kenova	188	38.23 N	82.34 W
Kenoza Lake	210	41.44 N	74.57 W
Kenoza Lake ⊜	283	42.47 N	71.03 W
Kenozero, ozero ⊜	24	62.03 N	38.14 E
Ken Rock	216	42.15 N	89.03 W
Kensal	198	47.18 N	98.43 W
Kense	86	46.49 N	68.20 E
Kensett	194	35.13 N	91.40 W
Kensico Lake ⊜	276	41.07 N	73.45 W
Kensico Reservoir ⊜[1]	210	41.05 N	73.46 W
Kensington, Austl.	274a	33.55 S	151.14 E
Kensington, P.E., Can.	186	46.26 N	63.38 W
Kensington, Ca., U.S.	226	37.54 N	122.16 W
Kensington, Ct., U.S.	207	41.38 N	72.46 W
Kensington, Ks., U.S.	198	39.46 N	99.01 W
Kensington, Md., U.S.	284c	39.01 N	77.04 W
Kensington, Oh., U.S.	214	40.44 N	80.57 W
Kensington ◆[8], S. Afr.	273d	26.12 S	28.06 E
Kensington ◆[8], N.Y., U.S.	276	40.39 N	73.58 W
Kensington ◆[8], Pa., U.S.	285	39.58 N	75.08 W
Kensington and Chelsea ◆[8]	260	51.29 N	0.11 W
Kensington Estates	284c	39.02 N	77.05 W
Kensington Metropolitan Park ♠	281	42.32 N	83.39 W
Kensington Park	220	27.22 N	82.31 W
Kent, S.L.	150	8.10 N	13.10 W
Kent, Ct., U.S.	207	41.43 N	73.28 W
Kent, N.Y., U.S.	210	43.20 N	78.08 W
Kent, Oh., U.S.	214	41.09 N	81.21 W
Kent, Or., U.S.	224	45.11 N	120.41 W
Kent, Wa., U.S.	224	47.22 N	122.14 W
Kent □[6], On., Can.	214	42.25 N	82.10 W
Kent □[6], Eng., U.K.	42	51.15 N	0.40 E
Kent □[6], De., U.S.	208	39.10 N	75.32 W
Kent □[6], Md., U.S.	208	39.13 N	76.04 W
Kent □[6], Mi., U.S.	216	42.56 N	85.33 W
Kent □[6], R.I., U.S.	207	41.40 N	71.38 W
Kent ≃	44	54.15 N	2.48 W
Kent, Vale of V	42	51.10 N	0.30 E
Kent Acres	208	39.07 N	75.31 W
Kentallen	46	56.39 N	5.15 W
Kentani	158	32.31 S	28.19 E
Kentau	85	43.36 N	68.36 E
Kent Bridge	214	42.31 N	82.04 W
Kent County Airport ⊠	216	42.54 N	85.39 W
Kentfield	282	37.57 N	122.33 W
Kent Group II	166	39.27 S	147.20 E
Kenthurst	274a	33.40 S	151.00 E
Kent Island I	208	38.55 N	76.20 W
Kent Lake ⊜	216	42.32 N	83.40 W
Kentland, In., U.S.	216	40.46 N	87.26 W
Kentland, Md., U.S.	284c	38.55 N	76.53 W
Kenton, Eng., U.K.	42	50.38 N	3.28 W
Kenton, De., U.S.	208	39.13 N	75.39 W
Kenton, Mi., U.S.	190	46.29 N	88.53 W
Kenton, Oh., U.S.	216	40.38 N	83.36 W
Kenton, Tn., U.S.	194	36.12 N	89.00 W
Kenton □[6]	218	38.56 N	84.33 W
Kent Park	283	42.06 N	70.41 W
Kent Park ♠	273d	26.08 S	28.04 E
Kent Peninsula ›[1]	176	68.30 N	107.00 W
Kent Point ›	208	38.50 N	76.22 W
Kentucky □[3]	178	37.30 N	85.15 W
Kentucky ≃	218	38.41 N	85.11 W
Kentucky, Middle Fork ≃	192	37.35 N	83.40 W
Kentucky, North Fork ≃	192	37.34 N	83.42 W
Kentucky, South Fork ≃	192	37.34 N	83.42 W
Kentucky Horse Park ♠	218	38.08 N	84.31 W
Kentucky Lake ⊜[1]	194	36.25 N	88.05 W
Kent Village	284c	38.55 N	76.53 W
Kentville	186	45.05 N	64.30 W
Kentwood, La., U.S.	194	30.56 N	90.30 W
Kentwood, Mi., U.S.	216	42.52 N	85.38 W
Kent Woodlands	282	37.57 N	122.34 W
Kenvil	276	40.52 N	74.37 W
Kenwick	168a	32.02 S	115.58 E
Kenwood, Ca., U.S.	226	38.25 N	122.33 W
Kenwood, Md., U.S.	284b	39.21 N	76.31 W
Kenwood, Oh., U.S.	218	39.12 N	84.22 W
Kenwood ◆[8]	278	41.49 N	87.36 W
Kenwood ⊥	260	51.34 N	0.10 W
Kenya □[1]	154	1.00 N	38.00 E
Kenya, Mount → Kirinyaga ∧	154	0.10 S	37.20 E
Kenyon, Eng., U.K.	262	53.27 N	2.34 W
Kenyon, Mn., U.S.	190	44.16 N	92.59 W
Kenyon, R.I., U.S.	207	41.26 N	71.37 W
Ken-zaki ›	268	35.08 N	139.41 E
Kenzingen	58	48.11 N	7.46 E
Kenzou	152	4.10 N	15.02 E
Keokea	229a	20.42 N	156.21 W
Keokuk	190	40.23 N	91.23 W
Keoladeo National Park ♠	124	27.10 N	77.20 E
Keonchi	124	22.38 N	81.47 E
Keo Neua, Col de)(	110	18.23 N	105.09 E
Keon Park	274b	37.42 S	145.01 E
Keosauqua	190	40.43 N	91.57 W
Keota, Ia., U.S.	190	41.21 N	91.57 W
Keota, Ok., U.S.	196	35.15 N	94.55 W
Keowee, Lake ⊜[1]	192	34.45 N	82.55 W
Kepa (Mittagskogel) ∧	61	46.31 N	13.57 E
Kepala Batas	114	5.31 N	100.26 E
Kepanjen	115a	8.07 S	112.34 E
Kepi	164	6.32 S	139.19 E
Kępice	30	54.15 N	16.52 E
Kepina	24	65.24 N	41.50 E
Keping Shan ϰ	85	40.00 N	77.10 E
Kępno	30	51.17 N	17.59 E
Kepo	112	2.56 S	106.33 E
Keppel Bay c	166	23.21 S	150.55 E
Keppel Harbour c	271c	1.16 N	103.50 E
Kepsut	130	39.41 N	28.09 E
Keptown	219	39.05 N	88.40 W
Kequan	98	36.04 N	114.00 E
Kerala □[3]	122	10.00 N	76.30 E
Keram ≃	164	4.07 S	144.07 E
Keramian, Pulau I	112	5.04 S	114.36 E
Kerandin	112	0.12 S	104.46 E
Kerang	166	35.44 S	143.55 E
Keranyo	144	5.04 N	38.18 E
Keratéa	38	37.48 N	23.59 E
Keratsínion	267c	37.58 N	23.37 E
Keraudren, Cape ›	162	19.57 S	119.45 E
Kerava	26	60.24 N	25.07 E
Keravat	164	4.19 S	152.01 E
Kerbat ≃	114	5.01 N	102.51 E
Kerbela → Karbalā'	128	32.36 N	44.02 E
Kerbi ≃	89	52.28 N	136.25 E
Kerby	202	42.11 N	123.39 W
Kerč'	78	45.22 N	36.27 E
Kerčel'	86	59.18 N	64.46 E
Kerčemja	24	61.28 N	53.50 E

Symbol	English	Deutsch	Español	Français	Português
≃	River	Fluß	Río	Rivière	Rio
≊	Canal	Kanal	Canal	Canal	Canal
ʟ	Waterfall, Rapids	Wasserfall, Stromschnellen	Cascada, Rápidos	Chute d'eau, Rapides	Cascata, Rápidos
ʯ	Strait	Meeresstraße	Estrecho	Détroit	Estreito
c	Bay, Gulf	Bucht, Golf	Bahía, Golfo	Baie, Golfe	Baía, Golfo
⊜	Lake, Lakes	See, Seen	Lago, Lagos	Lac, Lacs	Lago, Lagos
≡	Swamp	Sumpf	Pantano	Marais	Pântano
⊓	Ice Features, Glacier	Eis- und Gletscherformen	Accidentes Glaciales	Formes glaciaires	Acidentes glaciares
⍑	Other Hydrographic Features	Andere Hydrographische Objekte	Otros Elementos Hidrográficos	Autres données hydrographiques	Outros acidentes hidrográficos
✦	Submarine Features	Untermeerische Objekte	Accidentes Submarinos	Formes de relief sous-marin	Acidentes submarinos
□	Political Unit	Politische Einheit	Unidad Politica	Entité politique	Unidade política
ʊ	Cultural Institution	Kulturelle Institution	Institución Cultural	Institution culturelle	Institução cultural
⊥	Historical Site	Historische Stätte	Sitio Histórico	Site historique	Sitio histórico
♠	Recreational Site	Erholungs- und Ferienort	Sitio de Recreo	Centre de loisirs	Area de Lazer
⊠	Airport	Flughafen	Aeropuerto	Aéroport	Aeroporto
■	Military Installation	Militäranlage	Instalación Militar	Installation militaire	Instalação militar
◆	Miscellaneous	Verschiedenes	Misceláneo	Divers	Diversos

I · 86 Kerc-Kill

Name / Name	Page / Seite	Lat.°′ / Breite°′	Long.°′ / Länge°′ E = Ost
Kerčenskij poluostrov ≻[1]	78	45.15 N	36.00 E
Kerčenskij proliv ⊔	78	45.22 N	36.38 E
Kerčevskij	24	59.55 N	56.17 E
Kerch → Kerč'	78	45.22 N	36.27 E
Kerckhoff Lake ⊜[1]	226	37.09 N	119.31 W
Kéré	154	5.16 N	26.11 E
Kéré ≃	140	5.19 N	25.40 E
Kerec, mys ≻	24	65.20 N	39.40 E
Kerej, ozero ⊜	86	50.08 N	68.45 E
Kerema	164	8.00 S	145.45 E
Keremeos	182	49.12 N	119.50 W
Kerem Maharal	132	32.39 N	34.59 E
Kerempe Burnu ≻	130	42.01 N	33.21 E
Keren	144	15.46 N	38.28 E
Kerend	128	34.16 N	46.15 E
Kerens	222	32.07 N	96.13 W
Kerepes	264c	47.34 N	19.18 E
Keret'	24	66.16 N	33.34 E
Keret', ozero ⊜	24	65.55 N	32.56 E
Kerewan	150	13.29 N	16.10 W
Kerga	24	62.39 N	46.00 E
Kergez	84	40.18 N	49.38 E
Kerguélen, Îles II	6	49.15 S	69.10 E
Kerguelen Plateau ✢[3]	6	55.00 S	75.00 E
Kerhonkson	210	41.46 N	74.17 W
Kerian ≃	114	5.10 N	100.26 E
Kericho	154	0.22 S	35.17 E
Keri Kera	140	12.21 N	32.46 E
Kerikeri	172	35.13 S	173.58 E
Kerimäki	26	61.55 N	29.17 E
Kerinci, Gunung ∧	112	1.42 S	101.16 E
Kerio ≃	154	2.59 N	36.07 E
Keríon	38	37.40 N	20.48 E
Keritang	112	0.51 S	102.39 E
Keriya ≃	120	38.30 N	82.10 E
Kerka ≃	61	46.28 N	16.36 E
Kerkafalva	61	46.46 N	16.30 E
Kerkdriel	52	51.46 N	5.20 E
Kerkebet	144	16.18 N	37.24 E
Kerken	56	51.27 N	6.22 E
Kerkenna, Îles II	148	34.44 N	11.12 E
Kerkhove	50	50.48 N	3.30 E
Kerkhoven	198	45.11 N	95.19 W
Kerki, Ross.	24	63.43 N	54.05 E
Kerki, Turk.	128	37.50 N	65.12 E
Kérkira (Corfu)	38	39.36 N	19.56 E
Kérkira I	38	39.40 N	19.42 E
Kerkrade [-Holz]	56	50.52 N	6.04 E
Kerling	114	3.35 N	101.36 E
Kermadec Islands II	14	29.16 S	177.55 W
Kermadec Ridge ✢[3]	14	30.30 S	178.30 W
Kermadec Trench ✢[1]	14	30.00 S	177.00 W
Kermajärvi ⊜	26	62.28 N	28.40 E
Kermān, Īrān	128	30.17 N	57.05 E
Kerman, Ca., U.S.	226	36.43 N	120.04 W
Kermān □[4]	128	29.00 N	57.30 E
Kermit	196	31.51 N	103.05 W
Kermit Roosevelt Seamount ✢[3]	16	39.35 N	146.00 W
Kermode, Mount ∧	182	52.57 N	131.51 W
Kern □[6]	228	35.20 N	118.55 W
Kern ≃	204	35.13 N	119.17 W
Kern, South Fork ≃	204	35.40 N	118.27 W
Kern City	228	35.18 N	119.05 W
Kernersville	192	36.07 N	80.04 W
Kernforschungszentrum ʊ[3]	56	49.07 N	8.26 E
Kernhof	61	47.49 N	15.32 E
Kern Island Canal ≊	228	35.22 N	119.01 W
Kern Lake Bed ⊜	228	35.10 N	119.05 W
Kern River Channel ≃[1]	226	35.49 N	119.40 W
Kernville	204	35.45 N	118.25 W
Keroh	114	5.43 N	101.00 E
Keros	24	60.44 N	52.50 E
Kérou	150	10.50 N	2.06 E
Kérouané	150	9.16 N	9.01 W
Kerowagi	164	5.50 S	144.50 E
Kerpen	56	50.52 N	6.41 E
Kerpinen'	78	46.47 N	28.22 E
Kerr	214	41.03 N	78.25 W
Kerrera I	46	56.23 N	5.34 W
Kerridge	262	53.17 N	2.06 W
Kerridge Hill ∧[2]	262	53.17 N	2.06 W
Kerrobert	184	51.55 N	109.08 W
Kerrtown	214	41.38 N	80.10 W
Kerruish Park ♠	279a	41.26 N	81.34 W
Kerrville	196	30.02 N	99.08 W
Kerry	42	52.30 N	3.16 W
Kerry □[6]	48	52.10 N	9.30 W
Kerry Head ≻	48	52.25 N	9.57 W
Kersa	144	9.28 N	41.53 E
Kersbrook	168b	34.47 S	138.51 E
Kersey	214	41.21 N	78.35 W
Kershaw	192	34.33 N	80.35 W
Kersinyane	150	15.24 N	10.10 W
Kersley	182	52.49 N	122.25 W
Kerspestausee ⊜[1]	263	51.08 N	7.30 E
Kerstenhausen	56	51.04 N	9.13 E
Kert, Oued ≃	34	35.15 N	3.15 W
Kertamulia	112	0.23 S	109.09 E
Kerteh	114	4.31 N	103.27 E
Kerteminde	41	55.27 N	10.40 E
Kertosono	115a	7.35 S	112.06 E
Kerulen (Cherlen) (Herlen) ≃	90	48.48 N	117.00 E
Kerva	80	55.37 N	39.35 E
Kerzaz	148	29.30 N	1.37 W
Kerzendorf	264a	52.16 N	13.17 E
Keržеnec	80	56.28 N	44.26 E
Keržеnec ≃	80	56.05 N	45.03 E
Kerzers	58	46.58 N	7.12 E
Kesabpur	126	22.55 N	89.13 E
Ke Sach	110	9.46 N	105.59 E
Kesagami Lake ⊜	176	50.23 N	80.15 W
Kesälahti	26	61.54 N	29.50 E
Keşan	130	40.51 N	26.37 E
Keşap	130	40.55 N	38.31 E
Kesbern	263	51.20 N	7.42 E
Kesch, Piz ∧	58	46.38 N	9.52 E
Kesem ≃	144	9.14 N	40.06 E
Kesennuma	92	38.54 N	141.35 E
Kesh	48	54.32 N	7.43 W
Keshan	89	48.02 N	125.51 E
Keshena	190	44.53 N	88.38 W
Keshendeh	120	36.05 N	66.51 E
Keshequa Creek ≃	210	42.43 N	77.50 W
Keshod	120	21.18 N	70.15 E
Keşiş Dağları ⋏	130	39.50 N	39.45 E
Keskastel	56	48.58 N	7.02 E
Keskin	130	39.41 N	33.37 E
Keski-Suomen lääni □[4]	26	62.30 N	25.30 E
Keskozero	24	61.24 N	33.12 E
Keskuvejem, gora ∧	180	66.12 N	177.40 W
Kes'ma	76	58.27 N	37.04 E
Kesova Gora	76	57.35 N	37.17 E
Kespur	126	22.35 N	87.29 E
Kesra	36	35.49 N	9.22 E
Kessebüren	263	51.31 N	7.43 E
Kessel	56	51.08 N	4.37 E
Kesselsdorf	54	51.02 N	13.35 E
Kessingland	42	52.25 N	1.42 E
Kesswil	58	47.36 N	9.20 E
Kestel Gölü ⊜	130	37.24 N	30.28 E
Kestell	158	28.19 S	28.38 E
Kesten'ga	24	65.55 N	31.47 E
Kestilä	26	64.21 N	26.17 E
Keston ◆[8]	260	51.22 N	0.02 E
Keswick, On., Can.	212	44.15 N	79.28 W
Keswick, Eng., U.K.	44	54.37 N	3.08 W
Keszthely	30	46.46 N	17.15 E
Ket' ≃	86	58.55 N	81.32 E
Keta	150	5.55 N	1.00 E
Keta ≃	94	34.56 N	137.50 E
Keta, ozero ⊜	74	68.44 N	90.00 E
Ketaka	96	35.30 N	134.03 E
Keta Lagoon ⊂	150	5.54 N	0.56 E
Ketam, Pulau I	271c	1.24 N	103.57 E
Ketama	34	34.50 N	4.37 W
Ketang	100	22.58 N	115.28 E
Ketapang, Indon.	112	1.52 S	109.59 E
Ketapang, Indon.	115a	6.54 S	113.17 E
Ketapang, Indon.	115a	5.44 S	105.48 E
Ketaun	112	3.23 S	101.49 E
Ketčenery	80	47.18 N	44.31 E
Ketchikan	182	55.21 N	131.35 W
Ketchum	202	43.40 N	114.21 W
Kete Krachi	150	7.46 N	0.03 W
Ketelmeer ⊜	52	52.35 N	5.45 E
Keti Bandar	120	24.08 N	67.27 E
Ketingwan ∧	154	0.40 N	35.50 E
Ketoj, ostrov I	74	47.20 N	152.28 E
Kétou	150	7.22 N	2.36 E
Ketovo	86	55.21 N	65.18 E
Kętrzyn (Rastenburg)	30	54.06 N	21.23 E
Ketsch	56	49.22 N	8.31 E
Ketta	152	1.28 N	15.56 E
Kettering, Eng., U.K.	42	52.24 N	0.44 W
Kettering, Md., U.S.	284c	38.53 N	76.49 W
Kettering, Oh., U.S.	218	39.41 N	84.10 W
Kettinge	41	54.42 N	11.45 E
Kettle ≃, Mb., Can.	184	56.23 N	94.34 W
Kettle ≃, N.A.	182	48.42 N	118.07 W
Kettle ≃, Mn., U.S.	190	45.52 N	92.45 W
Kettle Creek ≃, On., Can.	212	42.40 N	81.13 W
Kettle Creek ≃, Pa., U.S.	210	41.18 N	77.51 W
Kettle Creek State Park ♠	214	41.23 N	77.56 W
Kettle Falls	202	48.36 N	118.03 W
Kettleman City	226	36.00 N	119.57 W
Kettleman Hills ⋏[2]	226	36.00 N	120.00 W
Kettle Rapids Dam ◆[6]	184	56.23 N	94.38 W
Kettlersville	216	40.22 N	84.16 W
Kettleshulme	262	53.19 N	2.01 W
Kettlewell	44	54.09 N	2.02 W
Kettwig	56	51.22 N	6.56 E
Kęty	30	49.53 N	19.13 E
Ketzin	54	52.28 N	12.50 E
Keudemane	114	5.15 N	96.55 E
Keudepasi	114	4.18 N	95.56 E
Keudeteunom	114	4.27 N	95.48 E
Keudeunga	114	5.01 N	95.22 E
Keuka Lake ⊜	210	42.27 N	77.10 W
Keuka Lake, West Branch ⊂	210	42.33 N	77.09 W
Keuka Park	210	42.37 N	77.06 W
Keukenhof ♠	52	52.16 N	4.33 E
Keul'	88	58.25 N	102.49 E
Keula	54	51.20 N	10.31 E
Keum ≃	86	59.32 N	70.35 E
Keurboomsrivier	158	34.00 S	23.24 E
Keurusselkä ⊜	26	62.10 N	24.40 E
Keuruu	26	62.16 N	24.42 E
Kevdo-Mel'sitovo	80	53.09 N	43.54 E
Kevelaer	52	51.35 N	6.15 E
Kevin	202	48.44 N	111.57 W
Kevsala	80	45.48 N	42.41 E
Kew, Austl.	169	37.49 S	145.02 E
Kew, T./C. Is.	238	21.54 N	72.02 W
Kewanee	190	41.14 N	89.55 W
Kewanna	216	41.01 N	86.25 W
Kewaunee	190	44.27 N	87.30 W
Keweenaw Bay ⊂	190	46.56 N	88.23 W
Keweenaw Peninsula ≻[1]	190	47.12 N	88.25 W
Keweenaw Point ≻	190	47.30 N	87.50 W
Kew Gardens ♠, On., Can.	275b	43.40 N	79.18 W
Kew Gardens ♠, Eng., U.K.	260	51.28 N	0.18 W
Keyala	154	4.27 N	32.52 E
Keyangkeer Shan ∧	120	31.20 N	87.13 E
Keya Paha ≃	198	42.54 N	99.00 W
Key Biscayne	220	25.42 N	80.10 W
Keyes, Ca., U.S.	226	37.33 N	120.54 W
Keyes, Ok., U.S.	196	36.48 N	102.15 W
Keyesport	219	38.44 N	89.17 W
Keyhole Reservoir ⊜[1]	198	44.21 N	104.51 W
Keyhole State Park ♠	198	44.19 N	104.48 W
Keyihe	89	50.40 N	122.27 E
Keyingham	44	53.42 N	0.07 W
Key Largo	220	25.04 N	80.28 W
Key Largo I	220	25.16 N	80.19 W
Keymer	42	50.55 N	0.08 W
Keynes Hill ∧[2]	168b	34.37 S	139.06 E
Keyneton	168b	34.34 S	139.08 E
Keynsham	42	51.26 N	2.30 W
Keynshamburg	154	19.15 S	29.39 E
Keyport, N.J., U.S.	276	40.25 N	74.12 W
Keyport, Wa., U.S.	224	47.42 N	122.38 W
Keyport Harbor ⊂	276	40.26 N	74.12 W
Keysborough	274b	38.00 S	145.10 E
Keysbrook	168a	32.26 S	115.59 E
Keyser	188	39.26 N	78.58 W
Keystone, In., U.S.	216	40.36 N	85.16 W
Keystone, Ia., U.S.	190	41.59 N	92.11 W
Keystone, S.D., U.S.	198	43.53 N	103.25 W
Keystone, W.V., U.S.	192	37.24 N	81.27 W
Keystone Lake ⊜[1], Ok., U.S.	196	36.15 N	96.25 W
Keystone Lake ⊜[1], Pa., U.S.	214	40.45 N	79.15 W
Keystone Peak ∧	200	31.53 N	111.13 W
Keystone Race Track ♠	285	40.07 N	74.57 W
Keystone State Park ♠	214	40.23 N	79.24 W
Keysville, Fl., U.S.	220	27.52 N	82.06 W
Keysville, Va., U.S.	192	37.02 N	78.29 W
Keytesville	194	39.26 N	92.56 W
Key West	220	24.33 N	81.46 W
Key West Island I	220	24.33 N	81.47 W
Key West Naval Air Station ■	220	24.34 N	81.41 W
Keyworth	42	52.52 N	1.05 W
Kez	80	57.53 N	53.43 E
Kezar Stadium ♠	282	37.46 N	122.27 W
Kezi	154	20.58 S	28.32 E
Kezilesu Zizhizhou □[8]	85	40.00 N	75.30 E
Kežma	88	58.59 N	101.09 E
Kežmarok	30	49.08 N	20.25 E
Kgalagadi □[5]	156	25.00 S	22.00 E
Kgatleng □[5]	156	24.28 S	26.05 E
Kgokgole ≃	158	26.44 S	22.28 E
Kgun Lake ⊜	180	61.32 N	163.45 W
Khaanziir, Ras ≻	144	10.55 N	45.47 E
Khabab	132	33.00 N	36.16 E
Khabīr, Kūh-e ∧	128	28.48 N	56.26 E
Khābūr, Nahr al- (Habur) ≃	130	35.08 N	40.26 E
Khādar	272a	28.33 N	77.22 E
Khadari, Wādī al- V	140	10.29 N	26.15 E
Khadaungnge Taung ∧	110	18.57 N	94.37 E
Khadki (Kirkee)	122	18.34 N	73.52 E
Khadra	34	36.15 N	0.35 E
Khafūrī, Wādī V	142	29.37 N	32.04 E
Khagaria	124	25.30 N	86.29 E
Khagdon ≃[1]	126	22.09 N	90.05 E
Khāgrāmuri	272b	22.26 N	88.14 E
Khaïdhárion	267c	37.33 N	22.53 E
Khair	124	27.57 N	77.50 E
Khairābād	124	27.32 N	80.45 E
Khairāgarh	120	21.25 N	80.58 E
Khairbani	126	24.14 N	87.05 E
Khairna	272c	19.06 N	73.01 E
Khairpur, Pāk.	120	27.32 N	68.46 E
Khairpur, Pāk.	123	29.35 N	72.14 E
Khairwāra	120	23.59 N	73.35 E
Khajrāho	120	24.50 N	79.58 E
Khajuri	126	21.52 N	87.58 E
Khajuri ◆[8]	272a	28.43 N	77.16 E
Kha Khaeng ≃	110	14.55 N	99.07 E
Khakhea	156	24.51 S	23.20 E
Khalándrion	267c	38.01 N	23.48 E
Khalatse	123	34.20 N	76.49 E
Khālidī, Khirbat al- ⊥	132	29.39 N	35.14 E
Khalkhāl	128	37.37 N	48.32 E
Khalkhalah	132	33.04 N	36.32 E
Khálki I	130	36.17 N	27.35 E
Khalkidhikí □[9]	38	40.25 N	23.27 E
Khalkís	38	38.28 N	23.36 E
Khālsar	120	34.31 N	77.41 E
Khambhāliya	120	22.12 N	69.39 E
Khambhāt	120	22.18 N	72.37 E
Khambhāt, Gulf of ⊂	122	21.00 N	72.30 E
Khāmgaon	122	20.41 N	76.34 E
Khamir	144	16.05 N	43.55 E
Khāmis, Ash-Shallāl al- (Fifth Cataract) ∟	140	18.23 N	33.47 E
Khamīs Mushayṭ	144	18.18 N	42.44 E
Khamkeut	110	18.15 N	104.43 E
Khamma	70	36.47 N	12.02 E
Khammam	122	17.15 N	80.09 E
Khamsah	142	30.25 N	32.23 E
Khan ≃, Lao	110	19.54 N	102.09 E
Khan ≃, Namibia	156	22.37 S	14.56 E
Khāna	126	23.20 N	87.44 E
Khānābād	120	36.41 N	69.07 E
Khān Abū Shāmāt	132	33.40 N	36.54 E
Khānākul	126	22.43 N	87.51 E
Khān al-Baghdādī	128	33.51 N	42.33 E
Khānaqīn	128	34.21 N	45.22 E
Khān Arnabah	132	33.11 N	35.53 E
Khancoban	171b	36.12 S	148.05 E
Khandaghosh	126	23.13 N	87.41 E
Khandela	120	27.36 N	75.30 E
Khandwa	124	21.50 N	76.20 E
Khān-e Chahār Bāgh, Afg.	120	35.58 N	69.38 E
Khān-e Chahār Bāgh, Afg.	128	37.00 N	65.14 E
Khāneh Khvodī	128	36.02 N	55.59 E
Khānewāl	123	30.18 N	71.56 E
Khāngāh Dogrān	123	31.50 N	73.37 E
Khāngarh, Pāk.	120	28.22 N	71.43 E
Khāngarh, Pāk.	123	29.55 N	71.10 E
Khangkhai	110	19.28 N	103.15 E
Khaniá	38	35.31 N	24.02 E
Khaníon, Kólpos ⊂	38	35.34 N	23.48 E
Khānkurda	126	22.00 N	87.25 E
Khanna	123	30.42 N	76.13 E
Khannā, Qā' ≍	132	32.04 N	36.26 E
Khānozai	120	30.37 N	67.19 E
Khānpur, India	272b	22.40 N	88.16 E
Khānpur, Pāk.	123	28.39 N	70.39 E
Khānpur ◆[8], India	272a	28.34 N	77.01 E
Khānpur ◆[8], India	272a	28.31 N	77.14 E
Khān Shaykhūn	130	35.26 N	36.38 E
Khanty-Mansiysk → Chanty-Mansijsk	74	61.00 N	69.06 E
Khān Yūnus	132	31.21 N	34.19 E
Khao Laem Reservoir ⊜[1]	110	14.50 N	98.30 E
Khao Saming	110	12.21 N	102.27 E
Khao Sok National Park ♠	110	8.55 N	98.35 E
Khao Yoi	110	13.14 N	99.50 E
Khapalu	123	35.10 N	76.20 E
Khaptad National Park ♠	124	29.28 N	81.10 E
Kharab, Ghoubet al ⊂	144	11.30 N	42.35 E
Kharabā	132	32.34 N	36.27 E
Kharagdiha	124	24.25 N	86.10 E
Kharagpur, India	124	25.07 N	86.33 E
Kharagpur, India	126	22.20 N	87.20 E
Kharak	123	33.07 N	71.06 E
Khārān	120	28.35 N	65.25 E
Kharānoq	128	32.20 N	54.39 E
Kharar, India	123	30.45 N	76.39 E
Kharar, India	126	22.42 N	87.41 E
Khāravli ∧[2]	272c	18.54 N	72.55 E
Kharāyij, Sabkhat al- ⊜	130	35.40 N	37.20 E
Kharaz, Jabal ∧	144	12.44 N	44.09 E
Kharbatā	132	31.57 N	35.04 E
Kharbine → Harbin	89	45.45 N	126.41 E
Khardaha	126	22.44 N	88.22 E
Khārghar	272c	19.03 N	73.04 E
Kharg Island → Khārk, Jazīreh-ye I	128	29.15 N	50.20 E
Khargon	120	21.49 N	75.36 E
Khāriān Cantonment	123	32.49 N	73.52 E
Khariār Road	122	20.54 N	82.31 E
Khārijah, Al-Wāḥāt al- ⊤[4]	140	25.20 N	30.35 E
Kharīm, Jabal ∧	132	30.17 N	33.58 E
Kharīṭ, Wādī al- V	140	24.26 N	33.03 E
Khārk, Jazīreh-ye (Kharg Island) I	128	29.15 N	50.20 E
Kharkov → Char'kov	78	50.00 N	36.15 E
Kharmān, Kūh-e ∧	128	29.13 N	53.35 E
Kharri	272b	22.55 N	88.14 E
Kharsāwān	124	22.48 N	85.50 E
Kharsia	124	21.58 N	83.07 E
Khartoum → Al-Kharṭūm	140	15.36 N	32.32 E
Khartoum North → Al-Kharṭūm Baḥrī	140	15.38 N	32.33 E
Khartum → Al-Kharṭūm	140	15.36 N	32.32 E
Kharumwa	154	3.12 S	32.39 E
Khāsbāti	272b	22.55 N	88.25 E
Khasebake	156	20.41 S	24.29 E
Khāsh, Afg.	128	31.31 N	62.52 E
Khāsh, Īrān	128	28.14 N	61.14 E
Khāsh ≃	128	31.11 N	62.05 E
Khāsh, Dasht-e ◆[2]	128	31.50 N	62.30 E
Khashab, Jabal al- ∧[2]	142	29.56 N	31.01 E
Khashm al-Qirbah	140	14.58 N	35.55 E
Khashm al-Qirbah, Khazzān ⊜[1]	140	14.40 N	35.55 E
Khashshab, Tur'at al- ≊	273c	29.53 N	31.17 E
Khashum	140	12.27 N	28.02 E
Khāş Konar	120	34.39 N	70.54 E
Khaskovo → Haskovo	38	41.56 N	25.33 E
Khatauli	124	29.17 N	77.43 E
Khātegaon	124	22.36 N	76.55 E
Khātra	126	22.59 N	86.51 E
Khatt, Oued al V	148	26.45 N	13.03 W
Khaur	123	33.16 N	72.28 E
Khāvda	120	23.51 N	69.43 E
Khawrah	144	14.26 N	46.09 E
Khawsa	110	15.03 N	97.50 E
Khayāla ◆[8]	272a	28.40 N	77.06 E
Khaybar, Ḥarrat ±[9]	128	25.30 N	39.45 E
Khayerpur	272b	22.35 N	88.33 E
Khayl, Kathīb al- ±[8]	142	30.33 N	32.28 E
Khayra Bil ⊜	272b	22.52 N	88.29 E
Khayrasole	126	23.48 N	87.16 E
Khayung ≃	110	15.07 N	104.42 E
Kheardaha	272b	22.29 N	88.28 E
Khe Bo	110	19.08 N	104.41 E
Khed	122	17.43 N	73.23 E
Khefapur	272a	28.30 N	77.05 E
Khejurdaha	272b	22.59 N	88.10 E
Khemis	148	36.16 N	2.13 E
Khemis el Khechna	34	36.39 N	3.20 E
Khemisset	148	33.50 N	6.03 W
Khemisset □[4]	148	33.50 N	6.05 W
Khem Karan	123	31.09 N	74.34 E
Khemmarat	110	16.03 N	105.13 E
Khenchla	148	35.28 N	7.11 E
Khenifra	148	33.00 N	5.40 W
Khenifra □[4]	148	32.35 N	5.10 W
Khenjān	120	35.36 N	70.59 E
Khenyen	272b	22.59 N	88.19 E
Khera ◆[8]	272a	28.46 N	77.08 E
Kheri	124	27.54 N	80.48 E
Kheri Branch ≊	124	28.11 N	80.25 E
Kherli	124	27.12 N	77.02 E
Kherrata	148	36.31 N	5.26 E
Khersān ≃	128	31.33 N	50.22 E
Kherson → Cherson	78	46.38 N	32.35 E
Khetia	120	21.40 N	74.35 E
Khevāj	120	38.13 N	71.02 E
Khewāri	120	26.36 N	68.52 E
Khewra	123	32.39 N	73.01 E
Kheyr Khāneh	128	34.57 N	63.37 E
Khichīwāra Plateau ⋏[1]	124	24.25 N	77.30 E
Khichripur ◆[8]	272a	28.37 N	77.19 E
Khilchipur	124	24.02 N	76.34 E
Khilkāpur	272b	22.46 N	88.29 E
Khimki → Chimki	82	55.54 N	37.26 E
Khíos	38	38.22 N	26.08 E
Khíos I	38	38.22 N	26.00 E
Khipro	120	25.50 N	69.22 E
Khirbat al-Ghazālah	132	32.44 N	36.12 E
Khirbat 'Awwād	132	32.19 N	36.43 E
Khirbat Qanāfār	132	33.38 N	35.43 E
Khirbat Umm as-Surab	132	32.26 N	36.19 E
Khirbitā	142	30.45 N	30.40 E
Khiri Mat	110	16.50 N	99.48 E
Khirpai	126	22.42 N	87.37 E
Khirr, Wādī al- V	128	31.51 N	44.29 E
Khisfīn	132	32.51 N	35.49 E
Khiuri Khala ∧	124	29.58 N	81.18 E
Khiva → Chiva	72	41.24 N	60.22 E
Khlong Khlung	110	16.12 N	99.43 E
Khlong Thom	110	7.56 N	99.09 E
Khlong Yai	110	11.46 N	102.54 E
Khlung	110	12.27 N	102.14 E
Khmel'nitskiy → Chmel'nickij	78	49.25 N	27.00 E
Khoai, Hon I	110	8.26 N	104.50 E
Khogali	140	6.08 N	27.47 E
Khojāng ∧	124	28.41 N	85.09 E
Khok Kloi	110	8.17 N	98.19 E
Khok Pho	110	6.43 N	101.06 E
Khoksa	126	23.48 N	89.17 E
Khok Samrong	110	15.04 N	100.44 E
Kholargós	267c	38.00 N	23.48 E
Kholm	120	36.42 N	67.41 E
Kholombidzo Falls ∟	154	15.54 S	34.44 E
Khomām	128	37.22 N	49.40 E
Khomas Hochland ⋏[1]	156	22.30 S	16.30 E
Khomeyn	128	33.38 N	50.04 E
Khomeynīshahr	128	32.41 N	51.31 E
Khomodimo	156	22.46 S	23.52 E
Khondmāl Hills ⋏[2]	122	20.20 N	84.00 E
Khong → Mekong ≃	12	10.33 N	105.24 E
Khoni	272c	19.10 N	73.07 E
Khon Kaen	110	16.26 N	102.50 E
Khóra	38	37.04 N	21.43 E
Khorāsān □[4]	128	35.00 N	58.00 E
Khóra Sfakíon	38	35.12 N	24.09 E
Khordha	120	20.11 N	85.37 E
Khorel	272b	22.42 N	88.19 E
Khorramābād	128	33.30 N	48.20 E
Khorram Daraq	128	36.26 N	48.36 E
Khorramshahr	128	30.25 N	48.11 E
Khoru	272b	22.51 N	88.31 E
Khossanto	150	13.08 N	11.58 W
Khouribga	148	32.54 N	6.57 W
Khouribga □[4]	148	32.50 N	6.30 W
Khowai	120	24.06 N	91.38 E
Khowāng	120	27.16 N	94.53 E
Khowst	120	33.22 N	69.57 E
Khrisokhoús, Kólpos ⊂	130	35.06 N	32.25 E
Khrisoúpolis	38	40.58 N	24.42 E
Khudiān	123	30.59 N	74.17 E
Khuff	128	24.57 N	44.42 E
Khugaung	110	26.07 N	98.18 E
Khūgīānī Šānī	120	31.31 N	66.12 E
Khuis	156	26.37 S	21.45 E
Khuīyāla	120	27.14 N	70.30 E
Khu Khan	110	14.42 N	104.12 E
Khulna	124	22.48 N	89.33 E
Khulna □[5]	126	22.45 N	89.30 E
Khŭm Bathéay	110	11.59 N	104.57 E
Khumbur Khūlē Ghar ∧	120	32.49 N	68.47 E
Khungdugang ∧	124	27.31 N	89.02 E
Khūnjerāb Pass)(	123	36.52 N	75.27 E
Khun Tan, Doi ∧	110	18.30 N	99.20 E
Khunti	124	23.05 N	85.17 E
Khūr	128	32.57 N	58.26 E
Khurai	124	24.03 N	78.19 E
Khuralji Khās ◆[8]	272a	28.39 N	77.17 E
Khuria Tank ⊜[1]	124	22.25 N	81.36 E
Khurigāchi	272b	22.49 N	88.20 E
Khurīyā Murīyā, Jazā'ir II	118	17.30 N	56.00 E
Khurja	124	28.15 N	77.51 E
Khurli	120	28.59 N	65.52 E
Khurramshahr → Khorramshahr	128	30.25 N	48.11 E
Khūsf	128	32.46 N	58.53 E
Khushāb	123	32.18 N	72.21 E
Khushālgarh	123	33.30 N	71.54 E
Khushk Khurd ◆[8]	272a	28.46 N	77.10 E
Khutubi ≃	86	44.45 N	86.25 E
Khuwayy	140	13.05 N	29.14 E
Khuzdār	120	27.48 N	66.37 E
Khūzestān □[4]	128	31.00 N	49.00 E
Khvāf	128	34.33 N	60.08 E
Khvājeh Moḥammad, Kūh-e ⋏	120	36.22 N	70.17 E
Khvājeh Ra'ūf	120	33.19 N	64.43 E
Khvor	128	33.47 N	55.03 E
Khvormūj	128	28.39 N	51.23 E
Khvoy	128	38.33 N	44.58 E
Khwae Noi ≃	110	14.01 N	99.32 E
Khyber Pass)(	123	34.05 N	71.10 E
Kia	175e	7.33 S	158.26 E
Kialwe	154	9.22 S	27.08 E
Kiama, Austl.	170	34.41 S	150.51 E
Kiama, Zaïre	152	7.15 S	17.44 E
Kiamba	116	5.59 N	124.37 E
Kiambi	154	7.20 S	28.01 E
Kiamboni, Kap → Jumbo, Raas ≻	144	1.39 S	41.36 E
Kiambu	154	1.10 S	36.50 E
Kiamesha Lake	210	41.41 N	74.40 W
Kiamichi ≃	194	33.57 N	95.14 W
Kiamika ≃	206	46.38 N	75.15 W
Kiamika, Barrage ◆[6]	206	46.37 N	75.08 W
Kiamika, Réservoir ⊜[1]	206	46.40 N	75.05 W
Kiamusze → Jiamusi	89	46.50 N	130.21 E
Kiana	180	66.59 N	160.25 W
Kiandra	171b	35.53 S	148.30 E
Kiangara	157b	17.58 S	47.02 E
Kiangarow, Mount ∧	166	26.49 S	151.33 E
Kiangsi → Jiangxi □[4]	100	28.00 N	116.00 E
Kiangsu → Jiangsu □[4]	90	33.00 N	120.00 E
Kian → Ji'an	100	27.07 N	114.58 E
Kiantajärvi ⊜	26	65.03 N	29.07 E
Kiaohsien → Jiaoxian	98	36.18 N	119.58 E
Kibæk	41	56.02 N	8.51 E
Kibaha	154	6.46 S	38.55 E
Kibali ≃	154	3.37 N	28.34 E
Kibali-Sturi Game Reserve ◆[4]	154	2.45 N	29.33 E
Kibamba	154	4.53 S	26.33 E
Kibanga Port	154	0.11 N	32.52 E
Kibangou	152	3.27 S	12.21 E
Kibanseke	273b	4.26 S	15.23 E
Kibar	120	32.20 N	78.01 E
Kibara	154	2.09 S	33.27 E
Kibāsī	128	30.34 N	47.50 E
Kibau Iyayi	154	8.52 S	34.32 E
Kibawe	116	7.34 N	125.00 E
Kibaya	154	5.18 S	36.34 E
Kibenga	152	7.55 S	17.35 E
Kibeni	164	7.25 S	143.48 E
Kiberashi	154	5.23 S	37.26 E
Kiberege	154	7.57 S	36.52 E
Kibi	150	6.10 N	0.33 W
Kibi-kōgen ⋏[1]	96	34.45 N	133.15 E
Kibila	154	8.14 S	26.23 E
Kibiti	154	7.44 S	38.57 E
Kibler Park	273d	26.18 S	28.00 E
Kiboga	154	1.02 N	30.58 E
Kiboko	154	2.15 S	37.42 E
Kibombo	154	3.54 S	25.55 E
Kibondo	154	3.35 S	30.42 E
Kibouendé, Congo	273b	4.19 S	15.11 E
Kibouendé, Congo	273b	4.17 S	15.09 E
Kibouendé I	273b	4.11 S	15.09 E
Kibouendé II	273b	4.12 S	15.09 E
Kibre Mengist	144	5.52 N	39.00 E
Kıbrısçık	130	40.25 N	31.51 E
Kıbrıs → Cyprus □[1]	130	35.00 N	33.00 E
Kibumbu	154	3.32 S	29.45 E
Kibungo	154	2.10 S	30.32 E
Kibuye, Bdi.	154	3.40 S	29.59 E
Kibuye, Rw.	154	2.03 S	29.21 E
Kibwesa	154	6.28 S	29.57 E
Kibwezi	154	2.25 S	37.58 E
Kibworth Harcourt	42	52.32 N	0.59 W
Kičevo	38	41.31 N	20.57 E
Kichčik	74	53.24 N	156.03 E
Kichijōji	268	35.42 N	139.35 E
Kickany	78	46.47 N	29.36 E
Kickapoo ≃	190	43.05 N	90.53 W
Kickapoo Creek ≃, Il., U.S.	194	40.08 N	89.27 W
Kickapoo Creek ≃, Il., U.S.	219	40.08 N	89.27 W
Kickapoo Creek ≃, Tx., U.S.	196	31.31 N	99.58 W
Kickapoo Creek ≃, Tx., U.S.	222	30.47 N	95.08 W
Kickapoo Creek ≃, Tx., U.S.	222	32.16 N	95.28 W
Kicking Horse Pass)(	182	51.27 N	116.18 W
Kičkino	80	47.05 N	44.02 E
Kičma	80	57.12 N	48.55 E
Kicman'	78	48.27 N	25.44 E
Kičmengskij Gorodok	24	59.59 N	45.48 E
Kičuj ≃	80	55.13 N	51.16 E
Kidal	150	18.26 N	1.24 E
Kidapawan	116	7.01 N	125.03 E
Kidatu	154	7.42 S	36.57 E
Kidbrooke ◆[8]	260	51.28 N	0.02 E
Kidderminster	42	52.23 N	2.14 W
Kidderpore ◆[8]	272b	22.31 N	88.19 E
Kidderpore Docks ◆[5]	272b	22.33 N	88.19 E
Kidd's Beach	158	33.09 S	27.42 E
Kidepo National Park ♠	154	3.50 N	33.40 E
Kidete, Tan.	154	6.25 S	37.16 E
Kidete, Tan.	154	6.39 S	36.42 E
Kidira	150	14.28 N	12.13 W
Kidlington	42	51.50 N	1.17 W
Kidnappers, Cape ≻	172	39.39 S	177.07 E
Kido	164	9.15 S	146.55 E
Kidričevo	61	46.24 N	15.47 E
Kidron	214	40.44 N	81.45 W
Kidsgrove	44	53.06 N	2.15 W
Kidston	166	18.53 S	144.10 E
Kidugallo	154	6.47 S	38.12 E
Kidul, Pegunungan ⋏	115a	8.13 S	111.30 E
Kidwelly	42	51.45 N	4.18 W
Kiefersfelden	64	47.37 N	12.11 E
Kiekebusch	264a	52.21 N	13.33 E
Kiel, Dtsch.	41	54.20 N	10.08 E
Kiel, Wi., U.S.	190	43.54 N	88.02 W
Kiel Canal → Nord-Ostsee-Kanal ≊	30	53.53 N	9.08 E
Kielce	30	50.52 N	20.37 E
Kielce □[4]	30	50.30 N	20.30 E
Kielder	44	55.14 N	2.35 W
Kielder Reservoir ⊜[1]	44	55.11 N	2.30 W
Kieler Bucht (Kiel Bay) ⊂	41	54.35 N	10.35 E
Kieler Förde ⊂	41	54.24 N	10.12 E
Kiembara	150	13.15 N	2.44 W
Kienberg	264a	52.40 N	12.54 E
Kienge	154	10.34 S	27.33 E
Kienitz	54	52.40 N	14.26 E
Kiens → Chienes	64	46.48 N	11.50 E
Kiental	58	46.35 N	7.43 E
Kierling	264b	48.19 N	16.17 E
Kierspe	56	51.08 N	7.35 E
Kierspe-Bahnhof	263	51.08 N	7.37 E
Kiester	190	43.32 N	93.42 W
Kieta	175e	6.13 S	155.38 E
Kietrz	30	50.05 N	18.01 E
Kietz	54	52.34 N	14.36 E
Kiev → Kijev	78	50.26 N	30.31 E
Kiev Station ◆[5]	265b	55.45 N	37.34 E
Kiew → Kijev	78	50.26 N	30.31 E
Kifaya	150	12.10 N	13.04 W
Kiffa	150	16.37 N	11.24 W
Kifisiá	38	38.04 N	23.48 E
Kifisós ≃, Ellás	38	38.26 N	23.15 E
Kifisós ≃, Ellás	267c	38.06 N	23.45 E
Kifrī	128	34.42 N	44.58 E
Kifrī, Jabal ∧	142	27.48 N	32.50 E
Kigač ≃	80	46.28 N	49.12 E
Kigali	154	1.57 S	30.04 E
Kiği	130	39.19 N	40.21 E
Kigille	140	8.40 N	34.02 E
Kigoma	154	4.52 S	29.38 E
Kigoma □[4]	154	4.30 S	30.30 E
Kigun, Cape ≻	180	52.00 N	175.21 W
Kigwa	154	5.10 S	33.08 E
Kihei	229a	20.47 N	156.27 W
Kihikihi	172	38.02 S	175.21 E
Kihniö	26	62.12 N	23.11 E
Kihnu I	76	58.08 N	24.00 E
Kiholo Bay ⊂	229d	19.52 N	155.56 W
Kihundo	154	9.25 S	38.59 E
Kihurio	154	4.28 S	38.04 E
Kii-hantō ≻[1]	92	34.00 N	135.45 E
Kiik	86	47.31 N	72.55 E
Kiikkaškan	86	49.28 N	77.04 E
Kiiminginjoki ≃	26	65.12 N	25.18 E
Kii-nagashima	92	34.12 N	136.20 E
Kiirun → Chilung	100	25.08 N	121.44 E
Kii-sanchi ⋏	92	34.00 N	135.50 E
Kii-suidō ⊔	96	33.55 N	134.55 E
Kija ≃	86	56.52 N	86.39 E
Kijabe	154	0.56 S	36.34 E
Kijakty, ozero ⊜	86	50.00 N	69.15 E
Kijal	114	4.21 N	103.29 E
Kijaly	86	54.17 N	69.41 E
Kijasovo	80	56.21 N	53.07 E
Kijev (Kiev)	78	50.26 N	30.31 E
Kijevka, Kaz.	86	50.16 N	71.34 E
Kijevka, Ross.	80	46.05 N	42.57 E
Kijevka, Ross.	80	50.46 N	48.28 E
Kijevskoje	78	45.03 N	37.52 E
Kijevskoje vodochranilišče ⊜[1]	78	51.00 N	30.25 E
Kijima-chosuichi ⊜	96	35.04 N	132.44 E
Kijimadaira	94	36.51 N	138.24 E
Kijima-dam ◆[6]	96	35.05 N	132.44 E
Kijma	86	51.35 N	67.34 E
Kijoka	174m	26.42 N	128.09 E
Kikagati	154	1.02 S	30.40 E
Kikai-shima I	93b	28.19 N	129.59 E
Kikale	154	7.50 S	39.12 E
Kikati ≃	152	14.48 S	12.28 E
Kikenka ≃	265a	59.52 N	30.04 E
Kikerino	76	59.28 N	29.35 E
Kikerk Lake ⊜	176	67.20 N	113.20 W
Kikimi	273b	4.26 S	15.25 E
Kikimorka	80	58.10 N	49.27 E
Kikinda	38	45.50 N	20.28 E
Kikládhes (Cyclades) II	38	37.30 N	25.00 E
Kiklah	146	32.05 N	12.41 E
Kiknur	80	57.19 N	47.14 E
Kikombo, Zaïre	152	5.59 S	18.09 E
Kikombo, Zaïre	152	5.40 S	18.48 E
Kikongo	152	4.16 S	17.11 E
Kikori	164	7.25 S	144.15 E
Kikori ≃	164	7.10 S	144.05 E
Kikorze	54	53.39 N	15.01 E
Kiku ≃	94	34.39 N	138.04 E
Kikuchi	96	32.59 N	130.49 E
Kikuchi ≃	96	32.56 N	130.35 E
Kikugawa, Nihon	94	34.45 N	138.05 E
Kikugawa, Nihon	96	34.07 N	131.02 E
Kikuka	96	33.02 N	130.46 E
Kikuma	96	34.03 N	132.53 E
Kikune	268	35.10 N	139.40 E
Kikusui	96	32.58 N	130.36 E
Kikvidze, Ross.	80	50.53 N	42.46 E
Kikvidze, Ross.	80	50.44 N	43.03 E
Kikvorsberg ⋏	158	31.17 S	25.20 E
Kikwit	152	5.02 S	18.49 E
Kil	26	59.30 N	13.19 E
Kilaån ≃	40	58.44 N	17.01 E
Kilafors	26	61.14 N	16.34 E
Kila Kila	164	9.30 S	147.10 E
Kīlakkarai	122	9.14 N	78.47 E
Kilambé, Cerro ∧	236	13.34 N	85.42 W
Kilauea	229b	22.12 N	159.24 W
Kilauea Crater ±[6]	229d	19.25 N	155.17 W
Kilauea Point ≻	229b	22.14 N	159.24 W
Kilb	61	48.06 N	15.24 E
Kilbaha	48	52.33 N	9.52 W
Kilbarchan	46	55.50 N	4.33 W
Kılbasan	130	37.20 N	33.12 E
Kilbeggan	48	53.22 N	7.29 W
Kilbirnie	46	55.46 N	4.41 W
Kilbourne, Il., U.S.	219	40.09 N	90.01 W
Kilbourne, Oh., U.S.	214	40.20 N	82.58 W
Kilbrannan Sound ⊔	46	55.40 N	5.25 W
Kilbride	46	57.05 N	7.27 W
Kilbuck Mountains ⋏	180	60.50 N	159.45 W
Kilbuck Run ≃	279b	40.31 N	80.08 W
Kilcar	48	54.38 N	8.35 W
Kilchberg	58	47.19 N	8.33 E
Kilchis ≃	224	45.30 N	123.52 W
Kilchoan	46	56.42 N	6.06 W
Kilchreest	48	53.10 N	8.38 W
Kilchrenan	46	56.21 N	5.11 W
Kilchu	98	40.58 N	129.20 E
Kilcock	48	53.24 N	6.40 W
Kilcolgan	48	53.13 N	8.52 W
Kilconnell	48	53.20 N	8.25 W
Kilcoole	48	53.06 N	6.04 W
Kilcormac	48	53.10 N	7.43 W
Kilcoy	171a	26.57 S	152.33 E
Kilcreggan	46	55.59 N	4.50 W
Kilcullen	48	53.08 N	6.45 W
Kildare (Saint-Ambroise-de-Kildare), P.Q., Can.	206	46.05 N	73.32 W
Kildare, Ire.	48	53.10 N	6.55 W
Kildare □[6]	48	53.15 N	6.45 W
Kildare, Cape ≻	186	46.52 N	63.58 W
Kildeer	278	42.10 N	88.03 W
Kil'din, ostrov I	24	69.22 N	34.12 E
Kil'dinstroj	24	68.48 N	33.06 E
Kildonan, B.C., Can.	182	49.00 N	125.00 W
Kildonan, Scot., U.K.	46	58.10 N	3.51 W
Kildonan, Zimb.	154	17.21 S	30.37 E
Kildonan, Strath of V	46	58.09 N	3.51 W
Kildorrery	48	52.14 N	8.26 W
Kildrummy Castle ⊥	46	57.14 N	2.52 W
Kildurk	164	16.26 S	129.37 E
Kilemary	80	56.47 N	46.52 E
Kilembe, Ug.	154	0.12 N	30.00 E
Kilembe, Zaïre	152	5.42 S	19.55 E
Kilfenora	48	52.59 N	9.13 W
Kilfinnane	48	52.21 N	8.28 W
Kilgard	224	49.03 N	122.12 W
Kilgarvan	48	51.45 N	9.26 W
Kilgore, Oh., U.S.	214	40.28 N	81.00 W
Kilgore, Tx., U.S.	222	32.23 N	94.52 W
Kilham	44	54.04 N	0.23 W
Kili I	14	5.39 N	169.04 E
Kilian Island I	176	73.35 N	107.53 W
Kilibo	150	8.34 N	2.36 E
Kılıç	130	40.38 N	29.23 E
Kilifi	154	3.38 S	39.51 E
Kilija	78	45.27 N	29.16 E
Kilikollūr	122	8.54 N	76.39 E
Kilima	154	0.59 S	29.12 E
Kilimanjaro □[4]	154	3.45 S	37.45 E
Kilimanjaro ∧	154	3.04 S	37.22 E
Kilimanjaro Game Reserve ◆[4]	154	3.05 S	37.20 E
Kilimatinde	154	5.51 S	34.57 E
Kilimavony	157b	23.48 S	43.41 E
Kilimli	130	41.28 N	31.50 E
Kilindoni	154	7.55 S	39.39 E
Kilingi-Nõmme	76	58.09 N	24.58 E
Kilis	130	36.44 N	37.05 E
Kilkare Woods	282	37.38 N	121.55 W
Kilkee	48	52.41 N	9.38 W
Kilkeel	48	54.04 N	6.00 W
Kilkelly	48	53.53 N	8.51 W
Kilkenny (Cill Chainnigh)	48	52.39 N	7.15 W
Kilkenny □[6]	48	52.40 N	7.20 W
Kilkerrin	48	53.33 N	8.34 W
Kilkhampton	42	50.53 N	4.29 W
Kilkieran	48	53.19 N	9.43 W
Kilkieran Bay ⊂	48	53.15 N	9.45 W
Kilkís	38	41.00 N	22.53 E
Killadoon	48	53.42 N	9.56 W
Killadysert	48	52.41 N	9.06 W
Killala	48	54.13 N	9.13 W
Killala Bay ⊂	48	54.15 N	9.10 W
Killaloe	48	52.48 N	8.27 W
Killaloe Station	190	45.33 N	77.25 W
Killam	182	52.47 N	111.51 W
Killara	274a	33.46 S	151.09 E
Killarney, Austl.	166	28.20 S	152.18 E
Killarney, Mb., Can.	184	49.12 N	99.42 W
Killarney, On., Can.	190	45.58 N	81.31 W
Killarney, Ire.	48	52.03 N	9.30 W
Killarney, Lake ⊜	240b	25.03 N	77.27 W
Killarney, Lakes of ⊜	48	52.01 N	9.30 W
Killarney Heights	274a	33.46 S	151.13 E
Killarney Provincial Park ♠	190	46.05 N	81.30 W
Killashandra	48	54.00 N	7.32 W
Killavally	48	53.45 N	9.23 W
Killawog	210	42.24 N	76.01 W
Killbear Provincial Park ♠	212	45.21 N	80.12 W
Kill Buck, N.Y., U.S.	210	42.10 N	78.41 W
Killbuck, Oh., U.S.	214	40.29 N	81.59 W
Killbuck Creek ≃, Il., U.S.	216	42.10 N	89.06 W
Killbuck Creek ≃, In., U.S.	218	40.07 N	85.41 W
Killbuck Creek ≃, Oh., U.S.	214	40.20 N	81.57 W
Killdeer	198	47.22 N	102.45 W
Killean	46	55.39 N	5.40 W
Killearn	46	56.03 N	4.22 W
Killeen	222	31.07 N	97.43 W
Killen	194	34.51 N	87.32 W

Symbols in the index entries represent the broad categories identified in the key at the right. Symbols with superior numbers (⋏[1]) identify subcategories (see complete key on page I · 1).

Symbole im Register stellen die rechts im Schlüssel erklärten Kategorien dar. Symbole mit hochgestellten Ziffern (⋏[1]) bezeichnen Unterabteilungen einer Kategorie (vgl. vollständiger Schlüssel auf Seite I · 1).

Los símbolos incluidos en el texto del índice representan las grandes categorías identificadas con la clave a la derecha. Los símbolos con números en su parte superior (⋏[1]) identifican las subcategorías (véase la clave completa en la página I · 1).

Les symboles de l'index représentent les catégories indiquées dans la légende à droite. Les symboles suivis d'un indice (⋏[1]) représentent des sous-catégories (voir légende complète à la page I · 1).

Os símbolos incluídos no texto do índice representam as grandes categorias identificadas com a chave à direita. Os símbolos com números em sua parte superior (⋏[1]) identificam as subcategorias (veja-se a chave completa à página I · 1).

∧ Mountain	Berg	Montaña	Montagne	Montanha
⋏ Mountains	Gebirge	Montañas	Montagnes	Montanhas
)(Pass	Paß	Paso	Col	Passo
V Valley, Canyon	Tal, Cañon	Valle, Cañón	Vallée, Canyon	Vale, Canhão
≍ Plain	Ebene	Llano	Plaine	Planície
≻ Cape	Kap	Cabo	Cap	Cabo
I Island	Insel	Isla	Île	Ilha
II Islands	Inseln	Islas	Îles	Ilhas
± Other Topographic Features	Andere Topographische Objekte	Otros Elementos Topográficos	Autres données topographiques	Outros acidentes topográficos

ESPAÑOL | FRANÇAIS | PORTUGUÊS

Nombre / Nom / Nome	Página / Page	Lat.°′	Long.°′ W = Oeste / W = Ouest
Killenaule	48	52.34 N	7.40 W
Killeter	48	54.40 N	7.41 W
Kılıdağ ∧	130	40.21 N	42.10 E
Killik ≃	180	69.00 N	153.58 W
Killilan	46	57.19 N	5.25 W
Killimor	48	53.10 N	8.17 W
Killin	46	56.28 N	4.19 W
Killington Peak ∧	188	43.36 N	72.49 W
Killingworth	207	41.21 N	72.33 W
Killíni	38	37.55 N	21.09 E
Killíni ∧	38	37.57 N	22.23 E
Killiniq Island I	176	60.24 N	64.40 W
Killinkoski	26	62.24 N	23.52 E
Killorglin	48	52.06 N	9.47 W
Killough	48	54.16 N	5.39 W
Killpecker Creek ≃	202	41.35 N	109.14 W
Killucan	48	53.31 N	7.07 W
Kill Van Kull ⊻	276	40.39 N	74.05 W
Killybegs	48	54.38 N	8.27 W
Killyleagh	48	54.24 N	5.39 W
Kilmacolm	46	55.54 N	4.38 W
Kilmacthomas	48	52.12 N	7.25 W
Kilmaine	48	53.34 N	9.09 W
Kilmallock	48	52.23 N	8.34 W
Kilmaluag	46	57.41 N	6.17 W
Kilmarnock, Scot., U.K.	46	55.36 N	4.30 W
Kilmarnock, Va., U.S.	208	37.42 N	76.22 W
Kilmartin	46	56.07 N	5.29 W
Kilmar Tor ∧ [2]	42	50.33 N	4.28 W
Kilmaurs	46	55.39 N	4.32 W
Kilmelford	46	56.16 N	5.29 W
Kil'mez', Ross.	80	56.57 N	51.04 E
Kil'mez', Ross.	80	57.04 N	51.21 E
Kil'mez' ≃	80	56.58 N	50.28 E
Kilmichael	194	33.26 N	89.34 W
Kilmichael Point >	48	52.44 N	6.10 W
Kilmore	169	37.18 S	144.57 E
Kilmore Creek ≃	216	40.20 N	86.38 W
Kilmory	46	57.03 N	6.22 W
Kilnaleck	48	53.52 N	7.19 W
Kilninver	46	56.20 N	5.31 W
Kilo	115b	8.21 S	118.24 E
Kilokri ◆ [8]	272a	28.35 N	77.16 E
Kiloli	154	6.50 S	33.23 E
Kilombero ≃	154	8.31 S	37.22 E
Kilomines	154	1.48 N	30.14 E
Kilondo	154	9.46 S	34.21 E
Kilosa	154	6.50 S	36.59 E
Kilpisjärvi	24	69.03 N	20.48 E
Kilrea	48	54.58 N	6.35 W
Kilrenny	46	56.14 N	2.41 W
Kilrush	48	52.39 N	9.30 W
Kilsbergen ⋏ [2]	40	59.20 N	14.47 E
Kilsmo	40	59.04 N	15.31 E
Kilsyth, Austl.	274b	37.48 S	145.19 E
Kilsyth, Scot., U.K.	46	55.59 N	4.04 W
Kiltealy	48	52.34 N	6.45 W
Kiltimagh	48	53.51 N	9.01 W
Kiltoom	48	53.28 N	8.01 W
Kilttān Island I	122	11.29 N	73.00 E
Kiltu-ri	98	34.35 N	127.20 E
Kilwa	154	9.18 S	28.25 E
Kilwa Island I	154	9.20 S	28.33 E
Kilwa Kivinje	154	8.45 S	39.24 E
Kilwa Masoko	154	8.56 S	39.31 E
Kilwinning	44	55.40 N	4.42 W
Kim	198	37.14 N	103.21 W
Kim ≃	152	5.28 N	11.07 E
Kima	154	1.26 S	26.43 E
Kimaam	164	7.58 S	138.53 E
Kimamba	154	6.47 S	37.08 E
Kimande	154	7.22 S	35.30 E
Kīmān Fāris (Crocodilopolis) (Arsinoe) ⊥	142	29.19 N	30.50 E
Kimba	166	33.09 S	136.25 E
Kimball, Mn., U.S.	190	45.19 N	94.18 W
Kimball, Ne., U.S.	198	41.14 N	103.39 W
Kimball, S.D., U.S.	198	43.44 N	98.57 W
Kimball, Mount ∧	180	63.14 N	144.39 W
Kimbanda	152	4.07 S	17.59 E
Kimbe	164	5.31 S	150.10 E
Kimbe Bay C	164	5.30 S	150.30 E
Kimberley, B.C., Can.	182	49.41 N	115.59 W
Kimberley, S. Afr.	158	28.43 S	24.46 E
Kimberley, Eng., U.K.	44	52.59 N	1.16 W
Kimberley Downs	162	17.24 S	124.22 E
Kimberley Plateau ⋏ [1]	160	17.00 S	127.00 E
Kimberling City	194	36.38 N	93.28 W
Kimberly, Id., U.S.	202	42.32 N	114.21 W
Kimberly, Wi., U.S.	190	44.16 N	88.20 W
Kimberton	208	40.08 N	75.34 W
Kimbolton, N.Z.	172	40.03 S	175.47 E
Kimbolton, Eng., U.K.	42	52.18 N	0.24 W
Kimbolton, Oh., U.S.	214	40.09 N	81.34 W
Kimbongo	152	6.08 S	18.01 E
Kimbwala	273b	4.22 S	15.12 E
Kimch'aek (Sŏngjin)	98	40.41 N	129.12 E
Kimch'ŏn	98	36.07 N	128.05 E
Kimerka ≃	82	56.52 N	37.22 E
Kimhae	98	35.14 N	128.52 E
Kimhwa	98	38.26 N	127.36 E
Kími	38	38.37 N	24.06 E
Kimil'tej	88	54.08 N	101.59 E
Kimito (Kemiö)	26	60.10 N	22.45 E
Kimito I	26	60.07 N	22.40 E
Kimi-tōge ∧ [2]	270	34.43 N	135.06 E
Kimi-tōge)(	96	34.23 N	135.37 E
Kimitsu	94	35.20 N	139.54 E
Kimiwan Lake ⊜	182	55.45 N	116.54 W
Kimje	98	35.48 N	126.52 E
Kim Kim ≃	271c	1.26 N	103.58 E
Kimmell	216	41.23 N	85.32 W
Kim-me-ni-oli Wash V	200	36.07 N	108.11 W
Kímolos I	38	36.48 N	24.34 E
Kimongo	152	4.29 S	12.58 E
Kimovsk	76	53.58 N	38.32 E
Kimpangu	152	5.51 S	15.01 E
Kim Plan	279b	40.20 N	79.44 W
Kimp'o	271b	37.37 N	126.43 E
Kimp'o Airport ⊠	271b	37.33 N	126.48 E
Kimpombo	273b	4.17 S	15.10 E
Kimpō-zan ∧	94	35.53 N	138.38 E
Kimry	82	56.52 N	37.21 E
Kimsquit	182	52.49 N	126.58 W
Kimstad	40	58.32 N	15.58 E
Kimu ≃	268	35.56 N	139.57 E
Kimuenza	273b	4.27 S	15.17 E
Kimvula	152	5.44 S	15.58 E
Kimwanga	154	7.08 S	28.42 E
Kin	174m	26.26 N	127.55 E
Kinabalian, Mount ∧	116	8.14 N	125.25 E
Kinabalu, Gunong ∧	112	6.05 N	116.33 E
Kinabalu National Park ♠	112	6.05 N	116.33 E
Kinabatangan ≃	112	5.42 N	118.23 E
Kınalı ◆ [8]	267b	40.55 N	29.03 E
Kınalı Ada I	267b	40.55 N	29.03 E
Kinangaly ∧	157b	19.12 S	45.40 E
Kinango	154	4.08 S	39.19 E
Kinapusan Island I	116	5.13 N	120.40 E
Kinara	164	2.16 S	132.44 E
Kinasa	94	36.42 N	138.01 E
Kinaūni	272a	28.39 N	77.23 E
Kinbasket Lake ⊜ [1]	182	51.58 N	118.03 W
Kinbrace	46	58.15 N	3.56 W
Kinbuck	46	56.13 N	3.57 W
Kincaid, Sk., Can.	184	49.39 N	107.00 W
Kincaid, Il., U.S.	219	39.35 N	89.24 W
Kincardine, On., Can.	190	44.11 N	81.38 W
Kincardine, Scot., U.K.	46	56.04 N	3.44 W
Kinchafoonee Creek ≃	192	31.38 N	84.10 W
Kinchang	110	26.32 N	98.02 E
Kinchara	272b	22.53 N	88.32 E
Kinchega National Park ♠	166	32.30 S	142.20 E
Kincheloe Air Force Base ■	190	46.15 N	84.28 W
Kincolith	182	55.00 N	129.57 W
Kincraig	46	57.08 N	3.55 W
Kinda, Zaïre	152	4.47 S	21.48 E
Kinda, Zaïre	154	9.18 S	25.04 E
Kindadal	112	1.35 S	123.11 E
Kindanba	152	3.44 S	14.31 E
Kindarun Mountain ∧	170	32.49 S	150.41 E
Kindberg	61	47.31 N	15.27 E
Kinde	190	43.56 N	82.59 W
Kindeje	152	7.07 S	13.44 E
Kindel'a	80	51.36 N	52.58 E
Kindel'a ≃	80	51.30 N	52.45 E
Kindelbrück	54	51.16 N	11.05 E
Kindele	152	8.39 S	24.11 E
Kinder	194	30.29 N	92.51 W
Kinderhook, Il., U.S.	219	39.42 N	91.09 W
Kinderhook, Mi., U.S.	216	41.48 N	85.00 W
Kinderhook, N.Y., U.S.	210	42.23 N	73.41 W
Kinderhook Creek ≃	210	42.19 N	73.45 W
Kinder Reservoir ⊜ [1]	262	53.23 N	1.55 W
Kinder Scout ∧	44	53.23 N	1.52 W
Kindersley	184	51.27 N	109.10 W
Kindia	150	10.04 N	12.51 W
Kindikan	88	56.02 N	115.15 E
Kinding	60	49.00 N	11.23 E
Kindley Field ⊠	240a	32.22 N	64.40 W
Kindred	198	46.38 N	97.01 W
Kindu	154	2.57 S	25.56 E
Kindykty, ozero ⊜	86	51.15 N	62.14 E
Kinel'	80	53.14 N	50.39 E
Kinel'-Čerkasy	80	53.29 N	51.29 E
Kinel'skije jary ⋏ [1]	80	53.42 N	52.00 E
Kineo, Mount ∧	188	45.42 N	69.44 W
Kinesi	154	1.28 S	33.52 E
Kinešma	80	57.26 N	42.09 E
Kineton	42	52.10 N	1.30 W
Kinfauns	46	56.22 N	3.21 W
King	192	36.16 N	80.21 W
King □ [6]	224	47.26 N	121.48 W
King ≃, Austl.	164	14.41 S	131.59 E
King ≃, Austl.	169	36.41 S	146.25 E
King, Lake ⊜	162	25.38 S	120.06 E
King, Mont ∧	212	45.29 N	75.52 W
King, Mount ∧	166	25.10 S	147.31 E
Kingabwa ◆ [8]	273b	4.19 S	15.20 E
King and Queen □ [6]	208	37.42 N	76.50 W
King and Queen Court House	208	37.40 N	76.52 W
Kingaroy	166	26.33 S	151.50 E
Kingarth	46	55.46 N	5.03 W
King City, On., Can.	212	43.56 N	79.32 W
King City, Ca., U.S.	226	36.12 N	121.07 W
King City, Mo., U.S.	194	40.03 N	94.31 W
King Cove	180	55.04 N	162.19 W
Kingdom City	219	38.58 N	91.56 W
King Edward ≃	164	14.14 S	126.35 E
Kingersheim	58	47.48 N	7.20 E
King Ferry	210	42.39 N	76.37 W
Kingfield	188	44.57 N	70.09 W
Kingfisher	196	35.51 N	97.55 W
King George	208	38.16 N	77.11 W
King George □ [6]	208	38.15 N	77.10 W
King George, Mount ∧	182	50.35 N	115.24 W
King George Bay C	254	51.33 S	60.37 W
King George Island I	9	62.00 S	58.15 W
King George Islands II	176	57.20 N	78.25 W
King George's Dock ◆ [5]	272b	22.32 N	88.18 E
King George Sound ⊻	162	35.03 S	117.57 E
King George's Reservoir ⊜ [1]	260	51.39 N	0.01 W
King Hill	202	43.00 N	115.12 W
Kinghorn	46	56.04 N	3.10 W
Kingie ≃	46	57.04 N	5.08 W
Kingisepp	76	59.22 N	28.36 E
King Island I, Austl.	166	39.50 S	144.00 E
King Island I, B.C., Can.	182	52.12 N	127.42 W
King Island I, Ak., U.S.	180	64.58 N	168.05 W
Kinglake National Park ♠	169	37.35 S	145.25 E
King Lear Peak ∧	204	41.12 N	118.34 W
King Leopold Ranges ⋏	160	17.30 S	125.45 E
Kingman, Az., U.S.	200	35.11 N	114.03 W
Kingman, Ks., U.S.	198	37.38 N	98.06 W
Kingman Reef ✦ [2]	14	6.24 N	162.22 W
King Mountain ∧, B.C., Can.	180	58.17 N	128.54 W
King Mountain ∧, Ok., U.S.	196	34.52 N	99.17 W
King Mountain ∧, Or., U.S.	202	42.42 N	123.14 W
King Mountain ∧, Or., U.S.	202	43.49 N	118.52 W
King of Prussia	208	40.05 N	75.23 W
King of Prussia Plaza ◆ [9]	285	40.05 N	75.25 W
Kingoma	152	5.11 S	13.34 E
Kingoma-Ngoma	152	5.50 S	16.49 E
Kingombe, Zaïre	154	3.56 S	26.35 E
Kingombe, Zaïre	154	7.24 S	26.11 E
Kingoonya	162	30.54 S	135.18 E
Kingoué	152	3.43 S	14.09 E
King Peak ∧	204	40.10 N	124.08 W
Kingri	120	30.27 N	69.49 E
Kings, Il., U.S.	216	42.00 N	89.06 W
Kings, Ms., U.S.	194	32.23 N	90.51 W
Kings □ [6], Ca., U.S.	226	36.20 N	119.39 W
Kings □ [6], N.Y., U.S.	210	40.42 N	74.00 W
Kings ≃, Ar., U.S.	194	36.29 N	93.35 W
Kings ≃, Ca., U.S.	226	36.03 N	119.49 W
Kings ≃, Nv., U.S.	204	41.31 N	118.08 W
Kings, Middle Fork ≃	204	36.50 N	118.52 W
Kings, North Fork ≃, Ca., U.S.	204	36.52 N	119.08 W
Kings, North Fork ≃, Ca., U.S.	226	36.18 N	119.52 W
Kings, South Fork ≃	226	36.18 N	119.52 W
King Salmon	180	58.41 N	156.39 W
King Salmon ≃	180	58.15 N	157.30 W
Kingsbarns	46	56.18 N	2.39 W
Kings Beach	226	39.14 N	120.01 W
Kingsbridge	42	50.17 N	3.46 W
Kingsburg	226	36.30 N	119.33 W
Kingsbury, Eng., U.K.	42	52.35 N	1.40 W
Kingsbury, In., U.S.	216	41.31 N	86.42 W
Kingsbury ◆ [8]	260	51.35 N	0.17 W
Kings Canyon National Park ♠	204	36.48 N	118.30 W
Kingsclere	42	51.20 N	1.14 W
Kingscote	168b	35.40 S	137.38 E
Kingscourt	48	53.53 N	6.48 W
Kings Creek	218	40.10 N	83.44 W
Kings Creek ≃, Austl.	171a	27.57 S	151.42 E
Kings Creek ≃, Tx., U.S.	222	32.25 N	96.15 W
King's Cross Station ◆ [5]	260	51.32 N	0.07 W
Kings Dominion ♠	208	37.51 N	77.27 W
Kingsdown, Eng., U.K.	42	51.11 N	1.25 E
Kingsdown, Eng., U.K.	260	51.21 N	0.17 E
Kings Falls ∟	212	43.55 N	75.38 W
Kingsford, Austl.	274a	33.56 S	151.14 E
Kingsford, Mi., U.S.	190	45.47 N	88.04 W
Kingsford Heights	216	41.29 N	86.42 W
Kingsford Smith Airport ⊠	170	33.57 S	151.11 E
Kingsgate	182	49.00 N	116.11 W
Kingsgrove	274a	33.57 S	151.06 E
Kingshill	241n	17.44 N	64.48 W
Kingshouse	46	56.21 N	4.19 W
Kings Island ♠	218	39.21 N	84.16 W
Kingskerswell	42	50.30 N	3.33 W
Kingsland, Eng., U.K.	42	52.15 N	2.47 W
Kingsland, Ar., U.S.	194	33.51 N	92.17 W
Kingsland, Ga., U.S.	192	30.47 N	81.41 W
Kingsland, Tx., U.S.	196	30.40 N	98.26 W
Kingsland, Va., U.S.	208	37.24 N	77.26 W
Kings Langley	42	51.43 N	0.28 W
Kingsley, S. Afr.	158	27.55 S	30.33 E
Kingsley, Eng., U.K.	42	53.01 N	1.59 W
Kingsley, Eng., U.K.	262	53.16 N	2.40 W
Kingsley, Ia., U.S.	198	42.35 N	95.58 W
Kingsley, Mi., U.S.	190	44.35 N	85.32 W
Kingsley, Pa., U.S.	210	41.46 N	75.45 W
Kingsley Dam ◆ [6]	198	41.11 N	101.39 W
King's Lynn	42	52.45 N	0.24 E
Kings Manor	285	40.05 N	75.21 W
Kingsmere Lake ⊜	184	54.06 N	106.27 W
Kings Mills	218	39.21 N	84.14 W
Kings Mountain	192	35.14 N	81.20 W
Kings Mountain National Military Park ♠	192	35.07 N	81.33 W
King Solomon's Mines → Mikhrot Shelomo Hamelekh ⊥	132	29.45 N	34.56 E
King Sound ⊻	162	17.00 S	123.30 E
Kings Park, N.Y., U.S.	210	40.53 N	73.16 W
Kings Park, Va., U.S.	284c	38.48 N	77.14 W
Kings Park ♠	168a	31.57 S	115.49 E
Kings Peak ∧	200	40.46 N	110.22 W
Kings Plaza ◆ [9]	276	40.37 N	73.55 W
King's Point, Nf., Can.	186	49.35 N	56.11 W
Kings Point, N.Y., U.S.	210	40.49 N	73.44 W
Kingsport	192	36.32 N	82.33 W
King's Sutton	42	52.01 N	1.16 W
Kingsteignton	42	50.33 N	3.35 W
King Sterndale	262	53.15 N	1.52 W
Kingsthorpe	171a	27.29 S	151.49 E
Kingston, Austl.	171a	27.40 S	153.07 E
Kingston, N.S., Can.	186	44.59 N	64.57 W
Kingston, On., Can.	212	44.14 N	76.30 W
Kingston, Jam.	241q	18.00 N	76.48 W
Kingston, N.Z.	172	45.20 S	168.42 E
Kingston, Norf. I.	174c	29.03 S	167.58 E
Kingston, Eng., U.K.	28	51.25 N	0.19 W
Kingston, Ga., U.S.	192	34.14 N	84.56 W
Kingston, Il., U.S.	216	42.06 N	88.46 W
Kingston, Ma., U.S.	207	41.59 N	70.43 W
Kingston, Mo., U.S.	194	39.38 N	94.02 W
Kingston, N.J., U.S.	276	40.22 N	74.36 W
Kingston, N.Y., U.S.	210	41.55 N	73.59 W
Kingston, Oh., U.S.	218	39.28 N	82.54 W
Kingston, Ok., U.S.	196	33.59 N	96.43 W
Kingston, Pa., U.S.	210	41.15 N	75.53 W
Kingston, R.I., U.S.	207	41.29 N	71.31 W
Kingston, Tn., U.S.	192	35.52 N	84.30 W
Kingston, Wa., U.S.	224	47.48 N	122.30 W
Kingston ◆ [8]	42	51.25 N	0.19 W
Kingston Bay C	283	42.00 N	70.42 W
Kingston Mills	212	44.17 N	76.27 W
Kingston Southeast	166	36.50 S	139.51 E
Kingston upon Hull	44	53.45 N	0.20 W
Kingston upon Thames ◆ [8]	260	51.25 N	0.19 W
Kingstown	241h	13.09 N	61.14 W
Kingstown → Dún Laoghaire	48	53.17 N	6.08 W
Kingstree	192	33.40 N	79.49 W
Kingsville, Austl.	274b	37.49 S	144.52 E
Kingsville, On., Can.	214	42.02 N	82.45 W
Kingsville, Md., U.S.	284b	39.26 N	76.25 W
Kingsville, Oh., U.S.	214	41.53 N	80.41 W
Kingsville, Tx., U.S.	196	27.30 N	97.51 W
Kingsville Naval Air Station ■	196	27.31 N	97.47 W
Kingswear	42	50.21 N	3.34 W
Kingswinford	42	52.29 N	2.10 W
Kingswood, Austl.	274a	33.46 S	150.43 E
Kingswood, S. Afr.	158	27.29 S	25.46 E
Kingswood, Eng., U.K.	42	51.27 N	2.22 W
Kingswood, Eng., U.K.	260	51.17 N	0.13 W
Kingswood Park	285	40.07 N	74.51 W
King's Worthy	42	51.06 N	1.18 W
Kingtechen → Jingdezhen	100	29.16 N	117.11 E
Kington	42	52.12 N	3.01 W
Kingunda	152	6.34 S	16.58 E
Kingungi	152	5.24 S	17.56 E
Kingussie	46	57.05 N	4.03 W
King William	208	37.41 N	77.00 W
King William □ [6]	208	37.42 N	77.05 W
King William Island I	176	69.00 N	97.30 W
King William's Town	158	32.51 S	27.22 E
Kingwood, Tx., U.S.	222	29.54 N	95.18 W
Kingwood, W.V., U.S.	188	39.28 N	79.41 W
Kinh Duc	110	11.49 N	107.58 E
Kinhwa → Jinhua	100	29.07 N	119.39 E
Kınık	130	39.05 N	27.23 E
Kinira ≃	158	31.12 S	29.17 E
Kinistino	184	52.57 N	105.00 W
Kinjar Khās	123	29.55 N	70.58 E
Kinkala	152	4.22 S	14.46 E
Kinker Creek ≃	282	38.02 N	121.52 W
Kinkony, Lac ⊜	157b	16.08 S	45.50 E
Kinkora	285	40.07 N	74.45 W
Kinleith	172	38.16 S	175.54 E
Kinloch	46	57.01 N	6.17 W
Kinlochbervie	46	58.28 N	5.03 W
Kinlocheil	46	56.51 N	5.20 W
Kinlochewe	46	57.36 N	5.20 W
Kinloch Hourn	46	57.06 N	5.22 W
Kinlochleven	46	56.42 N	4.58 W
Kinloch Rannoch	46	56.42 N	4.11 W
Kinloss	46	57.37 N	3.34 W
Kinmount	212	44.47 N	78.39 W
Kinmundy	219	38.46 N	88.50 W
Kinn	26	61.36 N	4.45 E
Kinna	26	57.30 N	12.41 E
Kinnaird	182	49.17 N	117.39 W
Kinnaird Head >	46	57.42 N	2.00 W
Kinnegad	48	53.26 N	7.05 W
Kinnekulle ∧ [2]	26	58.35 N	13.23 E
Kinnelon	210	40.59 N	74.23 W
Kinnel Water ≃	44	55.08 N	3.25 W
Kinneret	132	32.43 N	35.33 E
Kinneret, Yam (Sea of Galilee) ⊜	132	32.48 N	35.35 E
Kinneret-Negev Conduit ≅ [1]	132	32.52 N	35.32 E
Kinnerley	42	52.47 N	2.59 W
Kinniconick Creek ≃	218	38.37 N	83.09 W
Kinnula	26	63.22 N	24.58 E
Kino ≃	96	34.13 N	135.09 E
Kinoe	96	34.14 N	132.55 E
Kinogitan	116	9.00 N	124.48 E
Kinojévis ≃	190	48.23 N	78.21 W
Kinomoto	94	35.30 N	136.13 E
Kinonge ≃	206	45.39 N	74.55 W
Kinoni	154	0.39 S	30.27 E
Kinosaki	96	35.37 N	134.49 E
Kinpoku-san ∧	92	38.05 N	138.22 E
Kinrola	166	23.46 S	148.45 E
Kinross, S. Afr.	158	26.22 S	29.03 E
Kinross, Scot., U.K.	46	56.13 N	3.27 W
Kin-saki >	174m	26.26 N	127.57 E
Kinsale, Ire.	48	51.42 N	8.32 W
Kinsale, Va., U.S.	208	38.01 N	76.34 W
Kinsale, Old Head of >	48	51.36 N	8.32 W
Kinsale Harbour C	48	51.41 N	8.30 W
Kinsarvik	26	60.23 N	6.43 E
Kinschasa → Kinshasa	152	4.18 S	15.18 E
Kinshasa (Léopoldville), Zaïre	152	4.18 S	15.18 E
Kinshasa (Léopoldville), Zaïre	273b	4.18 S	15.18 E
Kinshasa □ [4]	152	4.18 S	15.18 E
Kinshasa (Ndolo) Airport ⊠, Zaïre	273b	4.20 S	15.19 E
Kinshasa (Ndjili) Airport ⊠, Zaïre	273b	4.23 S	15.27 E
Kinshasa-Est ◆ [8]	273b	4.18 S	15.18 E
Kinshasa-Ouest ◆ [8]	273b	4.20 S	15.15 E
Kinsley	198	37.55 N	99.24 W
Kinsman, Il., U.S.	216	41.11 N	88.34 W
Kinsman, Oh., U.S.	214	41.27 N	80.36 W
Kinston, Al., U.S.	194	31.12 N	86.10 W
Kinston, N.C., U.S.	192	35.15 N	77.34 W
Kintamani	115b	8.14 S	115.19 E
Kintamo, Rapides de ∟	273b	4.19 S	15.15 E
Kintampo	150	8.03 N	1.43 W
Kintap	112	3.51 S	115.13 E
Kintari, Mont ∧ [2]	273b	4.08 S	15.23 E
Kintélé	273b	4.09 S	15.21 E
Kintinian	150	11.36 N	9.23 W
Kintinku	154	5.53 S	35.14 E
Kintobongo-Bunge	154	8.54 S	26.23 E
Kintore	46	57.13 N	2.21 W
Kintore, Mount ∧	162	26.34 S	130.30 E
Kintore Range ⋏	162	23.25 S	129.20 E
Kintsana	273b	4.19 S	15.10 E
Kintus	86	60.09 N	71.25 E
Kintyre > [1]	46	55.32 N	5.35 W
Kintyre, Mull of >	46	55.17 N	5.55 W
Kinu ≃	94	35.56 N	139.57 E
Kinuseo Falls ∟	182	54.47 N	121.12 W
Kinuso	182	55.20 N	115.25 W
Kinvarra	48	53.08 N	8.55 W
Kinver	42	52.27 N	2.14 W
Kin-wan C	174m	26.25 N	127.54 E
Kinwood	222	29.56 N	95.23 W
Kinyangiri	154	4.27 S	34.37 E
Kinyeti ∧	154	3.57 N	32.54 E
Kinzia	152	3.36 S	18.26 E
Kinzig ≃, Dtsch.	56	50.08 N	8.54 E
Kinzig ≃, Dtsch.	58	48.37 N	7.49 E
Kinzua	202	44.59 N	120.03 W
Kinzua Creek ≃	214	41.47 N	78.50 W
Kinzua Dam ◆ [6]	214	41.50 N	79.01 W
Kioga-See → Kyoga, Lake ⊜	154	1.30 N	33.00 E
Kioshkokwi Lake ⊜	190	46.05 N	78.52 W
Kioto → Kyōto	94	35.00 N	135.45 E
Kiowa, Co., U.S.	198	39.20 N	104.27 W
Kiowa, Ks., U.S.	198	37.01 N	98.29 W
Kiowa, Ok., U.S.	196	34.43 N	95.53 W
Kiowa Creek ≃, U.S.	196	36.46 N	99.55 W
Kiowa Creek ≃, Co., U.S.	198	40.20 N	104.05 W
Kipahigan Lake ⊜	184	55.20 N	101.55 W
Kipandi	152	5.19 S	16.46 E
Kipanga	154	6.14 S	35.21 E
Kiparissía	38	37.14 N	21.40 E
Kiparissiakós Kólpos C	38	37.37 N	21.24 E
Kipatimu	154	8.29 S	38.56 E
Kipawa ≃	190	47.03 N	79.23 W
Kipawa, Lac ⊜	190	46.55 N	79.00 W
Kipawa, Réserve ♠	190	47.15 N	78.15 W
Kipembawe	154	7.39 S	33.24 E
Kipengere Range ⋏	154	9.10 S	34.15 E
Kiperčeny	78	47.32 N	28.50 E
Kipijevo	24	65.40 N	54.30 E
Kipili	154	7.26 S	30.36 E
Kipini	154	2.32 S	40.31 E
Kipling	184	50.10 N	102.38 W
Kipnuk	180	59.56 N	164.03 W
Kippax	44	53.46 N	1.22 W
Kippen	46	56.08 N	4.11 W
Kippenheim	58	48.17 N	7.49 E
Kippure ∧	48	53.10 N	6.18 W
Kípros → Cyprus □ [1]	130	35.00 N	33.00 E
Kipsdorf	54	50.47 N	13.32 E
Kipton	214	41.16 N	82.18 W
Kipushi	154	11.46 S	27.14 E
Kipushia, Zaïre	154	6.10 S	25.12 E
Kipushia, Zaïre	154	12.58 S	29.30 E
Kira, Nihon	94	34.49 N	137.05 E
Kir'a, Ross.	80	55.04 N	46.53 E
Kirakira	175e	10.27 S	161.55 E
Kirandul	122	18.40 N	81.16 E
Kirane	150	15.25 N	10.14 W
Kiranlık	130	39.07 N	41.41 E
Kiranomena	157b	18.17 S	46.03 E
Kīratpur	124	29.31 N	78.12 E
Kiraz	130	38.13 N	28.13 E
Kirazlı	130	40.02 N	26.41 E
Kırbaçbayırı ∧	267b	40.56 N	29.10 E
Kırbaşı	130	40.01 N	31.50 E
Kirbla	76	58.44 N	23.57 E
Kirby Muxloe	42	52.38 N	1.13 W
Kirbys Creek ≃	208	36.28 N	77.06 W
Kirbyville	194	30.39 N	93.53 W
Kırçal	130	41.39 N	35.16 E
Kırcasalih	130	41.23 N	26.48 E
Kirchardt	56	49.12 N	8.59 E
Kirchbach in Steiermark	61	46.54 N	15.44 E
Kirchberg, Dtsch.	54	50.37 N	12.32 E
Kirchberg, Dtsch.	56	49.12 N	9.58 E
Kirchberg, Dtsch.	56	49.56 N	7.24 E
Kirchberg, Dtsch.	60	48.54 N	13.11 E
Kirchberg, Schw.	58	47.05 N	7.35 E
Kirchberg, Schw.	58	47.25 N	9.03 E
Kirch-Berg ∧ [2]	264a	52.27 N	13.02 E
Kirchberg am Wagram	61	48.26 N	15.53 E
Kirchberg an der Pielach	61	48.02 N	15.26 E
Kirchberg in Tirol	64	47.27 N	12.19 E
Kirchbichl	64	47.31 N	12.05 E
Kirchderne ◆ [8]	263	51.33 N	7.30 E
Kirchdorf, Dtsch.	52	52.36 N	8.49 E
Kirchdorf, Dtsch.	54	54.00 N	11.26 E
Kirchdorf an der Krems	61	47.56 N	14.07 E
Kirchdorf im Wald	60	48.55 N	13.16 E
Kirchen	56	50.48 N	7.53 E
Kirchende	263	51.25 N	7.26 E
Kirchenlaibach	60	49.53 N	11.46 E
Kirchenlamitz	54	50.09 N	11.56 E
Kirchenthumbach	60	49.45 N	11.43 E
Kirchhain	56	50.49 N	8.55 E
Kirchham	60	48.21 N	13.16 E
Kirchheiligen	54	51.11 N	10.42 E
Kirchheimbolanden	56	49.40 N	8.00 E
Kirchheim in Schwaben	58	48.10 N	10.30 E
Kirchheim unter Teck	56	48.39 N	9.27 E
Kirchhellen	52	51.36 N	6.55 E
Kirchhellen Heide ◆ [3]	263	51.36 N	6.53 E
Kirchhofen	264a	52.22 N	13.53 E
Kirchhörde ◆ [8]	263	51.27 N	7.27 E
Kirchhundem	56	51.05 N	8.05 E
Kirchlengern	52	52.12 N	8.35 E
Kirchlinde ◆ [8]	263	51.32 N	7.22 E
Kirchlinteln	52	52.56 N	9.19 E
Kirchmöser	54	52.22 N	12.25 E
Kirchroth	60	48.57 N	12.33 E
Kirchschlag in der Buckligen Welt	61	47.31 N	16.18 E
Kirchveischede	56	51.05 N	7.59 E
Kirchwalsede	52	53.01 N	9.23 E
Kirchwerder ◆ [8]	52	53.25 N	10.11 E
Kirchzarten	58	47.58 N	7.56 E
Kircubbin	48	54.29 N	5.32 W
Kirda	85	41.06 N	69.00 E
Kirdāsah	142	30.02 N	31.07 E
Kireç	130	39.33 N	28.22 E
Kirej ≃	88	54.12 N	100.40 E
Kirejevo	80	50.01 N	44.29 E
Kirejevsk	76	53.56 N	37.56 E
Kirejkovo	76	53.38 N	35.49 E
Kirenga ≃	88	57.47 N	108.07 E
Kirensk	88	57.46 N	108.08 E
Kirghizia → Kyrgyzstan □ [1]	72	41.30 N	75.00 E
Kirgili	85	40.24 N	71.43 E
Kirgizija → Kyrgyzstan □ [1]	72	41.30 N	75.00 E
Kirgiziya → Kyrgyzstan □ [1]	72	41.30 N	75.00 E
Kirgiz-Mijaki	86	53.38 N	54.47 E
Kirgizskij chrebet ⋏	85	42.30 N	74.00 E
Kiri	152	1.27 S	19.00 E
Kiribati □ [1]	14	5.00 S	170.00 W
Kiribati II	14	0.30 S	174.00 E
Kiries West	158	26.34 S	19.00 E
Kiriga-mine ∧	94	36.06 N	138.12 E
Kırıkhan, Tür.	130	39.32 N	41.20 E
Kırıkhan, Tür.	130	36.32 N	36.19 E
Kirikiri Prisons ⊍	273a	6.27 N	3.19 E
Kırıkkale	130	39.50 N	33.31 E
Kirikovka	78	50.22 N	35.07 E
Kirillov	76	59.52 N	38.23 E
Kirillovka	265b	55.57 N	37.20 E
Kirillovo, Ross.	80	57.07 N	45.27 E
Kirillovo, Ross.	80	53.47 N	42.40 E
Kirillovskoje	76	60.28 N	29.17 E
Kirin → Jilin	89	43.51 N	126.33 E
Kirin → Jilin □ [4]	90	44.00 N	126.00 E
Kirinyaga (Mount Kenya) ∧	154	0.10 S	37.20 E
Kirishima-Yaku-kokuritsu-kōen ♠	92	31.55 N	130.51 E
Kirishima-yama ∧	92	31.56 N	130.52 E
Kiriši	76	59.27 N	32.02 E
Kiritimati (Christmas Island) I [1]	174o	1.52 N	157.20 W
Kiriwina Island I	164	8.35 S	151.05 E
Kiriwina Islands II	164	8.35 S	151.05 E
Kirizume-tōge ∧ [2]	270	34.56 N	135.16 E
Kirjanovskaja Kontora	88	58.18 N	104.13 E
Kırka	130	39.17 N	30.33 E
Kirkabister	46a	60.07 N	1.08 W
Kırkağaç	130	39.06 N	27.40 E
Kirkbride	44	54.54 N	3.12 W
Kirkburton	44	53.37 N	1.42 W
Kirkby ◆ [8]	44	53.29 N	2.54 W
Kirkby in Ashfield	44	53.06 N	1.15 W
Kirkby Lonsdale	44	54.13 N	2.36 W
Kirkby Malzeard	44	54.11 N	1.38 W
Kirkbymoorside	44	54.16 N	0.55 W
Kirkby Stephen	44	54.28 N	2.20 W
Kirkcaldy	46	56.07 N	3.10 W
Kirkcolm	44	54.58 N	5.05 W
Kirkconnel	44	55.23 N	4.00 W
Kirkcudbright	44	54.50 N	4.03 W
Kirkcudbright Bay C	44	54.48 N	4.04 W
Kirkdale ◆ [8]	262	53.26 N	2.59 W
Kirkeby	41	56.09 N	9.27 E
Kirkee → Khadki	122	18.34 N	73.52 E
Kirkenær	26	60.28 N	12.03 E
Kirkenes	24	69.40 N	30.03 E
Kirke Stillinge	41	55.26 N	11.15 E
Kirkham	44	53.47 N	2.53 W
Kirkhill	46	57.28 N	4.26 W
Kirkintilloch	46	55.57 N	4.10 W
Kirkjubæjarklaustur	24a	63.47 N	18.04 W
Kirkkonummi → Kyrkslätt	26	60.07 N	24.26 E
Kirkland, P.Q., Can.	275a	45.27 N	73.52 W
Kirkland, Il., U.S.	216	42.05 N	88.51 W
Kirkland, Tx., U.S.	196	34.23 N	100.04 W
Kirkland, Wa., U.S.	224	47.40 N	122.12 W
Kirkland Creek ≃	200	34.32 N	113.00 W
Kirkland Lake	190	48.09 N	80.02 W
Kırklar Dağı ∧	130	40.32 N	40.35 E
Kırklareli	130	41.44 N	27.12 E
Kırklareli □ [4]	130	41.40 N	27.30 E
Kirklees □ [8]	262	53.36 N	1.52 W
Kirkleyditch	262	53.18 N	2.12 W
Kirklin	194	40.11 N	86.21 W
Kirkliston	46	55.58 N	3.25 W
Kirk Michael, I. of Man	44	54.17 N	4.35 W
Kirkmichael, Scot., U.K.	46	56.43 N	3.29 W
Kirkmuirhill	46	55.40 N	3.55 W
Kirkness Lake ⊜	184	51.32 N	93.56 W
Kirkpatrick, Mount ∧	9	84.20 S	166.19 E
Kirkpatrick Lake ⊜	182	51.52 N	111.18 W
Kirk Sandall	44	53.33 N	1.04 W
Kirksville, Il., U.S.	219	39.34 N	88.40 W
Kirksville, Mo., U.S.	194	40.11 N	92.34 W
Kirkton of Culsalmond	46	57.23 N	2.34 W
Kirkton of Glenisla	46	56.44 N	3.17 W
Kirktown of Auchterless	46	57.27 N	2.28 W
Kirkūk	128	35.28 N	44.28 E
Kirkville	210	43.05 N	75.57 W
Kirkwall	46	58.59 N	2.58 W
Kirkwood, S. Afr.	158	33.24 S	25.26 E
Kirkwood, De., U.S.	208	39.34 N	75.41 W
Kirkwood, Il., U.S.	190	40.51 N	90.44 W
Kirkwood, Mo., U.S.	219	38.35 N	90.24 W
Kirkwood, N.J., U.S.	285	39.50 N	75.01 W
Kirkwood, N.Y., U.S.	210	42.02 N	75.48 W
Kirmir ≃	130	40.07 N	31.43 E
Kirn	56	49.47 N	7.28 E
Kirnāhar	126	23.45 N	87.52 E
Kirotshe	154	1.37 S	29.02 E
Kirov, Ross.	76	54.05 N	34.20 E
Kirov, Ross.	80	58.38 N	49.42 E
Kirova, zaliv C	84	39.09 N	49.03 E
Kirovabad → Gjandža	84	40.40 N	46.22 E
Kirovakan	84	40.48 N	44.30 E
Kirovgrad	86	57.26 N	60.04 E
Kirovka	86	47.07 N	82.00 E
Kirovo, Bela.	78	51.29 N	29.24 E
Kirovo, Ross.	86	55.33 N	63.46 E
Kirovo, Ukr.	78	47.41 N	35.46 E
Kirovo, Ukr.	83	48.23 N	37.55 E
Kirovo, Ukr.	83	48.50 N	38.03 E
Kirovo, Uzb.	85	40.26 N	70.34 E
Kirovo-Čepeck	80	58.33 N	50.01 E
Kirovograd	78	48.30 N	32.18 E
Kirovograd □ [8]	38	48.10 N	30.20 E
Kirovsk, Azer.	84	38.48 N	48.43 E
Kirovsk, Bela.	76	53.16 N	29.29 E
Kirovsk, Ross.	24	67.37 N	33.35 E
Kirovsk, Ross.	265a	59.52 N	31.00 E
Kirovsk, Turk.	128	37.42 N	60.23 E
Kirovsk, Ukr.	83	48.38 N	38.39 E
Kirovsk, Ukr.	83	49.01 N	37.56 E
Kirovskij, Azer.	84	40.26 N	49.51 E
Kirovskij, Kaz.	86	44.52 N	78.12 E
Kirovskij, Ross.	74	54.18 N	155.47 E
Kirovskij, Ross.	80	45.51 N	48.07 E
Kirovskij, Ross.	89	54.26 N	126.55 E
Kirovskij, Ross.	89	45.07 N	133.30 E
Kirovskije ostrova II	265a	59.58 N	30.15 E
Kirovskoje, Kyrg.	85	42.39 N	71.35 E
Kirovskoje, Ukr.	78	48.33 N	34.53 E
Kirovskoje, Ukr.	78	45.14 N	35.13 E
Kirovskoje, Ukr.	83	48.09 N	38.21 E
Kirov Stadium ♠	265a	59.58 N	30.14 E
Kirov Theatre ⊍	265a	59.55 N	30.18 E
Kirpičnyj Zavod	265a	60.01 N	30.48 E
Kirpil'skaja	78	45.23 N	39.43 E
Kirriemuir	46	56.41 N	3.01 W
Kirs	86	59.21 N	52.14 E
Kirsanov	80	52.38 N	42.43 E
Kirsanovka	80	52.30 N	52.53 E
Kirschau	54	51.04 N	14.27 E
Kırşehir	130	39.09 N	34.10 E
Kırşehir □ [4]	130	39.20 N	34.10 E
Kīrthar National Park ♠	120	25.50 N	67.40 E
Kīrthar Range ⋏	120	27.00 N	67.10 E
Kirtland, N.M., U.S.	200	36.44 N	108.21 W
Kirtland, Oh., U.S.	214	41.37 N	81.21 W
Kirtland Air Force Base ■	200	35.02 N	106.37 W
Kirtland Hills	214	41.37 N	81.24 W
Kirtle Water ≃	44	54.58 N	3.05 W
Kirton	42	52.56 N	0.04 W
Kirton in Lindsey	44	53.28 N	0.36 W
Kirton of Largo	46	56.13 N	2.55 W
Kirtorf	56	50.46 N	9.06 E
Kiruna	24	67.51 N	20.16 E
Kirundu	154	0.44 S	25.32 E
Kirurumo	154	5.53 S	34.11 E
Kirvin	222	31.46 N	96.20 W
Kirwan Heights	279b	40.22 N	80.06 W
Kirwee	172	43.30 S	172.13 E
Kirwin	198	39.40 N	99.07 W
Kirwin Reservoir ⊜ [1]	198	39.39 N	99.10 W
Kiryandongo	154	1.53 N	32.03 E
Kiryū	94	36.24 N	139.20 E
Kirza	86	54.14 N	81.40 E
Kiržač	82	56.09 N	38.52 E
Kiržač ≃	82	55.52 N	39.04 E
Kisa, Nihon	96	34.43 N	132.59 E
Kisa, Sve.	26	57.59 N	15.37 E
Kisai	94	36.06 N	139.35 E
Kisaichi	270	34.46 N	135.42 E
Kisakata	92	39.13 N	139.54 E
Kisaki	154	7.28 S	37.36 E
Kišaly	76	54.23 N	43.12 E
Kisambo	152	6.25 S	18.14 E
Kisanga	154	2.29 N	26.35 E
Kisangani (Stanleyville)	154	0.30 S	25.12 E
Kisantu	152	5.07 S	15.05 E
Kisar, Pulau I	112	8.05 S	127.10 E
Kisaralik ≃	180	60.51 N	161.16 W
Kisaran	114	2.59 N	99.37 E
Kisarawe	154	6.54 S	39.04 E
Kisarazu	94	35.23 N	139.55 E
Kisarazu-Kichi, Kōkū-jieitai ■	94	35.24 N	139.55 E
Kisawa	96	33.49 N	134.18 E
K.I. Sawyer Air Force Base ■	190	46.21 N	87.25 W
Kisbér	30	47.30 N	18.02 E
Kisbey	184	49.38 N	102.41 W
Kise ≃	94	35.06 N	138.53 E
Kiselevsk → Kisel'ovsk	86	54.00 N	86.39 E
Kisel'ovka	80	47.18 N	44.07 E
Kisel'ovsk	86	54.00 N	86.39 E
Kisengwa	154	6.00 S	25.50 E
Kisen-yama ∧ [2]	270	34.54 N	135.51 E
Kiser Lake ⊜	218	40.11 N	83.58 W
Kīsh, Jazīreh-ye I	128	26.32 N	53.56 E
Kishanda	154	1.42 S	31.34 E
Kishanganga ≃	123	34.22 N	73.30 E
Kishanganj	124	26.07 N	87.56 E
Kishangarh	120	27.52 N	70.34 E
Kishangarh ◆ [8]	272a	28.31 N	77.08 E
Kishangarh Bās	120	26.34 N	74.52 E
Kishb, Ḩarrat al- ⊥ [9]	144	23.00 N	41.25 E
Kishi, Nig.	150	9.05 N	3.52 E
Kishi, Zaïre	154	10.04 S	26.26 E
Kishida ≃	96	35.38 N	134.27 E
Kishigawa	96	34.13 N	135.20 E
Kishikas ≃	184	52.45 N	91.43 W
Kishimoto	96	35.23 N	133.25 E
Kishinev → Kišin'ov	78	47.00 N	28.50 E
Kishiwada	96	34.28 N	135.22 E
Kishorganj	124	24.26 N	90.46 E
Kishorn, Loch C	46	57.21 N	5.41 W
Kishtwār	123	33.19 N	75.46 E
Kishwaukee ≃	216	42.11 N	89.08 W
Kishwaukee, South Branch ≃	216	42.12 N	88.59 W
Kisia	152	4.35 S	18.22 E
Kisigo ≃	154	7.03 S	35.50 E
Kisii	154	0.41 S	34.46 E
Kisiju	154	7.24 S	39.20 E
Kiši-Karoj, ozero ⊜	86	54.03 N	71.20 E
Kisika-zaki >	93b	30.50 N	131.04 E
Kısıklı ◆ [8]	267b	41.01 N	29.03 E
Kišin	78	51.08 N	27.41 E
Kišin'ov (Kishinev)	78	47.00 N	28.50 E
Kısır Dağı ∧	84	40.58 N	43.04 E
Kısırkaya ◆ [8]	267b	41.14 N	28.58 E
Kısırmandıra ◆ [8]	267b	41.14 N	28.49 E
Kisiwada → Kishiwada	96	34.28 N	135.22 E
Kisiwani	154	4.08 S	37.57 E
Kisizi	154	1.00 S	29.56 E
Kiska Island I	181a	52.00 N	177.30 E
Kiskatinaw ≃	182	56.06 N	120.08 W
Kiska Volcano ∧ [1]	181a	52.07 N	177.36 E
Kis-Kevély ∧ [2]	264c	47.38 N	18.59 E
Kiski Lake ⊜	184	54.46 N	98.55 W
Kiskimere	279b	40.37 N	79.35 W
Kiskiminetas ≃	214	40.41 N	79.40 W
Kiskittogisu Lake ⊜	184	54.13 N	98.20 W
Kiskitto Lake ⊜	184	54.16 N	98.34 W
Kiskörei-víztároló ⊜ [1]	30	47.35 N	20.40 E
Kiskőrös	30	46.38 N	19.17 E
Kiskunfélegyháza	30	46.43 N	19.52 E
Kiskunhalas	30	46.26 N	19.30 E
Kiskunmajsa	30	46.30 N	19.45 E
Kiskunsági Nemzeti Park ♠	30	46.40 N	19.25 E
Kisl'akovka	78	46.44 N	31.59 E
Kisl'akovskaja	78	46.27 N	39.40 E
Kislovka	83	49.38 N	37.53 E
Kislovo	80	49.54 N	45.25 E
Kislovodsk	84	43.55 N	42.44 E
Kismaayo	144	0.22 S	42.32 E
Kismet	276	40.38 N	73.12 W
Kisnema	76	60.20 N	37.39 E
Kiso, Nihon	94	35.56 N	137.47 E
Kiso, Nihon	268	35.34 N	139.26 E
Kiso ≃	94	35.02 N	136.45 E
Kisofukushima	94	35.51 N	137.42 E
Kisogawa	94	35.20 N	136.47 E
Kisoripur	126	22.05 N	88.34 E
Kisoro	154	1.17 S	29.41 E
Kiso-sammyaku ⋏	94	35.43 N	137.50 E
Kisozaki	94	35.04 N	136.44 E
Kispest ◆ [8]	264c	47.27 N	19.08 E
Kispiox	182	55.21 N	127.41 W
Kispiox ≃	182	55.16 N	127.41 W
Kispiox Mountain ∧	182	55.25 N	127.57 W
Kissamos	38	35.30 N	23.38 E
Kissena Park ♠	276	40.45 N	73.49 W
Kisseynew Lake ⊜	184	54.58 N	101.35 W
Kissidougou	150	9.11 N	10.06 W
Kissimmee	220	28.17 N	81.24 W
Kissimmee ≃	220	27.10 N	80.53 W
Kissimmee, Lake ⊜	220	27.55 N	81.16 W
Kissing	60	48.18 N	10.59 E
Kississing	184	55.07 N	101.07 W
Kississing Lake ⊜	184	55.10 N	101.20 W
Kisslegg	58	47.47 N	9.53 E
Kissū, Jabal ∧	140	21.35 N	25.09 E
Kista	80	46.05 N	43.06 E
Kistanje	36	43.59 N	15.58 E
Kistarcsa	264c	47.33 N	19.16 E
Kistendej	80	52.08 N	43.39 E
Kistigan Lake ⊜	184	54.38 N	92.37 W
Kistler	214	40.22 N	77.51 W
Kisújszállás	30	47.13 N	20.46 E

Symbol	English	Deutsch	Español	Français	Português
≃	River	Fluß	Río	Rivière	Rio
≅	Canal	Kanal	Canal	Canal	Canal
∟	Waterfall, Rapids	Wasserfall, Stromschnellen	Cascada, Rápidos	Chute d'eau, Rapides	Cascata, Rápidos
⊻	Strait	Meeresstraße	Estrecho	Détroit	Estreito
C	Bay, Gulf	Bucht, Golf	Bahía, Golfo	Baie, Golfe	Baía, Golfo
⊜	Lake, Lakes	See, Seen	Lago, Lagos	Lac, Lacs	Lago, Lagos
≡	Swamp	Sumpf	Pantano	Marais	Pântano
⊓	Ice Features, Glacier	Eis- und Gletscherformen	Accidentes Glaciales	Formes glaciaires	Acidentes glaciares
⊤	Other Hydrographic Features	Andere Hydrographische Objekte	Otros Elementos Hidrográficos	Autres données hydrographiques	Outros acidentes hidrográficos
✦	Submarine Features	Untermeerische Objekte	Accidentes Submarinos	Formes de relief sous-marin	Acidentes submarinos
□	Political Unit	Politische Einheit	Unidad Politica	Entité politique	Unidade política
⊍	Cultural Institution	Kulturelle Institution	Institución Cultural	Institution culturelle	Instituição cultural
⊥	Historical Site	Historische Stätte	Sitio Histórico	Site historique	Sitio histórico
♠	Recreational Site	Erholungs- und Ferienort	Sitio de Recreo	Centre de loisirs	Area de Lazer
⊠	Airport	Flughafen	Aeropuerto	Aéroport	Aeroporto
■	Military Installation	Militäranlage	Instalación Militar	Installation militaire	Instalação militar
◆	Miscellaneous	Verschiedenes	Misceláneo	Divers	Diversos

Name	Page / Seite	Lat.°′ / Breite°′	Long.°′ / Länge°′ E = Ost
Kisuki	96	35.17 N	132.54 E
Kisumu	154	0.06 S	34.45 E
Kisvárda	30	48.13 N	22.05 E
Kiswere	154	9.26 S	39.33 E
Kita	150	13.03 N	9.29 W
Kita ◆[8], Nihon	268	35.45 N	139.44 E
Kita ◆[8], Nihon	270	34.45 N	135.08 E
Kita ◆[8], Nihon	270	34.42 N	135.30 E
Kita ◆[8], Nihon	270	35.03 N	135.45 E
Kitaaiki	94	36.04 N	138.34 E
Kita-Daitō-jima I	90	25.57 N	131.18 E
Kitafuji-enshūjō ■	94	35.25 N	138.48 E
Kitagata	94	35.26 N	136.41 E
Kitagawa	96	33.27 N	134.03 E
Kitagi-shima I	96	34.23 N	133.32 E
Kitaibaraki	94	36.48 N	140.45 E
Kitain Temple ʊ[1]	268	35.54 N	139.30 E
Kita-Iō-jima I	14	25.26 N	141.17 E
Kitairiso	268	35.50 N	139.26 E
Kitajima	96	34.05 N	134.35 E
Kitakami	92	39.18 N	141.07 E
Kitakami ≃	92	38.25 N	141.19 E
Kitakami-kōchi ⋀	92	39.30 N	141.30 E
Kitakata	92	37.39 N	139.52 E
Kitakyuschu → Kitakyūshū	96	33.53 N	130.50 E
Kitakyūshū	96	33.53 N	130.50 E
Kitakyushu-kokutei-kōen ♦	96	33.45 N	130.50 E
Kitale	154	1.01 N	35.00 E
Kitamachi ◆[8]	268	35.46 N	139.39 E
Kitamba ◆[8]	273b	4.19 S	15.14 E
Kitami	92a	43.48 N	143.54 E
Kitami-sanchi ⋀	92a	44.22 N	142.43 E
Kitamoto	94	36.02 N	139.32 E
Kita-Nagato-kaigan-kokutei-kōen ♦	96	34.24 N	131.16 E
Kitanakagusuku	174m	26.21 N	127.51 E
Kitanda, Zaïre	154	6.36 S	26.27 E
Kitanda, Zaïre	154	9.59 S	27.28 E
Kitangari	154	10.39 S	39.20 E
Kitangiri, Lake ⊜	154	4.05 S	34.19 E
Kitangua	152	6.17 S	20.22 E
Kitano, Nihon	96	33.20 N	130.35 E
Kitano, Nihon	268	35.47 N	139.26 E
Kitanoshinden	268	35.48 N	139.26 E
Kitatachibana	94	36.29 N	139.03 E
Kitatajima	268	35.56 N	139.30 E
Kitatawara	270	34.44 N	135.42 E
Kitaura	94	36.04 N	140.32 E
Kita-ura ⊜	94	36.00 N	140.34 E
Kitava Island I	164	8.40 S	151.20 E
Kitaya	154	10.39 S	40.10 E
Kit Carson, Ca., U.S.	226	38.41 N	120.07 W
Kit Carson, Co., U.S.	198	38.45 N	102.47 W
Kitchener, Austl.	162	31.02 S	124.11 E
Kitchener, On., Can.	212	43.27 N	80.29 W
Kitee	26	62.06 N	30.09 E
Kitega → Gitega	154	3.26 S	29.56 E
Kiteiyab	140	17.12 N	33.43 E
Kitenda	152	6.53 S	17.21 E
Kitenevo	82	56.21 N	36.13 E
Kitengo	152	7.26 S	24.08 E
Kitéssa	154	5.20 N	25.20 E
Kitgum	154	3.18 N	32.53 E
Kíthira	38	36.09 N	23.00 E
Kíthira I	38	36.20 N	22.58 E
Kíthnos	38	37.26 N	24.26 E
Kíthnos I	38	37.25 N	24.28 E
Kitimat	182	54.03 N	128.33 W
Kitimat ≃	182	54.06 N	128.38 W
Kitimat Ranges ⋀	182	53.30 N	128.50 W
Kitinen ≃	24	67.08 N	27.29 E
Kitíou, Akrotírion ›	130	34.48 N	33.36 E
Kitlope ≃	182	53.10 N	127.45 W
Kitlope Lake ⊜	182	53.07 N	127.47 W
Kitō, Nihon	94	34.42 N	138.03 E
Kitō, Nihon	96	33.46 N	134.12 E
Kitoj ≃	88	52.39 N	103.56 E
Kitridge Point ›	241g	13.09 N	59.25 W
Kitsap □[6]	224	47.41 N	122.44 W
Kitscoty	184	53.20 N	110.20 W
Kit's Coty House ʊ	260	51.19 N	0.30 E
Kitshua-Nseke	152	4.26 S	19.36 E
Kitsuki	92	33.25 N	131.37 E
Kitsuregawa	94	36.43 N	140.01 E
Kittanning	214	40.48 N	79.31 W
Kittatinny Mountain ∧	210	41.10 N	74.55 W
Kittatinny Tunnel ◆[5]	214	40.09 N	77.41 W
Kittendorf	54	53.37 N	12.54 E
Kittery	188	43.05 N	70.44 W
Kitt Green	262	53.33 N	2.41 W
Kittilä	24	67.40 N	24.54 E
Kittitas	202	46.59 N	120.24 W
Kittitas □[6]	224	47.13 N	121.01 W
Kitt Peak National Observatory ʊ[3]	200	31.58 N	111.36 W
Kittsee	61	48.05 N	17.04 E
Kitu	154	7.38 S	27.42 E
Kitui	154	1.22 S	38.01 E
Kitumbeine ∧[1]	154	2.44 S	36.16 E
Kitunda	154	6.48 S	33.13 E
Kitutu	154	3.17 S	28.05 E
Kitwanga	182	55.06 N	128.03 W
Kitwangar Indian Reserve ◆[4]	182	55.06 N	128.04 W
Kitwe	154	12.49 S	28.13 E
Kitwitwi	156	17.25 S	18.25 E
Kityang → Jieyang	100	23.35 N	116.21 E
Kitzbühel	64	47.27 N	12.23 E
Kitzbüheler Alpen ⋀	64	47.20 N	12.20 E
Kitzingen	56	49.44 N	10.09 E
Kitzscher	54	51.09 N	12.33 E
Kiukiang → Jiujiang	100	29.44 N	115.59 E
Kiukiu, Pointe ›	174x	9.47 S	139.09 W
Kiul	124	25.09 N	86.06 E
Kiunga, Kenya	154	1.45 S	41.29 E
Kiunga, Pap. N. Gui.	164	6.10 S	141.15 E
Kiuruvesi	26	63.39 N	26.37 E
Kiuschu → Kyūshū I	92	33.00 N	131.00 E
Kivak	180	64.16 N	172.57 W
Kivalina	180	67.44 N	164.33 W
Kivercy	78	50.50 N	25.27 E
Kiveriči	76	57.22 N	36.36 E
Kivijärvi	26	63.04 N	25.03 E
Kivijärvi ⊜	26	63.10 N	25.09 E
Kivik	26	55.41 N	14.15 E
Kiviõli	76	59.21 N	26.57 E
Kivu □[4]	154	2.30 S	27.00 E
Kivu, Lac ⊜	154	2.00 S	29.10 E
Kiwaba N'zogi	152	8.57 S	16.32 E
Kiwai Island I	164	8.30 S	143.25 E
Kiwalik	180	66.02 N	161.50 W
Kiwanis Lake	214	41.28 N	81.09 W
Kiyama	96	33.25 N	130.32 E
Kīyāmakī Dāgh ∧	84	38.47 N	45.51 E
Kiyan	174m	26.05 N	127.40 E
Kiyan-zaki ›	174m	26.05 N	127.39 E
Kıyıköy	130	41.38 N	28.05 E
Kiyiu Lake ⊜	184	51.38 N	108.55 W
Kiyl ≃	86	49.25 N	54.50 E
Kiyokawa	94	35.29 N	139.17 E
Kiyomi	94	36.07 N	137.11 E
Kiyosawa	94	35.03 N	138.15 E
Kiyose	94	35.47 N	139.32 E
Kiyosu	94	35.13 N	136.50 E
Kiyosumi-yama ∧	94	35.09 N	140.09 E
Kiyotani	270	34.52 N	134.59 E
Kiyotsu ≃	94	37.03 N	138.41 E
Kizel	86	59.03 N	57.40 E
Kizevatovo	80	53.13 N	45.18 E
Kızıl ≃	130	41.44 N	35.58 E
Kızıl Adalar II	130	40.52 N	29.05 E
Kızılcabölük	130	37.39 N	29.01 E
Kızılcadağ	130	37.01 N	29.58 E
Kızılcahamam	130	40.28 N	32.39 E
Kızılçakçak	84	40.46 N	43.37 E
Kızıldağ Milli Parkı ♦	130	37.58 N	31.28 E
Kızıldikme	130	39.05 N	37.01 E
Kızılhisar	130	37.33 N	29.18 E
Kızılırmak	130	40.21 N	33.59 E
Kızılören	130	37.52 N	32.07 E
Kizil'skoje	86	52.44 N	58.54 E
Kızılsu	130	37.28 N	42.13 E
Kiziltašskij liman ⊂	78	45.07 N	37.05 E
Kızıltepe	130	37.12 N	40.36 E
Kızıltoprak ◆[8]	267b	40.58 N	29.03 E
Kizil'unt	84	43.12 N	46.53 E
Kızılyaka	130	37.09 N	32.54 E
Kižimiz, gora ∧	24	63.12 N	58.48 E
Kizimkazi	154	6.27 S	39.28 E
Kižinga	88	51.51 N	109.55 E
Kizir ≃	86	53.51 N	93.06 E
Kızkalesi ⊥	130	36.28 N	34.04 E
Kızkulesi ◆[5]	267b	41.01 N	29.00 E
Kizl'ar	84	43.50 N	46.40 E
Kizl'arskij zaliv ⊂	84	44.33 N	46.55 E
Kizner	80	56.17 N	51.31 E
Kiz'oma	24	61.08 N	44.50 E
Kizu	96	34.44 N	135.49 E
Kizu ≃	94	34.53 N	135.42 E
Kizuki	268	35.34 N	139.40 E
Kizuri	270	34.39 N	135.34 E
Kizyl-Ajak	128	37.40 N	65.23 E
Kizyl-Arvat	128	38.58 N	56.15 E
Kizyl-Atrek	128	37.36 N	54.46 E
Kizyl-Su	128	39.48 N	53.01 E
Kjellerup	41	56.17 N	9.26 E
Kjøbenhavn → København	41	55.40 N	12.35 E
Kjustendil	38	42.17 N	22.41 E
Klaarstroom	158	33.20 S	22.32 E
Klaaswaal	52	51.46 N	4.26 E
Klabat, Gunung ∧	112	1.28 N	125.02 E
Kladanj	38	44.13 N	18.41 E
Kladbišči	80	55.32 N	45.33 E
Kläden	54	52.38 N	11.39 E
Kladkovo	82	55.24 N	38.51 E
Kladno	54	50.08 N	14.05 E
Kladovo	38	44.37 N	22.37 E
Kladow ◆[8]	264a	52.27 N	13.09 E
Kladruby	60	49.43 N	12.59 E
Klaeng	110	12.47 N	101.39 E
Klagan	112	5.58 N	117.27 E
Klagenfurt	61	46.37 N	14.18 E
Klågerup	41	55.36 N	13.15 E
Klagshamn	41	55.32 N	12.55 E
Klagstorp	41	55.24 N	13.22 E
Klahoose Indian Reserve ◆[4]	182	50.31 N	124.19 W
Klaipėda (Memel)	76	55.43 N	21.07 E
Klakah	115a	7.59 S	113.15 E
Klamath	204	41.31 N	124.02 W
Klamath ≃	204	41.33 N	124.04 W
Klamath Falls	202	42.13 N	121.46 W
Klamath Marsh ≋	202	42.54 N	121.44 W
Klamath Mountains ⋀	204	41.40 N	123.20 W
K. Lamido	146	9.21 N	11.12 E
Klämmingen ⊜	40	59.07 N	17.15 E
Klammpass)(	64	47.17 N	13.05 E
Klamono	164	1.08 S	131.30 E
Klangenan	115a	6.42 S	108.26 E
Klang → Kelang	114	3.02 N	101.27 E
Klangpi	110	22.59 N	93.20 E
Klarälven (Trysilelva) ≃	26	59.23 N	13.32 E
Kl'as'ma	265b	55.59 N	37.50 E
Klášterec	54	50.24 N	13.10 E
Kl'asticy	76	55.53 N	28.36 E
Klaten	115a	7.42 S	110.35 E
Klatovy	60	49.24 N	13.18 E
Klausdorf, Dtsch.	54	54.20 N	13.01 E
Klausdorf, Dtsch.	54	54.18 N	10.15 E
Klausenburg → Cluj-Napoca	38	46.47 N	23.36 E
Klausenpass)(	58	46.52 N	8.51 E
Kl'avlino	80	54.17 N	52.01 E
Klawer	158	31.44 S	18.36 E
Klawock	182	55.33 N	133.06 W
Klazienaveen	52	52.44 N	7.00 E
Kl'az'ma	82	55.58 N	37.27 E
Kl'az'ma ≃	80	56.10 N	42.58 E
Kl'az'minskoje vodochranilišče ⊜[1]	265b	55.59 N	37.35 E
Kleberg	222	32.40 N	96.37 W
Kleck	76	53.04 N	26.38 E
Kłecko	30	52.38 N	17.26 E
Kleczew	30	52.23 N	18.10 E
Kledering ◆[8]	264b	48.08 N	16.26 E
Kleef	263	51.11 N	6.56 E
Kleena Kleene	182	51.57 N	124.50 W
Kleinasien → Asia Minor □[9]	22	39.00 N	32.00 E
Kleinbeeren	264a	52.22 N	13.20 E
Kleinbegin	158	28.50 S	21.36 E
Klein-Blesbokspruit ≃	273d	26.16 S	28.29 E
Kleinbodungen	54	51.28 N	10.32 E
Klein Bonaire I	241s	12.10 N	68.18 W
Klein Bünzow	54	53.53 N	13.48 E
Kleinburg	275b	43.50 N	79.38 W
Klein Curaçao I	241s	12.00 N	68.40 W
Kleine Elster ≃	54	51.32 N	13.23 E
Kleine Emme ≃	58	47.04 N	8.17 E
Kleine Emscher ≃	263	51.31 N	6.43 E
Kleine Erlauf ≃	61	48.07 N	15.08 E
Kleineichen	263	51.08 N	7.21 E
Kleine Laber ≃	60	48.55 N	12.31 E
Kleinenberg	52	51.35 N	8.58 E
Kleinenbroich	263	51.12 N	6.35 E
Kleinengstingen	58	48.23 N	9.18 E
Kleiner Jasmunder Bodden ⊂	54	54.28 N	13.32 E
Kleiner Ravens-Berg ∧[2]	264a	52.22 N	13.04 E
Kleiner Wannsee ⊜	264a	52.25 N	13.10 E
Kleiner Zern-See ⊜	264a	52.26 N	12.55 E
Kleine Spree ≃	54	51.31 N	14.24 E
Kleines Walsertal V	64	47.23 N	10.12 E
Kleinfeltersville	208	40.18 N	76.15 W
Kleinglödnitz	61	46.51 N	14.08 E
Kleinhammer	263	51.14 N	7.46 E
Klein-Jukskei ≃	273d	26.08 S	27.56 E
Klein-Karas	156	27.32 S	18.06 E
Klein Karroo → Little Karroo ⋀[1]	158	33.45 S	21.30 E
Klein Kienitz	264a	52.18 N	13.29 E
Kleinlützel	58	47.26 N	7.25 E
Kleinmachnow	54	52.24 N	13.15 E
Klein Marzehns	54	52.01 N	12.37 E
Kleinmond	158	34.21 S	19.03 E
Klein-Olifants ≃	158	25.41 S	29.19 E
Kleinschönebeck	264a	52.29 N	13.43 E
Klein-Soutpan	158	30.26 S	22.26 E
Klein-Vis ≃	158	33.05 S	26.00 E
Klein Wanzleben	54	52.04 N	11.21 E
Klein Ziethen	264a	52.23 N	13.27 E
Klein Ziethener-Berge ∧[2]	264a	52.22 N	13.26 E
Klekovača ∧	36	44.26 N	16.31 E
Klementjevka	86	50.16 N	80.56 E
Klementjevo	82	55.38 N	36.01 E
Klemme	190	43.00 N	93.36 W
Klemtu	182	52.36 N	128.31 W
Klenovka	80	57.45 N	54.19 E
Klenovo	82	55.19 N	37.21 E
Klerksdorp	158	26.58 S	26.39 E
Klerkskraal	158	26.15 S	27.10 E
Klesov	78	51.19 N	26.54 E
Klésso	150	10.57 N	3.59 W
Klet' ∧	61	48.52 N	14.17 E
Kletn'a	76	53.23 N	33.12 E
Kletskij	80	49.19 N	43.04 E
Kletsko-Počtovskij	80	49.36 N	43.03 E
Klettgau ♦[1]	58	47.40 N	8.25 E
Klettwitz	54	51.32 N	13.53 E
Klevan'	78	50.44 N	26.02 E
Kleve	52	51.48 N	6.09 E
Klevenka	80	52.07 N	49.33 E
Kley ◆[8]	263	51.30 N	7.22 E
Klibreck, Ben ∧	46	58.14 N	4.22 W
Kličev	76	53.29 N	29.21 E
Klička	88	50.26 N	118.00 E
Klickitat	224	45.49 N	121.09 W
Klickitat □[6]	224	45.50 N	121.07 W
Klickitat ≃	224	45.42 N	121.17 W
Kliedbruch ◆[1]	263	51.22 N	6.33 E
Klietz	54	52.40 N	12.04 E
Klimino	88	58.39 N	98.42 E
Klimoviči	76	53.37 N	31.58 E
Klimovo, Ross.	76	52.23 N	32.11 E
Klimovo, Ross.	82	55.22 N	38.52 E
Klimovsk	82	55.22 N	37.32 E
Klimovskoje	82	54.42 N	37.48 E
Klimov Zavod	76	54.50 N	34.55 E
Klimpfjäll	24	65.04 N	14.52 E
Klin, Ross.	82	56.20 N	36.44 E
Klin, Ross.	82	55.19 N	36.20 E
Klinaklini ≃	182	51.05 N	125.36 W
Klin-Bel'din	82	54.45 N	39.13 E
Klincovka	80	51.41 N	49.11 E
Klincy	76	52.47 N	32.14 E
Kline Ditch ≋	279a	41.28 N	82.04 W
Kling	116	5.58 N	124.42 E
Klingbach ≃	56	50.17 N	9.22 E
Klingenberg	54	50.55 N	13.31 E
Klingenberg am Main	56	49.47 N	9.11 E
Klingenmünster	56	49.08 N	8.01 E
Klingenthal	54	50.21 N	12.28 E
Klinger Lake ⊜	216	41.47 N	85.33 W
Klingerstown	208	40.40 N	76.41 W
Klinghardtberge ∧	156	27.18 S	15.48 E
Klingnau	58	47.35 N	8.15 E
Klink	54	53.29 N	12.37 E
Klinkino	83	47.17 N	38.15 E
Klínovec ∧	54	50.24 N	12.58 E
Klinsko-Dmitrovskaja gr'ada ∧	82	56.15 N	37.30 E
Klintehamn	26	57.24 N	18.12 E
Klintsy → Klincy	76	52.47 N	32.14 E
Klip ≃, S. Afr.	158	27.03 S	29.03 E
Klip ≃, S. Afr.	273d	26.19 S	27.53 E
Klipbakken	158	28.50 S	21.21 E
Klipdale	158	34.19 S	19.57 E
Klipdam	158	27.35 S	19.56 E
Kliplev	41	54.56 N	9.25 E
Klippan	41	56.08 N	13.06 E
Klipplaat	158	33.02 S	24.21 E
Klippoortjie	273d	26.13 S	28.10 E
Klipriviersberg ⋀	273d	26.17 S	28.02 E
Kliptown	273d	26.17 S	27.53 E
Klipwerf	158	31.09 S	19.52 E
Kliškovcy	78	48.26 N	26.15 E
Klisura	38	42.42 N	24.27 E
Klitmøller	26	57.02 N	8.31 E
Klitten	54	51.20 N	14.36 E
Klixbüll	41	54.48 N	8.53 E
Ključ	36	44.32 N	16.47 E
Klobbicke	264a	52.46 N	13.48 E
Klobouky	61	49.00 N	16.52 E
Kłobuck	30	50.55 N	18.57 E
Klobuticy	76	58.35 N	29.35 E
Kłodawa	30	52.16 N	18.55 E
Kłodzko	30	50.27 N	16.39 E
Kløfta	26	60.04 N	11.09 E
Kłomnice	30	50.56 N	19.21 E
Klondike	216	40.28 N	86.57 W
Klondike □[9]	180	63.30 N	139.00 W
Klondike ≃	180	64.05 N	139.26 W
Klöntaler See ⊜	58	47.02 N	8.58 E
Klooga	76	59.19 N	24.16 E
Kloosterveen	52	52.59 N	6.33 E
Kloosterzande	52	51.22 N	4.02 E
Kloster	54	54.35 N	13.06 E
Klosterfelde	54	52.48 N	13.28 E
Klosterhardt ◆[8]	263	51.31 N	6.53 E
Klösterle	58	47.08 N	10.05 E
Klostermansfeld	54	51.35 N	11.29 E
Klosterneuburg	264b	48.18 N	16.20 E
Kloster Oesede	52	52.12 N	8.07 E
Klosters	58	46.54 N	9.53 E
Klostertal V	58	47.08 N	9.59 E
Kloster Zinna	54	52.01 N	13.07 E
Kloten, Schw.	58	47.27 N	8.35 E
Kloten, Sve.	40	59.54 N	15.17 E
Klotz, Lac ⊜	176	60.32 N	73.40 W
Klötze	54	52.38 N	11.10 E
Kloulklubed	175b	7.02 N	134.15 E
Klouto	150	6.57 N	0.34 E
Kluane ≃	180	61.53 N	139.43 W
Kluane Lake ⊜	180	61.15 N	138.40 W
Kluane National Park ♦	180	60.45 N	139.30 W
Kluang	112	2.41 S	103.54 E
Kl'učevaja	24	65.16 N	41.32 E
Kl'učevskaja Sopka, vulkan ∧[1]	74	56.04 N	160.38 E
Kl'učevskij	88	53.33 N	119.26 E
Kluchorskij, pereval)(	84	43.15 N	41.54 E
Kl'uči, Ross.	74	56.18 N	160.51 E
Kl'uči, Ross.	80	51.59 N	46.31 E
Kl'uči, Ross.	80	51.26 N	45.11 E
Kl'uči, Ross.	86	52.16 N	79.10 E
Kl'učovka, Kyrg.	85	42.34 N	71.48 E
Kl'učovka, Ross.	86	51.22 N	55.48 E
Kluczbork	30	50.59 N	18.13 E
Kluess	54	53.46 N	12.14 E
Kluet ≃	114	3.04 N	97.20 E
Kl'ukvenka	86	58.34 N	85.55 E
Klukwan	180	59.24 N	135.54 W
Klundert	52	51.40 N	4.32 E
Klungkung	115b	8.32 S	115.24 E
Klüppelberg	56	51.06 N	7.28 E
Klüterthöhle ±[5]	52	51.18 N	7.21 E
Klutina Lake ⊜	180	61.37 N	146.55 W
Klütz	54	53.58 N	11.10 E
Knaben gruver	26	58.39 N	7.04 E
Knaddah	130	35.45 N	36.12 E
Kn'aginino	80	55.49 N	45.03 E
Knaik ≃	46	56.14 N	3.52 W
Knapdaar	158	30.43 S	26.09 E
Knapdale ◆[1]	46	55.55 N	5.30 W
Knaphill	260	51.19 N	0.37 W
Knapp	190	44.57 N	92.04 W
Knapp Creek	210	42.00 N	78.30 W
Knappenberg	61	46.56 N	14.35 E
Knäred	26	56.32 N	13.19 E
Knaresborough	44	54.00 N	1.27 W
Knargram	126	24.01 N	87.59 E
Knauertown	285	40.10 N	75.44 W
Knauthain ◆[8]	54	51.16 N	12.18 E
Kn'ažaja Bajgora	76	52.23 N	40.02 E
Kn'azevka	86	57.35 N	74.10 E
Kn'ažji Gory	76	56.05 N	35.14 E
Kn'ažovo	76	59.40 N	43.54 E
Knebel	41	56.13 N	10.30 E
Knebworth	42	51.52 N	0.12 W
Kneehills Creek ≃	182	51.30 N	112.50 W
Knee Lake ⊜, Mb., Can.	184	55.03 N	94.40 W
Knee Lake ⊜, Sk., Can.	184	55.51 N	107.00 W
Knesebeck	54	52.41 N	10.42 E
Knesselare	50	51.08 N	3.25 E
Knetzgau	56	50.00 N	10.33 E
Knevicy	76	57.56 N	32.14 E
Kneža	38	43.30 N	24.05 E
Knić	38	43.55 N	20.43 E
Knickerbocker	196	31.16 N	100.38 W
Kniebis	58	48.28 N	8.17 E
Knife ≃	198	47.20 N	101.23 W
Knife Lake ⊜	184	53.47 N	91.20 W
Knife River Indian Historical Site ♦	198	47.21 N	101.23 W
Knight Inlet ⊂	182	50.41 N	125.40 W
Knight Island I	180	60.20 N	147.45 W
Knighton	42	52.21 N	3.03 W
Knightsen	226	37.58 N	121.40 W
Knights Landing	226	38.47 N	121.43 W
Knightstown	218	39.47 N	85.31 W
Knightville Dam ◆[6]	207	42.17 N	72.52 W
Knik Arm ⊂	180	61.25 N	149.45 W
Knin	36	44.02 N	16.12 E
Knippa	196	29.18 N	99.38 W
Knislinge	26	56.11 N	14.05 E
Knittelfeld	61	47.14 N	14.50 E
Knittlingen	56	49.01 N	8.45 E
Knivsbjerg ∧[2]	41	55.08 N	9.27 E
Knivsta	40	59.43 N	17.48 E
Knjaževac	38	43.34 N	22.16 E
Knob, Cape ›	162	34.32 S	119.16 E
Knobby Head ›	162	29.40 S	114.58 E
Knob Noster	194	38.45 N	93.33 W
Knob Peak ∧	116	12.28 N	121.21 E
Knoc	48	52.38 N	9.20 W
Knock	46	57.33 N	2.45 W
Knockholt	260	51.18 N	0.06 E
Knockholt Pound	260	51.19 N	0.08 E
Knocklayd ∧	48	55.09 N	6.15 W
Knocklong	48	52.26 N	8.24 W
Knockmealdown Mountains ⋀	48	52.10 N	8.00 W
Knokke	50	51.21 N	3.17 E
Knole ⊥	260	51.16 N	0.12 E
Knolls Green	262	53.19 N	2.18 W
Knollwood, Ct., U.S.	207	41.16 N	72.23 W
Knollwood, Il., U.S.	278	42.17 N	87.53 W
Knollwood, Md., U.S.	284c	39.02 N	76.58 W
Knollwood Park	216	42.14 N	84.22 W
Knon ⊜	40	60.12 N	13.40 E
Knossós ⊥	38	35.20 N	25.10 E
Knottingley	44	53.43 N	1.14 W
Knott's Berry Farm ♦	280	33.50 N	118.00 W
Knotts Island	208	36.31 N	75.56 W
Knotty Ash ◆[8]	262	53.25 N	2.54 W
Knotty Green	260	51.37 N	0.39 W
Knowland State Arboretum and Park ♦	282	37.45 N	122.09 W
Knowle	42	52.23 N	1.43 W
Knowlesville	210	43.14 N	78.19 W
Knowlton Lake ⊜	212	44.28 N	76.41 W
Knowltonwood	285	39.53 N	75.24 W
Knowsley ◆[8], Eng., U.K.	262	53.27 N	2.51 W
Knowsley ◆[8], Eng., U.K.	262	53.27 N	2.50 W
Knowsley Hall ʊ	262	53.26 N	2.50 W
Knowsley Park ♦	262	53.27 N	2.49 W
Knox, In., U.S.	216	41.17 N	86.37 W
Knox, N.Y., U.S.	210	42.40 N	74.07 W
Knox, Pa., U.S.	214	41.14 N	79.32 W
Knox □[6], Mo., U.S.	219	40.08 N	92.09 W
Knox □[6], Oh., U.S.	214	40.23 N	82.29 W
Knox, Cape ›	182	54.11 N	133.04 W
Knoxboro	210	42.58 N	75.36 W
Knox City, Mo., U.S.	219	40.08 N	92.00 W
Knox City, Tx., U.S.	196	33.25 N	99.49 W
Knox Coast ±[2]	9	66.30 S	105.00 E
Knox Dale	214	41.05 N	79.02 W
Knoxfield	274b	37.53 S	145.15 E
Knox Lake ⊜[1]	214	40.31 N	82.30 W
Knoxville, Ga., U.S.	192	32.43 N	83.59 W
Knoxville, Il., U.S.	190	40.54 N	90.17 W
Knoxville, Ia., U.S.	190	41.19 N	93.06 W
Knoxville, Pa., U.S.	210	41.57 N	77.26 W
Knoxville, Tn., U.S.	192	35.57 N	83.55 W
Knuckles ∧	122	7.24 N	80.48 E
Knudshoved Odde ›[1]	41	55.03 N	11.45 E
Knüll ∧	56	50.53 N	9.24 E
Knutby	40	59.55 N	18.15 E
Knuthenborg	41	54.50 N	11.30 E
Knutsford	44	53.19 N	2.22 W
Knysna	158	34.02 S	23.02 E
Knyszyn	30	53.19 N	22.55 E
Koala Sanctuary ◆[4]	274a	33.40 S	151.10 E
Koani	154	6.08 S	39.17 E
Kob'	88	55.25 N	101.24 E
Koba	112	2.29 S	106.24 E
Kob'aj	74	63.34 N	126.30 E
Kőbánya ◆[8]	264c	47.29 N	19.10 E
Kobarid	36	46.15 N	13.35 E
Kobar Sink ±[7]	144	13.35 N	40.50 E
Kobayashi	92	31.59 N	130.59 E
Kōbe, Nihon	96	34.41 N	135.10 E
Kōbe, Nihon	270	34.41 N	135.10 E
Kōbe-kō ⊂	270	34.40 N	135.12 E
Kobel'aki	78	49.09 N	34.12 E
København (Copenhagen)	41	55.40 N	12.35 E
København □[6]	41	55.45 N	12.25 E
Kōbe University ʊ[2]	270	34.43 N	135.14 E
Kobi	84	42.33 N	44.32 E
Koblenz, Dtsch.	56	50.21 N	7.35 E
Koblenz, Schw.	58	47.37 N	8.14 E
Koblenz □[5]	56	50.10 N	7.30 E
Kobo, Ityo.	144	12.11 N	39.33 E
Kobo, Zaïre	152	4.54 S	17.09 E
Ko-boke ♦	96	33.50 N	133.46 E
Koboko	154	3.25 N	30.58 E
Koboldo	89	52.58 N	132.42 E
Kobona	76	60.01 N	31.36 E
Kobou ≃	152	6.13 N	23.19 E
Kobowen Swamp ≋	144	5.38 N	33.54 E
Koboža	76	58.49 N	35.01 E
Koboža ≃	76	58.52 N	36.17 E
Kobra	24	60.03 N	50.44 E
Kobrin	76	52.13 N	24.21 E
Kobrinskoje	76	59.25 N	30.07 E
Kobroor, Pulau I	164	6.12 S	134.32 E
Kobuchizawa	94	35.52 N	138.19 E
Kobuga-hara ♦	94	36.40 N	139.35 E
Kobuk	180	66.54 N	156.52 W
Kobuk ≃	180	66.45 N	161.00 W
Kobuk Valley National Park ♦	180	67.20 N	159.00 W
Kobuleti	84	41.50 N	41.47 E
Kobushiga-take ∧	94	35.54 N	138.44 E
Kobylanka	54	53.19 N	14.50 E
Kobylin	30	51.43 N	17.13 E
Kobyl'nik	76	54.56 N	26.41 E
Kobyžča	78	50.49 N	31.30 E
Kocaali	130	41.03 N	30.52 E
Kocaaliler	130	37.19 N	30.44 E
Kocaavşar ≃	130	40.08 N	27.57 E
Kocaeli □[4]	130	40.55 N	29.55 E
Kocaeli → İzmit	130	40.46 N	29.55 E
Koçali	130	37.55 N	38.15 E
Kočani	38	41.55 N	22.25 E
Koçarlı	130	37.45 N	27.42 E
Kocasinan ◆[8]	267b	41.01 N	28.50 E
Koçbaşı Tepe ∧	84	39.25 N	43.21 E
Kočečum ≃	74	64.17 N	101.10 E
Kočelajevo	80	54.01 N	44.02 E
Kočemary	80	54.50 N	40.58 E
Kočen'ajevka	80	53.52 N	46.59 E
Kočen'ga, Ross.	76	60.09 N	43.33 E
Kočenga, Ross.	88	55.55 N	104.06 E
Kočenga ≃	88	55.55 N	104.06 E
Kočerdyk	86	54.35 N	62.58 E
Kočerga	88	55.15 N	103.46 E
Kočerov	78	50.21 N	29.21 E
Kočetovka, Ross.	80	55.16 N	46.07 E
Kočetovka, Ross.	80	52.58 N	40.29 E
Kočevar	76	60.26 N	42.11 E
Kočevje	36	45.38 N	14.52 E
Kočevo	86	59.36 N	54.18 E
Koch'am-ni	98	41.06 N	129.23 E
Kŏch'ang, Taehan	98	35.26 N	126.42 E
Kŏch'ang, Taehan	98	35.41 N	127.55 E
Kochanoviči	76	55.52 N	28.08 E
Kochanovo	76	54.28 N	30.01 E
Koch Bihār	124	26.19 N	89.26 E
Kochel	64	47.39 N	11.22 E
Kochelsee ⊜	64	47.38 N	11.20 E
Kochena	158	27.00 S	18.50 E
Kocher ≃	56	49.14 N	9.12 E
Kōchi, Nihon	96	34.28 N	132.53 E
Kōchi, Nihon	96	33.33 N	133.33 E
Kōchi □[5]	96	33.40 N	133.30 E
Kōchi-dani ♦	94	34.34 N	136.10 E
Kochinda	174m	26.08 N	127.43 E
Koch Island I	176	69.38 N	78.15 W
Kochiu → Gejiu	90	23.22 N	103.06 E
Kochma	80	56.56 N	41.06 E
Koch Peak ∧	202	45.02 N	111.28 W
Kochugaon	124	26.34 N	90.04 E
Kock	30	51.39 N	22.27 E
Kočki, Ross.	86	52.24 N	80.40 E
Kočki, Ross.	86	54.20 N	80.29 E
Kočkor-Ata	85	41.04 N	72.29 E
Kočkorka	85	42.14 N	75.45 E
Kocksoord	273d	26.13 S	27.39 E
Kočkurovo	80	54.02 N	45.26 E
Kočmes	24	66.12 N	60.44 E
Kočon'ovo	86	55.02 N	82.12 E
Kočov	60	49.49 N	12.44 E
Kočubej	84	44.24 N	46.33 E
Kočubejevskoje	84	44.41 N	41.41 E
Kōda, Nihon	94	34.52 N	137.10 E
Kōda, Nihon	96	34.42 N	132.45 E
Kodačdikost	24	63.11 N	55.49 E
Kodaikānal	122	10.14 N	77.29 E
Kodaira	94	35.44 N	139.29 E
Kodama	94	36.11 N	139.08 E
Kodar, chrebet ⋀	88	57.15 N	118.10 E
Kodāri	124	27.56 N	85.56 E
Kodarma	124	24.28 N	85.36 E
Kodera ◆[8]	270	34.41 N	135.04 E
Kodersdorf	54	51.15 N	14.53 E
Kodi	152	3.34 S	22.12 E
Kodiak	180	57.48 N	152.23 W
Kodiak Island I	180	57.30 N	153.30 W
Kodiang	114	6.24 N	100.18 E
Kodinār	120	20.47 N	70.42 E
Kodino	24	63.43 N	39.41 E
Kodo ≃	152	7.05 N	19.10 E
Kodo, Jabal ∧	140	12.26 N	23.38 E
Kodok	140	9.53 N	32.07 E
Kodori ≃	84	42.47 N	41.10 E
Kodorskij chrebet ⋀	84	43.00 N	42.00 E
Kodra	78	50.36 N	29.34 E
Kodry ⋀[2]	78	47.10 N	28.25 E
Kodyma	78	48.07 N	29.07 E
Kodyma ≃	78	48.01 N	30.48 E
Kodžori	84	41.40 N	44.41 E
Koegas	158	29.16 S	22.20 E
Koehn Lake ⊜	228	35.20 N	117.53 W
Koekelare	50	51.05 N	2.58 E
Koekenaap	158	31.30 S	18.18 E
Koeltztown	219	38.19 N	92.03 W
Koenigsmacker	56	49.24 N	6.17 E
Koersel	56	51.04 N	5.16 E
Koes	156	25.59 S	19.08 E
Kofa Mountains ⋀	200	33.20 N	114.00 W
Kofçaz	130	41.58 N	27.12 E
Kofeld	58	47.44 N	9.41 E
Köfering	60	48.56 N	12.12 E
Koffiefontein	158	29.30 S	25.00 E
Kofiau, Pulau I	164	1.11 S	129.50 E
Köflach	61	47.04 N	15.05 E
Koforidua	150	6.03 N	0.17 W
Kōfu, Nihon	94	35.39 N	138.35 E
Kōfu, Nihon	96	35.17 N	133.30 E
Koga, Nihon	94	36.11 N	139.43 E
Koga, Nihon	96	33.40 N	130.30 E
Koga, Tan.	154	6.14 S	32.25 E
Kogaluc ≃	176	59.40 N	77.35 W
Kogaluc, Baie ⊂	176	59.20 N	77.50 W
Kogaluk ≃	176	56.12 N	61.44 W
Kogan	166	27.03 S	150.46 E
Kogane	268	35.50 N	139.56 E
Koganei	94	35.42 N	139.32 E
Kogarah	274a	33.58 S	151.08 E
Kogarah Bay ⊂	274a	33.59 S	151.07 E
Køge, Dan.	41	55.27 N	12.11 E
Kōge, Nihon	96	35.24 N	134.15 E
Køge Bugt ⊂, Dan.	41	55.30 N	12.20 E
Køge Bugt ⊂, Kal. Nun.	176	65.00 N	40.30 W
Kogil'nik ≃	78	45.51 N	29.38 E
Kogin Baba	146	7.55 N	11.30 E
Koglhof	61	47.19 N	15.40 E
Kogon ≃	150	11.09 N	14.42 W
Kogoni	150	14.44 N	6.02 W
Kŏgŭm-do I	98	34.27 N	127.11 E
Kohak	128	25.44 N	62.33 E
Kohala Mountains ⋀	229d	20.05 N	155.45 W
Kohama-shima I	175d	24.19 N	123.59 E
Kohāt	123	33.35 N	71.26 E
Kohāt ≃	123	33.24 N	71.48 E
Kohatk Wash V	200	32.38 N	111.55 W
Kohila	76	59.10 N	24.45 E
Kohīma	120	25.40 N	94.07 E
Kohistān □[9]	123	35.03 N	72.52 W
Kohlberg ∧[2]	263	51.18 N	7.46 E
Kohler	190	43.44 N	87.46 W
Kohlstädt	52	51.50 N	8.52 E
Kohoku	94	35.26 N	136.15 E
Kōhoku ◆[8]	268	35.31 N	139.38 E
Kohren-Sahlis	54	51.01 N	12.36 E
Kohsān	128	34.39 N	61.12 E
Kohtla-Järve	76	59.24 N	27.15 E
Kohu → Kōfu	94	35.39 N	138.35 E
Kohukohu	172	35.21 S	173.32 E
Kohŭng	98	34.37 N	127.16 E
Kohunlich ⊥	232	18.27 N	89.01 W
Kohuratahi	172	39.06 S	174.46 E
Koide	94	37.13 N	138.57 E
Koidern	180	61.58 N	140.25 W
Koidu	150	8.38 N	10.59 W
Koigi	76	58.50 N	25.45 E
Koihoa	110	8.12 N	93.29 E
Koil-Aligarh → Alīgarh	124	27.53 N	78.05 E
Koimbani	157a	11.37 S	43.23 E
Koindu	150	8.26 N	10.19 W
Koin-ni	98	40.28 N	126.22 E
Koitere ⊜	26	62.58 N	30.45 E
Koito ≃	94	35.21 N	139.52 E
Kojandy	86	49.51 N	75.40 E
Kojda	24	66.23 N	42.31 E
Kŏje-do I	98	34.52 N	128.37 E
Kojetín	30	49.21 N	17.18 E
Kojgorodok	24	60.26 N	50.58 E
Ko-jima I	92a	41.22 N	139.48 E
Kojima-ko ⊜[1]	96	34.37 N	134.00 E
Kojŏ	98	38.57 N	127.51 E
Kojonup	162	33.50 S	117.09 E
Kojsary	85	42.33 N	78.10 E
Kojsug	83	47.07 N	39.41 E
Kojtas, Kaz.	86	51.32 N	76.15 E
Kojtaš, Uzb.	85	40.11 N	67.19 E
Kok (Hkok) ≃	110	20.14 N	100.09 E
Kōka	94	34.54 N	136.13 E
Koka, Lake ⊜[1]	144	8.23 N	39.05 E
Kokai ≃	94	35.52 N	140.08 E
K'okajgyr	85	40.43 N	75.37 E
Kokalaat	86	49.47 N	64.15 E
Kokand	85	40.33 N	70.57 E
Kokanee Glacier Provincial Park ♦	182	49.47 N	117.10 W
Kokankišlak	85	40.56 N	72.30 E
Kökar I	26	59.56 N	20.55 E
Kokas	164	2.42 S	132.26 E
Kokašice	60	49.53 N	12.57 E
Kokava nad Rimavicou	30	48.34 N	19.50 E
Kokawa	96	34.16 N	135.24 E
K'okbel'	85	40.17 N	72.55 E
Kokčetav	86	53.17 N	69.25 E
Kokčetavskaja vozvyšennost' ⋀[1]	86	52.50 N	69.00 E
Kokee State Park ♦	229b	22.08 N	159.40 W
Kokemäenjoki ≃	26	61.33 N	21.42 E
Kokemäki	26	61.15 N	22.21 E
Kokenau	164	4.43 S	136.26 E
Ko Kha	110	18.11 N	99.24 E
Kokhav HaYarden (Belvoir) ⊥	132	32.36 N	35.31 E
Kókhi, Ákra ›	267c	37.53 N	23.27 E
Koki	150	15.30 N	15.59 W
Kokinu	268	35.59 N	139.59 E
Kokiu → Gejiu	102	23.22 N	103.06 E
Kok-Jangak	85	41.02 N	73.12 E
Kokka	140	20.00 N	30.35 E
Kokkilai Lagoon ⊂	122	9.00 N	80.56 E
Kokkola (Karleby)	26	63.50 N	23.07 E
Kokku	98	40.22 N	128.44 E
Koknese	76	56.39 N	25.29 E
Koko	150	11.26 N	4.32 E
Kokoda	164	8.52 S	147.45 E
Koko Head ›	229c	21.16 N	157.42 W
Kokola	154	0.47 N	29.36 E
Kokole Point ›	229b	21.59 N	159.46 W
Kokolik ≃	180	69.46 N	163.00 W
Kokolopozo	150	5.08 N	6.05 W
K'ok'omeren ≃	85	41.43 N	73.54 E
Kokomo, Hi., U.S.	229a	20.52 N	156.18 W
Kokomo, In., U.S.	216	40.29 N	86.08 W
Kokomo, Ms., U.S.	194	31.11 N	90.00 W
Kokong	156	24.27 S	23.03 E
Kokonoe	96	33.10 N	131.10 E
Koko Nor → Qinghai Hu ⊜	102	36.50 N	100.20 E
Kokopo	164	4.20 S	152.15 E
Kokorevka	76	52.35 N	34.16 E
Kokosing ≃	214	40.22 N	82.12 W
Kokos-Inseln → Cocos (Keeling) Islands □[2]	14	12.10 S	96.55 E
Kokoškino	265b	55.38 N	37.11 E
Kokpāra Narsinghgarh	126	22.31 N	86.33 E
Kokpaš	86	51.12 N	87.45 E
Kokpekty	86	48.45 N	82.24 E
Kokrājhār	124	26.24 N	90.16 E
Kokrines	180	64.56 N	154.42 W
Kokrines Hills ⋀[2]	180	65.15 N	154.00 W
Koksa ≃	86	50.16 N	85.36 E
Kokšaalatau, chrebet ⋀	72	41.00 N	78.00 E
Koksan	98	38.46 N	126.40 E
Koksaraj	85	42.40 N	68.08 E
Kokšekol', ozero ⊜	86	46.05 N	62.00 E
Koksijde	50	51.07 N	2.38 E
Koksilah	224	48.40 N	123.38 W
Koksilah ≃	224	48.45 N	123.39 W
Koksoak ≃	176	58.32 N	68.10 W
Koksŏng	98	35.17 N	127.17 E
Koksovyj	78	48.12 N	40.39 E
Kokstad	158	30.32 S	29.29 E
Koksu, Kaz.	85	41.27 N	68.01 E
Koksu, Kaz.	86	44.59 N	77.56 E
Koktal	86	44.09 N	79.48 E
Koktas, Kaz.	86	47.33 N	70.55 E
Koktas, Kaz.	86	45.59 N	73.32 E
Kok-Taš, Kyrg.	85	41.12 N	72.25 E
Kokterek	80	49.25 N	49.15 E
Koktubek	86	48.07 N	56.51 E
Kokubu, Nihon	92	31.44 N	130.46 E
Kokubu, Nihon	96	34.56 N	132.07 E
Kokubunji, Nihon	94	36.22 N	139.51 E
Kokubunji, Nihon	96	34.18 N	133.58 E
Kokubunji, Nihon	268	35.42 N	139.29 E
Kokubunji Temple ʊ[1]	268	35.44 N	139.55 E
Kokufu	96	35.28 N	134.16 E
Kokuj	88	52.13 N	117.33 E
Kokujbel' ≃	85	38.21 N	72.46 E
Kokžar	86	49.01 N	60.10 E
Kol ≃	128	26.59 N	55.47 E
Kola, Indon.	164	5.26 S	134.29 E
Kola, Ross.	24	68.53 N	33.01 E
Kola ≃	24	68.53 N	33.02 E
Kolachel	122	8.10 N	77.15 E
Kolāchi ≃	120	27.08 N	67.02 E
Kol'adovka	83	49.05 N	39.12 E
Kolageran	84	40.58 N	44.37 E
Kolahun	150	8.24 N	10.02 W
Kolaka	112	4.03 S	121.36 E
Kolambo	152	7.34 S	21.58 E
Kolambugan	116	8.07 N	123.55 E
Kolangār	120	34.02 N	69.01 E
Kola Peninsula → Kol'skij poluostrov ›[1]	24	67.30 N	37.00 E
Kolār	122	13.08 N	78.08 E
Kolāras	124	25.14 N	77.36 E
Kolār Gold Fields	122	12.55 N	78.17 E
Kolari	24	67.20 N	23.48 E
Kolarovgrad → Šumen	38	43.16 N	26.55 E
Kolárovo	30	47.52 N	18.02 E
Kolašin	38	42.49 N	19.31 E
Kolāyat	120	27.50 N	72.57 E
Kolbači	89	54.22 N	123.02 E
Kolbäck	40	59.34 N	16.15 E
Kolbäcksån ≃	40	59.32 N	16.16 E
Kol'baj, gora ∧[2]	86	43.43 N	53.57 E
Kolbano	112	10.02 S	124.31 E
Kolbasna	78	47.47 N	29.13 E
Kolbča	76	53.39 N	29.14 E
Kolberg → Kołobrzeg	30	54.12 N	15.33 E
Kolbermoor	64	47.51 N	12.04 E
Kolbio	144	1.10 S	41.15 E
Kolbnitz	64	46.52 N	13.19 E
Kolbotn	26	59.49 N	10.48 E
Kolbuszowa	30	50.15 N	21.47 E
Kolby Kås	41	55.48 N	10.33 E
Kolchida ≋	84	42.15 N	42.00 E
Kolchozabad	120	37.27 N	68.31 E
Kol'covo	82	54.27 N	36.40 E
Kol'čuga	82	55.43 N	37.12 E
Kol'čugino	80	56.18 N	39.23 E
Kołczewo	54	53.58 N	14.38 E
Kolda	150	12.53 N	14.57 W
Kolda □[4]	150	12.50 N	14.50 W
Kolding	41	55.31 N	9.29 E
Kolding Fjord ⊂	41	55.30 N	9.35 E
Kole, Zaïre	152	3.27 S	22.29 E
Kole, Zaïre	154	2.07 N	25.26 E
Kolea	34	36.38 N	2.46 E
Kolebīra	124	22.43 N	84.42 E
Kole Kalyan ◆[8]	272c	19.06 N	72.51 E
Kolenfeld	52	52.24 N	9.27 E
Koleno	80	51.52 N	44.07 E
Kolenté	150	10.06 N	12.37 W
Kolenté (Great Scarcies) ≃	150	8.55 N	13.08 W
Kolga	76	59.32 N	25.42 E
Kolgujev, ostrov I	24	69.05 N	49.15 E
Kolhāpur, India	122	16.06 N	78.16 E
Kolhāpur, India	122	16.42 N	74.13 E
Kolho	26	62.08 N	24.31 E
Koli	76	59.30 N	34.30 E
Koli ∧[2]	26	63.06 N	29.48 E
Koli, Jabal ∧	140	14.05 N	25.31 E
Kolia	150	9.46 N	6.28 W
Koliba (Corubal) ≃	150	11.57 N	15.06 W
Koliganek	180	59.48 N	157.25 W
Kolima ⊜	26	63.16 N	25.50 E
Kolimbine ≃	150	14.26 N	11.23 W
Kolín	30	50.01 N	15.13 E
Kolka	76	57.45 N	22.35 E
Kølkær	41	56.04 N	9.06 E
Kolkasrags ›	76	57.47 N	22.36 E
Kolki, Ukr.	78	51.37 N	26.37 E
Kolki, Ukr.	78	51.07 N	25.41 E
Kolkwitz	54	51.45 N	14.15 E
Kollbach ≃	60	48.36 N	12.58 E
Kölleda	54	51.11 N	11.15 E
Kollegāl	122	12.09 N	77.07 E
Kolleru Lake ⊜	122	16.39 N	81.13 E
Kollum	52	53.16 N	6.09 E
Kollund	41	54.51 N	9.27 E

Symbols in the index entries represent the broad categories identified in the key at the right. Symbols with superior numbers (⋀[1]) identify subcategories (see complete key on page I · 1).

Symbole im Register stellen die rechts im Schlüssel erklärten Kategorien dar. Symbole mit hochgestellten Ziffern (⋀[1]) bezeichnen Unterabteilungen einer Kategorie (vgl. vollständiger Schlüssel auf Seite I · 1).

Los símbolos incluidos en el texto del índice representan las grandes categorías identificadas con la clave a la derecha. Los símbolos con números en su parte superior (⋀[1]) identifican las subcategorías (véase la clave completa en la página I · 1).

Les symboles de l'index représentent les catégories indiquées dans la légende à droite. Les symboles suivis d'un indice (⋀[1]) représentent des sous-catégories (voir légende complète à la page I · 1).

Os símbolos incluídos no texto do índice representam as grandes categorias identificadas com a chave à direita. Os símbolos com números em sua parte superior (⋀[1]) identificam as subcategorias (veja-se a chave completa à página I · 1).

	English	Deutsch	Español	Français	Português
∧	Mountain	Berg	Montaña	Montagne	Montanha
⋀	Mountains	Gebirge	Montañas	Montagnes	Montanhas
)(	Pass	Paß	Paso	Col	Passo
V	Valley, Canyon	Tal, Cañon	Valle, Cañón	Vallée, Canyon	Vale, Canhão
≍	Plain	Ebene	Llano	Plaine	Planície
›	Cape	Kap	Cabo	Cap	Cabo
I	Island	Insel	Isla	Île	Ilha
II	Islands	Inseln	Islas	Îles	Ilhas
♦	Other Topographic Features	Andere Topographische Objekte	Otros Elementos Topográficos	Autres données topographiques	Outros acidentes topográficos

ESPAÑOL — Nombre	FRANÇAIS — Nom	PORTUGUÊS — Nome	Página/Page	Lat.°′	Long.°′ W = Oeste / W = Ouest

Column 1

Nombre	Página	Lat.	Long.
Kolmanskop	156	26.40 S	15.12 E
Kolmården	40	58.40 N	16.23 E
Kolmården ⚓²	40	58.41 N	16.35 E
Kolmårdens Djurpark ♦	40	58.40 N	16.29 E
Kolmogorovo	86	59.15 N	91.20 E
Köln (Cologne)	56	50.56 N	6.59 E
Köln □⁵	56	50.55 N	6.40 E
Köln-Bonn, Flughafen ⚑	56	50.50 N	7.10 E
Kolno	30	53.25 N	21.56 E
Kolo, Niger	150	13.14 N	2.20 E
Koło, Pol.	30	52.12 N	18.38 E
Kolo, Tan.	154	4.44 S	35.50 E
Koloa	229b	21.54 N	159.28 W
Kolobovo	80	56.42 N	41.21 E
Kołobrzeg	30	54.12 N	15.33 E
Koloč	82	55.34 N	35.52 E
Kolochau	54	51.44 N	13.16 E
Kolodn'a	76	54.48 N	32.09 E
Kologriv	76	58.51 N	44.17 E
Kologrivovka	80	51.44 N	45.20 E
Kolojar	80	52.34 N	46.58 E
Kolok (Golok) ≃	114	6.15 N	102.05 E
Kolokani	110	13.35 N	8.02 W
Koloko	150	11.05 N	5.19 W
Kolokol'covka, Ross.	80	52.36 N	49.48 E
Kolokol'covka, Ross.	80	51.12 N	44.36 E
Kololo	144	7.29 N	41.58 E
Kolom'agi ⚓⁸	265a	60.00 N	30.17 E
Kolom'agi Airport ⚑	265a	60.01 N	30.17 E
Kolomak	78	49.50 N	35.18 E
Kolombangara Island I	175e	8.00 S	157.05 E
Kolomea → Kolomyja	78	48.32 N	25.04 E
Kolomenka ≃	82	55.06 N	38.46 E
Kolomenskaja Sloboda	82	54.22 N	38.15 E
Kolomenskoje ←⚓⁸	265b	55.40 N	37.41 E
Kolomna	82	55.05 N	38.49 E
Kolomyja	78	48.32 N	25.04 E
Kolondiéba	150	11.05 N	6.54 W
Kolonga	174w	21.08 S	175.04 W
Kolonia	174r	6.58 N	158.13 E
Kolon Stolp	264a	52.28 N	13.46 E
Kolono	112	4.18 S	122.41 E
Kolonodale	112	2.00 S	121.19 E
Kolora	272b	22.55 N	88.22 E
Kolosib	120	24.14 N	92.42 E
Kol'osnoje	78	46.02 N	29.56 E
Kolosovka	80	56.28 N	73.36 E
Kolovai	174w	21.06 S	175.20 W
Kolovertnoje	80	50.36 N	51.06 E
Kolowana Watobo, Teluk c	112	5.00 S	123.06 E
Kolozsvár → Cluj-Napoca	38	46.47 N	23.36 E
Kolp' ≃	76	59.20 N	36.49 E
Kolpaševo	86	58.20 N	82.50 E
Kolpino	76	59.45 N	30.36 E
Kölpinsee ⊜	54	53.30 N	12.34 E
Kolpny	76	52.15 N	37.02 E
Kölsa	54	51.28 N	12.13 E
Kol'skij poluostrov (Kola Peninsula) ⊁¹	24	67.30 N	37.00 E
Kolsnaren ⊜	40	59.02 N	16.01 E
Kolsva	40	59.36 N	15.50 E
Kol'togan ≃	85	43.51 N	67.25 E
Koltovskaja	80	52.47 N	44.16 E
Koltubanovskij	80	52.57 N	52.02 E
Koltuši	265a	59.56 N	30.40 E
Kol'ubakino	82	55.40 N	36.32 E
Kolubara ≃	38	44.40 N	20.15 E
Kol'učinskaja guba c	180	66.40 N	174.30 W
Koluèl Kayke	254	46.43 S	68.14 W
Kolumbien → Colombia □¹	246	4.00 N	72.00 W
Kol'upanovo	82	54.26 N	36.14 E
Koluškino	78	48.39 N	40.56 E
Koluszki	30	51.44 N	19.49 E
Koluton ≃	85	51.43 N	69.25 E
Koluton ≃	86	51.42 N	69.10 E
Kolva ≃	24	65.55 N	57.15 E
Kolvereid	24	64.51 N	11.32 E
Kølvrå	41	56.18 N	9.08 E
Kolwezi	154	10.43 S	25.28 E
Kolyberovo	82	55.16 N	38.44 E
Kolybelka	80	55.30 N	37.52 E
Kolyma ≃	74	69.30 N	161.00 E
Kolymskaja	74	68.44 N	158.44 E
Kolymskaja nizmennost' ≃	74	68.30 N	154.00 E
Kolyšlej	80	52.42 N	44.32 E
Kolyšovo	82	54.54 N	36.57 E
Kolyvan', Ross.	85	51.18 N	82.34 E
Kolyvan', Ross.	86	55.18 N	82.45 E
Kom ⚲	38	43.10 N	23.03 E
Kom ≃	152	2.18 N	11.40 E
Koma, Ityo.	144	8.27 N	36.52 E
Koma, Mya.	110	15.39 N	98.12 E
Koma, Ross.	86	55.05 N	51.10 E
Koma ≃	94	35.59 N	139.26 E
Komadougou Yobé (Komadugu Yobe) ≃	146	13.43 N	13.20 E
Komadugu Gana ≃	146	13.05 N	12.24 E
Komadugu Yobe (Komadougou Yobé) ≃	146	13.43 N	13.20 E
Komae	94	35.38 N	139.35 E
Komagane	94	35.43 N	137.55 E
Komaga-take ⚲, Nihon	92a	42.04 N	140.41 E
Komaga-take ⚲, Nihon	94	35.45 N	138.14 E
Komagome ←⚓⁸	268	35.44 N	139.45 E
Komaki	94	35.17 N	136.55 E
Komandorski ostrova II	74	55.00 N	167.00 E
Komandorski Village	226	37.43 N	121.54 W
Komariči	82	52.27 N	34.47 E
Komárno, Česko.	78	51.26 N	30.31 E
Komárnik	78	49.00 N	23.04 E
Komarno, Ukr.	78	47.45 N	18.09 E
Komárno, Česko.	30	47.46 N	18.08 E
Komárno, Ukr.	78	49.38 N	23.42 E
Komárom	30	47.44 N	18.08 E
Komárom-Esztergom □⁶	30	47.40 N	18.15 E
Komarovka	82	51.14 N	32.07 E
Komarovo	76	58.39 N	33.26 E
Komarovy	86	60.26 N	75.50 E
Komati (Incomáti) ≃	156	25.46 S	32.43 E
Komatipoort	156	25.26 S	31.55 E
Komatsu, Nihon	94	36.24 N	136.27 E
Komatsu, Nihon	94	35.33 N	133.07 E
Komatsu=kükō ⚑	94	36.23 N	136.24 E
Komatsushima	94	34.00 N	134.35 E
Kombissiri	150	12.04 N	1.20 W
Kombone	152	4.38 N	9.10 E
Komdhārā	272b	22.53 N	88.14 E
Kome Island I	154	0.06 S	32.45 E
Komenda	150	5.03 N	1.24 E
Komering ≃	112	2.59 S	104.50 E
Komfane	164	5.39 S	134.44 E
Komga	158	32.35 S	27.55 E
Komi Avtonomnaja Sovetskaja Socialističeskaja Respublika □³	24	64.00 N	54.00 E
Kominato → Amatsu-Kominato	94	35.07 N	140.10 E
Kominternovskoje	78	46.49 N	30.56 E
Komin Yanga	150	11.29 N	0.08 E

Column 2

Nom	Page	Lat.	Long.
Komi-Perm'ackij Avtonomnyj Okrug □⁸	24	60.00 N	54.30 E
Komissarovka, Ross.	83	48.07 N	40.09 E
Komissarovka, Ukr.	83	48.23 N	38.32 E
Komissarovo	89	44.59 N	131.46 E
Komissarovskij	80	47.29 N	42.59 E
Komkans	158	31.16 S	18.09 E
Komló	30	46.12 N	18.16 E
Kommadagga	158	33.09 S	25.55 E
Kommandodrif	158	27.30 S	26.14 E
Kommandokraal	158	33.05 S	22.51 E
Kommetjie	158	34.08 S	18.21 E
Kommunal'naja	88	52.03 N	115.06 E
Kommunar, Ross.	80	58.10 N	43.33 E
Kommunar, Ross.	106	21.23 N	119.08 E
Kommunarka	265b	55.34 N	37.29 E
Kommunarsk	83	48.30 N	38.47 E
Kommunary	26	50.54 N	29.47 E
Kommunizma, pik ⚲	85	38.57 N	72.01 E
Komo ⚲	152	0.09 N	9.50 E
Komodo	115b	8.35 S	119.30 E
Komodo, Pulau I	115b	8.36 S	119.30 E
Komoé ≃	150	5.12 N	3.44 W
Komoé, Parc National de la ♦	150	9.00 N	3.30 W
Komono, Congo	152	3.15 S	13.14 E
Komoran, Nihon	94	35.00 N	136.31 E
Komoran, Pulau I	164	8.18 S	138.45 E
Komoren → Comoros □¹	157a	12.10 S	44.10 E
Komorin, Kap → Comorin, Cape	122	8.04 N	77.34 E
Komorn → Komárno	30	47.45 N	18.09 E
Komoro	94	36.19 N	138.26 E
Komotau → Chomutov	54	50.28 N	13.26 E
Komotiní	38	41.08 N	25.25 E
Kompanejevka	78	48.15 N	32.12 E
Kompasberg ⚲	158	31.45 S	24.32 E
Kompiam	164	5.20 S	143.55 E
Kompot	112	0.24 N	124.10 E
Kom → Qom	128	34.39 N	50.54 E
Komrat	78	46.18 N	28.38 E
Komsomolabad	86	38.52 N	69.57 E
Komsomolec	86	53.45 N	62.02 E
Komsomolec, ostrov I	74	80.30 N	95.00 E
Komsomolec, zaliv c	80	45.30 N	52.45 E
Komsomol'sk, Ross.	80	57.02 N	40.21 E
Komsomol'sk, Ross.	86	57.27 N	86.02 E
Komsomol'sk, Ross.	86	55.38 N	88.11 E
Komsomol'skij, Kaz.	86	40.21 N	53.42 E
Komsomol'skij, Ross.	80	51.40 N	66.39 E
Komsomol'skij, Ross.	80	54.27 N	45.49 E
Komsomol'skij, Turk.	128	39.02 N	63.36 E
Komsomol'skij, Ukr.	83	47.40 N	37.26 E
Komsomol'sk-na-Amure	74	50.35 N	137.02 E
Komsomol'sk-na-Ust'urte	86	44.03 N	58.20 E
Komsomol'skoje, Ross.	80	55.16 N	47.33 E
Komsomol'skoje, Ross.	80	50.46 N	47.03 E
Komsomol'skoje, Ross.	88	52.29 N	111.06 E
Komsomol'skoje, Ukr.	78	49.43 N	28.40 E
Komsomol'skoje, Ukr.	83	47.40 N	38.05 E
Komsomol'skoj Pravdy, ostrova II	74	77.20 N	107.40 E
Kömun-do I	98	34.02 N	127.19 E
Kömürcüpınar ←⚓⁸	267b	41.15 N	28.51 E
Komusan	98	42.08 N	129.41 E
Komyšn'a	78	50.12 N	33.41 E
Kona, India	272b	22.37 N	88.18 E
Kona, Mali	150	14.57 N	3.53 W
Kona Coast ⚓²	229d	19.25 N	155.55 W
Konakovo	82	56.42 N	36.46 E
Konakpınar, Tür.	130	39.26 N	27.53 E
Konakpınar, Tür.	130	38.53 N	37.22 E
Konan, C. Iv.	150	8.21 N	8.00 W
Kōnan, Nihon	94	35.20 N	136.53 E
Kōnan, Nihon	94	34.56 N	136.11 E
Konar	268	32.39 S	139.35 E
Konar → Hüngnam	98	39.50 N	127.38 E
Konar (Kunar) ≃	123	34.25 N	70.32 E
Konārak	120	19.54 N	86.07 E
Konār Dam ⚒⁶	124	23.58 N	85.45 E
Konarhā □⁴	123	35.15 N	71.00 E
Konawa	196	34.57 N	96.45 W
Konaskeje-Suvorovskoje	76	58.39 N	34.04 E
Konceba	78	48.07 N	29.56 E
Konch	124	25.59 N	79.09 E
Konda ≃, Ross.	76	61.20 N	63.58 E
Konda ≃, Ross.	86	60.40 N	69.46 E
Kondagaon	122	19.36 N	81.40 E
Kondaparinga	160	34.00 S	138.58 E
Kondas ≃	80	58.10 N	55.20 E
Kondinin	162	32.30 S	118.16 E
Kondinskoje	86	59.40 N	67.22 E
Kondoa	154	4.54 S	35.47 E
Kondol'	80	52.49 N	45.03 E
Kondopoga	24	62.12 N	34.17 E
Kondorfa	61	46.54 N	16.24 E
Kondratjevo, Ross.	76	56.33 N	38.02 E
Kondratjevo, Ross.	88	57.21 N	98.11 E
Kondrovo	80	54.46 N	35.56 E
Kondúz □⁴	123	36.45 N	68.30 E
Koné, Passe de U	175l	21.08 S	164.12 E
Konecbor	78	66.00 N	60.30 E
Konevo	180	62.06 N	178.50 W
Konfara	150	9.09 N	4.37 W
Kong, C. Iv.	150	9.09 N	4.37 W
Kong, Dan.	41	56.01 N	11.50 E
Kong ≃	110	13.32 N	105.58 E
Kong, Kaoh I	110	11.20 N	103.00 E
Kong ≃	102	31.05 N	109.55 E
Kongcheng	102	31.02 N	117.05 E
Kongens Lyngby	100	27.58 N	116.53 E
Konggar	100	29.18 N	91.30 E
Konggyangas	106	30.31 N	84.27 E
Konghu	100	11.55 N	8.50 W
Kongjia ≃	102	32.10 N	113.10 E
Kongjiazhuang	105	40.47 N	114.48 E

Column 3

Nome	Página	Lat.	Long.
Kongō-Ikoma-kokutei-kōen ♦	96	34.28 N	135.40 E
Kongolo, Zaïre	154	5.26 S	24.49 E
Kongolo, Zaïre	154	5.23 S	27.00 E
Kongor	142	7.10 N	31.21 E
Kongō-sanchi ⚲	270	34.27 N	135.41 E
Kongoussi	150	13.19 N	1.32 W
Kongō-zan ⚲	96	34.25 N	135.41 E
Kongsberg	26	59.39 N	9.39 E
Kongsvinger	26	60.12 N	12.00 E
Kongsvoll	26	62.18 N	9.37 E
Kongtan	107	29.10 N	104.42 E
Kongur Shan ⚲, Zhg.	85	38.37 N	75.20 E
Kongur Shan ⚲, Zhg.	100	38.37 N	75.20 E
Kongwa	154	6.12 S	36.25 E
Kongyangcun	106	21.23 N	100.11 E
Kongzhen	106	31.29 N	119.00 E
Koni	154	10.42 S	27.15 E
Koni ≃	150	13.05 N	5.37 W
Koniakari	150	14.34 N	10.54 W
Konice	30	49.35 N	16.53 E
Koniecpol	30	50.48 N	19.41 E
Königgrätz → Hradec Králové	30	50.12 N	15.50 E
Königin Alexandra-Kette → Queen Alexandra Range ⚲	9	84.00 S	168.00 E
Königin Fabiola-Gebirge → Queen Fabiola Mountains ⚲	9	71.30 S	35.40 E
Königin Mary-Küste → Queen Mary Coast ⚹²	9	67.00 S	96.00 E
Königin Maud-Land → Queen Maud Land ⚹¹	9	72.30 S	12.00 E
König-Otto-Höhle ⚹⁵	60	49.15 N	11.42 E
Königsbach	60	48.58 N	8.36 E
Königsberg	56	50.05 N	10.34 E
Königsberg → Kaliningrad	76	54.43 N	20.30 E
Königsborn	263	51.33 N	7.41 E
Königsbrück	54	51.16 N	13.54 E
Königsbrunn, Dtsch.	58	48.16 N	10.53 E
Königsbrunn, Öst.	264b	48.21 N	16.25 E
Königsdorf	64	47.49 N	11.28 E
Königsee	54	50.39 N	11.05 E
Königsfelden ⚹¹	58	47.29 N	8.14 E
Königsfeld im Schwarzwald	58	48.08 N	8.25 E
Königshain	54	51.11 N	14.52 E
Königshardt ←⚓⁸	263	51.33 N	6.51 E
Königslutter	54	52.15 N	10.49 E
Königsmoor ←⚓³	52	53.15 N	9.40 E
Königssee	64	47.36 N	12.59 E
Königsstuhl ⚲⁴	54	55.01 N	14.04 E
Königstein, Dtsch.	56	50.55 N	14.04 E
Königstein, Dtsch.	56	50.11 N	8.29 E
Königstein, Dtsch.	60	49.37 N	11.38 E
Königstetten	264b	48.18 N	16.09 E
Königswalde	50	53.33 N	13.02 E
Königswartha	54	51.18 N	14.20 E
Königswiesen	58	48.24 N	14.50 E
Königswinter	56	50.40 N	7.11 E
Königs Wusterhausen	54	52.18 N	13.37 E
Konin	30	52.13 N	18.16 E
Konin ≃	30	52.20 N	18.20 E
Konispol	38	39.39 N	20.10 E
Kónitsa	38	40.03 N	20.45 E
Köniz	58	46.56 N	7.25 E
Konjic	38	43.39 N	17.57 E
Konka ≃	78	47.40 N	35.22 E
Könkämäälven ≃	24	68.29 N	22.17 E
Konkapot ≃	210	42.03 N	73.20 W
Konkiep ≃	156	28.00 S	17.21 E
Konkó	85	34.32 N	133.37 E
Kon'-Kolodez'	76	52.08 N	39.11 E
Konkouré ≃	150	9.58 N	13.42 W
Kon'kovo	83	47.20 N	38.10 E
Konkudera	88	57.33 N	112.30 E
Konkuk University ⚹²	271b	37.32 N	127.05 E
Konmagar	126	22.42 N	88.22 E
Konnern	54	51.40 N	11.46 E
Konnevesi	26	62.40 N	26.35 E
Konnur	122	16.12 N	74.45 E
Kono ≃	94	35.49 N	136.04 E
Konobejevo	82	55.24 N	38.40 E
Konoe ←⚓⁸	270	34.41 N	135.26 E
Konokke	270	34.42 N	135.37 E
Konolfingen	58	46.53 N	7.38 E
Konongo	150	6.37 N	1.13 W
Konoša	76	60.58 N	40.15 E
Kōno-shima I	96	34.28 N	133.31 E
Kōnosu	94	36.03 N	139.31 E
Konotop	78	51.14 N	33.12 E
Konovalovka	86	52.06 N	51.34 E
Konqi ≃	100	40.40 N	90.10 E
Konradshöhe ←⚓⁸	264a	52.35 N	13.15 E
Konradsreuth	54	50.16 N	11.50 E
Konsankoro	150	9.02 N	9.00 W
Konsen-daichi ⚲¹	92a	43.25 N	144.52 E
Końskie	30	51.12 N	20.26 E
Konstabel	158	30.36 S	20.17 E
Konstantinopel → İstanbul	130	41.01 N	28.58 E
Konstantinovka, Ross.	80	56.41 N	50.53 E
Konstantinovka, Ross.	265a	59.47 N	30.08 E
Konstantinovka, Ukr.	78	47.51 N	35.07 E
Konstantinovka, Ukr.	78	47.51 N	31.09 E
Konstantinovka, Ukr.	83	48.32 N	37.43 E
Konstantinovka, Ukr.	83	47.52 N	37.24 E
Konstantinovo	76	56.33 N	38.02 E
Konstantinovsk	78	47.35 N	41.06 E
Konstantinovskij	76	57.50 N	39.36 E
Konstantynów Łódzki	30	51.45 N	19.20 E
Konstanz	58	47.40 N	9.10 E
Kontagora	150	10.24 N	5.28 E
Kontcha	152	7.58 N	12.14 E
Kontejevo	80	58.26 N	41.21 E
Kontiolahti	26	62.46 N	29.51 E
Kontiomäki	26	64.21 N	28.09 E
Kon Tum	110	14.21 N	108.00 E
Kontum, Plateau du ⚲¹	110	14.30 N	108.00 E
Konuš	78	49.48 N	35.31 E
Konus, gora ⚲	88	67.34 N	178.10 E
Konya	130	37.52 N	32.31 E
Konya □⁴	130	37.30 N	33.00 E
Konyr	85	44.16 N	79.19 E
Konz	56	49.42 N	6.35 E
Konza	154	1.45 S	37.07 E
Konžakovskij Kamen', gora ⚲	76	59.38 N	59.08 E
Koocanusa, Lake ⊜¹	202	49.00 N	115.10 W
Koog [aan de Zaan]	52	52.27 N	4.49 E
Kookynie	162	29.20 S	121.29 E
Koolamarra	160	20.12 S	140.14 E
Koolatah	160	15.53 S	142.27 E
Koolau Range ⚲	229c	21.35 N	158.00 W
Kooloonong	160	34.53 S	143.09 E

Column 4

Nombre	Página	Lat.	Long.
Koolskamp	50	51.00 N	3.12 E
Koolyanobbing	162	30.50 S	119.35 E
Koolywurtie	168b	34.38 S	137.37 E
Koombana Bay c	168a	33.18 S	115.36 E
Koonap ≃	158	33.03 S	26.39 E
Koondrook	166	35.39 S	144.08 E
Koonga	76	58.35 N	24.12 E
Koonibba	162	31.58 S	133.27 E
Koontz Lake	216	41.25 N	86.29 W
Koontz Lake ⊜	216	41.25 N	86.28 W
Koopan-Noord	158	26.53 S	20.41 E
Koopan-Suid	158	27.15 S	20.22 E
Koopmansfontein	158	28.14 S	24.01 E
Koorawatha	166	34.02 S	148.33 E
Koorda	162	30.50 S	117.29 E
Koosa	76	58.33 N	27.07 E
Koosfontein	158	27.22 S	25.27 E
Koosharem	200	38.30 N	111.52 W
Koossa	202	46.06 N	115.58 W
Kootenai (Kootenay) ≃	182	49.15 N	117.39 W
Kootenai (Kootenay) ≃	182	49.15 N	117.39 W
Kootenay Indian Reserve ⚹⁴	182	49.37 N	115.45 W
Kootenay Lake ⊜	182	49.35 N	116.50 W
Kootenay National Park ♦	182	51.00 N	116.00 W
Kootjieskolk	158	31.15 S	20.21 E
Kootwijk	52	52.12 N	5.45 E
Koo-wee-rup	169	38.12 S	145.30 E
Kopa	85	43.32 N	75.50 E
Kopa ≃	85	43.40 N	76.15 E
Kopaganj	124	26.01 N	83.34 E
Kopaïl ≃	126	23.48 N	87.47 E
Kopajgorod	78	48.56 N	27.48 E
Kopanbulak	86	48.56 N	80.52 E
Kopang	115b	8.39 S	116.21 E
Kopanovka	80	47.27 N	46.48 E
Kopanskaja	78	46.17 N	38.29 E
Kopapan	80	50.20 N	50.26 E
Kopargaon	122	19.53 N	74.29 E
Koparkhairna	272c	19.06 N	72.59 E
Koparpāda	272c	19.02 N	73.04 E
Kopasker	24a	66.20 N	16.24 W
Kopatkeviči	76	52.19 N	28.49 E
Kopavogur	24a	64.06 N	21.50 W
Kopčany	54	54.14 N	28.19 E
Kopé, Mont ⚲	150	4.59 N	7.27 W
Kopejsk	86	55.07 N	61.37 E
Kopenhagen → København	41	55.40 N	12.35 E
Köpenick ←⚓⁸	54	52.27 N	13.34 E
Köpenick, Schloss ⚹	264a	52.27 N	13.34 E
Kopernitz	54	53.04 N	12.56 E
Kopervik	26	59.17 N	5.18 E
Kopetdag, chrebet ⚲	128	37.50 N	58.00 E
Kopeysk → Kopejsk	86	55.07 N	61.37 E
Kopice	54	50.44 N	14.32 E
Köping	40	59.31 N	16.00 E
Kopisty	50	50.34 N	13.35 E
Koplik	38	42.13 N	19.26 E
Kopmanholmen	38	63.10 N	18.34 E
Koppal	122	15.21 N	76.09 E
Koppang	26	61.34 N	11.04 E
Kopparberg ≃	40	60.20 N	15.06 E
Kopparberg	40	59.52 N	14.59 E
Kopparberg Län □⁶	26	61.00 N	14.30 E
Kopperå	26	63.24 N	11.51 E
Koppies	158	27.20 S	27.30 E
Koppom	26	59.43 N	12.09 E
Kopri	272c	19.11 N	72.58 E
Koprivnica	36	46.10 N	16.50 E
Köprü ≃	130	36.50 N	31.10 E
Köprülü Kanyon Milli Parkı ♦	130	37.20 N	31.18 E
Köprüören	130	39.29 N	29.47 E
Kopt'ovo	86	56.43 N	40.31 E
Kopyčincy	78	49.06 N	25.55 E
Kopyl'	76	53.09 N	27.05 E
Kopylovo, Ross.	86	60.35 N	45.02 E
Kopylovo, Ross.	88	56.16 N	85.13 E
Kor ≃	128	29.36 N	53.18 E
Kōra	94	36.12 N	136.15 E
Koraba ≃	128	30.05 N	49.40 E
Korab ⚲	38	41.47 N	20.34 E
Kor Aban	144	3.58 N	42.44 E
Korablino	80	53.55 N	40.01 E
Korahe	144	6.35 N	44.23 E
Kor'akovka	80	52.58 N	47.08 E
Kor'akskaja Sopka, vulkan ⚲¹	74	53.20 N	158.43 E
Kor'akskoje nagorje ⚲	74	62.30 N	172.00 E
Korakuen ⚹	270	34.39 N	133.55 E
Korakuen Stadium ♦	268	35.43 N	139.45 E
Koralbremer → Coral Sea ⚹²	14	20.00 S	158.00 E
Koralpe ⚲	58	46.50 N	14.58 E
Korannaberg ≃	158	27.25 S	22.32 E
Korapun	164	4.19 S	140.20 E
Korat → Nakhon Ratchasima	110	14.58 N	102.07 E
Kor'ažma	24	61.18 N	47.06 E
Korba, India	124	22.21 N	82.41 E
Korba, Tun.	34	36.35 N	10.52 E
Korbach	54	51.16 N	8.52 E
Korbol	146	10.28 N	17.03 E
Korbu, Gunong ⚲	114	4.43 N	101.17 E
Korbus ≃	86	58.20 N	62.05 E
Korčula	36	42.57 N	16.50 E
Korčula, Otok I	36	42.57 N	16.50 E
Korčulanski Kanal U	36	43.03 N	16.40 E
Korczyna	30	49.38 N	21.48 E
Kord Kūy	128	36.48 N	54.07 E
Korday	85	43.06 N	74.42 E
Korea, North □¹, Asia	98	40.00 N	127.00 E
Korea, South □¹, Asia	90	36.30 N	128.00 E
Korea Bay c	98	39.00 N	124.00 E
Korea University ⚹²	271b	37.36 N	127.02 E
Korec	78	50.37 N	27.09 E
Korekozevo	82	54.36 N	36.11 E
Koreliči	76	53.33 N	26.08 E
Koren	144	6.52 N	36.09 E
Korė (Die Wurzen) ×	64	46.31 N	13.45 E
Korf	74	60.18 N	166.00 E

Column 5

Nom	Page	Lat.	Long.
Korfovskij	89	48.13 N	135.03 E
Korga	158	30.12 S	20.28 E
Korgan	130	40.44 N	37.13 E
Korgašino	82	54.45 N	37.41 E
Körgessaare	76	58.59 N	22.28 E
Korgonskij chrebet ⚲	86	50.45 N	84.30 E
Korgus	140	19.13 N	33.29 E
Korhogo	150	9.27 N	5.38 W
Kōri	270	34.47 N	135.39 E
Koridhallós	267c	37.59 N	23.39 E
Korim	164	0.50 S	135.35 E
Korinda	169	37.10 S	145.39 E
Korienzé	130	15.24 N	3.47 W
Korim	164	0.54 S	136.02 E
Korinthiakós Kólpos c	38	38.19 N	22.04 E
Kórinthos (Corinth)	38	37.56 N	22.56 E
Korinthou, Dhiórix ≃	38	37.57 N	22.56 E
Kóris-hegy ⚲	30	47.18 N	17.45 E
Koritsa → Korçë	38	40.37 N	20.46 E
Koriukivka	78	51.44 N	32.15 E
Kōriyama → Yamato-Kōriyama	96	34.38 N	135.47 E
Korizo, Passe de ⚲	146	22.28 N	15.27 E
Korkino, Ross.	86	54.54 N	61.23 E
Korkino, Ross.	88	54.23 N	105.14 E
Korkinskoje, ozero ⊜	265a	59.55 N	30.44 E
Korkuteli	130	37.04 N	30.13 E
Korla	100	41.44 N	86.09 E
Korl'aki	80	57.06 N	46.57 E
Korliki	74	61.31 N	82.22 E
Korma, Bela.	76	52.21 N	31.31 E
Korma, Bela.	76	53.08 N	30.48 E
Körmend	61	47.01 N	16.37 E
Kormilovka	86	55.00 N	74.06 E
Kormovoje	86	46.17 N	43.30 E
Kornat, Otok I	36	43.50 N	15.16 E
Kornebach	263	51.35 N	7.38 E
Kornejevka, Kaz.	85	54.01 N	68.27 E
Kornejevka, Ross.	80	50.12 N	74.19 E
Kornelimünster	56	50.46 N	6.11 E
Körner, Dtsch.	54	51.13 N	10.35 E
Körner, Mt., U.S.	182	48.59 N	112.15 W
Kornešty	78	47.22 N	27.59 E
Korneuburg	264b	48.21 N	16.20 E
Körnik	30	52.17 N	17.04 E
Kornilovo	83	53.32 N	81.05 E
Kornis	80	45.33 N	13.44 E
Kornuchovo	80	55.33 N	49.53 E
Koro, C. Iv.	150	8.34 N	7.28 W
Koro, Mali	150	14.04 N	3.05 W
Koro Geçidi ⚲	86	40.03 N	40.33 E
Koroč ≃	56	53.44 N	14.32 E
Koroča	164	5.40 S	142.45 E
Korodougou Markala	150	12.26 N	6.17 W
Korogwe	154	5.09 S	38.29 E
Koroit	166	38.17 S	142.22 E
Korolenko, gora ⚲	86	58.15 N	115.01 E
Korolevskij Belok, gora ⚲	86	51.00 N	83.43 E
Koro Sea ⚹²	175j	18.00 S	179.50 E
Korosten'	78	50.57 N	28.39 E
Korostyšev	78	50.19 N	29.03 E
Korotojak	80	51.00 N	39.10 E
Koro Toro	146	16.05 N	18.30 E
Korotyš	76	52.12 N	36.08 E
Korovincy	78	50.23 N	33.20 E
Korovin Island I	180	55.25 N	160.15 W
Korovino, Ross.	82	54.43 N	38.52 E
Korovino, Ross.	88	57.55 N	97.51 E
Korovnik	81	43.50 N	116.16 E
Korovo	82	54.55 N	36.41 E
Koro Volcano ⚲¹	180	52.20 N	174.10 W
Koroyanitu ⚲	175j	17.37 S	177.35 E
Korpilahti	26	62.01 N	25.34 E
Korpo (Korppoo)	26	60.10 N	21.34 E
Korppoo (Korpo)	26	60.10 N	21.34 E
Korsakov	74	46.38 N	142.46 E
Korsakovo	82	53.25 N	36.41 E
Korschenbroich	56	51.11 N	6.31 E
Korsełbränna	26	64.27 N	15.35 E
Korsika → Corse I	36	42.00 N	9.00 E
Korsnäs, Suomi	26	62.47 N	21.12 E
Korsnäs, Sve.	40	60.32 N	15.20 E
Korsør	41	55.20 N	11.09 E
Korsør Nor c	41	55.19 N	11.11 E
Korsun'-Ševčenkovskij	78	49.26 N	31.16 E
Korsze	30	54.10 N	21.09 E
Kortemark	50	51.03 N	3.03 E
Kortgene	52	51.33 N	3.48 E
Kortkeros	24	61.49 N	51.28 E
Kortrijk (Courtrai)	50	50.50 N	3.16 E
Kortuz	88	55.30 N	94.57 E
Koruçam Burnu ⚲	130	35.40 N	32.50 E
Koruküyü → Jayapura	164	2.32 S	140.42 E
Korumburra	169	38.26 S	145.49 E
Korwai	124	24.07 N	78.04 E
Koryŏ	94	34.33 N	135.45 E
Koryŏ University ⚹²	271b	37.35 N	127.02 E
Koryst	78	51.37 N	26.50 E
Kos	38	36.53 N	27.19 E
Kos I	38	36.50 N	27.10 E
Kosa, Ross.	76	59.57 N	55.03 E
Kosa, Ross.	88	55.02 N	96.36 E
Kosa-Agač	86	50.00 N	88.40 E
Kosančič	38	42.49 N	21.45 E
Kosciuszko	30	52.05 N	18.40 E

Column 6

Nome	Página	Lat.	Long.
Kościerzyna	30	54.08 N	18.00 E
Kosciusko	194	33.03 N	89.35 W
Kosciusko □⁶	216	41.14 N	85.51 W
Kosciusko, Mount ⚲	171b	36.27 S	148.16 E
Kosciusko National Park ♦	166	36.10 S	148.15 E
Kös Dağı ⚲	130	40.59 N	34.25 E
Kosdaulet, peski ←⚓²	80	47.45 N	49.30 E
Kose, Eesti	76	59.11 N	25.10 E
Kose, Nihon	270	34.25 N	135.46 E
Köse, Tür.	130	40.11 N	39.39 E
Kösedağ ⚲	130	39.54 N	42.39 E
Kösefakii	130	39.36 N	34.09 E
Košelevka	82	55.09 N	38.05 E
Košelicha	80	55.02 N	43.33 E
Košerovo	82	55.38 N	38.22 E
Koserow	54	54.03 N	13.59 E
Koshen Stadium ♦	270	34.42 N	135.22 E
Koshigaya	94	35.54 N	139.48 E
Koshigoe	268	35.18 N	139.30 E
Koshikijima-rettō II	92	31.45 N	129.49 E
Koshino	94	36.02 N	135.01 E
Koshk-e Kohneh	128	34.52 N	62.31 E
Koshkonong	194	35.09 N	91.38 W
Koshkonong, Lake ⊜	216	42.52 N	88.58 W
Koshkonong Creek ≃	216	42.53 N	88.59 W
Koshlong Lake ⊜	212	44.58 N	78.29 W
Kōshoku	94	36.32 N	138.06 E
Koshu → Kwangju	98	35.09 N	126.54 E
Kosi ≃⁴	124	27.15 N	87.15 E
Kosi ≃	124	25.26 N	87.22 E
Košice	30	48.43 N	21.15 E
Kosigi	122	15.51 N	77.16 E
Kosi Kalan	124	27.48 N	77.26 E
Kosimeer ⊜	158	26.55 S	32.52 E
Kosino, Ross.	80	58.23 N	51.17 E
Kosino, Ross.	82	55.43 N	37.52 E
Kosju	24	65.38 N	59.03 E
Kosju ≃	24	66.18 N	59.53 E
Kosjuvom	24	66.17 N	59.50 E
Koskaecodde Lake ⊜	188	48.00 N	55.20 W
Koškar	80	47.27 N	53.29 E
Koški, Ross.	80	54.12 N	50.28 E
Koski, Suomi	26	60.39 N	23.09 E
Koškino	86	56.20 N	50.49 E
Koskuduk	86	44.06 N	77.22 E
Koskullskulle	24	67.12 N	20.50 E
Koslan	24	63.28 N	48.52 E
Köslin → Koszalin	30	54.12 N	16.09 E
Kosmonosy	54	50.26 N	15.00 E
Kosmonosy	54	50.26 N	15.00 E
Kosoba, gora ⚲	86	48.15 N	79.40 E
Kosogor	86	57.07 N	37.34 E
Kosoj, porog L, Ross.	88	57.44 N	96.20 E
Kosoj, porog L, Ross.	86	56.57 N	49.37 E
Kosolapovo	80	56.57 N	49.37 E
Kosong, C.M.I.K.	98	38.40 N	128.19 E
Kosong, Taehan	98	34.34 N	128.18 E
Kosovo	78	48.19 N	25.05 E
Kosovo-Metohija □⁴	38	42.35 N	21.00 E
Kosový potok ≃	60	49.46 N	12.48 E
Kosrae I	174c	5.19 N	162.59 E
Kösseine ⚲	130	49.51 N	11.59 E
Kossdorf	54	51.29 N	13.14 E
Kosse	222	31.17 N	96.38 W
Kössen	64	47.40 N	12.24 E
Kossindi	152	3.51 N	16.19 E
Kossol Passage U	175b	7.52 N	134.36 E
Kossol Reef ⚹²	175b	7.57 N	134.41 E
Kossou, Lac de ⊜¹	150	7.25 N	5.45 W
Kossovo	76	52.45 N	25.09 E
Kossuth	214	41.17 N	79.35 W
Kostajnica	36	45.14 N	16.33 E
Koš-Tegirmen	85	42.47 N	73.53 E
Kostelec nad Labem	54	50.13 N	14.35 E
Kostenec	38	42.16 N	23.49 E
Kostere	158	23.49 E	
Koster	158	25.51 S	26.54 E
Kösterberg	264b	53.36 N	9.49 E
Kostino, Ross.	88	57.47 N	87.07 E
Kostino, Ross.	80	58.16 N	52.44 E
Kostino-Otdelec	80	51.20 N	41.48 E
Kostjantynivka	83	48.33 N	37.42 E
Kostolac	38	44.43 N	21.11 E
Kostomuksa	24	64.41 N	30.49 E
Kostomłoty	54	51.07 N	16.29 E
Kostonjärvi ⊜	26	65.47 N	28.27 E
Kostopol'	78	50.53 N	26.27 E
Kostroma	76	57.46 N	40.55 E
Kostroma ≃	76	57.44 N	40.55 E
Kostrovo	82	55.53 N	36.42 E
Kostrzyn	30	52.37 N	14.39 E

Column 7

Nombre	Página	Lat.	Long.
Kostešty-Stynka, vodochranilišče (Lacul Stînca-Costești) ⊜¹	78	47.50 N	27.10 E
Koštice	54	50.24 N	13.55 E
Kostino, Ross.	80	52.11 N	51.20 E
Kostino, Ross.	88	56.27 N	148.16 E
Koš'ukovo	24	52.14 N	42.39 E
Kosu, India	124	26.56 N	83.29 E
Kota, India	124	25.11 N	75.50 E
Kota, India	124	25.11 N	75.50 E
Kota, Malay.	114	5.35 N	100.23 E
Kota Baharu, Malay.	114	6.08 N	102.15 E
Kota Bahru, Malay.	114	6.08 N	102.15 E
Kotabangun, Indon.	112	0.16 S	116.35 E
Kotabaru, Indon.	112	1.08 S	101.43 E
Kotabaru, Indon.	112	3.14 S	116.13 E
Kotabumi	112	4.49 S	104.54 E
Kota Kinabalu (Jesselton)	112	5.59 N	116.04 E
Kota Tinggi	114	1.44 N	103.54 E
Kotamobagu	112	0.46 N	124.19 E
Kot Diji	124	27.21 N	68.43 E
Kotdwāra	124	29.45 N	78.32 E
Kotel	38	42.53 N	26.27 E

Column 8

Nom	Page	Lat.	Long.
Kotabunan	112	0.49 N	124.38 E
Kota Sarang Semut	114	6.03 N	100.20 E
Kotaneemi, gora ⚲	88	67.43 N	77.18 E
Kōtaura	96	34.33 N	135.45 E

Column 9

Nome	Página	Lat.	Long.
Kotcho Lake ⊜	176	59.05 N	121.10 W
Kot Putli	124	27.43 N	76.12 E
Kotel	38	42.53 N	26.27 E

Symbols in the index entries represent the broad categories identified in the key at the right. Symbols with superior numbers (*) identify subcategories (see complete key on page 1).

Symbole im Register stellen die rechts im Schlüssel erklärten Kategorien dar. Symbole mit hochgestellten Zahlen (*) bezeichnen Unterabteilungen einer Kategorie (vgl. vollständiger Schlüssel auf Seite 1).

Les symboles de l'index représentent les catégories indiquées dans la légende à droite. Les symboles suivis d'un indice (*) représentent des sous-catégories (voir légende complète à la page 1).

Los símbolos incluidos en el texto del índice representan las grandes categorías identificadas en la clave a la derecha. Los símbolos con números en su parte superior (*) identifican las subcategorías (véase la clave completa en la página 1).

Os símbolos incluídos no texto do índice representam as grandes categorias identificadas com a chave à direita. Os símbolos com números com a sua parte superior (*) identificam as subcategorias (veja-se a chave completa na página 1).

^ Mountain	Berg	Montagne	Montaña	Montanha
^ Mountains	Gebirge	Montagnes	Montañas	Montanhas
) Pass	Paß	Col	Paso	Passo
V Valley, Canyon	Ebene	Vallée, Canyon	Vale, Cañon	Vale, Canhão
> Plain		Plaine	Planicie	Planicie
> Cape	Kap	Cap	Cabo	Cabo
I Island	Insel	Île	Isla	Ilha
II Islands	Inseln	Îles	Islas	Ilhas

Other Topographic Features / Andere Topographische Objekte / Autres données topographiques / Otros Elementos topográficos / Outros topográficos

ESPAÑOL

Nombre	Página	Lat.°′	Long.°′ W = Oeste
Krym	83	47.19 N	39.31 E
Krymsk	78	44.56 N	37.59 E
Krymskaja			
Avtonomnaja			
Sovetskaja			
Socialističeskaja			
Respublika □ 3	78	45.00 N	34.00 E
Krymskij	78	47.40 N	40.46 E
Krymskije gory ⋏	78	44.45 N	34.25 E
Krymskij poluostrov			
(Crimea) ≻ 1	78	45.00 N	34.00 E
Krymskij Zapovednik			
◆ 4	78	44.42 N	34.12 E
Krymskoje	83	48.45 N	38.48 E
Krynica	30	49.25 N	20.56 E
Krynka ≃	83	47.36 N	38.47 E
Kryžina, chrebet ⋏	88	54.00 N	95.00 E
Kryžopol'	78	48.23 N	28.52 E
Krzepice	30	50.58 N	18.44 E
Krzeszowice	30	50.09 N	19.39 E
Krzeszyce	54	52.36 N	15.01 E
Krzna ≃	30	52.08 N	23.31 E
Krzywiń	30	51.58 N	16.49 E
Krzyż	30	52.54 N	16.01 E
Ksar Chellala	148	35.13 N	2.18 E
Ksar el Barka	150	18.24 N	12.13 W
Ksar-el-Kebir	148	35.01 N	5.54 W
Ksar-el-Seghir	34	35.50 N	5.32 W
Ksar Hellal	36	35.39 N	10.54 E
Ksaverovka	78	50.03 N	30.12 E
Ksel, Djebel ∧	148	33.44 N	1.10 E
Kšen' ≃	76	52.23 N	37.44 E
Ksenjevka	88	53.34 N	118.44 E
Ksenofontova	24	60.58 N	56.12 E
Kšenskij	78	51.52 N	37.43 E
Książ Wielkopolski	30	52.05 N	17.14 E
Ksob, Oued ≃	36	35.49 N	7.53 E
Ksour, Monts des ⋏	148	32.45 N	0.30 W
Ksour Essaf	148	35.25 N	11.00 E
Kstovo	80	56.11 N	44.11 E
Kū', Wādī al- V	140	13.37 N	25.15 E
Kuah	114	6.19 N	99.51 E
Kuai ≃	100	33.09 N	117.32 E
Kuala, Indon.	112	2.55 N	105.48 E
Kuala, Indon.	114	3.32 N	98.24 E
Kualabee	114	4.24 N	96.03 E
Kuala Berang	114	5.04 N	103.01 E
Kualacenako	112	0.28 S	102.40 E
Kuala Kangsar	114	4.46 N	100.56 E
Kualakapuas	112	3.01 S	114.21 E
Kuala Kedah	114	6.06 N	100.18 E
Kuala Kelawang	114	2.56 N	102.05 E
Kuala Kerai	114	5.32 N	102.12 E
Kuala Kerau	114	3.43 N	102.22 E
Kualakeriau	112	0.50 N	113.20 E
Kuala Ketil	114	5.36 N	100.39 E
Kuala Kubu Baharu	114	3.34 N	101.39 E
Kuala Kurau	114	5.01 N	100.26 E
Kualakurun	112	1.07 S	113.53 E
Kualalangsa	114	4.32 N	98.01 E
Kuala Lipis	114	4.11 N	102.03 E
Kuala Lumpur	114	3.10 N	101.42 E
Kuala Lumpur □ 3	114	3.10 N	101.42 E
Kualamanjual	112	1.25 S	112.00 E
Kuala Nerang	114	6.15 N	100.36 E
Kualapesaguan	112	2.01 S	110.08 E
Kuala Pilah	114	2.44 N	102.15 E
Kualapuu	229a	21.09 N	157.02 W
Kuala Selangor	114	3.21 N	101.15 E
Kualasimpang	114	4.17 N	98.03 E
Kuala Terengganu	114	5.20 N	103.08 E
Kualu ≃	114	2.45 N	100.00 E
Kuamut	112	5.13 N	117.30 E
Kuamut ≃	112	5.13 N	117.32 E
Kuanbang	98	40.29 N	120.04 E
Kuancheng, Zhg.	98	40.37 N	118.31 E
Kuancheng, Zhg.	105	40.38 N	118.27 E
Kuandang	112	0.52 N	122.55 E
Kuandian	98	40.43 N	124.44 E
Kuando			
→ Cuando ≃	152	18.27 S	23.32 E
Kuanhsi	100	24.48 N	121.10 E
Kuanmiao	100	22.58 N	120.19 E
Kuanshan	100	23.03 N	121.09 E
Kuan Shan ∧	100	23.14 N	120.54 E
Kuantan	114	3.48 N	103.20 E
Kuantan ≃	114	3.50 N	103.17 E
Kuanyin	100	25.02 N	121.04 E
Kuanyün			
→ Guanyun	98	34.20 N	119.17 E
Kuanza			
→ Cuanza ≃	152	9.19 S	13.08 E
Kuba	84	41.22 N	48.31 E
Kuba			
→ Cuba □ 1	240p	21.30 N	80.00 W
Kuban' ≃	72	45.20 N	37.30 E
Kubatly	84	39.22 N	46.34 E
Kubbī	140	11.08 N	25.14 E
Kubbum	140	11.47 N	23.47 E
Kubena ≃	76	59.36 N	39.39 E
Kubenskoje	76	59.26 N	39.40 E
Kubenskoje, ozero ⊜	76	59.40 N	39.25 E
Kubiki	94	37.11 N	138.20 E
Kubinka	82	55.35 N	36.43 E
Kubitzer Bodden ⊂	54	54.24 N	13.12 E
Küblis	58	46.55 N	9.47 E
Kubn'a ≃	80	55.31 N	48.27 E
Kubokawa	96	33.12 N	133.08 E
Kubor, Mount ∧	164	6.05 S	144.45 E
Kubr' ≃	82	56.52 N	38.17 E
Kubrat	38	43.48 N	26.30 E
Kubu	115b	8.16 S	115.35 E
Kubuchaj	88	50.30 N	114.48 E
Kubu Gajah	114	5.10 N	100.41 E
Kubumesaai	112	1.31 N	115.06 E
Kubutambahan	115b	8.05 S	115.10 E
Kučema	24	65.37 N	42.28 E
Kučen'ajevo	80	54.44 N	46.24 E
Kučevo	38	44.27 N	21.44 E
Kuchaiburi	126	22.16 N	86.10 E
Kuchāman	120	27.09 N	74.52 E
Kuch'ang-ni	98	40.09 N	124.46 E
Kuchelebai	154	1.29 N	35.01 E
Kuchen Spitze ∧	58	47.03 N	10.14 E
Kuchinarai	110	16.32 N	104.04 E
Kuching	112	1.33 N	110.20 E
Kuchinoerabu-jima I	93b	30.28 N	130.12 E
Kuchino-shima I	93b	29.57 N	129.57 E
Kuchiwa	96	34.53 N	132.55 E
Kuchl	64	47.37 N	13.09 E
Kūchnay Darweyshān	128	30.59 N	64.11 E
Kuchterin Lug	89	52.25 N	128.05 E
Kuchtinka	82	54.29 N	38.10 E
Kučino	265b	55.45 N	37.58 E
Kučkak	85	40.15 N	70.20 E
Kučki	80	53.01 N	44.29 E
Kuçovë	38	40.48 N	19.54 E
Küçük Ağrı Dağı ∧	84	39.40 N	44.25 E
Küçükbahçe	130	38.33 N	26.24 E
Küçükbakkal ◆ 8	267b	40.58 N	29.06 E
Küçükçekmece ◆ 8	267b	40.59 N	28.46 E
Küçükçekmece Gölü			
⊜	267b	41.00 N	28.46 E
Küçükköy ◆ 8	267b	41.04 N	28.54 E
Küçükkuyu	130	39.32 N	26.36 E
Kučukskoje, ozero ⊜	86	52.42 N	79.46 E
Kucur, Tanjung ≻	115a	8.39 S	114.34 E
Kučurgan ≃	78	46.43 N	29.53 E
Kūd	123	33.05 N	75.17 E
Kuda ≃	88	52.25 N	104.08 E
Kudaka-jima I	174m	26.09 N	127.54 E
Kudamatsu	96	34.00 N	131.52 E
Kudanggou	104	41.06 N	124.00 E
Kudap	114	1.17 N	102.26 E
Kudara, Ross.	88	52.13 N	106.39 E
Kudara, Taj.	85	38.25 N	72.41 E
Kudara ≃	85	38.19 N	72.28 E
Kudara-Somon	88	50.10 N	107.25 E
Kudat	112	6.53 N	116.50 E
Kudbrooke ◆ 8	260	51.28 N	0.03 E

FRANÇAIS

Nom	Page	Lat.°′	Long.°′ W = Ouest
Kudejevskij	86	54.52 N	56.46 E
Kudene	164	6.14 S	134.39 E
Kudever'	76	56.47 N	29.23 E
Kudinovo	82	55.45 N	38.12 E
Kudirkos Naumiestis	76	54.46 N	22.53 E
Kudongho	98	35.31 N	126.29 E
Kudoyama	96	34.17 N	135.34 E
Kudremukh ∧	122	13.08 N	75.16 E
Kudrovo	265a	59.54 N	30.31 E
Kudus	115a	6.48 S	110.50 E
Kudyat al-Islām	142	27.32 N	30.45 E
Kudymkar	86	59.01 N	54.37 E
Kuee Ruins ⊥	229d	19.21 N	155.23 W
Kueishan Tao I	100	24.51 N	121.57 E
Kueisui			
→ Hohhot	102	40.51 N	111.40 E
Kueiyang			
→ Guiyang	102	26.35 N	106.43 E
Kuekvun' ≃	180	69.14 N	179.25 E
Kuënlun			
→ Kunlun Shan ⋏	120	36.30 N	88.00 E
Kuerbin	89	49.25 N	128.59 E
K'uerhlo			
→ Korla	90	41.44 N	86.09 E
Kufayr az-Zayt	132	33.26 N	35.44 E
Kufayr Yābūs	132	33.42 N	36.01 E
Kufrinjah	132	32.18 N	35.42 E
Kufstein	64	47.35 N	12.10 E
Kufūr Bilshāy	142	30.51 N	30.48 E
Kufūr Najm	142	30.44 N	31.35 E
Kuga, Nihon	96	34.05 N	132.05 E
Kuga, Nihon	96	33.56 N	132.16 E
Kuga, Zhg.	90	41.43 N	82.54 E
Kugaluk ≃	180	69.10 N	131.00 W
Kugaly	86	44.29 N	78.40 E
Kugarčino	80	55.33 N	50.29 E
Kugart ≃	85	40.52 N	72.53 E
Kugas	85	38.21 N	70.48 E
Kugej	83	46.53 N	39.19 E
Kugesi	80	56.02 N	47.18 E
Kugmallit Bay ⊂	180	69.33 N	133.25 W
Kugojeja ≃	78	46.34 N	39.38 E
Kuguno	94	36.03 N	137.16 E
Kuḥaylī	140	19.25 N	32.50 E
Kühbach	60	48.29 N	11.11 E
Kūhdasht	128	33.32 N	47.36 E
Kūh Lab, Ra's-e ≻	128	25.17 N	60.28 E
Kuḥlīyah, Wādī V	142	30.05 N	31.58 E
Kühlungsborn	54	54.09 N	11.43 E
Kuhmo	26	64.08 N	29.31 E
Kuhmoinen	26	61.34 N	25.11 E
Kühnhausen	54	51.02 N	10.58 E
Kühnsdorf	61	46.37 N	14.37 E
Kūhpāyeh	128	32.43 N	52.26 E
Kühren	54	51.20 N	12.50 E
Kuhstedt	52	53.23 N	8.58 E
Kui	164	7.30 S	147.15 E
Kuibyschew			
→ Samara	80	53.12 N	50.09 E
Kuidesu	98	41.46 N	119.29 E
Kuidou	100	25.10 N	118.11 E
Kuikkol', ozero ⊜	86	50.57 N	64.30 E
Kuikui, Lae o ≻	229a	20.36 N	156.35 W
Kuilāpāl	126	22.50 N	86.38 E
Kuinre	52	52.47 N	5.50 E
Kuiseb ≃	156	22.59 S	14.31 E
Kuishi-yama ∧, Nihon	96	33.51 N	133.35 E
Kuishi-yama ∧, Nihon	96	33.40 N	133.31 E
Kuitan	100	23.05 N	115.58 E
Kuito	152	12.22 S	16.56 E
Kuiu Island I	180	56.45 N	134.10 W
Kuivaniemi	26	65.35 N	25.11 E
Kuivastu	76	58.35 N	23.22 E
Kuja, Ross.	24	67.46 N	53.10 E
Kuja, Ross.	24	65.05 N	40.06 E
Kujal'nickij liman ⊜	78	46.40 N	30.42 E
Kujang	98	39.52 N	126.01 E
Kujani Game Reserve			
◆ 4	150	7.10 N	0.50 W
Kujawy ◆ 1	30	52.45 N	18.30 E
Kujbyšev	86	55.27 N	78.19 E
Kujbyševka	78	47.37 N	31.42 E
Kujbyševo, Ross.	83	47.49 N	38.55 E
Kujbyševo, Ukr.	78	44.38 N	33.52 E
Kujbyševo, Ukr.	78	47.22 N	36.39 E
Kujbyševo, Uzb.	85	40.22 N	71.17 E
Kujbyšev			
→ Samara	80	53.12 N	50.09 E
Kujbyševskij, Kaz.	86	53.15 N	66.51 E
Kujbyševskij, Uzb.	72	37.52 N	68.44 E
Kujbyševskij Zaton	80	55.09 N	49.12 E
Kujbyševskoje			
vodochranilišče ⊜ 1	80	54.30 N	48.30 E
Kujeda	86	56.26 N	55.35 E
Kujgan	86	45.25 N	74.10 E
Kujgenkol'	80	49.17 N	47.59 E
Kuji	92	40.11 N	141.46 E
Kuji ≃	94	36.29 N	140.37 E
Kujirai	268	35.56 N	139.27 E
Kujl'uk	85	41.15 N	69.20 E
Kujman'	76	52.52 N	39.16 E
Kujŏng-ni	98	37.53 N	125.54 E
Kujtun	88	54.21 N	101.29 E
Kujū	96	33.01 N	131.18 E
Kujūkuri	94	35.32 N	140.25 E
Kujūkuri-hama ♠ 2	94	35.35 N	140.30 E
Kujū-san ∧	96	33.05 N	131.15 E
Kuk ∧	64	46.16 N	13.45 E
Kuk ≃	180	70.36 N	160.00 W
Kukaklek Lake ⊜	180	59.09 N	155.20 W
Kukalaya ≃	236	13.39 N	83.37 W
Kukan	89	49.12 N	133.28 E
Kukarino	82	55.31 N	35.59 E
Kukawa	146	12.56 N	13.35 E
Kukerin	162	33.11 S	118.05 E
Kukës	38	42.05 N	20.24 E
Kuke Shan ⋏	85	40.00 N	75.00 E
Kuki	94	36.04 N	139.40 E
Kukipi	164	8.10 S	146.05 E
Kukkola	26	65.59 N	24.04 E
Kukmirn	61	47.04 N	16.13 E
Kukmor	80	56.13 N	50.54 E
Kukoboj	76	58.42 N	39.54 E
Kukol'	76	59.52 N	32.35 E
Kükong			
→ Shaoguan	100	24.50 N	113.37 E
Kukpowruk ≃	180	69.35 N	163.00 W
Kukpuk ≃	180	68.23 N	166.20 W
Kukshi	120	22.12 N	74.45 E
Kukuj	76	59.21 N	32.33 E
Kuku-Nor			
→ Qinghai Hu ⊜	102	36.50 N	100.20 E
Kukup	114	1.19 N	103.27 E
Kuku Point ≻	174a	19.18 N	166.34 E
Kukuri Mukuri Char I	126	21.56 N	90.39 E
Kukuštan	86	57.38 N	56.30 E
Kula, Blg.	38	43.53 N	22.31 E
Kula, Jugo.	38	45.36 N	19.32 E
Kula, Tür.	130	38.32 N	28.40 E
Kula, Hi., U.S.	229a	20.52 N	156.40 W
Kul'ab	120	37.55 N	69.46 E
Kulāchi	123	31.56 N	70.27 E
Kulagi	76	52.56 N	32.24 E
Kula Gulf ʯ	175e	8.05 S	157.18 E
Kulai	114	1.40 N	103.36 E
Kulaj	86	57.42 N	75.15 E
Kula Kangri ∧	124	28.03 N	90.27 E
Kulākh	144	21.18 N	40.41 E
Kulakovo, Ross.	82	55.06 N	37.28 E
Kulakovo, Ross.	86	58.06 N	93.57 E
Kulakši	86	47.12 N	55.24 E
Kulal, Mount ∧	154	2.43 N	36.56 E
Kulanak	85	41.22 N	75.31 E
Kulandy	86	46.08 N	59.31 E
Kulanutpes ≃	86	50.21 N	69.08 E
Kular	74	70.41 N	134.22 E
Kulassein Island I	116	6.25 N	120.41 E
Kulaura	120	24.32 N	92.03 E
Kulautuva	76	54.58 N	23.38 E
Kulaykilī	140	11.21 N	25.36 E

PORTUGUÊS

Nome	Página	Lat.°′	Long.°′ W = Oeste
Kul'či	89	53.33 N	139.36 E
Kuldīga	76	56.58 N	21.59 E
Kuldja			
→ Yining	86	43.54 N	81.21 E
Kul'dur	89	49.13 N	131.38 E
Kule	156	23.05 S	20.05 E
Kulebaki	80	55.24 N	42.32 E
Kulejevo	86	59.40 N	80.59 E
Kulen Vakuf	36	44.34 N	16.06 E
Kulešovka	83	47.05 N	39.33 E
Kulevčinskij	86	53.12 N	61.26 E
Kulgām	123	33.39 N	75.01 E
Kulgera	162	25.50 S	133.18 E
Kulgunino	86	53.35 N	56.56 E
Kuligi	80	58.11 N	53.46 E
Kulikov	78	49.58 N	24.04 E
Kulikovka, Ross.	80	52.14 N	47.36 E
Kulikovka, Ukr.	78	51.23 N	31.37 E
Kulikovo	76	52.14 N	39.35 E
Kulikovskij	80	50.51 N	42.34 E
Kulim	114	5.22 N	100.34 E
Kulin	162	32.40 S	118.10 E
Kuliushucun	105	40.07 N	116.34 E
Kulju	26	61.23 N	23.46 E
Kulkyne Creek ≃	166	30.16 S	144.12 E
Kullaberg ⋏ 2	41	56.18 N	12.30 E
Kullamaa	76	58.53 N	24.05 E
Küllenhahn ◆ 8	263	51.14 N	7.08 E
Küllstedt	56	51.16 N	10.17 E
Kullu	123	31.58 N	77.06 E
Kulm	198	46.18 N	98.57 W
Kulmbach	54	50.06 N	11.27 E
Kulnura	170	33.14 S	151.13 E
Kuloj, Ross.	24	64.58 N	43.28 E
Kuloj, Ross.	24	61.02 N	42.29 E
Kuloj ≃, Ross.	24	66.03 N	43.22 E
Kuloj ≃, Ross.	76	60.25 N	42.30 E
Kuloli	85	39.22 N	68.03 E
Kulongshan	98	41.43 N	116.54 E
Kulongshanpuzi	104	41.16 N	123.59 E
Kulotino	76	58.27 N	33.21 E
Kulp	130	38.30 N	41.02 E
Kulpahar	124	25.19 N	79.39 E
Kulpara	168b	34.04 S	138.02 E
Kulpawn ≃	150	10.21 N	1.05 W
Kulpi	126	22.06 N	88.15 E
Kul'pino	82	56.18 N	37.09 E
Kulpmont	208	40.47 N	76.28 W
Kulpsville	285	40.15 N	75.20 W
Kul'sary	86	46.59 N	54.01 E
Kulsbjerge ⋏ 2	41	55.01 N	12.01 E
Külsheim	56	49.40 N	9.31 E
Kültepe ⊥	130	38.44 N	35.34 E
Kulti	126	23.44 N	86.51 E
Kultikri	126	22.10 N	87.09 E
Kultuk	88	51.44 N	103.42 E
Kulu	130	39.06 N	33.05 E
Kuluha, Jabal ∧	140	15.31 N	23.25 E
Kulumadau	164	9.03 S	152.43 E
Kulunda	86	52.35 N	78.57 E
Kulunda ≃	86	52.59 N	79.48 E
Kulundinskaja step'			
≚	86	53.00 N	79.00 E
Kulundinskoje, ozero			
⊜	86	53.00 N	79.36 E
Kuluqi	89	50.23 N	124.13 E
Kulwin	166	35.02 S	142.33 E
Kum ≃	130	38.38 N	27.32 E
Kuma	96	33.39 N	132.54 E
Kuma ≃, Nihon	92	32.30 N	130.34 E
Kuma ≃, Ross.	72	44.56 N	47.00 E
Kuma ≃, Ross.	86	59.32 N	66.45 E
Kumagaya	94	36.08 N	139.23 E
Kumai, Indon.	112	3.23 S	112.33 E
Kumai, Indon.	112	2.44 S	111.43 E
Kumai, Teluk ⊂	112	3.00 S	111.43 E
Kumaishi	92a	42.08 N	139.59 E
Kumajri	84	40.48 N	43.50 E
Kumakanda	88	52.44 N	116.55 E
Kumalarang	116	7.44 N	123.08 E
Kumamba,			
Kepulauan II	164	1.36 S	138.45 E
Kumamoto	92	32.48 N	130.43 E
Kumamoto □ 5	96	32.58 N	130.55 E
Kumano, Nihon	92	33.54 N	136.05 E
Kumano, Nihon	96	34.20 N	132.34 E
Kumano ≃	92	33.44 N	136.01 E
Kumano-nada ⫟ 2	92	33.47 N	136.20 E
Kumanovo	38	42.08 N	21.43 E
Kumār ≃ 1, Bngl.	126	23.11 N	90.10 E
Kumār ≃ 1, Bngl.	126	23.31 N	89.28 E
Kumara, N.Z.	172	42.38 S	171.11 E
Kumara, Ross.	89	51.37 N	126.47 E
Kumārapālaiyam	122	11.28 N	77.43 E
Kumardhubi	126	23.48 N	86.43 E
Kumarganj	126	22.59 N	87.44 E
Kumārghāt	120	24.04 N	92.04 E
Kumārgrām	124	26.37 N	89.50 E
Kumāri ≃	126	22.57 N	86.48 E
Kumārkhāli	124	23.51 N	89.15 E
Kumarl	162	32.47 S	121.33 E
Kumasi	150	6.41 N	1.35 W
Kumatori	270	34.24 N	135.22 E
Kumawa,			
Pegunungan ⋏	164	3.50 S	132.50 E
Kumba	152	4.38 N	9.25 E
Kumbakonam	122	10.58 N	79.23 E
Kumba Pits	156	18.45 S	24.45 E
Kumbar	140	12.03 N	30.16 E
Kumbarilla	166	27.19 S	150.53 E
Kumbe	164	8.21 S	140.13 E
Kumbel'	85	42.30 N	73.11 E
Kŭmch'ŏn	98	38.10 N	126.29 E
Kum-Dag	128	39.16 N	54.35 E
Kumdah ⫟ 4	144	20.23 N	45.05 E
Kumdan ∧	123	35.09 N	77.35 E
Kumdanlı	130	38.19 N	30.59 E
Kume	96	35.03 N	133.54 E
Kume-jima I	93b	26.20 N	126.47 E
Kumenan	96	34.56 N	133.58 E
Kumeny	80	58.07 N	49.56 E
Kŭm-gang ≃	98	36.00 N	126.40 E
Kŭmgang-san ∧	98	38.35 N	128.10 E
Kŭmhwa	98	38.17 N	127.28 E
Kumi	154	1.29 N	33.56 E
Kumihama	96	35.36 N	134.55 E
Kuminovskoje	86	57.48 N	64.07 E
Kuminskij	86	58.40 N	66.04 E
Kumiyama	270	34.53 N	135.45 E
Kumizawa ◆ 8	268	35.23 N	139.31 E
Kumköy ◆ 8	267b	41.15 N	29.02 E
Kumla	40	59.08 N	15.08 E
Kumli	84	43.58 N	46.04 E
Kumlinge I	26	60.16 N	20.47 E
Kumluca, Tür.	130	36.22 N	30.18 E
Kumluca, Tür.	130	41.27 N	32.28 E
Kummelnäs	40	59.21 N	18.17 E
Kummerow	54	54.17 N	12.53 E
Kummerower See ⊜	54	53.49 N	12.52 E
Kümmersbruck	60	49.25 N	11.53 E
Kumo	146	10.03 N	11.13 E
Kŭmŏ-do I	98	34.31 N	127.45 E
Kumon Range ⋏	102	26.30 N	97.15 E
Kumora	88	55.53 N	111.13 E
Kumosō-yama ∧	96	33.54 N	134.18 E
Kumotori-yama ∧	94	35.51 N	138.57 E
Kumphawapi	110	17.07 N	103.01 E
Kumrābād	126	24.10 N	87.16 E
Kumru	130	40.53 N	37.17 E
Kŭmsan	98	36.07 N	127.30 E
Kŭmsan-ni	98	37.55 N	125.41 E
Kumsenga	154	3.47 S	30.25 E
Kumta	122	14.25 N	74.24 E
Kumu	154	3.04 N	25.09 E
Kumu ≃	114	1.24 N	100.43 E
Kumuch	84	42.11 N	47.07 E
Kumukahi, Cape ≻	229d	19.31 N	154.49 W
Kumukuli	120	37.33 N	88.50 E
Kumusi ≃	164	8.35 S	148.00 E
Kümüx	86	42.14 N	88.11 E

Kumzār	128	26.20 N	56.25 E
Kuna	202	43.29 N	116.25 W
Kunar (Konar) ≃	123	34.25 N	70.32 E
Kunašak	86	55.43 N	61.36 E
Kunashiri-tō			
→ Kunašir, ostrov I	92a	44.10 N	146.00 E
Kunašir, ostrov			
(Kunashiri-tō) I	92a	44.10 N	146.00 E
Kun'batar	84	44.17 N	45.34 E
Kuncheng Hu ⊜	106	31.35 N	120.45 E
Kunchhā	124	28.08 N	84.20 E
Kunc'ovo ◆ 8	265b	55.44 N	37.26 E
Kunda, Eesti	76	59.29 N	26.32 E
Kunda, Zaïre	154	3.57 S	26.35 E
Kunda Hills ⋏ 2	122	11.10 N	76.30 E
Kundahit	126	23.58 N	87.10 E
Kundam	124	23.13 N	80.21 E
Kundāpura	122	13.38 N	74.42 E
Kundar ≃	120	31.56 N	69.19 E
Kundat	86	55.14 N	87.51 E
Kundelungu, Parc			
National de ♠	154	10.30 S	27.45 E
Kunderu ≃	122	14.38 N	78.42 E
Kundi	154	1.08 S	40.41 E
Kundiān	123	32.27 N	71.28 E
Kundiawa	164	6.00 S	145.00 E
Kundima	164	4.14 S	143.52 E
Kundl	64	47.28 N	11.59 E
Kundla	120	21.20 N	71.18 E
Kundr'učje ≃	83	47.52 N	40.15 E
Kundur, Pulau I	112	0.45 N	103.26 E
Kunene (Cunene) ≃	152	17.20 S	11.50 E
Kunersdorf, Forst ◆ 3	264a	52.17 N	12.59 E
Kunes	24	70.21 N	26.31 E
Künes ≃	86	43.55 N	80.55 E
Kunga ≃ 1	126	21.45 N	89.30 E
Kungälv	26	57.52 N	11.58 E
Kungana	146	7.50 N	10.42 E
Kungchuling			
→ Huaide	89	43.32 N	124.50 E
Kungej-Alatau,			
chrebet ⋏	85	42.50 N	77.00 E
Kunggyü Yumco ⊜	124	30.35 N	82.09 E
Kunghit Island I	182	52.06 N	131.04 W
Kunghsi	100	24.37 N	121.16 E
Kung-pei-tien	269d	25.06 N	121.38 E
Kungrad	86	43.06 N	58.54 E
Kungsängen	40	59.29 N	17.45 E
Kungsängen flygplats			
⊠	40	58.36 N	16.15 E
Kungsbacka	26	57.29 N	12.04 E
Kungsgården	40	60.36 N	16.37 E
Kungshamn	26	58.22 N	11.15 E
Kungsör	40	59.25 N	16.05 E
Kungu	152	2.47 N	19.12 E
Kungur	86	57.25 N	56.57 E
Kunhār ≃	123	34.17 N	73.29 E
Kunhegyes	30	47.22 N	20.38 E
Kunhing	110	21.18 N	98.26 E
Kuni	94	36.35 N	138.38 E
Kunia	229c	21.29 N	158.07 W
Kunigami	174m	26.45 N	128.10 E
Kunimi	96	33.41 N	131.36 E
Kuningan	115a	6.59 S	108.29 E
Kunisaki	96	33.33 N	131.45 E
Kunisaki-hantō ≻ 1	96	33.30 N	131.40 E
Kunitachi	268	35.41 N	139.26 E
Kuni Vyselki	82	54.18 N	38.41 E
Kunja	76	56.18 N	30.59 E
Kunja ≃, Ross.	76	57.09 N	31.10 E
Kunja ≃, Ross.	82	56.31 N	38.12 E
Kunjāh	123	32.32 N	73.59 E
Kunje	83	49.23 N	37.15 E
Kunkle	216	41.38 N	84.30 W
Kunkletown	210	40.51 N	75.27 W
Kunkuri	124	22.45 N	83.57 E
Kunlong	110	23.25 N	98.39 E
Kunlun Shan ⋏	120	36.30 N	88.00 E
Kunming	102	25.05 N	102.40 E
Kunming Hu ⊜	271a	39.59 N	116.15 E
Kunmunya Aboriginal			
Reserve ◆ 4	164	15.45 S	124.45 E
Kunnamkulam	122	10.39 N	76.05 E
Kunost'	76	60.01 N	37.38 E
Kunovice	30	49.03 N	17.29 E
Kunow	54	53.00 N	12.07 E
Kunowice	54	52.20 N	14.50 E
Kunrau	54	52.35 N	11.01 E
Kunsan	98	35.58 N	126.41 E
Kunshan	106	31.23 N	120.57 E
Kunszentmárton	30	46.51 N	20.18 E
Kuntair	150	13.32 N	16.13 W
Kuntaur	150	13.40 N	14.48 W
Kuntiki	86	58.29 N	76.24 E
Kunting	100	29.48 N	121.56 E
Kuntshankoie	152	3.20 S	23.34 E
Kuntuolun	102	45.13 N	115.21 E
Kununurra	164	15.47 S	128.44 E
Kunwi	98	36.15 N	128.34 E
Kunya	150	12.14 N	8.34 E
Kunyo	144	6.17 N	42.33 E
Kunžak	61	49.07 N	15.11 E
Künzell	56	50.33 N	9.42 E
Künzelsau	56	49.16 N	9.41 E
Künzing	60	48.40 N	13.05 E
Kunzulu	152	3.29 S	16.09 E
Kuocang Shan ⋏	100	28.36 N	120.30 E
Kuohsing	100	24.02 N	120.51 E
Kuokegan	120	37.30 N	89.55 E
Kuolajarvi	24	66.58 N	29.12 E
Kuop I 1	175c	7.03 N	151.56 E
Kuopio	26	62.54 N	27.41 E
Kuopion lääni □ 4	26	63.00 N	27.30 E
Kuortane	26	62.48 N	23.30 E
Kupa ≃	36	45.28 N	16.24 E
Kup'abal	271b	37.37 N	126.54 E
Kupang	112	10.10 S	123.35 E
Kupang, Teluk ⊂	112	10.04 S	123.40 E
Kup'ansk	83	49.42 N	37.38 E
Kupanskoje	82	56.51 N	38.43 E
Kup'ansk-Uzlovoj	83	49.39 N	37.39 E
Kuparuk ≃	180	70.25 N	148.55 W
Kupava	80	51.07 N	42.57 E
Kupavna	265b	55.45 N	38.08 E
Kuper Island I	224	48.58 N	123.39 W
Kupferberg	263	51.09 N	7.27 E
Kupferdreh ◆ 8	263	51.23 N	7.05 E
Kupfermühle	41	54.50 N	9.24 E
Kupferzell	56	49.14 N	9.41 E
Kupiano	164	10.05 S	148.11 E
Kupičev	78	51.00 N	24.44 E
Kupino	86	54.22 N	77.18 E
Kupiškis	76	55.50 N	24.58 E
Küplü, Tür.	130	41.07 N	26.21 E
Küplü, Tür.	130	40.06 N	30.00 E
Kupol, gora ∧	180	68.38 N	174.45 E
Kuppenheim	56	48.49 N	8.15 E
Kupper Airport ⊠	276	40.31 N	74.36 W
Kupreanof	180	56.49 N	132.57 W
Kupreanof Island I	180	56.50 N	133.30 W
Kupreanof Point ≻	180	55.34 N	159.35 W
Kupres	36	44.00 N	17.17 E
Küps	54	50.11 N	11.16 E
Kupuri	89	54.44 N	130.30 E
Kur ≃	89	48.44 N	134.14 E
Kur, Pulau I	164	5.20 S	132.00 E
Kura (Kuruçay) ≃,			
Asia	84	39.24 N	49.19 E
Kura ≃, Ross.	84	44.06 N	44.57 E
Kurabuchi	94	36.25 N	138.48 E
Kur'ačeje	83	48.10 N	39.37 E
Kur'ačevka, Ukr.	83	49.39 N	38.42 E
Kur'ačevka, Ukr.	83	49.22 N	39.36 E
Kurach	84	41.36 N	47.46 E
Kurach ≃	84	41.40 N	48.11 E
Kurachovka	83	48.02 N	37.23 E
Kurachovo	83	47.59 N	37.16 E
Kuragaty	85	43.06 N	72.59 E
Kuragaty ≃	85	43.57 N	73.34 E
Kuragino	86	53.53 N	92.40 E

Kurahashi	96	34.06 N	132.30 E
Kurahashi-jima I	96	34.08 N	132.31 E
Kuraj	86	56.42 N	95.29 E
Kurajlysaj	80	50.07 N	51.51 E
Kurakaki	270	34.59 N	135.28 E
Kurakino, Ross.	80	52.33 N	44.03 E
Kurakino, Ross.	82	54.30 N	35.48 E
Kurakovo	82	54.05 N	37.14 E
Kūrāli	123	30.50 N	76.35 E
Kuram	85	43.33 N	78.08 E
Kuramā', Ḥarrat ♠ 9	128	24.30 N	40.15 E
Kurama-yama ∧	96	35.07 N	135.46 E
Kuraminskij chrebet ⋏	85	40.45 N	70.10 E
Kuramo Waters ⊂	273a	6.26 N	3.26 E
Kuranami	268	35.27 N	140.00 E
Kuraon	124	24.59 N	82.05 E
Kurar ◆ 8	272c	19.11 N	72.52 E
Kurašasaj	86	50.18 N	56.55 E
Kurashiki	96	34.35 N	133.46 E
Kurasiki			
→ Kurashiki	96	34.35 N	133.46 E
Kurate	96	33.47 N	130.41 E
Kurauli	124	27.24 N	78.59 E
Kuraymah	140	18.33 N	31.51 E
Kurayoshi	96	35.26 N	133.49 E
Kurayyimah	132	32.16 N	35.36 E
Kurba	80	57.34 N	39.32 E
Kurba ≃	88	52.02 N	108.30 E
Kurbağa Gölü ⊜	130	38.21 N	35.17 E
Kurbağalı ≃	267b	40.59 N	29.02 E
Kurbatovo	86	55.34 N	91.10 E
Kurbulik	88	53.45 N	108.57 E
Kurčaloj	84	43.12 N	46.05 E
Kurchatov	78	51.39 N	35.36 E
Kur-Čilik ≃	85	43.50 N	78.06 E
Kurčum	86	48.37 N	83.40 E
Kurdaj	85	43.21 N	74.59 E
K'urdamir	84	40.21 N	48.08 E
Kurdgelauri	84	41.58 N	45.32 E
Kurdistan □ 9	128	37.00 N	45.00 E
Kurdufān al-			
Janūbīyah □ 4	140	11.00 N	30.00 E
Kurdufān ash-			
Shamālīyah □ 4	140	14.00 N	29.45 E
Kurd'umovka	83	48.28 N	37.59 E
Kurduvādi	122	18.05 N	75.26 E
Kure, Austl.	164	15.27 S	124.33 E
Kure, Nihon	96	34.14 N	132.34 E
Küre, Tür.	130	41.48 N	33.43 E
Kure Atoll I 1	14	28.25 N	178.25 W
Küre Dağları ⋏	130	41.45 N	34.00 E
Kurejka ≃	74	66.30 N	87.12 E
Kurejskaja	88	58.56 N	111.20 E
Kuren'	78	51.09 N	32.44 E
Kurenalus	26	65.21 N	26.59 E
Kurenec	76	54.33 N	26.57 E
Kuresaare	76	58.15 N	22.28 E
Kurgal'džinskij	86	50.36 N	70.01 E
Kurgan	86	55.26 N	65.18 E
Kurgan Mečetnyj,			
gora ∧ 2	83	48.06 N	39.21 E
Kurgan-T'ube	120	37.50 N	68.48 E
Kurgasyn	86	49.15 N	66.43 E
Kurgatej	88	54.23 N	99.27 E
Kurgolovo	76	59.46 N	28.06 E
Kuria I	14	0.14 N	173.25 E
Kuria Muria Islands			
→ Khurīyā Murīyā,			
Jazā'ir II	118	17.30 N	56.00 E
Kuriasol	126	22.06 N	86.39 E
Kuridala	166	21.17 S	140.30 E
Kurīgrām	124	25.49 N	89.39 E
Kurihama	268	35.13 N	139.43 E
Kurihashi	94	36.08 N	139.42 E
Kurikka	26	62.37 N	22.25 E
Kurilen			
→ Kuril'skije			
ostrova II	74	46.10 N	152.00 E
Kurilen-Strasse			
→ Pervyj Kuril'skij			
proliv ʯ	74	50.50 N	156.36 E
Kuriles, Islas			
→ Kuril'skije			
ostrova II	74	46.10 N	152.00 E
Kuril Islands			
→ Kuril'skije			
ostrova II	74	46.10 N	152.00 E
Kurilovka	80	50.44 N	48.02 E
Kuril'sk	74	45.14 N	147.53 E
Kuril'skije ostrova			
(Kuril Islands) II	74	46.10 N	152.00 E
Kuril Strait			
→ Pervyj Kuril'skij			
proliv ʯ	74	50.50 N	156.36 E
Kuril Trench ⇼ 1	6	47.00 N	155.00 E
Kuřim	30	49.18 N	16.32 E
Kurimoto	94	35.49 N	140.30 E
Ku-Ring-Gai Chase			
National Park ♠	170	33.38 S	151.15 E
Kurinjippadi	122	11.34 N	79.36 E
Kurinskaja kosa ≻ 2	84	39.03 N	49.13 E
Kurinwás ≃	236	12.49 N	83.41 W
Kuripapango	172	39.23 S	176.21 E
Kuriyama, Nihon	92a	43.03 N	141.47 E
Kuriyama, Nihon	94	36.52 N	139.37 E
Kurja, Ross.	24	61.42 N	57.09 E
Kurja, Ross.	86	51.36 N	82.19 E
Kurjanovskaja	76	60.19 N	41.33 E
Kurkijoki	26	61.18 N	29.54 E
Kurkino, Ross.	76	53.26 N	38.40 E
Kurkino, Ross.	265b	55.53 N	37.23 E
Kurkliai	76	55.25 N	25.03 E
Kurl ◆ 8	263	51.35 N	7.35 E
Kurla ◆ 8	272c	19.05 N	72.53 E
Kurlackoje	83	47.21 N	39.03 E
Kurleja	88	52.11 N	119.11 E
Kurlin	80	51.48 N	51.00 E
Kurlovskij	80	55.27 N	40.36 E
Kurmanajevka	80	52.31 N	52.06 E
Kurmani	126	22.47 N	89.53 E
Kurmankol'	80	49.09 N	48.27 E
Kurmenty	85	42.48 N	78.15 E
Kurmuk	140	10.33 N	34.17 E
Kurnell	274a	34.01 S	151.13 E
Kurnell Peninsula ≻ 1	274a	34.02 S	15.11 E
Kurnool	122	15.50 N	78.03 E
Kurobane	94	36.51 N	140.07 E
Kurobe	94	36.51 N	137.26 E
Kurobe ≃	94	36.55 N	137.25 E
Kurobe-dam ◆ 6	94	36.36 N	137.38 E
Kurodashō	96	35.01 N	135.00 E
Kurogi	96	33.12 N	130.40 E
Kurohone	94	36.30 N	139.17 E
Kuroishi	92	40.38 N	140.36 E
Kuroiso	94	36.58 N	140.03 E
Kuroo-tōge)(	96	35.11 N	134.12 E
Kuropatkino, Ross.	80	46.32 N	45.20 E
Kuropatkino, Uzb.	85	39.57 N	67.27 E
Kurort-Darasun	88	51.12 N	113.44 E
Kurose	96	34.19 N	132.40 E
Kurose ≃	96	34.13 N	132.36 E
Kuro-shima I, Nihon	93b	30.50 N	129.57 E
Kuro-shima I, Nihon	175d	24.19 N	124.05 E
Kurosu	268	35.51 N	139.23 E
Kurovo	82	55.49 N	36.00 E
Kurovskoje	82	55.34 N	38.55 E
Kurow	172	44.44 S	170.28 E
Kuroya	268	35.55 N	139.44 E
Kurrajong	170	33.33 S	150.40 E
Kurram	120	30.06 N	66.31 E
Kurram ≃	123	32.36 N	71.20 E
Kurri Kurri	170	32.49 S	151.29 E
Kuršab ≃	85	40.46 N	73.06 E
Kursavka	84	44.28 N	42.31 E
Kursela	124	25.27 N	87.15 E
Kuršėnai	76	56.00 N	22.56 E
Kurseong	120	26.53 N	88.17 E
Kursk	78	51.42 N	36.12 E
Kursk □ 8	76	52.14 N	35.30 E
Kurskaja	84	44.03 N	44.27 E

Kurskaja kosa ≻ 2	76	55.18 N	21.00 E
Kurskij zaliv ⊂	76	55.00 N	21.00 E
Kursk Station ◆ 5	265b	55.46 N	37.40 E
Kuršumlija	38	43.08 N	21.17 E
Kurşunlu, Tür.	130	40.51 N	33.16 E
Kurşunlu, Tür.	130	38.40 N	37.51 E
Kurtalan	130	37.57 N	41.42 E
Kurtamyš	86	54.55 N	64.27 E
Kurtatsch			
→ Cortaccia	64	46.19 N	11.13 E
Kürten, Dtsch.	56	51.03 N	7.16 E
Kurten, Tx., U.S.	222	30.47 N	96.16 W
Kurthasanlı	130	38.20 N	32.11 E
Kurth Lake ⊜	222	31.26 N	94.42 W
Kūrtī	140	18.07 N	31.33 E
Kurtino	82	54.59 N	38.17 E
Kurtinskoje			
vodochranilišče ⊜ 1	85	43.50 N	76.20 E
Kurtistown	229d	19.36 N	155.03 W
Kurtoğlu Burnu ≻	130	36.35 N	28.50 E
Kurtušibinskij chrebet			
⋏	88	52.10 N	93.30 E
Kurty ≃	85	44.05 N	76.20 E
Kurtz	218	38.58 N	86.12 W
Kuru, Sūd.	140	7.43 N	26.31 E
Kuru, Suomi	26	61.52 N	23.44 E
Kuru ≃	140	9.08 N	26.57 E
Kurucaşile	130	41.50 N	32.43 E
Kuruçay	130	39.39 N	38.29 E
Kuruçay (Kura) ≃	84	39.24 N	49.19 E
Kuruçeşme ◆ 8	267b	41.03 N	29.02 E
Kuruktag ⋏	90	41.30 N	90.00 E
Kurum	164	4.45 S	145.55 E
Kuruman	158	27.28 S	23.28 E
Kuruman ≃	158	26.56 S	20.39 E
Kurumanheuwels ⋏ 2	158	27.40 S	23.25 E
Kurumdy, gora ∧	85	39.28 N	73.32 E
Kurume	96	33.19 N	130.31 E
Kurumkan	88	54.18 N	110.18 E
Kurun ≃	144	5.30 N	34.17 E
Kurunegala	122	7.29 N	80.22 E
Kurungbaja, Tanjung			
≻	115b	8.15 S	120.35 E
Kurung Tank ⊜ 1	124	22.19 N	82.14 E
Kurunzulaj	88	51.00 N	117.10 E
Kuruqi	89	48.58 N	123.50 E
Kurur, Jabal ∧	140	20.31 N	31.32 E
Kurusaj	85	40.35 N	69.24 E
Kurushima-kaikyo ʯ	96	34.07 N	133.00 E
Kuruson-zan ∧	96	34.12 N	130.58 E
Kurylys	86	48.38 N	60.47 E
Kuryongp'o	98	35.59 N	129.32 E
Kurzeme □ 9	76	56.50 N	22.30 E
Kusa	86	55.20 N	59.29 E
Kusabe	270	34.31 N	135.29 E
Kuşadası	130	37.51 N	27.15 E
Kuşadası Körfezi ⊂	130	37.50 N	27.08 E
Kusak ≃	86	47.50 N	75.45 E
Kušalino	76	57.07 N	36.05 E
Kusan-ni, Taehan	98	37.43 N	128.49 E
Kusan-ni, Taehan	271b	37.29 N	126.45 E
Kusatsu, Nihon	94	36.37 N	138.36 E
Kusatsu, Nihon	94	35.00 N	135.57 E
Kusawa Lake ⊜	180	60.20 N	136.15 W
Kusaybah, Bi'r ⫟ 4	140	22.41 N	29.55 E
Kuščovskaja	78	46.33 N	39.37 E
Kuse	96	35.04 N	133.45 E
Kusel	56	49.32 N	7.24 E
Kušen'ki	78	48.53 N	34.07 E
Kusey	54	52.36 N	11.05 E
Kuş Gölü ⊜	130	40.10 N	27.57 E
Kuş Gölü Milli Parkı ♠	130	40.15 N	27.55 E
Kushaka	150	10.32 N	6.48 E
Kushālgarh	120	23.10 N	74.27 E
Kusheriki	150	10.33 N	6.28 E
Kushi	174m	26.33 N	128.06 E
Kushida ≃	94	34.36 N	136.34 E
Kushigata	94	35.36 N	138.28 E
Kushihiki	268	35.55 N	139.36 E
Kushikino	92	31.44 N	130.16 E
Kushima	92	31.29 N	131.14 E
Kushimoto	92	33.28 N	135.47 E
Kushira	270	34.28 N	135.43 E
Kushiro	92a	42.58 N	144.23 E
Kushog Lake ⊜	212	45.05 N	78.48 W
Kushtia	124	23.55 N	89.07 E
Kushui	102	42.11 N	94.25 E
Kusiro			
→ Kushiro	92a	42.58 N	144.23 E
Kusiyāra ≃	120	24.36 N	91.44 E
Kuška	128	35.16 N	62.20 E
Kuška ≃	128	36.00 N	62.40 E
Kuskokwim ≃	180	60.17 N	162.27 W
Kuskokwim, North			
Fork ≃	180	63.06 N	154.37 W
Kuskokwim, South			
Fork ≃	180	63.06 N	154.37 W
Kuskokwim Bay ⊂	180	59.45 N	162.25 W
Kuskokwim			
Mountains ⋏	180	62.30 N	156.00 W
Kuskovo ◆ 8	265b	55.44 N	37.49 E
Kuškušara	24	64.58 N	40.21 E
Kuśmā	124	28.14 N	83.41 E
Kušmurun	86	52.27 N	64.36 E
Kušmurun, ozero ⊜	86	52.40 N	64.48 E
Küsnacht	58	47.19 N	8.35 E
Kušnarenkovo	86	55.06 N	55.22 E
Kušnica	78	48.27 N	23.14 E
Kusŏng	98	39.59 N	125.15 E
Kusria	272b	22.58 N	88.14 E
Kussharo-ko ⊜	92a	43.38 N	144.21 E
Küssnacht am Rigi	58	47.05 N	8.27 E
Kustanaj	86	53.10 N	63.35 E
Kustar'ovka	80	54.16 N	42.16 E
Küsten-Gebirge			
→ Coast			
Mountains ⋏	176	55.00 N	129.00 W
Küstenkanal ≊	52	52.57 N	7.18 E
Küsten-Ketten			
→ Coast Ranges ⋏	178	41.00 N	123.30 W
Kusthalia	126	23.29 N	87.03 E
Kūstī	140	13.10 N	32.40 E
Kusu, Nihon	94	34.55 N	136.38 E
Kusu, Nihon	96	33.16 N	131.09 E
Kušugum	78	47.42 N	35.14 E
Kušum ≃	80	48.54 N	50.32 E
Kusumba	272b	22.27 N	88.24 E
Kusumbāni ∧	126	21.57 N	86.26 E
Kušumskij	80	51.38 N	48.21 E
Kusung	98	36.18 N	128.55 E
Kusunoki	96	34.03 N	131.15 E
K'us'ur	74	70.39 N	127.15 E
Kušva	86	58.18 N	59.45 E
Kut, Ko I	110	11.40 N	102.35 E
Kuta	150	9.52 N	6.43 E
Kuta ≃	88	56.46 N	105.40 E
Kutabaru	112	0.44 S	102.56 E
Kutabuloh	114	3.28 N	97.04 E
Kutacane	114	3.30 N	97.48 E
Kütahya	130	39.25 N	29.59 E
Kütahya □ 4	130	39.20 N	29.30 E
Kutais	78	44.32 N	39.18 E
Kutaisi	84	42.15 N	42.40 E
Kutāmat al-Ghābah	142	30.55 N	30.54 E
Kutanibong	114	3.53 N	96.22 E
Kutaradja			
→ Banda Aceh	114	5.34 N	95.20 E
Kutarere	172	38.03 S	177.09 E
Kutasawang	114	5.08 N	96.54 E
Kutch, Rann of (Rann			
of Kachchh) ◆ 1	120	24.05 N	70.10 E
Kutchan	92a	42.54 N	140.45 E
Kutcharo-ko ⊜	92a	45.09 N	142.19 E
Kutejnikovo, Ross.	83	47.34 N	39.46 E
Kutejnikovo, Ukr.	83	47.49 N	38.18 E
Kutenholz	52	53.29 N	9.19 E
Kutima	88	57.10 N	108.16 E
Kutima ≃	88	57.08 N	108.14 E
Kutina	36	45.29 N	16.46 E
Kutiyāna	120	21.38 N	69.59 E

≃ River	Fluß	Río	Rivière	Rio	⇼ Submarine Features	Untermeerische Objekte
≊ Canal	Kanal	Canal	Canal	Canal	□ Political Unit	Politische Einheit
∟ Waterfall, Rapids	Wasserfall, Stromschnellen	Cascada, Rápidos	Chute d'eau, Rapides	Cascata, Rápidos	▾ Cultural Institution	Kulturelle Institution
ʯ Strait	Meeresstraße	Estrecho	Détroit	Estreito	⊥ Historical Site	Historische Stätte
⊂ Bay, Gulf	Bucht, Golf	Bahía, Golfo	Baie, Golfe	Baía, Golfo	♠ Recreational Site	Erholungs- und Ferienort
⊜ Lake, Lakes	See, Seen	Lago, Lagos	Lac, Lacs	Lago, Lagos	⊠ Airport	Flughafen
≚ Swamp	Sumpf	Pantano	Marais	Pântano	■ Military Installation	Militäranlage
⧈ Ice Features, Glacier	Eis- und Gletscherformen	Accidentes Glaciales	Formes glaciaires	Acidentes glaciares	◆ Miscellaneous	Verschiedenes
⫟ Other Hydrographic Features	Andere Hydrographische Objekte	Otros Elementos Hidrográficos	Autres données hydrographiques	Outros acidentes hidrográficos		

Accidentes Submarinos	Formes de relief sous-marin	Acidentes submarinos
Unidad Politica	Entité politique	Unidade política
Institución Cultural	Institution culturelle	Instituição cultural
Sitio Histórico	Site historique	Sítio histórico
Sitio de Recreo	Centre de loisirs	Area de Lazer
Aeropuerto	Aéroport	Aeroporto
Instalación Militar	Installation militaire	Instalação militar
Misceláneo	Divers	Diversos

ENGLISH

Name	Page	Lat.°′	Long.°′
Kutkai	110	23.27 N	97.56 E
Kutkašen	84	40.59 N	47.50 E
Kutluškino	80	55.14 N	50.24 E
Kutná Hora	30	49.57 N	15.16 E
Kutno	30	52.15 N	19.23 E
Kutoarjo	115a	7.43 S	109.54 E
Kutomara	88	51.06 N	118.49 E
Kutse Game Reserve ◆4	156	23.30 S	24.05 E
Kutsuki	94	35.21 N	135.55 E
Küttigen	58	47.25 N	8.03 E
Kuttura	24	68.24 N	26.28 E
Kuttusoja	24	67.46 N	28.50 E
Kuttuzi	265a	59.45 N	30.04 E
Kutu	152	2.44 S	18.09 E
Kutubdia Island I	120	21.50 N	91.52 E
Kutubu, Lake ⊜	164	6.23 S	143.18 E
Kutukovo	80	54.26 N	40.31 E
Kutulik	88	53.21 N	102.48 E
Kutulo, Lagh ≃	154	2.08 N	40.56 E
Kutuluk ≃	80	53.19 N	51.09 E
Kutum	140	14.12 N	24.40 E
Kutu-Moke	152	3.12 S	17.21 E
Kúty, Česko.	30	48.40 N	17.03 E
Kuty, Ukr.	78	48.16 N	25.10 E
Kutztown	210	40.31 N	75.46 W
Kuujjuaq	176	58.06 N	68.25 W
Kuuli-Majak	128	40.14 N	52.42 E
Kuurne	50	50.51 N	3.17 E
Kuusamo	26	65.58 N	29.11 E
Kuusankoski	26	60.54 N	26.38 E
Kuva	85	40.32 N	72.05 E
Kuvak-Nikol'skoje	80	53.37 N	43.30 E
Kuvandyk	86	51.28 N	57.21 E
Kuvango	152	14.28 S	16.20 E
Kuvasaj	85	40.18 N	71.58 E
Kuvet ≃	180	69.14 N	175.00 E
Kuvšinovo	76	57.02 N	34.10 E
Kuwabara	270	34.53 N	135.15 E
Kuwait (Al-Kuwayt) □1, Asia	118	29.30 N	47.45 E
Kuwait (Al-Kuwayt) □1, Asia	128	29.30 N	47.45 E
Kuwait → Al-Kuwayt	128	29.20 N	47.59 E
Kuwait Bay → Kuwayt, Jūn al- c	128	29.30 N	48.00 E
Kuwana	94	35.04 N	136.42 E
Kuwayt, Jūn al- (Kuwait Bay) c	128	29.30 N	48.00 E
Kuyāli	126	22.31 N	86.11 E
Kuybyshev → Samara	80	53.12 N	50.09 E
Kuye ≃	102	38.30 N	110.44 E
Kūysanjaq	128	36.05 N	44.38 E
Kuyucak, Tür.	130	37.51 N	38.21 E
Kuyucak, Tür.	130	37.55 N	28.28 E
Kuyuwini ≃	246	2.16 N	58.16 W
Kuyuyukak, Cape >	180	56.54 N	156.50 W
Kuzaranda	24	62.22 N	35.37 E
Kuze	94	35.33 N	136.30 E
Kuze ◆8	270	34.57 N	135.43 E
Kuzedejevo	86	53.20 N	87.10 E
Kuzemin	78	50.09 N	34.39 E
Kuzemovka	83	49.31 N	37.59 E
Kužener	80	56.48 N	48.56 E
Kuženkino	76	57.44 N	33.59 E
Kuzitrin ≃	180	65.10 N	165.28 W
Kuzkejevo	80	55.46 N	52.48 E
Kuz'miniči	76	54.16 N	33.42 E
Kuz'minka ≃	265a	59.48 N	30.31 E
Kuz'minki ◆8	265b	55.42 N	37.48 E
Kuz'mino, Ross.	82	55.09 N	37.53 E
Kuz'mino, Ross.	82	56.36 N	37.55 E
Kuzmiščevo	82	54.46 N	37.12 E
Kuz'movka	74	62.19 N	92.02 E
Kuznečicha	80	54.43 N	49.38 E
Kuznečikovo	82	56.13 N	36.35 E
Kuzneck	80	53.07 N	46.36 E
Kuzneckij Alatau ⋏	86	54.45 N	88.00 E
Kuzneck → Novokuzneck	86	53.45 N	87.06 E
Kuznečnoje	26	61.09 N	29.52 E
Kuznecova	89	46.16 N	138.03 E
Kuznecovka	76	56.18 N	28.33 E
Kuznecovo, Ross.	82	55.30 N	38.21 E
Kuznecovo, Ross.	82	55.27 N	36.57 E
Kuznecovo, Ross.	86	59.15 N	63.28 E
Kuznecovo-Michajlovka	83	47.27 N	38.13 E
Kuznecovskij	80	47.25 N	40.57 E
Kuznecy	82	55.51 N	38.40 E
Kuznetsk → Kuzneck	80	53.07 N	46.36 E
Kuznetsovsk	78	51.22 N	25.53 E
Kuzomen', Ross.	24	64.17 N	42.53 E
Kuzomen', Ross.	24	66.17 N	36.54 E
Kuzovatovo	80	53.33 N	47.41 E
Kuzucubelen	130	36.51 N	34.27 E
Kuzuha	270	34.52 N	135.41 E
Kuzuryū ≃	94	36.13 N	136.08 E
Kuzuu	94	36.24 N	139.37 E
Kuzyaka	130	41.14 N	33.44 E
Kvænangen c2	24	70.05 N	21.13 E
Kværndrup	41	55.10 N	10.32 E
Kvaisi	84	42.31 N	43.40 E
Kvaløy I	24	69.40 N	18.30 E
Kvaløya I	24	70.37 N	23.52 E
Kvam	26	61.40 N	9.42 E
Kvanløse	41	55.39 N	11.41 E
Kvanndal	26	60.29 N	6.36 E
Kvareli	84	41.56 N	45.54 E
Kvarner c	36	44.45 N	14.15 E
Kvarnerić ɥ	36	44.45 N	14.35 E
Kvarnsveden	40	60.31 N	15.24 E
Kvarntorp	40	59.08 N	15.15 E
Kvarsa	80	56.58 N	53.57 E
Kvarsebo	40	58.39 N	16.39 E
Kvašenki	82	56.48 N	37.33 E
Kvenna ≃	26	60.01 N	7.56 E
Kverkfjöll ∧	24a	64.43 N	16.38 W
Kvichak Bay c	180	58.48 N	157.30 W
Kvicksund	40	59.27 N	16.19 E
Kvidinge	41	56.08 N	13.04 E
Kvien ⊜	40	60.24 N	13.48 E
Kvikkjokk	24	66.55 N	17.50 E
Kvilda	60	49.01 N	13.35 E
Kvina ≃	26	58.17 N	6.56 E
Kvismare kanal ≊	40	59.12 N	15.11 E
Kvissleby	26	62.17 N	17.21 E
Kvistbro	40	59.09 N	14.49 E
Kvistgård	41	55.59 N	12.30 E
Kvitok	88	56.03 N	98.30 E
Kwa ≃	152	3.10 S	16.11 E
Kwachaga	154	5.38 S	38.08 E
Kwada	164	6.09 S	141.53 E
Kwahae-ri ◆8	271b	37.33 N	126.50 E
Kwahu Plateau ⋏1	150	6.30 N	0.30 W
Kwai → Khwae Noi ≃	110	14.00 N	99.33 E
Kwajalein I1	14	9.05 N	167.20 E
Kwajok	140	8.19 N	28.00 E
Kwakoegron	250	5.15 N	55.20 W
Kwale, Kenya	154	4.11 S	39.27 E
Kwale, Nig.	150	5.46 N	6.26 E
Kwambilo ≃	273b	4.26 S	15.20 E
Kwa-Mbonambi	158	28.36 S	32.05 E
Kwamisa ∧	150	7.08 N	1.53 W
Kwamouth	152	3.10 S	16.12 E
Kwa Mtoro	154	5.14 S	35.26 E
Kwanak-san ∧	271b	37.27 N	126.58 E
Kwando (Cuando) ≃	152	18.27 S	23.32 E
Kwangchow → Guangzhou	100	23.06 N	113.16 E
Kwangju	98	35.09 N	126.54 E
Kwangju □4	98	35.09 N	126.55 E
Kwango (Cuango) ≃	152	3.14 S	17.23 E
Kwangsi Chuang Autonomous Region → Guangxi Zhuangzu Zizhiqu □4	102	24.00 N	109.00 E
Kwangtung → Guangdong □4	90	23.00 N	113.00 E
Kwangwazi	154	7.47 S	38.15 E
Kwangyang	98	34.59 N	127.34 E
Kwania, Lake ⊜	154	1.45 N	32.45 E
Kwanmo-bong ∧	98	41.42 N	129.13 E
Kwansan-ni	271b	37.43 N	126.51 E
Kwanto Plain → Kantō-heiya ≍	94	36.00 N	139.30 E
Kwara □3	150	8.45 N	5.00 E
Kware	150	13.12 N	5.14 E
Kwa-Thema	273d	26.18 S	28.23 E
Kwatisore	164	3.15 S	134.57 E
Kweichow → Guizhou □4	102	27.00 N	107.00 E
Kweihwa → Hohhot	102	40.51 N	111.40 E
Kweijang → Guiyang	102	26.35 N	106.43 E
Kweilin → Guilin	102	25.17 N	110.17 E
Kweisui → Hohhot	102	40.51 N	111.40 E
Kweiyang → Guiyang	102	26.35 N	106.43 E
Kwekwe	154	18.55 S	29.49 E
Kweneng □5	156	24.00 S	24.00 E
Kwenge (Caengo) ≃	152	4.50 S	18.42 E
Kwesimintim	150	4.54 N	1.47 W
Kwethluk	180	60.49 N	161.27 W
Kwethluk ≃	180	60.46 N	161.26 W
Kwidzyn	30	53.45 N	18.56 E
Kwigillingok	180	59.51 N	163.08 W
Kwiguk	180	62.45 N	164.28 W
Kwiha	144	13.31 N	39.32 E
Kwikila	164	9.48 S	147.41 E
Kwilu (Cuilo) ≃	152	3.22 S	17.22 E
Kwinana	168a	32.15 S	115.48 E
Kwitaro ≃	246	3.19 N	58.47 W
Kwobrup	162	33.37 S	117.46 E
Kwoka, Gunung ∧	164	0.31 S	132.27 E
Kwolla	150	9.00 N	9.15 E
Kwun Tong	271d	22.19 N	114.12 E
Kyabé	146	9.27 N	18.57 E
Kyabra	166	26.18 S	143.10 E
Kyabra Creek ≃	166	25.36 S	142.55 E
Kyabram	166	36.19 S	145.03 E
Kyaikkami	110	16.04 N	97.34 E
Kyaiklat	110	16.26 N	95.44 E
Kyaikto	110	17.18 N	97.01 E
Kya-in	110	16.02 N	98.08 E
Kyaka	154	1.16 S	31.25 E
Kyalite	166	34.57 S	143.29 E
Kyancutta	166	33.08 S	135.34 E
Ky Anh	110	18.05 N	106.18 E
Kyat-aw	110	12.29 N	98.19 E
Kyaukhnyat	110	18.15 N	97.31 E
Kyaukkyi	110	18.19 N	96.46 E
Kyaukme	110	22.32 N	97.02 E
Kyaukpa	110	13.05 N	98.59 E
Kyaukpyu, Mya.	110	19.05 N	93.52 E
Kyaukpyu, Mya.	110	19.26 N	93.33 E
Kyaukse	110	21.36 N	96.08 E
Kyauktaw	110	20.51 N	92.59 E
Kyaunggon	110	17.06 N	95.11 E
Kybartai	76	54.39 N	22.45 E
Kybean	171b	36.22 S	149.25 E
Kybeyan Range ⋏	171b	36.10 S	149.30 E
Kyburz	226	38.47 N	120.18 W
Kydra	171b	36.27 S	149.23 E
Kyeamba	171b	35.26 S	147.37 E
Kyeamba Creek ≃	171b	35.06 S	147.29 E
Kyebang-san ∧	98	37.43 N	128.29 E
Kyegegwa	154	0.29 N	31.03 E
Kyeikdon	110	16.00 N	98.24 E
Kyeintali	110	18.00 N	94.29 E
Kyenjojo	154	0.37 N	30.38 E
Kyeryong-san Kukrip Kongwŏn ♦	98	36.21 N	127.13 E
Kyes Peak ∧	224	47.57 N	121.19 W
Kyffhäuser-Denkmal ⊥	54	51.23 N	11.06 E
Kyffhäuser Gebirge ⋏	54	51.23 N	11.05 E
Kyidaunggan	110	19.53 N	96.12 E
Kyindwe	110	20.58 N	93.51 E
Kyje ◆8	54	50.04 N	14.32 E
Kyjov	30	49.01 N	17.08 E
Kykladen → Kikládhes II	38	37.30 N	25.00 E
Kykotsmovi Village	200	35.52 N	110.37 W
Kykva	80	57.22 N	53.50 E
Kylās ∧	124	25.18 N	90.45 E
Kyle, Sk., Can.	184	50.50 N	108.02 W
Kyle, S.D., U.S.	198	43.25 N	102.10 W
Kyle, Tx., U.S.	196	29.59 N	97.52 W
Kyle □9	44	55.29 N	4.24 W
Kyle, Lake ⊜1	154	20.14 S	31.00 E
Kyleakin	46	57.16 N	5.44 W
Kyle of Lochalsh	46	57.17 N	5.43 W
Kylerhea	46	57.14 N	5.41 W
Kylertown	214	41.00 N	78.10 W
Kylestrome	46	58.16 N	5.02 W
Kyll ≃	56	49.48 N	6.42 E
Kyllburg	56	50.02 N	6.35 E
Kym ≃	42	52.14 N	0.17 W
Kymen lääni □4	26	61.00 N	28.00 E
Kymijoki ≃	26	60.30 N	26.52 E
Kyn	86	57.52 N	58.38 E
Kyndby	41	55.48 N	11.56 E
Kyneton	169	37.15 S	144.27 E
Kynnefjäll ∧2	26	58.42 N	11.41 E
Kynšperk nad Ohří	54	50.04 N	12.32 E
Kynuna	166	21.35 S	141.55 E
Kyodong-do I	98	37.45 N	126.16 E
Kyoga, Lake ⊜	154	1.30 N	33.00 E
Kyōga-misaki >	96	35.46 N	135.13 E
Kyogle	166	28.37 S	153.00 E
Kyoha-ri	271b	37.46 N	126.46 E
Kyohyŏn-ni	271b	37.43 N	126.58 E
Kyom ≃	140	8.58 N	28.13 E
Kyŏmip'o → Songnim	98	38.44 N	125.38 E
Kyonan	94	35.07 N	139.50 E
Kyondo	110	16.35 N	98.03 E
Kyŏnggi Do □4	98	37.30 N	127.15 E
Kyŏnggi-man c	98	37.25 N	126.00 E
Kyŏngju	98	35.51 N	129.14 E
Kyŏngju Kukrip Kongwŏn ♦	98	35.47 N	129.15 E
Kyŏngsan	98	35.48 N	128.43 E
Kyŏngsang Namdo □4	98	35.15 N	128.30 E
Kyŏngsang Pukdo □4	98	36.15 N	128.45 E
Kyŏngsŏng	98	41.35 N	129.36 E
Kyŏngsŏng → Sŏul	98	37.33 N	126.58 E
Kyŏngwŏn	98	42.48 N	130.09 E
Kyônkadun	110	16.04 N	95.38 E
Kyonmange	110	16.30 N	95.50 E
Kyonpyaw	110	17.18 N	95.12 E
Kyotera	154	0.33 S	31.19 E
Kyōto, Nihon	94	35.00 N	135.45 E
Kyōto, Nihon	270	35.00 N	135.45 E
Kyōto □5	94	35.05 N	135.45 E
Kyōto-bonchi ⋏	270	35.03 N	135.45 E
Kyōto Race Track ♦	270	34.54 N	135.44 E
Kyōto University ▾2	270	35.02 N	135.46 E
Kyōwa	94	36.19 N	140.03 E
Kyōyomi-dake ∧	96	33.31 N	131.02 E
Kypšak, ozero ⊜	86	50.09 N	68.28 E
Kyra	88	49.36 N	111.58 E
Kyra ≃	88	49.24 N	112.19 E
Kyrčany	80	57.37 N	50.10 E
Kyren	88	51.41 N	102.08 E
Kyrenia → Girne	130	35.20 N	33.19 E
Kyrgyzstan □1, Asia	72	41.30 N	75.00 E
Kyrgyzstan □1, Asia	85	41.30 N	75.00 E
Kyritz	54	52.56 N	12.23 E
Kyrkheden	40	60.10 N	13.29 E
Kyrkkazyk	85	42.30 N	72.20 E
Kyrksæterøra	26	63.17 N	9.06 E
Kyrkslätt (Kirkkonummi)	26	60.07 N	24.26 E
Kyrö	26	60.42 N	22.45 E
Kyrönjoki ≃	26	63.14 N	21.45 E
Kyrösjärvi ⊜	26	61.45 N	23.10 E
Kyröskoski	26	61.40 N	23.11 E
Kyrta	24	64.04 N	57.42 E
Kyrykkuduk	80	49.51 N	51.54 E
Ky Son	110	19.24 N	104.08 E
Kyštovka	86	56.33 N	76.38 E
Kyštym	86	55.42 N	60.34 E
Kysykkamys	80	49.14 N	50.19 E
Kyte ≃	190	42.00 N	89.19 W
Kytlym	86	59.30 N	59.12 E
Kytmanovo	86	53.28 N	85.28 E
Kyūhōji	270	34.38 N	135.35 E
Kyunchaung	110	15.33 N	98.15 E
Kyundon	110	20.31 N	95.44 E
Kyungyi I	110	15.04 N	97.44 E
Kyunhla	110	23.21 N	95.18 E
Kyuquot	182	50.02 N	127.23 W
Kyuquot Sound ɥ	182	50.05 N	127.15 W
Kyūroku-jima I	92	40.32 N	139.29 E
Kyū-shizudani-gakkō ⊥	96	34.45 N	134.13 E
Kyūshū I	92	33.00 N	131.00 E
Kyushu-Palau Ridge ✣3	14	20.00 N	136.00 E
Kyūshū-sanchi ⋏	92	32.35 N	131.17 E
Kywebwe	110	18.42 N	96.25 E
Kywong	166	34.59 S	146.44 E
Kyyjärvi	26	63.02 N	24.34 E
Kyyvesi ⊜	26	61.58 N	27.07 E
Kyzas	86	52.20 N	89.20 E
Kyzyl	88	51.42 N	94.27 E
Kyzylagadžskij zapovednik ◆4	84	39.10 N	49.00 E
Kyzylagaš	86	45.54 N	81.37 E
Kyzylaryk	85	43.57 N	70.42 E
Kyzylbejit	85	41.30 N	72.24 E
Kyzyl-Chaja	86	50.03 N	89.54 E
Kyzyl-Chem (Šišchid) ≃	88	51.21 N	96.58 E
Kyzyl-Džar	85	41.17 N	72.02 E
Kyzylemgek	85	41.57 N	74.56 E
Kyzylespe	86	47.27 N	73.53 E
Kyzylkak, ozero ⊜	86	53.25 N	73.48 E
Kyzyl-Kija	85	40.16 N	72.08 E
Kyzyl-Kommuna	86	48.44 N	67.32 E
Kyzylkum ◆2	72	42.00 N	64.00 E
Kyzylkup	128	40.38 N	53.58 E
Kyzyl-Mažalyk	86	51.10 N	90.32 E
Kyzylmazar	85	39.39 N	68.25 E
Kyzyloba	80	49.37 N	50.38 E
Kyzylsu ≃	85	39.17 N	71.23 E
Kyzyltas, gory ⋏	86	48.30 N	74.50 E
Kyzyltau	86	47.53 N	72.05 E
Kyzylt'ob'o	85	42.13 N	75.16 E
Kyzyltu, Kaz.	86	47.46 N	59.08 E
Kyzyltu, Kaz.	86	47.43 N	75.42 E
Kyzyltu, Kyrg.	85	42.11 N	76.40 E
Kyzyluj	86	48.07 N	65.28 E
Kyzylžar	86	48.17 N	69.39 E
Kzyl-Kuga	80	48.28 N	53.01 E
Kzyl-Orda	86	44.48 N	65.28 E
Kzyl-Orda □8	85	43.30 N	67.00 E
Kzyltu	86	53.38 N	72.20 E
L			
La'a	102	29.44 N	101.26 E
Laa an der Thaya	61	48.43 N	16.23 E
Laaben	61	48.06 N	15.52 E
Laaber	60	49.04 N	11.53 E
Laaberberg	60	48.46 N	12.01 E
Laab im Walde	264b	48.09 N	16.11 E
Laacher See ⊜	56	50.25 N	7.16 E
Laaerberg ∧2	264b	48.09 N	16.24 E
Laage	54	53.56 N	12.20 E
La Aguja, Cabo de >	246	11.18 N	74.12 W
Laakajärvi ⊜	26	63.50 N	27.55 E
Laaken ◆8	263	51.15 N	7.15 E
Laakirchen	64	47.58 N	13.49 E
La Albuera	34	38.43 N	6.49 W
La Alcarria ◆1	34	40.45 N	2.45 W
La Aldea	234	20.54 N	101.29 W
La Aldehuela	266a	40.18 N	3.36 W
La Algaba	34	37.28 N	6.01 W
La Almarcha	34	39.41 N	2.22 W
La Almunia de Doña Godina	34	41.29 N	1.22 W
Laanecoorie Reservoir ⊜1	169	36.52 S	143.53 E
La Antigua, Salina ≍	252	30.00 S	66.06 W
La Antorcha, Cerro ∧	234	21.43 N	102.45 W
Laar ◆8	263	51.28 N	6.43 E
La Araucanía □4	252	38.45 S	72.30 W
La Arena, Pan.	236	7.58 N	80.28 W
La Arena, Perú	248	5.20 S	80.44 W
Laas Caanood	144	8.28 N	47.21 E
La Ascensión	232	24.20 N	99.55 W
Laas Dawaco	144	10.28 N	49.05 E
Laas Dhaareed	144	10.10 N	45.59 E
Laase	54	53.04 N	11.18 E
Laas → Lasa	64	46.37 N	10.42 E
Laas Qoray	144	11.10 N	48.13 E
La Asunción	246	11.02 N	63.53 W
La Atravesada, Loma ∧2	232	29.57 N	112.12 W
Laatzen	52	52.19 N	9.47 E
Laau Point >	229a	21.06 N	157.19 W
La Aurora	286e	33.36 S	70.38 W
La Azufrosa	196	28.14 N	100.50 W
Laba ≃	78	45.11 N	39.42 E
La Babia	232	28.34 N	102.04 W
Labadie	219	38.31 N	90.51 W
Labadieville	194	29.50 N	90.57 W
La Baie	186	48.19 N	70.53 W
La Balme-de-Sillingy	58	45.58 N	6.02 E
La Balme-les-Grottes	62	45.51 N	5.20 E
Laban	208	37.24 N	76.17 W
La Banda	252	27.44 S	64.15 W
La Bandera, Cerro ∧	232	24.35 N	105.07 W
La Bañeza	34	42.18 N	5.54 W
La Barca	234	20.17 N	102.34 W
La Barceloneta ◆8	266d	41.22 N	2.11 E
La Barge	200	42.15 N	110.11 W
La Barge Creek ≃	200	42.14 N	110.10 W
La Barra	236	12.54 N	83.32 W
La Barre-en-Ouche	50	48.57 N	0.40 E
La Barrita	236	14.05 N	91.03 W
La Barr Meadows	226	39.11 N	121.02 W
Labason	116	8.04 N	122.31 E
La Bassée	50	50.32 N	2.48 E
Labastide-Murat	32	44.39 N	1.34 E
La Bastide-Puylaurent	62	44.36 N	3.54 E
La Bâte	261	48.35 N	2.01 E
La Baule-Escoublac	32	47.17 N	2.24 W
La Bazoche-Gouet	50	48.08 N	0.59 E
L'Abbé	261	48.34 N	1.50 E
Labdah (Leptis Magna) ⊥	146	32.38 N	14.18 E
Labé	150	11.19 N	12.17 W
Labe (Elbe) ≃	30	53.50 N	9.00 E
Labégude	62	44.39 N	4.22 E
La Bégude-Blanche	62	43.55 N	6.08 E
La Bégude-de-Mazenc	62	44.32 N	4.56 E
Labelle, P.Q., Can.	206	46.16 N	74.44 W
La Belle, Fl., U.S.	220	26.45 N	81.26 W
La Belle, Mo., U.S.	219	40.07 N	91.54 W
Labelle □6	206	46.20 N	75.00 W
Labelle, Lac ⊜, P.Q., Can.	206	46.13 N	74.52 W
La Belle, Lac ⊜, Wi., U.S.	216	43.08 N	88.31 W
Labengke, Pulau I	112	3.27 S	122.25 E
La Bérarde	62	44.56 N	6.18 E
Laberge, Lake ⊜	180	61.11 N	135.12 W
La Berra ∧	58	46.41 N	7.11 E
Laberweinting	60	48.48 N	12.19 E
La Besace	56	49.34 N	4.58 E
Labette Creek ≃	198	37.03 N	95.05 W
Labi	112	4.25 N	114.22 E
La Biche ≃	182	55.01 N	112.44 W
Labico	66	41.47 N	12.53 E
Labin	36	45.05 N	14.07 E
Labinsk	84	44.38 N	40.44 E
Labis	114	2.23 N	103.02 E
La Bisbal	34	41.57 N	3.03 E
Łabiszyn	30	52.57 N	17.55 E
Lablābah, Wādī al- V	273c	30.02 N	31.19 E
La Blanca	286e	33.31 S	70.41 W
La Blanca Grande, Laguna ⊜	252	38.26 S	63.55 W
Labná ⊥	232	20.11 N	89.34 W
Labo	116	14.09 N	122.51 E
Labo ≃	116	14.11 N	122.56 E
Labo, Mount ∧	116	14.01 N	122.48 E
Laboe	54	54.24 N	10.15 E
La Boissière	261	48.46 N	1.59 E
La Boissière-Ecole	261	48.41 N	1.39 E
La Bollène-Vésubie	62	43.59 N	7.20 E
La Bonneville-sur-Iton	50	49.00 N	1.02 E
Laboratory	214	40.09 N	80.13 W
Laborde, Arg.	252	33.09 S	62.51 W
La Borde, Fr.	261	48.32 N	2.50 E
Laborec ≃	30	48.36 N	22.00 E
Laborie	241f	13.45 N	61.00 W
Labouchere, Mount ∧	162	25.12 S	118.18 E
Labouheyre	32	44.13 N	0.55 W
Laboulaye	252	34.07 S	63.24 W
La Bouverie	50	50.24 N	3.52 E
La Boyera, Ven.	286c	10.25 N	66.50 W
La Boyera, Ven.	286c	10.23 N	66.57 W
Lābpur	126	23.50 N	87.49 E
Labrador ◆1	176	54.00 N	62.00 W
Labrador Basin ✣1	16	53.00 N	48.00 W
Labrador City	176	52.57 N	66.55 W
Labrador Sea ▾2	176	57.00 N	53.00 W
Lábrea, Bra.	248	7.16 S	64.47 W
La Brea, Trin.	241r	10.15 N	61.37 W
Labrède	32	44.41 N	0.31 W
La Bresse	58	48.00 N	6.53 E
La Brévine	58	46.59 N	6.36 E
Labrieville, Réserve ♦	186	49.20 N	69.40 W
La Brigue	62	44.04 N	7.37 E
La Brillanne	62	43.55 N	5.53 E
Labrit	32	44.07 N	0.33 W
La Broquerie	184	49.28 N	96.27 W
Labroye	50	50.17 N	1.59 E
Labry	56	49.10 N	5.52 E
Labuan, Pulau I	112	5.21 N	115.13 E
Labuha	164	0.37 S	127.29 E
Labuhan	115a	6.22 S	105.50 E
Labuhanbajo	115b	8.29 S	119.54 E
Labuhanbatu	114	2.12 N	100.12 E
Labuhanbilik	114	2.31 N	100.10 E
Labuhandeli	114	3.45 N	98.41 E
Labuhanhaji, Indon.	114	3.33 N	97.00 E
Labuhanhaji, Indon.	115b	8.42 S	116.34 E
Labuhanmarege	112	7.06 S	120.40 E
Labuhanmaringgai	115a	5.21 S	105.48 E
Labuhanruku	114	3.13 N	99.35 E
Labuk ≃	112	5.54 N	117.30 E
Labuk, Telukan c	116	6.07 N	117.46 E
Labu Kananga	115b	8.08 S	117.47 E
Labutta	110	16.09 N	94.46 E
Labytnangi	72	66.39 N	66.21 E
Lač, Ross.	24	63.18 N	54.28 E
Laç, Shq.	38	41.38 N	19.43 E
Lac □5	146	13.30 N	14.15 E
Lača, ozero ⊜	24	61.20 N	38.48 E
La Cadena	196	25.53 N	104.12 W
L'Acadie	275a	45.19 N	73.21 W
L'Acadie ≃	206	45.29 N	73.16 W
La Cadière-d'Azur	62	43.12 N	5.46 E
Lacadivas, Islas → Lakshadweep II	122	10.00 N	73.00 E
Laca Jahuira ≃	248	19.21 S	67.54 W
La Cal ≃	248	17.27 S	58.15 W
Lac-à-la-Tortue	206	46.37 N	72.38 W
La Calera, Chile	252	32.47 S	71.12 W
La Calera, Perú	286d	12.12 S	76.54 W
Lac-Allard	186	50.33 N	63.25 W
Lacamas Creek ≃	224	46.20 N	122.55 W
Lacamas Lake ⊜	224	45.37 N	122.26 W
La Campana, Esp.	34	37.34 N	5.26 W
La Campana, Méx.	234	22.45 N	105.35 W
La Cañada	234	20.37 N	100.19 W
La Cañada, Cerro ∧	234	21.24 N	99.13 W
La Canada Flintridge	228	34.12 N	118.12 W
La Canada Verde Creek ≃	280	33.52 N	118.02 W
Lacanau	32	44.59 N	1.05 W
Lacanau, Lac de c	32	44.58 N	1.07 W
La Candelaria, Arg.	252	26.06 S	65.06 W
La Candelaria, Méx.	200	31.07 N	106.29 W
La Cañiza	34	42.13 N	8.16 W
La Canourgue	32	44.26 N	3.13 E
Lacantún ≃	232	16.36 N	90.39 W
La Capelle-en-Thiérache	50	49.58 N	3.55 E
La Capelle-lès-Boulogne	50	50.44 N	1.42 E
Lacapelle-Marival	32	44.44 N	1.54 E
La Carlota, Arg.	252	33.26 S	63.18 W
La Carlota, Pil.	116	10.25 N	122.55 E
Lacarne	214	41.31 N	83.03 W
La Carolina	34	38.15 N	3.37 W
La Casita	234	23.43 N	104.46 W
La Castellana	116	10.20 N	123.03 E
Lacaune	32	43.43 N	2.42 E
Lac-Bellemare	206	46.34 N	72.55 W
Lac-Brome	206	45.13 N	72.31 W
Laccadive, Minicoy, and Amīndīvi → Lakshadweep □3	122	10.00 N	73.00 E
Laccadive Islands → Lakshadweep II	122	10.00 N	73.00 E
Laccadive Sea ▾2	12	7.00 N	76.00 E
Lacchiarella	62	45.19 N	9.08 E
Lacco Ameno	68	40.45 N	13.54 E
Lac Courte Oreilles Indian Reservation ◆4	190	45.55 N	91.19 W
Lac du Flambeau	190	45.59 N	89.51 W
Lac du Flambeau Indian Reservation ◆4	190	45.59 N	89.53 W
Laceby	44	53.32 N	0.10 W
Lacedonia	68	41.03 N	15.25 E
La Ceiba, Hond.	236	15.47 N	86.50 W
La Ceiba, Ven.	246	9.28 N	71.04 W
La Celle-les-Bordes	261	48.38 N	1.57 E
La Celle-Saint-Cloud	261	48.51 N	2.08 E
La Celle-Saint-Cyr	50	47.58 N	3.18 E
La Center, Ky., U.S.	194	37.04 N	88.58 W
La Center, Wa., U.S.	224	45.52 N	122.40 W
Lacepede Bay c	166	36.47 S	139.45 E
Lacerdónia	156	18.01 S	35.30 E
Laces (Latsch)	64	46.37 N	10.52 E
Lac-Etchemin	186	46.24 N	70.30 W
Lacey	224	47.02 N	122.49 W
Lacey Creek ≃	278	41.50 N	88.03 W
Laceyville	210	41.39 N	76.10 W
Lac-Frontière	186	46.42 N	70.00 W
La Chaise-Dieu	62	45.19 N	3.42 E
La Chambre	62	45.22 N	6.18 E
La Chapelle-d'Angillon	50	47.22 N	2.26 E
La Chapelle-en-Vercors	62	44.58 N	5.25 E
La Chapelle-Gauthier	261	48.33 N	2.54 E
La Chapelle-la-Reine	50	48.19 N	2.35 E
La Chapelle-Saint-Luc	50	48.20 N	4.03 E
La Chapelle-Vendômoise	50	47.40 N	1.15 E
La Charité-sur-Loire	50	47.11 N	3.01 E
La Chartre-sur-le-Loir	50	47.44 N	0.35 E
La Châtaigneraie	32	46.39 N	0.44 W
La Châtre	32	46.35 N	1.59 E
Lachaussée, Étang de ⊜	56	49.02 N	5.48 E
La Chaux-de-Fonds	58	47.06 N	6.50 E
Lachay, Punta >	248	11.18 S	77.39 W
Lach Dennis	262	53.15 N	2.26 W
Lachdenpochja	24	61.31 N	30.08 E
Lachen	58	47.12 N	8.51 E
Lachenaie	275a	45.42 N	73.34 W
Lachendorf	52	52.37 N	10.14 E
Lachhmangarh Sīkar	120	27.49 N	75.02 E
L'achi	80	55.20 N	41.56 E
Lachine	206	45.26 N	73.40 W
Lachine, Canal de ≊	275a	45.26 N	73.40 W
Lachine, Rapides de ↳	275a	45.25 N	73.36 W
La Chira, Punta >	286d	12.13 S	77.03 W
La Chivera	286c	10.37 N	66.54 W
Lachkaltsap Indian Reserve ◆4	182	55.03 N	129.34 W
Lachlan ≃	166	34.21 S	143.57 E
La Chorrera, Col.	246	0.44 S	73.01 W
La Chorrera, Pan.	236	8.53 N	79.47 W
L'achoviči, Bela.	76	53.02 N	26.16 E
L'achoviči, Bela.	76	52.23 N	27.55 E
L'achovskije ostrova II	74	73.30 N	141.00 E
La Choza	258	34.47 S	59.07 W
La Choza, Arroyo ≃	258	34.40 S	58.58 W
Lachta ◆8	265a	60.00 N	30.09 E
Lachtinskij Razliv, ozero ⊜	265a	60.00 N	30.11 E
Lachute	206	45.38 N	74.20 W
Lachva	78	52.13 N	27.04 E
La Ciénaga	252	27.30 S	66.57 W
La Ciénega	234	16.54 N	96.46 W
Lâçin	130	40.47 N	34.54 E
La Cinta Creek ≃	196	35.24 N	104.06 W
La Ciotat	62	43.10 N	5.36 E
La Cisterna	286e	33.33 S	70.41 W
La Citadelle ⊥	238	19.35 N	72.14 W
La Ciudad	234	23.44 N	105.42 W
Lack	48	54.33 N	7.35 W
Lackawanna	210	42.49 N	78.49 W
Lackawanna □6	210	41.24 N	75.40 W
Lackawanna ≃	210	41.21 N	75.47 W
Lackawanna, Lake ⊜	276	40.57 N	74.42 W
Lackawanna State Park ♦	210	41.33 N	75.44 W
Lackawaxen	210	41.29 N	74.59 W
Lackawaxen ≃	210	41.29 N	74.59 W
Lackey	208	37.14 N	76.33 W
Lackland Air Force Base ■	196	29.27 N	98.37 W
Läckö	26	58.41 N	13.13 E
Lackoje	76	58.05 N	38.08 E
Lac La Belle	216	43.09 N	88.32 W
Lac la Biche	182	54.46 N	111.58 W
Lac la Hache	182	51.49 N	121.28 W
Lac la Ronge Provincial Park ♦	184	55.15 N	104.55 W
La Clayette	32	46.18 N	4.19 E
Laclede, Id., U.S.	182	48.10 N	116.45 W
La Clede, Il., U.S.	219	38.53 N	88.43 W
Laclede, Mo., U.S.	194	39.47 N	93.09 W
La Clotilde	252	27.08 S	60.40 W
La Clusaz	58	45.54 N	6.25 E
La Cluse	58	46.10 N	5.34 E
La Cluse-et-Mijoux	58	46.53 N	6.23 E
Lacmalac	171b	35.19 S	148.19 E
Lac-Masson	206	46.02 N	74.04 W
Lac-Mégantic	188	45.36 N	70.53 W
Lacob ti-duyong, Mount ∧	116	17.35 N	121.09 E
La Cocha	252	27.47 S	65.34 W
Lacolle	206	45.05 N	73.22 W
Lacolle ≃	206	45.04 N	73.20 W
La Colle-sur-Loup	62	43.41 N	7.06 E
La Colmena	286a	19.36 N	99.18 W
La Colorada	232	28.41 N	110.25 W
La Columna → Bolívar, Pico ∧	246	8.30 N	71.02 W
La Coma	232	24.28 N	98.19 W
Lacombe, Ab., Can.	182	52.28 N	113.44 W
Lacombe, La., U.S.	194	30.18 N	89.56 W
Lacon	190	41.01 N	89.24 W
Lacona, Ia., U.S.	190	41.11 N	93.22 W
Lacona, N.Y., U.S.	212	43.38 N	76.04 W
La Concepción, Pan.	236	8.31 N	82.37 W
La Concepción, Ven.	246	10.38 N	71.50 W
La Condamine-Châtelard	62	44.27 N	6.45 E
Laconi	71	39.51 N	9.03 E
Laconia	188	43.31 N	71.28 W
La Conner	224	48.23 N	122.29 W
La Consulta	252	33.44 S	69.07 W
Lacoochee	220	28.27 N	82.10 W
La Coruña	34	43.22 N	8.23 W
La Coruña □4	34	43.00 N	8.35 W
Lacoste, Fr.	62	43.50 N	5.18 E
La Coste, Tx., U.S.	196	29.19 N	98.49 W
La Côte-Saint-André	62	45.23 N	5.15 E
La Courneuve	261	48.56 N	2.23 E
La Couronne	62	43.20 N	5.03 E
La Courtine	32	45.42 N	2.16 E
Lac qui Parle ≃	198	45.01 N	95.53 W
Lac qui Parle, West Branch ≃	198	44.55 N	96.02 W
La Crau	62	43.09 N	6.04 E
Lacre Punt >	241s	12.02 N	68.15 W
La Crescent	190	43.49 N	91.18 W
La Crescenta	228	34.13 N	118.14 W
La Croft	214	40.39 N	80.35 W
Lacroix-Saint-Ouen	50	49.21 N	2.47 E
La Crosse, In., U.S.	216	41.19 N	86.53 W
La Crosse, Ks., U.S.	198	38.31 N	99.18 W
La Crosse, Va., U.S.	192	36.41 N	78.05 W
Lacrosse, Wa., U.S.	202	46.49 N	117.53 W
La Crosse, Wi., U.S.	190	43.48 N	91.14 W
La Crosse ≃	190	43.49 N	91.16 W
La Cruz, Arg.	252	29.10 S	56.38 W
La Cruz, Col.	246	1.35 N	76.58 W
La Cruz, C.R.	236	11.04 N	85.39 W
La Cruz, Méx.	196	28.33 N	100.48 W
La Cruz, Ur.	258	33.56 S	56.15 W
La Cruz, Cerro ∧	234	17.55 N	101.31 W
La Cruz de Río Grande	236	13.06 N	84.10 W
Lac-Saguay	206	46.30 N	75.09 W
Lac Seul	184	50.20 N	92.16 W
Lac Seul Indian Reserve ◆4	184	50.15 N	92.10 W
La Cuchilla	234	18.54 N	103.19 W
La Cuesta, C.R.	236	8.30 N	82.50 W
La Cuesta, Méx.	234	20.10 N	104.51 W
La Cuesta, P.R.	240m	18.25 N	66.49 W
La Cumbre, Arg.	252	30.58 S	64.30 W
La Cumbre, Ven.	286c	10.32 N	66.57 W
La Cumbre, Volcán ∧1	246a	0.20 S	91.30 W
La Cure	58	46.28 N	6.05 E
Lacy Fork ≃	222	32.24 N	96.08 W
La Cygne	198	38.21 N	94.45 W
Lacy-Lakeview	222	31.37 N	97.06 W
Lada, Teluk c	115a	6.29 S	105.44 E
Ladainha	255	17.39 S	41.44 W
Ladākh □9	120	35.10 N	76.10 E

DEUTSCH

Name	Seite	Breite°′	Länge°′ E = Ost
Ladākh Range ⋏	120	34.00 N	78.00 E
Ladan	78	50.31 N	32.35 E
La Dang, Ko I	114	6.33 N	99.18 E
Ladang Jagor	114	4.42 N	101.35 E
Ladara	114	1.28 N	97.28 E
Ladário	248	19.01 S	57.35 W
Ladbergen	52	52.08 N	7.44 E
Ladby	41	55.26 N	10.38 E
Ladd	190	41.22 N	89.13 W
Ladder Creek ≃	198	38.48 N	100.52 W
Laddingford	260	51.12 N	0.25 E
Laddonia	219	39.14 N	91.38 W
Ladeburg	264a	52.42 N	13.35 E
La Défense ▾	261	48.53 N	2.15 E
La Dehesa	286e	33.22 S	70.33 W
La Dent d'Oche ∧	58	46.21 N	6.44 E
Ladera Heights	280	33.59 N	118.22 W
La Désirade I	241o	16.19 N	61.03 W
Ládhi	38	41.27 N	26.17 E
Ladhurka	126	23.22 N	86.32 E
La Digue I	138	4.21 S	55.50 E
Lâdik	130	40.55 N	35.55 E
Ladinger Spitze ∧	61	46.51 N	14.39 E
L'adiny	24	61.33 N	38.20 E
Ladismith	158	33.30 S	21.16 E
Ladispoli	66	41.56 N	12.05 E
Lādīz	128	28.56 N	61.19 E
Ladner	224	49.05 N	123.05 W
Lādnūn	120	27.39 N	74.23 E
Ladoga	194	39.54 N	86.48 W
Ladoga, Lake → Ladožskoje ozero ⊜	24	61.00 N	31.30 E
La Dolorita	286c	10.29 N	66.47 W
Ladon	50	48.00 N	2.32 E
Ladonia	196	33.25 N	95.56 W
La Dorada	246	5.27 N	74.40 W
La Dormida	252	33.21 S	67.55 W
Lado Sarāi ◆8	272a	28.32 N	77.12 E
L'adova ≃	78	48.28 N	27.37 E
Ladovskaja Balka	80	45.38 N	41.25 E
Ladožskaja	78	45.19 N	39.54 E
Ladožskoje Ozero	76	60.08 N	31.04 E
Ladožskoje ozero (Lake Ladoga) ⊜	24	61.00 N	31.30 E
Lādpur ◆8	272a	28.44 N	76.59 E
Ladrillero, Golfo c	254	49.20 S	75.37 W
Ladson	192	32.59 N	80.06 W
Ladue	219	38.38 N	90.23 W
Ladue ≃	180	63.09 N	140.25 W
Laduozong	102	31.27 N	97.19 E
Laduškin	76	54.36 N	20.11 E
Ladva	24	61.21 N	34.34 E
Ladva-Vetka	24	61.21 N	34.27 E
Lādwa	124	29.59 N	77.03 E
L'ady, Bela.	76	54.36 N	31.10 E
Lady, Fr.	261	48.35 N	2.54 E
L'ady, Ross.	76	58.38 N	28.47 E
Lady Ann Strait ɥ	176	75.40 N	79.50 W
Ladybank	46	56.16 N	3.08 W
Lady Barron	166	40.12 S	148.14 E
Ladybower Reservoir ⊜1	44	53.20 N	1.45 W
Ladybrand	158	29.19 S	27.25 E
Lady Elliot Island I	166	24.07 S	152.42 E
Lady Evelyn Lake ⊜	190	47.20 N	80.10 W
Lady Frere	158	31.44 S	27.16 E
Lady Grey	158	30.45 S	27.13 E
Lady Lake	220	28.55 N	81.55 W
Ladysmith, Austl.	171b	35.12 S	147.31 E
Ladysmith, B.C., Can.	182	48.58 N	123.49 W
Ladysmith, S. Afr.	158	28.34 S	29.45 E
Ladysmith, Wi., U.S.	190	45.27 N	91.06 W
Ladyženka	86	51.00 N	68.42 E
Ladyžin	78	48.41 N	29.15 E
Ladžanurges	84	42.37 N	42.50 E
Lae	164	6.45 S	147.00 E
Lae I1	14	8.56 N	166.14 E
Laem, Khao ∧	110	14.27 N	101.30 E
Laem Ngop	110	12.10 N	102.26 E
La Encantada	232	25.17 N	101.04 W
La Encarnacion	234	23.23 N	98.01 W
Laer	52	52.03 N	7.21 E
Laer ◆8	263	51.28 N	7.16 E
Lærdalsøyri	26	61.06 N	7.29 E
La Escondida	196	26.17 N	99.46 W
La Esmeralda, Méx.	232	27.17 N	103.39 W
La Esmeralda, Para.	252	22.13 S	62.38 W
La Esmeralda, Ven.	246	3.10 N	65.33 W
Læsø I	26	57.16 N	11.01 E
La Esperanza, Cuba	240p	22.46 N	83.44 W
La Esperanza, Hond.	236	14.20 N	88.10 W
La Esperanza, Méx.	196	26.46 N	104.00 W
La Esperanza, Méx.	200	32.06 N	114.47 W
La Esperanza, Perú	248	8.05 S	79.04 W
La Esperanza, P.R.	240m	18.22 N	66.07 W
La Estación ◆8	266a	40.27 N	3.48 W
La Estrada	34	42.41 N	8.29 W
La Estrella, Bol.	248	16.30 S	63.45 W
La Estrella, Ven.	286c	10.25 N	66.48 W
La Estrella, Cerro ∧	286a	19.20 N	99.05 W
Lafa	89	43.50 N	127.19 E
La Falda	252	31.05 S	64.30 W
La Farge	190	43.34 N	90.38 W
LaFargeville	212	44.11 N	75.57 W
Lafayette, Fr.	62	45.35 N	5.04 E
Lafayette, Al., U.S.	194	32.53 N	85.24 W
Lafayette, Ca., U.S.	226	37.53 N	122.07 W
Lafayette, Co., U.S.	198	39.59 N	105.05 W
Lafayette, Ga., U.S.	192	34.42 N	85.16 W
Lafayette, In., U.S.	216	40.25 N	86.52 W
Lafayette, La., U.S.	194	30.13 N	92.01 W
Lafayette, Mn., U.S.	190	44.26 N	94.23 W
Lafayette, N.J., U.S.	210	41.05 N	74.41 W
La Fayette, N.Y., U.S.	210	42.54 N	76.06 W
Lafayette, Oh., U.S.	216	40.46 N	83.57 W
Lafayette, Or., U.S.	224	45.14 N	123.06 W
La Fayette, R.I., U.S.	207	41.34 N	71.28 W
Lafayette, Tn., U.S.	194	36.31 N	86.01 W
La Fayette, Tx., U.S.	222	32.54 N	94.51 W
Lafayette, Mount ∧	188	44.10 N	71.38 W
Lafayette Hill	285	40.05 N	75.15 W
Lafayette Reservoir ⊜1	282	37.53 N	122.08 W
Lafayette Water Tunnel ◆5	282	37.54 N	122.12 W
La Fé	240p	21.45 N	82.45 W
La Fère	50	49.40 N	3.22 E
La Feria	196	26.09 N	97.49 W
Laferrere	288	34.45 S	58.35 W
La Ferrière-sur-Risle	50	48.59 N	0.48 E
La Ferté-Alais	50	48.29 N	2.21 E
La Ferté-Bernard	50	48.11 N	0.40 E
La Ferté-Frênel	50	48.50 N	0.30 E
La Ferté-Gaucher	50	48.47 N	3.18 E
La Ferté-Imbault	50	47.23 N	1.58 E
La Ferté-Macé	32	48.36 N	0.22 W
La Ferté-Milon	50	49.10 N	3.07 E
La Ferté-Saint-Aubin	50	47.43 N	1.56 E
La Ferté-sous-Jouarre	50	48.57 N	3.08 E
Laferté-sur-Amance	58	47.50 N	5.42 E
La Ferté-Vidame	50	48.37 N	0.55 E
La Ferté-Villeneuil	50	47.59 N	1.21 E
Lafferty	214	40.06 N	81.01 W
Laffrey	62	45.02 N	5.46 E
Lafia	150	8.30 N	8.30 E
Lafiagi	150	8.52 N	5.25 E
Laflamme ≃	190	48.56 N	77.18 W
Laflèche, P.Q., Can.	275a	45.30 N	73.28 W
Lafleche, Sk., Can.	184	49.43 N	106.35 W
La Flèche, Fr.	32	47.42 N	0.05 W
La Floresta	266d	41.27 N	2.04 E
La Florida, Chile	286e	33.33 S	70.34 W
La Florida, Esp.	266d	41.31 N	2.12 E
La Florida, Guat.	232	16.33 N	90.27 W
Lafnitz ≃	61	46.57 N	16.16 E
La Foa	175f	21.43 S	165.50 E
La Foce	62	44.08 N	9.47 E

Symbols in the index entries represent the broad categories identified in the key at the right. Symbols with superior numbers (⋏1) identify subcategories (see complete key on page *I · 1).*

Symbole im Register stellen die rechts im Schlüssel erklärten Kategorien dar. Symbole mit hochgestellten Ziffern (⋏1) bezeichnen Unterabteilungen einer Kategorie (vgl. vollständiger Schlüssel auf Seite *I · 1).*

Los símbolos incluídos en el texto del índice representan las grandes categorias identificadas con la clave a la derecha. Los símbolos con numeros en su parte superior (⋏1) identifican las subcategorías (véase la clave completa en la página *I · 1).*

Les symboles de l'index représentent les catégories indiquées dans la légende à droite. Les symboles suivis d'un indice (⋏1) représentent des sous-catégories (voir légende complète à la page *I · 1).*

Os símbolos incluídos no texto do índice representam as grandes categorias identificadas com a chave à direita. Os símbolos com números em sua parte superior (⋏1) identificam as subcategorias (veja-se a chave completa à página *I · 1).*

∧	Mountain	Berg	Montaña	Montagne	Montanha
⋏	Mountains	Gebirge	Montañas	Montagnes	Montanhas
×	Pass	Paß	Paso	Col	Passo
V	Valley, Canyon	Tal, Cañon	Valle, Cañón	Vallée, Canyon	Vale, Canhão
≍	Plain	Ebene	Llano	Plaine	Planície
>	Cape	Kap	Cabo	Cap	Cabo
I	Island	Insel	Isla	Île	Ilha
II	Islands	Inseln	Islas	Îles	Ilhas
⊥	Other Topographic Features	Andere Topographische Objekte	Otros Elementos Topográficos	Autres données topographiques	Outros acidentes topográficos

ESPAÑOL — Nombre	FRANÇAIS — Nom	PORTUGUÊS — Nome
Página · Lat.°' · Long.°' W=Oeste	Page · Lat.°' · Long.°' W=Ouest	Página · Lat.°' · Long.°' W=Oeste

Legend / symbols:

| River · Fluß · Río · Rivière · Rio | ≈ |
| Canal · Kanal · Canal · Canal · Canal |
| Waterfall, Rapids · Wasserfall, Stromschnellen · Cascada, Rápidos · Chute d'eau, Rapides · Cascata, Rápidos |
| Strait · Meeresstraße · Estrecho · Détroit · Estreito |
| Bay, Gulf · Bucht, Golf · Bahía, Golfo · Baie, Golfe · Baía, Golfo |
| Lake, Lakes · See, Seen · Lago, Lagos · Lac, Lacs · Lago, Lagos |
| Swamp · Sumpf · Pantano · Marais · Pântano |
| Ice Features, Glacier · Eis- und Gletscherformen · Otros Elementos · Formes glaciaires · Acidentes glaciares |
| Other Hydrographic Features · Andere Hydrographische Objekte · Otros Elementos Hidrográficos · Autres données hydrographiques · Outros acidentes hidrográficos |

| Submarine Features · Untermeerische Objekte · Accidentes Submarinos · Formes de relief sous-marin · Acidentes submarinos |
| Political Unit · Politische Einheit · Unidad Política · Entité politique · Unidade política |
| Cultural Institution · Kulturelle Institution · Institución Cultural · Institution culturelle · Instituição cultural |
| Historical Site · Historische Stätte · Sitio Histórico · Site historique · Sítio histórico |
| Recreational Site · Erholungs- und Ferienort · Sitio de Recreo · Centre de loisirs · Área de Lazer |
| Airport · Flughafen · Aeropuerto · Aéroport · Aeroporto |
| Military Installation · Militäranlage · Instalación Militar · Installation militaire · Instalação militar |
| Miscellaneous · Verschiedenes · Misceláneo · Divers · Diversos |

ENGLISH: Name — Page — Lat.°′ — Long.°′
DEUTSCH: Name — Seite — Breite°′ — Länge°′ E = Ost

Symbols in the index entries represent the broad categories identified in the key at the right. Symbols with superior numbers (⋏1) identify subcategories (see complete key on page *I · 1).*

Symbole im Register stellen die rechts im Schlüssel erklärten Kategorien dar. Symbole mit hochgestellten Ziffern (⋏1) bezeichnen Unterabteilungen einer Kategorie (vgl. vollständiger Schlüssel auf Seite *I · 1).*

Los símbolos incluídos en el texto del índice representan las grandes categorias identificadas con la clave a la derecha. Los símbolos con numeros en su parte superior (⋏1) identifican las subcategorías (véase la clave completa en la página *I · 1).*

Les symboles de l'index représentent les catégories indiquées dans la légende à droite. Les symboles suivis d'un indice (⋏1) représentent des sous-catégories (voir légende complète à la page *I · 1).*

Os símbolos incluídos no texto do índice representam as grandes categorias identificadas com a chave à direita. Os símbolos com números em sua parte superior (⋏1) identificam as subcategorias (veja-se a chave completa à página *I · 1).*

∧ Mountain	Berg	Montaña	Montagne	Montanha
⋏ Mountains	Gebirge	Montañas	Montagnes	Montanhas
)(Pass	Paß	Paso	Col	Passo
V Valley, Canyon	Tal, Cañon	Valle, Cañón	Vallée, Canyon	Vale, Canhão
≚ Plain	Ebene	Llano	Plaine	Planície
› Cape	Kap	Cabo	Cap	Cabo
I Island	Insel	Isla	Île	Ilha
II Islands	Inseln	Islas	Îles	Ilhas
⊥ Other Topographic Features	Andere Topographische Objekte	Otros Elementos Topográficos	Autres données topographiques	Outros acidentes topográficos

ESPAÑOL Nombre	Página	Lat.°′	Long.°′ W=Oeste
La Roche-sur-Foron	58	46.04 N	6.19 E
La Roche-sur-Yon	32	46.40 N	1.26 W
La Rochette, Fr.	62	45.28 N	6.07 E
La Rochette, Fr.	261	48.30 N	2.40 E
Larochette, Lux.	56	49.47 N	6.15 E
La Roda	34	39.13 N	2.09 W
La Romaine	186	50.13 N	60.40 W
La Romana	238	18.25 N	68.58 W
Larona	112	2.45 S	121.20 E
La Ronge	184	55.06 N	105.17 W
Laroquebrou	32	44.58 N	2.11 E
La Roquebrussanne	62	43.20 N	5.59 E
Larose	194	29.34 N	90.22 W
La Rosita	236	13.53 N	84.24 W
La Route	261	48.48 N	2.47 E
Larrabee State Park ♦	224	44.41 N	122.29 W
Larreynaga	236	12.40 N	86.34 W
Larrey Point ‣	162	19.58 S	119.07 E
Larrimah	164	15.35 S	133.12 E
Larringes	58	46.22 N	6.35 E
Larrison Creek ≃	222	31.27 N	95.03 W
Larroque	252	33.02 S	59.01 W
Larrys Creek ≃	210	41.13 N	77.13 W
Larrys River	186	45.13 N	61.23 W
Larsen Air Park ≃	281	42.11 N	83.33 W
Larsen Bay	180	57.33 N	154.00 W
Larsen Ice Shelf ⊠	9	68.30 S	62.30 W
Larteh Aheneasi	150	5.56 N	0.04 E
La Rubia	252	30.06 S	61.48 W
La Rue, Oh., U.S.	214	40.35 N	83.23 W
Larue, Tx., U.S.	222	32.07 N	95.41 W
La Rumorosa	204	32.34 N	116.06 W
Laruns	32	42.59 N	0.25 W
Larus Lake ⊜	184	51.17 N	94.40 W
Larvik	26	59.04 N	10.00 E
Larwill	216	41.10 N	85.37 W
Larzac, Causse du ♦	32	44.00 N	3.15 E
Lasa (Laas)	64	46.37 N	10.42 E
La Sabana	252	27.52 S	59.57 W
Las Adjuntas	286c	20.16 N	67.01 W
La Sagne	58	47.03 N	6.48 E
La Sal	200	38.18 N	109.14 W
La Salada, Laguna ⊜	234	22.28 N	98.20 W
La Salette-Fallavaux	62	44.51 N	5.59 E
La Salle, On., Can.	214	43.14 N	83.06 W
La Salle, P.Q., Can.	206	45.26 N	73.38 W
Lasalle, Fr.	62	44.03 N	3.51 E
La Salle, It.	62	45.45 N	7.04 E
La Salle, Co., U.S.	200	40.20 N	104.42 W
La Salle, Il., U.S.	216	41.20 N	89.06 W
La Salle, Mi., U.S.	216	41.21 N	88.51 W
La Salle ⊜6	184	49.45 N	97.08 W
Lasalle, Parc ♦	275a	45.26 N	73.40 W
La Salle College ⋎2	285	40.02 N	75.09 W
La Salle Gardens	281	42.39 N	83.21 W
Las Almejas, Bahía c	232	24.29 N	111.44 W
La Sal Mountains ⋏	200	38.30 N	109.10 W
Lasan	112	1.14 N	115.13 E
Lasanga Island I	164	7.25 S	147.16 E
Las Animas	198	38.04 N	103.13 W
La Santa, Cerro ⋏	240m	18.07 N	66.03 W
Las Arenas	240m	18.02 N	67.09 W
La Sarraz	58	46.40 N	6.31 E
La Sarre	190	48.48 N	79.12 W
La Sarre	58	48.43 N	79.16 W
Las Arrias	252	30.21 S	63.35 W
La Sauceda	58	28.26 N	100.38 W
La Sauce	62	44.25 N	6.01 E
Las Auras	196	26.25 N	99.20 W
Las Aves, Isla I	238	15.42 N	63.38 W
Las Aves, Islas II	246	12.00 N	67.30 W
Las Ballenas, Canal de ⯑	232	29.10 N	113.29 W
Lasberg	61	48.28 N	14.32 E
Las Blancas	196	25.42 N	97.35 W
Las Bonitas	246	7.52 N	65.40 W
Las Breñas	252	27.05 S	61.05 W
Låsby	41	56.09 N	9.49 E
Las Cabezas de San Juan	34	36.59 N	5.56 W
Las Cabras	252	34.18 S	71.19 W
Las Cañas ≃	252	22.29 N	105.36 W
Lascano	252	33.40 S	54.12 W
Lascar, Volcán ⋏1	252	23.23 S	67.45 W
Lascari	57	38.00 N	13.56 E
Las Casas — San Cristóbal de las Casas	234	16.45 N	92.38 W
Las Catitas	252	33.18 S	68.02 W
Las Catonas, Arroyo ≃	288	34.37 S	58.43 W
Lascaux, Grotte de ⋆ ♦	32	45.01 N	1.08 E
Las Cejas	252	26.53 S	64.44 W
L'Ascension	206	46.33 N	74.50 W
L'aščevka	78	49.33 N	32.41 E
Las Chacras	258	35.05 S	59.10 W
Las Choapas	234	17.55 N	94.05 W
La Scie	186	49.57 N	55.36 W
Las Coloradas	236	21.39 S	70.35 W
Las Condes	286e	33.22 S	70.31 W
Lascone, Monte ⋏2	267a	41.13 N	14.48 E
Las Cruces	200	32.18 N	106.46 W
Las Cuevas	232	29.38 N	101.19 W
Las Delicias	232	15.58 N	91.50 W
La Selle, Morne ⋏	238	18.22 N	71.59 W
La Selva Beach	226	36.55 N	121.51 W
Lasem	115a	6.42 S	111.26 E
La Serena	252	29.54 S	71.16 W
La Serena ✦1	34	38.45 N	5.30 W
La Seyne	32	43.06 N	5.53 E
La Seyne-sur-Mer	62	43.06 N	5.53 E
Las Flores, Arg.	252	36.03 S	59.07 W
Las Flores, Arg.	252	39.10 S	69.12 W
Las Flores, Méx.	234	18.22 N	93.10 W
Las Flores, P.R.	240m	18.03 N	66.22 W
Las Flores, Arroyo ≃	252	36.00 S	58.00 W
Las Flores, Cerro ⋏	234	16.43 N	95.30 W
Las Flores Canyon ⋎	280	34.20 N	118.38 W
Las Flores Chica, Laguna ⊜	258	35.30 S	59.01 W
Las Flores Grande, Laguna ⊜	258	35.34 S	59.02 W
Las Guacamayas	234	18.02 N	102.12 W
Las Guayabas	232	24.00 N	97.45 W
Lasham	42	51.11 N	1.03 W
Las Harquetas, Arroyo ≃	234	34.29 S	58.38 W
Lashburn	184	53.08 N	109.36 W
Las Heras, Arg.	252	32.51 S	68.49 W
Las Heras, Arg.	252	46.33 S	68.57 W
Lashio	110	22.56 N	97.45 E
Lashkar Gāh	128	31.35 N	64.21 E
Lashkar — Gwalior	124	26.13 N	78.10 E
Las Hormigas	232	25.30 N	98.44 W
Lasia	123	36.48 N	73.01 E
Lasia, Pulau I	114	2.10 N	96.39 E
La Sierra, Montaña ⋏	236	14.04 N	87.10 W
Las Iglesias	196	27.35 N	101.21 W
Lasithi	52	52.52 N	7.19 E
La Silla ≃	68	39.16 N	16.30 E
La Siligata	66	43.56 N	12.45 E
La Silla de Caracas ⋏	286c	10.32 N	66.50 W
Lasin	30	53.32 N	19.05 E
Łasin	80	58.16 N	49.52 E
Lāsjerd	128	35.24 N	53.04 E
Laskarzew	30	51.48 N	21.35 E
Ł'askel'a	24	61.45 N	30.59 E
Laško	36	46.09 N	15.14 E
L'aškoviči	78	52.07 N	28.09 E
Las Lajas, Arg.	252	38.31 S	70.22 W
Las Lajas, Pan.	236	8.15 N	81.52 W
Las Lajitas	252	24.41 S	64.15 W

FRANÇAIS Nom	Page	Lat.°′	Long.°′ W=Ouest
Las Lomas	246	4.40 S	80.15 W
Las Lomitas	252	24.42 S	60.36 W
Lašma	80	54.56 N	41.09 E
Las Malvinas	252	34.50 S	68.15 W
Lašmanka	80	54.44 N	51.28 E
Las Mareas	240m	17.56 N	66.09 W
Las Margaritas	232	16.19 N	91.59 W
Las Margaritas, Laguna ⊜	258	35.28 S	57.56 W
Las Marianas	258	35.04 S	59.31 W
Las Marias	240m	18.15 N	67.00 W
Las Marismas ⧗	34	37.00 N	6.15 W
Las Mayas	286c	10.26 N	66.56 W
Las Mercedes	246	9.07 N	66.24 W
Las Mesas de San Isidro	234	21.55 N	100.15 W
Las Minas	286	10.27 N	66.52 W
Las Minas, Cerro ⋏	236	14.33 N	88.39 W
Las Minillas, Cerro ⋏	236e	33.31 S	70.29 W
Las Moras Creek ≃	196	29.10 N	100.39 W
Las Mulas, Laguna ⊜	258	35.32 S	57.54 W
Las Navas	116	12.21 N	125.02 E
Las Nieves	232	26.24 N	105.22 W
Las Nopaleras, Cerro ⋏	232	25.08 N	103.14 W
La Solana	34	38.56 N	3.14 W
La Soledad, Cerro ⋏	232	26.32 N	107.17 W
Lasolo	112	3.29 S	122.04 E
Lasolo ≃	112	3.28 S	122.06 E
Las Ortegas, Arroyo ≃	288	34.45 S	58.32 W
Las Ovejas	252	37.01 S	70.45 W
Las Palmas, Arg.	252	27.04 S	58.42 W
Las Palmas, Arg.	258	34.05 S	59.10 W
Las Palmas, Pan.	236	8.08 N	81.27 W
Las Palmas, P.R.	240m	17.59 N	66.02 W
Las Palmas ≃	148	28.25 N	14.15 W
Las Palmas de Gran Canaria	148	28.06 N	15.24 W
Las Palomas	200	31.44 N	107.37 W
Las Perdices, Canal ☰	286e	33.31 S	70.33 W
La Spezia	62	44.07 N	9.50 E
La Spezia □4	62	44.11 N	9.42 E
Las Piedras, P.R.	240m	18.11 N	65.52 W
Las Piedras, Ur.	258	34.44 S	56.13 W
Las Piedras, Río de ≃	248	12.30 S	69.14 W
Las Piñas, Fr.	269f	14.29 N	120.59 E
Las Piñas, P.R.	240m	18.15 N	65.55 W
Las Plumas	254	43.43 S	67.15 W
Lasqueti Island I	182	49.29 N	124.17 W
Las Raices Creek ≃	196	28.09 N	99.02 W
Las Ratas, Cerro ⋏	234	18.37 N	103.37 W
Las Rejas	286e	33.28 S	70.44 W
Las Rosas, Arg.	252	32.28 S	61.34 W
Las Rosas, Chile	286e	33.35 S	70.37 W
Las Rosas, Méx.	232	16.24 N	92.23 W
Las Rozas de Madrid	286	40.29 N	3.52 W
Las Sales, Canal ☰	286a	29.15 N	99.03 W
Lassan	54	53.57 N	13.50 E
Lassance	255	17.54 S	44.34 W
Lassater	222	32.49 N	94.30 W
Lasse	58	48.26 N	0.30 W
Lassee	61	48.11 N	16.49 E
Lassellsville	210	43.03 N	74.36 W
Lassen Peak ⋏1	204	40.29 N	121.31 W
Lassen Volcanic National Park ♦	204	40.30 N	121.19 W
Lassigny	50	49.35 N	2.51 E
Lassnitz ≃	61	46.46 N	15.32 E
Lassnitzhöhe	61	47.03 N	15.35 E
Lasso ⋏2	174n	15.02 N	145.38 E
L'Assomption	206	45.48 N	73.35 W
L'Assomption □6	206	45.43 N	73.29 W
L'Assomption ≃	206	45.43 N	73.25 W
Lasswade	46	55.53 N	3.08 W
Lassy	261	49.06 N	2.27 E
Las Tablas	246	7.46 N	80.17 W
Lastarria, Parque Nacional ♦	254	44.50 S	72.05 W
Las Tinajas	252	27.27 S	62.55 W
Last Mountain ⋏	184	51.07 N	104.54 W
Last Mountain Lake ⊜	184	51.05 N	105.10 W
Lastoursville	152	0.49 S	12.42 E
Lastovo, Otok I	36	42.46 N	16.53 E
Lastra a Signa	66	43.46 N	11.06 E
Las Trampas Peak ⋏	282	37.50 N	122.03 W
Las Trampas Regional Park ♦	282	37.49 N	122.02 W
Las Trampas Ridge ⋏	282	37.50 N	122.00 W
Lastrup	40	58.54 N	17.18 E
Las Truchas	234	17.15 N	102.12 W
Lastrup	52	52.48 N	7.52 E
Las Tunas	240p	20.58 N	76.57 W
Las Tunas □4	240p	21.00 N	77.00 W
Las Tunas, Punta ‣	240m	18.30 N	66.38 W
Las Tunas Grandes, Laguna ⊜	252	35.58 S	62.25 W
La Suze	32	47.54 N	0.02 E
Las Varas, Méx.	234	21.10 N	105.18 W
Las Varas, Méx.	234	21.10 N	105.10 W
Las Varillas	252	31.52 S	62.43 W
Las Vegas, P.R.	240m	18.11 N	67.02 W
Las Vegas, Nv., U.S.	204	36.10 N	115.08 W
Las Vegas, N.M., U.S.	200	35.36 N	105.13 W
Las Vigas de Ramirez	234	19.38 N	97.05 W
La Tabatière	186	50.50 N	58.58 W
Latacunga	246	0.56 S	78.37 W
Latady Island I	9	70.45 S	74.35 W
La Tagua	246	0.03 S	74.40 W
Latakia □	130	35.30 N	36.00 E
Latakia — Al-Lādhiqīyah	130	35.31 N	35.47 E
Latamber	123	33.07 N	70.52 E
Lata Mountain ⋏	174v	14.14 S	169.29 W
La Tapona	232	23.45 N	104.59 W
Lätehausen ∟	263	51.24 N	7.19 E
Latehar	124	23.45 N	84.30 E
Lately Common	262	53.29 N	2.30 W
Laterina	66	43.31 N	11.43 E
Latham, Austl.	162	29.45 S	116.26 E
Latham, Il., U.S.	219	39.58 N	89.10 W
Latham, N.Y., U.S.	210	42.44 N	73.45 W
Latham, Oh., U.S.	218	39.06 N	83.15 W
Lathen	52	52.52 N	7.19 E
Lathi	122	21.43 N	71.23 E
Lathrop, Ca., U.S.	226	37.49 N	121.16 W
Lathrop, Mo., U.S.	194	39.32 N	94.19 W
Lathrup Village	281	42.30 N	83.14 W
La Thuile	62	45.43 N	6.57 E
Latham, Mount ⋏	286c	10.26 N	66.46 W
Latimer, Eng., U.K.	260	51.41 N	0.33 W
Latimer, Il., U.S.	190	42.45 N	93.22 W
Latisana	64	45.44 N	13.01 E

PORTUGUÊS Nome	Página	Lat.°′	Long.°′ W=Oeste
Latjuga	24	64.16 N	48.46 E
Latnaja	78	51.43 N	38.55 E
La Toma	252	33.03 S	65.37 W
Laton	226	36.26 N	119.41 W
Latorca	83	47.29 N	38.38 E
Latorica ≃	30	48.28 N	21.50 E
Latornell ≃	182	54.58 N	118.00 W
La Torrecilla ⋏	240m	18.12 N	66.20 W
La Tortuga, Isla I	246	10.56 N	65.20 W
Latouche Island I	180	60.00 N	147.55 W
Latouche Treville, Cape ‣	162	18.27 S	121.49 E
La Tour	162	43.57 N	7.11 E
La Tour-d'Aigues	62	43.44 N	5.33 E
La Tour-d'Auvergne	32	45.32 N	2.41 E
La Tour-de-Peilz	58	46.27 N	6.49 E
La Tour-du-Pin	62	45.34 N	5.27 E
La Tourette Park ♦	276	40.35 N	74.08 W
Lat Phrao, Khlong ≃	269a	13.48 N	100.35 E
La Tremblade	32	45.46 N	1.08 W
La Trimouille	32	46.28 N	1.02 E
La Trinidad, Arg.	252	27.24 S	65.31 W
La Trinidad, Nic.	236	12.58 N	86.14 W
La Trinidad, Pil.	116	16.28 N	120.35 E
La Trinidad, Ven.	286c	10.27 N	66.52 W
La Trinidad de Orichuna	246	7.07 N	69.45 W
La Trinitaria	232	16.07 N	92.03 W
La Trinité	246	14.44 N	60.58 W
Latrobe, Austl.	166	41.14 S	146.24 E
Latrobe, Pa., U.S.	214	40.19 N	79.22 W
La Trobe ≃	169	38.10 S	146.32 E
Latrobe University ⋎2	274b	37.43 S	145.03 E
La Tronche	62	45.12 N	5.44 E
Latronico	68	40.05 N	16.01 E
Latta	192	34.20 N	79.25 W
Lattarico	68	39.28 N	16.08 E
Lattasburg	214	40.53 N	82.06 W
Latterbach	58	46.40 N	7.35 E
Lattingtown	276	40.54 N	73.36 W
Latty	216	41.05 N	84.35 W
La Tuilerie	261	48.34 N	2.08 E
La Tuilière	62	44.11 N	5.32 E
Latuna	112	8.23 S	124.06 E
La Tuque	176	47.26 N	72.47 W
Lätür	122	18.24 N	76.35 E
La Turbie	62	43.45 N	7.24 E
Latvia (Latvija) ⊠1, Europe	22	57.00 N	25.00 E
Latvia (Latvija) ⊠1, Europe	22	57.00 N	25.00 E
Lau, Nig.	146	9.13 N	11.17 E
Lau, Pap. N. Gui.	164	5.50 S	151.20 E
Laubach	56	50.33 N	8.59 E
Lau Basin ◆1	14	20.00 S	177.00 W
Laubusch	54	51.28 N	14.10 E
Lauca, Parque Nacional ♦	248	18.20 S	115.45 E
Lauca ≃	248	18.50 S	96.55 W
Lauca Bay c	196	28.35 N	96.35 W
La Vachette	62	44.53 N	5.11 E
Lavagh More ⋏	48	54.45 N	8.05 W
Lavagna	62	44.18 N	9.20 E
Lavagna ≃	64	44.21 N	9.20 E
La Vall d'Uixó — La Vall d'Uixo	34	39.49 N	0.14 W
La Vallee	34	33.40 N	74.09 W
La Valley	200	37.06 N	105.20 W
Laval-Ouest ◆8	206	45.33 N	73.52 W
Laval, P.Q., Can.	206	45.35 N	73.45 W
Lavamünd	61	46.39 N	14.56 E
Lavant ≃	61	46.41 N	14.56 E
Lavaré	32	48.04 N	0.46 E
Lavaveix-les-Mines	32	46.07 N	2.12 E
La Vecchia ≃	34	42.51 N	5.24 W
La Vecilla de Curueño	34	42.51 N	5.24 W
La Vega, Col.	246	12.15 N	72.11 W
La Vela, Cabo de ‣	246	12.13 N	72.11 W
La Vela de Coro	246	11.27 N	69.34 W
Lavello	68	41.03 N	15.48 E
Lavelaire, Lac ⊜	186	50.46 N	66.22 W
Laven	41	56.07 N	9.43 E
La Venada	196	25.50 N	97.30 W
Lavenham	42	52.06 N	0.47 E
La Ventana ≃	234	16.59 N	93.46 W
La Venta ≃	234	18.08 N	94.03 W
La Ventura	232	24.38 N	100.54 W
Laver ≃	262	54.18 N	1.30 W
La Vera ✦1	34	40.07 N	5.30 W
La Verde, Arg.	252	27.08 S	59.23 W
La Verde, Arg.	252	34.44 S	59.16 W
Laverdière, Lac ⊜	206	46.50 N	74.28 W
L'Averdy, Cape ‣	175e	5.33 S	155.04 E
La Vérendrye, Réserve ♦	176	47.30 N	77.00 W
La Vergne	194	36.00 N	86.34 W
La Verne	228	34.06 N	117.46 W
Laveen	202	33.21 N	112.10 W
Lavelo ≃	50	47.05 N	0.05 W
Laverton, Austl.	162	28.38 S	122.25 E
Laverton, Austl.	169	37.52 S	144.45 E
Laverton Royal Australian Air Force Base ⋆	169	37.52 S	144.45 E

Nome	Página	Lat.°′	Long.°′
Laurel Ridge State Park ♦	188	39.58 N	79.23 W
Laurel River Lake ⊜1	192	36.55 N	84.15 W
Laurel Run	210	41.13 N	75.51 W
Laurel Run ≃	208	40.20 N	77.20 W
Laurel Springs	285	39.49 N	75.00 W
Laurelton	210	40.52 N	77.11 W
Laurelville, Oh., U.S.	188	39.28 N	82.44 W
Laurelville, Pa., U.S.	214	40.09 N	79.29 W
Laurenburg	56	50.20 N	7.54 E
Laurence Harbor	276	40.27 N	74.14 W
Laurencekirk	46	56.50 N	2.29 W
Laurens, Ia., U.S.	198	42.50 N	94.51 W
Laurens, S.C., U.S.	192	34.29 N	82.00 W
Laurentides	206	45.51 N	73.46 W
Laurentides, Les ⋏1	176	48.00 N	71.00 W
Laurentides, Parc Provincial des ♦	186	47.40 N	71.30 W
Laurenzana	68	40.02 N	15.58 E
La Vieux	68	40.02 N	15.50 E
Laurie Island I	9	60.45 S	44.35 W
Laurie Lake ⊜	184	56.34 N	101.54 W
Laurier, Mb., Can.	184	50.54 N	99.33 W
Laurier, P.Q., Can.	206	46.32 N	71.38 W
Laurière	32	46.05 N	1.28 E
Laurierville	206	46.18 N	71.39 W
Laurinburg	192	34.46 N	79.27 W
Laurino	68	40.20 N	15.20 E
Lauro	68	40.10 N	15.24 E
Lauritsala	26	61.04 N	28.16 E
Lauritzen Bay c	9	69.05 S	156.50 E
Laurium	190	47.14 N	88.26 W
Lauriya Nandangarh	124	26.59 N	84.24 E
Lauro, Monte ⋏	70	37.07 N	14.49 E
Laurys Station	208	40.43 N	75.32 W
Lausanne	58	46.31 N	6.38 E
Lausche ⋏	54	50.28 N	11.10 E
Laut	86	59.18 N	66.02 E
Laut, Pulau I, Indon.	112	3.40 S	116.10 E
Laut, Pulau I, Indon.	112	4.43 N	107.59 E
Laut, Selat ☰	112	3.25 S	116.03 E
Lautaro	252	38.31 S	72.27 W
Lautaro, Volcán ⋏1	254	49.00 S	73.32 W
Lautem	112	8.22 S	126.54 E
Lautenbach	58	47.57 N	7.09 E
Lautenthal	52	51.52 N	10.17 E
Lauter ≃, Dtsch.	56	49.39 N	7.35 E
Lauter ≃, Europe	56	48.58 N	8.11 E
Lauterach	58	47.29 N	9.44 E
Lauterbach, Dtsch.	56	50.38 N	9.24 E
Lauterbach, Dtsch.	58	48.14 N	8.20 E
Lauterbourg	58	48.59 N	8.11 E
Lauterbrunnen	58	46.36 N	7.55 E
Lauterecken	56	49.39 N	7.35 E
Lauterhofen	56	49.22 N	11.37 E
Lauter [Sachsen]	54	50.33 N	12.44 E
Laut Kecil, Kepulauan II	112	4.50 S	115.45 E
Lautoka	175g	17.37 S	177.27 E
Lauttakylä — Huittinen	26	61.11 N	22.42 E
Laut Tawar, Danau ⊜	114	4.38 N	96.54 E
Lauve	50	50.48 N	3.11 E
Lauwersee c	52	53.20 N	6.12 E
Lauzerte	32	44.15 N	1.08 E
Lauzon	206	46.50 N	71.10 W
Lava (Łyna) ≃	76	54.37 N	21.14 E
Lava, Nosy I	157b	14.33 S	47.36 E
Lava Beds National Monument ♦	204	41.42 N	121.30 W
Lavaca ≃	222	29.22 N	96.55 W
Lavaca ≃	196	28.35 N	96.36 W
Lavaca Bay c	196	28.35 N	96.35 W
Lavache	62	44.53 N	5.11 E
Lavava	112	3.25 S	122.56 E
Lavagh ≃	48	54.45 N	8.05 W
Lawa	150	10.39 S	2.52 W
Lawrence, N.Z.	175g	45.55 S	169.41 E
Lawrence, In., U.S.	218	39.50 N	86.01 W
Lawrence, Ks., U.S.	198	38.58 N	95.14 W
Lavaisse	252	33.49 S	65.25 W
Lawrence, Ma., U.S.	207	42.42 N	71.09 W
Lawrence, Mi., U.S.	216	42.13 N	86.03 W
Lawrence, Ne., U.S.	198	40.17 N	98.15 W
Lawrence, N.Y., U.S.	276	40.36 N	73.43 W
La Valette-du-Var	62	43.08 N	5.59 E
La Valette — Valletta	36	35.54 N	14.31 E
La Vall d'Uixo	34	39.49 N	0.14 W
Lavalle, Arg.	252	29.01 S	59.11 W
Lavalle, Arg.	252	28.12 S	65.08 W
Lavalleja — Minas	252	34.23 S	55.14 W
Lawrence Brook ≃	276	40.29 N	74.24 W
Laval, P.Q., Can.	206	45.35 N	73.45 W
Laval-Ouest ◆8	275a	45.33 N	73.52 W
Lavaltrie	206	45.53 N	73.17 W
Lavamünd	61	46.39 N	14.56 E
Låvän, Jazīreh-ye I	128	26.48 N	53.15 E
Lavan, Nahal V	132	30.52 N	34.21 E
Lavarano	157b	25.24 S	44.55 E
Lavapié, Punta ‣	254	37.09 S	73.35 W
Lávara	38	41.16 N	26.22 E
Lavaraty	157b	23.16 S	46.59 E
Lavardac	32	44.11 N	0.18 E
Lavarone	64	45.56 N	11.15 E
Lavassaare	26	58.31 N	24.22 E
Lava-Tudo ≃	252	28.26 S	50.25 W
Lavagga Peak ⋏	226	36.53 S	121.11 W
Lawrence Fork ≃	198	41.36 N	103.14 W
Lawrence Institute of Technology ⋎2	281	42.28 N	83.15 W
Lawrence Marsh ≃	276	40.36 N	73.42 W
Lawrence Municipal Airport ⋆	283	42.43 N	71.07 W
Lawrence Park	214	41.08 N	80.04 W
Lawrence, Lake ⊜	214	41.00 N	80.20 W
Lawrenceburg, In., U.S.	218	39.05 N	84.51 W
Lawrenceburg, Ky., U.S.	218	38.02 N	84.54 W
Lawrenceburg, Tn., U.S.	194	35.14 N	87.20 W
Lawrence, Mo., U.S.	194	37.40 N	93.52 W
Lawrenceville, Il.	194	38.43 N	87.40 W
Lawrenceville, N.J., U.S.	208	40.17 N	74.43 W
Lawrenceville, Pa., U.S.	210	42.00 N	77.08 W
Lawrenceville, Va., U.S.	192	36.45 N	77.50 W
Lawson, Austl.	170	33.43 S	150.26 E
Lawson, Mo., U.S.	194	39.26 N	94.12 W
Lawson Heights	208	40.18 N	79.23 W
Lawsonia ≃	208	37.58 N	75.50 W
Lawsons Creek ≃	285	32.35 S	149.43 E
Lawtey	192	30.02 N	82.04 W
Lawton, Ky., U.S.	218	38.16 N	83.13 W
Lawton, Mi., U.S.	216	42.10 N	85.50 W
Lawton, N.D., U.S.	198	48.18 N	98.22 W
Lawton, Ok., U.S.	196	34.36 N	98.23 W
Lawu, Gunung ⋏	115a	7.38 S	111.11 E
Lawyer Creek ≃	202	46.14 N	116.10 W
Lawz, Jabal al- ⋏	130	28.40 N	35.18 E
Laxá	40	58.59 N	14.37 E
Laxey	262	54.13 N	4.24 W
Laxford, Loch c	46	58.25 N	5.04 W
Lawu Kw'alaams	182	54.33 N	130.25 W
Laxou	58	48.41 N	6.09 E
Lay ≃	32	46.19 N	1.03 W
Lay, Col de ⋏	62	45.16 N	4.21 E
Laye ≃	62	44.33 N	6.10 E
La Yesca	234	21.19 N	104.02 W
Layhill	285	39.05 N	77.03 W
Layland	214	37.52 N	81.14 W
Laylow	285	21.30 N	158.02 W
Layou	241d	13.12 N	61.17 W
Layou ≃1	240d	15.21 N	61.26 W
La'youn □4	148	27.09 N	13.12 W
Laysan Island I	14	25.50 N	171.50 W
Laytonville	204	39.41 N	123.28 W
Laytown	204	53.40 N	6.14 W

Nome	Página	Lat.°′	Long.°′
Laviano	68	40.47 N	15.18 E
Lavic Lake ⊜	204	34.40 N	116.21 W
La Victoria, Perú	246d	12.04 S	77.02 W
La Victoria, Ven.	246	10.14 N	67.20 W
Lavieille, Lake ⊜	190	45.51 N	78.14 W
Lavik	26	61.06 N	5.30 E
La Vila Joiosa	34	38.30 N	0.14 W
La Villa	64	46.36 N	11.54 E
La Villa	236	7.59 N	80.23 W
La Ville-du-Bois	261	48.40 N	2.16 E
La Villeneuve-Saint-Martin	261	49.04 N	1.58 E
Lavillette	186	47.16 N	65.18 W
Lavin	58	46.46 N	10.06 E
La Viña, Arg.	252	25.27 S	65.35 W
Lavina, Mt., U.S.	206	46.17 N	108.56 W
Lavinio Lido di Enea	66	41.30 N	12.05 E
La Virginia	246	4.54 N	75.53 W
La Vista	198	41.09 N	96.01 W
Lavon	222	33.02 N	96.26 W
Lavonia	192	34.26 N	83.06 W
Lavon Lake ⊜1	222	33.05 N	96.28 W
La Voulte-sur-Rhône	62	44.48 N	4.47 E
Lavoûte-sur-Loire	62	45.07 N	3.54 E
Lavoutte, Anse c	241f	14.06 N	60.56 W
Lavradia	266c	38.40 N	9.03 W
Lavras	256	21.14 S	45.00 W
Lavras da Mangabeira	250	5.45 S	38.57 W
Lavras do Sul	252	30.49 S	53.55 W
Lavrentija	180	65.40 N	171.00 W
Lavrentija, zaliv c	180	65.40 N	171.15 W
Lavrinhas	256	22.35 S	44.54 W
Lavrio	38	37.44 N	24.04 E
Lavumisa	158	27.19 S	31.54 E
Lavushi Manda National Park ♦	154	12.20 S	30.50 E
Lawa	116	12.12 N	125.41 E
Lawang	222b	21.55 N	159.30 W
La Wantzenau	58	48.40 N	7.50 E
La Ward	222	28.51 N	96.28 W
Lawas ≃	112	4.51 N	115.24 E
Lawatu	112	2.53 S	120.18 E
Lawdar	144	13.53 N	45.52 E
Lawele	112	5.13 S	122.57 E
Lawers, Ben ⋏	46	56.33 N	4.13 W
Laweueng	114	5.31 N	95.52 E
Lawford Lake ⊜	184	54.30 N	96.43 W
Lawgi	166	24.34 S	150.39 E
Lawin	112	5.18 N	101.04 E
Lawit, Gunong ⋏	114	5.25 N	102.35 E
Lawksawk	110	21.15 N	96.52 E
Lawler	190	43.04 N	92.09 W
Lawlor, Mount ⋏	280	34.16 N	118.06 W
Lawn, Nf., Can.	186	46.57 N	55.32 W
Lawn, Pa., U.S.	208	40.13 N	76.32 W
Lawn, Tx., U.S.	196	32.08 N	99.49 W
Lawn Bay c	186	46.53 N	55.32 W
Lawndale, Ca., U.S.	228	33.53 N	118.21 W
Lawndale, Il., U.S.	219	40.13 N	89.17 W
Lawndale, N.C., U.S.	192	35.24 N	81.33 W
Lawndale ◆8, Il., U.S.	278	41.51 N	87.43 W
Lawnes Creek ≃	208	37.08 N	76.40 W
Lawn Hill	166	18.35 S	138.35 E
Lawn Hill Creek ≃	166	18.03 S	139.09 E
Lawn Hill National Park ♦	166	18.45 S	138.27 E
Lawnside	285	39.51 N	75.01 W
Lawowa	112	4.26 S	122.56 E
Lawqah	128	29.49 N	42.45 E
Lawra	150	10.39 N	2.52 W
Lawrence Hot Springs	202	42.37 N	112.00 W
La Valley	200	37.06 N	105.20 W
Lawrence Township ◆8	208	40.18 N	74.43 W
Lawz, Jabal al- ⋏	130	28.40 N	35.18 E
Laxe ≃	52	53.25 N	7.17 E
Laxou	58	48.41 N	6.09 E
Layang Layang	114	1.49 N	103.29 E
Laye ≃	62	44.33 N	6.10 E
La Yesca	234	21.19 N	104.02 W
Lazarevo	80	56.49 N	50.15 E
Lazarevskoje	84	43.55 N	39.20 E
Lazarino	157b	23.54 S	44.59 E
Lazaro Cárdenas, Méx.	196	25.23 N	103.10 W
Lázaro Cárdenas, Méx.	232	30.33 N	115.56 W
Lázaro Cárdenas, Méx.	234	17.57 N	102.12 W
Lázaro Cárdenas, Presa ⊜1	232	25.35 N	105.02 W
Lazdijai	76	54.14 N	23.31 E
Lazhui	102	26.26 N	101.50 E
Lazhulong	120	35.08 N	81.33 E
Lazi	116	9.08 N	123.38 E
Lazio □4	66	42.00 N	12.30 E
Lazise	64	45.30 N	10.44 E
Lazo	78	50.06 N	32.39 E
La Zorra, Quebrada ≃	286c	10.36 N	67.03 W
Lazovskij zapovednik ♦	89	43.00 N	133.55 E
Lazzaro	68	37.58 N	15.40 E
Lea ≃	42	51.30 N	0.01 E
Léach	110	12.21 N	103.46 E
Leach ≃	42	51.41 N	1.39 W
Leach Pond ⊜	283	42.10 N	71.09 W
Leachville	194	35.56 N	90.15 W
Leacock	208	40.05 N	76.12 W
Lead	198	44.21 N	103.45 W
Leadbetter Point ‣	224	46.38 N	124.03 W
Leadburn	46	55.47 N	3.14 W
Leadenham	44	53.05 N	0.34 W
Leaden Roding	260	51.48 N	0.19 E
Leader	184	50.53 N	109.31 W
Leader Water ≃	46	55.36 N	2.41 W
Leadgate	44	54.52 N	1.48 W
Lead Hill ≃2	194	36.25 N	92.56 W
Leadhills	46	55.25 N	3.47 W
Leadon ≃	42	51.53 N	2.16 W
Leadore	202	44.40 N	113.21 W
Leadville	200	39.15 N	106.17 W
Leaf ≃, Mn., U.S.	198	46.29 N	94.53 W
Leaf ≃, Ms., U.S.	194	31.00 N	88.45 W
Leaf Lake ⊜	184	53.02 N	102.07 W
Leaghur, Lake ⊜	166	33.35 S	143.04 E
League ≃	48	54.39 N	8.44 W
League City	222	29.30 N	95.05 W
Leakers, Ben ⋏	46	48.58 N	11.21 W
Leakey	196	29.43 N	99.45 W
Leakin Park ♦	284b	39.18 N	76.42 W
Leak Run ≃	279b	40.27 N	79.47 W
Leaksville	192	36.29 N	79.53 W
Lealman	192	27.49 N	82.40 W
Lealui	152	15.10 S	23.02 E
Leam ≃	42	52.17 N	1.14 W
Leamington	214	42.03 N	82.36 W
Leamington Spa — Royal Leamington Spa	42	52.18 N	1.31 W
Le'an	100	27.24 N	115.48 E
Leander Point ‣	236	15.47 N	87.20 W
Leandro	252	29.50 S	55.59 W
Leandro N. Alem	252	27.36 S	55.19 W
Leane, Lough ⊜	48	52.05 N	9.35 W
Leannan ≃	48	55.02 N	7.38 W
Leano, Monte ⋏	66	41.20 N	13.13 E
Learmonth	162	22.15 S	114.05 E
Leary	192	31.29 N	84.30 W
Leasde ≃8	275b	43.42 N	79.22 W
Leask	184	53.00 N	106.45 W
Leatherhead	42	51.18 N	0.20 W
Leatherman Peak ⋏	202	44.05 N	113.44 W
Leatherwood Creek ≃	218	38.49 N	86.30 W
Lea Town	262	53.46 N	2.48 W
Leavenworth, Ks., U.S.	198	39.18 N	94.55 W
Leavenworth, Wa., U.S.	224	47.35 N	120.39 W
Leavesden Aerodrome ⋆	260	51.42 N	0.27 W
Leavittsburg	214	41.14 N	80.52 W
Leawood	194	37.03 N	94.31 W
Łeba	30	54.47 N	17.33 E
Łeba ≃	54	54.47 N	17.33 E
Lebak	116	6.32 N	124.03 E
Lébamba	152	2.12 S	11.30 E
Lebango	152	0.22 N	14.49 E
Lebanon, Ct., U.S.	207	41.38 N	72.13 W
Lebanon, In., U.S.	218	40.02 N	86.28 W
Lebanon, Ks., U.S.	198	39.48 N	98.33 W
Lebanon, Ky., U.S.	218	37.34 N	85.15 W
Lebanon, Mo., U.S.	194	37.40 N	92.39 W
Lebanon, N.H., U.S.	188	43.38 N	72.15 W
Lebanon, N.J., U.S.	208	40.39 N	74.50 W
Lebanon, Oh., U.S.	218	39.26 N	84.12 W
Lebanon, Or., U.S.	204	44.32 N	122.54 W
Lebanon, Pa., U.S.	208	40.20 N	76.25 W
Lebanon, Tn., U.S.	194	36.12 N	86.17 W
Lebanon (Lubnān) □1, Asia	118	34.00 N	36.00 E
Lebanon, S.D., U.S.	198	45.04 N	99.46 W
Lebanon Junction	194	37.50 N	85.43 W
Lebanon Mountains — Lubnān, Jabal ⋏	132	34.00 N	36.00 E
Le Ban-Saint-Martin	261	49.07 N	6.09 E
Le Bar-sur-Loup	62	43.42 N	6.59 E
Le Beausset	62	43.12 N	5.48 E
Lébe	50	57.25 N	49.32 E
Le Béage	32	44.51 N	4.07 E
Lebec	228	34.50 N	118.52 W
Lebed' ≃	86	52.30 N	87.43 E
Lebedevka, Kaz.	80	51.07 N	53.07 E
Lebedevka, Ross.	86	50.09 N	54.07 E
Lebedi	150	6.51 N	1.31 W
Lebedin, Ukr.	78	48.50 N	34.30 E
Lebedin, Ukr.	80	50.35 N	34.29 E
Leben, Oued el V	148	34.37 N	10.01 E
Le Bessat	62	45.23 N	4.28 E
Le Bihan Falls ≃	158	30.00 N	26.59 E
Le Biot	58	46.16 N	6.38 E
Le Blanc	32	46.38 N	1.04 E
Le Blanc-Mesnil	261	48.56 N	2.28 E
Le Bleymard	32	44.29 N	3.44 E
Leblon	287a	22.59 S	43.13 W
Lebo, Zaire	150	5.30 N	5.35 E
Le Bois-de-Cise	50	50.05 N	1.26 E
Le Bois-Dieu	58	45.53 N	4.43 E
Le Bois-d'Oingt	58	45.56 N	4.35 E
Lebombo Mountains ⋏	158	26.00 S	32.00 E
Lebomboberge ⋏	158	26.30 S	31.50 E
Lebon Régis	252	26.56 S	50.42 W
Lebong	112	3.01 S	101.54 E
Lebork	30	54.33 N	17.44 E
Le Boulay	50	47.40 N	0.58 E
Le Bourg-d'Oisans	62	45.03 N	6.02 E
Le Bourget-du-Lac	62	45.39 N	5.52 E
Le Brassus	58	46.35 N	6.13 E

	River	Fluß	Río	Rivière	Rio
≈	Canal	Kanal	Canal	Canal	Canal
	Waterfall, Rapids	Wasserfall, Stromschnellen	Cascada, Rápidos	Chute d'eau, Rapides	Cascata, Rápidos
	Strait	Meeresstraße	Estrecho	Détroit	Estreito
	Bay, Gulf	Bucht, Golf	Bahía, Golfo	Baie, Golfe	Baía, Golfo
⊜	Lake, Lakes	See, Seen	Lago, Lagos	Lac, Lacs	Lago, Lagos
	Swamp	Sumpf	Pantano	Marais	Pântano
⊠	Ice Features, Glacier	Eis- und Gletscherformen	Accidentes Glaciares	Formes glaciaires	Acidentes glaciares
‣	Other Hydrographic Features	Andere Hydrographische Objekte	Otros Elementos Hidrográficos	Autres données hydrographiques	Outros acidentes hidrográficos

	Submarine Features	Untermeerische Objekte	Accidentes Submarinos	Formes de relief sous-marin	Formas de relevo submarino
□	Political Unit	Politische Einheit	Unidad Política	Entité politique	Unidade política
	Cultural Institution	Kulturelle Institution	Institución Cultural	Institution culturelle	Instituição Cultural
⊥	Historical Site	Historische Stätte	Sitio Histórico	Site historique	Sítio histórico
♦	Recreational Site	Erholungs- und Ferienort	Sitio de Recreo	Centre de loisirs	Área de Lazer
⋆	Airport	Flughafen	Aeropuerto	Aéroport	Aeroporto
	Military Installation	Militäranlage	Instalación Militar	Installation militaire	Instalação militar
	Miscellaneous	Verschiedenes	Misceláneo	Divers	Diversos

Symbols in the index entries represent the broad categories identified in the key at the right. Symbols with superior numbers (⋏[1]) identify subcategories (see complete key on page I · 1).

Symbole im Register stellen die rechts im Schlüssel erklärten Kategorien dar. Symbole mit hochgestellten Ziffern (⋏[1]) bezeichnen Unterabteilungen einer Kategorie (vgl. vollständiger Schlüssel auf Seite I · 1).

Los símbolos incluidos en el texto del índice representan las grandes categorías identificadas con la clave a la derecha. Los símbolos con números en su parte superior (⋏[1]) identifican las subcategorías (véase la clave completa en la página I · 1).

Les symboles de l'index représentent les catégories indiquées dans la légende à droite. Les symboles suivis d'un indice (⋏[1]) représentent des sous-catégories (voir légende complète à la page I · 1).

Os símbolos incluídos no texto do índice representam as grandes categorias identificadas com a chave à direita. Os símbolos com números em sua parte superior (⋏[1]) identificam as subcategorias (veja-se a chave completa à página I · 1).

English	Deutsch	Español	Français	Português
∧ Mountain	Berg	Montaña	Montagne	Montanha
⋏ Mountains	Gebirge	Montañas	Montagnes	Montanhas
)(Pass	Paß	Paso	Col	Passo
V Valley, Canyon	Tal, Cañon	Valle, Cañón	Vallée, Canyon	Vale, Canhão
≚ Plain	Ebene	Llano	Plaine	Planície
≻ Cape	Kap	Cabo	Cap	Cabo
I Island	Insel	Isla	Île	Ilha
II Islands	Inseln	Islas	Îles	Ilhas
± Other Topographic Features	Andere Topographische Objekte	Otros Elementos Topográficos	Autres données topographiques	Outros acidentes topográficos

Lesh-Ligu I · 97

ESPAÑOL Nombre	Página	Lat.°′	Long.°′ W = Oeste

FRANÇAIS Nom	Page	Lat.°′	Long.°′ W = Ouest

PORTUGUÊS Nome	Página	Lat.°′	Long.°′ W = Oeste

Les Haudères 58 46.05 N 7.31 E
Les Hautes-Rivières 56 49.53 N 4.50 E
Les Herbiers 32 46.52 N 1.01 W
Les Houches 62 45.53 N 6.48 E
Lesignano de'Bagni 64 44.39 N 10.18 E
Lésigny 261 48.45 N 2.37 E
Lesima, Monte ∧ 62 44.41 N 9.15 E
Lesina 68 41.52 N 15.21 E
Lesina, Lago di ⊂ 68 41.53 N 15.26 E
Les Islettes 56 49.06 N 5.00 E
Lesjaskog 26 62.15 N 8.22 E
Lesjöfors 40 59.59 N 14.11 E
Lesken 84 43.16 N 43.48 E
Les'ki 78 49.19 N 32.13 E
Lesko 30 49.29 N 22.21 E
Leskovac 38 42.59 N 21.57 E
Leskov Island I 18 56.40 S 28.10 W
Les Laumes 58 47.32 N 4.27 E
Les Lecques 62 43.11 N 5.40 E
Leslie, S. Afr. 158 26.27 S 28.55 E
Leslie, Scot., U.K. 46 56.12 N 3.13 W
Leslie, Ar., U.S. 194 35.49 N 92.33 W
Leslie, Ga., U.S. 192 31.57 N 84.05 W
Leslie, Mi., U.S. 216 42.27 N 84.25 W
Leslie, W.V., U.S. 188 38.02 N 80.43 W
Les Lilas 261 48.53 N 2.25 E
Les Loges 261 48.34 N 2.03 E
Les Loges-en-Josas 261 48.46 N 2.09 E
Lesmahagow 46 55.39 N 3.55 W
Les Marécottes 58 46.07 N 7.00 E
Les Mées 62 44.02 N 5.59 E
Les Mesnuls 50 48.45 N 1.50 E
Lesmo 266b 45.39 N 9.18 E
Les Molières 261 48.40 N 2.04 E
Les Monges ∧ 62 44.16 N 6.12 E
Lesmont 50 48.26 N 4.25 E
Les Mosses 58 46.24 N 7.07 E
Lesmurdie Falls National Park ♦ 168a 32.01 S 116.04 E
Les Mureaux 261 49.00 N 1.55 E
Leśna 30 51.02 N 15.16 E
Lesna ≃ 76 52.10 N 23.33 E
Lesnaja 76 52.59 N 25.46 E
Lesneven 32 48.34 N 4.19 W
Les Neyrolles 58 46.08 N 5.38 E
Lešnica 38 44.39 N 19.19 E
Lesnoj, Ross. 24 59.48 N 52.08 E
Lesnoj, Ross. 80 54.11 N 40.27 E
Lesnoj, Ross. 86 56.57 N 67.15 E
Lesnoj ✧[8] 265a 60.00 N 30.19 E
Lesnoje 76 58.17 N 35.32 E
Lesnoje Konobejevo 80 54.02 N 41.55 E
Lesnoje Mat'unino 80 53.27 N 47.26 E
Lesnoj Gorodok 265b 55.39 N 37.13 E
Lesnoj park ♦ 265a 59.59 N 30.21 E
Lesný ∧ 60 50.02 N 12.37 E
Lesnyje Pol'any, Ross. 24 58.58 N 52.26 E
Lesnyje Pol'any, Ross. 265b 55.57 N 37.53 E
Lesogorsk, Ross. 80 55.06 N 43.56 E
Lesogorsk, Ross. 88 56.03 N 99.33 E
Lesogorsk, Ross. 89 49.27 N 142.08 E
Lesogorskij 24 61.02 N 28.53 E
Lesong, Gunong ∧ 114 2.44 N 103.17 E
Lesopil'noje 89 46.44 N 134.20 E
Lesosibirsk 86 58.16 N 92.29 E
Lesotho □[1], Afr. 138 29.30 S 28.30 E
Lesotho □[1], Afr. 158 29.30 S 28.30 E
Lesovščina 78 50.47 N 28.35 E
Lesozavodsk 89 45.28 N 133.27 E
Lesozavodskij 24 66.44 N 32.49 E
Lesparre-Médoc 32 45.18 N 0.56 W
Les Pavillons-sous-Bois 261 48.55 N 2.30 E
Les Pieux 32 49.31 N 1.48 W
Les Planches-en-Montagne 58 46.40 N 6.01 E
Les Ponts-de-Martel 58 46.54 N 6.41 E
Les Posets ∧ 34 42.39 N 0.25 E
Les Praz-de-Chamonix 58 45.56 N 6.52 E
Lesquin 50 50.35 N 3.07 E
Les Riceys 50 47.59 N 4.22 E
Les Roches-l'Evêque 50 47.47 N 0.53 E
Les Rousses 58 46.29 N 6.04 E
Les Ruelles 261 48.40 N 1.37 E
Les Sables-d'Olonne 32 46.30 N 1.47 W
Lessach 64 47.11 N 13.49 E
Les Saintes II 241o 15.52 N 61.37 W
Les Salles-sur-Verdon 62 43.46 N 6.12 E
Lessay 32 49.13 N 1.32 W
Les Scaffarels 62 43.57 N 6.41 E
Lesse ≃ 56 50.14 N 4.54 E
Lessebo 26 56.45 N 15.16 E
Lessen → Lessines 50 50.43 N 3.50 E
Lesser Antilles II 238 15.00 N 61.00 W
Lesser Khingan Range → Xiao Hinggan Ling ⋏ 89 48.45 N 127.00 E
Lesser Slave ≃ 182 55.10 N 114.03 W
Lesser Slave Lake ⊜ 182 55.25 N 115.30 W
Lesser Sunda Islands → Tenggara, Nusa II 108 9.00 S 120.00 E
Lessines (Lessen) 50 50.43 N 3.50 E
Lessini, Monti ⋏ 64 45.41 N 11.13 E
L'Estaque 62 43.22 N 5.20 E
Leste ≃ 250 6.20 S 57.46 W
Lester, Pa., U.S. 285 39.52 N 75.17 W
Lester, Wa., U.S. 224 47.12 N 121.29 W
Lester B. Pearson International Airport ⊠ 212 43.41 N 79.38 W
Les Tessiers 62 44.24 N 4.16 E
Les Thilliers-en-Vexin 50 49.14 N 1.36 E
Lestijärvi 26 63.32 N 24.39 E
Lestijoki ≃ 26 64.04 N 23.38 E
Lestkov 60 49.54 N 12.52 E
Lestock 184 51.18 N 104.00 W
L'Estréchure 62 44.06 N 3.47 E
Les Trois-Îlets 240e 14.32 N 61.02 W
Les Trois Lacs ⊜ 206 45.48 N 71.54 W
Le Sueur 190 44.30 N 93.52 W
Le Sueur ≃ 190 44.07 N 94.03 W
Lesueur, Mount ∧[2] 162 30.10 S 115.11 E
Lešukonskoje 24 64.54 N 45.40 E
Les Ulis 261 48.41 N 2.11 E
Lesung, Tanjung › 115a 6.28 S 105.40 E
Lesunovo 80 55.40 N 43.07 E
Les Vans 62 44.24 N 4.08 E
Les Verrières 58 46.54 N 6.30 E
Lésvos I 38 39.10 N 26.20 E
Leszno 30 51.51 N 16.35 E
Leszno □[4] 30 51.45 N 16.45 E
Letälven ≃ 40 59.05 N 14.20 E
L'Étang-La-Ville 261 48.52 N 2.05 E
Letcher 198 43.53 N 98.08 W
Letchmore Heath 260 51.40 N 0.20 W
Letchworth 42 51.58 N 0.14 W
Letchworth State Park ♦ 210 42.42 N 77.56 W
Letea, Ostrovul I 38 45.20 N 29.20 E
Le Teil 62 44.33 N 4.41 E
Le Temple 261 49.00 N 1.58 E
Letenye 30 46.26 N 16.43 E
Le Tertre-Saint-Denis 261 48.56 N 1.36 E
Lethbridge, Austl. 274a 33.44 S 150.48 E
Lethbridge, Ab., Can. 182 49.42 N 112.50 W
Lethbridge, Nf., Can. 186 48.21 N 53.52 W
Le Theil-sur-Huisne 50 48.16 N 0.42 E
Lethem 246 3.23 N 59.48 W
Le Thillay 261 49.00 N 2.28 E
Le Thillot 58 47.53 N 6.46 E
Le Tholy 58 48.05 N 6.45 E
Le Thor 62 43.56 N 5.00 E
Le Thoronet 62 43.27 N 6.18 E
Leti, Kepulauan II 164 8.13 S 127.50 E
Leti, Pulau I 112 8.12 S 127.41 E
Letičev 78 49.23 N 27.37 E
Leticia 246 4.09 S 69.57 W
Leting 98 39.27 N 118.53 E
Letino 68 41.26 N 14.17 E
Letjiesbos 158 32.34 S 22.16 E
Letka 24 59.36 N 49.22 E
Letlhakane 156 21.27 S 25.30 E
Letlhakeng 156 24.08 S 25.02 E
Letmathe 56 51.22 N 7.37 E
Letn'aja Zolotica 24 64.57 N 36.50 E
Letnerečenskij 24 64.17 N 34.23 E
Le Touquet-Paris-Plage 50 50.31 N 1.35 E
Le Touvet 62 45.21 N 5.57 E
Letovo 265b 55.34 N 37.24 E
Letpadan 110 17.47 N 95.45 E
Le Trait 50 49.28 N 0.49 E
Le Trayas 62 43.28 N 6.55 E
Le Tremblay-sur-Mauldre 261 48.47 N 1.53 E
Le Tréport 50 50.04 N 1.22 E
Letschin 54 52.39 N 14.21 E
Letsôk-aw Kyun I 110 11.37 N 98.15 E
Letter 52 52.24 N 9.38 E
Letterfrack 48 53.33 N 10.00 W
Letterkenny 48 54.57 N 7.44 W
Lettermullan 48 53.13 N 9.42 W
Letterston 42 51.56 N 5.00 W
Lettonie → Latvia □[1] 72 57.00 N 25.00 E
Letts 218 39.14 N 85.35 W
Letung 112 2.58 N 105.42 E
Letzlingen 54 52.26 N 11.29 E
Leu 38 44.11 N 24.00 E
Léua 152 11.34 S 20.32 E
Leubnitz 54 50.43 N 12.21 E
Leubsdorf 54 50.48 N 13.08 E
Leuca 68 39.48 N 18.21 E
Leucadia 228 33.04 N 117.18 W
Leucate, Étang de ⊂ 32 42.51 N 3.00 E
Leuchars 46 56.23 N 2.53 W
Leuchtenberg 60 49.36 N 12.15 E
Leudeville 261 48.34 N 2.20 E
Leuenberger Forst ✧[3] 264a 52.40 N 13.53 E
Leuglay 58 47.49 N 4.48 E
Leuk 58 46.19 N 7.38 E
Leukerbad 58 46.23 N 7.38 E
Leulumoega 175a 13.49 S 171.55 W
Leumeah 274a 34.03 S 150.50 E
Leuna 54 51.19 N 12.01 E
Leupoldsgrün 54 50.17 N 11.47 E
Leura 170 33.43 S 150.20 E
Leura, Mount ∧[2] 169 38.15 S 143.09 E
Leuser, Gunung ∧ 114 3.45 N 97.11 E
Leušinskij Tuman, ozero ⊜ 86 59.42 N 65.35 E
Leutenberg 54 50.34 N 11.28 E
Leutersdorf 54 50.57 N 14.40 E
Leutershausen 56 49.18 N 10.24 E
Leutesdorf 56 50.27 N 7.23 E
Leutkirch 58 47.49 N 10.01 E
Leuven (Louvain) 56 50.53 N 4.42 E
Leuville-sur-Orge 261 48.37 N 2.16 E
Leuwiliang 115a 6.34 S 106.37 E
Leuze, Bel. 50 50.36 N 3.36 E
Leuze, Bel. 56 50.34 N 4.54 E
Levack 190 46.38 N 81.23 W
Levádhia 38 38.25 N 22.54 E
Levaja Mama ≃ 88 57.10 N 111.54 E
Le Val-d'Ajol 58 47.55 N 6.29 E
Le Val-d'Albian 261 48.45 N 2.11 E
Levallois-Perret 261 48.54 N 2.18 E
Le Val-Saint-Germain 261 48.34 N 2.04 E
Levan 200 39.33 N 111.51 W
Levanger 26 63.45 N 11.18 E
Levanna, Monte ∧ 62 45.24 N 7.12 E
Levant, Île du I 62 43.03 N 6.28 E
Levante, Riviera di •[2] 62 44.15 N 9.30 E
Levanto 62 44.10 N 9.38 E
Levanzo 70 37.59 N 12.20 E
Levanzo, Isola di I 70 38.00 N 12.20 E
Levaši 84 42.27 N 47.20 E
Le Vauclin 240e 14.33 N 60.51 W
Levdym 86 60.29 N 66.19 E
Leveaux Mountain ∧[2] 190 47.37 N 90.47 W
Levél 61 47.54 N 17.12 E
Level, Isla I 254 44.29 S 74.23 W
Level Green 279b 40.24 N 79.43 W
Levelland 196 33.35 N 102.22 W
Levelock 180 59.07 N 156.52 W
Level Park 216 42.22 N 85.18 W
Leven, Eng., U.K. 44 53.53 N 0.19 W
Leven, Scot., U.K. 46 56.12 N 3.00 W
Leven ≃, Eng., U.K. 44 54.14 N 3.01 W
Leven ≃, Eng., U.K. 44 54.31 N 1.21 W
Leven, Loch ⊜, Scot., U.K. 46 56.12 N 3.22 W
Leven, Loch ⊜, Scot., U.K. 46 56.41 N 5.07 W
Leven Point › 158 27.55 S 32.35 E
Levens 62 43.52 N 7.13 E
Levenshulme ✧[8] 262 53.27 N 2.10 W
Levent 130 38.27 N 37.52 E
Leventina, Valle V 58 46.25 N 9.52 E
Leveque, Cape › 162 16.24 S 122.56 E
Leverano 68 40.17 N 18.00 E
Leverburgh 46 57.45 N 7.00 W
Leveretts Chapel 222 32.19 N 94.55 W
Levering 190 45.38 N 84.47 W
Leverkusen 56 51.03 N 6.59 E
Levern 52 52.22 N 8.26 E
Lever Park ♦ 262 53.37 N 2.34 W
Le Vésinet 261 48.54 N 2.08 E
Le Vésuve → Vesuvio ∧[1] 68 40.49 N 14.26 E
Leviathan Peak ∧ 226 38.41 N 119.37 W
Levice 30 48.13 N 18.37 E
Levicha 86 57.36 N 59.55 E
Levick, Mount ∧ 9 74.08 S 163.12 E
Levico 64 46.01 N 11.18 E
Levie 36 41.42 N 9.07 E
Levier 58 46.57 N 6.08 E
Le Vigan 32 43.59 N 3.35 E
Levin 172 40.37 S 175.17 E
Levino 76 60.29 N 37.30 E
Lévis 206 46.48 N 71.11 W
Lévis □[6] 206 46.40 N 71.15 W
Levisa Fork ≃ 192 38.06 N 82.36 W
Lévis-Saint Nom 261 48.43 N 1.58 E
Levítha I 38 37.00 N 26.28 E
Levittown, P.R. 240m 18.27 N 66.14 W
Levittown, N.Y., U.S. 210 40.43 N 73.30 W
Levittown, Pa., U.S. 208 40.09 N 74.49 W
Levittown Discount World ✧[9] 285 40.09 N 74.49 W
Levittown → Willingboro 208 40.03 N 74.53 W
Lévka Óri ∧ 38 35.18 N 24.01 E
Levkás 38 38.50 N 20.41 E
Levkás I 38 38.39 N 20.27 E
Levkímmi 38 39.25 N 20.04 E
Levoča 30 49.02 N 20.36 E
Levokumskoje 84 44.48 N 44.39 E
Levroux 32 46.59 N 1.37 E
Levski 38 43.22 N 25.08 E
Lev Tolstoj 76 53.13 N 39.27 E
Levuka 175g 17.41 S 178.50 E
Lėvuo ≃ 76 56.04 N 24.23 E
Levyj Tuzlov ≃ 83 47.35 N 39.23 E
Lewapaku 115b 9.43 S 119.55 E
Lewbeach 210 42.00 N 74.47 W
Lewe 110 19.38 N 96.07 E
Lewedorp 52 51.30 N 3.45 E
Lewellen 198 41.19 N 102.08 W
Lewer ≃ 156 25.30 S 17.45 E
Lewes, Eng., U.K. 42 50.52 N 0.01 E
Lewes, De., U.S. 208 38.46 N 75.08 W
Lewin Brzeski 30 50.46 N 17.37 E
Lewis, Ia., U.S. 198 41.18 N 95.04 W
Lewis, Ks., U.S. 198 37.56 N 99.15 W
Lewis □[6], Ky., U.S. 218 38.32 N 83.21 W
Lewis □[6], Mo., U.S. 219 40.08 N 91.45 W
Lewis □[6], N.Y., U.S. 212 43.47 N 75.29 W
Lewis □[6], Wa., U.S. 224 46.35 N 122.22 W
Lewis ≃ 224 45.51 N 122.48 W
Lewis, Butt of › 46 58.31 N 6.16 W
Lewis, East Fork ≃ 224 45.52 N 122.43 W
Lewis, Isle of I 46 58.10 N 6.40 W
Lewis, Mount ∧ 204 40.24 N 116.51 W
Lewis and Clark ≃ 224 46.10 N 123.52 W
Lewis and Clark Cavern State Park ♦ 202 45.49 N 111.13 W
Lewis and Clark Lake ⊜[1] 198 42.50 N 97.45 W
Lewis and Clark Range ⋏ 202 47.30 N 113.00 W
Lewisberry 208 40.08 N 76.52 W
Lewisburg, Ky., U.S. 194 36.59 N 86.56 W
Lewisburg, Oh., U.S. 218 39.50 N 84.32 W
Lewisburg, Pa., U.S. 210 40.57 N 76.53 W
Lewisburg, Tn., U.S. 194 35.26 N 86.47 W
Lewisburg, W.V., U.S. 188 37.48 N 80.26 W
Lewis Center 214 40.12 N 83.01 W
Lewis Creek ≃, Ca., U.S. 226 35.17 N 120.58 W
Lewis Creek ≃, In., U.S. 218 39.22 N 85.51 W
Lewis Creek Reservoir ⊜[1] 222 30.26 N 95.32 W
Lewisdale 284c 38.58 N 76.58 W
Lewisetta 208 38.01 N 76.28 W
Lewis Gut ⊂ 276 41.09 N 73.09 W
Lewisham 273d 26.07 S 27.49 E
Lewisham ✧[8] 42 51.27 N 0.01 E
Lewisham Location 273d 26.10 S 27.47 E
Lewis-Lockport Airport ⊠ 278 41.36 N 88.05 W
Lewis Pass)(172 42.23 S 172.24 E
Lewisport 194 37.56 N 86.54 W
Lewisporte 186 49.15 N 55.03 W
Lewis Range ⋏, Austl. 162 20.20 S 128.40 E
Lewis Range ⋏, Mt., U.S. 202 48.35 N 113.40 W
Lewis Run 214 41.52 N 78.39 W
Lewis Run ≃ 279b 40.17 N 79.55 W
Lewis Smith Lake ⊜[1] 194 34.05 N 87.07 W
Lewiston, Ca., U.S. 204 40.43 N 122.48 W
Lewiston, Id., U.S. 202 46.25 N 117.01 W
Lewiston, Me., U.S. 188 44.06 N 70.12 W
Lewiston, Mi., U.S. 190 44.53 N 84.18 W
Lewiston, Mn., U.S. 190 43.59 N 91.52 W
Lewiston, N.Y., U.S. 210 43.10 N 79.02 W
Lewiston, Ut,. U.S. 200 41.58 N 111.51 W
Lewiston Orchards 202 46.23 N 116.59 W
Lewistown, Il., U.S. 194 40.23 N 90.09 W
Lewistown, Md., U.S. 208 39.32 N 77.24 W
Lewistown, Mo., U.S. 219 40.05 N 91.48 W
Lewistown, Mt., U.S. 202 47.03 N 109.25 W
Lewistown, Oh., U.S. 216 40.25 N 83.53 W
Lewistown, Pa., U.S. 208 40.35 N 77.34 W
Lewisville, N.B., Can. 186 46.06 N 64.46 W
Lewisville, Ar., U.S. 194 33.21 N 93.34 W
Lewisville, In., U.S. 218 39.48 N 85.21 W
Lewisville, Pa., U.S. 208 39.43 N 75.53 W
Lewisville, Tx., U.S. 222 33.02 N 96.59 W
Lewisville Dam ✧[6] 222 33.05 N 96.55 W
Lewisville Lake ⊜[1] 196 33.08 N 97.00 W
Lewoleba 112 8.23 S 123.24 E
Lewotobi-lakilaki, Ili ∧ 115b 8.32 S 122.46 E
Lewvan 184 50.00 N 104.06 W
Lexa 194 34.35 N 90.44 W
Lexington, Ga., U.S. 192 33.52 N 83.06 W
Lexington, Il., U.S. 216 40.38 N 88.47 W
Lexington, In., U.S. 218 38.39 N 85.37 W
Lexington, Ky., U.S. 218 38.02 N 84.30 W
Lexington, Ma., U.S. 207 42.26 N 71.13 W
Lexington, Mi., U.S. 190 43.16 N 82.31 W
Lexington, Ms., U.S. 194 33.06 N 90.03 W
Lexington, Mo., U.S. 194 39.11 N 93.52 W
Lexington, Ne., U.S. 198 40.46 N 99.44 W
Lexington, N.Y., U.S. 210 42.15 N 74.22 W
Lexington, N.C., U.S. 192 35.49 N 80.15 W
Lexington, Oh., U.S. 214 40.40 N 82.34 W
Lexington, Ok., U.S. 196 35.00 N 97.20 W
Lexington, Or., U.S. 202 45.26 N 119.41 W
Lexington, S.C., U.S. 192 33.58 N 81.14 W
Lexington, Tn., U.S. 194 35.39 N 88.23 W
Lexington, Tx., U.S. 222 30.25 N 97.01 W
Lexington, Va., U.S. 192 37.47 N 79.26 W
Lexington Park 208 38.16 N 76.27 W
Lexington Reservoir ⊜[1] 226 37.12 N 121.59 W
Lexton 169 37.17 S 143.31 E
Leybourne 260 51.18 N 0.25 E
Leyburn 44 54.19 N 1.49 W
Leyden → Leiden 52 52.09 N 4.30 E
Leye 102 24.48 N 106.34 E
Leyland 44 53.42 N 2.42 W
Leyond ≃ 184 51.40 N 96.32 W
Léyou ≃ 152 1.07 S 13.08 E
Leyre ≃ 32 44.39 N 1.01 W
Leysdown-on-Sea 42 51.24 N 0.55 E
Leysin 58 46.21 N 7.01 E
Leyte 116 11.23 N 124.29 E
Leyte □[4] 116 10.50 N 124.55 E
Leyte I 116 10.50 N 124.50 E
Leyte Gulf ⊂ 116 10.50 N 125.25 E
Leyu 106 31.55 N 120.43 E
Lèz ≃ 62 44.13 N 4.43 E
Lèz ≊ 62 43.31 N 3.55 E
Leža 76 58.56 N 40.45 E
Leža ≃ 76 59.15 N 40.10 E
Leżajsk 30 50.16 N 22.24 E
Lezama 246 9.43 N 66.24 W
Lézarde ≃ 240e 14.36 N 61.01 W
Lézat 58 46.30 N 5.56 E
Lèze ≃ 62 43.40 N 5.28 E
Lezhë 38 41.47 N 19.39 E
Lezhi 107 30.17 N 105.02 E
Ležn'ovo 80 56.46 N 40.53 E
Lezzeno 58 45.56 N 9.11 E
L'gov 78 51.43 N 35.17 E
Lhasa 120 29.40 N 91.09 E
Lhasa ≃ 120 29.21 N 90.45 E
L'Hautil 261 49.00 N 2.01 E
Lhazê 120 29.10 N 87.42 E
L'Hillil 34 35.41 N 0.19 E
Lhokkruet 114 4.52 N 95.24 E
Lhoknga 114 5.29 N 95.15 E
Lhokseumawe 114 5.10 N 97.08 E
Lhoksukon 114 5.03 N 97.19 E
L'Hôpital-sous-Rochefort 62 45.46 N 3.56 E
Lhorong 102 30.45 N 96.09 E
L'Hospitalet de Llobregat 34 41.22 N 2.08 E
Lhotse ∧ 124 27.57 N 86.56 E
Lhozhag 120 28.24 N 90.49 E
Lhuis 62 45.45 N 5.32 E
Lhuntsi Dzong 120 27.39 N 91.09 E
Lhünzê 120 28.25 N 92.31 E
Li 110 17.48 N 98.57 E
Li ≃, Thai 110 18.26 N 98.42 E
Li ≃, Zhg. 100 33.11 N 115.07 E
Li ≃, Zhg. 102 29.24 N 112.01 E
Lian ≃, Zhg. 100 24.02 N 113.18 E
Lian ≃, Zhg. 100 25.46 N 115.38 E
Lian ≃, Zhg. 102 24.02 N 113.18 E
Lian ≃, Zhg. 102 27.48 N 112.52 E
Liancheng 100 25.44 N 116.46 E
Liancourt 50 49.20 N 2.28 E
Liane ≃ 50 50.43 N 1.36 E
Liang 164 3.30 S 128.19 E
Lianga 116 8.38 N 126.06 E
Lianga Bay ⊂ 116 8.37 N 126.12 E
Liang'anchang 107 30.30 N 104.56 E
Liangbao 102 34.37 N 110.45 E
Liangbingbao 89 45.48 N 128.19 E
Liangbingtai 89 43.12 N 128.47 E
Liangbuaya 112 0.05 N 116.46 E
Liangchahe 107 29.03 N 106.18 E
Liangcheng 98 35.35 N 119.35 E
Liangcun 100 26.36 N 115.34 E
Liangdang 102 33.56 N 106.12 E
Liangdawa 105 40.39 N 117.37 E
Liangfengwu 107 30.11 N 105.22 E
Lianggezhuang 105 39.21 N 115.22 E
Lianghe, Zhg. 89 45.09 N 128.45 E
Lianghe, Zhg. 102 24.51 N 98.25 E
Liangheguan 102 32.52 N 109.19 E
Lianghekou, Zhg. 102 33.42 N 104.25 E
Lianghekou, Zhg. 102 29.14 N 108.40 E
Lianghekou, Zhg. 102 31.27 N 102.13 E
Lianghekou, Zhg. 107 28.55 N 106.03 E
Liangiu 98 35.12 N 117.47 E
Liangjia 107 29.29 N 105.33 E
Liangjiadian 98 39.10 N 121.54 E
Liangjiafang 98 41.04 N 117.18 E
Liangjianfang 105 40.45 N 117.20 E
Liangjiang 102 23.23 N 108.22 E
Liangjiangkou 98 42.38 N 128.05 E
Liangjiawazi 104 40.40 N 120.42 E
Liangjiazi 104 42.13 N 122.31 E
Liangkou 100 23.43 N 113.43 E
Lianglukou 107 29.18 N 106.15 E
Liangmen 98 35.34 N 114.54 E
Liangmentou 100 28.58 N 121.12 E
Liangmushi 106 30.46 N 119.35 E
Liangpa 102 24.10 N 106.13 E
Liangpeng 106 30.47 N 119.38 E
Liangping 102 30.41 N 107.49 E
Liang Shan ∧ 102 23.45 N 99.45 E
Liangshui ≃ 271a 39.49 N 116.40 E
Liangtian 100 25.37 N 113.00 E
Liangtinghe 100 30.20 N 116.12 E
Liangtoumen 100 29.31 N 120.45 E
Liangtun 98 40.14 N 122.34 E
Liangwangzhuang 105 39.01 N 116.58 E
Liangxiangzhen 105 39.44 N 116.08 E
Liangying 100 23.14 N 116.21 E
Liangyuan 100 32.00 N 117.34 E
Liangzhu 106 30.23 N 120.03 E
Liangzi Hu ⊜ 100 30.16 N 114.34 E
Lianhe 98 42.36 N 125.37 E
Lian Hu ⊜ 106 32.02 N 119.32 E
Lianhua 100 27.07 N 113.57 E
Lianhuachi 105 40.28 N 116.33 E
Lianhuapao 89 45.32 N 129.50 E
Lianhua Shan ⋏ 100 23.40 N 116.00 E
Lianjiang, Zhg. 100 26.12 N 119.31 E
Lianjiang, Zhg. 102 21.38 N 110.15 E
Lianjiechang 107 29.41 N 104.30 E
Liannan (Sanjiang) 102 24.38 N 112.10 E
Lianozovo ✧[8] 265b 55.54 N 37.35 E
Lianping 100 24.22 N 114.31 E
Lianpu 100 26.02 N 118.38 E
Lianshanguan 104 40.58 N 123.46 E
Lianshi 106 30.42 N 120.26 E
Lianshui 100 33.47 N 119.16 E
Liansiji 98 33.58 N 114.24 E
Liantang 106 31.37 N 120.38 E
Lianxian 102 24.48 N 112.25 E
Lianyin 89 53.28 N 123.51 E
Lianyuan (Lantian) 102 27.42 N 111.19 E
Lianyungang, Zhg. 98 34.44 N 119.30 E
Lianyungang (Xinpu), Zhg. 98 34.39 N 119.16 E
Lianyun Shan ∧ 100 28.32 N 113.50 E
Lianzhou → Hepu 102 21.39 N 109.11 E
Liao ≃ 90 40.50 N 121.48 E
Liaobinta 104 42.08 N 123.04 E
Liaocheng 98 36.30 N 115.59 E
Liaodong Bandao (Liaotung Peninsula) ›[1] 98 40.00 N 122.20 E
Liaodong Wan (Gulf of Liaotung) ⊂ 98 40.30 N 121.30 E
Liaohe Kou ⊂[1] 104 40.42 N 122.05 E
Liaojiangshi 100 26.05 N 113.17 E
Liaoning □[4] 90 41.00 N 123.00 E
Liaotung, Gulf of → Liaodong Wan ⊂ 98 40.30 N 121.30 E
Liaotung Peninsula → Liaodong Bandao ›[1] 98 40.00 N 122.20 E
Liaoyang 104 41.17 N 123.11 E
Liaoyangwopu 89 43.00 N 123.28 E
Liaoyuan 89 42.54 N 125.07 E
Liaozhong 104 41.31 N 122.44 E
Liapádhes 38 39.40 N 19.44 E
Liāquatpur 123 28.56 N 70.57 E
Liard ≃ 176 61.52 N 121.18 W
Liāri 120 25.41 N 66.29 E
Liart 50 49.46 N 4.20 E
Liat, Pulau I 112 2.53 S 107.05 E
Liathach ∧ 46 57.35 N 5.29 W
Lib I 14 8.19 N 167.25 E
Libagon 116 10.18 N 125.03 E
Libanga 152 0.19 N 18.41 E
Liban → Lebanon □[1] 128 34.00 N 36.00 E
Líbano 246 4.55 N 75.04 W
Libano → Lebanon □[1] 128 34.00 N 36.00 E
Libanon → Lebanon □[1] 128 34.00 N 36.00 E
Libau → Liepāja 76 56.31 N 21.01 E
Libby 202 48.23 N 115.33 W
Libby Dam ✧[6] 202 48.24 N 115.20 W
Libčeves 54 50.26 N 13.50 E
Libčice nad Vltavou 54 50.10 N 14.20 E
Liběchov 54 50.20 N 14.28 E
Libenge 152 3.39 N 18.38 E
Liberal, Ks., U.S. 198 37.02 N 100.55 W
Liberal, Mo., U.S. 194 37.33 N 94.31 W
Liberdade 256 22.01 S 44.19 W
Liberdade ✧[8] 287b 23.35 S 46.37 W
Liberdade ≃, Bra. 248 7.10 S 71.51 W
Liberdade ≃, Bra. 250 9.40 S 52.17 W
Liberec 30 50.46 N 15.03 E
Liberia 236 10.38 N 85.27 W
Liberia □[1], Afr. 134 6.30 N 9.30 W
Liberia □[1], Afr. 150 6.30 N 9.30 W
Liberta 240c 17.02 N 61.47 W
Libertad, Arg. 258 34.42 S 58.41 W
Libertad, Ur. 258 34.38 S 56.39 W
Libertad, Ven. 246 8.20 N 69.37 W
Libertad, Ven. 246 9.23 N 68.44 W
Libertador □[5] 286c 10.27 N 66.57 W
Libertador General Bernardo O'Higgins □[4] 252 34.30 S 71.00 W
Libertador General San Martín 252 23.48 S 64.48 W
Liberty, Il., U.S. 219 39.53 N 91.06 W
Liberty, In., U.S. 218 39.38 N 84.55 W
Liberty, Ky., U.S. 194 37.19 N 84.56 W
Liberty, Ms., U.S. 194 31.09 N 90.48 W
Liberty, Mo., U.S. 194 39.14 N 94.25 W
Liberty, Ne., U.S. 198 40.05 N 96.28 W
Liberty, N.Y., U.S. 210 41.48 N 74.44 W
Liberty, N.C., U.S. 192 35.51 N 79.34 W
Liberty, Pa., U.S. 210 41.34 N 77.06 W
Liberty, Pa., U.S. 279b 40.20 N 79.51 W
Liberty, S.C., U.S. 192 34.47 N 82.41 W
Liberty, Tx., U.S. 222 30.03 N 94.47 W
Liberty □[6] 222 30.12 N 94.50 W
Liberty Acres 280 34.04 N 118.12 W
Liberty Bell Race Track ♦ 285 40.05 N 74.58 W
Liberty Center, In., U.S. 216 40.41 N 85.16 W
Liberty Center, Oh., U.S. 216 41.26 N 84.00 W
Liberty City 222 32.27 N 94.57 W
Liberty Corner 276 40.39 N 74.34 W
Liberty Ditch ≊ 226 36.31 N 120.02 W
Liberty Farms 226 38.19 N 121.42 W
Liberty Hill 196 30.40 N 97.55 W
Liberty Island I 276 40.41 N 74.03 W
Liberty Lake ⊜[1] 208 39.25 N 76.53 W
Liberty Manor 284b 39.21 N 76.47 W
Liberty Mills 216 41.02 N 85.44 W
Liberty Park 216 41.26 N 87.22 W
Libertytown 208 39.29 N 77.14 W
Liberty Tree Mall ✧[9] 283 42.33 N 70.57 W
Liberty Tunnel ✧[5] 279b 40.26 N 80.01 W
Libertyville 216 42.16 N 87.57 W
Líbeznice 54 50.10 N 14.30 E
Libia → Libya □[1] 146 27.00 N 17.00 E
Libibi 152 14.42 S 17.44 E
Libishan 106 30.45 N 119.20 E
Lībīyah, Aṣ-Ṣaḥrā' al- (Libyan Desert) ✧[2] 136 24.00 N 25.00 E
Lībiyā → Libya □[1] 146 27.00 N 17.00 E
Liblín 60 49.55 N 13.32 E
Libni, Jabal ∧[2] 132 30.44 N 33.50 E
Libo 102 25.28 N 107.53 E
Libobo, Tanjung › 164 0.54 S 128.28 E
Liboc ≃ 54 50.10 N 13.31 E
Libochovice 54 50.22 N 14.03 E
Libode 158 31.33 S 29.02 E
Liboi 154 0.24 N 40.57 E
Liboko 152 2.43 N 21.28 E
Libomyšl 60 49.52 N 14.00 E
Libona 116 8.20 N 124.44 E
Liboumba ≃ 152 0.38 N 12.54 E
Libourne 32 44.55 N 0.14 W
Libramont 56 49.55 N 5.23 E
Library 214 40.18 N 80.02 W
Librazhd 38 41.11 N 20.19 E
Libres 234 19.28 N 97.41 W
Libreville 152 0.23 N 9.27 E
Librizzi 70 38.06 N 14.57 E
Libro Point › 116 11.26 N 119.29 E
Libu 102 23.41 N 111.30 E
Libucan Island I 116 11.54 N 124.39 E
Libuganon ≃ 116 7.27 N 125.47 E
Libunga 154 1.49 N 26.35 E
Liburung 112 3.55 S 120.09 E
Libušín 54 50.09 N 14.04 E
Libya (Lībiyā) □[1], Afr. 136 27.00 N 17.00 E
Libya (Lībiyā) □[1], Afr. 146 27.00 N 17.00 E
Libyan Desert → Lībīyah, Aṣ-Ṣaḥrā' al- ✧[2] 136 24.00 N 25.00 E
Libyan Plateau → Aḍ-Diffah ⋏[1] 140 30.30 N 25.30 E
Libye → Libya □[1] 146 27.00 N 17.00 E
Libyen → Libya □[1] 146 27.00 N 17.00 E
Libysche Wüste → Lībīyah, Aṣ-Ṣaḥrā' al- ✧[2] 136 24.00 N 25.00 E
Licancábur, Volcán ∧[1] 248 22.50 S 67.50 W
Licantén 252 34.59 S 72.00 W
Licata 70 37.06 N 13.56 E
Licciana Nardi 64 44.16 N 10.02 E
Lice 130 38.28 N 40.39 E
Lich 56 50.33 N 8.50 E
Lichačova, mys › 89 42.44 N 132.51 E
Lichaja ≃ 83 48.08 N 40.15 E
Lichang 107 28.53 N 104.26 E
Licheng 102 36.30 N 113.21 E
Lichères-Près-Aigremont 50 47.43 N 3.51 E
Lichfield 42 52.42 N 1.48 W
Lichinga 154 13.18 S 35.14 E
Lichitiseni 38 46.23 N 27.17 E
Lichoborka ≃ 265b 55.50 N 37.38 E
Lichoslavl' 76 57.07 N 35.28 E
Lichovka 78 48.41 N 33.55 E
Lichovskoj 83 48.07 N 40.12 E
Lichtaart 56 51.14 N 4.54 E
Lichte 54 50.31 N 11.10 E
Lichtenau 56 48.43 N 8.01 E
Lichtenberg, Dtsch. 54 50.23 N 11.40 E
Lichtenberg, Fr. 56 48.55 N 7.29 E
Lichtenberg ✧[8] 264a 52.31 N 13.29 E
Lichtenburg 158 26.08 S 26.08 E
Lichtendorf 263 51.28 N 7.37 E
Lichtenfels 56 50.09 N 11.04 E
Lichtenplatz ✧[8] 263 51.15 N 7.12 E
Lichtenrade ✧[8] 264a 52.23 N 13.25 E
Lichtensee 54 51.23 N 13.22 E
Lichtensteig 58 47.19 N 9.05 E
Lichtenstein 54 50.45 N 12.37 E
Lichtenstein, Schloss ʊ 58 48.24 N 9.15 E
Lichtentanne 54 50.42 N 12.25 E
Lichtenvoorde 52 51.59 N 6.34 E
Lichterfelde ✧[8] 264a 52.26 N 13.19 E
Lichtervelde 50 51.02 N 3.09 E
Lichuan, Zhg. 100 27.18 N 116.53 E
Lichuan, Zhg. 102 30.18 N 108.51 E
Lick Creek ≃, Il., U.S. 219 39.42 N 89.41 W
Lick Creek ≃, In., U.S. 218 38.33 N 86.31 W
Lick Creek ≃, Mo., U.S. 219 39.31 N 91.39 W
Lick Creek ≃, Oh., U.S. 216 41.21 N 84.25 W
Lick Creek ≃, Tn., U.S. 192 36.11 N 83.10 W
Lickershamn 26 57.50 N 18.31 E
Licking 194 37.29 N 91.51 W
Licking □[6] 214 40.10 N 82.30 W
Licking ≃, Ky., U.S. 188 39.06 N 84.30 W
Licking ≃, Oh., U.S. 214 40.03 N 82.20 W
Licking, North Fork ≃, Ky., U.S. 218 38.35 N 84.13 W
Licking, North Fork ≃, Oh., U.S. 214 40.03 N 82.23 W
Licking, South Fork ≃ 218 38.41 N 84.20 W
Lickingville 214 41.23 N 79.22 W
Lick Observatory ʊ[3] 226 37.22 N 121.37 W
Ličko Polje ≃ 36 44.35 N 15.25 E
Lick Run ≃, Pa., U.S. 210 41.12 N 77.32 W
Lick Run ≃, Pa., U.S. 279b 40.17 N 79.57 W
Licodia Eubea 70 37.09 N 14.42 E
Licosa, Punta › 68 40.15 N 14.54 E
Licun 98 38.32 N 117.08 E
Licungo ≃ 154 17.40 S 37.15 E
Lid' 76 59.39 N 35.05 E
Lida 76 53.53 N 25.18 E
Lidan ≃ 26 58.31 N 13.09 E
Lidao 98 37.15 N 122.32 E
Lidarentuncun 104 41.32 N 123.12 E
Lidcombe 274a 33.52 S 151.03 E
Liddel Water ≃ 44 55.04 N 2.57 W
Liddesdale V 44 55.12 N 2.46 W
Liddon Gulf ⊂ 176 75.03 N 113.00 W
Liden 26 62.42 N 16.48 E
Lidesi 100 33.33 N 115.53 E
Lidgerwood 198 46.04 N 97.09 W
Lidgetton 158 29.25 S 30.05 E
Lidian 107 28.57 N 103.44 E
Lídice, Bra. 256 22.51 S 44.12 W
Lídice, Pan. 236 8.45 N 79.54 W
Lidice ⊥ 54 50.03 N 14.08 E
Lidingö 40 59.22 N 18.08 E
Lidköping 26 58.30 N 13.10 E
Lido 64 45.25 N 12.22 E
Lido, Litorale di •[2] 64 45.23 N 12.21 E
Lido, Porto di ⊂ 64 45.26 N 12.25 E
Lido Beach 276 40.35 N 73.38 W
Lido di Camaiore 64 43.54 N 10.13 E
Lido di Castel Fusano ✧[8] 66 41.43 N 12.20 E
Lido di Iesolo 64 45.30 N 12.39 E
Lido di Metaponto 68 40.22 N 16.50 E
Lido di Ostia ✧[8] 66 41.44 N 12.14 E
Lido di Pomposa 66 44.45 N 12.14 E
Lido di Siponto 68 41.37 N 15.55 E
Lido Key I 220 27.19 N 82.35 W
Lidsjön ⊜ 40 58.55 N 16.51 E
Lidu 107 30.35 N 106.04 E
Lidzbark 30 53.17 N 19.49 E
Lidzbark Warmiński 30 54.09 N 20.35 E
Liebenau, Dtsch. 52 52.36 N 9.05 E
Liebenau, Öst. 61 48.32 N 14.49 E
Liebenbergsvlei ≃ 158 27.20 S 28.31 E
Liebenburg 52 52.01 N 10.26 E
Liebenwalde 54 52.52 N 13.23 E
Lieberhausen 56 51.03 N 7.40 E
Lieberose 54 51.59 N 14.17 E
Liebertwolkwitz 54 51.17 N 12.28 E
Liebig, Mount ∧ 162 23.18 S 131.22 E
Liebstadt 54 50.52 N 13.51 E
Liechtenstein □[1], Europe 22 47.09 N 9.35 E
Liechtenstein □[1], Europe 58 47.09 N 9.35 E
Liechtensteinklamm V 64 47.18 N 13.12 E
Liedberg 263 51.10 N 6.32 E
Liedekerke 50 50.52 N 4.05 E
Liège (Luik) 56 50.38 N 5.34 E
Liège □[4] 56 50.30 N 5.30 E
Liège, Aéroport ⊠ 56 50.39 N 5.30 E
Liegnitz → Legnica 30 51.13 N 16.09 E
Lieja → Liège 56 50.38 N 5.34 E
Lieksa 26 63.19 N 30.01 E
Lielais Liepu kalns ∧[2] 76 56.25 N 27.50 E
Lielupe ≃ 76 57.01 N 23.56 E
Lielvārde 76 56.43 N 24.51 E
Liemienzhen 107 30.29 N 106.05 E
Lienart 154 3.04 N 25.31 E
Lienchou → Hepu 102 21.39 N 109.11 E
Lienen 52 52.09 N 7.58 E
Lienz 64 46.50 N 12.47 E
Liepāja 76 56.31 N 21.01 E
Liepājas ezers ⊜ 76 56.27 N 21.03 E
Liepe 54 53.58 N 13.56 E
Liepna 76 57.25 N 27.25 E
Liepnitzsee ⊜ 264a 52.45 N 13.30 E
Lièpvre 58 48.16 N 7.17 E
Lier (Lierre) 50 51.08 N 4.34 E
Lierenfeld ✧[8] 263 51.13 N 6.51 E
Lierna 58 45.57 N 9.18 E
Liernais 50 47.12 N 4.17 E
Lierneux 56 50.18 N 5.48 E
Liershizhai 104 41.49 N 123.43 E
Liesborn 52 51.43 N 8.15 E
Lieser ≃, Dtsch. 56 49.55 N 7.01 E
Lieser ≃, Öst. 64 46.47 N 13.39 E
Lieshout 52 51.32 N 5.35 E
Liesing ✧[8] 264b 48.08 N 16.17 E
Liesing ≃ 264b 48.08 N 16.28 E
Liesingbach ≃ 61 47.20 N 15.02 E
Liesjärven Kansallispuisto ♦ 26 60.40 N 23.54 E
Lieskau 54 51.37 N 13.48 E
Liesse 50 49.37 N 3.48 E
Liessies 50 50.07 N 4.05 E
Liestal 58 47.29 N 7.44 E
Liești 38 45.38 N 27.32 E
Lietuva → Lithuania □[1] 72 56.00 N 24.00 E
Lietzow 54 54.29 N 13.30 E
Lieurey 50 49.14 N 0.29 E
Lieusaint 261 48.38 N 2.33 E
Lieutel ≃ 261 48.49 N 1.52 E
Lieutenant Robert J. Palenscar Memorial Airport ⊠ 285 39.51 N 75.03 W
Liévin 50 50.25 N 2.46 E
Lièvre, Rivière du ≃ 176 45.31 N 75.26 W
Lièvres, Île aux I 186 47.51 N 69.44 W
Liezen 61 47.35 N 14.15 E
Lifanga 152 0.19 N 21.57 E
Liffey ≃ 48 53.21 N 6.16 W
Liffol-le-Grand 58 48.19 N 5.35 E
Lifford 48 54.50 N 7.29 W
Liffré 32 48.13 N 1.30 W
Lifjell ∧ 26 59.30 N 8.52 E
Lifoku 152 0.04 S 21.18 E
Lifou I 175f 20.53 S 167.13 E
Lifoula 273b 4.06 S 15.25 E
Lifton 42 50.39 N 4.17 W
Liftwood 285 39.47 N 75.31 W
Lifune ≃ 152 8.21 S 13.22 E
Ligačovo 265b 55.56 N 37.15 E
Ligang 100 30.04 N 121.52 E
Ligao, Pil. 116 13.14 N 123.32 E
Ligao, Pil. 116 6.17 N 124.09 E
Ligasa 152 0.42 N 23.45 E
Līgatne 76 57.14 N 25.02 E
Ligezhuang, Zhg. 105 39.49 N 115.56 E
Ligezhuang, Zhg. 105 39.42 N 118.12 E
Light ≃ 168b 34.35 S 138.22 E
Lightfoot 208 37.20 N 76.45 W
Lighthouse Beach •[2] 273a 6.24 N 3.22 E
Lighthouse Point 220 26.16 N 80.05 W
Lighthouse Point ›, On., Can. 214 41.50 N 82.38 W
Lighthouse Point ›, Fl., U.S. 192 29.54 N 84.21 W
Lighthouse Point ›, Mi., U.S. 190 45.13 N 85.32 W
Lighthouse Reef ✢[2] 232 17.20 N 87.32 W
Lightning Creek ≃, Sk., Can. 184 49.12 N 101.43 W
Lightning Creek ≃, N.A. 224 48.50 N 121.03 W
Lightning Creek ≃, Wy., U.S. 198 43.11 N 104.44 W
Lightning Ridge 166 29.26 S 147.59 E
Lightstreet 210 41.02 N 76.25 W
Lightsville 216 40.18 N 84.42 W
Ligist 61 46.59 N 15.12 E
Lignano Pineta 64 45.40 N 13.07 E
Lignano Sabbiadoro 64 45.42 N 13.09 E
Lignières 32 46.45 N 2.11 E
Lignite 198 48.52 N 102.33 W
Lignon ≃ 62 45.44 N 4.08 E
Lignumvitae Key I 220 24.55 N 80.42 W
Ligny-en-Barrois 58 48.41 N 5.20 E
Ligny-en-Cambrésis 50 50.06 N 3.22 E
Ligny-le-Châtel 50 47.54 N 3.45 E
Ligny-le-Ribault 50 47.41 N 1.47 E
Ligonha ≃ 154 16.54 S 39.09 E
Ligonier, In., U.S. 216 41.27 N 85.35 W
Ligonier, Pa., U.S. 214 40.14 N 79.14 W
Ligovka 78 49.08 N 36.03 E
Ligovo 76 60.13 N 31.48 E
Ligovo ✧[8] 265a 59.50 N 30.12 E
Ligovskij kanal ≊ 265a 59.47 N 30.10 E
Liguantu 105 40.24 N 115.45 E
Ligueil 32 47.03 N 0.49 E
Ligui 232 25.43 N 111.16 W
Ligure, Mar → Ligurian Sea ⊤[2] 36 43.30 N 9.00 E
Liguria □[4] 62 44.30 N 8.50 E
Liguria, Mar de → Ligurian Sea ⊤[2] 36 43.30 N 9.00 E
Ligurian Sea ⊤[2] 36 43.30 N 9.00 E
Ligurisches Meer → Ligurian Sea ⊤[2] 36 43.30 N 9.00 E

≃	River	Fluß	Río	Rivière	Rio
≊	Canal	Kanal	Canal	Canal	Canal
⌊	Waterfall, Rapids	Wasserfall, Stromschnellen	Cascada, Rápidos	Chute d'eau, Rapides	Cascata, Rápidos
⊔	Strait	Meeresstraße	Estrecho	Détroit	Estreito
⊂	Bay, Gulf	Bucht, Golf	Bahía, Golfo	Baie, Golfe	Baía, Golfo
⊜	Lake, Lakes	See, Seen	Lago, Lagos	Lac, Lacs	Lago, Lagos
≡	Swamp	Sumpf	Pantano	Marais	Pântano
⊓	Ice Features, Glacier	Eis- und Gletscherformen	Accidentes Glaciales	Formes glaciaires	Acidentes glaciares
⊤	Other Hydrographic Features	Andere Hydrographische Objekte	Otros Elementos Hidrográficos	Autres données hydrographiques	Outros acidentes hidrográficos

✢	Submarine Features	Untermeerische Objekte	Accidentes Submarinos	Formes de relief sous-marin	Acidentes submarinos
□	Political Unit	Politische Einheit	Unidad Politica	Entité politique	Unidade política
ʊ	Cultural Institution	Kulturelle Institution	Institución Cultural	Institution culturelle	Instituição cultural
⊥	Historical Site	Historische Stätte	Sitio Histórico	Site historique	Sitio histórico
♦	Recreational Site	Erholungs- und Ferienort	Sitio de Recreo	Centre de loisirs	Area de Lazer
⊠	Airport	Flughafen	Aeropuerto	Aéroport	Aeroporto
■	Military Installation	Militäranlage	Instalación Militar	Installation militaire	Instalação militar
✧	Miscellaneous	Verschiedenes	Misceláneo	Divers	Diversos

Symbols in the index entries represent the broad categories identified in the key at the right. Symbols with superior numbers (⋏1) identify subcategories (see complete key on page *I · 1*).

Symbole im Register stellen die rechts im Schlüssel erklärten Kategorien dar. Symbole mit hochgestellten Ziffern (⋏1) bezeichnen Unterabteilungen einer Kategorie (vgl. vollständiger Schlüssel auf Seite *I · 1*).

Los símbolos incluidos en el texto del índice representan las grandes categorías identificadas con la clave a la derecha. Los símbolos con números en su parte superior (⋏1) identifican las subcategorías (véase la clave completa en la página *I · 1*).

Les symboles de l'index représentent les catégories indiquées dans la légende à droite. Les symboles suivis d'un indice (⋏1) représentent des sous-catégories (voir légende complète à la page *I · 1*).

Os símbolos incluídos no texto do índice representam as grandes categorias identificadas com a chave à direita. Os símbolos com números em sua parte superior (⋏1) identificam as subcategorias (veja-se a chave completa à página *I · 1*).

∧ Mountain	Berg	Montaña	Montagne	Montanha	
⋏ Mountains	Gebirge	Montañas	Montagnes	Montanhas	
x Pass	Paß	Paso	Col	Passo	
V Valley, Canyon	Tal, Cañon	Valle, Cañón	Vallée, Canyon	Vale, Canhão	
= Plain	Ebene	Llano	Plaine	Planície	
> Cape	Kap	Cabo	Cap	Cabo	
I Island	Insel	Isla	Île	Ilha	
II Islands	Inseln	Islas	Îles	Ilhas	
⊥ Other Topographic Features	Andere Topographische Objekte	Otros Elementos Topográficos	Autres données topographiques	Outros acidentes topográficos	

Litt-Locu I · 99

ESPAÑOL — Nombre / Página / Lat.°′ / Long.°′ W = Oeste
FRANÇAIS — Nom / Page / Lat.°′ / Long.°′ W = Ouest
PORTUGUÊS — Nome / Página / Lat.°′ / Long.°′ W = Oeste

Nombre	Página	Lat.°′	Long.°′ W = Oeste
Little Coco Island I	110	14.00 N	93.13 E
Little Colorado ≃	200	36.11 N	111.48 W
Little Compton	207	41.30 N	71.10 W
Little Cooley	214	41.44 N	79.53 W
Little Cottonwood ≃	198	44.15 N	94.20 W
Little Creek	208	39.10 N	75.26 W
Little Creek ≃	285	39.56 N	74.48 W
Little Creek Naval Amphibious Base ■	208	36.55 N	76.10 W
Little Creek Reservoir ⊜[1]	208	37.20 N	76.50 W
Little Cumbrae Island I	46	55.43 N	4.57 W
Little Current	190	45.58 N	81.56 W
Little Current ≃	176	50.57 N	84.36 W
Little Cypress Bayou ≃	194	32.41 N	94.15 W
Little Cypress Creek ≃	222	32.39 N	94.42 W
Little Darby Creek ≃	218	39.53 N	83.13 W
Little Dart ≃	42	50.54 N	3.51 W
Little Deep Creek ≃	198	48.35 N	100.52 W
Little Deer Creek ≃, In., U.S.	216	40.36 N	86.28 W
Little Deer Creek ≃, Pa., U.S.	279b	40.33 N	79.50 W
Little Deschutes ≃	202	43.51 N	121.27 W
Little Desert ⊸[2]	166	36.35 S	141.20 E
Little Desert National Park ♠	166	36.25 S	141.25 E
Little Diomede Island I	180	65.45 N	168.57 W
Little Don ≃	275b	43.42 N	79.20 W
Little Dry Creek ≃, Ca., U.S.	226	39.22 N	121.52 W
Little Dry Creek ≃, Mt., U.S.	202	47.21 N	106.22 W
Little Ease Run ≃	285	39.39 N	75.04 W
Little Eau Pleine ≃	190	44.40 N	89.41 W
Little Egg Harbor ⊂	208	39.35 N	74.18 W
Little Elkhart ≃	216	41.43 N	85.49 W
Little End	260	51.41 N	0.14 E
Little Etobicoke Creek ≃	275b	43.37 N	79.34 W
Little Exuma I	238	23.27 N	75.37 W
Little Fabius ≃	219	39.59 N	91.59 W
Little Falls, Mn., U.S.	190	45.58 N	94.21 W
Little Falls, N.J., U.S.	276	40.52 N	74.12 W
Little Falls, N.Y., U.S.	210	43.02 N	74.51 W
Little Falls ≃	208	39.36 N	76.38 W
Little Falls Dam ⊸[6]	284c	38.57 N	77.08 W
Little Farms	218	39.57 N	83.10 W
Little Ferry	276	40.51 N	74.02 W
Littlefield	196	33.55 N	102.19 W
Little Flatrock ≃	218	39.26 N	85.33 W
Littlefork	190	48.23 N	93.33 W
Little Fork ≃	190	48.31 N	93.35 W
Little Fort	182	51.25 N	120.12 W
Little Genesee	210	42.02 N	78.13 W
Little Gold ≃	162	18.01 S	126.29 E
Little Gunpowder Falls ≃	208	39.23 N	76.22 W
Littlehampton	42	50.48 N	0.33 W
Little Harbour Deep	186	50.15 N	56.33 W
Little Haw Creek ≃	192	29.23 N	81.24 W
Little Hawk Lake ⊜	212	45.10 N	78.42 W
Little Hoosic ≃	210	42.49 N	73.20 W
Little Hope	214	42.06 N	79.49 W
Little Hulton	262	53.32 N	2.25 W
Little Humboldt ≃	204	41.00 N	117.43 W
Little Humboldt, North Fork ≃	204	41.24 N	117.10 W
Little Humboldt, South Fork ≃	204	41.24 N	117.10 W
Little Hurricane Creek ≃	192	31.23 N	82.19 W
Little Inagua I	238	21.30 N	73.00 W
Little Indian Creek ≃, Il., U.S.	216	41.31 N	88.46 W
Little Indian Creek ≃, In., U.S.	218	38.12 N	86.08 W
Little Island Pond ⊜	283	42.43 N	71.17 W
Littlejohns Creek ≃	226	37.52 N	121.14 W
Little Juniata ≃	214	40.34 N	78.03 W
Little Juniata Creek ≃	208	40.23 N	77.02 W
Little Kanawha ≃	188	39.16 N	81.34 W
Little Kanawha, West Fork ≃	188	38.57 N	81.16 W
Little Karroo (Klein Karroo) ⋏[1]	158	33.45 S	21.30 E
Little Kentucky ≃	218	38.41 N	85.12 W
Little Klickitat ≃	224	45.51 N	121.04 W
Little Koniuji Island I	180	55.01 N	159.26 W
Little Lake ⊜, On., Can.	212	44.26 N	79.40 W
Little Lake ⊜, La., U.S.	194	29.30 N	90.10 W
Little Laramie ≃	200	41.28 N	105.44 W
Little Laver	260	51.46 N	0.14 E
Little Leigh	262	53.17 N	2.35 W
Little Lever	262	53.34 N	2.22 W
Little Limestone Lake ⊜	184	53.46 N	99.18 W
Little London	241q	18.15 N	78.13 W
Little Lost ≃	202	43.46 N	112.58 W
Little Lun ≃	116	6.02 N	125.17 E
Little Mahoning Creek ≃	214	40.49 N	79.00 W
Little Maitland ≃	212	43.52 N	81.18 W
Little Manatee ≃	220	27.42 N	82.28 W
Little Manatee, South Fork ≃	220	27.39 N	82.18 W
Little Manistee ≃	190	44.15 N	86.19 W
Little Manitou Lake ⊜	184	51.45 N	105.30 W
Little Marco Pass ⊂	220	26.01 N	81.46 W
Little Marsh	210	41.53 N	77.24 W
Little Meadows	210	41.59 N	76.08 W
Little Mecatina ≃	176	50.28 N	59.35 W
Little Medicine Bow ≃	200	41.58 N	106.18 W
Little Mexico	196	30.57 N	102.52 W
Little Miami ≃	218	39.05 N	84.26 W
Little Miami, East Fork ≃	218	39.09 N	84.18 W
Little Miami, North Fork ≃	218	39.48 N	83.47 W
Little Miami, Todd Fork ≃	218	39.21 N	84.08 W
Little Miami, Todd Fork, East Fork ≃	218	39.24 N	84.00 W
Littlemill	46	57.32 N	3.49 W
Little Mississippi ≃	212	45.17 N	77.35 W
Little Missouri ≃, U.S.	198	47.30 N	102.25 W
Little Missouri ≃, Ar., U.S.	194	33.49 N	92.54 W
Little Mountain ∧	208	40.47 N	76.40 W
Little Muddy ≃, Il., U.S.	194	37.50 N	89.11 W
Little Muddy ≃, N.D., U.S.	198	48.12 N	103.36 W
Little Mulberry Creek ≃	194	32.26 N	86.51 W
Little Naches ≃	224	46.58 N	121.08 W
Little Nahant	283	42.25 N	70.56 W
Little Namaqualand □[9]	156	29.00 S	17.00 E
Little Neck	283	42.42 N	70.48 W
Little Neck ⊸[8]	276	40.46 N	73.44 W
Little Neck Bay ⊂	276	40.47 N	73.46 W
Little Nemaha ≃	198	40.19 N	95.40 W
Little Neshaminy Creek ≃	285	40.15 N	75.02 W
Little Niangua ≃	194	38.04 N	92.54 W
Little Nicobar I	110	7.20 N	93.40 E
Little Ohoopee ≃	192	32.27 N	82.24 W
Little Osage ≃	194	38.02 N	94.14 W
Little Otter Creek ≃	212	42.44 N	80.51 W
Little Ouse ≃	42	52.30 N	0.22 E
Little Panoche Creek ≃	226	36.50 N	120.42 W
Little Patuxent ≃	284b	39.11 N	76.52 W
Little Paxton	42	52.15 N	0.15 W
Little Peconic Bay ⊂	207	40.59 N	72.24 W
Little Pee Dee ≃	192	33.42 N	79.11 W
Little Pic ≃	190	48.48 N	86.37 W
Little Pine and Lucky Man Indian Reserve ⊸[4]	184	52.56 N	109.05 W
Little Pine Creek ≃, Pa., U.S.	210	41.18 N	77.22 W
Little Pine Creek ≃, Pa., U.S.	279b	40.31 N	79.57 W
Little Pine Island I	220	26.36 N	82.05 W
Little Pine Key I	220	24.44 N	81.19 W
Little Pine State Park ♠	210	41.22 N	77.20 W
Little Pipe Creek ≃	208	39.36 N	77.16 W
Little Platte ≃	194	39.24 N	94.41 W
Little Plum Creek ≃	279b	40.30 N	79.51 W
Little Popo Aggie ≃	202	42.54 N	108.35 W
Little Porcupine Creek ≃, Mt., U.S.	202	48.02 N	106.04 W
Little Porcupine Creek ≃, Mt., U.S.	202	46.18 N	106.34 W
Littleport	42	52.28 N	0.19 E
Little Portage Creek ≃	216	42.00 N	85.27 W
Little Powder ≃	198	45.28 N	105.20 W
Little Pucketa Creek ≃	279b	40.33 N	79.45 W
Little Quill Lake ⊜	184	51.55 N	104.05 W
Little Rann of Kachchh ≚	120	23.25 N	71.15 E
Little Red ≃	194	35.11 N	91.27 W
Little Red, Middle Fork ≃	194	35.37 N	92.11 W
Little Red Deer ≃	182	52.04 N	114.09 W
Little Red River Indian Reserve ⊸[4]	184	53.30 N	105.58 W
Little Redstone Lake ⊜	212	45.13 N	78.34 W
Little River, Austl.	169	37.58 S	144.30 E
Little River, N.Z.	172	43.46 S	172.47 E
Little River, Ks., U.S.	198	38.23 N	98.00 W
Little River, Tx., U.S.	222	30.59 N	97.22 W
Little Rock, Ar., U.S.	194	34.44 N	92.17 W
Littlerock, Ca., U.S.	228	34.31 N	117.59 W
Little Rock, Il., U.S.	216	41.43 N	88.34 W
Little Rock, Ia., U.S.	198	43.26 N	95.52 W
Littlerock, Wa., U.S.	224	46.54 N	123.01 W
Little Rock ≃	198	43.16 N	96.15 W
Little Rock Air Force Base ■	194	34.55 N	92.10 W
Little Rock Creek ≃	228	34.28 N	118.01 W
Little Rock Wash V	228	34.42 N	118.02 W
Little Rocky Mountains ⋏	202	47.50 N	108.10 W
Little Rouge Creek ≃	212	43.48 N	79.08 W
Little Ruaha ≃	154	7.17 S	35.28 E
Little Sable Point ›	190	43.38 N	86.32 W
Little Sac ≃	194	37.39 N	93.46 W
Little Sachigo Lake ⊜	184	54.09 N	92.11 W
Little Saint Bernard Pass → Petit-Saint-Bernard, Col du)(	62	45.41 N	6.53 E
Little Salkehatchie ≃	192	32.37 N	80.53 W
Little Salmon ≃, Id., U.S.	202	45.25 N	116.19 W
Little Salmon ≃, N.Y., U.S.	212	43.32 N	76.16 W
Little Salmon, North Branch ≃	212	43.24 N	76.09 W
Little Salmon, South Branch ≃	212	43.24 N	76.09 W
Little Salmon Lake ⊜	180	62.12 N	134.45 W
Little Salt Lake ⊜	200	37.55 N	112.53 W
Little Sandy ≃	188	38.35 N	82.51 W
Little Sandy, East Fork ≃	188	38.30 N	82.50 W
Little Sandy Creek ≃	200	42.06 N	109.27 W
Little Sandy Desert ⊸[2]	162	24.20 S	120.50 E
Little Saskatchewan ≃	184	49.52 N	100.07 W
Little Scarcies ≃	150	8.51 N	13.09 W
Little Scioto ≃, Oh., U.S.	214	40.31 N	83.12 W
Little Scioto ≃, Oh., U.S.	218	38.46 N	82.53 W
Little Sewickley Creek ≃, Pa., U.S.	279b	40.15 N	79.45 W
Little Sewickley Creek ≃, Pa., U.S.	279b	40.33 N	80.12 W
Little Silver	276	40.20 N	74.02 W
Little Sioux ≃	198	41.49 N	96.04 W
Little Sioux, West Fork ≃	198	42.04 N	96.00 W
Little Sitkin Island I	181a	51.55 N	178.30 E
Little Smoky ≃	182	55.42 N	117.38 W
Little Snake ≃	200	40.27 N	108.26 W
Little Sodus Bay ⊂	210	43.20 N	76.43 W
Little Southwest Miramichi ≃	186	46.57 N	65.50 W
Little Stanney	262	53.15 N	2.53 W
Little Stony Creek ≃	226	39.20 N	122.31 W
Little Stour ≃	42	51.19 N	1.15 E
Littlestown	208	39.44 N	77.05 W
Little Stukeley	42	52.21 N	0.13 W
Little Sugarloaf ∧[2]	274b	37.41 S	145.19 E
Little Sur ≃	226	36.20 N	121.54 W
Little Sutton	262	53.17 N	2.57 W
Little Swatara Creek ≃	208	40.24 N	76.29 W
Little Tallapoosa ≃	192	33.18 N	85.34 W
Little Tanaga Island I	180	51.48 N	176.10 W
Little Tennessee ≃	192	35.47 N	84.15 W
Little Thurrock	260	51.28 N	0.21 E
Little Timber Creek ≃	285	39.53 N	75.08 W
Little Tinicum Island I	285	39.51 N	75.17 W
Little Tobago I, Br. Vir. Is.	240m	18.26 N	64.51 W
Little Tobago I, Trin.	241r	11.18 N	60.30 W
Little Toby Creek ≃	214	41.22 N	78.49 W
Littleton, Eng., U.K.	260	51.24 N	0.28 W
Littleton, Co., U.S.	200	39.36 N	105.00 W
Littleton, Ma., U.S.	207	42.32 N	71.30 W
Littleton, N.H., U.S.	188	44.18 N	71.46 W
Littleton, N.C., U.S.	192	36.26 N	77.54 W
Littleton, W.V., U.S.	188	39.41 N	80.31 W
Little Traverse Bay ⊂	190	45.24 N	85.03 W
Little Truckee ≃	226	39.25 N	120.05 W
Little Turtle ≃	184	48.46 N	92.36 W
Little Turtle State Recreation Area ♠	216	40.50 N	85.26 W
Little Valley	210	42.15 N	78.48 W
Little Vermilion ≃	216	41.20 N	89.05 W
Little Vermilion Lake ⊜	184	51.16 N	93.50 W
Little Vienna Estates	284c	38.54 N	77.18 W
Little Wabash ≃	194	37.54 N	88.05 W
Little Walsingham	42	52.54 N	0.51 E
Little Waltham	260	51.47 N	0.29 E
Little Warley	260	51.35 N	0.19 E
Little Washita ≃	196	34.58 N	97.51 W
Little Wellington, Isla I	254	48.30 S	74.45 W
Little White ≃	198	43.44 N	100.40 W
Little White Mountain ∧	182	49.42 N	119.20 W
Little White Salmon ≃	224	45.43 N	121.38 W
Little Wichita ≃	196	33.54 N	97.59 W
Little Wichita, East Fork ≃	196	33.52 N	98.07 W
Little Wind ≃	202	42.57 N	108.29 W
Little Wind, North Fork ≃	202	43.01 N	108.53 W
Little Wind, South Fork ≃	202	43.01 N	108.53 W
Little Wolf ≃	190	44.23 N	88.48 W
Little Wood ≃	202	42.57 N	114.21 W
Little York, In., U.S.	218	38.42 N	85.54 W
Little York, N.Y., U.S.	210	42.42 N	76.10 W
Little Zab (Zāb-e Kūchek) (Az-Zāb aṣ-Ṣaghīr) ≃	128	35.12 N	43.25 E
Littoral □[4]	152	4.13 N	10.25 E
Litunga	152	13.17 S	16.43 E
Litvínov	54	50.37 N	13.36 E
Litvinovka	83	49.18 N	39.27 E
Litvinovo	76	59.34 N	38.01 E
Litvinskoje	86	50.42 N	72.42 E
Litzmannstadt → Łódź	30	51.46 N	19.30 E
Liu ≃, Zhg.	98	41.48 N	122.43 E
Liu ≃, Zhg.	98	42.45 N	126.04 E
Liu ≃, Zhg.	98	40.38 N	118.09 E
Liu ≃, Zhg.	102	23.52 N	109.45 E
Liu ≃, Zhg.	105	40.38 N	118.09 E
Liu ≃, Zhg.	106	31.31 N	121.18 E
Liuanzhuang	105	39.14 N	117.11 E
Liuba	102	33.32 N	107.07 E
Liubotong	100	31.26 N	116.00 E
Liucao	106	31.07 N	121.41 E
Liuchen	102	23.09 N	110.29 E
Liucheng, Zhg.	100	24.03 N	115.08 E
Liucheng, Zhg.	100	28.36 N	119.34 E
Liucheng, Zhg.	102	24.32 N	109.21 E
Liuchengba	102	27.27 N	102.53 E
Liuch'iu Hsü I	100	22.21 N	120.22 E
Liuchow → Liuzhou	102	24.19 N	109.24 E
Liucun	106	30.44 N	119.23 E
Liucura	252	38.39 S	71.05 W
Liudaogou	98	41.34 N	127.12 E
Liudaohe	105	40.39 N	116.12 E
Liudongqiao	106	31.03 N	119.32 E
Liudu	100	26.44 N	119.33 E
Liuduo	100	34.01 N	120.17 E
Liuduzhuang	105	39.27 N	117.50 E
Liuerbao	104	41.13 N	122.55 E
Liufang	100	27.56 N	116.22 E
Liufangling	100	30.27 N	114.27 E
Liufentzu	269d	24.57 N	121.35 E
Liugezhuang, Zhg.	98	38.33 N	116.30 E
Liugezhuang, Zhg.	105	40.03 N	118.16 E
Liugou	105	40.57 N	118.18 E
Liugu ≃	98	40.22 N	120.26 E
Liuguan	100	29.56 N	113.08 E
Liuguantun	104	41.20 N	121.21 E
Liuhang	106	31.21 N	121.22 E
Liuhe, Zhg.	98	42.15 N	125.43 E
Liuhe, Zhg.	100	33.20 N	112.48 E
Liuhe, Zhg.	100	30.20 N	115.36 E
Liuhe, Zhg.	100	30.46 N	113.12 E
Liuhe, Zhg.	100	32.22 N	118.49 E
Liuhe, Zhg.	105	39.31 N	118.17 E
Liuhe, Zhg.	106	31.30 N	121.15 E
Liuhegou	104	41.56 N	122.44 E
Liuheita	104	42.09 N	123.56 E
Liuhejie	102	24.26 N	101.35 E
Liuhekou	105	40.39 N	118.09 E
Liuheng Dao I	100	29.43 N	122.08 E
Liuhuang	100	23.58 N	116.28 E
Liuhudang	104	42.31 N	122.22 E
Liujia	102	24.54 N	107.49 E
Liujiachang	107	29.46 N	103.49 E
Liujiachuan	105	40.07 N	114.47 E
Liujiadai	106	31.57 N	120.23 E
Liujiadian	89	50.07 N	124.17 E
Liujiadu	106	32.15 N	120.33 E
Liujiafen	105	39.58 N	115.47 E
Liujiagangzi	104	41.28 N	122.33 E
Liujiagou	98	37.47 N	120.53 E
Liujiahe, Zhg.	100	32.06 N	113.21 E
Liujiahe, Zhg.	104	40.40 N	123.58 E
Liujiang	98	40.04 N	119.34 E
Liujiashan	105	40.14 N	114.49 E
Liujiatun, Zhg.	104	41.52 N	122.44 E
Liujiatun, Zhg.	104	41.51 N	122.05 E
Liujiatun, Zhg.	104	42.08 N	122.44 E
Liujiawopeng	104	42.16 N	123.01 E
Liujiazhai	269b	31.21 N	121.27 E
Liujiazhen	106	32.04 N	121.30 E
Liujiazi, Zhg.	98	41.00 N	120.13 E
Liujiazi, Zhg.	104	42.36 N	122.15 E
Liujiazi, Zhg.	104	41.48 N	123.47 E
Liujingcun	105	39.27 N	115.26 E
Liujisu	105	40.01 N	117.13 E
Liukeshu	86	44.59 N	90.12 E
Liuku	102	25.48 N	98.52 E
Liuli	154	11.05 S	34.38 E
Liulicun	271a	39.56 N	116.28 E
Liulidian	106	31.31 N	119.17 E
Liuligou	104	41.24 N	121.29 E
Liulihezhen	105	39.36 N	116.01 E
Liulin	100	31.34 N	113.14 E
Liuliwei	100	24.20 N	114.03 E
Liulongtai	104	41.32 N	120.56 E
Liumachang	107	29.51 N	104.54 E
Liumaogou	89	48.12 N	127.13 E
Liupangtun	104	41.36 N	123.28 E
Liupan Shan ⋏	102	35.40 N	106.40 E
Liuqianhutun	104	42.01 N	123.41 E
Liuqiao	106	32.11 N	120.51 E
Liuquan, Zhg.	98	34.27 N	117.20 E
Liuquan, Zhg.	105	39.22 N	116.18 E
Liurenba	100	29.57 N	114.49 E
Liushi, Zhg.	98	38.33 N	115.44 E
Liushi, Zhg.	100	28.03 N	120.51 E
Liushilipu	100	32.45 N	115.58 E
Liushi Shan ∧	120	36.15 N	82.05 E
Liushouying	98	39.48 N	119.19 E
Liushudian	98	35.54 N	119.30 E
Liushudixia	104	42.26 N	121.14 E
Liushui	89	44.17 N	124.15 E
Liushuigou	100	31.34 N	112.27 E
Liushuquan	105	39.21 N	118.06 E
Liusiqiao	100	29.47 N	116.21 E
Liusong	105	39.40 N	117.08 E
Liuta	98	35.52 N	115.18 E
Liutai	98	41.20 N	113.43 E
Liutaizi	104	41.46 N	122.39 E
Liutang	102	24.58 N	110.21 E
Liutiaozhaicun	104	41.29 N	123.12 E
Liutuan	98	36.56 N	119.22 E
Liutuhutun	104	40.44 N	120.32 E
Liuwanglou	98	34.48 N	116.28 E
Liuwa Plain ≚	152	14.30 S	22.40 E
Liuwa Plain National Park ♠	152	14.30 S	22.40 E
Liuwei	106	32.16 N	119.28 E
Liuwudian	100	24.36 N	118.13 E
Liuxi ≃	100	23.22 N	112.54 E
Liuxia	106	30.15 N	120.03 E
Liuyang	100	28.09 N	113.38 E
Liuyang ≃	100	28.13 N	112.58 E
Liuyuan	98	36.10 N	114.34 E
Liuyuankou	98	34.54 N	114.20 E
Liuzhai	102	25.15 N	107.20 E
Liuzhou	102	24.19 N	109.24 E
Liuzhuang	100	33.10 N	120.19 E
Livada	38	47.52 N	23.07 E
Livadija	89	42.50 N	132.39 E
Livanátai	38	38.42 N	23.03 E
Līvāni	76	56.22 N	26.11 E
Livanjsko Polje ≚	36	43.55 N	16.45 E
Livanovka	86	52.06 N	61.59 E
Livarot	50	49.01 N	0.09 E
Lively, On., Can.	190	46.26 N	81.09 W
Lively, Va., U.S.	208	37.47 N	76.31 W
Lively Island I	254	52.02 S	58.30 W
Livengood	180	65.32 N	148.33 W
Livenka, Ross.	78	50.26 N	38.18 E
Livenka, Ross.	78	50.44 N	40.14 E
Livenza ≃	64	45.35 N	12.51 E
Live Oak, Ca., U.S.	226	39.16 N	121.39 W
Live Oak, Fl., U.S.	192	30.17 N	82.59 W
Live Oak Creek ≃	196	30.39 N	101.42 W
Liverdun	56	48.45 N	6.03 E
Liverdy-en-Brie	261	48.42 N	2.47 E
Livergnano	66	44.19 N	11.21 E
Liveringa	162	18.03 S	124.10 E
Livermore, Ca., U.S.	226	37.40 N	121.46 W
Livermore, Ia., U.S.	190	42.52 N	94.11 W
Livermore, Ky., U.S.	194	37.29 N	87.07 W
Livermore, Mount ∧	196	30.38 N	104.10 W
Livermore Falls	188	44.28 N	70.11 W
Liverpool, Austl.	170	33.54 S	150.56 E
Liverpool, N.S., Can.	186	44.02 N	64.43 W
Liverpool, Eng., U.K.	44	53.25 N	2.55 W
Liverpool, Eng., U.K.	262	53.25 N	2.55 W
Liverpool, In., U.S.	216	41.34 N	87.18 W
Liverpool, N.Y., U.S.	210	43.06 N	76.13 W
Liverpool, Pa., U.S.	208	40.34 N	76.59 W
Liverpool, Tx., U.S.	222	29.18 N	95.17 W
Liverpool □[8]	262	53.25 N	2.55 W
Liverpool ≃	164	12.02 S	134.13 E
Liverpool (Speke) Airport ⊠	44	53.21 N	2.52 W
Liverpool, Cape ›	176	73.38 N	78.06 W
Liverpool, University of ⊍[2]	262	53.24 N	2.58 W
Liverpool Bay ⊂, N.T., Can.	180	69.45 N	130.00 W
Liverpool Bay ⊂, N.S., Can.	186	44.02 N	64.41 W
Liverpool Bay ⊂, Eng., U.K.	44	53.30 N	3.16 W
Liverpool Football Ground ♠	262	53.26 N	2.57 W
Liverpool Heights	210	43.07 N	76.13 W
Liverpool Range ⋏	166	31.40 S	150.30 E
Liverpool Street Station ⊸[5]	260	51.31 N	0.05 W
Livet-et-Gavet	62	45.06 N	5.56 E
Livigno	64	46.32 N	10.04 E
Livilliers	261	49.06 N	2.06 E
Lívingston, Guat.	236	15.50 N	88.45 W
Livingston, Scot., U.K.	46	55.53 N	3.32 W
Livingston, Al., U.S.	194	32.35 N	88.11 W
Livingston, Ca., U.S.	226	37.23 N	120.43 W
Livingston, Il., U.S.	194	38.58 N	89.45 W
Livingston, Ky., U.S.	192	37.17 N	84.12 W
Livingston, La., U.S.	194	30.30 N	90.44 W
Livingston, Mt., U.S.	202	45.39 N	110.33 W
Livingston, N.J., U.S.	210	40.47 N	74.18 W
Livingston, N.Y., U.S.	210	42.09 N	73.47 W
Livingston, Tn., U.S.	194	36.23 N	85.19 W
Livingston, Tx., U.S.	222	30.42 N	94.55 W
Livingston, Wi., U.S.	190	42.54 N	90.25 W
Livingston □[6], Il., U.S.	216	40.53 N	88.38 W
Livingston □[6], Mi., U.S.	216	42.38 N	83.50 W
Livingston □[6], N.Y., U.S.	210	42.48 N	77.49 W
Livingstone	154	17.50 S	25.53 E
Livingstone, Chutes de (Livingstone Falls) ⌊	152	4.50 S	14.30 E
Livingstone, Lake ⊜[1]	222	30.50 N	95.30 W
Livingstone Falls → Livingstone, Chutes de ⌊	152	4.50 S	14.30 E
Livingstone Lake ⊜	212	45.22 N	78.43 W
Livingstonia	154	10.36 S	34.07 E
Livingston Island I	9	62.35 S	60.30 W
Livingston Mall ⊸[9]	276	40.47 N	74.21 W
Livingston Manor	210	41.54 N	74.49 W
Livno	36	43.50 N	17.01 E
Livny	76	52.25 N	37.37 E
Livojoki ≃	26	65.24 N	26.48 E
Livonia, In., U.S.	218	38.34 N	86.17 W
Livonia, La., U.S.	194	30.33 N	91.33 W
Livonia, Mi., U.S.	216	42.22 N	83.21 W
Livonia, N.Y., U.S.	210	42.49 N	77.40 W
Livonia Center	210	42.49 N	77.38 W
Livonia Mall ⊸[9]	281	42.26 N	83.20 W
Livorno (Leghorn)	66	43.33 N	10.19 E
Livorno □[4]	66	43.14 N	10.35 E
Livorno Ferraris	62	45.17 N	8.05 E
Livourne → Livorno	66	43.33 N	10.19 E
Livramento do Brumado	255	13.39 S	41.50 W
Livramento → Santana do Livramento	252	30.53 S	55.31 W
Livron-sur-Drôme	62	44.46 N	4.51 E
Livry-Gargan	261	48.56 N	2.33 E
Livry-sur-Seine	261	48.31 N	2.41 E
Liwa	112	5.04 S	104.06 E
Liwale	154	9.46 S	37.56 E
Liwale Chini	154	9.41 S	38.01 E
Liwan	154	4.54 N	35.40 E
Liwonde	154	14.52 S	35.28 E
Liwonde National Park ♠	154	14.50 S	35.20 E
Liwung ≃	115a	6.08 S	106.49 E
Lixi, Zhg.	100	29.15 N	114.46 E
Lixi, Zhg.	100	27.39 N	116.19 E
Lixian, Zhg.	98	38.29 N	115.34 E
Lixian, Zhg.	102	34.11 N	105.02 E
Lixian, Zhg.	102	29.30 N	111.37 E
Lixian, Zhg.	105	39.33 N	116.26 E
Lixian → Black ≃	110	21.15 N	105.20 E
Lixin, Zhg.	100	26.52 N	116.42 E
Lixin, Zhg.	100	33.06 N	116.08 E
Lixing	100	33.28 N	115.28 E
Lixingzhuang	105	39.25 N	117.56 E
Lixoúrion	38	38.12 N	20.26 E
Lixus ⊥	34	35.16 N	6.13 W
Liyang, Zhg.	98	37.28 N	113.37 E
Liyang, Zhg.	106	31.26 N	119.29 E
Liyuanbao	100	25.16 N	112.55 E
Liyujiang	100	25.57 N	113.15 E
Lizard	42	49.58 N	5.12 W
Lizarda	250	9.36 S	46.41 W
Lizard Head Peak ∧	200	42.47 N	109.11 W
Lizard Island I	164	14.40 S	145.28 E
Lizard Point ›	42	49.56 N	5.13 W
Lizard Point Indian Reserve ⊸[4]	184	50.40 N	100.57 W
Lize	107	30.08 N	106.11 E
Lizhai	106	31.34 N	121.45 E
Lizhou	102	28.08 N	102.10 E
Lizhu	100	29.56 N	120.30 E
Lizhuang, Zhg.	100	34.24 N	116.30 E
Lizhuang, Zhg.	107	28.47 N	104.46 E
Lizhuangqiao	106	31.48 N	119.37 E
Lizino	83	49.33 N	38.51 E
Lizinovka	78	50.08 N	39.28 E
Liziwei	107	30.19 N	106.39 E
Lizy-sur-Ourcq	50	49.01 N	3.02 E
Lizzana	64	45.51 N	11.03 E
Lizzanello	68	40.18 N	18.13 E
Lizzano	68	40.23 N	17.27 E
Lizzano in Belvedere	64	44.10 N	10.53 E
Ljalovo	82	56.03 N	37.14 E
Ljan	26	59.51 N	10.48 E
Ljubelj (Loiblpass))(	61	46.26 N	14.16 E
Ljubija	36	44.56 N	16.37 E
Ljubimec	38	41.50 N	26.05 E
Ljubinje	38	42.57 N	18.05 E
Ljubljana	36	46.03 N	14.31 E
Ljubovija	38	44.11 N	19.22 E
Ljubuški	36	43.12 N	17.33 E
Ljugarn	26	57.19 N	18.42 E
Ljunga	40	58.31 N	16.21 E
Ljungan ≃	26	62.19 N	17.23 E
Ljungaverk	26	62.29 N	16.03 E
Ljungby	26	56.50 N	13.56 E
Ljungbyhed	41	56.04 N	13.12 E
Ljungbyholm	26	56.38 N	16.10 E
Ljungdalen	26	62.51 N	12.47 E
Ljungsbro	26	58.31 N	15.30 E
Ljungskile	26	58.14 N	11.55 E
Ljusdal	26	61.50 N	16.05 E
Ljusfallshammar	40	58.47 N	15.29 E
Ljusnan ≃	26	61.12 N	17.08 E
Ljusnaren ⊜	40	59.51 N	14.56 E
Ljusne	26	61.13 N	17.08 E
Ljusterö I	40	59.31 N	18.37 E
Ljutomer	61	46.31 N	16.12 E
Llagas Creek ≃	226	36.58 N	121.31 W
Llaima, Volcán ∧[1]	252	38.43 S	71.43 W
Llamara, Salar de ≚	248	21.13 S	69.40 W
Llanaber	42	52.45 N	4.05 W
Llanaelhaearn	42	52.59 N	4.24 W
Llanarth	42	52.12 N	4.18 W
Llanarthney	42	51.52 N	4.09 W
Llanbedrog	42	52.52 N	4.29 W
Llanberis, Pass of V	44	53.06 N	4.04 W
Llanbister	42	52.21 N	3.27 W
Llanboidy	42	51.54 N	4.36 W
Llanbryde	46	57.37 N	3.13 W
Llanbrynmair	42	52.37 N	3.57 W
Llançà	34	42.22 N	3.09 E
Llancanelo, Laguna ⊜	252	35.35 S	69.09 W
Llandaff	42	51.30 N	3.14 W
Llandaff Cathedral ⊍[1]	42	51.29 N	3.15 W
Llanddewi Brefi	42	52.10 N	3.57 W
Llandeilo	42	51.52 N	3.59 W
Llandilo	274a	33.43 S	150.45 E
Llandinam	42	52.29 N	3.26 W
Llandissilio	42	51.53 N	4.44 W
Llandovery	42	51.59 N	3.48 W
Llandrindod Wells	42	52.15 N	3.23 W
Llandudno	44	53.19 N	3.49 W
Llandybie	42	51.50 N	4.00 W
Llandysul	42	52.02 N	4.19 W
Llanelli	42	51.42 N	4.10 W
Llanelltyd	42	52.45 N	3.54 W
Llanelly	169	36.44 S	143.51 E
Llanenddwyn	42	52.49 N	4.06 W
Llanerchymedd	44	53.20 N	4.22 W
Llanes	34	43.25 N	4.45 W
Llanfaethlu	44	53.21 N	4.32 W
Llanfair-Caereinion	42	52.39 N	3.20 W
Llanfairfechan	44	53.15 N	3.58 W
Llanfairpwllgwyngyll	44	53.13 N	4.12 W
Llanfrynach	42	51.56 N	3.21 W
Llanfyllin	42	52.46 N	3.17 W
Llanfynydd	42	51.56 N	4.06 W
Llanfyrnach	42	51.57 N	4.35 W
Llangadog	42	51.56 N	3.53 W
Llangefni	44	53.16 N	4.18 W
Llangennech	42	51.41 N	4.04 W
Llangollen	42	52.58 N	3.10 W
Llangollen Estates	208	39.39 N	75.37 W
Llangranog	42	52.09 N	4.29 W
Llangurig	42	52.25 N	3.36 W
Llangwyryfon	42	52.19 N	4.03 W
Llangynog	42	52.50 N	3.25 W
Llanharan	42	51.33 N	3.25 W
Llanidloes	42	52.27 N	3.32 W
Llanilar	42	52.21 N	4.01 W
Llanllyfni	44	53.03 N	4.17 W
Llano	196	30.45 N	98.40 W
Llano ≃	196	30.35 N	98.25 W
Llano Colorado	204	31.38 N	115.55 W
Llanon	42	52.17 N	4.10 W
Llanos ≚	246	5.00 N	70.00 W
Llanpumsaint	42	51.56 N	4.18 W
Llanquihue	254	41.15 S	73.01 W
Llanquihue, Lago ⊜	254	41.08 S	72.48 W
Llanrhaeadr-ym-Mochnant	42	52.51 N	3.17 W
Llanrhidian	42	51.37 N	4.11 W
Llanrhystud	42	52.18 N	4.09 W
Llanrwst	44	53.08 N	3.48 W
Llansantffraid-ym-Mechain	42	52.47 N	3.08 W
Llansawel	42	52.01 N	4.00 W
Llantrisant	42	51.33 N	3.23 W
Llantwit Major	42	51.25 N	3.30 W
Llanuwchllyn	42	52.52 N	3.41 W
Llanwenog	42	52.06 N	4.12 W
Llanwrda	42	51.58 N	3.53 W
Llanwrtyd Wells	42	52.07 N	3.38 W
Llanybydder	42	52.04 N	4.09 W
Llata	248	9.25 S	76.47 W
Llavallol ⊸[8]	288	34.48 S	58.28 W
Llay	44	53.06 N	2.59 W
Lleida	34	41.37 N	0.37 E
Lleida □[4]	34	42.00 N	1.10 E
Llentrisca, Cap ›	34	38.51 N	1.14 E
Llera de Canales	234	23.19 N	99.01 W
Llerena	34	38.14 N	6.01 W
Lleulleu, Lago ⊜	252	38.09 S	73.20 W
Lleyn Peninsula ›[1]	42	52.54 N	4.30 W
Llica	248	19.52 S	68.16 W
Llico	252	34.46 S	72.05 W
Lliria	34	39.38 N	0.36 W
Llivia	32	42.28 N	1.59 E
Llobregat ≃	34	41.19 N	2.09 E
Llobregat, Delta del ≚[2]	266d	41.17 N	2.08 E
Llorente	116	11.25 N	125.33 E
Llorente ≃	116	11.25 N	125.33 E
Llorona, Punta ›	236	8.39 N	83.45 W
Lloyd	218	38.37 N	82.51 W
Lloyd Harbor	210	40.54 N	73.27 W
Lloyd Harbor ⊂	276	40.55 N	73.27 W
Lloydminster	184	53.17 N	110.00 W
Lloyd Neck ›[1]	276	40.56 N	73.28 W
Lloyd Point ›	210	40.57 N	73.29 W
Lloyds ≃	186	48.33 N	57.13 W
Llucena	34	40.08 N	0.17 W
Llucmajor	34	39.29 N	2.54 E
Llullaillaco, Volcán ∧[1]	252	24.43 S	68.33 W
Llusco	248	14.21 S	72.07 W
Lluta ≃	248	18.24 S	70.19 W
Llyn Brianne Reservoir ⊜[1]	42	52.08 N	3.45 W
Llyswen	42	52.02 N	3.17 W
Llys-y-frân Reservoir ⊜[1]	42	51.53 N	4.51 W
Lnáře	60	49.28 N	13.47 E
Lo (Panlong) ≃	110	21.18 N	105.25 E
Loa	200	38.24 N	111.38 W
Loa ≃, Chile	244	21.26 S	70.04 W
Loa ≃, Congo	273b	4.20 S	15.11 E
Loami	194	39.40 N	89.51 W
Loanda, Bra.	255	22.54 S	53.10 W
Loanda, Gabon	152	0.55 S	9.00 E
Loanda → Luanda	152	8.48 S	13.14 E
Loande ≃	152	8.41 S	17.56 E
Loange (Luangue) ≃	152	4.17 S	20.02 E
Loango Buele	152	5.10 S	12.59 E
Loanhead	46	55.53 N	3.09 W
Loanja ≃	154	17.22 S	24.48 E
Loano	62	44.08 N	8.15 E
Loantaka Brook ≃	276	40.43 N	74.28 W
Lo Aranguiz	286e	33.23 S	70.40 W
Loay	116	9.36 N	124.01 E
Lob' ≃	82	56.29 N	35.51 E
Lobamba	158	26.27 S	31.12 E
Loban	24	65.44 N	45.25 E
Loban' ≃	80	56.58 N	51.12 E
Lobanovo	76	53.04 N	38.14 E
Lobanovskije Vyselki	82	54.18 N	38.58 E
Lo Barnechea	286e	33.21 S	70.31 W
Lobaski	80	54.38 N	45.09 E
Lobatos	234	22.49 N	103.24 W
Lobatse	156	25.11 S	25.40 E
Löbau	54	51.05 N	14.40 E
Lobau ≚	264b	48.10 N	16.32 E
Lobaye □[5]	152	4.00 N	18.30 E
Lobaye ≃	152	3.41 N	18.35 E
Lobbes	50	50.21 N	4.15 E
Lobbs Run ≃	279b	40.15 N	79.55 W
Lobdell Lake ⊜	216	42.48 N	83.48 W
Löbejün	54	51.38 N	11.53 E
Lobelville	194	35.46 N	87.47 W
Lo Benitez	286e	33.34 S	70.42 W
Lobenstein	54	50.26 N	11.38 E
Lobería	252	38.09 S	58.47 W
Lo Bernales	286e	33.34 S	70.34 W
Löberöd	41	55.47 N	13.30 E
Lobethal	168b	34.54 S	138.52 E
Łobez	30	53.39 N	15.36 E
Lobito	152	12.20 S	13.34 E
Lobitos	246	4.26 S	81.17 W
Lobitos Creek ≃	282	37.22 N	122.24 W
Lobkoviči	76	53.50 N	31.45 E
Lobn'a	82	56.01 N	37.30 E
Löbnitz, Dtsch.	54	51.35 N	12.28 E
Löbnitz, Dtsch.	54	54.17 N	12.43 E
Lobo, Indon.	164	3.45 S	134.05 E
Lobo, Pil.	116	13.39 N	121.13 E
Lobo ≃	150	6.02 N	6.47 W
Loboko	152	0.45 S	16.38 E
Lobos	258	35.11 S	59.06 W
Lobos, Cay I	238	22.24 N	77.32 W
Lobos, Isla I	232	27.20 N	110.36 W
Lobos, Isla de I, Esp.	148	28.45 N	13.49 W
Lobos, Isla de I, Méx.	234	21.27 N	97.13 W
Lobos, Laguna de ⊜	258	35.17 S	59.07 W
Lobos, Point ›	226	37.47 N	122.31 W
Lobos, Punta ›	248	21.01 S	70.11 W
Lobos de Afuera, Islas II	248	6.57 S	80.42 W
Lobos de Tierra, Isla I	248	6.27 S	80.52 W
Lo Boza	286e	33.23 S	70.46 W
Lobskoje	24	62.45 N	35.16 E
Lobstädt	54	51.08 N	12.29 E
Löbtau ⊸[8]	54	51.03 N	13.42 E
Loburg	54	52.07 N	12.05 E
Lobva	86	59.12 N	60.30 E
Łobżenica	30	53.16 N	17.15 E
Locana	62	45.25 N	7.27 E
Locana, Val di V	62	45.25 N	7.27 E
Locarno	58	46.10 N	8.48 E
Lo Castillo, Aeropuerto ⊠	286e	33.23 S	70.36 W
Locate Triulzi	62	45.21 N	9.13 E
Loccum	52	52.27 N	9.08 E
Loceri	71	39.51 N	9.35 E
Loch	169	38.22 S	145.43 E
Lochaber ⊸[1]	46	56.57 N	5.06 W
Lochailort	46	56.53 N	5.40 W
Lochaline	46	56.32 N	5.47 W
Locharbriggs	44	55.06 N	3.35 W
Lochar Water ≃	44	54.59 N	3.27 W
Lochboisdale	46	57.09 N	7.19 W
Lochcarron	46	57.24 N	5.30 W
Lochdon	46	56.26 N	5.41 W
Lochearn	284b	39.21 N	76.43 W
Lochearnhead	46	56.23 N	4.17 W
Lochem	52	52.09 N	6.25 E
Loches	50	47.08 N	1.00 E
Lochgair	46	56.03 N	5.20 W
Loch Garman → Wexford	48	52.20 N	6.27 W
Lochgelly	46	56.08 N	3.19 W
Lochgilphead	46	56.03 N	5.26 W
Lochgoilhead	46	56.10 N	4.54 W
Lochiel	168b	33.56 S	138.10 E
Lochindorb ⊜	46	57.24 N	3.43 W
Lochino	265b	55.42 N	37.19 E
Lochinvar National Park ♠	154	15.55 S	27.15 E
Lochinver	46	58.09 N	5.15 W
Lochmaben	44	55.08 N	3.27 W
Lochmaddy	46	57.36 N	7.11 W
Lochnagar ∧	46	56.57 N	3.16 W
Lochovice	60	49.51 N	13.59 E
Lochranza	46	55.42 N	5.18 W
Loch Raven Dam ⊸[6]	284b	39.26 N	76.33 W
Loch Raven Reservoir ⊜[1]	208	39.27 N	76.34 W
Lochristi	50	51.06 N	3.50 E
Lochsa ≃	202	46.08 N	115.36 W
Loch Sheldrake	210	41.46 N	74.39 W
Loch Sport	166	38.03 S	147.36 E
Lochvica	78	50.22 N	33.16 E
Lochwinnoch	46	55.48 N	4.39 W
Lochy, Loch ⊜	46	56.57 N	4.53 W
Lock	166	33.34 S	135.46 E
Lock and Dam No. 20 ⊸[6], U.S.	219	40.09 N	91.30 W
Lock and Dam No. 21 ⊸[6], U.S.	219	39.54 N	91.26 W
Lock and Dam No. 24 ⊸[6], U.S.	219	39.22 N	90.55 W
Lock and Dam No. 25 ⊸[6], U.S.	219	39.01 N	90.41 W
Lock and Dam No. 22 ⊸[6], U.S.	219	39.39 N	91.16 W
Locke, Ca., U.S.	226	38.15 N	121.31 W
Locke, In., U.S.	216	41.28 N	86.00 W
Locke, N.Y., U.S.	210	42.39 N	76.25 W
Lockeford	226	38.10 N	121.09 W
Lockenhaus	61	47.24 N	16.25 E
Lockeport	186	43.42 N	65.07 W
Lockerbie	44	55.07 N	3.22 W
Lockesburg	194	33.58 N	94.10 W
Lockhart, Austl.	166	35.14 S	146.43 E
Lockhart, Fl., U.S.	220	28.37 N	81.26 W
Lockhart, Tx., U.S.	222	29.53 N	97.40 W
Lockhart River Aboriginal Reserve ⊸[4]	164	13.00 S	143.15 E
Lock Haven	210	41.08 N	77.26 W
Lockheed Aircraft Corporation ⊍[3], Ca., U.S.	280	34.12 N	118.22 W
Lockheed Aircraft Corporation ⊍[3], Ca., U.S.	282	37.25 N	122.02 W
Lockington	216	40.12 N	84.13 W
Lock Mountain ∧	214	40.25 N	78.18 W
Lockney	196	34.07 N	101.26 W
Löcknitz	54	53.27 N	14.12 E
Löcknitz ≃, Dtsch.	54	53.07 N	11.16 E
Löcknitz ≃, Dtsch.	264a	52.25 N	13.49 E
Lockport, Mb., Can.	184	50.05 N	96.56 W
Lockport, Il., U.S.	216	41.35 N	88.03 W
Lockport, La., U.S.	194	29.39 N	90.32 W
Lockport, N.Y., U.S.	210	43.10 N	78.41 W
Lockport Lock ⊸[5]	278	41.35 N	88.04 W
Locks Heath	42	50.52 N	1.15 W
Locksley Park	210	42.45 N	78.52 W
Lockvattnet ⊜	40	59.03 N	17.05 E
Lockview	279b	40.10 N	79.55 W
Lockwood, Ca., U.S.	226	35.56 N	121.05 W
Lockwood, Mo., U.S.	194	37.23 N	93.57 W
Lockwood Corners	214	41.00 N	81.34 W
Lockyer Creek ≃	171a	27.25 S	152.36 E
Locminé	28	47.53 N	2.50 W
Loc Ninh	110	11.51 N	106.36 E
Loco, Bayou ≃	222	31.28 N	94.44 W
Locon	50	50.34 N	2.40 E
Locorotondo	68	40.45 N	17.20 E
Locri	68	38.14 N	16.16 E
Locri Epizefiri ⊥	68	38.12 N	16.13 E
Locroja	248	12.41 S	74.26 W
Locsin	116	13.09 N	123.43 E
Locumba	248	17.36 S	70.46 W
Locumba ≃	248	17.54 S	70.57 W
Locust	208	40.18 N	73.59 W
Locust Creek ≃	194	39.40 N	93.17 W
Locust Fork ≃	194	33.33 N	87.11 W
Locust Grove, N.Y., U.S.	276	40.48 N	73.30 W
Locust Grove, Ok., U.S.	196	36.12 N	95.10 W
Locust Lake State Park ♠	208	40.46 N	76.08 W
Locust Point ›	276	40.49 N	73.48 W
Locust Valley	210	40.53 N	73.36 W

Symbol	English	Deutsch	Español	Français	Português
≃	River	Fluß	Río	Rivière	Rio
≍	Canal	Kanal	Canal	Canal	Canal
⌊	Waterfall, Rapids	Wasserfall, Stromschnellen	Cascada, Rápidos	Chute d'eau, Rapides	Cascata, Rápidos
)(	Strait	Meeresstraße	Estrecho	Détroit	Estreito
⊂	Bay, Gulf	Bucht, Golf	Bahía, Golfo	Baie, Golfe	Baía, Golfo
⊜	Lake, Lakes	See, Seen	Lago, Lagos	Lac, Lacs	Lago, Lagos
≚	Swamp	Sumpf	Pantano	Marais	Pântano
⊓	Ice Features, Glacier	Eis- und Gletscherformen	Accidentes Glaciales	Formes glaciaires	Acidentes glaciares
⊤	Other Hydrographic Features	Andere Hydrographische Objekte	Otros Elementos Hidrográficos	Autres données hydrographiques	Outros acidentes hidrográficos
✢	Submarine Features	Untermeerische Objekte	Accidentes Submarinos	Formes de relief sous-marin	Acidentes submarinos
□	Political Unit	Politische Einheit	Unidad Politica	Entité politique	Unidade política
⊍	Cultural Institution	Kulturelle Institution	Institución Cultural	Institution culturelle	Instituição cultural
⊥	Historical Site	Historische Stätte	Sitio Histórico	Site historique	Sitio histórico
♠	Recreational Site	Erholungs- und Ferienort	Sitio de Recreo	Centre de loisirs	Area de Lazer
⊠	Airport	Flughafen	Aeropuerto	Aéroport	Aeroporto
■	Military Installation	Militäranlage	Instalación Militar	Installation militaire	Instalação militar
⊸	Miscellaneous	Verschiedenes	Misceláneo	Divers	Diversos

ENGLISH — Name, Page, Lat.°′, Long.°′
DEUTSCH — Name, Seite, Breite°′, Länge°′ E = Ost

Symbols in the index entries represent the broad categories identified in the key at the right. Symbols with superior numbers (⋏[1]) identify subcategories (see complete key on page I · 1).

Symbole im Register stellen die rechts im Schlüssel erklärten Kategorien dar. Symbole mit hochgestellten Ziffern (⋏[1]) bezeichnen Unterabteilungen einer Kategorie (vgl. vollständiger Schlüssel auf Seite I · 1).

Los símbolos incluídos en el texto del índice representan las grandes categorias identificadas con la clave a la derecha. Los símbolos con numeros en su parte superior (⋏[1]) identifican las subcategorías (véase la clave completa en la página I · 1).

Les symboles de l'index représentent les catégories indiquées dans la légende à droite. Les symboles suivis d'un indice (⋏[1]) représentent des sous-catégories (voir légende complète à la page I · 1).

Os símbolos incluídos no texto do índice representam as grandes categorias identificadas com a chave à direita. Os símbolos com números em sua parte superior (⋏[1]) identificam as subcategorias (veja-se a chave completa à página I · 1).

∧ Mountain	Berg	Montaña	Montagne	Montanha
⋏ Mountains	Gebirge	Montañas	Montagnes	Montanhas
)(Pass	Paß	Paso	Col	Passo
V Valley, Canyon	Tal, Cañon	Valle, Cañón	Vallée, Canyon	Vale, Canhão
≚ Plain	Ebene	Llano	Plaine	Planície
› Cape	Kap	Cabo	Cap	Cabo
I Island	Insel	Isla	Île	Ilha
II Islands	Inseln	Islas	Îles	Ilhas
⊥ Other Topographic Features	Andere Topographische Objekte	Otros Elementos Topográficos	Autres données topographiques	Outros acidentes topográficos

ESPAÑOL Nombre	Página	Lat.°′	Long.°′ W = Oeste
Lord Howe Seamounts ≈³	14	28.00 S	159.00 E
Lord Mayor Bay c	176	69.44 N	92.00 W
Lordsburg	200	32.21 N	108.42 W
Lord's Cricket Ground ♦	260	51.32 N	0.10 W
Lordstown	214	41.09 N	80.53 W
Lords Valley	210	41.23 N	75.04 W
Loreauville	194	30.03 N	91.44 W
Loreley ♦	56	50.08 N	7.44 E
Lorena, Bra.	256	22.44 S	45.08 W
Lorena, Tx., U.S.	222	31.23 N	97.13 W
Lorengau	164	2.00 S	147.15 E
Lorentz ≈	164	5.23 S	138.04 E
Lorentzen	56	48.57 N	7.10 E
Lorenzago di Cadore	64	46.29 N	12.28 E
Lorenzo	196	33.40 N	101.32 W
Lorenzo Geyres (Queguay)	252	32.05 S	57.55 W
Loreo	64	45.04 N	12.11 E
Lorestān □⁴	128	33.30 N	48.30 E
Loreto, Arg.	252	27.46 S	57.17 W
Loreto, Bol.	248	15.13 S	64.40 W
Loreto, Bra.	250	7.05 S	45.09 W
Loreto, It.	66	43.26 N	13.36 E
Loreto, Méx.	232	26.01 N	111.21 W
Loreto, Méx.	234	22.16 N	101.58 W
Loreto, Para.	252	23.16 S	57.11 W
Loreto, Pil.	116	8.12 N	125.45 E
Loreto, Pil.	116	10.21 N	125.34 E
Loreto □	246	3.00 S	75.00 W
Loreto Aprutino	66	42.26 N	13.59 E
Loreto Mocagua	246	3.48 S	70.15 W
Lorette, Mb., Can.	184	49.44 N	96.52 W
Lorette, Fr.	62	45.31 N	4.35 E
Loretteville	206	46.51 N	71.21 W
Loretto, Ky., U.S.	194	37.38 N	85.24 W
Loretto, Pa., U.S.	214	40.30 N	78.37 W
Loretto, Tn., U.S.	194	35.04 N	87.26 W
Loretto — Loreto	66	43.26 N	13.36 E
Lorgues	62	43.29 N	6.22 E
Lorian Swamp ⊞	154	0.40 N	39.35 E
Lorica	246	9.14 N	75.49 W
Lorida	220	27.26 N	81.15 W
Lorient	32	47.45 N	3.22 W
L'Original	206	45.37 N	74.42 W
Lorimer Park ♦	285	40.06 N	75.05 W
Lorimor	194	41.07 N	94.03 W
Loring, Aeródromo de □	266a	40.22 N	3.47 W
Loring Air Force Base ♦	186	46.57 N	67.54 W
Lorino	180	65.30 N	171.43 W
Loriol-sur-Drôme	62	44.45 N	4.49 E
Loris	192	34.03 N	78.53 W
Lorman	194	31.49 N	91.03 W
L'Orme	261	48.39 N	1.41 E
Lormes	50	47.17 N	3.49 E
Lorn, Firth of c¹	46	56.20 N	5.45 W
Lorna Glen	162	26.14 S	121.33 E
Lorne, Austl.	169	38.33 S	143.59 E
Lorne, N.B., Can.	186	47.53 N	66.08 W
Loro Ciuffenna	66	43.35 N	11.38 E
Loronyo	154	4.39 N	32.38 E
Lorquin	58	48.40 N	7.00 E
Lörrach	58	47.37 N	7.40 E
Lorraine □⁹	32	49.00 N	6.00 E
Lorrez-le-Bocage	50	48.14 N	2.54 E
Lorris	50	47.53 N	2.31 E
Lorsch	56	49.39 N	8.34 E
Lorsica	64	44.26 N	9.16 E
Lorup	52	52.55 N	7.38 E
Lorze ≈	58	47.15 N	8.25 E
Los	26	61.44 N	15.10 E
Los, Îles de �II	150	9.30 N	13.48 W
Losa, Nuraghe ⊥	71	40.07 N	8.46 E
Losada ≈	246	2.12 N	73.55 W
Los Aguacates	286c	10.35 N	66.48 W
Los Alamitos	280	33.48 N	118.04 W
Los Alamitos Armed Forces Reserve Center ♦	280	33.47 N	118.03 W
Los Alamitos Race Course ♦	280	33.48 N	118.03 W
Los Alamos, Ca., U.S.	204	34.44 N	120.16 W
Los Alamos, N.M., U.S.	200	35.53 N	106.19 W
Las Aldamas	232	26.03 N	99.11 W
Los Alerces, Parque Nacional ♦	254	42.50 S	71.52 W
Los Altos, Méx.	196	26.14 N	98.28 W
Los Altos, Ca., U.S.	226	37.23 N	122.06 W
Los Altos Hills	226	37.22 N	122.08 W
Los Amates, Guat.	238	15.16 N	89.06 W
Los Amates, Méx.	234	18.08 N	102.15 W
Los Americanos, Barra ⊞	232	24.50 N	97.35 W
Los Andes	252	32.50 S	70.37 W
Los Ángeles, Chile	252	37.28 S	72.21 W
Los Ángeles, Ca., U.S.	228	34.03 N	118.14 W
Los Ángeles, Ca., U.S.	280	34.03 N	118.14 W
Los Ángeles □⁶	228	34.03 N	118.14 W
Los Ángeles Aqueducto ≈¹	204	35.22 N	118.05 W
Los Angeles Coliseum and Sports Arena ♦	280	34.01 N	118.17 W
Los Angeles Convention Center ♦	280	34.03 N	118.17 W
Los Angeles County Fairgrounds ♦	280	34.05 N	117.46 W
Los Angeles County Museum of Art ✸	280	34.05 N	118.22 W
Los Angeles Harbor c	280	33.42 N	118.16 W
Los Angeles International Airport ⌖	228	33.56 N	118.24 W
Los Antiguos	254	46.33 S	71.37 W
Losantville	218	40.01 N	85.10 W
Losap I¹	14	6.54 N	152.44 E
Los Arabos	240p	22.44 N	80.43 W
Losarang	115a	6.24 S	108.10 E
Los Aros	234	22.46 N	102.57 W
Los Banos	226	37.03 N	120.50 W
Los Banos Creek ≈	226	37.20 N	120.57 W
Los Banos Creek, North Fork ≈	226	36.57 N	121.07 W
Los Banos Creek, South Fork ≈	226	36.57 N	121.07 W
Los Banos Reservoir ⊜¹	226	36.59 N	120.57 W
Los Berros	252	31.56 S	68.39 W
Los Blancos	252	23.35 S	62.36 W
Los Bolones, Cerro ∧, Méx.	232	16.50 N	92.38 W
Los Bolones, Cerro ∧, Méx.	196	16.39 N	92.34 W
Los Cardales	258	34.20 S	58.59 W
Los Cerrillos, Arg.	252	31.57 S	65.28 W
Los Cerrillos, Ur.	258	34.37 S	56.22 W
Los Cerrillos, Aeropuerto ⌖	286e	33.30 S	70.43 W
Los Cerritos Center ✸	280	33.52 N	118.05 W
Los Chacos	248	14.33 S	62.11 W
Löschenrod	56	50.30 N	9.41 E
Los Chiles	236	11.02 N	84.43 W
Los Conquistadores	252	30.34 S	58.28 W
Los Coronados, Islas II	204	32.25 N	117.15 W
Los Coyotes Indian Reservation ♦	204	33.20 N	116.35 W
Los Cuatro Álamos	286e	33.32 S	70.44 W

FRANÇAIS Nom	Page	Lat.°′	Long.°′ W = Ouest
Los Dos Caminos	286c	10.31 N	66.50 W
Los Ebanos	196	26.14 N	98.34 W
Loseley House ⊥	260	51.13 N	0.36 W
Los Esclavos ≈	236	13.50 N	90.20 W
Losevo	78	50.40 N	40.02 E
Los Flamencos, Laguna ⊜	258	35.36 S	58.42 W
Los Frailes, Picacho ∧	234	23.53 N	106.03 W
Los Frentones	252	26.25 S	61.25 W
Los Fresnos	196	26.04 N	97.29 W
Los Garzas	196	26.23 N	99.46 W
Los Gatos	226	37.13 N	121.58 W
Los Gatos Creek ≈, Ca., U.S.	226	36.13 N	120.08 W
Los Gatos Creek ≈, Ca., U.S.	226	37.20 N	121.54 W
Los Glaciares, Parque Nacional ♦	254	49.52 S	73.05 W
Los Guerras	196	26.25 N	99.05 W
Loshan — Leshan	107	29.34 N	103.45 E
Losheim	56	49.30 N	6.44 E
Los Hermanos, Islas II	246	11.45 N	64.25 W
Los Herreras	196	25.55 N	99.24 W
Los Huacales, Cerro ∧	234	22.19 N	101.34 W
Losi	30	52.14 N	22.43 E
Łosice	30	52.14 N	22.43 E
Los Idolos, Parque Arqueológico de ♦	246	1.55 N	76.10 W
Loší , Póln I	36	44.36 N	14.24 E
Losinoborskaja	86	58.27 N	89.28 E
Losino-Petrovskij	82	55.52 N	38.12 E
Los Jazmines, Presa ⊜	286a	19.25 N	99.16 W
Los Juríes	252	28.28 S	62.06 W
Loškar'ovka	78	47.57 N	34.12 E
Loskopdam ⊜¹	156	25.23 S	29.20 E
Loskop Dam Game Reserve ♦	156	25.23 S	29.20 E
Los Lagos	254	39.51 S	72.50 W
Los Lagos □⁴	254	41.45 S	73.00 W
Los Llanos	200m	10.40 N	66.24 W
Los Llanos [de Aridane]	148	28.39 N	17.54 W
Los Menucos	254	40.50 S	68.08 W
Los Micos, Laguna de c	236	15.55 N	87.36 W
Los'mino	76	55.04 N	34.24 E
Los Mochis	232	25.45 N	108.57 W
Los Molinos	204	40.01 N	122.05 W
Los Muermos	254	41.24 S	73.29 W
Los Naranjos	286c	10.27 N	66.48 W
Los Navalmorales	34	39.43 N	4.38 W
Los Nietos	280	33.58 N	118.04 W
Los Nogales	234	36.00 N	99.43 W
Losolava	175f	14.11 S	167.34 E
Los Olmos Creek ≈, Tx., U.S.	196	27.20 N	97.40 W
Los Olmos Creek ≈, Tx., U.S.	196	26.21 N	98.48 W
Los Osos	204	35.19 N	120.50 W
Los Oyameles	234	19.43 N	97.32 W
Los Padillas	200	34.58 N	106.41 W
Los Palacios, Arg.	252	29.22 S	68.11 W
Los Palacios, Cuba	240p	22.35 N	83.15 W
Los Palacios y Villafranca	34	37.10 N	5.56 W
Los Perros, Arroyo ≈	234	34.37 S	58.46 W
Los Pinos ≈	286b	23.04 N	82.23 W
Los Pinos ≈	200	36.56 N	107.36 W
Los Placeres del Oro	234	18.13 N	100.54 W
Los Polvorines	288	34.30 S	58.41 W
Los Quillayes	286e	33.34 S	70.37 W
Los Quiriquinchos	252	33.22 S	61.43 W
Los Ramones	240m	18.11 N	66.50 W
Los Ramones	196	25.42 N	99.37 W
Los Remedios ≈	286a	19.31 N	99.05 W
Los Reyes de Salgado	234	19.35 N	102.29 W
Los Reyes la Paz	286a	19.21 N	98.58 W
Los Ríos □⁴	246	1.30 S	79.25 W
Los Rodríguez	232	27.11 N	101.01 W
Los Roques, Islas II	246	11.50 N	66.45 W
Lossa ≈	54	51.13 N	11.25 E
Lossa ≈	54	51.18 N	11.10 E
Los Santos □⁴	236	7.55 N	80.25 W
Los Santos de Maimona	34	38.27 N	6.23 W
Los Sauces	252	37.58 S	72.50 W
Lossburg	58	48.25 N	8.27 E
Lössel	263	51.21 N	7.39 E
Losser	52	52.15 N	7.00 E
Los Serranos	286	23.59 N	117.42 W
Lossiemouth	46	57.43 N	3.18 W
Lössnitz	54	50.37 N	12.43 E
Lost ≈, In., U.S.	218	38.33 N	86.49 W
Lost ≈, Mn., U.S.	188	47.51 N	96.02 W
Lost ≈, W.V., U.S.	188	41.09 N	89.04 W
Lostant	218	41.09 N	89.04 W
Los Taques	246	11.50 N	70.16 W
Lost Bridge State Recreation Area ♦	216	40.45 N	85.37 W
Lost Creek ≈, Ar., U.S.	194	33.38 N	87.14 W
Lost Creek ≈, Oh., U.S.	194	34.10 N	92.31 W
Lost Creek ≈, Ut., U.S.	200	41.04 N	111.32 W
Lost Creek ≈, Wy., U.S.	200	42.01 N	108.11 W
Lost Draw V	196	32.58 N	102.02 W
Lost Telares	252	28.59 S	63.26 W
Lost Trail Pass)(	202	45.41 N	113.57 W
Lostwithiel	42	50.25 N	4.40 W
Losuia	164	8.32 S	151.04 E
Los Vilos	252	31.59 S	71.31 W
Los Yébenes	34	39.34 N	3.52 W
Lot □⁵	32	44.35 N	1.40 E
Lot ≈	32	44.18 N	0.20 E
Lotagipi Swamp (Lotikipi Plain) ≈	144	4.36 N	34.55 E
Lotak	112	0.11 S	115.54 E
Lotbinière □¹¹	206	46.30 N	71.40 W
Lotela, Lake ⊜	220	27.34 N	81.29 W
Loteni	26	60.49 N	11.19 E

FRANÇAIS Nom (cont.)	Page	Lat.°′	Long.°′
Lot-et-Garonne □⁵	32	44.20 N	0.20 E
Lotfābād	128	37.32 N	59.20 E
Lothair, S. Afr.	156	26.26 S	30.27 E
Lothair, Ky., U.S.	192	37.14 N	83.10 W
Lothian □⁴	46	55.55 N	3.05 W
Lothringen — Lorraine □⁹	32	49.00 N	6.00 E
Lotikipi Plain (Lotagipi Swamp) ≈	144	4.36 N	34.55 E
Loto ≈	152	2.49 S	22.29 E
Loto ≈	152	1.55 S	22.09 E
Lotofaga	175a	13.59 S	171.50 W
Lotoi ≈	152	1.35 S	18.30 E
Lotorp	40	58.44 N	15.50 E
Lotošino	76	56.14 N	35.38 E
Lotrului, Munții ∧	38	45.30 N	23.52 E
Lotsane ≈	156	22.41 S	28.11 E
Lötschberg Tunnel ⊽⁵	58	46.25 N	7.45 E
Lötschental V	58	46.25 N	7.50 E
Lotseninsel I	41	54.40 N	10.01 E
Lott	222	31.12 N	97.02 W
Lotta ≈	24	68.36 N	31.06 E
Lottaville	278	41.31 N	87.22 W
Lottinghausen ≈⁸	263	51.27 N	7.27 E
Lottrup	208	37.57 N	76.31 W
Lotts Creek ≈	192	32.09 N	81.47 W
Lottsford Branch ≈	284c	38.55 N	76.49 W
Lottstetten	58	47.38 N	8.34 E
Lotuke, Jabal ∧	154	4.07 N	33.48 E
Lotung	100	24.41 N	121.46 E
Lotzorai	71	39.58 N	9.39 E
Louang Namtha	110	20.57 N	101.25 E
Louangphrabang	110	19.52 N	102.08 E
L'Ouarsenis, Massif ∧	34	35.40 N	1.50 E
Loubaresse ≈	62	44.36 N	4.03 E
Loube, Montagne de la ∧	62	43.22 N	5.59 E
Loubetsi ≈	152	3.12 S	12.10 E
Louchi	26	66.04 N	33.00 E
Loučeň	60	49.22 N	15.07 E
Loučná ∧	54	50.39 N	13.37 E
Loude	96	35.54 N	117.18 E
Loudéac	32	48.10 N	2.45 W
Louden Cove c	276	41.05 N	73.43 W
Loudes	62	45.05 N	3.45 E
Loudima Poste	152	4.07 S	13.04 E
Loudon	192	35.43 N	84.20 W
Loudonville, N.Y., U.S.	210	42.42 N	73.45 W
Loudonville, Oh., U.S.	214	40.38 N	82.14 W
Loudoun □⁶	208	39.05 N	77.30 W
Loudun	32	47.01 N	0.05 E
Loué	48	48.00 N	0.09 W
Loue ≈	58	47.01 N	5.27 E
Louga	150	15.37 N	16.13 W
Louga □⁴	150	15.25 N	15.30 W
Louge ≈	252	36.57 S	61.40 W
Louggueré ≈	150	15.35 N	14.47 W
Loughborough	42	52.47 N	1.11 W
Loughborough Lake ⊜	212	44.23 N	76.30 W
Loughermore ∧²	48	54.59 N	7.05 W
Loughman	220	28.14 N	81.34 W
Loughor ≈	42	51.40 N	4.04 W
Loughor ≈	42	51.40 N	4.04 W
Loughrea	48	53.12 N	8.34 W
Loughros More Bay c	48	54.47 N	8.35 W
Loughton	260	51.39 N	0.03 E
Louhans	58	46.38 N	5.13 E
Louin	194	32.04 N	89.15 W
Louisa, Ky., U.S.	192	38.06 N	82.36 W
Louisa, Va., U.S.	208	38.01 N	78.00 W
Louisa, Lake ⊜, On., Can.	212	45.28 N	78.30 W
Louisa, Lake ⊜, Fl., U.S.	220	28.29 N	81.44 W
Louisa Bull Indian Reserve ♦⁴	182	52.53 N	113.31 W
Louisburg, Ks., U.S.	198	38.37 N	94.40 W
Louisburg, N.C., U.S.	192	36.05 N	78.18 W
Louisburgh	48	53.46 N	9.51 W
Louisdale	186	45.36 N	61.04 W
Louise, Ms., U.S.	194	32.58 N	90.35 W
Louise, Tx., U.S.	222	29.06 N	96.25 W
Louise, Lac ⊜, P.Q., Can.	206	45.46 N	74.25 W
Louise, Lac ⊜, P.Q., Can.	206	45.43 N	71.25 W
Louise, Lake ⊜	180	62.20 N	146.30 W
Louise Island I	182	52.58 N	131.50 W
Louiseville	206	46.15 N	72.57 W
Louis Gentil — Youssoufia	148	32.16 N	8.33 W
Louisiade Archipelago II	160	11.00 S	153.00 E
Louisiana □³, U.S.	219	39.26 N	91.03 W
Louisiana □³, U.S.	178	31.15 N	92.15 W
Louisiana □³, U.S.	41	55.58 N	12.33 E
Louis Trichardt	164	2.25 S	147.20 E
Louisvale	158	28.39 S	21.12 E
Louisville, On., Can.	214	42.28 N	82.07 W
Louisville, Al., U.S.	194	31.47 N	85.33 W
Louisville, Ga., U.S.	192	33.00 N	82.24 W
Louisville, Il., U.S.	194	38.46 N	88.30 W
Louisville, Ky., U.S.	218	38.15 N	85.45 W
Louisville, Ms., U.S.	194	33.07 N	89.03 W
Louisville, Ne., U.S.	198	41.00 N	96.09 W
Louisville, Oh., U.S.	214	40.50 N	81.15 W
Louisville Seamount ≈³	14	31.15 S	172.15 W
Louis-XIV, Pointe ⟩	176	54.37 N	79.45 W
Loukam	98	42.04 N	116.02 E
Loukkos, Oued ≈	34	35.12 N	6.09 W
Loukoua ≈	152	0.39 S	15.08 E
Loulé	34	37.08 N	8.02 W
Loulouni	150	11.08 N	5.36 W
Loumou	273b	4.05 S	15.09 E
Lount Lake ⊜	184	50.10 N	94.20 W
Loup ≈, Fr.	62	43.38 N	7.09 E
Loup ≈, Ne., U.S.	198	41.24 N	97.19 W
Loup, Gorge du V	62	43.50 N	6.59 E
Loup, Rivière du ≈	206	46.13 N	72.55 W
Loup City	198	41.16 N	98.57 W
Loups Marins, Lacs des ⊜	176	56.30 N	73.45 W
Lourches	50	50.19 N	3.21 E
Lourdes, Nf., Can.	186	48.39 N	59.00 W
Lourdes, Fr.	32	43.06 N	0.03 W
Lourenço	250	2.30 N	51.40 W
Lourenço Marques — Maputo	156	25.58 S	32.35 E
Loures	34	38.50 N	9.10 W
Lourical	34	40.07 N	8.45 W
Lourinhã	34	39.14 N	9.19 W
Lourmarin	62	43.46 N	5.22 E
Louny	60	50.20 N	13.48 E
Lousã, Port.	34	40.07 N	8.15 W
Lousã, Port.	266c	38.53 N	9.12 W
Lousada	34	41.17 N	8.17 W
Louth, Austl.	166	30.32 S	145.07 E
Louth, Ire.	48	53.57 N	6.33 W
Louth, Ire.	48	53.55 N	6.53 W
Louth, Eng., U.K.	44	53.22 N	0.01 W
Louth □⁶	48	53.55 N	6.30 W
Louth Bay c	166	34.34 S	136.02 E
Louti, Mayo ≈	146	9.38 N	13.56 E
Loutit Bay c	169	38.33 S	144.00 E
Loutra Aidhipsoú	38	38.51 N	23.02 E
Loutre ≈	219	38.42 N	91.25 W
Loutre, Bayou de ≈	194	32.41 N	92.08 W
Loutrópirgos	267c	38.02 N	23.28 E
Louvain — Leuven	56	50.53 N	4.42 E
Louveciennes	261	48.52 N	2.07 E
Louveigné	56	50.32 N	5.42 E
Louveira	256	23.04 S	46.58 W
Louviers, Fr.	50	49.13 N	1.10 E
Louviers, Co., U.S.	200	39.28 N	105.00 W
Louvre ✸	261	48.52 N	2.20 E
Louvres	50	49.02 N	2.30 E
Louvroil	50	50.16 N	3.58 E
Louwsburg	158	27.37 S	31.07 E
Lou Yaeger, Lake ⊜¹	219	39.10 N	89.37 W
Lövänger	26	64.22 N	21.18 E
Lovászi	61	46.33 N	16.34 E
Lovat' ≈	76	58.14 N	31.28 E
Lovcy	82	55.00 N	39.15 E
Love	184	53.29 N	104.09 W
Loveč	38	43.08 N	24.43 E
Love Clough	262	53.44 N	2.17 W
Lovedale	279b	40.17 N	79.52 W
Lovejoy	219	38.39 N	90.10 W
Lovelady	222	31.08 N	95.27 W
Loveland, Co., U.S.	200	40.23 N	105.05 W
Loveland, Oh., U.S.	218	39.16 N	84.16 W
Lovell	202	44.50 N	108.23 W
Lovell Island I	283	42.20 N	70.56 W
Lovelock	204	40.10 N	118.28 W
Lovely	192	37.49 N	82.24 W
Love Point ⟩	208	39.02 N	76.18 W
Lovere	64	45.49 N	10.04 E
Lovering, Lac ⊜	206	45.10 N	72.09 W
Lovero	64	46.14 N	10.14 E
Loves Green	260	51.43 N	0.24 E
Loves Park	216	42.19 N	89.03 W
Lovisa — Loviisa	26	60.27 N	26.14 E
Lovilia	190	41.08 N	92.54 W
Loving, N.M., U.S.	196	32.17 N	104.05 W
Loving, Tx., U.S.	196	33.16 N	98.31 W
Lovington, Il., U.S.	219	39.42 N	88.37 W
Lovington, N.M., U.S.	196	32.56 N	103.20 W
Lovisa (Loviisa)	26	60.27 N	26.14 E
Lovo	61	47.30 N	16.47 E
Lovoi ≈	152	8.30 N	17.50 E
Lovoi ≈	154	8.14 S	26.39 E
Lovosice	54	50.31 N	14.03 E
Lovozero, Ross.	24	68.00 N	35.00 E
Lovozero, Ross.	24	65.00 N	29.50 E
Lovozero, ozero ⊜	24	67.54 N	35.12 E
Lovrenc	61	46.32 N	15.23 E
Lövstabruk	40	60.24 N	17.53 E
Lövstabukten c	40	60.35 N	17.45 E
Lövstad slott ⊥	40	58.33 N	16.02 E
Lövua ≈	152	11.36 S	23.53 E
Lóvua, (Lóvua)	152	7.20 S	20.16 E
Lóvua (Lóvua) ≈	152	6.07 S	20.35 E
Low	188	45.78 N	75.57 W
Low, Cape ⟩	176	63.07 N	85.18 W
Lowa	154	1.24 S	25.51 E
Lowa ≈	154	1.24 S	25.51 E
Lowāda	126	22.27 N	87.37 E
Lowban — Lowa'	76	51.34 N	31.28 E
Lowden	190	41.51 N	90.55 W
Lowder Brook ≈	283	43.14 N	71.11 W
Lowell, Ar., U.S.	194	36.15 N	94.07 W
Lowell, In., U.S.	216	41.17 N	87.25 W
Lowell, Ma., U.S.	207	42.38 N	71.19 W
Lowell, Mi., U.S.	216	42.56 N	85.20 W
Lowell, Or., U.S.	202	43.55 N	122.46 W
Lowell, Lake ⊜	202	43.33 N	116.40 W
Lowell, University of ✸	283	42.39 N	71.20 W
Lowell-Dracut State Forest ♦	283	42.40 N	71.22 W
Lowelli	140	5.59 N	33.45 E
Lowellville	214	41.02 N	80.32 W
Löwen ≈	158	26.51 S	18.17 E
Löwenberg	54	52.54 N	13.08 E
Löwenbruch	264a	52.18 N	13.19 E
Löwen — Leuven	56	50.53 N	4.42 E
Löwenstein	56	49.06 N	9.22 E
Lowe Pond ⊜	283	42.41 N	70.59 W
Lower Arrow Lake ⊜	285	39.51 N	74.48 W
Lower Arrow Lake ⊜	182	49.40 N	118.08 W
Lower Bay c	208	40.33 N	74.02 W
Lower Bear River Reservoir ⊜¹	226	38.33 N	120.14 W
Lower Bershire Valley	276	40.54 N	74.37 W
Lower Beverley Lake ⊜	212	44.35 N	76.09 W
Lower Broughton ≈⁸	262	53.29 N	2.15 W
Lower Brule Indian Reservation ♦⁴	198	44.05 N	99.44 W
Lower Buckhorn Lake ⊜	212	44.33 N	78.17 W
Lower Burrell	214	40.35 N	79.45 W
Lower California — Baja California	232	28.00 N	113.30 W
Lower Chittering	168a	31.34 S	116.06 E
Lower Crystal Springs Reservoir ⊜¹	226	37.32 N	122.22 W
Lower Darwen	262	53.43 N	2.28 W
Lower Egypt □⁹	140	30.00 N	31.00 E
Lower Eltham Park ♦	274b	37.45 S	145.09 E
Lower Elwha Indian Reservation ♦	224	48.09 N	123.33 W
Lower Fort Garry National Historic Park ♦	184	50.07 N	96.55 W
Lower Ganga Canal ⟿	124	26.27 N	80.17 E
Lower Gap ≈	212	44.04 N	76.35 W
Lower Halstow	260	51.22 N	0.40 E
Lower Hay Lake ⊜	212	45.25 N	78.13 W
Lower Higham	260	51.26 N	0.28 E
Lower Hutt	172	41.13 S	174.55 E
Lower Kalskag	180	61.31 N	160.22 W
Lower Keechi Creek ≈	222	31.29 N	95.46 W
Lower Klamath Lake ⊜	204	41.55 N	121.42 W
Lower Lake	204	38.55 N	122.37 W
Lower Lake ⊜	204	41.15 N	120.02 W
Lower Loteni	158	29.32 S	29.36 E
Lower Manitou Lake ⊜	184	49.15 N	93.00 W
Lower Matecumbe Key I	220	24.51 N	80.43 W
Lower Merion	285	40.01 N	75.14 W
Lower Mystic Lake ⊜	283	42.26 N	71.09 W
Lower Nazeing	260	51.44 N	0.01 E
Lower Otay Lake ⊜	226	32.37 N	116.55 W
Lower Paia	229a	20.55 N	156.23 W
Lower Paudash Lake ⊜	212	44.58 N	78.01 W

PORTUGUÊS Nome	Página	Lat.°′	Long.°′ W = Oeste
Loutang	106	31.26 N	121.12 E
Loutézou, Île de I	273b	4.22 S	15.10 E
Louth, Austl.	166	30.32 S	145.07 E
Louth, Ire.	44	53.57 N	6.33 W
Louth, Ire.	44	53.55 N	6.53 W
Louth, Eng., U.K.	44	53.22 N	0.01 W
Louth □⁶	48	53.55 N	6.30 W
Louth Bay c	166	34.34 S	136.02 E
Louti, Mayo ≈	146	9.38 N	13.56 E
Loutit Bay c	169	38.33 S	144.00 E
Loutra Aidhipsoú	38	38.51 N	23.02 E
Loutre ≈	219	38.42 N	91.25 W
Loutre, Bayou de ≈	194	32.41 N	92.08 W
Loutrópirgos	267c	38.02 N	23.28 E
Louvain — Leuven	56	50.53 N	4.42 E
Louveciennes	261	48.52 N	2.07 E
Louveigné	56	50.32 N	5.42 E
Louveira	256	23.04 S	46.58 W
Louviers, Fr.	50	49.13 N	1.10 E
Louviers, Co., U.S.	200	39.28 N	105.00 W
Louvre ✸	261	48.52 N	2.20 E
Louvres	50	49.02 N	2.30 E
Louvroil	50	50.16 N	3.58 E
Louwsburg	158	27.37 S	31.07 E
Lou Yaeger, Lake ⊜¹	219	39.10 N	89.37 W
Lövänger	26	64.22 N	21.18 E
Lovászi	61	46.33 N	16.34 E
Lovat' ≈	76	58.14 N	31.28 E
Lovcy	82	55.00 N	39.15 E
Love	184	53.29 N	104.09 W
Loveč	38	43.08 N	24.43 E
Lowick	44	55.38 N	2.00 W
Łowicz	30	52.07 N	19.56 E
Lowman	210	42.02 N	76.54 W
Lowmoor	192	37.47 N	79.53 W
Lowood	171	27.28 S	152.35 E
Lowra (Pishīn Lora) ≈	120	29.09 N	64.55 E
Lowries Run ≈	279b	40.30 N	80.05 W
Low Rocky Point ⟩	166	43.00 S	145.30 E
Lowry Air Force Base ♦	198	39.43 N	104.53 W
Lowry City	44	38.08 N	93.43 W
Lowther, Me., U.S.	188	54.39 N	2.44 W
Lowther Hills ∧²	44	55.19 N	3.38 W
Lowton	262	53.28 N	2.35 W
Lowton Common	262	53.29 N	2.33 W
Lowville, N.Y., U.S.	212	43.47 N	75.29 W
Lowville, Pa., U.S.	214	40.21 N	79.49 W
Loxahatchee	220	26.49 N	80.13 W
Loxley	194	30.37 N	87.45 W
Loxstedt	52	53.28 N	8.38 E
Loxton	52	52.03 N	8.08 E
Loxton, Austl.	166	34.27 S	140.35 E
Loxton, S. Afr.	158	31.30 S	22.22 E
Loyal	190	44.44 N	90.29 W
Loyal, Loch ⊜	46	58.23 N	4.22 W
Loyalhanna	214	40.19 N	79.21 W
Loyalhanna Creek ≈	214	40.25 N	79.28 W
Loyalsock Creek ≈	210	41.14 N	76.56 W
Loyalton	204	39.40 N	120.14 W
Loyalty Islands — Loyauté, Îles II	175f	21.00 S	167.00 E
Loyang	271c	1.22 N	103.58 E
Loyang — Luoyang	102	34.41 N	112.28 E
Loyauté, Îles (Loyalty Islands) II	175f	21.00 S	167.00 E
Loyne, Loch ⊜	46	57.06 N	5.00 W
Loyola College ✸²	284b	39.21 N	76.37 W
Loyola University ✸², Ca., U.S.	280	33.58 N	118.25 W
Loyola University ✸², Il., U.S.	288	42.00 N	87.39 W
Loysburg	214	40.10 N	78.23 W
Loysville	208	40.22 N	77.21 W
Lozano	258	34.51 S	59.03 W
Lozère □⁵	32	44.30 N	3.30 E
Lozère, Mont ∧	32	44.30 N	3.46 E
Loznica	38	44.32 N	19.13 E
Loznikovo, Ross.	86	56.54 N	73.56 E
Loznoje, Ross.	78	49.22 N	44.17 E
Lozno-Aleksandrovka	78	49.50 N	38.44 E
Lozovaja, Kaz.	80	49.17 N	44.26 E
Lozovaja, Ukr.	78	53.17 N	77.45 E
Lozovaja, Ukr.	78	48.54 N	36.20 E
Lozovoje	78	49.18 N	27.18 E
Lozovoje, Ukr.	78	49.37 N	37.36 E
Lozovskij	83	48.53 N	44.54 E
Lozoyuela	34	40.55 N	3.37 W
Lozzo di Cadore	64	46.31 N	12.28 E
Lu	64	45.00 N	8.29 E
Lua ≈	152	2.46 N	18.26 E
Luabo	156	18.30 S	36.10 E
Luachimo ≈	152	2.46 S	18.19 E
Luaco	152	3.23 S	20.59 E
Luala-sibuha	110	0.31 S	98.28 E
Lualaba ≈	154	0.26 N	25.20 E
Luali	152	5.06 S	12.29 E
Luampa	152	15.02 S	24.24 E
Luan ≈	100	39.26 N	119.12 E
Luan Balu	152	9.00 S	13.15 E
Luancheng, Zhg.	98	30.43 N	114.39 E
Luancheng, Zhg.	102	37.54 N	114.38 E
Luanco	34	43.37 N	5.47 W
Luanda	152	8.48 S	13.14 E
Luanda □⁴	152	9.00 S	13.15 E
Luando, Réserve do ♦	152	11.10 S	17.30 E
Luang, Khao ∧	110	8.31 N	99.47 E
Luang, Thale ⊜	110	7.30 N	100.15 E
Luang Chiang Dao, Doi ∧	110	19.23 N	98.54 E
Luanginga (Luanguinga) ≈	152	15.11 S	22.56 E
Luang Prabang — Louangphrabang	110	19.52 N	102.08 E
Luang Prabang Range ∧	110	18.30 N	101.15 E
Luanguinga (Luanginga) ≈	152	15.11 S	22.56 E
Luangwa (Aruângua) ≈	152	15.36 S	30.25 E
Luanhaizi	104	34.27 N	93.12 E
Luanping (Bencheng)	98	40.57 N	117.44 E
Luanping	98	39.32 N	114.18 E
Luanshya	154	13.08 S	28.24 E
Luán Toro	252	36.12 S	65.06 W
Luapula ≈	154	9.26 S	28.33 E
Luar, Danau ⊜	112	0.54 N	112.15 E
Luarca	34	43.33 N	6.32 W
Luashi	152	10.56 S	23.37 E
Luashi	152	10.41 S	22.55 E
Luassinga ≈	152	15.47 S	18.50 E
Luati	152	14.35 S	21.13 E
Luatira	152	12.52 S	17.14 E
Luau	152	10.42 S	22.12 E
Lua-Vindu ≈	152	3.27 N	8.33 E
Lubaantun ⊥	232	16.17 N	88.58 W
Lubaczów	30	50.10 N	23.07 E
Lubalo	152	9.12 S	19.16 E
Lubān ≈	152	7.22 S	19.20 E
Lubamiti	152	2.29 S	17.47 E
Luban', Bela.	76	52.37 N	29.08 E
Luban', Bela.	76	52.48 N	27.59 E
Luban', Ross.	76	59.21 N	31.13 E
Lubānas ezers ⊜	76	56.54 N	26.43 E
Lubāns ⊜	76	56.46 N	26.53 E
Lubang Island I	116	13.52 N	120.07 E
Lubang Islands II	116	13.45 N	120.15 E
Lubango	152	14.55 S	13.30 E
Lubanowo	54	53.09 N	14.36 E
Lubansenshi ≈	154	11.21 S	30.35 E
Lub'any	80	56.02 N	51.24 E
Lubao	100	23.22 N	112.55 E
Lübars	264a	52.39 N	13.22 E
Lübars, Dtsch.	54	52.39 N	12.02 E
Lübars, Dtsch.	54	52.10 N	12.09 E
Lübars ≈⁸	264a	52.37 N	13.22 E
Lubartów	30	51.28 N	22.38 E
L'ubašovka	78	47.51 N	30.15 E
Lubawa	30	53.30 N	19.45 E
Lubayril, Bahr al- ≈	273c	29.56 N	31.11 E
Lübbecke	52	52.18 N	8.36 E
Lübbenau	54	51.56 N	13.53 E
Lübben	54	51.52 N	13.57 E
Lubber Brook ≈	283	42.33 N	71.09 W
Lubbers Run ≈	276	40.56 N	74.43 W
Lübbesee ⊜	54	53.30 N	13.34 E
Lubbock	196	33.34 N	101.51 W
Lübbow	54	52.54 N	11.10 E
Lubbub Creek ≈	194	33.04 N	88.10 W
Lübca ≈	76	53.45 N	26.03 E
L'ubeč, Ukr.	76	51.42 N	30.39 E
Lübeck	52	53.52 N	10.42 E
Lübecker Bucht c	54	54.00 N	10.55 E
Lubefu	152	4.43 S	24.25 E
Lubefu ≈	152	4.10 S	23.00 E
— Ljudinjana	36	46.03 N	14.31 E
Lubic Island I	116	10.58 N	120.44 E
L'ubickoje	80	51.46 N	49.19 E
Lubień Kujawski	30	52.25 N	19.10 E
Lubilash ≈	152	6.02 S	23.45 E
Lubile	154	2.55 S	26.45 E
Lubilhe ≈	154	3.17 S	26.52 E
L'ubimovka, Kaz.	86	58.22 N	40.41 E
L'ubimovka, Ross.	78	52.15 N	66.45 E
L'ubimovka, Ukr.	78	51.30 N	35.37 E
L'ubimovka, Ukr.	78	46.47 N	33.34 E
L'ubimyj	83	47.53 N	39.28 E
Lubin, Pol.	54	51.24 N	16.13 E
Lubin, Pol.	54	53.50 N	14.25 E
— Lubin	30	51.24 N	16.13 E
L'ubercy	82	55.41 N	37.53 E
Lubéron, Montagne du ∧	62	43.48 N	5.22 E
Lubersac	32	45.27 N	1.24 E
L'ubešov	78	51.46 N	25.31 E
Lübesse	54	53.29 N	11.28 E
Lubi ≈	152	4.58 S	23.26 E
— Ljubljana	36	46.03 N	14.31 E
Lubin, Pol.	54	51.24 N	16.13 E
L'ubercy	82	55.41 N	37.53 E
Lublin	30	51.15 N	22.35 E
Lublin □³	30	51.30 N	22.30 E
L'ublino ≈⁸	265b	55.40 N	37.44 E
Lubmin	54	54.08 N	13.37 E
Lubnān, Jabal ∧ (Lebanon Mountains) ∧	132	34.00 N	36.00 E
— Lebanon □¹	128	34.00 N	36.00 E
Lubny	78	50.01 N	33.00 E
Lubochna	76	53.33 N	34.23 E
Lubok Antu	112	1.05 N	111.50 E
Lubomierz	30	51.00 N	15.30 E
Lubon	30	51.14 N	24.01 E
Lubraniec	30	52.33 N	18.50 E
Lubrín	34	37.13 N	2.03 W
Lubsko	30	51.47 N	14.59 E
Lubuagan	116	17.21 N	121.10 E
Lubudi ≈	154	9.57 S	25.58 E
Lubudi, Zaïre	154	6.51 S	21.18 E
Lubudi, Zaïre	154	9.57 S	25.58 E
Lubudi ≈, Zaïre	154	4.03 S	21.23 E
Lubuk ≈	154	9.13 S	25.38 E
Lubukbalang	112	4.03 S	104.12 E
Lubukgadang	112	1.19 S	100.58 E
Lubuklinggau	112	3.18 S	102.52 E
Lubukpakam	112	3.33 N	98.52 E
Lubuksikaping	112	0.08 N	100.10 E
Lubumbashi (Élisabethville)	154	11.40 S	27.28 E
— Lubumbashi	154	11.40 S	27.28 E
Lubutu	154	0.44 S	26.35 E
Luby	34	58.49 N	33.23 E
L'ubytino	76	58.49 N	33.23 E
Lübz	54	53.28 N	12.01 E
Lucala	152	9.16 S	15.15 E
Lucala ≈, Ang.	152	8.38 S	13.12 E
Lucala ≈, Ang.	152	9.37 S	14.11 E
Lucan, On., Can.	190	43.11 N	81.24 W
Lucan, Ire.	48	53.22 N	6.27 W
Lucanas	248	14.36 S	74.15 W
Lucania, Mount ∧	180	61.01 N	140.28 W
Lucapa	152	8.25 S	20.44 E
Lucas, La., U.S.	194	41.01 N	93.27 W
Lucas, Ks., U.S.	198	39.03 N	98.32 W
Lucas, Oh., U.S.	214	40.42 N	82.25 W
Lucas, Tx., U.S.	222	33.05 N	96.35 W
Lucas González	252	32.25 S	59.32 W
Lucas Heights	274a	34.02 S	150.58 E
Lucasville	218	38.52 N	82.59 W
Lucca	66	43.50 N	10.29 E
Luccan	152	14.45 S	20.03 E
Luce ≈	44	54.55 N	4.49 W
Luce Sicula	50	48.26 N	13.18 E
Luce, Water of ≈	44	54.52 N	4.50 W
Luce Bay c	44	54.47 N	4.50 W

≈ River / Fluß / Rio / Rivière / Rio
≈ Canal / Kanal / Canal / Canal / Canal
ㄴ Waterfall, Rapids / Wasserfall, Stromschnellen / Cascada, Rápidos / Chute d'eau, Rapides / Cascata, Rápidos
) (Strait / Meeresstraße / Estrecho / Détroit / Estreito
c Bay, Gulf / Bucht, Golf / Bahía, Golfo / Baie, Golfe / Baía, Golfo
⊜ Lake, Lakes / See, Seen / Lago, Lagos / Lac, Lacs / Lago, Lagos
⊞ Swamp / Sumpf / Pantano / Marais / Pântano
⊟ Ice Features, Glacier / Eis- und Gletscherformen / Accidentes Glaciares / Formes glaciaires / Acidentes Glaciais
⊽ Other Hydrographic Features / Andere Hydrographische Objekte / Otros Elementos Hidrográficos / Autres données hydrographiques / Outros acidentes hidrográficos

□ Submarine Features / Untermeerische Objekte / Accidentes Submarinos / Formes de relief sous-marin / Acidentes submarinos
□ Political Unit / Politische Einheit / Unidad Política / Entité politique / Unidade política
⊥ Cultural Institution / Kulturelle Institution / Institución Cultural / Institution culturelle / Instituição Cultural
⊥ Historical Site / Historische Stätte / Sitio Histórico / Site historique / Sitio histórico
♦ Recreational Site / Erholungs- und Feriénort / Sitio de Recreo / Centre de loisirs / Area de Lazer
⌖ Airport / Flughafen / Aeropuerto / Aéroport / Aeroporto
♦ Military Installation / Militäranlage / Instalación Militar / Installation militaire / Instalação militar
✸ Miscellaneous / Verschiedenes / Misceláneo / Divers / Diversos

Symbols in the index entries represent the broad categories identified in the key at the right. Symbols with superior numbers (*) identify subcategories (see key on page 1·1).

Symbole im Register stellen die rechts im Schlüssel erklärten Kategorien dar. Symbole mit hochgestellten Ziffern (*) bezeichnen Unterteilungen einer Kategorie (vgl. vollständiger Schlüssel auf Seite 1·1).

Los símbolos incluidos en el texto del índice representan las grandes categorías identificadas en la clave a la derecha. Los símbolos con números superiores (*) identifican las subcategorías (véase la clave completa en la página 1·1).

Les symboles de l'index représentent les catégories indiquées dans la légende à droite. Les symboles suivis d'un indice (*) représentent des sous-catégories (voir légende complète à la page 1·1).

Os símbolos incluídos no texto do índice representam as grandes categorias identificadas com a chave à direita. Os símbolos com números em sua parte superior (*) identificam as subcategorias (veja-se a chave completa a página 1·1).

Features — Other Topographic Features — Andere Topographische Objekte — Autres Topographiques — Otros Elementos Topográficos — Outras acidentes topográficos

Symbol	English	Deutsch	Français	Español	Português
⊡	Island	Insel	Île	Isla	Ilha
≍	Plain	Ebene	Plaine	Llano	Planície
X	Pass	Paß	Col	Paso	Passo
V	Valley, Canyon	Tal, Cañon	Vallée, Canyon	Valle, Cañón	Vale, Canhão
▲	Mountain	Berg	Montagne	Montaña	Montanha
►	Mountains	Gebirge	Montagnes	Montañas	Montanhas

ESPAÑOL — Nombre | Página | Lat.°′ | Long.°′ W = Oeste
FRANÇAIS — Nom | Page | Lat.°′ | Long.°′ W = Ouest
PORTUGUÊS — Nome | Página | Lat.°′ | Long.°′ W = Oeste

Lyndon B. Johnson, Lake ⊜[1] 196 30.35 N 98.25 W
Lyndon B. Johnson Historical Park ⊥ 196 30.15 N 98.38 W
Lyndon B. Johnson Space Center ʋ[3] 222 29.34 N 95.05 W
Lyndonville, N.Y., U.S. 210 43.19 N 78.23 W
Lyndonville, Vt., U.S. 188 44.32 N 72.00 W
Lyndora 214 40.51 N 79.55 W
Lyne 260 51.23 N 0.33 W
Lyne ≃ 44 54.58 N 3.01 W
Lyneham 42 51.31 N 1.58 W
Lynemouth 44 55.12 N 1.31 W
Lyne Water ≃ 46 55.39 N 3.16 W
Lynga 80 57.17 N 53.04 E
Lyngdal 26 58.08 N 7.05 E
Lynge 41 55.51 N 12.17 E
Lyngen 24 69.34 N 20.10 E
Lyngen c[2] 24 69.58 N 20.30 E
Lyngør 26 58.38 N 9.10 E
Lynher ≃ 42 50.28 N 4.12 W
Lynmouth 42 51.15 N 3.50 W
Lynn, Al., U.S. 194 34.02 N 87.32 W
Lynn, In., U.S. 218 40.02 N 84.56 W
Lynn, Ma., U.S. 207 42.28 N 70.57 W
Lynn ≃ 212 42.47 N 80.12 W
Lynn Canal c 180 58.50 N 135.15 W
Lynndyl 200 39.31 N 112.22 W
Lynne Acres 284b 39.21 N 76.45 W
Lynnfield 207 42.32 N 71.02 W
Lynn Garden 192 36.34 N 82.34 W
Lynn Harbor c 283 42.27 N 70.57 W
Lynn Haven 194 30.14 N 85.38 W
Lynn Lake 184 56.51 N 101.03 W
Lynnville 190 41.34 N 92.47 W
Lynnwood, Pa., U.S. 210 41.14 N 75.56 W
Lynnwood, Pa., U.S. 214 40.07 N 79.51 W
Lynnwood, Wa., U.S. 224 47.49 N 122.18 W
Lynn Woods ♠ 283 42.29 N 70.59 W
Lynton 42 51.15 N 3.50 W
Lyntupy 76 55.03 N 26.19 E
Lynwood, Ca., U.S. 228 33.55 N 118.12 W
Lynwood, Il., U.S. 278 41.32 N 87.32 W
Lynx Lake ⊜ 176 62.25 N 106.15 W
Lyø I 41 55.02 N 10.10 E
Lyon 62 45.45 N 4.51 E
Lyon □[6] 226 39.00 N 119.15 W
Lyon ≃ 46 56.37 N 4.01 W
Lyon, Gare ◆[5] 261 48.51 N 2.23 E
Lyon, Glen V 46 56.35 N 4.20 W
Lyon, Loch ⊜ 46 56.32 N 4.36 W
Lyon Inlet c 176 66.32 N 83.53 W
Lyon Mountain 188 44.43 N 73.54 W
Lyon Mountain ∧ 188 44.41 N 73.53 W
Lyonnais □[9] 62 45.45 N 4.30 E
Lyonnais, Monts du ⋏ 62 45.40 N 4.30 E
Lyons, Co., U.S. 200 40.13 N 105.16 W
Lyons, Ga., U.S. 192 32.12 N 82.19 W
Lyons, Il., U.S. 216 41.48 N 87.49 W
Lyons, In., U.S. 194 38.59 N 87.04 W
Lyons, Ks., U.S. 198 38.20 N 98.12 W
Lyons, Mi., U.S. 216 42.58 N 84.56 W
Lyons, Ne., U.S. 198 41.56 N 96.28 W
Lyons, N.Y., U.S. 210 43.03 N 76.59 W
Lyons, Oh., U.S. 216 41.41 N 84.04 W
Lyons, Tx., U.S. 222 30.23 N 96.34 W
Lyons, Wi., U.S. 216 42.39 N 88.21 W
Lyons ≃ 162 25.02 S 115.09 E
Lyon-Satolas, Aéroport de ⊠ 62 45.43 N 5.04 E
Lyons Creek ≃ 284a 43.03 N 79.04 W
Lyons Falls 212 43.37 N 75.22 W
Lyons-la-Forêt 50 49.24 N 1.28 E
Lyons Plains 207 41.13 N 73.21 W
Lyons Run ≃ 279b 40.25 N 79.43 W
Lyon Station 208 40.28 N 75.45 W
Lyonsville 276 40.57 N 74.25 W
Lyracrumpane 48 52.20 N 9.30 W
Lyrestad 40 58.48 N 14.04 E
Lys (Leie) ≃, Europe 50 51.03 N 3.43 E
Lys ≃, It. 62 45.36 N 7.47 E
Lysá ∧ 60 49.29 N 12.42 E
Lysaja Gora 78 48.11 N 31.06 E
Lysaker 26 59.54 N 10.36 E
Lys'anka 78 49.16 N 30.50 E
Lysá pod Makytou 30 49.12 N 18.13 E
Lysefjorden c[2] 26 59.00 N 6.14 E
Lysekil 26 58.16 N 11.26 E
Łysica ∧ 30 50.54 N 20.55 E
Lysjön ⊜ 40 60.07 N 14.18 E
Lyskovo 80 56.04 N 45.02 E
Lysogorka 83 47.42 N 39.12 E
Lyss 58 47.04 N 7.18 E
Lysterfield 274b 37.56 S 145.18 E
Lysterfield ∧[2] 274b 37.56 S 145.16 E
Lysterfield Reservoir ⊜[1] 274b 37.58 S 145.18 E
Lyster Station 206 46.22 N 71.37 W
Lys'va 86 58.07 N 57.47 E
Lys'va ≃ 80 58.15 N 54.47 E
Lysyje Gory 80 51.32 N 44.46 E
Lytham Saint Anne's 44 53.45 N 2.57 W
Lytkarino 82 55.35 N 37.54 E
Lytle 196 29.13 N 98.47 W
Lytle Creek ≃ 228 34.09 N 117.23 W
Lyttelton, N.Z. 172 43.35 S 172.42 E
Lyttelton, S. Afr. 158 25.50 S 28.11 E
Lytton 182 50.14 N 121.34 W
Lytton Springs 222 30.00 N 97.37 W
Lyubertsy → L'ubercy 82 55.41 N 37.53 E

M

Ma ≃ 110 19.47 N 105.56 E
Ma, Oued el V, Alg. 148 27.45 N 7.45 W
Ma, Oued el V, Maur. 148 24.03 N 9.10 W
Maadid, Djebel ∧ 34 35.52 N 4.46 E
Maalaea Bay c 229a 20.47 N 156.29 W
Ma'alot-Tarshiha 132 33.01 N 35.17 E
Maam Cross 48 53.27 N 9.31 W
Ma'ān 132 30.12 N 35.44 E
Ma'ān □[8] 132 30.20 N 36.30 E
Maaninka 26 63.09 N 27.18 E
Ma'anshan, Zhg. 100 31.42 N 118.30 E
Maanshan, Zhg. 107 29.52 N 104.59 E
Ma-ao 116 10.29 N 122.59 E
Maap I 174q 9.35 N 138.11 E
Maar 140 6.54 N 31.33 E
Maardu 76 59.28 N 25.02 E
Maarianhamina → Mariehamn 26 60.06 N 19.57 E
Ma'ārik, Qārat al- ∧[2] 142 29.59 N 30.52 E
Ma'arrat an-Nu'mān 130 35.38 N 36.40 E
Ma'arrat Miṣrīn 130 36.01 N 36.40 E
Ma'arrat Ṣaydnāyā 132 33.41 N 36.23 E
Maarssen 52 52.08 N 5.08 E
Maas 48 54.50 N 8.22 W
Maas (Meuse) ≃ 30 51.49 N 5.01 E
Maasbracht 52 51.08 N 5.53 E
Maasdam 52 51.47 N 4.32 E
Maaseik 56 51.06 N 5.48 E
Maasholm 41 54.41 N 9.59 E
Maasin 116 10.08 N 124.50 E
Maasmechelen (Mechelen) 56 50.58 N 5.42 E
Maasniel 52 51.13 N 6.01 E
Maassluis 52 51.55 N 4.15 E
Maastricht 56 50.52 N 5.43 E
Maave 156 21.03 S 34.47 E
Ma-ayon ≃ 116 11.25 N 122.46 E
Maba 100 32.59 N 118.48 E
Maba, Ouadi V 146 15.10 N 21.00 E
Mababe Depression ⩡[7] 156 18.50 S 24.15 E
Mabaduan 164 9.16 S 142.44 E
Mabaho, Mount ∧ 116 9.15 N 125.42 E
Mabaia 152 7.13 S 14.03 E
Mabalacat 116 15.14 N 120.34 E
Mabalane 156 23.37 S 32.31 E
Mabana 224 48.05 N 122.24 W
Mabanga 152 1.30 N 19.06 E
Mabank 222 32.21 N 96.06 W
Mabaoquan 105 40.09 N 115.53 E
Ma'barot 132 32.22 N 34.54 E
Mabaruma 246 8.12 N 59.47 W
Mabashi 268 35.49 N 139.55 E
Mabau 112 2.14 S 111.54 E
Mabay 240p 20.16 N 76.40 W
Mabber, Ras › 144 9.28 N 50.50 E
Mabel Creek 162 29.01 S 134.17 E
Mabeleapodi 156 20.58 S 22.36 E
Mabel Lake ⊜ 182 50.35 N 118.44 W
Maben 194 33.33 N 89.05 W
Mabenga-Cité 152 3.39 S 18.40 E
Mabenge 152 4.14 N 24.09 E
Maberry, Loch ⊜ 44 55.02 N 4.41 W
Mabeti ≃ 92 40.31 N 141.31 E
Mabeul 36 36.27 N 10.46 E
Mabi, Nihon 96 34.38 N 133.41 E
Mabi, Zhg. 100 26.21 N 119.36 E
Mabi, Zhg. 102 35.59 N 112.15 E
Mabian 107 28.48 N 103.41 E
Mabian ≃ 107 29.08 N 103.58 E
Mablethorpe 44 53.21 N 0.15 E
Mableton 192 33.49 N 84.34 W
Mabole ≃ 150 9.01 N 12.44 W
Maboma 154 2.32 N 28.13 E
Mabonto 150 8.52 N 11.49 W
Mabote 156 22.03 S 34.09 E
Mabou 186 46.05 N 61.22 W
Mabrak, Jabal ∧ 132 30.13 N 35.29 E
Mabrous ⍑[4] 146 21.13 N 13.38 E
Mabrūk, Lībiyā 146 29.50 N 17.10 E
Mabrūk, Sūd. 140 8.07 N 29.25 E
Mabton 202 46.12 N 119.59 W
Mabuasehube Game Reserve ◆[4] 156 25.10 S 22.10 E
Mabuguai 100 29.49 N 112.42 E
Mabuki 154 2.59 S 33.11 E
Mabuni 174m 26.05 N 127.43 E
Mabwe 154 8.39 S 26.31 E
Mača, Ross. 74 59.54 N 117.35 E
Maca, Ven. 286c 10.28 N 66.48 W
Maca, Cerro ∧ 254 45.06 S 73.12 W
Macachín 252 37.09 S 63.39 W
Macaco, Morro do ∧[2] 287a 22.56 S 43.07 W
Macacos, Ilha dos I 250 1.20 S 50.35 W
Macacu ≃ 256 22.42 S 43.02 W
Macaé 255 22.23 S 41.47 W
Macaíba 250 5.51 S 35.21 W
Macajalar Bay c 116 8.37 N 124.38 E
Macajuba 255 12.09 S 40.22 W
Macalaya 116 12.53 N 123.46 E
Macalelon 116 13.45 N 122.08 E
Macalister 182 52.27 N 122.24 W
Macalister ≃ 166 38.02 S 146.59 E
Macalister, Mount ∧ 170 34.27 S 149.45 E
Macallum Lake ⊜ 184 55.02 N 108.25 W
Macaloge 154 12.25 S 35.25 E
MacAlpine Lake ⊜ 176 66.40 N 103.15 W
Macamic, Lac ⊜ 190 48.48 N 78.59 W
Macan, Kepulauan II 112 7.00 S 121.00 E
Macão 34 39.33 N 8.00 W
Macao → Macau □[2] 100 22.10 N 113.33 E
Macapá 250 0.02 N 51.03 W
Macará 246 4.23 S 79.57 W
Macarani 255 15.33 S 40.24 W
Macarao 286c 10.26 N 67.02 W
Macarao ≃ 286c 10.26 N 67.01 W
Macareo, Caño ≃[1] 246 9.47 N 61.37 W
Macari ≃ 250 1.52 N 50.31 W
MacArthur, Pil. 116 10.50 N 125.00 E
MacArthur, Il., U.S. 278 41.39 N 87.44 W
Macas 246 2.19 S 78.07 W
Macatawa ≃ 216 42.48 N 86.05 W
Macatawa, Lake c 216 42.47 N 86.10 W
Macaterick, Loch ⊜ 44 55.12 N 4.26 W
Macau, Bra. 250 5.07 S 36.38 W
Macau (Aomen), Macau 100 22.14 N 113.35 E
Macau □[2], Asia 90 22.10 N 113.33 E
Macau □[2], Asia 100 22.10 N 113.33 E
Macau, Ilha I 156 20.55 S 35.05 E
Macauã ≃ 248 9.13 S 68.44 W
Macaúbas 255 13.02 S 42.42 W
Macaya, Pic ∧ 238 18.25 N 74.00 W
Macaza ≃ 206 46.21 N 74.47 W
Maccarese ◆[8] 267a 41.53 N 12.13 E
Maccarese, Bonifica di ◆[1] 267a 41.51 N 12.13 E
Macchiagodena 66 41.33 N 14.24 E
MacClenny 192 30.16 N 82.07 W
Macclesfield, Austl. 168b 35.10 S 138.50 E
Macclesfield, Eng., U.K. 44 53.16 N 2.07 W
Macclesfield □[8] 262 53.17 N 2.15 W
Macclesfield Canal ≅ 262 53.24 N 2.03 W
Macclesfield Forest ◆[3] 262 53.15 N 2.03 W
Macdhui, Ben ∧ 158 30.39 S 27.58 E
MacDill Air Force Base ■ 220 27.51 N 82.29 W
Macdonald ≃ 170 33.23 S 150.59 E
Macdonald, Lake ⊜ 162 23.30 S 129.00 E
MacDonald Downs 162 22.27 S 135.13 E
MacDonald Lake ⊜ 212 45.14 N 78.34 W
MacDonald Pass)(202 46.34 N 112.18 W
Macdonald Range ⋏ 182 49.12 N 114.46 W
MacDonnell Ranges ⋏ 162 23.45 S 133.20 E
Macdonnel Peninsula ›[1] 168b 35.47 S 138.00 E
MacDowell Lake ⊜ 184 52.15 N 92.45 W
Macduff 46 57.40 N 2.29 W
Macdui, Ben ∧ 46 57.05 N 3.38 W
Mačecha 80 50.48 N 43.17 E
Mačechi 78 49.31 N 34.26 E
Maceday Lake ⊜ 281 42.42 N 83.26 W
Macedo de Cavaleiros 34 41.32 N 6.58 W
Macedon, Austl. 169 37.25 S 144.34 E
Macedon, N.Y., U.S. 210 43.04 N 77.17 W
Macedonia, Ct., U.S. 207 41.47 N 73.30 W
Macedonia, Oh., U.S. 214 41.18 N 81.30 W
Macedonia □[9] 38 41.00 N 23.00 E
Macedonia (Makedonija) □[1] 38 41.50 N 22.00 E
Macedonia Brook State Park ♠ 207 41.47 N 73.29 W
Maceió 250 9.40 S 35.43 W
Maceira 266c 38.52 N 9.19 W
Macenta 150 8.33 N 9.28 W
Maceo 246 6.33 N 74.47 W
Macerata 66 43.18 N 13.27 E
Macerata □[4] 66 43.12 N 13.10 E
Macerata Feltria 66 43.48 N 12.26 E
MacFarlane ≃ 176 59.12 N 107.58 W
Macfarlane, Lake ⊜ 166 31.55 S 136.42 E
Macfarlane, Mount ∧ 172 43.56 S 169.23 E
Macgillycuddy's Reeks ⋏ 48 51.55 N 9.45 W
MacGregor 184 49.57 N 98.49 W
Machacamarca 248 18.10 S 67.02 W
Machache ∧ 158 29.21 S 27.55 E
Machachi 246 0.30 S 78.34 W
Machačkala 84 42.58 N 47.30 E
Machada, Mata Nacional da ♠ 266c 38.36 N 9.02 W
Machadinho ≃ 248 9.00 S 61.52 W
Machado 256 21.41 S 45.56 W
Machado ≃, Bra. 248 8.03 S 62.52 W
Machado ≃, Bra. 256 21.38 S 45.52 W
Machadodorp 156 25.40 S 30.14 E
Machagai 252 26.56 S 60.03 W
Machaila 156 22.15 S 32.55 E
Machakos 154 1.31 S 37.16 E
Machala 246 3.16 S 79.58 W
Machalí 252 34.11 S 70.40 W
Machalilla, Parque Nacional ♠ 246 1.30 S 80.45 W
Machalino 80 53.05 N 46.14 E
Māchalpur 124 24.08 N 76.18 E
Machaneng 156 23.10 S 27.26 E
Machang, Malay. 114 5.46 N 102.13 E
Machang, Zhg. 98 34.06 N 119.02 E
Machang, Zhg. 98 42.05 N 119.42 E
Machanga 156 20.58 S 34.59 E
Machangcun 105 38.54 N 115.26 E
Machangfu 102 25.14 N 103.45 E
Machang Jianhe ≃ 105 39.00 N 117.40 E
Machaquilá ≃ 236 16.13 N 90.01 W
Machattie, Lake ⊜ 166 24.50 S 139.48 E
Machault 50 49.21 N 4.30 E
Machava 156 25.54 S 32.29 E
Machaze 156 20.51 S 33.26 E
Machecoul 32 47.00 N 1.50 W
Macheke 154 18.05 S 31.51 E
Machelen 50 50.55 N 4.26 E
Macheng 100 31.13 N 115.00 E
Macherio 266b 45.38 N 9.16 E
Mācherla 122 16.29 N 79.26 E
Machern 54 51.21 N 12.37 E
Machery 261 48.36 N 2.05 E
Machesna Mountain ∧ 226 35.17 N 120.14 W
Machesney Park 216 42.20 N 89.03 W
Māchhīwāra 123 30.55 N 76.12 E
Machhlīshahr 124 25.41 N 82.25 E
Machias, Me., U.S. 188 44.42 N 67.27 W
Machias, N.Y., U.S. 210 42.25 N 78.30 W
Machias ≃ 188 44.43 N 67.22 W
Machias Bay c 188 44.40 N 67.20 W
Machichaco, Cabo › 34 43.27 N 2.45 W
Machichi ≃ 184 57.03 N 92.06 W
Machico 148 32.42 N 16.46 W
Machida 94 35.32 N 139.27 E
Machile ≃ 154 17.26 S 25.02 E
Machilīpatnam (Bandar) 122 16.10 N 81.08 E
Machindžauri 84 41.40 N 41.43 E
Machiques 246 10.04 N 72.34 W
Machiya ≃ 94 35.01 N 136.42 E
Machkund ⊜[1] 122 18.26 N 82.35 E
Machmud-Mekteb 84 44.26 N 45.13 E
Machn'ovo 86 58.27 N 61.42 E
Macho, Arroyo del V 196 33.36 N 104.28 W
Machočen, porog ∟ 88 57.23 N 121.29 E
Machona, Laguna c 234 18.20 N 93.40 W
Machrihanish 46 55.26 N 5.45 W
Machtaly 85 41.22 N 68.02 E
Machupicchu 248 13.07 S 72.34 W
Machupicchu ⊥ 248 13.07 S 72.34 W
Machupo ≃ 248 12.34 S 64.25 W
Machynlleth 42 52.35 N 3.51 W
Maciá, Arg. 252 32.10 S 59.23 W
Macia, Moç. 156 25.03 S 33.10 E
Maciel, Arroyo ≃, Ur. 258 33.36 S 56.31 W
Maciel, Arroyo ≃, Ur. 258 33.42 S 57.59 W
Măcin 38 45.15 N 28.08 E
Macina → Massina ◆[1] 150 14.30 N 5.00 W
Macintyre ≃, Austl. 166 29.25 S 148.45 E
Macintyre ≃, Austl. 166 28.38 S 150.47 E
Maçka 130 40.48 N 39.38 E
Mačkassy 80 52.46 N 45.34 E
Mackay, Austl. 166 21.09 S 149.11 E
Mackay, Id., U.S. 202 43.54 N 113.36 W
MacKay ≃ 184 57.03 N 111.55 W
Mackay, Lake ⊜ 162 22.30 S 129.00 E
MacKay Lake ⊜ 176 63.55 N 110.25 W
Mackenrode 54 51.33 N 10.33 E
Mackenzie 246 6.00 N 58.17 W
Mackenzie ≃, Austl. 166 23.38 S 149.46 E
Mackenzie ≃, N.T., Can. 176 69.15 N 134.08 W
MacKenzie Bay c, Ant. 9 68.20 S 71.15 E
Mackenzie Bay c, Can. 180 69.00 N 136.30 W
Mackenzie Delta ≚[2] 180 68.50 N 135.25 W
Mackenzie Mountains ⋏ 180 64.00 N 130.00 W
Mackeyville 210 41.03 N 77.28 W
Mackinac, Straits of ʊ 190 45.49 N 84.42 W
Mackinac Bridge ◆[5] 190 45.50 N 84.45 W
Mackinac Island 190 45.50 N 84.37 W
Mackinac Island I 190 45.51 N 84.38 W
Mackinac Island State Park ♠ 190 45.52 N 84.40 W
Mackinaw 190 40.32 N 89.21 W
Mackinaw ≃ 194 40.33 N 89.44 W
Mackinaw City 190 45.47 N 84.43 W
Mackinnon Road 154 3.44 S 39.03 E
Macklin 184 52.20 N 109.56 W
Mačkovci 61 46.47 N 16.09 E
M'ačkovo, Ross. 82 55.13 N 38.40 E
M'ačkovo, Ross. 82 56.21 N 39.03 E
Macksville, Austl. 166 30.43 S 152.55 E
Macksville, Ks., U.S. 198 38.57 N 98.58 W
Maclean 166 29.28 S 153.13 E
Macleantown 158 32.47 S 27.45 E
Maclear 158 31.02 S 28.23 E
Macleay ≃ 166 30.52 S 153.01 E
Macleod 274b 37.43 S 145.04 E
Macleod, Lake ⊜ 162 24.00 S 113.35 E
Maclovia Herrera 232 29.05 N 105.08 W
Macmillan ≃ 180 62.52 N 135.55 W
Macocolo 152 6.47 S 16.08 E
Macolin 58 47.09 N 7.14 E
Macolla, Punta › 241s 12.06 N 70.13 W
Macolo 152 7.05 S 16.48 E
Macomb 190 40.27 N 90.40 W
Macomb □[6] 214 42.40 N 82.54 W
Macomb Mall ◆[9] 281 42.32 N 82.55 W
Macomer 71 40.16 N 8.47 E
Macomia 154 12.15 S 40.08 E
Macon, Bel. 50 50.03 N 4.13 E
Mâcon, Fr. 58 46.18 N 4.50 E
Macon, Ga., U.S. 192 32.50 N 83.37 W
Macon, Il., U.S. 219 39.42 N 88.59 W
Macon, Ms., U.S. 194 33.06 N 88.33 W
Macon, Mo., U.S. 194 39.44 N 92.28 W
Macon □[6], Il., U.S. 219 39.51 N 89.32 W
Macon □[6], Mo., U.S. 219 39.50 N 92.20 W
Macon, Bayou ≃ 194 31.55 N 91.33 W
Macon Creek ≃ 216 41.58 N 83.38 W
Macondo 152 12.35 S 23.44 E
Macondo ≃ 152 13.23 S 23.03 E
Mâconnais, Monts du ⋏ 58 46.18 N 4.45 E
Macorís, Cabo › 238 19.47 N 70.28 W
Macosquin 48 55.06 N 6.43 W
Macossa 156 17.52 S 33.56 E
Macouba, Pointe de › 240e 14.53 N 61.09 W
Macoun Lake ⊜ 184 56.32 N 103.50 W
Macoupin □[6] 219 39.17 N 89.53 W
Macoupin Creek ≃ 219 39.11 N 90.36 W
Macovane 156 21.28 S 35.04 E
Macpherson, Mount ∧[2] 162 21.49 S 121.35 E
Macquarie ≃, Austl. 166 41.44 S 147.08 E
Macquarie ≃, Austl. 166 30.07 S 147.24 E
Macquarie, Lake ⊜ 170 33.05 S 151.35 E
Macquarie Fields 274a 33.59 S 150.53 E
Macquarie Harbour c 166 42.19 S 145.23 E
Macquarie Island I 9 54.30 S 158.56 E
Macquarie Marshes ≡ 166 30.50 S 147.32 E
Macquarie Pass National Park ♠ 170 34.34 S 150.39 E
Macquarie Ridge ✣[3] 9 57.00 S 159.00 E
Macquarie University ʋ[2] 274a 33.46 S 151.06 E
MacRitchie Reservoir ⊜[1] 271c 1.21 N 103.50 E
Mac. Robertson Land ◆[1] 9 68.10 S 65.00 E
Macrohon 116 10.05 N 124.56 E
Macroom 48 51.54 N 8.57 W
Mactan Island I 116 10.18 N 123.58 E
MacTier 212 45.08 N 79.47 W
Macuco de Minas 256 21.46 S 44.47 W
Macucuau ≃ 246 0.37 S 61.24 W
Macuelizo 236 15.18 N 88.31 W
Macugnaga 58 45.58 N 7.58 E
Macujer 246 0.23 N 72.55 W
Macul 286e 33.30 S 70.34 W
Maculabo Island I 116 14.24 N 122.49 E
Macumba ≃ 162 27.52 S 137.12 E
Macungie 208 40.30 N 75.33 W
Macunqiao 100 33.50 N 116.13 E
Macuro 246 10.39 N 61.56 W
Macusani 248 14.05 S 70.26 W
Macuspana 234 17.46 N 92.36 W
Macusse 152 17.51 S 20.21 E
Macuto 286c 10.37 N 66.53 W
Macuze 156 17.42 S 37.11 E
Macy 216 40.57 N 86.07 W
Mad ≃, On., Can. 212 44.25 N 79.54 W
Mad ≃, Ca., U.S. 204 40.57 N 124.07 W
Mad ≃, N.Y., U.S. 212 43.20 N 75.44 W
Mad ≃, Oh., U.S. 188 39.46 N 84.11 W
Mad ≃, Vt., U.S. 188 44.18 N 72.41 W
Mada ≃ 150 7.59 N 7.55 E
Ma'dabā 132 31.43 N 35.48 E
Madagascar (Madagasikara) □[1], Afr. 138 19.00 S 46.00 E
Madagascar (Madagasikara) □[1], Afr. 157b 19.00 S 46.00 E
Madagascar Basin ✣[1] 12 27.00 S 53.00 E
Madagascar Plateau ✣[3] 10 30.00 S 45.00 E
Madagasikara → Madagascar □[1] 157b 19.00 S 46.00 E
Madagaskar → Madagascar □[1] 157b 19.00 S 46.00 E
Madagiz 84 40.19 N 46.44 E
Madagoi, Bohol V 144 0.44 N 42.56 E
Madā'in Ṣāliḥ 128 26.48 N 37.53 E
Madajevo 80 54.48 N 44.31 E
Madama 146 21.58 N 13.39 E
Madame, Isle I 186 45.33 N 61.02 W
Madan 38 41.30 N 24.57 E
Madanapalle 122 13.33 N 78.30 E
Madang, Pap. N. Gui. 164 5.15 S 145.50 E
Madang, Zhg. 100 29.58 N 116.40 E
Madang □[5] 164 5.00 S 145.30 E
Madanpur 272b 22.40 N 88.32 E
Madanpur Dabās ◆[8] 272a 28.43 N 77.02 E
Madaoua 150 14.05 N 5.58 E
Mādār Gāng ≃[1] 126 22.12 N 89.04 E
Mādāri Hāt 124 26.42 N 89.17 E
Mādārīpur 124 23.10 N 90.12 E
Madarounfa 150 13.18 N 7.09 E
Mādārpur 272b 22.54 N 88.27 E
Madau Island I 164 8.58 S 152.28 E
Madawaska, On., Can. 212 45.30 N 77.59 W
Madawaska, Me., U.S. 186 47.21 N 68.19 W
Madawaska ≃ 212 45.27 N 76.21 W
Madawaska Highlands ⋏[1] 212 45.15 N 77.35 W
Madawaska Lake ⊜ 212 45.20 N 78.23 W
Madaxmaroodi 144 2.39 N 44.36 E
Madaya, Mya. 110 22.13 N 96.07 E
Maḍāyā, Sūrīy. 132 33.41 N 36.06 E
Madbar 140 6.19 N 30.40 E
Mad Creek ≃ 210 42.55 N 77.59 W
Maddalena, Colle della (Col de Larche))(62 44.25 N 6.53 E
Maddalena, Isola I 71 41.14 N 9.25 E
Maddaloni 68 41.02 N 14.23 E
Maddela 116 16.21 N 121.41 E
Madden, Mount ∧ 162 33.12 S 119.51 E
Maddington 168a 32.03 S 115.59 E
Maddock 198 47.57 N 99.31 W
Maddy, Loch c 46 57.36 N 7.08 W
Made 52 51.41 N 4.46 E
Madeir 140 7.50 N 29.12 E
Madeira 218 39.11 N 84.21 W
Madeira I 148 32.44 N 17.00 W
Madeira ≃ 242 3.22 S 58.45 W
Madeira, Arquipélago da II 148 32.40 N 16.45 W
Madeira Beach 220 27.48 N 82.48 W
Madeirinha ≃ 248 8.31 S 60.46 W
Madeirinha, Paraná ≃[1] 246 3.25 S 58.51 W
M'adel' 76 54.53 N 26.57 E
Mädelegabel ∧ 58 47.18 N 10.18 E
Madeleine, Îles de la II 186 47.30 N 61.45 W
Madeleine, Pointe › 275a 45.27 N 73.57 W
Madeleine-Centre 186 49.15 N 65.21 W
Madeley, Eng., U.K. 42 52.59 N 2.20 W
Madeley, Eng., U.K. 42 52.39 N 2.28 W
Madelia 190 44.03 N 94.25 W
Madeline Island I 190 46.50 N 90.40 W
Maden, Tür. 130 38.23 N 39.40 E
Maden, Tür. 130 40.11 N 40.25 E
Madenijet 86 47.53 N 78.37 E
Madera, Méx. 232 29.12 N 108.07 W
Madera, Ca., U.S. 226 36.57 N 120.03 W
Madera, Pa., U.S. 214 40.49 N 78.26 W
Madera □[6] 226 37.15 N 119.45 W
Madera Canal ≅ 226 37.05 N 119.59 W
Madera Lake ⊜[1] 226 37.02 N 119.59 W
Madera Peak ∧ 226 37.32 N 119.23 W
Maderas, Islas → Madeira, Arquipélago da II 148 32.40 N 16.45 W
Maderas, Volcán ∧[1] 236 11.27 N 85.31 W
Maderno 64 45.38 N 10.35 E
Madgaon (Margao) 122 15.18 N 73.57 E
Madh ◆[8] 272c 19.08 N 72.47 E
Madhepura 124 25.55 N 86.47 E
Madhkūr, Bi'r ⍑[4] 142 30.42 N 32.32 E
Mādhopur 123 32.22 N 75.36 E
Madhubani 124 26.22 N 86.05 E
Madhudaha 272b 22.31 N 88.25 E
Madhugiri 122 13.40 N 77.12 E
Madhumati ≃[1] 126 22.53 N 89.52 E
Madhupar 126 22.54 N 86.28 E
Madhupur 126 24.16 N 86.39 E
Madhya Bhārat Pathār ◆[1] 124 25.00 N 77.00 E
Madhyamgrām 272b 22.42 N 88.27 E
Madhya Pradesh □[3] 118 23.00 N 79.00 E
Madia 154 7.08 S 26.00 E
Madian 106 32.15 N 119.58 E
Madibi 152 4.18 S 18.24 E
Madibira 154 8.12 S 34.49 E
Madibogo 158 26.25 S 25.10 E
Madida 98 42.57 N 130.48 E
Madidi ≃ 248 12.32 S 66.52 W
Madill 196 34.05 N 96.46 W
Madimba, Ang. 152 6.31 S 14.21 E
Madimba, Zaïre 152 4.58 S 15.08 E
Madina 150 13.24 N 8.51 W
Madina do Boé 150 11.45 N 14.13 W
Madinani 150 9.37 N 6.57 W
Madinat al-Abyār 146 32.11 N 20.36 E
Madīnat ash-Sha'b (Al-Ittiḥad) 144 12.50 N 44.56 E
Madīnat ath Thawrah 130 35.52 N 38.34 E
Madine, Lac de ⊜ 56 48.54 N 5.42 E
Madingo 152 4.07 S 11.22 E
Madingou 152 4.09 S 13.34 E
Madingzi 104 42.08 N 120.52 E
Madi Opei 154 3.37 N 33.05 E
Madirobe 157b 16.04 S 46.15 E
Madirovalo 157b 16.26 S 46.30 E
Madison, Al., U.S. 194 34.41 N 86.44 W
Madison, Ca., U.S. 226 38.41 N 121.58 W
Madison, Ct., U.S. 207 41.16 N 72.35 W
Madison, Fl., U.S. 192 30.28 N 83.24 W
Madison, Ga., U.S. 192 33.35 N 83.28 W
Madison, Il., U.S. 219 38.40 N 90.09 W
Madison, In., U.S. 218 38.44 N 85.22 W
Madison, Ks., U.S. 198 38.08 N 96.08 W
Madison, Me., U.S. 188 44.47 N 69.52 W
Madison, Md., U.S. 208 38.30 N 76.13 W
Madison, Mn., U.S. 198 45.00 N 96.11 W
Madison, Mo., U.S. 219 39.28 N 92.12 W
Madison, Ne., U.S. 198 41.49 N 97.27 W
Madison, N.J., U.S. 210 40.45 N 74.25 W
Madison, N.Y., U.S. 210 42.53 N 75.30 W
Madison, N.C., U.S. 192 36.23 N 79.57 W
Madison, Oh., U.S. 214 41.46 N 81.03 W
Madison, Pa., U.S. 279b 40.15 N 79.41 W
Madison, S.D., U.S. 198 44.00 N 97.06 W
Madison, Va., U.S. 188 38.22 N 78.15 W
Madison, W.V., U.S. 188 38.04 N 81.49 W
Madison, Wi., U.S. 216 43.04 N 89.24 W
Madison □[6], Il., U.S. 219 38.49 N 89.58 W
Madison □[6], In., U.S. 218 40.10 N 85.41 W
Madison □[6], N.Y., U.S. 210 43.05 N 75.42 W
Madison □[6], Oh., U.S. 218 39.53 N 83.27 W
Madison □[6], Tx., U.S. 222 30.58 N 95.55 W
Madison ≃ 202 45.56 N 111.30 W
Madison, West Fork ≃ 202 44.55 N 111.35 W
Madisonburg, Oh., U.S. 214 40.51 N 81.55 W
Madisonburg, Pa., U.S. 210 40.55 N 77.31 W
Madison Heights, Mi., U.S. 216 42.29 N 83.06 W
Madison Heights, Va., U.S. 192 37.25 N 79.07 W
Madison Mills 218 39.40 N 83.20 W
Madison-on-the-Lake 214 41.42 N 81.24 W
Madison Park 276 40.26 N 74.19 W
Madison Range ⋏ 202 45.15 N 111.20 W
Madison Square Garden ♠ 276 40.45 N 74.00 W
Madisonville, Ky., U.S. 194 37.19 N 87.29 W
Madisonville, La., U.S. 194 30.24 N 90.09 W
Madisonville, Tn., U.S. 192 35.31 N 84.21 W
Madisonville, Tx., U.S. 222 30.56 N 95.54 W
Madiun 115a 7.37 S 111.31 E
Madiun ≃ 115a 7.23 S 111.27 E
Madiyi 102 28.14 N 110.30 E
Madjingo 152 1.23 N 14.06 E
Madjoari 150 11.26 N 1.15 E
Madley, Mount ∧ 162 24.31 S 123.58 E
Madoc 212 44.30 N 77.28 W
Mado Gashi 154 0.44 N 39.10 E
Madoi 102 34.53 N 98.24 E
Madol 140 9.02 N 27.46 E
Madon ≃ 58 48.36 N 6.06 E
Madona 76 56.51 N 26.13 E
Madonna (Unserfrau) 64 46.43 N 10.52 E
Madonna della Guardia ʋ[1] 62 44.29 N 8.51 E
Madonna della Quercia ʋ[1] 66 42.25 N 12.06 E
Madonna dell'Olmo 62 44.25 N 7.32 E
Madonna del Sasso ʋ[1] 58 46.11 N 8.33 E
Madonna di Campiglio 64 46.14 N 10.49 E
Madonna di Tirano 64 46.13 N 10.09 E
Madora 76 53.09 N 30.11 E
Madougou 150 14.24 N 3.05 W
Madrakah 144 21.59 N 39.59 E
Madrakah, Ra's al- › 118 19.00 N 57.50 E
Madras, India 122 13.05 N 80.17 E
Madras, Or., U.S. 202 44.38 N 121.07 W
Madras → Tamil Nādu □[3] 122 11.00 N 78.15 E
Madre, Laguna c, Méx. 232 25.00 N 97.40 W
Madre, Laguna c, Tx., U.S. 196 27.00 N 97.35 W
Madre, Sierra ⋏ 116 16.20 N 122.00 E
Madre de Chiapas, Sierra ⋏ 232 15.30 N 92.35 W
Madre de Deus de Minas 256 21.29 S 44.20 W
Madre de Dios □[5] 248 12.00 S 70.15 W
Madre de Dios ≃ 248 10.23 S 65.24 W
Madre de Dios, Isla I 254 50.15 S 75.05 W
Madre del Sur, Sierra ⋏ 234 17.00 N 100.00 W
Madre Occidental, Sierra ⋏ 232 25.00 N 105.00 W
Madre Oriental, Sierra ⋏ 232 22.00 N 99.30 W
Madre Vieja ≃ 236 14.01 N 91.26 W
Madrid, Col. 246 4.44 N 74.16 W
Madrid, Esp. 34 40.24 N 3.41 W
Madrid, Esp. 266a 40.24 N 3.41 W
Madrid, Pil. 116 9.15 N 126.00 E
Madrid, Al., U.S. 194 31.02 N 85.23 W
Madrid, Ia., U.S. 190 41.52 N 93.49 W
Madrid, Ne., U.S. 198 40.51 N 101.32 W
Madrid □[4], Esp. 34 40.30 N 3.40 W
Madrid □[4], Esp. 34 40.30 N 3.40 W
Madridejos, Esp. 34 39.28 N 3.32 W
Madridejos, Pil. 116 11.18 N 123.44 E
Madrigalejo 34 39.09 N 5.37 W
Madrillon 284c 38.55 N 77.14 W
Madriz □[5] 236 13.30 N 86.30 W
Madroñera 34 39.26 N 5.46 W
Madruga 240p 22.55 N 81.51 W
Madrūsah 146 24.48 N 14.32 E
Madsen 184 50.58 N 93.55 W
Madsūs, Bi'r ⍑[4] 142 29.15 N 32.19 E
Maducang Island I 116 10.42 N 120.15 E
Maduda 152 4.55 S 13.06 E
Maduo 152 1.24 S 20.44 E
Madura 162 31.55 S 127.00 E
Madura I 115a 7.00 S 113.20 E
Madura, Selat ʊ 115a 7.25 S 113.25 E
Madurai 122 9.56 N 78.07 E
Madura → Madurai 122 9.56 N 78.07 E
Madurāntakam 122 12.31 N 79.54 E
Madureira, Serra de ⋏ 287a 22.49 S 43.31 W
Maduru ≃ 122 7.52 N 81.31 E
Madwar al-Bighāl ∧[2] 142 29.09 N 29.54 E
Madžalis 84 42.08 N 47.50 E
Mãe, Ilha da I 287a 22.59 S 43.04 W
Maeander Reef ✣[2] 116 8.05 N 119.18 E
Maebaru 92 33.33 N 130.12 E
Maebashi 94 36.23 N 139.04 E
Maeda 270 34.55 N 135.08 E
Mãe dos Homens 256 22.52 S 46.37 W
Maegye-ri 98 34.45 N 126.18 E
Mae Hong Son 110 19.16 N 97.56 E
Mae Klong ≃ 110 13.21 N 100.00 E
Maenclochog 42 51.54 N 4.48 W
Maengsan 98 39.40 N 126.30 E
Maeno ◆[8] 268 35.46 N 139.42 E
Maenza 66 41.31 N 13.11 E
Mae Ramat 110 16.58 N 98.31 E
Mae Rim 110 18.54 N 98.57 E
Maerkansu 85 39.19 N 73.53 E
Ma'erna 102 31.13 N 102.02 E
Maershan ∧ 102 26.18 N 100.20 E
Mae Sariang 110 18.10 N 97.56 E
Maeser 200 40.28 N 109.35 W
Mae Sot 110 16.43 N 98.34 E
Maesteg 42 51.37 N 3.40 W
Maestra, Sierra ⋏ 240p 20.00 N 76.45 W
Maestre de Campo Island I 116 12.56 N 121.42 E
Maestu 34 42.44 N 2.27 W
Mae Tha 110 18.28 N 99.08 E
Maevarano ≃ 157b 14.35 S 47.58 E
Maevatanana 157b 16.56 S 46.49 E
Maéwo I 175f 15.10 S 168.10 E
Ma'fan 146 25.55 N 14.29 E
Mafang 105 40.02 N 117.01 E
Mafangchang 107 29.24 N 106.06 E
Mafangcun 105 40.09 N 116.24 E
Ma Faro ✣[2] 122 5.50 N 73.26 E
Mafeking 184 52.41 N 101.06 W
Mafembage 152 14.32 S 21.42 E
Mafengtun 104 40.49 N 122.54 E
Mafeteng 158 29.51 S 27.15 E
Maffliers 261 49.05 N 2.19 E
Maffra 166 37.58 S 146.59 E
Mafia Channel ʊ 154 8.10 S 39.40 E
Mafia Island I 154 7.50 S 39.50 E
Mafikeng 156 25.53 S 25.39 E
Mafou ≃ 150 10.32 N 10.08 W
Mafra, Bra. 252 26.07 S 49.49 W
Mafra, Port. 34 38.56 N 9.20 W
Magadan 74 59.34 N 150.48 E
Magadi 154 1.54 S 36.17 E
Magadi, Lake ⊜ 154 1.52 S 36.17 E
Magaguadavic Lake ⊜ 186 45.43 N 67.12 W
Magai-butsu ʋ[1] 96 33.05 N 131.45 E
Magalhães Bastos ◆[8] 287a 22.53 S 43.23 W
Magalhães de Almeida 250 3.24 S 42.12 W
Magaliesberg ⋏ 158 25.50 S 27.30 E
Magallanes 116 12.50 N 123.50 E
Magallanes, Estrecho de (Strait of Magellan) ʊ 254 54.00 S 71.00 W
Magallanes → Punta Arenas 254 53.09 S 70.55 W
Magallanes y de la Antártica Chilena □[4] 254 53.00 S 72.00 W
Maganga 154 0.51 N 26.22 E
Magangué 246 9.14 N 74.45 W
Magansk 88 55.52 N 93.15 E
Maganuy ≃ 116 6.55 N 124.30 E
Magara, India 126 22.34 N 87.34 E
Mağara, Tür. 130 36.43 N 33.52 E
Magaramkent 84 41.37 N 48.21 E
Magaria 150 13.00 N 8.54 E
Magat ≃ 116 17.02 N 121.49 E
Magazine Mountain ∧ 194 35.10 N 93.38 W
Magazzolo ≃ 70 37.25 N 13.15 E
Magboro 273a 6.43 N 3.24 E
Magburaka 150 8.43 N 11.57 W
Magdagači 89 53.27 N 125.48 E
Magdalena, Arg. 258 35.04 S 57.32 W
Magdalena, Bol. 248 13.20 S 64.08 W
Magdalena, Méx. 234 20.55 N 103.57 W
Magdalena, Perú 248 6.21 S 77.49 W
Magdalena, Perú 286d 12.06 S 77.05 W
Magdalena, N.M., U.S. 200 34.07 N 107.14 W
Magdalena □[5] 246 10.00 N 74.00 W
Magdalena ≃, Col. 246 11.06 N 74.51 W
Magdalena ≃, Méx. 232 30.48 N 112.32 W
Magdalena, Bahía c 232 24.35 N 112.00 W
Magdalena, Isla I, Chile 254 44.40 S 73.10 W
Magdalena, Isla I, Méx. 232 24.55 N 112.15 W
Magdalena, Punta › 246 3.56 N 77.21 W
Magdalena Contreras ◆[8] 286a 19.18 N 99.17 W
Magdalena de Kino 232 30.38 N 110.57 W
Magdalena Peñasco 234 17.14 N 97.34 W
Magdalena Teitipac 234 16.54 N 96.34 W
Magdalena Tequisistlán 234 16.22 N 95.15 W
Magdalen Laver 260 51.45 N 0.11 E
Magdalinovka 78 48.55 N 34.54 E
Magdeborn 54 51.14 N 12.26 E
Magdeburg 54 52.07 N 11.38 E
Magdeburger Börde ≚ 54 52.00 N 11.30 E
Magdeburgo → Magdeburg 54 52.07 N 11.38 E
Magdiwang 116 12.30 N 122.31 E
Magdonskij, porog ∟ 88 57.45 N 100.55 E
Māge 110 26.33 N 98.33 E
Magé □[7] 287a 22.41 S 43.07 W
Magee 194 31.52 N 89.44 W
Magee, Island ›[1] 48 54.49 N 5.42 W
Magelang 115a 7.28 S 110.13 E
Magellan, Strait of → Magallanes, Estrecho de ʊ 254 54.00 S 71.00 W
Magellan-Strasse → Magallanes, Estrecho de ʊ 254 54.00 S 71.00 W
Magén 132 31.18 N 34.26 E
Magenta 62 45.28 N 8.53 E
Magenta, Lake ⊜ 162 33.26 S 119.10 E
Magerov 78 50.08 N 23.43 E
Magerøy I 24 71.03 N 25.45 E
Magetan 115a 7.39 S 111.20 E
Magezhuang 105 40.08 N 117.59 E
Maggia 58 46.15 N 8.42 E
Maggia ≃ 58 46.09 N 8.48 E
Maggia, Valle V 58 46.17 N 8.40 E
Maggie Creek ≃ 204 40.43 N 116.05 W
Maggiorasca, Monte ∧ 62 44.33 N 9.29 E
Maggiore ≃, It. 267a 41.54 N 12.16 E
Maggiore ≃, It. 267a 43.43 N 13.06 E
Maggiore, Lago ⊜ 36 46.00 N 8.40 E
Maggiore, Monte ∧ 68 41.14 N 14.12 E
Maghāghah 142 28.39 N 30.50 E
Maghama 150 15.31 N 12.51 W
Maghar 132 32.53 N 35.24 E
Maghdūshah 132 33.31 N 35.23 E
Maghera 48 54.51 N 6.40 W
Magherafelt 48 54.45 N 6.36 W
Maghniyya 148 34.50 N 1.50 W
Magholpur ◆[8] 272a 28.42 N 77.06 E
Maghull 44 53.32 N 2.57 W
Magician Lake ⊜ 216 42.04 N 86.10 W
Magic Mountain ♠ 228 34.26 N 118.36 W
Magic Reservoir ⊜[1] 202 43.17 N 114.23 W
Magill, Lac ⊜ 206 45.35 N 71.17 W
Magill Heights 279b 40.37 N 79.52 W
Magill Lake ⊜ 184 54.45 N 94.58 W
Mágina ∧ 34 37.43 N 3.28 W
Maginu 268 35.35 N 139.36 E
Magione 66 43.08 N 12.12 E
Magisano 68 39.01 N 16.27 E
Magiscatzín 234 22.48 N 98.42 W
Magiss Lake ⊜ 184 52.59 N 91.40 W
Maglaj 38 44.33 N 18.06 E
Magliana ◆[8] 267a 41.50 N 12.25 E
Magliana, Fosso ≃ 267a 41.49 N 12.25 E
Magliano dei Marsi 66 42.05 N 13.22 E
Magliano in Toscana 66 42.36 N 11.17 E
Magliano Sabina 66 42.22 N 12.29 E
Maglie 68 40.07 N 18.19 E
Maglód 264c 47.27 N 19.21 E
M'aglovo 265a 59.53 N 30.41 E
Magnago 266b 45.35 N 8.48 E
Magnanville 261 48.58 N 1.41 E
Magnet 184 51.19 N 99.30 W

Symbol	English	Deutsch	Español	Français	Português
≃	River	Fluß	Río	Rivière	Rio
≅	Canal	Kanal	Canal	Canal	Canal
∟	Waterfall, Rapids	Wasserfall, Stromschnellen	Cascada, Rápidos	Chute d'eau, Rapides	Cascata, Rápidos
ʊ	Strait	Meeresstraße	Estrecho	Détroit	Estreito
c	Bay, Gulf	Bucht, Golf	Bahía, Golfo	Baie, Golfe	Baía, Golfo
⊜	Lake, Lakes	See, Seen	Lago, Lagos	Lac, Lacs	Lago, Lagos
≡	Swamp	Sumpf	Pantano	Marais	Pântano
⍓	Ice Features, Glacier	Eis- und Gletscherformen	Accidentes Glaciales	Formes glaciaires	Acidentes glaciares
⍑	Other Hydrographic Features	Andere Hydrographische Objekte	Otros Elementos Hidrográficos	Autres données hydrographiques	Outros acidentes hidrográficos
✣	Submarine Features	Untermeerische Objekte	Accidentes Submarinos	Formes de relief sous-marin	Acidentes submarinos
□	Political Unit	Politische Einheit	Unidad Politica	Entité politique	Unidade política
ʋ	Cultural Institution	Kulturelle Institution	Institución Cultural	Institution culturelle	Instituição cultural
⊥	Historical Site	Historische Stätte	Sitio Histórico	Site historique	Sitio histórico
♠	Recreational Site	Erholungs- und Ferienort	Sitio de Recreo	Centre de loisirs	Area de Lazer
⊠	Airport	Flughafen	Aeropuerto	Aéroport	Aeroporto
■	Military Installation	Militäranlage	Instalación Militar	Installation militaire	Instalação militar
◆	Miscellaneous	Verschiedenes	Misceláneo	Divers	Diversos

Name	Page / Seite	Lat.°′ / Breite°′	Long.°′ / Länge°′ E = Ost
Magnetawan ≃	190	45.46 N	80.37 W
Magnetic Island I	166	19.08 S	146.50 E
Magnetic Springs	214	40.21 N	83.16 W
Magnetischer Nordpol → North Magnetic Pole ◆	16	77.19 N	101.49 W
Magnetischer Südpol → South Magnetic Pole ◆	9	65.18 S	139.30 E
Magnières	58	48.27 N	6.34 E
Magnitka	86	55.21 N	59.43 E
Magnitogorsk	86	53.27 N	59.04 E
Magnitostroj	80	51.43 N	53.05 E
Magnolia, Ar., U.S.	194	33.16 N	93.14 W
Magnolia, De., U.S.	208	39.04 N	75.28 W
Magnolia, Ma., U.S.	283	42.35 N	70.43 W
Magnolia, Mn., U.S.	198	43.38 N	96.04 W
Magnolia, Ms., U.S.	194	31.08 N	90.27 W
Magnolia, N.J., U.S.	285	39.51 N	75.02 W
Magnolia, Oh., U.S.	214	40.39 N	81.17 W
Magnolia, Tx., U.S.	222	30.13 N	95.45 W
Magnor	26	59.57 N	12.12 E
Magny-en-Vexin	50	49.09 N	1.47 E
Magny-le-Hongre	261	48.52 N	2.49 E
Magny-les-Hameaux	261	48.44 N	2.04 E
Mago	89	53.15 N	140.13 E
Magog	206	45.16 N	72.09 W
Magog ≃	206	45.24 N	71.54 W
Magog, Lake ⊜	206	45.18 N	72.03 W
Magoito	266c	38.52 N	9.26 W
Magome ◆[8]	268	35.35 N	139.43 E
Mago National Park ♦	144	5.30 N	36.15 E
Magonoy	116	6.54 N	124.33 E
Magoro	154	1.44 N	34.06 E
Magothy Bay c	208	37.10 N	75.55 W
Magothy River c	208	39.04 N	76.28 W
Magoúla	267c	38.04 N	23.32 E
Magoye	154	16.00 S	27.37 E
Magozal, Méx.	232	21.34 N	97.59 W
Magozal, Méx.	234	21.34 N	97.59 W
M'agozero	76	60.21 N	34.50 E
Magpie	186	50.19 N	64.30 W
Magpie ≃, On., Can.	190	47.56 N	84.50 W
Magpie ≃, P.Q., Can.	186	50.19 N	64.27 W
Magpie, Lac ⊜	186	51.00 N	64.41 W
Magpie Ouest ≃	186	51.02 N	64.42 W
Magra	126	22.59 N	88.22 E
Magra ≃	64	44.03 N	9.58 E
Magra Hāt	126	22.14 N	88.23 E
Magrath	182	49.25 N	112.52 W
Magrè (Margreid)	64	46.17 N	11.12 E
Magro ≃	34	39.11 N	0.25 W
Magruder Mountain ʌ	204	37.25 N	117.33 W
Magsaysay (Linugos)	116	9.01 N	125.11 E
Magsingal	116	17.41 N	120.25 E
Magu ≃	250	2.56 S	41.55 W
Maguan	102	22.59 N	104.19 E
Maguanying	271a	39.52 N	116.17 E
Maguari, Cabo ›	250	0.18 S	48.22 W
Magude	156	25.02 S	32.40 E
Magudu	158	27.31 S	31.40 E
Magueyes	196	25.44 N	97.47 W
Maguindanao □[4]	116	6.55 N	124.20 E
Magumeri	146	12.08 N	12.50 E
Māgura	124	23.29 N	89.25 E
Maguru	150	12.28 N	6.35 E
Maguse Lake ⊜	176	61.40 N	95.10 W
Maguzhan	120	31.15 N	88.00 E
Magway, Mya.	110	20.09 N	94.55 E
Magway, Mya.	110	20.30 N	94.30 E
Magwe	154	4.08 N	32.17 E
Magwood Park ♦	275b	43.39 N	79.30 W
Magyarország → Hungary □[1]	30	47.00 N	20.00 E
Mahābād	128	36.45 N	45.43 E
Mahābaleshwar	122	17.55 N	73.40 E
Mahabe	157b	17.05 S	45.20 E
Mahābhārat Lek ⩘	124	27.40 N	84.30 E
Mahabo, Madag.	157b	23.40 S	46.08 E
Mahabo, Madag.	157b	20.23 S	44.40 E
Mahād	122	18.05 N	73.25 E
Mahadday Weyn	144	2.58 N	45.32 E
Mahādebpur	126	23.51 N	89.53 E
Mahādeo Hills ⩘[2]	122	22.22 N	78.34 E
Mahādeo Range ⩘	122	17.50 N	74.15 E
Mahaffey	214	40.52 N	78.43 W
Mahagi	154	2.18 N	30.59 E
Mahagi Port	154	2.09 N	31.14 E
Mahai	102	38.17 N	94.13 E
Mahaica-Berbice □[4]	246	6.20 N	57.50 W
Mahaicony Village	246	6.36 N	57.48 W
Mahajamba ≃	157b	15.33 S	47.08 E
Mahajamba, Helodranon' i c	157b	15.24 S	47.05 E
Mahājan	123	28.47 N	73.50 E
Mahajanga	157b	15.43 S	46.19 E
Mahajanga □[4]	157b	17.00 S	46.00 E
Mahajilo ≃	157b	19.42 S	45.22 E
Mahajjah	132	32.57 N	36.14 E
Mahākālī □[8]	124	29.30 N	80.30 E
Mahākālī (Sārda) ≃	124	27.21 N	81.23 E
Mahakam ≃	112	0.35 S	117.17 E
Mahālandi	126	24.04 N	88.07 E
Mahalatswe	156	23.05 S	26.51 E
Mahalla el-Kubra → Al-Mahallah al-Kubrā	142	30.58 N	31.10 E
Mahallāt	128	33.55 N	50.27 E
Mahallat Kayl	142	31.01 N	30.17 E
Mahallat Marḥūm	142	30.48 N	30.57 E
Mahallat Minūf	142	30.53 N	30.58 E
Mahallat Zayyād	142	31.02 N	31.14 E
Maham	124	28.59 N	76.18 E
Mahamba	158	27.07 S	31.10 E
Mahānadi ≃	118	20.19 N	86.45 E
Mahānadpati	126	23.00 N	88.16 E
Mahānanda ≃	124	24.29 N	88.18 E
Mahanay Island I	116	10.12 N	124.14 E
Mahanoro	157b	19.54 S	48.48 E
Mahanoy City	208	40.48 N	76.08 W
Mahanoy Creek ≃	208	40.42 N	76.51 W
Mahantango Creek ≃	208	40.47 N	76.56 W
Mahantango Mountain ʌ	208	40.40 N	76.45 W
Mahao	89	43.10 N	127.59 E
Mahape	272c	19.07 N	73.01 E
Mahārājganj, India	124	27.09 N	83.34 E
Mahārājganj, India	124	26.07 N	84.29 E
Mahārājpur, India	124	25.01 N	79.44 E
Mahārājpur, India	272a	28.39 N	77.20 E
Mahārāshtra □[3]	122	19.00 N	76.00 E
Mahārīq, Wādī V	142	27.48 N	31.47 E
Mahārlū, Daryācheh-ye ⊜	128	29.25 N	52.50 E
Mahāsamund	120	21.06 N	82.06 E
Maha Sarakham	110	16.11 N	103.18 E
Maha Sawat, Khlong ≋	269a	13.47 N	100.28 E
Mahasoa	157b	22.12 S	46.06 E
Mahasolo	157b	19.07 S	46.22 E
Mahates	246	10.14 N	75.12 W
Mahatsinjo	157b	21.26 S	45.51 E
Mahattat al-Hafīf	132	32.12 N	37.08 E
Mahaut	240d	15.21 N	61.25 W
Mahavavy ≃, Madag.	157b	15.57 S	45.54 E
Mahavavy ≃, Madag.	157b	13.00 S	48.55 E
Mahaweli ≃	122	8.27 N	81.13 E
Mahaxai	110	17.25 N	105.12 E
Mahbas, Wādī al- V	140	15.50 N	29.45 E
Mahbūbābād	122	17.37 N	80.01 E
Mahbūbnagar	122	16.44 N	77.59 E
Mahd adh-Dhahab	128	23.30 N	40.52 E
Mahdāt, Bi'r al- ⊤[4]	142	30.44 N	32.32 E
Mahdia, Guy.	246	5.16 N	59.09 W
Mahdia, Tun.	148	35.30 N	11.04 E
Mahdia □[8]	148	35.18 N	10.45 E
Mahe	122	11.42 N	75.32 E
Mahébourg	157c	20.24 S	57.42 E
Mahé Island I	138	4.40 S	55.28 E
Mahendraganj	124	25.20 N	89.45 E
Mahendragarh	124	28.17 N	76.09 E
Mahendra Giri ʌ	122	18.58 N	84.21 E
Mahendranagar	124	28.52 N	80.17 E
Mahenge, Tan.	154	7.38 S	36.16 E
Mahenge, Tan.	154	8.41 S	36.43 E
Maheno	172	45.10 S	170.50 E
Mahesāna	120	23.36 N	72.24 E
Mahesgādi	272b	22.39 N	88.33 E
Maheshmunda	126	24.13 N	86.24 E
Maheshtala	272b	22.30 N	88.15 E
Maheshwar	120	22.11 N	75.35 E
Mahespur	124	23.21 N	88.55 E
Mahgawān	124	26.29 N	78.37 E
Mahi ≃	120	22.16 N	72.58 E
Mahia Peninsula ›[1]	172	39.10 S	177.53 E
Mahiāri	272b	22.35 N	88.14 E
Māhikpur	272b	22.32 N	88.14 E
Mahilāra	126	22.56 N	90.16 E
Māhīm ◆[8]	272c	19.03 N	72.49 E
Māhīm ≃	272c	19.03 N	72.51 E
Māhīm Bay c	272c	19.02 N	72.50 E
Mahina, Mali	150	13.46 N	10.51 W
Mahina, Poly. fr.	174s	17.31 S	149.30 W
Mahinerangi, Lake ⊜	172	45.51 S	169.57 E
Mahinog	116	9.09 N	124.47 E
Mahīshādal	126	22.11 N	87.59 E
Mahishdānga	272b	22.54 N	88.11 E
Mahlabatini	158	28.14 S	31.30 E
Mahlangasi	158	27.37 S	31.42 E
Mahlberg	58	48.17 N	7.48 E
Mahlow	54	52.22 N	13.24 E
Mahlsdorf	54	52.47 N	11.13 E
Mahlsdorf-Süd ◆[8]	264a	52.29 N	13.36 E
Mahmūdābād, India	124	27.18 N	81.07 E
Mahmūdābād, Īrān	128	36.38 N	52.15 E
Mahmūd-e Rāqī	120	35.01 N	69.20 E
Mahmūdīyah, Tur'at al- ≋	142	31.11 N	29.53 E
Mahmudiye	130	39.30 N	31.00 E
Mahmūdpur, India	272a	28.46 N	77.22 E
Mahmudpur, India	272b	22.41 N	88.09 E
Mahmutbey ◆[8]	267b	41.03 N	28.49 E
Mahmutşevketpaşa	130	41.05 N	29.19 E
Mahmutşevketpaşa ◆[8]	267b	41.09 N	29.11 E
Mahnomen	198	47.18 N	95.58 W
Mahoba	124	25.17 N	79.52 E
Mahogany Mountain ʌ	202	43.14 N	117.16 W
Mahomet	216	40.11 N	88.24 W
Mahone Bay	186	44.27 N	64.23 W
Mahone Bay c	186	44.30 N	64.15 W
Mahoning □[6]	214	41.06 N	80.39 W
Mahoning ≃	214	40.58 N	80.23 W
Mahoning, West Branch ≃	214	41.12 N	80.57 W
Mahoning Creek ≃	214	40.55 N	79.27 W
Mahoning Creek Lake ⊜[1]	214	40.50 N	79.10 W
Mahony Lake ⊜	180	65.30 N	125.20 W
Mahood Falls	182	51.50 N	120.39 W
Mahood Lake ⊜	182	51.55 N	120.24 W
Mahopac	210	41.22 N	73.44 W
Mahopac Falls	210	41.22 N	73.46 W
Mahora	34	39.13 N	1.44 W
Mahoras Brook ≃	276	40.25 N	74.08 W
Mahrāt, Jabal ⩘[1]	144	17.05 N	51.30 E
Mahrauli ◆[8]	272a	28.31 N	77.11 E
Mahrauni	124	24.35 N	78.43 E
Mähren → Morava □[9]	30	49.20 N	17.00 E
Mahres	148	34.32 N	10.30 E
Mähring	60	49.55 N	12.32 E
Mahuiling	100	29.24 N	115.48 E
Māhul ◆[8]	272c	19.01 N	72.53 E
Mahulia	126	22.39 N	86.24 E
Mahur Island I	164	2.50 S	152.40 E
Mahuta	154	10.52 S	39.27 E
Mahuva	120	21.05 N	71.48 E
Mahwa	124	27.03 N	76.56 E
Mahwah	276	41.06 N	74.09 W
Mahwah ≃	276	41.06 N	74.10 W
Mai, Île de I	275a	45.36 N	73.50 W
Maia, Am. Sam.	174y	14.13 S	169.28 W
Maia, Port.	34	41.14 N	8.37 W
Mai Aini	144	14.47 N	39.06 E
Maiala National Park ♦	171a	27.19 S	152.46 E
Maianga	152	14.12 S	21.45 E
Maiano	64	46.11 N	13.04 E
Maiauatá	250	1.51 S	49.02 W
Maicao	246	11.23 N	72.13 W
Maîche	58	47.15 N	6.48 E
Maichen	102	20.29 N	109.59 E
Maici ≃	248	6.30 S	61.43 W
Maicuru ≃	250	2.14 S	54.17 W
Maida	68	38.51 N	16.22 E
Maidan ♦	272b	22.33 N	88.21 E
Maiden	192	35.34 N	81.12 W
Maidenhead	42	51.32 N	0.44 W
Maiden Newton	42	50.46 N	2.35 W
Maidstone, Austl.	274b	37.47 S	144.52 E
Maidstone, On., Can.	214	42.13 N	82.53 W
Maidstone, Sk., Can.	184	53.06 N	109.18 W
Maidstone, Eng., U.K.	42	51.17 N	0.32 E
Maidstone □[8]	260	51.17 N	0.35 E
Maiduguri	146	11.51 N	13.10 E
Maie	154	2.46 N	30.34 E
Maiella, Montagna della ⩘	66	42.05 N	14.07 E
Maienfeld	58	47.00 N	9.32 E
Maierato	68	38.42 N	16.11 E
Maifeld □[9]	56	50.20 N	7.20 E
Maigatari	150	12.46 N	9.27 E
Maignelay	50	49.33 N	2.31 E
Maigo	116	8.10 N	123.57 E
Mai Gudo ʌ	144	7.29 N	37.12 E
Maihar	124	24.16 N	80.45 E
Maihara	94	35.19 N	136.17 E
Maijoma	196	28.55 N	104.21 W
Maikala Plateau ⩘[1]	124	22.30 N	81.00 E
Maikala Range ⩘	122	22.30 N	81.30 E
Maikammer	56	49.18 N	9.07 E
Maiko ≃	154	0.14 N	25.33 E
Maiko, Parc National de la ♦	154	3.30 N	27.45 E
Maikoor, Pulau I	164	6.15 S	134.15 E
Mailand → Milano	62	45.28 N	9.12 E
Mailāni	124	28.17 N	80.21 E
Mailasqui	256	23.33 S	47.04 W
Maili	229c	21.25 N	158.10 W
Maillane	62	43.50 N	4.47 E
Mailley-et-Chazelot	58	47.32 N	6.03 E
Maillezais	32	46.22 N	0.44 W
Mailly-le-Camp	50	48.40 N	4.13 E
Mailly-le-Château	50	47.36 N	3.38 E
Mailly-Maillet	50	50.04 N	2.36 E
Mailsi	123	29.48 N	72.11 E
Maimbung	116	5.56 N	121.02 E
Mai Mefales	144	14.59 N	38.16 E
Mā'īn	132	31.41 N	35.44 E
Main ≃, Dtsch.	30	50.00 N	8.18 E
Main ≃, N. Ire., U.K.	48	54.43 N	6.18 W
Maināguri	124	26.34 N	88.49 E
Mainau	58	47.42 N	9.11 E
Mainburg	60	48.38 N	11.47 E
Main Camp	174o	2.01 N	157.25 W
Main Canal ≋, Ca., U.S.	226	37.25 N	121.05 W
Main Canal ≋, Ca., U.S.	226	37.23 N	120.26 W
Main Canal ≋, Wa., U.S.	224	47.07 N	120.44 W
Main Channel ʊ	190	45.22 N	81.50 W
Maincourt-sur-Yvette	261	48.43 N	1.58 E
Main Creek ≃	276	40.34 N	74.11 W
Maincy	261	48.33 N	2.42 E
Mai-Ndombe, Lac ⊜	152	2.00 S	18.20 E
Main-Donau-Kanal ≋	60	49.02 N	11.36 E
Main Duck Island I	212	43.56 N	76.37 W
Maine	210	42.11 N	76.03 W
Maine □[9]	32	48.15 N	0.05 W
Maine □[3], U.S.	178	45.15 N	69.15 W
Maine □[3], U.S.	188	45.15 N	69.15 W
Maine ≃	48	52.09 N	9.45 W
Maine, Gulf of c	178	43.00 N	68.00 W
Mainebene □[9]	56	50.00 N	8.45 E
Maine-et-Loire □[5]	32	47.25 N	0.30 W
Mainesburg	210	41.47 N	77.07 W
Maïné-Soroa	146	13.12 N	12.02 E
Maineville	218	39.18 N	84.13 W
Mainguerin	261	48.32 N	1.51 E
Mainhardt	56	49.04 N	9.33 E
Mainit	116	9.32 N	125.32 E
Mainit, Lake ⊜	116	9.26 N	125.32 E
Mainland	285	40.15 N	75.22 W
Mainland I, Scot., U.K.	46	59.00 N	3.15 W
Mainland I, Scot., U.K.	46a	60.16 N	1.16 W
Mainleus	54	50.06 N	11.22 E
Mainoru	164	14.02 S	134.05 E
Mainpuri	124	27.14 N	79.01 E
Main Range National Park ♦	171a	28.01 S	152.22 E
Maintal	56	50.09 N	8.54 E
Maintenon	50	48.35 N	1.35 E
Maintirano	157b	18.03 S	44.01 E
Main Topsail ʌ	186	49.08 N	56.33 W
Mainvilliers	50	48.27 N	1.28 E
Mainz	56	50.01 N	8.16 E
Maio I	150a	15.15 N	23.10 W
Maiolati Spontini	66	43.28 N	13.06 E
Maiori	68	40.39 N	14.38 E
Maiori, Nuraghe ⊥	71	40.56 N	9.06 E
Maipa	164	8.21 S	146.33 E
Maipo ≃	252	33.37 S	71.39 W
Maipo, Volcán ʌ[1]	252	34.10 S	69.50 W
Maipú, Arg.	252	36.52 S	57.52 W
Maipú, Arg.	252	32.58 S	68.47 W
Maipú, Chile	252	33.31 S	70.46 W
Maiqihamiao	89	43.22 N	120.46 E
Maiquetía	246	10.36 N	66.57 W
Maira ≃	62	44.49 N	7.38 E
Maira, Valle V	62	44.30 N	7.08 E
Mairābāri	120	26.28 N	92.26 E
Mairi	250	11.43 S	40.08 W
Mairinque	256	23.33 S	47.10 W
Mairiporã	256	23.19 S	46.35 W
Mairiporã □[7]	287b	23.24 S	46.37 W
Mairipotaba	255	17.18 S	49.28 W
Maisach	60	48.13 N	11.16 E
Maisaka	94	34.41 N	137.37 E
Maishi	100	29.11 N	113.58 E
Maišiagala	76	54.52 N	25.04 E
Maiskhāl Island I	120	21.36 N	91.56 E
Maison de Pierre, Lac de la ⊜	206	46.53 N	74.42 W
Maisonneuve, Parc ♦	275a	45.33 N	73.34 W
Maisons-Alfort	261	48.48 N	2.26 E
Maisons-Laffitte	50	48.57 N	2.09 E
Maisons-Laffitte, Château de ⊥	261	48.57 N	2.09 E
Maisse	50	48.24 N	2.23 E
Maissin	56	49.58 N	5.11 E
Maitani	270	34.49 N	135.22 E
Maitengwe	156	20.06 S	27.13 E
Maitengwe ≃	156	19.59 S	26.26 E
Maithon Reservoir ⊜[1]	126	23.50 N	86.43 E
Maitland, Austl.	168b	34.22 S	137.40 E
Maitland, Austl.	170	32.44 S	151.33 E
Maitland, N.S., Can.	186	45.19 N	63.30 W
Maitland, On., Can.	212	44.38 N	75.37 W
Maitland, Fl., U.S.	220	28.37 N	81.21 W
Maitland ≃	190	43.45 N	81.43 W
Maitland, Lake ⊜	162	27.11 S	121.03 E
Maixie	100	27.38 N	115.29 E
Maíz ≃	236	11.17 N	83.52 W
Maíz, Islas del II	236	12.15 N	83.00 W
Maizefield	158	26.28 S	29.31 E
Maizhokunggar	120	29.50 N	91.45 E
Maizières-lès-Metz	56	49.13 N	6.09 E
Maizières-lès-Vic	58	48.43 N	6.46 E
Maizuru	96	35.28 N	135.24 E
Maja ≃, Ross.	74	60.24 N	134.30 E
Maja ≃, Ross.	89	54.31 N	134.41 E
Majābirah, Minqār al- ≗[4]	142	30.16 N	29.49 E
Majačka ≃	83	48.44 N	37.33 E
Majačnyj	86	52.41 N	55.44 E
Majadahonda	266a	40.29 N	3.52 W
Majagua	240p	21.55 N	79.00 W
Majagual	246	8.33 N	74.38 W
Majaki, Ukr.	78	46.25 N	30.16 E
Majaki, Ukr.	83	48.57 N	37.37 E
Majalaya	115a	7.03 S	107.45 E
Majalengka	115a	6.50 S	108.13 E
Majana, Ensenada de c	240p	22.41 N	82.45 W
Majanji	154	0.15 N	33.59 E
Majari ≃	246	3.29 N	60.58 W
Majayjay	116	14.09 N	121.28 E
Majchura	85	39.02 N	68.35 E
Majdantal	85	43.41 N	68.02 E
Majd el Kurūm	132	32.55 N	35.15 E
Majé	256	22.39 S	43.02 W
Majeigha	140	11.33 N	24.40 E
Majenang	115a	7.18 S	108.45 E
Majene	112	3.33 S	118.57 E
Majenica	216	40.46 N	85.27 W
Majevica ⩘	38	44.30 N	18.55 E
Maji	144	6.11 N	35.38 E
Majia	100	32.32 N	118.50 E
Majia ≃	98	38.09 N	117.53 E
Majiacun	106	30.08 N	119.58 E
Majiahe	102	35.20 N	104.46 E
Majian, Zhg.	100	29.19 N	119.36 E
Majian, Zhg.	100	29.43 N	120.00 E
Majiang, Zhg.	102	23.48 N	111.09 E
Majiang, Zhg.	110	26.28 N	107.28 E
Majiangzong	120	30.27 N	90.03 E
Majiaoba	102	32.14 N	104.35 E
Majiaping	102	36.31 N	103.20 E
Majiasi	105	39.03 N	117.05 E
Majiawopu	104	41.46 N	121.06 E
Majiayan	100	27.26 N	112.56 E
Majiazhai	104	42.22 N	124.04 E
Majiazhou	100	26.46 N	114.47 E
Majidun Creek ≃	273a	6.38 N	3.28 E
Majie, Zhg.	102	23.50 N	105.07 E
Majie, Zhg.	102	25.03 N	103.45 E
Majin	100	29.18 N	118.24 E
Majin ≃	100	29.00 N	118.21 E
Majinzhuangzi	104	41.55 N	123.53 E
Maji Shan I	106	31.26 N	120.06 E
Majītha	123	31.46 N	74.57 E
Majja	74	61.44 N	130.18 E
Majkain	86	51.27 N	75.52 E
Majkop	84	44.35 N	40.07 E
Majkor	86	59.01 N	55.54 E
Majlibaš	86	45.49 N	62.39 E
Majli-Saj	85	41.17 N	72.29 E
Majlispur	126	24.13 N	90.53 E
Majmak	85	42.40 N	71.15 E
Majna, Ross.	80	54.07 N	47.37 E
Majna, Ross.	86	53.00 N	91.28 E
Majnan	272b	22.59 N	88.09 E
Majnic, ozero ⊜	180	63.15 N	176.40 E
Majno-Gytkino	180	63.36 N	176.30 E
Majŏn-ni, C.M.I.K.	98	39.06 N	127.07 E
Majŏn-ni, Taehan	271b	37.36 N	126.41 E
Major, Puig ʌ	34	39.48 N	2.48 E
Majorca → Mallorca I	34	39.30 N	3.00 E
Major Creek ≃	169	36.51 S	145.05 E
Major Isidoro	250	9.32 S	37.00 W
Majorque, Île → Mallorca I	34	39.30 N	3.00 E
Majrūr	140	14.01 N	30.27 E
Majrūr, Wādī V	140	15.44 N	26.26 E
Majsk	86	57.49 N	77.16 E
Majskij, Ross.	83	47.43 N	40.03 E
Majskij, Ross.	84	43.38 N	44.04 E
Majskij, Ross.	89	52.18 N	129.38 E
Majskij, Ross.	89	49.00 N	140.10 E
Majskoje, Kaz.	86	50.55 N	78.15 E
Majskoje, Ross.	82	56.08 N	37.55 E
Majtan	86	45.46 N	74.20 E
Majtobe	85	43.01 N	70.35 E
Māju	126	22.37 N	88.05 E
Majuba Hill ⊥	158	27.28 S	29.51 E
Majuqiao	105	39.46 N	116.32 E
Majuro I[1]	14	7.09 N	171.12 E
Majuzigou	104	41.49 N	121.38 E
Maka	150	13.40 N	14.17 W
Makabana	152	2.48 S	12.29 E
Makabe	94	36.16 N	140.06 E
Makadasa ≃	116	7.22 N	124.36 E
Makaha, Hi., U.S.	229c	21.28 N	158.13 W
Makaha, Zimb.	154	17.17 S	32.37 E
Makaha Point ›	229b	22.08 N	159.44 W
Makah Indian Reservation ◆[4]	224	48.20 N	124.41 W
Makahuena Point ›	229b	21.52 N	159.27 W
Makak	152	3.33 N	11.02 E
Makala	273b	4.25 S	15.17 E
Makalamabedi	156	20.19 S	23.51 E
Makale	112	3.06 S	119.51 E
Makallé	252	27.13 S	59.17 W
Makālu ʌ	124	27.54 N	87.06 E
Makamba	154	4.08 S	29.49 E
Makanapur	272a	28.38 N	77.21 E
Makanči	86	46.48 N	82.00 E
Makanya	154	4.20 S	37.51 E
Makanza	152	1.36 N	19.07 E
Makaoo Indian Reserve ◆[4]	184	53.40 N	110.02 W
Makapu Point ›	174v	18.59 S	169.56 W
Makapuu Head ›	229c	21.19 N	157.39 W
Makarakomburu, Mount ʌ	175e	9.43 S	160.02 E
Makarakskij	86	55.36 N	88.03 E
Makarapan Mountain ʌ	246	4.00 N	58.51 W
Makarewa	172	46.20 S	168.21 E
Makari	146	12.35 N	14.28 E
Makar-Ib	24	63.39 N	49.24 E
Makaricha	24	66.15 N	58.20 E
Makarje	80	58.35 N	48.11 E
Makarjev	80	57.52 N	43.48 E
Makarjevo	80	56.06 N	45.06 E
Makarov, Ross.	89	48.38 N	142.48 E
Makarov, Ukr.	78	50.28 N	29.49 E
Makarovo, Ross.	80	52.18 N	43.20 E
Makarovo, Ross.	82	54.22 N	36.40 E
Makarovo, Ross.	88	57.29 N	107.52 E
Makarska	36	43.18 N	17.02 E
Makasar, Selat (Makassar Strait) ʊ	112	2.00 S	117.30 E
Makasar → Ujungpandang	112	5.07 S	119.24 E
Makaševka	80	51.30 N	42.36 E
Makassar Strait → Makasar, Selat ʊ	112	2.00 S	117.30 E
Makasuko	154	6.00 S	34.56 E
Makat	80	47.39 N	53.19 E
Makatea I	14	15.50 S	148.15 W
Makati	269f	14.34 N	121.02 E
Makaw, Mya.	110	26.27 N	96.42 E
Makaw, Zaïre	152	3.29 S	18.19 E
Makawao	229a	20.51 N	156.18 W
Makaweli	229b	21.55 N	159.38 W
Makay, Massif du ⩘	157b	21.15 S	45.15 E
Makaya	152	3.22 S	18.02 E
Makedonija → Macedonia □[1]	38	41.50 N	22.00 E
Makefu	174v	18.59 S	169.55 W
Makejevka, Ukr.	78	50.40 N	31.50 E
Makejevka, Ukr.	83	48.02 N	37.58 E
Makejevka, Ukr.	83	49.14 N	37.59 E
Makemie Park	208	37.55 N	75.34 W
Makemo I[1]	14	16.35 S	143.40 W
Makena	229a	20.39 N	156.27 W
Makeni	150	8.53 N	12.03 W
Makere	154	4.17 S	30.25 E
Maketu	172	37.46 S	176.27 E
Makeyevka → Makejevka	83	48.02 N	37.58 E
Makgadikgadi ≚	156	20.45 S	25.30 E
Makgadikgadi Pans Game Reserve ◆[4]	156	20.30 S	24.45 E
Makhachkala → Machačkala	84	42.58 N	47.30 E
Makhad	123	33.08 N	71.44 E
Makhaleng ≃	158	30.20 S	27.23 E
Mākhālpur	272b	22.56 N	88.10 E
Makham	110	12.40 N	102.12 E
Makhdūmnagar	124	26.28 N	82.46 E
Makhfar al-Quwayrah	132	29.48 N	35.19 E
Makhfar Ramn	132	29.42 N	35.25 E
Makhrūq, Wādī al- V	132	31.30 N	37.10 E
Makhyah, Wādī V	144	17.40 N	49.01 E
Maki, Indon.	164	3.11 S	134.14 E
Maki, Nihon	92	37.45 N	138.53 E
Maki, Nihon	94	37.05 N	138.23 E
Maki, Nihon	270	34.52 N	135.04 E
Makika, Lua ≗[6]	229a	20.34 N	156.34 W
Makikihi	172	44.38 S	171.09 E
Makilala	116	6.55 N	125.05 E
Makindu	154	2.17 S	37.49 E
Makino, Nihon	94	35.28 N	136.05 E
M'akino, Ross.	265b	55.48 N	37.22 E
Makinsk	86	52.37 N	70.26 E
Makio-dam ◆[6]	94	35.50 N	137.36 E
Makioka	94	35.45 N	138.43 E
Makira □[4]	175e	11.00 S	162.30 E
Makira Harbour c	175e	10.25 S	161.29 E
M'akiševo	76	56.34 N	28.53 E
M'akit	74	61.24 N	152.09 E
Makkah (Mecca)	144	21.27 N	39.49 E
Makkavejevo	88	51.44 N	113.58 E
Makkum	52	53.04 N	5.24 E
Makó, Magy.	30	46.13 N	20.29 E
Mako, Sén.	150	12.52 N	12.21 W
Makoaneng ʌ	158	29.47 S	28.57 E
Makobe Lake ⊜	190	47.27 N	80.25 W
Makoka	154	2.34 S	25.29 E
Makok-ni	271b	37.43 N	126.38 E
Makokou	152	0.34 N	12.52 E
Makoli	154	17.27 S	26.05 E
Makongai Island I	175g	17.27 S	178.58 E
Makongo	154	3.25 N	26.22 E
Makongolosi	154	8.24 S	33.09 E
Makopse	84	43.59 N	39.13 E
Makorako ʌ	172	39.09 S	176.02 E
Makoro	154	3.08 N	29.44 E
Makoshika State Park ♦	198	47.03 N	104.41 W
Makošino	78	51.27 N	32.18 E
Makotuku	172	40.07 S	176.14 E
Makoua	152	0.01 N	15.39 E
Makov	30	49.23 N	18.30 E
Makovskoje	86	58.12 N	90.52 E
Maków Mazowiecki	30	52.52 N	21.06 E
Maków Podhalański	30	49.44 N	19.41 E
Makrai	124	22.04 N	77.06 E
Makrampur	126	22.44 N	90.14 E
Makrāna	120	27.03 N	74.43 E
Makran Coast ≗[2]	128	25.15 N	61.00 E
M'aksa	76	58.54 N	38.12 E
Maksaticha	76	57.48 N	35.53 E
Maksimicha	88	53.15 N	108.43 E
Maksimkin Jar	86	58.42 N	86.48 E
Maksimoviči	78	51.13 N	29.37 E
Maksimovka, Ross.	80	52.59 N	51.10 E
Maksimovka, Ross.	89	46.04 N	137.51 E
Maksimovka, Ukr.	83	47.38 N	37.34 E
Maksimovo	82	56.20 N	35.58 E
Maksudangarh	124	24.03 N	77.15 E
Maktar	148	35.51 N	9.12 E
Maktau	154	3.24 S	38.08 E
Mākū, Īrān	128	39.17 N	44.31 E
Maku, Zhg.	105	39.33 N	114.46 E
Makuhari	268	35.39 N	140.03 E
Makuliro	154	9.35 S	37.26 E
Makumbako	154	8.51 S	34.50 E
Makumbi	152	5.51 S	20.41 E
Makung (P'enghu)	100	23.34 N	119.34 E
Makunudu I	122	6.25 N	72.41 E
Makunudu Atoll I[1]	122	6.20 N	72.36 E
Makuragi-san ʌ	96	35.32 N	133.08 E
Makurazaki	92	31.16 N	130.19 E
Makurdi	150	7.45 N	8.32 E
Makushin Volcano ʌ[1]	180	53.53 N	166.50 W
Makušino	86	55.13 N	67.13 E
Makuyuni	154	3.33 S	36.06 E
Makwa Lake ⊜	184	54.04 N	109.15 W
Makwassie	158	27.26 S	26.00 E
Makwende-Bayo	154	7.08 S	28.06 E
Makwiro	154	17.58 S	30.28 E
Māl, India	124	26.52 N	88.44 E
Mal, Maur.	150	16.58 N	13.23 W
Mala, Perú	248	12.39 S	76.38 W
Malå, Sve.	26	65.11 N	18.44 E
Mala ≃	248	12.40 S	76.41 W
Mala, Punta ›	246	7.28 N	80.00 W
Malabang	116	7.38 N	124.03 E
Malabar, Austl.	274a	33.58 S	151.15 E
Malabar, Fl., U.S.	220	28.00 N	80.33 W
Malabar Coast ≗[2]	122	11.00 N	75.00 E
Malabar Farm State Park ♦	214	40.38 N	82.25 W
Malabar Hill ʌ[2]	272c	18.57 N	72.48 E
Malabar Point ›	272c	18.57 N	72.47 E
Malabo	152	3.45 N	8.47 E
Mal Abrigo	258	34.09 S	56.57 W
Malabrigo Point ›	116	13.36 N	121.15 E
Malabuyoc	116	9.39 N	123.19 E
Malaca, Estrecho de → Malacca, Strait of ʊ	110	2.30 N	101.20 E
Malacacheta	255	17.50 S	42.05 W
Malacañang Palace ⊍	269f	14.36 N	120.59 E
Malacatepec, Volcán ʌ[1]	286a	19.10 N	99.16 W
Malacca, Strait of ʊ	110	2.30 N	101.20 E
Malachovka	82	55.39 N	38.00 E
Malachovo, Ross.	82	54.45 N	37.27 E
Malachovo, Ross.	82	54.22 N	37.31 E
Malachovskij	80	49.08 N	41.43 E
Malacky	30	48.27 N	17.00 E
Mālād ◆[8]	272c	19.11 N	72.51 E
Malad ≃	200	41.35 N	112.07 W
Malad City	202	42.11 N	112.15 W
Malad Creek ≃	272c	19.08 N	72.48 E
Malafede ≃	267a	41.47 N	12.24 E
Málaga, Col.	246	6.42 N	72.44 W
Málaga, Esp.	34	36.43 N	4.25 W
Malaga, Ca., U.S.	226	36.42 N	119.46 W
Malaga, N.J., U.S.	208	39.34 N	75.02 W
Malaga, N.M., U.S.	196	32.13 N	104.04 W
Málaga □[4]	34	36.50 N	4.40 W
Malagarasi	154	5.06 S	30.50 E
Malagarasi ≃	154	5.12 S	29.47 E
Malagash	186	45.46 N	63.23 W
Malagasy Republic → Madagascar □[1]	157b	19.00 S	46.00 E
Malago ≃	116	10.55 N	123.02 E
Malagón	34	39.10 N	3.51 W
Malagón ≃	34	37.35 N	7.29 W
Malagrotta ◆[8]	66	41.53 N	12.20 E
Mal'agurt	80	57.39 N	52.32 E
Malahat	224	48.32 N	123.34 W
Malahide	48	53.27 N	6.09 W
Malaimbandy	157b	20.20 S	45.36 E
Malaisie → Malaysia □[1]	112	2.30 N	112.30 E
Malaita □[4]	175e	9.00 S	161.00 E
Malaita I	175e	9.00 S	161.00 E
Malaja Beloz'orka	78	47.14 N	34.56 E
Malaja Bessergenovka	83	47.09 N	38.36 E
Malaja Borščovka	82	56.33 N	36.53 E
Malaja Bykovka	80	51.54 N	47.45 E
Malaja Čuja ≃	88	58.56 N	112.13 E
Malaja Devica	78	50.41 N	32.10 E
Malaja Doroginka	82	54.06 N	38.56 E
Malaja Dubna	82	55.52 N	38.58 E
Malaja Istra ≃	82	55.54 N	36.50 E
Malaja Ižmora	80	53.32 N	42.48 E
Malaja Janisol'	83	47.22 N	37.20 E
Malaja Jekaterinovka	80	51.26 N	44.17 E
Malaja Kinel' ≃	80	53.29 N	51.30 E
Malaja Kokšaga ≃	80	56.09 N	47.53 E
Malaja Konkudera ≃	88	57.26 N	112.37 E
Malaja Kuril'skaja Gr'ada (Habomai-Shotō) II	92a	43.30 N	146.10 E
Malaja Laba ≃	84	44.16 N	40.53 E
Malaja Neva ≃[1]	265a	59.57 N	30.15 E
Malaja Ochta ◆[8]	265a	59.56 N	30.24 E
Malaja Orlovka	80	47.18 N	41.24 E
Malaja Pera	24	64.11 N	54.47 E
Malaja Serdoba	80	52.28 N	44.56 E
Malaja Sestra ≃	82	56.17 N	35.57 E
Malaja Tokmačevka	78	47.32 N	35.54 E
Malaja Višera	76	58.51 N	32.14 E
Malaja Viska	78	48.39 N	31.38 E
Malaka, Sempitan ʊ	114	5.44 N	95.30 E
Malakāl	140	9.31 N	31.39 E
Malaka → Melaka	114	2.12 N	102.15 E
Malākand	123	34.34 N	71.56 E
Mala Kapela ⩘	36	44.50 N	15.30 E
Malakka, Strasse von → Malacca, Strait of ʊ	110	2.30 N	101.20 E
Malakoff, Fr.	261	48.49 N	2.19 E
Malakoff, Tx., U.S.	222	32.10 N	96.00 W
Malakpur ◆[8]	272a	28.42 N	77.12 E
Malakula □[8]	175f	16.20 S	167.20 E
Malakula I	175f	16.15 S	167.30 E
Malakwāl	123	32.34 N	73.13 E
Malala	164	5.15 S	147.10 E
Malalag	116	6.36 N	125.24 E
Malalbergo	64	44.43 N	11.32 E
Malamala	112	3.21 S	120.55 E
Mala Mala Game Reserve ◆[4]	156	24.52 S	31.30 E
Malamaui Island I	116	6.44 N	121.58 E
Malambo	246	10.52 N	74.47 W
Malambo, Arroyo ≃	258	33.43 S	58.46 W
Malambunga	116	9.02 N	117.38 E
Malamocco	64	45.22 N	12.20 E
Malampaya Sound ʊ	116	10.51 N	119.20 E
Malān	110	25.37 N	96.21 E
Malān, Rās ›	128	25.18 N	65.11 E
Malanao Island I	116	9.27 N	118.37 E
Malanas ≃	116	17.41 N	120.43 E
Mālancha	272b	22.55 N	88.26 E
Mālancha ≃[1]	126	21.40 N	89.20 E
Mālandighi	126	23.33 N	87.24 E
Malandji	152	5.56 S	22.18 E
Malang	115a	7.59 S	112.37 E
Malang, Gunung ʌ	115a	7.02 S	107.01 E
Malangali	154	8.34 S	34.51 E
Malangas	116	7.37 N	123.01 E
Malanggwā	124	26.52 N	85.34 E
Malangka, Tanjung ›	112	1.20 N	120.48 E
Malan Guan)(	105	40.16 N	117.39 E
Malanipa Island I	116	6.53 N	122.16 E
Malanje	152	9.32 S	16.20 E
Malanje □[5]	152	9.30 S	16.30 E
Malanut Bay c	116	9.16 N	117.59 E
Malanville	150	11.52 N	3.23 E
Malanyu	105	40.11 N	117.42 E
Malanzán	252	30.48 S	66.37 W
Mała Panew ≃	30	50.44 N	17.52 E
Malapantao, Mount ʌ	116	9.54 N	122.37 E
Malapardis Brook ≃	276	40.49 N	74.25 W
Mälaren ⊜	40	59.30 N	17.12 E
Malargüe	252	35.28 S	69.35 W
Mälar-See → Mälaren ⊜	40	59.30 N	17.12 E
Malartic	190	48.08 N	78.08 W
Malartic, Lac ⊜	190	48.15 N	78.07 W
Malasia → Malaysia □[1]	112	2.30 N	112.30 E
Malasiqui	116	15.55 N	120.25 E
Malaspina	254	44.56 S	66.54 W
Malaspina Glacier ⊓	180	59.50 N	140.30 W
Malaspina Strait ʊ	182	49.44 N	124.20 W
Malassis	261	48.38 N	2.03 E
Malāṭīyah	142	28.42 N	30.51 E
Malatya	130	38.21 N	38.19 E
Malatya □[4]	130	38.30 N	38.10 E
Malau	175f	15.10 S	166.48 E
Malaucène	62	44.10 N	5.08 E
Malaunay	50	49.32 N	1.02 E
Malaut	123	30.13 N	74.29 E
Malavalli	122	12.23 N	77.05 E
Malawali, Pulau I	116	7.03 N	117.18 E
Malawi □[1], Afr.	138	13.30 S	34.00 E
Malawi □[1], Afr.	154	13.30 S	34.00 E
Malawi, Lake → Nyasa, Lake ⊜	154	12.00 S	34.30 E
Malawiya	140	15.16 N	36.12 E
Malayagiri ʌ	120	21.23 N	85.16 E
Malayal	116	7.12 N	121.57 E
Malaya → Semenanjung Malaysia □[9]	114	4.00 N	102.00 E
Malaybalay	116	8.09 N	125.05 E
Malāyer	128	34.17 N	48.50 E
Malay Peninsula ›[1]	110	6.00 N	101.00 E
Malay Reef ✢[2]	166	17.59 S	149.18 E
Malaysia □[1], Asia	108	2.30 N	112.30 E
Malaysia □[1], Asia	112	2.30 N	112.30 E
Malazgirt	130	39.09 N	42.31 E
Malbaie ≃	186	47.39 N	70.09 W
Malbaie, La c	186	48.35 N	64.14 W
Malbon	166	21.04 S	140.18 E
Malbooma	162	30.41 S	134.11 E
Malborghetto Valbruna	64	46.30 N	13.26 E
Malbork	30	54.02 N	19.01 E
Malbrán	252	29.21 S	62.27 W
Malbuisson	58	46.48 N	6.18 E
Malbun	58	47.35 N	9.33 E
Malcesine	64	45.46 N	10.48 E
Mal'cevo	265b	55.56 N	37.57 E
Mal'čevskaja	78	49.04 N	40.21 E
Mal'čevsko-Polnenskaja	83	48.58 N	40.12 E
Malchanskij chrebet ⩘	88	50.45 N	109.30 E
Malchin	54	53.44 N	12.46 E
Malchiner See ⊜	54	53.43 N	12.38 E
Malching	60	48.19 N	13.12 E
Malchow	54	53.28 N	12.25 E
Malchow ◆[8]	264a	52.35 N	13.29 E
Malčir	88	49.44 N	93.18 E
Malcolm	162	28.56 S	121.30 E
Malcolm, Point ›	162	33.48 S	123.45 E
Malcolm Island I	182	50.40 N	127.00 W
Malcom	190	41.42 N	92.33 W
Malcompeth → Mahābaleshwar	122	17.55 N	73.40 E
Malcontenta	64	45.25 N	12.13 E
Malczyce	30	51.14 N	16.29 E
Māldah	124	25.02 N	88.09 E
Maldegem	50	51.13 N	3.27 E
Malden, Ma., U.S.	207	42.25 N	71.04 W
Malden, Mo., U.S.	194	36.33 N	89.57 W
Malden I	14	4.03 S	154.59 W
Malden ≃	283	42.24 N	71.05 W
Malden Bridge	210	42.28 N	73.35 W
Malden on Hudson	210	42.06 N	73.56 W
Maldivas → Maldives □[1]	12	3.15 N	73.00 E
Maldive Islands → Maldives □[1]	12	3.15 N	73.00 E
Mal di Ventre, Isola di I	71	39.59 N	8.18 E
Maldives □[1]	12	3.15 N	73.00 E
Maldon, Austl.	169	37.00 S	144.04 E
Maldon, Eng., U.K.	42	51.45 N	0.40 E
Maldon □[8]	260	51.43 N	0.40 E
Maldonado	252	34.54 S	54.57 W
Maldonado, Punta ›	234	16.20 N	98.35 W
Male, It.	64	46.21 N	10.55 E
Male, Mald.	12	4.10 N	73.30 E
Male, Mya.	110	23.02 N	95.58 E
Maléa, Ákra ›	38	36.26 N	23.12 E
Malea, Dolok ʌ	114	0.56 N	99.38 E
Malebo, Pool ⊜	152	4.17 S	15.20 E
Malediven → Maldives □[1]	12	3.15 N	73.00 E
Mālegaon	122	20.33 N	74.32 E
Malegno, It.	64	45.56 N	10.14 E
Malegno, It.	64	46.40 N	11.08 E
Malehra	124	24.34 N	79.19 E
Malein, Lake ⊜	140	7.55 N	28.35 E
Malejevka	78	47.29 N	32.43 E
Malek, Kaz.	85	40.47 N	68.37 E
Malek, Sūd.	140	6.04 N	31.36 E
Malé Karpaty ⩘	30	48.30 N	17.20 E
Malek Dīn	120	32.25 N	68.04 E
Malek Kandī	128	37.09 N	46.06 E
Malek Sīāh, Kūh-e ʌ	128	29.51 N	60.52 E
Malela, Zaïre	154	2.28 S	26.09 E
Malela, Zaïre	154	4.22 S	26.08 E
Malema	154	14.57 S	37.20 E
Malen'ga	24	63.50 N	36.25 E
Malengoya	154	3.32 N	25.25 E
Malente	54	54.10 N	10.33 E
Maleo	62	45.10 N	9.46 E
Māler Kotla	124	30.31 N	75.53 E
Malesco	58	46.08 N	8.30 E
Malesherbes	50	48.18 N	2.25 E
Malestroit	32	47.49 N	2.23 W
Maleta	88	50.50 N	108.25 E
Maletto	70	37.49 N	14.52 E
Malfa	70	38.35 N	14.50 E
Malgas	158	34.18 S	20.35 E
Malgersdorf	60	48.32 N	12.45 E
Malgobek	84	43.32 N	44.34 E
Malgomaj ⊜	26	64.47 N	16.12 E
Malha Wells	140	15.08 N	26.12 E
Malheur ≃	202	44.03 N	116.59 W
Malheur, North Fork ≃	202	43.45 N	118.04 W
Malheur, South Fork ≃	202	43.33 N	118.10 W
Malheureux, Cap ›	157c	19.59 S	57.36 E
Malheur Lake ⊜	202	43.20 N	118.45 W
Mali, Guinée	150	12.05 N	12.18 W
Mali, Zaïre	154	2.48 S	26.08 E
Mali □[1], Afr.	134	17.00 N	4.00 W
Mali □[1], Afr.	150	17.00 N	4.00 W
Mali ≃	102	25.43 N	97.29 E
Maliangping	102	31.29 N	111.20 E
Malianjingzi	102	41.32 N	95.23 E
Malibamatšo ≃	158	29.20 S	29.28 E
Malibu	228	34.02 N	118.42 W
Malibu Lake ⊜[1]	228	34.07 N	118.45 W
Malien ≃	269d	25.11 N	121.41 E
Malienkang	269d	25.10 N	121.39 E
Maligay Bay c	116	7.30 N	123.14 E
Malighati	126	22.33 N	87.40 E
Maligne ≃	182	52.56 N	118.02 W
Maligne Lake ⊜	182	52.40 N	117.31 W
Malihābād	124	26.55 N	80.43 E
Mālihah, Wādī V	142	29.21 N	32.35 E
Malik	112	0.34 S	123.14 E
Malik, Wādī al- V	140	18.02 N	30.58 E
Mali Kyun I	110	13.06 N	98.16 E
Malili	112	2.38 S	121.06 E
Målilla	26	57.23 N	15.48 E
Malimba, Monts ⩘	154	7.32 S	29.30 E
Malim Nawar	114	4.21 N	101.07 E
Malimono	116	9.34 N	125.25 E
Malin, Ire.	48	55.18 N	7.15 W

Symbols in the index entries represent the broad categories identified in the key at the right. Symbols with superior numbers (⩘[1]) identify subcategories (see complete key on page *I · 1).*

Symbole im Register stellen die rechts im Schlüssel erklärten Kategorien dar. Symbole mit hochgestellten Ziffern (⩘[1]) bezeichnen Unterabteilungen einer Kategorie (vgl. vollständiger Schlüssel auf Seite *I · 1).*

Los símbolos incluídos en el texto del índice representan las grandes categorias identificadas con la clave a la derecha. Los símbolos con numeros en su parte superior (⩘[1]) identifican las subcategorías (véase la clave completa en la página *I · 1).*

Les symboles de l'index représentent les catégories indiquées dans la légende à droite. Les symboles suivis d'un indice (⩘[1]) représentent des sous-catégories (voir légende complète à la page *I · 1).*

Os símbolos incluídos no texto do índice representam as grandes categorias identificadas com a chave à direita. Os símbolos com números em sua parte superior (⩘[1]) identificam as subcategorias (veja-se a chave completa à página *I · 1).*

	English	Deutsch	Español	Français	Português
ʌ	Mountain	Berg	Montaña	Montagne	Montanha
⩘	Mountains	Gebirge	Montañas	Montagnes	Montanhas
)(	Pass	Paß	Paso	Col	Passo
V	Valley, Canyon	Tal, Cañon	Valle, Cañón	Vallee, Canyon	Vale, Canhão
≚	Plain	Ebene	Llano	Plaine	Planície
›	Cape	Kap	Cabo	Cap	Cabo
I	Island	Insel	Isla	Île	Ilha
II	Islands	Inseln	Islas	Îles	Ilhas
≗	Other Topographic Features	Andere Topographische Objekte	Otros Elementos Topográficos	Autres données topographiques	Outros acidentes topográficos

ESPAÑOL

Nombre	Página	Lat.°'	Long.°' W = Oeste
Malin, Ukr.	78	50.46 N	29.15 E
Malin, Or., U.S.	202	42.00 N	121.24 W
Malinalco ⊥	234	18.57 N	99.30 W
Malinaltepec	234	17.03 N	98.40 W
Malinau	112	3.35 N	116.38 E
Malin Beg	48	54.40 N	8.48 W
Malindang, Mount ∧	116	8.13 N	123.38 E
Malindi	154	3.13 S	40.07 E
Malindi Marine National Park ♠	154	3.15 S	40.10 E
Malines → Mechelen	50	51.02 N	4.28 E
Malinga	152	2.25 S	12.14 E
Malingping	115a	6.46 S	106.01 E
Malingsbosjön ⊜	40	59.55 N	15.27 E
Malin Head ›	48	55.23 N	7.24 W
Malinki	82	54.05 N	38.59 E
Malinniki	82	56.17 N	38.24 E
Malino, Indon.	112	5.15 S	119.51 E
Malino, Ross.	82	55.06 N	38.11 E
Malino, Ross.	265b	55.58 N	37.13 E
Malino, Bukit ∧	112	0.45 N	120.47 E
Malinoa I	174w	21.02 S	175.08 W
Malinovka, Ross.	80	51.47 N	43.26 E
Malinovka, Ross.	86	53.24 N	87.17 E
Malinovka, Ukr.	78	49.47 N	36.43 E
Malinta	216	41.19 N	84.02 W
Malinyi	154	8.56 S	36.08 E
Malipāra	272b	22.57 N	88.14 E
Mali Rajinac ∧	36	44.48 N	15.02 E
Malita	116	6.25 N	125.36 E
Malitbog	116	10.10 N	125.00 E
Maliuchang	107	29.05 N	104.07 E
Maliuping	107	29.55 N	106.23 E
Ma Liu Shui	271d	22.25 N	114.12 E
Malivo	82	55.07 N	39.02 E
Maliwun	110	10.14 N	98.37 E
Malizhen	102	23.10 N	104.35 E
Maljamar	196	32.51 N	103.46 W
Malka, Ross.	74	53.20 N	157.30 E
Malka, Ross.	84	43.47 N	43.21 E
Malka ≃	84	43.44 N	44.15 E
Malkāpur	120	20.53 N	76.12 E
Malkara	130	40.53 N	26.54 E
Malkerns	158	26.32 S	31.11 E
Malko Târnovo	38	41.59 N	27.32 E
Mallāḥ	132	32.30 N	36.51 E
Mallaig, Ab., Can.	182	54.13 N	111.22 W
Mallaig, Scot., U.K.	46	57.00 N	5.50 W
Mallala	168b	34.26 S	138.30 E
Mallaoua	150	13.02 N	9.36 E
Mallapunyah	164	16.59 S	135.49 E
Mallaranny	48	53.54 N	9.49 W
Mallard Reservoir ⊜[1]	282	38.01 N	122.03 W
Mallawī	142	27.44 N	30.50 E
Mallee Cliffs National Park ♠	166	34.15 S	142.40 E
Mallemort	62	43.44 N	5.11 E
Mallersdorf	60	48.47 N	12.16 E
Mallery Lake ⊜	176	63.55 N	98.25 W
Malles Venosta (Mals)	64	46.41 N	10.32 E
Mallet	252	25.55 S	50.50 W
Mallig	116	17.08 N	121.41 E
Malligasta	252	29.11 S	67.26 W
Mallina	162	20.53 S	118.02 E
Malling	41	56.02 N	10.10 E
Mallnitz	64	46.59 N	13.10 E
Mallorca I	34	39.30 N	3.00 E
Mallorytown	212	44.29 N	75.53 W
Mallow	48	52.08 N	8.39 W
Mallwood	216	42.51 N	89.02 W
Malm	26	64.04 N	11.13 E
Malmbäck	26	57.35 N	14.28 E
Malmberget	24	67.10 N	20.40 E
Malmédy	56	50.25 N	6.02 E
Malmesbury, S. Afr.	158	33.28 S	18.44 E
Malmesbury, Eng., U.K.	42	51.36 N	2.06 W
Malmesbury, Vale of V	42	51.22 N	2.10 W
Malmköping	40	59.08 N	16.44 E
Malmlången ⊜	40	59.27 N	14.42 E
Malmö	41	55.36 N	13.00 E
Malmöhus Län □[6]	26	55.45 N	13.30 E
Malmsbury	169	37.12 S	144.23 E
Malmsbury Reservoir ⊜[1]	169	37.13 S	144.22 E
Malmslätt	26	58.25 N	15.30 E
Malmstrom Air Force Base ■	202	47.30 N	111.10 W
Malmyž	80	56.31 N	50.41 E
Malna	116	8.08 N	124.27 E
Malnate	62	45.48 N	8.53 E
Malnoue	261	48.50 N	2.36 E
Malo	64	45.39 N	11.24 E
Malo I	175f	15.40 S	167.11 E
Malo, Arroyo ≃	258	33.43 S	58.52 W
Maloarchangel'sk	76	52.24 N	36.30 E
Maloarchangel'skoje	88	50.24 N	108.50 E
Maloba	154	6.18 S	27.39 E
Malodel'skaja	80	50.11 N	43.53 E
Maloduša	78	52.09 N	30.14 E
Maloelap I[1]	14	8.45 N	171.03 E
Malo-Iljinovka ◆[8]	83	48.38 N	37.59 E
Maloja	58	46.24 N	9.41 E
Malojapass)(	58	46.24 N	9.41 E
Malojaroslavec	82	55.01 N	36.28 E
Malojaz	86	55.13 N	58.09 E
Maloje Goloustnoje	88	52.18 N	105.18 E
Malojekaterinovka	78	47.39 N	35.16 E
Maloje Kozino	80	56.26 N	43.41 E
Maloje Polesje ◆[1]	78	50.10 N	25.00 E
Maloje-Ščerbedino	80	51.59 N	42.50 E
Maloje Skuratovo	76	53.33 N	37.00 E
Malokirsanovka	83	47.28 N	38.31 E
Malokrasnojarka	86	56.28 N	76.01 E
Malo-les-Bains	50	51.03 N	2.24 E
Malolo	154	7.18 S	36.35 E
Malolos, Guam	174p	13.18 N	144.46 E
Malolos, Pil.	116	14.51 N	120.49 E
Malom	164	3.10 S	151.50 E
Maloma	158	27.00 S	31.40 E
Malombe, Lake ⊜	154	14.38 S	35.12 E
Malomichajlovka	78	48.06 N	36.23 E
Malonabatovskij	80	48.57 N	43.40 E
Malone, Fl., U.S.	192	30.57 N	85.09 W
Malone, N.Y., U.S.	188	44.50 N	74.17 W
Malone, Tx., U.S.	222	31.55 N	96.54 W
Malone, Wa., U.S.	224	46.58 N	123.20 W
Malonga	152	10.24 S	23.10 E
Malonno	64	46.07 N	10.18 E
Malonty	61	48.41 N	14.35 E
Małopolska ◆[1]	30	50.10 N	21.30 E
Malor'azancevo	83	48.53 N	38.23 E
Malorita	78	51.47 N	24.05 E
Malorossijskij	86	53.12 N	62.30 E
Malošujka	24	63.45 N	37.22 E
Malott	182	48.16 N	119.42 W
Måløv	41	55.45 N	12.20 E
Małowice	30	51.34 N	15.27 E
Måløy	26	61.56 N	5.07 E
Malozemel'skaja Tundra ◆[1]	24	67.50 N	51.00 E
Malpaisillo	236	12.35 N	86.41 W
Malpartida de Plasencia	34	39.59 N	6.02 W
Malpas, Austl.	166	34.43 S	140.37 E
Malpas, Eng., U.K.	44	53.01 N	2.46 W
Malpaso	234	22.37 N	102.46 W
Malpe	122	13.21 N	74.43 E
Malpelo, Isla de I	242	3.59 N	81.35 W
Malpensa, Aeroporto della ⊠	62	45.38 N	8.44 E
Malpeque Bay ⊂	186	46.30 N	63.47 W
Malprabha ≃	122	16.12 N	76.03 E
Mālpura	120	26.17 N	75.23 E
Mälsåker slott ⊥	40	59.23 N	17.18 E
Malsch	56	48.53 N	8.19 E
Malše (Maltsch) ≃	61	48.58 N	14.28 E

FRANÇAIS

Nom	Page	Lat.°'	Long.°' W = Ouest
Målselva ≃	24	69.14 N	18.30 E
Mals → Malles Venosta	64	46.41 N	10.32 E
Malta, Bra.	250	6.54 S	37.31 W
Malta, Lat.	76	56.21 N	27.10 E
Malta, Öst.	64	46.57 N	13.30 E
Malta, Il., U.S.	216	41.56 N	88.52 W
Malta, Mt., U.S.	202	48.21 N	107.52 W
Malta, Oh., U.S.	188	39.38 N	81.51 W
Malta □[1], Europe	22	35.50 N	14.35 E
Malta □[1], Europe	36	35.50 N	14.35 E
Malta I	36	35.53 N	14.27 E
Malta ≃	76	56.44 N	26.53 E
Malta Channel ⊔	36	36.20 N	15.00 E
Maltahöhe	156	24.50 S	17.00 E
Maltahöhe □[5]	156	25.00 S	16.30 E
Malta-Tal V	64	47.03 N	13.24 E
Maltby	44	53.26 N	1.11 W
Malte Brun ∧	172	43.34 S	170.18 E
Malte → Malta □[1]	36	35.50 N	14.35 E
Maltepe ◆[8]	267b	40.55 N	29.08 E
Malton	44	54.08 N	0.48 W
Malton ◆[8]	275b	43.42 N	79.38 W
Maltrata	234	18.48 N	97.16 W
Maltsch (Malše) ≃	61	48.58 N	14.28 E
Malugou	89	43.39 N	128.27 E
Maluku □[4]	164	5.00 S	130.00 E
Maluku (Moluccas) II	108	2.00 S	128.00 E
Maluku, Laut (Molucca Sea) ╤[2]	108	0.00	125.00 E
Maluku-Maes	152	4.06 S	15.31 E
Ma'lūlā	130	33.50 N	36.33 E
Ma'lūlā, Jabal ∧	132	33.54 N	36.36 E
Malu Mare	38	44.15 N	23.51 E
Malumfashi	150	11.47 N	7.37 E
Malunda	112	3.00 S	118.50 E
Malung	26	60.40 N	13.44 E
Maluso	116	6.33 N	121.53 E
Malūṭ	140	10.26 N	32.12 E
Maluti	126	24.09 N	87.41 E
Maluwe	150	8.40 N	2.17 W
Maluzhen	106	31.20 N	121.16 E
Malvaglia	58	46.25 N	8.59 E
Malvaglio	266b	45.31 N	8.47 E
Malvagna	70	37.55 N	15.04 E
Mālvan	122	16.04 N	73.28 E
Malveira	266c	38.45 N	9.27 W
Malvern, Austl.	274b	37.52 S	145.02 E
Malvern, Ar., U.S.	194	34.21 N	92.48 W
Malvern, Ia., U.S.	198	41.00 N	95.35 W
Malvern, Oh., U.S.	214	40.41 N	81.10 W
Malvern, Pa., U.S.	285	40.02 N	75.31 W
Malvern ◆[8]	273d	26.12 S	28.06 E
Malverne	276	40.40 N	73.40 W
Malvern Hills ⩘[2]	42	52.05 N	2.21 W
Malvérnia	156	22.06 S	31.42 E
Malvern Link	42	52.08 N	2.18 W
Malvinas	252	29.37 S	58.59 W
Malvinas, Islas → Falkland Islands □[2]	254	51.45 S	59.00 W
Malvito	68	39.36 N	16.03 E
Malwal	140	9.19 N	31.35 E
Mālwa Plateau ⩘[1]	124	23.50 N	77.30 E
Malybaj	85	43.30 N	78.25 E
Malý Dunaj ≃	30	47.45 N	18.09 E
Malyi Nesvetaj ≃	83	47.32 N	39.49 E
Malyj, ostrov I	76	60.02 N	28.02 E
Malyj An'uj ≃	74	68.30 N	160.49 E
Malyj Čeremšan ≃	80	54.18 N	50.01 E
Malyj Chamar-Daban, chrebet ⩘	88	51.00 N	105.00 E
Malyj Civil' ≃	80	55.54 N	47.28 E
Malyje Alabuchi	80	51.33 N	42.10 E
Malyje Čany, ozero ⊜	86	54.33 N	78.02 E
Malyje Gorod'atiči	76	52.33 N	28.20 E
Malyje Jagury	80	45.26 N	43.01 E
Malyje Kamkaly	86	44.44 N	71.31 E
Malyje Karmakuly	72	72.23 N	52.44 E
Malyje Porogi	265a	59.47 N	30.42 E
Malyj Irgiz ≃	80	52.12 N	47.58 E
Malyj Jenisej (Ka-Chem) ≃	88	51.43 N	94.26 E
Malyj Jugan ≃	86	60.40 N	73.54 E
Malyj Kavkaz ⩘	84	41.00 N	44.35 E
Malyj Kundyš ≃	80	56.22 N	47.53 E
Malyj Šantar, ostrov I	89	54.30 N	137.36 E
Malyj Sarybulak	86	52.10 N	72.35 E
Malyj Tajmyr, ostrov I	74	78.08 N	107.12 E
Malyj T'uters, ostrov I	76	59.49 N	26.56 E
Malyj Uran ≃	80	52.30 N	53.01 E
Malyj Uzen' ≃	80	48.50 N	49.39 E
Malyj Zelenčuk ≃	84	44.24 N	41.56 E
Malyn'	82	54.36 N	38.40 E
Malyševo	76	57.50 N	35.36 E
Malzéville	58	48.43 N	6.12 E
Mama	88	58.18 N	112.54 E
Mama ≃	88	58.18 N	112.55 E
Ma Ma Creek ≃	171a	27.35 S	152.13 E
Mamadyš	80	55.44 N	51.25 E
Mamagota	175e	6.46 S	155.24 E
Mamahuolang	104	42.24 N	124.12 E
Mamajiecun	104	41.26 N	122.51 E
Mamakan	88	57.48 N	114.01 E
Mamaku	172	38.06 S	176.05 E
Mamakwash Lake ⊜	184	51.38 N	92.56 W
Mamala Bay ⊂	229a	21.18 N	157.57 W
Mamalu Bay ⊂	229a	20.37 N	156.09 W
Mamanguape	250	6.50 S	35.07 W
Mama'o, Hakau ✢[2]	174w	21.00 S	175.12 W
Mamara	248	14.14 S	72.35 W
Mamaroneck	210	40.56 N	73.43 W
Mamaroneck ≃	276	40.57 N	73.44 W
Mamaroneck Harbor ⊂	276	40.56 N	73.43 W
Mamasa	112	2.56 S	119.22 E
Mamasa ≃	112	3.30 S	119.42 E
Mamba	94	36.07 N	138.55 E
Mambaí	255	14.28 S	46.07 W
Mambajao	116	9.15 N	124.43 E
Mambajao, Mount ∧	116	9.10 N	124.44 E
Mambali	154	4.33 S	32.41 E
Mambalot	116	8.51 N	117.55 E
Mambare ≃	164	8.20 S	147.55 E
Mambasa	154	1.21 N	29.03 E
Mamberamo ≃	164	1.26 S	137.53 E
Mambéré ≃	152	3.31 N	16.03 E
Mambili ≃	152	0.07 N	16.08 E
Mambrui	154	3.07 S	40.09 E
Mambucaba	256	23.01 S	44.31 W
Mambucaba ≃	256	23.02 S	44.32 W
Mamburao	116	13.14 N	120.35 E
Mambusao ≃	116	11.24 N	122.41 E
Mamdūḥ, Rujm ∧	132	32.14 N	36.15 E
Mamedkala	84	42.10 N	48.06 E
Mamehaktebo	112	0.08 N	115.32 E
Mamelodi	158	25.45 S	28.18 E
Ma-Me-O Beach	182	52.58 N	113.59 W
Mamera	286c	10.27 N	66.59 W
Mamera, Quebrada ≃	286c	10.27 N	66.59 W
Mamers	50	48.21 N	0.23 E
Mamfe	152	5.46 N	9.17 E
Mamiá ≃	250	1.55 S	55.07 W
Mamiá, Lago ⊜	246	4.15 S	63.03 W
Mamiao	98	35.04 N	116.10 E
Mamie	192	36.07 N	75.50 W
Mamiña	248	20.05 S	69.14 W
Maminigui	150	7.24 N	5.50 W
Mamirolle	58	47.12 N	6.10 E
Mamisonskij, pereval)(	84	42.43 N	43.48 E
Maml'utka	86	54.57 N	68.35 E
Mammendorf	60	48.12 N	11.09 E
Mammola	68	38.22 N	16.15 E
Mammoth, Az., U.S.	200	32.43 N	110.38 W
Mammoth, W.V., U.S.	188	38.15 N	81.22 W

PORTUGUÊS

Nome	Página	Lat.°'	Long.°' W = Oeste
Mammoth Cave National Park ♠	194	37.08 N	86.13 W
Mammoth Lakes	204	37.38 N	118.58 W
Mammoth Pool Reservoir ⊜[1]	226	37.20 N	119.20 W
Mammoth Spring	194	36.29 N	91.32 W
Mamoiada	71	40.13 N	9.17 E
Mamonovo, Ross.	76	54.28 N	19.57 E
Mamonovo, Ross.	265b	55.36 N	37.49 E
Mamonovo, Ross.	265b	55.41 N	37.19 E
Mamont	279b	40.29 N	79.36 W
Mamontovo, Ross.	86	52.43 N	81.37 E
Mamontovo, Ross.	86	51.45 N	81.25 E
Mamoré ≃	248	10.23 S	65.23 W
Mamori, Lago ⊜	246	3.38 S	60.07 W
Mamoriá ≃	248	7.30 S	66.21 W
Mamou, Guinée	150	10.23 N	12.05 W
Mamou, La., U.S.	194	30.38 N	92.25 W
Mamoutzou	157a	12.47 S	45.14 E
Mampikony	157b	16.06 S	47.38 E
Mampong	150	7.04 N	1.24 W
Mamraš	84	41.44 N	48.19 E
Mamre	158	33.30 S	18.29 E
Mamry, Jezioro ⊜	30	54.08 N	21.42 E
Mamuchi	98	35.41 N	118.17 E
Mamué	152	13.35 S	13.13 E
Mamuil, Paso de)(	254	39.35 S	71.28 W
Mamuju	112	2.41 S	118.54 E
Mamulique	196	26.08 N	100.20 W
Ma'mūn	140	12.15 N	22.41 E
Mamuno	156	22.16 S	20.01 E
Mamuripi (Manuripe) ≃	248	11.06 S	67.36 W
Mamuru ≃	250	2.42 S	56.44 W
Mamykovo	80	54.38 N	50.37 E
Mamyl'	24	61.57 N	56.41 E
Man, C. Iv.	150	7.24 N	7.33 W
Man, India	120	33.51 N	78.32 E
Man, W.V., U.S.	192	37.44 N	81.52 W
Man (Île de) → Isle of Man □[2]	44	54.15 N	4.30 W
Man, Isle of → Isle of Man □[2]	44	54.15 N	4.30 W
Mana, Guy. fr.	250	5.40 N	53.47 W
Mana, Hi., U.S.	229b	22.02 N	159.46 W
Mana ≃, Guy. fr.	250	5.44 N	53.54 W
Mana ≃, Ross.	86	55.57 N	92.28 E
Manabí □[4]	246	0.40 S	80.05 W
Manacacías ≃	246	4.23 N	72.04 W
Manacapuru	246	3.18 S	60.37 W
Manacapuru ≃	246	3.18 S	60.38 W
Manacle Point ›	42	50.03 N	5.03 W
Manacor	34	39.34 N	3.12 E
Manado	112	1.29 N	124.51 E
Managua	236	12.09 N	86.17 W
Managua □[5]	236	12.00 N	86.25 W
Managua, Aeropuerto ⊠	286b	23.00 N	82.17 W
Managua, Lago de ⊜	236	12.20 N	86.20 W
Manahawkin	208	39.41 N	74.15 W
Manahawkin Bay ⊂	208	39.40 N	74.12 W
Manaia	172	39.33 S	174.08 E
Manā'if, Bi'r al- ╤[4]	142	30.31 N	32.12 E
Manajenki	76	53.42 N	36.27 E
Manakalampona ∧	157b	15.23 S	48.50 E
Manakara	157b	22.08 S	48.01 E
Manakau	172	40.43 S	175.13 E
Manakau ∧	172	42.14 S	173.37 E
Manākhah	144	15.07 N	43.44 E
Manalapan Brook ≃	276	40.24 N	74.23 W
Manāli	123	32.15 N	77.10 E
Manama → Al-Manāmah	128	26.13 N	50.35 E
Manambaho ≃	157b	17.41 S	44.04 E
Manambato, Madag.	157b	13.14 S	49.54 E
Manambato, Madag.	157b	13.43 S	49.07 E
Manambolo ≃	157b	19.18 S	44.24 E
Manambolosy	157b	16.02 S	49.40 E
Manam Island I	164	4.05 S	145.05 E
Mánamo, Caño ≃[1]	246	9.55 N	62.16 W
Manamoc Island I	116	11.19 N	120.41 E
Manana Island I	229c	21.20 N	157.40 W
Mananantanana ≃	157b	21.25 S	45.33 E
Mananao	116	13.30 N	120.34 E
Mananara	157b	16.10 S	49.46 E
Mananara ≃	157b	23.21 S	47.42 E
Manandaza	157b	19.19 S	45.23 E
Mananjary	157b	21.13 S	48.20 E
Manankoro	150	10.28 N	7.27 W
Manantenina	157b	24.17 S	47.19 E
Manantiales Behr	254	45.41 S	67.31 W
Manaoag	116	16.03 N	120.29 E
Manáos → Manaus	246	3.08 S	60.01 W
Manapatrana	157b	21.40 S	47.35 E
Manapiare ≃	246	5.04 N	66.30 W
Manapire ≃	246	7.42 N	66.07 W
Manapla	116	10.58 N	123.07 E
Mana Point ›	229b	22.03 N	159.47 W
Mana Pools National Park ♠	154	16.00 S	28.35 E
Manapouri	172	45.34 S	167.36 E
Manapouri, Lake ⊜	172	45.30 S	167.30 E
Manappārai	122	10.36 N	78.25 E
Manaquiri, Lago ⊜	246	3.29 S	60.31 W
Manār ≃	122	18.39 N	77.44 E
Manaravolo	157b	23.59 S	45.39 E
Manas, Som.	144	2.57 N	43.28 E
Manas, Zhg.	86	44.18 N	86.13 E
Manās ≃, Asia	120	26.13 N	90.38 E
Manas ≃, Zhg.	86	45.38 N	85.12 E
Manas, gora ∧	85	42.18 N	71.01 E
Manasarowar Lake → Mapam Yumco ⊜	120	30.42 N	81.27 E
Manas Hu ⊜	86	45.45 N	85.55 E
Manāslu ∧	124	28.33 N	84.33 E
Manasota Key I	220	26.58 N	82.23 W
Manasquan	208	40.07 N	74.02 W
Manasquan ≃	208	40.06 N	74.02 W
Manassa	200	37.10 N	105.56 W
Manassas	208	38.45 N	77.28 W
Manassas National Battlefield Park ♠	208	38.50 N	77.32 W
Manassas Park	208	38.46 N	77.27 W
Manastash Creek ≃	224	46.59 N	120.35 W
Manastash Creek, North Fork ≃	224	46.57 N	120.44 W
Manastash Creek, South Fork ≃	224	46.57 N	120.44 W
Manastash Ridge ∧	224	46.55 N	120.30 W
Manatang	112	8.26 S	124.28 E
Manatawny	208	40.17 N	75.41 W
Manatawny Creek ≃	208	40.14 N	75.39 W
Manatee □[6]	220	27.26 N	82.25 W
Manatee ≃	220	27.32 N	82.38 W
Manatee, Lake ⊜[1]	220	27.29 N	82.20 W
Manatí, Col.	246	10.27 N	74.58 W
Manatí, Cuba	240p	21.19 N	76.56 W
Manatí, P.R.	240m	18.26 N	66.29 W
Manatí ≃	240p	21.40 N	79.50 W
Manatí, Bahía de ⊂	240p	21.24 N	76.48 W
Manatuto	112	8.30 S	126.01 E
Manaul	116	12.27 N	121.25 E
Manaung	110	18.51 N	93.44 E
Manaus	246	3.08 S	60.01 W
Manavgat	130	36.47 N	31.26 E
Manawa	190	44.27 N	88.55 W
Mānāwāla	123	31.35 N	73.41 E
Manawan Lake ⊜	184	55.24 N	103.14 W
Manāwar	120	22.14 N	75.05 E
Manawatu ≃	172	40.28 S	175.13 E
Manawoka, Pulau I	164	4.05 S	131.20 E
Manay	116	7.13 N	126.32 E
Manayunk ◆[8]	285	40.01 N	75.13 W
Manazuru	94	35.09 N	139.08 E
Manazuru-misaki ›	94	35.08 N	139.10 E
Manban	102	23.04 N	103.11 E
Mānbāzār	126	23.04 N	86.39 E
Manbian	102	24.19 N	100.32 E
Manbij	130	36.31 N	37.57 E
Manby	44	53.22 N	0.06 E
Mancelona	190	44.54 N	85.03 W
Mancha Blanca	254	40.47 S	65.27 W
Mancha Real	34	37.47 N	3.37 W
Manchaug	207	42.05 N	71.44 W
Manche □[5]	32	49.00 N	1.10 W
Mancheng	105	38.56 N	115.20 E
Mancherāl	122	18.52 N	79.26 E
Manchester, Eng., U.K.	44	53.28 N	2.15 W
Manchester, Eng., U.K.	262	53.28 N	2.15 W
Manchester, Ct., U.S.	207	41.46 N	72.31 W
Manchester, Ga., U.S.	192	32.51 N	84.37 W
Manchester, Il., U.S.	219	39.33 N	90.20 W
Manchester, Ia., U.S.	190	42.29 N	91.27 W
Manchester, Ky., U.S.	192	37.09 N	83.45 W
Manchester, Md., U.S.	208	39.39 N	76.53 W
Manchester, Ma., U.S.	207	42.34 N	70.46 W
Manchester, Mi., U.S.	216	42.09 N	84.02 W
Manchester, N.H., U.S.	188	42.59 N	71.27 W
Manchester, N.Y., U.S.	210	42.58 N	77.13 W
Manchester, Oh., U.S.	218	38.41 N	83.36 W
Manchester, Pa., U.S.	208	40.03 N	76.43 W
Manchester, Tn., U.S.	194	35.28 N	86.05 W
Manchester, Vt., U.S.	210	43.09 N	73.04 W
Manchester, Wa., U.S.	224	47.33 N	122.33 W
Manchester □[8]	262	53.27 N	2.13 W
Manchester Airport ⊠	44	53.21 N	2.15 W
Manchester Bridge	210	41.41 N	73.52 W
Manchester City Football Ground ♠	262	53.27 N	2.14 W
Manchester Docks ◆[5]	262	53.28 N	2.17 W
Manchester Race Course ♠	262	53.30 N	2.16 W
Manchester Ship Canal ≊	262	53.19 N	2.57 W
Manchester United Football Ground ♠	262	53.28 N	2.18 W
Manching	60	48.43 N	11.30 E
Manchioneal	241q	18.02 N	76.17 W
Manchón	236	14.23 N	92.02 W
Manchouli → Manzhouli	88	49.35 N	117.22 E
Manchuria □[9]	90	47.00 N	125.00 E
Manciano	66	42.35 N	11.31 E
Mancieulles	56	49.17 N	5.53 E
Máncora	246	4.06 S	81.05 W
Mancos	200	37.20 N	108.17 W
Mancos ≃	200	36.59 N	108.59 W
Mand	128	26.07 N	62.03 E
Mānd ≃, India	120	21.42 N	83.15 E
Mand ≃, Īrān	128	28.11 N	51.17 E
Manda, India	126	22.06 N	86.14 E
Manda, Tan.	154	7.58 S	32.26 E
Manda, Tan.	154	8.30 S	32.44 E
Manda, Tan.	154	10.28 S	34.35 E
Manda, Tchad	146	9.12 N	18.10 E
Manda, Jabal ∧	140	8.39 N	24.27 E
Mandabe, Madag.	157b	21.03 S	44.55 E
Mandabe, Madag.	157b	20.55 S	45.49 E
Mandach	102	44.28 N	108.11 E
Mandaguari	255	23.32 S	51.42 W
Mandai Orchard Gardens ♠	271c	1.24 N	103.47 E
Manda Island I	154	2.15 S	40.57 E
Mandal	26	58.02 N	7.27 E
Mandal, Jibāl ∧[2]	140	12.09 N	29.31 E
Mandala, Puncak ∧	164	4.44 S	140.20 E
Mandalay	110	22.00 N	96.05 E
Mandalay □[5]	110	21.00 N	96.00 E
Mandale	216	41.01 N	84.20 W
Mandale Station ◆[5]	272c	19.03 N	72.56 E
Mandalgov'	102	45.45 N	106.12 E
Mandalī	128	33.45 N	45.32 E
Mandalkia	272b	22.43 N	88.08 E
Mandal-Ovoo	102	44.35 N	104.05 E
Mandalselva ≃	26	58.02 N	7.28 E
Mandaluyong	269f	14.35 N	121.02 E
Mandan	198	46.49 N	100.53 W
Mandanici	70	38.00 N	15.19 E
Mandāoli ◆[8]	272a	28.38 N	77.18 E
Mandaon	116	12.14 N	123.17 E
Mandapur	126	23.00 N	88.29 E
Mandar, Teluk ⊂	112	3.40 S	119.15 E
Mandara Mountains (Monts Mandara) ⩘	146	10.45 N	13.40 E
Mandas	71	39.38 N	9.07 E
Mandatoriccio	68	39.28 N	16.50 E
Mandau ≃	114	0.48 N	101.47 E
Mandaue	116	10.20 N	123.56 E
Mandāwar	124	29.30 N	78.08 E
Mandeb, Bab el ⊔	144	12.40 N	43.20 E
Mandehu	104	42.07 N	121.33 E
Mandel	128	33.17 N	61.52 E
Mandélia	146	11.43 N	15.15 E
Mandelieu	62	43.33 N	6.56 E
Mandello del Lario	58	45.54 N	9.19 E
Mandera	154	3.56 N	41.52 E
Manderfeld	56	50.20 N	6.20 E
Manderscheid	56	50.05 N	6.49 E
Manderson	202	44.16 N	107.57 W
Mandeure	58	47.27 N	6.48 E
Mandeville, P.Q., Can.	206	46.22 N	73.22 W
Mandeville, Jam.	241q	18.02 N	77.30 W
Mandeville, N.Z.	172	46.00 S	168.49 E
Mandeville, La., U.S.	194	30.21 N	90.03 W
Mandi	123	31.43 N	76.55 E
Mandiana	150	10.38 N	8.41 W
Mandiangin	112	2.01 S	102.58 E
Mandi Angin, Gunong ∧	114	4.42 N	102.52 E
Mandi Bahāuddīn	123	32.35 N	73.30 E
Mandi Būrewāla	123	30.09 N	72.41 E
Mandi Dabwāli	123	29.58 N	74.42 E
Mandié	154	16.30 S	33.30 E
Mandimba	154	14.21 S	35.39 E
Mandini	158	29.09 S	31.25 E
Mandioli, Pulau I	108	0.44 S	127.14 E
Mandioré, Lagoa ⊜	248	18.08 S	57.33 W
Mandira ⊜[1]	124	22.20 N	84.35 E
Mandiri ≃	115a	7.02 S	106.32 E
Mandi Sādiqganj	123	30.10 N	73.44 E
Mandjafa	146	11.11 N	15.25 E
Mandjé, Lac ⊜	152	2.50 S	10.22 E
Mandji	152	1.36 S	10.26 E
Mandla	124	22.36 N	80.23 E
Mandora	162	19.44 S	120.51 E
Mandoto	157b	19.34 S	46.17 E
Mandoul ≃	146	8.56 N	17.58 E
Mandouri	150	10.51 N	0.49 E
Mándra, Ellás	267c	38.04 N	23.30 E
Māndrā, India	272b	22.55 N	88.07 E
Mandra, Pāk.	123	33.22 N	73.14 E
Mandrare ≃	157b	25.10 S	46.27 E
Mandres-les-Roses	261	48.42 N	2.33 E
Mandriola ◆[8]	267a	41.45 N	12.30 E
Mandriole	64	44.33 N	12.14 E
Mandrioli, Passo dei)(	64	43.48 N	11.55 E
Mandritsara	157b	15.50 S	48.49 E
Mandronarivo	157b	21.07 S	45.38 E
Mandsaur	120	24.04 N	75.04 E
Māndu	122	22.22 N	75.23 E
Mandu, Ribeirão do ≃	256	22.14 S	45.55 W
Manduba, Ponta ›	256	24.05 S	46.18 W
Manduhu	104	41.36 N	122.38 E
Mandun	102	22.17 N	100.05 E
Mandurah	168a	32.32 S	115.43 E
Manduria	68	40.24 N	17.38 E
Māndvi, India	120	21.15 N	73.18 E
Māndvi, India	120	22.50 N	69.22 E
Mandvi ◆[8]	272c	18.57 N	72.50 E
Mandya	122	12.33 N	76.54 E
Mané	150	12.59 N	1.21 W
Måne ≃	26	59.00 N	9.40 E
Manea	42	52.30 N	0.11 E
Manebach	54	50.41 N	10.51 E
Manek Urai	114	5.23 N	102.14 E
Manendragarh	124	23.13 N	82.13 E
Manera	157b	22.55 S	44.20 E
Manerbio	64	45.21 N	10.08 E
Manětin	60	49.59 N	13.14 E
Maneviči	78	51.17 N	25.33 E
Manfalūṭ	142	27.19 N	30.58 E
Manfredonia	68	41.38 N	15.55 E
Manfredonia, Golfo di ⊂	68	41.35 N	16.05 E
Manga, Bra.	255	14.46 S	43.56 W
Manga, Burkina	150	11.40 N	1.04 W
Manga, Ur.	258	34.49 S	56.06 W
Manga ◆[1]	146	15.00 N	14.00 E
Mangabeiras, Chapada das ⩘[2]	250	10.00 S	46.30 W
Mangagoy	116	8.11 N	126.21 E
Mangahao ≃	172	40.23 S	175.50 E
Mangai	164	2.45 S	151.05 E
Mangaia I	14	21.55 S	157.55 W
Mangakino	172	38.22 S	175.47 E
Mangala	152	1.02 N	23.50 E
Mangalagiri	122	16.26 N	80.33 E
Mangaldai	120	26.26 N	92.02 E
Mangaldan	116	16.04 N	120.24 E
Mangalia	38	43.50 N	28.35 E
Mangalkot	126	23.33 N	87.54 E
Mangalmé	146	12.21 N	19.37 E
Mangalore	122	12.52 N	74.53 E
Mangalpaita	126	23.19 N	89.11 E
Mangalvedha	122	17.31 N	75.28 E
Mangamahu	172	39.49 S	175.22 E
Manganês ≃	250	10.21 S	48.27 W
Manganji	268	35.40 N	139.26 E
Mangaoka	157b	12.19 S	49.07 E
Mangapehi	172	38.31 S	175.18 E
Mangaratiba	256	22.57 S	44.02 W
Mangart, Monte (Mangrt) ∧	64	46.25 N	13.40 E
Mangatarem	116	15.47 N	120.17 E
Mangawān	124	24.41 N	81.33 E
Mangaweka	172	39.48 S	175.47 E
Mangaweka ∧	172	39.49 S	176.05 E
Mangcao Point ›	116	11.02 N	123.54 E
Mangchang	102	25.08 N	107.31 E
Mangde ≃	124	27.35 N	90.28 E
Mange, S.L.	150	8.55 N	12.51 W
Mange, Zaïre	152	0.54 N	20.30 E
Mange, Zhg.	120	32.25 N	83.35 E
Mangeigne	146	10.31 N	21.19 E
Mangerton Mountain ∧	48	51.57 N	9.29 W
Mangfall ≃	64	47.51 N	12.08 E
Manggar	112	2.53 S	108.16 E
Manggeng	114	3.36 N	96.55 E
Manggonggri	164	3.30 S	133.19 E
Mangguar, Tanjung ›	164	2.53 S	134.51 E
Mangham	194	32.18 N	91.46 W
Mangichu ≃	126	23.24 N	90.48 E
Mangindrano	157b	14.17 S	48.58 E
Mangin Range ⩘	110	24.20 N	95.42 E
Mangkalihat, Tanjung ›	112	1.02 N	118.59 E
Mangkutana	112	2.24 S	120.48 E
Manglares, Cabo ›	246	1.36 N	79.02 W
Mangla Reservoir ⊜[1]	123	33.10 N	73.40 E
Manglaur	124	29.48 N	77.52 E
Manglisi	84	41.43 N	44.24 E
Mangnai	120	37.40 N	91.50 E
Mangniu ≃, Zhg.	104	41.45 N	120.53 E
Mangniu ≃, Zhg.	105	39.04 N	116.26 E
Mangnuiyingzi	104	41.37 N	120.43 E
Mango	220	28.00 N	82.19 W
Mangochi	154	14.28 S	35.16 E
Mango Island I	175g	17.27 S	179.09 W
Mangoky ≃, Madag.	157b	21.29 S	43.41 E
Mangoky ≃, Madag.	157b	23.27 S	45.13 E
Mangole, Pulau I	112	1.53 S	125.50 E
Mangombe	154	1.25 S	26.54 E
Mangone	68	39.12 N	16.20 E
Mangonia Park	220	26.46 N	80.05 W
Mangonui	172	34.59 S	173.32 E
Mangoplah	171b	35.23 S	147.15 E
Mangoro ≃	157b	20.00 S	48.45 E
Mangotsfield	42	51.28 N	2.28 W
Mangoupa	140	5.53 N	24.40 E
Mangrol	120	21.07 N	70.07 E
Mangrove Cay I	238	24.10 N	77.45 W
Mangrove Creek ≃	170	33.28 S	151.10 E
Mangrove Creek Dam ◆[6]	170	33.13 S	151.07 E
Mangrove Mountain	170	33.19 S	151.14 E
Mangrove Point ›	220	26.56 N	82.08 W
Mangrt (Monte Mangart) ∧	64	46.25 N	13.40 E
Mangrullo, Cuchilla ⩘[2]	258	34.34 S	56.42 W
Mangrūl Pīr	122	20.19 N	77.21 E
Mångsälven ≃	40	59.59 N	14.36 E
Mangsang	112	2.10 S	104.00 E
Mangu ≃	273b	4.24 S	15.24 E
Mangualde	34	40.36 N	7.46 W
Mangueira, Lagoa ⊂	252	33.06 S	52.48 W
Mangueirinha	252	25.57 S	52.09 W
Manguéni, Plateau du ⩘[1]	146	22.35 N	12.40 E
Mangui	89	52.03 N	122.13 E
Manguito	240p	22.35 N	80.55 W
Mangulile	236	15.03 N	86.49 W
Mangum	196	34.52 N	99.30 W
Mangungu	152	5.13 S	19.35 E
Mangut, Ross.	86	55.47 N	70.46 E
Mangut, Ross.	88	49.46 N	112.38 E
Mangya	90	37.40 N	90.50 E
Man'gyŏng	98	35.52 N	126.48 E
Mangyšlak □[8]	86	44.00 N	54.30 E
Manhan ≃	207	42.17 N	72.38 W
Manhartsberg ∧	61	48.32 N	15.44 E
Manhasset	276	40.47 N	73.42 W
Manhasset Bay ⊂	276	40.50 N	73.43 W
Manhasset Hills	276	40.46 N	73.41 W
Manhasset Neck ›[1]	276	40.50 N	73.42 W
Manhattan, Il., U.S.	216	41.25 N	87.59 W
Manhattan, Ks., U.S.	198	39.11 N	96.34 W
Manhattan, Mt., U.S.	202	45.51 N	111.19 W
Manhattan □[8]	276	40.46 N	73.55 W
Manhattan Beach	228	33.53 N	118.24 W
Manhattan Beach State Park ♠	280	33.54 N	118.25 W
Manhattan Bridge ◆[5]	276	40.42 N	73.59 W
Manhattan College ♁[2]	276	40.53 N	73.54 W
Manheim	208	40.09 N	76.23 W
Manhiça	156	25.24 S	32.48 E
Mān Hpāng	110	22.41 N	98.36 E
Manhuaçu	255	20.15 S	42.02 W
Manhuaçu ≃	255	19.30 S	41.06 W
Manhumirim	255	20.22 S	41.57 W
Maní, P.R.	240m	18.15 N	67.10 W
Mani, Zaïre	154	6.27 S	25.20 E
Māni', Jabal al- ∧	132	33.19 N	36.17 E
Mania ≃	157b	19.42 S	45.22 E
Maniago	64	46.10 N	12.43 E
Maniamba	154	12.43 S	35.00 E
Manianga	273b	4.10 S	15.19 E
Manica □[5]	156	19.00 S	33.15 E
Manicahan	116	7.01 N	122.12 E
Manicaland □[4]	154	19.30 S	32.15 E
Manicani Island I	116	10.59 N	125.38 E
Manicaragua	240p	22.09 N	79.58 W
Manic Deux, Réservoir ⊜[1]	186	49.25 N	68.25 W
Manicoré	248	5.49 S	61.17 W
Manicoré ≃	248	5.51 S	61.19 W
Manicouagan ≃	186	49.11 N	68.13 W
Manicouagan, Réservoir ⊜[1]	186	51.30 N	68.19 W
Manic Trois, Réservoir ⊜[1]	186	50.00 N	68.40 W
Manifold ≃	44	53.03 N	1.47 W
Maniganggo	102	32.01 N	99.11 E
Manignan	150	10.00 N	7.50 W
Manigotagan	184	51.06 N	96.18 W
Manigotagan ≃	184	51.07 N	96.20 W
Manihāri	124	25.21 N	87.38 E
Manihiki I[1]	14	10.24 S	161.01 W
Manika, Plateau de la ⩘[1]	154	10.00 S	26.00 E
Manikanāli	126	23.19 N	87.03 E
Mānikganj	124	23.52 N	90.00 E
Mānikpur	124	25.04 N	81.07 E
Manila, Pil.	116	14.35 N	121.00 E
Manila, Pil.	269f	14.35 N	121.00 E
Manila, Ar., U.S.	194	35.52 N	90.10 W
Manila, Ut,. U.S.	200	40.59 N	109.43 W
Manila Bay ⊂	116	14.30 N	120.45 E
Manila Cathedral ♁[1]	269f	14.35 N	120.59 E
Manila International Airport ⊠	269f	14.31 N	121.01 E
Manilla, Austl.	166	30.45 S	150.43 E
Manilla, In., U.S.	218	39.34 N	85.37 W
Manilla, Ia., U.S.	198	41.53 N	95.13 W
Manille → Manila	116	14.35 N	121.00 E
Manily	74	62.29 N	165.36 E
Mani Majra	123	30.43 N	76.50 E
Manimbaya, Tanjung ›	112	0.01 N	119.36 E
Manimpé	150	14.09 N	5.31 W
Maningory ≃	157b	17.13 S	49.28 E
Maningrida	164	12.03 S	134.13 E
Maninjau, Danau ⊜	112	0.20 S	100.11 E
Manino	76	53.58 N	34.20 E
Manipa, Pulau I	164	3.17 S	127.35 E
Manipa, Selat ⊔	164	3.20 S	127.23 E
Manipur □[3]	120	25.00 N	94.00 E
Manipur ≃	110	22.52 N	94.05 E
Manique de Baixo	266c	38.44 N	9.22 W
Maniquin Island I	116	11.36 N	121.45 E
Manirāmpur	126	23.01 N	89.14 E
Manisa	130	38.36 N	27.26 E
Manisa □[4]	130	38.50 N	28.10 E
Manissauá-Miçu ≃	250	10.58 S	53.20 W
Manistee	190	44.14 N	86.19 W
Manistee ≃	190	44.15 N	86.21 W
Manistique	190	45.57 N	86.14 W
Manistique ≃	190	45.57 N	86.15 W
Manistique, West Branch ≃	190	46.02 N	86.09 W
Manistique Lake ⊜	190	46.15 N	85.45 W
Manito	194	40.25 N	89.46 W
Manitoba □[4], Can.	176	54.00 N	97.00 W
Manitoba □[4], Can.	184	54.00 N	97.00 W
Manitoba, Lake ⊜	184	51.00 N	98.45 W
Manitou	184	49.15 N	98.31 W
Manitou ≃, On., Can.	184	48.58 N	93.20 W
Manitou ≃, P.Q., Can.	186	50.18 N	65.15 W
Manitou, Lac ⊜, P.Q., Can.	186	50.29 N	63.54 W
Manitou, Lac ⊜, P.Q., Can.	186	50.54 N	65.18 W
Manitou, Lac ⊜, P.Q., Can.	206	46.03 N	74.23 W
Manitou, Lake ⊜, On., Can.	190	45.48 N	82.00 W
Manitou, Lake ⊜, In., U.S.	216	41.03 N	86.11 W
Manitou Beach, Sk., Can.	184	51.43 N	105.26 W
Manitou Beach, Mi., U.S.	216	41.58 N	84.19 W
Manitou Lake ⊜, On., Can.	190	46.01 N	79.00 W
Manitou Lake ⊜, Sk., Can.	184	52.45 N	109.45 W
Manitoulin Island I	190	45.50 N	82.20 W
Manitou Springs	200	38.51 N	104.55 W
Manitouwabing Lake ⊜	212	45.29 N	79.54 W
Manitowaning	190	45.45 N	81.49 W
Manitowik Lake ⊜	190	48.10 N	84.24 W
Manitowish Waters	190	46.09 N	89.53 W
Manitowoc	190	44.05 N	87.39 W
Manitowoc ≃	190	44.05 N	87.39 W
Maniwaki	188	46.23 N	75.58 W
Ma'nīyā	142	30.50 N	30.39 E
Manizales	246	5.05 N	75.32 W
Manja, Madag.	157b	21.26 S	44.20 E
Manjā, Urd.	132	31.45 N	35.51 E
Manjacaze	156	24.44 S	33.53 E
Manjakandriana	157b	18.55 S	47.47 E
Manjeri	122	11.07 N	76.07 E
Manjiang	98	41.57 N	127.36 E
Manjimup	162	34.14 S	116.09 E
Manjing	107	29.55 N	104.07 E
Mānjra ≃	122	18.49 N	77.52 E
Manjuyod	116	9.41 N	123.09 E
Mank	61	48.06 N	15.20 E
Mankanaj	86	48.58 N	60.58 E
Månkarbo	40	60.14 N	17.28 E
Mān Kāt	110	22.05 N	98.01 E
Mankato, Ks., U.S.	198	39.47 N	98.12 W
Mankato, Mn., U.S.	190	44.09 N	93.59 W
Mankayane	158	26.42 S	31.00 E
Mankent	85	42.25 N	69.50 E
Mankera	123	31.23 N	71.26 E
Mankim	152	5.01 N	12.00 E
Mankinholes	262	53.42 N	2.03 W
Mankono	150	8.04 N	6.12 W
Mankota	184	49.25 N	107.04 W
Man'kovka, Ukr.	78	48.58 N	30.20 E
Man'kovka, Ukr.	83	49.34 N	38.27 E
Man'kovo	83	49.24 N	40.17 E
Man'kovo-Ber'ozovskaja	80	48.47 N	41.33 E
Mankoya	154	14.47 S	24.48 E
Mānkundu	272b	22.50 N	88.22 E
Mānkur, India	126	22.30 N	87.54 E
Mānkur, India	126	23.20 N	87.33 E
Manlaj	102	44.07 N	106.50 E
Manley	262	53.14 N	2.45 W
Manley Hot Springs	180	65.00 N	150.37 W
Manleys Corner	283	42.03 N	71.04 W
Manlius	210	43.00 N	75.58 W
Manlleu	34	42.00 N	2.17 E
Manly, Austl.	170	33.48 S	151.17 E
Manly, Austl.	171a	27.28 S	153.15 E
Manly, Ia., U.S.	190	43.17 N	93.12 W
Manly Warringah War Memorial Park ♠	274a	33.46 S	151.15 E
Manmād	122	20.15 N	74.27 E
Mann ≃	164	12.20 S	134.07 E
Mann, Mount ∧	162	25.59 S	129.42 E
Manna, Indon.	112	4.27 S	102.55 E
Mān Na, Mya.	110	23.27 N	97.14 E
Mannahill	166	32.26 S	139.59 E
Mannar	122	8.59 N	79.54 E
Mannar, Gulf of ⊂	122	8.30 N	79.00 E
Mannārgudi	122	10.40 N	79.26 E
Mannar Island I	122	9.03 N	79.50 E
Mann Creek ≃	281	42.32 N	83.44 W
Männedorf	58	47.15 N	8.42 E
Mannersdorf am Leithagebirge	61	47.58 N	16.36 E
Mannersdorf an der Rabnitz	61	47.25 N	16.31 E

Symbol	English	Deutsch	Español	Français	Português
≃	River	Fluß	Río	Rivière	Rio
≊	Canal	Kanal	Canal	Canal	Canal
ʟ	Waterfall, Rapids	Wasserfall, Stromschnellen	Cascada, Rápidos	Chute d'eau, Rapides	Cascata, Rápidos
⊔	Strait	Meeresstraße	Estrecho	Détroit	Estreito
⊂	Bay, Gulf	Bucht, Golf	Bahía, Golfo	Baie, Golfe	Baía, Golfo
⊜	Lake, Lakes	See, Seen	Lago, Lagos	Lac, Lacs	Lago, Lagos
⋿	Swamp	Sumpf	Pantano	Marais	Pântano
⊓	Ice Features, Glacier	Eis- und Gletscherformen	Accidentes Glaciales	Formes glaciaires	Acidentes glaciares
╤	Other Hydrographic Features	Andere Hydrographische Objekte	Otros Elementos Hidrográficos	Autres données hydrographiques	Outros acidentes hidrográficos
✢	Submarine Features	Untermeerische Objekte	Accidentes Submarinos	Formes de relief sous-marin	Acidentes submarinos
□	Political Unit	Politische Einheit	Unidad Politica	Entité politique	Unidade política
♁	Cultural Institution	Kulturelle Institution	Institución Cultural	Institution culturelle	Institução cultural
⊥	Historical Site	Historische Stätte	Sitio Histórico	Site historique	Sitio histórico
♠	Recreational Site	Erholungs- und Ferienort	Sitio de Recreo	Centre de loisirs	Area de Lazer
⊠	Airport	Flughafen	Aeropuerto	Aéroport	Aeroporto
■	Military Installation	Militäranlage	Instalación Militar	Installation militaire	Instalação militar
◆	Miscellaneous	Verschiedenes	Misceláneo	Divers	Diversos

Name	Page	Lat.°′	Long.°′
Mannford	196	36.09 N	96.23 W
Mannheim	56	49.29 N	8.29 E
Manni	120	34.48 N	87.15 E
Manning, Ia., U.S.	198	41.54 N	95.03 W
Manning, N.D., U.S.	198	47.13 N	102.46 W
Manning, S.C., U.S.	192	33.41 N	80.12 W
Manning, Cape ›	174o	2.02 N	157.26 W
Manning Provincial Park ♠	224	49.07 N	120.54 W
Manning Strait ʊ	175e	7.24 S	158.00 E
Mannington	188	39.31 N	80.20 W
Manningtree	42	51.57 N	1.04 E
Mannō	96	34.11 N	133.51 E
Mann Ranges ⋏	162	26.00 S	129.30 E
Mannsville	212	43.42 N	76.03 W
Mannswörth ◆[8]	264b	48.09 N	16.31 E
Mannu	71	39.18 N	8.58 E
Mannu ≃	71	40.50 N	8.23 E
Mannu, Capo ›	71	40.47 N	8.09 E
Mannu, Monte ∧	71	40.23 N	8.25 E
Mannum	166	34.55 S	139.18 E
Mannus	171b	35.48 S	147.57 E
Mannus Creek ≃	171b	35.58 S	148.03 E
Mannville	182	53.20 N	111.10 W
Mano	150	8.02 N	12.06 W
Mano ≃	150	6.56 N	11.31 W
Manoa	248	9.40 S	65.27 W
Manoel Ribas	252	24.31 S	51.39 W
Manohardi	126	24.08 N	90.43 E
Manoharpur, India	124	22.23 N	85.12 E
Manoharpur, India	126	21.59 N	87.18 E
Manokin ≃	208	38.05 N	75.55 W
Manokotak	180	58.40 N	159.09 W
Manokwari	164	0.52 S	134.05 E
Manolo Fortich (Maluko)	116	8.25 N	124.58 E
Manoma ≃	89	49.18 N	136.37 E
Manombo	157b	22.57 S	43.28 E
Manomet	207	41.55 N	70.34 W
Manomet Hill ∧[2]	207	41.55 N	70.36 W
Manong	114	4.36 N	100.53 E
Manonga ≃	154	4.08 S	34.12 E
Manono	154	7.18 S	27.25 E
Manono I	175a	13.50 S	172.05 W
Manoora	168b	34.00 S	138.49 E
Manoppello	66	42.15 N	14.03 E
Manor, Sk., Can.	184	49.36 N	102.05 W
Manor, Pa., U.S.	214	40.20 N	79.40 W
Manor, Tx., U.S.	222	30.20 N	97.33 W
Manorbier	42	51.39 N	4.48 W
Manorhamilton	48	54.18 N	8.10 W
Manorhaven	276	40.50 N	73.42 W
Manor Hill	214	40.38 N	77.55 W
Manori ◆[8]	272c	19.12 N	72.47 E
Manori Creek ⊂	272c	19.12 N	72.48 E
Manorina National Park ♠	171a	27.23 S	152.47 E
Manori Point ›	272c	19.11 N	72.47 E
Manoron	110	11.38 N	99.04 E
Manorville	214	40.47 N	79.31 W
Manosque	62	43.50 N	5.47 E
Manotick	212	45.13 N	75.41 W
Manouane ≃	186	49.30 N	71.11 W
Manouane, Lac ⊜	186	50.41 N	70.45 W
Manouanis ≃	186	50.28 N	70.08 W
Manouanis, Lac ⊜	186	50.51 N	70.20 W
Manown	279b	40.13 N	79.54 W
Manpaka	273b	4.18 S	15.12 E
Manpitou	100	22.17 N	112.52 E
Manp'o	98	41.10 N	126.17 E
Mānpur, India	122	20.22 N	80.43 E
Mānpur, India	124	23.46 N	81.08 E
Manqabād	142	27.12 N	31.07 E
Manqaṭīn	142	28.20 N	30.40 E
Manquehue, Cerro ∧	286e	33.21 S	70.36 W
Manra I[1]	14	4.27 S	171.15 W
Manresa	34	41.44 N	1.50 E
Manresa Island I	276	41.04 N	73.25 W
Mānsa, India	120	23.26 N	72.40 E
Mānsa, India	123	29.59 N	75.23 E
Mansa (Fort Rosebery), Zam.	154	11.12 S	28.53 E
Mansabá	150	12.18 N	15.15 W
Mansafīs	142	28.00 N	30.49 E
Mansalay	116	12.31 N	121.26 E
Mansara	150	13.20 N	4.39 W
Manse ≃	50	47.08 N	0.25 E
Manseau	206	46.22 N	72.00 W
Mānsehra	123	34.20 N	73.12 E
Mansein	110	25.12 N	95.58 E
Mansel Island I	176	62.00 N	79.50 W
Mansfeld	54	51.35 N	11.27 E
Mansfield, Austl.	169	37.03 S	146.05 E
Mansfield, Eng., U.K.	44	53.09 N	1.11 W
Mansfield, Ar., U.S.	194	35.04 N	94.13 W
Mansfield, Ga., U.S.	192	33.31 N	83.44 W
Mansfield, Il., U.S.	216	40.12 N	88.30 W
Mansfield, La., U.S.	194	32.02 N	93.42 W
Mansfield, Ma., U.S.	207	42.02 N	71.13 W
Mansfield, Mo., U.S.	194	37.06 N	92.34 W
Mansfield, N.J., U.S.	285	40.05 N	74.43 W
Mansfield, Oh., U.S.	214	40.45 N	82.30 W
Mansfield, Pa., U.S.	210	41.48 N	77.04 W
Mansfield, Tx., U.S.	222	32.33 N	97.08 W
Mansfield, Mount ∧	188	44.33 N	72.49 W
Mansfield Center	207	41.45 N	72.11 W
Mansfield Hollow Lake ⊜[1]	207	41.45 N	72.11 W
Mansfield Hollow State Park ♠	207	41.46 N	72.10 W
Mansfield Municipal Airport ⊠	283	42.00 N	71.12 W
Mansfield Woodhouse	44	53.11 N	1.12 W
Man Shan I	106	31.14 N	120.17 E
Mansieville Location	273d	26.05 S	27.45 E
Mānsinhapur	272b	22.39 N	88.09 E
Mansión	236	10.06 N	85.22 W
Manskoje belogorje ⋏	88	54.35 N	94.00 E
Mansle	32	45.53 N	0.11 E
Manso ≃	248	14.42 S	56.16 W
Mansôa	150	12.10 N	14.36 W
Manson, Ia., U.S.	198	42.32 N	94.32 W
Manson, Wa., U.S.	182	47.53 N	120.09 W
Manson ≃	182	55.42 N	123.47 W
Manson Creek	182	55.41 N	124.29 W
Mansonville	206	45.03 N	72.23 W
Mansourah	34	36.04 N	4.28 E
Mansucum	246	9.02 N	77.49 W
Mansura	194	31.03 N	92.02 W
Mansura → Al-Manṣūrah	142	31.03 N	31.23 E
Manṣūrīyah, Tur'at al- ≅	142	31.03 N	31.24 E
Mansurovo	82	55.52 N	36.36 E
Manta, Ec.	246	0.57 S	80.44 W
Manta, It.	62	44.37 N	7.29 E
Manta, Bahía de ⊂	246	0.54 S	80.42 W
Mantabuan Island I	116	5.02 N	120.13 E
Mantagao ≃	184	51.50 N	97.48 W
Mantalingajan, Mount ∧	116	8.48 N	117.40 E
Mantalingajan Range ⋏	116	8.46 N	117.40 E
Mantanani Besar, Pulau I	112	6.45 N	116.17 E
Mantangule Island I	116	8.10 N	117.10 E
Mantantale	152	2.10 S	20.06 E
Mantare	154	2.43 S	33.13 E
Mantaro ≃	248	12.15 S	73.58 W
Manteca	226	37.47 N	121.12 W
Mantecal	246	7.33 N	69.09 W
Mantel	60	49.39 N	12.03 E
Mantena	255	18.47 S	40.59 W
Manteno	216	41.15 N	87.49 W
Manteo	192	35.54 N	75.40 W
Mantes-Chérence, Aérodrome de ⊠	261	49.05 N	1.41 E
Mantes-la-Jolie	50	48.59 N	1.43 E
Mantes-la-Ville	261	48.58 N	1.42 E
Manteswar	126	23.26 N	88.06 E
Manteuil-le-Haudouin	50	49.08 N	2.48 E
Manthelan	50	47.08 N	0.47 E
Manti	200	39.16 N	111.38 W
Manticao	116	8.24 N	124.17 E
Mantilla ◆[8]	286b	23.04 N	82.20 W
Mantin	114	2.49 N	101.54 E
Mantiqueira, Serra da ⋏	256	22.00 S	44.45 W
Mantok	112	1.09 S	123.14 E
Manton	190	44.24 N	85.23 W
Mantorville	190	44.04 N	92.45 W
Mantos Blancos	252	23.25 S	70.05 W
Mantou	104	42.27 N	122.26 E
Mantova	64	45.09 N	10.48 E
Mantova □[4]	64	45.10 N	10.47 E
Māntri	126	21.39 N	86.49 E
Mänttä	26	62.02 N	24.38 E
Mantua, Cuba	240p	22.17 N	84.17 W
Mantua, N.J., U.S.	208	39.47 N	75.10 W
Mantua, Oh., U.S.	214	41.17 N	81.13 W
Mantua, Va., U.S.	284c	38.51 N	77.15 W
Mantua ≃	240p	22.12 N	84.25 W
Mantua Creek ≃	285	39.51 N	75.14 W
Mantua Creek, Chestnut Branch ≃	285	39.47 N	75.10 W
Mantua Creek, Porch Branch ≃	285	39.46 N	75.07 W
Mantua Hills	284c	38.51 N	77.16 W
Mantua → Mantova	64	45.09 N	10.48 E
Mantua Terrace	285	39.48 N	75.10 W
Manturovo, Ross.	78	51.28 N	37.07 E
Manturovo, Ross.	80	58.20 N	44.46 E
Mäntyharju	26	61.25 N	26.53 E
Mäntyluoto	26	61.35 N	21.29 E
Manu	248	12.15 S	70.50 W
Manú ≃	248	12.16 S	70.51 W
Manu, Parque Nacional del ♠	248	12.15 S	71.40 W
Manuae I[1], Cook Is.	14	19.21 S	158.56 W
Manuae I[1], Poly. fr.	14	16.30 S	154.40 W
Manua Islands II	174y	14.13 S	169.35 W
Manuel	234	22.44 N	98.19 W
Manuel Alves ≃	250	11.19 S	48.28 W
Manuel Alves Grande ≃	250	7.27 S	47.35 W
Manuel Antonio, Parque Nacional ♠	236	9.25 N	84.10 W
Manuel Avila Camacho, Presa ⊜[1]	234	18.55 N	98.10 W
Manuel Benavides	232	29.05 N	103.55 W
Manuel Derqui	252	27.50 S	58.48 W
Manuel Duarte	256	22.06 S	43.34 W
Manuel Ribeiro	256	22.54 S	42.47 W
Manuel Rodríguez, Isla I	254	52.35 S	73.50 W
Manuel Urbano	248	8.53 S	69.18 W
Manués-Açu ≃	250	3.22 S	57.44 W
Manuguru	122	17.59 N	80.43 E
Manuhangi I[1]	14	19.12 S	141.16 W
Manuherikia ≃	172	45.16 S	169.24 E
Manui, Pulau I	112	3.35 S	123.08 E
Manuilovskaja	76	60.29 N	40.40 E
Manu Island I	164	1.17 S	143.35 E
Manūjān	128	27.24 N	57.32 E
Manuk ≃	115a	6.14 S	108.13 E
Manuk, Pulau I	164	5.33 S	130.18 E
Manukan	116	8.31 N	123.06 E
Manukau	172	37.02 S	174.54 E
Manukau Harbour ⊂	172	37.01 S	174.44 E
Manulla ≃	48	53.57 N	9.12 W
Manulu Lagoon ⊂	174o	1.56 N	157.20 W
Manumuskin ≃	208	39.18 N	75.00 W
Manundi, Tanjung ›	164	0.38 S	135.22 E
Manunui	172	38.53 S	175.20 E
Manuoha ∧	172	38.39 S	177.07 E
Manuripe (Mamuripi) ≃	248	11.06 S	67.36 W
Manuripi ≃	248	11.42 S	67.16 W
Manursing Island I	276	40.58 N	73.40 W
Manursing Island Park ♠	276	40.58 N	73.40 W
Manus □[5]	164	2.00 S	147.00 E
Mānushmuria	126	22.22 N	86.47 E
Manus Island I	164	2.05 S	147.00 E
Manutahi	172	39.40 S	174.24 E
Manutuke	172	38.41 S	177.55 E
Manvel, N.D., U.S.	198	48.04 N	97.10 W
Manvel, Tx., U.S.	222	29.28 N	95.22 W
Manville, N.J., U.S.	210	40.32 N	74.35 W
Manville, R.I., U.S.	207	41.58 N	71.28 W
Mānwat	122	19.18 N	76.30 E
Many	194	31.34 N	93.29 W
Manyal Shīḥah	273c	29.57 N	31.14 E
Manyana	156	23.23 S	21.44 E
Manyani	154	3.05 S	38.30 E
Manyara, Lake ⊜	154	3.35 S	35.50 E
Manyas	130	40.02 N	27.58 E
Manyberries	184	49.24 N	110.42 W
Manyč ≃	72	47.15 N	40.00 E
Manyč-Gudilo, ozero ⊜	80	46.24 N	42.38 E
Manyeleti Game Reserve ◆[4]	156	25.42 S	31.30 E
Many Island Lake ⊜	184	50.08 N	110.03 W
Manyoni	154	5.45 S	34.50 E
Many Peaks	166	24.33 S	151.23 E
Manytsch → Manyč ≃	72	47.15 N	40.00 E
Manz'a	86	58.29 N	96.15 E
Mānzai	120	30.07 N	68.52 E
Manzanares	34	39.00 N	3.22 W
Manzanares ≃	34	40.19 N	3.32 W
Manzanares, Canal del ≅	266a	40.23 N	3.41 W
Manzanillo, Cuba	240p	20.21 N	77.07 W
Manzanillo, Méx.	234	19.03 N	104.20 W
Manzanillo, Bahía ⊂	234	19.04 N	104.22 W
Manzanillo, Bahía de ⊂	234	19.12 N	104.43 W
Manzanillo, Punta ›, Pan.	236	9.38 N	79.32 W
Manzanillo, Punta ›, Ven.	241s	11.32 N	69.17 W
Manzanillo Bay ⊂	238	19.45 N	71.46 W
Manzanita, Or., U.S.	224	45.43 N	123.56 W
Manzanita, Wa., U.S.	224	47.42 N	122.33 W
Manzano, It.	64	45.59 N	13.23 E
Manzano, N.M., U.S.	200	34.38 N	106.20 W
Manzanola	198	38.06 N	103.51 W
Manzano Peak ∧	200	34.35 N	106.26 W
Manželija	78	49.19 N	33.38 E
Manzhouli	88	49.35 N	117.22 E
Manziana	66	42.08 N	12.08 E
Manzil	128	29.15 N	63.05 E
Manzilah, Birkat al- ⊜	142	31.08 N	31.56 E
Manzilah, Buḥayrat al- ⊜	142	31.15 N	32.00 E
Manzini	158	26.30 S	31.25 E
Manzone	258	34.29 S	58.52 W
Manzurka	88	53.30 N	106.04 E
Maó, Esp.	34	39.53 N	4.15 E
Mao, Rep. Dom.	238	19.34 N	71.05 W
Mao, Tchad	136	14.07 N	15.19 E
Maoba	102	30.02 N	108.59 E
Maocifan	100	31.40 N	112.53 E
Maocun	98	34.25 N	117.16 E
Maodianzi, Zhg.	107	30.42 N	104.25 E
Maodianzi, Zhg.	107	29.45 N	104.55 E
Mao'ertuo	107	29.19 N	106.24 E
Maojiagou	104	40.58 N	120.51 E
Maojiaji	100	31.32 N	114.16 E
Maojiakou	100	29.53 N	112.58 E
Maojiaping	105	40.34 N	114.43 E
Maojiapuzi	104	41.10 N	123.32 E
Maojiatun	104	41.05 N	121.58 E
Maojiazao	98	39.53 N	113.26 E
Maoke, Pegunungan ⋏	164	4.00 S	138.00 E
Maolin, Zhg.	89	43.58 N	123.24 E
Maolin, Zhg.	100	30.32 N	118.14 E
Maomao Shan ∧	102	37.12 N	103.10 E
Maoming	102	21.39 N	110.54 E
Maomu	102	40.18 N	99.28 E
Ma On Shan ∧	271d	22.25 N	114.15 E
Ma On Shan Tsuen	271d	22.24 N	114.14 E
Maoping	102	30.23 N	110.33 E
Maopora, Pulau I	112	7.35 S	127.35 E
Maoshan	105	40.17 N	117.26 E
Mao Shan ⋏	106	31.43 N	119.17 E
Maoshi	100	26.57 N	113.05 E
Maospati	115a	7.36 S	111.26 E
Maouri, Dallol V	150	12.05 N	3.32 E
Maowen	102	31.30 N	103.39 E
Maoxing	89	45.32 N	124.33 E
Mao Yü I	100	23.19 N	119.19 E
Maozhou	105	38.51 N	116.06 E
Mapaga	112	0.06 S	119.48 E
Mapam Yumco ⊜	120	30.42 N	81.27 E
Mapan	112	2.21 S	111.10 E
Mapanda	152	9.32 S	24.16 E
Mapane	112	1.24 S	120.40 E
Mapanza	154	16.15 S	26.55 E
Mapaoni ≃	250	1.55 N	54.13 W
Mapari ≃, Bra.	246	1.49 S	66.48 W
Mapari ≃, Bra.	250	0.45 N	53.07 W
Mapastepec	234	15.26 N	92.54 W
Mapaville	219	38.14 N	90.29 W
Mapi	164	7.07 S	139.23 E
Mapi ≃	164	7.00 S	139.16 E
Mapia, Kepulauan II	108	0.50 N	134.20 E
Mapida	112	0.33 S	119.46 E
Mapimí	232	25.49 N	103.51 W
Mapimí, Bolsón de ◆[2]	232	26.30 N	104.00 W
Mapimí, Bufa de ∧	196	25.47 N	103.48 W
Maping, Zhg.	100	24.16 N	117.54 E
Maping, Zhg.	100	31.36 N	113.32 E
Mapinga	154	6.36 S	39.04 E
Mapinhane	156	22.19 S	35.03 E
Mapire	246	7.45 N	64.42 W
Mapiri	248	15.15 S	68.10 W
Mapiri ≃	248	9.52 S	66.21 W
Mapixari, Ilha I	246	2.10 S	65.08 W
Maple ◆[8]	275b	43.51 N	79.31 W
Maple ≃, U.S.	198	45.47 N	98.33 W
Maple ≃, Ia., U.S.	198	42.00 N	95.59 W
Maple ≃, Mi., U.S.	190	42.59 N	84.57 W
Maple ≃, Mn., U.S.	190	44.05 N	94.00 W
Maple ≃, N.D., U.S.	198	46.56 N	96.55 W
Maple Airfield ⊠	275b	43.51 N	79.32 W
Maple Bay	224	48.49 N	123.36 W
Maple Bluff	216	43.07 N	89.22 W
Maple Creek	184	49.55 N	109.27 W
Maple Creek ≃	198	41.33 N	96.27 W
Maplecrest	210	42.17 N	74.11 W
Maple Cross	260	51.37 N	0.30 W
Mapledale	214	41.23 N	79.51 W
Maple Falls	224	48.55 N	122.04 W
Maple Glen	285	40.11 N	75.11 W
Maple Grove, On., Can.	212	43.55 N	78.44 W
Maple Grove, P.Q., Can.	206	45.19 N	73.50 W
Maple Heights	214	41.24 N	81.33 W
Maple Lake	190	45.13 N	94.00 W
Maple Lake ⊜	212	45.06 N	78.40 W
Maple Lane	216	41.45 N	86.14 W
Maple Leaf Gardens ♠	275b	43.40 N	79.23 W
Maple Meadow Brook ≃	283	42.33 N	71.09 W
Maple Mount	194	37.42 N	87.26 W
Maple Park	216	41.55 N	88.36 W
Maples	216	41.01 N	84.58 W
Maple Shade	285	39.57 N	74.59 W
Maple Springs	214	42.12 N	79.25 W
Maplesville	194	32.47 N	86.52 W
Mapleton, S. Afr.	158	26.20 S	28.14 E
Mapleton, Ia., U.S.	198	42.09 N	95.47 W
Mapleton, Mn., U.S.	190	43.55 N	93.57 W
Mapleton, Or., U.S.	202	44.01 N	123.51 W
Mapleton, Ut,. U.S.	200	40.07 N	111.34 W
Mapleton Depot	214	40.24 N	77.57 W
Maple Valley	224	47.25 N	122.03 W
Mapleville	207	41.56 N	71.38 W
Maplewood, Mo., U.S.	219	38.36 N	90.19 W
Maplewood, N.J., U.S.	276	40.43 N	74.14 W
Maplewood, Oh., U.S.	216	40.23 N	84.02 W
Maplewood, Wa., U.S.	224	47.30 N	122.07 W
Maplewood Terrace	279b	40.17 N	79.32 W
Mapocho ≃	286e	33.25 S	70.47 W
Mapocho, Estación ◆[5]	286e	33.26 S	70.40 W
Mapoi	154	5.28 N	27.40 E
Mapoon Aboriginal Reserve ◆[4]	164	11.40 S	142.25 E
Mappsville	208	37.51 N	75.34 W
Maprik	164	3.40 S	143.05 E
Mapuera ≃	250	1.05 S	57.02 W
Mapujiang	105	40.24 N	114.56 E
Mapulanguene	156	24.29 S	32.06 E
Mapumulo	158	29.11 S	31.02 E
Maputa	158	26.59 S	32.46 E
Maputo	156	25.58 S	32.35 E
Maputo □[5]	156	26.00 S	32.25 E
Maputo (Great Usutu) (Lusutfu) ≃	158	26.11 S	32.42 E
Maputo, Baia de ⊂	158	25.48 S	32.51 E
Maqên Gangri ∧	102	34.55 N	99.18 E
Maqiangou	105	39.30 N	115.02 E
Maqiao, Zhg.	100	29.48 N	114.22 E
Maqiao, Zhg.	106	30.28 N	120.42 E
Maqna	128	28.24 N	34.45 E
Maqṭeïr ⊤[4]	148	22.10 N	10.50 W
Maquan ≃	124	29.35 N	84.10 E
Maqueda	34	40.04 N	4.22 W
Maqueda Bay ⊂	116	11.44 N	124.58 E
Maqueda Channel ʊ	116	13.42 N	124.01 E
Maquela do Zombo	152	6.03 S	15.07 E
Maquereau, Pointe au ›	186	48.12 N	64.47 W
Maquilaú ≃	246	1.23 N	63.24 W
Maquiling, Mount ∧	116	14.08 N	121.12 E
Maquinchao	254	41.15 S	68.44 W
Maquinchao ≃	254	41.13 S	69.25 W
Maquoketa	190	42.04 N	90.39 W
Maquoketa ≃	190	42.11 N	90.19 W
Maquoketa, North Fork ≃	190	42.05 N	90.40 W
Mar, Laguna ⊂	286b	23.05 N	82.30 W
Mar, Serra do ≗[4]	252	26.00 S	48.00 W
Mara, India	120	28.11 N	94.06 E
Mara, Perú	248	14.06 S	72.07 W
Mara, Zhg.	120	28.11 N	94.08 E
Mara □[4]	154	1.45 S	34.30 E
Mara ≃, Afr.	154	1.31 S	33.56 E
Mara ≃, Ross.	88	58.06 N	104.06 E
Maraã, Bra.	246	1.50 S	65.22 W
Maraa, Poly. fr.	174s	17.46 S	149.34 W
Marabá	250	5.21 S	49.07 W
Marabahan	112	3.00 S	114.45 E
Marabut	116	11.07 N	125.13 E
Maracá, Ilha de I, Bra.	246	3.25 N	61.40 W
Maracá, Ilha de I, Bra.	250	2.05 N	50.25 W
Maracaçumé ≃	250	1.23 S	45.42 W
Maracaí	255	22.36 S	50.39 W
Maracaibo	246	10.40 N	71.37 W
Maracaibo, Lago de ⊜	246	9.50 N	71.30 W
Maracaju	255	21.38 S	55.09 W
Maracaju, Serra de ⋏[2]	255	20.45 S	55.00 W
Maracalagonis	71	39.17 N	9.13 E
Maracanã	250	0.46 S	47.27 W
Maracanã ◆[8]	287a	22.54 S	43.14 W
Maracanã ≃	248	8.22 S	59.41 W
Maracanã, Estádio do ♠	287a	22.55 S	43.14 W
Maracanaú	250	3.52 S	38.38 W
Maracás	255	13.26 S	40.27 W
Maracay	246	10.15 N	67.36 W
Maracossic Creek ≃	208	37.53 N	77.11 W
Marādah	146	29.14 N	19.13 E
Maradi	150	13.29 N	7.06 E
Maradi □[5]	150	14.00 N	7.00 E
Maradi, Goulbin ≃	150	13.38 N	6.20 E
Marāghah, Sabkhat al- ⊜	130	35.39 N	37.39 E
Marāgheh	128	37.23 N	46.13 E
Maragiu, Capo ›	71	40.20 N	8.23 E
Maragogi	250	9.01 S	35.13 W
Maragogipe	255	12.46 S	38.55 W
Marahoué, Parc National de la ♠	150	7.00 N	6.00 W
Mārahra	124	27.44 N	78.35 E
Marahuaca, Cerro ∧	246	3.34 N	65.27 W
Maraial	250	8.47 S	35.50 W
Maraiche Lake ⊜	184	54.28 N	102.01 W
Marainviller	58	48.35 N	6.36 E
Maraisburg → Roodepoort-Maraisburg	273d	26.11 S	27.56 E
Marais des Cygnes ≃	194	38.02 N	94.14 W
Marais Temps Clair ⊜	219	38.54 N	90.24 W
Marajó, Baía de ⊂	250	1.00 S	48.30 W
Marajó, Ilha de I	250	1.00 S	49.30 W
Marakabei	158	29.32 S	28.09 E
Maʿrakah	132	33.16 N	35.18 E
Mārākand	84	38.52 N	45.14 E
Marakwini	164	3.42 S	141.31 E
Maralal	154	1.06 N	36.42 E
Maralaleng	156	25.47 S	22.45 E
Maralal Game Sanctuary ◆[4]	154	1.09 N	36.38 E
Maraldy	86	52.26 N	77.45 E
Marali	152	6.01 N	18.24 E
Maralik	84	40.35 N	43.52 E
Maralinga	162	30.10 S	131.35 E
Maralinga Lands ◆[4]	162	29.15 S	130.50 E
Maram	120	25.25 N	94.06 E
Maramag	116	7.46 N	125.00 E
Maramasike I	175e	9.32 S	161.27 E
Marambaia ≃	256	21.44 S	46.25 W
Marambaia, Ilha da I	256	23.04 S	43.58 W
Marambaia, Pico da ∧	256	23.04 S	43.59 W
Marambaia, Restinga de ≗[2]	256	23.04 S	43.45 W
Marambio ⊍[3]	9	64.14 S	56.43 W
Marampa	150	8.41 N	12.28 W
Maramsilli Reservoir ⊜[1]	122	20.32 N	81.41 E
Maramureș □[6]	38	47.40 N	24.00 E
Maran	114	3.35 N	102.46 E
Mārān, Koh-i- ∧	120	29.26 N	66.48 E
Marana, Mali	150	14.38 N	11.55 W
Marana, Az., U.S.	200	32.26 N	111.13 W
Maranalgo	162	29.23 S	117.48 E
Maranboy	164	14.30 S	132.45 E
Maranchón	34	41.03 N	2.12 W
Marand	128	38.26 N	45.46 E
Maranello	64	44.32 N	10.52 E
Marang, Malay.	114	5.12 N	103.13 E
Marang, Mya.	110	10.27 N	98.47 E
Marangá ≃	287a	22.51 S	43.23 W
Marangani	248	14.22 S	71.10 W
Marangas	116	8.40 N	117.38 E
Marange-Zondrange	56	49.07 N	6.32 E
Maranguape	250	3.53 S	38.40 W
Maranhão □[3]	250	5.00 S	45.00 W
Maranhão ≃	255	13.51 S	48.20 W
Marano	266b	45.38 N	8.38 E
Marano, Laguna di ⊂	64	45.44 N	13.10 E
Maranoa ≃	166	27.50 S	148.37 E
Marano di Napoli	68	40.54 N	14.11 E
Marano Lagunare	64	45.46 N	13.10 E
Marañón ≃	242	4.30 S	73.27 W
Marano sul Panaro	64	44.27 N	10.58 E
Marano Vicentino	64	45.41 N	11.25 E
Marans	32	46.19 N	1.00 W
Maraoli ◆[8]	272c	19.03 N	72.54 E
Marapanim	250	0.42 S	47.42 W
Marapendi, Lagoa de ⊂	287a	23.01 S	43.24 W
Marapi ≃	250	0.37 N	55.58 W
Marapicu, Morro do ∧	287a	22.50 S	43.36 W
Mararoa ≃	172	45.34 S	167.36 E
Mararui	154	1.56 S	41.18 E
Maras	248	13.20 S	72.09 W
Marasany	80	57.27 N	54.25 E
Marasende, Pulau I	112	5.08 S	118.09 E
Mărășești	38	45.52 N	27.14 E
Maraș → Kahramanmaraș	130	37.36 N	36.55 E
Maratasã ≃	250	4.14 S	42.15 W
Maratea	68	39.59 N	15.45 E
Marathon, Austl.	166	20.49 S	143.34 E
Marathon, On., Can.	190	48.43 N	86.23 W
Marathón, Ellás	38	38.10 N	23.58 E
Marathon, Fl., U.S.	220	24.42 N	81.05 W
Marathon, N.Y., U.S.	210	42.26 N	76.01 W
Marathon, Tx., U.S.	196	30.12 N	103.15 W
Marathon, Wi., U.S.	190	44.55 N	89.50 W
Maratua, Pulau I	112	2.15 N	118.36 E
Marau, Bra.	252	28.27 S	52.12 W
Maraú, Bra.	255	14.06 S	39.00 W
Marauiá ≃	246	0.23 S	65.13 W
Marausa	70	37.56 N	12.30 E
Maravari	175e	7.51 S	156.42 E
Maravatío de Ocampo	234	19.54 N	100.27 W
Maravilha	252	26.47 S	53.09 W
Maravillas	232	27.22 N	104.29 W
Maravillas Creek ≃	196	29.34 N	102.47 W
Mara Vista	207	41.33 N	70.34 W
Marav Lake ⊜	120	29.04 N	69.18 E
Maravovo	175e	9.17 S	159.38 E
Marāwah	146	32.29 N	21.25 E
Marawi, Pil.	116	8.01 N	124.18 E
Marawī, Sūd.	140	18.29 N	31.49 E
Marawwaḥ I	128	24.18 N	53.18 E
Maraye-en-Othe	50	48.10 N	3.51 E
Marayes	252	31.29 S	67.20 W
Marayong	274a	33.45 S	150.54 E
Maraza	84	40.33 N	48.56 E
Marazion	42	50.08 N	5.28 W
Marbach, Dtsch.	54	51.02 N	13.13 E
Marbach, Dtsch.	56	50.37 N	9.43 E
Marbach, Schw.	58	46.52 N	7.55 E
Marbach am Neckar	56	48.56 N	9.14 E
Marbache	56	48.48 N	6.05 E
Marbais	50	50.33 N	4.31 E
Marbeck	52	51.49 N	6.52 E
Marbella	34	36.31 N	4.53 W
Marble, Mn., U.S.	190	47.19 N	93.17 W
Marble, N.C., U.S.	192	35.10 N	83.55 W
Marble, Pa., U.S.	214	41.20 N	79.26 W
Marble Arch ⊥	146	30.29 N	18.35 E
Marble Bar	162	21.11 S	119.44 E
Marble Canyon V	200	36.30 N	111.50 W
Marble Falls	196	30.34 N	98.16 W
Marble Hall	156	24.57 S	29.13 E
Marblehead, Il., U.S.	219	39.50 N	91.22 W
Marblehead, Ma., U.S.	207	42.30 N	70.51 W
Marblehead, Oh., U.S.	214	41.32 N	82.44 W
Marblehead Neck ›[1]	283	42.29 N	70.51 W
Marble Hill	194	37.18 N	89.58 W
Marble Lake ⊜	216	41.54 N	84.54 W
Marblemount	224	48.31 N	121.26 W
Marble Rock	190	42.57 N	92.52 W
Marbleton	206	45.37 N	71.35 W

ENGLISH

Name	Page	Lat.°′	Long.°′
Marburg, Austl.	171a	27.34 S	152.35 E
Marburg, Dtsch.	56	50.49 N	8.46 E
Marburg, S. Afr.	158	30.44 S	30.26 E
Marburg, Lake ⊜[1]	208	39.48 N	76.53 W
Marburg an der Drau → Maribor	36	46.33 N	15.39 E
Marbury	208	38.34 N	77.09 W
Marc ≃	50	50.43 N	3.50 E
Marca, Ponta da ›	152	16.31 S	11.42 E
Marcal ≃	30	47.41 N	17.32 E
Marcala	236	14.07 N	88.00 W
Marcali	30	46.35 N	17.25 E
Marcallo con Casone	266b	45.29 N	8.52 E
Marcaria	64	45.07 N	10.32 E
Marceau, Lac ⊜	186	51.25 N	66.41 W
Marcedusa	68	39.02 N	16.50 E
Marcelin	184	52.55 N	106.47 W
Marceline	194	39.42 N	92.56 W
Marcelino Ramos	252	27.28 S	51.54 W
Marcella	276	40.59 N	74.28 W
Marcellina	66	42.01 N	12.48 E
Marcellus, Mi., U.S.	216	42.01 N	85.48 W
Marcellus, N.Y., U.S.	210	42.59 N	76.20 W
Marcellus Falls	210	43.00 N	76.20 W
Marcevo	83	47.15 N	38.53 E
March	42	52.33 N	0.06 E
March (Morava) ≃	30	48.10 N	16.59 E
Marcha	74	60.37 N	123.18 E
Marcha ≃	74	63.28 N	118.50 E
March Air Force Base ■	228	33.54 N	117.15 W
Marchais	261	48.31 N	2.03 E
Marchal	152	5.16 S	14.58 E
Marchamat	85	40.30 N	72.19 E
Marchand	214	40.51 N	79.02 W
Marchaux	58	47.19 N	6.08 E
Marche □[4]	66	43.30 N	13.15 E
Marche □[9]	32	46.05 N	2.10 E
Marche-en-Famenne	56	50.12 N	5.20 E
Marchegg	61	48.17 N	16.55 E
Marche-les-Dames	56	50.29 N	4.58 E
Marchémoret	261	49.03 N	2.46 E
Marchena	34	37.20 N	5.24 W
Marchena, Isla I	246a	0.21 N	90.29 W
Marchenoir	50	47.49 N	1.24 E
Marchesato	68	39.07 N	16.58 E
Marchfeld ◆[1]	264b	48.17 N	16.31 E
Marchienne-au-Pont	50	50.24 N	4.23 E
Marchinbar Island I	164	11.15 S	136.45 E
Marching	60	48.49 N	11.43 E
Mar Chiquita, Laguna ⊂	252	37.37 S	57.24 W
Mar Chiquita, Laguna ⊜	252	30.42 S	62.36 W
Marchtrenk	61	48.11 N	14.07 E
Marciana	66	42.47 N	10.10 E
Marciana Marina	66	42.48 N	10.12 E
Marcianise	68	41.02 N	14.17 E
Marciano della Chiana	66	43.18 N	11.47 E
Marčichina Buda	78	51.58 N	34.03 E
Marcigny	32	46.17 N	4.02 E
Marcillac-Vallon	32	44.29 N	2.28 E
Marcilloles	62	45.20 N	5.11 E
Marcilly	261	49.02 N	2.53 E
Marcilly-la-Campagne	50	48.50 N	1.13 E
Marcilly-le-Hayer	50	48.21 N	3.38 E
Marcilly-sur-Eure	50	48.49 N	1.21 E
Marck	50	50.57 N	1.57 E
Marckolsheim	58	48.10 N	7.33 E
Marco, Bra.	250	3.08 S	40.09 W
Marco, It.	64	45.51 N	11.01 E
Marco, Fl., U.S.	220	25.58 N	81.43 W
Marcoing	50	50.07 N	3.11 E
Marco Island I	220	25.55 N	81.45 W
Marcola	202	44.10 N	122.51 W
Marcolino, Igarapé ≃	250	11.03 S	58.35 W
Marcona	248	15.03 S	75.01 W
Marco Polo, Aeroporto ⊠	64	45.30 N	12.21 E
Marco Polo Bridge ◆[5]	271a	39.52 N	116.12 E
Marcos Juárez	252	32.42 S	62.06 W
Marcos Paz	258	34.46 S	58.50 W
Marcos Paz □[5]	288	34.49 S	58.49 W
Marcotte, Lac ⊜	206	46.47 N	73.12 W
Marcoussis	261	48.39 N	2.14 E
Marcq	261	48.52 N	1.49 E
Marcq-en-Barœul	50	50.40 N	3.05 E
Marčugi	82	55.21 N	38.33 E
Marcus	198	42.49 N	95.48 W
Marcus Baker, Mount ∧	180	61.26 N	147.45 W
Marcus Hook	208	39.49 N	75.25 W
Marcus Hook Creek ≃	285	39.49 N	75.25 W
Marcus Island → Minami-Tori-shima I	14	24.18 N	153.58 E
Marcy, Mount ∧	188	44.07 N	73.56 W
Marda	162	30.13 S	119.17 E
Mardakert	84	40.12 N	46.48 E
Mardalsfossen ⌊	26	62.30 N	8.07 E
Mardān	123	34.12 N	72.02 E
Mardarovka	78	47.32 N	29.44 E
Mar de Cães, Vala de ≅	266c	38.51 N	8.59 W
Mar de Espanha	256	21.52 S	43.00 W
Mardela Springs	208	38.27 N	75.45 W
Mar del Plata	252	38.00 S	57.33 W
Marden	42	51.10 N	0.29 E
Mardie	162	21.11 S	115.57 E
Mardin	130	37.18 N	40.44 E
Mardin □[4]	128	37.25 N	41.00 E
Mar Dyke ≃	260	51.29 N	0.14 E
Maré I	175f	21.30 S	168.00 E
Mare a Brăilei, Insula I	38	45.00 N	28.00 E
Marea de Portillo	240p	19.55 N	77.11 W
Marecchia ≃	66	44.04 N	12.34 E
Marechal Cândido Rondon	252	24.34 S	54.04 W
Marechal Deodoro	250	9.43 S	35.54 W
Marechal Taumaturgo	248	8.57 S	72.48 W
Maree, Loch ⊜	46	57.42 N	5.30 W
Mareeba	166	17.00 S	145.26 E
Mareetsane	158	26.09 S	25.25 E
Mareil-en-France	261	49.04 N	2.26 E
Mareil-le-Guyon	261	48.47 N	1.51 E
Mareil-Marly	261	48.53 N	2.05 E
Mare Island I	226	38.06 N	122.16 W
Mare Island Naval Shipyard ■	226	38.06 N	122.17 W
Mare Island Strait ʊ	282	38.06 N	122.17 W
Mareje, Gunung ∧	115b	8.46 S	116.08 E
Marek	112	4.48 S	120.21 E
Maremma ◆[1]	66	42.30 N	11.30 E
Marene	62	44.39 N	7.44 E
Marengo, Il., U.S.	216	42.14 N	88.36 W
Marengo, In., U.S.	218	38.22 N	86.20 W
Marengo, Ia., U.S.	190	41.47 N	92.04 W
Marengo, Mi., U.S.	216	42.17 N	84.51 W
Marengo, Oh., U.S.	214	40.24 N	82.49 W
Marengo ◆[1]	62	44.55 N	8.40 E
Marengo ⊥	62	44.49 N	8.40 E
Marengo Cave ≗[5]	218	38.23 N	86.21 W
Marenisco	190	46.22 N	89.41 W
Marennes	32	45.50 N	1.06 W
Marerano	157b	21.23 S	44.52 E
Maresias	256	23.48 S	45.33 W
Marettimo	70	37.58 N	12.04 E
Marettimo, Isola I	70	37.58 N	12.03 E
Mareuil-en-Brie	50	48.57 N	3.45 E
Mareuil-lès-Meaux	261	48.56 N	2.52 E
Mareuil-sur-Aÿ	50	49.03 N	4.02 E
Mareuil-sur-Belle	32	45.28 N	0.28 E
Marevo	76	57.19 N	32.05 E
Marey-sur-Tille	58	47.35 N	5.03 E
Marfa	196	30.18 N	104.01 W
Marfinka	83	47.36 N	38.32 E

DEUTSCH

Name	Seite	Breite°′	Länge°′ E = Ost
Marfino	80	46.25 N	48.44 E
Mar Forest ◆[3]	46	57.00 N	3.35 W
Margai Caka ⊜	120	35.00 N	87.00 E
Margam, Īrān	84	39.09 N	44.57 E
Margam, Wales, U.K.	42	51.34 N	3.44 W
Marganec	78	47.38 N	34.40 E
Margao → Madgaon	122	15.18 N	73.57 E
Margaree	186	46.24 N	61.05 W
Margaree Harbour	186	46.26 N	61.07 W
Margaret ≃	162	18.10 S	125.37 E
Margaret, Mount ∧	224	46.18 N	122.08 W
Margaret Bay	182	51.20 N	127.29 W
Margaret Creek ≃	166	29.26 S	137.07 E
Margarethenhöhe ◆[8]	263	51.26 N	6.58 E
Margaret River, Austl.	162	33.57 S	115.04 E
Margaret River, Austl.	162	18.38 S	126.52 E
Margaret Roding	260	51.47 N	0.19 E
Margaretting	260	51.41 N	0.25 E
Margarettsville	208	36.32 N	77.21 W
Margaretville	210	42.08 N	74.38 W
Margarita, Bahía → Marguerite Bay ⊂	9	68.30 S	68.30 W
Margarita, Isla I	246	9.05 N	74.30 W
Margarita, Isla de I	246	11.00 N	64.00 W
Margarita Belén	252	27.16 S	58.58 W
Margarita Peak ∧	228	33.26 N	117.23 W
Margaritovka	83	46.55 N	38.52 E
Margate, S. Afr.	158	30.55 S	30.15 E
Margate, Eng., U.K.	42	51.24 N	1.24 E
Margate, Fl., U.S.	220	26.14 N	80.12 W
Margate City	208	39.19 N	74.30 W
Margecany	30	48.54 N	21.01 E
Margelan → Margilan	85	40.28 N	71.44 E
Margeride, Monts de la ⋏	32	44.50 N	3.30 E
Margès	62	45.09 N	5.03 E
Mārgherita	120	27.17 N	95.41 E
Margherita di Savoia	68	41.23 N	16.09 E
Margherita → Jamaame	144	0.04 N	42.45 E
Margherita Peak ∧	154	0.22 N	29.51 E
Marghī	120	34.58 N	66.31 E
Marghita	38	47.21 N	22.21 E
Margi ≃	70	37.16 N	14.58 E
Margilan	85	40.28 N	71.44 E
Margit Híd ◆[5]	264c	47.31 N	19.02 E
Margit-sziget I	264c	47.32 N	19.03 E
Margny-lès-Compiègne	50	49.26 N	2.49 E
Margone	62	45.13 N	7.11 E
Margonin	30	52.59 N	17.05 E
Margos	248	10.04 S	76.26 W
Margosatubig	116	7.34 N	123.10 E
Margot Lake ⊜	184	52.28 N	93.10 W
Mārgow, Dasht-e ◆[2]	128	30.45 N	63.10 E
Margreid → Magrè	64	46.17 N	11.12 E
Marguerite, Pic → Margherita Peak ∧	154	0.22 N	29.51 E
Marguerite Bay ⊂	9	68.30 S	68.30 W
Marguerittes	62	43.51 N	4.27 E
Margut	56	49.35 N	5.16 E
Margyang	124	29.57 N	90.09 E
Mari	164	9.10 S	141.40 E
Maria	116	9.12 N	123.39 E
Maria, Îles II	14	21.48 S	154.41 W
Mariabrunn ◆[8]	264b	48.12 N	16.14 E
María Cleofas, Isla I	234	21.16 N	106.14 W
Maria da Fé	256	22.18 S	45.23 W
María Elena	252	22.21 S	69.40 W
Maria Enzersdorf	61	48.06 N	16.17 E
Maria Gail	64	46.36 N	13.52 E
Mariager	26	56.39 N	10.00 E
Mariāhu	124	25.37 N	82.37 E
María Ignacia (Vela)	252	37.24 S	59.30 W
Maria Island I, Austl.	164	14.52 S	135.40 E
Maria Island I, Austl.	166	42.39 S	148.04 E
Maria Island National Park ♠	166	42.39 S	148.06 E
Mariakani	154	3.52 S	39.28 E
Maria Laach ⊍[1]	56	50.24 N	7.14 E
María la Baja	246	9.59 N	75.17 W
Maria Lanzendorf	264b	48.06 N	16.25 E
Maria Luggau	64	46.42 N	12.45 E
María Madre, Isla I	234	21.35 N	106.33 W
María Magdalena, Isla I	234	21.25 N	106.24 W
Marian, Lake ⊜	220	27.52 N	81.06 W
Mariana	255	20.23 S	43.25 W
Mariana Basin ✢[1]	14	17.30 N	145.00 E
Mariana Islands II	108	16.00 N	145.30 E
Mariana Ridge ✢[3]	14	17.00 N	146.00 E
Mariana Trench ✢[1]	14	15.00 N	147.30 E
Mariāni	120	26.40 N	94.20 E
Marian Lake ⊜	176	63.00 N	116.10 W
Marianna, Ar., U.S.	194	34.46 N	90.45 W
Marianna, Fl., U.S.	192	30.46 N	85.13 W
Mariannelund	26	57.37 N	15.34 E
Mariannhill	158	29.52 S	30.50 E
Mariano Acosta	258	34.43 S	58.48 W
Mariano Comense	62	45.42 N	9.11 E
Mariano del Friuli	64	45.55 N	13.27 E
Mariano I. Loza	252	29.22 S	58.12 W
Mariano J. Haedo	288	34.38 S	58.36 W
Mariano Moreno	252	38.44 S	70.01 W
Mariano Moreno → Moreno	258	34.39 S	58.48 W
Marianopoli	70	37.36 N	13.55 E
Mariánské Lázně	60	49.59 N	12.43 E
Mariar	164	2.48 S	132.50 E
Mariarano	157b	15.29 S	46.42 E
Marias ≃	202	47.56 N	110.30 W
Marias, Dry Fork ≃	202	48.22 N	111.45 W
Marías, Islas II	234	21.25 N	106.28 W
Maria Saal	61	46.41 N	14.21 E
Marias Pass)(	202	48.19 N	113.21 W
Maria Stein	216	40.24 N	84.28 W
María Teresa	252	34.01 S	61.54 W
Maria-Theresiopel → Subotica	38	46.06 N	19.39 E
Mariato, Punta ›	246	7.13 N	80.53 W
Maria van Diemen, Cape ›	172	34.28 S	172.39 E
Mariaville	210	42.49 N	74.08 W
Mariazell	61	47.47 N	15.19 E
Ma'rib	144	15.30 N	45.20 E
Maribo	41	54.46 N	11.31 E
Maribojoc Bay ⊂	116	9.42 N	123.50 E
Maribor	61	46.33 N	15.39 E
Maribyrnong	274b	37.46 S	144.54 E
Marica, Blg.	38	42.02 N	25.50 E
Maricá, Bra.	256	22.55 S	42.49 W
Marica, Ross.	78	51.45 N	35.16 E
Maricá □[7]	287a	22.57 S	42.59 W
Marica (Évros) (Meriç) ≃	38	40.52 N	26.12 E
Maricá, Lagoa de ⊂	256	22.56 S	42.50 W
Maricaban Island I	116	13.39 N	120.53 E
Maricao	240m	18.11 N	66.59 W
Maricás, Ilhas II	256	23.01 S	42.55 W
Maricha Bil ⊜	272b	22.55 N	88.31 E
Marico ≃	156	24.12 S	26.52 E
Maricopa, Az., U.S.	200	33.03 N	112.02 W
Maricopa, Ca., U.S.	204	35.03 N	119.24 W
Maricopa Indian Reservation ◆[4]	200	33.02 N	112.05 W
Maricunga, Salar de ≚	252	26.55 S	69.05 W
Maridagao ≃	116	7.13 N	124.41 E
Marīdī	154	4.55 N	29.28 E
Maridi ≃	140	6.05 N	29.24 E
Marié ≃	246	0.27 S	66.26 W
Marie Byrd Land ◆[1]	9	80.00 S	120.00 W
Marie Curtis Park ♠	275b	43.35 N	79.33 W
Mariedamm	40	58.51 N	15.09 E

Symbols in the index entries represent the broad categories identified in the key at the right. Symbols with superior numbers (⋏[1]) identify subcategories (see complete key on page I · 1).

Symbole im Register stellen die rechts im Schlüssel erklärten Kategorien dar. Symbole mit hochgestellten Ziffern (⋏[1]) bezeichnen Unterabteilungen einer Kategorie (vgl. vollständiger Schlüssel auf Seite I · 1).

Los símbolos incluídos en el texto del índice representan las grandes categorias identificadas con la clave a la derecha. Los símbolos con numeros en su parte superior (⋏[1]) identifican las subcategorías (véase la clave completa en la página I · 1).

Les symboles de l'index représentent les catégories indiquées dans la légende à droite. Les symboles suivis d'un indice (⋏[1]) représentent des sous-catégories (voir légende complète à la page I · 1).

Os símbolos incluídos no texto do índice representam as grandes categorias identificadas com a chave à direita. Os símbolos com números em sua parte superior (⋏[1]) identificam as subcategorias (veja-se a chave completa à página I · 1).

∧ Mountain	Berg	Montaña	Montagne	Montanha
⋏ Mountains	Gebirge	Montañas	Montagnes	Montanhas
)(Pass	Paß	Paso	Col	Passo
V Valley, Canyon	Tal, Cañon	Valle, Cañón	Vallée, Canyon	Vale, Canhão
≚ Plain	Ebene	Llano	Plaine	Planície
› Cape	Kap	Cabo	Cap	Cabo
I Island	Insel	Isla	Île	Ilha
II Islands	Inseln	Islas	Îles	Ilhas
≗ Other Topographic Features	Andere Topographische Objekte	Otros Elementos Topográficos	Autres données topographiques	Outros acidentes topográficos

ESPAÑOL — Nombre | Página | Lat.°′ | Long.°′ W = Oeste
FRANÇAIS — Nom | Page | Lat.°′ | Long.°′ W = Ouest
PORTUGUÊS — Nome | Página | Lat.°′ | Long.°′ W = Oeste

Nombre	Página	Lat.°′	Long.°′ W = Oeste
Mariefred	40	59.16 N	17.13 E
Marie-Galante I	241o	15.56 N	61.16 W
Mariehamn	26	60.06 N	19.57 E
Marieholm	41	55.52 N	13.09 E
Mariel	240p	22.59 N	82.45 W
Marie Lake ⊜	184	54.37 N	110.18 W
Marie-Lefranc, Lac ⊜	206	46.08 N	75.00 W
Mariembourg	50	50.06 N	4.31 E
Marienbad → Mariánské Lázně	60	49.59 N	12.43 E
Marienbaum	52	51.41 N	6.22 E
Marienberg, Dtsch.	54	50.39 N	13.10 E
Marienberg, Dtsch.	56	50.39 N	7.57 E
Marienberg, Pap. N. Gui.	164	3.55 S	144.15 E
Marien-Berg ʌ [2]	264a	52.22 N	13.32 E
Marienborn	54	52.12 N	11.08 E
Marienburg → Malbork	30	54.02 N	19.01 E
Mariendorf ◆ [8]	264a	52.26 N	13.23 E
Marienfelde ◆ [8]	264a	52.25 N	13.22 E
Marienhafe	52	53.31 N	7.16 E
Marienheide	56	51.05 N	7.32 E
Mariental, Dtsch.	54	52.16 N	10.59 E
Mariental, Namibia	156	24.36 S	17.59 E
Mariental □ [5]	156	25.00 S	19.00 E
Marienville	214	41.28 N	79.07 W
Maries □ [6]	219	38.15 N	91.56 W
Maries ≃	194	38.30 N	92.01 W
Mariestad	40	58.43 N	13.51 E
Marieta ≃	246	5.02 N	66.38 W
Marietta, Ga., U.S.	192	33.57 N	84.33 W
Marietta, In., U.S.	218	39.26 N	85.53 W
Marietta, Mn., U.S.	198	45.00 N	96.25 W
Marietta, Oh., U.S.	188	39.24 N	81.27 W
Marietta, Ok., U.S.	196	33.56 N	97.06 W
Marietta, Pa., U.S.	208	40.03 N	76.33 W
Marietta, Tx., U.S.	222	33.10 N	94.33 W
Marietta, Wa., U.S.	224	48.47 N	122.34 W
Marieville	206	45.26 N	73.10 W
Mariga ≃	150	9.40 N	5.55 E
Marigliano	66	40.56 N	14.27 E
Marignane	62	43.25 N	5.13 E
Marignier	58	46.06 N	6.31 E
Marigny-le-Châtel	50	48.24 N	3.44 E
Marigny-L'Église	50	47.22 N	3.56 E
Marigot, Dom.	240d	15.32 N	61.18 W
Marigot, Guad.	238	18.04 N	63.06 W
Marihatag	116	8.48 N	126.18 E
Mariinsk	86	56.13 N	87.45 E
Mariinskoje	89	51.43 N	140.13 E
Marijampole	76	54.33 N	23.21 E
Marijec	80	56.32 N	49.50 E
Marijskaja Avtonomnaja Sovetskaja Socialističeskaja Respublika □ [3]	80	56.30 N	48.00 E
Marikana	158	25.42 S	27.30 E
Marikina	269f	14.38 N	121.06 E
Marikina ≃	269f	14.33 N	121.04 E
Marília	255	22.13 S	49.56 W
Marilla	210	42.50 N	78.33 W
Mari-Malmyž	80	56.30 N	50.52 E
Marimari ≃	246	3.58 S	58.49 W
Marimba	152	8.28 S	17.08 E
Marín	34	42.23 N	8.42 W
Marin □ [6]	226	38.03 N	122.33 W
Marina	226	36.41 N	121.48 W
Marina ◆ [8]	282	37.47 N	122.27 W
Marina del Rey	280	33.50 N	118.25 W
Marina del Rey ⊂	280	33.58 N	118.27 W
Marina di Andora	62	43.57 N	8.08 E
Marina di Campo	66	42.44 N	10.14 E
Marina di Caronia	70	38.02 N	14.28 E
Marina di Carrara	64	44.02 N	10.02 E
Marina di Cecina	66	43.18 N	10.29 E
Marina di Gioiosa Ionica	68	38.18 N	16.20 E
Marina di Grosseto	66	42.43 N	10.59 E
Marina di Massa	64	44.00 N	10.06 E
Marina di Minturno	66	41.16 N	13.45 E
Marina di Orosei	71	40.22 N	9.43 E
Marina di Palma ◆ [8]	70	37.10 N	13.43 E
Marina di Pietrasanta	64	43.56 N	10.12 E
Marina di Pisa	66	43.40 N	10.16 E
Marina di Ragusa	70	36.47 N	14.33 E
Marina di Ravenna	66	44.29 N	12.17 E
Marina Fall ∟	246	5.22 N	59.29 W
Marin City	282	37.52 N	122.21 W
Marinduque □ [4]	116	13.25 N	121.55 E
Marinduque Island I	116	13.24 N	121.58 E
Marine	219	38.47 N	89.46 W
Marine City	214	42.43 N	82.29 W
Marine-Ehrenmal ⊥	54	54.23 N	10.15 E
Marineland of the Pacific ʊ [3]	228	33.44 N	118.24 W
Marinella	70	37.35 N	12.50 E
Marine Museum ʊ	280	33.43 N	118.17 W
Marineo	70	37.57 N	13.25 E
Marine Park ♠	283	42.20 N	71.01 W
Marine Parkway Bridge ◆ [5]	276	40.34 N	73.53 W
Mariners Museum ʊ	208	37.03 N	76.30 W
Marines	50	49.09 N	1.59 E
Marinette	190	45.06 N	87.37 W
Marine World/Africa USA ♠	282	37.32 N	122.16 W
Maringá	255	23.25 S	51.55 W
Maringa ≃	152	1.14 N	19.48 E
Maringouin	194	30.29 N	91.31 W
Maríngué	154	17.55 S	34.24 E
Marinha Grande	34	39.45 N	8.56 W
Marinho ≃	287a	23.00 S	43.27 W
Marin Mall ◆ [9]	282	37.56 N	122.31 W
Marino, It.	66	41.46 N	12.39 E
Marino, Vanuatu	175f	15.00 S	168.09 E
Marinovka, Ross.	80	48.41 N	43.49 E
Marinovka, Ukr.	78	47.46 N	30.53 E
Marinovka, Ukr.	83	47.54 N	38.51 E
Marin Peninsula › [1]	282	37.51 N	122.31 W
Marinskij Posad	80	56.07 N	47.43 E
Marintu	112	0.34 N	110.00 E
Marinwood	226	38.02 N	122.32 W
Mario, Monte ʌ [2]	267a	41.55 N	12.27 E
Marion, Austl.	168b	35.01 S	138.34 E
Marion, Al., U.S.	194	32.37 N	87.19 W
Marion, Ar., U.S.	194	35.12 N	90.11 W
Marion, Ct., U.S.	207	41.33 N	72.55 W
Marion, Il., U.S.	194	37.43 N	88.55 W
Marion, In., U.S.	216	40.33 N	85.39 W
Marion, Ia., U.S.	190	42.02 N	91.35 W
Marion, Ks., U.S.	198	38.20 N	97.01 W
Marion, Ky., U.S.	194	37.19 N	88.04 W
Marion, La., U.S.	194	32.54 N	92.14 W
Marion, Ma., U.S.	207	41.42 N	70.45 W
Marion, Mi., U.S.	190	44.06 N	85.08 W
Marion, Ms., U.S.	194	32.25 N	88.38 W
Marion, N.Y., U.S.	210	43.08 N	77.11 W
Marion, N.C., U.S.	192	35.41 N	82.00 W
Marion, N.D., U.S.	198	46.36 N	98.19 W
Marion, Oh., U.S.	214	40.35 N	83.07 W
Marion, S.C., U.S.	192	34.10 N	79.24 W
Marion, S.D., U.S.	198	43.25 N	97.15 W
Marion, Va., U.S.	192	36.50 N	81.30 W
Marion, Wi., U.S.	190	44.40 N	88.53 W
Marion □ [6], Fl., U.S.	220	29.00 N	82.03 W
Marion □ [6], Il., U.S.	219	38.38 N	88.57 W
Marion □ [6], In., U.S.	218	39.46 N	86.09 W
Marion □ [6], Mo., U.S.	219	39.50 N	91.37 W
Marion □ [6], Oh., U.S.	214	40.35 N	83.08 W
Marion □ [6], Or., U.S.	224	45.06 N	122.47 W
Marion □ [6], Tx., U.S.	222	32.48 N	94.33 W
Marion, Lake ⊜	220	28.05 N	81.32 W
Marion, Lake ⊜ [1]	192	33.30 N	80.25 W
Marion Bay ⊂	166	42.48 S	147.55 E
Marion Center	214	40.46 N	79.03 W
Marion Downs	166	23.22 S	139.39 E
Marion Heights	210	40.48 N	76.28 W
Marion Hill	214	40.44 N	80.18 W
Marion Hills	278	41.45 N	87.57 W
Marion Junction	194	32.26 N	87.14 W
Marion Lake ⊜ [1]	198	38.24 N	97.08 W
Marion Reef ✢ [2]	166	19.10 S	152.17 E
Marion Station	208	38.02 N	75.46 W
Marionville	194	37.00 N	93.38 W
Marilópolis	252	26.20 S	52.33 W
Maripa	246	7.26 N	65.09 W
Maripá de Minas	256	21.48 S	42.58 W
Maripasoula	250	3.38 N	54.02 W
Maripipi Island I	116	11.47 N	124.19 E
Mariposa	226	37.29 N	119.57 W
Mariposa □ [6]	226	37.29 N	119.58 W
Mariposa Creek ≃	226	37.14 N	120.26 W
Mariposa Slough ≃	226	37.12 N	120.46 W
Mariquita	246	5.12 N	74.54 W
Marisa	112	0.28 N	121.56 E
Marisa ≃	112	0.28 N	121.56 E
Mariscal Estigarribia	252	22.02 S	60.38 W
Marisco, Ponta do ›	287a	23.01 S	43.17 W
Mariškino	82	55.21 N	38.37 E
Marissa	219	38.15 N	89.45 W
Maritime Alps (Alpes Maritimes) (Alpi Marittime) ʌʌ	62	44.15 N	7.10 E
Maritimes, Alpes → Maritime Alps ʌʌ	62	44.15 N	7.10 E
Marittime, Alpi → Maritime Alps ʌʌ	62	44.15 N	7.10 E
Mari-Turek	80	56.47 N	49.36 E
Maritzburg → Pietermaritzburg	158	29.37 S	30.16 E
Mariupol' (Ždanov)	83	47.06 N	37.33 E
Mariusa, Caño ≃ [1]	246	9.43 N	61.26 W
Mariusa, Isla I	241r	9.39 N	61.19 W
Marīvān	128	35.31 N	46.10 E
Mariveles	116	14.26 N	120.29 E
Märjamaa	76	58.54 N	24.26 E
Marjanovka, Ross.	86	54.58 N	72.38 E
Marjanovka, Ukr.	78	50.28 N	24.48 E
Marjanskaja	78	45.06 N	38.38 E
Marjevka	86	53.46 N	67.24 E
Marjina Gorka	76	53.31 N	28.09 E
Marjinka	83	47.56 N	37.31 E
Marjino, Ross.	82	54.28 N	37.12 E
Marjino, Ross.	89	48.31 N	130.38 E
Marjino, Ross.	265a	59.50 N	29.56 E
Marjino, Ross.	265a	59.54 N	31.00 E
Marjino, Ross.	265b	55.52 N	37.18 E
Marjinskaja	84	43.53 N	43.29 E
Marjinsko	76	58.49 N	28.32 E
Mār Jirjis, Jūn ⊂	132	33.54 N	35.33 E
Marj 'Uyūn	132	33.22 N	35.35 E
Marka, Som.	144	1.43 N	44.53 E
Mārkā, Urd.	132	31.59 N	35.59 E
Markā I	144	18.13 N	41.19 E
Mark Acres	279b	40.21 N	79.42 W
Markakol', ozero ⊜	86	48.45 N	85.48 E
Markala	150	13.41 N	6.05 W
Markam	102	29.40 N	98.30 E
Markansu	85	39.18 N	73.20 E
Mārkāpur	122	15.44 N	79.17 E
Markaryd	26	56.26 N	13.36 E
Markazī □ [4]	128	34.30 N	50.30 E
Markdale	212	44.19 N	80.39 W
Markdorf	58	47.43 N	9.23 E
Marked Tree	194	35.31 N	90.25 W
Markelo	52	52.14 N	6.30 E
Markelovo	86	56.42 N	83.33 E
Marken I	52	52.28 N	5.03 E
Markendorf	54	51.59 N	13.10 E
Markermeer ⊜	52	52.33 N	5.15 E
Markesan	190	43.42 N	88.59 W
Märket I	40	60.18 N	19.08 E
Market Bosworth	42	52.37 N	1.24 W
Market Deeping	42	52.41 N	0.19 W
Market Drayton	42	52.54 N	2.29 W
Market Harborough	42	52.29 N	0.55 W
Markethill	48	54.18 N	6.31 W
Market Lavington	42	51.18 N	1.59 W
Market Rasen	44	53.24 N	0.21 W
Market Weighton	44	53.52 N	0.40 W
Markfield	42	52.40 N	1.17 W
Markgröningen	56	48.54 N	9.05 E
Markham, On., Can.	212	43.52 N	79.16 W
Markham, Il., U.S.	278	41.35 N	87.41 W
Markham, Tx., U.S.	222	28.57 N	96.04 W
Markham ≃	164	6.35 S	146.25 E
Markham, Mount ʌ	9	82.51 S	161.21 E
Markham Bay ⊂	176	63.30 N	71.48 W
Markinch	46	56.12 N	3.08 W
Märkisch Buchholz	54	52.07 N	13.46 E
Markit	85	38.55 N	77.38 E
Markkleeberg	54	51.17 N	12.23 E
Markland Dam ◆ [6]	218	38.47 N	84.58 W
Markle, In., U.S.	216	40.50 N	85.20 W
Markle, Pa., U.S.	279b	40.34 N	79.39 W
Markleeville	226	38.41 N	119.46 W
Markleville	218	39.58 N	85.36 W
Markley Canyon V	282	38.00 N	121.50 W
Marknesse	52	52.43 N	5.52 E
Markneukirchen	54	50.18 N	12.19 E
Markoldendorf	52	51.48 N	9.46 E
Markópoulon	267c	37.54 N	23.54 E
Markounda	152	7.37 N	16.59 E
Markovka	83	49.31 N	39.34 E
Markovo, Ross.	74	64.40 N	170.25 E
Markovo, Ross.	80	57.01 N	40.30 E
Markovo, Ross.	82	55.52 N	39.17 E
Markovo, Ross.	88	57.20 N	107.04 E
Markoy	150	14.39 N	0.02 E
Markranstädt	54	51.18 N	12.13 E
Marks, Ross.	80	51.42 N	46.46 E
Marks, Ms., U.S.	194	34.15 N	90.16 W
Marks Tey	42	51.52 N	0.47 E
Marksuhl	56	50.55 N	10.11 E
Marksville	194	31.07 N	92.03 W
Markt Bibart	56	49.39 N	10.26 E
Marktbreit	56	49.40 N	10.08 E
Markt Erlbach	56	49.29 N	10.38 E
Marktheidenfeld	56	49.50 N	9.36 E
Markt Indersdorf	60	48.22 N	11.23 E
Marktl	60	48.15 N	12.51 E
Marktleugast	54	50.10 N	11.38 E
Marktleuthen	54	50.08 N	12.00 E
Marktoberdorf	58	47.47 N	10.37 E
Marktredwitz	30	50.00 N	12.06 E
Markt Rettenbach	58	47.57 N	10.23 E
Marktschellenberg	64	47.42 N	13.02 E
Markt Schwaben	60	48.11 N	11.51 E
Mark Twain Cave ⊥ [5]	219	39.42 N	91.21 W
Mark Twain Lake ⊜ [1]	219	39.30 N	91.45 W
Mark Twain State Park ♠	219	39.29 N	91.48 W
Markulešty	78	47.52 N	28.14 E
Markundi	140	11.33 N	23.49 E
Markvue Manor	279b	40.20 N	79.46 W
Mark West Creek ≃	226	38.30 N	122.42 W
Marl	52	51.38 N	7.05 E
Marlasi	164	5.30 S	134.38 E
Marlboro, Ab., Can.	182	53.33 N	116.45 W
Marlboro, N.J., U.S.	208	40.18 N	74.14 W
Marlboro, N.Y., U.S.	210	41.36 N	73.58 W
Marlboro, Oh., U.S.	214	40.53 N	81.12 W
Marlboro, Pa., U.S.	285	39.54 N	75.42 W
Marlborough, Austl.	166	22.49 S	149.53 E
Marlborough, Guy.	246	7.29 N	58.38 W
Marlborough, Eng., U.K.	42	51.26 N	1.43 W
Marlborough, Ct., U.S.	207	41.37 N	72.27 W
Marlborough, Ma., U.S.	207	42.20 N	71.33 W
Marlborough Downs ʌʌ [1]	42	51.30 N	1.45 W
Marldon	42	50.28 N	3.36 W
Marle	50	49.44 N	3.46 E
Marlenheim	58	48.37 N	7.30 E
Marles-en-Brie	261	48.44 N	2.53 E
Marles-les-Mines	50	50.30 N	2.31 E
Marlette	190	43.19 N	83.04 W
Marlette Lake ⊜	226	39.10 N	119.54 W
Marley, Il., U.S.	278	41.33 N	87.55 W
Marley, Md., U.S.	208	39.09 N	76.35 W
Marley Creek ≃	278	41.31 N	87.57 W
Marley Neck › [1]	284b	39.12 N	76.33 W
Marlieux	58	46.04 N	5.04 E
Marlin	222	31.18 N	96.53 W
Marlinton	188	38.13 N	80.05 W
Marl-Loemühle, Flughafen ⊠	263	51.39 N	7.10 E
Marlow, Dtsch.	54	54.09 N	12.34 E
Marlow, Eng., U.K.	42	51.35 N	0.48 W
Marlow, Ok., U.S.	196	34.38 N	97.57 W
Marlpit Hill	260	51.13 N	0.04 E
Marlton	208	39.53 N	74.55 W
Marlton Heights	285	39.40 N	75.21 W
Marly	50	50.20 N	3.32 E
Marly, Forêt de ♠	261	48.50 N	2.00 E
Marly-la-Ville	261	49.05 N	2.30 E
Marly-le-Roi	50	48.52 N	2.05 E
Marma, Sve.	26	61.16 N	16.52 E
Marma, Sve.	40	60.30 N	17.25 E
Marmaduke	194	36.11 N	90.22 W
Marmagne	58	46.50 N	4.21 E
Marmande	32	44.30 N	0.10 E
Marmara, Sea of → Marmara Denizi ⊤ [2]	130	40.40 N	28.15 E
Marmara Adası I	130	40.38 N	27.37 E
Marmara Denizi (Sea of Marmara) ⊤ [2]	130	40.40 N	28.15 E
Marmara Ereğlisi	130	40.58 N	27.57 E
Marmara Gölü ⊜	130	38.37 N	28.02 E
Marmaris	130	36.51 N	28.16 E
Marmarītā	130	34.47 N	36.15 E
Marmarth	198	46.17 N	103.55 W
Marmaton ≃	194	38.00 N	94.19 W
Marmelopolis	256	22.27 S	45.10 W
Marmelos	248	6.08 S	61.50 W
Marmelos, Rio dos ≃	248	6.06 S	61.46 W
Marmet	188	38.14 N	81.34 W
Marmion Lake ⊜ [1]	190	48.54 N	91.30 W
Marmirolo	64	45.13 N	10.45 E
Marmolada ʌ	64	46.26 N	11.51 E
Marmora, On., Can.	212	44.29 N	77.41 W
Marmora, N.J., U.S.	208	39.16 N	74.38 W
Marmore	66	42.33 N	12.43 E
Marmore ≃	62	45.44 N	7.37 E
Marmore, Cascàta delle ∟	66	42.33 N	12.43 E
Marmot Bay ⊂	180	58.00 N	152.20 W
Marmot Island I	180	58.13 N	151.51 W
Marmoutier	58	48.41 N	7.23 E
Mar Muerto, Laguna ⊂	234	16.10 N	94.10 W
Marnate	266b	45.38 N	8.54 E
Marnay	58	47.17 N	5.46 E
Marnaz	58	46.04 N	6.32 E
Marne, Dtsch.	52	53.57 N	9.00 E
Marne, Mi., U.S.	216	43.02 N	85.49 W
Marne □ [5]	32	48.55 N	4.10 E
Marne ≃, Austl.	168b	34.40 S	139.18 E
Marne ≃, Fr.	32	48.49 N	2.24 E
Marne à la Saône, Canal de la ≍	58	48.44 N	4.36 E
Marne au Rhin, Canal de la ≍	56	48.35 N	7.47 E
Marneuli	84	41.28 N	44.50 E
Marnhull	42	50.58 N	2.18 W
Marnitz	54	53.19 N	11.56 E
Maroa, Il., U.S.	219	40.02 N	88.57 W
Maroa, Ven.	246	2.43 N	67.33 W
Maroala	157b	15.23 S	47.59 E
Maroantsetra	157b	15.26 S	49.44 E
Marobi Raghza	120	32.36 N	69.52 E
Maroc → Morocco □ [1]	148	32.00 N	5.00 W
Maroelaboom	156	19.15 S	18.53 E
Marofandilia	157b	20.07 S	44.34 E
Maroglio ≃	70	37.03 N	14.15 E
Marokko → Morocco □ [1]	148	32.00 N	5.00 W
Marol ◆ [8]	272c	19.07 N	72.53 E
Marolambo	157b	20.02 S	48.07 E
Maroldsweisach	56	50.12 N	10.39 E
Marolles-en-Brie	261	48.44 N	2.33 E
Marolles-en-Hurepoix	261	48.34 N	2.18 E
Marolles-les-Braults	50	48.15 N	0.19 E
Maromandia	157b	14.13 S	48.08 E
Maromme	50	49.28 N	1.02 E
Maromokotro ʌ	157b	14.01 S	48.59 E
Marondera	154	18.10 S	31.36 E
Marone	64	45.44 N	10.05 E
Marong	102	31.07 N	99.20 E
Maronghi Creek ≃	171a	26.58 S	152.22 E
Maroni (Marowijne) ≃	250	5.45 N	53.58 W
Maroon	171a	28.10 S	152.44 E
Maroon, Mount ʌ	171a	28.13 S	152.44 E
Maroondah Aqueduct ≍ [1]	274b	37.42 S	145.01 E
Maros	112	5.00 S	119.34 E
Maros (Mureș) ≃	38	46.15 N	20.13 E
Maroseranana	157b	18.32 S	48.51 E
Marostica	64	45.45 N	11.39 E
Marosvásárhely → Tîrgu Mureș	38	46.33 N	24.33 E
Marotandrano	157b	16.10 S	48.50 E
Marotiri, Îles II	14	27.55 S	143.26 W
Marotta	66	43.46 N	13.08 E
Maroua	146	10.36 N	14.20 E
Maroubra	274a	33.57 S	151.16 E
Marouini ≃	250	3.18 N	54.04 W
Marovato, Madag.	157b	13.59 S	48.36 E
Marovato, Madag.	157b	15.48 S	48.05 E
Marovato, Madag.	157b	16.28 S	48.25 E
Marovoay	157b	16.06 S	46.39 E
Marovoay Nord	157b	16.57 S	44.34 E
Marowijne □ [5]	250	5.40 N	54.20 W
Marowijne (Maroni) ≃	250	5.45 N	53.58 W
Marpent	50	50.18 N	4.05 E
Marple	44	53.24 N	2.03 W
Marquam	224	45.04 N	122.41 W
Marquand	194	37.25 N	90.10 W
Marquard	158	28.54 S	27.28 E
Marquardt	54	52.27 N	12.57 E
Marquartstein	64	47.45 N	12.28 E
Marquesas Islands → Marquises, Îles II	6	9.00 S	139.30 W
Marquesas Keys II	220	24.34 N	82.08 W
Marquette, Ks., U.S.	198	38.33 N	97.50 W
Marquette, Mi., U.S.	190	46.32 N	87.23 W
Marquette Park ♠	278	41.46 N	87.42 W
Márquez, Perú	286d	11.57 S	77.08 W
Marquez, Tx., U.S.	222	31.14 N	96.15 W
Marquion	50	50.13 N	3.05 E
Marquis	241k	12.06 N	61.37 W
Marquis, Cape ›	241f	14.03 N	60.54 W
Marquise	50	50.49 N	1.42 E
Marquises, Îles (Marquesas Islands) II	6	9.00 S	139.30 W
Marrabel	168b	34.08 S	138.53 E
Marra Creek ≃	166	30.05 S	147.05 E
Marradi	66	44.04 N	11.37 E
Marradong	168a	32.52 S	116.27 E
Marrah, Jabal ʌ	140	13.04 N	24.21 E
Marra Hills ʌʌ [2]	140	6.05 N	27.33 E
Marrakech	148	31.38 N	8.00 W
Marrakech □ [4]	148	31.30 N	8.05 W
Marramarra National Park ♠	170	33.32 S	151.04 E
Marrawah	166	40.56 S	144.41 E
Marree	166	29.39 S	138.04 E
Marrero	194	29.53 N	90.06 W
Marrickville	274a	33.55 S	151.09 E
Marromeu	156	18.20 S	35.56 E
Marrowstone Island I	224	48.04 N	122.41 W
Marrubiu	71	39.45 N	8.38 E
Marruecos → Morocco □ [1]	148	32.00 N	5.00 W
Marrupa	154	13.08 S	37.30 E
Mars	214	40.41 N	80.00 W
Marsā al-Burayqah	146	30.25 N	19.34 E
Marsabit	154	2.20 N	37.59 E
Marsabit National Park ♠	154	2.20 N	38.00 E
Marsac-en-Livradois	62	45.29 N	3.44 E
Marṣafā wa Kafr Aḥmad Hashīsh	142	30.25 N	31.15 E
Marsal	56	48.48 N	6.36 E
Marsala	70	37.48 N	12.26 E
Marsā Maṭrūḥ	140	31.21 N	27.14 E
Marsā Maṭrūḥ □ [4]	142	29.00 N	30.00 E
Marsange ≃	261	48.43 N	2.45 E
Marsangue ≃	261	48.40 N	2.47 E
Marsannay-la-Côte	58	47.16 N	4.59 E
Marsanne	62	44.39 N	4.52 E
Marsassoum	150	12.50 N	16.00 W
Mars'aty	86	60.05 N	60.29 E
Marscheid ◆ [8]	263	51.14 N	7.14 E
Marsciano	66	42.54 N	12.20 E
Marsden, Austl.	166	33.45 S	147.32 E
Marsden, Eng., U.K.	262	53.36 N	1.56 W
Marsden, Point ›	168b	35.35 S	137.38 E
Marsden Park	274a	33.42 S	150.50 E
Marsdiep ʯ	52	52.59 N	4.45 E
Marseille	62	43.18 N	5.24 E
Marseille-en-Beauvaisis	50	49.35 N	1.57 E
Marseille-Marignane, Aéroport de ⊠	62	43.27 N	5.13 E
Marseilles, Il., U.S.	216	41.19 N	88.42 W
Marseilles, Oh., U.S.	214	40.42 N	83.23 W
Marsella → Marseille	62	43.18 N	5.24 E
Marsfield	274a	33.47 S	151.07 E
Marsfjället ʌ	24	65.05 N	15.28 E
Marshall, Liber.	150	6.10 N	10.23 W
Marshall, Ar., U.S.	194	35.54 N	92.37 W
Marshall, Il., U.S.	194	39.23 N	87.41 W
Marshall, Mi., U.S.	216	42.16 N	84.57 W
Marshall, Mn., U.S.	198	44.26 N	95.47 W
Marshall, Mo., U.S.	194	39.07 N	93.11 W
Marshall, N.C., U.S.	192	35.47 N	82.41 W
Marshall, Tx., U.S.	194	32.32 N	94.22 W
Marshall, Va., U.S.	188	38.51 N	77.51 W
Marshall, Wi., U.S.	216	43.10 N	89.04 W
Marshall □ [6], Il., U.S.	216	41.02 N	89.24 W
Marshall □ [6], In., U.S.	216	41.21 N	86.19 W
Marshall ≃	162	22.59 S	136.59 E
Marshall Bennett Islands II	164	8.50 S	151.50 E
Marshallberg	192	34.43 N	76.30 W
Marshall Canyon Regional Park ♠	280	34.09 N	117.43 W
Marshall Gold Discovery State Historical Park ♠	226	38.48 N	120.53 W
Marshall Hall	208	38.41 N	77.06 W
Marshall Islands □ [1]	14	11.00 N	168.00 E
Marshall Islands II	14	9.00 N	168.00 E
Marshalls Creek	210	41.03 N	75.08 W
Marshallton, De., U.S.	208	39.43 N	75.39 W
Marshallton, Pa., U.S.	210	40.47 N	76.33 W
Marshallton, Pa., U.S.	285	39.57 N	75.41 W
Marshalltown	190	42.02 N	92.54 W
Marshallville, Ga., U.S.	192	32.27 N	83.56 W
Marshallville, Oh., U.S.	214	40.54 N	81.44 W
Marshbank Metropolitan Park ♠	281	42.36 N	83.23 W
Marsh Creek ≃, Ca., U.S.	282	37.53 N	121.49 W
Marsh Creek ≃, Mi., U.S.	281	42.06 N	83.13 W
Marsh Creek ≃, Pa., U.S.	214	41.03 N	77.36 W
Marsh Creek ≃, Pa., U.S.	285	40.03 N	75.43 W
Marsh Creek ≃, Wi., U.S.	216	42.13 N	89.04 W
Marsh Creek Lake ⊜ [1]	208	40.04 N	75.44 W
Marshes Creek ≃	276	40.36 N	74.13 W
Marshfield, Eng., U.K.	42	51.28 N	2.19 W
Marshfield, Ma., U.S.	207	42.05 N	70.42 W
Marshfield, Mo., U.S.	194	37.20 N	92.54 W
Marshfield, Wi., U.S.	190	44.40 N	90.10 W
Marshfield Airport ⊠	283	42.06 N	70.40 W
Marshfield Center	283	42.07 N	70.43 W
Marshfield Hills	207	42.08 N	70.44 W
Marsh Harbour	238	26.33 N	77.03 W
Marsh Hill	210	41.29 N	76.58 W
Mars Hill, In., U.S.	218	39.43 N	86.09 W
Mars Hill, Me., U.S.	186	46.30 N	67.52 W
Mars Hill, N.C., U.S.	192	35.49 N	82.32 W
Marsh Island I	194	29.35 N	91.53 W
Marsh Lake ⊜	180	60.25 N	134.18 W
Marsh Peak ʌ	200	40.43 N	109.50 W
Marshside	262	53.40 N	2.58 W
Marshville	192	34.59 N	80.22 W
Marshyhope Creek ≃	208	38.32 N	75.45 W
Marsica ◆ [1]	66	41.50 N	13.45 E
Marsico Nuovo	68	40.25 N	15.44 E
Marsico Vetere	68	40.23 N	15.49 E
Marsillargues	62	43.40 N	4.11 E
Marsimang, Tanjung ›	164	3.27 S	130.49 E
Marsing	202	43.32 N	116.48 W
Marske-by-the-Sea	44	54.36 N	1.01 W
Mars-la-Tour	56	49.06 N	5.54 E
Marson	56	48.55 N	4.32 E
Marssum	52	53.12 N	5.42 E
Märsta	40	59.37 N	17.51 E
Marstal	41	54.51 N	10.31 E
Marsteller	214	40.39 N	78.48 W
Märstetten	58	47.36 N	9.04 E
Marston	262	53.16 N	2.30 W
Marston Moor ☷	44	53.57 N	1.17 W
Marston Moor Battlesite ⊥	44	53.57 N	1.17 W
Marstons Mills	207	41.39 N	70.25 W
Marstrand	26	57.53 N	11.35 E
Marsyāngdī ≃	124	28.05 N	84.28 E
Mart	222	31.32 N	96.50 W
Marta	66	42.32 N	11.55 E
Marta ≃	66	42.14 N	11.42 E
Martaban	110	16.32 N	97.37 E
Martaban, Gulf of ⊂	110	16.30 N	97.00 E
Martano	68	40.12 N	18.18 E
Martap	152	6.54 N	13.03 E
Martapura, Indon.	112	3.25 S	114.51 E
Martapura, Indon.	112	4.19 S	104.22 E
Marte	146	12.22 N	13.51 E
Marteg ≃	42	52.20 N	3.33 W
Martel, Fr.	32	44.56 N	1.37 E
Martel, Oh., U.S.	214	40.40 N	82.55 W
Martelange	56	49.50 N	5.44 E
Martell	226	38.22 N	120.48 W
Martello	64	46.34 N	10.47 E
Martello, Val V	64	46.31 N	10.45 E
Martemjanovskij	86	55.54 N	80.22 E
Marten ◆ [8]	263	51.31 N	7.23 E
Marten Lake ⊜	190	46.42 N	79.41 W
Marten Mountain ʌ	182	55.28 N	114.43 W
Marte R. Gomez, Presa ⊜ [1]	196	26.10 N	99.00 W
Martfeld	52	52.52 N	9.04 E
Marthaguy Creek ≃	166	30.16 S	147.35 E
Martha Lake	224	47.51 N	122.20 W
Marthall	262	53.17 N	2.18 W
Martham	42	52.42 N	1.38 E
Marthasville	219	38.37 N	91.03 W
Martha's Vineyard I	207	41.25 N	70.40 W
Martí, Cuba	240p	21.09 N	77.27 W
Martí, Cuba	240p	22.57 N	80.55 W
Martí, Pico ʌ	240p	20.01 N	76.35 W
Martignacco	64	46.05 N	13.08 E
Martignat	58	46.13 N	5.36 E
Martigny	58	46.06 N	7.04 E
Martigny-les-Bains	58	48.06 N	5.49 E
Martigues	62	43.24 N	5.03 E
Martil	34	35.37 N	5.17 W
Martim Francisco	256	22.31 S	46.57 W
Martin, Česko.	30	49.05 N	18.55 E
Martin, Ky., U.S.	192	37.34 N	82.45 W
Martin, Mi., U.S.	216	42.32 N	85.38 W
Martin, N.D., U.S.	198	47.49 N	100.06 W
Martin, Oh., U.S.	214	41.33 N	83.20 W
Martin, S.D., U.S.	198	43.10 N	101.43 W
Martin, Tn., U.S.	194	36.20 N	88.51 W
Martin □ [6]	220	27.07 N	80.31 W
Martín ≃	34	41.18 N	0.19 W
Martín, Arroyo ≃	288	34.51 S	58.04 W
Martin, Isle I	46	57.55 N	5.14 W
Martina	58	46.53 N	10.30 E
Martina Franca	68	40.42 N	17.21 E
Martinborough	172	41.13 S	175.28 E
Martín Chico, Punta ›	258	34.10 S	58.13 W
Martindale	196	29.50 N	97.51 W
Martindale Creek ≃, Austl.	170	32.32 S	150.42 E
Martindale Creek ≃, In., U.S.	218	39.48 N	85.09 W
Martindale Pond ⊜	284a	43.11 N	79.16 W
Martin-Église	50	49.54 N	1.09 E
Martinengo	62	45.34 N	9.46 E
Mărtinești	38	45.30 N	27.18 E
Martinez, Ca., U.S.	226	38.01 N	122.07 W
Martinez, Ga., U.S.	192	33.31 N	82.04 W
Martínez ◆ [8]	258	34.29 S	58.30 W
Martínez de la Torre	234	20.04 N	97.03 W
Martín García, Isla I	258	34.13 S	58.15 W
Martinho Campos	255	19.20 S	45.13 W
Martinica → Martinique □ [2]	240e	14.40 N	61.00 W
Martini Creek ≃	282	37.33 N	122.31 W
Martinique □ [2], N.A.	230	14.40 N	61.00 W
Martinique □ [2], N.A.	240e	14.40 N	61.00 W
Martinique Passage ʯ	238	15.10 N	61.15 W
Martin Lake ⊜ [1], Al., U.S.	194	32.50 N	85.55 W
Martin Lake ⊜ [1], Tx., U.S.	222	32.15 N	94.35 W
Martin Marietta Corporation ʊ [3]	284b	39.20 N	76.26 W
Martinniemi	26	65.13 N	25.18 E
Martinópole	250	3.15 S	40.41 W
Martin Peninsula › [1]	9	74.25 S	114.10 W
Martín Pérez ≃	286b	23.07 N	82.20 W
Martin Point ›	180	70.08 N	143.16 W
Martin Run ≃	279a	41.27 N	82.12 W
Martins	250	6.05 S	37.55 W
Martinsberg	61	48.22 N	15.09 E
Martins Brook ≃	283	42.34 N	71.06 W
Martinsburg, Mo., U.S.	219	39.06 N	91.38 W
Martinsburg, N.Y., U.S.	212	43.44 N	75.28 W
Martinsburg, Oh., U.S.	214	40.16 N	82.21 W
Martinsburg, Pa., U.S.	214	40.18 N	78.19 W
Martinsburg, W.V., U.S.	188	39.27 N	77.57 W
Martins Creek	208	40.47 N	75.11 W
Martins Creek ≃	210	41.37 N	75.46 W
Martinscroft	262	53.24 N	2.31 W
Martins Ferry	214	40.05 N	80.43 W
Martins Mills	222	32.25 N	95.47 W
Martins Pond ⊜	283	42.36 N	71.08 W
Martinstein	56	49.48 N	7.32 E
Martinsthal	56	50.03 N	8.07 E
Martinsville, Austl.	170	33.03 S	151.25 E
Martinsville, Il., U.S.	194	39.20 N	87.52 W
Martinsville, In., U.S.	218	39.25 N	86.25 W
Martinsville, N.J., U.S.	276	40.36 N	74.34 W
Martinsville, Oh., U.S.	218	39.19 N	83.48 W
Martinsville, Va., U.S.	192	36.41 N	79.52 W
Martinton	216	40.55 N	87.44 W
Martintown	206	45.09 N	74.42 W
Martin Van Buren National Historic Site ⊥	210	42.22 N	73.43 W
Martin Vaz, Ilhas II	244	20.30 S	28.51 W
Martis	71	40.47 N	8.49 E
Martisovo	76	56.34 N	31.55 E
Martock	42	50.59 N	2.46 W
Martofte	41	55.33 N	10.40 E
Marton, N.Z.	172	40.05 S	175.23 E
Marton, Eng., U.K.	262	53.12 N	2.13 W
Martorell	266d	41.28 N	1.56 E
Martorelles de Baix	266d	41.32 N	2.14 E
Martos	34	37.43 N	3.58 W
Martovaja	78	49.57 N	36.57 E
Martre, Lac la ⊜	176	63.15 N	117.55 W
Martti	24	67.28 N	28.28 E
Martūbah	146	32.35 N	22.46 E
Martuk	86	50.46 N	56.31 E
Martuni, Azer.	84	39.48 N	47.06 E
Martuni, Haya.	84	40.08 N	45.19 E
Martvili	84	42.25 N	42.22 E
Martville	210	43.17 N	76.38 W
Martynoviči	78	51.17 N	29.37 E
Martynovka	78	49.38 N	31.18 E
Martynovo	80	50.43 N	50.23 E
Martynovskij	80	50.29 N	42.18 E
Maru	150	12.22 N	6.22 E
Marua	164	9.30 S	149.20 E
Marudi	112	4.11 N	114.19 E
Marudu, Telukan ⊂	112	6.45 N	116.55 E
Marugame	96	34.17 N	133.47 E
Maruggio	68	40.19 N	17.34 E
Maruia	172	42.11 S	172.13 E
Maruia ≃	172	41.47 S	172.12 E
Maruim	250	10.45 S	37.05 W
Maruko	94	36.19 N	138.16 E
Marula	154	20.26 S	28.06 E
Marulan	170	34.43 S	150.00 E
Marulan South	170	34.46 S	150.02 E
Marum	52	53.08 N	6.16 E
Marum, Mont ʌ	175f	16.15 S	168.07 E
Marunga	152	17.27 S	20.02 E
Marungu	154	3.44 S	30.48 E
Marungu ʌʌ	154	7.42 S	30.00 E
Maruoka	94	36.09 N	136.16 E
Mårup	41	55.57 N	10.35 E
Marusino	265b	55.42 N	37.59 E
Maruškino	82	55.36 N	37.12 E
Ma'rūt	120	31.34 N	67.03 E
Marutea I [1]	14	17.00 S	143.10 W
Maruyama	94	35.01 N	139.58 E
Maruyama ≃	96	35.39 N	134.50 E
Marv Dasht	128	29.50 N	52.40 E
Marve ◆ [8]	272c	19.12 N	72.49 E
Marvejols	32	44.33 N	3.18 E
Marvell	194	34.33 N	90.54 W
Marvel Loch	162	31.28 S	119.28 E
Marviken	40	58.34 N	16.51 E
Marvila ◆ [8]	266c	38.44 N	9.06 W
Marville	56	49.27 N	5.27 E
Marvin Creek ≃	214	41.48 N	78.26 W
Marvine, Mount ʌ	200	38.40 N	111.39 W
Mar Vista ◆ [8]	280	34.00 N	118.27 W
Mārwār	120	25.44 N	73.36 E
Marwayne	184	53.32 N	110.20 W
Marwitz	264a	52.41 N	13.09 E
Marwitzer Heide ◆ [3]	264a	52.40 N	13.06 E
Marwood	214	40.48 N	79.47 W
Marxhagen	54	53.37 N	12.36 E
Marxloh ◆ [8]	263	51.31 N	6.46 E
Mary	128	37.36 N	61.50 E
Mary □ [8]	128	37.30 N	62.30 E
Mary ≃, Austl.	164	12.53 S	131.38 E
Mary ≃, Austl.	166	25.26 S	152.55 E
Mary Anne Group II	162	21.13 S	115.32 E
Maryborough, Austl.	166	25.32 S	152.42 E
Maryborough, Austl.	169	37.03 S	143.45 E
Maryborough → Port Laoise	48	53.02 N	7.17 W
Mary D	208	40.45 N	76.04 W
Marydale	158	29.23 S	22.05 E
Marydel	208	39.06 N	75.44 W
Maryfield	184	49.48 N	101.32 W
Maryhill	224	45.41 N	120.49 W
Mary Jane, Lake ⊜	220	28.22 N	81.11 W
Mary Kathleen	166	20.49 S	139.58 E
Maryknoll	210	41.11 N	73.50 W
Mary Lake ⊜	212	45.15 N	79.15 W
Maryland	210	42.32 N	74.53 W
Maryland □ [3], U.S.	178	39.00 N	76.45 W
Maryland □ [3], U.S.	188	39.00 N	76.45 W
Maryland, University of (Baltimore County Campus) ʊ [2], Md., U.S.	284b	39.15 N	76.43 W
Maryland, University of ʊ [2], Md., U.S.	284c	38.59 N	76.57 W
Maryland City	208	39.05 N	76.49 W
Maryland Gardens Park ♠	275b	43.47 N	79.32 W
Maryland Heights	219	38.42 N	90.25 W
Maryland Historical Society ʊ	284b	39.18 N	76.37 W
Maryland Line	208	39.42 N	76.39 W
Maryland Park	284c	38.53 N	76.54 W
Marylebone	262	53.34 N	2.38 W
Maryneal	196	32.14 N	100.27 W
Marypark	46	57.26 N	3.21 W
Maryport	44	54.43 N	3.30 W
Marys ≃, Il., U.S.	194	37.53 N	89.47 W
Marys ≃, Nv., U.S.	204	41.04 N	115.16 W
Marys Creek ≃	202	42.18 N	115.48 W
Mary's Igloo	180	65.09 N	165.04 W
Marys Peak ʌ	202	44.30 N	123.33 W
Marystown	186	47.10 N	55.09 W
Marysvale	200	38.26 N	112.13 W
Marysville, Austl.	169	37.31 S	145.45 E
Marysville, B.C., Can.	182	49.38 N	115.57 W
Marysville, N.B., Can.	186	45.59 N	66.35 W
Marysville, Ca., U.S.	226	39.08 N	121.35 W
Marysville, Ks., U.S.	198	39.50 N	96.38 W
Marysville, Mi., U.S.	214	42.54 N	82.29 W
Marysville, Oh., U.S.	214	40.14 N	83.22 W
Marysville, Pa., U.S.	208	40.20 N	76.55 W
Marysville, Wa., U.S.	224	48.03 N	122.10 W
Maryūṭ, Buḥayrat ⊜	142	31.08 N	29.56 E
Maryvale	171a	28.05 S	152.15 E
Maryvale ◆ [8]	275b	43.46 N	79.18 W
Maryville, Mo., U.S.	194	40.20 N	94.52 W
Maryville, Tn., U.S.	192	35.45 N	83.58 W
Marywell	46	57.02 N	2.42 W
Marywood	216	41.48 N	88.18 W
Marzabotto	64	44.20 N	11.12 E
Marzagão	255	17.59 S	48.39 W
Marzahn ◆ [8]	264a	52.33 N	13.33 E
Marzahna	54	52.00 N	12.46 E
Marzahne	54	52.31 N	12.31 E
Marzal, Aven de ⊥ [5]	62	44.22 N	4.31 E
Marzo, Punta ›	246	6.50 N	77.42 W
Marzolara	64	44.38 N	10.10 E
Marzūq	146	25.55 N	13.55 E
Marzūq, Ḥamādat ◆ [2]	146	26.10 N	12.45 E
Marzūq, Ṣaḥrā' ◆ [2]	146	24.30 N	13.00 E
Masa	152	3.45 S	15.29 E
Masachapa	236	11.47 N	86.31 W
Mas'adah (Cæsarea Philippi)	132	33.14 N	35.45 E
Masada → Meẓada, Ḥorvot ⊥	132	31.19 N	35.21 E
Más Afuera, Isla → Alejandro Selkirk, Isla I	244	33.45 S	80.46 W
Masagua	236	14.12 N	90.51 W
Masaguisi	116	12.41 N	121.32 E
Masai	114	1.29 N	103.53 E
Masai Mara Game Reserve ◆ [4]	154	1.15 S	35.15 E
Masai Steppe ʌʌ [1]	154	4.45 S	37.00 E
Masak	85	43.37 N	78.18 E
Masaka	154	0.20 S	31.44 E
Masaki, Nihon	96	33.47 N	132.42 E
Masaki, Nihon	268	35.13 N	140.02 E
Masalembu Besar, Pulau I	112	5.34 S	114.26 E
Masally	84	39.03 N	48.40 E
Masalok, Puntan ›	174n	15.01 N	145.41 E
Masamba	112	2.32 S	120.20 E
Masan	98	35.11 N	128.32 E
Masangwe ʌ	154	5.28 S	30.05 E
Masānjor	126	24.07 N	87.19 E
Masapelid Island I	116	9.42 N	125.39 E
Masapun	112	7.47 S	126.38 E
Masarah	142	27.29 N	30.50 E
Masaran	115a	7.28 S	110.55 E
Ma'ṣarat Samālūṭ	142	28.19 N	30.43 E
Masaryktown	220	28.26 N	82.27 W
Masasi	154	10.43 S	38.48 E
Masatepe	236	11.55 N	86.09 W
Más a Tierra, Isla → Róbinson Crusoe, Isla I	244	33.38 S	78.52 W
Masaya	236	11.58 N	86.06 W
Masaya □ [5]	236	12.00 N	86.10 W
Masba	146	11.30 N	13.00 E
Masbate	116	12.22 N	123.36 E
Masbate □ [4]	116	12.20 N	123.30 E
Masbate Island I	116	12.15 N	123.30 E
Masbate Pass ʯ	116	12.30 N	123.35 E
Mascali	70	37.45 N	15.12 E
Mascarene Basin ✢ [1]	12	15.00 S	56.00 E
Mascarene Islands II	157c	21.00 S	57.00 E
Mascarene Plateau ✢ [3]	12	10.00 S	60.00 E
Mascasín	252	31.22 S	66.59 W
Maschen	52	53.24 N	10.02 E
Maschito	68	40.54 N	15.50 E
Mascot, Austl.	274a	33.56 S	151.12 E
Mascot, Tn., U.S.	192	36.03 N	83.44 W
Mascota	234	20.32 N	104.49 W
Mascota ≃	234	20.38 N	104.59 W
Mascotte	220	28.35 N	81.53 W
Mascouche	206	45.45 N	73.36 W
Mascouche ≃	206	45.41 N	73.40 W
Mascoutah	219	38.29 N	89.47 W
Mascuppic Lake ⊜	283	42.41 N	71.23 W
Mase	102	27.16 N	104.08 E
Masefield	184	49.09 N	107.48 W
Masela, Pulau I	164	8.09 S	129.50 E
Masenberg ʌ	61	47.21 N	15.53 E
Maser	64	45.48 N	11.59 E
Maserada sul Piave	64	45.45 N	12.17 E
Maseru	158	29.28 S	27.30 E
Masevaux	58	47.47 N	7.00 E
Maševka	78	49.26 N	34.52 E
Maševo	78	52.06 N	32.48 E
Masha	100	27.26 N	117.50 E
Mashaba	154	20.02 S	30.29 E
Mashaba Mountains ʌʌ	154	18.45 S	30.32 E
Mash'abbe' Sade	132	31.00 N	34.47 E
Mashābih I	128	25.37 N	36.29 E
Mashalah	142	30.44 N	31.08 E
Masham	44	54.13 N	1.40 W
Mashan, Zhg.	89	45.13 N	130.35 E
Mashan, Zhg.	100	27.33 N	113.46 E
Mashan, Zhg.	102	23.50 N	108.16 E
Mashar	140	9.14 N	26.52 E
Mashbury	260	51.47 N	0.24 E
Mashel ≃	224	46.51 N	122.20 W

Symbol	English	Deutsch	Español	Français	Português
≃	River	Fluß	Río	Rivière	Rio
≍	Canal	Kanal	Canal	Canal	Canal
∟	Waterfall, Rapids	Wasserfall, Stromschnellen	Cascada, Rápidos	Chute d'eau, Rapides	Cascata, Rápidos
ʯ	Strait	Meeresstraße	Estrecho	Détroit	Estreito
⊂	Bay, Gulf	Bucht, Golf	Bahía, Golfo	Baie, Golfe	Baía, Golfo
⊜	Lake, Lakes	See, Seen	Lago, Lagos	Lac, Lacs	Lago, Lagos
☷	Swamp	Sumpf	Pantano	Marais	Pântano
⌂	Ice Features, Glacier	Eis- und Gletscherformen	Accidentes Glaciales	Formes glaciaires	Acidentes glaciares
⊤	Other Hydrographic Features	Andere Hydrographische Objekte	Otros Elementos Hidrográficos	Autres données hydrographiques	Outros acidentes hidrográficos
✢	Submarine Features	Untermeerische Objekte	Accidentes Submarinos	Formes de relief sous-marin	Acidentes submarinos
□	Political Unit	Politische Einheit	Unidad Politica	Entité politique	Unidade política
ʊ	Cultural Institution	Kulturelle Institution	Institución Cultural	Institution culturelle	Instituição cultural
⊥	Historical Site	Historische Stätte	Sitio Histórico	Site historique	Sitio histórico
♠	Recreational Site	Erholungs- und Ferienort	Sitio de Recreo	Centre de loisirs	Area de Lazer
⊠	Airport	Flughafen	Aeropuerto	Aéroport	Aeroporto
■	Military Installation	Militäranlage	Instalación Militar	Installation militaire	Instalação militar
◆	Miscellaneous	Verschiedenes	Misceláneo	Divers	Diversos

ENGLISH — DEUTSCH

Name	Page	Lat.°′	Long.°′
Mashenqiao	105	40.04 N	117.36 E
Masherbrum ∧	123	35.43 N	76.18 E
Mashgharah	132	33.32 N	35.39 E
Mashhad, Īrān	128	36.18 N	59.36 E
Mash-had, Yis.	132	32.44 N	35.19 E
Mashi, Nig.	150	13.00 N	7.54 E
Mashi, Zhg.	100	29.05 N	114.22 E
Mashi, Zhg.	100	25.01 N	114.09 E
Mashike	92a	43.51 N	141.31 E
Mashiko	94	36.28 N	140.06 E
Mashita ≃	94	35.40 N	137.10 E
Mashīz	128	29.56 N	56.37 E
Mashkai ≃	128	26.02 N	65.19 E
Māshkel, Hāmūn-i- ⊜	128	28.15 N	63.00 E
Māshkel, Rūd-i- (Māshkīd) ≃	128	28.02 N	63.25 E
Mashki Chāh	128	29.01 N	62.27 E
Māshkīd (Rūd-i-Māshkel) ≃	128	28.02 N	63.25 E
Mashonaland North □[4]	154	16.30 S	30.00 E
Mashonaland South □[4]	154	18.15 S	30.45 E
Mashpee	207	41.38 N	70.28 W
Mashra'ur-Raqq	140	8.25 N	29.16 E
Mashtūl as-Sūq	142	30.22 N	31.22 E
Mashū-ko ⊜	92a	43.35 N	144.32 E
Masibi	152	11.08 S	22.42 E
Masihi	114	2.47 N	99.40 E
Masīlah, Wādī al- V	144	15.10 N	51.08 E
Masi-Manimba	152	4.46 S	17.55 E
Masin	164	6.15 S	139.19 E
Masina	272b	22.55 N	88.32 E
Masindi	154	1.41 N	31.43 E
Masini Port	154	1.42 N	32.05 E
Masinloc	116	15.32 N	119.57 E
Masīr	142	31.03 N	31.00 E
Maşīrah I	118	20.25 N	58.50 E
Maşīrah, Khalīj c	118	20.10 N	58.15 E
Masis	84	40.00 N	44.29 E
Masisea	248	8.36 S	74.19 W
Masisi	154	1.24 S	28.49 E
Masjed-e Soleymān	128	31.58 N	49.18 E
Masjid Tanah	114	2.21 N	102.07 E
Mask, Lough ⊜	48	53.35 N	9.20 W
Maska	150	11.20 N	7.20 E
Maskan, Ras >	144	11.10 N	43.33 E
Maskanah	130	36.01 N	38.05 E
Maskin	128	23.35 N	56.39 E
Maškino	82	54.53 N	36.08 E
Maskinongé □[6]	206	46.35 N	73.30 W
Maskinongé ≃, P.Q., Can.	206	46.10 N	73.01 W
Maskinongé ≃, P.Q., Can.	206	45.49 N	74.40 W
Maskinongé, Lac ⊜	206	46.19 N	73.23 W
Maškoviči	82	54.11 N	36.17 E
Masku	26	60.34 N	22.06 E
Maskūtān	128	26.51 N	59.49 E
Maskwa ≃	184	50.33 N	96.08 W
Masl'anino	86	54.20 N	84.13 E
Masl'anskaja	86	55.56 N	70.08 E
Maslova	265a	59.47 N	30.48 E
Maslovka	78	51.33 N	39.14 E
Maslovo	86	60.07 N	60.30 E
Masnières	50	50.07 N	3.13 E
Maso	150	7.14 N	2.53 W
Masoala	157b	15.59 S	50.10 E
Masoala, Cap >	157b	15.59 S	50.13 E
Masoala, Presqu'île de >[1]	157b	15.40 S	50.12 E
Masoarivo	157b	19.03 S	44.19 E
Masomeloka	157b	20.17 S	48.37 E
Mason, Mi., U.S.	216	42.34 N	84.26 W
Mason, Oh., U.S.	218	39.21 N	84.18 W
Mason, Tn., U.S.	194	35.24 N	89.31 W
Mason, Tx., U.S.	196	30.44 N	99.13 W
Mason, W.V., U.S.	188	39.01 N	82.01 W
Mason □[6], Il., U.S.	219	40.18 N	90.04 W
Mason □[6], Ky., U.S.	218	38.35 N	83.48 W
Mason □[6], Wa., U.S.	224	47.20 N	123.09 W
Mason, Lake ⊜	162	27.39 S	119.34 E
Mason Bay c	172	46.56 S	167.44 E
Mason City, Il., U.S.	219	40.12 N	89.41 W
Mason City, Ia., U.S.	190	43.09 N	93.12 W
Mason City, Ne., U.S.	198	41.13 N	99.18 W
Masone	62	44.30 N	8.42 E
Masonicus Brook ≃	276	41.06 N	74.09 W
Mason Lake ⊜	224	47.20 N	122.57 W
Masons Creek ≃	285	39.59 N	74.51 W
Mason Valley V	226	39.07 N	119.10 W
Masonville, N.J., U.S.	285	39.59 N	74.52 W
Masonville, N.Y., U.S.	210	42.15 N	75.23 W
Maspeth ◆[8]	276	40.43 N	73.55 W
Masqat (Muscat)	128	23.37 N	58.35 E
Maşra'	142	27.14 N	31.02 E
Massa	64	44.01 N	10.09 E
Massa-Carrara □[4]	64	44.15 N	10.03 E
Massachusetts □[3], U.S.	178	42.15 N	71.50 W
Massachusetts □[3], U.S.	207	42.15 N	71.50 W
Massachusetts (Boston), University of υ[2]	283	42.19 N	71.03 W
Massachusetts Bay c	207	42.20 N	70.50 W
Massachusetts Correctional Institution υ	283	42.07 N	71.18 W
Massachusetts Institute of Technology υ[2]	283	42.21 N	71.06 W
Massaciuccoli, Lago di ⊜	66	43.50 N	10.20 E
Massacre Lake ⊜	204	41.39 N	119.35 W
Massa Fermana	66	43.09 N	13.28 E
Massa Fiscaglia	66	44.48 N	12.01 E
Massafra	68	40.35 N	17.07 E
Massaguet	146	12.28 N	15.26 E
Massakory	146	13.00 N	15.44 E
Massalassef	146	11.43 N	17.08 E
Massa Lombarda	66	44.27 N	11.49 E
Massa Lubrense	68	40.36 N	14.20 E
Massa Marittima	66	43.03 N	10.53 E
Massa Martana	66	42.46 N	12.31 E
Massandra	78	44.32 N	34.12 E
Massangano	152	9.37 S	14.15 E
Massangena	156	21.32 S	32.57 E
Massapê	250	3.31 S	40.19 W
Massapequa	210	40.40 N	73.28 W
Massapequa Park	276	40.40 N	73.27 W
Massapequa Reserve County Park ♠	276	40.42 N	73.27 W
Massapoag Brook ≃	283	42.09 N	71.09 W
Massapoag Lake ⊜	283	42.06 N	71.11 W
Massara	156	18.20 S	34.09 E
Massarosa	66	43.52 N	10.20 E
Massasoit State Park ♠	207	41.53 N	71.01 W
Massaua → Mitsiwa	144	15.38 N	39.28 E
Massawa → Mitsiwa	144	15.38 N	39.28 E
Massawippi ≃	206	45.22 N	71.51 W
Massawippi, Lake ⊜	206	45.14 N	72.00 W
Massay	50	47.09 N	2.00 E
Massé, Ruisseau ≃	275a	45.28 N	73.17 W
Massello	62	44.57 N	7.04 E
Massen	52	51.32 N	7.38 E
Massena, Ia., U.S.	198	41.15 N	94.46 W
Massena, N.Y., U.S.	206	44.55 N	74.53 W
Massenya	146	11.24 N	16.10 E
Masset	182	54.02 N	132.09 W
Masset Inlet c	182	53.42 N	132.20 W
Masseube	32	43.26 N	0.35 E
Massey	190	46.12 N	82.05 W
Massiac	32	45.15 N	3.12 E
Massiaru	76	58.00 N	24.35 E
Massico, Monte ∧	68	41.10 N	13.55 E
Massieville	218	39.16 N	82.58 W
Massif Central → Central, Massif ⋀	32	45.00 N	3.10 E
Massillon	214	40.48 N	81.32 W
Massima Camp	152	1.27 S	11.42 E
Massina	273b	4.22 S	15.22 E
Massina ◆[1]	150	14.30 N	5.00 W
Massinga	156	23.20 S	35.25 E
Massingir	156	23.51 S	32.04 E
Massive, Mount ∧	200	39.12 N	106.28 W
Masson, Lac ⊜	206	46.03 N	74.02 W
Masson Island I	9	66.08 S	96.34 E
Massy	261	48.44 N	2.17 E
Mastābah	144	20.49 N	39.20 E
Maštaga	84	40.32 N	50.00 E
Masterson	196	35.38 N	101.58 W
Masterton	172	40.57 S	175.40 E
Mas-Thibert	62	43.34 N	4.44 E
Mastic Point	192	25.03 N	77.57 W
Mastigouche ≃	206	46.20 N	73.24 W
Mastigouche Nord ≃	206	46.24 N	73.25 W
Mastūj	123	36.17 N	72.31 E
Mastūj ≃	123	35.54 N	71.49 E
Mastung	120	29.48 N	66.51 E
Mastūrah	128	23.06 N	38.50 E
Masu	146	12.10 N	13.19 E
Masua	126	24.16 N	90.46 E
Masuda	96	34.40 N	131.51 E
Masuho	94	35.34 N	138.28 E
Masuika	152	7.37 S	22.32 E
Masuku	154	17.12 S	27.07 E
Māsūleh	128	37.10 N	48.59 E
Masulipatam → Machilīpatnam	122	16.10 N	81.08 E
Masura	126	23.16 N	90.24 E
Masurai, Gunung ∧	112	2.30 S	101.51 E
Masury	214	41.12 N	80.32 W
Masvingo	154	20.05 S	30.50 E
Maşyāf	130	35.03 N	36.21 E
Maszewo, Pol.	30	53.29 N	15.02 E
Maszewo, Pol.	54	52.06 N	14.55 E
Mat ≃	38	41.39 N	19.34 E
Mata, Indon.	115b	8.12 S	122.56 E
Mata, Zaïre	152	7.53 S	21.58 E
Mata Amarilla	254	49.36 S	71.13 W
Mataba, Mount ∧	269f	14.42 N	121.10 E
Matabeleland North □[4]	154	19.00 S	27.15 E
Matabeleland South □[4]	154	21.00 S	29.15 E
Mātābhānga	124	26.20 N	89.13 E
Matabuena	34	41.10 N	3.40 W
Matachel ≃	34	38.50 N	6.17 W
Matachewan	190	47.56 N	80.39 W
Matacuni ≃	246	3.02 N	65.16 W
Matad	88	46.58 N	115.18 E
Mata de Plátano, Quebrada ≃	286c	10.35 N	66.46 W
Matadero Creek ≃	282	37.26 N	122.08 W
Mata de São João	255	12.31 S	38.17 W
Matadi	152	5.49 S	13.27 E
Matador	196	34.00 N	100.49 W
Matagalpa	236	12.55 N	85.55 W
Matagalpa □[5]	236	13.00 N	85.30 W
Matagami	176	49.45 N	77.38 W
Matag-ob	116	11.07 N	124.29 E
Matagorda	196	28.41 N	95.58 W
Matagorda □[6]	222	28.57 N	96.00 W
Matagorda Bay c	196	28.35 N	96.20 W
Matagorda Island I	196	28.15 N	96.30 W
Matagorda Peninsula >[1]	196	28.32 N	96.07 W
Mata Grande	250	9.07 S	37.44 W
Matahiae, Pointe >	174s	17.49 S	149.17 W
Mataiea	174s	17.45 S	149.23 W
Mataiva I[1]	14	14.53 S	148.40 W
Mataj	86	45.53 N	78.43 E
Matajing	107	29.32 N	104.00 E
Matak, Pulau I	112	3.18 N	106.16 E
Matakana, Austl.	166	33.00 S	145.54 E
Matakana, N.Z.	172	36.21 S	174.43 E
Matakana Island I	172	37.35 S	176.05 E
Matakitaki ≃	172	41.48 S	172.19 E
Matala	152	14.46 S	15.04 E
Matale	122	7.28 N	80.37 E
Matam	150	15.40 N	13.15 W
Matama	96	33.36 N	131.28 E
Matama, Cerro ∧	236	9.47 N	83.15 W
Matamata	172	37.49 S	175.47 E
Matameye	150	13.26 N	8.28 E
Matamoras	210	41.22 N	74.42 W
Matamoros, Méx.	232	25.53 N	97.30 W
Matamoros, Méx.	232	25.32 N	103.15 W
Matan	112	1.52 S	110.00 E
Matana	154	3.46 S	29.41 E
Matana, Danau ⊜	112	2.28 S	121.20 E
Matanalem, Cape >	164	2.28 S	149.57 E
Matandu ≃	154	8.45 S	39.19 E
Matane	186	48.51 N	67.32 W
Matang, Malay.	114	4.49 N	100.41 E
Matang, Zhg.	100	29.17 N	113.05 E
Matang, Zhg.	100	32.20 N	121.04 E
Matangi	172	37.49 S	175.25 E
Matani	84	42.06 N	45.13 E
Matanni	123	33.48 N	71.34 E
Matanuska ≃	180	61.30 N	149.15 W
Matanza, Aeródromo ⊠	288	34.44 S	58.30 W
Matanza, Río de la ≃	258	34.42 S	58.28 W
Matanzas, Cuba	240p	23.03 N	81.35 W
Matanzas, Méx.	234	21.37 N	101.38 W
Matanzas □[4]	240p	22.40 N	81.20 W
Matanzas, Bahía de c	240p	23.04 N	81.30 W
Matanza → San Justo	258	34.40 S	58.33 W
Matapa	156	23.11 S	24.39 E
Matapalo, Cabo >	236	8.23 N	83.19 W
Matape ≃	232	28.25 N	110.26 W
Matapédia	186	47.58 N	66.57 W
Matapédia, Lac ⊜	186	48.33 N	67.33 W
Matapi ≃	250	0.03 S	51.12 W
Mata Point >	174v	19.07 S	169.51 W
Matapu	172	39.29 S	174.14 E
Mataquito ≃	252	34.59 S	72.12 W
Matará, Perú	248	7.16 S	78.16 W
Matara, S. Lan.	122	5.56 N	80.33 E
Mataram	115b	8.35 S	116.07 E
Matarani	248	17.00 S	72.06 W
Mataranka	164	14.56 S	133.07 E
Matārimah, Ra's >	142	29.27 N	32.42 E
Matarinao Bay c	116	11.14 N	125.34 E
Mataró	34	41.32 N	2.27 E
Matarraña ≃	34	41.14 N	0.22 E
Matas ∧	266d	41.30 N	2.16 E
Matasiri, Pulau I	112	4.48 S	115.48 E
Mätäsvaara	26	63.26 N	29.36 E
Matata	172	37.53 S	176.45 E
Matatepai, Pointe >	174x	9.43 S	139.02 W
Matatiele	158	30.24 S	28.43 E
Mātātīla Dam ◆[6]	124	25.06 N	78.22 E
Matatindoc Point >	116	9.43 N	122.23 E
Matatula, Cape >	174u	14.15 S	170.34 W
Mataura	172	46.11 S	168.52 E
Matauráo ≃, Bra.	248	5.30 S	60.45 W
Mataura ≃, N.Z.	172	46.34 S	168.43 E
Matāutu	175a	13.57 S	171.56 W
Mataval, Baie de c	174s	17.30 S	149.30 W
Matavera	174k	21.13 S	159.44 W
Mataveri	174z	27.10 S	109.27 E
Mataveri Airstrip ⊠	174z	27.10 S	109.25 W
Matawai	172	38.21 S	177.32 E
Matawan	208	40.24 N	74.13 W
Matawin ≃	206	46.54 N	72.56 W
Matāy	142	28.25 N	30.46 E
Matbūl	142	31.05 N	31.02 E
Matča	85	39.27 N	69.39 E
Matchaponix Brook ≃	276	40.23 N	74.23 W
Matchi-Manitou, Lac ⊜	190	48.00 N	77.04 W
Matching	260	51.47 N	0.13 E
Matching Green	260	51.47 N	0.14 E
Matching Tye	260	51.47 N	0.12 E
Mateare	236	12.14 N	86.26 W
Mateba, Île de I	152	5.54 S	12.50 E
Matehuala	234	23.39 N	100.39 W
Mateke Hills ⋀[2]	154	21.48 S	31.00 E
Mateko	152	4.03 S	18.55 E
Matelica	66	43.15 N	13.00 E
Matemo, Ilha I	154	12.13 S	40.36 E
Matera	68	40.40 N	16.37 E
Matera □[4]	68	40.30 N	16.25 E
Materborn	52	51.46 N	6.06 E
Matese, Lago del ⊜	68	41.25 N	14.25 E
Matese, Monti del ⋀	66	41.27 N	14.22 E
Mátészalka	30	47.57 N	22.19 E
Matete ≃	273b	4.24 S	15.20 E
Matetsi	154	18.16 S	25.56 E
Mateur	148	37.03 N	9.40 E
Matewan	192	37.37 N	82.09 W
Matfield	207	42.02 N	70.59 W
Matfors	26	62.21 N	17.02 E
Matha	32	45.52 N	0.19 W
Mathbaria	126	22.18 N	89.57 E
Mathematicians Seamounts ✢[3]	16	15.00 N	111.00 W
Mather, Mb., Can.	184	49.06 N	99.07 W
Mather, Ca., U.S.	226	37.53 N	119.52 W
Mather, Pa., U.S.	188	39.56 N	80.04 W
Mather Air Force Base ■	226	38.34 N	121.18 W
Mather Gorge V	284c	38.59 N	77.15 W
Matheson	190	48.32 N	80.28 W
Matheson Island	184	51.44 N	96.56 W
Matheu	258	34.22 S	58.50 W
Mathews	208	37.26 N	76.19 W
Mathews □[6]	208	37.25 N	76.20 W
Mathews, Lake ⊜	228	33.51 N	117.26 W
Mathi	62	45.15 N	7.32 E
Mathis	196	28.05 N	97.49 W
Māthle	272b	22.35 N	88.14 E
Mathry	42	51.57 N	5.05 W
Mathura, India	122	10.57 N	78.27 E
Mathura, India	124	27.30 N	77.41 E
Mathura Bil ⊜	272b	22.56 N	88.29 E
Mathurai → Madurai	122	9.56 N	78.07 E
Mathurāpur, Bngl.	126	24.02 N	88.47 E
Mathurāpur, Bngl.	126	23.17 N	89.15 E
Mati	116	6.57 N	126.13 E
Matiacoali	150	12.22 N	1.02 E
Matiakhola	126	23.16 N	86.56 E
Mātiāli	124	26.56 N	88.49 E
Matiāri	120	25.36 N	68.27 E
Matias Barbosa	256	21.53 S	43.20 W
Matías Romero	234	16.53 N	95.02 W
Mātibhānga	126	22.49 N	89.56 E
Matícora ≃	246	11.03 N	71.09 W
Matiere	172	38.45 S	175.06 E
Matignon	32	48.36 N	2.18 W
Matiguás	236	12.50 N	85.28 W
Matinecock	276	40.53 N	73.38 W
Matinenda Lake ⊜	190	46.22 N	82.57 W
Matinha	250	3.06 S	45.02 W
Matinicock Point >	276	40.54 N	73.38 W
Matinicus Island I	188	43.54 N	68.55 W
Matino	68	40.02 N	18.08 E
Matipó	255	20.17 S	42.21 W
Maţir Ţāris	142	29.22 N	30.54 E
Matiyure ≃	246	7.36 N	67.39 W
Matjiesfontein	158	33.14 S	20.35 E
Matkasel'kja	26	61.58 N	30.33 E
Mātla ≃[1]	126	22.04 N	88.38 E
Matlab Bāzār	126	23.20 N	90.43 E
Matlacha	220	26.37 N	82.05 W
Matlacha Pass ɥ	220	26.37 N	82.04 W
Matlamanyane	156	19.33 S	25.57 E
Matlapa	234	21.15 N	98.50 W
M'atlevo	76	54.54 N	35.39 E
Mātli	120	25.02 N	68.39 E
Matlock, Eng., U.K.	44	53.08 N	1.32 W
Matlock, Wa., U.S.	224	47.14 N	123.25 W
Matlock, Mount ∧	169	37.35 S	146.11 E
Matmata	148	33.33 N	9.58 E
Matnog	116	12.35 N	124.05 E
Mato	154	8.01 S	24.55 E
Mato ≃	246	7.09 N	65.07 W
Mato, Cerro ∧	246	7.15 N	65.14 W
Matoaca	208	37.13 N	77.28 W
Matobe	112	2.42 S	100.11 E
Matočkin Šar	72	73.16 N	56.27 E
Matočkin Šar, proliv ɥ	72	73.20 N	55.21 E
Mato Grosso □[3]	242	12.00 S	57.00 W
Mato Grosso, Planalto do ⋀[1]	242	15.30 S	56.00 W
Mato Grosso do Sul □[3]	242	20.00 S	55.00 W
Matola-Rio	156	25.58 S	32.26 E
Matombo	154	7.03 S	37.46 E
Mato Mole, Serra do ⋀[2]	256	23.00 S	46.12 W
Matong	164	5.35 S	151.45 E
Matonipi ≃	186	51.21 N	69.45 W
Matope	154	15.20 S	34.59 E
Matopo Hills ⋀[2]	154	20.36 S	28.28 E
Matopos	154	20.24 S	28.28 E
Matos ≃	248	14.07 S	65.25 W
Matosinhos	34	41.11 N	8.42 W
Matoso, Ponta do >	287a	22.50 S	43.11 W
Matou, T'aiwan	100	23.11 N	120.14 E
Matou, Zhg.	98	36.29 N	114.26 E
Matou, Zhg.	100	29.49 N	115.35 E
Matou, Zhg.	100	25.14 N	118.22 E
Matou, Zhg.	100	30.48 N	118.29 E
Matou, Zhg.	105	39.46 N	116.49 E
Matou, Zhg.	105	39.18 N	116.45 E
Matou, Zhg.	105	39.33 N	116.07 E
Matouji	98	35.02 N	115.07 E
Matour	58	46.18 N	4.29 E
Matoury	250	4.51 N	52.20 W
Matouxi	107	30.15 N	106.31 E
Matouying	98	39.18 N	118.47 E
Matouzhen, Zhg.	98	34.39 N	118.18 E
Matouzhen, Zhg.	100	33.32 N	118.56 E
Mato Verde	255	15.23 S	42.52 W
Matozinhos	255	19.35 S	44.07 W
Mátra ⋀	30	47.55 N	20.00 E
Maţraḥ	128	23.38 N	58.34 E
Matraville	274a	33.54 S	151.18 E
Matrei am Brenner	64	47.08 N	11.27 E
Matrei in Osttirol	64	47.00 N	12.32 E
Matru	150	7.36 N	12.11 W
Matsap	158	28.38 S	22.47 E
Matsapha	158	26.29 S	31.23 E
Matsari	152	5.21 N	12.14 E
Matsena	150	13.05 N	10.05 E
Matsiatra ≃	157b	21.25 S	45.33 E
Matsieng	158	29.36 S	27.32 E
Matsknutsgårdarna	40	60.28 N	15.22 E
Matsqui	224	49.12 N	122.25 W
Matsubara	96	34.34 N	135.33 E
Matsubushi	268	35.55 N	139.49 E
Matsuda	94	35.21 N	139.09 E
Matsudai	94	37.08 N	138.37 E
Matsudo	94	35.47 N	139.54 E
Matsudo Race Track ♠	268	35.48 N	139.55 E
Matsue	96	35.28 N	133.04 E
Matsugasaki	268	35.53 N	139.58 E
Matsuida	94	36.19 N	138.48 E
Matsukawa, Nihon	94	36.25 N	137.51 E
Matsukawa, Nihon	94	35.36 N	137.55 E
Matsumae	92	41.26 N	140.07 E
Matsu → Matsu Tao I	100	26.09 N	119.56 E
Matsumoto	94	36.14 N	137.58 E
Matsuno	96	33.13 N	132.42 E
Matsunoyama	94	37.05 N	138.37 E
Matsuo	94	35.38 N	140.28 E
Matsuōji	268	35.08 N	140.01 E
Matsuoka	94	36.05 N	136.18 E
Matsuo-san ∧	270	34.38 N	135.44 E
Matsusaka	94	34.34 N	136.32 E
Matsushima	92	38.22 N	141.04 E
Matsu Tao I	100	26.09 N	119.56 E
Matsutō	94	36.31 N	136.34 E
Matsuura	92	33.22 N	129.42 E
Matsuyama	96	33.50 N	132.45 E
Matsuzaki	94	34.45 N	138.47 E
Matta ≃	208	38.07 N	77.26 W
Mattagami ≃	176	50.43 N	81.29 W
Mattagami Heights	190	48.29 N	81.22 W
Mattagami Lake ⊜	190	47.54 N	81.35 W
Mattamuskeet, Lake ⊜	192	35.30 N	76.11 W
Mattapan ◆[8]	283	42.16 N	71.06 W
Mattapoisett	207	41.39 N	70.49 W
Mattaponi	208	37.32 N	76.46 W
Mattaponi ≃	208	37.31 N	76.47 W
Mattarana	62	44.15 N	9.37 E
Mattarello	64	46.00 N	11.07 E
Mattawa, On., Can.	190	46.19 N	78.42 W
Mattawa, Wa., U.S.	202	46.44 N	119.54 W
Mattawa ≃	190	46.19 N	78.43 W
Mattawamkeag	188	45.30 N	68.21 W
Mattawamkeag ≃	188	45.30 N	68.24 W
Mattawan	216	42.12 N	85.47 W
Mattawana	214	40.30 N	77.44 W
Mattawoman Creek ≃	208	38.34 N	77.12 W
Matterhorn (Cervino) ∧, Europe	58	45.59 N	7.43 E
Matterhorn ∧, Nv., U.S.	204	41.49 N	115.23 W
Mattersburg	61	47.44 N	16.25 E
Mattertal V	58	46.10 N	7.49 E
Matteson	216	41.30 N	87.42 W
Matteson Lake ⊜	216	41.56 N	85.12 W
Matthew Flinders Memorial ⊥	169	38.19 S	145.04 E
Matthews	216	40.23 N	85.29 W
Matthews Mountain ∧[2]	194	37.29 N	90.21 W
Matthews Ridge	246	7.30 N	60.10 W
Matthew Town	238	20.57 N	73.40 W
Matthias Church υ[1]	264c	47.30 N	19.02 E
Matthiessen State Park ♠	216	41.17 N	89.01 W
Maţţī, Sabkhat ⊜	128	23.30 N	52.00 E
Mattie, Lake ⊜	220	28.08 N	81.46 W
Mattig ≃	60	48.10 N	13.07 E
Mattighofen	60	48.06 N	13.09 E
Mattinata	68	41.42 N	16.03 E
Mattishall	42	52.39 N	1.02 E
Mattituck	207	40.59 N	72.32 W
Mattole ≃	204	40.18 N	124.21 W
Mattoon, Il., U.S.	194	39.28 N	88.22 W
Mattoon, Wi., U.S.	190	45.00 N	89.02 W
Mattox Creek ≃	208	38.12 N	76.58 W
Mattox Draw V	198	38.03 N	101.11 W
Mattsee	64	47.58 N	13.06 E
Mattsee ⊜	60	47.59 N	13.07 E
Mattydale	210	43.05 N	76.08 W
Matu	112	2.41 N	111.32 E
Matua	112	2.59 S	110.45 E
Matuba	156	24.27 S	32.55 E
Matucana	248	11.51 S	76.24 W
Matudo → Matsudo	94	35.47 N	139.54 E
Matue → Matsue	96	35.28 N	133.04 E
Matuku Island I	175g	19.10 S	179.46 E
Matumoto → Matsumoto	94	36.14 N	137.58 E
Matungo ≃	152	16.25 S	21.27 E
Matunuck	207	41.23 N	71.32 W
Matuog	116	9.55 N	123.09 E
Matura Bay c	241r	10.38 N	61.01 W
Maturín	246	9.45 N	63.11 W
Maturino	76	59.06 N	37.55 E
Matusadona National Park ♠	154	16.25 S	28.35 E
Matusov	78	49.03 N	31.34 E
Matutina	255	19.13 S	45.58 W
Matuto	154	14.46 S	35.59 E
Matutum, Mount ∧	116	6.22 N	125.05 E
Matuzaka → Matsusaka	94	34.34 N	136.32 E
Matvejevka	80	53.32 N	53.29 E
Matvejev Kurgan	83	47.35 N	38.52 E
Matvejevo, Ross.	76	58.38 N	43.30 E
Matvejevo, Ross.	86	57.47 N	57.51 E
Mátyásföld ◆[8]	264c	47.31 N	19.13 E
Matyra ≃	76	52.38 N	39.38 E
Matyševo	80	50.49 N	44.12 E
Mau	124	25.17 N	81.23 E
Maú (Ireng) ≃	246	3.33 N	59.51 W
Mauá, Bra.	256	23.40 S	46.27 W
Maúa, Moç.	154	13.51 S	37.10 E
Mauá □[7]	287b	23.40 S	46.27 W
Mau Aimma	124	25.42 N	81.55 E
Mauban	116	14.12 N	121.44 E
Maubara	112	8.37 S	125.12 E
Maubeuge	50	50.17 N	3.58 E
Mauchamps	261	48.32 N	2.12 E
Mauchline	46	55.31 N	4.24 W
Maud, Scot., U.K.	46	57.31 N	2.06 W
Maud, Mo., U.S.	219	39.37 N	92.15 W
Maud, Oh., U.S.	218	39.21 N	84.23 W
Maud, Ok., U.S.	196	35.08 N	96.46 W
Maud, Tx., U.S.	194	33.20 N	94.21 W
Maud, Point >	162	23.06 S	113.45 E
Maudaha	124	25.41 N	80.07 E
Maude	166	34.28 S	144.18 E
Maudétour-en-Vexin	261	49.06 N	1.47 E
Mau-é-ele	156	24.21 S	34.07 E
Mauensee	58	47.10 N	8.04 E
Mauer ◆[8]	264b	48.09 N	16.16 E
Mauerbach	264b	48.15 N	16.10 E
Mauerbach ≃	264b	48.12 N	16.14 E
Mauerkirchen	60	48.11 N	13.08 E
Maués	250	3.24 S	57.42 W
Maués ≃	246	3.22 S	57.44 W
Maug ≃	116	8.20 N	125.53 E
Mauganj	124	24.41 N	81.53 E
Mauga Silisili ∧	175a	13.35 S	172.27 W
Maughold	44	54.18 N	4.17 W
Maug Islands II	108	20.01 N	145.13 E
Mauguio	62	43.37 N	4.01 E
Mauguio, Étang de c	62	43.35 N	4.02 E
Maui □[6]	229a	20.53 N	156.30 W
Maui I	229a	20.45 N	156.15 W
Mauk	115a	6.04 S	106.30 E
Mauke I	14	20.09 S	157.23 W
Maulbach	56	50.43 N	9.04 E
Maulbronn	56	49.00 N	8.49 E
Maulde	50	50.30 N	3.26 E
Mauldin	192	34.46 N	82.18 W
Mauldre ≃	261	48.58 N	1.49 E
Maule	50	48.55 N	1.51 E
Maule □[4]	252	35.30 S	71.30 W
Maule ≃	252	35.19 S	72.25 W
Maule, Laguna del ⊜	252	36.04 S	70.30 W
Mauléon	32	46.56 N	0.45 W
Mauléon-Licharre	32	43.14 N	0.53 W
Maulette	261	48.48 N	1.37 E
Maullín	254	41.38 S	73.37 W
Maulvi Bāzār	120	24.29 N	91.47 E
Maumaupaki ∧	172	36.58 S	175.35 E
Maumee	214	41.33 N	83.39 W
Maumee ≃	216	41.42 N	83.28 W
Maumee Bay c	214	41.43 N	83.26 W
Maumelle, Lake ⊜[1]	194	34.55 N	92.40 W
Maumere	115b	8.37 S	122.14 E
Maun	156	20.00 S	23.25 E
Maunabo	240m	18.01 N	65.54 W
Mauna Kea ∧[1]	229d	19.50 N	155.28 W
Maunaloa	229a	21.08 N	157.13 W
Mauna Loa ∧[1]	229d	19.29 N	155.36 W
Maunalua Bay c	229c	21.17 N	157.44 W
Maunath Bhanjan	124	25.57 N	83.33 E
Maunatlala	156	22.32 S	27.28 E
Maunesha ≃	216	43.13 N	88.57 W
Maungahaumi ∧	172	38.18 S	177.40 E
Maunga Roa ∧	174k	21.13 S	159.48 W
Maungatapere	172	35.45 S	174.12 E
Maungaturoto	172	36.06 S	174.22 E
Maungdaw	110	20.50 N	92.21 E
Maungmagan	110	14.09 N	98.06 E
Maungu	154	3.33 S	38.45 E
Maunoir, Lac ⊜	180	67.30 N	125.00 W
Maupihaa I[1]	14	16.50 S	153.55 W
Maupin	224	45.10 N	121.04 W
Maur	123	30.05 N	75.15 E
Mau Rānīpur	124	25.15 N	79.08 E
Maurecourt	261	49.00 N	2.04 E
Maure-de-Bretagne	32	47.54 N	1.59 W
Mauregard	261	49.02 N	2.35 E
Maurepas	261	48.45 N	1.55 E
Maurepas, Lake ⊜	194	30.15 N	90.30 W
Maures ⋀	62	43.16 N	6.23 E
Mauretanien → Mauritania □[1]	134	20.00 N	12.00 W
Mauri ≃	248	17.18 S	68.41 W
Mauria, Passo della)(	64	46.27 N	12.31 E
Mauriac	32	45.13 N	2.20 E
Maurice (Île) → Mauritius □[1]	157c	20.17 S	57.33 E
Maurice ≃	208	39.13 N	75.02 W
Maurice, Lake ⊜	162	29.28 S	130.58 E
Maurice K. Goddard State Park ♠	214	41.23 N	81.10 W
Mauricetown	208	39.17 N	74.58 W
Mauriceville	172	40.47 S	175.42 E
Mauricio → Mauritius □[1]	157c	20.17 S	57.33 E
Maurienne V	62	45.13 N	6.30 E
Maurino, Canal ≊	286e	33.34 S	70.32 W
Mauritania (Mauritanie) □[1]	134	20.00 N	12.00 W
Mauritanie → Mauritania □[1]	134	20.00 N	12.00 W
Mauriti	250	7.23 S	38.46 W
Mauritius □[1], Afr.	138	20.17 S	57.33 E
Mauritius □[1], Afr.	157c	20.17 S	57.33 E
Mauritius I	157c	20.17 S	57.33 E
Mauron	32	48.05 N	2.18 W
Maurs	32	44.43 N	2.11 E
Maurui	154	5.07 S	38.23 E
Maury ≃	192	37.37 N	79.27 W
Maury Channel ɥ	176	75.44 N	94.40 W
Maury Island >[1]	224	47.20 N	122.24 W
Maussane	62	43.43 N	4.48 E
Mauston	190	43.47 N	90.04 W
Mautala	126	22.25 N	89.05 E
Mautau, Pointe >	174x	9.42 S	138.58 W
Mautern an der Donau	61	48.24 N	15.35 E
Mauterndorf	64	47.08 N	13.40 E
Mautern in Steiermark	61	47.24 N	14.50 E
Mauth	60	48.53 N	13.35 E
Mauthausen	61	48.14 N	14.32 E
Mauthen	64	46.40 N	13.00 E
Mauvais Coulee V	198	48.21 N	99.06 W
Mauvaise Terre Creek ≃	219	39.43 N	90.38 W
Mauvaise Terre Lake ⊜[1]	219	39.42 N	90.12 W
Mauvezin	32	43.44 N	0.55 E
Mava	164	6.50 S	141.25 E
Mavaca ≃	246	2.31 N	65.11 W
Mavanza	156	22.43 S	35.08 E
Māvelikara	122	9.16 N	76.33 E
Maverick	200	33.43 N	109.32 W
Mavinga	152	15.50 S	20.21 E
Mavita	156	19.33 S	33.10 E
Mavonde	156	18.32 S	33.02 E
Mavuradona Mountains ⋀	154	16.30 S	31.20 E
Mawa	154	2.43 N	26.42 E
Mawai	114	1.52 N	103.57 E
Ma Wan I	271d	22.21 N	114.03 E
Mawāna	124	29.06 N	77.55 E
Mawangkanli Shan ∧	120	34.19 N	80.03 E
Mawangtang	106	30.42 N	120.42 E
Mawasangka	112	5.17 S	122.18 E
Mawchi	110	18.49 N	97.09 E
Maw-daung Pass)(	110	11.47 N	99.39 E
Mawdesley	262	53.38 N	2.46 W
Mawdesley Lake ⊜	184	54.01 N	100.39 W
Mawgan	42	50.06 N	5.06 W
Mawi	272a	28.39 N	77.25 E
Mawiwi	154	3.06 N	27.40 E
Māwiyah	144	13.35 N	44.21 E
Mawjib, Wādī al- V	132	31.28 N	35.34 E
Mawkhi	110	16.17 N	98.53 E
Mawlaik	110	23.38 N	94.24 E
Mawlamyaing → Mawlamyine	110	16.30 N	97.38 E
Mawlamyine (Moulmein)	110	16.30 N	97.38 E
Mawr, Wādī V	144	15.41 N	42.42 E
Mawshij	144	13.43 N	43.17 E
Mawson υ[3]	9	67.40 S	63.43 E
Mawson Escarpment ⊥[4]	9	73.05 S	68.10 E
Mawson Peninsula >[1]	9	68.35 S	154.11 E
Maw Taung ∧	110	11.39 N	99.35 E
Mawuba	102	29.50 N	108.11 E
Max	198	47.49 N	101.17 W
Maxaranguape	250	5.31 S	35.16 W
Maxatawny	208	40.33 N	75.41 W
Maxcanú	232	20.35 N	89.59 W
Maxéville	58	48.43 N	6.10 E
Maxglan, Flughafen ⊠	64	47.48 N	13.02 E
Maxhütte Haidhof	60	49.12 N	12.05 E
Maxiang	100	24.41 N	118.15 E
Maximo	214	40.53 N	81.11 W
Maximo Paz	258	34.56 S	58.37 W
Maxinkuckee, Lake ⊜	216	41.12 N	86.24 W
Maxixe	156	23.51 S	35.21 E
Maxon Creek ≃	196	29.53 N	102.24 W
Maxton	192	34.44 N	79.20 W
Maxville	206	45.17 N	74.51 W
Maxwell, Ca., U.S.	226	39.16 N	122.11 W
Maxwell, In., U.S.	218	39.51 N	85.46 W
Maxwell, Ia., U.S.	190	41.53 N	93.23 W
Maxwell, Ne., U.S.	198	41.04 N	100.31 W
Maxwell, N.M., U.S.	196	36.32 N	104.32 W
Maxwell, Tx., U.S.	222	29.53 N	97.48 W
Maxwell Air Force Base ■	194	32.23 N	86.21 W
Maxwell Bay c	176	74.35 N	89.00 W
May	196	31.59 N	98.55 W
May ≃, Austl.	162	17.07 S	123.50 E
May ≃, Ab., Can.	182	55.43 N	111.22 W
May ≃, Pap. N. Gui.	164	4.35 S	141.35 E
May, Cape >[1]	208	38.58 N	74.55 W
May, Isle of I	46	56.11 N	2.34 W
May, Mount ∧	182	54.02 N	119.58 W
Maya, Pulau I	112	1.10 S	109.35 E
May Aché	146	12.00 N	15.44 E
Mayaguana I	238	22.23 N	72.57 W
Mayaguana Passage ɥ	238	22.32 N	73.15 W
Mayagüez	240m	18.12 N	67.09 W
Mayagüez, Aeropuerto ⊠	240m	18.15 N	67.09 W
Mayagüez, Bahía de c	240m	18.12 N	67.10 W
Mayahi	150	13.58 N	7.40 E
Mayajigua	240p	22.14 N	79.04 W
Mayaka	152	5.17 S	16.52 E
Mayala	273b	4.21 S	15.09 E
Mayales, Punta >	236	11.52 N	85.26 W
Mayama	152	3.51 S	14.54 E
Mayamba	152	4.46 S	16.52 E
Mayāmey	128	36.24 N	55.42 E
Maya Mountains ⋀	232	16.40 N	88.50 W
Mayang	102	27.41 N	109.35 E
Mayang-do I	98	40.00 N	128.12 E
Mayantoc	116	15.37 N	120.23 E
Mayao	106	30.50 N	120.23 E
Mayapan ⊥	232	20.38 N	89.27 W
Māyāpur	272b	22.27 N	88.08 E
Mayarí	240p	20.40 N	75.41 W
Mayarí Arriba	240p	20.25 N	75.32 W
Mayaro Bay c	241r	10.15 N	60.58 W
Maya-san ∧	96	34.44 N	135.12 E
Maybee	216	42.00 N	83.30 W
Maybeury	192	37.22 N	81.22 W
Maybole	44	55.21 N	4.41 W
Maybrook	210	41.29 N	74.13 W
Maychew	144	13.02 N	39.34 E
Maydelle	222	31.48 N	95.18 W
Maydena	166	42.55 S	146.30 E
Maydh	144	11.00 N	47.07 E
Maydī	144	16.20 N	42.46 E
Maydolong	116	11.30 N	125.30 E
Maydūm	142	29.22 N	31.10 E
Mayen	56	50.19 N	7.13 E
Mayence → Mainz	56	50.01 N	8.16 E
Mayenne	32	48.18 N	0.37 W
Mayenne □[5]	32	48.05 N	0.40 W
Mayenne ≃	32	47.30 N	0.33 W
Mayer	200	34.23 N	112.14 W
Mayerling	61	48.03 N	16.06 E
Mayersville	194	32.54 N	91.03 W
Mayerthorpe	182	53.57 N	115.08 W
Mayet	50	47.46 N	0.17 E
Mayfair ◆[8], S. Afr.	273d	26.12 S	28.01 E
Mayfair ◆[8], Pa., U.S.	285	40.02 N	75.03 W
Mayfield, N.Z.	172	43.49 S	171.25 E
Mayfield, Eng., U.K.	42	51.01 N	0.15 E
Mayfield, Eng., U.K.	44	53.01 N	1.45 W
Mayfield, Scot., U.K.	46	55.52 N	3.02 W
Mayfield, In., U.S.	218	40.11 N	85.21 W
Mayfield, Ky., U.S.	194	36.44 N	88.38 W
Mayfield, N.Y., U.S.	210	43.06 N	74.15 W
Mayfield, Oh., U.S.	279a	41.33 N	81.26 W
Mayfield, Pa., U.S.	210	41.32 N	75.32 W
Mayfield, Ut., U.S.	200	39.06 N	111.42 W
Mayfield Creek ≃	194	36.57 N	89.05 W
Mayfield Dam ◆[6]	224	46.30 N	122.35 W
Mayfield Heights	214	41.31 N	81.27 W
Mayfield Lake ⊜[1]	224	46.31 N	122.32 W
Mayflower	194	34.57 N	92.25 W
Mayford	260	51.18 N	0.34 W
May Inlet c	176	76.15 N	100.45 W
Māyir, Sūrīy.	130	36.28 N	37.11 E
Māyir, Sūrīy.	130	36.23 N	37.02 E
May Jirgui	150	13.44 N	8.08 E
Maykop → Majkop	84	44.35 N	40.07 E
Mayland	42	51.39 N	0.47 E
Maymont	184	52.33 N	107.40 W
Maymūn, Wādī V	146	30.10 N	10.27 E
Maymyo	110	22.02 N	96.28 E
Mayna	126	22.14 N	87.47 E
Maynāmati	124	23.29 N	91.07 E
Maynard, Ia., U.S.	190	42.46 N	91.52 W
Maynard, Ma., U.S.	207	42.26 N	71.27 W
Maynard, Oh., U.S.	214	40.07 N	80.53 W
Maynardville	192	36.15 N	83.47 W
Mayne	224	48.51 N	123.18 W
Mayne ≃	166	23.34 S	141.18 E
Mayne Island I	224	48.51 N	123.17 W
Maynooth	48	53.23 N	6.35 W
Mayo, Yk., Can.	180	63.35 N	135.54 W
Mayo, Fl., U.S.	192	30.03 N	83.10 W
Mayo, Md., U.S.	208	38.53 N	76.30 W
Mayo □[6]	48	53.54 N	9.15 W
Mayo ≃, Arg.	254	45.46 S	69.43 W
Mayo ≃, Col.	246	1.40 N	77.21 W
Mayo ≃, Méx.	232	26.45 N	109.47 W
Mayo ≃, Perú	248	6.37 S	76.16 W
Mayoba	154	17.13 S	26.16 E
Mayo Bay c	116	6.56 N	126.22 E
Mayodan	192	36.24 N	79.58 W
Mayo Faran	146	8.57 N	12.04 E
Mayo-Kébbi □[5]	146	10.00 N	15.30 E
Mayoko, Congo	152	2.18 S	12.49 E
Mayoko, Zaïre	152	1.05 S	23.49 E
Mayola ≃	44	54.45 N	6.31 W
Mayo Lake ⊜	180	63.46 N	135.10 W
Mayo Ndaga	146	6.54 N	11.25 E
Mayon Volcano ∧[1]	116	13.15 N	123.41 E
Mayor Buratovich	252	39.15 S	62.37 W
Mayo Reservoir ⊜[1]	192	36.00 N	78.53 W
Mayor Island I	172	37.18 S	176.16 E
Mayor Pablo Lagerenza	248	19.58 S	60.45 W
Mayotte □[2], Afr.	138	12.50 S	45.10 E
Mayotte □[2], Afr.	157a	12.50 S	45.10 E
Mayoyao	116	16.59 N	121.14 E
Mayoyoque	246	0.41 N	75.18 W
Maypearl	222	32.19 N	97.01 W
May Pen	241q	17.58 N	77.14 W
Mayport Naval Station ■	192	30.22 N	81.24 W
Mayraira Point >	116	18.39 N	120.51 E
Mayrán, Desierto de ◆[2]	196	25.45 N	102.45 W
Mayres	62	44.40 N	4.07 E
Mayrhofen	64	47.10 N	11.52 E
Mays	218	39.45 N	85.26 W
Maysah, Tall al- ∧	132	31.08 N	35.40 E
Maysān □[4]	128	32.00 N	47.00 E
Maysfield	222	30.54 N	96.51 W
Mays Landing	208	39.27 N	74.43 W
Mays Lick	218	38.31 N	83.50 W
Maysville, Ky., U.S.	218	38.38 N	83.44 W
Maysville, Mo., U.S.	194	39.53 N	94.21 W
Maysville, N.C., U.S.	192	34.54 N	77.13 W
Maysville, Ok., U.S.	196	34.49 N	97.24 W
Maythalūn	132	32.21 N	35.16 E
Maytiguid Island I	116	11.03 N	119.36 E
Maytown	208	40.04 N	76.35 W
Mayu	100	27.48 N	120.26 E
Mayumba	152	3.25 S	10.39 E
Mayung	114	0.49 N	103.03 E
Māyūram	122	11.06 N	79.40 E
Mayville, Mi., U.S.	190	43.20 N	83.21 W
Mayville, N.Y., U.S.	214	42.15 N	79.30 W
Mayville, N.D., U.S.	198	47.29 N	97.19 W
Mayville, Wi., U.S.	190	43.29 N	88.32 W
Maywood, Ca., U.S.	280	33.59 N	118.11 W
Maywood, Il., U.S.	216	41.52 N	87.50 W
Maywood, Mo., U.S.	219	39.57 N	91.36 W
Maywood, Ne., U.S.	198	40.39 N	100.37 W
Maywood, N.J., U.S.	276	40.54 N	74.03 W
Maywood, N.Y., U.S.	210	42.42 N	73.52 W
Maywood Race Track ♠	278	41.44 N	87.50 W
Mayyit, Al-Baḥr al- → Dead Sea ⊜	132	31.30 N	35.30 E
Maza, Arg.	252	36.50 S	63.19 W
Maza, Ross.	80	57.14 N	44.13 E
Mazabuka	154	15.51 S	27.46 E
Mazagan → El-Jadida	148	33.16 N	8.30 W
Mazagão	250	0.07 S	51.17 W
Mazagaon ◆[8]	272c	18.57 N	72.50 E
Mazagão Velho	250	0.13 S	51.25 W
Ma'zah, Jabal ∧	130	35.51 N	40.38 E
Mazamet	32	43.30 N	2.24 E
Mazamitla	234	19.55 N	103.02 W
Mazán ≃	246	3.28 S	73.11 W
Māzandarān □[4]	128	36.30 N	53.30 E
Mazanovo	89	51.40 N	128.52 E
Mazār, Jabal ∧	132	33.34 N	36.03 E
Mazar, Oued V	148	31.50 N	1.36 E
Mazara, Val di ◆[1]	70	37.50 N	13.00 E
Mazara del Vallo	70	37.39 N	12.35 E
Mazār-e Sharīf	120	36.42 N	67.06 E
Mazargues	62	43.15 N	5.24 E
Mazaro ≃	70	37.39 N	12.35 E
Mazarredo	254	47.05 S	66.42 W
Mazarrón	34	37.36 N	1.19 W
Mazarrón, Golfo de c	34	37.30 N	1.18 W

Symbols in the index entries represent the broad categories identified in the key at the right. Symbols with superior numbers (⋀[1]) identify subcategories (see complete key on page *I · 1).*

Symbole im Register stellen die rechts im Schlüssel erklärten Kategorien dar. Symbole mit hochgestellten Ziffern (⋀[1]) bezeichnen Unterabteilungen einer Kategorie (vgl. vollständiger Schlüssel auf Seite *I · 1).*

Los símbolos incluídos en el texto del índice representan las grandes categorias identificadas con la clave a la derecha. Los símbolos con numeros en su parte superior (⋀[1]) identifican las subcategorías (véase la clave completa en la página *I · 1).*

Les symboles de l'index représentent les catégories indiquées dans la légende à droite. Les symboles suivis d'un indice (⋀[1]) représentent des sous-catégories (voir légende complète à la page *I · 1).*

Os símbolos incluídos no texto do índice representam as grandes categorias identificadas com a chave à direita. Os símbolos com números em sua parte superior (⋀[1]) identificam as subcategorias (veja-se a chave completa à página *I · 1).*

	English	Deutsch	Español	Français	Português
∧	Mountain	Berg	Montaña	Montagne	Montanha
⋀	Mountains	Gebirge	Montañas	Montagnes	Montanhas
)(	Pass	Paß	Paso	Col	Passo
V	Valley, Canyon	Tal, Cañon	Valle, Cañón	Vallée, Canyon	Vale, Canhão
≃	Plain	Ebene	Llano	Plaine	Planície
>	Cape	Kap	Cabo	Cap	Cabo
I	Island	Insel	Isla	Île	Ilha
II	Islands	Inseln	Islas	Îles	Ilhas
⊥	Other Topographic Features	Andere Topographische Objekte	Otros Elementos Topográficos	Autres données topographiques	Outros acidentes topográficos

ESPAÑOL Nombre / FRANÇAIS Nom / PORTUGUÊS Nome	Página / Page	Lat.°′	Long.°′ W = Oeste / W = Ouest
Mazarsu	85	41.56 N	72.40 E
Mazaruni ≃	246	6.25 N	58.38 W
Mazatenango	236	14.32 N	91.30 W
Mazatlán	234	23.13 N	106.25 W
Mazatlán Villa de Flores	234	18.02 N	96.54 W
Mazatzal Mountains ⋏	200	34.00 N	111.55 W
Mazatzal Peak ∧	200	34.03 N	111.28 W
Maze	94	35.52 N	137.10 E
Maze ≃	94	35.40 N	137.10 E
Mažeikiai	76	56.19 N	22.20 E
Mazenod	184	49.53 N	106.14 W
Mazeppa, Mn., U.S.	190	44.16 N	92.32 W
Mazeppa, Pa., U.S.	210	40.59 N	76.59 W
Mazha	100	23.27 N	114.00 E
Māzhān, Īrān	128	32.35 N	59.01 E
Mazhan, Zhg.	98	36.04 N	118.45 E
Mazhangfang, Zhg.	104	40.44 N	120.53 E
Mazhangfang, Zhg.	104	42.23 N	122.26 E
Mazhuang, Zhg.	98	37.47 N	115.17 E
Mazhuang, Zhg.	100	32.54 N	114.03 E
Mazhuang, Zhg.	105	39.11 N	116.15 E
Maẓhūr, Khubb al- ⩸ 8	128	27.45 N	43.55 E
Mazıdağı	130	37.30 N	40.30 E
Mazigou	105	40.28 N	114.48 E
Mazilovo ◆ 8	265b	55.44 N	37.26 E
Mazīnān	128	36.18 N	56.46 E
Mazinaw Lake ⊜	212	44.55 N	77.12 W
Mazirbe	76	57.41 N	22.21 E
Mazoco	154	11.40 S	35.48 E
Mazoe ≃	154	16.32 S	33.25 E
Mazomanie	190	43.10 N	89.47 W
Mazomba ≃	256	22.53 S	43.45 W
Mazon	216	41.14 N	88.25 W
Mazon ≃	216	41.21 N	88.25 W
Mazon, East Fork ≃	216	41.11 N	88.18 W
Mazon, West Fork ≃	216	41.15 N	88.21 W
Mazong Shan ∧	102	41.28 N	97.10 E
Mazong Shan ⋏	102	41.30 N	97.30 E
Mazou ≃	50	47.15 N	2.59 E
Mazraʿat-Bayt Jinn	132	33.19 N	35.55 E
Mazsalaca	76	57.52 N	25.03 E
Mazul'skij	86	56.16 N	90.28 E
Mazunga	154	21.45 S	29.52 E
Mazury ◆ 1	30	53.45 N	21.00 E
Mazzarino	70	37.18 N	14.13 E
Mazzarrà Sant'andrea	70	38.05 N	15.08 E
Mazzin	64	46.27 N	11.42 E
Mba	175g	17.33 S	177.41 E
Mbabala Island I	154	11.18 S	29.44 E
Mbabane	158	26.18 S	31.06 E
Mbabo, Tchabal ∧	152	7.16 N	12.09 E
Mbacké	150	14.48 N	15.55 W
Mbaéré ≃	152	3.47 N	17.31 E
Mbage	140	5.30 N	25.13 E
M'bahiakro	150	7.27 N	4.20 W
Mbaïki	152	3.53 N	18.00 E
Mbakaou, Barrage de ◆ 5	152	6.15 N	12.46 E
Mbala, Centraf.	152	7.48 N	20.51 E
Mbala (Abercorn), Zam.	154	8.50 S	31.22 E
Mbalam	152	2.13 N	13.49 E
Mbale	154	1.05 N	34.10 E
Mbali	152	2.50 S	16.12 E
Mbali ≃	152	4.26 N	18.20 E
Mbalizi	154	8.56 S	33.22 E
Mbalmayo	152	3.31 N	11.30 E
Mbalouro ≃	273b	4.09 S	15.21 E
Mbalourou	273b	4.09 S	15.21 E
Mbam ≃	152	4.24 N	11.17 E
Mbamba Bay	154	11.17 S	34.46 E
Mbamou, Île I	152	4.13 S	15.25 E
Mbamou, Pointe ≻	273b	4.16 S	15.19 E
Mbandaka (Coquilhatville)	152	0.04 N	18.16 E
Mbanga	152	4.30 N	9.34 E
Mbanika Island I	175e	9.05 S	159.12 E
M'banza Congo	152	6.16 S	14.15 E
Mbanza-Ngungu	152	5.15 S	14.52 E
Mbarangandu ≃	154	8.57 S	37.24 E
Mbarara	154	0.37 S	30.39 E
Mbari ≃	152	4.34 N	22.43 E
Mbarizunga Game Reserve ◆ 4	154	4.45 N	28.06 E
Mbashe ≃	158	32.15 S	28.53 E
Mbassay	146	7.39 N	15.40 E
Mbate	154	8.52 S	39.10 E
M'batto	150	6.28 N	4.22 W
Mbava Island I	175e	7.49 S	156.33 E
Mbé, Cam.	152	7.43 N	13.30 E
Mbé, Congo	152	3.18 S	15.54 E
Mbé ≃	152	0.27 N	9.41 E
Mbemba	154	10.03 S	38.36 E
Mbengga I	175g	18.23 S	178.08 E
M'bengué	150	10.00 N	5.54 W
Mbéré	146	10.49 N	15.44 E
Mbéré ≃	152	7.45 N	15.36 E
Mberengwa	154	20.30 S	29.53 E
Mbereshi Mission	154	9.45 S	28.46 E
Mberubu	150	6.10 N	7.38 E
Mbeya	154	8.54 S	33.27 E
Mbeya □ 4	154	8.00 S	33.30 E
Mbi ≃	152	4.26 N	18.16 E
Mbia	140	6.15 N	29.19 E
M'bigou	152	1.53 S	11.56 E
Mbinda	152	2.00 S	12.55 E
Mbindawina	152	15.57 S	23.18 E
Mbinga	154	10.56 S	35.01 E
Mbini	152	1.35 N	9.37 E
Mbini ≃	152	1.35 N	9.37 E
Mbirira	154	4.21 S	30.10 E
Mbirizi	154	0.23 S	31.27 E
Mbogo	154	7.26 S	33.26 E
Mboie	152	6.56 S	21.54 E
Mbola	175e	9.37 S	160.39 E
Mboli	152	4.08 N	23.09 E
Mbomou □ 5	152	5.00 N	23.30 E
Mbomou (Bomu) ≃	136	4.08 N	22.26 E
Mbonge	152	4.33 N	9.05 E
Mboro, Sén.	150	15.09 N	16.54 W
Mboro, Sūd.	140	6.18 N	28.45 E
Mborokua I	175e	9.00 S	158.40 E
Mborong	115b	8.49 S	120.37 E
Mboté	152	3.56 S	12.43 E
Mbotou ≃	152	6.49 N	24.14 E
Mbouda	152	5.38 N	10.15 E
Mboula	152	4.27 N	16.29 E
Mbour	150	14.24 N	16.58 W
Mbout	150	16.02 N	12.35 W
Mbrès	152	6.40 N	19.48 E
M'Bridge ≃	152	7.14 S	12.52 E
Mbua	175g	16.48 S	178.37 E
Mbua Bay ⊂	175g	16.49 S	178.35 E
Mbuji-Mayi (Bakwanga)	152	6.09 S	23.38 E
Mbulu	154	3.51 S	35.32 E
Mbulula	154	5.26 S	27.26 E
Mbuluzane ≃	158	26.08 S	31.52 E
Mbuluzi ≃	158	26.08 S	31.52 E
Mbuma	154	3.32 N	24.50 E
Mburucuyá	252	28.03 S	58.14 W
Mbutha	175g	16.39 S	179.50 E
Mbwemkuru ≃	154	9.29 S	39.39 E
McAdam	186	45.36 N	67.20 W
McAdam National Park ✦	164	7.15 S	145.40 E
McAdams Peak ∧ 2	219	38.58 N	90.32 W
McAdoo	210	40.54 N	75.59 W
McAdoo Heights	210	40.54 N	75.59 W
McAfee	210	41.10 N	74.32 W
McAlester	196	34.56 N	95.46 W
McAlisterville	208	40.38 N	77.16 W
McAllen	196	26.12 N	98.13 W
McAlpine	208	39.16 N	76.50 W
McAlpine Dam ◆ 6	218	38.16 N	85.47 W
McAlveys Fort	214	40.39 N	77.50 W
McArthur	188	39.14 N	82.28 W
McArthur ≃	164	15.54 S	136.40 E
McArthur River	164	16.27 S	136.07 E
McAuley	184	50.16 N	101.23 W
McBain	190	44.11 N	85.12 W
McBee	192	34.28 N	80.15 W
McBeth	222	29.11 N	95.30 W
McBeth Fjord ⊂ 2	176	69.38 N	68.30 W
McBride	182	53.18 N	120.10 W
McCall	202	44.54 N	116.05 W
McCall Creek	194	31.30 N	90.41 W
McCallum	186	47.38 N	56.15 W
McCallum Creek ≃	169	37.03 S	143.49 E
McCamey	196	31.08 N	102.13 W
McCammon	202	42.39 N	112.11 W
McCandless, Pa., U.S.	214	40.35 N	80.01 W
McCandless, Pa., U.S.	279b	40.34 N	80.02 W
McCarteney Creek ≃	202	47.13 N	120.05 W
McCarthy	180	61.26 N	142.55 W
McCauley Island I	182	53.40 N	130.15 W
McCaysville	192	34.59 N	84.22 W
McChord Air Force Base ■	224	47.08 N	122.29 W
McClarens Run ≃	279b	40.27 N	80.12 W
McClarty Lake ⊜	184	54.28 N	100.20 W
McCleary	224	47.03 N	123.15 W
McClees Creek ≃	276	40.22 N	74.03 W
McClellan Air Force Base ■	226	38.39 N	121.23 W
McClellan Creek ≃	196	35.22 N	100.34 W
McClellanville	192	33.05 N	79.27 W
McClintock, Mount ∧	9	80.13 S	157.26 E
McCloud	204	41.15 N	122.08 W
McCloud ≃	204	40.46 N	122.18 W
McClure, Il., U.S.	194	37.19 N	89.26 W
McClure, Oh., U.S.	216	41.22 N	83.56 W
McClure, Pa., U.S.	210	40.42 N	77.18 W
McClure, Lake ⊜ 1	226	37.37 N	120.16 W
McClusky	198	47.29 N	100.26 W
McColl	192	34.40 N	79.32 W
McComas	192	37.23 N	81.17 W
McComb, Ms., U.S.	194	31.14 N	90.27 W
McComb, Oh., U.S.	216	41.06 N	83.47 W
McConaughy, Lake ⊜ 1	198	41.15 N	101.50 W
McConnell Air Force Base ■	198	37.38 N	97.15 W
McConnell Range ⋏	180	64.00 N	123.50 W
McConnellsburg	188	39.55 N	77.59 W
McConnells Mill	279b	40.15 N	80.15 W
McConnells Mill State Park ✦	214	40.57 N	80.11 W
McConnellstown	214	40.27 N	78.05 W
McConnellsville	210	43.16 N	75.42 W
McConnelsville	188	39.38 N	81.51 W
McCook, Il., U.S.	278	41.48 N	87.50 W
McCook, Ne., U.S.	198	40.12 N	100.37 W
McCordsville	218	39.53 N	85.55 W
McCormick	192	33.54 N	82.17 W
McCormick Place ʋ	278	41.51 N	87.37 W
McCoy	224	45.03 N	123.13 W
McCoy Creek ≃	202	43.02 N	118.50 W
McCoy Lake ⊜	184	52.35 N	92.19 W
McCraney Creek ≃	219	39.39 N	91.12 W
McCreary	184	50.46 N	99.30 W
McCrory	194	35.15 N	91.12 W
McCulloch, Mount ∧	162	25.10 S	129.52 E
McCullom Lake	216	42.22 N	88.18 W
McCullough	279b	40.22 N	79.38 W
McCullough Mountain ∧	204	35.36 N	115.11 W
McCune	198	37.21 N	95.00 W
McCurtain	196	35.08 N	94.58 W
McCusker ≃	184	55.32 N	108.40 W
McCutchenville	214	40.59 N	83.15 W
McDade	222	30.17 N	97.15 W
McDavid	194	30.51 N	87.19 W
McDermitt	204	41.59 N	117.43 W
McDermott	218	38.50 N	83.03 W
McDonald, Ks., U.S.	198	39.47 N	101.22 W
McDonald, Pa., U.S.	214	40.22 N	80.14 W
McDonald, Lac ⊜	206	45.52 N	74.35 W
McDonald, Lake ⊜	202	48.35 N	113.55 W
McDonald Park ✦	282	37.18 N	122.17 W
McDonogh	284c	39.24 N	76.46 W
McDonough, Ga., U.S.	192	33.26 N	84.08 W
McDonough, N.Y., U.S.	210	42.30 N	75.46 W
McDouall Peak	162	29.51 S	134.55 E
McDougal, Mount ∧	200	42.54 N	110.36 W
McDowell Peak ∧	200	33.40 N	111.50 W
McElhattan	210	41.09 N	77.22 W
McElmo Creek ≃	200	37.13 N	109.12 W
Mc Ennen Airport ⊠	281	42.12 N	83.37 W
Mcensk	76	53.17 N	36.35 E
McEwen	194	36.06 N	87.37 W
McEwensville	210	41.05 N	76.49 W
McFadden	200	41.39 N	106.07 W
McFarland, Ca., U.S.	226	35.40 N	119.13 W
McFarland, Wi., U.S.	216	43.00 N	89.17 W
McGavock Lake ⊜	184	56.32 N	101.25 W
McGehee	194	33.37 N	91.23 W
McGill	204	39.24 N	114.46 W
McGill, Université ʋ 2	275a	45.30 N	73.35 W
McGillivray, Lac ⊜	190	46.04 N	77.06 W
McGinnis Slough Wildlife Refuge ◆ 4	278	41.39 N	87.52 W
McGovern	214	40.14 N	80.13 W
McGrann	214	40.47 N	79.31 W
McGrath	180	62.58 N	155.38 W
McGraw	210	42.35 N	76.05 W
McGregor, On., Can.	214	42.09 N	82.58 W
McGregor, S. Afr.	158	33.57 S	19.50 E
McGregor, Ia., U.S.	190	43.01 N	91.10 W
McGregor, Tx., U.S.	222	31.26 N	97.24 W
McGregor ≃	182	54.11 N	122.00 W
McGregor Creek ≃	214	42.24 N	82.11 W
McGregor Lake ⊜	182	50.31 N	112.53 W
McGregor Range ⋏	166	26.40 S	142.45 E
McGuffey	216	40.41 N	83.47 W
McGuire, Mount ∧	202	45.10 N	114.36 W
McGuire Air Force Base ■	208	40.02 N	74.35 W
McGuire Reservoir ⊜	224	45.19 N	123.26 W
M'Chedallah	34	36.21 N	4.16 E
McHenry, Il., U.S.	216	42.20 N	88.16 W
McHenry, Ms., U.S.	194	30.42 N	89.08 W
McHenry □ 6	216	42.19 N	88.27 W
Mcherrah ◆ 1	148	27.00 N	4.40 W
Mchinga	154	9.44 S	39.42 E
Mchinji	154	13.41 S	32.55 E
Mchungo	154	7.42 S	39.17 E
McInnes Lake ⊜	184	52.12 N	93.45 W
McIntosh, Al., U.S.	194	31.15 N	88.01 W
McIntosh, Il., U.S.	216	42.03 N	88.23 W
McIntosh, Mn., U.S.	198	47.38 N	95.53 W
McIntosh, S.D., U.S.	198	45.55 N	101.20 W
McIntosh Lake ⊜	184	55.45 N	105.08 W
McIntyre	214	40.34 N	79.17 W
McIntyre Bay ⊂	182	54.05 N	131.55 W
McKay, Mount ∧	162	22.26 S	120.01 E
McKay Creek ≃	202	45.40 N	118.50 W
McKean	214	41.59 N	80.09 W
McKean □ 6	214	41.49 N	78.27 W
McKeand ≃	176	65.26 N	68.10 W
McKee	192	37.25 N	83.59 W
McKee City	208	39.27 N	74.38 W
McKee Creek ≃	219	39.46 N	90.36 W
McKeesport	214	40.20 N	79.51 W
McKees Rocks	214	40.27 N	80.03 W
McKenna	224	46.56 N	122.33 W
McKenzie, Al., U.S.	194	31.32 N	86.42 W
McKenzie, Tn., U.S.	194	36.07 N	88.31 W
McKenzie ≃	202	44.07 N	123.06 W
McKenzie Bridge	202	44.10 N	122.09 W
McKenzie Creek ≃	212	43.02 N	79.53 W
McKenzie Island	184	51.05 N	93.48 W
McKenzie Lake ⊜, On., Can.	212	45.22 N	78.02 W
McKenzie Lake ⊜, Sk., Can.	184	54.12 N	102.30 W
McKerrow, Lake ⊜	172	44.26 S	168.03 E
McKillip Ditch ≡	216	40.50 N	86.51 W
McKinlay	166	21.16 S	141.17 E
McKinlay ≃	166	20.50 S	141.28 E
McKinley, Mount ∧	180	63.04 N	151.00 W
McKinley Airport ⊠	281	42.33 N	82.58 W
McKinley Park ✦	279b	40.25 N	80.00 W
McKinleyville, Ca., U.S.	204	40.56 N	124.05 W
McKinleyville, W.V., U.S.	214	40.15 N	80.36 W
McKinney	222	33.11 N	96.36 W
McKittrick, Ca., U.S.	226	35.18 N	119.37 W
McKittrick, Mo., U.S.	219	38.44 N	91.27 W
McKittrick Summit ∧	226	35.18 N	119.46 W
McKnight Lake ⊜	184	56.03 N	101.08 W
McKnightstown	208	39.52 N	77.20 W
McKnight Village	279b	40.31 N	80.00 W
McKownville	210	42.41 N	73.50 W
McLain	194	31.06 N	88.49 W
McLaren Vale	168b	35.14 S	138.32 E
McLarty Hills ⋏ 2	162	19.29 S	123.33 E
McLaughlin	198	45.48 N	100.48 W
McLaughlin ≃	184	53.46 N	97.38 W
McLaughlin Run ≃	279b	40.22 N	80.07 W
McLaurin	194	31.10 N	89.13 W
McLean, Sk., Can.	184	50.30 N	104.04 W
McLean, Il., U.S.	194	40.18 N	89.10 W
McLean, N.Y., U.S.	210	42.33 N	76.17 W
McLean, Tx., U.S.	196	35.13 N	100.35 W
McLean, Va., U.S.	208	38.56 N	77.10 W
McLean □ 6	216	40.29 N	88.45 W
McLean Hamlet	284c	38.56 N	77.13 W
McLean Lake ⊜	184	56.27 N	109.15 W
McLean Mountain ∧	186	47.07 N	68.50 W
McLeansboro	194	38.05 N	88.32 W
McLennan	182	55.42 N	116.54 W
McLennan □ 6	222	31.35 N	97.13 W
McLeod ≃	182	54.08 N	115.42 W
McLeod Bay ⊂	176	62.53 N	110.00 W
McLeodganj	123	30.15 N	73.42 E
McLeod Lake	182	54.59 N	123.02 W
M'Clintock Channel ʯ	176	72.00 N	102.00 W
McLoughlin, Mount ∧	202	42.27 N	122.19 W
McLoughlin Bay ⊂	176	67.50 N	99.00 W
McLoughlin House National Historic Site ⊥	224	45.20 N	122.33 W
McLouth	198	39.11 N	95.12 W
McLure	182	51.03 N	120.14 W
M'Clure Strait ʯ	176	74.30 N	116.00 W
McMahan	222	29.51 N	97.31 W
McMahon	184	50.05 N	107.32 W
McMasterville	206	45.33 N	73.15 W
McMichael Art Collection ʋ	275b	43.50 N	79.37 W
McMillan, Lake ⊜ 1	196	32.40 N	104.20 W
McMinnville, Or., U.S.	224	45.12 N	123.11 W
McMinnville, Tn., U.S.	194	35.41 N	85.46 W
McMurdo ʋ 3	9	77.50 S	166.25 E
McMurdo Sound ʯ	9	77.30 S	165.00 E
McMurray	214	40.17 N	80.05 W
McNair	222	29.48 N	95.02 W
McNary	200	34.04 N	109.51 W
McNeil, Ar., U.S.	194	33.20 N	93.12 W
McNeil, Tx., U.S.	222	30.27 N	97.43 W
McNeil, Mount ∧	182	54.35 N	130.14 W
McNeil Island I	224	47.13 N	122.41 W
McNeill	194	30.40 N	89.38 W
McNulty	224	45.50 N	122.50 W
McPhail ≃	184	52.44 N	96.31 W
McPhee Bay ⊂	212	44.35 N	79.19 W
McPhee Reservoir ⊜ 1	200	37.32 N	108.35 W
McPherson	198	38.22 N	97.39 W
McPherson Range ⋏	166	28.20 S	153.00 E
McQueeney	196	29.35 N	98.02 W
McRae, Ar., U.S.	194	35.06 N	91.49 W
McRae, Ga., U.S.	192	32.04 N	82.54 W
McRae, Mount ∧	162	22.17 S	117.35 E
McRae Point Provincial Park ✦	212	44.34 N	79.19 W
McRoberts	192	37.12 N	82.40 W
McSherrystown	208	39.48 N	77.00 W
McVeigh	192	37.32 N	82.15 W
McVeytown	214	40.30 N	77.44 W
McVickers Brook ≃	276	40.45 N	74.38 W
McVille	198	47.45 N	98.10 W
McWilliams	194	31.49 N	87.05 W
Mdandu	154	9.09 S	34.42 E
Mdantsana	158	32.56 S	27.42 E
M'Daourouch	36	36.05 N	7.49 E
Meacham	184	52.08 N	105.45 W
Mead	198	41.14 N	96.30 W
Mead, Lake ⊜ 1	200	36.05 N	114.25 W
Meade, Ks., U.S.	198	37.17 N	100.20 W
Meade, Mi., U.S.	214	42.43 N	82.52 W
Meade ≃	180	70.50 N	156.25 W
Meaden Peak ∧	200	40.46 N	107.03 W
Meade Peak ∧	202	42.30 N	111.15 W
Meadie, Loch ⊜	46	58.20 N	4.33 W
Meadow, Tx., U.S.	196	33.20 N	102.12 W
Meadow, Ut,. U.S.	200	38.53 N	112.24 W
Meadowbank Park ✦	274a	33.49 S	151.06 E
Meadowbrook, Il., U.S.	219	38.54 N	90.01 W
Meadowbrook, In., U.S.	216	41.03 N	85.03 W
Meadow Brook ≃, Ma., U.S.	283	42.03 N	70.58 W
Meadow Brook ≃, Pa., U.S.	285	40.07 N	75.04 W
Meadow Creek ≃	202	46.03 N	115.18 W
Meadowdale	278	41.32 N	87.21 W
Meadow Flat	170	33.26 S	149.56 E
Meadow Island I	276	40.36 N	73.33 W
Meadow Lake	184	54.08 N	108.26 W
Meadow Lake ⊜, Sk., Can.	184	54.07 N	108.20 W
Meadow Lake ⊜, N.Y., U.S.	276	40.44 N	73.50 W
Meadow Lake Provincial Park ✦	184	54.28 N	109.10 W
Meadow Lands	214	40.13 N	80.13 W
Meadowlands Sports Complex ✦	276	40.49 N	74.05 W
Meadowlark Airport ⊠	280	33.43 N	118.02 W
Meadowood, De., U.S.	285	39.43 N	75.47 W
Meadowood, Md., U.S.	284c	39.04 N	77.00 W
Meadows	168b	35.11 S	138.46 E
Meadows, Island of I	276	40.34 N	74.12 W
Meadows Field ⊠	226	35.26 N	119.03 W
Meadowvale ◆ 8	275b	43.37 N	79.43 W
Meadow Valley Wash V	204	36.39 N	114.35 W
Meadowview	192	36.46 N	81.52 W
Meadow Vista	226	39.06 N	121.01 W
Meads Creek ≃	210	42.10 N	77.07 W
Meadville, Ms., U.S.	194	31.28 N	90.53 W
Meadville, Mo., U.S.	194	39.47 N	93.18 W
Meadville, Pa., U.S.	214	41.38 N	80.09 W
Meaford	212	44.36 N	80.35 W
Meaghers Grant	186	44.55 N	63.15 W
Me-akan-dake ∧	92a	43.23 N	144.01 E
Mealasta Isle I	46	58.05 N	7.08 W
Mealhada	34	40.22 N	8.27 W
Méan	56	50.22 N	5.20 E
Meana	128	36.55 N	60.30 E
Meana Sardo	71	39.57 N	9.04 E
Meandarra	166	27.19 S	149.53 E
Meander Creek Reservoir ⊜ 1	214	41.09 N	80.47 W
Meander River	176	59.02 N	117.42 W
Mearim ≃	250	3.04 S	44.35 W
Measham	42	52.43 N	1.29 W
Meath □ 6	48	53.35 N	6.40 W
Meath □ 9	48	53.40 N	7.00 W
Meaux	50	48.57 N	2.52 E
Meaux-Esbly, Aérodrome de ⊠	261	48.55 N	2.50 E
Mebane	192	36.05 N	79.16 W
Mebisere	273a	6.42 N	3.31 E
Mebtoûh, Oued el ≃	34	35.16 N	0.32 W
Meča ≃	82	54.50 N	39.10 E
Meca, La → Makkah	144	21.27 N	39.49 E
Mecanhelas	154	15.12 S	35.54 E
Mecatán	234	21.32 N	105.08 W
Mecatlán	234	20.13 N	97.41 W
Mecaya ≃	246	0.29 N	75.11 W
Mecca → Makkah	144	21.27 N	39.49 E
Mečebilovo	78	49.04 N	36.41 E
Mečetinskaja	78	46.46 N	40.27 E
Mečetka	78	50.54 N	40.05 E
Mechanic Falls	188	44.06 N	70.23 W
Mechanicsburg, Il., U.S.	219	39.48 N	89.24 W
Mechanicsburg, In., U.S.	218	40.09 N	86.28 W
Mechanicsburg, Oh., U.S.	218	40.04 N	83.33 W
Mechanicsburg, Pa., U.S.	208	40.12 N	77.00 W
Mechanicstown, N.Y., U.S.	210	41.27 N	74.24 W
Mechanicstown, Oh., U.S.	214	40.37 N	80.57 W
Mechanicsville, Ia., U.S.	190	41.54 N	91.15 W
Mechanicsville, Md., U.S.	208	38.26 N	76.44 W
Mechanicsville, Va., U.S.	192	37.36 N	77.22 W
Mechanicville	210	42.54 N	73.41 W
Mechara	144	8.32 N	40.22 E
Mechelen (Malines)	50	51.02 N	4.28 E
Mechel'ta	84	42.48 N	46.30 E
Mechernich	56	50.35 N	6.38 E
Mechī □ 8	124	27.15 N	87.45 E
Mechī ≃	124	26.14 N	87.58 E
Mechita	252	35.04 S	60.24 W
Mechlin → Mechelen	50	51.02 N	4.28 E
Mechonskoje	86	56.09 N	64.34 E
Mechra Safsaf	34	34.52 N	2.36 W
Mechren'ga	24	61.46 N	40.57 E
Mechrenga ≃	24	63.15 N	41.20 E
Mechriyya	148	33.35 N	0.18 W
Mechroha	36	36.21 N	7.51 E
Mecidiye, Tür.	130	40.38 N	26.32 E
Mecidiye, Tür.	130	38.53 N	27.42 E
Mečigmen	180	65.28 N	172.05 W
Mečigmeskij zaliv ⊂	180	65.25 N	172.00 W
Meçitözü	130	40.31 N	35.19 E
Meckelfeld	52	53.25 N	10.01 E
Meckenbeuren	58	47.42 N	9.34 E
Meckenheim	56	50.37 N	7.07 E
Meckering	162	31.38 S	117.01 E
Meckesheim	56	49.19 N	8.49 E
Meckinghoven	263	51.37 N	7.19 E
Mecklenburg, Dtsch.	54	53.47 N	11.28 E
Mecklenburg, N.Y., U.S.	210	42.27 N	76.43 W
Mecklenburg □ 9	54	53.30 N	13.00 E
Mecklenburger Bucht ⊂	54	54.20 N	11.40 E
Mecklenburgische Seenplatte ◆ 1	54	53.30 N	12.00 E
Mecklenburg-Vorpommern □ 3	30	53.45 N	12.30 E
Meclov	60	49.31 N	12.52 E
Meco	210	43.03 N	74.23 W
Mecoacán	234	18.23 N	93.07 W
Mecoacán, Laguna ⊂	234	18.22 N	93.09 W
Meconta	154	14.49 S	39.50 E
Mecox Bay ⊂	207	40.54 N	72.20 W
Mecque, La → Makkah	144	21.27 N	39.49 E
Mecsek ⋏	30	46.15 N	18.05 E
Mecubúri	154	14.39 S	38.54 E
Mecubúri ≃	154	14.10 S	40.31 E
Mecúfi	154	13.17 S	40.30 E
Mecula	154	12.04 S	37.40 E
Meda, It.	62	45.40 N	9.09 E
Meda, Port.	34	40.58 N	7.16 W
Medak	122	18.02 N	78.16 E
Medākul	126	23.03 N	90.11 E
Médan, Fr.	261	48.57 N	2.00 E
Medan, Indon.	114	3.35 N	98.40 E
Medang	114	2.06 N	101.38 E
Medang, Pulau I	115b	8.09 S	117.23 E
Medang, Tanjung ≻	114	2.08 N	101.39 E
Médanos	252	38.50 S	62.41 W
Medanosa, Punta ≻	254	48.06 S	65.55 W
Medaryville	216	41.04 N	86.53 W
Mede	62	45.06 N	8.44 E
Medebach	56	51.12 N	8.42 E
Medeiros Neto	255	17.20 S	40.14 W
Medel, Val V	58	46.37 N	8.50 E
Medellín, Col.	246	6.15 N	75.35 W
Medellin, Pil.	116	11.08 N	123.58 E
Medelpad □ 9	26	62.40 N	16.15 E
Medemblik	52	52.46 N	5.06 E
Měděnec	54	50.25 N	13.05 E
Medenica	78	49.26 N	23.45 E
Médenine	148	33.21 N	10.30 E
Médenine □ 8	148	32.00 N	10.00 E
Mederdra	150	16.55 N	15.39 W
Medesano	64	44.45 N	10.08 E
Medevi	40	58.40 N	14.57 E
Medfield	207	42.11 N	71.18 W
Medford, Ma., U.S.	207	42.25 N	71.06 W
Medford, N.J., U.S.	208	39.54 N	74.49 W
Medford, N.Y., U.S.	210	40.49 N	73.00 W
Medford, Ok., U.S.	196	36.48 N	97.44 W
Medford, Or., U.S.	202	42.19 N	122.52 W
Medford, Wi., U.S.	190	45.08 N	90.20 W
Medford Farms	285	39.52 N	74.45 W
Medford Lakes	285	39.51 N	74.48 W
Medfra	180	63.06 N	154.44 W
Medgidia	38	44.15 N	28.16 E
Medgyes → Mediaș	38	46.10 N	24.21 E
Medi	154	5.04 N	30.44 E
Media	208	39.55 N	75.23 W
Mediapolis	190	41.00 N	91.09 W
Mediaș	38	46.10 N	24.21 E
Medical Lake	202	47.34 N	117.40 W
Medicina	66	44.28 N	11.38 E
Medicine Bow	200	41.53 N	106.12 W
Medicine Bow ≃	200	42.00 N	106.40 W
Medicine Bow Mountains ⋏	200	41.10 N	106.10 W
Medicine Bow Peak ∧	200	41.21 N	106.19 W
Medicine Creek ≃, Mo., U.S.	194	39.43 N	93.24 W
Medicine Creek ≃, Ne., U.S.	198	40.17 N	100.10 W
Medicine Creek ≃, S.D., U.S.	198	44.06 N	99.42 W
Medicine Hat	184	50.03 N	110.40 W
Medicine Knoll Creek ≃	198	44.19 N	100.05 W
Medicine Lake	198	48.30 N	104.30 W
Medicine Lodge	198	37.16 N	98.34 W
Medicine Lodge ≃	196	36.49 N	98.20 W
Medicine Rocks State Park ✦	198	46.01 N	104.35 W
Medina, Bra.	255	16.15 S	41.29 W
Medina, Pil.	116	8.55 N	125.01 E
Medina, N.Y., U.S.	210	43.13 N	78.23 W
Medina, N.D., U.S.	198	46.53 N	99.17 W
Medina, Oh., U.S.	214	41.08 N	81.51 W
Medina, Tx., U.S.	196	29.48 N	99.15 W
Medina, Wa., U.S.	224	47.37 N	122.13 W
Medina □ 6	214	41.08 N	81.52 W
Medina ≃	196	29.12 N	98.20 W
Medina → Al-Madīnah	128	24.28 N	39.36 E
Medinaceli	34	41.10 N	2.26 W
Medina del Campo	34	41.18 N	4.55 W
Medina de Ríoseco	34	41.53 N	5.02 W
Médina Gonasse	150	13.08 N	13.45 W
Medinah	278	41.59 N	88.01 W
Medina Lake ⊜ 1	196	29.35 N	98.58 W
Médina Sabak	150	13.36 N	15.35 W
Medina-Sidonia	34	36.27 N	5.55 W
Medinat al-Faiyum → Al-Fayyūm	142	29.19 N	30.50 E
Medininkai	76	54.32 N	25.40 E
Medinīpur	126	22.26 N	87.20 E
Medino	164	9.40 S	149.40 E
Medio, Arroyo del ≃	258	33.49 S	57.43 W
Medio, Punta ≻	252	27.07 S	70.57 W
Medio Creek ≃	196	28.19 N	97.19 W
Mediterranean Sea ⊤ 2	10	35.00 N	20.00 E
Mediterraneo, Mare → Mediterranean Sea ⊤ 2	10	35.00 N	20.00 E
Medjana	34	36.08 N	4.41 E
Medje	154	2.25 N	27.18 E
Medjerda, Monts de la ⋏	36	36.35 N	8.15 E
Medkovec	38	43.37 N	23.10 E
Mednogorsk	86	51.24 N	57.37 E
Mednoje	76	56.56 N	35.29 E
Mednyj, ostrov I	74	54.45 N	167.35 E
Médoc ◆ 1	32	45.20 N	1.00 W
Mêdog	120	29.20 N	95.15 E
Medolla	64	44.51 N	11.04 E
Medora, Il., U.S.	219	39.11 N	90.09 W
Medora, In., U.S.	218	38.49 N	86.10 W
Medora, N.D., U.S.	198	46.54 N	103.31 W
Médouneu	152	0.57 N	10.47 E
Medow	54	53.50 N	13.32 E
Medstead, Sk., Can.	184	53.19 N	108.02 W
Medstead, Eng., U.K.	42	51.08 N	1.04 W
Medua	126	22.38 N	90.44 E
Meductic	186	46.00 N	67.29 W
Medulla	220	27.58 N	81.58 W
Međumurje ◆ 1	61	46.25 N	16.30 E
Meduna ≃	64	45.49 N	12.34 E
Medveđa	38	42.50 N	21.35 E
Medvedevo, Ross.	76	60.02 N	43.01 E
Medvedevo, Ross.	80	56.37 N	47.47 E
Medvedevo, Ross.	86	60.37 N	77.21 E
Medvedevskoje	76	58.58 N	35.58 E
Medvedica ≃, Ross.	76	57.05 N	37.32 E
Medvedica ≃, Ross.	80	49.35 N	42.41 E
Medvedickij	80	50.47 N	44.43 E
Medvědí hora ∧	60	48.59 N	13.25 E
Medvedkovo ◆ 8	265b	55.53 N	37.38 E
Medvedok	80	57.23 N	50.05 E
Medvedovskaja	78	45.27 N	39.01 E
Medvenka, Ross.	78	51.26 N	36.07 E
Medvenka, Ross.	82	54.15 N	37.42 E
Medvežij, ostrov I	89	54.41 N	136.18 E
Medvežinka	83	48.10 N	39.31 E
Medvežje, ozero ⊜	86	55.07 N	68.00 E
Medvežjegorsk	24	62.55 N	34.23 E
Medvežji ostrova II	74	70.52 N	161.26 E
Medvežji ozera ⊜	265b	55.52 N	38.00 E
Medvežji Oz'ora	265b	55.52 N	37.59 E
Medvežskaja	24	64.57 N	57.34 E
Medviagalis ∧ 2	76	55.38 N	22.45 E
Medvin	78	49.23 N	30.47 E
Medv'onka ≃	265b	55.44 N	37.12 E
Medway, Ma., U.S.	207	42.08 N	71.23 W
Medway, Oh., U.S.	218	39.53 N	83.59 W
Medway □ 8	260	51.24 N	0.31 E
Medway ≃, N.S., Can.	186	44.08 N	64.36 W
Medway ≃, Eng., U.K.	42	51.27 N	0.44 E
Medyn'	82	54.58 N	35.52 E
Medynka ≃	82	54.44 N	36.02 E
Medynskij Zavorot, mys ≻	24	68.58 N	59.17 E
Medžibož	78	49.26 N	27.25 E
Medzilaborce	30	49.16 N	21.55 E
Meeberrie	162	26.58 S	115.58 E
Meekatharra	162	26.36 S	118.29 E
Meeker, Co., U.S.	200	40.02 N	107.54 W
Meeker, Oh., U.S.	214	40.39 N	83.18 W
Meeks Bay	226	39.02 N	120.08 W
Meelpaeg Lake ⊜ 1	186	48.16 N	56.35 W
Meenaar	168a	31.38 S	116.53 E
Meentheena	162	21.17 S	120.28 E
Meer	52	51.27 N	4.44 E
Meeralpen → Maritime Alps ⋏	62	44.15 N	7.10 E
Meerane	54	50.51 N	12.28 E
Meerbeck	263	51.28 N	6.39 E
Meerbeke	50	50.50 N	4.02 E
Meerbusch	56	51.15 N	6.41 E
Meerhout	56	51.08 N	5.05 E
Meerhusener Moor ◆ 3	52	53.35 N	7.30 E
Meerkerk	52	51.45 N	5.00 E
Meerle	52	51.28 N	4.48 E
Meersburg	58	47.41 N	9.16 E
Meerssen	56	50.53 N	5.45 E
Meerut	124	28.59 N	77.42 E
Meese ≃	42	52.40 N	2.39 W
Meeteetse	202	44.09 N	108.52 W
Mega, Indon.	164	0.41 S	131.53 E
Mega, Ityo.	144	4.07 N	38.16 E
Mega, Pulau I	112	4.00 S	101.02 E
Megalo	144	6.55 N	41.48 E
Megálon Khoríon	38	36.27 N	27.21 E
Megalópolis	38	37.24 N	22.08 E
Meganom, mys ≻	78	44.48 N	35.05 E
Mégantic □ 6	206	46.10 N	71.30 W
Mégantic, Lac ⊜	188	45.32 N	70.53 W
Mégantic, Mont ∧	206	45.28 N	71.09 W
Mégara	38	38.01 N	23.21 E
Megargel	196	33.27 N	98.56 W
Mégaron, Kólpos ⊂	267c	37.56 N	23.20 E
Megaruma ≃	154	13.28 S	40.32 E
Megasini ∧	126	21.38 N	86.21 E
Meget	88	52.24 N	104.03 E
Megève	62	45.52 N	6.37 E
Mégevette	58	46.12 N	6.30 E
Megezez ∧	144	9.17 N	39.32 E
Megget Reservoir ⊜ 1	46	55.29 N	3.17 W
Meghālaya □ 3	120	25.30 N	91.15 E
Meghna ≃	120	22.50 N	90.50 E
Megi-jima I	96	34.24 N	134.03 E
Mégiscane ≃	190	48.29 N	77.08 W
Mégiscane, Lac ⊜	190	48.35 N	75.55 W
Meglino, ozero ⊜	76	58.25 N	35.07 E
Megra, Ross.	24	66.09 N	41.37 E
Megra, Ross.	76	60.10 N	37.13 E
Megri	84	38.56 N	46.16 E
Meguro ◆ 8	268	35.38 N	139.42 E
Meguro ≃	268	35.37 N	139.45 E
Mehadia	38	44.55 N	22.22 E
Méhaigne ≃	56	50.32 N	5.13 E
Mehaïguene, Oued V	148	32.15 N	2.59 E
Mehakit	112	2.51 S	115.57 E
Mehar	120	27.11 N	67.49 E
Meharry, Mount ∧	162	22.59 S	118.35 E
Mehdia	148	35.25 N	1.45 E
Mehedeby	40	60.27 N	17.24 E
Mehedinți □ 6	38	44.30 N	22.50 E
Meheisa	140	19.38 N	32.57 E
Mehekar	122	20.09 N	76.34 E
Mehendiganj	124	22.49 N	90.42 E
Meherpur	124	23.46 N	88.38 E
Meherrin ≃	192	36.26 N	76.57 W
Mehetia I	14	17.52 S	148.03 W
Mehidpur	120	23.49 N	75.40 E
Mehikoorma	76	58.14 N	27.28 E
Mehlteuer	54	50.32 N	12.02 E
Mehlville	219	38.30 N	90.19 W
Mehnagar	124	25.53 N	83.07 E
Mehndāwal	124	26.59 N	83.07 E
Mehoopany	210	41.34 N	76.04 W
Mehoopany Creek ≃	210	41.34 N	76.03 W
Mehpālpur ◆ 8	272a	28.33 N	77.08 E
Mehr	52	51.43 N	6.29 E
Mehrābād	128	36.53 N	47.55 E
Mehrābād ◆ 8	267d	35.40 N	51.20 E
Mehram Nagar ◆ 8	272a	28.34 N	77.07 E
Mehrān	128	33.07 N	46.10 E
Mehrān ≃	128	26.52 N	55.24 E
Mehring	56	49.48 N	6.49 E
Mehrīz	128	31.35 N	54.28 E
Mehrow	264a	52.34 N	13.37 E
Mehrum	263	51.35 N	6.37 E
Mè-hsa-tè	110	19.33 N	97.38 E
Mehtarlām	120	34.39 N	70.10 E
Mehun-sur-Yèvre	50	47.09 N	2.13 E
Mei ≃, Zhg.	100	24.24 N	116.34 E
Mei ≃, Zhg.	100	26.00 N	115.23 E
Mei ≃, Zhg.	105	39.21 N	117.50 E
Meia Meia	154	5.49 S	35.48 E
Meia Ponte, Rio da ≃	255	18.32 S	49.36 W
Meichang	105	39.22 N	117.10 E
Meichuan	100	30.10 N	115.36 E
Meicun, Zhg.	100	25.30 N	116.56 E
Meicun, Zhg.	106	30.22 N	119.01 E
Meicun, Zhg.	106	30.40 N	119.04 E
Meicun, Zhg.	106	31.33 N	120.24 E
Meide	263	51.11 N	6.55 E
Meiderich ◆ 8	263	51.28 N	6.46 E
Meidling ◆ 8	264b	48.11 N	16.20 E
Meierij ◆ 1	52	51.35 N	5.40 E
Meierkaisong	120	30.54 N	84.31 E
Meiersberg	263	51.17 N	6.57 E
Meig ≃	46	57.34 N	4.41 W
Meiganga	152	6.31 N	14.11 E
Meigle	46	56.35 N	3.09 W
Meigs	192	31.04 N	84.05 W
Meigs Field ⊠	278	41.51 N	87.36 W
Meihsien → Meixian	100	24.21 N	116.08 E
Meihua	100	26.02 N	119.40 E
Meihuajie	100	25.14 N	113.05 E
Meijel	52	51.21 N	5.53 E
Meijino-Mori-Minō-kokutei-kōen ✦	94	34.51 N	135.29 E
Meiji Shrine ʋ 1	268	35.41 N	139.42 E
Meikeng	100	23.59 N	114.05 E
Meikle Millyea ∧	44	55.07 N	4.19 W
Meikle Says Law ∧	46	55.55 N	2.40 W
Meiktila	110	20.52 N	95.52 E
Meila	54	51.09 N	13.13 E
Meilen	58	47.16 N	8.38 E
Meili	106	31.42 N	120.53 E
Meilie	100	26.18 N	117.38 E
Meilin, Zhg.	100	23.18 N	115.58 E
Meilin, Zhg.	106	30.35 N	119.04 E
Meillerie	58	46.24 N	6.43 E
Meilong	100	22.56 N	115.17 E
Meilunyingzi	104	42.18 N	122.10 E
Meina	62	45.47 N	8.32 E
Meine	52	52.23 N	10.32 E
Meiners Oaks	228	34.26 N	119.17 W
Meinerzhagen	56	51.06 N	7.38 E
Meiningen	54	50.34 N	10.25 E
Meinung	100	22.54 N	120.32 E
Meio, Ilha do I	287a	23.02 S	43.17 W
Meiringen	58	46.43 N	8.12 E
Meisburg	56	50.06 N	6.41 E
Meisenheim	56	49.42 N	7.40 E
Meishan, Zhg.	106	31.06 N	119.43 E
Meishan, Zhg.	107	30.02 N	103.49 E
Meissen	54	51.10 N	13.28 E
Meissendorf	52	52.43 N	9.50 E
Meiss Lake ⊜	204	41.52 N	122.04 W
Meissner ∧	56	51.12 N	9.50 E
Meitan	102	27.46 N	107.35 E
Meitian	100	25.21 N	112.47 E
Meitingen	56	48.32 N	10.50 E
Meiwa	94	34.33 N	136.39 E
Meixi	106	30.48 N	119.45 E
Meixian, Zhg.	100	24.21 N	116.08 E
Meixian, Zhg.	100	28.52 N	113.38 E
Meiyao	89	49.37 N	124.30 E
Meiyino	140	6.12 N	34.40 E
Meizhai	102	25.30 N	108.50 E
Meizhou	100	23.50 N	117.20 E
Meizhou Dao I	100	25.06 N	119.07 E
Meizhou Wan ⊂	100	25.06 N	119.00 E
Meizhu	106	31.16 N	119.13 E
Meječkyn, ostrov I	180	65.26 N	178.00 W
Mejerda, Oued (Oued Medjerda) ≃	36	37.07 N	10.13 E
Mejez el Bab	148	36.39 N	9.37 E
Mejia	126	23.34 N	87.06 E
Mejicanos	236	13.43 N	89.12 W
Mejillones	252	23.06 S	70.27 W
Mejillones, Península ≻ 1	252	23.17 S	70.34 W
Mejillones del Sur, Bahía de ⊂	252	23.03 S	70.27 W
Mejnypil'gyno	74	62.32 N	177.02 E
Mejorada del Campo	266a	40.24 N	3.29 W
Meka	162	27.26 S	116.48 E
Mekada, Garaet el ≋	36	36.48 N	8.00 E
Mékambo	152	1.01 N	13.56 E
Mekele	144	13.33 N	39.30 E
Mekerra, Oued ≃	34	35.00 N	0.45 W
Mekhé	150	15.07 N	16.38 W
Mekhliganj	124	26.21 N	88.55 E
Mekhtar	120	30.28 N	69.22 E
Mékinac ≃	206	46.51 N	72.46 W
Mekka → Makkah	144	21.27 N	39.49 E
Meknès	148	33.53 N	5.37 W
Meknès □ 4	148	33.50 N	5.30 W
Mekong ≃	12	10.33 N	105.24 E
Mekongga, Gunung ∧	112	3.38 S	121.15 E
Mekongga, Pegunungan ⋏	112	3.35 S	121.15 E
Mékôngk → Mekong ≃	12	10.33 N	105.24 E
Mekoryuk	180	60.23 N	166.12 W
Mékrou ≃	150	12.24 N	2.49 E
Mel	64	46.04 N	12.05 E
Melado ≃	252	35.43 S	71.05 W
Melah, Oued el V, Alg.	148	28.21 N	6.00 E
Melah, Oued el V, Tun.	148	34.03 N	8.06 E
Melah, Sebkhet el ⊜	148	29.05 N	1.10 W
Melaka	114	2.12 N	102.15 E
Melaka □ 3	114	2.15 N	102.15 E
Melalap	112	5.14 N	116.00 E
Melandro ≃	68	40.37 N	15.27 E
Melanesia II	14	13.00 S	164.00 E
Melanesian Basin ✧ 1	14	0.05 N	160.35 E
Melappālaiyam	122	8.42 N	77.43 E
Melara	64	45.03 N	11.11 E
Melaune	54	51.11 N	14.44 E
Melawi ≃	112	0.05 N	111.29 E
Melayu ≃	271c	1.27 N	103.42 E
Melbern	216	41.28 N	84.39 W
Melbost	46	58.15 N	6.22 W
Melbourn	42	52.05 N	0.01 E
Melbourne, Austl.	169	37.49 S	144.58 E
Melbourne, Austl.	274b	37.49 S	144.58 E
Melbourne, On., Can.	214	42.49 N	81.33 W
Melbourne, Eng., U.K.	42	52.49 N	1.25 W
Melbourne, Ar., U.S.	194	36.03 N	91.54 W
Melbourne, Fl., U.S.	220	28.04 N	80.36 W

Symbol	English	Deutsch	Español	Français	Português
≃	River	Fluß	Río	Rivière	Rio
≡	Canal	Kanal	Canal	Canal	Canal
⸦	Waterfall, Rapids	Wasserfall, Stromschnellen	Cascada, Rápidos	Chute d'eau, Rapides	Cascata, Rápidos
ʯ	Strait	Meeresstraße	Estrecho	Détroit	Estreito
⊂	Bay, Gulf	Bucht, Golf	Bahía, Golfo	Baie, Golfe	Baía, Golfo
⊜	Lake, Lakes	See, Seen	Lago, Lagos	Lac, Lacs	Lago, Lagos
≋	Swamp	Sumpf	Pantano	Marais	Pântano
⊓	Ice Features, Glacier	Eis- und Gletscherformen	Accidentes Glaciales	Formes glaciaires	Acidentes glaciares
⊤	Other Hydrographic Features	Andere Hydrographische Objekte	Otros Elementos Hidrográficos	Autres données hydrographiques	Outros acidentes hidrográficos

Symbol	English	Deutsch	Español	Français	Português
✧	Submarine Features	Untermeerische Objekte	Accidentes Submarinos	Formes de relief sous-marin	Acidentes submarinos
□	Political Unit	Politische Einheit	Unidad Política	Entité politique	Unidade política
ʋ	Cultural Institution	Kulturelle Institution	Institución Cultural	Institution culturelle	Instituição cultural
⊥	Historical Site	Historische Stätte	Sitio Histórico	Site historique	Sitio histórico
✦	Recreational Site	Erholungs- und Ferienort	Sitio de Recreo	Centre de loisirs	Área de Lazer
⊠	Airport	Flughafen	Aeropuerto	Aéroport	Aeroporto
■	Military Installation	Militäranlage	Instalación Militar	Installation militaire	Instalação militar
◆	Miscellaneous	Verschiedenes	Misceláneo	Divers	Diversos

ESPAÑOL · FRANÇAIS · PORTUGUÊS

Nombre / Nom / Nome	Página / Page / Página	Lat.°′	Long.°′ W = Oeste / W = Ouest / W = Oeste
Metschow	54	53.49 N	12.58 E
Metsematluku	156	24.01 S	24.40 E
Metsera	154	2.35 S	26.07 E
Métsovon	38	39.46 N	21.11 E
Mettawa	278	42.14 N	87.56 W
Metten	60	48.52 N	12.55 E
Mettendorf	56	49.57 N	6.19 E
Metter	192	32.23 N	82.03 W
Mettet	56	50.19 N	4.40 E
Mettetal Airport ⊠	281	42.21 N	83.27 W
Mettingen	52	52.18 N	7.46 E
Mettlach	56	49.30 N	6.36 E
Mettmach	60	48.10 N	13.21 E
Mettmann	56	51.15 N	6.58 E
Mettray	50	47.27 N	0.39 E
Mettuppālaiyam	122	11.18 N	76.57 E
Mettūr	122	11.48 N	77.48 E
Metu	144	8.20 N	35.36 E
Metuchen	210	40.32 N	74.21 W
Metuge	154	12.58 S	40.20 E
Metulla	132	33.16 N	35.35 E
Metundo, Ilha I	154	11.10 S	40.41 E
Metz	56	49.08 N	6.10 E
Metzervisse	56	49.19 N	6.17 E
Metzger	224	45.26 N	122.45 W
Metzingen	56	48.32 N	9.17 E
Metzkausen	263	51.16 N	6.57 E
Metztitlán	234	20.36 N	98.45 W
Metztitlán, Laguna ⊜	234	20.40 N	98.50 W
Meu ≃	32	48.02 N	1.47 W
Meudon	261	48.48 N	2.14 E
Meudon, Bois de ♠	261	48.47 N	2.12 E
Meul ≃	158	27.56 S	28.50 E
Meulaboh	114	4.09 N	96.08 E
Meulan	50	49.01 N	1.54 E
Meulebeke	50	50.57 N	3.17 E
Meung-sur-Loire	50	47.50 N	1.42 E
Meureubo ≃	114	4.09 N	96.09 E
Meureudu	114	5.16 N	96.16 E
Meursault	58	46.59 N	4.46 E
Meurthe ≃	32	48.47 N	6.09 E
Meurthe-et-Moselle □[5]	32	48.35 N	6.10 E
Meuse	58	47.59 N	5.33 E
Meuse □[5]	56	49.00 N	5.30 E
Meuse (Maas) ≃	30	51.49 N	5.01 E
Meuselwitz	54	51.02 N	12.17 E
Meuvette ≃	50	48.45 N	1.08 E
Meux Creek ≃	212	44.07 N	81.02 W
Mevagissey	42	50.16 N	4.48 W
Mevang	152	0.07 N	11.05 E
Mewāt Plain ≚	124	27.40 N	77.15 E
Mexborough	44	53.30 N	1.17 W
Mexia	222	31.40 N	96.28 W
Mexia Lake ⊜[1]	222	31.39 N	96.36 W
Mexiana, Ilha I	250	0.02 S	49.35 W
Mexicali	232	32.40 N	115.29 W
Mexican Hat	200	37.09 N	109.52 W
Mexico, In., U.S.	216	40.49 N	86.06 W
Mexico, Me., U.S.	188	44.33 N	70.32 W
Mexico, Mo., U.S.	219	39.10 N	91.52 W
Mexico, N.Y., U.S.	212	43.27 N	76.13 W
Mexico, Pa., U.S.	208	40.32 N	77.21 W
México □[3]	234	19.20 N	99.45 W
Mexico (México) □[1], N.A.	230	23.00 N	102.00 W
Mexico (México) □[1], N.A.	232	23.00 N	102.00 W
México, Golfo de → Mexico, Gulf of ⊂	230	25.00 N	90.00 W
Mexico, Gulf of ⊂	230	25.00 N	90.00 W
Mexico Basin ✦[1]	16	25.00 N	92.00 W
Mexico Bay ⊂	212	43.31 N	76.17 W
Mexico Beach	192	29.58 N	85.24 W
Mexico City → Ciudad de México	234	19.24 N	99.09 W
Mexiko, Golf von → Mexico, Gulf of ⊂	230	25.00 N	90.00 W
Mexiko → Ciudad de México	234	19.24 N	99.09 W
Mexiko → Mexico □[1]	232	23.00 N	102.00 W
Meximieux	58	45.54 N	5.12 E
Mexique, Golfe du → Mexico, Gulf of ⊂	230	25.00 N	90.00 W
Mexique → Mexico □[1]	230	23.00 N	102.00 W
Mexticacán	234	21.13 N	102.43 W
Mey, Castle of ⊥	46	58.38 N	3.14 W
Meyanodas	164	7.38 S	131.38 E
Meycauayan	116	14.44 N	120.58 E
Meydan	130	38.21 N	41.47 E
Meydancık	130	41.25 N	42.14 E
Meydān-e Gel ≚	128	29.04 N	54.50 E
Meydān Khvolah	120	33.36 N	69.51 E
Meyenburg	54	53.18 N	12.14 E
Meyers Chuck	182	55.44 N	132.15 W
Meyersdale	188	39.48 N	79.01 W
Meyers Lake	214	40.52 N	81.24 W
Meyersville	222	28.55 N	97.21 W
Meyerton	158	26.33 S	28.01 E
Meyísti I	130	36.08 N	29.34 E
Meymac	32	45.32 N	2.09 E
Meymaneh	120	35.55 N	64.47 E
Meymeh	128	33.27 N	51.10 E
Meymeh ≃	128	32.05 N	47.16 E
Meynypilgino	180	62.32 N	177.02 E
Meyo Centre	152	2.33 N	11.02 E
Meyrargues	62	43.38 N	5.32 E
Meyrin	58	46.14 N	6.05 E
Meyronne	184	49.39 N	106.50 W
Meyrueis	32	44.10 N	3.26 E
Meyungs	175b	7.20 N	134.27 E
Meža ≃	61	46.35 N	15.02 E
Mezada, Horvot (Masada) ⊥	132	31.19 N	35.21 E
Mezapa	236	15.33 N	87.23 W
Mezcala	234	17.56 N	99.37 W
Mezcala ≃	234	18.00 N	99.47 W
Mezcalapa	234	17.37 N	93.22 W
Mezcalapa ≃	234	18.00 N	92.54 W
Mezdra	38	43.09 N	23.42 E
Meždurečensk	86	53.42 N	88.03 E
Meždurečenskij	86	59.36 N	65.53 E
Mèze	32	43.25 N	3.36 E
Mézel	62	43.59 N	6.12 E
Mezen′	24	65.50 N	44.13 E
Mezen′ ≃	24	66.11 N	43.59 E
Mézenc, Mont ∧	62	44.55 N	4.11 E
Mezenskaja guba ⊂	24	66.40 N	43.45 E
Meževaja	78	48.16 N	36.44 E
Mežgorje	78	48.32 N	23.30 E
Meziadin Lake ⊜	182	56.04 N	129.18 W
Mežica	61	46.31 N	14.52 E
Mézières-en-Brenne	32	46.49 N	1.13 E
Mézières-sur-Seine	261	48.58 N	1.48 E
Mézilhac	62	44.48 N	4.21 E
Mézin	32	44.03 N	0.16 E
Mezinovskij	76	55.30 N	40.21 E
Mežirič	78	50.43 N	34.29 E
Mezőberény	30	46.50 N	21.02 E
Mezőcsát	30	47.49 N	20.55 E
Mezőkovácsháza	30	46.25 N	20.55 E
Mezőkövesd	30	47.50 N	20.34 E
Mezőtúr	30	47.00 N	20.38 E
Mežoz′ornyj	86	54.09 N	59.23 E
Mezquital	234	23.29 N	104.23 W
Mezquital ≃	232	22.35 N	104.54 W
Mezquital del Oro	234	21.10 N	103.23 W
Mezquitic	234	22.23 N	103.41 W
Mezraa	130	41.12 N	35.08 E
Mézy	261	49.00 N	1.53 E
Mezzana	64	46.19 N	10.48 E
Mezzano	64	46.09 N	11.48 E
Mezzenile	62	45.17 N	7.23 E
Mezzocorona	64	46.13 N	11.07 E
Mezzoiuso	70	37.52 N	13.28 E
Mezzola, Lago di ⊜	58	46.12 N	9.26 E
Mezzoldo	58	46.01 N	9.40 E
Mezzolombardo	64	46.13 N	11.05 E
Mezzomerico	266b	45.37 N	8.36 E
Mfangano Island I	154	0.28 S	34.01 E
Mfolozi ≃	158	28.25 S	32.26 E
Mfou	152	3.43 N	11.38 E
Mfuwe	154	13.04 S	31.46 E
Mgači	89	51.05 N	142.17 E
Mgeni ≃	158	29.48 S	31.02 E
Mgeta	154	8.19 S	36.08 E
Mglin	76	53.04 N	32.51 E
M′goun, Irhil ∧	148	31.31 N	6.25 W
M′hai, B′nom ∧	110	11.21 N	107.50 E
Mhasvād	122	17.38 N	74.47 E
Mhlatuze ≃	158	28.47 S	32.06 E
Mhlume	158	26.02 S	31.50 E
Mholach, Beinn ∧[2]	46	56.45 N	4.18 W
Mhòr, Beinn ∧	46	57.17 N	7.19 W
Mhòr, Loch ⊜	46	57.14 N	4.26 W
Mhow	120	22.33 N	75.46 E
Mi ≃, Zhg.	98	37.12 N	119.10 E
Mi ≃, Zhg.	100	27.09 N	112.51 E
Mia, Oued V	148	30.47 N	4.54 E
Miacatlán	234	18.46 N	99.22 W
Mia-dong ◆[8]	271b	37.37 N	127.01 E
Miagao	116	10.39 N	122.14 E
Miahuatlán de Porfirio Díaz	234	16.20 N	96.36 W
Miajadas	34	39.09 N	5.54 W
Miaméré	146	8.52 N	19.50 E
Miami, Mb., Can.	184	49.21 N	98.11 W
Miami, Az., U.S.	200	33.23 N	110.52 W
Miami, Fl., U.S.	220	25.46 N	80.11 W
Miami, In., U.S.	216	40.36 N	86.06 W
Miami, Ok., U.S.	196	36.52 N	94.52 W
Miami, Tx., U.S.	196	35.42 N	100.38 W
Miami □[6], In., U.S.	216	40.45 N	86.04 W
Miami □[6], Oh., U.S.	218	40.02 N	84.13 W
Miami ≃	224	45.33 N	123.53 W
Miami Beach, On., Can.	212	44.13 N	79.29 W
Miami Beach, Fl., U.S.	220	25.47 N	80.07 W
Miami Canal ≊	220	25.47 N	80.15 W
Miami Creek ≃	226	37.21 N	119.44 W
Miami International Airport ⊠	220	25.48 N	80.17 W
Miami Lakes	220	25.53 N	80.18 W
Miamisburg	218	39.38 N	84.17 W
Miamisburg Mound State Memorial ⊥	218	39.38 N	84.17 W
Miami Shores	220	25.51 N	80.11 W
Miami Springs	220	25.49 N	80.17 W
Miami State Recreation Area ♠	216	40.40 N	85.55 W
Miamiville	218	39.13 N	84.18 W
Miān Channūn	123	30.27 N	72.22 E
Mianchi	102	34.48 N	111.49 E
Mīāndoāb	128	36.58 N	46.06 E
Miandrivazo	157b	19.31 S	45.28 E
Mianduhe	89	49.05 N	121.06 E
Miane	64	45.57 N	12.06 E
Mīāneh	128	37.26 N	47.42 E
Miang, Phu ∧	110	17.42 N	101.01 E
Miangas, Pulau I	108	5.35 N	126.35 E
Mianhu	100	23.28 N	116.09 E
Mianhuadi	104	41.15 N	120.49 E
Miāni	123	32.32 N	73.04 E
Miāni Hōr ⊂	120	25.34 N	66.19 E
Mianning	102	28.39 N	102.09 E
Mianus ≃	207	41.03 N	73.35 W
Mianus, East Branch ≃	276	41.06 N	73.35 W
Mianus Reservoir ⊜[1]	276	41.08 N	73.37 W
Miānwāli	123	32.35 N	71.33 E
Mianxian	102	33.09 N	106.48 E
Mianyang, Zhg.	100	30.23 N	113.25 E
Mianyang, Zhg.	102	31.30 N	104.49 E
Mianzhu	102	31.20 N	104.09 E
Miao Dao I	98	37.56 N	120.45 E
Miaodao Qundao II	98	38.10 N	120.40 E
Miao′ergou	86	45.32 N	83.52 E
Miaofengshan	105	40.04 N	116.13 E
Miaogou	104	41.12 N	120.40 E
Miaojiagou	104	42.16 N	123.22 E
Miaojiatun	104	40.54 N	120.55 E
Miaokou	98	35.48 N	114.09 E
Miaoli	100	24.34 N	120.49 E
Miao Ling ⋀	102	26.15 N	107.26 E
Miaopu	106	31.00 N	118.44 E
Miaoqian	100	30.33 N	117.44 E
Miaotou	106	30.58 N	120.33 E
Miaowan	100	33.07 N	114.41 E
Miaoyang	98	40.49 N	124.24 E
Miaozhen	106	31.43 N	121.21 E
Miaozigou	107	30.17 N	104.35 E
Miarayon	116	8.04 N	124.50 E
Miarinarivo, Madag.	157b	16.38 S	48.15 E
Miarinarivo, Madag.	157b	18.57 S	46.55 E
Miarinavaratra	157b	20.13 S	47.31 E
Miasa	94	36.34 N	137.53 E
Miass	86	54.59 N	60.06 E
Miass ≃	86	56.06 N	64.30 E
Miasteczko Krajeńskie	30	53.06 N	17.01 E
Miastko	30	54.01 N	17.00 E
Miboro-dam ◆[6]	94	36.08 N	136.55 E
Mibu	94	36.25 N	139.48 E
Mibu ≃	94	35.49 N	137.57 E
Mica	156	24.10 S	30.48 E
Mica Mountain ∧	200	32.13 N	110.33 W
Micang Shan ⋀	102	32.45 N	107.20 E
Micanopy	192	29.30 N	82.16 W
Micaúne	156	18.18 S	36.35 E
Mičavičevnik	24	64.14 N	57.58 E
Miccosukee, Lake ⊜[1]	192	30.34 N	83.58 W
Miccosukee Indian Reservation ◆[4]	220	26.10 N	80.50 W
Michael, Mount ∧	164	6.25 S	145.20 E
Michael J. Kirwan Reservoir ⊜[1]	214	41.10 N	81.10 W
Michajlo-Koc′ubinskoje	78	51.27 N	31.04 E
Michajlov	82	54.14 N	39.02 E
Michajlovka, Kaz.	85	42.50 N	75.42 E
Michajlovka, Kaz.	85	43.06 N	71.36 E
Michajlovka, Kaz.	86	53.51 N	76.32 E
Michajlovka, Kyrg.	85	42.37 N	78.20 E
Michajlovka, Ross.	78	49.53 N	39.38 E
Michajlovka, Ross.	80	47.38 N	46.54 E
Michajlovka, Ross.	80	50.05 N	43.15 E
Michajlovka, Ross.	86	51.49 N	79.45 E
Michajlovka, Ross.	86	56.26 N	78.53 E
Michajlovka, Ross.	88	50.26 N	104.10 E
Michajlovka, Ross.	88	55.30 N	114.09 E
Michajlovka, Ross.	88	51.07 N	119.20 E
Michajlovka, Ross.	88	52.57 N	103.18 E
Michajlovka, Ross.	89	49.13 N	129.56 E
Michajlovka, Ross.	89	43.56 N	132.00 E
Michajlovka, Ross.	265a	60.04 N	30.14 E
Michajlovka, Ross.	265a	59.43 N	30.01 E
Michajlovka, Ukr.	78	49.19 N	36.28 E
Michajlovka, Ukr.	78	47.16 N	35.14 E
Michajlovka, Ukr.	83	48.30 N	38.54 E
Michajlovka, Ukr.	83	48.09 N	37.22 E
Michajlovka, Ukr.	83	48.44 N	37.16 E
Michajlovo	80	56.56 N	45.04 E
Michajlovo-Aleksandrovskij	83	49.13 N	40.15 E
Michajlovskaja	80	50.58 N	41.52 E
Michajlovskaja Celina, zapovednik ♠	78	50.45 N	34.10 E
Michajlovskij, Kaz.	86	50.17 N	55.23 E
Michajlovskij, Ross.	76	60.05 N	43.29 E
Michajlovskij, Ross.	86	51.41 N	79.47 E
Michajlovskoje, Ross.	76	58.23 N	37.40 E
Michajlovskoje, Ross.	80	56.11 N	45.47 E
Michajlovskoje, Ross.	82	55.50 N	36.20 E
Michajlovskoje, Ross.	265b	55.35 N	37.35 E
Michalevo	82	55.27 N	38.26 E
Michali	82	55.17 N	39.05 E
Michalkovo	82	54.11 N	37.33 E
Michalovce	30	48.45 N	21.55 E
Michalovy Hory	60	49.55 N	12.47 E
Michanoviči	76	53.45 N	27.40 E
Michaud, Point ›	186	45.34 N	60.40 W
Micheal Peak ∧	182	53.35 N	126.26 W
Michejevo	88	57.10 N	104.53 E
Michel	182	49.43 N	114.49 W
Michelago	171b	35.43 S	149.10 E
Michelau	56	50.10 N	11.06 E
Micheldever	42	51.09 N	1.15 W
Micheldorf in Oberösterreich	61	47.52 N	14.08 E
Michelsneukirchen	60	49.08 N	12.33 E
Michelson, Mount ∧	180	69.19 N	144.17 W
Michel′sonovskij	265b	55.42 N	37.54 E
Michelstadt	56	49.41 N	9.00 E
Michendorf	54	52.18 N	13.01 E
Miches	238	18.59 N	69.03 W
Micheta	84	41.52 N	44.44 E
Michiana	216	41.46 N	86.48 W
Michiana Regional Airport ⊠	216	41.42 N	86.19 W
Michigamme ≃	190	46.04 N	88.13 W
Michigan	198	48.01 N	98.07 W
Michigan □[3], U.S.	178	44.00 N	85.00 W
Michigan □[3], U.S.	190	44.00 N	85.00 W
Michigan ≃	200	40.52 N	106.20 W
Michigan, Lake ⊜	190	44.00 N	87.00 W
Michigan, University of ⊎[2]	281	42.17 N	83.44 W
Michigan Center	216	42.13 N	84.19 W
Michigan City	216	41.42 N	86.53 W
Michigan International Speedway ♠	216	42.03 N	84.15 W
Michigan Stadium ♠	281	42.16 N	83.45 W
Michigan State Fair Grounds ♠	281	42.27 N	83.07 W
Michigantown	216	40.19 N	86.23 W
Michika	146	10.38 N	13.24 E
Michillinda	280	34.07 N	118.05 W
Michinmahuida, Volcán ∧[1]	254	42.49 S	72.28 W
Michipicoten Bay ⊂	190	47.55 N	84.56 W
Michipicoten Island I	190	47.45 N	85.45 W
Michnevo	82	55.07 N	37.58 E
Michninskaja	24	60.26 N	46.14 E
Michoacán	204	32.28 N	115.20 W
Michoacán □[3]	234	19.10 N	101.50 W
Michoacanejo	234	21.33 N	102.36 W
Michów	30	51.32 N	22.19 E
Michurinsk → Mičurinsk	80	52.54 N	40.30 E
Mickle Fell ∧	44	54.37 N	2.18 W
Mickleham	260	51.16 N	0.19 W
Mickleover	42	52.24 N	1.34 W
Mickleton	285	39.47 N	75.14 W
Mickle Trafford	262	53.13 N	2.50 W
Mickleyville	218	39.45 N	86.16 W
Mico ≃	236	12.11 N	84.16 W
Mico, Montañas del ⋀	236	15.30 N	88.55 W
Miconge	152	4.26 S	12.51 E
Micoud	241f	13.50 N	60.54 W
Micronesia II	14	11.00 N	159.00 E
Micronesia, Federated States of □[1]	14	5.00 N	152.00 E
Mičurin	38	42.10 N	27.51 E
Mičurinsk	80	52.54 N	40.30 E
Midai, Pulau I	112	3.00 N	107.47 E
Midale	184	49.22 N	103.27 W
Midar	148	34.58 N	3.30 W
Mid-Atlantic Ridge ✦[3]	8	0.00	20.00 W
Midbar Yehuda → Wilderness of Judæa ◆[2]	132	31.30 N	35.18 E
Middalya	162	23.55 S	114.45 E
Middelburg, Ned.	52	51.30 N	3.37 E
Middelburg, S. Afr.	158	31.30 S	25.00 E
Middelburg, S. Afr.	158	25.47 S	29.28 E
Middelfart	41	55.30 N	9.45 E
Middelharnis	52	51.45 N	4.11 E
Middelkerke	50	51.11 N	2.49 E
Middelkerke, Vliegveld ⊠	50	51.12 N	2.52 E
Middelpos	158	31.55 S	20.13 E
Middelstum	52	53.20 N	6.38 E
Middelwater	156	23.17 S	30.16 E
Middelwit	156	24.58 S	27.00 E
Middenbeemster	52	52.33 N	4.55 E
Middenin	158	27.43 S	28.02 E
Middenmeer	52	52.47 N	5.00 E
Middle ≃, B.C., Can.	182	54.50 N	125.08 W
Middle ≃, Ca., U.S.	226	38.03 N	121.31 W
Middle ≃, Ia., U.S.	194	41.29 N	93.24 W
Middle ≃, Mn., U.S.	198	48.22 N	97.04 W
Middle ≃, Mo., U.S.	219	38.39 N	91.53 W
Middle Alkali Lake ⊜	204	41.28 N	120.04 W
Middle America Trench ✦[1]	16	15.00 N	95.00 W
Middle Andaman I	110	12.30 N	92.50 E
Middle Barton	42	51.56 N	1.22 W
Middle Bass	214	41.41 N	82.50 W
Middle Bass Island I	214	41.41 N	82.49 W
Middle-Bay	186	51.28 N	57.30 W
Middle Bay ⊂	276	40.37 N	73.36 W
Middleboro	207	41.53 N	70.54 W
Middle Bosque ≃	222	31.31 N	97.16 W
Middlebourne	188	39.29 N	80.54 W
Middlebranch	214	40.54 N	81.20 W
Middle Breakwater ◆[5]	280	33.43 N	118.13 W
Middlebro	184	49.01 N	95.21 W
Middle Brook	186	48.45 N	54.13 W
Middle Brook ≃, N.J., U.S.	276	40.39 N	74.41 W
Middle Brook ≃, N.J., U.S.	276	40.33 N	74.33 W
Middle Brook, East Branch ≃	276	40.35 N	74.33 W
Middle Brook, West Branch ≃	276	40.35 N	74.33 W
Middleburg, Md., U.S.	208	39.35 N	77.12 W
Middleburg, N.Y., U.S.	210	42.36 N	74.20 W
Middleburg, Oh., U.S.	216	40.17 N	83.34 W
Middleburg, Pa., U.S.	208	40.47 N	77.02 W
Middleburg Heights	214	41.22 N	81.48 W
Middlebury, Ct., U.S.	207	41.31 N	73.07 W
Middlebury, In., U.S.	216	41.40 N	85.42 W
Middlebury, Vt., U.S.	188	44.00 N	73.10 W
Middlebush	276	40.29 N	74.32 W
Middle Caicos I	238	21.47 N	71.43 W
Middle Cape ›	220	25.09 N	81.09 W
Middle Castor ≃	212	45.16 N	75.24 W
Middle Channel ≃[1], N.T., Can.	180	69.21 N	135.33 W
Middle Channel ≃[1], Mi., U.S.	281	42.33 N	82.42 W
Middle Concho ≃	196	31.27 N	100.25 W
Middle Creek ≃, U.S.	208	39.41 N	76.18 W
Middle Creek ≃, Pa., U.S.	210	40.46 N	76.52 W
Middle Creek ≃, Pa., U.S.	210	41.28 N	75.11 W
Middle Fabius ≃	194	39.58 N	91.35 W
Middle Falls	210	43.07 N	73.32 W
Middlefield, Ct., U.S.	207	41.31 N	72.42 W
Middlefield, N.Y., U.S.	210	42.41 N	74.50 W
Middlefield, Oh., U.S.	214	41.27 N	81.04 W
Middle Fork Reservoir ⊜[1]	218	39.51 N	84.51 W
Middle Ground I	272c	18.55 N	72.51 E
Middle Ground ✦[2]	174g	28.15 N	177.25 W
Middle Grove, Mo., U.S.	219	39.24 N	92.16 W
Middle Grove, N.Y., U.S.	210	43.05 N	73.55 W
Middle Haddam	207	41.33 N	72.33 W
Middleham	44	54.17 N	1.49 W
Middle Harbour ⊂	274a	33.48 S	151.14 E
Middle Head ›	274a	33.50 S	151.16 E
Middle Hope	210	41.34 N	74.01 W
Middle Island	210	40.53 N	72.56 W
Middle Island I	162	34.07 S	123.12 E
Middle Level Main Drain ≊	42	52.43 N	0.22 E
Middle Loup ≃	198	41.17 N	98.23 W
Middle Maitland ≃	212	43.53 N	81.19 W
Middlemarch	172	45.31 S	170.07 E
Middlemount	166	22.49 S	148.40 E
Middle Musquodoboit	186	45.03 N	63.09 W
Middle Nodaway ≃	194	40.54 N	95.00 W
Middle Pease ≃	196	34.15 N	100.07 W
Middle Point	216	40.51 N	84.27 W
Middleport, N.Y., U.S.	210	43.12 N	78.28 W
Middleport, Oh., U.S.	188	39.00 N	82.02 W
Middleport, Pa., U.S.	208	40.44 N	76.05 W
Middle Raccoon ≃	198	41.34 N	94.12 W
Middle Reservoir ⊜[1]	283	42.27 N	71.07 W
Middle River	208	39.20 N	76.26 W
Middle River ⊂	208	39.19 N	76.25 W
Middle River Neck ›[1]	284b	39.22 N	76.23 W
Middle River Rouge ≃	281	42.20 N	83.15 W
Middle Rouge Parkway ♠	281	42.21 N	83.21 W
Middle Run ≃	285	39.41 N	75.43 W
Middlesboro	192	36.36 N	83.43 W
Middlesbrough	44	54.35 N	1.14 W
Middlesex, Belize	232	17.02 N	88.31 W
Middlesex, N.J., U.S.	276	40.34 N	74.29 W
Middlesex, N.Y., U.S.	210	42.42 N	77.16 W
Middlesex, N.C., U.S.	192	35.47 N	78.12 W
Middlesex □[6], On., Can.	212	43.00 N	81.08 W
Middlesex □[6], Ct., U.S.	207	41.33 N	72.39 W
Middlesex □[6], Ma., U.S.	207	42.30 N	71.25 W
Middlesex □[6], N.J., U.S.	208	40.29 N	74.27 W
Middlesex □[6], Va., U.S.	208	37.40 N	76.35 W
Middlesex Fells Reservation ♠	283	42.27 N	71.07 W
Middlesex Reservoir ⊜[1]	276	40.37 N	74.19 W
Middle Stewiacke	186	45.13 N	63.08 W
Middle Swan	168a	31.52 S	116.00 E
Middle Thames ≃	212	42.59 N	80.58 W
Middleton, Austl.	166	22.22 S	141.32 E
Middleton, N.S., Can.	186	44.57 N	65.04 W
Middleton, Eng., U.K.	42	52.43 N	0.28 E
Middleton, Eng., U.K.	44	53.33 N	2.13 W
Middleton, Ma., U.S.	207	42.35 N	71.01 W
Middleton, Mi., U.S.	190	43.11 N	84.42 W
Middleton, Tn., U.S.	194	35.03 N	88.53 W
Middleton, Wi., U.S.	216	43.05 N	89.30 W
Middleton-in-Teesdale	44	54.38 N	2.04 W
Middleton Island I	180	59.25 N	146.25 W
Middleton-on-the-Wolds	44	53.56 N	0.33 W
Middleton Pond ⊜	283	42.36 N	71.02 W
Middleton Reef I[1]	160	29.28 S	159.06 E
Middleton Saint George	44	54.30 N	1.28 W
Middletown, N. Ire., U.K.	48	54.18 N	6.50 W
Middletown, Ca., U.S.	226	38.45 N	122.36 W
Middletown, Ct., U.S.	207	41.33 N	72.39 W
Middletown, De., U.S.	208	39.26 N	75.43 W
Middletown, Il., U.S.	219	40.11 N	89.35 W
Middletown, In., U.S.	218	40.03 N	85.32 W
Middletown, Ky., U.S.	218	38.14 N	85.32 W
Middletown, Md., U.S.	208	39.26 N	77.32 W
Middletown, Mo., U.S.	219	39.07 N	91.24 W
Middletown, N.J., U.S.	208	40.23 N	74.07 W
Middletown, N.Y., U.S.	210	41.26 N	74.25 W
Middletown, Oh., U.S.	218	39.30 N	84.23 W
Middletown, Pa., U.S.	208	40.11 N	76.43 W
Middletown, R.I., U.S.	207	41.32 N	71.17 W
Middletown, Va., U.S.	188	39.01 N	78.16 W
Middletown Park	218	40.09 N	85.26 W
Middle Tuolumne ≃	226	37.50 N	120.01 W
Middleville, Mi., U.S.	216	42.42 N	85.27 W
Middleville, N.Y., U.S.	210	43.08 N	74.58 W
Middleville, N.Y., U.S.	276	43.08 N	74.58 W
Middlewich	44	53.11 N	2.27 W
Middle Yegua Creek ≃	222	30.19 N	96.47 W
Middle Yuba ≃	226	39.22 N	121.12 W
Midelt	148	32.41 N	4.43 W
Midfield	222	28.56 N	96.13 W
Midge Hall	262	53.42 N	2.45 W
Midgic	186	45.59 N	64.18 W
Mid Glamorgan □[6]	42	51.40 N	3.30 W
Midgley	262	53.44 N	1.58 W
Midhurst, On., Can.	212	44.27 N	79.44 W
Midhurst, Eng., U.K.	42	50.59 N	0.45 W
Midi, Aiguille du ∧	62	45.52 N	6.53 E
Midi, Canal du ≊	32	43.26 N	1.58 E
Midi de Bigorre, Pic du ∧	32	42.56 N	0.08 E
Mid Illovo	158	29.59 S	30.25 E
Mid-Indian Basin ✦[1]	12	10.00 S	80.00 E
Mid-Indian Ridge ✦[3]	6	30.00 S	75.00 E
Midland, Austl.	168a	31.53 S	116.00 E
Midland, On., Can.	212	44.45 N	79.53 W
Midland, Ca., U.S.	204	33.52 N	114.48 W
Midland, Mi., U.S.	190	43.36 N	84.14 W
Midland, N.C., U.S.	192	35.13 N	80.30 W
Midland, Oh., U.S.	218	39.18 N	83.54 W
Midland, Pa., U.S.	214	40.37 N	80.26 W
Midland, Pa., U.S.	214	40.37 N	80.26 W
Midland, S.D., U.S.	198	44.04 N	101.09 W
Midland, Tx., U.S.	196	31.59 N	102.04 W
Midland, Wa., U.S.	224	47.10 N	122.24 W
Midland Bay ⊂	212	44.47 N	79.52 W
Midland Beach ◆[8]	276	40.34 N	74.05 W
Midland City	219	40.09 N	89.08 W
Midland Park, Mi., U.S.	216	42.23 N	85.22 W
Midland Park, N.J., U.S.	276	40.59 N	74.08 W
Midland Park Lake ⊜	212	44.44 N	79.53 W
Midlands □[4]	154	19.00 S	29.45 E
Midleton	48	51.55 N	8.10 W
Midlothian, Il., U.S.	216	41.37 N	87.43 W
Midlothian, Tx., U.S.	222	32.28 N	96.59 W
Midlothian Creek ≃	278	41.39 N	87.40 W
Midlum	52	53.43 N	8.37 E
Midnapore	182	50.55 N	114.05 W
Midnapore Canal ≊	126	22.25 N	87.53 E
Midnapore Plain ≚	126	22.00 N	87.45 E
Mid-Ohio Sports Car Course ♠	214	40.40 N	82.38 W
Midongy Nord	157b	20.45 S	46.13 E
Midongy Sud	157b	23.35 S	47.01 E
Midori	96	34.43 N	132.37 E
Midori ◆[8]	268	35.32 N	139.34 E
Midori ≃	92	32.42 N	130.37 E
Midou ≃	32	43.54 N	0.30 W
Mid-Pacific Mountains ✦[3]	14	20.00 N	170.00 E
Midpines	226	37.32 N	119.55 W
Midreshet Ben Gurion	132	30.21 N	34.46 E
Midsayap	116	7.12 N	124.32 E
Midshipman Point ›	282	38.07 N	122.27 W
Midsland	52	53.22 N	5.16 E
Midsomer Norton	42	51.18 N	2.28 W
Midu	102	25.22 N	100.31 E
Midvale, De., U.S.	285	39.39 N	75.37 W
Midvale, Id., U.S.	202	44.28 N	116.44 W
Midvale, Oh., U.S.	214	40.26 N	81.22 W
Midville	192	32.49 N	82.14 W
Midway, B.C., Can.	182	49.01 N	118.47 W
Midway, B.C., Can.	202	49.01 N	118.46 W
Midway, Al., U.S.	194	32.04 N	85.31 W
Midway, In., U.S.	216	41.37 N	85.55 W
Midway, Ky., U.S.	218	38.09 N	84.41 W
Midway, Pa., U.S.	279b	40.22 N	80.17 W
Midway, Tx., U.S.	222	31.02 N	95.45 W
Midway, Ut,. U.S.	200	40.30 N	111.28 W
Midway City	280	33.45 N	118.00 W
Midway Islands □[2], Oc.	6	28.13 N	177.22 W
Midway Islands □[2], Oc.	174g	28.13 N	177.22 W
Midway Mall ◆[9]	279a	41.24 N	82.07 W
Midway Naval Station ■	174g	28.13 N	177.26 W
Midway Park	192	34.43 N	77.21 W
Midwest	200	43.24 N	106.16 W
Midwest City	196	35.26 N	97.23 W
Midwolda	52	53.12 N	7.00 E
Midyan ◆[1]	128	27.40 N	35.35 E
Midyat	130	37.25 N	41.23 E
Midyobe	152	1.21 N	10.18 E
Midžor (Midžur) ∧	38	43.23 N	22.42 E
Mie	96	32.58 N	131.35 E
Mie □[5]	92	34.30 N	136.30 E
Miechów	30	50.23 N	20.01 E
Miedwie, Jezioro ⊜	54	53.17 N	14.52 E
Międzybórz	30	51.24 N	17.40 E
Międzychód	30	52.36 N	15.55 E
Międzylesie	30	50.10 N	16.40 E
Międzyrzec Podlaski	30	52.00 N	22.47 E
Międzyrzecz	30	52.28 N	15.35 E
Międzyzdroje	30	53.55 N	14.28 E
Miehuapu	105	39.11 N	117.44 E
Miejska Górka	30	51.40 N	16.58 E
Miélan	32	43.26 N	0.19 E
Mielec	30	50.18 N	21.25 E
Mielno	30	54.16 N	16.01 E
Mien ⊜	26	56.25 N	14.51 E
Mienga	152	17.17 S	19.48 E
Mienhua Yü I	100	25.29 N	122.06 E
Mient′ienhuo Shan ∧	269d	25.11 N	121.30 E
Mier	232	26.26 N	99.09 W
Miercurea-Ciuc	38	46.22 N	25.48 E
Mieres	34	43.15 N	5.46 W
Mierlo	52	51.27 N	5.37 E
Mieroszów	30	50.41 N	16.10 E
Miersdorf	264a	52.20 N	13.37 E
Miersig	38	46.53 N	21.51 E
Mier y Noriega	234	23.25 N	100.07 W
Miesaituo	120	35.52 N	93.40 E
Miesbach	64	47.47 N	11.50 E
Miesenbach	61	47.22 N	15.46 E
Mieso	144	9.15 N	40.48 E
Mieste	54	52.28 N	11.11 E
Miesterhorst	54	52.27 N	11.09 E
Mieszkowice	30	52.46 N	14.30 E
Mifflin, Oh., U.S.	214	40.47 N	82.22 W
Mifflin, Pa., U.S.	208	40.34 N	77.24 W
Mifflin □[6]	210	40.40 N	77.33 W
Mifflinburg	210	40.55 N	77.02 W
Mifflintown	208	40.34 N	77.23 W
Mifflinville	210	41.01 N	76.18 W
Miftāḥ, Wādī V	142	30.15 N	31.46 E
Migdal	132	32.50 N	35.30 E
Migdal Ha′Emeq	132	32.41 N	35.15 E
Migdol	158	26.54 S	25.27 E
Migennes	50	47.58 N	3.31 E
Migliarino	66	44.46 N	11.56 E
Migliaro	64	44.48 N	11.58 E
Miglionico	68	40.34 N	16.30 E
Mignano Monte Lungo	68	41.23 N	13.58 E
Mignone ≃	66	42.11 N	11.44 E
Mignovillard	58	46.48 N	6.08 E
Migori ≃	154	0.59 S	34.15 E
Miguel Alemán, Presa ⊜[1]	234	18.13 N	96.32 W
Miguel Alves	250	4.10 S	42.54 W
Miguel Auza	232	24.18 N	103.25 W
Miguel Calmon	250	11.26 S	40.36 W
Miguel Couto	287a	22.43 S	43.27 W
Miguel de la Borda	236	9.09 N	80.19 W
Migueles, Arroyo de los ≃	266a	40.20 N	3.32 W
Miguelete	258	34.01 S	57.39 W
Miguelete, Arroyo ≃	258	34.14 S	57.54 W
Miguel Hidalgo, Presa ⊜[1]	232	26.30 N	108.35 W
Miguelópolis	255	20.12 S	48.03 W
Miguel Pereira	256	22.27 S	43.22 W
Miguel Riglos	252	36.51 S	63.42 W
Migulinskaja	80	49.42 N	41.16 E
Migvie	46	57.08 N	2.56 W
Migyaunglaung	110	14.40 N	98.09 E
Mihăești	38	45.07 N	25.00 E
Mihai Viteazu	38	44.39 N	28.41 E
Mihajlovgrad	38	43.25 N	23.13 E
Mihalgazi	130	40.02 N	30.34 E
Mihalıççık	130	39.52 N	31.30 E
Mihama, Nihon	94	34.46 N	136.54 E
Mihama, Nihon	94	35.36 N	135.56 E
Mihama, Nihon	96	33.54 N	135.08 E
Mihara, Nihon	96	34.24 N	133.05 E
Mihara, Nihon	96	34.17 N	134.46 E
Mihara, Nihon	96	34.32 N	135.34 E
Mihara-yama ∧	94	34.43 N	139.23 E
Mihla	54	51.04 N	10.20 E
Miho	94	36.00 N	140.18 E
Mihonoseki	96	35.34 N	133.19 E
Miho-wan ⊂	96	35.30 N	133.23 E
Mihuangzhuang	105	39.07 N	116.12 E
Mijaly	86	48.57 N	53.42 E
Mijares ≃	34	39.55 N	0.01 W
Mijdaḥah	144	14.00 N	48.26 E
Mijdrecht	52	52.13 N	4.52 E
Mijiang	98	43.01 N	130.08 E
Mijoux	58	46.22 N	6.00 E
Mikabo-yama ∧	94	36.09 N	138.55 E
Mikame	96	33.25 N	132.27 E
Mikamo, Nihon	96	35.09 N	133.37 E
Mikamo, Nihon	96	34.05 N	133.57 E
Mikasa	92a	43.14 N	141.53 E
Mikaševiči	78	52.13 N	27.28 E
Mikata	94	35.33 N	135.55 E
Mikata-ko ⊜	94	35.34 N	135.53 E
Mikatou	273b	4.16 S	15.08 E
Mikawa, Nihon	94	36.29 N	136.29 E
Mikawa, Nihon	96	33.37 N	132.58 E
Mikawa-wan ⊂	94	34.43 N	137.10 E
Mikawa-wan-kokutei-kōen ♠	94	34.42 N	137.10 E
Mikazuki	96	34.58 N	134.27 E
Mikese	154	6.46 S	37.54 E
Mikhaylov, Cape ›	9	66.51 S	118.33 E
Mikhrot Shelomo Hamelekh (Timna′) (King Solomon′s Mines) ⊥	132	29.45 N	34.56 E
Miki, Nihon	96	34.48 N	134.59 E
Miki, Nihon	96	34.17 N	134.05 E
Mikínai ⊥	38	37.44 N	22.45 E
Mikindani	154	10.17 S	40.07 E
Mikinduri	154	0.07 N	37.50 E
Mikkabi	94	34.48 N	137.33 E
Mikkaichi	270	34.26 N	135.35 E
Mikkeli	26	61.41 N	27.15 E
Mikkelin lääni □[4]	26	62.00 N	27.30 E
Mikkwa ≃	176	58.25 N	114.45 W
Mikołajki	30	53.49 N	21.36 E
Mikołów	30	50.11 N	18.55 E
Mikomeseng	152	2.08 N	10.37 E
Mikomoto-jima I	94	34.34 N	138.56 E
Míkonos	38	37.26 N	25.20 E
Míkonos I	38	37.29 N	25.25 E
Mikope	152	5.03 S	20.48 E
Mikre	38	43.02 N	24.31 E
Mikrí Préspa, Límni ⊜	38	40.46 N	21.04 E
Miksimil	126	22.52 N	89.23 E
Mikšino	76	57.15 N	35.43 E
Mikstat	30	51.32 N	17.59 E
Mikulášovice	54	50.58 N	14.20 E
Mikulincy	78	49.24 N	25.38 E
Mikulino	76	55.02 N	31.07 E
Mikulkin, mys ›	24	67.48 N	46.40 E
Mikulov	61	48.49 N	16.39 E
Mikumi	154	7.24 S	36.59 E
Mikumi National Park ♠	154	7.12 S	37.05 E
Mikun′	24	62.21 N	50.06 E
Mikuni	94	36.13 N	136.09 E
Mikuni-sammyaku ⋀	94	36.50 N	138.40 E
Mikuni-tōge)(	94	36.46 N	138.50 E
Mikuni-yama ∧	94	35.59 N	138.43 E
Mikura-jima I	92	33.52 N	139.36 E
Mila	34	36.27 N	6.16 E
Milaca	190	45.45 N	93.39 W
Miladummadulu Atoll I[1]	122	6.15 N	73.15 E
Milagre	256	21.18 S	47.00 W
Milagres	250	7.17 S	38.57 W
Milagro	246	2.07 S	79.36 W
Milagros	116	12.13 N	123.30 E
Milam □[6]	222	30.47 N	96.57 W
Milan, Ga., U.S.	192	32.01 N	83.03 W
Milan, In., U.S.	218	39.07 N	85.07 W
Milan, Mi., U.S.	216	42.05 N	83.40 W
Milan, Mn., U.S.	198	45.06 N	95.54 W
Milan, Mo., U.S.	194	40.12 N	93.07 W
Milan, N.M., U.S.	200	35.10 N	107.53 W
Milan, Oh., U.S.	214	41.17 N	82.36 W
Milan, Pa., U.S.	210	41.54 N	76.32 W
Milan, Tn., U.S.	194	35.55 N	88.45 W
Milando	152	8.45 S	17.36 E
Milan Federal Correctional Institution ⊎	281	42.06 N	83.40 W
Milang	168b	35.25 S	138.58 E
Milan → Milano	62	45.28 N	9.12 E
Milano (Milan), It.	62	45.28 N	9.12 E
Milano (Milan), It.	266b	45.28 N	9.12 E
Milano, Tx., U.S.	222	30.43 N	96.52 W
Milano □[4]	62	45.30 N	9.30 E
Milanoa	157b	13.35 S	49.47 E
Milano Marittima	66	44.16 N	12.21 E
Milanville	210	41.40 N	75.04 W
Milâs	130	37.19 N	27.47 E
Milaševiči	78	51.39 N	27.56 E
Mil′atino, Ross.	76	54.29 N	34.18 E
Mil′atino, Ross.	82	55.41 N	35.48 E
Milazzo	70	38.13 N	15.14 E
Milazzo, Capo di ›	70	38.16 N	15.14 E
Milazzo, Golfo di ⊂	70	38.15 N	15.20 E
Milbank	198	45.13 N	96.38 W
Milbanke Sound ∪	182	52.18 N	128.33 W
Milborne Port	42	50.58 N	2.27 W
Milbuk	116	6.10 N	124.16 E
Milburn	196	34.14 N	96.32 W
Milburn Creek ≃	276	40.38 N	73.36 W
Milden	184	51.30 N	107.31 W
Mildenau	54	50.35 N	13.04 E
Mildenhall	42	52.21 N	0.30 E
Milders	64	47.06 N	11.16 E
Mildmay	212	44.03 N	81.07 W
Mildred, Il., U.S.	219	39.46 N	89.38 W
Mildred, Pa., U.S.	210	41.28 N	76.22 W
Mildura	166	34.12 S	142.09 E
Mile	102	24.26 N	103.26 E
Miléai	38	39.20 N	23.09 E
Milena	70	37.28 N	13.44 E
Milendella	168b	34.49 S	139.12 E
Milepa	154	11.43 S	36.20 E
Miles, Austl.	166	26.40 S	150.11 E
Miles, Tx., U.S.	196	31.35 N	100.10 W
Miles ≃	283	42.40 N	70.51 W
Milesburg	214	40.56 N	77.47 W
Miles City	202	46.24 N	105.50 W
Miles Creek ⊂	208	38.46 N	76.12 W
Miles Creek ≃	226	37.12 N	120.21 W
Mile Seven Hundred Thirty Three	180	60.03 N	131.07 W
Milešovka ∧	54	50.33 N	13.56 E
Milestone	184	50.00 N	104.30 W
Milesville	279b	40.12 N	79.52 W
Milet (Miletus) ⊥	130	37.28 N	27.15 E
Mileto	68	38.36 N	16.04 E
Miletto, Monte ∧	68	41.27 N	14.22 E
Miletus → Milet ⊥	130	37.28 N	27.15 E
Mileura	162	26.23 S	117.20 E
Milevsko	30	49.27 N	14.22 E
Milford, Eng., U.K.	42	51.11 N	1.38 W
Milford, Ct., U.S.	207	41.13 N	73.04 W
Milford, De., U.S.	208	38.54 N	75.25 W
Milford, Il., U.S.	216	40.37 N	87.41 W
Milford, In., U.S.	216	41.24 N	85.50 W
Milford, Ia., U.S.	198	43.19 N	95.08 W
Milford, Ky., U.S.	218	38.34 N	84.09 W
Milford, Me., U.S.	188	44.56 N	68.38 W
Milford, Md., U.S.	284b	39.21 N	76.44 W
Milford, Ma., U.S.	207	42.08 N	71.31 W
Milford, Mi., U.S.	216	42.35 N	83.35 W
Milford, N.H., U.S.	207	42.50 N	71.38 W
Milford, N.J., U.S.	210	40.34 N	75.05 W
Milford, N.Y., U.S.	210	42.35 N	74.56 W
Milford, Oh., U.S.	218	39.10 N	84.17 W
Milford, Pa., U.S.	210	41.19 N	74.48 W
Milford, Tx., U.S.	222	32.07 N	96.57 W
Milford, Ut,. U.S.	200	38.23 N	113.00 W
Milford, Va., U.S.	208	38.01 N	77.22 W
Milford Brook ≃	276	40.19 N	74.17 W
Milford Center	218	40.10 N	83.26 W
Milford Cross Roads	285	39.43 N	75.44 W
Milford Haven	42	51.40 N	5.02 W
Milford Haven ⊂	42	51.42 N	5.03 W
Milford Lake ⊜[1]	198	39.15 N	97.00 W
Milford on Sea	42	50.44 N	1.36 W
Milford Ridge	284b	39.21 N	76.45 W
Milford Sound	172	44.40 S	167.54 E
Milford Sound ∪	172	44.35 S	167.47 E
Milford Station	186	45.03 N	63.26 W
Milgis ≃	154	1.48 N	38.06 E
Milgoo ∧	162	28.51 S	118.07 E
Mil′guvejem ≃	180	68.22 N	171.30 E
Milḥ, Baḥr al- ⊜	128	32.40 N	43.35 E
Milḥat Ashqar ⊜	128	35.18 N	41.55 E
Milḥat Ashqar ⁝⁝	130	35.18 N	41.55 E
Milhaud	62	43.47 N	4.18 E
Mili I[1]	14	6.08 N	171.55 E
Milian ≃	112	5.13 N	117.25 E
Milibangalala, Ponta ›	158	26.26 S	32.56 E
Milicia ≃	70	38.04 N	13.33 E
Milicz	30	51.32 N	17.17 E
Milieu, Rivière du ≃	206	46.47 N	73.56 W
Milīj	142	30.36 N	31.03 E
Milim	164	5.10 S	152.00 E
Milín	60	49.39 N	14.02 E
Miling	162	30.30 S	116.21 E
Milis	71	40.03 N	8.38 E
Militello in Val di Catania	70	37.16 N	14.48 E
Militello Rosmarino	70	38.03 N	14.41 E
Milk ≃	202	48.05 N	106.15 W

Symbol	English	Deutsch	Español	Français	Português
≃	River	Fluß	Río	Rivière	Rio
≊	Canal	Kanal	Canal	Canal	Canal
∟	Waterfall, Rapids	Wasserfall, Stromschnellen	Cascada, Rápidos	Chute d'eau, Rapides	Cascata, Rápidos
∪	Strait	Meeresstraße	Estrecho	Détroit	Estreito
⊂	Bay, Gulf	Bucht, Golf	Bahía, Golfo	Baie, Golfe	Baía, Golfo
⊜	Lake, Lakes	See, Seen	Lago, Lagos	Lac, Lacs	Lago, Lagos
⁝⁝	Swamp	Sumpf	Pantano	Marais	Pântano
⊓	Ice Features, Glacier	Eis- und Gletscherformen	Accidentes Glaciales	Formes glaciaires	Acidentes glaciares
⊤	Other Hydrographic Features	Andere Hydrographische Objekte	Otros Elementos Hidrográficos	Autres données hydrographiques	Outros acidentes hidrográficos
✦	Submarine Features	Untermeerische Objekte	Accidentes Submarinos	Formes de relief sous-marin	Acidentes submarinos
□	Political Unit	Politische Einheit	Unidad Politica	Entité politique	Unidade política
⊎	Cultural Institution	Kulturelle Institution	Institución Cultural	Institution culturelle	Instituição cultural
⊥	Historical Site	Historische Stätte	Sitio Histórico	Site historique	Sitio histórico
♠	Recreational Site	Erholungs- und Ferienort	Sitio de Recreo	Centre de loisirs	Area de Lazer
⊠	Airport	Flughafen	Aeropuerto	Aéroport	Aeroporto
■	Military Installation	Militäranlage	Instalación Militar	Installation militaire	Instalação militar
◆	Miscellaneous	Verschiedenes	Misceláneo	Divers	Diversos

Name	Page / Seite	Lat.°′ / Breite°′	Long.°′ / Länge°′ E = Ost
Milk Creek ≏, Co., U.S.	200	40.24 N	107.45 W
Milk Creek ≏, Or., U.S.	224	45.15 N	122.41 W
Milk Hill ʌ[2]	42	51.23 N	1.51 W
Mil'kovo	74	54.43 N	158.37 E
Milk River	182	49.09 N	112.05 W
Milk River Ridge Reservoir ⊜[1]	182	49.22 N	112.35 W
Mill	52	51.41 N	5.47 E
Mill ≏, Ct., U.S.	276	41.08 N	73.16 W
Mill ≏, Ma., U.S.	207	42.18 N	72.37 W
Mill ≏, Ma., U.S.	283	42.38 N	70.41 W
Mill ≏, Ma., U.S.	283	42.12 N	70.57 W
Mill ≏, Ma., U.S.	283	42.08 N	71.21 W
Mill ≏, Ma., U.S.	283	42.44 N	70.52 W
Mill ≏, N.Y., U.S.	276	40.38 N	73.39 W
Millard	198	41.13 N	96.07 W
Millau	32	44.06 N	3.05 E
Mill Bay	224	48.39 N	123.34 W
Millboro	192	37.59 N	79.36 W
Millbourne	285	39.58 N	75.15 W
Millbrae	226	37.35 N	122.23 W
Millbrook, On., Can.	212	44.09 N	78.27 W
Millbrook, Eng., U.K.	42	50.20 N	4.13 W
Millbrook, Ma., U.S.	283	42.03 N	70.41 W
Millbrook, N.J., U.S.	276	40.52 N	74.33 W
Millbrook, N.Y., U.S.	210	41.47 N	73.41 W
Mill Brook ≏, Ma., U.S.	283	42.31 N	71.18 W
Mill Brook ≏, N.J., U.S.	276	40.53 N	74.32 W
Mill Brook ≏, N.J., U.S.	276	40.25 N	74.06 W
Mill Brook ≏, N.J., U.S.	276	40.29 N	74.23 W
Millburn	276	40.44 N	74.18 W
Millbury, Ma., U.S.	207	42.11 N	71.45 W
Millbury, Oh., U.S.	214	41.33 N	83.25 W
Mill City	202	44.45 N	122.29 W
Mill Creek, Pa., U.S.	214	40.26 N	77.56 W
Millcreek, Ut,. U.S.	200	40.27 N	111.54 W
Mill Creek, W.V., U.S.	188	38.43 N	79.58 W
Mill Creek ≏, Austl.	274a	33.59 S	151.01 E
Mill Creek ≏, Ca., U.S.	226	36.49 N	119.21 W
Mill Creek ≏, Ca., U.S.	228	34.05 N	117.06 W
Mill Creek ≏, De., U.S.	285	39.42 N	75.39 W
Mill Creek ≏, Il., U.S.	219	39.50 N	91.24 W
Mill Creek ≏, In., U.S.	194	39.30 N	86.57 W
Mill Creek ≏, In., U.S.	216	41.01 N	86.36 W
Mill Creek ≏, Ia., U.S.	198	42.47 N	95.31 W
Mill Creek ≏, Ks., U.S.	198	39.55 N	96.56 W
Mill Creek ≏, Ky., U.S.	218	38.28 N	84.20 W
Mill Creek ≏, N.J., U.S.	276	40.48 N	74.03 W
Mill Creek ≏, N.J., U.S.	285	40.02 N	74.55 W
Mill Creek ≏, N.Y., U.S.	212	43.57 N	76.08 W
Mill Creek ≏, Oh., U.S.	214	41.06 N	80.40 W
Mill Creek ≏, Oh., U.S.	214	40.14 N	83.09 W
Mill Creek ≏, Oh., U.S.	218	39.06 N	84.32 W
Mill Creek ≏, Oh., U.S.	279a	41.25 N	81.38 W
Mill Creek ≏, Or., U.S.	224	45.36 N	121.11 W
Mill Creek ≏, Pa., U.S.	208	40.00 N	76.18 W
Mill Creek ≏, Pa., U.S.	210	41.53 N	77.08 W
Mill Creek ≏, Pa., U.S.	214	41.09 N	79.03 W
Mill Creek ≏, Pa., U.S.	285	40.03 N	75.16 W
Mill Creek ≏, Pa., U.S.	285	40.08 N	74.52 W
Mill Creek ≏, Tx., U.S.	222	32.46 N	95.46 W
Mill Creek ≏, Tx., U.S.	222	29.50 N	96.07 W
Mill Creek ≏, Tx., U.S.	222	30.08 N	95.37 W
Mill Creek ≏, Va., U.S.	208	38.09 N	77.10 W
Mill Creek, North Fork ≏	224	45.33 N	121.18 W
Mill Creek, South Fork ≏	224	45.36 N	121.12 W
Millcreek Township	214	42.05 N	80.10 W
Milldale	207	41.33 N	72.53 W
Milledgeville, Ga., U.S.	192	33.04 N	83.13 W
Milledgeville, Il., U.S.	190	41.57 N	89.46 W
Milledgeville, Oh., U.S.	218	39.36 N	83.35 W
Mille Îles, Rivière des ≏	206	45.42 N	73.32 W
Mille Lacs, Lac des ⊜	190	48.50 N	90.30 W
Mille Lacs Kathio State Park ♦	190	46.08 N	93.43 W
Mille Lacs Lake ⊜	190	46.15 N	93.40 W
Millemont	261	48.49 N	1.45 E
Millen	192	32.48 N	81.56 W
Millendon	168a	31.48 S	116.02 E
Miller, Mo., U.S.	194	37.13 N	93.50 W
Miller, S.D., U.S.	198	44.31 N	98.59 W
Miller □[6]	219	38.15 N	92.15 W
Miller, Mount ʌ	180	60.25 N	142.23 W
Miller City	216	41.06 N	84.08 W
Miller Creek ≏	282	38.02 N	122.30 W
Miller House	180	65.32 N	145.11 W
Miller Mountain ʌ	204	38.03 N	118.12 W
Millerovo, Ross.	78	48.55 N	40.25 E
Millerovo, Ross.	83	47.49 N	39.15 E
Miller Peak ʌ	200	31.23 N	110.17 W
Miller Place	210	40.58 N	73.00 W
Millers ≏	207	42.35 N	72.30 W
Millersburg, In., U.S.	216	41.31 N	85.41 W
Millersburg, In., U.S.	218	41.31 N	85.41 W
Millersburg, Ky., U.S.	218	38.18 N	84.08 W
Millersburg, Mi., U.S.	190	45.20 N	84.03 W
Millersburg, Oh., U.S.	214	40.33 N	81.55 W
Millersburg, Pa., U.S.	208	40.32 N	76.57 W
Millers Creek ≏	196	33.27 N	99.14 W
Miller Seamount ✢[3]	16	53.30 N	144.20 W
Millers Falls	207	42.34 N	72.29 W
Millers Ferry	194	32.05 N	87.22 W
Millers Flat	172	45.40 S	169.25 E
Millers Island	284b	39.14 N	76.24 W
Millers Pond ⊜	276	40.51 N	73.12 W
Millersport	188	39.54 N	82.32 W
Millers Run ≏	279b	40.22 N	80.07 W
Millerstown	210	40.32 N	77.09 W
Millersville, Il., U.S.	219	39.25 N	89.07 W
Millersville, Oh., U.S.	214	41.18 N	83.16 W
Millersville, Pa., U.S.	208	39.59 N	76.21 W
Millerton, N.Y., U.S.	210	41.57 N	73.30 W
Millerton, Pa., U.S.	210	41.59 N	76.56 W
Millerton Lake ⊜[1]	226	37.01 N	119.41 W
Millerton Lake State Recreation Area ♦	226	37.02 N	119.37 W
Millertown	186	48.49 N	56.33 W
Millertown Junction	186	49.01 N	56.21 W
Millesimo	62	44.22 N	8.12 E
Millet	182	53.06 N	113.28 W
Millett, Mi., U.S.	216	42.42 N	84.38 W
Millett, Tx., U.S.	196	28.35 N	99.12 W
Milleur Point ›	44	55.01 N	5.06 W
Millevaches, Plateau de ⋏[1]	32	45.30 N	2.10 E
Millford	48	55.07 N	7.43 W
Mill Green	260	51.41 N	0.22 E
Mill Grove	216	40.25 N	85.17 W
Mill Hall	210	41.06 N	77.29 W
Millheim	210	40.53 N	77.28 W
Mill Hill ◆[8]	260	51.37 N	0.13 W
Mill Hill ʌ[2]	262	53.25 N	1.54 W
Millhousen	218	39.13 N	85.26 W
Millican	222	30.28 N	96.12 W
Millicent	166	37.36 S	140.22 E
Milligan, Fl., U.S.	194	30.45 N	86.38 W
Milligan, Ne., U.S.	198	40.30 N	97.23 W
Milligan Gulch V	200	33.37 N	107.02 W
Milligantown	279b	40.33 N	79.41 W
Milliken	275b	43.49 N	79.18 W
Millingen aan de Rijn	52	51.52 N	6.02 E
Millington, Il., U.S.	216	41.34 N	88.36 W
Millington, Md., U.S.	208	39.15 N	75.50 W
Millington, Mi., U.S.	190	43.16 N	83.31 W
Millington, N.J., U.S.	210	40.40 N	74.31 W
Millington, Tn., U.S.	194	35.20 N	89.53 W
Millinocket	188	45.39 N	68.42 W
Millionnyj	89	54.30 N	126.19 E
Millis	207	42.10 N	71.21 W
Mill Island I, Ant.	9	65.30 S	100.40 E
Mill Island I, N.T., Can.	176	64.00 N	78.00 W
Millisle	48	54.36 N	5.32 W
Mill Lake ⊜	212	45.22 N	80.00 W
Millmerran	166	27.52 S	151.16 E
Millmont	210	40.53 N	77.08 W
Mill Neck	276	40.52 N	73.34 W
Mill Neck ›[1]	276	40.53 N	73.33 W
Mill Neck Creek ⊂	276	40.54 N	73.33 W
Millom	44	54.13 N	3.18 W
Mill Pond ⊜	276	40.53 N	73.22 W
Millport, Scot., U.K.	46	55.46 N	4.55 W
Millport, Al., U.S.	194	33.33 N	88.04 W
Millport, N.Y., U.S.	210	42.16 N	76.50 W
Millport, Pa., U.S.	214	41.55 N	78.07 W
Millrift	210	41.25 N	74.45 W
Mill River	207	42.06 N	73.16 W
Mill Run Acres	284c	38.58 N	77.17 W
Millry	194	31.38 N	88.18 W
Mills, Pa., U.S.	214	41.57 N	77.41 W
Mills, Wy., U.S.	202	42.50 N	106.21 W
Mills, Lake ⊜[1]	224	47.59 N	123.36 W
Millsboro	208	38.35 N	75.17 W
Mills Creek ≏, Austl.	166	22.23 S	143.05 E
Mills Creek ≏, Ca., U.S.	282	37.27 N	122.25 W
Mills Lake ⊜	176	61.30 N	118.10 W
Mills Mansion State Historic Site ⊥	210	41.52 N	73.57 W
Millstadt	219	38.27 N	90.05 W
Millstatt	64	46.48 N	13.35 E
Millstätter See ⊜	64	46.47 N	13.35 E
Millstone	276	40.29 N	74.35 W
Millstone ≏	276	40.33 N	74.34 W
Millstream, Austl.	162	21.35 S	117.04 E
Millstream, B.C., Can.	224	48.30 N	123.31 W
Millstream Chichester National Park ♦	162	21.25 S	117.20 E
Millstreet	48	52.03 N	9.04 W
Milltown, Scot., U.K.	46	57.14 N	2.52 W
Milltown, In., U.S.	218	38.20 N	86.16 W
Milltown, Mt., U.S.	202	46.52 N	113.52 W
Milltown, N.J., U.S.	208	40.27 N	74.26 W
Milltown, Wi., U.S.	190	45.31 N	92.30 W
Milltown Malbay	48	52.50 N	9.23 W
Millvale	279b	40.28 N	79.58 W
Mill Valley	226	37.54 N	122.32 W
Mill Village	214	41.53 N	79.58 W
Millville, Ma., U.S.	207	42.01 N	71.34 W
Millville, N.J., U.S.	208	39.24 N	75.02 W
Millville, Oh., U.S.	218	39.24 N	84.40 W
Millville, Pa., U.S.	210	41.07 N	76.31 W
Millville Lake	283	42.48 N	71.13 W
Millville Lake ⊜	283	42.48 N	71.13 W
Millwood, Md., U.S.	284c	38.53 N	76.53 W
Millwood, N.Y., U.S.	210	41.11 N	73.48 W
Millwood, Va., U.S.	188	39.04 N	78.02 W
Millwood Lake ⊜[1]	194	33.45 N	94.00 W
Milly-la-Forêt	50	48.24 N	2.28 E
Milly-Lamartine	58	46.21 N	4.42 E
Milmay	208	39.26 N	74.51 W
Milmersdorf	54	53.06 N	13.38 E
Milmine	219	39.54 N	88.39 W
Milmont Park	285	39.53 N	75.20 W
Milne Bay □[5]	164	10.00 S	152.30 E
Milne Bay ⊂	164	10.22 S	150.30 E
Milner	224	49.20 N	122.42 W
Milnesville	210	40.59 N	75.59 W
Milngavie	46	55.57 N	4.20 W
Milnor	198	46.15 N	97.27 W
Milnrow	44	53.37 N	2.06 W
Milnthorpe	44	54.14 N	2.46 W
Milo, Ab., Can.	182	50.34 N	112.53 W
Milo, Ia., U.S.	190	41.17 N	93.26 W
Milo, Me., U.S.	188	45.15 N	68.59 W
Milo ≏	150	11.04 N	9.14 W
Milon-la-Chapelle	261	48.44 N	2.03 E
Mílos	38	36.45 N	24.27 E
Mílos I	38	36.41 N	24.15 E
Miloslaviči	76	53.41 N	32.15 E
Miloslavskoje	76	53.34 N	39.24 E
Miłosław	30	52.13 N	17.29 E
Milow, Dtsch.	54	53.11 N	11.32 E
Milow, Dtsch.	54	52.31 N	12.18 E
Milpa Alta ◆[8]	286a	19.11 N	99.01 W
Milparinka	166	29.44 S	141.53 E
Milpitas	226	37.25 N	121.54 W
Milpitas Wash V	204	33.18 N	114.44 W
Milroy, In., U.S.	218	39.29 N	85.28 W
Milroy, Pa., U.S.	208	40.42 N	77.35 W
Milseburg ʌ	56	50.32 N	9.53 E
Mil'skaja ravnina ≚	84	40.00 N	48.00 E
Milspe	263	51.18 N	7.21 E
Miltach	60	49.09 N	12.46 E
Miltenberg	56	49.42 N	9.15 E
Miltitz	54	51.19 N	12.16 E
Milton, Austl.	170	35.19 S	150.26 E
Milton, On., Can.	212	43.31 N	79.53 W
Milton, N.Z.	172	46.07 S	169.58 E
Milton, Eng., U.K.	42	52.14 N	0.09 W
Milton, De., U.S.	208	38.46 N	75.18 W
Milton, Fl., U.S.	194	30.37 N	87.02 W
Milton, Il., U.S.	219	39.34 N	90.39 W
Milton, In., U.S.	218	39.47 N	85.09 W
Milton, In., U.S.	218	38.58 N	85.01 W
Milton, Ia., U.S.	190	40.40 N	92.09 W
Milton, Ky., U.S.	218	38.43 N	85.22 W
Milton, Ma., U.S.	207	42.15 N	71.05 W
Milton, N.J., U.S.	276	41.02 N	74.32 W
Milton, N.Y., U.S.	210	41.39 N	73.57 W
Milton, N.D., U.S.	198	48.37 N	98.02 W
Milton, Pa., U.S.	210	41.00 N	76.50 W
Milton, Vt., U.S.	188	44.38 N	73.06 W
Milton, Wa., U.S.	224	47.14 N	122.18 W
Milton, W.V., U.S.	188	38.26 N	82.07 W
Milton, Wi., U.S.	216	42.46 N	88.56 W
Milton, Lake ⊜	214	41.06 N	80.58 W
Milton Abbot	42	50.35 N	4.15 W
Milton-Freewater	202	45.55 N	118.23 W
Milton Harbor ⊂	276	40.57 N	73.42 W
Milton Keynes	42	52.02 N	0.42 W
Milton Point ›	276	40.57 N	73.42 W
Miltonvale	198	39.20 N	97.26 W
Miltou	146	10.14 N	17.26 E
Miltzow	54	54.12 N	13.13 E
Milumba	154	7.06 S	31.04 E
Miluo	100	28.50 N	113.04 E
Miluo ≏	100	28.50 N	113.06 E
Mil'utinskaja	80	48.38 N	41.40 E
Mil'utkej, gora ʌ	180	65.42 N	178.03 W
Milverton, On., Can.	212	43.34 N	80.55 W
Milverton, Eng., U.K.	42	51.02 N	3.16 W
Milwaukee	216	43.02 N	87.54 W
Milwaukee □[6]	216	43.02 N	87.58 W
Milwaukee ≏	190	43.02 N	87.54 W
Milwaukee Bay ⊂	216	43.02 N	87.53 W
Milwaukie	224	45.26 N	122.38 W
Mim	150	6.54 N	2.34 W
Mima	96	33.17 N	132.36 E
Mimasaka	96	35.00 N	134.10 E
Mimbres ≏	200	32.13 N	107.28 W
Mimbres Mountains ⋏	200	32.45 N	107.45 W
Mimi ≏	92	32.20 N	131.37 E
Mimico ◆[8]	275b	43.37 N	79.30 W
Mimico Creek ≏	275b	43.37 N	79.29 W
Mimizan	32	44.12 N	1.14 W
Mimmaya	92	41.12 N	140.26 E
Mimoň	54	50.40 N	14.44 E
Mimongo	152	1.11 S	11.36 E
Mimoso, Bra.	248	16.17 S	55.48 W
Mimoso, Bra.	255	15.10 S	48.05 W
Mimoso do Sul	255	21.04 S	41.22 W
Mims	220	28.39 N	80.50 W
Mimuro-yama ʌ	96	35.14 N	134.28 E
Min ≏, Zhg.	100	26.05 N	119.32 E
Min ≏, Zhg.	102	28.46 N	104.38 E
Mina, Méx.	196	26.01 N	100.32 W
Mina, Nv., U.S.	204	38.23 N	118.06 W
Mina ≏	112	10.09 S	124.12 E
Mîna, Oued ≏	34	35.47 N	0.30 E
Mīnā' al-Aḥmadī	128	29.04 N	48.08 E
Mīnāb	128	27.09 N	57.05 E
Mīnāb ≏	128	27.01 N	56.53 E
Minabe	96	33.46 N	135.19 E
Minabegawa	96	33.47 N	135.20 E
Mina El Limón	236	12.45 N	86.44 W
Minago ≏	184	54.34 N	98.08 W
Minahasa ›[1]	112	1.00 N	124.35 E
Mināj ≏[1]	126	22.31 N	89.22 E
Minakami	94	36.46 N	138.58 E
Minakuchi	94	34.58 N	136.10 E
Minam ≏	202	45.37 N	117.43 W
Minamata	92	32.13 N	130.24 E
Minami	94	35.39 N	136.57 E
Minami ◆[8], Nihon	268	35.24 N	139.36 E
Minami ◆[8], Nihon	270	34.40 N	135.31 E
Minami ◆[8], Nihon	270	34.58 N	135.45 E
Minami ≏	94	35.30 N	135.49 E
Minamiaiki	94	36.02 N	138.33 E
Minami-Alps-kokuritsu-kōen ♦	94	35.40 N	138.13 E
Minamiashigara	94	35.19 N	139.07 E
Minami-Bōsō-kokutei-kōen ♦	94	35.10 N	140.05 E
Minamichita	94	34.44 N	136.52 E
Minami-Daitō-jima I	90	25.50 N	131.15 E
Minami-Iō-jima I	14	24.14 N	141.28 E
Minamiizu	94	34.39 N	138.50 E
Minamimaki	94	36.00 N	138.30 E
Minaminasu	94	36.39 N	140.06 E
Minamisenju ◆[8]	268	35.44 N	139.48 E
Minamishinano	94	35.19 N	137.56 E
Minami-Tori-shima (Marcus Island) I	14	24.18 N	153.58 E
Minano	94	36.04 N	139.06 E
Mina Pirquitas	252	22.41 S	66.31 W
Minard, S. Afr.	158	31.17 S	27.35 E
Minard, Scot., U.K.	46	56.07 N	5.15 W
Minas, Cuba	240p	21.29 N	77.37 W
Minas, Indon.	114	0.50 N	101.29 E
Minas, Ur.	252	34.23 S	55.14 W
Minas, Sierra de las ⋏	236	15.10 N	89.40 W
Minas Basin ⊂	186	45.20 N	64.00 W
Minas Channel ⊔	186	45.15 N	64.45 W
Minas de Barroterán	232	27.40 N	101.20 W
Minas de Corrales	252	31.35 S	55.28 W
Minas de Matahambre	240p	22.35 N	83.57 W
Minas de Oro	236	14.46 N	87.20 W
Minas de Ríotinto	34	37.42 N	6.35 W
Minas Gerais □[3]	255	18.00 S	44.00 W
Minas Novas	255	17.15 S	42.36 W
Mînăstirea	38	44.13 N	26.54 E
Minatare	198	41.48 N	103.30 W
Minatitlán	234	17.59 N	94.31 W
Minato	268	35.13 N	139.52 E
Minato ◆[8], Nihon	268	35.39 N	139.45 E
Minato ◆[8], Nihon	270	34.39 N	135.26 E
Minato ≏	268	35.13 N	139.52 E
Minbāl	142	28.24 N	30.41 E
Minbu	110	20.11 N	94.52 E
Minbulak	85	41.30 N	75.53 E
Minbya	110	20.22 N	93.15 E
Minbyin	110	19.17 N	93.32 E
Minchinābād	123	30.10 N	73.34 E
Minchinhampton	42	51.42 N	2.10 W
Minchumina, Lake ⊜	180	63.52 N	152.15 W
Mincio ≏	64	45.04 N	10.59 E
Minco	196	35.18 N	97.56 W
Minčol ʌ	30	49.15 N	20.59 E
Mind'ak	86	54.02 N	58.48 E
Mindanao I	116	8.00 N	125.00 E
Mindanao ≏	116	7.07 N	124.24 E
Mindego Creek ≏	282	37.18 N	122.15 W
Mindego Hill ʌ[2]	282	37.18 N	122.13 W
Mindel ≏	58	48.31 N	10.23 E
Mindelheim	58	48.03 N	10.29 E
Mindelo	150a	16.53 N	25.00 W
Mindemoya	190	45.44 N	82.10 W
Minden, On., Can.	212	44.55 N	78.43 W
Minden, Dtsch.	52	52.17 N	8.55 E
Minden, La., U.S.	194	32.36 N	93.17 W
Minden, Ne., U.S.	198	40.29 N	98.56 W
Minden, Nv., U.S.	226	38.57 N	119.45 W
Minden, W.V., U.S.	188	37.58 N	81.07 W
Minden City	190	43.40 N	82.46 W
Mindenmines	194	37.28 N	94.35 W
Minderoo	162	22.00 S	115.02 E
Mindif	146	10.24 N	14.26 E
Mindiptana	164	5.45 S	140.42 E
Mindon	110	19.21 N	94.44 E
Mindoro I	116	12.50 N	121.05 E
Mindoro Occidental □[4]	116	13.00 N	121.00 E
Mindoro Oriental □[4]	116	13.00 N	121.20 E
Mindoro Strait ⊔	116	12.20 N	120.40 E
Mindouli	152	4.17 S	14.21 E
Mindourou, Cam.	152	4.06 N	14.34 E
Mindourou, Cam.	152	3.25 N	13.32 E
Minduri	256	21.41 S	44.37 W
Mindživan	84	39.03 N	46.42 E
Mine, Ityo.	144	8.20 N	40.09 E
Mine, Nihon	96	33.17 N	130.26 E
Mine, Nihon	96	34.10 N	131.13 E
Minear Lake ⊜	278	42.17 N	87.57 W
Minebank Run ≏	284b	39.25 N	76.32 W
Mine Brook ≏, Ma., U.S.	283	42.09 N	71.15 W
Mine Brook ≏, Ma., U.S.	283	42.08 N	71.26 W
Mine Brook ≏, N.J., U.S.	276	40.41 N	74.38 W
Mine Centre	190	48.45 N	92.37 W
Minehead	42	51.13 N	3.29 W
Mine Hill	210	40.52 N	74.35 W
Mineiros	255	17.34 S	52.34 W
Mineo	70	37.16 N	14.42 E
Mineola, N.Y., U.S.	210	40.44 N	73.38 W
Mineola, Tx., U.S.	222	32.39 N	95.29 W
Miner ≏	180	66.30 N	133.25 W
Mineral	224	46.43 N	122.10 W
Mineral City	214	40.36 N	81.21 W
Mineral Creek ≏	224	46.45 N	122.08 W
Mineral de Cucharas	234	22.52 N	105.19 W
Mineral del Monte	234	20.08 N	98.40 W
Mineral de Pozos	234	21.14 N	100.29 W
Mineral'nyje Vody	84	44.12 N	43.08 E
Mineral Point, Pa., U.S.	214	40.23 N	78.50 W
Mineral Point, Wi., U.S.	190	42.51 N	90.10 W
Mineral Ridge	214	41.08 N	80.46 W
Mineral Springs, Ar., U.S.	194	33.52 N	93.54 W
Mineral Springs, Pa., U.S.	214	41.00 N	78.22 W
Mineral Wells	196	32.48 N	98.06 W
Minerbe	64	45.14 N	11.20 E
Minerbio	64	44.37 N	11.29 E
Minersville, Pa., U.S.	208	40.41 N	76.16 W
Minersville, Ut,. U.S.	200	38.12 N	112.55 W
Mine Run ≏	285	40.15 N	75.28 W
Minerva, Ky., U.S.	218	38.42 N	83.55 W
Minerva, Oh., U.S.	214	40.43 N	81.06 W
Minerva, Tx., U.S.	222	30.46 N	96.59 W
Minerva, Embalse ⊜[1]	240p	22.25 N	79.48 W
Minerva Park	214	40.04 N	83.00 W
Minervino Murge	68	41.05 N	16.05 E
Minesing Swamp ≋	212	44.23 N	79.51 W
Minetto	210	43.23 N	76.28 W
Mineville	188	44.05 N	73.31 W
Mineyama	96	35.37 N	135.04 E
Minfeng	120	37.05 N	82.40 E
Minga	154	11.08 S	27.57 E
Mingala	152	5.06 N	21.49 E
Mingan	186	50.18 N	64.02 W
Mingan ≏	186	50.18 N	63.59 W
Mingan, Îles de II	186	50.12 N	63.35 W
Mingan Archipelago National Park ♦	186	50.12 N	63.35 W
Mingan Mountains ⋏	116	15.29 N	121.24 E
Mingāora	123	34.47 N	72.22 E
Mingardo ≏	68	40.02 N	15.18 E
Mingary	166	32.08 S	140.44 E
Mingcheng	89	43.11 N	125.59 E
Mingečaur	84	40.45 N	47.03 E
Mingečaurskoje vodochranilišče ⊜[1]	84	40.50 N	46.50 E
Mingela	166	19.53 S	146.38 E
Mingenew	162	29.11 S	115.26 E
Mingera Creek ≏	166	20.38 S	138.10 E
Minggang	100	32.29 N	114.03 E
Minggao	100	34.20 N	112.15 E
Minghuang	106	31.41 N	119.56 E
Mingin	110	22.52 N	94.39 E
Mingjuesi	106	31.34 N	118.53 E
Minglanilla	34	39.32 N	1.36 W
Ming Ming	164	5.30 S	146.10 E
Mingo, Congo	152	1.55 S	14.59 E
Mingo, Oh., U.S.	216	40.13 N	83.38 W
Mingo Creek ≏, Pa., U.S.	279b	40.13 N	79.57 W
Mingo Creek ≏, Pa., U.S.	285	40.10 N	75.32 W
Mingo Junction	214	40.19 N	80.36 W
Mingorría	34	40.45 N	4.40 W
Mingoville	214	40.56 N	77.39 W
Mingoyo	154	10.06 S	39.38 E
Mingrel'skaja	78	45.01 N	38.20 E
Mingshantou	100	29.18 N	112.33 E
Mingshui, Zhg.	89	47.10 N	125.55 E
Mingshui, Zhg.	102	42.06 N	96.04 E
Mingulay I	46	56.49 N	7.38 W
Mingwan	106	31.04 N	120.17 E
Mingxi	100	26.24 N	117.13 E
Mingyuegou	89	43.07 N	128.54 E
Mingyuelu	85	39.34 N	75.26 E
Minhang	106	31.01 N	121.24 E
Minhla, Mya.	110	19.58 N	95.03 E
Minhla, Mya.	110	17.59 N	95.43 E
Minho □[9]	34	41.40 N	8.30 W
Minho (Miño) ≏	34	41.52 N	8.51 W
Minhou	100	26.12 N	119.06 E
Minianko	150	9.58 N	8.22 W
Minićevo	38	43.41 N	22.18 E
Minicoy Island I	122	8.17 N	73.02 E
Minier	194	40.26 N	89.18 W
Minigwal, Lake ⊜	162	29.35 S	123.12 E
Minija ≏	76	55.21 N	21.17 E
Minilya	162	23.51 S	113.58 E
Minilya ≏	162	23.56 S	113.51 E
Minimarg	123	34.47 N	75.05 E
Minīn	132	33.39 N	36.18 E
Miniota	184	50.08 N	101.00 W
Minisinakwa Lake ⊜	190	47.40 N	81.43 W
Ministikwan Lake ⊜	184	54.01 N	109.39 W
Ministro Ramos Mexía	254	40.30 S	67.17 W
Ministro Rivadavia	288	34.51 S	58.22 W
Minitonas	184	52.07 N	101.00 W
Minj	164	5.54 S	144.39 E
Minjar	86	55.04 N	57.33 E
Minjary, Mount ʌ	171b	35.14 S	148.08 E
Minjiadianzi	104	41.35 N	121.41 E
Minjiaji	100	31.08 N	115.01 E
Minkamman	140	6.03 N	31.32 E
Min'kovo	76	59.42 N	43.28 E
Min-Kuš	85	41.41 N	74.28 E
Minlaton	168b	34.46 S	137.36 E
Minle, Zhg.	100	22.59 N	112.58 E
Minle, Zhg.	102	38.27 N	100.56 E
Minna	150	9.37 N	6.33 E
Minna Bluff ›[1]	9	78.32 S	166.30 E
Minna-shima I, Nihon	174m	26.39 N	127.49 E
Minna-shima I, Nihon	175d	24.45 N	124.42 E
Minneapolis, Ks., U.S.	198	39.07 N	97.42 W
Minneapolis, Mn., U.S.	190	44.58 N	93.15 W
Minnechaduza Creek ≏	198	42.54 N	100.29 W
Minnedosa	184	50.14 N	99.51 W
Minnehaha	224	45.39 N	122.37 W
Minnehaha, Lake ⊜	220	28.31 N	81.46 W
Minneola, Fl., U.S.	220	28.35 N	81.45 W
Minneola, Ks., U.S.	198	37.26 N	100.00 W
Minneola, Lake ⊜	220	28.34 N	81.46 W
Minneosa Creek ≏	196	35.31 N	102.48 W
Minneota	198	44.34 N	95.59 W
Minnertsga	52	53.15 N	5.35 E
Minnesota □[3]	178	46.00 N	94.15 W
Minnesota ≏	178	44.54 N	93.10 W
Minnesota Lake	190	43.50 N	93.49 W
Minnewanka, Lake ⊜	182	51.15 N	115.20 W
Minnewaukan	198	48.04 N	99.15 W
Minnie Creek	162	24.02 S	115.42 E
Minnigaff	44	54.58 N	4.30 W
Minnipa	162	32.51 S	135.09 E
Minnitaki Lake ⊜	184	49.58 N	92.00 W
Minnoch, Water of ≏	44	55.02 N	4.33 W
Mino, Nihon	94	35.32 N	136.55 E
Minō, Nihon	96	34.50 N	135.28 E
Miño (Minho) ≏, Europe	34	41.52 N	8.51 W
Minō ≏, Nihon	270	34.47 N	134.57 E
Minoa	210	43.04 N	76.00 W
Minobu	94	35.22 N	138.26 E
Minobu-san ʌ	94	35.24 N	138.25 E
Minobu-sanchi ⋏	94	35.14 N	138.20 E
Minocqua	190	45.52 N	89.42 W
Minokamo	94	35.26 N	137.01 E
Mino-Mikawa-kōgen ⋏[1]	94	35.11 N	137.23 E
Minong	190	46.05 N	91.49 W
Minonk	216	40.54 N	89.02 W
Minooka	216	41.27 N	88.16 W
Minorca → Menorca I	34	40.00 N	4.00 E
Minori	94	36.14 N	140.21 E
Minorsville	218	38.20 N	84.42 W
Minoshō	270	34.39 N	135.49 E
Minot, Ma., U.S.	283	42.14 N	70.45 W
Minot, N.D., U.S.	198	48.13 N	101.17 W
Minot Air Force Base ■	198	48.26 N	101.21 W
Minowa	94	35.55 N	137.59 E
Minqiao	100	32.53 N	119.13 E
Minqin	102	38.42 N	103.11 E
Minqing	100	26.12 N	118.51 E
Minquadale	285	39.42 N	75.34 W
Minquan	98	34.41 N	115.11 E
Minquiers, Plateau des II	32	48.57 N	2.09 W
Minsen	52	53.42 N	7.58 E
Min Shan ⋏	102	33.35 N	103.00 E
Minshāt adh-Dhahab	142	28.00 N	30.42 E
Minshat al-Amir Muhammad 'Ali	142	29.10 N	30.38 E
Minshāt al-Bakkārī	273c	30.01 N	31.08 E
Minshāt al-Ikhwah	142	30.56 N	31.21 E
Minshāt al-Mughālaqah	142	27.44 N	30.47 E
Minshāt Būlīn	142	31.11 N	30.10 E
Minshāt Sulṭān	142	30.32 N	30.55 E
Minsk	76	53.54 N	27.34 E
Minsk □[8]	24	54.30 N	28.00 E
Minskaja vozvyšennost' ⋏[1]	76	54.00 N	27.10 E
Mińsk Mazowiecki	30	52.11 N	21.34 E
Minster, Eng., U.K.	42	51.20 N	1.19 E
Minster, Eng., U.K.	42	51.26 N	0.49 E
Minster, Oh., U.S.	216	40.24 N	84.23 W
Minsterley	42	52.39 N	2.55 W
Minta	152	4.35 N	12.48 E
Mintaka Pass)(	123	37.00 N	74.50 E
Mintard	263	51.22 N	6.54 E
Mintaro	168b	33.55 S	138.43 E
Mint Canyon	228	34.26 N	118.25 W
Mintlaw	46	57.31 N	2.00 W
Minto, Austl.	274a	34.01 S	150.51 E
Minto, Mb., Can.	184	49.25 N	100.01 W
Minto, N.B., Can.	186	46.05 N	66.05 W
Minto, Yk., Can.	180	62.34 N	136.51 W
Minto, Ak., U.S.	180	65.09 N	149.21 W
Minto, N.D., U.S.	198	48.17 N	97.22 W
Minto, Lac ⊜	176	57.13 N	75.00 W
Minto, Mount ʌ	9	71.55 S	169.33 E
Minto Inlet ⊂	176	71.20 N	117.00 W
Mintom II	152	2.42 N	13.17 E
Minton	184	49.10 N	104.35 W
Mintoum	152	0.27 N	12.16 E
Minturn	200	39.35 N	106.25 W
Minturnae ⊥	68	41.14 N	13.45 E
Minturno	66	41.15 N	13.45 E
Minūf	142	30.28 N	30.56 E
Minulovo	265a	60.03 N	30.45 E
Minumadai-yōsui ≍	268	35.50 N	139.42 E
Minur'uk	85	40.56 N	73.22 E
Minusinsk	86	53.43 N	91.42 E
Minutang	120	28.13 N	96.32 E
Minute Man National Historical Park ♦	207	42.27 N	71.17 W
Minvoul	152	2.09 N	12.08 E
Minwakh	144	16.50 N	48.05 E
Minxian	102	34.26 N	104.02 E
Minya → Al-Minyā	142	28.06 N	30.45 E
Minyā al-Qamḥ	142	30.31 N	31.21 E
Minya Konka → Gongga Shan ʌ	102	29.35 N	101.51 E
Minyat an-Naṣr	142	31.07 N	31.39 E
Minyat as-Sīrij ◆[8]	273c	30.05 N	31.15 E
Minyat Sandūb	142	31.00 N	31.23 E
Minžir	78	46.40 N	28.19 E
Minzow	54	53.23 N	12.30 E
Mio	190	44.39 N	84.07 W
Mioglia	62	44.29 N	8.25 E
Mionica	38	44.15 N	20.05 E
Miory	76	55.37 N	27.38 E
Mipi	120	28.57 N	95.48 E
Miquan	86	44.06 N	87.35 E
Miquelon I	186	47.03 N	56.20 W
Miquihuana	234	23.34 N	99.47 W
Miquon	285	40.04 N	75.16 W
Mir, Bela.	76	53.27 N	26.28 E
Mir, Cuba	240p	20.46 N	76.36 W
Mīr, Miṣr	142	27.27 N	30.44 E
Mir, Niger	146	14.05 N	11.59 E
Mira	34	40.26 N	8.44 W
Mira ≏, N.S., Can.	186	46.03 N	60.00 W
Mira ≏, Col.	246	1.36 N	79.01 W
Mira ≏, Port.	34	37.43 N	8.47 W
Mīrābād	128	30.25 N	61.50 E
Mira Bay ⊂	186	46.02 N	59.56 W
Mirabeau	62	43.42 N	5.39 E
Mirabel	206	45.39 N	74.05 W
Mirabel, Aéroport International de ⊠	206	45.41 N	74.02 W
Mirabella Eclano	68	41.02 N	14.59 E
Mirabella Imbaccari	70	37.19 N	14.27 E
Mirabello, Ippodromo ♦	266b	45.36 N	9.17 E
Mirabello Monferrato	62	45.02 N	8.31 E
Miracema do Tocantins	250	9.33 S	48.24 W
Mirada Hills → La Mirada	228	33.54 N	118.01 W
Mirador	250	6.22 S	44.22 W
Mirador, Cerro ʌ	286d	11.57 S	77.02 W
Mirador, Paso de)(	254	40.42 S	71.56 W
Miradouro	255	20.53 S	42.21 W
Miraflores, Arg.	252	28.36 S	65.55 W
Miraflores, Col.	246	5.12 N	73.12 W
Miraflores, Col.	246	1.25 N	72.13 W
Miraflores, Perú	286d	12.07 S	77.02 W
Miraflores, Esclusas de ◆[5]	236	9.00 N	79.36 W
Miraflores, Palacio υ	286c	10.31 N	66.55 W
Mīrah, Wādī al- V	128	32.26 N	41.42 E
Miraí	256	21.12 S	42.37 W
Miraj	122	16.50 N	74.38 E
Miraki	85	39.02 N	67.10 E
Miraleste	228	33.46 N	118.19 W
Mira Loma	228	34.01 N	117.31 W
Miramar, Arg.	252	38.16 S	57.51 W
Miramar, Arg.	252	30.54 S	62.40 W
Miramar, C.R.	236	10.06 N	84.44 W
Miramar, Fr.	62	43.30 N	6.57 E
Miramar, Moç.	156	23.50 S	35.34 E
Miramar, Fl., U.S.	220	25.59 N	80.13 W
Miramar ◆[8]	286b	23.07 N	82.25 W
Miramar, Laguna ⊜	236	16.23 N	91.16 W
Miramare	66	44.02 N	12.38 E
Miramare, Aeroporto di ⊠	66	44.02 N	12.35 E
Miramare, Castello di ⊥	64	45.42 N	13.43 E
Miramar Naval Air Station ■	228	32.52 N	117.07 W
Miramas	62	43.35 N	5.00 E
Mirambeau	32	45.23 N	0.34 W
Miramichi Bay ⊂	186	47.08 N	65.08 W
Mira Monte	228	36.42 N	119.03 W
Mīram Shāh	120	33.01 N	70.04 E
Mīrān	123	31.24 N	70.43 E
Miranda, Austl.	274a	34.02 S	151.06 E
Miranda, Bra.	248	20.14 S	56.22 W
Miranda, Col.	246	3.15 N	76.14 W
Miranda, Ca., U.S.	204	40.14 N	123.49 W
Miranda □[3]	246	10.15 N	66.25 W
Miranda ≏	248	19.25 S	57.20 W
Miranda, Aerodromo ⊠	286c	10.29 N	66.50 W
Miranda de Ebro	34	42.41 N	2.57 W
Miranda do Douro	34	41.30 N	6.16 W
Mirande	32	43.31 N	0.25 E
Mirandela	34	41.29 N	7.11 W
Mirando City	196	27.26 N	99.00 W
Mirandola	64	44.53 N	11.04 E
Mirano	64	45.30 N	12.07 E
Mirantão	256	22.15 S	44.30 W
Mirante do Paranapanema	255	22.17 S	51.54 W
Mirapuxi ≏	255	13.06 S	51.10 W
Mirasaka	96	34.46 N	132.58 E
Mira Taglio	64	45.26 N	12.08 E
Miravalles, Volcán ʌ[1]	236	10.45 N	85.10 W
Miravete, Puerto de)(	34	39.43 N	5.43 W
Mīr Bacheh Kowt	120	34.45 N	69.08 E
Mir-Bašir	84	40.20 N	46.55 E
Mirbāṭ	118	17.00 N	54.45 E
Mirboo North	169	38.24 S	146.10 E
Mirebeau-sur-Bèze	58	47.24 N	5.19 E
Mirecourt	58	48.18 N	6.08 E
Miren	64	45.54 N	13.37 E
Mirfield	44	53.40 N	1.41 W
Mirgorod	78	49.58 N	33.36 E
Mirgorodka	80	50.58 N	53.33 E
Miri	112	4.23 N	113.59 E
Miriam Vale	166	24.20 S	151.34 E
Mirim, Lagoa (Laguna Merín) ⊂	252	32.45 S	52.50 W
Mirimichi, Lake ⊜	283	42.02 N	71.18 W
Mírina	38	39.52 N	25.04 E
Miriñay ≏	252	30.10 S	57.39 W
Mirinzal	250	2.01 S	44.43 W
Miritiparaná ≏	246	1.11 S	70.02 W
Miriyama	164	3.57 S	141.45 E
Mīrjāveh	128	29.01 N	61.28 E
Mirke ◆[8]	263	51.16 N	7.09 E
Mirna ≏	64	45.19 N	13.36 E
Mirnock ʌ	64	46.46 N	13.43 E
Mirnoje Ozero	86	57.44 N	78.45 E
Mirnyj, Ross.	74	62.33 N	113.53 E
Mirnyj, Ross.	80	53.30 N	50.18 E
Mirnyj, Ukr.	78	50.57 N	28.34 E
Mirnyy υ[3]	9	66.33 S	93.00 E
Mirond Lake ⊜	184	55.06 N	102.47 W
Mironeasa	38	46.58 N	27.25 E
Mironovka	78	49.39 N	30.59 E
Mironovo	88	58.19 N	109.38 E
Mironovskij	83	48.29 N	38.17 E
Miropol	78	50.07 N	27.41 E
Miropolje	78	51.02 N	35.16 E
Mirosław	61	48.57 N	16.18 E
Mirosławiec	30	53.21 N	16.05 E
Mirošov	60	49.41 N	13.40 E
Mirovice	60	49.31 N	14.02 E
Mirovoje	78	47.45 N	34.45 E
Mirovskoje	78	48.05 N	33.23 E
Mirow	54	53.16 N	12.49 E
Mīrpur, Bngl.	126	23.47 N	90.21 E
Mīrpur, Bngl.	126	23.56 N	88.59 E
Mīrpur, Pāk.	123	33.11 N	73.47 E
Mīrpur Batoro	120	24.44 N	68.16 E
Mīrpur Bībīwāri	120	28.32 N	67.44 E
Mīrpur Khās	120	25.32 N	69.00 E
Mīrpur Sakro	120	24.33 N	67.37 E
Mirria	150	13.43 N	9.07 E
Mirror	182	52.28 N	113.07 W
Mirror Lake ⊜, Ma., U.S.	283	42.05 N	71.20 W
Mirror Lake ⊜, N.J., U.S.	276	40.29 N	74.22 W
Mirtağ	130	38.23 N	41.56 E
Mirto	70	38.05 N	14.45 E
Mirtóön Pélagos ⩪[2]	38	36.51 N	23.18 E
Miryang	98	35.31 N	128.44 E
Miry Run ≏	285	40.15 N	74.49 W
Mirza-Aki	85	40.45 N	73.25 E
Mirzaani	84	41.23 N	46.09 E
Mirzāganj	126	22.21 N	90.14 E
Mīrzākalu	126	22.29 N	90.48 E
Mirzāpur, Bngl.	126	24.06 N	90.06 E
Mirzāpur, India	124	25.09 N	82.35 E
Mirzāpur, India	272b	22.50 N	88.24 E
Mis	64	46.12 N	11.57 E
Misa ≏	66	43.43 N	13.14 E
Misāḥah, Bi'r ⩪[4]	140	22.12 N	27.57 E
Misailovo	265b	55.34 N	37.49 E
Misaka	94	35.38 N	138.40 E
Misaka-tōge)(	96	33.42 N	132.52 E
Misaki, Nihon	94	35.18 N	140.22 E
Misaki, Nihon	96	33.23 N	132.07 E
Misaki, Nihon	96	34.19 N	135.09 E
Misaki → Miura	94	35.08 N	139.37 E
Misakubo	94	35.09 N	137.52 E
Misallah, Ra's ›	142	29.50 N	32.36 E
Misamis Occidental □[4]	116	8.20 N	123.42 E
Misamis Oriental □[4]	116	8.45 N	125.00 E
Misano Adriatico	66	43.57 N	12.39 E
Misantla	234	19.56 N	96.50 W
Misasa	96	35.24 N	133.54 E
Misasagi → Fujiidera	96	34.34 N	135.36 E
Misato, Nihon	94	36.23 N	138.57 E
Misato, Nihon	94	34.43 N	136.24 E
Misato, Nihon	94	36.15 N	137.54 E
Misato, Nihon	96	34.09 N	135.22 E
Misato, Nihon	268	35.50 N	139.53 E
Misawa	92	40.41 N	141.24 E
Misbourne ≏	260	51.34 N	0.29 W
Misburg	52	52.23 N	9.51 E
Miscou Centre	186	47.57 N	64.34 W
Miscou Island I	186	47.57 N	64.33 W
Miscou Point ›	186	48.03 N	64.32 W
Mišelevka	88	52.51 N	103.09 E
Misema ≏	190	47.54 N	79.53 W
Mi-sen ʌ	96	34.16 N	132.19 E
Misenheimer	192	35.29 N	80.17 W
Miseno	68	40.47 N	14.05 E
Misericórdia, Serra da ⋏	287a	22.51 S	43.17 W
Misery, Mount ʌ	169	37.24 S	143.36 E
Misgār	123	36.47 N	74.47 E
Mish'āb, Ra's al- ›	128	28.12 N	48.39 E
Mishagua ≏	248	11.13 S	72.59 W
Mishan	89	45.33 N	131.52 E
Mishawaka	216	41.39 N	86.09 W
Mishawum Lake ⊜	283	42.30 N	71.08 W
Mishbiḥ, Jabal ʌ	140	22.38 N	34.44 E
Misheguk Mountain ʌ	180	68.15 N	161.03 W
Mishe-Mokwa, Lake ⊜	285	39.52 N	74.48 W
Mishibishu Lake ⊜	190	48.05 N	85.25 W
Mishicot	190	44.14 N	87.38 W
Mishima	94	35.07 N	138.55 E
Mi-shima I	96	34.46 N	131.09 E
Mishima → Settsu	96	34.46 N	135.33 E
Mishmar HaNegev	132	31.21 N	34.43 E
Mishmi Hills ⋏[2]	120	29.00 N	96.00 E
Mishō	96	32.57 N	132.34 E
Mishqal, Jabal al- ʌ	132	31.53 N	36.08 E
Mišicha	88	51.38 N	105.35 E
Misikan	120	35.45 N	89.25 E
Misilmeri	70	38.02 N	13.27 E
Misima Island I	164	10.40 S	152.45 E
Misinto	266b	45.40 N	9.05 E
Misiones □[4]	252	27.00 S	55.00 W
Misiones □[5]	252	27.00 S	57.00 W
Misión San Francisco de Laishí	252	26.14 S	58.38 W
Misión San Vicente	232	31.20 N	116.15 W
Misirevo	82	56.16 N	36.45 E
Miskī	140	14.51 N	24.13 E
Miski, Enneri V	146	20.00 N	17.55 E
Miškino, Ross.	86	55.20 N	63.55 E
Miškino, Ross.	265a	59.42 N	30.45 E
Miskito Channel ⊔	236	14.20 N	83.08 W
Miskitos, Cayos II	236	14.23 N	82.46 W
Miskitos Reef ✢[2]	236	14.28 N	82.42 W
Miskolc	30	48.06 N	20.47 E
Misli	130	38.10 N	34.52 E
Mislinja	61	46.28 N	15.14 E
Mislinja ≏	61	46.35 N	15.02 E
Mislippi	146	10.00 N	15.37 E
Mislivna ʌ	61	48.40 N	14.44 E
Mismār	140	18.13 N	35.38 E
Mismār, Jabal ʌ	140	18.06 N	35.42 E
Mismi, Nevado ʌ	248	15.30 S	71.42 W
Mišn'ovo	76	53.58 N	36.21 E
Misoke	154	1.06 S	28.38 E
Misool, Pulau I	164	1.52 S	130.10 E
Mispillion ≏	208	38.57 N	75.20 W
Miscuamaebin Lake ⊜	184	53.30 N	91.05 W
Miscuamicut	207	41.20 N	71.49 W
Miṣr al-Jadīdah (Heliopolis) ◆[8]	273c	30.06 N	31.20 E
Miṣr al-Qadīmah (Old Cairo) ◆[8]	273c	30.00 N	31.14 E

Symbols in the index entries represent the broad categories identified in the key at the right. Symbols with superior numbers (⋏[1]) identify subcategories (see complete key on page I · 1).

Symbole im Register stellen die rechts im Schlüssel erklärten Kategorien dar. Symbole mit hochgestellten Ziffern (⋏[1]) bezeichnen Unterabteilungen einer Kategorie (vgl. vollständiger Schlüssel auf Seite I · 1).

Los símbolos incluídos en el texto del índice representan las grandes categorias identificadas con la clave a la derecha. Los símbolos con numeros en su parte superior (⋏[1]) identifican las subcategorías (véase la clave completa en la página I · 1).

Les symboles de l'index représentent les catégories indiquées dans la légende à droite. Les symboles suivis d'un indice (⋏[1]) représentent des sous-catégories (voir légende complète à la page I · 1).

Os símbolos incluídos no texto do índice representam as grandes categorias identificadas com a chave à direita. Os símbolos com números em sua parte superior (⋏[1]) identificam as subcategorias (veja-se a chave completa à página I · 1).

ʌ Mountain	Berg	Montaña	Montagne	Montanha
⋏ Mountains	Gebirge	Montañas	Montagnes	Montanhas
)(Pass	Paß	Paso	Col	Passo
V Valley, Canyon	Tal, Cañon	Valle, Cañón	Vallée, Canyon	Vale, Canhão
≚ Plain	Ebene	Llano	Plaine	Planície
› Cape	Kap	Cabo	Cap	Cabo
I Island	Insel	Isla	Île	Ilha
II Islands	Inseln	Islas	Îles	Ilhas
⊥ Other Topographic Features	Andere Topographische Objekte	Otros Elementos Topográficos	Autres données topographiques	Outros acidentes topográficos

ESPAÑOL

Nombre	Página	Lat.°′	Long.°′ W = Oeste
Misrātah	146	32.23 N	15.06 E
Mişr Baḩrī □[9]	140	31.00 N	31.00 E
Mişr → Egypt □[1]	140	27.00 N	30.00 E
Misrikh	124	27.27 N	80.31 E
Missanello	68	40.17 N	16.10 E
Missão Santa Cruz	152	16.14 S	21.57 E
Missão Velha	250	7.15 S	39.08 W
Misserghin	34	35.37 N	0.45 W
Missinaibi ≃	176	50.44 N	81.29 W
Missinaibi Lake ⊜	190	48.23 N	83.40 W
Missinaibi Lake Provincial Park ♠	190	48.25 N	83.35 W
Mission, S.D., U.S.	198	43.18 N	100.39 W
Mission, Tx., U.S.	196	26.12 N	98.19 W
Mission ◆[8]	282	37.45 N	122.25 W
Mission Bay ⊂	228	32.47 N	117.15 W
Mission Beach	166	17.52 S	146.06 E
Mission City	224	49.08 N	122.18 W
Mission Creek ≃	282	37.32 N	121.55 W
Mission Hills ◆[8]	280	34.16 N	118.27 W
Mission Mountain ∧[2]	194	36.02 N	94.35 W
Mission Peak ∧	282	37.31 N	121.53 W
Mission Range ⋏	202	47.30 N	113.55 W
Mission Texas State Historic Park ♠	222	31.33 N	95.15 W
Mission Valley	222	28.54 N	97.12 W
Mission Viejo	228	33.36 N	117.40 W
Missisquoi □[6]	206	45.10 N	72.55 W
Missisquoi ≃	206	45.00 N	73.08 W
Missisquoi Bay ⊂	206	45.05 N	73.10 W
Missisquoi-Nord ≃	206	45.02 N	72.26 W
Mississagagon Lake ⊜	212	44.52 N	77.05 W
Mississagi ≃	190	46.10 N	83.01 W
Mississagi Provincial Park ♠	190	46.35 N	82.45 W
Mississagua ≃	212	44.34 N	78.20 W
Mississagua Lake ⊜	212	44.42 N	78.19 W
Mississauga	212	43.35 N	79.39 W
Mississinewa ≃	216	40.46 N	86.02 W
Mississinewa Lake ⊜[1]	216	40.42 N	85.52 W
Mississippi □[3], U.S.	178	32.50 N	89.30 W
Mississippi □[3], U.S.	194	32.50 N	89.30 W
Mississippi ≃, On., Can.	212	45.26 N	76.16 W
Mississippi ≃, U.S.	178	29.00 N	89.15 W
Mississippi Bay ⊂	162	34.00 S	122.17 E
Mississippi Delta ≚[2]	194	29.10 N	89.15 W
Mississippi Lake ⊜	212	45.05 N	76.12 W
Mississippi Sound ⋓	194	30.15 N	88.40 W
Mississippi State	194	33.26 N	88.47 W
Missolonghi → Mesolóngion	38	38.21 N	21.17 E
Missoula	202	46.52 N	113.59 W
Missouri □[3], U.S.	178	38.30 N	93.30 W
Missouri □[3], U.S.	194	38.30 N	93.30 W
Missouri ≃	178	38.50 N	90.08 W
Missouri, Coteau du ⋏[2]	198	46.00 N	99.30 W
Missouri Buttes ∧	198	44.37 N	104.47 W
Missouri City	222	29.37 N	95.32 W
Missouri Creek ≃	219	40.07 N	90.43 W
Missouri Valley	198	41.33 N	95.53 W
Mistake, Mount ∧	171a	27.52 S	152.20 E
Mistake Creek	164	17.06 S	129.04 E
Mistake Creek ≃	166	21.38 S	146.50 E
Mistake Mountains ⋏	171a	27.52 S	152.22 E
Mistaken Point ›	186	46.38 N	53.10 W
Mistanipisipou ≃	186	51.32 N	61.50 W
Mistassibi ≃	176	48.53 N	72.13 W
Mistassibi Nord-Est ≃	186	49.50 N	71.56 W
Mistassini	176	50.25 N	73.52 W
Mistassini, Lac ⊜	176	51.00 N	73.37 W
Mistatim	184	52.52 N	103.22 W
Mistawasis Indian Reserve ◆[4]	184	53.06 N	106.48 W
Mistelbach, Dtsch.	60	49.55 N	11.31 E
Mistelbach, Öst.	61	48.34 N	16.35 E
Mistelgau	60	49.55 N	11.28 E
Misteln ⊜	40	59.07 N	16.57 E
Misterbianco	70	37.31 N	15.00 E
Misterei	140	13.07 N	22.09 E
Misteriosa Bank ✢[2]	238	18.50 N	83.50 W
Misterton, Eng., U.K.	42	50.52 N	2.47 W
Misterton, Eng., U.K.	44	53.27 N	0.51 W
Misti, Volcán ∧[1]	248	16.18 S	71.24 W
Mistikokan ≃	184	57.01 N	91.27 W
Mistley	42	51.56 N	1.05 E
Mistrás ⊥	38	37.04 N	22.21 E
Mistretta	70	37.56 N	14.22 E
Misugi	94	34.33 N	136.16 E
Misumi, Nihon	92	32.37 N	130.27 E
Misumi, Nihon	96	34.46 N	131.58 E
Misumi, Nihon	96	34.22 N	131.15 E
Misumi ≃	96	34.47 N	131.56 E
Misurina	64	46.35 N	12.15 E
Mišurin Rog	78	48.50 N	33.58 E
Mišutino, Ross.	76	59.31 N	36.01 E
Mišutino, Ross.	82	56.23 N	38.06 E
Mita, Punta ›	234	20.47 N	105.33 W
Mīt Abū Ghālib	142	31.17 N	31.40 E
Mita Hills Dam ◆[6]	154	14.15 S	29.06 E
Mit'ajevo, Ross.	82	55.16 N	36.32 E
Mit'ajevo, Ross.	86	60.17 N	61.06 E
Mitaka	94	35.40 N	139.33 E
Mitake, Nihon	94	35.25 N	137.08 E
Mitake, Nihon	94	35.51 N	137.37 E
Mit'akinka ≃	83	48.35 N	39.50 E
Mit'akino	82	54.24 N	38.50 E
Mit'akinskaja	83	48.36 N	39.47 E
Mīt al-ʿĀmil	142	30.54 N	31.21 E
Mitatib	140	16.03 N	36.11 E
Mitau → Jelgava	76	56.39 N	23.42 E
Mīt Badr Ḥalāwah	142	30.51 N	31.14 E
Mīt Bashshār	142	30.31 N	31.24 E
Mitcham, Austl.	168b	34.59 S	138.36 E
Mitcham, Austl.	274b	37.49 S	145.12 E
Mitcham ◆[8]	260	51.24 N	0.10 W
Mitcheldean	42	51.53 N	2.30 W
Mitchell, Austl.	166	26.29 S	147.58 E
Mitchell, On., Can.	212	43.28 N	81.12 W
Mitchell, Il., U.S.	219	38.46 N	90.06 W
Mitchell, In., U.S.	218	38.43 N	86.28 W
Mitchell, Ne., U.S.	198	41.56 N	103.48 W
Mitchell, Or., U.S.	202	44.34 N	120.09 W
Mitchell, S.D., U.S.	198	43.42 N	98.01 W
Mitchell ≃, Austl.	164	15.12 S	141.35 E
Mitchell ≃, Austl.	164	14.28 S	125.43 E
Mitchell ≃, Austl.	166	37.53 S	147.41 E
Mitchell, Lake ⊜[1]	194	32.50 N	86.30 W
Mitchell, Mount ∧	192	35.46 N	82.16 W
Mitchell and Alice Rivers National Park ♠	164	15.30 S	142.05 E
Mitchell Bay ⊂	214	42.28 N	82.26 W
Mitchell Corners	212	43.57 N	78.48 W
Mitchell Field ⊠	278	41.55 N	88.15 W
Mitchell Lake ⊜, B.C., Can.	182	52.53 N	120.36 W
Mitchell Lake ⊜, On., Can.	212	44.34 N	78.58 W
Mitchell Point ›	214	42.26 N	82.26 W
Mitchellville	190	41.40 N	93.21 W
Mitchelstown	48	52.16 N	8.16 W
Mīt Fāris	142	31.02 N	31.36 E
Mīt Ghamr	142	30.43 N	31.16 E
Mīt Halfah	273c	30.10 N	31.14 E
Mīt Ḥamal	142	30.26 N	31.32 E
Mithapur	120	22.25 N	69.00 E
Mitha Tiwāna	123	32.15 N	72.07 E
Mithi	120	24.44 N	69.48 E
Míthimna	38	39.22 N	26.10 E
Mitiaro I	14	19.49 S	157.43 W
Mitidja, Plaine de la ≚	34	36.45 N	3.00 E
Mitilíni	38	39.06 N	26.32 E

FRANÇAIS

Nom	Page	Lat.°′	Long.°′ W = Ouest
Mitino	265b	55.51 N	37.21 E
Mitis, Lac ⊜	186	48.17 N	67.45 W
Mitishto ≃	184	54.50 N	98.58 W
Mitiškovo	76	54.40 N	33.31 E
Mitiwanga	214	41.22 N	82.27 W
Mitkof Island I	180	56.45 N	132.50 W
Mitla ⊥	234	16.55 N	96.17 W
Mitla, Laguna ⊂	234	17.03 N	100.25 W
Mitla, Mamarr (Mitla Pass))(	142	30.00 N	32.53 E
Mitla Pass → Mitla, Mamarr)(	142	30.00 N	32.53 E
Mito, Nihon	94	34.49 N	137.19 E
Mito, Nihon	94	36.22 N	140.28 E
Mito, Nihon	96	34.40 N	131.59 E
Mitō, Nihon	96	34.13 N	131.21 E
Mito, Nihon	268	35.10 N	139.37 E
Mitomi	94	35.47 N	138.44 E
Mitoya	96	35.17 N	132.52 E
Mitra, Monte ∧	152	1.23 N	9.57 E
Mitra do Bispo ∧	256	22.10 S	44.34 W
Mitre ∧	172	40.48 S	175.27 E
Mitre, Península ›[1]	254	54.48 S	65.40 W
Mitre Peak ∧	172	44.38 S	167.50 E
Mitrofania Island I	180	55.51 N	158.49 W
Mitrofanovka	78	49.58 N	39.42 E
Mitrofanovo	24	63.13 N	56.00 E
Mīt Ruhaynah	273c	29.51 N	31.15 E
Mīt Ruhaynah (Memphis) ⊥	142	29.51 N	31.15 E
Mitry-le-Neuf	261	48.57 N	2.36 E
Mitry-Mory	261	48.59 N	2.37 E
Mitsamiouli	157a	11.23 S	43.18 E
Mitsinjo	157b	16.01 S	45.52 E
Mitsio, Nosy I	157b	12.54 S	48.36 E
Mitsiwa (Massawa)	144	15.38 N	39.28 E
Mitsiwa Channel ⋓	144	15.30 N	40.00 E
Mitsu, Nihon	96	34.47 N	134.33 E
Mitsu, Nihon	96	34.48 N	133.56 E
Mitsubori	268	35.56 N	139.56 E
Mitsue	94	34.29 N	136.10 E
Mitsugi	96	34.30 N	133.09 E
Mitsuike Park ♠	268	35.31 N	139.39 E
Mitsukaidō	94	36.01 N	139.59 E
Mitsuke	92	37.32 N	138.56 E
Mitsumarenge-dake ∧	94	36.23 N	137.35 E
Mitsushima	92	34.16 N	129.19 E
Mitsuzaku	268	35.25 N	140.00 E
Mitsuzawa Park Race Track ♠	268	35.27 N	139.36 E
Mitta, Oued el V	148	34.20 N	6.44 E
Mittagong	170	34.27 S	150.27 E
Mittagskogel (Kepa) ∧	61	46.31 N	13.57 E
Mittainville	261	48.40 N	1.39 E
Mitta Mitta ≃	171b	36.12 S	147.11 E
Mitte ◆[8]	264a	52.31 N	13.24 E
Mittelberg, Dtsch.	58	47.38 N	10.25 E
Mittelberg, Öst.	58	47.20 N	10.10 E
Mittelfischach	56	49.02 N	9.52 E
Mittelfranken □[5]	56	49.20 N	10.40 E
Mittellandkanal ≍	30	52.16 N	11.41 E
Mittelmeer → Mediterranean Sea ⊤[2]	10	35.00 N	20.00 E
Mittelsaida	54	50.46 N	13.18 E
Mittelstetten	60	48.15 N	11.06 E
Mittenwald	64	47.27 N	11.15 E
Mittenwalde, Dtsch.	54	53.11 N	13.39 E
Mittenwalde, Dtsch.	54	52.16 N	13.32 E
Mitterndorf	64	47.33 N	13.55 E
Mittersill	64	47.16 N	12.29 E
Mitterskirchen	60	48.21 N	12.44 E
Mitterteich	60	49.57 N	12.15 E
Mittewald an der Drau	64	46.46 N	12.36 E
Mittweida	54	50.59 N	12.59 E
Mitú	246	1.08 N	70.03 W
Mitumba, Monts ⋏	154	6.00 S	29.00 E
Mituo	107	28.53 N	105.37 E
Mitwaba	154	8.38 S	27.20 E
Mitwitz	56	50.15 N	11.12 E
Mityana	154	0.24 N	32.03 E
Mīt Yazīd	142	30.30 N	31.20 E
Mitzic	152	0.47 N	11.34 E
Miura	94	35.08 N	139.37 E
Miura-chosuichi ⊜[1]	94	35.49 N	137.23 E
Miura-dam ◆[6]	94	35.49 N	137.24 E
Miura-hantō ›[1]	94	35.15 N	139.39 E
Mius	80	51.26 N	47.56 E
Mius ≃	83	47.18 N	38.49 E
Miusinsk	83	48.05 N	38.53 E
Miusskij liman ⊂[1]	83	47.15 N	38.40 E
Miwa, Nihon	94	35.11 N	136.47 E
Miwa, Nihon	94	36.39 N	140.18 E
Miwa, Nihon	96	35.12 N	135.14 E
Miwa, Nihon	96	34.39 N	132.51 E
Miwa, Nihon	96	34.13 N	132.06 E
Miwa, Nihon	270	34.31 N	135.51 E
Mi-Wuk Village	226	38.05 N	120.13 W
Mixcoac ◆[8]	286a	19.23 N	99.12 W
Mixcoac, Presa de ⊜[1]	286a	19.22 N	99.14 W
Mixco Viejo ⊥	236	14.52 N	90.40 W
Mixian	100	34.31 N	113.22 E
Mixin	107	30.23 N	105.46 E
Mixquiahuala	234	20.14 N	99.13 W
Mixtán	234	17.55 N	95.51 W
Mixteco ≃	234	18.11 N	98.30 W
Mixtlán	234	20.26 N	104.25 W
Miya	94	36.05 N	137.15 E
Miya ≃, Nihon	94	34.32 N	136.44 E
Miya ≃, Nihon	94	36.28 N	137.15 E
Miyagawa, Nihon	94	36.19 N	137.09 E
Miyagawa, Nihon	94	34.22 N	136.21 E
Miyagi □[5]	92	38.22 N	140.52 E
Miyagi-jima I	174m	26.21 N	127.57 E
Miyāh, Wādī al- V	140	25.00 N	33.23 E
Miyahara	268	35.56 N	139.37 E
Miyajima	96	34.18 N	132.19 E
Miyake	270	34.35 N	135.47 E
Miyake-jima I	92	34.05 N	139.32 E
Miyako	92	39.38 N	141.57 E
Miyakojima ◆[8]	270	34.43 N	135.33 E
Miyako-jima I	175d	24.47 N	125.20 E
Miyakonojō	92	31.44 N	131.04 E
Miyako-rettō II	175d	24.24 N	125.00 E
Miyama, Nihon	92	34.06 N	136.14 E
Miyama, Nihon	94	36.00 N	136.22 E
Miyama, Nihon	94	35.33 N	136.45 E
Miyama, Nihon	96	35.16 N	135.33 E
Miyama, Nihon	96	33.59 N	135.22 E
Miyāni	120	21.51 N	69.23 E
Miyanojō	92	31.54 N	130.27 E
Miyanoura-dake ∧	93b	30.20 N	130.31 E
Miyara	175d	24.20 N	124.14 E
Miyata	96	33.44 N	130.40 E
Miyazaki, Nihon	92	31.54 N	131.26 E
Miyazaki, Nihon	94	35.56 N	136.05 E
Miyazakino-hana ›	96	34.04 N	135.05 E
Miyazu	96	35.32 N	135.11 E
Miyi	102	27.00 N	102.08 E
Miyoshi, Nihon	96	33.57 N	133.03 E
Miyoshi, Nihon	96	34.48 N	132.51 E
Miyoshi, Nihon	96	34.02 N	133.52 E
Miyoshi, Nihon	268	35.50 N	139.31 E
Miyota	94	36.18 N	138.30 E
Miyun	105	40.22 N	116.50 E
Miyun Shuiku ⊜[1]	105	40.30 N	116.58 E
Mizan Teferi	144	6.53 N	35.28 E
Mizdah	146	31.26 N	12.59 E
Mize	194	31.52 N	89.33 W
Mizen Head ›, Ire.	48	52.51 N	6.01 W
Mizen Head ›, Ire.	48	51.27 N	9.49 W
Miževiči	76	52.59 N	25.05 E
Mizhi	102	37.49 N	110.02 E
Mizil	38	45.00 N	26.26 E
Mizoč	78	50.24 N	26.09 E
Mizoguchi	96	35.21 N	133.26 E
Mizonokuchi	268	35.36 N	139.37 E

PORTUGUÊS

Nome	Página	Lat.°′	Long.°′ W = Oeste
Mizonuma	268	35.48 N	139.36 E
Mizoram □[3]	120	23.30 N	93.00 E
Mizpah	208	39.29 N	74.50 W
Mizpah Creek ≃	198	46.16 N	105.17 W
Miẓpé Ramon	132	30.36 N	34.48 E
Mizque	248	17.56 S	65.19 W
Mizque ≃	248	18.39 S	64.20 W
Mizue ◆[8]	268	35.41 N	139.54 E
Mizuho, Nihon	94	35.46 N	139.21 E
Mizuho, Nihon	96	35.10 N	135.22 E
Mizuho, Nihon	96	34.51 N	132.31 E
Mizukaidō → Mitsukaidō	94	36.01 N	139.59 E
Mizuko	268	35.50 N	139.34 E
Mizumaki	96	33.51 N	130.42 E
Mizunami	94	35.22 N	137.15 E
Mizunoko-jima I	96	33.02 N	132.11 E
Mizusawa	92	39.08 N	141.08 E
Mizushima-nada ⊂	96	34.25 N	133.40 E
Mizutori	270	34.47 N	135.45 E
Mizuwake-tōge)(	96	33.15 N	131.17 E
Mjälgen	40	60.33 N	15.07 E
Mjällom	26	62.59 N	18.26 E
Mjangad	86	48.15 N	91.57 E
Mjanyana	158	31.50 S	28.10 E
Mjölby	26	58.19 N	15.08 E
Mjøndalen	26	59.45 N	10.01 E
Mjörn ⊜	26	57.54 N	12.25 E
Mjøsa ⊜	26	60.40 N	11.00 E
Mkalama	154	4.07 S	34.38 E
Mkata	154	5.47 S	38.17 E
Mkhondvo ≃	158	26.39 S	31.25 E
Mkokotoni	154	5.52 S	39.15 E
Mkomazi ≃	158	30.12 S	30.50 E
Mkomazi Game Reserve ◆[4]	154	4.10 S	38.10 E
Mkulwe	154	8.35 S	32.19 E
Mkumvura ≃	154	15.55 S	31.07 E
Mkunumbi	154	2.18 S	40.42 E
Mkushi	154	13.40 S	29.20 E
Mkushi ≃	154	14.40 S	29.07 E
Mkushi River	154	13.32 S	29.45 E
Mkuze	158	27.37 S	32.02 E
Mkuze ≃	158	27.53 S	32.29 E
Mkuzi Game Reserve ◆[4]	158	27.40 S	32.15 E
Mkwaja	154	5.47 S	38.51 E
Mkwaya	154	10.06 S	39.40 E
Mladá Boleslav	54	50.23 N	14.59 E
Mladenovac	38	44.26 N	20.42 E
Mladotice	60	49.58 N	13.18 E
Mlala Hills ⋏[2]	154	6.47 S	31.45 E
M'Lang	116	6.55 N	124.53 E
M'Lang ≃	116	6.52 N	124.45 E
Mlanje Peak → Sapitwa ∧	154	15.57 S	35.36 E
Mlava ≃	38	44.45 N	21.13 E
Mława	30	53.06 N	20.23 E
Mlawula	158	26.11 S	32.01 E
Mliba	158	26.14 S	31.36 E
Mlinov	78	50.31 N	25.37 E
Mljet, Otok I	36	42.45 N	17.30 E
Mljet Nacionalni Park ♠	36	42.47 N	17.25 E
Mljetski Kanal ⋓	36	42.48 N	17.35 E
Mmabatho	138	25.51 S	25.38 E
Mmadinare	156	21.57 S	27.52 E
Mnazi	154	8.54 S	39.06 E
Mnevniki ◆[8]	265b	55.45 N	37.28 E
Mnichov	60	50.03 N	12.49 E
Mníšek pod Brdy	30	49.52 N	14.16 E
Mo	24	66.15 N	14.08 E
Mo ≃	150	8.45 N	0.11 E
Moa	240p	20.40 N	74.56 W
Moa ≃, Afr.	150	6.59 N	11.36 W
Moa ≃, Bra.	248	7.39 S	72.41 W
Moa, Pulau I	164	8.10 S	127.56 E
Moab	200	38.34 N	109.32 W
Moabi	152	2.15 S	11.00 E
Moaco ≃	248	7.41 S	68.18 W
Moa Island I	164	10.12 S	142.16 E
Moala Island I	175g	18.36 S	179.53 E
Moalboal	116	9.56 N	123.23 E
Moama	166	36.07 S	144.47 E
Moamba	156	25.35 S	32.13 E
Moana	168b	35.13 S	138.29 E
Moanda	152	1.34 S	13.11 E
Moanza	152	5.25 S	17.30 E
Moar Lake ⊜	184	52.00 N	95.09 W
Moate	48	53.24 N	7.58 W
Moatize	154	16.08 S	33.45 E
Moawhango	172	39.35 S	175.52 E
Moba, Nig.	273a	6.27 N	3.28 E
Moba, Zaïre	154	7.03 S	29.47 E
Mobara	94	35.25 N	140.18 E
Mobārakpur	126	22.58 N	89.10 E
Mobaye	152	4.19 N	21.11 E
Mobayi-Mbongo	152	4.18 N	21.11 E
Mobberley	262	53.19 N	2.20 W
Mobeetie	196	35.31 N	100.26 W
Mobeka	152	1.53 N	19.46 E
Mobenzélé	152	0.54 N	17.51 E
Moberly	194	39.25 N	92.26 W
Moberly ≃	182	56.12 N	120.55 W
Moberly Lake	182	55.48 N	121.45 W
Moberly Lake ⊜	182	55.49 N	121.45 W
Mobile, Al., U.S.	194	30.41 N	88.02 W
Mobile, Az., U.S.	200	33.03 N	112.16 W
Mobile ≃	194	30.29 N	88.01 W
Mobile Bay ⊂	194	30.25 N	88.00 W
Mobjack	208	37.23 N	76.21 W
Mobjack Bay ⊂	208	37.19 N	76.21 W
Mobridge	198	45.32 N	100.25 W
Moca, P.R.	240m	18.24 N	67.07 W
Moca, Rep. Dom.	238	19.24 N	70.31 W
Moča ≃	82	55.25 N	37.28 E
Mocajuba	250	2.35 S	49.30 W
Mocal ≃	236	14.00 N	88.33 W
Močalejevka	80	53.38 N	51.46 E
Močališče	80	56.21 N	48.23 E
Moçambique	154	15.03 S	40.45 E
Moçambique → Mozambique □[1]	138	18.15 S	35.00 E
Mocanaqua	210	41.08 N	76.08 W
Mocanguê Grande, Ilha I	287a	22.52 S	43.08 W
Mocassins, Lac des ⊜	206	46.35 N	74.25 W
Mo Cay	110	10.08 N	106.20 E
Moccasin, Ca., U.S.	226	37.49 N	120.18 W
Moccasin, Il., U.S.	219	39.09 N	88.45 W
Moc Chau	110	20.51 N	104.37 E
Moccoidumis	144	1.36 N	44.26 E
Mocha, Isla I	252	38.22 S	73.56 W
Mocha → Al-Makhā'	144	13.19 N	43.15 E
Moche ≃	248	8.10 S	79.03 W
Moche ⊥	248	8.06 S	79.05 W
Mocheng	106	31.35 N	120.43 E
Mochh	123	32.45 N	71.31 E
Mochigase	96	35.20 N	134.12 E
Mochitlan	234	17.30 N	99.18 W
Mochizuki	94	36.16 N	138.22 E
Mocho, Arroyo ≃	226	37.41 N	121.55 W
Mochov	54	50.08 N	14.50 E
Mochtín	60	49.22 N	13.21 E
Mochudi	156	24.28 S	26.05 E
Močily	82	54.20 N	38.41 E
Mocímboa da Praia	154	11.20 S	40.21 E
Mocímboa do Rovuma	154	11.20 S	39.18 E
Möckeln ⊜, Sve.	26	56.40 N	14.10 E
Möckeln ⊜, Sve.	40	59.18 N	14.30 E
Möckern	54	52.08 N	11.57 E
Mockfjärd	40	60.30 N	14.58 E
Mockhorn Island I	208	37.13 N	75.53 W
Möckmühl	56	49.19 N	9.22 E
Mockrehna	54	51.30 N	12.49 E
Mocksville	192	35.53 N	80.33 W
Moclips	224	47.14 N	124.12 W

Môco, Serra do ∧	152	12.28 S	15.10 E
Mocoa	246	1.09 N	76.37 W
Mococa	256	21.28 S	47.01 W
Mocoduene	156	23.40 S	35.10 E
Mocoretá	252	30.38 S	57.58 W
Mocorito	232	25.29 N	107.55 W
Moctezuma, Méx.	232	29.48 N	109.42 W
Moctezuma, Méx.	234	22.45 N	101.05 W
Moctezuma ≃, Méx.	232	29.09 N	109.40 W
Moctezuma ≃, Méx.	234	21.59 N	98.34 W
Mocuba	154	16.50 S	36.59 E
Močurica ≃	38	42.31 N	26.32 E
Modane	62	45.12 N	6.40 E
Modāsa	120	23.28 N	73.18 E
Modau ≃	56	49.49 N	8.28 E
Modbury	42	50.21 N	3.53 W
Modder ≃	158	29.02 S	24.37 E
Modderbee	273d	26.10 S	28.24 E
Modder East	273d	26.11 S	28.26 E
Modderfontein	273d	26.06 S	28.09 E
Modderfontein ≃	273d	26.13 S	28.10 E
Modderrivier	158	29.02 S	24.38 E
Model City	284a	43.11 N	78.59 W
Modena, It.	64	44.40 N	10.55 E
Modena, N.Y., U.S.	210	41.40 N	74.07 W
Modena □[4]	64	44.30 N	10.54 E
Moder ≃	56	48.49 N	8.06 E
Möderbrugg	61	47.17 N	14.29 E
Modern Art, Museum of ⊍	276	40.46 N	73.58 W
Modeste, Mount ∧	224	48.37 N	124.06 W
Modesto, Ca., U.S.	226	37.38 N	120.59 W
Modesto, Il., U.S.	219	39.29 N	89.59 W
Modesto City-County Airport ⊠	226	37.39 N	120.57 W
Modesto Main Canal ≍	226	37.39 N	120.27 W
Modesto Reservoir ⊜[1]	226	37.26 N	121.58 W
Modica	70	36.52 N	14.46 E
Modigliana	66	44.09 N	11.47 E
Modinagar	124	28.51 N	77.37 E
Modione ≃	70	37.34 N	12.49 E
Modjamboli	152	2.28 N	22.06 E
Modjeska	280	33.43 N	117.37 W
Mödling	264b	48.05 N	16.17 E
Mödling ≃	264b	48.04 N	16.22 E
Modoc	218	40.02 N	85.07 W
Modon ≃	50	47.16 N	1.27 E
Modowi	164	4.05 S	134.39 E
Modra, Česko.	30	48.21 N	17.17 E
Modra, Tchad	146	20.43 N	17.42 E
Modra špilja ⩍[5]	36	43.00 N	16.02 E
Mödrath	56	50.53 N	6.43 E
Modriča	38	44.57 N	18.18 E
Modřice	61	49.07 N	16.37 E
Mo Duc	110	14.57 N	108.53 E
Modugno	68	41.05 N	16.47 E
Moe	169	38.10 S	146.15 E
Moe ≃, Austl.	169	38.08 S	146.17 E
Moe ≃, P.Q., Can.	206	45.19 N	71.49 W
Moecherville	216	41.44 N	88.17 W
Moeda	255	20.20 S	44.03 W
Moehau ∧	172	36.35 S	175.24 E
Moel Fferna ∧	42	52.57 N	3.18 W
Moelv	26	60.56 N	10.42 E
Moema	255	19.50 S	45.24 W
Moen	50	50.46 N	3.24 E
Moen I	175c	7.26 N	151.52 E
Moena	64	46.22 N	11.39 E
Moengo	250	5.37 N	54.24 W
Moen-jo-Daro ⊥	120	27.18 N	68.15 E
Moenkopi	200	36.06 N	111.13 W
Moenkopi Wash V	200	35.54 N	111.26 W
Moeraki Point ›	172	45.22 S	170.52 E
Moerbeke, Bel.	50	50.45 N	3.55 E
Moerbeke, Bel.	50	51.10 N	3.56 E
Moerdijk	52	51.43 N	4.38 E
Moerewa	172	35.23 S	174.02 E
Moergestel	52	51.33 N	5.11 E
Moero, Lago → Mweru, Lake ⊜	154	9.00 S	28.45 E
Moers	56	51.27 N	6.37 E
Moersbach ≃	263	51.33 N	6.36 E
Moesa ≃	58	46.13 N	9.03 E
Moffat	44	55.20 N	3.27 W
Moffat Peak ∧	172	45.02 S	168.07 E
Moffatt	222	31.12 N	97.28 W
Moffatt, Lac ⊜	206	45.34 N	71.19 W
Moffat Water ≃	44	55.18 N	3.25 W
Moffet Point ›	180	55.26 N	162.32 W
Moffett Field Naval Air Station ■	226	37.24 N	122.03 W
Moffit	198	46.40 N	100.17 W
Mofoluku	273a	6.33 N	3.20 E
Moga	123	30.48 N	75.10 E
Mogadiscio → Muqdisho	144	2.04 N	45.22 E
Mogadishu → Muqdisho	144	2.04 N	45.22 E
Mogadore	214	41.02 N	81.23 W
Mogadore Reservoir ⊜[1]	214	41.04 N	81.21 W
Mogador → Essaouira	148	31.30 N	9.47 W
Mogadouro	34	41.20 N	6.39 W
Mogalakwena ≃	156	23.00 S	28.40 E
Mogalo	152	3.10 N	19.04 E
Mogami ≃	92	38.55 N	139.48 E
Mogan Shan ∧	106	30.36 N	119.52 E
Mogapinyana	156	22.19 S	27.27 E
Mogaung	110	25.18 N	96.56 E
Mogdy	89	50.35 N	133.51 E
Mogees	285	40.06 N	75.19 W
Møgeltønder	41	54.56 N	8.49 E
Mogenstrup	41	55.11 N	11.53 E
Mogent ≃	266d	41.33 N	2.15 E
Moggio Udinese	64	46.25 N	13.12 E
Mogi, Serra do ⋏	287b	23.47 S	46.20 W
Mogielnica	30	51.42 N	20.43 E
Mogila-Bel'mak, gora ∧[2]	78	47.20 N	36.35 E
Mogila-Mečetnaja, gora ∧[2]	83	48.16 N	38.53 E
Mogilev → Mogil'ov	76	53.54 N	30.21 E
Mogilno	30	52.40 N	17.58 E
Mogil'ov, Bela.	76	53.54 N	30.21 E
Mogil'ov, Ukr.	78	48.52 N	34.29 E
Mogil'ov-Podol'skij	78	48.27 N	27.48 E
Mogincual	154	15.35 S	40.25 E
Moglal, Wādī V	140	19.18 N	34.29 E
Moglia	64	44.56 N	10.55 E
Mogliano Veneto	64	45.33 N	12.14 E
Mogoča	88	53.44 N	119.44 E
Mogoča ≃	76	58.00 N	36.26 E
Mogočin	86	57.43 N	83.34 E
Mogod	88	48.24 N	103.00 E
Mogogh	140	8.26 N	31.19 E
Mogojto	88	54.25 N	110.27 E
Mogojtuj	88	51.17 N	114.55 E
Mogok	110	22.55 N	96.30 E
Mogollon Mountains ⋏	200	33.25 N	108.40 W
Mogollon Rim ⩍[4]	200	34.25 N	110.50 W
Mogor	120	32.52 N	67.47 E
Mogorella	71	39.52 N	8.51 E
Mogoro	71	39.41 N	8.47 E
Mogotes	246	6.30 N	72.58 W
Mogotón ∧	236	13.45 N	86.23 W
Mograt Island I	140	19.30 N	33.15 E
Mogroum	146	11.06 N	15.25 E
Moguer	34	37.16 N	6.50 W
Mogyoród	264c	47.36 N	19.15 E
Mogyoródi-patak ≃	264c	47.36 N	19.05 E
Mogzon	88	51.45 N	111.58 E
Mohács	30	45.59 N	18.42 E
Mohaka	172	39.07 S	177.11 E
Mohaka ≃	172	39.07 S	177.12 E
Mohall	198	48.45 N	101.30 W

Moḥammadābād	128	30.53 N	61.28 E
Mohammedia (Fedala)	148	33.44 N	7.24 W
Mohana	124	25.54 N	77.45 E
Mohangi	154	0.03 N	29.05 E
Mohania	124	25.11 N	83.37 E
Mohanpur, Bngl.	126	23.24 N	90.36 E
Mohanpur, India	126	21.51 N	87.26 E
Mohanpur, India	272a	28.44 N	77.10 E
Mohave, Lake ⊜[1]	204	35.25 N	114.38 W
Mohawk, Mi., U.S.	190	47.18 N	88.21 W
Mohawk, N.Y., U.S.	210	43.00 N	75.00 W
Mohawk ≃	210	42.47 N	73.42 W
Mohawk, East Branch ≃	212	43.22 N	75.28 W
Mohawk, Lake ⊜	276	41.02 N	74.41 W
Mohawk Dam ◆[6]	214	40.20 N	82.05 W
Mohawk Mountain ∧	207	41.49 N	73.17 W
Mohawk Point ›	212	42.51 N	79.29 W
Mohe	89	53.29 N	122.19 E
Moheda	26	57.00 N	14.34 E
Mohegan	207	41.28 N	72.06 W
Mohegan Lake	210	41.19 N	73.51 W
Mohelnice	30	49.46 N	16.55 E
Moher, Cliffs of ⩍[4]	48	52.57 N	9.26 W
Mohican ≃	214	40.22 N	82.09 W
Mohican, Black Fork ≃	214	40.35 N	82.17 W
Mohican, Cape ›	180	60.12 N	167.28 W
Mohican, Clear Fork ≃	214	40.35 N	82.12 W
Mohican, Jerome Fork ≃	214	40.45 N	82.23 W
Mohican, Lake Fork ≃	214	40.27 N	82.12 W
Mohican, Muddy Fork ≃	214	40.45 N	82.08 W
Mohican State Park ♠	214	40.37 N	82.16 W
Mohicanville Dam ◆[6]	214	40.44 N	82.09 W
Mohili ◆[8]	272c	19.06 N	72.53 E
Mohill	48	53.54 N	7.52 W
Mohlakeng	273d	26.13 S	27.42 E
Möhlau	54	51.44 N	12.21 E
Möhlin	58	47.34 N	7.51 E
Möhne ≃	52	51.27 N	7.57 E
Möhnestausee ⊜[1]	52	51.29 N	8.08 E
Mohns Ridge ✢[3]	16	72.30 N	5.00 E
Mohnton	208	40.17 N	75.59 W
Mohnyin	110	24.47 N	96.22 E
Moho ≃	236	16.04 N	88.52 W
Mohokare (Caledon) ≃	158	30.31 S	26.05 E
Moholm	40	58.37 N	14.02 E
Mohon	56	49.45 N	4.44 E
Mohorn	54	51.00 N	13.28 E
Mohoro	154	8.08 S	39.10 E
Möhringen	58	47.57 N	8.46 E
Mohrsville	208	40.28 N	75.59 W
Moi	26	58.28 N	6.32 E
Moiano, It.	68	40.39 N	14.28 E
Moiano, It.	68	41.05 N	14.32 E
Moindou	175f	21.42 S	165.41 E
Moinești	38	46.28 N	26.29 E
Moingbi	140	5.46 N	28.49 E
Moinkum	85	43.48 N	73.41 E
Mointy	86	47.13 N	73.21 E
Moio Alcantara	70	37.54 N	15.03 E
Moiporá	255	16.34 S	50.42 W
Moira	48	54.30 N	6.17 W
Moira ≃	212	44.09 N	77.23 W
Moiraba	250	2.27 S	49.25 W
Moira Lake ⊜	212	44.29 N	77.27 W
Moirans	62	45.20 N	5.34 E
Moirans-en-Montagne	58	46.26 N	5.44 E
Mõisaküla	76	58.06 N	25.11 E
Moisdon	32	47.37 N	1.22 W
Moisejeviči	76	53.13 N	28.17 E
Moisejevka, Ross.	86	58.05 N	76.16 E
Moisejevka, Ukr.	83	49.14 N	39.51 E
Moisejevo Alabuška	76	51.54 N	42.06 E
Moisenay	261	48.34 N	2.44 E
Moisés Ville	252	30.43 S	61.29 W
Moisie	186	50.11 N	66.05 W
Moisie ≃	176	50.11 N	66.05 W
Moisie, Baie de ⊂	186	50.16 N	65.56 W
Moisling ◆[8]	52	53.50 N	10.38 E
Moison Creek ≃	281	42.18 N	82.40 W
Moissac	32	44.06 N	1.05 E
Moïssala	146	8.21 N	17.46 E
Moisselles	261	49.03 N	2.20 E
Moisson	261	49.05 N	1.40 E
Moisson, Forêt de ♠	261	49.03 N	1.39 E
Moissy-Cramayel	261	48.38 N	2.36 E
Moita	34	38.39 N	8.59 W
Moitaco	246	8.01 N	64.21 W
Moivre ≃	56	48.52 N	4.28 E
Mojácar	34	37.08 N	1.51 W
Mojana, Brazo ≃[1]	246	9.02 N	74.46 W
Mojave	228	35.03 N	118.10 W
Mojave ≃	204	35.06 N	116.04 W
Mojave Desert ◆[2]	204	35.00 N	117.00 W
Mojave River Forks Reservoir ⊜[1]	228	34.20 N	117.15 W
Moji	85	38.59 N	74.24 E
Mojiang	102	23.28 N	101.39 E
Mojicuaçu ≃	255	20.53 S	48.10 W
Moji das Cruzes	256	23.31 S	46.11 W
Mojiguaçu	256	22.22 S	46.57 W
Mojimirim	256	22.26 S	46.57 W
Mojjero ≃	74	68.44 N	103.42 E
Mojnalyk	88	51.18 N	95.33 E
Mojo	144	8.36 N	39.07 E
Mojoagung	115a	7.34 S	112.21 E
Mojokerto	115a	7.28 S	112.26 E
Mojosari	115a	7.31 S	112.33 E
Mojstrana	64	46.27 N	13.56 E
Moju	250	1.53 S	48.46 W
Moju ≃	250	1.40 S	48.25 W
Mōka	94	36.26 N	140.01 E
Mokai	172	38.32 S	175.54 E
Mokāma	124	25.24 N	85.55 E
Mokambo	154	12.25 S	28.21 E
Mokane	219	38.40 N	91.52 W
Mokapu Peninsula ›[1]	229c	21.27 N	157.45 W
Mokaria	152	2.00 N	23.20 E
Mokarta, Castello di ⊥	70	37.48 N	12.45 E
Mokau	172	38.41 S	174.37 E
Mokau ≃	172	38.42 S	174.37 E
Moke	102	30.14 N	100.01 E
Mokelumne ≃	226	38.13 N	121.28 W
Mokelumne, Middle Fork ≃	226	38.22 N	120.37 W
Mokelumne, North Fork ≃	226	38.22 N	120.37 W
Mokelumne, South Fork ≃	226	38.23 N	120.35 W
Mokelumne Aqueduct ≍[1]	226	37.54 N	122.07 W
Mokelumne Hill	226	38.18 N	120.42 W
Mokena	216	41.31 N	87.53 W
Mokhotlong	158	29.22 S	29.02 E
Mokil I[1]	14	6.40 N	159.47 E
Mokimbo	154	6.20 S	28.42 E
Mokino	80	57.27 N	49.11 E
Moklakan	88	54.56 N	118.56 E
Möklinta	40	60.05 N	16.32 E
Moknine	148	35.38 N	10.54 E
Mokochu, Khao ∧	110	15.56 N	99.06 E
Mokohinau Islands II	172	35.55 S	175.07 E
Mokokchūng	120	26.20 N	94.32 E
Mokolo, Cam.	146	10.45 N	13.48 E
Mokolo, Zaïre	152	1.57 N	18.05 E
Mokolo ≃	156	23.14 S	27.43 E
Mokombe	152	0.14 S	23.48 E
Mokoreta ≃	172	46.21 S	168.51 E
Mokou	273b	4.13 S	15.13 E
Mokpalin	110	17.26 N	96.53 E
Mokp'o	98	34.48 N	126.22 E
Mokraja Jel'muta	80	46.51 N	41.41 E

Mokraja Ol'chovka	80	50.28 N	44.59 E
Mokraja Sura ≃	78	48.19 N	35.09 E
Mokraja Volnovacha ≃	83	47.30 N	37.15 E
Mokrany	78	51.50 N	24.14 E
Mokrisset	34	34.59 N	5.20 W
Mokro-Jelančik	83	47.42 N	38.31 E
Mokrous	80	51.14 N	47.37 E
Mokrousovo	86	55.48 N	66.45 E
Mokrušinskoje	86	57.31 N	93.11 E
Mokryje Jaly ≃	78	48.05 N	36.44 E
Mokryj Gašun	80	46.53 N	42.45 E
Mokryj Jelančik ≃	83	47.08 N	38.20 E
Mokryj Kor	82	54.34 N	37.58 E
Mokša ≃	80	54.44 N	41.53 E
Mokšan	80	53.26 N	44.37 E
Moku	154	2.57 N	29.22 E
Mokuleia	229c	21.35 N	158.09 W
Mokumbusu	152	1.44 N	21.04 E
Mokvin	78	50.57 N	26.48 E
Mokwa	150	9.20 N	5.02 E
Mol	56	51.11 N	5.06 E
Mola di Bari	68	41.04 N	17.05 E
Molale	144	10.08 N	39.42 E
Molalla	224	45.08 N	122.34 W
Molalla ≃	224	45.18 N	122.43 W
Molalla, North Fork ≃	224	45.05 N	122.29 W
Molanda	152	2.28 N	20.48 E
Molango	234	20.53 N	98.46 W
Molanosa	184	54.30 N	105.33 W
Moláoi	38	36.48 N	22.52 E
Molara, Isola I	71	40.52 N	9.43 E
Molaretto	62	45.10 N	7.00 E
Molat, Otok I	36	44.15 N	14.49 E
Molbergen	52	52.51 N	7.55 E
Molčanovka	83	46.52 N	38.37 E
Molčanovo	86	57.35 N	83.48 E
Mold	44	53.10 N	3.08 W
Moldary	86	50.47 N	78.29 E
Moldau → Vltava ≃	30	50.21 N	14.30 E
Moldavia □[9]	38	47.00 N	27.15 E
Moldavia → Moldova □[1]	78	47.00 N	29.00 E
Moldavija → Moldova □[1]	72	47.00 N	29.00 E
Molde	26	62.44 N	7.11 E
Moldotau, chrebet ⋏	85	41.35 N	74.40 E
Moldova □[1], Europe	22	47.00 N	29.00 E
Moldova □[1], Europe	78	47.00 N	29.00 E
Moldova ≃	38	46.54 N	26.58 E
Moldova Nouă	38	44.44 N	21.40 E
Moldoveanu, Vîrful ∧	38	45.36 N	24.44 E
Môle ≃, Fr.	62	43.15 N	6.32 E
Mole ≃, Eng., U.K.	42	50.57 N	3.54 W
Mole ≃, Eng., U.K.	42	51.24 N	0.21 W
Môle, Cap du ›	238	19.50 N	73.25 W
Mole Creek	166	41.33 S	146.24 E
Moledet	132	32.35 N	35.26 E
Molega Lake ⊜	186	44.22 N	64.53 W
Mole Game Reserve ◆[4]	150	9.30 N	2.00 W
Molegbe	152	4.14 N	20.53 E
Molenbeek-St.-Jean	50	50.51 N	4.19 E
Molepolole	156	24.25 S	25.30 E
Moléson ∧	58	46.33 N	7.01 E
Molėtai	76	55.14 N	25.25 E
Mole Valley □[8]	260	51.16 N	0.18 W
Molfetta	68	41.12 N	16.36 E
Molibagu	112	0.23 N	123.59 E
Molières-sur-Cèze	62	44.15 N	4.09 E
Molimiao	89	43.34 N	121.54 E
Molina	252	35.07 S	71.17 W
Molina de Aragón	34	40.51 N	1.53 W
Molina de Segura	34	38.03 N	1.12 W
Molina di Ledro	64	45.56 N	10.46 E
Molinara	68	41.18 N	14.54 E
Moline, Il., U.S.	190	41.30 N	90.30 W
Moline, Ks., U.S.	198	37.21 N	96.18 W
Moline, Mi., U.S.	216	42.44 N	85.39 W
Molinella	64	44.37 N	11.40 E
Molinges	58	46.21 N	5.46 E
Molingguan	106	31.50 N	118.50 E
Molini di Tures (Mühlen)	64	46.54 N	11.56 E
Molinière Point ›	241k	12.05 N	61.45 W
Molino	194	30.43 N	87.18 W
Molino de Rosas ◆[8]	286a	19.22 N	99.13 W
Molinos	252	25.25 S	66.19 W
Molins de Rei	34	41.25 N	2.01 E
Moliro	154	8.13 S	30.34 E
Molise □[4]	66	41.35 N	14.30 E
Moliterno	68	40.14 N	50.52 E
Mölkau	54	51.20 N	12.26 E
Molkom	40	59.36 N	13.43 E
Möll ≃	64	46.50 N	13.26 E
Mollahasan	130	39.22 N	42.37 E
Mollāhāt	126	22.56 N	89.48 E
Mollakendi	130	38.36 N	39.20 E
Mollaro	64	46.16 N	11.05 E
Möllbrücke	64	46.50 N	13.22 E
Mölle	41	56.17 N	12.29 E
Möllen	263	51.35 N	6.42 E
Möllenbeck, Dtsch.	54	53.17 N	11.44 E
Möllenbeck, Dtsch.	54	53.23 N	13.20 E
Mollendo	248	17.02 S	72.01 W
Möllensee ⊜	264a	52.26 N	13.51 E
Mollepata	248	13.31 S	72.32 W
Moller, Port ⊂	180	55.51 N	160.25 W
Möllersdorf	264b	48.02 N	16.18 E
Mollet del Vallès	266d	41.33 N	2.13 E
Mollia	62	45.49 N	8.02 E
Molliens-Vidame	50	49.53 N	2.01 E
Mollington	262	53.13 N	2.55 W
Mollis	58	47.05 N	9.04 E
Mölln, Dtsch.	54	53.37 N	10.41 E
Molln, Öst.	61	47.53 N	14.15 E
Mollösund	26	58.04 N	11.28 E
Mollusk	208	37.43 N	76.32 W
Molly Ann Brook ≃	276	40.55 N	74.11 W
Mölnbo	40	59.03 N	17.25 E
Mölndal	26	57.39 N	12.01 E
Mölnlycke	26	57.39 N	12.09 E
Mölntorp	40	59.33 N	16.15 E
Molocaboc Island I	116	10.58 N	123.34 E
Moločansk	78	47.12 N	35.36 E
Molochio	68	38.18 N	16.02 E
Moločnaja ≃	78	46.42 N	35.20 E
Moločnoje	76	59.17 N	39.41 E
Moločnoje, ozero ⊜	78	46.30 N	35.20 E
Molócuè ≃	154	17.03 S	38.52 E
Molodečno	76	54.19 N	26.49 E
Molodežnaja ⊍[3]	9	67.35 S	46.35 E
Molodi	82	55.17 N	37.31 E
Molodo	150	14.14 N	6.02 W
Molodogvardejsk	83	48.20 N	39.40 E
Molodoj Tud	76	56.26 N	33.36 E
Molod'ožnyj	89	50.23 N	136.48 E
Mologa ≃	76	58.50 N	37.11 E
Molokai I	229a	21.07 N	157.00 W
Molokai Fracture Zone ✢	14	23.00 N	148.00 W
Molokai Fracture Zone ✢	16	23.00 N	130.00 W
Molokča ≃	82	56.15 N	38.45 E
Molokini I	229a	20.38 N	156.30 W
Molokovo, Ross.	76	58.10 N	36.45 E
Molokovo, Ross.	82	55.34 N	37.52 E
Moloma ≃	24	58.20 N	48.28 E
Molong	166	33.06 S	148.52 E
Molonglo ≃	171b	35.15 S	148.58 E
Molopo ≃	156	28.30 S	20.13 E
Molotkoviči	78	52.07 N	25.56 E
Molotov → Perm'	86	58.00 N	56.15 E
Molotovsk → Severodvinsk	24	64.34 N	39.50 E
Molou	146	13.42 N	21.44 E
Moloundou	152	2.03 N	15.10 E
Molowaie	152	5.47 S	23.20 E

Symbol	English	Deutsch	Español	Français	Português
≃	River	Fluß	Río	Rivière	Rio
≍	Canal	Kanal	Canal	Canal	Canal
↳	Waterfall, Rapids	Wasserfall, Stromschnellen	Cascada, Rápidos	Chute d'eau, Rapides	Cascata, Rápidos
⋓	Strait	Meeresstraße	Estrecho	Détroit	Estreito
⊂	Bay, Gulf	Bucht, Golf	Bahía, Golfo	Baie, Golfe	Baía, Golfo
⊜	Lake, Lakes	See, Seen	Lago, Lagos	Lac, Lacs	Lago, Lagos
≚	Swamp	Sumpf	Pantano	Marais	Pântano
⌂	Ice Features, Glacier	Eis- und Gletscherformen	Accidentes Glaciales	Formes glaciaires	Acidentes glaciares
⊤	Other Hydrographic Features	Andere Hydrographische Objekte	Otros Elementos Hidrográficos	Autres données hydrographiques	Outros acidentes hidrográficos
✢	Submarine Features	Untermeerische Objekte	Accidentes Submarinos	Formes de relief sous-marin	Acidentes submarinos
□	Political Unit	Politische Einheit	Unidad Politica	Entité politique	Unidade política
⊍	Cultural Institution	Kulturelle Institution	Institución Cultural	Institution culturelle	Instituição cultural
⊥	Historical Site	Historische Stätte	Sitio Histórico	Site historique	Sitio histórico
♠	Recreational Site	Erholungs- und Ferienort	Sitio de Recreo	Centre de loisirs	Area de Lazer
⊠	Airport	Flughafen	Aeropuerto	Aéroport	Aeroporto
■	Military Installation	Militäranlage	Instalación Militar	Installation militaire	Instalação militar
◆	Miscellaneous	Verschiedenes	Misceláneo	Divers	Diversos

Name	Page	Lat.°′	Long.°′
Moloy	58	47.32 N	4.55 E
Molsheim	58	48.32 N	7.29 E
Molson Lake ⊜	184	54.12 N	96.45 W
Molteno	158	31.22 S	26.22 E
Moltrasio	58	45.52 N	9.05 E
Molu, Pulau I	164	6.45 S	131.33 E
Moluca, Mar de la → Maluku, Laut ±[2]	108	0.00	125.00 E
Molucas, Islas → Maluku II	108	2.00 S	128.00 E
Molucca Sea → Maluku, Laut ±[2]	108	0.00	125.00 E
Moluccas → Maluku II	108	2.00 S	128.00 E
Molukken → Maluku II	108	2.00 S	128.00 E
Molumbo	154	15.27 S	30.15 E
Molundo	116	7.56 N	124.23 E
Moluques → Maluku II	108	2.00 S	128.00 E
Molveno, Lago di ⊜	64	46.08 N	10.57 E
Molvoticy	76	57.25 N	32.20 E
Molžaninovo	82	55.56 N	37.22 E
Moma, Moç.	154	16.44 S	39.14 E
Moma, Zaïre	152	1.36 S	23.57 E
Moma ≃	74	66.26 N	143.06 E
Momanga	156	18.12 S	21.42 E
Momats ≃	164	5.20 S	137.47 E
Momax	234	21.56 N	103.19 W
Momba ≃	154	8.28 S	32.40 E
Mombaça	250	5.45 S	39.38 W
Mombaça, Corrego ≃	287b	23.46 S	46.47 W
Mombachito, Cerro ∧	236	12.24 N	85.34 W
Mombacho, Volcán ∧[1]	236	11.50 N	85.58 W
Mombango	152	1.45 N	24.26 E
Mombaruzzo	62	44.46 N	8.27 E
Mombasa	154	4.03 S	39.40 E
Mombetsu	92a	44.21 N	143.22 E
Mombo	154	4.53 S	38.17 E
Mombongo	152	1.39 N	23.09 E
Momboyo ≃	152	0.16 S	19.00 E
Mombuey	34	42.02 N	6.20 W
Mombum	164	8.23 S	138.51 E
Momčilgrad	38	41.32 N	25.25 E
Momence	216	41.10 N	87.39 W
Momfafa, Tanjung ›	164	0.18 S	131.20 E
Momi	175g	17.55 S	177.17 E
Momignies	50	50.02 N	4.10 E
Mommark	41	54.55 N	10.03 E
Mommenheim	56	48.45 N	7.39 E
Momo	152	1.52 N	11.48 E
Momotombo, Volcán ∧[1]	236	12.26 N	86.33 W
Momozaka	270	34.51 N	135.02 E
Mompog Island I	116	13.31 N	122.11 E
Mompog Pass ◡	116	13.34 N	122.13 E
Mompono	152	0.04 N	21.48 E
Mompós	246	9.14 N	74.26 W
Momskij chrebet ⋏	74	66.00 N	146.00 E
Mon	110	18.31 N	96.38 E
Mon □[8]	110	17.30 N	97.00 E
Møn I	41	55.00 N	12.20 E
Mon ≃	110	20.20 N	94.54 E
Mona	200	39.48 N	111.51 W
Mona, Canal de la ◡	238	18.30 N	67.45 W
Mona, Isla de I	238	18.05 N	67.54 W
Mona, Punta ›	236	9.38 N	82.37 W
Monaca	214	40.41 N	80.16 W
Monach, Sound of ◡	46	57.34 N	7.35 W
Monach Islands II	46	57.31 N	7.40 W
Monachovo	83	48.09 N	38.07 E
Monaci, Fiume dei ≃	70	37.24 N	14.48 E
Monaco	62	43.42 N	7.23 E
Monaco □[1], Europe	22	43.45 N	7.25 E
Monaco □[1], Europe	62	43.45 N	7.25 E
Monadhliath Mountains ⋏	46	57.10 N	4.00 W
Monadnock Mountain ∧	207	42.52 N	72.07 W
Monagas □[3]	246	9.20 N	63.00 W
Monaghan	48	54.15 N	6.58 W
Monaghan □[6]	48	54.10 N	7.00 W
Monagrillo	236	7.59 N	80.26 W
Monahans	196	31.35 N	102.53 W
Monahans Draw V	196	31.55 N	101.46 W
Monahans Sandhills State Park ♦	196	31.38 N	102.50 W
Monakino	89	43.24 N	133.29 E
Mona Lake ⊜	216	43.11 N	86.17 W
Monamolin	48	52.33 N	6.20 W
Monango	198	46.10 N	98.35 W
Monapo	154	14.57 S	40.17 E
Monapo ≃	154	15.07 S	40.33 E
Mona Quimbundo	152	9.55 S	19.58 E
Monar, Loch ⊜	46	57.25 N	5.06 W
Monarch	192	34.43 N	81.35 W
Monarch Mountain ∧	182	51.54 N	125.53 W
Monarch Pass)(	200	38.30 N	106.19 W
Monaro Range ⋏	171b	36.22 S	149.03 E
Monarto South	168b	35.08 S	139.08 E
Monaš	80	46.58 N	50.36 E
Monashee Mountains ⋏	182	50.30 N	118.30 W
Monashee Provincial Park ♦	182	50.28 N	118.11 W
Monash University ʊ[2]	274b	37.55 S	145.08 E
Monasterace	68	38.27 N	16.33 E
Monasterevin	48	53.07 N	7.02 W
Monasterolo di Savigliano	62	44.40 N	7.37 E
Monastir, It.	71	39.23 N	9.02 E
Monastir, Tun.	148	35.47 N	10.50 E
Monastir □[8]	148	35.15 N	10.45 E
Monastir → Bitola	38	41.01 N	21.20 E
Monastyrišče	78	49.00 N	29.49 E
Monastyriska	78	49.06 N	25.11 E
Monastyrščina	76	54.21 N	31.50 E
Monatélé	152	4.16 N	11.12 E
Mona Vale	170	33.41 S	151.18 E
Monbulk	274b	37.52 S	145.25 E
Monbulk Creek ≃	274b	37.54 S	145.15 E
Moncada	116	15.44 N	120.34 E
Moncalieri	62	45.00 N	7.41 E
Moncalvo	62	45.03 N	8.16 E
Monção, Bra.	250	3.30 S	45.15 W
Moncão, Port.	34	42.05 N	8.29 W
Monceau-sur-Sambre	50	50.25 N	4.22 E
Mončegorsk	24	67.54 N	32.58 E
Mönchdorf	61	48.21 N	14.48 E
Mönchengladbach	56	51.12 N	6.28 E
Mönchengladbach, Flughafen ⊠	263	51.14 N	6.29 E
Mönchhof	61	47.52 N	16.56 E
Monchique	34	37.19 N	8.33 W
Mönchweiler	58	48.06 N	8.25 E
Moncks Corner	192	33.11 N	80.00 W
Monclova	232	26.54 N	101.25 W
Moncontour	32	48.21 N	2.39 W
Moncoutant	32	46.43 N	0.35 W
Moncton	186	46.06 N	64.47 W
Mondaí	252	27.05 S	53.25 W
Mondaino	66	43.51 N	12.41 E
Mondavio	66	43.40 N	12.58 E
Monday ≃	252	25.33 S	54.41 W
Mondego ≃	34	40.09 N	8.52 W
Mondego, Cabo ›	34	40.11 N	8.55 W
Mondello	70	38.13 N	13.20 E
Mondeodo	112	3.33 S	122.12 E
Mondeor	273d	26.17 S	28.00 E
Mondimbi	152	1.43 N	22.58 E
Mondo, Tan.	154	4.59 S	35.54 E
Mondo, Tchad	146	13.47 N	15.32 E
Mondolè, Monte ∧	62	44.13 N	7.46 E
Mondolfo	66	43.45 N	13.06 E
Mondombe	152	0.53 S	22.45 E
Mondoñedo	34	43.26 N	7.22 W
Mondorf-les-Bains	56	49.31 N	6.16 E
Mondoro	150	14.40 N	1.57 W
Mondoubleau	50	47.59 N	0.54 E
Mondovi	190	44.34 N	91.40 W
Mondragon, Fr.	62	44.14 N	4.43 E
Mondragon, Pil.	116	12.31 N	124.45 E
Mondragone	68	41.07 N	13.53 E
Mondrain Island I	162	34.08 S	122.15 E
Mondsee	64	47.52 N	13.21 E
Mondsee ⊜	64	47.49 N	13.23 E
Monds Island I	285	39.50 N	75.19 W
Mondy	88	51.40 N	100.59 E
Monee	216	41.25 N	87.45 W
Moneglia	62	44.14 N	9.30 E
Monemvasía	38	36.41 N	23.03 E
Monero	200	36.54 N	106.52 W
Moneron, ostrov I	89	46.17 N	141.15 E
Monesiglio	62	44.28 N	8.07 E
Monessen	214	40.08 N	79.53 W
Monesterio	34	38.05 N	6.16 W
Monestier-de-Clermont	62	44.54 N	5.38 E
Monetnyj	86	57.03 N	60.53 E
Monett	194	36.55 N	93.55 W
Monette	194	35.53 N	90.20 W
Money Creek ≃	216	40.40 N	88.58 W
Moneygall	48	52.53 N	7.57 W
Moneymore	48	54.42 N	6.40 W
Monfalcone	64	45.49 N	13.32 E
Monferrato □[9]	62	44.55 N	8.05 E
Monflanquin	32	44.32 N	0.46 E
Monforte	34	39.03 N	7.26 W
Monforte de Lemos	34	42.31 N	7.30 W
Monforte San Giorgio	70	38.09 N	15.23 E
Monfort Heights	218	39.12 N	84.37 W
Monga	152	4.12 N	22.49 E
Mongaguá	256	24.06 S	46.37 W
Mongai-Musenge	152	4.04 S	19.34 E
Mongala ≃	152	1.53 N	19.46 E
Mongalla	154	5.12 N	31.46 E
Mongalla Game Reserve ◆[4]	154	5.12 N	31.33 E
Mongandjo	152	1.21 N	24.20 E
Mongarlowe ≃	170	35.15 S	149.52 E
Mongat	266d	41.28 N	2.17 E
Mongaup ≃	210	41.25 N	74.45 W
Mongaup Valley	210	41.40 N	74.47 W
Mongbwalu	154	1.57 N	30.02 E
Mongbyŏn-ni	271b	37.40 N	126.44 E
Mong Cai	110	21.32 N	107.58 E
Monge ∧	266c	38.46 N	9.26 W
Monger, Îles II	186	51.05 N	58.45 W
Mongeri	150	8.19 N	11.44 W
Mongers Lake ⊜	162	29.15 S	117.05 E
Monggon Qulu	89	48.35 N	119.49 E
Monggŭmp'o	98	38.09 N	124.47 E
Möng Hai	110	20.46 N	99.49 E
Möng Hawm	110	23.51 N	98.20 E
Monghidoro	66	44.13 N	11.19 E
Möng Hpāyak	110	20.53 N	99.54 E
Möng Hsat	110	20.32 N	99.15 E
Monghyr → Munger	124	25.23 N	86.28 E
Mongi ≃	164	6.35 S	147.35 E
Mongiana	68	38.31 N	16.19 E
Mongibello → Etna, Monte ∧[1]	70	37.46 N	15.00 E
Mongiuffi	70	37.55 N	15.17 E
Möng Küng	110	21.36 N	97.32 E
Möng Ma	110	21.37 N	99.54 E
Möng Mit	110	23.07 N	96.41 E
Möng Nai	110	20.31 N	97.52 E
Möng Nawng	110	21.39 N	98.08 E
Mongo, Tchad	146	12.11 N	18.42 E
Mongo, In., U.S.	216	41.41 N	85.17 W
Mongo ≃	150	9.34 N	12.11 W
Mongoj	88	53.57 N	113.50 E
Mongol Altajn nuruu ⋏	90	46.30 N	93.00 E
Mongol Ard Uls → Mongolia □[1]	90	46.00 N	105.00 E
Mongolei → Mongolia □[1]	90	46.00 N	105.00 E
Mongol els ◆[2]	88	47.45 N	94.30 E
Mongolia (Mongol Ard Uls) □[1]	90	46.00 N	105.00 E
Mongolie → Mongolia □[1]	90	46.00 N	105.00 E
Mongomo	152	1.38 N	11.19 E
Möngön Mor't	88	48.11 N	108.29 E
Mongororo	146	12.01 N	22.28 E
Mongoumba	152	3.38 N	18.36 E
Möng Pai	110	19.44 N	97.05 E
Möng Pan	110	20.19 N	98.22 E
Möng Pawn	110	20.49 N	97.28 E
Möng Ping	110	22.22 N	99.02 E
Mongpong ≃	116	12.44 N	120.48 E
Mongrando	62	45.31 N	8.00 E
Möng Si	110	23.40 N	98.23 E
Mong Tung Hang	271d	22.20 N	114.02 E
Mongu	152	15.15 S	23.09 E
Môngua	152	16.43 S	15.23 E
Monguelfo (Welsberg)	64	46.45 N	12.06 E
Monguno	146	12.40 N	13.38 E
Möng Yai	110	22.25 N	98.02 E
Möng Yawng	110	21.11 N	100.22 E
Monheim, Dtsch.	56	48.50 N	10.51 E
Monheim, Dtsch.	56	51.05 N	6.52 E
Moniaive	44	55.12 N	3.55 W
Mönichkirchen	61	47.31 N	16.02 E
Monico	190	45.34 N	89.09 W
Monida Pass)(	202	44.33 N	112.18 W
Mon Idée	50	49.53 N	4.23 E
Monie	152	4.00 S	17.22 E
Monie Bay ⊂	208	38.13 N	75.51 W
Monie Creek ≃	208	38.14 N	75.50 W
Monifieth	46	56.29 N	2.49 W
Monimail	46	56.18 N	3.08 W
Moninger	214	40.14 N	80.13 W
Monino	82	55.50 N	38.11 E
Moniquirá	246	5.52 N	73.36 W
Mõniste	76	57.35 N	26.33 E
Monistrol-d'Allier	62	44.57 N	3.38 E
Monistrol-sur-Loire	62	45.17 N	4.10 E
Monitor Range ⋏	204	38.45 N	116.30 W
Monitor Valley V	204	39.00 N	116.40 W
Monívea	48	53.23 N	8.43 W
Monjolo	256	22.49 S	42.57 W
Monk, Pointe ›	275a	45.29 N	73.57 W
Monkayo	116	7.50 N	126.03 E
Mönkebude	54	53.46 N	13.57 E
Monken Hadley ◆[8]	260	51.40 N	0.11 W
Monkey Bay	154	14.05 S	34.55 E
Monkey River	236	16.22 N	88.29 W
Mońki	30	53.24 N	22.49 E
Monkira	166	24.49 S	140.34 E
Monkoto	152	1.38 S	20.39 E
Monks Heath	262	53.16 N	2.14 W
Monkton	212	43.35 N	81.05 W
Monmouth, Wales, U.K.	42	51.50 N	2.43 W
Monmouth, Il., U.S.	190	40.54 N	90.38 W
Monmouth, In., U.S.	216	40.52 N	84.57 W
Monmouth, Or., U.S.	202	44.50 N	123.13 W
Monmouth □[6]	208	40.16 N	74.17 W
Monmouth Beach	276	40.19 N	73.58 W
Monmouth Hills	276	40.24 N	74.00 W
Monmouth Junction	208	40.22 N	74.32 W
Monmouth Mountain ∧	182	51.00 N	123.47 W
Monnickendam	52	52.27 N	5.02 E
Monnow ≃	42	51.48 N	2.42 W
Mono □[5]	150	6.45 N	1.50 E
Mono □[6]	226	38.18 N	119.22 W
Mono ≃	150	6.17 N	1.51 E
Mono, Caño ≃	246	4.25 N	67.47 W
Mono, Punta ›	236	11.36 N	83.39 W
Monobe	96	33.42 N	133.53 E
Monobe ≃	96	33.32 N	133.41 E
Monocacy ≃	208	39.13 N	77.27 W
Monocacy Station	208	40.16 N	75.46 W
Monogarovo	82	54.42 N	38.45 E
Mono Island I	175e	7.21 S	155.34 E
Mono Lake ⊜	204	38.00 N	119.00 W
Monolith	228	35.07 N	118.22 W
Monomoy Island I	207	41.35 N	69.59 W
Monomoy Point ›	207	41.33 N	70.02 W
Monon	216	40.52 N	86.52 W
Monona, Ia., U.S.	190	43.03 N	91.23 W
Monona, Wi., U.S.	216	43.03 N	89.20 W
Monona, Lake ⊜	216	43.03 N	89.22 W
Monongahela	214	40.12 N	79.55 W
Monongahela ≃	188	40.27 N	80.00 W
Monongahela Brook ≃	285	39.47 N	75.09 W
Monopoli	68	40.57 N	17.19 E
Monor	30	47.21 N	19.27 E
Mono Road Station	275b	43.51 N	79.51 W
Monòver	34	38.26 N	0.50 W
Monowai, Lake ⊜	172	45.52 S	167.27 E
Monponsett	207	42.01 N	70.50 W
Monponsett Pond ⊜	283	42.01 N	70.51 W
Monreal	34	42.42 N	1.30 W
Monreal del Campo	34	40.47 N	1.21 W
Monreale	70	38.05 N	13.17 E
Monreale, Castello di ⊥	71	39.38 N	8.49 E
Monroe, Ct., U.S.	207	41.19 N	73.12 W
Monroe, Fl., U.S.	220	25.52 N	81.06 W
Monroe, Ga., U.S.	192	33.47 N	83.42 W
Monroe, In., U.S.	216	40.44 N	84.56 W
Monroe, Ia., U.S.	190	41.31 N	93.06 W
Monroe, La., U.S.	194	32.30 N	92.07 W
Monroe, Mi., U.S.	214	41.54 N	83.23 W
Monroe, Ne., U.S.	198	41.28 N	97.35 W
Monroe, N.J., U.S.	276	41.06 N	74.38 W
Monroe, N.Y., U.S.	210	41.19 N	74.11 W
Monroe, N.C., U.S.	192	34.59 N	80.32 W
Monroe, Oh., U.S.	218	39.26 N	84.21 W
Monroe, Or., U.S.	202	44.18 N	123.17 W
Monroe, Ut,. U.S.	200	38.37 N	112.07 W
Monroe, Va., U.S.	192	37.30 N	79.07 W
Monroe, Wa., U.S.	224	47.51 N	121.58 W
Monroe, Wi., U.S.	190	42.36 N	89.38 W
Monroe □[6], Fl., U.S.	220	25.10 N	81.10 W
Monroe □[6], Il., U.S.	219	38.20 N	90.09 W
Monroe □[6], In., U.S.	218	39.10 N	86.26 W
Monroe □[6], Mi., U.S.	216	41.55 N	83.26 W
Monroe □[6], Mo., U.S.	219	39.30 N	92.00 W
Monroe □[6], N.Y., U.S.	210	43.10 N	77.36 W
Monroe □[6], Pa., U.S.	210	40.59 N	75.12 W
Monroe, Lake ⊜	220	28.52 N	81.16 W
Monroe Bridge	207	42.43 N	72.56 W
Monroe Center, Ct., U.S.	207	41.20 N	73.12 W
Monroe Center, Il., U.S.	216	42.06 N	89.00 W
Monroe City, In., U.S.	194	38.36 N	87.21 W
Monroe City, Mo., U.S.	219	39.39 N	91.44 W
Monroe City, Tx., U.S.	222	29.47 N	94.35 W
Monroe Lake ⊜[1]	218	39.05 N	86.25 W
Monroe Manor	216	41.36 N	86.40 W
Monroeton	210	41.43 N	76.30 W
Monroeville, Al., U.S.	194	31.31 N	87.19 W
Monroeville, In., U.S.	216	40.58 N	84.52 W
Monroeville, N.J., U.S.	208	39.37 N	75.09 W
Monroeville, Oh., U.S.	214	41.14 N	82.41 W
Monroeville, Pa., U.S.	214	40.26 N	79.47 W
Monroeville Mall ◆[9]	279b	40.26 N	79.48 W
Monrovia, Liber.	150	6.18 N	10.47 W
Monrovia, Ca., U.S.	228	34.08 N	117.59 W
Monrovia, In., U.S.	218	39.34 N	86.28 W
Monrovia Mountain Park ♦	280	34.10 N	118.10 W
Monrovia Peak ∧	280	34.13 N	117.58 W
Mons (Bergen), Bel.	50	50.27 N	3.56 E
Mons, Fr.	62	43.41 N	6.43 E
Monschau	56	50.33 N	6.14 E
Monse	112	4.07 S	123.15 E
Monsefú	248	6.52 S	79.52 W
Monselice	64	45.14 N	11.45 E
Monsenhor Hipólito	250	6.59 S	41.07 W
Monsenhor Paulo	256	21.46 S	45.33 W
Monsenhor Tabosa	250	4.47 S	40.04 W
Monserrato	71	39.15 N	9.08 E
Monsey	210	41.06 N	74.04 W
Monsheim, Dtsch.	56	49.38 N	8.12 E
Mönsheim, Dtsch.	56	48.52 N	8.52 E
Møns Klint ±[4]	41	54.58 N	12.33 E
Monsols	58	46.13 N	4.31 E
Monson, Me., U.S.	188	45.17 N	69.30 W
Monson, Ma., U.S.	207	42.06 N	72.19 W
Monster	52	52.02 N	4.10 E
Mönsterås	26	57.02 N	16.26 E
Monsummano Terme	66	43.52 N	10.49 E
Montà	62	44.48 N	7.57 E
Montabaur	56	50.26 N	7.50 E
Montabaur □[5]	56	50.30 N	7.40 E
Montafon V	58	47.02 N	9.57 E
Montagano	66	41.39 N	14.40 E
Montagnana	64	45.14 N	11.28 E
Montagnareale	70	38.07 N	14.57 E
Montagne d'Ambre, Parque National de la ♦	157b	12.40 S	49.05 E
Montagnola ⋏	66	43.17 N	11.11 E
Montagrier	32	45.16 N	0.29 E
Montagu	158	33.45 S	20.08 E
Montague, P.E., Can.	186	46.10 N	62.39 W
Montague, Ca., U.S.	204	41.43 N	122.31 W
Montague, Ma., U.S.	207	42.32 N	72.32 W
Montague, Mi., U.S.	190	43.25 N	86.21 W
Montague, Tx., U.S.	196	33.40 N	97.43 W
Montague, Isla I	232	31.45 N	114.48 W
Montague City	207	42.35 N	72.35 W
Montague Island I	180	60.00 N	147.30 W
Montague Peak ∧	180	60.15 N	147.01 W
Montagu Island I	18	58.25 S	26.20 W
Montaigle, Château de ⊥	56	50.18 N	4.49 E
Montaigu	32	46.59 N	1.19 W
Montaigut-en-Combraille	32	46.11 N	2.48 E
Montainville	261	48.53 N	1.52 E
Montaione	66	43.33 N	10.55 E
Montaj-Taš	85	42.06 N	68.58 E
Montalba	222	31.53 N	95.38 W
Montalbán	34	40.50 N	0.48 W
Montalbancito	286c	10.28 N	66.59 W
Montalbano Elicona	70	38.02 N	15.01 E
Montalbano Ionico	68	40.17 N	16.34 E
Montalcino	66	43.03 N	11.29 E
Montaldo di Cosola	62	44.40 N	9.11 E
Montale	66	43.56 N	11.01 E
Montalegre	34	41.49 N	7.48 W
Montalet-le-Bois	261	49.03 N	1.50 E
Montalieu-Vercieu	62	45.49 N	5.24 E
Montallegro	70	37.23 N	13.21 E
Mont Alto	208	39.50 N	77.33 W
Montalto ∧	68	38.10 N	15.55 E
Montalto delle Marche	66	42.59 N	13.36 E
Montalto di Castro	66	42.21 N	11.37 E
Montalto Ligure	62	43.56 N	7.51 E
Montalto Uffugo	68	39.25 N	16.10 E
Montalvin Manor	226	37.59 N	122.21 W
Montalvo	228	34.15 N	119.12 W
Montana, Schw.	58	46.18 N	7.29 E
Montana, Ak., U.S.	180	62.05 N	150.04 W
Montana □[3], U.S.	178	47.00 N	110.00 W
Montana □[3], U.S.	202	47.00 N	110.00 W
Montana de Oro State Park ♦	226	35.15 N	120.50 W
Montana Indian Reserve ◆[4]	182	52.43 N	113.25 W
Montanaro	62	45.14 N	7.51 E
Montánchez	34	39.13 N	6.09 W
Montandon	210	40.58 N	76.51 W
Montanha	255	18.08 S	40.21 W
Montano Antilia	68	40.10 N	15.22 E
Montara	226	37.33 N	122.31 W
Montara Beach ♦	282	37.33 N	122.31 W
Montara Mountain ⋏	282	37.32 N	122.27 W
Montargil	34	39.05 N	8.10 W
Montargis	50	48.00 N	2.45 E
Montataire	50	49.16 N	2.26 E
Montauban	32	44.01 N	1.21 E
Montauban, Lac ⊜	206	46.52 N	72.10 W
Montauban-les-Mines	206	46.50 N	72.20 W
Montauk	207	41.02 N	71.57 W
Montauk, Lake ⊜	207	41.04 N	71.55 W
Montauk Point ›	207	41.04 N	71.52 W
Montauroux	62	43.37 N	6.46 E
Monta Vista	226	37.19 N	122.03 W
Montazzoli	66	41.57 N	14.26 E
Montbard	50	47.37 N	4.20 E
Montbarrey	58	47.01 N	5.39 E
Montbazon	50	47.17 N	0.43 E
Montbéliard	58	47.31 N	6.48 E
Mont Belvieu	222	29.50 N	94.53 W
Montbenoît	58	46.59 N	6.28 E
Montblanc	34	41.22 N	1.10 E
Mont Blanc, Tunnel du ◆[5]	58	45.50 N	6.53 E
Mont-Bonvillers	56	49.20 N	5.51 E
Montbovon	58	46.29 N	7.03 E
Montbozon	58	47.28 N	6.16 E
Montbrison	62	45.36 N	4.03 E
Montbron	32	45.40 N	0.30 E
Montbronn	56	48.59 N	7.19 E
Montcada i Reixas	266d	41.29 N	2.11 E
Montcalm □[6]	206	46.20 N	74.20 W
Montceau-les-Mines	58	46.40 N	4.22 E
Montcenis	58	46.47 N	4.23 E
Mont Cenis, Col du)(	62	45.15 N	6.54 E
Mont Cenis, Lac du ⊜	62	45.14 N	6.55 E
Montcevelles, Lac ⊜	186	51.07 N	60.38 W
Montchanin, Fr.	58	46.45 N	4.27 E
Montchanin, De., U.S.	285	39.47 N	75.35 W
Montchauvet	261	48.54 N	1.38 E
Montclair, Ca., U.S.	228	34.06 N	117.41 W
Montclair, N.J., U.S.	210	40.49 N	74.12 W
Montclair State College ʊ[2]	276	40.51 N	74.12 W
Mont Clare	285	40.08 N	75.30 W
Montcornet	50	49.41 N	4.01 E
Montdale	210	41.32 N	75.37 W
Mont-de-Marsan	32	43.53 N	0.30 W
Montdidier	50	49.39 N	2.34 E
Mont-Dore	175f	22.16 S	166.34 E
Monte, Castel del ⊥	68	41.05 N	16.16 E
Monte, Laguna del ⊜, Arg.	252	37.00 S	62.28 W
Monte, Laguna del ⊜, Arg.	258	35.28 S	58.49 W
Montea ∧	68	39.40 N	15.57 E
Monte Adone, Galleria di ◆[5]	64	44.21 N	11.25 E
Monteagle	194	35.15 N	85.50 W
Monteagudo	248	19.49 S	63.59 W
Monte Albán ⊥	234	17.02 N	96.45 W
Monte Alegre, Bra.	250	2.01 S	54.04 W
Monte Alegre, Bra.	250	6.04 S	35.20 W
Monte Alegre de Goiás	255	13.14 S	47.10 W
Monte Alegre de Minas	255	18.52 S	48.52 W
Monte Alegre de Sergipe	250	10.02 S	37.33 W
Monte Alegre do Piauí	250	9.46 S	45.18 W
Monte Alegre do Sul	256	22.40 S	46.41 W
Monte Azul	255	15.09 S	42.53 W
Monte Azul Paulista	255	20.55 S	48.38 W
Montebello, P.Q., Can.	206	45.39 N	74.56 W
Montebello, It.	62	45.00 N	9.06 E
Montebello, P.R.	240m	18.22 N	66.31 W
Montebello, Ca., U.S.	228	34.00 N	118.06 W
Montebello Iónico	68	37.59 N	15.45 E
Monte Bello Islands II	162	20.25 S	115.32 E
Montebello Vicentino	64	45.27 N	11.23 E
Montebelluna	64	45.47 N	12.03 E
Monte Belo	256	21.20 S	46.23 W
Montebruno	62	44.31 N	9.15 E
Monte Buey	252	32.55 S	62.27 W
Montecalvo Irpino	68	41.11 N	15.02 E
Monte Campatri	267a	41.48 N	12.44 E
Montecarlo	252	26.34 S	54.47 W
Monte Carlo ◆[8]	62	43.44 N	7.25 E
Monte Carmelo	255	18.43 S	47.29 W
Montecarotto	66	43.31 N	13.04 E
Monte Caseros	252	30.15 S	57.39 W
Montecassiano	66	43.21 N	13.26 E
Montecassino, Abbazia di ʊ[1]	66	41.29 N	13.48 E
Montecastrilli	66	42.39 N	12.29 E
Montecatini-Terme	66	43.53 N	10.46 E
Monte Cavallo	66	42.59 N	13.00 E
Montecchio	66	43.51 N	12.46 E
Montecchio Emilia	64	44.42 N	10.27 E
Montecchio Maggiore	64	45.30 N	11.24 E
Montecelio	66	42.01 N	12.44 E
Montechiaro d'Asti	62	45.01 N	8.07 E
Montechiarugolo	64	44.42 N	10.25 E
Monte Chingolo ◆[8]	288	34.45 S	58.20 W
Monteciccardo	66	43.49 N	12.48 E
Montecilfone	66	41.54 N	14.50 E
Montecillos, Cordillera de ⋏	236	14.25 N	87.51 W
Montecito	204	34.26 N	119.37 W
Monte Comán	252	34.36 S	67.54 W
Montecorice	68	40.14 N	14.59 E
Montecorvino Pugliano	68	40.41 N	14.57 E
Montecorvino Rovella	68	40.42 N	14.59 E
Montecosaro	66	43.19 N	13.37 E
Monte Creek	182	50.39 N	119.57 W
Montecreto	64	44.14 N	10.41 E
Montecristi, Ec.	246	1.03 S	80.40 W
Monte Cristi, Rep. Dom.	238	19.52 N	71.39 W
Monte Cristo	248	14.43 S	61.14 W
Montecristo, Isola di I	36	42.20 N	10.19 E
Montecuccolo ʊ[1]	64	44.19 N	10.50 E
Montedinove	66	42.58 N	13.35 E
Monte di Procida	68	40.48 N	14.03 E
Monte do Carmo	250	10.45 S	48.07 W
Montedoro	70	37.27 N	13.49 E
Monte Escobedo	234	22.18 N	103.35 W
Monte Estoril	266c	38.42 N	9.24 W
Montefalcione	68	40.58 N	14.53 E
Montefalco	66	42.54 N	12.39 E
Montefalcone di Val Fortore	68	41.20 N	15.00 E
Montefano	66	43.25 N	13.26 E
Montefeltro ◆[1]	66	43.50 N	12.15 E
Montefiascone	66	42.32 N	12.02 E
Montefiorino	64	44.22 N	10.37 E
Monteforte d'Alpone	64	45.25 N	11.17 E
Monteforte Irpino	68	40.54 N	14.42 E
Montefrío	34	37.19 N	4.01 W
Montegallo	66	42.50 N	13.19 E
Montegiordano	68	40.02 N	16.32 E
Montegiorgio	66	43.08 N	13.32 E
Monte Giovi, Passo di (Jaufen Pass))(	64	46.50 N	11.19 E
Montego Bay	241q	18.28 N	77.55 W
Montegranaro	66	43.14 N	13.38 E
Monte Grande	252	30.06 S	70.31 W
Monte Grimano	66	43.52 N	12.29 E
Montegrotto Terme	64	45.19 N	11.46 E
Montegut	194	29.28 N	90.33 W
Monteiasi	68	40.30 N	17.23 E
Monteiro	250	7.53 S	37.07 W
Monteiro Lobato	256	22.58 S	45.50 W
Monteith, Mount ∧	182	55.45 N	122.30 W
Montejicar	34	37.34 N	3.30 W
Montejinni	164	16.40 S	131.45 E
Montelavar	266c	38.51 N	9.20 W
Monteleone di Puglia	68	41.10 N	15.15 E
Monteleone di Spoleto	66	42.39 N	12.58 E
Monteleone Rocco Doria	71	40.29 N	8.34 E
Monteleone Sabino	66	42.14 N	12.51 E
Montelepre	70	38.05 N	13.10 E
Montelíbano	246	8.05 N	75.29 W
Montélimar	62	44.34 N	4.45 E
Montelindo ≃	252	23.56 S	57.12 W
Montella	68	40.51 N	15.01 E
Montellano	34	37.00 N	5.34 W
Montello, Nv., U.S.	204	41.15 N	114.11 W
Montello, Wi., U.S.	190	43.47 N	89.19 W
Monteluco ʊ[1]	66	42.43 N	12.45 E
Montelungo	64	44.24 N	9.54 E
Montelupo Fiorentino	66	43.44 N	11.01 E
Montemaggiore Belsito	70	37.51 N	13.46 E
Montemagno	62	44.59 N	8.20 E
Monte Maíz	252	33.12 S	62.36 W
Montemarano	68	40.55 N	15.00 E
Montemarciano	66	43.38 N	13.19 E
Montemayor, Meseta de ⋏[1]	254	44.20 S	66.10 W
Montemesola	68	40.34 N	17.20 E
Montemiletto	68	41.01 N	14.54 E
Montemilone	68	41.02 N	15.38 E
Montemor	266c	38.49 N	9.12 W
Montemor ∧	266c	38.49 N	9.12 W
Montemorelos	232	25.12 N	99.49 W
Montemor-o-Novo	34	38.39 N	8.13 W
Montemor-o-Vehlo	34	40.10 N	8.41 W
Montemuro ∧	34	40.58 N	7.56 W
Montemurro	68	40.18 N	15.59 E
Montendre	32	45.17 N	0.24 W
Montenegro	252	29.42 S	51.28 W
Montenegro → Crna Gora □[3]	38	42.30 N	19.18 E
Montenero	66	43.30 N	10.21 E
Montenero ∧	68	39.13 N	16.35 E
Montenero di Bisaccia	66	41.57 N	14.47 E
Monteodorisio	66	42.05 N	14.39 E
Monte Oliveto Maggiore, Abbazia del ʊ[1]	66	43.12 N	11.32 E
Monte Pascoal, Parque Nacional de ♦	255	16.54 S	39.24 W
Monte Patria	252	30.42 S	70.58 W
Montepescali	66	42.53 N	11.05 E
Monte Porzio Catone	267a	41.49 N	12.43 E
Monteprandone	66	42.55 N	13.50 E
Montepuez	154	13.07 S	39.00 E
Montepuez ≃	154	12.32 S	40.27 E
Montepulciano	66	43.05 N	11.47 E
Monte Quemado	252	25.48 S	62.52 W
Monterado	112	0.45 N	109.08 E
Monterchi	66	43.29 N	12.07 E
Montereale	66	42.31 N	13.15 E
Montereale Valcellina	64	46.10 N	12.39 E
Montereau	50	47.51 N	2.34 E
Montereau-Faut-Yonne	50	48.23 N	2.57 E
Montereau-sur-le-Jard	261	48.35 N	2.40 E
Monterey, Ca., U.S.	226	36.36 N	121.53 W
Monterey, In., U.S.	216	41.09 N	86.28 W
Monterey, Ky., U.S.	218	38.25 N	84.52 W
Monterey, Ma., U.S.	207	42.10 N	73.12 W
Monterey, N.Y., U.S.	210	42.18 N	77.03 W
Monterey, Tn., U.S.	194	36.08 N	85.16 W
Monterey, Va., U.S.	188	38.24 N	79.34 W
Monterey □[6]	226	36.40 N	121.38 W
Monterey Bay ⊂	226	36.45 N	121.55 W
Monterey Park	228	34.03 N	118.07 W
Monterey Peninsula Airport ⊠	226	36.35 N	121.51 W
Montería	246	8.46 N	75.53 W
Monteriggioni	66	43.23 N	11.13 E
Montero	248	17.20 S	63.15 W
Monte Romano	66	42.16 N	11.54 E
Monteroni d'Arbia	66	43.14 N	11.25 E
Monteroni di Lecce	68	40.19 N	18.06 E
Monteros	252	27.10 S	65.30 W
Monterosso al Mare	62	44.09 N	9.39 E
Monterosso Almo	70	37.05 N	14.46 E
Monterosso Calabro	68	38.43 N	16.17 E
Monterotondo	66	42.03 N	12.37 E
Monterotondo Marittimo	66	43.09 N	10.51 E
Monterrey, Méx.	232	25.40 N	100.19 W
Monterrey, Méx.	234	16.05 N	93.23 W
Monterrico, Hipódromo de ♦	286d	12.06 S	76.59 W
Monterubbiano	66	43.05 N	13.43 E
Montes Altos	250	5.50 S	47.04 W
Monte San Biagio	66	41.21 N	13.21 E
Monte San Giovanni Campano	66	41.38 N	13.31 E
Montesano, It.	36	40.16 N	15.43 E
Montesano, Wa., U.S.	224	46.58 N	123.36 W
Montesano sulla Marcellana	68	40.16 N	15.42 E
Monte San Savino	66	43.20 N	11.43 E
Monte Santa Maria Tiberina	66	43.26 N	12.09 E
Monte Sant'Angelo	68	41.42 N	15.57 E
Monte Santo	250	10.26 S	39.20 W
Monte Santo de Minas	256	21.12 S	46.59 W
Monte Santu, Capo di ›	71	40.05 N	9.44 E
Montesarchio	68	41.04 N	14.38 E
Montescaglioso	68	40.33 N	16.40 E
Montes Claros	255	16.43 S	43.52 W
Montescudaio	66	43.18 N	10.40 E
Montese	64	44.16 N	10.56 E
Monte Sereno	226	37.15 N	122.01 W
Monte Sião	256	22.26 S	46.34 W
Montesilvano Marina	66	42.31 N	14.09 E
Montespaccato ◆[8]	267a	41.54 N	12.23 E
Montespertoli	66	43.38 N	11.04 E
Montespluga	58	46.30 N	9.21 E
Montets, Col des)(	58	46.00 N	6.55 E
Monteux	62	44.02 N	5.00 E
Montevago	70	37.42 N	12.58 E
Montevallo	194	33.06 N	86.51 W
Montevarchi	66	43.31 N	11.34 E
Monteverde	68	41.00 N	15.32 E
Monte Verde ≃	256	21.55 S	43.33 W
Monteverde Nuovo ◆[8]	267a	41.51 N	12.27 E
Montevergine, Santuario di ʊ[1]	68	40.55 N	14.45 E
Montevideo, Mn., U.S.	198	44.56 N	95.43 W
Montevideo, Ur.	258	34.53 S	56.11 W
Montevideo □[5]	258	34.50 S	56.12 W
Montevideo, Cerro de ∧[2]	258	33.54 S	56.15 W
Monte Vista	200	37.34 N	106.08 W
Montévrain	261	48.53 N	2.45 E
Montezemolo	62	44.22 N	8.08 E
Montezuma, Ca., U.S.	282	38.05 N	121.53 W
Montezuma, Ga., U.S.	192	32.18 N	84.01 W
Montezuma, In., U.S.	194	39.47 N	87.22 W
Montezuma, Ia., U.S.	190	41.35 N	92.31 W
Montezuma, Ks., U.S.	198	37.35 N	100.26 W
Montezuma, N.Y., U.S.	210	43.00 N	76.42 W
Montezuma, Oh., U.S.	216	40.29 N	84.33 W
Montezuma Castle National Monument ♦	200	34.38 N	110.49 W
Montezuma Creek ≃	200	37.17 N	109.20 W
Montezuma Hills ⋏[2]	282	38.07 N	121.51 W
Montezuma Slough ≃	226	38.04 N	121.52 W
Montfaucon, Fr.	56	49.17 N	5.08 E
Montfaucon, Fr.	62	45.10 N	4.18 E
Montfaucon, Schw.	58	47.17 N	7.03 E
Montfermeil	261	48.54 N	2.34 E
Montfleur	58	46.19 N	5.26 E
Montfort, Fr.	32	48.08 N	1.58 W
Montfort, Wi., U.S.	190	42.58 N	90.25 W
Montfort-l'Amaury	50	48.47 N	1.49 E
Montfort-le-Rotrou	50	48.03 N	0.25 E
Montfort-sur-Risle	50	49.18 N	0.40 E
Montfrin	62	43.53 N	4.36 E
Montgé	261	49.02 N	2.45 E
Montgenèvre	62	44.56 N	6.43 E
Montgenèvre, Col de)(	62	44.56 N	6.44 E
Montgeron	261	48.42 N	2.27 E
Montgeroult	261	49.05 N	2.00 E
Montgesoye	58	47.05 N	6.12 E
Montgomery, Wales, U.K.	42	52.33 N	3.03 W
Montgomery, Al., U.S.	194	32.23 N	86.18 W
Montgomery, Il., U.S.	216	41.43 N	88.20 W
Montgomery, La., U.S.	194	31.40 N	92.53 W
Montgomery, Mi., U.S.	216	41.46 N	84.48 W
Montgomery, Mn., U.S.	190	44.26 N	93.34 W
Montgomery, N.Y., U.S.	210	41.31 N	74.14 W
Montgomery, Oh., U.S.	218	39.13 N	84.21 W
Montgomery, Pa., U.S.	210	41.10 N	76.52 W
Montgomery, Tx., U.S.	222	30.23 N	95.42 W
Montgomery, W.V., U.S.	188	38.11 N	81.19 W
Montgomery □[6], Il., U.S.	219	39.09 N	89.29 W
Montgomery □[6], Md., U.S.	208	39.05 N	77.09 W
Montgomery □[6], Mo., U.S.	219	38.57 N	91.27 W
Montgomery □[6], N.Y., U.S.	210	42.57 N	74.22 W
Montgomery □[6], Oh., U.S.	218	39.45 N	84.15 W
Montgomery □[6], Pa., U.S.	208	40.07 N	75.21 W
Montgomery □[6], Tx., U.S.	222	30.18 N	95.30 W
Montgomery City	219	38.58 N	91.30 W
Montgomery Dam ◆[6]	214	40.39 N	80.24 W
Montgomery Knolls	284b	39.14 N	76.48 W
Montgomery Mall ◆[9]	284c	39.01 N	77.09 W
Montgomery → Sāhīwāl	123	30.40 N	73.06 E
Montgomery Square	284c	39.04 N	77.09 W
Montgomeryville	285	40.15 N	75.15 W
Montgomeryville Airport ⊠	285	40.15 N	75.14 W
Montguyon	32	45.13 N	0.11 W
Monthermé	56	49.53 N	4.44 E
Monthey	58	46.15 N	6.57 E
Monthois	56	49.19 N	4.43 E
Monthureux-sur-Saône	58	48.02 N	5.58 E
Monthyon	261	49.00 N	2.50 E
Monti	71	40.49 N	9.19 E
Monticelli d'Ongina	64	45.05 N	9.56 E
Monticello, Ar., U.S.	194	33.37 N	91.47 W
Monticello, Fl., U.S.	192	30.32 N	83.52 W
Monticello, Ga., U.S.	192	33.18 N	83.41 W
Monticello, Il., U.S.	194	40.01 N	88.34 W
Monticello, In., U.S.	216	40.44 N	86.45 W
Monticello, Ia., U.S.	190	42.14 N	91.11 W
Monticello, Ky., U.S.	194	36.49 N	84.50 W
Monticello, Mn., U.S.	190	45.18 N	93.47 W
Monticello, Ms., U.S.	194	31.33 N	90.06 W
Monticello, Mo., U.S.	219	40.07 N	91.42 W
Monticello, N.Y., U.S.	210	41.39 N	74.41 W
Monticello, Ut,. U.S.	200	37.52 N	109.20 W
Monticello, Wi., U.S.	190	42.44 N	89.35 W
Monticello ⊥	188	38.00 N	78.30 W
Monticello Conte Otto	64	45.35 N	11.35 E
Monticello Dam ◆[6]	226	38.30 N	122.07 W
Monticello Woods	284c	38.47 N	77.10 W
Montichiari	64	45.25 N	10.23 E
Monticiano	66	43.08 N	11.11 E
Montiel, Campo de ≃	34	38.46 N	2.44 W
Montier-en-Der	58	48.29 N	4.46 E
Montieri	66	43.08 N	11.01 E
Montieri, Poggio di ∧	66	43.08 N	11.00 E
Montiers-sur-Saulx	58	48.32 N	5.16 E
Montignac	32	45.04 N	1.10 E
Montigny	58	48.31 N	6.48 E
Montigny-Devant-Sassey	56	49.26 N	5.09 E
Montigny-le-Bretonneux	261	48.46 N	2.02 E
Montigny-le-Roi	58	48.00 N	5.30 E
Montigny-lès-Cormeilles	261	48.59 N	2.12 E
Montigny-lès-Metz	56	49.06 N	6.09 E
Montigny-sur-Aube	58	47.57 N	4.46 E
Montijo, Esp.	34	38.55 N	6.37 W
Montijo, Pan.	236	7.59 N	81.03 W
Montijo, Port.	34	38.42 N	8.58 W
Montijo, Aeroporto ⊠	266c	38.42 N	9.02 W
Montijo, Golfo de ⊂	246	7.40 N	81.07 W
Montilla	34	37.35 N	4.38 W
Montividiu	255	17.24 S	51.14 W
Montivilliers	50	49.33 N	0.12 E
Montjay-la-Tour	261	48.55 N	2.40 E
Montjoie, Lac ⊜, P.Q., Can.	206	46.17 N	75.08 W
Montjoie, Lac ⊜, P.Q., Can.	206	45.25 N	72.06 W
Mont-Joli	186	48.35 N	68.11 W
Montjovet	62	45.43 N	7.40 E
Montjuich, Estadio de ♦	266d	41.22 N	2.09 E
Montjuich, Faro de ◆[5]	266d	41.21 N	2.11 E
Montjuich, Parque de ♦	266d	41.21 N	2.09 E
Mont-Laurier	176	46.33 N	75.30 W
Montlebon	58	47.02 N	6.37 E
Montlhery	50	48.38 N	2.16 E
Montlhery, Tour de ʊ	261	48.38 N	2.16 E
Montlhery, Tour de ♦	261	48.38 N	2.16 E
Montlignon	261	49.01 N	2.17 E
Montlouet	261	48.31 N	1.43 E
Mont-Louis	32	42.31 N	2.07 E
Montlouis-sur-Loire	50	47.23 N	0.50 E
Montluçon	32	46.21 N	2.36 E
Montluel	62	45.51 N	5.03 E
Montmagny, P.Q., Can.	186	46.59 N	70.33 W
Montmagny, Fr.	261	48.58 N	2.21 E
Montmajour, Abbaye de ʊ[1]	62	43.43 N	4.40 E
Montmartre ◆[8]	261	48.53 N	2.21 E
Montmédy	56	49.31 N	5.22 E
Montmélian	62	45.30 N	6.04 E
Montmeló	266d	41.33 N	2.15 E
Montmerle-sur-Saône	58	46.05 N	4.46 E
Montmin	62	45.48 N	6.16 E

Symbols in the index entries represent the broad categories identified in the key at the right. Symbols with superior numbers (⋏[1]) identify subcategories (see complete key on page *I · 1).*

Symbole im Register stellen die rechts im Schlüssel erklärten Kategorien dar. Symbole mit hochgestellten Ziffern (⋏[1]) bezeichnen Unterabteilungen einer Kategorie (vgl. vollständiger Schlüssel auf Seite *I · 1).*

Los símbolos incluídos en el texto del índice representan las grandes categorias identificadas con la clave a la derecha. Los símbolos con numeros en su parte superior (⋏[1]) identifican las subcategorías (véase la clave completa en la página *I · 1).*

Les symboles de l'index représentent les catégories indiquées dans la légende à droite. Les symboles suivis d'un indice (⋏[1]) représentent des sous-catégories (voir légende complète à la page *I · 1).*

Os símbolos incluídos no texto do índice representam as grandes categorias identificadas com a chave à direita. Os símbolos com números em sua parte superior (⋏[1]) identificam as subcategorias (veja-se a chave completa à página *I · 1).*

	English	Deutsch	Español	Français	Português
∧	Mountain	Berg	Montaña	Montagne	Montanha
⋏	Mountains	Gebirge	Montañas	Montagnes	Montanhas
)(	Pass	Paß	Paso	Col	Passo
V	Valley, Canyon	Tal, Cañon	Valle, Cañón	Vallée Canyon	Vale, Canhão
≃	Plain	Ebene	Llano	Plaine	Planície
›	Cape	Kap	Cabo	Cap	Cabo
I	Island	Insel	Isla	Île	Ilha
II	Islands	Inseln	Islas	Îles	Ilhas
±	Other Topographic Features	Andere Topographische Objekte	Otros Elementos Topográficos	Autres données topographiques	Outros acidentes topográficos

ESPAÑOL Nombre	Página	Lat.	Long. W = Oeste
Montmirail, Fr.	50	48.52 N	3.32 E
Montmirail, Fr.	50	48.06 N	0.48 E
Montmirey-le-Château	58	47.13 N	5.32 E
Montmoreau-Saint-Cybard	32	45.24 N	0.08 E
Montmorenci	216	40.28 N	87.02 W
Montmorency, Austl.	274b	37.43 S	145.07 E
Montmorency, Fr.	261	49.00 N	2.20 E
Montmorency ≃	186	46.53 N	71.07 W
Montmorency, Forêt de ♦	261	49.02 N	2.16 E
Montmorency — Beauport	186	46.52 N	71.11 W
Montmorillon	32	46.26 N	0.52 E
Montmort	50	48.55 N	3.49 E
Monto	166	24.52 S	151.07 E
Montodine	62	45.17 N	9.42 E
Montoggio	62	44.31 N	9.03 E
Montoire-sur-le-Loir	50	47.45 N	0.52 E
Montone	66	43.22 N	12.20 E
Montone ≃, It.	64	44.24 N	12.14 E
Montone ≃, It.	66	43.22 N	12.20 E
Montopoli in Val d'Arno	66	43.40 N	10.45 E
Mont Orford, Parc du ♦	206	45.22 N	72.05 W

ENGLISH / DEUTSCH

Name	Page	Lat.°′	Long.°′
Mosby	26	58.14 N	7.54 E
Mosby Woods	284c	38.52 N	77.18 W
Moscavide	266c	38.47 N	9.06 W
Mosciano Sant'Angelo	66	42.45 N	13.53 E
Moščnyj, ostrov I	76	60.01 N	27.50 E
Moscos Islands II	110	14.00 N	97.45 E
Moscou → Moskva	82	55.45 N	37.35 E
Moscow, Id., U.S.	202	46.43 N	116.59 W
Moscow, In., U.S.	218	39.29 N	85.34 W
Moscow, Oh., U.S.	218	38.51 N	84.13 W
Moscow, Pa., U.S.	210	41.20 N	75.31 W
Moscow, Tx., U.S.	222	30.55 N	94.50 W
Moscow Air Terminal ⊠	265b	55.48 N	37.32 E
Moscow Circus ♦	265b	55.43 N	37.33 E
Moscow Mills	219	38.56 N	90.55 W
Moscow → Moskva	82	55.45 N	37.35 E
Moscow Station ◆[5]	265a	59.56 N	30.22 E
Moscow Victory Park ♦	265a	59.52 N	30.20 E
Moscow Zoo ♦	265b	55.46 N	37.34 E
Moscufo	66	42.25 N	14.03 E
Moscú → Moskva	82	55.45 N	37.35 E
Mosel	54	50.47 N	12.28 E
Mosel (Moselle) ≃	32	50.22 N	7.36 E
Moselebe ≃	156	25.03 S	23.13 E
Moselle, Ms., U.S.	194	31.30 N	89.16 W
Moselle, Mo., U.S.	219	38.23 N	90.54 W
Moselle □[5]	56	49.00 N	6.30 E
Moselle (Mosel) ≃	32	50.22 N	7.36 E
Moselotte ≃	58	48.01 N	6.38 E
Mošenskoje	76	58.31 N	34.35 E
Mosermandl ∧	64	47.12 N	13.24 E
Mosers River	186	44.59 N	62.15 W
Moses Lake	202	47.07 N	119.16 W
Moses Lake ⊜[1]	202	47.10 N	119.20 W
Moses Point	180	64.42 N	162.03 W
Moses Power Plant ◆[6]	284a	43.09 N	79.02 W
Mosetse	156	20.37 S	26.32 E
Mosgiel	172	45.53 S	170.21 E
Moshannon	214	41.02 N	78.00 W
Moshannon Creek ≃	214	41.04 N	78.06 W
Moshanpu	100	29.34 N	112.41 E
Moshaweng ≃	158	26.35 S	22.50 E
Mosheim, Tn., U.S.	192	36.11 N	82.57 W
Mosheim, Tx., U.S.	222	31.38 N	97.36 W
Moshi	154	3.21 S	37.20 E
Moshi ≃	150	9.18 N	4.38 E
Moshiyu	104	41.15 N	124.05 E
Mosier	224	45.41 N	121.23 W
Mosier Hill ∧[2]	214	40.06 N	80.24 W
Mosina	30	52.16 N	16.51 E
Mosinee	190	44.47 N	89.42 W
Mosjøen	24	65.50 N	13.10 E
Moskal'onki	86	54.59 N	71.54 E
Moskal'vo	89	53.35 N	142.30 E
Moskau → Moskva	82	55.45 N	37.35 E
Moskenesøya I	24	67.59 N	13.00 E
Moskháton	267c	37.57 N	23.41 E
Moškino	80	57.45 N	45.20 E
Moskito-Golf → Mosquitos, Golfo de los ⊂	236	9.00 N	81.15 W
Moškovo	86	55.18 N	83.37 E
Moskovskaja Slav'anka	265a	59.45 N	30.30 E
Moskovskaja vozvyšennost' ⋏[1]	76	56.15 N	37.30 E
Moskva (Moscow), Ross.	82	55.45 N	37.35 E
Moskva (Moscow), Ross.	265b	55.45 N	37.35 E
Moskva □[8]	82	55.45 N	37.30 E
Moskva ≃	76	55.05 N	38.50 E
Moskva, Gorod □[7]	265b	55.45 N	37.35 E
Moskva, pik ∧	85	38.57 N	71.49 E
Moskvy, kanal imeni ≅	82	56.43 N	37.08 E
Mosman	170	33.49 S	151.14 E
Mosman Park	168a	32.01 S	115.46 E
Mošny	78	49.32 N	31.44 E
Moso (Moos)	64	46.41 N	12.23 E
Moso in Passiria (Moos)	64	46.50 N	11.10 E
Mošok	80	55.48 N	41.17 E
Mosolovo	80	54.17 N	40.32 E
Mosomane	156	24.04 S	26.15 E
Mosoni-Duna ≃	61	47.54 N	17.17 E
Mosonmagyaróvár	30	47.51 N	17.17 E
Mosonszolnok	61	47.51 N	17.11 E
Mosopa	156	24.50 S	25.31 E
Mospino	83	47.53 N	38.03 E
Mosqueiro	250	1.10 S	48.28 W
Mosquera	246	2.30 N	78.29 W
Mosquero	196	35.46 N	103.57 W
Mosquic, Lac ⊜	206	46.39 N	74.28 W
Mosquito, Punta ›	246	9.07 N	77.53 W
Mosquito, Riacho ≃	252	22.02 S	57.57 W
Mosquito Brook ≃	283	42.40 N	71.02 W
Mosquito Creek ≃, Ia., U.S.	198	41.11 N	95.50 W
Mosquito Creek ≃, Oh., U.S.	214	41.10 N	80.45 W
Mosquito Creek ≃, Pa., U.S.	214	41.07 N	78.07 W
Mosquito Creek Lake ⊜[1]	214	41.22 N	80.45 W
Mosquito Creek State Park ♦	214	41.22 N	80.45 W
Mosquito Indian Reserve ◆[4]	184	52.30 N	108.15 W
Mosquito Lagoon ⊂	220	28.45 N	80.45 W
Mosquitos, Costa de □[9]	236	13.00 N	83.45 W
Mosquitos, Golfo de los ⊂	236	9.00 N	81.15 W
Moss	26	59.26 N	10.42 E
Mossaka	152	1.13 S	16.48 E
Mossâmedes	255	16.07 S	50.11 W
Mossbank, Sk., Can.	184	49.55 N	105.59 W
Moss Bank, Eng., U.K.	262	53.29 N	2.44 W
Mossbank, Scot., U.K.	46a	60.27 N	1.12 W
Moss Bank Park ♦	262	53.36 N	2.28 W
Moss Beach	282	37.32 N	122.31 W
Mossburn	172	45.40 S	168.15 E
Mosselbaai (Mossel Bay)	158	34.11 S	22.08 E
Mosselbaai ⊂	158	34.06 S	22.20 E
Mossendjo	152	2.57 S	12.44 E
Mosses, Col des)(	58	46.24 N	7.06 E
Mossgiel	166	33.15 S	144.34 E
Moss Hill	222	30.15 N	94.45 W
Mossig ≃	58	48.33 N	7.30 E
Mössingen	58	48.24 N	9.03 E
Moss Landing	226	36.48 N	121.47 W
Mossleigh	182	50.43 N	113.20 W
Mossley	262	53.32 N	2.02 W
Mossley Hill ◆[8]	262	53.23 N	2.55 W
Mossman	164	16.28 S	145.22 E
Mossmans Brook ≃	276	41.03 N	74.27 W
Moss Moor ◆[3]	262	53.37 N	2.00 W
Moss Mountain ∧	194	34.50 N	92.40 W
Mossø ⊜	41	56.02 N	9.48 E
Mosson ≃	62	43.33 N	3.54 E
Mossoró	250	5.11 S	37.20 W
Mosso Santa Maria	62	45.38 N	8.08 E
Moss Point	194	30.24 N	88.32 W
Moss Point ›	279a	41.37 N	81.32 W
Moss Side	262	53.46 N	2.57 W
Mossuril	154	14.58 S	40.42 E
Moss Vale	170	34.33 S	150.22 E
Mossy ≃, Mb., Can.	184	51.39 N	99.55 W
Mossy ≃, Sk., Can.	184	54.05 N	103.00 W
Mossyrock	224	46.31 N	122.29 W
Mossyrock Dam ◆[6]	224	46.32 N	122.25 W
Most	54	50.32 N	13.39 E
Mosta	80	56.32 N	42.10 E
Mostar	36	43.20 N	17.49 E
Mostardas, Bra.	252	31.06 S	50.57 W
Mostardas, Bra.	256	23.44 S	46.38 W
Møsting, Kap ›	176	64.00 N	41.00 W
Mostiska	78	49.48 N	23.09 E
Mostiștea ≃	38	44.15 N	27.10 E
Mostizzolo	64	46.24 N	11.01 E
Mostki	83	49.19 N	38.30 E
Most na Soči	64	46.09 N	13.44 E
Mostok	76	53.59 N	30.28 E
Móstoles	266a	40.19 N	3.51 W
Mostoos Hills ⋏[2]	184	55.00 N	109.15 W
Mostovaja	76	56.13 N	33.08 E
Mostovka	86	58.10 N	65.31 E
Mostovoje	78	47.24 N	30.59 E
Mostovskoj	84	44.25 N	40.48 E
Mostovskoje	86	55.46 N	66.22 E
Mostrim (Edgeworthstown)	48	53.42 N	7.36 W
Mostva ≃	78	52.00 N	27.33 E
Mosty	76	53.25 N	24.32 E
Mostyn, Malay.	112	4.40 N	118.11 E
Mostyn, Wales, U.K.	44	53.19 N	3.16 W
Mosul → Al-Mawșil	128	36.20 N	43.08 E
Møsvatnet ⊜	26	59.52 N	8.05 E
Mota	144	11.02 N	37.52 E
Mota I	175f	13.49 S	167.42 E
Motaba ≃	152	2.03 N	18.03 E
Mota del Cuervo	34	39.30 N	2.52 W
Mota del Marqués	34	41.38 N	5.10 W
Motagua ≃	236	15.44 N	88.14 W
Motala	26	58.33 N	15.03 E
Motala ström ≃	40	58.38 N	16.10 E
Mota Lava I	175f	13.40 S	167.40 E
Motane I	174x	9.59 S	138.49 W
Motatán	246	9.24 N	70.36 W
Motaze	156	24.48 S	32.52 E
Motegi	94	36.32 N	140.11 E
Mote Park ♦	260	51.17 N	0.34 E
Moteve, Cap ›	174x	9.58 S	139.02 W
Moth	124	25.43 N	78.57 E
Mother Brook ≅	283	42.15 N	71.10 W
Motherwell	46	55.48 N	4.00 W
Motihāri	124	26.39 N	84.55 E
Motilla del Palancar	34	39.34 N	1.53 W
Motiong	116	11.47 N	125.00 E
Motiti Island I	172	37.38 S	176.26 E
Motjärnshyttan	40	59.56 N	13.58 E
Motloutse	156	21.28 S	27.24 E
Motloutse ≃	156	22.15 S	29.00 E
Moto-ara ≃	94	35.53 N	139.50 E
Motobu	174m	26.39 N	127.54 E
Motol'	76	52.19 N	25.36 E
Motola, Monte ∧	68	40.22 N	15.26 E
Motopu	174x	9.55 S	139.03 W
Motor Island I	284a	42.58 N	78.56 W
Motorki	80	56.53 N	51.29 E
Motorovo	86	56.31 N	71.10 E
Motosu	94	35.29 N	136.40 E
Motosu-ko ⊜	94	35.28 N	138.35 E
Motou	106	32.18 N	120.34 E
Motovilovo	80	55.36 N	43.51 E
Motovun	64	45.20 N	13.50 E
Motoyama	96	33.45 N	133.35 E
Moto-yama ∧[2]	174f	24.48 N	141.20 E
Motozintla de Mendoza	232	15.22 N	92.14 W
Motril	34	36.45 N	3.31 W
Motrone	64	43.54 N	10.12 E
Motru	38	44.50 N	23.00 E
Mott	198	46.22 N	102.19 W
Motta	64	45.36 N	11.29 E
Motta Camastra	70	37.54 N	15.10 E
Motta d'Affermo	70	37.59 N	14.18 E
Motta di Livenza	64	45.47 N	12.36 E
Mottafollone	68	39.39 N	16.04 E
Motta Montecorvino	68	41.30 N	15.07 E
Motta San Giovanni	70	38.00 N	15.41 E
Motta Sant'Anastasia	70	37.31 N	14.58 E
Motta Visconti	62	45.17 N	8.59 E
Möttingen	56	48.48 N	10.35 E
Mottingham ◆[8]	260	51.26 N	0.03 E
Mottisfont	42	51.02 N	1.32 W
Mottola	68	40.38 N	17.03 E
Mottram in Longdendale	262	53.27 N	2.01 W
Motts Creek ≃	276	40.38 N	73.45 W
Mottville, Mi., U.S.	216	41.48 N	85.45 W
Mottville, N.Y., U.S.	210	42.59 N	76.27 W
Motu ≃	172	37.51 S	177.35 E
Motueka	172	41.07 S	173.00 E
Motueka ≃	172	41.05 S	173.01 E
Motul [de Felipe Carrillo Puerto]	232	21.06 N	89.17 W
Motu One I[1]	14	15.48 S	154.33 W
Motupe	248	6.09 S	79.44 W
Motupena Point ›	175e	6.32 S	155.09 E
Motutapu I	174k	21.14 S	159.43 W
Motygino	86	58.11 N	94.40 E
Motyklejka	74	59.26 N	148.38 E
Motyžin	78	50.23 N	29.55 E
Motyzlej	80	54.54 N	42.54 E
Mou	175f	21.05 S	165.26 E
Mouanko	152	3.39 N	9.49 E
Mouans-Sartoux	62	43.37 N	6.58 E
Mouaskar	148	35.45 N	0.01 E
Mouaskar □[5]	148	35.10 N	0.00
Mouchard	58	46.58 N	5.48 E
Mouchoir Bank ⊹[2]	238	20.57 N	70.42 W
Mouchoir Passage ⊔	238	21.10 N	71.00 W
Moúdhros	38	39.52 N	25.16 E
Mouding	102	25.24 N	101.35 E
Moudjéria	150	17.53 N	12.20 W
Moudon	58	46.40 N	6.48 E
Moudongouma ≃	152	1.36 N	17.24 E
Mouila	152	1.52 S	11.01 E
Mouit	150	16.35 N	13.05 W
Mouka	152	7.16 N	21.52 E
Moukden → Shenyang	104	41.48 N	123.27 E
Moulamein	166	35.05 S	144.02 E
Moulay-bou-Selham	34	34.53 N	6.15 W
Moulay-Idriss	148	34.02 N	5.27 W
Mouldsworth	262	53.14 N	2.44 W
Moule à Chique, Cap ›	241f	13.43 N	60.57 W
Moulhoulé	144	12.36 N	43.12 E
Moulin, Île du I	275a	45.41 N	73.32 W
Moulin-des-Ponts	58	46.20 N	5.19 E
Moulineaux	50	49.21 N	0.58 E
Moulinet	62	43.57 N	7.25 E
Moulins	32	46.34 N	3.20 E
Moulins-la-Marche	50	48.39 N	0.29 E
Moulmeingyun	110	16.23 N	95.16 E
Moulmein → Mawlamyine	110	16.30 N	97.38 E
Moulouya, Oued ≃	148	35.05 N	2.25 W
Moulton, Eng., U.K.	262	53.13 N	2.31 W
Moulton, Al., U.S.	194	34.28 N	87.17 W
Moulton, Ia., U.S.	190	40.41 N	92.40 W
Moulton, Tx., U.S.	222	29.34 N	97.09 W
Moultrie	192	31.10 N	83.47 W
Moultrie □[6]	219	39.36 N	88.37 W
Moultrie, Lake ⊜[1]	192	33.20 N	80.05 W
Mouly	175f	20.42 S	166.25 E
Mound	222	31.21 N	97.38 W
Mound Bayou	194	33.52 N	90.43 W
Mound City, Il., U.S.	194	37.05 N	89.09 W
Mound City, Ks., U.S.	198	38.08 N	94.48 W
Mound City, Mo., U.S.	194	40.07 N	95.13 W
Mound City, S.D., U.S.	198	45.43 N	100.04 W
Mound City Group National Monument ♦	218	39.23 N	83.00 W
Mound Lake ⊜	219	40.05 N	90.17 W
Moundou	146	8.34 N	16.05 E
Moundridge	198	38.12 N	97.31 W
Mounds, Il., U.S.	194	37.06 N	89.11 W
Mounds, Ok., U.S.	196	35.52 N	96.03 W
Mounds State Park ♦	218	40.07 N	85.37 W
Mounds State Recreation Area ♦	218	39.30 N	84.59 W
Moundsville	188	39.55 N	80.44 W
Moundville	194	32.59 N	87.37 W
Moungali ◆[8]	273b	4.15 S	15.17 E
Moung Roessei	110	12.46 N	103.27 E
Mounianzé ≃	152	0.32 N	12.52 E
Mounier, Mont ∧	62	44.09 N	6.58 E
Mounlapamôk	110	14.20 N	105.52 E
Mount Aetna	208	40.25 N	76.18 W
Mountain	190	45.11 N	88.28 W
Mountain □[4]	116	17.20 N	121.10 E
Mountain ≃	180	65.41 N	128.50 W
Mountainair	200	34.31 N	106.14 W
Mountainaire	200	35.05 N	111.39 W
Mountain Ash	42	51.42 N	3.24 W
Mountain Brook	194	33.30 N	86.45 W
Mountain Chute Dam ◆[6]	212	45.11 N	76.54 W
Mountain City, Ga., U.S.	192	34.55 N	83.23 W
Mountain City, Nv., U.S.	204	41.50 N	115.57 W
Mountain City, Tn., U.S.	192	36.28 N	81.48 W
Mountain Creek	194	32.43 N	86.29 W
Mountain Creek ≃, Pa., U.S.	208	40.09 N	77.11 W
Mountain Creek ≃, Tx., U.S.	222	32.42 N	96.58 W
Mountain Creek Lake ⊜[1]	222	32.43 N	96.58 W
Mountain Dale	210	41.41 N	74.31 W
Mountain Grove	194	37.07 N	92.15 W
Mountain Home, Ar., U.S.	194	36.20 N	92.23 W
Mountain Home, Id., U.S.	202	43.07 N	115.41 W
Mountainhome, Pa., U.S.	210	41.11 N	75.17 W
Mountain Home Air Force Base ■	202	43.03 N	115.52 W
Mountain Iron	190	47.31 N	92.37 W
Mountain Lake, Fl., U.S.	220	27.57 N	81.36 W
Mountain Lake, Mn., U.S.	198	43.56 N	94.55 W
Mountain Lake ⊜, On., Can.	212	44.42 N	81.03 W
Mountain Lake ⊜, On., Can.	212	44.59 N	78.43 W
Mountain Lake ⊜, N.J., U.S.	276	40.53 N	74.27 W
Mountain Lakes	210	40.53 N	74.26 W
Mountain Lodge	210	41.23 N	74.09 W
Mountain Nile (Baḥr al-Jabal) ≃	136	9.30 N	30.30 E
Mountain Park	182	52.55 N	117.14 W
Mountain Pine	194	34.34 N	93.10 W
Mountain Point	182	55.18 N	131.32 W
Mountain Ranch	226	38.14 N	120.33 W
Mountainside	208	40.40 N	74.21 W
Mountain Spring Lakes	276	41.02 N	74.23 W
Mountain Valley Lake ⊜	279b	40.18 N	79.35 W
Mountain View, Ar., U.S.	194	35.52 N	92.07 W
Mountain View, Ca., U.S.	226	37.23 N	122.04 W
Mountain View, Mo., U.S.	194	36.59 N	91.42 W
Mountain View, Ok., U.S.	196	35.05 N	98.44 W
Mountain View, Wy., U.S.	200	41.16 N	110.20 W
Mountain View, Wy., U.S.	200	42.51 N	106.23 W
Mountain View Acres	228	34.31 N	117.24 W
Mountain Village	180	62.05 N	163.44 W
Mountain Zebra National Park ♦	158	32.16 S	25.29 E
Mount Airy, Md., U.S.	208	39.22 N	77.09 W
Mount Airy, N.C., U.S.	192	36.29 N	80.36 W
Mount Airy ◆[8]	285	40.04 N	75.12 W
Mount Albert	212	44.08 N	79.19 W
Mount Alford	171a	28.04 S	152.36 E
Mount Alida	158	29.09 S	30.18 E
Mount Alverno	285	39.53 N	75.25 W
Mount Angel	224	45.04 N	122.47 W
Mount Ann Park ♦	283	42.37 N	70.44 W
Mount Arlington	210	40.55 N	74.38 W
Mount Assiniboine Provincial Park ♦	182	50.54 N	115.40 W
Mount Auburn	219	39.46 N	89.16 W
Mount Augustus	162	24.19 S	116.54 E
Mount Ayliff	158	30.54 S	29.20 E
Mount Ayr, In., U.S.	216	40.57 N	87.18 W
Mount Ayr, Ia., U.S.	198	40.42 N	94.14 W
Mount Baldy	280	34.14 N	117.40 W
Mount Barker, Austl.	162	34.38 S	117.40 E
Mount Barker, Austl.	168b	35.04 S	138.52 E
Mount Bellew Bridge	48	53.28 N	8.29 W
Mount Berry	194	34.17 N	85.11 W
Mount Bethel	210	40.54 N	75.07 W
Mount Blanchard	216	40.53 N	83.33 W
Mount Bold Reservoir ⊜[1]	168b	35.07 S	138.42 E
Mount Brydges	214	42.54 N	81.29 W
Mount Buffalo National Park ♦	166	36.45 S	146.45 E
Mount Buller	169	37.10 S	146.27 E
Mount Calm	222	31.45 N	96.53 W
Mount Carleton Provincial Park ♦	186	47.23 N	66.50 W
Mount Carmel, Nf., Can.	186	47.09 N	53.29 W
Mount Carmel, Il., U.S.	194	38.24 N	87.45 W
Mount Carmel, Ky., U.S.	218	38.29 N	83.38 W
Mount Carmel, Oh., U.S.	218	39.06 N	84.18 W
Mount Carmel, Pa., U.S.	208	40.47 N	76.24 W
Mount Carmel Heights	218	39.07 N	84.18 W
Mount Carroll	190	42.05 N	89.58 W
Mount Cavenagh	162	25.58 S	133.15 E
Mount Charles	275b	43.41 N	79.40 W
Mount Clare	188	39.13 N	80.21 W
Mount Clemens	214	42.35 N	82.52 W
Mount Colah	274a	33.41 S	151.07 E
Mount Compass	168b	35.22 S	138.37 E
Mount Cook	172	43.44 S	170.06 E
Mount Cook National Park ♦	172	43.35 S	170.15 E
Mount Coot-tha Park ♦	171a	27.28 S	152.56 E
Mount Cory	216	40.56 N	83.50 W
Mount Crawford	168b	34.40 S	138.57 E
Mount Crosby	171a	27.32 S	152.48 E
Mount Currie Indian Reserve ◆[4]	182	50.19 N	122.42 W
Mount Dandenong	274b	37.50 S	145.22 E
Mount Dennis ◆[8]	275b	43.42 N	79.30 W
Mount Desert Island I	188	44.20 N	68.20 W
Mount Diablo Creek ≃	282	38.02 N	122.02 W
Mount Diablo State Park ♦	226	37.51 N	121.55 W
Mount Dora	220	28.48 N	81.38 W
Mount Doreen	162	22.03 S	131.18 E
Mount Druitt	274a	33.46 S	150.49 E
Mount Eaton	214	40.42 N	81.42 W
Mount Eba	166	30.12 S	135.40 E
Mount Eden	226	37.38 N	122.06 W
Mount Edgecumbe	180	57.03 N	135.21 W
Mount Edwards	171a	28.01 S	152.31 E
Mount Elgon National Park ♦	154	1.07 N	34.44 E
Mount Elizabeth	164	16.15 S	126.12 E
Mount Emu Creek ≃	169	38.18 S	142.55 E
Mount Enterprise	222	31.55 N	94.41 W
Mount Ephraim	285	39.52 N	75.05 W
Mount Evelyn	274b	37.47 S	145.23 E
Mount Fern	276	40.52 N	74.34 W
Mount Field National Park ♦	166	42.40 S	146.35 E
Mount Fletcher	158	30.40 S	28.30 E
Mount Forest	212	43.59 N	80.44 W
Mount Freedom	210	40.49 N	74.34 W
Mount Frere	158	31.00 S	28.58 E
Mount Gambier	166	37.50 S	140.46 E
Mount Garnet	166	17.41 S	145.07 E
Mount Gay	188	37.51 N	82.00 W
Mount Gilead, N.C., U.S.	192	35.12 N	80.00 W
Mount Gilead, Oh., U.S.	214	40.32 N	82.49 W
Mount Gravatt	171a	27.33 S	153.06 E
Mount Greenwood ◆[8]	278	41.42 N	87.43 W
Mount Gunson	162	31.27 S	137.11 E
Mount Hagen	164	5.50 S	144.15 E
Mount Hawke	42	50.17 N	5.12 W
Mount Hawthorn	168a	31.55 S	115.50 E
Mount Healthy	218	39.14 N	84.32 W
Mount Hebron	284b	39.18 N	76.50 W
Mount Helena	168a	31.53 S	116.13 E
Mount Hermon, Ca., U.S.	226	37.03 N	122.04 W
Mount Hermon, Ma., U.S.	207	42.40 N	72.29 W
Mount Holly, N.J., U.S.	208	39.59 N	74.47 W
Mount Holly, N.C., U.S.	192	35.17 N	81.00 W
Mount Holly Springs	208	40.07 N	77.11 W
Mount Hope, Austl.	166	34.07 S	135.23 E
Mount Hope, On., Can.	212	43.09 N	79.55 W
Mount Hope, Ks., U.S.	198	37.52 N	97.39 W
Mount Hope, N.J., U.S.	276	40.56 N	74.33 W
Mount Hope, Oh., U.S.	214	40.38 N	81.47 W
Mount Hope, W.V., U.S.	188	37.53 N	81.09 W
Mount Hope Lake ⊜	276	40.56 N	74.32 W
Mount Horeb	190	43.00 N	89.44 W
Mount Houston	222	29.54 N	95.18 W
Mount Howitt	166	26.31 S	142.16 E
Mount Hunter Rivulet ≃	274a	34.02 S	150.40 E
Mount Ida	194	34.33 N	93.38 W
Mount Isa	166	20.44 S	139.30 E
Mount Jackson, Pa., U.S.	214	40.58 N	80.26 W
Mount Jackson, Va., U.S.	188	38.44 N	78.38 W
Mount Jewett	214	41.43 N	78.38 W
Mount Juliet	194	36.12 N	86.31 W
Mount Kaputar National Park ♦	166	30.16 S	150.10 E
Mount Kenya National Park ♦	154	0.09 S	37.19 E
Mount Kisco	210	41.12 N	73.43 W
Mount Kokeby	168a	32.13 S	116.58 E
Mountlake Terrace	224	47.47 N	122.18 W
Mount Laurel	285	39.56 N	74.54 W
Mount Lebanon	214	40.21 N	80.02 W
Mount Liberty	214	40.21 N	82.38 W
Mount Lofty Ranges ⋏	168b	34.45 S	139.00 E
Mount Magnet	162	28.04 S	117.49 E
Mount Manara	166	32.29 S	143.56 E
Mount Margaret, Austl.	162	28.47 S	122.11 E
Mount Margaret, Austl.	166	26.54 S	143.21 E
Mount Marion	210	42.02 N	73.59 W
Mount Martha	169	38.17 S	145.01 E
Mount Maunganui	172	37.37 S	176.11 E
Mount McKinley National Park → Denali National Park ♦	180	63.15 N	150.30 W
Mount Mee	171a	27.04 S	152.46 E
Mountmellick	48	53.07 N	7.20 W
Mount Misery Point ›	276	40.58 N	73.05 W
Mount Mistake National Park ♦	171a	27.53 S	152.20 E
Mount Molloy	164	16.41 S	145.20 E
Mount Monger	162	30.59 S	121.53 E
Mount Moorosi	158	30.16 S	27.53 E
Mount Morgan	166	23.39 S	150.23 E
Mount Morris, Il., U.S.	190	42.03 N	89.25 W
Mount Morris, Mi., U.S.	190	43.07 N	83.41 W
Mount Morris, N.Y., U.S.	210	42.43 N	77.52 W
Mount Morris Dam ◆[6]	210	42.44 N	77.53 W
Mount Mulligan	166	16.51 S	144.52 E
Mount Nebo	279b	40.33 N	80.06 W
Mountnessing	260	51.39 N	0.21 E
Mount Olive, Il., U.S.	219	39.04 N	89.43 W
Mount Olive, Ms., U.S.	194	31.45 N	89.39 W
Mount Olive, N.C., U.S.	192	35.11 N	78.04 W
Mount Oliver	279b	40.28 N	79.59 W
Mount Olivet	218	38.31 N	84.02 W
Mount Orab	218	39.01 N	83.55 W
Mount Penn	208	40.20 N	75.54 W
Mount Perry	166	25.11 S	151.39 E
Mount Pleasant, Austl.	168b	34.47 S	139.02 E
Mount Pleasant, On., Can.	212	43.05 N	80.19 W
Mount Pleasant, In., U.S.	218	38.07 N	86.31 W
Mount Pleasant, Ia., U.S.	190	40.57 N	91.33 W
Mount Pleasant, Mi., U.S.	190	43.35 N	84.46 W
Mount Pleasant, N.C., U.S.	192	35.23 N	80.26 W
Mount Pleasant, Oh., U.S.	214	40.11 N	80.48 W
Mount Pleasant, Pa., U.S.	214	40.08 N	79.32 W
Mount Pleasant, S.C., U.S.	192	32.47 N	79.51 W
Mount Pleasant, Tn., U.S.	194	35.32 N	87.12 W
Mount Pleasant, Tx., U.S.	222	33.09 N	94.58 W
Mount Pleasant, Ut., U.S.	200	39.32 N	111.27 W
Mount Pleasant Mills	208	40.43 N	77.01 W
Mount Pleasant Park ♦	284b	39.22 N	76.35 W
Mount Pocono	210	41.07 N	75.21 W
Mount Pritchard	274a	33.54 S	150.54 E
Mount Prospect, S. Afr.	158	27.29 S	29.53 E
Mount Prospect, Il., U.S.	216	42.03 N	87.56 W
Mount Pulaski	219	40.00 N	89.16 W
Mount Rainier	284c	38.56 N	76.57 W
Mount Rainier National Park ♦	224	46.52 N	121.43 W
Mountrath	48	53.00 N	7.27 W
Mount Repose	218	39.10 N	84.14 W
Mount Revelstoke National Park ♦	182	51.06 N	118.00 W
Mount Riddock	162	23.03 S	134.40 E
Mount Robson Provincial Park ♦	182	52.58 N	118.50 W
Mount Rogers National Recreation Area ♦	192	36.42 N	81.30 W
Mount Roskill	172	36.55 S	174.45 E
Mount Royal	285	39.49 N	75.13 W
Mount Rushmore National Memorial ⊥	198	43.50 N	103.24 W
Mount Saint Helens National Volcanic Monument ♦	224	46.12 N	122.11 W
Mount Sandiman	162	24.24 S	115.23 E
Mount Sarah	162	26.57 S	135.22 E
Mount Savage	188	39.41 N	78.52 W
Mount's Bay ⊂	42	50.03 N	5.25 W
Mount Selinda	154	20.25 S	32.43 E
Mount Selman	222	32.04 N	95.17 W
Mount Seymour Provincial Park ♦	182	49.23 N	122.57 W
Mount Shasta	204	41.18 N	122.18 W
Mount Sinai	276	40.57 N	73.02 W
Mount Sinai Harbor ⊂	276	40.57 N	73.02 W
Mount Sinai Ridge ∧	218	39.04 N	84.58 W
Mount Somers	172	43.43 S	171.24 E
Mountsorrel	42	52.44 N	1.07 W
Mount Spokane State Park ♦	202	47.58 N	117.13 W
Mount Sterling, Il., U.S.	219	39.59 N	90.45 W
Mount Sterling, Ky., U.S.	192	38.03 N	83.56 W
Mount Sterling, Mo., U.S.	219	38.28 N	91.38 W
Mount Sterling, Oh., U.S.	218	39.43 N	83.15 W
Mount Stewart, P.E., Can.	186	46.22 N	62.52 W
Mount Stewart, S. Afr.	158	33.10 S	24.26 E
Mount Stromlo Observatory ⊛[3]	171b	35.20 S	149.00 E
Mount Summit	218	40.00 N	85.23 W
Mount Surprise	166	18.09 S	144.19 E
Mount Sylvia	171a	27.44 S	152.14 E
Mount Tamalpais State Park ♦	226	37.54 N	122.34 W
Mount Torrens	168b	34.52 S	138.57 E
Mount Tremper	210	42.03 N	74.17 W
Mount Uniacke	186	44.54 N	63.50 W
Mount Union	214	40.23 N	77.52 W
Mount Upton	210	42.25 N	75.23 W
Mount Vernon, Austl.	162	24.13 S	118.14 E
Mount Vernon, Al., U.S.	194	31.05 N	88.00 W
Mount Vernon, Ga., U.S.	192	32.10 N	82.35 W
Mount Vernon, Il., U.S.	219	38.19 N	88.54 W
Mount Vernon, In., U.S.	194	37.55 N	87.53 W
Mount Vernon, Ia., U.S.	190	41.55 N	91.25 W
Mount Vernon, Ky., U.S.	192	37.21 N	84.20 W
Mount Vernon, Md., U.S.	208	38.14 N	75.49 W
Mount Vernon, Mo., U.S.	194	37.06 N	93.49 W
Mount Vernon, N.Y., U.S.	210	42.45 N	78.53 W
Mount Vernon, N.Y., U.S.	210	40.54 N	73.50 W
Mount Vernon, Oh., U.S.	214	40.23 N	82.29 W
Mount Vernon, Or., U.S.	202	44.25 N	119.06 W
Mount Vernon, Pa., U.S.	279b	40.17 N	79.48 W
Mount Vernon, S.D., U.S.	198	43.42 N	98.15 W
Mount Vernon, Tx., U.S.	222	33.11 N	95.13 W
Mount Vernon, Wa., U.S.	224	48.25 N	122.19 W
Mount Vernon ⊥	208	38.47 N	77.06 W
Mount Victoria	170	33.35 S	150.15 E
Mount Victory	216	40.32 N	83.31 W
Mount View	207	41.38 N	71.24 W
Mountville	208	40.02 N	76.26 W
Mount Vision	210	42.35 N	75.04 W
Mount Washington	284b	39.23 N	76.41 W
Mount Washington ◆[8]	284b	39.22 N	76.40 W
Mount Waverley	274b	37.53 S	145.08 E
Mount Wedge, Austl.	162	22.45 S	132.09 E
Mount Wedge, Austl.	162	33.29 S	135.10 E
Mount Wellington	172	36.54 S	174.51 E
Mount Wilhelm National Park ♦	164	5.45 S	145.05 E
Mount William National Park ♦	166	40.56 S	148.15 E
Mount Willoughby	162	27.58 S	134.08 E
Mount Wilson Observatory ⊛[3]	228	34.14 N	118.03 W
Mount Wolf	208	40.03 N	76.42 W
Mount Zion	219	39.46 N	88.53 W
Mounyaz	146	10.41 N	21.18 E
Moura, Austl.	166	24.35 S	149.58 E
Moura, Bra.	246	1.27 S	61.38 W
Moura, Port.	34	38.08 N	7.27 W
Moura, Tchad	146	13.47 N	21.13 E
Moura Brasil	256	22.07 S	43.09 W
Mouraya	146	11.27 N	20.59 E
Mourdi, Dépression du ⊥[7]	146	18.10 N	23.00 E
Mourdiah	150	14.28 N	7.28 W
Mouriès	62	43.41 N	4.52 E
Mourindi	152	2.32 S	10.48 E
Mourmelon-le-Grand	50	49.08 N	4.22 E
Mourne ≃	48	54.49 N	7.28 W
Mourne Beg ≃	48	54.41 N	7.39 W
Mourne Mountains ⋏	48	54.10 N	6.04 W
Mousa I	46a	60.00 N	1.11 W
Mouscron	50	50.44 N	3.13 E
Mousgougou	146	10.47 N	16.09 E
Moussa Ali ∧	144	12.28 N	42.24 E
Mousseaux-sur-Seine	261	49.03 N	1.39 E
Moussey	58	48.40 N	6.47 E
Moussoro	146	13.39 N	16.29 E
Moussy-le-Neuf	261	49.04 N	2.36 E
Moussy-le-Vieux	261	49.03 N	2.38 E
Moustiers-Sainte-Marie	62	43.51 N	6.13 E
Moustique, Morne ∧	241o	16.06 N	61.44 W
Mouthe	58	46.43 N	6.12 E
Mouthier-Haute-Pierre	58	47.02 N	6.16 E
Moutier	58	47.17 N	7.23 E
Moûtiers	62	45.29 N	6.32 E
Moutiers-au-Perche	50	48.29 N	0.51 E
Moutnice	61	49.02 N	16.46 E
Moutohora	172	38.17 S	177.32 E
Moutomoukadi	152	4.41 S	13.15 E
Moutong	112	0.28 N	121.13 E
Mouy	50	49.19 N	2.19 E
Mouydir ⋏	148	24.45 N	4.05 E
Mouyondzi	152	3.58 S	13.57 E
Mouzákion	38	39.26 N	21.40 E
Mouzarak	146	13.11 N	15.58 E
Mouzon	56	49.36 N	5.05 E
Mouzon ≃	58	48.21 N	5.41 E
Moville, Ire.	48	55.11 N	7.03 W
Moville, Ia., U.S.	198	42.29 N	96.04 W
Mowang	100	30.31 N	113.34 E
Moweaqua	219	39.37 N	89.01 W
Mowein	140	7.36 N	28.11 E
Mowry Slough ≃	282	37.29 N	122.03 W
Mowrystown	218	39.02 N	83.44 W
Mowu	100	26.50 N	117.42 E
Moxhe	56	50.38 N	5.05 E
Moxi	107	30.18 N	105.41 E
Moxico □[5]	152	13.00 S	20.30 E
Moxotó ≃	250	9.19 S	38.14 W
Moy	48	54.27 N	6.42 W
Moy ≃	48	54.12 N	9.08 W
Moy, Cnoc ∧[2]	46	55.22 N	5.46 W
Moya, Comores	157a	12.18 S	44.27 E
Moya, Perú	248	12.24 S	75.10 W
Moyagee	162	27.45 S	117.54 E
Moyahua	234	21.16 N	103.10 W
Moyale, Ityo.	144	3.30 N	39.07 E
Moyale, Kenya	154	3.32 N	39.03 E
Moyamba	150	8.10 N	12.26 W
Moycullen	48	53.21 N	9.09 W
Moydans	62	44.24 N	5.30 E
Moÿ-de-l'Aisne	50	49.45 N	3.22 E
Moye Dao I	98	36.55 N	122.32 E
Moyen Atlas ⋏	148	33.30 N	5.00 W
Moyen-Chari □[5]	146	9.00 N	18.00 E
Moyenmoutier	58	48.23 N	6.55 E
Moyenne-Sido	146	8.13 N	18.43 E
Moyenneville	50	50.04 N	1.45 E
Moyen-Ogooué □[4]	152	0.30 S	10.30 E
Moyenvic	56	48.47 N	6.33 E
Moyeuvre-Grande	56	49.15 N	6.02 E
Moyie	182	49.17 N	115.50 W
Moyie ≃	202	48.42 N	116.11 W
Moyie Springs	202	48.43 N	116.11 W
Moylan	285	39.54 N	75.23 W
Moyle ≃	48	52.24 N	7.39 W
Moyo	154	3.39 N	31.43 E
Moyo ≃	115b	8.26 S	117.28 E
Moyo, Pulau I	115b	8.15 S	117.34 E
Moyobamba	248	6.03 S	76.58 W
Moyock	208	36.31 N	76.10 W
Moyogalpa	236	11.32 N	85.42 W
Moyowosi ≃	154	4.50 S	31.24 E
Moyu	120	37.17 N	79.44 E
Moyuta, Volcán ∧[1]	236	14.02 N	90.06 W
M'oža ≃, Europe	76	55.27 N	30.43 E
M'oža ≃, Ross.	80	58.23 N	44.54 E
Možajevka	83	48.44 N	39.45 E
Možajsk	82	55.30 N	36.01 E
Možajskij	265a	59.43 N	30.07 E
Možajskoje vodochranilišče ⊜[1]	82	55.35 N	35.50 E
Mozambique (Moçambique) □[1]	138	18.15 S	35.00 E
Mozambique Channel ⊔	138	19.00 S	41.00 E
Mozambique → Moçambique	154	15.03 S	40.42 E
Mozambique Plateau ⊹[3]	10	32.00 S	35.00 E
Mozarlândia	255	14.47 S	50.35 W
Možarovka	86	51.09 N	59.05 E
Možarov Majdan	80	55.37 N	45.53 E
Možary	80	53.53 N	41.02 E
Mozdok	84	43.44 N	44.38 E
Možga	80	56.23 N	52.17 E
Mozhabong Lake ⊜	190	46.57 N	82.05 W
Mozia ⊥	70	37.52 N	12.28 E
Mozichang	107	29.20 N	103.53 E
Mozolevo	76	59.19 N	33.51 E
Mozu	270	34.34 N	135.29 E
Mozuli	76	56.36 N	28.11 E
Mozyr'	78	52.03 N	29.14 E
Mozzanica	62	45.29 N	9.41 E
Mozzano	66	42.50 N	13.31 E
Mozzate	266b	45.41 N	8.57 E
Mpaka	158	26.26 S	31.47 E
Mpala	154	6.45 S	29.31 E
Mpama ≃	152	0.57 S	15.39 E
Mpanda	154	6.22 S	31.02 E
Mpé	152	2.54 S	14.43 E
Mpese	152	5.14 S	15.33 E
Mpessoba	150	12.40 N	5.43 W
Mphoengs	154	21.10 S	27.51 E
Mpigi	154	0.13 N	32.42 E
Mpika	154	11.54 S	31.26 E
Mpila ◆[8]	273b	4.14 S	15.18 E
Mpoka	152	1.26 S	17.02 E
Mpoko ≃	152	4.19 N	18.33 E
Mporokoso	154	9.23 S	30.05 E
Mpouya	152	2.37 S	16.13 E
Mpraeso	150	6.35 N	0.44 W
Mpui	154	8.21 S	31.50 E
Mpulungu	154	8.46 S	31.07 E
Mpwapwa	154	6.21 S	36.29 E
Mqanduli	158	31.48 S	28.46 E
Mrągowo	30	53.52 N	21.19 E
Mrakovo	86	52.43 N	56.38 E
M'Raman	157a	12.21 S	44.32 E
Mrangger	115a	7.01 S	110.31 E
Mras-Su ≃	86	53.45 N	87.49 E
Mrhila, Jebel ∧	36	35.25 N	9.14 E
Mrijo	154	5.10 S	36.15 E
Mrkonjić Grad	36	44.25 N	17.05 E
Mrkopalj	36	45.19 N	14.51 E
Mrocza	30	53.14 N	17.36 E
Msagali	154	6.21 S	36.18 E
M'Saken	148	35.44 N	10.35 E
Msata	154	6.20 S	38.23 E
Mšec	54	50.10 N	13.54 E
Mšeno	54	50.27 N	14.38 E
M'Sila	148	35.46 N	4.31 E
M'Sila □[5]	148	35.00 N	4.20 E
M'Sila, Oued ≃	34	35.46 N	4.34 E
Mšinskaja	76	59.01 N	29.57 E
Msoro	154	13.36 S	31.55 E
Msta	76	57.55 N	34.29 E
Msta ≃	76	58.25 N	31.20 E
Mstera	80	56.23 N	41.56 E
Mstislavl'	76	54.02 N	31.42 E
Mstiž	76	54.34 N	28.10 E
Mszana Dolna	30	49.42 N	20.05 E
Mszczonów	30	51.58 N	20.31 E
Mtakataka	154	14.12 S	34.32 E
Mtakuja	154	7.22 S	30.37 E
Mtama	154	10.18 S	39.22 E
Mtamvuna ≃	158	31.06 S	30.12 E
Mtarazi National Park ♦	154	18.36 S	32.50 E
Mtata ≃	158	31.58 S	29.10 E
Mtelo ∧	154	1.39 N	35.23 E
Mtilikwe ≃	154	21.09 S	31.30 E
Mtito Andei	154	2.41 S	38.10 E
Mtowabaga	154	2.30 S	35.53 E
Mtsensk → Mcensk	76	53.17 N	36.35 E
Mtubatuba	158	28.30 S	32.08 E
Mtunzini	158	28.57 S	31.46 E
Mtwara	154	10.16 S	40.11 E
Mtwara □[4]	154	11.00 S	39.00 E
Mtyangimbori	154	10.16 S	35.31 E
Mu ≃, Mya.	110	21.56 N	95.38 E
Mu ≃, Nihon	92a	42.33 N	141.56 E
Mu, Cerro ∧	246	9.29 N	73.07 W
Mu'a	174w	21.11 S	175.07 W
Muacancala	152	10.02 S	19.40 E
Mualama	154	16.53 S	38.17 E
Mualang	112	0.42 N	111.18 E
Mu'allaqah, Lubnān	132	33.50 N	35.54 E
Mu 'Allaqah, Sūd.	140	13.28 N	23.57 E
Muan	98	34.58 N	126.26 E
Muaná	250	1.32 S	49.13 W
Muanda	152	5.56 S	12.21 E
Muangai	152	12.32 S	19.51 E
Muang Èng	110	20.22 N	101.44 E
Muang Hay	110	21.03 N	101.49 E
Muang Hinboun	110	17.35 N	104.36 E
Muang Hôngsa	110	19.43 N	101.20 E

Symbols in the index entries represent the broad categories identified in the key at the right. Symbols with superior numbers (⋏[1]) identify subcategories (see complete key on page *I · 1).*

Symbole im Register stellen die rechts im Schlüssel erklärten Kategorien dar. Symbole mit hochgestellten Ziffern (⋏[1]) bezeichnen Unterabteilungen einer Kategorie (vgl. vollständiger Schlüssel auf Seite *I · 1).*

Los símbolos incluídos en el texto del índice representan las grandes categorias identificadas con la clave a la derecha. Los símbolos con numeros en su parte superior (⋏[1]) identifican las subcategorías (véase la clave completa en la página *I · 1).*

Les symboles de l'index représentent les catégories indiquées dans la légende à droite. Les symboles suivis d'un indice (⋏[1]) représentent des sous-catégories (voir légende complète à la page *I · 1).*

Os símbolos incluídos no texto do índice representam as grandes categorias identificadas com a chave à direita. Os símbolos com números em sua parte superior (⋏[1]) identificam as subcategorias (veja-se a chave completa à página *I · 1).*

∧ Mountain	Berg	Montaña	Montagne	Montanha
⋏ Mountains	Gebirge	Montañas	Montagnes	Montanhas
)(Pass	Paß	Paso	Col	Passo
V Valley, Canyon	Tal, Cañon	Valle, Cañón	Vallée, Canyon	Vale, Canhão
⊻ Plain	Ebene	Llano	Plaine	Planície
› Cape	Kap	Cabo	Cap	Cabo
I Island	Insel	Isla	Île	Ilha
II Islands	Inseln	Islas	Îles	Ilhas
⊥ Other Topographic Features	Andere Topographische Objekte	Otros Elementos Topográficos	Autres données topographiques	Outros acidentes topográficos

ESPAÑOL

Nombre	Página	Lat.°′	Long.°′ W = Oeste
Muang Houn	110	20.09 N	101.27 E
Muang Hounxianghoung	110	21.37 N	102.18 E
Muang Huang	110	18.45 N	103.42 E
Muang Khammouan	110	17.24 N	104.48 E
Muang Khao	110	19.47 N	103.29 E
Muang Khi	110	18.27 N	101.46 E
Muang Không	110	14.07 N	105.51 E
Muang Khôngxédôn	110	15.34 N	105.49 E
Muang La	110	20.52 N	102.07 E
Muang Liap	110	18.29 N	101.40 E
Muang Long	110	20.57 N	100.48 E
Muang Meung	110	20.43 N	100.28 E
Muang Ngoy, Lao	102	20.43 N	102.41 E
Muang Ngoy, Lao	110	20.43 N	102.41 E
Muang Nong	110	16.22 N	106.30 E
Muang Ou Nua	110	22.18 N	101.48 E
Muang Ou Tai	110	22.07 N	101.48 E
Muang Pakbèng	110	19.54 N	101.08 E
Muang Pak-Lay	110	18.12 N	101.25 E
Muang Paktha	110	20.06 N	100.36 E
Muang Pakxan	110	18.22 N	103.39 E
Muang Peun	110	20.13 N	103.52 E
Muang Phalan	110	16.39 N	105.34 E
Muang Phiang	110	19.06 N	101.32 E
Muang Phônthong	110	15.05 N	105.39 E
Muang Phoun	110	19.07 N	102.43 E
Muang Sam Sip	110	15.31 N	104.44 E
Muang Sing	110	21.11 N	101.09 E
Muang Soum	110	18.45 N	102.36 E
Muang Souvannakhili	110	15.23 N	105.49 E
Muang Souy	110	19.33 N	102.52 E
Muang Sung	110	20.19 N	102.27 E
Muang Thadua	110	19.26 N	101.50 E
Muang Thatèng	110	15.26 N	106.23 E
Muang Thathôm	110	19.00 N	103.36 E
Muang Va	110	21.53 N	102.19 E
Muang Vangviang	110	18.56 N	102.27 E
Muang Vapi	110	15.40 N	105.55 E
Muang Xaignabouri	110	19.15 N	101.45 E
Muang Xamtong	110	19.51 N	103.51 E
Muang Xay	110	20.42 N	101.59 E
Muang Xépôn	110	16.41 N	106.14 E
Muang Xon	110	20.27 N	103.19 E
Muang Yo	110	21.31 N	101.51 E
Muang You	110	19.49 N	102.50 E
Muanza	156	18.59 S	34.48 E
Muar (Bandar Maharani)	114	2.02 N	102.34 E
Muar ≃	114	2.03 N	102.35 E
Muara	112	5.02 N	115.02 E
Muaraaman	112	3.07 S	102.12 E
Muaraancalung	112	0.27 N	116.41 E
Muarabeliti	112	3.15 S	103.02 E
Muarabenangin	112	0.58 S	115.19 E
Muarabinuangeun	115a	6.50 S	105.53 E
Muarabulian	112	1.43 S	103.15 E
Muarabungo	112	1.28 S	102.07 E
Muaradua	112	4.32 S	104.05 E
Muaraenim	112	3.39 S	103.48 E
Muaragusung	112	1.35 N	117.17 E
Muarajuloi	112	0.12 S	114.03 E
Muarakaman	112	0.09 S	116.43 E
Muarakelingi	112	3.05 S	103.14 E
Muarakumpe	112	1.24 S	104.00 E
Muaralabuh	112	1.29 S	101.03 E
Muaralakitan	112	2.51 S	103.19 E
Muaralasan	112	1.48 N	117.12 E
Muaralembu	112	0.24 S	101.21 E
Muaramawai	112	0.37 N	116.49 E
Muarapangean	112	2.38 N	116.41 E
Muarapantai	112	0.45 S	101.43 E
Muarapayang	112	1.32 S	115.48 E
Muararupit	112	2.44 S	102.54 E
Muarasabak	112	1.08 S	103.51 E
Muarasiberut	108	1.36 S	99.11 E
Muarasipongi	112	0.37 N	99.51 E
Muaratais	114	1.17 N	99.21 E
Muaratebo	112	1.30 S	102.26 E
Muarateladang	112	2.50 S	103.58 E
Muaratembesi	112	1.42 S	103.07 E
Muaratewe	112	0.57 S	114.53 E
Muaratuhup	112	0.37 S	114.50 E
Muaratunan	112	1.24 S	116.39 E
Muarawahau	112	1.02 N	116.52 E
Muāri, Rās ≻	120	24.49 N	66.40 E
Muasdale	46	55.36 N	5.41 W
Muá Ximica	152	9.50 S	18.41 E
Mubārakpur	124	26.05 N	83.18 E
Mubārakpur Dabās ⬥[8]	272a	28.43 N	77.03 E
Mubayyad Ŧ[4]	142	30.55 N	32.48 E
Mubende	154	0.35 N	31.23 E
Mubi	146	10.18 N	13.20 E
Mubur, Pulau I	112	3.20 N	106.12 E
Mucaitá ≃	250	6.59 S	42.40 W
Mucajaí ≃	246	2.25 N	60.52 W
Mucambo	250	3.54 S	40.44 W
Mucári	152	9.30 S	16.54 E
Muccan	162	20.38 S	120.04 E
Muccia	66	43.05 N	13.02 E
Much	56	50.54 N	7.25 E
Mucha	269d	24.59 N	121.34 E
Muchangpu	100	31.55 N	116.35 E
Muchanovo	82	56.31 N	38.20 E
Muchavec ≃	76	52.05 N	23.39 E
Much Dewchurch	42	51.59 N	2.46 W
Muchea	168a	31.35 S	115.59 E
Mücheln	54	51.18 N	11.48 E
Muchen	89	48.10 N	136.13 E
Muchengzhen	107	29.47 N	103.29 E
Much Hoole	262	53.42 N	2.48 W
Muchinga Escarpment ⊥[4]	154	14.45 S	29.30 E
Muchinga Mountains ⋏	154	12.20 S	31.00 E
Muchino, Ross.	80	58.11 N	51.02 E
Muchino, Ross.	89	52.16 N	127.14 E
Muchor-Konduj	88	52.25 N	113.16 E
Muchrani	84	41.56 N	44.35 E
Muchtadir	84	41.41 N	48.46 E
Muchtolovo	80	55.27 N	43.13 E
Muchuan	107	28.55 N	103.58 E
Much Wenlock	42	52.36 N	2.34 W
Mucifal	266c	38.48 N	9.26 W
Mučikan	88	53.02 N	120.27 E
Muck I	46	56.50 N	6.15 W
Mücka	54	51.18 N	14.40 E
Muckadilla	166	26.35 S	148.23 E
Muckalee Creek ≃	192	31.38 N	84.09 W
Muckamore	48	54.41 N	6.10 W
Mučkapskij	80	51.52 N	42.28 E
Mučkas	24	64.02 N	48.27 E
Mücke	56	50.38 N	9.03 E
Muckendorf an der Donau	264b	48.20 N	16.09 E
Mucking	260	51.30 N	0.26 E
Muckle Roe I	46a	60.22 N	1.27 W
Muckleshoot Indian Reservation ⬥[4]	224	47.16 N	122.09 W
Muckno Lough ⊜	48	54.07 N	6.42 W
Mucojo	154	12.04 S	40.28 E
Mucoma	152	15.18 S	13.39 E
Muconda	152	10.34 S	21.17 E
Mucope, Ang.	152	16.24 S	14.53 E
Mucope, Ang.	152	8.42 S	21.43 E
Mucrone, Monte ∧	62	45.36 N	7.56 E
Mucubela	154	16.55 S	37.52 E
Mucuchíes	246	8.45 N	70.55 W
M'uc'ucl'u	84	40.28 N	47.55 E
Mucugê	255	13.00 S	41.23 W
Mucuim ≃	248	6.33 S	64.18 W
Muculo	152	16.47 S	14.51 E
Muçum	252	29.10 S	51.53 W
Mucumbura	154	16.09 S	31.31 E
Mucun	100	26.44 N	114.00 E
Mucupia	156	18.01 S	36.48 E
Mucupina, Monte ∧	236	15.08 N	86.38 W
Mucur	130	39.04 N	34.23 E
Mucuri	255	18.05 S	39.34 W

FRANÇAIS

Nom	Page	Lat.°′	Long.°′ W = Ouest
Mucuri ≃	255	18.05 S	39.34 W
Mucusso	152	18.01 S	21.25 E
Mud ≃, Ky., U.S.	194	37.13 N	86.54 W
Mud ≃, W.V., U.S.	188	38.25 N	82.17 W
Muda ≃	114	5.33 N	100.22 E
Mudan ≃	89	46.22 N	129.33 E
Mudanjiang	89	44.35 N	129.36 E
Mudanya	130	40.22 N	28.52 E
Mudau	56	49.32 N	9.11 E
Mudaysīsāt, Jabal ∧	132	31.39 N	36.14 E
Mud Creek ≃, N.A.	206	45.01 N	72.24 W
Mud Creek ≃, U.S.	198	43.17 N	96.15 W
Mud Creek ≃, Il., U.S.	219	38.21 N	89.48 W
Mud Creek ≃, In., U.S.	216	41.06 N	86.21 W
Mud Creek ≃, In., U.S.	216	40.26 N	85.55 W
Mud Creek ≃, Ne., U.S.	198	41.01 N	98.54 W
Mud Creek ≃, N.Y., U.S.	210	42.17 N	77.13 W
Mud Creek ≃, N.Y., U.S.	210	42.59 N	77.23 W
Mud Creek ≃, N.Y., U.S.	210	43.05 N	78.43 W
Mud Creek ≃, Ok., U.S.	196	33.55 N	97.28 W
Mud Creek ≃, S.D., U.S.	198	45.11 N	98.24 W
Mud Creek ≃, Tx., U.S.	222	31.48 N	94.58 W
Muddus Nationalpark ♠	24	67.00 N	20.16 E
Muddy ≃, Nv., U.S.	204	36.27 N	114.22 W
Muddy ≃, Wa., U.S.	224	46.04 N	122.01 W
Muddy Boggy Creek ≃	196	34.03 N	95.47 W
Muddy Branch ≃	284c	39.03 N	77.18 W
Muddy Brook ≃	276	41.07 N	73.20 W
Muddy Creek ≃, U.S.	276	41.03 N	74.02 W
Muddy Creek ≃, Mo., U.S.	194	38.51 N	93.03 W
Muddy Creek ≃, Mt., U.S.	202	47.56 N	111.46 W
Muddy Creek ≃, Oh., U.S.	214	41.27 N	83.03 W
Muddy Creek ≃, Pa., U.S.	208	39.47 N	76.18 W
Muddy Creek ≃, Ut., U.S.	200	38.24 N	110.42 W
Muddy Creek ≃, Wy., U.S.	198	42.35 N	104.57 W
Muddy Creek ≃, Wy., U.S.	200	41.59 N	106.08 W
Muddy Creek ≃, Wy., U.S.	200	41.32 N	110.13 W
Muddy Creek ≃, Wy., U.S.	200	41.01 N	107.42 W
Muddy Creek ≃, Wy., U.S.	202	43.17 N	108.14 W
Muddy Fork ≃	224	46.22 N	121.34 W
Muddy Gut ⊂	284b	39.17 N	76.26 W
Muddy Peak ∧	204	36.18 N	114.42 W
Müden, Dtsch.	52	52.52 N	10.07 E
Müden, Dtsch.	54	52.31 N	10.22 E
Mudgee	166	32.36 S	149.35 E
Mudgeeraba	171a	28.04 S	153.22 E
Mudhol	122	16.21 N	75.17 E
Mud Island I	171a	27.20 S	153.15 E
Mud Islands II	169	38.17 S	144.45 E
Mudjatik ≃	184	56.02 N	107.36 W
Mudjuga	24	63.46 N	39.15 E
Mud Lake ⊜, Id., U.S.	202	43.53 N	112.24 W
Mud Lake ⊜, Nv., U.S.	204	37.52 N	117.04 W
Mud Lake ⊜, N.Y., U.S.	212	44.30 N	75.28 W
Mud Lake Reservoir ⊜[1]	198	45.50 N	98.10 W
Mudon	110	16.15 N	97.44 E
Mudongzhen	102	29.35 N	106.51 E
Mudu	106	31.15 N	120.30 E
Mudug □[4]	144	6.15 N	48.00 E
Mudurnu	130	40.28 N	31.13 E
Mudurnu ≃	130	40.49 N	30.33 E
M'ud'ur'um ≃	85	40.53 N	76.36 E
Mueda	154	11.39 S	39.33 E
Muelle de los Bueyes	236	12.04 N	84.32 W
Mueller, Mount ∧[2]	162	19.54 S	127.51 E
Muenster	196	33.39 N	97.23 W
Mu'er	107	29.48 N	106.37 E
Muerte, Valle de la → Death Valley V	204	36.30 N	117.00 W
Muerto ≃	252	23.02 S	62.29 W
Muerto, Mar → Dead Sea ⊜	132	31.30 N	35.30 E
Mufulira	154	12.33 S	28.14 E
Mufuma	152	9.04 S	17.06 E
Mufu Shan ∧	100	29.02 N	113.54 E
Mufu Shan ⋏	100	29.00 N	114.00 E
Mugang	100	29.44 N	115.14 E
Muganskaja ravnina ≚	84	39.40 N	48.15 E
Mugazine	158	26.07 S	32.30 E
Mugegawa	94	35.31 N	136.51 E
Mugello V	66	43.55 N	11.30 E
Mügeln	54	51.14 N	13.02 E
Muger ≃	144	9.54 N	37.57 E
Müggelberge ⋏[2]	264a	52.25 N	13.39 E
Müggelheim ⬥[8]	264a	52.25 N	13.40 E
Muggia	64	45.36 N	13.46 E
Muggio	266b	45.36 N	9.14 E
Mughal Sarāi	124	25.18 N	83.07 E
Mugi, Nihon	94	35.34 N	137.01 E
Mugi, Nihon	96	33.40 N	134.25 E
Mu Gia, Deo)(	110	17.40 N	105.47 E
Muginga	152	8.20 S	17.32 E
Muğla	130	37.12 N	28.22 E
Muğla □[4]	130	37.10 N	28.30 E
Mugodžarskaja	86	48.36 N	58.27 E
Mugodžary, gory ⋏[2]	86	49.00 N	58.40 E
Mugombazi	154	5.50 S	30.14 E
Mugo-ri	98	38.58 N	126.31 E
Mugrejevskij	80	56.36 N	42.21 E
Mugron	32	43.45 N	0.45 W
Mugu Karnālī ≃	124	29.38 N	81.52 E
Mugur-Aksy	86	50.21 N	90.30 E
Mūḥ, Sabkhat al- ⊜	130	34.30 N	38.20 E
Muhala	154	5.40 S	28.43 E
Muhamdi	124	27.57 N	80.13 E
Muḥammad, Ra's ≻	140	27.44 N	34.15 E
Muhammadābād	124	26.02 N	83.23 E
Muhammadpur	126	23.24 N	89.36 E
Muḥammad Qawl	140	20.54 N	37.05 E
Muḥayshir, Birkat ⊜	142	30.43 N	31.56 E
Muheza	154	5.10 S	38.47 E
Muḥīṭ, Maṣrif al- ≖	273c	30.07 N	31.06 E
Mühlacker	56	48.57 N	8.50 E
Mühlau	54	50.54 N	12.45 E
Mühlbach am Hochkönig	64	47.22 N	13.08 E
Muhlbach-sur-Munster	58	48.02 N	7.05 E
Mühlberg	54	51.26 N	13.13 E
Mühldorf	61	48.22 N	15.21 E
Mühldorf am Inn	60	48.15 N	12.32 E
Mühlenbeck	54	52.40 N	13.22 E
Mühlenbecker See ⊜	264a	52.41 N	13.24 E
Muhlenberg	210	41.14 N	76.09 W
Mühlen-Berg ∧[2]	264a	52.23 N	13.15 E
Mühlen Eichsen	54	53.45 N	11.15 E
Mühlenfliess ≃	264a	52.26 N	13.41 E
Mühlen → Molini di Tures	64	46.54 N	11.56 E
Mühlenrahmede	263	51.16 N	7.40 E
Mühlhausen, Dtsch.	54	51.12 N	10.27 E
Mühlhausen, Dtsch.	263	51.33 N	7.44 E
Mühlhausen im Täle	56	48.34 N	9.39 E
Mühlheim	56	50.07 N	8.50 E

PORTUGUÊS

Nome	Página	Lat.°′	Long.°′ W = Oeste
Mühlheim an der Donau	58	48.01 N	8.53 E
Mühlig-Hofmann Mountains ⋏	9	72.00 S	5.20 E
Mühlleiten	264b	48.10 N	16.34 E
Mühltroff	54	50.32 N	11.55 E
Mühlviertel ⬥[1]	30	48.25 N	14.10 E
Muhola	26	63.20 N	25.05 E
Muhoro	154	1.01 S	34.07 E
Muhos	26	64.48 N	25.59 E
Muḥradah	130	35.15 N	36.35 E
Mühringen	58	48.25 N	8.46 E
Muhu I	76	58.38 N	23.15 E
Muhula	154	13.53 S	39.30 E
Muhulu	154	1.03 S	27.17 E
Muhutwe	154	1.33 S	31.42 E
Muhu väin ʉ	76	58.45 N	23.20 E
Muhuwesi ≃	154	11.16 S	37.58 E
Muick, Loch ⊜	46	56.55 N	3.10 W
Muiden	52	52.19 N	5.04 E
Muiderslot ⊥	52	52.20 N	5.10 E
Muides-sur-Loire	50	47.40 N	1.31 E
Muié	152	14.25 S	20.36 E
Mui Hopohoponga Point ≻	174w	21.09 S	175.02 W
Muikaichi	96	34.21 N	131.56 E
Muikamachi	94	37.04 N	138.53 E
Muine Bheag	48	52.41 N	6.58 W
Muir, Mi., U.S.	216	42.59 N	84.56 W
Muir, Pa., U.S.	208	40.36 N	76.31 W
Muir, Mount ∧	180	61.06 N	148.24 W
Muir Beach	282	37.52 N	122.35 W
Muirdrum	46	56.31 N	2.42 W
Muirkirk, Scot., U.K.	46	55.31 N	4.04 W
Muirkirk, Md., U.S.	284c	39.03 N	76.53 W
Muir of Ord	46	57.31 N	4.27 W
Muiron Islands II	162	21.35 S	114.20 E
Muir Seamount ✦[3]	16	33.41 N	62.30 W
Muirtown	46	56.16 N	3.45 W
Muir Woods	282	37.53 N	122.34 W
Muir Woods National Monument ♠	226	37.54 N	122.33 W
Muiskraal	158	33.56 S	21.13 E
Muisne	246	0.36 N	80.02 W
Muite	154	14.02 S	39.00 E
Mui Wo	271d	22.16 N	113.59 E
Muizen	50	51.01 N	4.31 E
Muja, Ityo.	144	12.02 N	39.29 E
Muja, Ross.	88	56.24 N	115.39 E
Muja ≃	88	56.24 N	115.39 E
Mujāhidpur ⬥[8]	272a	28.34 N	77.13 E
Mujang-ni	98	35.26 N	126.32 E
Mujezerskij	24	63.57 N	31.55 E
Mujiapucun	104	41.06 N	122.48 E
Mujiayu	105	40.24 N	116.55 E
Mujimbeji Mission	154	12.11 S	24.57 E
Mujnak	86	43.48 N	59.02 E
Muju	98	36.02 N	127.40 E
Mujunkum, peski ⬥[2]	86	44.20 N	71.00 E
Mukačevo	78	48.27 N	22.45 E
Mukah	112	2.54 N	112.06 E
Mukaishima	96	34.20 N	133.10 E
Mukalla → Al-Mukallā	144	14.32 N	49.08 E
Mukandpur ⬥[8]	272a	28.44 N	77.11 E
Mukandwara	120	24.49 N	75.59 E
Mukawa	94	35.47 N	138.23 E
Mukāwir	132	31.34 N	35.38 E
Mukāwir ⊥	132	31.34 N	35.38 E
Mukawwar I	140	20.48 N	37.13 E
Mukdahan	110	16.32 N	104.43 E
Mukden → Shenyang	104	41.48 N	123.27 E
Muke Arba	144	8.57 N	42.09 E
Mukebo	154	6.49 S	28.03 E
Mukeriān	123	31.57 N	75.37 E
Mukharram al-Fawqānī	130	34.49 N	37.04 E
Mukhmās	132	31.52 N	35.17 E
Mukho	98	37.33 N	129.06 E
Mukilteo	224	47.56 N	122.18 W
Mukinbudin	162	30.54 S	118.13 E
Mukinge Hill	154	13.29 S	25.52 E
Mukō	96	34.56 N	135.42 E
Muko ≃	96	34.41 N	135.23 E
Mukomuko	112	2.35 S	101.07 E
Mukomwenze	154	6.52 S	27.16 E
Mukoshima-rettō II	14	27.37 N	142.10 E
Mukry	128	37.36 N	65.44 E
Muksi-ri	98	39.52 N	125.54 E
Muksu ≃	85	39.15 N	71.23 E
Muksūdpur	126	23.18 N	89.51 E
Muktāgācha	124	24.46 N	90.14 E
Muktsar	123	30.29 N	74.31 E
Mukuku	154	12.09 S	29.49 E
Mukuleshi ≃	154	10.21 S	24.30 E
Mukur	86	48.03 N	54.30 E
Mukusaki	115b	8.33 S	121.37 E
Mukutan	154	0.38 N	36.16 E
Mukutawa ≃	184	53.10 N	97.28 W
Mukwela	154	17.02 S	26.39 E
Mukwonago	216	42.51 N	88.19 W
Mūl	122	20.04 N	79.40 E
Mula, Esp.	34	38.03 N	1.30 W
Mula, Zhg.	102	29.40 N	100.39 E
Mula ≃, India	122	18.34 N	74.20 E
Mula ≃, India	122	19.32 N	74.50 E
Mūla ≃, Pāk.	120	27.57 N	67.36 E
Mulādi	126	22.54 N	90.25 E
Muladu I	122	7.01 N	72.59 E
Mulaly	86	45.27 N	78.19 E
Mulan	89	45.57 N	128.03 E
Muland ⬥[8]	272c	19.10 N	72.57 E
Mulanda	152	14.41 S	21.48 E
Mulanje, Malaŵi	154	16.03 S	35.31 E
Mulanje, Moç.	154	16.03 S	35.45 E
Mulargia, Lago ⊜	71	39.37 N	9.14 E
Mulas, Punta ≻	240m	18.09 N	65.27 W
Mulas, Punta de ≻	240p	21.01 N	75.35 W
Mulatos	232	28.39 N	108.51 W
Mulayit Taung ∧	110	16.11 N	98.32 E
Mulazzo	64	44.19 N	9.53 E
Mulbāgal	122	13.10 N	78.24 E
Mulben	46	57.31 N	3.06 W
Mulberry, Ar., U.S.	194	35.30 N	94.03 W
Mulberry, Fl., U.S.	220	27.53 N	81.58 W
Mulberry, In., U.S.	216	40.20 N	86.39 W
Mulberry, Oh., U.S.	218	39.11 N	84.14 W
Mulberry ≃	194	35.28 N	94.03 W
Mulberry Creek ≃, Al., U.S.	194	32.27 N	86.52 W
Mulberry Creek ≃, Tx., U.S.	196	34.37 N	100.55 W
Mulberry Fork ≃	194	33.33 N	87.11 W
Mulberry Grove	219	38.55 N	89.16 W
Mulberry Mountain ∧	194	35.42 N	92.56 W
Mulchatna ≃	180	59.39 N	157.08 W
Mulchén	252	37.43 S	72.14 W
Mulda, Dtsch.	54	50.48 N	13.25 E
Mul'da, Ross.	24	67.28 N	63.34 E
Mulde ≃	54	51.52 N	12.15 E
Muldenstein	54	51.40 N	12.19 E
Muldersdrif se Loop ≃	273d	26.06 S	27.51 E
Muldersvlei	158	30.41 S	22.13 E
Muldoon	222	29.49 N	97.04 W
Muldraugh	194	37.56 N	85.59 W
Muldrow	194	35.24 N	94.35 W
Mule, Lac la ⊜	186	51.33 N	65.35 W
Muleba	154	1.49 S	31.40 E
Mule Creek ≃	198	37.05 N	99.00 W
Mulegé	232	26.53 N	112.01 W
Mulegns	58	46.33 N	9.37 E
Mulei	86	43.49 N	90.11 E
Mules (Mauls)	64	46.51 N	11.31 E
Mules, Pulau I	115b	8.54 S	120.17 E
Muleshoe	196	34.13 N	102.43 W
Mulevala	154	16.30 S	37.30 E
Mulga Downs	162	22.08 S	118.26 E
Mulgathing	162	30.15 S	134.00 E

Mulgathing Rocks ∧	162	30.14 S	133.58 E
Mulghar	126	22.46 N	89.45 E
Mulgoa	170	33.50 S	150.40 E
Mulgoa Creek ≃	274a	33.46 S	150.39 E
Mulgowie	171a	27.43 S	152.22 E
Mulgrave, Austl.	274b	37.56 S	145.12 E
Mulgrave, N.S., Can.	186	45.37 N	61.23 W
Mulgrave Hills ⋏[2]	180	67.42 N	163.24 W
Mulgul	162	24.49 S	118.26 E
Mulhacén ∧	34	37.03 N	3.19 W
Mulhall	196	36.03 N	97.24 W
Mülhausen → Mulhouse	58	47.45 N	7.20 E
Mülheim	56	49.54 N	7.01 E
Mülheim an der Ruhr	56	51.24 N	6.54 E
Mülheimer Ruhrtalbrüke ⬥[5]	263	51.23 N	6.54 E
Mülheim-Karlich	56	50.21 N	7.28 E
Mulhouse (Mülhausen)	58	47.45 N	7.20 E
Muli	102	27.50 N	101.15 E
Muling, Zhg.	89	44.56 N	130.31 E
Muling, Zhg.	89	44.31 N	130.13 E
Muling ≃	89	45.53 N	133.30 E
Mulini, Capo ≻	70	37.34 N	15.10 E
Mulino	224	45.13 N	122.34 W
Mulinu'u, Cape ≻	175a	13.26 S	172.43 W
Mulita ≃	116	7.18 N	124.52 E
Mulkear ≃	48	52.40 N	8.33 W
Mūlki	122	13.06 N	74.48 E
Mull, Island of I	46	56.27 N	6.00 W
Mull, Sound of ʉ	46	56.32 N	5.50 W
Mullagh	48	53.49 N	6.57 W
Mullaghareirk Mountains ⋏	48	52.20 N	9.10 W
Mullaghcleevaun ∧	48	53.06 N	6.24 W
Mullaghmore ∧	48	54.52 N	6.51 W
Mullaloo Point ≻	168a	31.48 S	115.44 E
Mullan	202	47.28 N	115.48 W
Mullen	198	42.02 N	101.02 W
Müllenbach	56	50.19 N	6.55 E
Mullengudgery	166	31.41 S	147.26 E
Mullens	192	37.34 N	81.22 W
Muller, Pegunungan ⋏	112	0.40 N	113.50 E
Muller Creek ≃	162	22.29 S	134.30 E
Muller Range ⋏	164	5.35 S	142.15 E
Mullerup	41	55.30 N	11.13 E
Mullet Key I	220	27.37 N	82.44 W
Mullet Peninsula ≻[1]	48	54.12 N	10.00 W
Mullett Lake ⊜	190	45.30 N	84.30 W
Mullewa	162	28.33 S	115.31 E
Mull Head ≻, Scot., U.K.	46	59.23 N	2.54 W
Mull Head ≻, Scot., U.K.	46	58.58 N	2.43 W
Müllheim	58	47.48 N	7.38 E
Mullhyttan	40	59.09 N	14.41 E
Mullica ≃	208	39.33 N	74.25 W
Mullica, Alquatka Branch ≃	285	39.47 N	74.48 W
Mullica, Sleeper Branch ≃	285	39.39 N	74.40 W
Mullica Hill	208	39.44 N	75.13 W
Mulligan ≃	166	25.00 S	138.30 E
Mulliken	216	42.45 N	84.53 W
Mullin	196	31.33 N	98.40 W
Mullinahone	48	52.30 N	7.30 W
Mullinavat	48	52.21 N	7.10 W
Mullingar	48	53.32 N	7.20 W
Mullins	192	34.12 N	79.15 W
Mullinville	198	37.35 N	99.28 W
Mullion	42	50.01 N	5.15 W
Mulloon Creek ≃	171b	35.12 S	149.38 E
Mullovka	80	54.13 N	49.25 E
Müllrose	54	52.14 N	14.25 E
Mullsjö	26	57.55 N	13.53 E
Mullumbimby	166	28.33 S	153.30 E
Mullum Mullum Creek ≃	274b	37.44 S	145.10 E
Mulobezi	154	16.48 S	25.09 E
Mulonda Funda	154	11.06 S	25.28 E
Mulondo	152	15.39 S	15.14 E
Mulongo	154	7.50 S	27.00 E
Mulshi Lake ⊜	122	18.30 N	73.30 E
Multai	120	21.46 N	78.15 E
Multān	123	30.11 N	71.29 E
Multen ⊜	40	59.10 N	14.37 E
Multia	26	62.25 N	24.47 E
Multnomah □[6]	224	45.30 N	122.22 W
Multnomah Channel ≃[1]	224	45.51 N	122.52 W
Multnomah Falls ⌊	224	45.35 N	122.07 W
Mulu, Gunong ∧	112	4.04 N	114.56 E
Mulumbe, Monts ⋏	154	8.16 S	28.16 E
Mulungushi	154	14.40 S	28.50 E
Mulungushi Dam ⬥[6]	154	14.40 S	28.50 E
Mulvane	198	37.28 N	97.14 W
Mulwad	140	18.39 N	30.35 E
Mulyah Mountain ∧	166	30.37 S	144.31 E
Muma	152	3.24 N	23.15 E
Mumbles Head ≻	42	51.35 N	3.59 W
Mumbondo	152	10.09 S	14.15 E
Mumbra	272c	19.11 N	73.01 E
Mumbwa	154	14.59 S	27.04 E
Mumcular	130	37.05 N	27.40 E
Mume	154	9.40 S	27.26 E
Mumen	102	32.09 N	106.28 E
Mumeng	164	7.00 S	146.35 E
Mumford, N.Y., U.S.	210	42.59 N	77.52 W
Mumford, Tx., U.S.	222	30.44 N	96.34 W
Mumias	154	0.20 N	34.29 E
Mümling ≃	56	49.50 N	9.09 E
Mumoni ∧	154	0.31 S	38.01 E
Mumra	80	45.47 N	47.41 E
Mumu	140	12.06 N	23.42 E
Mumungwe	156	21.59 S	26.24 E
Mun ≃	110	15.19 N	105.30 E
Mun, Jabal ∧	140	14.08 N	22.42 E
Munā, Ar. Su.	144	21.25 N	39.52 E
Muna, Méx.	232	20.29 N	89.43 W
Muna ≃	74	67.52 N	123.06 E
Muna, Pulau I	112	5.00 S	122.30 E
Muna, Selat ʉ	112	5.15 S	122.10 E
Munā al-Amīr	142	29.54 N	31.15 E
Munābāo	120	25.45 N	70.17 E
Munajly	86	46.47 N	54.31 E
Munakata	96	33.50 N	130.35 E
Munam-ni	98	38.41 N	126.54 E
Munam-san ∧	98	40.26 N	127.22 E
Munbong-ni	271b	37.43 N	126.49 E
Muncar	115a	8.26 S	114.20 E
Münchberg	54	50.11 N	11.47 E
Müncheberg	54	52.30 N	14.08 E
Münchehofe	264a	52.30 N	13.40 E
München	60	48.08 N	11.34 E
Münchenbernsdorf	54	50.49 N	11.56 E
Münchenbuchsee	58	47.01 N	7.27 E
Münchendorf	264b	48.02 N	16.23 E
München-Gladbach → Mönchengladbach	56	51.12 N	6.28 E
München-Riem, Flughafen ⊠	60	48.08 N	11.41 E
Münchenstein	58	47.31 N	7.37 E
Münchhausen	56	50.57 N	8.43 E
Munchique, Cerro ∧	246	2.32 N	76.57 W
Munchique, Parque Nacional ♠	246	2.30 N	77.10 W
Munch'ŏn	98	39.16 N	127.15 E
Muncie	216	40.11 N	85.23 W
Muncusun	130	38.54 N	35.38 E
Muncy	210	41.12 N	76.47 W
Muncy Creek ≃	210	41.13 N	76.48 W
Muncy Valley	210	41.21 N	76.35 W
Mundare	182	53.36 N	112.20 W
Mundaring	168a	31.54 S	116.10 E
Munday	196	33.26 N	99.37 W
Mundelein	216	42.15 N	88.00 W
Mündelheim ⬥[8]	263	51.21 N	6.41 E

Münden	56	51.25 N	9.39 E
Munderfing	60	48.05 N	13.11 E
Munderkingen	58	48.14 N	9.38 E
Munderoo ∧	171b	35.48 S	147.47 E
Mundesley	42	52.53 N	1.26 E
Mundijong	168a	32.18 S	115.59 E
Mundiwindi	162	23.52 S	120.09 E
Mūndka ⬥[8]	272a	28.41 N	77.02 E
Mundo ≃	34	38.19 N	1.40 W
Mundolsheim	58	48.39 N	7.42 E
Mundon Hill	260	51.41 N	0.42 E
Mundo Novo	255	11.52 S	40.28 W
Mundra	120	22.51 N	69.44 E
Mundrabilla	162	31.52 S	127.51 E
Mundubbera	166	25.36 S	151.18 E
Mundybaš	86	53.14 N	87.19 E
Mundytau, gora ∧	85	38.00 N	68.27 E
Munene	154	20.38 S	30.03 E
Munenga	152	10.02 S	14.41 E
Munera	34	39.02 N	2.28 W
Munford	194	35.26 N	89.48 W
Munfordville	194	37.16 N	85.53 W
Mungallala	166	26.27 S	147.33 E
Mungallala Creek ≃	166	28.05 S	147.15 E
Mungana	166	17.07 S	144.24 E
Mungaoli	124	24.25 N	78.06 E
Mungári	154	17.12 S	33.31 E
Mungar Junction	166	25.36 S	152.36 E
Mungau	152	13.56 S	21.55 E
Mungbere	154	2.38 N	28.30 E
Mungeli	124	22.04 N	81.41 E
Munger	124	25.23 N	86.28 E
Mungeranie	162	28.00 S	138.36 E
Mungindi	166	28.58 S	148.59 E
Munglinup	162	33.43 S	120.51 E
Mungo	152	11.49 S	16.16 E
Mungo National Park ♠	166	33.44 S	143.02 E
Mungra Badshāhpur	124	25.40 N	82.11 E
Mungun-Tajga, gora ∧	86	50.16 N	90.05 E
Mun'gyŏng	98	36.44 N	128.07 E
Munhall	214	40.23 N	79.54 W
Munhamade	154	16.37 S	36.58 E
Munhango	152	12.12 S	18.42 E
Munhango ≃	152	11.20 S	19.50 E
Munhoz	256	22.37 S	46.22 W
Munhye-ri	98	38.10 N	127.19 E
Munich → München	60	48.08 N	11.34 E
Muniesa	34	41.02 N	0.48 W
Munim ≃	250	2.45 S	44.04 W
Munirka ⬥[8]	272a	28.34 N	77.10 E
Munising	190	46.24 N	86.38 W
Munith	216	42.23 N	84.15 W
Muñiz	258	34.33 S	58.42 W
Muniz Freire	255	20.28 S	41.25 W
Munkács → Mukačevo	78	48.27 N	22.45 E
Munka-Ljungby	41	56.15 N	12.58 E
Munkebjerg ∧[2]	41	55.41 N	9.37 E
Munkebo	41	55.27 N	10.34 E
Munkedal	26	58.29 N	11.41 E
Munkerud	40	59.50 N	13.31 E
Munkfors	40	59.50 N	13.32 E
Munksund	26	65.17 N	21.29 E
Munktorp	40	59.32 N	16.08 E
Munku-Sardyk, gora ∧	88	51.45 N	100.32 E
Munlochy	46	57.32 N	4.15 W
Münnerstadt	56	50.15 N	10.11 E
Munnsville	210	42.58 N	75.35 W
Muñoz	116	15.43 N	120.54 E
Munozero	24	67.05 N	34.12 E
Muñoz Gamero, Península ≻[1]	254	52.30 S	73.10 W
Munpal-li	271b	37.45 N	126.43 E
Munro ⬥[8]	288	34.32 S	58.31 W
Munroe Falls	214	41.08 N	81.26 W
Munro Lake ⊜	184	54.38 N	95.16 W
Munsan	98	37.51 N	126.48 E
Munsarpur	126	24.18 N	88.26 E
Munsey Park	276	40.48 N	73.41 W
Munshiganj	124	23.33 N	90.32 E
Münsing	64	47.54 N	11.22 E
Münsingen, Dtsch.	58	48.25 N	9.29 E
Münsingen, Schw.	58	46.53 N	7.34 E
Munsö I	40	59.23 N	17.35 E
Munson, Ab., Can.	182	51.34 N	112.45 W
Munson, Pa., U.S.	214	40.57 N	78.10 W
Munson Knob ∧[2]	214	40.40 N	81.54 W
Munsons Corners	210	42.35 N	76.13 W
Münster, Dtsch.	52	51.57 N	7.37 E
Munster, Dtsch.	52	52.59 N	10.05 E
Münster, Dtsch.	56	49.55 N	8.52 E
Munster, Fr.	56	48.55 N	6.54 E
Munster, Fr.	58	48.03 N	7.08 E
Münster, Schw.	58	46.29 N	8.16 E
Munster, In., U.S.	216	41.33 N	87.30 W
Münster □[6]	52	51.50 N	7.25 E
Munster □[9]	48	52.25 N	8.20 W
Munster ≃	48	52.33 N	7.12 W
Münsterkirche ʊ[1]	263	51.27 N	7.01 E
Münsterland ⬥[1]	52	52.00 N	7.30 E
Münsterlingen	58	47.38 N	9.14 E
Münstermaifeld	56	50.15 N	7.22 E
Muntadgin	162	31.45 S	118.34 E
Muntahak ∧	114	1.52 N	103.47 E
Munte	112	0.30 N	119.55 E
Muntele Mare, Vîrful ∧	38	46.29 N	23.14 E
Muntendam	52	53.07 N	6.53 E
Muntok	112	2.04 S	105.11 E
Mununzi	154	0.36 N	29.15 E
Munuscong Lake ⊜	190	46.10 N	84.08 W
Münzenberg	56	50.27 N	8.46 E
Münzkirchen	60	48.29 N	13.34 E
Munzur Dağları ⋏	130	39.30 N	39.10 E
Munzur Vadisi Milli Parkı ♠	130	39.25 N	39.30 E
Muojärvi ⊜	26	65.56 N	29.36 E
Muolea Point ≻	229a	20.41 N	156.01 W
Muong Het	110	20.49 N	104.01 E
Muong Hinh	110	19.49 N	105.03 E
Muong Khoua	110	21.05 N	102.31 E
Muong Saiapoun	110	18.24 N	101.31 E
Muong Te	110	22.28 N	102.37 E
Muonio	24	67.57 N	23.42 E
Muoro	36	40.20 N	9.20 E
Muotathal	58	46.59 N	8.46 E
Mupa	152	16.10 S	15.44 E
Mupa, Parque Nacional da ⬥[4]	152	16.00 S	15.35 E
Muping	98	37.24 N	121.35 E
Mupini	156	17.50 S	19.40 E
Mup'ungjang	98	35.58 N	127.49 E
Muqaddam, Wādī V	140	18.04 N	31.30 E
Muqaṭṭa'	140	14.40 N	35.51 E
Muqaybirah, Bi'r al- Ŧ[4]	142	30.53 N	32.50 E
Muqayshiṭ I	128	24.10 N	53.45 E
Muqdisho (Mogadishu)	144	2.04 N	45.22 E
Muqi	98	41.46 N	124.39 E
Muqsam, Jabal ∧	140	13.38 N	27.42 E
Muquequete	152	14.50 S	14.16 E
Muqui	255	20.57 S	41.20 W
Mur (Mura) ≃	30	46.18 N	16.53 E
Mura (Mur) ≃, Europe	30	46.18 N	16.53 E
Mura ≃, Ross.	88	58.27 N	98.34 E
Muradiye, Tür.	84	38.59 N	43.46 E
Muradiye, Tür.	130	38.39 N	27.21 E
Murādnagar	124	28.47 N	77.30 E
Murafa ≃	78	48.13 N	28.14 E
Murāgācha	126	23.32 N	88.24 E
Muraglione, Passo del)(	66	43.56 N	11.39 E
Murai Reservoir ⊜[1]	271c	1.24 N	103.41 E
Murajá	250	0.47 S	47.57 W

Murakami	92	38.14 N	139.29 E
Murallón, Cerro ∧	254	49.48 S	73.25 W
Murambi	154	1.46 S	30.23 E
Muramvya	154	3.16 S	29.37 E
Muráň	30	48.46 N	20.02 E
Murana	164	3.33 S	133.49 E
Murang'a	154	0.43 S	37.09 E
Murano, Isola di I	64	45.28 N	12.21 E
Muranskij porog ⌊	88	58.02 N	112.16 E
Muraoka	96	35.28 N	134.35 E
Muraši	24	59.24 N	48.55 E
Muraški	265b	55.59 N	37.45 E
Murat	32	45.07 N	2.52 E
Murat ≃	84	38.39 N	39.50 E
Murat Dağı ∧	130	38.55 N	29.43 E
Muratkovo	86	58.26 N	62.23 E
Muratlı	130	41.10 N	27.30 E
Muratovo	83	48.48 N	38.45 E
Muratpur	272b	22.59 N	88.27 E
Murau	61	47.07 N	14.10 E
Muravera	71	39.25 N	9.34 E
Muravjovka	89	49.50 N	127.44 E
Muravjovo	76	56.14 N	34.14 E
Murayama	92	38.28 N	140.22 E
Murayama-chosuichi ⊜[1]	268	35.45 N	139.25 E
Muraysah, Ra's al- ≻	146	31.55 N	25.02 E
Murča	34	41.24 N	7.27 W
Murcanyo	144	11.41 N	50.27 E
Mūrcheh Khvort	128	33.06 N	51.30 E
Murchin	54	53.54 N	13.44 E
Murchison, Austl.	166	36.37 S	145.14 E
Murchison, N.Z.	172	41.48 S	172.20 E
Murchison, Tx., U.S.	222	32.17 N	95.45 W
Murchison ≃	162	27.42 S	114.09 E
Murchison, Mount ∧, Austl.	162	26.46 S	116.25 E
Murchison, Mount ∧, N.Z.	172	43.01 S	171.22 E
Murchison Falls → Kabalega Falls ⌊	154	2.17 N	31.41 E
Murchison Range ⋏	162	20.11 S	134.26 E
Murcia, Esp.	34	37.59 N	1.07 W
Murcia, Pil.	116	10.36 N	123.02 E
Murcia □[4], Esp.	34	38.00 N	1.30 W
Murcia □[4], Esp.	34	38.00 N	1.30 W
Murcia □[4], Esp.	148	37.55 N	1.30 W
Murciélago, Islas II	236	10.51 N	85.57 W
Murcielagos Bay ⊂	116	8.39 N	123.33 E
Mur-de-Barrez	32	44.51 N	2.39 E
Murdeduke, Lake ⊜	169	38.11 S	143.53 E
Murder Creek ≃, Al., U.S.	194	31.04 N	87.06 W
Murder Creek ≃, N.Y., U.S.	210	43.05 N	78.31 W
Murderkill ≃	208	39.03 N	75.24 W
Murdo	198	43.53 N	100.42 W
Murdock	220	27.00 N	82.08 W
Mure	94	36.45 N	138.14 E
Mureaux, Aérodrome des ⊠	261	49.00 N	1.57 E
Mureck	61	46.42 N	15.46 E
Mürefte	130	40.40 N	27.14 E
Mureș □[6]	38	46.35 N	24.40 E
Mureș (Maros) ≃	38	46.15 N	20.13 E
Muret	32	43.28 N	1.21 E
Murewa	154	17.39 S	31.47 E
Murfreesboro, Ar., U.S.	194	34.03 N	93.41 W
Murfreesboro, N.C., U.S.	192	36.26 N	77.05 W
Murfreesboro, Tn., U.S.	194	35.50 N	86.23 W
Murg	58	47.33 N	8.01 E
Murg ≃	56	48.55 N	8.10 E
Murgab	85	38.10 N	73.59 E
Murgab (Morghāb) ≃, Asia	128	38.18 N	61.12 E
Murgab ≃, Taj.	120	38.20 N	72.30 E
Murgenella	164	11.33 S	132.55 E
Murgeni	38	46.12 N	28.01 E
Murgenthal	58	47.16 N	7.50 E
Murgha Faqīrzai	120	31.03 N	67.48 E
Murgha Kibzai	120	30.44 N	69.25 E
Murgon	166	26.15 S	151.57 E
Muri, Cook Is.	174k	21.14 S	159.43 W
Muri, Nig.	146	9.11 N	10.53 E
Muri, Schw.	58	46.56 N	7.29 E
Muri, Schw.	58	47.16 N	8.21 E
Muria, Gunung ∧	115a	6.36 S	110.53 E
Muriaé	255	21.08 S	42.22 W
Muriaé ≃	255	21.43 S	41.22 W
Murias de Paredes	34	42.51 N	6.11 W
Muribeca	250	10.26 S	36.59 W
Muribeca dos Guararapes	250	8.10 S	35.01 W
Murici	250	9.19 S	35.56 W
Muricizal ≃	250	6.40 S	48.40 W
Murīdke	123	31.48 N	74.16 E
Muriége	152	9.58 S	21.11 E
Muriel Lake ⊜	182	54.10 N	110.40 W
Murih, Pulau I	112	1.54 N	108.38 E
Murila	152	10.44 S	20.20 E
Murilo I[1]	14	8.40 N	152.11 E
Mūrinda	123	30.47 N	76.29 E
Murinja	88	54.47 N	107.21 E
Murino, Ross.	88	51.30 N	104.23 E
Murino, Ross.	265a	60.03 N	30.27 E
Murinskij ≃	265a	60.01 N	30.28 E
Muriqui	256	22.56 S	43.57 W
Muriqui ≃	287a	22.52 S	43.02 W
Murisengo	62	45.05 N	8.08 E
Mūrītāniyā → Mauritania □[1]	134	20.00 N	12.00 W
Müritz ⊜	54	53.25 N	12.43 E
Muriwai	172	38.46 S	177.55 E
Murkong Selek	120	27.49 N	95.16 E
Murlīganj	124	25.54 N	86.59 E
Murlo	66	43.09 N	11.23 E
Murmansk	24	68.58 N	33.05 E
Murmansk Rise ✦[3]	12	75.00 N	37.00 E
Murmerwoude	52	53.16 N	6.00 E
Murmino	80	54.36 N	40.03 E
Murnau	64	47.40 N	11.12 E
Murnei	140	12.57 N	22.52 E
Murō	94	34.34 N	136.02 E
Murō-Akame-Aoyama-kokutei-kōen ♠	94	34.30 N	136.10 E
Muro Lucano	68	40.45 N	15.29 E
Murom	80	55.34 N	42.02 E
Muromcevo	86	56.23 N	75.14 E
Muroran	92a	42.18 N	140.59 E
Muros	34	42.47 N	9.02 W
Muros y Noya, Ría de ⊂[1]	34	42.45 N	9.00 W
Muroto	96	33.18 N	134.09 E
Muroto-Anan-kaigan-kokutei-kōen ♠	96	33.41 N	134.32 E
Muroto-zaki ≻	96	33.15 N	134.11 E
Murovanyje Kurilovcy	78	48.43 N	27.31 E
Murowana Goślina	30	52.35 N	17.01 E
Murphy, Id., U.S.	202	43.13 N	116.33 W
Murphy, Mo., U.S.	219	38.29 N	90.29 W
Murphy, N.C., U.S.	192	35.05 N	84.02 W
Murphy Lake ⊜	182	52.03 N	121.14 W
Murphys	226	38.08 N	120.27 W
Murphysboro	194	37.45 N	89.20 W
Murphy Slough ≃	226	36.28 N	120.00 W
Murr ≃	56	48.57 N	9.16 E
Murr, Wādī V	142	28.27 N	32.18 E
Murrah, Qārat al- ∧[2]	142	30.00 N	32.41 E
Murrah al-Kubrā, Al-Buḥayrah al- (Great Bitter Lake) ⊜	142	30.20 N	32.23 E
Murrah aṣ-Ṣughrā, Al-Buḥayrah al- (Little Bitter Lake) ⊜	142	30.13 N	32.33 E

≃	River	Fluß	Río	Rivière	Rio	✦ Submarine Features	Untermeerische Objekte	Accidentes Submarinos	Formes de relief sous-marin	Acidentes submarinos
≖	Canal	Kanal	Canal	Canal	Canal	□ Political Unit	Politische Einheit	Unidad Politica	Entité politique	Unidade política
⌊	Waterfall, Rapids	Wasserfall, Stromschnellen	Cascada, Rápidos	Chute d'eau, Rapides	Cascata, Rápidos	ʊ Cultural Institution	Kulturelle Institution	Institución Cultural	Institution culturelle	Instituição cultural
ʉ	Strait	Meeresstraße	Estrecho	Détroit	Estreito	⊥ Historical Site	Historische Stätte	Sitio Histórico	Site historique	Sitio histórico
⊂	Bay, Gulf	Bucht, Golf	Bahía, Golfo	Baie, Golfe	Baía, Golfo	♠ Recreational Site	Erholungs- und Ferienort	Sitio de Recreo	Centre de loisirs	Area de Lazer
⊜	Lake, Lakes	See, Seen	Lago, Lagos	Lac, Lacs	Lago, Lagos	⊠ Airport	Flughafen	Aeropuerto	Aéroport	Aeroporto
≡	Swamp	Sumpf	Pantano	Marais	Pântano	■ Military Installation	Militäranlage	Instalación Militar	Installation militaire	Instalação militar
⊓	Ice Features, Glacier	Eis- und Gletscherformen	Accidentes Glaciales	Formes glaciaires	Acidentes glaciares	⬥ Miscellaneous	Verschiedenes	Misceláneo	Divers	Diversos
Ŧ	Other Hydrographic Features	Andere Hydrographische Objekte	Otros Elementos Hidrográficos	Autres données hydrographiques	Outros acidentes hidrográficos					

ENGLISH / DEUTSCH

Name	Page / Seite	Lat.°′ / Breite°′	Long.°′ / Länge°′ E = Ost
Murra Murra	166	28.16 S	146.48 E
Murrāt, Ābār ⊽⁴	140	21.03 N	32.55 E
Murray, Ia., U.S.	190	41.02 N	93.56 W
Murray, Ky., U.S.	194	36.36 N	88.18 W
Murray, Ut,. U.S.	200	40.40 N	111.53 W
Murray ≐, Austl.	166	35.22 S	139.22 E
Murray ≐, Austl.	168a	32.35 S	115.46 E
Murray ≐, B.C., Can.	182	55.40 N	121.10 W
Murray, Lake ⊜	164	7.00 S	141.30 E
Murray, Lake ⊜¹	192	34.04 N	81.23 W
Murray, Mount ∧, Yk., Can.	180	60.54 N	128.49 W
Murray, Mount ∧, Pap. N. Gui.	164	6.46 S	144.01 E
Murray Bay → La Malbaie	186	47.39 N	70.10 W
Murray Bridge	168b	35.07 S	139.17 E
Murray Canal ≊	212	44.04 N	77.35 W
Murray City	188	39.30 N	82.09 W
Murray Downs	162	21.04 S	134.40 E
Murray Fracture Zone ✦	16	34.00 N	135.00 W
Murray Harbour	186	46.00 N	62.31 W
Murray Head >	186	46.00 N	62.28 W
Murray Maxwell Bay ⊂	176	70.00 N	80.00 W
Murray Mouth ≐¹	168b	35.34 S	138.54 E
Murray River	186	46.01 N	62.37 W
Murraysburg	158	31.58 S	23.47 E
Murrayville, B.C., Can.	224	49.10 N	122.36 W
Murrayville, Il., U.S.	194	39.35 N	90.15 W
Murrébuè	154	13.02 S	40.30 E
Murree	123	33.54 N	73.24 E
Mürren	58	46.34 N	7.54 E
Murrhardt	56	48.59 N	9.34 E
Murrí ≐	246	6.33 N	76.52 W
Murrieta	228	33.33 N	117.12 W
Murro di Porca, Capo >	70	37.00 N	15.20 E
Murrumbidgee ≐	166	34.43 S	143.12 E
Murrumburrah	166	34.33 S	148.21 E
Murrupula	154	15.27 S	38.47 E
Murrurundi	166	31.46 S	150.50 E
Murry Hill	279b	40.17 N	80.09 W
Murrysville	279b	40.25 N	79.41 W
Mursal	130	39.11 N	37.59 E
Mursala, Pulau I	114	1.38 N	98.32 E
Murshidābād	126	24.11 N	88.16 E
Mürşitpınar	130	36.54 N	38.19 E
Murska Sobota	61	46.40 N	16.10 E
Murskij, porog ʟ	88	58.27 N	98.30 E
Mursko Središće	61	46.31 N	16.27 E
Murtajāpur	122	20.44 N	77.23 E
Murtal	266c	38.42 N	9.22 W
Murtee	166	31.35 S	143.30 E
Murten	58	46.56 N	7.07 E
Murtensee → Morat, Lac de ⊜	58	46.55 N	7.05 E
Murter, Otok I	36	43.48 N	15.37 E
Murtle Lake ⊜	182	52.08 N	119.38 W
Murtoa	166	36.37 S	142.28 E
Murton	44	54.49 N	1.24 W
Murtosa	34	40.44 N	8.38 W
Muru	140	6.36 N	29.15 E
Muru ≐	248	8.09 S	70.45 W
Muru, Capu di >	36	41.44 N	8.40 E
Murud	122	18.19 N	72.58 E
Murud, Gunong ∧	112	3.52 N	115.30 E
Murukta	74	67.46 N	102.01 E
Murung ≐	112	0.12 S	114.03 E
Murupara	172	38.28 S	176.42 E
Mururoa I¹	6	21.52 S	138.55 W
Murutinga	246	3.26 S	59.12 W
Murvaul, Lake ⊜¹	222	32.03 N	94.28 W
Murvaul Creek ≐	194	32.05 N	94.12 W
Murwāra	124	23.51 N	80.24 E
Murwillumbah	166	28.19 S	153.24 E
Mürz ≐	61	47.24 N	15.17 E
Mürzsteg	61	47.40 N	15.29 E
Mürzzuschlag	61	47.36 N	15.41 E
Muş	130	38.44 N	41.30 E
Muş ▫⁴	128	39.00 N	42.00 E
Musa	152	2.40 N	19.18 E
Mūša ≐, Europe	76	56.24 N	24.10 E
Musa ≐, Pap. N. Gui.	164	9.25 S	148.50 E
Mūsā, Jabal (Mount Sinai) ∧	140	28.32 N	33.59 E
Mūsā, ʿUyūn (Springs of Moses) ⊽⁴	142	29.52 N	32.39 E
Musabeyli	130	39.51 N	34.37 E
Musadi	152	2.34 S	22.47 E
Musaid	146	31.35 N	25.03 E
Mūsa Khel	123	32.38 N	71.44 E
Mūsa Khel Bāzār	120	30.52 N	69.49 E
Musala ∧	38	42.11 N	23.34 E
Musan	98	42.14 N	129.13 E
Musandam Peninsula >¹	128	26.18 N	56.24 E
Musao	154	7.43 S	26.17 E
Mūsā Qalʿeh	120	32.22 N	64.46 E
Mūsā Qalʿeh ≐	128	32.05 N	64.51 E
Musar	272b	22.54 N	88.14 E
Musasa	154	3.21 S	31.33 E
Musashi	96	33.30 N	131.43 E
Musashi → Iruma	94	35.50 N	139.24 E
Musashimurayama	268	35.45 N	139.23 E
Musashino	94	35.42 N	139.34 E
Musashino-daichi ∧∧¹	268	35.45 N	139.35 E
Musau	58	47.32 N	10.40 E
Musayʿīd	128	24.59 N	51.32 E
Musaymīr	144	13.27 N	44.37 E
Mūsāzai	120	30.23 N	66.32 E
Muscat and Oman → Oman ▫¹	118	22.00 N	58.00 E
Muscatatuck ≐	218	38.46 N	86.10 W
Muscatatuck, Grassy Fork ≐	218	38.45 N	85.07 W
Muscatatuck, Vernon Fork ≐	218	38.46 N	85.54 W
Muscatine	190	41.25 N	91.03 W
Muscat → Masqaṭ	128	23.37 N	58.35 E
Müsch	56	50.23 N	6.49 E
Mus-Chaja, gora ∧	74	62.35 N	140.50 E
Muschu Island I	164	3.25 S	143.35 E
Muschwitz	54	51.11 N	12.07 E
Muscle Shoals	194	34.44 N	87.40 W
Musclow, Mount ∧	182	53.17 N	127.09 W
Musclow Lake ⊜	184	51.25 N	94.56 W
Muscoda	190	43.11 N	90.26 W
Musconetcong ≐	210	40.36 N	75.11 W
Musconetcong, Lake ⊜	276	40.54 N	74.42 W
Muscongus Bay ⊂	188	43.55 N	69.20 W
Muscote Bay ⊂	212	44.06 N	77.18 W
Muscowpetung Indian Reserve ◆⁴	184	50.45 N	104.15 W
Muscoy	228	34.09 N	117.20 W
Muse	214	40.17 N	80.12 W
Musengezi ≐	154	15.43 S	31.14 E
Museum, Bergbau ❦	263	51.29 N	7.13 E
Musgrave, Austl.	164	14.47 S	143.30 E
Musgrave, B.C., Can.	224	48.45 N	123.32 W
Musgrave, Mount ∧	172	43.48 S	170.43 E
Musgrave Ranges ∧∧	162	26.10 S	131.50 E
Musgravetown	186	48.24 N	53.53 W
Mūshā	142	27.08 N	31.18 E
Mushābani	126	22.31 N	86.27 E
Mushāsh, Jabal al- ∧²	142	28.54 N	31.11 E
Mushenge	152	4.32 S	21.21 E
Mushie	152	3.01 S	16.54 E
Mushima	154	14.13 S	25.05 E
Mushin	150	6.32 N	3.22 E
Mūsi ≐, India	122	16.41 N	79.40 E
Musi ≐, Indon.	112	2.20 S	104.56 E
Musicians Seamounts ✦³	6	31.00 N	162.00 W
Muskauer Heide ◆³	54	51.25 N	14.40 E
Muskeg ≐	182	54.01 N	119.03 W
Muskeget Channel ʯ	207	41.25 N	70.20 W
Muskeget Island I	207	41.20 N	70.18 W
Muskeg Lake Indian Reserve ◆⁴	184	52.58 N	106.57 W
Muskego	216	42.54 N	88.08 W
Muskego Lake ⊜	216	42.53 N	88.07 W
Muskegon	216	43.14 N	86.14 W
Muskegon ▫⁶	216	43.12 N	86.08 W
Muskegon ≐	190	43.14 N	86.20 W
Muskegon County Airport ⊠	216	43.10 N	86.14 W
Muskegon Heights	216	43.12 N	86.14 W
Muskegon Lake ⊜	216	43.14 N	86.17 W
Muskegon State Park ♠	216	43.14 N	86.20 W
Mušketova, gora ∧	88	53.35 N	113.32 E
Muskingum ▫⁶	214	40.06 N	81.51 W
Muskingum ≐	188	39.27 N	81.30 W
Muskingum Brook ≐	285	39.48 N	74.44 W
Muskira	124	25.40 N	79.48 E
Muskö I	40	59.00 N	18.06 E
Muskoday Indian Reserve ◆⁴	184	53.06 N	105.30 W
Muskogee	196	35.44 N	95.22 W
Muskoka ▫⁶	212	45.05 N	79.03 W
Muskoka, Lake ⊜	212	45.00 N	79.25 W
Muskoka, North Branch ≐	212	45.02 N	79.19 W
Muskoka, South Branch ≐	212	45.02 N	79.19 W
Muskosh Channel ʯ	212	44.55 N	79.53 W
Muskowekwan Indian Reserve ◆⁴	184	51.19 N	104.06 W
Muskrat Creek ≐	202	43.09 N	108.11 W
Muskrat Dam Lake ⊜	184	53.25 N	91.40 W
Muskrat Lake ⊜	190	45.40 N	76.55 W
Muskwa ≐	176	58.45 N	122.35 W
Muskwa Lake ⊜	182	56.09 N	114.38 W
Muslimbāgh	120	30.49 N	67.45 E
Musl'umovo	80	55.18 N	53.12 E
Muşmuş	132	32.32 N	35.09 E
Musocco ◆⁸	266b	45.30 N	9.08 E
Musofu Mission	154	13.31 S	29.02 E
Musoma	154	1.30 S	33.48 E
Musone ≐, It.	64	45.50 N	11.55 E
Musone ≐, It.	66	43.28 N	13.38 E
Musoshi	154	11.54 S	27.46 E
Musquanousse, Lac ⊜	186	50.22 N	61.05 W
Musquapsink Brook ≐	276	40.59 N	74.01 W
Musquaro, Lac ⊜	186	50.38 N	61.05 W
Musquash ≐	212	44.57 N	79.52 W
Musquash Brook ≐	283	42.42 N	71.26 W
Musquashcut Pond ⊜	283	42.13 N	70.46 W
Musquodoboit Harbour	186	44.47 N	63.09 W
Mussau Island I	164	1.30 S	149.40 E
Musselburgh	46	55.57 N	3.04 W
Musselkanaal	52	52.56 N	7.00 E
Musselshell ≐	202	47.21 N	107.58 W
Mussende	152	10.32 S	16.05 E
Mussidan	32	45.02 N	0.22 E
Mussolo	152	9.59 S	17.19 E
Mussomeli	70	37.35 N	13.45 E
Mussoorie	124	30.27 N	78.05 E
Mussuco	152	17.08 S	19.05 E
Mussum	52	51.48 N	6.34 E
Mussuma	152	14.14 S	21.59 E
Mussy-sur-Seine	58	47.58 N	4.30 E
Mustafakemalpaşa	130	40.02 N	28.24 E
Mustafa Kemal Paşa ≐	130	40.07 N	28.33 E
Mustafino	80	55.01 N	53.38 E
Mustahil	144	5.12 N	44.17 E
Müstair	58	46.37 N	10.27 E
Mustajevo	80	51.48 N	53.25 E
Mustajõe	76	57.59 N	26.58 E
Mustāng	124	29.11 N	83.58 E
Mustang Draw V	196	32.12 N	101.36 W
Mustang Island I	196	28.00 N	96.55 W
Mustāy	142	30.37 N	31.09 E
Musters, Lago ⊜	254	45.27 S	69.13 W
Mustinka ≐	198	45.45 N	96.38 W
Mustjala	76	58.28 N	22.14 E
Mustla	76	58.14 N	25.52 E
Musṭurud	273c	30.08 N	31.17 E
Mustvee	76	58.51 N	26.56 E
Musu-dan >	98	40.50 N	129.43 E
Musun	84	39.42 N	43.49 E
Muswellbrook	166	32.16 S	150.53 E
Muszyna	30	49.21 N	20.54 E
Mūt, Miṣr	140	25.29 N	28.59 E
Mut, Tür.	130	36.39 N	33.27 E
Muta	61	46.37 N	15.10 E
Mutá, Ponta do >	255	13.52 S	38.56 W
Mu'tah	132	31.06 N	35.42 E
Mutalau	174v	18.56 S	169.50 W
Mutambara	154	19.36 S	32.33 E
Mutanchiang → Mudanjiang	89	44.35 N	129.36 E
Mutanda, Moç.	156	21.02 S	33.31 E
Mutanda, Zaïre	152	5.17 S	16.34 E
Mutanda Mission	154	12.24 S	26.16 E
Mutankiang → Mudanjiang	89	44.35 N	129.36 E
Mutarammil, Jabal al- ∧	132	31.04 N	36.06 E
Mutare	154	18.58 S	32.40 E
Mutbīn	132	33.09 N	36.15 E
Mutějovice	54	50.09 N	13.41 E
Mutha	154	1.48 S	38.26 E
Muthill	46	56.19 N	3.50 W
Mutiko	154	1.39 S	28.12 E
Muting	164	7.23 S	140.20 E
Mutis, Gunung ∧	112	9.34 S	124.14 E
Mutlu (Rezovska) ≐	130	41.59 N	28.01 E
Mutoko	154	17.24 S	32.13 E
Mutombo-Mukulu	152	7.58 S	24.00 E
Mutoraj	74	61.20 N	100.30 E
Mutoto	152	5.42 S	22.42 E
Mutouchengzi	98	41.20 N	119.59 E
Mutouhao	107	28.49 N	105.04 E
Mutsamudu	157a	12.09 S	44.25 E
Mutshatsha	152	10.39 S	24.27 E
Mutsu	92	41.17 N	141.10 E
Mutsuai	268	35.08 N	139.38 E
Mutsumi	96	34.26 N	131.34 E
Mutsuura ◆⁸	268	35.19 N	139.37 E
Mutsu-wan ⊂	92	41.05 N	140.55 E
Muttaburra	166	22.36 S	144.33 E
Mutte Kopf ∧	58	47.16 N	10.39 E
Muttenz	58	47.32 N	7.39 E
Mutters	64	47.14 N	11.23 E
Mutterstadt	56	49.26 N	8.21 E
Muttonbird Islands II	172	47.15 S	167.24 E
Muttontown	276	40.49 N	73.33 W
Muttra → Mathura	124	27.30 N	77.41 E
Mutual, Oh., U.S.	218	40.05 N	83.38 W
Mutual, Pa., U.S.	279b	40.14 N	79.30 W
Muṭūbis	142	31.18 N	30.31 E
Mutuca, Ribeirão da ≐	256	21.36 S	45.39 W
Mutuco, Lago ⊜	250	1.21 N	50.24 W
Mutuípe	255	13.15 S	39.31 W
Mutum	255	19.49 S	41.26 W
Mutum ≐	246	4.25 S	68.03 W
Mutum Biyu	146	8.38 N	10.46 E
Mutumbo	152	13.14 S	17.17 E
Mutunópolis	255	13.40 S	49.15 W
Muturi	164	2.06 S	133.43 E
Mututi, Ilha do I	250	0.45 S	51.00 W
Mutzig	58	48.32 N	7.28 E
Mutzschen	54	51.16 N	12.53 E
Mu Us Shamo ◆²	102	38.45 N	109.10 E
Muvattupula	122	9.58 N	76.35 E
Muvukoni	154	0.24 S	38.14 E
Muwopu	104	41.03 N	121.12 E
Muxaluando	152	8.07 S	14.17 E
Muxihe	100	31.03 N	115.21 E
Muxima	152	9.31 S	13.56 E
Muyaga	154	3.14 S	30.33 E
Muyang	100	27.06 N	119.34 E
Muyang ≐	100	27.00 N	119.41 E
Muyinga	154	2.51 S	30.20 E
Muymano ≐	248	11.27 S	69.03 W
Muy Muy	236	12.46 N	85.38 W
Muyua Island I	164	9.05 S	152.50 E
Muyuka	152	4.17 N	9.25 E
Muyumba	154	7.15 S	26.59 E
Mužač'	82	54.22 N	36.21 E
Muzaffarābād	123	34.22 N	73.28 E
Muzaffargarh	123	30.04 N	71.12 E
Muzaffarnagar	124	29.28 N	77.41 E
Muzaffarpur	124	26.07 N	85.24 E
Muzambinho	256	21.22 S	46.32 W
Muzambinho ≐	256	21.15 S	46.26 W
Muzambo ≐	256	21.17 S	46.16 W
Muzat ≐	90	41.15 N	83.27 E
Muzayrīb	132	32.42 N	36.01 E
Muzbek, gora ∧	85	40.23 N	69.39 E
Muzbel' ◆¹	86	50.15 N	70.50 E
Muzeze	152	15.03 S	17.43 E
Muzhen	100	30.43 N	117.56 E
Muži	74	65.22 N	64.40 E
Mužiči	84	43.03 N	44.59 E
Mužiksu	86	47.42 N	84.58 E
Muzillac	32	47.33 N	2.29 W
Muzkol, chrebet ∧∧	85	38.25 N	73.30 E
Muzoka	154	16.41 S	27.19 E
Muzon, Cape >	182	54.41 N	132.44 W
Muztag ∧, Zhg.	120	36.25 N	87.25 E
Muztag ∧, Zhg.	120	36.03 N	80.07 E
Muztagata ∧	85	38.17 N	75.11 E
Muz Tau ∧	86	43.50 N	85.40 E
Muzūrah	142	28.53 N	30.48 E
Muzzana del Turgnano	64	45.49 N	13.08 E
Mvam	152	0.13 S	9.39 E
Mvangan	152	2.38 N	11.44 E
Mvela	154	14.46 S	35.16 E
Mvengué	152	3.17 N	11.01 E
Mvolo	140	6.03 N	29.56 E
Mvomero	154	6.20 S	37.25 E
Mvoti ≐	158	29.24 S	31.22 E
Mvoung ≐	152	0.04 N	12.18 E
Mvouti	152	4.15 S	12.29 E
Mvuha	154	7.12 S	37.51 E
Mvuma	154	19.19 S	30.35 E
Mwadi-Kalumba	152	7.53 S	18.46 E
Mwadui	154	3.33 S	33.36 E
Mwali (Mohéli) I	157a	12.15 S	43.45 E
Mwami	154	16.40 S	29.46 E
Mwanangumune	152	15.31 S	23.30 E
Mwango	152	6.51 S	24.13 E
Mwanza, Malaŵi	154	15.37 S	34.31 E
Mwanza, Tan.	154	2.31 S	32.54 E
Mwanza, Zaïre	154	7.54 S	26.45 E
Mwanza, Zam.	152	17.02 S	24.27 E
Mwanza ▫⁴	154	2.45 S	32.45 E
Mwanza Gulf ⊂	154	2.35 S	32.51 E
Mwaya, Tan.	154	9.33 S	33.57 E
Mwaya, Tan.	154	8.55 S	36.50 E
Mweelrea ∧	48	53.38 N	9.50 W
Mwehu	154	5.44 S	26.40 E
Mweka	152	4.51 S	21.34 E
Mwemena	154	10.19 S	27.28 E
Mwenda	154	12.01 S	28.44 E
Mwendjila	152	7.12 S	18.51 E
Mwene-Ditu	152	7.03 S	23.27 E
Mwenezi	154	21.22 S	30.45 E
Mwenga	154	3.02 S	28.26 E
Mwepo	154	11.56 S	26.11 E
Mwerasandu	154	0.59 S	30.23 E
Mwereni	154	4.20 S	39.08 E
Mweru, Lake ⊜	154	9.00 S	28.45 E
Mweru Mantipa National Park ♠	154	8.45 S	29.30 E
Mweru Wantipa, Lake ⊜	154	8.45 S	29.40 E
Mwetshi	152	4.42 S	22.39 E
Mwilambwe	154	8.07 S	25.00 E
Mwilitau Islands II	164	2.50 S	146.20 E
Mwimbi	154	8.39 S	31.40 E
Mwingi	154	0.56 S	38.04 E
Mwinilunga	152	11.44 S	24.26 E
Mwitikira	154	6.31 S	35.39 E
Mwombezhi ≐	154	12.52 S	25.00 E
Myaing	110	21.37 N	94.51 E
Myājlār	120	26.15 N	70.23 E
Myakka ≐	220	26.56 N	82.11 W
Myakka, Lake ⊜	220	27.16 N	82.17 W
Myakka City	220	27.20 N	82.09 W
Myakka River State Park ♠	220	27.15 N	82.17 W
Myall Lakes National Park ♠	166	32.28 S	152.22 E
Myall Range ∧∧	170	32.58 S	151.22 E
Myanaung	110	18.17 N	95.19 E
Myanmar → Burma ▫¹	110	22.00 N	98.00 E
Myaungmya	110	16.36 N	94.56 E
Myawadi	110	16.41 N	98.31 E
Mybster	46	58.27 N	3.25 W
Myckelgensjö	26	63.34 N	17.37 E
Myebon	110	20.03 N	93.22 E
Myeik → Mergui	110	12.26 N	98.36 E
Myers, Ky., U.S.	218	38.21 N	83.57 W
Myers, N.Y., U.S.	210	42.32 N	76.32 W
Myerstown	208	40.22 N	76.19 W
Myingyan	110	21.28 N	95.23 E
Myinmoletkat Taung ∧	110	13.28 N	98.48 E
Myitkyinā	110	25.23 N	97.24 E
Myitnge ≐	110	21.52 N	95.59 E
Myitta	110	14.10 N	98.31 E
Myittha	110	21.25 N	96.03 E
Myittha ≐	110	23.12 N	94.17 E
Myjava	30	48.45 N	17.34 E
Myjeldino	24	61.46 N	54.43 E
Myjlybulak	86	48.57 N	75.13 E
Myla	24	65.25 N	50.43 E
Mylau	54	50.37 N	12.16 E
Myl'džino	86	59.03 N	78.29 E
Myllendonk, Schloss ⊥	263	51.13 N	6.29 E
Myllykoski	26	60.47 N	26.48 E
Myllymäki	26	62.32 N	24.17 E
Mylor	168b	35.03 S	138.45 E
Mymensingh	124	24.45 N	90.24 E
Mynämäki	26	60.40 N	22.00 E
Mynaral	86	45.25 N	73.41 E
Mynbulak, gora ∧	85	41.43 N	69.49 E
Mynfontein	158	30.55 S	23.57 E
Mynydd Bach ∧²	42	52.15 N	4.05 W
Mynydd Eppynt ∧	42	52.05 N	3.30 W
Mynydd Hiraethog ∧	44	53.05 N	3.33 W
Mynydd Pencarreg ∧²	42	52.04 N	4.04 W
Mynydd Preseli ∧	42	51.58 N	4.42 W
Myōgata	94	35.51 N	137.02 E
Myōgi	94	36.17 N	138.49 E
Myōgi-Arafune-Saku-kōgen-kokutei-kōen ♠	94	36.12 N	138.10 E
Myōgi-san ∧	94	36.17 N	138.44 E
Myo-gyi	110	21.27 N	96.22 E
Myohaung	110	20.36 N	93.10 E
Myohyang-san ∧	98	40.02 N	126.17 E
Myohyang-sanmaek ∧∧	98	40.30 N	127.00 E
Myōjin-dake ∧	270	34.57 N	135.56 E
Myōjin-san ∧	96	33.34 N	133.04 E
Myōken-san ∧	96	35.24 N	134.39 E
Myōken-zan ∧	270	34.56 N	135.28 E
Myōken-zan ∧²	270	34.30 N	134.57 E
Myōkō	94	36.56 N	138.13 E
Myōkō-kōgen	94	36.52 N	138.12 E
Myōkō-san ∧	94	36.52 N	138.07 E
Myŏnmong-ni ◆⁸	271b	37.35 N	127.05 E
Myponga	168b	35.24 S	138.28 E
Myponga Reservoir ⊜¹	168b	35.24 S	138.26 E
Myra ⊥	130	36.15 N	29.54 E
Mýrdalsjökull ⚑	24a	63.40 N	19.05 W
Myrnam	182	53.40 N	111.14 W
Myroodah	162	18.08 S	124.16 E
Myrskylä (Mörskom)	26	60.40 N	25.51 E
Myrtle Beach	192	33.41 N	78.53 W
Myrtle Beach Air Force Base ■	192	33.41 N	78.56 W
Myrtle Beach State Park ♠	192	33.37 N	78.58 W
Myrtle Creek	202	43.01 N	123.17 W
Myrtle Grove	194	30.25 N	87.18 W
Myrtle Point	202	43.03 N	124.08 W
Myrtle Springs	222	32.37 N	95.56 W
Myrtletowne	204	40.47 N	124.04 W
Myrtleville	170	34.29 S	149.49 E
Myšega	82	54.31 N	37.02 E
Mysen	26	59.33 N	11.20 E
Mysia ▫⁹	130	39.15 N	28.00 E
Mysingen ʯ	40	59.00 N	18.15 E
Myski	86	53.42 N	87.48 E
Myškino	76	57.47 N	38.27 E
Myśla ≐	54	52.40 N	14.29 E
Myślenice	30	49.51 N	19.56 E
Myślibórz	30	52.55 N	14.52 E
Mysłowice	30	50.15 N	19.07 E
Mysore	122	12.18 N	76.39 E
Mys Šmidta	180	68.56 N	179.26 W
Mystic, Ct., U.S.	207	41.21 N	71.58 W
Mystic, Ia., U.S.	190	40.46 N	92.56 W
Mystic ≐	283	42.23 N	71.03 W
Mystic Seaport ❦	207	41.22 N	71.58 W
Mys Vchodnoj	74	73.53 N	86.43 E
Mysy	24	60.34 N	53.57 E
Mys Želanija	72	76.56 N	68.35 E
Myszków	30	50.36 N	19.20 E
Myszyniec	30	53.24 N	21.21 E
Myt	80	56.48 N	42.21 E
My Tho	110	10.21 N	106.21 E
Mytholm	262	53.44 N	2.01 W
Mytholmroyd	262	53.44 N	1.59 W
Mytilene → Mitilíni	38	39.06 N	26.32 E
Mytišči	82	55.55 N	37.46 E
Mytishchi → Mytišči	82	55.55 N	37.46 E
Mytišino	76	54.48 N	34.01 E
Mýto	60	49.47 N	13.44 E
Myton	200	40.11 N	110.03 W
Mývatn ⊜	24a	65.37 N	16.58 W
Myzovo	78	51.22 N	24.31 E
M'zab, Oued V	148	32.19 N	5.24 E
Mže ≐	60	49.46 N	13.24 E
Mzenga	154	6.56 S	38.43 E
Mziha	154	5.54 S	37.47 E
Mzimba	154	11.52 S	33.34 E
Mzimkulu ≐	158	30.44 S	30.28 E
Mzimvubu ≐	158	31.38 S	29.32 E
Mzintlava ≐	158	31.12 S	29.18 E
Mzuzu	154	11.27 S	33.55 E
Mzymta ≐	84	43.27 N	39.56 E
N			
Na I	174r	6.52 N	158.22 E
Na (Tengtiao) ≐	110	22.05 N	103.09 E
Naab ≐	60	49.01 N	12.02 E
Naach, Jbel ∧	34	34.53 N	3.22 W
Naachtpunkt Brook ≐	276	40.54 N	74.15 W
Naaldwijk	52	52.00 N	4.12 E
Naalehu	229d	19.03 N	155.35 W
Naʿām	140	9.42 N	28.27 E
Na'âma, Sebkhet en ⩸	148	33.20 N	0.16 W
Naaman Creek ≐	285	39.48 N	75.27 W
Naaman Creek, South Branch ≐	285	39.49 N	75.27 W
Naamans Garden	285	39.49 N	75.31 W
Naantali	26	60.27 N	22.02 E
Naarden	52	52.17 N	5.09 E
Naarn ≐	61	48.11 N	14.49 E
Naas	48	53.13 N	6.39 W
Naas ≐	171b	35.36 S	149.04 E
Naast, Bel.	50	50.33 N	4.05 E
Naast, Scot., U.K.	46	57.47 N	5.39 W
Naʿaẕuẕ, Har ∧	132	30.01 N	35.00 E
Nabā, Jabal an- (Mount Nebo) ∧	132	31.46 N	35.45 E
Nababiep	156	29.36 S	17.46 E
Nabābpur	272b	22.42 N	88.12 E
Nabaganga ≐¹	126	22.59 N	89.34 E
Nabagram	126	24.12 N	88.06 E
Nabalat Al-Ḥajanah	140	13.13 N	29.02 E
Nabari	94	34.37 N	136.05 E
Nabari ≐	94	34.45 N	136.01 E
Nabarūh	142	31.06 N	31.18 E
Nabas	116	11.50 N	122.05 E
Nabasta	126	23.15 N	88.01 E
Nabawa	162	28.31 S	114.47 E
Nabb	218	38.36 N	85.38 W
Nabberu, Lake ⊜	162	25.36 S	120.30 E
Nabburg	60	49.28 N	12.11 E
Nabeina	174t	1.26 N	173.05 E
Naberera	154	4.12 S	36.56 E
Nabereżnoje	265b	55.57 N	37.58 E
Naberežnyje Čelny	80	55.42 N	52.19 E
Nabesna	180	62.22 N	143.00 W
Nabesna ≐	180	63.03 N	141.52 W
Nabeul	148	36.27 N	10.44 E
Nabeul ▫⁸	148	36.35 N	10.45 E
Nābha	123	30.22 N	76.09 E
Nab Hill ∧²	262	53.47 N	1.57 W
Nabigou	152	1.12 S	9.31 E
Nabī Hārūn, Jabal an- ∧	132	30.19 N	35.24 E
Nabileque ≐	248	20.55 S	57.49 W
Nabire	164	3.22 S	135.29 E
Nabī Shuʿayb, Jabal an- ∧	144	15.17 N	43.59 E
Nabisipi ≐	186	50.14 N	62.13 W
Nabiswera	154	1.28 N	32.16 E
Nabī Yūnus, Ra's an- >	132	33.39 N	35.24 E
Nabnasset	207	42.36 N	71.25 W
Nabnasset Pond ⊜	283	42.37 N	71.26 W
Nabogame	232	26.14 N	106.57 W
Naboomspruit	156	24.32 S	28.36 E
Nabordo	150	10.10 N	9.20 E
Nabou	150	11.27 N	2.43 W
Nabq	140	28.04 N	34.25 E
Nabua	116	13.24 N	123.22 E
Nabula	120	31.55 N	80.10 E
Nābulus	132	32.13 N	35.16 E
Nabunturan	116	7.35 N	125.58 E
Nacajuca	234	18.08 N	93.01 W
Nacala	154	14.34 S	40.41 E
Nacala-Velha	154	14.32 S	40.37 E
Načalovo	80	46.20 N	48.11 E
Nacaome	236	13.31 N	87.30 W
Nacastillo	234	19.35 N	104.55 W
Nacchie	144	7.23 N	40.10 E
Nacereddine	34	36.08 N	3.26 E
Nachabinka ≐	265b	55.51 N	37.12 E
Nachabino	82	55.51 N	37.11 E
Naches	224	46.43 N	120.41 W
Naches ≐	202	46.38 N	120.31 W
Nachičevan'	84	39.13 N	45.24 E
Nachičevanskaja Avtonomnaja Sovetskaja Socialističeskaja Respublika ▫³	84	39.20 N	45.30 E
Nachi-katsuura	92	33.30 N	135.55 E
Nāchinda	126	21.53 N	87.46 E
Nachingwea	154	10.23 S	38.46 E
Nāchna	120	27.30 N	71.43 E
Náchod	30	50.25 N	16.10 E
Nachodka	89	42.48 N	132.52 E
Nächstebreck ◆⁸	263	51.18 N	7.14 E
Nachterstedt	54	51.49 N	11.20 E
Nachuge	110	10.45 N	92.22 E
Nachvak Fiord ⊂²	176	59.03 N	63.45 W
Naci, Pil.	116	14.19 N	120.46 E
Naci, Pil.	116	6.19 N	124.46 E
Nacimiento	252	37.30 S	72.40 W
Nacimiento ≐	226	35.49 N	120.45 W
Nacimiento, Lake ⊜¹	226	35.45 N	121.00 W
Načinskij Golec, gora ∧	89	52.24 N	118.53 E
Nacka	40	59.18 N	18.10 E
Naco, Méx.	232	31.20 N	109.56 W
Naco, Az., U.S.	200	31.20 N	109.56 W
Nacogdoches	222	31.36 N	94.39 W
Nacogdoches ▫⁶	222	31.40 N	94.45 W
Nacogdoches, Lake ⊜¹	222	31.37 N	94.50 W
Nácori Chico	232	29.39 N	109.01 W
Nacozari de García	232	30.24 N	109.39 W
Ñacunday	252	26.01 S	54.46 W
Nada	222	29.24 N	96.23 W
Nada ◆⁸	270	34.44 N	135.14 E
Nadābhānga	272b	22.24 N	88.14 E
Nadachi	94	37.09 N	138.06 E
Nadaleen Mountain ∧	180	64.15 N	133.04 W
Nadasaki	96	34.32 N	133.52 E
Nádasd	61	46.58 N	16.37 E
Nadbai	124	27.14 N	77.12 E
Nadder ≐	42	51.03 N	1.48 W
Nadela	34	42.58 N	7.30 W
Nadelkap → Agulhas, Cape >	158	34.52 S	20.00 E
Naden Harbour ⊂	182	54.00 N	132.35 W
Nadeždinskoje	89	48.18 N	133.11 E
Nadi	140	18.40 N	33.42 E
Nadiād	120	22.42 N	72.52 E
Nādir, Miṣr	142	30.33 N	30.51 E
Nadir, Vir. Is., U.S.	240m	18.19 N	64.53 W
Nădlac	38	46.10 N	20.45 E
Nador	148	35.12 N	2.55 W
Nador ▫⁴	148	35.09 N	3.04 W
Nadporožje	76	60.28 N	34.17 E
Nadrin	56	50.10 N	5.41 E
Nadterečnaja	84	43.37 N	45.22 E
Nadvoicy	24	63.52 N	34.15 E
Nadvornaja	78	48.38 N	24.34 E
Nadym	72	65.35 N	72.42 E
Nadym ≐	74	66.12 N	72.00 E
Nadyrovo	80	54.53 N	52.28 E
Naeba-san ∧	94	36.51 N	138.41 E
Nae-dong	98	37.16 N	126.27 E
Naejang-san Kukrip Kongwŏn ♠	98	35.28 N	126.52 E
Naenwa	120	25.46 N	75.51 E
Nærbø	26	58.40 N	5.39 E
Næsby	41	55.25 N	10.22 E
Næstved	41	55.14 N	11.46 E
Nafada	146	11.08 N	11.20 E
Nafadji	150	12.37 N	11.37 W
Nafarros	266c	38.49 N	9.25 W
Nafāzah, ʿAlam ∧²	142	30.30 N	29.42 E
Näfels	58	47.06 N	9.04 E
Nafī	128	24.57 N	43.42 E
Nafīshah	142	30.34 N	32.15 E
Naftalan	84	40.31 N	46.50 E
Naftan, Puntan I >	174n	15.05 N	145.45 E
Nāfūrah	146	29.20 N	21.20 E
Nafūsah, Jabal ∧∧²	146	31.50 N	12.00 E
Nāg	120	27.24 N	65.08 E
Naga, Nihon	96	34.16 N	135.26 E
Naga, Pil.	116	13.37 N	123.11 E
Naga, Pil.	116	10.13 N	123.45 E
Nâga, Kreb en ±⁴	148	24.00 N	6.00 W
Naga, Oued en V	148	27.53 N	7.10 W
Nagaga	154	10.54 S	39.07 E
Nagahama, Nihon	94	35.23 N	136.16 E
Nagahama, Nihon	96	33.36 N	132.29 E
Nagahama, Nihon	174m	26.25 N	127.44 E
Naga Hills ∧∧	110	26.00 N	95.00 E
Nagai, Nihon	92	38.06 N	140.02 E
Nagai, Nihon	268	35.12 N	139.37 E
Nagai Island I	180	55.11 N	159.55 W
Nagai Park ♠	270	34.36 N	135.31 E
Nagaizumi	94	35.08 N	138.54 E
Nāgāland ▫³	120	26.00 N	95.00 E
Nagambie	169	36.47 S	145.10 E
Nagannu-shima I	174m	26.16 N	127.33 E
Nagano	94	36.39 N	138.11 E
Nagano ▫⁵	94	36.00 N	138.00 E
Nagano-dam ◆⁶	94	35.50 N	136.33 E
Naganohara	94	36.33 N	138.38 E
Nagao, Nihon	96	34.16 N	134.10 E
Nagao, Nihon	270	34.50 N	135.43 E
Nagao-hana >	96	35.32 N	134.01 E
Nagaoka	92	37.27 N	138.51 E
Nagaokakyō	94	34.55 N	135.42 E
Nagaon	120	26.20 N	92.40 E
Nāgappattinam	122	10.46 N	79.50 E
Nagar, India	123	32.07 N	77.10 E
Nagar, India	124	27.26 N	77.06 E
Nagara	270	34.26 N	135.44 E
Nagara ≐	94	35.01 N	136.43 E
Nagareyama	94	35.51 N	139.54 E
Nāgārjuna Sāgar ⊜¹	122	16.35 N	79.21 E
Nagarote	236	12.16 N	86.34 W
Nagar Pārkar	120	24.22 N	70.45 E
Nāgarpur	124	24.03 N	89.53 E
Nagar Untāri	124	24.17 N	83.30 E
Nagarzê	124	28.59 N	90.25 E
Nagas	116	13.06 N	123.18 E
Nagasaka	94	35.49 N	138.22 E
Nagasaki	92	32.48 N	129.55 E
Nagasawa	268	35.12 N	139.41 E
Nagashima	94	35.05 N	136.42 E
Naga-shima I, Nihon	96	33.49 N	132.05 E
Naga-shima I, Nihon	96	34.41 N	134.15 E
Nagashino ⊥	94	34.56 N	137.32 E
Nagasin Lake ⊜	190	47.44 N	83.37 W
Nagasu	96	32.56 N	130.27 E
Nagasu → Usa	96	33.31 N	131.22 E
Nagata ◆⁸	270	34.40 N	135.09 E
Nagataki	270	34.23 N	135.20 E
Nagatino ◆⁸	265b	55.41 N	37.41 E
Nagato, Nihon	94	36.15 N	138.16 E
Nagato, Nihon	96	34.21 N	131.10 E
Nagatsuda ◆⁸	268	35.32 N	139.30 E
Nāgaur	120	27.12 N	73.44 E
Nāgāvali ≐	122	18.13 N	83.56 E
Nagavskaja	80	47.47 N	42.50 E
Nagawa	94	36.05 N	137.41 E
Nagawicka Lake ⊜	216	43.05 N	88.23 W
Nagcarlan	116	14.08 N	121.25 E
Nagda	120	23.27 N	75.25 E
Nagele	52	52.37 N	5.44 E
Nāgercoil	122	8.10 N	77.26 E
Nagi	96	35.07 N	134.11 E
Nagiba	116	13.41 N	120.53 E
Nagibino	86	55.46 N	72.43 E
Nagichot	154	4.16 N	33.34 E
Nagīna	124	29.27 N	78.27 E
Nāgirāt	126	23.38 N	89.18 E
Nagi-san ∧	96	35.10 N	134.11 E
Nagiso	94	35.36 N	137.37 E
Nagla	272a	28.31 N	77.22 E
Naglarby	40	60.25 N	15.34 E
Nagles Mountains ∧∧	48	52.05 N	8.30 W
Nagłowice	30	50.41 N	20.06 E
Nago	174m	26.35 N	127.59 E
Nāgod	124	24.34 N	80.35 E
Nagog Pond ⊜	283	42.31 N	71.26 W
Nagoja → Nagoya	94	35.10 N	136.55 E
Nagold	56	48.33 N	8.43 E
Nagold ≐	56	48.52 N	8.42 E
Nagol'naja ≐	83	47.57 N	38.58 E
Nagol'no-Tarasovka	83	48.00 N	39.29 E
Nagorje	76	56.55 N	38.16 E
Nagornoje	78	45.26 N	28.27 E
Nagorno-Karabachskaja Avtonomnaja Oblast' ▫⁸	84	40.00 N	46.40 E
Nagornyj, Ross.	74	55.58 N	124.57 E
Nagornyj, Ross.	265a	59.43 N	30.16 E
Nagorsk	24	59.18 N	50.48 E
Nagorskoje	82	56.54 N	38.06 E
Nago-wan ⊂	174m	26.34 N	127.57 E
Nagoya	94	35.10 N	136.55 E
Nagoya-kūkō ⊠	94	35.15 N	136.55 E
Nāgpur	120	21.09 N	79.06 E
Nagqu	120	31.34 N	92.00 E
Nagrai	123	34.23 N	72.41 E
Nāgrākāta	124	26.54 N	88.55 E
Nagrota	123	32.03 N	76.05 E
Nagu I	26	60.10 N	21.48 E
Nagua	238	19.23 N	69.50 W
Naguabo	240m	18.13 N	65.44 W
Naguilian	116	17.01 N	121.50 E
Nagumbuaya Point >	116	13.34 N	124.21 E
Naguri	94	35.53 N	139.11 E
Naguri I	122	6.39 N	72.55 E
Nagyatád	30	46.14 N	17.22 E
Nagybajom	30	46.23 N	17.31 E
Nagybánya → Baia Mare	38	47.40 N	23.35 E
Nagycenk	61	47.36 N	16.42 E
Nagyecsed	30	47.52 N	22.24 E
Nagykállć	78	47.53 N	21.51 E
Nagykanizsa	30	46.27 N	17.00 E
Nagykáta	30	47.25 N	19.45 E
Nagy-Kevély ∧²	264c	47.37 N	18.59 E
Nagykőrös	30	47.02 N	19.43 E
Nagy-Milic ∧	30	48.35 N	21.28 E
Nagytarcsa	264c	47.32 N	19.17 E
Nagytétény ◆⁸	264c	47.24 N	18.58 E
Nagyvarad → Oradea	38	47.03 N	21.57 E
Naha	174m	26.13 N	127.40 E
Naha Airfield ⊠	174m	26.13 N	127.40 E
Nahabuan	112	0.49 N	114.05 E
Nahakki	123	34.25 N	71.20 E
Nahalal	132	32.41 N	35.12 E
Naḥal ʿOz	132	31.28 N	34.30 E
Naḥam	132	31.46 N	35.00 E
Nāhan	124	30.33 N	77.18 E
Nahang (Nihing) ≐	128	26.00 N	62.44 E
Nahanni National Park ♠	180	61.40 N	126.00 W
Nahant	207	42.25 N	70.55 W
Nahant Bay ⊂	207	42.27 N	70.55 W
Nahant Beach ±²	283	42.27 N	70.56 W
Nahari	96	33.25 N	134.01 E
Nahari ≐	96	33.25 N	134.01 E
Nahariyya	132	33.00 N	35.05 E
Naharpur ◆⁸	272a	28.42 N	77.07 E
Nahāta	126	23.20 N	89.31 E
Nahāvand	128	34.12 N	48.22 E
Nahcotta	224	46.30 N	124.02 W
Nahe	89	48.28 N	124.52 E
Nahe ≐	56	49.58 N	7.57 E
Naḥf	132	32.56 N	35.19 E
Nahma	190	45.50 N	86.39 W
Nahmer ◆⁸	263	51.20 N	7.35 E
Nahmer ≐	263	51.21 N	7.35 E
Nahoe	174x	9.45 S	138.55 W
Nahoï, Cap >	175f	14.39 S	166.37 E
Nahon ≐	50	47.14 N	1.39 E
Nahrīn	120	36.01 N	69.06 E
Nahr Ouassel, Oued ≐	148	35.42 N	2.33 E
Nahualate ≐	236	14.03 N	91.32 W
Nahuatzén	234	19.42 N	101.50 W
Nahuel Huapi	254	41.03 S	71.09 W
Nahuel Huapi, Lago ⊜	254	40.58 S	71.30 W
Nahuel Huapi, Parque Nacional ♠	254	41.00 S	71.48 W
Nahuel Niyeu	254	40.30 S	66.33 W
Nahunta	192	31.12 N	81.58 W
Nāhyā	142	30.03 N	31.07 E
Naia ≐	66	42.46 N	12.22 E
Naica	232	27.53 N	105.31 W
Naicam	184	52.25 N	104.30 W
Nai Ga	102	27.48 N	97.30 E
Naiguata, Pico ∧	286c	10.33 N	66.46 W
Naihāti, Bngl.	126	22.49 N	89.37 E
Naihāti, India	126	22.54 N	88.25 E
Naij Gol ≐, Zhg.	102	36.20 N	94.49 E
Naij Gol ≐, Zhg.	120	36.20 N	94.49 E
Naikliu	112	9.30 S	123.50 E
Naikoon Provincial Park ♠	182	53.50 N	131.50 W
Naila	54	50.19 N	11.42 E
Nailin	98	41.53 N	119.15 E
Nails Creek ≐	222	30.16 N	96.44 W
Nailsea	42	51.26 N	2.43 W
Nailsworth	42	51.42 N	2.14 W
Nā'im, Jabal an- ∧	132	31.04 N	35.55 E
Naiman Qi	89	42.55 N	120.43 E
Nain, Nf., Can.	176	56.32 N	61.41 W
Nā'īn, Īrān	128	32.52 N	53.05 E
Nain ⊜	40	60.14 N	13.50 E
Naini Tāl	124	29.23 N	79.27 E
Nainpur	124	22.26 N	80.07 E
Nairai I	175g	17.49 S	179.24 E
Nairn, Scot., U.K.	46	57.35 N	3.53 W
Nairn, La., U.S.	194	29.27 N	89.38 W
Nairn ≐	46	57.35 N	3.52 W
Nairne	168b	35.02 S	138.54 E
Nairobi	154	1.17 S	36.49 E
Nairobi Airport ⊠	276	41.08 N	74.21 W
Nairobi National Park ♠	154	1.24 S	36.50 E
Naissaar I	76	59.33 N	24.32 E
Naita ∧	144	5.30 N	35.18 E
Naitamba Island I	175g	17.31 S	179.17 W
Naivasha	154	0.43 S	36.26 E
Naivasha, Lake ⊜	154	0.46 S	36.21 E
Naivos	114	2.30 N	96.10 E
Naizifang	105	39.36 N	116.47 E
N'aizishen	89	43.41 N	127.29 E
Najac	32	44.13 N	1.59 E
Najafābād	128	32.37 N	51.21 E
Najafgarh ◆⁸	272a	28.37 N	76.59 E
Najafgarh Drain ≊	272a	28.43 N	77.14 E
Najasa ≐	240p	20.42 N	77.55 W
Najd ▫⁸	144	21.00 N	46.00 E
Najd ▫⁹	118	25.00 N	44.30 E
Nájera	34	42.25 N	2.44 W
Najhā	132	33.23 N	36.22 E
Najʿ Ḥammādī	140	26.03 N	32.15 E
Najībābād	124	29.38 N	78.20 E
Najin	98	42.15 N	130.18 E
Najinkouzi	89	50.23 N	126.57 E
Najio	270	34.50 N	135.18 E
Najsterjarvi	24	62.16 N	32.38 E
Naju	98	35.03 N	126.43 E
Najza, gora ∧	86	49.24 N	70.42 E
Naka, Nihon	94	36.27 N	140.30 E
Naka, Nihon	96	35.02 N	134.55 E
Naka, Nihon	268	35.49 N	140.03 E
Naka, Nihon	270	34.50 N	135.48 E
Naka, Nihon	270	34.42 N	135.45 E
Naka, Nihon	270	34.50 N	135.56 E
Naka ◆⁸	268	35.27 N	139.39 E
Naka ≐, Nihon	94	36.20 N	140.36 E
Naka ≐, Nihon	96	33.56 N	134.42 E
Nakadōri-shima I	92	32.57 N	129.04 E
Nakagami	268	35.49 N	139.21 E
Nakagawa	94	35.38 N	137.56 E
Nakagawa ◆⁸	268	35.33 N	139.35 E
Nakagō	94	36.58 N	138.14 E
Nakagusuku	174m	26.15 N	127.49 E

Symbols in the index entries represent the broad categories identified in the key at the right. Symbols with superior numbers (∧¹) identify subcategories (see complete key on page I · 1).

Symbole im Register stellen die rechts im Schlüssel erklärten Kategorien dar. Symbole mit hochgestellten Ziffern (∧¹) bezeichnen Unterabteilungen einer Kategorie (vgl. vollständiger Schlüssel auf Seite I · 1).

Los símbolos incluídos en el texto del índice representan las grandes categorías identificadas con la clave a la derecha. Los símbolos con numeros en su parte superior (∧¹) identifican las subcategorías (véase la clave completa en la página I · 1).

Les symboles de l'index représentent les catégories indiquées dans la légende à droite. Les symboles suivis d'un indice (∧¹) représentent des sous-catégories (voir légende complète à la page I · 1).

Os símbolos incluídos no texto do índice representam as grandes categorias identificadas com a chave à direita. Os símbolos com números em sua parte superior (∧¹) identificam as subcategorias (veja-se a chave completa à página I · 1).

∧ Mountain	Berg	Montaña	Montagne	Montanha
∧∧ Mountains	Gebirge	Montañas	Montagnes	Montanhas
✕ Pass	Paß	Paso	Col	Passo
V Valley, Canyon	Tal, Cañon	Valle, Cañón	Vallée, Canyon	Vale, Canhão
≐ Plain	Ebene	Llano	Plaine	Planície
> Cape	Kap	Cabo	Cap	Cabo
I Island	Insel	Isla	Île	Ilha
II Islands	Inseln	Islas	Îles	Ilhas
± Other Topographic Features	Andere Topographische Objekte	Otros Elementos Topográficos	Autres données topographiques	Outros acidentes topográficos

ESPAÑOL

Nombre	Página	Lat.°′	Long.°′ W = Oeste
Nakagusuku-wan ⊂	174m	26.14 N	127.53 E
Nakagyō ◆[8]	270	35.01 N	135.45 E
Nakaheji	96	33.47 N	135.31 E
Nakai	94	35.20 N	139.14 E
Nakaizu	94	34.57 N	139.00 E
Nakajima, Nihon	94	37.07 N	136.51 E
Nakajima, Nihon	96	33.58 N	132.07 E
Nakajima, Nihon	268	35.26 N	139.56 E
Nakajima, Nihon	268	35.18 N	139.58 E
Naka-jima I	96	33.58 N	132.37 E
Nakajō, Nihon	92	38.03 N	139.24 E
Nakajō, Nihon	94	36.36 N	138.02 E
Nakakawane	94	35.03 N	138.05 E
Nāka Khārari	120	25.15 N	66.44 E
Nakalele Point >	229a	21.02 N	156.35 W
Nākālia	126	24.02 N	89.40 E
Nakama, Nihon	96	33.50 N	130.43 E
Nakama, Nihon	174m	26.16 N	127.44 E
Nakaminato	94	36.21 N	140.36 E
Nakamura	96	32.59 N	132.56 E
Nakanai Mountains ʌʌ	164	5.35 S	151.10 E
Nakano, Nihon	94	36.45 N	138.22 E
Nakano, Nihon	268	35.20 N	139.54 E
Nakano, Nihon	270	34.58 N	135.58 E
Nakano ◆[8]	268	35.42 N	139.42 E
Nakanobu ◆[8]	268	35.36 N	139.43 E
Nakanojō	94	36.35 N	138.51 E
Nakano-shima I	93b	29.49 N	129.52 E
Nakanoshima-suidō ʊ	93b	29.44 N	129.49 E
Nakanougan-jima I	175d	24.11 N	123.33 E
Nakaosu	174m	26.37 N	128.02 E
Nakaōzō ◆[8]	270	34.51 N	135.11 E
Nakape	140	5.47 N	28.37 E
Nakashibetsu	92a	43.33 N	144.59 E
Nākāsipāra	126	23.35 N	88.21 E
Nakasongola	154	1.19 N	32.28 E
Nakatō	268	35.45 N	139.24 E
Nakatomi, Nihon	94	35.28 N	138.26 E
Nakatomi, Nihon	268	35.49 N	139.30 E
Nakatosa	96	33.20 N	133.14 E
Nakatsu, Nihon	96	33.34 N	131.13 E
Nakatsu, Nihon	96	33.57 N	135.18 E
Nakatsu, Nihon	268	35.30 N	139.20 E
Nakatsu ≃	94	37.00 N	138.39 E
Nakatsue	96	33.08 N	130.56 E
Nakatsugawa	94	35.29 N	137.30 E
Nakatsumine-yama ʌ	96	33.58 N	134.31 E
Nakauchigami	270	34.56 N	135.10 E
Naka-umi ⊂	96	35.28 N	133.12 E
Nakayama, Nihon	96	33.38 N	132.42 E
Nakayama, Nihon	96	35.31 N	133.35 E
Nakayama ◆[8]	268	35.31 N	139.33 E
Nakayama ≃	96	33.55 N	133.08 E
Nakazato, Nihon	94	36.05 N	138.50 E
Nakazato, Nihon	94	37.03 N	138.42 E
Nakazuma	268	35.58 N	139.35 E
Nakéty	175f	21.33 S	166.03 E
Nakfa	144	16.43 N	38.32 E
Nakhola	120	26.07 N	92.11 E
Nakhon Nayok	110	14.12 N	101.13 E
Nakhon Pathom	110	13.49 N	100.03 E
Nakhon Phanom	110	17.24 N	104.47 E
Nakhon Ratchasima	110	14.58 N	102.07 E
Nakhon Sawan	110	15.41 N	100.07 E
Nakhon Si Thammarat	110	8.26 N	99.58 E
Nakhon Thai	110	17.07 N	100.50 E
Nakhtarana	120	23.20 N	69.15 E
Nakina	176	50.10 N	86.42 W
Nakkaş ≃	267b	41.00 N	28.45 E
Nakło nad Notecią	30	53.08 N	17.35 E
Naknek	180	58.44 N	157.02 W
Naknek Lake ⊜	180	58.40 N	156.15 W
Nako	150	10.38 N	3.04 W
Nakodar	123	31.07 N	75.29 E
Nakonde	154	9.20 S	32.42 E
Nakoso-no-seki-ato ⊥	94	36.53 N	140.46 E
Nakou	100	27.09 N	117.38 E
Nakskov	41	54.50 N	11.09 E
Nakskov Fjord ⊂	41	54.50 N	11.02 E
Näkten ⊜	26	62.52 N	14.38 E
Naktong-gang ≃	98	35.07 N	128.57 E
Nakūr	124	29.55 N	77.18 E
Nakuru	154	0.17 S	36.04 E
Nakuru, Lake ⊜	154	0.22 S	36.05 E
Nakusp	182	50.15 N	117.48 W
Nāl ≃	120	26.02 N	65.19 E
Nālāgarh	123	31.03 N	76.43 E
Nalajch	88	47.45 N	107.16 E
Nālanda	124	25.07 N	85.25 E
Nalao	102	24.22 N	105.23 E
Nalázi	156	24.03 S	33.20 E
Nalbāri	120	26.25 N	91.26 E
Nalcayec, Isla I	254	46.06 S	73.49 W
Nalchik → Nal'čik	84	43.29 N	43.37 E
Nālchiti	124	22.38 N	90.17 E
Nal'čik	84	43.29 N	43.37 E
Naldānga	126	23.26 N	89.11 E
Nāldera	123	31.11 N	77.11 E
Näldsjön ⊜	26	63.23 N	14.17 E
Nałęczów	30	51.18 N	22.11 E
Nalgonda	122	17.03 N	79.16 E
Nalgora	126	22.52 N	90.39 E
Nalhāti	126	24.18 N	87.49 E
Naliagrām	126	23.36 N	89.37 E
Naliang	102	21.43 N	107.51 E
Nālikul	272b	22.49 N	88.11 E
Nalinnes	50	50.19 N	4.26 E
Nalisan	104	42.06 N	122.12 E
Nallamalla Hills ʌʌ	122	15.30 N	78.45 E
Nalles (Nals)	64	46.32 N	11.12 E
Nallıhan	130	40.11 N	31.21 E
Na Logu	64	46.23 N	13.45 E
Nalolo	152	15.35 S	23.07 E
Nalón ≃	34	43.32 N	6.04 W
Nalong	102	23.35 N	106.05 E
Nalusa	152	14.55 S	22.13 E
Nālūt	146	31.52 N	10.59 E
Nalžovské Hory	60	49.20 N	13.33 E
Nam ≃	110	21.33 N	98.38 E
Namaacha	156	25.58 S	32.01 E
Namachire	152	11.26 S	22.43 E
Namacunde	152	17.18 S	15.50 E
Namacurra	154	17.29 S	37.01 E
Namadgi National Park ♠	171b	35.45 S	148.57 E
Namak, Daryācheh-ye ⊜	128	34.30 N	51.50 E
Namak, Kavīr-e ◆[2]	128	34.45 N	57.45 E
Namakan Lake ⊜	190	48.27 N	92.35 W
Nāmakkal	122	11.14 N	78.10 E
Namaksār, Kowl-e ⊜	128	34.00 N	64.30 E
Namakula	174v	18.57 S	169.54 W
Namaland □[5]	156	25.50 S	18.00 E
Namamugi ◆[8]	268	35.29 N	139.41 E
Namanga	154	2.33 S	36.46 E
Namangan	85	41.00 N	71.40 E
Namanyere	154	7.31 S	31.03 E
Namapa	154	13.43 S	39.50 E
Namarodu, Cape >	164	3.38 S	152.30 E
Namarrói	154	15.58 S	36.55 E
Namasagali	154	1.01 N	32.57 E
Namatanai	164	3.40 S	152.25 E
Nambe Indian Reservation ◆[4]	200	35.52 N	105.57 W
Namber	164	1.04 S	134.49 E
Nambi	162	28.54 S	121.41 E
Nambour	166	26.38 S	152.58 E
Nambouwalu	175g	16.59 S	178.42 E
Nambuangongo	152	8.01 S	14.12 E
Nambucca Heads	166	30.39 S	153.00 E
Nam Can	110	8.46 N	104.59 E
Namcha Barwa → Namjagbarwa Feng ʌ	102	29.38 N	95.04 E
Namch'ang	98	35.26 N	129.16 E
Nam Co ⊜	120	30.42 N	90.30 E
Namdae-ch'ŏn ≃	98	40.26 N	128.57 E
Namdanak	85	41.11 N	69.42 E

FRANÇAIS

Nom	Page	Lat.°′	Long.°′ W = Ouest
Nam Dinh	110	20.25 N	106.10 E
Nämdö I	40	59.12 N	18.41 E
Nämdöfjärden ʊ	40	59.12 N	18.34 E
Nam Du, Quan Dao II	110	9.42 N	104.22 E
Namegawa	94	36.04 N	139.22 E
Nameh	112	2.34 N	116.21 E
Nameigos Lake ⊜	190	48.46 N	84.43 W
Namekagon ≃	190	46.05 N	92.06 W
Namen → Namur	56	50.28 N	4.52 E
Namerikawa	94	36.46 N	137.20 E
Náměšť'	61	49.12 N	16.10 E
Námestovo	30	49.25 N	19.30 E
Nametil	154	15.43 S	39.21 E
Namew Lake ⊜	184	54.13 N	101.56 W
Nam-gang ≃	98	39.03 N	125.52 E
Namhae	98	34.50 N	127.54 E
Namhae-do I	98	34.48 N	127.57 E
Namhan-gang ≃	98	37.31 N	127.18 E
Namhkam	110	23.50 N	97.41 E
Namho-ri	98	38.07 N	125.10 E
Namhsan	110	22.58 N	97.10 E
Namiai	94	35.22 N	137.41 E
Namib Desert ◆[2]	156	23.00 S	15.00 E
Namibe	152	15.10 S	12.09 E
Namibe □[5]	152	15.20 S	12.30 E
Namibia □[1], Afr.	138	22.00 S	17.00 E
Namibia □[1], Afr.	156	22.00 S	17.00 E
Namibie → Namibia □[1]	156	22.00 S	17.00 E
Namib-Naukluft Park ♠	156	23.30 S	15.30 E
Namie	92	37.29 N	141.00 E
Namies	158	29.18 S	19.13 E
Namīn	128	38.25 N	48.30 E
Naminga	88	56.33 N	118.41 E
Namjagbarwa Feng ʌ	102	29.38 N	95.04 E
Nāmja La)(	124	29.27 N	82.34 E
Namji-ri	98	35.23 N	128.29 E
Nāmkhāna	126	21.46 N	88.14 E
Nam Kwo Chau I	271d	22.15 N	114.21 E
Namlan	110	22.15 N	97.24 E
Nāmlāng ≃	124	29.28 N	82.50 E
Namlea	164	3.18 S	127.06 E
Namling	120	29.41 N	89.04 E
Namlos	58	47.21 N	10.40 E
Nam Ngum Reservoir ⊜[1]	110	18.30 N	102.40 E
Namnoi, Khao ʌ	110	10.36 N	98.38 E
Namo	112	1.24 S	119.57 E
Namoi ≃	166	30.00 S	148.07 E
Namoluk I[1]	14	5.55 N	153.08 E
Namonuito I[1]	14	8.46 N	150.02 E
Namorik I[1]	14	5.36 N	168.07 E
Namoruputh	154	4.34 N	35.57 E
Namounou	150	11.52 N	1.42 E
Namous, Oued en V	148	31.00 N	0.15 W
Namoya	154	4.01 S	27.34 E
Nampa, Ab., Can.	182	56.02 N	117.08 W
Nampa, Id., U.S.	202	43.32 N	116.33 W
Nampala	150	15.17 N	5.33 W
Nam Pat	110	17.43 N	100.41 E
Nampawng	110	22.45 N	97.52 E
Nam Phan □[9]	110	11.00 N	107.00 E
Nam Phong	110	16.42 N	102.52 E
Nampicuan	116	15.44 N	120.38 E
Namp'o	98	38.45 N	125.23 E
Nampont-Saint-Martin	50	50.21 N	1.45 E
Namp'ot'ae-san ʌ	98	41.44 N	128.24 E
Nampuecha	154	13.59 S	40.18 E
Nampula	154	15.07 S	39.15 E
Nampula □[5]	154	15.00 S	39.00 E
Namsang	110	20.53 N	97.43 E
Namsan Park ♠	271b	37.34 N	126.59 E
Namsanyŏng-ni	98	38.59 N	127.26 E
Namsen ≃	24	64.27 N	11.28 E
Namsi	98	39.54 N	124.36 E
Namsos	24	64.29 N	11.30 E
Nam Tok	110	14.14 N	99.04 E
Namtu	110	23.05 N	97.24 E
Namu	182	51.49 N	127.52 W
Namu I[1]	14	8.00 N	168.10 E
Namuka-I-Lau I	175g	18.51 S	178.38 W
Namúli, Serra ʌʌ	154	15.15 S	37.08 E
Namur, Bel.	56	50.28 N	4.52 E
Namur, P.Q., Can.	206	45.54 N	74.56 W
Namur □[4]	56	50.20 N	4.50 E
Namuruputh	154	4.34 N	35.57 E
Namutoni	156	18.49 S	16.55 E
Namwala	154	15.45 S	26.26 E
Namwera	154	14.22 S	35.30 E
Namwŏn	98	35.25 N	127.21 E
Namyang, C.M.I.K.	98	42.57 N	129.53 E
Namyang, Taehan	98	37.14 N	126.44 E
Namyit Island I	108	10.11 N	114.22 E
Namysłów	30	51.05 N	17.42 E
Nan	110	18.47 N	100.47 E
Nan ≃, Thai	110	15.42 N	100.09 E
Nan ≃, Zhg.	100	28.15 N	120.43 E
Nana ≃	152	5.00 N	15.50 E
Nana Barya ≃	146	7.59 N	17.43 E
Nana Barya, Réserve de Faune de la ◆[4]	146	7.30 N	17.30 E
Nanacamilpa	234	19.29 N	98.33 W
Nanaimo	224	49.10 N	123.56 W
Nanaimo ≃	224	49.08 N	123.54 W
Nanaimo Lakes ⊜	224	49.07 N	124.11 W
Nānakheri ◆[8]	272a	28.31 N	76.59 E
Nana Kru	150	4.50 N	8.44 W
Nanakuli	229c	21.23 N	158.09 W
Nanam	98	41.43 N	129.41 E
Nana-Mambéré □[5]	152	5.30 N	15.30 E
Nan'an	100	24.58 N	118.23 E
Nan'anba	107	28.46 N	104.38 E
Nanango	166	26.40 S	152.00 E
Nanantun	110	24.45 N	95.41 E
Nanao, Nihon	94	37.03 N	136.58 E
Nanao, T'aiwan	100	24.28 N	121.48 E
Nan'ao, Zhg.	100	23.27 N	117.02 E
Nan'ao Dao I	100	23.26 N	117.03 E
Nanao-wan ⊂	94	37.06 N	137.00 E
Nanas Channel ʊ	271c	1.25 N	103.58 E
Nanatsu-jima II	92	37.36 N	136.53 E
Nanatsuka	94	36.44 N	136.41 E
Nanay ≃	246	3.42 S	73.16 W
Nanba	102	32.20 N	104.58 E
Nanbaita	105	38.58 N	115.39 E
Nanbaixia	98	35.45 N	117.23 E
Nanbaozhen	106	31.32 N	121.37 E
Nanbu, Nihon	94	35.17 N	138.27 E
Nanbu, Zhg.	102	31.23 N	106.02 E
Nancaicun	105	39.28 N	117.01 E
Nancefield	273d	26.17 S	27.53 E
Nancha	89	47.08 N	129.19 E
Nanchang, Zhg.	100	28.41 N	115.53 E
Nanchang (Liantang), Zhg.	100	28.34 N	115.56 E
Nancheng, Zhg.	100	25.39 N	118.26 E
Nancheng, Zhg.	100	27.35 N	116.40 E
Nancheng → Hanzhong	102	33.08 N	107.02 E
Nanching → Nanjing	106	32.03 N	118.47 E
Nanchital	234	18.04 N	94.24 W
Nanchong	107	30.48 N	106.04 E
Nanchuan	102	29.08 N	107.07 E
Nanchuang	100	24.36 N	120.59 E
Nanch'ung → Nanchong	107	30.48 N	106.04 E
Nancowry Island I	110	7.59 N	93.32 E
Nancroix	62	45.32 N	6.46 E
Nancun, Zhg.	98	36.32 N	120.06 E
Nancun, Zhg.	98	39.46 N	114.07 E
Nancy	58	48.41 N	6.12 E
Nanda Devi ʌ	124	30.23 N	79.59 E
Nāndāha	272b	22.50 N	88.17 E
Nandaime	236	11.46 N	86.03 W
Nanda Kot ʌ	124	30.17 N	80.05 E
Nandan	96	34.15 N	134.43 E
Nandarivatu	175g	17.34 S	177.58 E

PORTUGUÊS

Nome	Página	Lat.°′	Long.°′ W = Oeste
Nandashan	100	29.01 N	112.43 E
Nānded	122	19.09 N	77.20 E
Nāndgaon, India	122	20.19 N	74.39 E
Nāndgaon, India	272c	18.58 N	73.08 E
Nandi	175g	17.48 S	177.25 E
Nandi Bay ⊂	175g	17.44 S	177.25 E
Nandi Drug ʌ	122	13.25 N	77.42 E
Nandigrām	126	22.01 N	87.58 E
Nandikotkūr	122	15.52 N	78.16 E
Nanding ≃, Asia	102	23.25 N	98.41 E
Nanding ≃, Asia	110	23.25 N	98.41 E
Nandlstadt	60	48.32 N	11.48 E
Nandom	150	10.51 N	2.45 W
N'andoma	24	61.40 N	40.12 E
Nandu	106	31.27 N	119.19 E
Nandu ≃	110	20.04 N	110.22 E
Nanduluohe	105	40.11 N	117.13 E
Nāndūra	122	20.50 N	76.27 E
Nandurbār	122	21.22 N	74.15 E
Nanduri	175g	16.27 S	179.09 E
Nandy	261	48.35 N	2.34 E
Nandyāl	122	15.29 N	78.29 E
Nanfangquan	106	31.26 N	120.16 E
Nanfen	104	41.06 N	123.44 E
Nanfeng, Zhg.	100	27.15 N	116.32 E
Nanfeng, Zhg.	100	29.16 N	116.32 E
Nangabadau	112	1.02 N	111.54 E
Nangade	154	11.05 S	39.36 E
Nanga Eboko	152	4.41 N	12.22 E
Nangahale	115b	8.34 S	122.32 E
Nangakelawit	112	0.23 N	112.26 E
Nāngal	123	31.24 N	76.14 E
Nangalangki	112	1.15 S	111.40 E
Nangalao Island I	116	11.27 N	120.11 E
Nangal Dewat ◆[8]	272a	28.33 N	77.06 E
Nangamau	112	0.06 S	111.55 E
Nangamesi, Teluk ⊂	115b	9.37 S	120.20 E
Nangamuntatai	112	0.22 S	112.23 E
Nangang	100	31.22 N	116.59 E
Nan Gang ⊂	100	23.30 N	117.00 E
Nan'gangwa	105	39.46 N	116.09 E
Nangaobat	112	0.57 N	113.13 E
Nangaocun	105	39.25 N	115.58 E
Nanga Parbat ʌ	123	35.15 N	74.36 E
Nangapinoh	112	0.20 S	111.44 E
Nangaraun	112	0.38 N	113.11 E
Nangarhār □[4]	120	34.15 N	70.30 E
Nangatayap	112	1.32 S	110.34 E
Nangezhuang	105	39.31 N	116.23 E
Nanggala Hill ʌ	175e	8.16 S	157.43 E
Nanggulan	115a	7.46 S	110.12 E
Nangi	272b	22.31 N	88.13 E
Nangin	110	10.31 N	98.31 E
Nangis	50	48.33 N	3.00 E
Nangka ≃	269f	14.41 N	121.06 E
Nanglal ≃	126	24.20 N	90.04 E
Nangloi ◆[8], India	272a	28.41 N	77.05 E
Nāngloi ◆[8], India	272a	28.40 N	77.02 E
Nangloi Jat ◆[8]	272a	28.41 N	77.04 E
Nangnim	98	40.58 N	127.08 E
Nangnim-sanmaek ʌʌ	98	40.00 N	127.00 E
Nangō, Nihon	92	31.32 N	131.23 E
Nangō, Nihon	94	37.13 N	139.33 E
Nangola	150	12.40 N	6.36 W
Nangoma	152	15.30 S	23.08 E
Nangong	98	37.24 N	115.22 E
Nangou	89	43.17 N	128.37 E
Nangō-yama-tunnel ◆[6]	94	35.12 N	139.10 E
Nangqên	102	32.22 N	96.21 E
Nang Rong	110	14.38 N	102.48 E
Nanguan	102	37.00 N	112.31 E
Nangweshi	152	16.26 S	23.17 E
Nanhai → Foshan	100	23.03 N	113.09 E
Nanhai → South China Sea ⫪[2]	108	10.00 N	113.00 E
Nanhe	98	37.01 N	114.41 E
Nanhedian	100	33.23 N	112.25 E
Nanhekan	107	30.24 N	103.27 E
Nanhezhao	105	39.05 N	115.56 E
Nanhsi	100	23.11 N	120.29 E
Nanhu	102	39.57 N	94.13 E
Nanhua	102	25.14 N	101.13 E
Nanhualou	104	42.30 N	123.53 E
Nanhuang	98	36.58 N	121.47 E
Nanhui	106	31.03 N	121.45 E
Nan Hulsan Hu ⊜	102	36.39 N	96.20 E
Nanhuta Shan ʌ	100	24.22 N	121.26 E
Nanhutou	89	43.44 N	128.55 E
Nanika Lake ⊜	182	53.45 N	127.40 W
Naniwa ◆[8]	270	34.39 N	135.30 E
Nanjangūd	122	12.06 N	76.42 E
Nanjemoy	208	38.27 N	77.13 W
Nanjemoy Creek ⊂	208	38.25 N	77.07 W
Nanji I	100	27.28 N	121.04 E
Nanjiang, Zhg.	100	32.44 N	120.52 E
Nanjiang, Zhg.	102	32.33 N	107.30 E
Nanjiangqiao	100	28.58 N	113.44 E
Nanjie	107	29.11 N	105.00 E
Nanjing, Zhg.	100	24.41 N	114.25 E
Nanjing, Zhg.	100	24.32 N	117.22 E
Nanjing (Nanking), Zhg.	106	32.03 N	118.47 E
Nanjing, Zhg.	107	28.49 N	105.12 E
Nanjinyi	107	30.02 N	104.42 E
Nanjirinji	154	9.39 S	39.04 E
Nanjō	94	35.50 N	136.13 E
Nanjuma ≃	105	39.24 N	115.43 E
Nankan	96	33.03 N	130.32 E
Nankāna Sāhib	123	31.27 N	73.42 E
Nankang	100	25.42 N	114.44 E
Nankang ◆[8]	269d	25.03 N	121.36 E
Nankin	214	40.55 N	82.17 W
Nanking → Nanjing	106	32.03 N	118.47 E
Nanko-kōen ♠	94	37.05 N	140.14 E
Nankoku	96	33.39 N	133.44 E
Nankou	100	26.38 N	117.24 E
Nankouzhen	105	40.14 N	116.07 E
Nanku	106	31.06 N	120.37 E
Nankye	110	14.20 N	98.11 E
Nanle	98	36.04 N	115.10 E
Nanling, Zhg.	100	30.56 N	118.20 E
Nanling, Zhg.	100	23.21 N	115.25 E
Nanling, Zhg.	104	41.37 N	120.56 E
Nan Ling ʌʌ	90	25.00 N	112.00 E
Nanlinqiao	100	29.35 N	114.19 E
Nanliu ≃	102	21.38 N	109.00 E
Nanliucun	105	40.10 N	116.04 E
Nanlongba	102	28.02 N	107.31 E
Nanlou Shan ʌ	89	43.27 N	126.42 E
Nanma	102	24.17 N	101.03 E
Nanmatang	106	32.18 N	120.38 E
Nanmeng	105	39.11 N	116.22 E
Nanmoku	94	36.10 N	138.44 E
Nannerch	262	53.13 N	3.15 W
Nannine	162	26.53 S	118.20 E
Nanning	102	22.48 N	108.20 E
Nanniwan	102	36.29 N	109.40 E
Nannō	94	35.13 N	136.36 E
Nannup	162	33.59 S	115.45 E
Nanny ≃	48	53.40 N	6.14 W
Na Noi	110	18.19 N	100.43 E
Nānole ◆[8]	272c	19.01 N	72.55 E
Nanoose Bay	224	49.16 N	124.12 W
Nanoose Harbour ⊂	224	49.20 N	124.10 W
Nanoshi	272c	18.56 N	73.05 E
Nanowin ≃	184	53.13 N	97.13 W
Nanpan ≃, Zhg.	102	25.07 N	106.00 E
Nanpan ≃, Zhg.	102	24.34 N	103.04 E
Nānpāra	124	27.52 N	81.30 E
Nanpengchang	107	29.21 N	106.38 E
Nanpi	98	38.02 N	116.42 E
Nanpiao	104	41.12 N	120.39 E
Nanping, Zhg.	89	43.24 N	129.05 E
Nanping, Zhg.	98	42.16 N	129.09 E
Nanping, Zhg.	100	26.38 N	118.10 E
Nanping, Zhg.	102	21.50 N	107.28 E

Nanping, Zhg.	102	33.07 N	104.20 E
Nanpingji	100	33.30 N	116.51 E
Nanpu	105	39.16 N	118.12 E
Nanpu ≃	100	27.02 N	118.18 E
Nanqingtuo	105	39.37 N	117.53 E
Nanqu	104	40.44 N	122.08 E
Nanquan	98	36.24 N	120.17 E
Nanri Dao I	100	25.13 N	119.30 E
Nansa ≃	34	43.22 N	4.29 W
Nansei	92	34.22 N	136.41 E
Nansei-shotō (Ryukyu Islands) II	90	26.30 N	128.00 E
Nansemond □[6]	208	36.43 N	76.40 W
Nansen, Lago ⊜	254	47.57 S	72.21 W
Nan Sha I	106	31.36 N	121.22 E
Nanshahe	98	35.03 N	117.12 E
Nanshan, Zhg.	100	26.38 N	118.20 E
Nanshan, Zhg.	105	39.21 N	115.34 E
Nanshanba	100	25.34 N	116.32 E
Nanshanchengzi	98	42.09 N	125.19 E
Nanshan Island I	108	10.45 N	115.49 E
Nanshankou	102	43.09 N	93.41 E
Nanshanlingcun	105	39.09 N	117.26 E
Nanshan → Qilian Shan ʌʌ	102	39.06 N	98.40 E
Nanshuang Dao I	100	26.35 N	120.08 E
Nanshui	100	22.02 N	113.16 E
Nansifa	105	39.27 N	116.27 E
Nansio	154	2.08 S	33.03 E
Nans-les-Pins	62	43.22 N	5.47 E
Nansunzhai	269b	31.21 N	121.27 E
Nant	32	44.01 N	3.18 E
Nant ≃	50	47.30 N	1.14 E
Nantai	104	40.55 N	122.47 E
Nantais, Lac ⊜	176	60.59 N	74.00 W
Nantai-san ʌ	94	36.43 N	140.26 E
Nantai-zan ʌ	94	36.46 N	139.29 E
Nantang	100	26.08 N	115.12 E
Nantangdun	106	31.15 N	120.56 E
Nantangmei	105	38.51 N	114.56 E
Nantasket Beach	283	42.16 N	70.52 W
Nantawarra	168b	34.00 S	138.14 E
Nant Bran ≃	42	51.57 N	3.28 W
Nanterre	50	48.53 N	2.12 E
Nantes	32	47.13 N	1.33 W
Nanteuil-le-Haudouin	50	49.08 N	2.48 E
Nanteuil-lès-Meaux	261	48.56 N	2.54 E
Nantian, Zhg.	100	27.57 N	119.56 E
Nantian, Zhg.	100	29.08 N	121.56 E
Nantianmen	104	40.56 N	123.04 E
Nanticoke, On., Can.	212	42.54 N	80.11 E
Nanticoke, Md., U.S.	208	38.16 N	75.54 W
Nanticoke, Pa., U.S.	210	41.12 N	76.00 W
Nanticoke ≃	208	38.16 N	75.56 W
Nanticoke Creek ≃, On., Can.	212	42.48 N	80.04 W
Nanticoke Creek ≃, N.Y., U.S.	210	42.05 N	76.05 W
Nantmeal Village	285	40.08 N	75.42 W
Nanto	92	34.20 N	136.31 E
Nanton	182	50.21 N	113.46 W
Nantong	106	32.02 N	120.53 E
Nant'ou, T'aiwan	100	23.55 N	120.41 E
Nantou, Zhg.	100	22.33 N	113.55 E
Nantouillet	261	49.00 N	2.42 E
Nantschang → Nanchang	100	28.41 N	115.53 E
Nantua	58	46.09 N	5.37 E
Nantuantingzhuang	105	40.17 N	118.17 E
Nantucket	207	41.17 N	70.06 W
Nantucket □[6]	207	41.17 N	70.06 W
Nantucket Island I	207	41.16 N	70.03 W
Nantucket Sound ʊ	207	41.30 N	70.15 W
Nantuego	154	11.21 S	38.24 E
Nantulo	154	12.17 S	39.03 E
Nantung → Nantong	106	32.02 N	120.53 E
Nantwich	44	53.04 N	2.32 W
Nanty Glo	214	40.28 N	78.50 W
Nant-y-Moch Reservoir ⊜[1]	42	52.27 N	3.50 W
Nanu	164	8.50 S	142.40 E
Nanuet	210	41.05 N	74.00 W
Nanuet Mall ◆[9]	276	41.06 N	74.01 W
Nanuku Passage ʊ	175g	16.45 S	179.15 W
Nanumanga I	14	6.18 S	176.20 E
Nanumea I[1]	14	5.39 S	176.08 E
Nanuque	255	17.50 S	40.21 W
Nānūr	126	23.42 N	87.52 E
Nanusa, Kepulauan II	108	4.42 N	127.06 E
Nanushuk ≃	180	69.18 N	151.00 W
Nanwan	100	32.09 N	113.57 E
Nan Wan ⊂	100	21.55 N	120.47 E
Nanwengkouzi	89	51.10 N	125.25 E
Nanwenquan	107	29.26 N	106.35 E
Nanxi, Zhg.	100	31.31 N	115.38 E
Nanxi, Zhg.	100	26.24 N	118.24 E
Nanxi, Zhg.	107	28.51 N	104.58 E
Nanxian	102	29.20 N	112.19 E
Nanxiang	106	31.17 N	121.18 E
Nanxikou	107	30.43 N	106.07 E
Nanxin, Zhg.	98	35.33 N	117.12 E
Nanxin, Zhg.	105	39.11 N	115.38 E
Nanxing Hu ⊜	106	31.08 N	120.48 E
Nanxinzhuang	98	36.39 N	115.15 E
Nanxiong	100	25.10 N	114.20 E
Nanxun	106	30.53 N	120.26 E
Nanya	100	26.52 N	118.19 E
Nanyandang Shan ʌ	100	27.36 N	120.04 E
Nanyang, Zhg.	100	27.24 N	119.39 E
Nanyang, Zhg.	100	33.00 N	112.32 E
Nanyang, Zhg.	100	33.25 N	120.13 E
Nanyangcun	106	31.53 N	121.43 E
Nanyanggangzi	89	48.43 N	125.27 E
Nanyang Hu ⊜	98	35.12 N	116.41 E
Nanyang Shan ʌ	106	31.20 N	120.28 E
Nanyang Technological Institute ʋ[2]	271c	1.21 N	103.41 E
Nanyi Hu ⊜	106	31.07 N	118.57 E
Nan-yō	92	38.03 N	140.10 E
Nanyu	100	25.59 N	119.14 E
Nanyuan	105	39.48 N	116.23 E
Nanyuan Airport ⊠	271a	39.47 N	116.23 E
Nanyue	100	27.13 N	112.43 E
Nanyuki	154	0.01 N	37.04 E
Nanyulin	105	40.09 N	115.23 E
Nanzamu	98	41.56 N	124.23 E
Nanzha	106	31.51 N	120.15 E
Nanzhai	106	31.34 N	120.02 E
Nanzhang, Zhg.	102	31.50 N	111.41 E
Nanzhang, Zhg.	105	39.03 N	115.46 E
Nanzhao	100	33.30 N	112.27 E
Nanzhaoji	100	32.38 N	115.58 E
Nanzhen	100	26.59 N	119.57 E
Nanzhenjie	106	31.48 N	119.17 E
Nanzhila	154	16.05 S	26.07 E
Nanzhuang, Zhg.	105	40.22 N	116.21 E
Nanzhuang, Zhg.	105	40.43 N	114.58 E
Nao	152	4.35 N	15.09 E
Naoābād	272b	22.28 N	88.27 E
Naoāpāra	126	22.45 N	89.39 E
Naococane, Lac ⊜	176	52.52 N	70.40 W
Naoetsu	94	37.11 N	138.15 E
Naogaon	124	24.47 N	88.56 E
Naoiri	96	33.04 N	131.23 E
Naokot	120	24.51 N	69.27 E
Naoli ≃	89	47.20 N	134.10 E
Naolinco	234	19.39 N	96.51 W
Não-me-Toque	252	28.28 S	52.49 W
Naong, Bukit ʌ	112	2.40 N	112.45 E
Nāopāra	126	24.09 N	88.54 E
Naopukuria	272b	22.55 N	88.16 E
Naosap Lake ⊜	184	54.51 N	101.24 W
Naoshima	96	34.27 N	133.59 E
Naours	50	50.02 N	2.17 E
Náousa	38	40.37 N	22.05 E
Naozhou Dao I	102	20.57 N	110.34 E
Napa	226	38.17 N	122.17 W
Napa □[6]	226	38.18 N	122.17 W

Napa ≃	226	38.07 N	122.18 W
Napacao Point >	116	9.43 N	124.31 E
Napajedla	30	49.10 N	17.31 E
Napakiak	180	60.42 N	161.57 W
Napaku	112	2.32 N	115.58 E
Na Pali Coast State Park ♠	229b	22.09 N	159.41 W
Napalkovo	74	70.03 N	73.47 E
Napamute	180	61.33 N	158.42 W
Napanee	212	44.15 N	76.57 W
Napanee ≃	212	44.12 N	77.02 W
Napanoch	210	41.44 N	74.22 W
Napareuli	84	42.03 N	45.31 E
Napas	86	59.53 N	81.58 E
Napaskiak	180	60.42 N	161.45 W
Napa Valley V	226	38.18 N	122.18 W
Napavine	224	46.34 N	122.54 W
Napayauan Island I	116	12.22 N	123.14 E
Napè	110	18.18 N	105.06 E
Napenay	252	26.44 S	60.37 W
Naperville	216	41.47 N	88.08 W
Napetipi ≃	186	51.21 N	58.08 W
Napf ʌ	58	47.00 N	7.56 E
Napido	164	0.41 S	135.23 E
Napiéolédougou	150	9.18 N	5.35 W
Napier, N.Z.	172	39.29 S	176.55 E
Napier, S. Afr.	158	34.29 S	19.53 E
Napier, Mount ʌ[2]	162	17.32 S	129.10 E
Napier Mountains ʌʌ	9	66.30 S	53.40 E
Napierville	206	45.11 N	73.25 W
Napierville □[6]	206	45.10 N	73.35 W
Napinka	184	49.17 N	100.50 W
Naplate	216	41.20 N	88.54 W
Naples, Fl., U.S.	220	26.08 N	81.47 W
Naples, Id., U.S.	202	48.34 N	116.23 W
Naples, Il., U.S.	219	39.45 N	90.36 W
Naples, N.Y., U.S.	210	42.36 N	77.24 W
Naples, Tx., U.S.	222	33.12 N	94.40 W
Naples → Napoli	68	40.51 N	14.17 E
Naples Park	220	26.16 N	81.48 W
Napo	102	23.16 N	105.54 E
Napo □[4]	246	0.30 S	77.00 W
Napo ≃	246	3.20 S	72.40 W
Napola	70	37.59 N	12.38 E
Napoleon, In., U.S.	218	39.12 N	85.19 W
Napoleon, Ky., U.S.	218	38.46 N	84.47 W
Napoleon, Mi., U.S.	216	42.10 N	84.15 W
Napoleon, N.D., U.S.	198	46.30 N	99.46 W
Napoleon, Oh., U.S.	216	41.23 N	84.07 W
Napoleonville	194	29.56 N	91.01 W
Nápoles → Napoli	68	40.51 N	14.17 E
Napoli (Naples)	68	40.51 N	14.17 E
Napoli □[4]	68	40.53 N	14.25 E
Napoli, Golfo di ⊂	68	40.43 N	14.10 E
Napopo	154	4.12 N	28.02 E
Nappamerry	166	27.36 S	141.07 E
Nappanee	216	41.26 N	86.00 W
Nappan Island I	212	44.23 N	77.49 W
Napton on the Hill	42	52.15 N	1.24 W
Napu	115b	9.24 S	119.56 E
Napudalutai Shan ʌ	89	51.06 N	122.13 E
Naqādah	140	25.54 N	32.43 E
Naqadeh	128	36.57 N	45.23 E
Naqb, Ra's an- ʌ	132	29.50 N	35.40 E
Nar ≃	42	52.45 N	0.24 E
Nara, Mali	150	15.10 N	7.17 W
Nara, Nihon	96	34.41 N	135.50 E
Nara □[5]	96	34.30 N	135.50 E
Nāra ≃, Pāk.	120	24.07 N	69.07 E
Nara ≃, Ross.	82	54.53 N	37.26 E
Nara-bonchi ≚[1]	270	34.38 N	135.50 E
Naracoorte	166	36.58 S	140.44 E
Naradhan	166	33.37 S	146.19 E
Narai ≃	94	36.20 N	137.55 E
Narāil	126	23.10 N	89.30 E
Naraina ◆[8]	272a	28.37 N	77.08 E
Naraini	124	25.11 N	80.29 E
Narainpur	126	24.03 N	86.36 E
Narakawa	94	35.59 N	137.50 E
Naramata	182	49.36 N	119.35 W
Naran	88	48.34 N	98.17 E
Naran Bulag	86	49.22 N	92.33 E
Nārang	123	31.54 N	74.31 E
Narangba	171a	27.12 S	152.58 E
Naranja	220	25.31 N	80.25 W
Naranjal, Ec.	246	2.42 S	79.37 W
Naranjal, Ven.	286c	10.28 N	67.02 W
Naranjito, Hond.	236	14.57 N	88.41 W
Naranjito, P.R.	240m	18.18 N	66.15 W
Naranjo	236	10.06 N	84.22 W
Naranjo ≃	236	14.30 N	92.11 W
Naranjo Islands II	116	12.23 N	124.03 E
Naranjos	234	21.21 N	97.41 W
Narao	92	32.50 N	129.04 E
Nara Park ♠	270	34.41 N	135.52 E
Narasannapeta	122	18.25 N	84.03 E
Narasapur	122	16.27 N	81.40 E
Narasaraopet	122	16.15 N	80.04 E
Narashino	94	35.41 N	140.02 E
Narasun	88	50.06 N	112.58 E
Narat	86	43.28 N	83.44 E
Narathiwat	110	6.26 N	101.50 E
Nara Visa	196	35.36 N	103.05 W
Nara Women's University ʋ[2]	270	34.42 N	135.49 E
Nārāyanganj	124	23.37 N	90.30 E
Nārāyaṇī □[8]	124	27.15 N	85.00 E
Nārāyaṇi ≃	124	25.39 N	85.13 E
Nārāyanpāra	272b	22.54 N	88.19 E
Nārāyanpet	122	16.44 N	77.30 E
Nārāyanpur	272b	22.29 N	88.34 E
Narazeni	84	42.27 N	41.57 E
Narberth, Wales, U.K.	42	51.48 N	4.45 W
Narberth, Pa., U.S.	285	40.00 N	75.15 W
Narbonne	32	43.11 N	3.00 E
Narcao	71	39.10 N	8.40 E
Narcea ≃	34	43.28 N	6.06 W
Narcondam Island I	110	13.20 N	94.16 E
Narcosli Creek ≃	182	52.49 N	122.28 W
Nardò	68	40.11 N	18.02 E
Nare ≃	246	6.12 N	74.35 W
Narellan	170	34.02 S	150.44 E
Narembeen	162	32.04 S	118.24 E
Narenbulake	89	49.52 N	120.23 E
Narendranagar	124	30.10 N	78.18 E
Nares Strait ʊ	16	80.30 N	68.00 W
Naretha	162	31.00 S	124.50 E
Narew ≃	30	52.26 N	20.42 E
Nargund	122	15.43 N	75.23 E
Narhan	272c	19.08 N	73.07 E
Nāri ≃	120	28.35 N	67.50 E
Naria	124	23.18 N	90.25 E
Nariai	270	34.53 N	135.38 E
Nariel	171b	36.26 S	147.50 E
Narijn ≃	88	50.20 N	93.24 E
Narijnteel	102	45.57 N	101.29 E
Nārikelbāria	126	23.17 N	89.21 E
Nariman	85	40.34 N	72.48 E
Narimanabad	84	38.53 N	48.52 E
Narimba, Her Majesty's Air Station (Royal Australian Navy Airfield) ■	274a	33.43 S	150.53 E
Narin ≃	120	36.54 N	92.51 E
Narince	130	37.52 N	38.46 E
Narinda, Baie de ⊂	157b	14.55 S	47.30 E
Nariño □[5]	246	1.30 N	78.00 W
Narita	94	35.47 N	140.19 E
Nariwa	96	34.47 N	133.33 E
Nariwa ≃	96	34.46 N	133.36 E
Nar'jan-Mar	24	67.39 N	53.00 E
Nārkanda	123	31.16 N	77.27 E
Narkatiāganj	124	27.06 N	84.28 E
Närke □[9]	40	59.06 N	15.03 E
Närkes Marieberg	40	59.12 N	15.10 E
Narlı	130	37.27 N	37.09 E
Narma	80	54.46 N	42.01 E

Narmada ≃	120	21.38 N	72.36 E
Narmada Valley V	124	22.30 N	77.00 E
Narmak ◆[8]	267d	35.43 N	51.29 E
Narman	130	40.21 N	41.52 E
Narmušad'	80	54.40 N	41.07 E
Nar-Nar-Goon	169	38.05 S	145.34 E
Nārnaul	124	28.03 N	76.07 E
Narni	66	42.31 N	12.31 E
Naro	70	37.18 N	13.47 E
Naro ≃	70	37.14 N	13.37 E
Naroč' ≃	76	54.26 N	26.39 E
Naroč', ozero ⊜	76	54.52 N	26.45 E
Narodiči	78	51.13 N	29.03 E
Narodnaja, gora ʌ	24	65.04 N	60.09 E
Naro-Fominsk	82	55.23 N	36.43 E
Naro Island I	116	11.53 N	123.40 E
Narok	154	1.05 S	35.52 E
Narol	30	50.22 N	23.21 E
Narón	34	43.32 N	8.10 W
Narooma	166	36.14 S	150.03 E
Naro-Osakovo	82	55.33 N	36.33 E
Narovčat	80	53.52 N	43.41 E
Narovl'a	78	51.48 N	29.29 E
Nārowāl	123	32.06 N	74.53 E
Närpes (Närpiö)	26	62.28 N	21.20 E
Närpiö → Närpes	26	62.28 N	21.20 E
Narrabeen	170	33.43 S	151.18 E
Narrabeen Lagoon ⊂	274a	33.43 S	151.17 E
Narrabri	166	30.19 S	149.47 E
Narragansett	207	41.25 N	71.27 W
Narragansett Bay ⊂	207	41.40 N	71.20 W
Narran ≃	166	29.45 S	147.20 E
Narra Narra ʌ	171b	35.50 S	147.27 E
Narrandera	166	34.45 S	146.33 E
Narraway ≃	182	54.48 N	119.56 W
Narraweena	274a	33.45 S	151.16 E
Narre Warren	274b	38.02 S	145.19 E
Narre Warren North	274b	37.59 S	145.19 E
Narrogin	162	32.56 S	117.10 E
Narromine	166	32.14 S	148.15 E
Narrows, Md., U.S.	208	38.58 N	76.15 W
Narrows, Va., U.S.	192	37.19 N	80.48 W
Narrowsburg	210	41.36 N	75.03 W
Närsen ⊜	40	60.17 N	14.23 E
Narsimhapur	124	22.57 N	79.12 E
Narsinghdi	124	23.55 N	90.43 E
Narsinghgarh	124	23.42 N	77.06 E
Narsīpatnam	122	17.40 N	82.37 E
Narskije Prudy, ozero ⊜[1]	82	55.32 N	36.36 E
Narssaq	176	60.54 N	46.00 W
Nartkala	84	43.33 N	43.50 E
Nartuby ≃	62	43.28 N	6.34 E
Naru	92	32.49 N	128.56 E
Narubis, Namibia	158	27.10 S	19.05 E
Narubis, Namibia	158	26.55 S	18.35 E
Naruko	92	38.44 N	140.43 E
Naruksovo	80	54.37 N	44.33 E
Naruo	270	34.43 N	135.23 E
Narusawa	94	35.29 N	138.41 E
Narutō, Nihon	94	35.36 N	140.25 E
Naruto, Nihon	96	34.11 N	134.37 E
Naruto-kaikyō ʊ	96	34.14 N	134.39 E
Narva, Eesti	76	59.23 N	28.12 E
Narva, Ross.	86	55.25 N	93.39 E
Narva ≃	76	59.27 N	28.02 E
Narvacan	116	17.25 N	120.28 E
Narva-Jõesuu	76	59.27 N	28.03 E
Narva laht (Narvskij zaliv) ⊂	76	59.30 N	27.40 E
Narvan	85	40.15 N	67.12 E
Narvik	24	68.26 N	17.25 E
Narvskij zaliv (Narva laht) ⊂	76	59.30 N	27.40 E
Narvskoje vodochranilišče ⊜[1]	76	59.18 N	28.14 E
Narwāna	124	29.37 N	76.07 E
Narwietooma	162	23.15 S	132.35 E
Narym	86	58.58 N	81.30 E
Naryn, Kyrg.	85	41.26 N	75.59 E
Naryn, Ross.	88	50.13 N	96.27 E
Naryn ≃	85	40.54 N	71.45 E
Narynkol	72	42.43 N	80.12 E
Naryntau, gory ʌʌ	85	41.25 N	76.50 E
Naryškino	76	52.58 N	35.44 E
Naryū-zaki >	96	35.36 N	135.28 E
Narzole	62	44.35 N	7.52 E
Nås, Sve.	40	60.27 N	14.29 E
Näs, Sve.	40	58.41 N	15.50 E
Nasadkino	82	56.29 N	37.21 E
Näsåker	26	63.26 N	16.54 E
Na San, Thai	110	8.48 N	99.22 E
Na San, Viet	110	21.12 N	104.02 E
Nasarawa	150	8.30 N	7.40 E
Năsăud	38	47.17 N	24.24 E
Nasawa	175f	15.13 S	168.09 E
NASA Wallops Station ʋ[3]	208	37.52 N	75.28 W
Nasbinals	32	44.40 N	3.03 E
Naschel	252	32.55 S	65.23 W
Naseby, N.Z.	172	45.02 S	170.09 E
Naseby, Eng., U.K.	42	52.25 N	0.58 W
Naselle	224	46.21 N	123.48 W
Naselle ≃	224	46.25 N	123.55 W
Nase → Naze	93b	28.23 N	129.30 E
Nash	194	33.27 N	94.08 W
Nashawena Island I	207	41.26 N	70.53 W
Nāshik	122	19.59 N	73.48 E
Nashoba Brook ≃	283	42.28 N	71.24 W
Nashport	214	40.04 N	82.09 W
Nashū', Wādī an- V	146	26.25 N	14.15 E
Nashua, Ia., U.S.	190	42.57 N	92.32 W
Nashua, Mt., U.S.	202	48.07 N	106.21 W
Nashua, N.H., U.S.	207	42.45 N	71.28 W
Nashua ≃	207	42.46 N	71.27 W
Nashuixi	102	30.09 N	108.40 E
Näshultasjön ⊜	40	59.14 N	16.21 E
Nashville, On., Can.	275b	43.50 N	79.40 W
Nashville, Ar., U.S.	194	33.56 N	93.50 W
Nashville, Ga., U.S.	192	31.12 N	83.15 W
Nashville, Il., U.S.	219	38.20 N	89.22 W
Nashville, In., U.S.	218	39.12 N	86.15 W
Nashville, Mi., U.S.	216	42.36 N	85.05 W
Nashville, N.C., U.S.	192	35.58 N	77.57 W
Nashville, Oh., U.S.	214	40.36 N	82.07 W
Nashville, Tn., U.S.	194	36.09 N	86.47 W
Nashwaak ≃	186	45.57 N	66.37 W
Nashwaaksis	186	45.59 N	66.39 W
Nashwah	142	30.30 N	31.29 E
Nashwauk	190	47.22 N	93.10 W
Nasia	150	10.09 N	0.48 W
Naṣīb	132	32.33 N	36.11 E
Našice	38	45.29 N	18.06 E
Nasielsk	30	52.36 N	20.48 E
Näsijärvi ⊜	26	61.37 N	23.42 E
Nāṣir	140	8.36 N	33.04 E
Nāṣir, Buḥayrat (Lake Nasser) ⊜[1]	140	22.40 N	32.00 E
Nasīrābād, India	120	26.18 N	74.44 E
Nasīrābād, Pāk.	120	28.23 N	68.24 E
Naskaftym	80	52.57 N	45.38 E
Naskaupi ≃	176	53.45 N	60.50 W
Näsnaren ⊜	40	58.51 N	16.18 E
Naso	70	38.07 N	14.47 E
Nasondoye	154	10.22 S	25.06 E
Naso Point >	116	10.25 N	121.57 E
Nasorolevu ʌ	175g	16.38 S	178.42 E
Nasosnyj	84	40.37 N	49.34 E
Naṣr	142	30.36 N	30.23 E
Naṣrābād	128	34.08 N	51.26 E
Naṣrānī, Jabal an- ʌ	130	34.06 N	37.24 E
Nasriddinbek	85	40.41 N	71.55 E
Nāsriganj	124	25.03 N	84.20 E
Nass ≃	182	55.00 N	129.50 W
Nassau, Ba.	240b	25.05 N	77.21 W
Nassau, Dtsch.	54	50.46 N	13.32 E
Nassau, Dtsch.	56	50.19 N	7.47 E
Nassau, N.Y., U.S.	210	42.30 N	73.36 W

≃ River	Fluß	Río	Rivière	Rio	
≊ Canal	Kanal	Canal	Canal	Canal	
ʟ Waterfall, Rapids	Wasserfall, Stromschnellen	Cascada, Rápidos	Chute d'eau, Rapides	Cascata, Rápidos	
ʊ Strait	Meeresstraße	Estrecho	Détroit	Estreito	
⊂ Bay, Gulf	Bucht, Golf	Bahía, Golfo	Baie, Golfe	Baía, Golfo	
⊜ Lake, Lakes	See, Seen	Lago, Lagos	Lac, Lacs	Lago, Lagos	
⊞ Swamp	Sumpf	Pantano	Marais	Pântano	
⍓ Ice Features, Glacier	Eis- und Gletscherformen	Accidentes Glaciales	Formes glaciaires	Acidentes glaciares	
⫪ Other Hydrographic Features	Andere Hydrographische Objekte	Otros Elementos Hidrográficos	Autres données hydrographiques	Outros acidentes hidrográficos	

⤈ Submarine Features	Untermeerische Objekte	Accidentes Submarinos	Formes de relief sous-marin	Acidentes submarinos	
□ Political Unit	Politische Einheit	Unidad Politica	Entité politique	Unidade política	
ʋ Cultural Institution	Kulturelle Institution	Institución Cultural	Institution culturelle	Instituição cultural	
⊥ Historical Site	Historische Stätte	Sitio Histórico	Site historique	Sitio histórico	
♠ Recreational Site	Erholungs- und Ferienort	Sitio de Recreo	Centre de loisirs	Area de Lazer	
⊠ Airport	Flughafen	Aeropuerto	Aéroport	Aeroporto	
■ Military Installation	Militäranlage	Instalación Militar	Installation militaire	Instalação militar	
◆ Miscellaneous	Verschiedenes	Misceláneo	Divers	Diversos	

ENGLISH — Name, Page, Lat.°′, Long.°′ · DEUTSCH — Name, Seite, Breite°′, Länge°′ E = Ost

Name	Page	Lat.°′	Long.°′
Nassau □[6]	210	40.45 N	73.38 W
Nassau, Bahía c	254	55.25 S	67.40 W
Nassau Bay	222	29.32 N	95.05 W
Nassau Coliseum ♦	276	40.43 N	73.36 W
Nassau International Airport ⊠	240b	25.02 N	77.28 W
Nassau Island I	14	11.33 S	165.25 W
Nassau Shores	276	40.39 N	73.26 W
Nassawadox	208	37.28 N	75.51 W
Nassawango Creek ≃	208	38.10 N	75.25 W
Nassenfels	60	48.48 N	11.16 E
Nassenheide	54	52.49 N	13.12 E
Nasser, Lake → Nāṣir, Buḥayrat ⊜[1]	140	22.40 N	32.00 E
Nassereith	58	47.19 N	10.50 E
Nassian	150	8.27 N	3.29 W
Nässjö	26	57.39 N	14.41 E
Nastapoca ≃	176	56.55 N	76.33 W
Nastapoka Islands II	176	57.00 N	76.50 W
Nastasjino	82	54.28 N	38.16 E
Nastaška	78	49.39 N	30.19 E
Nastätten	56	50.12 N	7.51 E
Nastauli	272a	28.43 N	77.22 E
Nastf, Bi'r ⊤[4]	142	30.18 N	30.28 E
Nasu	94	37.01 N	140.07 E
Nasu-dake ∧, Nihon	92	37.07 N	139.58 E
Nasu-dake ∧, Nihon	94	37.09 N	139.58 E
Nasugbu	116	14.05 N	120.38 E
Nasukoin Mountain ∧	202	48.48 N	114.35 W
Nasva	76	56.35 N	30.10 E
Nat ≃	190	48.48 N	82.07 W
Nata, Bots.	156	20.12 S	26.12 E
Natá, Pan.	236	8.20 N	80.31 W
Nata ≃	156	20.14 S	26.10 E
Natagaima	246	3.37 N	75.06 W
Nātāgarh	272b	22.42 N	88.25 E
Natal, Bra.	250	5.47 S	35.13 W
Natal, B.C., Can.	182	49.44 N	114.50 W
Natal, Indon.	110	0.33 N	99.07 E
Natal □[4]	158	28.40 S	30.40 E
Natal Basin ✦[1]	10	30.00 S	40.00 E
Natalia	196	29.11 N	98.51 W
Nataljevka	83	47.10 N	38.29 E
Nataljin Jar	80	51.46 N	50.35 E
Nataljino	80	52.56 N	49.02 E
Natalkuz Lake ⊜	182	53.26 N	125.20 W
Natalspruit ≃	273d	26.19 S	28.10 E
Natanes Plateau ⋏[1]	200	33.35 N	110.15 W
Natash, Wādī V	140	24.25 N	33.26 E
Natashō	96	35.24 N	135.38 E
Natashquan	186	50.12 N	61.49 W
Natashquan ≃	176	50.06 N	61.49 W
Natashquan, Pointe de >	186	50.06 N	61.44 W
Natashquan Est ≃	186	51.20 N	61.40 W
Natchez	194	31.33 N	91.24 W
Natchez Trace Parkway ♦	194	32.00 N	91.00 W
Natchitoches	194	31.45 N	93.05 W
Natco Lake ⊜	276	40.26 N	74.09 W
Natércia	256	22.07 S	45.30 W
Naters	58	46.20 N	7.59 E
Natewa Bay c	175g	16.35 S	179.40 E
Na Thawi	110	6.45 N	100.42 E
Nāthdwāra	120	24.56 N	73.49 E
Nathia Gali	123	34.04 N	73.24 E
Nathkaw	102	26.53 N	96.13 E
Nathula I	175g	16.53 S	177.25 E
Natick	207	42.17 N	71.21 W
Natick Laboratories ■	283	42.17 N	71.22 W
Natimuk	166	36.45 S	141.57 E
Nation ≃	182	55.28 N	123.35 W
National Agricultural Research Center ʊ[3]	284c	39.02 N	76.52 W
National Airport ⊠	281	42.19 N	83.25 W
National Arboretum ♦	284c	38.54 N	76.58 W
National Assembly ʊ	269a	13.46 N	100.31 E
National Baseball Hall of Fame and Museum ʊ	210	42.42 N	74.57 W
National City	228	32.40 N	117.05 W
National Gallery ʊ	260	51.31 N	0.08 W
National Institute of Health ʊ	284c	39.00 N	77.06 W
National Maritime Museum ʊ	260	51.29 N	0.00
National Park	285	39.51 N	75.10 W
National Taiwan Normal University ʊ[2]	269d	25.02 N	121.31 E
National Taiwan University ʊ[2]	269d	25.01 N	121.32 E
National Zoological Park ♦	284c	38.56 N	77.03 W
Natipi, Lac ⊜	186	51.27 N	71.23 W
Natisone ≃	64	45.57 N	13.22 E
Natitingou	150	10.19 N	1.22 E
Native Bay c	176	63.52 N	82.30 W
Natividade	250	11.43 S	47.47 W
Natividade da Serra	256	23.24 S	45.26 W
Natívitas ◆[8]	286a	19.14 N	99.05 W
Nativity, Church of the ʊ[1]	132	31.43 N	35.12 E
Natkyizin	110	14.55 N	97.57 E
Natl	132	31.39 N	35.52 E
Natoma	198	39.11 N	99.01 W
Natong	102	23.01 N	107.50 E
Nator	124	24.25 N	88.59 E
Natori	92	38.08 N	140.55 E
Natorp	263	51.30 N	7.38 E
Natron, Lake ⊜	154	2.25 S	36.00 E
Natrona Heights	214	40.37 N	79.43 W
Naṭrūn, Wādī an- ±[7]	142	30.25 N	30.13 E
Natsui ≃	94	37.03 N	140.59 E
Nattai ≃	170	34.05 S	150.25 E
Nattai River	170	34.04 S	150.27 E
Nattam	122	10.14 N	78.14 E
Nåttarö I	40	58.52 N	18.07 E
Nattaset ∧	24	68.12 N	27.20 E
Nattaung ∧	110	18.48 N	97.02 E
Natters	64	47.14 N	11.22 E
Nattwerder	264a	52.26 N	12.56 E
Natuchajevskaja	78	44.54 N	37.34 E
Nātudaha	126	23.39 N	88.41 E
Natukanaoka Pan ≚	156	18.40 S	15.45 E
Natuna Besar I	112	4.00 N	108.15 E
Natuna Besar, Kepulauan II	112	4.40 N	108.00 E
Natuna Selatan, Kepulauan II	112	2.45 N	109.00 E
Natural Bridge	212	44.04 N	75.29 W
Natural Bridge ♦	192	37.38 N	79.33 W
Natural Bridges National Monument ♦	200	37.30 N	110.08 W
Natural Bridge State Resort Park ♦	192	37.47 N	83.42 W
Naturaliste, Cape >	162	33.32 S	115.01 E
Naturaliste Channel ⊔	162	25.25 S	113.00 E
Naturita	200	38.13 N	108.34 W
Naturita Creek ≃	200	38.13 N	108.32 W
Naturno (Naturns)	64	46.39 N	11.00 E
Natzungen	52	51.36 N	9.14 E
Nau	85	40.09 N	69.22 E
Nau, Cap de la >	34	38.44 N	0.14 E
Naucalpan de Juárez	286a	19.28 N	99.14 W
Naucelle	32	44.12 N	2.20 E
Naučnyj	78	44.44 N	34.01 E
Naude	272c	19.03 N	73.06 E
Nauders	58	46.53 N	10.30 E
Nauen	54	52.36 N	12.52 E
Nauener Luch ≋	264a	52.37 N	12.55 E
Nauener Stadtforst ♦	264a	52.38 N	12.58 E
Naugachhia	124	25.24 N	87.06 E
Naugatuck	207	41.30 N	73.05 W
Naugatuck ≃	207	41.19 N	73.05 W
Naughton	190	46.24 N	81.12 W
Naugol'noje	82	56.22 N	38.11 E
Naui	140	18.28 N	30.43 E
Naujamiestis	76	55.41 N	24.04 E
Naujan	116	13.20 N	121.18 E
Naujan, Lake ⊜	116	13.10 N	121.21 E
Naujoji Akmenė	76	56.19 N	22.55 E
Naukan	180	66.01 N	169.43 W
Naulavaara ∧[2]	26	63.53 N	28.13 E
Naulila	152	17.12 S	14.42 E
Naumburg, Dtsch.	54	51.09 N	11.48 E
Naumburg, Dtsch.	56	51.15 N	9.10 E
Naumovščina	76	58.23 N	28.20 E
Naunak	86	59.00 N	80.13 E
Naundorf	54	50.56 N	13.25 E
Naunglon	110	16.48 N	97.45 E
Naungpale	110	19.33 N	97.08 E
Naunhof	54	51.16 N	12.35 E
Naupada ◆[8]	272c	19.04 N	72.50 E
Nā'ūr	132	31.53 N	35.50 E
Nauraushaun Brook ≃	276	41.03 N	73.59 W
Nauroth	56	50.42 N	7.52 E
Nauroz Kalāt	128	28.47 N	65.38 E
Naurskaja	84	43.38 N	45.19 E
Nauru □[1], Oc.	14	0.32 S	166.55 E
Nauru □[1], Oc.	174b	0.32 S	166.55 E
Naurzumskij zapovednik ♦	86	51.30 N	64.20 E
Naushahro Fīroz	120	26.50 N	68.07 E
Naushon Island I	207	41.29 N	70.45 W
Nauški	88	50.28 N	106.07 E
Nausori	175g	18.02 S	178.32 E
Naussac, Barrage de ◆[6]	62	44.46 N	3.49 E
Naustdal	26	61.31 N	5.43 E
Nauta	246	4.32 S	73.33 W
Nautanwa	124	27.26 N	83.25 E
Nautilus Park	207	41.22 N	72.05 W
Nautla	234	20.13 N	96.47 W
Nauvoo	190	40.33 N	91.23 W
Nava	232	28.25 N	100.46 W
Nava, Arroyo de la ≃	266a	40.31 N	3.46 W
Nava, Colle di)(	62	44.05 N	7.53 E
Nava del Rey	34	41.20 N	5.05 W
Navadwip	126	23.25 N	88.22 E
Navahermosa	34	39.38 N	4.28 W
Navajo	200	35.55 N	109.01 W
Navajo ≃	200	37.01 N	107.10 W
Navajo Creek ≃	200	36.59 N	111.24 W
Navajo Hopi Joint Use Area ◆[4]	200	36.15 N	110.30 W
Navajo Indian Reservation ◆[4]	200	36.25 N	110.00 W
Navajo Mountain ∧	200	37.02 N	110.52 W
Navajo National Monument ♦	200	36.40 N	110.33 W
Navajo Reservoir ⊜[1]	200	36.55 N	107.30 W
Naval	116	11.34 N	124.23 E
Navalmoral de la Mata	34	39.54 N	5.32 W
Naval Ordnance Test Station ■	228	35.32 N	117.05 W
Navalvillar de Pela	34	39.06 N	5.28 W
Navan	48	53.39 N	6.41 W
Navāpur	122	21.09 N	73.48 E
Navarin, mys >	180	62.16 N	179.10 E
Navarino, Isla I	254	55.05 S	67.40 W
Navarino → Pílos	38	36.55 N	21.43 E
Navarra □[4], Esp.	34	42.40 N	1.30 W
Navarra □[4], Esp.	34	42.45 N	1.30 W
Navarre, Austl.	169	36.54 S	143.07 E
Navarre, Oh., U.S.	214	40.43 N	81.31 W
Navarro	258	35.01 S	59.16 W
Navarro □[6]	222	32.05 N	96.30 W
Navarro ≃	204	39.11 N	123.45 W
Navarro, Cañada ≃	258	35.00 S	59.18 W
Navarro, Laguna ⊜	258	35.01 S	59.18 W
Navarro Mills Lake ⊜[1]	222	31.56 N	96.45 W
Navašino	80	55.32 N	42.12 E
Navasota	222	30.23 N	96.05 W
Navasota ≃	222	30.20 N	96.09 W
Navassa	192	34.15 N	78.00 W
Navassa Island I	238	18.24 N	75.01 W
Nave	64	45.35 N	10.17 E
Nävekvarn	40	58.38 N	16.49 E
Navenne	58	47.36 N	6.10 E
Naver ≃	46	58.32 N	4.15 W
Naver, Loch ⊜	46	58.17 N	4.23 W
Navesink	276	40.23 N	74.02 W
Navesink River c	276	40.23 N	73.58 W
Navesnoje	76	52.17 N	37.57 E
Nâves-Parmelan	58	45.56 N	6.11 E
Navesti ≃	76	58.30 N	24.54 E
Navestock	260	51.39 N	0.13 E
Navestock Side	260	51.39 N	0.16 E
Navia, Arg.	252	34.47 S	66.35 W
Navia, Esp.	34	43.32 N	6.43 W
Navia ≃	34	43.33 N	6.44 W
Navidad	252	33.57 S	71.50 W
Navidad ≃	196	28.41 N	96.35 W
Navidad, Bahía de c	234	19.17 N	104.50 W
Navidad Bank ✦[3]	238	20.00 N	68.50 W
Navio, Riacho do ≃	250	8.39 S	38.36 W
Naviraí	255	23.08 S	54.13 W
Navis	64	47.07 N	11.32 E
Naviti I	175g	17.07 S	177.15 E
Navl'a	76	52.51 N	34.30 E
Navl'a ≃	76	52.42 N	34.01 E
Năvodari	38	44.19 N	28.36 E
Navoi	72	40.15 N	65.15 E
Navojoa	232	27.06 N	109.26 W
Navolato	232	24.47 N	107.42 W
Navoloki	80	57.28 N	41.59 E
Navotas	269f	14.39 N	120.57 E
Návpaktos	38	38.23 N	21.50 E
Návplion	38	37.34 N	22.48 E
Navrongo	150	10.54 N	1.06 W
Navsāri	120	20.51 N	72.55 E
Navua	175g	18.14 S	178.10 E
Navy Island I	284a	43.04 N	79.01 W
Navy Pier ◆[5]	278	41.53 N	87.36 W
Navy Yard City	224	47.32 N	122.41 W
Nawa, Nihon	96	35.30 N	133.30 E
Nawá, Sūrīy.	132	32.53 N	36.03 E
Nawābganj, Bngl.	124	24.36 N	88.17 E
Nawābganj, Bngl.	126	23.40 N	90.10 E
Nawābganj, India	124	28.33 N	79.38 E
Nawābganj, India	124	26.52 N	82.08 E
Nawābganj, India	124	26.56 N	81.13 E
Nawābshāh	120	26.15 N	68.25 E
Nawāda	124	24.53 N	85.32 E
Nāwah	120	32.19 N	67.53 E
Nawa Kot	120	28.20 N	71.22 E
Nawalapitiya	122	7.03 N	80.32 E
Nawalgarh	120	27.51 N	75.16 E
Nawa → Naha	174m	26.13 N	127.40 E
Nawān Kot	123	31.06 N	71.32 E
Nawanshahr	123	31.07 N	76.08 E
Nawāpāra, Bngl.	126	23.02 N	89.23 E
Nawāpāra, India	122	20.58 N	81.51 E
Nawapārā, India	126	23.29 N	88.15 E
Nawasā al-Ghayṭ	142	30.58 N	31.19 E
Nawāshahr	123	34.10 N	73.16 E
Nawāṣīf, Harrat ±[9]	144	21.20 N	42.10 E
Nawāy	142	27.47 N	30.46 E
Nawiliwili Bay c	229b	21.57 N	159.21 W
Nawinda Kuta	152	16.25 S	24.28 E
Nawŏn-ni	98	36.25 N	126.40 E
Naxera	208	37.20 N	76.27 W
Naxi	107	28.47 N	105.22 E
Náxos	38	37.06 N	25.23 E
Náxos I	38	37.02 N	25.35 E
Naxos ⊥	70	37.49 N	15.17 E
Nayābās	272a	28.35 N	77.19 E
Nayāgaon	126	23.32 N	90.46 E
Nayāgarh	120	20.08 N	85.06 E
Nayāgrām	126	22.02 N	87.11 E
Nayak	120	34.44 N	66.57 E
Nayāpāra	126	21.35 N	87.01 E
Nayarit	204	32.20 N	115.19 W
Nayarit □[3]	234	22.00 N	105.00 W
Nayau Island I	175g	17.58 S	179.03 W
Nāy Band, Īrān	128	32.20 N	57.34 E
Nāy Band, Īrān	128	27.23 N	52.38 E
Nāy Band, Kūh-e ∧	128	32.26 N	57.22 E
Nayland	42	51.59 N	0.52 E
Naylor	194	36.34 N	90.36 W
Nayong	102	26.50 N	105.13 E
Nayoro	92a	44.21 N	142.28 E
Nazālī Ṭāhā'	142	28.11 N	30.42 E
Nazaré, Bra.	250	6.23 S	47.40 W
Nazaré, Bra.	255	13.02 S	39.00 W
Nazaré, Port.	34	39.36 N	9.04 W
Nazaré da Mata	250	7.44 S	35.14 W
Nazaré do Piauí	250	6.59 S	42.40 W
Nazareno	256	21.13 S	44.37 W
Nazaré Paulista	256	23.11 S	46.24 W
Nazareth, Bel.	50	50.58 N	3.36 E
Nazareth, Pa., U.S.	208	40.44 N	75.18 W
Nazareth, Vanuatu	175f	15.29 S	168.10 E
Nazareth Bank ✦[4]	12	14.30 S	60.45 E
Nazareth → Naẕerat	132	32.42 N	35.18 E
Nazário	255	16.36 S	49.54 W
Nazarjevo, Ross.	82	55.22 N	36.24 E
Nazarjevo, Ross.	265b	55.59 N	37.16 E
Nazarovo	86	56.01 N	90.26 E
Nazarovskij	78	49.33 N	40.56 E
Nazas	232	25.14 N	104.08 W
Nazas ≃	232	25.35 N	105.00 W
Nazca	248	14.50 S	74.57 W
Nazca Ridge ✦[3]	18	22.00 S	82.00 W
Naze	93b	28.23 N	129.30 E
Nazeing	260	51.44 N	0.03 E
N'azepetrovsk	86	56.03 N	59.36 E
Naẕerat (Nazareth)	132	32.42 N	35.18 E
Naẕerat 'Illit	132	32.42 N	35.19 E
Nazija	76	59.50 N	31.35 E
Nazik Gölü ⊜	130	38.50 N	42.16 E
Nazilli	130	37.55 N	28.21 E
Nazimicha	265b	55.59 N	38.08 E
Nazımiye	130	39.11 N	39.50 E
Nazimovo	86	59.30 N	90.58 E
Nazina	86	60.07 N	78.52 E
Nāzira	120	26.55 N	94.44 E
Nāzir Hāt	120	22.38 N	91.47 E
Nāzirpur	126	22.43 N	89.58 E
Nazko ≃	182	53.07 N	123.34 W
Nazlat al-'Amūdayn	142	28.14 N	30.42 E
Nazlat al-Badramān	142	27.40 N	30.44 E
Nazlat as-Sammān	273c	29.59 N	31.08 E
Nazlat Khalīfah	273c	30.01 N	31.10 E
Nazlat Quftan Bāshā	142	28.57 N	30.49 E
Nazlat Thābit	142	28.25 N	30.47 E
Nazran'	84	43.13 N	44.45 E
Nazret	144	8.33 N	39.16 E
Nazyvajevsk	86	55.34 N	71.21 E
N. B. C. Studios ʊ[3]	280	34.09 N	118.20 W
Nchanga	154	12.30 S	27.53 E
Nchelenge	154	9.20 S	28.50 E
Ncue	152	2.01 N	10.28 E
Ndabala	154	13.28 S	29.50 E
Ndala	154	4.46 S	33.16 E
N'dalatando	152	9.18 S	14.54 E
Ndali	150	9.51 N	2.43 E
Ndanda	152	5.12 N	22.21 E
Ndande	150	15.16 N	16.30 W
Ndarassa	152	6.49 N	22.15 E
Ndélé	146	8.24 N	20.39 E
Ndélélé	152	4.02 N	14.56 E
Ndemba	152	0.11 N	14.19 E
Ndendé	152	2.23 S	11.23 E
Ndikiniméki	152	4.46 N	10.50 E
Ndindi	152	3.46 S	11.09 E
N'Djamena	146	12.07 N	15.03 E
Ndji ≃	152	6.47 N	22.14 E
Ndjili ◆[8]	273b	4.20 S	15.22 E
Ndjili ≃	273b	4.19 S	15.24 E
Ndjili, Grande Île de la I	273b	4.19 S	15.24 E
Ndjim ≃	152	4.38 N	11.24 E
Ndjo	152	1.15 S	14.30 E
Ndjolé	152	0.11 S	10.45 E
Ndogo, Lagune c	152	2.35 S	10.00 E
Ndola	154	12.58 S	28.38 E
Ndolo ◆[8]	273b	4.19 S	15.19 E
Ndona	115b	8.46 S	121.45 E
Ndongo	152	2.19 S	13.38 E
Ndouba	152	0.11 S	14.09 E
Ndougou	152	1.39 S	9.40 E
Ndu	152	4.41 N	22.49 E
Nduguti	154	4.18 S	34.42 E
Nduindui	175f	15.24 S	167.46 E
Ndumbwe	154	10.14 S	39.58 E
Ndumu Game Reserve ◆[4]	158	26.53 S	32.15 E
Nduye	154	1.50 N	29.01 E
Ne	268	35.47 N	140.03 E
Nea ≃	26	63.13 N	11.02 E
Neabul Creek ≃	166	27.45 S	147.32 E
Néa Erithraía	267c	38.05 N	23.49 E
Néa Filadhélfia	267c	38.02 N	23.44 E
Neagari	94	36.27 N	136.27 E
Neagh, Lough ⊜	48	54.38 N	6.24 W
Neah Bay	224	48.22 N	124.37 W
Néa Ionía	267c	38.02 N	23.45 E
Neajlov ≃	38	44.11 N	26.12 E
Néa Khalkidhón	267c	38.02 N	23.43 E
Neale, Lake ⊜	162	24.22 S	130.00 E
Neales ≃	162	28.08 S	136.47 E
Neales Flat	168b	34.15 S	139.10 E
Néa Liósia	267c	38.02 N	23.42 E
Neamṭ □[6]	38	47.00 N	26.30 E
Neandertal, Naturschutzgebiet ♦	263	51.15 N	7.00 E
Néa Páfos (Paphos)	130	34.45 N	32.25 E
Neapel → Napoli	68	40.51 N	14.17 E
Néa Pendéli	267c	38.04 N	23.52 E
Néa Péramos	267c	38.00 N	23.26 E
Neápolis, Ellás	38	36.30 N	23.04 E
Neápolis, Ellás	38	35.15 N	25.37 E
Neapolis, Oh., U.S.	216	41.29 N	83.52 W
Néa Psará	38	38.23 N	23.48 E
Near Islands II	181a	52.40 N	173.30 E
Near North Side ◆[8]	278	41.54 N	87.38 W
Néa Smírni	267c	37.57 N	23.43 E
Neasons Hill	214	41.37 N	80.08 W
Neatahwanta, Lake ⊜	210	43.18 N	76.27 W
Neath	42	51.40 N	3.48 W
Neath ≃	42	51.37 N	3.50 W
Neauphle-le-Château	50	48.49 N	1.54 E
Neauphle-le-Vieux	261	48.49 N	1.52 E
Neavitt	208	38.43 N	76.16 W
Neba	94	35.15 N	137.35 E
Nebaj	236	15.24 N	91.08 W
Nebbou	150	11.18 N	1.53 W
Nebelhorn ∧	58	47.25 N	10.20 E
Nebesnaja, gora ∧	86	43.19 N	80.44 E
Nebeur	36	36.17 N	8.47 E
Nebine Creek ≃	166	29.07 S	146.56 E
Nebit-Dag (Krasnovodsk)	128	40.00 N	53.00 E
Nebit-Dag, Turk.	128	39.30 N	54.22 E
Neblina, Pico da ∧	246	0.48 N	66.02 W
Nebo	194	39.27 N	90 47 W
Nebo, Mount ∧	200	39.49 N	111 46 W
Nebo, Mount → Nabā, Jabal an- ∧	132	31.46 N	35.45 E
Nebolči	76	59.08 N	33.18 E
Nebra	54	51.17 N	11.34 E
Nebraska	218	39.04 N	85.28 W
Nebraska □[3], U.S.	178	41.30 N	100.00 W
Nebraska □[3], U.S.	198	41.30 N	100.00 W
Nebraska City	198	40.40 N	95.51 W
Nebrodi ⋏	70	37.54 N	14.35 E
Nebyloje	80	56.22 N	39.59 E
Nečajannoje	78	46.57 N	31.33 E
Nečajevka	80	53.17 N	44.27 E
Nečajevo	82	54.42 N	37.23 E
Necaxa ≃	234	20.16 N	97.27 W
Necedah	190	44.01 N	90.04 W
Nechajevskij	80	50.25 N	41.44 E
Nechako ≃	182	53.56 N	122.42 W
Nechako Plateau ⋏[1]	182	54.00 N	124.30 W
Nechako Range ⋏	182	53.20 N	124.30 W
Nechako Reservoir ⊜[1]	182	53.25 N	125.10 W
Neche	198	48.59 N	97.33 W
Neches	222	31.52 N	95.30 W
Neches ≃	194	29.55 N	93.52 W
Nechí	246	8.07 N	74.46 W
Nechí ≃	246	8.08 N	74.46 W
Nechisar National Park ♦	144	6.00 N	37.50 E
Nechmeya	36	36.36 N	7.31 E
Nechranická Přehradová Nádrž ⊜[1]	54	50.20 N	13.20 E
Nechvorošča	78	49.09 N	34.44 E
Neckar ≃	30	49.31 N	8.26 E
Neckarbischofsheim	56	49.17 N	8.57 E
Neckarelz	56	49.20 N	9.06 E
Neckargemünd	56	49.23 N	8.47 E
Neckarsteinach	56	49.25 N	8.53 E
Neckarsulm	56	49.12 N	9.13 E
Neckartailfingen	56	48.36 N	9.16 E
Neckartenzlingen	56	48.35 N	9.14 E
Neck Creek ≃	276	40.36 N	74.12 W
Necker	284b	39.23 N	76.29 W
Necker Island I, Br. Vir. Is.	240m	18.33 N	64.21 W
Necker Island I, Hi., U.S.	14	23.35 N	164.42 W
Necker Ridge ✦[3]	14	22.00 N	167.15 W
Necochea	252	38.33 S	58.45 W
Necrópolis ◆	266a	40.25 N	3.38 W
Nedalssjön ⊜	26	62.56 N	12.11 E
Nedančiči	78	51.30 N	30.37 E
Ned Brown Preserve ♦	278	42.02 N	88.01 W
Nedel'noje	82	54.50 N	36.39 E
Nederland	194	29.58 N	93.59 W
Nederland → Netherlands □[1]	30	52.15 N	5.30 E
Nederlandse Antillen → Netherlands Antilles □[2]	241s	12.15 N	69.00 W
Neder-Rijn ≃[1]	52	51.58 N	5.20 E
Nederweert	52	51.17 N	5.45 E
Nederzwalm-Hermelgem	50	50.53 N	3.41 E
Nedlands	168a	31.59 S	115.49 E
Nedlitz	54	52.04 N	12.14 E
Nedlitz ◆[8]	264a	52.26 N	13.03 E
Nêdong	120	29.14 N	91.46 E
Nedre Soppero	24	68.01 N	21.44 E
Nedre Vättern ⊜	40	59.49 N	15.40 E
Nedrigajlov	78	50.50 N	33.53 E
Nédroma	148	35.01 N	1.45 W
Nedrow	210	42.58 N	76.08 W
Nedstrand	26	59.21 N	5.51 E
Neebish Island I	190	46.16 N	84.09 W
Neede	52	52.08 N	6.36 E
Needham, In., U.S.	218	39.32 N	85.58 W
Needham, Ma., U.S.	207	42.17 N	71.14 W
Needham Market	42	52.09 N	1.03 E
Needhams Point >	241g	13.05 N	59.36 W
Needle Mountain ∧	202	44.05 N	109.37 W
Needles	204	34.50 N	114.36 W
Needling Hill ∧[2]	168a	31.53 S	116.56 E
Needville	222	29.23 N	95.50 W
Neelyton	214	40.10 N	77.50 W
Ñeembucú □[5]	252	27.00 S	58.00 W
Neenah	190	44.11 N	88.27 W
Neepawa	184	50.13 N	99.29 W
Neerabup National Park ♦	168a	31.41 S	115.43 E
Neerim South	169	38.01 S	145.58 E
Neermoor	52	53.18 N	7.26 E
Neeroeteren	56	51.05 N	5.42 E
Neerpelt	56	51.13 N	5.25 E
Neersen	263	51.15 N	6.29 E
Nee Soon	271c	1.24 N	103.49 E
Neetze	52	53.15 N	10.39 E
Neetze ≃	54	53.20 N	10.28 E
Nefedjevo, Ross.	82	54.39 N	37.56 E
Nefedjevo, Ross.	265b	55.54 N	37.10 E
Neffs	208	40.42 N	75.37 W
Neffsville	208	40.06 N	76.18 W
Nef'odovo	86	58.48 N	72.34 E
Nefta	148	33.52 N	7.33 E
Nefteabad	85	40.12 N	70.34 E
Neftečala	84	39.23 N	49.16 E
Neftegorsk	84	44.22 N	39.42 E
Neftekumsk	84	44.45 N	44.48 E
Nefyn	42	52.57 N	4.31 W
Nefza	36	36.58 N	9.05 E
Negage	152	7.45 S	15.16 E
Négala	150	12.52 N	8.27 W
Negapatam → Nāgappattinam	122	10.46 N	79.50 E
Negara, Indon.	112	2.37 S	115.06 E
Negara, Indon.	115a	8.22 S	114.37 E
Negara ≃	112	3.00 S	114.45 E
Negast	54	54.15 N	13.01 E
Negaunee	190	46.29 N	87.36 W
Negba	132	31.40 N	34.41 E
Negele	144	5.20 N	39.36 E
Negenborn	52	51.53 N	9.34 E
Negeribatin	112	4.35 S	104.32 E
Negeri Sembilan □[3]	114	2.45 N	102.10 E
Negev Desert → HaNegev ◆[1]	132	30.30 N	34.55 E
Negishi	268	35.51 N	139.23 E
Negley	214	40.47 N	80.32 W
Negola	152	14.10 S	14.30 E
Negomano	154	11.27 S	38.31 E
Negombo	122	7.13 N	79.50 E
Negonego I[1]	14	18.47 S	141.48 W
Negoreloje	76	53.36 N	27.04 E
Negotin	38	44.14 N	22.32 E
Negra, Laguna ⊜	252	34.03 S	53.40 W
Negra, Ponta >	256	22.58 S	42.42 W
Negra, Punta >, Belize	232	16.17 N	88.34 W
Negra, Punta >, Perú	248	6.06 S	81.09 W
Negrais	266c	38.53 N	9.17 W
Negras, Lomas ∧[2]	286d	11.55 S	77.06 W
Negreira	34	42.54 N	8.44 W
Nègres, Pointe des >	240e	14.36 N	61.06 W
Negrești	38	46.50 N	27.27 E
Negrești-Oaș	38	47.52 N	23.25 E
Negrine	148	34.30 N	7.30 E
Negritos	246	4.38 S	81.19 W
Negro ≃, Arg.	254	41.02 S	62.47 W
Negro ≃, Bol.	248	14.11 S	63.07 W
Negro ≃, Bol.	248	9.49 S	65.42 W
Negro ≃, Bra.	248	5.15 S	70.53 W
Negro ≃, Bra.	248	19.13 S	57.17 W
Negro ≃, Bra.	250	9.15 S	47.34 W
Negro ≃, Bra.	252	26.01 S	50.30 W
Negro ≃, Col.	246	5.44 N	74.39 W
Negro ≃, N.A.	236	13.02 N	87.17 W
Negro ≃, Para.	252	24.23 S	57.11 W
Negro ≃, S.A.	246	3.08 S	59.55 W
Negro ≃, S.A.	252	33.24 S	58.22 W
Negro, Baia del c	144	7.55 N	49.55 E
Negro, Cerro ∧, Arg.	254	46.55 S	70.12 W
Negro, Cerro ∧, Arg.	254	44.09 S	69.30 W
Negro, Cerro ∧, Méx.	234	17.19 N	97.25 W
Negro, Mar → Black Sea ⊤[2]	22	43.00 N	35.00 E
Negros I	116	10.00 N	123.00 E
Negros Occidental □[4]	116	10.20 N	123.00 E
Negros Oriental □[4]	116	9.40 N	123.00 E
Negru-Vodă	38	43.50 N	28.12 E
Neguac	186	47.15 N	65.05 W
Nehalem	224	45.43 N	123.53 W
Nehalem ≃	224	45.40 N	123.56 W
Nehawka	198	40.49 N	95.59 W
Nehbandān	128	31.32 N	60.02 E
Neheim-Hüsten	56	51.27 N	7.57 E
Nehonsey Brook ≃	285	39.49 N	75.18 W
Néhoué, Baie de c	175f	20.21 S	164.09 E
Nehru Planetarium ʊ	272c	18.59 N	72.49 E
Neiba	238	18.28 N	71.25 W
Neichiang → Neijiang	107	29.35 N	105.03 E
Neidpath	184	50.13 N	107.15 W
Neige, Crêt de la ∧	58	46.16 N	5.56 E
Neiges, Piton des ∧	157c	21.05 S	55.29 E
Neihart	202	46.56 N	110.44 W
Neihe ≃	100	22.54 N	115.38 E
Neihu	269d	25.05 N	121.34 E
Neihuang	98	35.59 N	114.55 E
Neijiang	107	29.35 N	105.03 E
Neikiang → Neijiang	107	29.35 N	105.03 E
Neilburg	184	52.50 N	109.38 W
Neillsville	190	44.33 N	90.35 W
Neilston	46	55.47 N	4.27 W
Neimen	263	51.29 N	7.48 E
Nei Monggol Zizhiqu (Inner Mongolia) □[4]	90	43.00 N	115.00 E
Nein	132	32.38 N	35.21 E
Neindorf	54	52.20 N	10.50 E
Neinstedt	54	51.45 N	11.05 E
Neiqiu	98	37.17 N	114.31 E
Neira	246	5.10 N	75.32 W
Neirone	62	44.27 N	9.11 E
Neishuishan	269d	25.09 N	121.43 E
Neisse (Nysa Łużycka) (Nisa) ≃	30	52.04 N	14.46 E
Neiva	246	2.56 N	75.18 W
Neiwufuquan	105	40.11 N	117.39 E
Neixiang	102	33.12 N	111.57 E
Neixpa ≃	234	18.05 N	102.46 W
Neizeng Shan ∧	100	24.02 N	117.32 E
Neja, Ross.	80	58.24 N	46.31 E
Neja, Ross.	80	58.18 N	43.54 E
Neja ≃	80	57.48 N	43.42 E
Nejapa de Madero	234	16.37 N	95.59 W
Nejdek	54	50.17 N	12.42 E
Nejd → Najd □[9]	118	25.00 N	44.30 E
Nejo	144	9.30 N	35.30 E
Nejva ≃	86	57.54 N	62.18 E
Nejvo-Šajtanskij	86	57.44 N	61.15 E
Nekalagba	154	2.50 N	28.01 E
Nekemte	144	9.02 N	36.31 E
Nekhab ⊥	140	25.10 N	32.48 E
Nekoosa	190	44.18 N	89.54 W
Nekor, Oued ≃	34	35.14 N	3.45 W
Neko-zaki >	96	35.40 N	134.46 E
Nekrasino	82	56.18 N	36.33 E
Nekrasovka	265b	55.41 N	37.56 E
Nekrasovo, Ross.	80	51.10 N	45.18 E
Nekrasovo, Ross.	82	54.30 N	38.57 E
Nekrasovskoje	80	57.41 N	40.22 E
Nekselø I	41	55.47 N	11.18 E
Neksø	26	55.04 N	15.09 E
Nela Park ♦	279a	41.33 N	81.33 W
Nel'aty	88	56.29 N	115.41 E
Nelichu ∧	140	6.08 N	34.25 E
Nelidovo	76	56.13 N	32.46 E
Neligh	198	42.07 N	98.01 W
Nel'kan	74	57.40 N	136.13 E
Nellie	214	40.20 N	82.04 W
Nellikuppam	122	11.46 N	79.41 E
Nellingen	56	48.33 N	9.47 E
Nellis Air Force Base ■	204	36.14 N	115.02 W
Nelliston	210	42.56 N	74.37 W
Nellis Weapons Range ■	204	37.15 N	116.20 W
Nellore	122	14.26 N	79.58 E
Nel'ma	89	47.39 N	139.09 E
Nelson, B.C., Can.	182	49.29 N	117.17 W
Nelson, N.Z.	172	41.17 S	173.17 E
Nelson, Eng., U.K.	44	53.51 N	2.13 W
Nelson, Ne., U.S.	198	40.12 N	98.04 W
Nelson, Pa., U.S.	210	41.59 N	77.14 W
Nelson ≃	184	57.04 N	92.30 W
Nelson, Cape >, Austl.	166	38.26 S	141.33 E
Nelson, Cape >, Pap. N. Gui.	164	9.00 S	149.15 E
Nelson, Estrecho ⊔	254	51.37 S	75.00 W
Nelson Creek ≃	222	30.56 N	95.31 W
Nelson House	184	55.47 N	98.51 W
Nelson Island I	180	60.35 N	164.45 W
Nelson-Kennedy Ledges State Park ♦	214	41.18 N	81.04 W
Nelson Lake ⊜	184	55.44 N	100.00 W
Nelson Lakes National Park ♦	172	41.50 S	172.40 E
Nelson Reservoir ⊜[1]	202	48.30 N	107.34 W
Nelson's Dockyard ⊥	240c	17.00 N	61.46 W
Nelsonville, N.Y., U.S.	210	41.25 N	73.57 W
Nelsonville, Oh., U.S.	188	39.27 N	82.14 W
Nelspoort	158	32.07 S	23.00 E
Nelspoortjie	158	29.58 S	22.25 E
Nelspruit	156	25.30 S	30.58 E
Néma, Maur.	150	16.37 N	7.15 W
Nema, Ross.	80	57.31 N	50.31 E
Néma, Ḍahr ±[4]	150	16.40 N	7.13 W
Nemadji ≃	190	46.41 N	92.02 W
Nemah	224	46.31 N	123.51 W
Nemaha	198	40.20 N	95.40 W
Neman	76	55.02 N	22.02 E
Neman (Nemunas) ≃	76	55.18 N	21.23 E
Nematābād ◆[8]	267d	35.38 N	51.21 E
Nembe	150	4.35 N	6.26 E
Nembrala	112	10.53 S	122.50 E
Nembro	62	45.45 N	9.45 E
Nemčinovka	265b	55.43 N	37.23 E
Nemda ≃, Ross.	80	57.35 N	48.56 E
Nemda ≃, Ross.	80	57.21 N	43.08 E
Nemegosenda ≃	190	48.31 N	82.53 W
Nemegt uul ⋏	102	43.40 N	101.10 E
Nemeiben Lake ⊜	184	55.20 N	105.20 W
Nemenčinė	76	54.51 N	25.29 E
Nementcha, Monts de ⋏	148	34.52 N	7.05 E
Nemeriči	76	53.51 N	33.59 E
Nemi	66	41.43 N	12.43 E
Nemi, Lago di ⊜	267a	41.43 N	12.42 E
Nemira Mare, Vîrful ∧	38	46.15 N	26.19 E
Nemirov, Ukr.	78	50.07 N	23.25 E
Nemirov, Ukr.	78	48.58 N	28.50 E
Nemirovo	82	55.54 N	36.12 E
Nemo	222	32.16 N	97.39 W
Nemoli	68	40.04 N	15.48 E
Nemor ≃	89	48.23 N	124.32 E
Nemours	50	48.16 N	2.42 E
Nemoviči	78	51.16 N	26.38 E
Nemrut Gölü ⊜	130	38.37 N	42.12 E
Nemuna, Bjeshkët e ⋏	38	42.27 N	19.47 E
Nemunas (Neman) ≃	76	55.18 N	21.23 E
Nemuro	92a	43.20 N	145.35 E
Nemuro-hantō >[1]	92a	43.21 N	145.42 E
Nemuro Strait ⊔	92a	44.00 N	145.20 E
Nemzeti Museum ʊ	264c	47.29 N	19.05 E
Nen ≃	89	45.25 N	124.40 E
Nena Creek ≃	224	45.07 N	121.07 W
Nenagh	48	52.52 N	8.12 W
Nenagh ≃	48	52.56 N	8.17 W
Nenana	180	64.34 N	149.07 W
Nenana ≃	180	64.30 N	149.00 W
Nenaševo	82	54.34 N	37.28 E
Nenasi	114	3.08 N	103.27 E
Nendaz	58	46.11 N	7.18 E
Nendeln	58	47.12 N	9.32 E
Nendo I	14	10.45 S	165.54 E
Nene ≃	42	52.48 N	0.13 E
Neneckij Avtonomnyj Okrug □[8]	24	67.30 N	54.00 E
Nenggiri ≃	114	4.53 N	101.48 E
Nengjia	104	41.38 N	120.46 E
Nengo ≃	152	14.27 S	22.09 E
Nenneper ≃	263	51.32 N	6.26 E
Neno	154	15.24 S	34.39 E
Nentón ≃	236	15.48 N	91.52 W
Nenzing	58	47.11 N	9.42 E
Neo	94	35.38 N	136.37 E
Neo ≃	94	35.24 N	136.34 E
Neodesha	198	37.25 N	95.40 W
Neoga	194	39.19 N	88.27 W
Neola, Ia., U.S.	198	41.26 N	95.36 W
Neola, Ut., U.S.	200	40.26 N	110.01 W
Neoneli	71	40.04 N	8.57 E
Néon Fáliron	267c	37.57 N	23.40 E
Néon Karlovásion	38	37.48 N	26.44 E
Néon Psikhikón	267c	38.00 N	23.47 E
Neopit	190	44.58 N	88.49 W
Neópolis	250	10.18 S	36.35 W
Neoshera	123	33.09 N	74.14 E
Neosho	194	36.52 N	94.22 W
Neosho ≃	194	35.48 N	95.18 W
Neotsu	224	45.00 N	123.58 W
Nepa ≃	88	59.16 N	108.16 E
Nepal (Nepāl) □[1], Asia	118	28.00 N	84.00 E
Nepal (Nepāl) □[1], Asia	124	28.00 N	84.00 E
Nepālganj	124	28.03 N	81.37 E
Nepa Nagar	120	21.28 N	76.23 E
Nepaug Reservoir ⊜[1]	207	41.48 N	72.57 W
Nepean	212	45.18 N	75.47 W
Nepean ≃	170	33.27 S	150.53 E
Nepean, Point >	169	38.18 S	144.39 E
Nepean Bay c	168b	35.42 S	137.44 E
Nepean Island I	174c	29.04 S	167.58 E
Nepean Reservoir ⊜[1]	170	34.22 S	150.35 E
Nepecino	82	55.12 N	38.37 E
Nepeña	248	9.10 S	78.23 W
Nepewassi Lake ⊜	190	46.20 N	80.40 W
Nephi	200	39.42 N	111.50 W
Nephin ∧	48	54.01 N	9.22 W
Nephin Beg Range ⋏	48	54.00 N	9.35 W
Nepi	66	42.14 N	12.21 E
Nepisiguit ≃	186	47.37 N	65.38 W
Nepisiguit Bay c	186	47.46 N	65.32 W
Népliget ♦	264c	47.29 N	19.07 E
Nepoko ≃	154	1.40 N	27.01 E
Nepomuceno	256	21.14 S	45.15 W
Nepomuk	60	49.29 N	13.36 E
Neponset ≃	283	42.17 N	71.02 W
Neponset Reservoir ⊜[1]	283	42.05 N	71.15 W
Neponset River Reservation ♦	283	42.13 N	71.08 W
Neppermin	54	53.56 N	14.02 E
Nepr'acva ≃	76	53.40 N	38.39 E
Nép-sziget I	264c	47.34 N	19.05 E
Neptune, N.J., U.S.	208	40.12 N	74.02 W
Neptune, Oh., U.S.	216	40.36 N	84.30 W
Neptune Beach	192	30.18 N	81.23 W
Neptune City	208	40.12 N	74.02 W
Neqarot, Naḥal V	132	30.40 N	35.15 E
Nera ≃, Europe	38	44.49 N	21.22 E
Nera ≃, It.	66	42.26 N	12.24 E
Nérac	32	44.08 N	0.20 E
Nerákion	267c	38.01 N	23.27 E
Nerang	171a	28.00 S	153.20 E
Nerang ≃	171a	28.03 S	153.17 E
Neratovice	54	50.14 N	14.31 E
Nerča ≃	88	51.56 N	116.40 E
Nerchau	54	51.16 N	12.47 E
Nerčinsk	88	51.58 N	116.35 E
Nerčinskij Zavod	88	51.19 N	119.36 E
Nère ≃	50	47.34 N	2.18 E
Nerechta	80	57.28 N	40.34 E
Nerenstetten	56	48.31 N	10.06 E
Neresheim	56	48.45 N	10.15 E
Nereta	76	56.13 N	25.18 E
Nereto	66	42.49 N	13.49 E
Neretva ≃	36	43.01 N	17.27 E
Nerevoznoje	80	56.53 N	53.54 E
Nerima ◆[8]	268	35.44 N	139.39 E
Neringa	76	55.18 N	21.01 E
Neris ≃	76	54.54 N	23.53 E
Nerito	66	42.32 N	13.28 E
Nerja	34	36.44 N	3.52 W
Nerka, Lake ⊜	180	59.30 N	158.45 W
Nerl', Ross.	76	57.03 N	37.59 E
Nerl', Ross.	80	56.40 N	40.24 E
Nerl' ≃, Ross.	76	57.07 N	37.39 E
Nerl' ≃, Ross.	80	56.11 N	40.34 E
Nero, ozero ⊜	80	57.07 N	39.27 E
Neroj	88	54.28 N	97.49 E
Néronde	62	45.50 N	4.14 E
Nérondes	32	47.00 N	2.49 E
Nerópolis	255	16.25 S	49.14 W
Nerriga	170	35.07 S	150.05 E
Nerrima	162	18.24 S	124.29 E
Nerrimunga Creek ≃	170	34.57 S	150.04 E
Nersingen	58	48.25 N	10.07 E
Nerskaja ≃	82	55.23 N	38.35 E
Nerul	272c	19.02 N	73.01 E
Nerus ≃	114	5.20 N	103.05 E
Nerussa ≃	76	52.33 N	33.47 E
Nerva	34	37.42 N	6.32 W
Nervi	62	44.23 N	9.02 E
Nervia ≃	62	43.47 N	7.38 E
Nerviano	266b	45.33 N	8.58 E
Nerville-la-Forêt	261	49.05 N	2.17 E
Nes, Ned.	52	53.04 N	5.51 E
Nes, Ned.	52	53.26 N	5.45 E
Nes, Nor.	26	60.34 N	9.59 E
Nes', Ross.	24	66.37 N	44.36 E
Nes, Har ∧	132	30.22 N	34.37 E
Nesbyen	26	60.34 N	9.09 E
Neščerdo, ozero ⊜	76	55.54 N	29.04 E
Neščeretovo	83	49.24 N	38.48 E
Nesco	208	39.38 N	74.41 W
Nescochague Creek ≃	285	39.39 N	74.41 W
Nescochague Creek, Great Swamp Branch ≃	285	39.41 N	74.43 W
Nesconset	276	40.51 N	73.09 W
Nescopeck	210	41.03 N	76.13 W
Nescopeck Creek ≃	210	41.03 N	76.14 W
Nescopeck Mountain ∧	210	41.03 N	76.05 W
Nesebâr	38	42.39 N	27.44 E
Neshaminy Creek ≃	208	40.04 N	74.55 W
Neshaminy Hills	285	40.10 N	74.57 W
Neshaminy Mall ◆[9]	285	40.08 N	74.57 W
Neshaminy State Park ♦	285	40.05 N	74.55 W
Neshaminy Woods	285	40.10 N	74.57 W
Neshannock Creek ≃	214	40.59 N	80.21 W
Nesher	132	32.46 N	35.03 E
Nesjøen ⊜[1]	26	63.02 N	12.01 E
Neškan	180	67.03 N	173.01 W
Neskaupstaður	24a	65.10 N	13.43 W
Neskowin	224	45.06 N	123.58 W
Neskynpil'gyn, laguna c	180	66.57 N	172.45 W
Nesle	50	49.46 N	2.55 E
Nesna	24	66.12 N	13.02 E
Nespelem	182	48.10 N	118.58 W
Nesque ≃	62	43.59 N	4.59 E
Nesquehoning	210	40.51 N	75.48 W
Ness	262	53.17 N	3.03 W
Ness, Loch ⊜	46	57.15 N	4.30 W
Ness City	198	38.27 N	99.54 W
Nesse ≃	54	50.59 N	10.32 E
Nesselrode, Mount ∧	180	58.58 N	134.18 W
Nesselwang	58	47.37 N	10.30 E
Nesselwängle	58	47.29 N	10.37 E
Nesslau	58	47.13 N	9.13 E
Nessmersiel	52	53.40 N	7.21 E
Nesso	58	45.55 N	9.08 E

Symbols in the index entries represent the broad categories identified in the key at the right. Symbols with superior numbers (⋏[1]) identify subcategories (see complete key on page *I · 1).*

Symbole im Register stellen die rechts im Schlüssel erklärten Kategorien dar. Symbole mit hochgestellten Ziffern (⋏[1]) bezeichnen Unterabteilungen einer Kategorie (vgl. vollständiger Schlüssel auf Seite *I · 1).*

Los símbolos incluídos en el texto del índice representan las grandes categorías identificadas con la clave a la derecha. Los símbolos con numeros en su parte superior (⋏[1]) identifican las subcategorías (véase la clave completa en la página *I · 1).*

Les symboles de l'index représentent les catégories indiquées dans la légende à droite. Les symboles suivis d'un indice (⋏[1]) représentent des sous-catégories (voir légende complète à la page *I · 1).*

Os símbolos incluídos no texto do índice representam as grandes categorias identificadas com a chave à direita. Os símbolos com números em sua parte superior (⋏[1]) identificam as subcategorias (veja-se a chave completa à página *I · 1).*

∧ Mountain	Berg	Montaña	Montagne	Montanha
⋏ Mountains	Gebirge	Montañas	Montagnes	Montanhas
)(Pass	Paß	Paso	Col	Passo
V Valley, Canyon	Tal, Cañon	Valle, Cañón	Vallée, Canyon	Vale, Canhão
≚ Plain	Ebene	Llano	Plaine	Planície
> Cape	Kap	Cabo	Cap	Cabo
I Island	Insel	Isla	Île	Ilha
II Islands	Inseln	Islas	Îles	Ilhas
± Other Topographic Features	Andere Topographische Objekte	Otros Elementos Topográficos	Autres données topographiques	Outros acidentes topográficos

ESPAÑOL

Nombre	Página	Lat.°′	Long.°′ W = Oeste
Neštěmice	54	50.40 N	14.07 E
Nesterkovo	76	59.10 N	30.33 E
Nesterov, Ross.	76	54.38 N	22.34 E
Nesterov, Ukr.	78	50.04 N	23.58 E
Nesterovka	80	52.26 N	53.42 E
Nesterovo, Ross.	80	54.31 N	41.49 E
Nesterovo, Ross.	82	56.45 N	36.30 E
Nesterovo, Ross.	88	52.22 N	107.53 E
Nestiary	80	56.34 N	45.21 E
Nestoita	78	47.47 N	29.21 E
Neston	44	53.18 N	3.04 W
Nestore ≃	66	43.21 N	12.15 E
Néstos (Mesta) ≃	38	40.41 N	24.44 E
Nesttun	26	60.19 N	5.20 E
Nestucca ≃	224	45.12 N	123.57 W
Nesvetaj	83	47.27 N	39.40 E
Nesviž	76	53.13 N	26.40 E
Nes Ẕiyyona	132	31.55 N	34.48 E
Netanya	132	32.20 N	34.51 E
Netarhāt	124	23.29 N	84.16 E
Netarts	224	45.26 N	123.56 W
Netarts Bay ⊂	224	45.24 N	123.56 W
Netcong	210	40.53 N	74.42 W
Nethan ≃	46	55.42 N	3.52 W
Nether Alderley	262	53.17 N	2.14 W
Netherdale	166	21.08 S	148.32 E
Netherlands (Nederland) □[1], Europe	22	52.15 N	5.30 E
Netherlands (Nederland) □[1], Europe	30	52.15 N	5.30 E
Netherlands Antilles (Nederlandse Antillen) □[2], N.A.	230	12.15 N	68.45 W
Netherlands Antilles (Nederlandse Antillen) □[2], N.A.	241s	12.15 N	68.45 W
Netherton	262	53.30 N	2.58 W
Nethy Bridge	46	57.16 N	3.38 W
Netia	154	14.48 S	39.59 E
Netley Marsh	42	50.53 N	1.21 W
Neto ≃	68	39.13 N	17.08 E
Netolice	61	49.03 N	14.12 E
Netphen	56	50.55 N	8.06 E
Netra	56	51.06 N	10.05 E
Netrakona	124	24.53 N	90.43 E
Netstal	58	47.03 N	9.03 E
Nettancourt	56	48.52 N	4.57 E
Nette	52	52.02 N	10.05 E
Nette ❖[8]	263	51.33 N	7.25 E
Nettelstedt	52	52.18 N	8.41 E
Nettetal	56	51.18 N	6.16 E
Nettilling Fiord ⊂[2]	176	66.02 N	68.12 W
Nettilling Lake ⊜	176	66.30 N	70.40 W
Nett Lake ⊜	190	48.10 N	93.10 W
Nett Lake Indian Reservation ❖[4]	190	48.06 N	93.10 W
Nettlebed	42	51.35 N	1.00 W
Nettle Creek ≃	218	40.03 N	83.48 W
Nettleden	260	51.47 N	0.32 W
Nettleham	44	53.16 N	0.29 W
Nettlestead	260	51.15 N	0.25 E
Nettlestead Green	260	51.14 N	0.25 E
Nettleton	194	34.05 N	88.37 W
Nettuno	66	41.27 N	12.39 E
Nettuno, Grotta di ⊥[5]	71	40.34 N	8.09 E
Netzschkau	54	50.36 N	12.14 E
Neualbenreuth	60	49.59 N	12.27 E
Neu-Anspach	56	50.17 N	8.29 E
Neuastenberg	56	51.10 N	8.29 E
Neubeckum	52	51.48 N	8.01 E
Neubrandenburg	54	53.33 N	13.15 E
Neubraunschweig → New Brunswick □[4]	186	46.30 N	66.15 W
Neubritannien → New Britain I	164	6.00 S	150.00 E
Neu Büddenstedt	54	52.10 N	10.31 E
Neubukow	54	54.02 N	11.40 E
Neuburg am Inn	60	48.30 N	13.27 E
Neuburg an der Donau	60	48.44 N	11.11 E
Neuchâtel	58	46.59 N	6.56 E
Neuchâtel □[3]	58	47.00 N	6.55 E
Neuchâtel, Lac de ⊜	58	46.52 N	6.50 E
Neu-Delhi → New Delhi	124	28.36 N	77.12 E
Neudenau	56	49.17 N	9.16 E
Neudietendorf	54	50.55 N	10.55 E
Neudorf, Sk., Can.	184	50.44 N	102.59 W
Neudorf, Dtsch.	54	50.29 N	12.58 E
Neudorf ❖[8]	263	51.25 N	6.47 E
Neudörfl	61	47.48 N	16.17 E
Neue Hebriden → Vanuatu □[1]	175f	16.00 S	167.00 E
Neuemühle	264a	52.18 N	13.39 E
Neuenburg, Dtsch.	52	53.23 N	7.57 E
Neuenbürg, Dtsch.	56	48.50 N	8.35 E
Neuenburg, Dtsch.	58	47.49 N	7.35 E
Neuenburg → Neuchâtel	58	46.59 N	6.56 E
Neuendettelsau	56	49.17 N	10.47 E
Neuendorf	54	54.31 N	13.05 E
Neuendorfer See ⊜	54	52.07 N	13.55 E
Neuenegg	58	46.54 N	7.18 E
Neuenhagen bei Berlin	54	52.32 N	13.41 E
Neuenhaus	52	52.30 N	6.59 E
Neuenhof ❖[8]	263	51.10 N	7.13 E
Neuenhoven	263	51.08 N	6.31 E
Neue Niers ≃	263	51.16 N	6.26 E
Neuenkamp ❖[8]	263	51.26 N	6.44 E
Neuenkirchen, Dtsch.	52	52.30 N	8.04 E
Neuenkirchen, Dtsch.	52	53.14 N	8.31 E
Neuenkirchen, Dtsch.	52	53.02 N	9.42 E
Neuenkirchen, Dtsch.	52	52.14 N	7.22 E
Neuenkirchen, Dtsch.	52	53.46 N	8.53 E
Neuenkirchen, Dtsch.	52	51.50 N	8.26 E
Neuenkirchen, Dtsch.	54	54.32 N	13.20 E
Neuenrade	56	51.17 N	7.47 E
Neuensalz	54	50.30 N	12.13 E
Neuenstadt am Kocher	56	49.14 N	9.20 E
Neuenwalde	52	53.40 N	8.40 E
Neuerburg	56	50.00 N	6.17 E
Neu-Erlaa ❖[8]	264b	48.08 N	16.19 E
Neues Palais ⊥	264a	52.24 N	13.01 E
Neu Fahrland	264a	52.26 N	13.03 E
Neufahrn bei Freising	60	48.19 N	11.40 E
Neufahrn in Niederbayern	60	48.44 N	12.11 E
Neuf-Brisach	58	48.01 N	7.32 E
Neufchâteau, Bel.	56	49.50 N	5.26 E
Neufchâteau, Fr.	58	48.21 N	5.42 E
Neufchâtel-en-Bray	50	49.44 N	1.27 E
Neufchâtel-sur-Aisne	50	49.26 N	4.02 E
Neufelden	61	48.29 N	14.00 E
Neuffen	56	48.33 N	9.22 E
Neuffossé, Canal de ≅	50	50.45 N	2.15 E
Neufmanil	56	49.49 N	4.48 E
Neuf-Marché	50	49.25 N	1.43 E
Neufmontiers-lès-Meaux	261	48.58 N	2.50 E
Neufundland → Newfoundland □[4]	176	52.00 N	56.00 W
Neufvilles	50	50.34 N	4.00 E
Neugersdorf	54	50.59 N	14.36 E
Neuglobsow	54	53.09 N	13.02 E
Neugraben-Fischbek ❖[8]	52	53.28 N	9.52 E
Neuguinea → New Guinea I	164	5.00 S	140.00 E
Neuharlingersiel	52	53.42 N	7.42 E
Neu-Hartmannsdorf	264a	52.22 N	13.51 E
Neuhaus, Dtsch.	54	50.30 N	11.08 E
Neuhaus, Dtsch.	54	53.17 N	10.55 E
Neuhaus, Dtsch.	58	47.48 N	8.34 E

FRANÇAIS

Nom	Page	Lat.°′	Long.°′ W = Ouest
Neuhaus, Öst.	61	47.47 N	15.11 E
Neuhaus an der Oste	52	53.48 N	9.02 E
Neuhausen, Dtsch.	54	50.41 N	13.28 E
Neuhausen, Dtsch.	58	47.58 N	8.55 E
Neuhausen, Schw.	58	47.41 N	8.37 E
Neuhaus im Solling	52	51.45 N	9.31 E
Neuhaus-Schierschnitz	54	50.19 N	11.14 E
Neuheum	114	5.34 N	95.32 E
Neuhof	56	50.27 N	9.40 E
Neuhof an der Zenn	56	49.27 N	10.38 E
Neuhofen	56	49.25 N	8.26 E
Neuhofen an der Krems	61	48.08 N	14.14 E
Neuillé-Pont-Pierre	50	47.33 N	0.33 E
Neuilly-en-Thelle	50	49.13 N	2.17 E
Neuilly-L'Évêque	58	47.55 N	5.26 E
Neuilly-Saint-Front	50	49.10 N	3.16 E
Neuilly-sur-Marne	261	48.51 N	2.32 E
Neuilly-sur-Seine	50	48.53 N	2.16 E
Neuirland → New Ireland I	164	3.20 S	152.00 E
Neu-Isenburg	56	50.03 N	8.41 E
Neukagran ❖[8]	264b	48.14 N	16.27 E
Neu-Kaledonien → New Caledonia □[2]	175f	21.30 S	165.30 E
Neukalen	54	53.49 N	12.47 E
Neu Kaliss	54	53.10 N	11.17 E
Neukieritzsch	54	51.10 N	12.25 E
Neukirch, Dtsch.	54	51.17 N	13.58 E
Neukirch, Dtsch.	54	51.05 N	14.20 E
Neukirch, Dtsch.	58	47.39 N	9.41 E
Neukirchen, Dtsch.	41	54.52 N	8.44 E
Neukirchen, Dtsch.	54	54.19 N	11.01 E
Neukirchen, Dtsch.	54	51.05 N	12.32 E
Neukirchen, Dtsch.	54	50.47 N	12.22 E
Neukirchen, Dtsch.	54	50.46 N	12.52 E
Neukirchen, Dtsch.	56	50.46 N	9.41 E
Neukirchen, Dtsch.	56	49.29 N	6.50 E
Neukirchen, Dtsch.	60	49.05 N	11.45 E
Neukirchen, Dtsch.	263	51.07 N	6.41 E
Neukirchen, Öst.	64	47.15 N	12.17 E
Neukirchen am Walde	60	48.24 N	13.46 E
Neukirchen bei Sulzbach-Rosenberg	60	49.32 N	11.38 E
Neukirchen-Vluyn	56	51.27 N	6.33 E
Neukloster	54	53.52 N	11.41 E
Neukölln ❖[8]	264a	52.29 N	13.27 E
Neu Kosenow	54	53.47 N	13.46 E
Neulangerwisch	264a	52.19 N	13.04 E
Neulengbach	61	48.12 N	15.55 E
Neulienken	54	53.27 N	14.22 E
Neu Lübbenau	54	52.04 N	13.53 E
Neulussheim	56	49.17 N	8.31 E
Neumagen	56	49.51 N	6.53 E
Neuman Creek ≃	284a	42.42 N	78.48 W
Neumark	54	50.39 N	12.21 E
Neumark ❖[1]	54	52.40 N	14.50 E
Neumarkt am Wallersee	64	47.57 N	13.14 E
Neumarkt im Hausruckkreis	60	48.16 N	13.45 E
Neumarkt in der Oberpfalz	60	49.16 N	11.28 E
Neumarkt in Steiermark	61	47.04 N	14.25 E
Neumarkt-Sankt Veit	60	48.22 N	12.30 E
Neumarkt → Tîrgu Mureș	38	46.33 N	24.33 E
Neumarkt → Tîrgu-Secuiesc	38	46.00 N	26.08 E
Neumünster	30	54.04 N	9.59 E
Neun ≃	110	19.42 N	104.03 E
Neunburg vorm Wald	60	49.21 N	12.24 E
Neundorf	54	51.49 N	11.34 E
Neung-sur-Beuvron	50	47.32 N	1.48 E
Neunkirchen, Dtsch.	56	50.32 N	8.06 E
Neunkirchen, Dtsch.	56	49.20 N	7.10 E
Neunkirchen, Dtsch.	56	50.48 N	8.00 E
Neunkirchen, Öst.	61	47.43 N	16.05 E
Neunkirchen am Brand	60	49.37 N	11.08 E
Neunkirchen am Potzberg	56	49.30 N	7.29 E
Neunkirchen-Seelscheid	56	50.51 N	7.20 E
Neuötting	60	48.14 N	12.42 E
Neupetershain	54	51.36 N	14.09 E
Neuquén	252	38.57 S	68.04 W
Neuquén □[4]	254	39.00 S	70.00 W
Neuquén ≃	252	38.59 S	68.00 W
Neurara	252	24.10 S	68.29 W
Neuravensburg	58	47.38 N	9.46 E
Neureisenberg	264b	48.01 N	16.30 E
Neurode → Nowa Ruda	30	50.35 N	16.31 E
Neuruppin	54	52.55 N	12.48 E
Neusalza-Spremberg	54	51.02 N	14.32 E
Neusalz → Nowa Sól	30	51.48 N	15.44 E
Neu Sankt Johann	58	47.14 N	9.12 E
Neusatz → Novi Sad	38	45.15 N	19.50 E
Neuschottland → Nova Scotia □[4]	186	45.00 N	63.00 W
Neuschwanstein, Schloss ᵿ	64	47.35 N	10.44 E
Neuse ≃	192	35.06 N	76.30 W
Neuseddin	264a	52.18 N	12.59 E
Neuseeland → New Zealand □[1]	172	41.00 S	174.00 E
Neusibirische Inseln → Novosibirskije ostrova II	74	75.00 N	142.00 E
Neusiedl am See	61	47.57 N	16.51 E
Neusiedler See (Fertő) ⊜	61	47.50 N	16.45 E
Neusohl → Banská Bystrica	30	48.44 N	19.07 E
Neusorg	60	49.56 N	11.58 E
Neuss	56	51.12 N	6.41 E
Neusserweyhe	263	51.13 N	6.39 E
Neustadt, On., Can.	212	44.05 N	81.00 W
Neustadt, Dtsch.	54	52.52 N	12.25 E
Neustadt, Dtsch.	54	51.01 N	14.13 E
Neustadt, Dtsch.	54	50.44 N	11.44 E
Neustadt, Dtsch.	56	50.51 N	9.07 E
Neustadt, Dtsch.	56	50.37 N	7.26 E
Neustadt ❖[8]	52	53.04 N	8.47 E
Neustadt am Rübenberge	52	52.30 N	9.28 E
Neustadt an der Aisch	56	49.34 N	10.37 E
Neustadt an der Donau	60	48.48 N	11.46 E
Neustadt an der Waldnaab	60	49.44 N	12.11 E
Neustadt an der Weinstrasse	56	49.21 N	8.08 E
Neustadt bei Coburg	56	50.19 N	11.07 E
Neustädter Bucht ⊂	54	54.02 N	10.50 E
Neustadt-Glewe	54	53.25 N	11.36 E
Neustadt in Holstein	54	54.06 N	10.48 E
Neustettin → Szczecinek	30	53.43 N	16.42 E
Neustift am Walde ❖[8]	264b	48.15 N	16.18 E
Neustift im Stubaital	64	47.07 N	11.19 E
Neustrelitz	54	53.21 N	13.04 E
Neu Töplitz	264a	52.27 N	12.54 E
Neutral Hills ⋏[2]	184	52.10 N	110.50 W
Neutraubling	60	48.59 N	12.12 E
Neutrebbin	54	52.40 N	14.13 E
Neu-Ulm	58	48.23 N	10.01 E
Neuve-Chapelle	50	50.35 N	2.47 E
Neuves-Maisons	58	48.37 N	6.06 E
Neuvic	32	45.23 N	2.16 E

PORTUGUÊS

Nome	Página	Lat.°′	Long.°′ W = Oeste
Neuville-aux-Bois	50	48.04 N	2.03 E
Neuville-de-Poitou	32	46.41 N	0.15 E
Neuville-en-Condroz	56	50.32 N	5.27 E
Neuville-lès-Dieppe	50	49.55 N	1.06 E
Neuville-sur-Oise	261	49.01 N	2.04 E
Neuville-sur-Saône	62	45.52 N	4.51 E
Neuvy-le-Roi	50	47.36 N	0.36 E
Neuvy-sur-Barangeon	50	47.19 N	2.15 E
Neuvy-sur-Loire	50	47.31 N	2.53 E
Neuwaldegg ❖[8]	264b	48.14 N	16.17 E
Neuwerk ❖[8]	263	51.13 N	6.28 E
Neuwerk I	52	53.55 N	8.30 E
Neuwied	56	50.25 N	7.27 E
Neuwiller-lès-Saverne	56	48.49 N	7.24 E
Neu Wulmstorf	52	53.28 N	9.48 E
Neuzelle	54	52.05 N	14.38 E
Neu Zittau	54	52.23 N	13.44 E
Neva ≃	265a	59.57 N	30.20 E
Névache	62	45.01 N	6.37 E
Nevada, Ia., U.S.	190	42.01 N	93.27 W
Nevada, Mo., U.S.	194	37.50 N	94.21 W
Nevada, Oh., U.S.	214	40.49 N	83.07 W
Nevada, Tx., U.S.	222	33.02 N	96.22 W
Nevada □[6]	226	39.16 N	121.01 W
Nevada □[3], U.S.	178	39.00 N	117.00 W
Nevada □[3], U.S.	204	39.00 N	117.00 W
Nevada, Sierra ⋏, Esp.	34	37.05 N	3.10 W
Nevada, Sierra ⋏, Ca., U.S.	204	38.00 N	119.15 W
Nevada City	226	39.15 N	121.00 W
Nevada Creek ≃	202	46.54 N	113.02 W
Nevado, Cerro ∧, Arg.	252	35.35 S	68.30 W
Nevado, Cerro ∧, Col.	246	3.59 N	74.04 W
Nevado de Colima, Parque Nacional del ♦	234	19.30 N	103.35 W
Nevado de Toluca, Parque Nacional ♦	234	19.10 N	99.44 W
Neval'cevo	86	58.38 N	81.53 E
Nevali	272c	19.01 N	73.07 E
Nevanka	88	56.30 N	98.54 E
Neve, Serra da ⋏	152	13.52 S	13.26 E
Nevel'	76	56.02 N	29.55 E
Nevel'sk	89	46.40 N	141.53 E
Nevel'skogo, proliv ʉ	89	52.05 N	141.35 E
Nevendon	260	51.36 N	0.30 E
Never	89	53.58 N	124.05 E
Neverkino	80	52.47 N	46.44 E
Neverovo	80	55.07 N	44.24 E
Nevers	32	47.00 N	3.09 E
Neversink ≃	210	41.21 N	74.42 W
Neversink Reservoir ⊜[1]	210	41.48 N	74.42 W
Nevertire	166	31.52 S	147.39 E
Neves	256	22.51 S	43.06 W
Nevesinje	38	43.15 N	18.07 E
Nevėžis ≃	76	54.56 N	23.46 E
Nevežkino	80	53.07 N	43.19 E
Neviano	68	40.06 N	18.06 E
Neviano degli Arduini	64	44.35 N	10.19 E
Neviges	56	51.19 N	7.05 E
Neville Island	279b	40.31 N	80.08 W
Neville Island I	279b	40.31 N	80.08 W
Nevinnomyssk	84	44.38 N	41.56 E
Nevis I	238	17.10 N	62.34 W
Nevis ≃	46	56.50 N	5.00 W
Nevis, Ben ∧	46	56.48 N	5.01 W
Nevis, Loch ⊂	46	57.01 N	5.43 W
Nevjansk	86	57.32 N	60.13 E
Nevlunghamn	26	58.58 N	9.52 E
Nevon	88	58.07 N	102.49 E
Nevşehir	130	38.38 N	34.43 E
Nevşehir □[4]	130	38.50 N	34.40 E
Nevskoje	76	58.08 N	30.26 E
New ≃, Belize	232	18.22 N	88.24 W
New ≃, Guy.	246	3.23 N	57.36 W
New ≃, N.A.	204	33.08 N	115.44 W
New ≃, Eng., U.K.	260	51.40 N	0.01 W
New ≃, U.S.	192	38.10 N	81.12 W
New ≃, Az., U.S.	200	33.31 N	112.18 W
New ≃, Fl., U.S.	192	29.50 N	84.40 W
New ≃, Fl., U.S.	192	29.55 N	82.25 W
New ≃, N.C., U.S.	192	34.32 N	77.20 W
New ≃, S.C., U.S.	192	32.09 N	80.50 W
New ≃, Tn., U.S.	192	36.25 N	84.38 W
New, North Fork ≃	192	36.33 N	81.21 W
Newabāgam	272b	22.48 N	88.24 E
New Abbey	44	54.59 N	3.38 W
New Addington ❖[8]	260	51.21 N	0.01 W
Newala	154	10.56 S	39.18 E
New Albany, In., U.S.	218	38.17 N	85.49 W
New Albany, Ms., U.S.	194	34.29 N	89.00 W
New Albany, Oh., U.S.	214	40.05 N	82.49 W
New Albany, Pa., U.S.	210	41.36 N	76.27 W
New Albin	190	43.29 N	91.17 W
New Alexandria, Oh., U.S.	214	40.17 N	80.40 W
New Alexandria, Pa., U.S.	214	40.24 N	79.25 W
New Alexandria, Va., U.S.	284c	38.47 N	77.03 W
New Alfa	140	15.10 N	35.40 E
New Almaden	226	37.11 N	121.49 W
New Alresford	42	51.06 N	1.10 W
New Amsterdam	246	6.15 N	57.31 W
New Angledool	166	29.07 S	147.57 E
Newark, Ar., U.S.	194	35.42 N	91.26 W
Newark, Ca., U.S.	226	37.31 N	122.02 W
Newark, De., U.S.	208	39.41 N	75.45 W
Newark, Il., U.S.	216	41.32 N	88.35 W
Newark, Md., U.S.	208	38.15 N	75.17 W
Newark, Mo., U.S.	219	39.59 N	91.59 W
Newark, N.J., U.S.	210	40.44 N	74.10 W
Newark, N.Y., U.S.	210	43.02 N	77.05 W
Newark, Oh., U.S.	214	40.04 N	82.24 W
Newark, Tx., U.S.	222	33.00 N	97.29 W
Newark Bay ⊂, U.S.	276	40.39 N	74.09 W
Newark Bay ⊂, N.J., U.S.	276	40.40 N	74.08 W
Newark Bay Bridge ❖[5]	276	40.42 N	74.07 W
Newark International Airport ⊠	210	40.42 N	74.10 W
Newark Lake ⊜	204	39.41 N	115.44 W
Newark-on-Trent	42	53.05 N	0.49 W
Newark Slough ≃	282	37.31 N	122.05 W
Newark Valley	210	42.13 N	76.11 W
New Athens, Il., U.S.	219	38.19 N	89.52 W
New Athens, Oh., U.S.	214	40.11 N	80.59 W
New Augusta	194	31.12 N	89.02 W
Newaukum, North Fork ≃	224	46.36 N	122.51 W
Newaukum, South Fork ≃	224	46.36 N	122.51 W
Newaygo	190	43.25 N	85.48 W
New Baden, Il., U.S.	219	38.32 N	89.42 W
New Baden, Tx., U.S.	222	31.03 N	96.26 W
New Baltimore, Mi., U.S.	214	42.40 N	82.44 W
New Baltimore, N.Y., U.S.	210	42.26 N	73.47 W
New Bavaria	216	41.12 N	84.10 W
New Bedford, Ma., U.S.	207	41.38 N	70.56 W
New Bedford, Pa., U.S.	214	41.06 N	80.30 W
New Bedford ≃	42	52.35 N	0.20 E
Newberg	224	45.18 N	122.58 W
New Berlin, Il., U.S.	219	39.43 N	89.54 W
New Berlin, N.Y., U.S.	210	42.37 N	75.19 W
New Berlin, Pa., U.S.	210	40.53 N	76.59 W
New Berlin, Wi., U.S.	216	42.58 N	88.06 W
New Berlinville	208	40.20 N	75.38 W
Newbern, Al., U.S.	194	32.35 N	87.31 W
Newbern, Il., U.S.	219	39.01 N	90.20 W
New Bern, N.C., U.S.	192	35.06 N	77.02 W
Newbern, Tn., U.S.	194	36.06 N	89.15 W
Newberry, Fl., U.S.	192	29.38 N	82.36 W
Newberry, Mi., U.S.	190	46.21 N	85.30 W
Newberry, S.C., U.S.	192	34.16 N	81.37 W
Newbery, Aeroparque ⊠, Arg.	258	34.35 S	58.24 W
Newbery, Aeroparque ⊠, Arg.	288	34.35 S	58.24 W
New Bethlehem	214	41.00 N	79.19 W
Newbiggin-by-the-Sea	44	55.11 N	1.30 W
New Bight	238	24.19 N	75.24 W
New Bloomfield, Mo., U.S.	219	38.43 N	92.05 W
New Bloomfield, Pa., U.S.	208	40.25 N	77.11 W
New Bloomington	214	40.35 N	83.19 W
Newbold Island I	285	40.08 N	74.45 W
Newboro	212	44.39 N	76.19 W
Newboro Lake ⊜	212	44.38 N	76.20 W
Newborough, Austl.	169	38.11 S	146.17 E
Newborough, Wales, U.K.	44	53.09 N	4.22 W
New Boston, Il., U.S.	190	41.10 N	90.59 W
New Boston, Mi., U.S.	216	42.09 N	83.24 W
New Boston, Oh., U.S.	218	38.45 N	82.56 W
New Boston, Tx., U.S.	194	33.27 N	94.24 W
New Braintree	207	42.19 N	72.07 W
New Braunfels	196	29.42 N	98.07 W
New Bremen	216	40.26 N	84.22 W
Newbridge → Droichead Nua	48	53.11 N	6.48 W
Newbridge on Wye	42	52.13 N	3.27 W
New Brighton, N.Z.	172	43.31 S	172.44 E
New Brighton, Eng., U.K.	262	53.26 N	3.03 W
New Brighton, Pa., U.S.	214	40.43 N	80.18 W
New Brighton ❖[8]	276	40.38 N	74.06 W
New Britain, Ct., U.S.	207	41.39 N	72.46 W
New Britain, Pa., U.S.	208	40.18 N	75.11 W
New Britain I	164	6.00 S	150.00 E
New Britain Trench ✣[1]	14	6.00 S	153.00 E
New Brockton	194	31.23 N	85.55 W
Newbrook	182	54.19 N	112.57 W
New Brooklyn County Park ♦	285	39.43 N	74.57 W
New Brunswick, In., U.S.	218	39.57 N	86.31 W
New Brunswick, N.J., U.S.	208	40.29 N	74.27 W
New Brunswick □[4], Can.	176	46.30 N	66.15 W
New Brunswick □[4], Can.	186	46.30 N	66.15 W
New Buffalo, Mi., U.S.	216	41.47 N	86.44 W
New Buffalo, Pa., U.S.	208	40.27 N	76.58 W
New Buildings	48	54.57 N	7.21 W
New Bullards Bar Lake ⊜[1]	226	39.25 N	121.08 W
Newburg, Mo., U.S.	194	37.54 N	91.54 W
Newburg, Pa., U.S.	208	40.08 N	77.32 W
Newburg, Pa., U.S.	214	40.31 N	78.25 W
Newburgh, On., Can.	212	44.19 N	76.52 W
Newburgh, Eng., U.K.	262	53.35 N	2.47 W
Newburgh, Scot., U.K.	46	57.18 N	2.00 W
Newburgh, Scot., U.K.	46	56.20 N	3.15 W
Newburgh, In., U.S.	194	37.56 N	87.24 W
Newburgh, N.Y., U.S.	210	41.30 N	74.00 W
Newburgh Heights	279a	41.27 N	81.39 W
Newburn	44	54.59 N	1.43 W
Newbury, On., Can.	214	42.41 N	81.48 W
Newbury, Eng., U.K.	42	51.25 N	1.20 W
Newbury, Ma., U.S.	207	42.49 N	70.53 W
Newbury Old Town	207	42.46 N	70.51 W
Newbury Park	228	34.11 N	118.53 W
Newburyport	207	42.48 N	70.52 W
Newby	44	54.20 N	0.28 W
Newby Bridge	44	54.16 N	2.58 W
New Caledonia (Nouvelle-Calédonie) □[2], Oc.	14	21.30 S	165.30 E
New Caledonia (Nouvelle-Calédonie) □[2], Oc.	175f	21.30 S	165.30 E
New Caledonia Basin ✣[1]	14	30.00 S	165.00 E
New Canaan	207	41.08 N	73.29 W
New Canada ❖[8]	273d	26.13 S	27.57 E
New Caney	222	30.09 N	95.13 W
New Canton	219	39.38 N	91.06 W
New-Carlisle, P.Q., Can.	186	48.01 N	65.20 W
New Carlisle, In., U.S.	216	41.42 N	86.30 W
New Carlisle, Oh., U.S.	218	39.56 N	84.01 W
New Carrollton	284c	38.58 N	76.52 W
New Cassel	276	40.45 N	73.34 W
Newcastle, Austl.	170	32.56 S	151.46 E
Newcastle, N.B., Can.	186	47.00 N	65.34 W
Newcastle, On., Can.	212	43.55 N	78.35 W
Newcastle, Ire.	48	52.16 N	7.48 W
Newcastle, S. Afr.	158	27.49 S	29.55 E
Newcastle, Eng., U.K.	42	52.26 N	3.06 W
Newcastle, N. Ire., U.K.	48	54.12 N	5.54 W
Newcastle, Ca., U.S.	226	38.53 N	121.08 W
New Castle, Co., U.S.	200	39.34 N	107.32 W
New Castle, De., U.S.	208	39.39 N	75.34 W
New Castle, In., U.S.	218	39.55 N	85.22 W
New Castle, Ky., U.S.	218	38.26 N	85.10 W
Newcastle, Ne., U.S.	198	42.33 N	96.42 W
Newcastle, Oh., U.S.	214	40.20 N	82.10 W
Newcastle, Ok., U.S.	196	35.15 N	97.36 W
New Castle, Pa., U.S.	214	41.00 N	80.20 W
Newcastle, Tx., U.S.	196	33.11 N	98.44 W
New Castle, Va., U.S.	192	37.30 N	80.06 W
Newcastle, Wy., U.S.	198	43.51 N	104.12 W
New Castle □[6]	208	39.44 N	75.33 W
Newcastle Airport ⊠	44	55.03 N	1.43 W
Newcastle Bay ⊂	164	10.50 S	142.37 E
Newcastle Bight ⊂[3]	170	32.51 S	151.54 E
Newcastle Creek ≃	164	17.20 S	133.23 E
Newcastle Emlyn	42	52.02 N	4.28 W
Newcastle Mine	182	51.28 N	112.46 W
Newcastleton	44	55.11 N	2.49 W
Newcastle-under-Lyme	44	53.00 N	2.14 W
Newcastle upon Tyne	44	54.59 N	1.35 W
Newcastle Waters	162	17.24 S	133.24 E
Newcastle West	48	52.27 N	9.03 W
New Centerville	285	40.04 N	75.26 W
Newcestown	48	51.47 N	8.51 W
New Chicago	216	41.34 N	87.16 W
Newchurch, Wales, U.K.	42	52.09 N	3.08 W
New Church, Va., U.S.	208	37.59 N	75.32 W
New City	210	41.08 N	73.59 W
Newclare ❖[8]	273d	26.11 S	27.58 E
New Columbia	210	41.02 N	76.52 W
New Columbus	210	41.10 N	76.18 W
Newcomerstown	214	40.16 N	81.36 W
New Concord	188	39.59 N	81.44 W
New Corydon	216	40.34 N	84.51 W
New Croton Aqueduct ≅[1]	276	41.11 N	73.49 W
New Croton Reservoir ⊜[1]	210	41.14 N	73.46 W
New Cumberland, Pa., U.S.	208	40.13 N	76.53 W
New Cumberland, W.V., U.S.	214	40.29 N	80.36 W
New Cumberland Dam ❖[6]	214	40.32 N	80.37 W
New Cumnock	44	55.24 N	4.12 W
New Dayton	182	49.25 N	112.23 W
New Deer	46	57.30 N	2.12 W
Newdegate	162	33.06 S	119.01 E
New Delhi, India	124	28.36 N	77.12 E
New Delhi, India	272a	28.36 N	77.12 E
New Delhi Railroad Station ❖[5]	272a	28.39 N	77.13 E
New Denver	182	49.59 N	117.22 W
New Derry	214	40.21 N	79.19 W
New Dundee	212	43.21 N	80.31 W
New Eagle	214	40.12 N	79.56 W
New Edinburg	194	33.45 N	92.14 W
New Effington	198	45.51 N	96.55 W
New Egypt	208	40.04 N	74.31 W
Newell, Ia., U.S.	198	42.36 N	95.00 W
Newell, S.D., U.S.	198	44.42 N	103.25 W
Newell, W.V., U.S.	214	40.37 N	80.36 W
Newell, Lake ⊜, Austl.	162	24.50 S	126.10 E
Newell, Lake ⊜, Ab., Can.	182	50.25 N	111.56 W
New Ellenton	192	33.25 N	81.41 W
Newellton	194	32.04 N	91.14 W
New Eltham ❖[8]	260	51.26 N	0.04 E
New England	198	46.32 N	102.52 W
New England National Park ♦	166	30.30 S	152.15 E
New England Range ⋏	166	30.00 S	151.50 E
Newenham, Cape >	180	58.37 N	162.12 W
Newent	42	51.56 N	2.24 W
New Enterprise	214	40.10 N	78.25 W
New Ermelo	158	26.32 S	30.02 E
New Falconwood	284a	42.59 N	78.58 W
Newfane, N.Y., U.S.	210	43.17 N	78.42 W
Newfane, Vt., U.S.	188	42.59 N	72.39 W
New Ferry	262	53.22 N	2.59 W
Newfield, N.J., U.S.	208	39.32 N	75.01 W
Newfield, N.Y., U.S.	210	42.22 N	76.35 W
Newfield Pond ⊜	283	42.38 N	71.22 W
New Florence, Mo., U.S.	219	38.54 N	91.26 W
New Florence, Pa., U.S.	214	40.22 N	79.04 W
New Forest ❖[3]	42	50.53 N	1.35 W
New Fork ≃	200	42.33 N	109.58 W
Newfound Gap)(	192	35.37 N	83.25 W
Newfoundland, N.J., U.S.	276	40.44 N	74.29 W
Newfoundland, Pa., U.S.	210	41.19 N	75.19 W
Newfoundland □[4]	176	52.00 N	56.00 W
Newfoundland I	186	48.30 N	56.00 W
Newfoundland Basin ✣[1]	8	45.00 N	40.00 W
Newfoundland Ridge ✣[3]	8	40.30 N	48.00 W
New Franklin	194	39.01 N	92.44 W
New Freedom	208	39.44 N	76.42 W
New Galilee	214	40.50 N	80.24 W
New Galloway	44	55.05 N	4.10 W
New Garden	285	39.49 N	75.45 W
Newgate	182	49.00 N	115.10 W
Newgate Street	260	51.44 N	0.07 W
New Georgia I	175e	8.15 S	157.30 E
New Georgia Group II	175e	8.30 S	157.20 E
New Georgia Sound ʉ	175e	8.00 S	158.10 E
New Germantown	208	40.18 N	77.34 W
New Germany	186	44.33 N	64.43 W
New Glarus	190	42.48 N	89.38 W
New Glasgow	186	45.35 N	62.39 W
New Gretna	208	39.35 N	74.27 W
New Guinea I	164	5.00 S	140.00 E
Newgulf	222	29.16 N	95.54 W
Newhalem	224	48.40 N	121.14 W
Newhalen	180	59.43 N	154.54 W
Newhall, Eng., U.K.	42	52.48 N	1.34 W
Newhall, Ca., U.S.	228	34.23 N	118.31 W
Newham ❖[8]	42	51.32 N	0.03 E
New Hamburg, On., Can.	212	43.23 N	80.42 W
New Hamburg, N.Y., U.S.	210	41.35 N	73.57 W
New Hampshire	216	40.33 N	83.57 W
New Hampshire □[3], U.S.	178	43.35 N	71.40 W
New Hampshire □[3], U.S.	188	43.35 N	71.40 W
New Hampton, Ia., U.S.	190	43.03 N	92.19 W
New Hampton, N.Y., U.S.	210	41.25 N	74.24 W
New Hanover, S. Afr.	158	29.28 S	30.28 E
New Hanover, Il., U.S.	219	38.23 N	90.13 W
New Hanover I	164	2.30 S	150.15 E
New Harmony	194	38.07 N	87.56 W
New Hartford, Ct., U.S.	207	41.52 N	72.58 W
New Hartford, Ia., U.S.	190	42.34 N	92.37 W
New Hartford, Mo., U.S.	219	39.12 N	91.16 W
New Hartford, N.Y., U.S.	210	43.04 N	75.18 W
Newhaven, Eng., U.K.	42	50.47 N	0.03 E
New Haven, Ct., U.S.	207	41.18 N	72.56 W
New Haven, Il., U.S.	194	37.54 N	88.07 W
New Haven, In., U.S.	216	41.04 N	85.00 W
New Haven, Ky., U.S.	194	37.39 N	85.35 W
New Haven, Mi., U.S.	214	42.43 N	82.48 W
New Haven, Mo., U.S.	219	38.36 N	91.13 W
New Haven, N.Y., U.S.	212	43.29 N	76.19 W
New Haven, Oh., U.S.	214	41.02 N	82.41 W
New Haven, W.V., U.S.	188	38.59 N	81.58 W
New Haven □[6]	207	41.18 N	72.56 W
New Hazelton	182	55.15 N	127.35 W
New Hebrides II	175f	16.00 S	167.00 E
New Hebrides Trench ✣[1]	14	22.30 S	170.00 E
New Hebrides → Vanuatu □[1]	175f	16.00 S	167.00 E
Newhebron	194	31.44 N	89.58 W
New Hempstead	276	41.08 N	74.03 W
New Hey	262	53.36 N	2.06 W
New Hogan Lake ⊜[1]	226	38.09 N	120.48 W
New Holland, Eng., U.K.	44	53.42 N	0.22 W
New Holland, Il., U.S.	219	40.11 N	89.36 W
New Holland, Oh., U.S.	218	39.33 N	83.15 W
New Holland, Pa., U.S.	208	40.06 N	76.05 W
New Holstein	190	43.57 N	88.05 W
New Hope, Al., U.S.	194	34.32 N	86.23 W
New Hope, Pa., U.S.	208	40.21 N	74.57 W
New Hudson	281	42.30 N	83.36 W
New Hyde Park	276	40.44 N	73.41 W
New Hythe	260	51.19 N	0.27 E
New Iberia	194	30.00 N	91.49 W
Newick	42	50.58 N	0.01 E
Newington, On., Can.	206	45.07 N	75.01 W
Newington, Eng., U.K.	42	51.05 N	1.08 E
Newington, Eng., U.K.	260	51.21 N	0.40 E
Newington, Ct., U.S.	207	41.42 N	72.43 W
Newinn	48	52.26 N	7.53 W
New Ipswich	207	42.44 N	71.51 W
New Ireland □[5]	164	3.00 S	151.30 E
New Ireland I	164	3.20 S	152.00 E
New Island I	126	21.31 N	88.12 E
New Jersey □[3], U.S.	178	40.15 N	74.30 W
New Jersey □[3], U.S.	188	40.15 N	74.30 W
New Jersey Institute of Technology ᵿ[2]	276	40.45 N	74.11 W
New Johnsonville	194	36.01 N	87.58 W
New Kensington	214	40.34 N	79.45 W
New Kent	208	37.31 N	76.58 W
New Kent □[6]	208	37.30 N	77.00 W
New Kingstown	208	40.13 N	77.07 W
Newkirk	196	36.52 N	97.03 W
Newkirk Estates	285	39.42 N	75.36 W
New Knoxville	216	40.29 N	84.18 W
New Kowloon (Xinjiulong)	271d	22.20 N	114.10 E
New Lagos ❖[8]	273a	6.30 N	3.22 E
New Lake ⊜	192	35.38 N	76.20 W
Newland	192	36.05 N	81.55 W
Newland Head >	168b	35.39 S	138.31 E
Newland Range ⋏	162	27.53 S	123.58 E
Newlands	166	21.11 S	147.54 E
Newlands ❖[8]	273d	26.11 S	27.58 E
New Lane	262	53.37 N	2.52 W
New Lebanon, N.Y., U.S.	210	42.27 N	73.23 W
New Lebanon, Oh., U.S.	218	39.45 N	84.23 W
New Lebanon, Pa., U.S.	214	41.25 N	80.04 W
New Lebanon Center	210	42.28 N	73.25 W
New Leipzig	198	46.22 N	101.56 W
New Lenox	216	41.30 N	87.57 W
New Lexington	188	39.42 N	82.12 W
New Liberty	218	38.36 N	84.54 W
New Lisbon	190	43.52 N	90.09 W
New Liskeard	190	47.30 N	79.40 W
Newllano	194	31.06 N	93.16 W
New London, Ct., U.S.	207	41.21 N	72.07 W
New London, Ia., U.S.	190	40.55 N	91.23 W
New London, Mn., U.S.	198	45.18 N	94.56 W
New London, Mo., U.S.	219	39.35 N	91.24 W
New London, N.H., U.S.	188	43.24 N	71.59 W
New London, Oh., U.S.	214	41.05 N	82.24 W
New London, Pa., U.S.	208	39.47 N	75.52 W
New London, Tx., U.S.	222	32.15 N	94.56 W
New London, Wi., U.S.	190	44.23 N	88.44 W
New London □[6]	207	41.21 N	72.07 W
New London Submarine Base ■	207	41.24 N	72.05 W
New Longton	262	53.44 N	2.45 W
Newlonsburg	279b	40.25 N	79.40 W
New Lyme	214	41.36 N	80.47 W
Newlyn, Austl.	169	37.25 S	143.59 E
Newlyn, Eng., U.K.	42	50.06 N	5.33 W
Newlyn East	42	50.22 N	5.03 W
Newmachar	46	57.16 N	2.11 W
New Machavie	158	26.48 S	26.57 E
New Madison	218	39.58 N	84.42 W
New Madrid	194	36.35 N	89.31 W
Newmains	44	55.47 N	3.53 W
Newman, Austl.	162	23.20 S	119.46 E
Newman, Ca., U.S.	226	37.18 N	121.01 W
Newman, Il., U.S.	194	39.47 N	87.59 W
Newman, Mount ∧	162	23.16 S	119.33 E
New Manchester	214	40.31 N	80.34 W
Newman Grove	198	41.45 N	97.46 W
Newmanstown	208	40.20 N	76.12 W
Newmansville	219	40.00 N	90.01 W
New Marion	218	39.00 N	85.22 W
Newmarket, Austl.	171a	27.25 S	153.01 E
Newmarket, On., Can.	212	44.03 N	79.28 W
Newmarket, Ire.	48	52.13 N	9.00 W
Newmarket, S. Afr.	273d	26.17 S	28.08 E
Newmarket, Eng., U.K.	42	52.15 N	0.25 E
New Market, Al., U.S.	194	34.54 N	86.25 W
New Market, Ia., U.S.	198	40.43 N	94.53 W
New Market, Md., U.S.	208	39.22 N	77.16 W
Newmarket, N.H., U.S.	188	43.04 N	70.56 W
New Market, N.J., U.S.	276	40.34 N	74.27 W
New Market, Va., U.S.	188	38.39 N	78.40 W
Newmarket on Fergus	48	52.45 N	8.53 W
Newmarket Race Course ♦	273d	26.17 S	28.08 E
New Marske	44	54.34 N	1.02 W
New Martinsville	188	39.38 N	80.51 W
New Meadows	202	44.58 N	116.16 W
New Melle	219	38.42 N	90.52 W
New Melones Lake ⊜[1]	226	38.00 N	120.32 W
New Memphis	219	38.29 N	89.41 W
New Mexico □[3]	178	34.30 N	106.00 W
New Miami	218	39.26 N	84.32 W
New Middletown	214	40.58 N	80.34 W
New Milford, Ct., U.S.	207	41.34 N	73.24 W
New Milford, Il., U.S.	216	42.11 N	89.04 W
New Milford, N.J., U.S.	276	40.56 N	74.01 W
New Milford, Pa., U.S.	210	41.52 N	75.43 W
New Millpond ⊜	276	40.50 N	73.13 W
New Millport	214	40.54 N	78.32 W
New Mills	44	53.23 N	2.00 W
Newmilns	46	55.37 N	4.20 W
New Milton	42	50.44 N	1.40 W
New Minden	219	38.26 N	89.22 W
New Munster	216	42.34 N	88.13 W
Newnan	192	33.22 N	84.47 W
Newnans Lake ⊜	192	29.39 N	82.13 W
Newnham	42	51.49 N	2.27 W
New Norcia	162	30.58 S	116.13 E
New Norfolk	166	42.47 S	147.03 E
New Norway	182	52.53 N	112.58 W
New Orleans	194	29.57 N	90.04 W
New Orleans Naval Air Station ■	194	29.51 N	90.01 W
New Oxford	208	39.51 N	77.03 W
New Palestine	218	39.43 N	85.53 W
New Paltz	210	41.44 N	74.05 W
New Paris, In., U.S.	216	41.30 N	85.49 W
New Paris, Oh., U.S.	218	39.51 N	84.47 W
New Paris, Pa., U.S.	214	40.06 N	78.39 W
New Philadelphia, Oh., U.S.	214	40.30 N	81.27 W
New Philadelphia, Pa., U.S.	208	40.43 N	76.06 W
New Pine Creek	202	41.59 N	120.17 W

≃	River	Fluß	Río	Rivière	Rio
≅	Canal	Kanal	Canal	Canal	Canal
↳	Waterfall, Rapids	Wasserfall, Stromschnellen	Cascada, Rápidos	Chute d'eau, Rapides	Cascata, Rápidos
ʉ	Strait	Meeresstraße	Estrecho	Détroit	Estreito
⊂	Bay, Gulf	Bucht, Golf	Bahía, Golfo	Baie, Golfe	Baía, Golfo
⊜	Lake, Lakes	See, Seen	Lago, Lagos	Lac, Lacs	Lago, Lagos
≡	Swamp	Sumpf	Pantano	Marais	Pântano
⊟	Ice Features, Glacier	Eis- und Gletscherformen	Accidentes Glaciales	Formes glaciaires	Acidentes glaciares
⊤	Other Hydrographic Features	Andere Hydrographische Objekte	Otros Elementos Hidrográficos	Autres données hydrographiques	Outros acidentes hidrográficos
✣	Submarine Features	Untermeerische Objekte	Accidentes Submarinos	Formes de relief sous-marin	Acidentes submarinos
□	Political Unit	Politische Einheit	Unidad Politica	Entité politique	Unidade política
ᵿ	Cultural Institution	Kulturelle Institution	Institución Cultural	Institution culturelle	Instituição cultural
⊥	Historical Site	Historische Stätte	Sitio Histórico	Site historique	Sitio histórico
♦	Recreational Site	Erholungs- und Ferienort	Sitio de Recreo	Centre de loisirs	Area de Lazer
⊠	Airport	Flughafen	Aeropuerto	Aéroport	Aeroporto
■	Military Installation	Militäranlage	Instalación Militar	Installation militaire	Instalação militar
❖	Miscellaneous	Verschiedenes	Misceláneo	Divers	Diversos

ENGLISH / DEUTSCH

Name / Name	Page / Seite	Lat.°′ / Breite°′	Long.°′ / Länge°′ E = Ost
New Pitsligo	46	57.35 N	2.11 W
New Pittsburg	214	40.50 N	82.06 W
New Plymouth, N.Z.	172	39.04 S	174.05 E
New Plymouth, Id., U.S.	202	43.58 N	116.49 W
New Point	218	39.18 N	85.19 W
New Point Comfort ›	208	37.18 N	76.17 W
Newport, Austl.	274a	33.40 S	151.19 E
Newport, Austl.	274b	37.51 S	144.53 E
Newport, P.Q., Can.	186	48.16 N	64.45 W
Newport, Ire.	48	52.42 N	8.24 W
Newport, Ire.	48	53.53 N	9.34 W
Newport, Eng., U.K.	42	50.42 N	1.18 W
Newport, Eng., U.K.	42	52.47 N	2.22 W
Newport, Eng., U.K.	42	51.59 N	0.15 E
Newport, Wales, U.K.	42	52.01 N	4.51 W
Newport, Wales, U.K.	42	51.35 N	3.00 W
Newport, Ar., U.S.	194	35.36 N	91.16 W
Newport, De., U.S.	208	39.42 N	75.36 W
Newport, In., U.S.	194	39.53 N	87.24 W
Newport, Ky., U.S.	218	39.05 N	84.29 W
Newport, Me., U.S.	188	44.50 N	69.16 W
Newport, Md., U.S.	208	38.25 N	76.54 W
Newport, Mi., U.S.	216	42.00 N	83.18 W
Newport, N.H., U.S.	188	43.21 N	72.10 W
Newport, N.J., U.S.	208	39.17 N	75.10 W
Newport, N.Y., U.S.	210	43.11 N	75.00 W
Newport, N.C., U.S.	192	34.47 N	76.51 W
Newport, Oh., U.S.	216	39.23 N	81.13 W
Newport, Or., U.S.	202	44.38 N	124.03 W
Newport, Pa., U.S.	208	40.28 N	77.07 W
Newport, R.I., U.S.	207	41.29 N	71.18 W
Newport, Tn., U.S.	192	35.58 N	83.11 W
Newport, Vt., U.S.	206	44.56 N	72.12 W
Newport, Wa., U.S.	202	48.11 N	117.02 W
Newport □[6]	207	41.35 N	71.15 W
Newport Bay ⊂	208	38.14 N	75.13 W
Newport Beach	228	33.37 N	117.55 W
Newport Center	206	44.57 N	72.18 W
Newport Hills	224	47.32 N	122.10 W
Newport News	208	36.58 N	76.25 W
Newport-on-Tay	46	56.26 N	2.55 W
Newport Pagnell	42	52.05 N	0.44 W
New Port Richey	220	28.14 N	82.43 W
Newportville	285	40.09 N	74.53 W
Newportville Terrace	285	40.07 N	74.54 W
New Prague	190	44.32 N	93.34 W
New Preston	207	41.40 N	73.21 W
New Providence, N.J., U.S.	210	40.41 N	74.24 W
New Providence, Pa., U.S.	208	39.56 N	76.12 W
New Providence, Tn., U.S.	194	36.32 N	87.23 W
New Providence I	240b	25.02 N	77.24 W
Newquay, Eng., U.K.	42	50.25 N	5.05 W
New Quay, Wales, U.K.	42	52.13 N	4.22 W
New Redruth	273d	26.16 S	28.07 E
New Richland	190	43.53 N	93.29 W
New-Richmond, P.Q., Can.	186	48.10 N	65.52 W
New Richmond, Oh., U.S.	218	38.56 N	84.16 W
New Richmond, Wi., U.S.	190	45.07 N	92.32 W
New Riegel	214	41.03 N	83.19 W
New Rim Ditch ≍	228	35.08 N	118.58 W
New Ringgold	208	40.41 N	76.00 W
New Road	186	44.45 N	63.28 W
New Roads	194	30.42 N	91.26 W
New Rochelle	210	40.54 N	73.46 W
New Rockford	198	47.40 N	99.08 W
New Romney	42	50.59 N	0.57 E
New Ross, N.S., Can.	186	44.44 N	64.27 W
New Ross, Ire.	48	52.24 N	6.56 W
New Rossington	44	53.29 N	1.04 W
Newry, N. Ire., U.K.	48	54.11 N	6.20 W
Newry, Pa., U.S.	214	40.24 N	78.26 W
Newry, S.C., U.S.	192	34.43 N	82.54 W
New Salem, In., U.S.	218	39.32 N	85.22 W
New Salem, N.D., U.S.	198	46.50 N	101.24 W
New Salisbury	218	38.19 N	86.06 W
New Sarum → Salisbury	42	51.05 N	1.48 W
New Schwabenland ◆[1]	9	72.30 S	1.00 E
New Scone	46	56.25 N	3.24 W
Newsham Park ♠	262	53.25 N	2.56 W
New Sharon	190	41.28 N	92.39 W
New Sheffield	214	40.36 N	80.17 W
New Shrewsbury	276	40.19 N	74.04 W
New Siberian Islands → Novosibirskoje ostrova II	74	75.00 N	142.00 E
New Smyrna Beach	220	29.01 N	80.55 W
Newsome	222	32.59 N	95.08 W
Newsoms	208	36.37 N	77.07 W
New South Wales □[3]	166	33.00 S	146.00 E
New South Wales, University of ʊ[2]	274a	33.55 S	151.14 E
New South Wales Lawn Tennis Association Courts ♠	274a	33.53 S	151.14 E
New Springfield	214	40.55 N	80.36 W
New Square	276	41.08 N	74.02 W
New Stanton	214	40.13 N	79.37 W
Newstead	169	37.07 S	144.04 E
New Stuyahok	180	59.29 N	157.20 W
New Suffolk	207	41.00 N	72.28 W
New Summerfield	222	31.59 N	95.06 W
New Tazewell	192	36.27 N	83.33 W
New Terrell City Lake ⊜[1]	222	32.44 N	96.14 W
New Territories □[8]	271d	22.24 N	114.10 E
New Thunderchild Indian Reserve ◆[4]	184	53.30 N	108.50 W
Newtok	180	60.56 N	164.38 W
Newton, Eng., U.K.	44	53.57 N	2.27 W
Newton, Eng., U.K.	262	53.16 N	2.43 W
Newton, Ga., U.S.	192	31.18 N	84.20 W
Newton, Il., U.S.	194	38.59 N	88.09 W
Newton, Ia., U.S.	190	41.41 N	93.02 W
Newton, Ks., U.S.	198	38.02 N	97.20 W
Newton, Ma., U.S.	207	42.20 N	71.12 W
Newton, Ms., U.S.	194	32.19 N	89.09 W
Newton, N.J., U.S.	210	41.03 N	74.45 W
Newton, N.C., U.S.	192	35.40 N	81.13 W
Newton, Tx., U.S.	194	30.50 N	93.45 W
Newton □[6]	216	40.46 N	87.27 W
Newton Abbot	42	50.32 N	3.36 W
Newton Arlosh	44	54.53 N	3.15 W
Newton Aycliffe	44	54.36 N	1.32 W
Newton Brook ◆[8]	275b	43.48 N	79.24 W
Newton Center	283	42.20 N	71.12 W
Newton Falls, N.Y., U.S.	188	44.12 N	74.59 W
Newton Falls, Oh., U.S.	214	41.11 N	80.58 W
Newton Ferrers	42	50.18 N	4.02 W
Newton Flotman	42	52.32 N	1.16 E
Newton Hamilton	214	40.24 N	77.51 W
Newton Highlands	283	42.19 N	71.13 W
Newton-le-Willows	44	53.28 N	2.37 W
Newton Longville	42	51.58 N	0.46 W
Newton Lower Falls	283	42.19 N	71.23 W
Newtonmore	46	57.04 N	4.08 W
Newton Stewart	44	54.57 N	4.29 W
Newtonsville	218	39.11 N	84.05 W
Newton Upper Falls	283	42.19 N	71.13 W
Newtonville, On., Can.	212	43.56 N	78.30 W
Newtonville, Ma., U.S.	283	42.21 N	71.13 W
Newtonville, N.J., U.S.	208	39.33 N	74.51 W
New Toronto ◆[8]	275b	43.36 N	79.30 W
Newtown, Austl.	169	38.09 S	144.20 E
Newtown, Nf., Can.	186	49.12 N	53.31 W
Newtown, Eng., U.K.	262	53.21 N	2.00 W
Newtown, Wales, U.K.	42	52.32 N	3.19 W
Newtown, Ct., U.S.	207	41.24 N	73.18 W
Newtown, In., U.S.	216	40.12 N	87.08 W
Newtown, Ky., U.S.	218	38.13 N	84.57 W
New Town, N.D., U.S.	198	47.58 N	102.29 W
Newtown, Pa., U.S.	208	40.14 N	74.56 W
Newtown ◆[8]	274a	33.54 S	151.11 E
Newtownabbey	48	54.42 N	5.54 W
Newtownards	48	54.36 N	5.41 W
Newtownbutler	48	54.12 N	7.23 W
Newtown Creek ≃, N.Y., U.S.	276	40.44 N	73.58 W
Newtown Creek ≃, Pa., U.S.	285	40.13 N	74.56 W
Newtown Crommelin	48	54.59 N	6.13 W
Newtown Forbes	48	53.46 N	7.50 W
Newtownhamilton	48	54.12 N	6.35 W
Newtown Mount Kennedy	48	53.05 N	6.07 W
Newtown Saint Boswells	46	55.34 N	2.40 W
Newtown Square	208	39.59 N	75.24 W
Newtownstewart	48	54.43 N	7.24 W
New Tredegar	42	51.43 N	3.14 W
New Tripoli	208	40.41 N	75.45 W
New Troy	216	41.53 N	86.33 W
New Truxton	219	38.58 N	91.15 W
New Ulm, Mn., U.S.	190	44.18 N	94.27 W
New Ulm, Tx., U.S.	222	29.53 N	96.29 W
New Utrecht ◆[8]	276	40.36 N	73.59 W
New Vernon	276	40.45 N	74.30 W
New Vienna	218	39.19 N	83.41 W
Newville, In., U.S.	216	41.21 N	84.51 W
Newville, Pa., U.S.	208	40.10 N	77.23 W
New Vineyard	188	44.48 N	70.07 W
New Waltham	44	53.32 N	0.04 W
New Washington, Pil.	116	11.39 N	122.26 E
New Washington, In., U.S.	218	38.33 N	85.32 W
New Washington, Oh., U.S.	214	40.57 N	82.51 W
New Waterford, N.S., Can.	186	46.15 N	60.05 W
New Waterford, Oh., U.S.	214	40.50 N	80.36 W
New Waverly, In., U.S.	216	40.46 N	86.12 W
New Waverly, Tx., U.S.	222	30.32 N	95.29 W
New Westminster	224	49.12 N	122.55 W
New Whiteland	218	39.33 N	86.05 W
New Wilmington	214	41.07 N	80.19 W
New Windsor, Md., U.S.	208	39.32 N	77.06 W
New Windsor, N.Y., U.S.	210	41.30 N	74.01 W
New Windsor → Windsor	42	51.29 N	0.38 W
New Woodbine Racetrack ♠	275b	43.43 N	79.36 W
New Woodstock	210	42.50 N	75.51 W
New World Island I	186	49.35 N	54.40 W
New Year Creek ≃	222	30.08 N	96.12 W
New York, N.Y., U.S.	210	40.43 N	74.01 W
New York, N.Y., U.S.	276	40.43 N	74.01 W
New York □[6]	276	40.47 N	73.58 W
New York □[3], U.S.	178	43.00 N	75.00 W
New York □[3], U.S.	188	43.00 N	75.00 W
New York, City College of ʊ[2]	276	40.49 N	73.57 W
New York, Polytechnic Institute of ʊ[2]	276	40.42 N	73.59 W
New York, State University of (Stony Brook) ʊ[2], N.Y., U.S.	276	40.55 N	73.08 W
New York, State University of (Buffalo) ʊ[2], N.Y., U.S.	284a	42.57 N	78.49 W
New York, State University of, College at Buffalo ʊ[2]	284a	42.56 N	78.53 W
New York at Buffalo, State University of ʊ[2]	284a	42.56 N	78.49 W
New York Mills, Mn., U.S.	198	46.31 N	95.22 W
New York Mills, N.Y., U.S.	210	43.06 N	75.18 W
New York State Barge Canal ≍	210	43.05 N	78.43 W
New York Stock Exchange ʊ	276	40.42 N	74.01 W
New Zealand □[1]	172	41.00 S	174.00 E
Nexapa ≃	234	18.07 N	98.46 W
Nexon	32	45.41 N	1.11 E
Ney	216	41.23 N	84.32 W
Neyagawa	96	34.46 N	135.38 E
Neye	263	51.07 N	7.22 E
Neyestausee ⊜[1]	263	51.08 N	7.24 E
Ney Lake ⊜	184	54.38 N	92.25 W
Neyland	42	51.43 N	4.57 W
Neylandville	222	33.12 N	96.00 W
Neyrīz	128	29.12 N	54.19 E
Neyshābūr	128	36.12 N	58.50 E
Neyyāttinkara	122	8.24 N	77.05 E
Nezahualcóyotl	234	19.27 N	99.03 W
Nezahualcóyotl, Presa ⊜[1]	234	17.10 N	93.40 W
Nezamajevskaja	78	46.09 N	40.16 E
Nezameno-toko ♠	94	35.46 N	137.42 E
Nežárka ≃	61	49.11 N	14.41 E
Nezavertajlovka	78	46.37 N	29.56 E
Nežin	78	51.03 N	31.54 E
Nezlobnaja	84	44.08 N	43.23 E
Neznanka ≃	265b	55.34 N	37.21 E
Neznanovo	80	54.02 N	40.06 E
Nezperce	202	46.14 N	116.14 W
Nez Perce Indian Reservation ◆[4]	202	46.20 N	116.30 W
Nez Perce National Historical Park ♠	202	45.50 N	116.15 W
Nezpique, Bayou ≃	194	30.12 N	92.35 W
Nezvěstice	60	49.39 N	13.32 E
Ngabang	112	0.23 N	109.57 E
Ngabé	152	3.12 S	16.11 E
Ngabordamlu, Tanjung ›	164	6.56 S	134.11 E
Ngadda ≃	146	12.40 N	13.50 E
Ngadirojo	115a	8.13 S	111.19 E
Ngadza	152	5.10 N	20.12 E
Ngahere	172	42.24 S	171.27 E
Ngala	146	12.20 N	14.10 E
Ngale	152	2.56 N	21.20 E
Ngali	152	2.27 S	19.20 E
Ngaliema, Baie de ⊂	273b	4.19 S	15.16 E
Ngalipaeng	112	3.24 N	125.37 E
Ngaloa Harbour ⊂	175g	19.06 S	178.11 E
Ngamaba	273b	4.14 S	15.16 E
Ngamba ◆[8]	273b	4.15 S	15.18 E
Ngambé	152	4.14 N	10.37 E
Ngamdu	146	11.48 N	12.18 E
Ngami, Lake ⊜	156	20.37 S	22.40 E
Ngamiland □[5]	156	19.09 S	22.47 E
Ngamo	154	19.08 S	27.32 E
Ngamouéri	273b	4.14 S	15.14 E
Ngamring	124	29.14 N	87.10 E
Nganda ∧	154	10.25 S	33.50 E
Ngangala	154	4.42 N	31.55 E
Ngangla Ringco ⊜	120	31.40 N	83.00 E
Nganglong Kangri ∧	120	32.45 N	81.12 E
Nganglong Kangri ⋏	120	32.00 N	83.00 E
Ngangzê Co ⊜	120	31.05 N	86.55 E
Nganjuk	115a	7.36 S	111.55 E
Ngao	110	18.46 N	99.59 E
Ngaoui, Mont ∧	152	6.40 N	14.57 E
Ngaoundéré	152	7.19 N	13.35 E
Ngapali	110	18.26 N	94.19 E
Ngapara	172	44.57 S	170.45 E
Ngape	110	20.04 N	94.38 E
Ngaputaw	110	16.32 N	94.42 E
Ngara	154	2.28 S	30.39 E
Ngaramasch	175b	6.54 N	134.08 E
Ngarimbi	154	8.28 S	38.36 E
Ngaruawahia	172	37.40 S	175.09 E
Ngaruroro ≃	172	39.34 S	176.56 E
Ngasamo	154	2.33 S	33.53 E
Ngat ≃	110	19.09 N	99.01 E
Ngatangiia	174k	21.14 S	159.43 W
Ngatangiia Harbour ⊂	174k	21.14 S	159.45 W
Ngatea	172	37.17 S	175.30 E
Ngathainggyaung	110	17.24 N	95.05 E
Ngatik I[1]	14	5.51 N	157.16 E
Ngau I	175g	18.02 S	179.18 E
Ngauruhoe, Mount ∧	172	39.09 S	175.38 E
Ngau Tau Kok → Kwun Tong	271d	22.19 N	114.12 E
Ngawen	115a	7.00 S	111.18 E
Ngawi	115a	7.24 S	111.26 E
Ngay Nua	110	21.50 N	101.54 E
Ngebel	115a	7.46 S	111.37 E
Ngele	152	0.29 S	20.25 E
Ngemelis Islands II	175b	7.07 N	134.15 E
Ngerengere	154	6.45 S	38.07 E
Ngerkeel	175b	7.25 N	134.30 E
Ngermechau	175b	7.35 N	134.39 E
Ngeruktabel I	175b	7.15 N	134.24 E
Ngetbong	175b	7.37 N	134.35 E
Ngetera	146	12.31 N	12.38 E
Nggamea Island I	175g	16.46 S	179.46 W
Nggatokae Island I	175e	8.46 S	158.11 E
Nggela Pile I	175e	9.05 S	160.15 E
Nggela Sule I	175e	9.05 S	160.15 E
Nggelelevu I	175g	16.05 S	179.09 W
Nggwavuma ≃	158	26.58 S	32.17 E
Nghia Dan	110	19.18 N	105.26 E
Nghia Hanh	110	15.03 N	108.47 E
Nghia Lo	110	21.36 N	104.31 E
Ngiap ≃	110	18.24 N	103.36 E
Ngidinga	152	5.37 S	15.17 E
Ngimbang	115a	7.17 S	112.12 E
Ng'iro ∧	154	2.08 N	36.51 E
Ngiro, Ewaso ≃, Kenya	154	2.04 S	36.07 E
Ng'iro, Ewaso ≃, Kenya	154	0.28 N	39.55 E
Ngo	152	2.29 S	15.45 E
Ngoangoa ≃	140	5.48 N	25.09 E
Ngoboli	154	4.57 N	32.37 E
Ngoko ≃, Afr.	152	1.40 N	16.03 E
Ngoko ≃, Congo	152	0.25 S	15.29 E
Ngol-Kedju Hill ∧[2]	152	6.20 N	9.45 E
Ngolo	146	9.56 N	22.16 E
Ngom ≃	102	31.11 N	97.15 E
Ngomahuru	154	20.26 S	30.43 E
Ngomba	154	8.23 S	32.53 E
Ngomba ∧	154	5.43 S	35.52 E
Ngombe, Zaïre	152	6.35 S	20.42 E
Ngombe, Zaïre	273b	4.24 S	15.11 E
Ngome	158	27.46 S	31.28 E
Ngomedzap	152	3.15 N	11.12 E
Ngomeni, Ras ›	154	2.59 S	40.14 E
Ngong	154	1.22 S	36.39 E
Ngongotaha	172	38.05 S	176.12 E
Ngono ≃	154	1.08 S	31.35 E
Ngonye Falls ⌊	152	16.40 S	23.35 E
Ngop	140	6.16 N	30.12 E
Ngora	154	1.27 N	33.46 E
Ngorengore	154	1.02 S	35.30 E
Ngoring Hu ⊜	102	34.50 N	97.35 E
Ngoro	115a	7.41 S	112.16 E
Ngorongoro Crater ⊥[6]	154	3.10 S	35.35 E
Ngote	154	2.14 N	30.48 E
Ngoto	152	4.00 N	17.21 E
Ngotwane ≃	156	23.35 S	26.58 E
Ngoulémakong	152	3.07 N	11.25 E
Ngouma	150	15.38 N	3.22 W
Ngounié □[4]	152	1.30 S	11.00 E
Ngounié ≃	152	0.37 S	10.18 E
Ngouri	146	13.38 N	15.22 E
Ngouroundou	152	6.27 N	22.37 E
Ngourti	146	15.19 N	13.12 E
Ngoywa	154	5.56 S	32.48 E
Ngozi	154	2.54 S	29.50 E
Ngqeleni	158	31.40 S	29.02 E
Ngudiabaka ≃	273b	4.25 S	15.11 E
Nguélémendouka	152	4.23 N	12.55 E
Ngugha ≃	156	19.21 S	23.15 E
Nguigmi	146	14.15 N	13.07 E
Nguila	152	4.43 N	11.41 E
Nguiu	164	11.45 S	130.38 E
Ngulu I[1]	108	8.27 N	137.29 E
Ngum ≃	110	18.09 N	103.06 E
Nguna, Île I	175f	17.26 S	168.21 E
Ngunga	154	3.41 S	33.34 E
Ngunju, Tanjung ›	115b	10.19 S	120.28 E
Ngunut	115a	8.06 S	112.01 E
Ngurore	146	9.18 N	12.14 E
Nguru	146	12.52 N	10.27 E
Ngwempisi ≃	158	26.42 S	31.26 E
Ngweni	158	27.56 S	32.15 E
Ngwenya ∧	158	26.11 S	31.02 E
Ngwerere	154	15.18 S	28.20 E
Ngweze ≃	154	17.40 S	25.07 E
Nha Be	269c	10.42 N	106.44 E
Nhabe ≃, Bots.	156	20.22 S	22.58 E
Nha Be ≃, Viet	269c	10.39 N	106.44 E
Nhacoongo	156	24.18 S	35.14 E
Nhamacolomo	156	18.05 S	34.26 E
Nhamundá	250	2.14 S	56.43 W
Nhamundá ≃	246	2.12 S	56.41 W
Nha Nam	110	21.27 N	106.06 E
Nhandeara	255	20.40 S	50.02 W
Nhareia	152	11.25 S	17.03 E
Nha Trang	110	12.15 N	109.11 E
Nhia ≃	152	10.15 S	14.12 E
Nhill	166	36.20 S	141.39 E
Nhlangano	158	27.06 S	31.12 E
Nhlazatshe	158	28.10 S	31.14 E
Nhoma ≃	156	18.52 S	20.53 E
Nhon Trach	269c	10.43 N	106.51 E
Nhulunbuy	164	12.11 S	136.47 E
Nhundo	152	14.25 S	21.23 E
Nhunguaçu	256	22.21 S	42.53 W
Niabembe	154	2.14 S	27.44 E
Niafounké	150	15.56 N	4.00 W
Niagara	190	45.46 N	87.59 W
Niagara □[6], On., Can.	212	43.05 N	79.20 W
Niagara □[6], N.Y., U.S.	210	43.10 N	78.42 W
Niagara ≃	212	43.15 N	79.04 W
Niagara County Historical Center ʊ	284a	43.10 N	78.43 W
Niagara Falls, On., Can.	212	43.06 N	79.04 W
Niagara Falls, On., Can.	284a	43.06 N	79.04 W
Niagara Falls, N.Y., U.S.	210	43.05 N	79.03 W
Niagara Falls, N.Y., U.S.	284a	43.05 N	79.03 W
Niagara Falls ⌊	212	43.05 N	79.04 W
Niagara Falls Airport ⊠	284a	43.02 N	79.08 W
Niagara Falls International Airport ⊠	284a	43.06 N	78.56 W
Niagara-on-the-Lake	212	43.15 N	79.04 W
Niagara University ʊ[2]	284a	43.08 N	79.02 W
Niagassola	150	12.19 N	9.07 W
Niah	112	3.52 N	113.44 E
Niakaramandougou	150	8.40 N	5.17 W
Niamey	150	13.31 N	2.07 E
Niamey □[5]	150	14.00 N	2.00 E
Niamtougou	150	9.46 N	1.06 E
Nianbadu	100	28.17 N	118.28 E
Niandan ≃	150	10.30 N	10.26 W
Niandan Koro	150	11.05 N	9.15 W
Nianforando	150	9.32 N	10.31 W
Niangara	154	3.42 N	27.52 E
Niangay, Lac ⊜	150	15.50 N	3.00 W
Niangmake	102	30.14 N	99.40 E
Niangnianggong	104	41.00 N	121.13 E
Niangniangmiao	98	42.34 N	118.05 E
Niangniangwa	105	40.33 N	117.30 E
Niangoloko	150	10.17 N	4.55 W
Niangua ≃	194	37.58 N	92.48 W
Niangzizhuang	105	40.02 N	118.05 E
Nia-Nia	154	1.24 N	27.36 E
Nianpan	104	41.48 N	124.02 E
Niantic, Ct., U.S.	207	41.19 N	72.11 W
Niantic, Il., U.S.	219	39.51 N	89.10 W
Nianyugou	104	42.00 N	123.59 E
Nianyushan	100	29.11 N	117.04 E
Nianzhuang	98	34.19 N	117.47 E
Nianzigang	100	31.03 N	114.18 E
Nianzishan	89	47.32 N	122.52 E
Niapu	154	2.25 N	26.28 E
Niari □[5]	152	3.15 S	12.30 E
Niari ≃	152	3.56 S	12.12 E
Niaro	140	10.38 N	31.31 E
Nias, Pulau I	114	1.05 N	97.35 E
Niassa □[5]	154	13.30 S	36.00 E
Niatupo	246	9.33 N	78.54 W
Nibbiano	62	44.54 N	9.19 E
Nibe	26	56.59 N	9.38 E
Nibong Tebal	114	5.10 N	100.29 E
Nibra	272b	22.36 N	88.16 E
Nīca	76	56.19 N	21.04 E
Nica ≃	86	57.29 N	64.33 E
Nicaea → İznik	130	40.26 N	29.43 E
Nicaragua □[1], N.A.	230	13.00 N	85.00 W
Nicaragua □[1], N.A.	236	13.00 N	85.00 W
Nicaragua, Lago de ⊜	236	11.30 N	85.30 W
Nicaro	240p	20.42 N	75.33 W
Nicastro	68	38.59 N	16.20 E
Ničatka, ozero ⊜	88	57.45 N	117.30 E
Nice	62	43.42 N	7.15 E
Nice-Côte d'Azur, Aéroport de ⊠	62	43.40 N	7.14 E
Niceville	194	30.31 N	86.28 W
Nichelino	62	44.59 N	7.38 E
Nicheng	106	30.55 N	121.49 E
Nichihara	96	34.33 N	131.50 E
Nichinan, Nihon	92	31.36 N	131.23 E
Nichinan, Nihon	96	35.09 N	133.16 E
Nicholas □[6]	218	38.20 N	84.02 W
Nicholas Channel ⊔	238	23.25 N	80.05 W
Nicholasville	192	37.52 N	84.34 W
Nicholls	192	31.31 N	82.38 W
Nicholl's Town	238	25.08 N	78.00 W
Nichols, Ca., U.S.	282	38.02 N	121.59 W
Nichols, Fl., U.S.	220	27.54 N	82.02 W
Nichols, N.Y., U.S.	210	42.01 N	76.22 W
Nichols Brook ≃	283	42.37 N	70.59 W
Nicholson, Austl.	162	18.02 S	128.54 E
Nicholson, Ky., U.S.	218	38.54 N	84.33 W
Nicholson, Ms., U.S.	194	30.28 N	89.41 W
Nicholson, Pa., U.S.	210	41.37 N	75.46 W
Nicholson ≃, Austl.	162	17.34 S	128.38 E
Nicholson ≃, Austl.	166	17.31 S	139.36 E
Nicholson Island I	212	43.56 N	77.31 W
Nicholson Range ⋏	162	27.15 S	116.45 E
Nicholson River Aboriginal Reserve ◆[4]	162	18.00 S	137.30 E
Nichols Run ≃	284b	39.03 N	77.18 W
Nickerie □[5]	250	5.40 N	56.50 W
Nickerie ≃	250	5.59 N	57.00 W
Nickerson	198	38.08 N	98.05 W
Nickol Bay ⊂	162	20.39 S	116.52 E
Nicktown	214	40.37 N	78.48 W
Nicobar Islands II	110	8.00 N	93.30 E
Nicola	182	50.10 N	120.40 W
Nicola ≃	182	50.25 N	121.18 W
Nicolae Bălcescu	38	47.34 N	26.52 E
Nicolai Mountain ∧	224	46.05 N	123.28 W
Nicola Lake ⊜	182	50.10 N	120.25 W
Nicola Mameet Indian Reserve ◆[4]	182	50.11 N	120.49 W
Nicolaus	226	38.54 N	121.35 W
Nicolet	206	46.13 N	72.37 W
Nicolet □[6]	206	46.15 N	72.20 W
Nicolet ≃	206	46.14 N	72.39 W
Nicolet, Lac ⊜	206	45.50 N	71.33 W
Nicolet, Lake ⊜	190	46.20 N	84.15 W
Nicolet Centre ≃	206	45.46 N	71.50 W
Nicolet Sud-Ouest ≃	206	46.13 N	72.36 W
Nicoll Bay ⊂	276	40.43 N	73.07 W
Nicollet	190	44.16 N	94.11 W
Nicoll Point ›	276	40.42 N	73.09 W
Nicolosi	70	37.37 N	15.01 E
Nicosia, It.	70	37.45 N	14.24 E
Nicosia (Levkosía), Kípros	130	35.10 N	33.22 E
Nicosia (Lefkoşa), Kıbrıs	130	35.10 N	33.22 E
Nicotera	68	38.34 N	15.57 E
Nicoya	236	10.09 N	85.27 W
Nicoya, Golfo de ⊂	236	9.47 N	84.48 W
Nicoya, Península de ›[1]	236	10.00 N	85.25 W
Nictheroy → Niterói	256	22.53 S	43.07 W
Nida ≃	30	50.18 N	20.52 E
Nidadavole	122	16.55 N	81.40 E
Nidau	58	47.07 N	7.14 E
Nidd ≃	44	54.01 N	1.12 W
Nidda	56	50.24 N	9.00 E
Nidda ≃	56	50.06 N	8.34 E
Nidder ≃	56	50.12 N	8.47 E
Nidderau	56	50.14 N	8.52 E
Nide	102	31.51 N	96.19 E
Nideggen	56	50.47 N	6.29 E
Nidelva ≃	26	58.24 N	8.48 E
Nidwalden □[3]	58	46.55 N	8.28 E
Nidž	84	40.56 N	47.41 E
Nidzica	30	53.22 N	20.26 E
Niebüll	41	54.48 N	8.50 E
Nied ≃	56	49.23 N	6.40 E
Nied Allemande ≃	56	49.10 N	6.26 E
Nieddu, Monte ∧	71	40.45 N	9.34 E
Niederanven	56	49.39 N	6.16 E
Niederau	54	51.10 N	13.32 E
Niederaula	56	50.48 N	9.36 E
Niederbayern □[5]	60	48.45 N	12.45 E
Niederbipp	58	47.16 N	7.39 E
Niederbobritzsch	54	50.54 N	13.26 E
Niederbonsfeld	263	51.23 N	7.08 E
Niederbronn-Les-Bains	56	48.57 N	7.38 E
Niederdonk	263	51.14 N	6.41 E
Niederelfringhausen	263	51.21 N	7.10 E
Niedere Tauern ⋏	30	47.18 N	14.00 E
Niederfinow	54	52.50 N	13.55 E
Niederfrohna	54	50.53 N	12.43 E
Niederhaverbeck	52	53.09 N	9.54 E
Niederheimbach	56	50.02 N	7.48 E
Niederhone	56	51.13 N	10.06 E
Niederkassel	56	50.49 N	7.02 E
Nieder-Kassel ◆[8]	263	51.14 N	6.45 E
Niederkrüchten	56	51.12 N	6.13 E
Niederlande → Netherlands □[1]	30	52.15 N	5.30 E
Niederländische Antillen → Netherlands Antilles □[2]	241s	12.15 N	69.00 W
Niederlausitz □[9]	54	51.40 N	14.15 E
Niederlehme	54	52.19 N	13.39 E
Niedermarsberg	56	51.28 N	8.50 E
Niedermarschacht	52	53.25 N	10.21 E
Nieder-Mörlen	56	50.23 N	8.43 E
Niederndodeleben	54	52.08 N	11.30 E
Nieder-Neuendorf	264a	52.37 N	13.12 E
Niedernhall	56	49.17 N	9.36 E
Niedernwöhren	52	52.21 N	9.08 E
Niederoderwitz	54	50.57 N	14.44 E
Nieder-Ohmen	56	50.38 N	9.02 E
Nieder-Olm	56	49.55 N	8.11 E
Niederorschel	54	51.22 N	10.25 E
Niederösterreich □[3]	61	48.20 N	15.50 E
Niedersachsen □[3]	30	52.40 N	9.00 E
Niedersachswerfen	54	51.33 N	10.46 E
Niederschöneweide ◆[8]	264a	52.27 N	13.31 E
Niederschönhausen ◆[8]	54	52.35 N	13.23 E
Niedersonthofen	58	47.38 N	10.13 E
Niederstetten	56	49.24 N	9.55 E
Niederstotzingen	56	48.32 N	10.14 E
Niedersulz	61	48.29 N	16.40 E
Niederurnen	58	47.07 N	9.03 E
Niederwald	58	46.26 N	8.12 E
Niederwalgern	56	50.44 N	8.41 E
Niederweningen	58	47.30 N	8.23 E
Niederwiesa	54	50.51 N	13.01 E
Niederwürschnitz	54	50.43 N	12.45 E
Nied Française ≃	56	49.10 N	6.26 E
Niedu	100	25.28 N	114.08 E
Niefang	152	1.50 N	10.14 E
Nieheim	52	51.48 N	9.06 E
Niekerkshoop	158	29.19 S	22.51 E
Niel	50	51.07 N	4.20 E
Niellé	150	10.12 N	5.38 W
Niellim	146	9.42 N	17.49 E
Niem	152	6.12 N	15.14 E
Niemba	154	5.57 S	28.26 E
Niemegk	54	52.04 N	12.41 E
Niemeyer ◆[8]	287a	23.00 S	43.15 W
Niemodlin	30	50.39 N	17.37 E
Niéna	150	11.26 N	6.21 W
Nienberge	52	52.00 N	7.34 E
Nienborg-Wigbold	52	52.08 N	7.06 E
Nienburg, Dtsch.	52	52.38 N	9.13 E
Nienburg, Dtsch.	54	51.50 N	11.46 E
Niendorf	54	53.59 N	10.50 E
Nienhagen, Dtsch.	52	52.33 N	10.05 E
Nienhagen, Dtsch.	54	51.57 N	11.09 E
Niénokoué, Mont ∧[2]	150	5.26 N	7.10 W
Niepkuhlen ≃	263	51.29 N	6.31 E
Niepołomice	30	50.03 N	20.13 E
Nieppe	50	50.42 N	2.50 E
Nier ≃	48	52.17 N	7.48 W
Niéré	146	14.30 N	21.09 E
Niéré, Hadjer ∧	146	14.21 N	21.40 E
Niéri Ko ≃	150	13.21 N	13.23 W
Niers ≃	52	51.43 N	5.57 E
Nierst	263	51.19 N	6.43 E
Nierstein	56	49.52 N	8.20 E
Niesen ∧	58	46.39 N	7.39 E
Niesky	54	51.17 N	14.49 E
Nieszawa	30	52.50 N	18.55 E
Nieto, Cañada de ≃	258	34.00 S	58.15 W
Nieu Bethesda	158	31.51 S	24.34 E
Nieuw-Amsterdam, Ned.	52	52.44 N	6.51 E
Nieuw Amsterdam, Sur.	250	5.53 N	55.05 W
Nieuw-Buinen	52	52.57 N	6.55 E
Nieuwefontein	158	28.01 S	19.06 E
Nieuwegein	52	52.03 N	5.05 E
Nieuwe-Niedorp	52	52.45 N	4.54 E
Nieuwe-Pekela	52	53.04 N	6.58 E
Nieuweschans	52	53.11 N	7.12 E
Nieuwkoop	52	52.08 N	4.47 E
Nieuw Nickerie	250	5.57 N	56.59 W
Nieuwolda	52	53.14 N	6.59 E
Nieuwoudtville	158	31.23 S	19.07 E
Nieuwpoort, Bel.	50	51.08 N	2.45 E
Nieuwpoort, Ned. Ant.	241s	12.03 N	68.49 W
Nieuwpoort-Bad	50	51.09 N	2.42 E
Nieuw-Schoonebeek	52	52.38 N	6.59 E
Nieuw-Vennep	52	52.16 N	4.38 E
Nieuw-Weerdinge	52	52.52 N	6.59 E
Nieva ≃	246	4.35 S	77.53 W
Nievenheim	56	51.07 N	6.46 E
Nievería	286d	11.59 S	76.55 W
Nièvre □[5]	32	47.05 N	3.30 E
Nièvre ≃	50	47.10 N	3.13 E
Niga	150	13.38 N	5.27 W
Nigan	126	23.30 N	87.59 E
Niğde	130	37.59 N	34.42 E
Niğde □[4]	130	38.15 N	34.15 E
Nigei Island I	182	50.55 N	127.50 W
Nigel	158	26.30 S	28.28 E
Niger □[3]	150	10.00 N	6.00 E
Niger □[1]	134	16.00 N	8.00 E
Niger ≃	150	5.33 N	6.33 E
Niger Delta ≚[2]	150	4.50 N	6.00 E
Nigeria □[1]	134	10.00 N	8.00 E
Nigerian Museum ʊ	273a	6.20 N	3.24 E
Nigg	46	57.43 N	4.00 W
Nighāsan	124	28.14 N	80.52 E
Nightcaps	172	45.58 S	168.02 E
Nighthawk	182	48.58 N	119.38 W
Night Hawk Lake ⊜	190	48.28 N	81.00 W
Nightingale Island I	10	37.24 S	12.28 W
Nightmute	180	60.29 N	164.43 W
Nigríta	38	40.55 N	23.30 E
Nihe	104	41.27 N	121.13 E
Nihing (Nahang) ≃	128	26.00 N	62.44 E
Nihoa I	14	23.06 N	161.58 W
Nihommatsu	92	37.35 N	140.26 E
Nihonbashi ◆[8]	268	35.41 N	139.47 E
Nihon → Japan □[1]	92	36.00 N	138.00 E
Nihon-kai → Japan, Sea of ∓[2]	90	40.00 N	135.00 E
Nihon University ʊ[2]	268	35.42 N	139.45 E
Nihtaur	124	29.20 N	78.23 E
Nihuil, Embalse del ⊜[1]	252	35.05 S	68.45 W
Niida ≃	96	33.11 N	132.58 E
Niigata	92	37.55 N	139.03 E
Niigata □[5]	94	37.08 N	138.30 E
Niihama	96	33.58 N	133.16 E
Niihari	94	36.07 N	140.09 E
Niiharu	94	36.41 N	138.55 E
Niihau I	229b	21.55 N	160.10 W
Nii-jima I	92	34.22 N	139.16 E
Niimi	96	34.59 N	133.28 E
Niinisalo	26	61.50 N	22.29 E
Niitsu	92	37.48 N	139.07 E
Niiza	94	35.48 N	139.34 E
Níjar	34	36.58 N	2.12 W
Nijiaqiao	269b	31.14 N	121.21 E
Nijil	132	30.31 N	35.33 E
Nijkerk	52	52.13 N	5.30 E
Nijlen	56	51.10 N	4.39 E
Nijmegen	52	51.50 N	5.50 E
Nijo Castle ⊥	270	35.01 N	135.45 E
Nijvel → Nivelles	50	50.36 N	4.20 E
Nijverdal	52	52.22 N	6.27 E
Níkaia	267c	37.58 N	23.39 E
Nikel'	24	69.24 N	30.12 E
Nikel'tau	86	50.23 N	58.13 E
Nikiforovo	265b	55.50 N	38.05 E
Nikiniki	112	9.49 S	124.28 E
Nikip Lake ⊜	184	52.53 N	91.53 W
Nikitovka, Ross.	78	50.23 N	38.25 E
Nikitovka, Ukr.	83	48.21 N	38.02 E
Nikitsch	61	47.32 N	16.40 E
Nikitskoje, Ross.	82	55.18 N	38.28 E
Nikitskoje, Ross.	82	55.13 N	35.46 E
Nikki	150	9.56 N	3.12 E
Nikkō	94	36.45 N	139.37 E
Nikkō-kokuritsu-kōen ♠	94	36.49 N	139.33 E
Niklā al-'Inab	142	30.55 N	30.46 E
Niklasdorf	61	47.24 N	15.10 E
Nikobaren → Nicobar Islands II	110	8.00 N	93.30 E
Nikolai	180	62.58 N	154.09 W
Nikolajev, Ukr.	78	49.32 N	23.58 E
Nikolajev, Ukr.	78	46.58 N	32.00 E
Nikolajevka, Kaz.	86	49.10 N	81.59 E
Nikolajevka, Ross.	80	46.21 N	47.44 E
Nikolajevka, Ross.	80	52.28 N	49.14 E
Nikolajevka, Ross.	80	52.11 N	48.04 E
Nikolajevka, Ross.	80	53.08 N	47.12 E
Nikolajevka, Ross.	83	47.18 N	38.50 E
Nikolajevka, Ross.	86	56.29 N	95.06 E
Nikolajevka, Ross.	86	54.57 N	75.44 E
Nikolajevka, Ross.	88	55.46 N	98.10 E
Nikolajevka, Ross.	89	48.34 N	134.47 E
Nikolajevka, Ukr.	78	47.38 N	33.12 E
Nikolajevka, Ukr.	78	47.06 N	34.14 E
Nikolajevka, Ukr.	78	44.58 N	33.37 E
Nikolajevka, Ukr.	78	46.23 N	29.24 E
Nikolajevka, Ukr.	78	47.33 N	30.25 E
Nikolajevka, Ukr.	78	51.04 N	34.02 E
Nikolajevka, Ukr.	83	48.46 N	38.20 E
Nikolajevka, Ukr.	83	47.39 N	37.41 E
Nikolajevka, Ukr.	83	48.51 N	37.46 E
Nikolajevo	76	58.16 N	29.29 E
Nikolajevo-Kozlovskij	83	47.13 N	38.21 E
Nikolajevsk	80	50.01 N	45.28 E
Nikolajevskaja	80	47.37 N	41.29 E
Nikolajevsk-Na-Amure	89	53.08 N	140.44 E
Nikolajevskoje, Ross.	78	45.08 N	39.36 E
Nikolajevskoje, Ross.	88	51.04 N	111.48 E
Nikolajevskoje, Ross.	88	52.21 N	117.00 E
Nikolassee ◆[8]	264a	52.26 N	13.12 E
Nikolayev → Nikolajev	78	46.58 N	32.00 E
Nikolo-Berezovec	76	58.38 N	42.17 E
Nikolo-Berjozovka	80	56.06 N	54.17 E
Nikolo-Chovanskoje	265b	55.36 N	37.27 E
Nikologory	80	56.09 N	41.59 E
Nikolo-Kropotki	82	56.44 N	37.55 E
Nikolo-L'vovsk	89	43.54 N	131.23 E
Nikolo-Makarovo	80	57.38 N	43.34 E
Nikolsdorf	64	46.47 N	12.55 E
Nikol'sk, Ross.	24	59.30 N	45.27 E
Nikol'sk, Ross.	80	53.45 N	46.05 E
Nikolski	180	52.56 N	168.52 W
Nikol'skij, Ross.	24	60.55 N	34.00 E
Nikol'skij, Ross.	86	56.18 N	68.58 E
Nikol'skij Toržok	76	59.53 N	38.46 E
Nikol'skoje, Ross.	74	55.12 N	166.00 E
Nikol'skoje, Ross.	76	52.39 N	36.04 E
Nikol'skoje, Ross.	76	55.26 N	35.04 E
Nikol'skoje, Ross.	76	59.23 N	44.36 E
Nikol'skoje, Ross.	76	59.30 N	42.32 E
Nikol'skoje, Ross.	78	50.35 N	41.10 E
Nikol'skoje, Ross.	80	52.37 N	43.49 E
Nikol'skoje, Ross.	80	47.46 N	46.24 E
Nikol'skoje, Ross.	82	55.15 N	36.04 E
Nikol'skoje, Ross.	82	56.09 N	36.43 E
Nikol'skoje, Ross.	82	55.53 N	36.26 E
Nikol'skoje, Ross.	82	54.51 N	35.53 E
Nikol'skoje, Ross.	82	54.27 N	36.24 E
Nikol'skoje, Ross.	82	54.30 N	36.50 E
Nikol'skoje, Ross.	82	54.03 N	37.10 E
Nikol'skoje, Ross.	82	54.18 N	35.53 E
Nikol'skoje, Ross.	82	55.37 N	36.41 E
Nikol'skoje, Ross.	86	57.12 N	84.21 E
Nikol'skoje, Ross.	86	52.02 N	55.43 E
Nikol'skoje, Ross.	265a	59.41 N	30.47 E
Nikol'skoje, Ross.	265b	55.46 N	37.54 E
Nikol'skoje, Ukr.	83	47.46 N	37.18 E
Nikol'skoje-na-Čeremšane	80	54.03 N	49.14 E
Nikol'skoje-na-Dnepre	78	48.12 N	35.12 E
Nikol'skoje-Ur'upino	265b	55.48 N	37.13 E
Nikonga ≃	154	4.40 S	31.28 E
Nikonorovka	83	49.07 N	39.59 E
Nikonova Gora	76	60.22 N	36.07 E
Nikonovskoje	82	55.17 N	38.10 E
Nikopol, Blg.	38	43.42 N	24.54 E
Nikopol', Ukr.	78	47.35 N	34.25 E
Niksar	130	40.36 N	36.58 E
Nīkshahr	128	26.13 N	60.12 E
Nikšić	38	42.46 N	18.56 E
Nikulino, Ross.	76	55.16 N	33.46 E
Nikulino, Ross.	80	58.05 N	44.14 E
Nikulino, Ross.	82	56.48 N	35.50 E
Nikulino ◆[8]	265b	55.40 N	37.28 E
Nikulkino	82	56.07 N	38.38 E
Nikul'skoje	82	55.10 N	38.41 E
Nikumaroro I[1]	14	4.40 S	174.32 W
Nikunau I	14	1.23 S	176.26 E
Nīl, Nahr an- → Nile ≃	140	30.10 N	31.06 E
Nila, Pulau I	164	6.44 S	129.31 E
Nilakka ⊜	26	63.07 N	26.33 E
Niland	204	33.14 N	115.31 W
Nil Blanc → White Nile ≃	140	15.38 N	32.31 E
Nile □[5]	154	3.00 N	31.30 E
Nile (Nahr an-Nīl) ≃	140	30.10 N	31.06 E
Niles, Il., U.S.	216	42.01 N	87.48 W
Niles, Mi., U.S.	216	41.49 N	86.15 W
Niles, Oh., U.S.	214	41.10 N	80.45 W
Niles Pond ⊜	283	42.35 N	70.40 W
Nilgani	272b	22.46 N	88.26 E
Nilgaut, Lac ⊜	190	46.36 N	77.15 W
Nīlgiri	126	21.28 N	86.46 E
Nilka	86	43.47 N	82.20 E
Nilkitkwa ≃	182	55.27 N	126.43 W
Nillahcootie, Lake ⊜[1]	169	36.54 S	146.00 E
Nil → Nile ≃	140	30.10 N	31.06 E
Nilo Azul → Blue Nile ≃	140	15.38 N	32.31 E
Nilo Blanco → White Nile ≃	140	15.38 N	32.31 E
Nilo → Nile ≃	140	30.10 N	31.06 E
Nilópolis	256	22.49 S	43.25 W
Nilópolis □[7]	287a	22.49 S	43.26 W
Nilphāmāri	124	25.56 N	88.51 E
Nilsiä	26	63.12 N	28.05 E
Niltepec	234	16.34 N	94.37 W
Nilüfer ≃	130	40.18 N	28.27 E
Nīlwāl ◆[8]	272a	28.40 N	76.59 E
Nilwood	219	39.24 N	89.49 W
Nima	96	35.09 N	132.24 E
Nīmach	120	24.28 N	74.52 E
Niman ≃	89	51.24 N	132.45 E
Nimančik	89	52.09 N	133.47 E
Nimba, Mount ∧	150	7.37 N	8.25 W
Nimbāhera	120	24.37 N	74.41 E
Nimba Range ⋏	150	7.30 N	8.30 W
Nimboran, Pegunungan ⋏	164	2.45 S	140.20 E
Nimelen ≃	89	52.27 N	136.32 E
Nîmes	62	43.50 N	4.21 E
Nimis	64	46.12 N	13.16 E
Nimishillen Creek ≃	214	40.38 N	81.22 W
Nimisila	214	40.56 N	81.34 W
Nimisila Reservoir ⊜[1]	214	40.57 N	81.31 W
Nīm Ka Thāna	120	27.44 N	75.48 E
Nimmitabel	166	36.31 S	149.16 E
Nimmonsburg	210	42.09 N	75.55 W
Nimpkish Lake ⊜	182	50.25 N	126.59 W
Nimrod Lake ⊜[1]	194	34.55 N	93.20 W
Nīmrūz □[4]	128	30.30 N	62.00 E
Nims ≃	56	49.51 N	6.28 E
Nimta	272b	22.40 N	88.25 E
Nimule	154	3.36 N	32.03 E
Nimule National Park ♠	154	3.50 N	31.35 E
Nimy	50	50.28 N	3.57 E
Niña Bonita, Presa ⊜[1]	286b	23.02 N	82.29 W
Nīnah, Wādī V	146	30.02 N	15.22 E
Nīnawā □[4]	128	36.10 N	42.35 E
Nīnawá (Nineveh) ⊥	128	36.25 N	43.10 E

Symbols in the index entries represent the broad categories identified in the key at the right. Symbols with superior numbers (⋏[1]) identify subcategories (see complete key on page *I · 1).*

Symbole im Register stellen die rechts im Schlüssel erklärten Kategorien dar. Symbole mit hochgestellten Ziffern (⋏[1]) bezeichnen Unterabteilungen einer Kategorie (vgl. vollständiger Schlüssel auf Seite *I · 1).*

Los símbolos incluídos en el texto del índice representan las grandes categorias identificadas con la clave a la derecha. Los símbolos con numeros en su parte superior (⋏[1]) identifican las subcategorías (véase la clave completa en la página *I · 1).*

Les symboles de l'index représentent les catégories indiquées dans la légende à droite. Les symboles suivis d'un indice (⋏[1]) représentent des sous-catégories (voir légende complète à la page *I · 1).*

Os símbolos incluídos no texto do índice representam as grandes categorias identificadas com a chave à direita. Os símbolos com números em sua parte superior (⋏[1]) identificam as subcategorias (veja-se a chave completa à página *I · 1).*

∧ Mountain	Berg	Montaña	Montagne	Montanha
⋏ Mountains	Gebirge	Montañas	Montagnes	Montanhas
)(Pass	Paß	Paso	Col	Passo
V Valley, Canyon	Tal, Cañon	Valle, Cañón	Vallée, Canyon	Vale, Canhão
≚ Plain	Ebene	Llano	Plaine	Planície
› Cape	Kap	Cabo	Cap	Cabo
I Island	Insel	Isla	Île	Ilha
II Islands	Inseln	Islas	Îles	Ilhas
⊥ Other Topographic Features	Andere Topographische Objekte	Otros Elementos Topográficos	Autres données topographiques	Outros acidentes topográficos

ESPAÑOL — Nombre | Página | Lat.°′ | Long.°′ W = Oeste
FRANÇAIS — Nom | Page | Lat.°′ | Long.°′ W = Ouest
PORTUGUÊS — Nome | Página | Lat.°′ | Long.°′ W = Oeste

Nombre / Nom / Nome	Página / Page	Lat.°′	Long.°′
Nin Bay c	116	12.13 N	123.15 E
Ninda	152	14.47 S	21.24 E
Nindigully	166	28.21 S	148.49 E
Nindirí	236	12.00 N	86.08 W
Nine Ashes	260	51.42 N	0.18 E
Nine Degree Channel ʮ	122	9.00 N	73.00 E
Ninemile Creek ≃, N.Y., U.S.	210	43.11 N	75.20 W
Ninemile Creek ≃, N.Y., U.S.	210	43.06 N	76.14 W
Ninemile Creek ≃, N.Y., U.S.	210	43.24 N	76.38 W
Nine Mile Creek ≃, Ut,. U.S.	200	39.50 N	109.53 W
Ninemile Island I	279b	40.29 N	79.52 W
Nine Mile Lake ⊜	212	44.57 N	79.34 W
Nine Mile Point >	212	44.09 N	76.34 W
Ninepin Group II	271d	22.16 N	114.21 E
Nineteen Hundred Five Memorial Cemetery ◆	265a	59.51 N	30.27 E
Ninette	184	49.24 N	99.38 W
Ninetyeast Ridge ✣[3]	6	4.00 S	90.00 E
Ninety Mile Beach ⍊[2], Austl.	166	38.13 S	147.23 E
Ninety Mile Beach ⍊[2], N.Z.	172	34.48 S	173.00 E
Ninety Six	192	34.10 N	82.01 W
Nineveh, In., U.S.	218	39.22 N	86.05 W
Nineveh, N.Y., U.S.	210	42.12 N	75.36 W
Nineveh → Nīnawá ⊥	128	36.25 N	43.10 E
Ninfa ⊥	66	41.36 N	12.58 E
Ninfas, Punta >	254	42.56 S	64.20 W
Ninfield	42	50.53 N	0.25 E
Ninga	184	49.13 N	99.51 W
Ningaloo	162	22.42 S	113.40 E
Ning'an	89	44.22 N	129.25 E
Ningari	150	14.40 N	3.16 W
Ningbo	100	29.52 N	121.31 E
Ningcheng (Tianyi)	98	41.33 N	119.20 E
Ningde	100	26.43 N	119.33 E
Ningdu	100	26.31 N	115.58 E
Ningerum	164	5.41 S	141.08 E
Ninggang	100	26.50 N	114.02 E
Ningguo	106	30.38 N	118.58 E
Ninghai	100	29.17 N	121.25 E
Ninghe (Lutai)	105	39.20 N	117.48 E
Ninghepu	105	40.43 N	116.07 E
Ninghua	100	26.15 N	116.38 E
Ningi	150	11.04 N	9.32 E
Ningjin, Zhg.	98	37.37 N	114.55 E
Ningjin, Zhg.	98	37.39 N	116.48 E
Ningjing Shan ⋏	102	29.45 N	98.45 E
Ningling	98	34.27 N	115.21 E
Ningming	102	22.07 N	107.05 E
Ningnan	102	27.11 N	102.36 E
Ningpo → Ningbo	100	29.52 N	121.31 E
Ningqiang	102	32.44 N	106.19 E
Ningshan	102	33.04 N	108.39 E
Ningsia Hui Autonomous Region → Ningxia Huizu Zizhiqu □[4]	102	37.00 N	106.00 E
Ningsia → Yinchuan	102	38.30 N	106.18 E
Ningwu	102	39.01 N	112.21 E
Ningxi	100	28.35 N	121.00 E
Ningxia Huizu Zizhiqu (Ningsia Hui) □[4]	102	37.00 N	106.00 E
Ningxian	102	35.31 N	108.01 E
Ningxiang	100	28.15 N	112.33 E
Ningyang	98	35.47 N	116.47 E
Ningyō-tōge)(	96	35.19 N	133.56 E
Ningyuan	102	25.37 N	111.46 E
Ningyuanbao	102	38.38 N	102.30 E
Ningyuanpu	105	40.44 N	114.54 E
Ninh Binh	110	20.15 N	105.59 E
Ninh Hoa	110	12.29 N	109.08 E
Ninhue	252	36.24 S	72.24 W
Ninigo Group II	164	1.15 S	144.15 E
Ninilchik	180	60.03 N	151.41 W
Ninnescah ≃	198	37.20 N	97.10 W
Ninnescah, North Fork ≃	198	37.34 N	97.42 W
Ninnescah, South Fork ≃	198	37.34 N	97.42 W
Ninnis Glacier Tongue ⍓	9	68.12 S	147.12 E
Ninohe	92	40.16 N	141.18 E
Ninomiya, Nihon	94	35.18 N	139.16 E
Ninomiya, Nihon	94	36.22 N	139.58 E
Ninove	50	50.50 N	4.01 E
Niny	84	44.29 N	43.57 E
Nio	96	34.12 N	133.39 E
Nioaque	248	21.08 S	55.48 W
Nioaque ≃	248	20.46 S	56.04 W
Niobe	214	42.01 N	79.27 W
Niobrara	198	42.45 N	98.01 W
Niobrara ≃	198	42.45 N	98.00 W
Nioka	154	2.10 N	30.39 E
Nioki	152	2.43 S	17.41 E
Niokolo Koba	150	13.04 N	12.43 W
Niokolo Koba, Parc National du ♦	150	13.00 N	13.00 W
Niono	150	14.15 N	6.00 W
Nionsamoridougou	150	8.43 N	8.50 W
Nioro du Rip	150	13.45 N	15.48 W
Nioro du Sahel	150	15.15 N	9.35 W
Niort	32	46.19 N	0.27 W
Niota	192	35.30 N	84.32 W
Nioût ╤[4]	150	16.03 N	6.52 W
Nipan	166	24.47 S	150.01 E
Nipāni	122	16.24 N	74.23 E
Nipawin	184	53.22 N	104.00 W
Nipawin Provincial Park ♦	184	54.00 N	104.40 W
Nipe, Bahía de c	240p	20.47 N	75.42 W
Nipekamew ≃	184	54.59 N	104.52 W
Nipekamew Lake ⊜	184	54.24 N	104.58 W
Nipepe	154	14.01 S	37.55 E
Nipigon	190	49.01 N	88.16 W
Nipigon, Lake ⊜	176	49.50 N	88.30 W
Nipigon Bay c	190	48.53 N	87.50 W
Nipin ≃	184	55.45 N	109.02 W
Nipisi Lake ⊜	182	55.47 N	114.57 W
Nipissing □[6]	212	45.30 N	78.50 W
Nipissing, Lake ⊜	190	46.17 N	80.00 W
Nipissis, Lac ⊜	186	51.02 N	66.10 W
Nipisso, Lac ⊜	186	50.52 N	65.50 W
Nipomo	204	35.02 N	120.28 W
Nippenicket, Lake ⊜	283	41.58 N	71.03 W
Nippers Harbour	186	49.48 N	55.52 W
Nippersink Creek ≃	216	42.23 N	88.22 W
Niqiu	100	33.25 N	115.38 E
Niquelândia	255	14.27 S	48.27 W
Niquero	240p	20.03 N	77.35 W
Niquivil	252	30.25 S	68.42 W
Nīr	128	38.02 N	47.59 E
Nīr, Jabal an- ⋏[2]	128	24.10 N	43.20 E
Nīra ≃	122	17.59 N	75.07 E
Nir'am	132	31.31 N	34.35 E
Nirasaki	94	35.42 N	138.27 E
Nirayama	94	35.03 N	138.57 E
Nirgua	246	10.09 N	68.34 W
Nirim	132	31.20 N	34.24 E
Nirmal	122	19.06 N	78.21 E
Nirmāli	124	26.19 N	86.35 E
Nirsa	126	23.47 N	86.43 E
Niš	38	43.19 N	21.54 E
Nisa	34	39.31 N	7.39 W
Nisa (Neisse) (Nysa Łużycka) ≃	30	52.04 N	14.46 E
Niṣāb, Ar. Su.	128	29.11 N	44.43 E
Niṣāb, Yaman	144	14.31 N	46.30 E
Nišava ≃	38	43.22 N	21.46 E
Nisbet	210	41.13 N	77.07 W
Niscemi	70	37.09 N	14.23 E
Nischintāpur	272b	22.26 N	88.22 E
Niṣf Thānī Bashbīsh	142	31.07 N	31.11 E
Nishan	120	33.35 N	85.30 E
Nishi ◆[8], Nihon	268	35.27 N	139.38 E
Nishi ◆[8], Nihon	270	34.41 N	135.30 E
Nishiarai ◆[8]	268	35.47 N	139.47 E
Nishiazai	94	35.31 N	136.10 E
Nishibetsuin	270	34.58 N	135.31 E
Nishi-Chūgoku-sanchi-kokutei-kōen ♦	96	34.40 N	132.10 E
Nishigō	94	37.09 N	140.10 E
Nishiiyayama	96	33.53 N	133.49 E
Nishiizu	94	34.46 N	138.47 E
Nishi-jima I	96	34.39 N	134.29 E
Nishikata	94	36.28 N	139.45 E
Nishikatsura	94	35.31 N	138.51 E
Nishiki	96	34.16 N	131.57 E
Nishiki ≃	96	34.09 N	132.15 E
Nishikiori	270	34.29 N	135.34 E
Nishikyō ◆[8]	270	34.59 N	135.40 E
Nishimori ◆[8]	270	34.45 N	135.01 E
Nishinari ◆[8]	270	34.38 N	135.28 E
Nishinasuno	94	36.53 N	139.59 E
Nishinomiya	96	34.43 N	135.20 E
Nishinoomote	93b	30.44 N	131.00 E
Nishio	94	34.52 N	137.03 E
Nishitoda ◆[8]	270	34.43 N	135.00 E
Nishitosa	96	33.09 N	132.47 E
Nishiwaki	96	34.59 N	134.58 E
Nishiyodogawa ◆[8]	270	34.42 N	135.27 E
Nish → Niš	38	43.19 N	21.54 E
Nisinomiya → Nishinomiya	96	34.43 N	135.20 E
Nísiros I	38	36.35 N	27.10 E
Niska Lake ⊜	184	55.35 N	108.38 W
Niskayuna	210	42.46 N	73.50 W
Nisling ≃	180	62.27 N	139.30 W
Nismes	56	50.05 N	4.33 E
Nispen	52	51.29 N	4.28 E
Nisporeny	78	47.06 N	28.11 E
Nisqually ≃	224	47.06 N	122.42 W
Nisqually Indian Reservation ◆[4]	224	47.02 N	122.42 W
Nisqually Reach c	224	47.07 N	122.45 W
Nissan ≃	26	56.40 N	12.51 E
Nissequogue	276	40.54 N	73.12 W
Nissequogue ≃	276	40.54 N	73.13 W
Nissequogue, Northeast Branch ≃	276	40.50 N	73.13 W
Nissequogue River State Park ♦	276	40.51 N	73.13 W
Nisser ⊜	26	59.10 N	8.30 E
Nisshin	94	35.08 N	137.02 E
Nissoria	70	37.39 N	14.27 E
Nissum Bredning c	26	56.38 N	8.22 E
Nissum Fjord c[2]	26	56.21 N	8.14 E
Nisswa	190	46.31 N	94.17 W
Nistelrode	52	51.43 N	5.33 E
Nister ≃	56	50.47 N	7.43 E
Nisutlin ≃	180	60.10 N	132.30 W
Nita, Indon.	115b	8.40 S	122.11 E
Nita, Nihon	96	35.12 N	133.01 E
Nitalas	272c	19.06 N	73.08 E
Nītaure	76	57.10 N	25.10 E
Niterói	256	22.53 S	43.07 W
Niterói □[7]	287a	22.56 S	43.04 W
Nith ≃, On., Can.	212	43.12 N	80.22 W
Nith ≃, Scot., U.K.	44	55.00 N	3.35 W
Nithāri	272a	28.35 N	77.21 E
Nithāri ◆[8]	272a	28.42 N	77.03 E
Nithi River	182	54.01 N	125.01 W
Nithsdale V	44	55.14 N	3.46 W
Nitibe	112	9.19 S	124.12 E
Nitinat	224	48.55 N	124.29 W
Nitinat ≃	224	48.49 N	124.37 W
Nitinat Lake ⊜	182	48.45 N	124.45 W
Niton	42	50.35 N	1.16 W
Nitra	30	48.20 N	18.05 E
Nitra ≃	30	47.46 N	18.10 E
Nitro	188	38.24 N	81.50 W
Nitry	50	47.40 N	3.53 E
Nítse Óros (Nidže) ʌ	38	40.58 N	21.49 E
Nitta	94	36.17 N	139.18 E
Nittälven ≃	40	59.51 N	14.50 E
Nittany Mountain ʌ	210	41.00 N	77.25 W
Nittedal	26	60.04 N	10.53 E
Nittenau	60	49.12 N	12.16 E
Nittendorf	60	49.02 N	11.58 E
Niu Aunfo Point >	174w	21.04 S	175.20 W
Niubaotun	105	39.46 N	116.41 E
Niubu	100	31.02 N	117.39 E
Niuchutuncun	104	41.28 N	122.58 E
Niudouguang	100	24.51 N	115.44 E
Niue □[2], Oc.	14	19.02 S	169.52 W
Niue □[2], Oc.	174v	19.02 S	169.52 W
Niu'erhe	89	51.30 N	121.49 E
Niufentai	89	47.05 N	120.02 E
Niufozhen	107	29.23 N	105.02 E
Niuhang	100	28.44 N	115.51 E
Niuhuaxi	107	29.29 N	103.48 E
Niujie	102	27.47 N	104.16 E
Niujingjie	110	25.46 N	100.33 E
Niuke	120	30.41 N	82.01 E
Niulakita I	14	10.45 S	179.30 E
Niulan ≃	102	27.28 N	103.10 E
Niulanshan	105	40.13 N	116.39 E
Niumaowu	98	40.58 N	124.59 E
Niupeng	106	31.32 N	121.50 E
Niupichang	107	30.35 N	103.40 E
Niushitun	98	35.18 N	114.24 E
Niut, Gunung ʌ	112	1.00 N	109.55 E
Niutan	107	29.05 N	105.21 E
Niutao I	14	6.06 S	177.17 E
Niuti	100	32.58 N	113.35 E
Niutian	100	27.17 N	115.44 E
Niutoushan	89	45.09 N	126.45 E
Niutou Shan I	100	29.07 N	121.56 E
Niutuo	105	39.15 N	116.20 E
Niutuoshan	106	31.04 N	119.37 E
Niuxichang	107	28.47 N	104.31 E
Niuxintai	104	41.21 N	123.53 E
Niuxintun	104	41.56 N	121.21 E
Niuyuanzi	105	40.20 N	117.47 E
Niuzhuang, Zhg.	98	37.21 N	118.29 E
Niuzhuang, Zhg.	104	40.58 N	122.32 E
Nivå	41	55.56 N	12.31 E
Nivala	26	63.55 N	24.58 E
Nive ≃, Austl.	166	26.02 S	146.25 E
Nive ≃, Fr.	32	43.30 N	1.29 W
Nivelles (Nijvel)	50	50.36 N	4.20 E
Nivernais □[9]	32	47.00 N	3.30 E
Nivernais, Canal du ≊	50	47.40 N	3.40 E
Niverville, Mb., Can.	184	49.37 N	97.01 W
Niverville, N.Y., U.S.	210	42.26 N	73.40 W
Nivillers	50	49.28 N	2.10 E
Nivnoje	76	53.11 N	32.35 E
Nivskij	24	67.16 N	32.23 E
Niwāno	128	26.22 N	62.43 E
Nixa	194	37.02 N	93.17 W
Nixi	102	27.58 N	99.27 E
Nixis	107	30.08 N	106.19 E
Nixizhen	107	29.02 N	104.16 E
Nixon, Nv., U.S.	204	39.49 N	119.21 W
Nixon, Pa., U.S.	214	40.45 N	79.56 W
Nixon, Tx., U.S.	222	29.16 N	97.45 W
Niyodo	96	33.32 N	133.08 E
Niyodo ≃	96	33.27 N	133.29 E
Niyor	114	2.05 N	103.17 E
Niyu Shan I	100	27.51 N	121.03 E
Niža	24	66.20 N	43.16 E
Nizāmābād	122	18.40 N	78.07 E
Nizamghāt	120	28.16 N	95.42 E
Nizām Sāgar ⊜[1]	122	18.10 N	77.55 E
Nižankoviči	78	49.40 N	22.47 E
Nīzgān ≃	128	33.13 N	63.40 E
Nizhniy Tagil → Nižnij Tagil	86	57.55 N	59.57 E
Nižin	76	52.38 N	28.10 E
Nizino	265a	59.50 N	29.53 E
Nizip	130	37.01 N	37.46 E
Nízke Tatry ⋏	30	48.54 N	19.40 E
Nízke Tatry, národní park ♦	30	47.48 N	19.35 E
Nižn'aja	80	56.34 N	49.07 E
Nižn'aja Čvorovaja	86	59.11 N	77.31 E
Nižnaja Dobrinka	80	50.18 N	45.42 E
Nižn'aja Duvanka	83	49.35 N	38.10 E
Nižn'aja-Gerasimovka	83	48.46 N	39.44 E
Nižn'aja Grajvoronka	78	51.47 N	37.45 E
Nižn'aja Irga	86	56.51 N	57.26 E
Nižn'aja Ivanovka ◆[8]	83	48.09 N	38.46 E
Nižn'aja Karelina	88	57.55 N	107.44 E
Nižn'aja Keul'skaja, šivera ᒪ	88	58.25 N	102.46 E
Nižn'aja Krynka	83	48.07 N	38.11 E
Nižnaja Matrenka	80	52.16 N	40.06 E
Nižn'aja-Ol'chovaja	83	48.44 N	39.35 E
Nižn'aja Omka	86	55.26 N	74.55 E
Nižn'aja Omra	24	62.46 N	55.46 E
Nižn'aja Ošma	80	55.44 N	51.18 E
Nižn'aja Peša	24	66.43 N	47.36 E
Nižn'aja Pojma	88	56.11 N	97.13 E
Nižn'aja Pokrovka	80	51.40 N	50.07 E
Nižn'aja Šachtama	88	51.24 N	117.40 E
Nižn'aja Salda	86	58.05 N	60.43 E
Nižn'aja Syzran'	80	53.04 N	48.34 E
Nižn'aja Tavda	86	57.40 N	66.12 E
Nižn'aja Tunguska ≃	74	65.48 N	88.04 E
Nižn'aja Tura	86	58.37 N	59.49 E
Nižn'aja Vol'dža	86	58.19 N	79.20 E
Nižn'aja Zaimka	88	56.09 N	98.14 E
Nižneangarsk	88	55.47 N	109.33 E
Nižnebakanskij	78	44.52 N	37.52 E
Nižne-Baranikovka	83	49.05 N	39.51 E
Nižnečujskij	85	43.12 N	74.21 E
Nižnedevick	78	51.33 N	38.20 E
Nižne-Gnilovskoj ◆[8]	83	47.11 N	39.36 E
Nižnegnutov	80	48.02 N	42.22 E
Nižnegorskij	78	45.27 N	34.44 E
Nižneilimsk	88	57.11 N	103.16 E
Nižneje	83	48.46 N	38.37 E
Nižneje Al'kejevo	80	54.46 N	50.03 E
Nižn'eje Gir'unino	88	51.12 N	116.58 E
Nižneje Kučukovo	80	56.13 N	52.57 E
Nižneje Kujto, ozero ⊜	24	64.58 N	31.38 E
Nižneje M'ačkovo	82	55.33 N	37.59 E
Nižneje Platino	83	48.48 N	39.30 E
Nižnejepravalje ≃	83	48.17 N	39.57 E
Nižneje Romanovo	86	59.47 N	69.35 E
Nižneje Sančelejevo	80	53.40 N	49.27 E
Nižnekamsk	80	55.32 N	51.58 E
Nižnekamskoje vodochranilišče ⊜[1]	24	55.50 N	53.00 E
Nižnekundr'učen-Skaja	80	47.45 N	40.57 E
Nižnelemskij	24	64.01 N	56.16 E
Nižne-Mit'akin Pervyj	83	48.41 N	40.02 E
Nižne-Nagol'naja	83	49.00 N	39.59 E
Nižneoz'ornoje	80	51.37 N	53.56 E
Nižne-Podpol'nyj	83	47.12 N	40.01 E
Nižne-Pokrovka	83	49.13 N	38.38 E
Nižnetambovskoje	89	50.54 N	138.13 E
Nižne-T'oploje	83	48.48 N	39.23 E
Nižnetroickij	80	54.20 N	53.41 E
Nižneudinsk	88	54.54 N	99.03 E
Nižnevartovsk	74	60.56 N	76.31 E
Nižnij Baskunčak	80	48.13 N	46.50 E
Nižnij Časučej	88	50.31 N	115.08 E
Nižnij Čir	80	48.22 N	43.03 E
Nižnij Čulym	86	54.37 N	78.56 E
Nižnije Černi	80	47.41 N	43.26 E
Nižnije Čeršely	80	54.40 N	52.08 E
Nižnije Ostrovcy	82	55.35 N	38.01 E
Nižnije Sergi	86	56.40 N	59.18 E
Nižnije Serogozy	78	46.50 N	34.23 E
Nižnije Timers'any	80	54.34 N	47.45 E
Nižnije V'azovyje	80	55.49 N	48.32 E
Nižnij Ingaš	88	56.12 N	96.31 E
Nižnij Kisl'aj	78	50.50 N	40.11 E
Nižnij Kuranach	74	58.49 N	125.32 E
Nižnij Lomov	80	53.32 N	43.41 E
Nižnij Mamon	78	50.11 N	40.30 E
Nižnij Novgorod (Gorky)	80	56.20 N	44.00 E
Nižnij Odes	24	63.40 N	54.52 E
Nižnij Ol'šan	78	50.45 N	38.55 E
Nižnij P'andž	120	37.08 N	68.32 E
Nižnij Paramonov	80	47.57 N	41.55 E
Nižnij Rogačik	78	47.21 N	34.02 E
Nižnij Serebr'akov	80	47.58 N	41.02 E
Nižnij Škaft	80	53.36 N	45.40 E
Nižnij Stan	88	52.18 N	115.44 E
Nižnij Tagil	86	57.55 N	59.57 E
Nižnij Takanyš	80	55.57 N	51.04 E
Nižnij Ufalej	86	55.55 N	59.59 E
Nižnij V'aloz'orskij	24	66.44 N	35.10 E
Nižnyj Nagol'čik	83	48.01 N	39.04 E
Nizwā	128	22.56 N	57.32 E
Nizy	78	50.47 N	34.46 E
Nizy-le-Comte	50	49.34 N	4.03 E
Nizza Monferrato	62	44.46 N	8.21 E
Nizzana	132	30.53 N	34.27 E
Nizzana, Naḥal V	132	30.57 N	34.23 E
Nizzanim	132	31.43 N	34.38 E
Njassa-See → Nyasa, Lake ⊜	154	12.00 S	34.30 E
Njazidja (Grande Comore) I	157a	11.35 S	43.20 E
Njinjo	154	8.48 S	38.54 E
Njoko ≃	152	17.10 S	24.05 E
Njombe	154	9.20 S	34.46 E
Njombe ≃	154	6.56 S	35.06 E
Njupeskär ᒪ	26	61.38 N	12.41 E
Njurunda	26	62.16 N	17.22 E
Nkambe	152	6.38 N	10.40 E
Nkandla	158	28.37 S	31.05 E
Nkawkaw	150	6.33 N	0.47 W
Nkayi	154	19.00 S	28.54 E
Nkhata Bay	154	11.33 S	34.18 E
Nkhotakota	154	12.57 S	34.17 E
Nkolabona	152	1.14 N	11.43 E
Nkomi, Lagune c	152	1.35 S	9.17 E
Nkongsamba	152	4.57 N	9.56 E
Nkonko	154	6.20 S	34.58 E
Nkoso	152	2.42 S	22.39 E
Nkoto	152	1.56 S	19.41 E
Nkunga	152	4.41 S	18.34 E
Nkurenkuru	152	17.38 S	18.35 E
Nkwalini	158	28.45 S	31.33 E
Nmai ≃	102	25.42 N	97.30 E
Nnewi	150	6.00 N	6.59 E
Nō	94	37.06 N	137.59 E
Noābād	272b	22.34 N	88.31 E
Noailles	50	49.20 N	2.12 E
Noākhāli	124	22.49 N	91.06 E
Noak Hill ◆[8]	260	51.37 N	0.14 E
Noale	64	45.32 N	12.04 E
Noāmundi	124	22.09 N	85.32 E
Noank	207	41.19 N	71.59 W
Noarlunga	168b	35.11 S	138.30 E
Noasca	62	45.27 N	7.19 E
Noatak	180	67.34 N	162.59 W
Noatak ≃	180	67.00 N	162.30 W
Nobby	171a	27.51 S	151.54 E
Nobel	212	45.25 N	80.06 W
Nobeoka	92	32.35 N	131.40 E
Nobidome	268	35.48 N	139.35 E
Nobidome-yōsui ≊[1]	268	35.44 N	139.27 E
Nōbi-heiya ≚	94	35.15 N	136.45 E
Nobili	150	11.33 N	1.12 W
Nobitz	54	50.58 N	12.29 E
Noble, Il., U.S.	194	38.41 N	88.13 W
Noble, Ok., U.S.	196	35.08 N	97.23 W
Noble □[6]	216	41.24 N	85.25 W
Noble Park	274b	37.58 S	145.10 E
Noblestown	279b	40.24 N	80.12 W
Noblesville	218	40.02 N	86.00 W
Nobleton, On., Can.	212	43.54 N	79.40 W
Nobleton, Fl., U.S.	220	28.38 N	82.15 W
Noboribetsu	92a	42.27 N	141.11 E
Noborito	268	35.37 N	139.34 E
Nobres	248	14.44 S	56.20 W
Nobsa	246	5.46 N	72.57 W
Nocatee	220	27.09 N	81.52 W
Noccundra	166	27.50 S	142.36 E
Nocé	50	48.22 N	0.42 E
Noce ≃	64	46.09 N	11.04 E
Nocera Inferiore	68	40.44 N	14.38 E
Nocera Superiore	68	40.44 N	14.40 E
Nocera Tirinese	68	39.02 N	16.09 E
Nocera Umbra	66	43.05 N	12.47 E
Noceto	64	44.48 N	10.11 E
Nochistlán	234	21.22 N	102.51 W
Nochten	54	51.26 N	14.36 E
Noci	68	40.48 N	17.08 E
Nociglia	68	40.02 N	18.20 E
Nockamixon Lake ⊜[1]	208	40.28 N	75.14 W
Nockamixon State Park ♦	208	40.27 N	75.16 W
Nockatunga	166	27.43 S	142.43 E
Nocona	196	33.47 N	97.43 W
Nocupétaro	234	18.48 N	101.04 W
Noda	94	35.56 N	139.52 E
Nodagawa	96	35.31 N	135.06 E
Nodaway ≃	194	39.54 N	94.58 W
Nodera	270	34.45 N	134.56 E
Nods	58	47.06 N	6.20 E
Noé, Ouadi V	146	15.39 N	21.19 E
Noel	194	36.32 N	94.29 W
Noenieput	158	27.29 S	20.06 E
Noepoli	68	40.05 N	16.20 E
Noer	41	54.27 N	10.00 E
Noetinger	252	32.22 S	62.19 W
Nœux-les-Mines	50	50.29 N	2.40 E
Nofels	58	47.15 N	9.34 E
Nogah	132	31.37 N	34.42 E
Nogajskaja step' ≚	84	44.17 N	46.05 E
Nogales, Chile	252	32.44 S	71.15 W
Nogales, Méx.	232	31.20 N	110.56 W
Nogales, Méx.	234	18.49 N	97.10 W
Nogales, Az., U.S.	200	31.20 N	110.56 W
Nogami	94	36.07 N	139.07 E
Nogangjin	98	39.30 N	125.23 E
Nogara, It.	64	45.11 N	11.04 E
Nogara, Ityo.	144	13.53 N	36.32 E
Nogaro	32	43.46 N	0.02 W
Nōgata	96	33.44 N	130.44 E
Nogent-en-Bassigny	58	48.02 N	5.21 E
Nogent-le-Roi	50	48.39 N	1.32 E
Nogent-le-Rotrou	50	48.19 N	0.50 E
Nogent-sur-Marne	261	48.50 N	2.29 E
Nogent-sur-Oise	50	49.16 N	2.28 E
Nogent-sur-Seine	50	48.29 N	3.30 E
Nogent-sur-Vernisson	50	47.51 N	2.45 E
Nogi	94	36.14 N	139.44 E
Nogies Creek ≃	212	44.35 N	78.31 W
Noginsk	82	55.51 N	38.27 E
Nogisaki	268	35.57 N	139.58 E
Nogliki	89	51.48 N	143.10 E
Nogmung	102	27.30 N	97.49 E
Nogoa ≃	166	23.33 S	148.32 E
Nōgohaku-san ʌ	94	35.46 N	136.31 E
Nogoon Nuur	86	49.33 N	90.17 E
Nogoyá	252	32.24 S	59.48 W
Nógrád □[6]	30	48.00 N	19.35 E
Noguera Pallaresa ≃	34	42.15 N	0.54 E
Noguera Ribagorzana ≃	34	41.40 N	0.43 E
Nohain ≃	50	47.24 N	2.55 E
Nohar	123	29.11 N	74.46 E
Noheji	92	40.52 N	141.08 E
Nohili Point >	229b	22.04 N	159.47 W
Nohjhīl	124	27.51 N	77.39 E
Nohta	124	23.40 N	79.34 E
Nohwa-do I	98	34.12 N	126.35 E
Noicattaro	68	41.02 N	16.59 E
Noichi	96	33.33 N	133.42 E
Noir, Causse ⋏[1]	32	44.10 N	3.15 E
Noir, Isla I	254	54.29 S	73.02 W
Noire ≃, P.Q., Can.	190	45.54 N	76.57 W
Noire ≃, P.Q., Can.	206	45.33 N	72.58 W
Noire ≃, P.Q., Can.	206	46.39 N	72.08 W
Noire, Mer du → Black Sea ╤[2]	22	43.00 N	35.00 E
Noire, Montagne ʌ	206	46.14 N	74.18 W
Noire, Montagne ⋏	32	43.28 N	2.18 E
Noirétable	62	45.49 N	3.46 E
Noirmoutier	32	47.00 N	2.14 W
Noirmoutier, Île de I	32	47.00 N	2.15 W
Noiseau	261	48.47 N	2.33 E
Noisiel	261	48.51 N	2.37 E
Noisy ≃	212	44.19 N	80.08 W
Noisy-le-Grand	261	48.51 N	2.33 E
Noisy-le-Roi	261	48.51 N	2.04 E
Noisy-le-Sec	261	48.53 N	2.28 E
Nojember'an	84	41.12 N	45.01 E
Nojima-zaki >	94	34.56 N	139.53 E
Nojiri-ko ⊜	94	36.49 N	138.13 E
Nojon	102	43.10 N	102.07 E
Nojon uul ⋏	102	43.10 N	101.30 E
Nokami	96	34.15 N	135.20 E
Nokaneng	156	19.40 S	22.16 E
Nōke	270	34.26 N	135.29 E
Nokha Mandi	120	27.35 N	73.29 E
Nokia	26	61.28 N	23.30 E
Nokilalaki, Bulu ʌ	112	1.13 S	120.08 E
Nok Kundi	128	28.46 N	62.46 E
Nokogiri-yama ʌ[2]	268	35.09 N	139.51 E
Nokomis, Sk., Can.	184	51.30 N	105.00 W
Nokomis, Fl., U.S.	220	27.07 N	82.26 W
Nokomis, Il., U.S.	219	39.18 N	89.17 W
Nokomis Lake ⊜	184	56.58 N	103.02 W
Nokou	146	14.35 N	14.47 E
Nokpan-ni ◆[8]	271b	37.36 N	126.56 E
Nokrek ʌ	124	25.27 N	90.20 E
Nokuku	175f	14.53 S	166.35 E
Nola, Centraf.	152	3.32 N	16.04 E
Nola, It.	68	40.55 N	14.33 E
Nolan ≃	222	32.07 N	97.26 W
Nolan Creek ≃	222	31.02 N	97.26 W
Nolanville	222	31.05 N	97.36 W
Nolay	58	46.57 N	4.38 E
Nole	62	45.15 N	7.35 E
Noli	62	44.12 N	8.26 E
Noli, Capo di >	62	44.12 N	8.25 E
Nolichucky ≃	192	36.07 N	83.14 W
Nolin ≃	194	37.13 N	86.15 W
Nolin Lake ⊜[1]	194	37.20 N	86.10 W
Nolinsk	80	57.33 N	49.57 E
Nomad	164	6.18 S	142.14 E
Nomahegan Brook ≃	276	40.41 N	74.18 W
Nomans Land I	207	41.15 N	70.49 W
Nombre de Dios, Méx.	234	23.51 N	104.14 W
Nombre de Dios, Pan.	236	9.35 N	79.28 W
Nombre de Dios, Cordillera ⋏	236	15.35 N	86.55 W
Nome	180	64.30 N	165.24 W
Nomény	56	48.54 N	6.14 E
Nomexy	58	48.18 N	6.23 E
Nomgon, Mong.	102	45.26 N	105.08 E
Nomgon, Mong.	102	42.50 N	105.07 E
Nomgon uul ⋏	102	42.50 N	104.20 E
Nomingue, Petit lac ⊜	206	46.21 N	75.00 W
Nomini Bay c	208	38.09 N	76.43 W
Nominingue	206	46.24 N	75.02 W
Nominingue, Lac ⊜	206	46.26 N	74.59 W
Nomoi Islands II	14	5.27 N	153.40 E
Nomoneas II	175c	7.24 N	151.53 E
Nomozaki	92	32.35 N	129.45 E
Nomtsas	156	24.22 S	16.47 E
Nomura	96	33.22 N	132.38 E
Nona, Lake ⊜	220	28.24 N	81.15 W
Nonacho Lake ⊜	176	61.42 N	109.40 W
Nonancourt	50	48.46 N	1.12 E
Nonant-le-Pin	50	48.42 N	0.13 E
Nonantola	64	44.41 N	11.02 E
Nonburg	24	65.34 N	50.32 E
Nonceveux	56	50.28 N	5.44 E
Nondalton	180	60.00 N	154.49 W
Nondwa	154	6.26 S	35.20 E
Nondweni	158	28.11 S	30.49 E
None	62	44.56 N	7.32 E
Nonette ≃	50	49.12 N	2.24 E
None-yama ʌ	96	33.29 N	134.10 E
Nong'an	89	44.25 N	125.10 E
Nong Bua Lamphu	110	17.11 N	102.25 E
Nong Han	110	17.21 N	103.07 E
Nong Hèt	110	19.29 N	103.59 E
Nong Khai	110	17.52 N	102.44 E
Nongoma	158	27.58 S	31.35 E
Nongpoh	120	25.54 N	91.53 E
Nongstoin	120	25.31 N	91.16 E
Nonnenhorn	58	47.34 N	9.36 E
Nonnevitz	54	54.39 N	13.17 E
Nonning	166	32.30 S	136.30 E
Nonnweiler	56	49.36 N	6.58 E
Nono	144	8.32 N	37.26 E
Nonoai	252	27.21 S	52.47 W
Nonoava	232	27.28 N	106.44 W
Nonoc Island I	116	9.51 N	125.37 E
Nono de Julho, Túnel ◆[5]	287b	23.34 S	46.39 W
Nonogasta	252	29.18 S	67.30 W
Nonoichi	94	36.32 N	136.37 E
Nonouti I[1]	14	0.40 S	174.21 E
Nonsan	98	36.12 N	127.05 E
Nonsuch Bay c	240c	17.03 N	61.42 W
Non Sung	110	15.11 N	102.16 E
Nonthaburi	110	13.50 N	100.29 E
Nonthaburi □[4]	269a	13.52 N	100.27 E
Nontron	32	45.32 N	0.40 E
Nonvianuk Lake ⊜	180	59.00 N	155.15 W
Noojee	169	37.55 S	146.00 E
Nookawarra	162	26.19 S	116.52 E
Nooksack	224	48.55 N	122.19 W
Nooksack ≃	224	48.46 N	122.35 W
Nooksack, Middle Fork ≃	224	48.50 N	122.08 W
Nooksack, North Fork ≃	224	48.50 N	122.11 W
Nooksack, South Fork ≃	224	48.50 N	122.11 W
Noonamah	164	12.38 S	131.04 E
Noonan	198	48.53 N	103.00 W
Noon Hill ʌ[2]	283	42.09 N	71.19 W
Noonkanbah	162	18.30 S	124.50 E
Noorat	169	38.12 S	142.56 E
Noord-Beveland I	52	51.35 N	3.45 E
Noord-Brabant □[4]	52	51.30 N	5.00 E
Noord-Holland □[4]	52	52.40 N	4.50 E
Noordhorn	52	53.16 N	6.24 E
Noordoewer	156	28.45 S	17.37 E
Noordoost Polder ◆[1]	52	52.42 N	5.45 E
Noordpunt >	241s	12.23 N	69.10 W
Noord-Scharwoude	52	52.43 N	4.47 E
Noordwijk aan Zee	52	52.14 N	4.26 E
Noordwijk-Binnen	52	52.13 N	4.27 E
Noordwijkerhout	52	52.15 N	4.30 E
Noordwolde	52	52.54 N	6.09 E
Noormarkku	26	61.35 N	21.52 E
Noorvik	180	66.50 N	161.12 W
Noosaville	166	26.24 S	153.04 E
Nootka Island I	182	49.32 N	126.42 W
Nootka Sound ʮ	182	49.33 N	126.38 W
Nopaltepec	234	18.17 N	95.59 W
No Point, Point >	276	41.09 N	73.08 W
Nóqui	152	5.51 S	13.25 E
Nora, Sve.	40	59.31 N	15.02 E
Nora, In., U.S.	218	39.55 N	86.08 W
Nora ≃	89	52.26 N	129.58 E
Nora ⊥	71	39.00 N	9.01 E
Nor Ačin	84	40.19 N	44.35 E
Norah Head >	170	33.17 S	151.35 E
Nora Islands II	144	16.02 N	40.03 E
Norala	116	6.28 N	124.38 E
Noralee	182	53.59 N	126.26 W
Noranda	190	48.15 N	79.02 W
Noraskög ⋏	40	59.39 N	14.50 E
Nora Springs	190	43.08 N	93.00 W
Norberg	40	60.04 N	15.56 E
Norberto de la Riestra	252	35.16 S	59.46 W
Norborne	194	39.18 N	93.40 W
Norcan Lake ⊜	212	45.10 N	76.53 W
Norcatur	198	39.50 N	100.11 W
Norchia ⊥	66	42.20 N	11.57 E
Norcia	66	42.48 N	13.05 E
Norco	228	33.56 N	117.33 W
Norcott, Mount ʌ	162	32.07 S	121.59 E
Norcross	192	33.56 N	84.12 W
Nord □[4]	146	9.00 N	13.30 E
Nord □[5]	50	50.20 N	3.40 E
Nord, Canal du ≊	50	50.16 N	3.05 E
Nord, Cap → Nordkapp >	24	71.11 N	25.48 E
Nord, Gare ◆[5]	261	48.53 N	2.21 E
Nord, Grand lac du ⊜	186	50.54 N	67.06 W
Nord, Petit lac du ⊜	186	50.50 N	67.10 W
Nord, Rivière du ≃	206	45.31 N	74.20 W
Nordamerika → North America ⍊[1]	16	45.00 N	100.00 W
Nordanholen	40	60.30 N	14.57 E
Nordausques	50	50.49 N	2.05 E
Nordaustlandet I	12	79.48 N	22.24 E
Nordbögge	263	51.37 N	7.44 E
Nordborg	41	55.03 N	9.45 E
Nordby	41	55.58 N	10.34 E
Nord Dakota → North Dakota □[3]	198	47.30 N	100.15 W
Norddeich	52	53.37 N	7.09 E
Nordegg	182	52.28 N	116.04 W
Nordegg ≃	182	52.53 N	115.18 W
Norden, Dtsch.	52	53.36 N	7.12 E
Norden, Eng., U.K.	262	53.38 N	2.13 W
Norden, Ca., U.S.	226	39.20 N	120.22 W
Nordendorf	56	48.36 N	10.50 E
Nordenham	52	53.29 N	8.28 E
Nordenšel'da, archipelag II	74	76.45 N	96.00 E
Nordenskiold ≃	180	62.05 N	136.18 W
Norderney	52	53.42 N	7.08 E
Norderney I	52	53.42 N	7.10 E
Norderstapel	41	54.21 N	9.14 E
Norderstedt	52	53.43 N	10.00 E
Nordfjord c[2]	26	61.54 N	5.12 E
Nordfjordeid	26	61.54 N	6.00 E
Nordfold	24	67.46 N	15.12 E
Nordfriesische Inseln → North Frisian Islands II	24	54.50 N	8.12 E
Nordfriesland ◆[1]	41	54.40 N	9.10 E
Nordgermersleben	54	52.13 N	11.20 E
Nordhalben	54	50.22 N	11.30 E
Nordhausen	54	51.30 N	10.47 E
Nordheim	222	28.55 N	97.36 W
Nordheim von der Rhön	56	50.28 N	10.11 E
Nordhelle ʌ[2]	263	51.09 N	7.46 E
Nordhorn	52	52.27 N	7.05 E
Nordic Park	278	41.57 N	88.02 W
Nordingrå	26	62.56 N	18.16 E
Nordirland → Northern Ireland □[8]	48	54.40 N	6.45 W
Nordiyya	132	32.19 N	34.54 E
Nordkanal ≊	263	51.10 N	6.42 E
Nordkapp >	24	71.11 N	25.48 E
Nordkinnhalvøya >[1]	24	70.55 N	27.45 E
Nordkirchen	52	51.44 N	7.31 E
Nordkjosbotn	24	69.13 N	19.30 E
Nord-Korea → Korea, North □[1]	98	40.00 N	127.00 E
Nordland	224	48.03 N	122.41 W
Nordland □[6]	24	67.00 N	14.40 E
Nördliche Dwina → Severnaja Dvina ≃	24	64.32 N	40.30 E
Nördliches Eismeer → Arctic Ocean ╤[1]	16	85.00 N	170.00 E
Nördlingen	56	48.51 N	10.30 E
Nordmaling	26	63.34 N	19.30 E
Nordmark	40	59.50 N	14.06 E
Nordmarka ◆[1]	26	60.00 N	10.25 E
Nordostrundingen >	16	81.36 N	12.09 W
Nord-Ostsee-Kanal ≊	30	53.53 N	9.08 E
Nord-Ouest □[4]	152	6.30 N	10.30 E
Nordpfälzer Bergland ⋏	56	49.40 N	7.40 E
Nordradde ≃	52	52.43 N	7.17 E
Nordreisa	24	69.46 N	21.03 E
Nordre Strømfjord c[2]	176	67.50 N	52.00 W
Nordrhein-Westfalen □[3]	30	51.30 N	7.30 E
Nordsee → North Sea ╤[2]	22	55.20 N	3.00 E
Nordstemmen	52	52.09 N	9.46 E
Nordstrand I	41	54.30 N	8.53 E
Nordstrandischmoor I	41	54.33 N	8.48 E
Nord-Trøndelag □[6]	24	64.25 N	12.00 E
Nordvik	74	74.02 N	111.32 E
Nordwalde	52	52.05 N	7.28 E
Nordwest-Kap → North West Cape >	162	21.45 S	114.10 E
Nore	26	60.10 N	9.01 E
Nore ≃	48	52.25 N	6.58 W
Noremberg → Nürnberg	60	49.27 N	11.04 E
Norf	263	51.09 N	6.43 E
Norf ≃	263	51.11 N	6.44 E
Norfolk, Ct., U.S.	207	41.59 N	73.12 W
Norfolk, Ma., U.S.	283	42.07 N	71.19 W
Norfolk, Ne., U.S.	198	42.02 N	97.25 W
Norfolk, Va., U.S.	208	36.50 N	76.17 W
Norfolk □[6], On., Can.	214	42.48 N	80.25 W
Norfolk □[6], Eng., U.K.	42	52.35 N	1.00 E
Norfolk □[6], Ma., U.S.	207	42.10 N	71.15 W
Norfolk Broads ◆[1]	42	52.40 N	1.30 E
Norfolk-Insel → Norfolk Island □[2]	174c	29.02 S	167.57 E
Norfolk International Airport ⊠	208	36.54 N	76.12 W
Norfolk Island □[2], Oc.	14	29.02 S	167.57 E
Norfolk Island □[2], Oc.	174c	29.02 S	167.57 E
Norfolk Island Aerodome ⊠	174c	29.03 S	167.56 E
Norfolk Naval Shipyard ■	208	36.49 N	76.18 W
Norfolk Naval Station ■	208	36.57 N	76.18 W
Norfolk Ridge ✣[3]	14	29.00 S	168.00 E
Norfork Lake ⊜[1]	194	36.25 N	92.10 W
Norg	52	53.04 N	6.27 E
Norge	208	37.22 N	76.46 W
Norge → Norway □[1]	24	62.00 N	10.00 E
Norham	44	55.43 N	2.10 W
Norheimsund	26	60.22 N	6.08 E
Noria de Ángeles	234	22.27 N	101.56 W
Norikura-dake ʌ	94	36.06 N	137.33 E
Noril'sk	74	69.20 N	88.06 E
Noring, Gunong ʌ	114	5.24 N	101.44 E
Norland, On., Can.	212	44.43 N	78.49 W
Norland, Fl., U.S.	220	25.57 N	80.12 W
Norlane	169	38.06 S	144.21 E
Norley	262	53.15 N	2.39 W
Norlina	192	36.26 N	78.11 W
Norma, It.	66	41.35 N	12.58 E
Norma, N.J., U.S.	208	39.29 N	75.05 W
Normal, Al., U.S.	194	34.47 N	86.34 W
Normal, Il., U.S.	216	40.30 N	88.59 W
Norman, Ar., U.S.	194	34.27 N	93.40 W
Norman, In., U.S.	218	38.57 N	86.16 W
Norman, Ok., U.S.	196	35.13 N	97.26 W
Norman ≃	166	17.28 S	140.49 E
Norman, Lake ⊜[1]	192	35.35 N	80.55 W
Normanby, Austl.	171a	27.28 S	153.01 E
Normanby, N.Z.	172	39.32 S	174.17 E
Normanby ≃	164	14.25 S	144.08 E
Normanby Island I	164	10.05 S	151.05 E
Norman Creek c	284b	39.18 N	76.25 W
Normandie □[9]	32	49.00 N	0.05 W
Normandie, Collines de ⋏[2]	32	48.40 N	0.30 W
Normandien	158	27.57 S	29.47 E
Normandy Heights	284b	39.17 N	76.48 W
Normandy → Normandie □[9]	32	49.00 N	0.05 W
Normandy Park	224	47.27 N	122.21 W
Normangee	222	31.02 N	96.07 W
Normanhurst	274a	33.43 S	151.06 E
Normanhurst, Mount ʌ	162	25.04 S	122.32 E
Norman Island I	240m	18.20 N	64.37 W
Normannische Inseln → Channel Islands II	28	49.20 N	2.20 W
Norman Park	192	31.16 N	83.41 W
Normans Kill ≃	210	42.36 N	73.44 W
Normanton, Austl.	166	17.40 S	141.05 E
Normanton, Eng., U.K.	44	53.41 N	1.27 W
Normanville	168b	35.27 S	138.19 E
Norman Wells	180	65.17 N	126.51 W
Nor Marsh ≡	260	51.24 N	0.38 E
Nornalup	162	35.00 S	116.49 E
Norogachi	232	27.15 N	107.07 W
Noroton ≃	276	41.03 N	73.31 W
Noroton Point >	276	41.03 N	73.26 W
Norovlin	88	48.40 N	112.00 E
Noroy-le-Bourg	58	47.37 N	6.18 E
Norphlet	194	33.18 N	92.39 W
Norquay	184	51.53 N	102.05 W
Ñorquinco	254	41.51 S	70.54 W
Norra Barken ⊜	40	60.07 N	15.31 E
Norra Björkfjärden c	40	59.27 N	17.28 E
Norrahammar	26	57.42 N	14.06 E
Norra Hörken ⊜	40	60.04 N	14.53 E
Norra Kvarken (Merenkurkku) ʮ	26	63.36 N	20.43 E
Norra Kvills Nationalpark ♦	26	57.44 N	15.37 E
Norrälgen ⊜	40	59.50 N	14.34 E
Norra Rörum	41	56.01 N	13.30 E
Norra Storfjället ʌ	24	65.52 N	15.18 E
Norra Yngern ⊜	40	59.09 N	17.22 E
Norrboda	40	60.28 N	18.25 E
Norrbotten □[9]	26	66.45 N	23.00 E
Norrbottens Län □[6]	24	66.00 N	20.00 E
Nørre Åby	41	55.27 N	9.54 E
Nørre Alslev	41	54.54 N	11.54 E
Nørre Broby	41	55.15 N	10.14 E
Nørre Nærå	41	55.34 N	10.17 E
Norrent-Fontes	50	50.35 N	2.24 E
Nørre Snede	41	55.58 N	9.25 E
Nørresundby	26	57.04 N	9.55 E
Nørre Vejrup	41	55.31 N	8.47 E
Norrfjärden	26	65.25 N	21.27 E
Norridge	216	41.57 N	87.49 W
Norridgewock	188	44.42 N	69.47 W
Norris	192	36.11 N	84.04 W
Norris, Lake ⊜	220	28.57 N	81.32 W
Norris Arm	186	49.05 N	55.15 W
Norris Bridge ◆[5]	208	37.37 N	76.26 W
Norris City	194	37.58 N	88.19 W
Norris Dam State Park ♦	192	36.14 N	84.07 W

Symbol	English	Deutsch	Español	Français	Português
≃	River	Fluß	Río	Rivière	Rio
≊	Canal	Kanal	Canal	Canal	Canal
ᒪ	Waterfall, Rapids	Wasserfall, Stromschnellen	Cascada, Rápidos	Chute d'eau, Rapides	Cascata, Rápidos
ʮ	Strait	Meeresstraße	Estrecho	Détroit	Estreito
c	Bay, Gulf	Bucht, Golf	Bahía, Golfo	Baie, Golfe	Baía, Golfo
⊜	Lake, Lakes	See, Seen	Lago, Lagos	Lac, Lacs	Lago, Lagos
≡	Swamp	Sumpf	Pantano	Marais	Pântano
⍓	Ice Features, Glacier	Eis- und Gletscherformen	Accidentes Glaciales	Formes glaciaires	Acidentes glaciares
╤	Other Hydrographic Features	Andere Hydrographische Objekte	Otros Elementos Hidrográficos	Autres données hydrographiques	Outros acidentes hidrográficos
✣	Submarine Features	Untermeerische Objekte	Accidentes Submarinos	Formes de relief sous-marin	Acidentes submarinos
□	Political Unit	Politische Einheit	Unidad Politica	Entité politique	Unidade política
⍦	Cultural Institution	Kulturelle Institution	Institución Cultural	Institution culturelle	Institução cultural
⊥	Historical Site	Historische Stätte	Sitio Histórico	Site historique	Sitio histórico
♦	Recreational Site	Erholungs- und Ferienort	Sitio de Recreo	Centre de loisirs	Area de Lazer
⊠	Airport	Flughafen	Aeropuerto	Aéroport	Aeroporto
■	Military Installation	Militäranlage	Instalación Militar	Installation militaire	Instalação militar
◆	Miscellaneous	Verschiedenes	Misceláneo	Divers	Diversos

Symbole im Register stellen die rechts im Schlüssel erklärten Kategorien dar. Symbole mit hochgestellten Ziffern (*) bezeichnen Unterabteilungen einer Kategorie (vgl. vollständiger Schlüssel auf Seite 1 · 1).

Los simbolos incluidos en el texto del índice representan las grandes categorías identificadas en la clave a la derecha. Los símbolos con números en su parte superior (*) identifican las subcategorías (véase la clave completa en la página 1 · 1).

Les symboles de l'index représentent les catégories indiquées dans la légende à droite. Les symboles suivis d'un indice (*) représentent des sous-catégories (voir légende complète à la page 1 · 1).

Symbols in the index entries represent the broad categories identified in the key at the right. Symbols with superior numbers (*) identify subcategories (see complete key on page 1 · 1).

Os símbolos incluídos no texto do índice representam as grandes categorias identificadas com a chave à direita. Os símbolos com números em sua parte superior (*) identificam as subcategorias (veja-se a chave completa à página 1 · 1).

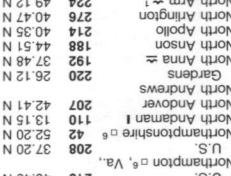
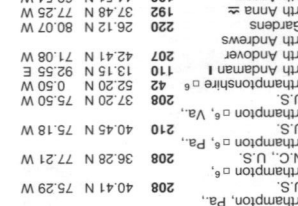

		topográficos	topographiques	Topográficos	Andere Topographische	Other Topographic
Outros acidentes	Autres données	Otros Elementos	Andere Elemente	Features
Ilhas	Iles	Islas	Inseln	Islands	II Island
Ilha	Ile	Isla	Insel	Island	> Cape
Cabo	Cap	Cabo	Kap	Cape
Planície	Plaine	Llano	Ebene	Plain	V Valley, Canyon
Vale, Canhão	Vallée, Canyon	Valle, Cañón	Tal, Cañon	Valley, Canyon
Passo	Col	Paso	Paß	Pass	✕ Pass
Montanhas	Montagnes	Montañas	Gebirge	Mountains
Montanha	Montagne	Montaña	Berg	Mountain	▲ Mountain, Peak

ESPAÑOL

Nombre	Página	Lat.°′	Long.°′ W = Oeste
Noto Antica ⊥	70	36.56 N	15.02 E
Notodden	26	59.34 N	9.17 E
Notogawa	94	35.10 N	136.10 E
Noto-hantō ≻[1]	92	37.20 N	137.00 E
Noto-hantō-kokutei-kōen ♠	94	37.10 N	136.50 E
Noto-jima	94	37.08 N	137.00 E
Noto-jima I	94	37.07 N	137.00 E
Nōtori-dake ∧	94	35.37 N	138.15 E
Notoro-ko ⊜	92a	44.05 N	144.10 E
Notozero, ozero ⊜	24	66.28 N	32.05 E
Notre-Dame	186	46.19 N	64.43 W
Notre-Dame ♥[1]	261	48.51 N	2.21 E
Notre-Dame, Bois ♠	261	48.45 N	2.35 E
Notre-Dame, Monts ⋌	186	48.10 N	68.00 W
Notre-Dame, Ruisseau ≃	275a	45.41 N	73.26 W
Notre Dame Bay c	186	49.45 N	55.15 W
Notre-Dame-de-Bellecombe	62	45.48 N	6.31 E
Notre-Dame-de-Lorette ♥[1]	50	50.25 N	2.42 E
Notre-Dame-de-Lourdes	184	49.32 N	98.33 W
Notre-Dame-de-Pierreville	206	46.06 N	72.53 W
Notre-Dame-des-Victoires ⬥[8]	275a	45.35 N	73.34 W
Notre-Dame-du-Haut ♥[1]	58	47.43 N	6.37 E
Notre-Dame-du-Laus	188	46.05 N	75.37 W
Notre-Dame-du-Nord	190	47.36 N	79.30 W
Notrees	196	31.55 N	102.45 W
Notreure ≃	50	47.41 N	2.36 E
Notsu	96	33.02 N	131.42 E
Notsuharu	96	33.09 N	131.32 E
Nottawa	216	41.55 N	85.27 W
Nottawa Creek ≃	216	42.01 N	85.24 W
Nottawasaga ≃	212	44.32 N	80.01 W
Nottawasaga Bay c	212	44.35 N	80.15 W
Nottaway ≃	176	51.22 N	79.55 W
Nottingham, Eng., U.K.	42	52.58 N	1.10 W
Nottingham, Pa., U.S.	208	39.45 N	76.01 W
Nottingham, Pa., U.S.	285	40.07 N	74.58 W
Nottingham Island I	176	63.20 N	77.55 W
Nottingham Park	278	41.46 N	87.48 W
Nottingham Road	158	29.22 S	30.00 E
Nottinghamshire □[6]	44	53.00 N	1.00 W
Notting Hill	274b	37.54 S	145.08 E
Nottleben	54	50.58 N	10.50 E
Nottoway	192	37.08 N	78.05 W
Nottoway ≃	192	36.33 N	76.55 W
Nottuln	52	51.55 N	7.22 E
Notukeu Creek ≃	184	49.55 N	106.30 W
Nouâdhibou	148	20.54 N	17.04 W
Nouâdhibou, Râs ≻	148	20.46 N	17.03 W
Nouakchott	150	18.06 N	15.57 W
Nouâmghâr	150	19.22 N	16.31 W
Nouan-le-Fuzelier	50	47.32 N	2.02 E
Nouans-les-Fontaines	50	47.08 N	1.18 E
Nouméa	175f	22.16 S	166.27 E
Noun ≃	152	4.55 N	11.06 E
Nouna	150	12.44 N	3.52 W
Nounsley	260	51.46 N	0.36 E
Noupoort	158	31.10 S	24.57 E
Nous	158	28.44 S	19.52 E
Nouveau Brunswick → New Brunswick □[4]	186	46.30 N	66.15 W
Nouveau Mexique → New Mexico □[3]	178	34.30 N	106.00 W
Nouveau-Québec, Cratère du ⏏[6]	176	61.17 N	73.40 W
Nouvelle	186	48.08 N	66.19 W
Nouvelle ≃	186	48.07 N	66.18 W
Nouvelle-Calédonie (New Caledonia) I	175f	21.30 S	165.30 E
Nouvelle-Calédonie → New Caledonia □[2]	175f	21.30 S	165.30 E
Nouvelle Écosse → Nova Scotia □[4]	186	45.00 N	63.00 W
Nouvelle-France, Cap de ≻	176	62.27 N	73.42 W
Nouvelle Galles du Sud → New South Wales □[3]	166	33.00 S	146.00 E
Nouvelle-Orléans → New Orleans	194	29.58 N	90.07 W
Nouvelles-Hébrides → Vanuatu □[1]	175f	16.00 S	167.00 E
Nouvelle Zélande → New Zealand □[1]	172	41.00 S	174.00 E
Nouvelle Zemble → Novaja Zeml'a II	72	74.00 N	57.00 E
Nouvion-en-Ponthieu	50	50.12 N	1.47 E
Nouvion-sur-Meuse	56	49.42 N	4.48 E
Nouzonville	56	49.49 N	4.45 E
Nova, Magy.	61	46.41 N	16.41 E
Nova, Oh., U.S.	214	41.02 N	82.18 W
Nova América	255	15.01 S	49.56 W
Nova Andradina	255	22.10 S	53.15 W
Novabad, Taj.	85	39.01 N	70.09 E
Novabad, Taj.	85	38.37 N	68.45 E
Nová Baňa	30	48.26 N	18.39 E
Nová Bystřice	61	49.01 N	15.06 E
Nova Cachoeirinha ⬥[8]	287b	23.28 S	46.40 W
Nova Caipemba	152	7.26 S	14.38 E
Novacella ♥[1]	64	46.44 N	11.39 E
Nova Era	255	19.45 S	43.03 W
Nova Esperança	255	23.08 S	52.13 W
Novafeltria	66	43.53 N	12.17 E
Nova Friburgo	256	22.16 S	42.32 W
Nova Goa → Panaji	122	15.29 N	73.50 E
Nova Gorica	64	45.57 N	13.39 E
Nova Gradiška	36	45.16 N	17.23 E
Nova Granada	255	20.29 S	49.19 W
Nova Iguaçu	256	22.45 S	43.27 W
Nova Iguaçu □[7]	287a	22.45 S	43.29 W
Novaja, Ross.	82	55.13 N	38.54 E
Novaja, Ross.	265b	55.48 N	38.03 E
Novaja ⬥[8]	265a	60.02 N	30.28 E
Novaja Astrachan'	83	49.07 N	38.36 E
Novaja Belaja	78	49.46 N	39.11 E
Novaja Belokoroviči	78	51.07 N	28.02 E
Novaja Binaradka	80	53.48 N	49.56 E
Novaja Borovaja	78	50.42 N	28.39 E
Novaja Čigla	78	51.13 N	40.28 E
Novaja Derevn'a, Ross.	82	54.01 N	38.53 E
Novaja Derevn'a, Ross.	88	57.15 N	103.08 E
Novaja Ivanovka	78	45.55 N	29.05 E
Novaja Janisol'	83	47.17 N	37.16 E
Novaja Kachovka	78	46.45 N	33.23 E
Novaja Kalitva	78	50.06 N	40.01 E
Novaja Kazanka	80	48.57 N	49.36 E
Novaja Kazmaska	80	56.49 N	53.31 E
Novaja Kriuša	78	50.16 N	41.16 E
Novaja Ladoga	76	60.05 N	32.16 E
Novaja L'al'a	86	59.03 N	60.36 E
Novaja Majačka	78	46.36 N	33.14 E
Novaja Maluksa	76	59.39 N	31.21 E
Novaja Malykla	80	54.13 N	49.57 E
Novaja Mojgora	82	54.27 N	38.32 E
Novaja Odessa	78	47.19 N	31.47 E
Novaja Porubežka	80	51.45 N	49.40 E
Novaja Praga	78	48.33 N	32.54 E
Novaja Ropša	265a	59.45 N	29.53 E
Novaja Sibir', ostrov I	74	75.00 N	149.00 E
Novaja Sloboda	78	51.23 N	34.08 E
Novaja Slobodka	82	54.56 N	36.47 E
Novaja Šul'ba	86	50.33 N	81.20 E
Novaja Uda	88	54.07 N	103.33 E
Novaja Ušica	78	48.49 N	27.16 E
Novaja Usman'	78	51.37 N	39.24 E

FRANÇAIS

Nom	Page	Lat.°′	Long.°′ W = Ouest
Novaja Vodolaga	78	49.43 N	35.52 E
Novaja Zburjevka	78	46.28 N	32.24 E
Novaja Zeml'a II	72	74.00 N	57.00 E
Nováky	30	48.43 N	18.34 E
Nova Lamego	150	12.19 N	14.11 W
Novale (Rauth)	64	46.24 N	11.30 E
Novalesa	62	45.11 N	7.01 E
Novaliches Reservoir ⊜[1]	269f	14.43 N	121.05 E
Nova Lima	255	19.59 S	43.51 W
Nova Lisboa → Huambo	152	12.44 S	15.47 E
Nova Lusitânia	156	19.54 S	34.35 E
Nova Mambone	156	20.59 S	35.01 E
Nova Milanese	266b	45.35 N	9.12 E
Nova Nabúri	154	16.46 S	38.57 E
Nova Odessa	256	23.09 S	46.51 W
Nova Olinda	250	7.06 S	39.40 W
Nova Olinda do Norte	246	3.45 S	59.03 W
Nová Paka	30	50.29 N	15.31 E
Nova Ponente (Deutschnofen)	64	46.25 N	11.25 E
Nova Ponte	255	19.08 S	47.41 W
Nova Prata	252	28.47 S	51.36 W
Novar	212	45.27 N	79.15 W
Novara	62	45.28 N	8.38 E
Novara □[4]	62	45.40 N	8.30 E
Novara di Sicilia	70	38.01 N	15.08 E
Nová Role	54	50.15 N	12.47 E
Nova Roma	255	13.51 S	46.57 W
Nova Russas	250	4.42 S	40.34 W
Nova Scotia □[4], Can.	176	45.00 N	63.00 W
Nova Scotia □[4], Can.	186	45.00 N	63.00 W
Nova Siri	68	40.09 N	16.32 E
Nova Sofala	156	20.09 S	34.42 E
Nova Soure	250	11.14 S	38.29 W
Novate Mezzola	58	46.15 N	9.27 E
Novate Milanese	266b	45.32 N	9.08 E
Nova Timboteua	250	1.12 S	47.24 W
Novato	226	38.06 N	122.34 W
Novato Creek ≃	282	38.06 N	122.29 W
Nova Vandúzi	156	18.57 S	33.16 E
Nova Varoš	38	43.28 N	19.48 E
Nova Venécia	255	18.43 S	40.24 W
Nova Viçosa	255	17.53 S	39.22 W
Nova Vida	248	10.11 S	62.47 W
Nova Vida, Cachoeira ⌊	248	9.25 S	63.36 W
Nova Zagora	38	42.29 N	26.01 E
Nove	64	45.43 N	11.40 E
Nové Hrady	61	48.47 N	14.37 E
Novelda	34	38.23 N	0.46 W
Novellara	64	44.51 N	10.44 E
Novelty	219	40.00 N	92.12 W
Nové Město	30	50.21 N	16.09 E
Nové Město nad Váhom	30	48.46 N	17.49 E
Nové Město na Moravě	30	49.34 N	16.04 E
Nové Mlýny, údolní nádrž ⊜[1]	61	48.54 N	16.34 E
Noventa di Piave	64	45.39 N	12.31 E
Noventa Padovana	64	45.24 N	11.58 E
Noventa Vicentina	64	45.17 N	11.32 E
Noves	62	43.52 N	4.54 E
Nové Sedlo	54	50.10 N	12.42 E
Nové Strašecí	54	50.07 N	13.53 E
Nové Údoli	60	48.48 N	13.48 E
Nové Zámky	30	47.59 N	18.11 E
Novgorod	76	58.31 N	31.17 E
Novgorodka	78	48.21 N	32.39 E
Novgorod-Severskij	78	51.59 N	33.16 E
Novgorodskoje	83	48.20 N	37.50 E
Novi	216	42.28 N	83.28 W
Novi Bečej	38	45.36 N	20.08 E
Novi Beograd	38	44.49 N	20.27 E
Novice	196	31.59 N	99.37 W
Novičicha	86	52.13 N	81.24 E
Novi di Modena	64	44.54 N	10.54 E
Novigrad, Cro.	36	45.19 N	13.34 E
Novigrad, Cro.	36	44.11 N	15.33 E
Novikovo, Ross.	86	58.15 N	80.39 E
Novikovo, Ross.	89	46.23 N	143.20 E
Novi Ligure	62	44.46 N	8.47 E
Noville	56	50.40 N	5.23 E
Novi Lyon Drain ≍	281	42.30 N	83.38 W
Novinger	194	40.13 N	92.42 W
Novinka	76	59.49 N	33.20 E
Novion-Porcien	50	49.36 N	4.25 E
Novi Pazar, Blg.	38	43.21 N	27.12 E
Novi Pazar, Jugo.	38	43.08 N	20.31 E
Novi Sad	38	45.15 N	19.50 E
Novi Vinodolski	36	45.08 N	14.48 E
Novka	76	55.27 N	30.24 E
Novki	80	56.22 N	41.06 E
Novl'anka	80	55.48 N	41.44 E
Novlenskoje	76	59.37 N	39.20 E
Novo ≃, Bra.	248	4.55 S	70.33 W
Novo ≃, Bra.	250	6.22 S	55.42 W
Novo ≃, Bra.	250	4.30 S	53.50 W
Novo ≃, Bra.	256	21.23 S	42.44 W
Novo, Lago ⊜	250	1.30 N	50.40 W
Novoachtyrka	83	48.55 N	38.49 E
Nôvo Acôrdo	255	13.10 S	46.48 W
Novoajdar	83	48.57 N	39.00 E
Novoaleksandrovka, Kaz.	86	51.47 N	68.49 E
Novoaleksandrovka, Ross.	80	51.56 N	52.26 E
Novoaleksandrovka, Ukr.	83	48.17 N	39.37 E
Novoaleksandrovka, Ukr.	83	49.08 N	39.17 E
Novoaleksandrovo	265b	55.59 N	37.33 E
Novoaleksandrovsk	80	45.29 N	41.16 E
Novoaleksejevka, Kaz.	86	52.47 N	74.54 E
Novoaleksejevka, Kaz.	86	52.56 N	64.41 E
Novoaleksejevka, Kaz.	86	50.08 N	55.39 E
Novoaleksejevka, Ukr.	78	46.06 N	32.30 E
Novoaleksejevka, Ukr.	78	46.13 N	34.39 E
Novoaltajsk	86	53.24 N	83.58 E
Novoamvrosijevskoje	83	47.49 N	38.29 E
Novoanninskij	80	50.32 N	42.41 E
Novoarchangel'sk	78	48.39 N	30.48 E
Novoarchangel'skoje	265b	55.55 N	37.33 E
Novo Aripuanã	246	5.08 S	60.22 W
Novoasbest	86	57.44 N	60.45 E
Novoazovsk	83	47.08 N	38.05 E
Novobachmutovka	83	48.15 N	37.48 E
Novobatajsk	83	46.54 N	39.47 E
Novobelaja	78	49.49 N	39.18 E
Novobessergenovka	83	47.11 N	38.51 E
Novobogatinskoje	80	47.22 N	51.11 E
Novobogdanovka	78	47.06 N	35.29 E
Novobogordskoje	80	53.11 N	53.56 E
Novoborovaja	83	49.15 N	38.33 E
Novo Brasil	255	16.11 S	50.38 W
Novobratcevskij	82	55.51 N	37.23 E
Novoburejskij	89	49.49 N	129.54 E
Novočeboksarsk	80	56.08 N	47.30 E
Novo Čeremšansk	80	54.21 N	50.10 E
Novočerkassk	83	47.25 N	40.06 E
Novočernorečenskij	86	56.16 N	91.06 E
Novocharitonovo	82	55.35 N	38.30 E
Novocherkassk → Novočerkassk	83	47.25 N	40.06 E
Novochop'orsk	80	51.07 N	41.37 E
Novochop'orskij	80	51.06 N	41.33 E
Novochovrino ⬥[8]	265b	55.52 N	37.30 E
Novociml'anskaja	80	47.59 N	42.17 E
Novo Cruzeiro	255	17.29 S	41.53 W
Novodanilovka	78	46.38 N	35.00 E
Novoderev'ankov-Skaja	78	46.19 N	38.45 E
Novoderkul	83	49.08 N	39.38 E

PORTUGUÊS

Nome	Página	Lat.°′	Long.°′ W = Oeste
Novodevičje	80	53.37 N	48.52 E
Novodolinka	86	51.12 N	72.33 E
Novodolinskij	86	49.44 N	72.45 E
Novodoroninskoje	88	51.08 N	112.08 E
Novodružesk	83	48.58 N	38.21 E
Novodubovoje	76	52.19 N	39.13 E
Novodugino	76	55.38 N	34.18 E
Novodvinsk	24	64.26 N	40.47 E
Novodžerelijevskaja	78	45.46 N	38.41 E
Novoekonomičeskoje	83	48.18 N	37.15 E
Novofetinino	82	56.14 N	39.17 E
Novogaritovo	80	52.47 N	40.07 E
Novogirejevo ⬥[8]	265b	55.45 N	37.49 E
Novogorbovo	82	55.43 N	36.29 E
Novogornyj	86	55.37 N	60.47 E
Novograd-Volynskij	78	50.36 N	27.36 E
Novogrigorjevka	78	46.24 N	34.59 E
Novogrigorjevskaja	80	49.26 N	43.37 E
Novogrodovka	83	48.13 N	37.20 E
Novogroznenskij	84	43.15 N	46.15 E
Novogrudok	76	53.36 N	25.50 E
Novogupalovka	78	48.02 N	35.26 E
Novo Hamburgo	252	29.41 S	51.08 W
Novo Horizonte	255	21.28 S	49.13 W
Novoignatjevka	83	47.38 N	37.41 E
Novoiljinsk	88	51.42 N	108.41 E
Novoiljinskij	86	57.54 N	55.30 E
Novoivanovka, Kaz.	85	43.08 N	71.26 E
Novoivanovka, Ukr.	78	49.44 N	33.28 E
Novoivanovka, Ukr.	83	47.41 N	38.23 E
Novoivanovskoje	265b	55.43 N	37.22 E
Novoizborsk	76	57.50 N	27.59 E
Novojampol'	89	52.55 N	127.38 E
Novojamskoje	76	52.14 N	34.28 E
Novoje, Ross.	82	55.38 N	38.55 E
Novoje, Ross.	86	58.53 N	68.40 E
Novoje Alechnovo	82	56.02 N	36.49 E
Novojegorjevskoje	86	51.46 N	80.53 E
Novojekaterinovka	83	47.43 N	38.07 E
Novoje Koval'ovo	265a	59.59 N	30.34 E
Novoje Leušino	80	56.48 N	40.32 E
Novojel'n'a	76	53.28 N	25.35 E
Novojenisejsk	86	58.16 N	92.24 E
Novoje Pavšino	82	54.15 N	37.07 E
Novoje Zarečje	76	57.43 N	34.22 E
Novokačalinsk	89	45.06 N	132.01 E
Novokadinsk	88	54.46 N	101.24 E
Novokamala	88	55.58 N	94.58 E
Novokarasuk	86	56.16 N	71.46 E
Novokaširovo	80	54.58 N	52.32 E
Novokaširsk	82	54.51 N	38.15 E
Novokazalinsk	86	45.50 N	62.10 E
Novokijevskij	80	50.27 N	43.08 E
Novokorsunskaja	78	45.38 N	39.09 E
Novokrasn'anka	83	49.08 N	38.18 E
Novokrasnoje	78	48.01 N	31.21 E
Novokručininskij	88	51.46 N	113.48 E
Novokubanka	86	51.40 N	70.44 E
Novokujbyševsk	80	53.07 N	49.58 E
Novokurovka	89	48.51 N	134.20 E
Novokuzneck	86	53.45 N	87.06 E
Novokuznetsk → Novokuzneck	86	53.45 N	87.06 E
Novolakskoje	84	43.07 N	46.29 E
Novolazarevskaja ♥[3]	9	70.45 S	11.50 E
Novoleuškovskaja	78	45.59 N	39.58 E
Novoli	68	40.23 N	18.03 E
Novolimarevka	83	49.17 N	39.36 E
Novolukoml'	76	54.40 N	29.08 E
Novol'vovsk	76	53.55 N	38.47 E
Novomalorossijskaja	78	45.38 N	39.53 E
Novomansurkino	80	53.52 N	51.52 E
Novomargaritovka	83	46.54 N	38.50 E
Novomariinka	88	55.27 N	96.01 E
Novomarkovka	86	51.44 N	72.17 E
Novomel'nikov	84	43.56 N	45.09 E
Novomelovatka	78	50.27 N	40.46 E
Novomelovoje	78	51.23 N	38.13 E
Novo Mesto	36	45.48 N	15.10 E
Novomichajlovka, Ross.	86	55.13 N	81.57 E
Novomichajlovka, Ukr.	78	47.19 N	36.04 E
Novomichajlovka, Ukr.	83	47.51 N	37.29 E
Novomichajlovskij	78	44.15 N	38.51 E
Novomichajlovskoje	82	55.25 N	37.10 E
Novominskaja	78	46.19 N	38.57 E
Novomirgorod	78	48.47 N	31.39 E
Novomoskovsk, Ross.	82	54.05 N	38.13 E
Novomoskovsk, Ukr.	78	48.37 N	35.12 E
Novomyšastovskaja	78	45.12 N	38.35 E
Novonagajevo	80	55.56 N	54.15 E
Novonikolajevka, Kaz.	85	42.26 N	70.28 E
Novonikolajevka, Ross.	83	46.59 N	39.36 E
Novonikolajevka, Ukr.	78	47.59 N	35.55 E
Novonikolajevka, Ukr.	78	46.13 N	32.45 E
Novonikolajevskij	80	50.58 N	42.22 E
Novonikolayevsk → Novosibirsk	86	55.02 N	82.55 E
Novonikol'skoje, Ross.	76	59.25 N	33.13 E
Novonikol'skoje, Ross.	80	49.09 N	45.00 E
Novonikol'skoje, Ross.	86	59.46 N	79.12 E
Novonikol'skoje, Ross.	265b	55.50 N	37.15 E
Novonikol'skoje, Ukr.	83	49.21 N	39.51 E
Novoomel'kovo	83	49.08 N	39.05 E
Novo Oriente	250	5.32 S	40.42 W
Novoorsk	86	51.23 N	58.58 E
Novopavlovka	88	51.13 N	109.14 E
Novopavlovskaja	84	43.58 N	43.38 E
Novopavlovskoje	88	50.56 N	111.35 E
Novopetrovo	86	57.11 N	69.10 E
Novopetrovskoje	82	55.59 N	36.28 E
Novopiscovo	76	57.19 N	41.54 E
Novopodrezkovo	82	55.57 N	37.21 E
Novopokrovka, Kaz.	86	50.41 N	80.28 E
Novopokrovka, Kaz.	86	53.43 N	67.45 E
Novopokrovka, Kyrg.	85	42.52 N	74.45 E
Novopokrovka, Ross.	89	45.52 N	134.28 E
Novopokrovka, Ukr.	78	48.03 N	34.37 E
Novopokrovskoje	80	51.35 N	43.36 E
Novopolevodino	80	51.46 N	47.29 E
Novopolock	76	55.31 N	28.38 E
Novopskov	83	49.33 N	39.05 E
Novorajčichinsk	89	49.47 N	129.38 E
Novor'ažsk	80	53.44 N	40.07 E
Novorepnoje	80	51.06 N	48.24 E
Novorossijka	85	42.44 N	76.07 E
Novorossijsk	78	44.45 N	37.45 E
Novorossijskoje	86	50.13 N	58.00 E
Novorossiysk → Novorossijsk	78	44.45 N	37.45 E
Novorossoš'	83	49.32 N	39.15 E
Novorudnyj	86	51.30 N	58.10 E
Novorybinka	86	51.51 N	71.14 E
Novorybnoje	74	72.50 N	105.50 E
Novoržev	76	57.02 N	29.20 E
Novošachtinsk	83	47.47 N	39.56 E
Novosaratovka	265a	59.50 N	30.32 E
Novoščerbinovskaja	78	46.28 N	38.38 E
Novosel'e	86	54.10 N	76.53 E
Novoselenginsk	88	51.06 N	106.37 E
Novoselica	78	48.14 N	26.17 E
Novoselickoje	84	44.45 N	43.26 E
Novoseliščе	78	49.48 N	25.03 E
Novoselje	265a	59.48 N	30.05 E
Novoselki, Ross.	82	55.08 N	37.33 E
Novoselki, Ross.	82	54.49 N	38.55 E
Novosel'nyj	86	50.00 N	54.38 E
Novoselovka Pervaja	83	48.12 N	37.31 E
Novoselovo	82	56.04 N	39.04 E
Novosel'skoje	78	45.20 N	28.33 E
Novosemejkino	80	53.23 N	50.22 E
Novosergijevka, Ross.	80	52.06 N	53.39 E
Novosergijevka, Ross.	265a	59.54 N	30.34 E
Novoseslavino	80	53.21 N	40.26 E
Novošešminsk	80	55.04 N	51.15 E
Novoshakhtinsk → Novošachtinsk	83	47.47 N	39.56 E
Novosibirsk	86	55.02 N	82.55 E
Novosibirskije ostrova II	74	75.00 N	142.00 E
Novosibirskoje vodochranilišče ⊜[1]	86	54.35 N	82.35 E
Novosil'	76	52.58 N	37.03 E
Novosil'skoje	78	51.56 N	38.31 E
Novosokol'niki	76	56.21 N	30.10 E
Novos'olki, Bela.	76	52.24 N	28.33 E
Novos'olki, Bela.	78	52.02 N	24.21 E
Novos'olki, Ross.	76	56.01 N	33.37 E
Novos'olki, Ross.	80	54.50 N	39.46 E
Novos'olki, Ross.	80	55.48 N	42.41 E
Novos'olki, Ross.	265a	59.42 N	30.17 E
Novos'olovka	83	49.04 N	37.42 E
Novos'olovo, Ross.	86	55.04 N	91.07 E
Novos'olovo, Ross.	88	56.04 N	107.42 E
Novos'olovskoje	78	45.26 N	33.34 E
Novospasovka	83	47.42 N	39.04 E
Novospasskoje	80	53.08 N	47.45 E
Novostrel'covka	83	49.20 N	39.55 E
Novostrojevo	76	54.27 N	21.50 E
Novosvetlovka	83	48.30 N	39.30 E
Novosysojevka	89	44.14 N	133.22 E
Novotavolžanka	78	50.22 N	36.50 E
Novotitarovskaja	78	45.14 N	39.00 E
Novotroick, Ross.	86	56.11 N	78.41 E
Novotroick, Ross.	86	51.12 N	58.20 E
Novotroickoje, Kaz.	85	43.42 N	73.46 E
Novotroickoje, Ross.	80	58.28 N	47.06 E
Novotroickoje, Ukr.	78	46.22 N	34.20 E
Novotroickoje, Ukr.	83	47.43 N	37.35 E
Novo-Troitsk → Novotroick	86	51.12 N	58.20 E
Novotulka, Ross.	80	52.38 N	48.45 E
Novotulka, Ross.	80	50.50 N	47.34 E
Novotul'skij	82	54.10 N	37.43 E
Novoukolovo	78	51.02 N	38.25 E
Novoukrainka	78	48.19 N	31.32 E
Novouljanovsk	80	54.08 N	48.24 E
Novoural'sk	86	51.15 N	57.16 E
Novouzensk	80	50.28 N	48.08 E
Novovaršavka	86	54.11 N	74.42 E
Novovasiljevka, Ukr.	78	46.51 N	36.46 E
Novovasiljevka, Ukr.	78	46.48 N	35.44 E
Novov'atsk	80	58.29 N	49.44 E
Novov'azniki	80	56.12 N	42.10 E
Novovolynsk	78	50.50 N	24.05 E
Novovoroncovka	78	47.29 N	33.54 E
Novovoronežskij	78	51.16 N	39.11 E
Novovoskresenovka	85	42.50 N	73.32 E
Novovoskresenskoje	78	47.21 N	33.37 E
Novozacharkino	80	52.11 N	48.29 E
Novozagorje	82	55.39 N	38.38 E
Novozavidovskij	82	56.33 N	36.26 E
Novožilovskaja	24	64.50 N	51.20 E
Novozizevka	80	50.48 N	49.08 E
Novozybkov	76	52.32 N	31.56 E
Novska	36	45.21 N	16.59 E
Nový Bohumín	30	49.56 N	18.20 E
Nový Bor	54	50.45 N	14.33 E
Novyj	86	55.39 N	86.39 E
Novyj Afon	84	43.06 N	40.48 E
Novyj Bor	24	66.43 N	52.16 E
Novyj Bug	78	47.41 N	32.30 E
Novyj Bujan	80	53.41 N	50.04 E
Novyj Bykov	78	50.36 N	31.39 E
Novyj Donbass ⬥[8]	83	48.05 N	38.46 E
Novyj Dvor	76	52.50 N	24.21 E
Novyje Ajbesi	80	54.49 N	47.02 E
Novyje Aneny	78	46.52 N	29.14 E
Novyje Basy	78	50.53 N	34.51 E
Novyje Burasy	80	52.08 N	46.06 E
Novyje Denisoviči	76	54.12 N	29.13 E
Novyje Gorki	80	56.42 N	41.06 E
Novyje Maty	80	55.15 N	54.04 E
Novyje Salty	80	54.06 N	53.26 E
Novyje Senžary	78	49.21 N	34.19 E
Novyje Z'atcy	80	57.27 N	52.36 E
Nový Jičín	30	49.36 N	18.00 E
Novyj Jaryčev	78	49.55 N	24.18 E
Novyj Jegorlyk	80	46.24 N	41.54 E
Novyj Karačaj	84	43.49 N	41.56 E
Novyj Karamass	80	56.11 N	48.58 E
Novyj Kiner	80	56.24 N	49.44 E
Novyj Multan	80	57.09 N	52.19 E
Novyj Nekouz	76	57.54 N	38.04 E
Novyj Oskol	78	50.46 N	37.53 E
Novyj Pogost	76	55.30 N	27.29 E
Novyj Port	74	67.40 N	72.52 E
Novyj Put'	85	43.29 N	73.52 E
Novyj Ropsk	76	52.18 N	32.19 E
Novyj Stan	82	56.18 N	37.00 E
Novyj Svet	83	47.48 N	38.00 E
Novyj Tap	86	57.04 N	67.49 E
Novyj Terek ≃	84	43.37 N	47.25 E
Novyj Tevriz	86	59.04 N	78.08 E
Novyj Uzen	72	43.18 N	52.48 E
Novyj Vas'ugan	86	58.34 N	76.29 E
Novy Torjal	80	57.00 N	48.44 E
Nowa Dęba	30	50.26 N	21.46 E
Nowaja Semlja → Novaja Zeml'a II	72	74.00 N	57.00 E
Nowa Ruda	30	50.35 N	16.31 E
Nowa Sól (Neusalz)	30	51.48 N	15.44 E
Nowata	196	36.42 N	95.38 W
Nowater Creek ≃	202	43.57 N	108.00 W
Nowbarān	128	35.08 N	48.42 E
Nowe	30	53.40 N	18.43 E
Nowe Miasto Lubawskie	30	53.27 N	19.35 E
Nowe Miasto nad Pilicą	30	51.38 N	20.35 E
Nowendoc	166	31.32 S	151.43 E
Nowe Warpno	30	53.44 N	14.16 E
Nowfel low Shātow	128	34.23 N	50.32 E
Nowgong	124	25.04 N	79.27 E
Nowingi	166	34.36 S	142.14 E
Nowitna ≃	180	65.55 N	154.17 W
Nowogard	30	53.40 N	15.08 E
Nowogród	30	53.15 N	21.53 E
Nowogrodziec	30	51.12 N	15.25 E
Nowokusnezk → Novokuzneck	86	53.45 N	87.06 E
Nowood ≃	202	44.17 N	107.58 W
Nowosibirsk → Novosibirsk	86	55.02 N	82.55 E
Nowra	170	34.53 S	150.36 E
Nowrangapur	122	19.14 N	82.33 E
Nowshāk ∧	123	36.26 N	71.50 E
Nowshera	123	34.01 N	71.59 E
Nowy Dwór Gdański	30	54.13 N	19.06 E
Nowy Dwór Mazowiecki	30	52.26 N	20.43 E
Nowy Sącz	30	49.38 N	20.42 E
Nowy Sącz □[4]	30	49.30 N	20.15 E
Nowy Staw	30	54.09 N	19.00 E
Nowy Targ	30	49.29 N	20.02 E
Nowy Tomyśl	30	52.20 N	16.07 E
Now Zād	120	32.24 N	64.28 E
Noxapater	194	32.59 N	89.03 W
Noxe ≃	50	48.33 N	3.35 E
Noxen	210	41.25 N	76.03 W
Noxon	202	48.00 N	115.47 W
Noxon Reservoir ⊜[1]	202	47.54 N	115.40 W
Noxubee ≃	194	32.50 N	88.10 W
Noy ≃	110	17.05 N	105.02 E
Noya	34	42.47 N	8.53 W
Noya ≃	152	0.58 N	9.48 E
Noyant	50	47.31 N	0.08 E
Noye ≃	50	49.51 N	2.20 E
Noyelles-sur Mer	50	50.11 N	1.43 E
Noyers	50	47.42 N	4.00 E
Noyers, Ruisseau des ≃	275a	45.21 N	73.22 W
Noyes Island I	182	55.30 N	133.40 W
Noyon	50	49.35 N	3.00 E
Nožaj-Jurt	84	43.05 N	46.24 E
Nozawa-onsen	94	36.55 N	138.27 E
Nozay, Fr.	32	47.34 N	1.38 W
Nozay, Fr.	261	48.40 N	2.14 E
Nozeroy	58	46.47 N	6.02 E
Nozori-dam ⬥[6]	94	36.43 N	138.39 E
Nozori-ko ⊜	94	36.42 N	138.39 E
Nozuta	268	35.35 N	139.27 E
Nqamakwe	158	32.12 S	27.56 E
Nqutu	158	28.13 S	30.32 E
N'Riquinha	152	15.45 S	21.42 E
N'Rougas	158	29.07 S	21.09 E
Nsa, Oued en ∨	148	32.28 N	5.24 E
Nsaba	150	5.39 N	0.45 W
Nsah	152	2.22 S	15.19 E
Nsang	152	2.02 N	10.56 E
Nsanje	154	16.55 S	35.12 E
Nsawam	150	5.50 N	0.20 W
Nsefu Game Reserve ⬥[4]	154	13.07 S	32.10 E
Nsele ≃	152	4.14 S	15.33 E
Nseleni	158	28.33 S	31.39 E
Nsok	152	1.08 N	11.16 E
Nsoko	158	27.02 S	31.57 E
Nsontin	152	3.09 S	18.00 E
Nsouélé	273b	4.12 S	15.11 E
Nsukka	150	6.52 N	7.24 E
Nsuta	150	5.17 N	1.58 W
Ntakat	150	16.49 N	11.43 W
Ntambanana	158	28.36 S	31.45 E
Ntandembele	152	2.11 S	17.08 E
Ntcheu	154	14.49 S	34.38 E
Ntem ≃	152	2.15 N	9.45 E
Ntoum	152	0.23 N	9.47 E
Ntsama	152	0.32 S	14.38 E
N'Tsaoueni	157a	11.27 S	43.18 E
Ntui	152	4.27 N	11.38 E
Ntumba	154	8.20 S	32.05 E
Ntusi	154	0.03 N	31.13 E
Ntwetwe Pan ≚	156	20.30 S	25.20 E
Nuala	154	13.27 S	28.16 E
Nuanchitang	104	41.02 N	120.41 E
Nuanetsi ≃	156	22.40 S	31.50 E
Nuangola	210	41.09 N	75.58 W
Nuanli	102	23.26 N	100.51 E
Nuannuan	269d	25.06 N	121.44 E
Nuanshui	100	28.53 N	117.51 E
Nuanzhouying	100	25.22 N	117.22 E
Nuasjärvi ⊜	26	64.10 N	28.05 E
Nuatabu	174t	1.33 N	172.59 E
Nuatja	150	6.57 N	1.10 E
Nuʻaymah	132	32.38 N	36.10 E
Nūbah	142	30.29 N	31.33 E
Nūbah, Jibāl an- ⋌	140	11.00 N	30.45 E
Nūbārīyah, Turʻat an- ≍	142	30.43 N	30.46 E
Nubian Desert ⬥[2]	140	20.30 N	33.00 E
Ñuble ≃	252	36.39 S	72.27 W
Nubra ≃	123	34.39 N	77.36 E
Nucet	38	46.28 N	22.35 E
Nucetto	62	44.20 N	8.04 E
Nucha → Šeki	84	41.12 N	47.12 E
Nuchatlitz Inlet c	182	49.45 N	126.55 W
N'uchča	24	63.27 N	46.28 E
Nuch'ŏn-ni	98	38.14 N	126.16 E
Nucla	200	38.16 N	108.32 W
Núcleo Colonial São Bento	287a	22.44 S	43.18 W
N'učpas	24	60.51 N	51.18 E
Nucuray ≃	246	5.02 S	75.34 W
Nuda, Monte la ∧	64	44.17 N	10.15 E
Nudaybah	142	30.59 N	30.22 E
Nudol' ≃	82	56.07 N	36.42 E
Nudol'-Šarino	82	56.06 N	36.31 E
Nudow	264a	52.20 N	13.10 E
Nueces ≃	196	27.50 N	97.30 W
Nueces Plains ≚	196	28.30 N	99.15 W
Nueltin Lake ⊜	176	60.20 N	99.50 W
Nuenen	52	51.29 N	5.33 E
Nü'er ≃	98	40.57 N	121.19 E
Nü'erhe	104	41.04 N	121.00 E
Nuestra Señora de Talavera	252	25.26 S	63.48 W
Nueva, Isla I	254	55.13 S	66.30 W
Nueva Antioquia	246	6.05 N	69.26 W
Nueva Asunción □[5]	248	21.00 S	61.00 W
Nueva Atzacoalco ⬥[8]	286a	19.29 N	99.05 W
Nueva Brunswick → New Brunswick □[4]	186	46.30 N	66.15 W
Nueva Caledonia → New Caledonia □[2]	175f	21.30 S	165.30 E
Nueva Chicago ⬥[8]	288	34.40 S	58.30 W
Nueva Ciudad Guerrero	232	26.35 N	99.15 W
Nueva Concepción	236	14.08 N	89.18 W
Nueva Cuadrilla	234	18.04 N	101.33 W
Nueva Ecija □[4]	116	15.35 N	121.00 E
Nueva Escocia → Nova Scotia □[4]	186	45.00 N	63.00 W
Nueva Esparta □[3]	246	11.00 N	64.00 W
Nueva Francia	252	28.11 S	64.12 W
Nueva Galia	252	35.07 S	65.15 W
Nueva Germania	252	23.54 S	56.45 W
Nueva Gerona	240p	21.53 N	82.48 W
Nueva Guinea, Isla → New Guinea I	164	5.00 S	140.00 E
Nueva Hébridas → Vanuatu □[1]	175f	16.00 S	167.00 E
Nueva Helvecia	258	34.19 S	57.13 W
Nueva Imperial	252	38.44 S	72.57 W
Nueva Italia de Ruiz	234	19.01 N	102.06 W
Nueva Loja	246	0.06 N	76.52 W
Nueva Lubecka	254	44.32 S	70.24 W
Nueva Ocotepeque	236	14.24 N	89.13 W
Nueva Palmira	258	33.53 S	58.25 W
Nueva Paz	240p	22.46 N	81.45 W
Nueva Pompeya ⬥[8]	288	34.39 S	58.25 W
Nueva Rosita	232	27.57 N	101.13 W
Nueva San Salvador	236	13.41 N	89.17 W
Nueva Segovia □[5]	236	13.40 N	86.10 W
Nueva Siberia, Islas → Novosibirskije ostrova II	74	75.00 N	142.00 E
Nueva Venecia	236	14.03 N	91.33 W
Nueva Vizcaya □[4]	116	16.25 N	121.10 E
Nueva Zelandia → New Zealand □[1]	172	41.00 S	174.00 E
Nueva Zembla, Isla de → Novaja Zeml'a II	72	74.00 N	57.00 E
Nueve, Canal Numero ≍	252	36.11 S	57.18 W
Nueve de Julio	252	35.27 S	60.52 W
Nuevitas	240p	21.33 N	77.16 W
Nuevitas, Bahía de c	240p	21.30 N	77.12 W
Nuevo	228	33.48 N	117.09 W
Nuevo, Bajo ⊹[4]	238	15.55 N	78.30 W
Nuevo, Cayo I	232	21.51 N	92.05 W
Nuevo, Golfo c	254	42.42 S	64.36 W
Nuevo Berlín	252	32.59 S	58.03 W
Nuevo Camarón	196	27.05 N	99.55 W
Nuevo Casas Grandes	232	30.25 N	107.55 W
Nuevo Chagres	236	9.14 N	80.05 W
Nuevo Delicias	232	26.15 N	102.50 W
Nuevo Laredo	232	27.30 N	99.31 W
Nuevo Léon	204	32.20 N	115.12 W
Nuevo León □[3]	232	25.40 N	100.00 W
Nuevo Morelos	234	17.31 N	95.02 W
Nuevo Necaxa	234	20.13 N	98.00 W
Nuevo Poblado el Oro	196	26.50 N	101.19 W
Nuevo Primero de Mayo	196	26.01 N	98.02 W
Nuevo Progreso	232	18.38 N	92.18 W
Nuevo Rocafuerte	246	0.56 S	75.24 W
Nuevo Saucillo	196	27.20 N	104.54 W
Nufcor	273d	26.17 S	27.44 E
Nugaal □[4]	144	8.30 N	49.00 E
Nugaaleed, Dooxo ∨	144	8.35 N	48.35 E
Nugget Point ≻	172	46.27 S	169.49 E
Nûgssuaq ≻[1]	176	70.25 N	52.30 W
Nugu ⊜[1]	122	11.58 N	76.28 E
Nuguria Islands II	14	3.20 S	154.45 E
Nūh	124	28.07 N	77.01 E
Nūh, Rās ≻	128	25.05 N	62.24 E
Nuhaka	172	39.03 S	177.45 E
Nuhaydāt as-Sūd, Jabal an- ∧	142	28.01 N	32.21 E
Nuhūd, Jabal an- ∧	140	14.50 N	29.53 E
Nui I[1]	14	7.15 S	177.10 E
Nuia	76	58.04 N	25.33 E
Nuits-Saint-Georges	58	47.08 N	4.57 E
Nuits-sur-Armançon	50	47.44 N	4.12 E
N'uja	74	60.32 N	116.14 E
N'uja ≃	74	60.32 N	116.20 E
Nujiang	102	29.58 N	97.25 E
N'uk, ozero ⊜	24	64.27 N	31.45 E
Nuka Island I	180	59.21 N	150.42 W
Nukan	175c	7.23 N	151.53 E
Nukata	94	34.55 N	137.17 E
Nukatl', chrebet ⋌	84	42.15 N	46.35 E
Nukey Bluff ⏏[4]	166	32.33 S	135.40 E
Nukhayb	128	32.02 N	42.15 E
Nukhaylah ⊤[4]	140	19.03 N	26.19 E
Nukhaylah, Wādī an- ∨	132	31.27 N	35.49 E
Nukiki	175e	6.46 S	156.28 E
N'uksenica	24	60.25 N	44.13 E
Nukuʻalofa	174w	21.08 S	175.12 W
Nukufetau I[1]	14	8.00 S	178.22 E
Nukuhu	164	5.35 S	149.25 E
Nukulaelae I[1]	14	9.23 S	179.52 E
Nukumanu Islands II	14	4.30 S	159.30 E
Nukunonu I	14	9.12 S	171.54 W
Nukunuku	174w	21.08 S	175.18 W
Nukuoro I[1]	14	3.51 N	154.58 E
Nukus	72	42.50 N	59.29 E
Nul	175f	16.49 S	168.24 E
Nulato	180	64.43 N	158.06 W
Nullagine	162	21.53 S	120.06 E
Nullagine ≃	162	20.43 S	120.33 E
Nullarbor	162	31.26 S	130.55 E
Nullarbor National Park ♠	162	31.30 S	130.30 E
Nullarbor Plain ≚	162	31.00 S	129.00 E
Nulltown	218	39.35 N	85.10 W
Nul'vand	85	38.16 N	70.32 E
Nulvi	71	40.47 N	8.45 E
Num, Mios I	164	1.30 S	135.13 E
Numabin Bay c	184	56.30 N	103.08 W
Numakuma	96	34.23 N	133.20 E
Numan	146	9.28 N	12.02 E
Numana	66	43.31 N	13.37 E
Numancia	116	9.52 N	125.58 E
Numancia ⊥	34	41.48 N	2.25 W
Numansdorp	52	51.44 N	4.26 E
Numara I	122	6.26 N	73.03 E
Numata, Nihon	92a	43.48 N	141.57 E
Numata, Nihon	94	36.38 N	139.03 E
Numata, Nihon	96	34.27 N	132.24 E
Numatinna ≃	140	7.14 N	27.37 E
Numazu	94	35.06 N	138.52 E
Numbargulme, Mount ∧	164	14.56 S	145.03 E
Number 5 Mine	214	41.08 N	80.11 W
Numedal ∨	26	60.06 N	9.06 E
Numeralla	171b	36.11 S	149.20 E
Numeralla ≃	171b	36.06 S	149.11 E
Numfoor, Pulau I	164	1.03 S	134.54 E
Numidia	210	40.53 N	76.24 W
Numila	229b	21.54 N	159.33 W
Nu Mine	214	40.48 N	79.18 W
Numto	74	63.40 N	71.20 E
Numurkah	166	36.06 S	145.26 E
Nun ≃[1]	150	4.20 N	6.00 E
Nun'amo	180	65.37 N	170.40 W
Nunapitchuk	180	60.54 N	162.29 W
Nunawading	169	37.49 S	145.10 E
Nünchritz	54	51.18 N	13.23 E
Nunda	210	42.34 N	77.56 W
Nundah	171a	27.24 S	153.04 E
Nundu	154	3.49 S	29.05 E
Nuneaton	42	52.32 N	1.28 W
Núñes, Isla I	254	53.31 S	73.48 W
Núñez ⬥[8]	288	34.33 S	58.27 W
Nunez ≃	150	10.36 N	14.40 W
Nungarin	162	31.11 S	118.06 E
Nungesser Lake ⊜	184	51.28 N	93.35 W
Nungwe	154	2.46 S	32.01 E
Nunica	216	43.04 N	86.04 W
Nunivak Island I	180	60.00 N	166.30 W
Nunjiang	89	49.10 N	125.11 E
Nunjikompita	162	32.16 S	134.19 E
Nunkini	232	20.20 N	90.11 W
Nunkun ∧	123	33.59 N	76.01 E
Nunligran	180	64.48 N	175.24 W
Nunnelly	194	35.51 N	87.28 W
Ñuñoa	286e	33.28 S	70.36 W
Nunshan	89	48.59 N	125.14 E
Nunspeet	52	52.23 N	5.46 E
Nuomin ≃	89	48.06 N	124.26 E
Nuomin Dashan ∧	89	50.15 N	122.46 E
Nuon ≃	150	6.30 N	8.36 W
Nuoro	71	40.19 N	9.20 E
Nuoro □[4]	71	40.10 N	9.20 E
Nuqruṣ, Jabal ∧	140	24.49 N	34.36 E
Nuquí	246	5.42 N	77.17 W
Nura	86	48.53 N	62.20 E
Nura ≃	86	50.30 N	69.59 E
Nurallao	71	39.47 N	9.05 E
Nuraminis	71	39.26 N	9.01 E
Nuratau, chrebet ⋌	85	40.20 N	67.15 E
Nuraxi, Nuraghe su ⊥	71	39.42 N	9.00 E
N'urba	74	63.17 N	118.20 E
Nürburg	56	50.21 N	6.57 E
Nürburgring ♠	56	50.21 N	6.58 E
Nur Dağları ⋌	130	36.45 N	36.20 E
Nure ≃	62	45.03 N	9.49 E
Nurek	85	38.23 N	69.19 E
Nurekskoje vodochranilišče ⊜[1]	85	38.30 N	69.30 E
Nuremberg	210	40.56 N	76.10 W
Nuremberg → Nürnberg	60	49.27 N	11.04 E
Nürenbei	107	30.11 N	106.04 E
Nūrestān □[9]	123	35.30 N	70.45 E
Nurettin	130	39.14 N	42.25 E
Nurhak	130	37.58 N	37.25 E
Nuria, Monte ∧	66	42.21 N	13.05 E
Nuriootpa	168b	34.29 S	139.00 E
Nurlat	80	54.26 N	50.46 E
Nurlaty	80	55.37 N	48.18 E
Nūrmahal	123	31.06 N	75.36 E
Nurmes	26	63.33 N	29.07 E
Nurmijärvi	26	60.28 N	24.48 E
Nūrnagar	126	22.20 N	89.03 E
Nürnberg	60	49.27 N	11.04 E
Nürnberg, Flughafen ⊠	60	49.30 N	11.06 E
Nūrpur, India	123	31.10 N	76.29 E
Nūrpur, India	123	32.18 N	75.54 E
Nurpur, India	126	22.13 N	88.05 E
Nūrpur, Pāk.	123	31.53 N	71.54 E
Nurrari Lakes ⊜	162	29.01 S	130.05 E
Nurri	71	39.43 N	9.14 E
Nurri, Mount ∧[2]	166	31.42 S	146.02 E
Nursery	222	28.56 N	97.06 W
Nürtingen	56	48.38 N	9.20 E
Nus	62	45.45 N	7.28 E

≃	River	Fluß	Río	Rivière	Rio
≍	Canal	Kanal	Canal	Canal	Canal
⌊	Waterfall, Rapids	Wasserfall, Stromschnellen	Cascada, Rápidos	Chute d'eau, Rapides	Cascata, Rápidos
⊔	Strait	Meeresstraße	Estrecho	Détroit	Estreito
c	Bay, Gulf	Bucht, Golf	Bahía, Golfo	Baie, Golfe	Baía, Golfo
⊜	Lake, Lakes	See, Seen	Lago, Lagos	Lac, Lacs	Lago, Lagos
≚	Swamp	Sumpf	Pantano	Marais	Pântano
⁂	Ice Features, Glacier	Eis- und Gletscherformen	Accidentes Glaciales	Formes glaciaires	Acidentes glaciares
⊤	Other Hydrographic Features	Andere Hydrographische Objekte	Otros Elementos Hidrográficos	Autres données hydrographiques	Outros acidentes hidrográficos

⊹	Submarine Features	Untermeerische Objekte	Accidentes Submarinos	Formes de relief sous-marin	Acidentes submarinos
□	Political Unit	Politische Einheit	Unidad Politica	Entité politique	Unidade política
♥	Cultural Institution	Kulturelle Institution	Institución Cultural	Institution culturelle	Instituição cultural
⊥	Historical Site	Historische Stätte	Sitio Histórico	Site historique	Sitio histórico
♠	Recreational Site	Erholungs- und Ferienort	Sitio de Recreo	Centre de loisirs	Area de Lazer
⊠	Airport	Flughafen	Aeropuerto	Aéroport	Aeroporto
■	Military Installation	Militäranlage	Instalación Militar	Installation militaire	Instalação militar
⬥	Miscellaneous	Verschiedenes	Misceláneo	Divers	Diversos

ENGLISH

DEUTSCH

Symbols in the index entries represent the broad categories identified in the key at the right. Symbols with superior numbers (⋏[1]) identify subcategories (see complete key on page *I · 1)*.

Symbole im Register stellen die rechts im Schlüssel erklärten Kategorien dar. Symbole mit hochgestellten Ziffern (⋏[1]) bezeichnen Unterabteilungen einer Kategorie (vgl. vollständiger Schlüssel auf Seite *I · 1)*.

Los símbolos incluídos en el texto del índice representan las grandes categorias identificadas con la clave a la derecha. Los símbolos con numeros en su parte superior (⋏[1]) identifican las subcategorías (véase la clave completa en la página *I · 1)*.

Les symboles de l'index représentent les catégories indiquées dans la légende à droite. Les symboles suivis d'un indice (⋏[1]) représentent des sous-catégories (voir légende complète à la page *I · 1)*.

Os símbolos incluídos no texto do índice representam as grandes categorias identificadas com a chave à direita. Os símbolos com números em sua parte superior (⋏[1]) identificam as subcategorias (veja-se a chave completa à página *I · 1)*.

∧ Mountain	Berg	Montaña	Montagne	Montanha
⋏ Mountains	Gebirge	Montañas	Montagnes	Montanhas
⋈ Pass	Paß	Paso	Col	Passo
V Valley, Canyon	Tal, Cañon	Valle, Cañón	Vallée, Canyon	Vale, Canhão
≡ Plain	Ebene	Llano	Plaine	Planície
› Cape	Kap	Cabo	Cap	Cabo
I Island	Insel	Isla	Île	Ilha
II Islands	Inseln	Islas	Îles	Ilhas
⊥ Other Topographic Features	Andere Topographische Objekte	Otros Elementos Topográficos	Autres données topographiques	Outros acidentes topográficos

ESPAÑOL

Nombre	Página	Lat.°′	Long.°′ W = Oeste
Oermten	263	51.29 N	6.27 E
Oesede	52	52.12 N	8.04 E
Oespel ◆[8]	263	51.30 N	7.23 E
Oeste, Canal del ≊	266a	40.32 N	3.42 W
Oeste, Parque del ♠	266a	40.26 N	3.44 W
Oesterdam ◆[5]	52	51.29 N	4.15 E
Oestrich	263	51.22 N	7.38 E
Oestrich ◆[8]	263	51.34 N	7.22 E
Oestrum ◆[8]	263	51.25 N	6.40 E
Ōetaka-yama ∧	96	35.04 N	132.26 E
Oettingen in Bayern	56	48.57 N	10.36 E
Oetz	58	47.12 N	10.54 E
Oeuf ≃	50	48.11 N	2.21 E
Oeventrop	56	51.23 N	8.08 E
Oeversee	41	54.42 N	9.26 E
Ōe-yama ∧	96	35.27 N	135.07 E
Oeyŏn-do I	98	36.14 N	126.05 E
Of	130	40.57 N	40.18 E
O'Fallon, Il., U.S.	219	38.35 N	89.54 W
O'Fallon, Mo., U.S.	219	38.48 N	90.41 W
O'Fallon Creek ≃	198	46.50 N	105.09 W
Ofanto ≃	68	41.22 N	16.13 E
Ofaqim	132	31.17 N	34.37 E
Ofenpass → Fuorn, Pass dal)(	58	46.37 N	10.15 E
Offa	150	8.09 N	4.44 E
Offaly □[6]	48	53.20 N	7.30 W
Offanengo	62	45.22 N	9.44 E
Offemont	58	47.40 N	6.53 E
Offenbach	56	50.08 N	8.47 E
Offenburg	58	48.28 N	7.57 E
Offendorf	58	48.43 N	7.55 E
Offerdal	26	63.28 N	14.00 E
Offham	260	51.17 N	0.23 E
Officer	274b	38.04 S	145.25 E
Officer Creek ≃	162	27.45 S	132.24 E
Offida	66	42.56 N	13.41 E
Offingen	58	48.29 N	10.21 E
Offranville	50	49.52 N	1.03 E
Offutt Air Force Base ■	198	41.08 N	95.56 W
Oficina Alemania	252	25.10 S	69.55 W
Oficina Alianza	248	20.46 S	69.42 W
Oficina Chile	252	25.09 S	69.54 W
Oficina Pedro de Valdivia	252	22.36 S	69.40 W
Oficina Victoria	248	20.44 S	69.42 W
Ofin	273a	6.33 N	3.30 E
Öflingen	58	47.35 N	7.55 E
Ofotfjorden c[2]	24	68.23 N	16.10 E
Oftringen	58	47.19 N	7.56 E
Ofu	174y	14.10 S	169.42 W
Ofu I	174y	14.11 S	169.42 W
Ōfukuroshinden	268	35.53 N	139.27 E
Ōfuna	268	35.21 N	139.32 E
Ōfunato	92	39.04 N	141.43 E
Oga	92	39.53 N	139.51 E
Ogaden ◆[1]	144	8.00 N	44.00 E
Oga-hantō ›[1]	92	39.55 N	139.50 E
Ōgaki, Nihon	94	35.21 N	136.37 E
Ōgaki, Nihon	96	34.06 N	132.30 E
Ogallala	198	41.07 N	101.43 W
Ogan ≃	112	3.01 S	104.44 E
Ogano	94	36.01 N	139.00 E
Ogasa	94	34.41 N	138.06 E
Ogasawara-guntō (Bonin Islands) II	14	27.00 N	142.10 E
Ōgata, Nihon	94	37.13 N	138.20 E
Ōgata, Nihon	96	33.01 N	133.01 E
Ogata, Nihon	96	32.58 N	131.29 E
Ōga-tō ∧	94	36.13 N	138.06 E
Ogatsu	92	38.31 N	141.28 E
Ogawa, Nihon	92	32.35 N	130.43 E
Ogawa, Nihon	94	36.10 N	140.21 E
Ogawa, Nihon	94	36.37 N	137.58 E
Ogawa, Nihon	94	36.03 N	139.16 E
Ogawa, Nihon	94	36.45 N	140.08 E
Ogawa, Nihon	268	35.44 N	139.28 E
Ogawara-ko ⊜	92	40.47 N	141.20 E
Ogbomosho	150	8.08 N	4.15 E
Ogden, Ia., U.S.	190	42.02 N	94.01 W
Ogden, Ks., U.S.	198	39.06 N	96.42 W
Ogden, Pa., U.S.	208	39.49 N	75.27 W
Ogden, Ut,. U.S.	200	41.13 N	111.58 W
Ogden, Mount ∧	180	58.26 N	133.23 W
Ogden Dunes	216	41.38 N	87.12 W
Ogden Island I	212	44.52 N	75.12 W
Ogden Reservoir ⊜[1]	262	53.42 N	2.22 W
Ogdensburg, N.J., U.S.	210	41.04 N	74.35 W
Ogdensburg, N.Y., U.S.	212	44.41 N	75.29 W
Ogeechee ≃	192	31.51 N	81.06 W
Ōge-jima I	96	34.12 N	134.38 E
Ogema	184	49.35 N	104.55 W
Oggersheim	56	49.29 N	8.22 E
Oghi Fort	123	34.31 N	73.01 E
Ogibalovo	76	60.34 N	39.40 E
Ogidaki Mountain ∧[2]	190	46.58 N	83.58 W
Ogies	158	26.02 S	29.04 E
Ogi-jima I	96	34.26 N	134.04 E
Ogijo	273a	6.42 N	3.31 E
Ogilvie, Austl.	162	28.09 S	114.38 E
Ogilvie, Mn., U.S.	190	45.49 N	93.25 W
Ogilvie ≃	180	65.52 N	137.16 W
Ogilvie Mountains ⋏	180	65.00 N	139.30 W
Ogilville	218	39.08 N	86.01 W
Ōgimi	174m	26.42 N	128.07 E
Ōgino-sen ∧	96	35.26 N	134.26 E
Ogle □[6]	216	42.01 N	89.20 W
Oglesby, Il., U.S.	216	41.17 N	89.03 W
Oglesby, Tx., U.S.	222	31.25 N	97.31 W
Oglethorpe	192	32.17 N	84.03 W
Ogliastra ◆[1]	71	39.56 N	9.37 E
Ogliastro Cilento	68	40.21 N	15.03 E
Oglio ≃	64	45.02 N	10.39 E
Ogmore	166	22.37 S	149.40 E
Ogmore ≃	42	51.28 N	3.38 W
Ogmore Vale	42	51.38 N	3.31 W
Ogni	86	51.54 N	88.31 E
Ognica	54	53.07 N	14.27 E
Ognon ≃	58	47.20 N	5.29 E
Ogn'ov Jar	86	58.23 N	76.29 E
Ogn'ovka	86	49.36 N	83.25 E
Ōgo	94	36.25 N	139.10 E
Ōgo ◆[8]	270	34.49 N	135.06 E
Ogo ≃	270	34.47 N	135.04 E
Ogoamas, Bulu ∧	112	0.40 N	120.12 E
Ogōchi-dam ◆[6]	94	35.47 N	139.04 E
Ogodža	89	52.44 N	132.31 E
Ogoja	150	6.40 N	8.48 E
Ogoki ≃	176	51.38 N	85.57 W
'Ogol, Khaṭṭ el V	150	20.01 N	15.29 W
Ogooué ≃	152	0.49 S	9.00 E
Ogooué-Ivindo □[4]	152	1.00 N	13.00 E
Ogooué-Lolo □[4]	152	1.00 S	12.30 E
Ogooué-Maritime □[4]	152	2.00 S	9.30 E
Ogōri, Nihon	96	33.22 N	130.32 E
Ogōri, Nihon	96	34.06 N	131.24 E
Ogorodnoje	78	45.53 N	28.50 E
Ogose	94	35.58 N	139.18 E
Ogosta ≃	38	43.45 N	23.51 E
Ogou ≃	150	7.50 N	1.19 E
Ogoyo	273a	6.26 N	3.29 E
Ogr	140	12.02 N	27.06 E
Ogre	76	56.51 N	24.36 E
Ogre ≃	76	56.48 N	24.36 E
Ogrodzieniec	30	50.27 N	19.31 E
Ogrosen	54	51.42 N	14.02 E
Ōguchi	94	35.20 N	136.55 E
Ŏgu-dong	98	38.57 N	126.56 E
Ogudu	273a	6.34 N	3.24 E
Ogulin	36	45.16 N	15.14 E
Ogun □[3]	150	6.45 N	3.25 E
Ogun ≃	150	6.36 N	3.27 E
Ogun Forest Reserve ♠	273a	6.37 N	3.26 E
Oguni, Nihon	92	38.04 N	139.45 E
Oguni, Nihon	96	33.07 N	131.04 E

FRANÇAIS

Nom	Page	Lat.°′	Long.°′ W = Ouest
Ogunlogun	273a	6.41 N	3.28 E
Ogunquit	188	43.14 N	70.35 W
Ogura-san ∧	94	36.02 N	138.37 E
Ogurčinskij, ostrov I	128	38.55 N	53.02 E
Oguta	150	5.44 N	6.44 E
Oğuz, Tür.	130	37.49 N	41.22 E
Oğuz, Tür.	130	39.32 N	38.51 E
Oğuzeli	130	36.59 N	37.30 E
Ogwashi-Uku	150	6.10 N	6.31 E
Ohakune	172	39.25 S	175.24 E
Ohanapecosh ≃	224	46.38 N	121.37 W
Ohanet	148	28.45 N	8.55 E
Ohār	124	27.21 N	84.37 E
Ōhara, Nihon	94	35.15 N	140.23 E
Ōhara, Nihon	96	35.07 N	134.20 E
Ōharano ◆[8]	270	34.58 N	135.40 E
Ōhara-tunnel ◆[5]	94	35.12 N	137.50 E
Ōhata	92	41.24 N	141.10 E
Ōhatake	268	35.57 N	139.46 E
Ohau, Lake ⊜	172	44.15 S	169.51 E
Ohaupo	172	37.55 S	175.19 E
Ohey	56	50.26 N	5.08 E
O'Higgins, Cabo ›	174z	27.05 S	109.15 W
O'Higgins, Cerro ∧	254	48.48 S	73.11 W
O'Higgins, Lago (Lago San Martín) ⊜	254	49.00 S	72.40 W
Ohingaiti	172	39.52 S	175.43 E
Ohio	190	41.34 N	89.28 W
Ohio □[6], In., U.S.	218	38.57 N	84.51 W
Ohio □[6], W.V., U.S.	214	40.09 N	80.35 W
Ohio □[3], U.S.	178	40.15 N	82.45 W
Ohio □[3], U.S.	188	40.15 N	82.45 W
Ohio ≃	178	36.59 N	89.08 W
Ohio Brush Creek ≃	218	38.41 N	83.27 W
Ohio Brush Creek, Baker Fork ≃	218	39.02 N	83.26 W
Ohio Brush Creek, Little West Fork ≃	218	38.58 N	83.34 W
Ohio Brush Creek, West Fork ≃	218	38.56 N	83.28 W
Ohio Canal ≊	279a	41.26 N	81.40 W
Ohio Caverns ⊥[5]	216	40.14 N	83.43 W
Ohio City	216	40.46 N	84.36 W
Ohio Peak ∧	200	38.49 N	107.07 W
Ohiopyle State Park ♠	188	39.50 N	79.31 W
Ohioville, N.Y., U.S.	210	41.45 N	74.03 W
Ohioville, Pa., U.S.	214	40.40 N	80.29 W
Ōhira	94	36.20 N	139.42 E
Ōhira-yama ∧	96	34.20 N	133.57 E
Ōhito	94	35.01 N	138.56 E
Ohlau → Oława	30	50.57 N	17.17 E
Ohligs ◆[8]	263	51.09 N	7.00 E
Ohlman	219	39.21 N	89.13 W
Ohlsdorf	64	47.57 N	13.47 E
Ohm ≃	56	50.51 N	8.48 E
Ōho	94	36.08 N	140.06 E
Ohoitom	164	5.56 S	132.41 E
'Ohonua	174w	21.20 S	174.57 W
Ohoopee ≃	192	31.54 N	82.07 W
Ōhori	268	35.20 N	139.52 E
Ohorn	54	51.10 N	14.02 E
Ohra Stausee ⊜[1]	54	50.46 N	10.42 E
Ohrdruf	54	50.50 N	10.44 E
Ohre ≃, Dtsch.	54	52.18 N	11.47 E
Ohře (Eger) ≃, Europe	54	50.32 N	14.08 E
Ohrid	38	41.07 N	20.47 E
Ohrid, Lake ⊜	38	41.02 N	20.43 E
Ohrigstad	156	24.49 S	30.33 E
Öhringen	56	49.12 N	9.29 E
Ohrnberg	56	49.15 N	9.27 E
Ohuira, Bahía c	232	25.38 N	108.58 W
Ohura	172	38.50 S	174.59 E
Ōi, Nihon	96	35.28 N	135.37 E
Ōi, Nihon	268	35.51 N	139.30 E
Oi ◆[8]	268	35.35 N	139.45 E
Ōi ≃, Nihon	94	34.46 N	138.18 E
Ōi ≃, Nihon	96	35.01 N	135.39 E
Oiapoque	250	3.50 N	51.50 W
Oiapoque (Oyapock) ≃	250	4.08 N	51.40 W
Oies, Île aux I	186	47.07 N	70.30 W
Ōigawa	94	34.48 N	138.17 E
Oignies	50	50.28 N	2.59 E
Oil Center	196	32.29 N	103.15 W
Oil City, La., U.S.	194	32.44 N	93.58 W
Oil City, Pa., U.S.	214	41.26 N	79.42 W
Oil Creek ≃	214	41.26 N	79.42 W
Oil Creek State Park ♠	214	41.33 N	79.40 W
Oildale	226	35.25 N	119.01 W
Oilmont	182	48.44 N	111.50 W
Oil Springs	214	42.47 N	82.07 W
Oilton, Ok., U.S.	196	36.05 N	96.35 W
Oilton, Tx., U.S.	196	27.33 N	98.59 W
Oil Trough	194	35.37 N	91.27 W
Oinville-sur-Montcient	261	49.02 N	1.51 E
Oir, Beinn an ∧	46	55.54 N	6.00 W
Oirschot	52	51.30 N	5.18 E
Oise □[5]	50	49.30 N	2.30 E
Oise ≃	50	49.00 N	2.04 E
Oise à l'Aisne, Canal de l' ≊	50	49.36 N	3.11 E
Oisemont	50	49.57 N	1.46 E
Ōiso, Nihon	94	35.18 N	139.19 E
Ōiso, Nihon	270	34.33 N	135.01 E
Oissel	50	49.20 N	1.06 E
Oissery	261	49.04 N	2.49 E
Oisterwijk	52	51.35 N	5.12 E
Oistins	241g	13.04 N	59.32 W
Ōita	96	33.14 N	131.36 E
Ōita □[5]	96	33.15 N	131.30 E
Ōita ≃	96	33.15 N	131.37 E
Oiticica	250	5.03 S	41.05 W
Oituz, Pasul)(	38	46.03 N	26.23 E
Ōiwa	270	34.53 N	135.33 E
Oiyung	124	29.39 N	89.46 E
Ōizumi, Nihon	94	36.15 N	139.25 E
Ōizumi, Nihon	94	35.52 N	138.23 E
Oizuruga-dake ∧	94	36.18 N	136.47 E
Öja I	40	58.45 N	17.52 E
Oja ≃	86	53.26 N	91.55 E
Ojai	228	34.26 N	119.14 W
Öjaren ⊜	40	60.43 N	16.50 E
Ojat' ≃	76	60.31 N	33.00 E
Ojcowski Park Narodowy ♠	30	50.15 N	19.50 E
Öje	26	60.49 N	13.51 E
Ojgon nuur ⊜	88	49.10 N	96.36 E
Ojgor	86	49.10 N	89.17 E
Ōji	96	34.35 N	135.42 E
Ōjima	94	36.15 N	139.20 E
Ojinaga	232	29.34 N	104.25 W
Ojiya	92	37.18 N	138.48 E
Ojm'akon	74	63.28 N	142.49 E
Ojocaliente	234	22.34 N	102.15 W
Ojo de la Casa	200	31.23 N	106.32 W
Ojo del Carrizo	232	29.58 N	105.16 W
Ojo de Liebre, Laguna c	232	27.45 N	114.15 W
Ojok	88	52.35 N	104.27 E
Ojos del Salado, Nevado ∧	252	27.06 S	68.32 W
Ojos Negros	232	31.52 N	116.16 W
Ojota	273a	6.35 N	3.23 E
Ojtal, Kaz.	85	42.55 N	73.17 E
Ojtal, Kyrg.	85	40.24 N	74.06 E
Oju	150	6.53 N	8.26 E
Ojuelos de Jalisco	234	21.52 N	101.35 W
Ojus	220	25.57 N	80.09 W
Oka	150	7.29 N	5.49 E
Oka ≃, Ross.	80	56.20 N	43.59 E
Oka ≃, Ross.	88	55.15 N	102.10 E
Okaba	164	8.06 S	139.42 E
Okabe, Nihon	94	36.12 N	139.15 E
Okabe, Nihon	94	34.55 N	138.17 E
Okagaki	96	33.50 N	130.38 E

PORTUGUÊS

Nome	Página	Lat.°′	Long.°′ W = Oeste
Okahandja	156	21.59 S	16.58 E
Okahandja □[5]	156	21.30 S	17.00 E
Okahukura	172	38.47 S	175.13 E
Okahumpka	220	28.45 N	81.54 W
Okaihau	172	35.19 S	173.47 E
Okalataka	152	0.20 S	14.59 E
Okaloacoochee Slough ≃	220	26.16 N	81.17 W
Okamoto	270	34.59 N	135.58 E
Okamoto ◆[8]	270	34.44 N	135.16 E
Okanagan (Okanogan) ≃	182	48.06 N	119.43 W
Okanagan Centre	182	50.03 N	119.27 W
Okanagan Falls	182	49.21 N	119.34 W
Okanagan Indian Reserve ◆[4]	182	50.21 N	119.17 W
Okanagan Lake ⊜	182	50.00 N	119.28 W
Okanagan Landing	182	50.14 N	119.22 W
Okanagan Mountain Provincial Park ♠	182	49.45 N	119.40 W
Okanagan Range (Okanogan Range) ⋏	182	49.00 N	120.00 W
Okanogan	202	48.21 N	119.34 W
Okanogan □[6]	224	48.39 N	120.41 W
Okanogan (Okanagan) ≃	182	48.06 N	119.43 W
Okanogan Range (Okanagan Range) ⋏	182	49.00 N	120.00 W
Okapilco Creek ≃	192	30.45 N	83.30 W
Okaputa	156	20.09 S	16.56 E
Okāra	123	30.49 N	73.27 E
Okarche	196	35.44 N	97.58 W
Okarito	172	43.14 S	170.11 E
Okasaki	270	34.46 N	135.52 E
Okatibbee Reservoir ⊜[1]	194	32.30 N	88.47 W
Okato	172	39.12 S	173.53 E
Okauchee	216	43.06 N	88.26 W
Okauchee Lake ⊜	216	43.07 N	88.26 W
Okaukuejo	156	19.10 S	15.54 E
Okavango (Cubango) ≃	138	18.50 S	22.25 E
Okavango Delta ≡[2]	156	18.45 S	22.45 E
Ōkawa, Nihon	92	33.12 N	130.23 E
Ōkawa, Nihon	94	35.05 N	138.15 E
Ōkawa, Nihon	96	33.47 N	133.26 E
Ōkawachi	96	35.04 N	134.45 E
Ōkawado	268	35.56 N	139.50 E
Okawville	219	38.26 N	89.33 W
Okaya	94	36.03 N	138.03 E
Okayama	96	34.39 N	133.55 E
Okayama □[5]	96	35.00 N	134.00 E
Okazaki	94	34.57 N	137.10 E
Okch'ŏn	98	36.20 N	127.34 E
Oke-Aro	273a	6.41 N	3.19 E
Okeechobee	220	27.14 N	80.49 W
Okeechobee □[6]	220	27.25 N	80.52 W
Okeechobee, Lake ⊜	220	26.55 N	80.45 W
O'Keefe Centre ʋ	275b	43.37 N	79.22 W
Okeene	196	36.06 N	98.19 W
Okefenokee Swamp ≡	192	30.42 N	82.20 W
Okegawa	94	36.00 N	139.35 E
Okehampton	42	50.44 N	4.00 W
Okeigbo	150	7.09 N	4.43 E
Okemah	196	35.25 N	96.18 W
Okement ≃	42	50.50 N	4.01 W
Okemos	216	42.43 N	84.25 W
Okene	150	7.33 N	6.15 E
Oke-Ode	150	8.33 N	5.02 E
Oke Ogbe	273a	6.24 N	3.23 E
Oker	52	51.54 N	10.29 E
Oker ≃	54	52.30 N	10.22 E
Okere ≃	154	2.07 N	33.55 E
Okhaldunggā	124	27.19 N	86.30 E
Okhla ◆[8]	272a	28.34 N	77.18 E
Okhotsk, Sea of (Ochotskoje more) ⫪[2]	74	53.00 N	150.00 E
Okhotsk Basin ✢[1]	12	53.00 N	148.00 E
Okiep	156	29.39 S	17.53 E
Okinawa	174m	26.20 N	127.50 E
Okinawa □[5]	93b	26.31 N	127.59 E
Okinawa-jima I	174m	26.30 N	128.00 E
Okinawa-shotō II	93b	26.40 N	128.00 E
Okino-Daitō-jima I	90	24.28 N	131.11 E
Okino-Erabu-shima I	93b	27.22 N	128.35 E
Okino-Kl'uči	88	50.36 N	107.06 E
Okino-shima I, Nihon	94	35.12 N	136.04 E
Okino-shima I, Nihon	96	34.07 N	135.06 E
Okino-Tori-shima (Parece Vela) I	90	20.25 N	136.00 E
Oki-shotō II	92	36.15 N	133.15 E
Okitipupa	150	6.29 N	4.46 E
Okitsu-zaki ›	96	33.09 N	133.14 E
Okkang-ni	98	40.18 N	124.42 E
Okkerbil' ≃	265a	59.56 N	30.26 E
Okladnevo	76	58.36 N	33.39 E
Oklahoma, Pa., U.S.	214	41.07 N	78.44 W
Oklahoma, Pa., U.S.	279b	40.35 N	79.35 W
Oklahoma □[3], U.S.	178	35.30 N	98.00 W
Oklahoma □[3], U.S.	196	35.30 N	98.00 W
Oklahoma City	196	35.28 N	97.30 W
Oklawaha	220	29.02 N	81.55 W
Oklawaha ≃, Fl., U.S.	192	29.28 N	81.41 W
Oklawaha ≃, Fl., U.S.	220	29.03 N	81.52 W
Oklee	198	47.50 N	95.51 W
Okmulgee	196	35.37 N	95.57 W
Oknica	78	48.24 N	27.29 E
Okno	78	48.34 N	25.58 E
Oko, Wādī V	140	21.15 N	35.56 E
Okobojo Creek ≃	198	44.38 N	100.28 W
Okok ≃	154	2.06 N	33.53 E
Okoka	152	2.57 S	23.27 E
Okola	152	4.01 N	11.23 E
Okollo	154	2.40 N	31.08 E
Okolo	152	3.46 S	23.55 E
Okolona, Ar., U.S.	194	33.59 N	93.20 W
Okolona, Ky., U.S.	194	38.08 N	85.41 W
Okolona, Ms., U.S.	194	34.00 N	88.45 W
Okombahe	156	21.23 S	15.22 E
Okondja	152	0.41 S	13.47 E
Okonek	30	53.33 N	16.50 E
Okonešnikovo	86	54.50 N	75.05 E
Okotoks	182	50.44 N	113.59 W
Okoyo	152	1.28 S	15.04 E
Okpara ≃	150	7.40 N	2.35 E
Okrika	150	4.47 N	7.04 E
Oksbøl	26	55.38 N	8.17 E
Okskij Zapovednik ◆[4]	80	54.45 N	40.45 E
Oksko-Donskaja ravnina ≍	80	53.00 N	40.30 E
Oksovskij	24	62.37 N	39.55 E
Oksskolten ∧	24	65.59 N	14.15 E
Oksu ≃, Asia	85	40.12 N	69.16 E
Oksu ≃, Taj.	120	38.09 N	73.57 E
Okt'abr', Kaz.	85	43.41 N	77.12 E
Okt'abr', Kaz.	86	45.45 N	61.34 E
Okt'abr', Ross.	76	57.50 N	37.26 E
Okt'abr'sk, Kaz.	86	49.28 N	57.25 E
Okt'abr'sk, Ross.	80	53.11 N	48.40 E
Okt'abr'skij, Bela.	76	52.38 N	28.53 E
Okt'abr'skij, Kaz.	86	52.35 N	62.40 E
Okt'abr'skij, Kaz.	86	49.38 N	83.35 E
Okt'abr'skij, Ross.	24	61.04 N	43.08 E
Okt'abr'skij, Ross.	24	59.29 N	48.50 E
Okt'abr'skij, Ross.	76	53.47 N	39.29 E
Okt'abr'skij, Ross.	78	44.56 N	39.00 E
Okt'abr'skij, Ross.	78	50.26 N	36.22 E
Okt'abr'skij, Ross.	80	54.28 N	53.28 E
Okt'abr'skij, Ross.	80	56.17 N	44.12 E
Okt'abr'skij, Ross.	80	57.08 N	40.20 E
Okt'abr'skij, Ross.	80	58.19 N	44.19 E
Okt'abr'skij, Ross.	80	56.35 N	53.58 E
Okt'abr'skij, Ross.	80	47.58 N	43.38 E
Okt'abr'skij, Ross.	82	55.37 N	37.58 E
Okt'abr'skij, Ross.	82	54.14 N	38.54 E
Okt'abr'skij, Ross.	83	47.28 N	40.04 E
Okt'abr'skij, Ross.	86	56.31 N	57.12 E
Okt'abr'skij, Ross.	88	50.04 N	118.04 E
Okt'abr'skij, Ross.	88	56.05 N	99.26 E
Okt'abr'skij, Ross.	89	53.01 N	128.37 E
Okt'abr'skij, Ross.	89	49.02 N	140.11 E
Okt'abr'skij, Taj.	85	38.33 N	68.22 E
Okt'abr'skoje, Kaz.	86	52.07 N	65.40 E
Okt'abr'skoje, Ross.	74	62.28 N	66.03 E
Okt'abr'skoje, Ross.	76	52.18 N	39.44 E
Okt'abr'skoje, Ross.	80	45.37 N	42.49 E
Okt'abr'skoje, Ross.	80	52.54 N	46.30 E
Okt'abr'skoje, Ross.	86	52.20 N	55.30 E
Okt'abr'skoje, Ross.	86	54.26 N	62.44 E
Okt'abr'skoje, Ukr.	78	48.38 N	33.04 E
Okt'abr'skoje, Ukr.	78	45.18 N	34.09 E
Okt'abr'skoje, Ukr.	83	48.28 N	37.22 E
Okt'abr'skoj Revol'ucii, ostrov I	74	79.30 N	97.00 E
Ok Tedi	164	5.44 S	141.09 E
Oktember'an	84	40.09 N	44.02 E
Oktong-ni	98	38.27 N	127.07 E
Oktwin	110	18.49 N	96.26 E
Oktyabr'skiy → Okt'abr'skij	80	54.28 N	53.28 E
Oku, Nihon	96	34.40 N	134.05 E
Oku, Nihon	174m	26.50 N	128.17 E
Ōkubo, Nihon	268	35.21 N	139.56 E
Ōkubo, Nihon	270	34.41 N	134.57 E
Ōkubo ◆[8]	268	35.24 N	139.35 E
Okučani	36	45.16 N	17.12 E
Ōkuchi, Nihon	92	32.04 N	130.37 E
Okuchi, Nihon	94	36.17 N	136.39 E
Okuku ≃	172	43.16 S	172.28 E
Okulovka	76	58.26 N	33.18 E
Okumi	84	42.43 N	41.45 E
Okundi	150	6.22 N	8.44 E
Okun'ov Nos	24	66.15 N	52.28 E
Ōkura-yama ∧	96	35.08 N	133.22 E
Okusawa ◆[8]	268	35.36 N	139.40 E
Okushiri	92a	42.10 N	139.31 E
Okushiri-tō I	92a	42.10 N	139.27 E
Ōkusu-yama ∧[2]	268	35.15 N	139.38 E
Okuta	150	9.14 N	3.15 E
Okutadami Dam ◆[6]	94	37.09 N	139.15 E
Okutama	94	35.47 N	139.02 E
Okutama-ko ⊜	94	35.47 N	139.02 E
Okutsu	96	35.14 N	133.56 E
Ōkuwa	94	35.41 N	137.40 E
Okwa (Chapman's) ≃	156	22.30 S	23.00 E
Okwoga	150	7.01 N	7.50 E
Olá, Pan.	236	8.25 N	80.39 W
Ola, Ross.	74	59.35 N	151.17 E
Ola, Ar., U.S.	194	35.01 N	93.13 W
Ola ≃	76	52.41 N	29.39 E
Ólafsfjörður	24a	66.06 N	18.38 W
Olambwe Valley Game Reserve ◆[4]	154	0.37 S	34.15 E
Olancha	204	36.16 N	118.00 W
Olancha Peak ∧	204	36.16 N	118.07 W
Olanchito	236	15.30 N	86.35 W
Olancho □[5]	236	14.45 N	86.00 W
Öland I	26	56.45 N	16.38 E
Olandsån ≃	40	60.20 N	18.14 E
Olango Island I	116	10.16 N	124.03 E
Olanta	192	33.56 N	79.55 W
Olar	192	33.10 N	81.11 W
Olarevo	76	59.22 N	40.04 E
Olaria, Bra.	256	21.52 S	43.56 W
Olaria, Bra.	287a	22.41 S	43.08 W
Olaria ◆[8]	287a	22.52 S	43.15 W
Olary	166	32.17 S	140.19 E
Olascoaga	252	35.12 S	60.36 W
Olasore	273a	6.40 N	3.17 E
Olathe, Co., U.S.	200	38.36 N	107.58 W
Olathe, Ks., U.S.	198	38.52 N	94.49 W
Olavarría	252	36.54 S	60.17 W
Olavinlinna ⊥	26	61.52 N	29.00 E
Oława	30	50.57 N	17.17 E
Olbernhau	54	50.39 N	13.20 E
Olbersdorf	54	50.52 N	14.46 E
Olbersleben	54	51.09 N	11.20 E
Olbia	71	40.55 N	9.31 E
Olbia, Golfo di c	71	40.55 N	9.39 E
Ølby Lyng	41	55.29 N	12.09 E
Olca, Volcán ∧[1]	248	20.57 S	68.30 W
Ol'chi	80	53.53 N	41.28 E
Olching	60	48.12 N	11.20 E
Ol'chon, ostrov I	88	53.09 N	107.24 E
Ol'chovaja ≃, Ross.	80	48.47 N	40.51 E
Ol'chovaja ≃, Ukr.	83	48.35 N	39.17 E
Ol'chovatka, Ross.	78	50.18 N	39.17 E
Ol'chovatka, Ukr.	83	48.15 N	38.25 E
Ol'chovka, Ross.	80	49.52 N	44.34 E
Ol'chovka, Ross.	86	56.22 N	63.46 E
Ol'chovoje	83	48.40 N	39.34 E
Olcott	210	43.20 N	78.42 W
Old ≃, Ca., U.S.	226	38.04 N	121.35 W
Old ≃, Tx., U.S.	222	30.25 N	96.19 W
Old Bahama Channel)(	238	22.30 N	78.50 W
Old Bedford ≃	42	52.35 N	0.20 E
Old Bennington	210	42.52 N	73.12 W
Old Bethpage	276	40.45 N	73.27 W
Old Bethpage Village ⊥	276	40.47 N	73.28 W
Old Brazoria	222	29.04 N	95.34 W
Old Bridge	276	40.24 N	74.21 W
Old Brookville	276	40.49 N	73.36 W
Oldbury	42	52.30 N	2.00 W
Old Cairo → Miṣr al-Qadīmah ◆[8]	273c	30.00 N	31.14 E
Oldcastle	48	53.46 N	7.10 W
Old Colwyn	44	53.18 N	3.43 W
Old Cork	166	22.56 S	141.52 E
Old Creek Estates	284c	38.50 N	77.16 W
Old Crow	180	67.35 N	139.50 W
Old Crow ≃	180	67.35 N	139.50 W
Oldeani	154	3.21 S	35.33 E
Oldebroek	52	52.26 N	5.54 E
Old Economy ⊥	279b	40.36 N	80.14 W
Olden, Nor.	26	61.50 N	6.49 E
Olden, Tx., U.S.	196	32.25 N	98.45 W
Oldenbrok	52	53.17 N	8.23 E
Oldenburg, Dtsch.	52	53.08 N	8.13 E
Oldenburg, In., U.S.	218	39.20 N	85.12 W
Oldenburg □[9]	52	53.00 N	8.00 E
Oldenburg in Holstein	54	54.17 N	10.52 E
Oldendorf	52	53.35 N	9.14 E
Oldenstadt	52	52.58 N	10.35 E
Oldenswort	41	54.22 N	8.56 E
Oldenzaal	52	52.19 N	6.56 E
Oldersum	52	53.20 N	7.20 E
Old Faithful Geyser ⫪[4]	202	44.30 N	110.45 W
Old Farm	284c	39.03 N	77.09 W
Old Field	276	40.57 N	73.08 W
Old Field Point ›	276	40.58 N	73.07 W
Old Forge, N.Y., U.S.	188	43.42 N	74.58 W
Old Forge, Pa., U.S.	210	41.22 N	75.44 W
Old Forge Village	276	40.49 N	74.29 W
Old Fort	214	41.15 N	83.09 W
Old Fort Erie ⊥	284a	42.53 N	78.56 W
Old Fort Henry ⊥	212	44.14 N	76.28 W
Old Fort Mountain ∧	182	55.05 N	126.30 W
Old Fort Niagara ⊥	284a	43.16 N	79.03 W
Old Fort Parker State Historic Site ⊥	222	31.34 N	96.34 W
Old Fort Point ›	240b	25.03 N	77.29 W
Old Greenwich	276	41.02 N	73.34 W
Oldham, Eng., U.K.	44	53.33 N	2.07 W
Oldham, S.D., U.S.	198	44.13 N	97.18 W
Oldham □[6]	218	38.23 N	85.27 W
Oldham □[8]	262	53.34 N	2.03 W
Oldham Pines	283	42.05 N	70.50 W
Oldham Pond ⊜	283	42.03 N	70.51 W
Oldham Village	207	42.04 N	70.49 W
Old Harbor	180	57.12 N	153.19 W
Old Harbour	241q	17.56 N	77.07 W
Old Hickory Lake ⊜[1]	194	36.18 N	86.30 W
Old Howe ≃	44	53.57 N	0.21 W
Oldisleben	54	51.18 N	11.10 E
Old Lyme	207	41.18 N	72.19 W
Old Malden ◆[8]	260	51.23 N	0.15 W
Oldman ≃	182	49.56 N	111.42 W
Old Man House ⊥	224	47.43 N	122.34 W
Old Man Mountain ∧	186	49.08 N	57.43 W
Old Manor	276	40.24 N	74.11 W
Oldmans Creek ≃	208	39.47 N	75.27 W
Oldmeldrum	46	57.20 N	2.20 W
Old Mkushi	154	14.22 S	29.22 E
Old Monroe	219	38.55 N	90.44 W
Old Mystic	207	41.23 N	71.57 W
Old Nene ≃	42	52.40 N	0.10 E
Old North Bridge ⊥	283	42.28 N	71.21 W
Old North Church ʋ[1]	283	42.22 N	71.03 W
Old Ocean	222	29.05 N	95.45 W
Ol Doinyo Sapuk National Park ♠	154	1.09 S	37.12 E
Ol'doj ≃	89	53.33 N	123.21 E
Old Orchard ◆[9]	278	42.04 N	87.45 W
Old Orchard Beach	188	43.31 N	70.22 W
Old Perlican	186	48.05 N	53.01 W
Old Place Creek ≃	276	40.38 N	74.12 W
Old Point Comfort ›	208	37.00 N	76.19 W
Old Rhodes Key I	220	25.22 N	80.14 W
Old Ripley	219	38.54 N	89.34 W
Old Road Bay c	284b	39.12 N	76.27 W
Old Road Bluff ›	240c	16.59 N	61.50 W
Old Round Rock	222	30.31 N	97.42 W
Olds	182	51.47 N	114.06 W
Old Saybrook	207	41.17 N	72.22 W
Oldsmar	220	28.02 N	82.39 W
Old Speck Mountain ∧	188	44.34 N	70.57 W
Old Sturbridge Village ⊥	207	42.07 N	72.07 W
Old Swamp ≃	283	42.11 N	70.57 W
Old Swedes Church ʋ[1]	285	39.44 N	75.32 W
Old Tampa Bay c	220	27.56 N	82.35 W
Old Tappan	276	41.00 N	73.59 W
Old Tate	156	21.22 S	27.46 E
Old Town	188	44.56 N	68.38 W
Old Trafford Cricket Ground ♠	262	53.28 N	2.17 W
Old Trap	192	36.15 N	76.02 W
Olduvai Gorge V	154	2.58 S	35.22 E
Old Westbury	276	40.47 N	73.37 W
Old Westbury Gardens ♠	276	40.46 N	73.36 W
Oldwick	210	40.40 N	74.44 W
Old Windsor	260	51.28 N	0.35 W
Old Wives Lake ⊜	184	50.06 N	106.00 W
Old Woman Creek ≃	198	43.19 N	104.21 W
Öldzijt, Mong.	88	48.07 N	102.34 E
Öldzijt, Mong.	102	45.18 N	106.12 E
Old Zoinsville	208	40.29 N	75.31 W
Olean	210	42.04 N	78.25 W
Olean Creek ≃	210	42.04 N	78.25 W
O'Leary	186	46.42 N	64.13 W
Olecko	30	54.03 N	22.30 E
Olegário Maciel	256	22.19 S	45.35 W
Oleggio	62	45.36 N	8.38 E
Olekma → Ol'okma ≃	74	60.22 N	120.42 E
Olema	24	64.30 N	46.08 E
Olen, Bel.	56	51.09 N	4.51 E
Ølen, Nor.	26	59.36 N	5.48 E
Ölen ⊜	40	59.13 N	14.31 E
Olenegorsk	24	68.09 N	33.15 E
Olenevka	78	45.23 N	32.32 E
Olenica	24	66.29 N	35.20 E
Olenij, ostrov I	74	72.25 N	77.45 E
Olenino	76	56.12 N	33.29 E
Olenja Rečka	86	52.48 N	93.14 E
Olen'kovo	82	54.34 N	38.06 E
Olen'ok	74	68.33 N	112.18 E
Olen'ok ≃	74	73.00 N	119.55 E
Olen'okskij zaliv c	74	73.20 N	121.00 E
Olentangy ≃	214	39.58 N	83.06 W
Olenty	80	50.02 N	52.07 E
Olenty ≃	80	49.50 N	52.03 E
Oleopolis	214	41.27 N	79.37 W
Oléron, Île d' I	32	45.56 N	1.15 W
Olesko	78	49.58 N	24.53 E
Olešná	60	49.46 N	13.48 E
Oleśnica	30	51.13 N	17.23 E
Olesno	30	50.53 N	18.25 E
Olevano Romano	66	41.52 N	13.02 E
Olevano sul Tusciano	68	40.40 N	15.01 E
Olevsk	78	51.13 N	27.39 E
Oley	208	40.23 N	75.47 W
Olfen	52	51.42 N	7.23 E
Ol'ga, Ross.	89	43.45 N	135.18 E
Olga, Wa., U.S.	224	48.37 N	122.50 W
Olga, Mount ∧, Austl.	162	25.19 S	130.46 E
Olga, Mount ∧, Vt., U.S.	207	42.51 N	72.48 W
Olgiata	267a	42.02 N	12.22 E
Olgiate Comasco	62	45.48 N	8.58 E
Olgiate Olona	62	45.38 N	8.53 E
Ölgij, Mong.	86	48.59 N	92.01 E
Ölgij, Mong.	86	48.56 N	89.57 E
Olginate	62	45.48 N	9.24 E
Ol'ginka, Ross.	78	44.14 N	38.53 E
Ol'ginka, Ukr.	83	47.42 N	37.31 E
Ol'gino	89	52.53 N	125.47 E
Ol'gino ◆[8]	265a	60.00 N	30.09 E
Ol'ginskaja, Ross.	78	45.57 N	38.34 E
Ol'ginskaja, Ross.	83	47.11 N	39.56 E
Ølgod	26	55.49 N	8.37 E
Ol'gopol'	78	48.12 N	29.29 E
Ol'govo	82	56.16 N	37.21 E
Olhão	34	37.02 N	7.50 W
Olho d'Água das Cunhãs	250	4.43 S	44.34 W
Olho d'Água das Flores	250	9.33 S	37.17 W
Oli ≃	150	9.45 N	4.38 E
Olib, Otok I	36	44.22 N	14.48 E
Oliden	258	35.11 S	57.57 W
Oliena	71	40.16 N	9.24 E
Olifants (Rio dos Elefantes) ≃, Afr.	156	24.10 S	32.40 E
Olifants ≃, Namibia	156	25.30 S	19.30 E
Olifants ≃, S. Afr.	158	31.42 S	18.12 E
Olifants ≃, S. Afr.	158	33.41 S	21.42 E
Olifants ≃, S. Afr.	158	29.39 S	21.10 E
Olifantshoek	158	27.57 S	22.42 E
Olifantsrivierberge ⋏	158	32.40 S	19.00 E
Oliki	265a	59.46 N	29.55 E
Olimarao I[1]	108	7.41 N	145.52 E
Olimbía ⊥	38	37.38 N	21.41 E
Ólimbos	38	35.44 N	27.11 E
Ólimbos ∧, Ellás	38	40.05 N	22.21 E
Ólimbos ∧, Kípros	130	34.56 N	32.52 E
Olímpia	255	20.44 S	48.54 W
Olímpico, Estadio ♠	286a	19.20 N	99.12 W
Olímpio Noronha	256	22.04 S	45.16 W
Olimpo → Ólimbos ∧	38	40.05 N	22.21 E
Olin	190	41.59 N	91.08 W
Olinalá	234	17.50 N	98.51 W
Olinda, Austl.	170	32.50 S	150.08 E
Olinda, Austl.	274b	37.51 S	145.22 E
Olinda, Bra.	250	8.01 S	34.51 W
Olinda, Bra.	256	22.49 S	43.25 W
Olinda, Mount ∧	274b	37.52 S	145.21 E
Olinda Creek ≃	274b	37.41 S	145.21 E
Olindina	250	11.22 S	38.21 W
Olinsk	88	52.24 N	116.13 E
Olio	166	21.54 S	143.13 E
Olišovka	78	51.13 N	31.18 E
Olite	34	42.29 N	1.39 W
Oliva, Arg.	252	32.03 S	63.34 W
Oliva, Esp.	34	38.55 N	0.07 W
Oliva de la Frontera	34	38.16 N	6.55 W
Olivais ◆[8]	266c	38.46 N	9.06 E
Olival Basto	266c	38.47 N	9.10 W
Olivares, Cerro de ∧	252	30.18 S	69.55 W
Olive Branch	194	34.57 N	89.49 W
Olivebridge	210	41.55 N	74.13 W
Olive Hill	218	38.18 N	83.10 W
Olivehurst	226	39.05 N	121.33 W
Oliveira	255	20.41 S	44.49 W
Oliveira dos Brejinhos	255	12.19 S	42.54 W
Oliveira Fortes	256	21.20 S	43.27 W
Olivelifuri I	122	5.17 N	73.35 E
Olive Mount ◆[8]	262	53.24 N	2.55 W
Olivença	154	11.47 S	35.13 E
Olivenza	34	38.41 N	7.06 W
Oliver	182	49.11 N	119.33 W
Olivera	258	34.38 S	59.15 W
Oliver Creek ≃	222	33.06 N	97.17 W
Oliver Ditch ≊	216	41.00 N	87.10 W
Oliverea	210	42.04 N	74.28 W
Oliver Estates	284c	38.59 N	77.18 W
Oliveri	70	38.07 N	15.03 E
Oliver Lake ⊜	184	56.56 N	103.22 W
Oliver Springs	192	36.02 N	84.20 W
Olivet, Fr.	50	47.52 N	1.54 E
Olivet, Mi., U.S.	216	42.26 N	84.55 W
Olivet, S.D., U.S.	198	43.14 N	97.40 W
Oliveto Citra	68	40.41 N	15.14 E
Oliveto Lucano	68	40.32 N	16.11 E
Olivette	219	38.39 N	90.22 W
Olivia	198	44.46 N	94.59 W
Olivine Range ⋏	172	44.18 S	168.30 E
Olivo	116	10.52 N	123.53 E
Olivo ≃	70	37.22 N	14.15 E
Olivone	58	46.32 N	8.57 E
Olivos ◆[8]	258	34.32 S	58.29 W
Öljaren ⊜	40	59.08 N	16.02 E
Olji Moron ≃	89	44.16 N	121.42 E
Olla	194	31.54 N	92.14 W
Ollagüe	248	21.14 S	68.16 W
Ollagüe, Volcán ∧[1]	248	21.18 S	68.12 W
Ollainville	261	48.35 N	2.13 E
Ollantaitambo	248	13.16 S	72.16 W
Ollatrim ≃	48	52.52 N	8.13 W
Ollei	175b	7.43 N	134.37 E
Ollerton	262	53.17 N	2.20 W
Ollerup	41	55.04 N	10.30 E
Olliergues	62	45.40 N	3.38 E
Ollioules	62	43.08 N	5.51 E
Ollomont	62	45.50 N	7.22 E
Ollon	58	46.18 N	7.00 E
Olloua	152	0.56 S	14.34 E
Olmedillo de Roa	34	41.47 N	3.56 W
Olmedo, Esp.	34	41.23 N	4.41 W
Olmedo, It.	71	40.39 N	8.23 E
Olmo al Brembo	58	45.58 N	9.39 E
Olmos	248	5.59 S	79.46 W
Olmsted	214	41.24 N	81.44 W
Olmsted Falls	279a	41.22 N	81.54 W
Olmütz → Olomouc	30	49.36 N	17.16 E
Olney, Eng., U.K.	42	52.09 N	0.42 W
Olney, Il., U.S.	194	38.43 N	88.05 W
Olney, Md., U.S.	208	39.09 N	77.04 W
Olney, Mo., U.S.	219	39.05 N	91.15 W
Olney, Mt., U.S.	182	48.32 N	114.34 W
Olney, Tx., U.S.	196	33.22 N	98.45 W
Olney ◆[8]	285	40.02 N	75.08 W
Oloči	89	51.21 N	119.55 E
Olofström	26	56.16 N	14.30 E
Oloj ≃	74	66.29 N	159.29 E
Ol'okma ≃	74	60.22 N	120.42 E
Ol'okminsk	74	60.24 N	120.24 E
Ol'okminskij Stanovik ⋏	88	54.30 N	120.00 E
Olokui ∧	229a	21.08 N	156.51 W
Olomane ≃	186	50.14 N	60.37 W
Olombo	152	1.18 S	15.53 E
Olomega, Laguna ⊜	236	13.19 N	88.04 W
Olomouc	30	49.36 N	17.16 E
Olona ≃	62	45.06 N	9.21 E
Olonec	24	61.00 N	32.57 E
Olongapo	116	14.50 N	120.16 E
Olonki	88	52.54 N	103.45 E
Olorgasailie National Monument ♠	154	1.40 S	36.22 E
Oloron, Gave d' ≃	32	43.33 N	1.05 W
Oloron-Sainte-Marie	32	43.12 N	0.36 W
Olosega	174y	14.11 S	169.39 W
Olosega I	174y	14.11 S	169.39 W
Olot	34	42.11 N	2.29 E
Olov'annaja, Ross.	88	50.56 N	115.35 E
Olov'annaja, Ross.	180	66.10 N	178.59 W
Oloví	54	50.11 N	12.33 E
Olpe, Dtsch.	56	51.02 N	7.52 E
Olpe, Ks., U.S.	198	38.15 N	96.10 W
Olperer ∧	64	47.03 N	11.39 E
Olsabach ≃	61	46.56 N	14.25 E
Ol'šana, Ukr.	78	49.47 N	37.46 E
Ol'šana, Ukr.	78	50.48 N	34.02 E
Ol'šana, Ukr.	78	49.13 N	31.13 E
Ol'šanka, Ross.	78	51.46 N	35.25 E
Ol'šanka, Ukr.	78	48.14 N	30.52 E
Ol'šany, Bela.	78	52.05 N	27.20 E
Olšany, Česko.	60	49.24 N	13.38 E
Ol'šany, Ukr.	78	50.03 N	35.53 E
Olsberg	56	51.21 N	8.29 E
Ølsemagle	41	55.30 N	12.10 E
Olshammar	40	58.45 N	14.48 E
Olst	52	52.20 N	6.06 E
Ølstykke	41	55.47 N	12.11 E
Olsufjevo	76	53.36 N	33.40 E
Olsztyn (Allenstein)	30	53.48 N	20.29 E
Olsztyn □[4]	30	53.50 N	20.40 E
Olsztynek	30	53.36 N	20.17 E
Olt □[6]	38	44.20 N	24.30 E
Olt ≃	38	43.43 N	24.51 E
Olta	252	30.37 S	66.16 W
Olten	58	47.21 N	7.54 E
Olteni	38	44.10 N	25.18 E
Oltenița	38	44.05 N	26.39 E
Olteț ≃	38	44.14 N	24.27 E
Olton	196	34.11 N	102.08 W
Oltre il Colle	64	45.54 N	9.46 E
Oltu	130	40.33 N	41.59 E
Oltu ≃	130	40.49 N	41.40 E
Oluan Pi ›	100	21.54 N	120.51 E
Olukonda	156	18.03 S	16.00 E
Olur	130	40.50 N	42.08 E
Olustee, Fl., U.S.	192	30.12 N	82.26 W
Olustee, Ok., U.S.	196	34.32 N	99.25 W
Olustee Creek ≃	192	29.57 N	82.32 W
Oluta	234	17.55 N	94.54 W
Olutanga (Suba Nipa)	116	7.26 N	122.54 E
Olutanga Island I	116	7.22 N	122.52 E
Olutayan Island I	116	11.39 N	122.50 E
Olute	273a	6.28 N	3.16 E
Ol'utorskij, mys ›	74	59.55 N	170.27 E
Ol'utorskij zaliv c	74	60.15 N	168.30 E
Oluwo	273a	6.42 N	3.18 E
Olvenstedt	54	52.09 N	11.34 E
Olvera	34	36.56 N	5.16 W
Olychovatka	78	50.12 N	37.31 E
Olyka	78	50.42 N	25.51 E
Olym	78	51.42 N	38.10 E
Olympe, Mont → Ólimbos ∧	38	40.05 N	22.21 E
Olympia	224	47.02 N	122.53 W
Olympia Fields	216	41.32 N	87.42 W
Olympia Heights	220	25.43 N	80.21 W
Olympia → Olimbía ⊥	38	37.38 N	21.41 E
Olympia Park ♠	273d	26.15 S	28.26 E
Olympia-Stadion ♠	264a	52.31 N	13.14 E
Olympic Mountains ⋏	224	47.50 N	123.45 W
Olympic National Park ♠	224	47.48 N	123.30 W
Olympic Valley	226	39.13 N	120.14 W
Olympic View	224	47.43 N	122.45 W
Olympieion ⊥	267c	37.58 N	23.44 E

≃ River	Fluß	Río	Rivière	Rio
≊ Canal	Kanal	Canal	Canal	Canal
ʟ Waterfall, Rapids	Wasserfall, Stromschnellen	Cascada, Rápidos	Chute d'eau, Rapides	Cascata, Rápidos
)(Strait	Meeresstraße	Estrecho	Détroit	Estreito
c Bay, Gulf	Bucht, Golf	Bahía, Golfo	Baie, Golfe	Baía, Golfo
⊜ Lake, Lakes	See, Seen	Lago, Lagos	Lac, Lacs	Lago, Lagos
≡ Swamp	Sumpf	Pantano	Marais	Pântano
⌂ Ice Features, Glacier	Eis- und Gletscherformen	Accidentes Glaciales	Formes glaciaires	Acidentes glaciares
⫪ Other Hydrographic Features	Andere Hydrographische Objekte	Otros Elementos Hidrográficos	Autres données hydrographiques	Outros acidentes hidrográficos

✢ Submarine Features	Untermeerische Objekte	Accidentes Submarinos	Formes de relief sous-marin	Acidentes submarinos
□ Political Unit	Politische Einheit	Unidad Politica	Entité politique	Unidade política
ʋ Cultural Institution	Kulturelle Institution	Institución Cultural	Institution culturelle	Institução cultural
⊥ Historical Site	Historische Stätte	Sitio Histórico	Site historique	Sitio histórico
♠ Recreational Site	Erholungs- und Ferienort	Sitio de Recreo	Centre de loisirs	Area de Lazer
⊠ Airport	Flughafen	Aeropuerto	Aéroport	Aeroporto
■ Military Installation	Militäranlage	Instalación Militar	Installation militaire	Instalação militar
◆ Miscellaneous	Verschiedenes	Misceláneo	Divers	Diversos

ENGLISH — Name, Page, Lat.°′, Long.°′
DEUTSCH — Name, Seite, Breite°′, Länge°′ E = Ost

Name	Page	Lat.°′	Long.°′
Olympique, Stade ♦	275a	45.33 N	73.33 W
Olymp → Ólimbos ∧	38	40.05 N	22.21 E
Olympus, Mount ∧	224	47.48 N	123.43 W
Olympus, Mount ∧[2]	192	38.03 N	83.39 W
Olympus, Mount → Ólimbos ∧	38	40.05 N	22.21 E
Olyphant	210	41.28 N	75.36 W
Olzai	71	40.11 N	9.09 E
Ol'zony	88	52.57 N	105.15 E
Om ≃, Pap. N. Gui.	164	5.09 S	142.22 E
Om' ≃, Ross.	86	54.59 N	73.22 E
Ōma	92	41.32 N	140.55 E
Ōmachi, Nihon	94	36.30 N	137.52 E
Ōmachi, Nihon	270	34.28 N	135.25 E
Omaezaki	94	34.35 N	138.13 E
Omae-zaki ›	94	34.36 N	138.14 E
Ōmagari	92	39.27 N	140.29 E
Omagh, On., Can.	275b	43.30 N	79.49 W
Omagh, N. Ire., U.K.	48	54.36 N	7.18 W
Ōmagi	268	35.52 N	139.42 E
Omaguas	246	4.08 S	73.15 W
Omaha, Ne., U.S.	198	41.15 N	95.56 W
Omaha, Tx., U.S.	222	33.11 N	94.45 W
Omaha Indian Reservation ◆[4]	198	42.08 N	96.22 W
Omak	202	48.24 N	119.31 W
Omakau	172	45.05 S	169.36 E
Omak Lake ⊜	202	48.16 N	119.23 W
Omalo	84	42.23 N	45.38 E
Ōmama	94	36.26 N	139.17 E
Oman ('Umān) □[1]	118	22.00 N	58.00 E
Oman, Gulf of ⊂	118	24.30 N	58.30 E
Omapere, Lake ⊜	172	35.21 S	173.47 E
Omar	192	37.45 N	81.59 W
Omarama	172	44.29 S	169.58 E
Omaruru	156	21.28 S	15.56 E
Omaruru □[5]	156	21.00 S	16.00 E
Omaruru ≃	156	22.07 S	14.15 E
Omas	248	12.31 S	76.17 W
Omatako ∧	156	21.07 S	16.43 E
Omatako ≃	156	17.59 S	20.30 E
Omate	248	16.41 S	70.59 W
Omatena	115b	9.53 S	119.47 E
Ōma-zaki ›	92	41.32 N	140.55 E
Ombai, Selat ʉ	112	8.30 S	125.00 E
Ombella-Mpoko □[5]	152	5.00 N	18.00 E
Omberg ∧[2]	26	58.20 N	14.39 E
Ombersley	42	52.17 N	2.13 W
Ombombo	156	18.43 S	13.53 E
Omboué	152	1.34 S	9.15 E
Ombrone ≃	66	42.39 N	11.00 E
Ombúes de Lavalle	258	33.55 S	57.47 W
Ombutosu ∧	156	21.22 S	16.50 E
Ombwe	154	4.22 S	25.35 E
Omčak	74	61.38 N	147.55 E
Omčaly	128	40.47 N	53.43 E
Omdraaisvlei	158	30.08 S	23.08 E
Omdurman → Umm Durmān	140	15.38 N	32.30 E
Ōme	94	35.47 N	139.15 E
Omega, Ga., U.S.	192	31.20 N	83.35 W
Omega, Oh., U.S.	218	39.09 N	82.55 W
Omegna	62	45.53 N	8.24 E
Omel'nik	78	49.12 N	33.32 E
Omemee	212	44.18 N	78.33 W
Omeo	166	37.06 S	147.36 E
Ömerköy	130	39.48 N	28.03 E
Ömerli	130	37.24 N	40.58 E
Ömerli Barajı ⊜[1]	130	41.00 N	29.20 E
Omerville	206	45.17 N	72.07 W
Ometepe, Isla de I	236	11.30 N	85.35 W
Ometepec	234	16.41 N	98.25 W
Ometepec ≃	234	16.30 N	98.45 W
Om Hajer	144	14.24 N	36.46 E
Omi, Nihon	94	36.27 N	138.03 E
Ōmi, Nihon	94	37.01 N	137.48 E
Ōmi, Nihon	94	35.20 N	136.24 E
Omigawa	94	35.51 N	140.37 E
Ōmi-hachiman	94	35.08 N	136.06 E
Ōminato → Mutsu	92	41.17 N	141.10 E
Omineca ≃	182	56.05 N	124.30 W
Omineca Mountains ⛰	182	56.00 N	125.00 W
Omin-ni ◆[8]	271b	37.27 N	127.01 E
Ōmino	270	34.32 N	135.33 E
Omišalj	36	45.13 N	14.34 E
Ōmi-shima I, Nihon	96	34.25 N	131.13 E
Omi-shima I, Nihon	96	34.15 N	133.00 E
Omitara	156	22.18 S	18.01 E
Omitlán ≃	234	17.06 N	99.34 W
Ōmiya, Nihon	94	36.33 N	140.25 E
Ōmiya, Nihon	94	35.54 N	139.38 E
Ōmiya, Nihon	96	35.35 N	135.06 E
Ōmiya-daichi ⛰[1]	268	35.56 N	139.38 E
Ōmiya Park Race Track ♦	268	35.55 N	139.38 E
Øm Kloster ⊥	41	56.03 N	9.45 E
Ommaney, Cape ›	180	56.10 N	134.39 W
Ommanney Bay ⊂	176	73.07 N	100.11 W
Omme ≃	41	55.53 N	8.40 E
Ommen	52	52.32 N	6.25 E
Ömnödelger	88	47.52 N	109.55 E
Ömnögov'	86	49.06 N	91.43 E
Ömnögov' □[4]	102	43.00 N	104.00 E
Omø I	41	55.09 N	11.10 E
Omo ≃	144	43.10 N	35.59 E
Omoa, Bahía de ⊂	236	15.45 N	88.10 W
Omodeo, Lago ⊜	71	40.08 N	8.55 E
Omogo	96	33.41 N	133.02 E
Omoi ≃	94	36.09 N	139.41 E
Omoko	150	5.20 N	6.39 E
Omole	273a	6.38 N	3.22 E
Omoloj ≃	74	71.10 N	132.08 E
Omolon ≃	74	68.42 N	158.36 E
Omo National Park ♦	144	6.00 N	35.45 E
Omono ≃	92	39.46 N	140.03 E
Omont	56	49.36 N	4.44 E
Omo Ranch	226	38.35 N	120.35 W
Ōmori ◆[8]	268	35.34 N	139.44 E
Omotegō	94	37.03 N	140.18 E
Omoy	152	1.21 S	13.09 E
Omrel'kaj ≃	180	68.34 N	170.30 E
Omro	190	44.02 N	88.44 W
Omsino	80	58.36 N	50.28 E
Omsk	86	55.00 N	73.24 E
Omsukčan	74	62.32 N	155.48 E
O-mu, Mya.	110	22.58 N	99.18 E
Ōmu, Nihon	92a	44.34 N	142.58 E
Omu-Aran	150	8.09 N	5.07 E
Ōmuda → Ōmuta	96	33.02 N	130.27 E
Omul, Vîrful ∧	38	45.26 N	25.26 E
Omulew ≃	30	53.05 N	21.32 E
Ōmura	92	32.54 N	129.57 E
Ōmura-wan ⊂	92	32.57 N	129.52 E
Ōmuro	268	35.54 N	139.58 E
Omurtag	38	43.06 N	26.25 E
Ōmuta	96	33.02 N	130.27 E
Omutinskij	86	56.31 N	67.41 E
Omutninsk	86	58.40 N	52.12 E
Ŏmyŏnbo	98	41.16 N	127.36 E
On	110	21.40 N	106.35 E
Ona, Nor.	26	62.52 N	6.34 E
Ona, Fl., U.S.	220	27.28 N	81.55 W
Ona ≃	86	52.34 N	89.50 E
Onabas	232	28.35 N	109.34 W
Ona → Bir'usa ≃	88	57.43 N	95.24 E
Onadikondo	152	3.52 S	24.10 E
Onaga	198	39.29 N	96.10 W
Onagawa	92	38.26 N	141.27 E
Onahama	94	36.57 N	140.54 E
Onalaska, Tx., U.S.	222	30.48 N	95.07 W
Onalaska, Wa., U.S.	224	46.34 N	122.43 W
Onamia	190	46.04 N	93.40 W
Onancock	208	37.42 N	75.44 W
Onangué, Lac ⊜	152	0.57 S	10.04 E
Onaping ≃	190	46.37 N	81.18 W
Onaping Lake ⊜	190	47.00 N	81.30 W
Onarga	216	40.42 N	88.00 W
Ōnari	268	35.55 N	139.37 E
Onatchiway, Lac ⊜	186	49.00 N	71.03 W
Onawa	198	42.01 N	96.05 W
Onaway	190	45.21 N	84.13 W
Oncativo	252	31.55 S	63.40 W
Once, Canal Numero ≚	252	36.09 S	58.36 W
Onchāi	272b	22.57 N	88.19 E
Onchan	44	54.11 N	4.27 W
Onch'ŏn-dong	98	40.51 N	129.07 E
Oncócua	152	16.34 S	13.28 E
Onda, Esp.	34	39.58 N	0.15 W
Onda, India	126	23.08 N	87.12 E
Ondangwa	156	17.55 S	16.00 E
Ondas, Rio de ≃	255	12.08 S	45.00 W
Ondava ≃	30	48.27 N	21.48 E
Onderdijk	52	52.45 N	5.07 E
Onderstedorings	158	30.13 S	20.37 E
Ondjiva	152	17.03 S	15.47 E
Ondo, Nig.	150	7.04 N	4.47 E
Ondo, Nihon	96	34.11 N	132.32 E
Ondo □[3]	150	7.00 N	5.15 E
Ondo-ōhashi ◆[5]	96	34.12 N	132.33 E
Öndörchaan	88	47.19 N	110.39 E
Öndörchangaj	88	49.20 N	94.50 E
Öndör-Önc	102	45.51 N	103.11 E
Öndöršireet	88	47.27 N	104.50 E
Öndör-Ulaan	88	48.03 N	100.30 E
Ondozero, ozero ⊜	24	63.48 N	33.20 E
O'Neals	226	37.08 N	119.42 W
One Arrow Indian Reserve ◆[4]	184	52.48 N	106.03 W
Oneco, Ct., U.S.	207	41.41 N	71.48 W
Oneco, Fl., U.S.	220	27.26 N	82.32 W
Onega	24	63.55 N	38.05 E
Onega ≃	24	63.58 N	37.55 E
Onega, Lake → Onežskoje ozero ⊜	24	61.30 N	35.45 E
Oneglia	62	43.53 N	8.02 E
One Hundred and Two ≃	194	39.44 N	94.43 W
One Hundred and Two, West Fork ≃	194	40.26 N	94.49 W
One Hundred Fifty Mile House	182	52.06 N	121.55 W
One Hundred Mile House	182	51.39 N	121.18 W
Oneida, Il., U.S.	190	41.04 N	90.13 W
Oneida, Ky., U.S.	192	37.16 N	83.38 W
Oneida, N.Y., U.S.	210	43.05 N	75.39 W
Oneida, Oh., U.S.	218	39.28 N	84.23 W
Oneida, Pa., U.S.	210	40.54 N	76.08 W
Oneida, Tn., U.S.	192	36.29 N	84.30 W
Oneida □[6]	210	43.10 N	75.20 W
Oneida ≃	210	43.12 N	76.17 W
Oneida Castle	210	43.05 N	75.40 W
Oneida County Airport ⊠	210	43.09 N	75.23 W
Oneida Creek ≃	210	43.10 N	75.44 W
Oneida Indian Reservation ◆[4]	190	44.30 N	88.10 W
Oneida Indian Reserve ◆[4]	214	42.49 N	81.24 W
Oneida Lake ⊜	210	43.13 N	76.00 W
O'Neil Forebay ⊜[1]	226	37.05 N	121.03 W
O'Neill	198	42.27 N	98.38 W
Onekama	190	44.21 N	86.12 W
Onekotan, ostrov I	74	49.25 N	154.45 E
Onema	152	4.33 S	24.31 E
Onemen, zaliv ⊂	180	64.45 N	176.35 E
Oneonta, Al., U.S.	194	33.56 N	86.28 W
Oneonta, N.Y., U.S.	210	42.27 N	75.03 W
Oneroa I	174k	21.15 S	159.43 W
One Tree Hill	168b	34.43 S	138.46 E
One Tree Hill ∧[2]	274b	37.52 S	145.19 E
One Tree Hill Lookout ♦	169	36.48 S	144.18 E
Onevai I	174w	21.05 S	175.07 W
Onex	58	46.10 N	6.06 E
Onežskaja guba ⊂	24	64.20 N	36.30 E
Onežskij poluostrov ›[1]	24	64.35 N	38.00 E
Onežskoje ozero (Lake Onega) ⊜	24	61.30 N	35.45 E
Onga ≃	96	33.54 N	130.39 E
Ongaonga	172	39.55 S	176.25 E
Ongarue	172	38.43 S	175.17 E
Ong Con, Cu Lao I	269c	10.45 N	106.50 E
Ongea Levu I	175g	19.08 S	178.24 W
Ongeluks ≃	158	32.24 S	19.46 E
Ongers ≃	158	31.04 S	23.13 E
Ongerup	162	33.58 S	118.29 E
Ongijn ≃	102	44.30 N	103.40 E
Ongjin	98	37.57 N	125.21 E
Ongoka	154	1.23 S	26.02 E
Ongole	122	15.31 N	80.04 E
Ongon	102	45.21 N	113.09 E
Ongudaj	86	50.45 N	86.09 E
Oni	84	42.34 N	43.27 E
Onich	46	56.42 N	5.13 W
Onida	198	44.42 N	100.03 W
Onifai	71	40.24 N	9.39 E
Oniferi	71	40.16 N	9.10 E
Onigajō-yama ∧	96	33.07 N	132.41 E
Onilahy ≃	157b	23.34 S	43.45 E
Onin, Jazirah ›[1]	164	2.50 S	132.05 E
Onion Creek ≃	222	30.12 N	97.35 W
Onion Peak ∧	224	45.49 N	123.53 W
Onishi	94	36.09 N	139.04 E
Onistagane, Lac ⊜	186	50.42 N	71.19 W
Onitsha	150	6.09 N	6.47 E
Onji	270	34.37 N	135.38 E
Onjuku	94	35.11 N	140.22 E
Onkaparinga ≃	168b	35.10 S	138.28 E
Onkivesi ⊜	26	63.18 N	27.18 E
Onko	152	4.07 S	19.59 E
Onley	208	37.41 N	75.42 W
Onna	174m	26.30 N	127.51 E
Onnaing	50	50.23 N	3.36 E
Onno	58	45.55 N	9.17 E
Onny ≃	42	52.23 N	2.45 W
Ōno, Nihon	94	35.59 N	136.29 E
Ōno, Nihon	94	35.28 N	136.38 E
Ōno, Nihon	96	34.18 N	132.17 E
Ono, Nihon	96	34.51 N	134.56 E
Ōno, Nihon	96	33.02 N	131.30 E
Ono, Nihon	270	34.57 N	135.14 E
Ono, Pa., U.S.	208	40.24 N	76.32 W
Ono I	175g	18.55 S	178.29 E
Ōno ≃	96	33.15 N	131.43 E
Onochoj	88	51.58 N	108.01 E
Onoda	96	33.59 N	131.11 E
Ōno-dam ◆[6]	96	35.15 N	135.27 E
Onogami	94	36.33 N	138.56 E
Ōnohara	96	34.05 N	133.40 E
Ono-I-Lau I	14	20.39 S	178.42 W
Ōnojō	96	33.32 N	130.28 E
Onolimbu	114	1.03 N	97.53 E
Ōnomi	96	33.21 N	133.09 E
Onomichi	96	34.25 N	133.12 E
Onon	88	49.08 N	112.38 E
Onon ≃	88	51.42 N	115.50 E
Onondaga, Mi., U.S.	216	42.26 N	84.33 W
Onondaga, N.Y., U.S.	210	43.00 N	76.11 W
Onondaga □[6]	210	43.03 N	76.09 W
Onondaga Creek ≃	210	43.04 N	76.11 W
Onondaga Indian Reservation ◆[4]	210	42.55 N	76.09 W
Onor	89	50.11 N	142.40 E
Onota Lake ⊜	207	42.28 N	73.17 W
Onoto	246	9.36 N	65.12 W
Onotoa I[1]	14	1.52 S	175.34 E
Onoway	182	53.42 N	114.12 W
Ons, Isla de I	34	42.23 N	8.56 W
Onsbjerg	41	55.51 N	10.35 E
Onseepkans	158	28.46 S	19.14 E
Onsen	96	35.33 N	134.29 E
Onset	207	41.44 N	70.39 W
Onslow	162	21.39 S	115.06 E
Onslow Bay ⊂	192	34.20 N	77.20 W
Onslow Village	260	51.14 N	0.36 W
Onsted	216	42.00 N	84.11 W
Onstmettingen	58	48.17 N	9.00 E
Onstwedde	52	53.02 N	7.02 E
On-take ∧	92	31.35 N	130.39 E
Ontake-san ∧	94	35.53 N	137.29 E
Ontario, Ca., U.S.	228	34.03 N	117.39 W
Ontario, In., U.S.	216	41.43 N	85.23 W
Ontario, N.Y., U.S.	210	43.13 N	77.17 W
Ontario, Oh., U.S.	214	40.45 N	82.35 W
Ontario, Or., U.S.	202	44.01 N	116.57 W
Ontario □[6]	210	42.54 N	77.17 W
Ontario □[4]	176	51.00 N	85.00 W
Ontario, Lake ⊜	212	43.45 N	78.00 W
Ontario Agricultural Museum ʊ	212	43.30 N	79.56 W
Ontario Center	210	43.14 N	77.19 W
Ontario International Airport ⊠	228	34.04 N	117.36 W
Ontario Place ♦	275b	43.38 N	79.25 W
Ontario Science Centre ʊ	275b	43.43 N	79.21 W
Ontelaunee, Lake ⊜	208	40.27 N	75.55 W
Ontinyent (Onteniente)	34	38.49 N	0.37 W
Ontojärvi ⊜	26	64.08 N	29.09 E
Ontonagon	190	46.52 N	89.18 W
Ontonagon ≃	190	46.52 N	89.20 W
Ontonagon, East Branch ≃	190	46.42 N	89.11 W
Ontonagon, Middle Branch ≃	190	46.42 N	89.10 W
Ontonagon, West Branch ≃	190	46.42 N	89.11 W
Ontong Java I[1]	175e	5.20 S	159.30 E
Onufrijevka	78	48.54 N	33.26 E
Onufrijevo	82	55.51 N	36.31 E
Ōnuma	268	35.32 N	139.25 E
Onverwacht	250	5.36 N	55.12 W
Onward	216	40.42 N	86.12 W
Ŏnyang, Taehan	98	36.47 N	127.00 E
Ŏnyang, Taehan	98	35.34 N	129.07 E
Onzain	50	47.30 N	1.11 E
Onzo ≃	152	8.12 S	13.16 E
Oobagooma	162	16.46 S	123.59 E
Oodnadatta	162	27.33 S	135.28 E
Ood Weyne	144	9.25 N	45.04 E
Ōoka	94	36.30 N	137.59 E
Ooldea	162	30.27 S	131.50 E
Oolitic	218	38.54 N	86.31 W
Oologah	196	36.26 N	95.42 W
Oologah Lake ⊜[1]	196	36.33 N	95.36 W
Ooma	174d	0.53 S	169.36 E
Oombergen	50	50.54 N	3.50 E
Oona River	182	53.57 N	130.18 W
Ooratippra	162	22.00 S	136.00 E
Ooratippra Creek ≃	162	21.55 S	136.05 E
Oorlogskloof ≃	158	31.52 S	19.01 E
Oos	56	48.47 N	8.11 E
Oos-Londen → East London	158	33.00 S	27.55 E
Oostakker	50	51.06 N	3.46 E
Oostburg, Ned.	52	51.20 N	3.30 E
Oostburg, Wi., U.S.	190	43.37 N	87.47 W
Oost-Cappel	50	50.55 N	2.36 E
Oostduinkerke	50	51.07 N	2.41 E
Oostelijk Flevoland ◆[1]	52	52.30 N	5.45 E
Oostende (Ostende)	50	51.13 N	2.55 E
Oosterbeek	52	52.00 N	5.50 E
Oosterend	52	53.05 N	4.52 E
Oosterhout	52	51.38 N	4.51 E
Oosterschelde ⊂	52	51.30 N	4.00 E
Oosterscheldedam ◆[6]	52	51.38 N	3.42 E
Oosterwolde	52	52.59 N	6.17 E
Oosterzele	50	50.57 N	3.48 E
Oosthuizen	52	52.35 N	5.00 E
Oostkamp	50	51.09 N	3.14 E
Oostmahorn	52	53.24 N	6.09 E
Oostmalle	56	51.18 N	4.44 E
Oostpunt ›	241s	12.02 N	68.45 W
Oostrozebeke	50	50.55 N	3.20 E
Oost-Souburg	52	51.27 N	3.35 E
Oost-Vlaanderen □[4]	50	51.00 N	3.45 E
Oostvleteren	50	50.56 N	2.44 E
Oost-Vlieland	52	53.17 N	5.04 E
Oostvoorne	52	51.55 N	4.06 E
Ootmarsum	52	52.25 N	6.54 E
Ootsa Lake	182	53.47 N	126.03 W
Ootsa Lake ⊜	182	53.49 N	126.18 W
Ootsi	156	25.02 S	25.45 E
Ootua, Mont ∧	174x	9.47 S	138.58 W
Opaka	38	43.27 N	26.10 E
Opala	152	0.37 S	24.21 E
Opalaca, Cordillera ⛰	236	14.30 N	88.20 W
Opal Cliffs	226	36.57 N	121.57 W
Opale, Côte d' ≛[2]	50	50.40 N	1.35 E
Opalenica	30	52.19 N	16.23 E
Opalicha	265b	55.49 N	37.15 E
Opa-Locka	220	25.54 N	80.15 W
Opari	154	3.56 N	32.03 E
Oparino	24	59.52 N	48.17 E
Opasatica, Lac ⊜	190	48.05 N	79.18 W
Opasatika Lake ⊜	190	49.04 N	83.08 W
Opasquia	184	53.16 N	93.35 W
Opasquia Lake ⊜	184	53.18 N	93.34 W
Opatija	36	45.21 N	14.19 E
Opatów	30	50.49 N	21.26 E
Opava	30	49.56 N	17.54 E
Opava ≃	30	49.50 N	18.13 E
Opečenskij Posad	76	58.16 N	34.07 E
Opeepeesway Lake ⊜	190	47.38 N	82.14 W
Opeilu	273a	6.42 N	3.18 E
Opelika	194	32.38 N	85.22 W
Opelousas	194	30.32 N	92.04 W
Open Bay ⊂	164	4.50 S	151.20 E
Open Door	258	34.30 S	59.05 W
Opeongo ≃	190	45.30 N	77.57 W
Opeongo Lake ⊜	190	45.42 N	78.23 W
Opequon Creek ≃	188	39.35 N	77.52 W
Opfikon	58	47.26 N	8.35 E
Ophain-Bois-Seigneur-Isaac	50	50.40 N	4.21 E
Ophasselt	50	50.49 N	3.53 E
Opheim	202	48.51 N	106.24 W
Opherdicke	263	51.29 N	7.38 E
Opheusden	52	51.56 N	5.38 E
Ophir, Ak., U.S.	180	63.10 N	156.31 W
Ophir, Or., U.S.	202	42.33 N	124.22 W
Ophirton ◆[8]	273d	26.14 S	28.01 E
Ophthalmia Range ⛰	162	23.17 S	119.30 E
Opi	66	41.47 N	13.50 E
Opienge	154	0.12 N	27.30 E
Opihikao	229d	19.25 N	154.53 W
Opinaca ≃	176	52.15 N	78.02 W
Opinan	46	57.43 N	5.47 W
Opinicon Lake ⊜	212	44.33 N	76.20 W
Opiscotéo, Lac ⊜	176	53.10 N	68.10 W
Opladen	56	51.04 N	7.00 E
Opmeer	52	52.43 N	4.56 E
Opobo	150	4.34 N	7.27 E
Opobo Town	150	4.30 N	7.30 E
Opočka	76	56.43 N	28.38 E
Opoczno	30	51.23 N	20.17 E
Opol	116	8.31 N	124.34 E
Opole (Oppeln)	30	50.41 N	17.55 E
Opole □[4]	30	50.30 N	17.45 E
Opole Lubelskie	30	51.09 N	21.58 E
Opon → Lapu-Lapu	116	10.19 N	123.57 E
Opopono, Lake ⊜	156	18.08 S	15.45 E
Opopeo	234	19.24 N	101.36 W
Oporto → Porto	34	41.11 N	8.36 W
Opošn'a	78	49.58 N	34.37 E
Opotiki	172	38.00 S	177.17 E
Opp	194	31.16 N	86.15 W
Oppach	54	51.03 N	14.30 E
Oppdal	26	62.36 N	9.40 E
Oppelhain	54	51.33 N	13.35 E
Oppeln → Opole	30	50.41 N	17.55 E
Oppenau	58	48.28 N	8.10 E
Oppenberg	61	47.29 N	14.16 E
Oppenheim, Dtsch.	56	49.51 N	8.21 E
Oppenheim, N.Y., U.S.	210	43.04 N	74.42 W
Oppenheim Park ♦	284a	43.06 N	78.54 W
Oppenhuizen	52	53.00 N	5.42 E
Oppido Lucano	68	40.47 N	16.00 E
Oppido Mamertina	68	38.16 N	16.00 E
Oppio	66	44.03 N	10.50 E
Oppland □[6]	26	61.10 N	9.40 E
Opportunity, Mt., U.S.	202	46.07 N	112.49 W
Opportunity, Wa., U.S.	202	47.39 N	117.14 W
Oppum ◆[8]	263	51.19 N	6.37 E
Opsa	76	55.32 N	26.47 E
Opsaheden	40	60.28 N	13.59 E
Optic Lake	184	54.46 N	101.13 W
Optima Lake ⊜[1]	196	36.40 N	101.10 W
Opua	172	35.19 S	174.07 E
Opunake	172	39.27 S	173.51 E
Opunohu, Baie d' ⊂	174s	17.30 S	149.51 W
Opuwo	152	18.03 S	13.45 E
Opwijk	50	50.58 N	4.11 E
Oquawka	190	40.55 N	90.56 W
Oquendo, Perú	286d	11.58 S	77.08 W
Oquendo, Pil.	116	12.08 N	124.32 E
O'Quinn	222	29.50 N	96.58 W
Or' ≃	86	51.12 N	58.30 E
Or, Côte d' ∧	58	47.10 N	4.50 E
Or, Étang d' ⊜	261	48.38 N	1.51 E
Ora (Auer), It.	64	46.21 N	11.18 E
Ora, Lībiyā	146	28.33 N	19.24 E
Ōra, Nihon	174m	26.33 N	128.02 E
Ora Banda	162	30.22 S	121.04 E
Oracle	200	32.36 N	110.46 W
Oradea	38	47.03 N	21.57 E
Oradell	276	40.57 N	74.02 W
Oradell Reservoir ⊜[1]	276	40.58 N	74.01 W
Öræfajökull ⊓	24a	64.03 N	16.38 W
Orahovica	38	45.31 N	17.53 E
Orai	124	25.59 N	79.28 E
Oraibi Wash V	200	35.26 N	110.49 W
Oraison	62	43.55 N	5.55 E
Oran	194	37.05 N	89.39 W
Oran, Sebkha d' ⊜	34	35.32 N	0.48 W
Orange, Austl.	166	33.17 S	149.06 E
Orange, Fr.	62	44.08 N	4.48 E
Orange, Ca., U.S.	228	33.47 N	117.51 W
Orange, Ct., U.S.	207	41.16 N	73.01 W
Orange, Ma., U.S.	207	42.35 N	72.18 W
Orange, N.J., U.S.	276	40.46 N	74.13 W
Orange, Oh., U.S.	279a	41.26 N	81.29 W
Orange, Tx., U.S.	194	30.05 N	93.44 W
Orange, Va., U.S.	188	38.14 N	78.06 W
Orange □[6], Ca., U.S.	228	33.43 N	117.54 W
Orange □[6], Fl., U.S.	220	28.32 N	81.16 W
Orange □[6], In., U.S.	218	38.33 N	86.28 W
Orange □[6], N.Y., U.S.	210	41.24 N	74.20 W
Orange (Oranje) ≃	156	28.41 S	16.28 E
Orange, Cabo ›	250	4.24 N	51.33 W
Orange Bowl ♦	220	25.46 N	80.14 W
Orangeburg, Ky., U.S.	218	38.35 N	83.39 W
Orangeburg, N.Y., U.S.	210	41.03 N	73.57 W
Orangeburg, S.C., U.S.	192	33.29 N	80.51 W
Orange City, Fl., U.S.	220	28.57 N	81.17 W
Orange City, Ia., U.S.	198	43.00 N	96.03 W
Orange County Airport ⊠	228	33.40 N	117.51 W
Orange Cove	226	36.37 N	119.19 W
Orange Free State (Oranje-Vrystaat) □[4]	158	28.30 S	27.00 E
Orange Grove	196	27.57 N	97.56 W
Orange Grove ◆[8]	273d	26.10 S	28.05 E
Orange Lake, Fl., U.S.	192	29.25 N	82.13 W
Orange Lake, N.Y., U.S.	210	41.33 N	74.06 W
Orange Lake ⊜	192	29.29 N	82.10 W
Orangemouth → Oranjemund	156	28.38 S	16.24 E
Orange Park	192	30.09 N	81.42 W
Orange Park Acres	280	33.48 N	117.47 W
Orange Reservoir ⊜[1]	276	40.46 N	74.17 W
Orangevale	226	38.40 N	121.13 W
Orangeville, On., Can.	212	43.55 N	80.06 W
Orangeville, Oh., U.S.	214	41.20 N	80.31 W
Orangeville, Pa., U.S.	210	41.05 N	76.25 W
Orangeville, Ut,. U.S.	200	39.13 N	111.03 W
Orange Walk	232	18.06 N	88.33 W
Orango Grande I	150	11.10 N	16.08 W
Orani, It.	71	40.15 N	9.11 E
Orani, Pil.	116	14.49 N	120.32 E
Oranienbaum	54	51.48 N	12.24 E
Oranienburg	54	52.45 N	13.14 E
Oranje	52	52.55 N	6.28 E
Oranjefontein	156	23.25 S	27.41 E
Oranje Gebergte ⛰	250	3.00 N	55.05 W
Oranjemund	156	28.38 S	16.24 E
Oranje → Orange ≃	156	28.41 S	16.28 E
Oranjerivier	158	29.40 S	24.12 E
Oranjestad	241s	12.33 N	70.06 W
Oranjeville	158	27.00 S	28.15 E
Oranki	80	55.53 N	43.44 E
Oranmore	48	53.16 N	8.54 W
Ŏran-ni	98	34.22 N	126.29 E
Oran → Wahran	148	35.43 N	0.43 W
Oranžerei	80	45.50 N	47.36 E
Or 'Aqiva	132	32.30 N	34.55 E
Orarak	140	6.15 N	32.23 E
Orari ≃	172	44.15 S	171.25 E
Oras	116	12.09 N	125.26 E
Oras ≃	116	12.08 N	125.26 E
Oras Bay ⊂	116	12.07 N	125.28 E
Orăștie	38	45.50 N	23.12 E
Orașul Stalin → Brașov	38	45.39 N	25.37 E
Oratório, Ribeirão do ≃	287b	23.37 S	46.32 W
Oratov	78	49.12 N	29.32 E
Oravais (Oravainen)	26	63.18 N	22.23 E
Oravița	38	45.02 N	21.41 E
Orawia	172	46.03 S	167.49 E
Orb ≃	32	43.15 N	3.18 E
Orba ≃	62	44.53 N	8.37 E
Orba Co ⊜	120	34.32 N	81.03 E
Orbassano	62	45.01 N	7.32 E
Orbe	58	46.43 N	6.32 E
Orbe ≃	58	46.47 N	6.39 E
Orbec-en-Auge	50	49.01 N	0.25 E
Orbetello	66	42.27 N	11.13 E
Orbetello, Laguna di ⊂	66	42.27 N	11.14 E
Orbey	58	48.08 N	7.10 E
Orbieu ≃	32	43.14 N	2.54 E
Orbigny	50	47.12 N	1.14 E
Órbigo ≃	34	41.58 N	5.40 W
Orbiquet ≃	50	49.09 N	0.14 E
Orbisonia	214	40.15 N	77.54 W
Orbost	166	37.42 S	148.27 E
Örbyhus	40	60.14 N	17.42 E
Orcadas ʊ[3]	9	60.45 S	44.43 W
Orcadas, Islas → Orkney Islands II	46	59.00 N	3.00 W
Orcadas del Sur, Islas → South Orkney Islands II	9	60.35 S	45.30 W
Orcades du Sud, Îles → South Orkney Islands II	9	60.35 S	45.30 W
Orcas	224	48.36 N	122.57 W
Orcas Island I	224	48.39 N	122.55 W
Orcemont	261	48.35 N	1.49 E
Orcera	34	38.19 N	2.39 W
Orchamps	58	47.09 N	5.40 E
Orchard, Ne., U.S.	198	42.20 N	98.14 W
Orchard, Tx., U.S.	222	29.36 N	95.58 W
Orchard City	200	38.49 N	107.58 W
Orchard Hills, Austl.	274a	33.47 S	150.43 E
Orchard Hills, Pa., U.S.	279b	40.35 N	79.32 W
Orchard Homes	202	46.51 N	114.02 W
Orchard Island	216	40.28 N	83.53 W
Orchard Lake ⊜	281	42.35 N	83.22 W
Orchard Lake Village	281	42.35 N	83.21 W
Orchard Mesa	200	39.02 N	108.33 W
Orchard Park	210	42.46 N	78.44 W
Orchard Park Airport ⊠	284a	42.48 N	78.45 W
Orchard Peak ∧	226	35.44 N	120.08 W
Orchards	224	45.40 N	122.33 W
Orchard Valley	200	41.05 N	104.48 W
Orchard View	285	40.04 N	74.53 W
Orchej	78	47.23 N	28.48 E
Orchha	124	25.21 N	78.39 E
Orchies	50	50.28 N	3.14 E
Orchon	88	49.09 N	105.21 E
Orchon ≃	88	50.21 N	106.05 E
Orchon Tuul	88	48.58 N	104.59 E
Orcia ≃	66	42.58 N	11.21 E
Orcières	62	44.41 N	6.20 E
Orčik ≃	78	49.10 N	35.04 E
Orco ≃	62	45.10 N	7.52 E
Ord	198	41.36 N	98.55 W
Ord ≃	160	15.30 S	128.21 E
Ord, Mount ∧	162	17.20 S	125.34 E
Orda	86	57.12 N	56.54 E
Ordenes	34	43.04 N	8.24 W
Orderville	200	37.16 N	112.38 W
Ordesa, Parque Nacional de ♦	34	42.39 N	0.02 E
Ord Mountain ∧	204	34.40 N	116.49 W
Ord Mountains ⛰	228	34.42 N	117.10 W
Ordoqui	252	35.54 S	61.10 W
Ord River	162	17.23 S	128.51 E
Ordu	130	41.00 N	37.53 E
Ordu □[4]	130	40.45 N	37.30 E
Ordubad	84	38.56 N	46.02 E
Ordway	198	38.13 N	103.45 W
Ordynskoje	86	54.22 N	81.56 E
Ordzhonikidze → Jenakijevo	83	48.14 N	38.13 E
Ordžhonikidze → Vladikavkaz, Ross.	84	43.03 N	44.40 E
Ordzhonikidze → Vladikavkaz, Ross.	84	43.03 N	44.40 E
Ordžonikidze, Azer.	84	40.53 N	47.23 E
Ordžonikidze, Kaz.	86	52.28 N	61.46 E
Ordžonikidze, Sak.	84	42.01 N	43.12 E
Ordžonikidze, Ukr.	78	47.40 N	34.04 E
Ordžonikidze, Ukr.	78	44.57 N	35.22 E
Ordžonikidzeabad	85	38.34 N	69.01 E
Ordžonikidzevskaja	84	43.18 N	45.03 E
Ordžonikidzevskij, Ross.	84	43.51 N	41.54 E
Ordžonikidzevskij, Ross.	86	54.46 N	88.59 E
Ore	150	6.44 N	4.52 E
Ore ≃	46	56.10 N	3.15 W
Öreälven ≃	26	63.32 N	19.44 E
Oreana	219	39.56 N	88.51 W
Örebro	40	59.17 N	15.13 E
Örebro Län □[6]	40	59.30 N	15.00 E
Orechov	78	47.34 N	35.47 E
Orechovka, Ross.	80	52.56 N	48.14 E
Orechovka, Ukr.	83	48.17 N	39.13 E
Orechovo	80	58.28 N	41.58 E
Orechovo-Zujevo	82	55.49 N	38.59 E
Orechovsk	76	54.41 N	30.30 E
Orechov'skij ◆[8]	83	48.01 N	38.42 E
Ore City	222	32.48 N	94.43 W
Oredež	76	58.49 N	30.20 E
Oredež ≃	76	58.49 N	30.00 E
Orefield	208	40.38 N	75.35 W
Oregon, Il., U.S.	190	42.00 N	89.19 W
Oregon, Mo., U.S.	194	39.59 N	95.08 W
Oregon, Oh., U.S.	214	41.38 N	83.29 W
Oregon, Wi., U.S.	216	42.55 N	89.23 W
Oregon □[3], U.S.	178	44.00 N	121.00 W
Oregon □[3], U.S.	202	44.00 N	121.00 W
Oregon Caves National Monument ♦	202	42.06 N	123.24 W
Oregon City	224	45.21 N	122.36 W
Oregon Creek ≃	226	39.23 N	121.05 W
Oregon Dunes National Recreation Area ♦	202	43.45 N	124.12 W
Oregon House	226	39.21 N	121.17 W
Öregrund	40	60.20 N	18.26 E
Öregrundsgrepen ⊂	40	60.27 N	18.18 E
Orehoved	41	54.57 N	11.52 E
Orekhovo-Zuyevo → Orechovo-Zujevo	82	55.49 N	38.59 E
Orel', ozero ⊜	89	53.30 N	139.42 E
Oreland	285	40.07 N	75.10 W
Orellana	248	6.54 S	75.04 W
Orellana, Embalse de ⊜[1]	34	39.00 N	5.25 W
Orel → Or'ol	76	52.59 N	36.05 E
Orem	200	40.17 N	111.41 W
Ören	130	37.02 N	27.57 E
Orenburg	86	51.54 N	55.06 E
Orenburg □[8]	80	52.38 N	53.00 E
Örencik	130	39.16 N	29.33 E
Oreng, Indon.	114	4.33 N	96.49 E
Oreng, Indon.	114	4.03 N	97.28 E
Orense, Arg.	252	38.40 S	59.47 W
Orense, Esp.	34	42.20 N	7.51 W
Orense □[4]	34	42.15 N	7.30 W
Örenşehir	130	39.00 N	36.39 E
Orepuki	172	46.17 S	167.44 E
Oreški	82	55.43 N	36.21 E
Oressa ≃	76	52.33 N	28.45 E
Orestes	216	40.16 N	85.43 W
Orestes Pereyra	232	26.31 N	105.40 W
Orestiás	38	41.30 N	26.31 E
Orestimba Creek ≃	226	37.25 N	121.00 W
Øresund → The Sound ʉ	41	55.50 N	12.40 E
Oreti ≃	172	46.28 S	168.17 E
Oreto ≃	70	38.06 N	13.24 E
Orewa	172	36.34 S	174.42 E
Oreye	56	50.44 N	5.22 E
Orfanoú, Kólpos ⊂	38	40.40 N	23.50 E
Orford, Eng., U.K.	42	52.06 N	1.31 E
Orford, Eng., U.K.	262	53.25 N	2.35 W
Orford, Mont ∧	206	45.19 N	72.15 W
Orford Ness ›	42	52.05 N	1.34 E
Orfordville	190	42.37 N	89.15 W
Organ Needle ∧	200	32.21 N	106.33 W
Organ Pipe Cactus National Monument ♦	200	32.00 N	112.55 W
Órgãos, Serra dos ⛰	256	22.22 S	42.45 W
Orgaz	34	39.39 N	3.54 W
Orge ≃	50	48.42 N	2.24 E
Orgelet	58	46.31 N	5.37 E
Orgères-en-Beauce	50	48.09 N	1.42 E
Orgerus	261	48.50 N	1.42 E
Orgeval	50	48.55 N	1.59 E
Orgeval ≃	261	49.00 N	1.54 E
Orgiano	64	45.21 N	11.28 E
Orgnac, Aven d' ≛[5]	62	44.19 N	4.27 E
Orgnac-l'Aven	62	44.19 N	4.27 E
Orgof	144	3.03 N	41.44 E
Orgon	62	43.47 N	5.02 E
Orgosolo	71	40.12 N	9.21 E
Orgtrud	80	56.12 N	40.37 E
Orgūn	120	32.51 N	69.07 E
Orhaneli	130	39.54 N	29.00 E
Orhangazi	130	40.30 N	29.18 E
Orhanlar	130	39.54 N	27.37 E
Oria, It.	68	40.30 N	17.38 E
Oria, Zaïre	154	3.17 N	30.41 E
Orica	236	14.41 N	86.56 W
Oriçanga, Rio do ≃	256	22.18 S	47.03 W
Orichuna ≃	246	7.25 N	68.58 W
Oriči	80	58.24 N	49.05 E
Orick	204	41.17 N	124.03 W
Oricola	66	42.02 N	13.02 E
Orient, Ia., U.S.	198	41.12 N	94.24 W
Orient, N.Y., U.S.	207	41.08 N	72.18 W
Orient, Oh., U.S.	218	39.48 N	83.09 W
Orient, Wa., U.S.	182	48.53 N	118.13 W
Oriental, Méx.	234	19.22 N	97.37 W
Oriental, N.C., U.S.	192	35.01 N	76.41 W
Oriental, Cordillera ⛰, Col.	246	6.00 N	73.00 W
Oriental, Cordillera ⛰, Perú	248	11.00 S	74.00 W
Oriental, Pico ∧	286c	10.32 N	66.50 W
Oriental de Zapata, Ciénaga ≖	240p	22.15 N	80.50 W
Oriental Park	214	42.09 N	79.22 W
Oriente	252	38.44 S	60.37 W
Orientos	166	28.05 S	141.14 E
Origgio	266b	45.36 N	9.01 E
Origny-en-Thiérache	50	49.54 N	4.01 E
Origny-Sainte-Benoite	50	49.50 N	3.30 E
Orillia	212	44.37 N	79.25 W
Orimattila	26	60.48 N	25.45 E
Orinda	226	37.52 N	122.10 W
Orinduik	246	4.42 N	60.01 W
Orini	172	37.34 S	175.18 E
Orinin	78	48.46 N	26.24 E
Orinoco ≃	246	8.37 N	62.15 W
Orinoco, Delta del ≛[2]	246	9.15 N	61.30 W
Oriola (Orihuela)	34	38.05 N	0.57 W
Oriole, Md., U.S.	208	38.10 N	75.48 W
Oriole, Pa., U.S.	210	41.08 N	77.13 W
Oriolo	68	40.03 N	16.27 E
Oriomo	164	8.50 S	143.15 E
Orion, Pil.	116	14.37 N	120.34 E
Orion, Il., U.S.	190	41.21 N	90.22 W
Oripää	26	60.51 N	22.41 E
Oriskany	210	43.09 N	75.19 W
Oriskany Battlefield State Historic Site ⊥	210	43.11 N	75.23 W
Oriskany Creek ≃	210	43.10 N	75.20 W
Oriskany Falls	210	42.56 N	75.27 W
Orissa □[3]	118	20.00 N	84.00 E
Orissaare	76	58.34 N	23.05 E
Orissa Coast Canal ≚	126	21.51 N	87.41 E
Oristano	71	39.54 N	8.36 E
Oristano □[4]	71	39.55 N	8.40 E
Oristano, Golfo di ⊂	71	39.50 N	8.29 E
Öriszentpéter	61	46.51 N	16.25 E
Orituco ≃	246	8.45 N	67.27 W
Orives	26	61.41 N	24.21 E
Orives ⊜	26	62.16 N	29.24 E
Oriximiná	250	1.45 S	55.52 W
Orizaba	234	18.51 N	97.06 W
Orizaba, Pico de (Volcán Citlatépetl) ∧[1]	234	19.01 N	97.16 W
Orizona	255	17.03 S	48.18 W
Orjahovo	38	43.45 N	23.57 E
Ørje	26	59.29 N	11.39 E
Orjen ∧	38	42.30 N	18.38 E
Orjiva	34	36.54 N	3.25 W
Ork, Ness of ›	46	59.05 N	2.48 W
Orkanger	26	63.19 N	9.52 E
Örkelljunga	41	56.17 N	13.17 E
Orken	263	51.06 N	6.34 E
Orkla ≃	26	63.18 N	9.50 E
Orkney, Sk., Can.	184	49.08 N	107.55 W
Orkney, S. Afr.	158	27.00 S	26.39 E
Orkney □[4]	46	59.00 N	3.00 W
Orkney Islands II	46	59.00 N	3.00 W
Orl'a	76	53.30 N	24.59 E
Orla ≃	54	50.46 N	11.31 E
Orlamünde	54	50.47 N	11.31 E
Orland, Ca., U.S.	204	39.44 N	122.11 W
Orland, In., U.S.	216	41.43 N	85.10 W
Orlândia	255	20.43 S	47.53 W
Orland Lake ⊜	278	41.38 N	87.52 W
Orlando, S. Afr.	273d	26.14 S	27.55 E
Orlando, Fl., U.S.	220	28.32 N	81.22 W
Orlando, Capo d' ›	70	38.10 N	14.45 E
Orlando Dam ⊜[1]	273d	26.16 S	27.56 E
Orlando International Airport ⊠	220	28.26 N	81.19 W
Orlando Naval Training Center ■	220	28.34 N	81.20 W
Orlando West Extension	273d	26.15 S	27.54 E
Orland Park	216	41.37 N	87.51 W
Orland Square ◆[9]	278	41.36 N	87.51 W
Orléanais □[9]	50	47.50 N	2.00 E
Orléans, On., Can.	212	45.28 N	75.31 W
Orléans, Fr.	50	47.55 N	1.54 E
Orleans, Ca., U.S.	204	41.18 N	123.32 W
Orleans, In., U.S.	218	38.39 N	86.27 W
Orleans, Ma., U.S.	207	41.47 N	69.59 W
Orleans, Ne., U.S.	198	40.07 N	99.27 W
Orleans, Vt., U.S.	188	44.48 N	72.12 W
Orleans □[6], N.Y., U.S.	210	43.15 N	78.12 W
Orleans □[6], Vt., U.S.	206	44.57 N	72.12 W
Orléans, Canal d' ≚	50	47.54 N	1.55 E
Orléans, Île d' I	186	46.55 N	70.58 W
Orléansville → Ech Cheliff	148	36.10 N	1.20 E
Orlik, Kaz.	80	48.17 N	51.32 E
Orlik, Ross.	88	52.30 N	99.55 E
Orlinaja, gora ∧	180	62.35 N	178.30 E
Orlinga	88	56.03 N	105.53 E
Orlinga ≃	88	56.03 N	105.53 E
Orlová	30	49.50 N	18.24 E
Orlov Gaj	80	50.57 N	48.12 E
Orlovista	220	28.32 N	81.28 W
Orlovka, Ross.	78	51.02 N	40.32 E
Orlovka, Ross.	86	59.03 N	85.59 E
Orlovka, Ukr.	78	51.54 N	32.47 E
Orlovka, Ukr.	78	45.40 N	33.21 E
Orlovka, Ukr.	83	48.10 N	37.39 E
Orlovka ≃	86	58.40 N	86.08 E
Orlovo, Ross.	78	51.45 N	39.35 E
Orlovo, Ross.	265b	55.38 N	37.23 E
Orlovskij	80	46.52 N	42.03 E
Orlu	150	5.47 N	7.02 E
Orly	261	48.45 N	2.24 E
Ormanlı	130	41.10 N	31.39 E
Ormāra	128	25.12 N	64.38 E
Ormāra, Rās ›	128	25.09 N	64.35 E
Orme, Rivière à l' ≃	275a	45.27 N	73.56 W
Ormea	62	44.09 N	7.54 E
Ormesby	44	54.33 N	1.11 W
Ormesby Saint Margaret	42	52.40 N	1.42 E
Ormiston	184	49.45 N	105.22 W
Ormoc	116	11.00 N	124.37 E
Ormoc Bay ⊂	116	10.58 N	124.35 E
Ormond	274b	37.54 S	145.03 E
Ormond Beach	192	29.17 N	81.03 W
Ormož	61	46.25 N	16.09 E
Ormsby	214	41.48 N	78.33 W
Ormsby □[6]	226	39.11 N	119.46 W
Ormsjön ⊜	26	64.23 N	16.03 E

Symbols in the index entries represent the broad categories identified in the key at the right. Symbols with superior numbers (⛰[1]) identify subcategories (see complete key on page I · 1).

Symbole im Register stellen die rechts im Schlüssel erklärten Kategorien dar. Symbole mit hochgestellten Ziffern (⛰[1]) bezeichnen Unterabteilungen einer Kategorie (vgl. vollständiger Schlüssel auf Seite I · 1).

Los símbolos incluídos en el texto del índice representan las grandes categorías identificadas con la clave a la derecha. Los símbolos con números en su parte superior (⛰[1]) identifican las subcategorías (véase la clave completa en la página I · 1).

Les symboles de l'index représentent les catégories indiquées dans la légende à droite. Les symboles suivis d'un indice (⛰[1]) représentent des sous-catégories (voir légende complète à la page I · 1).

Os símbolos incluídos no texto do índice representam as grandes categorias identificadas com a chave à direita. Os símbolos com números em sua parte superior (⛰[1]) identificam as subcategorias (veja-se a chave completa à página I · 1).

∧ Mountain	Berg	Montaña	Montagne	Montanha
⛰ Mountains	Gebirge	Montañas	Montagnes	Montanhas
✕ Pass	Paß	Paso	Col	Passo
V Valley, Canyon	Tal, Cañon	Valle, Cañón	Vallée, Canyon	Vale, Canhão
≖ Plain	Ebene	Llano	Plaine	Planície
› Cape	Kap	Cabo	Cap	Cabo
I Island	Insel	Isla	Île	Ilha
II Islands	Inseln	Islas	Îles	Ilhas
≛ Other Topographic Features	Andere Topographische Objekte	Otros Elementos Topográficos	Autres données topographiques	Outros acidentes topográficos

ESPAÑOL — Nombre | Página | Lat.°′ | Long.°′ W = Oeste
FRANÇAIS — Nom | Page | Lat.°′ | Long.°′ W = Ouest
PORTUGUÊS — Nome | Página | Lat.°′ | Long.°′ W = Oeste

Nombre / Nom / Nome	Página / Page	Lat.°′	Long.°′
Ormskirk	44	53.35 N	2.54 W
Ormstown	206	45.08 N	74.00 W
Ormtjernkampen Nasjonalpark ♠	26	61.12 N	9.48 E
Ornain ≃	58	48.46 N	4.47 E
Ornans	58	47.06 N	6.09 E
Ornäs	40	60.31 N	15.32 E
Ornavasso	58	45.58 N	8.24 E
Orne □[5]	32	48.40 N	0.05 E
Orne ≃, Fr.	32	49.19 N	0.14 W
Orne ≃, Fr.	50	48.08 N	0.11 E
Orne ≃, Fr.	56	49.17 N	6.11 E
Ornes	26	61.18 N	7.22 E
Orneta	30	54.08 N	20.08 E
Ornö I	40	59.04 N	18.24 E
Örnsköldsvik	26	63.18 N	18.43 E
Oro	98	40.02 N	127.26 E
Orø I	41	55.46 N	11.49 E
Orobie, Alpi ⋏	64	46.00 N	10.00 E
Oročanskij Golec, gora ∧	88	53.29 N	114.18 E
Oročen	74	58.28 N	125.26 E
Orocovis	240m	18.14 N	66.23 W
Orocué	246	4.48 N	71.20 W
Orocuina	236	13.26 N	87.06 W
Orodara	150	10.59 N	4.55 W
Orofino	202	46.28 N	116.15 W
Orogen Zizhiqi	89	50.34 N	123.40 E
Örög nuur ⊜, Mong.	86	50.10 N	91.00 E
Orog nuur ⊜, Mong.	102	45.03 N	100.42 E
Oro Grande	228	34.35 N	117.20 W
Orohena, Mont ∧	174s	17.37 S	149.28 W
Orok, Oldoinyo ∧	154	2.29 S	36.46 E
Oroku	174m	26.12 N	127.39 E
Or'ol, Ross.	76	52.59 N	36.05 E
Or'ol, Ross.	86	59.21 N	56.35 E
Or'ol □[8]	78	52.00 N	38.00 E
Or'ol' ≃	78	48.30 N	34.54 E
Oroluk I[1]	14	7.32 N	155.18 E
Oromocto	186	45.51 N	66.29 W
Oromocto Lake ⊜	186	45.36 N	67.00 W
Oron, Nig.	150	4.48 N	8.14 E
Oron, Ross.	88	57.11 N	116.28 E
Oron, ozero ⊜	88	57.06 N	116.30 E
Orona I[1]	14	4.29 S	172.10 W
Oron-la-Ville	58	46.34 N	6.50 E
Orono, On., Can.	212	43.59 N	78.37 W
Orono, Me., U.S.	188	44.52 N	68.40 W
Oronoque ≃	246	2.45 N	57.25 W
Oronsay I	46	56.01 N	6.16 W
Orontes → Asi ≃	130	36.02 N	35.58 E
Oropa, Santuario di ⊎[1]	62	45.38 N	7.58 E
Oropeo	234	18.50 N	101.48 W
Oroquieta	116	8.29 N	123.48 E
Orós	250	6.15 S	38.55 W
Orós, Açude ⊜[1]	250	6.15 S	39.05 W
Orosei	71	40.23 N	9.42 E
Orosei, Golfo di ⊂	71	40.15 N	9.44 E
Orosháza	30	46.34 N	20.40 E
Orosi	226	36.33 N	119.17 W
Orosí, Volcán ∧[1]	236	10.59 N	85.29 W
Oroszlány	30	47.30 N	18.19 E
Orotelli	71	40.18 N	9.07 E
Orote Peninsula ≻[1]	174p	13.26 N	144.38 E
Oroville, Ca., U.S.	226	39.30 N	121.33 W
Oroville, Wa., U.S.	202	48.56 N	119.26 W
Oroville, Lake ⊜[1]	204	39.32 N	121.25 W
Orowoc Creek ≃	276	40.43 N	73.13 W
Orpheus Island I	166	18.37 S	146.30 E
Orphin	261	48.35 N	1.47 E
Orpierre	62	44.19 N	5.41 E
Orpington ◆[8]	260	51.23 N	0.06 E
Orrefors	26	56.50 N	15.45 E
Orrell, Eng., U.K.	44	53.32 N	2.42 W
Orrell, Eng., U.K.	262	53.32 N	2.43 W
Orrick	194	39.12 N	94.07 W
Orrin	198	48.05 N	100.09 W
Orrin, Glen V	46	57.30 N	4.46 W
Orrin, Loch ⊜	46	57.30 N	4.45 W
Òrrius	266d	41.33 N	2.21 E
Orr Lake ⊜, Mb., Can.	184	56.07 N	97.11 W
Orr Lake ⊜, On., Can.	212	44.37 N	79.47 W
Orroroo	166	32.44 S	138.37 E
Orrs Island	188	43.45 N	69.58 W
Orrtanna	208	39.51 N	77.22 W
Orrville, Al., U.S.	194	32.18 N	87.14 W
Orrville, Oh., U.S.	214	40.50 N	81.45 W
Orrville, Pa., U.S.	279b	40.33 N	79.47 W
Orša, Bela.	76	54.30 N	30.24 E
Orsa, Sve.	26	61.07 N	14.37 E
Orša ≃	82	56.48 N	36.11 E
Orsago	64	45.56 N	12.25 E
Orsan	62	44.08 N	4.40 E
Oršanka	80	56.55 N	47.53 E
Orsara di Puglia	68	41.17 N	15.16 E
Orsasjön ⊜	26	61.07 N	14.34 E
Orsay	50	48.48 N	2.11 E
Orsett	260	51.31 N	0.22 E
Orsières	58	46.02 N	7.09 E
Orsjön ⊜	26	61.35 N	16.20 E
Orsk	86	51.12 N	58.34 E
Örskär I	40	60.31 N	18.23 E
Ørslev	41	55.02 N	11.59 E
Orsogna	66	42.13 N	14.17 E
Orsomarso	68	39.48 N	15.55 E
Orson	210	41.49 N	75.27 W
Orșova	38	44.42 N	22.24 E
Ørsta	26	62.12 N	6.09 E
Ørsted	41	55.20 N	10.04 E
Örsundaån ≃	40	59.44 N	17.21 E
Örsundsbro	40	59.44 N	17.18 E
Orta	130	40.38 N	33.06 E
Orta, Lago d' ⊜	62	45.49 N	8.24 E
Ortaca	130	36.49 N	28.47 E
Ortakent	130	37.02 N	27.21 E
Ortaklar	130	37.53 N	27.30 E
Ortaköy, Tür.	130	40.17 N	35.16 E
Ortaköy, Tür.	130	38.44 N	34.03 E
Ortaköy, Tür.	130	38.00 N	34.23 E
Ortaköy, Tür.	130	40.27 N	38.02 E
Ortaköy ◆[8]	267b	41.03 N	29.01 E
Orta Nova	68	41.19 N	15.42 E
Orta San Giulio	62	45.48 N	8.25 E
Orte	66	42.27 N	12.23 E
Ortega	246	3.56 N	75.13 W
Ortegal, Cabo ≻	34	43.45 N	7.53 W
Orteguaza ≃	246	0.43 N	75.16 W
Ortelsburg → Szczytno	30	53.34 N	21.00 E
Ortenberg, Dtsch.	56	50.21 N	9.02 E
Ortenberg, Dtsch.	58	48.27 N	7.58 E
Ortenburg	60	48.33 N	13.14 E
Orth	54	54.27 N	11.03 E
Orthez	32	43.29 N	0.46 W
Orthon ≃	248	10.50 S	66.04 W
Ortigalita Creek ≃	226	36.57 N	120.52 W
Ortigalita Peak ∧	226	36.48 N	120.55 W
Ortigara, Monte ∧	64	46.00 N	11.29 E
Ortigueira	34	43.41 N	7.51 W
Ortigueira, Ría de ⊂[1]	34	43.42 N	7.51 W
Orting	224	47.05 N	122.12 W
Ortisei (Sankt Ulrich)	64	46.34 N	11.40 E
Ortiz, Méx.	232	28.17 N	110.43 W
Ortiz, Ven.	246	9.37 N	67.17 W
Ortles (Otler) ∧	64	46.31 N	10.33 E
Örtofta	41	55.47 N	13.14 E
Ortolo ≃	71	41.30 N	8.55 E
Ortona	66	42.21 N	14.24 E
Ortona Lock ◆[5]	220	26.47 N	81.18 W
Orton Park ♠	275b	43.46 N	79.12 W
Ortonura	85	41.29 N	76.12 E
Ortonville, Mi., U.S.	216	42.51 N	83.26 W
Ortonville, Mn., U.S.	198	45.18 N	96.26 W
Ortonville State Recreation Area ♠	216	42.52 N	83.26 W
Ortoterek	85	41.56 N	71.21 E
Orto-Tokoj	85	42.21 N	76.01 E
Ortovero	62	44.03 N	8.07 E
Ortrand	54	51.22 N	13.45 E
Örträsk	26	64.08 N	18.59 E
Ortueri	71	40.02 N	8.59 E
Ortúzar, Canal ≊	286e	33.33 S	70.47 W
Örtze ≃	52	52.40 N	9.57 E
Oruanui	172	38.35 S	176.02 E
Oruba	273a	6.35 N	3.25 E
Orudjevo	82	56.26 N	37.32 E
Orūmīyeh (Reẕā'īyeh)	128	37.33 N	45.04 E
Orūmīyeh, Daryācheh-ye (Lake Urmia) ⊜	128	37.40 N	45.30 E
Orune	71	40.24 N	9.22 E
Oruro	248	17.59 S	67.09 W
Oruro □[5]	248	18.40 S	67.30 W
Or'us-Mijele ≃	88	58.35 N	121.30 E
Orust I	26	58.10 N	11.38 E
Orūzgān (Qala-i-Hazār Qadam)	120	32.56 N	66.38 E
Orūzgān □[4]	120	33.15 N	66.00 E
Orval, Abbaye d' ⊎[1]	56	49.38 N	5.22 E
Orvanne ≃	50	48.22 N	2.50 E
Orvieto	66	42.43 N	12.07 E
Orvilla	208	40.16 N	75.17 W
Orvilliers	261	48.52 N	1.39 E
Orvin ≃	50	48.28 N	3.23 E
Orvinio	66	42.08 N	12.56 E
Orviston	214	41.06 N	77.45 W
Orvyn, gora ∧	180	65.14 N	175.20 W
Orwell, On., Can.	214	42.46 N	81.02 W
Orwell, N.Y., U.S.	212	43.35 N	76.00 W
Orwell, Oh., U.S.	214	41.32 N	80.52 W
Orwell ≃	42	51.57 N	1.17 E
Orwigsburg	208	40.39 N	76.06 W
Orwin	208	40.35 N	76.31 W
Orxon ≃	88	49.00 N	117.41 E
Or Yehuda	132	32.01 N	34.51 E
Oryu-dong ◆[8]	271b	37.29 N	126.51 E
Oržev ≃	78	50.45 N	26.07 E
Orževka	80	52.43 N	42.55 E
Oržica	78	49.48 N	32.42 E
Orzinuovi	62	45.24 N	9.55 E
Orzyc ≃	30	52.47 N	21.13 E
Orzysz	30	53.49 N	21.56 E
Oš, Kyrg.	85	40.33 N	72.48 E
Os, Nor.	26	62.30 N	11.12 E
Ōsa, Nihon	96	35.05 N	133.34 E
Osa, Ross.	86	57.17 N	55.26 E
Osa, Ross.	88	53.24 N	103.53 E
Oša ≃	86	57.13 N	73.41 E
Osa, Península de ≻[1]	236	8.34 N	83.31 W
Osage, Ia., U.S.	190	43.17 N	92.48 W
Osage, Mo., U.S.	219	38.25 N	92.02 W
Osage, N.J., U.S.	285	39.51 N	75.01 W
Osage, Wy., U.S.	198	43.58 N	104.25 W
Osage □[6]	219	38.27 N	91.50 W
Osage ≃	194	38.35 N	91.57 W
Osage Beach	194	38.09 N	92.37 W
Osage City	198	38.38 N	95.49 W
Osaka, Nihon	94	35.57 N	137.16 E
Ōsaka, Nihon	96	34.40 N	135.30 E
Ōsaka, Nihon	270	34.40 N	135.30 E
Ōsaka □[5]	96	34.30 N	135.30 E
Osaka Castle ⊥	270	34.41 N	135.32 E
Ōsaka-heiya ≍	270	34.43 N	135.30 E
Ōsaka International Airport ⊠	270	34.47 N	135.26 E
Ōsaka-kō ⊂	270	34.38 N	135.26 E
Ōsaka-kokusai-kūkō ⊠	96	34.47 N	135.26 E
Osakarovka	86	50.32 N	72.39 E
Ōsaka-tōge)(	270	34.56 N	135.18 E
Osaka University ⊎[2]	270	34.42 N	135.30 E
Ōsaka-wan ⊂	96	34.30 N	135.18 E
Ōsakiga-hana ≻	96	35.11 N	132.25 E
Ōsaki-Kami-jima I	96	34.14 N	132.54 E
Osakis	198	45.52 N	95.09 W
Ōsaki-Shimo-jima I	96	34.10 N	132.50 E
Osâm ≃	38	43.42 N	24.51 E
Osan	98	37.11 N	127.04 E
Osanovo	82	54.12 N	38.41 E
Osasco	256	23.32 S	46.46 W
Osasco □[7]	287b	23.32 S	46.46 W
Ōsawano	94	36.34 N	137.12 E
Osawatomie	198	38.29 N	94.57 W
Ōsa-yama ∧	96	34.45 N	132.12 E
Osbaldeston	262	53.47 N	2.32 W
Osborne, Ks., U.S.	198	39.26 N	98.41 W
Osborne, Pa., U.S.	279b	40.32 N	80.10 W
Osburger Hochwald ◆[3]	56	49.40 N	6.50 E
Osburn	202	47.30 N	115.59 W
Osby	26	56.22 N	13.59 E
Osbyholm	41	55.51 N	13.36 E
Oscar Peak ∧	182	54.51 N	129.07 W
Oscarville	180	60.43 N	161.46 W
Oscawana Lake	210	41.23 N	73.52 W
Osceola, Ar., U.S.	194	35.42 N	89.58 W
Osceola, In., U.S.	216	41.39 N	86.04 W
Osceola, Ia., U.S.	190	41.02 N	93.45 W
Osceola, Mo., U.S.	194	38.02 N	93.42 W
Osceola, Ne., U.S.	198	41.10 N	97.32 W
Osceola, Pa., U.S.	210	41.59 N	77.21 W
Osceola, Tx., U.S.	222	32.08 N	97.14 W
Osceola, Wi., U.S.	190	45.19 N	92.42 W
Osceola □[6]	220	28.00 N	81.15 W
Osceola Mills	214	40.51 N	78.16 W
Oščepkovo	86	56.29 N	70.42 E
Oschatz	54	51.17 N	13.07 E
Oschersleben	54	52.01 N	11.13 E
Oschiri	71	40.43 N	9.06 E
Oscoda	190	44.26 N	83.20 W
Öse ≃	263	51.26 N	7.49 E
Osečenka	76	57.33 N	34.48 E
Osečina	38	44.23 N	19.36 E
Osejevskaja	82	55.53 N	38.10 E
Ošejkino	82	56.15 N	35.54 E
Osek	54	50.37 N	13.40 E
Ösel → Saaremaa I	76	58.25 N	22.30 E
Osen	24	64.17 N	10.30 E
Osetrovo	88	56.47 N	105.47 E
Ōse-zaki ≻	94	35.02 N	138.47 E
Osgood, In., U.S.	218	39.07 N	85.17 W
Osgood, Oh., U.S.	216	40.20 N	84.30 W
Osgoode	212	45.08 N	75.36 W
Oshamambe	92a	42.30 N	140.22 E
O'Shanassy ≃	166	18.59 S	138.46 E
O'Shaughnessy Dam ◆[6]	226	37.57 N	119.47 W
O'Shaughnessy Reservoir ⊜[1]	214	40.12 N	83.09 W
Oshawa	212	43.54 N	78.51 W
Oshawa Creek ≃	212	43.52 N	78.49 W
Oshibe ◆[8]	270	34.45 N	135.04 E
Oshigambo	156	17.47 S	16.05 E
Oshika, Nihon	92	38.16 N	141.32 E
Ōshika, Nihon	94	35.34 N	138.02 E
Oshika-hantō ≻[1]	92	38.20 N	141.30 E
Oshikango	156	17.25 S	15.56 E
Ōshima, Nihon	92	33.03 N	129.33 E
Ōshima, Nihon	94	37.07 N	138.30 E
Ōshima, Nihon	94	34.45 N	139.22 E
Ōshima, Nihon	96	33.55 N	132.15 E
Ō-shima I, Nihon	92a	41.30 N	139.22 E
Ō-shima I, Nihon	94	34.43 N	139.23 E
Ō-shima I, Nihon	94	36.15 N	136.07 E
Ō-shima I, Nihon	96	33.54 N	130.26 E
Ō-shima I, Nihon	96	33.38 N	134.30 E
Ō-shima I, Nihon	96	34.30 N	131.25 E
Ō-shima I, Nihon	96	34.00 N	133.22 E
Ō-shima I, Nihon	96	34.09 N	133.04 E
Oshima-hantō ≻[1]	92a	42.00 N	140.30 E
Oshimizu	94	36.49 N	136.46 E
Oshino	94	35.28 N	138.51 E
Oshivre ◆[8]	272c	19.09 N	72.51 E
Oshkosh, Ne., U.S.	198	41.24 N	102.20 W
Oshkosh, Wi., U.S.	190	44.01 N	88.32 W
Oshnovīyeh	128	37.02 N	45.06 E
Oshodi	273a	6.34 N	3.21 E
Oshoek	158	26.13 S	30.59 E
Oshogbo	150	7.47 N	4.34 E
Osh → Oš	85	40.33 N	72.48 E
Oshtemo	216	42.15 N	85.41 W
Oshtorān Kūh ∧	128	33.20 N	49.16 E
Oshtorīnān	128	34.01 N	48.38 E
Oshwe	152	3.24 S	19.30 E
Osi	150	8.08 N	5.14 E
Osica de Jos	38	44.15 N	24.17 E
Osich'ŏn-ni	98	41.25 N	128.16 E
Osiek	30	50.31 N	21.28 E
Osiglia	62	44.17 N	8.12 E
Osijek	38	45.33 N	18.41 E
Osilinka ≃	182	56.05 N	124.29 W
Osilo	71	40.45 N	8.40 E
Osimo	66	43.29 N	13.29 E
Osini	71	39.50 N	9.29 E
Osinki	80	52.51 N	49.30 E
Osinniki, Ross.	80	58.03 N	47.02 E
Osinniki, Ross.	86	53.37 N	87.21 E
Osinovka, Ross.	88	50.34 N	109.27 E
Osinovka, Ross.	88	56.19 N	101.56 E
Osinovka, Ukr.	83	49.34 N	39.05 E
Osinovskij chrebet ⋏	180	67.10 N	175.00 E
Osinów Dolny	54	52.48 N	14.10 E
Osintorf	76	54.42 N	30.39 E
Osio Sotto	62	45.36 N	9.35 E
Osipaonica	38	44.33 N	21.04 E
Osipenko	78	46.54 N	36.49 E
Osipenko → Berd'ansk	78	46.45 N	36.49 E
Osipoviči	76	53.18 N	28.38 E
Osipovo Selo	76	56.51 N	30.30 E
Osire	156	20.59 S	17.19 E
Osivān	120	26.43 N	72.55 E
Oskaloosa, Ia., U.S.	190	41.17 N	92.38 W
Oskaloosa, Ks., U.S.	198	39.12 N	95.18 W
Oskar-Fredriksborg	40	59.24 N	18.26 E
Oskarshamn	26	57.16 N	16.26 E
Oskarström	26	56.48 N	12.58 E
Os'kino	78	51.14 N	39.02 E
Oskol ≃	78	49.06 N	37.25 E
Oskolkovo	24	67.58 N	53.42 E
Oskū	128	37.55 N	46.06 E
Oskuj	76	59.17 N	32.05 E
Oskuja ≃	76	59.14 N	31.54 E
Osl'anka, gora ∧	86	59.10 N	58.33 E
Oslava ≃	61	49.05 N	16.22 E
Ösling ◆[1]	56	49.55 N	6.00 E
Oslo	26	59.55 N	10.45 E
Oslob	116	9.31 N	123.26 E
Oslofjorden ⊂[2]	26	59.20 N	10.35 E
Os'ma ≃, Ross.	76	54.55 N	33.24 E
Ošma ≃, Ross.	80	57.52 N	47.45 E
Osmānābād	122	18.10 N	76.02 E
Osmancık	130	40.59 N	34.49 E
Osmaneli	130	40.22 N	30.01 E
Osmaniye	130	37.05 N	36.14 E
Osmanpaşa	130	39.38 N	34.58 E
Ošm'anskaja vozvyšennost' ⋏[1]	76	54.20 N	26.00 E
Ošm'any	76	54.25 N	25.56 E
Osmeña	116	10.11 N	125.31 E
Osmington	42	50.38 N	2.22 W
Os'mino	76	59.01 N	29.06 E
Osminog, gora ∧	180	67.54 N	176.50 E
Ösmo	40	58.59 N	17.54 E
Osmond	198	42.21 N	97.35 W
Osmore ≃	248	17.33 S	71.12 W
Osmoy	261	48.52 N	1.43 E
Osmussaar I	76	59.18 N	23.22 E
Osnabrück	52	52.16 N	8.02 E
Ośno	30	52.28 N	14.50 E
Osny	261	49.04 N	2.04 E
Oso	224	48.16 N	121.56 W
Oso ≃	154	1.09 S	27.22 E
Oso, Gran Lago del → Great Bear Lake ⊜	176	66.00 N	120.00 W
Ošoba	85	40.44 N	70.26 E
Osogna	58	46.18 N	9.00 E
Osoppo	64	46.15 N	13.05 E
Osorakan-zan ∧	96	34.36 N	132.08 E
Osore-yama ∧	92	41.18 N	141.05 E
Osorio, Quebrada ≃	286c	10.36 N	66.56 W
Osório Fonseca	250	3.40 S	58.13 W
Osorno, Chile	254	40.34 S	73.09 W
Osorno, Esp.	34	42.24 N	4.22 W
Osorno, Volcán ∧[1]	254	41.06 S	72.30 W
Osorun	273a	6.33 N	3.29 E
Os'otr ≃	82	54.58 N	38.46 E
Osoyoos	182	49.02 N	119.28 W
Osoyoos Indian Reserve ◆[4]	182	49.08 N	119.30 W
Osoyoos Lake ⊜	182	49.00 N	119.26 W
Osøyra	26	60.11 N	5.28 E
Ospedaletti	62	43.48 N	7.43 E
Ospedaletto, It.	64	46.17 N	13.07 E
Ospedaletto, It.	64	46.03 N	11.33 E
Ospino	246	9.18 N	69.27 W
Ospitale di Cadore	64	46.20 N	12.19 E
Ospitaletto	64	45.33 N	10.04 E
Osprey	220	27.11 N	82.29 W
Osprey Reef ✣[2]	164	13.55 S	146.38 E
Ospwagan Lake ⊜	184	55.35 N	98.03 W
Oss	52	51.46 N	5.31 E
Ossa, Mount ∧	166	41.54 S	146.01 E
Ossabaw Island I	192	31.47 N	81.06 W
Osse ≃, Fr.	32	44.07 N	0.17 E
Osse ≃, Nig.	150	6.10 N	5.20 E
Ossenberg	263	51.34 N	6.35 E
Ossendrecht	52	51.24 N	4.19 E
Osseo, Mi., U.S.	216	41.53 N	84.33 W
Osseo, Wi., U.S.	190	44.34 N	91.13 W
Ossett	44	53.41 N	1.35 W
Ossi	71	40.40 N	8.35 E
Ossiacher See ⊜	64	46.40 N	13.55 E
Ossian, In., U.S.	216	40.52 N	85.09 W
Ossian, Ia., U.S.	190	43.08 N	91.45 W
Ossian, Loch ⊜	46	56.46 N	4.38 W
Ossining	210	41.09 N	73.51 W
Ossipee	188	43.41 N	71.07 W
Ossjøen ⊜	26	61.13 N	11.53 E
Ossling	54	51.21 N	14.09 E
Ossona	266b	45.30 N	8.54 E
Ossora	74	59.20 N	163.13 E
Ossum-Bösinghoven	263	51.18 N	6.39 E
Ošta	24	60.49 N	35.32 E
Ostaboningue, Lac ⊜	190	47.09 N	78.53 W
Östanå, Sve.	40	59.33 N	18.35 E
Östanå, Sve.	40	60.38 N	16.48 E
Östanbyn	40	60.39 N	16.48 E
Ostankino ◆[8]	265b	55.49 N	37.37 E
Östansjö	40	59.03 N	14.59 E
Ostapje	78	49.33 N	33.46 E
Ostaškov	76	57.09 N	33.06 E
Ostašovo	82	55.52 N	35.52 E
Ostbevern	52	52.02 N	7.50 E
Østbirk	41	55.58 N	9.46 E
Ostbüren	263	51.31 N	7.46 E
Østby	26	61.15 N	12.32 E
Ostchinesisches Meer → East China Sea ⫪[2]	90	30.00 N	126.00 E
Oste ≃	52	53.51 N	8.59 E
Osted	41	55.34 N	11.58 E
Osteen	220	28.50 N	81.09 W
Ostellato	66	44.45 N	11.56 E
Ostende → Oostende	50	51.13 N	2.55 E
Ostenfelde	52	51.52 N	8.04 E
Oster ≃	60	48.43 N	13.29 E
Osterath	56	51.16 N	6.37 E
Osterbönen	263	51.37 N	7.48 E
Osterburg, Dtsch.	54	52.47 N	11.44 E
Osterburg, Pa., U.S.	214	40.16 N	78.31 W
Osterburken	56	49.26 N	9.26 E
Österbybruk	40	60.12 N	17.54 E
Österbymo	26	57.50 N	15.16 E
Ostercappeln	52	52.20 N	8.13 E
Österdalälven ≃	26	60.33 N	15.08 E
Østerdalen V	26	61.15 N	11.10 E
Österfärnebo	40	60.18 N	16.48 E
Osterfeld	54	51.05 N	11.56 E
Osterfeld ◆[8]	263	51.30 N	6.53 E
Östergötland □[9]	26	58.24 N	15.34 E
Östergötlands Län □[6]	26	58.25 N	15.45 E
Österhaninge	40	59.08 N	18.12 E
Osterhofen	60	48.42 N	13.01 E
Øster Højst	41	55.00 N	9.03 E
Osterholz-Scharmbeck	52	53.14 N	8.47 E
Osterley Park ♠	260	51.30 N	0.21 W
Österlövsta	40	60.26 N	17.47 E
Ostermundigen	58	46.58 N	7.29 E
Osternienburg	54	51.48 N	12.01 E
Osterode	52	51.44 N	10.11 E
Osterode → Ostróda	30	53.43 N	19.59 E
Osterøya I	26	60.33 N	5.35 E
Österreich → Austria □[1]	30	47.20 N	13.20 E
Österreichisches Freilichtmuseum ⊎	61	47.10 N	15.19 E
Osterrönfeld	41	54.17 N	9.41 E
Östersjön → Baltic Sea ⫪[2]	24	57.00 N	19.00 E
Österskär	40	59.28 N	18.18 E
Östersund	26	63.11 N	14.39 E
Östervåla	40	60.11 N	17.11 E
Osterville	207	41.37 N	70.23 W
Osterwick	52	52.01 N	7.13 E
Osterwieck	54	51.58 N	10.42 E
Ostfeld ◆[8]	263	51.40 N	7.45 E
Østfold □[6]	26	59.20 N	11.30 E
Ostfriesische Inseln II	52	53.44 N	7.25 E
Ostfriesland □[9]	52	53.20 N	7.40 E
Ost-Ghats → Eastern Ghāts ⋏	122	14.00 N	78.50 E
Östhammar	40	60.16 N	18.22 E
Ostheim vor der Rhön	56	50.27 N	10.14 E
Osthofen	56	49.42 N	8.19 E
Ostia, Bonifica di ◆[1]	267a	41.46 N	12.18 E
Ostia Antica ⊥	66	41.45 N	12.16 E
Ostiano	64	45.13 N	10.15 E
Ostiglia	64	45.04 N	11.08 E
Ostki	78	51.16 N	27.22 E
Östliche Sierra Madre → Madre Oriental, Sierra ⋏	232	22.00 N	99.30 W
Östmark	26	60.17 N	12.45 E
Ost'or, Ross.	76	54.01 N	32.48 E
Ost'or, Ukr.	78	50.57 N	30.53 E
Ost'or ≃, Europe	76	53.47 N	31.46 E
Ost'or ≃, Ukr.	78	50.56 N	30.52 E
Ostpeene ≃	54	53.43 N	12.46 E
Ostra	66	43.37 N	13.09 E
Östraby	41	55.46 N	13.41 E
Ostrach	58	47.57 N	9.23 E
Ostrach ≃	58	48.04 N	9.24 E
Östra Grevie	41	55.28 N	13.08 E
Östra Husby	40	58.35 N	16.33 E
Östra Laxsjön ⊜	40	58.54 N	14.42 E
Östra Ljungby	41	56.11 N	13.04 E
Ostrander	214	40.15 N	83.12 W
Östra Ringsjön ⊜	41	55.52 N	13.32 E
Ostrau	54	51.12 N	13.09 E
Ostrau → Ostrava	30	49.50 N	18.17 E
Ostrava	30	49.50 N	18.17 E
Ostra Vetere	66	43.36 N	13.03 E
Ostrhauderfehn	52	53.08 N	7.37 E
Östrich	263	51.40 N	6.55 E
Ostricourt	50	50.27 N	3.02 E
Östringen	56	49.13 N	8.43 E
Ostritz	54	51.01 N	14.56 E
Ostróda	30	53.43 N	19.59 E
Ostrog	78	50.20 N	26.31 E
Ostrogožsk	78	50.52 N	39.05 E
Ostrokonje	76	59.52 N	42.02 E
Ostrołęka	30	53.06 N	21.34 E
Ostrołęka □[4]	30	53.00 N	21.30 E
Ostroróg	30	52.39 N	16.27 E
Ostrošickij Gorodok	76	54.04 N	27.42 E
Ostrov, Bela.	76	52.53 N	25.59 E
Ostrov, Česko.	54	50.17 N	12.57 E
Ostrov, Rom.	38	44.06 N	27.22 E
Ostrov, Ross.	76	57.20 N	28.22 E
Ostrov, Ross.	76	60.34 N	37.55 E
Ostrov, Ross.	265b	55.35 N	37.51 E
Ostrov I	30	47.55 N	17.35 E
Ostrov'anskij	80	46.45 N	42.13 E
Ostrovec	76	54.37 N	25.57 E
Ostrovki	265a	59.48 N	30.50 E
Ostrovno	76	55.08 N	29.53 E
Ostrovskaja	80	50.26 N	44.27 E
Ostrovskoje	80	57.48 N	42.15 E
Ostrov-Zalit	76	58.01 N	28.04 E
Ostrowiec Świętokrzyski	30	50.57 N	21.23 E
Ostrów Lubelski	30	51.30 N	22.52 E
Ostrów Mazowiecka	30	52.49 N	21.54 E
Ostrów Wielkopolski	30	51.39 N	17.49 E
Ostryna	76	53.44 N	24.32 E
Ostrzeszów	30	51.25 N	17.57 E
Ostseebad Ahrenshoop	54	54.23 N	12.25 E
Ostseebad Boltenhagen	54	54.00 N	11.12 E
Ostseebad Dierhagen	41	54.17 N	12.22 E
Ostseebad Graal-Müritz	54	54.15 N	12.12 E
Ostseebad Nienhagen	54	54.09 N	11.58 E
Ostseebad Rerik	54	54.06 N	11.37 E
Ostseebad Wustrow	54	54.21 N	12.23 E
Ostsee → Baltic Sea ⫪[2]	24	57.00 N	19.00 E
Ost-Sümmern	263	51.26 N	7.44 E
Osttirol ◆[1]	64	46.55 N	12.30 E
Ostúa ≃	236	14.17 N	89.33 W
Ostuacán	234	17.25 N	93.18 W
Ostula	234	18.30 N	103.28 W
Ostuni	68	40.44 N	17.35 E
Ostwald	58	48.33 N	7.43 E
Osu	98	35.31 N	127.18 E
Osuga	76	56.02 N	34.18 E
Osuga ≃	76	57.16 N	34.49 E
Ōsuka	94	34.41 N	137.59 E
O'Sullivan, Lac ⊜	190	47.37 N	76.05 W
Osum ≃	38	40.48 N	19.52 E
Ōsumi	270	34.50 N	135.45 E
Ōsumi-hantō ≻[1]	92	31.20 N	130.55 E
Ōsumi-kaikyō ꭒ	92	31.00 N	131.00 E
Ōsumi-shotō II	93b	30.30 N	130.00 E
Osuna	34	37.14 N	5.07 W
Osupugo ∧	154	1.40 N	35.49 E
Osvaldo Cruz	255	21.47 S	50.50 W
Osveja	76	56.01 N	28.06 E
Osvejskoje, ozero ⊜	76	56.03 N	28.08 E
Ošvor	24	66.58 N	62.53 E
Oswaldtwistle	44	53.43 N	2.26 W
Oswaldtwistle Moor ◆[3]	262	53.43 N	2.23 W
Oswald West State Park ♠	224	45.45 N	123.58 W
Oswayo	214	41.55 N	78.01 W
Oswayo Creek ≃	210	42.02 N	78.21 W
Oswegatchie ≃	188	44.42 N	75.30 W
Oswegatchie, Middle Branch ≃	212	44.07 N	75.19 W
Oswegatchie, West Branch ≃	188	44.18 N	75.20 W
Oswego, Il., U.S.	216	41.40 N	88.21 W
Oswego, In., U.S.	216	41.19 N	85.47 W
Oswego, Ks., U.S.	198	37.10 N	95.06 W
Oswego, N.Y., U.S.	212	43.27 N	76.30 W
Oswego □[6]	212	43.22 N	76.15 W
Oswego ≃, N.J., U.S.	208	39.40 N	74.32 W
Oswego ≃, N.Y., U.S.	212	43.28 N	76.31 W
Oswestry	42	52.52 N	3.04 W
Oświęcim	30	50.03 N	19.12 E
Osyka	194	31.00 N	90.28 W
Ota, Nihon	94	35.58 N	136.04 E
Ōta, Nihon	94	36.18 N	139.22 E
Ōta, Nihon	96	33.31 N	131.33 E
Ōta ◆[8]	268	35.34 N	139.43 E
Ōta ≃, Nihon	94	34.40 N	137.54 E
Ōta ≃, Nihon	96	34.22 N	132.25 E
Otago Peninsula ≻[1]	172	45.52 S	170.40 E
Otahuhu	172	36.57 S	174.51 E
Ōtake	96	34.12 N	132.13 E
Otaki, N.Z.	172	40.45 S	175.09 E
Ōtaki, Nihon	94	35.17 N	140.15 E
Ōtaki, Nihon	94	35.48 N	137.33 E
Ōtaki, Nihon	94	35.57 N	138.56 E
Ōtaki ≃	94	35.49 N	137.40 E
Ōtaki-yama ∧	96	34.07 N	134.08 E
Ōta-Koizumi-hikojō ♠	94	36.16 N	139.24 E
Otane	172	39.53 S	176.38 E
Otanmäki	26	64.07 N	27.06 E
Otar	85	43.33 N	75.13 E
Otari	94	36.46 N	137.54 E
Otaru	92a	43.13 N	141.00 E
Otatara	172	46.26 S	168.18 E
Otatitlán	234	18.12 N	96.02 W
Otautau	172	46.09 S	168.00 E
Otava	26	61.39 N	27.04 E
Otava ≃	30	49.27 N	14.12 E
Otavalo	246	0.14 N	78.16 W
Otavi	156	19.39 S	17.20 E
Ōtawara	94	36.52 N	140.02 E
Otawa-yama ∧	270	34.28 N	135.53 E
Otay	228	32.35 N	117.03 W
Otchinjau	152	16.30 S	13.57 E
Oteapan	234	18.00 N	94.39 W
Otego	210	42.23 N	75.10 W
Otego Creek ≃	210	42.25 N	75.07 W
Otélé	152	3.35 N	11.15 E
Otematata	172	44.37 S	170.16 E
Oteotea	175e	9.05 S	161.11 E
Otepää	76	58.03 N	26.30 E
Oteros ≃	232	26.55 N	108.22 W
Otford, Austl.	170	34.12 S	151.01 E
Otford, Eng., U.K.	42	51.19 N	0.12 E
Otgon	88	47.11 N	97.33 E
Otgon Tenger uul ∧	88	47.36 N	97.36 E
Otham	260	51.15 N	0.35 E
Othello	202	46.49 N	119.10 W
Othery	42	51.05 N	2.53 W
Othfresen	52	52.00 N	10.23 E
Óthiris, Óros ⋏	38	39.02 N	22.37 E
Othis	261	49.04 N	2.41 E
Othonoí I	38	39.50 N	19.26 E
Oti ≃	150	8.40 N	0.13 E
Otibanda	164	7.15 S	146.30 E
Otinapa	232	24.11 N	105.02 W
Otira	172	42.50 S	171.33 E
Otis, Co., U.S.	198	40.08 N	102.57 W
Otis, In., U.S.	216	41.36 N	86.54 W
Otis, Ks., U.S.	198	38.32 N	99.03 W
Otis, Ma., U.S.	207	42.11 N	73.05 W
Otisco	218	38.32 N	85.40 W
Otisco Lake ⊜	210	42.52 N	76.18 W
Otish, Monts ⋏	176	52.22 N	70.30 W
Otis Reservoir ⊜[1]	207	42.09 N	73.02 W
Otisville	210	41.28 N	74.32 W
Otjassy	80	53.14 N	41.39 E
Otjikondo	156	19.50 S	15.23 E
Otjimbingue	156	22.19 S	16.10 E
Otjinene	156	21.13 S	18.42 E
Otjiwarongo	156	20.29 S	16.36 E
Otjiwarongo □[5]	156	20.45 S	16.30 E
Otjozondjou ≃	156	20.18 S	20.50 E
Otley	44	53.54 N	1.41 W
Otmanlı	130	41.52 N	34.37 E
Otm'ok, pereval)(	85	42.20 N	73.10 E
Otmuchów	30	50.28 N	17.10 E
Otnes	26	61.45 N	11.14 E
Otnice	61	49.05 N	16.49 E
Ōtō	96	33.41 N	135.35 E
Otočac	36	44.52 N	15.14 E
Otog Qi	102	39.08 N	108.00 E
Ōtomi	175d	24.19 N	123.54 E
Oton	116	10.42 N	122.29 E
Otonabee ≃	212	44.08 N	78.14 W
Otoque, Isla I	236	8.36 N	79.36 W
Ōtori-kita	270	34.33 N	135.27 E
Otorma	80	53.32 N	42.32 E
Otoro ≃	236	15.00 N	88.16 W
Otorohanga	172	38.11 S	175.12 E
Otoskwin ≃	176	52.13 N	88.06 W
Otowa	94	34.51 N	137.18 E
Otowa-yama ∧	270	34.58 N	135.51 E
Otowa-yama-tunnel ◆[5]	94	34.58 N	135.51 E
Ōtoyo	96	33.46 N	133.40 E
Otra ≃	26	58.09 N	8.00 E
Otradnaja	84	44.23 N	41.31 E
Otradnoje	265a	59.47 N	30.49 E
Otradnyj	80	53.22 N	51.21 E
Otranto	68	40.09 N	18.30 E
Otranto, Capo d' ≻	68	40.06 N	18.31 E
Otranto, Strait of ꭒ	38	40.00 N	19.00 E
Otricoli	66	42.25 N	12.29 E
Otrokovice	30	49.13 N	17.31 E
Ötscher ∧	61	47.52 N	15.12 E
Otsego	216	42.27 N	85.41 W
Otsego □[6]	210	42.42 N	74.56 W
Otsego Lake ⊜	210	42.45 N	74.52 W
Otselic ≃	210	42.20 N	75.58 W
Ōtsu, Nihon	96	35.00 N	135.52 E
Ōtsu, Nihon	268	35.16 N	139.42 E
Ōtsu ≃	270	34.30 N	135.24 E
Ōtsuchi	92	39.21 N	141.54 E
Ōtsuki	94	35.36 N	138.57 E
Ōtsu-shima I	96	34.00 N	131.42 E
Otta, Nig.	150	6.42 N	3.10 E
Otta, Nor.	26	61.46 N	9.32 E
Otta ≃	26	61.46 N	9.31 E
Ottakring ◆[8]	264b	48.12 N	16.19 E
Ottana	71	40.14 N	9.02 E
Otta Pass ꭒ	175c	7.09 N	151.53 E
Ottarnic Pond ⊜	283	42.46 N	71.25 W
Ottati	68	40.28 N	15.19 E
Ottavia ◆[8]	267a	41.58 N	12.24 E
Ottaviano	68	40.51 N	14.28 E
Ottawa, On., Can.	212	45.25 N	75.42 W
Ottawa, Il., U.S.	216	41.20 N	88.50 W
Ottawa, Ks., U.S.	198	38.36 N	95.16 W
Ottawa, Oh., U.S.	216	41.01 N	84.02 W
Ottawa □[6], Mi., U.S.	216	42.57 N	86.02 W
Ottawa □[6], Oh., U.S.	214	41.31 N	82.56 W
Ottawa ≃, Can.	176	45.20 N	73.58 W
Ottawa ≃, Oh., U.S.	214	41.44 N	83.28 W
Ottawa ≃, Oh., U.S.	216	41.00 N	84.15 W
Ottawa-Carleton □[6]	212	45.15 N	75.45 W
Ottawa Hills	214	41.39 N	83.38 W
Ottawa International Airport ⊠	212	45.19 N	75.40 W
Ottawa Islands II	176	59.30 N	80.10 W
Ottbergen	52	51.42 N	9.18 E
Ottenby	26	56.14 N	16.25 E
Ottendorf-Okrilla	54	51.11 N	13.50 E
Ottenhöfen	58	48.34 N	8.09 E
Ottenschlag	61	48.25 N	15.13 E
Ottensheim	61	48.20 N	14.11 E
Ottenstein Stausee ⊜[1]	61	48.37 N	15.17 E
Otter ≃	42	50.46 N	3.17 W
Otterbach ≃	56	49.07 N	8.21 E
Otterbäcken	40	58.57 N	14.02 E
Otterbein	216	40.29 N	87.06 W
Otterburn	44	55.14 N	2.10 W
Otterburne	184	49.30 N	97.03 W
Otterburn Park	206	45.33 N	73.13 W
Otter Creek	192	29.19 N	82.46 W
Otter Creek ≃, On., Can.	212	44.06 N	81.07 W
Otter Creek ≃, Il., U.S.	219	39.18 N	90.07 W
Otter Creek ≃, In., U.S.	218	38.58 N	85.37 W
Otter Creek ≃, Ia., U.S.	190	41.20 N	93.30 W
Otter Creek ≃, Mo., U.S.	219	39.31 N	91.51 W
Otter Creek ≃, Mt., U.S.	202	45.36 N	106.17 W
Otter Creek ≃, N.Y., U.S.	212	43.43 N	75.23 W
Otter Creek ≃, Ut,. U.S.	200	38.10 N	112.02 W
Otter Creek ≃, Vt., U.S.	188	44.13 N	73.17 W
Otter Creek Reservoir ⊜[1]	200	38.12 N	111.59 W
Otterhöfen	56	48.33 N	8.12 E
Otter-Lake, P.Q., Can.	188	45.51 N	76.26 W
Otter Lake, Mi., U.S.	190	43.13 N	83.28 W
Otter Lake ⊜, On., Can.	212	44.47 N	76.07 W
Otter Lake ⊜, On., Can.	212	45.17 N	79.56 W
Otter Lake ⊜, Sk., Can.	184	55.35 N	104.39 W
Otter Lake ⊜[1]	219	39.26 N	89.54 W
Otterlo	52	52.06 N	5.45 E
Otterndorf	52	53.48 N	8.53 E
Otterøya I	26	62.42 N	6.48 E
Otter River	207	42.35 N	72.03 W
Ottersberg	52	53.06 N	9.08 E
Ottershaw	260	51.22 N	0.32 W
Ottersleben ◆[8]	54	52.05 N	11.34 E
Otter Tail ≃	198	46.16 N	96.36 W
Otter Tail Lake ⊜	198	46.23 N	95.40 W
Otterup	41	55.31 N	10.24 E
Otterville, On., Can.	212	42.55 N	80.36 W
Otterville, Il., U.S.	219	39.03 N	90.24 W
Otterville, Mo., U.S.	194	38.41 N	93.00 W
Ottery ≃	42	50.39 N	4.20 W
Ottery Saint Mary	42	50.45 N	3.17 W
Ottignies	56	50.40 N	4.34 E
Ottine	222	29.36 N	97.35 W
Ottleben	54	52.05 N	11.07 E
Ottmarsbocholt	52	51.49 N	7.32 E
Ottnang	60	48.06 N	13.40 E
Ottnaren ⊜	40	60.29 N	16.37 E
Otto, N.Y., U.S.	210	42.21 N	78.50 W
Otto, Tx., U.S.	222	31.27 N	96.49 W
Ottobeuren	58	47.56 N	10.18 E
Ottobeuren, Klosterkirche ⊎[1]	58	47.56 N	10.18 E
Ottobiano	62	45.09 N	8.50 E
Ottobrunn	60	48.04 N	11.40 E
Ottone	62	44.37 N	9.20 E
Ottoschwanden	58	48.12 N	7.52 E
Ottosdal	158	26.58 S	26.00 E
Ottoshoop	156	25.45 S	25.59 E
Ottoville	216	40.55 N	84.20 W
Ottuk, Kyrg.	85	42.18 N	76.18 E
Ottuk, Kyrg.	85	41.38 N	75.51 E
Ottumwa	190	41.00 N	92.22 W
Ottweiler	56	49.24 N	7.09 E
Otty Lake ⊜	212	44.50 N	76.13 W
Otu	150	8.14 N	3.24 E
Otukpa	150	7.09 N	7.41 E
Otumpa	252	27.19 S	62.13 W
Otun	273a	6.42 N	3.22 E
Otu → Ōtsu	96	35.00 N	135.52 E
Otuquis, Bañados de ≡	248	19.20 S	58.30 W
Oturkpo	150	7.14 N	8.08 E
Otway, Bahía ꭒ	254	53.20 S	74.00 W
Otway, Cape ≻	166	38.52 S	143.31 E
Otway, Seno ⊂	254	53.05 S	71.30 W
Otway Range ⋏	169	38.30 S	143.50 E
Otwock	30	52.07 N	21.16 E
Otyn'a	78	48.44 N	24.51 E
Ötztal V	64	47.05 N	10.55 E
Ötztaler Ache ≃	64	47.14 N	10.50 E
Ötztaler Alpen (Alpi Venoste) ⋏	64	46.45 N	10.55 E
Ou ≃, Lao	110	20.04 N	102.13 E
Ou ≃, Zhg.	100	26.02 N	113.09 E
Ou ≃, Zhg.	100	28.01 N	120.44 E
Oua ≃	152	0.43 N	12.55 E
Ouachita ≃	194	31.38 N	91.49 W
Ouachita, Lake ⊜[1]	194	34.40 N	93.25 W
Ouachita Mountains ⋏	194	34.40 N	94.25 W
Ouaco	175f	20.50 S	164.29 E
Ouadâne	148	20.56 N	11.37 W
Ouadda	152	8.04 N	22.24 E
Ouaddaï □[5]	146	13.00 N	21.00 E
Ouadey, Ouadi el V	146	13.34 N	18.03 E
Ouagadougou	150	12.22 N	1.31 W
Ouahigouya	150	13.35 N	2.25 W
Ouahran → Wahran	148	35.43 N	0.43 W
Ouaka □[5]	152	6.00 N	21.00 E
Ouaka ≃	152	4.59 N	19.56 E
Oualâta	150	17.18 N	7.02 W
Ouâlata, Dahr ⫠[4]	150	17.48 N	7.24 W
Oualé ≃	150	10.52 N	0.51 E
Oualidia	148	32.44 N	9.08 W
Ouallam	150	14.19 N	2.05 E
Ouallene	148	24.37 N	1.14 E
Oualto	150	9.01 N	10.06 W
Ouanary	250	4.13 N	51.40 W
Ouanda Djallé	146	8.54 N	22.48 E
Ouandago	146	7.10 N	18.42 E
Ouandja ≃	146	9.35 N	21.43 E
Ouandja-Vakaga, Réserve de la ◆[4]	146	9.00 N	21.30 E
Ouango	152	4.19 N	22.33 E
Ouangolodougou	150	9.58 N	5.09 W
Ouaninou	150	8.11 N	7.51 W
Ouanne ≃	50	47.57 N	2.47 E
Ouan Taredert	148	27.33 N	9.32 E
Ouaquaga	210	42.08 N	75.39 W
Ouara ≃	154	5.05 N	24.26 E
Ouarâne ◆[1]	134	21.00 N	10.30 W
Ouararda, Passe de)(	148	21.01 N	13.03 W
Ouareau ≃	206	45.56 N	73.25 W
Ouareau, Lac ⊜[1]	206	46.17 N	74.09 W
Ouargaye	150	11.32 N	0.01 E
Ouarkoye	150	12.05 N	3.40 W
Ouarkziz, Jbel ⋏	148	28.50 N	9.00 W
Ouarsenis, Djebel ∧	34	35.53 N	1.38 E
Ouarville	50	48.21 N	1.46 E
Ouarzazate	148	30.57 N	6.50 W
Ouarzazate □[4]	148	30.55 N	6.45 W
Ouassoulou ≃	150	11.35 N	8.11 W
Ouatcha	150	13.22 N	9.18 E
Oubangui (Ubangi) ≃	152	0.30 S	17.42 E
Ouche ≃	58	47.06 N	5.16 E
Oucques	50	47.49 N	1.18 E
Ōuda	94	34.28 N	135.56 E
Oudaze Lake ⊜	212	45.27 N	79.11 W
Oud-Beijerland	52	51.49 N	4.25 E
Ouddorp	52	51.18 N	3.56 E
Oude IJssel (Issel) ≃	52	52.00 N	6.10 E
Oudenaarde	50	50.51 N	3.36 E
Oudenbosch	52	51.35 N	4.31 E
Oudenburg	50	50.46 N	3.53 E
Oude-Pekela	52	53.04 N	6.58 E
Oude Rijn ≃	52	52.05 N	4.20 E
Oudeschild	52	53.02 N	4.50 E
Oude-Tonge	52	51.41 N	4.12 E

Symbol	English	Deutsch	Español	Français	Português
≃	River	Fluß	Río	Rivière	Rio
≊	Canal	Kanal	Canal	Canal	Canal
∟	Waterfall, Rapids	Wasserfall, Stromschnellen	Cascada, Rápidos	Chute d'eau, Rapides	Cascata, Rápidos
ꭒ	Strait	Meeresstraße	Estrecho	Détroit	Estreito
⊂	Bay, Gulf	Bucht, Golf	Bahía, Golfo	Baie, Golfe	Baía, Golfo
⊜	Lake, Lakes	See, Seen	Lago, Lagos	Lac, Lacs	Lago, Lagos
≡	Swamp	Sumpf	Pantano	Marais	Pântano
⌂	Ice Features, Glacier	Eis- und Gletscherformen	Accidentes Glaciales	Formes glaciaires	Acidentes glaciares
⫪	Other Hydrographic Features	Andere Hydrographische Objekte	Otros Elementos Hidrográficos	Autres données hydrographiques	Outros acidentes hidrográficos
✣	Submarine Features	Untermeerische Objekte	Accidentes Submarinos	Formes de relief sous-marin	Acidentes submarinos
□	Political Unit	Politische Einheit	Unidad Politica	Entité politique	Unidade política
⊎	Cultural Institution	Kulturelle Institution	Institución Cultural	Institution culturelle	Instituição cultural
⊥	Historical Site	Historische Stätte	Sitio Histórico	Site historique	Sitio histórico
♠	Recreational Site	Erholungs- und Ferienort	Sitio de Recreo	Centre de loisirs	Area de Lazer
⊠	Airport	Flughafen	Aeropuerto	Aéroport	Aeroporto
■	Military Installation	Militäranlage	Instalación Militar	Installation militaire	Instalação militar
◆	Miscellaneous	Verschiedenes	Misceláneo	Divers	Diversos

Symbols in the index entries represent the broad categories identified in the key at the right. Symbols with superior numbers (*) identify subcategories (see complete key on page 1-1).

Los símbolos incluidos en el texto del índice representan las grandes categorías identificadas con la clave a la derecha. Los símbolos con números en su parte superior (*) identifican las subcategorías (véase la clave completa en la página 1-1).

Les symboles de l'index représentent les catégories indiquées dans la légende à droite. Les symboles suivis d'un indice (*) identifient des sous-catégories (voir légende complète à la page 1-1).

Os símbolos incluídos no texto do índice representam as grandes categorias identificadas com a chave à direita. Os símbolos com números em su parte superior (*) identificam as subcategorias (veja-se a chave completa na página 1-1).

Symbole im Register stellen die rechts im Schlüssel erklärten Kategorien dar. Symbole mit hochgestellten Ziffern (*) bezeichnen Unterteilungen einer Kategorie (vgl. vollständiger Schlüssel auf Seite 1-1).

English	Español	Français	Português	Deutsch
▲ Mountain	Montaña	Montagne	Montanha	Berg
▲ Mountains	Montañas	Montagnes	Montanhas	Gebirge
⤒ Pass	Paso	Col	Passo	Paß
Plain	Llano	Plaine	Planície	Ebene
∨ Valley, Canyon	Valle, Cañón	Vallée, Canyon	Vale, Canhão	Tal, Cañon
► Cape	Cabo	Cap	Cabo	Kap
I Island	Isla	Île	Ilha	Insel
II Islands	Islas	Îles	Ilhas	Inseln
✦ Other Topographic Features	Otros Elementos Topográficos	Autres données topographiques	Outros acidentes topográficos	Andere Topographische Objekte

ESPAÑOL / FRANÇAIS / PORTUGUÊS

Nombre / Nom / Nome	Página / Page	Lat.°′	Long.°′ W = Oeste / W = Ouest
Pakokku	110	21.20 N	95.05 E
Pakość	30	52.49 N	18.05 E
Pakouabo	150	7.10 N	5.48 W
Pakowki Lake ⊜	184	49.22 N	110.57 W
Pākpattan	123	30.21 N	73.24 E
Pak Phanang	110	8.21 N	100.12 E
Pak Phayun	110	7.21 N	100.19 E
Pak Phraek	110	8.13 N	100.12 E
Pakrac	36	45.26 N	17.12 E
Pākrāganj	126	24.00 N	90.41 E
Pakruojis	76	55.58 N	23.52 E
Paks	30	46.39 N	18.53 E
Pak Sane → Muang Pakxan	110	18.22 N	103.39 E
Pāksey	126	24.05 N	89.03 E
Pak Thong Chai	110	14.43 N	102.01 E
Paktīā □[4]	120	33.30 N	69.30 E
Paktīkā □[4]	120	32.30 N	68.45 E
Pākundia	126	24.20 N	90.42 E
P'akupur ≃	74	65.00 N	77.48 E
Pakwach	154	2.28 N	31.30 E
Pakwash Lake ⊜	184	50.45 N	93.30 W
Pakxé	110	15.07 N	105.47 E
Pala, Mya.	110	12.51 N	98.40 E
Pala, Tchad	146	9.22 N	14.54 E
Pala, Ca., U.S.	228	33.22 N	117.05 W
Palaau State Park ♠	229a	21.11 N	157.00 W
Palabek	154	3.26 N	32.34 E
Palacca Point >	238	21.15 N	73.26 W
Palacios	196	28.42 N	96.13 W
Palacios ≃	248	16.36 S	64.18 W
Paladru	62	45.28 N	5.33 E
Palagano	64	44.20 N	10.39 E
Palagianello	68	40.37 N	16.58 E
Palagiano	68	40.35 N	17.02 E
Palagonia	70	37.19 N	14.45 E
Palagruža, Otoci II	36	42.24 N	16.15 E
Palai	122	9.44 N	76.41 E
Palai, Punta ∧	71	40.20 N	8.55 E
Palaia	66	43.36 N	10.46 E
Palaiá Epídhavros	38	37.38 N	23.09 E
Palaiá Psará	38	38.46 N	25.36 E
Palaikhóri	130	34.55 N	33.05 E
Pala Indian Reservation ◆[4]	228	33.21 N	117.04 W
Palaiokhóra	38	35.14 N	23.41 E
Palaión Fáliron	267c	37.55 N	23.41 E
Palaiseau	50	48.43 N	2.15 E
Pālakodu	122	16.32 N	81.44 E
Pālam ◆[8]	272a	28.35 N	77.05 E
Palam Airport ⊠	123	28.35 N	77.07 E
Palamás	38	39.28 N	22.05 E
Palamós	34	41.51 N	3.08 E
Pālampur	123	32.07 N	76.32 E
Palamuse	76	58.41 N	26.35 E
Palamut	130	38.59 N	27.41 E
Palana	74	59.07 N	159.58 E
Palanan, Mount ∧	116	17.03 N	122.15 E
Palanan Bay c	116	17.09 N	122.27 E
Palanan Point >	116	17.09 N	122.30 E
Palanas	116	12.09 N	123.55 E
Palandöken Dağları ⋏	130	39.47 N	41.15 E
Pālang	126	23.13 N	90.21 E
Pālang ≃[1]	126	23.15 N	90.21 E
Palanga	76	55.55 N	21.03 E
Palanganene	152	6.26 S	18.50 E
Palangkaraya	112	2.16 S	113.56 E
Palani	122	10.28 N	77.32 E
Pālanpur	120	24.10 N	72.26 E
Palanquinos	34	42.27 N	5.31 W
Palanzano	64	44.26 N	10.11 E
Palaoa Point >	229a	20.44 N	156.58 W
Palapag	116	12.33 N	125.07 E
Palapye	156	22.37 S	27.06 E
Pālār ≃	122	12.28 N	80.10 E
Palasan Island I	116	14.52 N	122.03 E
Palas de Rei	34	42.52 N	7.52 W
Palāshdānga	126	23.24 N	87.22 E
Palāspol	126	22.43 N	89.05 E
Palasthali	126	23.51 N	87.03 E
Palata	66	41.53 N	14.47 E
Palatcy	86	49.09 N	83.43 E
Palatine	216	42.06 N	88.02 W
Palatine Bridge	210	42.55 N	74.35 W
Palatka, Ross.	74	60.06 N	150.54 E
Palatka, Fl., U.S.	192	29.38 N	81.38 W
Palau, It.	71	41.11 N	9.23 E
Palau, Méx.	196	27.54 N	101.26 W
Palau □[2], Oc.	14	5.00 N	137.00 E
Palau (Belau) □[2], Oc.	175b	7.30 N	134.30 E
Palauig	116	15.26 N	119.54 E
Palaui Island I	116	18.33 N	122.08 E
Palau Islands II	175b	7.30 N	134.30 E
Palauk	110	13.16 N	98.38 E
Pal'avaam ≃	180	68.50 N	170.45 E
Pal'avaamskij chrebet ⋏	180	68.20 N	177.00 E
Palavas-les-Flots	62	43.32 N	3.56 E
Palaw	110	12.58 N	98.39 E
Palawai Basin ≚[1]	229a	20.47 N	156.55 W
Palawan □[4]	116	10.00 N	118.50 E
Palawan I	116	9.30 N	118.30 E
Palawan Passage ʮ	116	10.00 N	118.00 E
Palayan	116	15.33 N	121.06 E
Pālayankottai	122	8.43 N	77.44 E
Palazzo Adriano	70	37.41 N	13.23 E
Palazzolo Acreide	70	37.04 N	14.54 E
Palazzolo dello Stella	64	45.48 N	13.05 E
Palazzolo sull'Oglio	62	45.36 N	9.53 E
Palazzolo Vercellese	62	45.11 N	8.14 E
Palazzo San Gervasio	68	40.56 N	16.00 E
Palazzuolo sul Senio	66	44.07 N	11.33 E
P'albong-san ∧	98	40.16 N	127.57 E
Palca, Bol.	248	16.34 S	67.59 W
Palca, Perú	248	11.21 S	75.31 W
Palcamayo	248	11.18 S	75.46 W
Pal'co	76	53.17 N	34.56 E
Paldi	224	48.48 N	123.51 W
Paldiski	76	59.20 N	24.06 E
Pāldor ∧	124	28.16 N	85.11 E
Palech	80	56.48 N	41.51 E
Palel	120	24.27 N	94.02 E
Paleleh	112	1.04 N	121.57 E
Palembang	112	2.55 S	104.45 E
Palena	66	41.59 N	14.08 E
Palena ≃	254	43.50 S	72.59 W
Palena, Lago (Lago General Vintter) ⊜	254	43.55 S	71.40 W
Palencia	34	42.01 N	4.32 W
Palencia □[4]	34	42.25 N	4.35 W
Palen Lake ⊜	204	33.46 N	115.12 W
Palenque	232	17.31 N	91.58 W
Palenque ⊥	232	17.30 N	92.00 W
Palenque, Punta >	238	18.14 N	70.09 W
Palenville	210	42.10 N	74.01 W
Paleparto, Monte ∧	68	39.28 N	16.34 E
Palermo, Col.	246	2.54 N	75.26 W
Palermo, It.	70	38.07 N	13.21 E
Palermo, Ca., U.S.	226	39.26 N	121.33 W
Palermo, Ur.	252	33.48 S	55.59 W
Palermo □[4]	70	37.49 N	13.35 E
Palermo ◆[8]	288	34.35 S	58.25 W
Palermo, Golfo di c	70	38.08 N	13.26 E
Palese, Aeroporto di ⊠	68	41.10 N	16.47 E
Palestina, Bra.	255	20.23 S	49.25 W
Palestina, Méx.	196	29.10 N	100.55 W
Palestine, Ar., U.S.	194	34.58 N	90.54 W
Palestine, Il., U.S.	194	39.00 N	87.36 W
Palestine, Oh., U.S.	218	40.03 N	84.45 W
Palestine, Tx., U.S.	222	31.45 N	95.37 W
Palestine □[9]	132	32.00 N	35.15 E
Palestine, Lake ⊜[1]	222	32.06 N	95.27 W
Palestrina	66	41.50 N	12.53 E
Paletwa	110	21.18 N	92.51 E
Palézieux	58	46.33 N	6.50 E
Palfau	61	47.42 N	14.48 E
Palghāt	122	10.47 N	76.39 E
Palgrave, Mount ∧	162	23.22 S	115.58 E
Palgrave Point >	156	20.45 S	13.20 E
Palhais	266c	38.37 N	9.03 W
Palhano	250	4.44 S	37.57 W
Palhano ≃	250	4.33 S	37.42 W
Pāli, India	120	25.46 N	73.20 E
Pali, India	124	25.51 N	76.33 E
Paliano	66	41.48 N	13.03 E
Palikea ∧	229c	21.26 N	158.06 W
Palima	112	4.20 S	120.22 E
Palimanan	115a	6.42 S	108.26 E
Palimbang	116	6.12 N	124.12 E
Palimé	150	6.54 N	0.38 E
Palín	236	14.24 N	90.42 W
Palinges	32	46.33 N	4.13 E
Palinuro	68	40.02 N	15.17 E
Palinuro, Capo >	68	40.02 N	15.16 E
Palisade, Co., U.S.	200	39.06 N	108.21 W
Palisade, Ne., U.S.	198	40.20 N	101.06 W
Palisades, Id., U.S.	202	43.21 N	111.13 W
Palisades, N.Y., U.S.	276	41.01 N	73.55 W
Palisades Amusement Park ♠	276	40.50 N	73.59 W
Palisades Interstate Park ♠	210	40.56 N	73.55 W
Palisades Park, Mi., U.S.	216	42.18 N	86.19 W
Palisades Park, N.J., U.S.	276	40.50 N	73.59 W
Palisades Reservoir ⊜[1]	202	43.15 N	111.05 W
Paliseul	56	49.54 N	5.08 E
Pālitāna	120	21.31 N	71.50 E
Palivere	76	58.59 N	23.52 E
Palizada	232	18.15 N	92.05 W
Palizzi	68	37.58 N	15.59 E
Paljakka ∧[2]	26	64.41 N	28.08 E
Pälkäne	26	61.20 N	24.16 E
Palk Bay c	122	9.30 N	79.15 E
Palkino, Ross.	76	57.32 N	28.01 E
Palkino, Ross.	80	58.15 N	42.56 E
Pālkonda	122	18.36 N	83.45 E
Pālkonda Range ⋏	122	14.05 N	79.05 E
Palk Strait ʮ	122	10.00 N	79.45 E
Palla Bianca (Weisskugel) ∧	64	46.48 N	10.44 E
Pallagorio	68	39.18 N	16.54 E
Pallamana	168b	35.02 S	139.12 E
Pallasca	248	8.15 S	78.01 W
Pallas Grean	48	52.33 N	8.22 W
Pallaskenry	48	52.39 N	8.52 W
Pallas-Ounastunturin Kansallispuisto ♠	24	68.06 N	24.00 E
Pallasovka	80	50.03 N	46.53 E
Pallastunturi ∧	24	68.06 N	24.00 E
Pallejà	266d	41.25 N	2.00 E
Pallës, Bishti i >	38	41.24 N	19.24 E
Palling	182	54.21 N	125.55 W
Pallíni	267c	38.00 N	23.53 E
Pallinup ≃	162	34.29 S	118.54 E
Pallisa	154	1.10 N	33.42 E
Palliser, Cape >	172	41.37 S	175.17 E
Palliser Bay c	172	41.25 S	175.05 E
Pallu	123	28.56 N	74.13 E
Palluau	32	46.48 N	1.37 W
Palma, Bra.	255	21.22 S	42.19 W
Palma, Moç.	154	10.46 S	40.29 E
P'al'ma, Ross.	24	62.26 N	35.53 E
Palma ≃	255	12.33 S	47.52 W
Palma, Badia de c	34	39.27 N	2.35 E
Palmácia	250	4.08 S	38.50 W
Palma del Río	34	37.42 N	5.17 W
Palma [de Mallorca]	34	39.34 N	2.39 E
Palma di Montechiaro	70	37.11 N	13.46 E
Palmaḥim	132	31.56 N	34.42 E
Palma Pegada	234	22.42 N	101.48 W
Palmar ≃	246	10.10 N	71.50 W
Palmar, Lago Artificial del ⊜[1]	252	33.05 S	57.10 W
Palmar Camp	232	16.26 N	88.53 W
Palmar de Cariaco	286c	10.34 N	66.55 W
Palmar de los Sepúlveda	232	25.43 N	107.55 W
Palmar de Varela	246	10.45 N	74.45 W
Palmarejo	240m	18.03 N	67.05 W
Palmares, Bra.	250	8.41 S	35.36 W
Palmares, C.R.	236	10.03 N	84.26 W
Palmares, C.R.	236	9.21 N	83.40 W
Palmares do Sul	252	30.16 S	50.31 W
Palmaria, Isola I	62	44.02 N	9.51 E
Palmarito	246	7.37 N	70.10 W
Palmarola, Isola I	66	40.56 N	12.51 E
Palmar Sur	236	8.58 N	83.29 W
Palmas, Bra.	252	26.30 S	52.00 W
Palmas, Méx.	234	22.49 N	103.57 W
Palmas, Golfo di c	71	39.02 N	8.31 E
Palmas, Ilha das I, Bra.	287a	23.02 S	43.12 W
Palmas, Ilha das I, Bra.	287a	23.04 S	43.31 W
Palmas Bellas	236	9.14 N	80.05 W
Palmas de Monte Alto	255	14.16 S	43.10 W
Palma Sola	220	27.31 N	82.38 W
Palma Soriano	240p	20.13 N	76.00 W
Palm Bay	220	28.02 N	80.35 W
Palm Beach, Austl.	170	33.36 S	151.19 E
Palm Beach, Austl.	171a	28.08 S	153.28 E
Palm Beach, Fl., U.S.	220	26.42 N	80.02 W
Palm Beach □[6]	220	26.38 N	80.27 W
Palm Beach Gardens	220	26.49 N	80.06 W
Palm Beach International Airport ⊠	220	26.41 N	80.05 W
Palm City	220	27.09 N	80.16 W
Palmdale, Ca., U.S.	228	34.34 N	118.06 W
Palmdale, Fl., U.S.	220	26.56 N	81.18 W
Palmdale, Pa., U.S.	208	40.18 N	76.37 W
Palmdale, Lake ⊜[1]	228	34.33 N	118.07 W
Palm Desert	204	33.43 N	116.23 W
Palmeira, Bra.	252	25.25 S	50.00 W
Palmeira, C.V.	150a	16.46 N	22.59 W
Palmeira das Missões	252	27.55 S	53.17 W
Palmeira d'Oeste	255	20.23 S	50.47 W
Palmeira dos Índios	250	9.25 S	36.37 W
Palmeirais	250	5.58 S	43.04 W
Palmeiral	256	21.38 S	46.31 W
Palmeiras	255	12.31 S	41.34 W
Palmeiras ≃, Bra.	250	12.22 S	47.08 W
Palmeiras ≃, Bra.	255	15.25 S	51.10 W
Palmeirina	250	8.56 S	36.17 W
Palmeirinhas, Ponta das >	152	9.05 S	13.00 E
Palmela ≃	256	21.38 S	45.23 W
Palmelo	255	17.20 S	48.27 W
Palmer, Austl.	168b	34.51 S	139.10 E
Palmer, P.R.	240m	18.22 N	65.46 W
Palmer, Ak., U.S.	180	61.36 N	149.07 W
Palmer, Il., U.S.	219	39.27 N	89.24 W
Palmer, Ma., U.S.	207	42.09 N	72.19 W
Palmer, Ms., U.S.	194	31.16 N	89.15 W
Palmer, Ne., U.S.	198	41.13 N	98.15 W
Palmer, Tn., U.S.	194	35.21 N	85.34 W
Palmer, Tx., U.S.	222	32.26 N	96.40 W
Palmer ≃, Austl.	162	24.46 S	133.25 E
Palmer ≃, Austl.	164	15.34 S	142.26 E
Palmer ≃, P.Q., Can.	206	46.19 N	71.27 W
Palmer ◆[3]	9	64.46 S	64.03 W
Palmerah ◆[8]	269e	6.12 S	106.47 E
Palmer Heights	208	40.42 N	75.16 W
Palmer Lake	200	38.52 N	104.48 W
Palmer Land ◆[1]	9	71.30 S	65.00 W
Palmer Mill Brook ≃	283	41.58 N	70.52 W
Palmer Park	284c	38.55 N	76.52 W
Palmer Park ♠	281	42.26 N	83.07 W
Palmerston, On., Can.	212	43.50 N	80.51 W
Palmerston, N.Z.	172	45.29 S	170.43 E
Palmerston I[1]	14	18.04 S	163.10 W
Palmerston, Cape >	166	21.32 S	149.29 E
Palmerston Lake ⊜	212	45.01 N	76.50 W
Palmerston North	172	40.21 S	175.37 E
Palmerton	210	40.48 N	75.36 W
Palmerville	164	15.59 S	144.05 E
Palmetto, Fl., U.S.	220	27.31 N	82.34 W
Palmetto, Ga., U.S.	192	33.31 N	84.40 W
Palmetto, La., U.S.	194	30.43 N	91.54 W
Palmford	158	27.11 S	29.42 E
Palm Harbor	220	28.04 N	82.45 W
Palmi	68	38.21 N	15.51 E
Palminópolis	255	16.47 S	50.08 W
Palmira, Arg.	252	33.03 S	68.34 W
Palmira, Col.	246	3.32 N	76.16 W
Palmira, Cuba	240p	22.14 N	80.23 W
Palmira, Ec.	246	2.05 S	78.43 W
Palmira, Méx.	196	28.58 N	100.47 W
Palmitas	252	33.31 S	57.49 W
Palmitos	252	27.05 S	53.08 W
Palmnicken → Jantarnyj	76	54.52 N	19.57 E
Palmoli	66	41.56 N	14.32 E
Palm River	220	27.56 N	82.23 W
Palms ◆[8]	280	34.02 N	118.25 W
Palm Shores	220	28.11 N	80.35 W
Palm Springs, Ca., U.S.	204	33.49 N	116.32 W
Palm Springs, Fl., U.S.	220	26.39 N	80.06 W
Palmyra, Il., U.S.	219	39.26 N	89.59 W
Palmyra, In., U.S.	218	38.24 N	86.06 W
Palmyra, Mi., U.S.	216	41.52 N	83.56 W
Palmyra, Mo., U.S.	219	39.47 N	91.31 W
Palmyra, N.J., U.S.	208	40.00 N	75.01 W
Palmyra, N.Y., U.S.	210	43.03 N	77.14 W
Palmyra, Oh., U.S.	214	41.07 N	81.02 W
Palmyra, Pa., U.S.	208	40.18 N	76.35 W
Palmyra, Va., U.S.	192	37.51 N	78.15 W
Palmyra, Wi., U.S.	216	42.52 N	88.35 W
Palmyra ⊥	130	34.33 N	38.17 E
Palmyra Atoll I[1]	14	5.52 N	162.06 W
Palmyra → Tudmur	130	34.33 N	38.17 E
Palo, It.	66	41.56 N	12.06 E
Palo, Pil.	116	11.10 N	124.59 E
Palo Alto, Méx.	196	26.32 N	99.45 W
Palo Alto, Ca., U.S.	226	37.26 N	122.08 W
Palo Alto, Pa., U.S.	208	40.41 N	76.11 W
Palo Alto Airport ⊠	282	37.28 N	122.07 W
Palo Blanco, Méx.	196	26.45 N	101.32 W
Palo Blanco, P.R.	240m	18.26 N	66.39 W
Palo Blanco Creek ≃	196	27.10 N	97.52 W
Paločka	86	58.25 N	84.32 E
Palo del Colle	68	41.03 N	16.42 E
Palo Duro Canyon State Park ♠	196	34.55 N	101.42 W
Palo Duro Creek ≃, U.S.	196	36.39 N	100.58 W
Palo Duro Creek ≃, Tx., U.S.	196	35.00 N	101.55 W
Paloe, Pulau I	115b	8.20 S	121.43 E
Paloemeu ≃	250	3.21 N	55.26 W
Palo Flechado Pass)(	200	36.25 N	105.20 W
Paloh, Indon.	112	1.43 N	109.18 E
Paloh, Malay.	112	2.25 N	111.15 E
Paloh, Malay.	114	2.11 N	103.12 E
Paloich, Sūd.	140	6.45 N	30.08 E
Paloich, Sūd.	140	10.28 N	32.32 E
Palojoensuu	24	68.17 N	23.05 E
Paloma Creek ≃	226	36.15 N	121.26 W
Palomares Creek ≃	282	37.42 N	122.02 W
Palomar Mountain ∧	204	33.22 N	116.50 W
Palomar Mountain State Park ♠	228	33.19 N	116.53 W
Palomar Park	282	37.29 N	122.16 W
Palomas	196	28.43 N	103.45 W
Palomas Viejo	232	31.44 N	107.37 W
Palombara Sabina	66	42.04 N	12.46 E
Palominos, Isla I	240m	18.21 N	65.34 W
Palomonte	68	40.40 N	15.17 E
Palompon	116	11.03 N	124.23 E
Palo Negro	246	10.11 N	67.33 W
Palo Pinto	196	32.46 N	98.18 W
Palo Pinto Reservoir ⊜[1]	196	32.38 N	98.18 W
Palopo	112	3.00 S	120.12 E
Palora ≃	246	1.51 S	77.49 W
Palos	240p	22.48 N	81.44 W
Palos, Cabo de >	34	37.38 N	0.41 W
Palo Santo	252	25.34 S	59.21 W
Palos de la Frontera	34	37.14 N	6.53 W
Palos Gardens	278	41.40 N	87.48 W
Palos Heights	216	41.40 N	87.47 W
Palos Hills	278	41.41 N	87.49 W
Palos Hills ♠	278	41.42 N	87.53 W
Palos → Palos de la Frontera	34	37.14 N	6.53 W
Palos Park	278	41.40 N	87.49 W
Palos Verdes Estates	228	33.48 N	118.23 W
Palos Verdes Hills ⋏[2]	280	33.46 N	118.21 W
Palos Verdes Point >	228	33.47 N	118.26 W
Palotai-sziget I	264c	47.35 N	19.05 E
Paloúkia	267c	37.58 N	23.31 E
Palouse	202	46.54 N	117.04 W
Palouse ≃	202	46.35 N	118.13 W
Palouse, South Fork ≃	202	46.53 N	117.22 W
Palo Verde	204	33.25 N	114.43 W
Palo Verde, Parque Nacional ♠	236	10.15 N	85.10 W
P'alovskoje vodochranilišče ⊜[1]	82	56.03 N	37.40 E
Palpa	248	14.32 S	75.11 W
Palpalá	252	24.15 S	65.12 W
Pålsboda	40	59.04 N	15.20 E
Pālsit	126	23.12 N	88.03 E
Paltamo	26	64.25 N	27.50 E
Paltenbach ≃	61	47.34 N	14.20 E
Palu, Indon.	112	0.53 S	119.53 E
Palu, Tür.	130	38.42 N	39.57 E
Palu ≃	112	0.52 S	119.51 E
Palu, Teluk c	112	0.40 S	119.45 E
Paluan	116	13.25 N	120.28 E
Paluan Bay c	116	13.23 N	120.25 E
Palù del Fersina	64	46.08 N	11.21 E
Paludi	68	39.32 N	16.41 E
Paluga	24	65.16 N	45.11 E
Paluke	150	5.02 N	8.06 W
Paluška ∧	61	48.45 N	14.24 E
Paluxy ≃	196	32.15 N	97.43 W
Paluzza	64	46.32 N	13.01 E
Palvantaš	85	40.34 N	72.12 E
Palvār, Kūh-e ∧	128	30.04 N	57.28 E
Palvart	128	38.11 N	64.34 E
Palwal	124	28.09 N	77.20 E
Pal-Waukee Airport ⊠	278	42.07 N	87.54 W
Pam	175f	20.16 S	164.19 E
Pama	150	11.15 N	0.42 E
Pama ≃	152	4.23 N	18.27 E
Pamaluan	112	1.04 S	116.39 E
Pamanukan	115a	6.16 S	107.49 E
Pamarayan	115a	6.16 S	106.17 E
Pam'ati 0103 Borcov	86	56.13 N	92.20 E
Pam'atnaja	86	56.01 N	65.42 E
Pam'at' Parižskoj Kommuny	80	56.06 N	44.31 E
Pāmban Channel ʮ	122	9.17 N	79.10 E
Pāmban Island I	122	9.15 N	79.20 E
Pambeguwa	150	10.40 N	8.19 E
Pambuhan	116	13.59 N	123.05 E
Pambuhan ≃	116	12.34 N	124.55 E
Pambujan	116	12.34 N	124.56 E
Pamekasan	115a	7.10 S	113.28 E
Pamel	50	50.50 N	4.04 E
Pamenang	115a	8.24 S	116.06 E
Pamengpeuk	115a	7.38 S	107.43 E
Pamiers	32	43.07 N	1.36 E
Pamir ⋏	118	38.00 N	73.00 E
Pamlico ≃	192	35.20 N	76.30 W
Pamlico Sound ʮ	192	35.20 N	75.55 W
Pamotan	115a	6.46 S	111.29 E
Pampa	196	35.32 N	100.57 W
Pampã ≃	255	17.43 S	40.36 W
Pampa ◆[1]	252	35.00 S	63.00 W
Pampa Almirón	252	26.42 S	59.08 W
Pampacolca	248	15.43 S	72.33 W
Pampa del Castillo	254	45.48 S	68.05 W
Pampa del Chañar	252	30.11 S	68.43 W
Pampa del Indio	252	26.02 S	59.55 W
Pampa del Infierno	252	26.31 S	61.10 W
Pampa de los Guanacos	252	26.14 S	61.51 W
Pampa Grande	248	18.05 S	64.06 W
Pampana ≃	150	8.24 N	12.00 W
Pampanga □[4]	116	15.05 N	120.40 E
Pampanga ≃	116	14.47 N	120.39 E
Pampanua	112	4.14 S	120.08 E
Pamparato	62	44.17 N	7.55 E
Pampas	248	12.24 S	74.54 W
Pampas ≃	248	13.23 S	73.15 W
Pampas del Heath, Santuario Nacional ♠	248	12.40 S	68.15 W
Pampeluna → Pamplona	34	42.49 N	1.38 W
Pamphylia □[9]	130	37.00 N	31.00 E
Pamplico	192	33.59 N	79.34 W
Pamplona, Col.	246	7.23 N	72.39 W
Pamplona, Esp.	34	42.49 N	1.38 W
Pampoenpoort	158	31.03 S	22.40 E
Pampow	54	53.32 N	14.15 E
Pāmpur	123	34.01 N	74.56 E
Pamukkale (Hierapolis) ⊥	130	37.58 N	29.19 E
Pamukova	130	40.31 N	30.09 E
Pamunkey ≃	208	37.32 N	76.48 W
Pana	219	39.23 N	89.04 W
Panabá	232	21.17 N	88.16 W
Panabo	116	7.19 N	125.42 E
Panaca	204	37.47 N	114.23 W
Panacan	116	9.16 N	118.25 E
Panacea	192	30.02 N	84.23 W
Panache, Lake ⊜	190	46.15 N	81.20 W
Panadura	122	6.43 N	79.54 E
Panaeati Island I	164	10.40 S	152.20 E
Panāgar	124	23.18 N	79.59 E
Panagjurište	38	42.30 N	24.11 E
Panagtaran Point >	116	9.41 N	118.45 E
Panahan	112	1.44 S	111.49 E
Panaitan, Pulau I	115a	6.36 S	105.12 E
Panaitan, Selat ʮ	115a	6.40 S	105.16 E
Panaji (Panjim)	122	15.29 N	73.50 E
Pānākua	272b	22.23 N	88.21 E
Panamá, Bra.	255	18.11 S	49.21 W
Panamá, Pan.	236	8.58 N	79.32 W
Panama, Il., U.S.	219	39.02 N	89.32 W
Panama, N.Y., U.S.	214	42.04 N	79.29 W
Panama, Ok., U.S.	194	35.10 N	94.40 W
Panamá □[4]	236	8.48 N	79.55 W
Panama (Panamá) □[1], N.A.	230	9.00 N	80.00 W
Panama (Panamá) □[1], N.A.	246	9.00 N	80.00 W
Panamá, Bahía de c	246	8.50 N	79.20 W
Panamá, Canal de ≊	236	9.20 N	79.55 W
Panamá, Golfo de c	246	8.00 N	79.30 W
Panamá, Istmo de ⊻[3]	246	9.00 N	80.00 W
Panama Basin ✦[1]	18	5.00 N	83.30 W
Panama City	194	30.09 N	85.39 W
Panamá Vieja ⊥	236	9.00 N	79.29 W
Panambi	252	28.18 S	53.30 W
Panamint Range ⋏	204	36.30 N	117.20 W
Panamint Valley V	204	36.15 N	117.20 W
Pan'an	100	29.06 N	120.27 E
Panao, Perú	248	9.49 S	76.00 W
Pan'ao, Zhg.	107	30.09 N	103.37 E
Panaon Island I	116	10.03 N	125.13 E
Panarea, Isola I	70	38.38 N	15.04 E
Panaro ≃	64	44.55 N	11.25 E
Panarukan	115a	7.42 S	113.56 E
Panasoffkee, Lake ⊜	220	28.47 N	82.08 W
Panatinane Island I	164	11.15 S	153.10 E
Panay I	116	11.15 N	122.30 E
Panay ≃	116	11.35 N	122.43 E
Panay Gulf c	116	10.15 N	122.15 E
Panayía	38	39.56 N	25.20 E
Panay Island I	116	13.58 N	124.20 E
Pancalieri	62	44.50 N	7.35 E
Pancas	266c	38.48 N	8.55 W
Pančevo, Jugo.	38	44.52 N	20.39 E
Pančevo, Ukr.	78	48.44 N	31.51 E
Panchagarh	124	26.20 N	88.34 E
Pānchāl	126	23.15 N	87.18 E
Pānchet Hill ∧[2]	126	23.37 N	86.47 E
Pānchet Reservoir ⊜[1]	126	23.40 N	86.45 E
Pānchghara	272b	22.44 N	88.16 E
Panchgram	126	24.12 N	88.01 E
Panch'iao	269d	25.01 N	121.27 E
Panchla	126	22.32 N	88.09 E
Panchor	114	2.10 N	102.43 E
Pancho Simón ≃	286b	23.03 N	82.21 W
Pānchur	272b	22.32 N	88.16 E
Pānchuria	272b	22.33 N	88.29 E
Panciu	38	45.55 N	27.05 E
Panda	156	24.02 S	34.45 E
Pandakan	115a	7.39 S	112.41 E
Pandamatenga	156	18.35 S	25.42 E
Pandan, Malay.	112	3.09 N	113.22 E
Pandan, Pil.	116	11.43 N	122.06 E
Pandan, Pil.	116	14.03 N	124.10 E
Pandan, Selat ʮ	271c	1.15 N	103.44 E
Pandanan Island I	116	8.17 N	117.13 E
Pandan Bay c	116	11.43 N	122.04 E
Pandan Reservoir ⊜[1]	271c	1.19 N	103.44 E
Pandaria	124	22.14 N	81.25 E
Pandarochan Bay c	116	12.12 N	121.10 E
Pandasan	112	6.28 N	116.32 E
Pan de Azúcar	252	34.48 S	55.14 W
Pan de Azucar, Cerro ∧	286e	33.19 S	70.42 W
Pan de Azucar Island I	116	11.17 N	123.10 E
Pandegelang	115a	6.18 S	106.06 E
Pandėlys	76	56.01 N	25.13 E
Pāndharkawada	122	20.01 N	78.32 E
Pandharpur	122	17.40 N	75.20 E
Pāndhurna	122	21.36 N	78.31 E
Pandian	98	36.38 N	116.27 E
Pandino	62	45.24 N	9.33 E
Pando	252	34.43 S	55.57 W
Pando □[5]	248	11.20 S	67.40 W
Pando, Cerro ∧	236	8.55 N	82.43 W
Pandora	216	40.56 N	83.57 W
Pandu	152	5.01 N	19.16 E
Pandua, India	124	25.08 N	88.10 E
Pāndua, India	126	23.05 N	88.17 E
P'andž (Panj) ≃	120	37.06 N	68.20 E
Panebianco ≃	70	37.24 N	15.04 E
Panelas	250	8.40 S	36.01 W
Paneveggio	64	46.18 N	11.44 E
Panevėžys	76	55.44 N	24.21 E
Panfang	100	27.54 N	115.57 E
Panfilov	86	44.10 N	80.01 E
Panfilovo	80	50.26 N	42.55 E
Pang ≃	110	20.58 N	98.30 E
Panga	154	1.51 N	26.25 E
Pangai	152	3.15 N	14.34 E
Pangalanes, Canal des ≊	157b	22.40 S	47.50 E
Pangandaran	115a	7.41 S	108.39 E
Pangani	154	5.26 S	38.58 E
Pangani ≃	154	5.26 S	38.58 E
Panganiban	116	13.55 N	124.18 E
Pangantocan	116	7.50 N	124.49 E
Panganuran	116	7.24 N	122.03 E
Pangasinan □[4]	116	16.00 N	120.20 E
Pangbourne	42	51.29 N	1.05 W
Pangburn	194	35.25 N	91.50 W
Pange	56	49.05 N	6.22 E
Pangfou → Bengbu	100	32.58 N	117.24 E
Pangga, Tanjung >	115b	8.55 S	116.02 E
Panggezhuang, Zhg.	105	39.38 N	116.19 E
Panggezhuang, Zhg.	105	39.16 N	115.49 E
Panghkam	110	23.53 N	97.37 E
Pangi	154	3.11 S	26.38 E
Pangian	112	1.06 S	119.24 E
Pangjiabu	105	40.36 N	115.27 E
Pangkah	115a	6.58 S	109.10 E
Pangkajene	112	4.50 S	119.32 E
Pangkalanbrandan	114	4.01 N	98.17 E
Pangkalanbuun	112	2.41 S	111.37 E
Pangkalansusu	114	4.06 N	98.14 E
Pangkalaseang, Tanjung >	112	0.42 S	123.26 E
Pangkalpinang	112	2.08 S	106.08 E
Pangkatan	114	2.09 N	100.00 E
Pangke	114	1.01 N	103.10 E
Pangkor, Pulau I	114	4.13 N	100.33 E
Panglao	116	9.35 N	123.45 E
Panglao Island I	116	9.35 N	123.48 E
Pangman	184	49.39 N	104.38 W
Pangnirtung	176	66.08 N	65.44 W
Pango Aluquém	152	8.43 S	14.27 E
Pangŏjin	98	35.29 N	129.26 E
Pangong Tso ⊜	120	33.45 N	78.43 E
Pangp'u → Bengbu	100	32.58 N	117.24 E
Pāngsa	126	23.47 N	89.25 E
Pangtara	110	20.57 N	96.40 E
Pangubatan	116	6.57 N	125.47 E
Panguil Bay c	116	8.01 N	123.43 E
Panguipulli	254	39.38 S	72.20 W
Panguipulli, Lago ⊜	254	39.43 S	72.13 W
Panguiranan	116	12.04 N	123.19 E
Panguitch	200	37.49 N	112.26 W
Pangururan	114	2.37 N	98.42 E
Pangutaran	116	6.18 N	120.35 E
Pangutaran Group II	116	6.15 N	120.30 E
Pangutaran Island I	116	6.18 N	120.34 E
Pangutaran Passage ʮ	116	6.13 N	120.30 E
Pangzidian	107	30.38 N	105.04 E
Panhandle	196	35.20 N	101.22 W
Paniai, Danau ⊜	164	3.50 S	136.15 E
Pania-Mutombo	152	5.11 S	23.51 E
Paniau ∧	229b	21.57 N	160.05 W
Panié, Mont ∧	175f	20.36 S	164.46 E
Pānihāti	126	22.42 N	88.22 E
Panika	80	50.59 N	50.11 E
Panindícuaro	234	19.59 N	101.46 W
Panino, Ross.	76	56.25 N	34.34 E
Panino, Ross.	78	51.38 N	40.08 E
Panino-Nesterovo	82	55.23 N	38.11 E
Panīpāt	124	29.23 N	76.58 E
Paniqui	116	15.40 N	120.35 E
Panissières	62	45.47 N	4.20 E
Panitan	116	11.28 N	122.46 E
Panitian	116	9.05 N	118.05 E
Panj (P'andž) ≃	120	37.06 N	68.20 E
Panjāb	120	34.22 N	67.01 E
Panjang	115a	5.28 S	105.18 E
Panjang, Pulau I	112	2.44 N	108.55 E
Panjang, Selat ʮ	114	0.40 N	102.30 E
Panje	272c	18.54 N	72.57 E
Panjgūr	128	26.58 N	64.06 E
Panji	114	2.34 N	97.50 E
Panjiapie	100	32.54 N	120.42 E
Panjiatun	104	41.04 N	121.38 E
Panjim → Panaji	122	15.29 N	73.50 E
Pānjkora ≃	123	34.39 N	71.44 E
Panjnad ≃	123	28.57 N	70.30 E
Panjpāi	120	29.55 N	66.30 E
Panjshār ≃	120	34.38 N	69.42 E
Pankakoski	26	63.19 N	30.09 E
Panke ≃	264a	52.32 N	13.22 E
Panker	54	54.20 N	10.34 E
Pānkhāli	126	22.37 N	89.31 E
Pankof, Cape >	180	54.40 N	163.04 W
Pankow ◆[8]	54	52.34 N	13.25 E
Pankratovo	76	59.10 N	43.30 E
Pankshin	150	9.20 N	9.24 E
Panlong, Zhg.	100	25.52 N	114.52 E
Panlong, Zhg.	106	31.58 N	121.35 E
Panlong, Zhg.	106	31.11 N	121.16 E
Panlong (Lo) ≃	110	21.18 N	105.25 E
Panlongzhen	107	29.31 N	105.17 E
P'anmunjŏm	98	37.57 N	126.40 E
Panna	124	24.43 N	80.12 E
Pannawonica	162	21.44 S	116.22 E
Panni	68	41.13 N	15.16 E
Panningen	52	51.20 N	5.59 E
Pannonhalma ♁[1]	30	47.28 N	17.50 E
Panoche Creek ≃	226	36.44 N	120.31 W
Panola	194	31.58 N	86.23 W
Panola □[6]	222	32.07 N	94.30 W
Páno Lévkara	130	34.52 N	33.18 E
Panopah	112	1.56 S	111.11 E
Páno Panayiá	130	34.55 N	32.38 E
Páno Plátres	130	34.53 N	32.52 E
Panora	198	41.41 N	94.21 W
Panorama	255	21.21 S	51.51 W
Pánormos	38	37.38 N	25.02 E
Panovo, Ross.	24	59.48 N	46.27 E
Panovo, Ross.	88	58.58 N	101.58 E
P'anp'yŏng-ni	98	40.28 N	125.49 E
Panruti	122	11.46 N	79.33 E
Pansfelde	54	51.39 N	11.16 E
Panshan	104	41.12 N	122.04 E
Panshanger Aerodrome ⊠	260	51.48 N	0.08 W
Pansik, Rápido ⌞	236	14.30 N	85.15 W
Pansionat	265b	55.59 N	37.41 E
Pānskura	126	22.25 N	87.42 E
Pantabañgan	116	15.50 N	121.09 E
Pantajevka	78	48.41 N	32.53 E
Pantalica, Necropoli di ⊥	70	37.08 N	15.01 E
Pantanal Matogrossense, Parque Nacional do ♠	248	17.35 S	57.40 W
Pantanaw	110	16.59 N	95.28 E
Pântano	256	22.23 S	46.01 W
Pântano, Ribeirão do ≃	256	22.15 S	45.59 W
Pantar, Pulau I	112	8.25 S	124.07 E
Pantelejmonovka	83	48.12 N	37.59 E
Pantelleria	70	36.50 N	11.57 E
Pantelleria, Isola di I	70	36.47 N	12.00 E
Panteón Nacional ⊥	286c	10.31 N	66.55 W
Pantepec ≃	234	20.56 N	97.44 W
Pantha	110	23.49 N	94.33 E
Pantheon ⊥	267a	41.55 N	12.29 E
Panther Creek ≃, Id., U.S.	202	45.19 N	114.24 W
Panther Creek ≃, Ky., U.S.	194	37.45 N	87.19 W
Panther Creek, South Fork ≃	194	37.42 N	87.05 W
Panther Lake	210	43.19 N	75.54 W
Pantin	50	48.54 N	2.24 E
Pantitlán ◆[8]	286a	19.25 N	99.05 W
Panto, Tanjung >	115a	6.51 S	105.54 E
Panton, Mount ∧[2]	172	41.27 S	129.13 E
Pantonlabu	114	5.08 N	97.28 E
Pantry Brook ≃	283	42.24 N	71.22 W
Panu	152	3.48 S	19.07 E
Pánuco	234	22.03 N	98.10 W
Pánuco ≃	234	22.16 N	97.47 W
Panuke Lake ⊜	186	44.48 N	64.07 W
Panukulan	116	14.56 N	121.49 E
Pānuria	126	23.49 N	86.58 E
Pan'utino	78	48.56 N	36.17 E
Panvel	122	18.59 N	73.06 E
Panvel ≃	272c	19.01 N	73.04 W
Panvel Creek ≃	272c	18.59 N	73.00 E
Panwāri	124	25.27 N	79.29 E
Panxi	106	30.35 N	119.20 E
Panxian	102	25.50 N	104.36 E
Panxidu	98	35.39 N	115.52 E
Panyabungan	114	0.51 N	99.33 E
Panyam	150	9.25 N	9.13 E
Panyang	140	10.04 N	29.58 E
Panyčevo	86	57.05 N	81.49 E
Panyu	100	22.57 N	113.20 E
Panzerstausee ⊜[1]	263	51.11 N	7.16 E
Panzhuang	105	39.20 N	117.28 E
Panzi	152	7.13 S	17.58 E
Panzós	236	15.24 N	89.40 W
Pao ≃, Thai	110	16.13 N	103.43 E
Pao ≃, Ven.	246	8.33 N	68.01 W
Pao ≃, Ven.	246	8.06 N	64.17 W
Paochi → Baoji	102	34.23 N	107.09 E
Pão de Açúcar	250	9.45 S	37.26 W
Pão de Açúcar (Sugar Loaf) ∧	287a	22.57 S	43.09 W
Paoki → Baoji	102	34.23 N	107.09 E
Paola, It.	68	39.22 N	16.03 E
Paola, Ks., U.S.	198	38.34 N	94.52 W
Paoli, In., U.S.	218	38.33 N	86.28 W
Paoli, Pa., U.S.	208	40.02 N	75.28 W
Paoli, Wi., U.S.	216	42.56 N	89.32 W
Paonia	200	38.52 N	107.35 W
Pāonta Sāhib	124	30.27 N	77.37 E
Paopao	174s	17.31 S	149.49 W
Paoshenmiao	98	41.12 N	118.17 E
Paotai Yingzi	98	41.48 N	115.12 E
Paoting → Baoding	105	38.52 N	115.29 E
Paotow → Baotou	102	40.40 N	109.59 E
Paoua	152	7.15 N	16.26 E
Paoying → Baoying	100	33.16 N	119.20 E
P'aozero, ozero ⊜	24	66.05 N	30.58 E
Paozi	104	42.13 N	122.19 E
Pap	85	40.53 N	71.07 E
Pápa	30	47.19 N	17.28 E
Papa, Sound of ʮ	46a	60.18 N	1.41 W
Papagaio	250	6.01 S	45.21 W
Papagaio ≃, Bra.	246	1.53 S	62.35 W
Papagaio ≃, Bra.	248	12.56 S	58.18 W
Papagayo ≃	234	16.46 N	99.43 W
Papagayo, Golfo de c	236	10.42 N	85.50 W
Papago Indian Reservation ◆[4]	200	32.20 N	112.00 W
Papaikou	229d	19.47 N	155.05 W
Papakating Creek ≃	276	41.11 N	74.38 W
Papakura	172	37.04 S	174.57 E
Papalia	112	5.58 S	124.01 E
Papaloapan ≃	234	18.42 N	95.38 W
Papanoa	234	17.21 N	101.02 W
Papantla [de Olarte]	234	20.27 N	97.19 W
Papar, Indon.	115a	7.41 S	112.04 E
Papar, Malay.	112	5.44 N	115.56 E
Papara, Poly. fr.	174s	17.44 S	149.21 W
Papara, Sol.Is.	175e	7.02 S	156.48 E
Paparoa	172	36.06 S	174.14 E
Paparoa National Park ♠	172	42.05 S	171.25 E
Paparoa Range ⋏	172	42.00 S	171.35 E
Papasidero	68	39.52 N	15.54 E
Papa Stour I	46a	60.20 N	1.42 W
Papatoetoe	172	36.58 S	174.52 E
Papawai Point >	229a	20.47 N	156.33 W
Papa Westray I	46	59.21 N	2.54 W
Papeari	174s	17.45 S	149.21 W
Papeete	174s	17.32 S	149.34 W
Papelón	286c	10.27 N	66.47 W
Papenburg	52	53.05 N	7.23 E
Papendrecht	52	51.50 N	4.40 E
Papenoo	174s	17.30 S	149.25 W
Papenoo ≃	174s	17.30 S	149.25 W
Papetoai	174s	17.29 S	149.52 W
Papey I	24a	64.37 N	14.11 W
Paphlagonia □[9]	130	41.10 N	32.45 E
Paphos → Néa Páfos	130	34.45 N	32.25 E
Papilė	76	56.09 N	22.48 E
Papillion	198	41.09 N	96.02 W
Papineau	216	40.58 N	87.43 W
Papineau □[6]	206	45.50 N	75.00 W
Papineau, Lac ⊜	206	45.48 N	74.46 W
Papineau Creek ≃	212	45.13 N	77.43 W
Papineau-Labelle, Réserve ♠	188	45.55 N	75.20 W
Papineau Lake ⊜	212	45.20 N	77.50 W
Papineauville	206	45.37 N	75.01 W
Paposo	252	25.01 S	70.28 W
Papouasie Nouvelle-Guinée → Papua New Guinea □[1]	164	6.00 S	150.00 E
Papozze	64	44.59 N	12.02 E
Pappenheim, Dtsch.	54	50.47 N	10.27 E
Pappenheim, Dtsch.	56	48.56 N	10.58 E
Paps of Jura ∧	46	55.55 N	6.00 W
Papua, Gulf of c	164	8.30 S	145.00 E
Papua Neuguinea → Papua New Guinea □[1]	164	6.00 S	150.00 E
Papua New Guinea □[1]	164	6.00 S	147.00 E
Papuasia Nueva Guinea → Papua New Guinea □[1]	164	6.00 S	150.00 E
Papucaia	256	22.37 S	42.44 W
Papudo	252	32.31 S	71.27 W
Papulovo	24	60.34 N	48.00 E
Papun	110	18.04 N	97.27 E
Papunáua ≃	246	2.09 N	70.32 W
Papunya	162	23.16 S	131.54 E
Papurí ≃	246	0.36 N	69.11 W
Paquequer ≃	256	22.12 S	42.54 W
Paquequer, Serra do ⋏	256	22.12 S	42.40 W
Paquera	236	9.50 N	84.56 W
Paquetá, Ilha de I	287a	22.46 S	43.06 W
Par	42	50.21 N	4.43 W
Pará □[3]	250	4.00 S	53.00 W
Para □[5]	250	5.30 N	55.15 W
Pará ≃, Bra.	250	1.30 S	48.55 W
Pará ≃, Bra.	255	19.13 S	45.07 W
Para ≃, Ross.	80	54.23 N	40.52 E
Pará, Ilha do I	250	0.18 S	51.15 W
Para, Pulau I	112	3.05 N	125.30 E
Parabel'	86	58.43 N	81.31 E
Parabel' ≃	86	58.44 N	81.35 E
Pará → Belém	250	1.27 S	48.29 W
Parabiago	62	45.33 N	8.57 E
Parabita	68	40.03 N	18.08 E
Paraburdoo	162	23.14 S	117.48 E
Paracale	116	14.17 N	122.48 E
Paracambi	256	22.37 S	43.43 W
Paracari ≃	250	4.36 S	57.47 W
Paracas, Bahía de c	248	13.50 S	76.17 W
Paracas, Península de >	248	13.48 S	76.24 W
Paracatu	255	17.13 S	46.52 W
Paracatu ≃, Bra.	255	16.30 S	45.04 W
Paracatu ≃, Bra.	255	16.35 S	45.06 W
Paracel Islands → Xisha Qundao II	108	16.30 N	112.15 E
Parachilna	166	31.08 S	138.23 E
Pārachinār	120	33.54 N	70.06 E
Paracho de Verduzco	234	19.39 N	102.04 W
Parachute	200	39.27 N	108.03 W
Paraćin	38	43.52 N	21.24 E
Parácuaro	234	20.09 N	100.46 W
Paracuellos de Jarama	266a	40.30 N	3.32 W

Symbol	English	Deutsch	Español	Français	Português
≃	River	Fluß	Río	Rivière	Rio
≊	Canal	Kanal	Canal	Canal	Canal
⌞	Waterfall, Rapids	Wasserfall, Stromschnellen	Cascada, Rápidos	Chute d'eau, Rapides	Cascata, Rápidos
ʮ	Strait	Meeresstraße	Estrecho	Détroit	Estreito
c	Bay, Gulf	Bucht, Golf	Bahía, Golfo	Baie, Golfe	Baía, Golfo
⊜	Lake, Lakes	See, Seen	Lago, Lagos	Lac, Lacs	Lago, Lagos
≋	Swamp	Sumpf	Pantano	Marais	Pântano
⊓	Ice Features, Glacier	Eis- und Gletscherformen	Accidentes Glaciales	Formes glaciaires	Acidentes glaciares
≚	Other Hydrographic Features	Andere Hydrographische Objekte	Otros Elementos Hidrográficos	Autres données hydrographiques	Outros acidentes hidrográficos
✦	Submarine Features	Untermeerische Objekte	Accidentes Submarinos	Formes de relief sous-marin	Acidentes submarinos
□	Political Unit	Politische Einheit	Unidad Política	Entité politique	Unidade política
♁	Cultural Institution	Kulturelle Institution	Institución Cultural	Institution culturelle	Instituição cultural
⊥	Historical Site	Historische Stätte	Sitio Histórico	Site historique	Sitio histórico
♠	Recreational Site	Erholungs- und Ferienort	Sitio de Recreo	Centre de loisirs	Area de Lazer
⊠	Airport	Flughafen	Aeropuerto	Aéroport	Aeroporto
■	Military Installation	Militäranlage	Instalación Militar	Installation militaire	Instalação militar
◆	Miscellaneous	Verschiedenes	Misceláneo	Divers	Diversos

Symbols in the index entries represent the broad categories identified in the key at the right. Symbols with superior numbers (⋀[1]) identify subcategories (see complete key on page *I · 1).*

Symbole im Register stellen die rechts im Schlüssel erklärten Kategorien dar. Symbole mit hochgestellten Ziffern (⋀[1]) bezeichnen Unterabteilungen einer Kategorie (vgl. vollständiger Schlüssel auf Seite *I · 1).*

Los símbolos incluídos en el texto del índice representan las grandes categorías identificadas con la clave a la derecha. Los símbolos con numeros en su parte superior (⋀[1]) identifican las subcategorías (véase la clave completa en la página *I · 1).*

Les symboles de l'index représentent les catégories indiquées dans la légende à droite. Les symboles suivis d'un indice (⋀[1]) représentent des sous-catégories (voir légende complète à la page *I · 1).*

Os símbolos incluídos no texto do índice representam as grandes categorias identificadas com a chave à direita. Os símbolos com números em sua parte superior (⋀[1]) identificam as subcategorias (veja-se a chave completa à página *I · 1).*

∧ Mountain	Berg	Montaña	Montagne	Montanha
⋀ Mountains	Gebirge	Montañas	Montagnes	Montanhas
)(Pass	Paß	Paso	Col	Passo
V Valley, Canyon	Tal, Cañon	Valle, Cañón	Vallée, Canyon	Vale, Canhão
≍ Plain	Ebene	Llano	Plaine	Planície
› Cape	Kap	Cabo	Cap	Cabo
I Island	Insel	Isla	Île	Ilha
II Islands	Inseln	Islas	Îles	Ilhas
⊥ Other Topographic Features	Andere Topographische Objekte	Otros Elementos Topográficos	Autres données topographiques	Outros acidentes topográficos

ESPAÑOL / **FRANÇAIS** / **PORTUGUÊS**

Nombre / Nom / Nome	Página / Page	Lat.°′	Long.°′ W = Oeste / W = Ouest
Paulton, Pa., U.S.	279b	40.34 N	79.34 W
Pauma Indian Reservation ◆[4]	228	33.22 N	116.58 W
Pāunān	272b	22.57 N	88.17 E
Paung	110	16.37 N	97.28 E
Paungbyin	110	24.16 N	94.49 E
Paungde	110	18.29 N	95.30 E
Paunggyi	110	17.19 N	96.11 E
Paup	164	3.15 S	142.35 E
Paupack	210	41.24 N	75.14 W
Pauri	124	30.09 N	78.47 E
Pausa, Dtsch.	54	50.35 N	12.00 E
Pausa, Perú	248	15.16 S	73.20 W
Pausania	36	40.55 N	9.06 E
Pausin	264a	52.38 N	13.03 E
Paute	246	2.47 S	78.50 W
Paute ≃	246	2.46 S	78.16 W
Pauto ≃	246	5.09 N	70.55 W
Pautou → Baotou	102	40.40 N	109.59 E
Pauwalu Point ›	229a	20.52 N	156.08 W
Pauwela	229a	20.56 N	156.19 W
Pauwela Point ›	229a	20.57 N	156.19 W
Pavai ◆[8]	272c	19.07 N	72.55 E
Pavai Lake ⊜	272c	19.07 N	72.55 E
Pavda	86	59.15 N	59.30 E
Pāveh	128	35.03 N	46.22 E
Pavel'cevo	82	56.15 N	36.26 E
Pavelec	76	53.50 N	39.16 E
Pavelec Station ◆[5]	265b	55.44 N	37.38 E
Pavia	62	45.10 N	9.10 E
Pavia □[4]	62	45.07 N	9.08 E
Pavia, Naviglio di ≊	266b	45.27 N	9.11 E
Pavia di Udine	64	45.59 N	13.17 E
Pavilion, B.C., Can.	182	50.52 N	121.50 W
Pavilion, N.Y., U.S.	210	42.52 N	78.01 W
Pavilion Key I	220	25.42 N	81.22 W
Pavillion	200	43.14 N	108.41 W
Pavilly	50	49.34 N	0.58 E
Pāvilosta	76	56.53 N	21.14 E
Pavino	24	59.07 N	46.07 E
Pavione, Monte ∧	64	46.07 N	11.50 E
Pavlice	61	48.59 N	15.53 E
Pavlikeni	38	43.14 N	25.18 E
Pavliščevo, Ross.	82	55.11 N	35.59 E
Pavliščevo, Ross.	82	55.34 N	35.59 E
Pavlodar	86	52.18 N	76.57 E
Pavlof Bay c	180	55.30 N	161.32 W
Pavlof Volcano ∧[1]	180	55.24 N	161.52 W
Pavlograd	78	48.32 N	35.53 E
Pavlogradka	86	54.12 N	73.33 E
Pavlopol'	83	47.16 N	37.47 E
Pavlovka, Ross.	80	52.41 N	47.09 E
Pavlovka, Ross.	86	55.25 N	56.33 E
Pavlovka, Ross.	86	51.55 N	54.47 E
Pavlovka, Ukr.	78	47.45 N	37.14 E
Pavlovka, Ukr.	83	48.08 N	39.33 E
Pavlovka, Ukr.	83	49.36 N	38.42 E
Pavlovo, Ross.	76	60.05 N	45.17 E
Pavlovo, Ross.	80	55.58 N	43.04 E
Pavlovo, Ross.	265a	59.56 N	30.40 E
Pavlovo, Ross.	265a	59.49 N	30.54 E
Pavlovsk, Ross.	76	59.41 N	30.27 E
Pavlovsk, Ross.	78	50.27 N	40.08 E
Pavlovsk, Ross.	86	53.20 N	82.59 E
Pavlovskaja	78	46.08 N	39.48 E
Pavlovskaja Sloboda	82	55.49 N	37.05 E
Pavlovskij, Kaz.	86	52.32 N	63.06 E
Pavlovskij, Ross.	80	57.50 N	54.51 E
Pavlovskij Posad	82	55.47 N	38.40 E
Pavlyš	78	48.55 N	33.21 E
Pavne	272c	19.05 N	73.01 E
Pavo	192	31.02 N	84.04 W
Pavón, Arg.	258	34.23 S	59.03 W
Pavón, Col.	246	3.37 N	72.15 W
Pavón, Arroyo ≃	258	34.30 S	57.05 W
Pavona	267a	41.43 N	12.37 E
Pavonia	214	40.49 N	82.26 W
Pavšino	265b	55.49 N	37.21 E
Pavšozero	76	60.38 N	35.34 E
Pavullo nel Frignano	64	44.20 N	10.50 E
Pavuna, Arroio ≃	287a	22.58 S	43.23 W
Pavuvu Island I	175e	9.03 S	159.06 E
Pavy	76	58.03 N	29.30 E
Pawai, Pulau I	271c	1.12 N	103.43 E
Pawan ≃	112	1.51 S	109.57 E
Pawāyān	124	28.04 N	80.06 E
Pawcatuck	207	41.22 N	71.50 W
Paw Creek	192	35.16 N	80.56 W
Päwesin	54	52.31 N	12.42 E
Pawhuska	196	36.40 N	96.20 W
Pawling	210	41.33 N	73.36 W
Pawn ≃	110	18.53 N	97.19 E
Pawnee, Il., U.S.	219	39.35 N	89.34 W
Pawnee, Ok., U.S.	196	36.20 N	96.48 W
Pawnee ≃	198	38.10 N	99.06 W
Pawnee City	198	40.06 N	96.09 W
Pawnee Creek ≃	198	40.34 N	103.14 W
Pawnee Rock	198	38.15 N	98.58 W
Pawni	122	20.47 N	79.38 E
Pawota	110	17.46 N	97.17 E
Paw Paw, Il., U.S.	216	41.41 N	88.59 W
Paw Paw, Mi., U.S.	216	42.13 N	85.53 W
Paw Paw, W.V., U.S.	188	39.31 N	78.27 W
Paw Paw ≃	216	42.07 N	86.29 W
Paw Paw Creek ≃	216	40.52 N	85.58 W
Paw Paw Lake	216	42.12 N	86.15 W
Paw Paw Lake ⊜	216	42.12 N	86.16 W
Pawtucket	207	41.52 N	71.22 W
Pawtucket Falls ⌞	207	42.39 N	71.20 W
Paxoí I	38	39.12 N	20.12 E
Paxson	180	63.02 N	145.30 W
Paxton, Austl.	170	32.54 S	151.16 E
Paxton, Il., U.S.	216	40.27 N	88.05 W
Paxton, Ma., U.S.	207	42.18 N	71.55 W
Paxton, Ne., U.S.	198	41.07 N	101.21 W
Paxtonia	208	40.19 N	76.48 W
Paxtonville	208	40.46 N	77.05 W
Paya	236	15.37 N	85.17 W
Paya Besar	114	3.47 N	103.16 E
Payadapu	114	3.05 N	97.23 E
Payāgpur	124	27.25 N	81.48 E
Payagyi	110	17.29 N	96.32 E
Payakumbuh	112	0.14 S	100.38 E
Paya Lebar	271c	1.22 N	103.53 E
Paya Lebar Airport ⊠	271c	1.21 N	103.54 E
Payamlı	130	37.01 N	38.35 E
Payangan	115b	8.26 S	115.15 E
Payas, Cerro ∧	236	15.50 N	85.00 W
Payerne	58	46.49 N	6.56 E
Payeti	115b	9.41 S	120.20 E
Payette	202	44.04 N	116.55 W
Payette ≃	202	44.05 N	116.57 W
Payette, Middle Fork ≃	202	44.05 N	116.07 W
Payette, North Fork ≃	202	44.05 N	116.07 W
Payette, South Fork ≃	202	44.06 N	116.00 W
Payette Lake ⊜[1]	202	44.57 N	116.05 W
Paylampur	272b	22.47 N	88.16 E
Payne	216	41.04 N	84.43 W
Payne ≃	206	45.14 N	75.08 W
Payne, Lac ⊜	176	59.25 N	74.00 W
Payne Bay c	176	60.00 N	70.00 W
Payneham	168b	34.53 S	138.38 E
Paynes Creek ≃	204	40.16 N	122.11 W
Paynes Find	162	29.15 S	117.41 E
Paynesville, S. Afr.	273d	26.14 S	28.28 E
Paynesville, Mn., U.S.	198	45.22 N	94.42 W
Paynesville, Mo., U.S.	219	39.16 N	90.54 W
Paynetown State Recreation Area ♦	218	39.05 N	86.27 W
Paynton	184	53.01 N	108.56 W
Paysandú	252	32.19 S	58.05 W
Pays-Bas → Netherlands □[1]	30	52.15 N	5.30 E
Payson, Az., U.S.	200	34.13 N	111.19 W
Payson, Il., U.S.	219	39.49 N	91.14 W
Payson, Ut,. U.S.	200	40.02 N	111.43 W
Payún, Cerro ∧	252	36.30 S	69.18 W
Paz ≃	236	13.45 N	90.08 W
Paz, Cañada de la ≃	288	34.53 S	58.38 W
Paz, Rio da ≃	250	9.14 S	52.01 W
Pazar, Tür.	130	41.11 N	40.53 E
Pazar, Tür.	130	40.17 N	36.18 E
Pazarbaşi ›	130	41.10 N	30.11 E
Pazarcık	130	37.31 N	37.19 E
Pazardžik	38	42.12 N	24.20 E
Pazarköy, Tür.	130	40.55 N	32.11 E
Pazarköy, Tür.	130	39.51 N	27.24 E
Pazarören	130	38.41 N	36.11 E
Pazaryeri, Tür.	130	38.05 N	28.14 E
Pazaryeri, Tür.	130	40.00 N	29.54 E
Paz de Ariporo	246	5.53 N	71.54 W
Paz de Río	246	5.59 N	72.47 W
Pazifischer Ozean → Pacific Ocean ⍑[1]	6	10.00 S	150.00 W
P'ažijeva Sel'ga	24	61.29 N	34.29 E
Pazin	36	45.14 N	13.56 E
Pazña	248	18.36 S	66.55 W
Paznaun V	58	47.03 N	10.20 E
Pčevža	76	59.23 N	32.20 E
Pčevža ≃	76	59.21 N	31.54 E
Pchery	54	50.10 N	14.08 E
Pe	110	13.28 N	98.31 E
Pea	174w	21.10 S	175.14 W
Pea ≃	194	31.01 N	85.51 W
Peabody, Ks., U.S.	198	38.10 N	97.06 W
Peabody, Ma., U.S.	207	42.31 N	70.55 W
Peace ≃, Can.	176	59.00 N	111.25 W
Peace ≃, Fl., U.S.	220	26.55 N	82.05 W
Peace Arch ⊥	224	49.00 N	122.45 W
Peace Bridge ◆[5]	284a	42.54 N	78.55 W
Peace Canyon Dam ◆[6]	182	55.59 N	121.59 W
Peace Dale	207	41.27 N	71.29 W
Peacehaven	42	50.47 N	0.01 E
Peace River	182	56.14 N	117.17 W
Peach Creek	188	37.52 N	81.59 W
Peach Creek ≃, Tx., U.S.	222	30.07 N	95.10 W
Peach Creek ≃, Tx., U.S.	222	29.24 N	97.19 W
Peach Creek, Sandy Fork ≃	222	29.34 N	97.19 W
Peachdale	158	26.30 S	24.42 E
Peachland	182	49.46 N	119.44 W
Peach Orchard	192	33.28 N	82.04 W
Peach Springs	200	35.31 N	113.25 W
Peacock Hills ⋏[2]	176	66.05 N	110.45 W
Peacock Point ›, On., Can.	212	42.47 N	79.59 W
Peacock Point ›, Wake I.	174a	19.16 N	166.37 E
Peacock Sound ʉ	9	72.55 S	100.00 W
Pea Hill Branch ≃	284c	38.45 N	76.57 W
Peak Charles National Park ♦	162	32.55 S	121.06 E
Peak Crossing	171a	27.47 S	152.44 E
Peak Dale	262	53.17 N	1.52 W
Peak District National Park ♦	44	53.17 N	1.45 W
Peak Downs	166	22.12 S	148.10 E
Peake Creek ≃	162	28.05 S	136.07 E
Peaked Mountain ∧	186	46.34 N	68.49 W
Peak Forest	262	53.19 N	1.50 W
Peak Forest Canal ≊	262	53.29 N	2.06 W
Peak Hill, Austl.	162	25.38 S	118.43 E
Peak Hill, Austl.	166	32.44 S	148.12 E
Peakhurst	274a	33.58 S	151.04 E
Peakview	171b	36.04 S	149.24 E
Peäldoajvi ∧	24	69.11 N	26.36 E
Peale, Mount ∧	200	38.26 N	109.14 W
Peale Island I	174a	19.19 N	166.35 E
Peapack Brook ≃	276	40.41 N	74.39 W
Pearblossom	228	34.30 N	117.55 W
Pearce	200	31.54 N	109.49 W
Pearce, Royal Australian Air Force Station ■	168a	31.41 S	116.01 E
Pearce Point ›	164	14.25 S	129.21 E
Peard Bay c	180	70.51 N	159.10 W
Pea Ridge ∧	218	38.25 N	83.36 W
Pea Ridge National Military Park ♦	194	36.29 N	94.06 W
Pearisburg	192	37.19 N	80.44 W
Pearl, Il., U.S.	194	39.28 N	90.38 W
Pearl, Ms., U.S.	194	32.16 N	90.07 W
Pearl ≃	194	30.11 N	89.32 W
Pearl, Lake ⊜	283	42.04 N	71.21 W
Pearland	222	29.33 N	95.17 W
Pearl and Hermes Atoll I[1]	14	27.55 N	175.45 W
Pearl Bank ✢[4]	116	5.49 N	119.42 E
Pearl Beach	214	42.37 N	82.35 W
Pearl City	229c	21.23 N	157.58 W
Pearl Creek ≃	198	44.15 N	98.08 W
Pearl Harbor c	229c	21.22 N	157.58 W
Pearl Harbor Naval Station ■	229c	21.21 N	157.57 W
Pearl Peak ∧	204	40.14 N	115.32 W
Pearl River, La., U.S.	194	30.22 N	89.44 W
Pearl River, N.Y., U.S.	210	41.03 N	74.01 W
Pearns Point ›	240c	17.05 N	61.54 W
Pearsall	196	28.53 N	99.05 W
Pearse Island I	182	54.51 N	130.21 W
Pearsoll Peak ∧	202	42.18 N	123.50 W
Pearson	192	31.17 N	82.51 W
Pearson Lake ⊜	184	56.15 N	97.15 W
Pearston	158	32.35 S	25.08 E
Peary Land ◆[1]	16	83.00 N	35.00 W
Pease ≃	196	34.12 N	99.07 W
Pease Air Force Base ■	188	43.06 N	70.49 W
Peasedown Saint John	42	51.19 N	2.27 W
Peaster	222	32.52 N	97.52 W
Peat Inn	46	56.17 N	2.53 W
Pebane	154	17.10 S	38.08 E
Pebas	246	3.20 S	71.49 W
Pebble Beach	226	36.34 N	121.57 W
Pebble Island I	254	51.18 S	59.35 W
Peć	38	42.40 N	20.19 E
Pecan Bayou ≃	196	31.28 N	98.43 W
Pecangakan	115a	6.41 S	110.42 E
Pecan Gap	196	33.26 N	95.51 W
Peçanha	255	18.33 S	42.34 W
Peças, Ilha das I	252	25.26 S	48.19 W
Pecatonica	190	42.18 N	89.21 W
Pecatonica ≃	190	42.27 N	89.05 W
Pecatu	115b	8.50 S	115.07 E
Peccioli	66	43.33 N	10.43 E
Pécel	264c	47.29 N	19.21 E
Pečenegi	78	49.52 N	36.55 E
Peçenek	130	40.25 N	32.19 E
Pečenežin	78	48.32 N	24.54 E
Pečenga	24	69.33 N	31.07 E
Pečerniki	82	54.39 N	39.14 E
Pečernikovskije Vyselki	82	54.10 N	39.10 E
Pechanga Indian Reservation ◆[4]	228	33.27 N	117.04 W
Peche Island I	281	42.21 N	82.56 W
Pechincha ◆[8]	287a	22.56 S	43.21 W
Pechora → Pečora ≃	24	68.13 N	54.15 E
Pechorka ≃	265b	55.35 N	38.03 E
Pechra-Jakovlevskaja	265b	55.48 N	37.58 E
Pechra-Pokrovskoje	265b	55.50 N	37.57 E
Pechu	84	43.24 N	40.49 E
Peči	80	54.48 N	44.19 E
Pecica	38	46.10 N	21.05 E
Pečicy	82	55.36 N	38.27 E
Pecixe, Ilha de I	150	11.50 N	16.05 W
Peck	190	43.15 N	82.49 W
Peck Bay c	208	39.16 N	74.37 W
Peck-Berge ⋏[2]	264a	52.36 N	13.34 E
Peckeloh	52	52.01 N	8.07 E
Peckelsheim	52	51.36 N	9.07 E
Pecket Well	262	53.46 N	2.00 W
Peck Lake ⊜	210	43.07 N	74.25 W
Peckman ≃	276	40.53 N	74.13 W
Peconic ≃	207	40.55 N	72.37 W
Pečora, Ross.	24	65.10 N	57.11 E
Pečora, Ukr.	78	48.52 N	28.42 E
Pečora ≃	24	68.13 N	54.15 E
Pecora, Capo ›	71	39.27 N	8.23 E
Pecoraro, Monte ∧	68	38.32 N	16.20 E
Pečoro-Ilyčskij Zapovednik ◆[4]	24	62.20 N	59.00 E
Pečorskaja guba c	24	68.40 N	54.45 E
Pečorskoje more ⍑[2]	24	70.00 N	54.00 E
Pečory	76	57.49 N	27.36 E
Pecos, N.M., U.S.	200	35.34 N	105.40 W
Pecos, Tx., U.S.	196	31.25 N	103.29 W
Pecos ≃	178	29.42 N	101.22 W
Pecos National Monument ♦	200	35.26 N	105.56 W
Pecos Plains ≡	196	33.20 N	104.30 W
Pecq	50	50.41 N	3.20 E
Pecquencourt	50	50.23 N	3.13 E
Pecqueuse	261	48.39 N	2.03 E
Pécs	30	46.05 N	18.13 E
Pedana	122	16.16 N	81.10 E
Pedas	114	2.37 N	102.04 E
Pedasí	246	7.32 N	80.02 W
Pedaso	66	43.06 N	13.50 E
Peddāpuram	122	17.05 N	82.08 E
Pedder, Lake ⊜[1]	166	42.54 S	146.12 E
Peddie	158	33.12 S	27.07 E
Peddocks Island I	283	42.17 N	70.56 W
Pededze ≃	76	56.56 N	26.54 E
Pedernales, Arg.	252	35.15 S	59.39 W
Pedernales, Méx.	234	19.08 N	101.28 W
Pedernales, Rep. Dom.	238	18.02 N	71.45 W
Pedernales, Ven.	246	9.58 N	62.16 W
Pedernales ≃	196	30.26 N	98.04 W
Pedernales, Salar de ≡	252	26.15 S	69.10 W
Pedernales Falls State Park ♦	196	30.20 N	98.14 W
Pederobba	64	45.53 N	11.58 E
Pedersborg	41	55.27 N	11.34 E
Pederstrup	41	54.54 N	11.16 E
Pedesina	58	46.05 N	9.33 E
Pedhoulás	130	34.58 N	32.50 E
Pedja ≃	76	58.25 N	26.11 E
Pedley	228	33.59 N	117.28 W
Pé do Morro	256	22.20 S	44.57 W
Pedra	250	8.30 S	36.57 W
Pedra Azul	255	16.01 S	41.16 W
Pedra Bela	256	22.47 S	46.27 W
Pedra Branca	250	5.27 S	39.43 W
Pedra de Guaratiba ◆[8]	256	23.00 S	43.39 W
Pedra Grande, Recifes da ✢[2]	255	17.45 S	38.58 W
Pedra Lume	150a	16.46 N	22.54 W
Pedralva	256	22.14 S	45.28 W
Pedras	250	2.48 S	57.16 W
Pedras, Rio das ≃	287a	22.51 S	43.01 W
Pedras de Fogo	250	7.23 S	35.07 W
Pedra Selada	256	22.21 S	44.26 W
Pedras Negras	248	12.51 S	62.54 W
Pedras Salgadas	34	41.32 N	7.36 W
Pedraza	246	10.11 N	74.55 W
Pedregal, Pan.	236	8.22 N	82.26 W
Pedregal, Ven.	246	11.01 N	70.08 W
Pedregulho	255	20.16 S	47.29 W
Pedreira	256	22.43 S	46.55 W
Pedreira ≃	250	0.12 N	50.47 W
Pedreiras	250	4.34 S	44.39 W
Pedriceña	232	25.06 N	103.47 W
Pedricktown	208	39.46 N	75.24 W
Pedrinhas	250	11.12 S	37.41 W
Pedro, Point ›	122	9.50 N	80.14 E
Pedro Afonso	250	8.59 S	48.11 W
Pedro Antonio de los Santos	234	21.36 N	98.58 W
Pedro Avelino	250	5.31 S	36.23 W
Pedro Bay	180	59.47 N	154.07 W
Pedro Betancourt	240p	22.44 N	81.17 W
Pedro Cays II	238	17.00 N	77.50 W
Pedro de Olla, Cerro ∧	234	17.07 N	97.40 W
Pedro do Rio	256	22.20 S	43.09 W
Pedrógão Grande	34	39.55 N	8.09 W
Pedro Gomes	255	18.04 S	54.32 W
Pedro II	250	4.25 S	41.28 W
Pedro II, Ilha I	246	1.10 N	66.40 W
Pedro Juan Caballero	252	22.34 S	55.37 W
Pedro Leopoldo	255	19.38 S	44.03 W
Pedro Luro	252	39.29 S	62.41 W
Pedro Muñoz	34	39.24 N	2.58 W
Pedro Osório	252	31.51 S	52.45 W
Pedro R. Fernández	252	28.45 S	58.39 W
Pedro Teixeira	256	21.43 S	43.44 W
Pedro Velho	250	6.26 S	35.14 W
Peebinga	166	34.56 S	140.55 E
Peebles, Scot., U.K.	46	55.39 N	3.12 W
Peebles, Oh., U.S.	218	38.56 N	83.24 W
Peedamullah	162	21.50 S	115.38 E
Pee Dee ≃	192	34.43 N	79.52 W
Peekaboo Mountain ∧[2]	188	45.45 N	67.53 W
Peekskill	210	41.17 N	73.55 W
Peel, Austl.	170	33.19 S	149.38 E
Peel, I. of Man	44	54.13 N	4.40 W
Peel □[6]	212	43.45 N	79.47 W
Peel ≃	180	67.37 N	134.40 W
Peel Channel ≃[1]	180	68.13 N	135.00 W
Peel Fell ∧	44	55.17 N	2.35 W
Peel Inlet c	168a	32.35 S	115.44 E
Peel Island I	171a	27.30 S	153.22 E
Pe Ell	224	46.34 N	123.17 W
Peel Point ›	176	73.22 N	114.35 W
Peel Sound ʉ	176	73.15 N	96.30 W
Peene ≃	54	54.09 N	13.46 E
Peenemünde	54	54.08 N	13.46 E
Peepeekisis Indian Reserve ◆[4]	184	50.52 N	103.24 W
Peer	56	51.08 N	5.28 E
Peerless	202	48.46 N	105.49 W
Peers	182	53.40 N	116.00 W
Peesane	184	52.52 N	103.36 W
Peetz	198	40.57 N	103.06 W
Peetzsee ⊜	264a	52.26 N	13.50 E
Pefferlaw	212	44.19 N	79.12 W
Pefferlaw Brook ≃	212	44.15 N	79.13 W
Pegasus, Port c	172	47.12 S	167.41 E
Pegasus Bay c	172	43.20 S	173.00 E
Pegau	54	51.10 N	12.14 E
Pegli	62	44.26 N	8.48 E
Peglia, Monte ∧	66	42.49 N	12.13 E
Pegnitz	60	49.45 N	11.33 E
Pegnitz ≃	60	49.29 N	11.00 E
Pego	34	38.51 N	0.07 W
Pegolotte	64	45.12 N	12.02 E
Pegswood	44	55.11 N	1.38 W
Pegtymel' ≃	180	69.25 N	174.35 E
Pegtymel'skij chrebet ⋏	180	68.30 N	177.00 E
Pegu ≃	110	16.47 N	96.13 E
Pegu → Bago	110	17.20 N	96.29 E
Pegueros	234	20.57 N	102.40 W
Peguis Indian Reserve ◆[4]	184	51.20 N	97.35 W
Pegu Yoma ⋏	110	19.00 N	95.50 E
Pegwell Bay c	42	51.18 N	1.26 E
Pegyš	24	63.26 N	50.30 E
Pehčevo	38	41.46 N	22.54 E
Pehladpur ◆[8]	272a	28.35 N	77.06 E
Pehlivanköy	130	41.21 N	26.55 E
Pehowa	124	29.59 N	76.35 E
Pehuajó	252	35.48 S	61.53 W
Pehula	26	61.17 N	22.42 E
Peian → Bei'an	89	48.16 N	126.36 E
Peiching → Beijing	105	39.55 N	116.25 E
Peigan Indian Reserve ◆[4]	182	49.35 N	113.40 W
Peihai → Beihai	102	21.29 N	109.05 E
Peij	52	51.06 N	5.53 E
Peijiatun	98	39.19 N	121.41 E
Peikang	100	23.34 N	120.18 E
Peikang ≃	100	23.31 N	120.08 E
Peikant'ang Tao I	100	26.13 N	119.59 E
Peilstein im Mühlviertel	60	48.37 N	13.53 E
Peinan	100	22.47 N	121.07 E
Peinan ≃	100	22.46 N	121.10 E
Peine	52	52.19 N	10.13 E
Peine, Pointe à ›	240d	15.23 N	61.15 W
Peinnechaung I	110	19.59 N	93.04 E
Peio	64	46.22 N	10.40 E
Peip'ing → Beijing	105	39.55 N	116.25 E
Peipsi järv (Čudskoje ozero) ⊜	76	58.45 N	27.25 E
Peipus, Lake → Čudskoje ozero ⊜	76	58.45 N	27.25 E
Peïra-Cava	62	43.56 N	7.22 E
Peirce, Cape ›	180	58.35 N	161.47 W
Peisey-Nancroix	62	45.33 N	6.45 E
Peissenberg	64	47.48 N	11.04 E
Peissenberg ∧, Dtsch.	60	47.48 N	11.01 E
Peissenberg ∧, Dtsch.	64	47.48 N	11.01 E
Peiting	58	47.47 N	10.55 E
Peit'ou ◆[8]	269d	25.08 N	121.30 E
Peitz	54	51.51 N	14.24 E
Peixe	255	12.03 S	48.32 W
Peixe, Rio do ≃, Bra.	255	14.06 S	50.51 W
Peixe, Rio do ≃, Bra.	255	21.31 S	51.58 W
Peixe, Rio do ≃, Bra.	256	23.24 S	45.28 W
Peixe, Rio do ≃, Bra.	256	21.55 S	43.21 W
Peixe, Rio do ≃, Bra.	256	22.23 S	46.51 W
Peixe, Rio do ≃, Bra.	256	23.12 S	46.06 W
Peixe, Rio do ≃, Bra.	256	21.38 S	45.11 W
Peixe-Boi	250	1.12 S	47.18 W
Peixes, Rio dos ≃	250	10.42 S	57.56 W
Peixian (Yunhe), Zhg.	98	34.21 N	117.59 E
Peixian, Zhg.	98	34.44 N	116.59 E
Peixoto, Reprêsa de ⊜[1]	255	20.10 S	47.20 W
Peixoto de Azevedo ≃	250	10.06 S	55.31 W
Peiziyan	98	35.07 N	115.01 E
Pejantan, Pulau I	112	0.07 N	107.14 E
Pejelagartero	234	18.04 N	93.45 W
Pek ≃	38	44.46 N	21.33 E
Pekalongan	115a	6.53 S	109.40 E
Pekan	114	3.30 N	103.25 E
Pekanbaru	112	0.32 N	101.27 E
Pekanheran	112	0.21 S	102.26 E
Pekin, Il., U.S.	190	40.34 N	89.38 W
Pekin, In., U.S.	218	38.29 N	86.01 W
Pekin, N.Y., U.S.	284a	43.10 N	78.53 W
Pekin, Oh., U.S.	214	40.43 N	81.07 W
Pékin → Beijing	105	39.55 N	116.25 E
Peking → Beijing	105	39.55 N	116.25 E
Peking National Library ʋ	271a	39.56 N	116.22 E
Peking Railway Station ◆[5]	271a	39.54 N	116.26 E
Peking University ʋ[2]	271a	39.59 N	116.18 E
Peking Zoo ♦	271a	39.56 N	116.19 E
Peklino	76	53.33 N	33.32 E
Pekša ≃	80	55.53 N	39.40 E
Pektubajevo	80	57.02 N	48.23 E
Pekul'nej, chrebet ⋏	180	66.00 N	175.00 E
Pekul'nejskoje, ozero ⊜	180	62.40 N	177.00 E
Péla	150	7.37 N	9.07 W
Pelabuhandagang	112	1.08 S	103.05 E
Pelabuhan Kelang	114	3.00 N	101.24 E
Pelabuhanratu	115a	6.59 S	106.33 E
Pelabuhanratu, Teluk c	115a	7.03 S	106.27 E
Pel'a-Chovanskaja	80	54.36 N	44.56 E
Pelado, Volcán ∧[1]	286a	19.09 N	99.13 W
Pelagejevka	83	48.06 N	38.36 E
Pelagie, Isole II	70a	35.40 N	12.40 E
Pelago	66	43.46 N	11.30 E
Pelahatchie	194	32.18 N	89.47 W
Pelaihari	112	3.48 S	114.45 E
Pelalawan	112	0.27 N	102.05 E
Pelat, Mont ∧	62	44.16 N	6.42 E
Pelawan	114	2.47 N	102.55 E
Pełczyce	30	53.03 N	15.18 E
Pélé, Mont ∧	152	3.15 S	11.14 E
Peleaga, Vîrful ∧	38	45.22 N	22.54 E
Pelechuco	248	14.48 S	69.04 W
Peleduj	74	59.36 N	112.45 E
Pelée, Montagne ∧	240e	14.48 N	61.10 W
Pelee, Point ›	214	41.54 N	82.30 W
Pelee Island I	214	41.46 N	82.39 W
Pelee Passage ʉ	214	41.52 N	82.37 W
Pelekech ∧	154	3.48 N	35.04 E
Peleliu I	175b	7.01 N	134.15 E
Peleng, Pulau I	112	1.20 S	123.10 E
Peleng, Selat ʉ	112	1.10 S	122.45 E
Pelenija	78	47.53 N	27.50 E
Pelf, Monte ∧	64	46.14 N	12.12 E
Pelham, On., Can.	212	43.02 N	79.17 W
Pelham, Al., U.S.	194	33.17 N	86.48 W
Pelham, Ga., U.S.	192	31.07 N	84.09 W
Pelham, Ma., U.S.	207	42.23 N	72.24 W
Pelham, N.H., U.S.	207	42.44 N	71.19 W
Pelham, N.Y., U.S.	276	40.54 N	73.48 W
Pelham Bay c	276	40.52 N	73.47 W
Pelham Bay Park ♦	276	40.52 N	73.49 W
Pelham Manor	276	40.53 N	73.48 W
Pelhřimov	30	49.26 N	15.13 E
Pelican	180	57.57 N	136.14 W
Pelican ≃	198	46.17 N	96.08 W
Pelican, Punta ›	200	31.19 N	113.43 W
Pelican Bay c	184	52.45 N	100.20 W
Pelican Island I, Mo., U.S.	219	38.52 N	90.18 W
Pelican Island I, Tx., U.S.	222	29.20 N	94.48 W
Pelican Lagoon c	168b	35.50 S	137.47 E
Pelican Lake	190	45.30 N	89.10 W
Pelican Lake ⊜, Ab., Can.	182	55.47 N	113.15 W
Pelican Lake ⊜, Mb., Can.	184	53.50 N	96.08 W
Pelican Lake ⊜, Mb., Can.	184	52.30 N	100.20 W
Pelican Lake ⊜, Mb., Can.	184	49.20 N	99.35 W
Pelican Lake ⊜, Sk., Can.	184	55.08 N	103.00 W
Pelican Lake ⊜, Sk., Can.	184	50.32 N	106.00 W
Pelican Lake ⊜, Mn., U.S.	190	48.05 N	92.54 W
Pelican Lake ⊜, S.D., U.S.	198	44.52 N	97.11 W
Pelican Mountain ∧	182	55.35 N	113.40 W
Pelican Narrows	184	55.10 N	102.56 W
Pelican Point ›	168b	34.48 S	138.29 E
Pelican Rapids, Mb., Can.	184	52.45 N	100.42 W
Pelican Rapids, Mn., U.S.	198	46.34 N	96.04 W
Pelileo	246	1.19 S	78.32 W
Pelister ∧	38	41.00 N	21.12 E
Pelješac, Poluotok ›[1]	36	42.58 N	17.20 E
Pelkosenniemi	24	67.07 N	27.30 E
Pelkum, Dtsch.	52	51.39 N	7.46 E
Pelkum, Dtsch.	263	51.40 N	7.24 E
Pella, S. Afr.	158	29.01 S	19.06 E
Pella, Ia., U.S.	190	41.24 N	92.54 W
Pélla ⊥	38	40.45 N	22.33 E
Pellaro	68	38.01 N	15.39 E
Pell City	194	33.35 N	86.17 W
Pellechia, Monte ∧	66	42.07 N	12.52 E
Pellegrini	252	36.16 S	63.09 W
Pellegrini, Lago ⊜	252	38.40 S	68.00 W
Pellegrino, Cozzo ∧	68	39.45 N	16.03 E
Pellegrino, Monte ∧	70	38.10 N	13.21 E
Pellegrino Parmense	64	44.44 N	9.55 E
Pellendorf	264b	48.06 N	16.27 E
Peller, Monte ∧	64	46.18 N	10.57 E
Pellestrina, Litorale di ≗[2]	64	45.16 N	12.18 E
Pelletier Lake ⊜	184	56.30 N	97.00 W
Pellice ≃	62	44.50 N	7.38 E
Pellingen	56	49.40 N	6.40 E
Pell Lake	216	42.32 N	88.21 W
Pello	24	66.47 N	24.00 E
Pellston	190	45.33 N	84.47 W
Pellworm I	30	54.31 N	8.38 E
Pelly	184	51.52 N	101.55 W
Pelly ≃	180	62.47 N	137.19 W
Pelly Bay c	176	68.53 N	89.51 W
Pelly Crossing	180	62.50 N	136.35 W
Pelly Lake ⊜	176	65.59 N	101.12 W
Pelly Mountains ⋏	180	62.00 N	133.00 W
Pelón, Cerro ∧	234	20.05 N	99.55 W
Peloncillo Mountains ⋏	200	32.15 N	109.00 W
Pelopónnisos ›[1]	38	37.30 N	22.00 E
Peloritani, Monti ⋏	70	38.03 N	15.20 E
Pelotas	252	31.46 S	52.20 W
Pelotas ≃	252	27.28 S	51.55 W
Pelplin	30	53.56 N	18.42 E
Pelque ≃	254	51.03 S	70.58 W
Pelsin	54	53.48 N	13.40 E
Pelusium Bay → Ṭīnah, Khalīj aṭ- c	140	31.08 N	32.40 E
Pel'ušn'a	76	58.56 N	32.52 E
Pélussin	62	45.25 N	4.41 E
Pelvo d'Elva ∧	62	44.33 N	9.15 E
Pelym	86	59.38 N	63.05 E
Pemadumcook Lake ⊜	188	45.40 N	68.55 W
Pemalang	115a	6.54 S	109.22 E
Pemalang, Ujung ›	115a	6.47 S	109.29 E
Pemali ≃	115a	6.47 S	109.01 E
Pemangkat	112	1.10 N	108.58 E
Pematang	112	0.12 S	102.04 E
Pematangsiantar	114	2.57 N	99.03 E
Pematangtanahjawa	114	2.53 N	99.12 E
Pemba, Moç.	154	12.58 S	40.30 E
Pemba, Zam.	154	16.31 S	27.22 E
Pemba I	154	5.10 S	39.48 E
Pemba Channel ʉ	154	5.10 S	39.20 E
Pembarisan, Pegunungan ⋏	115a	7.13 S	108.45 E
Pemberton, Austl.	162	34.28 S	116.01 E
Pemberton, B.C., Can.	182	50.20 N	122.48 W
Pemberton, Eng., U.K.	262	53.32 N	2.41 W
Pemberton, N.J., U.S.	208	39.58 N	74.41 W
Pemberton, Oh., U.S.	216	40.18 N	84.02 W
Pemberton Airport ⊠	285	39.59 N	74.41 W
Pemberton Heights	285	39.58 N	74.41 W
Pemberville	214	41.24 N	83.27 W
Pembina	198	48.57 N	97.14 W
Pembina ≃, Ab., Can.	182	54.45 N	114.15 W
Pembina ≃, N.A.	184	48.57 N	97.14 W
Pembina Hills ⋏[2]	198	49.10 N	98.25 W
Pembine	190	45.38 N	87.59 W
Pembrey	42	51.42 N	4.16 W
Pembroke, On., Can.	190	45.49 N	77.07 W
Pembroke, Wales, U.K.	42	51.41 N	4.55 W
Pembroke, Ga., U.S.	192	32.08 N	81.37 W
Pembroke, Ky., U.S.	194	36.46 N	87.21 W
Pembroke, Me., U.S.	188	44.57 N	67.09 W
Pembroke, N.Y., U.S.	210	43.00 N	78.27 W
Pembroke, N.C., U.S.	192	34.40 N	79.11 W
Pembroke, Va., U.S.	192	37.19 N	80.38 W
Pembroke, Cape ›	176	62.56 N	81.55 W
Pembroke Castle ⊥	42	51.41 N	4.56 W
Pembroke Dock	42	51.42 N	4.56 W
Pembroke Pines	220	26.00 N	80.13 W
Pembrokeshire Coast National Park ♦	42	51.47 N	5.06 W
Pembuang	112	2.34 S	112.19 E
Pembuang ≃	112	3.24 S	112.33 E
Pembury	42	51.09 N	0.20 E
Pemfling	60	49.16 N	12.37 E
Pemichigamau Lake ⊜	184	56.16 N	99.33 W
Pemigewasset ≃	188	43.26 N	71.40 W
Pemmican Portage	184	53.56 N	102.17 W
Pemuco	252	36.58 S	72.06 W
Pemynoos Indian Reserve ◆[4]	182	50.29 N	121.15 W
Pemzašen	84	40.35 N	43.57 E
Pena, Parque de ♦	266c	38.47 N	9.23 W
Peña Barroza	248	22.10 S	67.25 W
Peña Blanca	236	8.27 N	81.40 W
Peñafiel, Esp.	34	41.36 N	4.07 W
Penafiel, Port.	34	41.12 N	8.17 W
Pen'agino	265b	55.50 N	37.21 E
Peña Gorda, Cerro ∧	234	20.44 N	104.50 W
Peña Grande ◆[8]	266a	40.29 N	3.44 W
Pen'akša	80	56.22 N	44.56 E
Peñalara ∧	34	40.51 N	3.57 W
Peñalolén	286e	33.29 S	70.32 W
Pena-Lunanga	154	4.16 S	28.10 E
Penalva	250	3.18 S	45.10 W
Penambulai, Pulau I	164	6.24 S	134.48 E
Penang → George Town	114	5.25 N	100.20 E
Penanjung, Teluk c	115a	7.45 S	108.37 E
Penápolis	255	21.24 S	50.04 W
Peñaranda de Bracamonte	34	40.54 N	5.12 W
Pen Argyl	210	40.52 N	75.15 W
Penaron	114	4.38 N	97.40 E
Peñarroya-Pueblonuevo	34	38.18 N	5.16 W
Penarth	42	51.27 N	3.11 W
Peñas, Cabo de ›	34	43.39 N	5.51 W
Penas, Golfo de c	254	47.22 S	74.50 W
Penasco	200	36.10 N	105.41 W
Peñasco, Rio ≃	196	32.45 N	104.19 W
Penataquit Creek ≃	276	40.43 N	73.14 W
Penbrook	208	40.16 N	76.50 W
Pencader	42	52.01 N	4.16 W
Pencahue	252	35.24 S	71.49 W
Pence	190	46.25 N	90.16 W
Pen Centre ◆[9]	284a	43.08 N	79.14 W
Penchard	261	48.59 N	2.52 E
Penck Trough V	9	73.00 S	2.45 W
Penco	252	36.44 S	72.59 W
Pencoed	42	51.32 N	3.30 W
Pendang, Indon.	112	1.28 S	114.51 E
Pendang, Malay.	114	6.00 N	100.28 E
Pendé ≃	146	7.55 N	16.36 E
Pendéli	267c	38.03 N	23.52 E
Pendelikón Óros ∧	267c	38.06 N	23.54 E
Pendembu, S.L.	150	8.06 N	10.42 W
Pendembu, S.L.	150	9.06 N	12.12 W
Pendências	250	5.15 S	36.43 W
Pendeng	114	4.06 N	97.36 E
Pender	198	42.06 N	96.42 W
Pender Bay c	162	16.45 S	122.42 E
Pendhar	272c	19.04 N	73.06 E
Pendik	267b	40.53 N	29.13 E
Pendjari ≃	150	10.54 N	0.51 E
Pendjari, Parc National de la ♦	150	11.20 N	1.15 E
Pendlebury	262	53.31 N	2.20 W
Pendle Hill	274a	33.48 S	150.57 E
Pendle Hill ∧[2]	44	53.52 N	2.17 W
Pendleton, In., U.S.	218	39.59 N	85.44 W
Pendleton, N.Y., U.S.	284a	43.05 N	78.44 W
Pendleton, Or., U.S.	202	45.40 N	118.47 W
Pendleton, S.C., U.S.	192	34.39 N	82.47 W
Pendleton □[6]	218	38.42 N	84.22 W
Pendolo	112	2.05 S	120.42 E
Pendopo	112	3.17 S	103.52 E
Pend Oreille ≃	202	49.04 N	117.37 W
Pend Oreille, Lake ⊜	202	48.10 N	116.11 W
Pend Oreille, Mount ∧	202	48.25 N	116.10 W
Pendotiba ≃	287a	22.53 S	43.02 W
Pendžikent	85	39.29 N	67.35 E
Penebel	115b	8.25 S	115.09 E
Penedo	250	10.17 S	36.36 W
Penedono	34	40.59 N	7.24 W
Penela	34	40.02 N	8.23 W
Penelope	222	31.52 N	96.56 W
Penetang Harbour c	212	44.47 N	79.57 W
Penetanguishene	212	44.47 N	79.55 W
Penfield, Il., U.S.	216	40.18 N	87.57 W
Penfield, N.Y., U.S.	210	43.07 N	77.28 W
Penfield, Oh., U.S.	214	41.10 N	82.08 W
Penfield, Pa., U.S.	214	41.13 N	78.34 W
Penganga ≃	122	19.53 N	79.09 E
Pengastulan	115b	8.11 S	114.55 E
Peng Chau I	271d	22.17 N	114.02 E
P'engchia Yü I	100	25.38 N	122.04 E
Penge, S. Afr.	156	24.22 S	30.13 E
Penge, Zaïre	154	5.31 S	24.37 E
Penge ◆[8]	260	51.25 N	0.04 W
Penggong	106	30.27 N	119.57 E
Penggongmiao	100	26.07 N	113.34 E
Penghu	100	25.24 N	118.11 E
P'enghu Ch'üntao (Pescadores) II	100	23.30 N	119.30 E
P'enghu Shuitao ʉ	100	23.30 N	119.50 E
Pengiki, Pulau I	112	0.15 N	108.03 E
Pengjiachang	107	30.36 N	103.53 E
Pengjialouzi	104	41.56 N	123.40 E
Pengjiawan	100	32.16 N	114.04 E
Pengjiawu	105	39.41 N	117.10 E
Pengkalan Baharu	114	4.28 N	100.38 E
Pengkou	100	25.32 N	116.42 E
Penglai (Dengzhou)	98	37.48 N	120.42 E
Penglaizhen	107	30.36 N	105.14 E
Penglang	106	31.23 N	121.05 E
Pengnan	107	30.25 N	105.53 E
Pengpu → Bengbu	100	32.58 N	117.24 E
Pengshan	107	30.13 N	103.52 E
Pengshi	100	30.28 N	113.10 E
Pengshui	102	29.18 N	108.09 E
Penguin	166	41.07 S	146.04 E
Pengwaluote Shan ∧	120	33.30 N	86.35 E
Pengxi	102	30.49 N	105.40 E
Pengxian	102	31.00 N	103.50 E
Pengze	100	29.53 N	116.33 E
Pengzhai	100	24.23 N	115.06 E
Pengzhuangzi	105	40.06 N	114.51 E
Penha	252	26.46 S	48.39 W
Penha ◆[8]	287a	22.49 S	43.17 W
Penha de França ◆[8]	287b	23.32 S	46.32 W
Penha Longa, Bra.	256	22.04 S	43.05 W
Penhalonga, Zimb.	154	18.54 S	32.40 E
Penhold	182	52.08 N	113.52 W
Penhold, Canadian Forces Base ■	182	52.12 N	113.53 W
Penhorn Creek ≃	276	40.45 N	74.05 W
Penhsi → Benxi	104	41.18 N	123.45 E
Peniche	34	39.21 N	9.23 W
Penicuik	46	55.50 N	3.14 W
Penida, Nusa I	115b	8.44 S	115.32 E
Penig	54	50.56 N	12.41 E
Peningo Neck ›[1]	276	40.57 N	73.41 W
Peninjai	112	1.26 S	101.50 E
Peninsula Lake ⊜	212	45.20 N	79.05 W
Peninsula State Park ♦	190	45.09 N	87.14 W
Peníscola	34	40.21 N	0.25 E
Penistone	44	53.32 N	1.37 W
Penitas	196	26.17 N	98.27 W
Penitencia Creek ≃	282	37.27 N	121.55 W
Penitente, Serra do ⋏[2]	250	8.45 S	46.20 W
Penjamillo [de Degollado]	234	20.06 N	101.54 W
Pénjamo	234	20.26 N	101.44 W
Penketh	262	53.23 N	2.40 W
Penki → Benxi	104	41.18 N	123.45 E
Penkino	82	54.50 N	38.53 E
Penkridge	42	52.44 N	2.07 W
Penkun	54	53.17 N	14.14 E
Pen Lake ⊜	212	45.28 N	78.23 W
Penllyn	285	40.10 N	75.15 W
Penmaenmawr	44	53.16 N	3.54 W
Penmarc'h, Pointe de ›	32	47.48 N	4.22 W
Penn	279b	40.20 N	79.38 W
Penna, Punta della ›	66	42.10 N	14.43 E
Pennabilli	66	43.49 N	12.16 E
Penn Acres	285	39.40 N	75.34 W
Pennant Hills	274a	33.44 S	151.04 E
Pennant Hills Park ♦	274a	33.45 S	151.06 E
Pennant Point ›	186	44.26 N	63.39 W
Pennant Station	184	50.33 N	108.12 W
Pennask Lake ⊜	182	50.00 N	120.05 W
Pennask Mountain ∧	182	49.53 N	120.07 W
Penn Brook ≃	283	42.44 N	70.59 W
Penn Cove c	224	48.14 N	122.41 W
Penn Cove Park	224	48.14 N	122.41 W
Penndel	285	40.09 N	74.55 W
Penne	66	42.27 N	13.55 E
Penne, Punta ›	68	40.41 N	17.56 E
Penne-d'Agenais	32	44.23 N	0.49 E
Pennedepie	50	49.25 N	0.11 E
Pennel Creek ≃	198	46.34 N	104.52 W
Penneru ≃	122	14.35 N	80.10 E
Pennes (Pens)	64	46.47 N	11.25 E
Pennes, Val di V	64	46.47 N	11.25 E
Penneshaw	168b	35.44 S	137.56 E
Penngrove	226	38.18 N	122.40 W
Penn Hills	214	40.28 N	79.51 W
Penn Hills Center ◆[9]	279b	40.28 N	79.50 W
Pennines ⋏	44	54.10 N	2.05 W
Pennines, Alpes ⋏	58	46.05 N	7.50 E
Penningby	40	59.41 N	18.40 E
Penningby slott ⊥	40	59.41 N	18.40 E
Pennington, N.J., U.S.	208	40.19 N	74.47 W
Pennington, Tx., U.S.	222	31.11 N	95.14 W
Pennington ≃[1]	150	4.45 N	5.35 E
Pennington Gap	192	36.45 N	83.01 W
Pennino, Monte ∧	66	43.06 N	12.53 E
Penn Run	214	40.37 N	79.01 W
Pennsauken	208	39.58 N	75.04 W
Pennsauken Creek ≃	285	39.59 N	75.03 W
Pennsauken Creek, North Branch ≃	285	39.58 N	75.01 W
Pennsauken Creek, South Branch ≃	285	39.58 N	75.01 W
Pennsboro	188	39.17 N	80.58 W
Penns Brook ≃	276	40.43 N	74.32 W
Pennsburg	208	40.23 N	75.29 W
Pennsbury Heights	285	40.12 N	74.49 W
Pennsbury Manor ⊥	285	40.08 N	74.46 W
Penn's Cave ≗[5]	210	40.53 N	77.36 W
Penns Creek	210	40.52 N	77.04 W
Penns Creek ≃	210	40.48 N	76.51 W
Pennsdale	210	41.15 N	76.48 W
Penns Grove	208	39.43 N	75.28 W

Symbol	English	Deutsch	Español	Français	Português
≃	River	Fluß	Río	Rivière	Rio
≊	Canal	Kanal	Canal	Canal	Canal
⌞	Waterfall, Rapids	Wasserfall, Stromschnellen	Cascada, Rápidos	Chute d'eau, Rapides	Cascata, Rápidos
ʉ	Strait	Meeresstraße	Estrecho	Détroit	Estreito
c	Bay, Gulf	Bucht, Golf	Bahía, Golfo	Baie, Golfe	Baía, Golfo
⊜	Lake, Lakes	See, Seen	Lago, Lagos	Lac, Lacs	Lago, Lagos
≡	Swamp	Sumpf	Pantano	Marais	Pântano
⌂	Ice Features, Glacier	Eis- und Gletscherformen	Accidentes Glaciales	Formes glaciaires	Acidentes glaciares
⍑	Other Hydrographic Features	Andere Hydrographische Objekte	Otros Elementos Hidrográficos	Autres données hydrographiques	Outros acidentes hidrográficos
✢	Submarine Features	Untermeerische Objekte	Accidentes Submarinos	Formes de relief sous-marin	Acidentes submarinos
□	Political Unit	Politische Einheit	Unidad Política	Entité politique	Unidade política
ʋ	Cultural Institution	Kulturelle Institution	Institución Cultural	Institution culturelle	Instituição cultural
⊥	Historical Site	Historische Stätte	Sitio Histórico	Site historique	Sitio histórico
♦	Recreational Site	Erholungs- und Ferienort	Sitio de Recreo	Centre de loisirs	Area de Lazer
⊠	Airport	Flughafen	Aeropuerto	Aéroport	Aeroporto
■	Military Installation	Militäranlage	Instalación Militar	Installation militaire	Instalação militar
◆	Miscellaneous	Verschiedenes	Misceláneo	Divers	Diversos

ENGLISH: Name | Page | Lat.°′ | Long.°′
DEUTSCH: Name | Seite | Breite°′ | Länge°′ E = Ost

Name	Page	Lat.°′	Long.°′
Pennside	208	40.20 N	75.53 W
Penns Neck	276	40.20 N	74.38 W
Pennsuco	220	25.53 N	80.22 W
Pennsville	208	39.39 N	75.31 W
Penns Woods	279b	40.21 N	79.46 W
Pennsylvania □3, U.S.	178	40.45 N	77.30 W
Pennsylvania □3, U.S.	188	40.45 N	77.30 W
Pennsylvania, University of ɤ2	285	39.57 N	75.12 W
Pennsylvania Canal ≊	285	40.13 N	74.47 W
Pennsylvania Station ◆5	276	40.45 N	74.00 W
Penn Valley, Ca., U.S.	226	39.12 N	121.11 W
Penn Valley, Pa., U.S.	285	40.01 N	75.16 W
Penn Valley Terrace	285	40.11 N	74.47 W
Pennville	216	40.29 N	85.08 W
Penn Wynne	285	39.59 N	75.16 W
Penny	182	53.50 N	121.17 W
Penn Yan	210	42.39 N	77.03 W
Pennycutaway ≃	184	56.43 N	92.44 W
Penny Hill	285	39.46 N	75.30 W
Penny Ice Cap ⊓	176	67.10 N	66.00 W
Pennypack Creek ≃	285	40.02 N	75.00 W
Pennypack Park ♠	285	40.04 N	75.03 W
Penny Strait ʯ	176	76.30 N	97.00 W
Peno	76	56.55 N	32.45 E
Penobscot	210	41.10 N	75.52 W
Penobscot ≃	188	44.30 N	68.50 W
Penobscot, East Branch ≃	186	45.35 N	68.32 W
Penobscot, West Branch ≃	188	45.35 N	68.32 W
Penobscot Bay ⊂	188	44.15 N	68.52 W
Peno Creek ≃	219	39.32 N	91.16 W
Pen'ok	86	55.30 N	81.34 E
Penola	166	37.23 S	140.50 E
Peñoles	196	25.39 N	104.30 W
Peñón Blanco	232	24.47 N	104.02 W
Penong	162	31.55 S	133.01 E
Penonomé	236	8.31 N	80.22 W
Penrhyn I1	14	9.00 S	158.00 W
Penrhyn Bay	44	53.19 N	3.45 W
Penrhyndeudraeth	42	52.56 N	4.04 W
Penrith, Austl.	170	33.45 S	150.42 E
Penrith, Eng., U.K.	44	54.40 N	2.44 W
Penryn, Eng., U.K.	42	50.09 N	5.06 W
Penryn, Ca., U.S.	226	38.51 N	121.10 W
Penryn, Pa., U.S.	208	40.12 N	76.22 W
Pensacola	194	30.25 N	87.13 W
Pensacola Bay ⊂	194	30.25 N	87.06 W
Pensacola Mountains ⋏	9	83.45 S	55.00 W
Pensacola Naval Air Station ■	194	30.21 N	87.19 W
Pensacola Seamount ✢3	14	18.17 N	157.20 W
Pensaukee ≃	190	44.49 N	87.55 W
Pensby	262	53.21 N	3.06 W
Pense	184	50.25 N	105.00 W
Penshaw	44	54.53 N	1.29 W
Pensiangan	112	4.33 N	116.19 E
Pensilva	42	50.30 N	4.25 W
Pensilvania	246	5.31 N	75.05 W
Pens → Pennes	64	46.47 N	11.25 E
Pentagna	256	22.09 S	43.45 W
Pentagon ɤ	284c	38.52 N	77.03 W
Pentagon Mountain ∧	202	47.56 N	113.07 W
Pentecost □8	175f	15.45 S	168.12 E
Pentecoste	250	3.48 S	39.17 W
Pentecôte I	175f	15.42 S	168.10 E
Pentecôte ≃	186	49.47 N	67.10 W
Pentecôte, Lac ⊜	186	49.53 N	67.20 W
Penticton	182	49.30 N	119.35 W
Penticton Indian Reserve ◆4	182	49.30 N	119.40 W
Pentire Point ›	42	50.36 N	4.55 W
Pentland	166	20.32 S	145.24 E
Pentland Firth ʯ	46	58.44 N	3.07 W
Pentland Hills ⋏2	46	55.48 N	3.23 W
Pentraeth	44	53.17 N	4.12 W
Pentre Halkyn	262	53.15 N	3.12 W
Pentucket, Lake ⊜	283	42.47 N	71.05 W
Pentucket Pond ⊜	283	42.44 N	71.00 W
Pentwater	190	43.46 N	86.25 W
Penuba	112	0.20 S	104.28 E
Peñuelas	240m	18.03 N	66.43 W
Penuguan	112	2.27 S	104.31 E
Penukonda	122	14.05 N	77.35 E
Penunjok, Tanjong ›	114	4.22 N	103.29 E
Pènwègon	110	18.13 N	96.34 E
Penwell	196	31.44 N	102.35 W
Peny	78	51.04 N	35.54 E
Penyagolosa ∧	34	40.13 N	0.21 W
Penyal d'Ifac ♠	34	38.38 N	0.05 E
Penyengat	114	0.54 N	102.20 E
Pen-y-Ghent ∧	44	54.09 N	2.14 W
Penygroes, Wales, U.K.	42	51.49 N	4.02 W
Penygroes, Wales, U.K.	44	53.04 N	4.17 W
Penyu, Kepulauan II	164	5.22 S	127.46 E
Penyu, Teluk ⊂	115a	7.45 S	109.15 E
Penza	80	53.13 N	45.00 E
Penza □8	76	53.30 N	43.00 E
Penzance	42	50.07 N	5.33 W
Penzberg	64	47.45 N	11.23 E
Penžina ≃	74	62.28 N	165.18 E
Penzing ◆8	264b	48.12 N	16.18 E
Penzino	80	52.07 N	50.27 E
Penžinskaja guba ⊂	74	61.00 N	162.00 E
Penžinskij chrebet ⋏	74	62.30 N	167.00 E
Penzlin	54	53.30 N	13.05 E
Péone	62	44.07 N	6.54 E
Peoples Creek ≃	202	48.24 N	108.19 W
Peoples Ditch ≊	226	36.15 N	119.41 W
Peoria, Az., U.S.	200	33.34 N	112.14 W
Peoria, Il., U.S.	190	40.41 N	89.35 W
Peoria, Oh., U.S.	216	40.19 N	83.27 W
Peoria Heights	190	40.44 N	89.34 W
Peotillos	234	22.30 N	100.37 W
Peotone	216	41.19 N	87.47 W
Peover Eye ≃	262	53.15 N	2.31 W
Peover Heath	262	53.15 N	2.19 W
Pepa	154	7.42 S	29.47 E
Pepacton Reservoir ⊜1	210	42.06 N	74.54 W
Pepaw ≃	184	52.40 N	102.23 W
Pepel	150	8.35 N	13.03 W
Peper	140	7.04 N	33.00 E
Pepin	190	44.26 N	92.08 W
Pepin, Lake ⊜	190	44.30 N	92.15 W
Pepinster	56	50.34 N	5.49 E
Péplos	130	40.58 N	26.16 E
Pepperdine University ɤ2	280	33.58 N	118.18 W
Pepperell	207	42.40 N	71.35 W
Pepper Park State Recreation Area ♠	220	27.30 N	80.18 W
Pepper Pike	279a	41.28 N	81.27 W
Peqi'in Hadasha	132	32.59 N	35.20 E
Pequin	38	41.03 N	19.45 E
Pequannock	210	40.57 N	74.17 W
Pequannock ≃	276	40.58 N	74.17 W
Pequanticut Brook ≃	283	42.01 N	71.08 W
Pequea Creek ≃	208	39.53 N	76.22 W
Pequeno ≃	287a	22.55 S	43.25 W
Pequeri	256	21.50 S	43.06 W
Pequest ≃	210	40.50 N	75.05 W
Pequez	208	39.53 N	76.22 W
Pequizeiro	250	8.32 S	48.58 W
Pequop Mountains ⋏	204	40.45 N	114.40 W
Pequot Lakes	190	46.36 N	94.18 W
Perabumulih	112	3.27 S	104.15 E
Perak □3	114	5.00 N	101.00 E
Perak ≃	114	3.58 N	100.53 E
Perak, Kuala ⊂	114	4.00 N	100.47 E
Peralba, Monte ∧	64	46.37 N	12.43 E
Perales de Alfambra	34	40.38 N	1.00 W
Perales del Rio	266a	40.19 N	3.38 W
Peralillo	252	34.29 S	71.29 W
Peralta	200	34.50 N	106.41 W
Pérama	267c	37.58 N	23.34 E
Perambalur	122	11.14 N	78.53 E
Perämeri (Bottenviken) ⊂	26	65.00 N	23.00 E
Peranāmbattu	122	12.56 N	78.43 E
Peraní, Ákra ›	267c	37.54 N	23.31 E
Perarolo di Cadore	64	46.24 N	12.21 E
Peräseinäjoki	26	62.34 N	23.04 E
Percé	186	48.31 N	64.13 W
Percée, Pointe ∧	58	45.57 N	6.33 E
Perch ≃	212	44.00 N	76.05 W
Perchas	240m	18.19 N	66.59 W
Perchau	61	47.06 N	14.27 E
Perchauer Sattel)(	61	47.07 N	14.27 E
Perche, Collines du ⋏2	50	48.25 N	0.40 E
Perche Creek ≃	194	38.49 N	92.24 W
Perch Lake ⊜	212	44.07 N	75.54 W
Perchtoldsdorf	264b	48.07 N	16.17 E
Perchuškovo	265b	55.41 N	37.10 E
Percival Lakes ⊜	162	21.25 S	125.00 E
Percy Creek ≃	212	44.15 N	77.49 W
Percy Isles II	166	21.39 S	150.16 E
Percy Lake ⊜	212	45.13 N	78.22 W
Percy Reach ⊜	212	44.15 N	77.45 W
Perdagangan-tomuon	114	3.09 N	99.20 E
Perdasdefogu	71	39.41 N	9.26 E
Perdeberg	158	28.59 S	25.05 E
Perdekop	158	27.13 S	29.38 E
Perdices, Arroyo de las ≃	288	34.41 S	58.22 W
Perdida ≃	250	9.13 S	47.59 W
Perdido	194	31.00 N	87.37 W
Perdido ≃, Bra.	248	22.10 S	57.33 W
Perdido ≃, U.S.	194	30.29 N	87.26 W
Perdido, Arroyo ≃	254	42.55 S	67.00 W
Perdido, Arroyo del ≃	258	33.37 S	57.23 W
Perdido, Cuchilla del ⋏2	258	33.43 S	57.17 W
Perdido, Monte ∧	34	42.40 N	0.05 E
Perdido Bay ⊂	194	30.21 N	87.27 W
Perdifumo	68	40.16 N	15.01 E
Perdix	208	40.22 N	76.57 W
Perdizes	255	19.21 S	47.17 W
Perdreauville	261	48.58 N	1.38 E
Perdu, Lac ⊜	186	50.44 N	70.14 W
Perdue	184	52.04 N	107.32 W
Perebrody	78	51.43 N	27.00 E
Perečin	78	48.44 N	22.26 E
Peredel	76	55.12 N	35.41 E
Peredel'cy	82	55.36 N	37.21 E
Peredelkino	265b	55.39 N	37.21 E
Peregino	76	57.27 N	31.21 E
Pereginskoje	78	48.49 N	24.12 E
Peregonovka	78	48.32 N	30.31 E
Pereira	246	4.49 N	75.43 W
Pereira Barreto	255	20.38 S	51.07 W
Pereiro	250	6.03 S	38.28 W
Perejaslav-Chmel'nickij	78	50.06 N	31.30 E
Perejaslavka	89	47.58 N	135.06 E
Perejaslavskaja	78	45.51 N	39.02 E
Perejezdnoje	83	48.47 N	38.04 E
Perejež'na	24	59.43 N	48.12 E
Perekopnoje	80	51.13 N	48.04 E
Perekopovka	78	50.37 N	33.25 E
Perekopskaja	80	49.21 N	43.20 E
Père-Lachaise, Cimetière du ◆	261	48.51 N	2.25 E
Perelazovskij	80	49.09 N	42.33 E
Perelazy	76	53.02 N	31.28 E
Perelesinskij	78	51.44 N	40.07 E
Perel'ub	80	51.52 N	50.22 E
Pere Marquette ≃	190	43.57 N	86.27 W
Pere Marquette, Big South Branch ≃	190	43.56 N	86.10 W
Pere Marquette State Park ♠	219	39.00 N	90.30 W
Perem'otnoje	80	51.11 N	50.49 E
Peremyšl'	82	54.16 N	36.10 E
Peremyšl'any	78	49.41 N	24.33 E
Perené ≃	248	11.09 S	74.18 W
Perenjori	162	29.26 S	116.17 E
Pereputje	92a	46.17 N	141.54 E
Pererov	78	52.04 N	28.00 E
Pereščepino	78	49.01 N	35.22 E
Pereščepnoje	80	50.32 N	45.06 E
Pereslavl'-Zalesskij	82	56.44 N	38.51 E
Peresypkino Pervoje	80	52.55 N	42.55 E
Peretrusovo	82	56.51 N	36.53 E
Pereval'sk	83	48.26 N	38.47 E
Perevoz, Ross.	80	55.36 N	44.32 E
Perevoz, Ross.	88	59.00 N	116.57 E
Perevoz, Ross.	265a	59.43 N	30.47 E
Pereyra, Arroyo ≃	288	34.47 S	58.08 W
Pereyra, Punta ›	258	34.14 S	58.04 W
Pérez	252	33.00 S	60.46 W
Perfugas	71	40.50 N	8.53 E
Perg	61	48.15 N	14.37 E
Pergamino	252	33.53 S	60.35 W
Pergamum ⊥	130	39.10 N	27.13 E
Pergau ≃	114	5.23 N	102.02 E
Pergine Valdarno	66	43.28 N	11.41 E
Pergine Valsugana	64	46.04 N	11.14 E
Pergola	66	43.34 N	12.50 E
Pergusa, Lago di ⊜	70	37.31 N	14.18 E
Perham	198	46.35 N	95.34 W
Perho	26	63.13 N	24.25 E
Peri	64	45.39 N	10.54 E
Peri ≃	130	38.50 N	39.35 E
Peribán de Ramos	234	19.32 N	102.28 W
Péribonca ≃	176	48.45 N	72.05 W
Péribonca, Lac ⊜	186	50.04 N	71.15 W
Perico, Arg.	252	24.23 S	65.06 W
Perico, Cuba	240p	22.46 N	81.01 W
Pericos	232	25.03 N	107.42 W
Pericumã ≃	250	2.17 S	44.42 W
Peridot	200	33.18 N	110.27 W
Périers	32	49.11 N	1.25 W
Perigiraja	112	0.16 S	103.30 E
Périgord □9	32	45.20 N	1.00 E
Perigoso, Canal ʯ	250	0.05 N	49.40 W
Périgueux	32	45.11 N	0.43 E
Perijá, Serranía De ⋏	246	10.00 N	73.00 W
Perim → Barīm I	144	12.39 N	43.25 E
Peri-Mirim	250	2.38 S	44.54 W
Perinaldo	62	43.52 N	7.40 E
Peringat	114	6.02 N	102.17 E
Periprava	38	45.24 N	29.32 E
Perisher Valley ♠	171b	36.23 S	145.24 E
Peristérion	267c	38.01 N	23.42 E
Perito	68	40.18 N	15.09 E
Perito Moreno	254	46.36 S	70.56 W
Peritoró	250	4.20 S	44.18 W
Perivale ◆8	260	51.32 N	0.19 W
Periyakulam	122	10.07 N	77.33 E
Periyār ≃	122	10.11 N	76.13 E
Perkasie	208	40.22 N	75.17 W
Perkins	196	35.58 N	97.02 W
Perkinsfield	212	44.42 N	79.57 W
Perkins Observatory ɤ3	214	40.14 N	83.02 W
Perkinston	194	30.46 N	89.08 W
Perkinsville, In., U.S.	218	40.09 N	85.52 W
Perkinsville, N.Y., U.S.	210	42.32 N	77.38 W
Perkiomen Creek ≃	208	40.07 N	75.28 W
Perkiomen Creek, East Branch ≃	208	40.15 N	75.27 W
Perkiomen Junction	285	40.21 N	75.28 W
Perkiomen Valley Airport ✈	285	40.12 N	75.25 W
Perl	56	49.28 N	6.36 E
Perlas, Archipiélago de las II	246	8.25 N	79.00 W
Perlas, Laguna de ⊂	236	12.30 N	83.40 W
Perlas, Punta de ›	236	12.23 N	83.30 W
Perleberg	54	53.04 N	11.51 E
Perlez	38	45.12 N	20.24 E
Perlis □3	114	6.30 N	100.15 E
Perl'ovka	78	51.51 N	38.51 E
Perm'	86	58.00 N	56.15 E
Perm' □8, Ross.	24	59.00 N	56.00 E
Perm' □8, Ross.	80	57.30 N	54.30 E
Permanente Creek ≃	282	37.25 N	122.05 W
Permas	24	59.20 N	45.34 E
Përmet	38	40.14 N	20.21 E
Permisi	80	54.06 N	45.48 E
Pernambuco □3	250	8.00 S	37.00 W
Pernambuco → Recife	250	8.03 S	34.54 W
Pernate	266b	45.27 N	8.41 E
Pernatty Lagoon ⊜	166	31.31 S	137.14 E
Pernay	50	47.27 N	0.30 E
Pernegg an der Mur	61	47.22 N	15.21 E
Pernes-les-Fontaines	62	44.00 N	5.03 E
Pernik	38	42.36 N	23.02 E
Pernink	54	50.20 N	12.45 E
Perniö	26	60.12 N	23.08 E
Pernitz	61	47.54 N	15.58 E
Pernovo	82	55.58 N	39.10 E
Pero	266b	45.31 N	9.05 E
Peroba, Ribeirão do ≃	287b	23.27 S	46.22 W
Pérols, Étang de ⊂	62	43.33 N	3.56 E
Peron, Cape ›	168a	32.17 S	115.41 E
Péronne	50	49.56 N	2.56 E
Péronnes	50	50.26 N	4.08 E
Peron Peninsula ›1	162	25.55 S	113.30 E
Pero Pinheiro	266c	38.51 N	9.20 W
Perosa Argentina	62	44.58 N	7.10 E
Perote	234	19.34 N	97.14 W
Peroto	248	14.50 S	64.31 W
Pérouges	58	45.54 N	5.11 E
Peroulaz	62	45.42 N	7.19 E
Pérou → Peru □1	242	10.00 S	76.00 W
Perovo ◆8	265b	55.44 N	37.46 E
Perow	182	54.31 N	126.26 W
Perpendicular, Point ›	170	35.06 S	150.48 E
Perpignan	32	42.41 N	2.53 E
Perranporth	42	50.20 N	5.09 W
Perrault Falls	184	50.19 N	93.11 W
Perray ≃	261	48.31 N	1.42 E
Perrero	62	44.56 N	7.05 E
Perriers-sur-Andelle	50	49.25 N	1.22 E
Perrignier	58	46.18 N	6.27 E
Perrigny	58	46.40 N	5.35 E
Perrin	196	33.02 N	98.04 W
Perrine	220	25.36 N	80.21 W
Perrineville	208	40.13 N	74.26 W
Perris	228	33.46 N	117.13 W
Perris, Lake ⊜1	228	33.50 N	117.10 W
Perro, Laguna del ⊜	200	34.40 N	105.57 W
Perro, Punta del ›	34	36.45 N	6.25 W
Perros, Bahía de ⊂	240p	22.25 N	78.30 W
Perros-Guirec	32	48.49 N	3.27 W
Perrot, Île I	206	45.22 N	73.57 W
Perry, Fl., U.S.	192	30.07 N	83.34 W
Perry, Ga., U.S.	192	32.27 N	83.43 W
Perry, Il., U.S.	219	39.47 N	90.45 W
Perry, Ia., U.S.	190	41.50 N	94.06 W
Perry, Ks., U.S.	198	39.04 N	95.23 W
Perry, Me., U.S.	186	44.58 N	67.04 W
Perry, Mi., U.S.	216	42.49 N	84.13 W
Perry, Mo., U.S.	219	39.25 N	91.40 W
Perry, N.Y., U.S.	210	42.42 N	78.00 W
Perry, Oh., U.S.	214	41.45 N	81.08 W
Perry, Ok., U.S.	196	36.17 N	97.17 W
Perry, Tx., U.S.	222	31.25 N	96.55 W
Perry, Ut,. U.S.	200	41.27 N	112.02 W
Perry □6	208	40.25 N	77.11 W
Perrydale	224	45.02 N	123.15 W
Perry Hall	208	39.24 N	76.27 W
Perry Heights	214	40.47 N	81.28 W
Perry-Jōriku-kinenhi ⊥	94	35.14 N	139.43 E
Perry Lake ⊜1	198	39.20 N	95.30 W
Perryman	208	39.28 N	76.12 W
Perrymont	279b	40.33 N	80.02 W
Perryopolis	214	40.05 N	79.45 W
Perry Park	218	38.33 N	85.00 W
Perry Point	208	39.33 N	76.04 W
Perrysburg, N.Y., U.S.	210	42.27 N	79.00 W
Perrysburg, Oh., U.S.	214	41.33 N	83.37 W
Perry's Landing Monument ⊥	268	35.13 N	139.43 E
Perry's Victory and International Peace Memorial ⊥	214	41.33 N	82.50 W
Perrysville, Oh., U.S.	214	40.39 N	82.18 W
Perrysville, Pa., U.S.	279b	40.32 N	80.01 W
Perryton	196	36.24 N	100.48 W
Perryville, Ak., U.S.	180	55.54 N	159.10 W
Perryville, Ar., U.S.	194	35.00 N	92.48 W
Perryville, Ky., U.S.	192	37.39 N	84.57 W
Perryville, Md., U.S.	208	39.33 N	76.04 W
Perryville, Mo., U.S.	194	37.43 N	89.51 W
Perryville, N.Y., U.S.	210	43.01 N	75.48 W
Peršaj	76	54.02 N	26.41 E
Persan	50	49.09 N	2.16 E
Perșani, Munții ⋏	38	45.40 N	25.15 E
Persberg	40	59.45 N	14.15 E
Perschling ≃	61	48.20 N	15.58 E
Perşembe	130	41.04 N	37.46 E
Persepolis → Takht-e Jamshīd ⊥	128	29.57 N	52.52 E
Perseverance, Mount ∧	171a	27.25 S	152.10 E
Perseverancia	248	14.44 S	62.48 W
Pershagen	40	59.10 N	17.39 E
Pershing	218	39.49 N	84.53 W
Pershore	42	52.07 N	2.05 W
Pershyttan	40	59.30 N	15.00 E
Persia	198	41.34 N	95.34 W
Persia → Iran □1	128	32.00 N	53.00 E
Persian Gulf (Arabian Gulf) ⊂	128	27.00 N	51.00 E
Pérsico, Golfo → Persian Gulf ⊂	128	27.00 N	51.00 E
Persimmon Creek ≃	194	31.31 N	86.50 W
Persique, Golfe → Persian Gulf ⊂	128	27.00 N	51.00 E
Persischer Golf → Persian Gulf ⊂	128	27.00 N	51.00 E
Peršotravensk, Ukr.	78	48.22 N	36.24 E
Peršotravensk, Ukr.	78	50.12 N	27.39 E
Peršotravnevoje, Ukr.	78	51.24 N	28.53 E
Peršotravnevoje, Ukr.	83	47.03 N	37.18 E
Perštejn	54	50.23 N	13.08 E
Perstorp	41	56.08 N	13.23 E
Pertandangan, Tanjung ›	114	2.41 N	100.14 E
Pertek	130	38.50 N	39.22 E
Perth, Austl.	168a	31.56 S	115.50 E
Perth, On., Can.	212	44.54 N	76.15 W
Perth, Scot., U.K.	46	56.24 N	3.28 W
Perth, N.Y., U.S.	210	43.03 N	74.12 W
Perth □6	[illegible]	[illegible]	[illegible]
Perth Amboy	210	40.30 N	74.15 W
Perth-Andover	186	46.45 N	67.42 W
Perth Basin ✢1	14	28.30 S	110.00 E
Perthes	58	48.39 N	4.49 E
Perth International Airport ✈	168a	31.57 S	115.58 E
Perthois ⋏1	58	48.40 N	4.45 E
Pertoka	144	16.59 N	37.28 E
Pertominsk	24	64.47 N	38.25 E
Pertovo	80	54.15 N	[illegible]
Pertuis	62	43.41 N	5.30 E
Pertusato, Capo ›	71	41.21 N	9.10 E
Peru, Il., U.S.	216	41.19 N	89.07 W
Peru, In., U.S.	216	40.45 N	86.04 W
Peru, Ne., U.S.	198	40.28 N	95.44 W
Peru, N.Y., U.S.	188	44.34 N	73.31 W
Peru (Perú) □1, S.A.	242	10.00 S	76.00 W
Peru (Perú) □1, S.A.	248	10.00 S	76.00 W
Peruaçu ≃	255	15.11 S	44.07 W
Peru Basin ✢1	18	15.00 S	85.00 W
Peruc	54	50.19 N	13.59 E
Perućac, Jezero ⊜1	38	43.55 N	19.10 E
Peru-Chile Trench ✢1	18	20.00 S	73.00 W
Perugia	66	43.08 N	12.22 E
Perugia □4	66	43.03 N	12.33 E
Perugorría	252	29.20 S	58.37 W
Peruíbe	252	24.19 S	47.00 W
Peruípe ≃	255	17.43 S	39.16 W
Perumalpār I1	122	11.10 N	72.04 E
Peruque Creek ≃	219	38.53 N	90.39 W
Perus ◆8	256	23.25 S	46.45 W
Perušić	36	44.39 N	15.23 E
Péruwelz	50	50.31 N	3.35 E
Pervaja Maja	86	48.55 N	67.25 E
Pervari	128	37.54 N	42.36 E
Pervenchères	50	48.26 N	0.26 E
Pervesinka	80	52.13 N	43.15 E
Pervijze	50	51.05 N	2.47 E
Pervoavgustovskij	76	52.14 N	35.03 E
Pervoje Pole	180	63.05 N	179.19 E
Pervomajka, Kaz.	86	51.17 N	70.08 E
Pervomajka, Ukr.	83	49.09 N	37.58 E
Pervomajka ◆8	83	48.17 N	39.50 E
Pervomajsk, Ross.	80	54.53 N	43.49 E
Pervomajsk, Ross.	88	58.02 N	94.05 E
Pervomajsk, Ukr.	78	48.04 N	30.52 E
Pervomajsk, Ukr.	83	48.37 N	38.35 E
Pervomajsk, Ukr.	83	49.05 N	39.37 E
Pervomajskij, Bela.	76	53.54 N	25.23 E
Pervomajskij, Kyrg.	85	42.51 N	74.04 E
Pervomajskij, Ross.	76	54.04 N	32.29 E
Pervomajskij, Ross.	80	53.22 N	51.38 E
Pervomajskij, Ross.	80	51.22 N	48.54 E
Pervomajskij, Ross.	80	53.15 N	40.18 E
Pervomajskij, Ross.	82	55.57 N	37.52 E
Pervomajskij, Ross.	82	54.03 N	37.32 E
Pervomajskij, Ross.	82	55.32 N	37.09 E
Pervomajskij, Ross.	86	51.32 N	55.06 E
Pervomajskij, Ross.	86	53.41 N	55.57 E
Pervomajskij, Ross.	86	54.52 N	61.08 E
Pervomajskij, Ross.	86	59.29 N	61.24 E
Pervomajskij, Ross.	88	51.44 N	115.39 E
Pervomajskij, Ukr.	78	49.24 N	36.12 E
Pervomajskij, Ukr.	83	47.58 N	38.47 E
Pervomajskoje, Kaz.	85	42.05 N	69.53 E
Pervomajskoje, Ross.	76	52.56 N	33.36 E
Pervomajskoje, Ross.	80	55.05 N	47.22 E
Pervomajskoje, Ross.	80	50.56 N	46.46 E
Pervomajskoje, Ross.	80	46.03 N	42.13 E
Pervomajskoje, Ross.	80	46.21 N	43.37 E
Pervomajskoje, Ross.	80	48.50 N	41.14 E
Pervomajskoje, Ross.	80	51.28 N	47.37 E
Pervomajskoje, Ross.	86	53.45 N	84.08 E
Pervomajskoje, Ross.	86	57.06 N	86.12 E
Pervomajskoje, Ukr.	78	45.43 N	33.51 E
Pervoural'sk	86	56.54 N	59.58 E
Pervušino	80	58.02 N	41.56 E
Pervyj Kuril'skij proliv ʯ	74	50.50 N	156.36 E
Perwenitz	264a	52.40 N	13.01 E
Pes'	76	58.55 N	34.19 E
Pes' ≃	76	59.08 N	35.18 E
Pesa ≃	66	43.44 N	11.01 E
Pes'akov, ostrov I	24	68.47 N	57.35 E
Pesangrohan ≃	269e	6.11 S	106.45 E
Pesaro	66	43.54 N	12.55 E
Pesaro e Urbino □4	66	43.40 N	12.38 E
Pesca	246	5.33 N	73.03 W
Pescadero	226	37.15 N	122.22 W
Pescadero Creek ≃, Ca., U.S.	226	36.42 N	121.17 W
Pescadero Creek ≃, Ca., U.S.	226	37.16 N	122.25 W
Pescadores, Punta ›, Méx.	232	23.46 N	109.43 W
Pescadores, Punta ›, Perú	248	16.21 S	73.15 W
Pescadores → P'enghu Ch'üntao II	100	23.30 N	119.30 E
Pescaglia	66	43.58 N	10.25 E
Pesčanaja	78	48.08 N	29.44 E
Pesčanka, Ross.	80	51.18 N	43.40 E
Pesčanka, Ukr.	78	48.12 N	28.53 E
Pesčanoje, Kaz.	86	53.01 N	76.19 E
Pesčanoje, Ross.	24	62.09 N	35.48 E
Pesčanoje, Ukr.	78	49.44 N	31.50 E
Pesčanoje, Ukr.	83	49.34 N	37.51 E
Pesčanokopskoje	80	46.12 N	41.04 E
Pescantina	64	45.29 N	10.51 E
Pesčanyj	83	47.02 N	37.28 E
Pesčanyje, ostrova II	83	46.52 N	38.17 E
Pescara	66	42.28 N	14.13 E
Pescara □4	66	42.20 N	13.57 E
Pescara ≃	66	42.28 N	14.13 E
Pescasseroli	66	41.48 N	13.47 E
Pesch	263	51.11 N	6.32 E
Pesch, Schloss ⊥	263	51.18 N	6.39 E
Peschici	68	41.57 N	16.01 E
Peschiera del Garda	64	45.26 N	10.42 E
Peschio, Monte ∧	267a	41.43 N	12.46 E
Pescia	66	43.54 N	10.41 E
Pescina	66	42.02 N	13.39 E
Pescocostanzo	66	41.53 N	14.04 E
Pescolanciano	66	41.41 N	14.20 E
Pescopagano	68	40.50 N	15.24 E
Pescorocchiano	66	42.12 N	13.09 E
Pesco Sannita	68	41.14 N	14.49 E
Pesé	236	7.54 N	80.37 W
Pesek, Pulau I	271c	1.17 N	103.41 E
Peseux	58	46.59 N	6.53 E
Peshastin	224	47.34 N	120.36 W
Peshastin Creek ≃	224	47.33 N	120.35 W
Peshāwar	123	34.01 N	71.33 E
Peshīn Jān	128	33.25 N	61.28 E
Peshkopi	38	41.41 N	20.26 E
Peshtigo	190	45.03 N	87.44 W
Peshtigo ≃	190	44.58 N	87.40 W
Pesio ≃	62	44.28 N	7.53 E
Pesjane	82	56.01 N	38.48 E
Peski, Bela.	76	53.21 N	24.38 E
Peski, Ross.	80	51.16 N	42.27 E
Peski, Ross.	82	55.13 N	38.46 E
Peški, Ross.	82	56.08 N	37.04 E
Peski, Ukr.	78	50.23 N	33.27 E
Peski, Ukr.	83	49.26 N	38.59 E
Peski-Rad'kovskije	83	49.17 N	37.36 E
Peskovatskoje	82	54.03 N	36.16 E
Peskovka, Ross.	86	59.04 N	52.22 E
Peskovka, Ukr.	78	50.42 N	29.38 E
Peškovo	83	47.02 N	39.24 E
Peškovo Grecovo	82	54.26 N	37.36 E
Peškovskoje	86	53.45 N	62.23 E
Pesmes	58	47.17 N	5.34 E
Pesnica	61	46.36 N	15.41 E
Pesnica ≃	61	46.24 N	16.05 E
Pešnoj, poluostrov ›2	80	46.52 N	51.42 E
Pesočenskij	82	54.10 N	36.06 E
Pesočin	78	49.57 N	36.06 E
Pesočn'a	80	54.07 N	40.50 E
Pesočnoje, Bela.	76	53.20 N	27.06 E
Pesočnoje, Ross.	80	58.01 N	39.10 E
Peso da Régua	34	41.10 N	7.47 W
Pespire	236	13.35 N	87.22 W
Pesqueira	250	8.22 S	36.42 W
Pesquería	196	25.47 N	100.03 W
Pesquería ≃	196	25.54 N	99.11 W
Pessac	32	44.48 N	0.38 W
Pessin	54	52.38 N	12.40 E
Pessinetto	62	45.17 N	7.24 E
Pest □6	30	47.25 N	19.20 E
Pest'aki	80	56.43 N	42.40 E
Peštera	38	42.02 N	24.18 E
Pesterzsébet ◆8	264c	47.26 N	19.07 E
Pesthidegkút ◆8	264c	47.34 N	18.58 E
Pestimre ◆8	264c	47.24 N	19.12 E
Pestlőrinc ◆8	264c	47.26 N	19.12 E
Pestovo, Ross.	76	58.36 N	35.48 E
Pestovo, Ross.	80	57.12 N	46.44 E
Pestovskoje vodochranilišče ⊜1	82	56.06 N	37.40 E
Pestravka	80	52.24 N	49.58 E
Pestrecy	80	55.46 N	49.39 E
Pestrikovo	82	55.05 N	38.53 E
Pestújhely ◆8	264c	47.32 N	19.07 E
Petacalco, Bahía ⊂	234	17.57 N	102.05 W
Petah Tiqwa	132	32.05 N	34.53 E
Petäjävesi	26	62.15 N	25.12 E
Petal	194	31.20 N	89.15 W
Petalcingo	232	17.17 N	92.27 W
Petaling Jaya	114	3.05 N	101.39 E
Petalión, Kólpos ⊂	38	37.59 N	24.02 E
Petaluma	226	38.13 N	122.38 W
Petaluma ≃	226	38.06 N	122.30 W
Pétange	56	49.34 N	5.52 E
Petare	246	10.29 N	66.49 W
Petatlán	234	17.31 N	101.16 W
Petauke	154	14.15 S	31.20 E
Petawawa	190	45.54 N	77.17 W
Petawawa ≃	190	45.55 N	77.15 W
Pété	146	10.58 N	14.30 E
Petegem	50	50.58 N	3.32 E
Petén □5	236	16.15 N	89.50 W
Petén Itzá, Lago ⊜	232	16.59 N	89.50 W
Petenwell Lake ⊜1	190	44.10 N	89.57 W
Peter and Paul Fortress ⊥	265a	59.57 N	30.19 E
Peterboro	210	42.58 N	75.41 W
Peterborough, Austl.	166	32.58 S	138.50 E
Peterborough, On., Can.	212	44.18 N	78.19 W
Peterborough, Eng., U.K.	42	52.35 N	0.15 W
Peterborough, N.H., U.S.	188	42.52 N	71.57 W
Peterborough □6	212	44.33 N	78.15 W
Peterculter	46	57.05 N	2.16 W
Peterhead	46	57.30 N	1.49 W
Peter Hill ∧	46	56.58 N	2.42 W
Peter I Island I	9	68.47 S	90.35 W
Peter Island I	240m	18.22 N	64.35 W
Peter Lake ⊜, N.T., Can.	176	63.08 N	92.48 W
Peter Lake ⊜, Sk., Can.	184	57.15 N	103.53 W
Peterlee	44	54.46 N	1.19 W
Peter Lougheed Provincial Park ♠	182	50.45 N	115.15 W
Peterman	194	31.35 N	87.15 W
Petermann Ranges ⋏	162	25.00 S	129.46 E
Petermann Reserve ◆4	162	25.00 S	130.15 E
Peter Pond Lake ⊜	184	55.55 N	108.44 W
Peter Pond Lake Indian Reserve ◆4	184	55.55 N	109.00 W
Petersberg	56	50.33 N	9.43 E
Peters Brook ≃	276	40.33 N	74.37 W
Petersburg, Ak., U.S.	180	56.49 N	132.57 W
Petersburg, Il., U.S.	219	40.00 N	89.50 W
Petersburg, In., U.S.	194	38.29 N	87.16 W
Petersburg, Mi., U.S.	216	41.54 N	83.42 W
Petersburg, Ne., U.S.	198	41.51 N	98.04 W
Petersburg, N.J., U.S.	208	39.15 N	74.43 W
Petersburg, N.Y., U.S.	210	42.44 N	73.20 W
Petersburg, Oh., U.S.	214	40.54 N	80.31 W
Petersburg, Pa., U.S.	214	40.34 N	78.03 W
Petersburg, Tn., U.S.	194	35.19 N	86.38 W
Petersburg, Tx., U.S.	196	33.52 N	101.36 W
Petersburg, Va., U.S.	208	37.13 N	77.24 W
Petersburg, W.V., U.S.	188	38.59 N	79.07 W
Petersburg National Battlefield ♠	208	37.14 N	77.22 W
Peters Canyon Reservoir ⊜1	280	33.47 N	117.45 W
Peters Creek ≃, Ca., U.S.	282	37.15 N	122.13 W
Peters Creek ≃, Pa., U.S.	279b	40.18 N	79.52 W
Peters Creek, Piney Fork ≃	279b	40.16 N	79.58 W
Petersdorf	54	54.29 N	11.04 E
Petersfield, S. Afr.	273d	26.14 S	28.26 E
Petersfield, Eng., U.K.	42	51.00 N	0.56 W
Petershagen, Dtsch.	52	52.23 N	8.58 E
Petershagen, Dtsch.	54	52.24 N	14.20 E
Petershagen bei Berlin	54	52.31 N	13.46 E
Petersham, Austl.	274a	33.54 S	151.09 E
Petersham, Ma., U.S.	207	42.29 N	72.11 W
Peters Hill ∧2	168b	34.11 S	138.50 E
Peterson	198	42.55 N	95.20 W
Peterson Air Force Base ■	198	38.49 N	104.42 W
Peters Pond ⊜	283	42.43 N	71.16 W
Peterswald Hill ∧2	162	26.43 S	123.39 E
Peter the Great Bay → Petra Velikogo, zaliv ⊂	89	42.40 N	132.00 E
Peter the Great Monument ⊥	265a	59.56 N	30.18 E
Pétervására	30	48.01 N	20.06 E
Petilia Policastro	68	39.07 N	16.47 E
Pétionville	238	18.31 N	72.17 W
Petit	273d	26.06 S	28.22 E
Petit Bois Island I	194	30.12 N	88.26 W
Petit-Bourg	241o	16.12 N	61.36 W
Petit-Canal	241o	16.23 N	61.29 W
Petitcodiac	186	45.56 N	65.10 W
Petitcodiac ≃	186	45.50 N	64.33 W
Petit Cul-de-Sac Marin ⊂	241o	16.12 N	61.33 W
Petite Nation, Rivière de la ≃	206	45.35 N	75.06 W
Petite Rivière du Chêne ≃	206	46.34 N	72.02 W
Petite Rivière Noire, Piton de la ∧	157c	20.24 S	57.24 E
Petite Rivière Rouge ≃	206	45.45 N	75.00 W
Petites-Anses	241o	15.51 N	61.39 W
Petite Sauldre ≃	50	47.27 N	2.05 E
Petite Terre, Îles de la II	241o	16.10 N	61.07 W
Petit Forte	186	47.24 N	54.40 W
Petit-Fort-Philippe	50	51.00 N	2.07 E
Petit-Goâve	238	18.26 N	72.52 W
Petit Jean ≃	194	35.10 N	92.56 W
Petit Jean State Park ♠	194	35.06 N	92.57 W
Petit Loango	152	2.16 S	9.35 E
Petit Loango, Parc National du ♠	152	2.15 S	9.36 E
Petit Mécatina, Île du I	186	50.33 N	59.20 W
Petit Morin ≃	50	48.56 N	3.07 E
Petitot ≃	176	60.14 N	123.29 W
Petit Piton ∧	241f	13.50 N	61.04 W
Petit Rhône ≃	62	43.27 N	4.24 E
Petit-Saint-Bernard, Col du)(	62	45.41 N	6.53 E
Petitsikapau Lake ⊜	176	54.45 N	66.25 W
Petkeljärven Kansallispuisto ♠	24	62.35 N	31.12 E
Petkus	54	51.59 N	13.21 E
Petlād	120	22.28 N	72.48 E
Petlalcingo	232	18.05 N	97.54 W
Peto	232	20.08 N	88.55 W
Petoh	114	2.53 N	103.15 E
Petone	172	41.13 S	174.52 E
Petorca	252	32.15 S	70.56 W
Petoskey	190	45.22 N	84.57 W
Petownikip Lake ⊜	184	52.56 N	92.02 W
Petra → Baṭrā ⊥	132	30.20 N	35.26 E
Petralia Soprana	70	37.47 N	14.06 E
Petralia Sottana	70	37.48 N	14.05 E
Petras, Mount ∧	9	75.52 S	128.38 W
Petra Velikogo, zaliv (Peter the Great Bay) ⊂	89	42.40 N	132.00 E
Petre, Point ›	212	43.50 N	77.09 W
Petrecovo	24	61.18 N	57.07 E
Petrella, Monte ∧	66	41.18 N	13.40 E
Petrella Salto	66	42.18 N	13.04 E
Petrella Tifernina	66	41.41 N	14.42 E
Petrič	38	41.24 N	23.13 E
Petrie	171a	27.16 S	152.59 E
Petrified Forest National Park ♠	200	34.55 N	109.49 W
Petrikov	78	52.08 N	28.30 E
Petrikovka	78	48.43 N	34.37 E
Petrila	38	45.27 N	23.25 E
Petrinja	36	45.26 N	16.17 E
Petriščevo, Ross.	82	54.37 N	36.57 E
Petriščevo, Ross.	82	55.30 N	36.18 E
Petrítis, Ákra ›	267c	37.56 N	23.24 E
Petrodvorec	76	59.53 N	29.54 E
Petroglyphs Provincial Park ♠	212	44.33 N	77.53 W
Petrogrado-Doneckoje ◆8	83	48.42 N	38.41 E
Petrograd → Sankt-Peterburg	76	59.55 N	30.15 E
Petrohué	254	41.08 S	72.25 W
Petrokrepost'	265a	59.57 N	31.02 E
Petrolândia	250	9.05 S	38.18 W
Petrólea	246	8.30 N	72.35 W
Petroleum	216	40.36 N	85.09 W
Petrolia, On., Can.	214	42.52 N	82.09 W
Petrolia, Pa., U.S.	214	41.01 N	79.43 W
Petrolia, Tx., U.S.	196	34.01 N	98.14 W
Petrolina	250	9.24 S	40.30 W
Petrolina de Goiás	255	16.06 S	49.20 W
Petronà	68	39.03 N	16.45 E
Petrona, Punta ›	240m	17.56 N	66.23 W
Petronila Creek ≃	196	27.32 N	97.32 W
Petropavlovka, Ross.	78	50.06 N	40.54 E
Petropavlovka, Ross.	88	50.38 N	105.19 E
Petropavlovka, Ukr.	78	48.27 N	36.26 E
Petropavlovka, Ukr.	83	49.43 N	37.42 E
Petropavlovsk, Kaz.	86	54.54 N	69.06 E
Petropavlovsk, Ross.	86	56.20 N	57.09 E
Petropavlovsk-Kamčatskij	74	53.01 N	158.39 E
Petropavlovskoje, Ross.	86	52.04 N	84.08 E
Petropavlovskoje, Ross.	88	58.13 N	108.59 E
Petrópolis	256	22.31 S	43.10 W
Petros	192	36.05 N	84.26 W
Petroșani	38	45.25 N	23.22 E
Petrosino	70	37.43 N	12.29 E
Petro-Slav'anka	265a	59.48 N	30.31 E
Petroso, Monte ∧	66	41.44 N	13.55 E
Petroúpolis	267c	38.03 N	23.41 E
Petrovac	38	44.22 N	21.27 E
Petrovgrad → Zrenjanin	38	45.23 N	20.24 E
Petrovka, Ross.	80	53.13 N	51.58 E
Petrovka, Ukr.	78	46.54 N	30.44 E
Petrovka, Ukr.	83	48.53 N	39.52 E
Petrovka, Ukr.	83	48.48 N	39.16 E
Petrovo, Ross.	76	58.22 N	35.09 E
Petrovo, Ross.	82	55.00 N	38.08 E
Petrovo, Ross.	88	54.30 N	105.15 E
Petrovo, Ukr.	78	48.20 N	33.16 E
Petrovo-Dal'neje	265b	55.45 N	37.11 E
Petrovo-Krasnoselje ◆8	83	48.18 N	38.52 E
Petrovsk	80	52.19 N	45.23 E
Petrovskaja	78	45.25 N	37.57 E
Petrovskij, Ross.	80	56.39 N	40.19 E
Petrovskij, Ross.	80	50.45 N	41.59 E
Petrovskij, Ross.	82	54.29 N	36.59 E
Petrovskoje, Ross.	80	52.39 N	40.15 E
Petrovskoje, Ross.	80	57.01 N	39.16 E
Petrovskoje, Ross.	82	55.27 N	38.21 E
Petrovskoje, Ross.	82	55.32 N	36.59 E
Petrovskoje, Ross.	265b	55.36 N	37.53 E
Petrovskoje, Ukr.	78	49.10 N	36.54 E
Petrovskoje, Ukr.	83	48.18 N	38.52 E
Petrovsko-Razumovskoje ◆8	265b	55.50 N	37.34 E
Petrovsk-Zabajkal'skij	88	51.17 N	108.50 E
Petrov Val	80	50.09 N	45.12 E
Petrozavodsk	24	61.47 N	34.20 E
Petrozseny → Petroșani	38	45.25 N	23.22 E
Petrun'	24	66.28 N	60.43 E
Petrusburg	158	29.08 S	25.27 E
Petrušino	265a	59.48 N	30.50 E
Petrus Steyn	158	27.38 S	28.08 E
Petrusville	158	30.05 S	24.41 E
Petschora → Pečora ≃	24	68.13 N	54.15 E
Petten	52	52.45 N	4.39 E
Pettenbach	61	47.57 N	14.01 E
Petteril ≃	44	54.54 N	2.55 W
Petticoat Creek ≃	275b	43.48 N	79.06 W
Pettigoe	48	54.33 N	7.50 W
Pettinascura, Monte ∧	68	39.22 N	16.37 E
Pettineo	70	37.58 N	14.17 E
Pettisville	216	41.31 N	84.13 W
Pettnau	64	47.18 N	11.08 E
Pettneu am Arlberg	58	47.09 N	10.20 E
Pettus	196	28.37 N	97.48 W
Petty Harbour	186	47.28 N	52.43 W
Petty Island I	285	39.58 N	75.07 W
Petua	272b	22.25 N	88.27 E
Petuchovo	86	55.06 N	67.58 E
Petuški	80	55.55 N	39.28 E
Petworth	42	50.59 N	0.38 W
Petzow	264a	52.21 N	12.56 E
Peudada	114	5.12 N	96.35 E
Peuerbach	60	48.21 N	13.56 E
Peuetsagoe, Gunung ∧	114	4.55 N	96.20 E
Peureulak	114	4.48 N	97.53 E
Peureulak ≃	114	4.54 N	97.53 E
Peureulak, Ujung ›	114	4.54 N	97.54 E
Peusangan ≃	114	5.16 N	96.51 E
Peusangan, Ujung ›	114	5.16 N	96.50 E
Pevek	74	69.42 N	170.17 E
Pevely	219	38.17 N	90.23 W
Pevensey	42	50.49 N	0.20 E
Pevensey Levels ≖	42	50.50 N	0.20 E
Peveragno	62	44.20 N	7.37 E
Pewamo	216	43.00 N	84.50 W
Pewaukee	216	43.04 N	88.15 W
Pewaukee Lake ⊜	216	43.04 N	88.19 W
Pewee Valley	218	38.18 N	85.29 W
Pews Creek ≃	276	40.27 N	74.06 W
Pewsey	42	51.21 N	1.46 W
Pewsey, Vale of ∨	42	51.20 N	1.48 W
Péyia	130	34.53 N	32.23 E
Peykjahlíð	24a	65.40 N	16.50 W
Peyrolles-en-Provence	62	43.39 N	5.35 E
Peyruis	62	44.02 N	5.56 E
Peza ≃	24	65.36 N	44.35 E
Pezas	86	54.39 N	87.46 E
Pezawa Taung ∧	110	19.33 N	94.31 E
Pézenas	32	43.27 N	3.25 E
Peženga	76	59.10 N	44.16 E
Pezinok	30	48.18 N	17.17 E
Pezu	123	32.19 N	70.44 E
Pezzana	62	45.16 N	8.29 E
Pfäfers	58	46.59 N	9.30 E
Pfaffenhausen	58	48.07 N	10.27 E
Pfaffenhofen an der Ilm	60	48.31 N	11.30 E

Symbols in the index entries represent the broad categories identified in the key at the right. Symbols with superior numbers (⋏1) identify subcategories (see complete key on page I · 1).

Symbole im Register stellen die rechts im Schlüssel erklärten Kategorien dar. Symbole mit hochgestellten Ziffern (⋏1) bezeichnen Unterabteilungen einer Kategorie (vgl. vollständiger Schlüssel auf Seite I · 1).

Los símbolos incluídos en el texto del índice representan las grandes categorías identificadas con la clave a la derecha. Los símbolos con números en su parte superior (⋏1) identifican las subcategorías (véase la clave completa en la página I · 1).

Les symboles de l'index représentent les catégories indiquées dans la légende à droite. Les symboles suivis d'un indice (⋏1) représentent des sous-catégories (voir légende complète à la page I · 1).

Os símbolos incluídos no texto do índice representam as grandes categorias identificadas com a chave à direita. Os símbolos com números em sua parte superior (⋏1) identificam as subcategorias (veja-se a chave completa à página I · 1).

	English	Deutsch	Español	Français	Português
∧	Mountain	Berg	Montaña	Montagne	Montanha
⋏	Mountains	Gebirge	Montañas	Montagnes	Montanhas
)(	Pass	Paß	Paso	Col	Passo
∨	Valley, Canyon	Tal, Cañon	Valle, Cañón	Vallée, Canyon	Vale, Canhão
≖	Plain	Ebene	Llano	Plaine	Planície
›	Cape	Kap	Cabo	Cap	Cabo
I	Island	Insel	Isla	Île	Ilha
II	Islands	Inseln	Islas	Îles	Ilhas
⊥	Other Topographic Features	Andere Topographische Objekte	Otros Elementos Topográficos	Autres données topographiques	Outros acidentes topográficos

ESPAÑOL Nombre	Página	Lat.°′	Long.°′ W=Oeste
Pfaffenhoffen	56	48.51 N	7.37 E
Pfaffenöden ⋏²	264b	48.04 N	16.33 E
Pfäffikersee ⊘	58	47.21 N	8.48 E
Pfäffikon	58	47.22 N	8.47 E
Pfaffnau	58	47.14 N	7.54 E
Pfaffstätten	264b	48.01 N	16.16 E
Pfalz ⊡⁵	56	49.20 N	8.00 E
Pfalzdorf	52	51.42 N	6.11 E
Pfalzel	56	49.47 N	6.41 E
Pfänder ⋏	58	47.30 N	9.47 E
Pfarrkirchen	60	48.27 N	12.56 E
Pfarrweisach	56	50.09 N	10.44 E
Pfastatt	58	47.47 N	7.18 E
Pfatter	60	48.58 N	12.23 E
Pfaueninsel, Schloss ⊥	264a	52.26 N	13.07 E
Pfeddersheim	56	49.38 N	8.16 E
Pfeffenhausen	60	48.40 N	11.58 E
Pfeiffer-Big Sur State Park ♦	226	36.15 N	121.47 W
Pferderennbahn ♦	263	51.31 N	7.32 E
Pflugerville	222	30.26 N	97.37 W
Pforzen	58	47.55 N	10.37 E
Pforzheim	56	48.54 N	8.42 E
Pfreimd ⋍	60	49.29 N	12.11 E
Pfrimm ⋍	56	49.39 N	8.22 E
Pfronten	58	47.34 N	10.33 E
Pfuhl	58	48.24 N	10.02 E
Pfullendorf	58	47.55 N	9.15 E
Pfullingen	58	48.28 N	9.13 E
Pfunds	58	46.58 N	10.33 E
Pfungstadt	56	49.48 N	8.36 E
Pfyn	56	47.36 N	8.57 E
Pha-an	110	16.53 N	97.38 E
Phachi	110	13.56 N	99.24 E
Phaéton, Port ⊂	174s	17.44 S	149.21 W
Phagwära	123	31.14 N	75.46 E
Phala	156	23.45 S	26.57 E
Phalaborwa	156	23.55 S	31.13 E
Phalanx	214	41.15 N	80.58 W
Phalempin	50	50.31 N	3.01 E
Phälia	123	32.26 N	73.35 E
Phalodi	120	27.08 N	72.22 E
Phalsbourg	56	46.46 N	7.16 E
Phalta	126	22.17 N	88.07 E
Phaltan	122	17.59 N	74.26 E
Phälti	272b	22.46 N	88.34 E
Phan	110	19.28 N	99.43 E
Phanat Nikhom	110	13.27 N	101.11 E
Phangan, Ko I	110	9.45 N	100.04 E
Phang Hoei, Khao ⋏	110	15.15 N	101.23 E
Phangnga	110	8.28 N	98.32 E
Phaniang ⋍	110	16.49 N	102.24 E
Phanom Dongrak, Thiu Khao ⋏	110	14.25 N	103.30 E
Phanom Thuan	110	14.07 N	99.42 E
Phan Rang	110	11.34 N	108.59 E
Phan Thiet	110	10.56 N	108.06 E
Phan Thong	110	13.28 N	101.06 E
Phantom Lake	216	42.52 N	88.21 W
Pharenda	124	27.06 N	83.17 E
Phariäro	120	27.12 N	68.59 E
Pharr	196	26.11 N	98.11 W
Phasi Charoen	269a	13.43 N	100.26 E
Phasi Charoen, Khlong ≊	269a	13.44 N	100.30 E
Phat Diem	110	20.06 N	106.06 E
Phato	110	9.48 N	98.48 E
Phatthalung	110	7.37 N	100.05 E
Phayao	110	19.10 N	99.55 E
Pheasant Creek ⋍	184	50.35 N	103.28 W
Pheba	110	33.35 N	88.56 W
Phelan	228	34.25 N	117.34 W
Phelps, N.Y., U.S.	210	42.57 N	77.03 W
Phelps, Tx., U.S.	222	30.42 N	95.27 W
Phelps, Wi., U.S.	190	46.03 N	89.05 W
Phelps Lake ⊘	192	35.46 N	76.27 W
Phenix City	192	32.28 N	85.00 W
Phepane ⋍	156	25.50 S	22.45 E
Phet Buri	110	13.13 N	99.59 E
Phetchabun	110	16.25 N	101.08 E
Phetchabun, Thiu Khao ⋏	110	16.20 N	100.55 E
Phetchaburi	110	13.06 N	99.57 E
Phetchaburi ⋍	110	13.15 N	100.05 E
Phichai	110	17.17 N	100.05 E
Phichit	110	16.26 N	100.22 E
Philadelphia, S. Afr.	158	33.40 S	18.36 E
Philadelphia, Il., U.S.	219	39.58 N	90.07 W
Philadelphia, Ms., U.S.	194	36.54 N	89.07 W
Philadelphia, Mo., U.S.	219	39.50 N	91.44 W
Philadelphia, N.Y., U.S.	212	44.09 N	75.42 W
Philadelphia, Pa., U.S.	208	39.57 N	75.09 W
Philadelphia, Pa., U.S.	208	39.57 N	75.09 W
Philadelphia, Tn., U.S.	192	35.40 N	84.24 W
Philadelphia ▫⁶	285	39.57 N	75.07 W
Philadelphia International Airport ⊠	208	39.53 N	75.14 W
Philadelphia Museum of Art ⊥	285	39.58 N	75.11 W
Philadelphia Naval Shipyard ⊥	285	39.53 N	75.11 W
Philae ⊥	140	24.01 N	32.53 E
Phil Campbell	194	34.21 N	87.42 W
Philip	198	44.02 N	101.39 W
Philipp	194	33.45 N	90.12 W
Pi ⋍	100	32.26 N	116.34 E
Pia	154	4.00 N	26.17 E
Pianau Pass ⋏	175c	7.21 N	116.44 E
Piabas	250	1.12 S	46.54 W
Piabetá	256	22.37 S	43.10 W
Piabonha ⋍	256	22.07 S	43.08 W
Piaçabuçu	250	10.24 S	36.25 W
Piacatuba	256	21.29 S	42.47 W
Piacenza	62	45.01 N	9.40 E
Piacenza ▫⁴	62	44.53 N	9.35 E
Piacouadie, Lac ⊘	186	51.16 N	71.30 W
Piadena	62	45.08 N	10.22 E
Piaggine	68	40.21 N	15.23 E
Piako ⋍	172	37.12 S	175.30 E
Pialba	166	25.17 S	152.51 E
Piäli ⋍	272b	22.35 N	88.28 E
Piana	70	41.22 N	8.13 E
Piana Crixia	62	44.29 N	8.18 E
Piana degli Albanesi	70	38.00 N	13.17 E
Piana degli Albanesi, Lago di ⊘	70	37.58 N	13.18 E
Piana Mwanga	154	7.40 S	28.10 E
Piancastagnaio	62	42.51 N	11.41 E
Piancó	250	7.12 S	37.57 W
Pian di Sco	66	43.38 N	11.33 E
Pianella	62	42.24 N	14.02 E
Pianello Val Tidone	62	44.57 N	9.24 E
Piangan	110	7.18 N	124.32 E
Pianjiaojie	102	26.01 N	100.32 E
Piankatank ⋍	208	37.32 N	76.18 W
Pianling	104	41.24 N	123.58 E
Piano d'Arta	64	46.29 N	13.01 E
Piano de Voglio	66	44.09 N	11.13 E
Pianosa, Isola I	66	42.35 N	10.04 E
Pianosa, Isola I, It.	36	45.55 N	15.02 E
Pianosinatico	66	44.07 N	10.44 E
Pianottoli-Caldarello, Fr.	71	41.29 N	9.03 E
Pians	58	47.08 N	10.30 E
Piapot	184	49.59 N	109.07 W

FRANÇAIS Nom	Page	Lat.°′	Long.°′ W=Ouest
Philmont	210	42.14 N	73.39 W
Philo, Il., U.S.	194	40.00 N	88.09 W
Philo, Oh., U.S.	188	39.51 N	81.54 W
Philomath	202	44.32 N	123.21 W
Philpots Island I	176	74.48 N	80.00 W
Phimai	110	15.13 N	102.30 E
Phinga	272b	22.41 N	88.25 E
Phitsanulok	110	16.50 N	100.15 E
Phnom Penh — Phnum Pénh	110	11.33 N	104.55 E
Phnum Pénh	110	11.33 N	104.55 E
Phnum Tbëng Méanchey	110	13.49 N	104.58 E
Pho ⋍	124	27.41 N	89.53 E
Phoenicia	210	42.05 N	74.18 W
Phoenix, Az., U.S.	200	33.26 N	112.04 W
Phoenix, Il., U.S.	278	41.36 N	87.38 W
Phoenix, Md., U.S.	208	39.30 N	76.36 W
Phoenix, N.Y., U.S.	210	43.13 N	76.18 W
Phoenix Islands II	14	4.00 S	172.00 W
Phoenix Lake ⊘¹	282	37.57 N	122.35 W
Phoenix Park ♦	281	42.24 N	83.27 W
Phoenixville	208	40.07 N	75.30 W
Phon	110	15.49 N	102.36 E
Phong ⋍	110	16.23 N	102.56 E
Phöngsali	110	21.41 N	102.06 E
Phong Tho	110	22.32 N	103.21 E
Phon Phisai	110	18.01 N	103.05 E
Phosphate Hill	166	21.52 S	139.51 E
Phrae	110	18.09 N	100.08 E
Phra Khanong ⋍⁸	269a	13.42 N	100.35 E
Phra Nakhon — Krung Thep	110	13.45 N	100.31 E
Phra Nakhon Si Ayutthaya	110	14.21 N	100.33 E
Phran Kratai	110	16.40 N	99.36 E
Phrao	110	19.22 N	99.13 E
Phra Pradaeng	269a	13.40 N	100.32 E
Phra Rop, Khao ⋏	110	13.11 N	99.31 E
Phrom Phiram	110	17.02 N	100.12 E
Phrygia ⊡¹	130	39.00 N	30.00 E
Prsar Réam	110	10.30 N	103.37 E
Phu Cat	110	14.01 N	109.03 E
Phu Huu, Viet	110	18.58 N	105.31 E
Phu Huu, Viet	269c	10.43 N	106.47 E
Phu Loc	110	16.16 N	107.53 E
Phücphür	124	25.33 N	62.06 E
Phuira	123	34.20 N	73.03 E
Phultala	110	22.59 N	89.28 E
Phu Ly	110	20.32 N	105.56 E
Phum Duang ⋍	110	9.10 N	99.20 E
Phumi Bǎ Khám	110	13.51 N	107.22 E
Phumi Banam	110	11.19 N	105.18 E
Phumi Bèng	110	13.05 N	104.18 E
Phumi Chämbák	110	11.14 N	104.49 E
Phumi Chämpho Ándëng	110	12.39 N	104.35 E
Phumi Chhuk	110	10.50 N	104.28 E
Phumi Chruóy Slëng	110	13.14 N	105.57 E
Phumi Dák Dám	110	12.25 N	107.45 E
Phumi Kämpóng Srálau	110	14.05 N	105.46 E
Phumi Kämpóng Trábák	110	13.06 N	105.14 E
Phumi Käntuót Sämraóng	110	14.12 N	104.37 E
Phumi Kaóh Kért	110	13.47 N	104.32 E
Phumi Kaôh Kông	110	11.26 N	103.11 E
Phumi Khpôb	110	11.02 N	105.12 E
Phumi Krêk	110	11.46 N	105.56 E
Phumi Lvéa Kraôm	110	11.23 N	102.54 E
Phumi Mörüng	110	11.33 N	103.33 E
Phumi Narüng	110	13.53 N	105.34 E
Phumi Phnum Srälau	110	11.03 N	103.42 E
Phumi Prêk Kák	110	12.15 N	105.22 E
Phumi Prey Toch	110	12.54 N	103.23 E
Phumi Puók Chäs	110	13.26 N	103.44 E
Phumi Sämraông	110	13.19 N	104.00 E
Phumi Sämraóng	110	14.11 N	103.31 E
Phumi Spœ Tbong	110	12.20 N	105.19 E
Phumi Srê Kôkir	110	13.08 N	106.04 E
Phumi Srê Rônéam	110	12.16 N	106.25 E
Phumi Thalabärivät	110	13.33 N	105.57 E
Phumi Thmâ Pôk	110	13.57 N	103.04 E
Phumi Tœk Choû	110	13.36 N	103.24 E
Phu My	110	14.10 N	109.03 E
Phung Hiep	110	9.49 N	105.50 E
Phuntsholing	124	26.52 N	89.23 E
Phuoc Binh	110	11.50 N	106.58 E
Phuoc Khanh	269c	10.40 N	106.48 E
Phuoc Long	110	11.50 N	106.44 E
Phuoc Long Xa	269c	10.49 N	106.46 E
Phuoc Luong	269c	10.48 N	106.48 E
Phu Quoc	110	10.13 N	103.58 E
Phu Quoc, Dao I	110	10.12 N	104.00 E
Phurphura	272b	22.44 N	88.08 E
Phu Tho	110	21.24 N	105.13 E
Phu Tho Hoa	269c	10.46 N	106.40 E
Phu Tho Race Track ♦	269c	10.46 N	106.40 E
Phutthaisong	110	15.32 N	103.01 E
Phu Vang	110	16.31 N	107.37 E
Phu Yen	110	21.16 N	104.39 E
Pi ⋍	100	32.26 N	116.34 E

PORTUGUÊS Nome	Página	Lat.°′	Long.°′ W=Oeste
Piapot Indian Reserve ⋪⁴	184	50.45 N	104.26 W
Piasa	219	39.07 N	90.07 W
Piasa Creek ⋍	219	38.56 N	90.17 W
Piaseczno	30	52.05 N	21.01 E
Piashti, Lac ⊘	186	50.29 N	62.52 W
Piaski	30	51.08 N	22.51 E
Piatã	255	13.09 S	41.48 W
Piatra-Neamţ	38	46.56 N	26.22 E
Piatra Olt	38	44.24 N	24.16 E
Piatt ▫⁶	219	40.00 N	88.35 W
Piau	256	21.31 S	43.19 W
Piaui ≈, Bra.	255	6.38 S	42.42 W
Piaui ⋍, Bra.	250	6.38 S	42.42 W
Piaui ≈, Bra.	255	16.41 S	41.53 W
Piaui, Morro do ⋏	255	14.59 S	47.31 W
Piave ⋍	64	45.32 N	12.44 E
Piawaning	162	30.51 S	116.22 E
Piaxtla ⋍	232	23.42 N	106.49 W
Piazza Armerina	70	37.23 N	14.22 E
Piazzi, Isla I	252	51.45 S	74.05 W
Piazzola sul Brenta	64	45.32 N	11.47 E
Piberegg	42	47.05 N	15.05 E
Pibor ⋍	140	8.26 N	33.13 E
Pibor Post	140	6.48 N	33.08 E
Pibroch	182	54.16 N	113.52 W
Pic ⋍	190	48.36 N	86.18 W
Pica	248	20.30 S	69.21 W
Picacho	200	32.42 N	111.29 W
Picacho, Cerro del ⋏	286a	19.35 N	99.08 W
Pičajevo	50	53.15 N	42.12 E
Picanoc ⋍	190	46.05 N	76.03 W
Picardie ⊡⁹	50	49.45 N	2.50 E
Picentini, Monti ⋏	68	40.45 N	15.00 E
Picerno	68	40.38 N	15.38 E
Piceance Creek ⋍	200	40.05 N	108.14 W
Piccadilly	186	48.34 N	58.55 W
Piccadilly Station ⋪⁵	262	53.28 N	2.14 W
Piccione	66	43.11 N	12.31 E
Piccolo, Mar (Taranto) ⋎²	68	40.29 N	17.16 E
Piccotts End	260	51.46 N	0.28 W
Pic de Tío ⋏	150	8.52 N	8.54 W
Piceno	68	42.53 N	13.35 E
Piçarra	62	45.03 N	11.41 E
Pich ⋍	123	34.52 N	71.09 E
Pichana ⋍	246	3.31 S	71.43 W
Pichanal	252	23.19 S	64.13 W
Picher	106	36.59 N	94.49 E
Pichhor	124	25.58 N	78.24 E
Pichi-Mahuída	252	38.50 S	64.57 W
Pichincha ▫⁴	246	0.10 S	78.40 W
Pichincha ⋏	246	0.10 S	78.40 W
Pichl bei Wels	60	48.11 N	13.54 E
Pichor	124	25.11 N	78.11 E
Pichtovka	86	56.00 N	82.42 E
Pichucalco	234	17.31 N	93.09 W
Picinguaba	256	23.22 S	44.50 W
Picinisco	66	41.39 N	13.52 E
Pic Island I	190	48.43 N	86.38 W
Pickardville	182	54.03 N	113.53 W
Pickaway ▫¹⁰	219	39.36 N	82.57 W
Pickens, Ms., U.S.	194	32.53 N	89.58 W
Pickens, S.C., U.S.	192	34.53 N	82.42 W
Pickens, W.V., U.S.	188	38.39 N	80.12 W
Pickensville	194	33.14 N	88.16 W
Pickerel ⋍	190	45.55 N	80.50 W
Pickerel Lake ⊘	184	52.36 N	99.30 W
Pickering, On., Can.	212	43.52 N	79.02 W
Pickering, Eng., U.K.	262	54.14 N	0.46 W
Pickering Beach	212	43.50 N	78.59 W
Pickering Brook	168a	32.03 S	116.08 E
Pickering Creek ⋍	285	40.08 N	75.30 W
Pickering Creek Reservoir ⊘¹	285	40.07 N	75.30 W
Pickett, Lake ⊘	220	28.36 N	81.07 W
Pickford	190	46.09 N	84.21 W
Pick'ajevo	50	54.17 N	42.27 E
Pickmere ⊘	262	53.17 N	2.29 W
Pickstown	198	43.04 N	98.31 W
Pickton	222	33.02 N	95.24 W
Pickwick Lake ⊘¹	194	35.00 N	88.10 W
Pickwick Landing Dam ⋎⁶	194	35.04 N	88.21 W
Picnic Point ⋗	274b	37.57 S	145.00 E
Pico	66	41.27 N	13.34 E
Pico, Il.	150a	14.56 N	24.21 W
Pico, Ponta do ⋏	148a	38.28 N	28.20 W
Pico de Orizaba, Parque Nacional ♦	246	0.30 N	66.00 W
Pico Rivera	228	33.58 N	118.05 W
Picos	250	7.05 S	41.28 W
Picota	248	6.55 S	76.20 W
Pico Truncado	252	46.48 S	67.58 W
Picquigny	50	49.57 N	2.09 E
Picton, Austl.	110	15.32 N	150.36 E
Picton, On., Can.	212	44.00 N	77.08 W
Picton, N.Z.	172	41.18 S	174.01 E
Picton, Eng., U.K.	262	53.14 S	2.51 W
Picton, Isla I	252	55.02 S	66.57 W
Picton Bay ⊂	212	44.03 N	77.08 W
Picton Junction	186	45.41 N	62.43 W
Pictou	186	45.41 N	62.43 W
Pictou Island I	186	45.50 N	62.34 W
Picture Butte	182	49.53 N	112.47 W
Pictured Rocks National Lakeshore ♦	190	46.35 N	86.20 W
Picture Rocks	208	41.17 N	76.43 W
Picúa, Punta ⋗	240m	18.25 N	65.46 W
Picui	250	6.31 S	36.21 W
Picunda	84	43.12 N	40.21 E
Picún Leufú	254	39.31 S	69.15 W
Picún Leufú, Arroyo ⋍	254	39.31 S	69.08 W
Picuris Indian Reservation ⋪⁴	200	36.12 N	105.42 W
Pidálion, Akrotírion ⋗	130	34.56 N	34.05 E
Pidarak	128	25.51 N	63.18 E
Piddle ⋍	262	50.42 N	2.04 W
Piddletrenthide	262	50.48 N	2.25 W
Pidie	112	5.23 N	95.56 E
Pidurutalagala ⋏	122	7.00 N	80.46 E
Piedade	287a	22.41 S	43.05 W
Piedade do Baruel	287b	23.37 S	46.18 W
Piedade do Rio Grande	256	21.28 S	44.12 W

Nome	Página	Lat.°′	Long.°′
Piedecuesta	246	6.59 S	73.03 W
Piedicavallo	62	45.42 N	7.57 E
Piedicroce	71	42.23 N	9.23 E
Piedimonte Etneo	70	37.48 N	15.12 E
Piedimonte Matese	68	41.21 N	14.22 E
Piedimonte San Germano	66	41.30 N	13.45 E
Piè di Ripa	66	44.07 N	10.44 E
Piedmont, Al., U.S.	194	33.55 N	85.37 W
Piedmont, Ca., U.S.	282	37.49 N	122.13 W
Piedmont, Mo., U.S.	194	37.09 N	90.41 W
Piedmont, S.C., U.S.	192	34.42 N	82.27 W
Piedmont, S.C., U.S.	192	34.54 N	82.27 W
Piedmont Lake ⊘¹	214	40.08 N	81.11 W

Nome	Página	Lat.°′	Long.°′
Piedra, C.R.	236	9.29 N	83.40 W
Piedra, Ca., U.S.	226	36.48 N	119.22 W
Piedra ⋍	200	37.01 N	107.24 W
Piedra, Cerro ⋏	252	37.41 S	73.07 W
Piedra Azul, Quebrada ⋍	286c	10.36 N	66.57 W
Piedrabuena	34	39.02 N	4.10 W
Piedra de Águila	254	40.03 S	70.05 W
Piedra del Águila, Embalse ⊘¹	254	40.30 S	70.20 W
Piedrafita, Puerto de ⋌	34	42.40 N	7.01 W
Piedrahita	34	40.28 N	5.19 W
Piedra Roja	236	8.38 N	81.48 W
Piedras, Arroyo de las ⋍	288	34.43 S	58.19 W
Piedras, Punta ⋗, Arg.	258	35.25 S	57.08 W
Piedras, Punta ⋗, Ven.	116	10.40 N	61.40 W
Piedras Blancas	252	31.11 S	59.56 W
Piedras Blancas, Point ⋗	226	35.40 N	121.17 W
Piedras Coloradas	252	32.23 S	57.36 W
Piedras Negras, Guat.	232	17.11 N	91.15 W
Piedras Negras, Méx.	232	28.42 N	100.31 W
Piedras Negras ⊥	232	17.12 N	91.15 W
Piedra Sola	252	32.04 S	56.21 W
Piediluco ⋍	62	42.58 N	12.05 E
Pie Island I	190	48.15 N	89.05 W
Pieksämäki	26	62.18 N	27.08 E
Piela	150	12.42 N	0.08 W
Pielach ⋍	42	48.15 N	15.22 E
Pielavesi	26	63.14 N	26.45 E
Pielavesi ⊘	26	63.18 N	26.35 E
Pieljekaise Nationalpark ♦	24	66.18 N	16.58 E
Piémonte ▫⁴	62	45.00 N	8.00 E
Pienaarsrivier	156	25.15 S	28.18 E
Piendamó	246	2.38 N	76.30 W
Pieniężno	30	54.15 N	20.08 E
Pieniński Park Narodowy ♦	30	49.25 N	20.25 E
Pieni-Salpausselkä ⋏	26	61.08 N	27.20 E
Pienza	62	43.04 N	11.41 E
Pierce, Co., U.S.	200	40.38 N	104.45 W
Pierce, Fl., U.S.	220	27.50 N	81.58 W
Pierce, Id., U.S.	202	46.29 N	115.47 W
Pierce, Ne., U.S.	198	42.11 N	97.31 W
Pierce, Tx., U.S.	222	29.14 N	96.12 W
Pierce City	194	36.56 N	94.00 W
Pierce Lake ⊘, Can.	184	54.10 N	92.56 W
Pierceton	214	41.12 N	85.42 W
Piermont	210	41.03 N	73.55 W
Pierowall	46	59.20 N	2.59 W
Pierpont, Oh., U.S.	214	41.45 N	80.34 W
Pierpont, S.D., U.S.	198	45.29 N	97.49 W
Pierre	198	44.22 N	100.21 W
Pierre, Bayou ⋍, Ms., U.S.	194	31.55 N	91.11 W
Pierre-Buffière	56	45.42 N	1.21 E
Pierreclos	58	46.53 N	5.15 E
Pierrefeu-du-Var	58	43.13 N	6.08 E
Pierrefitte-sur-Aire	50	48.58 N	5.20 E
Pierrefitte-sur-Sauldre	50	47.30 N	2.09 E
Pierrefonds, P.Q., Can.	206	46.04 N	72.49 W
Pierreville, Trin.	241r	10.18 N	61.00 W
Pierron	219	38.47 N	89.36 W
Pierron, Lac ⊘	204	34.55 N	88.10 W
Pierry	50	49.01 N	3.56 E
Pierson	192	29.14 N	81.27 W
Piesendorf	60	47.17 N	12.43 E
Piešt'any	30	48.36 N	17.50 E
Piesting ⋍	42	48.00 N	16.30 E
Pietarsaari — Jakobstad	26	63.40 N	22.42 E
Pieterburen	52	53.24 N	6.27 E
Pietermaritzburg	158	29.37 S	30.16 E
Pietersburg	156	23.54 S	29.25 E
Pietrabbondante	66	41.45 N	14.23 E
Pietracatella	66	41.35 N	14.52 E
Pietra del Pertusillo, Lago di ⊘	68	40.17 N	15.58 E
Pietragalla	68	40.49 N	15.53 E
Pietra Ligure	62	44.09 N	8.17 E
Pietralunga	66	43.26 N	12.26 E
Pietramala	66	44.10 N	11.20 E
Pietramelara	68	41.22 N	14.11 E
Pietramontecorvino	68	41.32 N	15.07 E
Pietrapaola	68	39.29 N	16.49 E
Pietrapertosa	68	40.31 N	16.04 E
Pietraperzia	70	37.25 N	14.08 E
Pietrasanta	62	43.57 N	10.14 E
Pietrelcina	68	41.12 N	14.51 E
Pietrosu, Vîrful ⋏, Rom.	38	47.36 N	25.09 E
Pietrosu, Vîrful ⋏, Rom.	38	47.08 N	25.11 E
Pieve	64	45.46 N	10.45 E
Pieve d'Alpago	64	46.09 N	12.22 E
Pieve di Cadore	64	46.26 N	12.22 E
Pieve di Cento	64	44.43 N	11.18 E
Pieve di Soligo	64	45.53 N	12.10 E
Pieve di Teco	62	44.03 N	7.56 E
Pieve Fosciana	66	44.08 N	10.25 E
Pievepelago	66	44.12 N	10.37 E
Pieve Santo Stefano	66	43.40 N	12.02 E
Piffard	210	42.50 N	77.51 W
Pigari	68	51.24 N	49.42 E
Pigeon, Mi., U.S.	190	43.49 N	83.16 W
Pigeon, Mi., U.S.	190	45.13 N	83.16 W

Nome	Página	Lat.°′	Long.°′
Pigeon Creek ⋍, Pa., U.S.	285	40.12 N	75.35 W
Pigeon Forge	192	35.47 N	83.33 W
Pigeon Lake ⊘, Ab., Can.	182	53.00 N	114.00 W
Pigeon Run ⋍	285	40.06 N	75.35 W
Pigeon Swamp ⋪	276	40.23 N	74.29 W
Pigezhuang	105	39.39 N	116.15 E
Pigg ⋍	192	37.00 N	79.29 W
Piggott	194	36.22 N	90.11 W
Piggs Peak	158	25.58 S	31.15 E
Pigkawagan	110	7.12 N	124.32 E
Piglio	66	41.49 N	13.08 E
Pigna	62	43.56 N	7.40 E
Pignans	62	43.18 N	6.13 E
Pignataro Maggiore	68	41.11 N	14.10 E
Pignola	68	40.34 N	15.47 E
Pigs, Bay of — Cochinos, Bahía de ⊂	240p	22.07 N	81.10 W
Pigüé	252	37.37 S	62.25 W
Pigüm-do I	98	34.45 N	125.55 E
Pihama	172	39.30 S	173.56 E
Piha Passage ⋎	174w	21.07 S	175.05 W
Pihäri	124	27.38 N	80.12 E
Pihlajavesi	26	61.45 N	28.50 E
Pihlava	26	61.33 N	21.36 E
Pihtipudas	26	63.23 N	25.34 E
Pihuamo	234	19.15 N	103.23 W
P'ihyön	98	40.01 N	124.37 E
Piikkiö	26	60.26 N	22.31 E
Piippola	26	64.10 N	25.58 E
Pijijiapan	234	15.42 N	93.14 W
Pijnacker	52	52.02 N	4.27 E
Pijol, Pic ⋏	236	15.06 N	87.35 W
Pikal'ovo	76	59.31 N	34.06 E
Pikangikum	184	51.49 N	94.00 W
Pikangikum Lake ⊘	184	51.48 N	94.00 W
Pike	210	42.33 N	78.09 W
Pike ▫⁶, Il., U.S.	219	39.36 N	90.48 W
Pike ▫⁶, Mo., U.S.	219	39.21 N	91.10 W
Pike ▫⁶, Oh., U.S.	218	39.05 N	83.06 W
Pike ▫⁶, Pa., U.S.	210	41.19 N	74.48 W
Pike, North Branch ⋍	190	45.26 N	87.52 W
Pike, South Branch ⋍	190	45.30 N	88.01 W
Pikes Peak	218	39.08 N	86.09 W
Pikes Peak ⋏	200	38.50 N	105.03 W
Pikes Rocks ⋏²	214	41.56 N	79.24 W
Pikesville	208	39.22 N	76.43 W
Piketberg	158	32.54 S	18.46 E
Piketon	218	39.04 N	83.00 W
Piketown	208	40.23 N	76.44 W
Pikeville, Ky., U.S.	192	37.28 N	82.31 W
Pikeville, Tn., U.S.	194	35.36 N	85.11 W
Pikiola	265a	59.42 N	30.08 E
Pikou	98	39.24 N	122.20 E
Pikounda	152	0.33 N	16.42 E
Pikwitonei	184	55.35 N	97.09 W
Pila (Schneidemühl), Pol.	30	53.10 N	16.44 E
Pita ⋍²	58	53.15 N	16.30 E
Pilanesberg ⋪	156	25.14 S	27.04 E
Pilanesberg Game Reserve ♦	156	25.15 S	27.05 E
Pilao Arcado	250	10.00 S	42.29 W
Pilar, Arg.	252	31.41 S	63.54 W
Pilar, Arg.	258	34.27 S	58.54 W
Pilar, Bra.	250	9.36 S	35.56 W
Pilar, Bra.	287a	22.26 S	43.00 W
Pilar, Para.	252	26.52 S	58.23 W
Pilar, Pil.	116	11.29 N	122.55 E
Pilar, Pil.	116	9.52 N	126.06 E
Pilar ⋪⁵	288	34.28 S	58.52 W
Pilar Bay ⊂	116	11.34 N	123.00 E
Pilarcitos Creek ⋍	282	37.33 N	122.25 W
Pilarcitos Lake ⊘	282	37.33 N	122.25 W
Pilar de Goiás	255	14.41 S	49.37 W
Pilar do Sul	255	23.49 S	47.43 W
Pilares	234	30.24 N	104.52 W
Pilas Group II	116	6.31 N	121.35 E
Pilas Island I	116	6.38 N	121.37 E
Pilawa	30	51.53 N	21.33 E
Pilaya ⋍	248	20.55 S	64.04 W
Pilcher Park ♦	278	41.32 N	88.01 W
Pilchuck ⋍	224	48.12 N	122.06 W
Pilchuck Creek ⋍	224	48.18 N	122.20 W
Pil'dozero	24	65.43 N	33.28 E
Piles Creek ⋍	276	40.37 N	74.12 W
Piliga	166	30.21 S	148.54 E
Pilgrim Gardens	285	39.57 N	75.19 W
Pilgrim Memorial Monument ⊥	207	42.03 N	70.10 W
Pilgrims Hatch	260	51.38 N	0.17 E
Pilgrims Rest	156	24.55 S	30.44 E
Pili	116	13.33 N	123.16 E
Pilica ⋍	30	51.52 N	21.17 E
Pilipinas — Philippines ▫¹	116	13.00 N	122.00 E
Pilis	30	47.17 N	19.33 E
Pilisborosjenő	264c	47.36 N	19.00 E
Pilkhua	124	28.43 N	77.39 E
Pillaro	246	1.10 S	78.32 W
Pillar Point ⋗¹	226	37.30 N	122.30 W
Pillau — Baltijsk	76	54.39 N	19.55 E
Pilley's Island I	186	49.31 N	55.44 W
Pilliga	166	30.21 S	148.54 E
Pillings Pond ⊘	207	42.31 N	71.02 W
Pilnitz ⋪	264a	51.00 N	13.52 E
Pilon, Col du ⋌	58	46.10 N	6.25 E
Pilón ⋍	240d	20.15 N	77.22 W
Pilos	72	36.55 N	21.43 E
Pilot ⋍	166	35.55 S	148.13 E
Pilot Butte	184	50.28 N	104.25 W
Pilot Grove	219	38.52 N	92.55 W
Pilot Hill	226	38.50 N	120.58 W
Pilot Knob	218	37.37 N	90.38 W
Pilot Knob ⋏, Id., U.S.	194	35.42 N	93.57 W
Pilot Mound	184	49.16 N	98.55 W
Pilot Peak ⋏, Wy., U.S.	204	44.58 N	109.52 W
Pilot Point, On., Can.	216	37.34 N	157.35 W
Pilot Point, Tx., U.S.	196	33.24 N	96.57 W
Pilot Rock	202	45.29 N	118.50 W

Nome	Página	Lat.°′	Long.°′
Pilot Rock ⋏	200	35.09 N	109.53 W
Pilot Station	180	61.56 N	162.54 W
Pilottown	194	29.10 N	89.15 W
Pilpah Range ⋪	166	20.23 S	138.34 E
Pilsen — Plzeň	60	49.45 N	13.23 E
Pilsensee ⊘	60	48.01 N	11.11 E
Pilsum	52	53.29 N	7.04 E
Piltene	76	57.13 N	21.40 E
Pilu ⋍	110	11.39 N	97.24 E
Piluchang	107	29.13 N	105.37 E
Pil'ugino	80	53.25 N	52.26 E
Pilusi	106	32.05 N	120.05 E
Pilzno	30	49.59 N	21.17 E
Pim ⋍	74	61.18 N	71.57 E
Pima	200	32.53 N	109.49 W
Pima ▫⁸	200	32.53 N	109.49 W
Pimah	110	15.36 N	107.25 E
Pimba	110	31.15 S	136.47 E
Pimelles	50	47.50 N	4.10 E
Pimenta Bueno	248	11.39 S	61.11 W
Pimenteira, Vereda ⋍	250	9.58 S	42.46 W
Pimenteiras	248	6.14 S	41.25 W
Pimentel, Bra.	250	3.43 S	45.30 W
Pimentel, Perú	248	6.50 S	79.57 W
Pimlico Race Course ♦	284b	39.21 N	76.40 W
Pimmit Hills	284c	38.54 N	77.12 W
Pimmit Run ⋍	284c	38.55 N	77.07 W
Pimu-Lendo	152	1.46 N	20.54 E
Pimville ⋍⁸	273d	26.16 S	27.54 E
Pina	34	41.29 N	0.32 W
Pina ⋍	78	52.10 N	26.14 E
Pinacanauan ⋍	116	17.37 N	121.44 E
Pinaculo, Cerro ⋏	254	50.45 S	72.16 W
Piñalón, Cerro ⋏	236	15.05 N	89.55 W
Pinamalayan	116	13.02 N	121.29 E
Pinang ⊡³	114	5.20 N	100.20 E
Pinang, Pulau I	114	5.23 N	100.15 E
Pinangah	112	5.12 N	116.50 E
Pinang — George Town	114	5.25 N	100.20 E
Pınarbaşı, Tür.	130	41.36 N	33.07 E
Pınarbaşı, Tür.	130	38.44 N	36.24 E
Pinar del Río	240p	22.25 N	83.42 W
Pinar del Río ▫⁴	240p	22.30 N	83.45 W
Pinardville	188	42.59 N	71.30 W
Pınarhisar	130	41.37 N	27.30 E
Pinarlar	130	38.53 N	39.25 E
Pinas, Arg.	252	31.09 S	65.29 W
Piñas, Ec.	246	3.42 S	79.42 W
Piñas, Cerro ⋏	236	15.25 N	85.47 W
Pinatubo, Mount ⋏	116	15.08 N	120.21 E
Pinazo, Arroyo ⋍	288	34.24 S	58.48 W
Pincher Creek	182	49.29 N	113.57 W
Pinchi Lake ⊘	182	54.35 N	124.20 W
Pinckney	216	42.27 N	83.56 W
Pinckney State Recreation Area ♦	216	42.25 N	84.04 W
Pinconning	190	43.51 N	83.58 W

ENGLISH Name · Page · Lat.°′ · Long.°′ — DEUTSCH Name · Seite · Breite°′ · Länge°′ E = Ost

Pine Hill, N.Y., U.S. 210 42.08 N 74.29 W
Pinehill, Tx., U.S. 222 32.06 N 94.36 W
Pine Hills 220 28.33 N 81.27 W
Pinehouse Lake 184 55.31 N 106.36 W
Pinehouse Lake ⊜ 184 55.32 N 106.35 W
Pinehurst, Ga., U.S. 192 32.11 N 83.45 W
Pinehurst, Id., U.S. 202 45.15 N 116.20 W
Pinehurst, Ma., U.S. 207 42.31 N 71.13 W
Pinehurst, N.Y., U.S. 284a 42.44 N 78.57 W
Pinehurst, N.C., U.S. 192 35.11 N 79.28 W
Pinehurst, Tx., U.S. 222 30.10 N 95.41 W
Pinehurst Lake ⊜ 182 54.39 N 111.25 W
Pine Island, Mn., U.S. 190 44.12 N 92.38 W
Pine Island, N.Y., U.S. 210 41.17 N 74.27 W
Pine Island I 220 26.35 N 82.06 W
Pine Island Bay c 9 74.50 S 102.05 W
Pine Island Bayou ≃ 194 30.10 N 94.07 W
Pine Island Creek ≃ 283 42.47 N 70.48 W
Pine Island Dam ◆⁶ 214 40.08 N 80.43 W
Pine Island Sound ⊔ 220 26.33 N 82.10 W
Pine Lake, In., U.S. 216 41.38 N 86.45 W
Pine Lake, Ma., U.S. 283 42.23 N 71.27 W
Pine Lake ⊜, On., Can. 212 44.57 N 79.27 W
Pine Lake ⊜, Mi., U.S. 281 42.35 N 83.20 W
Pine Lake ⊜, N.Y., U.S. 210 43.12 N 74.31 W
Pineland 194 31.14 N 93.58 W
Pine Lawn 219 38.41 N 90.16 W
Pinellas □⁶ 220 27.53 N 82.43 W
Pinellas, Point > 220 27.42 N 82.38 W
Pinellas Park 220 27.50 N 82.41 W
Pine Marsh ≡ 276 40.37 N 73.34 W
Pine Meadow Lake ⊜ 276 41.11 N 74.07 W
Pine Mountain ∧, U.S. 192 36.55 N 83.20 W
Pine Mountain ∧, Ca., U.S. 226 35.41 N 121.05 W
Pine Mountain ∧, Ca., U.S. 280 34.13 N 117.54 W
Pine Mountain ∧, Ct., U.S. 207 41.58 N 72.56 W
Pine Mountain ∧, Ga., U.S. 192 32.51 N 84.47 W
Pine Mountain ∧, Or., U.S. 202 43.47 N 120.54 W
Pine Mountain ∧, Wy., U.S. 200 41.02 N 109.01 W
Pine Nut Mountains ⋀ 226 39.00 N 119.25 W
Pine Orchard Meadows 284b 39.17 N 76.52 W
Pine Pass)(182 55.22 N 122.40 W
Pine Plains 210 41.59 N 73.40 W
Pine Point, Austl. 168b 34.34 S 137.52 E
Pine Point, N.T., Can. 176 61.01 N 114.15 W
Pine Point Park ♦ 275b 43.43 N 79.33 W
Pine Portage Dam ◆⁶ 176 49.18 N 88.19 W
Pine Prairie 194 30.47 N 92.25 W
Piner 218 38.50 N 84.32 W
Pine Rest 283 42.23 N 71.26 W
Pine Ridge, Pa., U.S. 285 39.55 N 75.22 W
Pine Ridge, S.D., U.S. 198 43.01 N 102.33 W
Pine Ridge, Va., U.S. 284c 38.52 N 77.14 W
Pine Ridge ∧ 198 42.40 N 103.00 W
Pine Ridge Estates 276 41.02 N 73.41 W
Pine Ridge Indian Reservation ◆⁴ 198 43.25 N 102.21 W
Pine River, Mb., Can. 184 51.47 N 100.32 W
Pine River, Mn., U.S. 190 46.43 N 94.24 W
Piñero 258 34.32 S 58.45 W
Pinerolo 62 44.53 N 7.21 E
Piñeros, Isla I 240m 18.15 N 65.35 W
Pinerovka 80 51.34 N 43.04 E
Pine Run ≃ 279b 40.37 N 79.35 W
Pines ≃ 283 42.27 N 70.58 W
Pines, Isle of → Juventud, Isla de la I 240p 21.40 N 82.50 W
Pines, Lake o' the ⊜¹ 222 32.46 N 94.35 W
Pines, Point of > 283 42.26 N 70.58 W
Pine Shores 220 27.17 N 82.32 W
Pines Lake ⊜ 276 41.00 N 74.16 W
Pines Run ≃ 285 39.50 N 75.05 W
Pine Swamp Knob ∧ 188 39.33 N 79.31 W
Pineto 66 42.36 N 14.04 E
Pinetop 200 34.07 N 109.56 W
Pinetops 192 35.47 N 77.38 W
Pinetown 158 29.52 S 30.46 E
Pine Tree Hill ∧ 114 3.43 N 101.42 E
Pine Valley, Md., U.S. 284b 39.26 N 76.39 W
Pine Valley, N.Y., U.S. 210 42.14 N 76.51 W
Pine Valley V 204 38.25 N 113.40 W
Pine Village 216 40.27 N 87.15 W
Pineville, Ky., U.S. 192 36.45 N 83.41 W
Pineville, La., U.S. 194 31.19 N 92.26 W
Pineville, Mo., U.S. 194 36.35 N 94.23 W
Pineville, N.C., U.S. 192 35.04 N 80.53 W
Pineville, Pa., U.S. 208 40.18 N 75.00 W
Pineville, W.V., U.S. 192 37.34 N 81.32 W
Pinewood, Fl., U.S. 220 25.53 N 80.14 W
Pinewood, S.C., U.S. 192 33.44 N 80.27 W
Piney 50 48.22 N 4.20 E
Piney ≃ 194 35.49 N 87.33 W
Piney Branch ≃ 284c 38.56 N 77.18 W
Piney Creek ≃, Tx., U.S. 222 31.03 N 94.34 W
Piney Creek ≃, Wy., U.S. 202 44.34 N 106.32 W
Piney Fork 214 40.15 N 80.50 W
Piney Point 222 29.46 N 95.31 W
Piney Point > 208 38.08 N 76.32 W
Piney Run ≃ 284c 38.58 N 77.17 W
Piney Woods 194 32.03 N 89.59 W
Pinfold 262 53.36 N 2.55 W
Ping ≃, Thai 110 15.42 N 100.09 E
Ping ≃, Zhg. 100 25.59 N 115.07 E
Pinga 154 1.01 S 28.42 E
Ping'an, Zhg. 89 45.20 N 123.42 E
Ping'an, Zhg. 104 41.11 N 123.26 E
Ping'an, Zhg. 107 30.36 N 104.42 E
Ping'anbu 98 41.45 N 116.13 E
Ping'ancheng 105 40.03 N 117.48 E
Ping'andi 104 42.34 N 121.52 E
Pingaring 162 32.45 S 118.37 E
Pingba, Zhg. 100 31.19 N 113.18 E
Pingba, Zhg. 102 26.22 N 106.09 E
Pingchang 102 31.35 N 107.03 E
Pingchao 106 32.07 N 120.45 E
Pingding 98 37.48 N 113.37 E
Pingdingpu 104 42.22 N 123.55 E
Pingdingshan, Zhg. 98 41.26 N 124.45 E
Pingdingshan, Zhg. 100 33.45 N 113.17 E
Pingding Shan ∧ 89 46.38 N 128.27 E
Pingdu 98 36.47 N 119.54 E
Pingelap I¹ 14 6.13 N 160.42 E
Pingelly 162 32.32 S 117.05 E
Pingfang, Zhg. 100 30.07 N 113.48 E
Pingfang, Zhg. 104 41.17 N 120.40 E
Pingfang, Zhg. 104 41.28 N 120.48 E
Pingfang, Zhg. 104 42.14 N 120.38 E
Pingfang, Zhg. 104 42.27 N 120.38 E
Pingfang, Zhg. 271a 39.56 N 116.33 E
Pingfangdu 104 41.45 N 121.12 E
Pingfangzi 104 41.31 N 121.21 E
Pinggau 61 47.27 N 16.04 E
Pinggu 105 40.09 N 117.07 E
Pingguo 102 23.19 N 107.39 E
Pinghai, Zhg. 100 25.14 N 119.15 E
Pinghai, Zhg. 100 22.39 N 114.53 E
Pinghe, Zhg. 100 24.25 N 117.22 E
Pinghe, Zhg. 102 22.51 N 102.30 E
Pinghe ≃ 100 24.25 N 116.36 E
P'inghsiang → Pingxiang 102 22.09 N 106.43 E
Pinghu, Zhg. 100 26.46 N 118.48 E
Pinghu, Zhg. 100 30.56 N 115.22 E
Pinghu, Zhg. 100 22.42 N 114.08 E
Pinghu, Zhg. 106 30.42 N 121.01 E
Pingjiang 100 28.44 N 113.34 E
Pingjing 105 39.20 N 116.06 E
Pinglan 100 22.22 N 113.27 E
Pingle, Zhg. 102 24.37 N 110.40 E
Pingle, Zhg. 102 24.31 N 106.59 E
Pingli 102 32.19 N 109.21 E
Pingliang 102 35.32 N 106.41 E
Pinglidian 98 37.17 N 119.59 E
Pingling 100 23.39 N 114.23 E
Pinglucheng 102 39.50 N 112.19 E
Pingluo 102 38.57 N 106.35 E
Pingluopu 104 41.56 N 123.20 E
Pingnan, Zhg. 100 26.56 N 119.02 E
Pingnan, Zhg. 102 23.30 N 110.30 E
Pingqiao 100 33.24 N 119.13 E
Pingquan 98 40.59 N 118.34 E
Pingrup 162 33.32 S 118.31 E
Ping Shan, H.K. 271d 22.27 N 114.00 E
Pingshan, Zhg. 100 25.36 N 117.52 E
Pingshan, Zhg. 100 23.26 N 113.15 E
Pingshan, Zhg. 100 22.43 N 114.22 E
Pingshan, Zhg. 102 38.15 N 114.10 E
Pingshang 98 35.11 N 119.07 E
Pingshi, Zhg. 100 32.32 N 113.03 E
Pingshi, Zhg. 100 25.20 N 113.02 E
Pingshui 100 29.53 N 120.38 E
Pingtaizi 105 40.44 N 116.25 E
Pingtan, Zhg. 100 25.31 N 119.47 E
Pingtan, Zhg. 100 23.04 N 114.38 E
Pingtan, Zhg. 107 29.38 N 105.16 E
Pingtan, Zhg. 107 29.50 N 105.56 E
Pingtan Dao I 100 25.33 N 119.48 E
Pingtang 102 25.50 N 107.19 E
Pingtian 100 25.19 N 113.31 E
P'ingtung 100 22.40 N 120.29 E
Pingües, Cayos II 240p 20.47 N 78.15 W
Pingwang 106 30.59 N 120.38 E
Pingwu 102 32.29 N 104.37 E
Pingxiang, Zhg. 100 27.38 N 113.50 E
Pingxiang, Zhg. 102 22.09 N 106.43 E
Pingyang, Zhg. 89 48.13 N 124.23 E
Pingyang, Zhg. 100 27.41 N 120.33 E
Pingyao, Zhg. 102 37.16 N 112.09 E
Pingyao, Zhg. 106 30.24 N 119.58 E
Pingyi 98 35.34 N 117.37 E
Pingyin 98 36.19 N 116.22 E
Pingyu 100 32.57 N 114.41 E
Pingyuan, Zhg. 98 37.11 N 116.25 E
Pingyuan, Zhg. 100 24.36 N 115.54 E
Pingzhai 102 24.07 N 104.22 E
Pingzhuang 98 42.03 N 119.22 E
Pinhal 256 22.12 S 46.45 W
Pinhal, Ribeirão do ≃ 256 22.42 S 46.42 W
Pinhal Novo 34 38.38 N 8.55 W
Pinhalzinho 256 22.46 S 46.36 W
Pinhão 250 10.34 S 37.44 W
Pinheiral 256 22.31 S 43.59 W
Pinheirinhos 256 22.26 S 44.59 W
Pinheiro 250 2.31 S 45.05 W
Pinheiro de Loures 266c 38.50 N 9.12 W
Pinheiro Machado 252 31.34 S 53.23 W
Pinheiros, Bra. 255 18.21 S 40.14 W
Pinheiros, Bra. 256 22.32 S 44.54 W
Pinheiros ≃ 287b 23.32 S 46.44 W
Pinhel 34 40.46 N 7.04 W
Pinhoe 42 50.44 N 3.27 W
Pinhuã ≃ 248 6.21 S 65.00 W
Pini, Pulau I 110 0.08 N 98.40 E
Pinillos 246 8.55 N 74.28 W
Piniós ≃ 38 39.54 N 22.45 E
Pinitos, Sierra de ⋀ 200 31.08 N 110.50 W
Pinjar, Lake ⊜ 168a 31.38 S 115.49 E
Pinjarra 168a 32.37 S 115.53 E
Pinjor Garden ♦ 123 30.47 N 76.47 E
Pinka ≃ 61 47.00 N 16.35 E
Pinkafeld 61 47.22 N 16.07 E
Pinkiang → Harbin 89 45.45 N 126.41 E
Pinlaung 110 20.08 N 96.47 E
Pinlebu 110 24.05 N 95.21 E
Pinn ≃ 260 51.31 N 0.29 W
Pinnacle ∧, N.Z. 172 41.49 S 173.17 E
Pinnacle ∧, N.Y., U.S. 188 43.13 N 74.23 W
Pinnacle ∧, Va., U.S. 188 39.08 N 78.26 W
Pinnacle Buttes ∧ 202 43.44 N 109.57 W
Pinnacle Island I 180 60.12 N 172.46 W
Pinnacle Peak ∧ 224 46.45 N 121.43 W
Pinnacles National Monument ♦ 226 36.28 N 121.19 W
Pinnaroo 166 35.16 S 140.55 E
Pinneberg 52 53.40 N 9.47 E
Pinner ◆⁸ 260 51.36 N 0.23 W
Pino, Sierra del ⋀ 196 28.15 N 103.03 W
Pin Oak Creek ≃ 222 31.57 N 96.28 W
Pinocchio 66 43.35 N 13.30 E
Pinochle Peak ∧ 224 45.43 N 123.36 W
Pinole 226 38.00 N 122.17 W
Pinole Creek ≃ 282 38.01 N 122.18 W
Pinole Point > 282 38.01 N 122.22 W
Pinole Ridge ∧ 282 37.59 N 122.15 W
Pinos 234 22.18 N 101.34 W
Pinos, Mount ∧ 228 34.50 N 119.09 W
Pinos, Point > 226 36.38 N 121.56 W
Pinos-Puente 34 37.15 N 3.45 W
Pinotepa de Don Luis 234 16.25 N 97.55 W
Pinrang 112 3.48 S 119.38 E
Pins, Île de → Juventud, Isla de la I 240p 21.40 N 82.50 W
Pins, Île des I 175f 22.37 S 167.30 E
Pins, Pointe aux > 214 42.15 N 81.51 W
Pins, Rivière des ≃ 206 46.01 N 72.03 W
Pinsk 78 52.07 N 26.04 E
Pinson 194 33.41 N 86.41 W
Pinsot 62 45.21 N 6.06 E
Pinta, Isla I 246a 0.35 N 90.44 W
Pintada Arroyo V 196 34.53 N 104.39 W
Pintado 258 33.50 S 56.18 W
Pintado ≃ 255 13.33 S 50.16 W
Pintado, Arroyo de ≃ 258 34.08 S 56.14 W
Pintado, Cuchilla del ⋀² 258 34.12 S 56.25 W
Pintados 248 20.37 S 69.38 W
Pintados, Salar de ≃ 248 20.30 S 69.42 W
Pintasan 112 5.26 N 117.43 E
Pinteus 266c 38.52 N 9.09 W
Pintlala Creek ≃ 194 32.21 N 86.30 W
Pinto Butte ∧ 184 49.22 N 107.25 W
Pinto Creek ≃, Ab., Can. 182 53.51 N 117.35 W
Pinto Creek ≃, Sk., Can. 184 49.40 N 106.42 W
Pintos, Arroyo de ≃ 258 33.55 S 56.51 W
Pintos Negreiros 256 22.18 S 45.13 W
Pintoyacu ≃, Ec. 246 2.07 S 76.03 W
Pintoyacu ≃, Perú 246 3.35 S 73.55 W
Pinturas ≃ 254 46.35 S 70.18 W
Pintuyan 116 9.57 N 125.15 E
Pin'ug 24 60.15 N 47.48 E
Pinukpuk 116 17.35 N 121.22 E
Pinwherry 44 55.09 N 4.50 W
Pinxton 42 53.06 N 1.19 W
Pinzano al Tagliamento 64 46.11 N 12.57 E
Pinzgau V 64 47.15 N 12.40 E
Pinzón, Isla I 246a 0.36 S 90.40 W
Piobbico 66 43.35 N 12.31 E
Pioche 204 37.55 N 114.27 W
Pio IX 250 6.50 S 40.37 W
Piolenc 62 44.11 N 4.46 E
Piombino 66 42.55 N 10.32 E
Piombino, Canale di ⊔ 66 42.53 N 10.30 E
Pioneer, Austl. 162 31.48 S 121.43 E
Pioneer, Ca., U.S. 226 38.25 N 120.33 W
Pioneer, Oh., U.S. 216 41.40 N 84.33 W
Pioneer Mine 182 50.46 N 122.46 W
Pioneer Mountains ⋀ 202 45.40 N 113.00 W
Pioneer Park ♦ 273d 26.14 S 28.04 E
Pioner, ostrov I 74 79.50 N 92.30 E
Pionerskij 76 54.57 N 20.20 E
Pionierbivak 164 2.16 S 138.02 E
Pionki 30 51.30 N 21.27 E
Pio Pico State Historical Monument ♦ 280 33.59 N 118.04 W
Piopio 172 38.28 S 175.01 E
Pioppo 70 38.03 N 13.14 E
Piora, Mount ∧ 164 6.45 S 146.00 E
Pioraco 66 43.11 N 12.59 E
Piorini ≃ 246 3.23 S 63.30 W
Piorini, Lago ⊜ 246 3.34 S 63.15 W
Piotrków Trybunalski 30 51.25 N 19.42 E
Piotrków Trybunalski □⁴ 30 51.30 N 19.45 E
Piotta 58 46.31 N 8.40 E
Pio V. Corpus (Limbujan) 116 11.53 N 124.03 E
Piove di Sacco 64 45.18 N 12.02 E
Piovene-Rocchette 64 45.45 N 11.25 E
Pio XII 250 3.53 S 45.17 W
Pipa 107 29.07 N 105.05 E
Pipalkoti 124 30.26 N 79.27 E
Pipanaco, Salar de ≃ 252 28.07 S 66.25 W
Pīpār 120 26.23 N 73.32 E
Piparia 124 22.45 N 78.21 E
Pīpar Road 120 26.27 N 73.27 E
Pipas 152 14.56 S 12.12 E
Pipe Creek ≃, In., U.S. 194 40.08 N 85.52 W
Pipe Creek ≃, In., U.S. 216 40.45 N 86.13 W
Pipe Creek ≃, In., U.S. 218 39.26 N 85.06 W
Piper City 216 40.45 N 88.11 W
Pipe Spring National Monument ♦ 200 36.43 N 112.33 W
Pipestem Creek ≃ 198 46.54 N 98.43 W
Pipestem State Park ♦ 192 37.32 N 81.00 W
Pipestone 198 44.00 N 96.19 W
Pipestone ≃ 176 52.53 N 89.23 W
Pipestone Creek ≃, Can. 184 49.42 N 100.45 W
Pipestone Creek ≃, Mi., U.S. 216 42.04 N 86.24 W
Pipestone National Monument ♦ 198 44.00 N 96.18 W
Pipi ≃ 146 7.27 N 22.48 E
Pipinas 258 35.32 S 57.20 W
Piping Brook ≃ 276 41.08 N 73.37 W
Pipiriki 172 39.29 S 175.03 E
Piplān 123 32.17 N 71.21 E
Piplūn 126 23.21 N 88.07 E
Pipmuacan, Réservoir ⊜¹ 186 49.35 N 70.30 W
Pipri 124 23.58 N 82.40 E
Pipriac 28 47.49 N 1.57 W
Piqiang 85 40.20 N 77.38 E
Piqiao 106 31.34 N 119.27 E
Piqua 218 40.08 N 84.14 W
Piquet Carneiro 250 5.48 S 39.25 W
Piquete 256 22.36 S 45.11 W
Piquete, Ribeirão ≃ 256 22.36 S 45.01 W
Piquiri ≃, Bra. 248 17.39 S 55.09 W
Piquiri ≃, Bra. 248 17.18 S 56.44 W
Piquiri ≃, Bra. 252 24.03 S 54.14 W
Pira 150 8.30 N 1.44 E
Piracaia 256 23.03 S 46.21 W
Piracanjuba 255 17.18 S 49.01 W
Piracanjuba ≃ 255 18.14 S 48.43 W
Piracão ≃ 287a 23.02 S 43.36 W
Piracicaba 255 22.43 S 47.33 W
Piracicaba ≃ 255 22.36 S 48.19 W
Piraçununga 255 21.59 S 47.25 W
Piracuruca 250 3.56 S 41.42 W
Pirae 174s 17.32 S 149.33 W
Piraeus → Piraiévs 38 37.57 N 23.38 E
Pirahmet 130 38.11 N 39.51 E
Piraí 256 22.38 S 43.54 W
Piraí ≃ 256 22.28 S 43.50 W
Piraí do Sul 252 24.31 S 49.56 W
Piraiévs (Piraeus) 38 37.57 N 23.38 E
Piraino 70 38.10 N 14.52 E
Piraju 255 23.12 S 49.23 W
Pirajuba 255 19.54 S 48.42 W
Pirajucara, Ribeirão ≃ 287b 23.34 S 46.43 W
Pirajuí 255 21.59 S 49.29 W
Pirakata 126 22.34 N 87.11 E
Piramida, gora ∧ 88 54.15 N 95.45 E
Piramidal'nyj, pik ∧ 85 39.34 N 69.57 E
Pirámide de Cuicuilco ⊥ 286a 19.18 N 99.11 W
Pirámide de Santa Cecilia ⊥ 286a 19.33 N 99.09 E
Pirámide de Tenayuca ⊥ 286a 19.32 N 99.11 W
Piram Island I 120 21.36 N 72.41 E
Piran 36 45.32 N 13.34 E
Piraña, Arroyo ≃ 288 34.24 S 58.30 W
Pirané 252 25.43 S 59.06 W
Piranga 255 20.41 S 43.18 W
Pirangaí 256 22.34 S 44.37 W
Piranguçu 256 22.31 S 45.30 W
Piranguinho 256 22.24 S 45.32 W
Piranhas 255 16.31 S 51.51 W
Piranhas ≃, Bra. 250 5.15 S 36.45 W
Piranhas ≃, Bra. 250 8.40 S 49.28 W
Piranhas ≃, Bra. 250 5.56 S 48.15 W
Piranji ≃ 250 4.23 S 37.48 W
Pīrān Shahr 128 36.41 N 45.08 E
Pirapemas 250 3.43 S 44.14 W
Pirapetinga ≃ 256 21.37 S 42.32 W
Pirapetinga, Ribeirão ≃ 256 21.49 S 43.36 W
Pirapó ≃ 255 22.30 S 52.01 W
Pirapora 255 17.21 S 44.56 W
Pirapora do Bom Jesus 256 23.24 S 47.00 W
Pirapora do Bom Jesus □⁷ 287b 23.24 S 46.56 W
Piraputanga 255 20.26 S 55.32 W
Piraquara 252 25.26 S 49.04 W
Piraquê ≃ 287a 23.01 S 43.37 W
Pirarajá 252 33.44 S 54.45 W
Pirata, Monte ∧² 240m 18.06 N 65.33 W
Pirate Creek ≃ 282 37.33 N 121.52 W
Pir'atin 78 50.15 N 32.30 E
Piratinga ≃ 255 15.41 S 46.07 W
Piratini 252 31.27 S 53.06 W
Piratini ≃ 252 28.06 S 55.27 W
Piratininga 287a 22.57 S 43.04 W
Piratininga, Lagoa c 256 22.57 S 43.05 W
Piratuba 252 27.27 S 51.48 W
Piratuba, Lago c 250 1.37 N 50.10 W
Piratucu ≃ 250 1.59 S 56.58 W
Piraúba 256 21.17 S 43.02 W
Piraube, Lac ⊜ 186 50.33 N 71.42 W
Piray ≃ 248 16.32 S 63.45 W
Piraziz 130 40.58 N 38.08 E
Pirbright 260 51.18 N 0.39 W
Pirdop 38 42.42 N 24.11 E
Pirenópolis 255 15.51 S 48.57 W
Pires, Ribeirão ≃ 287b 23.43 S 46.25 W
Pires do Rio 255 17.18 S 48.17 W
Pirgos 38 37.41 N 21.28 E
Piriá 250 1.40 S 50.32 W
Piriápolis 252 34.54 S 55.17 W
Piribebuy 252 25.29 S 57.33 W
Pirin ∧ 38 41.40 N 23.30 E
Pirinççi ◆⁸ 267b 41.10 N 28.50 E
Pirineos → Pyrenees ⋀ 34 42.40 N 1.00 E
Piripiri 250 4.16 S 41.47 W
Piritiba 250 11.44 S 40.34 W
Piritu, Ven. 246 9.23 N 69.12 W
Píritu, Ven. 246 11.22 N 69.08 W
Pirituba ◆⁸ 287b 23.29 S 46.43 W
Pirk 54 50.25 N 12.04 E
Pīr Mahal 123 30.46 N 72.26 E
Pirmasens 56 49.12 N 7.36 E
Pirna 54 50.58 N 13.56 E
Piroči 82 55.04 N 38.57 E
Pirogovka 78 51.54 N 33.18 E
Pirogovskij 265b 55.59 N 37.44 E
Pirogovskoje vodochranilišče ⊜¹ 82 55.58 N 37.40 E
Pirojpur 126 22.34 N 89.59 E
Pirón ≃ 34 41.23 N 4.31 W
Pirongia 172 38.00 S 175.12 E
Pirot 38 43.09 N 22.35 E
Pirovano 252 36.30 S 61.34 W
Pirovskoje 86 57.37 N 92.16 E
Pīr Panjāl Range ⋀ 123 33.37 N 74.32 E
Pirpirituba 250 6.46 S 35.30 W
Pirreşit Tepe ∧ 84 38.56 N 43.55 E
Pirsagat 84 39.54 N 49.24 E
Pirsagat ≃ 84 39.53 N 49.19 E
Pirtleville 200 31.22 N 109.34 W
Piru, Indon. 164 3.04 S 128.12 E
Piru, Ca., U.S. 228 34.25 N 118.48 W
Piru, Lake ⊜¹ 228 34.30 N 118.45 W
Piru, Teluk c 164 3.10 S 128.08 E
Piru Creek ≃ 228 34.23 N 118.47 W
Pisa 66 43.43 N 10.23 E
Pisa □⁴ 66 43.25 N 10.43 E
Pisa ∧² 26 63.13 N 28.18 E
Pisa ≃ 30 53.15 N 21.52 E
Pisa, Certosa di ☆¹ 66 43.45 N 10.31 E
Pisa, Mount ∧ 172 44.52 S 169.11 E
Pisagua 248 19.36 S 70.13 W
Pisam-bong ∧ 98 40.41 N 126.34 E
Pisang, Pulau I 164 1.23 S 128.55 E
Pisarevka 78 49.53 N 40.12 E
Pisarve 272c 19.06 N 73.05 E
Pisau, Tanjong > 116 6.04 N 118.03 E
Piščalje 80 58.14 N 48.42 E
Piscasaw Creek ≃ 216 42.16 N 88.49 W
Piscataway 210 40.29 N 74.23 W
Piscataway Creek ≃, Md., U.S. 208 38.42 N 77.02 W
Piscataway Creek ≃, Va., U.S. 208 37.54 N 76.50 W
Pişchia 38 45.55 N 21.20 E
Pisciotta 68 40.06 N 15.14 E
Pisco 248 13.42 S 76.13 W
Pisco ≃ 248 13.42 S 76.15 W
Pişcolt 38 47.35 N 22.18 E
Piscovo 80 57.11 N 40.32 E
Piseco Lake ⊜ 210 43.23 N 74.36 W
Písek 30 49.19 N 14.10 E
Pisgah, Md., U.S. 208 38.32 N 77.08 W
Pisgah, Oh., U.S. 218 39.19 N 84.22 W
Pisgah Forest 192 35.15 N 82.42 W
Pishan 120 37.37 N 78.18 E
Pishīn 120 30.35 N 67.00 E
Pishīn Lora (Lowrah) ≃ 120 29.09 N 64.55 E
Pisidia □⁹ 130 37.30 N 31.00 E
Pisinemo 200 32.02 N 112.18 W
Pising 112 5.05 S 121.54 E
Pis'mennoje 78 48.13 N 35.48 E
Pismo Beach 226 35.08 N 120.38 W
Pišnur 80 57.47 N 47.58 E
Piso, Lake ⊜ 150 6.48 N 11.17 W
Pisogne 64 45.48 N 10.06 E
Pisqui ≃ 248 7.45 S 75.01 W
Pissila 150 13.10 N 0.49 W
Pissos 32 44.19 N 0.47 W
Pistakee Highlands 216 42.25 N 88.11 W
Pistakee Lake ⊜ 216 42.23 N 88.12 W
Pisticci 68 40.23 N 16.34 E
Pistoia 66 43.55 N 10.54 E
Pistoia □⁴ 64 43.58 N 10.50 E
Pistolet Bay c 186 51.32 N 55.50 W
Pistuk Peak ∧ 180 59.43 N 159.42 W
Pisuerga ≃ 34 41.33 N 4.52 W
Pisz 30 53.38 N 21.49 E
Pit ≃ 204 40.45 N 122.22 W
Pit, North Fork ≃ 204 41.28 N 120.33 W
Pit, South Fork ≃ 204 41.28 N 120.33 W
Pita 150 11.05 N 12.24 W
Pital 246 2.16 N 75.49 W
Pitalito 246 1.51 N 76.02 W
Pitampura Kālan ◆⁸ 272a 28.42 N 77.08 E
Pitanga 252 24.46 S 51.44 W
Pitangueiras 255 21.02 S 48.13 W
Pitangueiras, Ribeirão das ≃ 256 21.27 S 44.27 W
Pitangui 255 19.40 S 44.54 W
Pitcairn 279b 40.24 N 79.46 W
Pitcairn □², Oc. 6 25.04 S 130.05 W
Pitcairn □², Oc. 174e 25.04 S 130.05 W
Pitcher 210 42.35 N 75.52 W
Pitch Place 260 51.16 N 0.36 W
Piteå 26 65.20 N 21.30 E
Piteälven ≃ 24 65.14 N 21.32 E
Piteglio 66 44.01 N 10.46 E
Pitelino 80 54.34 N 41.49 E
Piterka 80 50.42 N 47.27 E
Pitești 38 44.52 N 24.52 E
Pithapuram 122 17.07 N 82.16 E
Pithara 162 30.24 S 116.40 E
Pithiviers 50 48.10 N 2.15 E
Pithorāgarh 124 29.35 N 80.13 E
Piti, Lagoa ⊜ 158 26.34 S 32.53 E
Pitigliano 66 42.38 N 11.40 E
Pitim 80 53.12 N 42.21 E
Pitinga ≃ 246 1.32 S 59.49 W
Pitiquito 232 30.42 N 112.02 W
Pitjantjatjara Lands ◆⁴ 162 27.00 S 130.30 E
Pitk'aranta 24 61.34 N 31.27 E
Pitkas Point 180 62.02 N 163.17 W
Pitlochry 46 56.43 N 3.45 W
Pitman 208 39.43 N 75.07 W
Pitman Airport ⊠ 285 39.45 N 75.08 W
Pitmedden 46 57.20 N 2.11 W
Pitner Ditch ≍ 216 41.14 N 86.53 W
Pitogo 116 10.08 N 124.33 E
Pitomača 36 45.57 N 17.14 E
Pitou, Zhg. 100 25.01 N 114.35 E
Pitou, Zhg. 100 23.34 N 116.05 E
Pitou, Zhg. 100 24.26 N 114.22 E
Pitrufquén 254 38.59 S 72.39 W
Pitsea 260 51.34 N 0.31 E
Pitseng 158 28.58 S 28.16 E
Pitsford Reservoir ⊜¹ 42 52.20 N 0.52 W
Pitt ≃ 224 49.12 N 122.47 W
Pitt, Mount ∧ 174c 29.01 S 167.56 E
Pittem 50 51.00 N 3.16 E
Pitten ≃ 61 47.44 N 16.14 E
Pittenweem 46 56.12 N 2.44 W
Pitti Island I 122 10.50 N 72.38 E
Pitt Island I 182 53.35 N 129.45 W
Pitt Lake ⊜ 182 49.25 N 122.32 W
Pittsboro, In., U.S. 218 39.51 N 86.28 W
Pittsboro, Ms., U.S. 194 33.56 N 89.20 W
Pittsboro, N.C., U.S. 192 35.43 N 79.10 W
Pittsburg, Ca., U.S. 226 38.01 N 121.53 W
Pittsburg, In., U.S. 216 40.37 N 86.42 W
Pittsburg, Ks., U.S. 198 37.24 N 94.42 W
Pittsburg, N.H., U.S. 206 45.03 N 71.23 W
Pittsburg, Tx., U.S. 222 32.59 N 94.57 W
Pittsburgh, Pa., U.S. 214 40.26 N 79.59 W
Pittsburgh, Pa., U.S. 279b 40.26 N 79.59 W
Pittsburgh, University of ☆² 279b 40.27 N 79.58 W
Pittsburgh-Monroeville Airport ⊠ 279b 40.27 N 79.46 W
Pittsfield, Il., U.S. 219 39.36 N 90.48 W
Pittsfield, Me., U.S. 188 44.46 N 69.23 W
Pittsfield, Ma., U.S. 207 42.27 N 73.14 W
Pittsfield, N.H., U.S. 188 43.18 N 71.19 W
Pittsfield, Pa., U.S. 214 41.50 N 79.23 W
Pittsford, Mi., U.S. 216 41.52 N 84.28 W
Pittsford, N.Y., U.S. 210 43.05 N 77.31 W
Pitt Stadium ♦ 279b 40.27 N 79.58 W
Pittston 210 41.19 N 75.47 W
Pittsview 194 32.11 N 85.09 W
Pittsville 208 38.23 N 75.24 W
Pittsworth 166 27.43 S 151.38 E
Pitt Water c 170 33.37 S 151.18 E
Pituil 252 28.34 S 67.27 W
Pitumarca 248 13.59 S 71.25 W
Pituri Creek ≃ 166 22.58 S 138.50 E
Pitzbach ≃ 64 47.13 N 10.46 E
Pitztal V 58 47.07 N 10.47 E
Pium 250 10.27 S 49.11 W
Pium ≃ 250 10.12 S 49.57 W
Piura 248 5.12 S 80.38 W
Piura □⁵ 248 5.10 S 80.00 W
Piura ≃ 248 5.32 S 80.53 W
Piute Peak ∧ 204 35.27 N 118.24 W
Piute Reservoir ⊜¹ 200 38.17 N 112.12 W
Piva ≃ 38 43.21 N 18.51 E
Pivan' 89 50.29 N 137.06 E
Piverone 62 45.27 N 8.00 E
Pivijay 246 10.28 N 74.37 W
Piwniczna 30 49.27 N 20.42 E
Pixian 102 30.49 N 103.49 E
Pixley 226 35.58 N 119.17 W
Pižanka 80 57.28 N 48.33 E
Pižma 80 57.52 N 47.06 E
Pižma ≃ 80 57.37 N 48.58 E
Pizzighettone 62 45.11 N 9.47 E
Pizzillo, Monte ∧ 70 37.48 N 15.01 E
Pizzo 68 38.44 N 16.10 E
Pizzoferrato 66 41.55 N 14.14 E
Pizzoli 66 42.26 N 13.18 E
Pizzone 66 41.40 N 14.02 E
Pjalka 24 66.43 N 40.59 E
Pjana ≃ 80 55.40 N 45.57 E
Pjöngjang → P'yŏngyang 98 39.01 N 125.45 E
P. K. le Rouxdam ⊜¹ 158 30.12 S 24.54 E
Placanica 68 38.25 N 16.27 E
Place Bonaventure ◆⁹ 275a 45.30 N 73.34 W
Placentia, Nf., Can. 186 47.14 N 53.58 W
Placentia, Ca., U.S. 228 33.52 N 117.52 W
Placentia Bay c 186 47.15 N 54.30 W
Placer, Pil. 116 11.52 N 123.55 E
Placer, Pil. 116 9.39 N 125.36 E
Placer □⁶ 226 38.54 N 121.04 W
Placeres del Oro ≃ 234 18.27 N 100.57 W
Placeres de Picacho 234 23.11 N 105.42 W
Placerville 226 38.43 N 120.47 W
Placetas 240p 22.19 N 79.40 W
Place Versailles ◆⁹ 275a 45.35 N 73.32 W
Plachino 76 54.28 N 39.20 E
Plachtejevka 78 46.07 N 29.43 E
Placid, Lake ⊜ 220 27.14 N 81.22 W
Placida 220 26.49 N 82.15 W
Plácido de Castro 248 10.20 S 67.11 W
Plácido Rosas 252 32.45 S 53.44 W
Placita de Morelos 234 18.31 N 103.42 W
Plačkovica ⋀ 38 41.45 N 22.35 E
Plaffeien 58 46.44 N 7.17 E
Plages, Lac des ⊜ 206 45.59 N 74.54 W
Plage-Sainte-Cécile 50 50.34 N 1.35 E
Plailly 261 49.06 N 2.35 E
Plai Mat ≃ 110 15.22 N 102.45 E
Plain 224 47.46 N 120.39 W
Plain City, Oh., U.S. 214 40.06 N 83.16 W
Plain City, Ut,. U.S. 200 41.17 N 112.05 W
Plain Dealing 194 32.54 N 93.41 W
Plaines, Île aux I 275a 45.21 N 73.50 W
Plainfield, Ct., U.S. 207 41.40 N 71.54 W
Plainfield, Il., U.S. 216 41.37 N 88.12 W
Plainfield, In., U.S. 218 39.42 N 86.23 W
Plainfield, Ma., U.S. 207 42.30 N 72.55 W
Plainfield, N.J., U.S. 210 40.37 N 74.26 W
Plainfield, Oh., U.S. 214 40.13 N 81.43 W
Plainfield, Pa., U.S. 208 40.12 N 77.17 W
Plainfield, Wi., U.S. 190 44.12 N 89.29 W
Plainfield Heights 216 43.01 N 85.37 W
Plains, Ga., U.S. 192 32.02 N 84.23 W
Plains, Ks., U.S. 198 37.15 N 100.35 W
Plains, Mt., U.S. 202 47.27 N 114.52 W
Plains, Tx., U.S. 196 33.11 N 102.50 W
Plainsboro 208 40.20 N 74.36 W
Plainview, Ca., U.S. 226 36.08 N 119.08 W
Plainview, Il., U.S. 219 39.10 N 89.59 W
Plainview, Mn., U.S. 190 44.09 N 92.10 W
Plainview, Ne., U.S. 198 42.20 N 97.47 W
Plainview, N.Y., U.S. 210 40.46 N 73.28 W
Plainview, Tx., U.S. 196 34.11 N 101.42 W
Plainville, Ct., U.S. 207 41.40 N 72.51 W
Plainville, Il., U.S. 219 39.47 N 91.11 W
Plainville, In., U.S. 194 38.48 N 87.09 W
Plainville, Ks., U.S. 198 39.14 N 99.17 W
Plainville, Ma., U.S. 207 42.00 N 71.20 W
Plainville, N.Y., U.S. 210 43.10 N 76.27 W
Plainwell 216 42.26 N 85.38 W
Plaisance, Baie de c 186 47.18 N 61.53 W
Plaisir 261 48.49 N 1.57 E
Plaistow 207 42.50 N 71.05 W
Plaksino 76 56.11 N 30.42 E
Plamondon 182 54.51 N 112.19 W
Plampang 115b 8.48 S 117.48 E
Planá 60 49.52 N 12.44 E
Plana, Illa I 34 38.10 N 0.28 W
Planada 226 37.18 N 120.19 W
Planalto, Bra. 252 27.20 S 53.03 W
Planalto, Bra. 255 14.39 S 40.29 W
Planches 50 48.42 N 0.22 E
Plandome 276 40.48 N 73.42 W
Plandome Heights 276 40.48 N 73.42 W
Plandome Manor 276 40.49 N 73.42 W
Plan-d'Orgon 62 43.48 N 5.00 E
Plane ≃ 54 52.23 N 12.30 E
Planegg 60 48.06 N 11.25 E
Planerskoje 78 44.57 N 35.14 E
Planeta Rica 246 8.25 N 75.36 W
Plangeross 58 46.59 N 10.52 E
Plankenfels 60 49.53 N 11.20 E
Plankinton 198 43.42 N 98.29 W
Plano, Il., U.S. 216 41.39 N 88.32 W
Plano, Tx., U.S. 222 33.01 N 96.41 W
Plansee ⊜ 64 47.28 N 10.48 E
Plantagenet 206 45.32 N 75.00 W
Plantation, Fl., U.S. 220 26.07 N 80.14 W
Plantation, Fl., U.S. 220 24.59 N 80.33 W
Plantation, Ky., U.S. 218 38.17 N 85.36 W
Plantation Key I 220 24.58 N 80.33 W
Plant City 220 28.01 N 82.06 W
Plantersville, Al., U.S. 194 32.39 N 86.55 W
Plantersville, Ms., U.S. 194 34.12 N 88.39 W
Plantersville, Tx., U.S. 222 30.20 N 95.52 W
Planting Fields Arboretum State Park ♦ 276 40.52 N 73.33 W
Plantsite 200 33.03 N 109.19 W
Plantsville 207 41.35 N 72.53 W
Plaquemine 194 30.17 N 91.14 W
Plaridel, Pil. 116 10.32 N 124.46 E
Plaridel, Pil. 116 8.37 N 123.43 E
Plasencia 34 40.02 N 6.05 W
Plaški 36 45.05 N 15.22 E
Plassenburg ⊥ 60 50.06 N 11.28 E
Plassey 126 23.47 N 88.15 E
Plast 86 54.22 N 60.50 E
Plaster Rock 186 46.54 N 67.24 W
Plastovo 82 54.17 N 37.03 E
Plastun 89 44.45 N 136.19 E
Plastunovskaja 78 45.18 N 39.16 E
Plasy 60 49.56 N 13.24 E
Plata, Isla de la I 246 1.16 S 81.06 W
Plata, Río de la c¹ 258 35.00 S 57.00 W
Plata, Río de la ≃ 240m 18.29 N 66.15 W
Platani ≃ 70 37.24 N 13.16 E
Platania ≃ 68 39.00 N 16.19 E
Plátanos 288 34.47 S 58.11 W
Plátanos, Arroyo ≃ 288 34.45 S 58.08 W
Plate, Île I 275a 45.22 N 73.48 W
Platea 214 41.57 N 80.20 W
Plateau □³ 150 8.45 N 8.30 E
Plateau Creek ≃ 200 39.11 N 108.18 W
Plateaux □⁵ 152 2.15 S 15.30 E
Platì 68 38.13 N 16.03 E
Platinum 180 59.01 N 161.49 W
Platnirovskaja 78 45.23 N 39.23 E
Plato 246 9.47 N 74.47 W
Platono-Petrovka 83 46.59 N 39.28 E
Platonovka 80 52.43 N 41.57 E
Platón Sánchez 234 21.17 N 98.22 W
Platovo 83 48.05 N 39.53 E
Platrand 158 27.08 S 29.29 E
Platt 260 51.17 N 0.20 E
Platta 58 46.40 N 8.51 E
Platte 198 43.23 N 98.50 W
Platte ≃, U.S. 194 39.16 N 94.50 W
Platte ≃, Mn., U.S. 190 45.47 N 94.17 W
Platte ≃, Ne., U.S. 198 41.04 N 95.53 W
Platte ≃, Wi., U.S. 190 42.37 N 90.40 W
Platte Center 198 41.32 N 97.29 W
Platte City 194 39.22 N 94.46 W
Platte Creek ≃ 198 43.19 N 99.00 W
Platte Island I 138 5.52 S 55.23 E
Plattekill 210 41.37 N 74.05 W
Platteville, Co., U.S. 200 40.12 N 104.49 W
Platteville, Wi., U.S. 190 42.44 N 90.28 W
Platt Hall ⊥ 262 53.27 N 2.13 W
Plattling 60 48.47 N 12.53 E
Plattsburg 194 39.33 N 94.26 W
Plattsburgh 188 44.41 N 73.27 W
Plattsburgh Air Force Base ■ 188 44.40 N 73.28 W
Plattsmouth 198 41.00 N 95.52 W
Plattsville 212 43.18 N 80.37 W
Platveld 156 19.58 S 17.07 E
Plau 54 53.27 N 12.16 E
Plaue, Dtsch. 54 52.24 N 12.25 E
Plaue, Dtsch. 54 50.47 N 10.54 E
Plauen 54 50.30 N 12.08 E
Plauer See ⊜ 54 53.30 N 12.20 E
Plav 38 42.36 N 19.56 E
Plave 64 46.02 N 13.36 E
Pļaviņas 76 56.37 N 25.43 E
Plavsk 76 53.43 N 37.18 E
Plaxtol 260 51.15 N 0.18 E
Playa Azul 234 17.59 N 102.24 W
Playa Baracoa 286b 23.03 N 82.34 W
Playa Bonita 236 9.39 N 84.27 W
Playa de Fajardo 240m 18.20 N 65.38 W
Playa de Guayanés 240m 18.04 N 65.49 W
Playa de Guayanilla 240m 18.01 N 66.46 W
Playa del Carmen 232 20.36 N 87.06 W
Playa del Rey ◆⁸ 280 33.58 N 118.26 W
Playa de Naguabo 240m 18.12 N 65.43 W
Playa de Ponce 240m 17.59 N 66.37 W
Playa Noriega, Laguna ⊜ 232 29.10 N 111.50 W
Playas Lake ⊜ 200 31.50 N 108.34 W
Playa Vicente 234 17.50 N 95.49 W
Play Cu 110 13.59 N 108.00 E
Playford ≃ 162 19.03 S 135.35 E
Playgreen Lake ⊜ 184 54.00 N 98.10 W
Playland ♦ 276 40.58 N 73.41 W
Plaza 198 48.01 N 101.57 W
Plaza at Mid Island ◆⁹ 276 40.46 N 73.32 W
Plaza de Caisán 236 8.46 N 82.45 W
Plaza de Mayo ♦ 288 34.36 S 58.23 W
Plaza de Toros ♦ 266a 40.26 N 3.39 W
Plaza de Toros Las Arenas ♦ 266d 41.23 N 2.09 W
Plaza de Toros Monumental ♦ 266d 41.24 N 2.11 E
Plaza Huincul 252 38.55 S 69.09 W
Plaza Park 285 40.04 N 74.53 W
Plazas de Soberanía en el Norte de África → Spanish North Africa □² 34 35.53 N 5.19 W
Pleasant 275b 43.41 N 79.49 W
Pleasant, Lake ⊜¹ 200 33.53 N 112.16 W
Pleasant, Mount ∧ 192 37.44 N 79.10 W
Pleasant, Mount ∧² 186 45.26 N 66.49 W
Pleasant Bay 186 46.49 N 60.48 W
Pleasantdale, Sk., Can. 184 52.35 N 104.30 W
Pleasantdale, N.Y., U.S. 210 42.47 N 73.40 W
Pleasant Gap 214 40.52 N 77.44 W
Pleasant Garden 192 35.57 N 79.45 W
Pleasant Grove, Ca., U.S. 226 38.49 N 121.29 W
Pleasant Grove, Ut,. U.S. 200 40.21 N 111.44 W
Pleasant Grove Creek ≃ 226 38.48 N 121.32 W
Pleasant Hill, Ca., U.S. 226 37.56 N 122.03 W
Pleasant Hill, Il., U.S. 219 39.26 N 90.52 W
Pleasant Hill, La., U.S. 194 31.49 N 93.31 W
Pleasant Hill, Mo., U.S. 194 38.47 N 94.16 W
Pleasant Hill, N.C., U.S. 208 36.32 N 77.32 W
Pleasant Hill, Oh., U.S. 218 40.03 N 84.20 W
Pleasant Hill Lake ⊜¹ 214 40.38 N 82.21 W
Pleasant Hills 214 40.20 N 79.57 W
Pleasant Lake, In., U.S. 216 41.34 N 85.00 W
Pleasant Lake, Mi., U.S. 216 42.23 N 84.22 W
Pleasant Lake ⊜ 216 42.13 N 83.56 W
Pleasant Mills 216 40.47 N 84.51 W
Pleasant Mount 210 41.44 N 75.26 W
Pleasanton, Ca., U.S. 226 37.39 N 121.52 W
Pleasanton, Ks., U.S. 198 38.10 N 94.42 W
Pleasanton, Tx., U.S. 196 28.58 N 98.28 W
Pleasanton Ridge ∧ 282 37.40 N 121.55 W
Pleasant Plains, Il., U.S. 219 39.52 N 89.55 W
Pleasant Plains, N.J., U.S. 208 40.00 N 74.13 W
Pleasant Point 172 44.16 S 171.08 E
Pleasant Prairie 216 42.33 N 87.57 W
Pleasant Ridge 281 42.31 N 83.10 W
Pleasant Unity 214 40.15 N 79.28 W
Pleasant Valley, N.Y., U.S. 210 41.44 N 73.49 W
Pleasant Valley, Oh., U.S. 218 39.22 N 83.03 W
Pleasant Valley, Pa., U.S. 279b 40.31 N 75.18 W
Pleasantville, Ia., U.S. 190 41.23 N 93.16 W
Pleasantville, Md., U.S. 284b 39.11 N 76.38 W
Pleasantville, N.J., U.S. 208 39.23 N 74.31 W
Pleasantville, N.Y., U.S. 210 41.07 N 73.47 W
Pleasantville, Pa., U.S. 214 41.35 N 79.34 W
Pleasington 262 53.44 N 2.34 W
Pleasure Beach 207 41.18 N 72.08 W
Pleasure Ridge Park 218 38.09 N 85.51 W
Pleasureville 218 38.33 N 85.04 W
Pléaux 32 45.08 N 2.14 E
Plechanovo 82 54.14 N 37.33 E
Plechanovskoje 76 52.39 N 39.50 E
Plechovo 78 51.07 N 35.18 E
Plechý (Plöckenstein) ∧ 60 48.46 N 13.51 E
Pledger 222 29.11 N 95.55 W
Pleebo 150 4.35 N 7.40 W
Pleiku → Play Cu 110 13.59 N 108.00 E
Pleinfeld 56 49.06 N 10.59 E
Pleissa 54 50.50 N 12.46 E
Pleisse ≃ 54 51.20 N 12.22 E

Symbols in the index entries represent the broad categories identified in the key at the right. Symbols with superior numbers (⋀¹) identify subcategories (see complete key on page I · 1).

Symbole im Register stellen die rechts im Schlüssel erklärten Kategorien dar. Symbole mit hochgestellten Ziffern (⋀¹) bezeichnen Unterabteilungen einer Kategorie (vgl. vollständiger Schlüssel auf Seite I · 1).

Los símbolos incluidos en el texto del índice representan las grandes categorías identificadas con la clave a la derecha. Los símbolos con números en su parte superior (⋀¹) identifican las subcategorías (véase la clave completa en la página I · 1).

Les symboles de l'index représentent les catégories indiquées dans la légende à droite. Les symboles suivis d'un indice (⋀¹) représentent des sous-catégories (voir légende complète à la page I · 1).

Os símbolos incluídos no texto do índice representam as grandes categorias identificadas com a chave à direita. Os símbolos com números em sua parte superior (⋀¹) identificam as subcategorias (veja-se a chave completa à página I · 1).

∧ Mountain	Berg	Montaña	Montagne	Montanha
⋀ Mountains	Gebirge	Montañas	Montagnes	Montanhas
)(Pass	Paß	Paso	Col	Passo
V Valley, Canyon	Tal, Cañon	Valle, Cañón	Vallée, Canyon	Vale, Canhão
≡ Plain	Ebene	Llano	Plaine	Planície
> Cape	Kap	Cabo	Cap	Cabo
I Island	Insel	Isla	Île	Ilha
II Islands	Inseln	Islas	Îles	Ilhas
⊥ Other Topographic Features	Andere Topographische Objekte	Otros Elementos Topográficos	Autres données topographiques	Outros acidentes topográficos

ESPAÑOL / FRANÇAIS / PORTUGUÊS

Nombre / Nom / Nome	Página / Page / Página	Lat.°′	Long.°′ W = Oeste / W = Ouest / W = Oeste
Pléneuf	32	48.36 N	2.33 W
Plenty	184	51.47 N	108.36 W
Plenty ≐, Austl.	162	23.25 S	136.31 E
Plenty ≐, Austl.	274b	37.45 S	145.07 E
Plenty, Bay of c	172	37.40 S	177.00 E
Plentywood	198	48.46 N	104.33 W
Plered	115a	6.38 S	107.23 E
Pleščejevo, ozero ⊜	82	56.46 N	38.47 E
Pleščenicy	76	54.25 N	27.50 E
Pleseck	24	62.43 N	40.20 E
Plešivka	82	54.23 N	37.09 E
Plesna ≐	54	50.07 N	12.28 E
Pless	58	48.05 N	10.08 E
Plessa	54	51.28 N	13.37 E
Plessisville	206	46.14 N	71.47 W
Pless → Pszczyna	30	49.59 N	18.57 E
Pleszew	30	51.54 N	17.48 E
Pletenevka	82	54.31 N	36.06 E
Pleternica	38	45.17 N	17.48 E
Plétipi, Lac ⊜	176	51.44 N	70.06 W
Plet'onyj Tašlyk	78	48.29 N	31.40 E
Plettenberg	56	51.13 N	7.52 E
Plettenbergbaai	158	34.04 S	23.22 E
Pleurs	50	48.41 N	3.52 E
Pleven	38	43.25 N	24.37 E
Plevna, Mo., U.S.	219	39.58 N	92.05 W
Plevna, Mt., U.S.	198	46.25 N	104.31 W
Pleyben	32	48.14 N	3.58 W
Pleystein	60	49.39 N	12.25 E
Pliening	60	48.12 N	11.48 E
Pliezhausen	56	48.33 N	9.12 E
Plimmerton	172	41.05 S	174.52 E
Plimoth Plantation ⊥	207	41.57 N	70.38 W
Plintovka	265a	60.01 N	30.46 E
Pliski	78	51.07 N	32.24 E
Pliskov	78	49.23 N	29.18 E
Pliszka ≐	54	52.14 N	14.42 E
Plitvička Jezera Nacionalni Park ♠	36	44.53 N	15.38 E
Plješevica ⋏	36	44.40 N	15.45 E
Pljevlja	38	43.21 N	19.21 E
Ploaghe	71	40.40 N	8.45 E
Ploče	36	43.04 N	17.26 E
Plochingen	56	48.42 N	9.25 E
Płock	30	52.33 N	19.43 E
Płock □[4]	30	52.25 N	19.45 E
Plöckenpass)(	64	46.36 N	12.58 E
Plöckenstein (Plechý) ∧	60	48.46 N	13.51 E
Plockton	46	57.20 N	5.39 W
Pločno ∧	36	43.23 N	17.57 E
Plodorodnoje	80	46.44 N	41.06 E
Ploegsteert	50	50.43 N	2.53 E
Ploërmel	32	47.56 N	2.24 W
Ploești → Ploiești	38	44.56 N	26.02 E
Plogastel-Saint-Germain	28	47.59 N	4.16 W
Ploiești	38	44.56 N	26.02 E
Plomárion	38	38.59 N	26.22 E
Plomb du Cantal ∧	32	45.03 N	2.46 E
Plombières-les-Bains	58	47.58 N	6.29 E
Plombières-lès-Dijon	58	47.20 N	4.58 E
Plomer	258	34.48 S	59.02 W
Plomer, Point ≻	166	31.19 S	152.58 E
Plön	54	54.09 N	10.25 E
Plonge, Lac la ⊜	184	55.08 N	107.25 W
Płońsk	30	52.38 N	20.23 E
Pl'os	80	57.27 N	41.31 E
Plose, Cima delle ∧	64	46.42 N	11.44 E
Ploskij	78	46.17 N	40.15 E
Ploskoje	76	52.45 N	38.21 E
Ploskoš'	76	56.46 N	31.16 E
Pl'oso	76	59.47 N	35.43 E
Plotbišče	80	56.50 N	50.35 E
Plotina	83	48.33 N	40.05 E
Plotnica	78	52.03 N	26.39 E
Plottier	252	38.58 S	68.14 W
Płoty	30	53.49 N	15.16 E
Plötz	54	51.38 N	11.56 E
Plouay	32	47.55 N	3.20 W
Ploučnice ≐	54	50.47 N	14.13 E
Ploudalmézeau	32	48.32 N	4.39 W
Plouguenast	32	48.17 N	2.43 W
Plouha	32	48.41 N	2.56 W
Plovdiv	38	42.09 N	24.45 E
Plover ≐	190	44.29 N	89.35 W
Plover Islands II	180	71.15 N	155.30 W
Pluckemin	276	40.39 N	74.39 W
Plum, Pa., U.S.	214	40.31 N	79.45 W
Plum, Pa., U.S.	214	41.35 N	79.51 W
Plum, Tx., U.S.	222	29.56 N	96.58 W
Pluma Hidalgo	234	15.55 N	96.25 W
Plumas	184	50.25 N	99.02 W
Plumbridge	48	54.46 N	7.15 W
Plum Brook ≐	281	42.34 N	82.58 W
Plum Creek ≐, Il., U.S.	278	41.33 N	87.29 W
Plum Creek ≐, Ne., U.S.	198	41.52 N	96.44 W
Plum Creek ≐, Oh., U.S.	279a	41.18 N	82.09 W
Plum Creek ≐, Pa., U.S.	279b	40.31 N	79.51 W
Plum Creek ≐, S.D., U.S.	198	44.13 N	100.43 W
Plum Creek ≐, Tx., U.S.	196	29.38 N	97.36 W
Plum Creek, Clear Fork ≐	222	29.45 N	97.37 W
Plumerville	194	35.09 N	92.38 W
Plum Grove	222	30.15 N	95.05 W
Plum Grove Estates	278	42.04 N	88.02 W
Plum Island	283	42.49 N	70.59 W
Plum Island I, Ma., U.S.	207	42.45 N	70.48 W
Plum Island I, N.Y., U.S.	207	41.11 N	72.12 W
Plum Island Airport ⊠	283	42.48 N	70.50 W
Plum Island Sound ʯ	283	42.45 N	70.48 W
Plum Island State Park ♠	283	42.42 N	70.47 W
Plumley	262	53.17 N	2.25 W
Plummer	202	47.20 N	116.53 W
Plummers Landing	218	38.19 N	83.33 W
Plumper Sound ʯ	224	48.47 N	123.13 W
Plum Point ≻	276	40.50 N	40.43 W
Plumpton	274a	33.45 S	150.50 E
Plumridge Lakes ⊜	162	29.30 S	125.25 E
Plum Run ≐	279b	40.15 N	80.13 W
Plumsteadville	208	40.23 N	75.09 W
Plumtree	154	20.30 S	27.50 E
Plumville	214	40.48 N	79.11 W
Plumwood	218	40.01 N	83.23 W
Plungė	76	55.55 N	21.51 E
Pl'uskovo	76	52.46 N	33.49 E
Pl'ussa	76	58.26 N	29.21 E
Pl'ussa ≐	76	59.19 N	28.11 E
Plutarco Elías Calles, Presa ⊜[1]	232	29.10 N	109.40 W
Pluvigner	32	47.46 N	3.01 E
Plym ≐	42	50.12 N	4.07 W
Plymouth, Monts.	238	16.42 N	62.13 W
Plymouth, Trin.	241r	11.13 N	60.47 W
Plymouth, Eng., U.K.	42	50.23 N	4.10 W
Plymouth, Ca., U.S.	226	38.29 N	120.51 W
Plymouth, Ct., U.S.	207	41.40 N	73.03 W
Plymouth, Il., U.S.	194	40.17 N	90.55 W
Plymouth, In., U.S.	216	41.20 N	86.18 W
Plymouth, Ma., U.S.	207	41.57 N	70.40 W
Plymouth, Mi., U.S.	216	42.22 N	83.28 W
Plymouth, Ne., U.S.	198	40.18 N	96.59 W
Plymouth, N.H., U.S.	188	43.45 N	71.41 W
Plymouth, N.Y., U.S.	210	42.37 N	75.36 W
Plymouth, N.C., U.S.	192	35.52 N	76.44 W
Plymouth, Oh., U.S.	214	41.00 N	82.40 W
Plymouth, Pa., U.S.	210	41.14 N	75.56 W
Plymouth, Wi., U.S.	190	43.44 N	87.58 W
Plymouth □[6]	207	41.58 N	70.41 W
Plymouth ≐	283	42.12 N	70.54 W
Plymouth Airport ⊠	42	50.25 N	4.06 W
Plymouth Bay c	207	41.57 N	70.37 W
Plymouth Harbor c	283	41.58 N	70.39 W
Plymouth Meeting	285	40.06 N	75.16 W
Plymouth Meeting Mall ◆[9]	285	40.07 N	75.17 W
Plymouth Rock ⊥	207	41.57 N	70.39 W
Plymouth Valley	285	40.07 N	75.23 W
Plympton, Eng., U.K.	42	50.23 N	4.03 W
Plympton, Ma., U.S.	207	41.57 N	70.48 W
Plymptonville	214	41.03 N	78.28 W
Plymstock	42	50.22 N	4.04 W
Plynlimon ∧	42	52.28 N	3.47 W
Plzeň	60	49.45 N	13.23 E
Pniewy	30	52.31 N	16.15 E
Pô	150	11.10 N	1.09 W
Po ≐, It.	36	44.57 N	12.04 E
Po ≐, Zhg.	100	28.57 N	116.39 E
Po, Foci del ≐[1]	64	44.52 N	12.30 E
Pô, Parc National de ♠	150	11.30 N	1.15 W
Poá	256	23.32 S	46.20 W
Poá ≐	287b	23.37 S	46.45 W
Poana ≐	250	0.56 N	57.03 W
Poarta Orientală, Pasul)(	38	45.06 N	22.18 E
Poás, Volcán ∧[1]	236	10.11 N	84.13 W
Pobé, Bénin	150	6.58 N	2.41 E
Pobé, Burkina	150	13.53 N	1.45 W
Pobeda, gora ∧	74	65.12 N	146.12 E
Pobeda Ice Island I	9	64.30 S	97.00 E
Pobedino	74	49.51 N	142.49 E
Pobedy, pik ∧	72	42.02 N	80.05 E
Pobershau	54	50.38 N	13.13 E
Poběžovice	60	49.31 N	12.48 E
Poblado Cerro Gordo	240m	18.29 N	66.20 W
Poblado Jacaguas	240m	18.03 N	66.32 W
Poblado Mediania Alta	240m	18.26 N	65.50 W
Poblado Sábalos	240m	18.11 N	67.09 W
Poblado Santana	240m	18.27 N	66.40 W
Poblet	258	35.04 S	57.57 W
Pocahontas, Ar., U.S.	194	36.15 N	90.58 W
Pocahontas, Il., U.S.	219	38.49 N	89.32 W
Pocahontas, Ia., U.S.	198	42.44 N	94.40 W
Pocahontas State Park ♠	208	37.23 N	77.34 W
Počajev	78	50.01 N	25.31 E
Pocantico Hills	276	41.06 N	73.50 W
Pocantico Lake ⊜	276	41.07 N	73.50 W
Poção	250	8.11 S	36.42 W
Pocasset	207	41.41 N	70.37 W
Pocatalico ≐	188	38.29 N	81.49 W
Pocatello	202	42.52 N	112.26 W
Počep	76	52.56 N	33.27 E
Počepy	76	53.17 N	31.20 E
Pocé-sur-Cisse	50	47.26 N	0.59 E
Pöchlarn	61	48.12 N	15.13 E
Pochvistnevo	80	53.38 N	52.08 E
Pocinhos, Bra.	250	7.04 S	36.03 W
Pocinhos, Bra.	256	21.56 S	46.25 W
Počinki	80	54.42 N	44.51 E
Počinnaja Sopka	76	58.25 N	34.22 E
Počinok	76	54.25 N	32.27 E
Pocitos, Salar ≅	252	24.30 S	67.03 W
Pockau	54	50.40 N	13.27 E
Pocking	60	48.24 N	13.19 E
Pocklington	44	53.56 N	0.46 W
Pocoata	248	18.41 S	66.11 W
Poço da Cruz, Açude ⊜[1]	250	8.30 S	37.35 W
Poço do Bispo ◆[8]	266c	38.44 N	9.06 W
Poções	255	14.31 S	40.21 W
Poço Fundo	256	21.48 S	45.58 W
Poço Fundo, Cachoeira do ʟ	256	22.10 S	44.13 W
Pocol	64	46.31 N	12.07 E
Pocola	194	35.13 N	94.28 W
Pocomoke ≐	208	37.58 N	75.39 W
Pocomoke City	208	38.04 N	75.34 W
Pocomoke Sound ʯ	208	37.52 N	75.49 W
Pocona	248	17.39 S	65.24 W
Poconé	248	16.15 S	56.37 W
Pocono International Raceway ♠	210	41.03 N	75.31 W
Pocono Lake	210	41.06 N	75.31 W
Pocono Manor	210	41.06 N	75.22 W
Pocono Mountains ⋏[2]	210	41.10 N	75.20 W
Pocono Pines	210	41.05 N	75.29 W
Pocono Summit	210	41.07 N	75.25 W
Pocopson	285	39.54 N	75.37 W
Pocopson Creek ≐	285	39.54 N	75.37 W
Poço Redondo	250	9.49 S	37.41 W
Poços de Caldas	256	21.48 S	46.34 W
Poço Verde	250	10.42 S	38.11 W
Pocrane	255	19.37 S	41.37 W
Pocrí	236	8.16 N	80.33 W
Podbel'skaja	80	53.37 N	51.50 E
Podberezje, Ross.	76	56.57 N	30.38 E
Podberezje, Ross.	82	56.46 N	37.10 E
Podbořany	54	50.11 N	13.25 E
Podborki	82	54.11 N	35.56 E
Podborovje	76	59.30 N	35.02 E
Podbuž	78	49.22 N	23.15 E
Podbužje	76	53.30 N	34.56 E
Podčerje	24	63.57 N	57.34 E
Podchožeje	82	54.19 N	38.34 E
Podčinnyj	80	50.52 N	45.13 E
Poddębice	30	51.53 N	18.58 E
Poddemjur	24	64.05 N	53.26 E
Poddolgoje	76	53.12 N	38.04 E
Poddorje	76	57.28 N	31.07 E
Poděbrady	30	50.08 N	15.07 E
Po della Donzella ≐	64	44.48 N	12.25 E
Po delle Tolle ≐	64	44.50 N	12.28 E
Podensac	32	44.39 N	0.22 W
Podenzano	62	44.57 N	9.41 E
Podersdorf am See	61	47.51 N	16.50 E
Podgajcy	78	49.16 N	25.08 E
Podgorenskij	78	50.24 N	39.39 E
Podgorica → Titograd	38	42.26 N	19.14 E
Podgornaja	78	50.28 N	41.10 E
Podgornoje, Kaz.	85	42.55 N	72.25 E
Podgornoje, Ross.	78	51.43 N	39.07 E
Podgornoje, Ross.	78	50.27 N	39.37 E
Podgornoje, Ross.	80	46.33 N	43.07 E
Podgornoje, Ross.	86	57.47 N	82.36 E
Podgorodnaja	78	48.07 N	30.51 E
Podgorodnoje	78	48.34 N	35.08 E
Podhůří	60	49.28 N	13.40 E
Podi	112	1.08 S	121.16 E
Po di Goro ≐	64	44.48 N	12.27 E
Po di Volano ≐	64	44.49 N	12.15 E
Podjom-Michajlovka	80	52.49 N	50.32 E
Podjuchy ◆[8]	54	53.20 N	14.36 E
Podkamen'	78	49.57 N	25.19 E
Podkamennaja Tunguska	74	61.36 N	90.09 E
Podkamennaja Tunguska ≐	74	61.36 N	90.18 E
Podkoren	64	46.30 N	13.45 E
Podkumok ≐	84	44.14 N	43.36 E
Podlasie ◆[1]	30	52.30 N	23.00 E
Podlesnoje, Ross.	80	51.50 N	47.03 E
Podlesnoje, Ukr.	78	48.47 N	32.15 E
Podlopatki	88	50.55 N	107.05 E
Podmošje	82	56.23 N	37.24 E
Podol'sk	82	55.26 N	37.33 E
Podol'skaja vozvyšennost' ⋏[1]	78	49.00 N	27.00 E
Podor, Maur.	150	16.40 N	15.00 W
Podor, Sén.	150	16.40 N	14.57 W
Podora	24	62.22 N	54.19 E
Podosinovec	24	60.17 N	47.04 E
Podoz'orskij	80	57.14 N	40.20 E
Podporožje	24	60.53 N	34.07 E
Podravina ◆[1]	38	45.40 N	17.40 E
Podravska Slatina	38	45.42 N	17.42 E
Podrezčicha	24	59.22 N	51.28 E
Podstepnyj	80	51.08 N	51.28 E
Podsvilje	76	55.09 N	27.58 E
Podt'osovo	88	58.36 N	92.06 E
Pod'uga	24	61.06 N	40.53 E
Podujevo	38	42.55 N	21.11 E
Poduškino	265b	55.43 N	37.17 E
Podu Turcului	38	46.12 N	27.23 E
Podvoločisk	78	49.33 N	26.09 E
Podymachino	88	56.59 N	106.11 E
Podyvotje	78	52.03 N	34.08 E
Poe	216	40.56 N	85.05 W
Poechos, Embalse ⊜[1]	246	4.40 S	80.30 W
Poel I	54	54.00 N	11.26 E
Poeldijk	52	52.01 N	4.12 E
Poelela, Lagoa ⊜	156	24.38 S	35.00 E
Poelkapelle	50	50.55 N	2.57 E
Poestenkill	210	42.41 N	73.34 W
Poesten Kill ≐	210	42.43 N	73.42 W
Poetto	71	39.12 N	9.10 E
Pofadder	158	29.10 S	19.22 E
Pogamasing Lake ⊜	190	46.57 N	81.50 W
Pogan, Zhg.	100	27.40 N	116.46 E
Pogan, Zhg.	100	28.18 N	116.46 E
Pogăniș ≐	38	45.41 N	21.22 E
Pogar	76	52.33 N	33.16 E
Poge, Cape ≻	207	41.25 N	70.27 W
Poggendorf	54	54.03 N	13.07 E
Poggiardo	68	40.03 N	18.23 E
Poggibonsi	66	43.28 N	11.09 E
Poggio	64	44.30 N	10.00 E
Poggio Berni	66	44.02 N	12.24 E
Poggio Bustone	66	42.30 N	12.53 E
Poggio Imperiale	68	41.49 N	15.22 E
Poggiomarino	68	40.48 N	14.32 E
Poggio Mirteto	66	42.16 N	12.41 E
Poggio Moiano	66	42.12 N	12.53 E
Poggioreale	70	37.47 N	13.01 E
Poggio Renatico	64	44.46 N	11.29 E
Poggiorsini	68	40.55 N	16.15 E
Poggio Rusco	64	44.59 N	11.07 E
Poggio Sannita	66	41.47 N	14.25 E
Pöggstall	61	48.19 N	15.12 E
Pogibi	89	52.12 N	141.42 E
Pogil-to I	98	34.09 N	126.33 E
Pogliano	266b	45.32 N	8.59 E
Pogny	56	48.52 N	4.29 E
Pogoanele	38	44.54 N	27.00 E
Pogodajev	80	51.37 N	51.04 E
Pogoniani	38	40.00 N	20.25 E
Pogoreloje Gorodišče	76	56.08 N	34.56 E
Pogoso	152	6.46 S	17.12 E
Pogost, Bela.	76	52.51 N	27.39 E
Pogost, Bela.	76	53.51 N	29.09 E
Pogost, Ross.	80	57.39 N	42.33 E
Pogost, Ross.	82	56.52 N	39.04 E
Pogožeje	78	51.36 N	37.16 E
Pogradec	38	40.54 N	20.39 E
Po Grande ≐	64	44.57 N	12.26 E
Pograničnoje	80	50.32 N	48.38 E
Pograničnyj, Ross.	80	46.57 N	45.46 E
Pograničnyj, Ross.	89	44.25 N	131.24 E
Pogrebišče	78	49.29 N	29.16 E
Pogromni Volcano ∧[1]	180	54.33 N	164.45 W
Pogromnoje	80	52.35 N	52.32 E
Pogruznaja	80	54.14 N	50.29 E
Poh	112	0.46 S	122.49 E
P'ohang	98	36.03 N	129.20 E
Pohatcong Creek ≐	210	40.37 N	75.11 W
Pohénégamook	186	47.31 N	69.16 W
Pohick Creek ≐	284c	38.46 N	77.14 W
Pohick Creek, Rabbit Branch ≐	284c	38.48 N	77.17 W
Pohick Creek, Sideburn Branch ≐	284c	38.48 N	77.17 W
Pohjanmaa ◆[1]	26	64.00 N	25.00 E
Pohjois-Karjalan lääni □[4]	24	63.00 N	30.00 E
Pöhl, Talsperre ◆[6]	54	50.33 N	12.12 E
Pöhla	54	50.31 N	12.49 E
Pöhlde	52	51.37 N	10.18 E
Pohl-Göns	56	50.28 N	8.39 E
Pohlheim	56	50.34 N	8.45 E
Pohnpei I	174r	6.55 N	158.15 E
Pohořelice	61	48.59 N	16.32 E
Pohorje ⋏	36	46.30 N	15.20 E
Pohri	124	25.32 N	77.21 E
Pohsien → Boxian	100	33.53 N	115.45 E
Pohue Bay c	229d	19.00 N	155.48 W
Poiana Mare	38	43.55 N	23.04 E
Poiana Ruscă, Munții ⋏	38	45.41 N	22.30 E
Pöide	76	58.31 N	23.03 E
Poigny-la-Forêt	261	48.41 N	1.45 E
Poim	80	53.01 N	43.11 E
Poinsett, Cape ≻	9	65.42 S	113.18 E
Poinsett, Lake ⊜, Fl., U.S.	220	28.20 N	80.50 W
Poinsett, Lake ⊜, S.D., U.S.	198	44.34 N	97.05 W
Point	222	32.56 N	95.52 W
Point Arena	204	38.54 N	123.41 W
Point Au Fer Island I	194	29.15 N	91.15 W
Point Baker	180	56.21 N	133.37 W
Pointblank	222	30.45 N	95.13 W
Point Chautauqua	214	42.14 N	79.28 W
Point Comfort	196	28.41 N	96.33 W
Point Cook	274b	37.56 S	144.45 E
Point Cook Royal Australian Air Force Station ■	169	37.56 S	144.45 E
Point du Jour, Ruisseau du ≐	206	45.50 N	73.25 W
Pointe-à-la-Frégate	186	49.12 N	64.55 W
Pointe-à-la-Garde	186	48.05 N	66.32 W
Pointe a la Hache	194	29.34 N	89.47 W
Pointe-à-Maurier	186	50.20 N	59.48 W
Pointe-à-Pitre	241o	16.14 N	61.32 W
Pointe-à-Pitre-le Raizet, Aéroport de ⊠	241o	16.17 N	61.32 W
Pointe-au-Chêne	206	45.38 N	74.45 W
Pointe Aux Peaux Farms	216	41.57 N	83.16 W
Pointe-aux-Trembles	206	45.39 N	73.30 W
Pointe-Calumet	275a	45.30 N	73.58 W
Pointe-Claire	206	45.26 N	73.50 W
Pointe-des-Cascades	275a	45.20 N	73.58 W
Pointe-des-Galets → Le Port	157c	20.55 S	55.18 E
Pointe-du-Moulin	275a	45.22 N	73.52 W
Point Edward	214	43.00 N	82.24 W
Pointe-Noire, Congo	152	4.48 S	11.51 E
Pointe-Noire, Guad.	241o	16.14 N	61.47 W
Point Enterprise	222	31.40 N	96.26 W
Pointers	208	39.35 N	75.26 W
Point Fortin	241r	10.11 N	61.41 W
Point Hope	180	68.21 N	166.41 W
Point Imperial ∧	200	36.16 N	111.58 W
Point Independence	207	41.44 N	70.39 W
Point Lake ⊜	176	65.15 N	113.04 W
Point Leamington	186	49.20 N	55.24 W
Point Lookout, Md., U.S.	208	38.02 N	76.19 W
Point Lookout, N.Y., U.S.	276	40.35 N	73.35 W
Point Marion	188	39.44 N	79.53 W
Point McLeay	168b	35.32 S	139.06 E
Point Nepean National Park ♠	169	38.25 S	144.45 E
Point of Rocks	208	39.16 N	77.32 W
Point O'Woods	276	40.39 N	73.08 W
Point Pass	168b	34.05 S	139.03 E
Point Pelee National Park ♠	214	41.57 N	82.30 W
Point Peninsula ≻[1]	212	44.01 N	76.15 W
Point Pleasant, Md., U.S.	284b	39.11 N	76.35 W
Point Pleasant, N.J., U.S.	208	40.04 N	74.04 W
Point Pleasant, Oh., U.S.	218	38.54 N	84.14 W
Point Pleasant, Pa., U.S.	208	40.25 N	75.04 W
Point Pleasant, W.V., U.S.	188	38.50 N	82.08 W
Point Pleasant Beach	208	40.05 N	74.02 W
Point Reyes National Seashore ♠	204	38.00 N	122.58 W
Point Roberts	224	48.59 N	123.04 W
Point Salines International Airport ⊠	241k	12.01 N	61.47 W
Point Samson	162	20.36 S	117.12 E
Point Sapin	186	46.58 N	64.50 W
Point View Reservoir ⊜[1]	276	40.58 N	74.15 W
Point Whiteshed	180	60.28 N	145.57 W
Poirino	62	44.55 N	7.51 E
Poisevo	80	55.32 N	53.30 E
Poison Creek ≐	202	43.15 N	108.09 W
Poison Spider Creek ≐	200	42.46 N	106.31 W
Poisson Blanc, Réservoir du ⊜[1]	188	46.00 N	75.45 W
Poissonnier Point ≻	162	19.57 S	119.11 E
Poissons	58	48.25 N	5.13 E
Poissy	50	48.56 N	2.03 E
Poitiers	32	46.35 N	0.20 E
Poitou □[9]	32	46.20 N	0.30 W
Poix	50	49.47 N	1.59 E
Poix-Terron	56	49.39 N	4.39 E
Pojarkovo	89	49.38 N	128.38 E
Pojma ≐	88	56.54 N	97.48 E
Pojo	248	17.45 S	64.49 W
Pojoaque Valley	200	35.59 N	106.00 W
Pojuca	255	12.21 S	38.20 W
Pojuca ≐	255	12.34 S	38.03 W
Pokagon State Park ♠	216	41.43 N	85.01 W
Pokaran	120	26.55 N	71.55 E
Pokataroo	166	29.35 S	148.42 E
Pokatejeva	88	56.59 N	97.25 E
Pokatilovka, Kaz.	80	51.06 N	51.53 E
Pokatilovka, Kaz.	86	45.23 N	80.10 E
Poke Run ≐	279b	40.30 N	79.33 W
Pokharā	124	28.14 N	83.59 E
Pokharia	126	23.55 N	86.37 E
Poko, Sūd.	140	5.38 N	31.50 E
Poko, Zaïre	154	3.09 N	26.53 E
Pokoinu	174k	21.12 S	159.49 W
Pokojnoje	84	44.48 N	44.16 E
Pokok Sena	114	6.10 N	100.32 E
Pokol'ubiči	76	52.30 N	31.02 E
Pokrov	82	55.55 N	39.10 E
Pokrovka, Kaz.	86	54.17 N	68.15 E
Pokrovka, Kaz.	86	49.28 N	81.28 E
Pokrovka, Kyrg.	85	42.20 N	78.01 E
Pokrovka, Kyrg.	85	42.45 N	71.36 E
Pokrovka, Ross.	80	48.22 N	46.04 E
Pokrovka, Ross.	80	53.47 N	53.19 E
Pokrovka, Ross.	89	43.57 N	131.39 E
Pokrovo-Kirejevo	83	47.38 N	38.16 E
Pokrovsk	74	61.29 N	129.06 E
Pokrovskaja Arčada	80	52.56 N	44.13 E
Pokrovskij	78	46.32 N	31.38 E
Pokrovskoje, Ross.	76	52.38 N	36.51 E
Pokrovskoje, Ross.	80	54.04 N	43.37 E
Pokrovskoje, Ross.	80	53.54 N	40.26 E
Pokrovskoje, Ross.	82	56.25 N	37.03 E
Pokrovskoje, Ross.	82	55.53 N	36.19 E
Pokrovskoje, Ross.	83	47.25 N	38.54 E
Pokrovskoje, Ross.	86	57.14 N	66.48 E
Pokrovskoje, Ross.	265a	59.44 N	30.46 E
Pokrovskoje, Ukr.	78	49.44 N	38.13 E
Pokrovskoje, Ukr.	78	47.59 N	36.14 E
Pokrovskoje, Ukr.	83	48.37 N	38.09 E
Pokrovskoje ◆[8]	265b	55.37 N	37.37 E
Pokrovsko-Strešnevo ◆[8]	265b	55.49 N	37.29 E
Pokrovsk-Ural'skij	86	60.10 N	59.49 E
Pokur	74	61.02 N	75.26 E
Pola, Pil.	116	13.09 N	121.26 E
Pola, Ross.	76	57.56 N	31.50 E
Pola ≐	76	58.04 N	31.37 E
Pola Bay c	116	13.10 N	121.28 E
Polacca	200	35.50 N	110.22 W
Polacca Wash V	200	35.22 N	110.50 W
Pola de Laviana	34	43.15 N	5.34 W
Pola de Lena	34	43.10 N	5.49 W
Pola de Siero	34	43.23 N	5.40 W
Polān	128	25.35 N	61.12 E
Polanco	252	33.54 S	55.09 W
Poland, Kiribati	174o	1.59 N	157.32 W
Poland, N.Y., U.S.	210	43.13 N	75.03 W
Poland, Oh., U.S.	214	41.01 N	80.37 W
Poland (Polska) □[1], Europe	22	52.00 N	19.00 E
Poland (Polska) □[1], Europe	30	52.00 N	19.00 E
Polangui	116	13.17 N	123.29 E
Polanów	30	54.08 N	16.39 E
Polapare ≐	115b	9.43 S	119.06 E
Pola → Pula	64	44.52 N	13.50 E
Pol'arnik	180	67.03 N	178.53 W
Pol'arnyj, Ross.	24	69.12 N	33.22 E
Pol'arnyj, Ross.	74	69.10 N	178.48 E
Pol'arnyj Ural ⋏	24	66.55 N	64.30 E
Polatlı	130	39.36 N	32.09 E
Polba	272b	22.57 N	88.18 E
Polbain	46	58.02 N	5.23 W
Polbeth	46	55.52 N	3.33 W
Polch	56	50.18 N	7.18 E
Polcirkeln	24	66.34 N	21.05 E
Polcura	252	37.17 S	71.43 W
Połczyn Zdrój	30	53.46 N	16.06 E
Polden Hills ⋏[2]	42	51.08 N	2.50 W
Poldnevica	80	58.37 N	46.38 E
Pol'dorak	85	39.25 N	69.56 E
Poleang	112	4.42 S	121.46 E
Polebridge	182	48.45 N	114.17 W
Polecat Creek ≐	196	36.00 N	95.57 W
Poledník ∧	60	49.04 N	13.24 E
Polee, Pulau I	164	2.12 S	130.15 E
Polegate	42	50.49 N	0.15 E
Pol-e Khomrī	120	35.56 N	68.43 E
Pole Moor	262	53.39 N	1.54 W
Polenezköy ◆[8]	267b	41.07 N	29.12 E
Polen → Poland □[1]	30	52.00 N	19.00 E
Pol-e Safīd	128	36.06 N	53.01 E
Polesden Lacey ⊥	260	51.15 N	0.22 W
Polesella	64	44.58 N	11.45 E
Polesine □[9]	64	45.00 N	11.45 E
Polesine Parmense	64	45.01 N	10.04 E
Polesje	76	53.05 N	31.17 E
Polesje ◆[1]	72	52.00 N	27.00 E
Polessk [Labiau]	76	54.52 N	21.05 E
Polesskoje	78	51.14 N	29.22 E
Polesworth	42	52.37 N	1.36 W
Polevaja	78	51.37 N	36.30 E
Polevskoj	86	56.26 N	60.11 E
Polewali	112	3.25 S	119.20 E
Pol-e Žahāb	128	34.28 N	45.52 E
Polgár	30	47.52 N	21.08 E
Polgooth	42	50.19 N	4.48 W
Pŏlgyo	98	34.52 N	127.21 E
Poli, Cam.	146	8.29 N	13.15 E
Poli, Zhg.	98	35.43 N	119.47 E
Poli, Zhg.	98	35.57 N	118.17 E
Polia	68	38.45 N	16.19 E
Políaigos I	38	36.46 N	24.38 E
Policastro, Golfo di c	68	40.00 N	15.30 E
Policastro Bussentino	68	40.09 N	15.32 E
Police	30	53.35 N	14.33 E
Polička	30	49.43 N	16.16 E
Policoro	68	40.13 N	16.41 E
Polignac	62	45.04 N	3.52 E
Polignano a Mare	68	41.00 N	17.13 E
Poligny	58	46.50 N	5.43 E
Polihale State Park ♠	229b	22.05 N	159.45 W
Políkastron	38	41.00 N	22.34 E
Polikhnítos	38	39.05 N	26.11 E
Polillo	116	14.43 N	121.56 E
Polillo Island I	116	14.50 N	121.57 E
Polillo Islands II	116	14.50 N	122.05 E
Polillo Strait ʯ	116	14.44 N	121.51 E
Polinesia Francesa → French Polynesia □[2]	14	15.00 S	140.00 W
Polinik ∧	64	46.54 N	13.09 E
Polinyà de Vallès	266d	41.33 N	2.10 E
Pólis	130	35.02 N	32.25 E
Polist' ≐	76	58.06 N	31.31 E
Polistena	68	38.25 N	16.05 E
Politécnico Nacional, Instituto ʊ[2]	286a	19.30 N	99.08 W
Politotdel'skoje	83	47.33 N	39.05 E
Pölitz → Police	30	53.35 N	14.33 E
Polivanovo	80	53.36 N	47.23 E
Políyiros	38	40.23 N	23.27 E
Polizzi Generosa	70	37.49 N	14.00 E
Polizzo, Monte ∧	70	37.52 N	12.47 E
Polk, Ne., U.S.	198	41.04 N	97.47 W
Polk, Oh., U.S.	214	40.57 N	82.13 W
Polk, Pa., U.S.	214	41.22 N	79.55 W
Polk □[6], Fl., U.S.	220	28.01 N	81.37 W
Polk □[6], Or., U.S.	224	45.00 N	123.23 W
Polk □[6], Tx., U.S.	222	30.45 N	94.48 W
Polk City	220	28.10 N	81.49 W
Pol'kino	74	71.10 N	99.13 E
Polkton	192	35.00 N	80.12 W
Polla	68	40.30 N	15.30 E
Pollāchi	122	10.40 N	77.01 E
Pollanten	60	49.09 N	11.28 E
Pöllau	61	47.18 N	15.51 E
Pöllauberg	61	47.19 N	15.52 E
Polleben	54	51.34 N	11.36 E
Pollenfeld	60	48.57 N	11.12 E
Pollenza	66	43.16 N	13.21 E
Pollica	68	40.11 N	15.03 E
Pollina	70	37.59 N	14.09 E
Polling	64	47.48 N	11.09 E
Pollino, Monte ∧	68	39.55 N	16.11 E
Polloc Harbor c	116	7.23 N	124.12 E
Pollock, La., U.S.	194	31.31 N	92.24 W
Pollock, S.D., U.S.	198	45.54 N	100.17 W
Pollock Pines	226	38.46 N	120.34 W
Pollock Run ≐	279b	40.14 N	79.47 W
Pollok	222	31.27 N	94.52 W
Pollutri	66	42.08 N	14.35 E
Pollux ∧	172	44.14 S	168.53 E
Polmak	24	70.04 N	28.00 E
Polmont	46	55.59 N	3.42 W
Polná	30	49.29 N	15.43 E
Polnaja ≐	83	48.54 N	39.50 E
Pol'noje-Jaltunovo	80	53.59 N	41.52 E
Polnovo-Seliger	76	57.32 N	32.55 E
Polo, Il., U.S.	190	41.59 N	89.34 W
Polo, Mo., U.S.	194	39.33 N	94.02 W
Polochic ≐	236	15.28 N	89.22 W
Polock, Bela.	76	55.31 N	28.46 E
Polock, Ross.	86	52.46 N	59.42 E
Pologi	78	47.29 N	36.15 E
Pologne → Poland □[1]	30	52.00 N	19.00 E
Pologoje Zajmišče	80	48.29 N	45.57 E
Pologrudovo	86	57.07 N	74.13 E
Polom, Ross.	24	59.13 N	50.50 E
Polom, Ross.	80	57.47 N	53.29 E
Polo Magnético del Sur → South Magnetic Pole ◆	9	65.18 S	139.30 E
Pölömäki ∧[2]	26	63.21 N	27.03 E
Polomet' ≐	76	57.41 N	32.12 E
Polomolo	116	6.14 N	125.03 E
Polonia, Arroyo ≐	258	34.10 S	57.15 W
Polonia → Poland □[1]	30	52.00 N	19.00 E
Polonio, Cabo ≻	252	34.24 S	53.46 W
Polonnaruwa	122	7.56 N	81.00 E
Polonnaruwa ⊥	122	7.56 N	81.00 E
Polonnoje	78	50.07 N	27.30 E
Pološkovo	82	54.08 N	35.53 E
Polo Sur → South Pole ◆	9	90.00 S	0.00
Polotn'anyj	82	54.45 N	36.00 E
Polotsk → Polock	76	55.31 N	28.46 E
Polovinkino	83	49.14 N	38.55 E
Polovinnoje, Ross.	86	54.43 N	63.50 E
Polovinnoje, Ross.	86	53.46 N	79.15 E
Polovo	76	57.03 N	32.27 E
Polperro	42	50.19 N	4.31 W
Polruan	42	50.19 N	4.36 W
Pöls	61	47.11 N	14.45 E
Pölsbach ≐	61	47.11 N	14.45 E
Polska → Poland □[1]	30	52.00 N	19.00 E
Polski Trâmbeš	38	43.22 N	25.38 E
Polson	202	47.41 N	114.09 W
Polster ∧	61	47.32 N	14.58 E
Polsum	52	51.37 N	7.03 E
Poltava	78	49.35 N	34.34 E
Poltavka	86	54.22 N	71.45 E
Poltevy Pen'ki	80	54.35 N	42.06 E
Poltimore	188	45.47 N	75.43 W
Põltsamaa	76	58.38 N	25.58 E
Põltsamaa ≐	76	58.27 N	26.09 E
Poludino	86	54.51 N	69.55 E
Poluj ≐	74	66.31 N	66.33 E
Polunočnoje	72	60.52 N	60.25 E
Polur	122	12.30 N	79.08 E
Polur'adinki	82	54.51 N	38.41 E
Poluškino	265b	55.41 N	38.05 E
Pol'ustrovo ◆[8]	265a	59.58 N	30.25 E
Põlva	76	58.03 N	27.03 E
Polvaredas	258	35.35 S	59.30 W
Polverigi	66	43.31 N	13.23 E
Polvijärvi	26	62.51 N	29.22 E
Polvilho	287b	23.23 S	46.50 W
Polvoranca	266a	40.19 N	3.48 W
Polynesia II	14	4.00 S	156.00 W
Polynesian Cultural Center ʊ	229c	21.39 N	157.55 W
Polynésie française → French Polynesia □[2]	14	15.00 S	140.00 W
Polynnoje	80	46.51 N	46.56 E
Polysajevo	86	54.35 N	86.14 E
Pölzig	54	50.57 N	12.11 E
Poma, Lago ⊜[1]	70	37.55 N	13.06 E
Pomabamba	248	8.50 S	77.28 W
Pomacanchi	248	14.02 S	71.34 W
Pomahaka ≐	172	46.09 S	169.34 E
Pomarance	66	43.18 N	10.52 E
Pomarico	68	40.31 N	16.33 E
Pomarkku	26	61.42 N	22.00 E
Pomata	248	16.16 S	69.18 W
Pomáz	264c	47.39 N	19.02 E
Pomba ≐	256	21.24 S	42.32 W
Pombais, Ribeira de ≐	266c	38.48 N	9.07 W
Pombal, Bra.	250	6.46 S	37.47 W
Pombal, Port.	34	39.55 N	8.38 W
Pombia	266b	45.39 N	8.38 E
Pomellen	54	53.20 N	14.23 E
Pomene	156	22.53 S	35.33 E
Pomerania □[9]	30	54.00 N	16.00 E
Pomeranian Bay c	54	54.00 N	14.15 E
Pomerene	200	31.59 N	110.17 W
Pomerode	252	26.45 S	49.11 W
Pomeroon ≐	246	7.37 N	58.45 W
Pomeroon-Supenaam □[4]	246	7.20 N	58.50 W
Pomeroy, S. Afr.	158	28.33 S	30.26 E
Pomeroy, N. Ire., U.K.	48	54.36 N	6.55 W
Pomeroy, Ia., U.S.	198	42.33 N	94.41 W
Pomeroy, Oh., U.S.	188	39.01 N	82.02 W
Pomeroy, Pa., U.S.	208	39.58 N	75.53 W
Pomeroy, Wa., U.S.	202	46.28 N	117.36 W
Pomezia	66	41.40 N	12.30 E
Pomfret, S. Afr.	156	25.50 S	23.32 E
Pomfret, Ct., U.S.	207	41.53 N	71.57 W
Pomfret, Md., U.S.	208	38.34 N	77.01 W
Pomi	38	47.42 N	23.19 E
Pomigliano	66	40.54 N	14.23 E
Pominovo	82	55.26 N	39.11 E
Pomio	164	5.30 S	151.30 E
Pommard	58	47.01 N	4.47 E
Pomme de Terre ≐, Mn., U.S.	198	45.10 N	96.05 W
Pomme de Terre ≐, Mo., U.S.	194	38.11 N	93.24 W
Pomme de Terre Lake ⊜[1]	194	37.51 N	93.19 W
Pommera	50	50.10 N	2.26 E
Pommern → Pomerania □[9]	30	54.00 N	16.00 E
Pommersche Bucht → Pomeranian Bay c	54	54.00 N	14.15 E
Pommersfelden	56	49.46 N	10.49 E
Pomona, Namibia	156	27.09 S	15.18 E
Pomona, Ca., U.S.	228	34.03 N	117.45 W
Pomona, Ks., U.S.	198	38.36 N	95.27 W
Pomona, N.J., U.S.	208	39.28 N	74.34 W
Pomona, N.Y., U.S.	276	41.10 N	74.02 W
Pomona College ʊ[2]	280	34.06 N	117.44 W
Pomona Estates	273d	26.06 S	28.15 E
Pomona Lake ⊜[1]	198	38.40 N	95.35 W
Pomona Park	192	29.30 N	81.35 W
Pomongo	152	5.00 S	19.08 E
Pomor'any	78	49.38 N	24.56 E
Pomorie	38	42.33 N	27.39 E
Pomorskij proliv ʯ	24	68.30 N	50.00 E
Pomorze → Pomerania □[9]	30	54.00 N	16.00 E
Pomošnaja	78	48.14 N	31.26 E
Pomozdino	24	62.12 N	54.06 E
Pompano Beach	220	26.14 N	80.07 W
Pompano Beach Highlands	220	26.16 N	80.06 W
Pompei	68	40.45 N	14.30 E
Pompei ⊥	68	40.45 N	14.30 E
Pompéia	255	22.08 S	50.10 W
Pompejevka	89	48.23 N	130.46 E
Pompeston Creek ≐	285	40.01 N	75.01 W
Pompéu	255	19.12 S	44.59 W
Pompey, Fr.	56	48.46 N	6.07 E
Pompey, N.Y., U.S.	210	42.54 N	76.01 W
Pomponio Creek ≐	282	37.18 N	122.25 W
Pomponio State Beach ♠	282	37.17 N	122.24 W
Pomponne	261	48.53 N	2.41 E
Pompon-yama ∧	270	34.56 N	135.37 E
Pomposa	66	44.49 N	12.11 E
Pomposa, Abbazia di ʊ[1]	64	44.49 N	12.11 E
Pompton ≐	276	40.54 N	74.16 W
Pompton Lakes	210	41.00 N	74.17 W
Pompton Lakes ⊜	276	41.00 N	74.17 W
Pompton Plains	276	40.58 N	74.18 W
Pomquet	186	45.38 N	61.51 W
Pomssen	54	51.14 N	12.37 E
Ponape → Pohnpei I	174r	6.55 N	158.15 E
Ponask Lake ⊜	184	54.00 N	92.41 W
Ponass Lakes ⊜	184	52.18 N	103.58 W
Ponazyrevo	80	58.21 N	46.19 E
Ponca	198	42.33 N	96.42 W
Ponca City	196	36.42 N	97.05 W
Ponca Creek ≐	198	42.48 N	98.05 W
Ponce	240m	18.01 N	66.37 W
Ponce, Aeropuerto ⊠	240m	18.01 N	66.34 W
Ponce de Leon	194	30.43 N	85.56 W
Ponce de Leon Bay c	220	25.21 N	81.07 W
Ponce de Leon Inlet c	192	29.04 N	80.55 W
Poncé-sur-le-Loir	50	47.46 N	0.40 E
Poncha Pass)(	200	38.25 N	106.05 W
Ponchatoula	194	30.26 N	90.26 W
Poncin	58	46.05 N	5.24 E
Poncitlán	234	20.22 N	102.55 W
Pond ≐	194	37.32 N	87.21 W
Pond Brook ≐, N.J., U.S.	276	41.02 N	74.15 W
Pond Brook ≐, Oh., U.S.	279a	41.17 N	81.24 W
Pondcreek	196	36.40 N	97.48 W
Pond Creek ≐, U.S.	196	36.40 N	97.33 W
Pond Creek ≐, Tx., U.S.	222	31.02 N	96.46 W
Pond Eddy	210	41.27 N	74.49 W
Ponder	222	33.11 N	97.17 W
Pondera Coulee V	202	48.16 N	111.03 W
Ponders End ◆[8]	260	51.39 N	0.03 W
Pondicherry	122	11.56 N	79.53 E
Pondicherry □[8]	122	11.56 N	79.50 E
Pond Inlet	176	72.41 N	78.00 W
Pond Inlet c	176	72.46 N	77.00 W
Pondok Tanjong	114	5.00 N	100.44 E
Pondoland □[9]	158	31.10 S	29.30 E
Pondosa	204	41.12 N	121.41 W
Pond Run ≐	285	40.13 N	74.44 W
Poneas Island I	116	9.55 N	125.57 E
Ponente, Capo ≻	70a	35.31 N	12.31 E
Ponente, Riviera di •[2]	62	44.10 N	8.20 E
Ponérihouen	175f	21.05 S	165.24 E
Poneto	216	40.39 N	85.13 W
Ponežukaj	78	44.53 N	39.22 E
Ponferrada	34	42.33 N	6.35 W
Pong	110	19.10 N	100.17 E
Pongani	164	9.05 S	148.35 E
Pongara, Pointe ≻	152	0.21 N	9.21 E
Pongaroa	172	40.33 S	176.11 E
Pongau V	64	47.21 N	13.14 E
Pong Dam ◆[6]	123	31.59 N	75.57 E
Ponghyŏn	98	37.49 N	125.36 E
Pongo ≐	140	8.42 N	27.40 E
Pongolo ≐	158	26.57 S	32.17 E
Pon'goma	24	65.21 N	34.25 E
Pong Tamale	150	9.41 N	0.49 W
Ponhook Lake ⊜	186	44.19 N	64.53 W
Poni ≐	208	38.07 N	77.26 W
Poniatowa	30	51.11 N	22.05 E
Poniec	30	51.47 N	16.50 E
Ponil Creek ≐	196	36.29 N	104.48 W
Poninka	78	50.12 N	27.32 E
Ponino	80	58.16 N	52.49 E
Pönitz, Dtsch.	54	54.03 N	10.40 E
Ponitz, Dtsch.	54	50.51 N	12.25 E
Ponizovje	76	55.17 N	31.04 E
Ponkapog Pond ⊜	283	42.12 N	71.06 W
Pônley	110	12.26 N	104.27 E
Ponnaiyār ≐	122	11.46 N	79.47 E
Ponnāni	122	10.46 N	75.54 E
Ponnūru Nidubrolu	122	16.04 N	80.34 E
Pono	164	6.22 S	134.36 E
Ponoj	24	67.05 N	41.07 E
Ponoj ≐	24	66.59 N	41.17 E
Ponoka	182	52.42 N	113.35 W
Ponomar'ovka, Ross.	80	53.19 N	54.08 E
Ponomar'ovka, Ross.	86	56.08 N	82.23 E
Ponornica	78	51.43 N	32.49 E
Ponorogo	115a	7.52 S	111.27 E
Ponpāj	272b	22.56 N	88.15 E
Pons	32	45.35 N	0.33 W
Ponsacco	66	43.37 N	10.38 E
Ponson Island I	116	10.46 N	124.32 E

Symbol	English	Deutsch	Español	Français	Português
≐	River	Fluß	Río	Rivière	Rio
≅	Canal	Kanal	Canal	Canal	Canal
ʟ	Waterfall, Rapids	Wasserfall, Stromschnellen	Cascada, Rápidos	Chute d'eau, Rapides	Cascata, Rápidos
ʯ	Strait	Meeresstraße	Estrecho	Détroit	Estreito
c	Bay, Gulf	Bucht, Golf	Bahía, Golfo	Baie, Golfe	Baía, Golfo
⊜	Lake, Lakes	See, Seen	Lago, Lagos	Lac, Lacs	Lago, Lagos
≣	Swamp	Sumpf	Pantano	Marais	Pântano
⌓	Ice Features, Glacier	Eis- und Gletscherformen	Accidentes Glaciales	Formes glaciaires	Acidentes glaciares
⍑	Other Hydrographic Features	Andere Hydrographische Objekte	Otros Elementos Hidrográficos	Autres données hydrographiques	Outros acidentes hidrográficos
✢	Submarine Features	Untermeerische Objekte	Accidentes Submarinos	Formes de relief sous-marin	Acidentes submarinos
□	Political Unit	Politische Einheit	Unidad Politica	Entité politique	Unidade política
ʊ	Cultural Institution	Kulturelle Institution	Institución Cultural	Institution culturelle	Institução cultural
⊥	Historical Site	Historische Stätte	Sitio Histórico	Site historique	Sitio histórico
♠	Recreational Site	Erholungs- und Ferienort	Sitio de Recreo	Centre de loisirs	Area de Lazer
⊠	Airport	Flughafen	Aeropuerto	Aéroport	Aeroporto
■	Military Installation	Militäranlage	Instalación Militar	Installation militaire	Instalação militar
◆	Miscellaneous	Verschiedenes	Misceláneo	Divers	Diversos

ENGLISH / DEUTSCH

Name	Page / Seite	Lat.°′ / Breite°′	Long.°′ / Länge°′ E = Ost
Ponsul ≐	34	39.40 N	7.31 W
Pont	62	45.34 N	7.07 E
Pont-à-Celles	50	50.30 N	4.21 E
Ponta Delgada	148a	37.44 N	25.40 W
Ponta Delgada □[5]	148a	37.40 N	25.30 W
Ponta de Pedras	250	1.23 S	48.52 W
Ponta Grossa	252	25.05 S	50.09 W
Pontalete	256	21.27 S	45.40 W
Pontalina	255	17.31 S	49.27 W
Pontallier-sur-Saône	58	47.18 N	5.25 E
Pont-à-Marcq	50	50.31 N	3.07 E
Pont-à-Mousson	56	48.54 N	6.04 E
Ponta Negra	256	22.57 S	35.10 W
Pontão	34	39.55 N	8.22 W
Ponta Porã	255	22.32 S	55.43 W
Pontardawe	42	51.44 N	3.51 W
Pontardulais	42	51.43 N	4.03 W
Pontarlier	58	46.54 N	6.22 E
Pontas de Pedra	250	7.38 S	34.48 W
Pontassieve	66	43.46 N	11.26 E
Pontaubert	50	47.29 N	3.52 E
Pont-Audemer	50	49.21 N	0.31 E
Pontault-Combault	261	48.47 N	2.36 E
Pontaumur	32	45.52 N	2.40 E
Pont-Aven	32	47.51 N	3.45 W
Pontbriand	206	46.09 N	71.15 W
Pont Canavese	62	45.25 N	7.36 E
Pontcarré	261	48.48 N	2.42 E
Pontcharra	62	45.26 N	6.01 E
Pontchartrain	261	48.48 N	1.54 E
Pontchartrain, Lake ⊜	194	30.10 N	90.10 W
Pontchâteau	32	47.26 N	2.05 W
Pont-Croix	32	48.02 N	4.29 W
Pont-d'Ain	58	46.03 N	5.20 E
Pont d'Arc ♦	62	44.23 N	4.26 E
Pont-de-Bonne	56	50.27 N	5.17 E
Pont-de-Chéruy	62	45.45 N	5.11 E
Pont-de-l'Arche	50	49.18 N	1.10 E
Pont-de-Pany	58	47.18 N	4.49 E
Pont-de-Poitte	58	46.35 N	5.41 E
Pont-de-Roide	58	47.23 N	6.46 E
Pont-de-Ruan	50	47.15 N	0.35 E
Pont-de-Salars	32	44.17 N	2.44 E
Pont-de-Vaux	58	46.26 N	4.56 E
Pont-de-Veyle	58	46.16 N	4.53 E
Ponte a Elsa	66	43.41 N	10.54 E
Ponte Alta do Bom Jesus	255	12.06 S	46.29 W
Ponte Alta do Norte	250	10.45 S	47.34 W
Ponte a Moriano	66	43.54 N	10.31 E
Ponteareas	34	42.11 N	8.30 W
Pontebba	64	46.30 N	13.18 E
Ponte Branca	255	16.27 S	52.40 W
Ponte Caffaro	62	45.50 N	10.32 E
Pontecagnano	68	40.39 N	14.52 E
Ponte Caldelas	34	42.23 N	8.30 W
Pontecchio Marconi	64	44.25 N	11.15 E
Pontecchio Polesine	64	45.01 N	11.49 E
Pontecorvo	66	41.27 N	13.40 E
Pontecurone	62	44.57 N	8.56 E
Ponte da Barca	34	41.48 N	8.25 W
Ponte d'Arbia	66	43.10 N	11.28 E
Ponte delle Arche	64	46.02 N	10.52 E
Ponte dell'Olio	62	44.52 N	9.39 E
Pontedera	66	43.40 N	10.38 E
Ponte de Sor	34	39.15 N	8.01 W
Pontedeume	34	43.24 N	8.10 W
Ponte di Barbarano	64	45.23 N	11.34 E
Ponte di Legno	64	46.16 N	10.31 E
Ponte di Nava	62	44.08 N	7.53 E
Ponte di Piave	64	45.43 N	12.28 E
Ponte do Lima	34	41.46 N	8.35 W
Ponte do Púngoè	156	19.30 S	34.32 E
Pontefract	44	53.42 N	1.18 W
Ponte Galeria ❖[8]	267a	41.49 N	12.21 E
Ponte Gardena (Waidbruck)	64	46.36 N	11.32 E
Ponte Ghiereto	66	43.59 N	11.15 E
Pontegrande	58	45.59 N	8.09 E
Ponte in Valtellina	64	46.12 N	9.59 E
Ponteix	184	49.45 N	107.29 W
Pontelagoscuro	64	44.53 N	11.36 E
Ponteland	44	55.03 N	1.44 W
Pontelandolfo	68	41.17 N	14.41 E
Pontelongo	64	45.15 N	12.02 E
Ponte nell'Alpi	64	46.11 N	12.16 E
Ponte Nova	255	20.24 S	42.54 W
Pont-en-Royans	62	45.04 N	5.21 E
Ponte Nuovo	66	43.01 N	12.28 E
Pontenure	62	44.59 N	9.47 E
Pontepetri	66	44.02 N	10.53 E
Ponteríccioli	66	43.26 N	12.38 E
Ponte Rocchetta	64	46.14 N	11.04 E
Ponterwyd	42	52.25 N	3.50 W
Ponte San Giovanni	66	43.05 N	12.26 E
Ponte San Pietro	62	45.42 N	9.35 E
Pontesbury	42	52.39 N	2.54 W
Ponte Selva	64	45.52 N	9.54 E
Ponte Serrada	252	26.52 S	51.58 W
Pontestura	62	45.08 N	8.20 E
Ponte Tresa	58	45.58 N	8.52 E
Pontevedra, Arg.	258	34.45 S	58.42 W
Pontevedra, Esp.	34	42.26 N	8.38 W
Pontevedra, Pil.	116	10.22 N	122.52 E
Pontevedra □[4]	34	42.30 N	8.40 W
Pontevedra, Ría de ⊂[1]	34	42.22 N	8.45 W
Ponte Vedra Beach	192	30.14 N	81.23 W
Pont-Évêque	62	45.32 N	4.55 E
Pontevico	64	45.16 N	10.05 E
Pontfaverger-Moronvilliers	50	49.18 N	4.19 E
Pontgibaud	32	45.50 N	2.52 E
Ponthévrard	261	48.33 N	1.55 E
Ponthierry	261	48.32 N	2.33 E
Ponthierville → Ubundu	154	0.21 S	25.29 E
Pontiac, Il., U.S.	216	40.52 N	88.37 W
Pontiac, Mi., U.S.	216	42.38 N	83.17 W
Pontiac □[6]	212	46.30 N	77.00 W
Pontiac Lake	281	42.40 N	83.28 W
Pontiac Lake ⊜	281	42.40 N	83.28 W
Pontiac Lake State Recreation Area ♦	216	42.41 N	83.28 W
Pontiac Mall ❖[9]	281	42.39 N	83.20 W
Pontiac State Recreation Area ♦	281	42.41 N	83.28 W
Pontianak	112	0.02 S	109.20 E
Pontian Kechil	114	1.29 N	103.23 E
Pontida	62	45.43 N	9.30 E
Pontigny	50	47.55 N	3.43 E
Pontinha ❖[8]	266c	38.46 N	9.11 W
Pontinia	66	41.24 N	13.02 E
Pontivy	32	48.04 N	2.59 W
Pont-l'Abbé	32	47.52 N	4.13 W
Pont-lès-Moulins	58	47.19 N	6.22 E
Pont-l'Évêque	50	49.18 N	0.11 E
Pontlevoy	50	47.23 N	1.15 E
Pontoise	50	49.03 N	2.06 E
Pontoise-Cormeilles-en-Vexin, Aérodrome ⊠	261	49.06 N	2.02 E
Ponton Creek ≐	162	31.10 S	124.25 E
Pontonnyj	265a	59.47 N	30.38 E
Pontoon Beach	219	38.43 N	90.04 W
Pontorson	32	48.33 N	1.31 W
Pontotoc, Ms., U.S.	194	34.14 N	88.59 W
Pontotoc, Tx., U.S.	196	30.54 N	98.59 W
Pontremoli	62	44.22 N	9.53 E
Pont-Remy	50	50.03 N	1.55 E
Pontresina	58	46.28 N	9.53 E
Pontrhydfendigaid	42	52.17 N	3.51 W
Pont-Rouge	206	46.45 N	71.42 W
Pont-Royal	62	43.43 N	5.11 E
Ponts	34	41.55 N	1.12 E
Pont-Sainte-Marie	50	48.19 N	4.06 E
Pont-Sainte-Maxence	50	49.18 N	2.36 E
Pont-Saint-Esprit	62	44.15 N	4.39 E
Pont-Saint-Martin	62	45.36 N	7.48 E
Pont-Scorff	28	47.50 N	3.24 W
Ponts Quentin, Ruisseau des ≐	261	48.44 N	1.48 E
Pont-sur-Yonne	50	48.17 N	3.12 E
Pontuda, Ilha I	287a	23.02 S	43.18 W
Pontus □[9]	130	40.15 N	38.00 E
Pontvallain	50	47.45 N	0.12 E
Pont-Viau ❖[8]	275a	45.34 N	73.41 W
Pontyberem	42	51.47 N	4.09 W
Pontycymer	42	51.37 N	3.34 W
Pontypool	42	51.43 N	3.02 W
Pontypridd	42	51.37 N	3.22 W
Pony	202	45.39 N	111.53 W
Ponyri	76	52.19 N	36.20 E
Ponza	66	40.54 N	12.58 E
Ponza, Isola di I	66	40.55 N	12.57 E
Ponziane, Isole II	66	40.55 N	12.58 E
Ponzone	62	44.35 N	8.27 E
Poochera	162	32.43 S	134.51 E
Pool □[5]	152	3.30 S	15.00 E
Poole	42	50.43 N	1.59 W
Poole, Mount ∧	166	29.37 S	141.46 E
Poole Bay ⊂	42	50.42 N	1.52 W
Pooler	192	32.06 N	81.14 W
Poole's Cavern ≐[5]	262	53.14 N	1.56 W
Pooles Island I	208	39.17 N	76.16 W
Poolesville	208	39.08 N	77.25 W
Poolewe	46	57.45 N	5.37 W
Pooley Island I	182	52.44 N	128.16 W
Pool's Cove	186	47.41 N	55.26 W
Poolville	222	32.58 N	97.52 W
Poona → Pune	122	18.32 N	73.52 E
Pooncarie	166	33.23 S	142.34 E
Poondinna, Mount ∧	162	27.20 S	129.59 E
Poopo	248	18.23 S	66.59 W
Poopó, Lago ⊜	248	18.45 S	67.07 W
Pooraka	168b	34.50 S	138.37 E
Poor Knights Islands II	172	35.30 S	174.45 E
Poor Man Indian Reserve ❖[4]	184	51.30 N	104.23 W
Poor Meadow Brook ≐	283	42.01 N	70.55 W
Poortjie	158	30.13 S	22.44 E
Poowong	169	38.21 S	145.46 E
Popa, Isla I	236	9.11 N	82.07 W
Popasnaja	83	48.37 N	38.20 E
Popasnoje	78	48.48 N	35.31 E
Popayán	246	2.27 N	76.36 W
Pope	194	34.12 N	89.56 W
Pope Creek ≐	226	38.37 N	122.17 W
Popel'n'a	78	49.57 N	29.27 E
Popel'nastoje	78	48.39 N	33.43 E
Popereĉnoje	88	52.23 N	110.42 E
Poperinge	50	50.51 N	2.43 E
Popeşti	38	47.14 N	22.25 E
Popeşti-Leordeni	38	44.23 N	26.10 E
Pope Valley	226	38.37 N	122.26 W
Popham Bay ⊂	176	64.10 N	65.10 W
Popigaj	74	71.55 N	110.47 E
Popigaj ≐	74	72.54 N	106.36 E
Popiltah Lake ⊜	166	33.10 S	141.43 E
Popinci	38	42.25 N	24.17 E
Popki	80	50.11 N	44.30 E
Popkum	224	49.12 N	121.44 W
Poplar, Ca., U.S.	226	36.03 N	119.08 W
Poplar, Mt., U.S.	198	48.06 N	105.11 W
Poplar, Wi., U.S.	190	46.35 N	91.47 W
Poplar ❖[8]	260	51.31 N	0.01 W
Poplar ≐, Can.	184	53.00 N	97.24 W
Poplar ≐, N.A.	198	48.05 N	105.11 W
Poplar ≐, Mn., U.S.	198	47.51 N	96.04 W
Poplar, West Fork ≐	198	48.31 N	105.43 W
Poplar Bluff	194	36.45 N	90.23 W
Poplar Grove	216	42.22 N	88.49 W
Poplar Heights	284c	38.53 N	77.12 W
Poplar Hill	184	52.05 N	94.18 W
Poplar Mountain ∧	194	36.43 N	85.03 W
Poplar Point	184	50.04 N	97.57 W
Poplar Ridge	210	42.44 N	76.37 W
Poplar Springs	208	39.21 N	77.06 W
Poplarville	194	30.50 N	89.32 W
Poplevinskij	76	53.41 N	39.33 E
Popocatépetl, Volcán ∧[1]	234	19.02 N	98.38 W
Popof Island I	180	55.17 N	160.25 W
Popoh	115a	8.15 S	111.48 E
Popokabaka	152	5.42 S	16.35 E
Popoli	66	42.10 N	13.50 E
Popondetta	164	8.46 S	148.14 E
Popova	89	42.58 N	131.42 E
Popovka, Ross.	78	50.03 N	33.39 E
Popovka, Ross.	80	49.14 N	41.12 E
Popovkino	82	56.07 N	36.01 E
Popovo	38	43.21 N	26.13 E
Poppberg ∧	60	49.25 N	11.35 E
Poppel	56	51.27 N	5.02 E
Poppenbüttel ❖[8]	52	53.39 N	10.04 E
Poppenhausen	56	50.06 N	10.08 E
Poppi	66	43.43 N	11.46 E
Popple ≐	190	45.50 N	88.21 W
Poprad	30	49.03 N	20.18 E
Poprad ≐	30	49.38 N	20.42 E
Popricani	38	47.18 N	27.31 E
Popsong	98	35.22 N	126.27 E
Poptong	98	38.59 N	127.05 E
Poptún	236	16.21 N	89.26 W
Populonia	66	42.59 N	10.29 E
Poputnaja	84	44.31 N	41.27 E
Poquessing Creek ≐	285	40.03 N	74.58 W
Poquetanuck	207	41.29 N	72.02 W
Poquonock	207	41.54 N	72.40 W
Poquonock Bridge	207	41.20 N	72.01 W
Poquoson	208	37.07 N	76.21 W
Poquoson ≐	208	37.10 N	76.24 W
Poquott	276	40.57 N	73.05 W
Porādaha	126	23.51 N	89.01 E
Porāli Nai ≐	120	25.58 N	66.26 E
Poranga	250	4.44 S	40.55 W
Porangahau	172	40.18 S	176.37 E
Porangatu	255	13.26 S	49.10 W
Porbandar	120	21.38 N	69.36 E
Porce ≐	246	7.28 N	74.53 W
Porchaman	128	33.08 N	63.51 E
Porcher Island I	182	53.57 N	130.30 W
Porcheville	261	48.58 N	1.47 E
Porchov	76	57.46 N	29.34 E
Porcia	64	45.57 N	12.36 E
Porciuncula	255	20.58 S	42.02 W
Porco	248	19.50 S	65.59 W
Porcos, Rio dos ≐	255	12.42 S	45.07 W
Porcuna	34	37.52 N	4.11 W
Porcupine ≐	180	66.35 N	145.15 W
Porcupine Brook ≐	283	42.46 N	71.13 W
Porcupine Creek ≐	202	48.07 N	106.20 W
Porcupine Creek, Middle Fork ≐	202	48.31 N	106.30 W
Porcupine Creek, West Fork ≐	202	48.31 N	106.30 W
Porcupine Dome ∧	180	65.31 N	145.31 W
Porcupine Hills ∧[2]	184	52.30 N	101.45 W
Porcupine Mountains State Park ♦	190	46.47 N	89.50 W
Pordenone	64	45.57 N	12.39 E
Pordenone □[4]	64	46.00 N	12.45 E
Pordim	38	43.23 N	24.51 E
Poreč	36	45.13 N	13.37 E
Porecatu	255	22.43 S	51.24 W
Porečje, Bela.	76	53.55 N	24.07 E
Porečje, Ross.	76	55.43 N	35.33 E
Porečje, Ross.	76	56.06 N	30.29 E
Porečje-Rybnoje	80	57.06 N	39.23 E
Poreckoje	80	55.12 N	46.20 E
Porez	80	57.40 N	51.10 E
Pori	26	61.29 N	21.47 E
Poricy Brook ≐	276	40.21 N	74.05 W
Poringland	42	52.33 N	1.21 E
Porirua	172	41.08 S	174.51 E
Porjaguba	24	66.47 N	33.45 E
Porkkala	26	59.59 N	24.26 E
Porlamar	246	10.57 N	63.51 W
Porlezza	58	46.03 N	9.07 E
Porlock	42	51.14 N	3.36 W
Porma ≐	34	42.29 N	5.28 W
Pornassio	62	44.04 N	7.52 E
Pörnbach	60	48.37 N	11.28 E
Pornic	32	47.07 N	2.06 W
Poro ∧	154	1.14 N	36.37 E
Porog, Ross.	24	63.50 N	38.29 E
Porog, Ross.	76	59.16 N	33.24 E
Porogi	265a	59.46 N	30.47 E
Poro Island I	116	10.40 N	124.27 E
Porokylä	26	63.33 N	29.06 E
Poroma	248	18.29 S	65.30 W
Poronaj ≐	89	49.14 N	143.06 E
Poronajsk	89	49.14 N	143.04 E
Porong	115a	7.32 S	112.41 E
Porong ≐	115a	7.32 S	112.51 E
Poropotank ≐	208	37.27 N	76.42 W
Poroškovo	78	48.41 N	22.45 E
Porosozero	24	62.43 N	32.42 E
Poroto Mountains ∧	154	9.00 S	33.45 E
Porozovo	76	52.56 N	24.22 E
Porožskij	88	56.04 N	101.46 E
Porpoise Bay ⊂	9	66.30 S	128.30 E
Porpoise Channel ⊻	276	40.55 N	73.09 W
Porquerolles	62	43.00 N	6.12 E
Porquerolles, Île de I	62	43.00 N	6.13 E
Porrentruy	58	47.25 N	7.05 E
Porretta Terme	64	44.09 N	10.59 E
Porsangen ⊂[2]	24	70.58 N	27.00 E
Porsangerhalvøya >[1]	24	70.50 N	25.00 E
Porsea	114	2.27 N	99.09 E
Porsgrunn	26	59.09 N	9.40 E
Porsuk ≐	130	39.42 N	31.59 E
Portachuelo	248	17.21 S	63.24 W
Portaclay	48	54.19 N	9.48 W
Port Adelaide	168b	34.51 S	138.30 E
Portadown	48	54.26 N	6.27 W
Portaferry	48	54.23 N	5.33 W
Portage, In., U.S.	216	41.34 N	87.10 W
Portage, Mi., U.S.	216	42.12 N	85.34 W
Portage, Oh., U.S.	216	41.20 N	83.39 W
Portage, Pa., U.S.	214	40.23 N	78.40 W
Portage, Ut., U.S.	200	41.58 N	112.14 W
Portage, Wi., U.S.	190	43.32 N	89.27 W
Portage □[6]	214	41.09 N	81.15 W
Portage ≐, Mi., U.S.	216	41.57 N	85.38 W
Portage ≐, Oh., U.S.	214	41.31 N	83.05 W
Portage, East Branch ≐	216	41.17 N	83.31 W
Portage, Middle Branch ≐	216	41.22 N	83.28 W
Portage, North Branch ≐	216	41.25 N	83.27 W
Portage, South Branch ≐	216	41.22 N	83.30 W
Portage Bay ⊂	184	51.33 N	98.50 W
Portage Des Sioux	219	38.55 N	90.20 W
Portage Lake ⊜, Mi., U.S.	190	47.04 N	88.30 W
Portage Lake ⊜, Mi., U.S.	216	42.25 N	83.54 W
Portage Lake ⊜, Mi., U.S.	216	42.03 N	85.31 W
Portage Lakes	214	40.59 N	81.32 W
Portage Lakes ⊜	214	40.59 N	81.32 W
Portage Lakes State Park ♦	214	40.57 N	81.32 W
Portage-la-Prairie	184	49.59 N	98.18 W
Portage Park ❖[8]	278	41.57 N	87.46 W
Portageville, Mo., U.S.	194	36.25 N	89.41 W
Portageville, N.Y., U.S.	210	42.34 N	78.02 W
Portal, Ga., U.S.	192	32.32 N	81.55 W
Portal, N.D., U.S.	198	48.59 N	102.32 W
Portal del Infierno ⊻	236	14.22 N	85.38 W
Portalegre, Bra.	250	6.02 S	38.00 W
Portalegre, Port.	34	39.17 N	7.26 W
Portales	196	34.11 N	103.20 W
Port Alexander	180	56.15 N	134.39 W
Port Alfred (Kowie)	158	33.36 S	26.55 E
Port Alice	182	50.23 N	127.27 W
Port Allegany	214	41.48 N	78.16 W
Port Allen	194	30.27 N	91.12 W
Port Alma, Austl.	166	23.35 S	150.51 E
Port Alma, On., Can.	214	42.11 N	82.15 W
Port Alsworth	180	60.12 N	154.20 W
Port Angeles	224	48.07 N	123.25 W
Port Angeles Harbor ⊂	224	48.07 N	123.24 W
Port Anson	186	49.32 N	55.50 W
Port Antonio	241q	18.11 N	76.28 W
Port Aransas	196	27.50 N	97.04 W
Portarlington, Austl.	169	38.07 S	144.39 E
Portarlington, Ire.	48	53.10 N	7.11 W
Port Arthur, Austl.	166	43.09 S	147.51 E
Port Arthur, Tx., U.S.	194	29.53 N	93.55 W
Port Arthur → Lüshun	98	38.48 N	121.16 E
Port Arthur → Thunder Bay	190	48.23 N	89.15 W
Port Ashton	180	60.04 N	148.01 W
Port Askaig	46	55.51 N	6.07 W
Port Augusta	166	32.30 S	137.46 E
Port au Port	186	48.33 N	58.44 W
Port au Port Bay ⊂	186	48.40 N	58.45 W
Port au Port Peninsula >[1]	186	48.35 N	59.00 W
Port-au-Prince	238	18.32 N	72.20 W
Port-au-Prince, Baie de ⊂	238	18.40 N	72.30 W
Port Austin	190	44.02 N	82.59 W
Port-aux-Basques → Channel-Port-aux-Basques	186	47.34 N	59.09 W
Portavogie	48	54.27 N	5.27 W
Porta Westfalica	52	52.14 N	8.55 E
Porta Westfalica ♦	52	52.14 N	8.55 E
Port Bannatyne	46	55.52 N	5.05 W
Port Barre	194	30.33 N	91.57 W
Port Bell	154	0.17 N	32.39 E
Port-Bergé	157b	15.33 S	47.40 E
Port Blair	110	11.40 N	92.45 E
Port Blakely	224	47.37 N	122.28 W
Port Blandford	186	48.21 N	54.10 W
Port Bolivar	222	29.22 N	94.46 W
Port Borden	186	46.15 N	63.42 W
Port-Bouët	150	5.15 N	3.58 W
Port Broughton	166	33.36 S	137.56 E
Port Burwell	212	42.39 N	80.49 W
Port Byron, Il., U.S.	190	41.36 N	90.20 W
Port Byron, N.Y., U.S.	210	43.02 N	76.37 W
Port Campbell	169	38.37 S	143.00 E
Port Campbell National Park ♦	169	38.38 S	142.55 E
Port Canning	126	22.18 N	88.40 E
Port Carbon	208	40.42 N	76.10 W
Port Carling	212	45.07 N	79.35 W
Port-Cartier	186	50.01 N	66.52 W
Port-Cartier Sept-Îles, Réserve ♦	186	50.35 N	67.10 W
Port Chalmers	172	45.49 S	170.37 E
Port Charlotte	220	26.58 N	82.05 W
Port Chester	210	41.00 N	73.39 W
Port Chester Harbor ⊂	276	40.59 N	73.40 W
Port Chicago	226	38.03 N	122.01 W
Port Clements	182	53.42 N	132.11 W
Port Clinton, Austl.	168b	34.13 S	138.01 E
Port Clinton, Oh., U.S.	214	41.30 N	82.56 W
Port Clinton, Pa., U.S.	208	40.35 N	76.02 W
Port Clyde	188	43.55 N	69.15 W
Port Colborne	212	42.53 N	79.14 W
Port Colden	210	40.45 N	74.57 W
Port Columbus International Airport ⊠	218	40.00 N	82.53 W
Port Coquitlam	224	49.16 N	122.46 W
Port Costa	226	38.03 N	122.11 W
Port Crane	210	42.10 N	75.50 W
Port Credit	212	43.33 N	79.35 W
Port-Cros	62	43.00 N	6.23 E
Port-Cros, Île de I	62	43.00 N	6.24 E
Port-Cros, Parc National de ♦	62	43.01 N	6.24 E
Port-Daniel, Réserve ♦	186	48.18 N	64.55 W
Port-de-Bouc	62	43.24 N	4.59 E
Port-de-Paix	238	19.57 N	72.50 W
Port Deposit	208	39.36 N	76.06 W
Port Dickinson	210	42.08 N	75.53 W
Port Dickson	114	2.31 N	101.48 E
Porte Crayon, Mount ∧	188	38.56 N	79.27 W
Port Edward, B.C., Can.	182	54.14 N	130.18 W
Port Edward, S. Afr.	158	31.02 S	30.13 E
Port Edwards	190	44.21 N	89.51 W
Port Edward → Weihai	98	37.28 N	122.07 E
Portegolpe	236	10.20 N	85.46 W
Porteiras	250	7.31 S	39.07 W
Porteirinha	255	15.44 S	43.02 W
Portel, Bra.	250	1.57 S	50.49 W
Portel, Port.	34	38.18 N	7.42 W
Portela, Aeroporto da ⊠	266c	38.46 N	9.08 W
Port Elgin, N.B., Can.	186	46.03 N	64.05 W
Port Elgin, On., Can.	190	44.26 N	81.24 W
Port Elizabeth, St. Vin.	241h	13.03 N	61.13 W
Port Elizabeth, S. Afr.	158	33.58 S	25.40 E
Port Elizabeth, N.J., U.S.	208	39.18 N	74.58 W
Port Ellen	46	55.39 N	6.12 W
Port Elliot	168b	35.32 S	138.41 E
Port-en-Bessin	32	49.21 N	0.45 W
Porter, In., U.S.	216	41.36 N	87.04 W
Porter, Ok., U.S.	196	35.52 N	95.31 W
Porter, Tx., U.S.	222	30.06 N	95.14 W
Porter, Wa., U.S.	224	46.56 N	123.18 W
Porter □[6]	216	41.28 N	87.04 W
Port'Ercole	66	42.23 N	11.12 E
Porter Corners	210	43.09 N	73.53 W
Porter Creek ≐	279a	41.41 N	81.56 W
Port Erin	44	54.06 N	4.44 W
Porter Lake ⊜	184	56.21 N	107.20 W
Porter Point >	241h	13.23 N	61.11 W
Porter Springs	222	31.16 N	95.36 W
Porters Retreat	170	34.00 S	149.48 E
Porters Run ≐	279b	40.27 N	79.33 W
Portersville	214	40.56 N	80.09 W
Porterville, S. Afr.	158	33.00 S	19.00 E
Porterville, Ca., U.S.	204	36.03 N	119.00 W
Porterville, Ms., U.S.	194	32.41 N	88.28 W
Portes-lès-Valence	62	44.52 N	4.53 E
Port Essington	182	54.09 N	129.57 W
Portete, Bahía ⊂	246	12.13 N	71.55 W
Port-Étienne → Nouâdhibou	148	20.54 N	17.04 W
Port Ewen	210	41.54 N	73.58 W
Port-Eynon	42	51.33 N	4.13 W
Port-Eynon Point >	42	51.32 N	4.12 W
Portezuelo	234	20.25 N	102.31 W
Port Fairy	166	38.23 S	142.14 E
Port Fitzroy	172	36.10 S	175.21 E
Port Gamble	224	47.51 N	122.34 W
Port Gamble Indian Reservation ❖[4]	224	47.53 N	122.34 W
Port Gentil	152	0.43 S	8.47 E
Port Germein	166	33.01 S	138.00 E
Port Gibson, Ms., U.S.	194	31.57 N	90.59 W
Port Gibson, N.Y., U.S.	210	43.02 N	77.09 W
Port Glasgow	46	55.57 N	4.41 W
Portglenone	48	54.52 N	6.29 W
Port Graham	180	59.21 N	151.50 W
Port Greville	186	45.24 N	64.33 W
Porth	42	51.38 N	3.25 W
Port Hacking	274a	34.04 S	151.08 E
Port Hacking Point >	170	34.05 S	151.10 E
Port Hammond	224	49.13 N	122.39 W
Port Harcourt	150	4.43 N	7.05 E
Port Hardy	182	50.43 N	127.29 W
Port Hawkesbury	186	45.37 N	61.21 W
Porthcawl	42	51.29 N	3.43 W
Port Hedland	162	20.19 S	118.34 E
Port Heiden	180	56.55 N	158.41 W
Port Henry	188	44.02 N	73.27 W
Port Hill	186	46.35 N	63.53 W
Porthleven	42	50.05 N	5.19 W
Porthmadog	42	52.55 N	4.08 W
Porth Neigwl ⊂	42	52.48 N	4.34 W
Port Hood	186	46.01 N	61.32 W
Port Hope, On., Can.	212	43.57 N	78.18 W
Port Hope, Mi., U.S.	190	43.56 N	82.42 W
Port Howe	238	24.15 N	75.21 W
Port Hueneme	228	34.08 N	119.11 W
Port Hughes	168b	34.04 S	137.32 E
Port Huron	216	42.58 N	82.25 W
Portici	68	40.49 N	14.20 E
Portico di Romagna	66	44.01 N	11.47 E
Portigliola	68	38.14 N	16.13 E
Port-Iljič	84	38.53 N	48.48 E
Portimão	34	37.08 N	8.32 W
Portinho, Rio do ≐	287a	23.03 S	43.35 W
Port Isaac	42	50.35 N	4.49 W
Port Isabel	196	26.04 N	97.12 W
Portishead	42	51.30 N	2.46 W
Port Jefferson, N.Y., U.S.	210	40.56 N	73.03 W
Port Jefferson, Oh., U.S.	216	40.19 N	84.05 W
Port Jefferson Harbor ⊂	276	40.58 N	73.05 W
Port Jefferson Station	210	40.55 N	73.02 W
Port Jervis	210	41.22 N	74.41 W
Port Julia	168b	34.40 S	137.52 E
Port-Katon	83	46.52 N	38.46 E
Port Kembla	170	34.29 S	150.54 E
Port Kennedy	285	40.06 N	75.25 W
Port Kenny	162	33.10 S	134.42 E
Portknockie	46	57.41 N	2.51 W
Port Lairge → Waterford	48	52.15 N	7.06 W
Port Lambton	214	42.39 N	82.30 W
Portland, Austl.	166	38.21 S	141.36 E
Portland, Austl.	170	33.22 S	150.00 E
Portland, N.Z.	172	35.48 S	174.19 E
Portland, Ar., U.S.	194	33.14 N	91.30 W
Portland, Ct., U.S.	207	41.34 N	72.38 W
Portland, In., U.S.	216	40.26 N	84.58 W
Portland, Me., U.S.	188	43.39 N	70.15 W
Portland, Mi., U.S.	216	42.52 N	84.54 W
Portland, Mo., U.S.	219	38.42 N	91.43 W
Portland, N.Y., U.S.	214	42.22 N	79.28 W
Portland, N.D., U.S.	198	47.29 N	97.22 W
Portland, Or., U.S.	224	45.31 N	122.40 W
Portland, Pa., U.S.	210	40.55 N	75.06 W
Portland, Tn., U.S.	194	36.34 N	86.30 W
Portland, Tx., U.S.	196	27.52 N	97.19 W
Portland, Wi., U.S.	216	43.12 N	88.58 W
Portland, Bill of >	42	50.31 N	2.27 W
Portland, Cape >	166	40.45 S	147.57 E
Portland, Isle of I	42	50.33 N	2.27 W
Portland Bay ⊂	241q	17.48 N	77.08 W
Portland Bight ⊂[3]	241q	17.53 N	77.08 W
Portland Canal ⊂	182	55.11 N	130.08 W
Portland Creek Pond ⊜	186	50.12 N	57.34 W
Portland Inlet ⊂	182	54.50 N	130.15 W
Portland International Airport ⊠	224	45.35 N	122.36 W
Portland Island I	172	39.17 S	177.52 E
Portland Mills	214	41.23 N	78.50 W
Portland Point >	241q	17.42 N	77.11 W
Portlandville	210	42.32 N	74.58 W
Port Laoise (Maryborough)	48	53.02 N	7.17 W
Port Lavaca	196	28.36 N	96.37 W
Portlaw	48	52.17 N	7.19 W
Port → Le Port	157c	20.55 S	55.18 E
Port-Lesney	58	47.00 N	5.49 E
Portlethen	46	57.03 N	2.06 W
Port Leyden	212	43.35 N	75.21 W
Port Lincoln	166	34.44 S	135.52 E
Port Lions	180	57.52 N	152.53 W
Portlock Reefs ❖[2]	164	9.30 S	144.45 E
Port Logan	44	54.43 N	4.56 W
Port Loko	150	8.46 N	12.47 W
Port-Louis, Fr.	32	47.43 N	3.21 W
Port-Louis, Guad.	241o	16.25 N	61.32 W
Port Louis, Maus.	157c	20.10 S	57.30 E
Port Ludlow	224	47.55 N	122.40 W
Port-Lyautey → Kenitra	148	34.16 N	6.40 W
Port MacDonnell	166	38.03 S	140.42 E
Port Macquarie	166	31.26 S	152.55 E
Port Madison Indian Reservation ❖[4]	224	47.45 N	122.35 W
Portmahomack	46	57.49 N	3.50 W
Port Maitland, N.S., Can.	186	43.59 N	66.09 W
Port Maitland, On., Can.	214	42.52 N	79.34 W
Port Maria	241q	18.22 N	76.54 W
Portmarnock	48	53.25 N	6.08 W
Port Matilda	214	40.48 N	78.03 W
Port Mayaca	220	27.08 N	80.12 W
Port McNeill	182	50.35 N	127.06 W
Port McNicoll	212	44.45 N	79.49 W
Port Melbourne	274b	37.51 S	144.56 E
Port Mellon	182	49.32 N	123.29 W
Port-Menier	186	49.48 N	64.20 W
Port Moller	180	55.59 N	160.34 W
Port Monmouth	276	40.25 N	74.05 W
Port Moody	224	49.17 N	122.51 W
Port Morant	241q	17.54 N	76.19 W
Portmore	241q	17.58 N	76.53 W
Port Moresby	164	9.30 S	147.10 E
Port Moresby □[5]	164	9.30 S	147.10 E
Port Morien	186	46.08 N	59.52 W
Port Morris	276	40.54 N	74.41 W
Port Mouton	186	43.56 N	64.51 W
Port Murray	210	40.47 N	74.54 W
Portnaguran	46	58.17 N	6.13 W
Portnahaven	46	55.41 N	6.31 W
Port Neches	194	29.59 N	93.57 W
Port Neill	166	34.07 S	136.20 E
Port Nelson	184	57.03 N	92.36 W
Portneuf	206	46.42 N	71.53 W
Portneuf □[6]	206	46.45 N	72.00 W
Portneuf ≐, P.Q., Can.	186	48.38 N	69.05 W
Portneuf ≐, P.Q., Can.	206	46.42 N	71.53 W
Portneuf ≐, Id., U.S.	202	42.58 N	112.35 W
Portneuf, Lac ⊜	186	49.08 N	70.18 W
Portneuf-Station	206	46.43 N	71.54 W
Portneuf-sur-Mer	186	48.37 N	69.06 W
Port Neville	182	50.29 N	126.05 W
Port Noarlunga	168b	35.09 S	138.28 E
Port Nolloth	156	29.17 S	16.51 E
Port Norris	208	39.14 N	75.02 W
Porto, Bra.	250	3.54 S	42.42 W
Porto, Port.	34	41.11 N	8.36 W
Porto, Bonifica di ❖[1]	267a	41.48 N	12.16 E
Porto Acre	248	9.34 S	67.31 W
Porto Alegre, Bra.	252	30.04 S	51.11 W
Porto Alegre, S. Tom./P.	152	0.02 N	6.32 E
Porto Amboim	152	10.44 S	13.44 E
Porto Azzurro	66	42.46 N	10.24 E
Portobello	46	55.58 N	3.07 W
Porto Belo, Bra.	252	27.10 S	48.33 W
Portobelo, Pan.	236	9.33 N	79.39 W
Porto Calvo	250	9.04 S	35.24 W
Porto Ceresio	58	45.54 N	8.55 E
Port O'Connor	196	28.27 N	96.24 W
Porto das Caixas	256	22.42 S	42.53 W
Porto d'Ascoli	66	42.55 N	13.53 E
Porto das Flôres	256	22.05 S	43.34 W
Porto das Gabarras	250	3.07 S	44.34 W
Pôrto de Mós	34	39.36 N	8.39 W
Porto de Moz	250	1.45 S	52.14 W
Porto de Pedras	250	9.10 S	35.17 W
Porto di Potenza Picena	66	43.21 N	13.42 E
Porto di Traiano, Necropoli del ⊥	267a	41.46 N	12.16 E
Porto dos Gaúchos	250	11.29 S	57.22 W
Porto Empedocle	70	37.17 N	13.32 E
Porto Esperança	248	19.37 S	57.27 W
Porto Esperidião	248	15.51 S	58.28 W
Porto Farina	36	37.10 N	10.12 E
Porto Feliz	255	23.13 S	47.32 W
Portoferraio	66	42.49 N	10.19 E
Porto Ferreira	255	21.51 S	47.28 W
Portofino	62	44.18 N	9.12 E
Port of Ness	46	58.29 N	6.13 W
Porto Franco	250	6.20 S	47.24 W
Port of Spain	241r	10.39 N	61.31 W
Porto Garibaldi	64	44.41 N	12.14 E
Porto Grande	250	0.42 N	51.24 W
Portogruaro	64	45.47 N	12.50 E
Porto Inglês	150a	15.08 N	23.13 W
Portola	226	39.48 N	120.28 W
Portola State Park ♦	226	37.15 N	122.13 W
Portola Valley	226	37.23 N	122.13 W
Porto Lucena	252	27.51 S	55.01 W
Pörtom (Pirttikylä)	26	62.42 N	21.37 E
Portomaggiore	64	44.42 N	11.48 E
Porto Maurizio	62	43.52 N	8.01 E
Porto Mendes	252	24.30 S	54.20 W
Porto Murtinho	248	21.42 S	57.52 W
Porto Nacional	250	10.42 S	48.25 W
Porto-Novo, Bénin	150	6.29 N	2.37 E
Porto Novo, Bra.	256	23.40 S	45.28 W
Porto Novo, India	122	11.29 N	79.46 E
Porto Novo Creek ⊂	273a	6.26 N	3.20 E
Portopalo, It.	70	36.41 N	15.08 E
Porto Palo, It.	70	37.34 N	12.54 E
Port Orange	192	29.06 N	80.59 W
Port Orchard	224	47.32 N	122.38 W
Porto Real	256	22.25 S	44.20 W
Porto Real do Colégio	250	10.11 S	36.49 W
Porto Recanati	66	43.26 N	13.40 E
Port Orford	202	42.44 N	124.29 W
Porto Rico	152	6.08 S	12.30 E
Porto Rico → Puerto Rico □[2]	240m	18.15 N	66.30 W
Portorož	64	45.31 N	13.36 E
Porto Salvo	266c	38.43 N	9.18 W
Porto San Giorgio	66	43.11 N	13.48 E
Porto Santana	250	0.03 S	51.11 W
Porto Sant'Elpidio	66	43.15 N	13.45 E
Porto Santo I	148	33.04 N	16.20 W
Porto Santo Stefano	66	42.26 N	11.07 E
Porto São José	255	22.43 S	53.10 W
Portoscuso	71	39.12 N	8.23 E
Porto Seguro, Bra.	255	16.26 S	39.05 W
Porto-Séguro, Togo	150	6.12 N	1.29 E
Porto Torres	71	40.50 N	8.24 E
Porto União	252	26.15 S	51.05 W
Porto Valter	248	8.15 S	72.45 W
Porto Valtravaglia	58	45.58 N	8.41 E
Porto-Vecchio	36	41.35 N	9.16 E
Porto Velho	248	8.46 S	63.54 W
Porto Velho do Cunha	256	21.50 S	42.32 W
Portovenere	62	44.03 N	9.51 E
Portoviejo	246	1.03 S	80.27 W
Portpatrick, Scot., U.K.	44	54.51 N	5.07 W
Port Patrick, Vanuatu	175f	20.08 S	169.47 E
Port Penn	208	39.31 N	75.34 W
Port Perry	212	44.06 N	78.57 W
Port Phillip Bay ⊂	169	38.07 S	144.48 E
Port Pirie	166	33.11 S	138.01 E
Port Providence	285	40.08 N	75.30 W
Portraine	48	53.30 N	6.07 W
Port Reading	276	40.33 N	74.15 W
Portree	46	57.24 N	6.12 W
Port Renfrew	224	48.33 N	124.25 W
Port Republic	208	39.31 N	74.29 W
Port Rextor	186	48.23 N	53.20 W
Port Richey	220	28.16 N	82.43 W
Port Richmond	208	37.33 N	76.49 W
Port Robinson	284a	43.02 N	79.13 W
Port Rowan	214	42.37 N	80.28 W
Port Royal, Jam.	241q	17.56 N	76.51 W
Port Royal, Ky., U.S.	218	38.33 N	85.04 W
Port Royal, Pa., U.S.	208	40.32 N	77.23 W
Port Royal, S.C., U.S.	192	32.22 N	80.41 W
Port Royal, Va., U.S.	208	38.10 N	77.11 W
Port-Royal-des-Champs, Abbaye de ⊍[1]	261	48.45 N	2.01 E
Port Royal National Historic Park ♦	186	44.44 N	65.40 W
Portrush	48	55.12 N	6.40 W
Port Said → Būr Saʿīd	142	31.16 N	32.18 E
Port-Sainte-Marie	32	44.15 N	0.24 E
Port Saint Joe	192	29.49 N	85.18 W
Port Saint Johns	158	31.38 S	29.33 E
Port-Saint-Louis	62	43.23 N	4.48 E
Port Saint Lucie	220	27.20 N	80.20 W
Port Saint Mary	44	54.05 N	4.43 W
Port-Saint-Servan	186	51.19 N	58.02 W
Port Salerno	220	27.08 N	80.12 W
Portsalon	48	55.13 N	7.37 W
Port Sanilac	190	43.25 N	82.32 W
Port Saunders	186	50.39 N	57.18 W
Pörtschach	61	46.37 N	14.08 E
Portsea	169	38.19 S	144.43 E
Port Seton	46	55.58 N	2.57 W
Port Shepstone	158	30.46 S	30.22 E
Portslade	42	50.50 N	0.11 W
Portsmouth, Dom.	240d	15.35 N	61.28 W
Portsmouth, Eng., U.K.	42	50.48 N	1.05 W
Portsmouth, N.H., U.S.	188	43.04 N	70.45 W
Portsmouth, Oh., U.S.	218	38.43 N	82.59 W
Portsmouth, R.I., U.S.	207	41.36 N	71.15 W
Portsmouth, Va., U.S.	208	36.50 N	76.17 W
Portsmouth Naval Shipyard ■	188	43.05 N	70.45 W
Portsoy	46	57.41 N	2.41 W
Port Stanley	214	42.40 N	81.13 W
Port Stanley → Stanley	254	51.42 S	57.51 W
Portstewart	48	55.11 N	6.43 W
Port Sudan → Būr Sūdān	140	19.37 N	37.14 E
Port Sulphur	194	29.28 N	89.41 W
Port Sunlight	262	53.21 N	2.59 W
Port-sur-Saône	58	47.41 N	6.03 E
Port Talbot	42	51.36 N	3.47 W
Port Taufiq → Būr Tawfīq	128	29.57 N	32.34 E
Porttipahdan tekojärvi ⊜[1]	24	68.08 N	26.40 E
Port Tobacco River ⊂	208	38.27 N	77.02 W
Port Townsend	224	48.07 N	122.45 W
Port Trevorton	208	40.42 N	76.52 W
Portugal □[1], Europe	22	39.30 N	8.00 W
Portugal □[1], Europe	34	39.30 N	8.00 W
Portugal, Cachoeira ⊻	248	9.55 S	64.16 W
Portugal Cove South	186	46.42 N	53.15 W
Portugalete	34	43.19 N	3.01 W
Portuguesa □[3]	246	9.10 N	69.15 W
Portuguesa ≐	246	7.57 N	67.32 W
Portuguese Guinea → Guinea-Bissau □[1]	150	12.00 N	15.00 W
Portumna	48	53.06 N	8.13 W
Port Union, Nf., Can.	186	48.30 N	53.05 W
Port Union, On., Can.	275b	43.47 N	79.08 W
Port-Vendres	32	42.31 N	3.07 E
Port Victoria → Victoria	138	4.38 S	55.27 E
Port Vila	175f	17.44 S	168.19 E
Portville	210	42.02 N	78.20 W
Port Vincent	168b	34.47 S	137.51 E
Port Vue	279b	40.20 N	79.52 W
Port Waikato	172	37.23 S	174.44 E
Port Wakefield, Austl.	168b	34.11 S	138.09 E
Port Wakefield, Ak., U.S.	180	58.03 N	153.03 W
Port Washington, B.C., Can.	224	48.49 N	123.19 W
Port Washington, N.Y., U.S.	210	40.49 N	73.41 W
Port Washington, Oh., U.S.	214	40.27 N	81.37 W
Port Washington, Wi., U.S.	190	43.23 N	87.52 W
Port Weld	114	4.50 N	100.38 E
Port Welshpool	169	38.42 S	146.28 E
Port Wentworth	192	32.08 N	81.09 W
Port William, Scot., U.K.	44	54.46 N	4.35 W
Port William, Oh., U.S.	218	39.33 N	83.47 W
Port Wing	190	46.46 N	91.23 W
Porum	196	35.21 N	95.15 W
Porus	241q	18.02 N	77.25 W
Porvenir, Chile	254	53.18 S	70.22 W
Porvenir, Méx.	232	31.15 N	105.51 W
Porvoo (Borgå)	26	60.24 N	25.40 E
Porvoonjoki ≐	26	60.23 N	25.40 E
Porz	56	50.53 N	7.03 E
Porzdni	80	57.00 N	42.33 E
Porzuna	34	39.09 N	4.09 W
Posada	71	40.38 N	9.43 E
Posada ≐	71	40.39 N	9.45 E
Posadas, Arg.	252	27.23 S	55.53 W
Posadas, Esp.	34	37.48 N	5.06 W
Posavina ⋁	36	45.10 N	17.20 E
Poščharv	85	38.24 N	71.10 E
Poschiavino ≐	58	46.12 N	10.10 E
Poschiavo	58	46.18 N	10.04 E
Pošechonje-Volodarsk	76	58.30 N	39.07 E
Posen, Il., U.S.	278	41.37 N	87.40 W
Posen, Mi., U.S.	190	45.15 N	83.41 W
Posen → Poznań	30	52.25 N	16.55 E
Poseritz	54	54.18 N	13.16 E
Posesión, Bahía ⊂	254	52.17 S	69.14 W
Posevnaja	86	54.18 N	83.20 E
Poshan → Boshan	98	36.29 N	117.50 E
Poshiwu	106	30.22 N	119.36 E
Posieux	58	46.46 N	7.06 E
Posina	64	45.47 N	11.15 E
Pösing	60	49.14 N	12.33 E
Posio	26	66.06 N	28.09 E
Positano	68	40.38 N	14.29 E
Posjet	89	42.39 N	130.50 E
Poso	112	1.23 S	120.44 E
Poso, Danau ⊜	112	1.52 S	120.35 E
Poso, Teluk ⊂	112	1.15 S	120.55 E
Poso Creek ≐	226	35.41 N	119.22 W

Symbols in the index entries represent the broad categories identified in the key at the right. Symbols with superior numbers (∧[1]) identify subcategories (see complete key on page I · 1).

Symbole im Register stellen die rechts im Schlüssel erklärten Kategorien dar. Symbole mit hochgestellten Ziffern (∧[1]) bezeichnen Unterabteilungen einer Kategorie (vgl. vollständiger Schlüssel auf Seite I · 1).

Los símbolos incluídos en el texto del índice representan las grandes categorías identificadas con la clave a la derecha. Los símbolos con numeros en su parte superior (∧[1]) identifican las subcategorías (véase la clave completa en la página I · 1).

Les symboles de l'index représentent les catégories indiquées dans la légende à droite. Les symboles suivis d'un indice (∧[1]) représentent des sous-catégories (voir légende complète à la page I · 1).

Os símbolos incluídos no texto do índice representam as grandes categorias identificadas com a chave à direita. Os símbolos com números em sua parte superior (∧[1]) identificam as subcategorias (veja-se a chave completa à página I · 1).

∧ Mountain	Berg	Montaña	Montagne	Montanha
∧ Mountains	Gebirge	Montañas	Montagnes	Montanhas
✕ Pass	Paß	Paso	Col	Passo
V Valley, Canyon	Tal, Cañon	Valle, Cañón	Vallée, Canyon	Vale, Canhão
≃ Plain	Ebene	Llano	Plaine	Planície
> Cape	Kap	Cabo	Cap	Cabo
I Island	Insel	Isla	Île	Ilha
II Islands	Inseln	Islas	Îles	Ilhas
≐ Other Topographic Features	Andere Topographische Objekte	Otros Elementos Topográficos	Autres données topographiques	Outros acidentes topográficos

≃ River	Fluß	Río	Rivière	Rio	↦ Submarine Features	Untermeerische Objekte	Accidentes Submarinos	Formes de relief sous-marin	Acidentes submarinos
↳ Canal	Kanal	Canal	Canal	Canal	◻ Political Unit	Politische Einheit	Unidad Política	Entité politique	Unidade política
↧ Waterfall, Rapids	Wasserfall, Stromschnellen	Cascada, Rápidos	Chute d'eau, Rapides	Cascata, Rápidos	⊹ Cultural Institution	Kulturelle Institution	Institución Cultural	Institution culturelle	Instituição cultural
⊂ Strait	Meeresstraße	Estrecho	Détroit	Estreito	⊥ Historical Site	Historische Stätte	Sitio Histórico	Site historique	Sítio histórico
⊂ Bay, Gulf	Bucht, Golf	Bahía, Golfo	Baie, Golfe	Baía, Golfo	♦ Recreational Site	Erholungs- und Ferienort	Centro de loisirs	Centre de loisirs	Área de Lazer
⊜ Lake, Lakes	See, Seen	Lago, Lagos	Lac, Lacs	Lago, Lagos	⊹ Airport	Flughafen	Aeropuerto	Aéroport	Aeroporto
⊻ Swamp	Sumpf	Pantano	Marais	Pântano	⊞ Military Installation	Militäranlage	Instalación Militar	Installation militaire	Instalação militar
⊠ Ice Features, Glacier	Eis- und Gletscherformen	Accidentes Glaciares	Formes glaciaires	Acidentes glaciares	⊙ Miscellaneous	Verschiedenes	Misceláneo	Divers	Diversos
➝ Other Hydrographic Features	Andere Hydrographische Objekte	Otros Elementos Hidrográficos	Autres données hydrographiques	Outros acidentes hidrográficos					

Name	Page	Lat.°′	Long.°′
Princetown	42	50.33 N	4.00 W
Princeville, P.Q., Can.	206	46.10 N	71.53 W
Princeville, Il., U.S.	190	40.56 N	89.45 W
Princeville, N.C., U.S.	192	35.53 N	77.31 W
Prince William □[6]	208	38.42 N	77.27 W
Prince William Forest Park ♠	208	38.36 N	77.23 W
Prince William Sound ʯ	180	60.40 N	147.00 W
Príncipe I	152	1.37 N	7.25 E
Príncipe Alberto, Montes → Prince Albert Mountains ⋌	9	76.00 S	161.30 E
Príncipe Carlos, Montes → Prince Charles Mountains ⋌	9	72.00 S	67.00 E
Principe Channel ʯ	182	53.28 N	130.00 W
Príncipe da Beira	248	12.25 S	64.25 W
Príncipe de Gales, Isla → Prince of Wales Island I, Austl.	164	10.40 S	142.10 E
Príncipe de Gales, Isla → Prince of Wales Island I, N.T., Can.	176	72.40 N	99.00 W
Príncipe Eduardo, Isla → Prince Edward Island □[4]	186	46.20 N	63.20 W
Príncipe Olav, Costa → Prince Olav Coast ≗[2]	9	68.30 S	42.30 E
Príncipe Patricio, Isla → Prince Patrick Island I	16	76.45 N	119.30 W
Prineville	202	44.18 N	120.51 W
Prineville Reservoir ⊜[1]	202	44.08 N	120.42 W
Prineville Southeast	202	44.17 N	120.53 W
Pringgabaja	115b	8.34 S	116.37 E
Pringsewu	112	5.24 S	104.55 E
Pringy	261	48.31 N	2.34 E
Prinsenbeek	52	51.36 N	4.42 E
Prinses Margrietkanaal ≊	52	53.10 N	5.55 E
Prinshof	158	32.06 S	20.53 E
Prinzapolka	236	13.24 N	83.34 W
Prinzapolka ≃	236	13.24 N	83.34 W
Prinzessin Astrid-Küste → Princess Astrid Coast ≗[2]	9	70.45 S	12.30 E
Prinzessin Charlotte Bucht → Princess Charlotte Bay c	164	14.25 S	144.00 E
Prinzessin Martha-Küste → Princess Martha Coast ≗[2]	9	72.00 S	7.30 W
Prinzessin Ragnhild-Küste → Princess Ragnhild Coast ≗[2]	9	70.15 S	27.30 E
Priobskoje plato ⋌[1]	86	52.40 N	83.00 E
Prioksko-Terrasnyj Zapovednik ◆[4]	82	54.51 N	37.36 E
Priolo Gargallo	70	37.09 N	15.11 E
Prior, Cabo ≻	34	43.34 N	8.19 W
Priort	264a	52.31 N	12.58 E
Priozernyj	80	47.23 N	45.14 E
Prioz'ornyj	86	47.50 N	84.13 E
Prioz'orsk	24	61.02 N	30.04 E
Prip'at' ≃	78	51.21 N	30.09 E
Pripet Marshes → Polesje ◆[1]	72	52.00 N	27.00 E
Pripet → Prip'at' ≃	78	51.21 N	30.09 E
Pripol'arnyj Ural ⋌	24	65.00 N	60.00 E
Priputni	78	50.57 N	32.14 E
Prirečje	88	55.07 N	101.03 E
Prirečnyj	80	51.03 N	52.26 E
Přísečnice	54	50.27 N	13.06 E
Priselje	76	55.09 N	32.49 E
Prišib, Azer.	84	39.08 N	48.36 E
Prišib, Ukr.	78	47.16 N	35.21 E
Prislon	82	56.48 N	37.16 E
Pristan'-Prževal'sk	85	42.34 N	78.18 E
Pristen', Ross.	78	51.15 N	36.41 E
Pristen', Ukr.	83	49.36 N	37.38 E
Priština	38	42.39 N	21.10 E
Pritchett	198	37.22 N	102.51 W
Přítluky	61	48.51 N	16.46 E
Pritzerbe	54	52.30 N	12.27 E
Pritzier	54	53.22 N	11.04 E
Pritzwalk	54	53.09 N	12.10 E
Priural'nyj	80	51.29 N	53.06 E
Privas	62	44.44 N	4.36 E
Priverno	66	41.28 N	13.11 E
Privetnoje	78	44.50 N	34.41 E
Privodino	24	61.05 N	46.28 E
Privokzal'nyj, Ross.	82	55.59 N	35.56 E
Privokzal'nyj, Ross.	86	58.53 N	60.43 E
Privolje, Ukr.	83	49.01 N	38.18 E
Privolje, Ukr.	83	48.52 N	37.16 E
Privol'naja	78	46.09 N	38.42 E
Privol'n'anskij ◆[8]	83	48.41 N	38.28 E
Privol'noje, Ross.	80	50.57 N	46.06 E
Privol'noje, Ukr.	78	47.29 N	32.17 E
Privolžje	80	52.52 N	48.37 E
Privolžsk	80	57.23 N	41.17 E
Privolžskaja vozvyšennost' ⋌[1]	80	52.00 N	46.00 E
Privolžskij, Ross.	80	46.24 N	48.00 E
Privolžskij, Ross.	80	51.24 N	46.02 E
Privolžskoje	80	51.06 N	45.57 E
Prizren	38	42.12 N	20.44 E
Prizzi	70	37.43 N	13.26 E
Prizzi, Lago di ⊜	70	37.44 N	13.25 E
Prnjavor	36	44.52 N	17.40 E
Probolinggo	115a	7.45 S	113.13 E
Proboštov	54	50.39 N	13.50 E
Probstzella	54	50.32 N	11.22 E
Probus	42	50.17 N	4.57 W
Procchio	66	42.47 N	10.15 E
Prochladnoje	86	48.30 N	82.41 E
Prochladnyj	84	43.46 N	44.00 E
Prochorkino	86	59.34 N	79.26 E
Prochorovka	82	54.07 N	38.11 E
Prochowice	30	51.17 N	16.22 E
Procida	68	40.46 N	14.02 E
Procida, Isola di I	68	40.45 N	14.01 E
Procter	182	49.37 N	116.57 W
Proctor, Mn., U.S.	190	46.44 N	92.13 W
Proctor, Vt., U.S.	188	43.39 N	73.02 W
Proctor Brook ≃	283	42.32 N	70.54 W
Proctor Lake ⊜	228	35.07 N	118.21 W
Proctor Lake ⊜	222	32.02 N	98.32 W
Proddatūr	122	14.44 N	78.33 E
Proença-a-Nova	34	39.45 N	7.55 W
Profen	54	51.07 N	12.13 E
Pro Football Hall of Fame ◆	214	40.49 N	81.25 W
Prognoj	83	48.45 N	39.51 E
Progreso, Méx.	196	27.28 N	100.59 W
Progreso, Méx.	232	21.17 N	89.40 W
Progreso, Méx.	234	23.48 N	103.18 W
Progreso, Méx.	234	20.15 N	99.12 W
Progreso, Ur.	258	34.40 S	56.13 W
Progress, Ross.	89	49.42 N	129.39 E
Progress, Or., U.S.	224	45.28 N	122.47 W
Progress, Pa., U.S.	208	40.18 N	76.34 W
Project City	204	40.41 N	122.21 W
Prokopjeva	88	58.03 N	100.39 E
Prokopjevsk	86	53.53 N	86.45 E
Prokopyevsk → Prokopjevsk	86	53.53 N	86.45 E
Prokuplje	38	43.14 N	21.36 E
Prokuševo	76	59.55 N	34.56 E
Prokutkino	86	56.19 N	69.46 E
Proletarij	76	58.26 N	31.44 E
Proletarsk, Ross.	80	46.42 N	41.44 E
Proletarsk, Taj.	85	40.10 N	69.30 E
Proletarsk, Ukr.	78	48.56 N	38.23 E
Proletarsk ◆[8]	83	48.56 N	38.23 E
Proletarskij, Ross.	78	50.47 N	35.47 E
Proletarskij, Ross.	82	55.01 N	37.23 E
Proletarskij ◆[8]	83	48.08 N	39.18 E
Prolysovo	76	52.54 N	34.09 E
Prome (Pyè)	110	18.49 N	95.13 E
Promised Land State Park ♠	210	41.18 N	75.11 W
Promissão	255	21.32 S	49.52 W
Promitorio	267a	42.03 N	12.39 E
Promontogno	58	46.21 N	9.34 E
Prompton	210	41.35 N	75.19 W
Prompton Lake ⊜[1]	210	41.36 N	75.20 W
Prompton Lake State Park ♠	210	41.37 N	75.22 W
Promyšlennaja	86	54.55 N	85.40 E
Promyšlennovskij	86	55.29 N	86.12 E
Promyšlennyj	24	67.35 N	63.55 E
Promyslovka	80	45.44 N	47.10 E
Pron'a ≃, Bela.	76	53.25 N	31.01 E
Pron'a ≃, Ross.	80	54.21 N	40.24 E
Pron'a Gorodišče	82	54.15 N	38.43 E
Pronin	80	49.12 N	42.11 E
Pronsfeld	56	50.10 N	6.20 E
Pronsk	76	54.07 N	39.37 E
Prony, Baie du c	175f	22.22 S	166.53 E
Prophet ≃	176	58.45 N	122.45 W
Prophetstown	190	41.40 N	89.56 W
Propriá	250	10.13 S	36.51 W
Propriano	36	41.40 N	8.55 E
Prorer Wiek c	54	54.27 N	13.38 E
Prorva	86	46.03 N	53.15 E
Proryvnoje	86	54.23 N	64.26 E
Pros'anaja	78	48.07 N	36.23 E
Pros'anov	78	49.42 N	35.47 E
Prösen	54	51.25 N	13.30 E
Proserpine	166	20.24 S	148.34 E
Prosigk	54	51.42 N	12.03 E
Proskurov → Chmel'nickij	78	49.25 N	27.00 E
Prosna ≃	30	52.10 N	17.39 E
Prosnica	80	58.26 N	50.15 E
Prosotsáni	38	41.10 N	23.59 E
Prospect, Austl.	168b	34.54 S	138.35 E
Prospect, Austl.	274a	33.48 S	150.56 E
Prospect, Ct., U.S.	207	41.30 N	72.58 W
Prospect, N.Y., U.S.	210	43.18 N	75.09 W
Prospect, Oh., U.S.	214	40.27 N	83.11 W
Prospect, Pa., U.S.	214	40.54 N	80.03 W
Prospect Bay c	208	38.56 N	76.14 W
Prospect Creek ≃	274a	33.55 S	150.59 E
Prospect Heights	278	42.05 N	87.56 W
Prospect Hill	168b	35.13 S	138.44 E
Prospect Hill ∧[2], Ma., U.S.	207	41.21 N	70.45 W
Prospect Hill ∧[2], Ma., U.S.	283	42.23 N	71.15 W
Prospect Hill Park ♠	283	42.23 N	71.15 W
Prospect Meadows	278	42.05 N	87.57 W
Prospect Park, N.J., U.S.	276	40.56 N	74.10 W
Prospect Park, Pa., U.S.	214	41.31 N	78.13 W
Prospect Park, Pa., U.S.	285	39.53 N	75.18 W
Prospect Park ♠	276	40.40 N	73.58 W
Prospect Park Lake ⊜	276	40.39 N	73.57 W
Prospect Plains	276	40.19 N	74.28 W
Prospect Point	276	40.58 N	74.38 W
Prospect Point ≻	276	40.52 N	73.43 W
Prospect Reservoir ⊜[1]	274a	33.49 S	150.54 E
Prospectville	285	40.13 N	75.11 W
Prosper	222	33.14 N	96.48 W
Prosperi Airport ⊠	278	41.33 N	87.47 W
Prosperidad	116	8.34 N	125.52 E
Prosser	202	46.12 N	119.46 W
Prosser Creek Reservoir ⊜[1]	226	39.22 N	120.08 W
Prostějov	30	49.29 N	17.07 E
Prostki	30	53.43 N	22.26 E
Proston	166	26.10 S	151.36 E
Proszowice	30	50.12 N	20.18 E
Protasovo, Ross.	82	54.48 N	38.35 E
Protasovo, Ross.	82	56.08 N	37.36 E
Protasovo, Ross.	82	54.11 N	37.00 E
Protasy	76	52.47 N	29.05 E
Protea	273d	26.17 S	27.51 E
Protection	198	37.12 N	99.29 W
Protection Island I	224	48.07 N	122.55 W
Protem	158	34.16 S	20.05 E
Protivín	61	49.12 N	14.13 E
Protoka ≃	78	45.43 N	37.46 E
Protva	82	55.01 N	36.41 E
Protva ≃	82	54.51 N	37.16 E
Protville	36	36.54 N	10.01 E
Prötzel	54	52.38 N	13.59 E
Proud Lake State Recreation Area ♠	281	42.34 N	83.33 W
Proulxville	206	46.40 N	72.30 W
Provadija	38	43.11 N	27.26 E
Provencal	194	31.39 N	93.12 W
Provence □[9]	62	44.00 N	6.00 E
Provence, Alpes de ⋌	62	43.40 N	6.00 E
Provenchères-sur-Fave	58	48.19 N	7.05 E
Providence, Ky., U.S.	194	37.23 N	87.45 W
Providence, R.I., U.S.	207	41.49 N	71.24 W
Providence, Ut,. U.S.	200	41.42 N	111.48 W
Providence □[6]	207	41.52 N	71.36 W
Providence ≃	207	41.43 N	71.21 W
Providence Forge	208	37.26 N	77.02 W
Providence Island I	138	9.14 S	51.02 E
Providência, Bra.	256	21.40 S	42.35 W
Providencia, Chile	286e	33.26 S	70.37 W
Providencia, Méx.	196	27.06 N	103.32 W
Providencia, Isla de I	236	13.21 N	81.22 W
Providenciales I	238	21.47 N	72.17 W
Providenija	180	64.23 N	173.18 W
Providenija, buchta c	180	64.30 N	173.20 W
Provincetown	207	42.03 N	70.10 W
Provins	50	48.33 N	3.18 E
Provo	200	40.14 N	111.39 W
Provo ≃	200	40.14 N	111.44 W
Provost	184	52.21 N	110.16 W
Provost, Lac ⊜	206	46.22 N	74.00 W
Prozor	36	43.49 N	17.37 E
Pru ≃	150	7.58 N	0.53 W
Prud'anka	78	50.14 N	36.09 E
Prudentópolis	252	25.12 S	50.57 W
Prudentov	80	49.39 N	46.19 E
Prudhoe	44	54.58 N	1.51 W
Prudhoe Bay c	180	70.20 N	148.20 W
Prudhoe Island I	166	21.19 S	149.40 E
Prudišči	82	54.24 N	38.25 E
Prudki	82	54.46 N	36.29 E
Prudnik	30	50.19 N	17.34 E
Prudy	76	53.47 N	26.32 E
Pruggern	64	47.25 N	13.52 E
Prüm	56	50.12 N	6.25 E
Prüm ≃	56	49.49 N	6.28 E
Pruna, Punta sa ≻	71	40.11 N	9.26 E
Prunay-le-Temple	261	48.52 N	1.40 E
Prunay-sous-Ablis	261	48.32 N	1.48 E
Prunedale	226	36.47 N	121.40 W
Pruneřov	54	50.25 N	13.16 E
Prunières	62	44.33 N	6.20 E
Prunn, Schloss ⊥	60	48.57 N	11.44 E
Pruszków	30	52.11 N	20.48 E
Prut ≃	78	45.30 N	28.12 E
Pruth → Prut ≃	78	45.30 N	28.12 E
Prutting	64	47.53 N	12.11 E
Prutz	58	47.05 N	10.40 E
Pružany	76	52.33 N	24.28 E
Prydz Bay c	9	69.00 S	76.00 E
Pryor	196	36.19 N	95.19 W
Pryor Creek ≃	202	45.54 N	108.19 W
Pryor Mountain ∧[2]	222	31.43 N	95.12 W
Prysor ≃	42	52.56 N	4.00 W
Przasnysz	30	53.01 N	20.55 E
Przedbórz	30	51.06 N	19.53 E
Przemków	30	51.32 N	15.48 E
Przemocze	54	53.27 N	14.55 E
Przemyśl	30	49.47 N	22.47 E
Przemyśl □[4]	30	50.00 N	22.40 E
Przeworsk	30	50.05 N	22.29 E
Przewóz	54	51.29 N	14.59 E
Przybiernów	54	53.46 N	14.46 E
Przysucha	30	51.22 N	20.38 E
Pšagar	85	39.58 N	68.08 E
Psakhná	38	38.35 N	23.38 E
Psará I	38	38.35 N	25.37 E
Psárion	38	37.20 N	21.51 E
Psebaj	84	44.07 N	40.47 E
Pšecha ≃	78	44.47 N	39.48 E
Psekups ≃	78	45.00 N	39.09 E
Pselec	78	51.17 N	36.32 E
Psikhikón	267c	38.01 N	23.46 E
Pšiš ≃	78	45.01 N	39.18 E
Pšiš, gora ∧	84	43.24 N	41.12 E
Psittália I	267c	37.56 N	23.35 E
Pskem	85	41.56 N	70.22 E
Pskem ≃	85	41.38 N	70.01 E
Pskent	85	40.54 N	69.20 E
Pskov	76	57.50 N	28.20 E
Pskovskoje ozero ⊜	76	58.00 N	28.00 E
Pskowsee → Pskovskoje ozero ⊜	76	58.00 N	28.00 E
Ps'ol ≃	78	49.02 N	33.33 E
Pšov	54	50.10 N	13.29 E
Pszczyna	30	49.59 N	18.57 E
Ptarmigan, Cape ≻	176	71.04 N	118.07 W
Ptič'	78	52.09 N	28.52 E
Ptič' ≃	76	52.09 N	28.52 E
Ptolemais	38	40.31 N	21.41 E
Ptolemais ⊥	146	32.43 N	20.57 E
Ptuj	61	46.25 N	15.52 E
Pu ≃, Zhg.	104	41.21 N	122.47 E
Pu ≃, Zhg.	107	30.25 N	103.49 E
Puah, Pulau I	112	0.30 S	122.34 E
Puakonikai	174d	0.52 S	169.36 E
Puamau, Baie c	174x	9.46 S	138.52 W
Puán, Arg.	252	37.33 S	62.43 W
Puan, Taehan	98	35.45 N	126.44 E
Pubāil	126	23.56 N	90.29 E
Pubnico	186	43.42 N	65.47 W
Pucallpa	248	8.23 S	74.32 W
Pucara	248	18.43 S	64.11 W
Pucarani	248	16.23 S	68.30 W
Puccha ≃	248	9.05 S	76.54 W
Puccia, Serra di ∧	70	37.44 N	13.56 E
Puce	214	42.18 N	82.47 W
Puces ≃	281	42.18 N	82.47 W
Pučevejem ≃	180	68.48 N	170.30 E
Pučež	80	56.59 N	43.11 E
Puchberg am Schneeberg	61	47.47 N	15.54 E
Pucheng, Zhg.	100	27.55 N	118.31 E
Pucheng, Zhg.	102	34.59 N	109.29 E
Pucheta	252	29.54 S	57.34 W
Puchheim	60	48.09 N	11.20 E
Púchov	30	49.08 N	18.20 E
Puchoviči	76	53.32 N	28.15 E
Pucioasa	38	45.04 N	25.26 E
Pucio Point ≻	116	11.46 N	121.51 E
Pučišća	36	43.21 N	16.44 E
Puck	30	54.44 N	18.27 E
Puckapunyal	169	37.01 S	145.03 E
Pucketa Creek ≃	279b	40.33 N	79.45 W
Pudahuel	286e	33.26 S	70.46 W
Pudding ≃	224	45.18 N	122.43 W
Puddingstone Reservoir ⊜[1]	280	34.05 N	117.48 W
Puddington	262	53.15 N	3.00 W
Puddletown	42	50.45 N	2.21 W
Pūdeh Tal ≃	128	31.03 N	62.15 E
Pudem	80	58.18 N	52.10 E
Pudi	102	27.58 N	99.05 E
Pudimoe	158	27.26 S	24.44 E
Puding	102	26.21 N	105.40 E
Pudino	86	57.34 N	79.24 E
Pudops Dam ◆[6]	186	48.09 N	56.50 W
Pudož	24	61.48 N	36.32 E
Pudsey	44	53.48 N	1.40 W
Pudu ≃	102	26.19 N	102.45 E
Puduari ≃	246	2.08 S	61.15 W
Puduhe	102	25.39 N	102.39 E
Pudukkottai	122	10.23 N	78.49 E
Puebla □[3]	234	18.50 N	98.00 W
Puebla de Alcocer	34	38.59 N	5.15 W
Puebla de Don Fadrique	34	37.58 N	2.26 W
Puebla de Don Rodrigo	34	39.05 N	4.37 W
Puebla de Sanabria	34	42.03 N	6.38 W
Puebla de Trives	34	42.20 N	7.15 W
Puebla [de Zaragoza]	234	19.03 N	98.12 W
Pueblito de Ponce	240m	18.26 N	66.58 W
Pueblo	198	38.15 N	104.36 W
Pueblo Libertador	252	30.13 S	59.23 W
Pueblo Libre	286d	12.05 S	77.04 W
Pueblo Mountain ∧	202	42.06 N	118.39 W
Pueblo Nuevo, Col.	246	8.31 N	75.15 W
Pueblo Nuevo, Méx.	234	20.31 N	101.22 W
Pueblo Nuevo, Nic.	236	13.23 N	86.29 W
Pueblo Nuevo, P.R.	240m	18.28 N	66.51 W
Pueblo Nuevo, Ur.	258	34.26 S	56.29 W
Pueblo Nuevo, Ven.	246	11.58 N	69.55 W
Pueblo Nuevo ◆[8]	266a	40.26 N	3.39 W
Pueblo Nuevo Tiquisate	236	14.17 N	91.22 W
Pueblo of Acoma	200	35.03 N	107.35 W
Pueblo Reservoir ⊜[1]	198	38.15 N	104.45 W
Puebloviejo, Ec.	246	1.34 S	79.30 W
Pueblo Viejo, Méx.	234	17.33 N	100.05 W
Pueblo Viejo, Méx.	234	16.14 N	94.39 W
Pueblo Viejo, Laguna c	234	22.10 N	97.53 W
Pueblo Yaqui	232	27.19 N	110.01 W
Puelches	252	38.09 S	65.55 W
Puente Alto	252	33.37 S	70.35 W
Puente de Arganda	266a	40.19 N	3.31 W
Puente de Ixtla	234	18.37 N	99.20 W
Puente-Genil	34	37.23 N	4.47 W
Puente Hills ⋌[2]	280	34.00 N	117.55 W
Puente Hills Mall ◆[9]	280	33.59 N	117.56 W
Puente la Reina	34	42.40 N	1.49 W
Puente Nuevo, Embalse de ⊜[2]	34	38.00 N	5.00 W
Puente Piedra	286d	11.57 S	77.05 W
Pueo Point ≻	229b	21.54 N	160.04 W
Pu'er	102	23.07 N	101.02 E
Puerca, Punta ≻	240m	18.14 N	65.36 W
Puerco ≃	200	34.53 N	110.07 W
Puerco, Rio ≃	200	34.22 N	106.50 W
Pu'erdu	102	28.08 N	104.24 E
Puerto Acosta	248	15.32 S	69.15 W
Puerto Adela	252	24.33 S	54.22 W
Puerto Aisén	254	45.24 S	72.42 W
Puerto Alegre	248	13.53 S	61.36 W
Puerto Ángel	234	15.40 N	96.29 W
Puerto Arista	234	15.56 N	93.48 W
Puerto Armuelles	236	8.17 N	82.52 W
Puerto Asís	246	0.30 N	76.31 W
Puerto Ayacucho	246	5.40 N	67.35 W
Puerto Ayora, Ec.	246a	0.45 S	90.19 W
Puerto Ayora, Ec.	246a	0.45 S	90.19 W
Puerto Bahía Negra	248	20.15 S	58.12 W
Puerto Baquerizo Moreno	246a	0.54 S	89.36 W
Puerto Barrios	236	15.43 N	88.36 W
Puerto Bermejo	252	26.56 S	58.30 W
Puerto Bermúdez	248	10.20 S	74.54 W
Puerto Berrío	246	6.29 N	74.24 W
Puerto Bolívar, Col.	246	12.15 N	71.58 W
Puerto Bolívar, Ec.	246	3.16 S	79.59 W
Puerto Boyacá	246	5.45 N	74.39 W
Puerto Busch	248	20.02 S	57.55 W
Puerto Cabello	246	10.28 N	68.01 W
Puerto Cabezas	236	14.02 N	83.23 W
Puerto Carreño	246	6.12 N	67.22 W
Puerto Casado	252	22.20 S	57.55 W
Puerto Castilla	236	16.01 N	86.01 W
Puerto Chicama	248	7.42 S	79.27 W
Puerto Colombia	246	10.59 N	74.58 W
Puerto Constanza	258	33.50 S	59.03 W
Puerto Cortés	236	15.48 N	87.56 W
Puerto Cumarebo	246	11.29 N	69.21 W
Puerto de Eten	248	6.54 S	79.52 W
Puerto Delicia	252	26.12 S	54.35 W
Puerto de Lomas	248	15.34 S	74.50 W
Puerto Delón	236	14.22 N	85.53 W
Puerto del Rosario	148	28.30 N	13.52 W
Puerto Deseado	254	47.45 S	65.54 W
Puerto El Triunfo	236	13.17 N	88.33 W
Puerto Escondido	234	15.50 N	97.10 W
Puerto Espãna → Port of Spain	241r	10.39 N	61.31 W
Puerto Esperanza	252	26.01 S	54.39 W
Puerto Felipe, Bahía → Port Phillip Bay c	169	38.07 S	144.48 E
Puerto Fonciere	252	22.29 S	57.48 W
Puerto Francisco de Orellana	246	0.28 S	76.58 W
Puerto Gonzalo Moreno	248	11.06 S	66.10 W
Puerto Guaraní	248	21.18 S	57.55 W
Puerto Heath	248	12.30 S	68.40 W
Puerto Iguazú	252	25.34 S	54.34 W
Puerto Inca	248	9.22 S	74.58 W
Puerto Ingeniero Ibáñez	254	46.18 S	71.56 W
Puerto Inírida	246	3.53 N	67.52 W
Puerto Jiménez	236	8.33 N	83.19 W
Puerto Juárez	232	21.11 N	86.49 W
Puerto la Cruz	246	10.13 N	64.38 W
Puerto la Plata, Zona Nacional □[5]	288	34.52 S	57.52 W
Puerto Leda	248	20.41 S	58.02 W
Puerto Leguízamo	246	0.12 S	74.46 W
Puerto Lempira	236	15.13 N	83.47 W
Puerto Libertad, Arg.	252	25.55 S	54.36 W
Puerto Libertad, Méx.	232	29.55 N	112.43 W
Puerto Limón, Col.	246	3.23 N	73.30 W
Puerto Limón, C.R.	236	10.00 N	83.02 W
Puertollano	34	38.41 N	4.07 W
Puerto Lobos	254	42.00 S	65.06 W
Puerto López	246	4.05 N	72.58 W
Puerto Madero	236	14.44 N	92.25 W
Puerto Madryn	254	42.46 S	65.03 W
Puerto Maldonado	248	12.36 S	69.11 W
Puerto Manatí	240p	21.22 N	76.50 W
Puerto Mihanovich	248	20.52 S	57.59 W
Puerto Montt	254	41.28 S	72.57 W
Puerto Morazán	236	12.51 N	87.11 W
Puerto Morelos	232	20.50 N	86.52 W
Puerto Nariño	246	4.56 N	67.48 W
Puerto Natales	254	51.44 S	72.31 W
Puerto Nuevo, Punta ≻	240m	18.30 N	66.24 W
Puerto Octay	254	40.58 S	72.54 W
Puerto Ordaz → Ciudad Guayana	246	8.22 N	62.40 W
Puerto Padre	240p	21.12 N	76.36 W
Puerto Páez	246	6.13 N	67.28 W
Puerto Palmer, Pico ∧	196	27.08 N	101.47 W
Puerto Peñasco	232	31.20 N	113.33 W
Puerto Pilón	236	9.22 N	79.48 W
Puerto Pinasco	252	22.43 S	57.50 W
Puerto Pirámide	254	42.34 S	64.17 W
Puerto Piray	252	26.28 S	54.42 W
Puerto Píritu	246	10.04 N	65.03 W
Puerto Plata	238	19.48 N	70.41 W
Puerto Portillo	248	9.46 S	72.45 W
Puerto Princesa, Pil.	116	9.44 N	118.44 E
Puerto Princesa, Pil.	116	10.06 N	125.29 E
Puerto Real, Esp.	34	36.32 N	6.11 W
Puerto Real, P.R.	240m	18.05 N	67.11 W
Puerto Rico, Arg.	252	26.48 S	55.02 W
Puerto Rico, Bol.	248	11.05 S	67.38 W
Puerto Rico, Col.	246	1.54 N	75.10 W
Puerto Rico □[2], N.A.	230	18.15 N	66.30 W
Puerto Rico □[2], N.A.	240m	18.15 N	66.30 W
Puerto Rico Trench ✢[1]	16	20.00 N	66.00 W
Puerto Rondón	246	6.17 N	71.06 W
Puerto Saavedra	252	38.47 S	73.24 W
Puerto Salgar	246	5.28 N	74.39 W
Puerto Sandino	236	12.12 N	86.46 W
Puerto San José	236	13.55 N	90.49 W
Puerto San Julián	254	49.18 S	67.43 W
Puerto Santa Cruz	254	50.01 S	68.31 W
Puerto Sastre	252	22.06 S	57.59 W
Puerto Siles	248	12.48 S	65.05 W
Puerto Suarez	248	18.57 S	57.51 W
Puerto Supe	248	10.49 S	77.45 W
Puerto Tejada	246	3.14 N	76.24 W
Puerto Tolosa	246	0.59 S	74.09 W
Puerto Umbría	246	0.52 N	76.33 W
Puerto Vallarta	234	20.37 N	105.15 W
Puerto Varas	254	41.19 S	72.59 W
Puerto Victoria, Arg.	252	26.20 S	54.39 W
Puerto Victoria, Perú	248	9.54 S	74.58 W
Puerto Viejo, C.R.	236	10.26 N	83.59 W
Puerto Viejo, C.R.	236	9.39 N	82.45 W
Puerto Villamil	246a	0.56 S	91.01 W
Puerto Villamizar	246	8.19 N	72.26 W
Puerto Villarroel	248	16.50 S	64.47 W
Puerto Visser	254	45.24 S	67.08 W
Puerto Wilches	246	7.21 N	73.54 W
Puerto Williams	254	54.56 S	67.37 W
Puerto Ybapobó	252	23.42 S	57.12 W
Pueyrredón, Lago (Lago Cochrane) ⊜	254	47.20 S	72.00 W
Puffendorf	56	50.56 N	6.13 E
Puffing Billy Railroad Station ◆[5]	274b	37.55 S	145.21 E
Pugačov	80	52.01 N	48.50 E
Pugač'ovo	80	56.35 N	53.02 E
Puge, Tan.	154	4.45 S	33.07 E
Puge, Zhg.	102	27.28 N	102.31 E
Puget, Cape ≻	180	59.52 N	148.26 W
Puget Island I	224	46.10 N	123.23 W
Puget Sound ʯ	224	47.50 N	122.30 W
Puget Sound Naval Shipyard ■	224	47.33 N	122.38 W
Puget-sur-Argens	62	43.27 N	6.41 E
Puget-Théniers	62	43.57 N	6.54 E
Puget-Ville	62	43.17 N	6.08 E
Pugh Mountain ∧	224	48.08 N	121.22 W
Pughtown	285	40.10 N	75.40 W
Puglia □[4]	68	41.15 N	16.15 E
Pugong-ni	271b	37.43 N	126.58 E
Pugŏ-ri	98	42.01 N	129.59 E
Pugwash	186	45.51 N	63.40 W
Puhe	104	41.57 N	123.36 E
Puhi	229b	21.58 N	159.23 W
Puhja	76	58.20 N	26.19 E
Puhos	26	62.05 N	29.54 E
Puhosjärvi ⊜	26	65.19 N	27.55 E
Puica	248	15.04 S	72.42 W
Puieşti	38	46.25 N	27.33 E
Puigcerdà	34	42.26 N	1.56 E
Puigmal ∧	34	42.23 N	2.07 E
Puimoisson	62	43.52 N	6.08 E
Puinahua, Canal de ≃	248	5.20 S	74.13 W
Puināñ	272b	22.56 N	84.13 E
Puir	89	53.10 N	141.25 E
Puisaye, Collines de la ⋌[2]	50	47.40 N	3.15 E

ENGLISH Name	Page	Lat.°′	Long.°′

Name	Page	Lat.°′	Long.°′
Puiseaux	50	48.12 N	2.28 E
Puiseaux ≃	50	48.00 N	2.44 E
Puiseux-en-France	261	49.04 N	2.29 E
Puiseux-Pontoise	261	49.03 N	2.01 E
Puisieux	50	50.07 N	2.42 E
Puits ≃	50	48.31 N	4.15 E
Pujada Bay c	116	6.51 N	126.14 E
Pujehun	150	7.21 N	11.42 W
Puji, Zhg.	100	27.59 N	113.25 E
Puji, Zhg.	100	29.58 N	112.32 E
Pujiang, Zhg.	100	29.28 N	119.53 E
Pujiang, Zhg.	107	30.12 N	103.30 E
Pujilí	246	0.57 S	78.41 W
Pujon	115a	7.50 S	112.28 E
Pujun	112	1.20 S	114.20 E
Pujut	114	1.25 N	100.39 E
Pujut, Tanjung ≻	115a	5.52 S	106.02 E
Pukaki, Lake ⊜	172	44.07 S	170.10 E
Pukalani	229a	20.50 N	156.20 W
Pukaskwa ≃	190	48.00 N	85.53 W
Pukaskwa National Park ♠	190	48.20 N	85.50 W
Pukch'ang	98	39.36 N	126.17 E
Pukchin	98	40.10 N	125.43 E
Pukch'ŏn	98	36.13 N	126.45 E
Pukch'ŏng	98	40.15 N	128.20 E
Pukë	38	42.03 N	19.54 E
Pukeashun Mountain ∧	182	51.12 N	119.14 W
Pukekohe	172	37.12 S	174.55 E
Puketeraki Range ⋌	172	42.58 S	172.12 E
Puketoi Range ⋌	172	40.30 S	176.05 E
Pukeuri Junction	172	45.02 S	171.02 E
Pukhan-gang ≃	98	37.31 N	127.18 E
Pŭkhan-san ∧	271b	37.41 N	127.00 E
Pukhrāyān	124	26.14 N	79.51 E
Pukoo	229d	21.04 N	156.48 W
Pukou, Zhg.	100	26.16 N	119.35 E
Pukou, Zhg.	106	32.07 N	118.43 E
Puksoozero	24	62.38 N	40.36 E
Puksubaek-san ∧	98	40.42 N	127.44 E
Puktae-ch'ŏn ≃	98	40.28 N	129.00 E
Pula, Cro.	64	44.52 N	13.50 E
Pula, It.	71	39.01 N	9.00 E
Pulacayo	248	20.25 S	66.41 W
Pulandian Wan c	98	39.18 N	121.35 E
Pulanduta Point ≻	116	11.54 N	123.10 E
Pulangi ≃	116	7.18 N	124.50 E
Pulangpisau	112	2.46 S	114.14 E
Pulap I[1]	14	7.35 N	149.24 E
Púlar, Cerro ∧	252	24.11 S	68.04 W
Pulaski, In., U.S.	216	40.59 N	86.40 W
Pulaski, Mi., U.S.	216	42.07 N	84.40 W
Pulaski, N.Y., U.S.	212	43.34 N	76.07 W
Pulaski, Oh., U.S.	216	41.30 N	84.26 W
Pulaski, Pa., U.S.	214	41.07 N	80.26 W
Pulaski, Tn., U.S.	194	35.11 N	87.01 W
Pulaski, Va., U.S.	192	37.02 N	80.46 W
Pulaski, Wi., U.S.	190	44.40 N	88.14 W
Pulaski □[6]	216	41.03 N	86.36 W
Pulau ≃	164	5.50 S	138.15 E
Pulaukida	112	2.44 S	102.34 E
Pulaukijang	112	0.42 S	103.12 E
Pulaumerak, Indon.	115a	5.56 S	106.00 E
Pulaumerak, Indon.	115a	5.56 S	106.00 E
Pulauraja	114	2.42 N	99.37 E
Puławy	30	51.25 N	21.57 E
Pulborough	42	50.58 N	0.30 W
Pul'chakim	85	38.10 N	67.21 E
Pulehu Gulch V	229a	20.50 N	156.28 W
Pulfero	64	46.11 N	13.29 E
Pulga	123	31.59 N	77.26 E
Pulgaon	122	20.44 N	78.20 E
Pulham Market	42	52.26 N	1.14 E
Pulheim	56	51.00 N	6.47 E
Puli	100	23.58 N	120.57 E
Pulicat	122	13.25 N	80.19 E
Pulicat Lake c	122	13.40 N	80.10 E
Pulichatum	128	35.57 N	61.07 E
Puliciano	66	43.23 N	11.51 E
Puliyangudi	122	9.10 N	77.25 E
Pulj → Pula	64	44.52 N	13.50 E
Pulkau	61	48.42 N	15.51 E
Pulkau ≃	61	48.43 N	16.21 E
Pulkkila	26	64.16 N	25.52 E
Pulkovo ◆[8]	265a	59.46 N	30.20 E
Pullman, Mi., U.S.	216	42.29 N	86.05 W
Pullman, Wa., U.S.	202	46.43 N	117.10 W
Pullman ◆[8]	278	41.43 N	87.36 W
Púllo	248	15.14 S	73.50 W
Pully	58	46.31 N	6.39 E
Pul'mo	78	51.31 N	23.47 E
Pulo ⊥	68	41.12 N	16.34 E
Pulo Anna I	108	4.40 N	131.58 E
Pulog, Mount ∧	116	16.36 N	120.54 E
Pulogadung ◆[8]	269e	6.11 S	106.54 E
Pulon'ga	24	66.17 N	40.02 E
Púlpito do Sul	152	15.46 S	12.00 E
Pulsano	68	40.23 N	17.22 E
Pulsen	54	51.23 N	13.26 E
Pulsnitz	54	51.11 N	14.01 E
Pulsnitz ≃	54	51.27 N	13.30 E
Pulteney	210	42.31 N	77.10 W
Pultneyville	210	43.17 N	77.11 W
Pułtusk	30	52.43 N	21.05 E
Pulü, Zhg.	107	29.50 N	106.11 E
Pulu, Zhg.	120	36.11 N	81.30 E
Pulupandan	116	10.31 N	122.48 E
Pulur	130	40.10 N	39.53 E
Pulusuk I	14	6.42 N	149.19 E
Pulversheim	58	47.51 N	7.18 E
Puma Yumco ⊜	124	28.35 N	90.20 E
Pumbi	152	3.26 N	22.11 E
Pumei	102	23.28 N	105.15 E
Pumphrey	284b	39.13 N	76.38 W
Pumpkin Buttes ∧	200	43.44 N	105.54 W
Pumpkin Center	228	35.18 N	119.05 W
Pumpkin Creek ≃, Mt., U.S.	198	46.15 N	105.45 W
Pumpkin Creek ≃, Ne., U.S.	198	41.38 N	103.01 W
Pumsaint	42	52.03 N	3.58 W
Pumsi	80	57.12 N	51.39 E
Puná, Isla I	246	2.50 S	80.08 W
Punaauia	174s	17.38 S	149.36 W
Punaauia, Pointe de ≻	174s	17.38 S	149.36 W
Punakha	124	27.37 N	89.52 E
Punaluu	229c	21.35 N	157.53 W
Punan, Indon.	112	1.20 N	115.34 E
Punan, Indon.	112	3.24 N	116.16 E
Punan, Zhg.	100	24.39 N	117.41 E
Punata	248	17.32 S	65.50 W
Pūnch	123	33.46 N	74.06 E
Pūnch ≃	123	33.12 N	73.40 E
Punchaw	182	53.28 N	123.13 W
Punchbowl	274a	33.56 S	151.03 E
Pundaguitan	116	6.22 N	126.10 E
Punda Maria	156	22.40 S	31.05 E
Pünderich	56	50.02 N	7.07 E
Pundri	124	29.45 N	76.33 E
Punduga	24	60.08 N	40.12 E
Pune (Poona)	122	18.32 N	73.52 E
P'ungam-ni	98	37.43 N	128.11 E
Pungan	85	40.45 N	70.49 E
Punganūru	122	13.22 N	78.35 E
Pungeşti	38	46.42 N	27.20 E
Punggol	271c	1.25 N	103.55 E
Punggol ≃	271c	1.25 N	103.54 E
Pungki	114	4.17 N	96.13 E
Pungo ≃	192	35.23 N	76.33 W
Pungo Andongo	154	9.40 S	15.35 E
Pungoé ≃	154	19.50 S	34.48 E
P'ungsan, C.M.I.K.	98	40.47 N	128.10 E
P'ungsan, C.M.I.K.	98	38.28 N	125.01 E
P'ungsong-ni	98	39.56 N	127.11 E
Punia	154	1.28 S	26.27 E
Punilla, Sierra de la ⋌	252	28.55 S	69.00 W
Puning	100	23.18 N	116.12 E

DEUTSCH Name	Seite	Breite°′	Länge°′ E = Ost

Name	Seite	Breite°′	Länge°′ E = Ost
Punitaqui	252	30.50 S	71.16 W
Punjab □[3]	123	31.00 N	75.30 E
Punjab □[4]	120	31.00 N	72.00 E
Punkaharju ◆	26	61.47 N	29.20 E
Punkalaidun	26	61.07 N	23.06 E
Punnichy	184	51.23 N	104.18 W
Puno	248	15.50 S	70.02 W
Puno □[5]	248	15.00 S	70.00 W
Punta, Castillo de la ⊥	286b	23.09 N	82.21 W
Punta, Cerro de ∧	240m	18.10 N	66.36 W
Punta Alegre	240p	22.23 N	78.49 W
Punta Alta	254	38.53 S	62.05 W
Punta Arenas	254	53.09 S	70.55 W
Punta Banda, Cabo ≻	232	31.45 N	116.45 W
Punta Brava ◆[8]	286b	23.01 N	82.30 W
Punta Cardón	246	11.38 N	70.14 W
Punta Colnett	232	31.05 N	116.05 W
Punta de Agua Creek (Tramperos Creek) ≃	196	35.32 N	102.27 W
Punta de Bombón	248	17.11 S	71.48 W
Punta de Díaz	252	28.03 S	70.37 W
Punta del Cobre	252	27.30 S	70.16 W
Punta del Este	252	34.58 S	54.57 W
Punta Delgada	254	42.46 S	63.38 W
Punta de los Llanos	252	30.09 S	66.33 W
Punta de Mata	246	9.43 N	63.38 W
Punta de Piedras	246	10.54 N	64.06 W
Punta Flecha	116	7.23 N	123.25 E
Punta Gorda, Belize	232	16.07 N	88.48 W
Punta Gorda, Nic.	236	11.31 N	83.47 W
Punta Gorda, Fl., U.S.	220	26.55 N	82.02 W
Punta Gorda ≃	236	11.30 N	83.47 W
Punta Gorda, Bahía de c	236	11.15 N	83.45 W
Punta Negra, Salar de ≚	252	24.35 S	69.00 W
Punta Prieta	232	28.58 N	114.17 W
Punta Raisi, Aeroporto di ⊠	70	38.11 N	13.06 E
Puntarenas	236	9.58 N	84.50 W
Puntarenas □[4]	236	9.00 N	83.15 W
Punta Santiago	240m	18.10 N	65.45 W
Puntas del Sauce	258	33.51 S	57.01 W
Punto Fijo	246	11.42 N	70.13 W
Puntzi Lake ⊜	182	52.12 N	124.02 W
Punung	115a	8.08 S	111.01 E
Punxsutawney	214	40.56 N	78.58 W
Puolanka	26	64.52 N	27.40 E
Puolo Point ≻	229b	21.54 N	159.36 W
Puper	164	0.10 S	131.18 E
Pup'yŏng	271b	37.30 N	126.43 E
Puqi, Zhg.	100	28.11 N	121.01 E
Puqi, Zhg.	100	29.43 N	113.53 E
Puqian, Zhg.	100	23.34 N	114.38 E
Puqian, Zhg.	102	20.03 N	110.36 E
Puquio	248	14.42 S	74.08 W
Pur ≃	74	67.31 N	77.55 E
Purabiya Plain ≚	124	25.50 N	82.30 E
Puracé, Volcán ∧[1]	246	2.21 N	76.23 W
Purandarpur	126	23.51 N	87.36 E
Pūranpur	124	28.31 N	80.09 E
Purari ≃	164	7.25 S	145.05 E
Purba	114	2.54 N	98.42 E
Purbashthāli	126	23.28 N	88.21 E
Purbeck, Isle of I	42	50.38 N	2.00 W
Purbolinggo	115a	7.24 S	109.22 E
Purcell	196	35.00 N	97.21 W
Purcell Mountains ⋌	182	50.00 N	116.30 W
Purcellville	188	39.08 N	77.42 W
Purchase	276	41.02 N	73.43 W
Purchena	34	37.21 N	2.22 W
Purdon	222	31.57 N	96.37 W
Purdoški	80	54.40 N	43.32 E
Purdy	194	36.49 N	93.55 W
Purech	80	56.39 N	43.05 E
Pureora ∧	172	38.33 S	175.38 E
Purépero	234	19.55 N	102.01 W
Purfleet	42	51.29 N	0.15 E
Purga	171a	27.43 S	152.44 E
Purga Creek ≃	171a	27.42 S	152.45 E
Purgatoire ≃	198	38.04 N	103.10 W
Purgatory Brook ≃	283	42.11 N	71.11 W
Purgg	61	47.32 N	14.04 E
Purgstall an der Erlauf	61	48.03 N	15.08 E
Puri	120	19.48 N	85.51 E
Purial, Sierra del ⋌	240p	20.12 N	74.42 W
Purificación, Col.	246	3.51 N	74.55 W
Purificación, Méx.	234	19.43 N	104.38 W
Purificación ≃, Méx.	232	23.58 N	98.42 W
Purificación ≃, Méx.	234	19.18 N	104.54 W
Purikari neem ≻	76	59.40 N	25.43 E
Purísima	196	29.09 N	100.46 W
Purísima, Sierra de la ⋌	196	26.30 N	101.44 W
Purisima Creek ≃	282	37.24 N	122.26 W
Purísima de Bustos	234	21.02 N	101.52 W
Purkersdorf	264b	48.12 N	16.11 E
Purleigh	260	51.41 N	0.40 E
Purley	222	33.05 N	95.16 W
Purley ◆[8]	260	51.20 N	0.07 W
Purling	210	42.17 N	74.00 W
Purmerend	52	52.31 N	4.57 E
Pūrna ≃, India	122	19.07 N	77.02 E
Pūrna ≃, India	122	21.05 N	76.00 E
Pūrnia	124	25.47 N	87.31 E
Puronga	76	60.09 N	40.54 E
Purranque	254	40.55 S	73.10 W
Purrorumba Hill ∧	171b	35.10 S	149.23 E
Purros	156	18.38 S	12.59 E
Purrumbete, Lake ⊜	169	38.17 S	143.14 E
Pursat → Poŭthĭsăt	110	12.32 N	103.55 E
Purton	42	51.36 N	1.52 W
Puruándiro	234	20.05 N	101.30 W
Puruarán	234	19.06 N	101.32 W
Puruí ≃	246	1.40 S	68.08 W
Purukcahu	112	0.35 S	114.35 E
Puruliya	126	23.20 N	86.22 E
Puruni ≃	246	6.00 N	59.12 W
Purus (Purús) ≃	242	3.42 S	61.28 W
Puruvesi ⊜	26	61.50 N	29.27 E
Purvis	194	31.08 N	89.24 W
Purwakarta	115a	6.34 S	107.26 E
Purwantoro	115a	7.51 S	111.15 E
Purwareja	115a	7.28 S	109.25 E
Purwodadi, Indon.	115a	7.49 S	110.00 E
Purwodadi, Indon.	115a	7.05 S	110.54 E
Purwokerto	115a	7.25 S	109.14 E
Purworejo	115a	7.43 S	110.01 E
Pusa	112	1.36 N	111.17 E
Pusad	122	19.54 N	77.35 E
Pusan	98	35.06 N	129.03 E
Pusan □[4]	98	35.10 N	129.05 E
Pūsa Road	124	25.59 N	85.41 E
Pusat Gayo, Pegunungan ⋌	114	4.15 N	97.05 E
Puščino	82	54.50 N	37.36 E
Pusgo Point ≻	116	13.31 N	122.38 E
Pushang	98	36.08 N	119.42 E
Pushkar	120	26.30 N	74.33 E
Pushkin Airport ⊠	265a	59.41 N	30.21 E
Pushkin Drama Theatre ◆	265a	59.56 N	30.21 E
Pushkin → Puškin	76	59.43 N	30.25 E
Pushthrough	186	47.39 N	56.10 W
Puškar'ovka	78	48.40 N	34.16 E
Puskiakiwenin Indian Reserve ◆[4]	184	53.57 N	110.26 W
Puškin	76	59.43 N	30.25 E
Puškino, Azer.	84	39.27 N	48.33 E
Puškino, Ross.	80	51.14 N	46.59 E
Puškino, Ross.	82	56.01 N	37.51 E
Puškino, Ross.	82	56.36 N	35.46 E
Puškinskij	265a	59.43 N	30.18 E
Puškinskije Gory	76	57.01 N	28.54 E
Puskwaskau ≃	182	55.29 N	118.10 W

Symbols in the index entries represent the broad categories identified in the key at the right. Symbols with superior numbers (⋌[1]) identify subcategories (see complete key on page I · 1).

Symbole im Register stellen die rechts im Schlüssel erklärten Kategorien dar. Symbole mit hochgestellten Ziffern (⋌[1]) bezeichnen Unterabteilungen einer Kategorie (vgl. vollständiger Schlüssel auf Seite I · 1).

Los símbolos incluidos en el texto del índice representan las grandes categorías identificadas con la clave a la derecha. Los símbolos con números en su parte superior (⋌[1]) identifican las subcategorías (véase la clave completa en la página I · 1).

Les symboles de l'index représentent les catégories indiquées dans la légende à droite. Les symboles suivis d'un indice (⋌[1]) représentent des sous-catégories (voir légende complète à la page I · 1).

Os símbolos incluídos no texto do índice representam as grandes categorias identificadas com a chave à direita. Os símbolos com números em sua parte superior (⋌[1]) identificam as subcategorias (veja-se a chave completa à página I · 1).

	English	Deutsch	Español	Français	Português
∧	Mountain	Berg	Montaña	Montagne	Montanha
⋌	Mountains	Gebirge	Montañas	Montagnes	Montanhas
⋈	Pass	Paß	Paso	Col	Passo
V	Valley, Canyon	Tal, Cañon	Valle, Cañón	Vallée, Canyon	Vale, Canhão
≚	Plain	Ebene	Llano	Plaine	Planície
≻	Cape	Kap	Cabo	Cap	Cabo
I	Island	Insel	Isla	Île	Ilha
II	Islands	Inseln	Islas	Îles	Ilhas
◆	Other Topographic Features	Andere Topographische Objekte	Otros Elementos Topográficos	Autres données topographiques	Outros acidentes topográficos

ESPAÑOL: Nombre | Página | Lat.°′ | Long.°′ W = Oeste
FRANÇAIS: Nom | Page | Lat.°′ | Long.°′ W = Ouest
PORTUGUÊS: Nome | Página | Lat.°′ | Long.°′ W = Oeste

Puslinch Lake ⊜ 212 43.25 N 80.16 W
Pusŏng-ni 98 40.19 N 127.19 E
Püspökladány 30 47.19 N 21.07 E
Pussay 50 48.21 N 2.00 E
Püssi 76 59.24 N 27.01 E
Puster-Tal ∨ 64 46.45 N 12.20 E
Pustin' 76 59.54 N 35.32 E
Pustomyty 78 49.42 N 23.56 E
Pustoš' 76 60.07 N 42.45 E
Pustoška 76 56.20 N 29.22 E
Pustozersk 24 67.33 N 52.27 E
Pusur ≃ [1] 126 21.45 N 89.30 E
Puszczykowo 30 52.17 N 16.52 E
Putaendo 252 32.38 S 70.44 W
Putah Creek ≃ 226 38.33 N 121.42 W
Putai 100 23.23 N 120.09 E
Putana, Volcán ∧ [1] 252 22.43 S 67.54 W
Putang ≃ 269e 6.13 S 106.54 E
Putangqiao 106 31.34 N 118.59 E
Putao 102 27.21 N 97.24 E
Putaruru 172 38.03 S 175.47 E
Put'atin 89 42.52 N 132.25 E
Put'atino 80 54.10 N 41.07 E
Putbus 54 54.21 N 13.28 E
Puteaux 261 48.53 N 2.14 E
Puteran, Pulau I 115a 7.05 S 114.00 E
Putfontein Landbouhoewes 273d 26.08 S 28.24 E
Putgarten 54 54.40 N 13.25 E
Puth Kalān ◆ [8] 272a 28.43 N 77.05 E
Putian, Zhg. 100 29.16 N 114.58 E
Putian, Zhg. 100 25.26 N 119.01 E
Putifigari 71 40.34 N 8.27 E
Putignano 68 40.51 N 17.07 E
Putila 78 48.01 N 25.03 E
Putilkovo 265b 55.52 N 37.23 E
Putina 248 14.55 S 69.52 W
Put-in-Bay 214 41.39 N 82.49 W
Putincevo 86 49.50 N 84.22 E
Puting, Tanjung ≻ 112 3.31 S 111.46 E
Putivl' 78 51.21 N 33.52 E
Putla de Guerrero 234 17.02 N 97.56 W
Putlitz 54 53.15 N 12.02 E
Putnam, Ct., U.S. 207 41.54 N 71.54 W
Putnam, Tx., U.S. 196 32.22 N 99.12 W
Putnam □ [6], N.Y., U.S. 210 41.26 N 73.41 W
Putnam □ [6], Oh., U.S. 216 41.01 N 84.03 W
Putnam Lake 210 41.28 N 73.35 W
Putnam Lake ⊜ 276 41.05 N 73.38 W
Putnam Valley 210 41.20 N 73.52 W
Putnamville Reservoir ⊜ [1] 283 42.36 N 70.57 W
Putney, Ga., U.S. 192 31.29 N 84.07 W
Putney, Vt., U.S. 188 42.58 N 72.31 W
Putney ◆ [8] 260 51.28 N 0.13 W
Putney Island I 126 21.42 N 89.20 E
Puto 175e 5.41 S 154.43 E
Putorana, plato ⌃ [1] 74 69.00 N 95.00 E
Putorino 172 39.08 S 177.00 E
Putre 248 18.12 S 69.35 W
Putri Narrows Ʉ 271c 1.27 N 103.42 E
Putsonderwater 158 29.09 S 21.51 E
Pütt 263 51.11 N 6.59 E
Puttalam 122 8.02 N 79.49 E
Puttalam Lagoon c 122 8.07 N 79.47 E
Putte, Bel. 56 51.04 N 4.38 E
Putte, Ned. 52 51.22 N 4.23 E
Puttelange-lès-Farschviller 56 49.03 N 6.56 E
Putten 52 52.15 N 5.36 E
Putten I 52 51.50 N 4.15 E
Puttgarden 41 54.30 N 11.13 E
Püttlingen 56 49.17 N 6.53 E
Puttūr 122 13.27 N 79.33 E
Putty 170 32.57 S 150.40 E
Putty Creek ≃ 170 33.05 S 150.37 E
Putú 252 35.13 S 72.17 W
Putumayo □ [8] 246 0.30 N 76.00 W
Putumayo (Içá) ≃ 246 3.07 S 67.58 W
Putuo 100 29.58 N 122.17 E
Putu Range ⌃ 150 5.30 N 8.10 W
Pütürge 130 38.12 N 38.53 E
Putussibau 112 0.50 N 112.56 E
Putzkau 54 51.06 N 14.13 E
Putzu Idu 71 40.02 N 8.25 E
Pu'uhonua o Honaunau National Historical Park ♦ 229d 19.25 N 155.54 W
Puu Kaaumakua ∧ 229c 21.30 N 157.54 W
Puu Keahiakahoe ∧ 229c 21.23 N 157.49 W
Puukohola Heiau National Historic Site ⊥ 229d 20.00 N 155.46 W
Puukolii 229a 20.56 N 156.40 W
Puu Kukui ∧ 229a 20.52 N 156.35 W
Puula ⊜ 26 61.50 N 26.42 E
Puumala 26 61.32 N 28.11 E
Puunene 229a 20.51 N 156.27 W
Pu'upu'a 175a 13.34 S 172.09 W
Puurmani 76 58.34 N 26.17 E
Puurs 50 51.05 N 4.17 E
Puuwai 229b 21.54 N 160.12 W
Puxi 100 25.10 N 119.08 E
Puxian 102 36.30 N 111.02 E
Puxico 194 36.56 N 90.09 W
Puxingchang 107 30.41 N 105.06 E
Puyallup 224 47.11 N 122.17 W
Puyallup ≃ 224 47.15 N 122.24 W
Puyang 98 35.42 N 114.59 E
Puyang ≃ 100 30.05 N 120.11 E
Puyango (Tumbes) ≃ 246 3.30 S 80.27 W
Puy-de-Dôme □ [5] 32 45.45 N 3.05 E
Puyehue 254 40.40 S 72.37 W
Puyehue, Volcán ∧ [1] 254 40.35 S 72.08 W
Puylaurens 32 43.34 N 2.01 E
Puy-l'Évêque 32 44.30 N 1.08 E
Puyloubier 62 43.31 N 5.41 E
Puymorens, Col de)(32 42.30 N 1.50 E
Puyo, Ec. 246 1.28 S 77.59 W
Puyŏ, Taehan 98 36.18 N 126.54 E
Puysegur Point ≻ 172 46.09 S 166.36 E
Puyuan 106 30.41 N 120.38 E
Puyuguapi, Canal Ʉ 254 44.45 S 72.48 W
Puyun-dong 98 41.55 N 129.30 E
Pūzak, Hāmūn-e ⊜ 128 31.30 N 61.45 E
Puzhen 106 32.09 N 118.41 E
Puzzle Creek ≃ 162 17.58 S 135.41 E
Puzzle Lake ⊜, On., Can. 212 44.36 N 76.58 W
Puzzle Lake ⊜, Fl., U.S. 220 28.41 N 81.02 W
Pwalagu 150 10.35 N 0.50 W
Pwani □ [4] 154 7.00 S 39.00 E
Pweto 154 8.28 S 28.54 E
Pwinbyu 110 20.22 N 94.40 E
Pwllheli 42 52.53 N 4.25 W
Pyalo 110 19.09 N 95.11 E
Pyalong 169 37.07 S 144.54 E
Pyamalaw ≃ [1] 110 15.49 N 94.42 E
Pyapon 110 16.17 N 95.41 E
Pyatigorsk → P'atigorsk 84 44.03 N 43.04 E
Pyawbwe 110 20.35 N 96.04 E
Pyaye 110 19.15 N 95.06 E
Pyčas 80 56.29 N 52.28 E
Pye Islands II 180 59.22 N 150.25 W
Pygmalion Point ≻ 110 6.45 N 93.49 E
Pyhäjärvi ⊜, Suomi 26 61.53 N 30.00 E
Pyhäjärvi ⊜, Suomi 26 61.00 N 22.18 E
Pyhäjärvi ⊜, Suomi 26 62.46 N 25.30 E
Pyhäjärvi ⊜, Suomi 26 63.35 N 25.57 E
Pyhäjärvi ⊜, Suomi 26 61.28 N 23.35 E
Pyhäjoki 26 64.28 N 24.14 E
Pyhäjoki ≃ 26 64.28 N 24.13 E
Pyhämaa I 26 60.57 N 21.20 E
Pyhän-Häkin kansallispuisto ♦ 26 62.52 N 25.30 E
Pyhäsalmi 26 63.41 N 25.59 E
Pyhäselkä 26 62.26 N 29.58 E

Pyhäselkä ⊜ 26 62.26 N 29.58 E
Pyhätunturi ∧ 24 67.01 N 27.09 E
Pyhätunturin Kansallispuisto ♦ 24 67.01 N 27.10 E
Pyhra 61 48.10 N 15.41 E
Pyhtää (Pyttis) 26 60.29 N 26.32 E
Pyinbongyi 110 17.34 N 96.34 E
Pyingaing 110 23.09 N 94.51 E
Pyinkayaing 110 15.58 N 94.24 E
Pyinmana 110 19.44 N 96.13 E
Pyle 42 51.32 N 3.42 W
Pylos → Pílos 38 36.55 N 21.43 E
Pymatuning Creek ≃ 214 41.18 N 80.27 W
Pymatuning Reservoir ⊜ [1] 214 41.37 N 80.30 W
Pymatuning State Park ♦, Oh., U.S. 214 41.38 N 80.33 W
Pymatuning State Park ♦, Pa., U.S. 214 41.30 N 80.27 W
Pymble 274a 33.45 S 151.09 E
Pyngopil'gyn, laguna c 180 67.24 N 175.10 W
Pyŏktong 98 40.35 N 125.20 E
Pyŏlch'ang-ni 98 39.17 N 126.26 E
P'yŏngan Namdo □ [4] 98 39.20 N 126.00 E
P'yŏngan Pukdo □ [4] 98 40.10 N 125.20 E
P'yŏngch'ang 98 37.23 N 128.22 E
P'yŏngdong-ni 98 37.10 N 128.02 E
P'yŏnggang 98 38.26 N 127.16 E
P'yonghae 98 36.46 N 129.28 E
P'yŏngsan 98 38.19 N 126.23 E
P'yŏngt'aek 98 37.00 N 127.05 E
P'yŏngyang 98 39.01 N 125.45 E
P'yŏngyang □ [4] 98 39.05 N 125.50 E
Pyŏrha-ri 98 40.48 N 126.32 E
Pyote 196 31.32 N 103.08 W
Pyramid Head ≻ 228 32.49 N 118.21 W
Pyramid Lake ⊜ 204 40.00 N 119.35 W
Pyramid Lake ⊜ [1] 228 34.39 N 118.47 W
Pyramid Lake Indian Reservation ◆ [4] 204 40.20 N 119.35 W
Pyramid Peak ∧, Ca., U.S. 226 38.50 N 120.19 W
Pyramid Peak ∧, Wa., U.S. 224 47.07 N 121.24 W
Pyramid Peak ∧, Wy., U.S. 200 43.27 N 110.28 W
Pyramid Point ≻ 174h 2.52 S 171.37 W
Pyramids of Giza → Jīzah, Ahrāmāt al- ⊥ 142 29.59 N 31.08 E
Pyrenäen → Pyrenees ⌃ 34 42.40 N 1.00 E
Pyrenees ⌃ 34 42.40 N 1.00 E
Pyrénées-Atlantiques □ [5] 32 43.15 N 0.50 W
Pyrénées Occident, Parc National des ♦ 32 42.48 N 0.08 W
Pyrénées-Orientales □ [5] 32 42.30 N 2.20 E
Pyre Peak ∧ 180 52.20 N 172.31 W
Pyrford 260 51.19 N 0.30 W
Pyrgi ⊥ 66 42.01 N 11.58 E
Pyrgos → Pírgos 38 37.41 N 21.28 E
Pyrkanajjan, gora ∧ 180 69.14 N 175.50 E
Pyrkino 80 53.29 N 45.07 E
Pyrmont 216 40.28 N 86.41 W
Pyrzyce 30 53.10 N 14.55 E
Pyšma 86 56.56 N 63.13 E
Pyšma ≃ 86 57.08 N 66.18 E
Pytalovo 76 57.04 N 27.56 E
Pythonga, Lac ⊜ 190 46.23 N 76.25 W
Pyu 110 18.29 N 96.26 E
Pyuntaza 110 17.52 N 96.44 E
Pyūṭhān 124 28.06 N 82.54 E
Pyvėsa ≃ 76 56.06 N 24.27 E
Pyzdry 30 52.11 N 17.41 E

Q

Qabāṭīyah 132 32.25 N 35.17 E
Qabbāsīn 130 36.25 N 37.34 E
Qabb Ilyās 132 33.48 N 35.49 E
Qabr Hūd 144 16.08 N 49.37 E
Qacentina (Constantine) 148 36.22 N 6.37 E
Qacentina □ [5] 148 36.20 N 6.40 E
Qaddīs Anṭūn, Dayr al- (Monastery of Saint Anthony) ℧ [1] 142 28.55 N 32.21 E
Qaddīs Būlus, Dayr al- (Monastery of Saint Paul) ℧ [1] 142 28.52 N 32.33 E
Qāderābād 128 30.17 N 53.16 E
Qādiān 123 31.49 N 75.23 E
Qā'emshahr 128 36.28 N 52.53 E
Qā'en 128 33.44 N 59.11 E
Qāfilah 142 31.04 N 30.16 E
Qagan 88 49.14 N 118.08 E
Qagan Nur ⊜, Zhg. 98 41.23 N 113.55 E
Qagan Nur ⊜, Zhg. 102 43.37 N 114.40 E
Qahā 142 30.17 N 31.12 E
Qahar Youyi Zhongqi 102 41.09 N 112.38 E
Qahbûna 142 30.48 N 31.54 E
Qaidam ≃ 102 36.39 N 96.20 E
Qaidam Pendi ⊻ [1] 120 37.00 N 95.00 E
Qakar 120 36.32 N 80.43 E
Qala' an-Naḥl 140 13.38 N 34.57 E
Qalabshū 142 31.26 N 31.19 E
Qalamshāh 142 29.10 N 30.50 E
Qalandīyah 132 31.50 N 35.14 E
Qalandūl 142 27.49 N 30.50 E
Qalāt 120 32.07 N 66.54 E
Qal'at ash-Shaqīf (Beaufort Castle) ⊥ 132 33.19 N 35.32 E
Qal'at Bīshah 144 20.01 N 42.36 E
Qal'at Ṣāliḥ 128 31.31 N 47.16 E
Qal'at Sukkar 128 31.51 N 46.05 E
Qal'eh Shahr 120 35.33 N 65.34 E
Qal'eh-ye Deh-e Bārez 128 27.26 N 57.12 E
Qal'eh-ye Now, Afg. 120 35.27 N 67.08 E
Qal'eh-ye Now, Afg. 128 34.59 N 63.08 E
Qal'eh-ye Panjeh 123 37.00 N 72.36 E
Qal'eh-ye Sarkārī 120 35.54 N 67.17 E
Qallābāt, Sūd. 140 12.43 N 23.26 E
Qallābāt, Sūd. 140 12.58 N 36.09 E
Qallīn 142 31.03 N 30.51 E
Qalqilīya 132 32.11 N 34.58 E
Qalyūb 142 30.11 N 31.12 E
Qamar, Ghubbat al- c 118 16.00 N 52.30 E
Qamata 158 32.00 S 27.21 E
Qamdo 102 31.11 N 97.15 E
Qamīnis 146 31.39 N 20.03 E
Qamr-ud-dīn Kārez 120 31.39 N 68.25 E
Qamṣar 128 33.45 N 51.26 E
Qanā, Ar. Su. 128 27.47 N 41.25 E
Qānā, Lubnān 132 33.13 N 35.18 E
Qanāyah 132 33.01 N 36.11 E
Qandahār 120 31.32 N 65.30 E
Qandahār □ [4] 120 31.00 N 65.45 E
Qandala 144 11.28 N 49.52 E
Qanṭarah, Jabal ∧ [2] 142 30.09 N 30.15 E
Qantur 140 9.45 N 25.52 E
Qārah, Ar. Su. 128 29.52 N 40.15 E
Qārah, Sūrīy. 130 34.09 N 36.44 E
Qarah Bāgh 128 34.56 N 61.46 E
Qarak 85 38.23 N 76.58 E
Qarāvol 120 37.14 N 68.46 E
Qardho 144 9.30 N 49.05 E
Qareh ≃ 128 34.52 N 51.25 E
Qareh Sū ≃ 128 39.27 N 47.23 E
Qareh Ẕīā' od Dīn 84 38.54 N 45.02 E
Qarqan ≃ 90 39.25 N 88.20 E
Qarqīn 120 37.25 N 66.03 E

Qarṭabā 130 34.06 N 35.51 E
Qārūn, Birkat (Lake Moeris) ⊜ 142 29.28 N 30.40 E
Qaryat al-Qaddāḥīyah 146 31.22 N 15.14 E
Qaryat al-Zuwaytīnah 146 30.58 N 20.07 E
Qaṣa-e Qand 128 26.12 N 60.45 E
Qāsh, Nahr al- (Gash) ≃ 140 16.48 N 35.51 E
Qashqeh, Kūh-e ∧ 128 28.23 N 55.18 E
Qāsim 132 32.59 N 36.05 E
Qāsimwāla 123 30.09 N 73.50 E
Qaṣr ad-Dayr, Jabal ∧ 132 30.48 N 35.34 E
Qaṣr al-Azraq ⊥ 132 31.53 N 36.49 E
Qasr al-Dubārā (Garden City) ◆ [8] 273c 30.02 N 31.14 E
Qaṣr al-Farāfirah 140 27.03 N 27.58 E
Qaṣr al-Jibālī 142 29.20 N 30.38 E
Qaṣr al-Kharānah ⊥ 132 31.44 N 36.28 E
Qaṣr al-Mushāsh ⊥ 132 31.49 N 36.19 E
Qaṣr al-Mushattā ⊥ 132 31.44 N 36.01 E
Qaṣr al Qarābūllī 146 32.45 N 13.43 E
Qaṣr 'Amrah ⊥ 132 31.48 N 36.35 E
Qaṣr aṭ-Ṭūbah ⊥ 132 31.20 N 36.34 E
Qaṣr Baghdād 142 30.44 N 30.53 E
Qaṣr Bū-Hādī 146 31.03 N 16.40 E
Qaṣr Ḍab'ah ⊥ 132 31.36 N 36.03 E
Qaṣr-e Fīrūzeh 267d 35.40 N 51.32 E
Qasr el-Boukhari 148 35.51 N 2.52 E
Qaṣr-e Shīrīn 128 34.31 N 45.35 E
Qaṣr Qārūn 142 29.25 N 30.25 E
Qa'ṭabah 144 13.51 N 44.42 E
Qaṭanā 132 33.26 N 36.05 E
Qatar (Qaṭar) □ [1], Asia 118 25.00 N 51.10 E
Qatar (Qaṭar) □ [1], Asia 128 25.00 N 51.10 E
Qaṭia, Bi'r ⍑ [4] 142 30.58 N 32.45 E
Qaṭmah 130 36.36 N 36.57 E
Qaṭrānī, Jabal ∧ [2] 142 29.41 N 30.35 E
Qaṭṭāntyah, Ghurd al- ⊻ [8] 142 29.50 N 30.17 E
Qattara Depression → Qaṭṭārah, Munkhafaḍ al- ⊻ [7] 140 30.00 N 27.30 E
Qaṭṭārah, Munkhafaḍ al- (Qattara Depression) ⊻ [7] 140 30.00 N 27.30 E
Qaṭṭīnah, Buḥayrat ⊜ [1] 130 34.39 N 36.34 E
Qawz Rajab 140 16.04 N 35.34 E
Qāy 142 29.09 N 30.57 E
Qayṭah 132 33.04 N 36.08 E
Qāzigund 123 33.38 N 75.09 E
Qazvīn 128 36.16 N 50.00 E
Qeh 102 42.18 N 100.59 E
Qena → Qinā 140 26.10 N 32.43 E
Qeqertaq I 176 71.55 N 55.30 W
Qesari, Ḥorbat (Cæsarea) ⊥ 132 32.30 N 34.53 E
Qeshm 128 26.58 N 56.16 E
Qeshm, Jazīreh-ye I 128 26.45 N 55.45 E
Qetura 132 29.58 N 35.03 E
Qeydār 128 36.07 N 48.35 E
Qeyṣār 120 35.41 N 64.17 E
Qezel Owzan ≃ 128 36.45 N 49.22 E
Qezel Qeshlāq 84 39.08 N 45.21 E
Qi ≃, Zhg. 98 35.30 N 114.17 E
Qi ≃, Zhg. 100 30.09 N 115.20 E
Qi ≃, Zhg. 107 30.38 N 105.26 E
Qi ≃, Zhg. 107 29.15 N 106.24 E
Qiakemake 85 40.05 N 75.24 E
Qian ≃ 102 23.25 N 110.10 E
Qian'an, Zhg. 89 45.00 N 124.01 E
Qian'an, Zhg. 98 39.59 N 118.40 E
Qiancaijiatun 104 41.14 N 121.38 E
Qiandiwu 105 39.16 N 116.38 E
Qiandong 100 23.41 N 116.55 E
Qiandun 106 31.16 N 121.00 E
Qianertaizi 104 42.04 N 122.42 E
Qianfang 100 28.32 N 116.13 E
Qian Gorlos 89 45.08 N 124.47 E
Qiangzilu 105 40.26 N 117.13 E
Qianhonghepu 104 41.23 N 123.07 E
Qianhuang 106 31.36 N 119.58 E
Qianji 100 33.55 N 118.56 E
Qianjiadian 89 43.42 N 122.35 E
Qianjiang, Zhg. 100 30.25 N 112.51 E
Qianjiang, Zhg. 102 23.37 N 109.00 E
Qianjian'gangzi 104 41.34 N 122.26 E
Qianjiangtai 104 41.46 N 122.03 E
Qianjiaqiao 106 30.53 N 121.31 E
Qianjiaying 105 39.35 N 118.21 E
Qianjiazhuang 106 32.16 N 120.17 E
Qianjing 106 31.33 N 121.15 E
Qianjinmiao 100 25.09 N 118.20 E
Qiankeng 106 30.43 N 119.47 E
Qiankoutou 105 39.42 N 117.01 E
Qianlijiazhuang 105 39.25 N 118.17 E
Qianluanshanzi 104 42.17 N 122.27 E
Qianmajiagushanzi 104 42.23 N 123.33 E
Qianmintun 104 41.49 N 123.15 E
Qianning 102 30.30 N 101.31 E
Qianpai 102 22.22 N 111.11 E
Qianqi 100 27.20 N 120.20 E
Qianqianjianglugou 104 41.59 N 120.58 E
Qiansandaoliangzi 104 42.06 N 120.44 E
Qianshahezi 104 41.46 N 123.01 E
Qianshan, Zhg. 100 30.38 N 116.33 E
Qianshan, Zhg. 100 22.16 N 113.33 E
Qianshan, Zhg. 106 31.06 N 120.24 E
Qian Shan ⌃ 104 40.52 N 123.25 E
Qianshuangshanzi 104 41.22 N 121.13 E
Qiansuo 100 28.44 N 121.27 E
Qiantang ≃ 106 30.23 N 120.33 E
Qiantangzhen 107 30.12 N 106.18 E
Qianwei, Zhg. 98 40.12 N 120.06 E
Qianwei, Zhg. 107 29.12 N 103.57 E
Qianxi, Zhg. 102 26.57 N 106.00 E
Qianxi, Zhg. 105 40.09 N 118.19 E
Qianxiatazi 104 42.23 N 123.53 E
Qianyamen 104 42.04 N 121.26 E
Qianyang 102 27.11 N 110.04 E
Qianyaopu 104 42.02 N 123.37 E
Qi'anzhen 106 32.11 N 121.03 E
Qianzhou 106 31.42 N 120.13 E
Qiaodun 100 27.29 N 120.18 E
Qiaoershan ⌃ 102 31.48 N 99.10 E
Qiaogou 100 32.26 N 115.45 E
Qiaohengjin 102 29.30 N 99.50 E
Qiaojia 102 26.57 N 102.52 E
Qiaojiang 269b 31.15 N 121.19 E
Qiaokou 100 25.55 N 113.10 E
Qiaolima 120 34.35 N 81.00 E
Qiaolin 100 31.57 N 118.32 E
Qiaomu 98 39.34 N 114.27 E
Qiaopurikebazha 85 38.48 N 76.19 E
Qiaoqi 106 31.49 N 120.18 E
Qiaoshe 100 28.48 N 115.58 E
Qiaosi 106 30.21 N 120.18 E
Qiaotou, Zhg. 100 33.05 N 112.46 E
Qiaotou, Zhg. 102 28.17 N 99.22 E
Qiaotou, Zhg. 104 41.13 N 123.44 E
Qiaotou, Zhg. 106 32.11 N 119.14 E
Qiaotou, Zhg. 107 29.18 N 104.39 E
Qiaotoucun 106 30.36 N 119.08 E
Qiaotouji 100 31.45 N 117.34 E
Qiaotoupu 106 30.33 N 118.50 E
Qiaotouyi 100 28.24 N 112.58 E
Qiaotouzhen 106 30.49 N 119.13 E
Qiaowan 102 40.36 N 96.55 E
Qiaowei 102 22.51 N 109.50 E
Qiaoxia 106 31.09 N 119.35 E
Qiaoxiajie 100 28.10 N 120.34 E
Qiaozhen 106 31.39 N 121.24 E
Qibao 106 31.09 N 121.20 E
Qibyā 132 31.59 N 35.01 E
Qichun 100 30.17 N 115.26 E

Qiddīsah Kātrīnā, Dayr al- (Monastery of Saint Catherine) ℧ [1] 140 28.29 N 34.01 E
Qidong, Zhg. 102 26.44 N 112.04 E
Qidong, Zhg. 106 31.49 N 121.40 E
Qidu 100 30.16 N 117.46 E
Qiemo 120 38.08 N 85.32 E
Qiesanglinzi 104 41.42 N 123.30 E
Qieshikou 271a 39.59 N 116.24 E
Qiezixi 107 29.25 N 106.30 E
Qifosi 107 29.27 N 105.58 E
Qifṭ (Coptos) 140 26.00 N 32.49 E
Qigong 102 28.38 N 100.38 E
Qigongtai 104 41.50 N 123.08 E
Qihe (Yancheng) 98 36.48 N 116.44 E
Qiji 98 37.16 N 115.21 E
Qijiadian 89 46.48 N 125.36 E
Qijian 107 30.14 N 106.09 E
Qijiang 107 29.02 N 106.39 E
Qijiapuzi 104 40.54 N 122.31 E
Qijiawan 100 30.53 N 114.13 E
Qijiawopeng 104 41.02 N 121.26 E
Qijiazi 104 41.54 N 122.58 E
Qika 89 50.35 N 119.16 E
Qikou 98 38.35 N 117.31 E
Qila Abdullāh 120 30.43 N 66.38 E
Qila Dīdār Singh 123 32.08 N 74.01 E
Qilaguganni Shan ∧ 124 28.46 N 87.38 E
Qila Lādgasht 128 27.54 N 62.57 E
Qila Saifullāh 120 30.43 N 68.21 E
Qila Sobha Singh 123 32.14 N 74.46 E
Qilian 102 38.05 N 100.12 E
Qilian Shan ∧ 102 39.12 N 98.35 E
Qilian Shan ⌃ 102 39.06 N 98.40 E
Qili Hai ≡ 105 39.19 N 117.33 E
Qilihe, Zhg. 104 41.21 N 121.16 E
Qilihe, Zhg. 104 41.30 N 121.15 E
Qilihezi 104 40.56 N 121.02 E
Qiling 100 24.05 N 115.27 E
Qilingzicun 104 41.05 N 123.06 E
Qilinmen 106 32.04 N 118.55 E
Qilinzhen 106 31.56 N 121.21 E
Qiliping 100 31.27 N 114.39 E
Qiliqiao 106 31.35 N 120.48 E
Qilizhen, Zhg. 102 35.43 N 108.59 E
Qilizhen, Zhg. 106 32.19 N 121.05 E
Qilṭ, 'Ayn al- ⍑ [4] 132 31.50 N 35.23 E
Qimafang 98 40.08 N 114.31 E
Qiman al-'Arūs 142 29.18 N 31.10 E
Qimen, Zhg. 100 29.52 N 117.42 E
Qimen, Zhg. 100 25.18 N 113.15 E
Qimoudi 105 39.35 N 115.32 E
Qimu Jiao ≻ 98 37.46 N 120.12 E
Qin ≃, Zhg. 100 23.58 N 115.47 E
Qin ≃, Zhg. 100 26.16 N 115.52 E
Qin ≃, Zhg. 102 35.01 N 113.25 E
Qinā 140 26.10 N 32.43 E
Qinā, Wādī ∨, Miṣr 140 26.12 N 32.44 E
Qinā, Wādī ∨, Miṣr 142 29.39 N 31.53 E
Qincaigou 104 40.38 N 120.37 E
Qing ≃, Zhg. 98 42.26 N 123.50 E
Qing ≃, Zhg. 102 30.22 N 111.20 E
Qing'an 89 46.52 N 127.30 E
Qingbaikou 105 40.01 N 115.50 E
Qingcaoge 100 30.50 N 116.46 E
Qingcheng 98 37.12 N 117.40 E
Qingchengzi 104 40.44 N 123.36 E
Qingchuan 102 32.36 N 105.09 E
Qingcungang 106 30.56 N 121.34 E
Qingdao (Tsingtao) 98 36.06 N 120.19 E
Qingdian 105 39.51 N 117.22 E
Qingduizi, Zhg. 98 39.50 N 123.18 E
Qingduizi, Zhg. 104 41.28 N 121.53 E
Qingfeng 98 35.54 N 115.07 E
Qingfengtuo 98 40.59 N 116.04 E
Qingfu 102 28.29 N 104.35 E
Qinggang 89 46.43 N 126.07 E
Qingguang 105 39.11 N 117.02 E
Qingguji 98 34.45 N 115.47 E
Qinghai (Tsinghai) □ [4] 90 36.00 N 96.00 E
Qinghai Hu ⊜ 102 36.50 N 100.20 E
Qinghai Nanshan ⌃ 102 37.06 N 99.05 E
Qinghe, Zhg. 86 46.36 N 90.39 E
Qinghe, Zhg. 98 40.02 N 122.35 E
Qinghe, Zhg. 104 42.32 N 124.09 E
Qinghe, Zhg. 105 40.01 N 116.20 E
Qinghecheng 104 41.28 N 124.15 E
Qinghechengzi 104 41.44 N 121.25 E
Qinghemen 104 41.45 N 121.25 E
Qinghezhen 98 37.16 N 117.39 E
Qinghu 100 28.40 N 118.34 E
Qinghua 100 29.24 N 117.46 E
Qinghuayuan 105 40.00 N 116.19 E
Qinghuazhen 100 32.55 N 112.19 E
Qingjian 102 37.10 N 110.00 E
Qingjiang, Zhg. 100 28.05 N 115.29 E
Qingjiang, Zhg. 100 33.35 N 119.02 E
Qingjiang, Zhg. 100 28.16 N 121.06 E
Qingjiang, Zhg. 107 29.17 N 105.34 E
Qingjujie 107 30.42 N 106.07 E
Qinglian 100 24.27 N 112.45 E
Qingliu 100 26.12 N 116.52 E
Qingliuzhen 107 29.56 N 105.19 E
Qinglong, Zhg. 98 40.24 N 118.54 E
Qinglong, Zhg. 100 25.28 N 114.28 E
Qinglong, Zhg. 102 25.50 N 105.10 E
Qinglong ≃, Zhg. 98 39.51 N 118.51 E
Qinglong ≃, Zhg. 105 39.35 N 117.46 E
Qinglongchang, Zhg. 107 28.50 N 106.31 E
Qinglongchang, Zhg. 107 29.51 N 105.40 E
Qinglongchang, Zhg. 107 30.20 N 103.51 E
Qinglonggang 106 31.51 N 121.15 E
Qinglongguan 107 30.25 N 104.48 E
Qinglongji 98 34.05 N 116.37 E
Qinglongwan ≃ 105 39.19 N 117.32 E
Qingmuguan 107 29.41 N 106.18 E
Qingningsi 106 31.16 N 121.33 E
Qingping, Zhg. 98 36.47 N 116.06 E
Qingping, Zhg. 107 29.00 N 106.21 E
Qingping, Zhg. 107 30.14 N 106.12 E
Qingpu 106 31.09 N 121.06 E
Qingshan, Zhg. 100 31.33 N 116.22 E
Qingshan, Zhg. 100 30.38 N 114.23 E
Qingshan, Zhg. 106 30.43 N 120.03 E
Qingshan, Zhg. 106 30.36 N 119.41 E
Qingshan, Zhg. 106 30.15 N 119.52 E
Qingshanpu 100 29.27 N 114.01 E
Qingshen 107 29.50 N 103.50 E
Qingshui, Zhg. 102 39.23 N 99.09 E
Qingshui, Zhg. 102 34.42 N 106.21 E
Qingshui, Zhg. 107 30.10 N 104.03 E
Qingshui ≃, Zhg. 102 37.30 N 105.30 E
Qingshui ≃, Zhg. 102 27.08 N 109.36 E
Qingshuihe 86 44.12 N 80.45 E
Qingshuijian 105 39.59 N 115.58 E
Qingshuilang Shan ⌃ 102 26.15 N 99.35 E
Qingshuixi 102 29.09 N 103.55 E
Qingtan 100 31.48 N 112.48 E
Qingtang, Zhg. 100 26.28 N 115.48 E
Qingtang, Zhg. 100 24.14 N 113.51 E
Qingtian 100 28.10 N 120.17 E
Qingtong 107 29.28 N 103.27 E
Qingtongxia 102 37.53 N 105.54 E
Qingtuosi 98 35.29 N 118.20 E
Qingtuozi, Zhg. 104 41.05 N 121.28 E
Qingtuozi, Zhg. 105 39.08 N 117.45 E
Qingxi, Zhg. 89 49.19 N 127.10 E
Qingxi, Zhg. 100 31.40 N 118.00 E
Qingxi, Zhg. 107 30.40 N 106.14 E
Qingxian 98 38.34 N 116.46 E
Qingxizhen 107 29.09 N 103.55 E
Qingyang, Zhg. 89 45.20 N 128.47 E
Qingyang, Zhg. 100 30.38 N 117.48 E
Qingyang, Zhg. 102 36.06 N 107.47 E
Qingyangzhen 106 31.46 N 120.15 E
Qingyi ≃ 107 29.34 N 103.42 E
Qingyuan, Zhg. 98 42.13 N 124.56 E
Qingyuan, Zhg. 100 27.38 N 119.04 E
Qingyuan, Zhg. 100 23.42 N 113.02 E

Qingyuan → Baoding 105 38.52 N 115.29 E
Qingyun (Xiejiaji) 98 37.52 N 117.21 E
Qingyunbao 104 42.34 N 123.50 E
Qingyundian 105 39.38 N 116.29 E
Qing Zang Gaoyuan ⌃ [1] 12 33.00 N 92.00 E
Qingzhen, Zhg. 102 26.29 N 106.22 E
Qingzhen, Zhg. 106 30.45 N 120.30 E
Qingzhou 100 23.39 N 116.57 E
Qinhuai ≃ 106 32.01 N 118.50 E
Qinhuangdao (Chinwangtao) 98 39.56 N 119.36 E
Qinjia 89 46.47 N 127.00 E
Qinlan 100 32.37 N 119.08 E
Qin Ling (Tsinlingshan) ⌃ 102 34.00 N 108.00 E
Qinnan 100 33.16 N 119.55 E
Qinshui 102 35.41 N 112.11 E
Qintong 100 32.39 N 120.08 E
Qinxian 102 36.48 N 112.41 E
Qinyang 102 35.06 N 112.57 E
Qinyuan 102 36.30 N 112.15 E
Qinzhou 102 21.59 N 108.36 E
Qionghai (Jiaji) 110 19.20 N 110.30 E
Qionglai 107 30.25 N 103.27 E
Qionglaishan ⌃ 102 31.21 N 102.50 E
Qionglong Shan ∧ 106 31.15 N 120.25 E
Qiongzhong, Zhg. 90 19.02 N 109.49 E
Qiongzhong, Zhg. 110 19.04 N 109.48 E
Qiongzhou Haixia Ʉ 102 20.10 N 110.15 E
Qipandi 105 39.46 N 115.12 E
Qipanshan 98 42.05 N 117.30 E
Qiqian 89 52.12 N 120.49 E
Qiqihar (Tsitsihar) 89 47.19 N 123.55 E
Qira 120 37.00 N 80.47 E
Qir'awn, Buḥayrat al- ⊜ [1] 132 33.34 N 35.42 E
Qiryat 132 32.49 N 35.06 E
Qiryat 'Anavim 132 31.48 N 35.07 E
Qiryat Ata 132 32.48 N 35.06 E
Qiryat Bialik 132 32.50 N 35.05 E
Qiryat Gat 132 31.36 N 34.46 E
Qiryat Ḥayyim 132 32.49 N 35.04 E
Qiryat Mal'akhi 132 31.44 N 34.44 E
Qiryat Motzkin 132 32.50 N 35.04 E
Qiryat Ono 132 32.04 N 34.51 E
Qiryat Shemona 132 33.13 N 35.34 E
Qiryat Tiv'on 132 32.43 N 35.08 E
Qiryat Yam 132 32.51 N 35.04 E
Qirzah, Wādī ∨ 146 30.56 N 14.31 E
Qiseqi Shan ∧ 89 48.37 N 122.32 E
Qishn 144 15.26 N 51.40 E
Qishon ≃ 132 32.49 N 35.02 E
Qishrān I 144 20.14 N 40.05 E
Qishudang 107 29.13 N 104.39 E
Qishuyan 106 31.44 N 120.04 E
Qiṣrāyā 130 34.53 N 36.26 E
Qitai 86 44.01 N 89.28 E
Qitaihe 89 45.48 N 130.53 E
Qitaizi 104 41.33 N 122.11 E
Qitamu 89 44.22 N 126.20 E
Qitangzhen 107 29.47 N 106.16 E
Qiting 100 31.02 N 114.44 E
Qitingqiao 106 31.26 N 119.52 E
Qitou 100 24.54 N 117.29 E
Qiubei 102 24.07 N 104.12 E
Qiuchang 107 28.59 N 104.42 E
Qiuji 100 33.51 N 118.01 E
Qiujia 106 31.49 N 121.51 E
Qiujiatun 104 41.20 N 121.00 E
Qiujin 100 29.10 N 115.42 E
Qiuxi ≃ 107 29.58 N 104.40 E
Qiuxizhen 107 29.56 N 104.41 E
Qiweigang 106 32.01 N 119.59 E
Qixia 98 37.17 N 120.48 E
Qixian (Zhaoge), Zhg. 98 35.38 N 114.11 E
Qixian, Zhg. 100 34.33 N 114.47 E
Qixianji 100 33.28 N 117.01 E
Qixiashan 106 32.10 N 118.57 E
Qi Xia Si ℧ [1] 106 32.12 N 118.58 E
Qixingqiao 106 30.49 N 120.51 E
Qiyahe 89 53.02 N 120.33 E
Qiyang 102 26.29 N 111.43 E
Qiyi 100 32.30 N 112.54 E
Qiying 102 36.38 N 106.25 E
Qizhou 100 30.04 N 115.20 E
Qizil Jilga 120 35.21 N 78.52 E
Qizil Langar 120 35.13 N 77.59 E
Qnadsa 148 31.48 N 2.26 W
Qogir Feng (K2) ∧ 123 35.53 N 76.30 E
Qolhak ◆ [8] 267d 35.47 N 51.26 E
Qom 128 34.39 N 50.54 E
Qom ≃ 128 34.48 N 51.02 E
Qomolangma Feng → Everest, Mount ∧ 124 27.59 N 86.56 E
Qomsheh 128 32.01 N 51.52 E
Qondūz ≃ 120 37.00 N 68.16 E
Qorveh 128 35.10 N 47.48 E
Qoṭbābād 128 28.42 N 53.34 E
Qoṭūr 128 38.28 N 44.25 E
Qu ≃, Zhg. 100 29.12 N 119.27 E
Qu ≃, Zhg. 102 30.01 N 106.24 E
Quabbin Reservoir ⊜ [1] 207 42.22 N 72.18 W
Quaddick Reservoir ⊜ [1] 207 41.57 N 71.49 W
Quadra Island I 182 50.08 N 125.16 W
Quadraro ◆ [8] 267a 41.51 N 12.33 E
Quadrath-Ichendorf 56 50.56 N 6.41 E
Quadros, Lagoa dos c 252 29.42 S 50.05 W
Quāidābād 123 32.20 N 71.52 E
Quail Lake ⊜ [1] 228 34.47 N 118.45 W
Quail Valley 228 33.43 N 117.15 W
Quairading 162 32.01 S 117.25 E
Quakake 210 40.51 N 76.02 W
Quakenbrück 52 52.40 N 7.57 E
Quaker Hill, Ct., U.S. 207 41.22 N 72.06 W
Quaker Hill, N.Y., U.S. 210 41.35 N 73.33 W
Quakers Hill 170 33.43 S 150.53 E
Quakers Knob ∧ [2] 214 40.21 N 80.24 W
Quaker Street 210 42.44 N 74.11 W
Quakertown, N.J., U.S. 210 40.33 N 74.56 W
Quakertown, Pa., U.S. 208 40.26 N 75.20 W
Qualicum Beach 182 49.21 N 124.27 W
Quambatook 166 35.51 S 143.31 E
Quanah 196 34.17 N 99.44 W
Quanbao Shan ∧ 102 34.09 N 111.29 E
Quangang 100 28.10 N 115.34 E
Quang Ngai 110 15.07 N 108.48 E
Quang Trach 110 17.45 N 106.27 E
Quanjiang 100 27.43 N 113.59 E
Quanjiao 100 32.06 N 118.16 E
Quan Long → Ca Mau 110 9.11 N 105.08 E
Quanmian 104 42.02 N 122.13 E
Quannan 100 24.44 N 114.31 E
Quannapowitt, Lake ⊜ 283 42.31 N 71.05 W
Quanshang 100 26.25 N 116.55 E
Quanshengpu 104 41.59 N 123.22 E
Quanshui 104 41.18 N 124.11 E
Quanshuitou 105 40.24 N 116.39 E
Quantico, Md., U.S. 208 38.22 N 75.44 W
Quantico, Va., U.S. 208 38.31 N 77.17 W
Quantico Marine Corps Air Station ■ 208 38.31 N 77.19 W
Quantock Hills ⌃ [2] 42 51.07 N 3.10 W
Quantou 89 42.52 N 124.07 E
Quanxishi 100 26.51 N 112.45 E
Quanyanhezi 104 40.52 N 123.26 E
Quanzhou (Chuanchou) 100 24.54 N 118.35 E
Quanzhou Gang c 100 24.52 N 118.37 E
Qu'Appelle 184 50.33 N 103.52 W

Qu'Appelle ≃ 184 50.25 N 101.20 W
Qu'Appelle Dam ◆ [6] 184 51.00 N 106.25 W
Quaraí 252 30.23 S 56.27 W
Quaraí ≃ 252 30.12 S 57.36 W
Quaregnon 50 50.26 N 3.51 E
Quarles, Pegunungan ⌃ 112 2.55 S 119.30 E
Quarrata 66 43.51 N 10.58 E
Quarré-les-Tombes 50 47.22 N 3.59 E
Quarry 222 30.18 N 96.30 W
Quarry Heights 276 41.04 N 73.45 W
Quarryville, Ct., U.S. 207 41.51 N 72.25 W
Quarryville, Pa., U.S. 208 39.53 N 76.09 W
Quartu Sant'Elena 71 39.14 N 9.11 E
Quartz Hill 228 34.39 N 118.13 W
Quartz Lake ⊜ 176 70.55 N 80.33 W
Quartz Mountain ∧ 202 43.10 N 122.40 W
Quartzsite 200 33.39 N 114.13 W
Quatis 256 22.25 S 44.16 W
Quatre, Isle à I 241h 12.57 N 61.15 W
Quatsino Sound Ʉ 182 50.25 N 127.55 W
Qubei 124 28.18 N 86.53 E
Qūchān 128 37.06 N 58.30 E
Quchijie 102 28.03 N 111.53 E
Qudaym 130 35.03 N 38.25 E
Qudi 98 37.06 N 117.15 E
Qudsia Gardens ♦ 272a 28.40 N 77.13 E
Quê ≃ 152 14.45 S 14.45 E
Queanbeyan 171b 35.21 S 149.14 E
Queanbeyan ≃ 171b 35.20 S 149.14 E
Québec 206 46.49 N 71.14 W
Québec □ [6] 206 46.50 N 71.20 W
Québec □ [4] 176 52.00 N 72.00 W
Quebec Airport ⊠ 206 46.47 N 71.23 W
Quebec House ⊥ 260 51.14 N 0.05 E
Quebeck 194 35.49 N 85.34 W
Quebra-Anzol ≃ 255 19.09 S 47.38 W
Quebra-Cangalha, Serra do ⌃ 256 22.55 S 45.10 W
Quebracho 252 31.57 S 57.53 W
Quebrada Seca 240m 18.14 N 65.40 W
Quebradillas 240m 18.29 N 66.56 W
Quebrangulo 250 9.20 S 36.29 W
Quecholac 234 18.57 N 97.40 W
Quechultenango 234 17.25 N 99.13 W
Quecreek 214 40.06 N 79.05 W
Quedal, Cabo ≻ 254 40.59 S 73.59 W
Quedas 156 19.30 S 33.29 E
Quedlinburg 54 51.48 N 11.09 E
Queen 214 40.16 N 78.31 W
Queen Alexandra Range ⌃ 9 84.00 S 168.00 E
Queen Alia International Airport ⊠ 132 31.44 N 35.59 E
Queen Anne 208 38.55 N 75.57 W
Queen Anne Creek ≃ 285 40.08 N 74.53 W
Queen Annes □ [6] 208 39.03 N 76.04 W
Queen Bess, Mount ∧ 182 51.16 N 124.34 W
Queenborough 42 51.26 N 0.45 E
Queen Charlotte 182 53.16 N 132.05 W
Queen Charlotte Bay c 254 51.50 S 60.40 W
Queen Charlotte Islands II 182 53.00 N 132.00 W
Queen Charlotte Mountains ⌃ 182 53.00 N 132.00 W
Queen Charlotte Sound Ʉ 182 51.30 N 129.30 W
Queen Charlotte Strait Ʉ 182 50.50 N 127.25 W
Queen City, Mo., U.S. 194 40.24 N 92.34 W
Queen City, Tx., U.S. 194 33.08 N 94.09 W
Queen Elizabeth II Reservoir ⊜ [1] 260 51.23 N 0.24 W
Queen Elizabeth Islands II 16 78.00 N 95.00 W
Queen Fabiola Mountains ⌃ 9 71.30 S 35.40 E
Queen Mary ◆ 280 33.45 N 118.12 W
Queen Mary Coast ⊻ [2] 9 67.00 S 96.00 E
Queen Mary Reservoir ⊜ [1] 260 51.25 N 0.28 W
Queen Maud Gulf c 176 68.25 N 102.30 W
Queen Maud Land ◆ [1] 9 72.30 S 12.00 E
Queen Maud Mountains ⌃ 9 86.00 S 160.00 W
Queens □ [6] 210 40.34 N 73.52 W
Queensbury 44 53.46 N 1.50 W
Queens Channel Ʉ, Austl. 164 14.46 S 129.24 E
Queens Channel Ʉ, N.T., Can. 176 76.11 N 96.00 W
Queenscliff 169 38.16 S 144.40 E
Queensferry, Scot., U.K. 46 55.59 N 3.25 W
Queensferry, Wales, U.K. 44 53.12 N 3.01 W
Queensland □ [3] 160 22.00 S 145.00 E
Queensland Plateau ✢ [3] 14 17.00 S 150.00 E
Queens Park ♦, Austl. 274a 33.54 S 151.16 E
Queens Park ♦, On., Can. 275b 43.40 N 79.24 W
Queens Park ♦, Eng., U.K. 262 53.30 N 2.13 W
Queens Park ♦, Eng., U.K. 262 53.35 N 2.27 W
Queen's Park ♦, Eng., U.K. 262 53.44 N 2.28 W
Queensport 186 45.20 N 61.16 W
Queens Sound Ʉ 182 51.55 N 128.11 W
Queenston 284a 43.10 N 79.03 W
Queenston Chippawa Power Canal ≅ 284a 43.08 N 79.03 W
Queenstown, Austl. 166 42.05 S 145.33 E
Queenstown, Guy. 246 7.12 N 58.29 W
Queenstown, N.Z. 172 45.02 S 168.40 E
Queenstown, S. Afr. 158 31.52 S 26.52 E
Queenstown, Md., U.S. 208 38.59 N 76.09 W
Queenstown → Cobh 48 51.51 N 8.17 W
Queensville 212 44.08 N 79.28 W
Queen Victoria Park ♦ 284a 43.05 N 79.05 W
Que'er'ao I 100 28.48 N 121.51 E
Queerhe 104 40.57 N 121.35 E
Queets 224 47.32 N 124.19 W
Queets ≃ 224 47.33 N 124.21 W
Queguay Grande ≃ 252 32.09 S 58.09 W
Queich ≃ 56 49.14 N 8.23 E
Queige 62 45.43 N 6.28 E
Queimada, Ilha I 250 0.10 S 50.50 W
Queimada Nova 250 8.35 S 41.25 W
Queimadas 250 10.58 S 39.38 W
Queimados 256 22.42 S 43.34 W
Queiros, Cap ≻ 175f 14.55 S 167.01 E
Quela 152 9.16 S 17.02 E
Quelimane 156 17.53 S 36.51 E
Quelizhen 106 30.54 N 121.26 E
Quelle 52 52.00 N 8.29 E
Quellendorf 54 51.45 N 12.07 E
Quellón 254 43.07 S 73.37 W
Quelo 152 6.27 S 12.48 E
Quelpart Island → Cheju-do I 90 33.20 N 126.30 E
Queluz, Bra. 256 22.32 S 44.46 W
Queluz, Port. 266c 38.45 N 9.15 W
Queluz → Conselheiro Lafaiete 255 20.40 S 43.48 W
Quemado, N.M., U.S. 200 34.20 N 108.29 W
Quemado, Tx., U.S. 196 28.56 N 100.38 W

Symbol	English	Deutsch	Español	Français	Português
≃	River	Fluß	Río	Rivière	Rio
≅	Canal	Kanal	Canal	Canal	Canal
↳	Waterfall, Rapids	Wasserfall, Stromschnellen	Cascada, Rápidos	Chute d'eau, Rapides	Cascata, Rápidos
Ʉ	Strait	Meeresstraße	Estrecho	Détroit	Estreito
c	Bay, Gulf	Bucht, Golf	Bahía, Golfo	Baie, Golfe	Baía, Golfo
⊜	Lake, Lakes	See, Seen	Lago, Lagos	Lac, Lacs	Lago, Lagos
≡	Swamp	Sumpf	Pantano	Marais	Pântano
⊼	Ice Features, Glacier	Eis- und Gletscherformen	Accidentes Glaciales	Formes glaciaires	Acidentes glaciares
⍑	Other Hydrographic Features	Andere Hydrographische Objekte	Otros Elementos Hidrográficos	Autres données hydrographiques	Outros acidentes hidrográficos

Symbol	English	Deutsch	Español	Français	Português
✢	Submarine Features	Untermeerische Objekte	Accidentes Submarinos	Formes de relief sous-marin	Acidentes submarinos
□	Political Unit	Politische Einheit	Unidad Politica	Entité politique	Unidade política
℧	Cultural Institution	Kulturelle Institution	Institución Cultural	Institution culturelle	Instituição cultural
⊥	Historical Site	Historische Stätte	Sitio Histórico	Site historique	Sitio histórico
♦	Recreational Site	Erholungs- und Ferienort	Sitio de Recreo	Centre de loisirs	Area de Lazer
⊠	Airport	Flughafen	Aeropuerto	Aéroport	Aeroporto
■	Military Installation	Militäranlage	Instalación Militar	Installation militaire	Instalação militar
◆	Miscellaneous	Verschiedenes	Misceláneo	Divers	Diversos

Name	Page	Lat.°′	Long.°′
Quemado, Punta de ›	240p	20.13 N	74.08 W
Quemado de Güines	240p	22.48 N	80.15 W
Quemahoning Reservoir ⊜[1]	214	40.09 N	78.57 W
Quembo ≃	152	14.57 S	20.22 E
Quemchi	254	42.09 S	73.29 W
Quemoy → Chinmen Tao I	100	24.27 N	118.23 E
Quemú Quemú	252	36.03 S	63.33 W
Quend	50	50.19 N	1.38 E
Quend Plage	50	50.19 N	1.33 E
Queñi, Nevado de ∧	254	40.14 S	71.49 W
Quenouilles, Lac aux ⊜	206	46.10 N	74.23 W
Quentin	208	40.17 N	76.26 W
Quepos	236	9.27 N	84.09 W
Quepos, Punta ›	236	9.23 N	84.10 W
Quequén	252	38.32 S	58.42 W
Querary ≃	246	1.04 N	69.51 W
Quercianella	66	43.27 N	10.22 E
Quercy □[9]	32	44.30 N	1.25 E
Querecotillo	248	4.50 S	80.40 W
Querenburg ◆[8]	263	51.27 N	7.16 E
Querenhorst	54	52.20 N	10.57 E
Querétaro	234	20.36 N	100.23 W
Querétaro □[3]	234	21.00 N	99.55 W
Querfurt	54	51.23 N	11.36 E
Quero	64	45.55 N	11.56 E
Querobabi	232	30.03 N	111.01 W
Quesada, C.R.	236	10.19 N	84.26 W
Quesada, Esp.	34	37.51 N	3.04 W
Queset Brook ≃	283	42.02 N	71.04 W
Queshan	100	32.48 N	114.01 E
Quesnel	182	52.59 N	122.30 W
Quesnel ≃	182	53.00 N	122.30 W
Quesnel Lake ⊜	182	52.32 N	121.05 W
Quesnoy	50	50.43 N	3.00 E
Que Son	110	15.40 N	108.14 E
Questa	200	36.42 N	105.35 W
Questembert	32	47.40 N	2.27 W
Quetico Lake ⊜	190	48.34 N	91.52 W
Quetico Provincial Park ♣	190	48.30 N	91.30 W
Quetta	120	30.12 N	67.00 E
Quettehou	32	49.36 N	1.18 W
Quetzala ≃	234	16.35 N	98.30 W
Quetzaltenango	236	14.50 N	91.31 W
Quetzaltenango □[5]	236	14.45 N	91.40 W
Quevedo	246	1.02 S	79.29 W
Quezaltepeque, El Sal.	236	13.50 N	89.17 W
Quezaltepeque, Guat.	236	14.38 N	89.27 W
Quezon, Pil.	116	15.34 N	120.49 E
Quezon, Pil.	116	14.01 N	122.11 E
Quezon □[4]	116	13.58 N	122.02 E
Quezon City	116	14.38 N	121.03 E
Quezon Memorial ⊥	269f	14.39 N	121.03 E
Qufu	98	35.36 N	117.02 E
Qugou, Zhg.	102	36.10 N	100.56 E
Qugou, Zhg.	105	39.17 N	116.15 E
Quibala	152	10.46 S	14.59 E
Quibaxi	152	8.29 S	14.36 E
Quibdó	246	5.42 N	76.40 W
Quiberon	32	47.29 N	3.07 W
Quiberville	50	49.54 N	0.55 E
Quíbor	246	9.56 N	69.37 W
Quibray Bay ⊂	274a	34.01 S	151.11 E
Quibú ≃	286b	23.05 N	82.27 W
Quiçama, Parque Nacional de ♣	152	9.45 S	13.30 E
Qui Chau	110	19.33 N	105.06 E
Quiches	248	8.25 S	77.27 W
Quickborn	52	53.44 N	9.53 E
Quiculungo	152	8.31 S	15.19 E
Quidapil Point ›	116	6.49 N	123.57 E
Quidnessett	207	41.37 N	71.27 W
Quidnick	207	41.41 N	71.32 W
Quiechapa ≃	234	16.37 N	95.59 W
Quien Sabe Creek ≃	226	36.43 N	121.09 W
Quiévrain	50	50.24 N	3.41 E
Quiévy	50	50.10 N	3.25 E
Quiindy	252	25.58 S	57.16 W
Quila	232	24.23 N	107.13 W
Quilalí	236	13.34 N	86.02 W
Quilates, Cap ›	34	35.20 N	3.45 W
Quilcene	224	47.49 N	122.52 W
Quilenda	152	10.33 S	14.22 E
Quilengues	152	14.05 S	14.04 E
Quileute Indian Reservation ◆[4]	224	47.55 N	124.38 W
Quilicura	286e	33.22 S	70.45 W
Quilimarí	252	32.07 S	71.30 W
Quilino	252	30.12 S	64.29 W
Quillabamba	248	12.49 S	72.43 W
Quillacollo	248	17.26 S	66.17 W
Quillagua	248	21.39 S	69.33 W
Quillan	32	42.52 N	2.11 E
Quillebeuf-sur-Seine	50	49.29 N	0.31 E
Quill Lake	184	52.05 N	104.15 W
Quillota	252	32.53 S	71.16 W
Quilmes	258	34.44 S	58.16 W
Quilmes □[5]	288	34.44 S	58.16 W
Quilmes, Aeródromo ⊠	288	34.42 S	58.15 W
Quilombo ≃	256	23.52 S	46.21 W
Quilon	122	8.53 N	76.36 E
Quilotosa Wash V	200	32.56 N	112.46 W
Quilpie	166	26.37 S	144.15 E
Quilpué	252	33.03 S	71.27 W
Quilty	48	52.47 N	9.26 W
Quimarí, Alto de ∧	246	8.07 N	76.23 W
Quimbango	152	11.01 S	17.26 E
Quimbaya	246	4.38 N	75.47 W
Quimbele	152	6.28 S	16.13 E
Quimbo	152	13.59 S	16.05 E
Quimbonge	152	8.36 S	18.30 E
Quimbumbe	152	7.50 S	14.03 E
Quimby	198	42.37 N	95.38 W
Quime	248	17.02 S	67.15 W
Quimichis	234	22.21 N	105.32 W
Quimilí	252	27.38 S	62.25 W
Quimper	32	48.00 N	4.06 W
Quimperlé	32	47.52 N	3.33 W
Quinalasag Island I	116	13.56 N	123.38 E
Quinault	224	47.28 N	123.50 W
Quinault ≃	224	47.23 N	124.18 W
Quinault, North Fork ≃	224	47.32 N	123.40 W
Quinault Indian Reservation ◆[4]	224	47.24 N	124.10 W
Quinault Lake ⊜	224	47.28 N	123.52 W
Quinby Inlet ⊂	208	37.28 N	75.40 W
Quincampoix	50	49.32 N	1.11 E
Quince Mil	248	13.16 S	70.38 W
Quinches	248	12.13 S	76.05 W
Quincy, Ca., U.S.	204	39.56 N	120.56 W
Quincy, Fl., U.S.	192	30.35 N	84.35 W
Quincy, Il., U.S.	219	39.56 N	91.24 W
Quincy, Ky., U.S.	218	38.37 N	83.07 W
Quincy, Ma., U.S.	207	42.15 N	71.00 W
Quincy, Mi., U.S.	216	41.56 N	84.53 W
Quincy, Oh., U.S.	216	40.17 N	83.58 W
Quincy, Or., U.S.	224	46.08 N	123.09 W
Quincy, Pa., U.S.	208	39.48 N	77.35 W
Quincy, Wa., U.S.	202	47.14 N	119.51 W
Quincy Bay ⊂	283	42.17 N	70.58 W
Quincy-sous-Sénart	261	48.40 N	2.33 E
Quincy-Voisins	261	48.54 N	2.53 E
Quindanning	168a	33.03 S	116.34 E
Quindío □[5]	246	4.30 N	75.40 W
Quinebaug	207	42.01 N	71.57 W
Quinebaug ≃	207	41.33 N	72.03 W
Quines	252	32.13 S	65.48 W
Quinga	154	15.49 S	40.15 E
Quingey	58	47.06 N	5.53 E
Quingyi ≃	100	31.12 N	118.29 E
Quinhagak	180	59.45 N	161.43 W
Qui Nhon	110	13.46 N	109.14 E
Quiniluban Islands II	116	11.27 N	120.48 E
Quinjenje	152	12.49 S	14.55 E
Quinlan	222	32.55 N	96.08 W
Quinn ≃	204	40.52 N	119.03 W
Quiñones, Arroyo de los ≃	266a	40.33 N	3.34 W
Quinson	62	43.42 N	6.02 E
Quinta da Boa Vista ♣	287a	22.54 S	43.15 W
Quintanar de la Orden	34	39.34 N	3.03 W
Quintana Roo □[3]	232	19.40 N	88.30 W
Quinta Normal	286e	33.27 S	70.42 W
Quinta Normal de Agricultura ʋ[2]	286e	33.27 S	70.42 W
Quinte, Bay of ⊂	212	44.07 N	77.15 W
Quinter	198	39.04 N	100.13 W
Quintero	252	32.47 S	71.32 W
Quintette Mountain ∧	182	54.52 N	120.53 W
Quintin	32	48.24 N	2.55 W
Quintino Sella, Canale ≋	266b	45.29 N	8.38 E
Quinto	34	41.25 N	0.29 W
Quinto ≃	252	34.14 S	64.10 W
Quinto Creek ≃	226	37.11 N	121.02 W
Quinto de Noviembre, Presa ◆[6]	236	13.59 N	88.44 W
Quinton, Sk., Can.	184	51.23 N	104.24 W
Quinton, N.J., U.S.	208	39.32 N	75.24 W
Quinton, Ok., U.S.	196	35.07 N	95.22 W
Quinto Romano ◆[8]	266b	45.29 N	9.05 E
Quinzano d'Oglio	64	45.19 N	10.00 E
Quinzáu	152	6.51 S	12.46 E
Quinze, Lac des ⊜	190	47.35 N	79.05 W
Quionga	154	10.37 S	40.30 E
Quipapá	250	8.50 S	36.02 W
Quipar ≃	34	38.14 N	1.36 W
Quipeio	152	12.26 S	15.30 E
Quipemba	152	7.12 S	15.06 E
Quipit ≃	116	8.04 N	122.29 E
Quipungo	152	14.51 S	14.30 E
Quiquive ≃	248	14.39 S	67.38 W
Quirauk Mountain ∧	208	39.42 N	77.31 W
Quiriguá ⊥	236	15.17 N	89.04 W
Quirihue	252	36.17 S	72.32 W
Quirima	152	10.48 S	18.09 E
Quirimba, Ilha I	154	12.20 S	40.36 E
Quirimbo	152	10.36 S	14.12 E
Quirindi	166	31.31 S	150.41 E
Quirino □[4]	116	16.25 N	121.35 E
Quirinópolis	255	18.32 S	50.30 W
Quiriquire	246	9.59 N	63.13 W
Quiriri ≃	152	15.13 S	18.47 E
Quiririm	256	23.02 S	45.38 W
Quirke Lake ⊜	190	46.28 N	82.33 W
Quiroga, Esp.	34	42.29 N	7.16 W
Quiroga, Méx.	234	19.40 N	101.32 W
Quirós	252	28.47 S	65.07 W
Quirpon Island I	186	51.35 N	55.25 W
Quirra, Salto di ◆[1]	71	39.35 N	9.33 E
Quissac	62	43.55 N	4.00 E
Quissanga	154	12.25 S	40.29 E
Quissico	156	24.42 S	34.44 E
Quissongo	152	10.01 S	15.07 E
Quistello	64	45.00 N	10.59 E
Quitapa	152	10.23 S	18.14 E
Quitaque	196	34.22 N	101.04 W
Quitasueño ◆[4]	236	14.20 N	81.15 W
Quiterajo	154	11.48 S	40.25 E
Quitilipi	252	26.52 S	60.13 W
Quitman, Ga., U.S.	192	30.47 N	83.33 W
Quitman, Ms., U.S.	194	32.02 N	88.43 W
Quitman, Tx., U.S.	222	32.47 N	95.27 W
Quitman, Lake ⊜[1]	222	32.52 N	95.27 W
Quito	246	0.13 S	78.30 W
Quitzdorf, Speicherbecken ⊜[1]	54	51.17 N	14.45 E
Quivilla	248	9.32 S	76.41 W
Quixadá	250	4.58 S	39.01 W
Quixeramobim	250	5.12 S	39.17 W
Quixeré	250	5.05 S	37.59 W
Quixico	152	7.59 S	14.25 E
Quixinge	152	9.52 S	14.23 E
Quixito ≃	246	4.29 S	70.18 W
Quizenga	152	9.21 S	15.28 E
Qujiadian	89	43.13 N	123.53 E
Qujiang, Zhg.	100	28.15 N	115.45 E
Qujiang, Zhg.	100	24.41 N	113.35 E
Qujiang, Zhg.	100	24.48 N	113.17 E
Qujing	102	25.32 N	103.41 E
Qujiu	102	22.28 N	107.40 E
Qukou	105	39.46 N	117.07 E
Qulayʻah, Ra's al- ›	128	28.53 N	48.18 E
Qulin	194	36.35 N	90.14 W
Qulubbā	142	27.45 N	30.50 E
Qulūd, Jabal ∧[2]	140	11.41 N	29.31 E
Qulūṣanā	142	28.21 N	30.44 E
Qulzum, Baḥr al- ⊂	142	29.55 N	32.31 E
Qumar ≃, Zhg.	90	34.42 N	94.50 E
Qumar ≃, Zhg.	120	34.39 N	95.00 E
Qumarlêb	102	34.35 N	95.27 E
Qumbu	158	31.10 S	28.48 E
Qumrān, Khirbat ⊥	132	31.44 N	35.27 E
Qunayfidhah, Nafūd ⊥[8]	128	24.45 N	45.30 E
Qunbush Al-Ḥamrā'	142	29.00 N	30.59 E
Qungtag	120	29.59 N	87.33 E
Qunshen'guan	105	39.49 N	117.59 E
Quobba, Point ›	162	24.23 S	113.24 E
Quoich ≃	176	64.00 N	93.30 W
Quoich, Loch ⊜	46	57.04 N	5.17 W
Quoile ≃	48	54.21 N	5.42 W
Quoin Point ›	158	34.46 S	19.37 E
Quonochontaug	207	41.21 N	71.43 W
Quorn	166	32.21 S	138.03 E
Quorndon	42	52.45 N	1.09 W
Quoxo ≃	156	22.16 S	24.02 E
Qurayyah, Wādī V	132	30.26 N	34.01 E
Qurayyāt	128	23.17 N	58.55 E
Qurdūd	140	10.17 N	29.56 E
Qurrāṣah	140	14.38 N	32.12 E
Qurūn Ḥarḥash ∧[2]	142	28.09 N	31.42 E
Qūṣ	140	25.55 N	32.45 E
Quṣayr ad-Daffah ⊥	146	30.20 N	23.57 E
Qūshchī	128	37.59 N	45.03 E
Qushui	107	30.41 N	106.02 E
Qutang	100	32.30 N	120.21 E
Qutbapur ◆[8]	272a	28.35 N	77.01 E
Qutb Minar ʋ[1]	272a	28.32 N	77.11 E
Qutdligssat	176	70.04 N	53.01 W
Quthing	158	30.30 S	27.36 E
Quṭūr	142	30.59 N	30.57 E
Quwaysinā	142	30.34 N	31.09 E
Quxi, Zhg.	100	28.00 N	120.31 E
Quxi, Zhg.	100	23.36 N	116.26 E
Quxia	106	32.06 N	120.09 E
Quxian, Zhg.	100	28.58 N	118.52 E
Quxian, Zhg.	102	30.51 N	106.59 E
Quxingji	98	34.52 N	114.39 E
Quxiong	102	31.09 N	96.00 E
Qüxü	120	29.22 N	90.43 E
Quyang	98	38.34 N	114.42 E
Qūyjāq-e-Bālā	84	39.16 N	47.07 E
Quyon	188	45.31 N	76.14 W
Quyquyó	252	26.14 S	57.01 W
Quzaymah, Jabal ∧	132	30.34 N	36.21 E
Quzhou	98	36.46 N	114.57 E
Quzong	102	30.08 N	96.00 E
R			
Råå	41	56.00 N	12.44 E
Raab	60	48.21 N	13.39 E
Raab (Rába) ≃	30	47.42 N	17.38 E
Raab → Győr	30	47.42 N	17.38 E
Raabs an der Thaya	61	48.51 N	15.30 E
Raadt ◆[8]	263	51.24 N	6.56 E
Raahe	26	64.41 N	24.29 E
Rääkkylä	26	62.19 N	29.37 E
Raalte	52	52.24 N	6.16 E
Raamsdonksveer	52	51.42 N	4.56 E
Raʻananna	132	32.11 N	34.53 E
Raas, Pulau I	115a	7.09 S	114.32 E
Raasay I	46	57.23 N	6.04 W
Raasay, Sound of ⊔	46	57.27 N	6.06 W
Raasdorf	264b	48.15 N	16.34 E
Raasiku	76	59.22 N	25.11 E
Rab	36	44.46 N	14.46 E
Rab, Otok I	36	44.47 N	14.45 E
Raba	115b	8.27 S	118.46 E
Rába (Raab) ≃, Europe	30	47.42 N	17.38 E
Raba ≃, Pol.	30	50.09 N	20.30 E
Rabaable	144	8.17 N	48.18 E
Rabaçal ≃	34	41.30 N	7.12 W
Rábade	34	43.07 N	7.37 W
Rábahidvég	61	47.04 N	16.45 E
Rabai	154	3.58 S	39.37 E
Rabak	140	13.09 N	32.44 E
Rabal	164	6.22 S	134.52 E
Rabaraba	164	10.00 S	149.50 E
Rabat, Magreb	148	34.02 N	6.51 W
Rabat (Victoria), Malta	36	36.02 N	14.14 E
Rabat, Malta	36	35.52 N	14.25 E
Rabat □[4]	148	33.57 N	6.50 W
Rabaul	164	4.12 S	152.12 E
Rabbit ≃	216	42.38 N	86.06 W
Rabbit, Lac ⊜	190	47.30 N	78.22 W
Rabbit Creek ≃, S.D., U.S.	198	45.13 N	102.10 W
Rabbit Creek ≃, Tx., U.S.	222	32.26 N	94.47 W
Rabbit Ears Pass)(	200	40.23 N	106.37 W
Rabbit Lake ⊜, On., Can.	190	47.00 N	79.37 W
Rabbit Lake ⊜, Ca., U.S.	228	34.27 N	117.01 W
Rabbs Creek ≃	222	29.59 N	96.55 W
Rábca ≃	61	47.43 N	17.17 E
R'abcevo	76	54.39 N	32.19 E
Rabeira, Ponta da ›	287a	22.49 S	43.10 W
Rabenau	54	50.57 N	13.38 E
Rabette, Ruisseau la ≃	261	48.35 N	2.00 E
Rābiʻ, Ash-Shallāl ar- (Fourth Cataract) ∟	140	18.47 N	32.03 E
Rābigh	128	22.48 N	39.01 E
Rabinal	236	15.06 N	90.27 W
Rabiusa ≃	58	46.48 N	9.20 E
Rabka	30	49.36 N	19.56 E
Rabkavi Banhatti	122	16.28 N	75.06 E
Rabnābād Channel ⊔	126	21.50 N	90.19 E
Rabnābād Islands II	126	21.58 N	90.24 E
Rabočeostrovsk	24	64.59 N	34.48 E
Rabočij	86	59.07 N	79.00 E
Rabong, Gunong ∧	114	4.48 N	102.07 E
Rabotki	80	56.03 N	44.38 E
R'abovskij	80	50.01 N	41.53 E
Rabun Bald ∧	192	34.58 N	83.18 W
Rabwāh	123	31.44 N	72.50 E
Raby	262	53.19 N	3.02 W
Rabyānah ⍑[4]	146	24.15 N	22.00 E
Rabyānah, Ṣaḥrā' ◆[2]	146	24.30 N	21.00 E
Racale	68	39.57 N	18.06 E
Racalmuto	70	37.24 N	13.44 E
Răcari	38	44.38 N	25.45 E
Racconigi	62	44.46 N	7.46 E
Raccoon ≃	194	41.35 N	93.37 W
Raccoon Creek ≃, N.J., U.S.	208	39.48 N	75.23 W
Raccoon Creek ≃, Oh., U.S.	188	38.43 N	82.11 W
Raccoon Creek ≃, Oh., U.S.	214	40.02 N	82.24 W
Raccoon Creek ≃, Pa., U.S.	214	40.38 N	80.22 W
Raccoon Creek ≃, Pa., U.S.	285	39.48 N	75.23 W
Raccoon Creek ≃, Va., U.S.	208	36.48 N	77.10 W
Raccoon Creek, South Branch ≃	285	39.44 N	75.15 W
Raccoon Creek State Park ♣	214	40.30 N	80.27 W
Raccoon Island I	285	39.49 N	75.22 W
Raccuia	70	38.03 N	14.54 E
Race, Cape ›	186	46.40 N	53.10 W
Raceland	194	29.43 N	90.35 W
Race Point ›	207	42.04 N	70.14 W
Racette, Lac ⊜	206	46.34 N	74.03 W
Racette, Ruisseau ≃	206	46.36 N	74.04 W
Raceview	273d	26.17 S	28.08 E
Rach'a	76	60.05 N	30.49 E
Rach Gia	110	10.01 N	105.05 E
Rach Gia, Vinh ⊂	110	10.00 N	105.00 E
Rachmanovka, Ross.	80	51.57 N	49.29 E
Rachmanovka, Ukr.	78	47.48 N	33.13 E
Rachmanovo	82	55.44 N	38.37 E
Rachny Lesovyje	78	48.47 N	28.29 E
Rachov	78	48.03 N	24.12 E
Raciąż	30	52.47 N	20.06 E
Racibórz (Ratibor)	30	50.06 N	18.13 E
Racine, Pa., U.S.	214	40.49 N	80.20 W
Racine, Wi., U.S.	216	42.43 N	87.46 W
Racine □[6]	216	42.45 N	88.05 W
Racines	64	46.52 N	11.18 E
Račinskij chrebet ⋏	84	42.30 N	43.30 E
Rackerby	226	39.26 N	121.20 W
Ráckeve	30	47.10 N	18.56 E
Rackwick	46	58.52 N	3.23 W
R'ad	76	57.56 N	35.04 E
Råda	40	60.00 N	13.36 E
Radama, Nosy II	157b	14.00 S	47.47 E
Radama, Presqu'île ›[1]	157b	14.16 S	47.53 E
Rådasjön ⊜	40	59.58 N	13.38 E
Radaur	124	30.02 N	77.09 E
Rădăuți	38	47.51 N	25.55 E
Radbuza ≃	60	49.46 N	13.24 E
Radčenskoje	78	49.48 N	40.32 E
Radcliff	194	37.50 N	85.56 W
Radcliffe	44	53.34 N	2.20 W
Radcliffe on Trent	42	52.57 N	1.03 W
Radda in Chianti	66	43.29 N	11.22 E
Raddusa	70	37.28 N	14.32 E
Råde	26	59.21 N	10.51 E
Radebaugh	279b	40.19 N	79.35 W
Radeberg	54	51.07 N	13.55 E
Radebeul	54	51.06 N	13.40 E
Radeburg	54	51.13 N	13.43 E
Radeče	36	46.04 N	15.11 E
Radechov	78	50.18 N	24.37 E
Radegast	54	51.39 N	12.05 E
Radenci	61	46.38 N	16.03 E
Radenthein	64	46.48 N	13.43 E
Radevormwald	56	51.12 N	7.21 E
Radford	192	37.07 N	80.34 W
Rādhānagar, India	126	23.09 N	87.19 E
Rādhānagar, India	272b	22.27 N	88.28 E
Rādhanpur	120	23.50 N	71.36 E
Radici, Foce delle)(	64	44.12 N	10.31 E
Radicofani	66	42.54 N	11.46 E
Radicondoli	66	43.16 N	11.02 E
Rădinești	38	44.48 N	23.46 E
Radiščevo	80	52.51 N	47.53 E
Radisson	184	52.27 N	107.23 W
Radiumbad Brambach	54	50.13 N	12.19 E
Radium Hot Springs	182	50.38 N	116.03 W
Rad'kovka	78	51.06 N	36.58 E
Radlett	42	51.42 N	0.20 W
Radlett Aerodrome ⊠	260	51.43 N	0.19 W
Radley Run ≃	285	39.54 N	75.37 W
Radlje ob Dravi	61	46.37 N	15.13 E
Rådmansö ›[1]	40	59.45 N	18.55 E
Radnevo	38	42.18 N	25.56 E
Radnice	60	49.51 N	13.37 E
Radnor, Oh., U.S.	214	40.23 N	83.09 W
Radnor, Pa., U.S.	285	40.02 N	75.21 W
Radnor Forest ∧	42	52.18 N	3.10 W
Radnor Mere ⊜	262	53.17 N	2.14 W
Radofinnikovo	76	59.09 N	30.55 E
Radogošča	76	59.47 N	34.51 E
Radoj'a	78	47.44 N	28.09 E
Radolfzell	58	47.44 N	8.58 E
Radom, Pol.	30	51.25 N	21.10 E
Radom, Il., U.S.	219	38.17 N	89.12 W
Radom □[4]	30	51.25 N	21.15 E
Radomicko	54	52.10 N	14.58 E
Radomir	38	42.33 N	22.58 E
Radomka	78	51.56 N	32.32 E
Radomka ≃	30	51.43 N	21.26 E
Radomsko	30	51.05 N	19.25 E
Radomyšl'	78	50.30 N	29.14 E
Radomyśl Wielki	30	50.12 N	21.16 E
Radošice	60	49.33 N	13.39 E
Radoškoviči	76	54.09 N	27.14 E
Radotin	30	50.00 N	14.22 E
Radovicy	80	55.06 N	39.32 E
Radoviš	38	41.38 N	22.28 E
Radovljica	36	46.21 N	14.11 E
Radstadt	64	47.23 N	13.27 E
Radstädter Tauern)(	64	47.15 N	13.24 E
Radstock	42	51.18 N	2.28 W
Radstock, Cape ›	162	33.12 S	134.20 E
Raduha ∧	61	46.25 N	14.45 E
Radul'	78	51.49 N	30.42 E
Radun'	76	54.03 N	25.00 E
Radušnoje	78	47.49 N	33.29 E
Radutino	76	52.39 N	33.57 E
Radvaniči	78	52.02 N	24.02 E
Radviliškis	76	55.50 N	23.31 E
Radville	184	49.27 N	104.17 W
Radway	182	54.04 N	112.57 W
Radykovskoje	80	45.56 N	41.57 E
Radymno	30	49.57 N	22.48 E
Radyr	42	51.31 N	3.15 W
Radziejów	30	52.38 N	18.32 E
Radzyń Chełmiński	30	53.24 N	18.56 E
Radzyń Podlaski	30	51.48 N	22.38 E
Rae	176	62.50 N	116.03 W
Rae ≃	176	67.55 N	115.30 W
Rāe Bareli	124	26.13 N	81.14 E
Raeford	192	34.58 N	79.13 W
Rae Isthmus ⊥[3]	176	66.55 N	86.10 W
Rāenda	126	22.18 N	89.51 E
Raeren	56	50.41 N	6.07 E
Raesfeld	52	51.46 N	6.50 E
Raeside, Lake ⊜	162	29.30 S	122.00 E
Rae Strait ⊔	176	68.45 N	95.00 W
Raetihi	172	39.26 S	175.17 E
Rafaela	252	31.16 S	61.29 W
Rafael Calzada	258	34.48 S	58.22 W
Rafael Castillo	288	34.43 S	58.37 W
Rafael Perazza	258	34.32 S	56.47 W
Rafaḥ	132	31.18 N	34.15 E
Rafaï	152	4.58 N	23.56 E
Rafalovka	78	51.22 N	25.52 E
Raffadali	70	37.24 N	13.32 E
Raffelberg, Rennbahn ♣	263	51.26 N	6.50 E
Raffili Mission	140	6.53 N	27.58 E
Rafḥā'	128	29.42 N	43.30 E
Rafinesque, Mount ∧[2]	210	42.47 N	73.37 W
Rafsanjān	128	30.24 N	56.01 E
Raft ≃	202	42.37 N	113.15 W
Raft River Mountains ⋏	200	41.55 N	113.25 W
Rafz	58	47.37 N	8.32 E
Raga	140	8.28 N	25.41 E
Ragada	64	46.10 N	10.38 E
Ragang, Mount ∧	116	7.43 N	124.32 E
Ragay	116	13.49 N	122.47 E
Ragay Gulf ⊂	116	13.30 N	122.45 E
Rågeleje	41	56.06 N	12.10 E
Rägelin	54	53.01 N	12.38 E
Ragewitz	54	51.14 N	12.51 E
Ragged, Mount ∧	162	33.27 S	123.25 E
Ragged Island I	238	22.12 N	75.44 W
Ragged Island Range II	238	22.40 N	75.54 W
Ragged Lake ⊜	212	45.28 N	78.38 W
Ragged Top Mountain ∧	200	41.27 N	105.20 W
Raghabpur	272b	22.25 N	88.21 E
Rāghogarh	124	24.27 N	77.12 E
Raghumāthbāri	126	22.22 N	87.47 E
Raghunāthpur, Bngl.	126	23.12 N	89.31 E
Raghunāthpur, India	126	23.33 N	86.40 E
Raglan, Austl.	170	33.26 S	149.36 E
Raglan, N.Z.	172	37.48 S	174.53 E
Raglan, Wales, U.K.	42	51.47 N	2.51 W
Ragland	194	33.44 N	86.09 W
Ragnitz	61	46.50 N	15.35 E
Rago Nasjonalpark ♣	24	67.26 N	16.00 E
Ragow	264a	52.17 N	13.33 E
Ragozino	86	59.15 N	77.52 E
Rågsveden	40	60.29 N	14.05 E
Raguda, Ghubbet ⊂	144	10.45 N	46.34 E
Raguhn	54	51.42 N	12.17 E
Raguli	80	45.38 N	43.42 E
Ragusa	70	36.55 N	14.44 E
Ragusa □[4]	70	36.55 N	14.36 E
Ragusa → Dubrovnik	38	42.38 N	18.07 E
Raguva	76	55.34 N	24.36 E
Raha	112	4.51 S	122.43 E
Rahad, Nahr ar- (Rahad) ≃	140	14.28 N	33.31 E
Rahad al-Bardī	140	11.18 N	23.53 E
Rahad Game Reserve ◆[4]	140	13.06 N	35.05 E
Rahaṭ, Ḥarrat ⊥[9]	144	22.20 N	40.05 E
Rahatgaon	124	22.15 N	77.14 E
Rāhatgarh	124	23.47 N	78.22 E
Raḥbah	130	34.30 N	36.09 E
Rahden	52	52.26 N	8.36 E
Rahimatpur	122	17.36 N	74.12 E
Rahīm Ki Bāzār	120	24.19 N	69.09 E
Rahīmyār Khān	120	28.25 N	70.18 E
Rahlstedt ◆[8]	52	53.36 N	10.09 E
Rahm	263	51.26 N	6.26 E
Rahm ◆[8], Dtsch.	263	51.32 N	7.23 E
Rahm ◆[8], Dtsch.	263	51.21 N	6.47 E
Rahmer See ⊜	264a	52.45 N	13.25 E
Rahns	285	40.12 N	75.27 W
Rahnsdorf ◆[8]	264a	52.26 N	13.42 E
Rāhon	123	31.03 N	76.07 E
Rahotu	172	39.20 S	173.48 E
Rahouia	34	35.32 N	1.01 E
Rāhwāli	123	32.15 N	74.10 E
Rahway	210	40.36 N	74.16 W
Rahway ≃	276	40.35 N	74.12 W
Rahway, East Branch ≃	276	40.42 N	74.18 W
Rahway, Robinsons Branch ≃	276	40.37 N	74.17 W
Rahway, South Branch ≃	276	40.36 N	74.17 W
Rahway, West Branch ≃	276	40.42 N	74.18 W
Rahway River Parkway ♣	276	40.41 N	74.19 W
Raiano	66	42.06 N	13.49 E
Raiatea I	14	16.50 S	151.25 W
Rāichūr	122	16.12 N	77.22 E
Raidak ≃	124	26.22 N	89.45 E
Rāidighi	126	22.00 N	88.26 E
Raiding	61	47.34 N	16.32 E
Raiford	192	30.03 N	82.14 W
Raiganj	124	25.37 N	88.07 E
Raigarh	122	21.54 N	83.24 E
Raijua, Pulau I	112	10.37 S	121.36 E
Rāikot	123	30.39 N	75.36 E
Railroad	208	39.46 N	76.42 W
Railroad Canyon Reservoir ⊜[1]	228	33.42 N	117.16 W
Railroad Creek ≃	224	48.12 N	120.36 W
Rail Road Flat	226	38.20 N	120.30 W
Railroad Valley V	204	38.25 N	115.40 W
Railton	166	41.21 S	146.25 E
Raimangal ≃	126	21.47 N	89.08 E
Rain	56	48.41 N	10.55 E
Rainbach im Innkreis	60	48.27 N	13.32 E
Rainbow	228	33.24 N	117.10 W
Rainbow Bridge ◆[5]	284a	43.05 N	79.04 W
Rainbow Bridge National Monument ♣	200	37.06 N	110.57 W
Rainbow Falls ∟	182	52.23 N	119.59 W
Rainbow Lakes	276	40.52 N	74.28 W
Rainbow Park ♣	278	41.46 N	87.33 W
Rainbow Shores	212	43.37 N	76.12 W
Rainelle	188	37.58 N	80.46 W
Rainford	44	53.30 N	2.48 W
Rainham	42	51.23 N	0.36 E
Rainham ◆[8]	260	51.31 N	0.12 E
Rainhill	262	53.26 N	2.46 W
Rainhill Stoops	262	53.24 N	2.45 W
Rainier, Or., U.S.	224	46.05 N	122.56 W
Rainier, Wa., U.S.	224	46.53 N	122.41 W
Rainier, Mount ∧	224	46.52 N	121.46 W
Rainow	262	53.17 N	2.04 W
Rains □[6]	222	32.50 N	95.47 W
Rainsboro	218	39.13 N	83.25 W
Rainsford Island I	283	42.18 N	70.57 W
Rains → Riva di Tures	64	46.57 N	12.04 E
Rainworth	44	53.07 N	1.08 W
Rainy ≃, N.A.	184	48.50 N	94.41 W
Rainy ≃, Mi., U.S.	190	45.27 N	84.13 W
Rainy Lake ⊜, On., Can.	212	45.32 N	79.30 W
Rainy Lake ⊜, N.A.	184	48.42 N	93.10 W
Rainy Pass)(	224	48.32 N	120.39 W
Rainy River	190	48.43 N	94.34 W
Rāipur, Bngl.	126	23.03 N	90.46 E
Raipur, India	122	21.14 N	81.38 E
Raipur, India	124	30.19 N	78.06 E
Raipur, India	126	22.48 N	86.57 E
Raipur, India	272a	28.32 N	77.20 E
Raipur, India	272b	22.24 N	88.09 E
Rāipura	126	23.59 N	90.53 E
Raipur Uplands ⋏[1]	122	21.00 N	82.20 E
Rairākhol	120	21.04 N	84.21 E
Ra'īs	128	23.34 N	38.36 E
Raisdorf	54	54.17 N	10.16 E
Raisen	124	23.20 N	77.48 E
Ráisi, Punta ›	70	38.11 N	13.06 E
Raisin	226	36.36 N	119.54 W
Raisin ≃, On., Can.	206	45.08 N	74.29 W
Raisin ≃, Mi., U.S.	216	41.53 N	83.20 W
Rāisinghnagar	123	29.32 N	73.27 E
Raismes	50	50.23 N	3.29 E
Raita	126	24.07 N	88.57 E
Raitenbuch	60	49.01 N	11.08 E
Raití	236	14.35 N	85.02 W
Raivavae I	14	23.52 S	147.40 W
Rāiwind	123	31.15 N	74.13 E
Raizeux	261	48.37 N	1.41 E
Raja, Gili I	115a	7.14 S	113.47 E
Raja, Ujung ›	114	3.45 N	96.33 E
Rājābāri	126	23.23 N	90.28 E
Rajabasa	112	5.25 S	104.24 E
Rājābhāt Khāwa	124	26.37 N	89.32 E
Rājābhita	126	23.52 N	86.20 E
Rājahmundry	122	16.59 N	81.47 E
Rajāj	140	10.55 N	24.43 E
Rāja Jang	123	31.13 N	74.16 E
Raja-Jooseppi	24	68.28 N	28.21 E
Rājākhera	124	26.55 N	78.11 E
Rājaldesar	120	28.02 N	74.28 E
Raj-Aleksandrovka	83	48.48 N	37.51 E
Rājāluka	126	22.09 N	86.38 E
Rajamäki	26	60.32 N	24.45 E
Rājampet	122	14.11 N	79.10 E
Rajang ≃	112	2.04 N	111.12 E
Rājanpur	120	29.06 N	70.19 E
Rājapālaiyam	122	9.27 N	77.34 E
Rājāpur, Bngl.	126	22.34 N	90.09 E
Rājāpur, India	122	16.40 N	73.31 E
Rājāpur, India	124	25.23 N	81.09 E
Rājāpur, India	272b	22.39 N	88.11 E
Rājapur Canal ≋	272b	22.30 N	88.07 E
Rājasthān □[3]	120	27.00 N	74.00 E
Rājauri	123	33.23 N	74.18 E
Rājbāri, Bngl.	124	23.46 N	89.39 E
Rājbāri, India	126	22.25 N	88.48 E
Raj Bhavan ʋ	272b	22.34 N	88.21 E
Rājbirāj	124	26.32 N	86.44 E
Rajčichinsk	89	49.46 N	129.25 E
Rājendrapur	126	24.06 N	90.27 E
Rajevskij	86	54.04 N	54.56 E
Rāj Gangpur	124	22.11 N	84.36 E
Rājganj ≃[1]	126	22.21 N	90.16 E
Rājgarh, India	123	28.38 N	75.23 E
Rājgarh, India	124	23.56 N	76.58 E
Rājgarh, India	124	27.14 N	76.38 E
Rajghat ʋ[1]	272a	28.39 N	77.15 E
Rājgīr	124	25.02 N	85.25 E
Rajgorod	80	48.26 N	44.55 E
Rajgorodka, Ukr.	83	49.22 N	37.57 E
Rajgorodka, Ukr.	83	48.50 N	39.04 E
Rajgorodok, Kaz.	80	48.48 N	52.53 E
Rajgorodok, Ukr.	83	48.54 N	37.43 E
Rajgród	30	53.44 N	22.42 E
Rājhāt	272b	22.56 N	88.21 E
Rajhrad	61	49.05 N	16.37 E
Rājibpur	272b	22.49 N	88.34 E
Rajik	112	2.36 S	105.56 E
Rajka	61	48.02 N	17.11 E
Rājkot	120	22.18 N	70.47 E
Rajkuzi	265a	59.47 N	29.57 E
Rājmahāl	124	25.03 N	87.50 E
Rājmahāl Hills ⋏[2]	124	24.40 N	87.25 E
Rājnagar	126	23.57 N	87.19 E
Rāj Nāndgaon	120	21.06 N	81.02 E
Rajokri ◆[8]	272a	28.31 N	77.07 E
Rājpipla	120	21.47 N	73.34 E
Rājpur, India	120	21.56 N	75.08 E
Rājpur, India	126	22.25 N	88.25 E
Rājpur, India	272a	28.44 N	77.22 E
Rājpur ◆[8]	272a	28.41 N	77.12 E
Rājpura	124	30.29 N	76.36 E
Rājshāhi	124	24.22 N	88.36 E
Rājshāhi □[5]	124	25.15 N	89.15 E
Rajskoje	83	48.34 N	37.25 E
Rājula	122	21.03 N	71.26 E
Raka	124	29.26 N	85.50 E
Raka ≃	124	29.24 N	87.58 E
Rakaia	172	43.45 S	172.01 E
Rakaia ≃	172	43.56 S	172.13 E
Rakamaz	30	48.08 N	21.30 E
Rakaposhi ∧	123	36.10 N	74.30 E
Rakata, Pulau I	115a	6.10 S	105.26 E
Rakha La)(	124	27.53 N	87.34 E
Rakhawt, Wādī V	144	17.40 N	51.40 E
Rakhine □[8]	110	19.00 N	94.15 E
Rakhneh	128	31.39 N	59.13 E
Rakhni	120	30.03 N	69.55 E
Rakhshān ≃	128	27.10 N	63.25 E
Rākīn	132	31.14 N	35.42 E
Rakitnoje, Ross.	78	50.51 N	35.50 E
Rakitnoje, Ross.	89	45.36 N	134.17 E
Rakitnoje, Ukr.	78	49.42 N	30.27 E
Rakitnoje, Ukr.	78	51.17 N	27.14 E
Rakke	76	58.59 N	26.15 E
Rakkestad	26	59.26 N	11.21 E
Rakoniewice	30	52.10 N	16.16 E
Rakops	156	21.00 S	24.32 E
Rákoscsaba ◆[8]	264c	47.29 N	19.17 E
Rákoshegy ◆[8]	264c	47.28 N	19.14 E
Rákoskeresztúr ◆[8]	264c	47.29 N	19.15 E
Rákoskert ◆[8]	264c	47.28 N	19.19 E
Rákosliget ◆[8]	264c	47.30 N	19.16 E
Rákospalota ◆[8]	264c	47.34 N	19.08 E
Rákos-patak ≃	264c	47.33 N	19.04 E
Rákosszentmihály ◆[8]	264c	47.32 N	19.11 E
Rakovnická plošina ⋏[1]	54	50.08 N	13.47 E
Rakovník	54	50.05 N	13.43 E
Rakovski	38	42.18 N	24.58 E
Rakša	80	53.33 N	41.37 E
Raksakiny	86	60.37 N	73.52 E
Rakuša	80	47.03 N	52.47 E
Råkvåg	26	63.46 N	10.05 E
Rakvere	76	59.22 N	26.20 E
Rakwa	164	2.42 S	134.30 E
Raleigh, Nf., Can.	186	51.34 N	55.44 W
Raleigh, Ms., U.S.	194	32.02 N	89.31 W
Raleigh, N.C., U.S.	192	35.46 N	78.38 W
Raleigh Hills	224	45.29 N	122.45 W
Raleighvallen Voltz Berg, Natuurreservaat ♣, Sur.	246	4.45 N	56.05 W
Raleighvallen Voltz Berg, Natuurreservaat ♣, Sur.	250	4.50 N	55.10 W
Ralik Chain II	14	8.00 N	167.00 E
Ralls	196	33.40 N	101.23 W
Ralls □[6]	219	39.34 N	91.30 W
Ralsko ∧	54	50.42 N	14.47 E
Ralston, Ne., U.S.	198	41.12 N	96.02 W
Ralston, Pa., U.S.	210	41.31 N	76.57 W
Ram ≃	182	52.23 N	115.25 W
Rama, Nic.	236	12.09 N	84.15 W
Rama, Yis.	132	32.56 N	35.22 E
Rama ≃	236	12.08 N	84.13 W
Ramacca	70	37.23 N	14.42 E
Rāmachandrapuram	122	16.51 N	82.01 E
Ramādah	144	13.38 N	43.56 E
Ramah	200	35.07 N	108.29 W
Ramah Indian Reservation ◆[4]	200	34.50 N	108.25 W
Rama Indian Reserve ◆[4]	212	44.41 N	79.15 W
Ramales de la Victoria	34	43.15 N	3.27 W
Rām Allāh	132	31.54 N	35.12 E
Rāman	123	29.58 N	74.58 E
Rāmanagaram	122	12.43 N	77.18 E
Rāmanāthapuram	122	9.23 N	78.50 E
Ramanāthpur	272b	22.41 N	88.14 E
Ramanpāti	272b	22.47 N	88.08 E
Rāmānuj Ganj	124	23.48 N	83.42 E
Ramapo	276	41.08 N	74.10 W
Ramapo ≃	276	40.58 N	74.17 W
Ramapo Lake ⊜	276	41.02 N	74.16 W
Ramapo Mountains ⋏	276	41.08 N	74.12 W
Ramapo Valley Airport ⊠	276	41.06 N	74.02 W
Ramas, Cape ›	122	15.07 N	73.55 E
Ramasaig	46	57.24 N	6.44 W
Ramasucha	76	52.46 N	33.33 E
Ramat Gan	132	32.05 N	34.49 E
Ramat HaSharon	132	32.09 N	34.50 E
Ramat HaShofét	132	32.37 N	35.06 E
Ramathlabama	156	25.40 S	25.35 E
Ramatuelle	62	43.13 N	6.37 E
Rama VI Bridge ◆[5]	269a	13.48 N	100.31 E
Rāmban	123	33.15 N	75.15 E
Rambervillers	58	48.21 N	6.38 E
Rambi I	175g	16.30 S	179.59 E
Rambipuji	115a	8.13 S	113.36 E
Rambleton Acres	208	39.39 N	75.38 W
Ramblewood	285	39.55 N	74.56 W
Rambouillet	50	48.39 N	1.50 E
Rambouillet, Château de ⊥	261	48.39 N	1.49 E
Rambouillet, Forêt de ♣	261	48.40 N	1.50 E
Rambutyo Island I	164	2.20 S	147.50 E
Rām Dās	123	31.58 N	74.54 E
Rāmdia	126	23.42 N	89.32 E
Rāmdurg	122	15.57 N	75.18 E
Ramea	186	47.31 N	57.23 W
Ramea Islands II	186	47.31 N	57.21 W
Rāmechhāp	124	27.20 N	86.05 E
Rame Head ›, Transkei	158	31.48 S	29.22 E
Rame Head ›, Eng., U.K.	42	50.19 N	4.13 W
Rämen ⊜	40	60.18 N	15.10 E
Ramenje, Ross.	76	60.17 N	43.46 E
Ramenje, Ross.	82	56.34 N	37.13 E
Ramenka ◆[8]	265b	55.41 N	37.30 E
Ramenskoje	82	55.34 N	38.14 E
Ramer	194	32.03 N	86.13 W
Ramerupt	50	48.31 N	4.18 E
Rameški	76	57.21 N	36.03 E
Rāmeswaram	122	9.17 N	79.18 E
Ramey	214	40.48 N	78.24 W
Rāmganj	126	23.06 N	90.51 E
Rāmgarh, Bngl.	120	22.59 N	91.44 E
Rāmgarh, India	120	27.22 N	70.30 E
Rāmgarh, India	120	27.15 N	75.11 E
Rāmgarh, India	124	23.38 N	85.31 E
Rāmgarh, India	124	24.34 N	87.15 E
Rāmgarh, India	126	22.42 N	87.04 E
Rāmgarh Hills ⋏[2]	124	22.50 N	83.10 E
Ram Head ›	240m	18.18 N	64.42 W
Rāmhormoz	128	31.16 N	49.36 E
Ramingining	164	12.19 S	135.03 E
Ramingstein	64	47.04 N	13.50 E
Ramírez, Méx.	196	27.20 N	100.58 W
Ramírez, Méx.	196	25.57 N	97.46 W
Ramiriquí	246	5.24 N	73.20 W
Ramis ≃	144	7.59 N	41.34 E
Rāmjībanpur	126	22.50 N	87.37 E
Rāmkānāli	126	23.35 N	86.45 E
Raml, Qārat ar- ∧[2]	142	30.02 N	30.39 E
Ramla	132	31.55 N	34.52 E
Ramlu ∧	144	13.24 N	41.51 E
Ramm, Jabal ∧	132	29.35 N	35.24 E
Rämmen	40	60.07 N	14.08 E
Rāmnagar, India	123	32.49 N	75.19 E
Rāmnagar, India	124	25.17 N	83.02 E
Rāmnagar, India	124	29.24 N	79.07 E
Rāmnagar, India	126	21.41 N	87.33 E
Rāmnagar, India	272b	22.23 N	88.19 E
Ramnäs	40	59.46 N	16.12 E
Ramo	144	6.42 N	41.23 E
Ramon'	78	51.54 N	39.20 E
Ramon, Har ∧	132	30.30 N	34.38 E
Ramon, Makhtésh ⊥[7]	132	30.36 N	34.49 E
Ramon, Naḥal V	132	30.36 N	34.55 E
Ramona, Ca., U.S.	228	33.02 N	116.52 W
Ramona, Ok., U.S.	196	36.31 N	95.55 W
Ramona, S.D., U.S.	198	44.07 N	97.12 W
Ramor, Lough ⊜	48	53.49 N	7.05 W
Ramos	234	22.50 N	101.55 W
Ramos ◆[8]	287a	22.51 S	43.15 W
Ramos ≃[1]	150	5.08 N	5.22 E
Ramosch	58	46.50 N	10.22 E
Ramos Island I	116	8.06 N	117.02 E
Ramos Mejía	258	34.38 S	58.34 W
Ramot	132	32.46 N	35.40 E
Ramotswa	156	24.56 S	25.50 E
Rāmpāl	126	22.34 N	89.39 E
Rampart	180	65.30 N	150.11 W
Ramparts ≃	180	66.11 N	129.03 W
Rampillon	50	48.33 N	3.04 E
Rampside	44	54.05 N	3.10 W
Rāmpur, India	120	31.27 N	77.38 E
Rāmpur, India	123	29.49 N	77.27 E
Rāmpur, India	124	28.49 N	79.02 E
Rāmpura	120	24.28 N	75.26 E
Rāmpura Phūl	123	30.17 N	75.14 E
Rampur Boalia → Rājshāhi	124	24.22 N	88.36 E
Rāmpur Hāt	126	24.10 N	87.47 E
Ramrath	263	51.06 N	6.41 E
Ramree Island I	110	19.06 N	93.48 E
Rāmsāgar	126	23.05 N	87.17 E

Symbols in the index entries represent the broad categories identified in the key at the right. Symbols with superior numbers (⋏[1]) identify subcategories (see complete key on page I · 1).

Symbole im Register stellen die rechts im Schlüssel erklärten Kategorien dar. Symbole mit hochgestellten Ziffern (⋏[1]) bezeichnen Unterabteilungen einer Kategorie (vgl. vollständiger Schlüssel auf Seite I · 1).

Los símbolos incluidos en el texto del índice representan las grandes categorías identificadas con la clave a la derecha. Los símbolos con números en su parte superior (⋏[1]) identifican las subcategorías (véase la clave completa en la página I · 1).

Les symboles de l'index représentent les catégories indiquées dans la légende à droite. Les symboles suivis d'un indice (⋏[1]) représentent des sous-catégories (voir légende complète à la page I · 1).

Os símbolos incluídos no texto do índice representam as grandes categorias identificadas com a chave à direita. Os símbolos com números em sua parte superior (⋏[1]) identificam as subcategorias (veja-se a chave completa à página I · 1).

English	Deutsch	Español	Português	Français	
∧ Mountain	Berg	Montaña	Montanha	Montagne	
⋏ Mountains	Gebirge	Montañas	Montanhas	Montagnes	
)(Pass	Paß	Paso	Passo	Col	
V Valley, Canyon	Tal, Cañon	Valle, Cañón	Vale, Canhão	Vallée, Canyon	
≚ Plain	Ebene	Llano	Planície	Plaine	
› Cape	Kap	Cabo	Cabo	Cap	
I Island	Insel	Isla	Ilha	Île	
II Islands	Inseln	Islas	Ilhas	Îles	
⊥ Other Topographic Features	Andere Topographische Objekte	Otros Elementos Topográficos	Outros acidentes topográficos	Autres données topographiques	

ESPAÑOL — Nombre / Página / Lat.°′ / Long.°′ W = Oeste
FRANÇAIS — Nom / Page / Lat.°′ / Long.°′ W = Ouest
PORTUGUÊS — Nome / Página / Lat.°′ / Long.°′ W = Oeste

Nombre	Página	Lat.°′	Long.°′ W = Oeste
Ramsau	64	47.36 N	12.54 E
Ramsay Range ⋀	162	18.31 S	127.03 E
Ramsbeck	56	51.18 N	8.24 E
Ramsberg	40	59.46 N	15.17 E
Ramsbottom	44	53.40 N	2.19 W
Ramsden Bellhouse	260	51.37 N	0.29 E
Ramsden Heath	260	51.38 N	0.28 E
Ramsdorf	52	51.54 N	6.55 E
Ramsele	26	63.33 N	16.29 E
Ramsenthal	60	50.01 N	11.35 E
Ramseur	192	35.44 N	79.39 W
Ramsey, I. of Man	44	54.20 N	4.21 W
Ramsey, Eng., U.K.	42	51.56 N	1.14 E
Ramsey, Eng., U.K.	42	52.27 N	0.07 W
Ramsey, Il., U.S.	219	39.08 N	89.06 W
Ramsey, N.J., U.S.	210	41.03 N	74.08 W
Ramsey Bay ⊂	44	54.20 N	4.20 W
Ramsey Brook ≏	276	41.02 N	74.08 W
Ramsey Creek ≏	219	39.03 N	89.04 W
Ramsey Island I	42	51.52 N	5.10 W
Ramsey Lake ⊜	190	47.15 N	82.16 W
Ramsey Lake State Park ♠	219	39.10 N	89.08 W
Ramsgate, Austl.	274a	33.59 S	151.08 E
Ramsgate, S. Afr.	158	30.55 S	30.20 E
Ramsgate, Eng., U.K.	42	51.20 N	1.25 E
Rāmshai	124	26.44 N	88.51 E
Rāmshīr	128	30.54 N	49.24 E
Ramshorn Peak ∧	202	45.09 N	111.06 W
Rämshyttan	40	60.18 N	15.13 E
Ramsjö	26	62.11 N	15.39 E
Ramsloh	52	53.06 N	7.40 E
Ramstein	56	49.27 N	7.33 E
Rāmtek	120	21.24 N	79.20 E
Rāmu, Bngl.	120	21.25 N	92.07 E
Ramu, Kenya	154	3.56 N	41.13 E
Ramu ≏	164	4.02 S	144.41 E
Ramuševo	76	57.50 N	31.37 E
Ramvik	26	62.49 N	17.51 E
Ramville, Îlet I	240e	14.42 N	60.53 W
Ramygala	76	55.31 N	24.18 E
Ramzaj	80	53.18 N	44.44 E
Rānāghāt	126	23.11 N	88.35 E
Rana Kao, Volcán ∧[1]	174z	27.11 S	109.27 W
Ranalt	64	47.02 N	11.13 E
Rāna Pratāp Sāgar ⊜[1]	120	24.50 N	75.35 E
Rånäs	40	59.48 N	18.17 E
Ranau	112	5.58 N	116.41 E
Ranau, Danau ⊜	112	4.50 S	103.55 E
Ranbīrsinghpura	123	32.38 N	74.44 E
Ranburne	194	33.31 N	85.20 W
Ranburn Woods	278	41.33 N	87.22 W
Rancabali	115a	7.08 S	107.21 E
Rancagua	252	34.10 S	70.45 W
Rancah	115a	7.12 S	108.30 E
Rance ≏	32	48.31 N	1.59 W
Rancevo, Ross.	76	56.56 N	34.03 E
Rancevo, Ross.	76	56.40 N	33.02 E
Rancharia	255	22.15 S	50.55 W
Rancheria	180	60.05 N	130.40 W
Ranchería ≏	246	11.34 N	72.54 W
Rancheria Rock ∧	202	44.53 N	120.08 W
Ranches of Taos	200	36.22 N	105.37 W
Ranchester	202	44.54 N	107.09 W
Rānchi	124	23.21 N	85.20 E
Ranchillos	252	26.57 S	65.03 W
Rānchi Plateau ⋀[1]	124	23.20 N	84.50 E
Ranch Lake ⊜	184	52.30 N	104.46 W
Rancho Colorado, Presa de ⊜[1]	286a	19.29 N	99.17 W
Rancho Cordova	226	38.35 N	121.18 W
Rancho Del Mar	226	38.10 N	122.15 W
Rancho Nuevo, Méx.	196	26.22 N	99.54 W
Rancho Nuevo, Méx.	234	23.12 N	97.48 W
Rancho Palos Verdes	228	33.45 N	118.24 W
Rancho Rinconado	226	37.18 N	122.01 W
Rancho Santa Fe	228	33.01 N	117.12 W
Rancho Veloz	240p	22.53 N	80.23 W
Ranchuelo	240p	22.23 N	80.09 W
Ranco, Lago ⊜	254	40.14 S	72.24 W
Rancocas	208	40.00 N	74.52 W
Rancocas Creek ≏	285	40.02 N	74.59 W
Rancocas Creek, North Branch ≏	208	40.00 N	74.52 W
Rancocas Creek, South Branch ≏	208	40.00 N	74.52 W
Rancocas Creek, Southwest Branch ≏	285	39.57 N	74.48 W
Rancocas Heights	285	39.59 N	74.51 W
Rancocas State Park ♠	285	40.00 N	74.50 W
Rancocas Woods	285	39.59 N	74.51 W
Rancul	252	35.03 S	64.42 W
Rand	166	35.36 S	146.35 E
Rand (Germiston) Airport ⊠	273d	26.15 S	28.09 E
Randa	58	46.07 N	7.47 E
Randall Lake ⊜	216	41.57 N	85.02 W
Randall Park Mall ◆[9]	279a	41.26 N	81.32 W
Randalls Island I	276	40.48 N	73.55 W
Randallstown	284b	39.22 N	76.48 W
Randalstown	48	54.45 N	6.19 W
Randan	32	46.01 N	3.21 E
Rāndaveswar	126	23.43 N	87.17 E
Randazzo	70	37.53 N	14.57 E
Randbøl	41	55.42 N	9.16 E
Randburg	273d	26.06 S	27.59 E
Randers	26	56.28 N	10.03 E
Randfontein	158	26.11 S	27.42 E
Randfontein □[5]	273d	26.13 S	27.40 E
Randgate	273d	26.11 S	27.41 E
Randhurst ◆[9]	278	42.05 N	87.56 W
Randle	224	46.32 N	121.57 W
Randleman	192	35.49 N	79.48 W
Randlett	196	34.10 N	98.27 W
Randolph, Az., U.S.	200	32.55 N	111.30 W
Randolph, Me., U.S.	188	44.13 N	69.46 W
Randolph, Ma., U.S.	207	42.09 N	71.02 W
Randolph, Ne., U.S.	198	42.22 N	97.21 W
Randolph, N.Y., U.S.	210	42.09 N	78.58 W
Randolph, Oh., U.S.	214	41.01 N	81.14 W
Randolph, Ut,. U.S.	200	41.39 N	111.10 W
Randolph, Vt., U.S.	188	43.55 N	72.39 W
Randolph, Wi., U.S.	190	43.32 N	89.00 W
Randolph □[6], In., U.S.	218	40.10 N	85.00 W
Randolph □[6], Mo., U.S.	219	39.22 N	92.20 W
Randolph Air Force Base ■	196	29.32 N	98.16 W
Randolph Hills	284c	39.03 N	77.05 W
Randolph Village	284c	38.53 N	76.52 W
Random Island I	186	48.08 N	53.45 W
Random Lake	190	43.33 N	87.57 W
Randow ≏	54	53.41 N	14.04 E
Randowaya	164	1.52 S	136.31 E
Randowbruch ≋	54	53.15 N	14.10 E
Randsburg	228	35.22 N	117.39 W
Randse Afrikaanse Universiteit ʊ[2]	273d	26.11 S	27.50 E
Randsfjorden ⊜	26	60.25 N	10.24 E
Rand Stadium ♠	273d	26.14 S	28.03 E
Randublatung	115a	7.12 S	111.23 E
Randudongkal	115a	7.06 S	109.19 E
Randwick	170	33.55 S	151.15 E
Randwick Racecourse ♠	274a	33.54 S	151.14 E
Råneå	26	65.52 N	22.18 E
Ranelagh	258	34.48 S	58.12 W
Rāner	123	28.53 N	73.17 E
Ranérou	150	15.18 N	13.58 W
Rāneswar	126	24.02 N	87.25 E
Raneue	114	5.03 N	95.20 E
Ranford	168a	32.48 S	116.31 E
Ranfurly, N.Z.	172	45.08 S	170.06 E
Ranfurly, Scot., U.K.	46	55.52 N	4.33 W
Rangae	114	6.17 N	101.44 E
Rāngāmāti	120	22.38 N	92.12 E
Rangantemiang	112	0.35 S	113.19 E
Rangas, Tanjung ›	112	2.38 S	118.49 E
Rangasa, Tanjung ›	112	3.33 S	118.56 E
Rangaunu Bay ⊂	172	34.50 S	173.15 E
Range Creek ≏	200	39.18 N	110.04 W
Range Indian Reserve ◆[4]	182	49.09 N	119.50 W
Rangeley	188	44.57 N	70.38 W
Rangely	200	40.05 N	108.48 W
Ranger	196	32.28 N	98.40 W
Ranger Lake ⊜	190	46.54 N	83.35 W
Rangersdorf	64	46.51 N	12.58 E
Ranghe	100	33.43 N	112.51 E
Rangia	120	26.28 N	91.38 E
Rangiora	172	43.18 S	172.36 E
Rangitaiki ≏	172	37.54 S	176.53 E
Rangitata ≏	172	44.12 S	171.30 E
Rangitikei ≏	172	40.18 S	175.14 E
Rangitukia	172	37.46 S	178.27 E
Rangkasbitung	115a	6.21 S	106.15 E
Rangkul'	85	38.29 N	74.22 E
Rangoon ≏	110	16.29 N	96.21 E
Rangoon → Yangon	110	16.47 N	96.10 E
Rangpo	124	27.11 N	88.32 E
Rangpur, Bngl.	124	25.45 N	89.15 E
Rangpur, Pāk.	123	30.31 N	71.34 E
Rangpuri ⊥	272a	28.33 N	77.08 E
Rangsang, Pulau I	114	1.00 N	102.55 E
Rangsdorf	54	52.17 N	13.25 E
Rangsdorfer See ⊜	264a	52.17 N	13.24 E
Ranguana Cay I	236	16.20 N	88.09 W
Ranguana Entrance ʮ	236	16.19 N	88.09 W
Rangun → Yangon	110	16.47 N	96.10 E
Ranholas	266c	38.47 N	9.22 W
Rānībāndh	126	22.52 N	86.47 E
Rānībennur	122	14.37 N	75.37 E
Rānīganj	126	23.37 N	87.08 E
Rānikhet	124	29.39 N	79.25 E
Ranino	80	52.58 N	40.15 E
Ranis	54	50.39 N	11.34 E
Rānīwāra	120	24.45 N	72.13 E
Rāniyah	128	36.15 N	44.53 E
Rankamhaeng National Park ♠	110	17.10 N	99.58 E
Ranken ≏	166	20.31 S	137.36 E
Ranken Store	166	19.35 S	136.55 E
Rankin, Il., U.S.	216	40.27 N	87.53 W
Rankin, Mi., U.S.	216	42.55 N	83.46 W
Rankin, Pa., U.S.	279b	40.24 N	79.52 W
Rankin, Tx., U.S.	196	31.13 N	101.56 W
Rankin Inlet	176	62.45 N	92.10 W
Rankins Springs	166	33.50 S	146.16 E
Rankūs	132	33.45 N	36.23 E
Rankweil	58	47.17 N	9.39 E
Ranlo	192	35.17 N	81.07 W
Ranneje	80	51.29 N	52.37 E
Rannersdorf	264b	48.08 N	16.28 E
Rannoch, Loch ⊜	46	56.41 N	4.20 W
Rannoch Moor ◆[3]	46	56.38 N	4.40 W
Rann of Kutch → Kutch, Rann of ◆[1]	120	24.05 N	70.10 E
Ranobe ≏	157b	17.10 S	44.08 E
Ranohira	157b	22.29 S	45.24 E
Ranomafana, Madag.	157b	18.57 S	48.50 E
Ranomafana, Madag.	157b	24.36 S	46.58 E
Ranomena	157b	23.25 S	47.17 E
Ranong	110	9.58 N	98.38 E
Ranongga Island I	175e	8.05 S	156.34 E
Ranopiso	157b	25.03 S	46.40 E
Ranot	110	7.46 N	100.19 E
Ranotsara Nord	157b	22.48 S	46.36 E
Rānsai	272c	18.53 N	73.05 E
Ransäter	40	59.46 N	13.26 E
Ransiki	164	1.30 S	134.10 E
Ransom, Il., U.S.	216	41.09 N	88.39 W
Ransom, Ks., U.S.	198	38.38 N	99.56 W
Ransom, Pa., U.S.	210	41.24 N	75.50 W
Ransom Creek ≏	284a	43.04 N	78.45 W
Ransomville	210	43.14 N	78.54 W
Ranson	188	39.17 N	77.51 W
Ransta	40	59.48 N	16.38 E
Ranstadt	56	50.21 N	8.59 E
Rantabe	157b	15.42 S	49.39 E
Rantasalmi	26	62.04 N	28.18 E
Rantau, Indon.	112	2.56 S	115.09 E
Rantau, Malay.	114	2.35 N	101.58 E
Rantaukampar	114	1.24 N	100.59 E
Rantaupanjang, Indon.	112	1.51 S	102.19 E
Rantaupanjang, Indon.	112	1.16 S	101.49 E
Rantaupanjang, Indon.	114	0.58 N	99.13 E
Rantauprapat	114	2.06 N	99.50 E
Rantekombola, Bulu ∧	112	3.21 S	120.01 E
Ranten	61	47.09 N	14.05 E
Rantepao	112	2.59 S	119.54 E
Rantigny	50	49.20 N	2.26 E
Rantoul	216	40.09 N	88.20 W
Rantsila	26	64.31 N	25.39 E
Rantzau	54	54.15 N	10.30 E
Ranua	26	65.55 N	26.32 E
Rānvād	272c	18.53 N	72.55 E
Ranwanalenaus	156	19.35 S	22.47 E
Råö	26	57.24 N	11.56 E
Rao'er	100	28.48 N	117.40 E
Raohe	89	46.47 N	134.00 E
Raon-L'Étape	58	48.24 N	6.51 E
Raon-sur-Plaine	58	48.31 N	7.06 E
Raoping	100	23.43 N	117.01 E
Raoui, 'Erg er ◆[2]	148	29.17 N	2.20 W
Raoul	192	34.27 N	83.36 W
Raoul Island I	14	29.16 S	177.54 W
Raoyang	98	38.16 N	115.44 E
Raoyang ≏	104	41.50 N	122.35 E
Raoyanghe	104	41.46 N	122.26 E
Rapa I	14	27.36 S	144.20 W
Rapa, Ponta do ›	252	27.22 S	48.26 W
Rapallo	62	44.21 N	9.14 E
Rapang	112	3.50 S	119.48 E
Rāpar	120	23.34 N	70.38 E
Raparo, Monte ∧	68	40.12 N	15.59 E
Rapatovo	80	55.04 N	54.37 E
Rāpch ≏	128	25.28 N	59.21 E
Rapel ≏	252	33.55 S	71.51 W
Rapel, Embalse ⊜[1]	252	34.12 S	71.30 W
Rapelli	252	26.24 S	64.29 W
Raphoe	48	54.52 N	7.36 W
Rapid ≏, Mi., U.S.	190	45.55 N	86.58 W
Rapid ≏, Mn., U.S.	198	48.42 N	94.26 W
Rapid ≏, Wa., U.S.	224	47.48 N	121.18 W
Rapidan ≏	188	38.22 N	77.37 W
Rapid Bay	168b	35.32 S	138.12 E
Rapid City, Mb., Can.	184	50.08 N	100.02 W
Rapid City, Mi., U.S.	190	44.50 N	85.16 W
Rapid City, S.D., U.S.	198	44.04 N	103.13 W
Rapid Creek ≏	198	43.54 N	102.37 W
Rapide Taureau, Barrage du ◆[6]	206	46.52 N	73.39 W
Rapid River	190	45.55 N	86.58 W
Räpina	76	58.06 N	27.27 E
Rapkan	85	40.22 N	70.40 E
Rapla	76	59.01 N	24.47 E
Rapness	46	59.14 N	2.51 W
Rapolano Terme	66	43.17 N	11.36 E
Rapolla	68	40.58 N	15.41 E
Rapone	68	40.51 N	15.30 E
Raposo ∧[2]	266c	38.40 N	9.11 W
Rappahannock ≏	208	37.34 N	76.18 W
Rappbodestausee ⊜[1]	54	51.09 N	10.58 E
Rappenlochschlucht ʟ	58	47.23 N	9.47 E
Rappottenstein	61	48.31 N	15.05 E
Rāptī □[8]	124	28.15 N	82.30 E
Rāpti (Raptī) ≏, Asia	124	26.18 N	83.41 E
Rāptī ≏, Nepāl	124	27.33 N	84.07 E
Rapulo ≏	248	13.43 S	65.32 W
Rapu-Rapu	116	13.11 N	124.08 E
Rapu Rapu Island I	116	13.12 N	124.09 E
Raqabah, Khashm ar- ∧[2]	142	28.18 N	31.43 E
Raquette ≏	206	45.00 N	74.42 W
Raraka I[1]	14	16.10 S	144.54 W
Rara National Park ♠	124	29.35 N	82.05 E
Rārh Plains ≚	126	23.13 N	87.20 E
Rāribahāl	126	24.05 N	87.21 E
Raritan	210	40.34 N	74.38 W
Raritan ≏	208	40.29 N	74.17 W
Raritan, North Branch ≏	210	40.33 N	74.41 W
Raritan, South Branch ≏	210	40.33 N	74.41 W
Raritan Bay ⊂	208	40.28 N	74.12 W
Raroïa I	14	16.01 S	142.27 W
Raron	58	46.19 N	7.48 E
Rarotonga I	174k	21.14 S	159.46 W
Rarotonga International Airport ⊠	174k	21.12 S	159.49 W
Rarz	85	39.23 N	68.44 E
Rasa, Ilha I	287a	23.04 S	43.09 W
Rasa, Punta ›, Arg.	252	36.17 S	56.47 W
Rasa, Punta ›, Arg.	254	40.51 S	62.19 W
Rašaant	88	49.07 N	101.25 E
Rasa de Guaratiba, Ilha I	256	23.05 S	43.34 W
Rasa Island I	116	9.14 N	118.27 E
Ra's al-'Ayn	130	36.51 N	40.04 E
Ra's al-Barr	142	31.31 N	31.50 E
Ra's al-Khalīj	142	31.15 N	31.39 E
Ra's al-Khaymah	128	25.47 N	55.57 E
Ra's al-Unūf	146	30.31 N	18.34 E
Ra's al-Ushsh ◆[8]	142	31.08 N	32.18 E
Ra's an-Naqb, Miṣr	132	29.36 N	34.51 E
Ra's an-Naqb, Urd.	132	30.00 N	35.29 E
Rasawi	164	2.04 S	134.01 E
Ra's Ba'labakk	130	34.15 N	36.25 E
Rasbo	40	59.57 N	17.53 E
Raschau	54	50.32 N	12.50 E
Ras Dashen Terara ∧	144	13.16 N	38.24 E
Rasdorf	56	50.43 N	9.53 E
Raseborg	26	59.59 N	23.39 E
Raseiniai	76	55.24 N	23.07 E
Râs el Aïoun	36	35.30 N	8.18 E
Ras el Ma, Alg.	148	34.31 N	0.46 W
Râs el Mâ, Mali	150	16.37 N	4.28 W
Ras el Oued	34	35.57 N	5.03 E
Rasen-Antholz → Anterselva di Sopra	64	46.52 N	12.08 E
Raševka	78	50.14 N	33.54 E
Rashād	140	11.51 N	31.04 E
Rāshayyā	132	33.30 N	35.51 E
Rashīd (Rosetta)	142	31.24 N	30.25 E
Rashīd, Far' (Rosetta Branch) ≏	142	31.30 N	30.21 E
Rashīd, Maṣabb (Rosetta Mouth) ≏[1]	142	31.30 N	30.20 E
Rashīd Qal'eh	120	31.31 N	67.31 E
Rashin → Najin	98	42.15 N	130.18 E
Rasht	128	37.16 N	49.36 E
Rashtrapati Bhawan ʊ	272a	28.37 N	77.12 E
Rasina ≏	38	43.37 N	21.22 E
Rāsipuram	122	11.28 N	78.10 E
Rasi Salai	110	15.20 N	104.09 E
Rāsk	128	26.13 N	61.25 E
Raška	38	43.17 N	20.37 E
Rask Mølle	41	55.52 N	9.37 E
Rās Koh ∧	128	28.50 N	65.12 E
Raškov	78	47.57 N	28.50 E
Raskunda	126	22.48 N	87.26 E
Rasm al-Arwām, Sabkhat ⊜	130	35.53 N	37.40 E
R'asna	76	54.01 N	31.12 E
R'asnopol'	78	47.04 N	31.12 E
Raso, Cabo ›	266c	38.43 N	9.29 W
Raso, Ilhéu I	150a	16.37 N	24.36 W
Rasocolmo, Capo ›	70	38.18 N	15.31 E
Rason Lake ⊜	162	28.46 S	124.20 E
Raspberry Peak ∧	194	34.23 N	94.01 W
Raspopinskaja	80	49.24 N	42.52 E
Rasra	124	25.51 N	83.51 E
Rass Jebel	36	37.13 N	10.09 E
Rasskazovka	265b	55.38 N	37.20 E
Rasskazovo	80	52.40 N	41.53 E
Rassua, ostrov I	74	47.45 N	153.01 E
Rassudovo	82	55.29 N	36.54 E
Rassvet, Ross.	84	43.58 N	46.44 E
Rassvet, Ross.	84	43.58 N	46.44 E
Rassvet, Ross.	86	57.02 N	91.34 E
Rassvet, Ross.	88	57.02 N	91.34 E
Rassypnaja	80	51.35 N	53.37 E
Rassypnoje	83	48.08 N	38.34 E
Rast	38	43.53 N	23.17 E
Rastälven ≏	40	59.37 N	14.56 E
Ra's Tannūrah	128	26.42 N	50.06 E
Rastatt	56	48.51 N	8.12 E
Rastavica ≏	78	49.44 N	30.01 E
Rastede	52	53.15 N	8.11 E
Rastegai'sa ∧	24	70.00 N	26.18 E
Rastenberg	54	51.10 N	11.25 E
Rastenburg → Kętrzyn	30	54.06 N	21.23 E
Rastorf	54	54.16 N	10.19 E
Rastorgujevo	82	55.33 N	37.41 E
Rastovcy	82	56.39 N	37.35 E
Rastunovo	82	55.16 N	37.50 E
Rasu, Monte ∧	71	40.25 N	9.00 E
Rasūl	123	32.42 N	73.34 E
Rasūlnagar	123	32.20 N	73.47 E
Rasulpur	272a	28.37 N	77.22 E
Rasulpur ◆[8]	272a	28.42 N	77.01 E
Rasun di sopra	64	46.48 N	12.03 E
Rasun di sotto	64	46.47 N	12.02 E
Rasura	58	46.06 N	9.33 E
Råsvalen ⊜	40	59.40 N	15.10 E
Răsvani	38	44.25 N	26.53 E
Rat ≏, Mb., Can.	184	55.41 N	99.04 W
Rat ≏, Mb., Can.	184	49.35 N	97.08 W
Ratahan	112	1.04 N	124.48 E
Ratak Chain II	14	9.00 N	171.00 E
Ratangarh	120	28.05 N	74.36 E
Ratanpur, India	126	23.07 N	87.04 E
Ratanpur, India	272b	22.50 N	88.14 E
Rätansbyn	26	62.29 N	14.32 E
Rat Burana	269a	13.41 N	100.30 E
Ratčino, Ross.	80	53.02 N	39.55 E
Ratčino, Ross.	82	55.16 N	38.39 E
Ratcliff	222	31.24 N	95.08 W
Rateče	64	46.30 N	13.43 E
Ratekau	54	53.57 N	10.44 E
Rāth	124	25.35 N	79.34 E
Rath ◆[8]	263	51.17 N	6.49 E
Rathangan	48	53.12 N	6.59 W
Rathbone	210	42.08 N	77.19 W
Rathbun Lake ⊜	212	44.47 N	78.12 W
Rathbun Lake ⊜[1]	190	40.54 N	93.05 W
Rathcoole	48	53.16 N	6.28 W
Rathcormack	48	52.05 N	8.17 W
Rathdowney, Austl.	171a	28.12 S	152.52 E
Rathdowney, Ire.	48	52.50 N	7.34 W
Rathdrum, Ire.	48	52.56 N	6.13 W
Rathdrum, Id., U.S.	202	47.48 N	116.53 W
Rathebur	54	53.44 N	13.46 E
Ratheim	52	51.04 N	6.10 E
Rathen	46	57.38 N	2.02 W
Rathenow	54	52.36 N	12.20 E
Rathfriland	48	54.14 N	6.10 W
Rathkeale	48	52.32 N	8.56 W
Rathlin Island I	48	55.18 N	6.13 W
Rathlin Sound ʮ	48	55.15 N	6.15 W
Ráth Luirc (Charleville)	48	52.21 N	8.41 W
Rathmecke	263	51.15 N	7.38 E
Rathmelton	48	55.02 N	7.38 W
Rathmore	48	52.03 N	9.13 W
Rathmullan	48	55.06 N	7.33 W
Rathnew	48	53.00 N	6.05 W
Ratho	46	55.55 N	3.22 W
Rathowen	48	53.40 N	7.31 W
Rathstock	54	52.31 N	14.32 E
Rathwell	184	49.40 N	98.32 W
Ratibor → Racibórz	30	50.06 N	18.13 E
Raticosa, Passo della)(	66	44.10 N	11.20 E
Rätikon ⋀	58	47.03 N	9.40 E
Ratingen	56	51.18 N	6.51 E
Ratisbon → Regensburg	60	49.01 N	12.06 E
Rätische Alpen → Rhaetian Alps ⋀	58	46.30 N	10.00 E
Rat Island I	181a	51.55 N	178.20 E
Rat Islands II	181a	51.40 N	178.30 E
Rat'kovo	82	56.01 N	38.38 E
Rat Lake ⊜	184	56.10 N	99.40 W
Ratlām	120	23.19 N	75.04 E
Ratmanova, ostrov I	180	65.46 N	169.02 W
Ratnāgiri	122	16.59 N	73.18 E
Ratnapura	122	6.41 N	80.24 E
Ratno	78	51.40 N	24.31 E
Ratodero	120	27.48 N	68.18 E
Ratomka	76	53.56 N	27.21 E
Raton	196	36.54 N	104.26 W
Raton Pass)(	196	36.59 N	104.29 W
Ratqah, Wādī ar- V	130	34.25 N	40.55 E
Ratt ≏	224	47.27 N	124.21 W
Rattanaburi	110	15.19 N	103.51 E
Rattaphum	110	7.08 N	100.16 E
Ratten	61	47.29 N	15.43 E
Rattlesnake	202	46.56 N	113.59 W
Rattlesnake Creek ≏, Ks., U.S.	198	38.13 N	98.22 W
Rattlesnake Creek ≏, Oh., U.S.	218	39.16 N	83.23 W
Rattlesnake Creek ≏, Or., U.S.	202	42.44 N	117.47 W
Rattlesnake Creek ≏, Wa., U.S.	224	46.45 N	120.55 W
Rattlesnake Creek ≏, Wa., U.S.	224	45.48 N	121.29 W
Rattlesnake Mountain ∧	207	41.42 N	72.50 W
Rattlesnake Peak ∧	280	34.16 N	117.47 W
Rattling Brook	186	49.38 N	56.10 W
Rattling Run ≏	279b	40.33 N	79.32 W
Rattray	46	56.35 N	3.19 W
Rattray Head ›	46	57.37 N	1.49 W
Rattu	123	35.08 N	74.48 E
Rättvik	26	60.53 N	15.06 E
Ratz, Mount ∧	180	57.23 N	132.19 W
Ratzeburg	54	53.42 N	10.46 E
Ratzeburger See ⊜	54	53.45 N	10.47 E
Rätzlingen	54	52.23 N	11.08 E
Rau	112	0.34 N	100.01 E
Raub, Malay.	114	3.48 N	101.52 E
Raub, In., U.S.	216	40.44 N	87.29 W
Raubsville	208	40.38 N	75.12 W
Rauch	252	36.46 S	59.06 W
Raucheck ∧	64	47.30 N	13.14 E
Rauchenwarth	264b	48.05 N	16.32 E
Rauchtown	210	41.07 N	77.14 W
Raucourt-et-Flaba	56	49.36 N	4.57 E
Rauen	54	52.20 N	14.01 E
Rauenstein	54	50.24 N	11.03 E
Raufarhöfn	24a	66.30 N	15.57 W
Raufoss	26	60.43 N	10.37 E
Rauhe Ebrach ≏	56	49.50 N	10.56 E
Raukumara Range ⋀	172	37.47 S	178.02 E
Raul Soares	255	20.05 S	42.22 W
Rauma	26	61.08 N	21.30 E
Rauma ≏	26	62.33 N	7.43 E
Raumünzach	56	48.38 N	8.21 E
Rauna	76	57.20 N	25.43 E
Raunds	42	52.21 N	0.33 W
Raung, Gunung ∧	115a	8.08 S	114.03 E
Raunheim	56	50.01 N	8.28 E
Raupal'an	180	65.28 N	171.59 W
Raurimu	172	39.07 S	175.24 E
Rauris	64	47.13 N	13.00 E
Raurkela	124	22.13 N	84.53 E
Rauschenberg	56	50.53 N	8.55 E
Rausu	92a	44.01 N	145.12 E
Rautalampi	26	62.38 N	26.50 E
Rāutara	272b	22.51 N	88.28 E
Rautavaara	26	63.29 N	28.18 E
Ravahere I[1]	14	18.14 S	142.09 W
Ravalgaon	122	20.38 N	74.25 E
Ravanica, Manastir ʊ[1]	38	43.58 N	21.26 E
Ravānsar	128	34.43 N	46.40 E
Ravanusa	70	37.16 N	13.58 E
Rāvar	128	31.15 N	56.53 E
Ravarano	64	44.35 N	10.04 E
Ravarino	64	44.44 N	11.06 E
Rava-Russkaja	78	50.14 N	23.37 E
Ravascletto	64	46.32 N	12.57 E
Ravat	85	39.54 N	70.12 E
Ravello	68	40.39 N	14.37 E
Ravelo	248	18.48 S	65.32 W
Raven	192	37.05 N	81.51 W
Ravena	210	42.28 N	73.49 W
Ravenglass	44	54.21 N	3.24 W
Raven Lake ⊜	212	45.13 N	78.51 W
Ravenna, It.	66	44.25 N	12.12 E
Ravenna, Ky., U.S.	192	37.41 N	83.57 W
Ravenna, Mi., U.S.	216	43.11 N	85.56 W
Ravenna, Ne., U.S.	198	41.01 N	98.54 W
Ravenna, Oh., U.S.	214	41.09 N	81.14 W
Ravenna □[4]	66	44.25 N	11.59 E
Ravensbourne	171a	27.22 S	152.10 E
Ravensbourne National Park ♠	171a	27.21 S	152.15 E
Ravensburg	58	47.47 N	9.37 E
Ravenscrag	184	49.30 N	109.05 W
Ravensdale	224	47.21 N	121.58 W
Ravenshoe	166	17.37 S	145.29 E
Ravensthorpe, Austl.	162	33.35 S	120.02 E
Ravensthorpe, Eng., U.K.	44	53.42 N	1.35 W
Ravenswood, S. Afr.	273d	26.11 S	28.15 E
Ravenswood, Mi., U.S.	216	42.45 N	84.36 W
Ravenswood, W.V., U.S.	188	38.56 N	81.45 W
Ravenswood Park ♠	283	42.36 N	70.42 W
Ravenswood Point ›	282	37.30 N	122.08 W
Ravensworth	284c	38.48 N	77.13 W
Rāver	120	21.15 N	76.02 E
Ravernet ≏	48	54.30 N	6.04 W
Rāvi ≏	123	30.35 N	71.49 E
Ravières	50	47.45 N	4.17 E
Ravine	208	40.34 N	76.24 W
Ravine Lake ⊜[1]	276	40.43 N	74.38 W
Ravinia Park ♠	278	42.09 N	87.46 W
Ravna Gora	36	45.23 N	14.57 E
Ravne	61	46.33 N	14.58 E
Ravnina	128	37.57 N	62.40 E
Ravsted	41	55.01 N	9.08 E
Rāwah	128	34.28 N	41.55 E
Rawaki I[1]	14	3.43 S	170.43 W
Rāwala Kot	123	33.52 N	73.46 E
Rāwalpindi	123	33.36 N	73.04 E
Rawa Mazowiecka	30	51.46 N	20.16 E
Rāwāndūz	128	36.37 N	44.31 E
Rawang	114	3.19 N	101.35 E
Rawas ≏	112	2.42 S	103.24 E
Rāwatsar	123	29.17 N	74.23 E
Rawāwiṣ, Wādī V	146	30.26 N	15.24 E
Rawḍah ⊜	130	35.15 N	41.05 E
Rawḍah, Wādī ar- V	130	34.22 N	37.21 E
Rawd al-Faraj ◆[8]	273c	30.05 N	31.14 E
Rawḍaw, Jazīrat ar- I	273c	30.01 N	31.13 E
Rawdon	206	46.03 N	73.43 W
Rawene	172	35.24 S	173.30 E
Rawḥah	144	19.28 N	41.48 E
Rawhide Creek ≏	198	42.06 N	104.20 W
Rawhide Lake ⊜	190	46.39 N	82.37 W
Rawhide Mountain ∧	204	38.17 N	116.25 W
Rawi	112	2.07 S	113.56 E
Rawi, Ko I	114	6.33 N	99.14 E
Rawicz	30	51.37 N	16.52 E
Rawlinna	162	31.01 S	125.20 E
Rawlins	200	41.47 N	107.14 W
Rawlinson, Mount ∧	162	25.58 S	127.28 E
Rawlinson Range ⋀	162	24.51 S	128.00 E
Rawmarsh	44	53.27 N	1.21 W
Rawreth	260	51.37 N	0.35 E
Rawson, Arg.	252	34.36 S	60.04 W
Rawson, Arg.	254	43.18 S	65.06 W
Rawson, Oh., U.S.	216	40.57 N	83.47 W
Rawsonville	158	33.41 S	19.20 E
Rawtenstall	44	53.42 N	2.18 W
Rawu	102	29.30 N	96.45 E
Rax ⋀	61	47.42 N	15.43 E
Raxāul	124	26.59 N	84.51 E
Ray, Il., U.S.	219	40.12 N	90.29 W
Ray, In., U.S.	216	41.45 N	84.53 W
Ray, N.D., U.S.	198	48.20 N	103.09 W
Ray ≏	42	51.48 N	1.15 W
Ray, Cape ›	186	47.40 N	59.18 W
Raya	112	1.05 N	118.32 E
Raya, Bukit ∧	112	0.40 S	112.41 E
Raya, Gunong ∧	114	6.22 N	99.49 E
Raya, Pulau I	114	4.52 N	95.22 E
Rāyachoti	122	14.03 N	78.45 E
Rāyadurg	122	14.42 N	76.52 E
Rāyagarha	122	19.10 N	83.25 E
Rayburn	222	30.25 N	94.56 W
Rayen, Dtsch.	263	51.28 N	6.32 E
Rāyen, Īrān	128	29.34 N	57.26 E
Ray Hubbard, Lake ⊜[1]	222	32.53 N	96.35 W
Rāyikhah I	128	26.12 N	36.21 E
Rayland	214	40.11 N	80.41 W
Rayleigh	42	51.36 N	0.36 E
Raymond, Ab., Can.	182	49.27 N	112.39 W
Raymond, Ca., U.S.	226	37.13 N	119.54 W
Raymond, Il., U.S.	219	39.19 N	89.34 W
Raymond, Mn., U.S.	198	45.00 N	95.14 W
Raymond, Ms., U.S.	194	32.15 N	90.25 W
Raymond, Oh., U.S.	216	40.20 N	83.28 W
Raymond, Wa., U.S.	224	46.41 N	123.43 W
Raymond Terrace	170	32.46 S	151.44 E
Raymondville	196	26.29 N	97.47 W
Raymore	184	51.25 N	104.31 W
Ray Mountains ⋀	180	65.45 N	151.30 W
Rāyna	126	23.05 N	87.54 E
Rayne	194	30.14 N	92.16 W
Raynham	207	41.56 N	71.04 W
Raynham Dog Track ♠	283	41.59 N	71.04 W
Rayón, Méx.	232	29.43 N	110.35 W
Rayón, Méx.	234	17.12 N	93.00 W
Rayón, Méx.	234	21.51 N	99.40 W
Rayones	232	25.01 N	100.05 W
Rayong	110	12.40 N	101.17 E
Rāypur	272b	22.25 N	88.31 E
Rayrah ⫪[4]	140	15.21 N	34.41 E
Rayse Creek ≏	219	38.13 N	89.00 W
Raystown Lake ⊜[1]	214	40.20 N	78.05 W
Rayton	158	25.45 S	28.32 E
Raytown	194	39.00 N	94.27 W
Rayville	194	32.28 N	91.45 W
Raywood	222	30.02 N	94.40 W
Raz, Pointe du ›	32	48.02 N	4.44 W
Raza, Punta ›	234	21.02 N	105.20 W
Razan, Īrān	128	35.23 N	49.02 E
R'azan', Ross.	80	54.38 N	39.44 E
R'azan □[8]	82	54.15 N	39.00 E
R'azancevo	82	56.42 N	39.12 E
Ražanj	38	43.40 N	21.33 E
R'azanovo	82	55.29 N	37.31 E
Razbegaj	265a	59.47 N	29.56 E
Războeni	38	47.05 N	26.32 E
Razdan	84	40.30 N	44.46 E
Razdan ≏	84	39.58 N	44.27 E
Razdel'naja	78	46.51 N	30.05 E
Razdolinsk	86	58.25 N	94.38 E
Razdolje	88	52.27 N	103.13 E
Razdol'noje, Ross.	89	43.30 N	131.52 E
Razdol'noje, Ukr.	78	45.47 N	33.29 E
Razdol'noje, Ukr.	83	47.37 N	38.01 E
Razdol'nyj	80	46.38 N	42.57 E
Razdorskaja	78	47.33 N	40.38 E
Razdory, Ross.	265b	55.45 N	37.18 E
Razdory, Ukr.	78	48.21 N	35.42 E
R'aženoje	83	47.31 N	38.52 E
Raževo	86	56.09 N	68.25 E
Razgrad	38	43.32 N	26.31 E
Razim, Lacul ⊜	38	44.54 N	28.57 E
Razlog	38	41.53 N	23.28 E
Razmachnino	88	51.47 N	115.28 E
Razmitelevo	265a	59.54 N	30.41 E
Raznočinovka	80	46.37 N	47.57 E
Raznomojka	86	52.29 N	55.52 E
Razorback Mountain ∧	182	51.35 N	124.42 W
R'ažsk	80	53.43 N	40.04 E
Razvil'noje	80	46.14 N	41.18 E
Razzoli, Isola I	71	41.18 N	9.21 E
Ré, Île de I	32	46.12 N	1.25 W
Rea ≏	42	52.18 N	2.32 W
Read	262	53.49 N	2.21 W
Reading, Eng., U.K.	42	51.28 N	0.59 W
Reading, Il., U.S.	216	41.05 N	88.51 W
Reading, Ks., U.S.	198	38.31 N	95.57 W
Reading, Ma., U.S.	207	42.31 N	71.05 W
Reading, Mi., U.S.	216	41.50 N	84.44 W
Reading, Oh., U.S.	218	39.13 N	84.26 W
Reading, Pa., U.S.	208	40.20 N	75.55 W
Reading Center	210	42.26 N	76.56 W
Reading Station ◆[5]	285	39.57 N	75.10 W
Readington	210	40.34 N	74.44 W
Readlyn	190	42.42 N	92.13 W
Readsboro	207	42.46 N	72.56 W
Readstown	190	43.26 N	90.45 W
Reagan	222	31.13 N	96.47 W
Real	116	14.40 N	121.36 E
Real ≏	250	11.27 S	37.22 W
Real, Cordillera ⋀	248	19.00 S	66.30 W
Real, Estero ≏	236	12.55 N	87.23 W
Real del Padre	252	34.50 S	67.46 W
Real de San Carlos	258	34.26 S	57.53 W
Realengo ◆[8]	256	22.53 S	43.25 W
Real Felipe, Museo Histórico del ⊥	286d	12.04 S	77.09 W
Realicó	252	35.02 S	64.15 W
Realitos	196	27.27 N	98.32 W
Realmonte	70	37.18 N	13.28 E
Reamstown	208	40.12 N	76.07 W
Reana del Roiale	64	46.12 N	13.13 E
Reardan	202	47.40 N	117.52 W
Reata	232	26.08 N	101.05 W
Reatini, Monti ⋀	66	42.28 N	13.00 E
Réau	261	48.37 N	2.38 E
Reay	46	58.33 N	3.47 W
Reay Forest ◆[3]	46	58.19 N	4.47 W
Rebecca, Lake ⊜	162	29.53 S	122.10 E
Rebecq-Rognon	50	50.40 N	4.08 E
Rebeida, Wādī V	140	20.45 N	34.06 E
Rebel Hill	285	40.04 N	75.20 W
Rebersburg	210	40.57 N	77.27 W
Rebi	164	6.23 S	134.06 E
Rebiana Sand Sea → Rabyānah, Ṣaḥrā' ◆[2]	146	24.20 N	20.37 E
Rebild Bakker ♠	26	56.50 N	9.51 E
Reboly	24	63.50 N	30.47 E
Rebouças	252	25.36 S	50.42 W
Reboucas, Túnel ◆[5]	287a	22.56 S	43.14 W
Rebricha	86	53.05 N	82.20 E
Rebun-tō I	92a	45.23 N	141.02 E
Recalde	252	36.39 S	61.05 W
Recanati	66	43.24 N	13.32 E
Rečane	76	56.25 N	31.39 E
Recco	62	44.22 N	9.09 E
Recey-sur-Ource	58	47.47 N	4.52 E
Rēchah Lām	120	34.58 N	70.51 E
Rechberghausen	56	48.44 N	9.38 E
Recherche, Archipelago of the II	162	34.05 S	122.45 E
Recherche, Cape ›	175e	10.11 S	161.19 E
Réchicourt-le-Château	58	48.40 N	6.51 E
Rechlin	54	53.21 N	12.43 E
Rechna Doāb ⋀[1]	123	31.35 N	73.30 E
Rechnitz	61	47.18 N	16.27 E
Rečica, Bela.	76	52.22 N	30.25 E
Rečica, Bela.	78	51.52 N	26.48 E
Recife	250	8.03 S	34.54 W
Recife, Kaap ›	158	34.02 S	25.44 E
Recinto	252	36.48 S	71.44 W
Recke	52	52.22 N	7.43 E
Rečki	78	51.07 N	34.30 E
Recklinghausen	52	51.36 N	7.13 E
Recknitz ≏	54	54.14 N	12.28 E
Recoaro Terme	64	45.42 N	11.13 E
Recogne	56	49.55 N	5.22 E
Recoleta	286e	33.23 S	70.38 W
Recologne	58	47.16 N	5.50 E
Reconquista	252	29.09 S	59.39 W
Reconquista, Río de la ≏	288	34.25 S	58.35 W
Recovery Glacier ⍓	9	81.10 S	28.00 W
Recreio	255	21.32 S	42.28 W
Recreo	252	29.16 S	65.04 W
Rector	194	36.15 N	90.17 W
Rectorville	218	38.34 N	83.39 W
Recuay	248	9.43 S	77.28 W
Recz	30	53.16 N	15.33 E
Red (Hong) (Yuan) ≏, Asia	110	20.17 N	106.34 E
Red ≏, N.A.	178	50.24 N	96.48 W
Red ≏, U.S.	178	31.00 N	91.40 W
Red ≏, U.S.	194	36.32 N	87.22 W
Red ≏, Ky., U.S.	192	37.51 N	84.05 W
Red ≏, N.M., U.S.	200	36.39 N	105.42 W
Red ≏, Wi., U.S.	190	44.49 N	88.38 W
Red, Elm Fork ≏	196	34.53 N	99.19 W
Red, North Fork ≏	196	34.24 N	99.14 W
Red, Prairie Dog Town Fork ≏	196	34.35 N	99.58 W
Red, Salt Fork ≏	196	34.27 N	99.22 W
Red, South Fork ≏	194	36.41 N	86.56 W
Red, West Fork ≏	194	36.32 N	87.21 W
Reda	30	54.37 N	18.21 E
Redang, Pulau I	114	5.47 N	103.00 E
Redange	56	49.46 N	5.54 E
Redang Panjang	114	5.07 N	100.47 E
Red Bank, N.J., U.S.	208	40.20 N	74.03 W
Red Bank, Tn., U.S.	194	35.07 N	85.17 W
Red Bank Battle Monument ⊥	285	39.52 N	75.11 W
Redbank Creek ≏	214	40.58 N	79.33 W
Red Banks	194	34.49 N	89.33 W
Red Bay, Nf., Can.	186	51.44 N	56.25 W
Red Bay, Al., U.S.	194	34.26 N	88.08 W
Redbay, Fl., U.S.	194	30.35 N	85.56 W
Red Bay ⊂	48	55.04 N	6.02 W
Redberry Lake ⊜	184	52.40 N	107.10 W
Redbird	214	41.48 N	81.06 W
Red Bluff	204	40.10 N	122.14 W
Red Bluff Reservoir ⊜[1]	196	31.57 N	103.56 W
Red Boiling Springs	194	36.31 N	85.50 W
Redbourn	42	51.48 N	0.24 W
Redbridge ◆[8]	42	51.34 N	0.05 E
Red Bud	219	38.12 N	89.59 W
Red Canyon V	198	43.18 N	103.49 W
Redcar	44	54.37 N	1.04 W
Red Cedar ≏, Mi., U.S.	216	42.43 N	84.33 W
Red Cedar ≏, Wi., U.S.	190	44.42 N	91.53 W
Red Cedar Lake ⊜	190	46.45 N	79.54 W
Red Clay Creek ≏	285	39.43 N	75.39 W
Red Clay Creek, East Branch ≏	285	39.49 N	75.42 W
Red Clay Creek, West Branch ≏	285	39.49 N	75.42 W
Redcliff, Ab., Can.	184	50.05 N	110.47 W
Red Cliff, Co., U.S.	200	39.31 N	106.22 W
Redcliff, Zimb.	154	19.02 S	29.50 E
Redcliffe	171a	27.14 S	153.07 E
Redcliffe, Mount ∧	162	28.25 S	121.32 E
Red Cliff Indian Reservation ◆[4]	190	46.50 N	90.47 W
Red Cliffs	166	34.19 S	142.11 E
Red Cloud	198	40.05 N	98.31 W
Red Creek	210	43.14 N	76.43 W
Red Creek ≏	194	30.41 N	88.40 W
Red Cross Lake ⊜	184	55.05 N	92.55 W
Red Deer	182	52.16 N	113.48 W
Red Deer ≏, Can.	176	50.56 N	109.54 W
Red Deer ≏, Can.	184	52.53 N	101.01 W
Red Deer Creek ≏	196	35.56 N	100.24 W
Red Deer Lake ⊜, Ab., Can.	182	52.43 N	113.02 W
Red Deer Lake ⊜, Mb., Can.	184	52.56 N	101.20 W
Reddersburg	158	29.38 S	26.07 E
Red Devil	180	61.46 N	157.18 W
Red Dial	44	54.48 N	3.10 W
Reddick	216	41.06 N	88.15 W
Redding, Ca., U.S.	204	40.35 N	122.23 W
Redding, Ct., U.S.	207	41.18 N	73.23 W
Redding Ridge	207	41.18 N	73.21 W
Reddish	262	53.26 N	2.09 W
Redditch	42	52.19 N	1.56 W
Rede ≏	44	55.08 N	2.13 W
Redefin	54	53.21 N	11.11 E
Redelinghuys	158	32.30 S	18.33 E
Redenção	250	4.13 S	38.43 W
Redenção da Serra	256	23.16 S	45.33 W
Redesdale V	44	55.17 N	2.16 W
Redes Mere ⊜	262	53.15 N	2.14 W
Redeye ≏	198	46.26 N	94.49 W
Redfield, Ia., U.S.	198	41.35 N	94.11 W
Redfield, N.Y., U.S.	212	43.32 N	75.49 W
Redfield, S.D., U.S.	198	44.52 N	98.31 W
Redfish Lake ⊜	202	44.07 N	114.56 W
Redford	196	29.47 N	104.10 W
Redford ◆[8]	281	42.25 N	83.16 W
Redford Township	216	42.25 N	83.16 W
Red Fox Forest	284c	38.49 N	77.15 W
Redhead	241r	10.47 N	60.57 W
Red Hill, Austl.	162	21.59 S	116.03 E
Redhill, Eng., U.K.	42	51.14 N	0.11 W
Red Hill, Ca., U.S.	280	33.45 N	117.48 W
Red Hill, Pa., U.S.	208	40.22 N	75.29 W
Red Hill ∧	172	41.38 S	173.04 E
Redhill Aerodrome ⊠	260	51.12 N	0.07 W
Red Hill Branch ≏	284b	39.14 N	76.51 W
Red Hook	210	41.59 N	73.52 W
Redhouse Creek ≏	284b	39.18 N	76.31 W
Rédics	61	46.36 N	16.30 E
Red Indian Lake ⊜	186	48.40 N	56.50 W
Redinger Lake ⊜[1]	226	37.09 N	119.26 W
Redington Beach	220	27.49 N	82.49 W
Redington Shores	220	27.50 N	82.50 W
Red Island I	186	47.23 N	54.11 W
Redja ≏	76	58.05 N	31.33 E
Redkey	216	40.21 N	85.09 W
Redkino	82	56.38 N	36.17 E
Red Lake, On., Can.	184	51.03 N	93.49 W
Redlake, Mn., U.S.	198	47.53 N	95.01 W
Red Lake ⊜, On., Can.	184	51.01 N	94.05 W

Symbol	English	Deutsch	Español	Français	Português
≏	River	Fluß	Río	Rivière	Rio
⩧	Canal	Kanal	Canal	Canal	Canal
ʟ	Waterfall, Rapids	Wasserfall, Stromschnellen	Cascada, Rápidos	Chute d'eau, Rapides	Cascata, Rápidos
ʮ	Strait	Meeresstraße	Estrecho	Détroit	Estreito
⊂	Bay, Gulf	Bucht, Golf	Bahía, Golfo	Baie, Golfe	Baía, Golfo
⊜	Lake, Lakes	See, Seen	Lago, Lagos	Lac, Lacs	Lago, Lagos
≋	Swamp	Sumpf	Pantano	Marais	Pântano
⍓	Ice Features, Glacier	Eis- und Gletscherformen	Accidentes Glaciales	Formes glaciaires	Acidentes glaciares
⫪	Other Hydrographic Features	Andere Hydrographische Objekte	Otros Elementos Hidrográficos	Autres données hydrographiques	Outros acidentes hidrográficos
◆	Submarine Features	Untermeerische Objekte	Accidentes Submarinos	Formes de relief sous-marin	Acidentes submarinos
□	Political Unit	Politische Einheit	Unidad Politica	Entité politique	Unidade política
ʊ	Cultural Institution	Kulturelle Institution	Institución Cultural	Institution culturelle	Instituição cultural
⊥	Historical Site	Historische Stätte	Sitio Histórico	Site historique	Sitio histórico
♠	Recreational Site	Erholungs- und Ferienort	Sitio de Recreo	Centre de loisirs	Area de Lazer
⊠	Airport	Flughafen	Aeropuerto	Aéroport	Aeroporto
■	Military Installation	Militäranlage	Instalación Militar	Installation militaire	Instalação militar
◆	Miscellaneous	Verschiedenes	Misceláneo	Divers	Diversos

ENGLISH — Name · Page · Lat.°′ · Long.°′ | DEUTSCH — Name · Seite · Breite°′ · Länge°′ E = Ost

Red Lake ⊜, Az., U.S. 200 35.40 N 114.04 W
Red Lake ⊜, S.D., U.S. 198 43.44 N 99.13 W
Red Lake ⊜[1] 222 31.40 N 95.58 W
Red Lake ≃ 198 47.55 N 97.01 W
Red Lake Falls 198 47.52 N 96.16 W
Red Lake Indian Reservation ⊸[4] 198 48.05 N 95.05 W
Red Lake Road 184 49.58 N 93.22 W
Redland, Scot., U.K. 46 59.05 N 3.05 W
Redland, Tx., U.S. 222 31.25 N 94.43 W
Redland Bay 171a 27.37 S 153.18 E
Redlands, S. Afr. 158 29.52 S 22.57 E
Redlands, Ca., U.S. 228 34.01 N 117.12 W
Redlands, Co., U.S. 200 39.04 N 108.38 W
Red Level 194 31.24 N 86.36 W
Red Lick 194 31.47 N 90.58 W
Redlin 54 53.22 N 12.01 E
Red Lion, Pa., U.S. 208 39.54 N 76.36 W
Red Lion, Pa., U.S. 285 39.53 N 75.41 W
Red Lion Airport ⊠ 285 39.54 N 74.45 W
Red Lodge 202 45.11 N 109.14 W
Red Mill 206 46.25 N 72.28 W
Redmond, Or., U.S. 202 44.16 N 121.10 W
Redmond, Ut., U.S. 200 39.00 N 111.51 W
Redmond, Wa., U.S. 224 47.40 N 122.07 W
Red Mountain 228 35.21 N 117.36 W
Red Mountain ∧, Ca., U.S. 204 41.35 N 123.06 W
Red Mountain ∧, Ca., U.S. 228 35.21 N 117.36 W
Red Mountain ∧, Mt., U.S. 202 47.07 N 112.44 W
Red Mountain Pass)(200 37.54 N 107.43 W
Rednitz ≃ 56 49.28 N 10.59 E
Red Oak, Ia., U.S. 198 41.00 N 95.13 W
Red Oak, Ok., U.S. 196 34.57 N 95.04 W
Red Oak, Tx., U.S. 222 32.31 N 96.48 W
Red Oak Creek ≃ 222 32.28 N 96.30 W
Red Oaks Mill 210 41.40 N 73.53 W
Redon 32 47.39 N 2.05 W
Redonda I 238 16.55 N 62.19 W
Redonda, Ilha I 256 23.04 S 43.12 W
Redonda, Isla I 241r 9.52 N 61.35 W
Redonda Islands II 182 50.13 N 124.48 W
Redondela 34 42.17 N 8.36 W
Redondo, Port. 34 38.39 N 7.33 W
Redondo, Wa., U.S. 224 47.20 N 122.19 W
Redondo, Mount ∧ 116 10.21 N 125.38 E
Redondo Beach 228 33.50 N 118.23 W
Redondo Beach State Park ♠ 280 33.50 N 118.24 W
Redoubt, Mount ∧ 224 48.57 N 121.18 W
Redoubt Volcano ∧[1] 180 60.29 N 152.45 W
Red Pass 182 52.59 N 118.59 W
Red Pheasant Indian Reserve ⊸[4] 184 52.30 N 108.07 W
Red Pine Lake ⊜ 212 45.12 N 78.42 W
Red Point › 170 34.29 S 150.55 E
Red Rock, B.C., Can. 182 53.39 N 122.41 W
Red Rock, On., Can. 190 48.58 N 88.15 W
Red Rock, Tx., U.S. 222 29.58 N 97.27 W
Red Rock I 282 37.56 N 122.26 W
Red Rock ≃ 202 44.59 N 112.52 W
Red Rock, Lake ⊜[1] 190 41.30 N 93.02 W
Red Rock Canyon State Park ♠ 228 35.23 N 118.00 W
Red Rock Creek ≃ 196 36.36 N 97.03 W
Red Rocks Point › 162 32.13 S 127.32 E
Red Root Creek ≃ 276 40.30 N 74.19 W
Red Run ≃, Md., U.S. 284b 39.24 N 76.47 W
Red Run ≃, Mi., U.S. 281 42.34 N 82.58 W
Redruth 42 50.13 N 5.14 W
Red Sea ⊤[2] 136 20.00 N 38.00 E
Red Springs 192 34.48 N 79.11 W
Redstone 182 52.08 N 123.42 W
Redstone ≃, N.T., Can. 180 64.17 N 124.33 W
Redstone ≃, On., Can. 190 48.27 N 81.03 W
Redstone Arsenal ■ 194 34.38 N 86.38 W
Redstone Creek ≃ 198 44.04 N 98.05 W
Redstone Lake ⊜ 212 45.11 N 78.32 W
Red Sucker ≃ 184 55.19 N 92.31 W
Red Sucker Lake ⊜ 184 54.09 N 93.40 W
Reduction 279b 40.11 N 79.46 W
Redut 80 47.22 N 51.53 E
Redvers 184 49.33 N 101.39 W
Redwater 182 53.57 N 113.06 W
Redwater ≃ 198 48.03 N 105.13 W
Red Wharf Bay ⊂ 44 53.18 N 4.10 W
Redwillow ≃ 182 55.04 N 119.21 W
Red Willow Creek ≃ 198 40.13 N 100.29 W
Red Wing 190 44.33 N 92.32 W
Redwood 212 44.18 N 75.48 W
Redwood ≃ 198 44.34 N 95.05 W
Redwood City 226 37.29 N 122.14 W
Redwood Creek ≃, Ca., U.S. 204 41.18 N 124.05 W
Redwood Creek ≃, Ca., U.S. 226 38.18 N 122.18 W
Redwood Creek ≃, Ca., U.S. 282 37.31 N 122.12 W
Redwood Creek ≃, Ca., U.S. 282 37.52 N 122.35 W
Redwood Estates 226 37.10 N 121.59 W
Redwood Falls 198 44.32 N 95.07 W
Redwood National Park ♠ 204 41.30 N 124.05 W
Redwood Point › 282 37.32 N 122.12 W
Redwood Regional Park ♠ 282 37.38 N 122.10 W
Redwood Terrace 282 37.19 N 122.18 W
Redwood Valley 204 39.15 N 123.12 W
Ree, Lough ⊜ 48 53.35 N 8.00 W
Reed City 190 43.52 N 85.30 W
Reeder 198 46.06 N 102.56 W
Reeders 210 41.01 N 75.20 W
Reed Lake ⊜, Mb., Can. 184 54.37 N 100.30 W
Reed Lake ⊜, Sk., Can. 184 50.24 N 107.05 W
Reedley 226 36.35 N 119.26 W
Reedsburg, Oh., U.S. 214 40.49 N 82.07 W
Reedsburg, Wi., U.S. 190 43.31 N 90.00 W
Reeds Peak ∧ 200 33.09 N 107.51 W
Reedsport 202 43.42 N 124.05 W
Reedsville, Pa., U.S. 208 40.39 N 77.35 W
Reedsville, Wi., U.S. 190 44.09 N 87.57 W
Reedurban 214 40.47 N 81.26 W
Reedville 208 37.50 N 76.16 W
Reedy Creek ≃ 220 28.04 N 81.21 W
Reedy Creek Swamp ⊞ 220 28.17 N 81.31 W
Reedy Lake ⊜ 220 27.44 N 81.22 W
Reefton 172 42.07 S 171.52 E
Reelfoot Lake ⊜ 194 36.25 N 89.22 W
Reepham 42 52.46 N 1.07 E
Reersø I[1] 41 55.31 N 11.06 E
Rees 52 51.45 N 6.23 E
Reese 190 43.27 N 83.41 W
Reese ≃ 204 40.39 N 116.54 W
Reese Air Force Base ■ 196 33.36 N 102.02 W
Reeseville 190 43.18 N 88.50 W
Reesville 218 39.29 N 83.41 W
Reetz 54 53.11 N 11.52 E
Refaa, Djebel ∧ 34 35.34 N 5.52 E
Refahiye 130 39.54 N 38.46 E
Reform 194 33.22 N 88.00 W
Reforma de Pineda 234 16.24 N 94.28 W
Refton 208 39.57 N 76.14 W
Refuge Cove 182 50.07 N 124.50 W
Refugio 196 28.18 N 97.16 W
Refugio, Isla I 254 43.58 S 73.12 W
Refugio Creek ≃ 282 38.01 N 122.17 W
Rega ≃ 30 54.10 N 15.18 E
Regaïa 34 35.38 N 5.46 W

Regalbuto 70 37.39 N 14.38 E
Regau 64 47.59 N 13.41 E
Regen 60 48.59 N 13.07 E
Regen ≃ 60 49.01 N 12.06 E
Regência 255 19.36 S 39.49 W
Regency Estates 284c 39.03 N 77.10 W
Regeneração 250 6.15 S 42.41 W
Regensburg 60 49.01 N 12.06 E
Regensdorf 58 47.26 N 8.28 E
Regenstauf 60 49.08 N 12.08 E
Regent, Austl. 274b 37.44 S 145.00 E
Regent, N.D., U.S. 198 46.25 N 102.33 W
Regent Park 284c 39.03 N 77.10 W
Regents Park 274a 33.53 S 151.02 E
Regents Park ⊸[8] 273d 26.15 S 28.04 E
Regent's Park ♠ 260 51.32 N 0.09 W
Regentville 274a 33.47 S 150.40 E
Reggâne 148 26.42 N 0.10 E
Regge ≃ 52 52.31 N 6.22 E
Reggello 66 43.41 N 11.32 E
Reggio di Calabria 68 38.07 N 15.39 E
Reggio di Calabria □[4] 68 38.10 N 16.00 E
Reggiolo 64 44.55 N 10.48 E
Reggio nell'Emilia 64 44.43 N 10.36 E
Reggio nell'Emilia □[4] 64 44.37 N 10.37 E
Regharen ⊜ 40 58.54 N 15.46 E
Reghin 38 46.47 N 24.42 E
Regina, Sk., Can. 184 50.25 N 104.39 W
Régina, Guy. fr. 250 4.19 N 52.08 W
Regina, S. Afr. 158 27.02 S 26.30 E
Regina Beach 184 50.47 N 105.00 W
Regina Elena, Canale ≍ 266b 45.41 N 8.39 E
Región Metropolitana □[4] 252 33.30 S 70.30 W
Regis-Breitingen 54 51.05 N 12.26 E
Registro 252 24.30 S 47.50 W
Registro do Araguaia 255 15.44 S 51.50 W
Regiwar 120 25.57 N 65.44 E
Regla ⊸[8] 286b 23.08 N 82.20 W
Regnéville 32 49.01 N 1.33 W
Regnitz ≃ 56 49.54 N 10.49 E
Rego Park ⊸[8] 276 40.44 N 73.52 W
Regozero 24 65.28 N 31.10 E
Regresso, Cachoeira do ∟ 250 0.58 S 54.51 W
Regstrup 41 55.40 N 11.37 E
Reguengos de Monsaraz 34 38.25 N 7.32 W
Reh 263 51.22 N 7.33 E
Rehau 54 50.15 N 12.02 E
Rehbach ≃ 56 49.27 N 8.27 E
Rehberg 54 52.43 N 12.10 E
Rehberge ⋏[2] 264a 52.35 N 13.11 E
Rehberge, Volkspark ♠ 264a 52.33 N 13.20 E
Rehburg 52 52.28 N 9.13 E
Rehden 52 52.37 N 8.29 E
Rehe 56 50.38 N 8.07 E
Rehefeld-Zaunhaus 54 50.43 N 13.42 E
Rehfelde 54 52.30 N 13.54 E
Rehli 124 23.38 N 79.05 E
Rehme 52 52.12 N 8.49 E
Rehna 54 53.47 N 11.03 E
Rehoboth, Namibia 156 17.53 S 15.04 E
Rehoboth, Namibia 156 23.18 S 17.03 E
Rehoboth □[5] 156 23.30 S 17.00 E
Rehoboth Bay ⊂ 208 38.40 N 75.06 W
Rehoboth Beach 208 38.43 N 75.04 W
Rehoboth Seamount ✦[3] 16 37.30 N 59.50 W
Réhon 56 49.30 N 5.45 E
Reḥovot 132 31.54 N 34.49 E
Rehti 124 22.44 N 77.26 E
Reiche Ebrach ≃ 56 49.49 N 10.58 E
Reiche Liesing ≃ 264b 48.08 N 16.16 E
Reichelsheim 56 49.43 N 8.50 E
Reichenau, Dtsch. 58 47.41 N 9.03 E
Reichenau, Schw. 58 46.49 N 9.24 E
Reichenau an der Rax 61 47.42 N 15.50 E
Reichenbach, Dtsch. 54 50.37 N 12.18 E
Reichenbach, Dtsch. 54 51.08 N 14.48 E
Reichenbach, Schw. 58 46.38 N 7.42 E
Reichenbach → Dzierżoniów 30 50.44 N 16.39 E
Reichenberg → Liberec 30 50.46 N 15.03 E
Reichenhofen 58 47.50 N 9.58 E
Reichensachsen 56 51.09 N 9.59 E
Reichen Spitze ∧ 64 47.09 N 12.07 E
Reichertshausen 60 48.28 N 11.31 E
Reichertsheim 60 48.12 N 12.17 E
Reichertshofen 60 48.40 N 11.28 E
Reichraming 61 47.53 N 14.27 E
Reichsbrücke ⊸[5] 264b 48.14 N 16.25 E
Reichshoffen 56 48.56 N 7.40 E
Reid 162 30.49 S 128.26 E
Reid, Mount ∧, Austl. 162 17.58 S 130.38 E
Reid, Mount ∧, Ak., U.S. 182 55.42 N 131.15 W
Reid Lake ⊜[1] 184 50.02 N 108.05 W
Reidsville, Ga., U.S. 192 32.05 N 82.07 W
Reidsville, N.C., U.S. 192 36.21 N 79.39 W
Reiffton 208 40.19 N 75.53 W
Reigate 42 51.14 N 0.13 W
Reigate and Banstead □[8] 260 51.17 N 0.12 W
Reignac-sur-Indre 50 47.13 N 0.55 E
Reignier 58 46.08 N 6.16 E
Reigoldswil 58 47.24 N 7.41 E
Reihoku 92 32.31 N 130.02 E
Reillanne 62 43.53 N 5.40 E
Reims 50 49.15 N 4.02 E
Reims, Montagne de ⋏[2] 50 49.08 N 4.00 E
Reina Alejandra → Queen Alexandra Range ⋏ 9 84.00 S 168.00 E
Reina Carlota, Estrecho de la → Queen Charlotte Sound ⩌ 182 51.30 N 129.30 W
Reinach, Schw. 58 47.30 N 7.35 E
Reinach, Schw. 58 47.15 N 8.11 E
Reina Fabiola → Queen Fabiola Mountains ⋏ 9 71.30 S 35.40 E
Reina Maria, Costa de la → Queen Mary Coast ⩡[2] 9 67.00 S 96.00 E
Reina Maud, Tierras de la → Queen Maud Land ⩡[2] 9 72.30 S 12.00 E
Reinbeck 190 42.19 N 92.35 W
Reinbek 52 53.31 N 10.14 E
Reinberg 54 54.12 N 13.15 E
Reindeer ≃ 184 55.36 N 103.11 W
Reindeer Island I 184 52.25 N 98.00 W
Reindeer Lake ⊜ 176 57.15 N 102.40 W
Reindeer Station 180 68.42 N 134.06 W
Reine Charlotte, Détroit de la → Queen Charlotte Sound ⩌ 182 51.30 N 129.30 W
Reinerton 208 40.36 N 76.34 W
Reinfeld 52 53.49 N 10.28 E
Reinga, Cape › 172 34.25 S 172.41 E
Reinhardswald ⋏[3] 52 51.30 N 9.30 E
Reinhardtsdorf 54 50.53 N 14.11 E
Reinheim 56 49.49 N 8.50 E
Reinickendorf ⊸[8] 264a 52.35 N 13.21 E
Reinosa 34 43.00 N 4.08 W
Reino Unido → United Kingdom □[1] 28 54.00 N 2.00 W
Reinsdorf, Dtsch. 54 50.42 N 12.33 E
Reinsdorf, Dtsch. 54 51.54 N 12.37 E
Reinshagen ⊸[8] 263 51.10 N 7.09 E

Reinstorf 54 53.50 N 11.38 E
Reis 130 38.16 N 31.35 E
Reisach 64 46.39 N 13.09 E
Reisaelva ≃ 24 69.48 N 21.00 E
Reischach 60 48.17 N 12.44 E
Reisdorf 56 49.53 N 6.15 E
Reisdorf, Camp ■ 273b 4.21 S 15.15 E
Reisholz ⊸[8] 263 51.11 N 6.52 E
Reisjärvi 26 63.37 N 24.54 E
Reiss 46 58.28 N 3.10 W
Reisterstown 208 39.28 N 76.49 W
Reisterstown Road Plaza ⊸[9] 284b 39.02 N 76.42 W
Reitano 70 37.58 N 14.20 E
Reitdiep ≍ 52 53.20 N 6.18 E
Reith bei Seefeld 64 47.18 N 11.12 E
Reit im Winkl 64 47.40 N 12.28 E
Reitz 158 27.53 S 28.31 E
Reitzenhain 54 50.33 N 13.13 E
Reivilo 158 27.36 S 24.08 E
Rejinagar 126 23.53 N 88.15 E
Rejmyra 40 58.50 N 15.55 E
Rejowiec Fabryczny 30 51.08 N 23.13 E
Rejštejn 60 49.09 N 13.31 E
Rekarne 40 59.26 N 16.20 E
Rekarne □[9] 40 59.17 N 16.25 E
Reken 52 51.50 N 7.02 E
Rekjoāti 272b 22.37 N 88.28 E
Reliance, N.T., Can. 176 62.42 N 109.08 W
Reliance, Wy., U.S. 200 41.40 N 109.11 W
Relief Reservoir ⊜[1] 226 38.16 N 119.44 W
Religione, Punta › 70 36.42 N 14.46 E
Reliz Creek ≃ 226 36.19 N 121.18 W
Rellingen 52 53.39 N 9.49 E
Rellinghausen ⊸[8] 263 51.25 N 7.04 E
Reloncaví, Seno ⊂ 254 41.40 S 72.35 W
Remada 148 32.19 N 10.24 E
Remagen 56 50.34 N 7.13 E
Rémalard 50 48.26 N 0.47 E
Remanso 250 9.37 S 42.07 W
Remarde ≃ 261 48.35 N 2.15 E
Remarkable, Mount ∧ 162 32.48 S 138.10 E
Rembang 115a 6.42 S 111.20 E
Rembau 114 2.35 N 102.06 E
Rembia 114 2.20 N 102.13 E
Remchi 34 35.04 N 1.26 W
Remecó 252 37.38 S 63.39 W
Remedios, Col. 246 7.02 N 74.41 W
Remedios, Cuba 240p 22.30 N 79.33 W
Remedios, Pan. 236 8.14 N 81.51 W
Remedios, Punta › 236 13.31 N 89.49 W
Remedios, Santuario de los ♥[1] 286a 19.28 N 99.15 W
Remedios de Escalada ⊸[8] 258 34.43 S 58.23 W
Remels 52 53.18 N 7.44 E
Remennicy 82 56.43 N 36.36 E
Remer 190 47.03 N 93.54 W
Remeshk 128 26.50 N 58.49 E
Remhoogte 158 29.33 S 23.01 E
Remich 56 49.33 N 6.22 E
Remich Airport ⊠ 279b 40.36 N 79.49 W
Rémigny, Lac ⊜ 190 47.51 N 79.12 W
Rémilly 56 49.01 N 6.24 E
Reminderville 214 41.20 N 81.23 W
Remington, In., U.S. 216 40.45 N 87.09 W
Remington, Va., U.S. 188 38.32 N 77.48 W
Rémire 250 4.53 N 52.17 W
Remiremont 58 48.01 N 6.35 E
Remo □[8] 273a 6.42 N 3.29 E
Remolá, Estany del ⊂ 266d 41.17 N 2.04 E
Remollon 62 44.28 N 6.10 E
Remontnoje 80 46.33 N 43.39 E
Remoray 58 46.46 N 6.14 E
Remoulins 62 43.56 N 4.34 E
Removka ⊸[8] 83 47.59 N 38.43 E
Rempang, Pulau I 114 0.51 N 104.10 E
Remptendorf 54 50.31 N 11.39 E
Rems ≃ 56 48.52 N 9.16 E
Remscheid 56 51.11 N 7.11 E
Remscheider-Stausee ⊜[1] 263 51.10 N 7.14 E
Remsen, Ia., U.S. 198 42.48 N 95.58 W
Remsen, N.Y., U.S. 210 43.19 N 75.11 W
Remsfeld 56 51.00 N 9.29 E
Remuna 126 21.33 N 86.54 E
Remus 190 43.36 N 85.09 W
Rémuzat 62 44.24 N 5.21 E
Rena 26 61.08 N 11.22 E
Renaix → Ronse 50 50.45 N 3.36 E
Renāla Khurd 123 30.53 N 73.36 E
Rena Point › 116 16.10 N 119.45 E
Renard Islands II 164 10.50 S 153.05 E
Renata 182 49.26 N 118.06 W
Renaud Island I 9 65.40 S 66.00 W
Renca 286e 33.24 S 70.44 W
Renca, Cerro ∧ 286e 33.23 S 70.43 W
Rencēni 76 57.44 N 25.26 E
Renchen 56 48.35 N 8.01 E
Rencontre East 186 47.38 N 55.12 W
Rencun 98 36.19 N 113.50 E
Renda, Ityo. 144 14.30 N 39.53 E
Renda, Lat. 76 57.09 N 22.22 E
Rende 68 39.19 N 16.11 E
Rendena, Valle V 58 46.08 N 10.42 E
Rend Lake ⊜[1] 194 38.05 N 88.58 W
Rendova Island I 175e 8.32 S 157.20 E
Rendsburg 41 54.18 N 9.40 E
Renens 58 46.32 N 6.35 E
Renesse 52 51.44 N 3.46 E
Renews 186 46.56 N 52.56 W
Renfrew, On., Can. 212 45.28 N 76.41 W
Renfrew, Scot., U.K. 46 55.53 N 4.24 W
Renfrew, Pa., U.S. 214 40.46 N 79.58 W
Renfrew □[6] 212 45.25 N 77.05 W
Rengam 114 1.53 N 103.24 E
Ren'gang 106 32.01 N 120.50 E
Rengasdengklok 115a 6.09 S 107.17 E
Rengat 112 0.24 S 102.33 E
Rengel 115a 7.04 S 112.00 E
Rengen ⊜ 26 64.05 N 14.03 E
Rengezhuang 105 39.45 N 118.13 E
Rengit 114 1.41 N 103.09 E
Rengkang 112 1.07 N 112.10 E
Rengo 252 34.25 S 70.52 W
Rengsdorf 56 50.30 N 7.29 E
Reng Tlang ∧ 120 21.59 N 92.36 E
Renhe, Zhg. 100 33.32 N 114.02 E
Renhe, Zhg. 100 27.41 N 115.15 E
Renhechang 107 30.30 N 105.06 E
Renheji 100 31.56 N 115.07 E
Renhua 100 25.06 N 113.44 E
Renhuai 102 27.48 N 106.18 E
Reni 78 45.27 N 28.17 E
Renick 188 37.59 N 80.21 W
Renish Point › 46 57.44 N 6.59 W
Renjiawopeng 104 41.27 N 122.18 E
Renjiaxu 106 30.49 N 121.00 E
Renju 100 24.51 N 115.54 E
Renko 26 60.54 N 24.17 E
Renkum 52 51.58 N 5.45 E
Renliuchang 107 29.30 N 106.28 E
Renlong 107 30.32 N 105.14 E
Renmark 166 34.11 S 140.45 E
Renmei 100 25.50 N 117.56 E
Renmin 89 46.37 N 125.32 E
Renna, Monte ∧ 70 36.52 N 14.41 E
Rennau 54 52.17 N 10.55 E
Renne, Lac du → Reindeer Lake ⊜ 176 57.15 N 102.40 W
Renne, Rivière le ≃ 206 45.41 N 72.39 W
Rennell I 160 11.40 S 160.10 E
Rennell, Islas II 254 52.00 S 74.00 W
Rennell Sound ⩌ 182 53.23 N 132.40 W
Renner 222 32.59 N 96.47 W
Rennerdale 279b 40.24 N 80.08 W
Rennerod 56 50.36 N 8.04 E
Renner Springs 162 18.20 S 133.48 E
Rennertshofen 60 48.45 N 11.02 E

Rennes 32 48.05 N 1.41 W
Rennick Bay ⊂ 9 70.18 S 161.45 E
Rennick Glacier ⩍ 9 70.30 S 161.45 E
Rennie 184 49.51 N 95.33 W
Rennie's Mill 271d 22.18 N 114.15 E
Renningen 56 48.46 N 8.56 E
Renntier-See → Reindeer Lake ⊜ 176 57.15 N 102.40 W
Rennweg 64 47.01 N 13.37 E
Reno, Nv., U.S. 226 39.31 N 119.48 W
Reno, Pa., U.S. 214 41.25 N 79.45 W
Reno, Tx., U.S. 222 32.56 N 97.05 W
Reno ≃ 64 44.37 N 12.16 E
Reno Beach 214 41.40 N 83.15 W
Reno Hill ∧ 200 42.35 N 106.03 W
Reno International Airport ⊠ 226 39.30 N 119.46 W
Renoster ≃ 158 31.37 S 20.37 E
Renous 186 46.49 N 65.48 W
Renous ≃ 183 46.50 N 65.50 W
Renovo 214 41.19 N 77.45 W
Renqiao 100 33.27 N 117.16 E
Renqiu 98 38.43 N 116.05 E
Rens 41 54.54 N 9.06 E
Renshan 100 22.50 N 114.48 E
Renshou, Zhg. 100 27.08 N 117.51 E
Renshou, Zhg. 107 30.00 N 104.08 E
Rensjön 24 68.05 N 19.49 E
Rensselaer, In., U.S. 216 40.56 N 87.09 W
Rensselaer, Mo., U.S. 219 39.40 N 91.33 W
Rensselaer, N.Y., U.S. 210 42.38 N 73.44 W
Rensselaer □[6] 210 42.43 N 73.40 W
Rensselaer Falls 212 44.35 N 75.19 W
Rensselaerville 210 42.30 N 74.08 W
Rentería 34 43.19 N 1.54 W
Rentfort ⊸[8] 263 51.35 N 6.57 E
Renton 224 47.28 N 122.12 W
Rentuo 107 29.14 N 106.23 E
Rentweinsdorf 56 50.04 N 10.47 E
Renun ≃ 114 3.05 N 97.55 E
Renville 198 44.47 N 95.12 W
Renwez 56 49.50 N 4.36 E
Renwick, N.Z. 172 41.30 S 173.50 E
Renwick, Ia., U.S. 190 42.49 N 93.58 W
Renyichang 107 29.29 N 105.28 E
Renziehalusen Park ♠ 279b 40.21 N 79.50 W
Réo, Burkina 150 12.19 N 2.28 W
Reo, Indon. 115b 8.19 S 120.30 E
Reola ⊸[8] 272a 28.34 N 76.59 E
Repartimento ≃ 250 6.06 S 50.40 W
Repaupo 285 39.48 N 75.18 W
Repbäcken 40 60.31 N 15.20 E
Répce ≃ 30 47.41 N 17.03 E
Repentigny 206 45.44 N 73.28 W
Repetek 128 38.34 N 63.11 E
Repino 76 60.10 N 29.52 E
Repjovka, Ross. 78 51.05 N 38.39 E
Repjovka, Ross. 80 53.09 N 48.06 E
Repki 78 51.48 N 31.05 E
Repolka 76 59.16 N 29.34 E
Repolovo 86 60.40 N 69.50 E
Reporoa 172 38.26 S 176.21 E
Reposaari 26 61.37 N 21.27 E
Repton 194 31.24 N 87.14 W
Republic, Ks., U.S. 198 39.55 N 97.49 W
Republic, Mi., U.S. 190 46.24 N 87.58 W
Republic, Mo., U.S. 194 37.07 N 93.28 W
Republic, Oh., U.S. 214 41.07 N 83.00 W
Republic, Wa., U.S. 202 48.38 N 118.44 W
República Centroafricana → Central African Republic □[1] 136 7.00 N 21.00 E
Republic Airport ⊠ 276 40.44 N 73.25 W
Republican ≃ 198 39.03 N 96.48 W
Republican, North Fork ≃ 198 40.01 N 101.59 W
Republican, South Fork ≃ 198 40.03 N 101.31 W
Republic Observatory ♥[3] 273d 26.11 S 28.05 E
Republic Steel Corporation ♥[3] 279a 41.28 N 81.40 W
République centrafricaine → Central African Republic □[1] 136 7.00 N 21.00 E
Repueblo de Oriente 196 25.51 N 99.39 W
Repulse Bay 176 66.32 N 86.15 W
Repulse Bay ⊂ 166 20.36 S 148.43 E
Repvåg 24 70.45 N 25.41 E
Requena, Esp. 34 39.29 N 1.06 W
Requena, Perú 248 4.58 S 73.50 W
Réquista 32 44.02 N 2.32 E
Rère ≃ 50 47.22 N 1.50 E
Reriutaba 250 4.10 S 40.35 W
Reşadiye 130 40.24 N 37.21 E
Reşadiye ⊸[8] 267b 41.05 N 29.15 E
Reşadiye Yarımadası ›[1] 130 36.40 N 27.45 E
Resang, Tanjong › 114 2.35 N 103.51 E
Resarö 40 59.26 N 18.20 E
Rescalda 266b 45.38 N 8.56 E
Rescaldina 266b 45.37 N 8.57 E
Reschenpass (Passo di Resia))(64 46.50 N 10.30 E
Reschenscheideck)(64 46.51 N 10.31 E
Rescue 208 36.59 N 76.33 W
Research 274b 37.42 S 145.11 E
Reseda ⊸[8] 280 34.12 N 118.31 W
Resen 38 41.05 N 21.00 E
Resende 256 22.28 S 44.27 W
Reserva 252 24.38 S 50.52 W
Reserva, Parque de la ♠ 286d 12.04 S 77.02 W
Reserve, La., U.S. 194 30.03 N 90.33 W
Reserve, N.M., U.S. 200 33.42 N 108.45 W
Reserve Township 279b 40.29 N 79.59 W
Reservoir 274b 37.43 S 145.00 E
Reservoir Pond ⊜ 283 42.10 N 71.07 W
Rešetilovka 78 49.34 N 34.04 E
Rešetnikovo 82 56.27 N 36.34 E
Reshi 98 42.09 N 119.18 E
Reshuitang 102 24.10 N 103.09 E
Resia, Passo di (Reschenpass))(64 46.50 N 10.30 E
Resipol, Beinn ∧ 46 56.43 N 5.39 W
Resistencia 252 27.27 S 58.59 W
Reşiţa 38 45.17 N 21.53 E
Resiutta 64 46.23 N 13.13 E
Resko 30 53.47 N 15.25 E
Rešma 80 57.24 N 42.34 E
Reš'ovka 78 49.47 N 27.25 E
Resolute 176 74.41 N 94.54 W
Resolution Island I, N.T., Can. 176 61.30 N 65.00 W
Resolution Island I, N.Z. 172 45.40 S 166.40 E
Resolven 42 51.42 N 3.42 W
Resort, Loch ⊂ 46 58.03 N 7.06 W
Rešoty 76 57.09 N 28.30 E
Resplandes 250 6.17 S 45.13 W
Resplendor 255 19.20 S 41.15 W
Ressa ≃ 54 55.45 N 35.10 E
Ressaca, Ribeirão da ≃ 287b 23.38 S 46.51 W
Resse ⊸[8] 263 51.34 N 7.07 E
Resseta ≃ 76 53.49 N 35.15 E
Ressons-sur-Matz 50 49.33 N 2.45 E
Resta ≃ 76 53.36 N 30.56 E
Resthaven 216 41.16 N 88.09 W
Restigouche (Ristigouche) ≃ 186 48.04 N 66.20 W
Restín, Punta › 246 4.17 S 81.15 W
Restinga 34 35.42 N 5.23 W
Restinga Seca 252 29.49 S 53.23 W
Reston, Mb., Can. 184 49.35 N 101.02 W
Reston, Scot., U.K. 46 55.51 N 2.11 W

Reston, Va., U.S. 208 38.58 N 77.20 W
Restoule Lake ⊜ 190 46.03 N 79.47 W
Restrepo, Col. 246 4.15 N 73.33 W
Restrepo, Col. 246 3.48 N 76.31 W
Resuttano 70 37.41 N 14.02 E
Retalhuleu 236 14.32 N 91.41 W
Retalhuleu □[5] 236 14.20 N 91.50 W
Retamosa 252 33.35 S 54.44 W
Retem, Oued er V 148 33.30 N 5.45 E
Řetenice 54 50.38 N 13.46 E
Retezat, Parcul Național ♠ 38 45.20 N 22.50 E
Retezatului, Munții ⋏ 38 45.25 N 23.00 E
Rethel 50 49.31 N 4.22 E
Rethem 52 52.45 N 9.23 E
Réthimnon 38 35.22 N 24.29 E
Retiche, Alpi → Rhaetian Alps ⋏ 58 46.30 N 10.00 E
Retie 56 51.16 N 5.04 E
Retiers 28 47.55 N 1.23 W
Retiro, Estacion ⊸[5] 288 34.36 S 58.22 W
Retiro, Parque del ♠ 266a 40.25 N 3.41 W
Retournac 62 45.12 N 4.02 E
Retreat 222 32.03 N 96.29 W
Retreat ≃ 170 34.07 S 149.38 E
Retsof 210 42.50 N 77.53 W
Rettenberg 58 47.35 N 10.17 E
Rettendon 260 51.39 N 0.33 E
Rettendon Place 260 51.38 N 0.34 E
Rettichovka 89 44.10 N 132.47 E
Rettin 54 54.06 N 10.53 E
Return Creek ≃ 226 37.56 N 119.28 W
Retz 61 48.45 N 15.57 E
Retzow 54 52.37 N 12.41 E
Reuden 54 52.04 N 12.18 E
Reungeut 114 4.34 N 96.22 E
Reunion (Réunion) □[2], Afr. 138 21.06 S 55.36 E
Reunion (Réunion) □[2], Afr. 157c 21.06 S 55.36 E
Reus 34 41.09 N 1.07 E
Reuschenberg 263 51.10 N 6.42 E
Reusel 52 51.21 N 5.22 E
Reusrath 263 51.06 N 6.57 E
Reuss ≃ 58 47.28 N 8.14 E
Reut ≃ 78 47.15 N 29.09 E
Reuterstadt Stavenhagen 54 53.42 N 12.53 E
Reutlingen 58 48.29 N 9.11 E
Reutov 82 55.46 N 37.52 E
Reutte 58 47.29 N 10.43 E
Reuver 52 51.17 N 6.05 E
Revadim 132 31.46 N 34.48 E
Rev'akino 82 54.22 N 37.40 E
Reval → Tallinn 76 59.25 N 24.45 E
Revda, Ross. 24 67.58 N 34.32 E
Revda, Ross. 86 56.48 N 59.57 E
Réveillon, Ruisseau le ≃ 261 48.42 N 2.30 E
Revel 62 45.11 N 5.52 E
Revelganj 124 25.47 N 84.40 E
Revelstoke 182 50.59 N 118.12 W
Reventazón 248 6.10 S 80.58 W
Reventazón ≃ 236 10.17 N 83.24 W
Revere, It. 64 45.03 N 11.08 E
Revere, Ma., U.S. 207 42.24 N 71.00 W
Revere, Pa., U.S. 208 40.31 N 75.10 W
Revere Beach ⩡[2] 283 42.25 N 70.59 W
Revermont ⋏[2] 58 46.27 N 5.25 E
Revesby 274a 33.57 S 151.01 E
Revest-du-Bion 62 44.05 N 5.33 E
Révia 154 13.23 S 36.31 E
Reviga 38 44.42 N 27.06 E
Revigny-sur-Ornain 56 48.50 N 4.59 E
Revilla del Campo 34 42.13 N 3.32 W
Revillagigedo, Islas II 232 19.00 N 111.30 W
Revillagigedo Channel ⩌ 182 55.10 N 131.13 W
Revillagigedo Island I 182 55.35 N 131.23 W
Revillo 198 45.01 N 96.34 W
Revin 56 49.56 N 4.38 E
Revloc 214 40.29 N 78.45 W
Řevničov 54 50.08 N 13.45 E
Revò 64 46.23 N 11.03 E
Revol'ucii, pik ∧ 85 38.31 N 72.21 E
Revolución Mexicana 234 16.03 N 93.04 W
Revolution, Museum of the ♥ 265b 55.46 N 37.36 E
Revsundssjön ⊜ 26 62.49 N 15.17 E
Revúboè ≃ 154 16.13 S 33.37 E
Revuè ≃ 156 19.49 S 34.00 E
Rew 214 41.54 N 78.32 W
Rewa 124 24.32 N 81.18 E
Rewa ≃ 246 3.53 N 58.45 W
Rewāri 124 28.11 N 76.37 E
Rewataya, Taka ✦[2] 112 6.05 S 118.55 E
Rex, Mount ∧ 9 74.57 S 76.00 W
Rexburg 202 43.49 N 111.47 W
Rexdale ⊸[8] 275b 43.43 N 79.35 W
Rexford, Ks., U.S. 198 39.28 N 100.44 W
Rexford, Mt., U.S. 202 48.52 N 115.13 W
Rexhame 283 42.06 N 70.40 W
Rexton 186 46.39 N 64.52 W
Rexville, In., U.S. 278 41.31 N 87.21 W
Rexville, N.Y., U.S. 210 42.05 N 77.40 W
Rey, Arroyo del ≃ 288 34.46 S 58.27 W
Rey, Embalse del ⊜[1] 266a 40.18 N 3.32 W
Rey, Estrecho del → King Sound ⩌ 162 17.00 S 123.30 E
Rey, Isla del I 246 8.22 N 78.55 W
Rey, Laguna del ⊜ 196 27.01 N 103.26 W
Rey Bouba 146 8.40 N 14.11 E
Reyes 248 14.19 S 67.23 W
Reyes, Point › 204 38.00 N 123.01 W
Reyes Peak ∧ 228 34.38 N 119.17 W
Reyhanlı 130 36.18 N 36.32 E
Rey Jorge, Estrecho → King George Sound ⩌ 162 35.03 S 117.57 E
Rey Jorge, Isla → King George Island I 9 62.00 S 58.15 W
Reykjanes ›[1] 24a 63.49 N 22.43 W
Reykjanes Ridge ✦[3] 10 62.00 N 27.00 W
Reykjavík 24a 64.09 N 21.51 W
Reynella 168b 35.06 S 138.32 E
Reyno 194 36.21 N 90.45 W
Reynolds, Ga., U.S. 192 32.33 N 84.05 W
Reynolds, In., U.S. 216 40.44 N 86.52 W
Reynolds, N.D., U.S. 198 47.57 N 97.45 W
Reynolds Channel ⩌ 276 40.36 N 73.40 W
Reynolds Creek ≃, Austl. 171a 27.56 S 152.36 E
Reynolds Creek ≃, On., Can. 212 43.00 N 80.58 W
Reynoldsville 214 41.05 N 78.53 W
Reynosa 232 26.07 N 98.18 W
Reyssouze ≃ 58 46.27 N 4.54 E
Rež 86 57.23 N 61.24 E
Rež ≃ 86 57.54 N 62.18 E
Reza, gora (Kūh-e Rīzeh) ∧ 128 37.47 N 58.05 E
Rezé 32 47.12 N 1.34 W
Rēzekne 76 56.30 N 27.19 E
Rēzekne ≃ 76 56.46 N 26.28 E
Rezeny 78 46.46 N 28.54 E
Rezina 78 47.44 N 28.58 E
Rezino 86 55.51 N 75.18 E
Rēznas ezers ⊜ 76 56.20 N 27.27 E
Rezovo 38 41.59 N 28.02 E
Rezovska (Mutlu) ≃ 130 41.59 N 28.01 E
Rezvānshahr 128 37.33 N 49.09 E
Rezzato 64 45.31 N 10.19 E
Rezzoaglio 62 44.32 N 9.23 E
Rezzonico 58 46.04 N 9.16 E
Rhade 52 53.19 N 9.07 E
Rhadeswood Reservoir ⊜[1] 262 53.29 N 1.56 W

Rhaetian Alps (Rätische Alpen) (Alpi Retiche) ⋏ 58 46.30 N 10.00 E
Rhallamane, Sebkha de ≚ 148 23.41 N 9.50 W
Rhame 198 46.13 N 103.39 W
Rharbi, Île I 148 34.39 N 11.03 E
Rharbi, Zahrez ⊜ 148 34.50 N 2.50 E
Rhauderfehn 52 53.08 N 7.35 E
Rhaunen 56 49.52 N 7.20 E
Rhayader 42 52.18 N 3.30 W
Rhea Creek ≃ 202 45.30 N 119.46 W
Rheda-Wiedenbrück 52 51.50 N 8.18 E
Rhede, Dtsch. 52 53.03 N 7.16 E
Rhede, Dtsch. 52 51.50 N 6.11 E
Rheden 52 52.01 N 6.02 E
Rheems 208 40.08 N 76.34 W
Rheem Valley 226 37.52 N 122.07 W
Rheidol ≃ 42 52.25 N 4.05 W
Rheims → Reims 50 49.15 N 4.02 E
Rhein 184 51.22 N 102.10 W
Rheinau 56 48.41 N 7.56 E
Rheinbach 56 50.37 N 6.57 E
Rheinberg 52 51.33 N 6.35 E
Rheinböllen 56 50.00 N 7.40 E
Rheinbrohl 56 50.30 N 7.19 E
Rheinbrücke ⊸[5] 263 51.12 N 6.44 E
Rheindürkheim 56 49.42 N 8.21 E
Rheine 52 52.17 N 7.26 E
Rheineck 58 47.28 N 9.35 E
Rheinen 263 51.27 N 7.38 E
Rheinfall ∟ 58 47.41 N 8.38 E
Rheinfelden, Dtsch. 58 47.33 N 7.47 E
Rheinfelden, Schw. 58 47.33 N 7.48 E
Rheinhausen 56 51.24 N 6.44 E
Rhein-Herne-Kanal ≍ 263 51.27 N 6.47 E
Rheinhessen □[5] 56 49.40 N 8.40 E
Rheinkamp 52 51.30 N 6.37 E
Rheinland-Pfalz □[3] 56 50.00 N 7.00 E
Rhein → Rhine ≃ 30 51.52 N 6.02 E
Rheinsberg 54 53.06 N 12.53 E
Rheinstadion ♠ 263 51.16 N 6.44 E
Rheinstein, Burg ⊥ 56 50.00 N 7.50 E
Rheinwald V 58 46.32 N 9.17 E
Rheinwaldhorn ∧ 58 46.30 N 9.02 E
Rheirs, Oued V 148 30.39 N 4.26 W
Rhêmes-Notre-Dame 62 45.34 N 7.07 E
Rhenen 52 51.57 N 5.34 E
Rhens 56 50.17 N 7.37 E
Rheurdt 263 51.27 N 6.28 E
Rheydt 56 51.10 N 6.25 E
Rheydt, Schloss ⊥ 263 51.11 N 6.29 E
Rhin ≃ 54 52.59 N 12.55 E
Rhinau 58 48.19 N 7.42 E
Rhine 192 31.59 N 83.12 W
Rhine (Rhein) (Rhin) ≃ 30 51.52 N 6.02 E
Rhinebeck 210 41.55 N 73.54 W
Rhinecliff 210 41.55 N 73.57 W
Rhineland 219 38.43 N 91.31 W
Rhinelander 190 45.38 N 89.24 W
Rhin Kanal ≍ 54 52.47 N 12.24 E
Rhinluch ≡ 54 52.50 N 12.50 E
Rhinns of Kells ⋏ 44 55.07 N 4.22 W
Rhinns Point › 46 55.40 N 6.30 W
Rhino Camp 154 2.58 N 31.24 E
Rhinow 54 52.45 N 12.20 E
Rhin → Rhine ≃ 30 51.52 N 6.02 E
Rhiou, Oued ≃ 34 36.00 N 0.55 E
Rhir, Cap › 148 30.38 N 9.55 W
Rhis, Oued ≃ 34 35.14 N 3.57 W
Rhiw ≃ 42 52.36 N 3.11 W
Rho 62 45.32 N 9.02 E
Rhode Island □[3], U.S. 178 41.40 N 71.30 W
Rhode Island □[3], U.S. 207 41.40 N 71.30 W
Rhode Island I 207 41.33 N 71.15 W
Rhode Island Sound ⩌ 207 41.25 N 71.15 W
Rhoden 52 51.28 N 9.00 E
Rhodes, Austl. 274a 33.50 S 151.05 E
Rhodes, S. Afr. 158 30.47 S 27.59 E
Rhodes, Eng., U.K. 262 53.33 N 2.14 W
Rhodesia → Zimbabwe □[1] 154 20.00 S 30.00 E
Rhodes Inyanga National Park ♠ 154 18.12 S 32.45 E
Rhodes Matopos National Park ♠ 154 20.33 S 28.20 E
Rhodes Park ♠ 273d 26.12 S 28.06 E
Rhodes Peak ∧ 202 46.41 N 114.47 W
Rhodes → Ródhos 38 36.26 N 28.13 E
Rhodes → Ródhos I 38 36.10 N 28.00 E
Rhodes' Tomb ⊥ 154 20.30 S 28.30 E
Rhododendron 224 45.20 N 121.55 W
Rhododendron State Park ♠ 207 42.47 N 72.12 W
Rhodon 261 48.43 N 2.04 E
Rhodon, Ruisseau le ≃ 261 48.42 N 2.04 E
Rhodope Mountains ⋏ 38 41.30 N 24.30 E
Rhodt 56 49.16 N 8.07 E
Rhome 222 33.03 N 97.28 W
Rhondda 42 51.40 N 3.27 W
Rhône □[5] 32 45.55 N 4.40 E
Rhône ≃ 32 43.20 N 4.50 E
Rhône à Sète, Canal du ≍ 62 43.25 N 3.42 E
Rhône au Rhin, Canal du ≍ 58 47.06 N 5.19 E
Rhoose 42 51.24 N 3.20 W
Rhosesmor 262 53.12 N 3.10 W
Rhosllanerchrugog 44 53.00 N 3.03 W
Rhosneigr 44 53.14 N 4.31 W
Rhos-on-Sea 44 53.19 N 3.45 W
Rhossili 42 51.34 N 4.17 W
Rhourde-El-Baguel 148 31.24 N 6.57 E
Rhuddlan 44 53.18 N 3.27 W
Rhue ≃ 42 45.23 N 2.29 E
Rhum I 46 57.00 N 6.20 W
Rhum, Sound of ⩌ 46 56.56 N 6.14 W
Rhyl 44 53.19 N 3.29 W
Rhymney 42 51.46 N 3.18 W
Rhymney ≃ 42 51.28 N 3.10 W
Rhynie 46 57.19 N 2.50 W
Riaba 152 3.23 N 8.46 E
Riace 68 38.25 N 16.29 E
Riachão 250 7.22 S 46.37 W
Riachão do Dantas 250 11.04 S 37.44 W
Riachão do Jacuípe 250 11.48 S 39.21 W
Riacho de Santana 255 13.37 S 42.57 W
Riacho Grande 256 23.48 S 46.35 W
Riachos, Islas de los II 254 40.10 S 62.08 W
Riachuelo, Bra. 250 10.44 S 37.11 W
Riachuelo, Chile 254 40.49 S 73.21 W
Riachuelo, Ur. 258 34.28 S 57.43 W
Riachuelo ≃ 288 34.38 S 58.22 W
Riachuelo, Arroyo ≃ 258 34.27 S 57.44 W
Rialma 255 15.18 S 49.34 W
Rialto, Bra. 256 22.35 S 44.16 W
Rialto, Ca., U.S. 228 34.06 N 117.22 W
Riamkanan, Waduk ⊜[1] 112 3.30 S 115.05 E
Rianápolis 255 15.29 S 49.28 W
Riāng 120 27.32 N 92.56 E
Riangnom 140 9.55 N 30.01 E
Riaño 34 42.58 N 5.01 W
Rians 62 43.37 N 5.45 E
Riansares ≃ 34 39.32 N 3.18 W
Riāsi 123 33.05 N 74.50 E
Riau □[4] 112 1.00 N 102.00 E
Riau, Kepulauan II 112 1.00 N 104.30 E
Riaz 58 46.38 N 7.04 E

Symbols in the index entries represent the broad categories identified in the key at the right. Symbols with superior numbers (⋏[1]) identify subcategories (see complete key on page I · 1).

Los símbolos incluidos en el texto del índice representan las grandes categorías identificadas con la clave a la derecha. Los símbolos con números en su parte superior (⋏[1]) identifican las subcategorías (véase la clave completa en la página I · 1).

Os símbolos incluídos no texto do índice representam as grandes categorias identificadas com a chave à direita. Os símbolos com números em sua parte superior (⋏[1]) identificam as subcategorias (veja-se a chave completa à página I · 1).

Symbole im Register stellen die rechts im Schlüssel erklärten Kategorien dar. Symbole mit hochgestellten Ziffern (⋏[1]) bezeichnen Unterabteilungen einer Kategorie (vgl. vollständiger Schlüssel auf Seite I · 1).

Les symboles de l'index représentent les catégories indiquées dans la légende à droite. Les symboles suivis d'un indice (⋏[1]) représentent des sous-catégories (voir légende complète à la page I · 1).

∧ Mountain	Berg	Montaña	Montagne	Montanha
⋏ Mountains	Gebirge	Montañas	Montagnes	Montanhas
)(Pass	Paß	Paso	Col	Passo
V Valley, Canyon	Tal, Cañon	Valle, Cañón	Vallée, Canyon	Vale, Canhão
≚ Plain	Ebene	Llano	Plaine	Planície
› Cape	Kap	Cabo	Cap	Cabo
I Island	Insel	Isla	Île	Ilha
II Islands	Inseln	Islas	Îles	Ilhas
◆ Other Topographic Features	Andere Topographische Objekte	Otros Elementos Topográficos	Autres données topographiques	Outros acidentes topográficos

ESPAÑOL — Nombre | Página | Lat.°′ | Long.°′ W = Oeste
FRANÇAIS — Nom | Page | Lat.°′ | Long.°′ W = Ouest
PORTUGUÊS — Nome | Página | Lat.°′ | Long.°′ W = Oeste

Riaza 34 41.17 N 3.28 W
Riaza ≃ 34 41.42 N 3.55 W
Ribadavia 34 42.17 N 8.08 W
Ribadeo 34 43.32 N 7.02 W
Ribadesella 34 43.28 N 5.04 W
Ribas de Jarama 266a 40.23 N 3.31 W
Ribas do Rio Pardo 255 20.27 S 53.46 W
Ribauè 154 14.57 S 38.17 E
Ribble ≃ 44 53.44 N 2.50 W
Ribbleton 262 53.46 N 2.40 W
Ribble Valley □[8] 262 53.48 N 2.31 W
Ribbon Fall ʟ 226 37.44 N 119.39 W
Ribchester 262 53.49 N 2.32 W
Ribe 41 55.21 N 8.46 E
Ribe □[6] 41 55.35 N 8.50 E
Ribe Å ≃ 41 55.21 N 8.40 E
Ribeauvillé 58 48.12 N 7.19 E
Ribécourt 50 49.31 N 2.55 E
Ribeira 252 24.40 S 49.01 W
Ribeira do Iguape ≃ 252 24.40 S 47.24 W
Ribeira do Pombal 250 10.50 S 38.32 W
Ribeira Grande, C.V. 150a 17.11 N 25.04 W
Ribeira Grande, Port. 148a 37.49 N 25.31 W
Ribeirão 250 8.31 S 35.23 W
Ribeirão das Lajes, Represa do ⊜[1] 256 22.45 S 43.55 W
Ribeirão de São Joaquim 256 22.17 S 44.11 W
Ribeirão do Pinhal 255 23.24 S 50.18 W
Ribeirão Pires 256 23.43 S 46.25 W
Ribeirão Preto 255 21.10 S 47.48 W
Ribeirao Vermelho 255 21.11 S 45.03 W
Ribeirãozinho 255 16.27 S 52.35 W
Ribeiro Gonçalves 250 7.32 S 45.14 W
Ribeiro Junqueira 256 21.28 S 42.31 W
Ribeiros 256 21.59 S 45.35 W
Ribemont 50 49.48 N 3.28 E
Ribera 70 37.30 N 13.16 E
Ribérac 32 45.15 N 0.20 E
Riberalta 248 10.59 S 66.06 W
Riberão Pires □[7] 287b 23.43 S 46.21 W
Ribiers 62 44.14 N 5.52 E
Rib Lake 190 45.19 N 90.12 W
Ribnica, Slo. 36 45.44 N 14.44 E
Ribnica, Slo. 61 46.32 N 15.16 E
Ribnitz-Damgarten 54 54.15 N 12.28 E
Ribstone Creek ≃ 184 52.51 N 110.05 W
Ricadi 68 38.37 N 15.52 E
Ricarda, Estany de la c 266d 41.18 N 2.07 E
Ricardo Flores Magón 232 29.58 N 106.58 W
Ricaurte 246 1.13 N 77.59 W
Riccall 44 53.50 N 1.04 W
Riccarton 172 43.32 S 172.36 E
Riccia 66 41.29 N 14.50 E
Riccione 66 43.59 N 12.39 E
Rice 222 32.15 N 96.30 W
Rice Creek ≃ 216 42.16 N 84.57 W
Rice Lake 190 45.30 N 91.44 W
Rice Lake ⊜, On., Can. 190 47.42 N 82.08 W
Rice Lake ⊜, On., Can. 212 44.08 N 78.13 W
Rice Lake Indian Reserve ◆[4] 212 44.10 N 78.12 W
Riceville, Ia., U.S. 190 43.22 N 92.33 W
Riceville, Pa., U.S. 214 41.47 N 79.48 W
Riceville, Tn., U.S. 192 35.23 N 84.41 W
Rich, Cape > 212 44.43 N 80.38 W
Richan 184 49.59 N 92.49 W
Richard B. Russell Lake ⊜[1] 192 34.05 N 82.39 W
Richard Collinson Inlet c 176 72.45 N 113.45 W
Richards 222 30.32 N 95.51 W
Richard's Bay 158 28.47 S 32.06 E
Richard's Bay c 158 28.50 S 32.02 E
Richards-Gebaur Air Force Base ■ 194 38.51 N 94.33 W
Richard's Harbour 186 47.37 N 56.24 W
Richards Island I 180 69.20 N 134.30 W
Richardson 222 32.56 N 96.43 W
Richardson ≃ 176 58.30 N 111.30 W
Richardson, Mount ∧ 162 28.49 S 119.59 E
Richardson Bay c 282 37.52 N 122.29 W
Richardson Mountains ⋏, Can. 180 67.15 N 136.30 W
Richardson Mountains ⋏, N.Z. 172 44.45 S 168.31 E
Richardson Park 285 39.44 N 75.35 W
Richardsville 214 41.14 N 79.01 W
Richard-Toll 150 16.28 N 15.41 W
Richardton 198 46.53 N 102.18 W
Rîchât, Guelb er ∧[2] 148 21.07 N 11.24 W
Richboro 208 40.13 N 75.01 W
Richburg 210 42.05 N 78.09 W
Riche, Pointe > 186 50.42 N 57.25 W
Richebourg 261 48.49 N 1.38 E
Richelieu, P.Q., Can. 206 45.27 N 73.15 W
Richelieu, Fr. 32 47.01 N 0.19 E
Richelieu □[6] 206 45.55 N 73.00 W
Richelieu ≃ 206 46.03 N 73.07 W
Richer 184 49.39 N 96.28 W
Richey 198 47.38 N 105.04 W
Richfield, Id., U.S. 202 43.02 N 114.09 W
Richfield, Mn., U.S. 190 44.53 N 93.16 W
Richfield, Oh., U.S. 214 41.14 N 81.39 W
Richfield, Pa., U.S. 208 40.41 N 77.07 W
Richfield, Ut,. U.S. 200 38.46 N 112.05 W
Richfield Springs 210 42.51 N 74.59 W
Richford, N.Y., U.S. 210 42.21 N 76.12 W
Richford, Vt., U.S. 206 44.59 N 72.40 W
Rich Fountain 219 38.24 N 91.53 W
Richgrove 226 35.48 N 119.07 W
Richhill, N. Ire., U.K. 48 54.23 N 6.33 W
Rich Hill, Mo., U.S. 194 38.05 N 94.12 W
Richibucto 186 46.41 N 64.52 W
Richisau 58 47.02 N 8.54 E
Richland, Ga., U.S. 192 32.05 N 84.40 W
Richland, Mi., U.S. 216 42.22 N 85.27 W
Richland, Mo., U.S. 194 37.51 N 92.24 W
Richland, N.J., U.S. 208 39.29 N 74.52 W
Richland, N.Y., U.S. 212 43.34 N 76.03 W
Richland, Pa., U.S. 208 40.21 N 76.16 W
Richland, Tx., U.S. 222 31.56 N 96.26 W
Richland, Tx., U.S. 222 32.57 N 95.49 W
Richland, Wa., U.S. 202 46.17 N 119.17 W
Richland □[6] 214 40.46 N 82.31 W
Richland Center 190 43.20 N 90.23 W
Richland Creek ≃, Il., U.S. 219 38.14 N 89.54 W
Richland Creek ≃, Tn., U.S. 194 35.02 N 86.55 W
Richland Creek ≃, Tx., U.S. 222 31.58 N 96.03 W
Richlands, N.C., U.S. 192 34.53 N 77.32 W
Richlands, Va., U.S. 192 37.05 N 81.47 W
Richland Springs 196 31.16 N 98.57 W
Richmond, Austl. 166 20.44 S 143.08 E
Richmond, Austl. 170 33.36 S 150.46 E
Richmond, Austl. 274b 37.49 S 145.00 E
Richmond, B.C., Can. 224 49.09 N 123.06 W
Richmond, On., Can. 212 45.11 N 75.50 W
Richmond, P.Q., Can. 206 45.40 N 72.09 W
Richmond, N.Z. 172 41.20 S 173.11 E
Richmond, S. Afr. 158 31.23 S 23.56 E
Richmond, S. Afr. 158 29.54 S 30.08 E
Richmond, Eng., U.K. 44 54.24 N 1.44 W
Richmond, Ca., U.S. 226 37.56 N 122.20 W
Richmond, Il., U.S. 216 42.28 N 88.18 W
Richmond, In., U.S. 218 39.49 N 84.53 W
Richmond, Ks., U.S. 198 38.24 N 95.15 W
Richmond, Ky., U.S. 192 37.44 N 84.17 W
Richmond, Me., U.S. 188 44.05 N 69.47 W
Richmond, Ma., U.S. 207 42.22 N 73.22 W
Richmond, Mi., U.S. 214 42.48 N 82.45 W
Richmond, Mn., U.S. 190 45.27 N 94.31 W
Richmond, Mo., U.S. 194 39.16 N 93.58 W
Richmond, Oh., U.S. 214 40.26 N 80.46 W

Richmond, Tx., U.S. 222 29.34 N 95.45 W
Richmond, Ut,. U.S. 200 41.55 N 111.48 W
Richmond, Vt., U.S. 188 44.24 N 72.59 W
Richmond, Va., U.S. 208 37.33 N 77.27 W
Richmond □[6], P.Q., Can. 206 45.40 N 72.00 W
Richmond □[6], N.Y., U.S. 210 40.38 N 74.05 W
Richmond □[6], Va., U.S. 208 37.32 N 77.28 W
Richmond ◆[8], Eng., U.K. 42 51.28 N 0.18 W
Richmond ◆[8], Ca., U.S. 282 37.46 N 122.29 W
Richmond ◆[8], Pa., U.S. 285 39.59 N 75.06 W
Richmond, Mount ∧ 172 41.29 S 173.24 E
Richmond, Point > 282 37.55 N 122.23 W
Richmond Beach 224 47.46 N 122.23 W
Richmond Creek ≃ 276 40.34 N 74.11 W
Richmond Heights, Fl., U.S. 220 25.37 N 80.22 W
Richmond Heights, Mo., U.S. 219 38.37 N 90.19 W
Richmond Heights, Oh., U.S. 214 41.33 N 81.30 W
Richmond Highlands 224 47.45 N 122.20 W
Richmond Hill, On., Can. 212 43.52 N 79.27 W
Richmond Hill, Ga., U.S. 192 31.56 N 81.18 W
Richmond Hill ◆[8] 276 40.42 N 73.49 W
Richmond International Airport ⊠ 208 37.30 N 77.19 W
Richmond Mall ◆[9] 279a 41.32 N 81.30 W
Richmond National Battlefield Park ✦ 208 37.25 N 77.23 W
Richmond Park ✦ 260 51.26 N 0.16 W
Richmond Peak ∧ 241h 13.17 N 61.13 W
Richmond Range ⋏ 172 41.27 S 173.30 E
Richmond Royal Australian Air Force Base ■ 170 33.37 S 150.48 E
Richmond-San Rafael Bridge ◆[5] 282 37.56 N 122.27 W
Richmondtown Restoration ⊥ 276 40.34 N 74.09 W
Richmond Valley ◆[8] 276 40.31 N 74.13 W
Richmondville 210 42.38 N 74.33 W
Richrath 263 51.08 N 6.56 E
Rich Square 192 36.16 N 77.17 W
Rich Stadium ✦ 284a 42.57 N 78.47 W
Richtenberg 54 54.12 N 12.53 E
Richterswil 58 47.13 N 8.42 E
Richton 194 31.20 N 88.56 W
Richton Park 216 41.29 N 87.42 W
Richvale, On., Can. 212 43.51 N 79.26 W
Richvale, Ca., U.S. 226 39.30 N 121.45 W
Richview 219 38.23 N 89.11 W
Richville, N.Y., U.S. 212 44.25 N 75.23 E
Richville, Oh., U.S. 214 40.45 N 81.27 W
Richwood, N.J., U.S. 285 39.43 N 75.10 W
Richwood, Oh., U.S. 214 40.25 N 83.17 W
Richwood, W.V., U.S. 188 38.13 N 80.32 W
Richwood Village 222 29.04 N 95.25 W
Ricinskij zapovednik ✦ 84 43.25 N 40.30 E
Rickenbacker Air Force Base ■ 218 39.48 N 82.56 W
Rickenpass)(58 47.14 N 9.02 E
Ricken Tunnel ◆[5] 58 47.12 N 9.05 E
Ricketts Glen State Park ✦ 210 41.20 N 76.18 W
Ricketts Point > 274b 38.00 S 145.02 E
Rickleån ≃ 26 64.05 N 20.56 E
Rickling 54 54.01 N 10.13 E
Rickmansworth 42 51.39 N 0.29 W
Rico 200 37.41 N 108.01 W
Ricoa ≃ 241s 11.30 N 69.12 W
Ricobayo, Embalse de ⊜[1] 34 41.30 N 5.55 W
Ricupe 152 14.37 S 21.25 E
Ridā' 144 14.38 N 44.54 E
Ridanna (Ridnaun) 64 46.55 N 11.15 E
Riddarhyttan 40 59.48 N 15.33 E
Ridderkerk 52 51.52 N 4.36 E
Riddes 58 46.10 N 7.13 E
Riddle 202 42.57 N 123.21 W
Riddle Mountain ∧ 202 43.07 N 118.30 W
Riddlesburg 214 40.10 N 78.15 W
Riddlewood 285 39.54 N 75.26 W
Riddon, Loch c 46 55.58 N 5.12 W
Rideau ≃ 212 45.27 N 75.42 W
Ridge, Eng., U.K. 260 51.41 N 0.15 W
Ridge, N.Y., U.S. 207 40.54 N 72.53 W
Ridge, Tx., U.S. 222 31.09 N 96.19 W
Ridge Acres 276 40.41 N 74.32 W
Ridgecrest, Ca., U.S. 204 35.37 N 117.40 W
Ridgecrest, Wa., U.S. 224 47.45 N 122.21 W
Ridgedale 184 53.04 N 104.09 W
Ridge Farm 194 39.53 N 87.39 W
Ridgefield, Ct., U.S. 207 41.16 N 73.29 W
Ridgefield, Il., U.S. 216 42.16 N 88.22 W
Ridgefield, N.J., U.S. 210 40.50 N 74.00 W
Ridgefield, Wa., U.S. 224 45.48 N 122.44 W
Ridgefield Park 276 40.51 N 74.01 W
Ridgeland, Ms., U.S. 194 32.25 N 90.07 W
Ridgeland, S.C., U.S. 192 32.28 N 80.58 W
Ridgely, Md., U.S. 208 38.56 N 75.53 W
Ridgely, Tn., U.S. 194 36.15 N 89.29 W
Ridge Manor 220 28.31 N 82.10 W
Ridgemont 210 43.13 N 77.43 W
Ridgetown 214 42.26 N 81.54 W
Ridgeville, Mb., Can. 184 49.04 N 97.01 W
Ridgeville, In., U.S. 216 40.17 N 85.01 W
Ridgeville, S.C., U.S. 192 33.05 N 80.18 W
Ridgeville Corners 216 41.26 N 84.15 W
Ridgeway, On., Can. 284a 42.53 N 79.03 W
Ridgeway, Mi., U.S. 216 41.59 N 83.51 W
Ridgeway, Mo., U.S. 194 40.22 N 93.56 W
Ridgeway, N.J., U.S. 208 40.01 N 74.17 W
Ridgeway, Oh., U.S. 216 40.30 N 83.34 W
Ridgeway, Tx., U.S. 222 33.11 N 95.46 W
Ridgeway, Wi., U.S. 190 43.00 N 89.59 W
Ridgeway Ditch ≊ 279a 41.25 N 82.05 W
Ridgewood 210 40.58 N 74.07 W
Ridgewood ◆[8] 276 40.42 N 73.53 W
Ridgewood Farm 285 39.57 N 75.34 W
Ridgewood Reservoir ⊜[1] 276 40.41 N 73.53 W
Ridgway, Co., U.S. 200 38.09 N 107.46 W
Ridgway, Il., U.S. 194 37.47 N 88.15 W
Ridgway, Pa., U.S. 214 41.25 N 78.43 W
Riding Mountain ∧ 184 50.37 N 99.37 W
Riding Mountain National Park ✦ 184 50.55 N 100.25 W
Ridīwajār 124 27.57 N 83.26 E
Ridley Creek ≃ 285 39.51 N 75.21 W
Ridley Creek State Park ✦ 285 39.57 N 75.27 W
Ridley Park 285 39.52 N 75.19 W
Ridnaun → Ridanna 64 46.55 N 11.15 E
Riebeek-Kasteel 158 33.23 S 18.53 E
Riebeek-Oos 158 33.10 S 26.10 E
Riebeek-Wes 158 33.21 S 18.52 E
Riecawr, Loch ⊜ 44 55.13 N 4.27 W
Riedau 60 48.18 N 13.38 E
Riedelbach 56 50.18 N 8.23 E
Rieden 60 49.19 N 11.57 E
Riedenburg 60 48.58 N 11.41 E
Rieder 54 51.44 N 11.10 E
Riederalp 58 46.23 N 8.01 E
Riedern 56 49.40 N 9.23 E
Ried im Innkreis 60 48.13 N 13.30 E
Ried im Oberinntal 58 47.03 N 10.39 E
Riedisheim 58 47.45 N 7.22 E
Riedlingen 58 48.09 N 9.28 E
Riedstadt 56 49.50 N 8.30 E

Riegel 58 48.09 N 7.45 E
Riegelsville, N.J., U.S. 210 40.49 N 74.52 W
Riegelsville, Pa., U.S. 208 40.36 N 75.12 W
Riegelwood 192 34.20 N 78.15 W
Riegersburg 61 47.00 N 15.56 E
Riegersburg, Schloss ⊥ 61 47.01 N 15.56 E
Riegersdorf 64 46.33 N 13.47 E
Riehen 58 47.35 N 7.39 E
Rieka → Rijeka 36 45.20 N 14.27 E
Rielasingen 58 47.44 N 8.50 E
Riemke ◆[8] 263 51.30 N 7.13 E
Riemst 56 50.48 N 5.36 E
Rieneck 56 50.05 N 9.38 E
Rienza (Rienz) ≃ 64 46.43 N 11.39 E
Rienzi 194 34.45 N 88.31 W
Riesa 54 51.18 N 13.17 E
Riesco, Isla I 254 53.00 S 72.30 W
Rieseby 41 54.32 N 9.48 E
Riesel 222 31.28 N 96.56 W
Riesenbeck 52 52.16 N 7.37 E
Riese Pio X 64 45.44 N 11.55 E
Riesi 70 37.17 N 14.05 E
Riestedt 54 51.29 N 11.21 E
Riet ≃, S. Afr. 158 29.00 S 23.54 E
Riet ≃, S. Afr. 158 31.20 S 20.17 E
Rietavas 76 55.44 N 21.56 E
Rietberg 52 51.47 N 8.25 E
Rietbron 158 32.54 S 23.10 E
Rietfontein 156 21.58 S 20.58 E
Riethuiskraal 158 34.20 S 21.22 E
Rieti 66 42.24 N 12.51 E
Rieti □[4] 66 42.18 N 12.52 E
Rietschen 54 51.23 N 14.47 E
Rietspruit ≃, S. Afr. 273d 26.19 S 28.18 E
Rietspruit ≃, S. Afr. 273d 26.06 S 27.39 E
Rietvlei 158 30.29 S 29.51 E
Rietzer See ⊜ 54 52.22 N 12.39 E
Rievaulx Abbey ♁[1] 44 54.16 N 1.07 W
Riez 62 43.49 N 6.06 E
Riezlern 58 47.21 N 10.11 E
Rif ⋏ 148 35.00 N 4.00 W
Riffe Lake ⊜[1] 224 46.30 N 122.20 W
Rifflart 273b 4.25 S 15.21 E
Rifiano (Riffian) 64 46.42 N 11.11 E
Rifle 200 39.32 N 107.46 W
Rifle ≃ 190 44.00 N 83.49 W
Rifstangi > 24a 66.35 N 16.10 W
Rifton 210 41.50 N 74.03 W
Rift Valley □[4] 154 0.30 N 36.00 E
Rift Valley V 10 3.00 S 29.00 E
Rift Valley Lakes National Park ✦ 144 7.30 N 38.30 E
Rīga, Lat. 76 56.57 N 24.06 E
Riga, Ross. 88 56.36 N 106.17 E
Riga, Mi., U.S. 216 41.49 N 83.50 W
Riga, Gulf of (Rīgas jūras līcis) (Riia laht) c 76 57.30 N 23.35 E
Riga, Mount ∧ 162 21.59 S 116.25 E
Rigacikun 150 10.40 N 7.28 E
Rigaih 114 4.40 N 95.34 E
Rīgān 128 28.37 N 58.58 E
Rīgas jūras līcis → Riga, Gulf of c 76 57.30 N 23.35 E
Rīga Station ◆[5] 265b 55.48 N 37.38 E
Rigaud 206 45.29 N 74.18 W
Rigaud ≃ 206 45.29 N 74.18 W
Rigby 202 43.40 N 111.54 W
Rīgestān ◆[1] 128 31.00 N 65.00 E
Riggins 202 45.25 N 116.18 W
Riggisberg 58 46.48 N 7.29 E
Riggston 219 39.42 N 90.25 W
Righedo, Passo del)(64 44.27 N 9.55 E
Rigi ∧ 58 47.05 N 8.30 E
Rignano Flaminio 66 42.12 N 12.29 E
Rignano Garganico 68 41.40 N 15.35 E
Rignano sull'Arno 66 43.43 N 11.27 E
Rigney 58 47.23 N 6.11 E
Rigney Bluff 210 43.19 N 77.38 W
Rigny-Ussé 50 47.15 N 0.18 E
Rigo 164 9.47 S 147.34 E
Rigolet 176 54.20 N 58.35 W
Rig-Rig 146 14.16 N 14.21 E
Rigside 46 55.36 N 3.47 W
Riguldi 76 59.08 N 23.33 E
Rīḥ, Jazīrat ar- I 140 18.10 N 38.27 E
Riḥāb 132 32.19 N 36.06 E
Rihand ≃ 124 24.33 N 82.59 E
Rihand Dam ◆[6] 124 24.05 N 82.45 E
Riihimäki 26 60.45 N 24.46 E
Riiser-Larsen Peninsula >[1] 9 68.55 S 34.00 E
Rijau 150 11.07 N 5.14 E
Riječki Zaljev c 36 45.15 N 14.25 E
Rijeka 36 45.20 N 14.27 E
Rijen 52 51.35 N 4.55 E
Rijkevorsel 56 51.21 N 4.46 E
Rijksdorp 52 52.09 N 4.25 E
Rijn → Rhine ≃ 30 51.52 N 6.02 E
Rijnsburg 52 52.12 N 4.27 E
Rijssel → Lille 50 50.38 N 3.04 E
Rijssen 52 52.18 N 6.30 E
Rijswijk 52 52.04 N 4.20 E
Rike 144 10.42 N 39.55 E
Rikers Island I 276 40.47 N 73.53 W
Rikers Island Channel ʊ 276 40.47 N 73.52 W
Rikkavesi ⊜ 26 62.50 N 28.44 E
Riksgränsen 24 68.24 N 18.12 E
Rikuchū-kaigan-kokuritsu-kōen ✦ 92 39.25 N 141.57 E
Rikuzen-takata 92 39.01 N 141.38 E
Rila ⋏ 38 42.08 N 23.33 E
Riley 198 39.17 N 96.49 W
Riley, Mount ∧ 200 31.55 N 107.07 W
Riley, Point > 168b 33.53 S 137.36 E
Riley Creek ≃ 216 41.02 N 84.00 W
Riley Lake ⊜ 212 44.50 N 79.11 W
Rileys Range ⋏ 170 34.21 S 150.10 E
Rilievo 70 37.55 N 12.33 E
Rillieux 62 45.49 N 4.54 E
Rillington 44 54.09 N 0.42 W
Rillito 200 32.24 N 111.09 W
Rillton 214 40.17 N 79.44 W
Rilly-la-Montagne 50 49.10 N 4.03 E
Rilski manastir ♁[1] 38 42.08 N 23.20 E
Rima ≃ 150 13.04 N 5.10 E
Rímac 286d 12.03 S 77.03 W
Rímac ≃ 248 12.02 S 77.09 W
Rimachi, Laguna ⊜ 246 4.25 S 76.43 W
Rimāḥ, Jabal ar- ∧ 132 32.19 N 36.52 E
Rima San Giuseppe 62 45.52 N 8.00 E
Rimatara I 14 22.38 S 152.51 W
Rimavská Sobota 30 48.23 N 20.02 E
Rimbey 182 52.38 N 114.14 W
Rimbo 40 59.45 N 18.22 E
Rimé, Ouadi V 146 14.02 N 18.03 E
Rimersburg 214 41.02 N 79.30 W
Rimforsa 26 58.08 N 15.40 E
Rimi 150 12.58 N 7.43 E
Rimini 66 44.04 N 12.34 E
Rîmna ≃ 38 45.39 N 27.19 E
Rîmnicu Sărat 38 45.23 N 27.03 E
Rîmnicu Vîlcea 38 45.06 N 24.22 E
Rimo Glacier ⊓ 123 35.25 N 77.30 E
Rimogne 56 49.50 N 4.33 E
Rimouski 186 48.26 N 68.33 W
Rimouski ≃ 186 48.27 N 68.32 W
Rimouski, Réserve ✦ 186 48.03 N 68.15 W
Rimpar 56 49.51 N 9.57 E
Rimrock Lake ⊜[1] 224 46.38 N 121.12 W
Rimsko-Korsakovka 80 51.34 N 48.31 E
Rinbung 124 29.21 N 89.57 E
Rinca 115b 8.37 S 119.48 E
Rinca, Pulau I 115b 8.41 S 119.42 E

Rinchnach 60 48.57 N 13.12 E
Rinčin Lchumbe 88 51.07 N 99.40 E
Rincón, C.R. 236 8.42 N 83.29 W
Rincón, P.R. 240m 18.20 N 67.15 W
Rincon, Ga., U.S. 192 32.17 N 81.14 W
Rincon, N.M., U.S. 200 32.40 N 107.03 W
Rincón, Bahía de c 240m 17.58 N 66.20 W
Rinconada 252 22.26 S 66.10 W
Rinconada, Hipódromo de la ✦ 286c 10.26 N 66.56 W
Rincón de la Vieja, Parque Nacional ✦ 236 10.48 N 85.18 W
Rincón del Bonete, Lago Artificial de ⊜[1] 252 32.45 S 56.00 W
Rincón del Ocote, Cerro ∧ 236 13.36 N 87.10 W
Rincón de Romos 234 22.14 N 102.18 W
Rincon Indian Reservation ◆[4] 228 33.15 N 116.57 W
Rincon Valley 226 38.28 N 122.39 W
Rindal 26 63.03 N 9.13 E
Rindown Castle ⊥ 48 53.32 N 7.59 W
Rīngas 120 27.21 N 75.34 E
Ringdove 175f 16.38 S 168.09 E
Ringe 41 55.14 N 10.29 E
Ringebu 26 61.31 N 10.10 E
Ringenwalde 54 53.03 N 13.42 E
Ringertown 279b 40.25 N 79.36 W
Ringford 44 54.54 N 4.03 W
Ringgau ◆[1] 56 51.04 N 10.04 E
Ringgit, Gunung ∧ 115a 7.43 S 113.50 E
Ringgold, Ga., U.S. 192 34.54 N 85.06 W
Ringgold, La., U.S. 194 32.19 N 93.16 W
Ringgold, Pa., U.S. 214 41.00 N 79.10 W
Ringgold Isles II 175g 16.15 S 179.25 W
Ringim 150 12.08 N 9.10 E
Ringkøbing 26 56.05 N 8.15 E
Ringkøbing □[6] 41 56.10 N 8.50 E
Ringkøbing Fjord c[2] 26 56.00 N 8.15 E
Ringlet 114 4.25 N 101.23 E
Ringling 196 34.10 N 97.35 W
Ringling Museums ♁ 220 27.23 N 82.34 W
Ringmer 42 50.53 N 0.04 E
Ringoes 208 40.26 N 74.52 W
Rings Island 283 42.49 N 70.52 W
Ringsted, Dan. 41 55.27 N 11.49 E
Ringsted, Ia., U.S. 198 43.17 N 94.30 W
Ringtown 210 40.51 N 76.14 W
Ringvassøy I 24 69.55 N 19.15 E
Ringville 48 52.02 N 7.34 W
Ringwood, Austl. 169 37.49 S 145.14 E
Ringwood, Eng., U.K. 42 50.51 N 1.47 W
Ringwood, N.J., U.S. 210 41.06 N 74.14 W
Ringwood Manor ⊥ 276 41.08 N 74.15 W
Ringwood North 274b 37.48 S 145.14 E
Ringwood State Park ✦ 210 41.08 N 74.16 W
Riñihue 254 39.49 S 72.27 W
Riñihue, Lago ⊜ 254 39.50 S 72.18 W
Rinjani, Gunung ∧ 115b 8.24 S 116.28 E
Rinkenæs 41 54.54 N 9.34 E
Rinkerode 52 51.50 N 7.41 E
Rinnes, Ben ∧ 46 57.23 N 3.15 W
Rinnthal 56 49.13 N 7.55 E
Rín → Rhine ≃ 30 51.52 N 6.02 E
Rinsumageest 52 53.18 N 5.57 E
Rinteln 52 52.11 N 9.04 E
Rinxent 50 50.48 N 1.44 E
Rio, Fl., U.S. 220 27.13 N 80.14 W
Rio, Wi., U.S. 190 43.26 N 89.14 W
Rio Azul 252 25.43 S 50.47 W
Riobamba 246 1.40 S 78.38 W
Río Blanco, Chile 252 32.55 S 70.19 W
Río Blanco (Tenango de Rio Blanco), Méx. 234 18.50 N 97.09 W
Rio Bonito 256 22.43 S 42.37 W
Rio Bonito ◆[8] 287b 23.43 S 46.41 W
Rio Branco, Bra. 248 9.58 S 67.48 W
Río Branco, Ur. 252 32.34 S 53.25 W
Río Bravo, Méx. 196 28.17 N 100.55 W
Río Bravo, Méx. 232 25.59 N 98.06 W
Rio Brilhante 255 21.48 S 54.33 W
Río Bueno 254 40.19 S 72.58 W
Río Caribe 246 10.42 N 63.07 W
Rio Casca 255 20.13 S 42.39 W
Río Cauto 240p 20.33 N 76.55 W
Río Ceballos 252 31.10 S 64.20 W
Río Chico, Arg. 254 41.43 S 70.30 W
Río Chico, Ven. 246 10.18 N 65.59 W
Rio Claro, Bra. 255 22.24 S 47.33 W
Rio Claro, Bra. 256 22.43 S 44.09 W
Rio Claro, Trin. 241r 10.18 N 61.11 W
Rio Claro, Represa do ⊜[1] 256 23.39 S 45.54 W
Río Colorado 252 39.01 S 64.05 W
Rio Comprido ◆[8] 287a 22.55 S 43.12 W
Río Cuarto 252 33.08 S 64.21 W
Rio das Flores 256 22.10 S 43.35 W
Rio das Pedras 156 23.12 S 35.23 E
Rio de Contas 255 13.36 S 41.48 W
Rio de Janeiro, Bra. 256 22.54 S 43.14 W
Rio de Janeiro, Bra. 287a 22.54 S 43.14 W
Rio de Janeiro □[3] 255 22.00 S 42.30 W
Rio de Janeiro □[7] 287a 22.55 S 43.30 W
Río de Jesús 236 7.59 N 81.10 W
Rio Dell 204 40.29 N 124.06 W
Rio de Mouro 266c 38.46 N 9.20 W
Río de Oro 246 8.17 N 73.23 W
Rio do Prado 255 16.35 S 40.34 W
Rio do Sul 252 27.13 S 49.39 W
Rio Douro 287a 22.39 S 43.32 W
Rio Espera 255 20.51 S 43.29 W
Río Gallegos 254 51.38 S 69.13 W
Río Grande, Arg. 254 53.47 S 67.42 W
Rio Grande, Bra. 252 32.02 S 52.05 W
Río Grande, Méx. 234 15.59 N 97.27 W
Río Grande, Méx. 234 23.50 N 103.02 W
Río Grande, Nic. 236 12.53 N 86.32 W
Río Grande, P.R. 240m 18.23 N 65.50 W
Rio Grande, N.J., U.S. 208 39.00 N 74.52 W
Río Grande, Ven. 286c 10.35 N 66.57 W
Rio Grande, Ponte do ◆[5] 287b 23.46 S 46.31 W
Rio Grande City 196 26.22 N 98.49 W
Rio Grande Da Serra, Bra. 256 23.44 S 46.24 W
Rio Grande da Serra, Bra. 287b 23.44 S 46.24 W
Rio Grande da Serra □[7] 287b 23.45 S 46.23 W
Rio Grande do Norte □[3] 250 5.45 S 36.00 W
Rio Grande do Sul □[3] 252 30.00 S 54.00 W
Rio Grande do Sul → Rio Grande 252 32.02 S 52.05 W
Rio Grande → Grande, Rio ≃ 178 25.57 N 97.09 W
Riograndina 256 22.11 S 42.30 W
Ríohacha 246 11.33 N 72.55 W
Río Hato 236 8.23 N 80.10 W
Río Hondo, Méx. 286a 19.25 N 99.16 W
Rio Hondo, Tx., U.S. 196 26.14 N 97.34 W
Rioja 248 6.05 S 77.09 W
Rio Jaguari, Reservatório do ⊜[1] 256 22.55 S 46.25 W
Río Jueyes 240m 18.01 N 66.20 W
Riola 64 44.16 N 11.04 E
Río Lagartos 232 21.36 N 88.10 W
Riolândia 255 19.59 S 49.40 W
Rio Largo 250 9.29 S 35.51 W
Riola Sardo 71 39.59 N 8.32 E
Rio Linda 226 38.41 N 121.26 W
Riolo Terme 66 44.16 N 11.43 E
Río Luján 258 34.17 S 58.54 W
Riom 32 45.54 N 3.07 E
Riomaggiore 62 44.06 N 9.44 E

Rio Marina 66 42.49 N 10.25 E
Río Mayo 254 45.41 S 70.16 W
Rio Mulatos 248 19.42 S 66.47 W
Río Muni □[4] 152 1.30 N 10.30 E
Riondel 182 49.46 N 116.52 W
Rio Negro, Bra. 252 26.06 S 49.48 W
Rio Negro, Bra. 255 19.27 S 54.58 W
Río Negro, Chile 254 40.47 S 73.14 W
Ríonegro, Col. 246 6.09 N 75.22 W
Ríonegro, Col. 246 7.16 N 73.09 W
Río Negro □[4] 254 40.00 S 67.00 W
Rio Negro, Pantanal do ⁝ 248 19.00 S 56.00 W
Rionero in Vulture 68 40.56 N 15.41 E
Rionero Sannitico 66 41.42 N 14.08 E
Rioni ≃ 84 42.08 N 41.39 E
Rio Novo 256 21.29 S 43.08 W
Rio Novo do Sul 255 20.52 S 40.56 W
Riópar 34 38.30 N 2.27 W
Rio Pardo 252 29.59 S 52.22 W
Rio Pardo de Minas 255 15.37 S 42.33 W
Río Pico 254 44.13 S 71.21 W
Río Piedras, Arg. 252 25.18 S 64.54 W
Río Piedras, P.R. 240m 18.24 N 66.03 W
Río Pilcomayo, Parque Nacional ✦ 252 25.10 S 58.00 W
Rio Piracicaba 255 19.55 S 43.11 W
Rio Pomba 256 21.17 S 43.11 W
Rio Prêto 256 22.06 S 43.50 W
Rio Prêto → São José do Rio Prêto 256 22.10 S 42.57 W
Rio Rancho 200 35.14 N 106.38 W
Rio Real 250 11.28 S 37.56 W
Rio Saliceto 64 44.49 N 10.49 E
Río San Juan □[5] 236 11.10 N 84.30 W
Río Segundo 252 31.40 S 63.55 W
Ríosucio, Col. 246 5.25 N 75.42 W
Ríosucio, Col. 246 7.27 N 77.07 W
Río Tercero 252 32.11 S 64.06 W
Rio Tinto 250 6.48 S 35.05 W
Riotord 62 45.14 N 4.24 E
Rio Tuba 116 8.30 N 117.25 E
Riou, Île de I 62 43.11 N 5.24 E
Rioveggio 64 44.17 N 11.14 E
Rio Verde, Bra. 255 17.43 S 50.56 W
Ríoverde, Méx. 234 21.56 N 99.59 W
Rio Verde de Mato Grosso 255 18.56 S 54.52 W
Rio Vermelho 255 18.18 S 43.00 W
Rio Vista, Ca., U.S. 226 38.09 N 121.41 W
Rio Vista, Tx., U.S. 222 32.14 N 97.23 W
Rioz 58 47.25 N 6.04 E
Riozinho ≃, Bra. 246 2.55 S 67.07 W
Riozinho ≃, Bra. 250 10.22 S 49.50 W
Riozinho ≃, Bra. 250 7.06 S 51.40 W
Riozinho ≃, Bra. 250 8.25 S 45.43 W
Řip ∧ 54 50.24 N 14.18 E
Ripacandida 68 40.55 N 15.43 E
Ripalti, Punta dei > 66 42.42 N 10.25 E
Ripatransone 66 43.00 N 13.46 E
Ripley, Eng., U.K. 42 53.03 N 1.24 W
Ripley, Eng., U.K. 260 51.18 N 0.29 W
Ripley, Il., U.S. 219 40.01 N 90.38 W
Ripley, In., U.S. 216 41.06 N 86.39 W
Ripley, Ms., U.S. 194 34.43 N 88.57 W
Ripley, N.Y., U.S. 214 42.16 N 79.42 W
Ripley, Oh., U.S. 218 38.44 N 83.50 W
Ripley, Tn., U.S. 194 35.44 N 89.31 W
Ripley, W.V., U.S. 188 38.49 N 81.42 W
Ripley □[6] 218 39.04 N 85.15 W
Ripoll 34 42.12 N 2.12 E
Ripoll ≃ 266d 41.29 N 2.12 E
Ripollet 266d 41.30 N 2.10 E
Ripon, P.Q., Can. 206 45.47 N 75.06 W
Ripon, Eng., U.K. 44 54.08 N 1.31 W
Ripon, Ca., U.S. 226 37.44 N 121.07 W
Ripon, Wi., U.S. 190 43.50 N 88.50 W
Riposto 70 37.44 N 15.12 E
Rippling Ridge 284b 39.11 N 76.37 W
Ripponden 44 53.41 N 1.57 W
Rippowam ≃ 276 41.03 N 73.33 W
Riquewihr 58 48.10 N 7.18 E
Ririba, Laga ≃ 154 3.34 N 37.15 E
Ririe 202 43.37 N 111.46 W
Risālpur Cantonment 123 34.04 N 72.00 E
Risaralda □[5] 246 5.00 N 76.00 W
Risasi 154 0.25 S 25.44 E
Risbäck 26 64.42 N 15.32 E
Risca 42 51.37 N 3.07 W
Rischenau 52 51.53 N 9.17 E
Riscle 32 43.40 N 0.05 W
Risco, Ilha do I 246 3.07 S 58.19 W
Rishā', Wādī ar- V 128 25.33 N 44.05 E
Rīshahr 128 28.55 N 50.50 E
Rishīkesh 124 30.07 N 78.19 E
Rishiri-Rebun-Sarobetsu-kokuritsu-kōen ✦ 92a 45.10 N 141.35 E
Rishiri-suidō ʊ 92a 45.10 N 141.25 E
Rishiri-tō I 92a 45.11 N 141.15 E
Rishiri-zan ∧ 92a 45.11 N 141.15 E
Rishmayyā 132 33.44 N 35.36 E
Rishon LeẔiyyon 132 31.58 N 34.48 E
Rishpon 132 32.12 N 34.49 E
Rishra 272b 22.43 N 88.21 E
Rishrāsh, Wādī V 142 29.29 N 31.16 E
Rishton 262 53.46 N 2.25 W
Rishworth 262 53.40 N 1.57 W
Rishworth Moor ◆[3] 262 53.39 N 2.01 W
Risinge 40 58.42 N 15.51 E
Rising Star 196 32.05 N 98.57 W
Rising Sun, In., U.S. 218 38.56 N 84.51 W
Rising Sun, Md., U.S. 208 39.41 N 76.03 W
Risingsun, Oh., U.S. 214 41.16 N 83.25 W
Risle ≃ 50 49.26 N 0.23 E
Risnjak ∧ 36 45.26 N 14.37 E
Rîşnov 38 45.36 N 25.28 E
Risø 41 55.42 N 12.06 E
Rison, Ar., U.S. 194 33.57 N 92.11 W
Rison, Md., U.S. 208 38.32 N 77.10 W
Risør 26 58.43 N 9.14 E
Ris-Orangis 50 48.39 N 2.25 E
Riss ≃ 58 48.17 N 9.49 E
Rissani 148 31.23 N 4.09 W
Risskov ◆[8] 41 56.11 N 10.14 E
Risstissen 58 48.16 N 9.49 E
Risti 76 58.59 N 24.03 E
Ristigouche (Restigouche) ≃ 186 48.04 N 66.20 W
Ristiina 26 61.30 N 27.16 E
Ristijärvi 26 64.44 N 28.24 E
Ristinge 41 54.50 N 10.38 E
Ristna 76 58.56 N 22.05 E
Risum-Lindholm 41 54.45 N 8.53 E
Rita Blanca Creek ≃ 196 35.40 N 102.29 W
Ritchie, S. Afr. 158 29.02 S 24.38 E
Ritchie, Md., U.S. 284c 38.52 N 76.52 W
Ritchie Branch ≃ 284c 38.53 N 76.52 W
Rithāla ◆[8] 272a 28.43 N 77.06 E
Ritidian Point > 174p 13.39 N 144.51 E
Ritscher Upland ⋏[1] 9 73.20 S 9.30 W
Ritsumeikan University ♁[2] 270 35.01 N 135.46 E
Ritsurin-kōen ✦ 96 34.21 N 134.02 E
Ritta Island I 220 26.44 N 80.48 W
Ritter, Mount ∧ 226 37.42 N 119.12 W
Ritterhude 52 53.11 N 8.45 E
Rittersgrün 54 50.29 N 12.47 E
Rittman 214 40.58 N 81.46 W
Rittō 94 35.01 N 136.00 E
Ritzleben 54 52.50 N 11.21 E
Ritzville 202 47.07 N 118.22 W
Riu 120 28.19 N 95.03 E
Riva 208 38.57 N 76.35 W
Rivadavia, Arg. 252 35.28 S 62.57 W
Rivadavia, Arg. 252 33.11 S 68.28 W
Rivadavia, Arg. 252 24.11 S 62.53 W
Rivadavia, Arg. 252 31.33 S 68.37 W
Rivadavia, Chile 252 29.58 S 70.34 W

Riva del Garda 64 45.53 N 10.50 E
Riva del Sole 66 42.46 N 10.52 E
Riva di Tures (Rain) 64 46.57 N 12.04 E
Rivanazzano 62 44.56 N 9.01 E
Rivanna ≃ 192 37.45 N 78.10 W
Rivare 216 40.49 N 84.50 W
Rivarolo Canavese 62 45.19 N 7.43 E
Rivarolo Mantovano 64 45.04 N 10.26 E
Rivas 236 11.26 N 85.50 W
Rivas □[5] 236 11.25 N 85.50 W
Rivasdale 273d 26.17 S 27.56 E
Rīvash 128 35.26 N 58.26 E
Rivas-Vaciamadrid 266a 40.20 N 3.31 W
Riva Trigoso 62 44.16 N 9.26 E
Rive, Île de la I 273b 4.21 S 15.26 E
Rive d'Arcano 64 46.08 N 13.02 E
Rive-de-Gier 62 45.32 N 4.37 E
Rivello 68 40.04 N 15.45 E
Rivera, Arg. 252 37.12 S 63.14 W
Rivera, Col. 246 2.47 N 75.15 W
Rivera, Ur. 252 30.54 S 55.31 W
Riverbank 226 37.44 N 120.56 W
River Cess 150 5.28 N 9.32 W
Riverdale, Ca., U.S. 226 36.25 N 119.51 W
Riverdale, Il., U.S. 278 41.38 N 87.37 W
Riverdale, Md., U.S. 284c 38.57 N 76.55 W
Riverdale, N.J., U.S. 276 40.59 N 74.18 W
Riverdale, N.D., U.S. 198 47.29 N 101.22 W
Riverdale, Or., U.S. 224 45.27 N 122.41 W
Riverdale ◆[8] 276 40.54 N 73.54 W
Riverdale Heights 284c 38.58 N 76.55 W
Riverdale Park ✦ 275b 43.40 N 79.21 W
River Drive Park 212 44.08 N 79.31 W
River Edge, N.J., U.S. 276 40.55 N 74.02 W
River Edge, Oh., U.S. 279a 41.25 N 81.51 W
River Falls, Al., U.S. 194 31.21 N 86.32 W
River Falls, Wi., U.S. 190 44.51 N 92.37 W
River Forest 278 41.53 N 87.48 W
Rivergaro 62 44.55 N 9.36 E
River Grove 278 41.55 N 87.50 W
Riverhaven 216 41.05 N 85.02 W
Riverhead, Eng., U.K. 260 51.17 N 0.10 E
Riverhead, N.Y., U.S. 207 40.55 N 72.39 W
River Hébert 186 45.42 N 64.23 W
River Hill 279b 40.12 N 79.54 W
River Hills 216 43.10 N 87.55 W
Riverhurst 184 50.53 N 106.52 W
Riverina ◆[1] 166 35.30 S 145.30 E
River John 186 45.45 N 63.03 W
River Jordan 224 48.25 N 124.03 W
Riverlea 214 40.05 N 83.02 W
River Lea Navigation ≊ 260 51.32 N 0.02 W
River Meadow Brook ≃ 283 42.38 N 71.17 W
Rivermont 192 35.13 N 77.38 W
Rivero, Isla I 254 45.37 S 74.20 W
River Oaks 284c 38.57 N 77.11 W
River of Ponds 186 50.32 N 57.24 W
River Pines, Ca., U.S. 226 38.33 N 120.45 W
River Pines, Ma., U.S. 207 42.33 N 71.17 W
River Plaza 208 40.21 N 74.05 W
River Ridge Estates 284c 38.47 N 77.00 W
River Road 202 44.03 N 123.05 W
River Rouge 216 42.16 N 83.08 W
River Rouge Park ✦ 281 42.22 N 83.15 W
Rivers 184 50.02 N 100.12 W
Rivers □[3] 150 4.30 N 6.30 E
Rivers, Lake of the ⊜ 184 49.45 N 105.45 W
Riversdale, N.Z. 172 45.54 S 168.45 E
Riversdale, S. Afr. 158 34.07 S 21.15 E
Riverside, Ca., U.S. 228 33.57 N 117.23 W
Riverside, Ct., U.S. 276 41.02 N 73.35 W
Riverside, Il., U.S. 278 41.50 N 87.49 W
Riverside, Ia., U.S. 190 41.28 N 91.34 W
Riverside, Mi., U.S. 216 42.11 N 86.23 W
Riverside, Mi., U.S. 216 42.17 N 84.29 W
Riverside, N.J., U.S. 208 40.01 N 74.57 W
Riverside, N.Y., U.S. 210 42.55 N 73.40 W
Riverside, N.Y., U.S. 210 42.08 N 77.01 W
Riverside, Pa., U.S. 210 40.57 N 76.38 W
Riverside, Tx., U.S. 222 30.57 N 95.24 W
Riverside, Wa., U.S. 182 48.30 N 119.30 W
Riverside □[6] 228 33.45 N 117.10 W
Riverside ◆[8] 281 42.20 N 82.57 W
Riverside International Raceway ✦ 228 33.57 N 117.17 W
Riverside Manors 284a 43.11 N 79.03 W
Riverside Park ✦, Mi., U.S. 281 42.22 N 83.26 W
Riverside Park ✦, N.Y., U.S. 284a 42.57 N 78.54 W
Rivers Inlet 182 51.41 N 127.15 W
Rivers Inlet c 182 51.39 N 127.30 W
Riversleigh 166 19.02 S 138.44 E
Riverstone 170 33.40 S 150.52 E
Riverton, Austl. 168b 34.09 S 138.45 E
Riverton, Mb., Can. 184 50.59 N 96.59 W
Riverton, N.Z. 172 46.21 S 168.01 E
Riverton, Il., U.S. 219 39.51 N 89.33 W
Riverton, Ne., U.S. 198 40.05 N 98.45 W
Riverton, N.J., U.S. 208 40.00 N 75.00 W
Riverton, Ut,. U.S. 200 40.31 N 111.56 W
Riverton, Va., U.S. 188 38.56 N 78.11 W
Riverton, Wy., U.S. 200 43.01 N 108.22 W
Riverton Heights 224 47.28 N 122.18 W
River Vale 276 40.59 N 74.00 W
Riverview, S. Afr. 158 28.27 S 32.10 E
River View, Al., U.S. 194 32.47 N 85.08 W
Riverview, Fl., U.S. 220 27.51 N 82.19 W
Riverview, Ks., U.S. 198 37.47 N 97.22 W
Riverview, Mi., U.S. 216 42.10 N 83.10 W
Riverview Park ✦ 279b 40.29 N 80.01 W
Riverwood, Austl. 274a 33.57 S 151.03 E
Riverwood, In., U.S. 218 40.06 N 85.58 W
Riverwoods 278 42.10 N 87.54 W
Rives, Fr. 62 45.21 N 5.30 E
Rives, Tn., U.S. 194 36.21 N 89.02 W
Rivesaltes 32 42.46 N 2.52 E
Rives Junction 216 42.23 N 84.27 W
Rive Sud, Canal de la ≊ 275a 45.25 N 73.41 W
Rivesville 188 39.31 N 80.07 W
Riviera, Az., U.S. 204 35.04 N 114.35 W
Riviera, Tx., U.S. 196 27.18 N 97.49 W
Riviera V 58 46.15 N 8.58 E
Riviera Beach, Fl., U.S. 220 26.46 N 80.03 W
Riviera Beach, Md., U.S. 208 39.10 N 76.30 W
Rivière-à-Claude 186 49.13 N 65.54 W
Rivière-au-Tonnerre 186 50.16 N 64.47 W
Rivière-Bleue 186 47.26 N 69.03 W
Rivière-Bois-Clair 206 46.34 N 71.50 W
Rivière-de-la-Chaloupe 186 49.08 N 62.32 W
Rivière-des-Prairies ◆[8] 275a 45.39 N 73.33 W
Rivière-du-Loup 186 47.50 N 69.32 W
Rivière du Rempart 157c 20.06 S 57.41 E
Rivière-Matane 186 48.39 N 67.20 W
Rivière-Mékinac 206 46.47 N 72.48 W
Rivière-Pentecôte 186 49.47 N 67.10 W
Rivière-Pilote 240e 14.29 N 60.54 W
Rivière-Salée 240e 14.32 N 60.59 W
Rivière-Verte 186 47.19 N 68.09 W
Riviersonderend 158 34.09 S 19.55 E
Rivignano 64 45.52 N 13.03 E
Rivington 262 53.37 N 2.34 W
Rivington Reservoirs ⊜[1] 262 53.37 N 2.34 W
Rivisondoli 66 41.52 N 14.04 E
Rivoli 62 45.04 N 7.31 E
Rivoli Bay c 166 37.32 S 140.04 E
Rivolta d'Adda 62 45.28 N 9.31 E
Rivoltella 64 45.27 N 10.33 E
Riwaka 172 41.05 S 173.00 E

≃ River	Fluß	Río	Rivière	Rio
≊ Canal	Kanal	Canal	Canal	Canal
ʟ Waterfall, Rapids	Wasserfall, Stromschnellen	Cascada, Rápidos	Chute d'eau, Rapides	Cascata, Rápidos
ʊ Strait	Meeresstraße	Estrecho	Détroit	Estreito
c Bay, Gulf	Bucht, Golf	Bahía, Golfo	Baie, Golfe	Baía, Golfo
⊜ Lake, Lakes	See, Seen	Lago, Lagos	Lac, Lacs	Lago, Lagos
⁝ Swamp	Sumpf	Pantano	Marais	Pântano
⊓ Ice Features, Glacier	Eis- und Gletscherformen	Accidentes Glaciales	Formes glaciaires	Acidentes glaciares
⊤ Other Hydrographic Features	Andere Hydrographische Objekte	Otros Elementos Hidrográficos	Autres données hydrographiques	Outros acidentes hidrográficos

✣ Submarine Features	Untermeerische Objekte	Accidentes Submarinos	Formes de relief sous-marin	Acidentes submarinos
□ Political Unit	Politische Einheit	Unidad Politica	Entité politique	Unidade política
♁ Cultural Institution	Kulturelle Institution	Institución Cultural	Institution culturelle	Institução cultural
⊥ Historical Site	Historische Stätte	Sitio Histórico	Site historique	Sitio histórico
✦ Recreational Site	Erholungs- und Ferienort	Sitio de Recreo	Centre de loisirs	Area de Lazer
⊠ Airport	Flughafen	Aeropuerto	Aéroport	Aeroporto
■ Military Installation	Militäranlage	Instalación Militar	Installation militaire	Instalação militar
◆ Miscellaneous	Verschiedenes	Misceláneo	Divers	Diversos

ENGLISH / DEUTSCH

Symbols in the index entries represent the broad categories identified in the key at the right. Symbols with superior numbers (⋏[1]) identify subcategories (see complete key on page *I · 1*).

Symbole im Register stellen die rechts im Schlüssel erklärten Kategorien dar. Symbole mit hochgestellten Ziffern (⋏[1]) bezeichnen Unterabteilungen einer Kategorie (vgl. vollständiger Schlüssel auf Seite *I · 1*).

Los símbolos incluídos en el texto del índice representan las grandes categorias identificadas con la clave a la derecha. Los símbolos con numeros en su parte superior (⋏[1]) identifican las subcategorías (véase la clave completa en la página *I · 1*).

Les symboles de l'index représentent les catégories indiquées dans la légende à droite. Les symboles suivis d'un indice (⋏[1]) représentent des sous-catégories (voir légende complète à la page *I · 1*).

Os símbolos incluídos no texto do índice representam as grandes categorias identificadas com a chave à direita. Os símbolos com números em sua parte superior (⋏[1]) identificam as subcategorias (veja-se a chave completa à página *I · 1*).

∧	Mountain	Berg	Montaña	Montagne	Montanha
⋏	Mountains	Gebirge	Montañas	Montagnes	Montanhas
)(	Pass	Paß	Paso	Col	Passo
V	Valley, Canyon	Tal, Cañon	Valle, Cañón	Vallée, Canyon	Vale, Canhão
≚	Plain	Ebene	Llano	Plaine	Planície
›	Cape	Kap	Cabo	Cap	Cabo
I	Island	Insel	Isla	Île	Ilha
II	Islands	Inseln	Islas	Îles	Ilhas
⊥	Other Topographic Features	Andere Topographische Objekte	Otros Elementos Topográficos	Autres données topographiques	Outros acidentes topográficos

ESPAÑOL — Nombre · Página · Lat.°′ · Long.°′ W = Oeste
FRANÇAIS — Nom · Page · Lat.°′ · Long.°′ W = Ouest
PORTUGUÊS — Nome · Página · Lat.°′ · Long.°′ W = Oeste

Romiley 262 53.25 N 2.05 W
Romilly, Mount ∧[2] 162 20.27 S 126.34 E
Romilly-sur-Seine 50 48.31 N 3.43 E
Romit 85 38.44 N 69.17 E
Romit, zapovednik ♠ 85 38.52 N 69.20 E
Romita 234 20.52 N 101.31 W
Romitorio 267a 42.01 N 12.39 E
Rommani 148 34.34 N 6.37 W
Romme 40 60.26 N 15.30 E
Rommerskirchen 56 51.02 N 6.40 E
Romney, In., U.S. 216 40.14 N 86.54 W
Romney, W.V., U.S. 188 39.20 N 78.45 W
Romney Marsh ⁝ 42 51.03 N 0.55 E
Romny, Ross. 89 50.44 N 129.15 E
Romny, Ukr. 78 50.45 N 33.30 E
Rømø I 26 55.08 N 8.31 E
Romodan 78 49.59 N 33.19 E
Romodanovo 80 54.26 N 45.20 E
Romoland 228 33.45 N 117.10 W
Romont 58 46.42 N 6.55 E
Romorantin-Lanthenay 50 47.22 N 1.45 E
Rompin, Malay. 114 2.42 N 102.31 E
Rompin, Malay. 114 2.48 N 103.29 E
Rompin ≃ 114 2.49 N 103.29 E
Romrod 56 50.43 N 9.13 E
Rom → Roma 66 41.54 N 12.29 E
Romsdalen V 26 62.15 N 8.05 E
Romsdalsfjorden ⊂[2] 26 62.39 N 7.15 E
Romsey, Austl. 169 37.21 S 144.45 E
Romsey, Eng., U.K. 42 50.59 N 1.30 W
Romsø I 41 55.31 N 10.48 E
Romulus, Mi., U.S. 216 42.13 N 83.23 W
Romulus, N.Y., U.S. 210 42.45 N 76.50 W
Røn, Nor. 26 61.03 N 9.03 E
Ron, Viet 110 17.53 N 106.27 E
Ron, Mui ≻ 110 18.07 N 106.27 E
Rona, Schw. 58 46.34 N 9.38 E
Rona, Zaïre 154 2.14 N 30.52 E
Rona I, Scot., U.K. 46 57.34 N 5.59 W
Rona I, Scot., U.K. 46 59.07 N 5.49 W
Ronald 224 47.14 N 121.01 W
Ronan 202 47.31 N 114.06 W
Ronas Hill ∧[2] 46a 60.31 N 1.28 W
Ronas Voe ⊂ 46a 60.32 N 1.29 W
Ronay I 46 57.29 N 7.11 W
Roncade 64 45.38 N 12.22 E
Roncador, Cayos de ✧[4] 236 13.32 N 80.03 W
Roncador, Serra do ⋏[1] 242 12.00 S 52.00 W
Roncador Reef ✧[2] 175e 6.13 S 159.22 E
Roncegno 64 46.03 N 11.25 E
Roncesvalles 34 43.01 N 1.19 W
Ronceverte 192 37.44 N 80.27 W
Ronchamp 58 47.42 N 6.39 E
Ronchi dei Legionari 64 45.50 N 13.30 E
Ronchin 50 50.36 N 3.06 E
Ronchis 64 45.49 N 13.00 E
Ronciglione 66 42.17 N 12.13 E
Ronco 58 46.08 N 8.44 E
Ronco Canavese 62 45.30 N 7.32 E
Roncofreddo 66 44.02 N 12.20 E
Roncone 64 45.59 N 10.40 E
Ronco Scrivia 62 44.37 N 8.59 E
Roncq 50 50.45 N 3.07 E
Rond, Sommet ∧ 206 45.05 N 72.33 W
Ronda 34 36.44 N 5.10 W
Ronda, Serranía de ⋏ 34 36.44 N 5.03 W
Rondane ∧ 26 61.55 N 9.45 E
Rondane Nasjonal Park ♠ 26 61.50 N 9.50 E
Rønde 41 56.18 N 10.29 E
Ronde, Pointe ≻ 240d 15.33 N 61.29 W
Rondeau Harbour ⊂ 214 42.18 N 81.53 W
Rondeau Provincial Park ♠ 214 42.16 N 81.51 W
Rondebult 273d 26.18 S 28.14 E
Ronde Island I 241k 12.18 N 61.35 W
Rondissone 62 45.15 N 7.58 E
Rondon 255 23.23 S 52.48 W
Rondônia □[3] 248 11.00 S 63.00 W
Rondonópolis 255 16.28 S 54.38 W
Rondout 278 42.17 N 87.53 W
Rondout Creek ≃ 210 41.55 N 73.53 W
Rondout Reservoir ⊜[1] 210 41.50 N 74.29 W
Rone ≃ 50 50.46 N 3.27 E
Ronehamn 26 57.10 N 18.29 E
Rong ≃ 102 24.32 N 109.15 E
Ronga 80 56.43 N 48.32 E
Rongai 154 0.10 S 35.51 E
Rong'an 102 25.10 N 109.20 E
Rongbaca 102 31.48 N 99.40 E
Rongchang 107 29.24 N 105.36 E
Rongcheng, Zhg. 98 37.08 N 122.23 E
Rongcheng, Zhg. 105 39.03 N 115.52 E
Rongding 107 28.57 N 103.40 E
Ronge, Lac la ⊜ 184 55.10 N 105.00 W
Rongelap I[1] 14 11.20 N 166.50 E
Rongjiang 102 25.52 N 108.37 E
Rongkop 115a 8.10 S 110.45 E
Rongola 158 27.22 S 31.37 E
Rongotea 172 40.18 S 175.25 E
Rõngu 76 58.09 N 26.15 E
Rongui, Ilha I 154 10.50 S 40.40 E
Rongwanshi 100 28.10 N 112.57 E
Rongxian, Zhg. 102 22.50 N 110.38 E
Rongxian, Zhg. 107 29.28 N 104.25 E
Ronkiti Harbor ⊂ 174r 6.48 N 158.10 E
Ronkonkoma 276 40.48 N 73.06 W
Ronkonkoma, Lake ⊜ 276 40.50 N 73.07 W
Rønne 26 55.06 N 14.42 E
Rönne ≃ 41 56.16 N 12.50 E
Ronneburg 54 50.51 N 12.10 E
Ronneby 26 56.12 N 15.18 E
Ronne Entrance ⊂ 9 72.30 S 74.00 W
Ronne Ice Shelf ⊓ 9 78.30 S 61.00 W
Ronnenberg 52 52.20 N 9.40 E
Rönneshytta 40 58.56 N 15.02 E
Rönninge 40 59.12 N 17.44 E
Ronroni 175e 9.37 S 159.58 E
Rönsahl 263 51.07 N 7.30 E
Ronsdorf ◆[8] 263 51.14 N 7.12 E
Ronse (Renaix-Gleiche) 50 50.45 N 3.36 E
Röntgenmuseum ⊍ 263 51.12 N 7.16 E
Ronuro ≃ 255 11.56 S 53.33 W
Roodepoort □[5] 273d 26.10 S 27.52 E
Roodepoort-Maraisburg 158 26.11 S 27.54 E
Roodeschool 52 53.25 N 6.45 E
Roodhouse 219 39.29 N 90.22 W
Roof Butte ∧ 200 36.28 N 109.05 W
Rooiberge ∧ 158 28.27 S 28.26 E
Rooiboklaagte ≃ 156 20.50 S 21.00 E
Rooidam 158 28.07 S 21.15 E
Rooilyf 158 28.49 S 21.57 E
Rooiwal 158 27.18 S 27.32 E
Rooks Creek ≃ 216 40.57 N 88.44 W
Rookwood Cemetery ◆ 274a 33.53 S 151.04 E
Roon, Pulau I 164 2.23 S 134.33 E
Rooniu, Mont ∧ 174s 17.49 S 149.12 W
Roordahuizum 52 53.06 N 5.46 E
Roorkee 124 29.52 N 77.53 E
Roosboom 158 28.36 S 29.44 E
Roosendaal 52 51.32 N 4.28 E
Roosevelt, Az., U.S. 200 33.40 N 111.08 W
Roosevelt, Mn., U.S. 198 48.48 N 95.05 W
Roosevelt, N.J., U.S. 208 40.13 N 74.28 W
Roosevelt, N.Y., U.S. 276 40.40 N 73.35 W
Roosevelt, Ok., U.S. 196 34.50 N 99.01 W
Roosevelt, Ut,. U.S. 200 40.17 N 109.59 W
Roosevelt ≃ 248 7.35 S 60.20 W
Roosevelt Beach 210 43.19 N 78.52 W
Roosevelt Campobello International Park ♠ 186 44.52 N 66.58 W
Roosevelt Field ◆[9] 276 40.45 N 73.37 W
Roosevelt Island I 9 79.30 S 162.00 W
Roosevelt Park 216 43.11 N 86.15 W
Roosevelt Park ♠ 276 40.33 N 74.21 W
Roosevelt Raceway ♠ 276 40.44 N 73.36 W
Roosevelt Roads Naval Station ■ 240m 18.15 N 65.38 W
Roosevelt Terrace 226 38.08 N 122.16 W
Root 58 47.07 N 8.23 E
Root ≃, N.T., Can. 180 62.50 N 123.40 W
Root ≃, Mn., U.S. 190 43.46 N 91.15 W
Root ≃, Wi., U.S. 216 42.44 N 87.47 W
Root, North Branch ≃ 190 43.49 N 92.10 W
Root, South Branch ≃ 190 43.44 N 91.58 W
Root Lake ⊜ 184 54.04 N 101.24 W
Rootstown 214 41.05 N 81.14 W
Rooty Hill 170 33.46 S 150.50 E
Ropang 115b 8.52 S 117.29 E
Ropaži 76 57.08 N 24.30 E
Ropča 24 63.02 N 52.16 E
Ropczyce 30 50.03 N 21.37 E
Roper 192 35.52 N 76.36 W
Roper ≃ 164 14.43 S 135.27 E
Roper Bar 164 14.44 S 134.44 E
Roper Valley 164 14.56 S 134.00 E
Ropes Creek ≃ 274a 33.43 S 150.47 E
Ropesville 196 33.26 N 102.09 W
Roppe 58 47.40 N 6.55 E
Ropša 265a 59.44 N 29.52 E
Roque 250 3.01 S 45.23 W
Roquebillière 62 44.01 N 7.18 E
Roquebrune-Cap-Martin 62 43.46 N 7.28 E
Roquebrune-sur-Argens 62 43.26 N 6.38 E
Roquefavour, Aqueduc de ≡[1] 62 43.31 N 5.19 E
Roquefort 32 44.02 N 0.19 W
Roquemaure 62 44.03 N 4.47 E
Roque Pérez 258 35.25 S 59.20 W
Roquestéron 62 43.52 N 7.00 E
Roquevaire 62 43.21 N 5.36 E
Rora Head ≻ 46 58.52 N 3.25 W
Roraima □[3] 246 1.00 N 61.00 W
Roraima, Mount ∧ 246 5.12 N 60.44 W
Rörbäcksnäs 26 61.08 N 12.49 E
Roreto Chisone 62 44.59 N 7.06 E
Rorey Lake ⊜ 180 66.55 N 128.25 W
Rorke Lake ⊜ 184 54.33 N 92.30 W
Rorke's Drift ⊥ 158 28.20 S 30.32 E
Rorketon 184 51.26 N 99.32 W
Røros 26 62.35 N 11.20 E
Rorschach 58 47.29 N 9.30 E
Rørvig 41 55.57 N 11.46 E
Rørvik 24 64.51 N 11.14 E
Ros' ≃ 78 49.39 N 31.35 E
Rosà, It. 64 45.43 N 11.45 E
Rosa, Zam. 154 9.38 S 31.21 E
Rosa, Cap ≻ 36 36.58 N 8.14 E
Rosa, Lake ⊜ 238 21.00 N 73.30 W
Rosa, Monte ∧ 58 45.55 N 7.53 E
Rosairinho 266c 38.40 N 9.01 W
Rošal' 80 55.40 N 39.51 E
Rosales, Méx. 232 28.12 N 105.33 W
Rosales, Pil. 116 15.54 N 120.38 E
Rosalia 202 47.14 N 117.22 W
Rosalie, Lake ⊜ 220 27.58 N 81.28 W
Rosalind Bank ✧[4] 238 16.30 N 80.30 W
Rosamond, Ca., U.S. 228 34.51 N 118.09 W
Rosamond, Il., U.S. 219 39.23 N 89.10 W
Rosamond Lake ⊜ 228 34.50 N 118.04 W
Rosamorada 234 22.08 N 105.12 W
Rosana 255 22.33 S 53.00 W
Rosander, Mount ∧ 224 48.46 N 124.42 W
Rosanky 222 29.56 N 97.18 W
Rosanna 274b 37.45 S 145.04 E
Rosans 62 44.23 N 5.28 E
Rosario, Arg. 252 32.57 S 60.40 W
Rosário, Bra. 250 2.57 S 44.14 W
Rosario, Méx. 232 27.37 N 109.16 W
Rosario, Méx. 234 23.00 N 105.52 W
Rosario, Para. 252 24.27 S 57.03 W
Rosario, Pil. 116 13.51 N 121.12 E
Rosario, Pil. 116 16.14 N 120.29 E
Rosario, Ur. 258 34.19 S 57.21 W
Rosario, Ven. 246 10.19 N 72.19 W
Rosario ≃, Arg. 252 24.50 S 65.43 W
Rosario ≃, Ur. 258 34.26 S 57.21 W
Rosario, Bahía ⊂ 232 29.52 N 115.45 W
Rosario, Cayo el I 240p 21.38 N 81.53 W
Rosario, Islas del II 246 10.10 N 75.46 W
Rosario Bank ✧[2] 238 18.30 N 84.05 W
Rosario de Arriba 232 30.01 N 115.40 W
Rosario de la Frontera 252 25.48 S 64.58 W
Rosario de Lerma 252 24.59 S 65.35 W
Rosario del Tala 252 32.18 S 59.09 W
Rosário de Minas 256 21.43 S 43.38 W
Rosário do Sul 252 30.15 S 54.55 W
Rosário Oeste 248 14.50 S 56.25 W
Rosario Strait ⋓ 224 48.30 N 122.45 W
Rosarito, Méx. 204 32.20 N 117.02 W
Rosarito, Méx. 232 26.27 N 111.38 W
Rosarito, Embalse de ⊜[1] 34 40.05 N 5.15 W
Rosarno 68 38.29 N 15.59 E
Rosas 196 26.09 N 103.27 W
Rosazza 62 45.41 N 7.58 E
Rošča 82 54.47 N 36.51 E
Roščino 76 60.15 N 29.37 E
Rosciolo 66 42.07 N 13.20 E
Roscoe, Il., U.S. 216 42.25 N 89.01 W
Roscoe, N.Y., U.S. 210 41.55 N 74.54 W
Roscoe, Pa., U.S. 214 40.04 N 79.51 W
Roscoe, S.D., U.S. 198 45.26 N 99.20 W
Roscoe, Tx., U.S. 196 32.26 N 100.32 W
Roscoe ≃ 180 69.40 N 120.57 W
Roscoe Village ⊥ 214 40.18 N 81.54 W
Roscoff 32 48.44 N 3.59 E
Roscommon, Ire. 48 53.38 N 8.11 W
Roscommon, Mi., U.S. 190 44.29 N 84.35 W
Roscommon □[6] 48 53.45 N 8.15 W
Roscrea 48 52.57 N 7.47 W
Rosdorf 52 51.30 N 9.53 E
Rose, It. 68 39.24 N 16.17 E
Rose, N.Y., U.S. 210 43.09 N 76.53 W
Rose, Monte ∧ 70 37.39 N 13.25 E
Rose, Mount ∧ 226 39.21 N 119.55 W
Rose, Pointe de la ≻ 240e 14.40 N 60.53 W
Roseau, Dom. 240d 15.18 N 61.24 W
Roseau, Mn., U.S. 198 48.50 N 95.45 W
Roseau ≃, Dom. 240d 15.18 N 61.24 W
Roseau ≃, N.A. 198 49.08 N 97.15 W
Roseau ≃, St. Luc. 241f 13.58 N 61.02 W
Rosebank ◆[8] 273d 26.09 S 28.02 E
Rosebank Station 275b 43.47 N 79.07 W
Roseberry Lakes ⊜ 184 52.40 N 92.30 W
Roseberth 166 25.47 S 139.37 E
Rosebery 166 41.46 S 145.32 E
Rosebery ◆[8] 274a 33.55 S 151.12 E
Rose-Blanche 186 47.37 N 58.41 W
Roseboom 210 42.45 N 74.47 W
Roseboro 192 34.57 N 78.30 W
Rose Bowl ♠ 280 34.10 N 118.09 W
Rosebud, Austl. 169 38.21 S 144.54 E
Rosebud, Mo., U.S. 219 38.23 N 91.24 W
Rosebud, Mt., U.S. 202 46.16 N 106.26 W
Rose Bud, Pa., U.S. 214 40.45 N 78.33 W
Rosebud, S.D., U.S. 198 43.13 N 100.51 W
Rosebud, Tx., U.S. 222 31.04 N 96.58 W
Rosebud ≃ 182 51.25 N 112.37 W
Rosebud Creek ≃ 202 46.16 N 106.28 W
Rosebud Indian Reservation ◆[4] 198 43.25 N 100.28 W
Roseburg 202 43.13 N 123.20 W
Rosebush 190 43.41 N 84.46 W
Rose City 190 44.25 N 84.07 W
Rose Creek ≃, U.S. 198 40.04 N 97.07 W
Rose Creek ≃, Ca., U.S. 226 38.07 N 120.24 W
Rosecroft Raceway ♠ 284c 38.48 N 76.58 W
Rosedale, Austl. 166 24.38 S 151.55 E
Rosedale, Ab., Can. 182 51.25 N 112.38 W
Rosedale, B.C., Can. 224 49.11 N 121.48 W
Rosedale, In., U.S. 194 39.37 N 87.17 W
Rosedale, La., U.S. 194 30.27 N 91.27 W
Rosedale, Md., U.S. 284b 39.19 N 76.30 W
Rosedale, Ms., U.S. 194 33.51 N 91.01 W
Rosedale ◆[8], On., Can. 275b 43.41 N 79.22 W
Rosedale ◆[8], N.Y., U.S. 276 40.39 N 73.45 W
Rosedale Estates 284c 38.47 N 76.58 W
Rosedale Hills 218 39.42 N 86.07 W
Rosedene 158 32.01 S 22.07 E
Rosehall 246 6.16 N 57.21 W
Rosehearty 46 57.42 N 2.07 W
Rose-Hill, Maus. 157c 20.14 S 57.27 E
Rose Hill, N.C., U.S. 192 34.49 N 78.01 W
Rose Hill, Va., U.S. 192 36.40 N 83.22 W
Rose Hill, Wa., U.S. 224 47.42 N 122.10 W
Rosehill Cemetery ◆ 278 41.59 N 87.41 W
Rosehill Racecourse ♠ 274a 33.49 S 151.02 E
Rose Hills Memorial Park ◆ 280 34.01 N 118.02 W
Roseira 256 22.54 S 45.18 W
Rose Island I, Am. Sam. 14 14.32 S 168.08 W
Rose Island I, Ba. 192 25.06 N 77.14 W
Rose Lake 182 54.24 N 126.02 W
Roseland, Ca., U.S. 226 38.30 N 122.55 W
Roseland, In., U.S. 216 41.42 N 86.15 W
Roseland, La., U.S. 194 30.45 N 90.30 W
Roseland, N.J., U.S. 276 40.49 N 74.17 W
Roseland, Oh., U.S. 214 40.47 N 82.32 W
Roseland ◆[8] 278 41.42 N 87.38 W
Roselawn 216 41.09 N 87.19 W
Roselle, Il., U.S. 216 41.59 N 88.04 W
Roselle, N.J., U.S. 276 40.39 N 74.15 W
Roselle Field ⊠ 278 41.59 N 88.06 W
Rosellen 263 51.08 N 6.43 E
Roselle Park 276 40.39 N 74.15 W
Rosellerheide 263 51.07 N 6.44 E
Rose Lodge 224 45.01 N 123.52 W
Rosemary 182 50.46 N 112.05 W
Rosemary Brook ≃ 283 42.19 N 71.15 W
Rosemead 280 34.04 N 118.04 W
Rosemère 206 45.38 N 73.48 W
Rosemont, Ca., U.S. 226 38.34 N 121.20 W
Rosemont, Il., U.S. 278 41.59 N 87.52 W
Rosemont, Ky., U.S. 218 38.01 N 84.32 W
Rosemont, Oh., U.S. 214 41.03 N 80.53 W
Rosemont, Pa., U.S. 285 40.01 N 75.19 W
Rosemont Horizon ♠ 278 42.00 N 87.53 W
Rosenberg 222 29.33 N 95.48 W
Rosendaël 50 51.02 N 2.24 E
Rosendal, Nor. 26 59.59 N 6.01 E
Rosendal, S. Afr. 158 28.30 S 27.55 E
Rosendale 210 41.51 N 74.05 W
Roseneath 273d 26.17 S 28.11 E
Rosenfeld 58 48.17 N 8.43 E
Rosengarten 52 53.23 N 9.54 E
Rosenhayn 208 39.28 N 75.07 W
Rosenheim 64 47.51 N 12.07 E
Rosenhügel ◆[8] 263 51.10 N 7.12 E
Rosenthal, Dtsch. 54 50.51 N 14.04 E
Rosenthal, Dtsch. 56 50.58 N 8.52 E
Rosenthal ◆[8] 264a 52.36 N 13.23 E
Rose Peak ∧ 200 33.26 N 109.22 W
Rosepine 194 30.55 N 93.17 W
Rose Point ≻ 182 54.13 N 131.35 W
Rosersberg 40 59.35 N 17.53 E
Rosersberg ⊥ 40 59.34 N 17.50 E
Roses, Golf de ⊂ 34 42.10 N 3.15 E
Roseto 210 40.52 N 75.12 W
Roseto Capo Spulico 68 39.59 N 16.36 E
Roseto degli Abruzzi 66 42.41 N 14.01 E
Roseto Valfortore 68 41.22 N 15.06 E
Rosetown 184 51.33 N 108.00 W
Rose Tree 285 39.56 N 75.23 W
Rose Tree Park ♠ 285 39.56 N 75.24 W
Rosetta Branch → Rashīd, Far'≃ 142 31.30 N 30.21 E
Rosetta Mouth → Rashīd, Maṣabb ≃[1] 142 31.30 N 30.20 E
Rosetta → Rashīd 142 31.24 N 30.25 E
Rosettenville ◆[8] 273d 26.15 S 28.03 E
Rosevale 171a 27.51 S 152.29 E
Rose Valley, Sk., Can. 184 52.18 N 103.50 W
Rose Valley, Pa., U.S. 285 39.53 N 75.23 W
Rose Valley, Pa., U.S. 285 40.10 N 75.13 W
Rose Valley, Wa., U.S. 224 46.06 N 122.50 W
Roseville, Austl. 274a 33.47 S 151.11 E
Roseville, Ca., U.S. 226 38.45 N 121.17 W
Roseville, Il., U.S. 190 40.43 N 90.39 W
Roseville, Mi., U.S. 214 42.29 N 82.56 W
Roseville, Mn., U.S. 190 45.00 N 93.09 W
Roseville, Oh., U.S. 188 39.48 N 82.04 W
Roseville, Pa., U.S. 210 41.51 N 76.57 W
Roseville Park 285 39.42 N 75.43 W
Rosewood, Austl. 171a 27.39 S 152.35 E
Rosewood, Austl. 171b 35.41 S 147.52 E
Rosewood, Oh., U.S. 216 40.13 N 83.58 W
Rosewood Heights 219 38.53 N 90.05 W
Roseworthy 168b 34.32 S 138.44 E
Roshanara Gardens ♠ 272a 28.40 N 77.12 E
Rosharon 222 29.21 N 95.28 W
Rosheim 58 48.30 N 7.28 E
Rosherville Dam ⊜[1] 273d 26.14 S 28.07 E
Rosh Ha'Ayin 132 32.06 N 34.57 E
Rosholt, S.D., U.S. 198 45.52 N 96.43 W
Rosholt, Wi., U.S. 190 44.37 N 89.18 W
Rosh Pinna 132 32.58 N 35.32 E
Rosica ≃ 38 43.15 N 25.42 E
Rosice 30 49.11 N 16.23 E
Rosiclare 194 37.25 N 88.20 W
Rosières-aux-Salines 58 48.36 N 6.20 E
Rosières-en-Santerre 50 49.49 N 2.43 E
Rosiers, Rivière des ≃ 206 45.59 N 72.07 W
Rosignano Marittimo 66 43.24 N 10.28 E
Rosignano Solvay 66 43.23 N 10.26 E
Rosignol 246 6.17 N 57.32 W
Roșiori de Vede 38 44.07 N 25.00 E
Rositz 54 51.01 N 12.22 E
Roskilde 41 55.39 N 12.05 E
Roskilde □[6] 41 55.30 N 12.05 E
Roskilde Fjord ⊂ 41 55.56 N 12.00 E
Roskow 54 52.28 N 12.42 E
Roslagen □[9] 40 59.30 N 18.40 E
Roslags-Bro 40 59.50 N 18.44 E
Rosl'akovo 24 69.03 N 33.09 E
Rosl'atino 76 59.46 N 44.15 E
Roslavl' 76 53.57 N 32.52 E
Roslev 26 56.42 N 8.59 E
Roslindale ◆[8] 283 42.18 N 71.07 W
Roslyn, N.Y., U.S. 276 40.48 N 73.39 W
Roslyn, Pa., U.S. 208 40.07 N 75.08 W
Roslyn, Pa., U.S. 285 39.57 N 75.36 W
Roslyn, Wa., U.S. 224 47.13 N 120.59 W
Roslyn Estates 276 40.47 N 73.40 W
Roslyn Harbor 276 40.49 N 73.38 W
Roslyn Heights 276 40.47 N 73.38 W
Rosmalen 52 51.43 N 5.22 E
Rosman 192 35.08 N 82.49 W
Rosmead 158 31.29 S 25.08 E
Ros Mhic Thriúin → New Ross 48 52.24 N 6.56 W
Røsnæs ≻[1] 41 55.44 N 10.59 E
Rosne, Ruisseau le ≃ 261 48.58 N 2.25 E
Rosneath 46 56.01 N 4.49 W
Rosny-sous-Bois 261 48.53 N 2.29 E
Rosny-sur-Seine 50 49.00 N 1.38 E
Rosolina 64 45.05 N 12.15 E
Rosolini 70 36.49 N 14.57 E
Rošore 85 38.20 N 72.19 E
Rosporden 32 47.58 N 3.50 W
Rösrath 56 50.54 N 7.11 E
Ross, Austl. 166 42.02 S 147.29 E
Ross', Bela. 76 53.17 N 24.24 E
Ross, N.Z. 172 42.54 S 170.49 E
Ross, Ca., U.S. 226 37.55 N 122.32 W
Ross, In., U.S. 278 41.32 N 87.23 W
Ross, Oh., U.S. 218 39.19 N 84.39 W
Ross □[6] 218 39.20 N 83.06 W
Ross ≃ 180 61.59 N 132.26 W
Ross, Cape ≻ 116 10.56 N 119.13 E
Ross, Mount ∧ 172 41.28 S 175.21 E
Ross, Point ≻ 174c 29.04 S 167.56 E
Ross, Pointe ≻ 275a 45.21 N 73.48 W
Rossa 58 46.22 N 9.08 E
Rossach 56 50.09 N 10.56 E
Rossano 68 39.35 N 16.39 E
Rossasna 76 54.39 N 30.53 E
Rossau 54 52.47 N 11.38 E
Rossbach 54 51.15 N 11.53 E
Ross Behy 48 52.02 N 9.58 W
Ross-Béthio 150 16.16 N 16.08 W
Rossburg 216 40.17 N 84.38 W
Rossburn 184 50.40 N 100.52 W
Ross Carbery 48 51.35 N 9.01 W
Rosscott Manor 285 39.39 N 75.44 W
Ross Dam ◆[6] 224 48.44 N 121.04 W
Rossdorf 56 49.51 N 8.45 E
Rosseau 212 45.16 N 79.39 W
Rosseau, Lake ⊜ 212 45.10 N 79.35 W
Rossel, Cap ≻ 175f 20.23 S 166.36 E
Rossell y Rius 252 33.11 S 55.42 W
Rossen ⊜ 40 60.19 N 16.26 E
Rossendale □[8] 262 53.43 N 2.14 W
Rosser 222 32.28 N 96.27 W
Rosses Bay ⊂ 48 55.10 N 8.27 W
Rosses Point 48 54.18 N 8.33 W
Rossford 214 41.37 N 83.33 W
Ross Fork Creek ≃ 202 47.05 N 109.43 W
Rosshaupten 58 47.39 N 10.43 E
Rosshyttan 40 60.04 N 16.21 E
Ross Ice Shelf ⊓ 9 81.30 S 175.00 W
Rossiglione 62 44.34 N 8.40 E
Rossignol, Lake ⊜ 186 44.10 N 65.10 W
Rossija → Russia □[1] 72 60.00 N 80.00 E
Rössing 156 22.31 S 14.52 E
Rossio, Estação do ◆[5] 266c 38.43 N 9.09 W
Ross Island I, Ant. 9 77.30 S 168.00 E
Ross Island I, Mb., Can. 184 54.14 N 97.45 W
Rossiter 214 40.53 N 78.55 W
Rossitten → Rybačij 76 55.09 N 20.51 E
Rossiya → Russia □[1] 72 60.00 N 80.00 E
Rossla 54 51.28 N 11.04 E
Ross Lake ⊜[1] 224 48.53 N 121.04 W
Ross Lake National Recreation Area ♠ 224 48.45 N 121.00 W
Rossland 182 49.05 N 117.48 W
Rosslare 48 52.17 N 6.23 W
Rosslare Harbour 48 52.15 N 6.22 W
Rosslau 54 51.53 N 12.14 E
Rosslea 48 54.14 N 7.11 W
Rossleben 54 51.17 N 11.25 E
Rosslyn Farms 279b 40.26 N 80.05 W
Rossmoor 280 33.47 N 118.05 W
Rossmore 274a 33.57 S 150.46 E
Rossmoyne 208 40.13 N 76.57 W
Rosso 150 16.30 N 15.49 W
Rossön 26 63.55 N 16.21 E
Ross-on-Wye 42 51.55 N 2.35 W
Rossony 76 55.53 N 28.49 E
Rossoš', Ross. 78 51.08 N 38.29 E
Rossoš', Ross. 78 50.12 N 39.34 E
Rossouw 158 31.09 S 27.18 E
Ross R. Barnett Reservoir ⊜[1] 194 32.30 N 90.00 W
Ross River 180 61.59 N 132.27 W
Ross-Schelfeis → Ross Ice Shelf ⊓ 9 81.30 S 175.00 W
Ross Sea ⊤[2] 9 76.00 S 175.00 W
Rosstal 56 49.25 N 10.52 E
Rosston 218 40.03 N 86.17 W
Rossu, Capu ≻ 36 42.14 N 8.33 E
Røssvatnet ⊜ 24 65.45 N 14.00 E
Rossville, Ga., U.S. 192 34.58 N 85.17 W
Rossville, Il., U.S. 216 40.22 N 87.40 W
Rossville, In., U.S. 216 40.25 N 86.35 W
Rossville, Ks., U.S. 198 39.08 N 95.57 W
Rossville, Md., U.S. 284b 39.20 N 76.29 W
Rosswein 54 51.03 N 13.10 E
Røst II 24 67.28 N 11.59 E
Rostāg 120 37.07 N 69.49 E
Röstånga 41 56.00 N 13.17 E
Rosthern 184 52.40 N 106.17 W
Rostherne 262 53.21 N 2.23 W
Rostherne Mere ⊜ 262 53.21 N 2.23 W
Roštkala 120 37.16 N 71.49 E
Rostock 54 54.05 N 12.07 E
Rostov 80 57.11 N 39.25 E
Rostov □[8] 83 47.30 N 39.30 E
Rostov-na-Donu 83 47.14 N 39.42 E
Rostrataville 158 26.49 S 25.39 E
Rostraver Airport ⊠ 279b 40.13 N 79.50 W
Rostrevor 48 54.06 N 6.12 W
Rosvinskoje 24 66.32 N 52.26 E
Roswell, Ga., U.S. 192 34.01 N 84.21 W
Roswell, N.M., U.S. 196 33.23 N 104.31 W
Roswell, Oh., U.S. 214 40.28 N 81.21 W
Rosyth 46 56.03 N 3.26 W
Rot ≃ 58 48.19 N 9.54 E
Rota 34 36.37 N 6.21 W
Rota I 108 14.10 N 145.12 E
Rot am See 56 49.15 N 10.01 E
Rotan 196 32.51 N 100.27 W
Rotanda 156 19.33 S 32.50 E
Rotary Island I 285 40.14 N 74.49 W
Rotbach ≃ 263 51.34 N 6.41 E
Rotberg 264a 52.21 N 13.31 E
Rote-Erde, Stadion ♠ 263 51.30 N 7.27 E
Rotenburg 52 53.06 N 9.24 E
Rotenburg an der Fulda 56 51.00 N 9.45 E
Roter Main ≃ 54 50.04 N 11.24 E
Rotes Meer → Red Sea ⊤[2] 136 20.00 N 38.00 E
Roth, Dtsch. 56 50.46 N 7.42 E
Roth, Dtsch. 60 49.15 N 11.06 E
Roth ≃ 58 48.27 N 10.10 E
Rötha 54 51.12 N 12.25 E
Rothaargebirge ⋏ 56 51.05 N 8.15 E
Rothbury 44 55.19 N 1.55 W
Rothbury Forest ◆[3] 44 55.18 N 1.54 W
Rothemühl 54 53.36 N 13.49 E
Röthenbach, Dtsch. 58 47.37 N 9.59 E
Röthenbach, Schw. 58 46.51 N 7.45 E
Röthenbach an der Pegnitz 60 49.29 N 11.15 E
Rothenburg 54 51.20 N 14.58 E
Rothenburg ob der Tauber 56 49.23 N 10.10 E
Rothenkirchen 54 50.33 N 12.30 E
Rothenschirmbach 54 51.27 N 11.33 E
Rothenstein ∧[2] 263 51.07 N 7.41 E
Rother ≃ 42 50.57 N 0.32 W
Rothera ⊍[3] 9 67.34 S 68.08 W
Rotherham, N.Z. 172 42.42 S 172.57 E
Rotherham, Eng., U.K. 44 53.26 N 1.20 W
Rothes 46 57.31 N 3.13 W
Rothesay, N.B., Can. 186 45.23 N 66.00 W
Rothesay, Scot., U.K. 46 55.51 N 5.03 W
Roth-Neusiedl ◆[8] 264b 48.08 N 16.23 E
Rothrist 58 47.19 N 7.53 E
Rothsay, Austl. 162 29.17 S 116.53 E
Rothsay, Mn., U.S. 198 46.28 N 96.16 W
Rothschild 190 44.53 N 89.37 W
Rothsville 208 40.09 N 76.15 W
Rothwell, N.B., Can. 186 46.04 N 66.04 W
Rothwell, Eng., U.K. 42 52.25 N 0.48 W
Rothwell, Eng., U.K. 44 53.46 N 1.29 W
Roti, Pulau I 112 10.45 S 123.10 E
Roti, Selat ⋓ 112 10.25 S 123.25 E
Roto 166 33.03 S 145.28 E
Rotoiti, Lake ⊜, N.Z. 172 41.50 S 172.50 E
Rotoiti, Lake ⊜, N.Z. 172 38.02 S 176.25 E
Rotomanu 172 42.39 S 171.32 E
Rotonda 68 39.57 N 16.02 E
Rotondella 68 40.10 N 16.32 E
Rotondo, Monte ∧ 36 42.13 N 9.03 E
Rotoroa, Lake ⊜ 172 41.52 S 172.38 E
Rotorua 172 38.09 S 176.15 E
Rotorua, Lake ⊜ 172 38.05 S 176.16 E
Rotowaro 172 37.36 S 175.05 E
Rott 64 47.54 N 10.59 E
Rott ≃ 60 48.27 N 13.26 E
Rottach-Egern 64 47.41 N 11.46 E
Rott am Inn 64 47.59 N 12.07 E
Rotten ≃ 58 46.17 N 7.33 E
Röttenbach 60 49.09 N 11.02 E
Rottenbach-Tremersdorf 56 50.21 N 10.56 E
Rottenbuch 64 47.44 N 10.58 E
Rottenburg am Neckar 58 48.28 N 8.56 E
Rottenburg an der Laaber 60 48.42 N 12.02 E
Rottenmann 61 47.31 N 14.22 E
Rotterdam, Ned. 52 51.55 N 4.28 E
Rotterdam, N.Y., U.S. 210 42.48 N 73.59 W
Rotterdam, Luchthaven ⊠ 52 51.58 N 4.30 E
Rotterdam Junction 210 42.52 N 74.03 W
Rotthalmünster 60 48.21 N 13.12 E
Rotthausen ◆[8] 263 51.30 N 7.05 E
Rottingdean 42 50.48 N 0.04 W
Röttingen 56 49.30 N 9.58 E
Rottleberode 54 51.31 N 10.57 E
Rottnest Island I 168a 32.00 S 115.30 E
Rottofreno 62 45.03 N 9.34 E
Rottum 263 51.36 N 7.42 E
Rottumeroog I 52 53.30 N 6.30 E
Rottumerplaat I 52 53.32 N 6.30 E
Rottweil 58 48.10 N 8.37 E
Rotuma I 14 12.30 S 177.05 E
Rotwand ∧ 64 47.39 N 11.56 E
Rötz 60 49.21 N 12.32 E
Roubaix 50 50.42 N 3.10 E
Roubideau Creek ≃ 200 38.44 N 108.10 W
Roubidoux Creek ≃ 194 37.51 N 92.13 W
Roubion ≃ 62 44.31 N 4.42 E
Rouceux 58 48.22 N 5.41 E
Roudnice [nad Labem] 54 50.22 N 14.16 E
Rouen 50 49.26 N 1.05 E
Rougé 32 47.47 N 1.27 W
Rouge ≃, On., Can. 212 43.48 N 79.07 W
Rouge ≃, P.Q., Can. 206 45.39 N 74.42 W
Rouge ≃, P.Q., Can. 206 45.33 N 74.20 W
Rouge, Bell Branch ≃ 281 42.23 N 83.16 W
Rouge, Lac ⊜ 206 46.56 N 74.38 W
Rouge, Mer → Red Sea ⊤[2] 136 20.00 N 38.00 E
Rouge, River ≃ 281 42.17 N 83.06 W
Rougeau, Forêt de ♠ 261 48.35 N 2.30 E
Rougemont, Fr. 58 47.29 N 6.21 E
Rougemont, Schw. 58 46.29 N 7.12 E
Rougemont-le-Château 58 47.44 N 6.58 E
Rouge → Red ≃ 178 31.00 N 91.40 W
Rough ≃ 194 37.29 N 87.08 W
Rough And Ready 226 39.14 N 121.08 W
Rough River Lake ⊜[1] 194 37.40 N 86.25 W
Rouiba 34 36.44 N 3.17 E
Rouillac 32 45.47 N 0.04 W
Rouillon 261 48.33 N 2.00 E
Roulans 58 47.19 N 6.14 E
Rouleau 184 50.11 N 104.55 W
Roulers → Roeselare 50 50.57 N 3.08 E
Roulette 214 41.46 N 78.09 W
Roumanie → Romania □[1] 38 46.00 N 25.30 E
Round Harbour 186 49.51 N 55.40 W
Roundhead 216 40.34 N 83.50 W
Round Hill Head ≻ 166 24.10 S 151.53 E
Round Hill Regional Park ♠ 279b 40.15 N 79.51 W
Round Knowe ∧[2] 48 55.08 N 6.55 W
Round Lake, Il., U.S. 278 42.21 N 88.05 W
Round Lake, Mn., U.S. 198 43.32 N 95.28 W
Round Lake, N.Y., U.S. 210 42.56 N 73.47 W
Round Lake ⊜, Nf., Can. 186 51.08 N 56.33 W
Round Lake ⊜, On., Can. 190 45.38 N 77.32 W
Round Lake ⊜, On., Can. 212 44.30 N 77.52 W
Round Lake ⊜, On., Can. 212 45.28 N 79.24 W
Round Lake ⊜, Sk., Can. 184 50.33 N 102.23 W
Round Lake ⊜, Il., U.S. 278 42.22 N 88.05 W
Round Lake ⊜, Mi., U.S. 216 41.58 N 84.17 W
Round Lake Beach 216 42.22 N 88.05 W
Round Lake Park 216 42.21 N 88.04 W
Round Mound ∧[2] 198 38.55 N 99.39 W
Round Mountain 204 38.42 N 117.04 W
Round Mountain ∧, Austl. 166 30.27 S 152.14 E
Round Mountain ∧, Austl. 171b 36.15 S 148.34 E
Round Pond ⊜, Nf., Can. 186 48.10 N 56.00 W
Round Pond ⊜, Ma., U.S. 283 42.36 N 70.49 W
Round Rock 222 30.30 N 97.40 W
Roundstone 48 53.23 N 9.53 W
Round Top 210 42.16 N 74.02 W
Round Top ∧[2] 208 40.30 N 76.42 W
Round Top Regional Park ♠ 282 37.51 N 122.12 W
Roundup 202 46.26 N 108.32 W
Round Valley Indian Reservation ◆[4] 204 39.50 N 123.20 W
Round Valley Reservoir ⊜[1] 210 40.36 N 74.50 W
Roundwood 48 53.04 N 6.13 W
Roura 250 4.44 N 52.20 W
Rourkela → Raurkela 124 22.13 N 84.53 E
Rousay I 46 59.10 N 3.02 W
Rouse Hill 274a 33.41 S 150.56 E
Rouses Point 206 45.00 N 73.22 W
Rouseville 214 41.28 N 79.41 W
Rousies 50 50.16 N 4.00 E
Rousseau, Lake ⊜[1] 220 29.02 N 82.32 W
Rousset, Col de)(62 44.50 N 5.24 E
Roussigny 261 48.39 N 2.06 E
Roussillon, Fr. 62 45.22 N 4.49 E
Roussillon, Fr. 62 43.54 N 5.17 E
Roussillon □[9] 32 42.30 N 2.30 E
Roussy-le-Village 56 49.27 N 6.10 E
Routhierville 186 48.11 N 67.09 W
Routot 50 49.23 N 0.44 E
Rouveen 52 52.36 N 6.11 E
Rouvignies 50 50.20 N 3.26 E
Rouville □[6] 206 45.23 N 73.04 W
Rouvray 50 47.25 N 4.06 E
Rouvray, Lac ⊜ 186 49.18 N 70.49 W
Rouxville 158 30.29 S 26.46 E
Rouyn 190 48.15 N 79.01 W
Rouzerville 208 39.44 N 77.32 W
Rovaniemi 24 66.34 N 25.48 E
Rovasenda 62 45.32 N 8.19 E
Rovato 64 45.34 N 10.00 E
Rovbickskaja 76 52.40 N 24.05 E
Rove, Tunnel du ◆[5] 62 43.22 N 5.17 E
Rovegno 62 44.35 N 9.17 E
Rovellasca 62 45.40 N 9.03 E
Rovello Porro 62 45.39 N 9.02 E
Roven'ki, Ross. 78 49.56 N 38.54 E
Roven'ki, Ukr. 83 48.05 N 39.21 E
Rovenskaja Sloboda 78 52.13 N 30.19 E
Roverbella 64 45.16 N 10.46 E
Rovere 66 42.10 N 13.31 E
Roverè della Luna 64 46.15 N 11.10 E
Roveredo 58 46.14 N 9.08 E
Rovereto 64 45.53 N 11.02 E
Roverè Veronese 64 45.36 N 11.03 E
Rövershagen 54 54.10 N 12.15 E
Roversi 252 27.35 S 61.57 W
Roverud 26 60.15 N 12.03 E
Roviano 66 42.01 N 13.00 E
Rovigo 64 45.04 N 11.47 E
Rovigo □[4] 64 45.02 N 11.50 E
Rovinj 36 45.05 N 13.38 E
Rovira 246 4.14 N 75.14 W
Rovno 78 50.37 N 26.15 E
Rovnoje, Kyrg. 85 42.53 N 73.32 E
Rovnoje, Ross. 80 50.47 N 46.05 E
Rovnoje, Ukr. 78 48.15 N 31.45 E
Rovubu (Ruvubu) ≃ 154 2.23 S 30.47 E
Rovuma (Ruvuma) ≃ 154 10.29 S 40.28 E
Rów 54 52.58 N 14.45 E
Rowan □[6] 218 38.17 N 83.26 W
Rowan Lake ⊜ 184 49.18 N 93.32 W
Rowanty Creek ≃ 208 36.58 N 77.21 W
Rowena, Austl. 166 29.49 S 148.54 E
Rowena, Tx., U.S. 196 31.39 N 100.03 W
Rowe Park ♠ 273a 6.30 N 3.23 E
Rowhill 273d 26.14 S 28.26 E
Rowland, N.C., U.S. 192 34.32 N 79.17 W
Rowland, Pa., U.S. 210 41.28 N 75.03 W
Rowland Flat 168b 34.35 S 138.56 E
Rowland Heights 280 33.58 N 117.54 W
Rowlands Gill 44 54.54 N 1.45 W
Rowlesburg 188 39.20 N 79.40 W
Rowlett 222 32.54 N 96.33 W
Rowlett, Isla I 254 44.48 S 74.25 W
Rowlett Creek ≃ 222 32.49 N 96.31 W
Rowley 207 42.43 N 70.52 W
Rowley ≃, N.T., Can. 176 70.16 N 77.45 W
Rowley ≃, Ma., U.S. 283 42.43 N 70.49 W
Rowley Island I 176 69.08 N 78.50 W
Rowley Regis 42 52.29 N 2.03 W
Rowley Shoals ✧[2] 162 17.30 S 119.00 E
Rowntree Mill Park ♠ 275b 43.45 N 79.35 W
Rowsburg 214 40.52 N 82.10 W
Rowville 274b 37.56 S 145.14 E
Roxa, Ilha I 150 11.15 N 15.40 W
Roxana 219 38.50 N 90.04 W
Roxas, Pil. 108 11.35 N 122.45 E
Roxas, Pil. 116 17.08 N 121.36 E
Roxas, Pil. 116 12.35 N 121.31 E
Roxas, Pil. 116 10.20 N 119.21 E
Roxas (Capiz), Pil. 116 11.35 N 122.45 E
Roxboro, P.Q., Can. 275a 45.31 N 73.48 W
Roxboro, N.C., U.S. 192 36.23 N 78.58 W
Roxborough 241r 11.15 N 60.35 W
Roxborough ◆[8] 285 40.02 N 75.13 W
Roxburgh, N.Z. 172 45.32 S 169.19 E
Roxburgh, Scot., U.K. 46 55.34 N 2.30 W
Roxbury, Ct., U.S. 207 41.33 N 73.18 W
Roxbury, N.Y., U.S. 210 42.17 N 74.33 W
Roxbury, Pa., U.S. 214 40.07 N 77.40 W
Roxbury, Va., U.S. 208 37.28 N 77.09 W
Roxbury ◆[8], Ma., U.S. 283 42.20 N 71.06 W
Roxbury ◆[8], N.Y., U.S. 276 40.34 N 73.54 W
Roxby Downs 162 30.43 S 136.46 E
Roxel 52 51.57 N 7.32 E
Roxen ⊜ 26 58.30 N 15.41 E
Roxie 194 31.30 N 91.04 W
Roxo, Cap ≻ 150 12.20 N 16.43 W
Roxton 196 33.33 N 95.44 W
Roxton Pond (Sainte-Pudentienne) 206 45.29 N 72.40 W
Roxwell 260 51.45 N 0.23 E
Roy, N.M., U.S. 196 35.56 N 104.11 W
Roy, Ut,. U.S. 200 41.09 N 112.01 W
Roy, Wa., U.S. 224 47.00 N 122.32 W
Roya (Roia) ≃ 62 43.48 N 7.35 E
Royal 198 43.03 N 95.17 W
Royal Albert Hall ⊍ 260 51.30 N 0.11 W
Royal Australian Naval College ⊍[2] 170 35.07 S 150.42 E
Royal Bangkok Sports Club ♠ 269a 13.44 N 100.33 E
Royal Botanic Gardens ♠, Austl. 274a 33.52 S 151.13 E
Royal Botanic Gardens ♠, Austl. 274b 37.50 S 144.59 E
Royal Canal ≡ 48 53.21 N 6.15 W
Royal Center 216 40.51 N 86.29 W
Royal Chitwan National Park ♠ 124 27.30 N 84.30 E
Royal City 202 46.54 N 119.38 W
Royale, Isle I 190 48.00 N 89.00 W
Royal Festival Hall ⊍ 260 51.30 N 0.07 W
Royal Gorge V 200 38.17 N 105.45 W
Royal Island I 192 25.31 N 76.51 W
Royalla 171b 35.31 S 149.09 E
Royal Leamington Spa 42 52.18 N 1.31 W
Royal Natal National Park ♠ 158 28.45 S 28.57 E
Royal National Park ♠ 170 34.10 S 151.05 E
Royal Naval College ■ 260 51.29 N 0.01 W
Royal Oak, B.C., Can. 224 48.30 N 123.23 W
Royal Oak, Md., U.S. 208 38.44 N 76.10 W
Royal Oak, Mi., U.S. 216 42.29 N 83.08 W
Royal Oak Township 281 42.27 N 83.10 W
Royal Ontario Museum ⊍ 275b 43.40 N 79.24 W
Royal Opera House ⊍ 260 51.30 N 0.08 W
Royal Palms State Beach ♠ 280 33.44 N 118.19 W
Royal Park ♠ 274b 37.47 S 144.57 E
Royal Roads ⊂ 224 48.26 N 123.26 W
Royalton, In., U.S. 218 39.56 N 86.21 W
Royalton, Mn., U.S. 190 45.49 N 94.17 W
Royalton, Pa., U.S. 208 40.11 N 76.44 W
Royal Tunbridge Wells 42 51.08 N 0.16 E
Royal Turf Club ♠ 269a 13.46 N 100.32 E
Royan 32 45.37 N 1.01 W
Royaume-Uni → United Kingdom □[1] 28 54.00 N 2.00 W
Roybon 62 45.15 N 5.15 E
Royce Brook ≃ 276 40.32 N 70.35 W
Roydon, Eng., U.K. 42 51.46 N 0.03 E
Roydon, Eng., U.K. 42 52.50 N 0.32 E
Roye 50 49.42 N 2.48 E
Royersford 208 40.11 N 75.32 W

Symbol	English	Deutsch	Español	Français	Português
≃	River	Fluß	Río	Rivière	Rio
≡	Canal	Kanal	Canal	Canal	Canal
∟	Waterfall, Rapids	Wasserfall, Stromschnellen	Cascada, Rápidos	Chute d'eau, Rapides	Cascata, Rápidos
⋓	Strait	Meeresstraße	Estrecho	Détroit	Estreito
⊂	Bay, Gulf	Bucht, Golf	Bahía, Golfo	Baie, Golfe	Baía, Golfo
⊜	Lake, Lakes	See, Seen	Lago, Lagos	Lac, Lacs	Lago, Lagos
⁝	Swamp	Sumpf	Pantano	Marais	Pântano
⊓	Ice Features, Glacier	Eis- und Gletscherformen	Accidentes Glaciales	Formes glaciaires	Acidentes glaciares
⊤	Other Hydrographic Features	Andere Hydrographische Objekte	Otros Elementos Hidrográficos	Autres données hydrographiques	Outros acidentes hidrográficos

Symbol	English	Deutsch	Español	Français	Português
✧	Submarine Features	Untermeerische Objekte	Accidentes Submarinos	Formes de relief sous-marin	Acidentes submarinos
□	Political Unit	Politische Einheit	Unidad Politica	Entité politique	Unidade política
⊍	Cultural Institution	Kulturelle Institution	Institución Cultural	Institution culturelle	Instituição cultural
⊥	Historical Site	Historische Stätte	Sitio Histórico	Site historique	Sitio histórico
♠	Recreational Site	Erholungs- und Ferienort	Sitio de Recreo	Centre de loisirs	Area de Lazer
⊠	Airport	Flughafen	Aeropuerto	Aéroport	Aeroporto
■	Military Installation	Militäranlage	Instalación Militar	Installation militaire	Instalação militar
◆	Miscellaneous	Verschiedenes	Misceláneo	Divers	Diversos

Other Topographic Features	Features Topographiques	Otros Elementos Topográficos	Andere Topographische Objekte	Outros acidentes topográficos
II Islands	Îles	Islas	Inseln	Ilhas
1 Island	Île	Isla	Insel	Ilha
1 Cape	Cap	Cabo	Kap	Cabo
2 Plain	Plaine	Llano	Ebene	Planície
⊀ Valley, Canyon	Vallée, Cañon	Valle, Cañón	Tal, Cañon	Vale, Canhão
x Pass	Col	Paso	Paß	Passo
▲ Mountain	Montagne	Montaña	Berg	Montanha
▲ Mountains	Montagnes	Montañas	Gebirge	Montanhas

Symbols in the index entries represent the broad categories identified in the key at the right. Symbols with superior numbers (¹) identify subcategories (see complete key on page I·1).

Les symboles de l'index représentent les catégories indiquées dans la légende à droite. Les symboles suivis d'un indice (¹) identifient des sous-catégories (voir légende complète à la page I·1).

Los símbolos incluidos en el texto del índice repre- sentan las grandes categorías identificadas con la clave a la derecha. Los símbolos con números en su parte superior (¹) identifican las subcategorías (véase la clave completa en la página I·1).

Symbole im Register stellen die rechts im Schlüssel erklärten Kategorien dar. Symbole mit hochgestellten Ziffern (¹) bezeichnen Unterab- teilungen einer Kategorie (vgl. vollständiger Schlüssel auf Seite I·1).

Os símbolos incluídos no texto do índice repre- sentam as grandes categorias identificadas com a chave à direita. Os símbolos com números em sua parte superior (¹) identificam as subcategorias (veja- se a chave completa à página I·1).

ESPAÑOL: Nombre · Página · Lat.°′ · Long.°′ W = Oeste
FRANÇAIS: Nom · Page · Lat.°′ · Long.°′ W = Ouest
PORTUGUÊS: Nome · Página · Lat.°′ · Long.°′ W = Oeste

Nombre / Nom / Nome	Página / Page	Lat.°′	Long.°′
Sacandaga, West Branch ≃	210	43.22 N	74.17 W
Sacandica	152	5.58 S	15.56 E
Sacaola	152	12.57 S	22.25 E
Sacariúna ≃	248	12.52 S	57.22 W
Sacaton	200	33.04 N	111.44 W
Sacavém	266c	38.47 N	9.06 W
Sačchere	84	42.21 N	43.23 E
Sac City	198	42.25 N	94.59 W
Sacco ≃	66	41.31 N	13.32 E
Sacedón	34	40.29 N	2.43 W
Săcele	38	45.37 N	25.42 E
Şaç Geçidi)(	130	39.54 N	42.22 E
Šacha ≃	82	56.45 N	39.10 E
Sachalin □[8]	89	50.00 N	143.00 E
Sachalin, ostrov (Sakhalin) I	89	51.00 N	143.00 E
Sachalinskij zaliv c	89	53.45 N	141.30 E
Šachand	85	40.54 N	71.28 E
Šachayoj	252	26.41 S	61.50 W
Šachbuz	84	39.25 N	45.34 E
Šachdagskij chrebet ⩘	84	40.24 N	45.35 E
Saché	50	47.14 N	0.33 E
Šache ≃	84	43.47 N	39.27 E
Sachicapa	152	10.21 S	19.59 E
Sachigo ≃	176	55.06 N	88.58 W
Sachigo Lake ⊜	184	53.49 N	92.08 W
Sachimbo	152	9.14 S	20.16 E
Šachnovščina	78	49.08 N	35.53 E
Šachovskaja	76	56.02 N	35.29 E
Sachrang	64	47.41 N	12.15 E
Šachrichan	85	40.44 N	72.03 E
Šachrinau	85	38.34 N	68.20 E
Šachrisabz	72	39.03 N	66.50 E
Šachristan	85	39.47 N	68.49 E
Šachristan, pereval)(	85	39.33 N	68.33 E
Šachrovka	80	58.34 N	52.12 E
Sachse	222	32.59 N	96.36 W
Sachseln	58	46.52 N	8.15 E
Sachsen □[3]	30	51.00 N	13.00 E
Sachsen □[9]	30	52.45 N	9.30 E
Sachsen-Anhalt □[3]	30	52.00 N	11.30 E
Sachsenbrunn	54	50.27 N	10.56 E
Sachsenburg	64	46.50 N	13.21 E
Sachsenhagen	52	52.24 N	9.16 E
Sachsenhausen, Dtsch.	54	52.47 N	13.14 E
Sachsenhausen, Dtsch.	56	51.15 N	9.00 E
Sachs Harbour	176	72.00 N	125.00 W
Sächsische Schweiz ✦[1]	54	50.55 N	14.10 E
Šachterskij	180	64.42 N	177.40 E
Šachtinsk	86	49.40 N	72.37 E
Šachtnoje	83	47.57 N	38.17 E
Šacht'orsk, Ross.	89	49.11 N	142.07 E
Šacht'orsk, Ukr.	83	48.03 N	38.28 E
Šacht'orskij ✦[8]	83	48.09 N	39.08 E
Šachty	83	47.42 N	40.13 E
Šachunja	80	57.40 N	46.37 E
Sachy	56	49.40 N	5.08 E
Sacile	64	45.57 N	12.30 E
Šack, Bela.	76	53.25 N	27.41 E
Šack, Ross.	80	54.01 N	41.43 E
Šack, Ukr.	78	51.31 N	23.57 E
Sackets Harbor	212	43.56 N	76.07 W
Sackville	186	45.54 N	64.22 W
Saclay	261	48.44 N	2.10 E
Saclay, Étang de ⊜	261	48.45 N	2.10 E
Saco, Me., U.S.	188	43.30 N	70.26 W
Saco, Mt., U.S.	202	48.27 N	107.20 W
Saco ≃	188	43.27 N	70.22 W
Saco Bay c	188	43.30 N	70.15 W
Sacol Island I	116	6.58 N	122.13 E
Sacotes	266c	38.48 N	9.20 W
Sacra, Isola I	267a	41.45 N	12.15 E
Sacra Familia do Tinguá	256	22.29 S	43.36 W
Sacramento, Bra.	255	19.53 S	47.27 W
Sacramento, Ca., U.S.	226	38.34 N	121.29 W
Sacramento □[6]	226	38.35 N	121.30 W
Sacramento ≃, Ca., U.S.	204	38.03 N	121.56 W
Sacramento ≃, N.M., U.S.	200	32.16 N	105.31 W
Sacramento, Pampa del ≋	248	8.00 S	75.50 W
Sacramento Metropolitan Airport ⊠	226	38.42 N	121.37 W
Sacramento Mountains ⩘	200	32.45 N	105.30 W
Sacramento River Deep Water Ship Channel ≅	226	38.15 N	121.40 W
Sacramento South	226	38.32 N	121.26 W
Sacramento Valley V	204	39.15 N	122.00 W
Sacramento Wash V	200	34.43 N	114.28 W
Sacre ≃	248	12.56 S	58.18 W
Sacré-Cœur ʋ[1]	261	48.53 N	2.21 E
Sacred Heart	198	44.47 N	95.21 W
Sacriston	44	54.49 N	1.37 W
Sacro, Monte ʌ	68	40.13 N	15.20 E
Sacro Monte ʋ[1]	62	45.49 N	8.15 E
Sacrow ✦[8]	264a	52.26 N	13.06 E
Sacrower See ⊜	264a	52.27 N	13.06 E
Săcueni	38	47.21 N	22.06 E
Sacul	222	31.50 N	94.56 W
Sacupana	246	8.35 N	61.39 W
Sada, Esp.	34	43.21 N	8.15 W
Sada, Nihon	96	35.15 N	132.43 E
Sádaba	34	42.17 N	1.16 W
Sadābād, India	124	27.27 N	78.03 E
Sa'dābād, Īrān	128	29.23 N	51.07 E
Sa'dābād, Īrān	128	34.51 N	50.36 E
Şadad	130	34.18 N	36.56 E
Şa'dah	144	16.52 N	43.37 E
Sadaik Taung ʌ	110	15.09 N	98.12 E
Sadali	71	39.49 N	9.16 E
Sada-misaki >	96	33.20 N	132.01 E
Sada-misaki-hantō >[1]	96	33.26 N	132.13 E
Sadamitsu	96	34.02 N	134.04 E
Sadane ≃	115a	6.01 S	106.37 E
Sadang ≃	112	3.43 S	119.27 E
Sadanga	116	17.09 N	121.02 E
Sadani	154	6.03 S	38.47 E
Sadao	110	6.38 N	100.26 E
Sadarpur, Bngl.	126	23.28 N	90.02 E
Sādarpur, India	272a	28.33 N	77.21 E
Sadčikovka	86	53.01 N	63.27 E
Sadda	120	33.42 N	70.20 E
Saddle ≃	276	40.52 N	74.07 W
Saddleback ʌ	44	54.38 N	3.03 W
Saddleback, Mount ʌ	168a	32.58 S	116.28 E
Saddle Brook	276	40.54 N	74.06 W
Saddlebunch Keys II	220	24.37 N	81.37 W
Saddle Lake Indian Reserve ✦[4]	182	54.00 N	111.40 W
Saddle Mountain ʌ, Co., U.S.	200	38.50 N	105.28 W
Saddle Mountain ʌ, Or., U.S.	224	45.58 N	123.41 W
Saddle Mountains ⩘	202	46.50 N	119.55 W
Saddle Mountain State Park ♦	224	45.58 N	123.41 W
Saddle Peak ʌ	110	13.09 N	93.01 E
Saddle River	276	40.54 N	74.05 W
Saddle Rock	276	40.48 N	73.45 W
Saddleworth, Austl.	168b	34.05 S	138.47 E
Saddleworth, Eng., U.K.	262	53.33 N	1.59 W
Saddleworth Moor ✦[3]	262	53.33 N	1.57 W
Sa Dec	110	10.18 N	105.46 E
Sadelkow	54	53.36 N	13.26 E
Sādhaura	124	30.23 N	77.13 E
Sādhuhāti	126	23.34 N	89.01 E
Sadieville	218	38.23 N	84.32 W
Sadiola	150	13.53 N	11.42 W
Sādiqābād	120	28.18 N	70.08 E
Sadiya	120	27.50 N	95.40 E
Sa'dīyah, Wādī V	144	20.35 N	39.38 E
Sa'dīyāt, Ra's as- >	132	33.41 N	35.25 E
Sadler Lake ⊜	184	55.17 N	103.45 W
Sado I	92	38.00 N	138.25 E
Sado ≃	34	38.29 N	8.55 W
Sado-kaikyō ʊ	92	37.50 N	138.40 E
Sadon	84	42.51 N	44.00 E
Sadovoje, Ross.	80	46.56 N	44.23 E
Sadovoje, Ross.	80	47.46 N	44.30 E
Sadovoje Pervoje	78	51.33 N	40.29 E
Sadowara	92	32.02 N	131.26 E
Sādri	120	25.11 N	73.26 E
Šadrina	89	51.33 N	130.22 E
Šadrino	86	55.52 N	91.06 E
Šadrinsk	86	56.05 N	63.38 E
Sadsburyville	208	39.59 N	75.53 W
Sādulpur	123	28.38 N	75.24 E
Sädvaluspen	24	66.24 N	16.51 E
Sæby, Dan.	26	57.20 N	10.32 E
Sæby, Dan.	41	55.33 N	11.19 E
Saegertown	214	41.43 N	80.09 W
Sae Islands II	164	0.45 S	145.15 E
Saeki, Nihon	96	34.22 N	132.11 E
Saeki, Nihon	96	34.51 N	134.06 E
Saeki → Saiki	96	32.57 N	131.54 E
Saengil-to I	98	34.19 N	126.59 E
Saerbeck	52	52.10 N	7.38 E
Saerluojia Hu ⊜	120	33.55 N	86.55 E
Særslev, Dan.	41	55.31 N	10.11 E
Særslev, Dan.	41	55.43 N	11.23 E
Saeul	56	49.44 N	5.59 E
Şafā, Tulūl aş- ʌ[1]	132	33.02 N	37.12 E
Safad → Ẕefat	132	32.58 N	35.30 E
Safājah, Jazīrat I	140	26.45 N	33.59 E
Safakulevo	86	54.59 N	62.33 E
Şafānīyah	142	28.49 N	30.48 E
Šafárikovo	30	48.27 N	20.20 E
Safdar Jang Airport ⊠	272a	28.37 N	77.13 E
Safdar Jang's Tomb ⊥	272a	28.36 N	77.13 E
Safed Koh Range ⩘	123	33.58 N	70.25 E
Safe Harbor Dam ✦[6]	208	39.59 N	76.28 W
Safenbach ≃	61	47.06 N	16.05 E
Safety Bay	168a	32.18 S	115.43 E
Safety Harbor	220	27.59 N	82.41 W
Säffle	26	59.08 N	12.56 E
Safford	200	32.50 N	109.42 W
Saffron Walden	42	52.01 N	0.15 E
Safi	148	32.20 N	9.17 W
Safi □[4]	148	32.05 N	9.00 W
Safia	164	9.35 S	148.40 E
Şafīābād	128	36.45 N	57.58 E
Safīd ≃	120	36.44 N	65.38 E
Safīd Kūh, Selseleh-ye ⩘	128	34.30 N	63.30 E
Safidon	124	29.25 N	76.40 E
Safiental V	58	46.40 N	9.18 E
Safioune, Sebkhet ≋	148	32.16 N	5.27 E
Safipur	126	23.01 N	90.22 E
Şāfītā	130	34.49 N	36.07 E
Safonovo, Ross.	24	65.42 N	47.39 E
Safonovo, Ross.	76	55.06 N	33.15 E
Safonovo, Ross.	82	55.33 N	38.17 E
Safrakköyü ✦[8]	267b	41.00 N	28.47 E
Safranbolu	130	41.15 N	32.45 E
Şaft al-'Inab	142	30.49 N	30.41 E
Şaft al-Khammār	142	28.02 N	30.42 E
Şaft al-Laban	273c	30.02 N	31.10 E
Şaft al-Mulūk	142	30.49 N	30.41 E
Şaft Rāshīn	142	28.58 N	30.55 E
Şaft Turāb	142	30.54 N	31.07 E
Şafwān	128	30.07 N	47.43 E
Saga, Kaz.	86	50.23 N	64.15 E
Saga, Kaz.	86	49.25 N	55.17 E
Saga, Nihon	92	33.15 N	130.18 E
Saga, Nihon	96	33.05 N	133.06 E
Saga, Zhg.	120	29.30 N	85.22 E
Saga □[5]	96	33.21 N	130.28 E
Sagaba	152	11.17 S	23.07 E
Sagae	92	38.22 N	140.17 E
Sagaing	110	21.52 N	95.59 E
Sagaing □[8]	110	24.00 N	95.00 E
Sagak, Cape >	180	52.48 N	169.08 W
Şagalaherang	115a	6.40 S	107.39 E
Šagalakasa	80	46.54 N	50.43 E
Sagamāthā □[8]	124	27.15 N	86.45 E
Sagami ≃	94	35.19 N	139.22 E
Sagamihara	94	35.34 N	139.23 E
Sagamihara-daichi ⩘[1]	268	35.27 N	139.27 E
Sagamiko	94	35.37 N	139.12 E
Sagami-ko ⊜	94	35.35 N	139.16 E
Sagami-nada c	94	35.00 N	139.30 E
Sagami-wan c	94	35.15 N	139.25 E
Sagamore, Ma., U.S.	207	41.46 N	70.31 W
Sagamore, Pa., U.S.	214	40.46 N	79.13 W
Sagamore Beach	207	41.47 N	70.31 W
Sagamore Hill National Historic Site ⊥	276	40.53 N	73.30 W
Şagamore Hills	279a	41.02 N	81.26 W
Šagan ≃, Kaz.	86	50.37 N	79.15 E
Sagån ≃, Sve.	40	59.35 N	16.54 E
Saganaga Lake ⊜	190	48.14 N	90.52 W
Saganashkee Slough ≃	278	41.41 N	87.53 W
Saganash Lake ⊜	190	49.04 N	82.35 W
Saganoseki	96	33.15 N	131.53 E
Şaganthit Kyun I	110	11.56 N	98.29 E
Šagany, ozero ⊜	78	45.43 N	29.53 E
Sagan → Żagań	30	51.37 N	15.19 E
Sagaon	272c	19.12 N	73.06 E
Sāgar, India	122	14.10 N	75.02 E
Sāgar, India	124	23.50 N	78.43 E
Sagara	94	34.41 N	138.12 E
Sagaranten	115a	7.13 S	106.52 E
Sagard	54	54.31 N	13.33 E
Sāgardīghi	126	24.17 N	88.06 E
Sagaredžo	84	41.44 N	45.20 E
Sāgar Island I	126	21.43 N	88.06 E
Sagarmatha → Everest, Mount ʌ	124	27.59 N	86.56 E
Sagarmatha National Park ♦	124	27.50 N	86.45 E
Sāgar Plateau ⩘[1]	124	23.30 N	78.30 E
Sagavanirktok ≃	180	70.20 N	148.00 W
Sagay	116	10.57 N	123.25 E
Sage, Mount ʌ	240m	18.25 N	64.39 W
Sage Creek ≃, N.A.	202	48.58 N	110.06 W
Sage Creek ≃, U.S.	202	44.50 N	108.26 W
Sage Creek ≃, Mt., U.S.	202	47.16 N	109.43 W
Sage Creek ≃, Mt., U.S.	202	48.20 N	110.03 W
Sagemace Bay c	184	51.49 N	100.03 W
Sagerton	196	33.05 N	99.58 W
Saggaubach ≃	61	46.43 N	15.24 E
Sag Harbor	207	40.59 N	72.17 W
Şaghbīn	132	33.37 N	35.42 E
Şaghīr, Al-Baḩr aş- ≅	142	31.09 N	31.56 E
Sagil	86	50.20 N	91.40 E
Saginaw, Mi., U.S.	190	43.25 N	83.56 W
Saginaw, Tx., U.S.	222	32.52 N	97.22 W
Saginaw ≃	190	43.39 N	83.51 W
Saginaw Bay c	190	43.50 N	83.40 W
Sagiz, Kaz.	80	47.31 N	53.16 E
Sagiz, Kaz.	86	48.12 N	54.56 E
Sagiz ≃	86	47.32 N	53.20 E
Sağkaya	130	37.11 N	35.41 E
Sagleipie	150	7.00 N	8.52 W
Şaglek Bay c	176	58.35 N	63.00 W
Šaglyteniz, ozero ⊜	86	54.08 N	69.52 E
Šagonar	86	51.32 N	92.48 E
Sagra ʌ	34	37.57 N	2.34 W
Sagrado	64	45.52 N	13.29 E
Sagres	34	37.00 N	8.56 W
Sag Sag	164	5.35 S	148.20 E
Sagsaj	86	48.54 N	89.37 E
Sagsajn ≃	102	44.50 N	96.26 E
Sagu, Indon.	112	8.15 S	123.13 E
Şagu, Rom.	38	46.03 N	21.17 E
Saguache	200	38.05 N	106.05 W
Saguache Creek ≃	200	37.52 N	105.51 W
Sagua de Tánamo	240p	20.35 N	75.14 W
Sagua la Chica ≃	240p	22.45 N	79.39 W
Sagua la Grande	240p	22.49 N	80.05 W
Saguaro National Monument ♦	200	32.12 N	110.38 W
Saguenay ≃	176	48.08 N	69.44 W
Saguna	272b	22.59 N	88.29 E
Sagunay Lake	216	41.43 N	86.34 W
Sagunovka	78	49.17 N	32.23 E
Sagunt	34	39.41 N	0.16 W
Saguny	78	50.36 N	39.43 E
Sagutjevo	76	52.28 N	33.28 E
Sāgwāra	120	23.41 N	74.01 E
Sagy	261	49.03 N	1.57 E
Sa'gya	120	28.55 N	88.05 E
Sagyndyk, mys >	84	44.02 N	50.52 E
Sah	150	15.38 N	4.03 W
Saḩāb	132	31.53 N	36.00 E
Sahaba	140	18.55 N	30.28 E
Sahagún, Col.	246	8.57 N	75.27 W
Sahagún, Esp.	34	42.22 N	5.02 W
Saḩam	132	32.42 N	35.47 E
Saḩam al-Jawlān	132	32.46 N	35.56 E
Sahana Ambodipont	157b	14.37 S	50.11 E
Sahand, Kūh-e ʌ	128	37.44 N	46.27 E
Sahara ✦[2]	10	26.00 N	13.00 E
Sahāranpur	124	29.58 N	77.33 E
Sahara Occidentale → Western Sahara □[2]	148	24.30 N	13.00 W
Sahara Occidental → Western Sahara □[2]	148	24.30 N	13.00 W
Saharsa	124	25.53 N	86.36 E
Sahasinaka	157b	21.49 S	47.49 E
Sahasrail	126	23.19 N	89.43 E
Sahaswān	124	28.05 N	78.45 E
Sahel, Canal du ≅	150	13.44 N	6.05 W
Sahel, Oued ≃	34	36.26 N	4.33 E
Sahel → Sudan ✦[1]	134	10.00 N	20.00 E
Sāhibabad	272a	28.40 N	77.22 E
Sahibābad ✦[8]	272a	28.45 N	77.05 E
Sāhibganj	124	25.15 N	87.39 E
Sāhibi ≃	124	28.29 N	76.44 E
Şahin	130	41.01 N	26.50 E
Sāhīwāl, Pāk.	123	31.58 N	72.20 E
Sāhīwāl, Pāk.	123	30.40 N	73.06 E
Sahlenburg	52	53.52 N	8.38 E
Şaḩneh	128	34.29 N	47.41 E
Şaḩrā', Bi'r ⊤[4]	140	22.52 N	28.37 E
Şahrajat al-Kubrā wa Kafr Jirjis Yūsuf	142	30.38 N	31.17 E
Sahtlam	224	48.48 N	123.54 W
Sahuaripa	232	29.03 N	109.14 W
Sahuarita	200	31.57 N	110.58 W
Sahuayo de José María Morelos	234	20.04 N	102.43 W
Sahul Shelf ✢[4]	14	12.30 S	125.00 E
Sa Huynh	110	14.40 N	109.04 E
Şahwat al-Qamḩ	132	32.36 N	36.23 E
Šahy	30	48.05 N	18.57 E
Saï	150	13.50 N	5.00 W
Sai ≃, India	124	25.39 N	82.47 E
Sai ≃, Nihon	94	36.36 N	136.35 E
Sai ≃, Nihon	94	36.37 N	138.14 E
Saibai Island I	164	9.24 S	142.40 E
Sai Buri	110	6.42 N	101.37 E
Sai Buri ≃	110	6.43 N	101.39 E
Saïda	148	34.50 N	0.09 E
Saïda □[5]	148	33.00 N	0.30 W
Saidābād, Bngl.	126	24.18 N	89.43 E
Sa'īdābād, Īrān	267d	35.40 N	51.11 E
Saidaiji	96	34.39 N	134.02 E
Saïdia	148	35.04 N	2.15 W
Sa'īdīyeh	128	36.26 N	48.48 E
Saido	268	35.52 N	139.41 E
Saidor	164	5.35 S	146.30 E
Saidpur, Bngl.	124	25.47 N	88.54 E
Saidpur, India	124	25.33 N	83.11 E
Saidu	123	34.45 N	72.21 E
Saigawa	96	33.39 N	130.57 E
Saignelégier	58	47.15 N	7.00 E
Saignon	62	43.52 N	5.26 E
Saigō	92	36.12 N	133.20 E
Sai Gon ≃	269c	10.45 N	106.45 E
Saigon → Thanh Pho Ho Chi Minh	269c	10.45 N	106.40 E
Saihaku	96	35.20 N	133.20 E
Saihan Toroi	102	41.41 N	100.26 E
Saijō, Nihon	96	33.55 N	133.11 E
Saijō, Nihon	96	34.56 N	133.07 E
Saijō ≃	96	34.48 N	132.51 E
Saikai-kokuritsu-kōen ♦	92	33.12 N	129.22 E
Sai Keng	271d	22.26 N	114.16 E
Saiki	96	32.57 N	131.54 E
Saiki-wan c	96	33.00 N	131.58 E
Sai Kung	271d	22.23 N	114.15 E
Saileati	85	38.57 N	74.45 E
Sailkupa	126	23.41 N	89.15 E
Saillans	62	44.42 N	5.11 E
Sailly	261	49.02 N	1.48 E
Sailmouille, Ruisseau ≃	261	48.37 N	2.17 E
Sailolof	164	1.15 S	130.46 E
Sailor Creek ≃	202	42.56 N	115.29 W
Şail-sous-Couzan	62	45.44 N	3.57 E
Šaim	86	60.21 N	64.14 E
Saima	98	41.00 N	124.14 E
Saimaa ⊜	26	61.15 N	28.15 E
Saimaa Canal ≅	26	61.05 N	28.18 E
Saimbeyli	130	38.00 N	36.06 E
Saín Alto	234	23.35 N	103.15 W
Saindak	128	29.17 N	61.34 E
Şā'īn Dezh	128	36.40 N	46.33 E
Sainghin-en-Weppes	50	50.33 N	2.54 E
Sainjang	98	39.15 N	125.51 E
Sainō-ha'iji ⊥	96	35.29 N	133.39 E
Sains-du-Nord	50	50.06 N	4.00 E
Sains-en-Gohelle	50	50.27 N	2.41 E
Sains-Richaumont	50	49.49 N	3.42 E
Saint Abb's Head >	46	55.54 N	2.09 W
Sainte-Adèle	206	45.57 N	74.07 W
Sainte-Adresse	50	49.30 N	0.05 E
Saint-Adrien	206	45.49 N	71.43 W
Saint-Affrique	32	43.57 N	2.53 E
Saint-Agapit	206	46.34 N	71.27 W
Saint Agatha	212	43.26 N	80.36 W
Sainte-Agathe, Mb., Can.	184	49.34 N	97.10 W
Sainte-Agathe, Fr.	62	45.49 N	3.37 E
Sainte-Agathe [-de-Lotbinière]	206	46.23 N	71.24 W
Sainte-Agathe-des-Monts	206	46.03 N	74.17 W
Sainte-Agnès, Fr.	62	43.48 N	7.28 E
Saint Agnes, Eng., U.K.	42	50.18 N	5.13 W
Saint Agnes I	42a	49.54 N	6.20 W
Saint-Agrève	62	45.01 N	4.24 E
Saint-Aignan	50	47.16 N	1.23 E
Saint-Aimé (Massueville)	206	45.55 N	72.56 W
Saint Albans, Austl.	169	37.44 S	144.48 E
Saint Albans, Austl.	170	33.17 S	150.59 E
Saint Alban's, Nf., Can.	186	47.52 N	55.51 W
Saint Albans, Eng., U.K.	42	51.46 N	0.21 W
Saint Albans, Mo., U.S.	219	38.35 N	90.46 W
Saint Albans, Vt., U.S.	188	44.48 N	73.05 W
Saint Albans, W.V., U.S.	188	38.23 N	81.50 W
Saint Albans □[8]	260	51.45 N	0.20 W
Saint Albans ✦[8]	276	40.42 N	73.46 W
Saint Albans, Cape >	168b	35.49 S	138.07 E
Saint Albans Cathedral ʋ[1]	260	51.45 N	0.20 W
Saint Albert, Ab., Can.	182	53.38 N	113.38 W
Saint-Albert, P.Q., Can.	206	46.00 N	72.05 W
Saint Aldhelm's Head >	42	50.34 N	2.04 W
Saint-Alexandre-de-Kamouraska	186	47.41 N	69.38 W
Saint-Alexis-des-Monts	206	46.28 N	73.08 W
Saint-Amable	275a	45.39 N	73.18 W
Saint-Amand	56	48.49 N	4.36 E
Saint-Amand-en-Puisaye	50	47.31 N	3.04 E
Saint-Amand-les-Eaux	50	50.26 N	3.26 E
Saint-Amand-Longpré	50	47.41 N	1.01 E
Saint-Amand-Montrond	32	46.44 N	2.30 E
Saint-Amant-Roche-Savine	62	45.34 N	3.38 E
Saint-Amarin	58	47.53 N	7.01 E
Saint-Ambroix	62	44.15 N	4.11 E
Sainte-Amélie	184	50.59 N	99.21 W
Saint-Amour	58	46.26 N	5.21 E
Saint-André	157c	20.57 S	55.39 E
Saint-André, Cap >	157b	16.11 S	44.27 E
Saint-André, Ruisseau ≃	275a	45.22 N	73.29 W
Saint-André-Avellin	206	45.43 N	75.03 W
Saint-André-de-l'Eure	50	48.54 N	1.17 E
Saint-André-de-Valborgne	62	44.09 N	3.41 E
St.-André-Est	206	45.34 N	74.20 W
Saint-André-les-Alpes	62	43.58 N	6.30 E
Saint-André-les-Vergers	50	48.17 N	4.03 E
Saint Andrew	241g	13.15 N	59.33 W
Saint Andrew, Mount ʌ	241h	13.11 N	61.13 W
Saint Andrew Lakes ⊜	212	44.36 N	76.40 W
Saint Andrews, N.B., Can.	186	45.05 N	67.03 W
Saint Andrews, Scot., U.K.	46	56.20 N	2.48 W
Saint Andrews, S.C., U.S.	192	32.46 N	79.59 W
Saint Andrews Bay c	46	56.22 N	2.50 W
Saint Andrew's Cathedral ʋ[1]	271c	1.18 N	103.51 E
Saint Andrews Channel ʊ	186	46.03 N	60.38 W
Saint Ann	219	38.43 N	90.22 W
Sainte-Anne, Guad.	241o	16.14 N	61.23 W
Saint Anne, Guernsey	43b	49.42 N	2.12 W
Sainte-Anne, Mart.	240e	14.26 N	60.53 W
Saint Anne, Il., U.S.	216	41.01 N	87.42 W
Sainte-Anne ≃	206	46.33 N	72.12 W
Saint Anne, Cathedral of ʋ[1]	273b	4.18 S	15.19 E
Sainte Anne, Lac ⊜, Ab., Can.	182	53.43 N	114.27 W
Sainte-Anne, Lac ⊜, P.Q., Can.	186	50.05 N	67.50 W
Sainte-Anne-de-Beaupré	186	47.02 N	70.56 W
Sainte-Anne-de-Bellevue	275a	45.24 N	73.57 W
Sainte-Anne-de-la-Pérade	206	46.35 N	72.12 W
Sainte-Anne-de-Madawaska	186	47.15 N	68.02 W
Sainte-Anne-des-Chênes	184	49.40 N	96.40 W
Sainte-Anne-des-Monts	186	49.08 N	66.30 W
Sainte-Anne-des-Plaines	206	46.46 N	73.48 W
Saint Anne of the Congo ʋ[1]	273b	4.16 S	15.17 E
Saint Anne's	44	53.45 N	3.02 W
Saint Ann's Bay	241q	18.26 N	77.08 W
Saint Anns Bay c	186	46.20 N	60.30 W
Saint Ann's Head >	42	51.41 N	5.10 W
Saint-Anselme	186	46.37 N	70.58 W
Saint Ansgar	190	43.22 N	92.55 W
Saint-Anthème	62	45.31 N	3.55 E
Saint Anthony, N.B., Can.	186	46.22 N	64.45 W
Saint Anthony, Nf., Can.	186	51.22 N	55.35 W
Saint Anthony, Id., U.S.	202	43.57 N	111.40 W
Saint-Antoine, P.Q., Can.	206	45.46 N	73.59 W
Saint-Antoine, Fr.	62	45.10 N	5.13 E
Saint-Antonin	32	44.09 N	1.45 E
Saint-Apollinaire (Francoeur)	206	46.37 N	71.31 W
Saint Arnaud, Austl.	166	36.37 S	143.15 E
Saint Arnaud, N.Z.	172	41.48 S	172.50 E
Saint-Arnoult, Forêt de ♦	261	48.35 N	1.55 E
Saint-Arnoult-en-Yvelines	50	48.34 N	1.56 E
Saint Arvans	42	51.40 N	2.41 W
Saint Asaph	44	53.16 N	3.26 W
Saint-Astier	32	45.09 N	0.32 E
Saint Athan	42	51.24 N	3.25 W
Saint-Auban	62	43.51 N	6.44 E
Saint-Aubert, Mont ʌ[2]	50	50.39 N	3.24 E
Saint Aubert Island I	219	38.40 N	91.52 W
Saint-Aubin, Fr.	50	49.53 N	0.53 E
Saint-Aubin, Fr.	58	47.02 N	5.20 E
Saint Aubin, Jersey	43b	49.11 N	2.10 W
Saint-Aubin, Schw.	58	46.54 N	6.47 E
Saint-Aubin-d'Aubigné	32	48.15 N	1.36 W
Saint-Aubin-lès-Elbeuf	50	49.18 N	1.01 E
Saint-Aubin-sur-Aire	58	48.42 N	5.27 E
Saint-Augustin	157b	23.33 S	43.46 E
Saint-Augustin ≃	176	51.14 N	58.41 W
Saint-Augustin-Deux-Montagnes	275a	45.38 N	73.59 W
Saint Augustine	192	29.53 N	81.18 W
Saint-Augustin Nord-Ouest ≃	186	51.16 N	58.42 W
Saint-Augustin-Saguenay	186	51.14 N	58.39 W
Saint-Aulaye	32	45.12 N	0.08 E
Saint Austell	42	50.20 N	4.48 W
Saint-Avertin	50	47.22 N	0.44 E
Saint-Avold	56	49.06 N	6.42 E
Saint-Ay	50	47.51 N	1.45 E
Saint-Aygulf	62	43.23 N	6.44 E
Saint Barbe	186	51.12 N	56.46 W
Saint Barnabas Chapel ʋ[1]	174c	29.02 S	167.55 E
Saint-Barthélemy I	238	17.54 N	62.50 W
Saint-Basile	186	47.21 N	68.14 W
Saint-Basile-de-Portneuf	206	46.45 N	71.49 W
Saint-Basile-le-Grand	206	45.32 N	73.17 W
Saint Bathans, Mount ʌ	172	44.44 S	169.46 E
Sainte-Baume, Chaîne de la ⩘	62	43.20 N	5.45 E
Saint-Béat	32	42.55 N	0.42 E
Saint Bees	44	54.30 N	3.37 W
Saint Bees Head >	44	54.32 N	3.38 W
Saint Benedict	214	40.38 N	78.44 W
Saint-Benoît, Fr.	261	48.40 N	1.55 E
Saint-Benoît, Réu.	157c	21.02 S	55.43 E
Saint-Benoît-du-Sault	32	46.27 N	1.23 E
Saint-Benoît-en-Woëvre	56	48.59 N	5.47 E
Saint Bernard	218	39.10 N	84.29 W
Saint-Bernard, Île I	275a	45.23 N	73.45 W
Saint-Bernard-de-Dorchester	206	46.30 N	71.08 W
Saint-Béron	62	45.30 N	5.43 E
Saint-Blaise, P.Q., Can.	206	45.13 N	73.17 W
Saint-Blaise, Schw.	58	47.01 N	6.59 E
Saint-Blaise-la-Roche	58	48.24 N	7.10 E
Saint Blaize, Cape >	158	34.11 S	22.10 E
Saint Blazey	42	50.22 N	4.43 W
Saint-Blin	58	48.16 N	5.25 E
Saint-Bonaventure, P.Q., Can.	206	45.58 N	72.41 W
Saint Bonaventure, N.Y., U.S.	210	42.05 N	78.28 W
Saint-Boniface-de-Shawinigan	206	46.30 N	72.49 W
Saint-Bonnet	62	44.41 N	6.05 E
Saint-Bonnet-de-Joux	58	46.29 N	4.27 E
Saint-Bonnet-le-Château	62	45.25 N	4.04 E
Saint-Bonnet-le-Froid	62	45.09 N	4.27 E
Saint Boswells	46	55.34 N	2.39 W
Saint Brendan's	186	48.52 N	53.40 W
Saint-Brice-sous-Forêt	261	49.00 N	2.21 E
Saint Bride, Mount ʌ	182	51.30 N	115.57 W
Saint Bride's	186	46.55 N	54.10 W
Saint Brides Bay c	42	51.48 N	5.15 W
Saint Bride's Major	42	51.28 N	3.38 W
Saint-Brieuc	32	48.31 N	2.47 W
Saint-Brieux	184	52.38 N	104.52 W
Saint-Broing-Les-Moines, Fr.	58	47.41 N	4.50 E
Saint-Broing-les-Moines, Fr.	58	48.32 N	6.36 E
Saint-Bruno	206	45.32 N	73.21 W
Saint-Bruno, Mont ʌ[2]	275a	45.33 N	73.19 W
Saint-Calais	50	47.55 N	0.45 E
Saint-Calixte-de-Kilkenny	206	45.57 N	73.51 W
Saint-Cannat	62	43.37 N	5.18 E
Saint-Casimir	206	46.40 N	72.08 W
Saint-Cassien, Lac de ⊜[1]	62	43.35 N	6.48 E
Saint Catharines	212	43.10 N	79.15 W
Saint Catharines Airport ⊠	284a	43.11 N	79.10 W
Saint Catherine	220	28.37 N	82.08 W
Saint Catherine, Monastery of → Qiddīsah Kātrīnā, Dayr al- ʋ[1]	140	28.29 N	34.01 E
Saint Catherine, Mount ʌ	241k	12.10 N	61.40 W
Sainte-Catherine-de-Fierbois	50	47.09 N	0.39 E
Saint Catherines Island I	192	31.38 N	81.10 W
Saint Catherine's Point >	42	50.34 N	1.15 W
Saint-Célestin (Annaville)	206	46.13 N	72.26 W
Saint-Céré	32	44.52 N	1.53 E
Saint-Cergue	58	46.27 N	6.09 E
Saint-Césaire	206	45.25 N	73.00 W
Saint-Cézaire-sur-Siagne	62	43.39 N	6.48 E
Saint-Chamas	62	43.33 N	5.02 E
Saint-Chamond	62	45.28 N	4.30 E
Saint-Chaptes	62	43.58 N	4.17 E
Saint Charles, Ar., U.S.	194	34.22 N	91.08 W
Saint Charles, Id., U.S.	202	42.06 N	111.23 W
Saint Charles, Il., U.S.	216	41.54 N	88.18 W
Saint Charles, Md., U.S.	208	38.36 N	76.56 W
Saint Charles, Mi., U.S.	190	43.17 N	84.08 W
Saint Charles, Mn., U.S.	190	43.58 N	92.03 W
Saint Charles, Mo., U.S.	219	38.47 N	90.28 W
Saint Charles □[6]	219	38.47 N	90.43 W
Saint-Charles ≃	275a	45.40 N	73.27 W
Saint-Charles, Lac ⊜	206	46.55 N	71.23 W
Saint-Charles-de-Drummond	206	45.54 N	72.28 W
Saint Charles Mesa	198	38.15 N	104.32 W
Saint-Charles-sur-Richelieu	206	45.41 N	73.11 W
Saint-Chef	62	45.38 N	5.22 E
Saint-Chély-d'Apcher	32	44.48 N	3.17 E
Saint-Chéron	261	48.33 N	2.07 E
Saint-Christophe-en-Bazelle	50	47.11 N	1.43 E
Saint-Christophe-Nevis → Saint Kitts and Nevis □[1]	238	17.20 N	62.45 W
Saint Christopher (Saint Kitts) I	238	17.20 N	62.45 W
Saint Christopher-Nevis → Saint Kitts and Nevis □[1]	238	17.20 N	62.45 W
Saint-Chrysostome	206	45.06 N	73.46 W
Saint-Ciers-sur-Gironde	32	45.18 N	0.37 W
Saint Clair, Mi., U.S.	214	42.48 N	82.29 W
Saint Clair, Mo., U.S.	219	38.20 N	90.58 W
Saint Clair, Pa., U.S.	208	40.43 N	76.11 W
Saint Clair, Pa., U.S.	279b	40.16 N	79.33 W
Saint Clair □[6], Il., U.S.	219	38.31 N	90.00 W
Saint Clair □[6], Mi., U.S.	214	42.50 N	82.42 W
Saint Clair ≃	214	42.37 N	82.31 W
Saint Clair, Lake ⊜	214	42.25 N	82.41 W
Saint Clair Beach	281	42.19 N	82.51 W
Saint Clair Flats	214	42.32 N	82.37 W
Saint Clair Flats ≋	281	42.35 N	82.36 W
Saint Clair Flats Canal ≅	214	42.20 N	82.58 W
Saint Clair Flats State Wildlife Area ✦[4]	281	42.36 N	82.40 W
Saint Clair Haven	214	42.34 N	82.47 W
Saint Clair Shores	214	42.29 N	82.53 W
Saint-Clair-sur-Epte	50	49.12 N	1.41 E
Saint Clairsville, Oh., U.S.	214	40.04 N	80.54 W
Saint Clairsville, Pa., U.S.	214	40.09 N	78.31 W
Saint Clair Tunnel ✦[5]	214	42.57 N	82.25 W
Saint-Claud	32	45.53 N	0.23 E
Saint-Claude, Mb., Can.	184	49.40 N	98.22 W
Saint-Claude, Fr.	58	46.23 N	5.52 E
Saint-Claude, Guad.	241o	16.02 N	61.42 W
Saint-Claude, Ruisseau ≃	275a	45.25 N	73.28 W
Saint Clears	42	51.50 N	4.30 W
Saint Clements	212	43.31 N	80.39 W
Saint Clements Bay c	208	38.17 N	76.42 W
Sainte-Clothilde	206	45.59 N	72.14 W
Sainte-Clotilde-de-Châteauguay	206	45.10 N	73.41 W
Saint-Cloud, Fr.	50	48.50 N	2.11 E
Saint Cloud, Fl., U.S.	220	28.14 N	81.16 W
Saint Cloud, Mn., U.S.	190	45.33 N	94.09 W
Saint-Cloud, Parc de ♦	261	48.50 N	2.13 E
Saint-Colomban-des-Villards	62	45.18 N	6.14 E
Sainte-Colombe	58	47.52 N	4.32 E
Saint Columb Major	42	50.26 N	5.03 W
Saint Combs	46	57.39 N	1.54 W
Saint-Constant	206	45.22 N	73.37 W
Saint-Cosme-en-Vairais	50	48.16 N	0.28 E
Sainte-Croix, P.Q., Can.	206	46.38 N	71.44 W
Sainte-Croix, Schw.	58	46.49 N	6.31 E
Saint Croix I	241n	17.45 N	64.45 W
Saint Croix ≃, N.A.	186	45.10 N	67.10 W
Saint Croix ≃, U.S.	190	44.45 N	92.49 W
Sainte-Croix-aux-Mines	58	48.16 N	7.13 E
Saint Croix Falls	190	45.24 N	92.38 W
Saint Croix Island I	158	33.48 S	25.45 E
Saint Croix Island National Monument ♦	188	45.08 N	67.08 W
Saint Croix National Scenic Riverway ♦	190	46.00 N	92.25 W
Saint Croix State Park ♦	190	46.00 N	92.40 W
Sainte-Croix-Vallée-Francaise	62	44.11 N	3.44 E
Saint-Cuthbert	206	46.09 N	73.14 W
Saint-Cyprien	32	44.52 N	1.02 E
Saint-Cyrille-de-Wendover	206	45.56 N	72.26 W
Saint-Cyr-L'École	50	48.48 N	2.04 E
Saint-Cyr-l'École, Aérodrome de ⊠	261	48.49 N	2.04 E
Saint Cyr Range ⩘	180	61.10 N	131.10 W
Sainte-Cyr-sous-Dourdan	261	48.34 N	2.02 E
Saint-Cyr-sur-Loire	50	47.24 N	0.40 E
Saint-Cyr-sur-Mer	62	43.11 N	5.43 E
Saint-Dalmas-de-Tende	62	44.03 N	7.35 E
Saint-Damien-de-Brandon	206	46.20 N	73.29 W
Saint David, Az., U.S.	200	31.54 N	110.12 W
Saint David, Il., U.S.	190	40.29 N	90.02 W
Saint David's, Nf., Can.	186	48.12 N	58.52 W
Saint Davids, On., Can.	284a	43.10 N	79.06 W
Saint David's, Wales, U.K.	42	51.54 N	5.16 W
Saint Davids, Pa., U.S.	285	40.02 N	75.22 W
Saint David's Cathedral ʋ[1]	42	51.54 N	5.16 W
Saint David's Head >	42	51.55 N	5.19 W
Saint David's Island I	240a	32.22 N	64.39 W
Saint Day	42	50.14 N	5.11 W
Saint-Denis, Fr.	50	48.56 N	2.22 E
Saint-Denis, Réu.	157c	20.52 S	55.28 E
Saint-Denis, Basilique ʋ[1]	261	48.56 N	2.22 E
Saint-Denis-de-l'Hôtel	50	47.52 N	2.07 E
Saint-Denis-en-Bugey	58	45.57 N	5.20 E
Saint-Denis-Rivière-Richelieu	206	45.47 N	73.09 W
Saint Dennis	42	50.23 N	4.53 W
Saint-Didier-en-Velay	62	45.18 N	4.17 E
Saint-Didier-les-Bains	62	44.00 N	5.07 E
Saint-Dié	58	48.17 N	6.57 E
Saint-Disdier	62	44.44 N	5.54 E
Saint-Dizier	58	48.38 N	4.57 E
Saint Dogmaels	42	52.05 N	4.40 W
Saint-Donat-de-Montcalm	206	46.19 N	74.13 W
Saint-Donat-sur-l'Herbasse	62	45.07 N	5.00 E
Sainte-Dorothée ✦[8]	275a	45.32 N	73.49 W
Saint-Dyé-sur-Loire	50	47.39 N	1.29 E
Saint-Édouard-de-Maskinongé	206	46.20 N	73.09 W
Saint Edward	198	41.34 N	97.52 W
Saint-Égrève	62	45.14 N	5.41 E
Saint Eleanor's	186	46.25 N	63.49 W
Saint Elias, Cape >	180	59.52 N	144.30 W
Saint Elias, Mount ʌ	180	60.18 N	140.55 W
Saint Elias Mountains ⩘	180	60.30 N	139.30 W
Saint-Élie	250	4.50 N	53.17 W
Saint Elmo	219	39.01 N	88.50 W
Saint-Éloi	186	48.02 N	69.14 W
Saint-Émile-de-Montcalm	206	46.06 N	74.00 W
Saint-Émile-de-Québec	206	46.52 N	71.20 W
Saint-Émile-de-Suffolk	206	45.56 N	74.55 W
Sainte-Enimie	32	44.22 N	3.26 E
Saint-Épain	50	47.08 N	0.32 E
Saint-Esprit ≃	206	45.52 N	73.27 W
Saint-Étienne	62	45.26 N	4.24 E
Saint-Étienne-de-Lugdarès	62	44.39 N	3.57 E
Saint-Étienne-de-Saint-Geoirs	62	45.20 N	5.21 E
Saint-Étienne-des-Grès	206	46.26 N	72.46 W
Saint-Étienne-de-Tinée	62	44.15 N	6.55 E
Saint-Étienne-du-Rouvray	50	49.23 N	1.06 E
Saint-Étienne-en-Dévoluy	62	44.42 N	5.56 E
Saint-Étienne-le-Laus	62	44.30 N	6.10 E
Saint-Étienne-les-Orgues	62	44.03 N	5.47 E
Saint-Étienne-lès-Remiremont	58	48.02 N	6.37 E
Saint-Eugène	206	45.30 N	74.28 W
Saint-Eustache	206	45.34 N	73.54 W
Saint-Evroult-Notre-Dame-du-Bois	50	48.48 N	0.28 E
Saint-Fabien	186	48.18 N	68.52 W
Saint Faith's	158	30.30 S	30.12 E
Saint-Fargeau	50	47.38 N	3.04 E
Saint-Fargeau-Ponthierry	261	48.33 N	2.32 E
Saint-Félicien, P.Q., Can.	176	48.39 N	72.26 W
Saint-Félicien, Fr.	62	45.05 N	4.38 E
Sainte-Félicité	186	48.54 N	67.20 W
Saint-Félix	62	45.48 N	5.58 E
Saint-Félix-de-Kingsey	206	45.48 N	72.12 W
Saint-Félix-de-Valois	206	46.10 N	73.26 W
Saint-Ferdinand (Bernierville)	206	46.06 N	71.34 W
Saintfield	48	54.28 N	5.50 W
Saint Fillans	46	56.23 N	4.07 W
Saint-Firmin	62	44.47 N	6.02 E
Saint-Firmin-sur-Loire	50	47.37 N	2.44 E
Saint-Flavien	206	46.31 N	71.36 W
Saint-Florent	36	42.41 N	9.18 E
Saint-Florentin	50	48.00 N	3.44 E
Saint-Florent-sur-Cher	32	46.59 N	2.15 E
Saint-Floris, Parc National ♦	146	9.40 N	21.35 E
Saint-Flour	32	45.02 N	3.05 E

Symbol	English	Deutsch	Español	Français	Português
≃	River	Fluß	Río	Rivière	Rio
≅	Canal	Kanal	Canal	Canal	Canal
ᒪ	Waterfall, Rapids	Wasserfall, Stromschnellen	Cascada, Rápidos	Chute d'eau, Rapides	Cascata, Rápidos
ʊ	Strait	Meeresstraße	Estrecho	Détroit	Estreito
c	Bay, Gulf	Bucht, Golf	Bahía, Golfo	Baie, Golfe	Baía, Golfo
⊜	Lake, Lakes	See, Seen	Lago, Lagos	Lac, Lacs	Lago, Lagos
≋	Swamp	Sumpf	Pantano	Marais	Pântano
⊼	Ice Features, Glacier	Eis- und Gletscherformen	Accidentes Glaciales	Formes glaciaires	Acidentes glaciares
⊤	Other Hydrographic Features	Andere Hydrographische Objekte	Otros Elementos Hidrográficos	Autres données hydrographiques	Outros acidentes hidrográficos
✢	Submarine Features	Untermeerische Objekte	Accidentes Submarinos	Formes de relief sous-marin	Acidentes submarinos
□	Political Unit	Politische Einheit	Unidad Politica	Entité politique	Unidade política
ʋ	Cultural Institution	Kulturelle Institution	Institución Cultural	Institution culturelle	Instituição cultural
⊥	Historical Site	Historische Stätte	Sitio Histórico	Site historique	Sitio histórico
♦	Recreational Site	Erholungs- und Ferienort	Sitio de Recreo	Centre de loisirs	Area de Lazer
⊠	Airport	Flughafen	Aeropuerto	Aéroport	Aeroporto
■	Military Installation	Militäranlage	Instalación Militar	Installation militaire	Instalação militar
✦	Miscellaneous	Verschiedenes	Misceláneo	Divers	Diversos

Name	Page	Lat. °′	Long. °′
Saint-Fons	62	45.42 N	4.52 E
Saint-Fortunat	206	45.58 N	71.36 W
Sainte-Foy	206	46.47 N	71.17 W
Sainte-Foy-la-Grande	32	44.50 N	0.13 E
Sainte-Foy-l'Argentière	62	45.42 N	4.28 E
Sainte-Foy-lès-Lyon	62	45.44 N	4.48 E
Sainte-Foy-Tarentaise	62	45.35 N	6.53 E
Saint Francis, Ks., U.S.	198	39.46 N	101.47 W
Saint Francis, S.D., U.S.	198	43.08 N	100.54 W
Saint Francis, Wi., U.S.	216	42.58 N	87.52 W
Saint Francis ≃, N.A.	186	47.10 N	68.57 W
Saint Francis ≃, U.S.	194	34.38 N	90.35 W
Saint Francis, Cape ≻, Nf., Can.	186	47.50 N	52.47 W
Saint Francis, Cape ≻, S. Afr.	158	34.14 S	24.49 E
Saint Francis, Lake ⊜	206	45.08 N	74.25 W
Saint Francis Bay c	158	34.35 S	25.10 E
Saint Francisville	194	30.46 N	91.22 W
Saint-François	241o	16.15 N	61.17 W
Saint-François ≃	206	46.07 N	72.55 W
Saint-François, Lac ⊜	206	45.55 N	71.10 W
Saint-François de Boundji	152	1.03 S	15.22 E
Saint-François-de-Laval ◆[8]	275a	45.40 N	73.34 W
Saint-François-du-Lac	206	46.04 N	72.50 W
Saint Francois Mountains ʌ[2]	194	37.30 N	90.35 W
Saint-François-sur-Bugeon	62	45.24 N	6.21 E
Saint-Front	62	44.59 N	4.08 E
Saint-Gabriel	206	46.17 N	73.23 W
Saint-Gabriel-de-Gaspé	186	48.31 N	64.32 W
Saint-Gabriel-de-Rimouski	186	48.25 N	68.10 W
Saint-Gall → Sankt Gallen	58	47.25 N	9.23 E
Saint-Galmier	62	45.35 N	4.19 E
Sainte-Gauburge-Sainte-Colombe	50	48.42 N	0.26 E
Saint-Gaudens	32	43.07 N	0.44 E
Saint-Gaudens National Historic Site ⊥	188	43.29 N	72.19 W
Saint-Gaultier	32	46.38 N	1.25 E
Saint-Gély-du-Fesc	62	43.42 N	3.48 E
Saint-Genest-Lerpt	62	45.27 N	4.20 E
Saint-Genest-Malifaux	62	45.20 N	4.25 E
Sainte-Geneviève, P.Q., Can.	275a	45.29 N	73.52 W
Sainte Genevieve, Mo., U.S.	194	37.59 N	90.03 W
Sainte-Geneviève-de-Batiscan	206	46.32 N	72.20 W
Sainte-Geneviève-des-Bois	50	48.38 N	2.20 E
Saint-Gengoux-le-National	58	46.37 N	4.39 E
Saint-Genis-de-Saintonge	32	45.29 N	0.34 W
Saint-Genis-Laval	62	45.41 N	4.48 E
Saint-Genis-Pouilly	58	46.15 N	6.01 E
Saint-Genix-sur-Guiers	62	45.36 N	5.38 E
Saint-Geoire-en-Valdaine	62	45.27 N	5.38 E
Saint George, Austl.	166	28.02 S	148.35 E
Saint George, Ber.	240a	32.22 N	64.40 W
Saint George, N.B., Can.	186	45.08 N	66.49 W
Saint George, On., Can.	212	43.15 N	80.15 W
Saint George, Pa., U.S.	214	41.15 N	79.47 W
Saint George, S.C., U.S.	192	33.11 N	80.34 W
Saint George, Ut,. U.S.	200	37.06 N	113.34 W
Saint George ◆[8]	276	40.39 N	74.05 W
Saint George, Cape ≻, Nf., Can.	186	48.27 N	59.15 W
Saint George, Cape ≻, Pap. N. Gui.	164	4.52 S	152.52 E
Saint George, Cape ≻, Fl., U.S.	192	29.35 N	85.04 W
Saint George, Point ≻	204	41.47 N	124.15 W
Saint George Island, Ak., U.S.	180	56.36 N	169.32 W
Saint George Island, Md., U.S.	208	38.07 N	76.29 W
Saint George Island I, Ak., U.S.	180	56.35 N	169.35 W
Saint George Island I, Fl., U.S.	192	29.39 N	84.55 W
Saint George's, Nf., Can.	186	48.26 N	58.29 W
Saint-Georges, P.Q., Can.	188	46.07 N	70.40 W
Saint-Georges, P.Q., Can.	206	46.37 N	72.40 W
Saint-Georges, Fr.	58	48.40 N	6.56 E
Saint George's, Gren.	241k	12.03 N	61.45 W
Saint-Georges, Guy. fr.	250	3.54 N	51.48 W
Saint Georges, De., U.S.	208	39.33 N	75.39 W
Saint Georges Basin c	170	35.07 S	150.36 E
Saint George's Bay c, Nf., Can.	186	48.20 N	59.00 W
Saint Georges Bay c, N.S., Can.	186	45.50 N	61.45 W
Saint George's Channel ꭒ, Europe	28	52.00 N	6.00 W
Saint George's Channel ꭒ, Pap. N. Gui.	164	4.30 S	152.30 E
Saint-Georges-de-Reneins	58	46.04 N	4.43 E
Saint-Georges-de-Windsor	206	45.42 N	71.50 W
Saint-Georges-en-Couzan	62	45.42 N	3.56 E
Saint Georges Head ≻	170	35.12 S	150.42 E
Saint George's Island I	240a	32.22 N	64.40 W
Saint George Sound ꭒ	192	29.47 N	84.42 W
Saint-Gérard, Bel.	56	50.21 N	4.45 E
Saint-Gérard, P.Q., Can.	206	45.46 N	71.25 W
Saint-Germain	32	48.54 N	2.05 E
Saint-Germain ≃	206	45.55 N	72.30 W
Saint-Germain, Forêt de ♠	261	48.55 N	2.05 E
Saint-Germain-de-Calberte	62	44.13 N	3.48 E
Saint-Germain-de-Grantham	206	45.50 N	72.34 W
Saint-Germain-de-Joux	58	46.11 N	5.44 E
Saint-Germain-des-Champs	50	47.25 N	3.55 E
Saint-Germain-du-Bois	58	46.45 N	5.15 E
Saint-Germain-du-Plain	58	46.42 N	4.58 E
Saint-Germain-en-Laye	50	48.54 N	2.05 E
Saint-Germain-en-Laye, Château de ⊥	261	48.54 N	2.06 E
Saint-Germain-Laval	62	45.50 N	4.01 E
Saint-Germain-Laxis	261	48.35 N	2.43 E
Saint-Germain-Lembron	32	45.28 N	3.14 E
Saint-Germain-lès-Arlay	58	46.46 N	5.34 E
Saint-Germain-lès-Corbeil	261	48.37 N	2.29 E
Saint-Germain-l'Herm	32	45.28 N	3.33 E
Saint-Germain-sur-Morin	261	48.53 N	2.51 E
Saint Germans	42	50.24 N	4.18 W
Saint-Germer-de-Fly	50	49.27 N	1.47 E
Saint-Gervais-d'Auvergne	32	46.02 N	2.49 E
Saint-Gervais-les-Bains	62	45.54 N	6.43 E
Saint-Gervasy	62	43.53 N	4.29 E
Saint-Géry	32	44.29 N	1.35 E
Saint-Gilles, Bel.	50	50.49 N	4.20 E
Saint-Gilles, P.Q., Can.	206	46.31 N	71.22 W
Saint-Gilles, Fr.	62	43.41 N	4.26 E
Saint-Gilles-Croix-de-Vie	32	46.42 N	1.57 W
Saint-Gingolph	58	46.24 N	6.52 E
Saint-Girons	32	42.59 N	1.09 E
Saint-Gobain	50	49.36 N	3.23 E
Saint Gotthard Pass → San Gottardo, Passo del)(	58	46.33 N	8.34 E
Saint Govan's Head ≻	42	51.36 N	4.55 W
Saint-Gratien	261	48.58 N	2.17 E
Saint-Grégoire (Larochelle)	206	46.16 N	72.30 W
Saint Gregory, Mount ʌ	186	49.19 N	58.13 W
Saint-Guénolé	32	47.49 N	4.20 W
Saint-Guillaume-d'Upton	206	45.53 N	72.46 W
Saint-Héand	62	45.31 N	4.22 E
Saint Helena	226	38.30 N	122.28 W
Saint Helena □[2]	10	15.57 S	5.42 W
Saint Helena, Mount ʌ	226	38.40 N	122.38 W
Saint Helena Sound ꭒ	192	32.27 N	80.25 W
Sainte-Hélène, Île I	275a	45.31 N	73.32 W
Sainte-Hélène-de-Bagot	206	45.44 N	72.44 W
Saint Helens, Austl.	166	41.20 S	148.15 E
Saint Helens, Eng., U.K.	42	50.42 N	1.06 W
Saint Helens, Eng., U.K.	44	53.28 N	2.44 W
Saint Helens, Or., U.S.	224	45.51 N	122.48 W
Saint Helens □[8]	262	53.28 N	2.45 W
Saint Helens, Mount ʌ[1]	224	46.12 N	122.11 W
Saint Helens Canal ≅	262	53.27 N	2.42 W
Saint Helier	43b	49.11 N	2.06 W
Saint Henry	216	40.25 N	84.38 W
Sainte-Hermine	32	46.33 N	1.04 W
Saint-Hilaire-du-Harcouët	32	48.35 N	1.06 W
Saint-Hilarion	261	48.37 N	1.44 E
Saint-Hippolyte, Fr.	58	47.19 N	6.49 E
Saint-Hippolyte, Fr.	62	43.38 N	4.45 E
Saint-Hippolyte-de-Kilkenny	206	45.56 N	74.01 W
Saint-Hippolyte-du-Fort	62	43.58 N	3.51 E
Saint-Honorat, Mont ʌ	62	44.05 N	6.46 E
Saint-Hubert, Bel.	56	50.01 N	5.23 E
Saint-Hubert, P.Q., Can.	206	45.30 N	73.25 W
Saint-Hubert, Étang de ⊜	261	48.43 N	1.51 E
Saint-Hubert-le-Roi	261	48.43 N	1.52 E
Saint-Hugues	206	45.48 N	72.52 W
Saint-Hyacinthe	206	45.37 N	72.57 W
Saint-Hyacinthe □[6]	206	45.40 N	73.05 W
Saint-Ignace, N.B., Can.	186	46.42 N	65.05 W
Saint Ignace, Mi., U.S.	190	45.52 N	84.43 W
Saint Ignace Island I	190	48.48 N	87.55 W
Saint Ignatius, Guy.	246	3.20 N	59.47 W
Saint Ignatius, Mt., U.S.	202	47.19 N	114.05 W
Saint-Imier	58	47.09 N	7.00 E
Saint-Imier, Vallon de V	58	47.10 N	7.00 E
Saint-Isidore	186	47.33 N	65.03 W
Saint-Isidore-d'Auckland	206	45.16 N	71.31 W
Saint-Isidore-de-Laprairie	275a	45.18 N	73.41 W
Saint Ives, Austl.	274a	33.44 S	151.10 E
Saint Ives, Eng., U.K.	32	50.12 N	5.29 W
Saint Ives, Eng., U.K.	42	52.20 N	0.05 W
Saint Ives Bay c	42	50.14 N	5.28 W
Saint Jacob	219	38.43 N	89.46 W
Saint Jacobs	212	43.32 N	80.33 W
Saint-Jacques	206	45.57 N	73.34 W
Saint-Jacques ≃	275a	45.26 N	73.29 W
Saint James, Il., U.S.	219	38.57 N	88.51 W
Saint James, Mi., U.S.	190	45.45 N	85.30 W
Saint James, Mn., U.S.	198	43.58 N	94.37 W
Saint James, Mo., U.S.	194	37.59 N	91.36 W
Saint James, N.Y., U.S.	210	40.52 N	73.09 W
Saint James, Cape ≻	182	51.56 N	131.01 W
Saint James City	220	26.29 N	82.04 W
Saint James Islands II	240m	18.19 N	64.50 W
Saint James Palace ʊ	260	51.30 N	0.08 W
Saint-Janvier	275a	45.43 N	73.56 W
Saint-Jean □[6]	206	45.15 N	73.20 W
Saint-Jean ≃, P.Q., Can.	186	48.46 N	64.26 W
Saint-Jean ≃, P.Q., Can.	186	50.17 N	64.20 W
Saint-Jean, Île I	275a	45.41 N	73.39 W
Saint-Jean, Lac ⊜	176	48.35 N	72.05 W
Saint-Jean, Rapides de ⌊	275a	45.19 N	73.15 W
Saint-Jean Airport ⊠	275a	45.18 N	73.17 W
Saint-Jean-aux-Bois	50	49.21 N	2.55 E
Saint-Jean-Baptiste	184	49.16 N	97.21 W
Saint-Jean-Baptiste-de-Rouville	206	45.31 N	73.07 W
Saint-Jean-Cap-Ferrat	62	43.41 N	7.20 E
Saint-Jean-d'Angély	32	45.57 N	0.31 W
Saint-Jean-d'Assé	50	48.09 N	0.07 E
Saint-Jean-de-Bournay	62	45.29 N	5.08 E
Saint-Jean-de-Braye	50	47.54 N	1.58 E
Saint-Jean-de-la-Ruelle	50	47.55 N	1.52 E
Saint-Jean-de-Losne	58	47.06 N	5.15 E
Saint-Jean-de-Luz	32	43.23 N	1.40 W
Saint-Jean-de-Maurienne	62	45.17 N	6.21 E
Saint-Jean-de-Monts	32	46.48 N	2.03 W
Saint-Jean-des-Piles	206	46.41 N	72.45 W
Saint-Jean-du-Gard	62	44.06 N	3.53 E
Saint-Jean-en-Royans	62	45.01 N	5.18 E
Saint-Jean-Pied-de-Port	32	43.10 N	1.14 W
Saint-Jean-Port-Joli	186	47.13 N	70.16 W
Saint-Jean-Soleymieux	62	45.30 N	4.02 E
Saint-Jean-sur-Richelieu	206	45.19 N	73.16 W
Saint-Jeoire	58	46.09 N	6.28 E
Saint-Jérôme	206	45.47 N	74.00 W
Saint Jo	196	33.41 N	97.31 W
Saint Joachim	214	42.16 N	82.38 W
Saint Joe	216	41.18 N	84.54 W
Saint Joe ≃	202	47.21 N	116.42 W
Saint John, N.B., Can.	186	45.16 N	66.03 W
Saint John, Jersey	43b	49.15 N	2.08 W
Saint John, In., U.S.	216	41.27 N	87.28 W
Saint John, Ks., U.S.	198	38.00 N	98.45 W
Saint John, N.D., U.S.	198	48.56 N	99.42 W
Saint John, Wa., U.S.	202	47.05 N	117.34 W
Saint John I	240m	18.20 N	64.45 W
Saint John ≃, Liber.	150	6.40 N	9.10 W
Saint John ≃, N.A.	186	45.15 N	66.04 W
Saint John, Cape ≻	186	50.00 N	55.32 W
Saint John, Lake ⊜, Nf., Can.	186	48.23 N	54.41 W
Saint John, Lake ⊜, On., Can.	212	44.41 N	79.20 W
Saint John Bay c	186	50.54 N	57.08 W
Saint John Island I	186	50.49 N	57.14 W
Saint John's, Antig.	240c	17.06 N	61.51 W
Saint John's, Nf., Can.	186	47.34 N	52.43 W
Saint John's, I. of Man	44	54.13 N	4.38 W
Saint Johns, Az., U.S.	200	34.30 N	109.21 W
Saint Johns, Mi., U.S.	216	43.00 N	84.33 W
Saint Johns, Mo., U.S.	219	38.42 N	90.20 W
Saint Johns, Oh., U.S.	216	40.33 N	84.05 W
Saint Johns ≃, Ca., U.S.	226	36.25 N	119.25 W
Saint Johns ≃, Fl., U.S.	192	30.24 N	81.24 W
Saint Johnsburg	210	43.05 N	78.53 W
Saint Johnsbury	188	44.25 N	72.00 W
Saint Johns Creek ≃	219	38.34 N	91.01 W
Saint John's Jerusalem ⊥	260	51.25 N	0.14 E
Saint Johns Marsh ≡	220	27.45 N	80.40 W
Saint John's Point ≻	48	54.13 N	5.40 W
Saint Johns → Saint-Jean-sur-Richelieu	206	45.19 N	73.16 W
Saint John's University ʊ[2]	276	40.43 N	73.48 W
Saint Johnsville	210	42.59 N	74.41 W
Saint Joseph, N.B., Can.	186	45.59 N	64.34 W
Saint Joseph, Dom.	240d	15.26 N	61.26 W
Saint-Joseph, Mart.	240e	14.40 N	61.03 W
Saint-Joseph, N. Cal.	175f	20.27 S	166.36 E
Saint-Joseph, Réu.	157c	21.22 S	55.36 E
Saint Joseph, Il., U.S.	194	40.06 N	88.02 W
Saint Joseph, La., U.S.	194	31.55 N	91.14 W
Saint Joseph, Mi., U.S.	216	42.05 N	86.29 W
Saint Joseph, Mn., U.S.	190	45.33 N	94.19 W
Saint Joseph, Mo., U.S.	194	39.46 N	94.50 W
Saint Joseph, Tn., U.S.	194	35.02 N	87.30 W
Saint Joseph □[6], In., U.S.	216	41.41 N	86.15 W
Saint Joseph □[6], Mi., U.S.	216	41.55 N	85.31 W
Saint Joseph ≃, U.S.	216	42.07 N	86.29 W
Saint Joseph ≃, U.S.	216	41.05 N	85.08 W
Saint Joseph, East Branch ≃	216	41.39 N	84.34 W
Saint-Joseph, Île I	275a	45.41 N	73.42 W
Saint-Joseph, Lac ⊜	206	46.54 N	71.38 W
Saint Joseph, Lake ⊜	176	51.05 N	90.35 W
Saint Joseph, West Branch ≃	216	41.39 N	84.34 W
Saint Joseph Bay c	192	29.47 N	85.21 W
Saint Joseph Channel ꭒ	190	46.19 N	84.04 W
Saint-Joseph-d'Alma → Alma	186	48.33 N	71.39 W
Saint-Joseph-de-Beauce	186	46.18 N	70.53 W
Saint-Joseph-de-Mékinac	206	46.55 N	72.42 W
Saint-Joseph-de-Sorel	206	46.02 N	73.07 W
Saint-Joseph-du-Lac	275a	45.32 N	74.00 W
Saint Joseph Island I	190	46.13 N	83.57 W
Saint Joseph's University ʊ[2]	285	40.00 N	75.14 W
Saint-Jouin-Bruneval	50	49.39 N	0.10 E
Saint-Jovite	206	46.07 N	74.36 W
Sainte-Julie	206	45.35 N	73.19 W
Saint-Julien	58	46.23 N	5.27 E
Saint-Julien-Chapteuil	62	45.02 N	4.04 E
Saint-Julien-du-Sault	50	48.02 N	3.18 E
Saint-Julien-du-Verdon	62	43.55 N	6.32 E
Saint-Julien-en-Beauchêne	62	44.37 N	5.42 E
Saint-Julien-en-Born	32	44.04 N	1.14 W
Saint-Julien-en-Genevois	58	46.08 N	6.05 E
Saint-Julien-en-Jarez	62	45.28 N	4.31 E
Saint-Julien-les-Villas	50	48.16 N	4.06 E
Saint-Julien-Molin-Molette	62	45.19 N	4.37 E
Sainte-Julienne	206	45.58 N	73.43 W
Saint-Junien	32	45.53 N	0.54 E
Saint Just, P.R.	240m	18.23 N	66.00 W
Saint Just, Eng., U.K.	42	50.07 N	5.42 W
Saint-Just-en-Chaussée	50	49.30 N	2.26 E
Saint-Just-en-Chevalet	32	45.55 N	3.50 E
Saint-Justin	206	46.15 N	73.05 W
Saint-Just-Malmont	62	45.20 N	4.19 E
Saint-Just-sur-Loire	62	45.29 N	4.16 E
Saint Keverne	42	50.03 N	5.06 W
Saint Kilda, Austl.	168b	34.44 S	138.32 E
Saint Kilda, Austl.	169	37.52 S	144.59 E
Saint Kilda, N.Z.	172	45.54 S	170.30 E
Saint Kilda I	28	57.49 N	8.36 W
Saint Kitts	168b	34.21 S	139.04 E
Saint Kitts and Nevis □[1], N.A.	230	17.20 N	62.45 W
Saint Kitts and Nevis □[1], N.A.	238	17.20 N	62.45 W
Saint Kitts → Saint Christopher I	238	17.20 N	62.45 W
Saint-Lambert, P.Q., Can.	206	45.30 N	73.30 W
Saint-Lambert, Fr.	261	48.44 N	2.01 E
Saint Landry	194	30.50 N	92.15 W
Saint-Laurent, Mb., Can.	184	50.24 N	97.56 W
Saint-Laurent, P.Q., Can.	206	45.30 N	73.40 W
Saint-Laurent, Fr.	58	48.09 N	6.27 E
Saint-Laurent-Blangy	50	50.18 N	2.48 E
Saint-Laurent-de-Chamousset	62	45.44 N	4.28 E
Saint-Laurent-du-Maroni	250	5.30 N	54.02 W
Saint-Laurent-du-Maroni □[8]	250	4.00 N	53.30 W
Saint-Laurent-du-Pont	62	45.23 N	5.44 E
Saint-Laurent-du-Var	62	43.40 N	7.11 E
Saint-Laurent-en-Caux	50	49.45 N	0.53 E
Saint-Laurent-en-Grandvaux	58	46.35 N	5.57 E
Saint-Laurent-et-Benon	32	45.09 N	0.49 W
Saint-Laurent-les-Bains	62	44.37 N	3.58 E
Saint-Laurent → Saint Lawrence ≃	176	49.30 N	67.00 W
Saint-Laurent-sur-Saône	58	46.18 N	4.50 E
Saint Lawrence, Austl.	166	22.21 S	149.31 E
Saint Lawrence, Nf., Can.	186	46.55 N	55.24 W
Saint Lawrence □[6]	212	44.30 N	75.27 W
Saint Lawrence ≃	176	49.30 N	67.00 W
Saint Lawrence, Cape ≻	186	47.03 N	60.37 W
Saint Lawrence, Gulf of c	186	48.00 N	62.00 W
Saint Lawrence, Lake ⊜	206	44.56 N	75.04 W
Saint Lawrence Island I	180	63.30 N	170.30 W
Saint Lawrence Islands National Park ♠	212	44.18 N	76.08 W
Saint-Lawrence Seaway ≅	275a	45.43 N	73.25 W
Saint-Lazare	184	50.26 N	101.16 W
Saint-Lazare, Gare ◆[5]	261	48.53 N	2.20 E
Saint-Léandre	186	48.44 N	67.36 W
Saint-Léger-en-Yvelines	261	48.43 N	1.46 E
Saint-Léger-sur-Dheune	58	46.51 N	4.38 E
Saint Leo	220	28.20 N	82.15 W
Saint Leon	218	39.17 N	84.57 W
Saint-Léonard, N.B., Can.	186	47.10 N	67.56 W
Saint-Léonard, P.Q., Can.	206	45.35 N	73.35 W
Saint Leonard, Md., U.S.	208	38.28 N	76.30 W
Saint-Léonard-d'Aston	206	46.06 N	72.22 W
Saint-Léonard-de-Noblat	32	45.50 N	1.29 E
Saint Leonards, Eng., U.K.	42	50.49 N	1.51 W
Saint Leonards, Eng., U.K.	42	50.51 N	0.34 E
Saint-Leu-d'Esserent	50	49.13 N	2.25 E
Saint-Leu-la-Forêt	50	49.01 N	2.15 E
Saint-Liboire	206	45.39 N	72.46 W
Saint-Lô	32	49.07 N	1.05 W
Saint-Louis, Sk., Can.	184	52.56 N	105.49 W
Saint-Louis, Fr.	58	47.35 N	7.34 E
Saint-Louis, Guad.	241o	15.57 N	61.19 W
Saint-Louis, Réu.	157c	21.16 S	55.25 E
Saint-Louis, Sén.	150	16.02 N	16.30 W
Saint Louis, Mi., U.S.	190	43.24 N	84.36 W
Saint Louis, Mo., U.S.	219	38.37 N	90.11 W
Saint Louis, Tx., U.S.	222	32.18 N	95.20 W
Saint-Louis □[4]	150	16.00 N	14.30 W
Saint Louis □[6]	219	38.39 N	90.25 W
Saint-Louis ≃, P.Q., Can.	275a	45.19 N	73.53 W
Saint Louis ≃, U.S.	190	46.45 N	92.06 W
Saint-Louis, Lac ⊜	206	45.24 N	73.48 W
Saint-Louis, Pointe ≻	275a	45.19 N	73.53 W
Saint Louis Crossing	218	39.19 N	85.51 W
Saint-Louis-de-Champlain	206	46.25 N	72.36 W
Saint-Louis-de-Kent	186	46.44 N	64.58 W
Saint Louis Park	190	44.56 N	93.20 W
Saint Louisville	214	40.10 N	82.25 W
Saint-Loup-sur-Aujon	58	47.53 N	5.05 E
Saint-Loup-sur-Semouse	58	47.53 N	6.16 E
Saint-Luc, P.Q., Can.	206	45.22 N	73.18 W
Saint-Luc, Schw.	58	46.13 N	7.36 E
Sainte-Luce	240e	14.28 N	60.56 W
Saint Lucia □[1], N.A.	230	13.53 N	60.58 W
Saint Lucia □[1], N.A.	241f	13.53 N	60.58 W
Saint Lucia, Cape ≻	158	28.25 S	32.25 E
Saint Lucia, Lake ⊜	158	28.05 S	32.26 E
Saint Lucia Channel ꭒ	238	14.09 N	60.57 W
Saint Lucia Estuary	158	28.22 S	32.25 E
Saint Lucia Game Reserve ◆[4]	158	28.10 S	32.28 E
Sainte-Lucie, Fr.	36	41.42 N	9.22 E
Saint Lucie, Fl., U.S.	220	27.29 N	80.20 W
Saint Lucie □[6]	220	27.23 N	80.26 W
Saint Lucie Canal ≅	220	27.10 N	80.15 W
Saint Lucie Inlet c	220	27.10 N	80.10 W
Saint Lucie Lock ◆[5]	220	27.07 N	80.17 W
Saint-Lucien	261	48.39 N	1.38 E
Saint-Lupicin	58	46.24 N	5.47 E
Sainte-Magnance	50	47.27 N	4.04 E
Saint Magnus Bay c	46a	60.24 N	1.34 W
Saint Magnus Cathedral ʊ[1]	46	58.58 N	2.57 W
Saint-Malo, P.Q., Can.	206	45.12 N	71.30 W
Saint-Malo, Fr.	32	48.39 N	2.01 W
Saint-Malo, Golfe de c	32	48.45 N	2.00 W
Saint-Mamert-du-Gard	62	43.53 N	4.12 E
Saint-Mammès	50	48.23 N	2.49 E
Saint-Mandé	261	48.50 N	2.25 E
Saint-Mandrier-sur-Mer	62	43.04 N	5.56 E
Saint-Marc	238	19.07 N	72.42 W
Saint-Marc, Canal de ꭒ	238	18.50 N	72.45 W
Saint-Marc-des-Carrières	206	46.41 N	72.03 W
Saint-Marcel	58	46.47 N	4.54 E
Saint-Marcellin	62	45.09 N	5.19 E
Saint-Marcelline-de-Kildare	206	46.07 N	73.36 W
Saint-Marc-sur-Richelieu	275a	45.41 N	73.12 W
Saint-Mard	261	49.02 N	2.42 E
Saint Margaret Bay c	186	51.01 N	56.58 W
Saint Margaret's at Cliffe	42	51.09 N	1.24 E
Saint Margarets Bay c	186	44.35 N	64.00 W
Saint Margaret's Hope	46	58.49 N	2.57 W
Sainte-Marguerite ≃	176	50.09 N	66.36 W
Sainte-Marguerite, Baie c	186	50.06 N	66.36 W
Sainte-Marguerite-sur-Mer	50	49.55 N	0.57 E
Sainte-Marie	240e	14.47 N	61.00 W
Sainte-Marie, Cap ≻	157b	25.36 S	45.08 E
Sainte-Marie-aux-Mines (Markirch)	58	48.15 N	7.11 E
Saint Maries	202	47.18 N	116.33 W
Saint Maries ≃	202	47.19 N	116.33 W
Saint-Marin → San Marino □[1]	66	43.56 N	12.25 E
Saint Marks, S. Afr.	158	32.01 S	27.22 E
Saint Marks, Fl., U.S.	192	30.09 N	84.12 W
Saint Marks ≃	192	30.08 N	84.12 W
Sainte-Marthe-de-Gaspé	186	49.12 N	66.10 W
Sainte-Marthe-sur-le-Lac	275a	45.32 N	73.56 W
Saint-Martin (Sint Maarten) I	238	18.04 N	63.04 W
Saint-Martin, Cap ≻	240e	14.52 N	61.13 W
Saint Martin, Lake ⊜	184	51.37 N	98.29 W
Saint-Martin-Boulogne	50	50.43 N	1.38 E
Saint-Martin-d'Ardèche	62	44.18 N	4.35 E
Saint-Martin-d'Auxigny	50	47.12 N	2.25 E
Saint-Martin-de-Belleville	62	45.23 N	6.30 E
Saint-Martin-de-Bossenay	50	48.26 N	3.41 E
Saint-Martin-de-Bréthencourt	261	48.31 N	1.56 E
Saint-Martin-de-Crau	62	43.38 N	4.49 E
Saint-Martin-de-Londres	62	43.47 N	3.44 E
Saint-Martin-de-Nigelles	261	48.37 N	1.37 E
Saint-Martin-d'Entraunes	62	44.08 N	6.46 E
Saint-Martin-des-Champs	261	48.53 N	1.43 E
Saint-Martin-de-Valamas	62	44.56 N	4.22 E
Saint-Martin-d'Hères	62	45.10 N	5.46 E
Saint-Martin-du-Puy	50	47.20 N	3.52 E
Saint-Martin-du-Tertre	261	49.06 N	2.21 E
Saint-Martin-du-Var	62	43.49 N	7.12 E
Sainte-Martine	206	45.15 N	73.48 W
Saint-Martin-en-Bresse	58	46.49 N	5.04 E
Saint-Martin-la-Garenne	261	49.02 N	1.41 E
Saint-Martin-la-Plaine	62	45.32 N	4.36 E
Saint Martins, N.B., Can.	186	45.21 N	65.32 W
Saint Martin's, Eng., U.K.	42	52.55 N	2.59 W
Saint Martin's I	42a	49.58 N	6.20 W
Saint Martins Keys II	220	28.47 N	82.44 W
Saint-Martin-Vésubie	62	44.04 N	7.15 E
Saint Martinville	194	30.07 N	91.49 W
Saint Mary	194	37.52 N	89.58 W
Saint Mary ≃, B.C., Can.	182	49.37 N	115.38 W
Saint Mary ≃, N.A.	182	49.37 N	112.52 W
Saint Mary, Cape ≻	150	13.28 N	16.40 W
Saint Mary, Mount ʌ	164	8.10 S	147.00 E
Saint Mary Bourne	42	51.16 N	1.24 W
Saint Mary Cray ◆[8]	260	51.23 N	0.07 E
Saint Mary Lake ⊜	202	48.40 N	113.30 W
Saint Marylebone ◆[8]	260	51.31 N	0.10 W
Saint Mary of the Lake Seminary ʊ[2]	278	42.17 N	88.00 W
Saint Mary Peak ʌ	166	31.30 S	138.33 E
Saint Mary Reservoir ⊜[1]	182	49.19 N	113.12 W
Saint Marys, Austl.	166	41.35 S	148.10 E
Saint Marys, Austl.	170	33.47 S	150.47 E
Saint Mary's, Nf., Can.	186	46.55 N	53.34 W
Saint Mary's, On., Can.	212	43.16 N	81.08 W
Saint Marys, Ak., U.S.	180	62.04 N	163.10 W
Saint Marys, Ga., U.S.	192	30.43 N	81.32 W
Saint Marys, Ks., U.S.	198	39.11 N	96.04 W
Saint Marys, Oh., U.S.	216	40.32 N	84.23 W
Saint Marys, Pa., U.S.	214	41.25 N	78.33 W
Saint Marys, W.V., U.S.	188	39.23 N	81.12 W
Saint Marys □[6]	208	38.17 N	76.38 W
Saint Mary's I	42a	49.55 N	6.18 W
Saint Marys ≃, N.S., Can.	186	45.02 N	61.54 W
Saint Marys ≃, N.A.	190	45.58 N	83.54 W
Saint Marys ≃, U.S.	192	30.43 N	81.27 W
Saint Marys ≃, U.S.	216	41.05 N	85.08 W
Saint Marys ≃, Md., U.S.	208	38.06 N	76.26 W
Saint Mary's, Cape ≻, Nf., Can.	186	46.49 N	54.12 W
Saint Marys, Cape ≻, N.S., Can.	186	44.05 N	66.13 W
Saint Marys, North Prong ≃	192	30.22 N	82.06 W
Saint Marys, South Prong ≃	192	30.22 N	82.06 W
Saint Mary's Bay	42	51.00 N	0.58 E
Saint Mary's Bay c, Nf., Can.	186	46.50 N	53.47 W
Saint Marys Bay c, N.S., Can.	186	44.25 N	66.10 W
Saint Marys City	208	38.11 N	76.26 W
Saint Mary's Hoo	260	51.28 N	0.36 E
Saint Marys Lake ⊜	278	42.17 N	87.59 W
Saint Mary's Marshes ≡	260	51.28 N	0.35 E
Saint-Mathieu	32	45.42 N	0.46 E
Saint-Mathieu, Pointe de ≻	32	48.20 N	4.46 W
Saint-Mathieu-de-Laprairie	275a	45.19 N	73.31 W
Saint Matthew Island I	180	60.30 N	172.45 W
Saint Matthews, Ky., U.S.	218	38.15 N	85.39 W
Saint Matthews, S.C., U.S.	192	33.39 N	80.46 W
Saint Matthias Group II	164	1.30 S	149.40 E
Saint-Maur-des-Fossés	50	48.48 N	2.30 E
Sainte-Maure-de-Touraine	32	47.07 N	0.37 E
Saint-Maurice, Fr.	261	48.49 N	2.25 E
Saint-Maurice, Schw.	58	46.13 N	7.00 E
Saint-Maurice □[6]	206	46.35 N	73.00 W
Saint-Maurice ≃	176	46.21 N	72.31 W
Saint-Maurice, Parc de ♠	206	46.52 N	73.10 W
Saint-Maurice-en-Montagne	58	46.34 N	5.50 E
Saint-Maurice-Montcouronne	261	48.35 N	2.07 E
Saint Mawes	42	50.09 N	5.01 W
Saint Mawgan	42	50.28 N	4.58 W
Saint-Max	58	48.42 N	6.13 E
Sainte-Maxime	62	43.18 N	6.38 E
Saint-Maximin-la-Sainte-Baume	62	43.27 N	5.52 E
Saint-Méen-le-Grand	32	48.11 N	2.12 W
Saint Meinrad	194	38.10 N	86.48 W
Sainte-Menehould	56	49.05 N	4.54 E
Saint-Menges	56	49.44 N	4.56 E
Sainte-Mère-Église	32	49.25 N	1.19 W
Saint Merryn	42	50.31 N	4.58 W
Saint-Méry	261	48.35 N	2.50 E
Sainte-Mesme	261	48.32 N	1.58 E
Saint-Mesmes	261	48.59 N	2.42 E
Saint Michael, Ak., U.S.	180	63.29 N	162.02 W
Saint Michael, Pa., U.S.	214	40.20 N	78.46 W
Saint Michaels	208	38.47 N	76.13 W
Saint-Michel, Fr.	50	49.55 N	4.08 E
Saint-Michel, Fr.	62	45.13 N	6.28 E
Saint-Michel ◆[8]	275a	45.35 N	73.35 W
Saint-Michel-de-Napierville	206	45.14 N	73.34 W
Saint-Michel-des-Saints	206	46.41 N	73.55 W
Saint-Michel-sur-Meurthe	58	48.19 N	6.54 E
Saint-Michel-sur-Orge	261	48.38 N	2.18 E
Saint-Mihiel	56	48.54 N	5.33 E
Saint Monance	46	56.12 N	2.46 W
Sainte-Monique-des-Deux-Montagnes	275a	45.40 N	74.00 W
Sainte-Montaine	50	47.29 N	2.19 E
Saint-Moritz → Sankt Moritz	58	46.30 N	9.50 E
Saint-Narcisse	206	46.34 N	72.28 W
Saint-Nazaire	32	47.17 N	2.12 W
Saint-Nazaire-en-Royans	62	45.04 N	5.15 E
Saint-Nazaire-le-Désert	62	44.34 N	5.17 E
Saint Nazianz	190	44.00 N	87.55 W
Saint Neots	42	52.14 N	0.17 W
Saint-Nicéphore	206	45.50 N	72.25 W
Saint-Nicolas, Bel.	56	50.38 N	5.32 E
Saint-Nicolas, P.Q., Can.	206	46.42 N	71.24 W
Saint-Nicolas-aux-Bois	50	49.36 N	3.25 E
Saint-Nicolas-d'Aliermont	50	49.53 N	1.13 E
Saint-Nicolas → Sint-Niklaas	50	51.10 N	4.08 E
Saint-Nizier-du-Moucherotte	62	45.10 N	5.38 E
Saint-Nom-la-Bretèche	261	48.51 N	2.01 E
Saint Nora Lake ⊜	212	45.08 N	78.49 W
Saint-Norbert-d'Arthabaska	206	46.07 N	71.50 W
Sainte-Odile ʊ[1]	58	48.26 N	7.24 E
Saint-Omer	50	50.45 N	2.15 E
Saintonge □[9]	32	45.30 N	0.30 W
Saint-Ouen, Fr.	50	50.02 N	2.03 E
Saint-Ouen, Fr.	261	48.54 N	2.20 E
Saint-Ouen-l'Aumône	50	49.03 N	2.06 E
Saint-Pacôme	186	47.24 N	69.57 W
Saint-Pamphile	186	46.58 N	69.47 W
Saint Pancras ◆[8]	260	51.32 N	0.07 W
Saint Pancras Station ◆[5]	260	51.32 N	0.08 W
Saint Paris	218	40.07 N	83.57 W
Saint-Pascal	186	47.32 N	69.49 W
Saint-Paterne	50	48.24 N	0.07 E
Saint-Pathus	261	49.04 N	2.48 E
Saint-Patrice, Lac ⊜	190	46.22 N	77.20 W
Saint Paul, Ab., Can.	182	53.59 N	111.17 W
Saint-Paul, Fr.	62	43.42 N	7.07 E
Saint-Paul, Fr.	62	44.31 N	6.45 E
Saint-Paul, Réu.	157c	21.00 S	55.16 E
Saint Paul, In., U.S.	218	39.25 N	85.28 W
Saint Paul, Ks., U.S.	198	37.31 N	95.10 W
Saint Paul, Mn., U.S.	190	44.57 N	93.05 W
Saint Paul, Ne., U.S.	198	41.13 N	98.27 W
Saint Paul, Or., U.S.	224	45.12 N	122.58 W
Saint Paul, Va., U.S.	192	36.54 N	82.18 W
Saint-Paul ≃, Can.	176	51.26 N	57.40 W
Saint Paul ≃, Liber.	150	6.23 N	10.48 W
Saint Paul, Cape ≻	150	5.49 N	0.57 E
Saint-Paul, Île I	6	38.43 S	77.29 E
Saint-Paul, Lac ⊜	206	46.18 N	72.29 W
Saint Paul Bay c	116	10.14 N	118.54 E
Saint-Paul-de-Chester (Chesterville)	206	45.57 N	71.49 W
Saint-Paul-en-Jarez	62	45.29 N	4.35 E
Saint-Paul-et-Valmalle	62	43.38 N	3.40 E
Saint-Paulien	62	45.08 N	3.49 E
Saint-Paulin	206	46.25 N	73.01 W
Saint Paul Island	180	57.07 N	170.17 W
Saint Paul Island I, N.S., Can.	186	47.15 N	60.10 W
Saint Paul Island I, Ak., U.S.	180	57.10 N	170.15 W
Saint Pauls	192	34.48 N	78.58 W
Saint Paul's Cathedral ʊ[1]	260	51.31 N	0.06 W
Saint Paul's Cray ◆[8]	260	51.24 N	0.07 E
Saint Pauls Inlet c	186	49.50 N	57.45 W
Saint Paul's Point ≻	174e	25.04 S	130.05 W
Saint-Paul-Trois-Châteaux	62	44.21 N	4.46 E
Saint-Péravy-la-Colombe	50	48.00 N	1.42 E
Saint-Péray	62	44.57 N	4.50 E
Saint-Père	50	47.28 N	3.46 E
Saint Peter, Il., U.S.	219	38.52 N	88.51 W
Saint Peter, Mn., U.S.	190	44.19 N	93.57 W
Saint Peter, Lake ⊜	212	45.18 N	78.02 W
Saint Peter Island I	162	32.17 S	133.35 E
Saint Peter Port	43b	49.27 N	2.32 W
Saint Peters, N.S., Can.	186	45.40 N	60.52 W
Saint Peters, Mo., U.S.	219	38.48 N	90.37 W
Saint Peters, Pa., U.S.	285	40.11 N	75.44 W
Saint Peters Bay	186	46.25 N	62.35 W
Saint Petersburg, Fl., U.S.	220	27.46 N	82.40 W
Saint Petersburg, Pa., U.S.	214	41.10 N	79.37 W
Saint Petersburg Beach	220	27.43 N	82.44 W
Saint Petersburg → Sankt-Peterburg	76	59.55 N	30.15 E
Saint Peter's College ʊ[2]	276	40.44 N	74.05 W
Saint-Philippe-d'Argenteuil	206	45.37 N	74.25 W
Saint-Philippe-de-Laprairie	275a	45.21 N	73.28 W
Saint-Pie	206	45.30 N	72.54 W
Saint-Pierre, P.Q., Can.	275a	45.27 N	73.39 W
Saint-Pierre, Fr.	62	45.40 N	3.45 E
Saint-Pierre, It.	62	45.42 N	7.14 E
Saint-Pierre, Mart.	240e	14.45 N	61.11 W
Saint-Pierre, Réu.	157c	21.19 S	55.29 E
Saint-Pierre, St. P./M.	186	46.47 N	56.11 W
Saint-Pierre I	186	46.47 N	56.11 W
Saint-Pierre ≃	275a	45.23 N	73.34 W
Saint-Pierre, Lac ⊜, P.Q., Can.	186	50.08 N	68.26 W
Saint-Pierre, Lac ⊜, P.Q., Can.	206	46.12 N	72.52 W
Saint Pierre and Miquelon (Saint-Pierre-et-Miquelon) □[2], N.A.	176	46.55 N	56.20 W
Saint Pierre and Miquelon (Saint-Pierre-et-Miquelon) □[2], N.A.	186	46.55 N	56.20 W
Saint-Pierre-d'Albigny	62	45.34 N	6.09 E
Saint-Pierre-de-Bœuf	62	45.22 N	4.45 E
Saint-Pierre-de-Broughton	206	46.15 N	71.12 W
Saint-Pierre-de-Chartreuse	62	45.20 N	5.49 E
Saint-Pierre-des-Corps	50	47.23 N	0.44 E
Saint-Pierre-de-Vacquière	62	43.52 N	4.13 E
Saint-Pierre-du-Vauvray	50	49.14 N	1.13 E
Saint-Pierre-Église	32	49.40 N	1.24 W
Saint-Pierre-en-Port	50	49.48 N	0.29 E
Saint-Pierre-et-Miquelon → Saint Pierre and Miquelon □[2]	186	46.55 N	56.20 W
Saint Pierre Island I	138	9.19 S	50.43 E
Saint Pierre-Jolys	184	49.26 N	96.59 W
Saint Pierre-le-Moûtier	32	46.48 N	3.07 E
Saint-Pierre-lès-Elbeuf	50	49.16 N	1.03 E
Saint-Pierre-sur-Dives	28	49.01 N	0.02 W
Saint-Pierreville	62	44.49 N	4.29 E
Saint-Point, Lac de ⊜	58	46.49 N	6.19 E
Saint-Pol-de-Léon	32	48.41 N	3.59 W
Saint-Pol-sur-Mer	50	51.02 N	2.21 E

Symbols in the index entries represent the broad categories identified in the key at the right. Symbols with superior numbers (ʌ[1]) identify subcategories (see complete key on page I · 1).

Symbole im Register stellen die rechts im Schlüssel erklärten Kategorien dar. Symbole mit hochgestellten Ziffern (ʌ[1]) bezeichnen Unterabteilungen einer Kategorie (vgl. vollständiger Schlüssel auf Seite I · 1).

Los símbolos incluídos en el texto del índice representan las grandes categorias identificadas con la clave a la derecha. Los símbolos con numeros en su parte superior (ʌ[1]) identifican las subcategorías (véase la clave completa en la página I · 1).

Les symboles de l'index représentent les catégories indiquées dans la légende à droite. Les symboles suivis d'un indice (ʌ[1]) représentent des sous-catégories (voir légende complète à la page I · 1).

Os símbolos incluídos no texto do índice representam as grandes categorias identificadas com a chave à direita. Os símbolos com números em sua parte superior (ʌ[1]) identificam as subcategorias (veja-se a chave completa à página I · 1).

English	Deutsch	Español	Français	Português
ʌ Mountain	Berg	Montaña	Montagne	Montanha
ʌ Mountains	Gebirge	Montañas	Montagnes	Montanhas
)(Pass	Paß	Paso	Col	Passo
V Valley, Canyon	Tal, Cañon	Valle, Cañón	Vallée, Canyon	Vale, Canhão
≃ Plain	Ebene	Llano	Plaine	Planície
≻ Cape	Kap	Cabo	Cap	Cabo
I Island	Insel	Isla	Île	Ilha
II Islands	Inseln	Islas	Îles	Ilhas
♠ Other Topographic Features	Andere Topographische Objekte	Otros Elementos Topográficos	Autres données topographiques	Outros acidentes topográficos

ESPAÑOL Nombre	Página	Lat.	Long. W=Oeste	FRANÇAIS Nom	Page	Lat.	Long. W=Ouest	PORTUGUÊS Nome	Página	Lat.	Long. W=Oeste

ESPAÑOL

Nombre	Página	Lat.	Long. W=Oeste
Saint-Pol-sur-Ternoise	50	50.23 N	2.20 E
Saint-Polycarpe	206	45.18 N	74.18 W
Saint-Pons	32	43.29 N	2.46 E
Saint-Pourçain-sur-Sioule	32	46.19 N	3.17 E
Saint-Prex	58	46.29 N	6.28 E
Saint-Priest	62	45.42 N	4.57 E
Saint-Priest-en-Jarez	62	45.28 N	4.22 E
Saint-Prix	261	49.01 N	2.16 E
Saint-Prosper-de-Dorchester	188	46.13 N	70.29 W
Saint-Quentin, N.B., Can.	186	47.30 N	67.23 W
Saint-Quentin, Fr.	50	49.51 N	3.17 E
Saint-Quentin, Canal de ≖	50	49.36 N	3.11 E
Saint-Quentin, Étang de ⌧	261	48.47 N	2.01 E
Saint-Rambert-d'Albon	62	45.17 N	4.49 E
Saint-Rambert-en-Bugey	58	45.57 N	5.26 E
Saint-Rambert-sur-Loire	62	45.30 N	4.15 E
Saint-Raphaël	62	43.25 N	6.46 E
Saint-Raymond	206	46.54 N	71.50 W
Saint-Rédempteur-de-Lévis	206	46.42 N	71.17 W
Saint Regis	202	47.17 N	115.06 W
Saint-Régis ≖, P.Q., Can.	275a	45.24 N	73.34 W
Saint Regis ≖, N.A.	188	45.00 N	74.39 W
Saint Regis ≖, Mt., U.S.	202	47.18 N	115.05 W
Saint Regis, West Branch ≖	188	44.47 N	74.46 W
Saint Regis Falls	188	44.40 N	74.32 W
Saint Regis Indian Reservation ◄⁴	206	44.58 N	74.39 W
Saint-Rémi	206	45.16 N	73.37 W
Saint-Rémi-d'Amherst	206	46.01 N	74.46 W
Saint-Rémy (lès-Chevreuse), Fr.	50	48.42 N	2.05 E
Saint-Rémy, Fr.	58	46.46 N	4.50 E
Saint Remy, N.Y., U.S.	210	41.54 N	74.01 W
Saint-Rémy-de-Provence	62	43.47 N	4.50 E
Saint-Rémy-en-Bouzemont	58	48.38 N	4.39 E
Saint-Rémy-lès-Chevreuse	261	48.42 N	2.05 E
Saint-Rémy-l'Honoré	261	48.45 N	1.53 E
Saint-Rémy-sur-Avre	50	48.46 N	1.15 E
Saint-Renan	32	48.26 N	4.37 W
Saint-Révérien	50	47.13 N	3.30 E
Saint-Rhémy	62	45.50 N	7.11 E
Saint-Riquier	50	50.08 N	1.57 E
Saint Robert	194	37.50 N	92.09 W
Saint-Roch-de-l'Achigan	206	45.51 N	73.36 W
Saint-Romain-de-Colbosc	50	49.32 N	0.22 E
Saint-Romain-le-Puy	62	45.33 N	4.07 E
Saint-Romans	62	45.07 N	5.19 E
Saint-Romuald	206	46.45 N	71.14 W
Sainte-Rosalie	206	45.38 N	72.54 W
Sainte-Rose	241d	16.20 N	61.42 W
Sainte-Rose ◄⁸	275a	45.36 N	73.47 W
Sainte-Rose-du-Lac	184	51.03 N	99.32 W
Saintry-sur-Seine	261	48.36 N	2.30 E
Saintes, Bel.	50	50.42 N	4.10 E
Saintes, Fr.	50	45.45 N	0.38 W
Saintes ⌧	194	49.40 N	1.17 E
Saint Sampson	43b	49.29 N	2.31 W
Saint-Saturnin-d'Apt	62	43.56 N	5.23 E
Saint-Sauveur, Fr.	50	47.37 N	3.12 E
Saint-Sauveur, Fr.	58	47.48 N	6.23 E
Saint-Sauveur-des-Monts	206	45.52 N	74.10 W
Saint-Sauveur-sur-Tinée	62	44.05 N	7.06 E
Saint Savin	32	46.34 N	0.52 E
Sainte-Savine	50	48.18 N	4.03 E
Saint-Savinien	32	45.53 N	0.41 W
Saint Saviour	43b	49.11 N	2.06 W
Saint Sebastian Bay	158	34.25 S	21.00 E
Saint-Sébastien, Cap ►	157b	12.26 S	48.44 E
Saint Séverin	50	50.32 N	5.25 E
Saint Shotts	186	46.38 N	53.35 W
Saint-Sigolène	62	45.14 N	4.15 E
Saint-Siméon	186	47.50 N	69.53 W
Saint-Simon	50	49.45 N	3.10 E
Saint Simons Island	192	31.09 N	81.22 W
Saint Simons Island ◄	192	31.14 N	81.21 W
Saint-Sixte ≖	206	45.39 N	75.08 W
Saintes-Maries, Golfe des ◌	62	43.25 N	4.31 E
Saintes-Maries-de-la-Mer	62	43.27 N	4.26 E
Sainte-Sophie-de-Mégantic	206	46.09 N	71.42 W
Saint-Soupplets	261	49.02 N	2.48 E
Saint-Stanislas Bay	174o	1.53 N	157.30 W
Saint-Stanislas-de-Kostra	206	45.11 N	74.08 W
Saint Stephen, N.B., Can.	186	45.12 N	67.17 W
Saint Stephen, S.C., U.S.	192	33.24 N	79.55 W
Saint-Sulpice-de-Favières	261	48.33 N	2.11 E
Sainte-Suzanne	32	46.19 N	1.22 E
Sainte-Sylvestre	206	46.41 N	71.14 W
Saint-Symphorien, Fr.	32	44.26 N	0.30 W
Saint-Symphorien, Fr.	261	48.31 N	1.46 E
Saint-Symphorien-d'Ozon	62	45.38 N	4.52 E
Saint-Symphorien-sur-Coise	62	45.38 N	4.27 E
Sainte-Thècle	206	46.49 N	72.31 W
Saint-Théodore-d'Acton	206	45.41 N	72.35 W
Sainte-Thérèse	206	45.38 N	73.51 W
Sainte-Thérèse, Île ◄, P.Q., Can.	275a	45.41 N	73.28 W
Sainte-Thérèse, Île ◄, P.Q., Can.	275a	45.22 N	73.15 W
Saint-Thibault-des-Vignes	261	48.52 N	2.41 E
Saint Thomas, On., Can.	212	42.47 N	81.12 W
Saint Thomas, Mo., U.S.	219	38.22 N	92.13 W
Saint Thomas, N.D., U.S.	198	48.37 N	97.26 W
Saint Thomas	240m	18.21 N	64.55 W
Saint Thomas — Charlotte Amalie	240m	18.21 N	64.56 W
Saint-Timothée	206	45.18 N	74.02 W
Saint-Tite	206	46.44 N	72.34 W
Saint-Tite-des-Caps	186	47.08 N	70.47 W
Saint-Trivier-de-Courtes	58	46.28 N	5.05 E
Saint-Trivier-sur-Moignans	62	46.04 N	4.54 E
Saint-Tropez	62	43.16 N	6.38 E
Saint Tudy	42	50.33 N	4.43 W
Sainte-Tulle	62	43.47 N	5.49 E
Saint-Ubald	206	46.45 N	72.16 W
Saint-Urbain-de-Charlevoix	186	47.33 N	70.32 W
Saint-Ursanne	58	47.22 N	7.10 E
Saint-Uze	62	45.11 N	4.52 E
Saint-Valérien	62	48.11 N	3.06 E
Saint-Valéry-en-Caux	50	49.52 N	0.44 E
Saint-Valéry-sur-Somme	50	50.11 N	1.38 E
Saint-Vallier, Fr.	58	46.38 N	4.22 E
Saint-Vallier, Fr.	62	45.10 N	4.49 E
Saint-Vallier-de-Thiey	62	43.42 N	6.51 E
Saint-Varent	32	46.53 N	0.14 W
Saint-Venant	50	50.37 N	2.33 E
Saint-Véran	62	44.42 N	6.52 E
Sainte-Victoire, Montagne ▲	62	43.32 N	5.39 E
Saint-Victoret	62	43.25 N	5.14 E
Saint Vincent	198	48.58 N	97.13 W
Saint Vincent ◄	241h	13.15 N	61.12 W
Saint-Vincent, Baie de ◌	175f	22.00 S	166.05 E
Saint-Vincent, Cap ►	157b	21.57 S	43.16 E
Saint-Vincent, Cape ►	166	43.18 S	145.50 E
Saint-Vincent, Cape — São Vicente, Cabo de ►	34	37.01 N	9.00 W
Saint-Vincent, Gulf ⊂	168b	35.00 S	138.05 E
Saint Vincent and the Grenadines ◻¹, N.A.	230	13.15 N	61.12 W
Saint Vincent and the Grenadines ◻¹, N.A.	241h	13.15 N	61.12 W
Saint-Vincent-de-Paul	275a	45.37 N	73.39 W
Saint-Vincent-de-Tyrosse	32	43.40 N	1.18 W
Saint Vincent Passage ʯ	238	13.30 N	61.00 W
Saint Vincent's	186	46.48 N	53.38 W
Saint-Vith	58	47.11 N	5.49 E
Saint-Vith	56	50.17 N	6.08 E
Saint-Vivien-de-Médoc	32	45.26 N	1.02 W
Saint-Vrain	261	48.33 N	2.20 E
Saint Walburg	184	53.39 N	109.12 W
Saint-Wandrille-Rançon	50	49.32 N	0.46 E
Saint-Wenceslas ≖	206	46.18 N	72.23 W
Saint Williams	206	42.40 N	80.25 W
Saint-Witz	261	49.05 N	2.34 E
Saint-Yrieix-la-Perche	32	45.31 N	1.12 E
Saint-Yvon	186	49.10 N	64.48 W
Saint-Zacharie	62	43.23 N	5.43 E
Saint-Zénon	206	46.33 N	73.49 W
Säinthiya	126	23.57 N	87.40 E
Saipan	174n	15.12 N	145.45 E
Saipan Channel ʯ	174n	15.05 N	145.41 E
Saipan International Airport ⌧	174n	15.07 N	145.43 E
Saiqi	100	27.00 N	119.43 E
Saishu-to — Cheju-do ◄	90	33.20 N	126.30 E
Saita	96	34.08 N	133.49 E
Saitama ≖	96	34.08 N	133.38 E
Saitama University ⌆²	268	35.52 N	139.36 E
Saito	96	32.06 N	131.24 E
Saiwai ◄⁸	268	35.33 N	139.41 E
Saiwa Swamp National Park ◆	154	1.06 N	35.12 E
Saiydān ◄⁸	272a	28.40 N	77.05 E
Sai'Yok	110	14.27 N	99.08 E
Sajak	86	47.02 N	72.22 E
Sajam	164	0.53 S	132.41 E
Sajama	248	17.37 S	69.00 W
Sajama, Nevado ▲	248	18.06 S	68.54 W
Sajanogorsk	86	53.08 N	91.29 E
Sajano-Šušenskoje vodochranilišče ⌧¹	86	52.20 N	92.25 E
Sajan — Sayan Mountains ↗	88	52.45 N	96.00 E
Sajantuj	88	51.44 N	107.30 E
Sajasan	88	43.03 N	46.17 E
Sajat	128	38.47 N	63.53 E
Sajch	88	48.40 N	102.39 E
Sajchandulaan	102	44.40 N	109.01 E
Sajchan-Ovoo	102	45.27 N	103.54 E
Sajchin	88	48.50 N	46.47 E
Sajen	115a	7.40 N	112.31 E
Šajgino	92	57.46 N	46.51 E
Sajhān	144	16.52 N	41.50 E
Šajmak'	120	37.24 N	74.44 E
Sajnšand	102	44.52 N	110.09 E
Sajó ≖	30	47.56 N	21.08 E
Sajószentpéter	30	48.13 N	20.44 E
Sajram	85	42.18 N	69.45 E
Sajukino	85	42.14 N	45.10 E
Säjūr (Bağırsak) ≖	130	36.40 N	38.05 E
Saka, Kenya	154	0.09 S	39.20 E
Saka, Nihon	96	34.20 N	132.31 E
Sakado	96	35.57 N	139.24 E
Sakae, Nihon	96	36.58 N	138.15 E
Sakae, Nihon	96	35.49 N	140.24 E
Sakaide	96	34.19 N	133.52 E
Sakaigawa	96	35.35 N	138.37 E
Sakaiminato	96	35.33 N	133.14 E
Sakākah	128	29.59 N	40.06 E
Sakakawea, Lake ⌧¹	198	47.50 N	102.20 W
Sakaki	96	36.28 N	138.11 E
Sakakita	94	35.23 N	138.01 E
Sakala, Pulau ◄	112	6.54 S	116.15 E
Sakami, Kenya	154	0.06 S	39.20 E
Sakami, Lac ⌧	176	53.40 N	76.40 W
Sakania	154	12.45 S	28.34 E
Sakar	128	38.55 N	63.53 E
Sakarahâ	157b	22.55 S	44.32 E
Sakar-Çaga	85	37.38 N	61.40 E
Sakar Island ◄	164	5.25 S	148.05 E
Sakartvelo — Georgia ◻¹	22	42.00 N	44.00 E
Sakarya ◻⁴	130	40.45 N	30.35 E
Sakarya ≖	130	41.07 N	30.39 E
Sakashita	94	35.34 N	137.32 E
Sakassou	150	7.27 N	5.18 W
Sakata	94	38.55 N	139.50 E
Sakauchi	94	35.39 N	136.25 E
Sakawa	96	33.30 N	133.17 E
Sakchu	98	40.23 N	125.01 E
Sakesar	123	32.31 N	71.56 E
Sakété	150	6.43 N	2.40 E
Sakhalin — Sachalin, ostrov ◄	89	51.00 N	143.00 E
Sakhi Sarwar	120	29.59 N	70.18 E
Sakhnīn	132	32.52 N	35.17 E
Sakht Sar	128	36.53 N	50.41 E
Šaki	128	41.12 N	47.10 E
Saki ≖	272c	19.06 N	72.53 E
Sakai	76	33.17 N	35.49 E
Sakai	86	54.17 N	23.03 E
Sakya Bendera, Pulau ◄	271c	1.13 N	103.51 E
Sakijang Pelepah, Pulau ◄	271c	1.13 N	103.52 E
Sakishima-shotō ◄	175d	24.46 N	124.00 E

FRANÇAIS

Nom	Page	Lat.	Long. W=Ouest
Sakito	92	33.02 N	129.32 E
Sakkara — Saqqārah	142	29.51 N	31.13 E
Sakmara ≖	86	51.46 N	55.01 E
Sako	270	34.53 N	135.47 E
Sakon Nakhon	110	17.10 N	104.09 E
Sakonnet	207	41.28 N	71.12 W
Sakonnet Point ►	207	41.27 N	71.12 W
Sakoyra	150	14.17 N	1.24 E
Sakra, Pulau ◄	271c	1.16 N	103.42 E
Sakrand	120	26.08 N	68.16 E
Sakrivier	158	30.54 S	20.28 E
Sakrow-Paretzer Kanal ≖	264a	52.28 N	12.55 E
Saks	194	33.42 N	85.52 W
Saksagan' ≖	78	47.53 N	33.18 E
Saksauldala ◄²	86	44.30 N	73.00 E
Sakskøbing	41	54.48 N	11.39 E
Sakti	124	22.02 N	82.58 E
Saku, Nihon	94	36.09 N	138.30 E
Saku, Nihon	94	36.13 N	138.29 E
Sakubva	154	19.00 S	32.10 E
Sakugi	96	34.52 N	132.43 E
Sakuma	94	35.05 N	137.48 E
Sakuma-dam ◄⁶	94	35.05 N	137.47 E
Sakuma-ko ◄¹	94	35.08 N	137.47 E
Sakura	94	35.43 N	140.14 E
Sakura ≖	94	36.05 N	140.14 E
Sakurae	94	34.57 N	132.20 E
Sakurai	96	34.30 N	135.51 E
Sakura-tōge ⋊	270	34.36 N	135.53 E
Sakutō	96	35.01 N	134.14 E
Sakwaso Lake ⌧	184	53.01 N	91.55 W
Säkylä	26	61.02 N	22.20 E
Sakyŏ ◄⁸	270	35.02 N	135.48 E
Sal ◄	150a	16.45 N	22.55 W
Sal, Cay ◄	238	23.42 N	80.24 W
Sal, Ponta do ►	266c	38.41 N	9.22 W
Sal, Punta ►	236	15.53 N	87.37 W
Šal'a, Česko.	30	48.09 N	17.52 E
Šal'a, Ross.	86	57.15 N	58.43 E
Sala, Sve.	40	59.55 N	16.36 E
Sala, Ouadi ⌄	146	17.00 N	20.53 E
Sala Baganza	64	44.43 N	10.14 E
Salabangka, Kepulauan ◄◄	112	3.02 S	122.25 E
Salaberry, Île de ◄	206	45.17 N	74.07 W
Salaberry-de-Valleyfield	206	45.15 N	74.08 W
Salaca ≖	76	57.45 N	24.21 E
Salacgrīva	76	57.45 N	24.21 E
Sala Consilina	68	40.24 N	15.36 E
Salada, Laguna ⌧, Arg.	258	35.17 S	59.24 W
Salada, Laguna ⌧, Méx.	232	32.20 N	115.40 W
Saladas	252	28.15 S	58.38 W
Saladillo ≖, Arg.	252	35.38 S	59.46 W
Saladillo ≖, Arg.	252	33.25 S	63.02 W
Saladillo ≖, Arg.	252	29.05 S	63.25 W
Saladillo, Arroyo ≖	258	35.33 S	59.04 W
Saladillo de Rodríguez, Arroyo ≖	258	35.29 S	59.01 W
Saladillo Dulce, Arroyo ≖	252	31.25 S	60.33 W
Salado, Arg.	252	28.18 S	67.15 W
Salado, Tx., U.S.	222	30.57 N	97.32 W
Salado ≖, Arg.	252	28.49 S	64.57 W
Salado ≖, Arg.	252	29.13 S	66.34 W
Salado ≖, Arg.	252	31.42 S	60.44 W
Salado ≖, Cuba	240p	20.36 N	76.56 W
Salado ≖, Méx.	232	26.52 N	99.19 W
Salado ≖, Méx.	234	17.55 N	96.58 W
Salado, Arroyo ≖, Arg.	254	41.37 S	65.02 W
Salado, Arroyo ≖, Arg.	252	40.35 S	66.33 W
Salado, Río ≖	200	34.16 N	106.52 W
Salado Creek ≖, Tx., U.S.	196	29.14 N	98.25 W
Salado Creek ≖, Tx., U.S.	222	30.59 N	97.25 W
Salāh	150	32.38 N	36.46 E
Salāh ad-Dīn ◻⁴	128	34.15 N	43.55 E
Sala'īlua	175a	13.41 S	172.34 W
Salair	86	54.13 N	85.47 E
Salairskij kr'až ↗	86	54.15 N	85.30 E
Salaj ◻⁶	78	47.15 N	23.00 E
Salak ◄	114	2.34 N	98.20 E
Salak, Gunung ▲	115a	6.42 S	106.44 E
Salakas	76	55.35 N	26.08 E
Salakuša	24	62.15 N	40.17 E
Salala	146	14.51 N	17.13 E
Salala, Chile	252	30.41 S	71.32 W
Salala, Liber.	150	6.40 N	10.05 W
Salālah, Süd.	140	16.30 N	36.13 E
Salālah, 'Umān	140	17.00 N	54.06 E
Salamá, Guat.	236	15.06 N	90.16 W
Salamá, Méx.	234	14.50 N	86.36 W
Salamajärven kansallispuisto ◆	26	63.20 N	24.40 E
Salamanca, Chile	252	31.47 S	70.58 W
Salamanca, Esp.	34	40.58 N	5.39 W
Salamanca, Méx.	234	20.34 N	101.12 W
Salamanca, Perú	248	15.31 S	72.50 W
Salamanca, N.Y., U.S.	210	42.09 N	78.42 W
Salamanca ◻⁴	34	40.45 N	6.00 W
Salamat ◻⁴	148	11.00 N	20.30 E
Salamat, Bahr ≖	146	9.27 N	18.06 E
Salāmbek	146	10.58 N	20.09 E
Salamina	246	5.24 N	75.29 W
Salamís, Órmos ⊂	267c	37.56 N	23.28 E
Salamis ◄	130	35.10 N	33.54 E
Salamiyah	130	35.01 N	37.03 E
Salamīyah	144	16.57 N	43.37 E
Salang Khān	146	13.47 N	20.20 E
Salamonie ≖	214	40.50 N	85.43 W
Salamonie Lake ⌧¹	214	40.46 N	85.37 W
Salang, Tünel-e ⋊⁵	120	35.19 N	69.02 E
Salani	175a	14.00 S	171.33 W
Salar ≖	85	41.21 N	69.22 E
Salard	38	47.13 N	22.03 E
Salas	34	43.25 N	6.16 W
Salas de los Infantes	34	42.01 N	3.17 W
Salat ≖	32	43.10 N	1.08 E
Salatiga	115a	7.19 S	110.30 E
Salavat	85	53.21 N	55.55 E
Salaverry	248	8.14 S	78.58 W
Salavina	252	28.48 S	63.25 W
Salawati ◄	164	1.07 S	130.52 E
Salay	112	8.52 N	124.47 E
Salāya	120	22.19 N	69.35 E
Sala y Gómez, Isla ◄	18	26.28 S	105.28 W
Sala y Gomez Ridge ◄⁺³	18	25.00 S	98.00 W
Salazar'	80	54.07 N	43.09 E
Salbani	88	53.14 N	92.36 E
Salbosjön ⌧	126	22.38 N	87.20 E
Salbohed	40	59.55 N	16.19 E
Salbris	50	47.26 N	2.03 E
Šalbuzdag, gora ▲	84	41.19 N	47.48 E
Salcajá	236	14.53 N	91.27 W
Salcantay, Nevado ▲	248	13.20 S	72.33 W
Salcedo, Pil.	116	11.09 N	125.40 E
Salcedo, Rep. Dom.	238	19.23 N	70.25 W
Salcha ≖	180	64.29 N	147.00 W
Salching	60	48.49 N	12.34 E
Šalčia ≖	76	54.18 N	25.23 E
Šalčininkai	76	54.18 N	25.23 E
Salcombe	42	50.13 N	3.47 W
Saldaña	34	42.31 N	4.44 W
Saldaña ≖	246	4.01 N	74.52 W
Saldanha	158	33.00 S	17.56 E
Saldanhabaai ⊂	158	33.04 S	18.00 E
Saldê	80	16.52 N	14.46 E
Saldungaray	252	38.12 S	61.47 W
Saldus	76	56.40 N	22.30 E
Sale, Austl.	166	38.06 S	147.04 E
Sale, It.	62	44.59 N	8.48 E
Salé, Magreb	148	34.04 N	6.50 W
Sale, Eng., U.K.	44	53.26 N	2.19 W
Saleabu, Pulau ◄	108	3.51 N	126.32 E
Salebard	74	66.33 N	66.40 E
Sale Creek	194	35.22 N	85.06 W
Salée, Rivière ʯ	241o	16.17 N	61.33 W
Saleh, Teluk ⊂	115b	8.34 S	117.57 E
Salelologa	175a	13.44 S	172.14 W
Salem, Ont., Can.	212	43.42 N	80.27 W
Salem, Dtsch.	58	47.46 N	9.16 E
Salem, India	122	11.39 N	78.10 E
Salem, S. Afr.	158	33.28 S	26.29 E
Salem, Sve.	40	59.13 N	17.44 E
Salem, Ar., U.S.	194	36.22 N	91.49 W
Salem, Il., U.S.	219	38.37 N	88.56 W
Salem, In., U.S.	218	38.36 N	86.15 W
Salem, Ia., U.S.	190	40.51 N	91.37 W
Salem, Ky., U.S.	190	37.15 N	88.14 W
Salem, Ma., U.S.	207	42.31 N	70.53 W
Salem, Mi., U.S.	281	42.24 N	83.34 W
Salem, Mo., U.S.	194	37.38 N	91.32 W
Salem, N.H., U.S.	207	42.47 N	71.12 W
Salem, N.J., U.S.	208	39.34 N	75.28 W
Salem, N.Y., U.S.	210	43.10 N	73.19 W
Salem, Oh., U.S.	214	40.54 N	80.51 W
Salem, Or., U.S.	224	44.56 N	123.02 W
Salem, S.D., U.S.	198	43.43 N	97.23 W
Salem, Ut., U.S.	200	40.03 N	111.40 W
Salem, Va., U.S.	192	37.17 N	80.03 W
Salem, W.V., U.S.	188	39.16 N	80.33 W
Salem, Wi., U.S.	214	42.33 N	88.06 W
Salem ◻⁶	208	39.34 N	75.20 W
Salem Airfield ⌧	281	42.25 N	83.34 W
Sale Marasino	64	45.43 N	10.06 E
Salem Canal ≖	285	39.41 N	75.31 W
Salem Depot	283	42.47 N	71.12 W
Salem Harbor ⊂	283	42.31 N	70.53 W
Salem Heights	214	40.54 N	80.53 W
Salem Maritime National Historic Site ◻	207	42.31 N	70.53 W
Salem State College	283	42.30 N	70.54 W
Salem Upland ◄¹	194	37.25 N	91.30 W
Salen, Sve.	40	61.10 N	13.16 E
Salen, Scot., U.K.	46	56.43 N	5.47 W
Salen, Scot., U.K.	46	56.31 N	5.57 W
Salentina, Penisola ► ◄³	68	40.25 N	18.00 E
Salentina, Murge ◄¹	68	40.02 N	18.13 E
Salerno	68	40.41 N	15.11 E
Salernes	62	43.33 N	6.14 E
Salerno, N.A.	188	40.41 N	14.47 E
Salerno, Ct., U.S.	207	41.29 N	72.29 W
Salerno, Golfo di ⊂	68	40.32 N	14.42 E
Salers	32	45.08 N	2.30 E
Salesbury	262	53.47 N	2.30 W
Salesópolis	255	23.32 S	45.51 W
Salève, Mont ▲	62	46.08 N	6.10 E
Salford ◻⁸	262	53.28 N	2.18 W
Salford	44	53.28 N	2.23 W
Salgar	246	8.04 N	75.16 W
Salgir ≖	78	45.38 N	35.01 E
Salgótarján	30	48.07 N	19.48 E
Salgueiro	250	8.04 S	39.06 W
Sali, Cro.	64	43.56 N	15.10 E
Šali, Ross.	84	55.41 N	49.40 E
Šali, Ross.	84	55.44 N	49.40 E
Salice Salentino	68	40.23 N	17.58 E
Salice Terme	64	44.55 N	9.01 E
Salida, Ca., U.S.	226	37.44 N	121.05 W
Salida, Co., U.S.	200	38.32 N	105.59 W
Salies-de-Béarn	32	43.29 N	0.55 W
Salignac-Eyvignes	144	23.41 N	42.40 E
Salihli	130	38.29 N	28.09 E
Salihorsk	76	52.48 N	27.32 E
Šalikovo	82	55.30 N	36.13 E
Salima	154	13.47 S	34.26 E
Salimah, Wāhat ⊽	142	21.22 N	28.33 E
Salin	110	20.34 N	94.38 E
Salimbatu	112	2.57 N	117.21 E
Salina, Ks., U.S.	196	38.50 N	97.36 W
Salina, Ut., U.S.	200	38.57 N	111.51 W
Salina, Isola ◄	68	38.34 N	14.50 E
Salina Cruz	234	16.10 N	95.12 W
Salina Point ►	238	22.13 N	74.18 W
Salinas, Bra.	255	16.10 S	42.17 W
Salinas, Ec.	248	2.13 S	80.58 W
Salinas, P.R.	240m	17.59 N	66.18 W
Salinas, Ca., U.S.	226	36.40 N	121.39 W
Salinas ≖, Bra.	255	16.37 S	42.18 W
Salinas (Chixoy) ≖, N.A.	236	16.28 N	90.33 W
Salinas ≖, Ca., U.S.	226	36.45 N	121.48 W
Salinas, Pampa de las ◌	252	31.58 S	66.42 W
Salinas, Ponta das ►	154	12.50 S	12.56 E
Salinas, Sierra de ↗	226	36.18 N	121.20 W
Salinas de Garci Mendoza	248	19.38 S	67.43 W
Salinas de Hidalgo	234	22.38 N	101.43 W
Salinas del Rey	196	27.38 N	101.20 W
Salinas Municipal Airport ⌧	226	36.40 N	121.40 W
Salinas National Monument ◻	200	34.05 N	106.14 W
Salinas Valley ⌄	226	36.15 N	121.15 W
Salinas Victoria	196	25.53 N	100.19 W
Saline-de-Giraud	62	43.24 N	4.43 E
Salindres	62	44.10 N	4.10 E
Saline, La., U.S.	194	32.09 N	92.58 W

PORTUGUÊS

Nome	Página	Lat.	Long. W=Oeste
Saline, Mi., U.S.	216	42.10 N	83.46 W
Saline ≖, Ar., U.S.	194	33.44 N	93.58 W
Saline ≖, Ar., U.S.	194	33.10 N	92.08 W
Saline ≖, Il., U.S.	194	37.35 N	88.08 W
Saline ≖, Ks., U.S.	198	38.51 N	97.30 W
Saline ≖, Mi., U.S.	216	41.59 N	83.37 W
Saline, North Fork ≖	194	37.44 N	88.19 W
Saline ≖, Mi., U.S.	194	31.45 N	92.58 W
Saline Bayou ≖	194	31.45 N	92.58 W
Salines, Point ►	241k	12.00 N	61.48 W
Salines, Pointe des ►	240e	14.24 N	60.53 W
Salineville	214	40.37 N	80.51 W
Salingyi	110	22.13 N	95.03 E
Šalinopolis	250	0.37 S	47.20 W
Šalinskoje	86	55.43 N	93.46 E
Salina ≖, U.S.	202	43.08 N	111.02 W
Salisbury, Austl.	168b	34.46 S	138.38 E
Salisbury, Dom.	240d	15.26 N	61.27 W
Salisbury, Eng., U.K.	42	51.05 N	1.48 W
Salisbury, Ct., U.S.	207	41.59 N	73.25 W
Salisbury, Md., U.S.	208	38.21 N	75.35 W
Salisbury, Ma., U.S.	207	42.50 N	70.51 W
Salisbury, Mo., U.S.	194	39.25 N	92.48 W
Salisbury, N.C., U.S.	192	35.40 N	80.28 W
Salisbury, Pa., U.S.	188	39.45 N	79.04 W
Salisbury Cathedral ◣¹	42	51.05 N	1.48 W
Salisbury Center	210	43.09 N	74.47 W
Salisbury Hall ◣	260	51.43 N	0.16 W
Salisbury — Harare	154	17.50 S	31.03 E
Salisbury Island ◄, Austl.	162	34.21 S	123.32 E
Salisbury Island ◄, N.T., Can.	176	63.30 N	77.00 W
Salisbury Mills	210	41.26 N	74.08 W
Salisbury Plain ≖	42	51.12 N	1.55 W
Salisbury Plain ◄	283	42.02 N	70.58 W
Salish Mountains ↗	202	48.15 N	114.45 W
Salito	70	37.29 N	13.46 E
Salitpa	194	31.37 N	88.01 W
Saljany	84	39.34 N	48.58 E
Šalkar, Kaz.	84	48.03 N	46.56 E
Šalkar, Kaz.	80	50.32 N	51.51 E
Šalkar, ozero ⌧	80	50.33 N	51.40 E
Šalkar-Jega-Kara, ozero ⌧	86	50.45 N	60.54 E
Salkehatchie ≖	192	32.37 N	80.53 W
Salkhad	132	32.29 N	36.43 E
Salkhia	172b	22.35 N	88.21 E
Salkum	224	46.31 N	122.37 W
Salla	24	66.50 N	28.40 E
Salladasburg	210	41.17 N	77.14 W
Sallanches	62	45.56 N	6.38 E
Salland ◄¹	52	52.20 N	6.20 E
Salles-Curan	32	44.11 N	2.47 E
Salles-sous-Bois	62	44.27 N	4.56 E
Sallgast	54	51.36 N	13.51 E
Salliqueló	252	36.45 S	62.56 W
Sallisaw	196	35.27 N	94.47 W
Salluit	70	62.14 N	75.38 W
Sallūm	140	31.34 N	25.09 E
Sallūm, Khalīj as- ⊂	146	31.40 N	25.21 E
Salm ≖, Bel.	56	50.12 N	5.52 E
Salm ≖, Dtsch.	58	49.51 N	6.51 E
Salmās	128	38.11 N	44.47 E
Salme	76	58.10 N	22.15 E
Salmi	24	61.22 N	31.53 E
Salmo	182	49.12 N	117.17 W
Salmon	182	45.11 N	113.53 W
Salmon ≖, B.C., Can.	182	54.05 N	122.34 W
Salmon ≖, N.B., Can.	182	54.05 N	122.34 W
Salmon, On., Can.	212	44.11 N	77.15 W
Salmon ≖, N.A.	188	45.04 N	74.31 W
Salmon ≖, Ct., U.S.	207	41.29 N	72.29 W
Salmon ≖, Id., U.S.	202	45.51 N	116.46 W
Salmon, North Branch ≖	212	43.16 N	75.48 W
Salmon, South Fork ≖	182	44.46 N	115.31 W
Salmon Arm	182	50.42 N	119.16 W
Salmon-Bear ≖	186	51.26 N	57.36 W
Salmon Creek ≖, N.Y., U.S.	210	43.16 N	77.14 W
Salmon Falls Creek ≖	202	42.43 N	114.51 W
Salmon Falls Creek Reservoir ⌧¹	202	42.08 N	114.45 W
Salmon Gums	162	32.59 S	121.38 E
Salmon Mountain ▲	188	44.49 N	78.28 W
Salmon Mountain ▲	226	41.08 N	123.30 W
Salmon Peak ▲	196	29.45 N	100.10 W
Salmon Point ►	212	43.52 N	77.14 W
Salmon River Mountains ↗	202	44.45 N	115.30 W
Salmon River Reservoir ⌧¹	210	43.32 N	75.52 W
Salmon Valley	182	54.05 N	122.41 W
Salo, It.	64	45.36 N	10.31 E
Salo, Centraf.	152	5.36 N	16.07 E
Salome	200	33.46 N	113.36 W
Salomon, Cap ►	240e	14.30 N	61.06 W
Salomón, Islas — Solomon Islands ◻¹	175e	8.00 S	159.00 E
Salomón, Monte ▲	267a	41.47 N	12.44 E
Salomone-Inseln — Solomon Islands	175e	8.00 S	159.00 E
Salon (Salum)	64	45.36 N	10.31 E
Salon-de-Provence	62	43.38 N	5.06 E
Salonga, Parc National de la ◆	152	1.45 S	21.20 E
Salonika — Thessaloníki	38	40.38 N	22.56 E
Salonta	38	46.48 N	21.40 E
Salor ≖	34	39.39 N	7.03 W
Salovka	265b	55.47 N	38.12 E
— El Salvador ◻¹	236	13.50 N	88.55 W
Salween ≖	130	40.59 N	39.12 E
Sal Rei	150a	16.11 N	22.55 W
Salsacate	252	31.19 S	65.05 W
Salsette Island ◄	272c	19.10 N	72.53 E
Salsilgo, Qawz ≖⁸	140	10.49 N	22.54 E
Salsipuedes, Canal ʯ	232	28.37 N	113.00 W
Salsipuedes, Punta ►, C.R.	236	8.28 N	83.37 W
Salsipuedes, Punta ►, Méx.	232	32.05 N	116.53 W
Sal'sk	80	46.28 N	41.33 E
Šal'skij	80	46.28 N	41.33 E
Sal'sko-Manyčskaja gr'ada ↗	80	46.40 N	42.30 E
Salso ≖	70	37.06 N	13.57 E
Salsomaggiore Terme	64	44.49 N	9.59 E
Salt ≖, U.S.	202	43.08 N	111.02 W
Salt ≖, Az., U.S.	200	33.23 N	112.18 W
Salt ≖, Il., U.S.	194	38.00 N	85.57 W
Salt ≖, Ky., U.S.	281	42.29 N	82.47 W
Salt ≖, Mo., U.S.	194	39.28 N	91.53 W
Salt, Elk Fork ≖	281	39.28 N	91.49 W
Salt, Middle Fork ≖	219	39.28 N	91.49 W
Salt, North Fork ≖	219	39.30 N	91.47 W
Salt, South Fork ≖	219	39.28 N	91.49 W
Salta	252	24.47 S	65.25 W
Salta ◻⁴	252	25.00 S	64.30 W
Saltaim, ozero ⌧	86	56.10 N	71.45 E
Saltair	224	40.46 N	112.09 W
Saltaire	276	40.39 N	73.12 W
Saltanovka	76	54.17 N	34.17 E
Saltara	66	43.45 N	12.54 E
Salt Ash, Austl.	170	32.47 S	151.51 E
Saltash, Eng., U.K.	42	50.24 N	4.12 W
Saltbæk Vig ⊂	41	55.43 N	11.12 E
Salt Basin ◌	200	31.50 N	105.00 W
Saltburn-by-the-Sea	44	54.35 N	0.58 W
Salt Cay ◄	240b	21.20 N	71.12 W
Saltcoats, Sk., Can.	184	51.03 N	102.12 W
Saltcoats, Scot., U.K.	46	55.38 N	4.47 W
Salt Creek ≖, Ca., U.S.	204	36.15 N	116.49 W
Salt Creek ≖, Il., U.S.	194	40.08 N	89.50 W
Salt Creek ≖, Il., U.S.	278	41.49 N	87.50 W
Salt Creek ≖, In., U.S.	216	41.37 N	87.09 W
Salt Creek ≖, In., U.S.	218	38.50 N	86.32 W
Salt Creek ≖, Ks., U.S.	198	39.06 N	97.44 W
Salt Creek ≖, N.M., U.S.	196	33.35 N	104.23 W
Salt Creek ≖, Ok., U.S.	196	36.32 N	96.43 W
Salt Creek ≖, Or., U.S.	202	43.43 N	122.26 W
Salt Creek ≖, Wy., U.S.	202	43.24 N	106.20 W
Salt Creek, Middle Fork ≖	218	39.04 N	86.15 W
Salt Creek, North Fork ≖, Il., U.S.	216	40.13 N	88.50 W
Salt Creek, North Fork ≖, In., U.S.	218	39.08 N	86.21 W
Salt Creek, West Branch ≖	278	42.02 N	88.01 W
Salt Creek South ≖	218	39.09 N	86.16 W
Salt Draw ⌄	196	31.19 N	103.28 W
Saltee Islands ◄◄	48	52.07 N	6.36 W
Saltholm ◄	41	55.38 N	12.46 E
Saltillo, Méx.	232	25.25 N	101.00 W
Saltillo, Pa., U.S.	194	34.22 N	88.40 W
Saltillo, Tn., U.S.	194	35.23 N	88.12 W
Salt Island ◄	240m	18.22 N	64.31 W
Salt Lake City	200	40.45 N	111.53 W
Salto, Ur.	252	31.23 S	57.58 W
Salto, Ur. ◻⁴	252	31.23 S	57.58 W
Salto, Lago del ⌧	66	42.13 N	12.54 E
Salto da Divisa	255	16.00 S	39.57 W
Salto de las Rosas	252	34.45 S	68.20 W
Salto del Fraile ►	286d	12.11 S	77.03 W
Salto del Guairá	252	24.03 S	54.17 W
Salto Grande	255	22.54 S	49.59 W
Salto Grande, Embalse ⌧¹	252	31.15 S	57.55 W
Salton City	204	33.19 N	115.59 W
Salton Sea ⌧	204	33.19 N	115.50 W
Salton Sea State Recreation Area ◆	204	33.29 N	115.53 W
Salto Santiago, Represa de ⌧¹	255	25.52 S	52.30 W
Salt Pan Creek ≖	274a	33.59 S	151.02 E
Saltpond	150	5.12 N	1.04 W
Salt Range ↗	123	32.45 N	72.00 E
Salt River Indian Reservation ◄⁴	200	33.31 N	111.48 W
Saltsjöbaden	40	59.17 N	18.18 E
Salta ◄	70	37.24 N	13.43 E
Saltspring Island ◄	224	48.47 N	123.30 W
Salt Springs	192	29.21 N	81.44 W
Salt Wells Creek ≖	202	41.45 N	108.44 W
Saltykovka, Ross.	265b	55.46 N	37.55 E
Saltykovka, Ross.	84	51.07 N	44.49 E
Saluda, S.C., U.S.	192	34.00 N	81.46 W
Saluda, Va., U.S.	208	37.36 N	76.35 W
Saluda ≖	192	34.01 N	81.04 W
Saludecio	66	43.52 N	12.40 E
Saluen — Salween ≖	12	16.31 N	97.37 E
Salue Timpaus, Selat ʯ	112	1.55 S	124.00 E
Salug	116	8.07 N	122.47 E
Saluggia	62	45.14 N	8.00 E
Salūm	144	21.29 N	42.10 E
Salur	124	18.31 N	83.13 E
— Salorno	64	46.14 N	11.13 E
Salutaris	256	22.15 S	8.07 E
Saluzzo	62	44.39 N	7.29 E
Salvación, Bahía ⊂	254	50.15 S	75.20 W
Salvador, Mount ▲	162	25.15 S	121.01 E
Salvador, Bahia ◄	250	13.00 S	38.30 W
Salvador, Lake ⌧	194	29.45 N	90.15 W
Salvador Island ◄	116	15.31 N	119.55 E
Salvador María	252	35.18 S	59.10 W

Símbolo	English	Deutsch	Español	Français	Português
≈	River	Fluß	Río	Rivière	Rio
⊞	Canal	Kanal	Canal	Canal	Canal
ʯ	Waterfall, Rapids	Wasserfall, Stromschnellen	Cascada, Rápidos	Cascade, Rápidos	Cascata, Rápidos
ʮ	Strait	Meerestraße	Estrecho	Détroit	Estreito
◌	Bay, Gulf	Bucht, Golf	Bahía, Golfo	Baie, Golfe	Baía, Golfo
⌧	Lake, Lakes	See, Seen	Lago, Lagos	Lac, Lacs	Lago, Lagos
⌇	Swamp	Sumpf	Pantano	Marais	Pântano
⊠	Ice Features, Glacier	Eis- und Gletscherformen	Accidentes Glaciales	Formes glaciaires	Acidentes glaciares
⟿	Other Hydrographic Features	Andere Hydrographische Objekte	Otros Elementos Hidrográficos	Autres éléments hydrographiques	Outros acidentes hidrográficos
◄	Submarine Features	Untermeerische Objekte	Accidentes Submarinos	Formes de relief sous-marin	Acidentes submarinos
◻	Political Unit	Politische Einheit	Unidad Política	Entité politique	Unidade política
◣	Cultural Institution	Kulturelle Institution	Institución Cultural	Institution culturelle	Instituição cultural
◆	Historical Site	Historische Stätte	Sitio Histórico	Site historique	Sítio histórico
◆	Recreational Site	Erholungs- und Ferienort	Sitio de Recreo	Centre de loisirs	Área de Lazer
⌧	Airport	Flughafen	Aeropuerto	Aéroport	Aeroporto
	Military Installation	Militäranlage	Instalación Militar	Installation militaire	Instalação militar
	Miscellaneous	Verschiedenes	Misceláneo	Divers	Diversos

ENGLISH — Name / Page / Lat.°′ / Long.°′ DEUTSCH — Name / Seite / Breite°′ / Länge°′ E = Ost

Symbols in the index entries represent the broad categories identified in the key at the right. Symbols with superior numbers (∧∧1) identify subcategories (see complete key on page I · 1).

Symbole im Register stellen die rechts im Schlüssel erklärten Kategorien dar. Symbole mit hochgestellten Ziffern (∧∧1) bezeichnen Unterabteilungen einer Kategorie (vgl. vollständiger Schlüssel auf Seite I · 1).

Los símbolos incluidos en el texto del índice representan las grandes categorías identificadas con la clave a la derecha. Los símbolos con numeros en su parte superior (∧∧1) identifican las subcategorías (véase la clave completa en la página I · 1).

Les symboles de l'index représentent les catégories indiquées dans la légende à droite. Les symboles suivis d'un indice (∧∧1) représentent des sous-catégories (voir légende complète à la page I · 1).

Os símbolos incluídos no texto do índice representam as grandes categorias identificadas com a chave à direita. Os símbolos com números em sua parte superior (∧∧1) identificam as subcategorias (veja-se a chave completa à página I · 1).

∧ Mountain	Berg	Montaña	Montagne	Montanha
∧∧ Mountains	Gebirge	Montañas	Montagnes	Montanhas
)(Pass	Paß	Paso	Col	Passo
V Valley, Canyon	Tal, Cañon	Valle, Cañón	Vallée, Canyon	Vale, Canhão
≚ Plain	Ebene	Llano	Plaine	Planície
› Cape	Kap	Cabo	Cap	Cabo
I Island	Insel	Isla	Île	Ilha
II Islands	Inseln	Islas	Îles	Ilhas
≐ Other Topographic Features	Andere Topographische Objekte	Otros Elementos Topográficos	Autres données topographiques	Outros acidentes topográficos

Nombre	Página	Lat.º′	Long.º′ W = Oeste
Sandusky □⁶	214	41.21 N	83.07 W
Sandusky ≃	214	41.21 N	83.00 W
Sandusky Bay c	214	41.21 N	82.52 W
Sand ul ʌ	102	43.27 N	104.04 E
Sandvig	26	55.17 N	14.47 E
Sandvika	26	59.54 N	10.31 E
Sandviken	40	60.37 N	16.46 E
Sandweiler	56	49.37 N	6.13 E
Sandwich, Eng., U.K.	42	51.17 N	1.20 E
Sandwich, Il., U.S.	216	41.38 N	88.37 W
Sandwich, Ma., U.S.	207	41.45 N	70.29 W
Sandwich Bay c, Nf., Can.	176	53.35 N	57.15 W
Sandwich Bay c, Namibia	156	23.22 S	14.30 E
Sandwich del Sur, Islas — South Sandwich Islands II	18	57.45 S	26.30 W
Sandwich, B.C., Can.	182	49.42 N	124.59 W
Sandwich, Scot., U.K.	46a	60.00 N	1.15 W
Sand Wick c	46a	60.42 N	0.52 W
Sandwîp	124	22.29 N	91.26 E
Sandwîp Channel ʋ	124	22.30 N	91.35 E
Sandwîp Island I	124	22.30 N	91.25 E
Sandy, Eng., U.K.	42	52.08 N	0.18 W
Sandy, Or., U.S.	224	45.23 N	122.15 W
Sandy, Pa., U.S.	214	41.07 N	78.47 W
Sandy, Ut., U.S.	200	40.35 N	111.53 W
Sandy ≃, Me., U.S.	188	44.45 N	69.52 W
Sandy ≃, Or., U.S.	224	45.34 N	122.24 W
Sandy ≃, Va., U.S.	192	36.35 N	79.25 W
Sandy Bay c, Nic.	236	14.28 N	83.16 W
Sandy Bay c, Ma., U.S.	283	42.40 N	70.37 W
Sandy Bay Indian Reserve ◆⁴	184	50.33 N	98.40 W
Sandy Bay Mountain ʌ	188	45.47 N	70.25 W
Sandy Beach	210	43.04 N	78.55 W
Sandy Branch ≃	284c	39.03 N	77.16 W
Sandy Cape ›, Austl.	166	24.42 S	153.17 E
Sandy Cape ›, Austl.	166	41.25 S	144.45 E
Sandy Creek ≃	212	43.38 N	76.05 W
Sandy Creek ≃, Austl.	166	32.10 S	144.39 E
Sandy Creek ≃, U.S.	196	34.25 N	99.35 W
Sandy Creek ≃, U.S.	196	36.50 N	98.10 W
Sandy Creek ≃, Il., U.S.	219	39.34 N	90.35 W
Sandy Creek ≃, N.Y., U.S.	212	43.44 N	76.15 W
Sandy Creek ≃, N.Y., U.S.	212	43.20 N	77.55 W
Sandy Creek ≃, N.C., U.S.	192	36.08 N	78.02 W
Sandy Creek ≃, Pa., U.S.	214	40.38 N	81.26 W
Sandy Creek ≃, Tx., U.S.	214	41.18 N	79.51 W
Sandy Creek ≃, Tx., U.S.	196	30.34 N	98.26 W
Sandy Creek ≃, Tx., U.S.	222	29.02 N	96.33 W
Sandy Creek, East Branch ≃	210	43.17 N	78.03 W
Sandy Creek, North Branch ≃	212	43.51 N	75.58 W
Sandy Creek, West Branch ≃	214	43.17 N	78.03 W
Sandy Desert ◆²	128	28.40 N	62.30 E
Sandy Hook, Ct., U.S.	207	41.25 N	73.16 W
Sandy Hook, Ky., U.S.	192	38.05 N	83.07 W
Sandy Hook, Ms., U.S.	194	31.02 N	89.48 W
Sandy Hook › ²	208	40.27 N	74.00 W
Sandy Hook Bay c	276	40.26 N	74.03 W
Sandykači	128	36.33 N	62.34 E
Sandy Key I	220	25.02 N	81.01 W
Sandy Lake	214	41.20 N	80.04 W
Sandy Lake ⊜, Nf., Can.	186	49.16 N	57.00 W
Sandy Lake ⊜, On., Can.	184	53.02 N	93.00 W
Sandy Lake ⊜, On., Can.	212	44.33 N	78.24 W
Sandy Lick Creek ≃	214	41.09 N	79.05 W
Sandy Point ›, Austl.	168b	34.16 S	138.09 E
Sandy Point ›, Trin.	112r	11.09 N	60.50 W
Sandy Point ›, R.I., U.S.	207	41.14 N	71.35 W
Sandy Point Town	238	17.22 N	62.50 W
Sandy Pond ⊜	283	42.26 N	71.19 W
Sandy Ridge	214	40.49 N	78.14 W
Sandy Springs	192	33.55 N	84.22 W
Sandyville, Md., U.S.	208	39.31 N	76.55 W
Sandyville, Oh., U.S.	214	40.38 N	81.23 W
Sandžak ◆¹	38	43.10 N	19.30 E
San Eladio	258	34.46 S	59.11 W
San Elizario	200	31.35 N	106.16 W
San Emigdio Creek ≃	228	35.02 N	119.11 W
San Emilio	116	17.14 N	120.37 E
Sanen	115a	8.23 S	113.37 E
San Enrique	252	35.47 S	60.22 W
San Estanislao	252	24.39 S	56.26 W
San Esteban	236	15.17 N	85.52 W
San Esteban, Isla I	232	28.42 N	112.36 W
San Esteban de Gormaz	34	41.35 N	3.12 W
San Fele	68	40.49 N	15.32 E
San Felice (Sankt Felix)	64	46.30 N	11.08 E
San Felice Circeo	66	41.14 N	13.05 E
San Felice sul Panaro	64	44.50 N	11.08 E
San Felipe, Chile	252	32.45 S	70.44 W
San Felipe, Col.	246	1.55 N	67.06 W
San Felipe, Méx.	232	31.00 N	114.52 W
San Felipe, Méx.	234	21.29 N	101.13 W
San Felipe, Pil.	116	15.04 N	120.04 E
San Felipe, Tx., U.S.	222	29.48 N	96.06 W
San Felipe, Ven.	246	10.20 N	68.44 W
San Felipe, Castillo de I	236	15.39 N	89.01 W
San Felipe, Cayos de II	240p	21.58 N	83.30 W
San Felipe Aztatán	234	22.23 N	105.24 W
San Felipe Creek ≃	204	33.09 N	115.46 W
San Felipe de Vichayal	248	4.52 S	81.05 W
San Felipe Indian Reservation ◆⁴	200	35.26 N	106.26 W
San Felipe Jalapa de Díaz	234	18.04 N	96.32 W
San Felipe Nuevo Mercurio	232	24.22 N	102.06 W
San Felipe Pueblo	200	35.27 N	106.28 W
San Félix ≃	236	8.10 N	81.51 W
San Félix, Isla I	244	26.17 S	80.05 W
San Ferdinando di Puglia	68	41.18 N	16.04 E
San Fermín	36	26.20 N	104.49 W
San Fernando, Arg.	258	34.26 S	58.34 W
San Fernando, Chile	252	34.35 S	71.00 W
San Fernando, Esp.	34	36.28 N	6.12 W
San Fernando, Méx.	196	28.32 N	100.54 W
San Fernando, Méx.	232	24.50 N	98.10 W
San Fernando, Méx.	234	16.52 N	93.13 W
San Fernando, Pil.	116	16.37 N	120.19 E
San Fernando, Pil.	116	12.30 N	123.46 E
San Fernando, Pil.	116	15.01 N	120.41 E
San Fernando, Trin.	241r	10.17 N	61.28 W
San Fernando, U.S.	228	34.17 N	118.26 W
San Fernando, Ven.	246	7.54 N	67.28 W
San Fernando □⁵	288	34.28 S	58.34 W

Nom	Page	Lat.º′	Long.º′ W = Ouest
San Fernando, Aeródromo ◆²	288	34.27 S	58.35 W
San Fernando Airport ◆	280	34.17 N	118.25 W
San Fernando Creek ≃	196	27.28 N	97.46 W
San Fernando de Atabapo	246	4.03 N	67.42 W
San Fernando de Henares	266a	40.26 N	3.32 W
San Fernando del Valle de Catamarca	252	28.28 S	65.47 W
San Fernando Mission v¹	280	34.16 N	118.28 W
San Fernando Point ›	116	16.38 N	120.17 E
San Fernando Valley ∨	280	34.13 N	118.27 W
San Fili	68	39.20 N	16.09 E
San Filippo del Mela ∨	70	38.10 N	15.17 E
Sånfjället ʌ	26	62.17 N	13.32 E
Sånfjällets Nationalpark ◆	26	62.20 N	13.40 E
San Floriano	64	46.02 N	12.18 E
Sanford, Co., U.S.	200	37.15 N	105.54 W
Sanford, Fl., U.S.	220	28.48 N	81.16 W
Sanford, Me., U.S.	188	43.26 N	70.46 W
Sanford, Mi., U.S.	190	43.40 N	84.22 W
Sanford, N.C., U.S.	192	35.28 N	79.10 W
Sanford, Va., U.S.	196	35.42 N	101.32 W
Sanford ≃	162	27.22 S	115.53 E
Sanford, Mount ʌ	180	62.13 N	144.09 W
San Francesco, Convento v¹, It.	66	42.28 N	12.45 E
San Francesco, Convento v¹, It.	267a	42.03 N	12.46 E
San Francisco, Arg.	252	31.26 S	62.05 W
San Francisco, Col.	246	1.11 N	76.53 W
San Francisco, C.R.	236	9.49 N	85.15 W
San Francisco, El Sal.	236	13.42 N	88.06 W
San Francisco, Pan.	236	8.15 N	80.58 W
San Francisco, Pil.	116	8.30 N	125.56 E
San Francisco, Pil.	116	10.04 N	125.09 E
San Francisco, Ca., U.S.	226	37.46 N	122.25 W
San Francisco ≃, U.S.	196	32.10 N	114.25 W
San Francisco □⁶	226	37.45 N	122.22 W
San Francisco ≃, Arg.	252	23.16 S	64.03 W
San Francisco ≃, U.S.	200	32.59 N	109.22 W
San Francisco, Arroyo ≃	288	34.43 S	58.19 W
San Francisco, Paso de ⋋	252	26.53 S	68.19 W
San Francisco, University v²	282	37.46 N	122.26 W
San Francisco Bay c	226	37.43 N	122.17 W
San Francisco Creek ≃	196	29.53 N	102.19 W
San Francisco Culhuacán ◆⁸	286a	19.20 N	99.08 W
San Francisco de Borja	232	27.53 N	106.41 W
San Francisco de Horizonte	196	25.56 N	103.26 W
San Francisco de Lajas	234	23.07 N	105.07 W
San Francisco de la Paz	236	14.55 N	86.14 W
San Francisco del Chañar	252	29.47 S	63.56 W
San Francisco del Monte de Oro	252	32.36 S	66.08 W
San Francisco del Rincón	234	21.01 N	101.51 W
San Francisco Libre	236	12.30 N	86.18 W
San Francisco Maritime State Historical Park ◆	282	37.48 N	122.27 W
San Francisco State Fish and Game Refuge ◆⁴	282	37.35 N	122.25 W
San Francisco State University v²	282	37.43 N	122.28 W
San Francisco Tlaltelalpa	234	19.18 N	99.46 W
San Francisco Tlaltenco ◆⁸	286a	19.17 N	99.01 W
San Francisco Zoological Gardens ⌘	282	37.44 N	122.30 W
San Francisquito Creek ≃	282	37.28 N	122.07 W
San Franco, Cerro ʌ	252	25.51 S	87.18 W
San Fratello	70	38.01 N	14.36 E
San Fratello ≃	70	38.02 N	14.34 E
Sanga, Ang.	152	11.07 S	15.22 E
Sanga, Burkina	150	11.10 N	0.10 E
Sanga, Mali	150	14.28 N	3.19 W
Sanga, Zaïre	154	7.02 S	28.21 E
San Gabriel, Ec.	246	0.36 N	77.49 W
San Gabriel, Ca., U.S.	280	34.05 N	118.06 W
San Gabriel ≃, Ca., U.S.	280	33.45 N	118.07 W
San Gabriel ≃, Tx., U.S.	222	30.46 N	97.01 W
San Gabriel, Isla I	232	24.26 N	110.19 W
San Gabriel, North Fork ≃, Ca., U.S.	280	34.15 N	117.52 W
San Gabriel, North Fork ≃, Tx., U.S.	196	30.38 N	97.41 W
San Gabriel, South Fork ≃	196	30.38 N	97.41 W
San Gabriel Arcangel, Mission v¹	280	34.06 N	118.06 W
San Gabriel Chilac	234	18.19 N	97.21 W
San Gabriel Dam ◆⁶	280	34.13 N	117.52 W
San Gabriel Mountains ʌ	280	34.20 N	118.00 W
San Gabriel Peak ʌ	280	34.13 N	118.06 W
San Gabriel Reservoir ⊜¹	228	34.13 N	117.51 W
Sangačal, mys ›	84	40.13 N	49.30 E
San Galgano, Abbazia di v¹	66	43.10 N	11.10 E
Šangaly	24	61.08 N	43.19 E
Sangamankanda Point ›	122	6.29 N	81.52 E
Sangamner	122	19.34 N	74.13 E
Sangamon ≃	219	39.37 N	90.40 W
Sangamon, South ≃	194	40.07 N	90.20 W

Nome	Página	Lat.º′	Long.º′ W = Oeste
Sanga Sanga Island I	116	5.04 N	119.47 E
Sangat	123	30.05 N	74.50 E
Sangatte	50	50.56 N	1.45 E
San Gavino Monreale	71	39.33 N	8.47 E
Sangay ʌ¹	246	2.00 S	78.20 W
Sangay, Parque Nacional ◆	246	1.50 S	78.20 W
Sangayán, Isla I	248	13.51 S	76.28 W
Sang Bast	128	35.59 N	59.46 E
Sangbê	152	6.03 N	12.28 E
Sangchris Lake ⊜¹	219	39.35 N	89.30 W
Sangchris Lake State Park ◆	219	39.38 N	89.28 W
Sangchungshih	100	25.04 N	121.29 E
Sangeang, Pulau I	115b	8.12 S	119.04 E
Sang-e Māsheh	120	33.08 N	67.27 E
San Gemini	66	42.37 N	12.33 E
San Genesio Atesino	64	46.32 N	11.20 E
Sangenjaya ◆⁸	268	35.38 N	139.40 E
Sanger, Ca., U.S.	228	36.42 N	119.33 W
Sanger, Tx., U.S.	196	33.21 N	97.10 W
Sangerhausen	54	51.28 N	11.17 E
San Germán	240m	18.05 N	67.03 W
San Germano	62	45.21 N	8.15 E
San Gerónimo	226	38.01 N	122.39 W
San Gerónimo, Arroyo ≃	258	33.57 S	56.05 W
Sangerville	188	45.10 N	69.21 W
Sanggan ≃	90	40.21 N	115.21 E
Sanggar, Teluk c	115b	8.20 S	118.18 E
Sanggau	112	0.08 N	110.36 E
Sanggé-ri ◆⁸	271b	37.41 N	127.05 E
Sanggin Dalai	102	38.11 N	105.17 E
Sanggona	112	3.52 S	121.46 E
Sangha □⁵, Centraf.	152	3.35 N	16.20 E
Sangha □⁵, Congo	152	1.00 N	15.30 E
Sangha ≃	152	1.13 S	16.49 E
Sanghar	120	26.02 N	68.57 E
San Giacomo (Sankt Jakob in Pfitsch)	64	46.57 N	11.36 E
San Giacomo Filippo	64	46.20 N	9.21 E
Sanghe, Kepulauan II	112	3.00 N	125.30 E
Sanghe, Pulau I	112	3.35 N	125.32 E
Sangin dalaj nuur ⊜	88	49.17 N	99.00 E
San Gil	246	6.33 N	73.08 W
Sangilen, chrebet ʌ	88	50.18 N	96.30 E
San Gimignano	64	43.28 N	11.02 E
San Ginesio	66	43.06 N	13.19 E
San Gion	58	46.38 N	8.50 E
San Giorgio	68	40.51 N	14.23 E
San Giorgio Canavese	62	45.20 N	7.48 E
San Giorgio della Richinvelda	64	46.03 N	12.52 E
San Giorgio del Sannio	68	41.04 N	14.51 E
San Giorgio di Lomellina	62	45.10 N	8.47 E
San Giorgio di Nogaro	64	45.50 N	13.13 E
San Giorgio di Piano	64	44.39 N	11.22 E
San Giorgio Ionico	68	40.27 N	17.23 E
San Giorgio la Molara	68	41.16 N	14.55 E
San Giorgio Lucano	68	40.07 N	16.23 E
San Giorgio Monferrato	62	45.07 N	8.23 E
San Giorgio Morgeto	68	38.23 N	16.06 E
San Giorgio Piacentino	64	44.57 N	9.44 E
San Giorgio su Legnano	266b	45.34 N	8.55 E
San Giovanni (Sankt Johann)	64	46.38 N	11.44 E
San Giovanni al Timavo (Sankt Johann in Ahrn)	64	46.58 N	11.57 E
San Giovanni a Piro	68	40.03 N	15.27 E
San Giovanni-Bianco	58	45.52 N	9.39 E
San Giovanni d'Asso	66	43.09 N	11.35 E
San Giovanni Gemini	70	37.38 N	13.39 E
San Giovanni Ilarione	64	45.30 N	11.15 E
San Giovanni in Croce	64	45.05 N	10.22 E
San Giovanni in Fiore	68	39.15 N	16.42 E
San Giovanni in Laterano v¹	267a	41.53 N	12.30 E
San Giovanni in Persiceto	64	44.38 N	11.11 E
San Giovanni la Punta	70	37.35 N	15.07 E
San Giovanni Lupatoto	64	45.23 N	11.03 E
San Giovanni Rotondo	68	41.42 N	15.44 E
San Giovanni Suergiu	71	39.07 N	8.31 E
San Giovanni Valdarno	68	43.34 N	11.32 E
San Giuliano, Lago di ⊜	68	40.37 N	16.30 E
San Giuliano Milanese	266b	45.24 N	9.17 E
San Giuliano Terme	64	43.46 N	10.26 E
San Giuseppe, It.	62	44.22 N	8.18 E
San Giuseppe, It.	70	37.58 N	13.11 E
San Giuseppe Vesuviano	68	40.50 N	14.30 E
San Giusto	66	43.33 N	12.10 E
San Giusto, Aeroporto di ⊼	66	43.11 N	10.21 E
San Giusto Canavese	62	45.19 N	7.49 E
Sangju	98	36.26 N	128.09 E
Sangkapura	115a	5.52 S	112.40 E
Sãngké ≃	110	13.13 N	103.41 E
Sangkhla	110	14.39 N	103.52 E
Sangkulirang	112	0.59 N	117.58 E
Sãngla	123	31.43 N	73.23 E
Sangley Point ›	269†	14.30 N	120.55 E
Sãngli	122	16.52 N	74.34 E
Sangliuoshu	98	37.31 N	117.43 E
Sangmélima	152	2.56 N	11.59 E
Sangngagqoiling	102	28.33 N	93.00 E
Sangnyŏng-ni	98	38.14 N	126.54 E
Sango	270	34.36 S	135.42 E
San Godenzo	66	43.55 N	11.37 E
Sangolquí	246	0.19 S	78.27 W
San Gorgonio Mountain ʌ	204	34.06 N	116.50 W
San Gottardo, Passo del ⋋	58	46.33 N	8.34 E
Sangou	98	41.02 N	118.11 E
Sangre de Cristo Mountains ʌ	200	37.30 N	105.15 W
San Gregorio, Arg.	252	34.19 S	62.02 W
San Gregorio, It.	62	42.19 N	13.29 E
San Gregorio, Ur.	252	32.37 S	55.40 W
San Gregorio, Ur.	258	33.57 S	56.45 W
San Gregorio ◆⁸	286a	19.15 N	99.03 W
San Gregorio, Arroyo ≃	258	33.59 S	56.50 W
San Gregorio Creek ≃	226	37.19 N	122.25 W
San Gregorio Magno	68	40.39 N	15.24 E
San Gregorio State Beach ◆	226	38.03 N	122.24 W
Sangre Grande	241†	10.35 N	61.07 W
Sangro ≃	66	42.14 N	14.32 E
Sangrūr	123	30.14 N	75.50 E
Sangsues, Lac aux ⊜	190	46.29 N	77.57 W
Sanguanmiao	100	32.25 N	114.04 E
Sanguanyingzi	104	41.39 N	120.44 E

Nome	Página	Lat.º′	Long.º′ W = Oeste
Sangudo	182	53.53 N	114.54 W
Sangue, Rio do ≃	248	11.01 S	58.39 W
Sangüesa	34	42.35 N	1.17 W
Sanguinetto	64	45.11 N	11.09 E
Sanguli	104	40.45 N	124.14 E
Sânguli	272c	18.56 N	73.07 E
Sangutane ≃	156	24.07 S	33.47 E
Sangvor, Taj.	85	38.47 N	71.12 E
Sangvor, Taj.	85	38.53 N	71.06 E
Sangwa	154	5.30 S	26.00 E
Sangya	120	30.52 N	91.40 E
Sangyuanbao	106	31.37 N	118.53 E
Sangyuanzhen	107	30.30 N	103.26 E
Sangzhi	102	29.18 N	110.02 E
Sangzidian	98	36.46 N	116.55 E
Sanhe, Zhg.	100	24.24 N	116.34 E
Sanhe, Zhg.	105	39.59 N	117.04 E
Sanhechang, Zhg.	107	31.22 N	106.48 E
Sanhechang, Zhg.	107	30.04 N	105.01 E
Sanhecun	98	42.28 N	129.29 E
Sanheji	100	32.42 N	117.55 E
Sanhekou	106	31.50 N	120.08 E
Sanhetun	104	42.38 N	123.38 E
Sanhezhen	89	52.34 N	126.02 E
Sanhezhuang	105	40.04 N	116.18 E
Sanhui, Zhg.	100	30.06 N	106.36 E
Sanhui, Zhg.	100	27.55 N	115.24 E
Sanhür	142	29.25 N	30.46 E
Sanhür al-Madīnah	142	29.51 N	30.40 E
Sani	142	24.25 N	120.46 E
Sanibel	220	26.26 N	82.01 W
Sanibel Island I	220	26.27 N	82.06 W
Sãnī Bherī ≃	124	28.42 N	82.16 E
San Ignacio, Arg.	252	27.16 S	55.32 W
San Ignacio, C.R.	236	9.48 N	84.09 W
San Ignacio, Hond.	236	14.38 N	87.02 W
San Ignacio, Méx.	234	27.27 N	112.51 W
San Ignacio, Méx.	234	23.12 N	100.12 W
San Ignacio, Méx.	234	23.55 N	106.25 W
San Ignacio, Para.	252	26.52 S	57.03 W
San Ignacio, Perú	248	5.08 S	78.59 W
San Ignacio, Isla I	232	25.25 N	108.54 W
San Ignacio, Laguna ⊜	232	26.54 N	113.13 W
San Ignacio de Moxo	248	14.53 S	65.36 W
San Ignacio de Velasco	248	16.23 S	60.59 W
San Ildefonso, Cape ›	116	16.02 N	121.59 E
San Ildefonso, Cerro ʌ	236	15.31 N	88.17 W
San Ildefonso Indian Reservation ◆⁴	200	35.53 N	106.08 W
San Ildefonso o La Granja	34	40.54 N	4.00 W
San Ildefonso Peninsula › ¹	116	16.10 N	122.05 E
San Ildefonso Villa Alta	234	17.21 N	96.09 W
San'in-kaigan-kokuritsu-kōen ◆	96	35.38 N	134.38 E
Sanis	246	5.59 N	29.54 E
Sani Pass ⋋	158	29.34 S	29.19 E
San Isidro, Arg.	258	28.27 S	65.44 W
San Isidro, Arg.	258	34.27 S	58.30 W
San Isidro, C.R.	236	9.22 N	83.42 W
San Isidro, Méx.	196	31.31 N	106.18 W
San Isidro, Nic.	236	12.56 N	86.12 W
San Isidro, Perú	288	12.07 S	77.03 W
San Isidro, Pil.	116	11.24 N	124.21 E
San Isidro ≃, Tx., U.S.	196	26.42 N	98.27 W
San Isidro □⁵	288	34.29 S	58.33 W

Nome	Página	Lat.º′	Long.º′ W = Oeste
San Jorge, Bahía de c	200	31.12 N	113.15 W
San Jorge, Cabo ›	254	45.47 S	67.21 W
San Jorge, Canal de — Saint George's Channel ʋ	28	52.00 N	6.00 W
San Jorge, Golfo c	254	46.00 S	67.00 W
San Jorge Island I	175e	8.27 S	159.35 E
San José, Arg.	252	27.46 S	55.47 W
San José, C.R.	236	9.56 N	84.05 W
San José, N. Mar. Is.	174n	15.09 N	145.43 E
San José, Para.	258	25.33 S	56.45 W
San José, Pil.	116	10.45 N	121.56 E
San José, Pil.	116	15.48 N	121.00 E
San José, Pil.	116	12.27 N	121.03 E
San José, Ca., U.S.	226	37.20 N	121.53 W
San José, Ca., U.S.	282	37.20 N	121.53 W
San José, Il., U.S.	194	40.18 N	89.36 W
San José, N.M., U.S.	200	35.23 N	105.28 W
San José, Ven.	286c	10.34 N	66.57 W
San José □⁷	236	9.40 N	84.00 W
San José ≃	258	34.15 S	56.45 W
San José □⁷	286b	22.57 N	82.14 W
San José ≃, B.C., Can.	182	52.14 N	122.15 W
San José ≃, Ur.	258	34.38 S	56.29 W
San José, Arroyo ≃	282	38.03 N	122.30 W
San José, Golfo c	254	42.20 S	64.18 W
San José, Isla I, Méx.	232	25.00 N	110.38 W
San José, Isla I, Pan.	246	8.15 N	79.07 W
San José, Laguna ⊜	240m	18.25 N	66.01 W
San José, Mission v¹	282	37.32 N	121.55 W
San José, Rio ≃	200	34.52 N	107.01 W
San José Ayquila	234	17.58 N	97.57 W
San José Batuc	232	29.15 N	109.44 W
San José Buenavista	236	13.49 N	90.19 W
San José Creek ≃	280	34.01 N	118.03 W
San José de Bácum	196	27.34 N	101.23 W
San José de Buan	116	12.02 N	125.01 E
San José de Chiquitos	248	17.51 S	60.47 W
San José de Copán	236	14.54 N	88.44 W
San José de Feliciano	252	30.23 S	58.45 W
San José de Galipán	240p	10.35 N	66.54 W
San José de Gracia	200	10.37 N	66.54 W
San José de Guanipa	246	8.54 N	64.09 W
San José de Guaribe	246	9.52 N	65.48 W
San José de Iturbide	234	21.00 N	100.23 W
San José de Jáchal	252	30.14 S	68.45 W
San José de la Esquina	252	33.06 S	61.42 W
San José de la Parilla	234	23.44 N	104.07 W
San José de la Popa	196	26.10 N	100.47 W
San José de las Flores	234	17.20 N	95.24 W
San José de las Lajas	240p	22.58 N	82.09 W
San José de las Raíces	234	24.35 N	100.14 W
San José del Cabo	232	23.03 N	109.41 W
San José del Guaviare	246	2.35 N	72.38 W
San José de Llanetes	234	23.03 N	103.16 W
San José de Lourdes	248	23.18 N	103.01 W
San José del Valle	234	23.20 N	98.24 W
San José del Mayo	234	34.20 S	56.42 W
San José de Ocuné	246	4.15 N	70.20 W
San José de Sisa	248	6.37 S	76.39 W
San José el Real, Catedral de v¹	266a	40.25 N	3.42 W
San José Hills ʌ²	280	34.04 N	117.49 W
San José Island I	196	28.10 N	96.45 W
San José Municipal Airport ⊼	282	37.22 N	121.56 W
San Jose State University v²	282	37.20 N	121.53 W
San Juan, Arg.	252	31.32 S	68.31 W
San Juan, Guat.	236	15.52 N	88.53 W
San Juan, Méx.	196	31.04 N	104.36 W
San Juan, Perú	248	15.21 S	75.10 W
San Juan, Pil.	116	13.50 N	121.24 E
San Juan, Pil.	116	16.40 N	120.20 E
San Juan, Pil.	116	8.25 N	126.20 E
San Juan, P.R.	240m	18.28 N	66.07 W
San Juan ≃	232	31.00 S	69.00 W
San Juan □⁶	252	48.34 S	122.59 W
San Juan ≃, Arg.	252	32.17 S	67.22 W

Nome	Página	Lat.º′	Long.º′ W = Oeste
San Juan de los Lagos	234	21.18 N	102.33 W
San Juan de los Morros	246	9.55 N	67.21 W
San Juan del Río, Méx.	232	24.47 N	104.27 W
San Juan del Río, Méx.	234	20.23 N	100.00 W
San Juan del Salado	234	23.18 N	101.56 W
San Juan del Sur	236	11.15 N	85.52 W
San Juan de Lurigancho	286d	11.59 S	77.01 W
San Juan de Micay ≃	246	3.05 N	77.32 W
San Juan de Miraflores	286d	12.11 S	76.57 W
San Juan de Payara	246	7.39 N	67.36 W
San Juan de Sabinas	196	27.55 N	101.18 W
San Juan Evangelista	234	17.54 N	95.08 W
San Juan Guichicovi	234	16.58 N	95.08 W
San Juanico	232	26.15 N	112.24 W
San Juanillo	236	10.02 N	85.44 W
San Juan Indian Reservation ◆⁴	200	36.03 N	106.04 W
San Juan Island I	224	48.32 N	123.05 W
San Juan Island National Historical Park ◆	224	48.28 N	123.00 W
San Juan Islands II	224	48.36 N	122.50 W
San Juanito	224	21.43 N	106.38 W
San Juan Ixcaquixtla	234	18.27 N	97.49 W
San Juan Ixtayopan ◆⁸	286a	19.14 N	99.00 W
San Juan Lachao	234	16.14 N	97.09 W
San Juan Mazatlán	234	17.02 N	95.25 W
San Juan Mountains ʌ	200	37.35 N	107.10 W
San Juan Nepomuceno, Col.	246	9.57 N	75.05 W
San Juan Nepomuceno, Para.	252	26.06 S	55.58 W
San Juan Peyotán	234	22.24 N	104.21 W
San Juan Quiahije	234	16.17 N	97.20 W
San Juan Sacatepéquez	236	14.43 N	90.39 W
San Juan y Martínez	240p	22.16 N	83.50 W
San Julián, Pil.	116	11.45 N	125.27 E
San Julian, Quebrada ≃	286c	10.37 N	66.51 W
San Justo, Arg.	252	30.47 S	60.35 W
San Justo, Arg.	258	34.40 S	58.33 W
San Justo, Aeródromo ⊼	288	34.44 S	58.36 W
Sankanbiaiwa ʌ	150	8.56 N	10.48 W
Sankarani ≃	150	11.20 N	8.19 W
Sankarankovil	122	9.10 N	77.33 E
Sankarpur	272b	22.51 N	88.27 E
Sãnkdaha	126	22.46 N	89.10 E
Sankeng	100	23.36 N	112.48 E
Sankertown	214	40.28 N	78.35 W
Sankeshu	104	42.38 N	122.25 E
Sankey Brook ≃	262	53.22 N	2.38 W
Sankh ≃	124	22.15 N	84.48 E
Sankheda	120	22.10 N	73.35 E
Sankosh ≃	124	26.48 N	89.56 E
Sãnkra	120	21.18 N	82.39 E
Sãnkrail	272b	22.34 N	88.14 E
Sankt Aegyd am Neuwalde	61	52.52 N	15.35 E
Sankt Andrä	61	46.46 N	14.49 E
Sankt Andrä vor dem Hagenthale	264b	48.19 N	16.13 E
Sankt Andreasberg	54	51.43 N	10.31 E
Sankt Anton am Arlberg	58	47.08 N	10.16 E
Sankt Antönien	58	46.58 N	9.49 E
Sankt Gallen, Ost.	61	47.41 N	14.37 E
Sankt Gallen, Schw.	58	47.25 N	9.23 E
Sankt Gallen □³	58	47.25 N	9.21 E
Sankt Gallenkirch	58	47.01 N	9.59 E
Sankt Georgen, Dtsch.	58	48.07 N	8.20 E
Sankt Georgen, Dtsch.	54	53.59 N	7.47 E
Sankt Georgen, Ost.	61	46.43 N	14.55 E
Sankt Georgen im Attergau	64	47.56 N	13.29 E
Sankt Gertraud — Santa Gertrude	64	46.29 N	10.53 E
Sankt Gilgen	64	47.46 N	13.22 E
Sankt Goar	58	50.09 N	7.43 E
Sankt Goarshausen	56	50.09 N	7.44 E
Sankt Helena — Saint Helena □²	18	15.57 S	5.42 W
Sankt Hubert	56	51.23 N	6.26 E
Sankt Jakob im Lesachtal	64	46.41 N	12.56 E
Sankt Jakob im Rosental	61	46.33 N	14.03 E
Sankt Jakob in Defereggen	64	46.55 N	12.20 E
Sankt Jakob — San Giacomo	64	46.57 N	11.36 E
Sankt Johann am Tauern	64	47.21 N	14.29 E
Sankt Johann im Pongau	64	47.21 N	13.12 E
Sankt Johann im Walde	64	46.54 N	12.37 E
Sankt Johann in Tirol	64	47.31 N	12.26 E
Sankt Johann — San Giovanni	64	46.38 N	11.44 E
Sankt Kanzian	61	46.37 N	14.34 E
Sankt Leonhard am Forst	64	48.09 N	15.17 E
Sankt Leonhard im Pitztal	58	47.04 N	10.51 E
Sankt Leonhard — San Leonardo	52	46.49 N	11.15 E
Sankt Lorenz ◆⁸	64	53.51 N	10.40 E
Sankt Lorenzen im Lesachtal	64	46.42 N	12.47 E
Sankt Lorenzen — San Lorenzo di Sebato	64	46.47 N	11.54 E
Sankt Lorenz-Golf — Saint Lawrence, Gulf of	186	48.00 N	62.00 W
Sankt Lorenz-Insel — Saint Lawrence Island I	180	63.30 N	170.30 W
Sankt Mang	58	47.44 N	10.21 E
Sankt Margarethen an der Raab	61	47.03 N	15.45 E
Sankt Margrethen	58	47.27 N	9.36 E
Sankt Martin an der Raab	61	46.55 N	16.08 E
Sankt Martin in Gsies — San Martino in Casies	64	46.49 N	12.14 E

	Español	Deutsch	Español	Français	Português
≃	River	Fluß	Río	Rivière	Rio
⌇	Canal	Kanal	Canal	Canal	Canal
↯	Waterfall, Rapids	Wasserfall, Stromschnellen	Cascada, Rápidos	Chute d'eau, Rapides	Cascata, Rápidos
ʋ	Strait	Meeresstraße	Estrecho	Détroit	Estreito
c	Bay, Gulf	Bucht, Golf	Bahía, Golfo	Baie, Golfe	Baía, Golfo
⊜	Lake, Lakes	See, Seen	Lago, Lagos	Lac, Lacs	Lago, Lagos
≋	Swamp	Sumpf	Pantano	Marais	Pântano
⌘	Ice Features, Glacier	Eis- und Gletscherformen	Accidentes Glaciares	Formes glaciares	Acidentes glaciares
�⊽	Other Hydrographic Features	Andere Hydrographische Objekte	Otros Elementos Hidrográficos	Autres données hydrographiques	Outros acidentes hidrográficos
◆	Submarine Features	Untermeerische Objekte	Accidentes Submarinos	Formes de relief sous-marin	Acidentes submarinos
□	Political Unit	Politische Einheit	Unidad Política	Entité politique	Unidade política
v	Cultural Institution	Kulturelle Institution	Institución Cultural	Institution culturelle	Instituição cultural
⌐	Historical Site	Historische Stätte	Sitio Histórico	Site historique	Sítio histórico
≍	Recreational Site	Erholungs- und Ferienort	Sitio de Recreo	Centre de loisirs	Area de Lazer
⊼	Airport	Flughafen	Aeropuerto	Aéroport	Aeroporto
⊡	Military Installation	Militäranlage	Instalación Militar	Installation militaire	Instalação militar
◆	Miscellaneous	Verschiedenes	Misceláneo	Divers	Diversos

ENGLISH — Name, Page, Lat.°′, Long.°′ / DEUTSCH — Name, Seite, Breite°′, Länge°′ E = Ost

Symbols in the index entries represent the broad categories identified in the key at the right. Symbols with superior numbers (⋏[1]) identify subcategories (see complete key on page *I · 1).*

Symbole im Register stellen die rechts im Schlüssel erklärten Kategorien dar. Symbole mit hochgestellten Ziffern (⋏[1]) bezeichnen Unterabteilungen einer Kategorie (vgl. vollständiger Schlüssel auf Seite *I · 1).*

Los símbolos incluídos en el texto del índice representan las grandes categorias identificadas con la clave a la derecha. Los símbolos con numeros en su parte superior (⋏[1]) identifican las subcategorías (véase la clave completa en la página *I · 1).*

Les symboles de l'index représentent les catégories indiquées dans la légende à droite. Les symboles suivis d'un indice (⋏[1]) représentent des sous-catégories (voir légende complète à la page *I · 1).*

Os símbolos incluídos no texto do índice representam as grandes categorias identificadas com a chave à direita. Os símbolos com números em sua parte superior (⋏[1]) identificam as subcategorias (veja-se a chave completa à página *I · 1).*

Symbol	English	Deutsch	Español	Français	Português
∧	Mountain	Berg	Montaña	Montagne	Montanha
⋏	Mountains	Gebirge	Montañas	Montagnes	Montanhas
)(	Pass	Paß	Paso	Col	Passo
V	Valley, Canyon	Tal, Cañon	Valle, Cañón	Vallée, Canyon	Vale, Canhão
≃	Plain	Ebene	Llano	Plaine	Planície
›	Cape	Kap	Cabo	Cap	Cabo
I	Island	Insel	Isla	Île	Ilha
II	Islands	Inseln	Islas	Îles	Ilhas
◆	Other Topographic Features	Andere Topographische Objekte	Otros Elementos Topográficos	Autres données topographiques	Outros acidentes topográficos

ESPAÑOL

Nombre	Página	Lat.°′	Long.°′ W = Oeste
Santa Cruz Meyehualco ◆[8]	286a	19.20 N	99.03 W
Santa Cruz Mountains ⋏	226	37.15 N	122.00 W
Santa Cruz Point >	116	15.44 N	119.52 E
Santa Cruz Tacache de Mina	234	17.51 N	98.07 W
Santadi	71	39.05 N	8.43 E
Santa Domenica Talao	68	39.49 N	15.51 E
Santa Domenica Vittoria	70	37.55 N	14.58 E
Sant Adrià de Besòs	266d	41.25 N	2.14 E
Santa Elena, Arg.	252	30.57 S	59.48 W
Santa Elena, Ec.	246	2.14 S	80.51 W
Santa Elena, El Sal.	236	13.22 N	88.25 W
Santa Elena, Méx.	196	27.59 N	103.56 W
Santa Elena, Méx.	232	27.28 N	102.33 W
Santa Elena, Méx.	234	18.39 N	101.34 W
Santa Elena ≃	248	15.42 S	67.13 W
Santa Elena, Bahía de ⊂	246	2.06 S	80.53 W
Santa Elena, Golfo de ⊂	236	10.59 N	85.50 W
Santa Elena, Punta >, C.R.	236	10.54 N	85.57 W
Santa Elena, Punta >, Ec.	246	2.11 S	81.00 W
Santa Elena del Gomero	286e	33.29 S	70.46 W
Santa Elena de Uairén	246	4.37 N	61.08 W
Santa Elisabetta	70	37.26 N	13.33 E
Santa Eufemia	34	38.36 N	4.54 W
Santa Eugenia	34	42.33 N	9.00 W
Santa Eulalia, Esp.	34	40.34 N	1.19 W
Santa Eulalia, Guat.	236	15.45 N	91.29 W
Santa Eulària del Riu	34	38.59 N	1.31 E
Santa Fe, Arg.	252	31.38 S	60.42 W
Santa Fé, Bra.	255	15.40 S	51.16 W
Santa Fé, Bra.	255	23.01 S	51.48 W
Santa Fe, Esp.	34	37.11 N	3.43 W
Santa Fe, Hond.	236	15.55 N	86.05 W
Santa Fé, Pan.	236	8.31 N	81.05 W
Santa Fe, Pil.	116	11.09 N	123.47 E
Santa Fe, Pil.	116	16.10 N	120.57 E
Santa Fe, Pil.	116	12.10 N	122.00 E
Santa Fe, Mo., U.S.	219	39.22 N	91.49 W
Santa Fe, N.M., U.S.	200	35.41 N	105.56 W
Santa Fe □[4]	252	31.00 S	61.00 W
Santa Fé ◆[8]	286b	23.05 N	82.31 W
Santa Fe ≃, Fl., U.S.	192	29.53 N	82.53 W
Santa Fe ≃, N.M., U.S.	200	35.36 N	106.20 W
Santa Fé, Aeropuerto ⊠	286b	23.04 N	82.28 W
Santa Fe, Isla I	246a	0.49 S	90.04 W
Santa Fé, Ribeirão ≃	287b	23.24 S	46.48 W
Santa Fe Baldy ∧	200	35.50 N	105.46 W
Santa Fe Dam ◆[6]	280	34.07 N	117.58 W
Santa Fe de Bogotá	246	4.36 N	74.05 W
Santa Fe de Minas	255	16.42 S	45.26 W
Santa Fé do Sul	255	20.13 S	50.56 W
Santa Fe Flood Control Basin ≊[1]	280	34.07 N	117.58 W
Santa Fe Springs	280	33.56 N	118.04 W
Santa Filomena	250	9.07 S	45.56 W
Santa Fiora	66	42.50 N	11.35 E
Santa Flavia	70	38.05 N	13.31 E
Sant'Agata Bolognese	64	44.40 N	11.08 E
Sant'Agata de'Goti	68	41.05 N	14.30 E
Sant'Agata del Bianco	68	38.05 N	16.05 E
Sant'Agata di Militello	70	38.04 N	14.38 E
Sant'Agata di Puglia	68	41.09 N	15.23 E
Sant'Agata Feltria	66	43.52 N	12.12 E
Sant'Agata sul Santerno	66	44.26 N	11.51 E
Santa Gertrude (Sankt Gertraud)	64	46.29 N	10.53 E
Santa Gertrudis	196	26.09 N	98.44 W
Santa Giusta, Stagno di ⊜	71	39.52 N	8.35 E
Sant'Agostino	64	44.48 N	11.23 E
Sāntāhār	124	24.48 N	88.59 E
Santa Helena	250	2.14 S	45.18 W
Santa Helena de Goiás	255	17.43 S	50.35 W
Santai, Zhg.	85	39.14 N	77.42 E
Santai, Zhg.	86	44.35 N	81.18 E
Santai, Zhg.	102	31.10 N	105.02 E
Santai, Zhg.	104	41.48 N	121.53 E
Santai, Zhg.	104	41.56 N	123.11 E
Santai, Zhg.	105	38.58 N	115.49 E
Santa Inês	255	13.17 S	39.48 W
Santa Inés, Bahía ⊂	232	26.59 N	111.59 W
Santa Inés, Isla I	254	53.45 S	72.45 W
Santa Inés Ahuatempan	234	18.25 N	98.01 W
Santa Iria de Azóia	266c	38.51 N	9.05 W
Santa Isabel, Arg.	252	36.15 S	66.56 W
Santa Isabel, Arg.	252	33.54 S	61.42 W
Santa Isabel, Bra.	256	23.19 S	46.14 W
Santa Isabel, Ec.	246	3.21 S	79.19 W
Santa Isabel, Méx.	234	23.15 N	100.52 W
Santa Isabel, P.R.	240m	17.58 N	66.24 W
Santa Isabel I	175e	8.00 S	159.00 E
Santa Isabel ≃	236	15.59 N	90.00 W
Santa Isabel, Pico de ∧	152	3.35 N	8.46 E
Santa Isabel Creek ≃	196	27.39 N	99.38 W
Santa Isabel de Sihuas	248	16.20 S	72.06 W
Santa Isabel do Araguaia	250	6.07 S	48.19 W
Santa Isabel do Rio Prêto	256	22.14 S	44.05 W
Santa Isabel → Malabo	152	3.45 N	8.47 E
Santaizi	104	41.21 N	121.36 E
Santa Josefa	116	8.02 N	125.57 E
Santa Julia	286e	33.30 S	70.38 W
Santa Juliana	255	19.19 S	47.32 W
Sant'Alberto	66	44.32 N	12.09 E
Sant'Alfio	70	37.44 N	15.08 E
Sāntalpur	120	23.45 N	71.10 E
Santa Luce	66	43.28 N	10.34 E
Santa Lucía, Arg.	252	28.59 S	59.06 W
Santa Lucía, Arg.	252	31.32 S	68.29 W
Santa Lucía, Cuba	240p	21.02 N	76.00 W
Santa Lucía, Cuba	240p	22.40 N	83.58 W
Santa Lucia, It.	64	46.28 N	10.21 E
Santa Lucía, Ur.	258	34.27 S	56.24 W
Santa Lucía, Ven.	246	8.07 N	69.46 W
Santa Lucía ≃	258	34.48 S	56.22 W
Santa Lucia, Cabo → Saint Lucia, Cape >	158	28.25 S	32.25 E
Santa Lucía, Cuchilla ⋏[2]	258	34.09 S	56.11 W
Santa Lucía Chico ≃	258	34.21 S	56.20 W
Santa Lucía Cotzumalguapa	236	14.20 N	91.01 W
Santa Lucia Creek ≃	226	36.13 N	121.30 W
Santa Lucia del Mela	70	38.09 N	15.17 E
Santa Lucia di Piave	64	45.51 N	12.17 E
Santa Lucia Range ⋏	226	36.00 N	121.20 W
Santa Lucía → Saint Lucia □[1]	241f	13.53 N	60.58 W
Santaluz	250	11.15 S	39.22 W
Santa Luzia, Bra.	250	6.53 S	36.56 W
Santa Luzia, Port.	34	37.44 N	8.24 W
Santa Luzia I	150a	16.46 N	24.45 W
Santa Magdalena	252	34.30 S	63.56 W
Santa-Manza, Golfu di ⊂	71	41.37 N	9.22 E
Santa Margarita	226	35.23 N	120.36 W
Santa Margarita ≃	228	33.14 N	117.25 W

FRANÇAIS

Nom	Page	Lat.°′	Long.°′ W = Ouest
Santa Margarita, Isla I	232	24.27 N	111.50 W
Santa Margarita Lake ⊜[1]	226	35.20 N	120.28 W
Santa Margarita Mountains ⋏	228	33.30 N	117.25 W
Santa Margherita di Belice	70	37.41 N	13.01 E
Santa Margherita Ligure	62	44.20 N	9.12 E
Santa María, Arg.	252	26.41 S	66.02 W
Santa Maria, Bra.	252	29.41 S	53.48 W
Santa Maria, C.V.	150a	16.36 N	22.54 W
Santa María, C.R.	236	9.39 N	83.57 W
Santa María, Méx.	196	28.02 N	101.38 W
Santa María, Pan.	236	8.07 N	80.40 W
Santa Maria, Pil.	116	17.22 N	120.29 E
Santa María, P.R.	240m	18.09 N	65.26 W
Santa Maria, Schw.	58	46.16 N	9.09 E
Santa Maria, Schw.	58	46.36 N	10.24 E
Santa Maria, Ca., U.S.	204	34.57 N	120.26 W
Santa Maria I, Port.	148a	36.58 N	25.06 W
Santa Maria I, Vanuatu	175f	14.15 S	167.30 E
Santa Maria ≃, Bra.	252	29.48 S	54.56 W
Santa Maria ≃, Bra.	252	21.50 S	54.53 W
Santa María ≃, Méx.	232	31.00 N	107.14 W
Santa María ≃, Méx.	234	21.48 N	99.10 W
Santa María ≃, Pan.	236	8.06 N	80.29 W
Santa Maria ≃, Az., U.S.	200	34.19 N	113.31 W
Santa María, Bahía ⊂	232	25.04 N	108.06 W
Santa María, Cabo >	252	34.40 S	54.10 W
Santa Maria, Cabo de >, Ang.	152	13.25 S	12.32 E
Santa Maria, Cabo de >, Port.	34	36.58 N	7.54 W
Santa Maria, Cabo → Sainte-Marie, Cap >	157b	25.36 S	45.08 E
Santa Maria, Cape >	238	23.41 N	75.19 W
Santa María, Cayo I	240p	22.40 N	79.00 W
Santa María, Cerro ∧	286d	11.56 S	76.57 W
Santa Maria, Giogo di (Pass Umbrail))(	64	46.34 N	10.25 E
Santa María, Isla I, Chile	252	37.02 S	73.33 W
Santa María, Isla I, Ec.	246a	1.17 S	90.26 W
Santa Maria, Isola I	71	41.17 N	9.22 E
Santa María, Laguna de ⊜	200	31.07 N	107.16 W
Santa Maria, Ribeirão ≃	250	7.10 S	49.13 W
Santa María, Volcán ∧[1]	236	14.45 N	91.33 W
Santa María Ajoloapan	234	19.58 N	99.03 W
Santa Maria a Monte	66	43.42 N	10.42 E
Santa María Asunción Tlaxiaco	234	17.16 N	97.41 W
Santa Maria a Vico	68	41.02 N	14.29 E
Santa María Ayoquezco	234	16.41 N	96.50 W
Santa Maria Capua Vetere	68	41.05 N	14.15 E
Santa María Chimalapa	234	16.55 N	94.41 W
Santa María Colotepec	234	15.53 N	96.55 W
Santa Maria da Boa Vista	250	8.49 S	39.49 W
Santa Maria da Vitória	255	13.24 S	44.12 W
Santa Maria degli Angeli	66	43.03 N	12.34 E
Santa María de Huazamoto	234	22.30 N	104.30 W
Santa María de Ipire	246	8.49 N	65.19 W
Santa Maria de Itabira	255	19.27 S	43.08 W
Santa Maria del Cedro	68	39.45 N	15.50 E
Santa Maria della Versa	62	44.59 N	9.18 E
Santa Maria delle Grazie ψ[1]	266b	45.27 N	9.10 E
Santa María del Oro	232	25.56 N	105.22 W
Santa María de los Ángeles	234	22.11 N	103.14 W
Santa María del Refugio	234	23.44 N	101.14 W
Santa María del Río	234	21.48 N	100.45 W
Santa María del Valle	234	20.54 N	102.22 W
Santa Mariá de Mohovano	232	26.42 N	103.39 W
Santa Maria di Galeria ◆[8]	267a	42.01 N	12.19 E
Santa Maria di Leuca, Capo >	68	39.47 N	18.22 E
Santa Maria di Licodia	70	37.37 N	14.53 E
Santa Maria di Siponto ψ[1]	68	41.40 N	15.51 E
Santa Maria do Suaçuí	255	18.12 S	42.25 W
Santa María Huazolotitlán	234	16.17 N	97.56 W
Santa María Jalapa del Marqués	234	16.30 N	95.28 W
Santa María la Real de Nieva	34	41.04 N	4.24 W
Santa Maria Madalena	255	21.57 S	42.01 W
Santa Maria Maggiore	58	46.08 N	8.28 E
Santa Maria Maggiore ψ[1]	267a	41.53 N	12.30 E
Santa Maria Nuova	66	43.29 N	13.18 E
Santa-Maria-Siché	36	41.52 N	8.59 E
Santa María Tulpetlac	286a	19.34 N	99.03 W
Santa María Xadani	234	15.56 N	96.04 W
Santa María Zoquitlán	234	16.33 N	96.23 W
Santa Marinella	66	42.02 N	11.51 E
Santa Marta, Col.	246	11.15 N	74.13 W
Santa Marta, Guat.	236	13.58 N	91.18 W
Santa Marta, Cabo de >, Ang.	152	13.52 S	12.25 E
Santa Marta, Cabo de >, Moç.	158	26.05 S	32.58 E
Santa Marta, Cerro ∧	234	18.19 N	94.48 W
Santa Marta, Ciénaga Grande ⊂	246	10.50 N	74.25 W
Santa Marta Grande, Cabo de >	252	28.38 S	48.45 W
Sant'Ambrogio	64	45.31 N	10.50 E
Santa Mónica, Méx.	196	28.12 N	100.37 W
Santa Monica, Ca., U.S.	228	34.01 N	118.29 W
Santa Mónica ◆[8]	286c	10.29 N	66.53 W
Santa Monica Bay ⊂	228	33.54 N	118.25 W
Santa Monica Beach State Park ♠	280	34.01 N	118.30 W
Santa Monica Mountains ⋏	228	34.05 N	118.40 W
Santa Monica Mountains National Recreation Area ♠	228	34.05 N	118.45 W
Santa Monica Municipal Airport ⊠	280	34.01 N	118.27 W
Santan	112	0.03 S	117.28 E
Santana	255	12.59 S	44.03 W
Santana ◆[8]	287b	23.29 S	46.38 W
Santana ≃	255	19.43 S	51.02 W
Santana, Coxilha de ⋏[2]	252	31.15 S	55.15 W
Santana, Ilha de I	250	2.18 S	43.41 W
Santana, Ribeirão ≃	250	9.47 S	50.13 W

PORTUGUÊS

Nome	Página	Lat.°′	Long.°′ W = Oeste
Santana da Boa Vista	252	30.52 S	53.07 W
Santana da Vargem	256	21.15 S	45.30 W
Santana de Caldas	256	21.50 S	46.24 W
Santana de Cataguases	256	21.17 S	42.33 W
Santana de Parnaíba	256	23.27 S	46.55 W
Santana de Parnaíba □[7]	287b	23.27 S	46.54 W
Santana do Campestre	256	21.16 S	42.56 W
Santana do Capivari	256	22.14 S	44.56 W
Santana do Cariri	250	7.11 S	39.44 W
Santana do Deserto	256	21.57 S	43.11 W
Santana do Garambéu	256	21.36 S	44.06 W
Santana do Ipanema	250	9.22 S	37.14 W
Santana do Livramento	252	30.53 S	55.31 W
Santana do Matos	250	5.57 S	36.39 W
Santander, Col.	246	3.01 N	76.28 W
Santander, Esp.	34	43.28 N	3.48 W
Santander, Pil.	116	9.25 N	123.20 E
Santander □[5]	246	7.00 N	73.15 W
Santander Jiménez	232	24.13 N	98.28 W
Sant'andrea, Isola I	68	40.03 N	17.57 E
Sant'Andrea Frius	71	39.29 N	9.10 E
Sant Andreu de la Barca	266d	41.27 N	1.59 E
Santa Nella	226	37.03 N	121.02 W
Santanésia	256	22.30 S	43.49 W
Santang	100	28.44 N	116.32 E
Sant'Angelo, Castel ⊥	267a	41.55 N	12.28 E
Sant'Angelo, Monte ∧	267a	41.56 N	12.49 E
Sant'Angelo dei Lombardi	68	40.56 N	15.11 E
Sant'Angelo in Vado	66	43.40 N	12.25 E
Sant'Angelo Lodigiano	62	45.14 N	9.24 E
Sant'Angelo Muxard	70	37.28 N	13.32 E
Sant'Angelo Romano	267a	42.02 N	12.42 E
Santanghu	102	44.13 N	93.22 E
Santanilla, Islas II	238	17.25 N	83.55 W
Santa Ninfa	70	37.46 N	12.53 E
Sant'Antimo	68	40.56 N	14.14 E
Sant'antine, Nuraghe ⊥	71	40.29 N	8.46 E
Sant'Antioco	71	39.04 N	8.27 E
Sant'Antioco, Isola di I	71	39.02 N	8.25 E
Sant Antoni de Portmany	34	38.58 N	1.18 E
Sant'Antonio Abate	68	40.43 N	14.32 E
Sant'Antonio di Santadi	71	39.43 N	8.29 E
Sant'Antonio Morignone	64	46.24 N	10.21 E
Santanyi	34	39.22 N	3.07 E
Santa Panagia, Capo >	70	37.07 N	15.18 E
Santa Paula	228	34.21 N	119.03 W
Santa Paula Creek ≃	228	34.21 N	119.03 W
Santa Perpètua de Mogoda	266d	41.32 N	2.11 E
Santapogue Creek ≃	276	40.40 N	73.21 W
Santa Pola, Cap de >	34	38.12 N	0.31 W
Sant'Apollinare in Classe ψ[1]	66	44.22 N	12.15 E
Santaquin	200	39.58 N	111.47 W
Santa Quitéria	250	4.20 S	40.10 W
Santa Quitéria do Maranhão	250	3.31 S	42.32 W
Sant'Arcangelo	68	40.15 N	16.17 E
Santarcangelo di Romagna	66	44.04 N	12.27 E
Sant'Arcangelo Trimonte	68	41.10 N	14.56 E
Santarém, Bra.	250	2.26 S	54.42 W
Santarém, Port.	34	39.14 N	8.41 W
Santarém □[5]	266c	38.50 N	8.56 W
Santaren Channel ⊔	238	24.00 N	79.30 W
Santa Rita, Bra.	250	7.08 S	34.58 W
Santa Rita, Bra.	287a	22.41 S	43.28 W
Santa Rita, Col.	246	0.33 N	73.58 W
Santa Rita, Hond.	236	15.09 N	87.53 W
Santa Rita, Méx.	196	27.29 N	100.33 W
Santa Rita, Méx.	232	28.34 N	111.42 W
Santa Rita, Pil.	116	11.27 N	124.56 E
Santa Rita, Mt., U.S.	182	48.42 N	112.19 W
Santa Rita, Ven.	246	10.32 N	71.32 W
Santa Rita, Punta >	258	34.28 S	57.52 W
Santa Rita de Caldas	256	22.02 S	46.20 W
Santa Rita de Catuna	252	30.57 S	66.13 W
Santa Rita de Jacutinga	256	22.09 S	44.06 W
Santa Rita del Rucio	234	23.04 N	100.19 W
Santa Rita do Araguaia	255	17.20 S	53.12 W
Santa Rita do Ibitipoca	256	21.33 S	43.55 W
Santa Rita do Sapucaí	256	22.15 S	45.42 W
Santa Rita do Weil	246	3.29 S	69.19 W
Santa Rita Park	226	37.02 N	120.35 W
Santa Rosa, Arg.	252	36.37 S	64.17 W
Santa Rosa, Arg.	252	23.22 S	64.30 W
Santa Rosa, Bol.	248	14.10 S	66.53 W
Santa Rosa, Bol.	248	10.36 S	67.25 W
Santa Rosa, Bol.	248	17.07 S	63.35 W
Santa Rosa, Bra.	252	27.52 S	54.29 W
Santa Rosa, Bra.	255	15.01 S	47.13 W
Santa Rosa, Col.	246	2.31 N	68.13 W
Santa Rosa, C.R.	236	10.51 N	85.38 W
Santa Rosa, Ec.	246	3.27 S	79.58 W
Santa Rosa, Méx.	204	31.59 N	116.45 W
Santa Rosa, Méx.	234	22.18 N	104.24 W
Santa Rosa, Para.	248	21.46 S	61.43 W
Santa Rosa, Para.	252	26.52 S	56.49 W
Santa Rosa, Ca., U.S.	226	38.26 N	122.42 W
Santa Rosa, N.M., U.S.	196	34.56 N	104.40 W
Santa Rosa, Tx., U.S.	196	26.15 N	97.50 W
Santa Rosa, Ur.	258	34.30 S	56.03 W
Santa Rosa, Ven.	246	7.03 N	68.28 W
Santa Rosa, Ven.	246	8.26 N	69.24 W
Santa Rosa, Ven.	286c	10.30 N	66.46 W
Santa Rosa □[5]	236	14.10 N	90.18 W
Santa Rosa, Mount ∧[2]	174p	13.32 N	144.55 E
Santa Rosa, Parque Nacional ♠	236	10.50 N	85.45 W
Santa Rosa, Presa ⊜[1]	234	20.58 N	103.35 W
Santa Rosa Beach	194	30.23 N	86.13 W
Santa Rosa Creek ≃	226	35.34 N	121.06 W
Santa Rosa de Aguán	236	15.57 N	85.43 W
Santa Rosa de Amanadona	246	1.29 N	66.55 W
Santa Rosa [de Copán]	236	14.47 N	88.46 W
Santa Rosa de Huechuraba	286e	33.21 S	70.41 W
Santa Rosa del Conlara	252	32.20 S	65.12 W
Santa Rosa de Leales	252	27.09 S	65.15 W
Santa Rosa de Lima	236	13.37 N	87.53 W
Santa Rosa de Locobe	286e	33.26 S	70.33 W
Santa Rosa del Palmar	248	16.54 S	62.24 W
Santa Rosa de Osos	246	6.39 N	75.28 W
Santa Rosa de Río Primero	252	31.09 S	63.23 W
Santa Rosa de Sucumbíos	246	0.22 N	77.10 W
Santa Rosa de Viterbo	246	5.53 N	72.59 W
Santa Rosa Indian Reservation ◆[4]	204	33.35 N	116.35 W
Santa Rosa Island I, Ca., U.S.	204	33.58 N	120.06 W
Santa Rosa Island I, Fl., U.S.	194	30.22 N	86.55 W
Santa Rosa Jáuregui	234	20.44 N	100.27 W
Santa Rosalía, Méx.	196	26.08 N	98.59 W
Santa Rosalía, Méx.	232	27.19 N	112.17 W
Santa Rosalía, Ven.	246	9.02 N	69.01 W
Santa Rosa Range ⋏	204	41.35 N	117.40 W
Santa Rosa Wash ∨	200	33.00 N	112.00 W
Santa Rosita	286d	12.03 S	76.59 W
Sant'Arsenio	68	40.28 N	15.29 E
Šantarskije ostrova II	74	55.00 N	137.36 E
Santa Severa	66	42.02 N	11.57 E
Santa Severina	68	39.09 N	16.55 E
Santa Sofia	66	43.57 N	11.54 E
Santa Susana	228	34.16 N	118.43 W
Santa Susana Mountains ⋏	228	34.20 N	118.42 W
Santa Sylvina	252	27.49 S	61.09 W
Santa Tecla → Nueva San Salvador	236	13.41 N	89.17 W
Santa Teresa, Bra.	255	19.55 S	40.36 W
Santa Teresa, Méx.	196	29.34 N	104.39 W
Santa Teresa, Méx.	200	30.52 N	111.33 W
Santa Teresa, Méx.	232	25.17 N	97.51 W
Santa Teresa, Méx.	234	22.28 N	104.44 W
Santa Teresa ≃	255	11.47 S	48.37 W
Santa Teresa, Embalse de ⊜[1]	34	40.40 N	5.30 W
Santa Teresa de lo Ovalle	286e	33.23 S	70.47 W
Santa Teresa di Riva	70	37.57 N	15.22 E
Santa Teresa Gallura	71	41.14 N	9.11 E
Santa Tereza de Goiás	255	13.38 S	49.01 W
Santa Terezinha	250	10.28 S	50.31 W
Santa Valburga (Sankt Wallburg)	64	46.33 N	11.00 E
Santa Venerina	70	37.41 N	15.08 E
Santa Venetia	226	38.01 N	122.31 W
Santa Vitória	255	18.50 S	50.08 W
Santa Vitória do Palmar	252	33.31 S	53.21 W
Santa Vittoria, Monte ∧	71	39.45 N	9.18 E
Santa Vittoria in Matenano	66	43.01 N	13.29 E
Santa Ynez ≃	204	34.41 N	120.36 W
Santa Ynez Canyon ∨	280	34.04 N	118.34 W
Santa Ysabel Indian Reservation ◆[4]	204	33.11 N	116.41 W
Sant Bartomeu de la Quadra	266d	41.26 N	2.02 E
Sant Boi de Llobregat	266d	41.21 N	2.03 E
Sant Carles de la Ràpita	34	40.37 N	0.36 E
Sant Climent de Llobregat	266d	41.20 N	2.00 E
Sant Cugat del Vallès	266d	41.28 N	2.05 E
Santee	228	32.50 N	116.58 W
Santee ≃	192	33.14 N	79.28 W
Santee Dam ◆[6]	192	33.24 N	80.12 W
Santee Indian Reservation ◆[4]	198	42.45 N	97.50 W
Sant'Egidio alla Vibrata	66	42.49 N	13.42 E
Sant'Elena	64	45.12 N	11.43 E
Sant'Elia a Pianisi	66	41.38 N	14.52 E
Sant'Elia Fiumerapido	66	41.32 N	13.52 E
Sant'Elpidio a Mare	66	43.14 N	13.41 E
Santena	62	44.57 N	7.45 E
Santenay	58	46.55 N	4.41 E
Santeny	261	48.43 N	2.34 E
San Teodoro, It.	70	37.51 N	14.42 E
San Teodoro, It.	71	40.46 N	9.39 E
Santermo in Colle	68	40.48 N	16.45 E
Santerno ≃	66	44.34 N	11.58 E
Santerre □[9]	50	49.40 N	2.40 E
Sant'Eufemia, Golfo di ⊂	68	38.50 N	16.00 E
Sant'Eufemia a Maiella	66	42.07 N	14.02 E
Sant'Eufemia d'Aspromonte	68	38.16 N	15.52 E
Sant'Eufemia Lamezia	68	38.55 N	16.15 E
Sant Feliu de Guíxols	34	41.47 N	3.02 E
Sant Feliu de Llobregat	266d	41.23 N	2.03 E
Sant Fost de Campsentelles	266d	41.31 N	2.14 E
Sānthia, Bngl.	126	24.03 N	89.33 E
Santhià, It.	62	45.22 N	8.10 E
Santiago, Bol.	248	18.19 S	59.34 W
Santiago, Bra.	252	29.11 S	54.53 W
Santiago, Chile	252	33.27 S	70.40 W
Santiago, Chile	286e	33.27 S	70.40 W
Santiago, Méx.	232	23.28 N	109.43 W
Santiago, Pan.	236	8.06 N	80.59 W
Santiago, Para.	252	27.09 S	56.47 W
Santiago, Perú	248	14.11 S	75.44 W
Santiago, Pil.	116	16.41 N	121.33 E
Santiago I	150a	15.05 N	23.40 W
Santiago ≃, Arg.	288	34.50 S	57.57 W
Santiago ≃, Méx.	232	25.11 N	105.26 W
Santiago ≃, S.A.	246	4.27 S	77.38 W
Santiago, Cape >	116	13.46 N	120.39 E
Santiago, Cerro ∧	236	8.33 N	81.44 W
Santiago, Isla I, Arg.	288	34.50 S	57.53 W
Santiago, Isla I, Ec.	246a	0.14 S	90.45 W
Santiago, Serranía de ⋏	248	18.25 S	59.25 W
Santiago Atitlán	236	14.38 N	91.14 W
Santiago Chazumba	234	18.12 N	97.40 W
Santiago Choapan	234	17.20 N	95.57 W
Santiago Creek ≃, Ca., U.S.	228	35.06 N	119.17 W
Santiago Creek ≃, Ca., U.S.	228	33.46 N	117.54 W
Santiago Dam ◆[6]	280	33.47 N	117.43 W
Santiago de Cao	248	7.58 S	79.15 W
Santiago de Chocorvos	248	13.50 S	75.16 W
Santiago de Chuco	248	8.09 S	78.11 W
Santiago de Compostela	34	42.53 N	8.33 W
Santiago de Cuba	240p	20.01 N	75.49 W
Santiago de Cuba □[4]	240p	20.10 N	75.55 W
Santiago de Huari	248	19.00 S	66.48 W
Santiago de Huata	248	16.06 S	68.53 W
Santiago de la Peña	234	20.57 N	97.24 W
Santiago de las Vegas ◆[8]	286b	22.58 N	82.23 W
Santiago del Estero	252	27.47 S	64.16 W
Santiago del Estero □[4]	252	28.00 S	63.30 W
Santiago [de los Caballeros]	238	19.27 N	70.42 W
Santiago de Machaca	248	17.05 S	69.16 W
Santiago de Méndez	246	2.43 S	78.19 W
Santiago de Surco	286d	12.09 S	77.01 W
Santiago do Cacém	34	38.01 N	8.42 W
Santiago Island I	116	16.24 N	119.56 E
Santiago Ixcuintla	234	21.49 N	105.13 W
Santiago Ixtayutla	234	16.33 N	97.39 W
Santiago Jamiltepec	234	16.17 N	97.49 W
Santiago Juxtlahuaca	234	17.20 N	98.01 W
Santiago Lachiguirí	234	16.41 N	95.32 W
Santiago Larre	258	35.34 S	59.10 W
Santiago Maravatío	234	20.10 N	101.00 W
Santiago Papasquiaro	232	25.03 N	105.25 W
Santiago Peak ∧, Ca., U.S.	228	33.42 N	117.32 W
Santiago Peak ∧, Tx., U.S.	196	29.47 N	103.25 W
Santiago Pinotepa Nacional	234	16.19 N	98.01 W
Santiago Reservoir ⊜[1]	228	33.47 N	117.43 W
Santiago → Santiago de Compostela	34	42.53 N	8.33 W
Santiago Tepalcatlapan ◆[8]	286a	19.15 N	99.08 W
Santiago Tulantepec	234	20.02 N	98.22 W
Santiago Tutla	234	17.10 N	95.26 W
Santiago Tuxtla	234	18.28 N	95.18 W
Santiago Vázquez	258	34.48 S	56.21 W
Santiago Yaveo	234	17.19 N	95.42 W
Santiago Zacatepec	234	17.11 N	95.51 W
Santiaguillo, Laguna ⊜	232	24.48 N	104.48 W
Santiam Pass)(	202	44.25 N	121.51 W
San Tian Zhu (Three Indian Temples) ψ[1]	106	30.15 N	120.08 E
Santiao Chiao >	100	25.02 N	121.59 E
Santiaoqiao	106	31.36 N	121.22 E
Santi Filippo e Giacomo	70	37.51 N	12.31 E
Santiguila	150	12.42 N	7.26 W
Sant'Ilario d'Enza	64	44.46 N	10.27 E
San Timoteo	246	9.48 N	71.04 W
San Timoteo Canyon ∨	228	34.04 N	117.17 W
Säntis ∧	58	47.15 N	9.21 E
Santissima Trinita di Saccargia ψ[1]	71	40.41 N	8.42 E
Santíssimo ◆[8]	287a	22.53 S	43.31 W
Santisteban del Puerto	34	38.15 N	3.12 W
Sant Joan de Labritja	34	39.05 N	1.30 E
Sant Joan Despí	266d	41.22 N	2.04 E
Sant Jordi, Golf de ⊂	34	40.53 N	1.00 E
Sant Just Desvern	266d	41.23 N	2.05 E
Sant Mateu del Maestrat	34	40.28 N	0.11 E
Santō, Nihon	94	35.21 N	136.22 E
Santō, Nihon	96	35.19 N	134.53 E
Santo, Tx., U.S.	196	32.36 N	98.13 W
Santo, Vanuatu	175f	15.32 S	167.08 E
Santo Aleixo	256	22.34 S	43.04 W
Santo Amaro, Bra.	250	2.33 S	43.14 W
Santo Amaro, Bra.	255	12.32 S	38.43 W
Santo Amaro ◆[8]	287b	23.39 S	46.42 W
Santo Amaro, Ilha de I	256	23.57 S	46.14 W
Santo Amaro das Brotas	250	10.47 S	37.04 W
Santo Anastácio	255	21.58 S	51.39 W
Santo André	256	23.40 S	46.31 W
Santo Ângelo	252	28.18 S	54.16 W
Santo Antão I	150a	17.05 N	25.10 W
Santo Antônio, Bra.	250	6.18 S	35.27 W
Santo António, S. Tom./P.	152	1.39 N	7.26 E
Santo Antônio ≃, Bra.	250	11.31 S	48.37 W
Santo Antônio ≃, Bra.	255	17.30 S	45.37 W
Santo Antônio ≃, Bra.	287a	22.42 S	43.37 W
Santo António, Ilha de I	156	21.58 S	35.28 E
Santo Antônio da Charneca	266c	38.37 N	9.02 W
Santo Antônio da Patrulha	252	29.50 S	50.32 W
Santo Antônio de Jesus	255	12.58 S	39.16 W
Santo Antônio de Pádua	255	21.32 S	42.11 W
Santo Antonio de Posse	256	22.36 S	46.55 W
Santo Antônio do Amparo	255	20.57 S	44.55 W
Santo Antônio do Aventureiro	256	21.45 S	42.49 W
Santo Antônio do Içá	246	3.05 S	67.57 W
Santo Antônio do Jardim	256	22.07 S	46.41 W
Santo Antônio do Leverger	248	15.52 S	56.05 W
Santo Antônio do Pinhal	256	22.47 S	45.41 W
Santo Antônio do Rio Verde	255	17.57 S	47.27 W
Santo Antônio do Sudoeste	252	26.02 S	53.44 W
Santo Augusto	252	27.51 S	53.47 W
Santo Corazón	248	17.59 S	58.51 W
Santo Domingo, Cuba	240p	22.35 N	80.15 W
Santo Domingo, Méx.	196	25.38 N	101.05 W
Santo Domingo, Méx.	196	25.48 N	104.28 W
Santo Domingo, Méx.	232	25.32 N	112.02 W
Santo Domingo, Nic.	236	12.16 N	85.05 W
Santo Domingo, Rep. Dom.	238	18.28 N	69.54 W
Santo Domingo ≃, Méx.	234	16.41 N	93.00 W
Santo Domingo ≃, Méx.	234	17.40 N	98.07 W
Santo Domingo ≃, Méx.	234	18.10 N	96.08 W
Santo Domingo ≃, Méx.	236	16.15 N	91.17 W
Santo Domingo, Arroyo ≃	204	30.43 N	116.03 W
Santo Domingo, Isla → Hispaniola I	238	19.00 N	71.00 W
Santo Domingo de la Calzada	34	42.26 N	2.57 W
Santo Domingo de los Colorados	246	0.15 S	79.09 W
Santo Domingo Indian Reservation ◆[4]	200	35.30 N	106.25 W
Santo Domingo Nuxaá	234	17.08 N	97.02 W
Santo Domingo Pueblo	200	35.30 N	106.21 W
Santo Domingo Tehuantepec	234	16.20 N	95.14 W
Santo Domingo Teojomulco	234	16.36 N	97.14 W
Santo Domingo Zanatepec	234	16.29 N	94.21 W
Santo Estêvão	255	12.26 S	39.13 W
Sant'Olcese	62	44.30 N	8.58 E
Santolea, Embalse de ⊜[1]	34	40.47 N	0.19 W
Santo / Malo □[8]	175f	15.20 S	166.55 E
San Tomé	246	8.58 N	64.08 W
San Tommaso	66	42.11 N	13.58 E
Sant'Omobono Imagna	62	45.48 N	9.32 E
Santoña	34	43.27 N	3.27 W
Santong ≃	98	42.39 N	126.03 E
Santo Nino Island I	116	11.55 N	124.27 E
Sant' Onofrio ◆[8]	267a	41.56 N	12.25 E
Santo Onofre ≃	255	12.34 S	43.12 W
Santop, Pic ∧	175f	18.39 S	169.03 E
Sant'Oreste	66	42.14 N	12.32 E
Santorini → Thíra I	38	36.24 N	25.29 E
Santorso	64	45.44 N	11.23 E
Santos	256	23.57 S	46.20 W
Santos, Arroyo de los ≃	258	35.28 S	57.29 W
Santos, Baía de ⊂	256	24.00 S	46.21 W
Santos Dumont	256	21.28 S	43.34 W
Santos Dumont, Aeroporto ⊠	256	22.55 S	43.10 W
Santoshpur	272b	22.40 N	88.10 E
Santo Stefano, Isola I	66	40.47 N	13.27 E
Santo Stefano Belbo	62	44.43 N	8.14 E
Santo Stefano d'Aveto	62	44.35 N	9.27 E
Santo Stefano di Cadore	64	46.33 N	12.32 E
Santo Stefano di Camastra	70	38.01 N	14.21 E
Santo Stefano di Magra	64	44.10 N	9.55 E
Santo Stefano Quisquina	70	37.37 N	13.29 E
Santo Stino di Livenza	64	45.44 N	12.41 E
Santos Tomás del Norte	236	13.11 N	86.56 W
Santo Tirso	34	41.21 N	8.28 W
Santo Tomás, Col.	246	10.46 N	74.45 W
Santo Tomás, Méx.	232	31.33 N	116.24 W
Santo Tomás, Nic.	236	12.04 N	85.05 W
Santo Tomás, Perú	248	6.36 S	77.48 W
Santo Tomás, Perú	248	14.29 S	72.06 W
Santo Tomas, Pil.	116	7.29 N	125.38 E
Santo Tomás ≃, Méx.	204	31.32 N	116.40 W
Santo Tomás ≃, Perú	248	13.47 S	72.09 W
Santo Tomás, Punta >	232	31.34 N	116.42 W
Santo Tomas, University of ψ[2]	269f	14.37 N	120.59 E
Santo Tomás, Volcán ∧[1]	246a	0.48 S	91.07 W
Santo Tomás y Principe → Sao Tome and Principe □[1]	152	1.00 N	7.00 E
Santo Tomé, Arg.	252	28.33 S	56.03 W
Santo Tomé, Arg.	252	31.40 S	60.46 W
Santo Tomé de Guayana → Ciudad Guayana	246	8.22 N	62.40 W
Sant' Pietro, Lago di ⊜	68	41.01 N	15.30 E
Santpoort	52	52.25 N	4.38 E
Sant Quirze de la Serra	266d	41.32 N	2.05 E
Santuanjiang	106	30.54 N	121.43 E
Santuario de Quillacas	248	19.14 S	66.58 W
Santu Lussurgiu	71	40.08 N	8.39 E
Santunying	105	40.14 N	118.12 E
Sant Vicenç dels Horts	266d	41.24 N	2.01 E
San Ubaldo	236	11.51 N	85.20 W
Sanuki	268	35.16 N	139.53 E
Sanuki-sammyaku ⋏	96	34.09 N	134.11 E
Şānūr	132	32.21 N	35.15 E
San Valentino in Abruzzo Citeriore	66	42.14 N	13.59 E
San Valentino Torio	68	40.48 N	14.36 E
San Venanzo	66	42.52 N	12.16 E
San Vendemiano	64	45.54 N	12.20 E
San Vicente, Arg.	252	28.30 S	64.09 W
San Vicente, Arg.	258	34.58 S	58.22 W
San Vicente, El Sal.	236	13.38 N	88.48 W
San Vicente □[5]	288	34.56 S	58.24 W
San Vicente, Cabo → São Vicente, Cabo de >	34	37.01 N	9.00 W
San Vicente, Volcán de ∧[1]	236	13.36 N	88.51 W
San Vicente Creek ≃	282	37.32 N	122.31 W
San Vicente de Alcántara	34	39.21 N	7.08 W
San Vicente de Cañete	248	13.05 S	76.24 W
San Vicente de Chucurí	246	6.54 N	73.25 W
San Vicente de la Barquera	34	43.26 N	4.24 W
San Vicente del Caguán	246	2.07 N	74.46 W
San Vicente de Tagua-Tagua	252	34.26 S	71.05 W
San Vicente Mountain ∧	280	34.08 N	118.31 W
San Vicente Reservoir ⊜[1]	228	32.55 N	116.55 W
San Vicente → Saint Vincent and the Grenadines □[1]	241h	13.15 N	61.12 W
San Vicente Tancuayalab	234	21.44 N	98.34 W
San Vigilio	64	45.34 N	10.41 E
San Vigilio ψ[1]	64	46.37 N	11.07 E
San Vincenzo	66	43.06 N	10.32 E
San Vito, C.R.	236	8.50 N	82.58 W
San Vito, It.	71	39.26 N	9.32 E
San Vito, Capo >	70	38.11 N	12.44 E
San Vito, Serralta di ∧	68	38.46 N	16.22 E
San Vito al Tagliamento	64	45.54 N	12.52 E
San Vito Chietino	66	42.18 N	14.27 E
San Vito dei Normanni	68	40.39 N	17.42 E
San Vito lo Capo	70	38.10 N	12.45 E
San Vito Romano	66	41.53 N	12.59 E
San Vito sullo Ionio	68	38.43 N	16.25 E
Sanwa, Nihon	94	37.07 N	138.21 E
Sanwa, Nihon	94	36.12 N	139.49 E
Sanwa, Nihon	96	34.42 N	133.15 E
San Xavier Indian Reservation ◆[4]	200	32.05 N	111.08 W
Sanxi, Zhg.	100	30.22 N	118.25 E
Sanxi, Zhg.	100	27.42 N	120.04 E
Sanxing, Zhg.	106	31.47 N	121.35 E
Sanxing, Zhg.	106	31.58 N	121.07 E
Sanxingchang, Zhg.	107	30.19 N	104.09 E
Sanxingchang, Zhg.	107	30.32 N	104.38 E
Sanxingjie	106	32.06 N	121.01 E
Sanyang, Zhg.	100	28.37 N	116.15 E
Sanyang, Zhg.	100	31.20 N	113.10 E
Sanyang, Zhg.	100	27.57 N	114.22 E
Sanyangzhen	106	31.55 N	121.29 E
Sanyanjing	104	41.28 N	122.27 E
Sanyanqiao	100	28.39 N	113.43 E
Sanyati ≃	154	16.49 S	28.45 E
San Ygnacio	196	27.03 N	99.27 W
Sanyō, Nihon	96	34.45 N	134.01 E
Sanyō, Nihon	96	34.02 N	131.10 E
Sanyuan	102	34.35 N	108.54 E
Sanyuanpu	98	42.02 N	125.44 E
Sanyuhao	98	42.30 N	117.34 E
Sanyuzhen	106	32.08 N	121.19 E
Sanza	68	40.15 N	15.33 E
Sanzao Dao I	100	22.03 N	113.21 E
Sanza Pombo	152	7.19 S	15.59 E
Sanzar ≃	85	40.00 N	67.40 E
San Zeno di Montagna	64	45.37 N	10.43 E
Sanzha	98	41.44 N	114.39 E
Sanzhan, Zhg.	89	49.42 N	125.20 E
Sanzhan, Zhg.	89	49.36 N	126.38 E
Sanzuodian	98	41.36 N	118.49 E
São Benedito	250	4.03 S	40.53 W
São Benedito ≃	250	9.11 S	57.02 W
São Benedito das Areias	256	21.19 S	47.02 W
São Benedito do Rio Preto	250	3.20 S	43.35 W
São Bento	250	2.42 S	44.50 W
São Bento ≃	256	21.42 S	45.18 W
São Bento, Mosteiro de ψ[1]	287a	22.54 S	43.11 W

≃	River	Fluß	Río	Rivière	Rio
≊	Canal	Kanal	Canal	Canal	Canal
⌊	Waterfall, Rapids	Wasserfall, Stromschnellen	Cascada, Rápidos	Chute d'eau, Rapides	Cascata, Rápidos
⊔	Strait	Meeresstraße	Estrecho	Détroit	Estreito
⊂	Bay, Gulf	Bucht, Golf	Bahía, Golfo	Baie, Golfe	Baía, Golfo
⊜	Lake, Lakes	See, Seen	Lago, Lagos	Lac, Lacs	Lago, Lagos
≡	Swamp	Sumpf	Pantano	Marais	Pântano
⊓	Ice Features, Glacier	Eis- und Gletscherformen	Accidentes Glaciales	Formes glaciaires	Acidentes glaciares
⊤	Other Hydrographic Features	Andere Hydrographische Objekte	Otros Elementos Hidrográficos	Autres données hydrographiques	Outros acidentes hidrográficos

✣	Submarine Features	Untermeerische Objekte	Accidentes Submarinos	Formes de relief sous-marin	Acidentes submarinos
□	Political Unit	Politische Einheit	Unidad Politica	Entité politique	Unidade política
ψ	Cultural Institution	Kulturelle Institution	Institución Cultural	Institution culturelle	Instituição cultural
⊥	Historical Site	Historische Stätte	Sitio Histórico	Site historique	Sitio histórico
♠	Recreational Site	Erholungs- und Ferienort	Sitio de Recreo	Centre de loisirs	Area de Lazer
⊠	Airport	Flughafen	Aeropuerto	Aéroport	Aeroporto
■	Military Installation	Militäranlage	Instalación Militar	Installation militaire	Instalação militar
◆	Miscellaneous	Verschiedenes	Misceláneo	Divers	Diversos

Name (ENGLISH) / Name (DEUTSCH)	Page / Seite	Lat.°′ / Breite°′	Long.°′ / Länge°′ E = Ost
São Bento Abade	256	21.35 S	45.04 W
São Bento de Caldas	256	22.08 S	46.18 W
São Bento do Norte	250	5.04 S	36.02 W
São Bento do Sapucaí	256	22.42 S	45.43 W
São Bento do Sul	252	26.15 S	49.23 W
São Bento do Una	250	8.32 S	36.22 W
São Bernardino	287a	22.40 S	43.26 W
São Bernardo	250	3.22 S	42.24 W
São Bernardo do Campo	256	23.42 S	46.33 W
São Bernardo do Campo □7	287b	23.44 S	46.33 W
São Borja	252	28.39 S	56.00 W
São Brás	250	10.05 S	36.55 W
São Brás de Alportel	34	37.09 N	7.53 W
São Braz, Cabo de ›	152	9.59 S	13.19 E
São Caetano de Odivelas	250	0.45 S	48.02 W
São Caetano do Sul	256	23.36 S	46.34 W
São Caetano do Sul □7	287b	23.37 S	46.33 W
São Carlos	255	22.01 S	47.54 W
São Cristóvão	250	11.01 S	37.12 W
São Cristóvão ◂8	287a	22.54 S	43.14 W
Saodatun	104	42.02 N	123.31 E
São Domingos, Bra.	252	26.34 S	52.32 W
São Domingos, Bra.	255	13.24 S	46.19 W
São Domingos, Bra.	256	21.41 S	42.47 W
São Domingos, Gui.-B.	150	12.22 N	16.08 W
São Domingos ≃, Bra.	248	12.28 S	64.13 W
São Domingos ≃, Bra.	255	13.24 S	47.12 W
São Domingos ≃, Bra.	255	19.13 S	50.44 W
São Domingos ≃, Bra.	255	20.03 S	53.13 W
São Domingos da Bocaina	256	21.50 S	44.01 W
São Domingos do Capim	250	1.41 S	47.47 W
São Domingos do Maranhão	250	5.42 S	44.22 W
São Felipe	255	14.49 S	41.23 W
São Félix de Balsas	250	7.08 S	44.52 W
São Félix do Araguaia	250	11.36 S	50.39 W
São Félix do Piauí	250	5.56 S	42.07 W
São Filipe	150a	14.54 N	24.31 W
São Francisco	255	15.57 S	44.52 W
São Francisco ≃, Bra.	242	10.30 S	36.24 W
São Francisco ≃, Bra.	255	16.09 S	40.39 W
São Francisco ≃, Bra.	256	21.50 S	42.42 W
São Francisco ≃, Bra.	287a	22.57 S	43.20 W
São Francisco, Baía de c	252	26.10 S	48.34 W
São Francisco, Ilha de I	252	26.18 S	48.37 W
São Francisco de Assis	252	29.33 S	55.08 W
São Francisco de Goiás	255	15.55 S	49.16 W
São Francisco de Paula	252	29.27 S	50.35 W
São Francisco do Croará	287a	22.42 S	43.08 W
São Francisco do Maranhão	250	6.15 S	42.52 W
São Francisco do Piauí	250	7.15 S	42.32 W
São Francisco do Sul	252	26.14 S	48.39 W
São Francisco Xavier	256	22.54 S	45.58 W
São Gabriel	252	30.20 S	54.19 W
São Gabriel da Palha	255	19.01 S	40.32 W
São Gabriel de Goiás	255	15.12 S	47.34 W
São Gonçalo, Bra.	256	21.36 S	46.19 W
São Gonçalo, Bra.	256	22.51 S	43.04 W
São Gonçalo □7	287a	22.48 S	43.01 W
São Gonçalo do Abaeté	255	18.20 S	45.49 W
São Gonçalo do Sapucaí	256	21.54 S	45.36 W
São Gonçalo dos Campos	255	12.25 S	38.58 W
Sao Hill	154	8.20 S	35.12 E
São Jerônimo	252	29.58 S	51.43 W
São Jerônimo, Serra de ⋀1	255	16.30 S	54.50 W
São Jerônimo da Serra	255	23.43 S	50.44 W
São João	150	11.32 N	15.26 W
São João ≃, Bra.	255	12.27 S	51.07 W
São João ≃, Bra.	256	22.33 S	42.29 W
São João da Barra	255	21.38 S	41.03 W
São João da Boa Vista	256	21.58 S	46.47 W
São João D'Aliança	255	14.42 S	47.32 W
São João da Madeira	34	40.54 N	8.30 W
São João da Mata	256	21.56 S	45.56 W
São João da Ponte	255	15.56 S	44.01 W
São João da Serra	256	21.28 S	43.27 W
São João das Lampas	266c	38.52 N	9.24 W
São João de Côrtes	250	2.12 S	44.32 W
São João del-Rei	255	21.09 S	44.16 W
São João de Meriti	256	22.48 S	43.22 W
São João de Meriti □7	287a	22.48 S	43.21 W
São João de Meriti ≃	287a	22.48 S	43.18 W
São João do Araguaia	250	5.23 S	48.46 W
São João do Jaguaribe	250	5.16 S	38.16 W
São João do Paraíso	255	15.19 S	42.01 W
São João do Piauí	250	8.21 S	42.15 W
São João do Sabugi	250	6.43 S	37.12 W
São João dos Patos	250	6.30 S	43.42 W
São João Evangelista	255	18.32 S	42.45 W
São João Nepomuceno	256	21.33 S	43.01 W
São João Novo	256	23.33 S	47.01 W
São Joaquim	252	28.18 S	49.56 W
São Joaquim, Parque Nacional de ♦	252	28.15 S	49.57 W
São Joaquim da Barra	255	20.35 S	47.53 W
São Jorge I	148a	38.38 N	28.03 W
São Jorge, Castelo de ⊥	266c	38.43 N	9.08 W
São José, Bra.	252	27.38 S	48.39 W
São José, Bra.	256	22.43 S	42.36 W
São José ≃, Bra.	255	19.10 S	40.12 W
São José ≃, Bra.	287a	22.39 S	43.27 W
São José, Ponta de ›	152	12.36 S	13.12 E
São José da Laje	250	9.01 S	36.03 W
São José de Anauá	246	1.00 N	61.23 W
São José de Encoge	152	7.38 S	14.41 E
São José de Mipibu	250	6.05 S	35.15 W
São José de Piranhas	250	7.07 S	38.30 W
São José do Alegre	256	22.19 S	45.32 W
São José do Barreiro	256	22.38 S	44.35 W
São José do Belmonte	250	7.52 S	38.46 W
São José do Campestre	250	6.18 S	35.42 W
São José do Cedro	252	26.30 S	53.30 W
São José do Egito	250	7.28 S	37.16 W
São José do Gurupi	250	1.36 S	46.13 W
São José do Norte	252	32.01 S	52.03 W
São José do Peixe	250	7.24 S	42.34 W
São José do Piriá	250	1.17 S	46.18 W
São José do Rio Parto	256	21.36 S	46.54 W
São José do Rio Preto, Bra.	255	20.48 S	49.23 W
São José do Rio Prêto, Bra.	256	22.10 S	42.57 W
São José dos Campos	256	23.11 S	45.53 W
São José dos Lopes	256	21.48 S	43.53 W
São José dos Pinhais	252	25.31 S	49.13 W
São José do Turvo	256	22.21 S	43.59 W
São Julião da Barra	266c	38.40 N	9.21 W
São Julião do Tojal	266c	38.51 N	9.08 W
São Leopoldo	252	29.46 S	51.09 W
São Lourenço	256	22.07 S	45.03 W
São Lourenço, Pantanal de ≡	248	17.30 S	56.30 W
São Lourenço da Serra	256	23.52 S	46.57 W
São Lourenço do Oeste	252	26.24 S	52.46 W
São Lourenço do Sul	252	31.22 S	51.58 W
São Luís	250	2.31 S	44.16 W
São Luís de Montes Belos	255	16.32 S	50.20 W
São Luís do Curu	250	3.40 S	39.14 W
São Luís Do Paraitinga	256	23.14 S	45.20 W
São Luís do Quitunde	250	9.20 S	35.33 W
São Luís Gonzaga	252	28.24 S	54.58 W
São Mamede	250	6.56 S	37.06 W
São Manuel	255	22.44 S	48.34 W
São Manuel ≃	242	7.21 S	58.03 W
São Manuel do Guaiaçu	256	21.20 S	42.51 W
São Marcos ≃	255	18.15 S	47.37 W
São Mateus, Bra.	255	18.44 S	39.51 W
São Mateus, Bra.	256	22.49 S	43.23 W
São Mateus, Port.	148a	38.26 N	28.27 W
São Mateus, Braço Norte ≃	255	18.37 S	40.05 W
São Mateus de Minas	256	22.42 S	46.03 W
São Mateus do Sul	252	25.52 S	50.23 W
São Miguel	250	6.13 S	38.30 W
São Miguel I	148a	37.47 N	25.30 W
São Miguel ≃	255	16.26 S	41.00 W
São Miguel do Araguaia	255	13.19 S	50.13 W
São Miguel d'Oeste	252	26.45 S	53.34 W
São Miguel do Guamá	250	1.37 S	47.27 W
São Miguel dos Campos	250	9.47 S	36.05 W
São Miguel dos Macacos	250	1.11 S	50.28 W
São Miguel do Tapuio	250	5.30 S	41.20 W
São Miguel Paulista (Baquiriru) ◂8	256	23.30 S	46.26 W
Saona, Isla I	238	18.09 N	68.40 W
Saonara	64	45.22 N	11.59 E
Saône ≃	58	45.44 N	4.50 E
Saône-et-Loire □5	32	46.42 N	4.45 E
Saonek	164	0.28 S	130.47 E
Saoner	120	21.23 N	78.54 E
São Nicolau I	150a	16.35 N	24.15 W
São Nicolau ≃	250	5.45 S	42.02 W
São Paulo, Bra.	256	23.32 S	46.37 W
São Paulo, Bra.	287b	23.32 S	46.37 W
São Paulo □3	255	22.00 S	49.00 W
São Paulo □7	287b	23.33 S	46.38 W
São Paulo, Ribeirão de ≃	256	22.16 S	46.37 W
São Paulo de Olivença	246	3.27 S	68.48 W
São Paulo do Potengi	250	5.55 S	35.45 W
São Pedro	255	19.53 S	51.55 W
São Pedro ≃	255	16.30 S	41.17 W
São Pedro de Caldas	256	21.49 S	46.16 W
São Pedro de Viseu	250	2.33 S	49.33 W
São Pedro do Estoril	266c	38.42 N	9.22 W
São Pedro do Piauí	250	5.56 S	42.43 W
São Pedro do Sul, Bra.	252	29.37 S	54.10 W
São Pedro do Sul, Port.	34	40.45 N	8.04 W
São Rafael	250	5.47 S	36.55 W
São Raimundo das Mangabeiras	250	7.01 S	45.29 W
São Raimundo Nonato	250	9.01 S	42.42 W
Saorge	62	43.59 N	7.33 E
Saori	94	35.11 N	136.44 E
São Romão	255	16.22 S	45.04 W
São Roque, Bra.	256	23.32 S	47.08 W
São Roque, Bra.	256	23.06 S	44.42 W
São Roque, Cabo de ›	250	5.29 S	35.16 W
São Roque da Fartura	256	21.51 S	46.45 W
São Salvador → Salvador	255	12.59 S	38.31 W
São Sebastião	256	23.48 S	45.25 W
São Sebastião, Canal de u	256	23.48 S	45.23 W
São Sebastião, Ilha de I	256	23.50 S	45.18 W
São Sebastião, Pico de ∧	256	23.52 S	45.23 W
São Sebastião, Ponta ›	156	22.07 S	35.30 E
São Sebastião da Bela Vista	256	22.10 S	45.45 W
São Sebastião da Boa Vista	250	1.42 S	49.31 W
São Sebastião da Grama	256	21.43 S	46.49 W
São Sebastião da Vitória	256	21.14 S	44.25 W
São Sebastião do Barreado	256	22.04 S	43.38 W
São Sebastião do Maranhão	255	18.05 S	42.35 W
São Sebastião do Paraíso	255	20.55 S	47.00 W
São Sebastião do Rio Claro	255	15.45 S	51.30 W
São Sebastião do Rio Verde	256	22.13 S	44.58 W
São Sebastião dos Robertos	256	22.13 S	46.32 W
São Sebastião do Umbuzeiro	250	8.09 S	37.01 W
São Sepé	252	30.10 S	53.34 W
São Silvestre do Jacare22	256	23.23 S	46.01 W
São Simão, Bra.	255	18.56 S	50.30 W
São Simão, Bra.	255	21.30 S	47.33 W
São Simão, Reprêsa de ⊜1	255	18.40 S	50.00 W
São Tiago	255	20.55 S	44.30 W
São Timóteo	255	13.51 S	42.11 W
São Tomé, Bra.	250	5.58 S	36.04 W
São Tomé, S. Tom./P.	152	0.20 N	6.44 E
São Tomé I	152	0.12 N	6.39 E
São Tomé ≃, Bra.	250	8.10 S	58.13 W
São Tomé ≃, Bra.	256	21.26 S	46.02 W
São Tomé, Cabo de ›	255	21.59 S	40.59 W
São Tomé, Pico de ∧	152	0.16 N	6.33 E
Sao Tome and Principe (São Tomé e Principe) □1, Afr.	138	1.00 N	7.00 E
Sao Tome and Principe (São Tomé e Principe) □1, Afr.	152	1.00 N	7.00 E
São Tomé das Letras	256	21.43 S	44.59 W
Sao Tomé-et-Principe → Sao Tome and Principe □1	152	1.00 N	7.00 E
Saou	62	44.39 N	5.04 E
Saoura, Oued V	148	29.00 N	0.55 W
São Valério ≃	250	11.20 S	48.28 W
São Vicente	256	23.58 S	46.23 W
São Vicente I	150a	16.50 N	25.00 W
São Vicente, Cabo de (Cape Saint Vincent) ›	34	37.01 N	9.00 W
São Vicente, Ribeirão ≃	256	21.59 S	45.40 W
São Vicente de Minas	256	21.42 S	44.27 W
São Vicente Ferrer	250	7.35 S	35.30 W
Sa Pa	110	22.21 N	103.50 E
Sápai	38	41.02 N	25.41 E
Sapanca	130	40.41 N	30.16 E
Sapang Baho ≃	269f	14.33 N	121.06 E
Sapao	116	10.01 N	126.02 E
Sapão ≃	250	11.01 S	45.32 W
Saparua, Pulau I	164	3.34 S	128.40 E
Sapatgrām	124	26.20 N	90.08 E
Sapé, Bra.	250	7.06 S	35.13 W
Sape, Indon.	115b	8.34 S	118.59 E
Sapé ≃	287a	22.52 S	43.02 W
Sape, Selat u	115b	8.39 S	119.18 E
Sapele	150	5.54 N	5.41 E
Sapello ≃	200	35.47 N	104.59 W
Sapelo Island I	192	31.28 N	81.15 W
Saperkino	80	54.05 N	51.38 E
Şaphane	130	39.01 N	29.14 E
Şapian Bay c	116	11.33 N	122.37 E
Sapindji	152	9.39 S	23.12 E
Şapitwa ∧	154	15.57 S	35.36 E
Šapki	76	59.36 N	31.14 E
Šapkina ≃	24	66.44 N	52.25 E
Šapkino	80	51.42 N	42.24 E
Šapkovo, Ross.	76	55.47 N	33.20 E
Sapkovo, Ross.	82	54.34 N	39.10 E
Sa Pobla	34	39.46 N	3.01 E
Sapodilla Cays I	236	16.08 N	88.15 W
Saponara	70	38.11 N	15.26 E
Saponé	150	12.03 N	1.36 W
Sap'o-ri	98	40.49 N	129.31 E
Sap'ornaja	265a	59.46 N	30.41 E
Saporoschje → Zaporožje	78	47.50 N	35.10 E
Saposoa	248	6.56 S	76.48 W
Sapou	175c	7.18 N	151.53 E
Sapožok	80	53.56 N	40.41 E
Sappa Creek ≃	198	40.07 N	99.38 W
Sappa Creek, Middle Fork ≃	198	39.40 N	100.53 W
Sappa Creek, North Fork ≃	198	39.47 N	100.35 W
Sappa Creek, South Fork ≃	198	39.47 N	100.35 W
Sappada	64	46.34 N	12.41 E
Sapphire Mountains ⋀	202	46.20 N	113.45 W
Sappho	224	48.04 N	124.16 W
Sappington	219	38.32 N	90.22 W
Sapporo	92a	43.03 N	141.21 E
Şapri	68	40.04 N	15.38 E
Šapša	76	60.34 N	34.01 E
Sap Songkhla, Thale c	110	7.13 N	100.30 E
Šapsugskaja	78	44.45 N	38.05 E
Saptajev	86	47.55 N	67.28 E
Saptakośī ≃	124	26.31 N	86.58 E
Sapta-ri	271b	37.43 N	126.44 E
Sapu	152	12.29 S	19.26 E
Sapucaí	256	22.19 S	46.42 W
Sapucaí ≃	256	21.33 S	45.40 W
Sapucaia	256	22.00 S	42.54 W
Sapucaí-Mirim	256	22.44 S	45.45 W
Sapucaí-Mirim ≃	256	22.12 S	45.53 W
Sapudi, Pulau I	115a	7.06 S	114.20 E
Sapulpa	196	35.59 N	96.06 W
Sapulu	115a	6.54 S	112.57 E
Sapuran	115a	7.28 S	109.58 E
Sapwe	154	10.57 S	28.10 E
Sāq, Jabal ∧2	128	26.17 N	43.16 E
Sāqiat al-ʿAbd	140	20.48 N	30.19 E
Sāqiyat Makkī	142	30.00 N	31.13 E
Şaqqārah	142	29.51 N	31.13 E
Şaqqārah (Step Pyramid) ⊥	142	29.52 N	31.13 E
Saqqez	128	36.14 N	46.16 E
Saquarema	256	22.56 S	42.30 W
Saquarema, Lagoa de c	256	22.55 S	42.33 W
Saquena	248	4.40 S	73.31 W
Saquish Neck ›1	283	42.00 N	70.37 W
Saquisilí	246	0.51 S	78.40 W
Sāra, Bngl.	126	24.07 N	89.02 E
Sara, Burkina	150	11.43 N	3.50 W
Sara, Pil.	116	11.16 N	123.01 E
Sara, Ross.	80	54.38 N	46.46 E
Sarāb	128	37.56 N	47.32 E
Sarabia, Méx.	234	20.31 N	101.05 W
Sarabia, Méx.	234	17.03 N	95.01 W
Sarabia ≃	234	17.11 N	94.56 W
Sarābiyūm	142	30.23 N	32.17 E
Saraburi	110	14.32 N	100.55 E
Saracena	68	39.46 N	16.09 E
Saraceno, Monte ∧	66	41.27 N	14.44 E
Saracura ≃	255	12.18 S	40.07 W
Saracuruna ≃	287a	22.41 S	43.13 W
Saraféré	150	15.50 N	3.42 W
Saragosa	196	31.01 N	103.39 W
Saragossa → Zaragoza	34	41.38 N	0.53 W
Saraguay ◂8	275a	45.31 N	73.45 W
Saraguro	246	3.36 S	79.13 W
Sarai	80	53.44 N	41.00 E
Sarāi Alamgir	123	32.54 N	73.45 E
Saraikela	124	22.43 N	85.57 E
Sarāi Naurang	123	32.50 N	70.47 E
Saraipāli	120	21.20 N	83.00 E
Säräisniemi	26	64.27 N	26.47 E
Sarajas de Madrid ◂8	266a	40.28 N	3.35 W
Sarajčik	80	47.30 N	51.43 E
Sarajevo	38	43.52 N	18.25 E
Saraj-Gir	80	53.36 N	53.24 E
Saraji	166	22.21 S	148.18 E
Sarajskij	80	47.19 N	40.45 E
Sarakhs	128	36.32 N	61.11 E
Saraktaš	86	51.50 N	56.22 E
Sarala	86	54.52 N	89.14 E
Şaraland	194	30.49 N	88.04 W
Šaraldaj	88	51.01 N	107.38 E
Saralžinskaja	80	49.12 N	48.55 E
Saramacca □5	250	5.40 N	55.40 W
Saramacca ≃	250	5.51 N	55.53 W
Saramaguacán ≃	240p	21.30 N	77.17 W
Saran, Fr.	50	47.57 N	1.53 E
Şaran', Kaz.	86	49.46 N	72.52 E
Šaran, Ross.	80	54.49 N	54.00 E
Saran, Gunung ∧	112	0.25 S	111.18 E
Saranac	216	42.55 N	85.12 W
Saranac ≃	188	44.42 N	73.27 W
Saranac Lake	188	44.19 N	74.07 W
Saranakan, gora ∧	88	52.35 N	113.50 E
Şaranap	226	37.53 N	122.06 W
Šaranbaš-Kn'azevo	80	54.58 N	54.09 E
Saranda	154	5.43 S	34.59 E
Sarandapótamos ≃	267c	38.26 N	23.54 E
Sarandë	38	39.52 N	20.00 E
Sarandi	252	27.56 S	52.55 W
Sarandí ◂8	258	34.40 S	58.21 W
Sarandí del Yi	252	33.21 S	55.38 W
Sarandí Grande	258	33.44 S	56.20 W
Şarandira	256	21.50 S	43.11 W
Šaranga	80	57.11 N	46.34 E
Sarangani Bay c	116	5.57 N	125.11 E
Sarangani Island I	116	5.27 N	125.28 E
Sarangani Islands II	116	5.25 N	125.26 E
Sarangani Strait u	116	5.31 N	125.23 E
Sārangarh	120	21.36 N	83.05 E
Sārangpur	124	23.34 N	76.28 E
Sārankhola	126	22.18 N	89.47 E
Saranley	144	2.22 N	42.17 E
Saranpaul'	24	64.14 N	60.53 E
Saransk	80	54.11 N	45.11 E
Sarantina, Valle V	64	46.35 N	11.25 E
Sara Peak ∧	150	9.41 N	9.17 E
Saraphi	110	18.43 N	99.03 E
Sarapiquí ≃	236	10.43 N	83.56 W
Şarapó ≃	287a	22.46 S	43.37 W
Šarapovo, Ross.	80	55.17 N	44.42 E
Šarapovo, Ross.	82	55.11 N	37.16 E
Sarapuí ≃	287a	22.46 S	43.24 W
Sarapuí, Canal de ≋	287a	22.44 S	43.16 W
Sarapul	80	56.28 N	53.48 E
Sarapul'skaja vozvyšennost' ⋀1	80	56.15 N	53.30 E
Sarapul'skoje	89	48.52 N	135.59 E
Sarāqib	130	35.52 N	36.48 E
Sarare	246	9.47 N	69.10 W
Sarare ≃	246	7.18 N	70.41 W
Sarar Plain ≚	144	9.25 N	46.17 E
Sara Sara, Nevado ∧	248	15.19 S	73.27 W
Sarasota	220	27.20 N	82.31 W
Sarasota □6	220	27.10 N	82.21 W
Sarasota Bay c	220	27.23 N	82.39 W
Sarasota-Bradenton Airport ⊠	220	27.24 N	82.33 W
Sarasota Springs	220	27.17 N	82.28 W
Saraswati ≃	272b	22.59 N	88.22 E
Sarata	78	46.02 N	29.38 E
Sarath	126	24.14 N	86.50 E
Saratoga, Austl.	170	33.28 S	151.21 E
Saratoga, Ca., U.S.	226	37.15 N	122.01 W
Saratoga, In., U.S.	216	40.14 N	84.55 W
Saratoga, Tx., U.S.	222	30.17 N	94.31 W
Saratoga, Wy., U.S.	200	41.27 N	106.48 W
Saratoga □6	210	43.00 N	73.51 W
Saratoga Battlefield Monument ⊥	210	43.05 N	75.36 W
Saratoga Creek ≃	282	37.25 N	121.58 W
Saratoga Lake ⊜	210	43.01 N	73.39 W
Saratoga National Historical Park ♦	210	43.00 N	73.38 W
Saratoga Passage u	224	48.10 N	122.30 W
Saratoga Spa State Park ♦	210	43.03 N	73.50 W
Şaratoga Springs	210	43.04 N	73.47 W
Šara-Togot	88	53.01 N	106.43 E
Saratok	112	1.44 N	111.20 E
Saratov	80	51.34 N	46.02 E
Saratov □8	76	52.00 N	42.40 E
Saratovka	86	51.12 N	54.54 E
Saratovskoje vodochranilišče ⊜1	80	52.45 N	48.30 E
Saraurcu ∧	246	0.06 S	77.55 W
Sarāvān, Īrān	128	27.15 N	62.40 E
Saravan, Lao	110	15.43 N	106.25 E
Sarawak □3	112	2.30 N	113.30 E
Saray	130	41.26 N	27.55 E
Saraya, Guinée	150	10.46 N	10.24 W
Saraya, Sén.	150	12.50 N	11.45 W
Sarāyān	128	33.51 N	58.31 E
Saraycık	130	40.57 N	35.08 E
Saraydüzü	130	41.20 N	34.52 E
Sarā-ye Aḥmadī	128	27.56 N	56.42 E
Sarayevo → Sarajevo	38	43.52 N	18.25 E
Sarayköy	130	37.55 N	28.58 E
Sarayönü	130	38.17 N	32.25 E
Sarbaj	80	53.39 N	51.34 E
Sarbāz	128	26.39 N	61.15 E
Sarbinowo	54	52.40 N	14.40 E
Sárbogárd	30	46.53 N	18.38 E
Sarca ≃	64	45.52 N	10.52 E
Sarce ≃	50	48.09 N	4.18 E
Sarcee Indian Reserve ◂4	182	50.58 N	114.06 W
Sarcelle, Passe de la u	175f	22.29 S	167.12 E
Sarcelles	50	49.00 N	2.23 E
Sarche di Calavino	64	46.03 N	10.57 E
Sarcidano ◂1, It.	36	39.55 N	9.05 E
Şarcidano ◂1, It.	71	39.49 N	9.10 E
Šarčino	86	53.09 N	81.45 E
Sarclet	46	58.22 N	3.07 W
Sarcoxie	194	37.04 N	94.06 W
Sārda (Mahākālī) ≃	124	27.22 N	81.23 E
Sard āb)(	123	36.40 N	71.32 E
Sārda Canal ≋	124	28.08 N	80.24 E
Sardagna	64	46.03 N	11.06 E
Sardah	124	24.18 N	88.44 E
Sardaq	128	34.48 N	58.07 E
Sardara	71	39.37 N	8.49 E
Sardār Chāh	128	27.58 N	64.50 E
Sardārpur	120	22.39 N	74.59 E
Sardārshahr	120	28.26 N	74.29 E
Sar Dasht, Īrān	128	36.09 N	45.28 E
Sar Dasht, Īrān	128	32.32 N	48.52 E
Sardegna □4	71	40.00 N	9.00 E
Sardegna (Sardinia) I	71	40.00 N	9.00 E
Sardeh Band	120	33.17 N	68.39 E
Sardhana	124	29.09 N	77.37 E
Sardiha	126	22.22 N	87.09 E
Sardinal	236	10.31 N	85.39 W
Sardinata	246	8.05 N	72.48 W
Sardinia, N.Y., U.S.	210	42.32 N	78.31 W
Sardinia, Oh., U.S.	218	39.00 N	83.48 W
Sardinia → Sardegna I	71	40.00 N	9.00 E
Sardinien → Sardegna I	71	40.00 N	9.00 E
Sardis, B.C., Can.	224	49.08 N	121.57 W
Sardis, Al., U.S.	194	32.17 N	86.59 W
Sardis, Ga., U.S.	192	32.58 N	81.45 W
Sardis, Ky., U.S.	218	38.31 N	83.57 W
Sardis, Ms., U.S.	194	34.26 N	89.55 W
Sardis, Pa., U.S.	279b	40.29 N	79.42 W
Sardis, Tn., U.S.	194	35.27 N	88.18 W
Sardis Lake ⊜1	194	34.27 N	89.43 W
Şardona, Piz ∧	58	46.55 N	9.15 E
Šardonem'	24	63.56 N	44.37 E
Sarek ∧	24	67.25 N	17.46 E
Sareks Nationalpark ♦	24	67.15 N	17.30 E
Sārenga, India	126	22.46 N	87.02 E
Sārenga, India	272b	22.31 N	88.13 E
Sarentino (Sarnthein)	64	46.38 N	11.21 E
Sar-e Pol	120	36.14 N	65.55 E
Sarepta	194	32.53 N	93.26 W
Sarezzo	64	45.39 N	10.12 E
Sargans	58	47.03 N	9.26 E
Sargasso Sea ⊤2	8	30.00 N	50.00 W
Sargasso Sea ⊤2	8	30.00 N	50.00 W
Sargatskoje	86	55.37 N	73.30 E
Sargé-lès-le-Mans	50	48.02 N	0.14 E
Sargent, Ga., U.S.	192	33.25 N	84.52 W
Sargent, Ne., U.S.	198	41.38 N	99.22 W
Sargent Creek ≃	226	35.57 N	120.52 W
Şargodha	123	32.05 N	72.40 E
Šargol'džin	88	52.21 N	114.42 E
Šargorod	78	48.44 N	28.05 E
Sargou ≃	85	43.25 N	73.50 E
Şargul', ozero ⊜	86	54.35 N	78.51 E
Šargun	85	38.37 N	67.53 E
Sarh	146	9.09 N	18.23 E
Sarhli, Djebel ∧	34	36.06 N	0.40 E
Sārī	128	36.34 N	53.04 E
Saría I	38	35.50 N	27.15 E
Saribi, Tanjung ›	164	1.36 S	135.25 E
Sarıbuğday	130	40.35 N	35.35 E
Saric	232	31.08 N	111.23 W
Saricumbe	152	12.12 S	19.46 E
Sarigan I	108	16.42 N	145.47 E
Sarıgazi ◂8	267b	41.01 N	29.12 E
Sarıgöl	130	38.14 N	28.43 E
Sarıkamış	130	40.20 N	42.35 E
Sarıkaya, Tür.	130	38.47 N	32.15 E
Sarıkaya, Tür.	130	39.30 N	35.24 E
Sarikei	112	2.07 N	111.31 E
Sarıköy	130	40.12 N	27.36 E
Sarilhos Grandes	266c	38.41 N	8.58 W
Sarilhos Pequenos	266c	38.41 N	8.59 W
Sarim	154	0.23 S	40.58 E
Sarimbun, Pulau I	271c	1.26 N	103.41 E
Sarina	166	21.26 S	149.13 E
Sarine ≃	58	46.54 N	7.14 E
Sariñena	34	41.48 N	0.10 W
Sarıoğlan	130	39.05 N	35.59 E
Saripul'	85	38.26 N	70.08 E
Sarīr	146	27.36 N	22.32 E
Sarısu	84	39.01 N	42.55 E
Sarita	196	27.13 N	97.47 W
Sariwŏn	98	38.31 N	125.44 E
Sarıyar Barajı ⊜1	130	40.02 N	31.40 E
Şarız	130	38.30 N	36.30 E
Šarja	80	58.24 N	45.30 E
Sarju (Babaī) ≃	124	27.42 N	81.16 E
Sark I	43b	49.26 N	2.21 W
Sark ≃	44	54.58 N	3.04 W
Şarkad	30	46.44 N	21.23 E
Šarkan	80	57.18 N	53.53 E
Sarkand	86	45.26 N	79.54 E
Şarkikaraağaç	130	38.04 N	31.23 E
Şarkışla	130	39.21 N	36.26 E
Šarkovščina	76	55.22 N	27.28 E
Şarköy	130	40.37 N	27.06 E
Şarlat-la-Canéda	32	44.53 N	1.13 E
Šarlauk	128	38.13 N	55.38 E
Şarles	198	48.56 N	98.59 W
Šarlyk	86	52.55 N	54.35 E
Sarmakovo	84	43.43 N	43.12 E
Sarmanovo	80	55.15 N	52.36 E
Sărmaşu	38	46.46 N	24.11 E
Sarmathura	124	26.31 N	77.22 E
Sarmatskaja ≃	83	47.20 N	38.48 E
Sármellék	30	46.44 N	17.10 E
Sarmi	164	1.51 S	138.44 E
Sarmiento	254	45.36 S	69.05 W
Sarmiento ≃	288	34.25 S	58.35 W
Sarmiento de Gambia, Cerro ∧	254	54.27 S	70.50 W
Sarmiento de Gamboa, Cerro I	9	22.48 S	43.12 W
Sarmiento de Gamboa, Lago ⊜	254	51.04 S	72.45 W
Särna	26	61.41 N	13.08 E
Sarna, ozero ⊜	80	48.24 N	44.38 E
Sarnano	66	43.02 N	13.18 E
Sārnāth ⊥	124	25.24 N	83.01 E
Sarnen	58	46.54 N	8.15 E
Sârnena ⋀	38	42.35 N	25.10 E
Sarner See ⊜	58	46.52 N	8.13 E
Sarnia	214	42.58 N	82.23 W
Sarnico	64	45.40 N	9.57 E
Sarno	68	40.49 N	14.37 E
Sarnow	54	53.45 N	13.37 E
Sarnowa	30	51.38 N	16.54 E
Sarnthein → Sarentino	64	46.38 N	11.21 E
Šarnutovskij	80	47.40 N	43.46 E
Sarny	78	51.21 N	26.36 E
Şaroako	112	2.31 S	121.22 E
Šaroargun ≃	84	43.02 N	45.44 E
Sarolangun	112	2.18 S	102.42 E
Saroma-ko ⊜	92a	44.08 N	143.50 E
Saron	158	33.11 S	19.01 E
Saronikós Kólpos c	38	37.54 N	23.12 E
Saronno	62	45.38 N	9.02 E
Saros Körfezi c	130	40.30 N	26.20 E
Sárospatak	30	48.19 N	21.34 E
Šarovka	78	50.01 N	35.27 E
Sarowbī	120	34.36 N	69.43 E
Sarpa	80	47.07 N	45.29 E
Şarpa, ozero ⊜	80	47.18 N	45.20 E
Šarpajevka	78	48.34 N	40.59 E
Sar Passage u	175b	7.12 N	134.23 E
Şarpinskije ozera ⊜	80	47.30 N	45.00 E
Šar Planina ⋀	38	42.05 N	20.50 E
Sarpsborg	26	59.17 N	11.07 E
Sarpy Creek ≃	202	46.15 N	107.09 W
Sárrabus ◂1	71	39.23 N	9.21 E
Sarralbe	56	49.00 N	7.01 E
Sarras	62	45.11 N	4.48 E
Sarrath, Oued V	36	35.59 N	8.23 E
Sarratt	260	51.41 N	0.29 W
Sarre	62	45.43 N	7.15 E
Sarre (Saar) ≃	56	49.42 N	6.34 E
Sarre Blanche ≃	56	48.41 N	7.01 E
Sarrebourg	58	48.44 N	7.03 E
Sarrebruck → Saarbrücken	56	49.14 N	6.59 E
Sarreguemines	56	49.06 N	7.03 E
Sarre Rouge ≃	56	48.41 N	7.01 E
Sarre-Union	56	48.56 N	7.05 E
Sarria	34	42.47 N	7.24 W
Sarriá ◂8	266d	41.24 N	2.08 E
Sarro	150	13.43 N	5.15 W
Sarroch	71	39.04 N	9.00 E
Sars	86	56.33 N	57.07 E
Sarsfield	212	45.27 N	75.21 W
Sarsina	66	43.55 N	12.08 E
Sarsol	272c	19.02 N	73.01 E
Sarstedt	52	52.14 N	9.51 E
Sarstein ∧	64	47.36 N	13.41 E
Sarstoon (Sarstún) ≃	236	15.53 N	88.55 W
Sarstún (Sarstoon) ≃	236	15.53 N	88.55 W
Sarsuna	272b	22.28 N	88.18 E
Sart	56	50.31 N	5.56 E
Sartang ≃	74	67.44 N	133.12 E
Sarteano	66	42.59 N	11.52 E
Sartell	190	45.37 N	94.12 W
Sartène	36	41.36 N	8.59 E
Sarthe □5	32	48.00 N	0.05 E
Sarthe ≃	32	47.30 N	0.32 W
Sartičala	84	41.43 N	45.10 E
Sartilly	32	48.45 N	1.27 W
Sartirana Lomellina	62	45.07 N	8.39 E
Sartlan, ozero ⊜	86	55.00 N	78.35 E
Sartol'gen	80	48.57 N	47.03 E
Sartrouville	261	48.57 N	2.10 E
Saru	85	42.20 N	77.55 E
Sarufutsu	92a	45.16 N	142.12 E
Saruhanlı	130	38.44 N	27.34 E
Şarūr	128	23.22 N	58.07 E
Šar Us ≃	88	47.08 N	97.38 E
Saru-shima I	268	35.17 N	139.42 E
Sarvadyk	80	46.07 N	44.07 E
Sárvár	30	47.15 N	16.57 E
Sarver	214	40.44 N	79.45 W
Sarvestān	128	29.16 N	53.13 E
Sárvíz ≃	30	46.24 N	18.41 E
Saryagač	85	41.27 N	69.10 E
Saryassija	85	38.25 N	67.57 E
Sarybarak	85	43.24 N	71.30 E
Sarybasat	86	46.38 N	60.27 E
Sarybulak, Kaz.	86	49.27 N	76.27 E
Sarybulak, Kyrg.	85	40.54 N	73.49 E
Saryč, mys ›	78	44.23 N	33.45 E
Sarychosor	85	38.32 N	69.49 E
Sarydala	85	41.11 N	70.27 E
Saryg-Sep	88	51.30 N	95.36 E
Sary-Išikotrau ◂2	86	45.30 N	76.00 E
Sarykamskoje, ozero ⊜	72	41.56 N	57.25 E
Sarykoby	85	43.44 N	72.35 E
Sarykol'skij chrebet ⋀	120	38.00 N	74.30 E
Sarykomej	86	45.12 N	74.11 E
Sarykopa, ozero ⊜	86	50.22 N	64.08 E
Sarymogol	85	39.55 N	72.47 E
Sarymoin, ozero ⊜	86	51.36 N	64.30 E
Şaryozek	86	44.22 N	77.59 E
Šarypovo	86	55.33 N	89.12 E
Saryšagan	86	46.07 N	73.38 E
Sarysu	86	48.23 N	69.59 E
Sarysu ≃	86	45.12 N	66.36 E
Sary-Taš	85	39.44 N	73.15 E
Sarytau	86	49.54 N	76.41 E
Saryžaz	72	42.55 N	79.38 E
Sarzana	64	44.07 N	9.58 E
Sarzanello, Fortezza di ⊥	64	44.08 N	9.58 E
Sarzeau	32	47.32 N	2.46 W
S'as' ≃	76	60.09 N	32.30 E
Saʿsaʿ, Sūrīy.	132	33.17 N	36.02 E
Sasa, Yis.	132	33.02 N	35.24 E
Sasabe	200	31.27 N	111.31 W
Sasabe ≃	200	30.41 N	111.56 W
Sasabeneh	144	7.55 N	43.39 E
Sasaga-mine ∧	96	33.49 N	133.17 E
Sasaginnigak Lake ⊜	184	51.36 N	95.40 W
Sasago-tunnel ◂5	94	35.38 N	138.47 E
Sasaguri	96	33.37 N	130.32 E
Sasak	110	0.01 S	99.42 E
Sasakwa	196	34.56 N	96.31 W
Sasamungga	175e	7.02 S	156.47 E
Sasao	270	34.57 N	135.20 E
Sasar, Tanjung ›	115b	9.17 S	119.56 E
Sāsarām	124	24.57 N	84.02 E
Sasayama	96	35.04 N	135.13 E
Sasa-yama ∧	96	33.03 N	132.40 E
Sasbach	58	48.08 N	7.37 E
Sasco Brook ≃	276	41.07 N	73.18 W
Sásd	30	46.15 N	18.06 E
Sasebo	92	33.10 N	129.43 E
Sasebo Naval Base ■	92	33.09 N	129.45 E
Saseenos	224	48.24 N	123.40 W
Saseginaga, Lac ⊜	190	47.06 N	78.35 W
Sashalom ◂8	264c	47.31 N	19.11 E
Sas-hegy ∧2	264c	47.23 N	19.18 E
Sashiki	174m	26.10 N	127.47 E
Sashima	94	36.08 N	139.51 E
Saskatchewan □4, Can.	176	54.00 N	105.00 W
Saskatchewan □4, Can.	184	54.00 N	105.00 W
Saskatchewan ≃	184	53.12 N	99.16 W
Saskatoon	184	52.07 N	106.38 W
Saskylach	74	71.55 N	114.01 E
Saslaya, Cerro ∧	238	13.45 N	85.03 W
Sasmik, Cape ›	180	51.36 N	177.55 W
Sāsni	124	27.43 N	78.05 E
Sasolburg	158	26.48 S	27.45 E
Sason	130	38.20 N	41.25 E
Sasovo	80	54.21 N	41.54 E
Saspamco	196	29.14 N	98.18 W
Saspul Gompa	123	34.15 N	77.09 E
Sassafras, Austl.	274b	37.52 S	145.21 E
Sassafras, Ky., U.S.	192	37.14 N	83.06 W
Sassafras ≃	208	39.23 N	76.02 W
Sassafras Mountain ∧	192	35.03 N	82.48 W
Sassafras Neck ›1	208	39.25 N	75.55 W
Sassandra	150	4.58 N	6.05 W
Sassandra ≃	150	4.58 N	6.05 W
Sassano	68	40.20 N	15.33 E
Sassari	71	40.44 N	8.33 E
Sassari □4	71	40.40 N	9.00 E
Sassbach ≃	61	46.43 N	15.48 E
Sasse ≃	62	44.15 N	5.55 E
Sassello	62	44.29 N	8.30 E
Sassenage	62	45.12 N	5.40 E
Sassenberg	52	51.59 N	8.02 E
Sassenheim	52	52.13 N	4.31 E
Sassnitz	54	54.31 N	13.38 E
Sassocorvaro	66	43.47 N	12.30 E
Sasso di Castalda	68	40.30 N	15.40 E
Sassoferrato	66	43.26 N	12.51 E
Sasso Marconi	64	44.24 N	11.15 E
S'as'stro	76	60.08 N	32.34 E
Sassuolo	64	44.33 N	10.47 E
Sastobe	85	42.34 N	70.00 E
Sastown	150	4.40 N	8.26 W
Sastre	252	31.45 S	61.50 W
Sas van Gent	52	51.14 N	3.47 E
Sasyk, ozero ⊜	78	45.12 N	33.31 E
Sasykkol', ozero ⊜	86	46.35 N	81.00 E
Şasykoli	80	47.33 N	47.00 E
Šat ≃	82	54.08 N	37.47 E
Satadougou	150	12.21 N	10.07 W
Satah Mountain ∧	182	52.29 N	124.41 W
Şatakunta ◂1	26	61.30 N	23.00 E
Šatalovka	78	51.09 N	38.16 E
Šatalovo	76	54.20 N	32.27 E
Sata-misaki ›	92	30.59 N	130.40 E
Satāna	122	20.35 N	74.12 E
Satanov	78	49.15 N	26.16 E
Satanta	198	37.26 N	100.59 W
Sátão	34	40.44 N	7.44 W
Sātāra, India	122	17.41 N	73.59 E
Satara, S. Afr.	156	24.29 S	31.47 E
Sataua	175a	13.28 S	172.40 W
Sātbāria, Bngl.	126	23.52 N	89.26 E
Sātbāria, India	272b	22.25 N	88.33 E
Satélite	232	31.43 N	106.23 W
Satellite Beach	220	28.10 N	80.35 W
Satellite Channel u	224	48.43 N	123.30 W
Satema	152	4.18 N	21.42 E
Satengar, Pulau I	112	7.31 S	117.17 E
Säter	40	60.21 N	15.45 E
Sātgāchia	126	23.16 N	88.08 E
Sātghara	272b	22.44 N	88.21 E
Saticoy	228	34.17 N	119.09 W
Satilla ≃	192	30.59 N	81.28 W
Satilpa Creek ≃	194	31.39 N	88.05 W
Satin	222	31.21 N	97.02 W
Satipo	248	11.16 S	74.37 W
Sátiro Dias	250	11.36 S	38.36 W
Satis	80	55.02 N	43.48 E
Satīt (Tekeze) ≃	140	14.20 N	35.50 E
Satka	86	55.03 N	59.01 E
Satkānia	120	22.04 N	92.03 E
Şātkhira	124	22.43 N	89.06 E
Šatki	80	55.11 N	44.08 E
Satla Bīl ≡	126	22.54 N	90.04 E
Satluj → Sutlej ≃	120	29.23 N	71.02 E
Satna	124	24.35 N	80.50 E
Sato, Cañada de ≃	288	34.35 S	58.38 W
Satomi	94	36.43 N	140.30 E
Şátoraljaújhely	30	48.24 N	21.39 E
Šatov	61	48.48 N	16.01 E
Šatovo	82	54.56 N	37.14 E
Satow	54	53.59 N	11.51 E
Sātpura Range ⋀	122	22.00 N	78.00 E
Sätrabrunn	40	59.51 N	16.27 E
Şatriano di Lucania	68	40.33 N	15.33 E
Šatrovo	86	56.31 N	64.38 E
Satrup	41	54.41 N	9.35 E
Satsop ≃	224	47.03 N	123.30 W
Satsop, Middle Fork ≃	224	47.05 N	123.30 W
Satsop, West Fork ≃	224	47.02 N	123.32 W
Satsuma	194	30.51 N	88.03 W
Satsuma-hantō ›1	92	31.25 N	130.25 E
Satsunan-shotō II	93b	29.00 N	130.00 E
Sattahip	110	12.40 N	100.54 E
Sāttānkulam	122	8.27 N	77.56 E
Satte	94	36.04 N	139.43 E
Sattel	58	47.05 N	8.42 E
Sattenapalle	122	16.24 N	80.11 E
Satthwa	110	17.46 N	94.30 E
Sattledt	61	48.04 N	14.03 E
Satui	112	3.47 S	115.27 E
Sātuli	272b	22.33 N	88.34 E
Satu Mare	38	47.48 N	22.53 E
Satu Mare □6	38	47.40 N	23.00 E
Şatun	110	6.37 N	100.04 E
Šatura	80	55.34 N	39.32 E
Saturna	224	48.43 N	123.11 W
Saturna Island I	224	48.47 N	123.08 W
Şaturnino M. Laspiur	252	31.42 S	62.29 W
Šaturtorf	76	55.34 N	39.26 E
Satus Creek ≃	202	46.16 N	120.07 W
Satus Peak ∧	224	46.15 N	120.45 W
Satyamangalam	122	11.31 N	77.15 E
Satzkorn	264a	52.29 N	12.59 E
Sau ≃	269c	10.46 N	106.48 E
Sauble ≃	212	44.40 N	81.17 W
Sauce, Arg.	252	30.05 S	58.46 W
Sauce, Perú	248	6.44 S	76.10 W
Sauce, Ur.	258	34.39 S	56.04 W
Sauce, Arroyo ≃	258	34.26 S	57.28 W
Sauce, Arroyo del ≃	288	34.41 S	58.50 W

Symbols in the index entries represent the broad categories identified in the key at the right. Symbols with superior numbers (⋀1) identify subcategories (see complete key on page *I · 1).*

Symbole im Register stellen die rechts im Schlüssel erklärten Kategorien dar. Symbole mit hochgestellten Ziffern (⋀1) bezeichnen Unterabteilungen einer Kategorie (vgl. vollständiger Schlüssel auf Seite *I · 1).*

Los símbolos incluídos en el texto del índice representan las grandes categorias identificadas con la clave a la derecha. Los símbolos con numeros en su parte superior (⋀1) identifican las subcategorías (véase la clave completa en la página *I · 1).*

Les symboles de l'index représentent les catégories indiquées dans la légende à droite. Les symboles suivis d'un indice (⋀1) représentent des sous-catégories (voir légende complète à la page *I · 1).*

Os símbolos incluídos no texto do índice representam as grandes categorias identificadas com a chave à direita. Os símbolos com números em sua parte superior (⋀1) identificam as subcategorias (veja-se a chave completa à página *I · 1).*

∧ Mountain	Berg	Montaña	Montagne	Montanha
⋀ Mountains	Gebirge	Montañas	Montagnes	Montanhas
)(Pass	Paß	Paso	Col	Passo
V Valley, Canyon	Tal, Cañon	Valle, Cañón	Vallée, Canyon	Vale, Canhão
≚ Plain	Ebene	Llano	Plaine	Planície
› Cape	Kap	Cabo	Cap	Cabo
I Island	Insel	Isla	Île	Ilha
II Islands	Inseln	Islas	Îles	Ilhas
⊥ Other Topographic Features	Andere Topographische Objekte	Otros Elementos Topográficos	Autres données topographiques	Outros acidentes topográficos

ESPAÑOL				FRANÇAIS				PORTUGUÊS			
Nombre	Página	Lat.°′	Long.°′ W = Oeste	Nom	Page	Lat.°′	Long.°′ W = Ouest	Nome	Página	Lat.°′	Long.°′ W = Oeste

The body of this page is a multilingual geographic index (gazetteer) arranged in six columns across three languages (Español, Français, Português), each listing place names with page numbers and latitude/longitude coordinates, followed by a fourth group of columns running from "Schäftlarn" through "Schweizer-Reneke" on the right side of the page. The dense entries cover names from "Sauce Corto, Arroyo" through "Schweizer-Reneke."

Bottom legend (symbols key):

≃	River	Fluß	Río	Rivière	Rio	◻ Submarine Features	Untermeerische Objekte
≍	Canal	Kanal	Canal	Canal	Canal	⬩ Political Unit	Politische Einheit
レ	Waterfall, Rapids	Wasserfall, Stromschnellen	Cascada, Rápidos	Chute d'eau, Rapides	Cascata, Rápidos	⊥ Cultural Institution	Kulturelle Institution
ﬤ	Strait	Meeresstraße	Estrecho	Détroit	Estreito	⊥ Historical Site	Historische Stätte
@	Bay, Gulf	Bucht, Golf	Bahía, Golfo	Baie, Golfe	Baía, Golfo	♣ Recreational Site	Erholungs- und Feriënort
@	Lake, Lakes	See, Seen	Lago, Lagos	Lac, Lacs	Lago, Lagos	✈ Airport	Flughafen
≋	Swamp	Sumpf	Pantano	Marais	Pântano	✠ Military Installation	Militäranlage
⊟	Ice Features, Glacier	Eis- und Gletscherformen	Accidentes Glaciares	Formes glaciaires	Acidentes glaciares	⊠ Miscellaneous	Verschiedenes
◻	Other Hydrographic Features	Andere Hydrographische Objekte	Otros Elementos Hidrográficos	Autres données hydrographiques	Outros acidentes hidrográficos		

Accidentes Submarinos	Unidad Política	Formes de relief sous-marin	Accidentes submarinos
Institución Cultural	Kulturelle Institution	Entité politique	Unidade política
Sitio Histórico	Historische Stätte	Institution culturelle	Instituição cultural
Centro de Recreo	Erholungs- und Feriënort	Site historique	Sítio histórico
Aeropuerto	Flughafen	Centre de loisirs	Área de Lazer
Instalación Militar	Militäranlage	Aéroport	Aeroporto
Misceláneo	Verschiedenes	Installation militaire	Instalação militar
		Divers	Diversos

ENGLISH: Name — Page — Lat.°′ — Long.°′
DEUTSCH: Name — Seite — Breite°′ — Länge°′ E = Ost

Symbols in the index entries represent the broad categories identified in the key at the right. Symbols with superior numbers (⋏[1]) identify subcategories (see complete key on page *I · 1).*

Symbole im Register stellen die rechts im Schlüssel erklärten Kategorien dar. Symbole mit hochgestellten Ziffern (⋏[1]) bezeichnen Unterabteilungen einer Kategorie (vgl. vollständiger Schlüssel auf Seite *I · 1).*

Los símbolos incluídos en el texto del índice representan las grandes categorias identificadas con la clave a la derecha. Los símbolos con numeros en su parte superior (⋏[1]) identifican las subcategorías (véase la clave completa en la página *I · 1).*

Les symboles de l'index représentent les catégories indiquées dans la légende à droite. Les symboles suivis d'un indice (⋏[1]) représentent des sous-catégories (voir légende complète à la page *I · 1).*

Os símbolos incluídos no texto do índice representam as grandes categorias identificadas com a chave à direita. Os símbolos com números em sua parte superior (⋏[1]) identificam as subcategorias (veja-se a chave completa à página *I · 1).*

∧ Mountain	Berg	Montaña	Montagne	Montanha
⋏ Mountains	Gebirge	Montañas	Montagnes	Montanhas
)(Pass	Paß	Paso	Col	Passo
V Valley, Canyon	Tal, Cañon	Valle, Cañón	Vallée Canyon	Vale, Canhão
≚ Plain	Ebene	Llano	Plaine	Planície
› Cape	Kap	Cabo	Cap	Cabo
I Island	Insel	Isla	Île	Ilha
II Islands	Inseln	Islas	Îles	Ilhas
± Other Topographic Features	Andere Topographische Objekte	Otros Elementos Topográficos	Autres données topographiques	Outros acidentes topográficos

Semi-Sha I · 159

ESPAÑOL / FRANÇAIS / PORTUGUÊS

Nombre / Nom / Nome	Página / Page / Página	Lat.°′	Long.°′ W = Oeste / W = Ouest / W = Oeste
Semibratovo	80	57.18 N	39.32 E
Semibugry	80	46.11 N	48.16 E
Semichi Islands II	181a	52.42 N	174.00 E
Semides'atnoje	78	51.21 N	38.44 E
Semidi Islands II	180	56.07 N	156.44 W
Semigorsk	88	56.42 N	104.41 E
Semijarka	86	50.54 N	78.20 E
Semikarakorsk	80	47.31 N	40.48 E
Semilej	80	53.57 N	45.21 E
Semilovo	80	55.04 N	42.10 E
Semiluki	78	51.41 N	39.02 E
Semily	30	50.36 N	15.20 E
Seminara	68	38.20 N	15.52 E
Seminary	194	31.33 N	89.29 W
Seminoe Reservoir ⊜[1]	200	42.00 N	106.50 W
Seminoe State Park ♠	202	42.05 N	106.55 W
Seminole, Fl., U.S.	220	27.50 N	82.47 W
Seminole, Ok., U.S.	196	35.13 N	96.40 W
Seminole, Tx., U.S.	196	32.43 N	102.38 W
Seminole □[6]	220	28.45 N	81.13 W
Seminole, Lake ⊜[1]	192	30.46 N	84.50 W
Seminole Draw V	196	32.27 N	102.20 W
Seminole Park	220	27.52 N	82.45 W
Seminskij chrebet ⋏	86	51.05 N	85.50 E
Semiozerje	88	49.52 N	110.23 E
Semioz'ornoje	86	52.22 N	64.08 E
Semioz'ornyj	88	53.44 N	120.25 E
Semipalatinsk	86	50.28 N	80.13 E
Semipolka	86	54.07 N	67.16 E
Semipolki	78	50.43 N	30.56 E
Semirara Island I	116	12.04 N	121.23 E
Semisopochnoi Island I	181a	52.00 N	179.35 E
Semitau	112	0.33 N	111.58 E
Semizbugy	86	50.12 N	74.48 E
Semizbugy, gora ∧	86	50.10 N	74.56 E
Semjany	80	56.02 N	45.59 E
Semli Kalān	124	24.10 N	76.39 E
Seml'ovo	76	55.03 N	33.58 E
Semmens Lake ⊜	184	55.03 N	94.11 W
Semmering	61	47.38 N	15.49 E
Semnān	128	35.33 N	53.24 E
Semnān □[4]	128	35.30 N	54.00 E
Semois ≃	56	49.53 N	4.45 E
Šemonaicha	86	50.39 N	81.54 E
Sem'ono-Aleksandrovka	78	51.03 N	40.12 E
Sem'onov	24	56.48 N	44.30 E
Sem'onovka, Kaz.	86	51.20 N	70.46 E
Sem'onovka, Kyrg.	85	42.43 N	77.32 E
Sem'onovka, Ukr.	78	49.36 N	33.10 E
Sem'onovka, Ukr.	78	52.10 N	32.35 E
Sem'onovskoje, Ross.	82	55.03 N	37.46 E
Sem'onovskoje, Ross.	82	55.18 N	38.21 E
Šemordan	80	56.11 N	50.26 E
Sempach	58	47.08 N	8.11 E
Sempacher See ⊜	58	47.09 N	8.09 E
Sempang Mangayau, Tanjong ›	112	7.02 N	116.45 E
Semple Lake ⊜	184	55.02 N	95.38 W
Sempol	115a	8.01 S	114.08 E
Semporna	112	4.28 N	118.36 E
Sempu, Pulau I	115a	8.26 S	112.42 E
Semuda	112	2.51 S	112.58 E
Semuliki ≃	154	1.14 N	30.28 E
Semur-en-Auxois	50	47.29 N	4.20 E
Šemurša	80	54.53 N	47.32 E
Šemyšejka	80	52.54 N	45.24 E
Semža	24	66.09 N	44.08 E
Sên ≃	110	12.32 N	104.28 E
Sena, Bol.	248	11.32 S	67.11 W
Seňa, Česko.	30	48.34 N	21.15 E
Sena, Moç.	154	17.27 S	35.00 E
Senador Amaral	256	22.35 S	46.11 W
Senador Canedo	255	16.43 S	49.05 W
Senador Côrtes	256	21.48 S	42.56 W
Senador Firmino	255	20.55 S	43.06 W
Senador Guiomard	248	10.14 S	67.36 W
Senador José Bento	256	22.10 S	46.10 W
Senador José Porfirio	250	2.39 S	51.55 W
Senador Pompeu	250	5.35 S	39.22 W
Senago	266b	45.35 N	9.07 E
Senahú	236	15.24 N	89.50 W
Senai	114	1.36 N	103.39 E
Senainville	261	48.30 N	1.37 E
Senaja	112	6.45 N	117.03 E
Senaki	84	42.17 N	42.04 E
Senale	64	46.31 N	11.06 E
Senales, Val di V	64	46.45 N	10.50 E
Sena Madureira	248	9.04 S	68.40 W
Senamaninik	114	0.45 N	100.47 E
Senanayake Samudra ⊜[1]	122	7.11 N	81.29 E
Senang, Pulau I	271c	1.11 N	103.44 E
Senanga	152	16.06 S	23.16 E
Sénart, Forêt de ♠	261	48.40 N	2.30 E
Sénas	62	43.45 N	5.05 E
Sena → Seine ≃	32	49.26 N	0.26 E
Senate	184	49.18 N	109.41 W
Senath	194	36.08 N	90.09 W
Senatobia	194	34.37 N	89.58 W
Šenbertal	86	48.43 N	60.20 E
Senča	78	50.16 N	33.20 E
Send	260	51.17 N	0.31 W
Sendafa	144	9.07 N	39.00 E
Sendai, Nihon	92	31.49 N	130.18 E
Sendai, Nihon	92	38.15 N	140.53 E
Sendai ≃, Nihon	92	31.51 N	130.12 E
Sendai ≃, Nihon	96	35.32 N	134.11 E
Sendai-heiya ≚	92	38.15 N	141.00 E
Sendelingsdrif	156	28.12 S	16.53 E
Senden, Dtsch.	52	51.51 N	7.29 E
Senden, Dtsch.	58	48.19 N	10.03 E
Sendenhorst	52	51.50 N	7.49 E
Šender	86	49.46 N	66.09 E
Sendhwa	120	21.41 N	75.06 E
Sêndo	102	31.42 N	95.16 E
Sendurjana	120	21.32 N	78.17 E
Senduruhan	112	1.00 S	110.46 E
Sene ≃	150	7.30 N	0.33 W
Senebui, Tanjung ›	114	2.17 N	101.03 E
Senec	30	48.14 N	17.24 E
Seneca, Il., U.S.	216	41.18 N	88.36 W
Seneca, Ks., U.S.	198	39.50 N	96.03 W
Seneca, Md., U.S.	284c	39.04 N	77.17 W
Seneca, Mo., U.S.	194	36.50 N	94.36 W
Seneca, Or., U.S.	202	44.08 N	118.58 W
Seneca, Pa., U.S.	214	41.23 N	79.42 W
Seneca, S.C., U.S.	192	34.41 N	82.57 W
Seneca □[6], N.Y., U.S.	210	42.54 N	76.52 W
Seneca □[6], Oh., U.S.	214	41.07 N	83.11 W
Seneca ≃	210	43.12 N	76.17 W
Seneca, Mount ∧	210	42.01 N	78.49 W
Seneca Castle	210	42.53 N	77.06 W
Seneca Caverns ⊥[5]	214	41.11 N	82.53 W
Seneca Creek ⊂	284b	39.19 N	76.22 W
Seneca Creek ≃	196	36.36 N	102.52 W
Seneca Falls	210	42.54 N	76.47 W
Seneca Lake ⊜	210	42.40 N	76.57 W
Seneca Mall ◆[9]	284a	42.50 N	78.47 W
Seneca State Park ♠	208	39.08 N	77.15 W
Senecaville Lake ⊜[1]	188	39.55 N	81.25 W
Seneffe	50	50.31 N	4.15 E
Senegal (Sénégal) □[1], Afr.	134	14.00 N	14.00 W
Senegal (Sénégal) □[1], Afr.	150	14.00 N	14.00 W
Sénégal ≃	150	15.48 N	16.32 W
Seneghe	71	40.05 N	8.36 E
Senekal	158	28.19 S	27.36 E
Senerchia	68	40.44 N	15.12 E
Senetosa, Capu di ›	71	41.33 N	8.47 E
Sénez	62	43.55 N	6.24 E
Senežskoje, ozero ⊜	82	56.12 N	37.00 E
Senftenberg	54	51.31 N	14.00 E
Senga Hill	154	9.22 S	31.12 E
Sengbachstausee ⊜[1]	263	51.08 N	7.09 E
Sengejskij, ostrov I	24	68.27 N	51.05 E
Šengel'šij	86	48.33 N	57.28 E
Sengés	255	24.06 S	49.29 W
Senggarang	114	1.45 N	103.03 E
Sênggê ≃	120	32.28 N	79.44 E
Senghenydd	42	51.36 N	3.16 W
Sengilej	80	53.58 N	48.46 E
Sengkamang	114	0.42 N	101.55 E
Sengsengbirge ⋏	61	47.47 N	14.15 E
Senguer ≃	254	45.32 S	68.54 W
Sengwa ≃	154	17.07 S	28.05 E
Sengwarden	52	53.35 N	8.02 E
Senhāti	126	22.53 N	89.33 E
Senhor do Bonfim	250	10.27 S	40.11 W
Senica	30	48.41 N	17.22 E
Senigallia	66	43.43 N	13.13 E
Senirkent	130	38.07 N	30.33 E
Senise	68	40.09 N	16.18 E
Senj	36	44.59 N	14.54 E
Senja I	24	69.20 N	17.30 E
Senjitu	98	41.56 N	116.25 E
Senjō-san ∧	96	35.26 N	133.36 E
Senkevičevka	78	50.32 N	25.02 E
Senkobo	154	17.38 S	25.58 E
Sen'kovo	83	49.31 N	37.43 E
Şenköy	130	36.05 N	36.05 E
Šenkursk	24	62.08 N	42.53 E
Senlac	184	52.29 N	109.41 W
Şenlikköy ◆[8]	267b	40.59 N	28.47 E
Senlis	50	49.12 N	2.35 E
Senlisse	261	48.41 N	1.59 E
Senmonorom	110	12.27 N	107.12 E
Senn, Dahr ou ⊥[4]	150	18.30 N	11.00 W
Sennaja	78	45.15 N	37.01 E
Sennan	96	34.22 N	135.17 E
Senne(Zenne) ≃	50	51.04 N	4.26 E
Sennecey-le-Grand	58	46.39 N	4.52 E
Senne II → Sennestadt	52	51.59 N	8.37 E
Sennen	42	50.04 N	5.42 W
Sennestadt	52	51.59 N	8.37 E
Senneterre	190	48.23 N	77.15 W
Senneville	275a	45.27 N	73.57 W
Sennevoy-le-Bas	50	47.48 N	4.17 E
Senno	76	54.49 N	29.43 E
Sennoj, Ross.	80	52.11 N	46.57 E
Sennoj, Ross.	80	50.16 N	43.37 E
Sennokura-yama ∧	94	36.49 N	138.50 E
Sennori	71	40.47 N	8.35 E
Sennwald	58	47.16 N	9.30 E
Sennybridge	42	51.57 N	3.34 W
Senoia	192	33.18 N	84.33 W
Senonches	50	48.33 N	1.02 E
Senones	58	48.24 N	6.59 E
Senorbì	71	39.32 N	9.08 E
Sénou	150	12.31 N	6.56 W
Sénouire ≃	62	45.16 N	3.25 E
Şenpazar	130	41.48 N	33.16 E
Senqunyane ≃	158	30.03 S	28.10 E
Senqu → Orange ≃	156	28.41 S	16.28 E
Senriyama	270	34.47 N	135.30 E
Sens	50	48.12 N	3.17 E
Sense ≃	58	46.54 N	7.14 E
Sensée ≃	50	50.16 N	3.06 E
Sensée, Canal de la ≊	50	50.14 N	3.17 E
Sensuntepeque	236	13.52 N	88.38 W
Senta	38	45.56 N	20.04 E
Šentala	80	54.27 N	51.29 E
Sentani, Danau ⊜	164	2.36 S	140.34 E
Sentarum, Danau ⊜	112	0.51 N	112.06 E
Sentas	86	49.19 N	82.28 E
Sentelek	86	51.13 N	83.44 E
Sentery	154	5.22 S	25.45 E
Šentilj	61	46.41 N	15.40 E
Sentinel	196	35.09 N	99.10 W
Sentinel Butte ∧	198	46.53 N	103.50 W
Sentinel Peak ∧	182	54.54 N	121.57 W
Sentinel Range ⋏	9	78.10 S	85.30 W
Sentino ≃	66	43.24 N	12.59 E
Šentjur	36	46.13 N	15.24 E
Sentolo	115a	7.50 S	110.13 E
Sentosa I	271c	1.15 N	103.50 E
Sento Sé	250	9.51 S	41.51 W
Sentsū-zan ∧	96	35.09 N	133.11 E
Senyavin Islands II	14	6.55 N	158.00 E
Senye	152	1.34 N	9.50 E
Şenyurt	130	37.06 N	40.40 E
Senzaki-wan ⊂	96	34.24 N	131.15 E
Sen-zan ∧	96	34.21 N	134.51 E
Senzig	54	52.17 N	13.39 E
Senzu-dake ∧	270	34.57 N	135.52 E
Seo de Urgel	34	42.21 N	1.28 E
Seohāra	124	29.13 N	78.35 E
Seolag-san Kukrip Kongwŏn ♠	98	38.09 N	128.24 E
Seon	58	47.21 N	8.10 E
Seonāth ≃	122	21.44 N	82.28 E
Seoni	124	22.05 N	79.32 E
Seoni Mālwa	124	22.27 N	77.28 E
Seorīnārāyan	120	21.44 N	82.35 E
Seoul Bridge ◆[5]	271b	37.32 N	126.56 E
Seoul National University ɤ[2]	271b	37.28 N	126.57 E
Seoul → Sŏul	98	37.33 N	126.58 E
Seoul Stadium ♠	271b	37.35 N	127.02 E
Seoul Station ◆[5]	271b	37.34 N	126.58 E
Sepahat	114	1.34 N	101.53 E
Sepang	114	2.42 N	101.45 E
Sepanjang, Pulau I	112	7.10 S	115.50 E
Separation Creek ≃	200	41.59 N	107.28 W
Separation Point ›	172	40.47 S	173.00 E
Sepasu	112	0.43 N	117.35 E
Sepatini ≃	248	7.36 S	65.24 W
Sépeaux	50	47.57 N	3.14 E
Sepetiba ◆[8]	256	22.58 S	43.42 W
Sepetiba, Baía de ⊂	256	23.00 S	43.48 W
Šepetovka	78	50.11 N	27.04 E
Sepi	175e	8.33 S	159.50 E
Sepik ≃	164	3.51 S	144.34 E
Sepino	66	41.24 N	14.37 E
Sep'o	98	38.39 N	127.22 E
Sępólno Krajeńskie	30	53.28 N	17.32 E
Sépone → Muang Xépôn	110	16.41 N	106.14 E
Sepopa	156	18.13 S	22.13 E
Sępopol	30	54.15 N	21.00 E
Sepoti ≃	248	6.43 S	61.38 W
Sepotuba ≃	248	15.56 S	57.39 W
Seppeltsfield	168b	34.30 S	138.54 E
Seppenrade	52	51.46 N	7.23 E
Sepphoris → Ẓippori	132	32.45 N	35.17 E
Seppois-le-Bas	58	47.33 N	7.10 E
Septeuil	261	48.54 N	1.41 E
Sept Frères, Lac des ⊜	206	46.20 N	75.10 W
Sept-Îles (Seven Islands)	186	50.12 N	66.23 W
Septvaux	50	49.34 N	3.23 E
Sepulga ≃	194	31.11 N	86.46 W
Sepúlveda	34	41.18 N	3.45 W
Sepulveda ◆[8]	280	34.13 N	118.28 W
Sepulveda Dam ◆[6]	280	34.10 N	118.29 W
Sepulveda Flood Control Basin ≚[1]	228	34.11 N	118.29 W
Seputih ≃	112	4.42 S	105.54 E
Sepyč	80	58.11 N	54.08 E
Sequals	64	46.10 N	12.50 E
Sequatchie ≃	192	35.02 N	85.38 W
Sequeros	34	40.31 N	6.01 W
Sequillo ≃	34	41.45 N	5.30 W
Sequim	224	48.04 N	123.06 W
Sequim Bay ⊂	224	48.03 N	123.02 W
Sequoia National Park ♠	204	36.30 N	118.30 W
Sera	96	34.36 N	133.03 E
Sera, Pulau I	164	7.40 S	131.05 E
Šerabad	128	37.40 N	67.01 E
Serachs	128	36.32 N	61.13 E
Serafettin Dağları ⋏	130	39.05 N	41.10 E
Serafimovič	80	49.36 N	42.43 E
Šeragul	88	54.29 N	100.56 E
Seraidi	36	36.55 N	7.41 E
Seraing	56	50.36 N	5.29 E
Seraja ≃	82	56.15 N	38.45 E
Seram (Ceram) I	164	3.00 S	129.00 E
Seram, Laut (Ceram Sea) ⊤[2]	108	2.30 S	128.00 E
Serampore	126	22.45 N	88.21 E
Serang	115a	6.07 S	106.09 E
Serang ≃	115a	6.43 S	110.35 E
Serangoon	271c	1.22 N	103.54 E
Serangoon ≃	271c	1.24 N	103.56 E
Serangoon, Pulau I	271c	1.25 N	103.56 E
Serangoon Harbour ⊂	271c	1.23 N	103.57 E
Serapo	66	41.13 N	13.34 E
Serasan, Pulau I	112	2.30 N	109.03 E
Serasan, Selat ⊍	112	2.20 N	109.00 E
Seravalle Sesia	62	45.41 N	8.19 E
Seravezza	64	43.59 N	10.13 E
Seraya, Pulau I	271c	1.16 N	103.43 E
Serayevo → Sarajevo	38	43.52 N	18.25 E
Serayu ≃	115a	7.41 S	109.06 E
Šerbakul'	86	54.38 N	72.24 E
Serbeulangit, Pegunungan ⋏	114	3.45 N	97.50 E
Serbia → Srbija □[3]	38	44.00 N	21.00 E
Serchio ≃	64	43.47 N	10.16 E
Serdce-Kamen', mys ›	180	66.57 N	171.40 W
Serdež	80	57.17 N	48.17 E
Serditoje	83	48.02 N	38.24 E
Serdo	144	11.58 N	41.18 E
Serdoba ≃	80	52.34 N	44.01 E
Serdobsk	80	52.28 N	44.13 E
Séré'ama, Mont ∧	175f	13.47 S	167.29 E
Serebr'anka, Ross.	86	57.13 N	70.42 E
Serebr'anka, Ross.	265b	55.45 N	37.55 E
Serebr'anka, Ukr.	83	48.55 N	38.08 E
Serebr'anka ≃	265b	55.47 N	37.42 E
Serebr'ansk	86	49.43 N	83.20 E
Serebr'anyj Bor ◆[8]	265b	55.48 N	37.25 E
Serebr'anyje Prudy	82	54.28 N	38.44 E
Serebrovo	88	55.24 N	97.52 E
Serechoviči	78	51.25 N	24.40 E
Sered'	30	48.17 N	17.44 E
Sereda, Ross.	76	55.54 N	35.31 E
Sereda, Ross.	80	58.00 N	40.27 E
Šeredar' ≃	82	55.56 N	39.04 E
Seredejskij	76	54.03 N	35.14 E
Serediči	76	53.35 N	35.51 E
Seredina-Buda	78	52.11 N	34.01 E
Serednikovo, Ross.	80	55.15 N	39.40 E
Serednikovo, Ross.	265b	55.56 N	37.14 E
Seredn'ovo	265b	55.35 N	37.18 E
Seredžius	76	55.05 N	23.25 E
Şereflikoçhisar	130	38.56 N	33.33 E
Šeregeš	86	52.57 N	88.02 E
Seregno	62	45.39 N	9.12 E
Serein ≃	50	47.55 N	3.31 E
Seremban	114	2.43 N	101.56 E
Šeremetjevka	80	55.23 N	51.32 E
Šeremetjevo, Aeroport ⊠	82	55.59 N	37.24 E
Šeremetjevskij	82	55.59 N	37.30 E
Seremuk ≃	164	1.36 S	131.46 E
Serena	216	41.29 N	88.44 W
Seren del Grappa	64	45.59 N	11.51 E
Serengeti National Park ♠	154	2.20 S	34.50 E
Serengeti Plain ≚	154	2.50 S	35.00 E
Serengka	112	1.40 S	110.40 E
Serenje	154	13.15 S	30.14 E
Sereno	256	21.19 S	42.39 W
Šereševo	76	52.33 N	24.13 E
Seret ≃	78	48.38 N	25.52 E
Serfaus	58	47.02 N	10.36 E
Ser'ga	86	57.46 N	56.52 E
Sergač	80	55.32 N	45.28 E
Sergeant	214	41.38 N	78.45 W
Sergeant Bluff	198	42.24 N	96.21 W
Sergeja Kirova, ostrova II	74	77.12 N	89.30 E
Sergejeviči	76	53.30 N	27.45 E
Sergejevka, Kaz.	86	51.39 N	68.13 E
Sergejevka, Kaz.	86	53.51 N	67.25 E
Sergejevka, Ross.	89	44.22 N	131.39 E
Sergejevka, Ross.	89	43.21 N	133.22 E
Sergejevka, Ukr.	83	48.40 N	37.22 E
Sergejevo	86	57.18 N	86.02 E
Sergen	130	41.42 N	27.42 E
Sergijevka	78	51.46 N	41.05 E
Sergijev Posad (Zagorsk)	82	56.18 N	38.08 E
Sergijevskaja, Ross.	76	60.16 N	43.54 E
Sergijevskaja, Ross.	80	50.16 N	43.47 E
Sergijevskij	80	51.56 N	51.54 E
Sergili	85	41.13 N	69.14 E
Sergines	50	48.20 N	3.15 E
Serginskij	72	62.30 N	65.38 E
Sergipe □[3]	250	10.30 S	37.30 W
Sergokala	84	42.27 N	47.40 E
Sergozero, ozero ⊜	24	66.47 N	36.42 E
Seria	112	4.39 N	114.23 E
Serian	112	1.10 N	110.34 E
Seriana, Valle V	64	45.55 N	9.55 E
Seriate	62	45.41 N	9.43 E
Seribu, Kepulauan II	115a	5.36 S	106.33 E
Seribudolok, Indon.	114	2.56 N	98.37 E
Seribudolok, Indon.	114	2.51 N	99.04 E
Sericho	154	1.05 N	39.05 E
Seridó ≃	250	6.12 S	37.10 W
Sérifontaine	50	49.21 N	1.46 E
Sérifos	38	37.09 N	24.31 E
Sérifos I	38	37.11 N	24.31 E
Sérignan-du-Comtat	62	44.11 N	4.51 E
Sérigny ≃	176	56.47 N	66.00 W
Serik	130	36.55 N	31.06 E
Seringat, Pulau I	271c	1.14 N	103.51 E
Serino	68	40.51 N	14.52 E
Serinyol	130	36.24 N	36.11 E
Serio ≃	62	45.16 N	9.45 E
Seritinga	256	21.54 S	44.30 W
Serjol	24	60.02 N	48.58 E
Serkhe, Cerro ∧	248	17.22 S	69.22 W
Serkout, Djebel ∧	148	23.30 N	6.48 E
Serkovo	82	54.28 N	38.46 E
Serles ∧	64	47.08 N	11.23 E
Šerlovaja Gora	88	50.34 N	116.15 E
Serm ◆[8]	263	51.21 N	6.42 E
Sermaise	261	48.32 N	2.05 E
Sermaises	50	48.18 N	2.12 E
Sermaize-les-Bains	56	48.47 N	4.55 E
Serman	80	53.34 N	46.22 E
Sermata, Pulau I	164	8.13 S	128.55 E
Sermide	64	45.00 N	11.18 E
Sermilik ⊂[2]	176	65.37 N	38.03 W
Sermizelles	50	47.32 N	3.48 E
Sermoneta	66	41.33 N	12.59 E
Šerna ≃	82	55.51 N	38.34 E
Sernambetiba, Pontal de ›	287a	23.02 S	43.27 W
Sernambitiba	287a	22.41 S	42.59 W
Serniki	78	51.49 N	26.14 E
Sernovodsk	80	53.56 N	51.17 E
Sernur	80	56.56 N	49.09 E
Sernyy Zavod	128	39.59 N	58.50 E
Séro	150	14.48 N	11.04 W
Serodino	252	32.37 S	60.57 W
Ser'odka	76	58.10 N	28.12 E
Seroglazka	80	47.01 N	47.29 E
Ser'ogovo	24	62.20 N	50.36 E
Serooskerke	52	51.42 N	3.50 E
Seropédica	256	22.44 S	43.43 W
Serov	86	59.29 N	60.31 E
Serovo	85	40.27 N	71.12 E
Serowe	156	22.25 S	26.44 E
Ser'oža ≃	80	55.34 N	42.29 E
Serpa	34	37.56 N	7.36 W
Serpeddì, Punta ∧	71	39.22 N	9.18 E
Serpejsk	76	54.20 N	34.59 E
Serpent, Rivière au ≃	186	49.33 N	71.14 W
Serpentine	168a	32.22 S	115.59 E
Serpentine ≃, Austl.	168a	32.33 S	115.46 E
Serpentine ≃, B.C., Can.	224	49.05 N	122.50 W
Serpentine Lakes ⊜	162	28.32 S	129.09 E
Serpentine National Park ♠	168a	32.22 S	116.01 E
Serpentine Reservoir ⊜[1]	168a	32.25 S	116.08 E
Serpent Mound State Memorial ⊥	218	39.02 N	83.26 W
Serpents Mouth ⊍	241r	10.00 N	62.00 W
Serpnevoje	78	46.18 N	29.02 E
Serpuchov	82	54.55 N	37.25 E
Serpukhov → Serpuchov	82	54.55 N	37.25 E
Serqo → Sark I	43b	49.26 N	2.21 W
Serra	255	20.07 S	40.18 W
Serra, Monte ∧	66	43.46 N	10.33 E
Serra Branca	250	7.29 S	36.40 W
Serracapriola	68	41.48 N	15.09 E
Serrada	64	45.53 N	11.09 E
Serra da Canastra, Parque Nacional da ♠	255	20.10 S	46.40 W
Serra da Capivara, Parque Nacionl da ♠	250	8.40 S	42.15 W
Serra d'aiello	68	39.05 N	16.08 E
Serra de'Conti	66	43.33 N	13.02 E
Serra di Corvo, Lago di ⊜[1]	68	40.51 N	16.14 E
Serradifalco	70	37.27 N	13.53 E
Serra do Navio	250	0.59 N	52.03 W
Serra dos Aimorés	255	17.46 S	40.15 W
Serra do Salitre	255	19.06 S	46.41 W
Serra dos Órgãos, Parque Nacional da ♠	256	22.26 S	43.02 W
Sérrai	38	41.05 N	23.32 E
Serramanna	71	39.25 N	8.55 E
Serramazzoni	64	44.25 N	10.47 E
Serramonte Center ◆[9]	282	37.40 N	122.28 W
Serrana	255	21.14 S	47.36 W
Serrana, Cayo de ✦[4]	236	14.23 N	80.12 W
Serra Negra	256	22.36 S	46.42 W
Serra Negra do Norte	250	6.40 S	37.24 W
Serrânia	255	21.33 S	46.03 W
Serranilla, Cayo de ✦[4]	236	15.50 N	79.50 W
Serranópolis	255	18.16 S	52.00 W
Serranos	256	21.51 S	44.30 W
Serrara	68	40.42 N	13.54 E
Serra San Bruno	68	38.35 N	16.20 E
Serra San Quirico	66	43.27 N	13.01 E
Serrastretta	68	39.01 N	16.25 E
Serrat, Cap ›	36	37.14 N	9.13 E
Serra Talhada	250	7.59 S	38.18 W
Serravalle, It.	66	43.57 N	12.30 E
Serravalle, It.	66	42.47 N	13.01 E
Serravalle all'Adige	64	45.49 N	11.01 E
Serravalle Scrivia	62	44.43 N	8.51 E
Serre	68	40.35 N	15.11 E
Serre ≃	50	49.41 N	3.23 E
Serrenti	71	39.29 N	8.58 E
Serre-Ponçon, Barrage de ◆[6]	62	44.33 N	6.30 E
Serre-Ponçon, Lac de ⊜[1]	62	44.30 N	6.17 E
Serres	62	44.26 N	5.43 E
Serrezuela	252	30.38 S	65.23 W
Serri	71	39.42 N	9.08 E
Serrières	62	45.19 N	4.45 E
Serrinha	250	11.39 S	39.00 W
Serriola, Bocca)(	66	43.31 N	12.21 E
Serris	261	48.51 N	2.47 E
Serrita	250	7.56 S	39.19 W
Serro	255	18.37 S	43.23 W
Sersale	68	39.01 N	16.44 E
Šerstin	76	52.39 N	31.03 E
Šerstobitovo	86	57.16 N	78.52 E
Sertã	34	39.48 N	8.06 W
Sertânia	250	8.05 S	37.16 W
Sertãozinho	256	22.19 S	46.03 W
Sertig-Dörfli	58	46.44 N	9.51 E
Sertung, Pulau I	115a	6.06 S	105.24 E
Seru	144	7.50 N	40.28 E
Serua, Pulau I	164	6.18 S	130.01 E
Šerubaj-Nura ≃	86	49.54 N	72.31 E
Serui	164	1.53 S	136.14 E
Seruini ≃	248	7.42 S	66.42 W
Serule	156	21.58 S	27.20 E
Serutu, Pulau I	112	1.42 S	108.45 E
Seruwai	114	4.21 N	98.10 E
Sérvia	38	40.11 N	22.00 E
Servi Burnu ›	130	41.40 N	28.06 E
Servigliano	66	43.05 N	13.29 E
Servon	261	48.43 N	2.35 E
Servoz	58	45.56 N	6.46 E
Serwaru	112	8.10 S	127.42 E
Sêrxü	102	33.04 N	97.45 E
Seryševo	89	51.08 N	128.20 E
Şes, Muntele ⋏	38	47.05 N	22.30 E
Šešan	180	66.46 N	171.26 W
Sesayap ≃	112	3.36 N	117.15 E
Sesayap Lama	112	3.36 N	117.03 E
Sešča	76	53.45 N	33.23 E
Sese Islands II	154	0.20 S	32.20 E
Seseke ≃	263	51.37 N	7.32 E
Sesfontein	156	19.07 S	13.39 E
Sesheke	152	17.28 S	24.18 E
Seshu	105	39.33 N	115.37 E
Sesia ≃	62	45.05 N	8.37 E
Sesia, Val V	62	45.47 N	8.05 E
Sesibu	112	4.02 N	116.33 E
Sesimbra	34	38.26 N	9.06 W
Seskar, ostrov I	76	60.02 N	28.23 E
Seskarö	26	65.44 N	23.44 E
Šešma ≃	80	55.27 N	51.05 E
Sesmarias ≃	256	22.28 S	44.27 W
Sesoko-jima I	174m	26.38 N	127.52 E
Sespe	228	34.23 N	118.58 W
Sespe Creek ≃	204	34.23 N	118.57 W
Sessa	152	13.56 S	20.38 E
Sessa Aurunca	68	41.14 N	13.56 E
Ses Salines, Cap de ›	34	39.16 N	3.03 E
Séssé	146	11.30 N	17.34 E
Sessenheim	56	48.48 N	7.59 E
Sesta Godano	62	44.17 N	9.40 E
Šestakovka	78	48.32 N	31.58 E
Šestakovo, Ross.	82	56.21 N	35.49 E
Šestakovo, Ross.	88	56.29 N	103.59 E
Sestao	34	43.18 N	3.00 W
Šestern'a	78	47.33 N	33.16 E
Sestino	66	43.42 N	12.18 E
Sesto (Sexten)	64	46.42 N	12.21 E
Sesto Calende	62	45.44 N	8.38 E
Sesto Fiorentino	66	43.50 N	11.12 E
Sestola	64	44.14 N	10.46 E
Sesto San Giovanni	62	45.32 N	9.14 E
Sestra ≃, Ross.	80	52.11 N	49.36 E
Sestra ≃, Ross.	82	56.43 N	37.14 E
Sestriere	62	44.57 N	6.53 E
Sestri Levante	62	44.16 N	9.24 E
Sestri Ponente	62	44.25 N	8.51 E
Sestroreck	76	60.06 N	29.58 E
Sestroreckij Razliv, ozero ⊜	265a	60.04 N	30.00 E
Sestu	71	39.18 N	9.05 E
Šešupe ≃	76	55.03 N	22.12 E
Šešurga	80	57.29 N	47.35 E
Šešuvis ≃	76	55.13 N	22.15 E
Šėta, Liet.	76	55.17 N	24.15 E
Seta, Nihon	270	34.58 N	135.55 E
Seta ≃	270	34.56 N	135.54 E
Setagaya ◆[8]	268	35.39 N	139.40 E
Setail ≃	115a	8.30 S	114.21 E
Setaka	96	33.09 N	130.28 E
Setana	92a	42.26 N	139.51 E
Setapak	114	3.11 N	101.42 E
Setauket	210	40.57 N	73.07 W
Sète	62	43.24 N	3.41 E
Sete Barras	252	24.23 S	47.55 W
Sete Cidades, Parque Nacional de ♠	250	3.50 S	41.40 W
Sete de Setembro ≃	255	12.56 S	52.51 W
Sete Lagoas	255	19.27 S	44.14 W
Sete Pontes	256	22.51 S	43.05 W
Sete Quedas, Cachoeira das ∟	250	9.27 S	56.41 W
Sete Quedas, Parque Nacional de ♠	252	24.02 S	54.12 W
Sete Rios ◆[8]	266c	38.45 N	9.10 W
Setesdal V	26	59.25 N	7.25 E
Seth Ward	196	34.13 N	101.42 W
Setī □[8]	124	29.15 N	81.00 E
Setī ≃	124	28.58 N	81.06 E
Setlagodi	158	26.16 S	25.06 E
Set Net, Punta ›	236	12.28 N	83.30 W
Seto, Nihon	94	35.14 N	137.06 E
Seto, Nihon	96	33.27 N	132.15 E
Seto, Nihon	96	34.44 N	134.02 E
Setoda	96	34.18 N	133.05 E
Seto-naikai ⊤[2]	96	34.20 N	133.30 E
Seto-naikai-kokuritsu-kōen ♠	96	34.15 N	133.28 E
Seton Hall University ɤ[2]	276	40.45 N	74.15 W
Seton Lake ⊜	182	50.45 N	122.05 W
Seton Portage	182	50.43 N	122.18 W
Seto-saki ›	174m	26.51 N	128.18 E
Setouchi	93b	28.10 N	129.15 E
Seto-zaki ›	96	33.40 N	135.20 E
Setraki	78	49.23 N	40.49 E
Setta ≃	64	44.22 N	11.14 E
Settat	148	33.04 N	7.37 W
Settat □[4]	148	33.05 N	7.30 W
Sette Bagni ≃	267a	42.00 N	12.31 E
Setté Cama	152	2.32 S	9.45 E
Settecamini ◆[8]	267a	41.56 N	12.37 E
Sette-Daban, chrebet ⋏	74	62.00 N	138.00 E
Settee Lake ⊜	184	57.03 N	96.55 W
Settepani, Monte ∧	62	44.15 N	8.12 E
Settimo Milanese	266b	45.29 N	9.03 E
Settimo San Pietro	71	39.17 N	9.11 E
Settimo Torinese	62	45.09 N	7.46 E
Settimo Vittone	62	45.33 N	7.50 E
Settingiano	68	38.55 N	16.31 E
Setting Lake ⊜	184	55.00 N	98.38 W
Settle	44	54.04 N	2.16 W
Settlement Point ›	169	38.25 S	145.25 E
Settlers	156	25.02 S	28.30 E
Settlers Cabin Regional Park ♠	279b	40.26 N	80.10 W
Settons, Lac des ⊜	50	41.11 N	4.04 E
Settsu	96	34.46 N	135.33 E
Setúbal	34	38.32 N	8.54 W
Setúbal □[5]	266c	38.37 N	9.00 W
Setúbal, Baía de ⊂	34	38.27 N	8.53 W
Setun' ≃	265b	55.44 N	37.33 E
Seui	71	39.50 N	9.19 E
Seul, Lac ⊜	184	50.20 N	92.30 W
Seul Choix Point ›	190	45.56 N	85.52 W
Seulimeum	114	5.22 N	95.35 E
Seulo	71	39.52 N	9.14 E
Seúl → Sŏul	98	37.33 N	126.58 E
Seumanyam	114	3.45 N	96.38 E
Seurre	58	47.00 N	5.09 E
Seuzach	58	47.32 N	8.44 E
Sev ≃	76	52.24 N	34.10 E
Sevan	84	40.34 N	44.57 E
Sevan, ozero ⊜	84	40.20 N	45.20 E
Sévaré	150	14.32 N	4.06 W
Sevastopol'	78	44.36 N	33.32 E
Sevastopol'skij	86	53.08 N	65.44 E
Ševčenko	72	43.35 N	51.05 E
Ševčenkovo, Ukr.	78	49.41 N	37.10 E
Ševčenkovo, Ukr.	78	51.40 N	33.39 E
Ševčenkovo, Ukr.	78	45.33 N	29.20 E
Ševčenkovo Vtoroje	78	47.29 N	36.08 E
Sevelen, Dtsch.	52	51.29 N	6.25 E
Sevelen, Schw.	58	47.07 N	9.29 E
Ševelevskaja	24	60.52 N	44.12 E
Ševelevskij Majdan	80	54.25 N	42.15 E
Seven ≃	44	54.11 N	0.52 W
Seven Caves ⊥[5]	218	39.13 N	83.23 W
Seven Creeks ≃	169	36.43 S	145.34 E
Seven Harbors	216	42.40 N	83.34 W
Sevenhill	168b	33.53 S	138.38 E
Seven Hills, Austl.	274a	33.46 S	150.57 E
Seven Hills, Oh., U.S.	214	41.23 N	81.40 W
Seven Islands → Sept-Îles	186	50.12 N	66.23 W
Seven Kings ◆[8]	260	51.34 N	0.05 E
Seven Mile	218	39.28 N	84.33 W
Seven Mile Beach National Park ♠	170	34.49 S	150.46 E
Sevenmile Bridge ◆[5]	220	24.41 N	81.11 W
Sevenmile Creek ≃	218	39.28 N	84.33 W
Sevenoaks, Eng., U.K.	42	51.16 N	0.12 E
Seven Oaks, Tx., U.S.	222	30.51 N	94.51 W
Sevenoaks □[8]	260	51.18 N	0.10 E
Sevenoaks Weald	260	51.14 N	0.12 E
Seven Palm Lake ⊜	220	25.12 N	80.44 W
Seven Persons	184	49.52 N	110.54 W
Seven Sisters	42	51.46 N	3.43 W
Seven Sisters Peaks ⋏	182	54.58 N	128.10 W
Seventy Mile House	182	51.18 N	121.24 W
Seven Valleys	208	39.51 N	76.46 W
Sévérac-le-Château	32	44.19 N	3.04 E
Severance Center ◆[9]	279a	41.31 N	81.33 W
Sever'anskij les ♠	83	48.55 N	38.00 E
Severka ≃	82	55.10 N	38.45 E
Severn, S. Afr.	158	26.36 S	22.52 E
Severn, Md., U.S.	208	39.08 N	76.41 W
Severn, N.C., U.S.	208	36.30 N	77.11 W
Severn, Va., U.S.	208	37.17 N	76.24 W
Severn ≃, On., Can.	176	56.02 N	87.36 W
Severn ≃, On., Can.	212	44.52 N	79.41 W
Severn ≃, U.K.	42	51.35 N	2.40 W
Severn, Mouth of the ≃	42	51.25 N	3.00 W
Severnaja Dvina ≃	24	64.32 N	40.30 E
Severnaja Sos'va ≃	72	64.10 N	65.28 E
Severnaja Zeml'a II	74	79.30 N	98.00 E
Severna Park	208	39.04 N	76.32 W
Severn Bridge ◆[5]	42	51.39 N	2.42 W
Severn Lake ⊜	184	53.54 N	90.48 W
Severnoje, Ross.	80	58.02 N	41.26 E
Severnoje, Ross.	80	54.06 N	52.32 E
Severnoje, Ross.	84	44.49 N	42.51 E
Severnoje, Ross.	86	56.21 N	78.23 E
Severnoje, Ukr.	83	48.04 N	38.44 E
Severn River ⊂, Md., U.S.	208	38.58 N	76.28 W
Severn River ⊂, Va., U.S.	208	37.19 N	76.25 W
Severn Tunnel ◆[5]	42	51.35 N	2.44 W
Severnyj, Ross.	24	67.38 N	64.06 E
Severnyj, Ross.	265b	55.56 N	37.33 E
Severnyje uvaly ⋏[2]	24	59.30 N	49.00 E
Severnyj Kommunar	80	58.23 N	54.02 E
Severnyj Prijut	84	43.16 N	41.51 E
Severnyj Ural ⋏	24	63.00 N	59.00 E
Severo-Bajkal'skoje nagorje ⋏[1]	88	57.00 N	111.00 E
Severočeský Kraj □[4]	30	50.30 N	14.00 E
Severodoneck	83	48.58 N	38.27 E
Severodvinsk	24	64.34 N	39.50 E
Severo-Dvinskij kanal ≊	76	59.45 N	38.22 E
Severo-Jenisejskij	74	60.22 N	93.01 E
Severo-Kazachstanskaja Oblast' □[8]	86	54.30 N	69.00 E
Severo-Kuril'sk	74	50.40 N	156.08 E
Severomoravský Kraj □[4]	30	49.45 N	17.50 E
Severomorsk	24	69.05 N	33.24 E
Severo-Mujskij chrebet ⋏	88	56.30 N	114.00 E
Severo-Osetinskaja Avtonomnaja Sovetskaja Socialističeskaja Respublika □[3]	84	43.00 N	44.15 E
Severo-Sibirskaja nizmennost' ≚	74	73.00 N	100.00 E
Severoural'sk	86	60.09 N	59.57 E
Severo-Zadonsk	82	54.02 N	38.24 E
Severskaja	78	44.51 N	38.42 E
Severskij Donec ≃	72	47.35 N	40.54 E
Severskij Donec-Donbass, kanal ≊	83	48.55 N	37.45 E
Severucha	86	58.28 N	63.25 E
Severy	198	37.37 N	96.13 W
Seveso	62	45.39 N	9.09 E
Seveso ≃	266b	45.30 N	9.12 E
Ševětin	61	49.06 N	14.35 E
Sevettijärvi	24	69.26 N	28.38 E
Sevier ≃	200	39.04 N	113.06 W
Sevier, East Fork ≃	200	38.14 N	112.12 W
Sevier Bridge Reservoir ⊜[1]	200	39.21 N	111.57 W
Sevier Desert ◆[2]	200	39.25 N	112.50 W
Sevier Lake ⊜	200	38.55 N	113.09 W
Sevierville	192	35.52 N	83.33 W
Sevilla, Col.	246	4.16 N	75.57 W
Sevilla (Seville), Esp.	34	37.23 N	5.59 W
Sevilla □[4]	34	37.25 N	5.35 W
Sevilla, Isla I	236	8.14 N	82.24 W
Seville, Fl., U.S.	192	29.19 N	81.29 W
Seville, Oh., U.S.	214	41.00 N	81.51 W
Seville → Sevilla	34	37.23 N	5.59 W
Sevir	130	39.12 N	38.13 E
Şevketiye	130	40.05 N	27.51 E
Ševli ≃	89	54.08 N	133.04 E
Sevlievo	38	43.01 N	25.06 E
Sevran	50	48.56 N	2.32 E
Sevrej	102	43.35 N	102.12 E
Sèvres	50	48.49 N	2.12 E
Sévrier	58	45.52 N	6.08 E
Sevsk	78	52.09 N	34.30 E
Ševykan	88	54.20 N	106.49 E
Sewa ≃	150	7.18 N	12.08 W
Sewanee	194	35.04 N	85.55 W
Sewāni	123	28.55 N	75.37 E
Seward, Ak., U.S.	180	60.06 N	149.26 W
Seward, Ne., U.S.	198	40.54 N	97.05 W
Seward, N.Y., U.S.	210	42.43 N	74.37 W
Seward, Pa., U.S.	214	40.25 N	79.01 W
Seward Glacier ⊼	180	60.22 N	140.15 W
Seward Peninsula ›[1]	180	65.00 N	164.00 W
Sewaren	276	40.33 N	74.15 W
Sewekow	54	53.15 N	12.39 E
Sewell, Chile	252	34.05 S	70.23 W
Sewell, N.J., U.S.	208	39.45 N	75.08 W
Sewen	58	47.48 N	6.54 E
Sewernaja-Semlja → Severnaja Zeml'a II	74	79.30 N	98.00 E
Seweweekspoort	158	33.22 S	21.25 E
Sewickley	214	40.32 N	80.11 W
Sewickley Creek ≃	279b	40.14 N	79.47 W
Sewickley Heights	279b	40.33 N	80.09 W
Sewickley Hills	279b	40.34 N	80.08 W
Sewri ◆[8]	272c	19.00 N	72.51 E
Sexcello	152	3.58 S	11.38 E
Sexsmith	182	55.21 N	118.47 W
Sexten → Sesto	64	46.42 N	12.21 E
Sextin ≃	232	25.44 N	105.14 W
Sexton	218	39.42 N	85.27 W
Sexton Island I	276	40.39 N	73.14 W
Seya ◆[8], Nihon	268	35.29 N	139.29 E
Seya ◆[8], Nihon	268	35.27 N	139.30 E
Seybaplaya	232	19.39 N	90.40 W
Seybothenreuth	60	49.54 N	11.43 E
Seybouse, Oued ≃	148	36.54 N	7.47 E
Seychellen → Seychelles □[1]	138	4.35 S	55.40 E
Seychelles □[1]	138	4.35 S	55.40 E
Seychelles Bank ✦[4]	12	4.45 S	55.30 E
Seyches	32	44.33 N	0.18 E
Seyda	54	51.53 N	12.53 E
Seydim	130	40.33 N	34.45 E
Seydişehir	130	37.25 N	31.51 E
Seydisfjörður	24a	65.16 N	14.00 W
Seyfe Gölü ⊜	130	39.13 N	34.23 E
Seyhan ≃	130	36.43 N	34.53 E
Seyhan Barajı ⊜[1]	130	37.05 N	35.15 E
Seyitgazi	130	39.27 N	30.43 E
Seylac	144	11.21 N	43.29 E
Seymour, Austl.	169	37.02 S	145.08 E
Seymour, Ciskei	158	32.33 S	26.46 E
Seymour, Ct., U.S.	207	41.23 N	73.04 W
Seymour, In., U.S.	218	38.57 N	85.53 W
Seymour, Ia., U.S.	190	40.40 N	93.07 W
Seymour, Mo., U.S.	194	37.08 N	92.46 W
Seymour, Tx., U.S.	196	33.35 N	99.15 W
Seymour, Wi., U.S.	190	44.30 N	88.19 W
Seymour ≃	182	51.05 N	126.50 W
Seymour Inlet ⊂	182	51.03 N	127.10 W
Seymour Johnson Air Force Base ■	192	35.21 N	77.58 W
Seymour Range ⋏	224	48.40 N	124.00 W
Seymourville	194	30.27 N	91.29 W
Seyne	62	44.21 N	6.21 E
Seynod	58	45.53 N	6.05 E
Seyring	264b	48.20 N	16.29 E
Seyssel	58	45.57 N	5.49 E
Şeytan ≃	267b	41.06 N	28.59 E
Sežana	36	45.42 N	13.52 E
Sézanne	50	48.43 N	3.43 E
Sezela	158	30.24 S	30.42 E
Šežim	24	62.07 N	58.21 E
Sezimovo Ústí	30	49.23 N	14.42 E
Sezze	66	41.30 N	13.03 E
Sfax	148	34.44 N	10.46 E
Sfax □[8]	148	34.50 N	10.20 E
Sferracavallo ◆[8]	70	38.12 N	13.17 E
Sfîntu-Gheorghe	38	45.52 N	25.47 E
Sfîntu Gheorghe, Brațul ≃[1]	38	44.53 N	29.36 E
Sfîntu Gheorghe, Ostrovul I	38	45.07 N	29.22 E
Sfizef	148	35.14 N	0.15 W
Sforzesco, Castello ⊥	266b	45.28 N	9.11 E
's-Gravendeel	52	51.46 N	4.37 E
's-Gravenhage (The Hague)	52	52.06 N	4.18 E
's-Gravenzande	52	52.00 N	4.10 E
Sgritheall, Beinn ∧	46	57.08 N	5.35 W
Sgurgola	66	41.40 N	13.09 E
Sha ≃, Zhg.	98	37.31 N	117.50 E
Sha ≃, Zhg.	100	33.39 N	114.38 E
Sha ≃, Zhg.	100	26.35 N	118.02 E
Sha ≃, Zhg.	104	41.21 N	123.07 E

Symbol	English	Deutsch	Español	Français	Português
≃	River	Fluß	Río	Rivière	Rio
≊	Canal	Kanal	Canal	Canal	Canal
∟	Waterfall, Rapids	Wasserfall, Stromschnellen	Cascada, Rápidos	Chute d'eau, Rapides	Cascata, Rápidos
⊍	Strait	Meeresstraße	Estrecho	Détroit	Estreito
⊂	Bay, Gulf	Bucht, Golf	Bahía, Golfo	Baie, Golfe	Baía, Golfo
⊜	Lake, Lakes	See, Seen	Lago, Lagos	Lac, Lacs	Lago, Lagos
≡	Swamp	Sumpf	Pantano	Marais	Pântano
⊼	Ice Features, Glacier	Eis- und Gletscherformen	Accidentes Glaciales	Formes glaciaires	Acidentes glaciares
⊤	Other Hydrographic Features	Andere Hydrographische Objekte	Otros Elementos Hidrográficos	Autres données hydrographiques	Outros acidentes hidrográficos
✦	Submarine Features	Untermeerische Objekte	Accidentes Submarinos	Formes de relief sous-marin	Acidentes submarinos
□	Political Unit	Politische Einheit	Unidad Politica	Entité politique	Unidade política
ɤ	Cultural Institution	Kulturelle Institution	Institución Cultural	Institution culturelle	Institução cultural
⊥	Historical Site	Historische Stätte	Sitio Histórico	Site historique	Sitio histórico
♠	Recreational Site	Erholungs- und Ferienort	Sitio de Recreo	Centre de loisirs	Area de Lazer
⊠	Airport	Flughafen	Aeropuerto	Aéroport	Aeroporto
■	Military Installation	Militäranlage	Instalación Militar	Installation militaire	Instalação militar
◆	Miscellaneous	Verschiedenes	Misceláneo	Divers	Diversos

ENGLISH				DEUTSCH			
Name	Lat.°'	Long.°'	Page	Name	Seite	Breite°	Länge° E=Ost

ESPAÑOL — Nombre | Página | Lat.°′ | Long.°′ W = Oeste
FRANÇAIS — Nom | Page | Lat.°′ | Long.°′ W = Ouest
PORTUGUÊS — Nome | Página | Lat.°′ | Long.°′ W = Oeste

Nombre / Nom / Nome	Página / Page	Lat.°′	Long.°′
Sher Shāh	123	30.06 N	71.21 E
Shertallai	122	9.42 N	76.20 E
's-Hertogenbosch	52	51.41 N	5.19 E
Sherway Centre ◆ [9]	275b	43.37 N	79.33 W
Sherwood, On., Can.	275b	43.50 N	79.31 W
Sherwood, P.E., Can.	186	46.17 N	63.08 W
Sherwood, Ar., U.S.	194	34.48 N	92.13 W
Sherwood, Md., U.S.	208	38.36 N	76.19 W
Sherwood, Mi., U.S.	216	42.00 N	85.14 W
Sherwood, N.D., U.S.	198	48.57 N	101.37 W
Sherwood, Oh., U.S.	216	41.17 N	84.33 W
Sherwood, Or., U.S.	224	45.21 N	122.50 W
Sherwood, Tn., U.S.	194	35.04 N	85.55 W
Sherwood, Lake ⊜	281	42.36 N	83.33 W
Sherwood Forest, Ca., U.S.	226	37.57 N	122.17 W
Sherwood Forest, Md., U.S.	284c	39.05 N	77.01 W
Sherwood Forest ◆ [3]	44	53.08 N	1.08 W
Sherwood Island State Park ♣	276	41.07 N	73.20 W
Sherwood Manor	207	42.01 N	72.38 W
Sherwood Park, Ab., Can.	182	53.31 N	113.19 W
Sherwood Park, De., U.S.	285	39.44 N	75.39 W
Sherwood Park, N.Y., U.S.	210	42.36 N	73.43 W
Sherwood Park ♣	275b	43.43 N	79.24 W
Sherwood Point ›	276	41.07 N	73.20 W
Sherwood Shores	196	30.36 N	98.22 W
She Shan ∧ [2]	106	31.06 N	121.11 E
Sheshea ≃	248	9.36 S	74.10 W
Shesh Gāv	120	33.45 N	68.33 E
Shet Bandar	272c	18.58 N	72.56 E
Shetek, Lake ⊜	198	44.08 N	95.42 W
Shetland □ [4]	46a	60.30 N	1.15 W
Shetland del Sur, Islas → South Shetland Islands II	9	62.00 S	58.00 W
Shetland Islands II	46a	60.30 N	1.15 W
Shetou	106	31.39 N	119.27 E
Shetrunji ≃	120	21.19 N	72.07 E
Shetucket ≃	207	41.31 N	72.05 W
Sheva	272c	18.56 N	72.57 E
Sheva Nhava	272c	18.58 N	72.58 E
Shevaroy Hills ⩘ [2]	122	11.50 N	78.16 E
Shevington	262	53.34 N	2.42 W
Shevington Moor	262	53.35 N	2.41 W
Shewa □ [4]	144	9.00 N	39.00 E
Shewa Gimira	144	7.00 N	35.50 E
Shexian, Zhg.	98	36.33 N	113.40 E
Shexian, Zhg.	100	29.53 N	118.26 E
Sheyang, Zhg.	100	33.20 N	119.38 E
Sheyang, Zhg.	100	33.46 N	120.18 E
Sheyenne	198	47.49 N	99.07 W
Sheyenne ≃	198	47.05 N	96.50 W
Sheykhābād	120	34.05 N	68.45 E
Shey-Phoksundo National Park ♣	124	29.30 N	82.45 E
Shezhu	106	31.19 N	119.16 E
Shḥīm	132	33.37 N	35.29 E
Shi ≃, Zhg.	100	32.18 N	114.31 E
Shi ≃, Zhg.	100	32.32 N	115.52 E
Shiant, Sound of Ʊ	46	57.55 N	6.25 W
Shiant Islands II	46	57.53 N	6.21 W
Shiawassee □ [6]	216	42.56 N	84.09 W
Shiawassee ≃	216	43.06 N	84.10 W
Shiawassee, South Branch ≃	216	42.49 N	83.56 W
Shiba	100	32.45 N	118.07 E
Shiba ≃	268	35.47 N	139.44 E
Shibadu	102	28.01 N	110.51 E
Shibakawa	94	35.13 N	138.33 E
Shibām	144	15.56 N	48.38 E
Shiban	107	30.18 N	104.28 E
Shibanxi	107	29.17 N	103.51 E
Shibaocheng	102	39.48 N	96.10 E
Shibarni	140	14.50 N	24.25 E
Shibasaki	268	35.39 N	139.34 E
Shibata	92	37.57 N	139.20 E
Shibayama	94	35.41 N	140.25 E
Shibayama-gata ⊜	94	36.21 N	136.23 E
Shibden Hall	262	53.44 N	1.51 W
Shibecha	92a	43.17 N	144.36 E
Shibetsu, Nihon	92a	43.40 N	145.08 E
Shibetsu, Nihon	92a	44.10 N	142.23 E
Shibi	100	26.43 N	120.02 E
Shibīn al-Kawm	142	30.33 N	31.01 E
Shibīn al-Qanāṭir	142	30.19 N	31.19 E
Shibing	102	26.50 N	108.04 E
Shibishan	100	29.21 N	116.45 E
Shiblanjah	142	30.28 N	31.16 E
Shibu	98	36.45 N	119.27 E
Shibukawa	94	36.29 N	139.00 E
Shibure-yama ∧	270	34.45 N	135.05 E
Shibushi	92	31.28 N	131.07 E
Shibutsu-san ∧	94	36.54 N	139.11 E
Shibuya ◆ [8]	268	35.40 N	139.42 E
Shibuzi	98	36.09 N	119.06 E
Shicha	100	28.24 N	115.50 E
Shichangyu	104	41.12 N	123.14 E
Shicheng, Zhg.	98	40.39 N	124.17 E
Shicheng, Zhg.	100	25.18 N	119.21 E
Shicheng, Zhg.	100	26.22 N	116.22 E
Shicheng Dao I	98	39.31 N	123.02 E
Shichisō	94	35.33 N	137.07 E
Shickley	198	40.25 N	97.43 W
Shickshinny	210	41.09 N	76.09 W
Shidai	100	30.20 N	117.56 E
Shidao	98	36.53 N	122.23 E
Shideng	102	26.44 N	99.11 E
Shidler	196	36.46 N	96.39 W
Shido	96	34.19 N	134.10 E
Shidong, Zhg.	107	28.59 N	105.27 E
Shidong, Zhg.	107	30.25 N	105.20 E
Shidongzigou	105	40.41 N	118.23 E
Shiel, Loch ⊜	46	56.47 N	5.35 W
Shiel Bridge	46	57.12 N	5.25 W
Shieldaig	46	57.31 N	5.39 W
Shieldhill	46	55.58 N	3.46 W
Shields ≃	202	45.43 N	110.28 W
Shiercun	106	30.31 N	119.34 E
Shi'er Shan ∧	100	29.18 N	118.08 E
Shi'erwei	106	32.15 N	119.14 E
Shifang	100	25.01 N	116.14 E
Shifnal	42	52.40 N	2.21 W
Shifo	107	29.58 N	103.50 E
Shifobao	104	41.28 N	121.27 E
Shifochang	107	30.19 N	105.07 E
Shifodian	100	32.06 N	115.46 E
Shifosi	104	42.08 N	123.20 E
Shifoya	98	40.12 N	123.10 E
Shiga, Nihon	94	36.20 N	137.59 E
Shiga, Nihon	94	35.09 N	135.55 E
Shiga □ [5]	96	35.15 N	136.00 E
Shigaib	140	15.01 N	23.36 E
Shigang, Zhg.	100	32.13 N	120.58 E
Shigang, Zhg.	106	32.14 N	121.00 E
Shigangmen	269b	31.21 N	121.17 E
Shigaopu	107	30.16 N	104.01 E
Shigar ≃, Asia	123	34.39 N	75.51 E
Shigar ≃, Pāk.	123	34.39 N	75.51 E
Shigaraki	94	34.52 N	136.03 E
Shigaraki-gū ʋ [1]	94	34.54 N	136.04 E
Shigenobu	96	33.48 N	132.50 E
Shigenobu ≃	96	33.48 N	132.41 E
Shigezhuang, Zhg.	105	38.57 N	116.19 E
Shigezhuang, Zhg.	105	38.59 N	115.36 E
Shigezhuang, Zhg.	105	39.18 N	116.53 E
Shigouyi	102	37.44 N	106.26 E
Shigu, Zhg.	100	29.27 N	117.14 E
Shigu, Zhg.	102	26.50 N	99.55 E
Shiguaigou	102	40.42 N	110.20 E
Shiguantun	104	41.38 N	123.39 E
Shigulingyu	105	40.38 N	116.54 E
Shīḥān ∧	132	31.23 N	35.44 E
Shihchiachuang → Shijiazhuang	98	38.03 N	114.28 E
Shihch'i → Zhongshan	100	22.31 N	113.22 E
Shihe	98	39.19 N	121.52 E
Shihengyuanyu	106	31.50 N	121.45 E
Shihezi	86	44.18 N	86.02 E
Shihkiachwang → Shijiazhuang	98	38.03 N	114.28 E
Shihlin ◆ [8]	269d	25.06 N	121.31 E
Shihti	269d	25.02 N	121.44 E
Shihting	269d	24.59 N	121.39 E
Shihu, Zhg.	98	41.29 N	126.18 E
Shihu, Zhg.	105	40.04 N	117.17 E
Shihuajie	102	32.20 N	111.25 E
Shihudang	106	30.58 N	121.07 E
Shihuixi	107	29.02 N	105.04 E
Shihuiyaozi	104	42.08 N	123.47 E
Shihuxia	105	40.48 N	117.22 E
Shiida	96	33.39 N	131.04 E
Shijiaba	107	30.18 N	104.46 E
Shijiagangzi	104	42.19 N	123.34 E
Shijiagou	104	42.27 N	123.28 E
Shijiao	100	23.36 N	112.59 E
Shijiaqiao, Zhg.	106	30.46 N	120.06 E
Shijiaqiao, Zhg.	106	32.18 N	119.26 E
Shijiawu	105	39.21 N	116.15 E
Shijiaxiang	107	29.38 N	104.59 E
Shijiayaozhuang	106	32.13 N	120.29 E
Shijiazhai, Zhg.	98	38.56 N	114.18 E
Shijiazhai, Zhg.	269b	31.23 N	121.30 E
Shijiazhen	106	31.51 N	121.10 E
Shijiazhuang	98	38.03 N	114.28 E
Shijiazi, Zhg.	104	42.39 N	122.06 E
Shijiazi, Zhg.	104	42.07 N	122.18 E
Shijiedu	106	30.57 N	119.13 E
Shijing, Zhg.	98	35.30 N	118.57 E
Shijing, Zhg.	100	24.40 N	118.24 E
Shijing, Zhg.	105	39.54 N	114.58 E
Shijingshan	105	39.56 N	116.07 E
Shijiu Hu ⊜	106	31.28 N	118.53 E
Shijiusuo	98	35.24 N	119.29 E
Shijiu Tuo I	98	39.11 N	118.56 E
Shijōnawate	270	34.45 N	135.39 E
Shijūmagari-tōge)(	96	35.11 N	133.32 E
Shika	94	37.01 N	136.47 E
Shikami-yama ∧	270	34.47 N	135.10 E
Shikano	96	35.28 N	134.04 E
Shikārpur, India	122	14.16 N	75.21 E
Shikārpur, India	124	28.17 N	78.01 E
Shikārpur, Pāk.	120	27.57 N	68.38 E
Shikatsu	94	35.14 N	136.53 E
Shikengkong ∧	100	24.56 N	113.00 E
Shikewusumiao	102	40.13 N	108.52 E
Shiki	94	35.50 N	139.35 E
Shikishima	94	35.41 N	138.32 E
Shikohābād	124	27.06 N	78.36 E
Shikoku I	92	33.45 N	133.30 E
Shikoku-sanchi ⩘	96	33.47 N	133.30 E
Shikoma	268	35.11 N	139.56 E
Shikotsu-ko ⊜	92a	42.45 N	141.20 E
Shikotsu-Tōya-kokuritsu-kōen ♣	92a	42.47 N	141.00 E
Shikuang	106	31.54 N	121.24 E
Shil	272c	19.09 N	73.03 E
Shilabo	144	6.05 N	44.48 E
Shilbottle	44	55.23 N	1.42 W
Shildon	44	54.38 N	1.39 W
Shiliangji	100	33.54 N	115.14 E
Shilibao	105	39.55 N	116.29 E
Shiliguri	124	26.42 N	88.26 E
Shilihe	104	41.31 N	123.22 E
Shiling	106	30.26 N	119.35 E
Shilipeng	106	31.14 N	119.35 E
Shilipu, Zhg.	105	39.29 N	116.18 E
Shilipu, Zhg.	105	39.11 N	115.59 E
Shilipu, Zhg.	105	40.15 N	117.58 E
Shiliuban	100	24.08 N	117.33 E
Shillelagh	48	52.45 N	6.32 W
Shillingstone	42	50.54 N	2.14 W
Shillington	208	40.18 N	75.57 W
Shillong	120	25.34 N	91.53 E
Shilo, Canadian Forces Base ■	184	49.49 N	99.38 W
Shiloh, Il., U.S.	219	38.34 N	89.54 W
Shiloh, N.J., U.S.	208	39.27 N	75.17 W
Shiloh, Oh., U.S.	214	40.58 N	82.36 W
Shiloh, Oh., U.S.	218	39.49 N	84.13 W
Shiloh, Oh., U.S.	218	39.49 N	84.13 W
Shiloh, Pa., U.S.	208	39.59 N	76.49 W
Shiloh National Military Park ♣	194	35.06 N	88.21 W
Shiloh → Saylūn, Khirbat ⊥	132	32.03 N	35.17 E
Shilong, Zhg.	100	23.07 N	113.48 E
Shilong, Zhg.	102	23.54 N	109.40 E
Shilong, Zhg.	107	30.15 N	106.34 E
Shilou	100	22.58 N	113.29 E
Shima, Nihon	92	34.13 N	136.51 E
Shima, Nihon	270	34.59 N	135.20 E
Shima, Zhg.	100	24.27 N	117.49 E
Shima, Zhg.	107	29.38 N	105.50 E
Shimabara	92	32.47 N	130.22 E
Shimachang, Zhg.	107	28.59 N	105.55 E
Shimachang, Zhg.	107	29.03 N	105.36 E
Shimada, Nihon	94	34.49 N	138.11 E
Shimada, Nihon	268	35.59 N	139.25 E
Shimagahara	94	34.46 N	136.03 E
Shima-hantō › [1]	94	34.26 N	136.33 E
Shimamiao	106	32.08 N	119.20 E
Shimamoto	96	34.53 N	135.40 E
Shimane □ [5]	96	35.00 N	132.30 E
Shimane-hantō › [1]	96	35.30 N	133.00 E
Shimantan	100	33.17 N	113.28 E
Shimanto ≃	96	32.56 N	133.00 E
Shimata ≃	96	33.57 N	131.55 E
Shimber Berris ∧	144	10.44 N	47.15 E
Shimei	106	32.14 N	120.10 E
Shimen, Zhg.	98	39.44 N	118.52 E
Shimen, Zhg.	102	29.28 N	111.17 E
Shimen, Zhg.	105	40.06 N	117.42 E
Shimen, Zhg.	106	30.37 N	120.26 E
Shimen, Zhg.	107	29.36 N	106.27 E
Shimen, Zhg.	107	29.09 N	106.02 E
Shimencun, Zhg.	106	31.21 N	119.34 E
Shimencun, Zhg.	106	30.23 N	119.41 E
Shimendong	100	28.16 N	120.07 E
Shimengou	104	40.40 N	123.43 E
Shimenjie	100	29.34 N	116.44 E
Shimenlou	100	28.58 N	114.51 E
Shimenying	105	39.54 N	116.05 E
Shimenzi	89	48.30 N	121.31 E
Shimian	102	29.18 N	102.22 E
Shimiaozi	104	40.39 N	123.31 E
Shimizu, Nihon	92	35.01 N	138.29 E
Shimizu, Nihon	92a	43.01 N	142.53 E
Shimizu, Nihon	94	36.02 N	136.09 E
Shimizu, Nihon	94	35.01 N	138.29 E
Shimizu, Nihon	96	34.05 N	135.26 E
Shimizu → Tosa-shimizu	92	32.46 N	132.57 E
Shimizu-tunnel ◆ [5]	94	36.52 N	138.55 E
Shimla	123	31.06 N	77.10 E
Shimminato	94	36.47 N	137.04 E
Shimobe	94	35.27 N	138.29 E
Shimoda	94	34.40 N	138.57 E
Shimodate	94	36.18 N	139.59 E
Shimofusa	94	35.52 N	140.21 E
Shimofusa-daichi ⩘ [1]	268	35.45 N	139.58 E
Shimofusa-kōkūkichi, Kaijō-jieitai- ■	94	35.50 N	140.05 E
Shimofusa Naval Air Base ■	268	35.48 N	140.01 E
Shimoga	122	13.55 N	75.34 E
Shimogawara	268	35.56 N	139.21 E
Shimogōri	268	35.21 N	140.03 E
Shimogyō ◆ [8]	270	34.59 N	135.45 E
Shimohōya	268	35.45 N	139.34 E
Shimoichi	96	34.22 N	135.47 E
Shimoigusa ◆ [8]	268	35.43 N	139.37 E
Shimoji	175d	24.45 N	125.16 E
Shimoji-jima I	175d	24.49 N	125.09 E
Shimojō	94	35.24 N	137.47 E
Shimokawa	92a	44.18 N	142.39 E
Shimokita-hantō › [1]	92	41.15 N	141.00 E
Shimomatsu	270	34.27 N	135.23 E
Shimomizo	268	35.31 N	139.23 E
Shimoni	154	4.39 S	39.23 E
Shimoniikura	268	35.47 N	139.38 E
Shimonita	94	36.13 N	138.47 E
Shimonoseki	96	33.57 N	130.57 E
Shimookudomi	268	35.53 N	139.26 E
Shimoryūzu-zaki ›	96	33.30 N	133.34 E
Shimosakamoto	270	35.03 N	135.53 E
Shimosuwa	94	36.04 N	138.05 E
Shimotajiri	270	34.57 N	135.28 E
Shimotomi	268	35.50 N	139.29 E
Shimotsu	96	34.10 N	135.08 E
Shimotsuchidana	268	35.24 N	139.27 E
Shimotsui	96	34.26 N	133.47 E
Shimotsuma	94	36.11 N	139.58 E
Shimotsuruma	268	35.29 N	139.28 E
Shimoya	268	35.23 N	139.21 E
Shimoyama	94	35.02 N	137.19 E
Shimoyugi	268	35.38 N	139.23 E
Shimura ◆ [8]	268	35.46 N	139.41 E
Shin, Loch ⊜	46	58.06 N	4.34 W
Shinagawa ◆ [8]	268	35.37 N	139.45 E
Shinan	102	22.43 N	109.54 E
Shinano	94	36.48 N	138.13 E
Shinano ≃	92	37.56 N	139.03 E
Shinarā	142	28.47 N	30.46 E
Shināṣ	128	24.46 N	56.28 E
Shinawari	123	33.32 N	70.48 E
Shinbārī	273c	30.07 N	31.09 E
Shīndand	128	33.18 N	62.08 E
Shindenbaru-kichi, Kōkū-jieitai- ■	92	32.04 N	131.30 E
Shindo	268	35.21 N	139.21 E
Shiner	222	29.25 N	97.10 W
Shingbwiyang	110	26.41 N	96.13 E
Shingishū → Sinŭiju	98	40.05 N	124.24 E
Shinglehouse	214	41.57 N	78.11 W
Shingle Springs	226	38.40 N	120.56 W
Shing Mun Reservoir ⊜ [1]	271d	22.23 N	114.08 E
Shingo	96	34.59 N	133.23 E
Shingū, Nihon	92	33.44 N	135.59 E
Shingū, Nihon	96	34.55 N	134.33 E
Shingū, Nihon	96	33.56 N	133.38 E
Shingwidzi	156	23.05 S	31.25 E
Shingwidzi (Singuédeze) ≃	156	23.53 S	32.17 E
Shinichi	96	34.33 N	133.16 E
Shining Tor ∧	262	53.16 N	2.01 W
Shinīrah	132	32.22 N	36.45 E
Shinji	96	35.24 N	132.54 E
Shinji-ko ⊜	96	35.27 N	132.58 E
Shinjō, Nihon	92	38.46 N	140.18 E
Shinjō, Nihon	270	34.30 N	135.44 E
Shinjuku ◆ [8]	268	35.41 N	139.42 E
Shinkawa	94	35.09 N	136.50 E
Shīnkay	120	31.57 N	67.26 E
Shinkolobwe	154	11.02 S	26.35 E
Shinmachi	94	36.16 N	139.07 E
Shinminato ≃	270	34.38 N	135.09 E
Shinnārah, Minqār • [4]	142	28.52 N	30.38 E
Shinnayō	96	34.04 N	131.47 E
Shinnecock Bay ⊂	207	40.52 N	72.28 W
Shinnel Water ≃	44	55.13 N	3.49 W
Shinness	46	58.05 N	4.28 W
Shinnston	188	39.23 N	80.18 W
Shino-jima I	94	34.39 N	137.00 E
Shinsai-bashi ◆ [8]	270	34.40 N	135.31 E
Shinshār	130	34.36 N	36.44 E
Shinshiro	94	34.54 N	137.30 E
Shinshū-shinmachi	94	36.34 N	138.01 E
Shintone	94	35.50 N	140.20 E
Shinyanga	154	3.40 S	33.26 E
Shinyanga □ [4]	154	3.45 S	33.00 E
Shin-yōdo ≃ [1]	270	34.41 N	135.26 E
Shio	94	36.52 N	136.48 E
Shiobara	94	36.58 N	139.49 E
Shiocton	190	44.26 N	88.34 W
Shiogama	92	38.19 N	141.01 E
Shiojiri	94	36.06 N	137.58 E
Shiojiri-tōge)(	94	36.05 N	138.02 E
Shiomi-dake ∧	94	35.34 N	138.12 E
Shionoe	96	34.10 N	134.05 E
Shiono-misaki ›	92	33.26 N	135.45 E
Shioya	94	36.46 N	139.51 E
Shioya ◆ [8]	270	34.38 N	135.06 E
Shioya-zaki ›, Nihon	92	33.26 N	135.45 E
Shioya-zaki ›, Nihon	94	36.59 N	140.59 E
Shiozawa	94	37.02 N	138.51 E
Shipai, Zhg.	100	23.08 N	113.21 E
Shipai, Zhg.	106	31.30 N	120.55 E
Shipanpu	107	30.28 N	104.23 E
Shipantuo	107	30.25 N	106.13 E
Ship Bottom	208	39.38 N	74.10 W
Shipbourne	260	51.15 N	0.17 E
Ship Cove	186	47.06 N	54.05 W
Shipdham	42	52.37 N	0.53 E
Shiping, Zhg.	102	28.20 N	107.42 E
Shiping, Zhg.	102	23.47 N	102.30 E
Shipley	44	53.50 N	1.47 W
Shipman, Il., U.S.	219	39.07 N	90.03 W
Shipman, Va., U.S.	192	37.43 N	78.50 W
Shippan Point ›	276	41.01 N	73.32 W
Shippegan	186	47.45 N	64.42 W
Shippensburg	208	40.03 N	77.31 W
Shippenville	214	41.15 N	79.28 W
Shippingport	214	40.38 N	80.25 W
Shippō	94	35.10 N	136.48 E
Shiprock	200	36.47 N	108.41 W
Ship Rock ∧	200	36.42 N	108.50 W
Shipshaw ≃	186	48.27 N	71.12 W
Shipshewana	216	41.40 N	85.34 W
Shipston-on-Stour	42	52.04 N	1.37 W
Shipton-under-Wychwood	42	51.51 N	1.35 W
Shipu, Zhg.	100	29.13 N	121.55 E
Shipu, Zhg.	106	31.15 N	121.03 E
Shiqian	102	27.31 N	108.20 E
Shiqiao, Zhg.	100	33.12 N	112.36 E
Shiqiao, Zhg.	100	26.58 N	114.23 E
Shiqiao, Zhg.	106	30.30 N	119.11 E
Shiqiao, Zhg.	107	30.25 N	104.31 E
Shiqiaopu	107	30.05 N	105.23 E
Shiqiaozi	104	41.27 N	123.43 E
Shiqi → Zhongshan	100	22.31 N	113.22 E
Shiqma ≃	132	31.36 N	34.30 E
Shiquan, Zhg.	102	33.03 N	108.17 E
Shiquan, Zhg.	106	30.30 N	120.48 E
Shirahama, Nihon	94	34.54 N	139.54 E
Shirahama, Nihon	96	33.40 N	135.20 E
Shirahata-yama ∧	96	34.54 N	134.23 E
Shiraitono-taki ᒪ	94	35.18 N	138.38 E
Shirakami-misaki ›	92a	41.24 N	140.12 E
Shirakawa, Nihon	94	37.07 N	140.13 E
Shirakawa, Nihon	94	35.35 N	137.12 E
Shirakawa, Nihon	94	36.16 N	136.54 E
Shirakawa-no-seki-ato ⊥	94	37.03 N	140.15 E
Shirakawa-tōge ∧ [2]	270	34.42 N	135.07 E
Shirako	94	35.26 N	140.23 E
Shirākol	126	22.18 N	88.16 E
Shirakura-yama ∧	94	35.00 N	137.46 E
Shirama-yama ∧	96	34.01 N	135.23 E
Shiramine	94	36.10 N	136.37 E
Shirane	94	35.38 N	138.28 E
Shirane-san ∧, Nihon	94	36.38 N	138.32 E
Shirane-san ∧, Nihon	94	36.48 N	139.22 E
Shirane-san (Kita-dake) ∧, Nihon	94	35.40 N	138.15 E
Shiranuka	92a	42.57 N	144.05 E
Shiraoi	92a	42.33 N	141.21 E
Shiraoka	94	36.01 N	139.40 E
Shiraone	272c	19.03 N	73.01 E
Shirasawa	94	36.40 N	139.08 E
Shirati	154	1.08 S	33.59 E
Shīrāz	128	29.36 N	52.32 E
Shirbīn	142	31.11 N	31.32 E
Shirdley Hill	262	53.36 N	2.58 W
Shire (Chire) ≃	154	17.42 S	35.19 E
Shirebrook	44	53.12 N	1.13 W
Shiremanstown	208	40.13 N	76.57 W
Shiretoko-hantō › [1]	92a	44.00 N	145.00 E
Shiretoko-kokuritsu-kōen ♣	92a	44.08 N	145.10 E
Shiretoko-misaki ›	92a	44.14 N	145.17 E
Shīrīn ≃	120	36.49 N	65.01 E
Shīr Kūh ∧	128	31.34 N	54.04 E
Shirland	216	42.27 N	89.12 W
Shirley, B.C., Can.	224	48.23 N	123.54 W
Shirley, Il., U.S.	216	40.24 N	89.04 W
Shirley, In., U.S.	218	39.53 N	85.34 W
Shirley, Ma., U.S.	207	42.32 N	71.39 W
Shirley Plantation ⊥	208	37.21 N	77.15 W
Shirleysburg	214	40.18 N	77.53 W
Shiro	222	30.37 N	95.53 W
Shiroi	94	35.48 N	140.04 E
Shiroishi	92	38.00 N	140.37 E
Shirokawa	96	33.23 N	132.46 E
Shirone	92	37.46 N	139.01 E
Shirotori, Nihon	94	35.53 N	136.52 E
Shirotori, Nihon	96	34.15 N	134.20 E
Shirouma-dake ∧	94	36.45 N	137.46 E
Shiroyama	94	35.35 N	139.19 E
Shiro-yama ∧	270	34.38 N	135.53 E
Shirpur	120	21.21 N	74.53 E
Shirrell Heath	42	50.55 N	1.12 W
Shirshābah	142	30.47 N	31.10 E
Shīrvān	128	37.24 N	57.55 E
Shisaka-jima I	96	34.07 N	133.11 E
Shisanling	105	40.19 N	116.16 E
Shi San Ling (Ming Tombs) ⊥	105	40.19 N	116.13 E
Shisanzhan	89	51.21 N	125.43 E
Shisha Hai ⊜	271a	39.57 N	116.22 E
Shishaldin Volcano ∧ [1]	180	54.45 N	163.57 W
Shishan	104	41.16 N	121.30 E
Shishi	100	24.48 N	118.38 E
Shishikui	96	33.34 N	134.18 E
Shishi Shan ∧	100	24.44 N	117.54 E
Shishmaref	180	66.14 N	166.09 W
Shishmaref Inlet ⊂	180	66.07 N	165.50 W
Shishou	102	29.43 N	112.19 E
Shisht al-An'ām	142	30.52 N	30.44 E
Shisiazhan	89	51.36 N	125.42 E
Shisixian	104	40.53 N	122.59 E
Shisler Point ›	284a	42.52 N	79.08 W
Shisui	94	35.43 N	140.16 E
Shitai	100	30.13 N	117.27 E
Shitan, Zhg.	100	27.44 N	112.42 E
Shitan, Zhg.	100	23.10 N	113.47 E
Shitang, Zhg.	100	28.16 N	121.36 E
Shitang, Zhg.	102	25.38 N	110.50 E
Shitangwan	106	31.40 N	120.13 E
Shitara	94	35.05 N	137.35 E
Shithāthah	128	32.33 N	43.29 E
Shiting, Zhg.	100	27.36 N	113.16 E
Shiting, Zhg.	105	39.31 N	115.41 E
Shitoufangzi	89	48.38 N	126.08 E
Shitougouzi	89	49.19 N	125.55 E
Shitoumiao	102	41.41 N	106.50 E
Shitoumiaozi	104	41.38 N	121.26 E
Shitoushan	105	40.27 N	116.13 E
Shitoushuangmiao	98	41.28 N	118.55 E
Shituan	107	30.09 N	105.01 E
Shitunwei	104	41.07 N	121.31 E
Shiv	120	26.11 N	71.15 E
Shivalya	126	23.50 N	89.47 E
Shively	218	38.12 N	85.49 W
Shivering, Mount ∧	170	34.08 S	150.02 E
Shivpuri	124	25.26 N	77.39 E
Shivta, Ḥorvot (Subeita) ⊥	132	30.53 N	34.38 E
Shivwits Plateau ⩘ [1]	200	36.15 N	113.40 W
Shiwaku-shotō II	96	34.20 N	133.45 E
Shiwan, Zhg.	100	27.17 N	112.57 E
Shiwan, Zhg.	100	28.12 N	113.49 E
Shiwan, Zhg.	100	23.01 N	113.04 E
Shiwan, Zhg.	102	37.35 N	109.01 E
Shiwenchang	104	41.43 N	123.54 E
Shiwu	89	43.48 N	124.13 E
Shixi, Zhg.	100	28.16 N	117.45 E
Shixi, Zhg.	100	28.16 N	115.36 E
Shixia	105	40.20 N	114.59 E
Shixian	89	43.05 N	129.47 E
Shixiancun	106	31.12 N	120.29 E
Shixiechang	107	29.51 N	106.41 E
Shixing	100	24.58 N	114.03 E
Shixun	100	24.44 N	118.11 E
Shiyachang	107	30.27 N	106.31 E
Shiyan, Zhg.	102	32.38 N	110.44 E
Shiyan, Zhg.	107	30.22 N	104.27 E
Shiyangchang, Zhg.	107	29.56 N	105.37 E
Shiyangchang, Zhg.	107	30.42 N	105.57 E
Shiyanqiao	107	29.19 N	105.22 E
Shiyiwei	106	31.59 N	120.43 E
Shiyizhan	89	51.13 N	125.52 E
Shiyu	107	29.46 N	106.06 E
Shizhangzi	98	40.24 N	119.48 E
Shizheng	100	24.32 N	115.50 E
Shizhenjie	100	28.51 N	116.56 E
Shizhong, Zhg.	100	24.57 N	117.06 E
Shizhong, Zhg.	106	30.44 N	120.16 E
Shizhongtan	107	30.26 N	104.35 E
Shizhu, Zhg.	100	28.48 N	120.06 E
Shizhu, Zhg.	102	29.56 N	108.09 E
Shizhuang	106	32.08 N	120.31 E
Shizhuangzi, Zhg.	104	42.24 N	122.53 E
Shizhuangzi, Zhg.	105	40.38 N	116.59 E
Shizhuzi	104	41.18 N	121.35 E
Shizichang	107	29.32 N	106.14 E
Shizigu	105	39.23 N	118.08 E
Shizikou	100	24.12 N	113.38 E
Shizilin	106	31.26 N	121.25 E
Shizipo	105	40.21 N	115.07 E
Shizipu	106	30.59 N	119.07 E
Shizuchi-kokutei-kōen ♣	96	33.45 N	133.08 E
Shizugawa	92	38.40 N	141.27 E
Shizui, Zhg.	89	43.08 N	126.06 E
Shizui, Zhg.	98	38.52 N	113.42 E
Shizuma ≃	96	35.12 N	132.28 E
Shizunai	92a	42.20 N	142.22 E
Shizuoka	94	34.58 N	138.23 E
Shizuoka □ [5]	94	35.00 N	138.00 E
Shkodër	38	42.05 N	19.30 E
Shkumbin ≃	38	41.01 N	19.26 E
Shō ≃	94	36.47 N	137.04 E
Shoal ≃	194	30.41 N	86.39 W
Shoal Cape ›	162	33.53 S	121.07 E
Shoal Creek ≃, U.S.	194	34.50 N	87.33 W
Shoal Creek ≃, U.S.	194	37.05 N	94.42 W
Shoal Creek ≃, U.S.	194	40.28 N	92.42 W
Shoal Creek ≃, Il., U.S.	219	38.28 N	89.35 W
Shoal Creek ≃, Mo., U.S.	194	39.44 N	93.32 W
Shoal Creek, East Fork ≃	219	38.51 N	89.30 W
Shoal Creek, Middle Fork ≃	219	39.05 N	89.33 W
Shoal Creek, West Fork ≃	219	39.05 N	89.33 W
Shoal Harbour	186	48.11 N	53.59 W
Shoalhaven ≃	170	34.52 S	150.44 E
Shoalhaven Bight ⊂ [3]	170	34.52 S	150.47 E
Shoal Lake	184	50.26 N	100.34 W
Shoal Lake ⊜	184	49.32 N	95.00 W
Shoal Point ›	276	41.08 N	73.15 W
Shoals	194	38.39 N	86.47 W
Shoals, Bay of ⊂	168b	35.37 S	137.37 E
Shoalwater Bay ⊂	166	22.02 S	150.25 E
Shōbara	96	34.51 N	133.01 E
Shōboku	96	35.06 N	134.07 E
Shobonier	219	38.52 N	89.05 W
Shōbu	94	36.04 N	139.36 E
Shōdai	270	34.51 N	135.42 E
Shōdo-shima I	96	34.30 N	134.17 E
Shoeburyness	42	51.32 N	0.48 E
Shoe Cove	186	49.55 N	55.33 W
Shoemakersville	208	40.30 N	75.58 W
Shōgawa	94	36.34 N	136.59 E
Shogunle	273a	6.35 N	3.21 E
Shohola	210	41.28 N	74.55 W
Shohola Creek ≃	210	41.28 N	74.55 W
Shokambetsu-dake ∧	92a	43.43 N	141.31 E
Shokan	210	41.58 N	74.13 W
Shōkawa	94	36.02 N	136.57 E
Sholingnur	122	13.07 N	79.25 E
Shomera	132	33.05 N	35.17 E
Shomolu	273a	6.32 N	3.23 E
Shōmyō-no-taki ᒪ	94	36.35 N	137.24 E
Shona, Eilean I	46	56.47 N	5.52 W
Shōnai	96	33.11 N	131.26 E
Shōnai ≃	94	35.04 N	136.50 E
Shōnan	268	35.50 N	140.02 E
Shongum	276	40.50 N	74.33 W
Shongum Lake ⊜	276	40.51 N	74.32 W
Shongwe	158	27.24 S	32.25 E
Shōō	96	35.02 N	134.08 E
Shooters Hill	170	33.54 S	149.52 E
Shooters Island I	276	40.39 N	74.10 W
Shopiere	216	42.34 N	88.57 W
Shoranūr	122	10.46 N	76.17 E
Shorāpur	122	16.31 N	76.45 E
Shoreacres, B.C., Can.	182	49.26 N	117.32 W
Shore Acres, Ca., U.S.	226	38.02 N	121.58 W
Shore Acres, Ma., U.S.	207	42.12 N	70.44 W
Shore Acres, N.J., U.S.	208	40.01 N	74.06 W
Shoreacres, Tx., U.S.	222	29.37 N	95.01 W
Shoreditch ◆ [8]	260	51.32 N	0.05 W
Shoreham, Austl.	169	38.25 S	145.03 E
Shoreham, Eng., U.K.	260	51.20 N	0.11 E
Shoreham, Mi., U.S.	216	42.03 N	86.30 W
Shoreham-by-Sea	42	50.49 N	0.16 W
Shorewood, Il., U.S.	216	41.32 N	88.12 W
Shorewood, Wi., U.S.	216	43.05 N	87.53 W
Shorewood Hills	216	43.04 N	89.26 W
Shorkot	123	30.50 N	72.04 E
Shorkot Road	123	30.47 N	72.15 E
Shorne	260	51.25 N	0.26 E
Short Acres	226	36.21 N	119.38 W
Short Beach	207	41.15 N	72.50 W
Short Creek	214	40.11 N	80.55 W
Shortland Islands II	175e	6.55 S	155.53 E
Short Mountain ∧	192	36.23 N	83.10 W
Shortsville	210	42.57 N	77.13 W
Shoshone	202	42.56 N	114.24 W
Shoshone ≃	202	44.52 N	108.11 W
Shoshone, North Fork ≃	202	44.29 N	109.18 W
Shoshone, South Fork ≃	202	44.27 N	109.14 W
Shoshone Basin ≚ [1]	202	43.05 N	108.05 W
Shoshone Lake ⊜	202	44.22 N	110.43 W
Shoshone Mountains ⩘	204	39.00 N	117.30 W
Shoshone Peak ∧	204	36.56 N	116.16 W
Shoshone Range ⩘	204	40.20 N	116.50 W
Shoshong	156	22.59 S	26.30 E
Shoshoni	200	43.14 N	108.06 W
Shostka → Šostka	78	51.52 N	33.30 E
Shotley Gate	42	51.58 N	1.15 E
Shotton	262	53.12 N	3.02 W
Shotton Colliery	44	54.44 N	1.20 W
Shotts	46	55.49 N	3.48 W
Shotwick	262	53.14 N	2.59 W
Shou'anzhen	107	30.16 N	103.37 E
Shouchang	100	29.22 N	119.13 E
Shoufeng	100	23.52 N	121.30 E
Shouguang	98	36.53 N	118.42 E
Shouning	100	27.27 N	119.30 E
Shournagh ≃	48	51.53 N	8.35 W
Shoushan	104	41.12 N	123.03 E
Shouwangfen	105	40.35 N	117.48 E
Shouxian	100	32.35 N	116.47 E
Shouyang	102	37.59 N	113.09 E
Shōwa, Nihon	94	36.37 N	139.04 E
Shōwa, Nihon	96	34.43 N	133.39 E
Showell	208	38.23 N	75.12 W
Show Low	200	34.15 N	110.01 W
Shqipëri → Albania □ [1]	38	41.00 N	20.00 E
Shreve	214	40.40 N	82.01 W
Shreveport	194	32.30 N	93.44 W
Shrevewood	284c	38.53 N	77.13 W
Shrewsbury, Eng., U.K.	42	52.43 N	2.45 W
Shrewsbury, Ma., U.S.	207	42.17 N	71.42 W
Shrewsbury, N.J., U.S.	208	40.19 N	74.03 W
Shrewsbury, Pa., U.S.	208	39.46 N	76.40 W
Shrewsbury River ⊂	276	40.21 N	74.00 W
Shrewton	42	51.12 N	1.55 W
Shri Dūngargarh	120	28.05 N	74.00 E
Shri Mohangarh	120	27.17 N	71.14 E
Shriner Mountain ∧	210	40.56 N	77.20 W
Shrīrangapattana	122	12.25 N	76.42 E
Shrivenham	42	51.36 N	1.39 W
Shropshire □ [6]	42	52.40 N	2.40 W
Shropshire Union Canal ≡	262	53.17 N	2.53 W
Shrub Oak	210	41.20 N	73.49 W
Shrule	48	53.30 N	9.08 W
Shu ≃	98	34.07 N	118.30 E
Shuajingsi	102	32.00 N	103.05 E
Shuanfeng Shan ∧	107	29.26 N	105.47 E
Shuang ≃	269d	25.00 N	121.31 E
Shuangbai	102	24.54 N	101.32 E
Shuangcheng	89	45.21 N	126.17 E
Shuangchengzi	105	40.11 N	118.03 E
Shuangdian	100	32.23 N	120.51 E
Shuangdun	106	32.13 N	121.08 E
Shuangfeng, Zhg.	102	27.24 N	112.05 E
Shuangfeng, Zhg.	106	31.31 N	121.02 E
Shuangfeng, Zhg.	106	31.31 N	121.01 E
Shuangfeng Shan ∧	100	24.28 N	114.43 E
Shuangfengyi	107	29.27 N	105.09 E
Shuangfu	105	39.48 N	117.44 E
Shuangfuchang, Zhg.	107	29.41 N	103.31 E
Shuangfuchang, Zhg.	107	30.08 N	103.32 E
Shuanggang, Zhg.	89	45.07 N	122.59 E
Shuanggang, Zhg.	100	28.11 N	117.30 E
Shuanggetun	89	48.58 N	129.57 E
Shuanggou, Zhg.	98	34.03 N	117.37 E
Shuanggou, Zhg.	100	32.12 N	112.21 E
Shuanggou, Zhg.	100	33.16 N	118.10 E
Shuanggufen	107	29.38 N	104.11 E
Shuanghe, Zhg.	100	31.33 N	116.46 E
Shuanghe, Zhg.	100	31.41 N	112.46 E
Shuanghe, Zhg.	107	29.40 N	104.48 E
Shuanghe, Zhg.	107	30.07 N	105.10 E
Shuanghe, Zhg.	107	30.15 N	104.44 E
Shuanghechang, Zhg.	107	28.51 N	104.51 E
Shuanghechang, Zhg.	107	29.25 N	106.17 E
Shuanghechang, Zhg.	107	29.12 N	105.43 E
Shuanghechang, Zhg.	107	29.18 N	105.36 E
Shuang-hsi	269d	25.01 N	121.39 E
Shuangji ≃	100	34.05 N	114.24 E
Shuangjiang, Zhg.	100	26.48 N	116.28 E
Shuangjiang, Zhg.	102	23.37 N	99.41 E
Shuangjiang, Zhg.	107	30.13 N	105.45 E
Shuangjiangqiao	102	25.19 N	98.51 E
Shuangjianji	100	33.12 N	116.40 E
Shuangjingzi	104	42.28 N	123.42 E
Shuangkou	105	39.15 N	117.02 E
Shuangliao	89	43.31 N	123.30 E
Shuanglin	106	30.47 N	120.19 E
Shuanglingzi, Zhg.	104	40.54 N	124.10 E
Shuanglingzi, Zhg.	104	40.50 N	123.06 E
Shuangliu	107	30.34 N	103.55 E
Shuangliushu	100	31.56 N	115.12 E
Shuanglongtai	104	40.56 N	122.39 E
Shuangmiao, Zhg.	100	28.24 N	120.45 E
Shuangmiao, Zhg.	100	32.09 N	116.52 E
Shuangmiaozi, Zhg.	104	42.25 N	122.17 E
Shuangmiaozi, Zhg.	104	42.02 N	121.52 E
Shuangpai	110	25.57 N	111.32 E
Shuangpaishi	106	31.24 N	118.59 E
Shuangqiao, Zhg.	100	32.29 N	116.41 E
Shuangqiao, Zhg.	105	39.54 N	116.37 E
Shuangqiao, Zhg.	106	30.59 N	118.47 E
Shuangshanzi	98	40.21 N	119.08 E
Shuangshipu	107	29.14 N	104.42 E
Shuangshiqiao, Zhg.	107	29.22 N	105.51 E
Shuangshiqiao, Zhg.	107	29.23 N	104.29 E
Shuangshu	105	39.34 N	117.01 E
Shuangshutai	89	43.50 N	121.15 E
Shuangtaizi, Zhg.	104	41.34 N	121.12 E
Shuangtaizi, Zhg.	104	42.21 N	124.10 E
Shuangtaizi, Zhg.	104	42.25 N	123.11 E
Shuangtaizi, Zhg.	104	41.00 N	122.34 E
Shuangtaizi, Zhg.	104	41.11 N	121.14 E
Shuangtaizi ≃	104	40.59 N	121.51 E
Shuangtaizihe Kou ≃ [1]	104	40.55 N	121.50 E
Shuangtang, Zhg.	100	28.01 N	116.44 E
Shuangtang, Zhg.	105	39.03 N	116.17 E
Shuangtang, Zhg.	105	38.53 N	116.54 E
Shuangtangdian	106	30.59 N	118.51 E
Shuangtuo	105	39.14 N	117.20 E
Shuangtuozhen	105	39.29 N	118.23 E
Shuangxi, Zhg.	100	27.01 N	119.03 E
Shuangxi, Zhg.	106	30.24 N	119.50 E
Shuangyang	89	43.32 N	125.42 E
Shuangyangdian	104	41.07 N	121.16 E
Shuangyaocun	105	38.55 N	117.03 E
Shuangyashan	89	46.37 N	131.22 E
Shu'ayb, Wādī V	132	31.54 N	35.38 E
Shu'ayt, Wādī V	144	18.15 N	52.00 E
Shubenacadie ≃	186	45.20 N	63.30 W
Shublik Mountains ⩘	180	69.31 N	145.40 W
Shubrā al-Khaymah	142	30.06 N	31.15 E
Shubrā Bābil	142	30.54 N	31.11 E
Shubrā Khalfūn	142	30.29 N	31.05 E
Shubrā Khīt	142	31.02 N	30.43 E
Shubuta	194	31.51 N	88.41 W
Shucheng	100	31.27 N	116.57 E
Shufu	85	39.27 N	75.52 E
Shufuka Shan ∧	89	50.28 N	123.10 E
Shugudali	89	52.47 N	124.02 E
Shuheyingzi	104	42.18 N	122.16 E
Shuhezhen	106	31.35 N	121.35 E
Shūhō	96	34.13 N	131.18 E
Shuhong	100	28.39 N	120.09 E
Shuibatang	102	28.39 N	107.03 E
Shuibei, Zhg.	100	28.04 N	115.01 E
Shuibei, Zhg.	106	31.40 N	119.39 E
Shuichaoyang	100	26.22 N	117.57 E
Shuicheng	102	26.41 N	104.50 E
Shuidao	98	37.10 N	121.33 E
Shuidiangou	89	47.43 N	122.40 E
Shuidong, Zhg.	106	31.23 N	119.37 E
Shuidong, Zhg.	106	30.47 N	118.57 E
Shuidongjie	106	31.07 N	119.33 E
Shuiduixia	106	30.17 N	118.50 E
Shuihai	100	33.02 N	120.26 E
Shuihouling	100	30.43 N	116.26 E
Shuiji	100	27.26 N	118.20 E
Shuijiahuangdi	104	42.14 N	123.28 E
Shuijian	105	40.09 N	115.58 E
Shuijing	102	26.10 N	99.09 E
Shuijingtang	102	28.50 N	108.11 E
Shuikou, Zhg.	100	26.59 N	117.41 E
Shuikou, Zhg.	100	26.22 N	118.44 E
Shuikou, Zhg.	100	26.18 N	113.46 E
Shuikou, Zhg.	100	24.00 N	115.55 E
Shuikou, Zhg.	102	25.54 N	109.06 E
Shuikou, Zhg.	107	29.29 N	103.42 E
Shuikouchang	107	29.33 N	103.40 E
Shuikouguan	102	22.30 N	106.34 E
Shuikoushan	102	26.30 N	112.30 E
Shuikouxu	100	25.09 N	114.28 E
Shuiliandong	98	42.12 N	125.09 E
Shuimenzi	98	39.36 N	122.19 E
Shuimingqiao	106	31.03 N	119.09 E
Shuimoqipan	85	39.51 N	76.42 E
Shuiquan'gou	104	41.58 N	121.50 E
Shuiquanzi, Zhg.	104	42.15 N	121.32 E
Shuiquanzi, Zhg.	104	40.53 N	121.05 E
Shuitangzi	102	29.18 N	101.10 E
Shuiting	100	29.10 N	119.14 E
Shuitou, Zhg.	100	24.43 N	118.25 E
Shuitou, Zhg.	100	23.53 N	113.37 E
Shuitou, Zhg.	100	27.38 N	120.16 E
Shuitouwei	100	26.06 N	115.28 E
Shuituzhen	107	29.47 N	106.31 E
Shuiyang	106	31.14 N	118.47 E
Shuiyang ≃	106	31.14 N	118.48 E
Shuiye	98	36.08 N	114.07 E
Shuizhai	98	36.54 N	117.24 E
Shuizhuyang	100	26.59 N	119.13 E
Shujāābād	123	29.53 N	71.18 E
Shujālpur	124	23.24 N	76.43 E
Shujiawazi	104	42.20 N	121.57 E
Shuksan, Mount ∧	224	48.50 N	121.36 W
Shulan	89	44.27 N	126.57 E
Shulaps Peak ∧	182	50.57 N	122.31 W
Shule	85	39.23 N	76.06 E
Shule ≃	102	40.50 N	94.10 E
Shūlgareh	120	36.19 N	66.53 E
Shullsburg	190	42.34 N	90.13 W
Shulu (Xinji)	98	37.54 N	115.13 E
Shumagin Islands II	180	55.07 N	159.45 W
Shumatuscacant ≃	283	42.03 N	70.51 W
Shumen → Šumen	38	43.16 N	26.55 E
Shūnah, Wādī ash- V	142	29.38 N	32.13 E
Shun'an	100	30.57 N	117.57 E
Shūnat Nimrīn	132	31.54 N	35.37 E
Shunayn, Sabkhat ⊜	146	30.30 N	21.00 E
Shunchang	100	26.50 N	117.48 E
Shunde	100	22.50 N	113.14 E
Shundian	100	34.15 N	113.20 E
Shundianqiao	106	31.24 N	120.41 E
Shunge	102	37.25 N	95.27 E
Shungnak	180	66.53 N	157.02 W
Shunhechang	107	29.57 N	104.42 E
Shunlongchang	107	30.04 N	103.27 E
Shunshanpu	104	42.08 N	122.21 E
Shuntianhu	100	24.08 N	114.48 E
Shunyi	105	40.08 N	116.38 E
Shuoduzong	102	30.48 N	95.47 E
Shuojiaji	100	33.42 N	119.44 E
Shuping	107	29.19 N	104.43 E
Shupiyan	123	33.43 N	74.50 E
Shuqayyiqah, Nafūd • [8]	128	25.45 N	43.55 E
Shuqualak	194	32.58 N	88.34 W
Shūr ≃, Īrān	128	30.57 N	57.42 E
Shūr ≃, Īrān	128	35.57 N	56.24 E
Shūr ≃, Īrān	128	31.45 N	55.15 E
Shūr ≃, Īrān	128	34.38 N	51.46 E
Shuri	174m	26.13 N	127.43 E
Shurkhua	110	22.15 N	93.38 E
Shurugwi	154	19.40 S	30.00 E
Shūsf	128	31.48 N	60.01 E
Shūsh	128	32.11 N	48.15 E
Shushan	210	43.05 N	73.21 W
Shushan Hu ⊜	98	35.36 N	116.27 E
Shūshtar	128	32.03 N	48.51 E

≃	River	Fluß	Río	Rivière	Rio
≡	Canal	Kanal	Canal	Canal	Canal
ᒪ	Waterfall, Rapids	Wasserfall, Stromschnellen	Cascada, Rápidos	Chute d'eau, Rapides	Cascata, Rápidos
Ʊ	Strait	Meeresstraße	Estrecho	Détroit	Estreito
⊂	Bay, Gulf	Bucht, Golf	Bahía, Golfo	Baie, Golfe	Baía, Golfo
⊜	Lake, Lakes	See, Seen	Lago, Lagos	Lac, Lacs	Lago, Lagos
⩦	Swamp	Sumpf	Pantano	Marais	Pântano
⊓	Ice Features, Glacier	Eis- und Gletscherformen	Accidentes Glaciales	Formes glaciaires	Acidentes glaciares
⊤	Other Hydrographic Features	Andere Hydrographische Objekte	Otros Elementos Hidrográficos	Autres données hydrographiques	Outros acidentes hidrográficos
✦	Submarine Features	Untermeerische Objekte	Accidentes Submarinos	Formes de relief sous-marin	Acidentes submarinos
□	Political Unit	Politische Einheit	Unidad Politica	Entité politique	Unidade política
ʋ	Cultural Institution	Kulturelle Institution	Institución Cultural	Institution culturelle	Instituição cultural
⊥	Historical Site	Historische Stätte	Sitio Histórico	Site historique	Sitio histórico
♣	Recreational Site	Erholungs- und Ferienort	Sitio de Recreo	Centre de loisirs	Area de Lazer
⊠	Airport	Flughafen	Aeropuerto	Aéroport	Aeroporto
■	Military Installation	Militäranlage	Instalación Militar	Installation militaire	Instalação militar
◆	Miscellaneous	Verschiedenes	Misceláneo	Divers	Diversos

ENGLISH: Name · Page · Lat.°′ · Long.°′ — DEUTSCH: Name · Seite · Breite°′ · Länge°′ E = Ost

Name	Page	Lat.°′	Long.°′
Shuswap ≃	182	50.50 N	119.00 W
Shuswap Lake ⊜	182	50.57 N	119.15 W
Shuṭab	142	27.08 N	31.14 E
Shutendōji-yama ∧	96	33.06 N	130.54 E
Shuteye Peak ∧	226	37.21 N	119.25 W
Shutlingsloe ∧	262	53.13 N	2.02 W
Shūtō	96	34.05 N	132.05 E
Shuwak	140	14.23 N	35.52 E
Shuwaykah	132	32.20 N	35.02 E
Shuya	174m	26.40 N	128.06 E
Shuyak Island I	180	58.35 N	152.30 W
Shuyang	98	34.08 N	118.47 E
Shuya → Šuja	24	61.55 N	34.12 E
Shuyūkh Fawqānī	130	36.46 N	38.03 E
Shuzenji	94	34.58 N	138.56 E
Shwangliao → Liaoyuan	89	42.54 N	125.07 E
Shwebo	110	22.34 N	95.42 E
Shwegun	110	17.09 N	97.39 E
Shwegyin	110	17.55 N	96.53 E
Shweli (Longchuan) ≃	102	23.56 N	96.17 E
Shwenyaung	110	20.46 N	96.57 E
Shyamdih	126	23.47 N	86.56 E
Shyok	120	34.11 N	78.08 E
Shyok ≃	120	35.13 N	75.53 E
Si ≃	98	35.11 N	116.42 E
Sia	164	6.49 S	134.19 E
Siabu	114	1.01 N	99.29 E
Siachen Glacier ⊓	123	35.30 N	77.00 E
Sīād Kuh, Kavīr-e ≚	128	32.40 N	53.52 E
Siagne ≃	62	43.32 N	6.57 E
Siāhān Range ⩘	128	27.25 N	64.30 E
Sīāh Kūh, Selseleh-ye ⩘	128	34.00 N	64.00 E
Siak ≃	114	1.13 N	102.09 E
Siak Kecil ≃	114	1.16 N	102.08 E
Siak Sri Indrapura	114	0.46 N	102.04 E
Sialang	114	1.31 N	99.27 E
Sialejevskaja P'atina	80	53.49 N	44.32 E
Siālkot	123	32.30 N	74.31 E
Sialsūk	120	23.24 N	92.45 E
Siam, Gulf of → Thailand, Gulf of ⊂	110	10.00 N	101.00 E
Siamanna	71	39.55 N	8.46 E
Siam → Thailand □1	110	15.00 N	100.00 E
Si'an	106	30.54 N	119.39 E
Siangtan → Xiangtan	100	27.51 N	112.54 E
Sianhala	150	10.03 N	6.51 W
Sianów	30	54.15 N	16.16 E
Siantan, Pulau I	112	3.10 N	106.15 E
Sian → Xi'an	102	34.15 N	108.52 E
Sianzhuang	100	33.05 N	119.13 E
Siapa ≃	246	2.07 N	66.28 W
Siargao Island I	116	9.53 N	126.02 E
Siari	123	34.56 N	76.44 E
Siasconset	207	41.15 N	69.58 W
Siasi	116	5.33 N	120.49 E
Siasi Island I	116	5.33 N	120.51 E
Šiaškotan, ostrov I	74	48.49 N	154.06 E
Siátista	38	40.16 N	21.33 E
Siaton	116	9.04 N	123.02 E
Siaton ≃	116	9.02 N	123.02 E
Siaton Point ›	116	9.03 N	123.01 E
Siau, Pulau I	112	2.42 N	125.24 E
Siaugues-Saint-Romain	62	45.06 N	3.38 E
Šiauliai	76	55.56 N	23.19 E
Siazan'	84	41.05 N	49.06 E
Sibago Island I	116	6.45 N	122.24 E
Sibāʿī, Jabal as- ∧	140	25.43 N	34.09 E
Sibaj	86	52.42 N	58.39 E
Sibalom	116	10.47 N	122.01 E
Sibanicú	240p	21.14 N	77.31 W
Sibao	100	25.55 N	116.42 E
Sibari, Piana di ≚	68	39.45 N	16.25 E
Sibasa	156	22.53 S	30.33 E
Sibati	86	47.12 N	88.15 E
Sibayi ⊜	158	27.20 S	32.40 E
Sibay Island I	116	11.51 N	121.29 E
Sibbald	184	51.23 N	110.09 W
Sibbald Point Provincial Park ♦	212	44.19 N	79.19 W
Šibbe	85	39.53 N	72.05 E
Sibbo	26	60.22 N	25.16 E
Sibchar	126	23.21 N	90.09 E
Šibenik	36	43.44 N	15.54 E
Siberia Occidental, Llanura de → Zapadno-Sibirskaja ravnina ≚	72	60.00 N	75.00 E
Siberia → Sibir' ⬥1	74	65.00 N	110.00 E
Sibérie Occidentale, Dépression de la → Zapadno-Sibirskaja ravnina ≚	72	60.00 N	75.00 E
Siberut, Pulau I	108	1.20 S	98.55 E
Sibi	120	29.33 N	67.53 E
Sibiči	89	46.04 N	135.22 E
Sibidiri	164	9.00 S	142.15 E
Sibigo	114	2.51 N	95.55 E
Sibillini, Monti ⩘	66	42.54 N	13.13 E
Sibir' (Siberia) ⬥1	74	65.00 N	110.00 E
Sibir'akova, ostrov I	74	72.50 N	79.00 E
Sibircevo	89	44.12 N	132.26 E
Sibiti	152	3.41 S	13.21 E
Sibiti ≃	154	3.49 S	34.46 E
Sibiu	38	45.48 N	24.09 E
Sibiu □6	38	46.00 N	24.15 E
Sible Hedingham	42	51.58 N	0.35 E
Sibley, Il., U.S.	216	40.35 N	88.23 W
Sibley, Ia., U.S.	198	43.23 N	95.45 W
Sibley, La., U.S.	194	32.33 N	93.18 W
Sibley, Ms., U.S.	194	31.22 N	91.23 W
Sibley Peninsula ›1	190	48.25 N	88.45 W
Sibley Provincial Park ♦	190	48.25 N	88.49 W
Siboa	112	0.30 N	120.02 E
Sibochi	107	28.50 N	104.32 E
Sibolga	114	1.45 N	98.48 E
Siborang	114	1.08 N	99.26 E
Siborongborong	114	2.13 N	98.59 E
Sibpur, Bngl.	124	24.02 N	90.44 E
Sibpur, India	272b	22.24 N	88.33 E
Sibpur, India	272b	22.34 N	88.19 E
Sibsa ≃1	126	22.01 N	89.30 E
Sibsāgar	120	26.59 N	94.39 E
Sibu	112	2.18 N	111.49 E
Sibu, Pulau I	114	2.13 N	104.04 E
Sibuatan, Gunung ∧	114	2.56 N	98.24 E
Sibuguey ≃	116	7.38 N	122.48 E
Sibuguey Bay ⊂	116	7.30 N	122.40 E
Sibut	152	5.44 N	19.05 E
Sibuti	112	4.03 N	113.48 E
Sibutu Island I	112	4.46 N	119.29 E
Sibutu Passage ʮ	112	4.50 N	119.35 E
Sibuyan Island I	116	12.25 N	122.34 E
Sibuyan Sea ⩡2	116	12.50 N	122.40 E
Siby	150	12.23 N	8.20 W
Sibyŏn	98	38.19 N	126.41 E
Sicamous	182	50.50 N	119.00 W
Sicapoo, Mount ∧	116	18.01 N	120.56 E
Siccus ≃	166	31.26 S	139.30 E
Šichakou	98	41.39 N	116.26 E
Šichany	80	52.07 N	47.13 E
Sichifulo ≃	154	17.26 S	25.02 E
Si Chon	110	9.00 N	99.54 E
Sichote-Alin' ⩘	89	48.00 N	138.00 E
Sichote-Alinskij zapovednik ♦	89	45.15 N	136.15 E
Šichtovo	76	55.43 N	32.18 E
Sichuan (Szechwan) □4	102	31.00 N	105.00 E
Sichuan Pendi ≚1	102	30.00 N	105.00 E
Sichuanzhai	102	23.02 N	101.44 E
Sicié, Cap ›	62	43.03 N	5.51 E
Sicignano degli Alburni	68	40.34 N	15.18 E
Sicilia □4	36	37.30 N	14.00 E
Sicilia (Sicily) I	70	37.30 N	14.00 E
Sicilia, Isla de → Sicilia I	70	37.30 N	14.00 E
Sicily, Strait of ʮ	36	37.20 N	11.20 E
Sicily Island	194	31.50 N	91.39 W
Sicily → Sicilia I	70	37.30 N	14.00 E
Sickingmühle	263	51.42 N	7.07 E
Sicklerville	208	39.43 N	74.58 W
Sicogon Island I	116	11.27 N	123.16 E
Sico Tinto ≃	236	15.58 N	84.58 W
Sicuani	248	14.16 S	71.13 W
Siculiana	70	37.20 N	13.25 E
Šicun	106	31.55 N	119.18 E
Šid	38	45.08 N	19.13 E
Sīdah, Qārat ∧2	142	30.16 N	29.58 E
Sidamo □4	144	5.00 N	39.00 E
Sidao	271a	39.51 N	116.26 E
Sidaohe	105	40.24 N	117.17 E
Sidareja	115a	7.29 S	108.47 E
Sidas	112	0.24 N	109.46 E
Sidcup ⬥8	260	51.25 N	0.06 E
Siddeburen	52	53.25 N	6.52 E
Siddhapur	120	23.55 N	72.23 E
Siddinghausen	263	51.32 N	7.48 E
Siddington	262	53.14 N	2.14 W
Siddipet	122	18.06 N	78.51 E
Sideia Island I	164	10.35 S	150.50 E
Sidel'kino	80	54.32 N	51.08 E
Sidéradougou	150	10.40 N	4.15 W
Siderno	68	38.16 N	16.18 E
Sideróplis	252	28.35 S	49.26 W
Šiderty ≃, Kaz.	80	50.10 N	52.20 E
Šiderty ≃, Kaz.	86	52.32 N	74.50 E
Sidhauli	124	27.17 N	80.50 E
Sídheros, Ákra ›	38	35.19 N	26.19 E
Sidhi	124	24.25 N	81.53 E
Sidhirókastron	38	41.14 N	23.22 E
Sīdī ʿAbd ar-Raḥmān	140	30.58 N	29.44 E
Sidi Aïch	34	36.37 N	4.42 E
Sidi Aïssa	148	35.53 N	3.48 E
Sidi Akacha	34	36.28 N	1.18 E
Sidi Ali	34	36.06 N	0.25 E
Sidi Ali, Oued V	148	34.07 N	2.05 W
Sidi Ali Ben Nasrallah	36	35.15 N	9.50 E
Sīdī Barrānī	140	31.36 N	25.55 E
Sidi bel Abbès	148	35.13 N	0.10 W
Sidi Bel Abbes □5	148	35.00 N	1.00 W
Sidi Bennour	148	32.30 N	8.30 W
Sidi Bou Zid	148	35.02 N	9.30 E
Sidi Bou Zid □8	148	35.00 N	9.15 E
Sidi Daoud	36	37.00 N	10.55 E
Sidi el Hani, Sebkhet ⊜	36	35.33 N	10.25 E
Sīdī Ghāzī	142	31.12 N	31.03 E
Sīdī Ḥunaysh	140	31.10 N	27.37 E
Sidi Ifni	148	29.24 N	10.12 W
Sidi Kacem	148	34.15 N	5.39 W
Sidikalang	114	2.45 N	98.19 E
Sidimo	144	2.27 N	41.58 E
Sidi Mohammed Ben Ali	34	36.09 N	0.51 E
Sidi Moussa, Oued V	148	26.58 N	3.54 E
Sidi Okba	148	34.48 N	5.54 E
Sīdī Sālim	142	31.17 N	30.48 E
Sidi Slimane	148	34.15 N	5.49 W
Sidi Smaïl	148	32.49 N	8.30 W
Sidlaghatta	122	13.23 N	77.52 E
Sidlaw Hills ⩘2	46	56.30 N	3.10 W
Sidley, Mount ∧	9	77.02 S	126.00 W
Sidli	124	26.33 N	90.28 E
Sidman	214	40.20 N	78.45 W
Sidmouth	42	50.41 N	3.15 W
Sidnaw	190	46.30 N	88.42 W
Sidney, B.C., Can.	224	48.39 N	123.24 W
Sidney, Il., U.S.	194	40.01 N	88.04 W
Sidney, In., U.S.	216	41.06 N	85.45 W
Sidney, Ia., U.S.	198	40.44 N	95.38 W
Sidney, Mt., U.S.	198	47.43 N	104.09 W
Sidney, Ne., U.S.	198	41.08 N	102.58 W
Sidney, N.Y., U.S.	210	42.18 N	75.23 W
Sidney, Oh., U.S.	216	40.17 N	84.09 W
Sidney Center	210	42.17 N	75.15 W
Sidney Island I	224	48.37 N	123.18 W
Sidney Lanier, Lake ⊜1	192	34.15 N	83.57 W
Sido	150	11.40 N	7.36 W
Sidoan	112	0.16 N	120.12 E
Sidoarjo	115a	7.27 S	112.43 E
Sidon	194	33.24 N	90.12 W
Sidon → Ṣaydā	132	33.33 N	35.22 E
Sidorovo	76	58.48 N	40.58 E
Sidory	80	50.08 N	43.19 E
Sidr, Ra's as- ›	142	29.36 N	32.40 E
Sidr, Wādī V	142	29.40 N	32.41 E
Sidra, Gulf of → Surt, Khalīj ⊂	146	31.30 N	18.00 E
Sidrolândia	255	20.55 S	54.58 W
Sidu, Zhg.	100	23.48 N	117.18 E
Sidu, Zhg.	100	24.12 N	115.15 E
Siduan	106	30.59 N	121.48 E
Siebengebirge ⩘2	56	50.40 N	7.14 E
Siebenlehn	54	51.01 N	13.18 E
Sieber	52	51.42 N	10.25 E
Siebnen	58	47.11 N	8.54 E
Siedenbollentin	54	53.44 N	13.23 E
Siedenburg	52	52.41 N	8.56 E
Siedlce	30	52.11 N	22.16 E
Siedlce □4	30	52.15 N	22.00 E
Sieg ≃	56	50.45 N	7.05 E
Siegburg	56	50.47 N	7.12 E
Siegen	56	50.52 N	8.02 E
Siegenburg	60	48.45 N	11.51 E
Siegendorf im Burgenland	61	47.47 N	16.33 E
Siegenfeld	264b	48.02 N	16.10 E
Sieghartskirchen	61	48.15 N	16.01 E
Siegler Springs	226	38.54 N	122.39 W
Siegsdorf	64	47.46 N	12.39 E
Sielbeck	54	54.11 N	10.37 E
Sielenbach	60	48.24 N	11.10 E
Siemens, Cape ›	164	1.21 S	149.34 E
Siemensstadt ⬥8	264a	52.32 N	13.17 E
Siemianowice Śląskie	30	50.19 N	19.01 E
Siemiatycze	30	52.26 N	22.53 E
Siĕmpang	110	14.07 N	106.23 E
Siĕmréab	110	13.22 N	103.51 E
Siems-Dänischburg ⬥8	54	53.55 N	10.44 E
Siena	66	43.19 N	11.21 E
Siena □4	66	43.13 N	11.24 E
Sieniawa	30	50.11 N	22.36 E
Sienna → Siena	66	43.19 N	11.21 E
Sienyang → Xianyang	102	34.22 N	108.42 E
Sieradz	30	51.36 N	18.45 E
Sieradz □4	30	51.40 N	18.45 E
Sieraków	30	52.39 N	16.04 E
Sierck-les-Bains	56	49.26 N	6.21 E
Sierksdorf	54	54.04 N	10.46 E
Sierning	61	48.03 N	14.19 E
Sierpc	30	52.52 N	19.41 E
Si'erpu	104	40.47 N	120.41 E
Sierra □6	226	39.30 N	120.30 W
Sierra Blanca	200	31.11 N	105.21 W
Sierra Blanca Peak ∧	200	33.23 N	105.48 W
Sierra-Bullones	116	9.51 N	124.20 E
Sierra Chica	252	36.50 S	60.13 W
Sierra City	226	39.33 N	120.37 W
Sierra Colorada	254	40.35 S	67.48 W
Sierra de Agua	232	17.32 N	88.54 W
Sierra de Outes	34	42.51 N	8.54 W
Sierra Gorda	252	22.54 S	69.19 W
Sierra Leona → Sierra Leone □1	150	8.30 N	11.30 W
Sierra Leone □1, Afr.	134	8.30 N	11.30 W
Sierra Leone □1, Afr.	150	8.30 N	11.30 W
Sierra Leone Basin ✢1	10	5.00 N	17.00 W
Sierra Leone Rise ✢3	10	5.30 N	21.00 W
Sierra Madre	228	34.09 N	118.03 W
Sierra Mojada	196	27.17 N	103.42 W
Sierra Nevada, Parque Nacional ♦	246	8.36 N	70.50 W
Sierra Peak ∧	280	33.51 N	117.39 W
Sierra San Pedro Mártir, Parque Nacional ♦	204	31.00 N	115.30 W
Sierras Bayas	252	36.57 S	60.09 W
Sierraville	226	39.35 N	120.21 W
Sierra Vista	200	31.33 N	110.18 W
Sierre	58	46.18 N	7.32 E
Siersleben	54	51.36 N	11.32 E
Siesta Key	220	27.19 N	82.34 W
Siesta Key I	220	27.16 N	82.33 W
Siete Puntas ≃	252	23.34 S	57.20 W
Siethen	264a	52.17 N	13.13 E
Siethener See ⊜	264a	52.17 N	13.12 E
Sietow	54	53.26 N	12.35 E
Sieve ≃	66	43.46 N	11.26 E
Sievering ⬥8	264b	48.15 N	16.20 E
Siezenheim	64	47.48 N	12.59 E
Sifahandra	114	1.30 N	97.21 E
Sifangtai, Zhg.	89	46.55 N	127.00 E
Sifangtai, Zhg.	104	41.33 N	121.19 E
Sifangtai, Zhg.	104	41.02 N	122.46 E
Sifangtai, Zhg.	104	41.35 N	122.57 E
Sifen	100	27.32 N	113.30 E
Sifeni	144	12.16 N	40.21 E
Sifentoudun	106	32.18 N	121.21 E
Siffu ≃	116	17.12 N	121.48 E
Sifié	150	7.59 N	6.55 W
Sífnos I	38	36.59 N	24.40 E
Sifón Villanueva	196	27.17 N	100.17 W
Sifton	184	51.21 N	100.07 W
Sig, Alg.	34	35.32 N	0.11 W
Sig, Ross.	24	65.35 N	34.13 E
Si Galangang	114	1.15 N	99.20 E
Šigali	80	55.33 N	48.02 E
Sigean	32	43.02 N	2.59 E
Sigel	214	41.17 N	79.07 W
Sigep	110	1.02 S	98.49 E
Siggebohyttan	40	59.37 N	15.01 E
Sighetu Marmației	38	47.56 N	23.54 E
Sighișoara	38	46.13 N	24.48 E
Sighty Crag ∧	44	55.07 N	2.37 W
Sigillo	66	43.20 N	12.44 E
Sigiriya	122	7.57 N	80.45 E
Siglan	74	59.02 N	152.25 E
Siglerville	208	40.44 N	77.31 W
Sigli	114	5.23 N	95.57 E
Sigli, Cap ›	34	36.54 N	4.46 E
Sigloy	50	47.50 N	2.14 E
Siglufjörður	24a	66.10 N	18.56 W
Sigmaringen	58	48.05 N	9.13 E
Sigmaringendorf	58	48.04 N	9.15 E
Signa	66	43.47 N	11.05 E
Signachi	84	41.37 N	45.54 E
Signalberg ∧	60	49.28 N	12.32 E
Signal Hill, Ca., U.S.	280	33.47 N	118.09 W
Signal Hill, Il., U.S.	219	38.34 N	90.05 W
Signal Hill National Historic Park ♦	186	47.35 N	52.40 W
Signal Mountain	194	35.07 N	85.20 W
Signal Mountain ∧	188	44.12 N	72.20 W
Signal Peak ∧	200	37.19 N	113.29 W
Signau	58	46.55 N	7.43 E
Signes	62	43.18 N	5.52 E
Signy ✿3	9	60.43 S	45.36 W
Signy-l'Abbaye	50	49.42 N	4.25 E
Signy-Le-Petit	50	49.54 N	4.17 E
Šigony	80	53.23 N	48.42 E
Sigourney	190	41.20 N	92.12 W
Sigre ≃	236	15.49 N	84.38 W
Sigriswil	58	46.43 N	7.42 E
Sígsig	246	3.01 S	78.45 W
Sigtuna	40	59.37 N	17.43 E
Siguanea, Ensenada de la ⊂	240p	21.38 N	83.05 W
Siguatepeque	236	14.32 N	87.49 W
Siguel ≃	116	5.58 N	125.06 E
Sigüenza	34	41.04 N	2.38 W
Sigües	34	42.38 N	1.00 W
Siguiri	150	11.25 N	9.10 W
Sigulda	76	57.09 N	24.51 E
Sigurd	200	38.50 N	111.58 W
Siguri Falls ⌞	154	8.31 S	37.23 E
Sihabuhabu, Dolok ∧	114	2.10 N	99.21 E
Sihai	105	40.33 N	116.24 E
Sihala → Sri Lanka □1	122	7.00 N	81.00 E
Sihanoukville → Kâmpóng Saôm	110	10.38 N	103.30 E
Sihecun	105	39.56 N	117.07 E
Sihepeng	114	1.06 N	99.27 E
Sihl ≃	58	47.23 N	8.32 E
Sihlepu	158	27.42 S	32.06 E
Sihlsee ⊜	58	47.07 N	8.47 E
Sihong	100	33.28 N	118.11 E
Sihor	120	21.42 N	71.58 E
Sihorā	124	23.29 N	80.07 E
Sihu	98	34.38 N	117.59 E
Sihuas	248	8.34 S	77.37 W
Sihuas ≃	248	16.37 S	72.19 W
Sihui	102	23.19 N	112.40 E
Sihŭng ⬥8	271b	37.28 N	126.54 E
Šiiči	78	52.15 N	29.14 E
Siikajoki ≃	26	64.50 N	24.44 E
Siilinjärvi	26	63.05 N	27.40 E
Siʿīr	132	31.35 N	35.09 E
Siirt	130	37.56 N	41.57 E
Siirt □4	128	38.00 N	42.00 E
Sija	24	63.38 N	41.38 E
Sijā ≃	124	29.08 N	81.35 E
Sijbekarspel	52	52.43 N	4.59 E
Sijiaba	106	32.02 N	121.18 E
Sijianfang	104	42.29 N	122.17 E
Sijiao Shan I	100	30.41 N	122.28 E
Sijiazi	98	41.47 N	120.06 E
Sijing	106	31.07 N	121.16 E
Sijunjung	112	0.42 S	100.58 E
Sijupu	107	30.02 N	106.18 E
Sik	114	5.49 N	100.44 E
Sika	115b	8.45 S	122.12 E
Sikalongo	154	16.46 S	27.07 E
Sikandarābād	124	28.27 N	77.42 E
Sikandarpur, India	272a	28.42 N	77.21 E
Sikandarpur, India	272b	22.57 N	88.12 E
Sikandra	124	24.57 N	86.02 E
Sikandra Rao	124	27.42 N	78.24 E
Sikanni Chief ≃	176	58.20 N	121.50 W
Sikao	110	7.34 N	99.21 E
Sīkar	120	27.37 N	75.09 E
Sikarpur	272b	22.36 N	88.32 E
Sikasso	150	11.19 N	5.40 W
Sikasso □4	150	10.55 N	7.00 W
Sikéai	38	36.46 N	22.56 E
Sikelenge	152	14.50 S	24.14 E
Sikeli	112	5.16 S	121.48 E
Sikensi	150	5.40 N	4.34 W
Sikeshu	86	44.25 N	84.14 E
Sikeston	194	36.52 N	89.35 W
Sikfors	40	59.48 N	14.35 E
Si Khiu	110	14.53 N	101.44 E
Sikiá	38	40.02 N	23.56 E
Sikiang → Xi ≃	102	22.25 N	113.23 E
Sikijang	114	4.22 N	98.02 E
Siking → Xi'an	102	34.15 N	108.52 E
Síkinos	38	36.39 N	25.06 E
Síkinos I	38	36.39 N	25.06 E
Sikión ⊥	38	37.59 N	22.44 E
Sikkim □3	124	27.35 N	88.35 E
Siklós ⊥	30	45.52 N	18.28 E
Sikonge	154	5.38 S	32.46 E
Šikosi	156	17.59 S	23.19 E
Šikotan, ostrov (Shikotan-tō) I	92a	43.47 N	146.45 E
Sikrod	272a	28.43 N	77.11 E
Sikt'ach	74	69.55 N	125.02 E
Sikuati	112	6.53 N	116.40 E
Sikutu	112	0.53 N	120.37 E
Šil ≃	34	42.27 N	7.43 W
Šila	86	56.33 N	93.02 E
Silacayoapan	234	17.30 N	98.09 W
Sila Grande ⩘	68	39.22 N	16.30 E
Sila Greca ⩘	68	39.30 N	16.30 E
Silai ≃	126	22.41 N	87.46 E
Šilalahi	114	2.48 N	98.32 E
Šilalė	76	55.28 N	22.12 E
Silam, Gunong ∧	116	4.58 N	118.10 E
Silāmpur ⬥8	272a	28.40 N	77.16 E
Silandro (Schlanders)	64	46.38 N	10.46 E
Silang	116	14.14 N	120.58 E
Silangcheng	98	42.19 N	115.43 E
Silanus	71	40.17 N	8.53 E
Silao	234	20.56 N	101.26 W
Sila Piccola ⩘	68	39.05 N	16.35 E
Silas	194	31.45 N	88.19 W
Silat	112	0.21 N	111.47 E
Sīlat az-Ẓahr	132	32.19 N	35.11 E
Silau ≃	114	2.58 N	99.48 E
Silaut	112	2.22 S	101.08 E
Silaw Aihagam, Gunung ∧	114	5.25 N	95.40 E
Silay	116	10.48 N	122.58 E
Silay, Mount ∧	116	10.47 N	123.14 E
Silba	36	44.23 N	14.42 E
Silbertal	58	47.05 N	9.59 E
Silchar	120	24.49 N	92.48 E
Šilda, India	126	22.37 N	86.49 E
Šil'da, Ross.	86	51.46 N	59.45 E
Šile	130	41.11 N	29.36 E
Šile ≃	64	45.33 N	12.27 E
Šileby	42	52.43 N	1.06 W
Šilega	24	64.03 N	44.01 E
Silenrieux	50	50.14 N	4.24 E
Silent Lake ⊜	212	44.55 N	78.04 W
Silent Lake Provincial Park ♦	212	44.54 N	78.05 W
Siler City	192	35.43 N	79.27 W
Sileru ≃	122	17.47 N	81.24 E
Silesia □9	30	51.00 N	16.45 E
Silet	148	22.44 N	4.37 E
Siletz	202	44.43 N	123.55 W
Siletz ≃	202	44.54 N	124.00 W
Silex	219	39.07 N	91.03 W
Silgaḍhī	124	29.16 N	80.59 E
Silghāt	120	26.37 N	92.56 E
Silhouette I	138	4.29 S	55.14 E
Siliana	148	36.05 N	9.22 E
Siliana □8	148	36.00 N	9.20 E
Siliana, Oued ≃	36	36.33 N	9.25 E
Silifke	130	36.22 N	33.56 E
Šilijiang	105	39.43 N	117.28 E
Šilikty	86	47.10 N	84.32 E
Silingan, Mount ∧	116	7.46 N	122.30 E
Siling Co ⊜	120	31.50 N	89.00 E
Siliqua	71	39.18 N	8.48 E
Silistra	38	44.07 N	27.16 E
Šilivri	130	41.04 N	28.15 E
Šiljak ∧	38	43.45 N	21.50 E
Siljan ⊜	26	60.50 N	14.45 E
Šiljansnäs	26	60.45 N	14.42 E
Šilka	88	51.51 N	116.02 E
Šilka ≃	74	53.22 N	121.32 E
Silkāripāra	126	24.14 N	87.28 E
Silkeborg	41	56.10 N	9.34 E
Silkworth	210	41.16 N	76.05 W
Sill ≃	64	47.16 N	11.25 E
Sillamäe	76	59.24 N	27.45 E
Sillānwāli	123	31.50 N	72.33 E
Sillaro ≃	66	44.34 N	11.51 E
Sille	130	37.56 N	32.26 E
Sillem Island I	176	70.55 N	71.30 W
Sillen ⊜	40	58.59 N	17.22 E
Sillenstede	52	53.34 N	7.59 E
Sillery, P.Q., Can.	206	46.46 N	71.15 W
Sillery, Fr.	50	49.12 N	4.08 E
Silli	150	11.36 N	2.30 W
Sillian	64	46.45 N	12.25 E
Sillil	144	10.59 N	43.26 E
Sillon de Talbert ›1	32	48.53 N	3.05 W
Silloth	44	54.52 N	3.23 W
Sillustani ⊥	248	15.45 S	70.05 W
Silly-le-Long	261	49.06 N	2.48 E
Šil'naja Balka	80	50.34 N	49.01 E
Silnice	60	48.54 N	13.44 E
Siloam Springs	194	36.11 N	94.32 W
Siloam Springs State Park ♦	219	39.53 N	90.54 W
Šilogui	110	1.14 S	99.00 E
Šilovići	76	55.24 N	32.33 E
Šilovka	80	54.03 N	48.40 E
Šilovo, Ross.	76	55.00 N	33.46 E
Šilovo, Ross.	80	54.19 N	40.53 E
Silowana Plains ≚	152	17.00 S	23.15 E
Silphuh	126	23.44 N	86.22 E
Silsbee	194	30.20 N	94.10 W
Silsby Lake ⊜	184	55.29 N	95.46 W
Silschede	263	51.21 N	7.19 E
Silsden	44	53.55 N	1.55 W
Sils im Engadin	58	46.22 N	9.46 E
Silton	184	50.48 N	104.55 W
Siluas	112	1.17 N	109.51 E
Šiluko	150	6.31 N	5.09 E
Šilutė	76	55.21 N	21.29 E
Silvacane, Abbaye de ✿1	62	43.44 N	5.20 E
Silvan (Miyafarkin)	130	38.08 N	41.01 E
Silvana	224	48.12 N	122.15 W
Sīlvāneh	128	37.25 N	44.51 E
Silvânia	255	16.42 S	48.38 W
Silvano d'Orba	62	44.41 N	8.40 E
Silvan Reservoir ⊜1	169	37.50 S	145.25 E
Silvaplana	58	46.26 N	9.47 E
Silvassa	122	20.17 N	73.00 E
Silveiras	256	22.40 S	44.52 W
Silver	196	32.04 N	100.40 W
Silverado	228	33.45 N	117.35 W
Silver Bank ✢2	238	20.30 N	69.45 W
Silver Bank Passage ʮ	238	20.45 N	70.15 W
Silver Bay	190	47.17 N	91.15 W
Silver Bell	200	32.23 N	111.29 W
Silver City, N.M., U.S.	200	32.46 N	108.16 W
Silver City, N.C., U.S.	192	35.00 N	79.12 W
Silver Creek, Ms., U.S.	194	31.36 N	89.59 W
Silver Creek, Ne., U.S.	198	41.18 N	97.39 W
Silver Creek, N.Y., U.S.	214	42.32 N	79.10 W
Silver Creek ≃, Az., U.S.	200	34.44 N	110.02 W
Silver Creek ≃, Ca., U.S.	226	38.47 N	120.35 W
Silver Creek ≃, Ca., U.S.	226	36.36 N	120.41 W
Silver Creek ≃, Il., U.S.	219	38.20 N	89.52 W
Silver Creek ≃, Il., U.S.	278	41.54 N	87.50 W
Silver Creek ≃, In., U.S.	218	38.17 N	85.47 W
Silver Creek ≃, In., U.S.	218	39.36 N	84.59 W
Silver Creek ≃, Ky., U.S.	192	37.48 N	84.30 W
Silver Creek ≃, Or., U.S.	202	43.16 N	119.13 W
Silver Creek ≃, Wa., U.S.	224	46.32 N	121.55 W
Silver Creek, Muddy Fork ≃	218	38.25 N	86.44 W
Silver Creek, South Fork ≃	226	38.49 N	120.27 W
Silverdale, B.C., Can.	224	49.09 N	122.24 W
Silverdale, N.Z.	172	36.37 S	174.40 E
Silverdale, Eng., U.K.	44	54.10 N	2.49 W
Silverdale, Pa., U.S.	208	40.21 N	75.16 W
Silverdale, Wa., U.S.	224	47.38 N	122.41 W
Silverdalen	26	57.32 N	15.44 E
Silverdome ♦	281	42.39 N	83.15 W
Silver End	42	51.51 N	0.37 E
Silver Falls State Park ♦	202	44.48 N	122.50 W
Silverfields	273d	26.07 S	27.49 E
Silver Fork ≃	219	39.06 N	92.21 W
Silver Grove	218	39.02 N	84.23 W
Silver Hill	284c	38.50 N	76.56 W
Silverhope Creek ≃	224	49.18 N	121.27 W
Silver Lake, Ca., U.S.	226	38.38 N	120.07 W
Silver Lake, In., U.S.	216	41.04 N	85.53 W
Silver Lake, Ks., U.S.	198	39.06 N	95.51 W
Silver Lake, Ma., U.S.	207	42.34 N	71.11 W
Silver Lake, Mn., U.S.	190	44.54 N	94.11 W
Silver Lake, Oh., U.S.	214	41.09 N	81.27 W
Silver Lake, Or., U.S.	202	43.07 N	121.02 W
Silverlake, Wa., U.S.	224	46.17 N	122.48 W
Silver Lake, Wi., U.S.	216	42.32 N	88.09 W
Silver Lake ⊜, Ca., U.S.	226	38.39 N	120.07 W
Silver Lake ⊜, De., U.S.	208	39.11 N	75.32 W
Silver Lake ⊜, Ma., U.S.	283	42.01 N	70.48 W
Silver Lake ⊜, N.Y., U.S.	210	42.42 N	78.02 W
Silver Lake ⊜, N.Y., U.S.	276	41.03 N	73.45 W
Silver Lake ⊜, Or., U.S.	202	43.06 N	120.53 W
Silver Lake ⊜, Or., U.S.	202	43.22 N	119.24 W
Silver Lake ⊜, Wa., U.S.	224	46.17 N	122.47 W
Silver Lake ⊜, Wa., U.S.	224	48.58 N	122.04 W
Silver Lake Park ♦	276	41.03 N	73.45 W
Silver Lake Reservoir ⊜1, Ca., U.S.	280	34.06 N	118.16 W
Silver Lake Reservoir ⊜1, N.Y., U.S.	276	40.37 N	74.06 W
Silvermine ≃	276	41.08 N	73.26 W
Silver Mine Bay ⊂	271d	22.16 N	114.00 E
Silvermine Brook ≃	276	41.08 N	73.27 W
Silvermine Mountains ⩘	48	52.45 N	8.15 W
Silvermines	48	52.47 N	8.13 W
Silver Mountain ∧	280	34.12 N	117.52 W
Silver Peak ∧	228	33.28 N	118.35 W
Silver Peak Range ⩘	204	37.35 N	117.45 W
Silver Spring, Md., U.S.	208	38.59 N	77.01 W
Silver Spring, Pa., U.S.	208	40.04 N	76.26 W
Silver Springs, Nv., U.S.	226	39.24 N	119.13 W
Silver Springs, N.Y., U.S.	210	42.39 N	78.05 W
Silver Springs State Park ♦	216	41.38 N	88.32 W
Silver Star Mountain ∧	224	48.33 N	120.35 W
Silver Star Provincial Park ♦	182	50.22 N	119.05 W
Silverstone	42	52.05 N	1.02 W
Silver Streams	158	28.20 S	23.33 E
Silverthrone Mountain ∧	182	51.31 N	126.06 W
Silvertip Mountain ∧	202	47.47 N	113.15 W
Silverton, Austl.	166	31.53 S	141.13 E
Silverton, B.C., Can.	182	49.57 N	117.21 W
Silverton, Eng., U.K.	42	50.48 N	3.28 W
Silverton, Co., U.S.	200	37.48 N	107.39 W
Silverton, N.J., U.S.	208	40.00 N	74.08 W
Silverton, Oh., U.S.	218	39.12 N	84.24 W
Silverton, Or., U.S.	224	45.00 N	122.46 W
Silverton, Tx., U.S.	196	34.28 N	101.19 W
Silverwood Lake ⊜1	228	34.18 N	117.19 W
Silves	34	37.11 N	8.26 W
Silvi	66	42.34 N	14.05 E
Silvia	246	2.37 N	76.21 W
Silvianópolis	256	22.02 S	45.50 W
Silvícola	164	8.39 S	126.59 E
Silvies ≃	202	43.22 N	118.48 W
Silview	285	39.42 N	75.37 W
Silvolde	52	51.54 N	6.53 E
Silvretta Gruppe ⩘	58	46.50 N	10.10 E
Sim	86	54.59 N	57.41 E
Sim, Cap ›	148	31.23 N	9.51 W
Sima, Comores	157a	12.11 S	44.17 E
Sima, Ross.	80	56.41 N	39.33 E
Simaltala	124	24.43 N	86.33 E
Simanggang	112	1.15 N	111.26 E
Simangumban	114	1.42 N	99.10 E
Šimanoviči	76	53.05 N	28.38 E
Šimanovsk	89	52.00 N	127.42 E
Simao	102	22.50 N	101.00 E
Simão Dias	250	10.44 S	37.49 W
Simão Pereira	256	21.58 S	43.19 W
Simara Island I	116	12.48 N	122.03 E
Simard, Lac ⊜	190	47.37 N	78.41 W
Simaria Kalān	124	24.04 N	84.56 E
Simatang, Pulau I	112	1.04 N	120.23 E
Simav	130	39.05 N	28.59 E
Simav ≃	130	40.23 N	28.31 E
Simav Gölü ⊜	130	39.09 N	28.55 E
Simaxis	71	39.56 N	8.41 E
Simba, Kenya	154	2.10 S	37.36 E
Simba, Tan.	154	1.44 S	34.13 E
Simba, Zaïre	152	0.36 N	22.55 E
Simbach	60	48.34 N	12.45 E
Simbach am Inn	60	48.16 N	13.01 E
Simbario	68	38.37 N	16.20 E
Simberi Island I	164	2.40 S	152.00 E
Simbirsk → Uljanovsk	80	54.20 N	48.24 E
Simbo, Tan.	154	4.53 S	29.44 E
Simbo, Tan.	154	4.40 S	33.27 E
Simbo Island I	175e	8.17 S	156.33 E
Simbruini, Monti ⩘	66	41.55 N	13.15 E
Simcoe	212	42.50 N	80.18 W
Simcoe □6	212	44.25 N	79.50 W
Simcoe, Lake ⊜	212	44.20 N	79.20 W
Simcoe Creek ≃	224	46.22 N	120.36 W
Simcoe Island I	212	44.10 N	76.31 W
Simcoe Point ›	275b	43.49 N	79.01 W
Simdega	124	22.37 N	84.31 E
Simeiz	78	44.26 N	34.01 E
Simen	104	40.44 N	123.49 E
Simeng	107	29.56 N	103.44 E
Simen Mountains National Park ♦	144	13.08 N	38.15 E
Simenti	150	13.00 N	13.25 W
Simeri ≃	68	38.52 N	16.43 E
Simeria	38	45.51 N	23.01 E
Simeto ≃	70	37.24 N	15.06 E
Simeulue, Pulau I	114	2.33 N	96.05 E
Simferopol'	78	44.57 N	34.06 E
Sími	38	36.36 N	27.50 E
Sími I	38	36.35 N	27.52 E
Simi, Arroyo ≃	228	34.16 N	118.39 W
Simiane	62	43.25 N	5.26 E
Simianshan	107	28.49 N	105.09 E
Simikoṭ	124	29.58 N	81.50 E
Similkameen ≃	182	48.56 N	119.26 W
Simingchang	107	29.02 N	105.45 E
Simiri	150	14.08 N	2.08 E
Simisa Island I	116	5.57 N	121.35 E
Simití	246	7.58 N	73.57 W
Simi Valley	228	34.16 N	118.47 W
Simiyu ≃	154	2.33 S	33.25 E
Simizu → Shimizu	94	35.01 N	138.29 E
Simla, India	272b	22.47 N	88.16 E
Simla, India	272b	22.54 N	88.22 E
Simla, Co., U.S.	198	39.08 N	104.05 W
Simla ⬥3	272b	22.35 N	88.22 E
Simlāpāl	126	22.55 N	87.05 E
Şimleu Silvaniei	38	47.14 N	22.48 E
Šimlipālgarh	126	21.51 N	86.23 E
Simme ≃	58	46.41 N	7.38 E
Simmelsdorf	60	49.36 N	11.21 E
Simmental V	58	46.37 N	7.25 E
Simmerath	56	50.36 N	6.18 E
Simmerberg	58	47.35 N	9.56 E
Simmering ⬥8	264b	48.11 N	16.25 E
Simmern	56	49.59 N	7.31 E
Simmesport	194	30.59 N	91.48 W
Simmie	184	49.57 N	108.06 W
Simmons Island I	282	38.06 N	121.58 W
Simmons Point ›	282	38.03 N	121.56 W
Simmonswood Moss ⬥3	262	53.30 N	2.50 W
Simms	202	47.29 N	111.55 W
Simnas	76	54.24 N	23.39 E
Simoca	252	27.16 S	65.21 W
Simões	250	7.36 S	40.49 W
Simojärvi ⊜	26	66.06 N	27.03 E
Simojoki ≃	26	65.37 N	25.03 E
Simojovel	234	17.12 N	92.38 W
Simon, Lac ⊜, P.Q., Can.	206	45.58 N	75.05 W
Simon, Lac ⊜, P.Q., Can.	206	46.10 N	74.45 W
Simón Bolívar, Aeropuerto Internacional ⊠	286c	10.37 N	66.59 W
Simoneti	84	42.14 N	42.52 E
Simonette ≃	182	55.07 N	118.00 W
Simonhouse Lake ⊜	184	54.30 N	101.10 W
Simonicha	80	56.31 N	53.50 E
Simoniči	78	51.53 N	28.04 E
Simonoseki → Shimonoseki	96	33.57 N	130.57 E
Simonsbath	42	51.09 N	3.45 W
Simonson Brook ≃	276	40.26 N	74.37 W
Simonstone	262	53.48 N	2.20 W
Simonstorp	40	58.47 N	16.09 E
Simon's Town	158	34.14 S	18.26 E
Simonton Lake	216	41.44 N	85.59 W
Šimoom Sound	182	50.45 N	126.29 W
Šimorskoje	80	55.19 N	42.02 E
Simpang, Indon.	112	1.16 S	104.05 E
Simpang, Indon.	112	1.03 S	110.06 E
Simpang, Indon.	112	0.09 N	103.15 E
Simpangampat	114	2.55 N	99.43 E
Simpang Empat	114	6.20 N	100.11 E
Simpang-kanan ≃	114	2.21 N	97.51 E
Simpang-kiri ≃	114	2.21 N	97.51 E
Simpang Rengam	114	1.50 N	103.19 E
Simpangtiga	114	2.23 N	99.47 E
Simpangulim	114	5.06 N	97.32 E
Simpele	26	61.26 N	29.22 E
Simplício Mendes	250	7.51 S	41.54 W
Simplon Pass)(	58	46.15 N	8.02 E
Simplon Tunnel ⬥5	58	46.15 N	8.05 E
Simpnäs	40	59.52 N	19.04 E
Simp'o-ri	98	38.36 N	127.41 E
Simpson, La., U.S.	194	31.14 N	93.00 W
Simpson, Pa., U.S.	210	41.35 N	75.29 W
Simpson ≃	254	45.25 S	72.32 W
Simpson, Isla I	254	45.53 S	73.48 W
Simpson Desert ⬥2	162	25.00 S	137.00 E
Simpson Desert National Park ♦	162	25.40 S	138.15 E
Simpson Island I	190	48.48 N	87.40 W
Simpson Lake ⊜	180	68.10 N	126.35 W
Simpson Peak ∧	180	59.44 N	131.27 W
Simpson Peninsula ›1	176	68.34 N	88.45 W
Simpsons Gap National Park ♦	162	23.40 S	133.45 E
Simpson Strait ʮ	176	68.27 N	97.45 W
Simpsonville, Ky., U.S.	218	38.13 N	85.21 W
Simpsonville, Md., U.S.	208	39.11 N	76.52 W
Simpsonville, S.C., U.S.	192	34.44 N	82.15 W
Simrishamn	26	55.33 N	14.20 E
Sims	216	40.30 N	85.51 W
Šimsbury	207	41.52 N	72.48 W
Šimsk	76	58.13 N	30.43 E
Simssee ⊜	64	47.52 N	12.14 E
Simunjan	112	1.23 N	110.45 E
Simurāli	126	23.03 N	88.30 E
Simušir, ostrov I	74	46.58 N	152.02 E
Sīnā' □4	142	30.15 N	32.40 E
Sīna ≃	122	17.22 N	75.54 E
Sīnā', Shibh Jazīrat (Sinai Peninsula) ›1	140	29.30 N	34.00 E
Sinabang	114	2.29 N	96.23 E
Sinabelkirchen	61	47.06 N	15.50 E
Sinabung, Gunung ∧	114	3.10 N	98.24 E
Sinadhago	144	5.22 N	46.20 E
Sinagra	70	38.05 N	14.51 E
Sinai, Mount ∧	241k	12.04 N	61.42 W
Sinai, Mount → Mūsā, Jabal ∧	140	28.32 N	33.59 E
Sinaia	38	45.21 N	25.33 E
Sinai Peninsula → Sīnā', Shibh Jazīrat ›1	140	29.30 N	34.00 E
Sin'aja ≃, Europe	76	57.10 N	28.31 E
Sin'aja ≃, Ross.	74	61.06 N	126.50 E
Sinajana	174p	13.28 N	144.45 E
Sinako, Mount ∧	116	7.30 N	125.17 E
Sinaloa □3	232	25.00 N	107.30 W
Sinaloa ≃	232	25.18 N	108.30 W
Sinalunga	66	43.12 N	11.44 E
Sinamaica	246	11.05 N	71.51 W
Sinamary ≃	250	5.27 N	53.00 W
Sinan, Tür.	130	37.52 N	41.00 E
Sinan, Zhg.	102	27.54 N	108.18 E
Sinanju	98	39.36 N	125.36 E
Sinanpaşa	130	38.45 N	30.15 E
Sīnarū	142	29.22 N	30.45 E
Sinatle	84	42.28 N	43.04 E
Sin'avka, Bela.	76	52.58 N	26.29 E
Sin'avka, Ross.	83	47.17 N	39.17 E
Sīnāwin	146	31.02 N	10.36 E
Sinbad Creek ≃	282	37.35 N	121.53 W
Sinbaungwe	110	19.43 N	95.10 E
Sinbo	110	24.46 N	97.03 E
Sinbokchang	98	41.01 N	128.54 E
Sincan, Tür.	130	39.28 N	37.54 E
Sincan, Tür.	130	39.59 N	32.26 E
Sincé	246	9.15 N	75.09 W
Sincelejo	246	9.18 N	75.24 W
Sinch'ang, C.M.I.K.	98	40.07 N	128.28 E
Sinch'ang, C.M.I.K.	98	40.19 N	125.27 E
Sinch'ŏn	98	38.22 N	125.28 E
Sinch'ŏn-ni	271b	37.27 N	126.48 E
Sinclair	200	41.46 N	107.06 W
Sinclair, Lake ⊜1	192	33.11 N	83.16 W
Sinclair, Point ›	162	32.06 S	133.00 E
Sinclair Island I	224	48.37 N	122.40 W
Sinclair Mills	182	54.02 N	121.41 W
Sinclair's Bay ⊂	46	58.30 N	3.07 W
Sinclairville	214	42.15 N	79.15 W
Sind □4	120	25.30 N	69.00 E
Sind ≃	124	26.26 N	79.13 E
Sinda	89	48.57 N	136.18 E
Sindal	26	57.28 N	10.13 E
Sindangan	116	8.14 N	123.00 E
Sindangan ≃	116	8.13 N	123.00 E
Sindangan Bay ⊂	116	8.11 N	122.50 E
Sindangan Point ›	116	8.10 N	122.40 E

Symbols in the index entries represent the broad categories identified in the key at the right. Symbols with superior numbers (⩘1) identify subcategories (see complete key on page *I · 1*).

Symbole im Register stellen die rechts im Schlüssel erklärten Kategorien dar. Symbole mit hochgestellten Ziffern (⩘1) bezeichnen Unterabteilungen einer Kategorie (vgl. vollständiger Schlüssel auf Seite *I · 1*).

Los símbolos incluídos en el texto del índice representan las grandes categorias identificadas con la clave a la derecha. Los símbolos con numeros en su parte superior (⩘1) identifican las subcategorias (véase la clave completa en la página *I · 1*).

Les symboles de l'index représentent les catégories indiquées dans la légende à droite. Les symboles suivis d'un indice (⩘1) représentent des sous-catégories (voir légende complète à la page *I · 1*).

Os símbolos incluídos no texto do índice representam as grandes categorias identificadas com a chave à direita. Os símbolos com números em sua parte superior (⩘1) identificam as subcategorias (veja-se a chave completa à página *I · 1*).

	English	Deutsch	Español	Français	Português
∧	Mountain	Berg	Montaña	Montagne	Montanha
⩘	Mountains	Gebirge	Montañas	Montagnes	Montanhas
)(	Pass	Paß	Paso	Col	Passo
V	Valley, Canyon	Tal, Cañon	Valle, Cañón	Vallée, Canyon	Vale, Canhão
≚	Plain	Ebene	Llano	Plaine	Planície
›	Cape	Kap	Cabo	Cap	Cabo
I	Island	Insel	Isla	Île	Ilha
II	Islands	Inseln	Islas	Îles	Ilhas
⊥	Other Topographic Features	Andere Topographische Objekte	Otros Elementos Topográficos	Autres connées topographiques	Outros acidentes topográficos

ESPAÑOL — Nombre | Página | Lat.°′ | Long.°′ W = Oeste
FRANÇAIS — Nom | Page | Lat.°′ | Long.°′ W = Ouest
PORTUGUÊS — Nome | Página | Lat.°′ | Long.°′ W = Oeste

Nombre / Nom / Nome	Página / Page	Lat.°′	Long.°′ W = Oeste / Ouest
Sindangbarang	115a	7.27 S	107.08 E
Sindara	152	1.02 S	10.40 E
Sindari	120	25.35 N	71.55 E
Sindelfingen	56	48.42 N	9.00 E
Sindèr	150	14.29 N	1.22 E
Sindhnūr	122	15.47 N	76.46 E
Sindhulī Māńdi	124	27.16 N	85.58 E
Sindi	76	58.24 N	24.40 E
Sindia	71	40.18 N	8.39 E
Sindingale	110	18.17 N	94.25 E
Sındıran	130	39.17 N	32.41 E
Sındırgı	130	39.14 N	28.10 E
Sindiyūn	142	30.15 N	31.12 E
Sin-do I	98	39.48 N	124.14 E
Sindŏk	98	36.47 N	126.10 E
Sindor	24	62.50 N	51.57 E
Sindou	150	10.40 N	5.10 W
Sindri	126	23.45 N	86.42 E
Sind Sāgar Doāb ⩕[1]	123	31.30 N	71.30 E
Sine ∨	150	14.10 N	16.28 W
Sinegorje	24	59.42 N	50.40 E
Sinegorsk	89	47.10 N	142.30 E
Sinegorskij	78	48.00 N	40.53 E
Šine-Ider	88	48.56 N	99.33 E
Sinekçi	130	40.16 N	27.24 E
Sinekli	130	41.14 N	28.12 E
Sinel'nikovo	78	48.20 N	35.31 E
Sinendé	150	10.21 N	2.23 E
Sinen'kije	80	51.15 N	45.46 E
Sinepuxent Bay c	208	38.16 N	75.09 W
Sines	34	37.57 N	8.52 W
Sines, Cabo de ›	34	37.57 N	8.53 W
Sinevir	78	48.30 N	23.38 E
Sinevka	78	50.33 N	34.06 E
Sinewit, Mount ∧	164	4.40 S	152.00 E
Sinez'orki	76	53.02 N	34.26 E
Sinfra	150	6.37 N	5.55 W
Singair	126	23.49 N	90.08 E
Singako	146	9.50 N	19.29 E
Singal	123	36.06 N	73.53 E
Singalamwe	156	17.41 S	23.23 E
Singālila ∧	124	27.13 N	88.01 E
Singālila Range ⩕	124	27.25 N	88.05 E
Singaparna	115a	7.21 S	108.06 E
Singapore, Sing.	114	1.17 N	103.51 E
Singapore, Sing.	271c	1.17 N	103.51 E
Singapore □[1], Asia	108	1.22 N	103.48 E
Singapore □[1], Asia	114	1.22 N	103.48 E
Singapore I	271c	1.23 N	103.48 E
Singapore ≃	271c	1.17 N	103.51 E
Singapore, National University of ʊ[2]	271c	1.18 N	103.46 E
Singapore Station ◆[5]	271c	1.17 N	103.50 E
Singapore Strait ʉ	112	1.15 N	104.00 E
Singapour → Singapore □[1]	114	1.22 N	103.48 E
Singapur → Singapore	114	1.17 N	103.51 E
Singapur → Singapore □[1]	114	1.22 N	103.48 E
Singaraja	115b	8.07 S	115.06 E
Singarka ≃	265a	59.53 N	29.54 E
Singāti	126	22.44 N	89.43 E
Singatoka	175g	18.08 S	177.30 E
Sing Buri	110	14.53 N	100.25 E
Singe	272b	22.57 N	88.26 E
Singen (Hohentwiel)	58	47.46 N	8.50 E
Singer	194	30.39 N	93.24 W
Singhi	126	23.37 N	87.48 E
Singida	154	4.49 S	34.45 E
Singida □[4]	154	5.30 S	34.30 E
Singing, India	102	28.59 N	94.50 E
Singing, India	120	28.53 N	94.47 E
Singing Tower ♠	220	27.57 N	81.34 W
Singkaling Hkāmti	110	26.00 N	95.42 E
Singkang	112	4.08 S	120.01 E
Singkawang	112	0.54 N	109.00 E
Singkep, Pulau I	112	0.30 S	104.25 E
Singkil	114	2.17 N	97.49 E
Singkuang	114	1.03 N	98.56 E
Singleton, Austl.	170	32.34 S	151.10 E
Singleton, Eng., U.K.	42	50.55 N	0.46 W
Singleton, Mount ∧, Austl.	162	29.28 S	117.18 E
Singleton, Mount ∧, Austl.	162	22.00 S	130.49 E
Singleton Ditch ≊	216	41.10 N	87.37 W
Singlewell or Ifield	260	51.25 N	0.23 E
Singö	40	60.10 N	18.44 E
Singö I	40	60.11 N	18.46 E
Singora → Songkhla	110	7.12 N	100.36 E
Şingorkai	164	5.55 S	146.55 E
Šingoža	86	47.45 N	80.40 E
Singpāra	272b	22.40 N	88.31 E
Singrāmau	124	25.57 N	82.23 E
Singuédeze (Shingwidzi) ≃	156	23.53 S	32.17 E
Singur	126	22.49 N	88.14 E
Sin'gye	98	38.36 N	126.30 E
Sinhai → Lianyungang	98	34.39 N	119.16 E
Sinh Ho	110	22.22 N	103.14 E
Sinhŭng	98	40.11 N	127.34 E
Siniaka-Minia, Réserve de ■	146	10.30 N	18.00 E
Sinicha	83	49.31 N	37.34 E
Sinička ≃	265b	55.50 N	37.19 E
Sinije gory ⩕[2]	80	51.10 N	49.25 E
Sinije Lip'agi	78	51.23 N	38.29 E
Siniloan	116	14.25 N	121.27 E
Sining → Xining	102	36.38 N	101.55 E
Siniscola	71	40.34 N	9.41 E
Sinj	36	43.42 N	16.38 E
Sinjah	140	13.09 N	33.56 E
Sinjai	112	5.07 S	120.15 E
Sinjang-ni	98	39.04 N	127.46 E
Sinjār	128	36.19 N	41.52 E
Sinjār, Jabal ⩕	130	36.25 N	41.40 E
Sinji-do I	98	34.20 N	126.50 E
Sinkan	110	24.08 N	97.01 E
Sinkāt	140	18.50 N	36.50 E
Sinkiang → Xinjiang Uygur Zizhiqu □[4]	90	40.00 N	85.00 E
Sinking ≃	48	53.37 N	8.52 W
Sinking Creek ≃	210	40.51 N	77.34 W
Sinking Spring, Oh., U.S.	218	39.04 N	83.23 W
Sinking Spring, Pa., U.S.	208	40.19 N	76.02 W
Şin'kok-ni	271b	37.37 N	126.46 E
Šinkovo, Ross.	76	56.03 N	31.31 E
Sin'kovo, Ross.	82	54.37 N	38.56 E
Sin'kovo, Ross.	82	56.26 N	36.04 E
Sin'kovo, Ross.	82	56.23 N	37.19 E
Sinks Canyon State Park ♠	200	42.45 N	108.50 W
Sin-le-Noble	50	50.22 N	3.07 E
Sinmak	98	38.25 N	126.14 E
Sinmi-do I	98	39.33 N	124.53 E
Sinn ≃	56	50.03 N	9.42 E
Sinnahwā	142	30.25 N	31.21 E
Sínnai	71	39.18 N	9.12 E
Sinnamahoning	214	41.19 N	78.06 W
Sinnamary	250	5.23 N	52.57 W
Sinnar	122	19.51 N	74.00 E
Sinnemahoning Creek ≃	210	41.15 N	77.54 W
Sinnemahoning Creek, Bennett Branch ≃	210	41.20 N	78.08 W
Sinnemahoning Creek, Driftwood Branch ≃	210	41.20 N	78.08 W
Sinnemahoning Creek, First Fork ≃	210	41.19 N	78.05 W
Sinnersdorf	56	51.01 N	6.49 E
Sinnes	26	58.56 N	6.50 E
Sinni ≃	68	40.09 N	16.42 E
Sînnicolau Mare	38	46.05 N	20.38 E
Sinntal	56	50.18 N	9.38 E
Sinnūris	142	29.25 N	30.52 E
Sinnyŏng	98	36.04 N	128.46 E
Sino, Pedra do ∧	256	22.30 S	43.03 W
Sinoie, Lacul ⊜	38	44.38 N	28.53 E
Sinop, Bra.	250	11.55 S	55.35 W
Sinop, Tür.	130	42.01 N	35.09 E
Sinop □[4]	130	41.40 N	34.50 E
Sinop Burnu ›	130	42.02 N	35.12 E
Sinp'a	98	41.24 N	127.46 E
Sinp'o	98	40.03 N	128.12 E
Sins	58	47.11 N	8.23 E
Sinsang	98	39.38 N	127.25 E
Sinsen	263	51.40 N	7.11 E
Sinsheim	56	49.15 N	8.53 E
Sinsiang → Xinxiang	98	35.20 N	113.51 E
Sinsin	56	50.17 N	5.15 E
Sinsi-ri	98	39.59 N	124.58 E
Sinskoje	74	61.08 N	126.48 E
Sinspelt	56	49.58 N	6.19 E
Sint-Amandsberg	50	51.04 N	3.45 E
Sintana	38	46.21 N	21.30 E
Sint-Andries	50	51.12 N	3.10 E
Sintang	112	0.04 N	111.30 E
Sint Annaland	52	51.36 N	4.06 E
Sint Annaparochie	52	53.16 N	5.39 E
Sint Anthonis	52	51.37 N	5.52 E
Sint Christoffelberg ∧[2]	241s	12.20 N	69.08 W
Sint-Denijs-Westrem	50	51.01 N	3.40 E
Sint Eustatius I	238	17.30 N	62.59 W
Sint-Gillis-Waas	50	51.13 N	4.08 E
Sint Helenabaai c	158	32.43 S	18.05 E
Sint-Joris-Weert	56	50.48 N	4.39 E
Sint-Joris-Winge	56	50.55 N	4.52 E
Sint-Katelijne-Waver	56	51.04 N	4.32 E
Sint-Kruis, Bel.	50	51.13 N	3.15 E
Sint Kruis, Ned. Ant.	241s	12.18 N	69.08 W
Sint-Lenaarts	56	51.21 N	4.41 E
Sint Maarten	52	52.46 N	4.44 E
Sint Maarten (Saint-Martin) I	238	18.04 N	63.04 W
Sint Maartensdijk	52	51.33 N	4.05 E
Sint-Michiels	50	51.11 N	3.12 E
Sint Michielsgestel	52	51.38 N	5.21 E
Sint Nicolaas	241s	12.27 N	69.52 W
Sint-Niklaas (Saint-Nicolas)	50	51.10 N	4.08 E
Sint-Oedenrode	52	51.34 N	5.27 E
Sinton	196	28.02 N	97.30 W
Sintong	114	1.31 N	100.58 E
Sint Pancras	52	52.39 N	4.46 E
Sint-Pieters-Leeuw	50	50.47 N	4.14 E
Sintra	34	38.48 N	9.23 W
Sintra, Serra de ⩕[2]	266c	38.47 N	9.25 W
Sintra Granjo do Marquez, Aeroporto ⊠	266c	38.49 N	9.20 W
Sint-Truiden	56	50.48 N	5.12 E
Sint Willebrord	52	51.33 N	4.35 E
Sinú ≃	246	9.24 N	75.49 W
Sin'ucha ≃, Ross.	84	44.45 N	40.58 E
Sin'ucha ≃, Ukr.	78	48.03 N	30.51 E
Sin'uga	88	57.45 N	115.13 E
Sinŭiju	98	40.05 N	124.24 E
Sinujif	144	8.33 N	48.59 E
Sinŭp, C.M.I.K.	98	39.54 N	126.47 E
Sinŭp, Taehan	98	37.54 N	127.12 E
Sinwŏn-ni	98	38.13 N	125.44 E
Sinzig	56	50.32 N	7.15 E
Sinzing	60	49.00 N	12.02 E
Sió ≃, Magy.	30	46.20 N	18.55 E
Sio ≃, Togo	150	6.17 N	1.13 E
Siocon	116	7.42 N	122.08 E
Siófok	30	46.54 N	18.04 E
Sioma	152	16.39 S	23.30 E
Sioma Ngweze National Park ♠	152	17.15 S	23.20 E
Sion (Sitten)	58	46.14 N	7.21 E
Sionascaig, Loch ⊜	46	58.04 N	5.11 W
Sion Mills	48	54.47 N	7.29 W
Sioule ≃	32	46.22 N	3.19 E
Sioux Center	198	43.04 N	96.10 W
Sioux City	198	42.30 N	96.24 W
Sioux Falls	198	43.33 N	96.42 W
Sioux Lookout	184	50.06 N	91.55 W
Sioux Narrows	184	49.25 N	94.06 W
Sioux Rapids	198	42.53 N	95.09 W
Sipalay	116	9.45 N	122.24 E
Sipalay ≃	116	9.46 N	122.24 E
Sipaliwini □[5]	250	4.00 N	56.00 W
Sipaliwini ≃	250	2.22 N	56.50 W
Sipaozi	104	41.26 N	122.13 E
Sipapo ≃	246	5.03 N	67.48 W
Siparia	241r	10.08 N	61.30 W
Šipčenski prohod)(	38	42.46 N	25.19 E
Şipek	130	40.14 N	41.29 E
Sipes	220	28.48 N	81.14 W
Sipesville	214	40.06 N	79.06 W
Šipicyno, Ross.	24	61.17 N	46.28 E
Šipicyno, Ross.	86	56.04 N	77.18 E
Šipilovo	82	54.49 N	37.32 E
Siping	89	43.12 N	124.20 E
Sipingjie	98	42.31 N	125.08 E
Sipirok	114	1.37 N	99.16 E
Sipitang	112	5.05 N	115.33 E
Sipiwesk	184	55.27 N	97.24 W
Sipiwesk Lake ⊜	184	55.05 N	97.35 W
Siple ʊ[3]	9	75.56 S	84.15 W
Siple, Mount ∧	9	73.15 S	126.06 W
Siple Coast ⏏[2]	9	82.00 S	153.00 W
Sipocot	116	13.46 N	122.58 E
Sipofaneni	158	26.41 S	31.41 E
Sipot	114	4.31 N	96.02 E
Šipoteny	78	47.18 N	28.11 E
Šipovatoje	78	49.56 N	37.24 E
Sipplingen	58	47.47 N	9.05 E
Si Prachan	110	14.37 N	100.09 E
Sipsey ≃	194	33.00 N	88.10 W
Sipsey Creek ≃	194	33.53 N	88.17 W
Sipu	98	40.48 N	113.43 E
Şipul	164	5.50 S	148.45 E
Šipunovo	86	52.13 N	82.17 E
Šipunskij, mys ›	74	53.06 N	160.02 E
Sipupus	114	1.25 N	99.31 E
Sipura, Pulau I	112	2.12 S	99.40 E
Siqian, Zhg.	100	22.31 N	112.52 E
Siqian, Zhg.	100	24.40 N	114.06 E
Siqueira Campos	255	23.42 S	49.50 W
Siquia ≃	236	12.09 N	84.13 W
Siquijor	116	9.13 N	123.30 E
Siquijor □[4]	116	9.11 N	123.34 E
Siquijor Island I	116	9.11 N	123.34 E
Siquirres	236	10.06 N	83.30 W
Siquisique	246	10.34 N	69.42 W
Sīra, India	122	13.45 N	76.54 E
Şira, Nor.	26	58.25 N	6.38 E
Šira, Ross.	86	54.29 N	89.56 E
Sira ≃	26	58.17 N	6.24 E
Si Racha	110	13.10 N	100.56 E
Siracuas	248	21.03 S	61.46 W
Siracusa (Syracuse)	70	37.04 N	15.17 E
Siracusa □[4]	70	37.03 N	15.00 E
Sir Adam Beck II Reservoir ⊜[1]	284a	43.08 N	79.04 W
Şirāhā	124	26.39 N	86.12 E
Šir'aj	80	49.34 N	44.07 E
Šir'ajevo	78	47.23 N	30.13 E
Sirājganj	124	24.27 N	89.43 E
Sir Alexander, Mount ∧	182	53.56 N	120.23 W
Sirāmpur	126	24.08 N	86.20 E
Şiran	130	40.12 N	39.08 E
Sirasso	150	9.16 N	6.06 W
Sirault	50	50.30 N	3.47 E
Siraway	116	7.34 N	122.08 E
Sirba ≃	150	13.46 N	1.40 E
Şīr Banī Yās I	128	24.19 N	52.37 E
Sir Colin Mackenzie Wildlife Sanctuary ◆[4]	169	37.40 S	145.32 E
Sirdalsvatn ⊜	26	58.33 N	6.41 E
Sīrdān	128	36.39 N	49.12 E
Şirdar	182	49.15 N	116.37 W
Širdkoje	78	48.08 N	34.49 E
Sir Douglas, Mount ∧	182	50.44 N	115.20 W
Sire	144	9.00 N	36.55 E
Sir Edward Pellew Group II	164	15.40 S	136.48 E
Širega	76	60.10 N	41.15 E
Sireniki	180	64.25 N	173.57 W
Sirente, Monte ∧	66	42.09 N	13.36 E
Siret	38	47.57 N	26.04 E
Siret ≃	38	45.24 N	28.01 E
Sirevåg	26	58.30 N	5.47 E
Sir Francis Drake, Mount ∧	182	50.48 N	124.47 W
Sir Francis Drake Channel ʉ	240m	18.25 N	64.30 W
Sirghāyā	132	33.48 N	36.09 E
Sirḥān, Wādī as- ∨	128	30.30 N	38.00 E
Sirhind	124	30.39 N	76.23 E
Sirhind Canal ≊	123	30.47 N	76.01 E
Siria → Syria □[1]	128	35.00 N	38.00 E
Sirik, Tanjong ›	112	2.46 N	111.19 E
Sirikit Reservoir ⊜[1]	110	17.50 N	100.30 E
Şírina I	130	36.21 N	26.42 E
Širinquši	80	53.51 N	42.46 E
Sirino, Monte ∧	68	40.08 N	15.50 E
Siriya-zaki ›	92	41.26 N	141.28 E
Sir James MacBrien, Mount ∧	180	62.07 N	127.41 W
Sīrjān	128	29.27 N	55.40 E
Sir Joseph Banks Group II	166	34.32 S	136.17 E
Sirkābād	126	23.16 N	86.12 E
Sirkeli	130	40.09 N	32.52 E
Sirmaur	124	24.51 N	81.23 E
Şirmione	64	45.30 N	10.36 E
Širmovka	78	49.34 N	29.06 E
Sirnach	58	47.28 N	9.00 E
Siro, Jabal ∧	140	14.23 N	24.23 E
Şirohi	120	24.54 N	72.51 E
Širokaja Pad'	89	50.14 N	142.09 E
Širokij	89	49.45 N	129.30 E
Širokij Bujerak	80	52.07 N	47.46 E
Širokino	83	47.06 N	37.49 E
Širokoje, Ukr.	78	47.41 N	33.14 E
Širokoje, Ukr.	83	47.58 N	38.13 E
Širokolanovka	78	47.10 N	31.24 E
Širokovo	88	55.27 N	99.23 E
Sirolo	66	43.32 N	13.37 E
Sirombu	114	0.57 N	97.25 E
Sironj	124	24.06 N	77.42 E
Síros I	38	37.26 N	24.54 E
Síros → Ermoúpolis	38	37.26 N	24.56 E
Sirotino, Bela.	76	55.23 N	29.37 E
Sirotino, Ukr.	83	48.55 N	38.31 E
Sirotinskaja	80	49.16 N	43.39 E
Siroua, Jebel ∧	148	30.41 N	7.37 W
Sırpsındığı	130	41.46 N	26.29 E
Sirrah, Nafūd as- ⏏[8]	128	23.05 N	44.25 E
Sīrrī, Jazīreh-ye I	128	25.55 N	54.32 E
Sirsa, India	123	29.32 N	75.01 E
Sirsa, India	126	22.14 N	86.38 E
Sirsāganj	124	27.03 N	78.42 E
Sirs al-Layyānah	142	30.26 N	30.58 E
Sir Sandford, Mount ∧	182	51.40 N	117.52 W
Sirsi	122	14.37 N	74.51 E
Sirsilla	122	18.23 N	78.50 E
Sirsinā, Mişr	142	30.36 N	30.54 E
Sirsinā, Mişr	142	29.24 N	30.58 E
Sirsiri	154	4.24 N	31.53 E
Sir Thomas, Mount ∧	162	27.10 S	129.45 E
Siruma	116	14.00 N	123.15 E
Sirupa ≃	232	29.10 N	108.35 W
Şirvan	130	38.02 N	42.00 E
Şīrvān (Diyālā) ≃	128	33.14 N	44.31 E
Širvanskaja ravnina ≡	84	40.15 N	48.00 E
Širvintos	76	55.03 N	24.57 E
Sir Wilfrid Laurier, Mount ∧	182	52.47 N	119.45 W
Sir Wilfrid Laurier's Birthplace National Historic Site ⊥	206	45.51 N	73.45 W
Sirykrabet ⊥	86	44.07 N	62.35 E
Şís ≃, Guat.	236	14.09 N	91.39 W
Šiš ≃, Ross.	86	57.19 N	73.23 E
Sisa, Mount ∧	164	6.08 S	142.45 E
Sisaba ∧	154	6.09 S	29.48 E
Sisaiya Thāna	124	27.35 N	81.20 E
Sisak	36	45.29 N	16.23 E
Şi Sa Ket	110	15.07 N	104.20 E
Šišaki	78	49.53 N	34.00 E
Šišakovo	76	60.02 N	41.30 E
Şi Satchanalai	110	17.31 N	99.46 E
Šišchid (Kyzyl-Chem) ≃	88	51.21 N	96.58 E
Šiševka	76	58.52 N	38.52 E
Sishangcun	105	40.16 N	116.33 E
Sishen	158	27.55 S	22.59 E
Sishili	106	32.09 N	120.45 E
Sishilijie	100	29.08 N	116.44 E
Sishilipu	105	40.12 N	118.08 E
Sishuang Liedao II	100	26.42 N	120.24 E
Sishui	98	35.39 N	117.15 E
Sisian	84	39.32 N	46.02 E
Şisib Lake ⊜	184	52.35 N	99.22 W
Šišicy	76	53.13 N	27.32 E
Sisikon	58	46.57 N	8.42 E
Sisim ≃	88	55.09 N	91.54 E
Şisipuk Lake ⊜	184	55.45 N	101.50 W
Šiškejevo	80	54.12 N	44.45 E
Šiškino	88	52.18 N	113.35 E
Siskiyou Mountains ⩕	204	41.55 N	123.15 W
Siskiyou Pass)(	202	42.03 N	122.36 W
Şişli ◆[8]	267b	41.04 N	28.59 E
Šišlovo	82	54.14 N	38.33 E
Sison	116	9.40 N	125.31 E
Sisŏphŏn	110	13.35 N	102.59 E
Sisquoc ≃	204	34.54 N	120.18 W
Sissa ≃	115b	8.29 S	121.18 E
Sissach	58	47.28 N	7.49 E
Sissano	164	3.00 S	142.05 E
Sisséla	150	10.49 N	10.37 W
Sisseton	198	45.39 N	97.02 W
Sisseton Indian Reservation ◆[4]	198	45.40 N	97.02 W
Sissili ≃	150	10.16 N	1.15 W
Sisson Branch Reservoir ⊜[1]	186	47.16 N	67.20 W
Sissonne	50	49.34 N	3.54 E
Sissonville	188	38.31 N	81.37 W
Sīstān ◆[1]	128	30.30 N	62.00 E
Sīstān va Balūchestān □[4]	128	28.30 N	60.30 E
Sister Bay	190	45.11 N	87.07 W
Sister Lakes	216	42.05 N	86.12 W
Sisteron	62	44.12 N	5.56 E
Sisters	202	44.17 N	121.32 W
Sistersville	188	39.33 N	80.59 W
Sistig	56	50.29 N	6.30 E
Sisto ≃	66	41.18 N	13.10 E
Sistranda	26	63.43 N	8.50 E
Sit' ≃, Ross.	76	59.59 N	40.10 E
Sit' ≃, Ross.	76	58.16 N	37.54 E
Sitabamba	248	8.02 S	77.44 W
Sitai, Zhg.	85	39.23 N	77.56 E
Sitai, Zhg.	98	41.16 N	114.23 E
Sitaizi, Zhg.	104	42.29 N	123.20 E
Sitaizi, Zhg.	104	41.17 N	122.16 E
Sitaizui	105	40.49 N	115.20 E
Sitakili	150	13.07 N	11.14 W
Sitalike	154	6.38 S	31.08 E
Sitalkuchi	124	26.10 N	89.11 E
Sītāmarhi	124	26.36 N	85.29 E
Sitampiky	157b	16.41 S	46.06 E
Si Tangkay	112	4.40 N	119.24 E
Sītāpur	124	27.34 N	80.41 E
Sītāpur Branch ≊	124	28.10 N	80.25 E
Sitārāmpur	126	23.43 N	86.53 E
Siteki	158	26.32 S	31.58 E
Sites	226	39.19 N	122.20 W
Si Thep ⊥	110	15.30 N	101.10 E
Sithoniá	38	35.12 N	26.07 E
Sithoniá ›[1]	38	40.10 N	23.47 E
Sitidgi Lake ⊜	180	68.32 N	132.42 W
Sítio D'Abadia	255	14.48 S	46.16 W
Sítio Novo	250	5.51 S	46.43 W
Sitka	180	57.03 N	135.02 W
Sitkalidak Island I	180	57.10 N	153.14 W
Sitka National Historical Park ♠	180	57.05 N	135.15 W
Sitka Point ›	180	57.00 N	135.49 W
Sitka Sound ʉ	180	57.00 N	135.30 W
Sitkinak Island I	180	56.35 N	154.12 W
Şitkinak Strait ʉ	180	56.39 N	154.06 W
Šitkino	88	56.23 N	98.21 E
Sitkovcy	78	48.54 N	29.12 E
Sitna ≃	38	47.37 N	27.08 E
Sitn'a-Ščelkanovo	82	54.58 N	37.59 E
Sitnica ≃	38	42.45 N	21.01 E
Sitniki	80	56.27 N	44.06 E
Sitnikovo	86	56.23 N	67.53 E
Sitobela	158	26.53 S	31.36 E
Sitona	144	14.28 N	37.27 E
Sitrah	128	26.09 N	50.38 E
Sitrah ₸[4]	140	28.42 N	26.54 E
Sittard	56	51.00 N	5.53 E
Sittendorf	264b	48.05 N	16.10 E
Sittensen	52	53.17 N	9.30 E
Sitten → Sion	58	46.14 N	7.21 E
Sitter ≃	58	47.29 N	9.14 E
Sittingbourne	42	51.21 N	0.44 E
Sittoung ≃	110	17.10 N	96.58 E
Sittwe (Akyab)	110	20.09 N	92.54 E
Situ	105	39.20 N	115.39 E
Situbondo	115a	7.42 S	114.00 E
Siufaalele Point ›	174y	14.17 S	169.29 W
Si'ufage	174y	14.14 S	169.32 W
Siulakderas	112	1.55 S	101.18 E
Siu Lek Yuen	271d	22.23 N	114.12 E
Siumbatu	112	2.45 S	122.03 E
Siumpu, Pulau I	112	5.40 S	122.31 E
Siuna	236	13.44 N	84.46 W
Siurgus Donigala	71	39.35 N	9.12 E
Siuri	126	23.55 N	87.32 E
Siusi (Seis)	64	46.32 N	11.34 E
Siuslaw ≃	202	44.01 N	124.08 W
Siva ≃	80	56.48 N	53.55 E
Sivaganga	122	9.52 N	78.29 E
Sivakāsi	122	9.27 N	77.49 E
Sivaki	89	52.39 N	126.45 E
Sīvand ≃	128	29.51 N	52.46 E
Sivas	130	39.45 N	37.02 E
Sivas □[4]	130	39.30 N	37.15 E
Sivaš ʉ	78	46.00 N	34.30 E
Sivaslı	130	38.30 N	29.42 E
Sivašskoje	78	46.23 N	34.34 E
Şivé	150	15.42 N	13.12 W
Šiveluč, vulkan ∧[1]	74	56.39 N	161.18 E
Siverek	130	37.45 N	39.19 E
Siverskij	76	59.21 N	30.05 E
Sivkovo	82	55.26 N	35.53 E
Sivomaskinskij	24	66.40 N	62.35 E
Sivri Ada I	267b	40.54 N	28.59 E
Sivrice	130	38.27 N	39.19 E
Sivrihisar	130	39.27 N	31.34 E
Sivry-Courtry	261	48.32 N	2.45 E
Sivry-sur-Meuse	56	49.19 N	5.16 E
Sīwah	140	29.12 N	25.31 E
Sīwah, Wāḥat ₸[4]	140	29.12 N	25.31 E
Siwalik Range ⩕	120	31.00 N	78.00 E
Siwān	124	26.13 N	84.22 E
Siwang ≃	107	29.25 N	103.50 E
Sixaola ≃	236	9.34 N	82.34 W
Six Flags Great America ♠	216	42.21 N	87.55 W
Six Flags over Mid-America ♠	219	38.31 N	90.40 W
Six Flags Over Texas ♠	222	32.45 N	97.05 W
Six-Fours-la-Plage	62	43.06 N	5.51 E
Sixian	100	33.30 N	117.56 E
Sixitou	100	27.31 N	119.57 E
Six Mile Creek ≃, On., Can.	284a	43.15 N	79.10 W
Sixmile Creek ≃, Ky., U.S.	218	38.26 N	84.58 W
Sixmile Creek ≃, N.Y., U.S.	284a	43.17 N	78.58 W
Sixmilecross	48	54.34 N	7.08 W
Six Mile Lake ⊜	212	44.55 N	79.45 W
Sixmile Run ≃	276	40.28 N	74.35 W
Six Mile Water ≃	48	54.42 N	6.14 W
Six Nations Indian Reserve ◆[4]	212	43.03 N	80.07 W
Sixshooter Draw ∨	196	30.51 N	102.33 W
Sixteen Mile Creek ≃, On., Can.	275b	43.27 N	79.40 W
Sixteenmile Creek ≃, Mt., U.S.	202	46.06 N	111.23 W
Sixth Cataract → Sablūkah, Ash-Shallāl as- ᒪ	140	16.20 N	32.42 E
Siyāl, Jazā'ir II	140	22.47 N	36.12 E
Siyāna	124	28.38 N	78.03 E
Siyang	100	33.43 N	118.41 E
Si Yat ≃	110	13.42 N	101.26 E
Siyeteb	140	18.00 N	35.01 E
Siz'absk	24	65.05 N	53.49 E
Sizaja	88	58.07 N	100.38 E
Sizhijian	98	42.25 N	114.36 E
Siziano	62	45.20 N	9.12 E
Sizilien → Sicilia I	70	37.30 N	14.00 E
Siziman	89	50.43 N	140.26 E
Siziwang Qi	102	41.33 N	111.31 E
Sizun	32	48.24 N	4.05 W
Sizuoka → Shizuoka	94	34.58 N	138.23 E
Sjælland I	41	55.30 N	11.45 E
Sjællands Odde ›[1]	41	55.58 N	11.22 E
Själevad	26	63.18 N	18.36 E
Sjanovo	82	54.59 N	37.25 E
Sjenica	38	43.16 N	20.00 E
Sjeništa ∧	38	43.42 N	18.37 E
Sjoa ≃	26	61.41 N	9.33 E
Sjöbo	41	55.38 N	13.42 E
Sjøholt	26	62.29 N	6.48 E
Sjösa	40	58.46 N	17.04 E
Sjötorp	40	58.50 N	13.59 E
Skaby	264a	52.19 N	13.51 E
Skaby-Berge ⩕[2]	264a	52.19 N	13.49 E
Skåde	41	56.06 N	10.13 E
Skadovsk	78	46.08 N	32.54 E
Skælskør	41	55.15 N	11.19 E
Skærbæk, Dan.	41	55.31 N	9.38 E
Skærbæk, Dan.	41	55.09 N	8.46 E
Skævinge	41	55.55 N	12.10 E
Skaftafell National Park ♠	24a	64.15 N	17.00 W
Skaftung	26	62.07 N	21.22 E
Skagafjörður c	24a	65.55 N	19.35 W
Skagen	26	57.44 N	10.36 E
Skagern ⊜	40	58.59 N	14.17 E
Skagerrak ʉ	26	57.45 N	9.00 E
Skagersvik	40	58.58 N	14.06 E
Skaggs Creek ≃	194	36.54 N	86.04 W
Skagit □[6]	224	48.29 N	121.45 W
Skagit ≃	224	48.20 N	122.25 W
Skagit Bay c	224	48.19 N	122.24 W
Skagway	180	59.28 N	135.19 W
Skaidi	24	70.25 N	24.30 E
Skaistkalne	76	56.23 N	24.39 E
Skála Oropoú	38	38.20 N	23.46 E
Skala-Podol'skaja	78	48.51 N	26.12 E
Skalat	78	49.26 N	25.59 E
Skalbmierz	30	50.19 N	20.25 E
Skälderviken	41	56.17 N	12.50 E
Skälderviken c	41	56.18 N	12.38 E
Skalica	30	48.51 N	17.14 E
Skalino	76	58.32 N	40.13 E
Skalistaja, gora ∧	84	42.48 N	45.08 E
Skalistyj, gora ∧	180	68.12 N	178.10 E
Skalistyj chrebet ⩕	84	43.15 N	43.00 E
Skalistyj Golec, gora ∧	88	56.24 N	119.12 E
Skalka ⊜	24	66.50 N	18.46 E
Skalka, údolní nádrž ⊜[1]	54	50.06 N	12.19 E
Skalná	54	50.07 N	12.23 E
Skal'nyj	86	58.22 N	57.59 E
Skamania	224	45.37 N	122.02 W
Skamania □[6]	224	45.58 N	121.53 W
Skamlingsbanke ∧[2]	41	55.25 N	9.34 E
Skamokawa	224	46.16 N	123.27 W
Skanderborg	41	56.02 N	9.56 E
Skanderborg Sø ⊜	41	56.01 N	9.56 E
Skåne □[9]	41	55.59 N	13.30 E
Skaneateles	210	42.56 N	76.25 W
Skaneateles Falls	210	43.00 N	76.27 W
Skaneateles Lake ⊜	210	42.53 N	76.24 W
Skånevik	26	59.44 N	5.59 E
Skänninge	26	58.24 N	15.05 E
Skanör	26	55.25 N	12.52 E
Skara	26	58.22 N	13.25 E
Skaraborgs Län □[6]	26	58.20 N	13.30 E
Skaramagás	267c	38.01 N	23.36 E
Skärblacka	40	58.34 N	15.54 E
Skarđ	24a	64.03 N	19.50 W
Skardhø ∧	26	62.30 N	8.45 E
Skārdu	123	35.18 N	75.37 E
Skärhamn	26	58.00 N	11.33 E
Skarhult	41	55.49 N	13.23 E
Skarnes	26	60.15 N	11.41 E
Skarø I	41	55.00 N	10.29 E
Skärplinge	40	60.28 N	17.46 E
Skarszewy	30	54.05 N	18.27 E
Skårup	41	55.05 N	10.42 E
Skaryszew	30	51.19 N	21.15 E
Skarżysko-Kamienna	30	51.08 N	20.53 E
Skášov	60	49.31 N	13.26 E
Skate Creek ≃	224	46.37 N	121.41 W
Skattkärr	40	59.25 N	13.41 E
Skaudvilė	76	55.24 N	22.35 E
Skaugum	26	59.51 N	10.26 E
Skawina	30	49.59 N	19.49 E
Skebobruk	40	59.58 N	18.36 E
Skebokvarn	40	59.04 N	16.42 E
Skedviken ⊜	40	59.46 N	18.16 E
Skedvisjön ⊜	40	59.35 N	15.40 E
Skeena ≃	182	54.09 N	130.02 W
Skeena Crossing	182	55.06 N	127.49 W
Skeena Mountains ⩕	176	57.00 N	128.30 W
Skeen Peak ∧	222	32.59 N	97.48 W
Skegness	44	53.10 N	0.21 E
Skegrie	41	55.24 N	13.04 E
Skei	26	61.38 N	6.30 E
Skeikampen	26	61.20 N	10.07 E
Skelde	41	54.51 N	9.44 E
Skeleton Coast ⏏[2]	156	19.15 S	12.30 E
Skeleton Coast Park ♠	156	19.25 S	12.55 E
Skeleton Creek ≃	196	35.58 N	97.25 W
Skeleton Lake ⊜	212	45.15 N	79.27 W
Skellefteå	26	64.46 N	20.57 E
Skellefteälven ≃	26	64.42 N	21.06 E
Skelleftehamn	26	64.41 N	21.14 E
Skellig Rocks II[1]	48	51.48 N	10.31 W
Skellytown	196	35.34 N	101.11 W
Skelmersdale	44	53.33 N	2.48 W
Skelmorlie	46	55.51 N	4.53 W
Skelton, Eng., U.K.	44	54.43 N	2.51 W
Skelton, Eng., U.K.	44	54.33 N	0.59 W
Skene	26	57.29 N	12.38 E
Skene, Mount ∧	169	37.25 S	146.23 E
Skepptuna	40	59.43 N	18.05 E
Skerne ≃	44	54.29 N	1.34 W
Skerpioensdrif	158	31.05 S	21.33 E
Skerries	48	53.35 N	6.07 W
Skerryvore I[2]	46	56.19 N	7.07 W
Skewen	42	51.40 N	3.51 W
Skhíza I	38	36.44 N	21.46 E
Ski	26	59.43 N	10.50 E
Skíathos	38	39.10 N	23.29 E
Skíathos I	38	39.10 N	23.28 E
Skiatook	196	36.22 N	96.00 W
Skibbereen	48	51.33 N	9.15 W
Skibby	41	55.45 N	11.58 E
Skibotn	24	69.24 N	20.16 E
Skiddaw ∧	44	54.38 N	3.08 W
Skidegate	182	53.15 N	132.00 W
Skidegate Inlet c	182	53.14 N	132.00 W
Skidel'	76	53.34 N	24.15 E
Skidmore	196	28.15 N	97.41 W
Skien	26	59.12 N	9.36 E
Skierniewice	30	51.58 N	20.08 E
Skierniewice □[4]	30	52.10 N	20.15 E
Skiftet ʉ	26	60.15 N	21.05 E
Skihist Mountain ∧	182	50.11 N	121.54 W
Skikda (Philippeville)	148	36.50 N	6.58 E
Skikda □[5]	148	36.45 N	7.00 E
Skilak Lake ⊜	180	60.25 N	150.25 W
Skillet Fork ≃	194	38.08 N	88.07 W
Skillingaryd	26	57.26 N	14.05 E
Skillman	276	40.25 N	74.42 W
Škin'	82	55.11 N	38.30 E
Skinnastaður	24a	66.07 N	16.24 W
Skinner Reservoir ⊜[1]	228	33.35 N	117.03 W
Skinnskatteberg	40	59.50 N	15.41 E
Skippack	285	40.14 N	75.24 W
Skippack Creek ≃	285	40.09 N	75.27 W
Skippack Creek, West Branch ≃	285	40.14 N	75.23 W
Skippers	208	36.37 N	77.38 W
Skipskop	158	34.33 S	20.25 E
Skipton, Austl.	169	37.41 S	143.22 E
Skipton, Eng., U.K.	44	53.58 N	2.01 W
Skirfare ≃	44	54.07 N	2.01 W
Skirmish Point ›	171a	27.05 S	153.13 E
Skíros	38	38.53 N	24.33 E
Skíros I	38	38.53 N	24.32 E
Skivarp	41	55.25 N	13.34 E
Skive	26	56.34 N	9.02 E
Skjálfandafljót ≃	24a	65.57 N	17.38 W
Skjálfandi c	24a	66.08 N	17.38 W
Skjeberg	26	59.14 N	11.12 E
Skjern	26	55.57 N	8.30 E
Skjern Å ≃	41	55.57 N	8.40 E
Şklad	74	71.55 N	123.33 E
Šklov	76	54.13 N	30.18 E
Skniga ≃	82	54.53 N	37.24 E
Skobeleva, pik ∧	85	39.49 N	72.44 E
Şkoby	40	60.02 N	18.01 E
Škocjanske jame ⏏[7]	36	45.40 N	14.00 E
Skodborg	41	55.25 N	9.09 E
Skodsborg	41	55.49 N	12.34 E
Şkoenmakerskop	158	34.02 S	25.33 E
Škofije	64	45.34 N	13.48 E
Škofja Loka	36	46.10 N	14.18 E
Skoganvarre	24	69.47 N	25.06 E
Skoghall	40	59.19 N	13.26 E
Skogstorp	40	59.20 N	16.28 E
Skokholm Island I	42	51.42 N	5.16 W
Skoki	30	52.41 N	17.10 E
Skokie	216	42.02 N	87.44 W
Skokie ≃	216	42.05 N	87.46 W
Skokie Lagoons c	278	42.07 N	87.47 W
Skokloster ⊥	40	59.42 N	17.37 E
Skokomish, North Fork ≃	224	47.18 N	123.14 W
Skokomish, South Fork ≃	224	47.18 N	123.14 W
Skokomish Indian Reservation ◆[4]	224	47.21 N	123.12 W
Sköldinge	40	59.02 N	16.26 E
Skole	78	49.02 N	23.29 E
Sköllersta	40	59.09 N	15.20 E
Skolsta	40	59.40 N	17.14 E
Skolwin	54	53.32 N	14.35 E
Skomer Island I	42	51.44 N	5.17 W
Skomoroški, Ross.	82	54.05 N	36.57 E
Skomoroški, Ukr.	78	49.20 N	29.26 E
Skón	110	12.04 N	105.04 E
Skookumchuck ≃	224	46.41 N	123.00 W
Skookumchuck Reservoir ⊜[1]	224	47.47 N	122.42 W
Skoonspruit ≃	158	27.00 S	26.38 E
Skootamatta ≃	212	44.32 N	77.20 W
Skootamatta Lake ⊜	212	44.50 N	77.15 W
Skópelos, Ellás	38	39.07 N	23.43 E
Skópelos, Ellás	38	39.02 N	26.26 E
Skópelos I	38	39.10 N	23.40 E
Skopin	76	53.51 N	39.33 E
Skopje	38	41.59 N	21.26 E
Skórcz	30	53.48 N	18.32 E
Skorodnoje, Bela.	78	51.38 N	28.49 E
Skorodnoje, Ross.	78	51.05 N	37.14 E
Skørping	26	56.50 N	9.53 E
Skotfoss	26	59.12 N	9.30 E
Şkotovataja	83	48.13 N	37.54 E
Škotovo	89	43.20 N	132.21 E
Skotterud	26	59.59 N	12.07 E
Skovby	41	54.53 N	10.00 E
Skövde	26	58.24 N	13.50 E
Skovlund	41	55.44 N	8.43 E
Skovorodino	89	53.59 N	123.55 E
Skowhegan	188	44.45 N	69.43 W
Skownan	184	51.57 N	99.36 W
Skradin	36	43.49 N	15.56 E
Skreen	48	54.15 N	8.45 W
Skreia	26	60.39 N	10.56 E
Skriplivka	76	57.32 N	30.38 E
Skrīveri	76	56.39 N	25.08 E
Skromberga	41	56.00 N	12.58 E
Skrudaļiena	76	55.49 N	26.43 E
Skrunda	76	56.41 N	22.01 E
Skruv	26	56.41 N	15.22 E
Skrydstrup	41	55.14 N	9.15 E
Skudeneshavn	26	59.09 N	5.17 E
Skukuza	156	25.01 S	31.38 E
Skuleberget ∧[2]	26	63.05 N	18.21 E
Skulforp	26	58.21 N	13.49 E
Skull	48	51.32 N	9.33 W
Skull Creek ≃	222	29.32 N	96.24 W
Skull Valley	200	34.30 N	112.41 W
Skull Valley Indian Reservation ◆[4]	200	40.24 N	112.45 W
Skultuna	40	59.43 N	16.25 E
Skuna ≃	194	33.54 N	89.41 W
Şkunk ≃	190	40.42 N	91.07 W
Škunovka	86	50.45 N	55.27 E
Skuodas	76	56.16 N	21.32 E
Şkuratovskij	82	54.07 N	37.36 E
Škurinskaja	78	46.35 N	39.22 E
Skurišenskaja	80	49.52 N	42.57 E
Skurup	41	55.28 N	13.30 E
Skutskär	40	60.38 N	17.25 E
Skvira	78	49.44 N	29.40 E
Skwentna	180	61.58 N	151.11 W
Skwentna ≃	180	62.00 N	151.08 W
Skwierzyna	30	52.36 N	15.30 E
Skye, Island of I	46	57.18 N	6.15 W
Sky Harbor Airport ⊠	278	42.09 N	87.51 W
Skykomish	224	47.42 N	121.21 W
Skykomish ≃	224	47.50 N	122.03 W
Skykomish, North Fork ≃	224	47.47 N	121.33 W
Skykomish, South Fork ≃	224	47.47 N	121.33 W
Sky Lake	220	28.28 N	81.24 W
Sky Lake ⊜	212	44.48 N	81.15 W
Skyland, Nv., U.S.	226	39.01 N	119.56 W
Skyland, N.C., U.S.	192	35.29 N	82.31 W
Skylight	218	38.25 N	85.31 W
Skyline	284c	38.50 N	76.54 W
Skyline Lakes ⊜	276	41.04 N	74.16 W
Skyllberg	40	58.57 N	14.59 E
Skyring, Península ›[1]	254	45.58 S	74.53 W
Skyring, Seno ʉ	254	52.35 S	72.00 W
Sky Sailing Airport ⊠	282	37.30 N	121.58 W
Skytop	210	41.14 N	75.15 W
Skyttorp	40	60.05 N	17.44 E
Skyway	224	47.29 N	122.14 W
Slackhall	262	53.20 N	1.53 W
Slackwood	208	40.15 N	74.44 W
Slade Green ◆[8]	260	51.28 N	0.12 E
Sladkij	80	46.10 N	42.17 E
Sladkovo	86	55.32 N	70.20 E
Slagelse	41	55.24 N	11.22 E
Slagnäs	24	65.34 N	18.05 E
Slagoviščí	76	53.57 N	35.54 E
Slaithwaite	262	53.37 N	1.53 W
Slamannan	46	55.56 N	3.50 W
Slamet, Gunung ∧	115a	7.14 S	109.12 E
Slancy	76	59.06 N	28.04 E
Slaney ≃	48	52.21 N	6.30 W
Slangerup	41	55.51 N	12.11 E
Slănic	38	45.15 N	25.57 E
Slănic Moldova	38	46.13 N	26.26 E
Slano	36	42.47 N	17.54 E
Slanské vrchy ⩕	30	48.50 N	21.30 E
Şlaný	54	50.11 N	14.04 E
Šlapanice	30	49.10 N	16.44 E
Slaščevskaja	80	49.52 N	42.21 E
Śląsk → Silesia □[9]	30	51.00 N	16.45 E
Slastucha	80	51.57 N	44.32 E
Slate Bottom Creek ≃	284a	42.53 N	78.45 W
Slate Creek ≃, Ks., U.S.	198	37.08 N	97.09 W
Slate Creek ≃, Pa., U.S.	279b	40.28 N	79.32 W
Slatedale	208	40.45 N	75.40 W
Slate Hill	210	41.23 N	74.29 W
Slater, Ia., U.S.	190	41.52 N	93.40 W
Slater, Mo., U.S.	194	39.13 N	93.04 W
Slater Creek ≃	200	40.59 N	107.23 W
Slatersville	207	42.00 N	71.34 W
Slaterville Springs	210	42.24 N	76.21 W
Slatina	38	44.26 N	24.22 E
Slatington	208	40.44 N	75.36 W
Slatino	78	50.12 N	36.11 E
Slaton	196	33.26 N	101.38 W
Slattocks	262	53.35 N	2.10 W
Slaughter	194	30.43 N	91.08 W
Slaung	115a	8.02 S	111.24 E
Slautnoje	74	63.00 N	167.59 E
Slava	89	52.08 N	129.24 E
Slav'anka, Ross.	89	42.53 N	131.21 E
Slav'anka, Ukr.	78	48.24 N	36.43 E
Slav'anka, Uzb.	85	40.40 N	68.32 E
Slav'anka ≃	265a	59.50 N	30.32 E
Slav'anogorsk	83	49.02 N	37.31 E
Slav'anoserbsk	83	48.42 N	38.59 E
Slav'ansk	83	48.52 N	37.37 E
Slav'ansk-na-Kubani	78	45.15 N	38.08 E
Slave ≃	176	61.18 N	113.39 W
Slave Coast ⏏[2]	150	6.25 N	3.00 E
Slave Lake	182	55.17 N	114.46 W
Slavgorod, Bela.	76	53.27 N	31.00 E
Slavgorod, Ross.	86	53.00 N	78.40 E
Slavgorod, Ukr.	78	50.36 N	35.21 E
Slavgorod, Ukr.	78	48.06 N	35.31 E
Slavitino	82	56.41 N	39.13 E
Slavkino	80	52.58 N	47.11 E
Slavkoviči	76	57.39 N	29.05 E
Slavkovský les ⩕	54	50.07 N	12.45 E

≃ River	Fluß	Río	Rivière	Rio	✤ Submarine Features	Untermeerische Objekte	Accidentes Submarinos	Formes de relief sous-marin	Acidentes submarinos
≊ Canal	Kanal	Canal	Canal	Canal	□ Political Unit	Politische Einheit	Unidad Politica	Entité politique	Unidade política
ᒪ Waterfall, Rapids	Wasserfall, Stromschnellen	Cascada, Rápidos	Chute d'eau, Rapides	Cascata, Rápidos	ʊ Cultural Institution	Kulturelle Institution	Institución Cultural	Institution culturelle	Instituição cultural
ʉ Strait	Meeresstraße	Estrecho	Détroit	Estreito	⊥ Historical Site	Historische Stätte	Sitio Histórico	Site historique	Sitio histórico
c Bay, Gulf	Bucht, Golf	Bahía, Golfo	Baie, Golfe	Baía, Golfo	♠ Recreational Site	Erholungs- und Ferienort	Sitio de Recreo	Centre de loisirs	Area de Lazer
⊜ Lake, Lakes	See, Seen	Lago, Lagos	Lac, Lacs	Lago, Lagos	⊠ Airport	Flughafen	Aeropuerto	Aéroport	Aeroporto
≡ Swamp	Sumpf	Pantano	Marais	Pântano	■ Military Installation	Militäranlage	Instalación Militar	Installation militaire	Instalação militar
⊼ Ice Features, Glacier	Eis- und Gletscherformen	Accidentes Glaciales	Formes glaciaires	Acidentes glaciares	◆ Miscellaneous	Verschiedenes	Misceláneo	Divers	Diversos
₸ Other Hydrographic Features	Andere Hydrographische Objekte	Otros Elementos Hidrográficos	Autres données hydrographiques	Outros acidentes hidrográficos					

Symbols in the index entries represent the broad categories identified in the key at the right. Symbols with superior numbers (⋀1) identify subcategories (see complete key on page *I · 1).*

Symbole im Register stellen die rechts im Schlüssel erklärten Kategorien dar. Symbole mit hochgestellten Ziffern (⋀1) bezeichnen Unterabteilungen einer Kategorie (vgl. vollständiger Schlüssel auf Seite *I · 1).*

Los símbolos incluídos en el texto del índice representan las grandes categorias identificadas con la clave a la derecha. Los símbolos con numeros en su parte superior (⋀1) identifican las subcategorías (véase la clave completa en la página *I · 1).*

Les symboles de l'index représentent les catégories indiquées dans la légende à droite. Les symboles suivis d'un indice (⋀1) représentent des sous-catégories (voir légende complète à la page *I · 1).*

Os símbolos incluídos no texto do índice representam as grandes categorias identificadas com a chave à direita. Os símbolos com números em sua parte superior (⋀1) identificam as subcategorias (veja-se a chave completa à página *I · 1).*

English	Deutsch	Español	Français	Português
∧ Mountain	Berg	Montaña	Montagne	Montanha
⋀ Mountains	Gebirge	Montañas	Montagnes	Montanhas
)(Pass	Paß	Paso	Col	Passo
V Valley, Canyon	Tal, Cañon	Valle, Cañón	Vallée, Canyon	Vale, Canhão
≚ Plain	Ebene	Llano	Plaine	Planície
⟩ Cape	Kap	Cabo	Cap	Cabo
I Island	Insel	Isla	Île	Ilha
II Islands	Inseln	Islas	Îles	Ilhas
⊥ Other Topographic Features	Andere Topographische Objekte	Otros Elementos Topográficos	Autres données topographiques	Outros acidentes topográficos

ESPAÑOL · FRANÇAIS · PORTUGUÊS

Nombre / Nom / Nome	Página / Page	Lat.°′	Long.°′ W = Oeste / Ouest
Solus, Mount ∧	168a	32.28 S	116.13 E
Solutré-Pouilly	58	46.18 N	4.43 E
Solva	42	51.52 N	5.11 W
Solva ≏	42	51.52 N	5.17 W
Solvang	204	34.36 N	120.08 W
Solvarbo	40	60.24 N	15.40 E
Solvay	210	43.03 N	76.12 W
Sölvesborg	26	56.03 N	14.33 E
Sol'vyčegodsk	24	61.21 N	46.52 E
Solway Firth ⊂[1]	44	54.50 N	3.35 W
Solwezi	154	12.11 S	26.25 E
Soly	76	54.31 N	26.11 E
Solymár	264c	47.36 N	18.56 E
Solza	24	64.33 N	39.29 E
Sōma, Nihon	92	37.48 N	140.57 E
Soma, Tür.	130	39.10 N	27.36 E
Somabula	154	19.41 S	29.41 E
Sōmahara-chūtonchi, Rikujō-jieitai- ■	94	36.23 N	138.58 E
Somain	50	50.22 N	3.17 E
Somalia (Somaliya) □[1], Afr.	136	6.00 N	48.00 E
Somalia (Somaliya) □[1], Afr.	144	6.00 N	48.00 E
Somali Basin ✢[1]	12	0.00	52.00 E
Somalie → Somalia □[1]	144	6.00 N	48.00 E
Somaliland → Somalia □[1]	144	6.00 N	48.00 E
Somali Republic → Somalia □[1]	144	6.00 N	48.00 E
Somaliya → Somalia □[1]	144	6.00 N	48.00 E
Somalomo	152	3.23 N	12.44 E
Sŏman	98	41.20 N	128.54 E
Somanga	154	8.24 S	39.17 E
Sombernon	58	47.18 N	4.42 E
Sombo	152	8.42 S	20.57 E
Sombor	38	45.46 N	19.07 E
Sombra	214	42.43 N	82.29 W
Sombrerete	234	23.38 N	103.39 W
Sombreretillo	196	26.19 N	99.58 W
Sombrero I	238	18.36 N	63.26 W
Sombrero Channel ⊔	110	7.41 N	93.35 E
Sombrio	252	29.07 S	49.40 W
Sombrio, Lagoa do ⊂	252	29.12 S	49.42 W
Șomcuta-Mare	38	47.31 N	23.29 E
Šomdari	120	25.49 N	72.35 E
Somenos	224	48.49 N	123.44 W
Somercotes	44	53.04 N	1.22 W
Somerdale, N.J., U.S.	208	39.50 N	75.01 W
Somerdale, Oh., U.S.	214	40.34 N	81.22 W
Someren	52	51.24 N	5.44 E
Somero	26	60.37 N	23.32 E
Sõmerpalu	76	57.51 N	26.48 E
Somers, Austl.	169	38.24 S	145.10 E
Somers, Ct., U.S.	207	41.59 N	72.26 W
Somers, Mt., U.S.	202	48.04 N	114.13 W
Somers, Wi., U.S.	216	42.38 N	87.54 W
Somersby	170	33.25 S	151.17 E
Somerset, Austl.	166	41.03 S	145.49 E
Somerset, Mb., Can.	184	49.24 N	98.39 W
Somerset, Co., U.S.	200	38.55 N	107.28 W
Somerset, Ky., U.S.	192	37.05 N	84.36 W
Somerset, Md., U.S.	284c	38.58 N	77.05 W
Somerset, Ma., U.S.	207	41.46 N	71.07 W
Somerset, N.J., U.S.	208	40.44 N	74.34 W
Somerset, Oh., U.S.	188	39.48 N	82.17 W
Somerset, Pa., U.S.	188	40.00 N	79.04 W
Somerset, Tx., U.S.	196	29.13 N	98.40 W
Somerset, Wi., U.S.	190	45.07 N	92.40 W
Somerset □[6], Eng., U.K.	42	51.08 N	3.00 W
Somerset □[6], Md., U.S.	208	38.12 N	75.41 W
Somerset □[6], N.J., U.S.	208	40.34 N	74.37 W
Somerset □[6], Pa., U.S.	214	40.09 N	79.00 W
Somerset Airport ⊠	276	40.37 N	74.40 W
Somerset Center	216	42.03 N	84.25 W
Somerset East	158	32.42 S	25.35 E
Somerset Hills Airport ⊠	276	40.41 N	74.32 W
Somerset Island I, Ber.	240a	32.17 N	64.52 W
Somerset Island I, N.T., Can.	176	73.15 N	93.30 W
Somerset Reservoir ⊜[1]	171a	27.03 S	152.35 E
Somerset West	158	34.08 S	18.50 E
Somersham	42	52.23 N	0.01 E
Somers Point	208	39.19 N	74.35 W
Somersworth	188	43.15 N	70.51 W
Somerton, Eng., U.K.	42	51.03 N	2.44 W
Somerton, Az., U.S.	200	32.35 N	114.42 W
Somerton ◆[8]	285	40.06 N	75.01 W
Somerton Creek ≏	208	36.32 N	76.55 W
Somervell □[6]	222	32.15 N	97.45 W
Somerville, Austl.	169	38.13 S	145.10 E
Somerville, Ma., U.S.	207	42.23 N	71.06 W
Somerville, N.J., U.S.	210	40.34 N	74.36 W
Somerville, Oh., U.S.	218	39.33 N	84.38 W
Somerville, Tn., U.S.	194	35.14 N	89.21 W
Somerville, Tx., U.S.	222	30.20 N	96.31 W
Somerville Lake ⊜[1]	222	30.18 N	96.40 W
Someș (Szamos) ≏	38	48.07 N	22.22 E
Someșu Cald ≏	38	46.44 N	23.22 E
Someșul Mare ≏	38	47.12 N	24.12 E
Someșul Mic ≏	38	47.09 N	23.55 E
Someșul Rece ≏	38	46.44 N	23.22 E
Somino	76	59.21 N	34.52 E
Somis	228	34.16 N	119.00 W
Sŏmjin-gang ≏	98	34.58 N	127.46 E
Somma	66	42.40 N	12.44 E
Sommacampagna	64	45.24 N	10.50 E
Somma Lombardo, It.	62	45.41 N	8.42 E
Somma Lombardo, It.	266b	45.41 N	8.42 E
Sommariva	166	26.24 S	146.36 E
Sommariva del Bosco	62	44.46 N	7.47 E
Sommatino	70	37.20 N	13.59 E
Somme □[5]	50	49.55 N	2.30 E
Somme ≏, Fr.	50	49.01 N	4.12 E
Somme ≏, Fr.	50	50.11 N	1.39 E
Somme, Baie de la ⊂	50	50.14 N	1.33 E
Somme, Canal de la ≖	50	49.55 N	2.43 E
Sommedieue	56	49.05 N	5.28 E
Sommelsdijk	52	51.45 N	4.09 E
Sommen ⊜	26	58.01 N	15.15 E
Sommepy-Tahure	56	49.15 N	4.33 E
Sommerberg ◆[8]	263	51.27 N	7.32 E
Sömmerda	54	51.10 N	11.07 E
Sommersdorf	54	53.17 N	14.11 E
Sommersted	41	55.19 N	9.19 E
Sommesous	50	48.44 N	4.12 E
Somme Woods ♠	278	42.09 N	87.49 W
Somnitel'nyj	89	52.12 N	139.04 E
Somo ≏	190	45.29 N	89.48 W
Somogy □[6]	30	46.25 N	17.35 E
Somonauk	216	41.38 N	88.40 W
Somonauk Creek ≏	216	41.32 N	88.41 W
Somosierra, Puerto de)(	34	41.09 N	3.35 W
Somosomo	175g	16.46 S	179.58 W
Somosomo Strait ⊔	175g	16.47 S	179.58 E
Somotillo	236	13.02 N	86.55 W
Somoto	236	13.28 N	86.35 W
Somovo, Ross.	76	52.53 N	34.58 E
Somovo, Ross.	78	51.44 N	39.23 E
Sompeta	122	18.56 N	84.36 E
Somplago	64	46.21 N	13.04 E
Sompolno	30	52.24 N	18.31 E
Somport, Puerto de)(	34	42.48 N	0.31 W
Sompuis	50	48.41 N	4.23 E
Somuncurá, Meseta de ⋏[1]	254	41.30 S	67.15 W
Somvix	58	46.44 N	8.56 E
Šomyškol'	86	46.30 N	59.53 E
Son, Ned.	52	51.31 N	5.30 E
Son, Nor.	26	59.31 N	10.42 E
Son ≏	124	25.42 N	84.52 E
Soná	236	8.01 N	81.19 W
Sona-Bata	152	4.54 S	15.09 E
Sonādugi	126	22.47 N	90.40 E
Sonaguera	236	15.38 N	86.20 W
Sonahula	124	25.05 N	87.09 E
Sonāmarg	123	34.18 N	75.18 E
Sonāmukhi	126	23.18 N	87.25 E
Sonāpur	126	23.42 N	89.30 E
Sonar	164	2.33 S	133.00 E
Sonār ≏	124	24.24 N	79.56 E
Sonari	272c	18.52 N	72.59 E
Sonarpur	272b	22.26 N	88.25 E
Sonātikri	272b	22.57 N	88.20 E
Sonceboz	58	47.11 N	7.11 E
Sonchamp	261	48.35 N	1.53 E
Sŏnch'ŏn	98	39.48 N	124.55 E
Soncino	62	45.24 N	9.52 E
Sondags ≏, S. Afr.	158	33.44 S	25.51 E
Sondags ≏, S. Afr.	158	28.43 S	30.16 E
Sondalo	64	46.20 N	10.19 E
Sønderå ≏	41	54.53 N	8.59 E
Sønderborg	41	54.55 N	9.47 E
Sønderby	41	55.47 N	10.01 E
Sønder Felding	41	55.57 N	8.47 E
Sønderhav	41	54.51 N	9.30 E
Sønderjylland □[6]	41	55.10 N	9.15 E
Sønder Nærå	41	55.18 N	10.30 E
Sønder Omme	41	55.50 N	8.54 E
Sondershausen	54	51.22 N	10.52 E
Søndersø	41	55.29 N	10.16 E
Sondi	114	2.58 N	98.52 E
Søndre Strømfjord	176	66.59 N	50.40 W
Søndre Strømfjord ⊂[2]	176	66.30 N	52.15 W
Sondrio	64	46.10 N	9.52 E
Sondrio □[4]	58	46.10 N	10.03 E
Sonduga	76	60.08 N	41.55 E
Sone ≏	126	21.34 N	86.54 E
Sonepur	120	20.50 N	83.55 E
Sonestown	210	41.21 N	76.33 W
Song, Malay.	112	2.01 N	112.33 E
Song, Nig.	146	9.50 N	12.38 E
Song, Thai	110	18.28 N	100.11 E
Song ≏	100	27.02 N	118.18 E
Song'ao	100	29.36 N	121.41 E
Songbahutun	104	41.28 N	121.11 E
Song Bay Hap, Cua ⊂	110	8.46 N	104.52 E
Songbu	100	31.05 N	114.48 E
Sŏngbyŏn-ni	98	38.03 N	125.18 E
Song Cau	110	13.27 N	109.13 E
Sŏng-ch'ŏn-gang ≏	98	39.48 N	127.35 E
Songcun	106	30.26 N	119.43 E
Songe	26	58.41 N	9.00 E
Songea	154	10.41 S	35.39 E
Songeons	50	49.33 N	1.52 E
Songgaizhen	107	29.03 N	105.54 E
Songgang	100	22.49 N	113.51 E
Songgato ≏	164	3.26 S	140.22 E
Songhe	100	31.10 N	113.20 E
Songhua ≏	89	47.44 N	132.32 E
Songhuahu ⊜	89	43.20 N	127.07 E
Songhuajiang	89	44.46 N	125.54 E
Songhwa	98	38.21 N	125.08 E
Songino	88	48.54 N	95.54 E
Sŏngjang-ni	98	41.02 N	126.50 E
Songjiachang	107	28.47 N	104.55 E
Songjiang	106	31.01 N	121.14 E
Songjiangzhen	98	42.12 N	126.56 E
Songjiapu	107	29.38 N	104.44 E
Songjiaying	105	40.38 N	115.14 E
Sŏngjin → Kimch'aek	98	40.41 N	129.12 E
Songjŏng	98	35.10 N	126.46 E
Sŏngju	98	35.55 N	128.16 E
Songkan	102	28.27 N	106.50 E
Songkhla	110	7.12 N	100.36 E
Songkhram ≏	110	17.39 N	104.28 E
Songkou, Zhg.	100	25.48 N	118.36 E
Songkou, Zhg.	100	24.32 N	116.24 E
Songlinba	100	24.00 N	115.59 E
Songlindian	105	39.25 N	115.54 E
Songling	89	48.02 N	121.12 E
Song Ling ⋏	98	41.10 N	120.09 E
Songmen	100	28.19 N	121.34 E
Songming	102	25.24 N	102.59 E
Sŏngmo-do I	98	37.42 N	126.18 E
Sŏngnae-ri	98	39.28 N	126.59 E
Sŏngnam	98	37.26 N	127.08 E
Sŏng-ni	98	39.38 N	127.06 E
Songnim	98	38.44 N	125.38 E
Songo	152	7.22 S	14.51 E
Songololo	152	5.42 S	14.02 E
Songot ∧	154	3.59 N	34.28 E
Songpan	102	32.40 N	103.24 E
Song Phi Nong	110	14.13 N	100.03 E
Sŏngsa-ri	271b	37.38 N	126.52 E
Songshancun	104	41.02 N	121.09 E
Songshu	98	39.50 N	122.06 E
Songshugou	105	41.02 N	117.49 E
Songtangmiao	106	31.08 N	119.16 E
Songtao	102	28.06 N	109.05 E
Șongtun	98	39.54 N	123.56 E
Šonguj	24	68.47 N	33.00 E
Songu-ri	98	37.49 N	127.09 E
Songwe, Zaïre	154	3.24 S	26.16 E
Songwe, Zaïre	154	12.25 S	29.40 E
Songwe ≏	154	9.43 S	33.56 E
Songxi, Zhg.	100	27.33 N	118.46 E
Songxi, Zhg.	100	26.16 N	116.59 E
Songxia, Zhg.	100	25.44 N	119.36 E
Songxia, Zhg.	100	30.07 N	120.51 E
Songxian	102	34.10 N	112.05 E
Songyan	98	37.13 N	113.43 E
Songyin	106	30.54 N	121.13 E
Songyin ≏	100	28.18 N	119.44 E
Songzhangzi	98	41.13 N	119.08 E
Songzhuang	106	32.06 N	121.17 E
Son Ha	110	15.03 N	108.34 E
Soni, Ehi ∧	146	20.49 N	17.23 E
Sonico	64	46.10 N	10.21 E
Sonid Youqi	102	42.44 N	112.40 E
Sonid Zuoqi	102	43.58 N	113.59 E
Sonīpat	124	28.59 N	77.01 E
Sonkach	124	22.59 N	76.21 E
Sonk'ol', ozero ⊜	85	41.50 N	75.08 E
Sonkovo	76	57.47 N	37.09 E
Son La	110	21.19 N	103.54 E
Sonmiāni	120	25.26 N	66.36 E
Sonmiāni Bay ⊂	120	25.15 N	66.30 E
Sonnberg ∧	264b	48.20 N	16.15 E
Sonneberg	54	50.22 N	11.10 E
Sonnefeld	56	50.13 N	11.08 E
Sonnen	60	48.41 N	13.43 E
Sonnenberg ∧[2]	61	47.52 N	16.28 E
Sonnewalde	54	51.42 N	13.38 E
Sonning Common	42	51.31 N	0.59 W
Sonningdale	184	52.24 N	107.40 W
Sonnino	66	41.25 N	13.14 E
Sonntagberg	61	47.59 N	14.45 E
Sono	270	34.48 N	135.55 E
Sono, Rio do ≏, Bra.	250	8.58 S	48.11 W
Sono, Rio do ≏, Bra.	255	17.02 S	45.32 W
Sonobe	96	35.06 N	135.28 E
Sonogno	58	46.21 N	8.47 E
Sonoita Creek ≏	200	31.30 N	110.58 W
Sonoma	226	38.17 N	122.27 W
Sonoma □[6]	226	38.26 N	122.35 W
Sonoma Creek ≏	226	38.10 N	122.24 W
Sonoma Mountains ⋏	226	38.17 N	122.35 W
Sonoma Peak ∧	204	40.52 N	117.36 W
Sonoma State Historical Park ♠	226	38.18 N	122.28 W
Sononder	158	29.43 S	21.51 E
Sonop	158	25.39 S	27.42 E
Sonora, Ca., U.S.	226	37.59 N	120.22 W
Sonora, Tx., U.S.	196	30.34 N	100.38 W
Sonora □[3]	232	29.20 N	110.40 W
Sonora ≏	232	28.48 N	111.33 W
Sonoran Desert ◆[2]	16	30.00 N	113.00 W
Sonora Pass)(	226	38.19 N	119.37 W
Sonostrov	24	66.09 N	34.10 E
Sonoyta	232	31.51 N	112.50 W
Sonoyta ≏	200	31.16 N	113.26 W
Sonpār Hills ⋏[2]	124	24.20 N	82.15 E
Sonqor	128	34.47 N	47.36 E
Sŏnsan	98	36.16 N	128.17 E
Sonsbeck	52	51.37 N	6.22 E
Sonseca	34	39.42 N	3.57 W
Sonskyn	158	30.47 S	26.28 E
Sonsón	246	5.42 N	75.18 W
Sonsonate	236	13.43 N	89.44 W
Sonsorol Islands II	108	5.20 N	132.13 E
Sonstorp	40	58.45 N	15.36 E
Sonstraal	158	27.07 S	22.28 E
Sontag	194	31.39 N	90.12 W
Son Tay	110	21.08 N	105.30 E
Sonthofen	58	47.31 N	10.17 E
Sontra	56	51.04 N	9.56 E
Sonwān	124	27.40 N	81.45 E
Sonyea	210	42.41 N	77.50 W
Soochow → Suzhou	106	31.18 N	120.37 E
Sooke	224	48.23 N	123.43 W
Sooke ≏	224	48.23 N	123.42 W
Sooke Basin ⊂	224	48.23 N	123.40 W
Sooke Lake ⊜	224	48.33 N	123.42 W
Sooner Lake ⊜[1]	196	36.26 N	97.02 W
Soonwald ⋏	56	49.55 N	7.40 E
Soo → Sault Sainte Marie	190	46.29 N	84.20 W
Sooyaac	144	0.03 N	42.17 E
Sopa Sopa Head ≻	164	1.58 S	146.35 E
Sopchoppy	192	30.03 N	84.29 W
Soperton	192	32.22 N	82.35 W
Sop Hao	110	20.33 N	104.27 E
Sophia	192	37.42 N	81.15 W
Sopki	76	57.06 N	30.55 E
Sopockin	76	53.50 N	23.39 E
Sopot	30	54.28 N	18.34 E
Sop Pong	110	22.04 N	102.03 E
Sop Prap	110	17.53 N	99.20 E
Soprabolzano	64	46.32 N	11.24 E
Sopron	61	47.41 N	16.36 E
Sopronhorpács	61	47.29 N	16.44 E
Șopronkövesd	61	47.33 N	16.45 E
Šoptykol'	86	51.16 N	75.45 E
Sopur	123	34.18 N	74.28 E
Sŏp'yŏng-ni	98	35.01 N	127.24 E
Soquel	226	36.59 N	121.57 W
Soquel Creek ≏	226	36.58 N	121.57 W
Sor, Ribeira de ≏	34	39.00 N	8.17 W
Sora	66	41.43 N	13.37 E
Sorada	122	19.45 N	84.26 E
Sorae-san ∧	271b	37.27 N	126.47 E
Soraga	64	46.22 N	11.39 E
Soragna	64	44.56 N	10.07 E
Söråker	26	62.31 N	17.30 E
Șorano	66	42.41 N	11.43 E
Šorapani	84	42.05 N	43.05 E
Soras	248	14.07 S	73.37 W
Sorata	248	15.47 S	68.40 W
Soratte, Monte ∧	66	42.15 N	12.30 E
Sorau → Żary	30	51.38 N	15.09 E
Soraya	248	14.10 S	73.19 W
Șorbas	34	37.07 N	2.07 W
Šorbas, gora ∧	86	47.25 N	84.12 E
Sorbhog	120	26.30 N	90.52 E
Sorbie	44	54.48 N	4.26 W
Sorbo ≏	85	38.45 N	69.20 E
Sorbolo	64	44.51 N	10.28 E
Sorbonne ʋ[2]	261	48.51 N	2.21 E
Sorcier, Lac au ⊜	206	46.42 N	73.24 W
Sordevolo	62	45.34 N	7.59 E
Sore	32	44.20 N	0.35 W
Sorel	206	46.02 N	73.07 W
Sorell	166	42.47 S	147.33 E
Sorell, Cape ≻	166	42.12 S	145.10 E
Sorel Point ≻	43b	49.16 N	2.10 W
Sörenberg	58	46.50 N	8.03 E
Sorento	219	39.00 N	89.34 W
Soreq ≏	132	31.56 N	34.42 E
Soresina	64	45.17 N	9.51 E
Sörfjärden ⊂	40	59.24 N	16.50 E
Sørfjorden ⊂[2]	26	60.24 N	6.40 E
Sørfold	24	67.28 N	15.22 E
Sörforsa	26	61.40 N	17.00 E
Sorge ≏	41	54.21 N	9.25 E
Sorgono	71	40.01 N	9.06 E
Sorgues	62	44.00 N	4.52 E
Sorgun	130	39.49 N	35.11 E
Sori	62	44.22 N	9.06 E
Soria	34	41.46 N	2.28 W
Soria □[4]	34	41.35 N	2.35 W
Soriano	252	33.24 S	58.19 W
Soriano □[5]	258	33.45 S	57.45 W
Soriano Calabro	68	38.36 N	16.14 E
Soriano nel Cimino	66	42.25 N	12.14 E
Sorico	58	46.10 N	9.22 E
Sorido	164	1.09 S	136.03 E
Sori-do I	98	34.26 N	127.48 E
Sørli	26	64.15 N	13.45 E
Sormonne ≏	56	49.46 N	4.40 E
Sorn	46	55.30 N	4.18 W
Sorne ≏	58	47.22 N	7.22 E
Sorø, Dan.	41	55.26 N	11.34 E
Soro, India	120	21.17 N	86.40 E
Soro, Monte ∧	70	37.56 N	14.42 E
Sorocaba	255	23.29 S	47.27 W
Sorocabuçu ≏	256	23.38 S	47.13 W
Soročinka	80	47.30 N	51.44 E
Soročinsk	80	52.26 N	53.10 E
Soročkino	86	57.02 N	68.52 E
Soroco	240m	18.22 N	65.38 W
Sorok	88	52.20 N	100.12 E
Sorok ≏	61	47.07 N	16.50 E
Soroka	78	48.09 N	28.17 E
Sorokino, Ross.	86	53.45 N	84.58 E
Sorokino, Ross.	86	54.13 N	91.31 E
Sorokošiči	78	51.12 N	30.35 E
Soroksár ◆[8]	264c	47.24 N	19.07 E
Sorol I[1]	108	8.08 N	140.23 E
Soron	124	27.53 N	78.45 E
Sorong	164	0.53 S	131.15 E
Sororó ≏	250	5.24 S	49.07 W
Sorot' ≏	76	57.04 N	28.50 E
Soroti	154	1.43 N	33.37 E
Sorovskije	86	59.53 N	71.34 E
Sørøya I	24	70.36 N	22.46 E
Sorpestausee ⊜[1]	56	51.20 N	7.56 E
Sorraia ≏	34	38.56 N	8.53 W
Sorrento, Austl.	169	38.20 S	144.45 E
Sorrento, It.	68	40.37 N	14.22 E
Sorrento, Fl., U.S.	220	28.48 N	81.33 W
Sorrento, La., U.S.	194	30.11 N	90.51 W
Sorris Sorris	156	20.57 S	14.50 E
Sør Rondane Mountains ⋏	9	72.00 S	25.00 E
Sorsakoski	26	62.27 N	27.39 E
Sorsatunturi ∧	24	67.24 N	29.38 E
Sorsele	24	65.30 N	17.30 E
Sorsk	86	54.01 N	90.12 E
Sorso	71	40.48 N	8.34 E
Sorsogon	116	12.58 N	124.00 E
Sorsogon □[4]	116	12.50 N	123.55 E
Sorsogon Bay ⊂	116	12.55 N	123.55 E
Sörstafors	40	59.35 N	16.13 E
Šorsu	85	40.17 N	70.48 E
Șort	34	42.24 N	1.08 E
Šortandy	86	51.42 N	71.00 E
Sortat	46	58.33 N	3.13 W
Sortavala	24	61.42 N	30.41 E
Sortino	70	37.09 N	15.02 E
Sortland	24	68.40 N	15.20 E
Sør-Trøndelag □[6]	26	63.00 N	10.40 E
Sorunda	40	59.01 N	17.48 E
Sörup	41	54.43 N	9.40 E
Sõrve neem ≻	76	57.54 N	22.03 E
Sörvik	40	60.11 N	15.09 E
Sorviži	80	57.52 N	48.32 E
Sosa, Dtsch.	54	50.30 N	12.39 E
Șosa, Taehan	271b	37.29 N	126.47 E
Šoša ≏	82	56.31 N	36.05 E
Sŏsan	98	36.47 N	126.26 E
Sösdala	41	56.02 N	13.40 E
Sos del Rey Católico	34	42.30 N	1.13 W
Sosedka	80	53.15 N	42.40 E
Sosedno	76	58.14 N	28.42 E
Sosenka ≏, Ross.	265b	55.35 N	37.23 E
Sosenka ≏, Ross.	265b	55.47 N	37.42 E
Sosenki	82	55.34 N	37.26 E
Sösetalsperre ◆[6]	52	51.44 N	10.20 E
Soshigaya ◆[8]	268	35.39 N	139.36 E
Șösjöfjällen ⋏	26	63.53 N	13.15 E
Šoška	24	62.42 N	50.40 E
Soskovo	76	52.45 N	35.23 E
Sosna ≏	76	52.42 N	38.55 E
Sosneado, Cerro ∧	252	34.45 S	69.59 W
Sosnica	78	51.32 N	32.28 E
Sosnicy	76	57.38 N	30.25 E
Sosnogorsk	24	63.37 N	53.51 E
Sosnovaja Maza	80	52.30 N	47.53 E
Sosnovaja Pol'ana ◆[8]	265a	59.50 N	30.09 E
Sosnovec	24	64.26 N	34.27 E
Sosnovica	76	60.21 N	40.50 E
Sosnovka, Kaz.	86	51.26 N	79.28 E
Sosnovka, Kyrg.	85	42.40 N	73.55 E
Sosnovka, Ross.	24	66.30 N	40.32 E
Sosnovka, Ross.	80	56.13 N	47.13 E
Sosnovka, Ross.	80	57.48 N	51.43 E
Sosnovka, Ross.	80	57.16 N	53.31 E
Sosnovka, Ross.	80	54.06 N	46.38 E
Sosnovka, Ross.	80	56.17 N	51.17 E
Sosnovka, Ross.	80	53.14 N	41.22 E
Sosnovka, Ross.	80	52.26 N	43.29 E
Sosnovka, Ross.	82	54.31 N	38.08 E
Sosnovka, Ross.	82	54.54 N	38.41 E
Sosnovka, Ross.	86	59.10 N	81.18 E
Sosnovka, Ross.	88	54.09 N	109.35 E
Sosnovo, Ross.	76	60.33 N	30.15 E
Sosnovo, Ross.	80	56.42 N	54.35 E
Sosnovoborsk	80	53.18 N	46.16 E
Sosnovoje	78	50.49 N	27.00 E
Sosnovo-Oz'orskoje	88	52.31 N	111.30 E
Sosnovskij	86	54.36 N	73.10 E
Sosnovskoje	80	55.48 N	43.10 E
Sosnovyj Bor, Bela.	76	52.32 N	29.36 E
Sosnovyj Bor, Ross.	76	59.55 N	29.07 E
Sosnovyj Bor, Ross.	86	57.07 N	55.03 E
Sosnovyj Solonec	80	53.17 N	49.33 E
Sosnowiec	30	50.18 N	19.08 E
Soso	194	31.45 N	89.16 W
Sosok	112	0.17 N	110.14 E
Sospel	62	43.53 N	7.27 E
Sospirolo	64	46.09 N	12.04 E
Șossusvlei ⊜	156	24.40 S	15.23 E
Šoštanj	61	46.23 N	15.03 E
Šostka	78	51.52 N	33.30 E
Sŏsura	98	42.16 N	130.37 E
Sos'va, Ross.	72	63.40 N	62.06 E
Sos'va, Ross.	86	59.10 N	61.50 E
Sos'va ≏	86	59.32 N	62.20 E
Sosyka ≏	78	46.35 N	39.05 E
Sot' ≏	80	58.00 N	40.39 E
Sota ≏	150	11.52 N	3.24 E
Sotik	154	0.41 S	35.21 E
Sotkamo	26	64.08 N	28.25 E
Sotnicyno	80	54.17 N	41.49 E
Soto de Aldovea	266a	40.26 N	3.27 W
Soto de Pajares	266a	40.17 N	3.32 W
Soto la Marina	234	23.46 N	98.13 W
Soto La Marina ≏	234	23.45 N	97.45 W
Soto la Marina, Barra I	232	24.10 N	97.43 W
Sotomayor	248	19.18 S	65.03 W
Sotonera, Embalse de ⊜[1]	34	42.05 N	0.48 W
Sotouboua	150	8.34 N	0.59 E
Sotta, Fr.	71	41.32 N	9.12 E
Sotta, Fr.	71	41.32 N	9.12 E
Sottens	58	46.39 N	6.44 E
Sottern ⊜	40	59.02 N	15.29 E
Sotteville	50	49.25 N	1.06 E
Sottile, Punta ≻	70a	35.30 N	12.38 E
Sottomarina	64	45.13 N	12.17 E
Sottrum	52	53.06 N	9.14 E
Sottrup	41	54.57 N	9.43 E
Sottunga I	26	60.08 N	20.40 E
Souain-Perthes-lès-Hurlus	56	49.11 N	4.32 E
Souanké	152	2.05 N	14.03 E
Soubakaniédougou	150	10.28 N	5.01 W
Soubré	150	5.47 N	6.36 W
Soudan	166	20.05 S	137.00 E
Soudan → Sudan □[1]	140	15.00 N	30.00 E
Soude ≏	50	48.52 N	4.10 E
Soudersburg	208	40.01 N	76.09 W
Souderton	208	40.18 N	75.19 W
Souesmes	50	47.27 N	2.10 E
Soufflay	152	2.01 N	14.54 E
Soufflenheim	56	48.50 N	7.58 E
Soufflot, Lac ⊜	190	47.24 N	78.31 W
Souflíon	38	41.12 N	26.18 E
Soufrière	241f	13.52 N	61.04 W
Soufrière ∧, Guad.	241o	16.03 N	61.40 W
Soufrière ∧, St. Vin.	241h	13.20 N	61.11 W
Soufrière Bay ⊂, Dom.	240d	15.14 N	61.22 W
Soufrière Bay ⊂, St. Luc.	241f	13.51 N	61.04 W
Sougahatchee Creek ≏	194	32.38 N	85.50 W
Sougne-Remouchamps	56	50.29 N	5.40 E
Souguer	148	35.12 N	1.30 E
Souhegan ≏	188	42.51 N	71.29 W
Souillac	32	44.54 N	1.29 E
Souilly	56	49.01 N	5.17 E
Souk-el-Arba-des-Beni-Hassan	34	35.16 N	5.20 W
Souk-Khemis-du-Sahel	34	35.17 N	6.05 W
Souk Larbat Gharb	148	34.43 N	6.01 W
Sŏul (Seoul), Taehan	98	37.33 N	126.58 E
Sŏul (Seoul), Taehan	271b	37.33 N	126.58 E
Sŏul □[4]	98	37.34 N	127.00 E
Soulac-sur-Mer	32	45.31 N	1.07 W
Soulaines-Dhuys	58	48.22 N	4.44 E
Soulanges □[6]	206	45.20 N	74.15 W
Soulanges, Canal de ≖	275a	45.20 N	73.58 W
Soulougou	150	13.01 N	0.23 E
Soulsbyville	226	37.59 N	120.16 W
Soultzeren	58	48.04 N	7.06 E
Soultz-Haut-Rhin	58	47.53 N	7.14 E
Soultzmatt	58	47.58 N	7.14 E
Soultz-sous-Forêts	56	48.56 N	7.53 E
Soummam, Oued ≏	34	36.45 N	5.04 E
Sound Beach	210	40.57 N	72.58 W
Sounding Creek ≏	184	52.06 N	110.28 W
Sounding Lake ⊜	184	52.08 N	110.29 W
Sound View Park ♠	276	40.49 N	73.52 W
Soúnion, Ákra ≻	38	37.39 N	24.02 E
Soup Harbour ⊂	212	43.51 N	77.11 W
Souppes-sur-Loing	50	48.11 N	2.44 E
Souq Ahras	148	36.23 N	8.00 E
Sources, Mont aux ∧	158	28.46 S	28.52 E
Soure, Bra.	250	0.44 S	48.31 W
Soure, Port.	34	40.03 N	8.38 W
Sour el Ghozlane	148	36.10 N	3.45 E
Souris, Mb., Can.	184	49.38 N	100.15 W
Souris, P.E., Can.	186	46.21 N	62.15 W
Souris ≏	198	49.39 N	99.34 W
Sourlake	194	30.09 N	94.25 W
Sourland Mountain ∧[2]	208	40.29 N	74.43 W
Sourou ≏	150	12.45 N	3.25 W
Souroukaha	150	8.13 N	5.08 W
Souš	54	50.32 N	13.34 E
Sous, Oued V	148	30.27 N	9.31 W
Sousa	250	6.45 S	38.14 W
Sousânia	255	16.11 S	49.05 W
Sousas	256	22.52 S	46.59 W
Sousel	34	38.57 N	7.40 W
Sous-le-Vent, Îles → Leeward Islands II	238	17.00 N	63.00 W
Sousse	148	35.49 N	10.38 E
Sousse □[8]	148	35.40 N	10.30 E
Sout ≏, S. Afr.	158	31.35 S	18.24 E
Sout ≏, S. Afr.	158	33.03 S	23.28 E
Sout ≏, S. Afr.	158	28.56 S	20.40 E
South ≏, Ia., U.S.	190	41.29 N	93.20 W
South ≏, Ma., U.S.	283	42.10 N	70.43 W
South ≏, Mo., U.S.	219	39.52 N	91.26 W
South ≏, N.J., U.S.	208	40.29 N	74.23 W
South ≏, N.C., U.S.	192	34.20 N	78.03 W
South ≏, Va., U.S.	192	37.46 N	79.23 W
South ≏, Va., U.S.	208	38.02 N	77.23 W
South Acton	207	42.27 N	71.27 W
South Africa (Suid-Afrika) □[1], Afr.	138	30.00 S	26.00 E
South Africa (Suid-Afrika) □[1], Afr.	156	30.00 S	26.00 E
Southall ◆[8]	260	51.31 N	0.23 W
South Alligator ≏	164	12.15 S	132.24 E
Southam	42	52.15 N	1.23 W
South Amboy	208	40.28 N	74.17 W
South America ⊥[1]	4	15.00 S	60.00 W
South America ⊥[1]	18	15.00 S	60.00 W
South Amherst, Ma., U.S.	207	42.20 N	72.30 W
South Amherst, Oh., U.S.	214	41.22 N	82.14 W
Southampton, N.S., Can.	186	45.35 N	64.15 W
Southampton, On., Can.	212	44.29 N	81.23 W
Southampton, Eng., U.K.	42	50.55 N	1.25 W
Southampton, Ma., U.S.	207	42.13 N	72.43 W
Southampton, N.Y., U.S.	207	40.53 N	72.23 W
Southampton, Pa., U.S.	285	40.10 N	75.02 W
Southampton □[6]	208	36.42 N	77.05 W
Southampton (Eastleigh) Airport ⊠	42	50.57 N	1.21 W
Southampton, Cape ≻	176	62.09 N	83.40 W
Southampton Island I	176	64.20 N	84.40 W
South Andaman I	110	11.45 N	92.45 E
South Anna ≏	192	37.48 N	77.25 W
South Apopka	220	28.39 N	81.31 W
Southard	208	40.08 N	74.14 W
Southards Pond ⊜	276	40.43 N	73.20 W
South Ashburnham	207	42.36 N	71.56 W
South Aulatsivik Island I	176	56.45 N	61.30 W
South Australia □[3]	162	30.00 S	135.00 E
South Australian Basin ✢[1]	14	38.00 S	126.00 E
Southaven	194	34.59 N	90.02 W
South Bald Mountain ∧	200	40.45 N	105.41 W
South Baldy ∧	200	33.59 N	107.11 W
South Banda Basin ✢[1]	14	6.30 S	127.30 E
Southbank	182	54.02 N	125.46 W
South Barre	207	42.23 N	72.05 W
South Barrington	278	42.06 N	88.07 W
South Barrule ∧[2]	44	54.12 N	4.40 W
South Bass Island I	214	41.39 N	82.49 W
South Bay	220	26.39 N	80.42 W
South Bay ⊂, Mb., Can.	184	56.43 N	99.00 W
South Bay ⊂, N.T., Can.	176	63.58 N	83.30 W
South Bay ⊂, On., Can.	190	45.38 N	81.50 W
South Bay ⊂, On., Can.	212	43.55 N	77.03 W
South Bay ⊂, On., Can.	212	44.52 N	79.47 W
South Bay ⊂, Fl., U.S.	220	26.42 N	80.45 W
South Bay ⊂, Va., U.S.	208	37.14 N	75.52 W
South Bay ⊂, Wa., U.S.	224	46.53 N	124.04 W
South Baymouth	190	45.33 N	82.01 W
South Beach ♠	276	40.35 N	74.05 W
South Beacon Mountain ∧	210	41.29 N	73.57 W
South Bedias Creek ≏	222	30.54 N	95.42 W
South Bellingham	207	42.03 N	71.28 W
South Belmar	208	40.10 N	74.02 W
South Beloit	216	42.29 N	89.02 W
South Bend, In., U.S.	216	41.41 N	86.15 W
South Bend, Wa., U.S.	224	46.40 N	123.48 W
South Benfleet	42	51.33 N	0.34 E
South Bentinck Arm ⊂	182	52.15 N	126.50 W
South Bethlehem	214	41.00 N	79.20 W
South Bihar Plains ≋	124	25.15 N	84.30 E
South Bloomfield	218	39.43 N	82.59 W
Southborough, Eng., U.K.	42	51.10 N	0.15 E
Southborough, Ma., U.S.	207	42.18 N	71.31 W
South Bosque ≏	222	31.29 N	97.16 W
South Boston	192	36.41 N	78.54 W
South Boston ◆[8]	283	42.20 N	71.03 W
South Bound Brook	276	40.33 N	74.32 W
South Bradenton	220	27.27 N	82.35 W
South Branch, Nf., Can.	186	47.55 N	59.02 W
South Branch, N.J., U.S.	276	40.33 N	74.42 W
South Brent	42	50.25 N	3.50 W
Southbridge, N.Z.	172	43.49 S	172.15 E
Southbridge, Ma., U.S.	207	42.04 N	72.02 W
South Britain	207	41.28 N	73.15 W
Southbrook, Austl.	171a	27.41 S	151.43 E
Southbrook, N.Z.	172	43.20 S	172.36 E
South Brook ≏	285	39.52 N	75.44 W
South Brookfield	186	44.23 N	64.58 W
South Brooklyn ◆[8]	276	40.41 N	73.59 W
South Bruny Island I	166	43.23 S	147.17 E
South Buganda □[5]	154	0.30 S	31.35 E
South Burlington	188	44.28 N	73.10 W
Southbury	207	41.28 N	73.12 W
South Butler	210	43.08 N	76.46 W
South Byfield	283	42.44 N	70.54 W
South Byron	210	43.03 N	78.04 W
South Cairo	210	42.17 N	73.57 W
South Canaan	210	41.30 N	75.25 W
South Cape ≻	175g	17.01 S	179.55 E
South Carolina □[3], U.S.	178	34.00 N	81.00 W
South Carolina □[3], U.S.	192	34.00 N	81.00 W
South Carver	207	41.50 N	70.44 W
South Castor ≏	212	45.15 N	75.23 W
South Cave	44	53.46 N	0.35 W
South Cerney	42	51.40 N	1.56 W
South Chagrin Reservation ♠	279a	41.25 N	81.25 W
South Channel ⊔, Pil.	116	14.20 N	120.37 E
South Channel ⊔, Mi., U.S.	190	45.38 N	84.32 W
South Channel ≏[1]	281	42.32 N	82.40 W
South Chaplin	207	41.46 N	72.07 W
South Charleston, Oh., U.S.	218	39.49 N	83.38 W
South Charleston, W.V., U.S.	188	38.22 N	81.41 W
South Chatham	207	41.40 N	70.01 W
South Chelmsford	283	42.34 N	71.23 W
South Chicago ◆[8]	278	41.44 N	87.33 W
South China Basin ✢[1]	12	15.00 N	115.00 E
South China Sea ⊤[2]	108	10.00 N	113.00 E
South Cle Elum	224	47.11 N	120.56 W
South Coast Botanic Garden ♠	280	33.47 N	118.21 W
South Coatesville	208	39.58 N	75.49 W
South Coffeyville	196	36.59 N	95.37 W
South Concho ≏	196	31.21 N	100.28 W
South Corinth	210	43.12 N	73.51 W
South Corning	210	42.07 N	77.02 W
South Cotabato □[4]	116	6.15 N	125.00 E
South Creek ≏	170	33.36 S	150.50 E
South Crest	273d	26.15 S	28.07 E
South Dakota □[3], U.S.	178	44.15 N	100.00 W
South Dakota □[3], U.S.	198	44.15 N	100.00 W
South Dandalup ≏	168a	32.35 S	115.53 E
South Dandalup Dam ◆[6]	168a	32.38 S	116.04 E
South Darenth	260	51.24 N	0.15 E
South Dartmouth	207	41.35 N	70.56 W
South Dayton	210	42.21 N	79.03 W
South Deerfield	207	42.28 N	72.36 W
South Dennis, Ma., U.S.	207	41.41 N	70.09 W
South Dennis, N.J., U.S.	208	39.10 N	74.49 W
South Dorset	210	43.13 N	73.04 W
South Dorset Downs ⋏[1]	42	50.40 N	2.25 W
South Dos Palos	226	36.57 N	120.39 W
South Downs ⋏[1]	42	50.55 N	0.25 W
South Dum Dum	126	22.37 N	88.25 E
South Duxbury	207	42.01 N	70.41 W
South East □[5]	156	25.00 S	25.45 E
Southeast Asia Treaty Organization Headquarters ʋ	269a	13.45 N	100.31 E
South East Cape ≻, Austl.	166	43.39 S	146.50 E
Southeast Cape ≻, Ak., U.S.	180	62.55 N	169.42 W
Southeast Indian Ridge ✢[3]	6	50.00 S	110.00 E
South Easton	207	42.02 N	71.04 W
Southeast Pacific Basin ✢[1]	6	60.00 S	115.00 W
South East Point ≻, Austl.	166	39.00 S	146.20 E
South East Point ≻, Kiribati	174o	1.40 N	157.10 W
South Egg Harbor	208	39.31 N	74.39 W
South Egremont	207	42.09 N	73.25 W
South Elgin	216	41.59 N	88.17 W
South Elkhorn Creek ≏	218	38.13 N	84.48 W
South El Monte	280	34.03 N	118.02 W
Southend	44	55.20 N	5.38 W
Southend Municipal Airport ⊠	42	51.34 N	0.41 E
Southend-on-Sea	42	51.33 N	0.43 E
Southend-on-Sea □[8]	260	51.33 N	0.41 E
Southend Pier ◆[5]	260	51.31 N	0.44 E
South English ≏	190	41.30 N	91.56 W
Southern □[4], Malaŵi	154	15.30 S	35.00 E
Southern □[4], S.L.	150	8.00 N	12.15 W
Southern □[4], Zam.	154	16.30 S	27.00 E
Southern □[5], Bots.	156	24.45 S	24.00 E
Southern □[5], Ug.	154	0.30 S	30.30 E
Southern Alps ⋏	172	43.30 S	170.30 E
Southern California, University of ʋ[2]	280	34.02 N	118.17 W
Southern Cook Islands II	14	20.00 S	159.00 W
Southern Cross	162	31.13 S	119.19 E
Southern Ghāts ⋏	122	9.30 N	77.00 E
Southern Highlands □[5]	164	6.00 S	143.30 E
Southern Indian Lake ⊜	176	57.10 N	98.40 W
Southern Leyte □[4]	116	10.50 N	124.55 E
Southern Lueti ≏	152	16.14 S	23.13 E
Southern Pines	192	35.10 N	79.23 W
Southern Ute Indian Reservation ◆[4]	200	37.05 N	107.45 W
Southern View	219	39.46 N	89.39 W
Southern Yemen → Yemen □[1]	144	15.00 N	47.00 E
Southery	42	52.32 N	0.23 E
South Esk ≏, Austl.	166	41.25 S	147.08 E
South Esk ≏, Scot., U.K.	46	56.42 N	2.32 W
South Esk ≏, Scot., U.K.	46	55.53 N	3.04 W
Southesk Tablelands ⋏[1]	162	20.50 S	126.40 E
South Essex	207	42.38 N	70.46 W
South Euclid	214	41.31 N	81.31 W
Southey	184	50.56 N	104.30 W
South Fabius ≏	219	39.54 N	91.30 W
South Fallsburg	210	41.42 N	74.37 W
South Farmbridge	260	51.38 N	0.41 E
South Farmingdale	276	40.43 N	73.26 W
Southfield, Ma., U.S.	207	42.06 N	73.14 W
Southfield, Mi., U.S.	216	42.28 N	83.13 W
Southfields	210	41.15 N	74.11 W
South Fiji Basin ✢[1]	14	26.00 S	175.00 E
Southfleet	260	51.25 N	0.19 E
South Floral Park	276	40.43 N	73.42 W
South Foreland ≻	42	51.09 N	1.23 E
South Fork, Co., U.S.	200	37.40 N	106.38 W
South Fork, Pa., U.S.	214	40.22 N	78.47 W
South Fort George	182	53.54 N	122.45 W
South Forty Foot Drain ≖	42	52.56 N	0.15 W
South Fox Island I	190	45.25 N	85.50 W
South Fulton	194	36.30 N	88.52 W
South Gate, Ca., U.S.	228	33.57 N	118.12 W
Southgate, Fl., U.S.	220	27.18 N	82.32 W
Southgate, Mi., U.S.	216	42.12 N	83.11 W
Southgate, Wa., U.S.	224	47.10 N	122.30 W
Southgate ◆[8]	260	51.38 N	0.08 W
Southgate U.S.A. ◆[9]	279a	41.25 N	81.32 W
South Georgia I	244	54.15 S	36.45 W
South Georgia and the South Sandwich Islands □[2]	244	54.00 S	38.00 W
South Gibson	210	41.44 N	75.38 W
South Glamorgan □[6]	42	51.30 N	3.25 W
South Glastonbury	207	41.40 N	72.35 W
South Glens Falls	210	43.17 N	73.38 W
South Grafton	207	42.11 N	71.42 W
South Grand ≏	194	38.18 N	93.28 W
South Grand Island Bridge ◆[5]	284a	43.00 N	78.56 W
South Green	260	51.37 N	0.26 E
South Greensburg	214	40.17 N	79.33 W
South Hackensack	276	40.51 N	74.02 W
South Hadley, Ma., U.S.	188	42.15 N	72.34 W
South Hadley, Ma., U.S.	207	42.15 N	72.34 W
South Hadley Falls	207	42.13 N	72.36 W
South Hamilton	207	42.36 N	70.52 W

Symbol	English	Deutsch	Español	Français	Português
≏	River	Fluß	Río	Rivière	Rio
≖	Canal	Kanal	Canal	Canal	Canal
⌞	Waterfall, Rapids	Wasserfall, Stromschnellen	Cascada, Rápidos	Chute d'eau, Rapides	Cascata, Rápidos
⊔	Strait	Meeresstraße	Estrecho	Détroit	Estreito
⊂	Bay, Gulf	Bucht, Golf	Bahía, Golfo	Baie, Golfe	Baía, Golfo
⊜	Lake, Lakes	See, Seen	Lago, Lagos	Lac, Lacs	Lago, Lagos
≋	Swamp	Sumpf	Pantano	Marais	Pântano
⊓	Ice Features, Glacier	Eis- und Gletscherformen	Accidentes Glaciales	Formes glaciaires	Acidentes glaciares
⊤	Other Hydrographic Features	Andere Hydrographische Objekte	Otros Elementos Hidrográficos	Autres données hydrographiques	Outros acidentes hidrográficos
✢	Submarine Features	Untermeerische Objekte	Accidentes Submarinos	Formes de relief sous-marin	Acidentes submarinos
□	Political Unit	Politische Einheit	Unidad Política	Entité politique	Unidade política
ʋ	Cultural Institution	Kulturelle Institution	Institución Cultural	Institution culturelle	Instituição cultural
⊥	Historical Site	Historische Stätte	Sitio Histórico	Site historique	Sitio histórico
♠	Recreational Site	Erholungs- und Ferienort	Sitio de Recreo	Centre de loisirs	Area de Lazer
⊠	Airport	Flughafen	Aeropuerto	Aéroport	Aeroporto
■	Military Installation	Militäranlage	Instalación Militar	Installation militaire	Instalação militar
◆	Miscellaneous	Verschiedenes	Misceláneo	Divers	Diversos

Other Topographic Features	Andere Topographische Objekte	Otros Elementos Topográficos	Outros Elementos Topográficos	
Islands	Inseln	Islas	Ilhas	
Island	Insel	Isla	Ilha	
Cape	Kap	Cabo	Cabo	
Plain	Ebene	Llano	Planície	
Valley, Canyon	Tal, Cañon	Valle, Cañón	Vale, Canhão	
Pass	Paß	Paso	Passo	
Mountains	Gebirge	Montañas	Montanhas	
Mountain	Berg	Montaña	Montanha	

Name	Lat.°	Long.°		Name	Page
				Länge° E=Ost	Seite
				Breite°	

ESPAÑOL

Nombre	Página	Lat.°′	Long.°′ W = Oeste
Springs	**158**	26.13 S	28.25 E
Springs □[5]	**273d**	26.14 S	28.30 E
Springs Aerodrome ⊠	**273d**	26.15 S	28.24 E
Springside	**285**	40.04 N	74.51 W
Springs Junction	**172**	42.19 S	172.11 E
Springsure	**166**	24.07 S	148.05 E
Springton	**168b**	34.43 S	139.05 E
Springtown	**222**	32.58 N	97.41 W
Springvale, Austl.	**162**	17.48 S	127.41 E
Springvale, Austl.	**166**	23.33 S	140.42 E
Springvale, Austl.	**169**	37.57 S	145.09 E
Springvale, Me., U.S.	**188**	43.28 N	70.47 W
Springvale South	**274b**	37.58 S	145.09 E
Spring Valley, Ca., U.S.	**228**	32.44 N	116.59 W
Spring Valley, Il., U.S.	**190**	41.19 N	89.11 W
Spring Valley, Mn., U.S.	**190**	43.41 N	92.23 W
Spring Valley, N.Y., U.S.	**210**	41.06 N	74.02 W
Spring Valley, Oh., U.S.	**218**	39.36 N	84.00 W
Spring Valley, Tx., U.S.	**222**	29.47 N	95.31 W
Spring Valley, Wi., U.S.	**190**	44.50 N	92.14 W
Spring Valley V	**204**	39.15 N	114.25 W
Spring Valley Creek ≃	**204**	39.20 N	114.25 W
Springview	**198**	42.49 N	99.44 W
Springville, Al., U.S.	**194**	33.46 N	86.28 W
Springville, Ca., U.S.	**204**	36.08 N	118.49 W
Springville, Ia., U.S.	**190**	42.03 N	91.26 W
Springville, N.J., U.S.	**285**	39.56 N	74.52 W
Springville, N.Y., U.S.	**210**	42.30 N	78.40 W
Springville, Pa., U.S.	**210**	41.42 N	75.55 W
Springville, Ut,. U.S.	**200**	40.09 N	111.36 W
Springwater	**210**	42.38 N	77.35 W
Springwood	**170**	33.42 S	150.33 E
Sprint ≃	**44**	54.22 N	2.45 W
Sprite Creek ≃	**210**	43.08 N	74.44 W
Sproat Lake ⊜	**182**	49.16 N	125.03 W
Sprockhövel	**56**	51.22 N	7.15 E
Sprogels Run ≃	**285**	40.14 N	75.37 W
Sprogø I	**41**	55.20 N	10.58 E
Sprötze	**52**	53.18 N	9.49 E
Sproul	**214**	40.16 N	78.28 W
Sprout Brook ≃	**276**	40.54 N	74.05 W
Spruce ≃	**184**	53.15 N	105.43 W
Spruce Brook	**186**	48.45 N	58.11 W
Spruce Creek	**214**	40.37 N	78.08 W
Spruce Creek ≃	**210**	43.07 N	74.46 W
Spruce Grove	**182**	53.32 N	113.55 W
Spruce Knob ∧	**188**	38.42 N	79.32 W
Spruce Knob-Seneca Rocks National Recreation Area ♠	**188**	38.50 N	79.20 W
Spruce Lake	**184**	53.32 N	109.05 W
Spruce Mountain ∧, Az., U.S.	**200**	34.28 N	112.24 W
Spruce Mountain ∧, Nv., U.S.	**204**	40.33 N	114.49 W
Spruce Pine, Al., U.S.	**194**	34.23 N	87.43 W
Spruce Pine, N.C., U.S.	**192**	35.54 N	82.03 W
Spruce Run Reservoir ⊜[1]	**210**	40.40 N	74.57 W
Spruce Run State Park ♠	**210**	40.40 N	74.56 W
Spruce Woods Provincial Park ♠	**184**	49.42 N	99.05 W
Spry	**208**	39.55 N	76.41 W
Spry Lake ⊜	**212**	44.44 N	81.15 W
Spulico, Capo ›	**68**	39.58 N	16.39 E
Spur	**196**	33.28 N	100.51 W
Spurfield	**182**	55.13 N	114.16 W
Spurger	**194**	30.42 N	94.11 W
Spurn Head ›	**44**	53.34 N	0.07 E
Spurr, Mount ∧	**180**	61.18 N	152.15 W
Sputendorf	**264a**	52.20 N	13.13 E
Spuzzum	**182**	49.41 N	121.25 W
Spy Hill	**184**	50.36 N	101.41 W
Spy Pond ⊜	**283**	42.24 N	71.09 W
Squally Channel ⊔	**182**	53.10 N	129.15 W
Squamish	**182**	49.42 N	123.09 W
Squamish ≃	**182**	49.45 N	123.09 W
Squam Lake ⊜	**188**	43.45 N	71.32 W
Square Butte Creek ≃	**198**	46.55 N	100.55 W
Square Lake ⊜	**186**	47.03 N	68.20 W
Squatec	**186**	47.53 N	68.43 W
Squaw Cap Mountain ∧	**186**	47.53 N	66.53 W
Squaw Creek ≃, Id., U.S.	**202**	43.51 N	116.22 W
Squaw Creek ≃, Il., U.S.	**278**	42.21 N	88.07 W
Squaw Creek ≃, Or., U.S.	**202**	44.27 N	121.20 W
Squaw Creek Lake ⊜[1]	**222**	32.19 N	97.47 W
Squaw Harbor	**180**	55.11 N	160.30 W
Squaw Hill ∧	**200**	41.48 N	105.02 W
Squaw Island I	**284a**	42.56 N	78.54 W
Squaw Peak ∧, Ca., U.S.	**226**	39.11 N	120.16 W
Squaw Peak ∧, Mt., U.S.	**202**	47.10 N	114.21 W
Squaw Rapids	**184**	53.41 N	103.20 W
Squaw Rapids Dam ◆[6]	**184**	53.40 N	103.25 W
Squaw Run ≃	**279b**	40.29 N	79.52 W
Squaw Valley State Recreation Area ♠	**226**	39.12 N	120.15 W
Squibnocket Point ›	**207**	41.18 N	70.47 W
Squilax	**182**	50.52 N	119.35 W
Squillace	**68**	38.47 N	16.31 E
Squillace, Golfo di ⊂	**68**	38.50 N	16.50 E
Squinzano	**68**	40.26 N	18.03 E
Squire	**192**	37.14 N	81.36 W
Squires, Mount ∧	**162**	26.12 S	127.28 E
Squirrel ≃	**180**	66.57 N	160.27 W
Squirrel Hill ◆[8]	**279b**	40.26 N	79.55 W
Squirrel Hill Tunnel ◆[5]	**279b**	40.26 N	79.55 W
Squirrel's Heath ◆[8]	**260**	51.35 N	0.13 E
Şragen	**115a**	7.26 S	111.02 E
Šramkovka	**78**	50.10 N	32.05 E
Srbija (Serbia) □[3]	**38**	44.00 N	21.00 E
Srbobran	**38**	45.33 N	19.48 E
Srê Âmběl	**110**	11.07 N	103.46 E
Sredinnyj chrebet ⩘	**74**	56.00 N	158.00 E
Sredna Gora ⩘	**38**	42.30 N	25.00 E
Sredn'aja Achtuba	**80**	48.43 N	44.52 E
Sredn'aja Mokla ≃	**88**	55.01 N	119.37 E
Sredn'aja Nanaki, gora ∧	**89**	52.26 N	132.50 E
Sredn'aja Ol'okma	**88**	55.26 N	120.33 E
Srednegorje	**76**	60.34 N	29.25 E
Sredneje Kujto, ozero ⊜	**24**	65.08 N	31.15 E
Srednekolymsk	**74**	67.27 N	153.41 E
Srednerusskaja vozvyšennost' ⩘[1]	**72**	52.00 N	38.00 E
Srednesibirskoje ploskogorje ⩘[1]	**74**	65.00 N	105.00 E
Srednij Ikorec	**78**	51.05 N	39.45 E
Srednij Kalar	**88**	55.51 N	117.24 E
Srednij Ural ⩘	**86**	58.00 N	59.00 E
Srednij Urgal	**89**	51.09 N	132.59 E
Srednij Vas'ugan	**86**	59.16 N	78.15 E
Srednyj	**83**	48.09 N	39.50 E
Srê Khtŭm	**110**	12.10 N	106.52 E
Śrem	**30**	52.08 N	17.01 E
Srê Moăt	**110**	13.18 N	107.10 E
Sremska Mitrovica	**38**	44.58 N	19.37 E
Sremski Karlovci	**38**	45.12 N	19.57 E
Srêng ≃	**110**	13.21 N	103.27 E
Srêpŏk ≃	**110**	13.33 N	106.16 E
Sretensk	**88**	52.15 N	117.43 E

FRANÇAIS

Nom	Page	Lat.°′	Long.°′ W = Ouest
Sretenskoje	**88**	56.28 N	96.25 E
Srīdharpur	**126**	23.04 N	89.25 E
Sri Hargobindpur	**123**	31.41 N	75.39 E
Sri Jayawardenepura (Kotte)	**122**	6.54 N	79.54 E
Srīkākulam	**122**	18.18 N	83.54 E
Sri Kālahasti	**122**	13.45 N	79.43 E
Sri Lanka □[1], Asia	**118**	7.00 N	81.00 E
Sri Lanka □[1], Asia	**122**	7.00 N	81.00 E
Srīnagar, Bngl.	**126**	23.32 N	90.18 E
Srīnagar, India	**123**	34.05 N	74.49 E
Srīnagar, India	**124**	30.13 N	78.47 E
Srīnagar Airport ⊠	**123**	34.00 N	74.52 E
Srīpur, Bngl.	**126**	24.12 N	90.29 E
Srīpur, Bngl.	**126**	23.36 N	89.24 E
Srīrampur, India	**122**	19.34 N	74.34 E
Srirāmpur, India	**272b**	22.49 N	88.29 E
Srīrangam	**122**	10.52 N	78.41 E
Srīvardhan	**122**	18.02 N	73.01 E
Srīvilliputtūr	**122**	9.31 N	77.38 E
Środa Śląska	**30**	51.10 N	16.36 E
Środa Wielkopolski	**30**	52.14 N	17.17 E
Srpska Crnja	**38**	45.43 N	20.42 E
Ssangmun-ni ◆[8]	**271b**	37.39 N	127.02 E
Ssuchunghsi	**100**	22.06 N	120.44 E
Ssup'ing → Siping	**89**	43.12 N	124.20 E
Staaken ◆[8]	**264a**	52.32 N	13.08 E
Staaten ≃	**164**	16.24 S	141.17 E
Staaten River National Park ♠	**164**	16.40 S	143.00 E
Staatsburg	**210**	41.50 N	73.55 W
Staatz	**61**	48.40 N	16.29 E
Stabbursdalen Nasjonalpark ♠	**24**	70.06 N	24.30 E
Staberhuk ›	**54**	54.24 N	11.19 E
Stabroek	**50**	51.20 N	4.22 E
Stachanov	**83**	48.34 N	38.40 E
Stachy	**60**	49.06 N	13.40 E
Stack, Loch ⊜	**46**	58.20 N	4.55 W
Stackpoie Head ›	**42**	51.37 N	4.54 W
Stack Skerry I[2]	**46**	59.01 N	4.31 W
Stacksteads	**262**	53.41 N	2.13 W
Stacyville	**190**	43.26 N	92.46 W
Stad-Delden	**52**	52.16 N	6.42 E
Stade	**52**	53.36 N	9.28 E
Staden, Bel.	**50**	50.59 N	3.01 E
Staden, Dtsch.	**56**	50.20 N	8.54 E
Städjan ∧	**26**	61.55 N	12.52 E
Stadl an der Mur	**61**	47.05 N	13.58 E
Stadlandet ›[1]	**26**	62.07 N	5.18 E
Stadlau ◆[8]	**264b**	48.14 N	16.28 E
Stadl-Paura	**64**	48.05 N	13.53 E
Stadskanaal	**52**	53.00 N	6.55 E
Stadtallendorf	**56**	50.50 N	9.01 E
Stadtbergen	**58**	48.22 N	10.50 E
Stadt Haag	**30**	48.07 N	14.34 E
Stadthagen	**52**	52.19 N	9.13 E
Stadtilm	**54**	50.47 N	11.05 E
Städtische Rahmede	**263**	51.17 N	7.40 E
Stadtkyll	**56**	50.21 N	6.32 E
Stadtlauringen	**56**	50.11 N	10.22 E
Stadtlengsfeld	**56**	50.47 N	10.07 E
Stadtlohn	**52**	51.59 N	6.55 E
Stadtoldendorf	**52**	51.53 N	9.37 E
Stadtprozelten	**56**	49.47 N	9.25 E
Stadtroda	**54**	50.51 N	11.44 E
Stadtsteinach	**54**	50.09 N	11.30 E
Stadt Wehlen	**54**	50.58 N	14.02 E
Stadum	**41**	54.44 N	9.03 E
Stäfa	**58**	47.15 N	8.44 E
Staffa I	**46**	56.25 N	6.20 W
Staffanstorp	**41**	55.38 N	13.13 E
Staffelberg ∧	**56**	50.06 N	11.02 E
Staffelde	**264a**	52.44 N	13.00 E
Staffelsee ⊜	**64**	47.42 N	11.10 E
Staffelstein	**56**	50.06 N	11.00 E
Staffin	**46**	57.37 N	6.12 W
Staffora ≃	**62**	45.04 N	9.01 E
Stafford, Eng., U.K.	**42**	52.48 N	2.07 W
Stafford, Ct., U.S.	**207**	41.59 N	72.17 W
Stafford, Ks., U.S.	**198**	37.57 N	98.36 W
Stafford, N.Y., U.S.	**210**	42.59 N	78.04 W
Stafford, Tx., U.S.	**222**	29.37 N	95.34 W
Stafford, Va., U.S.	**208**	38.25 N	77.24 W
Stafford □[6]	**208**	38.25 N	77.30 W
Staffordshire □[6]	**28**	52.50 N	2.00 W
Stafford Springs	**207**	41.57 N	72.18 W
Staffordsville	**188**	37.49 N	82.50 W
Staffordville	**207**	41.59 N	72.15 W
Stagen	**112**	3.18 S	116.10 E
Stag Pond ⊜	**276**	40.59 N	74.42 W
Stahl-Berg ∧[2]	**264a**	52.21 N	13.46 E
Stahlbrode	**54**	54.14 N	13.17 E
Stahle	**52**	51.50 N	9.25 E
Stahnsdorf	**54**	52.23 N	13.13 E
Stahringen	**58**	47.47 N	8.58 E
Staicele	**76**	57.50 N	24.45 E
Staines	**42**	51.26 N	0.31 W
Staines Reservoirs ⊜[1]	**260**	51.27 N	0.30 W
Stainforth	**44**	53.36 N	1.01 W
Staining	**44**	53.49 N	2.59 W
Stainland	**262**	53.40 N	1.53 W
Stainmore Forest ◆[3]	**44**	54.30 N	2.10 W
Stains	**261**	48.57 N	2.23 E
Stainz	**61**	46.54 N	15.16 E
Stairtown	**222**	29.43 N	97.44 W
Stajki	**78**	50.05 N	30.54 E
Staked Plain → Estacado, Llano ≚	**196**	33.30 N	102.40 W
Stäket	**40**	59.28 N	17.48 E
Stakroge	**41**	55.53 N	8.51 E
Stalać	**38**	43.40 N	21.25 E
Stalbridge	**42**	50.58 N	2.23 W
Stalden	**58**	46.14 N	7.52 E
Stalettì	**68**	38.46 N	16.32 E
Stalham	**42**	52.47 N	1.31 E
Stalheim	**26**	60.50 N	6.40 E
Stalhofen	**61**	47.05 N	15.16 E
Stalinabad → Dušanbe	**85**	38.35 N	68.48 E
Stalin → Brașov	**38**	45.39 N	25.37 E
Stalin → Kuçovë	**38**	40.48 N	19.54 E
Stalingrad → Volgograd	**80**	48.44 N	44.25 E
Stalino → Doneck	**83**	48.00 N	37.48 E
Stalinogorsk → Novomoskovsk	**82**	54.05 N	38.13 E
Stalinsk → Novokuzneck	**86**	53.45 N	87.06 E
Stalin → Varna	**38**	43.13 N	27.55 E
Stallarholmen	**40**	59.22 N	17.12 E
Ställberg	**40**	59.59 N	14.55 E
Ställdalen	**40**	59.56 N	14.56 E
Stallwang	**60**	49.03 N	12.40 E
Stalowa Wola	**30**	50.35 N	22.02 E
Stalybridge, Eng., U.K.	**44**	53.29 N	2.03 W
Stalybridge, Eng., U.K.	**262**	53.29 N	2.04 W
Stambaugh	**190**	46.04 N	88.37 W
Stamford, Austl.	**166**	21.16 S	143.49 E
Stamford, Eng., U.K.	**42**	52.39 N	0.29 W
Stamford, Ct., U.S.	**207**	41.03 N	73.32 W
Stamford, N.Y., U.S.	**210**	42.24 N	74.36 W
Stamford, Tx., U.S.	**196**	32.56 N	99.48 W
Stamford, Vt., U.S.	**207**	42.45 N	73.04 W
Stamford, Lake ⊜[1]	**196**	33.05 N	99.35 W
Stamford Bridge	**44**	53.59 N	0.55 W
Stamford Brige Stadium ♠	**260**	51.29 N	0.11 W
Stamford Harbor ⊂	**276**	41.02 N	73.32 W
Stamford Museum ⊍	**276**	41.07 N	73.33 W
Stammbach	**54**	50.09 N	11.41 E

PORTUGUÊS

Nome	Página	Lat.°′	Long.°′ W = Oeste
Stammersdorf ◆[8]	**264b**	48.18 N	16.25 E
Stammham	**60**	48.15 N	12.53 E
Stammheim, Dtsch.	**56**	48.41 N	8.46 E
Stammheim, Schw.	**58**	47.38 N	8.47 E
Stampede Reservoir ⊜[1]	**226**	39.29 N	120.07 W
Stamping Ground	**218**	38.16 N	84.41 W
Stampriet	**156**	24.20 S	18.28 E
Stamps	**194**	33.21 N	93.29 W
Stams	**64**	47.16 N	10.59 E
Stanaford	**188**	37.48 N	81.09 W
Stanardsville	**188**	38.17 N	78.26 W
Stanberry	**194**	40.13 N	94.32 W
Stanborough	**260**	51.47 N	0.13 W
Stancija-Gorčakovo	**85**	40.25 N	71.45 E
Stancionno-Ojašinskij	**86**	55.28 N	83.53 E
Standard, Ab., Can.	**182**	51.07 N	112.59 W
Standard, Ak., U.S.	**180**	64.47 N	148.32 W
Standard, Ca., U.S.	**226**	37.59 N	120.20 W
Standard, Pa., U.S.	**214**	40.10 N	79.32 W
Standard Oil Company Refinery ⊍[3]	**282**	37.57 N	122.24 W
Standard Shaft	**279b**	40.10 N	79.32 W
Standedge Canal Tunnel ◆[5]	**262**	53.34 N	2.00 W
Standedge Railway Tunnel ◆[5]	**262**	53.34 N	2.00 W
Standerton	**158**	26.58 S	29.07 E
Standiford Field ⊠	**218**	38.11 N	85.44 W
Standing Rock Indian Reservation ◆[4]	**198**	45.50 N	101.10 W
Standing Stone Creek ≃	**214**	40.30 N	78.00 W
Standing Stones ⊥	**46**	58.12 N	6.48 W
Standish, Eng., U.K.	**44**	53.36 N	2.41 W
Standish, Mi., U.S.	**190**	43.58 N	83.57 W
Standish Monument ⊥	**283**	42.01 N	70.41 W
Standon	**42**	51.53 N	0.02 E
Stanfield, Az., U.S.	**200**	32.52 N	111.57 W
Stanfield, Or., U.S.	**202**	45.46 N	119.12 W
Stanford, S. Afr.	**158**	34.26 S	19.29 E
Stanford, Ca., U.S.	**226**	37.25 N	122.08 W
Stanford, Ky., U.S.	**192**	37.31 N	84.39 W
Stanford, Mt., U.S.	**202**	47.09 N	110.13 W
Stanford Center ◆[9]	**282**	37.27 N	122.10 W
Stanford Heights	**210**	42.46 N	73.53 W
Stanford le Hope	**42**	51.31 N	0.26 E
Stanford Linear Accelerator ⊍[3]	**282**	37.25 N	122.12 W
Stanford Rivers	**260**	51.41 N	0.13 E
Stanford University ⊍[2]	**282**	37.26 N	122.10 W
Stanfordville	**210**	41.52 N	73.43 W
Stånga	**26**	57.17 N	18.28 E
Stångån ≃	**26**	58.27 N	15.37 E
Stångby	**41**	55.46 N	13.10 E
Stange	**26**	60.43 N	11.11 E
Stanger	**158**	29.27 S	31.14 E
Stanghella	**64**	45.08 N	11.45 E
Stanhope, Eng., U.K.	**44**	54.45 N	2.01 W
Stanhope, Ia., U.S.	**190**	42.17 N	93.47 W
Stanhope, N.J., U.S.	**210**	40.54 N	74.42 W
Staničnо-Luganskoje	**83**	48.39 N	39.30 E
Stanislaus □[6]	**226**	37.39 N	121.00 W
Stanislaus ≃	**226**	37.40 N	121.14 W
Stanislaus, Clark Fork ≃	**226**	38.22 N	119.52 W
Stanislaus, Middle Fork ≃	**226**	38.09 N	120.21 W
Stanislaus, North Fork ≃	**226**	38.09 N	120.21 W
Stanislaus, South Fork ≃	**226**	38.04 N	120.25 W
Stanislav	**78**	46.34 N	32.09 E
Stanislavčik	**78**	48.58 N	28.07 E
Stanislav → Ivano-Frankovsk	**78**	48.55 N	24.43 E
Stanisławów → Ivano-Frankovsk	**78**	48.55 N	24.43 E
Stanke Dimitrov	**38**	42.16 N	23.07 E
Staňkov	**60**	49.34 N	13.04 E
Stanley, Austl.	**166**	40.46 S	145.18 E
Stanley, N.B., Can.	**186**	46.17 N	66.44 W
Stanley, Falk. Is.	**254**	51.42 S	57.51 W
Stanley, H.K.	**271d**	22.13 N	114.12 E
Stanley, Eng., U.K.	**44**	54.52 N	1.42 W
Stanley, Scot., U.K.	**46**	56.28 N	3.27 W
Stanley, N.Y., U.S.	**210**	42.49 N	77.06 W
Stanley, N.C., U.S.	**192**	35.21 N	81.05 W
Stanley, N.D., U.S.	**198**	48.19 N	102.23 W
Stanley, Va., U.S.	**188**	38.34 N	78.30 W
Stanley, Wi., U.S.	**190**	44.57 N	90.56 W
Stanley ≃	**171a**	27.09 S	152.32 E
Stanley, Mont ∧[2]	**273b**	4.19 S	15.15 E
Stanley Bay ⊂	**271d**	22.12 N	114.12 E
Stanley Falls ∟	**154**	0.30 N	25.12 E
Stanley Mills	**275b**	43.46 N	79.44 W
Stanley Mound ∧	**271d**	22.14 N	114.12 E
Stanley Park ♠, B.C., Can.	**224**	49.19 N	123.09 W
Stanley Park ♠, Eng., U.K.	**262**	53.26 N	2.57 W
Stanley Park ♠, Eng., U.K.	**262**	53.49 N	3.02 W
Stanley Reservoir ⊜[1]	**122**	11.54 N	77.50 E
Stanleyville → Kisangani	**154**	0.30 N	25.12 E
Stanlow	**44**	53.17 N	2.52 W
Stanmore ◆[8]	**260**	51.37 N	0.19 W
Stannards	**210**	42.05 N	77.55 W
Stannington	**44**	55.06 N	1.40 W
Stanovoj chrebet ⩘	**74**	56.20 N	126.00 E
Stanovoje nagorje (Stanovoy Mountains) ⩘	**88**	56.00 N	114.00 E
Stanovoj Kolodez'	**76**	52.51 N	36.16 E
Stanovoy Mountains → Stanovoje nagorje ⩘	**88**	56.00 N	114.00 E
Stans	**58**	46.57 N	8.22 E
Stansbury	**168b**	34.55 S	137.47 E
Stansmore Range ⩘	**162**	21.23 S	128.33 E
Stansstad	**58**	46.59 N	8.20 E
Stanstead	**206**	45.01 N	72.05 W
Stanstead □[6]	**206**	45.10 N	72.00 W
Stanstead Abbots	**42**	51.47 N	0.01 E
Stansted	**260**	51.20 N	0.18 E
Stansted Mountfitchet	**42**	51.54 N	0.12 E
Stanthorpe	**166**	28.39 S	151.57 E
Stanton, Eng., U.K.	**42**	52.19 N	0.53 E
Stanton, Ca., U.S.	**228**	33.48 N	117.59 W
Stanton, De., U.S.	**208**	39.43 N	75.37 W
Stanton, Ia., U.S.	**198**	41.05 N	95.11 W
Stanton, Ky., U.S.	**192**	37.50 N	83.51 W
Stanton, Mi., U.S.	**190**	43.17 N	85.04 W
Stanton, Mo., U.S.	**219**	38.16 N	91.06 W
Stanton, Ne., U.S.	**198**	41.57 N	97.13 W
Stanton, N.D., U.S.	**198**	47.19 N	101.22 W
Stanton, Tn., U.S.	**194**	35.27 N	89.24 W
Stanton, Tx., U.S.	**196**	32.07 N	101.47 W
Stantonsburg	**192**	35.36 N	77.49 W
Stanwell	**260**	51.27 N	0.29 W
Stanwell Moor	**260**	51.28 N	0.30 W
Stanwood	**224**	48.14 N	122.22 W
Stanwood Gardens	**285**	40.07 N	74.57 W
Stanwyck Estates	**285**	39.42 N	75.33 W
Stanzach	**58**	47.23 N	10.34 E
Stanz im Mürztal	**61**	47.28 N	15.30 E
Stapelburg	**54**	51.53 N	10.40 E
Stapelfeld	**52**	53.36 N	10.13 E
Staphorst	**52**	52.37 N	6.12 E
Stapleford	**42**	52.56 N	1.16 W
Stapleford Abbotts	**260**	51.38 N	0.10 E
Stapleford Aerodrome ⊠	**260**	51.39 N	0.08 E
Stapleford Tawney	**260**	51.40 N	0.11 E
Staplehurst	**42**	51.10 N	0.33 E
Staples	**198**	46.21 N	94.47 W
Stapleton, Al., U.S.	**194**	30.44 N	87.47 W
Stapleton, Ne., U.S.	**198**	41.28 N	100.30 W
Stąporków	**30**	51.09 N	20.34 E
Star', Ross.	**76**	53.37 N	34.09 E
Star, Ms., U.S.	**194**	32.05 N	90.02 W
Star, N.C., U.S.	**192**	35.24 N	79.47 W
Stará Boleslav	**54**	50.12 N	14.42 E
Starachowice	**30**	51.03 N	21.04 E
Stara Fužina	**64**	46.17 N	13.54 E
Staraja	**265a**	59.55 N	30.38 E
Staraja Belica, Bela.	**76**	54.42 N	29.38 E
Staraja Belica, Ross.	**78**	51.59 N	35.13 E
Staraja Belogorka	**80**	52.05 N	53.17 E
Staraja Derevn'a ◆[8]	**265a**	59.59 N	30.15 E
Staraja Duginka	**82**	54.20 N	38.45 E
Staraja Kriuša	**78**	50.12 N	41.09 E
Staraja Kulatka	**80**	52.43 N	47.37 E
Staraja Kupavna	**82**	55.48 N	38.10 E
Staraja Majačka	**78**	46.30 N	33.11 E
Staraja Majna	**80**	54.36 N	48.57 E
Staraja Poltavka	**80**	50.28 N	46.28 E
Staraja Porubežka	**80**	52.03 N	49.11 E
Staraja Račejka	**80**	53.22 N	48.03 E
Staraja Rudn'a	**76**	52.50 N	30.17 E
Staraja Russa	**76**	58.00 N	31.23 E
Staraja Ruza	**82**	55.39 N	36.20 E
Staraja Sachča	**80**	54.25 N	49.58 E
Staraja Sin'ava	**78**	49.36 N	27.37 E
Staraja Sitn'a	**82**	54.56 N	38.09 E
Staraja Terizmorga	**80**	54.16 N	44.32 E
Staraja Toropa	**76**	56.17 N	31.40 E
Staraja Ušica	**78**	48.35 N	27.07 E
Staraja Veduga	**78**	51.48 N	38.31 E
Staraja Vičuga	**80**	57.16 N	41.53 E
Staraja Vyževka	**78**	51.27 N	24.24 E
Staranzano	**64**	45.49 N	13.30 E
Stara Pazova	**38**	44.59 N	20.10 E
Stara Planina (Balkan Mountains) ⩘	**38**	42.45 N	25.00 E
Stará Role	**54**	50.14 N	12.47 E
Starav, Ben ∧	**46**	56.32 N	5.03 W
Stará Voda	**60**	50.00 N	12.36 E
Stara Zagora	**38**	42.25 N	25.38 E
Starbejevo	**265b**	55.55 N	37.28 E
Starbrick	**214**	41.50 N	79.12 W
Starbuck, Mb., Can.	**184**	49.46 N	97.36 W
Starbuck, Mn., U.S.	**198**	45.36 N	95.31 W
Starbuck, Wa., U.S.	**202**	46.31 N	118.07 W
Starbuck I	**14**	5.37 S	155.53 W
Starčenkovo	**78**	47.17 N	36.59 E
Star City, Sk., Can.	**184**	52.53 N	104.21 W
Star City, Ar., U.S.	**194**	33.56 N	91.50 W
Star City, In., U.S.	**216**	40.58 N	86.33 W
Starcross	**42**	50.38 N	3.27 W
Stare Czarnowo	**54**	53.16 N	14.45 E
Staré Sedliště	**60**	49.45 N	12.42 E
Starford	**214**	40.42 N	78.58 W
Stargard Szczeciński (Stargard in Pommern)	**30**	53.20 N	15.02 E
Stargo	**200**	33.04 N	109.21 W
Star Harbour ⊂	**175e**	10.47 S	162.18 E
Stari Bar	**38**	42.06 N	19.08 E
Starica, Ross.	**76**	56.30 N	34.56 E
Starica, Ross.	**76**	59.04 N	29.30 E
Starica, Ross.	**80**	48.13 N	45.56 E
Stari Grad	**36**	43.11 N	16.36 E
Starij R'ad	**76**	58.05 N	34.54 E
Starina	**76**	59.37 N	44.42 E
Stari Vlah ◆[1]	**38**	43.35 N	20.15 E
Star Junction	**214**	40.04 N	79.46 W
Stark □[6]	**214**	40.48 N	81.22 W
Starke	**192**	29.56 N	82.06 W
Starke □[6]	**216**	41.18 N	86.37 W
Starkey	**210**	42.32 N	76.56 W
Starkville	**194**	33.27 N	88.49 W
Star Lake	**224**	47.22 N	122.18 W
Star Mountains ⩘	**164**	5.05 S	141.05 E
Starnberg	**60**	48.00 N	11.20 E
Starnberger See ⊜	**64**	47.55 N	11.18 E
Starnikovo	**82**	55.22 N	38.24 E
Staroalejskoje	**86**	51.00 N	82.01 E
Starobačaty	**86**	54.14 N	86.07 E
Starobaltačevo	**86**	56.01 N	55.56 E
Starobel'sk	**83**	49.16 N	38.56 E
Starobeševo	**83**	47.44 N	38.03 E
Starobin	**76**	52.44 N	27.28 E
Staročerkasskaja	**83**	47.15 N	40.03 E
Starocuruchajtuj	**88**	50.12 N	119.15 E
Staroderev'ankov-Skaja	**78**	46.08 N	38.58 E
Starodub	**76**	52.35 N	32.46 E
Starod'umejevo	**80**	55.16 N	54.22 E
Starogan'kino	**80**	53.55 N	52.15 E
Starogard Gdański	**30**	53.59 N	18.33 E
Staroignatjevka	**83**	47.32 N	37.47 E
Staroje	**76**	59.16 N	40.40 E
Staroje Bajsarovo	**80**	55.31 N	53.54 E
Staroje Drožžanoje	**80**	54.44 N	47.34 E
Staroje Ibrajkino	**80**	54.52 N	51.02 E
Staroje Jaškino	**80**	52.49 N	52.57 E
Staroje Jermakovo	**80**	54.04 N	51.59 E
Staroje Oleničevo	**80**	45.34 N	47.11 E
Staroje Rachino	**76**	58.08 N	32.39 E
Staroje Šajgovo	**80**	54.18 N	44.26 E
Staroje Šajmurzino	**80**	54.45 N	47.58 E
Staroje Selo	**76**	55.14 N	29.54 E
Staroje Sindrovo	**80**	54.25 N	44.06 E
Staroje Slavkino	**80**	52.34 N	45.08 E
Staroje Ustje	**80**	53.28 N	41.51 E
Starojurjevo	**80**	53.21 N	40.42 E
Starokazačje	**78**	46.21 N	29.59 E
Starokonstantinov	**78**	49.46 N	27.13 E
Starokuručevo	**80**	55.09 N	54.04 E
Starolaspa	**83**	47.34 N	37.59 E
Staroleuškovskaja	**78**	45.59 N	39.44 E
Staromichajlovka	**83**	47.58 N	37.36 E
Starominskaja	**78**	46.31 N	39.04 E
Staromlinovka	**78**	47.42 N	36.49 E
Staromušta	**80**	55.49 N	54.14 E
Staronikolajevo	**82**	55.37 N	36.16 E
Staro-Podgorodneje	**82**	54.46 N	38.57 E
Staropokrovka	**85**	42.50 N	75.18 E
Staroščerbinovskaja	**78**	46.37 N	38.40 E
Staroseslavino	**80**	53.12 N	40.25 E
Starošešminsk	**80**	55.22 N	51.15 E
Starosiedle	**54**	51.50 N	14.50 E
Starosoldatskoje	**86**	56.12 N	72.37 E
Starosubchangulovo	**86**	53.06 N	57.26 E
Starotimoškino	**24**	53.43 N	47.32 E
Starotitarovskaja	**78**	45.14 N	37.09 E
Staroutkinsk	**86**	57.14 N	59.20 E
Staroverovka	**78**	49.33 N	35.42 E
Starožilovo	**80**	54.14 N	39.55 E
Starožil'sk	**80**	56.34 N	47.17 E
Star Peak ∧	**204**	40.32 N	118.10 W
Starr	**214**	41.32 N	79.22 W
Starrucca	**210**	41.54 N	75.28 W
Start Bay ⊂	**42**	50.17 N	3.36 W
Start Point ›	**42**	50.13 N	3.38 W
Startup	**224**	47.52 N	121.44 W
Starvation Reservoir ⊜[1]	**200**	40.15 N	110.30 W
Starved Rock State Park ♠	**216**	41.19 N	88.58 W
Staryj Ajbesi	**80**	54.57 N	47.03 E
Staryj-Ajdar	**83**	48.43 N	39.11 E
Staryj Bagr'až	**80**	54.54 N	51.39 E
Staryj Bir'uz'ak	**84**	44.47 N	46.54 E
Staryj Bol'ševik	**265b**	55.57 N	37.47 E
Staryj Čartorijsk	**78**	51.15 N	25.54 E
Staryj Chop'or	**80**	51.30 N	42.58 E
Staryj Čindant	**88**	50.33 N	115.33 E
Staryje Burasy	**80**	52.16 N	46.09 E
Staryje Dorogi	**76**	53.02 N	28.16 E
Staryje Maty	**80**	55.14 N	53.55 E
Staryje Popel'uchi	**78**	48.18 N	28.55 E
Staryje Senžary	**78**	49.25 N	34.27 E
Staryje Turdaki	**80**	53.55 N	45.29 E
Staryje Z'atcy	**80**	57.21 N	52.39 E
Staryj Kazangal	**80**	50.15 N	47.39 E
Staryj Kistruss	**80**	54.28 N	40.34 E
Staryj Krym, Ukr.	**78**	45.03 N	35.05 E
Staryj Krym, Ukr.	**83**	47.10 N	37.30 E
Staryj Lesken	**84**	43.20 N	43.55 E
Staryj Medved'	**76**	58.18 N	30.30 E
Staryj Merčik	**78**	49.58 N	35.46 E
Staryj Oskol	**78**	51.19 N	37.51 E
Staryj Sambor	**78**	49.27 N	22.59 E
Staryj Terek ≃	**84**	44.00 N	47.24 E
Staryj Tukšum	**80**	53.42 N	48.33 E
Starý Plzenec	**60**	49.42 N	13.28 E
Stary Sącz	**30**	49.34 N	20.38 E
Stassfurt	**54**	51.51 N	11.34 E
Staszów	**30**	50.34 N	21.20 E
State Center	**190**	42.01 N	93.09 W
State College	**214**	40.47 N	77.51 W
State Fair Grounds ♠	**284b**	39.27 N	76.38 W
Stateline, Ca., U.S.	**226**	38.57 N	119.57 W
State Line, Ms., U.S.	**194**	31.26 N	88.28 W
Stateline, Nv., U.S.	**204**	38.58 N	119.56 W
Staten Island I	**276**	40.35 N	74.09 W
Staten Island Mall ◆[9]	**276**	40.35 N	74.10 W
Statenville	**192**	30.42 N	83.01 W
State Park Place	**219**	38.40 N	90.03 W
State Road	**192**	36.19 N	80.52 W
Statesboro	**192**	32.26 N	81.47 W
Statesville	**192**	35.46 N	80.53 W
Stateville Correctional Center ⊍	**278**	41.35 N	88.06 W
Station Peak	**162**	21.10 S	118.11 E
Statte	**68**	40.34 N	17.12 E
Statue of Liberty National Monument ♠	**210**	40.41 N	74.03 W
Staubbachfall ∟	**58**	46.35 N	7.55 E
Staufen	**58**	47.53 N	7.44 E
Staufenberg	**56**	50.40 N	8.43 E
Staughton Vale	**169**	37.51 S	144.17 E
Staunton, Il., U.S.	**219**	39.00 N	89.47 W
Staunton, Va., U.S.	**188**	38.08 N	79.04 W
Staunton → Roanoke ≃	**192**	35.56 N	76.43 W
Stavanger	**26**	58.58 N	5.45 E
Stave ≃	**224**	49.10 N	122.26 W
Stave Lake ⊜	**182**	49.15 N	122.21 W
Staveley	**44**	53.16 N	1.20 W
Stavelot	**56**	50.23 N	5.56 E
Stavely, Ab., Can.	**182**	50.10 N	113.38 W
Stavely, Eng., U.K.	**44**	54.22 N	2.49 W
Staveren	**52**	52.53 N	5.22 E
Stavern	**26**	59.00 N	10.02 E
Stavišče	**78**	49.23 N	30.12 E
Stavnoje	**78**	48.59 N	22.40 E
Stavropol'	**72**	45.02 N	41.59 E
Stavropol' □[8]	**84**	44.38 N	43.30 E
Stavropol → Toljatti	**80**	53.31 N	49.26 E
Stavrovo	**80**	56.08 N	40.00 E
Stavsnäs	**40**	59.17 N	18.41 E
Stawell	**166**	37.04 S	142.46 E
Stawell ≃	**166**	20.38 S	142.55 E
Stawiski	**30**	53.23 N	22.09 E
Stawiszyn	**30**	51.55 N	18.07 E
Staxigoe	**46**	58.28 N	3.04 W
Stayner	**212**	44.25 N	80.05 W
Stayton	**202**	44.48 N	122.47 W
Stazzema	**64**	43.59 N	10.19 E
Steamboat	**226**	39.22 N	119.44 W
Steamboat Creek ≃	**226**	39.31 N	119.42 W
Steamboat Mountain ∧	**200**	41.58 N	108.58 W
Steamboat Slough ≃	**226**	38.11 N	121.40 W
Steamboat Springs	**200**	40.29 N	106.49 W
Steamburg	**210**	42.07 N	78.54 W
Stearns	**192**	36.41 N	84.28 W
Stearns Pond ⊜	**283**	42.37 N	71.04 W
Stębark	**30**	53.30 N	20.08 E
Stebbins	**180**	63.32 N	162.18 W
Stebl'ov	**78**	49.24 N	31.06 E
Stechow	**54**	52.38 N	12.28 E
Steckborn	**58**	47.40 N	8.55 E
Stederdorf	**52**	52.21 N	10.15 E
Stedten	**54**	51.26 N	11.41 E
Stedum	**52**	53.18 N	6.41 E
Steeg	**58**	47.14 N	10.17 E
Steel ≃	**190**	48.46 N	86.54 W
Steel City	**210**	40.38 N	75.20 W
Steele, Mo., U.S.	**194**	36.05 N	89.49 W
Steele, N.D., U.S.	**198**	46.51 N	99.54 W
Steele ◆[8]	**263**	51.27 N	7.05 E
Steele, Mount ∧	**200**	41.50 N	107.00 W
Steele Creek ≃, Tx., U.S.	**222**	31.13 N	96.19 W
Steele Creek ≃, Tx., U.S.	**222**	32.01 N	97.28 W
Steeles Corners	**275b**	43.48 N	79.25 W
Steeleville	**194**	38.00 N	89.39 W
Steelhead	**224**	49.13 N	122.19 W
Steel's Drift	**158**	27.21 S	29.30 E
Steels Point ›	**174c**	29.02 S	168.00 E
Steels Run ≃	**279b**	40.25 N	79.38 W
Steelton, N.Y., U.S.	**284a**	42.47 N	78.49 W
Steelton, Pa., U.S.	**208**	40.14 N	76.50 W
Steelville	**194**	37.58 N	91.21 W
Steenbergen	**52**	51.35 N	4.19 E
Steenburg Lake ⊜	**212**	44.50 N	77.41 W
Steenderen	**52**	52.04 N	6.11 E
Steens Mountain ⩘	**202**	42.35 N	118.40 W
Steenvoorde	**50**	50.48 N	2.35 E
Steenwijk	**52**	52.47 N	6.08 E
Steepbank ≃	**184**	57.01 N	111.28 W
Steephill Lake ⊜	**184**	55.58 N	103.08 W
Steep Holm I	**42**	51.21 N	3.07 W
Steeping ≃	**44**	53.06 N	0.18 E
Steeple Claydon	**42**	51.56 N	0.59 W
Steep Point ›	**162**	26.08 S	113.08 E
Steep Rock	**184**	51.26 N	98.48 W
Stefanie, Lake (Chew Bahir) ⊜	**144**	4.40 N	36.50 E
Stefansson Island I	**176**	73.20 N	105.45 W
Ştefan Vodă	**38**	44.19 N	27.19 E
Šteffisburg	**58**	46.47 N	7.39 E
Steg	**58**	47.21 N	8.56 E
Stegalovka	**76**	52.24 N	38.19 E
Stege	**41**	54.59 N	12.18 E
Stegeborg	**26**	58.26 N	16.35 E
Stege Bugt ⊂	**41**	55.01 N	12.50 E
Stegelitz	**54**	53.08 N	13.51 E
Steger	**216**	41.28 N	87.38 W
Stegersbach	**61**	47.10 N	16.10 E
Steglitz ◆[8]	**264a**	52.28 N	13.19 E
Stehag	**41**	55.54 N	13.23 E
Stehekin	**224**	48.18 N	120.39 W
Stehekin ≃	**224**	48.21 N	120.40 W
Steiermark □[3]	**30**	47.10 N	15.10 E
Steigerwald ⩘	**56**	49.40 N	10.20 E
Steigra	**54**	51.18 N	11.39 E
Steilacoom	**224**	47.10 N	122.36 W
Steimbke	**52**	52.40 N	9.22 E
Stein, Dtsch.	**60**	49.25 N	11.01 E
Stein, Ned.	**56**	50.57 N	5.46 E
Stein, Schw.	**58**	47.33 N	7.58 E
Steina	**54**	51.12 N	14.01 E
Steinach, Dtsch.	**54**	50.25 N	11.10 E
Steinach, Dtsch.	**58**	48.18 N	8.04 E
Steinach, Öst.	**64**	47.05 N	11.28 E
Steinach ≃	**56**	50.11 N	11.12 E
Steinamanger → Szombathely	**61**	47.14 N	16.38 E
Stein am Rhein	**58**	47.40 N	8.51 E
Steinau	**56**	50.23 N	9.27 E
Steinbach, Mb., Can.	**184**	49.32 N	96.41 W
Steinbach, Dtsch.	**56**	48.43 N	8.10 E
Steinbach-Hallenberg	**54**	50.42 N	10.34 E
Steinberg ∧[2]	**263**	51.05 N	7.27 E
Steinberger Slough ≃	**282**	37.33 N	122.13 W
Steinbourg	**56**	48.46 N	7.25 E
Steindorf	**61**	46.42 N	14.01 E
Steinen	**58**	47.38 N	7.44 E
Steinernes Meer ⩘	**64**	47.30 N	12.58 E
Steinfeld, Dtsch.	**52**	52.35 N	8.12 E
Steinfeld, Dtsch.	**54**	50.22 N	10.44 E
Steinfeld, Öst.	**64**	46.45 N	13.15 E
Steinfort	**56**	49.40 N	5.55 E
Steinforth	**263**	51.09 N	6.32 E
Steinfurt	**52**	52.09 N	7.21 E
Steingaden	**58**	47.42 N	10.51 E
Steinhagen, Dtsch.	**52**	52.00 N	8.24 E
Steinhagen, Dtsch.	**54**	54.13 N	12.59 E
Steinhatchee ≃	**192**	29.40 N	83.24 W
Steinhausen	**156**	21.49 S	18.20 E
Steinhausen ⊍[1]	**58**	48.01 N	9.41 E
Steinheid	**54**	50.28 N	11.04 E
Steinheim, Dtsch.	**52**	51.52 N	9.05 E
Steinheim, Dtsch.	**56**	48.58 N	9.16 E
Steinheim, Dtsch.	**58**	48.01 N	10.09 E
Steinhöfel	**54**	52.24 N	14.10 E
Steinhöring	**60**	48.05 N	12.02 E
Steinhude	**52**	52.27 N	9.21 E
Steinhuder Meer ⊜	**52**	52.28 N	9.19 E
Steinkjer	**26**	64.01 N	11.30 E
Steinkopf	**156**	29.18 S	17.43 E
Steinloge	**52**	52.54 N	8.19 E
Stein-Neukirch	**56**	50.41 N	8.03 E
Steinpass)(	**64**	47.39 N	12.45 E
Steinsdorf	**54**	52.02 N	14.40 E
Steinshamn	**26**	62.47 N	6.29 E
Steinstücken ◆[8]	**264a**	52.23 N	13.08 E
Steinwiesen	**54**	50.17 N	11.28 E
Stekene	**50**	51.12 N	4.02 E
Stekl'anka	**76**	59.08 N	41.37 E
Steklino	**76**	56.51 N	32.10 E
Steksovo	**80**	55.17 N	43.25 E
Stella, It.	**62**	44.24 N	8.30 E
Stella, S. Afr.	**158**	26.38 S	24.48 E
Stella, Ne., U.S.	**198**	40.13 N	95.46 W
Stella Niagara	**210**	43.12 N	79.02 W
Stella-Plage	**50**	50.29 N	1.35 E
Stellaquo Indian Reserve ◆[4]	**182**	54.03 N	124.55 W
Stellarton	**186**	45.34 N	62.40 W
Stelle	**52**	53.23 N	10.06 E
Stellenbosch	**158**	33.58 S	18.50 E
Steller, Mount ∧	**180**	60.30 N	143.02 W
Stelvio, Parco Nazionale dello ♠	**58**	46.30 N	10.40 E
Stelvio, Passo dello)(	**58**	46.32 N	10.27 E
Stemwede	**52**	52.25 N	8.27 E
Stenay	**56**	49.29 N	5.11 E
Stendal	**54**	52.36 N	11.51 E
Stende	**76**	57.09 N	22.33 E
Stenden	**263**	51.25 N	6.27 E
Stenhammar slott ⊥	**40**	59.03 N	16.31 E
Stenhouse Bay	**166**	35.17 S	136.56 E
Stenhousemuir	**46**	56.02 N	3.48 W
Stenico	**64**	46.03 N	10.51 E
Stenlille	**41**	55.32 N	11.36 E
Stenløse	**41**	55.46 N	12.12 E
Stenness, Loch of ⊜	**46**	59.00 N	3.15 W
Stenón	**267c**	37.58 N	22.20 E
Stenón Návstathmou ⊔	**267c**	37.58 N	23.33 E
Stensätra	**40**	60.36 N	16.44 E
Stensele	**24**	65.05 N	17.09 E
Stenstorp	**26**	58.16 N	13.43 E
Stenstrup	**41**	55.07 N	10.31 E
Stentrop	**263**	51.30 N	7.49 E
Stenungsund	**26**	58.05 N	11.49 E
Stepan'	**78**	51.10 N	26.18 E
Stepanakert	**84**	39.49 N	46.44 E
Stepanavan	**84**	41.00 N	44.23 E
Stepancevo, Ross.	**80**	56.08 N	41.42 E
Stepancevo, Ross.	**82**	56.22 N	36.10 E
Stepancy	**78**	49.42 N	31.18 E
Stepano-Krynka	**83**	47.55 N	38.21 E
Stepanovka, Ross.	**80**	52.04 N	53.02 E
Stepanovka, Ross.	**86**	57.13 N	67.26 E
Stepanovka, Ukr.	**78**	50.58 N	34.37 E
Stepanovo	**82**	55.43 N	38.28 E
Stepanovskoje	**265b**	55.47 N	37.10 E
Stepan Razin	**84**	40.24 N	49.59 E
Stepanščino	**82**	55.15 N	38.30 E
Stepenitz ≃	**54**	53.48 N	11.10 E
Stephans-Dom ⊍[1]	**264b**	48.12 N	16.23 E
Stephanskirchen	**64**	47.51 N	12.11 E
Stephen	**198**	48.27 N	96.52 W
Stephen A. Forbes State Park ♠	**219**	38.44 N	88.46 W
Stephen F. Austin State Historic Park ♠	**222**	29.48 N	96.05 W
Stephens	**194**	33.24 N	93.04 W
Stephens, Cape ›	**172**	40.42 S	173.57 E
Stephens, Port ⊂	**166**	32.45 S	152.05 E
Stephens City	**188**	39.05 N	78.13 W
Stephens Creek	**166**	31.50 S	141.30 E
Stephens Island I	**182**	54.10 N	130.45 W
Stephens Knob ∧[2]	**192**	36.37 N	84.20 W
Stephens Lake ⊜[1]	**184**	56.26 N	95.07 W
Stephens Mills	**210**	42.23 N	77.38 W
Stephenson	**190**	45.24 N	87.36 W
Stephenson, Lake ⊜	**222**	29.35 N	94.40 W
Stephenson, Mount ∧	**9**	69.49 S	69.43 W
Stephens Passage ⊔	**180**	57.50 N	133.50 W
Stephentown	**210**	42.33 N	73.23 W
Stephentown Center	**210**	42.34 N	73.25 W
Stephenville, Nf., Can.	**186**	48.33 N	58.35 W
Stephenville, Tx., U.S.	**196**	32.13 N	98.12 W
Stephenville Crossing	**186**	48.30 N	58.26 W
Stepn'ak	**86**	52.50 N	70.50 E
Stepney ◆[8]	**260**	51.31 N	0.02 W
Stepnica	**54**	53.40 N	14.36 E
Stepnoj	**80**	48.56 N	45.36 E
Stepnoje, Ross.	**80**	51.24 N	46.52 E
Stepnoje, Ross.	**84**	44.17 N	44.36 E
Step Pyramid → Şaqqārah ⊥	**142**	29.52 N	31.14 E
Steps Point ›	**174u**	14.22 S	170.45 W
Steptoe Valley V	**204**	39.25 N	114.45 W
Stepurino	**76**	56.24 N	35.16 E
Sterdyń	**30**	52.35 N	22.18 E
Sterkaar	**158**	31.05 S	23.42 E
Sterkrade ◆[8]	**263**	51.31 N	6.51 E
Sterkspruit	**158**	30.32 S	27.22 E
Sterkstroom	**158**	31.32 S	26.32 E
Sterlibaševo	**86**	53.28 N	55.15 E
Sterling, S. Afr.	**158**	31.16 S	21.28 E
Sterling, Ak., U.S.	**180**	60.32 N	150.48 W
Sterling, Co., U.S.	**198**	40.37 N	103.12 W
Sterling, Ct., U.S.	**207**	41.42 N	71.49 W
Sterling, Il., U.S.	**190**	41.47 N	89.41 W
Sterling, Ks., U.S.	**198**	38.12 N	98.12 W
Sterling, Ma., U.S.	**207**	42.26 N	71.45 W
Sterling, Mi., U.S.	**190**	44.02 N	84.01 W
Sterling, Ne., U.S.	**198**	40.27 N	96.22 W
Sterling, N.Y., U.S.	**210**	43.20 N	76.39 W
Sterling, Oh., U.S.	**214**	40.58 N	81.51 W
Sterling, Ok., U.S.	**196**	34.45 N	98.10 W
Sterling, Va., U.S.	**208**	39.00 N	77.25 W
Sterling City	**196**	31.50 N	100.59 W
Sterling Creek ≃	**210**	43.20 N	76.42 W
Sterling Forest Lake ⊜	**276**	41.10 N	74.16 W
Sterling Heights	**214**	42.34 N	83.01 W
Sterling Junction	**207**	42.24 N	71.46 W
Sterling Park	**282**	37.41 N	122.26 W
Sterling Run	**214**	41.25 N	78.12 W
Sterlington	**194**	32.41 N	92.05 W
Sterlitamak	**86**	53.37 N	55.58 E
Šternberg	**54**	53.43 N	11.49 E
Šternberk	**30**	49.44 N	17.18 E
Šternstein ∧	**61**	48.34 N	14.16 E
Šterovka	**83**	48.19 N	38.57 E
Sterup	**41**	54.44 N	9.44 E

Symbol	English	Deutsch	Español	Français	Português
≃	River	Fluß	Río	Rivière	Rio
≚	Canal	Kanal	Canal	Canal	Canal
∟	Waterfall, Rapids	Wasserfall, Stromschnellen	Cascada, Rápidos	Chute d'eau, Rapides	Cascata, Rápidos
⊔	Strait	Meeresstraße	Estrecho	Détroit	Estreito
⊂	Bay, Gulf	Bucht, Golf	Bahía, Golfo	Baie, Golfe	Baía, Golfo
⊜	Lake, Lakes	See, Seen	Lago, Lagos	Lac, Lacs	Lago, Lagos
≡	Swamp	Sumpf	Pantano	Marais	Pântano
⊓	Ice Features, Glacier	Eis- und Gletscherformen	Accidentes Glaciales	Formes glaciaires	Acidentes glaciares
⍑	Other Hydrographic Features	Andere Hydrographische Objekte	Otros Elementos Hidrográficos	Autres données hydrographiques	Outros acidentes hidrográficos
⊹	Submarine Features	Untermeerische Objekte	Accidentes Submarinos	Formes de relief sous-marin	Acidentes submarinos
□	Political Unit	Politische Einheit	Unidad Politica	Entité politique	Unidade política
⊍	Cultural Institution	Kulturelle Institution	Institución Cultural	Institution culturelle	Institução cultural
⊥	Historical Site	Historische Stätte	Sitio Histórico	Site historique	Sitio histórico
♠	Recreational Site	Erholungs- und Ferienort	Sitio de Recreo	Centre de loisirs	Area de Lazer
⊠	Airport	Flughafen	Aeropuerto	Aéroport	Aeroporto
■	Military Installation	Militäranlage	Instalación Militar	Installation militaire	Instalação militar
◆	Miscellaneous	Verschiedenes	Misceláneo	Divers	Diversos

ESPAÑOL

Nombre	Página	Lat.°′	Long.°′ W = Oeste
Stura di Viù ≃	62	45.16 N	7.26 E
Sturbridge	207	42.06 N	72.04 W
Sturdee	162	31.52 S	132.23 E
Sturge Island I	9	67.27 S	164.18 E
Sturgeon, Mo., U.S.	219	39.14 N	92.16 W
Sturgeon, Pa., U.S.	279b	40.23 N	80.13 W
Sturgeon ≃, On., Can.	190	46.19 N	79.58 W
Sturgeon ≃, Sk., Can.	184	53.12 N	105.53 W
Sturgeon ≃, Mi., U.S.	190	45.24 N	84.38 W
Sturgeon ≃, Mi., U.S.	190	45.50 N	86.41 W
Sturgeon ≃, Mi., U.S.	190	47.02 N	88.30 W
Sturgeon Bay	190	44.50 N	87.22 W
Sturgeon Bay ⊂	184	52.00 N	97.50 W
Sturgeon Falls	190	46.22 N	79.55 W
Sturgeon Lake ⊜, Ab., Can.	182	55.06 N	117.30 W
Sturgeon Lake ⊜, On., Can.	184	55.25 N	90.55 W
Sturgeon Lake ⊜, On., Can.	212	44.28 N	78.42 W
Sturgeon Lake ⊜, Wa., U.S.	224	45.44 N	122.48 W
Sturgeon Lake Indian Reserve ◆[4], Ab., Can.	182	55.04 N	117.29 W
Sturgeon Lake Indian Reserve ◆[4], Sk., Can.	184	53.25 N	106.05 W
Sturgeon Landing	184	54.16 N	101.49 W
Sturgeon Point ›	212	42.42 N	79.03 W
Sturgis, Sk., Can.	184	51.58 N	102.32 W
Sturgis, Ky., U.S.	194	37.32 N	87.59 W
Sturgis, Mi., U.S.	216	41.47 N	85.25 W
Sturgis, Ms., U.S.	194	33.20 N	89.02 W
Sturgis, S.D., U.S.	198	44.24 N	103.30 W
Sturla	62	44.24 N	8.59 E
Sturminster Newton	42	50.50 N	2.19 W
Štúrovo	30	47.48 N	18.49 E
Sturry	42	51.18 N	1.07 E
Sturt, Mount ∧	166	29.33 S	141.42 E
Sturt Creek	162	19.10 S	128.10 E
Sturt Creek ≃	162	20.08 S	127.24 E
Sturtevant	216	42.41 N	87.53 W
Sturt National Park ♠	166	29.00 S	141.40 E
Sturt Stony Desert ◆[2]	166	28.30 S	141.00 E
Sturup flygplats ⊠	41	55.34 N	13.21 E
Stürzelberg	263	51.08 N	6.49 E
Stutterheim	158	32.33 S	27.28 E
Stuttgart, Dtsch.	56	48.46 N	9.11 E
Stuttgart, Ar., U.S.	194	34.30 N	91.33 W
Stuttgart □[5]	56	49.00 N	9.45 E
Stuttgart, Flughafen ⊠	56	48.41 N	9.12 E
Stützengrün	54	50.32 N	12.31 E
Stützerbach	54	50.38 N	10.51 E
Stuyvesant	210	42.24 N	73.47 W
Stuyvesant Falls	210	42.21 N	73.44 W
Stviga ≃	78	52.04 N	27.54 E
Styal	262	53.21 N	2.15 W
Stykkishólmur	24a	65.06 N	22.48 W
Styla	83	47.41 N	37.50 E
Styr' ≃	78	52.07 N	26.35 E
Styrum ◆[8]	263	51.27 N	6.51 E
Styx ≃, On., Can.	212	44.11 N	80.57 W
Styx ≃, Al., U.S.	194	30.31 N	87.27 W
Suaçuí Grande ≃	255	18.50 S	41.46 W
Suai	112	3.48 N	113.38 E
Suain	164	3.20 S	142.55 E
Suaita	246	6.07 N	73.27 W
Suakin Archipelago II	140	18.42 N	38.30 E
Sual	116	16.04 N	120.05 E
Suan	98	38.42 N	126.22 E
Suao, T'aiwan	100	24.36 N	121.51 E
Su'ao, Zhg.	100	25.38 N	119.42 E
Suapure ≃	246	6.25 N	66.23 W
Suaqui Grande	232	28.24 N	109.54 W
Suār	124	29.02 N	79.03 E
Suātala	124	23.09 N	79.02 E
Suatima	114	4.13 N	96.04 E
Šubač	76	60.22 N	38.14 E
Subačius	76	55.46 N	24.47 E
Subah	115a	6.58 S	109.52 E
Subaio	256	22.30 S	42.50 W
Subang	115a	6.34 S	107.45 E
Subansiri ≃	120	26.48 N	93.50 E
Šubarkuduk	86	49.13 N	56.34 E
Subar Laut, Pulau I	271c	1.13 N	103.50 E
Subarnapur	272b	22.58 N	88.34 E
Subarnarekha ≃	120	21.34 N	87.24 E
Šubarši	86	48.35 N	57.12 E
Subashi	85	38.22 N	74.57 E
Subasio, Monte ∧	66	43.03 N	12.40 E
Subata	76	56.01 N	25.56 E
Subay', 'Urūq as- ◆[2]	144	22.15 N	43.05 E
Subbiano	66	43.34 N	11.52 E
Subbotino	86	53.04 N	91.55 E
Subchankulovo	80	54.34 N	53.49 E
Subei	102	39.27 N	95.03 E
Subeita → Shivta, Ḥorvot ⊥	132	30.53 N	34.38 E
Suben	60	48.25 N	13.26 E
Subhepur	272a	28.45 N	77.16 E
Subi, Pulau I	112	2.55 N	108.50 E
Subiaco	66	41.55 N	13.06 E
Subic	116	14.53 N	120.14 E
Subic Bay ⊂	116	14.45 N	120.13 E
Subic Bay Naval Base (U.S.) ■	116	14.47 N	120.16 E
Subipur	272b	22.54 N	88.08 E
Subk al-Ahad	142	30.18 N	31.02 E
Sublette	198	37.28 N	100.50 W
Sublett Range ⋀	202	42.20 N	112.50 W
Sublime	222	29.29 N	96.48 W
Subotica	38	46.06 N	19.39 E
Suburban Airport ⊠	284c	39.05 N	76.50 W
Suburban Village	285	39.58 N	75.34 W
Suca	144	6.31 N	39.14 E
Sucarnoochee ≃	194	32.25 N	88.02 W
Succasunna	210	40.52 N	74.38 W
Succor Creek ≃	202	43.38 N	116.56 W
Suceava	38	47.39 N	26.19 E
Suceava □[6]	38	47.30 N	25.45 E
Suceava ≃	38	47.32 N	26.32 E
Sucha [Beskidzka]	30	49.44 N	19.36 E
Suchaja	88	52.32 N	107.06 E
Suchaja Volnovacha ≃	83	47.37 N	38.01 E
Suchań	30	53.17 N	15.19 E
Suchana	74	68.45 N	118.00 E
Suchang	107	30.34 N	103.34 E
Suchan → Partizansk	89	43.08 N	133.09 E
Süchbaatar	88	50.15 N	106.12 E
Süchbaatar □[4]	102	45.30 N	114.00 E
Suchdol ◆[8]	54	50.08 N	14.21 E
Suchdol nad Lužnicí	61	48.54 N	14.53 E
Suchedniów	30	51.03 N	20.51 E
Suchetgarh	123	32.34 N	74.40 E
Suchiapa	234	16.37 N	93.05 W
Suchiapa ≃	234	16.36 N	93.01 W
Súchil	234	23.38 N	103.55 W
Suchiniči	76	54.06 N	35.20 E
Suchitepéquez □[5]	236	14.25 N	91.20 W
Suchitlán	234	19.22 N	103.43 W
Suchitoto	236	13.56 N	89.02 W
Suchobezvodnoje	80	57.03 N	44.50 E
Suchoborka	24	59.06 N	49.58 E
Suchodol, Ross.	80	53.55 N	51.14 E
Suchodol, Ross.	82	54.27 N	37.22 E
Suchodol'skij	76	53.43 N	38.17 E
Suchodrev ≃	82	54.44 N	35.59 E
Suchoj	80	47.06 N	41.21 E
Suchoj Jelančik ≃	83	47.16 N	38.25 E
Suchoj Log	86	56.55 N	62.01 E
Suchoj Pit	86	58.48 N	92.49 E
Suchoj Sambek ≃	83	47.23 N	39.07 E
Suchoj Torec ≃	83	48.49 N	37.36 E

FRANÇAIS

Nom	Page	Lat.°′	Long.°′ W = Ouest
Suchona ≃	24	60.46 N	46.24 E
Suchorečka	80	52.49 N	52.27 E
Suchotinka	80	52.31 N	41.35 E
Suchou → Suzhou	106	31.18 N	120.37 E
Suchoverkovo	76	56.37 N	35.35 E
Suchov Pervyj	80	49.59 N	43.28 E
Süchow → Xuzhou	98	34.16 N	117.11 E
Süchteln	56	51.17 N	6.22 E
Suchumi	84	43.01 N	41.02 E
Sucio ≃	246	7.27 N	77.07 W
Suck ≃	48	53.16 N	8.03 W
Sucker Creek ≃	212	44.09 N	77.08 W
Sucker Creek Indian Reserve ◆[4]	182	55.28 N	116.10 W
Sucker Lake ⊜	212	44.46 N	78.16 W
Suckling, Mount ∧	164	9.45 S	148.55 E
Sucre, Arg.	258	34.30 S	59.07 W
Sucre, Bol.	248	19.02 S	65.17 W
Sucre, Col.	246	8.49 N	74.44 W
Sucre, Ec.	246	1.16 S	80.26 W
Sucre □[3]	246	10.25 N	63.30 W
Sucre □[5], Col.	246	9.00 N	75.00 W
Sucre □[5], Ven.	286c	10.25 N	66.50 W
Sucúa	246	2.28 S	78.10 W
Sucuaro	246	4.34 N	68.50 W
Sucumbíos □[4]	246	0.06 N	76.52 W
Sucunduri ≃	248	5.50 S	59.32 W
Sucuriju	250	1.39 N	49.57 W
Sucuriú ≃	255	20.47 S	51.38 W
Sucy-en-Brie	50	48.46 N	2.32 E
Sud, Canal du ⋓	238	18.40 N	73.05 W
Sud, Grand Récif ✦[2]	175f	23.00 S	167.02 E
Sud, Pointe ›	157a	11.53 S	43.49 E
Sud, Rivière du ≃	206	45.08 N	73.15 W
Suda	76	59.09 N	37.33 E
Suda ≃	76	59.11 N	37.30 E
Südafrika → South Africa □[1]	156	30.00 S	26.00 E
Sudaj	76	58.58 N	43.08 E
Sudak	78	44.52 N	34.59 E
Südamerika → South America ●[1]	18	15.00 S	60.00 W
Sudan	196	34.04 N	102.31 W
Sudan (As-Sūdān) □[1], Afr.	136	15.00 N	30.00 E
Sudan (As-Sūdān) □[1], Afr.	140	15.00 N	30.00 E
Sudan ◆[1]	10	10.00 N	20.00 E
Sudañez	248	19.06 S	64.44 W
Sudarsan	272b	22.59 N	88.17 E
Südbahnhof ◆[5]	264b	48.11 N	16.23 E
Sudberg ◆[8]	263	51.11 N	7.08 E
Sudbišči	76	52.57 N	37.39 E
Sud'bodarovka	80	52.19 N	54.07 E
Südbrookmerland	52	53.29 N	7.24 E
Sudbury, On., Can.	190	46.30 N	81.00 W
Sudbury, Eng., U.K.	42	52.02 N	0.44 E
Sudbury, Ma., U.S.	207	42.23 N	71.25 W
Sudbury ≃	283	42.28 N	71.22 W
Sudbury Center	283	42.23 N	71.25 W
Sudbury Reservoir ⊜[1]	207	42.19 N	71.31 W
Südchinesisches Meer → South China Sea ⊤[2]	108	10.00 N	113.00 E
Sud Dakota → South Dakota □[3]	198	44.15 N	100.00 W
Sudd an-Na'ām, Jabal ∧	142	29.49 N	31.43 E
Sudd → As-Sudd ◆[1]	140	8.00 N	31.00 E
Suddie	246	7.07 N	58.29 W
Sude ≃	54	53.22 N	10.45 E
Süderbrarup	41	54.38 N	9.46 E
Süderlügum	41	54.52 N	8.55 E
Suderwich	263	51.37 N	7.15 E
Sudeten → Sudety ⋀	30	50.30 N	16.00 E
Sudety ⋀	30	50.30 N	16.00 E
Süd-Georgien → South Georgia I	244	54.15 S	36.45 W
Sudi	154	10.06 S	39.57 E
Sudislavl'	80	57.53 N	41.43 E
Südkamen	263	51.35 N	7.39 E
Süd-Korea → Korea, South □[1]	98	36.30 N	128.00 E
Sudlersville	208	39.11 N	75.51 W
Südlicher Bug → Južnyj Bug ≃	78	46.59 N	31.58 E
Südlicher Indianer-See → Southern Indian Lake ⊜	176	57.10 N	98.40 W
Sudnikovo	82	55.53 N	36.02 E
Sudogda	80	55.57 N	40.50 E
Sudomskaja vozvyšennost' ⋀[1]	76	57.25 N	29.25 E
Sudong, Pulau I	271c	1.13 N	103.44 E
Süd-Orkney-Inseln → South Orkney Islands II	9	60.35 S	45.30 W
Sudost' ≃	76	52.19 N	33.24 E
Sud-Ouest □[4]	152	5.10 N	9.00 E
Sud-Ouest, Pointe du ›	186	49.23 N	63.36 W
Sudovaja Višn'a	78	49.49 N	23.22 E
Südradde ≃	52	52.41 N	7.34 E
Süd-Sandwich-Inseln → South Sandwich Islands II	18	57.45 S	26.30 W
Süd-Shetland-Inseln → South Shetland Islands II	9	62.00 S	58.00 W
Sudūd	142	30.25 N	30.54 E
Südwest-Kap → South West Cape ›	166	43.34 S	146.02 E
Sudweyhe	52	52.59 N	8.53 E
Sudža	78	51.12 N	35.16 E
Sue	96	33.35 N	130.30 E
Sue ≃	140	7.41 N	28.03 E
Sueca	34	39.12 N	0.19 W
Suecia → Sweden □[1]	24	62.00 N	15.00 E
Sue Creek ⊂	284b	39.17 N	76.24 W
Suedberg	208	40.32 N	76.28 W
Suède → Sweden □[1]	24	62.00 N	15.00 E
Suemez Island I	182	55.17 N	133.21 W
Suèvres	50	47.40 N	1.28 E
Suez, Gulf of → Suways, Khalīj as- ⊂	140	29.00 N	32.50 E
Suez → As-Suways	142	29.58 N	32.33 E
Suez Canal → Suways, Qanāt as- ≊	142	29.55 N	32.33 E
Sūf	132	32.19 N	35.50 E
Şufaynah	128	23.09 N	40.32 E
Suffern	210	41.06 N	74.09 W
Suffern Park	276	41.07 N	74.07 W
Suffield, Ab., Can.	184	50.12 N	111.10 W
Suffield, Ct., U.S.	207	41.58 N	72.39 W
Suffield, Oh., U.S.	214	41.01 N	81.21 W
Suffield, Canadian Forces Base ■	184	50.15 N	111.10 W
Suffolk	208	36.43 N	76.35 W
Suffolk □[6], Eng., U.K.	42	52.10 N	1.00 E
Suffolk □[6], Ma., U.S.	207	42.21 N	71.04 W
Suffolk □[6], N.Y., U.S.	210	40.55 N	72.40 W
Suffolk, Ruisseau ≃	206	45.48 N	74.59 W
Suffolk Downs Race Track ♠	283	42.23 N	71.00 W
Şūfīān	128	38.17 N	45.59 E

PORTUGUÊS

Nome	Página	Lat.°′	Long.°′ W = Oeste
Sufi-Kurgan	85	40.02 N	73.30 E
Sufu → Kashi	85	39.29 N	75.59 E
Suga-jima I	94	34.29 N	136.53 E
Sugana, Val V	64	46.00 N	11.40 E
Sugandha	272b	22.54 N	88.20 E
Sugandy	85	43.27 N	74.38 E
Sugano	268	35.44 N	139.56 E
Sugar ≃, U.S.	190	42.26 N	89.12 W
Sugar ≃, N.H., U.S.	188	43.24 N	72.24 W
Sugar ≃, N.Y., U.S.	212	43.31 N	75.19 W
Sugar City	202	43.52 N	111.44 W
Sugarcreek, Oh., U.S.	214	40.30 N	81.39 W
Sugarcreek, Pa., U.S.	214	41.25 N	79.52 W
Sugar Creek ≃, U.S.	216	40.47 N	87.45 W
Sugar Creek ≃, Il., U.S.	194	40.09 N	89.38 W
Sugar Creek ≃, Il., U.S.	219	38.28 N	89.37 W
Sugar Creek ≃, Il., U.S.	219	39.48 N	89.32 W
Sugar Creek ≃, In., U.S.	194	39.51 N	87.21 W
Sugar Creek ≃, In., U.S.	218	39.21 N	86.00 W
Sugar Creek ≃, Mi., U.S.	281	42.06 N	83.36 W
Sugar Creek ≃, N.Y., U.S.	210	42.38 N	77.09 W
Sugar Creek ≃, Oh., U.S.	214	40.31 N	81.28 W
Sugar Creek ≃, Oh., U.S.	216	40.57 N	84.11 W
Sugar Creek ≃, Oh., U.S.	218	39.27 N	83.25 W
Sugar Creek ≃, Ok., U.S.	196	35.05 N	98.10 W
Sugar Creek ≃, Pa., U.S.	210	41.47 N	76.27 W
Sugar Creek ≃, Wi., U.S.	216	42.43 N	88.19 W
Sugar Grove, Il., U.S.	216	41.45 N	88.27 W
Sugargrove, Pa., U.S.	214	41.59 N	79.21 W
Sugar Grove, Va., U.S.	192	36.46 N	81.24 W
Sugar Hill	192	34.06 N	84.02 W
Sugar Island I, On., Can.	212	44.26 N	77.17 W
Sugar Island I, Mi., U.S.	190	46.25 N	84.12 W
Sugar Land	222	29.37 N	95.38 W
Sugar Loaf	210	41.19 N	74.17 W
Sugarloaf ∧[2]	214	41.24 N	81.06 W
Sugarloaf Hill ∧[2]	274b	37.58 S	145.19 E
Sugarloaf Key I	220	24.40 N	81.32 W
Sugarloaf Mountain ∧, Ky., U.S.	218	38.13 N	83.32 W
Sugarloaf Mountain ∧, Me., U.S.	188	45.01 N	70.22 W
Sugar Loaf Mountain ∧, Md., U.S.	208	39.16 N	77.23 W
Sugar Loaf Mountain ∧, Ok., U.S.	194	35.02 N	94.28 W
Sugarloaf Mountain ∧[2]	220	28.39 N	81.44 W
Sugar Loaf → Pão de Açúcar ∧	287a	22.57 S	43.09 W
Sugarloaf Peak ∧	280	34.14 N	117.38 W
Sugarloaf Point ›, Austl.	166	32.26 S	152.33 E
Sugar Loaf Point ›, On., Can.	284a	42.52 N	79.17 W
Sugarloaf Reservoir ⊜[1]	169	37.41 S	145.18 E
Sugarloaf Ridge State Park ♠	226	38.26 N	122.29 W
Sugar Notch	210	41.11 N	75.55 W
Sugar Pine Point State Park ♠	226	39.03 N	120.07 W
Sugartown	285	40.00 N	75.31 W
Sugauli	124	26.46 N	84.44 E
Sugbai Passage ⋓	116	5.22 N	120.33 E
Sugbay	116	7.31 N	123.19 E
Sugbuhan Point ›	116	10.04 N	126.04 E
Suggi Lake ⊜	184	54.22 N	102.47 W
Suginami ◆[8]	268	35.42 N	139.38 E
Sugita ◆[8]	268	35.23 N	139.38 E
Sugito	94	36.02 N	139.44 E
Şuğla Gölü ⊜	130	37.20 N	32.02 E
Šugnou	85	38.35 N	70.20 E
Sugod	116	12.03 N	124.09 E
Sugoj ≃	74	64.15 N	154.29 E
Šugonovo	82	54.41 N	36.41 E
Šugozero	76	59.55 N	34.12 E
Šugurovo, Ross.	80	53.25 N	46.29 E
Šugurovo, Ross.	80	54.31 N	52.06 E
Sugut ≃	112	6.26 N	117.43 E
Suguta ≃	154	2.03 N	36.33 E
Suguti	154	1.44 S	33.39 E
Suhai Hu ⊜	102	38.50 N	94.00 E
Suhaitu	102	44.50 N	93.39 E
Şuḥār	128	24.22 N	56.45 E
Suheli Island I[1]	122	10.03 N	72.17 E
Suhl	54	50.37 N	10.41 E
Suhlendorf	54	52.55 N	10.46 E
Suhopolje	36	45.48 N	17.30 E
Suhr	58	47.22 N	8.05 E
Suhr ≃	58	47.25 N	8.04 E
Suhum	150	6.05 N	0.27 W
Şuhut	130	38.32 N	30.33 E
Šūi	120	28.37 N	69.19 E
Suiá-Miçu ≃	250	11.13 S	53.15 W
Suianzhan	89	53.07 N	125.20 E
Suiattle ≃	224	48.20 N	121.33 W
Suichang	100	28.34 N	119.14 E
Suichuan	100	26.26 N	114.32 E
Suichuan ≃	100	26.30 N	114.45 E
Suid Afrika → South Africa □[1]	156	30.00 S	26.00 E
Suide	102	37.32 N	110.12 E
Suiding	86	44.03 N	80.49 E
Suido-suigenchi ⊜[1]	270	34.54 N	135.17 E
Suidvaal	158	26.52 S	29.47 E
Suifenhe	89	44.24 N	131.10 E
Suifu	94	36.37 N	140.29 E
Suifu → Yibin	107	28.47 N	104.38 E
Suigō-kokutei-kōen ♠	94	36.05 N	140.20 E
Suigō-Tsukuba-kokutei-kōen ♠	94	36.00 N	140.20 E
Suihua	89	46.37 N	127.00 E
Suijiang	102	28.31 N	104.07 E
Suileng	89	47.18 N	127.10 E
Suining, Zhg.	100	33.54 N	117.56 E
Suining, Zhg.	102	26.21 N	110.00 E
Suining, Zhg.	107	30.31 N	105.34 E
Suipacha	252	34.45 S	59.41 W
Suiping	100	33.10 N	113.57 E
Suippe ≃	50	49.25 N	3.57 E
Suippes	56	49.08 N	4.32 E
Suir ≃	48	52.15 N	7.00 W
Suisse → Switzerland □[1]	58	47.00 N	8.00 E
Suisun Bay ⊂	226	38.06 N	122.00 W
Suisun City	226	38.14 N	122.02 W
Suisun Creek ≃	226	38.12 N	122.06 W
Suita	96	34.45 N	135.32 E
Suitland	284c	38.50 N	76.55 W
Suixi, Zhg.	100	33.56 N	116.46 E
Suixi, Zhg.	102	21.25 N	110.15 E
Suixian, Zhg.	98	34.26 N	115.05 E
Suixian, Zhg.	100	31.42 N	113.20 E
Suiyang, Zhg.	89	44.26 N	130.53 E
Suiyang, Zhg.	102	27.56 N	107.18 E
Suiyangdian	100	32.04 N	112.55 E
Suiza → Switzerland □[1]	58	47.00 N	8.00 E
Suize ≃	58	48.08 N	5.08 E

Suizhong	98	40.20 N	120.19 E
Šuja, Ross.	24	61.55 N	34.12 E
Šuja, Ross.	80	56.50 N	41.23 E
Šuja ≃, Ross.	24	61.54 N	34.15 E
Šuja ≃, Ross.	80	57.56 N	43.15 E
Sujānagar	126	23.57 N	89.25 E
Sujāngarh	120	27.42 N	74.28 E
Sujāwal	120	24.36 N	68.05 E
Suji	107	29.35 N	103.37 E
Sujiabu	100	31.38 N	116.22 E
Sujiaqiao	105	39.24 N	116.10 E
Sujiatun	104	41.40 N	123.22 E
Sujiawan	107	29.48 N	104.57 E
Sujiawu	105	39.17 N	115.55 E
Sujiazui	100	33.40 N	119.29 E
Šujskoje	76	59.22 N	40.59 E
Sujutkina Kosa, mys ›	84	44.13 N	47.15 E
Sukabihanawa	112	9.30 S	124.57 E
Sukabumi	115a	6.55 S	106.56 E
Sukadana, Indon.	112	1.15 S	109.57 E
Sukadana, Indon.	115a	5.05 S	105.33 E
Sukadana, Teluk ⊂	112	1.24 S	109.50 E
Sukagawa	92	37.17 N	140.23 E
Sukamandi	115a	6.20 S	107.39 E
Sukamara	112	2.43 S	111.11 E
Sukanegara	115a	7.06 S	107.07 E
Sukapura	115a	7.52 S	113.03 E
Sukaraja, Indon.	112	2.21 S	110.37 E
Sukaraja, Indon.	115a	7.27 S	108.12 E
Sukaraja, Indon.	115a	7.27 S	109.17 E
Sukarno, Pegunungan → Jaya, Puncak ∧	164	4.05 S	137.11 E
Sukau	112	5.32 N	118.17 E
Sukchar	272b	22.42 N	88.22 E
Sukch'ŏn	98	39.24 N	125.38 E
Sukematsu	270	34.31 N	135.26 E
Sukeva	26	63.52 N	27.26 E
Sukhnah, 'Ayn ⊤[4]	142	29.35 N	32.15 E
Sukhothai	110	17.01 N	99.49 E
Sukhumi → Suchumi	84	43.01 N	41.02 E
Sukkertoppen (Maniitsoq)	176	65.25 N	52.53 W
Sukkozero	24	63.11 N	32.18 E
Sukkur	120	27.42 N	68.52 E
Sukkwan Island I	182	55.05 N	132.45 W
Suklāra	126	23.11 N	86.21 E
Sukmanovka	78	51.47 N	41.34 E
Sukodadi	115a	7.06 S	112.19 E
Sukoharjo	115a	7.41 S	110.50 E
Sukovo	82	54.54 N	38.19 E
Sukroml'a	76	56.53 N	34.44 E
Sukses	156	21.01 S	16.52 E
Suksun	86	57.07 N	57.24 E
Sukumo	92	32.56 N	132.44 E
Sukun, Pulau I	115b	8.07 S	122.08 E
Sukunka ≃	182	55.37 N	121.37 W
Sul, Baía ⊂	252	27.40 S	48.35 W
Sul, Canal do ⋓	250	0.10 S	49.30 W
Sula I	26	61.08 N	4.55 E
Sula ≃, Ross.	24	67.16 N	52.07 E
Sula ≃, Ukr.	78	49.40 N	32.41 E
Sula, Kepulauan II	112	1.52 S	125.22 E
Sulaco ≃	236	15.01 N	87.44 W
Sulaimān Khel	123	33.41 N	71.01 E
Sulaimān Range ⋀	120	30.30 N	70.10 E
Sulak, Ross.	80	51.52 N	48.21 E
Sulak, Ross.	84	43.16 N	47.32 E
Sulak ≃	84	43.20 N	47.34 E
Sulakyurt	130	40.10 N	33.44 E
Sulang	115a	6.48 S	111.23 E
Sulat	116	11.49 N	125.27 E
Sulauan Point ›	116	8.37 N	124.29 E
Sulawesi (Celebes) I	112	2.00 S	121.00 E
Sulawesi Selatan □[4]	112	3.30 S	120.00 E
Sulawesi Tengah □[4]	112	1.00 N	123.00 E
Sulawesi Tenggara □[4]	112	4.00 S	122.00 E
Sulawesi Utara □[4]	112	0.30 N	124.00 E
Sulaymān, Birak (Solomon's Pools) ⊥	132	31.41 N	35.10 E
Sulby	44	54.18 N	4.29 W
Sulcis ◆[1]	71	39.04 N	8.41 E
Suldalsvatnet ⊜	26	59.35 N	6.45 E
Sūldeh	128	36.34 N	52.01 E
Sulechów	30	52.06 N	15.37 E
Sulęcin	30	52.26 N	15.08 E
Suleja	86	55.09 N	58.50 E
Sulejów	30	51.22 N	19.53 E
Sulejówek	30	52.14 N	21.17 E
Sulen, Mount ∧	164	3.25 S	142.15 E
Sule Skerry I[2]	46	59.05 N	4.26 W
Suleymaniye Mosque ʊ[1]	267b	41.00 N	28.57 E
Süleymanlı	130	37.54 N	36.50 E
Şülfeld	52	53.48 N	10.14 E
Šul'ginka	83	49.08 N	38.56 E
Šul'gino, Ross.	82	54.33 N	37.35 E
Sulğino, Ross.	82	55.50 N	35.55 E
Sulia	154	1.32 S	26.33 E
Suliki	112	0.06 S	100.27 E
Sulima	150	6.58 N	11.35 W
Sulin	83	48.54 N	40.07 E
Sulina	38	45.09 N	29.40 E
Sulina, Brațul ≃[1]	38	45.09 N	29.41 E
Sulincheer	102	42.41 N	109.20 E
Sulingen	52	52.41 N	8.47 E
Sulinskij	83	47.52 N	40.06 E
Sulitelma ∧	24	67.08 N	16.24 E
Sulkava	26	61.47 N	28.23 E
Sullana	248	4.53 S	80.41 W
Sullane ≃	48	51.53 N	8.56 W
Sulligent	194	33.54 N	88.08 W
Sullivan, Il., U.S.	194	39.35 N	88.36 W
Sullivan, In., U.S.	194	39.06 N	87.24 W
Sullivan, Mo., U.S.	219	38.12 N	91.09 W
Sullivan, Oh., U.S.	214	41.02 N	82.13 W
Sullivan, Wi., U.S.	216	43.00 N	88.35 W
Sullivan □[6], N.Y., U.S.	210	41.39 N	74.42 W
Sullivan □[6], Pa., U.S.	210	41.25 N	76.29 W
Sullivan Canyon V	280	34.03 N	118.30 W
Sullivan Creek ≃	226	37.53 N	120.25 W
Sullivan Lake ⊜	182	52.00 N	112.00 W
Sullivan Stadium ♠	283	42.05 N	71.16 W
Sullivanville	210	42.14 N	76.46 W
Sully-sur-Loire	50	47.46 N	2.22 E
Sulm ≃	61	46.45 N	15.34 E
Sulmona	66	42.03 N	13.55 E
Sulot' ≃	82	56.41 N	38.01 E
Sulphur, Yk., Can.	180	63.47 N	138.53 W
Sulphur, In., U.S.	218	38.14 N	86.28 W
Sulphur, Ky., U.S.	218	38.29 N	85.16 W
Sulphur, La., U.S.	194	30.14 N	93.22 W
Sulphur, Ok., U.S.	196	34.30 N	96.58 W
Sulphur ≃, Ab., Can.	182	53.50 N	119.10 W
Sulphur ≃, U.S.	194	33.07 N	93.52 W
Sulphur Creek ≃	198	44.46 N	102.25 W
Sulphur Draw V	196	33.12 N	102.17 W
Sulphur Springs, In., U.S.	218	40.00 N	85.26 W
Sulphur Springs, Oh., U.S.	214	40.52 N	82.52 W
Sulphur Springs, Tx., U.S.	222	33.08 N	95.36 W
Sulphur Springs Draw V	196	32.12 N	101.36 W
Sulphur Springs Valley V	200	31.50 N	109.50 W
Sulsul	144	5.06 N	44.55 E
Sultan	224	47.51 N	121.48 W
Sultan ≃	224	47.52 N	121.49 W
Sultana	226	36.33 N	119.20 W
Sultanahmet Mosque ʊ[1]	267b	41.00 N	28.58 E
Sultan Alonto, Lake ⊜	116	7.53 N	124.15 E

Sultana Point ›	168b	35.08 S	137.45 E
Sultanatābād ◆[8]	267d	35.46 N	51.28 E
Sultançiftligi ◆[8]	267b	41.02 N	29.13 E
Sultandağı	130	38.32 N	31.14 E
Sultan Dağı ∧	130	38.58 N	27.26 E
Sultanhanı	130	38.15 N	33.33 E
Sultanhisar	130	37.53 N	28.10 E
Sultan Kudarat	116	7.17 N	124.16 E
Sultan Kudarat □[4]	116	6.20 N	124.20 E
Sultan Mosque ʊ[1]	271c	1.18 N	103.52 E
Sultānpur, India	123	31.13 N	75.11 E
Sultānpur, India	124	26.16 N	82.04 E
Sultānpur Dabās ◆[8]	272a	28.46 N	77.03 E
Sultan sa Barongis	116	6.46 N	124.38 E
Sultan-Saly	83	47.21 N	39.35 E
Sulu	164	5.25 S	151.00 E
Sulu □[4]	116	6.00 N	121.00 E
Suluan Island I	116	10.46 N	125.57 E
Sulu Archipelago II	116	6.00 N	121.00 E
Sulu Basin ✦[1]	12	8.00 N	121.30 E
Sulu Chi ⊜	124	30.12 N	86.20 E
Sülüklü	130	39.05 N	30.58 E
Sul'ukta	85	39.56 N	69.34 E
Sululta	144	9.10 N	38.48 E
Suluntah	146	32.36 N	21.43 E
Suluova (Suluca)	130	40.47 N	35.42 E
Sulūq	146	31.39 N	20.15 E
Sulusaj	85	38.50 N	67.05 E
Sulusaray	130	40.00 N	36.06 E
Sulu Sea ⊤[2]	116	8.00 N	120.00 E
Suly	86	53.45 N	66.30 E
Sulz	58	48.18 N	7.51 E
Sulz am Neckar	58	48.21 N	8.37 E
Sulzano	64	45.41 N	10.05 E
Sulzbach	56	49.18 N	7.07 E
Sulzbach ≃	60	48.36 N	13.02 E
Sulzbach am Kocher	56	48.58 N	9.50 E
Sulzbach-Rosenberg	60	49.30 N	11.45 E
Sulzberger Bay ⊂	9	77.00 S	152.00 W
Sulzbrunn	58	47.41 N	10.20 E
Sulzburg	58	47.50 N	7.42 E
Şülze	52	52.46 N	10.02 E
Šum, Ross.	76	59.52 N	31.46 E
Šum, Ross.	88	54.51 N	95.18 E
Šuma ◆[8]	270	34.39 N	135.08 E
Šum'ači	76	53.52 N	32.25 E
Šumadija ◆[1]	38	44.10 N	20.50 E
Sumalata	112	0.59 N	122.30 E
Sumallo ≃	224	49.14 N	121.05 W
Şumampa	252	29.22 S	63.28 W
Šumanaj	86	42.37 N	59.08 E
Sumangat, Tanjong ›	116	6.35 N	117.33 E
Sumano-ura ♠	96	34.38 N	135.08 E
Sūmār	128	33.52 N	45.39 E
Sumarokovo	82	55.46 N	35.55 E
Sumas	202	49.00 N	122.15 W
Sumas ≃	224	49.09 N	122.12 W
Sumatera (Sumatra) I	108	0.05 S	102.00 E
Sumatera Barat □[4]	112	0.30 S	100.30 E
Sumatera Selatan □[4]	112	3.00 S	104.00 E
Sumatera Utara □[4]	114	2.20 N	99.00 E
Sum'atino	82	55.00 N	36.21 E
Sumatou	107	30.28 N	104.03 E
Sumatra → Sumatera I	108	0.05 S	102.00 E
Sumava Resorts	216	41.10 N	87.26 W
Sumayḥ	140	12.43 N	30.50 E
Sumba I	115b	10.00 S	120.00 E
Sumba, Île I	152	1.44 N	19.32 E
Sumba, Selat ⋓	115b	9.05 S	120.00 E
Sumbar ≃	128	38.00 N	55.17 E
Sumbawa I	115b	8.40 S	118.00 E
Sumbawa Besar	115b	8.30 S	117.26 E
Sumbawanga	154	7.58 S	31.37 E
Sumbay	248	15.58 S	71.23 W
Sumbe	152	11.13 S	13.50 E
Sümber	90	46.21 N	108.20 E
Sumbilla	34	43.10 N	1.40 W
Sumbing, Gunung ∧	115a	7.23 S	110.04 E
Sumbu National Park ♠	154	8.50 S	30.25 E
Sumburgh Head ›	46a	59.53 N	1.20 W
Sumburgh Roost ⋓	46a	59.49 N	1.19 W
Šumbut	80	55.33 N	50.41 E
Sumbuya	150	7.39 N	11.58 W
Sumdo	120	35.01 N	78.41 E
Sumé	250	7.39 S	36.55 W
Sumedang	115a	6.52 S	107.55 E
Sümeg	30	46.59 N	17.17 E
Šumek	86	48.42 N	85.32 E
Šumen	38	43.16 N	26.55 E
Sumène	62	43.59 N	3.43 E
Sumenep	115a	7.01 S	113.52 E
Šumerl'a	80	55.30 N	46.26 E
Sumgait	84	40.36 N	49.38 E
Sumgait ≃	84	40.37 N	49.37 E
Šumicha	86	55.14 N	63.19 E
Sumida ◆[8]	268	35.42 N	139.48 E
Sumida ≃	268	35.40 N	139.47 E
Sumidouro	256	22.03 S	42.41 W
Sumilao	116	8.18 N	124.57 E
Šumilino	76	55.18 N	29.37 E
Šumilinskaja	80	49.58 N	41.26 E
Suminoe ◆[8]	270	34.36 N	135.28 E
Sumisu-jima I	90	31.27 N	140.03 E
Sumiswald	58	47.02 N	7.45 E
Sumiyoshi ◆[8]	270	34.36 N	135.31 E
Sumki	86	55.03 N	65.44 E
Sumkino	86	58.09 N	68.21 E
Sumlog ≃	116	6.53 N	126.02 E
Summer Bridge	44	54.03 N	1.41 W
Summerdale	208	40.18 N	76.56 W
Summerfield, Fl., U.S.	220	29.00 N	82.02 W
Summerfield, Mo., U.S.	219	38.17 N	91.49 W
Summerfield, N.C., U.S.	192	36.12 N	79.54 W
Summerford, Nf., Can.	186	49.29 N	54.47 W
Summerford, Oh., U.S.	218	39.55 N	83.29 W
Summerhill, Ire.	48	53.29 N	6.44 W
Summerhill, Pa., U.S.	214	40.22 N	78.46 W
Summer Island I	190	45.34 N	86.39 W
Summer Isles II	46	58.02 N	5.28 W
Summer Lake ⊜	202	42.50 N	120.45 W
Summerland	182	49.36 N	119.41 W
Summerland Reserve ◆[4]	169	38.31 S	145.10 E
Sümmern	56	51.25 N	7.43 E
Summer Palace ʊ	265a	59.53 N	29.55 E
Summerseat	262	53.38 N	2.19 W
Summerside	186	46.24 N	63.47 W
Summersville, Mo., U.S.	194	37.10 N	91.39 W
Summersville, W.V., U.S.	188	38.16 N	80.51 W
Summerton	192	33.36 N	80.21 W
Summertown	194	35.26 N	87.18 W
Summerville, On., Can.	275b	43.37 N	79.34 W
Summerville, Ga., U.S.	192	34.28 N	85.20 W
Summerville, Pa., U.S.	214	41.06 N	79.11 W
Summerville, S.C., U.S.	192	33.00 N	80.11 W
Summit, Eng., U.K.	262	53.40 N	2.05 W
Summit, Ak., U.S.	180	63.20 N	149.08 W
Summit, Ca., U.S.	228	34.20 N	117.25 W
Summit, Il., U.S.	216	41.47 N	87.48 W
Summit, Ms., U.S.	194	31.17 N	90.28 W
Summit, N.J., U.S.	210	40.44 N	74.21 W
Summit, N.Y., U.S.	210	42.35 N	74.35 W
Summit, S.D., U.S.	198	45.18 N	97.02 W
Summit, Wa., U.S.	224	47.10 N	122.21 W
Summit □[6]	214	41.05 N	81.31 W
Summit Creek ≃	224	46.00 N	121.10 W
Summit Farms	284b	39.19 N	76.32 W

Summit Hill	210	40.49 N	75.52 W
Summit Lake	182	54.17 N	122.38 W
Summit Lake ⊜	224	47.04 N	123.07 W
Summit Mountain ∧	204	39.23 N	116.28 W
Summit Park	276	41.09 N	74.03 W
Summit Park Mall ◆[9]	284a	43.05 N	78.56 W
Summit Peak ∧	200	37.21 N	106.42 W
Summit Rock ∧	172	45.25 S	170.04 E
Summit Station	208	40.34 N	76.12 W
Summitville, In., U.S.	216	40.20 N	85.38 W
Summitville, N.Y., U.S.	210	41.37 N	74.27 W
Summitville, Oh., U.S.	214	40.41 N	80.53 W
Summt	264a	52.41 N	13.22 E
Summter See ⊜	264a	52.42 N	13.23 E
Šumná	61	48.56 N	15.52 E
Sumnal	120	35.45 N	78.40 E
Sumner, Ia., U.S.	190	42.50 N	92.05 W
Sumner, Ms., U.S.	194	33.58 N	90.22 W
Sumner, Wa., U.S.	224	47.12 N	122.14 W
Sumner, Lake ⊜	172	42.42 S	172.13 E
Sumner, Lake ⊜[1]	196	34.38 N	104.25 W
Sumner Lake State Park ♠	196	34.38 N	104.24 W
Sumner Strait ⋓	180	56.15 N	133.45 W
Sumoto	96	34.21 N	134.54 E
Sumpangbinangae	112	4.24 S	119.36 E
Šumperk	30	49.58 N	16.58 E
Sumpiuh	115a	7.37 S	109.21 E
Sumprabum	110	26.33 N	97.34 E
Sumpter	281	42.10 N	83.29 W
Sumrall	194	31.25 N	89.32 W
Sumsar	85	41.18 N	71.19 E
Š'umsi	80	57.07 N	51.37 E
Šumskij	88	54.48 N	99.09 E
Šumskij Posad	24	64.15 N	35.25 E
Šumskoje	78	50.07 N	26.07 E
Šumšu, ostrov I	74	50.45 N	156.20 E
Sumter	192	33.55 N	80.20 W
Sumter □[6]	220	28.38 N	82.08 W
Sumusṭā al-Waqf	142	28.55 N	30.51 E
Sumy	78	50.55 N	34.45 E
Sumy □[8]	76	52.10 N	33.40 E
Sumzom	102	29.45 N	96.10 E
S'un' ≃, Ross.	80	55.44 N	54.16 E
Sun ≃, Mt., U.S.	202	47.30 N	111.19 W
Sun ≃, Zhg.	107	29.13 N	106.21 E
Suna, Kenya	154	1.05 S	34.26 E
Suna, Ross.	80	57.51 N	50.05 E
Suna ≃	24	62.08 N	34.12 E
Sunagawa	92a	43.29 N	141.55 E
Sun al-Heteimi ⊤[4]	132	31.05 N	34.00 E
Sun' al-Menī'i ⊤[4]	132	31.07 N	34.12 E
Sunām	123	30.08 N	75.48 E
Sunāmganj	120	25.04 N	91.24 E
Sunami	94	35.25 N	136.40 E
Sunan	98	39.13 N	125.41 E
Sunapee Lake ⊜	188	43.23 N	72.03 W
Sunart, Loch ⊜	46	56.41 N	5.43 W
Sunashinden	268	35.53 N	139.30 E
Sunbāṭ	142	30.48 N	31.12 E
Sunbright	192	36.14 N	84.40 W
Sunburst	202	48.52 N	111.54 W
Sunbury, Austl.	169	37.35 S	144.44 E
Sunbury, Eng., U.K.	260	51.25 N	0.26 W
Sunbury, N.C., U.S.	192	36.26 N	76.36 W
Sunbury, Oh., U.S.	214	40.14 N	82.51 W
Sunbury, Pa., U.S.	210	40.51 N	76.47 W
Sunchales	252	30.56 S	61.34 W
Sunch'ang	98	35.23 N	127.07 E
Sunchild Indian Reserve ◆[4]	182	52.43 N	115.24 W
Sünching	60	48.53 N	12.21 E
Suncho Corral	252	27.56 S	63.27 W
Sunch'ŏn, C.M.I.K.	98	39.26 N	125.54 E
Sunch'ŏn, Taehan	98	34.57 N	127.28 E
Sun City, Az., U.S.	200	33.35 N	112.16 W
Sun City, Ca., U.S.	228	33.42 N	117.11 W
Sun City, Fl., U.S.	220	27.40 N	82.28 W
Sun City Center	220	27.43 N	82.21 W
Suncook	188	43.07 N	71.27 W
Suncook ≃	188	43.08 N	71.28 W
Sunda, Selat (Sunda Strait) ⋓	112	6.00 S	105.45 E
Sundance	198	44.24 N	104.22 W
Sundar	112	4.54 N	115.12 E
Sundar ∧	124	28.26 N	84.20 E
Sundarbans ◆[1]	126	22.00 N	89.00 E
Sundargarh	124	22.07 N	84.02 E
Sundarnagar	123	31.32 N	76.53 E
Sunda Shelf ✦[4]	14	5.00 N	107.00 E
Sunda Strait → Sunda, Selat ⋓	112	6.00 S	105.45 E
Sunday Creek ≃	169	37.02 S	145.05 E
Sundby, Dan.	41	54.42 N	11.48 E
Sundby, Sve.	40	59.23 N	17.03 E
Sundbyberg	40	59.22 N	17.58 E
Sundbyholm	40	59.27 N	16.37 E
Sundbyholm slott ⊥	40	59.27 N	16.37 E
Sunde	26	59.50 N	5.43 E
Sunderland, On., Can.	212	44.16 N	79.04 W
Sunderland, Eng., U.K.	44	54.55 N	1.23 W
Sunderland, Ma., U.S.	207	42.28 N	72.34 W
Sunderland, Vt., U.S.	210	43.06 N	73.06 W
Sundern	56	51.20 N	8.00 E
Sünderup	41	54.46 N	9.27 E
Sundhausen	54	50.56 N	10.40 E
Sundhouse	58	48.15 N	7.36 E
Sundi-Lutete	152	4.34 S	14.14 E
Sundown, Austl.	162	26.14 S	133.12 E
Sundown, N.Y., U.S.	210	41.53 N	74.28 W
Sundown, Tx., U.S.	196	33.27 N	102.29 W
Sundra	273d	26.11 S	28.33 E
Sundre	182	51.48 N	114.38 W
Sundridge, On., Can.	190	45.46 N	79.24 W
Sundridge, Eng., U.K.	260	51.17 N	0.18 E
Sunds	41	56.12 N	9.01 E
Sundsbruk	26	62.27 N	17.22 E
Sundsvall	26	62.23 N	17.18 E
Sundwig	263	51.23 N	7.47 E
Suneori	268	35.56 N	139.24 E
Sunfield	216	42.45 N	84.59 W
Sunfish Creek ≃	218	39.01 N	83.03 W
Sunflower	194	33.32 N	90.32 W
Sunflower, Mount ∧	198	39.04 N	102.01 W
Sungaianyar	112	2.55 S	116.18 E
Sungaiapit	114	1.09 N	102.10 E
Sungaibamban	114	3.26 N	99.09 E
Sungaibatu	112	0.48 N	110.45 E
Sungai Bayor	114	5.15 N	100.47 E
Sungaibuntu	115a	6.03 S	107.24 E
Sungaidareh	112	0.58 S	101.30 E
Sungaigerong	112	2.59 S	104.52 E
Sungaiguntung	112	0.18 N	103.37 E
Sungaikakap	112	0.04 S	109.10 E
Sungai Kolok	114	6.02 N	101.58 E
Sungailangsat	112	0.52 S	101.18 E
Sungai Lembing	114	3.55 N	103.02 E
Sungailiat	112	1.51 S	106.08 E
Sungailimau	112	0.31 S	100.03 E
Sungaimanasip	114	1.49 N	100.54 E
Sungainipah	114	0.57 N	98.57 E
Sungaipakning	114	1.20 N	102.09 E
Sungaipenuh	112	2.05 S	101.23 E
Sungaipenyu	112	0.16 N	109.04 E
Sungai Petani	114	5.39 N	100.30 E
Sungaipinang	112	0.48 S	114.04 E
Sungairampah	114	3.29 N	99.09 E
Sungairotan, Indon.	112	1.39 S	102.51 E
Sungairotan, Indon.	112	3.06 S	104.18 E
Sungaisalak	112	0.27 S	102.59 E
Sungaiselan	112	2.24 S	105.59 E
Sungai Siput	114	4.49 N	101.04 E
Sungaitampang	114	2.20 N	100.07 E
Şungaitiram	112	0.47 S	117.12 E
Šungaj	80	48.32 N	46.46 E

≃	River	Fluß	Río	Rivière	Rio
≊	Canal	Kanal	Canal	Canal	Canal
⌊	Waterfall, Rapids	Wasserfall, Stromschnellen	Cascada, Rápidos	Chute d'eau, Rapides	Cascata, Rápidos
⋓	Strait	Meeresstraße	Estrecho	Détroit	Estreito
⊂	Bay, Gulf	Bucht, Golf	Bahía, Golfo	Baie, Golfe	Baía, Golfo
⊜	Lake, Lakes	See, Seen	Lago, Lagos	Lac, Lacs	Lago, Lagos
⩨	Swamp	Sumpf	Pantano	Marais	Pântano
⊓	Ice Features, Glacier	Eis- und Gletscherformen	Accidentes Glaciales	Formes glaciaires	Acidentes glaciares
⊤	Other Hydrographic Features	Andere Hydrographische Objekte	Otros Elementos Hidrográficos	Autres données hydrographiques	Outros acidentes hidrográficos
✦	Submarine Features	Untermeerische Objekte	Accidentes Submarinos	Formes de relief sous-marin	Acidentes submarinos
□	Political Unit	Politische Einheit	Unidad Politica	Entité politique	Unidade política
ʊ	Cultural Institution	Kulturelle Institution	Institución Cultural	Institution culturelle	Instituição cultural
⊥	Historical Site	Historische Stätte	Sitio Histórico	Site historique	Sitio histórico
♠	Recreational Site	Erholungs- und Ferienort	Sitio de Recreo	Centre de loisirs	Area de Lazer
⊠	Airport	Flughafen	Aeropuerto	Aéroport	Aeroporto
■	Military Installation	Militäranlage	Instalación Militar	Installation militaire	Instalação militar
◆	Miscellaneous	Verschiedenes	Misceláneo	Divers	Diversos

ENGLISH

Name	Page	Lat.°	Long.°

DEUTSCH

Name	Page	Breite° Lat.°	Länge° Long.° E=Ost

Sydn-Tala I · 171

ESPAÑOL Nombre	Página	Lat.°′	Long.°′ W = Oeste

FRANÇAIS Nom	Page	Lat.°′	Long.°′ W = Ouest

PORTUGUÊS Nome	Página	Lat.°′	Long.°′ W = Oeste

Sydney Lake ⊜ 184 50.40 N 94.24 W
Sydney Mines 186 46.14 N 60.14 W
Sydney Point › 174d 0.53 S 169.36 E
Syferbult 158 26.00 S 27.20 E
Sygan 279b 40.21 N 80.08 W
Syke 52 52.54 N 8.49 E
Sykesville, Md., U.S. 208 39.22 N 76.58 W
Sykesville, Pa., U.S. 214 41.03 N 78.49 W
Sykkylven 26 62.24 N 6.35 E
Syktyvkar 24 61.40 N 50.46 E
Sylacauga 194 33.10 N 86.15 W
Sylarna ∧ 26 63.02 N 12.13 E
Sylhet 120 24.54 N 91.52 E
Syloga 24 63.50 N 43.39 E
Sylt I 30 54.54 N 8.20 E
Sylva 192 35.22 N 83.13 W
Sylva ≏ 86 57.39 N 56.54 E
Sylvan 224 45.30 N 122.41 W
Sylvan Beach 210 43.11 N 75.43 W
Sylvan Glen 285 40.11 N 75.42 W
Sylvan Grove 198 39.00 N 98.23 W
Sylvan Hills 194 34.50 N 92.13 W
Sylvania, Austl. 274a 34.01 S 151.07 E
Sylvania, Ga., U.S. 192 32.45 N 81.38 W
Sylvania, Oh., U.S. 214 41.43 N 83.42 W
Sylvania, Pa., U.S. 210 41.48 N 76.51 W
Sylvania Heights 274a 34.02 S 151.06 E
Sylvan Lake, Ab., Can. 182 52.19 N 114.05 W
Sylvan Lake, Il., U.S. 278 42.15 N 88.03 W
Sylvan Lake, Mi., U.S. 281 42.37 N 83.20 W
Sylvan Lake ⊜, Ab., Can. 182 52.21 N 114.10 W
Sylvan Lake ⊜, In., U.S. 216 41.29 N 85.20 W
Sylvan Lake ⊜, Mi., U.S. 281 42.37 N 83.20 W
Sylvan Pass)(202 44.28 N 110.08 W
Sylvan Shores 220 28.49 N 81.41 W
Sylvensteinsee ⊜[1] 64 47.34 N 11.32 E
Sylvester, Ga., U.S. 192 31.31 N 83.50 W
Sylvester, Tx., U.S. 196 32.43 N 100.15 W
Sylvester, Mount ∧[2] 186 48.11 N 55.04 W
Sylvia 198 37.57 N 98.24 W
Sym 74 60.20 N 88.23 E
Symmes Creek ≏ 188 38.26 N 82.27 W
Syn'a 24 65.22 N 57.42 E
Syndal 274b 37.53 S 145.09 E
Synkovo 82 55.21 N 37.38 E
Synnyr, chrebet ⋀ 88 56.50 N 111.10 E
Syntul 80 55.00 N 41.18 E
Synžereja 78 47.38 N 28.09 E
Syon House ⊥ 260 51.29 N 0.19 W
Syosset 210 40.49 N 73.30 W
Syowa ⊍[3] 9 69.00 S 39.35 E
Syracuse, In., U.S. 216 41.25 N 85.45 W
Syracuse, Ks., U.S. 198 37.58 N 101.45 W
Syracuse, Ne., U.S. 198 40.39 N 96.11 W
Syracuse, N.Y., U.S. 210 43.02 N 76.08 W
Syracuse Hancock International Airport ⊠, N.Y., U.S. 210 43.07 N 76.07 W
Syracuse Hancock International Airport ⊠, N.Y., U.S. 212 43.07 N 76.07 W
Syracuse → Siracusa 70 37.04 N 15.18 E
Syrčan 80 57.22 N 50.15 E
Syrdarja 85 40.52 N 68.38 E
Syrdarja (Syr Darya) ≏ 72 46.03 N 61.00 E
Syr-Darya → Syrdarja ≏ 72 46.03 N 61.00 E
Syre 46 58.22 N 4.14 W
Syre ≏ 56 49.35 N 6.08 E
Syria (Sūrīyah) □[1], Asia 118 35.00 N 38.00 E
Syria (Sūrīyah) □[1], Asia 128 35.00 N 38.00 E
Syriam 110 16.46 N 96.15 E
Syrian Desert → Shām, Bādiyat ash- ✦[2] 128 32.00 N 40.00 E
Syrien → Syria □[1] 128 35.00 N 38.00 E
Syrie → Syria □[1] 128 35.00 N 38.00 E
Syrskij 76 52.34 N 39.29 E
Sysert' 86 56.29 N 60.49 E
Sysmä 26 61.30 N 25.41 E
Sysola ≏ 24 61.42 N 50.53 E
Sysslebäck 26 60.44 N 12.52 E
Syston 42 52.42 N 1.04 W
Systyg-Chem 88 52.40 N 95.30 E
Syt'kovo 76 56.31 N 34.01 E
Sytykanskij, porog ∟ 88 57.49 N 118.33 E
Syukunoshō 270 34.50 N 135.32 E
Syväri ⊜ 26 63.16 N 28.06 E
Syzran' 80 53.09 N 48.27 E
Syzran' ≏ 80 53.04 N 48.26 E
Szabadka → Subotica 38 46.06 N 19.39 E
Szabolcs-Szatmár-Bereg □[6] 30 48.00 N 22.10 E
Szada 264c 47.38 N 19.19 E
Szamocin 30 53.02 N 17.08 E
Szamos (Someș) ≏ 38 48.07 N 22.20 E
Szamotuły 30 52.37 N 16.35 E
Szarvas 30 46.52 N 20.34 E
Szatmárnémeti → Satu Mare 38 47.48 N 22.53 E
Százhalombatta 264c 47.20 N 18.56 E
Szczawnica 30 49.26 N 20.30 E
Szczecin (Stettin) 30 53.24 N 14.32 E
Szczecin □[4] 30 53.45 N 15.00 E
Szczecinek (Neustettin) 30 53.43 N 16.42 E
Szczeciński, Zalew (Oderhaff) ⊂ 54 53.46 N 14.14 E
Szczekociny 30 50.38 N 19.50 E
Szczuczyn 30 53.34 N 22.18 E
Szczytno 30 53.34 N 21.00 E
Szechwan Basin → Sichuan Pendi ⊻[1] 102 30.00 N 105.00 E
Szechwan → Sichuan □[4] 102 31.00 N 105.00 E
Szécsény 30 48.06 N 19.31 E
Szeged 30 46.15 N 20.09 E
Szeghalom 30 47.01 N 21.11 E
Székesfehérvár 30 47.12 N 18.25 E
Szekszárd 30 46.21 N 18.42 E
Szemenyecsörnye 61 46.30 N 16.37 E
Szentendre 30 47.40 N 19.05 E
Szentendrei-Duna ≏[1] 264c 47.36 N 19.05 E
Szentendrei-sziget I 264c 47.39 N 19.07 E
Szentes 30 46.39 N 20.16 E
Szentgotthárd 61 46.57 N 16.17 E
Szentpéterfa 61 47.06 N 16.29 E
Szeping → Siping 89 43.12 N 124.20 E
Szépművészeti Museum ⊍ 264c 47.31 N 19.05 E
Szerencs 30 48.09 N 21.13 E
Szigethalom 264c 47.20 N 19.00 E
Szigetszentmiklós 264c 47.21 N 19.03 E
Szilas-patak ≏ 264c 47.36 N 19.06 E
Szlichtyngowa 30 51.43 N 16.15 E
Szob 30 47.50 N 18.52 E
Szolnok 30 47.10 N 20.12 E
Szombathely 61 47.14 N 16.38 E
Szprotawa 30 51.34 N 15.33 E
Sztum 30 53.56 N 19.01 E
Szubin 30 53.00 N 17.44 E
Szydłowiec 30 51.14 N 20.51 E
Szypliszki 30 54.15 N 23.05 E

T

Ta ≏ 94 36.17 N 139.54 E
Taacyn ≏ 102 45.09 N 101.27 E
Taal 116 13.53 N 120.55 E
Taal, Lake ⊜ 116 13.55 N 121.00 E
Taalintehdas → Dalsbruk 26 60.02 N 22.31 E
Taan ≏ 100 24.24 N 120.36 E
Taancan Point › 116 10.00 N 125.01 E
Taavetti 26 60.55 N 27.34 E
Tabacal 252 23.16 S 64.15 W
Tabacal, Quebrada ≏ 286c 10.31 N 67.02 W
Tabaco 116 13.23 N 123.44 E
Tabacundo 246 0.03 N 78.12 W
Tabai ≏ 164 3.01 S 135.52 E
Tabalosos 248 6.21 S 76.41 W
Tabanan 115b 8.32 S 115.08 E
Tabango 116 11.19 N 124.22 E
Tabankulu 158 30.58 S 29.19 E
Tábara 34 41.49 N 5.57 W
Tabar Island I 164 2.55 S 152.05 E
Tabar Islands II 164 2.50 S 152.00 E
Tabarka 148 36.57 N 8.45 E
Tabarz 54 50.52 N 10.31 E
Ṭabas 128 33.36 N 56.54 E
Tabasará ≏ 236 8.00 N 81.39 W
Tabasco □[3] 232 18.15 N 93.00 W
Ṭabas Masīnā 128 32.48 N 60.14 E
Tabat 86 52.57 N 90.43 E
Tabatinga ≏ 255 17.24 S 43.18 W
Tabayama 94 35.47 N 138.55 E
Tabayin 110 22.42 N 95.19 E
Tabb 208 37.08 N 76.29 W
Tabei 98 39.44 N 122.29 E
Tabelbala 148 29.23 N 3.15 W
Tabelbala, Kahal ⊥[8] 148 28.30 N 2.00 W
Taber 182 49.47 N 112.08 W
Taberg, Sve. 26 57.41 N 14.05 E
Taberg, Sve. 40 59.50 N 14.08 E
Taberg, N.Y., U.S. 210 43.18 N 75.37 W
Tabernacle 285 39.50 N 74.42 W
Tabi 152 8.10 S 13.18 E
Tabiang 174d 0.52 S 169.35 E
Tabiano Terme 64 44.48 N 10.21 E
Tabira 250 7.35 S 37.33 W
Tabiteuea 174t 1.25 N 173.07 E
Tabiteuea I[1] 14 1.20 S 174.50 E
Tabla 150 13.46 N 3.01 E
Tabla, Cerro de la ∧ 240m 18.03 N 66.08 W
Tablada 288 34.42 S 58.32 W
Tablas, Cabo › 252 31.51 S 71.34 W
Tablas Island I 116 12.24 N 122.02 E
Tablas Plateau ⋀[1] 116 9.43 N 122.43 E
Tablas Strait ʊ 116 12.40 N 121.48 E
Tablat 34 36.24 N 3.19 E
Table Bay ⊂ 158 33.53 S 18.27 E
Table Cape › 172 39.06 S 178.00 E
Tableland 162 17.17 S 127.00 E
Table Mountain ∧, Nf., Can. 186 47.43 N 59.13 W
Table Mountain ∧, S. Afr. 158 33.57 S 18.25 E
Table Mountain ∧, Az., U.S. 200 32.49 N 110.31 W
Table Rock 198 40.10 N 96.05 W
Table Rock Lake ⊜[1] 194 36.35 N 93.30 W
Tabletop ∧, Austl. 162 22.32 S 123.55 E
Table Top ∧, Az., U.S. 200 32.46 N 112.07 W
Tabletop Mountain ∧ 171b 35.58 S 148.30 E
Tabley Mere ⊜ 262 53.17 N 2.25 W
Tabligbo 150 6.35 N 1.30 E
Tablones 240m 18.15 N 65.45 W
Taboan ≏ 116 17.57 N 122.11 E
Taboão, Ribeirão do ≏ 287b 23.40 S 46.28 W
Taboão da Serra 256 23.38 S 46.46 W
Taboco ≏ 248 19.53 S 55.58 W
Taboga 236 8.48 N 79.33 W
Tabogon 116 10.57 N 124.02 E
Tábor, Česko. 30 49.25 N 14.41 E
Tabor, Ross. 74 71.16 N 150.12 E
Tabor, Ia., U.S. 198 40.53 N 95.40 W
Tabor, N.J., U.S. 276 40.52 N 74.29 W
Tabor, S.D., U.S. 198 42.56 N 97.39 W
Tabor, Mount → Tavor, Har ∧ 132 32.41 N 35.23 E
Tabora 154 5.01 S 32.48 E
Tabora □[4] 154 5.15 S 32.45 E
Tabor City 192 34.08 N 78.52 W
Tabory 86 58.31 N 64.33 E
Tabou 150 4.25 N 7.21 W
Tabrīz 128 38.05 N 46.18 E
Tábua, Riacho da ≏ 250 9.12 S 44.25 W
Tabuaço 34 41.07 N 7.34 W
Tabuaeran I[1] 14 3.52 N 159.20 W
Tabuão 256 21.59 S 44.02 W
Tábuas 256 22.12 S 43.37 W
Tabu-dong 98 36.03 N 128.31 E
Tabuelan 116 10.49 N 123.52 E
Tabūk, Ar. Su. 128 28.23 N 36.35 E
Tabuk, Pil. 116 17.24 N 121.25 E
Tabuleiro 256 21.22 S 43.15 W
Tabuleiro do Norte 250 5.15 S 38.07 W
Tabuny 86 52.46 N 78.45 E
Tabuse 96 33.57 N 132.03 E
Tabuyung 114 0.51 N 99.00 E
Tabwémasana, Mont ∧ 175f 15.20 S 166.44 E
Täby 40 59.30 N 18.03 E
Tacagua, Quebrada ≏ 286c 10.37 N 67.02 W
Tacámbaro de Codallos 234 19.14 N 101.28 W
Tacaná 236 15.14 N 92.05 W
Tacaná, Volcán ∧[1] 236 15.08 N 92.06 W
Tacañitas 252 28.38 S 62.36 W
Tacaratu 250 9.06 S 38.10 W
Taceno 58 46.02 N 9.21 E
T'ačev 78 48.02 N 23.34 E
Taché, Lac ⊜ 176 64.00 N 120.00 W
Tacheng (Qoqek) 86 46.45 N 82.57 E
Tacherting 60 48.05 N 12.34 E
Tachia 100 24.21 N 120.37 E
Tachia ≏ 100 24.20 N 120.33 E
Tachiaochang Airport ⊠ 107 32.01 N 118.47 E
Tachiataš 72 42.22 N 59.35 E
Tachibana, Nihon 96 33.11 N 130.36 E
Tachibana, Nihon 96 33.54 N 132.17 E
Tachie ≏ 182 54.40 N 124.50 W
Tachikawa 94 35.42 N 139.25 E
Tachikawa Air Base ■ 268 35.43 N 139.25 E
Tachinger See ⊜ 60 47.58 N 12.45 E
Táchira □[3] 246 7.50 N 72.05 W
Tachoshui 100 24.20 N 121.44 E
Tachov 60 49.48 N 12.38 E
Tachta, Ross. 80 45.54 N 42.07 E
Tachta, Ross. 89 53.08 N 139.53 E
Tachta-Bazar 128 35.57 N 62.50 E
Tachtabrod 86 52.38 N 67.34 E
Tachtakupyr 86 43.02 N 60.17 E
Tachtamygda 89 54.06 N 123.34 E
Tacima 250 6.30 S 35.39 W
Taciņa ≏ 68 38.56 N 16.53 E
Tacinskij 80 48.13 N 41.17 E
Taciuã, Lago ≏ 246 4.29 S 60.35 W
Tacloban 116 11.15 N 125.00 E
Taclobo 116 12.20 N 122.34 E
Tacna, Perú 248 18.01 S 70.15 W
Tacna, Az., U.S. 200 32.41 N 113.57 W
Tacna □[5] 248 17.40 S 70.20 W
Tacoignières 261 48.50 N 1.40 E
Tacoma 224 47.15 N 122.26 W
Tacoma Narrows Bridge ✦[5] 224 47.16 N 122.33 W
Taconic 207 42.02 N 73.24 W
Taconic Range ⋀ 210 42.30 N 73.20 W
Taconic State Park ♦ 210 42.05 N 73.34 W
Tacony ✦[8] 285 40.02 N 75.03 W
Tacony Creek ≏ 285 40.01 N 75.06 W
Tacony Creek Park ♦ 285 40.02 N 75.07 W
Tacony Palmyra Bridge ✦[5] 285 40.01 N 75.02 W
Taco Pozo 252 25.37 S 63.17 W
Tacotalpa 234 17.36 N 92.49 W
Tacotalpa ≏ 234 17.50 N 92.52 W
Tacuarembó 252 31.44 S 55.59 W
Tacuarembó ≏ 252 32.25 S 55.29 W
Tacuarí ≏ 252 32.46 S 53.18 W
Tacuatí 252 23.27 S 56.35 W
Tacuba ✦[8] 286a 19.28 N 99.12 W
Tacubaya ✦[8] 286a 19.25 N 99.12 W
Tacuparé, Cachoeira ∟ 250 5.20 S 55.50 W
Tacurong 116 6.42 N 124.42 E
Tacuru, Bra. 252 23.43 N 55.02 W
Tacuru, Bra. 255 23.38 S 55.01 W
Tacurú, Laguna ⊜ 258 34.58 S 58.25 W
Tacutu (Takutu) ≏ 246 3.01 N 60.29 W
Tadain 270 34.52 N 135.24 E
Tadami 92 37.21 N 139.19 E
Tadaoka 270 34.29 N 135.24 E
Tadasuni 71 40.06 N 8.53 E
Tadcaster 44 53.53 N 1.16 W
Tademaït, Plateau du ⋀[1] 148 28.30 N 2.00 E
Tadenac Lake ⊜ 212 45.03 N 79.56 W
Tādepallegūdem 122 16.50 N 81.30 E
Tadía, Ciénaga de ⊜ 246 6.48 N 76.49 W
Tadine 175f 21.33 S 167.52 E
Tadio, Lagune ⊂ 150 5.11 N 5.15 W
Tadjemout 148 25.37 N 3.48 E
Tadjenanet 34 36.08 N 5.59 E
Tadjeraout, Oued ∨ 148 21.17 N 1.19 E
Tadjoura 144 11.47 N 42.54 E
Tadjoura, Golfe de ⊂ 144 11.42 N 43.00 E
Tadley 42 51.21 N 1.08 W
Tado 94 35.08 N 136.38 E
Tadok 114 3.58 N 96.19 E
Tadotsu 96 34.16 N 133.45 E
Tadoule Lake ⊜ 176 58.36 N 98.20 W
Tadoussac 186 48.09 N 69.43 W
Tādpatri 122 14.55 N 78.01 E
Taduno 112 1.55 S 123.05 E
Tadworth 42 51.17 N 0.14 W
Tadzhikistan → Tajikistan □[1] 72 39.00 N 71.00 E
Tadzhikstan → Tajikistan □[1] 72 39.00 N 71.00 E
Tadžikabad 85 39.07 N 70.50 E
T'aean 98 36.46 N 126.16 E
T'aebaek-san ∧ 98 37.06 N 128.55 E
T'aebaek-sanmaek ⋀ 98 37.40 N 128.50 E
Taebu-do I 98 37.15 N 126.35 E
Taech'ŏn 98 36.22 N 126.34 E
Taech'ŏng-do I 98 37.49 N 124.43 E
Taedong 98 39.05 N 125.31 E
Taedong-gang ≏ 98 38.42 N 125.15 E
Taegu 98 35.52 N 128.35 E
Taegu □[4] 98 35.50 N 128.35 E
Taegwan 98 40.13 N 125.12 E
Taehan-Min'guk → Korea, South □[1] 98 36.30 N 128.00 E
Taehŭksan-do I 98 34.40 N 125.25 E
Taehŭng 98 40.06 N 126.56 E
Taehwajŏn 271b 37.36 N 126.52 E
T'aein 98 35.40 N 126.55 E
Taejin 98 36.34 N 129.24 E
Taejŏn 98 36.20 N 127.26 E
Taejujŏm 98 38.24 N 127.58 E
T'aemo-san ∧ 271b 37.27 N 127.04 E
Taeng ≏ 110 19.06 N 98.57 E
Taer 102 34.09 N 98.50 E
Ta'erwan 100 31.49 N 113.25 E
Taeryanghwa 98 41.14 N 129.42 E
Tafahi I 14 15.51 S 173.43 W
Tafahnā al-ʿAzab 142 30.36 N 31.15 E
Tafalla 34 42.31 N 1.40 W
Tafanlieh 100 21.58 N 120.46 E
Ṭafas 132 32.44 N 36.04 E
Tafāsīkh, Ghurd at- ⊥[8] 142 29.43 N 29.45 E
Tafassasset, Oued (Oued Tafassâsset) ∨ 148 20.56 N 10.12 E
Tafassâsset, Ténéré du ✦[2] 146 21.00 N 11.00 E
Tafea □[8] 175f 19.30 S 169.00 E
Tafelbaai → Table Bay ⊂ 158 33.53 S 18.27 E
Tafelberg ∧ 250 3.55 N 56.10 W
Tafermaar 164 6.51 S 134.06 E
Taff ≏ 42 51.27 N 3.09 W
Tafiré 150 9.04 N 5.10 W
Tafí Viejo 252 26.44 S 65.16 W
Taflan 130 41.25 N 36.09 E
Tafna, Oued ≏ 34 35.17 N 1.30 W
Tafo 150 6.13 N 0.22 W
Tafraoute 148 29.40 N 8.58 W
Taft, Īrān 128 31.45 N 54.14 E
Taft, Pil. 116 11.54 N 125.25 E
Taft, Ca., U.S. 204 35.08 N 119.27 W
Taft, Fl., U.S. 220 28.23 N 81.24 W
Taft, Ok., U.S. 196 35.45 N 95.32 W
Taft, Tx., U.S. 196 27.58 N 97.23 W
Taftān, Kūh-e ∧ 128 28.36 N 61.08 E
Tafton 210 41.25 N 75.11 W
Taga, Nihon 94 35.13 N 136.17 E
Taga, Nihon 270 34.49 N 135.49 E
Taga, W. Sam. 175a 13.46 S 172.28 W
Tagabukid 116 7.00 N 126.21 E
Taga Dzong 124 27.04 N 89.53 E
Tagagawik ≏ 180 66.30 N 159.00 W
Tagaj 80 54.18 N 47.39 E
Tagajō 92 38.20 N 141.00 E
Tagan 86 54.57 N 77.18 E
Tagana-an 116 9.42 N 125.35 E
Taganrog 83 47.12 N 38.56 E
Taganrogskij zaliv ⊂ 78 47.00 N 38.23 E
Tagant □[4] 150 18.20 N 11.30 W
Tagânt ✦[1] 150 18.00 N 12.00 W
Tagapula Island I 116 12.04 N 124.12 E
Tågarp 41 55.56 N 12.57 E
Tagauayan Island I 116 10.58 N 121.13 E
Tagawa 96 33.38 N 130.49 E
Tagaytay 116 14.06 N 120.56 E
Tagbara 152 5.56 N 21.09 E
Tagbilaran 116 9.39 N 123.51 E
Tagdempt → Tihert 148 35.28 N 1.21 E
Tage 164 6.20 S 143.20 E
Tageren Canal ≊ 174q 9.33 N 138.09 E
Taggia 62 43.52 N 7.51 E
Taghit 148 30.55 N 2.02 W
Taghkanic Creek ≏ 210 42.13 N 73.45 W
Taghmon 48 52.18 N 6.39 W
Tagig 269f 14.32 N 121.04 E
Tagig ≏ 269f 14.31 N 121.05 E
T'aginka 78 46.47 N 33.04 E
Tagish Lake ⊜ 180 59.45 N 134.15 W
Tagliacozzo 66 42.04 N 13.14 E
Tagliamento ≏ 64 45.38 N 13.06 E
Tagliata, Monte della ∧ 64 44.34 N 9.48 E
Taglio di Po 64 45.00 N 12.12 E
Tagna 88 53.36 N 101.54 E
Tagna ≏ 88 53.38 N 101.53 E
Tago 116 9.02 N 126.13 E
Tago ≏ 116 9.01 N 126.14 E
Tagoloan 116 8.32 N 124.45 E
Tagolo Point › 116 8.44 N 123.23 E
Tagon Harbour ⊂ 162 33.53 S 123.00 E
Tagounit 148 29.58 N 5.36 W
Tagourâret ⊤[4] 150 17.45 N 7.43 W
Tagow Bāy 120 35.42 N 66.03 E
Tagrina, Oued ∨ 148 21.00 N 6.16 E
Taguatinga 255 12.25 S 46.26 W
Tagubanhan Island I 116 11.08 N 123.07 E
Tagudin 116 16.56 N 120.27 E
Taguedoufat ∨ 150 14.50 N 7.42 E
Taguke 120 32.07 N 84.35 E
Tagul ≏ 88 55.35 N 97.45 E
Tagula Island I 160 11.30 S 153.30 E
Tagum 116 7.28 N 125.48 E
T'agun 86 53.56 N 85.38 E
Tagun Bay ⊂ 116 13.55 N 123.46 E
Tagus (Tejo) (Tajo) ≏ 34 38.40 N 9.24 W
T'agyŏng-ni 98 38.04 N 126.03 E
Tah, Sebkha ⊜ 148 27.45 N 12.42 W
Taha 89 47.33 N 124.14 E
Tahaa I 14 16.38 S 151.30 W
Tahakopa 172 46.31 S 169.23 E
Tahala 148 34.04 N 4.20 W
Tahan, Gunong ∧ 114 4.38 N 102.14 E
Tahanaoute 148 31.24 N 7.54 W
Tahāneh-ye Ney Basteh 128 32.59 N 60.53 E
Tahara 94 34.40 N 137.16 E
Tahart 148 22.51 N 5.12 E
Tahat ∧ 148 23.18 N 5.47 E
Taheke 172 35.27 S 173.39 E
Ṭāherī 128 27.42 N 52.21 E
Tahgong, Puntan › 174n 15.06 N 145.39 E
Tahifet 148 22.58 N 5.55 E
Tahiryuak Lake ⊜ 176 70.56 N 112.20 W
Tahiti I 174s 17.37 S 149.27 W
Tahkuna neem › 76 59.07 N 22.36 E
Tāhlāb (Ṭālāb) ≏ 128 28.09 N 62.45 E
Tahlequah 196 35.54 N 94.58 W
Ṭahmā wa Minshāt ʿAbd as-Sayyid 142 29.38 N 31.14 E
Tahmoor 170 34.13 S 150.36 E
Tahneta Pass)(180 61.53 N 147.20 W
Tahoe, Lake ⊜ 226 39.07 N 120.03 W
Tahoe City 226 39.10 N 120.08 W
Tahoe Lake ⊜ 176 70.15 N 108.45 W
Tahoe Paradise 226 38.52 N 120.01 W
Tahoe Valley 226 38.55 N 120.00 W
Tahoka 196 33.10 N 101.47 W
Taholah 224 47.20 N 124.17 W
Tahoua 150 14.54 N 5.16 E
Tahoua □[5] 150 16.00 N 5.00 E
Tahquamenon ≏ 190 46.34 N 85.02 W
Tahquamenon Falls State Park ♦ 190 46.29 N 85.05 W
Tahsi 100 24.57 N 121.53 E
Tahsis 182 49.55 N 126.39 W
Ṭahṭā 140 26.46 N 31.30 E
Tahtaköprü 130 39.57 N 29.39 E
Tahtsa Lake ⊜ 182 53.42 N 127.26 W
Tahtsa Peak ∧ 182 53.33 N 127.47 W
Tahu 100 24.26 N 120.52 E
Tahuamanu ≏ 248 11.06 S 67.36 W
Tahuata I 174x 9.57 S 139.05 W
Tahulandang, Pulau I 112 2.20 N 125.25 E
Tahuna 112 3.37 N 125.29 E
Tahuofang ⊜[1] 104 41.55 N 124.07 E
Tahuya ≏ 224 47.23 N 123.03 W
Ṭahwāy 142 30.22 N 30.52 E
Taï, C. Iv. 150 5.52 N 7.27 W
Tai, It. 64 46.25 N 12.20 E
Tai, Nihon 270 34.31 N 135.26 E
Tai ✦[8] 270 34.45 N 135.00 E
Taiaçupeba 256 23.40 S 46.11 W
Tai'an, Zhg. 98 36.12 N 117.07 E
Tai'an, Zhg. 104 41.23 N 122.27 E
Tai'an, Zhg. 107 30.05 N 105.47 E
Tai'angang 106 31.43 N 121.40 E
Taiarapu, Presqu'île de ›[1] 174s 17.47 S 149.14 W
Taibai 102 34.00 N 107.18 E
Taibai Shan ∧, Zhg. 98 39.19 N 114.11 E
Taibai Shan ∧, Zhg. 102 33.54 N 107.46 E
Taibilla, Sierra de ⋀ 34 38.10 N 2.10 W
Taibon Agordino 64 46.18 N 12.00 E
Taibus Qi (Baochang) 98 41.56 N 115.22 E
Taicang 106 31.26 N 121.07 E
T'aichou → Taizhou 100 32.30 N 119.58 E
T'aichung 100 24.09 N 120.41 E
Taichu → T'aichung 100 24.09 N 120.41 E
Taicunzhen 106 31.27 N 119.03 E
Taiden → Taejŏn 98 36.20 N 127.26 E
Taiei 94 35.49 N 140.25 E
Taieri ≏ 172 46.03 S 170.11 E
Taif → Aṭ-Ṭā'if 144 21.16 N 40.24 E
Taigu 102 37.28 N 112.30 E
Tai Hang 271d 22.17 N 114.11 E
Taihang Shan ⋀ 102 38.00 N 114.00 E
Taihape 172 39.40 S 175.48 E
Taihe, Zhg. 100 33.11 N 115.36 E
Taihe, Zhg. 100 26.49 N 114.55 E
Taihe, Zhg. 107 30.10 N 105.56 E
Taihezhen, Zhg. 89 44.47 N 123.29 E
Taihezhen, Zhg. 107 30.07 N 103.50 E
Taihezhen, Zhg. 107 30.06 N 106.03 E
Taiho 174m 26.39 N 128.07 E
Taihoku → T'aipei 100 25.03 N 121.30 E
T'aihsi 100 23.42 N 120.11 E
T'aihsien → Taizhou 100 32.30 N 119.58 E
Taihu 100 30.26 N 116.16 E
Tai Hu ⊜ 106 31.15 N 120.10 E
Taijiang 102 26.32 N 108.22 E
Taijimiao 98 40.55 N 113.46 E
Taijüan → Taiyuan 102 37.55 N 112.30 E
Taikang 98 34.04 N 114.50 E
Taikkyi 110 17.19 N 95.58 E
Taikou 102 31.53 N 111.07 E
Taiko-yama ∧ 96 35.46 N 135.12 E
Taikyu → Taegu 98 35.52 N 128.35 E
Tailai 89 46.23 N 123.27 E
Tai Lam Chung 271d 22.22 N 114.01 E
Tai Lam Chung Reservoir ⊜[1] 271d 22.23 N 114.01 E
Tailem Bend 166 35.16 S 139.27 E
Tailfingen 58 48.15 N 9.01 E
Tai Long, H.K. 271d 22.25 N 114.22 E
Tai Long, H.K. 271d 22.13 N 113.59 E
Tai Long Bay ⊂ 271d 22.24 N 114.24 E
Taima, Nihon 96 34.30 N 135.42 E
T'aima, T'aiwan 100 22.37 N 120.59 E
Taimba 74 60.18 N 98.58 E
Taimei 100 23.19 N 114.29 E
Tai Mong Tsai 271d 22.24 N 114.18 E
Tai Mo Shan ∧ 271d 22.25 N 114.07 E
Taimyr-Halbinsel → Tajmyr, poluostrov ›[1] 74 76.00 N 104.00 E
Tain 46 57.48 N 4.04 W
Tainaka 270 34.36 N 135.37 E
T'ainan 100 23.00 N 120.12 E
Taínaron, Ákra › 38 36.22 N 22.30 E
Taining 100 26.54 N 117.09 E
Tain-l'Hermitage 62 45.04 N 4.51 E
Tai O, H.K. 100 22.15 N 113.51 E
Taio, It. 64 46.20 N 11.04 E
Taiobeiras 255 15.49 S 42.14 W
Tai Pang Wan ⊂ 100 22.30 N 114.24 E
T'aipei, T'aiwan 100 25.03 N 121.30 E
T'aipei, T'aiwan 269d 25.03 N 121.30 E
T'aipei □[6] 269d 25.00 N 121.40 E
Taipei Bridge ✦[5] 269d 25.04 N 121.30 E
T'aipeihsien 100 25.00 N 121.27 E
Taipei Institute of Technology ⊍[2] 269d 25.02 N 121.32 E
Taipei New Park ♦ 269d 25.03 N 121.31 E
T'aipei Shih □[7] 269d 25.05 N 121.33 E
Taiping, Malay. 114 4.51 N 100.44 E
Taiping, Zhg. 100 22.49 N 113.41 E
Taiping, Zhg. 100 30.18 N 118.12 E
Taiping, Zhg. 102 22.40 N 107.05 E
Taiping, Zhg. 107 30.24 N 103.37 E
Taipingchang, Zhg. 102 27.25 N 103.04 E
Taipingchang, Zhg. 107 29.33 N 103.33 E
Taipingchang, Zhg. 107 29.53 N 106.04 E
Taipingchang, Zhg. 107 29.55 N 103.49 E
Taipingchang, Zhg. 107 30.10 N 106.21 E
Taipingchang, Zhg. 107 30.25 N 103.46 E
Taipingchang, Zhg. 107 30.39 N 105.54 E
Taipingchuan, Zhg. 89 44.23 N 123.11 E
Taipingchuan, Zhg. 98 42.36 N 127.20 E
Taipingdian 102 32.08 N 111.45 E
Taipingkou 100 29.50 N 113.35 E
Taipingling 89 43.26 N 128.09 E
Taipingshan, Zhg. 98 40.34 N 122.25 E
Taipingshan, Zhg. 104 41.36 N 123.41 E
Taipingshao 98 40.54 N 125.08 E
Taipingsi 107 29.24 N 103.34 E
Taipingxigou 104 42.36 N 121.13 E
Taipingzhai 104 42.14 N 124.07 E
Taipingzhen, Zhg. 89 46.44 N 130.44 E
Taipingzhen, Zhg. 102 35.42 N 107.37 E
Taipingzhen, Zhg. 107 29.24 N 105.47 E
Taipingzhen, Zhg. 107 30.26 N 104.12 E
Taipingzhuang, Zhg. 104 42.38 N 123.45 E
Taipingzhuang, Zhg. 105 40.03 N 116.24 E
Taipingzhuang, Zhg. 105 40.08 N 117.36 E
Tai Po Hoi ⊂ 271d 22.26 N 114.12 E
Tai Po Tsai 271d 22.21 N 114.15 E
Taipu 250 5.37 S 35.36 W
Taira 94 36.26 N 136.57 E
Taira → Iwaki 94 37.03 N 140.55 E
Tairetá 256 22.36 S 43.42 W
Tairiqiao 106 30.59 N 121.33 E
Tais 112 4.06 S 102.34 E
Taisen-zan ∧ 96 33.06 N 131.17 E
Taisha 96 35.24 N 132.40 E
Taisha → Izumo 96 35.22 N 132.46 E
Taishaku-kyō ♦ 96 34.53 N 133.13 E
Taishaku-zan ∧, Nihon 94 36.58 N 139.28 E
Taishaku-zan ∧, Nihon 270 34.47 N 135.07 E
Taishan, Zhg. 98 39.01 N 113.36 E
Taishan, Zhg. 102 22.16 N 112.44 E
Taishanchang 107 30.32 N 106.42 E
Taishi, Nihon 96 34.50 N 134.33 E
Taishi, Nihon 270 34.31 N 135.39 E
Taishō 96 33.12 N 132.58 E
Taishō ✦[8] 270 34.38 N 135.27 E
Tai Shui Hang 271d 22.25 N 14.13 E
Taishun 100 27.33 N 119.43 E
Tai Tam Bay ⊂ 271d 22.13 N 114.13 E
Taitao, Peninsula de ›[1] 254 46.30 S 74.25 W
Taitapu 172 43.40 S 172.33 E
Taitō ✦[8] 268 35.43 N 139.47 E
Tai Tong 271d 22.25 N 114.01 E
Taitouying 98 40.02 N 119.12 E
Taitō-zaki › 94 35.18 N 140.25 E
T'aitung 100 22.45 N 121.09 E
Taivalkoski 26 65.34 N 28.15 E
Tai Wan 271d 22.10 N 114.15 E
Taiwan (T'aiwan) □[1], Asia 90 23.30 N 121.00 E
Taiwan (T'aiwan) □[1], Asia 100 23.30 N 121.00 E
T'aiwan I 100 23.30 N 121.00 E
Taiwan Strait ʊ 100 24.00 N 119.00 E
Tai Wan Tau 271d 22.18 N 114.17 E
Taixi 100 24.42 N 116.56 E
Taixian 100 32.31 N 120.09 E
Taixing 106 32.11 N 120.01 E
Taixizhen 106 31.03 N 119.49 E
Taiyang 100 30.12 N 119.19 E
Taiyanggong 271a 39.58 N 116.25 E
Taiyetos Óros ⋀ 38 37.16 N 22.12 E
Ṭaiyiba 132 32.16 N 35.01 E
Taiyuan 102 37.55 N 112.30 E
Taizhao 120 30.01 N 93.08 E
Taizhou 100 32.30 N 119.58 E
Taizhou Liedao II 100 28.30 N 121.53 E
Taizi ≏ 98 41.00 N 122.26 E
Taʿizz 144 13.38 N 44.04 E
Tāj al-ʿIzz 142 30.57 N 31.35 E
Tajarḥī 146 24.21 N 14.28 E
Tajbola 24 68.26 N 33.19 E
Tajdakovo 82 54.29 N 37.32 E
Tajerouine 36 35.54 N 8.34 E
Tajetteret, Oued ∨ 148 21.20 N 7.22 E
Tajga 86 56.04 N 85.37 E
Tajgonos, mys › 74 60.35 N 160.08 E
Tajgonos, poluostrov ›[1] 74 61.20 N 161.00 E
Tajikistan □[1], Asia 72 39.00 N 71.00 E
Tajikistan □[1], Asia 85 39.00 N 71.00 E
Tajikstan → Tajikistan □[1] 72 39.00 N 71.00 E
Tajima 94 37.12 N 139.46 E
Tajimi 94 35.19 N 137.08 E
Tajique 200 34.45 N 106.17 W
Tajiri 270 34.24 N 135.18 E
Tajitos 232 30.58 N 112.18 W
Tajlakdžegen 86 43.54 N 60.29 E
Tajlakovy 86 59.20 N 74.04 E
Tāj Mahal ⊥ 124 27.10 N 78.03 E
Tajmura ≏ 72 63.46 N 98.01 E
Tajmyr, ozero ⊜ 74 74.30 N 102.30 E
Tajmyr, poluostrov ›[1] 74 76.00 N 104.00 E
Tajna 88 56.27 N 95.30 E
Tajninka 265b 55.54 N 37.45 E
Tajo → Tagus ≏ 34 38.40 N 9.24 W
Tajožnyj, Ross. 86 56.09 N 94.29 E
Tajožnyj, Ross. 88 56.13 N 94.55 E
Tajpur, India 124 25.51 N 85.41 E
Tajpur, India 124 29.10 N 78.29 E
Tājpur, India 272b 22.44 N 88.16 E
Tajpur Khurd ✦[8] 272a 28.35 N 77.03 E
Tajšet 88 55.57 N 98.00 E
Tajsojgan 80 48.19 N 53.29 E
Tajturka 88 52.51 N 103.28 E
Tajumulco, Volcán ∧[1] 236 15.02 N 91.55 W
Tajuña ≏ 34 40.07 N 3.35 W
Tājūrā', Lībiyā 146 32.53 N 13.21 E
Tajura, Ross. 88 57.00 N 106.35 E
Tajura ≏ 88 57.00 N 106.35 E
Tajžina 86 53.38 N 87.28 E
Tak 110 16.52 N 99.08 E
Takāb 128 36.24 N 47.07 E
Takabanare-jima I 174m 26.22 N 127.59 E
Takabara 150 11.50 N 11.30 W
Takachiho 92 32.42 N 131.18 E
Takachu 156 22.37 S 21.58 E
Takada → Bungo-takada 96 33.33 N 131.27 E
Takada → Yamato-takada 96 34.31 N 135.45 E
Takagi 268 35.56 N 139.35 E
Takahagi 94 36.43 N 140.43 E
Takahama, Nihon 94 34.55 N 136.59 E
Takahama, Nihon 94 37.00 N 136.46 E
Takahama, Nihon 96 35.29 N 135.33 E
Takahara ≏ 94 36.28 N 137.15 E
Takahashi 96 34.47 N 133.37 E
Takahashi ≏ 96 34.31 N 133.42 E
Takahe, Mount ∧ 9 76.16 S 112.14 W
Takaido ✦[8] 268 35.40 N 139.37 E
Takaishi 96 34.32 N 135.26 E
Takaka 172 40.51 S 172.48 E
Takakkaw Falls ∟ 182 51.30 N 116.28 W
Takalaou 146 10.07 N 19.48 E
Takalar 112 5.28 S 119.24 E
Takamatsu, Nihon 94 36.46 N 136.43 E
Takamatsu, Nihon 96 34.20 N 134.03 E
Takami-shima I 96 34.19 N 133.41 E
Takamiya 96 34.47 N 132.44 E
Takami-yama ∧ 94 34.25 N 136.05 E
Takamori 94 35.33 N 137.53 E
Takanabe 92 32.08 N 131.30 E
Takanawa-hantō ›[1] 96 33.58 N 132.56 E
Takanawa-san ∧ 96 33.56 N 132.51 E
Takane, Nihon 94 36.02 N 137.29 E
Takane, Nihon 94 35.50 N 138.25 E
Takanezawa 94 36.37 N 139.59 E
Takano 96 35.02 N 132.55 E
Takanosu 92 40.13 N 140.22 E
Takaoka 94 36.45 N 137.01 E
Takao → Kaohsiung 100 22.38 N 120.17 E
Takao-kokutei-kōen ♦ 94 35.38 N 139.15 E
Takao-san ∧, Nihon 94 35.38 N 139.15 E
Takao-san ∧, Nihon 270 34.49 N 135.51 E
Takapau 172 40.02 S 176.21 E
Takapuna 172 36.47 S 174.47 E
Takara-jima I 93b 29.09 N 129.13 E
Takarazuka 270 34.49 N 135.21 E
Takasago 96 34.45 N 134.48 E
Takasaki 94 36.20 N 139.01 E
Takase 96 34.10 N 133.45 E
Takase ≏ 94 36.28 N 137.52 E
Takashima, Nihon 92 32.39 N 129.45 E
Takashima, Nihon 94 35.18 N 136.01 E
Taka-shima I 96 34.50 N 131.50 E
Takashippu 174m 26.24 N 127.44 E
Takasu 94 35.57 N 136.53 E
Takata 96 33.06 N 130.28 E
Takata → Joetsu 94 37.06 N 138.15 E
Takata → Rikuzen-takata 92 39.01 N 141.38 E
Takatō 94 35.50 N 138.04 E
Takatomi 94 35.29 N 136.47 E
Takatori 96 34.27 N 135.48 E
Takatori-yama ∧ 96 33.18 N 130.43 E
Takatori-yama ∧[2] 268 35.18 N 139.37 E
Takatsu ≏ 96 34.42 N 131.49 E
Takatsuki, Nihon 94 35.28 N 136.14 E
Takatsuki, Nihon 96 34.51 N 135.37 E
Takaungu 154 3.41 S 39.51 E
Ta-kaw 110 21.36 N 98.56 E
Takayama, Nihon 94 36.08 N 137.15 E
Takayama, Nihon 94 36.37 N 138.57 E
Takayama, Nihon 94 36.40 N 138.21 E
Takayama, Nihon 270 34.45 N 135.44 E
Takayanagi, Nihon 94 37.13 N 138.38 E
Takayanagi, Nihon 268 35.25 N 139.57 E
Tak Bai 114 6.16 N 102.03 E
Takčijan 85 38.32 N 68.03 E
Takebe 96 34.52 N 133.54 E
Takefu 94 35.54 N 136.10 E
Takehara 96 34.21 N 132.55 E
Takeli 85 40.30 N 69.25 E
Takenake 120 34.11 N 81.20 E
Takengon 114 4.38 N 96.50 E
Takeno ≏ 96 35.45 N 135.06 E
Takenotsuka ✦[8] 268 35.48 N 139.48 E
Takeo 92 33.12 N 130.01 E
Takeoka 268 35.12 N 139.51 E
Tåkern ⊜ 26 58.21 N 14.48 E
Takeshi 94 36.17 N 138.14 E
Take-shima I 93b 30.49 N 130.26 E
Take-shima (Tok-to) II 92 37.17 N 131.53 E
Tākestān 128 36.04 N 49.43 E
Taketa 96 32.58 N 131.24 E
Taketoyo 94 34.51 N 136.55 E
Takêv 110 10.59 N 104.47 E
Take-yama ∧[2] 268 35.13 N 139.39 E
Takhādīd ⊤[4] 128 29.59 N 44.30 E
Takhār □[4] 120 36.30 N 69.30 E
Takhatpur 124 22.09 N 81.52 E
Takhli 110 15.15 N 100.21 E
Ta Khoa 110 21.13 N 104.18 E
Takht-e Jamshīd ⊥ 128 29.57 N 52.52 E
Takht-i-Bhāi 123 34.17 N 71.56 E
Tāki, India 126 22.36 N 88.55 E
Taki, Nihon 94 34.30 N 136.33 E
Taki, Nihon 96 35.16 N 132.38 E
Taki, Pap. N. Gui. 175e 6.29 S 155.50 E
Takijuk Lake ⊜ 176 66.15 N 113.05 W
Takikawa 92a 43.33 N 141.54 E
Takino 96 34.56 N 134.58 E
Takipur 126 24.19 N 87.58 E
Takitimu Mountains ⋀ 172 45.41 S 167.53 E
Takla Lake ⊜ 182 55.25 N 125.53 W
Takla Landing 182 55.29 N 125.58 W
Takla Makan → Taklimakan Shamo ✦[2] 90 39.00 N 83.00 E
Taklimakan Shamo ✦[2] 90 39.00 N 83.00 E
Tako 94 35.44 N 140.28 E
Takob 85 38.50 N 68.57 E
Tako-bana › 96 35.36 N 133.06 E
Takolekaju, Pegunungan ⋀ 112 2.00 S 121.00 E
Takoma Park 284c 38.58 N 77.00 W
Takoradi → Sekondi-Takoradi 150 4.59 N 1.43 W
Takotna 180 62.56 N 156.04 W
Takow → Kaohsiung 100 22.38 N 120.17 E
Takpochao, Okso ∧ 174n 15.11 N 145.45 E
Takrouna 36 36.09 N 10.20 E
Taksimo 88 51.03 N 107.50 E
Taksino 82 56.19 N 36.10 E
Takslesluk Lake ⊜ 180 61.04 N 162.55 W
Taksony 264c 47.20 N 19.04 E
Taku 92 33.17 N 130.08 E
Taku ≏ 180 58.26 N 133.59 W
Takuan, Mount ∧ 175e 6.27 S 155.36 E
Takua Pa 110 8.53 N 98.21 E
Taku Glacier ⊓ 180 58.35 N 134.10 W
Takum 150 7.17 N 9.59 E
Takuma 96 34.13 N 133.40 E
Takundi 152 4.45 S 16.34 E
Takutea I 14 19.49 S 158.18 W
Takut Tangub Bay ⊂ 116 6.33 N 122.15 E
Takutu (Tacutu) ≏ 246 3.01 N 60.29 W
Takuu Islands II 14 4.45 S 157.00 E
Takysie Lake 182 53.54 N 125.53 W
Tāl 123 34.55 N 72.13 E
Tala, Bngl. 126 22.46 N 89.16 E
Tāla, India 124 23.43 N 81.02 E
Tala, Méx. 234 20.40 N 103.42 W
Talā, Miṣr 142 30.41 N 30.56 E
Tala, Ur. 252 34.21 S 55.46 W
Tala, Arroyo del ≏ 258 33.37 S 56.34 W
Ṭālāb (Tāhlāb) ≏ 128 28.09 N 62.45 E
Talacogon 116 8.28 N 125.46 E
Talaga 112 2.11 S 125.53 E
Talagang 123 32.55 N 72.25 E
Talagante 252 33.40 S 70.56 W
Talagou 104 41.37 N 120.32 E
Ta Lai 110 11.24 N 107.23 E
Talaimannar 122 9.05 N 79.44 E
Talāja 120 21.21 N 72.03 E
Talak ✦[1] 150 18.20 N 6.00 E
Talakag 116 8.16 N 124.37 E
Talakan 89 49.38 N 133.18 E
Talakovka 83 47.10 N 37.43 E
Tālāla 120 21.02 N 70.32 E
Talalajevka 78 50.51 N 33.08 E
Talamanca, Cordillera de ⋀ 236 9.30 N 83.40 W
Talamba 123 30.32 N 72.14 E
Talamone 66 42.33 N 11.08 E
Talana, It. 71 40.02 N 9.30 E
Talana, S. Afr. 158 28.10 S 30.15 E
Talandža 89 49.27 N 131.35 E
Talang, Gunung ∧ 112 0.58 S 100.39 E
Talangbatu 112 4.06 S 105.29 E
Talangbetutu 112 2.53 S 104.41 E
Talangpadang 112 5.21 S 104.11 E
Talangrimbo 112 3.29 S 105.25 E
Talant 58 47.19 N 5.00 E
Talap 80 48.26 N 48.03 E

Symbol	English	Deutsch	Español	Français	Português
≏	River	Fluß	Río	Rivière	Rio
≊	Canal	Kanal	Canal	Canal	Canal
∟	Waterfall, Rapids	Wasserfall, Stromschnellen	Cascada, Rápidos	Chute d'eau, Rapides	Cascata, Rápidos
ʊ	Strait	Meeresstraße	Estrecho	Détroit	Estreito
⊂	Bay, Gulf	Bucht, Golf	Bahía, Golfo	Baie, Golfe	Baía, Golfo
⊜	Lake, Lakes	See, Seen	Lago, Lagos	Lac, Lacs	Lago, Lagos
⋿	Swamp	Sumpf	Pantano	Marais	Pântano
⊓	Ice Features, Glacier	Eis- und Gletscherformen	Accidentes Glaciales	Formes glaciaires	Acidentes glaciares
⊤	Other Hydrographic Features	Andere Hydrographische Objekte	Otros Elementos Hidrográficos	Autres données hydrographiques	Outros acidentes hidrográficos
✛	Submarine Features	Untermeerische Objekte	Accidentes Submarinos	Formes de relief sous-marin	Acidentes submarinos
□	Political Unit	Politische Einheit	Unidad Politica	Entité politique	Unidade política
⊍	Cultural Institution	Kulturelle Institution	Institución Cultural	Institution culturelle	Instituição cultural
⊥	Historical Site	Historische Stätte	Sitio Histórico	Site historique	Sitio histórico
♦	Recreational Site	Erholungs- und Ferienort	Sitio de Recreo	Centre de loisirs	Area de Lazer
⊠	Airport	Flughafen	Aeropuerto	Aéroport	Aeroporto
■	Military Installation	Militäranlage	Instalación Militar	Installation militaire	Instalação militar
✦	Miscellaneous	Verschiedenes	Misceláneo	Divers	Diversos

I · 172 Tala-Taqu

ENGLISH / DEUTSCH

Name	Page	Lat.°′	Long.°′
Talara	246	4.34 S	81.17 W
Talarrubias	34	39.02 N	5.14 W
Talas	85	42.32 N	72.14 E
Talas ≃	85	44.02 N	69.37 E
Talasea	164	5.20 S	150.05 E
Talasskij-Alatau, chrebet ⋏	85	42.10 N	72.00 E
Talatakoh, Pulau I	112	0.22 S	122.05 E
Tal‘at al-Jamā‘ah, Rujm ∧	132	30.23 N	35.30 E
Talata Mafara	150	12.35 N	6.04 E
Talaud, Kepulauan II	108	4.20 N	126.50 E
Talavera	116	15.35 N	120.55 E
Talavera de la Reina	34	39.57 N	4.50 W
Talawdī	140	10.38 N	30.23 E
Talayan	116	6.55 N	124.24 E
Tālbāndh	126	22.03 N	86.20 E
Talbingo	171b	35.34 S	148.18 E
Talbingo Reservoir ⊜[1]	171b	35.43 S	148.20 E
Talbot	169	37.11 S	143.43 E
Talbot ≃	212	44.28 N	79.10 W
Talbot, Cape ›	164	13.48 S	126.43 E
Talbot Brook	168a	32.01 S	116.40 E
Talbot Brook ≃	168a	32.10 S	116.49 E
Talbot Islands II	164	9.15 S	142.08 E
Talbot Lake ⊜, Mb., Can.	184	54.00 N	99.55 W
Talbot Lake ⊜, On., Can.	212	44.42 N	78.51 W
Talbotton	192	32.40 N	84.32 W
Talbotville Royal	214	42.48 N	81.15 W
Talbragar ≃	166	32.12 S	148.37 E
Talca	252	35.26 S	71.40 W
Talcahuano	252	36.43 S	73.07 W
Tālcher	120	20.57 N	85.13 E
Talchichitle, Isla I	232	24.59 N	108.04 W
Talco	196	33.21 N	95.06 W
Talcottville	207	41.49 N	72.30 W
Talcy, Château de ⊥	50	47.46 N	1.27 E
Taldan	89	53.40 N	124.48 E
Tāldāngra	126	23.02 N	87.06 E
Taldom	82	56.44 N	37.32 E
Taldyapan, Kaz.	80	48.07 N	47.08 E
Taldyapan, Kaz.	80	49.46 N	50.14 E
Taldyk, pereval)(	85	39.47 N	73.11 E
Taldykuduk	80	50.09 N	49.33 E
Taldy-Kurgan	86	45.00 N	78.23 E
Taldy-Kurgan □[8]	85	44.00 N	78.00 E
Tale	150	9.26 N	1.07 W
Taleex	144	9.09 N	48.26 E
Talence	32	44.49 N	0.35 W
Talent	202	42.14 N	122.47 W
Tālesh	128	37.48 N	48.55 E
Taley	152	6.40 N	16.23 E
Talgar	85	43.18 N	77.18 E
Talgar, pik ∧	85	43.05 N	77.20 E
Talgarreg	42	52.08 N	4.18 W
Talgarth	42	52.00 N	3.15 W
Ṭalḥ, ‘Ilw aṭ- ∧[2]	142	28.30 N	29.38 E
Talhār	120	24.53 N	68.49 E
Tali, Pointe de ›	241o	15.56 N	61.12 W
Talia, Austl.	162	33.19 S	134.54 E
Talia, Méx.	196	25.44 N	102.26 W
Taliabu, Pulau I	112	1.48 S	124.48 E
Talian Dao I	98	39.03 N	122.52 E
Talibon	116	10.09 N	124.19 E
Talibong, Ko I	110	7.15 N	99.23 E
Talica, Ross.	76	58.44 N	41.34 E
Talica, Ross.	80	58.01 N	51.30 E
Talica, Ross.	86	57.00 N	63.43 E
Talickij Čamlyk	80	52.02 N	40.32 E
Talien → Dalian	98	38.53 N	121.35 E
Talihina	196	34.45 N	95.02 W
Tālīkota	122	16.29 N	76.19 E
Talikud Island I	116	6.56 N	125.42 E
Talim Island I	116	14.21 N	121.14 E
Talimuashili	85	39.08 N	77.03 E
Taling Chan	269a	13.46 N	100.27 E
Taliouine	148	30.36 N	7.49 W
Taliparamba	122	12.03 N	75.21 E
Tali Post	140	5.54 N	30.47 E
Talisay, Pil.	116	14.08 N	122.55 E
Talisay, Pil.	116	10.15 N	123.51 E
Talisay, Pil.	116	10.44 N	122.58 E
Talisayan	116	9.00 N	124.55 E
Talisei, Pulau I	112	1.51 N	125.05 E
Talish-Mikeyli	84	39.23 N	48.22 E
Talish Mountains (Kūhhā-ye Ṭavālesh ⋏	128	38.42 N	48.18 E
Talisker	46	57.17 N	6.27 W
Taliwang	115b	8.44 S	116.52 E
Tal'ka	76	53.22 N	28.21 E
Talkeetna	180	62.20 N	150.07 W
Talkeetna Mountains ⋏	180	62.10 N	148.15 W
Ṭalkhā	142	31.03 N	31.22 E
Talkheh ≃	128	37.52 N	45.53 E
Talladale	46	57.42 N	5.29 W
Talladega	194	33.26 N	86.06 W
Tall ‘Afar	128	36.22 N	42.27 E
Tallaght	48	53.26 N	6.21 W
Tal Lah, India	126	22.19 N	87.18 E
Tallah, Miṣr	142	28.05 N	30.44 E
Tallahaga Creek ≃	194	32.55 N	88.58 W
Tallahala Creek ≃	194	31.12 N	89.05 W
Tallahassee	192	30.26 N	84.16 W
Tallahatchie ≃	194	33.33 N	90.10 W
Tall al-Abyaḍ	130	36.41 N	38.57 E
Tall al-‘Amārnah (Akhetatem) ⊥	142	27.38 N	30.54 E
Tall al-Maskhūtah (Succotah) ⊥	142	30.33 N	32.07 E
Tall al-Muqayyar (Ur) ⊥	128	30.57 N	46.09 E
Tallanalla	168a	33.06 S	116.07 E
Tallangatta	166	36.13 S	147.15 E
Tallangatta Creek ≃	171b	36.15 S	147.13 E
Tallapoosa	194	33.44 N	85.17 W
Tallapoosa ≃	194	32.30 N	86.16 W
Tallard	62	44.28 N	6.03 E
Talla Reservoir ⊜[1]	46	55.29 N	3.24 W
Tall ar-Ratābah (Pithom) ⊥	142	30.32 N	32.06 E
Tall ar-Rub‘ (Mendes) ⊥	142	30.58 N	31.31 E
Tallassee	194	32.32 N	85.53 W
Tall as-Sulṭān ⊥	132	31.52 N	35.27 E
Tall Banī ‘Umrān	142	27.40 N	30.54 E
Tall Basṭah (Bubastis) ⊥	142	30.34 N	31.31 E
Tällberg	26	60.49 N	15.00 E
Tall Bīsah	130	34.50 N	36.44 E
Tall-e Khosrow-ye Soflá	128	30.37 N	51.35 E
Talleyville	208	39.48 N	75.32 W
Tallinn	76	59.25 N	24.45 E
Tall Kalakh	130	34.40 N	36.15 E
Tall Kayf	128	36.29 N	43.08 E
Tall Kūjik	130	36.48 N	42.04 E
Tallmadge	214	41.06 N	81.27 W
Tallman	276	41.07 N	74.06 W
Tallman Mountain State Park ♦	276	41.01 N	73.54 W
Talloires	62	45.51 N	6.13 E
Tallong	170	34.44 S	150.05 E
Tallow	48	52.05 N	8.00 W
Tallowa Dam ◆[6]	170	34.47 S	150.18 E
Tall Rāk	142	30.54 N	31.43 E
Tall Rif‘at	130	36.28 N	37.06 E
Tall Salḥab	130	35.15 N	36.22 E
Tall Tamir	130	36.39 N	40.22 E
Tallula	219	39.56 N	89.56 W
Tallulah	194	32.24 N	91.11 W
Tally	80	53.08 N	53.04 E
Tally Ho	274b	37.52 S	145.09 E
Tālma	126	23.29 N	89.54 E
Talmage, Ca., U.S.	204	39.08 N	123.10 W
Talmage, Ne., U.S.	198	40.31 N	96.01 W
Talmage, Pa., U.S.	208	40.07 N	76.13 W
Talmalmo	171b	35.56 S	147.30 E
Talmas	50	50.02 N	2.20 E
Talmazy	78	46.38 N	29.40 E
Tal'menka	86	53.51 N	83.35 E
Talmine	46	58.31 N	4.26 W
Talmont	32	46.28 N	1.37 W
Tal'niki	88	52.47 N	102.24 E
Tal'noje	78	48.53 N	30.42 E
Talo ∧	144	10.44 N	37.55 E
Taloda	120	21.34 N	74.13 E
Talofofo	174p	13.21 N	144.45 E
Talofofo Bay c	174p	13.20 N	144.46 E
Taloga	196	36.02 N	98.57 W
Taloje	88	55.24 N	95.40 E
Taloje Budrukh	272c	19.05 N	73.05 E
Talok	112	1.03 N	118.48 E
Talon, Lake ⊜	190	46.18 N	79.05 W
Talonan, Tano ›	115b	9.07 S	117.02 E
Tāloqān	120	36.44 N	69.33 E
Taloro ≃	71	40.08 N	8.58 E
Talovaja	78	51.06 N	40.44 E
Talovka, Kaz.	80	50.25 N	47.35 E
Talovka, Ross.	80	49.58 N	45.01 E
Talovka, Ross.	84	44.14 N	46.36 E
Talovka, Ross.	86	51.27 N	81.54 E
Talovka, Ross.	86	57.10 N	93.09 E
Talovoje	83	48.18 N	39.40 E
Talpa	196	31.47 N	99.43 W
Talpa de Allende	234	20.23 N	104.51 W
Talquin, Lake ⊜[1]	192	30.26 N	84.33 W
Tālsa	272b	22.49 N	88.33 E
Talsarnau	42	52.54 N	4.03 W
Talsi	76	57.15 N	22.36 E
Talšik	86	53.42 N	71.53 E
Taltal	252	25.24 S	70.29 W
Taltapin Lake ⊜	182	54.19 N	125.20 W
Taltson ≃	176	61.23 N	112.45 W
Talu	112	0.14 N	99.59 E
Taludaa	112	0.20 N	123.28 E
Taluk	112	0.32 S	101.35 E
Talumphuk, Laem ›	110	8.30 N	100.10 E
Taluti, Teluk c	164	3.21 S	129.45 E
Talvik'ul'a	24	68.45 N	29.19 E
Talwandi Bhāi	123	30.51 N	74.56 E
Talwood	166	28.30 S	149.30 E
Taly	78	49.51 N	40.04 E
Ṭalyā	142	30.16 N	31.00 E
Tal-y-bont	42	52.29 N	3.59 W
Tama, Arg.	252	30.31 S	66.32 W
Tama, Nihon	94	35.37 N	139.27 E
Tama, Ia., U.S.	190	41.58 N	92.34 W
Tama ≃	94	35.32 N	139.47 E
Tama Cemetery ◆	268	35.41 N	139.31 E
Tamacuarí, Pico ∧	246	1.15 N	64.45 W
Tamadjert	148	25.36 N	7.20 E
Tamagawa, Nihon	94	37.12 N	140.24 E
Tamagawa, Nihon	96	34.01 N	132.56 E
Tamagawa ◆[8]	268	35.37 N	139.39 E
Tamagawa-josui ≃	268	35.42 N	139.35 E
Tamakautonga	174v	19.05 S	169.55 W
Tamaki	94	34.29 N	136.38 E
Tāmākośī ≃	124	27.22 N	85.59 E
Tama-kyūryō ⋏[2]	268	35.35 N	139.30 E
Tamala, Austl.	162	26.42 S	113.45 E
Tamala, Ross.	80	52.33 N	43.16 E
Tamalameque	246	8.52 N	73.49 W
Tamalave, Sierra ⋏	234	22.45 N	99.15 W
Ṭamalāy	142	30.30 N	30.51 E
Tamale	150	9.25 N	0.50 W
Tamalea	112	2.29 S	119.19 E
Tamalpais, Mount ∧	226	37.56 N	122.35 W
Tamalpais Valley	226	37.53 N	122.32 W
Tamamura	94	36.18 N	139.07 E
Taman, Indon.	115a	7.25 S	112.41 E
Taman', Ross.	78	45.13 N	36.43 E
Tamana	92	32.55 N	130.33 E
Tamana I	14	2.29 S	175.59 E
Tamaná, Cerro ∧	246	5.02 N	76.17 W
Tamana, Mount ∧[2]	241r	10.28 N	61.12 W
Tamanaco ≃	246	9.25 N	65.23 W
Tamanan	115a	8.01 S	113.49 E
Tamanar	148	31.00 N	9.35 W
Tamandourirt, Oued V	150	19.39 N	2.04 W
Tamanduateí ≃	287b	23.36 S	46.35 W
Tamanhint	146	27.13 N	14.36 E
Tamani	150	13.20 N	6.50 W
Tamaniquá	246	2.38 S	65.44 W
Taman Negara ♦	114	4.43 N	102.23 E
Tamano	96	34.30 N	133.56 E
Tamanquaré, Ilha I	246	0.28 S	64.55 W
Tamanskij zaliv c	78	45.18 N	36.45 E
Tamanthi	110	25.19 N	95.18 E
Tamanusi	112	1.48 S	121.18 E
Tamapatz	234	21.35 N	99.09 W
Tamaqua	208	40.47 N	75.58 W
Tamar ≃, Austl.	166	41.04 S	146.47 E
Tamar ≃, Nepāl	124	26.55 N	87.10 E
Tamar ≃, Eng., U.K.	42	50.22 N	4.10 W
Támara	246	5.50 N	72.10 W
Tamarac ≃	198	48.29 N	97.07 W
Tamarack Lake ⊜[1]	214	41.35 N	80.05 W
Tamarite de Litera	34	41.52 N	0.26 E
Tamaroa	194	38.08 N	89.14 W
Tamarome	164	2.54 S	133.38 E
Tamarugal, Pampa del ≚	248	21.00 S	69.25 W
Tamashima	96	34.32 N	133.40 E
Tamási	30	46.38 N	18.18 E
Tamaské	150	14.49 N	5.39 E
Tamatsukuri	94	36.06 N	140.25 E
Tamaulipas □[3]	232	24.00 N	98.45 W
Tamaya ≃	248	8.31 S	74.13 W
Tamayu	96	35.25 N	133.01 E
Tama Zoological Park ♦	268	35.39 N	139.24 E
Tamazula	232	24.57 N	106.57 W
Tamazula de Gordiano	234	19.38 N	103.15 W
Tamazulapan del Progreso	234	17.41 N	97.34 W
Tamazunchale	234	21.16 N	98.47 W
Tamba	96	35.09 N	135.25 E
Tambach-Dietharz	54	50.48 N	10.36 E
Tambacounda	150	13.47 N	13.40 W
Tambacounda □[4]	150	14.00 N	13.00 W
Tamba Dabatou	150	11.48 N	10.40 W
Tambak	115a	5.45 S	112.37 E
Tambakboyo	115a	6.48 S	111.50 E
Tamba-kōchi ⋏[1]	92	35.20 N	135.30 E
Tambakrejo	115a	7.16 S	111.36 E
Tambalan	112	3.08 N	115.34 E
Tambangsawah	112	3.02 S	102.11 E
Tambara, Moç.	154	16.45 S	34.15 E
Tambara, Nihon	96	33.54 N	133.04 E
Tāmbaram	122	12.55 N	80.07 E
Tambaú ≃	256	21.34 S	47.05 W
Tambault, Île à I	275a	45.20 N	73.51 W
Tambea	112	4.12 S	121.36 E
Tambej	74	71.30 N	71.50 E
Tambelan, Kepulauan II	112	1.00 N	107.30 E
Tambelan Besar, Pulau I	112	0.58 N	107.34 E
Tambellup	162	34.02 S	117.39 E
Tamberías	252	31.28 S	69.25 W
Tambisan, Pulau I	116	5.27 N	119.10 E
Tambler	116	6.03 N	125.09 E
Tambo, Austl.	166	24.53 S	146.15 E
Tambo, Perú	248	12.56 S	74.01 W
Tambo ≃, Austl.	166	37.51 S	147.48 E
Tambo ≃, Perú	248	17.10 S	71.51 W
Tambo ≃, Perú	248	10.43 S	73.45 W
Tamboara	255	23.09 S	52.33 W
Tambo Grande	248	4.56 S	80.21 W
Tambohorano	157b	17.30 S	43.58 E
Tamboli	112	3.57 S	121.20 E
Tambolongang, Pulau I	112	6.36 S	120.24 E
Tambopata ≃	248	12.36 S	69.11 W
Tambor	236	9.43 N	85.01 W
Tambora, Gunung ∧	115b	8.14 S	117.55 E
Tamboril	250	4.50 S	40.20 W
Tamborine	171a	27.53 S	153.08 E
Tamborine Mountain ∧[2]	171a	27.55 S	153.10 E
Tamboritha, Mount ∧	166	37.28 S	146.41 E
Tamboryacu ≃	246	2.31 S	73.40 W
Tambov	80	52.43 N	41.25 E
Tambov □[8]	78	51.45 N	41.20 E
Tambovka, Ross.	80	47.18 N	47.23 E
Tambovka, Ross.	89	50.06 N	128.04 E
Tambre ≃	34	42.49 N	8.53 W
Tambu	112	0.02 S	119.52 E
Tambu, Teluk c	112	0.02 N	119.45 E
Tambulian Point ›	116	7.22 N	123.27 E
Tambunan	112	5.40 N	116.22 E
Tambura	140	5.36 N	27.28 E
Tamchaket	150	17.15 N	10.40 W
Tam Chuak, Laem ›	110	8.33 N	98.12 E
Tamdhas	124	28.04 N	83.14 E
Tame	246	6.28 N	71.44 W
Tame ≃	262	53.25 N	2.09 W
Tameapa	232	25.39 N	107.22 W
Tamedda, Djebel ∧	148	32.48 N	0.05 E
Tâmega ≃	34	41.05 N	8.21 W
Tameghza	148	34.23 N	7.57 E
Tamel Aike	254	48.19 S	70.58 W
Tamelelt	148	31.50 N	7.29 W
Tamenghest	148	22.56 N	5.30 E
Tamenghest □[5]	148	25.00 N	5.00 E
Tamenghest, Oued V	148	22.10 N	0.10 E
Tamenuen	164	6.27 S	139.48 E
Tamerton Foliot	42	50.26 N	4.08 W
Tamesí ≃	234	22.13 N	97.52 W
Tameside □[8]	262	53.29 N	2.03 W
Tamga, Kyrg.	85	42.09 N	77.32 E
Tamga, Ross.	89	45.34 N	133.36 E
Tamgak, Monts ⋏	150	19.11 N	8.42 E
Tamgué, Massif du ⋏	150	12.00 N	12.18 W
Tamiahua	234	21.16 N	97.27 W
Tamiahua, Laguna de c	234	21.35 N	97.35 W
Tamiami Canal ≋	220	25.47 N	80.15 W
Tamiang ≃	114	4.25 N	98.16 E
Tamica	24	64.10 N	38.05 E
Tamil Harbor c	174q	9.30 N	138.09 E
Tamil Nādu □[3]	122	11.00 N	78.15 E
Tamiment	210	41.09 N	75.02 W
Tamina	222	30.11 N	96.26 W
Tamir	88	50.24 N	107.25 E
Tamiryn ≃	88	47.48 N	102.36 E
Tamiš (Timiș) ≃	38	44.51 N	20.39 E
Tamitatoala ≃	255	11.56 S	53.36 W
Ṭāmīyah	142	29.29 N	30.58 E
Tamkūhi	124	26.41 N	84.11 E
Tam Ky	110	15.34 N	108.29 E
Tamlūk	126	22.18 N	87.55 E
Tāmma	120	25.11 N	93.42 E
Tammaro ≃	68	41.09 N	14.50 E
Tammerfors → Tampere	26	61.30 N	23.45 E
Tammisaari → Ekenäs	26	59.58 N	23.26 E
Tamms	194	37.14 N	89.16 W
Ṭammūh	273c	29.56 N	31.16 E
Tāmna	126	23.15 N	86.21 E
Tämnarån ≃	40	60.31 N	17.39 E
Tämnaren ⊜	40	60.10 N	17.20 E
Tamnum	144	15.07 N	50.49 E
Tamon ◆[8]	270	34.39 N	135.04 E
Tampa, Ang.	152	15.30 S	13.27 E
Tampa, Fl., U.S.	220	27.56 N	82.27 W
Tampa Bay c	220	27.45 N	82.35 W
Tampa International Airport ⊠	220	27.59 N	82.32 W
Tampamachoco, Laguna c	234	21.00 N	97.21 W
Tampang	112	5.54 S	104.43 E
Tampaón ≃	234	21.59 N	98.36 W
Tamparan	116	8.27 N	117.13 E
Tampere	26	61.30 N	23.45 E
Tampico, Méx.	234	22.13 N	97.51 W
Tampico, Il., U.S.	190	41.37 N	89.47 W
Tampico, In., U.S.	218	38.48 N	85.58 W
Tampin	114	2.28 N	102.14 E
Tampiquito	234	23.52 N	98.14 W
Tampulonanjing, Gunung ∧	114	1.46 N	99.24 E
Tam Quan	110	14.35 N	109.03 E
Tamra	132	32.51 N	35.12 E
Tamrau, Pegunungan ⋏	164	0.30 S	132.27 E
Tamri	148	30.43 N	9.43 W
Tamsagbulag	88	47.14 N	117.21 E
Tamsalu	76	59.10 N	26.06 E
Tamshiyacu	246	4.05 S	72.58 W
Tamsweg	64	47.08 N	13.48 E
Tamu	110	24.13 N	94.18 E
Tamuín	234	21.59 N	98.45 W
Tamuk Island I	116	6.27 N	121.49 E
Tamuning	174p	13.29 N	144.46 E
Tamura	268	35.22 N	139.22 E
Tamusuke	85	38.03 N	76.53 E
Tamworth, Austl.	166	31.05 S	150.55 E
Tamworth, On., Can.	212	44.29 N	77.00 W
Tamworth, Eng., U.K.	42	52.39 N	1.40 W
Tamyang	98	35.21 N	126.58 E
Tan ≃	100	23.57 N	115.47 E
Tana, Chile	248	19.27 S	69.57 W
Tana, Nor.	24	70.28 N	28.18 E
Tana ≃, Cuba	240p	20.42 N	77.25 W
Tana (Teno) ≃, Europe	24	70.30 N	28.23 E
Tana ≃, Kenya	154	2.32 S	40.31 E
T'an'a ≃, Ross.	88	58.40 N	120.30 E
Tana, Lake ⊜	144	12.00 N	37.20 E
Tanabe, Nihon	96	34.49 N	135.46 E
Tanabe, Nihon	96	33.44 N	135.22 E
Tanabi	255	20.37 S	49.37 W
Tanacross	180	63.23 N	143.21 W
Tanafjorden c[2]	24	70.54 N	28.40 E
Tanaga Island I	180	51.50 N	178.00 W
Tanaga Volcano ∧[1]	180	51.53 N	178.09 W
Tanagro ≃	68	40.38 N	15.14 E
Tanaguarena	286c	10.37 N	66.49 W
Tanagura	94	37.02 N	140.23 E
Tanah, Tanjung ›	115a	6.29 S	108.32 E
Tanahbala, Pulau I	110	0.25 S	98.25 E
Tanahgrogot	112	1.55 S	116.12 E
Tanahjampea, Pulau I	112	7.05 S	120.42 E
Tanahmasa, Pulau I	110	0.12 S	98.27 E
Tanahmerah, Indon.	112	3.41 N	117.31 E
Tanahmerah, Indon.	164	6.05 S	140.17 E
Tanah Merah, Malay.	114	5.48 N	102.09 E
Tanah Merah, Malay.	114	2.36 N	101.48 E
Tanahputih	114	1.41 N	101.03 E
Tanaka ◆[8]	270	34.42 N	134.59 E
Tanakeke, Pulau I	112	5.30 S	119.16 E
Tanakpur	124	29.05 N	80.07 E
Tan‘am	128	23.09 N	56.29 E
Tanami	162	19.59 S	129.43 E
Tanami Desert ◆[2]	162	20.00 S	129.30 E
Ṭanān, Miṣr	142	30.15 N	31.14 E
Tan An, Viet	110	8.46 N	105.11 E
Tan An, Viet	110	10.32 N	106.25 E
Tanana	180	65.10 N	152.05 W
Tanana ≃	180	65.09 N	151.55 W
Tananarive → Antananarivo	157b	18.55 S	47.31 E
Tanapag	174n	15.14 N	145.45 E
Tanapag, Lagunan c	174n	15.14 N	145.44 E
Tanaro ≃	62	45.01 N	8.47 E
Tanārūt, Wādī V	146	30.08 N	9.59 E
Tanashi	94	35.44 N	139.33 E
Tanat ≃	42	52.46 N	3.07 W
Tanauan	116	11.07 N	125.01 E
Tanbar	166	25.50 S	141.55 E
Tanbidī	142	28.38 N	30.47 E
Tan Binh	269c	10.48 N	106.40 E
Tanbu, Zhg.	98	35.51 N	118.17 E
Tanbu, Zhg.	100	28.08 N	114.12 E
Tancarville	50	49.29 N	0.28 E
Tancarville, Canal de ≋	50	49.28 N	0.28 E
Tancha	174m	26.28 N	127.50 E
Tan Chau	110	10.48 N	105.15 E
Tancheng	98	34.37 N	118.23 E
Tanchoj	88	51.33 N	105.07 E
Tanch'ŏn	98	40.27 N	128.54 E
Tancítaro	234	19.20 N	102.22 W
Tancítaro, Pico de ∧	234	19.23 N	102.13 W
Tancochapa ≃	234	17.59 N	94.04 W
Tanda, C. Iv.	150	7.48 N	3.10 W
Tānda, India	123	31.42 N	75.38 E
Tānda, India	124	28.59 N	78.56 E
Tānda, India	124	26.33 N	82.39 E
Tānda, Pāk.	123	32.42 N	74.22 E
Tandag	116	9.04 N	126.12 E
Tandah	142	27.41 N	30.46 E
Tandai	154	19.36 S	32.48 E
Tandaj	80	47.33 N	51.30 E
Tandala	154	9.23 S	34.14 E
Tandaltī	140	13.01 N	31.52 E
Ţăndărei	38	44.38 N	27.40 E
Tandaué	152	17.00 S	18.06 E
Tandian	98	40.39 N	124.46 E
Tandil	252	37.19 S	59.09 W
Tandjilé □[5]	146	9.45 N	16.30 E
Tandjilé ≃	146	9.45 N	15.50 E
Tāndliānwāla	123	31.02 N	73.08 E
Tando Ādam	120	25.46 N	68.40 E
Tando Allāhyār	120	25.28 N	68.43 E
Tando Bāgo	120	24.47 N	68.58 E
Tando Muhammad Khān	120	25.08 N	68.32 E
Tandou Bougou	152	3.32 S	10.53 E
Tandou Lake ⊜	166	32.38 S	142.05 E
Tandovo, ozero ⊜	86	55.07 N	78.02 E
Tando Zinze	152	5.22 S	12.26 E
Tandragee	48	54.20 N	6.25 W
Tandridge	260	51.14 N	0.02 W
Tandridge □[8]	260	51.17 N	0.05 W
Tandslet	41	54.55 N	9.59 E
Tandubas	116	5.10 N	120.20 E
Tandubatu Island I	116	5.13 N	120.17 E
Tandula Tank ⊜[1]	122	20.40 N	81.12 E
Tandun	112	0.36 N	100.38 E
Tāndūr	122	17.14 N	77.35 E
Tanduy ≃	115a	7.41 S	108.47 E
Taneatua	172	38.04 S	177.01 E
Tanega-shima I	93b	30.40 N	131.00 E
Taneichi	92	40.26 N	141.43 E
Tan Emellel	148	27.30 N	9.45 E
Tanete	112	4.32 S	119.36 E
Taneum Creek ≃	224	47.10 N	120.40 W
Tanew ≃	30	50.31 N	22.16 E
Taneytown	208	39.39 N	77.10 W
Tanezrouft ◆[2]	148	24.00 N	0.45 W
Tanezzuft, Wādī V	146	25.51 N	10.19 E
Tanforan Park ◆[9]	282	37.38 N	122.25 W
Tang ≃, Zhg.	98	38.45 N	115.35 E
Tang ≃, Zhg.	100	32.09 N	112.25 E
Tang ≃, Zhg.	100	33.18 N	117.46 E
Tang ≃, Zhg.	104	41.15 N	123.21 E
Tang ≃, Zhg.	105	40.43 N	116.38 E
Tanga, Ross.	88	51.02 N	111.33 E
Tånga, Sve.	41	56.12 N	12.46 E
Tanga, Tan.	154	5.04 S	39.06 E
Tanga □[4]	154	5.00 S	38.15 E
Tangail	124	24.15 N	89.55 E
Tangainony	157b	22.42 S	47.45 E
Tanga Islands II	14	3.30 S	153.15 E
Tanga Langua ›	241k	12.14 N	61.39 W
Tangalla	122	6.01 N	80.48 E
Tangamong Lake ⊜	212	44.43 N	77.51 W
Tangancícuaro [de Arista]	234	19.54 N	102.08 W
Tanganika, Lago → Tanganyika, Lake ⊜	154	6.00 S	29.30 E
Tanganjika-See → Tanganyika, Lake ⊜	154	6.00 S	29.30 E
Tanganyika, Lake ⊜	154	6.00 S	29.30 E
Tangarana ≃	246	3.02 S	75.08 W
Tangarare	175e	9.35 S	159.39 E
Tanga-shima I	96	34.40 N	134.35 E
Tangba	107	30.00 N	105.46 E
Tangchi	89	47.00 N	123.46 E
Tangchigou	104	41.04 N	124.11 E
Tangcun, Zhg.	100	29.50 N	118.54 E
Tangcun, Zhg.	100	25.26 N	113.10 E
Tangdaohe	98	40.38 N	118.58 E
Tanger (Tangier)	148	35.48 N	5.45 W
Tanger □[4]	148	35.35 N	5.50 W
Tanger ≃	54	52.33 N	11.59 E
Tangerang	115a	6.11 S	106.37 E
Tangerhütte	54	52.26 N	11.48 E
Tangerine	220	28.47 N	81.38 W
Tang'erli	105	39.09 N	116.43 E
Tangermünde	54	52.32 N	11.58 E
Tangfang, Zhg.	102	27.00 N	101.08 E
Tangfang, Zhg.	104	41.20 N	120.34 E
Tangfang, Zhg.	105	39.29 N	118.01 E
Tangfangqiao	106	31.45 N	120.50 E
Tangfeng	98	38.07 N	115.30 E
Tanggangzi	104	41.01 N	122.54 E
Tanggeasinua, Pegunungan ⋏	112	3.24 S	121.42 E
Tanggengtou	106	30.55 N	119.03 E
Tanggou	100	33.59 N	118.57 E
Tanggu	105	39.01 N	117.40 E
Tangguantun	98	38.43 N	116.55 E
Tanggul	115a	8.10 S	113.26 E
Tanggulashan (Tuotuoheyan)	120	34.05 N	92.45 E
Tanggula Shan ⋏	120	33.00 N	92.00 E
Tanggula Shankou)(	120	32.59 N	91.45 E
Tanggushiluke	120	38.45 N	80.55 E
Tanghe	100	32.43 N	112.48 E
Tanghekou	105	40.44 N	116.38 E
Tanghu	105	39.11 N	115.24 E
Tanghuang	106	31.41 N	119.25 E
Tangi	123	34.18 N	71.40 E
Tangier, N.S., Can.	186	44.48 N	62.42 W
Tangier, Va., U.S.	208	37.49 N	75.59 W
Tangier Island I	208	37.50 N	76.00 W
Tangier Sound ʯ	208	38.02 N	75.58 W
Tangier → Tanger	148	35.48 N	5.45 W
Tangijatuo	107	29.36 N	106.39 E
Tangipahoa ≃	194	30.20 N	90.18 W
Tangjia	100	22.23 N	113.36 E
Tangjiagou	100	30.48 N	117.28 E
Tangjiang	100	25.51 N	114.44 E
Tangjiapao	104	41.59 N	122.14 E
Tangjiaqiao	106	31.24 N	119.12 E
Tangjin	98	36.54 N	126.37 E
Tangjiqiaozhen	106	31.13 N	121.31 E
Tangkahan	112	1.36 S	113.52 E
Tangkak	114	2.16 N	102.33 E
Tangkou	100	30.06 N	118.11 E
Tanglad	115b	8.47 S	115.35 E
Tanglewood, Fl., U.S.	220	26.37 N	81.53 W
Tanglewood, Tx., U.S.	222	30.30 N	96.59 W
Tanglewood ♦	207	42.21 N	73.20 W
Tangling	100	26.14 N	119.24 E
Tanglitun	104	41.45 N	123.57 E
Tangmai	102	30.08 N	95.11 E
Tangmarg	123	34.02 N	74.26 E
Tangmazhai	104	41.10 N	122.44 E
Tang Nhon Phu	269c	10.50 N	106.47 E
Tang-ni	98	34.12 N	126.52 E
Tango	96	35.44 N	135.06 E
Tango-hantō ›[1]	96	35.40 N	135.10 E
Tangowahine	172	35.52 S	173.56 E
Tangpu, Zhg.	100	29.51 N	120.47 E
Tangpu, Zhg.	100	28.28 N	114.58 E
Tangqi	106	30.29 N	120.11 E
Tangqiao	106	31.13 N	119.15 E
Tangra Yumco ⊜	120	31.00 N	86.20 E
Tangsanying	98	41.38 N	117.40 E
Tangschan → Tangshan	105	39.38 N	118.11 E
Tangse	114	5.01 N	95.55 E
Tangshan, Zhg.	105	40.10 N	116.22 E
Tangshan, Zhg.	105	39.38 N	118.11 E
Tangshan, Zhg.	106	32.05 N	119.03 E
Tang Shan ∧	106	32.03 N	119.02 E
Tangshi	106	31.33 N	120.51 E
Tangtou, Zhg.	98	35.16 N	118.35 E
Tangtou, Zhg.	102	27.42 N	108.17 E
Tangtou, Zhg.	106	31.38 N	120.19 E
Tangtouxia	100	22.50 N	114.06 E
Tangtse	120	34.02 N	78.11 E
Tanguá	256	22.44 S	42.43 W
Tangub	116	8.03 N	123.44 E
Tanguiéta	150	10.37 N	1.16 E
Tanguip Point ›	116	7.43 N	126.32 E
Tanguj	88	55.23 N	100.58 E
Tangulbei	154	0.48 N	36.17 E
Tangusu, Telukan c	116	5.27 N	119.03 E
Tangwang ≃	89	46.40 N	129.54 E
Tangxi	100	29.04 N	119.23 E
Tangxian	98	38.45 N	114.58 E
Tangxianzhen	100	31.59 N	113.07 E
Tangyan	110	22.29 N	98.24 E
Tangyi	98	36.32 N	115.47 E
Tangyin, Zhg.	98	35.55 N	114.21 E
Tangyin, Zhg.	100	27.32 N	116.16 E
Tangyuan	89	46.42 N	129.55 E
Tangzha	106	32.05 N	120.49 E
Tanhuato	234	20.17 N	102.20 W
Taniantaweng Shan ⋏	102	30.00 N	98.00 E
Tanigami ◆[8]	270	34.46 N	135.10 E
Tanigawa-dake ∧	94	36.50 N	138.56 E
Tanigumi	94	35.31 N	136.36 E
Tanimbar, Kepulauan II	164	7.30 S	131.30 E
Taninges	58	46.07 N	6.36 E
Tanintharyi □[8]	110	12.00 N	99.00 E
Tanır	130	38.26 N	36.55 E
Tanis (Zoan) ⊥	142	30.57 N	31.53 E
Tanishpa ∧	120	31.10 N	68.24 E
Tanjay	116	9.31 N	123.09 E
Tanjiafang	98	36.41 N	118.36 E
Tanjiahe	100	31.58 N	113.56 E
Tanjiang	100	24.07 N	116.32 E
Tanjiaqiao	100	30.11 N	118.15 E
Tanjil ≃	169	38.08 S	146.17 E
Tanjong Dawai	114	5.41 N	100.22 E
Tanjong Malim	114	3.41 N	101.31 E
Tanjore → Thanjāvūr	122	10.48 N	79.09 E
Tanjung, Indon.	112	2.11 S	115.23 E
Tanjung, Indon.	115a	6.52 S	108.52 E
Tanjung, Indon.	115b	8.21 S	116.09 E
Tanjungbalai	114	2.58 N	99.48 E
Tanjungbatu, Indon.	112	0.45 N	117.26 E
Tanjungbatu, Indon.	112	2.17 N	118.05 E
Tanjungbatu, Indon.	112	0.38 N	103.26 E
Tanjungenim	112	3.45 S	103.48 E
Tanjungkarang-Telukbetung	115a	5.27 S	105.16 E
Tanjunglabu	112	2.57 S	106.54 E
Tanjungmedan, Indon.	114	1.26 N	100.34 E
Tanjungmedan, Indon.	114	2.06 N	100.14 E
Tanjungmengedar	114	2.39 N	100.01 E
Tanjungpandan	112	2.45 S	107.39 E
Tanjungpinang	112	0.55 N	104.27 E
Tanjungpriok ◆[8]	269e	6.06 S	106.53 E
Tanjungpura	114	3.54 N	98.26 E
Tanjungpusu	112	0.01 S	113.30 E
Tanjungraja	112	3.21 S	104.40 E
Tanjungredep	112	2.09 N	117.29 E
Tanjungsamak	114	0.52 N	103.03 E
Tanjungselor	112	2.51 N	117.22 E
Tanjungslamat	114	3.49 N	98.20 E
Tanjunguban	112	1.03 N	104.14 E
Tānk	120	32.13 N	70.23 E
Tan Kena	148	26.33 N	9.35 E
Tan Kien	269c	10.42 N	106.35 E
Tankou	100	25.48 N	114.50 E
Tankwa ≃	158	32.20 S	19.33 E
Tanlay	50	47.50 N	4.05 E
Tann	56	50.38 N	10.01 E
Tanna	54	50.30 N	11.51 E
Tanna I	175f	19.30 S	169.20 E
Tannan	96	35.05 N	135.10 E
Tännäs	26	62.27 N	12.40 E
Tanna-tunnel ◆[5]	94	35.06 N	139.00 E
Tannay	50	47.21 N	3.36 E
Tanne	54	51.41 N	10.42 E
Tannenberg → Stębark	30	53.30 N	20.08 E
Tannenbergsthal	54	50.26 N	12.27 E
Tanner	194	34.43 N	86.58 W
Tanner, Mount ∧	182	49.40 N	118.34 W
Tannersville, N.Y., U.S.	210	42.12 N	74.08 W
Tannersville, Pa., U.S.	210	41.03 N	75.18 W
Tännesberg	60	49.32 N	12.20 E
Tännforsen ʟ	26	63.27 N	12.44 E
Tannhausen	56	48.59 N	10.21 E
Tannheim	58	47.30 N	10.31 E
Tannila	26	65.29 N	25.59 E
Tannis Bugt c	26	57.40 N	10.15 E
Tannu-Ola, chrebet ⋏	74	51.00 N	94.00 E
Tannūrah, Ra's ›	128	26.40 N	50.30 E
Tano, Nihon	96	33.26 N	134.00 E
Tano, Nihon	270	34.57 N	135.36 E
Tano ≃	150	5.07 N	2.56 W
Tanon Strait ʯ	116	10.20 N	123.30 E
Tânout	150	14.58 N	8.53 E
Tanpok ≃	250	3.27 N	54.00 W
Tanque de Dolores	234	23.40 N	101.10 W
Tanque Grande, Ribeirão ≃	287b	23.25 S	46.28 W
Tan Qui Dong	269c	10.44 N	106.42 E
Tanquinho	255	11.58 S	39.06 W
Tansania → Tanzania □[1]	154	6.00 S	35.00 E
T'an' Šan' → Tien Shan ⋏	90	42.00 N	80.00 E
Tansboro	285	39.46 N	74.55 W
Tānsen	124	27.52 N	83.33 E
Tanshui	100	25.10 N	121.26 E
Tanshui ≃	100	25.11 N	121.25 E
Tansilla	150	12.26 N	4.23 W
Tánsin, Isla de I	236	15.17 N	83.54 W
Tánsin, Laguna de c	236	15.19 N	83.58 W
Tan Son Nhut Airport ⊠	269c	10.49 N	106.40 E
Tansyk	86	47.20 N	79.52 E
Ṭanṭā	142	30.47 N	31.00 E
Tantabogue Creek ≃	222	31.00 N	95.21 W
Tan-Tan	148	28.26 N	11.06 W
Tan-Tan □[4]	148	28.05 N	11.00 W
Tantangara Reservoir ⊜[1]	171b	35.45 S	148.39 E
Tan Thoi Nhut	269c	10.50 N	106.36 E
Tan Thuan Dong	269c	10.45 N	106.44 E
Tāntipāra	126	23.54 N	87.22 E
Tantō	96	35.29 N	135.00 E
Tantonville	58	48.28 N	6.08 E
Tantou, Zhg.	100	29.07 N	121.09 E
Tantou, Zhg.	100	26.03 N	119.35 E
Tantou, Zhg.	100	26.53 N	115.26 E
Tantou Shan I	100	29.11 N	122.01 E
Tantoyuca	234	21.21 N	98.14 W
Tanuku	122	16.45 N	81.42 E
Tanuma	94	36.22 N	139.35 E
Tanumshede	26	58.44 N	11.19 E
Tanunda	168b	34.32 S	138.57 E
Tan'urer ≃	180	64.44 N	174.15 E
Tanushimaru	96	33.21 N	130.41 E
Tanvald	30	50.45 N	15.19 E
Tanwax Creek ≃	224	46.52 N	122.27 W
Tanworth-in-Arden	42	52.20 N	1.50 W
Tanxi	100	28.58 N	115.38 E
Tanxia	100	23.58 N	115.34 E
Tanxu Shan I	106	30.37 N	121.37 E
Tanyang	98	36.57 N	128.21 E
Tanyeri	130	39.37 N	39.50 E
Tanyi	98	35.14 N	118.09 E
Tanymas ≃	85	38.25 N	72.39 E
Tanzania □[1], Afr.	138	6.00 S	35.00 E
Tanzania □[1], Afr.	154	6.00 S	35.00 E
Tanzanie → Tanzania □[1]	154	6.00 S	35.00 E
Tanzawa-Ōyama-kokutei-kōen ♦	94	35.30 N	139.10 E
Tanzawa-san ∧	94	35.28 N	139.10 E
Tao ≃, Zhg.	100	25.56 N	115.06 E
Tao ≃, Zhg.	102	35.52 N	103.16 E
Tao, Ko I	110	10.05 N	99.52 E
Tao'an	89	45.22 N	122.47 E
Taochong	100	31.04 N	118.06 E
Taochuan	102	25.07 N	111.06 E
Taocun	98	37.10 N	121.05 E
Taodigou	105	40.52 N	116.14 E
Tao'er ≃	89	45.42 N	124.05 E
Taoerdeng	98	40.44 N	119.02 E
Taohe	105	39.12 N	116.50 E
Taohua	106	31.23 N	120.04 E
Taohuachiyingzi	104	42.18 N	121.06 E
Taohua Dao I	100	29.48 N	122.17 E
Taohuanbuligai	104	42.13 N	122.14 E
Taohuatu	104	41.40 N	120.40 E
Taohuayuan	106	30.34 N	118.42 E
Taohuazhen	105	40.04 N	114.59 E
Taojiagou	107	29.48 N	104.48 E
Taojiahe	100	30.55 N	115.56 E
Taojialiang	104	42.36 N	121.25 E
Taolahusu	98	42.34 N	116.48 E
Taolaizhao	89	44.51 N	125.57 E
Taolakepa	120	32.05 N	85.22 E
Taole	102	38.46 N	106.40 E
Taolin	98	34.30 N	118.30 E
Taoling	100	30.21 N	118.16 E
Taoluo	98	35.17 N	119.24 E
T'aonan → Tao'an	89	45.22 N	122.47 E
Taongi I[1]	14	14.37 N	168.58 E
Taormina	70	37.51 N	15.17 E
Taos, Mo., U.S.	219	38.30 N	92.04 W
Taos, N.M., U.S.	200	36.24 N	105.34 W
Taos Pueblo	200	36.26 N	105.32 W
Taoudenni	148	22.40 N	4.00 W
Taougrite	34	36.15 N	0.55 E
Taounate	148	34.25 N	4.39 W
Taounate □[4]	148	34.30 N	4.40 W
Taoura	36	36.09 N	8.03 E
Taourirt	148	34.25 N	2.53 W
Taourirt ∧	148	24.03 N	5.02 E
Taoussa	150	16.55 N	0.35 W
Taowu	106	31.47 N	118.46 E
Taoxi, Zhg.	100	31.33 N	117.00 E
Taoxi, Zhg.	100	25.18 N	116.05 E
Taoxi, Zhg.	100	28.44 N	119.36 E
Taoxiantun	104	41.39 N	123.27 E
Taoyuan, Zhg.	100	25.48 N	117.32 E
Taoyuan, Zhg.	102	28.46 N	111.20 E
Taozhu	100	28.50 N	121.31 E
Taozhuang	106	30.58 N	120.48 E
Tapa, Eesti	76	59.16 N	25.58 E
Tapa, India	123	30.19 N	75.21 E
Tapaan Island I	116	5.28 N	120.44 E
Tapacari	248	17.31 S	66.36 W
Tapachula	232	14.54 N	92.17 W
Tapaga, Cape ›	175a	14.01 S	171.23 W
Tapah	114	4.11 N	101.16 E
Tapah Road	114	4.10 N	101.12 E
Tapaje ≃	246	2.44 N	78.07 W
Tapajós ≃	250	2.24 S	54.41 W
Tapaktuan	114	3.16 N	97.11 E
Tapalpa	234	19.57 N	103.46 W
Tapalqué	252	36.21 S	60.01 W
Tapan	112	2.10 S	101.04 E
Tapanahony ≃	250	4.22 N	54.27 W
Tapanui	172	45.57 S	169.16 E
Tapanuli, Teluk c	114	1.38 N	98.45 E
Tapasi	126	23.40 N	87.08 E
Tapauá	248	5.45 S	63.04 W
Tapauá ≃	248	5.40 S	64.21 W
Tapawera	172	41.24 S	172.49 E
Tapaz	116	11.16 N	122.32 E
Tapejara	252	28.04 S	52.00 W
Tapera	252	28.38 S	52.52 W
Taperas	248	17.54 S	60.23 W
Taperoá, Bra.	250	7.12 S	36.49 W
Taperoá, Bra.	255	13.31 S	39.06 W
Tapes	252	30.40 S	51.23 W
Tapeta	150	6.29 N	8.51 W
Taphan Hin	110	16.13 N	100.26 E
Taphoen ≃	110	14.07 N	99.25 E
Tāpi ≃, India	120	21.06 N	72.41 E
Ta Pi ≃, Thai	110	9.05 N	99.12 E
Tapiales	288	34.42 S	58.31 W
Tapiantana Channel ʯ	116	6.23 N	122.00 E
Tapiantana Group II	116	6.20 N	122.00 E
Tapiantana Island I	116	6.18 N	121.59 E
Tapiche ≃	248	4.59 S	73.51 W
Tapili	154	3.25 N	27.40 E
Tapilula	234	17.14 N	93.02 W
Taping (Daying) ≃	102	24.17 N	97.14 E
Tapini	164	8.20 S	147.00 E
Tapiraí	255	19.52 S	46.01 W
Tapirapé ≃	250	10.41 S	50.38 W
Tapiratiba	256	21.28 S	46.45 W
Tapis, Gunong ∧	114	4.03 N	102.54 E
Tapiutan Island I	116	11.12 N	119.16 E
Tapiwa	174d	0.52 S	169.35 E
Taplan National Park ♦	110	14.20 N	102.20 E
Tāplejungg	124	27.21 N	87.40 E
Tapoa ≃	150	12.36 N	2.29 E
Tapol	146	8.31 N	15.35 E
Tapolca	30	46.53 N	17.27 E
Tappahannock	208	37.55 N	76.51 W
Tappal	124	28.03 N	77.35 E
Tappan	210	41.01 N	73.56 W
Tappan, Lake ⊜[1]	276	41.01 N	73.59 W
Tappan Lake ⊜[1]	214	40.21 N	81.11 W
Tappan Zee c	276	41.06 N	73.53 W
Tappan Zee Bridge ◆[5]	276	41.04 N	73.54 W
Tappen	198	46.52 N	99.38 W
Tappernøje	41	55.10 N	11.59 E
Tappi-zaki ›	92	41.15 N	140.21 E
Tappo	150	10.12 N	2.38 W
Tapps, Lake ⊜	224	47.13 N	122.09 W
Tapsiā ◆[8]	272b	22.32 N	88.22 E
Tapuaenuku ∧	172	42.00 S	173.40 E
Tapuio ≃	250	3.41 S	44.16 W
Tapul Group II	116	5.30 N	121.00 E
Tapul Island I	116	5.43 N	120.55 E
Tapun	110	18.22 N	95.27 E
Tapurucuara	246	0.24 S	65.02 W
Taputapu, Cape ›	174u	14.19 S	170.50 W
Taqāṭu‘ Hayyā	140	18.20 N	36.22 E
Taqian	100	29.03 N	117.03 E
Taqiao, Zhg.	100	31.28 N	118.25 E
Taqiao, Zhg.	100	28.24 N	117.02 E
Ṭaqṭaq	128	35.53 N	44.35 E
Taquara	252	29.39 S	50.47 W
Taquara ◆[8]	287a	22.55 S	43.21 W
Taquara, Serra da ∧	256	22.12 S	43.53 W
Taquaras, Ponta das ›	252	27.01 S	48.34 W
Taquari, Bra.	252	29.48 S	51.51 W
Taquari, Bra.	255	17.50 S	53.17 W
Taquari ≃, Bra.	248	19.15 S	57.17 W
Taquari ≃, Bra.	252	29.56 S	51.44 W
Taquari, Pantanal do ≚	248	18.20 S	56.30 W
Taquaritinga	255	21.24 S	48.30 W

DEUTSCH: Name · Seite · Breite°′ · Länge°′ E = Ost

Symbols in the index entries represent the broad categories identified in the key at the right. Symbols with superior numbers (⋏[1]) identify subcategories (see complete key on page *I · 1*).

Symbole im Register stellen die rechts im Schlüssel erklärten Kategorien dar. Symbole mit hochgestellten Ziffern (⋏[1]) bezeichnen Unterabteilungen einer Kategorie (vgl. vollständiger Schlüssel auf Seite *I · 1*).

Los símbolos incluídos en el texto del índice representan las grandes categorías identificadas con la clave a la derecha. Los símbolos con numeros en su parte superior (⋏[1]) identifican las subcategorías (véase la clave completa en la página *I · 1*).

Les symboles de l'index représentent les catégories indiquées dans la légende à droite. Les symboles suivis d'un indice (⋏[1]) représentent des sous-catégories (voir légende complète à la page *I · 1*).

Os símbolos incluídos no texto do índice representam as grandes categorias identificadas com a chave à direita. Os símbolos com números em sua parte superior (⋏[1]) identificam as subcategorias (veja-se a chave completa à página *I · 1*).

∧ Mountain	Berg	Montaña	Montagne	Montanha
⋏ Mountains	Gebirge	Montañas	Montagnes	Montanhas
)(Pass	Paß	Paso	Col	Passo
V Valley, Canyon	Tal, Cañon	Valle, Cañón	Vallée, Canyon	Vale, Canhão
≚ Plain	Ebene	Llano	Plaine	Planície
› Cape	Kap	Cabo	Cap	Cabo
I Island	Insel	Isla	Île	Ilha
II Islands	Inseln	Islas	Îles	Ilhas
⊥ Other Topographic Features	Andere Topographische Objekte	Otros Elementos Topográficos	Autres données topographiques	Outros acidentes topográficos

ESPAÑOL Nombre	Página	Lat.°′	Long.°′ W = Oeste
Taquaruçu ≃, Bra.	248	20.30 S	55.49 W
Taquaruçu ≃, Bra.	255	21.35 S	52.07 W
Tar ≃, Kyrg.	85	40.38 N	73.26 E
Tar ≃, N.C., U.S.	192	35.33 N	77.05 W
Tara, Austl.	166	27.17 S	150.28 E
Tara, On., Can.	212	44.28 N	81.09 W
Tara, Ross.	86	56.54 N	74.22 E
Tara, Zam.	154	16.56 S	26.47 E
Tara ≃	38	43.55 N	19.25 E
Tara ≃, Europe	38	43.21 N	18.51 E
Tara ≃, Ross.	86	56.42 N	74.36 E
Taraba ≃	146	8.30 N	10.15 E
Tarabine, Oued ti-n- ∨	148	20.50 N	7.25 E
Tarabuco	248	19.10 S	64.57 W
Tarābulus (Tripoli), Libiyā	146	32.54 N	13.11 E
Tarābulus (Tripoli), Lubnān	130	34.26 N	35.51 E
Tarābulus (Tripolitania) □ 9	146	31.00 N	15.00 E
Tarabya ◆ 8	267b	41.08 N	29.03 E

[The full page is a multilingual (Español, Français, Português) geographic gazetteer index with latitude and longitude coordinates arranged in numerous columns. The remaining entries continue in the same format across all columns.]

Bottom legend:

≃ River	Fluß	Río	Rivière	Rio	◆ Submarine Features	Untermeerische Objekte	Accidentes Submarinos	Formes de relief sous-marin	Acidentes submarinos
≍ Canal	Kanal	Canal	Canal	Canal	□ Political Unit	Politische Einheit	Unidad Política	Entité politique	Unidade política
⊔ Waterfall, Rapids	Wasserfall, Stromschnellen	Cascada, Rápidos	Chute d'eau, Rapides	Cascata, Rápidos	⌁ Cultural Institution	Kulturelle Institution	Institución Cultural	Institution culturelle	Instituição cultural
⊐ Strait	Meeresstraße	Estrecho	Détroit	Estreito	⌁ Historical Site	Historische Stätte	Sitio Histórico	Site historique	Sítio histórico
c Bay, Gulf	Bucht, Golf	Bahía, Golfo	Baie, Golfe	Baía, Golfo	⌁ Recreational Site	Erholungs- und Ferienort	Sitio de Recreo	Centre de loisirs	Área de Lazer
≈ Lake, Lakes	See, Seen	Lago, Lagos	Lac, Lacs	Lago, Lagos	✈ Airport	Flughafen	Aeropuerto	Aéroport	Aeroporto
⊒ Swamp	Sumpf	Pantano	Marais	Pântano	⚔ Military Installation	Militäranlage	Instalación Militar	Installation militaire	Instalação militar
❄ Ice Features, Glacier	Eis- und Gletscherformen	Accidentes Glaciares	Formes glaciaires	Acidentes glaciares	◆ Miscellaneous	Verschiedenes	Misceláneo	Divers	Diversos
◆ Other Hydrographic Features	Andere Hydrographische Objekte	Otros Elementos Hidrográficos	Autres données hydrographiques	Outros acidentes hidrográficos					

Name	Page	Lat.°'	Long.°'
Teheran — Tehrān	128	35.40 N	51.26 E
Téhini	150	9.36 N	3.40 W
Tehoohaivei, Cap ▸	174x	9.49 S	138.54 W
Te Hope O Te Keho, Cap ▸	174x	10.02 S	139.06 W
Tehoru	164	3.23 S	129.30 E
Tehrān, Īrān	128	35.40 N	51.26 E
Tehrān, Īrān	267d	35.40 N	51.26 E
Tehrān □⁴	128	35.30 N	51.30 E
Tehrān, University of ◉²	267d	35.41 N	51.24 E
Tehrān International Airport ⇄	267d	35.41 N	51.19 E
Tehrān Pārs ⊶⁸	267d	35.44 N	51.32 E
Tehrathum	124	27.07 N	87.32 E
Tehri	124	30.23 N	78.29 E
Tehuacán	234	18.27 N	97.23 W
Tehuacana	234	31.44 N	96.33 W
Tehuacana Creek ≃, Tx., U.S.	222	31.31 N	97.02 W
Tehuacana Creek ≃, Tx., U.S.	222	31.50 N	95.59 W
Tehuantepec	234	18.41 N	103.17 W
Tehuantepec	234	16.10 N	95.07 W
Tehuantepec, Golfo de ⊂	234	16.00 N	94.50 W
Tehuantepec, Istmo de	234	17.00 N	95.00 W
Tehuantepec Ridge ⊹³	16	13.30 N	95.00 W
Tehuelches	254	46.56 S	67.27 W
Tehuipango	234	18.31 N	97.04 W
Tehuitzingo	234	18.21 N	98.17 W
Teià	266d	41.30 N	2.19 E
Teichl ≃	61	47.46 N	14.10 E
Teichröda	54	50.45 N	11.18 E
Teichwolframsdorf	54	50.43 N	12.14 E
Teide, Parque Nacional del ♠	148	28.15 N	16.30 W
Teide, Pico de ∧	148	28.16 N	16.38 W
Teifi ≃	42	52.07 N	4.42 W
Teifisidw ≃¹	42	52.02 N	4.22 W
Teiga Plateau ⚹¹	140	15.38 N	25.40 E
Teign ≃	42	50.33 N	3.29 W
Teignmouth	42	50.33 N	3.30 W
Teise ≃	260	51.13 N	0.25 E
Teisendorf	54	47.51 N	12.49 E
Teisnach	60	49.02 N	13.00 E
Teith ≃	46	56.08 N	3.59 W
Teixeira	250	7.13 S	37.15 W
Teixeira Pinto	150	12.10 N	13.55 W
Teixeira Soares	252	25.22 S	50.27 W
Teixeira ∧	115b	8.05 S	115.20 E
Tejamén	232	24.48 N	105.07 W
Tejkovo	80	56.52 N	40.34 E
Tejon Creek ≃	228	35.08 N	118.53 W
Tejon Pass)(	228	34.48 N	118.52 W
Tejo — Tagus ≃	34	38.40 N	9.24 W
Tejupan, Punta ▸	234	18.20 N	103.32 W
Tejupilco de Hidalgo	234	18.54 N	100.09 W
Te Kaha	172	37.44 S	177.41 E
Tekai ≃	114	4.14 N	102.23 E
Tékakwitha, Île ⤸	275a	45.25 N	73.42 W
Tekam ≃	114	3.52 N	102.27 E
Tekamah	198	41.46 N	96.13 W
Te Kao	172	34.39 S	172.57 E
Tekapo, Lake ◎	172	43.53 S	170.31 E
Te Karaka	172	38.28 S	177.52 E
Tekāri	124	24.56 N	84.50 E
Te Kauwhata	172	37.24 S	175.09 E
Tekax	232	20.12 N	89.17 W
Teke	130	41.04 N	39.39 E
Teke, ozero ◎	86	53.48 N	73.00 E
Teke Burnu ▸	130	35.26 N	26.36 E
Tekeli	86	44.48 N	78.57 E
Tekeli Dağı ∧	130	40.09 N	37.28 E
Tekes ≃	86	43.10 N	81.43 E
Tekes ≃	86	43.36 N	82.32 E
Tekeze (Satīt) ≃	140	14.20 N	35.50 E
Tekirdağ	130	40.59 N	27.31 E
Tekirdağ □⁴	130	41.00 N	27.30 E
Tekkali	122	18.37 N	84.14 E
Tekke	130	40.43 N	36.12 E
Tekke Burnu ▸	130	42.26 N	26.10 E
Tekkiraz	130	40.59 N	37.08 E
Tekman	130	39.38 N	41.31 E
Tekoa	202	47.13 N	117.04 W
Tekong, Pulau Ⅰ	271c	1.24 N	104.03 E
Tekonsha	216	42.05 N	84.59 W
Te Kopuru	172	36.02 S	173.56 E
Tekouiat, Oued ∨	146	22.25 N	2.35 E
Tékro ⸜⁴	146	19.30 N	20.58 E
Tekstil'ščiki	82	55.57 N	37.49 E
Tekstil'ščiki ⊶⁸	265b	52.47 N	37.44 E
Teku	112	0.46 S	123.26 E
Te Kuiti	172	38.20 S	175.10 E
Tekukor, Pulau Ⅰ	271c	1.14 N	103.50 E
Tel ≃	122	20.50 N	83.54 E
Tela, Hond.	236	15.44 N	87.27 W
Tela, India	272a	28.44 N	77.20 E
Tela, Bahía de ⊂	236	15.48 N	87.30 W
Telaga	116	6.51 N	117.03 E
Telaga, Teluk ⊂	114	2.10 N	98.00 E
Telaga-kulon	115a	6.58 S	108.18 E
Télagh	148	34.47 N	0.34 W
Telavåg	26	60.16 N	4.49 E
Telavi	84	41.55 N	45.28 E
Tel Aviv □⁵	132	32.05 N	34.48 E
Tel Aviv-Yafo	132	32.03 N	34.46 E
Telč	60	49.11 N	15.27 E
Tel'č'je	76	53.13 N	36.20 E
Telde	148	28.00 N	15.25 W
Tele ≃, Afr.	158	4.00 N	27.33 E
Tele ≃, Russia	52	2.48 N	23.54 E
Telechany	76	52.31 N	25.51 E
Telecote, ozero ◎	86	51.35 N	87.40 E
Telefomin	164	5.10 S	141.35 E
Telegapulang	112	2.55 S	112.25 E
Telegino	80	52.55 N	44.34 E
Telegrafo, Pizzo ∧	78	37.37 N	13.10 E
Telegraph Canyon ∨	280	33.55 N	117.45 W
Telegraph Cove	180	50.33 N	126.50 W
Telegraph Creek	180	57.55 N	131.10 W
Telêmaco Borba	252	24.20 S	50.40 W
Telemark □⁹	26	59.30 N	8.40 E
Telemba	88	52.43 N	113.16 E
Telembi ≃	246	1.50 N	78.16 W
Telén	252	36.16 S	65.30 W
Telenešty	78	47.30 N	28.22 E
Teleno ∧	34	42.21 N	6.23 W
Teleorman □⁹	38	44.00 N	25.15 E
Teleorman ≃	38	43.49 N	25.26 E
Téléphone, Île du Ⅰ	273b	4.20 S	15.12 E
Telertheba, Djebel ∧	148	24.10 N	6.51 E
Telescope Peak ∧	204	36.10 N	117.05 W
Telescope Point ▸	241k	12.08 N	61.36 W
Telese	68	41.13 N	14.32 E
Telesterion ⊥	267c	38.02 N	23.32 E
Telferner	222	28.51 N	96.53 W
Telford, Eng., U.K.	42	52.40 N	2.28 W
Telford, Pa., U.S.	208	40.19 N	75.19 W
Telfs	52	47.19 N	11.04 E
Telgte	52	51.59 N	7.47 E
Telica ≃	236	14.43 N	86.08 W
Telica, Volcán ∧¹	236	12.36 N	86.50 W
Telida	180	63.23 N	153.16 W
Telika	60	52.35 N	43.17 E
Télimélé	150	10.54 N	13.02 W
Telixtlahuaca	234	17.18 N	96.54 W
Telizi	265a	59.42 N	29.59 E
Teljo, Jabal ∧	140	14.05 N	25.35 E

Name	Page	Lat.°'	Long.°'
Telkwa	182	54.42 N	127.03 W
Telkwa ≃	182	54.41 N	127.02 W
Tel Lakhish ⊥	132	31.34 N	34.51 E
Tellaro ≃	70	36.50 N	15.06 E
Tell City	194	37.57 N	86.46 W
Teller	180	65.16 N	166.22 W
Tellicherry	122	11.45 N	75.32 E
Tellico ≃	192	35.36 N	84.13 W
Tellico Plains	192	35.21 N	84.17 W
Tellier	254	47.39 S	66.03 W
Tellier, Lac ◎	206	46.23 N	74.00 W
Tello	246	3.04 N	75.08 W
Telluride	200	37.56 N	107.48 W
Tel'ma	88	52.43 N	103.41 E
Tel'manovo	83	48.30 N	39.18 E
Tel'manovo	83	47.24 N	38.02 E
Tel Megiddo (Armageddon) ⊥	132	32.35 N	35.11 E
Telmen	88	48.38 N	97.37 E
Telmen nuur ◎	88	48.50 N	97.18 E
Tel Mond	132	32.15 N	34.56 E
Tel'novskij	89	49.22 N	142.05 E
Telo	116	0.03 N	98.16 E
Teloekbetoeng — Tanjungkarang-Telukbetung	115a	5.27 S	105.16 E
Telogia Creek ≃	192	30.16 N	84.44 W
Telok Anson	114	4.02 N	101.01 E
Telok Datok	114	2.49 N	101.31 E
Telolapan	234	18.21 N	99.51 W
Telpaneca	236	13.32 N	86.17 W
Telsen	254	42.24 S	66.57 W
Telsen, Arroyo ≃	254	42.51 S	66.48 W
TelŠiai	76	55.59 N	22.15 E
Telti	71	40.52 N	9.21 E
Teltow	54	52.23 N	13.16 E
Teltow ⊶⁸	264a	52.18 N	13.25 E
Teltower Hochfläche ⋯	264a	52.22 N	13.20 E
Teltowkanal ≋	264a	52.26 N	13.35 E
Telukbatang	112	1.00 S	109.46 E
Telukbayur, Indon.	112	2.09 N	117.24 E
Telukbayur, Indon.	112	1.00 S	100.22 E
Telukbrombang	114	2.03 N	100.52 E
Telukbutun	112	4.13 N	108.12 E
Telukdalem	114	0.34 N	97.49 E
Telukkuljut	112	0.09 N	103.29 E
Telukkuala	114	1.51 N	101.44 E
Telukmerbau	114	2.04 N	100.38 E
Telukpambang	114	1.28 N	102.28 E
Teluk Punggur, Ujung ▸	112	3.53 S	102.17 E
Telumengtang Shan ∧	120	30.33 N	86.27 E
Teluša	76	53.03 N	29.31 E
Tem'	88	55.21 N	100.44 E
Tema	150	5.38 N	0.01 E
Temae	174s	17.29 S	149.46 W
Temagami, Lake ◎	206	47.00 N	80.05 W
Temanggung, Pulau Ⅰ	112	0.29 N	108.52 E
Temalacacingo	234	17.52 N	98.41 W
Temali Bendi ≃⁶	267b	41.04 N	29.06 E
Te Manga ∧	174k	21.13 S	159.45 W
Temanggung Baharu	112	5.42 N	102.09 E
Temangga	112	0.27 N	111.21 E
Temanggung	115a	7.18 S	110.10 E
Temascalcingo, Méx.	234	23.24 N	104.14 W
Temascal, Méx.	234	18.15 N	96.20 W
Tem'asovo	86	52.59 N	58.06 E
Temastián	234	21.53 N	103.28 W
Tematagi ∧¹	114	21.41 S	140.40 W
Tembakul, Pulau Ⅰ	271c	1.14 N	103.52 E
Tembe ≃	114	0.16 S	28.14 E
Tembe	158	26.03 S	32.26 E
Tembeling	114	4.04 N	102.19 E
Tembeling ≃	114	4.04 N	102.20 E
Tembenči ≃	74	64.36 N	99.58 E
Tembilahan	112	0.19 S	103.09 E
Tembisa	161	25.58 S	28.14 E
Temblador	246	8.59 N	62.44 W
Tembleque	34	39.42 N	3.30 W
Temblor Range ∧	226	35.20 N	119.55 W
Tembo Aluma	152	7.42 S	17.17 E
Tembué	154	14.52 S	32.58 E
Tembuland □⁹	158	31.30 S	27.40 E
Teme ≃	42	52.09 N	2.18 W
Temecula	234	33.29 N	117.08 W
Temecula Creek ≃	228	33.28 N	117.08 W
Temelli	234	39.44 N	32.22 E
Temengor	114	5.19 N	101.22 E
Temengor, Tasek ◎¹	114	5.30 N	101.20 E
Temerin	38	45.24 N	19.53 E
Temerloh	114	3.27 N	102.25 E
Temescal Canyon ∨	280	34.04 N	118.32 W
Temescal Wash ∨	228	33.40 N	117.20 W
Temesvár — Timişoara	38	45.45 N	21.13 E
Temiang, Pulau Ⅰ	112	0.19 N	104.23 E
Teminabuan	164	1.26 S	132.01 E
Temir	86	49.08 N	57.06 E
Temirgojevskaja	78	45.07 N	40.16 E
Temirjansk	86	42.26 N	69.17 E
Temirtau, Kaz.	86	50.05 N	72.56 E
Temirtau, Russia	86	53.08 N	87.28 E
Témiscamie ≃	206	53.08 N	72.12 W
Témiscamie, Lac ◎	186	51.11 N	72.12 W
Témiscaming	190	46.43 N	79.06 W
Témiscouata, Lac ◎	186	47.41 N	68.49 W
Temistʻan	234	18.50 N	99.14 W
Temnik ≃	88	51.00 N	106.18 E
Temnikov	80	54.38 N	43.12 E
Temninskij chrebet ∧	265b	55.43 N	38.01 E
Temo ≃	71	40.21 N	8.47 E
Temoaya	234	19.28 N	99.35 W
Temoe Ⅰ	166	34.26 S	147.32 E
Temosachic	234	28.57 N	107.51 W
Temósachic ≃	232	29.30 N	107.31 W
Tempaleo	200	33.24 N	111.54 W
Tempe, Danau ◎	112	4.06 S	119.57 E
Tempe	200	33.25 N	111.55 W
Tempelfelde	264a	52.43 N	13.43 E
Tempelhof ⊶⁸	264a	52.28 N	13.23 E
Temperance	216	41.46 N	83.34 W
Temperanceville	208	37.53 N	75.32 W
Temperley ∧	264c	34.47 S	58.24 W
Tempest, Mount ∧²	171a	27.10 S	153.26 E
Tempilang	112	2.07 S	105.40 E
Tempino	112	1.42 S	103.31 E
Tempio di Clitunno ⊥	66	42.48 N	12.45 E
Tempio Pausania	71	40.54 N	9.06 E
Tempisque ≃	236	10.12 N	85.14 W
Temple, Ok., U.S.	196	34.16 N	98.14 W
Temple, Pa., U.S.	208	40.24 N	75.55 W
Temple, Tx., U.S.	222	31.05 N	97.20 W
Temple City	234	34.06 N	118.03 W
Templecombe	42	51.00 N	2.25 W
Temple Ewell	260	51.09 N	1.16 E
Temple Hills Park	284c	38.48 N	76.57 W
Templemore	44	52.48 N	7.50 W
Templers	168b	34.35 S	138.45 E
Temple Sowerby	40	54.39 N	2.35 W
Temple Terrace	192	28.02 N	82.23 W
Templeton, Ca., U.S.	226	35.33 N	120.42 W
Templeton, In., U.S.	216	40.33 N	87.12 W
Templeton, Ma., U.S.	208	42.33 N	72.04 W
Templeton, P.Q., Can.	212	45.29 N	75.33 W
Templeuve, Bel.	50	50.32 N	3.10 E
Templeuve, Valle del ∧	70	37.17 N	13.35 E
Templin	54	53.07 N	13.30 E
Templiner See ◎	264a	52.22 N	13.03 E
Tempoal Island Ⅰ	116	13.09 N	122.52 E
Tempoal de Sánchez	234	21.31 N	98.23 W
Tempy	82	56.38 N	37.18 E
Tem'uk	82	33.45 N	118.15 W

Name	Page	Lat.°'	Long.°'
Temr'ukskij zaliv ⊂	78	45.24 N	37.20 E
Temse	50	51.08 N	4.13 E
Temü	64	46.15 N	10.28 E
Temuco	252	38.44 S	72.36 W
Temuka	172	44.15 S	171.17 E
Temwen Ⅰ	174r	6.52 N	158.19 E
Tena	246	0.59 S	77.49 W
Tenabo	232	20.03 N	90.14 W
Tenafly	210	40.55 N	73.57 W
Tenaha	194	31.57 N	94.15 W
Tenakee Springs	180	57.47 N	135.13 W
Tenakill Brook ≃	276	40.59 N	73.58 W
Tena Kourou ∧²	150	10.45 N	5.25 W
Tenāli	122	16.15 N	80.35 E
Tenamaxtlán	234	20.13 N	104.10 W
Tenancingo [de Degollado]	234	18.58 N	99.36 W
Tenango de Arista	234	19.07 N	99.33 W
Tenasillahe Island Ⅰ	224	46.14 N	123.27 W
Tenasserim	110	12.05 N	99.01 E
Tenay	58	45.55 N	5.30 E
Tenaya Creek ≃	226	37.44 N	119.35 W
Tenbury Wells	42	52.19 N	2.35 W
Tenby	42	51.41 N	4.43 W
Tench Island Ⅰ	164	1.40 S	150.40 E
Tencin	58	45.19 N	5.58 E
Tenda, Colle di (Col de Tende))(	62	44.09 N	7.34 E
Tendaho	144	11.48 N	40.52 E
Tendai-san ∧	270	34.55 N	135.28 E
Tende	62	44.05 N	7.36 E
Tende, Col de (Colle di Tenda))(	62	44.09 N	7.34 E
Tende, Tunnel de ≃⁵	62	44.09 N	7.34 E
Ten Degree Channel ᴗ	110	10.00 N	93.00 E
Tendeka	158	27.44 S	30.54 E
Tendō	92	38.21 N	140.22 E
Tendrara	148	33.04 N	1.59 W
Tendrovskaja kosa ⸜²	78	46.12 N	31.50 E
Tendrovskij zaliv ⊂	78	46.15 N	31.55 E
Tendŭlecak Dâgi ∧	84	39.22 N	43.52 E
Tênenkou	150	14.28 N	4.55 W
Tenente Marques ≃	248	11.10 S	59.56 W
Tenente Portela	252	27.22 S	53.45 W
Ténéré, Erg du ⸜⁸	146	17.35 N	10.55 E
Ténéré, Erg du ⸜⁸	146	17.35 N	10.55 E
Ténès	34	36.31 N	1.14 E
Ténès, Cap ▸	34	36.33 N	1.21 E
Tenexpa	234	17.11 N	100.43 W
Tenextepango	234	18.43 N	98.57 W
Teng ≃	110	19.52 N	97.45 E
Tengah, Kepulauan Ⅱ	112	7.30 S	117.30 E
Tengah, Sungai Ⅰ	104	41.05 N	122.49 E
Tengchong	102	25.04 N	98.29 E
Tengeh Reservoir ◎	271c	1.21 N	103.39 E
Tengen	52	47.49 N	8.40 E
Tenggara, Nusa (Lesser Sunda Islands) Ⅱ	108	9.00 S	120.00 E
Tenggarong	112	0.24 S	116.58 E
Tengger Shamo ⸜²	102	38.00 N	104.40 E
Tenggol, Pulau Ⅰ	114	4.48 N	103.38 E
Tenghilan	116	6.14 N	116.19 E
Tengi ≃	114	3.24 N	101.10 E
Tengiz, ozero ◎	86	50.26 N	68.56 E
Tengjiabao	110	18.22 N	109.46 E
Tengréla	150	10.29 N	6.24 W
Tengtian	100	27.04 N	115.40 E
Tengxian (Na) ≃	112	22.05 N	103.09 E
Tengxian, Zhg.	98	35.08 N	117.10 E
Tengxian, Zhg.	102	23.21 N	110.53 E
Teniente Rodolfo Marsh ⸜¹	9	62.12 S	58.54 W
Tenigerbad	64	39.42 N	8.57 E
Tenino	226	46.51 N	122.51 W
Tenis, ozero ◎	86	56.09 N	71.56 E
Teniya-zaki ▸	174m	26.33 N	128.09 E
Teniz, ozero ◎	86	54.08 N	64.34 E
Tenjin ≃	96	35.33 N	133.50 E
Tenjo, Mount ∧²	174p	13.25 N	144.42 E
Tenkäsi	122	8.58 N	77.18 E
Tenke, Zaïre	154	10.35 S	26.07 E
Tenke, Zaïre	154	11.26 S	26.45 E
Tenkeli	74	70.01 N	140.58 E
Tenkergynpil'gyn, laguna ⊂	180	68.30 N	178.00 W
Ten'ki	80	55.26 N	49.00 E
Tenkiller Ferry Lake ◎	196	35.43 N	95.00 W
Tenkodogo	150	11.47 N	0.22 W
Tenmile ≃, Ma., U.S.	283	41.58 N	71.20 W
Tenmile ≃, N.Y., U.S.	210	41.40 N	73.31 W
Ten Mile ≃, On., Can.	284a	43.07 N	79.11 W
Ten Mile Creek ≃, Ky., U.S.	218	38.43 N	84.46 W
Tenmile Creek ≃, Oh., U.S.	216	41.42 N	83.33 W
Tenmile Creek ≃, Pa., U.S.	188	40.08 N	80.22 W
Ten Mile Creek ≃, Tx., U.S.	222	32.34 N	96.34 W
Ten Mile Lake ◎	186	51.06 N	56.41 W
Tenmile Run ≃	276	40.27 N	74.35 W
Tenmile Wash ∨	200	32.52 N	113.28 W
Tennmoku-san ∧	94	35.33 N	138.47 E
Tennant ≃	46	55.14 N	13.47 E
Tennant Creek	162	19.40 S	134.10 E
Tennenbronn	48	48.11 N	8.20 E
Tennengau ⸜¹	64	47.30 N	13.15 E
Tennengebirge ∧	64	47.30 N	13.15 E
Tennent	208	40.18 N	74.20 W
Tennessee ≃	178	35.50 N	85.30 W
Tennessee □³	178	35.50 N	88.33 W
Tennessee Colony	222	31.50 N	95.50 W
Tennille	192	32.56 N	82.48 W
Tennyson	168	33.52 S	146.33 E
Tenō ∧	148	29.01 N	13.32 W
Tenōji ⊶⁸	270	34.39 N	135.31 E
Tenom	116	5.08 N	115.57 E
Tenosique	234	17.29 N	91.26 W
Teno (Tana) ≃	252	30.28 S	70.30 W
Tenosique de Pino Suárez	234	17.29 N	91.26 W
Ténos, Pointe ▸	240e	14.48 N	61.00 W
Tenosique	234	17.29 N	91.26 W
Tenryū	94	34.52 N	137.49 E
Tenryū, Nihon	94	34.52 N	137.49 E
Tenryū ≃	94	34.39 N	137.47 E
Tensas ≃	194	31.38 N	91.49 W
Tensed	202	47.09 N	116.55 W
Tensift, Oued ≃	148	32.02 N	9.03 W
Ten Sleep	202	44.02 N	107.27 W
Tensta	30	60.05 N	17.40 E
Tente ∧¹	263	51.18 N	7.14 E
Tenteksor ⊥	80	47.13 N	48.20 E
Tentena	112	1.47 S	120.39 E
Tenterden	42	51.05 N	0.42 E
Tent Hill	166	29.13 S	135.44 E
Tenthill Creek ≃	171a	27.34 S	152.14 E
Ten Thousand Islands Ⅱ	192	25.50 N	81.25 W
Tentolomatinan, Gunung ∧	112	0.56 N	121.48 E
Tentudia ∧	34	38.05 N	6.20 W
Teocaltiche	234	21.26 N	102.35 W
Teocelo	234	19.23 N	96.58 W
Teocuitatlán de Corona	234	20.07 N	103.24 W

Name	Page	Lat.°'	Long.°'
Teófilo Cunha	287a	22.39 S	43.34 W
Teófilo Otoni	255	17.51 S	41.30 W
Teofipol'	78	49.50 N	26.25 E
Teohotepapa, Pointe ▸	174x	9.46 S	138.48 W
Teohotupa, Pointe ▸	174x	9.46 S	138.50 W
Teo Lakes ◎	184	51.30 N	109.21 W
Teolo	64	45.21 N	11.40 E
Teomabal Island Ⅰ	116	6.20 N	120.51 E
Teor	64	45.51 N	13.03 E
Teora	68	40.51 N	15.15 E
Teotihuacán ⊥	234	19.44 N	98.50 W
Teotitlán de Flores Magón	234	18.08 N	97.05 W
Teotitlán del Valle	234	17.02 N	96.30 W
Tepa, Ghana	150	7.00 N	2.10 W
Tepa, Indon.	164	7.52 S	129.31 E
Tepalcatepec	234	19.11 N	102.51 W
Tepalcingo	234	18.36 N	98.51 W
Tepa Point ▸	174v	19.07 S	169.56 W
Tepatitlán de Morelos	234	20.49 N	102.44 W
Tepatlaxco [de Hidalgo]	234	19.04 N	97.58 W
Tepe	130	37.48 N	40.47 E
Tepeaca	234	18.58 N	97.54 W
Tepeapulco	234	19.47 N	98.33 W
Tepebaşı	130	36.40 N	32.45 E
Tepechitlán	234	21.40 N	103.20 W
Tepeguaje	196	25.40 N	99.50 W
Tepeguajes	234	23.30 N	97.50 W
Tepehan	130	38.06 N	38.45 E
Tepehuanes	234	25.21 N	105.44 W
Tepehuanes ≃	232	25.10 N	105.25 W
Tepeji de Ocampo	234	19.54 N	99.21 W
Tepelenë	38	40.18 N	20.01 E
Tepelmeme de Morelos	234	17.51 N	97.21 W
Tepeören	130	41.04 N	35.30 E
Tepepan ⸜⁸	286a	19.16 N	99.08 W
Tepe Saif	267d	35.36 N	51.18 E
Tepetiltic, Volcán ∧¹	234	21.15 N	104.43 W
Tepetixtla	234	17.13 N	100.08 W
Tepetlixpa	234	19.02 N	98.49 W
Tepi	144	7.10 N	35.23 E
Tepic	234	21.30 N	104.54 W
Tepko	168b	34.58 S	139.11 E
Teplá	54	49.59 N	12.52 E
Teplá ≃	54	50.14 N	12.52 E
Teplice	54	50.39 N	13.48 E
Teplitz — Teplice	54	50.39 N	13.48 E
Teploozʻorsk	89	49.04 N	131.48 E
Teplovka	80	51.33 N	51.33 E
Teplovo	80	55.25 N	42.56 E
Tepoca, Bahía ⊂	232	30.16 N	112.51 W
Tepoca, Punta ▸	232	29.55 N	112.46 W
Te Pohue	172	39.15 S	176.41 E
Tepopa, Cabo ▸	232	29.22 N	112.27 W
Te Puke	172	37.47 S	176.20 E
Tepuzhuacán	234	20.02 N	100.13 W
Tequila	234	20.54 N	103.47 W
Tequisquita Slough ≃	226	36.58 N	121.27 W
Tequixquitla	234	19.19 N	97.40 W
Tequma	132	31.27 N	34.35 E
Ter ≃, Esp.	34	42.01 N	3.12 E
Ter ≃, Ityo.	144	7.10 N	35.23 E
Ter ≃, Eng., U.K.	42	51.50 N	0.36 E
Téra	150	14.01 N	0.45 E
Tera ≃	34	41.54 N	5.44 W
Teradomari	92	33.38 N	138.46 E
Terai ◣	124	26.36 N	86.30 E
Ter'ajevo	82	56.07 N	36.07 E
Terakhāda	126	22.56 N	89.40 E
Teralba	170	32.58 S	151.37 E
Teramo	66	42.39 N	13.42 E
Teramo □⁶	66	42.30 N	13.41 E
Terang	166	38.14 S	142.55 E
Teranum	114	3.44 N	101.49 E
Ter Apel	52	52.53 N	7.04 E
Teraruma	164	8.00 S	141.50 E
Teras	112	1.00 N	101.49 E
Teratak	112	0.55 N	101.32 E
Terborg	52	51.55 N	6.21 E
Terbury	76	52.08 N	38.17 E
Tercan	130	39.47 N	40.24 E
Terceira Ⅰ	148a	38.43 N	27.13 W
Tercero ≃	252	32.55 S	62.19 W
Tercero de Febrero, Parque ∧	288	34.34 S	58.25 W
Terdal	122	16.30 N	75.03 E

Name	Seite	Breite°'	Länge°' E = Ost
Terminal Island Coast Guard Base ⋆	280	33.43 N	118.17 W
Termini Imerese	70	37.59 N	13.42 E
Termini Imerese, Golfo di ⊂	70	38.01 N	13.45 E
Terminillo, Monte ∧	66	42.28 N	13.00 E
Términos, Laguna de ⊂	232	18.37 N	91.33 W
Termit, Massif de ∧	146	16.15 N	11.17 E
Termoli	66	42.00 N	15.00 E
Termonde — Dendermonde	50	51.02 N	4.07 E
Tern ≃	42	52.47 N	2.32 W
Ternate, Indon.	108	0.48 N	127.24 E
Ternate, Pil.	116	14.17 N	120.43 E
Ternberg	61	47.58 N	14.22 E
Ternej	89	45.03 N	136.37 E
Terneuzen	52	51.20 N	3.50 E
Terni	66	42.34 N	12.37 E
Terni □⁴	66	42.41 N	12.19 E
Ternitz	61	47.44 N	16.03 E
Ternois ≃	50	50.23 N	2.01 E
Ternopol'	78	49.34 N	25.36 E
Ternovatoje	78	47.50 N	36.09 E
Ternovka, Ross.	78	51.40 N	41.37 E
Ternovka, Ross.	80	53.09 N	45.02 E
Ternovka, Ukr.	78	48.32 N	29.58 E
Ternovka, Ukr.	78	47.02 N	32.01 E
Ternovoje	78	50.03 N	43.43 E
Ternovskaja	78	45.53 N	40.24 E
Terok	114	3.53 N	101.23 E
Terong	114	4.43 N	100.44 E
Terontola	66	43.13 N	12.02 E
Terpe	54	51.32 N	14.19 E
Terpenija, mys ▸	89	48.39 N	144.44 E
Terpenija, zaliv ⊂	89	49.00 N	143.30 E
Terra Alta	188	39.26 N	79.32 W
Terra Bella	204	35.58 N	119.03 W
Terrace	182	54.31 N	128.35 W
Terrace Bay	190	48.47 N	87.06 W
Terracina	66	41.17 N	13.15 E
Terra del Sole	66	44.11 N	11.57 E
Terral	196	33.53 N	97.56 W
Terralba	71	39.43 N	8.39 E
Terra Linda	226	38.01 N	122.32 W
Terra Nova Bay ⊂	9	74.45 S	164.30 E
Terranova da Sibari	68	39.39 N	16.18 E
Terranova di Pollino	68	39.59 N	16.18 E
Terranova di Sicilia — Gela	70	37.04 N	14.15 E
Terra Nova Lake ◎	186	48.30 N	54.20 W
Terra Nova National Park ♠	186	48.37 N	53.56 W
Terranova — Newfoundland □⁴	176	52.00 N	56.00 W
Terranuova Bracciolini	66	43.33 N	11.35 E
Terra Rica	255	22.43 S	52.38 W
Terrarossa, Foce di)(	64	44.12 N	10.26 E
Terra Roxa	252	24.08 S	53.59 W
Terra, Pinhal do ⸜³	266c	38.59 N	9.02 W
Terra Santa	250	2.06 S	56.29 W
Terrasini	70	38.09 N	13.05 E
Terrassa	34	41.34 N	2.01 E
Terrasse-Vaudreuil	206	45.24 N	73.59 W
Terrasson-la-Villedieu	58	45.08 N	1.18 E
Terravecchia	68	39.29 N	16.58 E
Terrebonne	206	45.42 N	73.38 W
Terrebonne □⁴	206	46.00 N	74.10 W
Terrebonne Bay ⊂	194	29.10 N	90.35 W
Terre-Neuve — Newfoundland □⁴	176	52.00 N	56.00 W
Terre Noire Creek ≃	194	33.49 N	92.55 W
Terre Rouge Creek ≃	194	33.49 N	93.11 W
Terres australes et antarctiques françaises — French Southern and Antarctic Territories □²	6	49.30 S	69.30 E
Terre Hill	208	40.09 N	76.03 W
Terre Haute	194	39.28 N	87.24 W
Terre Hommes ⋆	275a	45.31 N	73.32 W
Terrell	222	32.44 N	96.16 W
Terrell, Lake ◎	224	48.52 N	122.41 W
Terrell Hills	196	29.28 N	98.27 W
Terrenceville	186	47.40 N	54.44 W
Tersa ≃	80	51.00 N	42.55 E
Tersakkan ≃	86	50.39 N	66.55 E
Tersana, Punta ▸	252	23.23 S	70.38 W
Terschelling Ⅰ	52	53.24 N	5.20 E
Tersef	146	13.10 N	18.10 E
Terskej-Alatau, chrebet ∧	102	42.15 N	78.40 E
Terskij bereg ⸜²	26	66.05 N	38.30 E
Terskol	84	43.15 N	42.30 E
Terter ≃	84	40.21 N	47.10 E
Tertenia	71	39.42 N	9.34 E
Teruel	34	40.21 N	1.06 W
Teruel, Col.	246	4.44 N	75.33 W
Teruel, Esp. □⁴	34	40.35 N	0.55 W
Tervakoski	28	60.48 N	24.37 E
Tervola	28	66.05 N	24.48 E
Tervuren	50	50.49 N	4.31 E
Terwagne	50	50.27 N	5.26 E
Terwolde	52	52.16 N	6.06 E
Terzaghi Dam ⸜⁶	182	50.49 N	122.12 W
Teržola	84	42.12 N	43.01 E
Tes ≃	88	50.27 N	93.30 E
Tesa, Magy.	60	48.02 N	18.51 E
Teša, Ross.	80	55.30 N	42.11 E
Teša ≃	80	55.47 N	42.11 E

Name	Seite	Breite°'	Länge°' E = Ost
Tešanj	38	44.37 N	18.00 E
Tes-Chem (Tesijn) ≃	88	50.28 N	93.04 E
Tescott	198	39.00 N	97.52 W
Tešečoakán ≃	234	18.31 N	95.42 W
Teseney	144	15.07 N	36.41 E
Tesero	64	46.17 N	11.31 E
Teshekpuk Lake ◎	180	70.35 N	153.30 W
Teshikaga	92a	43.29 N	144.28 E
Te-shima Ⅰ, Nihon	96	34.29 N	134.05 E
Te-shima Ⅰ, Nihon	96	34.31 N	133.40 E
Teshio	92a	44.53 N	141.44 E
Teshio ≃	92a	44.53 N	141.44 E
Teshio-sanchi ∧	92a	44.15 N	142.05 E
Tešig	88	49.56 N	102.34 E
Tesijn (Tes-Chem) ≃	88	50.28 N	93.04 E
Tesimo (Tisens)	64	46.34 N	11.10 E
Teslin	180	60.09 N	132.45 W
Teslin ≃	180	61.34 N	134.54 W
Teslin Lake ◎	180	60.15 N	132.57 W
Tesouro	255	14.36 S	50.51 W
Tesouro	255	16.04 S	53.34 W
Tesovo	82	55.34 N	36.05 E
Tesperhude	52	53.24 N	10.26 E
Tessa, Oued ≃	36	36.34 N	8.54 E
Tessa-Araral, Oued ∨	148	26.18 N	1.58 E
Tessala	34	35.17 N	0.48 W
Tessala, Monts du ∧	34	35.25 N	0.45 W
Tessalit	150	20.12 N	1.00 E
Tessancourt-sur-Aubette	261	49.02 N	1.55 E
Tessaoua	150	13.45 N	7.59 E
Tessei	96	34.56 N	133.20 E
Tessenderlo	54	51.04 N	5.05 E
Tesserete	58	46.04 N	8.58 E
Tessin ≃	54	54.01 N	12.28 E
Tessin — Ticino □³	58	46.20 N	8.45 E
Tessy-sur-Vire	32	48.58 N	1.04 W
Testa	42	50.55 N	1.29 W
Testa, Capo ▸	71	41.15 N	9.09 E
Teston, On., Can.	275b	43.52 N	79.32 W
Teston, Eng., U.K.	260	51.15 N	0.26 E
Tesuque	200	35.45 N	105.55 W
Têt ≃	32	42.44 N	3.02 E
Tetachuck Lake ◎	182	53.20 N	125.50 W
Tetagouche ≃	186	47.35 N	65.41 W
Tetas, Punta ▸	252	23.31 S	70.38 W
Tetbury	42	51.39 N	2.10 W
Tete	154	16.13 S	33.35 E
Tete □⁵	154	15.15 S	32.40 E
Tété ≃	146	12.19 N	20.29 E
Tête-à-la-Baleine	186	50.41 N	59.20 W
Tête du Parmelan ∧	58	45.57 N	6.14 E
Tête-Jaune-Cache	182	52.57 N	119.26 W
Te Teko	172	38.02 S	176.48 E
Tetepare Island Ⅰ	175a	8.43 S	157.33 E
Tétépisca, Lac ◎	186	51.00 N	69.25 W
Teterboro	276	40.52 N	74.03 W
Teterboro Airport ⇄	276	40.51 N	74.04 W
Teterchen	50	49.14 N	6.34 E
Teterow	54	53.46 N	12.34 E
Teteven	38	42.55 N	24.16 E
Tetiaroa Ⅰ¹	174s	17.05 S	149.32 W
Tetica ∧	34	37.15 N	2.25 W
Tetijev	78	49.23 N	29.41 E
Tetiš ≃	74	73.40 N	84.35 E
Tetlin	180	63.08 N	142.31 W
Tetlin Lake ◎	180	63.05 N	142.45 W
Teton ≃	202	43.53 N	111.40 W
Teton ≃, Id., U.S.	202	43.53 N	111.40 W
Teton ≃, Mt., U.S.	202	47.56 N	110.31 W
Tetonia	202	43.49 N	111.09 W
Teton Range ∧	202	43.45 N	110.50 W
Tétouan	148	35.34 N	5.23 W
Tetovo	38	42.01 N	20.58 E
Tétreauville ⸜⁸	275a	45.35 N	73.32 W
Tetri-Ckaro	84	41.34 N	44.28 E
Tetschen — Děčín	54	50.48 N	14.13 E
Tetsuta	96	34.56 N	132.08 E
Tettau	54	50.28 N	11.16 E
Tettenhall	262	52.36 N	2.09 W
Tettens	52	53.38 N	7.53 E
Tettnang	48	47.40 N	9.35 E
Tetuán — Tétouan	148	35.34 N	5.23 W
Tetufera, Mont ∧	174s	17.40 S	149.26 W
Teulbäria	126	22.35 N	90.37 E
Teulia □⁴	126	22.15 N	90.37 E
Teturi	154	1.04 N	29.08 E
Tet'uškoje	80	54.18 N	48.03 E
Teublitz	60	49.13 N	12.05 E
Teuchern	54	51.07 N	12.01 E
Teuco ≃	252	25.38 S	60.12 W
Teufels-Insel — Diable, Île du Ⅰ	250	5.17 N	52.35 W
Teufelsmoor ⸜³	52	53.15 N	8.50 E
Teufen	61	47.23 N	9.23 E
Teunom	114	4.48 N	95.44 E
Teunom ≃	114	4.49 N	95.48 E
Teupitz	54	52.08 N	13.37 E
Teureubangan-cut	114	4.26 N	95.48 E
Teuri-tō Ⅰ	92a	44.25 N	141.19 E
Teuschnitz	54	50.24 N	11.23 E
Teutopolis	194	39.08 N	88.28 W
Teutschenthal	54	51.25 N	11.48 E
Teuva	28	62.29 N	21.44 E
Tevere ≃	66	41.44 N	12.14 E
Teverya (Tiberias)	132	32.47 N	35.32 E
Teviot ≃	46	55.36 N	2.26 W
Teviot Brook ≃	171a	27.51 S	152.57 E
Teviotdale ∧	58	46.15 S	172.32 E
Tevli	76	52.09 N	24.15 E
Teviz	82	55.34 N	72.24 E
Te Waewae Bay ⊂	172	46.15 S	167.32 E
Tewah	112	1.05 S	113.42 E
Tewkesbury	42	51.59 N	2.09 W
Tew-Mac Airport ⇄	283	42.38 N	71.12 W
Têwo	102	34.02 N	103.05 E
Texada Island Ⅰ	182	49.40 N	124.24 W
Texana	222	29.07 N	96.34 W
Texarkana, Ar., U.S.	194	33.25 N	94.02 W
Texarkana, Tx., U.S.	194	33.26 N	94.03 W
Texas ≃	171a	28.51 S	151.11 E
Texas □³	178	31.30 N	99.00 W
Texas City	222	29.23 N	94.54 W
Texcaltitlán	234	18.58 N	99.52 W
Texcoco, Lago de ◎	234	19.30 N	99.00 W
Texhoma	196	36.30 N	101.47 W
Texico	196	34.23 N	103.03 W
Texline	196	36.22 N	103.01 W
Teyateyaneng	158	29.09 S	27.34 E
Teyeä	96	37.29 N	22.24 E

Symbols in the index entries represent the broad categories identified in the key at the right. Symbols with superior numbers (⸜¹) identify subcategories (see complete key on page I · 1).

Symbole im Register stellen die rechts im Schlüssel erklärten Kategorien dar. Symbole mit hochgestellten Ziffern (⸜¹) bezeichnen Unterteilungen einer Kategorie (vgl. vollständigen Schlüssel auf Seite I · 1).

Los símbolos incluidos en el texto del índice representan las grandes categorías identificadas en la clave a la derecha. Los símbolos con números en su parte superior (⸜¹) identifican las subcategorías (véase la clave completa en la página I · 1).

Les symboles de l'index représentent les catégories identifiées dans la légende à droite. Les symboles suivis d'un indice (⸜¹) représentent des sous-catégories (voir légende complète à la page I · 1).

Os símbolos incluídos no texto do índice representam as grandes categorias identificadas com a chave à direita. Os símbolos com números em sua parte superior (⸜¹) identificam as subcategorias (veja-se a chave completa à página I · 1).

∧	Mountain	Berg	Montaña	Montagne	Montanha
∧	Mountains	Gebirge	Montañas	Montagnes	Montanhas
)(	Pass	Paß	Paso	Col	Passo
∨	Valley, Canyon	Tal, Cañon	Valle, Cañón	Vallée, Canyon	Vale, Canhão
▸	Plain	Ebene	Llano	Plaine	Planície
▸	Cape	Kap	Cabo	Cap	Cabo
Ⅰ	Island	Insel	Isla	Île	Ilha
Ⅱ	Islands	Inseln	Islas	Îles	Ilhas
⊥	Other Topographic Features	Andere Topographische Objekte	Otros Elementos Topográficos	Autres données topographiques	Outros acidentes topográficos

ESPAÑOL

Nombre	Página	Lat.°′	Long.°′ W = Oeste
Teynham	42	51.20 N	0.50 E
Teywarah	120	33.21 N	64.25 E
Teza ≃	80	56.32 N	41.53 E
Teziutlán	234	19.49 N	97.21 W
Težler, gora ∧	84	40.42 N	44.37 E
Tezoatlán de Segura y Luna	234	17.42 N	97.49 W
Tezpur	120	26.37 N	92.48 E
Tezu	120	27.53 N	96.11 E
Tezzeron Lake ⊜	182	54.41 N	124.25 W
Tha ≃	110	20.07 N	100.36 E
Tha-anne ≃	176	60.31 N	94.37 W
Thabana-Ntlenyana ∧	158	29.28 S	29.16 E
Thaba Nchu	158	29.17 S	26.52 E
Thabankulu ∧	158	27.30 S	30.20 E
Thaba-Putsoa Range ⩘	158	29.45 S	27.55 E
Thabaung	110	17.02 N	94.48 E
Thabawleikkyi	110	12.01 N	99.12 E
Thabazimbi	156	24.41 S	27.21 E
Thabor, Mont ∧	62	45.07 N	6.34 E
Thabyu	110	15.36 N	98.29 E
Thacher Island I	207	42.38 N	70.35 W
Thādiq	128	25.18 N	45.52 E
Thagyettaw	110	13.45 N	98.09 E
Thai Binh	110	20.27 N	106.20 E
Thailand (Prathet Thai) □[1], Asia	108	15.00 N	100.00 E
Thailand (Prathet Thai) □[1], Asia	110	15.00 N	100.00 E
Thailand, Gulf of c	110	10.00 N	101.00 E
Thaïlande → Thailand □[1]	110	15.00 N	100.00 E
Thailandia → Thailand □[1]	110	15.00 N	100.00 E
Thai Muang	110	8.24 N	98.16 E
Thai Nguyen	110	21.36 N	105.50 E
Thak	120	30.32 N	70.13 E
Thakhek → Muang Khammouan	110	17.24 N	104.48 E
Thākurdwāra	124	29.12 N	78.51 E
Thākurdwāri	272b	22.34 N	88.28 E
Thākurgaon	124	26.02 N	88.28 E
Thākurpukur	272b	22.28 N	88.19 E
Thākurvādi	272c	18.54 N	73.04 E
Thal, Dtsch.	54	50.55 N	10.23 E
Thal, Pāk.	123	33.22 N	70.33 E
Tha'l, Jabal ∧	140	14.13 N	24.14 E
Thala	36	35.35 N	8.40 E
Thalang	110	8.01 N	98.19 E
Thal-Assling	64	46.47 N	12.38 E
Thalāthah	142	30.35 N	32.20 E
Thal Desert ◆[2]	123	31.30 N	71.40 E
Thale	54	51.45 N	11.02 E
Thalfang	56	49.45 N	6.59 E
Thalgau	64	47.50 N	13.15 E
Thalheim	54	50.42 N	12.51 E
Thalheim bei Wels	61	48.09 N	14.02 E
Tha Li	110	17.37 N	101.25 E
Thalia	196	33.59 N	99.32 W
Thālith, Ash-Shallāl ath- (Third Cataract) ∟	140	19.49 N	30.19 E
Thalitter	56	51.13 N	8.53 E
Thalkirch	58	46.38 N	9.16 E
Thallon	166	28.38 S	148.52 E
Thallwitz	54	51.26 N	12.40 E
Thalmah, Marsā c	142	29.03 N	32.38 E
Thalmässing	60	49.05 N	11.13 E
Thalwil	58	47.17 N	8.34 E
Thamar, Jabal ∧	144	13.53 N	45.12 E
Thame	42	51.45 N	0.59 W
Thames	172	37.08 S	175.33 E
Thames ≃, On., Can.	190	42.19 N	82.27 W
Thames ≃, Eng., U.K.	42	51.28 N	0.43 E
Thames ≃, Ct., U.S.	207	41.18 N	72.05 W
Thames, Firth of c	172	37.00 S	175.25 E
Thames Barrier ◆[6]	260	51.29 N	0.03 E
Thames Ditton	260	51.23 N	0.21 W
Thames Estuary c[1]	260	51.30 N	0.40 W
Thamesford	212	43.04 N	81.00 W
Thames Haven	260	51.30 N	0.31 E
Thamesville	214	42.33 N	81.59 W
Thāmit, Wādī V	146	31.15 N	16.06 E
Thammasat University ʋ[2]	269a	13.45 N	100.30 E
Thamūd, Bi'r ⍑[4]	144	17.17 N	49.56 E
Thāna, India	122	19.12 N	72.58 E
Thāna, Pāk.	128	28.55 N	63.45 E
Thāna Creek c	272c	19.00 N	72.57 E
Thāna Gāzi	124	27.25 N	76.19 E
Thāna Kasba	124	25.13 N	77.20 E
Thanbyuzayat	110	15.58 N	97.44 E
Thandaung	110	19.04 N	96.41 E
Thānedārwāla	123	32.36 N	71.07 E
Thānesar	124	29.59 N	76.49 E
Thanet, Isle of I	42	51.22 N	1.20 E
Thanet Lake ⊜	212	44.47 N	77.46 W
Thang Binh	110	15.44 N	108.22 E
Thangoo	162	18.10 S	122.22 E
Thangool	166	24.29 S	150.35 E
Thanh Hoa	110	19.48 N	105.46 E
Thanh My Tay	269c	10.49 N	106.46 E
Thanh Pho Ho Chi Minh (Saigon), Viet	110	10.45 N	106.40 E
Thanh Pho Ho Chi Minh (Saigon), Viet	269c	10.45 N	106.40 E
Thanjāvūr	122	10.48 N	79.09 E
Thann	58	47.49 N	7.05 E
Thannhausen	58	48.17 N	10.28 E
Thāno Bula Khān	120	25.22 N	67.50 E
Than Uyen	110	22.00 N	103.54 E
Thaoge ≃	156	20.27 S	22.36 E
Thaon-les-Vosges	58	48.15 N	6.25 E
Tha Pla	110	17.48 N	100.32 E
Thap Than ≃	110	15.21 N	104.06 E
Tharabwin West	110	12.17 N	99.03 E
Tharād	120	24.24 N	71.38 E
Tharandt	54	50.59 N	13.35 E
't Harde	52	52.25 N	5.53 E
Thar Desert (Great Indian Desert) ◆[2]	120	27.00 N	71.00 E
Thargomindah	166	28.00 S	143.49 E
Thāri Pātan ∧	124	28.58 N	82.04 E
Thar Nhom	140	7.26 N	30.29 E
Tharptown	210	40.48 N	76.34 W
Tharr, Wüste → Thar Desert ◆[2]	120	27.00 N	71.00 E
Tharrawaddy	110	17.39 N	95.48 E
Tharrawaw	110	17.41 N	95.28 E
Tharros ⊥	71	39.52 N	8.26 E
Tharsuinn, Beinn ∧	46	57.47 N	4.21 W
Tharthār, Buḥayrat ath- ⊜	128	34.00 N	43.05 E
Tharthār, Wādī ath- V	128	33.59 N	43.12 E
Tharwa	171b	35.31 S	149.04 E
Tha Sala	110	8.40 N	99.56 E
Thásos	38	40.47 N	24.42 E
Thásos I	38	40.41 N	24.47 E
Thásos ⊥	38	40.46 N	24.33 E
Tha Tako	110	15.38 N	100.29 E
Thatcham	42	51.25 N	1.15 W
Thatch Cay I	240m	18.22 N	64.52 W
Thatcher	200	32.50 N	109.45 W
Thatch Island I	276	40.38 N	73.23 W
That Khe	110	22.16 N	106.28 E
Thaton	110	16.55 N	97.22 E
That Phanom	110	16.57 N	104.44 E
Thatto Heath	262	53.26 N	2.45 W
Tha Tum	110	15.19 N	103.41 E
Thau, Bassin de c	32	43.23 N	3.36 E
Thaungdut	110	24.26 N	94.42 E
Thaungyin ≃	110	17.50 N	97.42 E
Tha Uthen	110	17.34 N	104.36 E
Thawville	216	40.41 N	88.07 W
Thaxted	42	51.57 N	0.20 E
Thaya (Dyje) ≃	61	48.37 N	16.56 E

FRANÇAIS

Nom	Page	Lat.°′	Long.°′ W = Ouest
Thayawthadangyi Kyun I	110	12.20 N	98.00 E
Thayer, Il., U.S.	219	39.32 N	89.46 W
Thayer, In., U.S.	216	41.10 N	87.20 W
Thayer, Ks., U.S.	198	37.29 N	95.28 W
Thayer, Mo., U.S.	194	36.31 N	91.32 W
Thayetchaung	110	13.52 N	98.16 E
Thayetmyo	110	19.19 N	95.11 E
Thayngen	58	47.45 N	8.42 E
Thazi	110	20.51 N	96.05 E
The Aldermen Islands II	172	36.58 S	176.05 E
Theale	42	51.27 N	1.04 W
Thealka	192	37.49 N	82.47 W
The Basin	274b	37.51 S	145.19 E
Thebes	194	37.13 N	89.28 W
Thebes ⊥	140	25.42 N	32.37 E
Thebes → Thívai	38	38.21 N	23.19 E
The Birket ≃	262	53.24 N	3.01 W
The Bluffs ⏏[4]	210	43.22 N	76.40 W
The Bourne ≃	260	51.22 N	0.29 W
The Calvados Chain II	164	11.10 S	152.40 E
The Camels Hump ∧	169	37.23 S	144.35 E
The Capital ʋ	284c	38.53 N	77.00 W
The Cheviot ∧	44	55.28 N	2.09 W
The Citadel ⊥, Magy.	264c	47.29 N	19.03 E
The Citadel ⊥, Mişr	273c	30.02 N	31.15 E
The Cloisters ʋ	276	40.52 N	73.56 W
The Colony	222	33.05 N	96.52 W
The Coorong c	168b	35.40 S	139.15 E
The Coteau ⩘[2]	184	51.10 N	107.30 W
The Curragh ♠	48	53.10 N	6.52 W
The Dalles	224	45.35 N	121.10 W
The Dalles Dam ◆[6]	224	45.37 N	121.08 W
The Deeps c	46a	60.09 N	1.23 W
Thedford	198	41.58 N	100.34 W
Thedinghausen	52	52.58 N	9.01 E
The Downs ⍑[3]	42	51.13 N	1.27 E
Theebine	166	25.57 S	152.33 E
The English Companys Islands II	164	11.50 S	136.32 E
The Entrance	170	33.21 S	151.30 E
Theessen	54	52.14 N	12.02 E
The Everglades ☷	220	26.00 N	80.40 W
The Fens ◆[1]	42	52.38 N	0.02 E
The Fishing Lakes ⊜	184	50.45 N	103.51 W
The Flash ⊜	262	53.29 N	2.33 W
The Flat Tops ⩘	200	40.00 N	107.10 W
The Forest of Nisene Marks State Park ♠	226	37.03 N	121.53 W
The Glenkens ◆[1]	44	55.10 N	4.15 W
Thègon	110	18.39 N	95.25 E
The Granites	162	20.35 S	130.21 E
The Granites ∧	162	20.35 S	130.20 E
The Graves II	283	42.22 N	70.52 W
The Grove	222	31.16 N	97.32 W
The Hague → 's-Gravenhage	52	52.06 N	4.18 E
The Heads ›	202	42.44 N	124.31 W
The Hermitage ʋ	265a	59.56 N	30.20 E
The Home Park ♠	260	51.28 N	0.36 W
The Hunters Hills ⩘[2]	172	44.30 S	170.50 E
Theinkun	110	11.53 N	99.09 E
The Isles Lagoon c	174o	1.50 N	157.23 W
Theissen	54	51.05 N	12.06 E
Theiss → Tisa ≃	38	45.15 N	20.17 E
The Key Indian Reserve ◆[4]	184	51.45 N	102.08 W
The Lake Fleet Islands II	212	44.18 N	76.07 W
The Lakes National Park ♠	166	38.05 S	147.40 E
The Little Minch ʉ	46	57.35 N	6.55 W
Thelon ≃	176	64.16 N	96.05 W
The Long Mynd ∧	42	52.35 N	2.48 W
The Lower Hope ≃[1]	260	51.28 N	0.28 E
Thelwall	262	53.23 N	2.32 W
The Lynd	166	18.56 S	144.30 E
Them	41	56.06 N	9.33 E
The Machars ◆[1]	44	54.50 N	4.33 W
The Mall in Columbia ◆[9]	284b	39.13 N	76.52 W
Themar	54	50.30 N	10.37 E
The Meadows Race Track ♠	279b	40.13 N	80.12 W
The Mere ⊜	262	53.20 N	2.24 W
Théméricourt	261	49.05 N	1.54 E
The Minch ʉ	46	58.10 N	5.50 W
The Mumbles	42	51.34 N	4.00 W
Then	123	32.26 N	75.44 E
The Narrows ʉ	276	40.37 N	74.03 W
The Navy Islands II	212	44.21 N	76.03 W
The Naze ›	42	51.53 N	1.16 E
The Needles ›	42	50.39 N	1.34 W
Thénezay	32	46.43 N	0.02 W
Thenia	148	36.43 N	3.34 E
Theniet el Hadd	148	35.47 N	2.01 E
The Oa ›[1]	46	55.37 N	6.16 W
The Oaks, Austl.	170	34.04 S	150.34 E
The Oaks, Ca., U.S.	226	39.13 N	121.05 W
Theodore, Austl.	166	24.57 S	150.05 E
Theodore, Sk., Can.	184	51.25 N	102.54 W
Theodore, Al., U.S.	194	30.32 N	88.10 W
Theodore Francis Green Airport ⊠	207	41.44 N	71.26 W
Theodore Roosevelt Inaugural National Historical Site ⊥	284a	42.54 N	78.52 W
Theodore Roosevelt Island I	284c	38.54 N	77.03 W
Theodore Roosevelt Lake ⊜[1]	200	33.42 N	111.07 W
Theodore Roosevelt National Park (South Unit) ♠, N.D., U.S.	198	46.55 N	103.26 W
Theodore Roosevelt National Park (North Unit) ♠, N.D., U.S.	198	47.34 N	103.24 W
Theodor-Heuss-Brücke ◆[5]	263	51.15 N	6.45 E
Theog	123	31.07 N	77.21 E
Theólogos	38	40.39 N	24.41 E
The Orchards	284b	39.18 N	76.50 W
Théoule-sur-Mer	62	43.31 N	6.57 E
The Oval ⊥	260	51.29 N	0.07 W
The Pages II	168b	35.47 S	138.17 E
The Paps ∧	48	52.00 N	9.17 W
The Pas	184	53.50 N	101.15 W
The Peak ∧	192	36.24 N	81.39 W
Thepha	110	6.52 N	100.58 E
The Pinnacle ∧[2]	219	39.22 N	90.55 W
Thérain ≃	50	49.15 N	2.27 E
The Rajah ∧	182	53.15 N	118.31 W
The Rand → Witwatersrant ◆[1]	158	26.00 S	27.00 E
The Range	154	19.00 S	31.04 E
Theresa	212	44.12 N	75.47 W
Theresa Creek ≃	166	23.26 S	148.09 E
Theresa Park	274a	34.01 S	150.39 E
Theresienstadt → Terezín	54	50.31 N	14.08 E
The Rhins ›[1]	44	54.50 N	5.00 W
The Rip c	169	38.17 S	144.37 E
Thermaïkós Kólpos c	38	40.23 N	22.47 E
Thermalito	226	39.31 N	121.36 W
Thermopílai ⊥	38	38.48 N	22.33 E
Thermopolis	200	43.38 N	108.12 W
Thermopylae → Thermopílai ⊥	38	38.48 N	22.33 E
The Road c	42a	49.56 N	6.20 W
The Rock	166	35.16 S	147.07 E
The Rockies ∧	224	46.39 N	122.22 W
Theron Mountains ⩘	9	79.05 S	28.15 W

PORTUGUÊS

Nome	Página	Lat.°′	Long.°′ W = Oeste
The Rope ⏏[4]	174e	25.04 S	130.05 W
Thérouanne	50	50.38 N	2.15 E
The Savannahs ⊜	220	27.19 N	80.17 W
Theseion ⊥	267c	37.58 N	23.43 E
Thesiger Bay c	176	71.30 N	124.05 W
The Sisters ∧[2]	162	26.17 S	126.40 E
The Slot → New Georgia Sound ʉ	175e	8.00 S	158.10 E
The Sluice ≋	262	53.41 N	2.57 W
The Sny ≃	219	39.16 N	90.44 W
The Solent ʉ	42	50.46 N	1.20 W
The Sound (Øresund) ʉ	41	55.50 N	12.40 E
The Springs	207	40.52 N	72.32 W
Thesprotikón	38	39.15 N	20.47 E
Thessalía □[9]	38	39.30 N	22.00 E
Thessalon	190	46.15 N	83.34 W
Thessaloníki (Salonika)	38	40.38 N	22.56 E
Thessalonique → Thessaloníki	38	40.38 N	22.56 E
The Storr ∧	46	57.31 N	6.12 W
The Swale ʉ	42	51.22 N	0.56 E
Thet ≃	42	52.27 N	0.33 E
The Tauride Palace ʋ	265a	59.57 N	30.23 E
The Terraces ⏏[4]	162	28.40 S	121.30 E
Thetford	42	52.25 N	0.45 E
Thetford-Mines	206	46.05 N	71.18 W
The Thorofare ʉ	208	37.15 N	75.54 W
The Thumbs ∧	172	43.36 S	170.44 E
Thetis Island	224	49.59 N	123.40 W
Thetis Island I	224	49.00 N	123.41 W
The Twelve Pins ∧	48	53.31 N	9.50 W
The Twins ∧	172	41.14 S	172.39 E
Theunissen	158	28.30 S	26.41 E
Theux	56	50.32 N	5.49 E
The Valley	238	18.13 N	63.04 W
Thevenard	162	32.09 S	133.38 E
Thevenard Island I	162	21.27 S	115.00 E
The Wash c	42	52.55 N	0.15 E
The Weald ◆[1]	42	51.05 N	0.05 E
The Whirlpool ≃	284a	43.07 N	79.04 W
The Winehead ∧	210	40.58 N	77.28 W
The Woodlands	222	30.09 N	95.27 W
The Wrekin ∧[2]	42	52.41 N	2.34 W
Theydon Bois	260	51.40 N	0.06 E
Theys	62	45.18 N	6.00 E
Thiais	261	48.46 N	2.23 E
Thiant	50	50.18 N	3.27 E
Thiaucourt-Regniéville	56	48.57 N	5.52 E
Thibaudeau	184	57.05 N	94.08 W
Thiberville	50	49.08 N	0.27 E
Thibodaux	194	29.47 N	90.49 W
Thicket	222	30.24 N	94.38 W
Thicket Portage	184	55.19 N	97.42 W
Thiéblemont-Farémont	58	48.41 N	4.44 E
Thief ≃	198	48.08 N	96.10 W
Thief Lake ⊜	198	48.30 N	95.55 W
Thief River Falls	198	48.07 N	96.10 W
Thièle ≃	58	47.03 N	7.05 E
Thiel Mountains ⩘	9	85.15 S	91.00 W
Thielsen, Mount ∧	202	43.09 N	122.04 W
Thiendorf	54	51.17 N	13.44 E
Thiene	64	45.42 N	11.29 E
Thiensville	216	43.14 N	87.58 W
Thier	263	51.05 N	7.22 E
Thiérache, Collines de la ⩘[2]	50	49.50 N	3.50 E
Thierhaupten	56	48.34 N	10.54 E
Thiers	62	45.51 N	3.34 E
Thiersheim	54	50.04 N	12.07 E
Thierville-sur-Meuse	56	49.10 N	5.21 E
Thiès	150	14.48 N	16.56 W
Thiès □[4]	150	14.45 N	16.50 W
Thiesi	71	40.31 N	8.43 E
Thiessow	54	54.16 N	13.43 E
Thieux	261	49.01 N	2.40 E
Thieveley Pike ∧[2]	262	53.45 N	2.12 W
Thika	154	1.03 S	37.05 E
Thikombia Island I	175g	15.44 S	179.55 W
Thilay	56	49.52 N	4.49 E
Thilenius, Cape ›	164	1.35 S	149.57 E
Thimphu	124	27.28 N	89.39 E
Thines	62	44.29 N	4.03 E
Thingvallavatn ⊜	24a	64.12 N	21.10 W
Thingvellir	24a	64.17 N	21.07 W
Thingvellir National Park ♠	24a	64.17 N	21.06 W
Thio	175f	21.37 S	166.14 E
Thionville	56	49.22 N	6.10 E
Thiou	150	13.48 N	2.40 W
Thíra	38	36.25 N	25.26 E
Thíra I	38	36.24 N	25.29 E
Third ≃	276	40.49 N	74.08 W
Third Cataract → Thālith, Ash-Shallāl ath- ∟	140	19.49 N	30.19 E
Third Cliff ⏏[4]	283	42.11 N	70.43 W
Third Creek ≃, Mo., U.S.	219	38.26 N	91.40 W
Third Creek ≃, N.C., U.S.	192	35.47 N	80.31 W
Third Han-gang Bridge ◆[5]	271b	37.32 N	127.00 E
Third Herring Brook ≃	283	42.07 N	70.48 W
Third Lake ⊜	206	45.14 N	71.12 W
Third Street Station ◆[5]	282	37.46 N	122.23 W
Thirlmere	170	34.12 S	150.34 E
Thirlmere ⊜	44	54.33 N	3.04 W
Thirlmere Lakes National Park ♠	170	34.14 S	150.32 E
Thiron	50	48.19 N	0.59 E
Thironne ≃	50	48.17 N	1.15 E
Thirroul	170	34.19 S	150.56 E
Thirsk	44	54.14 N	1.20 W
Thirtieth Street Station ◆[5]	285	39.57 N	75.11 W
Thirtymile Creek ≃	198	46.22 N	102.03 W
Thirtymile Point ›	210	43.22 N	78.29 W
Thiruvārūr	122	10.46 N	79.39 E
Thisted	26	56.57 N	8.42 E
Thistilfjörður c	24a	66.20 N	15.25 W
Thistledown Race Track ♠	279a	41.26 N	81.32 W
Thistle Island I	166	35.00 S	136.09 E
Thistletown ◆[8]	275b	43.44 N	79.33 W
Thithia Island I	175g	17.45 S	179.18 W
Thívai (Thebes)	38	38.21 N	23.19 E
Thiverval-Grignon	261	48.51 N	1.55 E
Thiviers	32	45.25 N	0.56 E
Thizy	32	46.02 N	4.19 E
Thjórsá ≃	24a	63.47 N	20.48 W
Thlewiaza ≃	176	60.28 N	94.45 W
Thoa ≃	176	60.30 N	109.47 W
Tho Chu, Dao II	110	9.20 N	103.28 E
Thoen	110	17.36 N	99.12 E
Thohoyandou	156	23.00 S	30.29 E
Thoi Binh	110	9.21 N	105.05 E
Thoirette	58	46.16 N	5.32 E
Thoiry	261	48.52 N	1.48 E
Thoissey	58	46.10 N	4.48 E
Tholen	52	51.32 N	4.12 E
Tholen I	52	51.35 N	4.05 E
Tholey	56	49.29 N	7.02 E
Thollon	58	46.23 N	6.43 E
Thomas, Ok., U.S.	196	35.44 N	98.44 W
Thomas, Pa., U.S.	279b	40.15 N	80.06 W
Thomas, Wa., U.S.	224	47.21 N	122.13 W
Thomas, W.V., U.S.	188	39.08 N	79.29 W
Thomasboro	216	40.15 N	88.11 W
Thomas Creek ≃	202	44.40 N	122.56 W
Thomas Hill Reservoir ⊜[1]	194	39.40 N	92.40 W
Thomas J. O'Brien Lock and Dam ◆[5]	278	41.39 N	87.35 W
Thomas Lake ⊜	184	57.00 N	96.43 W

Thomas Mountains ⩘	9	75.32 S	70.57 W
Thomas Point ›	208	38.54 N	76.28 W
Thomaston, Al., U.S.	194	32.15 N	87.37 W
Thomaston, Ct., U.S.	207	41.40 N	73.04 W
Thomaston, Ga., U.S.	192	32.53 N	84.19 W
Thomaston, Me., U.S.	188	44.04 N	69.10 W
Thomaston, N.Y., U.S.	276	40.47 N	73.43 W
Thomaston, Tx., U.S.	222	29.00 N	97.09 W
Thomastown, Austl.	274b	37.41 S	145.01 E
Thomastown, Ire.	48	52.31 N	7.08 W
Thomasville, Al., U.S.	194	31.54 N	87.44 W
Thomasville, Ga., U.S.	192	30.50 N	83.58 W
Thomasville, N.C., U.S.	192	35.52 N	80.04 W
Thomasville, Pa., U.S.	208	39.56 N	76.51 W
Thomes Creek ≃	204	39.59 N	122.06 W
Thom Lake ⊜	184	55.24 N	96.08 W
Thomlinson, Mount ∧	182	55.33 N	127.29 W
Thompson, Mb., Can.	184	55.45 N	97.45 W
Thompson, Ct., U.S.	207	41.57 N	71.51 W
Thompson, Ia., U.S.	190	43.22 N	93.46 W
Thompson, Mo., U.S.	219	39.11 N	91.59 W
Thompson, N.D., U.S.	198	47.46 N	97.06 W
Thompson, Oh., U.S.	214	41.41 N	81.03 W
Thompson, Pa., U.S.	210	41.52 N	75.31 W
Thompson ≃, B.C., Can.	182	50.15 N	121.33 W
Thompson ≃, U.S.	194	39.45 N	93.36 W
Thompson Creek ≃, U.S.	198	45.04 N	104.25 W
Thompson Creek ≃, Ms., U.S.	194	31.10 N	88.54 W
Thompson Falls	202	47.35 N	115.20 W
Thompson Island I	283	42.23 N	71.01 W
Thompson Pass ⟩⟨	180	61.08 N	145.45 W
Thompson Peak ∧	204	41.00 N	123.03 W
Thompson Place	224	47.03 N	122.45 W
Thompson Ridge	210	41.34 N	74.20 W
Thompson Run ≃	279b	40.24 N	79.50 W
Thompsons	222	29.30 N	95.36 W
Thompsons Creek ≃	284a	43.03 N	79.08 W
Thompson Sound ʉ	172	45.09 S	166.57 E
Thompsontown	208	40.33 N	77.14 W
Thompsonville	190	44.31 N	85.56 W
Thomsen ≃	176	74.08 N	119.35 W
Thomson, Ga., U.S.	192	33.28 N	82.30 W
Thomson, Il., U.S.	190	41.58 N	90.06 W
Thomson, N.Y., U.S.	210	43.07 N	73.35 W
Thomson ≃, Austl.	166	25.11 S	142.53 E
Thomson ≃, Austl.	169	37.58 S	146.32 E
Thomson, Lake ⊜[1]	169	37.45 S	146.22 E
Thomson Lake ⊜[1]	184	49.45 N	106.35 W
Thon ≃	50	49.53 N	3.55 E
Thon Buri	110	13.43 N	100.29 E
Thônes	62	45.53 N	6.20 E
Thong	260	51.24 N	0.24 E
Thong Hoe	271c	1.25 N	103.42 E
Thong Tay Hoi	269c	10.50 N	106.39 E
Thongwa	110	16.46 N	96.32 E
Thon Lac Nghiep	110	11.20 N	108.54 E
Thonnance-lès-Joinville	58	48.27 N	5.10 E
Thonon-les-Bains	58	46.22 N	6.29 E
Thonotosassa	220	28.03 N	82.18 W
Thonze	110	17.38 N	95.47 E
Thorah Island I	212	44.27 N	79.14 W
Thorame-Haute	62	44.06 N	6.33 E
Thorburn	186	45.34 N	62.33 W
Thoreau	200	35.24 N	108.13 W
Thorembais-les-Béguines	56	50.40 N	4.49 E
Thorenc	62	43.48 N	6.49 E
Thorens-Glières	58	45.59 N	6.15 E
Thorhild	182	54.10 N	113.07 W
Thorial	140	8.40 N	29.56 E
Thorigny-sur-Marne	261	48.53 N	2.42 E
Thorigny-sur-Oreuse	50	48.17 N	3.24 E
Thórisvatn ⊜	24a	64.50 N	19.26 W
Thörl	61	47.31 N	15.13 E
Thorlákshöfn	24a	63.53 N	21.18 W
Thormanby	44	54.10 N	1.14 W
Thorn	52	51.10 N	5.50 E
Thornaby-on-Tees	44	54.34 N	1.18 W
Thornapple ≃, Mi., U.S.	216	42.56 N	85.28 W
Thornapple ≃, Wi., U.S.	190	45.28 N	91.16 W
Thornapple Lake ⊜	216	42.37 N	85.11 W
Thornburg	279b	40.26 N	80.05 W
Thornbury, Austl.	274b	37.45 S	145.00 E
Thornbury, On., Can.	212	44.34 N	80.26 W
Thornbury, N.Z.	172	46.17 S	168.06 E
Thornbury, Eng., U.K.	42	51.37 N	2.32 W
Thorn Creek ≃	278	41.36 N	87.35 W
Thorndale, On., Can.	212	43.06 N	81.08 W
Thorndale, Tx., U.S.	222	30.36 N	97.12 W
Thorndike	207	42.11 N	72.20 W
Thorndon	42	52.17 N	1.08 E
Thorne	44	53.37 N	0.58 W
Thorne ≃	184	54.56 N	90.35 W
Thorne Bay	182	55.44 N	132.32 W
Thorney	42	52.37 N	0.07 W
Thorngumbald	44	53.43 N	0.10 W
Thornhill, On., Can.	275b	43.48 N	79.25 W
Thornhill, S. Afr.	273d	26.07 S	28.09 E
Thornhill, Scot., U.K.	44	55.15 N	3.46 W
Thornhurst	210	41.11 N	75.35 W
Thornleigh	274a	33.44 S	151.05 E
Thornton, Austl.	171a	27.49 S	152.23 E
Thornton, Eng., U.K.	44	53.53 N	3.02 W
Thornton, Eng., U.K.	262	53.30 N	3.00 W
Thornton, Eng., U.K.	262	53.47 N	1.51 W
Thornton, Scot., U.K.	46	56.10 N	3.09 W
Thornton, Ar., U.S.	194	33.46 N	92.29 W
Thornton, Ca., U.S.	226	38.14 N	121.25 W
Thornton, Co., U.S.	200	39.52 N	104.58 W
Thornton, Il., U.S.	278	41.35 N	87.37 W
Thornton, Pa., U.S.	285	39.54 N	75.32 W
Thornton, Tx., U.S.	222	31.24 N	96.34 W
Thornton Beach ♠	282	37.42 N	122.30 W
Thornton Dale	44	54.14 N	0.43 W
Thornton Hough	262	53.19 N	3.03 W
Thornton-le-Moors	262	53.16 N	2.50 W
Thorntonville	196	31.34 N	102.55 W
Thorn → Toruń	30	53.02 N	18.35 E
Thornwood	210	41.07 N	73.46 W
Thornwood Common	260	51.43 N	0.08 E
Thorny Mountain ∧[2]	194	37.06 N	91.10 W
Thorofare	285	39.50 N	75.11 W
Thorold	212	43.07 N	79.12 W
Thorold South	284a	43.06 N	79.12 W
Thoronet, Abbaye du ʋ[1]	62	43.28 N	6.16 E
Thorp, Wa., U.S.	224	47.04 N	120.40 W
Thorp, Wi., U.S.	190	44.57 N	90.47 W
Thorpe	260	51.24 N	0.32 W
Thorpe-le-Soken	42	51.52 N	1.10 E
Thorp Spring	222	32.28 N	97.49 W
Thorsby, Ab., Can.	182	53.14 N	114.03 W
Thorsby, Al., U.S.	194	32.54 N	86.42 W
Thorshavn → Tórshavn	22	62.01 N	6.46 W
Thórshöfn	24a	66.13 N	15.17 W
Thorsø	41	56.18 N	9.48 E
Thorsteinson Lake ⊜	184	57.15 N	97.30 W
Thorton Moor Reservoir ⊜[1]	262	53.47 N	1.55 W
Thot Not	110	10.16 N	105.32 E
Thouars	32	46.59 N	0.13 W
Thouin, Cape ›	162	20.20 S	118.12 E
Thoune → Thun	58	46.45 N	7.37 E
Thourotte	50	49.29 N	2.53 E
Thousand Islands II	212	44.15 N	76.12 W

Thousand Islands International Bridge ◆[5]	212	44.20 N	75.58 W
Thousand Lake Mountain ∧	200	38.25 N	111.29 W
Thousand Oaks	228	34.10 N	118.50 W
Thousand Ships Bay c	175e	8.25 S	159.40 E
Thousand Springs Creek ≃	200	41.17 N	113.51 W
Thowa ≃	154	1.33 S	40.03 E
Thowgla Creek ≃	171b	36.10 S	147.57 E
Thrace □[9]	38	41.20 N	26.45 E
Thrakikón Pélagos ⍑[2]	38	40.15 N	24.28 E
Thrall	222	30.35 N	97.18 W
Thrapston	42	52.24 N	0.32 W
Thrasher Lake ⊜	212	44.55 N	78.58 W
Thread Creek ≃	216	43.01 N	83.42 W
Thredbo Village	171b	36.29 S	148.19 E
Three Bridges	208	40.31 N	74.47 W
Three Brothers ∧	224	47.23 N	120.45 W
Three Brothers Mountain ∧	224	49.10 N	120.46 W
Three Creek ≃	208	36.47 N	77.10 W
Three Fathoms Cove c	271d	22.26 N	114.17 E
Three Fingered Jack ∧	202	44.29 N	121.50 W
Three Fingers ∧	224	48.10 N	121.41 W
Three Fools Creek ≃	224	48.53 N	120.57 W
Three Forks	202	45.53 N	111.33 W
Three Hills	182	51.42 N	113.16 W
Three Hummock Island I	166	40.26 S	144.55 E
Three Kings Islands II	172	34.10 S	172.05 E
Three Lakes	190	45.47 N	89.09 W
Three M Airport ⊠	285	40.08 N	74.51 W
Three Mile Bay	212	44.04 N	76.11 W
Three Mile Plains	186	44.58 N	64.07 W
Three Oaks	216	41.47 N	86.36 W
Three Pagodas Pass ⟩⟨	110	15.18 N	98.23 E
Threepoint Lake ⊜	184	55.41 N	98.56 W
Three Points, Cape ›	150	4.45 N	2.06 W
Three Rivers, Austl.	162	25.07 S	119.09 E
Three Rivers, Ma., U.S.	207	42.10 N	72.21 W
Three Rivers, Mi., U.S.	216	41.56 N	85.37 W
Three Rivers, Tx., U.S.	196	28.27 N	98.10 W
Three Rivers □[8]	260	51.40 N	0.27 W
Three Rivers → Trois-Rivières	206	46.21 N	72.33 W
Three Sisters	158	31.54 S	23.06 E
Three Sisters ∧	202	44.10 N	121.46 W
Three Sisters Islands II	175e	10.10 S	161.57 E
Three Springs, Austl.	162	29.32 S	115.45 E
Three Springs, Pa., U.S.	214	40.12 N	77.59 W
Threlkeld	44	54.38 N	3.03 W
Throat ≃	184	51.48 N	93.30 W
Throckley	44	54.59 N	1.45 W
Throckmorton	196	33.10 N	99.10 W
Throgs Neck ◆[8]	276	40.49 N	73.49 W
Throgs Neck Bridge ◆[5]	276	40.48 N	73.48 W
Throgs Point ›	276	40.48 N	73.48 W
Throop	210	41.27 N	75.36 W
Throssel, Lake ⊜	162	27.27 S	124.16 E
Throssell Range ⩘	162	22.03 S	121.43 E
Thrushel ≃	42	50.39 N	4.15 W
Thruway Mall ◆[9]	284a	42.55 N	78.46 W
Thu, Cu Lao I	110	10.33 N	108.57 E
Thuan Chau	110	21.26 N	103.41 E
Thu Dau Mot	110	10.58 N	106.39 E
Thu Duc	269c	10.51 N	106.45 E
Thueyts	62	44.41 N	4.13 E
Thuilley-aux-Groseilles	58	48.34 N	5.58 E
Thuin	50	50.20 N	4.17 E
Thul	120	28.14 N	68.46 E
Thulaythiwāt, Tilāl ath- ∧	132	30.58 N	36.40 E
Thulba ≃	56	50.11 N	9.52 E
Thule	16	76.34 N	68.47 W
Thulī Bherī ≃	124	28.42 N	82.16 E
Thum	54	50.40 N	12.57 E
Thumb Peak ∧	116	9.48 N	118.36 E
Thumby	41	54.35 N	9.54 E
Thun	58	46.45 N	7.37 E
Thun Chang	110	19.25 N	100.53 E
Thunder Bay	190	48.23 N	89.15 W
Thunder Bay c, On., Can.	190	48.24 N	89.00 W
Thunder Bay c, On., Can.	212	44.48 N	80.03 W
Thunder Bay c, Mi., U.S.	190	45.00 N	83.22 W
Thunder Bay ≃	190	45.04 N	83.25 W
Thunder Bay, North Branch ≃	190	45.08 N	83.35 W
Thunderbird, Lake ⊜[1]	196	35.15 N	97.20 W
Thunderbolt	192	32.02 N	81.03 W
Thunder Butte ∧	198	45.19 N	101.53 W
Thunder Butte Creek ≃	198	45.13 N	101.42 W
Thunder Creek ≃, Sk., Can.	184	50.23 N	105.32 W
Thunder Creek ≃, Wa., U.S.	224	48.40 N	121.05 W
Thunder Hills ⩘[2]	184	54.30 N	106.00 W
Thunder Mountain ∧[2]	216	42.16 N	86.20 W
Thundersley	260	51.34 N	0.35 E
Thunersee ⊜	58	46.40 N	7.45 E
Thüngen	56	49.56 N	9.51 E
Thung Song	110	8.09 N	99.41 E
Thung Wa	110	7.06 N	99.46 E
Thur ≃, Fr.	58	48.05 N	7.23 E
Thur ≃, Schw.	58	47.36 N	8.35 E
Thurcroft	44	53.24 N	1.16 W
Thurgau □[3]	58	47.35 N	9.00 E
Thurgovie → Thurgau □[3]	58	47.35 N	9.00 E
Thüringen	58	47.12 N	9.45 E
Thüringen □[3]	30	51.00 N	11.00 E
Thüringer Wald ⩘	30	50.40 N	10.50 E
Thürkow	54	53.50 N	12.33 E
Thurles	48	52.41 N	7.49 W
Thurmont	208	39.37 N	77.24 W
Thurn, Pass ⟩⟨	64	47.19 N	12.24 E
Thurnau	60	50.01 N	11.23 E
Thurnham	260	51.17 N	0.36 E
Thurnscoe	44	53.31 N	1.19 W
Thurnwald Range ⩘	164	4.45 S	141.15 E
Thurø	41	55.03 N	10.40 E
Thurrock □[8]	260	51.30 N	0.21 E
Thursby	44	54.51 N	3.03 W
Thursday Island	164	10.35 S	142.13 E
Thurso, P.Q., Can.	206	45.36 N	75.15 W
Thurso, Scot., U.K.	46	58.35 N	3.32 W
Thurso ≃	46	58.36 N	3.30 W
Thurstaston	262	53.21 N	3.08 W
Thurston	42	52.15 N	0.49 E
Thurston □[6]	224	46.59 N	122.42 W
Thurston Island I	9	72.20 S	99.00 W
Thusis	58	46.42 N	9.26 E
Thwaites Iceberg Tongue ⊓	9	74.45 S	106.30 W
Thy ◆[1]	26	57.00 N	8.30 E
Thyborøn	26	56.42 N	8.13 E
Thylungra	166	26.04 S	143.28 E
Thyolo	154	16.10 S	35.10 E
Thyregod	41	55.54 N	9.16 E
Thysville → Mbanza-Ngungu	152	5.15 S	14.52 E
Tiadiaye	150	14.25 N	16.42 W
Tía Juana	246	10.16 N	71.22 W

Tian ≃	105	40.42 N	116.33 E
Tiana, Esp.	266d	44.29 N	2.16 E
Tiana, It.	71	40.04 N	9.08 E
Tian'anmen Square ⊥	271a	39.55 N	116.23 E
Tianbao	100	24.36 N	117.35 E
Tianchang	100	32.41 N	119.01 E
Tiancunpu	105	39.06 N	115.41 E
Tiandeng	102	23.09 N	107.10 E
Tiandong	102	23.36 N	107.08 E
Tian'e	102	25.01 N	107.20 E
Tianeti	84	42.07 N	44.59 E
Tianfanjie	100	29.20 N	116.50 E
Tiangang, Zhg.	89	43.55 N	127.00 E
Tiangang, Zhg.	89	43.24 N	125.54 E
Tiangongsi	105	39.14 N	115.53 E
Tianguá	250	3.44 S	40.59 W
Tianhe	100	27.01 N	114.30 E
Tianhekou	100	32.08 N	113.25 E
Tianhelong	89	43.56 N	120.39 E
Tianhuang	98	35.29 N	117.18 E
Tianjara, Mount ∧	170	35.11 S	150.18 E
Tianjia, Zhg.	104	41.07 N	122.03 E
Tianjia, Zhg.	107	29.40 N	105.08 E
Tianjiaba	102	32.08 N	110.03 E
Tianjiatun	104	41.39 N	123.44 E
Tianjiawopu	104	42.28 N	122.38 E
Tianjiazhen	100	29.56 N	115.26 E
Tianjin (Tientsin)	105	39.08 N	117.12 E
Tianjing	106	31.27 N	120.46 E
Tianjin Shi (Tientsin Shih) □[7]	98	39.30 N	117.15 E
Tianjun	102	37.25 N	98.58 E
Tiankai	105	39.38 N	115.51 E
Tiankoura	150	10.46 N	3.16 W
Tiankoye	150	12.35 N	12.40 W
Tianlin, Zhg.	102	24.14 N	106.03 E
Tianlin, Zhg.	107	29.49 N	105.19 E
Tian Ling ∧	89	44.22 N	129.52 E
Tianmashan	106	31.04 N	121.08 E
Tianmen	100	30.39 N	113.06 E
Tianmu Shan ⩘	100	30.25 N	119.30 E
Tianpu	106	31.56 N	121.07 E
Tianqiaochang	104	40.52 N	121.02 E
Tianqiaoling	89	43.26 N	129.38 E
Tianquan	102	30.10 N	102.48 E
Tian Shan → Tien Shan ⩘	90	42.00 N	80.00 E
Tianshenggang	106	32.03 N	120.45 E
Tianshifu	98	41.17 N	124.21 E
Tianshui	102	34.30 N	105.58 E
Tianshuijing, Zhg.	102	40.17 N	95.21 E
Tianshuijing, Zhg.	104	41.19 N	121.48 E
Tianshuituo	105	39.20 N	118.12 E
Tianshuizhan	104	41.00 N	123.34 E
Tiantai	100	29.09 N	121.02 E
Tiantang	102	22.32 N	111.55 E
Tiantou, Zhg.	100	28.48 N	120.39 E
Tiantou, Zhg.	100	26.19 N	115.57 E
Tianwangsi	106	31.45 N	119.12 E
Tianxin, Zhg.	100	27.53 N	113.06 E
Tianxin, Zhg.	100	28.11 N	114.35 E
Tianxin, Zhg.	102	27.21 N	111.00 E
Tianxingqiao	106	32.05 N	119.57 E
Tianxiyang	100	26.31 N	118.33 E
Tianyang	102	23.51 N	106.34 E
Tianyangping	107	29.11 N	105.16 E
Tianyar	115b	8.12 S	115.30 E
Tianzhen	98	40.28 N	114.06 E
Tianzhongying	100	33.13 N	115.22 E
Tianzhu, Zhg.	102	37.14 N	102.59 E
Tianzhu, Zhg.	102	26.50 N	109.00 E
Tianzhuang, Zhg.	100	25.43 N	113.40 E
Tianzhuang, Zhg.	105	39.25 N	117.54 E
Tianzhuangtai	104	40.50 N	122.08 E
Tiao ≃	106	30.56 N	120.11 E
Tiaodengchang	107	30.47 N	106.22 E
Tiarel	174s	17.32 S	149.20 W
Tiarno	64	45.53 N	10.40 E
Tiaro	166	25.44 S	152.35 E
Tiassalé	150	5.54 N	4.50 W
Tiati ∧	154	1.19 N	35.56 E
Ti'avea	175a	13.57 S	171.24 W
Tiawichi Creek ≃	222	32.19 N	94.44 W
Tiba → Chiba	94	35.36 N	140.07 E
Tibaji	252	24.30 S	50.24 W
Tibaji ≃	252	22.47 S	51.01 W
Tibari	154	5.01 N	31.43 E
Tibasti, Sarīr ◆[2]	146	24.00 N	17.00 E
Tibati	152	6.27 N	12.38 E
Tibbermore	46	56.22 N	3.32 W
Tibbie	194	31.21 N	88.14 W
Tibe	144	9.03 N	37.08 E
Tibel'ti	88	51.46 N	103.11 E
Tiberias, Lake → Kinneret, Yam ⊜	132	32.48 N	35.35 E
Tiberias → Teverya	132	32.47 N	35.32 E
Tiberina, Val V	66	43.31 N	12.10 E
Tiber → Tevere ≃	66	41.44 N	12.14 E
Tibesti ⩘	146	21.30 N	17.30 E
Tibet, Lake ⊜	220	28.27 N	81.31 W
Tibet, Plateau of → Qing Zang Gaoyuan ⩘[1]	12	33.00 N	92.00 E
Tibet → Xizang Zizhiqu □[4]	90	32.00 N	88.00 E
Tibiao	116	11.17 N	122.02 E
Tibiao Point ›	116	11.18 N	122.02 E
Tibidabo ∧	266d	41.25 N	2.07 E
Tibiri, Niger	150	13.06 N	4.00 E
Tibiri, Niger	150	13.34 N	7.04 E
Tibirke	41	56.03 N	12.07 E
Tiblawan	116	6.29 N	126.06 E
Tiblemont, Lac ⊜	190	48.14 N	77.18 W
Tibnah	132	32.59 N	36.13 E
Tibnīn	132	33.12 N	35.25 E
Tibooburra	166	29.26 S	142.01 E
Tibro	26	58.26 N	14.10 E
Tiburon	226	37.52 N	122.27 W
Tiburón, Cabo ›	246	8.42 N	77.24 W
Tiburón, Isla I	232	29.00 N	112.23 W
Tiburon Peninsula ›[1]	282	37.53 N	122.28 W
Tiča, jazovir ⊜[1]	38	43.05 N	26.45 E
Ticao Island I	116	12.31 N	123.42 E
Ticao Pass ʉ	116	12.38 N	123.47 E
Tice	220	26.40 N	81.48 W
Tice Creek ≃	282	37.53 N	122.03 W
Ticehurst	42	51.03 N	0.25 E
Tichigan	216	42.50 N	88.12 W
Tichigan Lake ⊜	216	42.49 N	88.13 W
Tîchît	150	18.28 N	9.30 W
Tîchît, Dahr ⏏[4]	150	18.30 N	9.25 W
Tichmenevo, Ross.	76	58.00 N	38.36 E
Tichmenevo, Ross.	89	49.12 N	142.54 E
Ticho	144	7.50 N	39.32 E
Tichon	24	59.23 N	46.38 E
Tichonova Pustyn'	82	54.38 N	36.09 E
Tichonoviči	78	51.56 N	32.09 E
Tichonovka	88	53.13 N	104.13 E
Tichookeanskij	89	43.00 N	132.24 E
Tichoreck	78	45.51 N	40.09 E
Tichtozero	24	65.35 N	30.27 E
Tichvin	76	59.39 N	33.31 E
Tichvinskaja gr'ada ∧	76	59.30 N	34.30 E
Ticino □[3]	58	46.20 N	8.45 E
Ticino ≃	36	45.09 N	9.14 E
Tickfaw	194	30.34 N	90.28 W
Tickfaw ≃	194	30.20 N	90.28 W
Tickhill	44	53.26 N	1.06 W
Ticomán ◆[8]	286a	19.31 N	99.08 W
Ticonderoga	188	43.50 N	73.25 W
Ticul	232	20.24 N	89.32 W
Tīdah	142	31.15 N	30.50 E
Tidaholm	26	58.11 N	13.57 E
Tidan ≃	40	58.42 N	13.58 E
Tiddim	110	23.23 N	93.39 E
Tide Lake ⊜	184	50.33 N	111.20 W

	English	Deutsch	Español	Français	Português
≃	River	Fluß	Río	Rivière	Rio
≋	Canal	Kanal	Canal	Canal	Canal
∟	Waterfall, Rapids	Wasserfall, Stromschnellen	Cascada, Rápidos	Chute d'eau, Rapides	Cascata, Rápidos
ʉ	Strait	Meeresstraße	Estrecho	Détroit	Estreito
c	Bay, Gulf	Bucht, Golf	Bahía, Golfo	Baie, Golfe	Baía, Golfo
⊜	Lake, Lakes	See, Seen	Lago, Lagos	Lac, Lacs	Lago, Lagos
☷	Swamp	Sumpf	Pantano	Marais	Pântano
⊓	Ice Features, Glacier	Eis- und Gletscherformen	Accidentes Glaciales	Formes glaciaires	Acidentes glaciares
⍑	Other Hydrographic Features	Andere Hydrographische Objekte	Otros Elementos Hidrográficos	Autres données hydrographiques	Outros acidentes hidrográficos
✣	Submarine Features	Untermeerische Objekte	Accidentes Submarinos	Formes de relief sous-marin	Acidentes submarinos
□	Political Unit	Politische Einheit	Unidad Politica	Entité politique	Unidade política
ʋ	Cultural Institution	Kulturelle Institution	Institución Cultural	Institution culturelle	Instituição cultural
⊥	Historical Site	Historische Stätte	Sitio Histórico	Site historique	Sitio histórico
♠	Recreational Site	Erholungs- und Ferienort	Sitio de Recreo	Centre de loisirs	Area de Lazer
⊠	Airport	Flughafen	Aeropuerto	Aéroport	Aeroporto
■	Military Installation	Militäranlage	Instalación Militar	Installation militaire	Instalação militar
◆	Miscellaneous	Verschiedenes	Misceláneo	Divers	Diversos

ENGLISH Name / DEUTSCH Name	Page / Seite	Lat.°' / Breite°'	Long.°' / Länge°' E = Ost
Tideswell	44	53.16 N	1.46 W
Tidewater	208	37.51 N	76.42 W
Tidewater ◂¹	208	37.45 N	77.00 W
Tidikelt ≚	148	26.54 N	1.20 E
Tidioute	214	41.41 N	79.24 W
Tidirhine, Jebel ∧	148	34.50 N	4.30 W
Tidjikja	150	18.33 N	11.25 W
Tidö	40	59.30 N	16.28 E
Tidone ≃	62	45.04 N	9.32 E
Tidore	108	0.40 N	127.26 E
Tiébissou	150	7.10 N	5.13 W
Tiechang, Zhg.	98	41.44 N	126.11 E
Tiechang, Zhg.	100	24.10 N	115.30 E
Tiechang, Zhg.	102	26.34 N	103.58 E
Tiechang, Zhg.	105	40.04 N	118.12 E
Tiechangpu	107	29.29 N	104.20 E
Tiefenbach	60	49.26 N	12.35 E
Tiefenbroich	263	51.18 N	6.49 E
Tiefencastel	58	46.40 N	9.35 E
Tiefensee	54	52.41 N	13.50 E
Tiefo	107	29.45 N	104.33 E
T'iehling → Tieling	104	42.18 N	123.49 E
Tiekou	98	37.16 N	121.13 E
Tiel	52	51.54 N	5.25 E
Tieli	89	46.59 N	128.02 E
Tieling	104	42.18 N	123.49 E
Tielt	50	51.00 N	3.19 E
Tielutou	100	27.49 N	115.48 E
Tiémé	150	9.33 N	7.19 W
T'ienching → Tianjin	105	39.08 N	117.12 E
T'ienchung	100	23.52 N	120.35 E
Tienen	56	50.48 N	4.57 E
Tiengen	58	47.38 N	8.16 E
Tiénigboué	150	8.11 N	5.43 W
Tienko	150	10.14 N	7.29 W
Tien Shan ⋏	90	42.00 N	80.00 E
T'ienshui → Tianshui	102	34.30 N	105.58 E
Tientsin → Tianjin	105	39.08 N	117.12 E
Tien Yen	110	21.20 N	107.24 E
Tiepido ≃	64	44.30 N	10.59 E
Tie Plant	194	33.44 N	89.47 W
Tierga	34	41.37 N	1.36 W
Tiergarten ◂⁸	264a	52.31 N	13.21 E
Tiergarten ♦	264a	52.31 N	13.21 E
Tieroko, Tarso ∧	146	20.45 N	17.52 E
Tierp	40	60.20 N	17.30 E
Tierpark ♦	264a	52.30 N	13.32 E
Tierra Amarilla, Chile	252	27.29 S	70.17 W
Tierra Amarilla, N.M., U.S.	200	36.42 N	106.32 W
Tierra Blanca, Méx.	196	27.12 N	104.53 W
Tierra Blanca, Méx.	234	18.25 N	96.20 W
Tierra Blanca Creek ≃	196	34.58 N	101.55 W
Tierra Buena	226	39.09 N	121.40 W
Tierra Colorada, Méx.	234	17.10 N	99.35 W
Tierra Colorada, Méx.	234	17.56 N	92.39 W
Tierra Colorada, Bajo de la ≚¹	254	42.52 S	66.48 W
Tierra de Campos ◂¹	34	42.10 N	4.50 W
Tierra del Fuego □⁸	254	54.00 S	67.00 W
Tierra del Fuego, Isla Grande de I	254	54.00 S	69.00 W
Tierra del Fuego, Parque Nacional ♦	254	54.39 S	68.30 W
Tierra del Norte → Severnaja Zeml'a II	74	79.30 N	98.00 E
Tierralta	246	8.11 N	76.04 W
Tierra Redonda Mountain ∧	226	35.47 N	120.59 W
Tierras Australes y Antárticas Francesas → French Southern and Antarctic Territories □²	6	49.30 S	69.30 E
Tieshan	100	30.14 N	114.52 E
Tieshanguan	100	23.30 N	113.54 E
Tiétar ≃	34	39.50 N	6.01 W
Tietê	255	23.07 S	47.43 W
Tietê ≃	255	20.40 S	51.35 W
Tiéti	175f	20.57 S	165.19 E
Tieton	224	46.42 N	120.45 W
Tieton ≃	224	46.45 N	120.45 W
Tieton, South Fork ≃	224	46.38 N	121.08 W
Tietzow	264a	52.43 N	12.56 E
Tif	148	27.00 N	1.37 E
Tiffany Mountain ∧	202	48.40 N	119.56 W
Tiffin	214	41.07 N	83.11 W
Tiffin ≃	216	41.17 N	84.23 W
Tiflis → Tbilisi	84	41.43 N	44.49 E
Tifton	192	31.27 N	83.30 W
Tiftona	192	35.05 N	85.10 W
Tiga, Île I	175f	21.07 S	167.49 E
Tiga, Pulau I	112	5.43 N	115.39 E
Tigalda Island I	180	54.05 N	165.05 W
Tigapuluh, Pegunungan ⋏	112	1.05 S	102.30 E
Tigard	224	45.25 N	122.46 W
Tigasaki → Chigasaki	94	35.19 N	139.24 E
Tigbauan	116	10.41 N	122.22 E
Tigeaux	261	48.50 N	2.54 E
Tiger Lake ◎	220	27.53 N	81.22 W
Tiger Stadium ♦	281	42.20 N	83.04 W
Tigery	261	48.38 N	2.31 E
Tighennif	148	35.20 N	0.21 E
Tighvein ∧²	46	55.30 N	5.10 W
Tigil'	74	57.48 N	158.40 E
Tiglid	148	28.31 N	10.15 W
Tiglione ≃	62	44.48 N	8.27 E
Tignale	64	45.44 N	10.44 E
Tignall	192	33.52 N	82.44 W
Tignère	152	7.22 N	12.39 E
Tignes	62	45.30 N	6.55 E
Tignish	186	46.57 N	64.02 W
Tignousti, Jebel ∧	148	31.31 N	6.44 W
Tigoda ≃	76	59.22 N	31.54 E
Tigray □⁴	144	13.40 N	40.00 E
Tigre, Arg.	258	34.25 S	58.34 W
Tigre, Col.	246	2.28 N	68.15 W
Tigre □⁵	288	34.24 S	58.37 W
Tigre ≃, Arg.	288	34.25 S	58.35 W
Tigre ≃, Méx.	234	22.43 N	97.51 W
Tigre ≃, Perú	246	4.26 S	74.05 W
Tigre ≃, Ven.	246	9.20 N	62.30 W
Tigre, Cerro ∧	236	8.31 N	83.28 W
Tigre, Isla del I	258	34.47 S	56.23 W
Tigre, Punta del >	258	34.46 S	56.33 W
Tigres, Baía dos c	152	16.38 S	11.46 E
Tigre → Tigris ≃	128	31.00 N	47.25 E
Tigris (Dicle) (Dijlah) ≃	128	31.00 N	47.25 E
Tiguabos	240p	20.14 N	75.21 W
Tiguentourine	148	27.50 N	9.18 E
Tiguesmat ⋏²	148	24.54 N	8.14 W
Tigy	50	47.48 N	2.12 E
Tigyaing	110	23.46 N	96.08 E
Tigzert, Oued V	148	28.20 N	9.35 W
Tigzirt	34	36.54 N	4.08 E
Tīh, Jabal at- ⋏¹	140	29.30 N	34.00 E
Tihāmah ≚	128	26.00 N	36.30 E
Tihany ⊥	30	46.54 N	17.53 E
Tihert	148	35.28 N	1.21 E
Tihert □⁵	148	35.00 N	1.45 E
Ţihnāwī, Wādī aṭ- V	142	28.11 N	30.46 E
Tihuatlán	234	20.43 N	97.32 W
Tihua → Ürümqi	86	43.48 N	87.35 E
Tiilikkajärven kansallispuisto ♦	26	63.38 N	28.20 E
Tijamuchi ≃	248	14.10 S	64.58 W
Tijesno	36	43.48 N	15.39 E
Tījī	146	32.01 N	11.22 E
Tijuana	232	32.32 N	117.01 W
Tijuana ≃	204	32.33 N	117.07 W
Tijuca ◂⁸	287a	22.56 S	43.14 W
Tijuca, Barra da ʊ	287a	23.01 S	43.18 W
Tijuca, Lagoa da c	287a	22.59 S	43.20 W
Tijuca, Parque Nacional da ♦	287a	22.58 S	43.15 W
Tijuca, Pico da ∧	287a	22.56 S	43.17 W
Tijucas	252	27.14 S	48.38 W
Tijucas do Sul	252	25.55 S	49.12 W
Tijuco ≃	255	18.40 S	50.05 W
Tikal ⊥	232	17.20 N	89.39 W
Tīkamgarh	124	24.44 N	78.50 E
Tikaré	150	13.17 N	1.43 W
Tikchik Lakes ◎	180	60.07 N	158.35 W
Tikei, Île I	14	14.58 S	144.32 W
Tikhand ◂⁸	272a	28.31 N	77.17 E
Tikhoretsk → Tichoreck	78	45.51 N	40.09 E
Tikitiki	172	37.48 S	178.24 E
Tiko	152	4.05 N	9.22 E
Tikokino	172	39.49 S	176.27 E
Tikrīt	128	34.36 N	43.42 E
Tikša	24	64.07 N	32.27 E
Tikšeozero, ozero ◎	24	66.16 N	31.53 E
Tiksi	74	71.36 N	128.48 E
Tiku	112	0.24 S	99.56 E
Til	130	38.44 N	41.49 E
Tiladummati Atoll I¹	122	6.50 N	73.05 E
Tilamuta	112	0.30 N	122.20 E
Tilarán	236	10.28 N	84.59 W
Tilbalakan, Laguna c	236	15.30 N	84.17 W
Tilbānah	142	30.59 N	31.27 E
Tilburg	52	51.34 N	5.05 E
Tilbury, On., Can.	214	42.16 N	82.26 W
Tilbury, Eng., U.K.	42	51.28 N	0.23 E
Tilcara	252	23.34 S	65.22 W
Tilcha	166	29.36 S	140.54 E
Til-Châtel	58	47.31 N	5.10 E
Tilden, Il., U.S.	219	38.12 N	89.40 W
Tilden, Ne., U.S.	198	42.02 N	97.50 W
Tilden, Tx., U.S.	196	28.28 N	98.33 W
Tilden Lake ◎	226	38.07 N	119.36 W
Tilden Woods	284c	39.03 N	77.09 W
Tilemsès	150	15.37 N	4.44 E
Tilemsi, Vallée du V	150	16.15 N	0.02 E
Tilff	56	50.34 N	5.35 E
Tilghman Island I	208	38.42 N	76.20 W
Tilhar	124	27.59 N	79.44 E
Tilia, Oued V	148	27.27 N	0.01 W
Tiligul ≃	78	47.04 N	30.57 E
Tiligulo-Berezanka	78	46.52 N	31.24 E
Tiligul'skij liman ◎	78	46.48 N	31.08 E
Tiliktino	82	56.06 N	36.36 E
Tilimsen	148	34.52 N	1.15 W
Tilimsen □⁵	148	35.00 N	2.00 W
Tilin	110	21.42 N	94.04 E
Tilisarao	252	32.44 S	65.18 W
Till ≃, Eng., U.K.	44	55.41 N	2.12 W
Till ≃, Eng., U.K.	44	53.16 N	0.37 W
Tillaberi	150	14.13 N	1.27 E
Tillamook	202	45.27 N	123.50 W
Tillamook □⁶	224	45.25 N	123.39 W
Tillamook ≃	224	45.28 N	123.53 W
Tillamook Bay c	224	45.30 N	123.53 W
Tillamook Head >	224	45.57 N	124.00 W
Tillanchāng Dwīp I	110	8.30 N	93.37 E
Tillberga	40	59.41 N	16.37 E
Tille ≃	58	47.07 N	5.21 E
Tillery, Lake ◎¹	192	35.17 N	80.05 W
Tilley	182	50.27 N	111.39 W
Tilli	126	23.57 N	89.57 E
Tillia	150	16.08 N	4.47 E
Tillicoultry	46	56.09 N	3.45 W
Tillicum	224	47.08 N	122.33 W
Tillières-sur-Avre	50	48.46 N	1.04 E
Tilling Bourne ≃	260	51.13 N	0.34 W
Tillmans Corner	194	30.43 N	88.05 W
Tillson	210	41.49 N	74.04 W
Tillsonburg	212	42.51 N	80.44 W
Tillyfourie	46	57.11 N	2.35 W
Tilogne	150	15.58 N	13.36 W
Tilomar	112	9.21 S	125.08 E
Tílos I	38	36.25 N	27.25 E
Tilpa	166	30.57 S	144.24 E
Tilrhemt	148	33.10 N	3.21 E
Tilsit → Sovetsk	76	55.05 N	21.53 E
Tilt ≃	46	56.46 N	3.50 W
Tilton, Il., U.S.	194	40.05 N	87.38 W
Tilton, Ky., U.S.	218	38.22 N	83.45 W
Tilton, N.H., U.S.	188	43.26 N	71.35 W
Tilton ≃	224	46.33 N	122.33 W
Tiltonsville	214	40.10 N	80.41 W
Tilzapotla	234	18.29 N	99.16 W
Tim	78	51.37 N	37.07 E
Tim ≃	76	52.15 N	37.22 E
Ţimā	140	26.54 N	31.26 E
Timah, Bukit ∧²	271c	1.21 N	103.47 E
Timahoe	48	53.20 N	6.49 W
Timaná	246	1.58 N	75.56 W
Timane ≃	248	20.34 S	59.15 W
Timanskij kr'až ∧	24	65.00 N	51.00 E
Timar	84	38.49 N	43.27 E
Timaricha	80	57.33 N	44.47 E
Timaru	172	44.24 S	171.15 E
Timaševo, Ross.	80	53.21 N	51.12 E
Timaševo, Ross.	82	55.08 N	36.29 E
Timaševsk	78	45.37 N	38.57 E
Timau, It.	64	46.35 N	13.00 E
Timau, Kenya	154	0.05 N	37.14 E
Timavo San Giovanni	64	45.48 N	13.37 E
Timay al-Amdīd	142	30.57 N	31.32 E
Timbákion	38	35.04 N	24.46 E
Timbalier Bay c	194	29.10 N	90.20 W
Timbaúba	250	7.31 S	35.19 W
Timbavati Game Reserve ◂⁴	156	24.27 S	31.27 E
Timbedgha	150	16.15 N	8.10 W
Timber	224	45.43 N	123.17 W
Timber Creek	164	15.39 S	130.29 E
Timber Creek ≃	198	44.49 N	98.17 W
Timber Lake, Il., U.S.	278	42.14 N	88.07 W
Timberlake, Oh., U.S.	214	41.41 N	81.25 W
Timber Lake, S.D., U.S.	198	45.26 N	101.04 W
Timber Run ≃	284b	39.27 N	76.52 W
Timber Trails	278	41.52 N	87.57 W
Timberview	284b	39.13 N	76.45 W
Timbío	246	2.20 N	76.40 W
Timbiras	250	4.15 S	43.57 W
Timblin	214	40.58 N	79.12 W
Timbó, Bra.	252	26.50 S	49.18 W
Timbo, Guinée	150	10.38 N	11.50 W
Timbo, Liber.	150	5.37 N	9.43 W
Timbó ≃	287a	22.52 S	43.16 W
Timboon	169	38.29 S	142.59 E
Timbuctoo	285	40.00 N	74.49 W
Timbuktu → Tombouctou	150	16.46 N	3.01 W
Timbun Mata, Pulau I	112	4.39 N	118.28 E
Timel'ga	86	58.53 N	76.42 E
Timelkam	60	48.00 N	13.36 E
Times Square ♦	276	40.45 N	74.00 W
Timétrine	150	19.27 N	0.26 W
Timétrine ⋏	150	19.20 N	0.42 W
Timeu Creek ≃	182	54.28 N	114.27 W
Timewell	219	40.00 N	90.52 W
Timgad ⊥	148	35.29 N	6.28 E
Timimoun	148	29.14 N	0.16 E
Timimoun, Sebkha de ◎	148	29.00 N	0.05 E
Timinar	140	19.02 N	30.29 E
Timi Ouli, Ehi ∧	146	21.08 N	16.31 E
Timir'azevo	76	55.05 N	21.37 E
Timir'azevskij	86	56.29 N	84.54 E
Timirevo	82	55.08 N	39.10 E
Timirist, Râs >	150	19.23 N	16.32 W
Timiș □⁶	38	45.40 N	21.20 E
Timiș (Tamiš) ≃	38	44.51 N	20.39 E
Timiskaming, Lake ◎	190	47.10 N	79.25 W
Timișoara	38	45.45 N	21.13 E
Timkoviči	76	53.03 N	27.00 E
Timkovo	82	55.56 N	38.37 E
Timmendorfer Strand	54	54.00 N	10.46 E
Timmernabben	26	56.58 N	16.26 E
Timmins	190	48.28 N	81.20 W
Timmonsville	192	34.08 N	79.56 W
Timms Hill ∧²	190	45.27 N	90.11 W
Timok ≃	38	44.13 N	22.40 E
Timon	250	5.06 S	42.49 W
Timonovo	82	56.13 N	37.02 E
Timor I	112	9.00 S	125.00 E
Timor Sea ⫧²	14	11.00 S	128.00 E
Timor Timur □⁴	112	8.35 S	126.00 E
Timor Trough ⟡¹	14	9.50 S	126.00 E
Timošino, Ross.	76	60.05 N	36.10 E
Timošino, Ross.	80	57.50 N	44.25 E
Timotes	246	8.59 N	70.44 W
Timothy Lake ◎¹	224	45.07 N	121.47 W
Timoudi	148	29.19 N	1.09 W
Timousserarène ≃	150	16.21 N	8.07 E
Timpanogos Cave National Monument ♦	200	40.18 N	111.52 W
Timpas Creek ≃	198	38.02 N	103.38 W
Timpaus, Pulau I	112	1.51 S	124.01 E
Timperley	262	53.24 N	2.19 W
Timpson	194	31.54 N	94.23 W
Timpton ≃	74	58.43 N	127.12 E
Timrå	26	62.31 N	17.22 E
Timsāh, Buḩayrat at- (Lake Timsah) ◎	142	30.34 N	32.17 E
Timsah, Lake → Timsāh, Buḩayrat at- ◎	142	30.34 N	32.17 E
Timšer	24	62.06 N	54.40 E
Tims Ford Lake ◎¹	194	35.15 N	86.10 W
Timun	114	0.50 N	103.22 E
Timur	85	42.50 N	68.26 E
Timur, Banjaran ⋏	114	5.00 N	102.30 E
Timurni	124	22.22 N	77.22 E
Tīn, Ra's at- >	146	32.37 N	23.08 E
Tina ≃	158	31.18 S	29.14 E
Tinaca Point >	116	5.33 N	125.20 E
Tinaco	246	9.42 N	68.26 W
Tinaga Island I	116	14.28 N	122.56 E
Ţīnah, Khalīj aṭ- c	140	31.08 N	32.40 E
Tinahely	48	52.48 N	6.28 W
Tinaja, Punta >	248	16.14 S	73.39 W
Tinalmud	116	13.36 N	122.53 E
Tinambac	116	13.49 N	123.19 E
Tinambung	112	3.31 S	119.01 E
Ti-n-Amzi V	150	18.20 N	4.32 E
Tinapagee	166	29.28 S	144.23 E
Tinaquillo	246	9.55 N	68.18 W
Tindari, Capo >	70	38.10 N	15.03 E
Tinderry Peak ∧	171b	35.42 S	149.16 E
Tindila	150	10.16 N	8.15 W
Tindis	126	21.35 N	86.44 E
Tindivanam	122	12.15 N	79.39 E
Tindouf	148	27.50 N	8.04 W
Tindouf, Hamada de ◂¹	148	27.30 N	9.00 W
Tindouf, Sebkha de ≚	148	27.45 N	7.15 W
Tineba, Pegunungan ⋏	112	1.40 S	120.25 E
Tinée ≃	62	43.55 N	7.11 E
Tineg ≃	116	17.38 N	120.37 E
Tineo	34	43.20 N	6.25 W
Ting ≃	100	24.24 N	116.35 E
Tinga ∧	146	9.21 N	23.38 E
Tingambato	234	19.30 N	101.52 W
Tinggi, Pulau I	114	2.18 N	104.07 E
Tingha	166	29.57 S	151.13 E
Tinghert, Hamādat (Plateau du Tinghert) ⋏¹	148	29.00 N	9.00 E
Tinghert, Plateau du (Hamādat Tinghert) ⋏¹	148	29.00 N	9.00 E
Tinghsien → Dingxian	98	38.32 N	114.59 E
Tingkar ∧	116	5.20 N	117.06 E
Ting Kau	271d	22.22 N	114.05 E
Tingkawk Sakan	110	26.04 N	96.44 E
Tingkou	98	36.34 N	119.46 E
Tinglev	41	54.56 N	9.15 E
Tinglin	106	30.53 N	121.17 E
Tingliuhe	98	39.34 N	118.49 E
Tingloy	116	13.40 N	120.52 E
Tingmerkpuk Mountain ∧	180	68.34 N	162.28 W
Tingo de Saposoa	248	7.07 S	76.38 W
Tingo María	248	9.09 S	75.56 W
Tingo María, Parque Nacional ♦	248	9.15 S	76.05 W
Tingqian	100	30.10 N	115.54 E
Tingri, Zhg.	120	28.35 N	86.38 E
Tingri, Zhg.	120	28.38 N	87.04 E
Tingsiqiao	100	29.50 N	114.12 E
Tingsryd	26	56.32 N	14.59 E
Tingstäde	26	57.44 N	18.36 E
Tingsted	41	54.49 N	11.56 E
Tinguá	256	22.36 S	43.26 W
Tingüindín	234	19.45 N	102.29 W
Tinguiririca, Volcán ∧¹	252	34.49 S	70.21 W
Tingvoll	26	62.54 N	8.12 E
Tingvollfjorden c²	26	62.50 N	8.11 E
Tingwick	206	45.50 N	71.58 W
Tingwon Group II	164	2.35 S	149.45 E
Tingzitou	106	30.12 N	119.46 E
Tinharé, Ilha de I	255	13.30 S	38.58 W
Tinh Bien	110	10.36 N	104.57 E
Tinian	174n	14.58 N	145.38 E
Tinian I	174n	15.00 N	145.38 E
Tinian Harbor c	174n	14.57 N	145.36 E
Tinié	150	14.20 N	1.28 W
Tiniguiban	116	11.22 N	119.30 E
Tinitian	116	10.04 N	119.12 E
Tinjar ≃	112	4.04 N	114.18 E
Tinjil, Pulau I	115a	6.58 S	105.47 E
Tinker Air Force Base ■	196	35.25 N	97.24 W
Tinkers Creek ≃, Md., U.S.	284c	38.46 N	76.57 W
Tinkers Creek ≃, Oh., U.S.	214	41.22 N	81.37 W
Tinkertown	283	42.01 N	70.44 W
Tinkisso ≃	150	11.21 N	9.10 W
Tinley Creek ≃	278	41.39 N	87.45 W
Tinley Creek Woods ♦	278	41.39 N	87.47 W
Tinley Park	216	41.34 N	87.47 W
Tinniswood, Mount ∧	182	50.19 N	123.50 W
Tinnoset	26	59.43 N	9.02 E
Tinnsjø ◎	26	59.54 N	8.55 E
Tinogasta	252	28.04 S	67.34 W
Tinompo	112	2.09 S	121.17 E
Tínos	38	37.32 N	25.10 E
Tínos I	38	37.38 N	25.10 E
Tinquipaya	248	19.11 S	65.51 W
Tin Rerhoh, Tassili ⋏	150	19.40 N	4.00 E
Tinrhir	148	31.28 N	5.30 W
Tin Sam	271d	22.22 N	114.11 E
Tinskoj	88	56.10 N	96.55 E
Tinsley	194	32.43 N	90.27 W
Tinsukia	120	27.30 N	95.22 E
Tintagel, B.C., Can.	182	54.12 N	125.35 W
Tintagel, Eng., U.K.	42	50.40 N	4.45 W
Tintagel Head >	42	50.41 N	4.46 W
Tintaldra	171b	36.03 S	147.56 E
Tintas, Rio das ≃	287a	22.52 S	43.28 W
Tinte, Cerro ∧	248	22.40 S	67.02 W
Tintern Abbey ♁¹	42	51.41 N	2.40 W
Tintern Parva	42	51.42 N	2.40 W
Tintigny	56	49.41 N	5.31 E
Tintina	252	27.02 S	62.43 W
Tintinara	166	35.54 S	140.03 E
Tintioulé	150	10.13 N	9.12 W
Tinto ∧	46	55.36 N	3.39 W
Tinto ≃	34	37.12 N	6.55 W
Ti-n-Toumma ◂¹	146	16.04 N	12.40 E
Tintwistle	262	53.28 N	1.58 W
Tinui	172	40.53 S	176.04 E
Tinwald	172	43.55 S	171.43 E
Ti-n-Zaouatene	150	19.55 N	2.52 E
Tinzap ≃	120	38.23 N	77.24 E
Tio	144	14.42 N	40.58 E
Tioga, Il., U.S.	219	40.13 N	91.21 W
Tioga, N.D., U.S.	198	48.23 N	102.56 W
Tioga, Pa., U.S.	210	41.55 N	77.08 W
Tioga □⁶, N.Y., U.S.	210	42.06 N	76.16 W
Tioga □⁶, Pa., U.S.	210	41.45 N	77.17 W
Tioga ◂⁸	285	40.00 N	75.10 W
Tioga ≃	210	42.09 N	77.05 W
Tioga Center	210	42.04 N	76.21 W
Tioga Pass)(	226	37.54 N	119.16 W
Tioga Terrace	210	42.03 N	76.07 W
Tiojala	24	61.10 N	23.52 E
Tioman, Pulau I	114	2.48 N	104.10 E
Tiona	214	41.45 N	79.03 W
Tione di Trento	64	46.02 N	10.43 E
Tionesta	214	41.30 N	79.27 W
Tionesta Creek ≃	214	41.28 N	79.22 W
Tionesta Lake ◎¹	214	41.28 N	79.28 W
Tioor, Pulau I	164	4.45 S	131.45 E
Tior	140	6.23 N	31.11 E
Tioro	112	4.41 S	122.36 E
Tioro, Selat ʊ	112	4.40 S	122.20 E
Tioroniaradougou	150	9.21 N	5.38 W
Tioughnioga ≃	210	42.14 N	75.51 W
Tioughnioga, East Branch ≃	210	42.36 N	76.10 W
Tipasa	34	36.35 N	2.27 E
Tipitapa	236	12.12 N	86.06 W
Tipoca, Monter ∧²	250	3.34 N	51.20 W
Tipp City	218	39.57 N	84.10 W
Tippecanoe, In., U.S.	216	41.12 N	86.06 W
Tippecanoe, Oh., U.S.	214	40.16 N	81.17 W
Tippecanoe □⁶	216	40.25 N	86.53 W
Tippecanoe ≃	216	40.31 N	86.47 W
Tippecanoe, Lake ◎	216	41.20 N	85.46 W
Tippecanoe Battlefield State Memorial ⊥	216	40.31 N	86.52 W
Tippecanoe River State Park ♦	216	41.07 N	86.36 W
Tipperary, Austl.	164	13.44 S	131.02 E
Tipperary, Ire.	48	52.29 N	8.10 W
Tipperary □⁶	48	52.40 N	8.20 W
Tipton, Eng., U.K.	42	52.32 N	2.05 W
Tipton, Ca., U.S.	226	36.03 N	119.18 W
Tipton, In., U.S.	216	40.16 N	86.02 W
Tipton, Ia., U.S.	190	41.46 N	91.07 W
Tipton, Mi., U.S.	216	42.01 N	84.04 W
Tipton, Mo., U.S.	194	38.39 N	92.46 W
Tipton, Ok., U.S.	196	34.30 N	99.08 W
Tipton, Pa., U.S.	214	40.38 N	78.18 W
Tipton □⁶	216	40.17 N	86.02 W
Tipton, Mount ∧	200	35.32 N	114.12 W
Tiptonville	194	36.22 N	89.28 W
Tip Top Mountain ∧	190	48.16 N	85.59 W
Tiptree	42	51.49 N	0.45 E
Tiptūr	122	13.16 N	76.29 E
Tiputini ≃	246	0.47 S	75.32 W
Tiquicheo	234	18.53 N	100.44 W
Tīra	132	32.14 N	34.57 E
Tira Chapéu, Morro ∧	256	22.45 S	44.39 W
Tiradentes	255	21.07 S	44.11 W
Tīrah, Baḩr ≚	142	31.03 N	31.15 E
Tīrān I	128	27.56 N	34.34 E
Tīrān, Maḑīq ʊ	140	27.58 N	34.28 E
Tiran, Strait of → Tīrān, Maḑīq ʊ	140	27.58 N	34.28 E
Tirana → Tiranë	38	41.20 N	19.50 E
Tiranë	38	41.20 N	19.50 E
Tirano	64	46.13 N	10.10 E
Tiraque	248	17.37 S	65.04 W
Tirari Desert ◂²	162	28.00 S	138.20 E
Tiraspol'	78	46.51 N	29.38 E
Tirat Karmel	132	32.46 N	34.58 E
Tirat Ẕevi	132	32.25 N	35.32 E
Tirau	172	37.59 S	175.45 E
Tire	130	38.04 N	27.45 E
Tirebolu	130	41.00 N	38.48 E
Tiree I	46	56.31 N	6.49 W
Tire Hill	214	40.16 N	78.55 W
Tires (Tiers), It.	64	46.28 N	11.31 E
Tires, Port.	266c	38.43 N	9.21 W
Tires ◂¹	148	23.30 N	13.10 W
Tîrgoviște	38	44.56 N	25.27 E
Tîrgu Bujor	38	45.52 N	27.54 E
Tîrgu-Cărbunești	38	44.58 N	23.31 E
Tîrgu-Frumos	38	47.13 N	27.00 E
Tîrgu Jiu	38	45.02 N	23.17 E
Tîrgu-Lăpuș	38	47.27 N	23.52 E
Tîrgu Mureș	38	46.33 N	24.33 E
Tîrgu-Neamț	38	47.12 N	26.22 E
Tîrgu Ocna	38	46.15 N	26.37 E
Tîrgu Secuiesc	38	46.00 N	26.08 E
Tîrgusor	38	44.28 N	28.25 E
Tirhahart, Oued V	148	23.45 N	3.10 E
Tiria, Monte ∧	71	40.23 N	9.16 E
Tirich Mīr ∧	123	36.15 N	71.50 E
Tiriro	150	10.27 N	8.39 W
Tiris Zemmour □⁴	148	24.10 N	9.30 W
Tirl'anskij	86	54.14 N	58.35 E
Tirna ≃	122	18.04 N	76.57 E
Tîrnava Mare ≃	38	46.09 N	23.42 E
Tîrnava Mică ≃	38	46.11 N	23.55 E
Tîrnăveni	38	46.20 N	24.17 E
Tírnavos	38	39.45 N	22.17 E
Tirnovo → Veliko Târnovo	38	43.04 N	25.39 E
Tiro	214	40.54 N	82.46 W
Tirodi	120	21.41 N	79.42 E
Tirol □³	64	47.15 N	11.20 E
Tiroler Ache (Grossache) ≃	60	47.51 N	12.30 E
Tirolo (Tirol)	64	46.42 N	11.10 E
Tiros	255	19.00 S	45.58 W
Tiroungoulou	146	9.34 N	22.09 E
Tīr Pol	128	34.36 N	61.15 E
Tirrenia	66	43.38 N	10.17 E
Tirreno, Mare → Tyrrhenian Sea ⫧²	36	40.00 N	12.00 E
Tirry ≃	46	58.02 N	4.26 W
Tirsā, Miṣr	142	29.25 N	30.49 E
Tirsā, Miṣr	273c	29.58 N	31.12 E
Tirschenreuth	60	49.53 N	12.21 E
Tirso ≃	71	39.53 N	8.32 E
Tirsted	41	54.44 N	11.21 E
Tirstrup	41	56.18 N	10.42 E
Tīrthahalli	122	13.42 N	75.14 E
Tirua Point >	172	38.23 S	174.38 E
Tiruchchirāppalli	122	10.49 N	78.41 E
Tiruchengodu	122	11.23 N	77.56 E
Tirukkalukkunram	122	12.37 N	80.04 E
Tirukkovilūr	122	11.57 N	79.12 E
Tiruliai	76	55.47 N	23.22 E
Tirumangalam	122	9.50 N	77.59 E
Tirunelveli	122	8.44 N	77.42 E
Tirupati	122	13.39 N	79.25 E
Tiruppattūr, India	122	12.30 N	78.34 E
Tiruppattūr, India	122	10.08 N	78.37 E
Tiruppur	122	11.06 N	77.21 E
Tirūr	122	10.54 N	75.55 E
Tiruttani	122	13.11 N	79.38 E
Tirutturaippūndi	122	10.32 N	79.39 E
Tiruvalla	122	9.23 N	76.34 E
Tiruvallūr	122	13.09 N	79.55 E
Tiruvannāmalai	122	12.13 N	79.04 E
Tiruvettipuram	122	12.40 N	79.33 E
Tirūvottiyūr	122	13.09 N	80.18 E
Tiruvur	122	17.06 N	80.38 E
Tisa (Tisza) ≃	38	45.15 N	20.17 E
Tis'ah	142	30.02 N	32.35 E
Tisaiyanvilai	122	8.20 N	77.53 E
Tisaren ◎	40	59.00 N	15.08 E
Tisbury	42	51.04 N	2.03 W
Tisdale	184	52.51 N	104.04 W
Tishomingo, Ms., U.S.	194	34.38 N	88.13 W
Tishomingo, Ok., U.S.	196	34.14 N	96.40 W
Tisisat Falls ∟	144	11.29 N	37.35 E
Ţīsīyah	132	32.24 N	36.27 E
Tisjön ◎	26	60.55 N	12.58 E
Tiskilwa	190	41.17 N	89.30 W
Tiskino	86	58.05 N	83.10 E
Tiškovka	78	48.29 N	30.56 E
Tiškovo, Ross.	80	46.02 N	48.36 E
Tiškovo, Ross.	82	56.05 N	37.44 E
Tisma	236	12.05 N	86.01 W
Tisnaren ◎	40	58.57 N	15.57 E
Tišnevo	82	55.10 N	36.17 E
Tišnov	30	49.21 N	16.25 E
Tisovec	30	48.43 N	19.57 E
Tissa	146	7.26 N	10.16 E
Tissemsilt	148	35.35 N	1.50 E
Tissø ◎	41	55.35 N	11.18 E
Tīsta ≃	124	25.23 N	89.43 E
Tisul'	86	55.45 N	88.19 E
Tisvildeleje	41	56.03 N	12.05 E
Tisza (Tisa) ≃	38	45.15 N	20.17 E
Tiszaföldvár	30	46.59 N	20.15 E
Tiszafüred	30	47.37 N	20.46 E
Tiszavasvári	30	47.58 N	21.22 E
Tit	148	23.00 N	5.10 E
Titaf	148	27.26 N	0.13 W
Titāgarh	126	22.45 N	88.22 E
Titano, Monte ∧	66	43.55 N	12.28 E
Titao	150	13.46 N	2.04 W
Tit-Ary	74	71.58 N	127.01 E
Titel	38	45.12 N	20.18 E
Tithwāl	123	34.24 N	73.47 E
Titicaca, Lago ◎	248	15.50 S	69.20 W
Titicus	207	41.18 N	73.30 W
Titi Karangan	114	5.31 N	100.37 E
Titikaveka	174k	21.15 S	159.45 W
Titilāgarh	122	20.18 N	83.09 E
Titisee-Neustadt	58	47.54 N	8.13 E
Titlis ∧	58	46.47 N	8.25 E
Tito	68	40.35 N	15.40 E
Titograd	38	42.26 N	19.14 E
Titonka	190	43.14 N	94.02 W
Titou	100	29.52 N	112.42 E
Titova Korenica	36	44.45 N	15.43 E
Titova Mitrovica	38	42.53 N	20.52 E
Titovka	83	48.59 N	39.44 E
Titovo, Ross.	80	53.17 N	43.41 E
Titovo, Ross.	82	54.19 N	36.56 E
Titovo, Ross.	82	55.35 N	39.07 E
Titovo Užice	38	43.51 N	19.51 E
Titovo Velenje	61	46.22 N	15.07 E
Titov Veles	38	41.41 N	21.48 E
Titov vrh ∧	38	42.00 N	20.51 E
Titran	26	63.40 N	8.18 E
Tittabawassee ≃	190	43.23 N	83.59 W
Titteri ⋏	34	36.00 N	3.30 E
Titterstone Clee Hill ∧²	42	52.23 N	2.35 W
Titting	60	49.00 N	11.13 E
Tittling	60	48.44 N	13.23 E
Tittmoning	60	48.04 N	12.46 E
Titu	38	44.41 N	25.32 E
Titule	154	3.17 N	25.32 E
Titus □⁶	222	33.05 N	94.58 W
Titusville, Fl., U.S.	220	28.36 N	80.48 W
Titusville, N.J., U.S.	208	40.18 N	74.52 W
Titusville, Pa., U.S.	214	41.37 N	79.40 W
Titz	56	51.01 N	6.25 E
Tiu Chung Chau I	271d	22.20 N	114.19 E
Tiumpan Head >	46	58.16 N	6.09 W
Tiuni	120	30.57 N	77.51 E
Tiva ≃	154	2.20 S	38.48 E
Tivaouane	150	14.57 N	16.49 W
Tiveden ⋏²	40	58.45 N	14.40 E
Tiverton, Eng., U.K.	42	50.55 N	3.29 W
Tiverton, R.I., U.S.	207	41.37 N	71.12 W
Tivoli, Gren.	241k	12.10 N	61.37 W
Tivoli, It.	66	41.58 N	12.48 E
Tivoli, N.Y., U.S.	210	42.03 N	73.54 W
Tivoli, Tx., U.S.	196	28.27 N	96.53 W
Tivoli ♦	41	55.40 N	12.34 E
Ţiwāl, Wādī V	146	10.22 N	22.43 E
Ţiwāl al-'Abā ∧	130	36.20 N	39.22 E
Tiwi, Pil.	116	13.27 N	123.41 E
Ţīwī, 'Umān	128	22.49 N	59.16 E
Tiwuronto	115b	8.48 S	120.09 E
Tixtla de Guerrero	234	17.35 N	99.26 W
Tiyās	130	34.33 N	37.40 E
Tiyo, Pegunungan ⋏	164	4.00 S	135.30 E
Tizapán ◂⁸	286a	19.20 N	99.13 W
Tizapán El Alto	234	20.10 N	103.04 W
Tizimín	232	21.10 N	88.10 W
Tizi-Ouzou	148	36.48 N	4.02 E
Tizi Ouzou □⁵	148	36.40 N	4.10 E
Tizmant ash-Sharqīyah	142	29.03 N	31.03 E
Tiznados ≃	246	8.16 N	67.47 W
Tiznit	148	29.43 N	9.44 W
Tiznit □⁴	148	29.40 N	9.45 W
Tizoc	196	25.41 N	101.59 W
Tjällmo	40	58.43 N	15.21 E
Tjeukemeer ◎	52	52.54 N	5.50 E
Tjilatjap → Cilacap	115a	7.44 S	109.00 E
Tjirebon → Cirebon	115a	6.44 S	108.34 E
Tjolotjo	154	19.47 S	27.46 E
Tjøme I	26	59.07 N	10.24 E
Tjörn I	26	58.00 N	11.38 E
Tjörnarp	41	56.00 N	13.37 E
Tkibuli	84	42.21 N	42.59 E
Tkvarčeli	84	42.51 N	41.41 E
Tlachichuca	234	19.06 N	97.25 W
Tlacoapa	234	17.09 N	98.52 W
Tlacotalpan	234	18.37 N	95.40 W
Tlacotepec	234	17.46 N	99.59 W
Tlacuitapan	234	21.14 N	102.12 W
Tláhuac ◂⁸	286a	19.16 N	99.00 W
Tlahualilo de Zaragoza	232	26.07 N	103.27 W
Tlahuelilpan	234	20.08 N	99.14 W
Tlahuitoltepec	234	17.04 N	95.59 W
Tlajomulco de Zúñiga	234	20.28 N	103.27 W
Tlalchapa	234	18.24 N	100.28 W
Tlalcozotitlán	234	17.54 N	99.15 W
Tlalixtac de Cabrera	234	17.04 N	96.39 W
Tlalixtaquilla	234	17.21 N	98.28 W
Tlalnepantla	234	19.33 N	99.12 W
Tlalnepantla ≃	286a	19.31 N	99.16 W
Tlalpan ◂⁸	286a	19.17 N	99.10 W
Tlalpujahua	234	19.48 N	100.10 W
Tlaltenango de Sánchez Román	234	21.47 N	103.19 W
Tl'ančetamak	80	55.28 N	52.37 E
Tlapacoyan	234	19.58 N	97.13 W
Tlapa de Comonfort	234	17.33 N	98.33 W
Tlapaneco ≃	234	18.05 N	98.48 W
Tlapehuala	234	18.13 N	100.31 W
Tlapeng	156	23.15 S	21.49 E
Tlaquepaque	234	20.39 N	103.19 W
Tl'arata	84	42.07 N	46.22 E
Tlatlauquitepec	234	19.51 N	97.29 W
Tlaxcala □³	234	19.25 N	98.10 W
Tlaxcala [de Xicoténcatl]	234	19.19 N	98.14 W
Tlaxcoapan	234	20.05 N	99.13 W
Tlaxco [de Morelos]	234	19.37 N	98.07 W
Tlaxmalac	234	18.21 N	99.25 W
Tlazazalca	234	19.58 N	102.04 W
Tletat ed Douair	34	35.59 N	2.55 E
Tlētē Ouāte Gharbī, Jabal ∧	130	35.20 N	39.13 E
Tlevak Strait ʊ	182	55.03 N	132.58 W
Tlhakgameng	158	26.27 S	24.21 E
Tloch	84	42.38 N	46.28 E
Tlučiná	60	49.44 N	13.14 E
Tlumač	78	48.52 N	25.01 E
Tłuszcz	30	52.26 N	21.26 E
Tmassah	146	26.22 N	15.47 E
Tmīsān	146	27.32 N	13.19 E
Tnâot ≃	110	11.29 N	104.57 E
Tnekvejem ≃	180	65.50 N	177.31 E
Toa ≃	240p	20.23 N	74.32 W
Toa Alta	240m	18.23 N	66.15 W
Toab	46a	59.53 N	1.19 W
Toa Baja	240m	18.27 N	66.15 W
Toabré ≃	236	8.56 N	80.33 W
Toachi ≃	246	0.08 N	79.18 W
Toahayaná	232	26.08 N	107.44 W
Toamasina	157b	18.10 S	49.23 E
Toamasina □⁴	157b	18.00 S	48.40 E
Toandonggu	98	40.33 N	127.35 E
Toandos Peninsula >¹	224	47.43 N	122.47 W
Toano, It.	64	44.23 N	10.34 E
Toano, Va., U.S.	208	37.22 N	76.48 W
Toano Draw V	204	41.27 N	114.35 W
Toano Range ⋏	204	40.50 N	114.20 W
Toast	192	36.30 N	80.37 W
Toa Vaca, Embalse ◎¹	240m	18.06 N	66.28 W
Toay	252	36.40 S	64.21 W
Toba, Mali	150	11.52 N	7.28 W
Toba, Nihon	94	34.29 N	136.51 E
Toba, Zhg.	102	31.18 N	97.40 E
Toba ≃	182	50.30 N	124.15 W
Toba, Danau ◎	114	2.35 N	98.50 E
Tobacco ≃	190	43.49 N	84.24 W
Tobacco Plains Indian Reserve ◂⁴	182	49.04 N	115.06 W
Tobacco Root Mountains ⋏	202	45.35 N	112.00 W
Tobago I	241r	11.15 N	60.40 W
Toba Inlet c	182	50.20 N	124.50 W
Toba Kākar Range ⋏	120	31.15 N	68.00 E
Tobalaba Eulogio Sánchez, Aeródromo ⊠	286e	33.27 S	70.33 W
Tobalai, Pulau I	164	1.37 S	128.20 E
Tobarra	34	38.35 N	1.41 W
Tobas	252	28.08 S	62.42 W
Tobašino	80	56.56 N	47.40 E
Toba Tek Singh	123	30.58 N	72.29 E
Tobe	96	33.44 N	132.47 E
Tobejuba, Isla I	246	9.20 N	60.52 W
Tobekuduk	86	49.50 N	54.15 E
Tobelo	108	1.44 N	128.01 E
Tobelombang	112	0.57 S	122.00 E
Tobercurry	48	54.03 N	8.43 W
Tobermorey	166	22.15 S	138.00 E
Tobermory, Austl.	166	27.17 S	143.41 E
Tobermory, On., Can.	190	45.15 N	81.40 W
Tobermory, Scot., U.K.	46	56.37 N	6.05 W
Toberonochy	46	56.13 N	5.38 W
Tōbetsu	92a	43.13 N	141.31 E
Tobi I	108	3.00 N	131.10 E
Tobias	198	40.25 N	97.20 W
Tobias Barreto	250	11.11 S	38.01 W
Tobiishi-bana >	174f	24.45 N	141.17 E
Tobin, Mount ∧	204	40.22 N	117.32 W
Tobin Lake ◎, Austl.	162	21.45 S	125.49 E
Tobin Lake ◎, Sk., Can.	184	53.40 N	103.35 W
Tobique ≃	186	46.46 N	67.42 W
Tobi-shima I	92	39.12 N	139.34 E
Toblach → Dobbiaco	64	46.44 N	12.14 E
Tobo, Indon.	164	3.34 S	130.11 E
Tobo, Sve.	40	60.16 N	17.39 E
Toboali	112	3.00 S	106.30 E
Tobol	86	52.40 N	62.39 E
Tobol ≃	86	58.10 N	68.12 E
Toboli	112	0.43 S	120.05 E
Tobol'sk	86	58.12 N	68.16 E
Tobong-san ∧	271b	37.42 N	127.01 E
Tobor	150	12.39 N	16.16 W
Toboso	116	10.43 N	123.31 E
Tobré	150	10.12 N	2.08 E
Tobruk → Ţubruq	146	32.05 N	23.59 E
Tobseda	24	68.36 N	52.14 E
Tōbu	94	36.21 N	138.20 E
Toburdanovo	80	55.22 N	47.38 E
Toby, Mount ∧	207	42.29 N	72.32 W
Tobyhanna	210	41.10 N	75.25 W
Tobyhanna Creek ≃	210	41.07 N	75.39 W
Tobyhanna State Park ♦	210	41.13 N	75.25 W
Tobyš ≃	24	65.30 N	51.00 E
Toca Grande, Morro da ∧	287a	22.58 S	43.31 W
Tocantínia	250	9.33 S	48.22 W
Tocantinópolis	250	6.20 S	47.25 W
Tocantins □³	250	10.00 S	48.00 W
Tocantins ≃, Bra.	242	1.45 S	49.10 W
Tocantins ≃, Bra.	250	5.21 S	55.58 W
Tocantinzinho ≃	255	13.57 S	48.20 W
Toccoa	192	34.34 N	83.19 W
Toccoa (Ocoee) ≃	192	35.12 N	84.40 W
Toce ≃	58	45.56 N	8.29 E
Tochapan	234	18.54 N	97.37 W
Tochcha Lake ◎	182	54.56 N	125.54 W
Tochigi	94	36.23 N	139.44 E
Tochigi □⁵	94	36.45 N	139.45 E
Tochimilco	234	18.54 N	98.34 W
Tochio	92	37.28 N	139.00 E
Tochoj	88	50.30 N	105.00 E
Tochta	24	62.14 N	48.48 E
Tochtamyš	120	37.50 N	74.39 E
Tockholes	262	53.42 N	2.31 W
Tockoje	80	52.32 N	52.45 E
Töcksfors	26	59.30 N	11.50 E
Točnik	60	49.27 N	13.19 E
Toco, Chile	252	22.05 S	69.35 W
Toco, Trin.	241r	10.50 N	60.57 W
Tocoa	236	15.41 N	86.03 W
Tócome ≃	286c	10.29 N	66.49 W
Toconao	252	23.11 S	68.01 W
Tocopilla	252	22.05 S	70.12 W
Tocos do Moji	256	22.22 S	46.06 W
Tocuco ≃	246	9.36 N	72.15 W
Tocumwal	166	35.49 S	145.34 E
Tocuyo ≃	246	11.03 N	68.23 W
Tocuyo de la Costa	246	11.02 N	68.23 W
Toda	94	35.48 N	139.41 E
Toda Bhīm	124	26.55 N	76.49 E
Todaiji Temple ♁¹	270	34.42 N	135.51 E
Todang-ni	271b	37.37 N	126.50 E
Toda Rāisingh	120	26.01 N	75.29 E
Todd	214	40.16 N	78.04 W
Todd ≃	162	24.52 S	135.48 E
Todd Estates	285	39.40 N	75.43 W
Toddington	42	51.57 N	0.32 W
Todd Point >	284b	39.15 N	76.27 W
Toddville, Md., U.S.	208	38.17 N	76.04 W
Toddville, N.Y., U.S.	210	41.17 N	73.53 W
Todeli	112	1.40 S	124.29 E
Todenyang	154	4.32 N	35.56 E
Todi	66	42.47 N	12.24 E
Tödi ∧	58	46.49 N	8.56 E
Todmorden, Austl.	162	27.08 S	134.48 E
Todmorden, Eng., U.K.	44	53.43 N	2.05 W
Todoga-saki >	92	39.33 N	142.05 E
Todoromi	270	34.53 N	135.28 E
Todos Santos, Bol.	248	16.48 S	65.08 W
Todos Santos, Méx.	232	23.27 N	110.13 W
Todos Santos, Bahía c	232	31.48 N	116.42 W
Todro	154	3.21 N	30.14 E
Todtenhausen	52	52.20 N	8.56 E
Todtmoos	58	47.44 N	8.00 E

Symbols in the index entries represent the broad categories identified in the key at the right. Symbols with superior numbers (⋏¹) identify subcategories (see complete key on page I · 1).

Symbole im Register stellen die rechts im Schlüssel erklärten Kategorien dar. Symbole mit hochgestellten Ziffern (⋏¹) bezeichnen Unterabteilungen einer Kategorie (vgl. vollständiger Schlüssel auf Seite I · 1).

Los símbolos incluidos en el texto del índice representan las grandes categorías identificadas con la clave a la derecha. Los símbolos con números en su parte superior (⋏¹) identifican las subcategorías (véase la clave completa en la página I · 1).

Les symboles de l'index représentent les catégories indiquées dans la légende à droite. Les symboles suivis d'un indice (⋏¹) représentent des sous-catégories (voir légende complète à la page I · 1).

Os símbolos incluídos no texto do índice representam as grandes categorias identificadas com a chave à direita. Os símbolos com números em sua parte superior (⋏¹) identificam as subcategorias (veja-se a chave completa à página I · 1).

English	Deutsch	Español	Français	Português
∧ Mountain	Berg	Montaña	Montagne	Montanha
⋏ Mountains	Gebirge	Montañas	Montagnes	Montanhas
)(Pass	Paß	Paso	Col	Passo
V Valley, Canyon	Tal, Cañon	Valle, Cañón	Vallée, Canyon	Vale, Canhão
≚ Plain	Ebene	Llano	Plaine	Planície
> Cape	Kap	Cabo	Cap	Cabo
I Island	Insel	Isla	Île	Ilha
II Islands	Inseln	Islas	Îles	Ilhas
♦ Other Topographic Features	Andere Topographische Objekte	Otros Elementos Topográficos	Autres données topographiques	Outros acidentes topográficos

ESPAÑOL

Nombre	Página	Lat.°′	Long.°′ W = Oeste
Todtmoos Au	58	47.42 N	7.58 E
Todtnau	58	47.50 N	7.56 E
Toe Head >	46	57.50 N	7.08 W
Tōei	94	35.04 N	137.41 E
T'oejo	98	39.54 N	127.46 E
Toéssé	150	11.50 N	1.16 W
Toetoes Bay ⊂	172	46.38 S	168.43 E
Tofield	182	53.22 N	112.40 W
Tofino	182	49.09 N	125.54 W
Töfsingdalens Nationalpark ♠	26	62.09 N	12.30 E
Tofte	26	59.33 N	10.34 E
Toften ⊜	40	59.03 N	14.36 E
Tofterup	41	55.39 N	8.50 E
Toftlund	41	55.11 N	9.04 E
Toga	94	36.27 N	137.02 E
Toga I	175f	13.26 S	166.42 E
Togakushi	94	36.44 N	138.05 E
Togakushi-yama ʌ	94	36.46 N	138.04 E
Toganas	80	50.49 N	52.02 E
Tōgane	94	35.33 N	140.22 E
Togauchi	96	34.34 N	132.13 E
Togdheer □[4]	144	9.00 N	46.00 E
Toggenburg V	58	47.15 N	9.10 E
Togho	152	6.01 N	17.26 E
Togi	94	37.08 N	136.44 E
Togiak	180	59.04 N	160.24 W
Togiak Bay ⊂	180	59.00 N	160.30 W
Togian, Kepulauan II	112	0.20 S	122.00 E
Togian, Pulau I	112	0.22 S	121.56 E
Töging am Inn	60	48.15 N	12.35 E
Togliatti → Toljatti	80	53.31 N	49.26 E
Togni	140	18.04 N	35.13 E
Tōgō, Nihon	94	35.05 N	137.03 E
Tōgō, Nihon	96	35.28 N	133.53 E
Togo □[1], Afr.	134	8.00 N	1.10 E
Togo □[1], Afr.	150	8.00 N	1.10 E
Togochale	144	9.33 N	43.18 E
Tōgō-ike ⊜	96	35.28 N	133.54 E
Togoron	116	12.35 N	123.37 E
Tögrög, Mong.	102	45.46 N	94.48 E
Tögrög, Mong.	102	45.32 N	102.59 E
Togtoh	102	40.22 N	111.11 E
Togučin	86	55.16 N	84.23 E
Togur	86	58.24 N	82.49 E
Togura	94	36.29 N	138.09 E
Toguzak ≃	86	54.06 N	62.50 E
Toguzbulak	85	42.06 N	76.44 E
Togwotee Pass)(	202	43.45 N	110.04 W
Tŏgyu-san ʌ	98	35.46 N	127.40 E
Tŏgyu-san Kukrip Kongwŏn ♠	98	35.52 N	127.45 E
Togyz	86	47.34 N	60.33 E
Tōhaku	96	35.30 N	133.40 E
Tohakum Peak ʌ	204	40.11 N	119.27 W
Tohāna	124	29.42 N	75.54 E
Tohiea, Mont ʌ	174s	17.33 S	149.49 W
Tohma ≃	130	38.31 N	38.25 E
Toholampi	26	63.46 N	24.15 E
Tohopekaliga, Lake ⊜	220	28.12 N	81.23 W
Tohor, Tanjong >	114	1.51 N	102.42 E
T'ohyŏn-ni	98	39.53 N	124.52 E
Toi, Nihon	94	34.54 N	138.47 E
Toi, Niue	174v	18.57 S	169.51 W
Toijala	26	61.10 N	23.52 E
Toili	112	1.27 S	122.24 E
Toi-misaki >	92	31.20 N	131.22 E
Tōin	94	35.05 N	136.35 E
Toinya	140	6.17 N	29.44 E
Toi Sar	120	31.06 N	69.54 E
Toiyabe Range ⋀	204	39.10 N	117.10 W
Tojg	128	32.04 N	61.48 E
To-jima I	96	33.12 N	132.22 E
Tojo, Indon.	112	1.17 S	121.11 E
Tōjō, Nihon	96	34.53 N	133.16 E
Tōjō, Nihon	270	34.55 N	135.04 E
Tojtepa	85	41.03 N	69.22 E
Tōju-in ɤ[1]	94	35.19 N	136.04 E
Tok	180	63.19 N	142.59 W
Tok ≃	80	52.46 N	52.22 E
Tokaanu	172	38.58 S	175.46 E
Tokachi ≃	92a	42.44 N	143.42 E
Tokachi-dake ʌ	92a	43.25 N	142.41 E
Tokachi-heiya ≚	92a	43.00 N	143.30 E
Tōkagi	268	35.42 N	139.56 E
Tokai, Malay.	114	6.01 N	100.24 E
Tōkai, Nihon	94	36.27 N	140.34 E
Tōkai, Nihon	94	35.00 N	136.53 E
Tokaj ≃	78	51.18 N	41.04 E
Tokala	112	1.47 S	121.43 E
Tōkamachi	94	37.08 N	138.46 E
Tokanui	172	46.34 S	168.56 E
Tokara-kaikyō ⊔	93b	30.10 N	130.10 E
Tokara-rettō II	93b	29.36 N	129.43 E
Tokarevka	86	50.08 N	73.12 E
Tokar Game Reserve ➤[4]	140	18.15 N	37.45 E
Tokar'ovka	80	51.59 N	41.09 E
Tokar'ovo, Ross.	76	55.17 N	35.04 E
Tokar'ovo, Ross.	265b	55.38 N	37.55 E
Tokashiki-jima I	93b	26.11 N	127.21 E
Tokat	130	40.19 N	36.34 E
Tokat □[4]	130	40.25 N	36.30 E
Tŏkchŏk-kundo II	98	37.14 N	126.07 E
Tŏkch'ŏn	98	39.46 N	126.19 E
Tokeland	224	46.42 N	123.58 W
Tokelau □[2]	14	9.00 S	171.45 W
Tokelau-Inseln → Tokelau □[2]	14	9.00 S	171.45 W
Tokeneke Brook ≃	276	41.03 N	73.28 W
Tŏkhŭng-ni	98	40.02 N	127.08 E
Toki	94	35.21 N	137.11 E
Toki ≃	94	35.12 N	136.52 E
Tokio → Tōkyō	94	35.42 N	139.46 E
Toki Point >	174a	19.19 N	166.35 E
Tokiwadaira	268	35.48 N	139.57 E
Tokke ⊜	26	59.01 N	9.15 E
Tokko	74	59.59 N	119.52 E
Tokko ≃	88	58.42 N	119.50 E
Toklar	130	38.26 N	36.01 E
Toklat ≃	180	64.27 N	150.17 W
Tokma	88	58.13 N	105.42 E
Tokmak, Kyrg.	85	42.55 N	75.18 E
Tokmak, Ukr.	78	47.15 N	35.43 E
Toko	172	39.20 S	174.24 E
Tököl	264c	47.19 N	18.58 E
Tokolimbu	112	2.48 S	121.34 E
Tokomaru	172	40.28 S	175.30 E
Tokomaru Bay	172	38.08 S	178.18 E
Tokoname	94	34.53 N	136.51 E
Toko Range ⋀	166	23.05 S	138.20 E
Tokoro ≃	92a	44.07 N	144.05 E
Tokoroa	172	38.14 S	175.52 E
Tokorozawa	94	35.47 N	139.28 E
Tokovskoje	78	47.38 N	33.59 E
Tokrau ≃	86	46.48 N	75.24 E
Toksook Bay	180	60.32 N	165.06 W
Toksovo	76	60.09 N	30.31 E
Tok-to (Take-shima) II	92	37.17 N	131.53 E
Toktogul	85	41.50 N	72.50 E
Toktogul'skoje vodochranilišče ⊜[1]	85	41.50 N	72.55 E
Toku Island I	14	18.10 S	174.11 W
Tokuji	96	34.11 N	131.40 E
Tokul Creek ≃	224	47.35 N	121.50 W
Tokung	112	0.18 S	114.28 E
Tokuno-shima I	93b	27.45 N	128.58 E
Tokur	89	53.10 N	132.53 E
Tokura	270	34.58 N	135.18 E
Tokura-tōge)(	96	35.17 N	134.31 E
Tokusaga-mine ʌ	96	34.26 N	131.41 E
Tokushima	96	34.04 N	134.34 E
Tokushima □[5]	96	33.45 N	134.00 E
Tokuyama, Nihon	94	35.42 N	136.29 E
Tokuyama, Nihon	96	34.03 N	131.49 E
Tokwe ≃	154	21.09 S	31.30 E
Tōkyō, Nihon	94	35.42 N	139.46 E
Tōkyō, Nihon	268	35.42 N	139.46 E

FRANÇAIS

Nom	Page	Lat.°′	Long.°′ W = Ouest
Tōkyō □[5]	94	35.45 N	139.30 E
Tokyo Bay → Tōkyō-wan ⊂	94	35.25 N	139.47 E
Tōkyō-daigaku-uchūkūkan-kenkyūsho ɤ[3]	92	31.17 N	131.05 E
Tokyo Disneyland ♠	268	35.37 N	139.53 E
Tōkyō-kō ⊂	268	35.37 N	139.47 E
Tōkyō-kokusai-kūkō ⊠	94	35.45 N	140.21 E
Tokyo Station ➤[5]	268	35.41 N	139.46 E
Tokyo Tower ɤ	268	35.39 N	139.45 E
Tokyo University ɤ[2]	268	35.42 N	139.46 E
Tokyo University of Education ɤ[2]	268	35.43 N	139.44 E
Tōkyō-wan (Tokyo Bay) ⊂	94	35.25 N	139.47 E
Tokzār	120	35.52 N	66.26 E
Tol I	175c	7.22 N	151.37 E
Tolaga Bay	172	38.22 S	178.18 E
Tolala	112	2.56 S	121.06 E
Tolang	114	1.56 N	99.26 E
Tolbert	52	53.10 N	6.21 E
Tolbo Nuur	86	48.25 N	90.17 E
Tolbuchino	80	57.51 N	40.03 E
Tolderol Point >	168b	35.22 S	139.10 E
Toldo, Pico del ʌ	240p	20.30 N	74.54 W
Tole, Kaz.	85	42.40 N	70.08 E
Tolé, Pan.	236	8.14 N	81.41 W
Toledo, Bol.	248	18.10 S	67.25 W
Toledo, Bra.	252	24.44 S	53.45 W
Toledo, Bra.	256	22.44 S	46.23 W
Toledo, Col.	246	7.19 N	72.28 W
Toledo, Esp.	34	39.52 N	4.01 W
Toledo, Pil.	116	10.23 N	123.38 E
Toledo, Il., U.S.	194	39.16 N	88.14 W
Toledo, Ia., U.S.	190	41.59 N	92.34 W
Toledo, Oh., U.S.	214	41.39 N	83.33 W
Toledo, Or., U.S.	202	44.37 N	123.56 W
Toledo, Wa., U.S.	224	46.26 N	122.50 W
Toledo, Ur.	258	34.45 S	56.05 W
Toledo □[4]	34	39.45 N	4.00 W
Toledo □[5]	236	16.20 N	88.55 W
Toledo, Montes de ⋀	34	39.33 N	4.20 W
Toledo Bend Reservoir ⊜[1]	194	31.30 N	93.45 W
Toledo Express Airport ⊠	216	41.35 N	83.49 W
Tolentino	66	43.12 N	13.17 E
Tolfa	66	42.09 N	11.56 E
Tolfa, Monti della ⋀	66	42.08 N	11.54 E
Tolga, Alg.	148	34.46 N	5.22 E
Tolga, Nor.	26	62.25 N	11.00 E
Toli	86	45.57 N	83.37 E
Toliara	157b	23.21 S	43.40 E
Toliara □[4]	157b	24.00 S	45.00 E
Tolima □[5]	246	3.45 N	75.15 W
Tolima, Nevado del ʌ	246	4.40 N	75.19 W
Tolimán, Méx.	234	19.36 N	103.55 W
Tolimán, Méx.	234	20.55 N	99.56 W
Tolitoli	112	1.02 N	120.49 E
Toljatti (Togliatti)	80	53.31 N	49.26 E
Tol'ka	74	64.02 N	81.55 E
Tolkmicko	30	54.20 N	19.31 E
Tolland	207	41.52 N	72.22 W
Tolland □[6]	207	41.52 N	72.22 W
Tollarp	26	55.56 N	13.59 E
Tollense ≃	54	53.54 N	13.02 E
Tollensesee ⊜	54	53.30 N	13.11 E
Tollesboro	218	38.33 N	83.34 W
Tollesbury	42	51.46 N	0.50 E
Tolleson	200	33.27 N	112.15 W
Tollhouse	226	37.01 N	119.23 W
Tolloche	252	25.30 S	63.32 W
Tølløse	41	55.37 N	11.45 E
Tollygunge ➤[8]	272b	22.30 N	88.21 E
Tolmači	76	57.26 N	35.41 E
Tolmačovo	76	58.52 N	29.55 E
Tolmezzo	64	46.24 N	13.01 E
Tolmin	36	46.11 N	13.44 E
Tolna	30	46.26 N	18.46 E
Tolna □[6]	30	46.30 N	18.35 E
Tolo	152	2.56 S	18.34 E
Tolo, Teluk ⊂	112	2.00 S	122.30 E
Toloa, Houma >	174w	21.17 S	175.08 W
Toločin	76	54.25 N	29.42 E
Tolokiwa Island I	164	5.20 S	147.40 E
Tolomo	89	50.03 N	137.45 E
Tolong Bay ⊂	116	9.20 N	122.49 E
Tolongoina	157b	21.33 S	47.31 E
Tolono	194	39.59 N	88.15 W
Tolosa	34	43.08 N	2.04 W
Tolosa, Aeródromo ⊠	288	34.53 S	57.58 W
Tolovana ≃	180	64.51 N	149.45 W
Tolpuddle	42	50.45 N	2.18 W
Tolsan-do I	98	34.38 N	127.45 E
Tol'skij Majdan	80	54.57 N	44.39 E
Tolsta Head >	46	58.20 N	6.10 W
Tolstoj, mys >	74	59.10 N	155.12 E
Tolstoje	78	48.50 N	25.44 E
Tolstopal'cevo	265b	55.38 N	37.13 E
Tolt, North Fork ≃	224	47.42 N	121.49 W
Toltén	254	39.13 S	73.14 W
Tolten ≃	254	39.15 S	73.14 W
Tolti	123	35.02 N	76.06 E
Toltry ⋀[1]	78	49.00 N	26.10 E
Tolt-Seattle Water Supply Reservoir ⊜[1]	224	47.42 N	121.39 W
Tolú	246	9.31 N	75.35 W
Toluca	216	41.00 N	89.08 W
Toluca, Nevado de ʌ[1]	234	19.08 N	99.44 W
Toluca [de Lerdo]	234	19.17 N	99.40 W
Tolvajarvi	24	62.17 N	31.27 E
Tolvdalselva ≃	26	58.10 N	8.00 E
Tolve	68	40.42 N	16.01 E
Tolwa	140	6.38 N	32.37 E
Tolworth ➤[8]	260	51.23 N	0.17 W
Tolyatti → Toljatti	80	53.31 N	49.26 E
Tolybaj	86	50.31 N	62.19 E
Tom' ≃, Ross.	86	56.50 N	84.27 E
Tom' ≃, Ross.	89	51.00 N	127.54 E
Toma	150	12.46 N	2.53 W
Tomago	170	32.50 S	151.44 E
Tomah	190	43.58 N	90.30 W
Tomahawk	190	45.28 N	89.43 W
Tomakomai	92a	42.38 N	141.36 E
Tomakovka	78	47.48 N	34.44 E
Tomani	112	4.50 N	115.55 E
Tomanivi ʌ	175g	17.37 S	178.01 E
Tomar, Kaz.	86	46.24 N	75.03 E
Tomar, Port.	34	39.36 N	8.25 W
Tomari	89	47.47 N	142.03 E
Tomarovka	78	50.41 N	36.14 E
Tomarza	130	38.27 N	35.49 E
Tomás Barrón (Eucaliptus)	248	17.35 S	67.31 W
Tomasboda ʌ[2]	40	59.24 N	14.58 E
Tomás Gomensoro	252	30.26 S	57.26 W
Tomašgorod	78	51.19 N	27.02 E
Tomasine ≃	190	46.40 N	76.16 W
Tomás Jofré	258	34.43 S	59.19 W
Tomášov	61	48.09 N	17.16 E
Tomašpol'	78	48.33 N	28.31 E
Tomaszów Lubelski	30	50.28 N	23.25 E
Tomaszów Mazowiecki	30	51.32 N	20.01 E
Tomatin	46	57.20 N	3.59 W
Tomatlán	234	19.56 N	105.15 W
Tomatlán ≃	234	19.50 N	105.23 W
Tomave	248	20.06 S	66.35 W
Tomazina	255	23.46 S	49.58 W
Tomba di Nerone ➤[8]	267a	41.57 N	12.27 E
Tombadonkéa	150	11.00 N	14.23 W
Tombador, Serra do ⋀[1]	248	12.00 S	57.40 W
Tomball	222	30.06 N	95.37 W
Tombe	140	5.49 N	31.41 E

PORTUGUÊS

Nome	Página	Lat.°′	Long.°′ W = Oeste
Tombigbee ≃	194	31.04 N	87.58 W
Tombo, Punta >	254	44.03 S	65.11 W
Tombôco	152	6.48 S	13.18 E
Tombolo	64	45.38 N	11.50 E
Tombos	255	20.55 S	42.02 W
Tombouctou (Timbuktu)	150	16.46 N	3.01 W
Tombouctou □[4]	150	18.20 N	3.50 W
Tombs of the Caliphs ⊥	273c	30.03 N	31.17 E
Tombstone	200	31.42 N	110.04 W
Tombstone Mountain ʌ	180	64.25 N	138.30 W
Tombua	152	15.49 S	11.53 E
Tom Burke	156	23.05 S	28.00 E
Tomdoun	46	57.04 N	5.03 W
Tomé	252	36.37 S	72.57 W
Tomea, Pulau I	112	5.45 S	123.56 E
Tomé-Açu	250	2.25 S	48.09 W
Tömek	130	38.02 N	32.41 E
Tomelilla	26	55.33 N	13.57 E
Tomelloso	34	39.10 N	3.01 W
Tomerong	170	35.04 S	150.35 E
Tomhannock Reservoir ⊜[1]	210	42.51 N	73.33 W
Tomi ≃	152	5.07 N	19.19 E
Tomich	46	57.18 N	4.48 W
Tomichi Creek ≃	200	38.31 N	106.58 W
Tomifobia ≃	206	45.11 N	72.02 W
Tomiko Lake ⊜	190	46.32 N	79.49 W
Tomilino	265b	55.39 N	37.57 E
Tomini	112	0.30 N	120.32 E
Tomini, Teluk ⊂	112	0.20 S	121.00 E
Tominian	150	13.17 N	4.35 W
Tomintoul	46	57.14 N	3.22 W
Tomio ≃	270	34.35 N	135.44 E
Tomioka	94	36.15 N	138.54 E
Tomisato	94	35.44 N	140.19 E
Tomiura	94	35.03 N	139.50 E
Tomiyama, Nihon	94	35.11 N	137.48 E
Tomiyama, Nihon	94	35.05 N	139.51 E
Tomizawa	94	35.14 N	138.29 E
T'omkino	76	55.05 N	35.01 E
Tomkins Cove	210	41.15 N	73.59 W
Tomkinson Ranges ⋀	162	26.11 S	129.05 E
Tomkinsville	208	38.19 N	76.53 W
Tomlinson Run State Park ♠	214	40.33 N	80.34 W
Tommerup Stationsby	41	55.19 N	10.13 E
Tommot	74	58.58 N	126.19 E
Tomnavoulin	46	57.18 N	3.19 W
T'omnyj	88	53.24 N	118.31 E
Tomo ≃	246	5.20 N	67.48 W
Tomobe	94	36.20 N	140.20 E
Tomogashima-suidō ⊔	96	34.17 N	135.00 E
Tomohon	112	1.19 N	124.49 E
Tömör Bulag	88	49.16 N	100.15 E
Tomori	174m	26.08 N	127.44 E
Tomori, Teluk ⊂	112	1.58 S	121.28 E
Tompa	88	55.08 N	109.47 E
Tompkins, Nf., Can.	186	47.48 N	59.13 W
Tompkins, Sk., Can.	184	50.04 N	108.47 W
Tompkins □[6]	210	42.27 N	76.30 W
Tompkins County Airport ⊠	210	42.29 N	76.57 W
Tompkinsville	194	36.42 N	85.41 W
Tompo	112	0.56 N	120.20 E
Tom Price	162	22.41 S	117.43 E
Tom Price, Mount ʌ	162	22.39 S	117.40 E
Tomptokan	74	57.06 N	133.59 E
Tomra	26	62.35 N	6.56 E
Toms ≃	208	39.57 N	74.07 W
Toms, Ridgeway Branch ≃	208	40.00 N	74.14 W
Toms Cove ⊂	208	37.53 N	75.22 W
Toms Creek ≃	208	39.38 N	77.17 W
Tomsk	86	56.30 N	84.58 E
Toms River	208	39.58 N	74.12 W
Tom Steed Reservoir ⊜[1]	196	34.45 N	99.00 W
Tomtabacken ʌ[2]	26	57.30 N	14.28 E
Tömük	130	36.41 N	34.22 E
Tomuzlovka ≃	84	44.46 N	44.10 E
Ton	64	46.15 N	11.04 E
Tonadico	64	46.11 N	11.50 E
Tonaki-shima I	93b	26.21 N	127.09 E
Tonalá, Méx.	234	16.04 N	93.45 W
Tonalá, Méx.	234	20.37 N	103.14 W
Tonalá ≃	234	18.13 N	94.11 W
Tonale, Passo del)(	64	46.16 N	10.35 E
Tonami	94	36.38 N	136.54 E
Tonantins	246	2.47 S	67.47 W
Tonantins ≃	246	2.47 S	67.47 W
Tonara	71	40.02 N	9.10 E
Tonasket	202	48.42 N	119.26 W
Tonate	250	4.55 N	52.22 W
Tonatico	234	18.47 N	99.41 W
Tonawanda	210	43.01 N	78.52 W
Tonawanda Channel ≃[1]	284a	43.04 N	79.00 W
Tonawanda Creek ≃	210	43.02 N	78.53 W
Tonawanda Indian Reservation ➤[4]	210	43.05 N	78.27 W
Tonawanda Island I	284a	43.02 N	78.53 W
Tonbara	96	35.05 N	132.47 E
Tonbo	110	18.31 N	95.05 E
Tonbridge	42	51.12 N	0.16 E
Tonbridge and Malling □[8]	260	51.16 N	0.20 E
Tonda	270	34.50 N	135.36 E
Tonda ≃	96	33.38 N	135.24 E
Tondabayashi	96	34.30 N	135.36 E
Tondano	112	1.19 N	124.54 E
Tønder	41	54.56 N	8.54 E
Tondhre	272c	19.05 N	73.08 E
Tondi	122	9.44 N	79.01 E
Tondibi	150	16.39 N	0.14 W
Tondidji	150	13.06 N	10.20 W
Tondi Kiwindi	150	14.28 N	2.02 E
Tondoro	156	17.45 S	18.50 E
Tone, Nihon	94	36.42 N	139.13 E
Tone, Nihon	94	35.51 N	140.09 E
Tone ≃	94	35.44 N	140.51 E
Tonekābon	128	36.49 N	50.53 E
Tone-unga ≍	268	35.54 N	139.53 E
Tonež	78	51.49 N	27.48 E
Tonga, Cam.	152	4.58 N	10.42 E
Tonga, Sūd.	140	9.28 N	31.03 E
Tonga □[1]	14	20.00 S	175.00 W
Tongaat	158	29.37 S	31.03 E
Tonga Islands II	14	20.00 S	175.00 W
Tong'an	100	24.46 N	118.08 E
Tonganoxie	198	39.06 N	95.05 W
Tong'anqiao	106	31.22 N	120.27 E
Tonga Ridge ✢[3]	14	21.00 S	175.00 W
Tongariro, Mount ʌ	172	39.08 S	175.38 E
Tongariro National Park ♠	172	39.15 S	175.30 E
Tongas	115a	7.44 S	113.06 E
Tongatapu □[8]	174w	21.10 S	175.10 W
Tongatapu I	174w	21.10 S	175.10 W
Tongatapu Group II	14	21.10 S	175.10 W
Tonga Trench ✢[1]	14	20.00 S	173.00 W
Tongbai, Zhg.	100	32.22 N	113.24 E
Tongbai, Zhg.	105	39.35 N	116.44 E
Tongbai Shan ʌ	100	32.20 N	113.14 E
Tongbai Shan ⋀	100	32.20 N	113.15 E
Tongbei	89	47.45 N	126.46 E
Tongcheng, Zhg.	100	29.11 N	113.49 E
Tongcheng, Zhg.	100	31.03 N	116.58 E
Tongcheng, Zhg.	100	32.53 N	118.58 E
Tongchengzha	100	31.30 N	118.07 E
Tongchengzhuang	105	39.22 N	117.36 E
T'ongch'ŏn	98	38.54 N	127.54 E
Tongchuan	102	35.01 N	109.01 E
Tongdao	102	26.23 N	109.23 E
Tongde	102	35.17 N	100.42 E
Tongerbao	104	41.26 N	123.02 E
Tongeren	56	50.47 N	5.28 E
Tongerlo	56	51.07 N	4.54 E
Tonggou	98	41.53 N	125.46 E
Tonggu, Zhg.	100	28.33 N	114.21 E
Tonggu, Zhg.	100	21.53 N	112.55 E
Tongguan, Zhg.	100	28.29 N	112.48 E
Tongguan, Zhg.	102	34.38 N	110.20 E
Tongguan, Zhg.	102	23.18 N	101.23 E
Tongguanyi	107	29.20 N	106.23 E
Tonghai	102	24.07 N	102.49 E
Tonghaikou	100	30.14 N	113.08 E
Tonghe, Zhg.	89	45.59 N	128.45 E
Tonghe, Zhg.	100	32.56 N	112.45 E
Tongho-ri	98	35.49 N	127.54 E
Tonghua, Zhg.	98	41.41 N	125.55 E
Tonghua (Kuaidamao), Zhg.	98	41.40 N	125.44 E
Tonghui ≃	271a	39.53 N	116.41 E
Tongi	126	23.53 N	90.24 E
Tong Island I	164	2.05 S	147.50 E
Tongjiang, Zhg.	89	47.40 N	132.30 E
Tongjiang, Zhg.	102	31.58 N	107.14 E
Tongjiangchang	107	29.37 N	103.43 E
Tongjiangkou	104	42.37 N	123.41 E
Tongjing	100	31.47 N	118.33 E
Tongjosŏn-man ⊂	98	39.30 N	128.00 E
Tongjuzhen	98	38.36 N	117.11 E
Tongken ≃	89	46.31 N	126.22 E
Tongli	106	31.10 N	120.43 E
Tongliang	107	29.51 N	106.03 E
Tongliao	89	43.39 N	122.14 E
Tongling, Zhg.	100	30.53 N	117.46 E
Tongling, Zhg.	102	23.28 N	109.40 E
Tonglu	100	29.48 N	119.40 E
Tonglü Yunhe ≍	106	32.04 N	121.40 E
Tongmang-ni	98	37.37 N	126.26 E
Tongmu, Zhg.	100	27.57 N	113.55 E
Tongmu, Zhg.	102	24.09 N	110.04 E
Tongnae	98	35.12 N	129.05 E
Tongnan	107	30.11 N	105.48 E
Tongno-gang ≃	98	40.58 N	126.04 E
Tongo	166	30.30 S	143.45 E
Tongoa I	175f	16.54 S	168.34 E
Tongobory	157b	23.32 S	44.20 E
Tongololo Creek ≃	162	22.06 S	121.08 E
Tongoy	252	30.15 S	71.30 W
Tongqin	100	28.52 N	119.56 E
Tongquansi	107	30.23 N	104.50 E
Tongquil Island I	116	6.02 N	121.51 E
Tongren, Zhg.	102	27.38 N	109.03 E
Tongren, Zhg.	102	35.32 N	101.54 E
Tongrengchang	107	30.02 N	106.42 E
Tongsa ≃	124	26.52 N	90.57 E
Tongsa Dzong	124	27.31 N	90.30 E
Tongsan-ni	271b	37.38 N	126.53 E
Tongshan	100	29.38 N	114.29 E
Tongshi	98	35.26 N	117.43 E
Tongshuping	100	27.17 N	114.54 E
Tongta	110	21.20 N	99.16 E
Tongtai	100	32.38 N	120.47 E
Tongtan	107	28.56 N	105.17 E
Tongtian ≃	102	33.25 N	96.32 E
Tongue	46	58.28 N	4.25 W
Tongue ≃, U.S.	202	46.24 N	105.52 W
Tongue ≃, N.D., U.S.	198	48.56 N	97.18 W
Tongue ≃, Tx., U.S.	196	34.07 N	100.25 W
Tongue, Kyle of ⊂	46	58.30 N	4.26 W
Tongue of the Ocean ✢[1]	238	24.30 N	77.30 W
Tongue River Reservoir ⊜[1]	202	45.06 N	106.47 W
Tongwei	102	35.07 N	105.27 E
Tongxi	107	29.59 N	106.08 E
Tongxian	105	39.55 N	116.39 E
Tongxianchang	107	30.14 N	105.24 E
Tongxiang	106	30.38 N	120.32 E
Tongxin	102	37.02 N	106.09 E
Tongxinchang	107	29.42 N	106.26 E
Tongxing	107	30.35 N	106.12 E
Tongxu	98	34.29 N	114.28 E
Tongyang-ni	98	39.08 N	126.52 E
Tongyang Yunhe ≍	106	32.02 N	120.48 E
Tongyu	89	44.48 N	123.05 E
Tongyuan, Zhg.	100	28.04 N	116.08 E
Tongyuan, Zhg.	106	30.28 N	120.52 E
Tongyuanpu	104	40.49 N	123.54 E
Tongzhaipu	100	32.48 N	112.44 E
Tongzi	102	28.08 N	106.49 E
Tongzidixia	104	41.08 N	120.34 E
Tonica	216	41.12 N	89.04 W
Tonila	234	19.26 N	103.31 W
Tönisberg	263	51.25 N	6.30 E
Tönisheide	263	51.19 N	7.03 E
Tönisvorst	56	51.19 N	6.29 E
Tonj	140	7.17 N	28.45 E
Tonk	120	26.10 N	75.47 E
Tonkawa	196	36.40 N	97.18 W
Tonkin, Gulf of ⊂	110	20.00 N	108.00 E
Tonkin → Bac Phan □[9]	110	22.00 N	105.00 E
Tonkino	80	57.23 N	46.28 E
Tonkou, Mont ʌ	150	7.27 N	7.39 W
Tonkwa	110	23.36 N	96.58 E
Tônlé Sab, Bœng ⊜	110	13.00 N	104.00 E
Tonle Sap → Tônlé Sab, Bœng ⊜	110	13.00 N	104.00 E
Tonnay-Boutonne	32	45.58 N	0.42 W
Tonneins	32	44.23 N	0.19 E
Tonner Canyon V	280	33.58 N	117.48 W
Tonnerre	50	47.51 N	3.58 E
Tönnet	40	60.14 N	13.30 E
Tönning	41	54.19 N	8.56 E
Tōno	92	39.19 N	141.32 E
Tonogaya	268	35.46 N	139.22 E
Tonopah	204	38.04 N	117.13 W
Tōnoshō, Nihon	94	35.49 N	140.42 E
Tonoshō, Nihon	96	34.29 N	134.11 E
Tonosí	246	7.24 N	80.27 W
Tonota	156	21.29 S	27.29 E
Tonquish Creek ≃	281	42.21 N	83.22 W
Tons ≃	124	25.17 N	82.04 E
Tonšajevo	80	57.44 N	47.00 E
Tønsberg	26	59.17 N	10.25 E
Tönsholt	263	51.38 N	6.58 E
Tonstad	26	58.40 N	6.43 E
Tonto Creek ≃	200	33.46 N	111.15 W
Tontogany	216	41.25 N	83.44 W
Tonto National Monument ♠	200	33.34 N	111.02 W
Tonya	130	40.53 N	39.16 E
Tonypandy	42	51.38 N	3.27 W
Tonyrefail	42	51.36 N	3.25 W
Toobeah	166	28.25 S	149.52 E
Toodyay	168a	31.33 S	116.28 E
Tooele	200	40.31 N	112.17 W
Toogoolawah	171a	27.06 S	152.23 E
Tool	222	32.16 N	96.10 W
Toolik ≃	180	69.55 N	149.30 W
Tooma	171b	35.58 S	148.03 E
Tooma ≃	171b	36.04 S	148.00 E
Tooma Reservoir ⊜[1]	171b	36.04 S	148.16 E
Toomebridge	48	54.45 N	6.27 W
Toompine	166	27.13 S	144.22 E
Toomsboro	192	32.49 N	83.04 W
Toomyvara	48	52.50 N	8.02 W
Toongabbie	274a	33.47 S	150.57 E
Toora	169	38.40 S	146.20 E
Toora-Chem	88	52.28 N	96.17 E
Toorak	274b	37.51 S	145.01 E
Toormakeady	48	53.39 N	9.24 W
Toosey Indian Reserve ➤[4]	182	51.56 N	122.29 W
Toot Hill	260	51.42 N	0.12 E
Tootias	144	3.57 N	43.57 E
Tootie, Mount ʌ	170	33.28 S	150.30 E
Tootsi	76	58.34 N	24.47 E
Toowoomba	171a	27.33 S	151.57 E
Topanga	228	34.06 N	118.36 W
Topanga Canyon V	280	34.05 N	118.36 W
Topanga State Park ♠	280	34.06 N	118.33 W
Topar	86	49.32 N	72.50 E
Topawa	200	31.48 N	111.49 W
Topaz Lake ⊜	226	38.41 N	119.32 W
Topçam	130	40.38 N	37.48 E
Topchānchi	126	23.54 N	86.12 E
Töpchin	54	52.10 N	13.34 E
Topčicha	86	52.49 N	83.10 E
Topeka, In., U.S.	216	41.32 N	85.32 W
Topeka, Ks., U.S.	198	39.02 N	95.40 W
Töpen	54	50.23 N	11.52 E
Topia	232	25.13 N	106.34 W
Topilejo ➤[8]	286a	19.12 N	99.09 W
Topino ≃	66	43.02 N	12.30 E
Topkanovo	82	54.43 N	38.29 E
Topkapı ➤[8]	267b	41.02 N	28.54 E
Topkapi Palace ⊥	267b	41.00 N	28.59 E
Topki	86	55.16 N	85.36 E
Topko, gora ʌ	74	57.08 N	137.24 E
Topl'a ≃	30	48.45 N	21.45 E
Topley	182	54.30 N	126.18 W
Toplica ≃	38	43.13 N	21.49 E
Toplița	38	46.55 N	25.21 E
T'oploje, Ross.	76	53.13 N	38.53 E
T'oploje, Ross.	76	53.37 N	37.36 E
T'oploje ≃	83	48.47 N	39.19 E
T'oplyj Stan	80	53.58 N	50.10 E
T'oplyj Stan ➤[8]	265b	55.37 N	37.30 E
Topo ≃	286c	10.33 N	67.00 W
Topocalma, Punta >	252	34.08 S	72.01 W
Top of Hebers	262	53.34 N	2.12 W
Topo Infiernito ʌ	286c	10.33 N	66.55 W
Topol'čany	30	48.34 N	18.10 E
Topoli	80	47.59 N	51.36 E
Topolobampo	232	25.36 N	109.03 W
Topolog	38	44.53 N	28.22 E
Topolovățu Mare	38	45.46 N	21.37 E
Topolovgrad	38	42.05 N	26.20 E
Toporok	76	58.33 N	33.28 E
Topozero, ozero ⊜	24	65.40 N	32.00 E
Toppenish	202	46.22 N	120.18 W
Toppenish Creek ≃	202	46.20 N	120.11 W
Toppenish Ridge ʌ	224	46.18 N	120.40 W
Toppings	262	53.37 N	2.25 W
Toprakkale	130	37.06 N	36.07 E
Tops, Mount ʌ	162	21.50 S	134.00 E
Topsa	24	62.39 N	43.34 E
Topsfield	207	42.38 N	70.57 W
Topsham, Eng., U.K.	42	50.41 N	3.27 W
Topsham, Me., U.S.	188	43.55 N	69.58 W
Top Springs	164	16.38 S	131.50 E
Topton	208	40.30 N	75.42 W
Toquima Range ⋀	204	38.45 N	116.55 W
Toquop Wash V	204	36.45 N	114.11 W
Tor	144	7.51 N	33.35 E
Torahime	94	35.25 N	136.16 E
Torano Castello	68	39.30 N	16.08 E
Torawitan, Tanjung >	112	1.46 N	124.58 E
Toraya	248	14.03 S	73.18 W
Torbalı	130	38.10 N	27.21 E
Torbat-e Ḩeydarīyeh	128	35.16 N	59.13 E
Torbat-e Jām	128	35.14 N	60.36 E
Torbay	186	47.40 N	52.44 W
Torbay □[9]	42	50.26 N	3.34 W
Tor Bay ⊂	42	50.25 N	3.30 W
Torbejevo, Ross.	80	54.05 N	43.15 E
Torbejevo, Ross.	82	54.44 N	36.11 E
Torbert, Mount ʌ	180	61.25 N	152.24 W
Torbino	76	58.35 N	32.53 E
Torbole	64	45.52 N	10.52 E
Torbreck, Mount ʌ	169	37.21 S	145.57 E
Torbrook	186	44.55 N	64.59 W
Torch ≃	184	53.50 N	103.05 W
Torchany	80	55.34 N	46.36 E
Torchiarolo	68	40.29 N	18.03 E
Torch Lake ⊜	190	45.00 N	85.19 W
Torčin	78	50.46 N	24.59 E
Torcy	261	48.51 N	2.39 E
Torda → Turda	38	46.34 N	23.47 E
Tordera ≃	34	41.39 N	2.47 E
Tordesillas	34	41.30 N	5.00 W
Tordino ≃	66	42.44 N	13.59 E
Tor di Quinto ➤[8]	267a	41.56 N	12.28 E
Töre	26	65.54 N	22.39 E
Töreboda	40	58.43 N	14.08 E
Torej	88	50.33 N	104.50 E
Torekov	26	56.26 N	12.37 E
Toreno	34	42.42 N	6.30 W
Torez	83	48.01 N	38.37 E
Torfou	261	48.32 N	2.14 E
Torgau	54	51.34 N	13.00 E
Torgelow	54	53.37 N	14.00 E
Torgelower See ⊜	54	53.34 N	12.47 E
Torgo	88	58.28 N	119.50 E
Torgun ≃	80	50.15 N	46.18 E
Torhamn	26	56.05 N	15.50 E
Torhout	50	51.04 N	3.06 E
Toribulu	112	0.19 S	120.01 E
Toride	94	35.53 N	140.04 E
Torigakubi-misaki >	94	37.10 N	138.06 E
Torigoe	94	36.21 N	136.36 E
Toriido	270	34.25 N	135.43 E
Torii-tōge)(	94	36.29 N	138.24 E
Toriki	265a	59.47 N	30.07 E
Torino (Turin)	62	45.03 N	7.40 E
Torino □[4]	62	45.08 N	7.22 E
Torino di Sangro Marina	66	42.11 N	14.32 E
Torío ≃	34	42.35 N	5.34 W
Toriparu	255	16.20 S	53.55 W
Torit	154	4.24 N	32.34 E
Toritto	68	41.00 N	16.41 E
Toriya	94	36.59 N	136.54 E
Torjun	115a	7.10 S	113.13 E
Torkestān, Selseleh-ye Band-e ⋀	128	35.25 N	64.15 E
Torkoviči	76	58.52 N	30.20 E
Torlino	86	58.53 N	63.46 E
Torment, Point >	162	17.02 S	123.36 E
Tormentine, Cape >	186	46.07 N	63.47 W
Tormes ≃	34	41.18 N	6.29 W
Tormestorp	41	56.07 N	13.44 E
Tormey	282	38.03 N	122.15 W
Tormini	64	45.36 N	10.29 E
Tormosin	80	48.12 N	42.42 E
Torna	24	68.04 N	44.10 E
Torna ʌ	122	18.16 N	73.37 E
Tornado Mountain ʌ	182	49.58 N	114.39 W
Tornareccio	66	42.02 N	14.24 E
Tornberget ʌ[2]	40	59.08 N	18.01 E
Torne ≃	44	53.36 N	0.44 W
Torneälven (Tornionjoki) ≃	24	65.48 N	24.08 E
Torne Brook ≃	276	41.08 N	74.10 W
Tornesch	52	53.41 N	9.43 E
Torneträsk ⊜	24	68.20 N	19.10 E
Torngat Mountains ⋀	176	59.00 N	64.00 W
Tornillo	200	31.27 N	106.05 W
Tornillo Creek ≃	196	29.11 N	103.00 W
Tornimparte	66	42.17 N	13.18 E
Torning	41	56.17 N	9.20 E
Tornio	26	65.51 N	24.08 E
Tornionjoki (Torneälven) ≃	24	65.48 N	24.08 E
Tornquist	252	38.06 S	62.14 W
T'orny, Ukr.	78	48.09 N	33.33 E
T'orny, Ukr.	78	50.59 N	33.59 E
T'orny, Ukr.	83	49.05 N	37.57 E
Tornyiszentmiklós	61	46.31 N	16.34 E
Toro	34	41.31 N	5.24 W
Torö I	40	58.50 N	17.50 E
Toro, Arroyo ≃	288	34.27 S	58.52 W
Toro, Cañada del ≃	258	35.16 S	59.05 W
Toro, Cerro ʌ	234	19.10 N	104.27 W
Toro, Lago del ⊜	254	51.14 S	72.45 W
Toro, Punta >	252	33.47 S	71.49 W
Torobuku	112	4.25 S	122.26 E
Torodi	150	13.18 N	1.40 E
Toro-iseki ⊥	94	34.57 N	138.24 E
Torok	146	10.03 N	14.33 E
Torokina	175e	6.14 S	155.03 E
Törökszentmiklós	30	47.11 N	20.25 E
Torola ≃	236	13.52 N	88.30 W
Torom	89	54.32 N	135.50 E
Torom ≃	89	54.36 N	135.46 E
Toroni, Nevado ʌ	248	19.43 S	68.41 W
Toronto, Austl.	170	33.01 S	151.36 E
Toronto, On., Can.	212	43.39 N	79.23 W
Toronto, On., Can.	275b	43.39 N	79.23 W
Toronto, Ks., U.S.	198	37.47 N	95.56 W
Toronto, Oh., U.S.	214	40.27 N	80.36 W
Toronto, S.D., U.S.	198	44.34 N	96.38 W
Toronto □[6]	275b	43.44 N	79.24 W
Toronto, Canadian Forces Base ■	212	43.45 N	79.28 W
Toronto, University of ɤ[2]	275b	43.40 N	79.24 W
Toronto Harbour ⊂	275b	43.38 N	79.22 W
Toronto Island Airport ⊠	275b	43.38 N	79.24 W
Toronto Lake ⊜[1]	198	37.46 N	95.57 W
Toronto Reservoir ⊜[1]	210	41.38 N	74.51 W
Toronto Zoo, Metro ♠	275b	43.49 N	79.11 W
Toro Peak ʌ	204	33.32 N	116.25 W
Toropec	76	56.30 N	31.39 E
Toropovo	82	54.21 N	36.07 E
Tororo	154	0.42 N	34.11 E
Toros (Acho), Plaza de ♠	286d	12.02 S	77.02 W
Toros Dağları (Taurus Mountains) ⋀	130	37.00 N	33.00 E
Torošino	76	57.56 N	28.36 E
Torosozero	24	62.30 N	38.10 E
Torotoro	248	18.07 S	65.46 W
Toroume ʌ[2]	174k	21.15 S	159.45 W
Torpa ⊥	26	57.39 N	13.16 E
Torpè	71	40.38 N	9.40 E
Torphins	46	57.06 N	2.37 W
Tor Pignatara ➤[8]	267a	41.52 N	12.32 E
Torpo	26	60.40 N	8.43 E
Torpoint	42	50.22 N	4.11 W
Torpy ≃	182	53.44 N	120.55 W
Torquay, Austl.	169	38.21 S	144.19 E
Torquay, Sk., Can.	184	49.08 N	103.31 W
Torquay, Eng., U.K.	42	50.28 N	3.30 W
Torquemada	34	42.02 N	4.19 W
Torraca	68	40.07 N	15.38 E
Torraccia, Fosso ≃	267a	42.00 N	12.30 E
Torrance, Ca., U.S.	228	33.50 N	118.20 W
Torrance, Pa., U.S.	214	40.25 N	79.14 W
Torrance Lake ⊜	184	57.04 N	98.12 W
Torrance Municipal Airport ⊠	280	33.48 N	118.20 W
Torrão	34	38.18 N	8.13 W
Torre Annunziata	68	40.45 N	14.27 E
Torre Baja	34	40.07 N	1.15 W
Torrebelvicino	64	45.43 N	11.18 E
Torre Beretti	62	45.04 N	8.40 E
Torreblanca	34	40.13 N	0.12 E
Torrebruna	66	41.52 N	14.33 E
Torrecilla ʌ	34	37.36 N	2.31 W
Torrecilla en Cameros	34	42.16 N	2.37 W
Torre del Campo	34	37.46 N	3.53 W
Torre del Greco	68	40.47 N	14.22 E
Torre del Lago Puccini	66	43.50 N	10.17 E
Torre de Moncorvo	34	41.10 N	7.03 W
Torre de'Passeri	66	42.14 N	13.56 E
Torre di Mosto	64	45.41 N	12.43 E
Torre di Santa Maria	64	46.14 N	9.51 E
Torredonjimeno	34	37.46 N	3.57 W
Torre Faro ➤[8]	70	38.16 N	15.39 E
Torre Gaia ➤[8]	267a	41.51 N	12.39 E
Torregrotta	70	38.11 N	15.21 E
Torrejon Air Base ■	266a	40.28 N	3.28 W
Torrejoncillo	34	39.54 N	6.28 W
Torrejón de Ardoz	34	40.27 N	3.29 W
Torrejón-Tajo, Embalse de ⊜[1]	34	39.50 N	5.50 W
Torrelaguna	34	40.50 N	3.32 W
Torrelavega	34	43.21 N	4.03 W
Torrellas, Riera de ≃	266d	41.23 N	2.01 E
Torrelles de Llobregat	266d	41.21 N	1.59 E
Torrelletes	266d	41.21 N	1.57 E
Torremaggiore	68	41.41 N	15.17 E
Torremolinos	34	36.37 N	4.30 W
Torrenieri	66	43.05 N	11.33 E
Torrens ≃	168b	34.56 S	138.30 E
Torrens, Lake ⊜	166	31.00 S	137.50 E
Torrens, Mount ʌ	168b	34.52 S	138.56 E
Torrens Creek	166	20.46 S	145.02 E
Torrens Creek ≃	166	22.22 S	145.09 E
Torrens Island I	168b	34.48 S	138.32 E
Torrent, Arg.	252	28.50 S	56.28 W
Torrent, Esp.	34	39.26 N	0.28 W
Torreões	256	21.52 S	43.33 W
Torreón	232	25.33 N	103.26 W
Torre Orsaia	68	40.08 N	15.28 E
Torre Pedrera	66	44.06 N	12.31 E
Torre Pellice	62	44.49 N	7.13 E
Torreperogil	34	38.02 N	3.17 W
Torres, Arg.	258	34.26 S	59.08 W
Torres, Bra.	252	29.21 S	49.44 W
Torres, Arroyo ≃	288	34.39 S	58.45 W
Torres, Îles II	175f	13.15 S	166.37 E
Torre Santa Susanna	68	40.28 N	17.44 E
Torresdale ➤[8]	285	40.03 N	75.00 W
Torres de Alcalá	34	35.10 N	4.16 W
Torres Martinez Indian Reservation ➤[4]	204	33.35 N	116.02 W
Torres Novas	34	39.29 N	8.32 W
Torres Strait ⊔	164	10.25 S	142.10 E
Torres Vedras	34	39.06 N	9.16 W
Torretta	68	38.08 N	13.14 E
Torrette di Fano	66	43.47 N	13.07 E
Torrevella	34	37.59 N	0.41 W
Torricella	68	40.21 N	17.29 E
Torricella in Sabina	66	42.16 N	12.52 E
Torricella Peligna	66	42.01 N	14.15 E
Torricella Sicura	66	42.39 N	13.39 E
Torricelli Mountains ⋀	164	3.25 S	142.20 E
Torridge ≃	42	51.03 N	4.11 W
Torridon	46	57.33 N	5.31 W
Torridon, Loch ⊂	46	57.35 N	5.46 W
Torriglia	62	44.31 N	9.10 E
Torrijos, Esp.	34	39.59 N	4.17 W
Torrijos, Pil.	116	13.19 N	122.05 E
Torrild	41	55.59 N	10.04 E
Torrimpietra ➤[8]	267a	41.56 N	12.13 E
Torrin	46	57.12 N	6.02 W
Tørring	41	55.51 N	9.29 E
Torrington, Ct., U.S.	207	41.48 N	73.07 W
Torrington, Wy., U.S.	198	42.03 N	104.10 W
Torrinha	255	22.26 S	48.09 W
Torrita di Siena	66	43.10 N	11.46 E
Torröjen ⊜	26	63.55 N	12.56 E
Torrox	34	36.46 N	3.58 W
Torrvarpen ⊜	40	59.42 N	14.30 E
Torsåker	40	60.31 N	16.29 E
Tor Sapienza ➤[8]	267a	41.54 N	12.35 E
Torsås	26	56.24 N	16.00 E
Torsburgen ⊥	26	57.25 N	18.43 E
Torsby	26	60.08 N	13.00 E
Tors Cove	186	47.13 N	52.51 W
Torshälla	40	59.25 N	16.28 E
Tórshavn	22	62.01 N	6.46 W
Torside Reservoir ⊜[1]	262	53.29 N	1.54 W
Torsö	40	58.47 N	13.48 E
Torsö I	40	58.48 N	13.50 E
Torteval	43b	49.27 N	2.38 W
Torto ≃	70	37.58 N	13.46 E
Tortola I	240m	18.27 N	64.36 W
Tórtolas, Cerro de las ʌ	252	29.56 S	69.54 W
Tortolì	71	39.55 N	9.39 E

≃	River	Fluß	Río	Rivière	Rio
≍	Canal	Kanal	Canal	Canal	Canal
⌊	Waterfall, Rapids	Wasserfall, Stromschnellen	Cascada, Rápidos	Chute d'eau, Rapides	Cascata, Rápidos
⊔	Strait	Meeresstraße	Estrecho	Détroit	Estreito
⊂	Bay, Gulf	Bucht, Golf	Bahía, Golfo	Baie, Golfe	Baía, Golfo
⊜	Lake, Lakes	See, Seen	Lago, Lagos	Lac, Lacs	Lago, Lagos
⊞	Swamp	Sumpf	Pantano	Marais	Pântano
⊓	Ice Features, Glacier	Eis- und Gletscherformen	Accidentes Glaciales	Formes glaciaires	Acidentes glaciares
⊤	Other Hydrographic Features	Andere Hydrographische Objekte	Otros Elementos Hidrográficos	Autres données hydrographiques	Outros acidentes hidrográficos

✢	Submarine Features	Untermeerische Objekte	Accidentes Submarinos	Formes de relief sous-marin	Acidentes submarinos
□	Political Unit	Politische Einheit	Unidad Politica	Entité politique	Unidade política
ɤ	Cultural Institution	Kulturelle Institution	Institución Cultural	Institution culturelle	Instituição cultural
⊥	Historical Site	Historische Stätte	Sitio Histórico	Site historique	Sítio histórico
♠	Recreational Site	Erholungs- und Ferienort	Sitio de Recreo	Centre de loisirs	Área de Lazer
⊠	Airport	Flughafen	Aeropuerto	Aéroport	Aeroporto
■	Military Installation	Militäranlage	Instalación Militar	Installation militaire	Instalação militar
➤	Miscellaneous	Verschiedenes	Misceláneo	Divers	Diversos

Name	Page	Lat.°′	Long.°′
Tortona	62	44.54 N	8.52 E
Tortora	68	39.56 N	15.48 E
Tortoreto	66	42.48 N	13.55 E
Tortorici	70	38.02 N	14.49 E
Tortosa	34	40.48 N	0.31 E
Tortosa, Cap de ›	34	40.43 N	0.55 E
Tortue ≃	186	50.18 N	65.23 W
Tortue, Île de la I	238	20.04 N	72.49 W
Tortue, Rivière de la ≃	206	45.24 N	73.32 W
Tortuguero ≃	236	10.34 N	83.31 W
Tortuguero, Laguna ⊂	240m	18.28 N	66.26 W
Tortuguero, Parque Nacional ♦	236	10.25 N	83.55 W
Tortuguitas	288	34.28 S	58.46 W
Tortum	130	40.19 N	41.35 E
Toru ≃	114	1.26 N	98.46 E
Toruajgyr	85	42.32 N	76.26 E
Torue	112	0.58 S	120.18 E
Torugart, pereval)(	85	40.33 N	75.20 E
Torul	130	40.35 N	39.18 E
Toruń	30	53.02 N	18.35 E
Toruń □[4]	30	53.20 N	19.00 E
Torunos	246	8.30 N	70.04 W
Torup, Sve.	26	56.58 N	13.05 E
Torup, Sve.	41	55.34 N	13.12 E
Tõrva	76	58.00 N	25.56 E
Tory	88	51.47 N	103.00 E
Tory Island I	48	55.16 N	8.14 W
Torysa ≃	30	48.39 N	21.21 E
Tory Sound ɰ	48	55.14 N	8.14 W
Toržok	76	57.03 N	34.58 E
Torzym	30	52.20 N	15.04 E
Tosa, Nihon	96	33.29 N	133.25 E
Tosa, Nihon	96	33.44 N	133.32 E
T'oša ≃	80	55.38 N	42.09 E
T'osan	98	38.18 N	126.43 E
Tosari	115a	7.53 S	112.54 E
Tosa-shimizu	92	32.46 N	132.57 E
Tosa-wan ⊂	96	33.20 N	133.40 E
Tosayama	96	33.38 N	133.32 E
Tosa-yamada	96	33.36 N	133.41 E
Tosca	156	25.53 S	23.58 E
Toscaig	46	57.24 N	5.50 W
Toscana (Tuscany) □[4]	36	43.25 N	11.00 E
Toscano ≃	234	18.01 N	102.32 W
Toscolano	64	45.38 N	10.37 E
Tösens	58	47.01 N	10.36 E
Toses, Collada de)(	34	42.19 N	2.01 E
Tōshi-jima I	94	34.31 N	136.53 E
Toshima ●[8]	268	35.44 N	139.43 E
To-shima I	94	34.31 N	139.17 E
Tōshō-gū ʊ[1]	94	36.46 N	139.36 E
Tosi, Indon.	115b	9.35 S	118.57 E
Tosi, It.	66	43.45 N	11.31 E
Tosilei	144	1.25 N	41.24 E
Toškalykaja, gora ∧	86	50.38 N	89.30 E
Toškovskij	83	48.46 N	38.34 E
Tosna ≃	265a	59.46 N	30.46 E
Tosno	76	59.33 N	30.53 E
Toson Cengel	88	48.47 N	98.15 E
Toson Hu ⊜	102	35.18 N	98.54 E
T'osovo	76	55.37 N	34.30 E
T'osovo-Netyl'skij	76	58.57 N	31.04 E
T'osovskij	76	58.48 N	30.52 E
Töss ≃	58	47.33 N	8.33 E
Tossens	52	53.34 N	8.16 E
Tossicia	66	42.33 N	13.39 E
Tostado	252	29.14 S	61.46 W
Tõstamaa	76	58.20 N	24.00 E
Tostedt	52	53.17 N	9.42 E
Tosterön I	40	59.25 N	17.00 E
Tostu	85	41.34 N	71.34 E
Tost uul ⋀	102	43.15 N	100.30 E
Tosu	96	33.22 N	130.31 E
Tosya	130	41.01 N	34.02 E
Totagatic ≃	190	46.05 N	92.11 W
Totak ⊜	26	59.42 N	7.57 E
Totana	34	37.46 N	1.30 W
Totānāla	126	22.05 N	87.40 E
Totatiche	234	21.56 N	103.27 W
Totban	80	46.47 N	49.06 E
Toteng	156	20.22 S	22.58 E
Tôtes	50	49.41 N	1.03 E
Totes Gebirge ⋀	30	47.42 N	13.55 E
T'otkino	78	51.17 N	34.16 E
Tot'ma	76	59.57 N	42.45 E
Totnes	42	50.25 N	3.41 W
Totness	250	5.53 N	56.19 W
Toto	152	7.08 S	14.16 E
Totonicapán	236	14.55 N	91.22 W
Totonicapán □[5]	236	15.00 N	91.20 W
Totopotomoy Creek ≃	208	37.41 N	77.13 W
Totora, Bol.	248	17.42 S	65.09 W
Totora, Bol.	248	17.49 S	68.07 W
Totoras	252	32.35 S	61.11 W
Totos	248	13.31 S	74.30 W
Tototlán	234	20.33 N	102.48 W
Totowa	210	40.54 N	74.12 W
Totoya Island I	175g	18.57 S	179.50 W
Totson Mountain ∧	180	64.26 N	157.15 W
Totsuka ●[8]	268	35.24 N	139.32 E
Tottenham, Austl.	166	32.14 S	147.21 E
Tottenham, On., Can.	212	44.01 N	79.49 W
Tottenham ●[8]	260	51.35 N	0.04 W
Tottenham Hotspur Football Ground ♦	260	51.36 N	0.04 W
Totten Inlet ⊂	224	47.07 N	123.02 W
Tottenville ●[8]	276	40.31 N	74.15 W
Totteridge ●[8]	260	51.38 N	0.12 W
Tottington	44	53.37 N	2.20 W
Totton	42	50.56 N	1.29 W
Tottori	96	35.30 N	134.14 E
Tottori □[5]	96	35.30 N	134.00 E
Tottori-sakyū ∧[2]	96	35.31 N	134.15 E
Totuskey Creek ≃	208	37.52 N	76.45 W
Tou, Motu I	174k	21.11 S	159.48 W
Touba, C. Iv.	150	8.17 N	7.41 W
Touba, Sén.	150	14.51 N	15.53 W
Toubei	100	26.44 N	116.05 E
Toubéré Bafal	150	14.23 N	13.32 W
Toubkal, Jebel ∧	148	31.05 N	7.55 W
Toubkal, Parc National du ♦	148	31.05 N	7.55 W
Toubori	146	13.59 N	12.18 E
Touboro	152	7.43 N	15.12 E
T'ouch'eng	100	24.52 N	121.49 E
Touchet ≃	202	46.02 N	118.41 W
Touchwood Hills ⋀[2]	184	51.35 N	104.17 W
Touchwood Lake ⊜, Ab., Can.	182	54.50 N	111.23 W
Touchwood Lake ⊜, Mb., Can.	184	54.29 N	95.00 W
Toucy	50	47.44 N	3.18 E
Toudao ≃	98	42.36 N	127.11 E
Toudaogou, Zhg.	98	42.46 N	129.12 E
Toudaogou, Zhg.	104	41.37 N	121.40 E
Toudaogou, Zhg.	105	40.58 N	117.59 E
Touët-sur-Var	62	43.57 N	7.00 E
Tougan	150	13.04 N	3.04 W
Touggourt	148	33.10 N	6.00 E
Toughkenamon	285	39.50 N	75.46 W
Tougouri	150	13.19 N	0.31 W
Tougué	150	11.27 N	11.41 W
Touho	175f	20.47 S	165.14 E
Touiel, Oued ∨	148	31.30 N	4.46 E
Touil, Oued ∨	148	35.30 N	2.33 E
Touisset	207	41.43 N	71.13 W
Toukansi	100	29.22 N	119.06 E
Toukley	170	33.16 S	151.33 E
Toukoto	150	13.27 N	9.53 W
Toul	58	48.41 N	5.54 E
Toulépleu	150	6.35 N	8.25 W
Touliu	100	23.43 N	120.32 E
Toulnustouc ≃	186	49.35 N	68.24 W
Toulnustouc Nord-Est ≃	186	50.56 N	67.44 W
Toulon, Fr.	62	43.07 N	5.56 E
Toulon, Il., U.S.	190	41.05 N	89.51 W
Toulon Lake ⊜	204	40.01 N	118.40 W
Toulon-sur-Arroux	32	46.42 N	4.08 E
Touloubre ≃	62	43.33 N	5.02 E
Toulourenc ≃	62	44.14 N	5.09 E
Toulouse	32	43.36 N	1.26 E
Toumen Shan I	100	28.41 N	121.46 E
Toumfafi	150	15.02 N	5.38 E
Toumodi	150	6.33 N	5.01 W
Tounan	100	23.41 N	120.28 E
Tounassine, Hamada ●[2]	148	28.30 N	5.00 W
Toungo	146	8.07 N	12.03 E
Toungoo	110	18.56 N	96.26 E
Toupeng	106	30.19 N	120.31 E
Touques	50	49.22 N	0.06 E
Touques ≃	50	49.22 N	0.06 E
Tour, Étang de la ⊜	261	48.40 N	1.53 E
Toura, Monts du ⋀	150	7.40 N	7.25 W
Touraine	188	45.34 N	75.47 W
Touraine □[9]	50	47.12 N	1.30 E
Tourakom	110	18.26 N	102.32 E
Tourane → Da Nang	108	16.04 N	108.13 E
Tourassine ⊤[4]	148	24.37 N	11.23 W
Tourbe ≃	56	49.10 N	4.52 E
Tourcoing	50	50.43 N	3.09 E
Touriñan, Cabo ›	34	43.03 N	9.18 W
Tournai	50	50.36 N	3.23 E
Tournan-en-Brie	50	48.44 N	2.46 E
Tourndo, Oued ∨	148	22.15 N	10.28 E
Tournesac ≃	50	47.15 N	4.12 E
Tournhout	56	51.19 N	4.57 E
Tournon	62	45.04 N	4.50 E
Tournus	58	46.34 N	4.54 E
Touros	250	5.12 S	35.28 W
Tou Rout	110	16.24 N	107.00 E
Tourouvre	50	48.35 N	0.40 E
Tourrette-Levens	62	43.47 N	7.16 E
Tours	50	47.23 N	0.41 E
Tours-sur-Marne	50	49.03 N	4.07 E
Tours-sur-Meymont	62	45.40 N	3.35 E
Tourteron	56	49.32 N	4.39 E
Tourves	62	43.24 N	5.56 E
Toury	50	48.12 N	1.56 E
Toussaint Creek ≃	214	41.35 N	83.04 W
Toussidé, Pic ∧	146	21.02 N	16.25 E
Toussoro, Mont ∧	146	9.18 N	23.28 E
Toussus-le-Noble	261	48.45 N	2.07 E
Toussus-le-Noble, Aéroport de ⊠	261	48.45 N	2.10 E
Toustain	36	36.40 N	8.15 E
Toutai, Zhg.	89	45.40 N	124.50 E
Toutai, Zhg.	104	41.41 N	121.11 E
Toutaizi	104	42.19 N	122.49 E
Toutle	224	46.20 N	122.41 W
Toutle ≃	224	46.17 N	122.55 W
Toutle, North Fork ≃	224	46.23 N	122.34 W
Toutle, South Fork ≃	224	46.20 N	122.44 W
Toutle Mountain Range ⋀	224	46.20 N	122.30 W
Toutuohe	100	31.06 N	116.25 E
Touws ≃	158	33.45 S	21.11 E
Touwsrivier	158	33.20 S	20.00 E
Touzhan	89	49.27 N	119.41 E
Toužim	60	50.04 N	13.00 E
Töv □[4]	88	47.30 N	106.30 E
Tova	24	65.58 N	40.45 E
Tovar	246	8.20 N	71.46 W
Tovarkovo	82	54.42 N	35.57 E
Tovarkovskij	76	53.40 N	38.14 E
Tove ≃	42	52.05 N	0.38 W
Tovey	219	39.35 N	89.27 W
Tow	196	30.53 N	98.28 W
Tōwa	96	33.13 N	132.53 E
Towaco	210	40.55 N	74.20 W
Towada	92	40.37 N	141.13 E
Towada-Hachimantai-kokuritsu-kōen ♦	92	40.35 N	140.53 E
Towada-ko ⊜	92	40.28 N	140.55 E
Towai	172	35.29 S	174.08 E
Towamencin Creek ≃	285	40.13 N	75.23 W
Towanda, Il., U.S.	216	40.34 N	88.54 W
Towanda, Ks., U.S.	198	37.47 N	96.59 W
Towanda, Pa., U.S.	210	41.46 N	76.26 W
Towanda Creek ≃	210	41.45 N	76.26 W
Towan Head ›	42	50.25 N	5.07 W
Towar Gardens	216	42.45 N	84.28 W
Towari	112	4.36 S	121.29 E
Towcester	42	52.08 N	1.00 W
Tower	190	47.48 N	92.16 W
Tower City, N.D., U.S.	198	46.55 N	97.40 W
Tower City, Pa., U.S.	208	40.35 N	76.33 W
Tower Hamlets ●[8]	42	51.32 N	0.03 W
Tower Hill, Austl.	166	22.03 S	144.36 E
Tower Hill, Il., U.S.	219	39.23 N	88.57 W
Towerhill Creek ≃	166	22.29 S	144.39 E
Tower of London ⊥	260	51.30 N	0.05 W
Tower Peak ∧	226	38.09 N	119.33 W
Towers of Silence ʊ[1]	272c	18.58 N	72.48 E
Tower Soudan State Park ♦	190	47.50 N	92.15 W
Towla, Mount ∧	154	21.22 S	29.52 E
Tow Law	44	54.44 N	1.49 W
Towlī	84	39.11 N	47.32 E
Town ≃	283	42.00 N	70.57 W
Town and Country	202	47.42 N	117.23 W
Town Bank	208	39.00 N	74.56 W
Town Creek ≃, Al., U.S.	194	34.46 N	87.25 W
Town Creek ≃, Al., U.S.	194	34.24 N	86.11 W
Town Creek ≃, Oh., U.S.	216	41.05 N	84.25 W
Town Creek Manor	208	38.19 N	76.27 W
Towneley Hall ⊥	262	53.46 N	2.13 W
Towner	198	48.20 N	100.24 W
Town Estates	285	40.04 N	74.52 W
Town Hill ∧[2]	240a	32.19 N	64.44 W
Townline Tunnel ●[5]	284a	42.57 N	79.15 W
Town of Niagara	284a	43.06 N	78.59 W
Town of Pines	216	41.41 N	86.58 W
Town of Tonawanda	210	42.59 N	78.52 W
Townsend, On., Can.	212	42.54 N	80.07 W
Townsend, De., U.S.	208	39.23 N	75.41 W
Townsend, Ma., U.S.	207	42.40 N	71.42 W
Townsend, Mt., U.S.	202	46.19 N	111.31 W
Townsend, Va., U.S.	208	37.11 N	75.57 W
Townsend, Mount ∧	171b	36.25 S	148.15 E
Townsend Island I	276	40.38 N	73.26 W
Townsends Inlet ⊂	208	39.07 N	74.43 W
Townshend Island I	166	22.15 S	150.30 E
Township Line Run ≃	279b	40.13 N	79.33 W
Townsville	166	19.16 S	146.48 E
Townville	214	41.41 N	79.53 W
Towrang	170	34.42 S	149.51 E
Towrang, Mount ∧	170	34.46 S	149.51 E
Towra Point ›	274a	34.00 S	151.10 E
Towr Kham	123	34.08 N	71.05 E
Towrzī, Afg.	120	30.11 N	65.59 E
Towrzī, Afg.	128	32.38 N	65.53 E
Towson	208	39.24 N	76.36 W
Towson State College ʊ[2]	284b	39.24 N	76.37 W
Towuti, Danau ⊜	112	2.45 S	121.32 E
Toxkan (Aksaj) ≃, Asia	85	40.55 N	78.16 E
Toxkan ≃, Zhg.	90	41.08 N	80.11 E
Toyah	196	31.19 N	103.47 W
Toyah Creek ≃	196	31.18 N	103.27 W
Tōya-ko ⊜	92a	42.35 N	140.51 E
Toyama	94	36.41 N	137.13 E
Toyama □[5]	94	36.30 N	137.30 E
Toyama-heiya ≚	94	36.40 N	137.15 E
Toyama-wan ⊂	94	36.50 N	137.10 E
Toyapakeh	115b	8.41 S	115.29 E
Tōyo, Nihon	96	33.55 N	133.05 E
Tōyō, Nihon	96	33.30 N	134.16 E
Toyo ≃	94	34.47 N	137.20 E
Toyoake	94	35.03 N	137.01 E
Toyoda, Nihon	94	34.45 N	137.49 E
Toyoda, Nihon	268	35.39 N	139.23 E
Toyofuta	268	35.53 N	139.57 E
Toyohama	96	34.04 N	133.38 E
Toyohara	175d	24.15 N	123.48 E
Toyohashi	94	34.46 N	137.23 E
Toyohira	96	34.40 N	132.24 E
Toyokawa	94	34.49 N	137.24 E
Toyo-kawa-yōsui ≋	94	34.35 N	137.03 E
Toyonaka, Nihon	96	34.09 N	133.42 E
Toyonaka, Nihon	96	34.47 N	135.28 E
Toyone	94	35.09 N	137.43 E
Toyono	94	36.43 N	138.16 E
Toyooka, Nihon	94	35.33 N	137.54 E
Toyooka, Nihon	94	34.50 N	137.52 E
Toyooka, Nihon	96	35.32 N	134.50 E
Toyooka, Nihon	268	35.11 N	139.58 E
Toyosaka, Nihon	92	37.56 N	139.13 E
Toyosaka, Nihon	96	34.34 N	132.50 E
Toyosato	94	36.06 N	140.02 E
Toyoshina	94	36.18 N	137.54 E
Toyota, Nihon	94	35.05 N	137.09 E
Toyota, Nihon	94	36.46 N	138.19 E
Toyota, Nihon	96	34.12 N	131.04 E
Toyota-ko ⊜	96	34.14 N	131.08 E
Toyotomi	94	35.34 N	138.33 E
Toyotsu	96	33.40 N	130.58 E
Toyoura	96	34.08 N	130.58 E
Toy's Hill	260	51.14 N	0.06 E
Tozer, Mount ∧	164	12.45 S	143.13 E
Tozeur	148	33.55 N	8.08 E
Tozi, Mount ∧	180	65.41 N	150.58 W
Tozitna ≃	180	65.08 N	152.23 W
Tpig	84	41.47 N	47.36 E
Traar ●[8]	263	51.23 N	6.36 E
Trabaria, Bocca)(	66	43.36 N	12.14 E
Traben-Trarbach	56	49.57 N	7.06 E
Trabia	70	37.59 N	13.39 E
Trabiju	255	22.03 S	48.18 W
Trabuco, Arroyo ≃	228	33.31 N	117.40 W
Trabzon	130	41.00 N	39.43 E
Trabzon □[4]	130	40.50 N	39.50 E
Tracadie	186	47.31 N	64.54 W
Trachselwald	58	47.01 N	7.45 E
Tra Cu	110	9.42 N	106.16 E
Tracy, P.Q., Can.	206	46.01 N	73.09 W
Tracy, Ca., U.S.	226	37.44 N	121.25 W
Tracy, Mn., U.S.	198	44.14 N	95.37 W
Tracy City	194	35.15 N	85.44 W
Tracyton	224	47.36 N	122.39 W
Tradate	62	45.43 N	8.54 E
Trade Lake ⊜	184	55.22 N	103.44 W
Tradewater ≃	194	37.31 N	88.03 W
Trading Bay ⊂	212	45.15 N	78.55 W
Tradinghouse Creek Reservoir ⊜[1]	222	31.35 N	96.55 W
Traditional Cultures, Museum of ʊ	269f	14.31 N	121.00 E
Trælleborg ⊥	41	55.23 N	11.17 E
Traer	190	42.11 N	92.27 W
Traessu, Monte ∧	71	40.28 N	8.40 E
Trafalgar, Austl.	169	38.12 S	146.09 E
Trafalgar, On., Can.	275b	43.29 N	79.43 W
Trafalgar, In., U.S.	218	39.24 N	86.09 W
Trafalgar, Cabo ›	34	36.11 N	6.02 W
Trafaria	266c	38.40 N	9.14 W
Trafford	214	40.23 N	79.45 W
Trafford □[8]	262	53.24 N	2.21 W
Trafford, Lake ⊜	220	26.25 N	81.30 W
Trafford Park	262	53.28 N	2.20 W
Trafoi	64	46.33 N	10.31 E
Tragacete	34	40.21 N	1.51 W
Tragliata ●[8]	267a	41.58 N	12.15 E
Tragwein	61	48.20 N	14.37 E
Traição, Córrego ≃	287b	23.36 S	46.41 W
Traid	34	40.40 N	1.49 W
Traiguén	252	38.15 S	72.41 W
Traiguén, Isla I	254	45.35 S	73.42 W
Trail	182	49.06 N	117.42 W
Trail Creek	216	41.41 N	86.51 W
Trailer Estates	220	27.24 N	82.34 W
Trail Ridge ∧	192	30.35 N	82.05 W
Traînel	50	48.25 N	3.27 E
Trainer	285	39.50 N	75.25 W
Traipu	250	9.58 S	37.01 W
Traíra (Taraira) ≃	246	1.04 S	69.26 W
Trairão ≃	250	7.20 S	51.14 W
Traíras ≃	255	14.07 S	48.31 W
Trairi	250	3.17 S	39.15 W
Traisen	61	48.02 N	15.37 E
Traisen ≃	61	48.22 N	15.46 E
Traiskirchen	61	48.01 N	16.18 E
Traismauer	61	48.21 N	15.44 E
Traîtres, Baie des ⊂	174x	9.50 S	139.02 W
Trajouce	266c	38.44 N	9.20 W
Trakai	76	54.38 N	24.56 E
Trakt	24	62.44 N	51.11 E
Träkvista	40	59.16 N	17.47 E
Tralee	48	52.16 N	9.42 W
Tralee Bay ⊂	48	52.15 N	9.59 W
Trá Lí → Tralee	48	52.16 N	9.42 W
Tramatza	71	40.00 N	8.39 E
Tramayes	58	46.18 N	4.36 E
Tramelan	58	47.13 N	7.06 E
Tra Mi	110	15.20 N	108.13 E
Tramin → Termeno	64	46.20 N	11.14 E
Trammel	192	37.00 N	82.17 W
Trammel Creek ≃	194	36.52 N	86.23 W
Tramonti di sopra	64	46.18 N	12.47 E
Tramore	48	52.10 N	7.10 W
Tramperos Creek (Punta de Agua Creek) ≃	196	35.32 N	102.27 W
Tramping Lake ⊜	184	52.08 N	108.49 W
Tramutola	68	40.19 N	15.47 E
Trân	38	42.50 N	22.39 E
Tranås	26	58.03 N	14.59 E
Trancão ≃	266c	38.48 N	9.06 W
Trancas	252	26.13 S	65.17 W
Trancoso	34	40.47 N	7.21 W
Trand	123	34.38 N	72.59 E
Tranderup	41	54.52 N	10.22 E
Tranebjerg	41	55.50 N	10.36 E
Tranekær	41	55.00 N	10.51 E
Tranemo	26	57.29 N	13.21 E
Tranent	46	55.57 N	2.58 W
Tränental	158	27.09 S	19.33 E
Trang	110	7.33 N	99.36 E
Trangahy	157b	19.07 S	44.43 E
Trangan, Pulau I	164	6.35 S	134.20 E
Trangie	166	32.02 S	147.59 E
Tran Grande ≃	116	6.43 N	124.01 E
Trängslet	26	61.25 N	13.40 E
Trani	68	41.17 N	16.26 E
Tranmere	262	53.23 N	3.01 W
Trannon ≃	42	52.31 N	3.25 W
Tranoroa	157b	24.42 S	45.04 E
Tranquebar	122	11.02 N	79.51 E
Tranqueras	252	31.12 S	55.45 W
Tranquility	218	38.58 N	83.32 W
Tranquillity	226	36.38 N	120.15 W
Transantarctic Mountains ⋀	9	85.00 S	175.00 W
Trans-en-Provence	62	43.30 N	6.29 E
Transfer	214	41.20 N	80.26 W
Transit Airport ⊠	284a	43.06 N	78.44 W
Transkei □[1], Afr.	138	31.20 S	29.00 E
Transkei □[1], Afr.	158	31.20 S	29.00 E
Transquaking ≃	208	38.22 N	76.00 W
Transsylvanische Alpen → Carpații Meridionali ⋀	38	45.30 N	24.15 E
Transtrand	26	61.05 N	13.19 E
Transtrandsfjällen ∧	26	61.17 N	13.00 E
Transvaal □[4]	156	25.00 S	29.00 E
Transylvania □[9]	38	46.30 N	24.00 E
Transylvanian Alps → Carpații Meridionali ⋀	38	45.30 N	24.15 E
Tranters Creek ≃	192	35.33 N	77.05 W
Traona	58	46.09 N	9.31 E
Trapalcó, Salinas de ≚	254	39.45 S	66.45 W
Trapani	70	38.01 N	12.31 E
Trapani □[4]	70	37.50 N	12.40 E
Traphole Brook ≃	283	42.10 N	71.11 W
Trappe, Md., U.S.	208	38.39 N	76.03 W
Trappe, Pa., U.S.	208	40.12 N	75.29 W
Trappenkamp	54	54.03 N	10.16 E
Trapper Peak ∧	202	45.54 N	114.18 W
Trappes	50	48.47 N	2.00 E
Trappeto	70	38.04 N	13.03 E
Trapuá ≃	287b	23.36 S	46.17 W
Traralgon	169	38.12 S	146.32 E
Traralgon Creek ≃	169	38.10 S	146.31 E
Traras, Monts des ⋀	34	35.10 N	1.40 W
Trarza □[4]	150	17.45 N	15.45 W
Trârza ●[1]	150	18.00 N	15.00 W
Trasacco	66	41.57 N	13.32 E
Trasadingen	58	47.40 N	8.26 E
Trascăului, Munții ⋀	38	46.23 N	23.33 E
Trasimeno, Lago ⊜	66	43.08 N	12.06 E
Trask ≃	224	45.28 N	123.53 W
Träslövsläge	26	57.04 N	12.16 E
Trasna	82	54.45 N	38.42 E
Trás-os-Montes □[9]	34	41.30 N	7.15 W
Trassem	56	49.34 N	6.31 E
Trâstenik	38	43.31 N	24.28 E
Trat	110	12.14 N	102.30 E
Tratalias	71	39.06 N	8.34 E
Tratzberg, Schloss ⊥	64	47.23 N	11.44 E
Trauchgau	58	47.38 N	10.49 E
Traun	61	48.13 N	14.14 E
Traun ≃, Dtsch.	60	48.00 N	12.32 E
Traun ≃, Öst.	30	48.16 N	14.22 E
Traunkirchen	64	47.50 N	13.47 E
Traunreut	64	47.56 N	12.35 E
Traunsee ⊜	64	47.51 N	13.48 E
Traunstein, Dtsch.	64	47.52 N	12.38 E
Traunstein, Öst.	61	48.26 N	15.07 E
Traunstein ∧	64	47.52 N	13.50 E
Trautenstein	54	51.41 N	10.43 E
Travagliato	64	45.31 N	10.05 E
Trave ≃	54	53.54 N	10.50 E
Travedona	62	45.48 N	8.40 E
Travellers Lake ⊜	166	33.18 S	142.00 E
Travemünde ●[8]	54	53.57 N	10.52 E
Traver	226	36.27 N	119.29 W
Travers, Mount ∧	172	42.01 S	172.44 E
Travers, Val de ∨	58	46.57 N	6.38 E
Traverse, Lake ⊜	198	45.43 N	96.40 W
Traverse Bay ⊂	184	50.40 N	96.25 W
Traverse City	190	44.45 N	85.37 W
Traversella	62	45.30 N	7.45 E
Traverse Peak ∧	180	65.10 N	159.12 W
Traversetolo	64	44.38 N	10.23 E
Travers Reservoir ⊜[1]	182	50.14 N	112.51 W
Tra Vinh	110	9.56 N	106.20 E
Travis	222	31.08 N	97.00 W
Travis □[6]	222	30.18 N	97.40 W
Travis, Lake ⊜[1]	196	30.27 N	98.00 W
Travis Air Force Base ■	226	38.16 N	121.55 W
Travnik	36	44.14 N	17.40 E
Trawalla	169	37.26 S	143.29 E
Trawbreaga Bay ⊂	48	55.17 N	7.18 W
Trawick	222	31.46 N	94.45 W
Trawsfynydd	42	52.54 N	3.55 W
Trayning	162	31.07 S	117.48 E
Trazegnies	50	50.28 N	4.19 E
Trbovlje	36	46.10 N	15.03 E
Treadwell	210	42.21 N	75.03 W
Treales	262	53.47 N	2.51 W
Treasure Island	220	27.46 N	82.46 W
Treasure Island I	226	37.48 N	122.22 W
Treasure Island Naval Station ■	282	37.49 N	122.22 W
Trebatsch	54	52.05 N	14.09 E
Trebbia ≃	62	45.04 N	9.41 E
Trebbin	54	52.13 N	13.13 E
Třebechovice pod Orebem	30	50.12 N	16.00 E
Trebel	54	52.59 N	11.20 E
Trebel ≃	54	53.55 N	13.01 E
Trebelsee ⊜	54	52.28 N	12.47 E
Třebenice	54	50.29 N	14.00 E
Trebgast	60	50.04 N	11.33 E
Třebíč	30	49.13 N	15.53 E
Trebinje	38	42.43 N	18.20 E
Trebisacce	68	39.52 N	16.32 E
Trebišov	30	48.40 N	21.47 E
Trebitz	54	51.45 N	12.44 E
Trebizond → Trabzon	130	41.00 N	39.43 E
Trebjerg ∧[2]	41	55.10 N	10.14 E
Třebkov	60	49.22 N	14.04 E
Treble Mountain ∧	182	55.50 N	129.51 W
Treblinka	30	52.39 N	22.03 E
Třeboň	61	49.00 N	14.47 E
Třebouň ∧	60	50.01 N	12.59 E
Trebsen	54	51.17 N	12.45 E
Trebur	56	49.56 N	8.25 E
Trecastagni	70	37.37 N	15.05 E
Trecate	62	45.26 N	8.44 E
Trecchina	68	40.02 N	15.46 E
Trece Martires	116	14.16 N	120.50 E
Trecenta	64	45.02 N	11.28 E
Tred Avon River ⊂	208	38.42 N	76.08 W
Tredegar	42	51.47 N	3.16 W
Tredici Archi, Ponte ●[5]	66	41.32 N	14.57 E
Treene ≃	41	54.22 N	9.05 E
Trees Mills	279b	40.23 N	80.13 W
Treffen	64	46.40 N	13.52 E
Treffort	58	46.16 N	5.22 E
Treffurt	56	51.08 N	10.14 E
Trèfle, Lac du ⊜	206	46.36 N	73.55 W
Tregaron	42	52.13 N	3.55 W
Tregnago	64	45.31 N	11.10 E
Tregosse Islets II	166	17.41 S	150.43 E
Tregubovo	76	58.59 N	31.33 E
Tréguier	32	48.47 N	3.14 W
Treharris	42	51.41 N	3.16 W
Treherne	184	49.38 N	98.41 W
Trehörningsjö	26	63.42 N	18.48 E
Treia, Dtsch.	41	54.30 N	9.17 E
Treia, It.	66	43.19 N	13.19 E
Treig, Loch ⊜[1]	46	56.50 N	4.44 W
Treinta y Tres	252	33.14 S	54.23 W
Treis	56	50.10 N	7.17 E
Trekkopje	156	22.18 S	14.53 E
Trélazé	32	47.27 N	0.28 W
Trelde Næs ›	41	55.37 N	9.52 E
Trelew	254	43.15 S	65.18 W
Trelleborg	41	55.22 N	13.10 E
Treloar	219	38.39 N	91.10 W
Tremadog	42	52.56 N	4.09 W
Tremadog Bay ⊂	42	52.52 N	4.15 W
Tremblant, Lac ⊜	206	46.15 N	74.38 W
Tremblant, Mont ∧	206	46.16 N	74.35 W
Tremblay, Hippodrome du ♦	261	48.50 N	2.29 E
Tremblay-lès-Gonesse	261	48.59 N	2.34 E
Trembleur Lake ⊜	182	54.51 N	125.07 W
Tremedal	255	14.58 S	41.24 W
Tremembé	256	22.58 S	45.33 W
Tremezzo	58	45.59 N	9.15 E
Tremino	88	56.42 N	98.04 E
Tremiti, Isole II	66	42.07 N	15.30 E
Tremo La)(	124	27.44 N	89.12 E
Tremont, Il., U.S.	190	40.31 N	89.29 W
Tremont, In., U.S.	216	41.39 N	87.02 W
Tremont, Pa., U.S.	208	40.37 N	76.23 W
Tremont ●[8]	276	40.51 N	73.55 W
Tremont City	218	40.00 N	83.50 W
Tremonton	200	41.42 N	112.09 W
Třemošna	60	49.49 N	13.20 E
Třemošná ≃	60	49.52 N	13.32 E
Tremp	34	42.10 N	0.54 E
Trempealeau	190	44.00 N	91.26 W
Trempealeau ≃	190	44.02 N	91.32 W
Tremsbüttel	52	53.44 N	10.18 E
Trena	144	10.45 N	40.38 E
Trenčín	30	48.54 N	18.04 E
Trendelburg	52	51.34 N	9.25 E
Trenel	252	35.42 S	64.08 W
Trêng	110	12.49 N	102.54 E
Trenggalek	115a	8.03 S	111.43 E
Trenque Lauquen	252	35.58 S	62.42 W
Trent	54	54.31 N	13.15 E
Trent ≃, On., Can.	212	44.06 N	77.34 W
Trent ≃, Eng., U.K.	28	53.42 N	0.41 W
Trent ≃, N.C., U.S.	192	35.05 N	77.02 W
Trent, Vale of ∨	42	52.44 N	1.50 W
Trent and Mersey Canal ≋	262	53.19 N	2.39 W
Trente et un Milles, Lac des ⊜	188	46.12 N	75.49 W
Trentham	169	37.23 S	144.19 E
Trentino-Alto Adige □[4]	64	46.30 N	11.20 E
Trento	64	46.04 N	11.08 E
Trento □[4]	64	46.08 N	11.07 E
Trentola-Ducenta	68	40.59 N	14.10 E
Trenton, N.S., Can.	186	45.37 N	62.38 W
Trenton, On., Can.	212	44.06 N	77.35 W
Trenton, Fl., U.S.	192	29.36 N	82.49 W
Trenton, Ga., U.S.	192	34.52 N	85.30 W
Trenton, Il., U.S.	219	38.36 N	89.40 W
Trenton, Ky., U.S.	194	36.43 N	87.15 W
Trenton, Mi., U.S.	216	42.08 N	83.10 W
Trenton, Mo., U.S.	194	40.04 N	93.36 W
Trenton, Ne., U.S.	198	40.10 N	101.00 W
Trenton, N.J., U.S.	208	40.13 N	74.44 W
Trenton, N.C., U.S.	192	35.04 N	77.21 W
Trenton, Oh., U.S.	218	39.29 N	84.28 W
Trenton, Tn., U.S.	194	35.58 N	88.56 W
Trenton, Tx., U.S.	196	33.26 N	96.20 W
Trenton, Canadian Forces Base ■	190	44.07 N	77.33 W
Trenton Channel ≃[1]	281	42.06 N	83.11 W
Trent → Trento	64	46.04 N	11.08 E
Trentwood	202	47.42 N	117.13 W
Trepalade	64	45.34 N	12.24 E
Trepassey	186	46.44 N	53.22 W
Trepassey Bay ⊂	186	46.37 N	53.20 W
Treptow ●[8]	54	52.29 N	13.29 E
Trepuzzi	68	40.24 N	18.05 E
Trequanda	66	43.11 N	11.40 E
Tresa ≃	58	46.00 N	8.43 E
Tres Algarrobos	252	35.12 S	62.46 W
Tres Árboles	252	32.24 S	56.43 W
Tres Arroyos	252	38.23 S	60.17 W
Tres Cerros	254	48.13 S	67.33 W
Treščevo	82	54.11 N	37.55 E
Tresckow	210	40.54 N	75.58 W
Tresco I	42a	49.57 N	6.19 W
Três Corações	256	21.42 S	45.16 W
Trescore Balneario	62	45.41 N	9.50 E
Três Coroas	252	29.32 S	50.48 W
Tres de Febrero □[5]	288	34.36 S	58.35 W
Tres de Febrero → Caseros	258	34.36 S	58.33 W
Três de Maio	252	27.47 S	54.14 W
Tresenda	64	46.10 N	10.05 E
Tres Esquinas	246	0.43 N	75.16 W
Três Fronteiras	255	20.13 S	50.55 W
Treshnish Isles II	46	56.30 N	6.24 W
Treshnish Point ›	46	56.33 N	6.21 W
Tre Signori, Picco dei (Dreiherrnspitze) ∧	64	47.04 N	12.15 E
Três Ilhas	256	22.04 S	43.29 W
Tresinaro ≃	64	44.39 N	10.47 E
Tres Isletas	252	26.21 S	60.26 W
Treskino	80	52.40 N	44.40 E
Três Lagoas	255	20.48 S	51.43 W
Tres Lagos	254	49.37 S	71.30 W
Tres Lomas	252	36.27 S	62.51 W
Três Marias	255	18.12 S	45.14 W
Três Marias, Represa de ⊜[1]	255	18.12 S	45.15 W
Tres Montes, Golfo ⊂	254	46.54 S	75.00 W
Tres Montes, Península ›[1]	254	46.50 S	75.30 W
Tres Montosas ∧	200	34.06 N	107.28 W
Tres Morros, Alto de ∧	246	7.08 N	76.11 W
Tresnuraghes	71	40.15 N	8.31 E
Tres Padres, Pico ∧	286a	19.35 N	99.08 W
Tres Palacios ≃	196	28.45 N	96.09 W
Tres Palos, Laguna ⊂	234	16.46 N	99.44 W
Três Passos	252	27.27 S	53.56 W
Tres Picos	234	15.52 N	93.32 W
Tres Picos, Cerro ∧, Arg.	252	38.09 S	61.57 W
Tres Picos, Cerro ∧, Méx.	234	16.12 N	93.37 W
Tres Pinos	226	36.48 N	121.19 W
Tres Pinos Creek ≃	226	36.47 N	121.21 W
Três Pontas	256	21.22 S	45.31 W
Três Pontas, Cabo das ›	152	10.23 S	13.32 E
Tres Puntas, Cabo ›, Arg.	254	47.06 S	65.53 W
Tres Puntas, Cabo ›, Guat.	236	15.56 N	88.37 W
Três Ranchos	255	18.22 S	47.47 W
Tres Reyes Islands II	116	13.14 N	121.51 E
Três Rios, Bra.	256	22.07 S	43.12 W
Tres Ríos, C.R.	236	9.54 N	83.58 W
Tressancourt	261	48.55 N	2.00 E
Třešť	30	49.18 N	15.30 E
Tresta	46a	60.14 N	1.21 W
Tres Valles	234	18.15 N	96.08 W
Tres Vírgenes, Volcán de las ∧[1]	232	27.27 N	112.34 W
Tres Zapotes ⊥	234	18.28 N	95.24 W
Tret'akovskaja Galereja ʊ	265b	55.45 N	37.37 E
Tretet	114	4.40 N	96.51 E
Trets	62	43.27 N	5.41 E
Tretten	26	61.19 N	10.19 E
Treuchtlingen	56	48.57 N	10.54 E
Treuen	54	50.32 N	12.18 E
Treuenbrietzen	54	52.06 N	12.52 E
Treuhandgebiet Pazifische Inseln → Trust Territory of the Pacific Islands □[2]	14	5.00 N	137.00 E
Trevelín	254	43.04 S	71.28 W
Trèves → Trier	56	49.45 N	6.38 E
Trevi	66	42.52 N	12.45 E
Treviglio	62	45.31 N	9.35 E
Trevignano Romano	66	42.09 N	12.15 E
Treviño	34	42.44 N	2.45 W
Treviso	64	45.40 N	12.15 E
Treviso □[4]	64	45.50 N	12.13 E
Trevor	216	42.30 N	88.07 W
Trevorton	208	40.46 N	76.40 W
Trevose	208	40.08 N	74.58 W
Trevose Head ›	42	50.33 N	5.01 W
Trevose Heights	285	40.09 N	74.59 W
Trévoux	58	45.56 N	4.46 E
Trexlertown	208	40.33 N	75.36 W
Trezevant	194	36.00 N	88.37 W
Trezzano sul Naviglio	266b	45.25 N	9.04 E
Trezzo sull'Adda	62	45.36 N	9.31 E
Trgovište	38	42.21 N	22.05 E
Trhomné	60	49.55 N	13.05 E
Trhové Sviny	61	48.51 N	14.39 E
Triabunna	166	42.30 S	147.55 E
Triadelphia Reservoir ⊜[1]	208	39.13 N	77.01 W
Trialeti	84	41.33 N	44.07 E
Trialetskij chrebet ⋀	84	41.45 N	43.50 E
Triana	66	42.47 N	11.33 E
Triánda	38	36.24 N	28.10 E
Triangle, Eng., U.K.	262	53.42 N	1.56 W
Triangle, Va., U.S.	208	38.32 N	77.20 W
Triangle Lake	210	42.32 N	74.13 W
Triangul'atorov, pik ∧	88	53.45 N	97.00 E
Triángulos, Arrecifes ✢[2]	232	20.57 N	92.16 W
Triaucourt-en-Argonne	56	48.59 N	5.04 E
Tribeni	126	22.59 N	88.24 E
Triberg	58	48.08 N	8.13 E
Tribes Hill	210	42.57 N	74.17 W
Tribobó	287a	22.52 S	43.01 W
Triborough Bridge ●[5]	276	40.47 N	73.55 W
Tri Brata, porog ⌞	86	57.25 N	95.39 E
Tribsees	54	54.05 N	12.45 E
Tribugá, Ensenada de ⊂	246	5.45 N	77.20 W
Tribune, Sk., Can.	184	49.15 N	103.50 W
Tribune, Ks., U.S.	198	38.28 N	101.45 W
Tribune Channel ɰ	182	50.50 N	126.16 W
Tribuswinkel	264b	48.00 N	16.16 E
Tricarico	68	40.37 N	16.09 E
Tricase	68	39.56 N	18.22 E
Tricesimo	64	46.10 N	13.13 E
Trichardt	158	26.28 S	29.13 E
Trichiana	64	46.05 N	12.07 E
Trichinopoly → Tiruchchirāppalli	122	10.49 N	78.41 E
Trichūr	122	10.31 N	76.13 E
Tri Cities	222	32.09 N	95.56 W
Tricot	50	49.34 N	2.35 E
Tri County Supply Canal ≋	198	40.49 N	100.06 W
Trida	166	33.01 S	145.01 E
Trident Peak ∧	204	41.54 N	118.25 W
Triduby	78	48.06 N	30.24 E
Trieben	61	47.29 N	14.30 E
Triebes	54	50.41 N	12.01 E
Triel-sur-Seine	261	48.59 N	2.00 E
Trient → Trento	64	46.04 N	11.08 E
Triepkendorf	54	53.17 N	13.20 E
Trier	56	49.45 N	6.38 E
Trier □[5]	56	50.00 N	6.40 E
Triesen	58	47.06 N	9.31 E
Trieste (Triest)	64	45.40 N	13.46 E
Trieste □[4]	64	45.30 N	13.50 E
Trieste, Gulf of ⊂	64	45.40 N	13.35 E
Triesting ≃	264b	48.05 N	16.24 E
Trieux	56	49.20 N	5.56 E
Triftern	60	48.24 N	13.01 E
Trigal	248	18.17 S	64.08 W
Triggiano	68	41.04 N	16.55 E
Triglav ∧	64	46.23 N	13.50 E
Triglitz	54	53.12 N	12.05 E
Trigna, Pizzo ∧	70	37.58 N	13.34 E
Trigno ≃	66	42.04 N	14.48 E
Trigueros	34	37.23 N	6.50 W
Tríkala	38	39.34 N	21.46 E
Trikhonís, Límni ⊜	38	38.34 N	21.28 E
Trikora, Puncak (Wilhelmina Peak) ∧	164	4.15 S	138.45 E
Tri-Lakes	216	41.14 N	85.26 W
Trilbardou	261	48.57 N	2.48 E
Trilby	220	28.27 N	82.11 W
Trilesy	78	49.59 N	29.50 E
Trillick	48	54.27 N	7.30 W
Trilport	50	48.57 N	2.57 E
Trim	48	53.34 N	6.47 W
Triman	120	29.38 N	69.05 E
Trimbach	58	47.22 N	7.54 E
Trimble □[6]	218	38.37 N	85.20 W
Trim Creek ≃	216	41.10 N	87.38 W
Trimdon	44	54.42 N	1.25 W
Trimont	198	43.45 N	94.42 W
Trimonte	256	21.43 S	42.35 W
Trin	58	46.50 N	9.22 E
Trinchera Creek ≃	200	37.19 N	105.45 W
Trincheras, Méx.	196	25.37 N	101.55 W
Trincheras, Méx.	232	30.24 N	111.32 W
Trincomalee	122	8.34 N	81.14 E
Trincomali Channel ɰ	224	48.02 N	123.30 W
Trindade	255	16.40 S	49.30 W
Trindade I	244	20.31 S	29.19 W
Třinec	30	49.41 N	18.40 E
Tring	42	51.48 N	0.40 W
Trinidad, Bol.	248	14.47 S	64.47 W
Trinidad, Col.	246	5.25 N	71.40 W
Trinidad, Cuba	240p	21.48 N	79.59 W
Trinidad, Hond.	236	14.57 N	88.45 W
Trinidad, Co., U.S.	198	37.10 N	104.30 W
Trinidad, Tx., U.S.	222	32.08 N	96.05 W
Trinidad, Ur.	252	33.32 S	56.54 W
Trinidad I	241r	10.30 N	61.15 W
Trinidad ≃	234	17.49 N	95.09 W
Trinidad, Golfo ⊂	254	49.55 S	75.25 W
Trinidad, Isla I	252	39.08 S	61.58 W
Trinidad and Tobago □[1], N.A.	230	11.00 N	61.00 W
Trinidad and Tobago □[1], N.A.	241r	11.00 N	61.00 W
Trinità	62	44.30 N	7.45 E
Trinità, Lago della ⊜	70	37.43 N	12.46 E
Trinità d'agultu	71	40.59 N	8.54 E
Trinitapoli	68	41.21 N	16.05 E
Trinité, Havre de la ⊂	240e	14.44 N	60.58 W
Trinity, Nf., Can.	186	48.59 N	53.55 W
Trinity, Tx., U.S.	222	30.56 N	95.22 W
Trinity □[6]	222	31.07 N	95.10 W
Trinity ≃, Ca., U.S.	204	41.11 N	123.42 W
Trinity ≃, Tx., U.S.	222	29.47 N	94.42 W
Trinity, Clear Fork ≃	196	32.46 N	97.21 W
Trinity, East Fork ≃	222	32.30 N	96.30 W
Trinity, Elm Fork ≃	222	32.47 N	96.54 W
Trinity, South Fork ≃	204	40.54 N	123.35 W
Trinity, West Fork ≃	196	32.48 N	96.51 W
Trinity Bay ⊂, Nf., Can.	186	48.00 N	53.40 W
Trinity Bay ⊂, Tx., U.S.	222	29.40 N	94.45 W
Trinity Islands II	180	56.33 N	154.25 W
Trinity Mountain ∧	202	43.36 N	115.26 W
Trinity Mountains ⋀	204	41.00 N	122.30 W
Trinity Park ♦	275b	43.39 N	79.25 W
Trinity Peak ∧	204	40.14 N	118.45 W
Trinity Site ⊥	200	33.41 N	106.28 W
Trinkat Island I	110	8.05 N	93.30 E
Trinkitat	140	18.41 N	37.43 E
Trino	62	45.12 N	8.18 E
Trins	64	47.05 N	11.25 E
Trinway	214	40.08 N	82.00 W
Triolet	157c	20.03 S	57.32 E
Triolo ≃	66	41.40 N	15.34 E
Trion	192	34.32 N	85.18 W
Trionto ≃	68	39.37 N	16.45 E
Trionto, Capo ›	68	39.37 N	16.45 E
Triora	62	43.59 N	7.46 E
Tripa ≃	114	3.53 N	96.23 E
Tripi	70	38.03 N	15.06 E
Triplett Creek ≃	218	38.10 N	83.27 W
Triplett Creek, North Fork ≃	218	38.10 N	83.31 W
Tripoli	190	42.48 N	92.15 W
Trípolis	38	37.31 N	22.21 E
Tripolis ⊥	130	37.58 N	28.59 E
Tripolis → Ṭarābulus	146	32.54 N	13.11 E
Tripolitania → Ṭarābulus □[9]	146	31.00 N	15.00 E
Tripoli → Ṭarābulus, Lībiyā	146	32.54 N	13.11 E
Tripoli → Ṭarābulus, Lubnān	130	34.26 N	35.51 E
Tripolje	78	50.07 N	30.46 E

Symbols in the index entries represent the broad categories identified in the key at the right. Symbols with superior numbers (⋀[1]) identify subcategories (see complete key on page *I · 1*).

Symbole im Register stellen die rechts im Schlüssel erklärten Kategorien dar. Symbole mit hochgestellten Ziffern (⋀[1]) bezeichnen Unterabteilungen einer Kategorie (vgl. vollständiger Schlüssel auf Seite *I · 1*).

Los símbolos incluídos en el texto del índice representan las grandes categorias identificadas con la clave a la derecha. Los símbolos con numeros en su parte superior (⋀[1]) identifican las subcategorías (véase la clave completa en la página *I · 1*).

Les symboles de l'index représentent les catégories indiquées dans la légende à droite. Les symboles suivis d'un indice (⋀[1]) représentent des sous-catégories (voir légende complète à la page *I · 1*).

Os símbolos incluídos no texto do índice representam as grandes categorias identificadas com a chave à direita. Os símbolos com números em sua parte superior (⋀[1]) identificam as subcategorias (veja-se a chave completa à página *I · 1*).

ENGLISH	DEUTSCH	ESPAÑOL	FRANÇAIS	PORTUGUÊS
∧ Mountain	Berg	Montaña	Montagne	Montanha
⋀ Mountains	Gebirge	Montañas	Montagnes	Montanhas
)(Pass	Paß	Paso	Col	Passo
∨ Valley, Canyon	Tal, Cañon	Valle, Cañón	Vallée, Canyon	Vale, Canhão
≍ Plain	Ebene	Llano	Plaine	Planície
› Cape	Kap	Cabo	Cap	Cabo
I Island	Insel	Isla	Île	Ilha
II Islands	Inseln	Islas	Îles	Ilhas
♦ Other Topographic Features	Andere Topographische Objekte	Otros Elementos Topográficos	Autres données topographiques	Outros acidentes topográficos

ESPAÑOL / FRANÇAIS / PORTUGUÊS

Nombre / Nom / Nome	Página / Page	Lat.°′	Long.°′ W = Oeste / W = Ouest
Triponzo	66	42.50 N	12.56 E
Tripp	198	43.13 N	97.57 W
Trips Subdivision	281	42.34 N	83.25 W
Triptis	54	50.44 N	11.52 E
Tripura □[3]	120	24.00 N	92.00 E
Triquet, Lac ⊜	186	50.42 N	59.47 W
Trisanna ≃	58	47.07 N	10.30 E
Tristan da Cunha Group II	10	37.15 S	12.30 W
Tristan Island I	10	37.05 S	12.17 W
Tristán Suárez	258	34.53 S	58.34 W
Tristao, Îles II	150	10.53 N	14.58 W
Tristate Village	278	41.44 N	87.57 W
Triste	34	42.23 N	0.43 W
Triste, Golfo ⊂	246	10.40 N	68.10 W
Triśuli Gaṅggā ≃	124	27.49 N	84.47 E
Tri Ton	110	10.25 N	105.00 E
Tritriva	157b	22.46 S	46.07 E
Trittau	52	53.37 N	10.25 E
Trittenheim	56	49.49 N	6.54 E
Triuggio	266b	45.40 N	9.16 E
Triumph	194	29.20 N	89.28 W
Triunfo, Igarapé ≃	250	6.22 S	52.25 W
Trivandrum	122	8.29 N	76.55 E
Trivento	66	41.47 N	14.33 E
Trivero	62	45.40 N	8.10 E
Trivigno	68	40.35 N	15.59 E
Trkmanka ≃	61	48.47 N	16.50 E
Trnava	30	48.23 N	17.35 E
Trnovo → Veliko Târnovo	38	43.04 N	25.39 E
Tr'ochgolovyj Golec, gora ∧	88	53.22 N	107.03 E
Tr'ochizbenka	83	48.45 N	38.58 E
Tr'ochsv'atskoje	82	56.29 N	37.03 E
Trochtelfingen	58	48.18 N	9.14 E
Trochu	182	51.50 N	113.13 W
Troense	41	55.02 N	10.39 E
Trofa, Arroyo de ≃	266a	40.30 N	3.45 W
Trofaich	61	47.25 N	15.00 E
Trofarello	62	44.59 N	7.44 E
Trögd >[1]	40	59.31 N	17.15 E
Trogen	58	47.24 N	9.28 E
Trogir	36	43.31 N	16.15 E
Troglav ∧	36	43.57 N	16.36 E
Tröglitz	54	51.04 N	12.11 E
Troia	68	41.22 N	15.18 E
Troica	76	54.24 N	40.14 E
Troice-Lykovo ◆[8]	265b	55.47 N	37.24 E
Troick, Ross.	86	54.06 N	61.35 E
Troick, Ross.	88	57.25 N	94.50 E
Troickaja	78	45.08 N	38.07 E
Troickij, Ross.	80	50.14 N	43.05 E
Troickij, Ross.	80	50.14 N	43.03 E
Troickij, Ross.	86	50.41 N	54.38 E
Troickij, Ross.	86	57.03 N	63.43 E
Troickij, Ross.	88	54.36 N	113.09 E
Troickije Rosl'ai	80	53.21 N	41.24 E
Troickij Sungur	80	53.17 N	47.37 E
Troickij Zavod	88	53.27 N	102.09 E
Troicko-Charcyzsk	83	47.58 N	38.16 E
Troickoje, Ross.	78	51.17 N	41.28 E
Troickoje, Ross.	80	46.26 N	44.15 E
Troickoje, Ross.	80	53.06 N	52.32 E
Troickoje, Ross.	80	53.22 N	48.23 E
Troickoje, Ross.	80	53.23 N	52.48 E
Troickoje, Ross.	82	55.23 N	37.25 E
Troickoje, Ross.	82	54.52 N	37.07 E
Troickoje, Ross.	83	47.22 N	38.53 E
Troickoje, Ross.	86	52.58 N	84.40 E
Troickoje, Ross.	86	59.07 N	58.25 E
Troickoje, Ross.	86	52.19 N	56.23 E
Troickoje, Ross.	89	49.27 N	136.36 E
Troickoje, Ukr.	78	49.55 N	38.19 E
Troickoje, Ukr.	78	47.38 N	30.19 E
Troickoje, Ukr.	83	48.32 N	38.23 E
Troicko-Pečorsk	24	62.44 N	56.06 E
Troina	70	37.47 N	14.36 E
Troina ≃	70	37.49 N	14.46 E
Troisdorf	56	50.49 N	7.08 E
Trois Fourches, Cap des >	148	35.26 N	2.58 W
Trois-Pistoles	186	48.07 N	69.10 W
Trois Pitons, Morne ∧	240d	15.22 N	61.20 W
Trois Ponts	56	50.22 N	5.52 E
Trois-Rivières, P.Q., Can.	206	46.21 N	72.33 W
Trois-Rivières, Guad.	241o	15.59 N	61.39 W
Trois-Rivières-Ouest	206	46.19 N	72.35 W
Troisvierges	56	50.08 N	6.00 E
Trojan	38	42.51 N	24.43 E
Trojanov	78	50.07 N	28.31 E
Trojanova Tabla ⊥	38	44.37 N	22.20 E
Trojanovka	78	51.20 N	25.17 E
Trojebratskij	86	54.28 N	66.01 E
Trojekurovo, Ross.	76	53.00 N	38.58 E
Trojekurovo, Ross.	76	53.25 N	39.43 E
Troldhede	41	55.59 N	8.45 E
Trolleholm	41	55.54 N	13.15 E
Trollhättan	26	58.16 N	12.18 E
Trollheimen ∧	26	62.51 N	9.05 E
Trombay ◆[8]	272c	19.02 N	72.57 E
Trombetas ≃	250	1.55 S	55.35 W
Tromelin, Île I	138	15.52 S	54.25 E
Tromello	62	45.12 N	8.52 E
Tromper Wiek ⊂	54	54.37 N	13.24 E
Trompia, Val V	64	45.44 N	10.12 E
Trompsburg	158	30.01 S	25.46 E
Troms □[6]	24	69.15 N	19.40 E
Tromsø	24	69.40 N	18.58 E
Trona	204	35.45 N	117.22 W
Tronador, Monte ∧	254	41.10 S	71.54 W
Troncoso	234	22.44 N	102.22 W
Trondheim	26	63.25 N	10.25 E
Trondheimsfjorden ⊂[2]	26	63.39 N	10.49 E
Trondheimsleia ʊ	26	63.30 N	9.00 E
Tronto ≃	66	42.54 N	13.55 E
Tronville-en-Barrois	56	48.43 N	5.17 E
Tronzano Vercellese	62	45.21 N	8.10 E
Troo	50	47.47 N	0.47 E
Troödos	130	34.55 N	32.53 E
Trooilapspan	158	28.40 S	21.25 E
Troon, Eng., U.K.	42	50.12 N	5.16 W
Troon, Scot., U.K.	46	55.32 N	4.40 W
Trooper	285	40.09 N	75.24 W
Troparevo	82	55.23 N	35.54 E
Tropar'ovo ◆[8]	265b	55.39 N	37.29 E
Tropas, Rio das ≃	250	6.07 S	57.28 W
Tropea	68	38.41 N	15.54 E
Trophy Mountain ∧	182	51.47 N	119.48 W
Tropic	200	37.37 N	112.04 W
Tropojë	38	42.24 N	20.10 E
Troppau → Opava	30	49.56 N	17.54 E
Trosa	40	58.54 N	17.33 E
Troškovo	80	57.19 N	46.05 E
Troškūnai	76	55.36 N	24.51 E
Trosna	76	52.26 N	35.46 E
Trossingen	58	48.04 N	8.38 E
Trostan ∧	48	55.03 N	6.09 W
Trost'anec, Ukr.	78	50.28 N	34.59 E
Trost'anec, Ukr.	78	48.31 N	29.12 E
Tröstau	60	50.01 N	11.57 E
Trostberg	60	48.01 N	12.32 E
Trostenskoje, ozero ⊜	82	55.52 N	36.29 E
Trotha ◆[8]	54	51.31 N	11.58 E
Trottiscliffe	260	51.19 N	0.21 E
Trotuș ≃	38	46.03 N	27.14 E
Trotwood	218	39.47 N	84.18 W
Troublesome Creek ≃	219	39.54 N	91.37 W
Troubridge Point >	168b	35.11 S	137.41 E
Trou-du-Nord	238	19.38 N	72.01 W
Troup	222	32.08 N	95.07 W
Troup Head >	46	57.41 N	2.18 W
Troupsburg	210	42.03 N	77.33 W
Trout	194	31.41 N	92.10 W
Trout ≃, N.T., Can.	176	61.19 N	119.51 W
Trout ≃, N.A.	206	45.05 N	74.10 W
Trout Brook ≃, Ma., U.S.	283	42.16 N	71.18 W
Trout Brook ≃, Ma., U.S.	283	42.39 N	71.16 W
Trout Creek, Mi., U.S.	190	46.28 N	89.00 W
Trout Creek, Mt., U.S.	182	47.50 N	115.35 W
Trout Creek, N.Y., U.S.	210	42.12 N	75.17 W
Trout Creek ≃, Az., U.S.	200	34.56 N	113.36 W
Trout Creek ≃, Or., U.S.	202	44.48 N	121.03 W
Trout Creek ≃, Or., U.S.	202	42.23 N	118.36 W
Trout Creek ≃, Pa., U.S.	285	40.07 N	75.24 W
Trout Creek ≃, Wa., U.S.	224	46.02 N	121.12 W
Trout Creek Pass)(	200	38.54 N	105.58 W
Troutdale	224	45.32 N	122.23 W
Trout Lake	224	45.59 N	121.31 W
Trout Lake ⊜, B.C., Can.	182	50.35 N	117.26 W
Trout Lake ⊜, N.T., Can.	176	60.35 N	121.10 W
Trout Lake ⊜, On., Can.	184	51.13 N	93.20 W
Trout Lake ⊜, On., Can.	190	46.18 N	79.20 W
Trout Lake ⊜, On., Can.	190	46.13 N	80.35 W
Trout Lake Creek ≃	224	46.00 N	121.30 W
Trout Peak ∧	202	44.36 N	109.32 W
Trout River	186	49.29 N	58.08 W
Trout Run	210	41.23 N	77.03 W
Troutville, Pa., U.S.	214	41.02 N	78.47 W
Troutville, Va., U.S.	192	37.25 N	79.52 W
Trouville-sur-Mer	50	49.22 N	0.05 E
Trowbridge	42	51.20 N	2.13 W
Troxelville	210	40.48 N	77.12 W
Troy, Al., U.S.	194	31.48 N	85.58 W
Troy, Id., U.S.	202	46.44 N	116.46 W
Troy, Il., U.S.	219	38.43 N	89.52 W
Troy, In., U.S.	194	37.59 N	86.47 W
Troy, Ks., U.S.	198	39.46 N	95.05 W
Troy, Mi., U.S.	214	42.34 N	83.09 W
Troy, Mo., U.S.	219	38.58 N	90.58 W
Troy, Mt., U.S.	202	48.27 N	115.53 W
Troy, N.H., U.S.	207	42.49 N	72.10 W
Troy, N.Y., U.S.	210	42.43 N	73.41 W
Troy, N.C., U.S.	192	35.21 N	79.53 W
Troy, Oh., U.S.	218	40.02 N	84.12 W
Troy, Pa., U.S.	210	41.47 N	76.47 W
Troy, Tn., U.S.	194	36.20 N	89.09 W
Troy, Tx., U.S.	222	31.12 N	97.18 W
Troy Brook ≃	276	40.50 N	74.22 W
Troyes	50	48.18 N	4.05 E
Troy Grove	216	41.28 N	89.05 W
Troy Hills	210	40.51 N	74.23 W
Troy Lake ⊜	204	34.49 N	116.33 W
Troy Meadows ⩨	276	40.50 N	74.22 W
Troy Peak ∧	204	38.19 N	115.30 W
Troy → Truva ⊥	130	39.57 N	26.15 E
Trpanj	36	43.00 N	17.17 E
Trstená	30	49.22 N	19.37 E
Trstenik	38	43.37 N	21.00 E
Trst → Trieste	64	45.40 N	13.46 E
Truax	184	49.55 N	104.58 W
Trubč'ovsk	76	52.37 N	33.44 E
Trubetčino	76	52.53 N	39.33 E
Trubino, Ross.	82	54.58 N	36.42 E
Trubino, Ross.	82	55.59 N	38.08 E
Trub'ož ≃	82	56.44 N	38.51 E
Truchas	200	36.02 N	105.48 W
Truchas Peak ∧	200	35.58 N	105.39 W
Truchtersheim	58	48.40 N	7.36 E
Trucial States → United Arab Emirates □[1]	128	24.00 N	54.00 E
Truckee	226	39.19 N	120.10 W
Truckee ≃	204	39.51 N	119.24 W
Trucksville	210	41.18 N	75.56 W
Trud	76	57.37 N	33.58 E
Trudfront	80	45.56 N	47.41 E
Trudnovo	86	56.39 N	91.30 E
Trudovaja	83	48.21 N	38.04 E
Trudovoj	80	51.42 N	52.43 E
Trues Creek ≃	276	40.41 N	73.17 W
Truganina	274b	37.49 S	144.43 E
Truim ≃	46	57.02 N	4.10 W
Truite, Lac à la ⊜	190	47.16 N	78.17 W
Trujillo, Col.	246	4.10 N	76.19 W
Trujillo, Esp.	34	39.28 N	5.53 W
Trujillo, Hond.	236	15.55 N	86.00 W
Trujillo, Méx.	234	23.10 N	103.13 W
Trujillo, Perú	248	8.07 S	79.02 W
Trujillo, Ven.	246	9.22 N	70.26 W
Trujillo □[3]	246	9.25 N	70.30 W
Trujillo Alto	240m	18.22 N	66.01 W
Trujillo Creek ≃	196	35.28 N	102.52 W
Truk Islands II	175c	7.25 N	151.47 E
Truk Lagoon ⊂	175c	7.25 N	151.45 E
Trull Brook ≃	283	42.39 N	71.15 W
Truman	198	43.49 N	94.26 W
Trumann	194	35.40 N	90.30 W
Trumansburg	210	42.32 N	76.39 W
Trumbauersville	208	40.25 N	75.23 W
Trumbull	207	41.14 N	73.12 W
Trumbull □[6]	214	41.14 N	80.52 W
Trumbull, Mount ∧	200	36.25 N	113.10 W
Trumon	114	2.49 N	97.38 E
Trun, Fr.	50	48.51 N	0.02 E
Trun, Schw.	58	46.45 N	8.58 E
Trundle	166	32.55 S	147.43 E
Trung Luong	110	13.57 N	109.15 E
Trung Phan □[9]	110	15.00 N	108.00 E
Trunovskoje	80	45.29 N	42.08 E
Truro, Austl.	168b	34.25 S	139.07 E
Truro, N.S., Can.	186	45.22 N	63.16 W
Truro, Eng., U.K.	42	50.16 N	5.03 W
Truro, Ma., U.S.	207	41.59 N	70.03 W
Trusan ≃	112	4.58 N	115.11 E
Truscott	196	33.45 N	99.49 W
Trušeny	78	47.04 N	28.41 E
Trușești	38	47.46 N	27.01 E
Trusetal	54	50.47 N	10.25 E
Truskavec	78	49.16 N	23.33 E
Truslejka	80	53.54 N	46.24 E
Trus Madi, Gunong ∧	112	5.33 N	116.31 E
Trust Territory of the Pacific Islands □[2]	14	5.00 N	137.00 E
Truth or Consequences (Hot Springs)	200	33.07 N	107.15 W
Trutnov	30	50.34 N	15.55 E
Truva (Troy) ⊥	130	39.57 N	26.15 E
Truxall	279b	40.33 N	79.33 W
Truxton, Mo., U.S.	219	39.00 N	91.14 W
Truxton, N.Y., U.S.	210	42.43 N	76.02 W
Truxton Wash V	200	35.38 N	114.04 W
Truyère ≃	32	44.39 N	2.34 E
Trwyn Cilan >	42	52.46 N	4.30 W
Tryon, Ne., U.S.	198	41.33 N	100.57 W
Tryon, N.C., U.S.	192	35.12 N	82.14 W
Tryonville	214	41.42 N	79.47 W
Trysil	26	61.19 N	12.16 E
Trysilelva (Klarälven) ≃	26	59.23 N	13.32 E
Tryškiai	76	56.04 N	22.35 E
Tryweryn ≃	42	52.55 N	3.35 W
Trzcianka	30	53.03 N	16.28 E
Trzciel	30	52.23 N	15.52 E
Trzcińsko-Zdrój	30	52.58 N	14.35 E
Trzebiatów	30	54.04 N	15.14 E
Trzebiel	54	51.37 N	14.50 E
Trzebież	30	53.42 N	14.31 E
Trzebinia	30	50.10 N	19.18 E
Trzebnica	30	51.19 N	17.03 E
Trzemeszno	30	52.35 N	17.50 E
Trzęsacz	54	54.05 N	14.58 E
Tržič	61	46.22 N	14.19 E
Tsacha Lake ⊜	182	53.05 N	124.40 W
Tsala Apopka Lake ⊜	220	28.52 N	82.20 W
Tsamkong → Zhanjiang	102	21.16 N	110.28 E
Tsandi	156	17.42 S	14.50 E
Tsangano	154	15.08 S	34.32 E
Ts'anghsien → Cangzhou	98	38.19 N	116.51 E
T'sangwu → Wuzhou	102	23.30 N	111.27 E
Ts'aot'un	100	23.59 N	120.41 E
Tsarabaria	157b	13.46 S	49.58 E
Tsaramandroso	157b	16.22 S	47.02 E
Tsaratanana	157b	16.47 S	47.39 E
Tsaratanana, Massif du ⩘	157b	14.00 S	49.00 E
Tsaraxaibis	158	27.25 S	19.22 E
Tsaritsyn → Volgograd	80	48.44 N	44.25 E
Tsau	156	20.12 S	22.22 E
Tsaukaib	156	26.37 S	15.31 E
Tsavo	154	2.59 S	38.28 E
Tsavo East National Park ♠	154	2.11 S	38.25 E
Tsavo West National Park ♠	154	2.55 S	37.55 E
Tsawwassen	224	49.01 N	123.06 W
Tsaydaychuz Peak ∧	182	53.02 N	126.35 W
Tsayta Lake ⊜	182	55.25 N	125.30 W
Tschad → Chad □[1]	146	15.00 N	19.00 E
Tschad-See → Chad, Lake ⊜	146	13.20 N	14.00 E
Tschagguns	58	47.05 N	9.54 E
Tschamut	58	46.40 N	8.42 E
Tschangscha → Changsha	100	28.12 N	112.58 E
Tschangtschun → Changchun	89	43.53 N	125.19 E
Tschechoslowakei → Czechoslovakia □[1]	30	49.30 N	17.00 E
Tscheljuskin, Kap → Čel'uskin, mys >	74	77.45 N	104.20 E
Tschengtu → Chengdu	107	30.39 N	104.04 E
Tschenstochau → Częstochowa	30	50.49 N	19.06 E
Tschernitz	54	51.35 N	14.37 E
Tscheschkaja-Bucht → Češskaja guba ⊂	24	67.30 N	46.30 E
Tschida, Lake ⊜[1]	198	46.36 N	101.54 W
Tschingtau → Qingdao	98	36.06 N	120.19 E
Tschittagong → Chittagong	120	22.20 N	91.50 E
Tschuktschen-Meer → Chukchi Sea ⍑[2]	16	69.00 N	171.00 W
Tschungking → Chongqing	107	29.34 N	106.35 E
Tsekanyani	156	19.52 S	26.39 E
Tsembeyi	158	31.36 S	27.03 E
Ts'engwen ≃	100	23.03 N	120.03 E
Tsenke ≃	273b	4.24 S	15.26 E
Tses	156	25.58 S	18.08 E
Tsévié	150	6.25 N	1.13 E
Tshabong	156	26.03 S	22.29 E
Tshabuta	152	7.47 S	23.16 E
Tshane	156	24.05 S	21.54 E
Tshaneni	158	26.00 S	31.47 E
Tshangalele, Lac ⊜	154	10.55 S	27.03 E
Tshangu ≃	273b	4.25 S	15.23 E
Tshela	152	4.59 S	12.56 E
Tshesebe	156	21.51 S	27.35 E
Tshibeke	154	2.44 S	28.36 E
Tshibinda	154	2.19 S	28.45 E
Tshibomba	152	9.02 S	22.34 E
Tshidilamolomo	156	25.50 S	24.41 E
Tshikapa	152	6.25 S	20.48 E
Tshilenge	152	6.15 S	23.46 E
Tshimbulu	152	6.29 S	22.51 E
Tshindjamba	152	10.54 S	22.41 E
Tshinota	152	7.01 S	20.57 E
Tshinsenda	154	12.18 S	27.58 E
Tshisuku	152	6.26 S	19.55 E
Tshitadi	152	6.45 S	21.45 E
Tshoa	152	5.34 S	12.41 E
Tshofa	154	5.14 S	25.15 E
Tshopo ≃	154	0.33 N	25.07 E
Tshuapa ≃	152	0.14 S	20.42 E
Tshukudu	156	22.30 S	23.22 E
Tshumbiri	152	2.39 S	16.14 E
Tshwaane	156	22.29 S	22.03 E
Tsiafajavona ∧	157b	19.21 S	47.15 E
Tsianaloka	157b	18.08 S	44.50 E
Tsiémé ≃	273b	4.15 S	15.18 E
Tsiga	152	1.32 S	10.11 E
Tsihombe	157b	25.18 S	45.29 E
Tsilmamo	144	6.01 N	35.17 E
Tsimanampetsotsa, Lac ⊜	157b	24.08 S	43.46 E
Tsimilofo	157b	24.59 S	45.10 E
Tsimpsean Indian Reserve ◆[4]	182	54.30 N	130.22 W
Tsinan → Jinan	98	36.40 N	116.57 E
Tsineng	158	27.06 S	23.04 E
Tsinghai → Qinghai □[4]	90	36.00 N	96.00 E
Tsingkiang → Qingjiang	100	33.35 N	119.02 E
Tsingtao → Qingdao	98	36.06 N	120.19 E
Tsing Yi I	271d	22.21 N	114.05 E
Tsingyuan → Baoding	105	38.52 N	115.29 E
Tsining → Jining	98	35.25 N	116.36 E
Tsinjoarivo	157b	19.37 S	47.40 E
Tsinjomitondraka	157b	15.36 S	47.08 E
Tsinling Shan → Qin Ling ⩘	102	34.00 N	108.00 E
Tsintsabis	156	18.45 S	17.51 E
Tsiribihina ≃	157b	19.42 S	44.31 E
Tsiroanomandidy	157b	18.46 S	46.02 E
Tsitondroina	157b	21.19 S	46.00 E
Tsitsihar → Qiqihar	89	47.19 N	123.55 E
Tsitsikama Forest and Coastal National Park ♠	158	33.57 S	23.53 E
Tsitsutl Peak ∧	182	52.44 N	125.47 W
Tsivory	157b	24.04 S	46.05 E
Tskhinvali → Cchinvali	84	42.13 N	43.56 E
Tsna → Cna ≃	80	54.32 N	42.05 E
Tsobis	156	19.27 S	17.30 E
Tsolo	158	31.18 S	28.37 E
Tsomo	158	32.00 S	27.42 E
Tsomo ≃	158	32.25 S	27.50 E
Tsoying	100	22.41 N	120.17 E
Tsu	94	34.43 N	136.31 E
Tsubakuro-dake ∧	94	36.24 N	137.42 E
Tsubame	92	37.39 N	138.56 E
Tsubata	94	36.40 N	136.44 E
Tsuboro-suigenchi ⊜[1]	270	34.24 N	135.54 E
Tsuchiura	94	36.05 N	140.12 E
Tsuchiyama	94	34.56 N	136.17 E
Tsuda, Nihon	96	34.17 N	134.15 E
Tsuda, Nihon	270	34.49 N	135.43 E
Tsuen Wan (Quanwan)	271d	22.22 N	114.07 E
Tsugaru-hantō >[1]	92	41.00 N	140.30 E
Tsugaru-heiya ≚	92	40.49 N	140.27 E
Tsugaru-kaikyō ʊ	92a	41.35 N	141.00 E
Tsuge	94	34.37 N	135.57 E
Tsugu	94	35.10 N	137.37 E
Tsuha	174m	26.14 N	127.47 E
Tsuiki	96	33.40 N	131.03 E
Tsujidō	268	35.20 N	139.27 E
Tsukahara	268	35.18 N	139.58 E
Tsukechi	94	35.38 N	137.26 E
Tsuken-jima I	174m	26.15 N	127.57 E
Tsukigase	94	34.42 N	136.02 E
Tsukinowa-kofun ⊥	96	34.55 N	134.11 E
Tsukiyono	94	36.41 N	138.59 E
Tsukuba	94	36.13 N	140.06 E
Tsukuba-san ∧	94	36.13 N	140.06 E
Tsukude	94	34.59 N	137.25 E
Tsukui	94	35.35 N	139.16 E
Tsukumi	96	33.04 N	131.52 E
Tsukumono ◆[8]	270	34.50 N	135.11 E
Tsukushi-heiya ≚	96	33.20 N	130.30 E
Tsukushi-sanchi ⩘	92	33.30 N	130.30 E
Tsumagoi	94	36.31 N	138.32 E
Tsumeb	156	19.13 S	17.42 E
Tsumeb □[5]	156	19.00 S	17.30 E
Tsumeki-zaki >	94	34.39 N	138.59 E
Tsumis Park	156	23.43 S	17.28 E
Tsumkwe	156	19.41 S	20.30 E
Tsuna	96	34.26 N	134.54 E
Tsunan	94	37.01 N	138.39 E
Tsunashima ◆[8]	268	35.32 N	139.38 E
Tsunekami-misaki >	94	35.38 N	135.49 E
Tsuni → Zunyi	102	27.39 N	106.57 E
Tsuno-shima I	96	34.21 N	130.51 E
Tsuru	94	35.33 N	138.55 E
Tsuruga	94	35.39 N	136.04 E
Tsurugaoka-hachimangu Shrine ⚲[1]	268	35.19 N	139.33 E
Tsurugashima	268	35.56 N	139.24 E
Tsuruga-wan ⊂	94	35.45 N	136.04 E
Tsurugi	94	36.27 N	136.38 E
Tsurugi-dake ∧	94	36.37 N	137.37 E
Tsurugi-san ∧	96	33.51 N	134.06 E
Tsurugi-san-kokutei-kōen ♠	96	33.50 N	134.06 E
Tsuruhara	270	34.26 N	135.20 E
Tsuruma	268	35.51 N	139.33 E
Tsurumi ◆[8]	268	35.30 N	139.41 E
Tsurumi ≃	94	35.29 N	139.41 E
Tsurumi-dake ∧	96	33.17 N	131.26 E
Tsuruoka	92	38.44 N	139.50 E
Tsushima, Nihon	94	35.10 N	136.43 E
Tsushima, Nihon	96	33.05 N	132.30 E
Tsushima II	92	34.30 N	129.22 E
Tsushima-kaikyō (Eastern Channel) ʊ	92	34.00 N	129.00 E
Tsuwano	96	34.28 N	131.46 E
Tsuyama	96	35.03 N	134.00 E
Tsuyazaki	96	33.47 N	130.28 E
Ttruchchendūr	122	8.29 N	78.07 E
Tua	152	3.38 S	16.36 E
Tua ≃	34	41.13 N	7.26 W
Tua, Tanjung >	115a	5.54 S	105.44 E
Tua Chau	110	21.55 N	103.21 E
Tuakau	172	37.16 S	174.57 E
Tual	164	5.40 S	132.45 E
Tualatin	224	45.23 N	122.45 W
Tualatin ≃	224	45.20 N	122.39 W
Tuam	48	53.31 N	8.50 W
Tuamarina	172	41.26 S	173.57 E
Tuamotu, Îles (Tuamotu Archipelago) II	14	19.00 S	142.00 W
Tuamotu Ridge ✦[3]	14	17.00 S	145.00 W
Tuan, Tanjong >	114	2.23 N	101.52 E
Tuanan	112	2.07 S	114.24 E
Tuanfeng	100	30.38 N	114.51 E
Tuan Giao	110	21.35 N	103.25 E
Tuangku, Pulau I	114	2.10 N	97.16 E
Tuanlin	98	39.35 N	119.15 E
Tuannian	107	29.55 N	106.03 E
Tuanpi	100	30.44 N	115.13 E
Tuanshan	98	40.02 N	123.34 E
Tuanwang	98	36.45 N	120.38 E
Tuanxi	102	27.28 N	107.08 E
Tuapa	174v	18.57 S	169.54 W
Tuapeka Mouth	172	46.01 S	169.31 E
Tuapse	84	44.07 N	39.05 E
Tuaran	112	6.11 N	116.14 E
Tuas	114	1.19 N	103.38 E
Tuasivi	175a	13.40 S	172.07 W
Tuasivi, Cape >	175a	13.40 S	172.07 W
Tuatapere	172	46.08 S	167.41 E
Tuath, Loch ʊ	46	56.30 N	6.12 W
Tuba	88	57.24 N	102.48 E
Tuba ≃	86	53.57 N	91.31 E
Tubac	200	31.36 N	111.02 W
Tuba City	200	36.08 N	111.14 W
T'ub'ak-Čekurča	80	56.05 N	49.56 E
Tubalan Head >	116	6.30 N	125.35 E
Tuban	115a	6.54 S	112.03 E
Tubarão	252	28.30 S	49.01 W
Ţūbās	132	32.19 N	35.22 E
Tubau	112	3.08 N	113.42 E
Tubbataha Reefs ✦[2]	116	8.51 N	119.56 E
Tubbergen	52	52.25 N	6.46 E
Tubbs Island I	282	38.08 N	122.26 W
Ţubhār	142	29.19 N	30.42 E
Tubig ≃	116	11.54 N	125.25 E
Tubigan Island I	116	6.26 N	120.47 E
Tubingantan Point >	116	5.54 N	120.55 E
Tübingen	58	48.31 N	9.02 E
Tübingen □[5]	58	48.10 N	9.30 E
Tubinskij	86	52.53 N	58.13 E
Tubize	50	50.41 N	4.12 E
T'ub-Karagan, mys >	84	44.39 N	50.18 E
T'ub-Karagan, poluostrov >[1]	84	44.30 N	50.30 E
Tubli	116	13.56 N	124.09 E
Tubod	116	8.03 N	123.48 E
Tubre	64	46.39 N	10.27 E
Ţubruq (Tobruk)	146	32.05 N	23.59 E
Tuburan, Pil.	116	10.44 N	123.49 W
Tuburan, Pil.	116	6.39 N	122.16 E
Tubusereia	164	9.33 S	147.18 E
Tubutama	200	30.53 N	111.29 W
Tucacas	246	10.48 N	68.19 W
Tucacas, Punta >	246	10.50 N	68.14 W
Tucalota Creek ≃	228	33.32 N	117.10 W
Tucannon ≃	202	46.33 N	118.11 W
Tucano	250	10.58 S	38.48 W
Tucava ≃	248	18.37 S	58.59 W
T'uch'ang	100	24.35 N	121.29 E
Tucheim	54	52.17 N	12.11 E
Tüchen	54	53.04 N	12.05 E
T'uch'eng, T'aiwan	269d	24.59 N	121.26 E
Tucheng, Zhg.	98	38.53 N	121.15 E
Tucheng, Zhg.	102	28.12 N	105.58 E
Tuchengzi, Zhg.	98	41.20 N	116.29 E
Tuchengzi, Zhg.	98	40.29 N	124.24 E
Tuchengzi, Zhg.	104	42.27 N	122.44 E
Tuchengzicun	104	41.52 N	120.41 E
Tuchengziwuhao	98	40.56 N	113.58 E
Tuchlovice	54	50.06 N	14.00 E
Tuchola	30	53.35 N	17.50 E
Tuchów	30	49.54 N	21.03 E
T'uchtet	86	56.32 N	89.19 E
Tuckahoe, N.J., U.S.	208	39.17 N	74.45 W
Tuckahoe, N.Y., U.S.	276	40.57 N	73.49 W
Tuckahoe ≃	208	39.17 N	74.39 W
Tuckahoe Creek ≃	208	38.49 N	75.53 W
Tuckanarra	162	27.07 S	118.05 E
Tucker Heights	210	42.55 N	73.55 W
Tuckerman	194	35.43 N	91.11 W
Tuckernuck Island I	207	41.18 N	70.15 W
Tuckerton, N.J., U.S.	208	39.36 N	74.20 W
Tuckerton, Pa., U.S.	208	40.25 N	75.57 W
Tuckfield, Mount ∧	162	18.44 S	124.54 E
Tučkovo	82	55.36 N	36.28 E
Tucson	200	32.13 N	110.55 W
Tucumã ≃[1]	246	3.58 S	66.26 W
Tucumán □[4]	252	27.00 S	65.30 W
Tucumán → San Miguel de Tucumán	252	26.49 S	65.13 W
Tucumcari	196	35.10 N	103.43 W
Tucumcari Mountain ∧	196	35.08 N	103.42 W
Tucunuco	252	30.36 S	68.38 W
Tucupido	246	9.17 N	65.47 W
Tucupita	246	9.04 N	62.03 W
Tucuruí	250	3.42 S	49.27 W
Tucuruí, Represa de ⊜[1]	250	4.40 S	49.20 W
Tucuruvi ◆[8]	287b	23.28 S	46.35 W
Tuczna	30	51.54 N	23.26 E
Tud ≃	42	52.38 N	1.15 E
Tudameda	112	10.52 S	122.55 E
Tudcum	252	30.14 S	69.15 W
Tudeå ≃	41	55.23 N	11.13 E
Tudela, Esp.	34	42.05 N	1.36 W
Tudela, Pil.	116	8.15 N	123.50 E
Tudela de Duero	34	41.35 N	4.35 W
Tudian	106	30.35 N	120.37 E
Tudichang	107	30.06 N	103.56 E
Tuditang	100	30.12 N	114.18 E
Tudmur (Palmyra)	130	34.33 N	38.17 E
Tudu	76	59.11 N	26.51 E
Tudweiliog	42	52.54 N	4.35 W
Tuela ≃	34	41.30 N	7.12 W
Tuen Mun	271d	22.24 N	113.58 E
Tuenno	64	46.20 N	11.01 E
Tueré ≃	250	2.48 S	50.59 W
Tuergate	85	40.28 N	75.21 E
Tufanbeyli	130	38.16 N	36.13 E
Tufānganj	124	26.19 N	89.40 E
Tuffé	50	48.07 N	0.31 E
Tufi	164	9.05 S	149.20 E
Tufo	68	41.00 N	14.47 E
Tufts University ⚲[2]	283	42.24 N	71.07 W
Tufu Point >	174y	14.13 S	169.32 W
Tugaske	184	50.53 N	106.16 W
Tugela	158	29.09 S	31.29 E
Tugela ≃	158	29.14 S	31.30 E
Tugela Falls ∟	158	28.45 S	28.58 E
Tugela Ferry	158	28.44 S	30.27 E
Tug Fork ≃	192	38.06 N	82.36 W
Tuggerah Lake ⊂	170	33.18 S	151.30 E
Tughlakābād ◆[8]	272a	28.31 N	77.16 E
Tugidak Island I	180	56.30 N	154.36 W
Tuğköyü	130	38.27 N	42.16 E
Tuglie	68	40.04 N	18.05 E
Tugnug Point >	116	11.21 N	125.38 E
Tugolesskij Bor	80	55.33 N	39.49 E
Tugolukovo	80	51.56 N	41.40 E
Tugubun Point >	116	7.00 N	126.27 E
Tuguegarao	116	17.37 N	121.44 E
Tugulym	86	57.04 N	64.39 E
Tugun	171a	28.09 S	153.30 E
Tugur	89	53.48 N	136.48 E
Tugur ≃	89	53.48 N	136.44 E
Tugurskij poluostrov >[1]	89	54.00 N	137.24 E
Tuguša	88	55.57 N	96.26 E
Tugutuj	88	52.40 N	104.50 E
Tuhai ≃	98	37.55 N	118.05 E
Tuhepu	104	40.54 N	122.49 E
Tuhuangba	102	31.40 N	108.21 E
Tuibo	89	44.01 N	127.47 E
Tuichi ≃	248	14.36 S	67.35 W
Tuim	86	54.20 N	89.55 E
Tuineje	148	28.19 N	14.03 W
Tuira ≃	246	8.21 N	78.03 W
Tuirc, Beinn an ∧[2]	46	55.34 N	5.34 W
Tuitán	234	21.08 N	103.48 W
Tuitui	256	22.47 S	46.42 W
Tuj ≃	86	57.33 N	72.31 E
T'ujabuguz	85	40.58 N	69.15 E
Tujemojnak	86	49.20 N	62.55 E
Tuji-ri	98	41.31 N	127.12 E
Tujmazy	80	54.36 N	53.42 E
Tüjn Gol ≃	102	45.04 N	100.46 E
Tujunga ◆[8]	280	34.15 N	118.17 W
Tujunga Valley V	280	34.17 N	118.20 W
Tujunga Wash V	280	34.09 N	118.24 W
Tukaj	86	55.24 N	90.49 E
T'ukalinsk	86	55.52 N	72.12 E
Tukan	86	53.50 N	57.26 E
Tukan ≃	86	60.02 N	71.36 E
Tukangbesi, Kepulauan II	112	5.40 S	123.50 E
Ţūkh, Mişr	142	27.41 N	30.49 E
Ţūkh, Mişr	142	30.21 N	31.12 E
Ţūkh al-Aqlām	142	30.52 N	31.26 E
Ţūkh al-Khayl	142	28.06 N	30.40 E
Tukituki ≃	172	39.36 S	176.57 E
Tuk Méas	110	10.40 N	104.34 E
Tukolon'	88	55.24 N	107.42 E
Tukosméra, Mont ∧	175f	19.35 S	169.22 E
Tukpo	154	4.25 N	25.52 E
Tūkrah	146	32.32 N	20.34 E
Tuktoyaktuk	180	69.27 N	133.02 W
Tuktoyaktuk Peninsula >[1]	180	69.45 N	131.20 W
Tukuj-Mekteb	84	44.20 N	45.11 E
Tukums	76	57.00 N	23.10 E
Tukuran	116	7.51 N	123.35 E
Tukuringra, chrebet ⩘	89	54.20 N	126.20 E
Tukuyu	154	9.15 S	33.39 E
T'uk'u Yüeh ∧	269d	25.02 N	121.38 E
Tukwila	224	47.28 N	122.15 W
Tula, Am. Sam.	174u	14.15 S	170.34 W
Tula, It.	71	40.44 N	8.59 E
Tula, Méx.	234	23.00 N	99.43 W
Tula, Nig.	146	9.50 N	11.28 E
Tula, Ross.	82	54.12 N	37.37 E
Tula □[8]	82	54.23 N	37.47 E
Tula ≃, Kenya	154	0.50 S	39.51 E
Tula ≃, Méx.	234	20.40 N	99.30 W
Tula ⊥	234	20.06 N	99.19 W
Tula de Allende	234	20.03 N	99.21 W
Tulaghi	175e	9.06 S	160.09 E
Tulagt Ar ≃	120	36.35 N	92.20 E
Tulai Nanshan ⩘	102	38.44 N	98.20 E
Tūlak	128	33.58 N	63.44 E
Tulalip Indian Reservation ◆[4]	224	48.06 N	122.15 W
Tulancingo	234	20.05 N	98.22 W
Tulangbawang ≃	112	4.24 S	105.52 E
Tulaodian	104	41.13 N	121.27 E
T'ul'apsy	86	57.28 N	89.38 E
Tulare, Ca., U.S.	226	36.12 N	119.20 W
Tulare, S.D., U.S.	198	44.44 N	98.30 W
Tulare □[6]	226	36.20 N	119.18 W
Tulare Canal ≅	226	36.08 N	119.25 W
Tulare Lake Bed ⊜	226	36.03 N	119.49 W
Tulare Lake Canal ≅	226	36.04 N	119.39 W
Tularosa	200	33.04 N	106.01 W
Tularosa ≃	200	33.41 N	108.46 W
Tularosa Valley ≚[1]	200	32.45 N	106.10 W
Tulbagh	158	33.17 S	19.09 E
Tulbing	264b	48.16 N	16.09 E
Tulbinger Kogel ∧	264b	48.17 N	16.09 E
Tulcán	246	0.48 N	77.43 W
Tulcea	38	45.11 N	28.48 E
Tulcea □[6]	38	45.00 N	29.00 E
Tul'čin	78	48.39 N	28.52 E
Tulcingo de Valle	234	18.03 N	98.26 W
Tule ≃, Nic.	236	11.20 N	84.52 W
Tule ≃, Ca., U.S.	226	36.03 N	119.50 W
Tule, North Branch ≃	226	36.06 N	119.22 W
Tule, South Branch ≃	226	36.05 N	119.29 W
Tule Canal ≅	226	38.37 N	121.35 W
Tule Creek ≃	196	34.40 N	101.14 W
T'ulek	85	41.56 N	75.41 E
Tulelake	204	41.57 N	121.29 W
Tule Lake Sump ⊜[1]	204	41.54 N	121.32 W
Tulemalu Lake ⊜	176	62.58 N	99.25 W
T'ulenij, mys >	84	40.12 N	50.22 E
T'ulenij, ostrov I	84	44.28 N	47.30 E
Tule River Indian Reservation ◆[4]	204	36.02 N	118.42 W
Tulette	62	44.17 N	4.56 E
Tule Valley V	200	39.20 N	113.25 W
T'ul'gan	86	52.22 N	56.12 E
Tul'goviči	78	51.47 N	29.38 E
Tuli	154	21.59 S	29.15 E
Tuli ≃	154	21.48 S	29.04 E
Tulia	196	34.32 N	101.45 W
Tuliahan ≃	269f	14.41 N	120.58 E
Tulica ≃	82	54.12 N	37.37 E
Tulik Volcano ∧[1]	180	53.22 N	168.03 W
Tuling	100	25.11 N	118.50 E
Tuliszków	30	52.05 N	18.17 E
Ţūlkarm	132	32.19 N	35.02 E
T'ul'kino	86	59.49 N	56.30 E
T'ul'kubas	85	42.28 N	70.02 E
Tulla	48	52.52 N	8.45 W
Tullahoma	194	35.21 N	86.12 W
Tullamarine	274b	37.41 S	144.52 E
Tullamarine International Airport ⊠, Austl.	169	37.40 S	144.50 E
Tullamarine International Airport ⊠, Austl.	274b	37.40 S	144.50 E
Tullamore, Austl.	166	32.38 S	147.34 E
Tullamore, On., Can.	275b	43.47 N	79.46 W
Tullamore, Ire.	48	53.16 N	7.30 W
Tullaroop Creek ≃	169	36.53 S	143.53 E
Tullaroop Reservoir ⊜[1]	169	37.07 S	143.52 E
Tull Bay ⊂	208	36.30 N	76.04 W
Tulle	32	45.16 N	1.46 E
Tullgarn	40	58.57 N	17.35 E
Tullibigeal	166	33.25 S	146.44 E
Tullinge	40	59.12 N	17.53 E
Tullins	62	45.18 N	5.29 E
Tulln	61	48.20 N	16.03 E
Tullner Feld ◆[1]	264b	48.19 N	16.10 E
Tulloch Reservoir ⊜[1]	226	37.53 N	120.35 W
Tullock Creek ≃	202	46.08 N	107.27 W
Tullos	194	31.49 N	92.19 W
Tullow	48	52.48 N	6.44 W
Tullus	140	11.03 N	24.33 E
Tully, Austl.	166	17.56 S	145.56 E
Tully, N.Y., U.S.	210	42.47 N	76.06 W
Tully Dam ◆[6]	207	42.39 N	72.11 W
Tullytown	208	40.09 N	74.49 W
Ţulmaythah	146	32.43 N	20.57 E
Tuloma ≃	24	68.52 N	32.49 E
Tulpfontein	158	32.44 S	19.43 E
Tulsa	196	36.09 N	95.59 W
Tulsequah	176	58.35 N	133.35 W
Tulsī Lake ⊜	272c	19.11 N	72.55 E
Tulsīpur	124	28.07 N	82.18 E
Tulsk	48	53.47 N	8.16 W
Tul'skij	84	44.31 N	40.10 E
Tulstrup	41	56.07 N	9.46 E
Tultepec	234	19.41 N	99.08 W
Tultitlán	286a	19.39 N	99.09 W
Tuluá	246	4.06 N	76.11 W
Tuluksak	180	61.06 N	160.58 W
Tulum	232	20.13 N	87.28 W
Tulum ⊥	232	20.12 N	87.26 W
Tulumayo ≃	248	11.10 S	75.16 W
Tulun	88	54.35 N	100.33 E
Tulungagung	115a	8.04 S	111.54 E
Tulungselapan	112	3.15 S	105.19 E
Tuluran Island I	116	10.59 N	119.17 E
Tulu Welel ∧	144	8.53 N	34.47 E
Tulyehualco ◆[8]	286a	19.15 N	99.01 W
Tum	164	3.38 S	130.23 E
Tuma	80	55.09 N	40.34 E
Tuma ≃	236	13.03 N	84.44 W
Tumacacori National Monument ♠	200	31.25 N	111.01 W
Tumaco	246	1.49 N	78.46 W
Tumaco, Rada de ⊂	246	1.55 N	78.45 W
Tumak	80	46.14 N	48.31 E
Tumalykol'	86	48.21 N	60.03 E
Tuman'an	84	41.00 N	44.40 E
Tuman-gang (Tumen) ≃	98	42.18 N	130.41 E
Tumannaja, gora ∧	180	66.33 N	179.43 E
Tumanovo	76	55.25 N	34.39 E
Tumanšet ≃	88	55.53 N	97.30 E
Tumanskij	180	63.58 N	178.12 E
Tumany	74	60.56 N	155.56 E
Tumarbong	116	10.23 N	119.27 E
T'um'ati → Sklad	74	71.55 N	123.33 E
Tumatumari	246	5.22 N	59.00 W
Tumauini	116	17.17 N	121.49 E
Tumba	40	59.12 N	17.49 E
Tumba, Lac ⊜	152	0.48 S	18.03 E
Tumbarumba	171b	35.47 S	148.01 E
Tumbarumba Creek ≃	171b	35.58 S	148.03 E
Tumbes	246	3.34 S	80.28 W
Tumbes □[5]	246	3.50 N	80.30 W
Tumbes (Puyango) ≃	246	3.30 S	80.27 W
Tumbes, Punta >	252	36.37 S	73.07 W
Tumbiscatio de Ruiz	234	18.31 N	102.21 W
Tumble Mountain ∧	202	45.19 N	110.02 W
Tumbler Ridge	182	55.07 N	120.55 W
Tumblong	171b	35.09 S	148.00 E
Tumbotino	80	55.59 N	43.02 E
Tumbur	154	4.20 N	31.34 E
Tumby Bay	166	34.22 S	136.06 E
Tumča ≃	24	66.36 N	30.48 E
Tŭmch'on-ni ◆[8]	271b	37.34 N	126.51 E
T'umen', Ross.	86	57.09 N	65.32 E
Tumen, Zhg.	98	42.58 N	129.49 E
T'umen □[8]	24	65.00 N	62.00 E
Tumen (Tuman-gang) ≃	98	42.18 N	130.41 E
T'umen'-Aryk	86	44.02 N	67.01 E
T'umencevo	86	53.20 N	81.31 E
T'umenec, porog ∟	88	56.38 N	99.00 E
Tumenpu	107	29.49 N	103.39 E
Tumenskoje	82	55.00 N	38.32 E
Tumenzi	102	37.43 N	103.09 E
Tumeremo	246	7.18 N	61.30 W
Tumiritinga	255	18.58 S	41.38 W
Tumkūr	122	13.21 N	77.05 E
Tummel ≃	46	56.38 N	3.40 W
Tumnin ≃	89	49.18 N	140.22 E
Tumon Bay ⊂	174p	13.31 N	144.48 E
Tumos ≃	156	22.55 S	14.37 E
Tumoteqi	102	40.52 N	111.28 E
Tumpang	115a	8.00 S	112.46 E
Tumpat	114	6.12 N	102.10 E
Tumsar	120	21.23 N	79.44 E
Tumtum	182	47.53 N	117.40 W
Tumu, Ghana	150	10.52 N	1.59 W
Tumu, Zhg.	105	40.23 N	115.36 E
Tumuc-Humac Mountains ⩘	250	2.20 N	55.00 W
Tumut	171b	35.18 S	148.13 E
Tumut ≃	171b	35.07 S	148.13 E
Tumut Pond Reservoir ⊜[1]	171b	35.59 S	148.25 E
Tumutuk	80	55.02 N	53.19 E
Tumwater	224	47.00 N	122.54 W
Tun ≃	110	17.25 N	98.42 E
Tuna Canyon V	280	34.03 N	118.36 W
Tunago Lake ⊜	180	66.18 N	125.50 W
Tuna-Hästberg	40	60.20 N	15.11 E
Tunapuna	241r	10.38 N	61.23 W
Tunari, Cerro ∧	248	17.18 S	66.22 W
Tunas Creek ≃	196	31.01 N	102.11 W
Tunas de Zaza	240p	21.38 N	79.33 W
Tūnat al-Jabal, Mişr	142	27.46 N	30.44 E

≃ River	Fluß	Río	Rivière	Rio
≅ Canal	Kanal	Canal	Canal	Canal
∟ Waterfall, Rapids	Wasserfall, Stromschnellen	Cascada, Rápidos	Chute d'eau, Rapides	Cascata, Rápidos
ʊ Strait	Meeresstraße	Estrecho	Détroit	Estreito
⊂ Bay, Gulf	Bucht, Golf	Bahía, Golfo	Baie, Golfe	Baía, Golfo
⊜ Lake, Lakes	See, Seen	Lago, Lagos	Lac, Lacs	Lago, Lagos
⩨ Swamp	Sumpf	Pantano	Marais	Pântano
⍓ Ice Features, Glacier	Eis- und Gletscherformen	Accidentes Glaciales	Formes glaciaires	Acidentes glaciares
⍑ Other Hydrographic Features	Andere Hydrographische Objekte	Otros Elementos Hidrográficos	Autres données hydrographiques	Outros acidentes hidrográficos
✦ Submarine Features	Untermeerische Objekte	Accidentes Submarinos	Formes de relief sous-marin	Acidentes submarinos
□ Political Unit	Politische Einheit	Unidad Politica	Entité politique	Unidade política
⚲ Cultural Institution	Kulturelle Institution	Institución Cultural	Institution culturelle	Instituição cultural
⊥ Historical Site	Historische Stätte	Sitio Histórico	Site historique	Sitio histórico
♠ Recreational Site	Erholungs- und Ferienort	Sitio de Recreo	Centre de loisirs	Area de Lazer
⊠ Airport	Flughafen	Aeropuerto	Aéroport	Aeroporto
■ Military Installation	Militäranlage	Instalación Militar	Installation militaire	Instalação militar
◆ Miscellaneous	Verschiedenes	Misceláneo	Divers	Diversos

Name	Page	Lat.°′	Long.°′
Tūnat al-Jabal, Miṣr	142	28.13 N	30.43 E
Tunaydah	140	25.31 N	29.21 E
Tunbridge Wells → Royal Tunbridge Wells	42	51.08 N	0.16 E
Tunçbilek	130	39.37 N	29.29 E
Tunceli	130	39.07 N	39.32 E
Tunceli □[4]	130	39.10 N	39.30 E
Tunchang	110	19.28 N	110.08 E
T'unch'i → Tunxi	100	29.44 N	118.18 E
Tunda, Pulau I	115a	5.49 S	106.16 E
Tundazi ∧	154	17.33 S	28.05 E
Tündern	52	52.04 N	9.22 E
Tūndla	124	27.12 N	78.17 E
Tundubai ▾[4]	140	18.31 N	28.33 E
Tunduru	154	11.07 S	37.21 E
Tundyk ≃	86	51.04 N	77.24 E
Tundža ≃	38	41.40 N	26.34 E
Tune	41	55.36 N	12.11 E
Tunesien → Tunisia □[1]	148	34.00 N	9.00 E
T'unež	82	54.37 N	38.29 E
Túnez → Tunis	148	36.48 N	10.11 E
Túnez → Tunisia □[1]	148	34.00 N	9.00 E
T'ung ≃	74	63.46 N	121.35 E
Tunga	150	8.00 N	9.19 E
Tunga ≃	122	14.00 N	75.41 E
Tungabhadra ≃	122	15.57 N	78.15 E
Tungabhadra Reservoir ⊜[1]	122	15.16 N	76.21 E
Tungaru	140	10.14 N	30.42 E
Tungauan Bay c	116	7.28 N	122.21 E
Tungchi University ʊ[2]	269b	31.18 N	121.29 E
Tungchi Yü I	100	23.15 N	119.40 E
T'ungchou → Tongxian	105	39.55 N	116.39 E
Tungch'üan Tao I	100	25.58 N	119.58 E
T'ungch'uan → Tongchuan	102	35.01 N	109.01 E
Tungelsta	40	59.06 N	18.02 E
Tung Hai → East China Sea ▾[2]	90	30.00 N	126.00 E
Tungho	100	22.58 N	121.18 E
T'unghsien → Tongxian	105	39.55 N	116.39 E
T'unghua → Tonghua	98	41.41 N	125.55 E
Tunghwa → Tonghua	98	41.41 N	125.55 E
Tungir ≃	88	55.24 N	120.32 E
Tungirskij chrebet ⋏	88	54.40 N	119.40 E
Tungkal ≃	112	0.49 S	103.29 E
Tungkang	100	22.28 N	120.26 E
Tungkillo	168b	34.49 S	139.04 E
Tungku	112	5.01 N	118.53 E
Tungla	236	13.18 N	84.26 W
T'ungliao → Tongliao	89	43.39 N	122.14 E
Tung Lung Island I	271d	22.15 N	114.17 E
Tung O	271d	22.12 N	114.08 E
Tungokočen	88	53.33 N	115.36 E
Tungsha Tao (Pratas Island) I	90	20.42 N	116.43 E
Tungshih	100	24.15 N	120.49 E
Tungsten	180	61.57 N	128.16 W
Tungsunga, Jabal ∧	140	11.29 N	23.21 E
Tungting Tao I	100	24.10 N	118.14 E
Tungurahua □[4]	246	1.15 S	78.35 W
Tungurahua ∧[1]	246	1.27 S	78.26 W
Tungyin Tao I	100	26.22 N	120.30 E
Tuni	122	17.21 N	82.33 E
Tunia ≃	246	1.13 N	72.44 W
Tunica	194	34.41 N	90.22 W
Tunis	148	36.48 N	10.11 E
Tunis □[8]	148	36.50 N	10.15 E
Tunis, Golfe de c	36	37.00 N	10.30 E
Tunis et Banlieue □[8]	36	36.48 N	10.10 E
Tunisia (Tunisie) □[1], Afr.	134	34.00 N	9.00 E
Tunisia (Tunisie) □[1], Afr.	148	34.00 N	9.00 E
Tunisie → Tunisia □[1]	148	34.00 N	9.00 E
Tunis Sud □[8]	148	36.30 N	10.00 E
Tūnis → Tunisia □[1]	148	34.00 N	9.00 E
Tunitas Creek ≃	282	37.21 N	122.24 W
Tunja	246	5.31 N	73.22 W
Tunjang	114	6.16 N	100.21 E
Tunka	88	51.45 N	102.32 E
Tunkás	232	20.54 N	88.45 W
Tunkhannock	210	41.32 N	75.56 W
Tunkhannock Creek ≃	210	41.32 N	75.57 W
Tunkhannock Creek, East Branch ≃	210	41.38 N	75.43 W
Tunliu	102	36.19 N	112.54 E
Tunnel	210	42.13 N	75.44 W
Tunnel Hill, Ga., U.S.	192	34.50 N	85.02 W
Tunnelhill, Pa., U.S.	214	40.29 N	78.33 W
Tunnelton, In., U.S.	218	38.46 N	86.21 W
Tunnelton, W.V., U.S.	188	39.23 N	79.44 W
Tunnsjøen ⊜	24	64.43 N	13.24 E
Tunø I	41	55.57 N	10.26 E
Tuntenhausen	64	47.56 N	12.01 E
Tuntum	250	5.14 S	44.39 W
Tuntutuliak	180	60.22 N	162.38 W
Tununak	180	60.35 N	165.16 W
Tunungayualok Island I	176	56.05 N	61.05 W
Tunuyán	252	33.34 S	69.01 W
Tunuyán ≃	252	34.03 S	66.45 W
Tunxi	100	29.44 N	118.18 E
Tuo ≃, Zhg.	100	33.16 N	117.45 E
Tuo ≃, Zhg.	102	28.57 N	105.27 E
Tuobalage	120	31.37 N	88.10 E
Tuobuja	74	62.00 N	122.02 E
Tuocheng	100	24.05 N	115.13 E
Tuoe Shan ∧	102	24.20 N	103.32 E
Tuoheji	100	33.26 N	117.26 E
Tuoj-Chaja	74	62.32 N	111.18 E
Tuoji Dao I	98	38.09 N	120.14 E
Tuokedingling	120	32.45 N	84.55 E
Tuokusidawan Ling ∧	120	37.14 N	85.47 E
Tuoli	105	39.46 N	116.01 E
Tuolumne	226	37.57 N	120.14 W
Tuolumne □[6]	226	37.59 N	120.23 W
Tuolumne ≃	226	37.36 N	121.10 W
Tuolumne, Lyell Fork ≃	226	37.53 N	119.23 W
Tuolumne, North Fork ≃	226	37.54 N	120.15 W
Tuolumne, South Fork ≃	226	37.50 N	120.03 W
Tuolunduo	89	50.35 N	120.05 E
Tuong Duong	110	19.16 N	104.27 E
Tuotuo ≃	120	34.15 N	93.11 E
Tuowu	102	28.58 N	102.13 E
T'up	85	42.44 N	78.22 E
Tupã	255	21.56 S	50.30 W
Tupaciguara	255	18.35 S	48.42 W
Tupana ≃	246	4.25 S	60.05 W
Tupanciretã	252	29.05 S	53.51 W
Tuparro ≃	246	5.13 N	67.50 W
Tupelo, Ms., U.S.	194	34.15 N	88.42 W
Tupelo, Ok., U.S.	196	34.36 N	96.25 W
Tupelo National Battlefield ⊥	194	34.13 N	88.44 W
Tupi	116	6.19 N	124.57 E
Tupičov	78	51.46 N	31.26 E
Tupik	88	54.26 N	119.57 E
Tupilac	116	7.40 N	122.30 E
Tupinambarana, Ilha I	246	3.00 S	58.00 W
Tupi Paulista	255	21.24 S	51.34 W
Tupiraçaba	255	14.29 S	48.34 W
Tupiza	248	21.27 S	65.43 W
Tuplice	30	51.41 N	14.50 E
Tupman	226	35.17 N	119.21 W
Tupper	182	55.31 N	120.02 W
Tupper Lake	188	44.13 N	74.29 W
Tupperville	214	42.36 N	82.16 W
Tupuai, Île I	14	23.18 S	149.30 W
Tupungato	252	33.22 S	69.08 W
Tupungato, Cerro ∧	252	33.22 S	69.47 W
Tuqiao, Zhg.	106	31.56 N	119.03 E
Tuqiao, Zhg.	106	31.39 N	120.24 E
Tuqiao, Zhg.	107	30.24 N	105.28 E
Tuqiaozhen	107	30.32 N	104.50 E
Tuquan	89	45.26 N	121.50 E
Túquerres	246	1.05 N	77.37 W
Tuquiaochang	107	29.47 N	106.01 E
Tura, India	124	25.31 N	90.13 E
Ṭurā, Miṣr	142	29.56 N	31.16 E
Tura, Ross.	74	64.17 N	100.15 E
Tura ≃, Ross.	86	57.12 N	66.56 E
Tura ≃, Ross.	88	51.36 N	114.09 E
Turabah	144	21.13 N	41.39 E
Turabah ▾[4]	128	28.15 N	42.55 E
Turābah, 'Ayn at- ▾[4]	132	31.36 N	35.25 E
Turāg ≃	126	23.45 N	90.21 E
Turaiyūr	122	11.10 N	78.37 E
Turakina	172	40.02 S	175.13 E
Turakina ≃	172	40.04 S	175.08 E
Turama ≃	164	6.50 S	143.05 E
Turambhe	272c	19.04 N	73.01 E
Turan, Ross.	88	51.38 N	101.40 E
Turan, Ross.	88	52.08 N	93.55 E
Turangi	172	39.00 S	175.49 E
Turano ≃	66	42.26 N	12.47 E
Turanskaja nizmennost' ≚	86	44.30 N	63.00 E
Ṭurāq al-'Ilab ⋏[2]	130	33.55 N	38.18 E
Turate	266b	45.39 N	9.00 E
Tur'at Ghunaym	142	31.16 N	31.29 E
Ṭurayf	128	31.44 N	38.33 E
Turbaco	246	10.20 N	75.25 W
Turbacz ∧	30	49.33 N	20.08 E
Turbat	128	25.59 N	63.04 E
Turbenthal	58	47.27 N	8.51 E
Turbigo	62	45.32 N	8.44 E
Turbio ≃	234	20.19 N	101.37 W
Turbo	246	8.06 N	76.43 W
Turbotville	210	41.06 N	76.46 W
Turbov	78	49.21 N	28.44 E
Turčasovo	24	63.06 N	39.12 E
Turchi, Balata dei ≻	70	36.43 N	12.02 E
Turčiansky Svätý Martin → Martin	30	49.05 N	18.55 E
Turckheim	58	48.05 N	7.17 E
Turda	38	46.34 N	23.47 E
Turdej	76	53.22 N	38.01 E
Turee Creek	162	23.37 S	118.39 E
Turee Creek ≃	162	23.35 S	117.25 E
Turek	30	52.02 N	18.30 E
Turen	115a	8.10 S	112.41 E
Turenki	26	60.55 N	24.38 E
Turfan Depression → Turpan Pendi ⊥[7]	86	42.40 N	89.10 E
Turfan → Turpan	86	42.56 N	89.10 E
Turffontein ◆[8]	273d	26.15 S	28.02 E
Turffontein Race Course ♠	273d	26.14 S	28.03 E
Turgaj, Kaz.	86	51.46 N	72.44 E
Turgaj, Kaz.	86	49.38 N	63.28 E
Turgaj ≃	86	48.01 N	62.45 E
Turgajskaja ložbina V	86	51.00 N	64.30 E
Turgajskaja Oblast' □[8]	86	50.00 N	65.20 E
Turgajskoje plato ⋏[1]	86	51.00 N	64.00 E
Turgen', Kaz.	85	43.24 N	77.36 E
Türgen, Mong.	86	50.04 N	91.36 E
Turgen' ≃	85	43.50 N	77.38 E
Turgenevka	88	53.02 N	105.41 E
Turgenevo	80	54.50 N	46.19 E
Turginovo	82	56.30 N	36.00 E
Turgojak	86	55.10 N	60.07 E
Turgoš	76	59.18 N	35.10 E
Tŭrgovishte → Târgovište	38	43.15 N	26.34 E
Turgut, Tür.	130	38.37 N	31.49 E
Turgut, Tür.	130	37.22 N	28.02 E
Turgutlu	130	38.30 N	27.43 E
Turgwi ≃	154	20.28 S	32.18 E
Turhal	130	40.24 N	36.06 E
Türi, Eesti	76	58.48 N	25.26 E
Turi, It.	68	40.55 N	17.01 E
Turia ≃	34	39.27 N	0.19 W
Turiaçu	250	1.41 S	45.21 W
Turiaçu ≃	250	1.36 S	45.19 W
Turiančajskij zapovednik ♠	84	40.40 N	47.35 E
Turij Rog	89	45.14 N	131.58 E
Turijsk	78	51.07 N	24.31 E
Turilovka	83	49.06 N	40.13 E
Turimetta Head ≻	274a	33.42 S	151.19 E
Turimiquire, Cerro ∧	246	10.07 N	63.53 W
Turin, Ab., Can.	182	49.58 N	112.31 W
Turin, N.Y., U.S.	212	43.38 N	75.25 W
Turinge	40	59.12 N	17.27 E
Turinsk	86	58.03 N	63.42 E
Turinskaja Sloboda	86	57.37 N	64.25 E
Turin → Torino	62	45.03 N	7.40 E
Turja ≃	78	51.48 N	24.52 E
Turka, Ross.	88	52.57 N	108.13 E
Turka, Ukr.	78	49.10 N	23.02 E
Turka ≃	88	52.56 N	108.13 E
Turkana, Lake → Rudolf, Lake ⊜	144	3.30 N	36.05 E
Türkei → Turkey □[1]	22	39.00 N	35.00 E
Türkeli Adası I	130	40.30 N	27.30 E
Turkestan	85	43.18 N	68.15 E
Turkestanskij chrebet ⋏	85	39.35 N	69.15 E
Turkestanskij kanal ≊	85	42.44 N	69.00 E
Túrkeve	30	47.06 N	20.45 E
Turkey	196	34.23 N	100.53 W
Turkey (Türkiye) □[1], Asia	22	39.00 N	35.00 E
Turkey (Türkiye) □[1], Asia	130	39.00 N	35.00 E
Turkey ≃	190	42.43 N	91.01 W
Turkey Branch ≃	284c	38.52 N	76.48 W
Turkey City	214	41.11 N	79.37 W
Turkey Creek	164	17.02 S	128.12 E
Turkey Creek ≃, On., Can.	281	42.14 N	83.06 W
Turkey Creek ≃, U.S.	198	39.58 N	96.02 W
Turkey Creek ≃, In., U.S.	278	41.31 N	87.18 W
Turkey Creek ≃, Ia., U.S.	198	41.20 N	95.05 W
Turkey Creek ≃, Ks., U.S.	198	38.53 N	97.11 W
Turkey Creek ≃, Ne., U.S.	198	40.23 N	96.53 W
Turkey Creek ≃, Ok., U.S.	196	35.58 N	97.56 W
Turkey Creek ≃, Tx., U.S.	222	30.39 N	97.05 W
Turkey Island I	284c	38.58 N	77.12 W
Turkey Point ≻, On., Can.	212	42.40 N	80.21 W
Turkey Point ≻, Fl., U.S.	220	25.26 N	80.19 W
Turkey Point Provincial Park ♠	212	42.40 N	80.22 W
Turkey Run State Park ♠	194	39.54 N	87.13 W
Turkeytown	279b	40.12 N	79.44 W
Türkheim	58	48.03 N	10.38 E
Turki	80	51.59 N	43.16 E
Turkish Republic of Northern Cyprus → Cyprus, North □[1]	130	35.15 N	33.40 E
Türkiye → Turkey □[1]	22	39.00 N	35.00 E
Turkmān Deh	267d	35.40 N	51.36 E
Turkmenia → Turkmenistan □[1]	72	40.00 N	60.00 E
Turkmenija → Turkmenistan □[1]	72	40.00 N	60.00 E
Turkmenistan □[1], Asia	72	40.00 N	60.00 E
Turkmenistan □[1], Asia	128	39.00 N	60.00 E
Turkmeniya → Turkmenistan □[1]	72	40.00 N	60.00 E
Turkmen-Kala	128	37.26 N	62.20 E
Turkmenskij zaliv c	128	38.54 N	53.48 E
Turk Mine	154	19.45 S	28.50 E
Türkoğlu	130	37.31 N	36.49 E
Turks and Caicos Islands □[2], N.A.	230	21.45 N	71.35 W
Turks and Caicos Islands □[2], N.A.	238	21.45 N	71.35 W
Turks Island Passage ʮ	238	21.25 N	71.19 W
Turks Islands II	238	21.24 N	71.07 W
Turks-und Caicos-Inseln → Turks and Caicos Islands □[2]	238	21.45 N	71.35 W
Turku (Åbo)	26	60.27 N	22.17 E
Turkwel ≃	154	3.06 N	36.06 E
Turlan	85	43.36 N	69.03 E
Turley	196	36.14 N	95.58 W
Turlock	226	37.29 N	120.50 W
Turlock Lake ⊜[1]	226	42.17 N	73.21 W
Turmalina	255	17.17 S	42.45 W
Turmantas	76	55.42 N	26.27 E
Turmerito, Quebrada ≃	286c	10.26 N	66.55 W
Turnagain ≃	180	59.06 N	127.35 W
Turnagain, Cape ≻	172	40.29 S	176.37 E
Turnagain Arm c	180	61.00 N	150.00 W
Turnagain Island I	164	9.34 S	142.18 E
Turna nad Bodvou	30	48.37 N	20.53 E
Turnau	61	47.33 N	15.20 E
Turnbull, Mount ∧	200	33.04 N	110.16 W
Turnbull, Mount ∧[2]	162	21.03 S	131.57 E
Turneffe Islands II	232	17.22 N	87.51 W
Turner, Austl.	162	17.50 S	128.17 E
Turner, Mt., U.S.	202	48.50 N	108.24 W
Turner, Or., U.S.	202	44.50 N	122.57 W
Turner ≃	162	20.21 S	118.25 E
Turner Field ⊠	285	40.13 N	75.13 W
Turners Falls	207	42.36 N	72.33 W
Turners Peninsula ≻[1]	150	7.22 N	12.22 W
Turnersville, N.J., U.S.	285	39.46 N	75.03 W
Turnersville, Tx., U.S.	222	31.37 N	97.44 W
Turner Valley	182	50.40 N	114.17 W
Turnhout	52	51.19 N	4.57 E
Türnitz	61	47.57 N	15.30 E
Turnor Lake ⊜	184	56.32 N	108.38 W
Turnov	30	50.35 N	15.10 E
Tŭrnovo → Veliko Târnovo	38	43.04 N	25.39 E
Turnpike Lake ⊜	283	42.01 N	71.19 W
Turnu-Măgurele	38	43.45 N	24.53 E
Turnu Roșu, Pasul)(	38	45.33 N	24.16 E
Turnu-Severin → Drobeta-Turnu Severin	38	44.38 N	22.39 E
Turobin	30	50.50 N	22.45 E
Turočak	86	52.16 N	87.08 E
Turon	198	37.48 N	98.25 W
Turon ≃	170	33.03 S	149.43 E
Turopin	78	51.00 N	24.27 E
Turopolje ≚	36	45.40 N	16.05 E
Tuross ≃	171b	36.09 S	149.39 E
Turov	78	52.04 N	27.44 E
Turovo	82	54.52 N	37.49 E
Turpan	86	42.56 N	89.10 E
Turpan Pendi (Turfan Depression) ⊥[7]	86	42.40 N	89.10 E
Turques et Caicos, Îles → Turks and Caicos Islands □[2]	238	21.45 N	71.35 W
Turquía → Turkey □[1]	22	39.00 N	35.00 E
Turquie → Turkey □[1]	22	39.00 N	35.00 E
Turquino, Pico ∧	240p	19.59 N	76.50 W
Turrach	64	46.57 N	13.52 E
Turramurra	274a	33.44 S	151.08 E
Turrell	194	35.22 N	90.15 W
Turret Peak ∧	200	34.15 N	111.53 W
Turriaco	64	45.49 N	13.26 E
Turrialba	236	9.54 N	83.41 W
Turrialba, Volcán ∧[1]	236	10.02 N	83.46 W
Turriers	62	44.24 N	6.10 E
Turriff	46	57.32 N	2.28 W
Turritano ◆[1]	71	40.45 N	8.35 E
Turrubares, Cerro ∧	236	9.47 N	84.28 W
Tursi	68	40.15 N	16.28 E
Tursunzade	85	38.32 N	68.13 E
Turtas ≃	86	59.06 N	68.52 E
Turtipār	124	26.10 N	83.54 E
Turtle ≃, Mb., Can.	184	51.07 N	99.39 W
Turtle ≃, On., Can.	184	48.51 N	92.45 W
Turtle, North Branch ≃	198	47.57 N	97.35 W
Turtle Creek, N.B., Can.	186	45.58 N	64.53 W
Turtle Creek, Pa., U.S.	214	40.24 N	79.49 W
Turtle Creek ≃, Pa., U.S.	279b	40.23 N	79.51 W
Turtle Creek ≃, S.D., U.S.	198	44.55 N	98.29 W
Turtle Creek ≃, Wi., U.S.	216	42.29 N	89.03 W
Turtle-Flambeau Flowage ⊜[1]	190	46.05 N	90.11 W
Turtleford	184	53.23 N	108.56 W
Turtle Harbor Channel ʮ	220	25.15 N	80.18 W
Turtle Islands II	150	7.37 N	13.02 W
Turtle Lake, N.D., U.S.	198	47.31 N	100.53 W
Turtle Lake, Wi., U.S.	190	45.23 N	92.08 W
Turtle Lake ⊜	184	53.35 N	108.40 W
Turtle Mountain ∧[2]	184	49.00 N	100.15 W
Turtle Mountain Indian Reservation ◆[4]	198	48.51 N	99.45 W
Turtle Mountain Provincial Park ♠	184	49.03 N	100.15 W
Turtmann	58	46.18 N	7.41 E
Turton and Entwistle Reservoir ⊜[1]	262	53.39 N	2.25 W
Turton Bottoms	262	53.38 N	2.24 W
Turton Moor ◆[3]	262	53.40 N	2.29 W
Turton Tower ʊ	262	53.38 N	2.25 W
Turu ≃	74	64.38 N	100.00 E
Turua	172	37.14 S	175.34 E
Turuchan ≃	74	65.56 N	87.42 E
Turuchansk	74	65.49 N	87.59 E
Turuntajevo, Ross.	86	56.38 N	85.59 E
Turuntajevo, Ross.	88	52.12 N	107.37 E
Turusele ∧	71	40.09 N	9.34 E
Turvo	252	28.56 S	49.41 W
Turvo ≃, Bra.	255	17.46 S	50.12 W
Turvo ≃, Bra.	255	19.56 S	49.55 W
Turvo ≃, Bra.	256	22.04 S	45.42 W
Turvo ≃, Bra.	256	22.29 S	44.15 W
Turvo Grande ≃	256	21.42 S	44.22 W
Turvolândia	256	21.47 S	45.47 W
Turvo Pequeno ≃	256	21.42 S	44.22 W
Turyu-san ∧	98	41.10 N	128.47 E
Turzovka	30	49.25 N	18.39 E
Tusa	70	37.59 N	14.14 E
Tusa ≃	70	38.01 N	14.16 E
Tusas, Rio ≃	200	36.23 N	106.03 W
Tuscaloosa	194	33.12 N	87.34 W
Tuscaloosa, Lake ⊜[1]	194	33.20 N	87.35 W
Tuscania	66	42.25 N	11.52 E
Tuscany → Toscana □[4]	36	43.25 N	11.00 E
Tuscarawas	214	40.24 N	81.25 W
Tuscarawas □[6]	214	40.30 N	81.27 W
Tuscarawas ≃	214	40.17 N	81.52 W
Tuscarora, N.Y., U.S.	210	42.38 N	77.52 W
Tuscarora, Pa., U.S.	208	40.46 N	76.02 W
Tuscarora Creek ≃, N.Y., U.S.	210	42.07 N	77.14 W
Tuscarora Creek ≃, Pa., U.S.	208	40.32 N	77.23 W
Tuscarora Creek, North Branch ≃	210	42.05 N	77.18 W
Tuscarora Indian Reservation ◆[4]	210	43.09 N	78.57 W
Tuscarora Mountain ∧	188	40.10 N	77.45 W
Tuscarora Mountains ⋏	204	41.00 N	116.20 W
Tuscarora State Park ♠	208	40.48 N	76.01 W
Tuscarora Tunnel ◆[5]	214	40.05 N	77.50 W
Tuscola, Il., U.S.	194	39.47 N	88.16 W
Tuscola, Tx., U.S.	196	32.12 N	99.48 W
Tuscolo ⊥	267a	41.48 N	12.42 E
Tuscumbia, Al., U.S.	194	34.43 N	87.42 W
Tuscumbia, Mo., U.S.	194	38.13 N	92.27 W
Tuse	41	55.43 N	11.37 E
Tushan	98	34.14 N	117.51 E
Tušino ◆[8]	265b	55.50 N	37.26 E
Tuskegee	194	32.25 N	85.41 W
Tusker Rock II[1]	42	51.27 N	3.40 W
Tussey Mountain ∧	214	40.25 N	78.07 W
Tüssling	60	48.13 N	12.36 E
Tustin	228	33.44 N	117.49 W
Tustin Marine Corps Air Station (Helicopter) ■	280	33.43 N	117.50 W
Tustumena Lake ⊜	180	60.12 N	150.50 W
Tuszyn	30	51.37 N	19.34 E
Tut	130	37.48 N	37.55 E
Tuta	152	14.37 S	20.45 E
Tutaekuri ≃	172	39.30 S	176.54 E
Tutaizi	104	41.01 N	122.38 E
Tutajev	80	57.53 N	39.32 E
Tutak	84	39.32 N	42.46 E
Tutang	100	29.21 N	116.24 E
Tutbury	42	52.51 N	1.41 W
Tuthills Creek ≃	276	40.45 N	73.02 W
Tuticorin	122	8.47 N	78.08 E
Tutin	38	42.59 N	20.20 E
T'ut'kovo	82	54.37 N	38.32 E
Tutóia	250	2.45 S	42.16 W
Tutoko, Mount ∧	172	44.36 S	168.00 E
Tutong	112	4.50 N	114.40 E
Tutova ≃	38	46.06 N	27.32 E
Tutrakan	38	44.03 N	26.37 E
Tu → Tsu	94	34.43 N	136.31 E
Tuttle, N.D., U.S.	198	47.08 N	99.59 W
Tuttle, Ok., U.S.	196	35.17 N	97.48 W
Tuttle Creek Lake ⊜[1]	198	39.22 N	96.40 W
Tuttlingen	58	47.59 N	8.49 E
Tutuala	112	8.24 S	127.15 E
Tutuban Station ◆[5]	269f	14.37 N	120.58 E
Tutu Bay c	116	5.55 N	121.12 E
Tutubu	154	5.30 S	32.41 E
Tutuí ≃	250	2.39 S	54.10 W
Tutuila I	174u	14.18 S	170.42 W
Tuṭūn	142	29.09 N	30.46 E
Tütüncü	130	40.04 N	27.43 E
Tutupaca, Volcán ∧[1]	248	17.01 S	70.22 W
Tutura	88	54.46 N	105.15 E
Tututalak Mountain ∧	180	67.46 N	161.10 W
Tutwiler	194	34.00 N	90.25 W
Tutzing	64	47.54 N	11.17 E
Tuul ≃	90	48.57 N	104.48 E
Tuupovaara	26	62.29 N	30.36 E
Tuurun-Poorin lääni □[4]	26	61.20 N	22.30 E
Tuusniemi	26	62.49 N	28.30 E
Tuutapu, Cerro ∧	174z	27.08 S	109.24 W
T'uva-Guba	24	69.08 N	33.32 E
Tuvalu □[1]	14	8.00 S	178.00 E
Tuvinskaja Avtonomnaja Sovetskaja Socialističeskaja Respublika □[3]	88	53.00 N	96.00 E
Tuvutha Island I	175g	17.40 S	178.48 W
Tuwang	107	29.06 N	105.48 E
Ṭuwayq, Jabal ⋏	118	23.00 N	46.00 E
Ṭuwayyil ash-Shihāq ∧[2]	132	30.36 N	36.08 E
Tuxedo Park, De., U.S.	285	39.43 N	75.37 W
Tuxedo Park, N.Y., U.S.	210	41.11 N	74.11 W
Tuxer Hauptkamm ∧	64	47.10 N	11.45 E
Tuxer Vorberge ⋏	64	47.10 N	11.45 E
Tuxford, Sk., Can.	184	50.35 N	105.35 W
Tuxford, Eng., U.K.	44	53.13 N	0.53 W
Tuxiaqiao	100	28.47 N	121.29 E
Tuxpan, Méx.	234	20.57 N	97.24 W
Tuxpan, Méx.	234	19.33 N	103.24 W
Tuxpan, Méx.	234	19.34 N	100.28 W
Tuxpan, Méx.	234	21.57 N	105.18 W
Tuxpan ≃	234	20.59 N	97.18 W
Tuxsun	86	42.47 N	88.38 E
Tuxtepec	234	18.06 N	96.07 W
Tuxtla Gutiérrez	234	16.45 N	93.07 W
Tuy	34	42.03 N	8.38 W
Tuy ≃	246	10.24 N	65.59 W
Tuy An	110	13.17 N	109.16 E
Tuyen Hoa	110	17.50 N	106.10 E
Tuyen Quang	110	21.49 N	105.13 E
Tuy Hoa	110	13.05 N	109.18 E
Tūysarkān	128	34.33 N	48.27 E
Tuyün → Duyun	102	26.12 N	107.31 E
Ṭuyūr, Burj aṭ- ∧[2]	140	20.55 N	27.55 E
Tuža	80	57.37 N	47.57 E
T'uzašu, pereval)(	85	42.21 N	73.48 E
T'uzbel'	85	40.34 N	73.21 E
Tuzdykol', ozero ⊜	80	49.36 N	52.20 E
Tuz Gölü ⊜	130	38.45 N	33.25 E
Tuzigoot National Monument ♠	200	34.49 N	112.01 W
Ṭūz Khurmātū	128	34.53 N	44.38 E
Tuzla, Bos.	38	44.32 N	18.41 E
Tuzla, Tür.	130	36.42 N	35.05 E
Tuzla ≃	130	39.43 N	40.16 E
Tuzla Gölü ⊜	130	39.02 N	35.50 E
Tuzlagözü	130	38.11 N	41.34 E
Tuzlov ≃	83	47.23 N	40.08 E
Tuzluca	84	40.03 N	43.40 E
Tuzlukçu	130	38.28 N	31.38 E
Tuzly	78	45.52 N	30.05 E
Tuzuntla ≃	234	18.51 N	100.44 W
Tvărdica, Blg.	38	43.42 N	25.52 E
Tvardica, Mol.	78	46.09 N	28.58 E
Tvedestrand	26	58.37 N	8.55 E
Tveitsund	26	59.01 N	8.32 E
Tver' (Kalinin)	82	56.52 N	35.55 E
Tver' □[8]	82	56.45 N	36.30 E
Tverca ≃	76	56.52 N	35.55 E
Twain Harte	226	38.02 N	120.14 W
Twann	58	47.06 N	7.10 E
Twardogóra	30	51.22 N	17.28 E
Tweed	212	44.29 N	77.19 W
Tweed ≃	44	55.46 N	2.00 W
Tweeddale V	46	55.40 N	3.10 W
Tweede Exloërmond	52	52.55 N	6.58 E
Tweed Heads	171a	28.10 S	153.31 E
Tweedmouth	44	55.45 N	2.01 W
Tweedsmuir Provincial Park ♠	182	52.55 N	126.05 W
Tweedy Mountain ∧	202	45.29 N	112.58 W
Tweeling	158	27.38 S	28.31 E
Twee Rivieren	158	26.27 S	20.37 E
Tweespruit	158	29.11 S	27.01 E
Twello	52	52.14 N	6.06 E
Twelve Mile	216	40.52 N	86.13 W
Twelve Mile Creek ≃, On., Can.	212	43.11 N	79.16 W
Twelvemile Creek ≃, N.Y., U.S.	210	43.18 N	78.51 W
Twelvemile Island I	279b	40.32 N	79.51 W
Twelve Mile Lake ⊜, On., Can.	212	45.02 N	78.43 W
Twelve Mile Lake ⊜, Sk., Can.	184	49.29 N	106.14 W
Tweng	64	47.11 N	13.36 E
Twente ◆[1]	52	52.17 N	6.40 E
Twentekanaal ≊	52	52.15 N	6.40 E
Twentieth Century Fox Studios ʊ[3]	280	34.03 N	118.25 W
Twentyfive Mile Wash V	200	37.33 N	111.07 W
Twenty Mile Creek ≃	212	43.10 N	79.22 W
Twentynine Palms	204	34.08 N	116.03 W
Twentynine Palms Marine Corps Center ■	204	34.25 N	116.10 W
Tweya	152	0.54 S	19.05 E
Twickenham ◆[8]	260	51.27 N	0.20 W
Twilight Cove c	162	32.16 S	126.03 E
Twilight Park	210	42.11 N	74.05 W
Twillingate	186	49.39 N	54.46 W
Twin Beach	216	42.34 N	83.24 W
Twinberg	61	46.55 N	14.50 E
Twin Bridge Farm	285	39.57 N	75.33 W
Twin Bridges	202	45.32 N	112.19 W
Twin Butte Creek ≃	198	38.46 N	100.56 W
Twin Buttes ∧	202	44.20 N	122.15 W
Twin Buttes Reservoir ⊜[1]	196	31.20 N	100.35 W
Twin City	192	32.34 N	82.09 W
Twin Creek ≃	218	39.33 N	84.21 W
Twin Falls	202	42.33 N	114.27 W
Twin Heads ⋏	162	20.13 S	126.30 E
Twin Hills	180	59.23 N	159.58 W
Twin Lakes, Ca., U.S.	226	36.58 N	122.00 W
Twin Lakes, Ga., U.S.	192	30.42 N	83.12 W
Twin Lakes, In., U.S.	216	41.19 N	86.23 W
Twin Lakes, Mi., U.S.	216	42.02 N	86.04 W
Twin Lakes, Oh., U.S.	214	41.11 N	81.21 W
Twin Lakes, Pa., U.S.	210	41.24 N	74.54 W
Twin Lakes, Wi., U.S.	216	42.31 N	88.14 W
Twin Lakes ⊜, Ca., U.S.	226	38.09 N	119.21 W
Twin Lakes ⊜, Ct., U.S.	207	42.02 N	73.26 W
Twin Lakes ⊜, Wa., U.S.	224	47.55 N	120.51 W
Twin Oaks, Il., U.S.	278	42.03 N	87.50 W
Twin Oaks, Pa., U.S.	208	39.51 N	75.26 W
Twin Peak Islands II	162	34.00 S	122.50 E
Twin Peaks	228	34.12 N	117.12 W
Twin Peaks ⋏, Ca., U.S.	282	37.45 N	122.27 W
Twin Peaks ⋏, Id., U.S.	202	44.35 N	114.29 W
Twin Rocks, Or., U.S.	224	45.36 N	123.57 W
Twin Rocks, Pa., U.S.	214	40.29 N	78.51 W
Twinsburg	214	41.18 N	81.26 W
Twin Valley	198	47.15 N	96.15 W
Twisp	202	48.21 N	120.07 W
Twiss Green	262	53.27 N	2.32 W
Twist	52	52.38 N	7.03 E
Twiste ≃	52	51.29 N	9.09 E
Twistringen	52	52.48 N	8.38 E
Twitchell Reservoir ⊜[1]	204	35.00 N	120.19 W
Twitya ≃	180	64.10 N	128.12 W
Two, Channel ʮ	220	24.50 N	80.45 W
Two Butte Creek ≃	198	38.02 N	102.08 W
Twofold Bay c	166	37.06 S	149.55 E
Two Harbors	190	47.01 N	91.40 W
Two Hills	182	53.43 N	111.45 W
Two Lakes ⊜	224	46.22 N	121.27 W
Two Medicine ≃	202	48.29 N	112.14 W
Two Mile Creek ≃, On., Can.	284a	43.16 N	79.06 W
Twomile Creek ≃, N.Y., U.S.	284a	43.01 N	78.55 W
Twong	140	8.18 N	28.20 E
Two Penny Run ≃	285	39.41 N	75.26 W
Two River Lake ⊜	184	53.52 N	91.27 W
Two Rivers	190	44.09 N	87.34 W
Two Rivers Reservoir ⊜[1]	196	33.17 N	104.45 W
Two Thumb Range ⋏	172	43.45 S	170.43 E
Two Wells	168b	34.36 S	138.30 E
Twrch ≃, Wales, U.K.	42	52.42 N	3.29 W
Twrch ≃, Wales, U.K.	42	51.46 N	3.46 W
Twyford, Eng., U.K.	42	51.29 N	0.53 W
Twyford, Eng., U.K.	42	51.01 N	1.19 W
Twymyn ≃	42	52.38 N	3.44 W
Tyabb	169	38.16 S	145.11 E
Tybee Island	192	32.01 N	80.51 W
Tybju	24	60.37 N	50.20 E
Tychy	30	50.09 N	18.59 E
Tyczyn	30	49.58 N	22.02 E
Tydal	26	63.04 N	11.34 E
Tye	196	32.27 N	99.52 W
Tyende Creek ≃	200	36.50 N	109.43 W
Tyendinaga Indian Reserve ◆[4]	212	44.11 N	77.07 W
Tyers ≃	169	38.10 S	146.26 E
Tyfors	40	60.09 N	14.12 E
Tygarts Creek ≃	218	38.43 N	82.57 W
Tygda	89	53.07 N	126.20 E
Tygda ≃	89	52.35 N	127.55 E
Tygelsjö	41	55.31 N	13.00 E
Tygh Valley	224	45.14 N	121.10 W
Tyin ⊜	26	61.17 N	8.13 E
Tyja ≃	88	55.36 N	109.20 E
Tylden	158	32.07 S	27.05 E
Tyldesley	44	53.31 N	2.28 W
Tyler, Mn., U.S.	198	44.16 N	96.08 W
Tyler, Pa., U.S.	214	41.14 N	78.32 W
Tyler, Tx., U.S.	222	32.21 N	95.18 W
Tyler □[6]	222	30.47 N	94.32 W
Tyler, Lake ⊜[1]	222	32.13 N	95.10 W
Tyler East, Lake ⊜[1]	222	32.15 N	95.10 W
Tyler Park	284c	38.52 N	77.12 W
Tylersburg	214	41.23 N	79.19 W
Tyler State Park ♠, Pa., U.S.	208	40.14 N	74.59 W
Tyler State Park ♠, Tx., U.S.	222	32.29 N	95.14 W
Tylersville	210	41.00 N	77.25 W
Tylerton	208	37.58 N	76.01 W
Tylertown	194	31.06 N	90.08 W
Tylla	40	60.28 N	15.33 E
Tylösand	26	56.39 N	12.44 E
Tylöskog ⋏[2]	40	58.45 N	15.20 E
Tylovaj	80	57.30 N	53.47 E
Tym ≃, Ross.	74	59.25 N	80.04 E
Tym' ≃, Ross.	89	51.51 N	143.10 E
Tymna, laguna c	180	64.00 N	178.30 E
Tymochtee Creek ≃	214	40.57 N	83.16 W
Tymovskoje	89	50.51 N	142.39 E

Name	Seite	Breite°′	Länge°′ E = Ost
Tymsk	86	59.24 N	80.18 E
Tynagh	48	53.09 N	8.22 W
Tyndall	198	42.59 N	97.51 W
Tyndall Air Force Base ■	194	30.04 N	85.35 W
Tyndaris ⊥	70	38.09 N	15.03 E
Tyndinskij	74	55.10 N	124.43 E
Tyndrum	46	56.27 N	4.44 W
Tyne ≃, Eng., U.K.	44	55.01 N	1.26 W
Tyne ≃, Scot., U.K.	46	56.01 N	2.37 W
Tyne and Wear □[6]	44	54.55 N	1.35 W
Tynemouth	44	55.01 N	1.24 W
Tyner	216	41.24 N	86.24 W
Tyngsboro	283	42.40 N	71.25 W
Tyngsjö	40	60.18 N	13.53 E
Tynica	78	51.08 N	32.54 E
Týn nad Vltavou	30	49.14 N	14.26 E
Tynnelsö	40	59.25 N	17.06 E
Tynset	26	62.17 N	10.47 E
Tyonek	180	61.02 N	151.17 W
Typta	88	54.35 N	104.31 E
Tyr	89	52.57 N	139.48 E
Tyre	214	40.26 N	80.16 W
Tyresö	40	59.14 N	18.18 E
Tyre → Ṣūr	132	33.16 N	35.11 E
Tyret'	88	53.41 N	102.19 E
Tyrgetuj	88	51.27 N	113.46 E
Tyrifjorden ⊜	26	60.02 N	10.08 E
Tyringe	41	56.10 N	13.35 E
Tyringham	207	42.14 N	73.12 W
Tyrka	88	54.30 N	107.09 E
Tyrma	89	50.03 N	132.12 E
Tyrma ≃	89	50.29 N	131.18 E
Tyrnovo	78	48.10 N	27.40 E
Tyrnyauz	84	43.23 N	42.56 E
Tyrone, Ky., U.S.	218	38.01 N	84.50 W
Tyrone, N.Y., U.S.	210	42.25 N	77.03 W
Tyrone, Ok., U.S.	196	36.57 N	101.03 W
Tyrone, Pa., U.S.	214	40.40 N	78.14 W
Tyrone Lake ⊜	281	42.42 N	83.43 W
Tyrrell, Lake ⊜	166	35.21 S	142.50 E
Tyrrellspass	48	53.23 N	7.22 W
Tyrrhenian Sea (Mare Tirreno) ▾[2]	36	40.00 N	12.00 E
Tyrrhenisches Meer → Tyrrhenian Sea ▾[2]	36	40.00 N	12.00 E
Tysmenica	78	48.54 N	24.49 E
Tysnesøy I	26	60.00 N	5.35 E
Tysons Corner	284c	38.55 N	77.14 W
Tysons Corner Center ◆[9]	284c	38.55 N	77.13 W
Tysons Green	284c	38.55 N	77.15 W
Tysse	26	60.22 N	5.45 E
Tyssedal	26	60.07 N	6.34 E
Tysslingen ⊜	40	59.19 N	15.02 E
Tystberga	40	58.52 N	17.15 E
Tystrup Sø ⊜	41	55.22 N	11.35 E
Tytherington	262	53.17 N	2.08 W
Tytuvėnai	76	55.36 N	23.12 E
Ty Ty	192	31.28 N	83.38 W
Tyumen' → T'umen'	86	57.09 N	65.32 E
Tyvrov	78	49.01 N	28.30 E
Tywa ≃	54	53.13 N	14.29 E
Tywardreath	42	50.22 N	4.41 W
Tywi ≃	42	51.46 N	4.22 W
Tywyn	42	52.35 N	4.05 W
Tzaneen	156	23.50 S	30.09 E
Tzekung → Zigong	107	29.24 N	104.47 E
Tzeliutsing → Zigong	107	29.24 N	104.47 E
Tzucacab	232	20.04 N	89.03 W
Tzukung → Zigong	107	29.24 N	104.47 E
Tzupo → Boshan	98	36.29 N	117.50 E
Tzupo → Zibo	98	36.47 N	118.01 E

U

Name	Seite	Breite°′	Länge°′
Uaboe	174b	0.31 S	166.55 E
Uac, Mount ∧	116	12.12 N	123.40 E
Uaçá ≃	250	4.13 N	51.32 W
Uagadugu → Ouagadougou	150	12.22 N	1.31 W
Uamba	152	7.12 S	16.25 E
Uamba (Wamba) ≃, Afr.	152	3.56 S	17.12 E
Uamba ≃, Ang.	152	7.58 S	17.09 E
Uampochane	158	26.23 S	32.41 E
Uaoa Bay c	229a	20.56 N	156.16 W
Uaran → Ouarâne ◆[1]	134	21.00 N	10.30 W
Uato-Lari	112	8.45 S	126.34 E
Uatumã ≃	246	2.26 S	57.37 W
Uauá	250	9.50 S	39.28 W
Uaupés (Vaupés) ≃	246	0.02 N	67.16 W
Uaxactún ⊥	232	17.24 N	89.39 W
Ubá	255	21.07 S	42.56 W
Uba ≃	86	50.15 N	81.41 E
Übach-Palenberg	56	50.55 N	6.07 E
Ubagan ≃	86	54.24 N	64.45 E
Ubai	164	5.40 S	150.40 E
Ubaidullaganj	124	22.59 N	77.36 E
Ubaitaba	255	14.18 S	39.20 W
Ubajara	250	3.51 S	40.56 W
Ubajara, Parque Nacional de ♠	250	3.47 S	40.56 W
Ubangi (Oubangui) ≃	152	0.30 S	17.42 E
Ubatã	255	14.12 S	39.31 W
Ubaté	246	5.19 N	73.49 W
Ubatuba	256	23.26 S	45.04 W
Ubatuba, Baía de c	256	23.27 S	45.02 W
Ubauro	120	28.10 N	69.44 E
Ubay	116	10.03 N	124.28 E
Ubaye	62	44.28 N	6.22 E
Ubaye ≃	62	44.28 N	6.18 E
Ubayyiḍ, Wādī al- V	128	32.34 N	43.48 E
Ubby	41	55.37 N	11.13 E
Ube	96	33.56 N	131.15 E
Ubed' ≃	78	51.27 N	32.29 E
Úbeda	34	38.01 N	3.22 W
Uberaba	255	19.45 S	47.55 W
Uberaba ≃	255	20.07 S	48.31 W
Uberaba, Lagoa ⊜	248	17.30 S	57.45 W
Überackern	60	48.11 N	12.52 E
Über dem Wind, Inseln → Leeward Islands II	238	17.00 N	63.00 W
Uberlândia	255	18.56 S	48.18 W
Überlingen	58	47.46 N	9.10 E
Überlinger See c	58	47.45 N	9.09 E
Übersee	64	47.49 N	12.28 E
Ubiaja	150	6.38 N	6.21 E
Ubili	154	1.07 S	26.55 E
Ubin, Pulau I	271c	1.24 N	103.58 E
Ubinskoje	86	55.19 N	79.41 E
Ubinskoje, ozero ⊜	86	55.30 N	80.05 E
Ubl'a	30	48.55 N	22.23 E
Ubly	190	43.42 N	82.55 W
Uboldo	266b	45.37 N	9.00 E
Ubombo	158	27.33 S	32.00 E
Ubondo	154	0.52 S	25.37 E
Ubon Ratchathani	110	15.14 N	104.54 E
Úborsko	60	49.20 N	13.09 E
Ubort' ≃	78	52.06 N	28.28 E
Ubrique	34	36.41 N	5.27 W
Ubudiah, Masjid ʊ[1]	114	4.46 N	100.56 E
Ubundu (Ponthierville)	154	0.21 S	25.29 E
Ubur-Tochtor	88	50.06 N	113.37 E
Uča ≃, Ross.	82	56.02 N	37.37 E
Uča ≃, Ross.	265b	55.56 N	37.57 E
Ucacha	252	33.02 S	63.31 W

Symbols in the index entries represent the broad categories identified in the key at the right. Symbols with superior numbers (⋏[1]) identify subcategories (see complete key on page I · 1).

Symbole im Register stellen die rechts im Schlüssel erklärten Kategorien dar. Symbole mit hochgestellten Ziffern (⋏[1]) bezeichnen Unterabteilungen einer Kategorie (vgl. vollständiger Schlüssel auf Seite I · 1).

Los símbolos incluídos en el texto del índice representan las grandes categorías identificadas con la clave a la derecha. Los símbolos con numeros en su parte superior (⋏[1]) identifican las subcategorías (véase la clave completa en la página I · 1).

Les symboles de l'index représentent les catégories indiquées dans la légende à droite. Les symboles suivis d'un indice (⋏[1]) représentent des sous-catégories (voir légende complète à la page I · 1).

Os símbolos incluídos no texto do índice representam as grandes categorias identificadas com a chave à direita. Os símbolos com números em sua parte superior (⋏[1]) identificam as subcategorias (veja-se a chave completa à página I · 1).

	English	Deutsch	Español	Français	Português
∧	Mountain	Berg	Montaña	Montagne	Montanha
⋏	Mountains	Gebirge	Montañas	Montagnes	Montanhas
)(	Pass	Paß	Paso	Col	Passo
V	Valley, Canyon	Tal, Cañon	Valle, Cañón	Vallée, Canyon	Vale, Canhão
≚	Plain	Ebene	Llano	Plaine	Planície
≻	Cape	Kap	Cabo	Cap	Cabo
I	Island	Insel	Isla	Île	Ilha
II	Islands	Inseln	Islas	Îles	Ilhas
⊥	Other Topographic Features	Andere Topographische Objekte	Otros Elementos Topográficos	Autres données topographiques	Outros acidentes topográficos

ESPAÑOL — Nombre | Página | Lat.°′ | Long.°′ W = Oeste
FRANÇAIS — Nom | Page | Lat.°′ | Long.°′ W = Ouest
PORTUGUÊS — Nome | Página | Lat.°′ | Long.°′ W = Oeste

Uč-Adži 128 38.05 N 62.48 E
Učaly 86 54.19 N 59.27 E
Učami 74 63.50 N 96.29 E
Učaral 86 46.10 N 80.56 E
Ucayali □ [5] 248 9.00 S 74.00 W
Ucayali ≃ 242 4.30 S 73.27 W
Uccellina, Monti dell' ʌʌ 66 42.38 N 11.05 E
Uccle 50 50.48 N 4.19 E
Uch 123 29.14 N 71.03 E
Uchab 156 19.47 S 17.42 E
Uchāna 124 29.28 N 76.10 E
Uchaud 62 43.45 N 4.16 E
Uchee Creek ≃ 192 32.18 N 84.57 W
Uchihara 94 36.22 N 140.21 E
Uchihata 270 34.25 N 135.27 E
Uchiko 96 33.33 N 132.39 E
Uchi Lake 184 51.05 N 92.35 W
Uchinada 94 36.39 N 136.39 E
Uchinomi 96 34.30 N 134.20 E
Uchinoura 92 31.16 N 131.05 E
Uchiumi 96 33.01 N 132.30 E
Uchiura-wan c 92a 42.20 N 140.40 E
Uchiza 248 8.29 S 76.23 W
Uchoa 255 20.56 S 49.13 W
Ucholovo 80 53.47 N 40.29 E
Uchra ≃ 80 58.20 N 39.00 E
Uchta, Ross. 24 61.12 N 38.32 E
Uchta, Ross. 24 63.33 N 53.38 E
Uchte 52 52.30 N 8.54 E
Uchte ≃ 54 52.46 N 11.45 E
Uchtoma 76 60.10 N 38.02 E
Uchtspringe 54 52.32 N 11.36 E
Učinskij Rybоučastok 86 60.02 N 65.10 E
Učinskoje vodochranilišče ⊜ [1] 82 56.02 N 37.45 E
Uckange 56 49.18 N 6.09 E
Ückendorf ⬥ [8] 263 51.30 N 7.07 E
Uckermark ⬥ [1] 54 53.10 N 13.35 E
Uckfield 42 50.58 N 0.06 E
Üçköşe 130 40.13 N 41.00 E
Uckro 54 51.51 N 13.37 E
Učkupr'uk 85 40.33 N 71.04 E
Učkurgan 85 41.07 N 72.05 E
Ucluelet 182 48.57 N 125.33 W
Ucon 202 43.35 N 111.57 W
Üçpınar 130 37.08 N 32.16 E
Ucria 70 38.03 N 14.53 E
Üçtepeler ʌ 130 39.39 N 42.41 E
Učterek 85 41.45 N 73.12 E
Úcua ≃ 152 8.35 S 13.40 E
Učujevskij Majdan 80 54.33 N 44.30 E
Učur ≃ 74 58.48 N 130.35 E
Uda ≃, Ross. 88 56.05 N 99.34 E
Uda ≃, Ross. 88 51.47 N 107.33 E
Uda ≃, Ross. 89 54.42 N 135.14 E
Udagamandalam 122 11.24 N 76.42 E
Udaipur 120 24.35 N 73.41 E
Udaj ≃ 78 50.05 N 33.07 E
Udala 126 21.35 N 86.34 E
Udalguri 120 26.46 N 92.08 E
Udall 198 37.23 N 97.06 W
Udamalpet 122 10.35 N 77.15 E
Udankudi 122 8.26 N 78.01 E
Udaquiola 252 36.34 S 58.31 W
Udarnyj 89 49.07 N 142.09 E
Udaypur 124 26.56 N 86.31 E
Udbina 36 44.32 N 15.46 E
Udby 41 55.05 N 11.57 E
Uddeholm 40 60.01 N 13.37 E
Uddel 52 52.15 N 5.46 E
Uddevalla 26 58.21 N 11.55 E
Uddingston 46 55.50 N 4.06 W
Uddjaure ⊜ 24 65.55 N 17.49 E
Udel'naja 82 55.38 N 38.03 E
Udel'naja ⬥ [8] 265a 60.01 N 30.19 E
Uden 52 51.40 N 5.36 E
Udenhout 52 51.37 N 5.08 E
Uder 56 51.22 N 10.05 E
Üdersdorf 56 50.09 N 6.49 E
Udgīr 122 18.23 N 77.07 E
Udhampur 123 32.56 N 75.08 E
Udhruḥ 132 30.20 N 35.36 E
Udi 150 6.19 N 7.25 E
Udimskij 24 61.09 N 45.52 E
Udine 64 46.03 N 13.14 E
Udine □ [4] 64 46.10 N 13.00 E
Udmurtskaja Avtonomnaja Sovetskaja Socialističeskaja Respublika □ [3] 80 57.00 N 53.00 E
Udokan, chrebet ʌʌ 88 56.20 N 118.10 E
Udoml'a 76 57.52 N 35.01 E
Udone-jima I 94 34.28 N 139.18 E
Udono 92 33.44 N 136.01 E
Udon Thani 110 17.26 N 102.46 E
Udor, Mount ʌ 162 23.30 S 131.01 E
Udot I 175c 7.23 N 151.43 E
Udskaja guba c 89 54.50 N 135.45 E
Udskoje 89 54.32 N 134.26 E
Udubo 146 11.57 N 10.38 E
Udupi 122 13.21 N 74.45 E
Udy 78 50.24 N 36.03 E
Udyl', ozero ⊜ 89 52.06 N 139.48 E
Udža 74 71.14 N 117.10 E
Udžary 84 40.31 N 47.39 E
Uebigau 54 51.35 N 13.18 E
Uebonti 112 0.55 S 121.38 E
Uebonti, Teluk c 112 0.50 S 121.45 E
Uecker ≃ 54 53.45 N 14.04 E
Ueckeritz 54 54.00 N 14.02 E
Ueckermünde 54 53.44 N 14.03 E
Ueckermünder Heide ⬥ [3] 54 53.40 N 14.10 E
Ueda 94 36.24 N 138.16 E
Uedem 52 51.40 N 6.16 E
Uedesheim 263 51.10 N 6.48 E
Uegō 268 35.13 N 139.56 E
Ueharu 175d 24.25 N 123.46 E
Uehlfeld 56 49.40 N 10.43 E
Uele ≃ 136 4.09 N 22.26 E
Uelen 180 66.10 N 169.48 W
Uel'kal' 180 65.32 N 179.17 W
Uelsen 52 52.30 N 6.53 E
Uelzen, Dtsch. 52 52.58 N 10.33 E
Uelzen, Dtsch. 263 51.33 N 7.44 E
Ueno, Nihon 94 36.05 N 138.47 E
Ueno, Nihon 94 34.45 N 136.08 E
Ueno, Nihon 270 34.53 N 135.14 E
Uenohara 94 35.37 N 139.07 E
Ueno Park ♦ 268 35.43 N 139.46 E
Uenoshiba 270 34.33 N 135.28 E
Uerdingen ⬥ [8] 263 51.21 N 6.39 E
Uere ≃ 154 3.42 N 25.24 E
Uetersen 52 53.41 N 9.39 E
Uettingen 56 49.48 N 9.43 E
Uetz 264a 52.28 N 12.56 E
Uetze 52 52.28 N 10.11 E
Ufa 86 54.44 N 55.56 E
Ufa ≃ 86 54.40 N 56.00 E
Ufala, Punta › 70 38.22 N 14.59 E
Uffculme 42 50.54 N 3.20 W
Uffenheim 56 49.32 N 10.14 E
Ufita ≃ 68 41.09 N 14.56 E
Ufra 128 40.00 N 53.02 E
Uft'uga ≃ 76 59.46 N 39.21 E
Ugab ≃ 156 21.08 S 13.40 E
Ugak Bay c 180 57.25 N 152.45 W
Ugāle 76 57.16 N 22.02 E
Ugalla ≃ 154 5.08 S 30.42 E
Ugamskij chrebet ʌʌ 85 42.00 N 70.20 E
Uganda □ [1] 154 1.00 N 32.00 E
Uganik Island I 180 57.53 N 153.28 W
Ugârčin 38 43.06 N 24.25 E
Ugarit ⊥ 130 35.35 N 35.45 E
Ugashik 180 57.32 N 157.25 W
Ugashik Bay c 180 57.34 N 157.38 W
Ugatkyn ≃ 180 68.24 N 171.30 E
Ugento 68 39.56 N 18.10 E
Ugep 150 5.48 N 8.05 E
Ugerløse 41 55.35 N 11.40 E
Uggiano la Chiesa 68 40.06 N 18.27 E
Ughaybish 140 10.52 N 31.05 E
Ughelli 150 5.29 N 5.59 E
Ugie 158 31.10 S 28.13 E
Ugie ≃ 46 57.30 N 1.47 W
Ugíjar 34 36.57 N 3.03 W
Ugine 62 45.45 N 6.25 E
Uglegorsk, Ross. 89 49.02 N 142.03 E
Uglegorsk, Ukr. 83 48.19 N 38.17 E
Uglekamensk 89 43.13 N 133.11 E
Uglezavodsk 89 47.21 N 142.38 E
Uglič 76 57.32 N 38.19 E
Ugljan, Otok I 36 44.05 N 15.10 E
Uglovaja 80 57.01 N 52.57 E
Uglovka 76 58.14 N 33.31 E
Uglovoje 89 43.20 N 132.06 E
Uglovskoje 86 51.23 N 80.12 E
Ugly-Zavod 78 52.11 N 32.53 E
Ugnev 78 50.23 N 23.44 E
Ugodiči 80 57.10 N 39.30 E
Ugodskij Zavod 82 55.02 N 36.45 E
Ugol'naja, buchta c 180 63.00 N 179.20 E
Ugolnyy 180 62.58 N 179.17 E
Ugoma ʌ 154 4.00 S 28.45 E
Ugovizza 64 46.31 N 13.29 E
Ugra 76 54.47 N 34.17 E
Ugra ≃ 82 54.30 N 36.07 E
Ugrojedy 78 50.52 N 35.17 E
Ugr'umovo 82 55.09 N 37.40 E
Ugtaal Cajdam 88 48.17 N 105.25 E
Uguj 86 56.02 N 76.03 E
Uğurludağ 130 40.27 N 34.28 E
Ug'ut 85 41.24 N 74.50 E
Ugyak, Cape › 180 58.17 N 154.04 W
Uh (Už) ≃ 30 48.34 N 22.00 E
Uha-dong 98 40.41 N 125.38 E
Uḥayjibah, Jabal al- ʌ 132 30.11 N 34.33 E
Uherčice 61 48.55 N 15.38 E
Uherské Hradiště 30 49.05 N 17.28 E
Uherský Brod 30 49.02 N 17.39 E
Uhingen 56 48.42 N 9.35 E
Úhlava ≃ 60 49.43 N 13.23 E
Uhlenhorst 156 23.45 S 17.55 E
Ühlingen 58 47.43 N 8.19 E
Uhlman Lake ⊜ 184 56.40 N 98.23 W
Uhlstädt 54 50.44 N 11.28 E
Uhrichsville 214 40.23 N 81.20 W
Uhyst, Dtsch. 54 51.11 N 14.13 E
Uhyst, Dtsch. 54 51.24 N 14.30 E
Uiche 152 12.03 S 21.02 E
Ui-do I 98 34.37 N 125.51 E
Uig 46 57.35 N 6.22 W
Uíge 152 7.37 S 15.03 E
Uíge □ [5] 152 7.00 S 15.30 E
Ŭijŏngbu 98 37.44 N 127.03 E
Ŭiju 98 40.12 N 124.32 E
Uil 86 49.05 N 54.40 E
Uil ≃ 80 48.36 N 52.30 E
Uilpata, gora ʌ 84 42.48 N 43.48 E
Uimaharju 26 62.55 N 30.15 E
Uinebona ≃ 246 5.04 N 63.01 W
Uinskoje 86 56.53 N 56.35 E
Uinta ≃ 200 40.14 N 109.51 W
Uintah and Ouray Indian Reservation ⬥ [4] 200 40.20 N 110.20 W
Uinta Mountains ʌʌ 200 40.45 N 110.05 W
Uiraúna 250 6.31 S 38.25 W
Uis 156 21.08 S 14.49 E
Ŭisŏng 98 36.22 N 128.41 E
Uitenhage 158 33.40 S 25.28 E
Uitgeest 52 52.32 N 4.43 E
Uithoorn 52 52.14 N 4.50 E
Uithuizen 52 53.24 N 6.40 E
Uithuizermeeden 52 53.24 N 6.42 E
Uitspanning 158 26.46 S 29.56 E
Uj ≃, Asia 86 54.17 N 64.58 E
Uj ≃, Ross. 86 57.06 N 74.12 E
Ujae I [1] 14 9.05 N 165.40 E
Ujaly 86 44.37 N 60.57 E
Ujandina ≃ 74 68.23 N 145.50 E
Ujar 86 55.48 N 94.20 E
Ujarrás ⊥ 236 9.51 N 83.50 W
Ujedinenija, ostrov I 72 77.28 N 82.28 E
Ujelang I [1] 14 9.49 N 160.55 E
Ujemskij 24 64.29 N 40.50 E
Újezd, Česko. 54 50.03 N 14.44 E
Újezd, Česko. 60 49.26 N 13.27 E
Újezd u Brna 61 49.06 N 16.45 E
Újfehértó 30 47.48 N 21.40 E
Ujgursaj 85 40.53 N 71.03 E
Ujhāni 124 28.01 N 79.01 E
Uji 96 34.53 N 135.48 E
Uji ≃ 96 34.53 N 135.42 E
Uji-guntō II 92 31.11 N 129.27 E
Ujiie 94 36.41 N 139.58 E
Ujiji 154 4.55 S 29.41 E
Uji-tawara 96 34.51 N 135.52 E
Uji-yamada → Ise 94 34.29 N 136.42 E
Ujjain 120 23.11 N 75.46 E
Újkér 61 47.28 N 16.49 E
'Ujmān 128 25.25 N 55.27 E
Újpest ⬥ [8] 264c 47.34 N 19.06 E
Ujście 30 53.04 N 16.43 E
Ujskoje 86 54.22 N 60.00 E
Ujum 85 38.22 N 70.51 E
Ujung 112 7.04 S 120.46 E
Ujungbatu 114 0.43 N 100.31 E
Ujungbatu, Pulau I 114 2.20 N 97.24 E
Ujungberung 115a 6.55 S 107.42 E
Ujunggading 110 0.16 N 99.33 E
Ujunggenteng 115a 7.22 S 106.24 E
Ujungkulon, Semenanjung › [1] 115a 6.45 S 105.20 E
Ujungkulon National Park ♦ 115a 6.40 S 105.20 E
Ujunglamuru 112 4.40 S 119.58 E
Ujungpandang (Makasar) 112 5.07 S 119.24 E
Újvidék → Novi Sad 38 45.15 N 19.50 E
Uk 88 55.04 N 98.52 E
Uka, Nihon 174m 26.48 N 128.14 E
Uka, Ross. 74 57.50 N 162.06 E
Ukamas 158 28.02 S 19.45 E
Ukara Island I 154 1.50 S 33.03 E
Ukerewe Island I 154 2.03 S 33.00 E
Ukhayḍir, Wādī V 132 30.55 N 37.01 E
Ukhra 126 23.39 N 87.14 E
Ukhrul 120 25.07 N 94.22 E
Ukhta → Uchta 24 63.33 N 53.38 E
Ukiah, Ca., U.S. 204 39.09 N 123.12 W
Ukiah, Or., U.S. 202 45.08 N 118.55 W
Ukibaru-jima I 174m 26.18 N 128.00 E
Ukiha 96 33.19 N 130.47 E
Uki Ni Masi Island I 175e 10.15 S 161.45 E
Ukmergė 76 55.15 N 24.45 E
Ukolnoi Island I 180 55.14 N 161.34 W
Ukraina → Ukraine □ [1] 22 49.00 N 32.00 E
Ukraine □ [1], Europe 22 49.00 N 32.00 E
Ukraine □ [1], Europe 78 49.00 N 32.00 E
Ukrainka 86 54.39 N 71.20 E
Ukrainsk 83 48.06 N 37.18 E
Ukrina ≃ 36 45.05 N 17.56 E
Uks'anskoje 86 55.57 N 63.01 E
Uktuz 86 55.38 N 68.30 E
Uktym 24 62.38 N 48.52 E
Uku 152 11.24 S 14.15 E
Ukui 112 0.09 S 102.11 E
Ukurejskij 88 52.24 N 116.49 E
Ukuti 154 3.39 S 33.32 E
Ukyō ⬥ [8] 270 35.03 N 135.42 E
Ukyr 88 49.28 N 108.52 E
Ula, India 272b 22.43 N 88.33 E
Ula, Tür. 130 37.05 N 28.26 E
Ulaanbaatar 88 47.55 N 106.53 E
Ulaanbaatar □ [8] 88 47.55 N 106.53 E
Ulaanbadrach 102 44.07 N 110.11 E
Ulaan Chus 86 49.02 N 89.23 E
Ulaangom 86 49.58 N 92.02 E
Ulaan nuur ⊜ 102 44.30 N 103.35 E
Ulaan Tajga ʌʌ 88 50.45 N 98.30 E
Ula-Chuduk 80 47.39 N 45.34 E
Ulak Island I 181a 51.22 N 179.00 W
Ulakmedan 114 2.43 N 99.38 E
Ulamba 152 9.07 S 23.40 E
Ulamona 164 5.00 S 151.15 E
Ulan, Austl. 166 32.17 S 149.44 E
Ulan, Zhg. 102 36.59 N 98.26 E
Ulan Bator → Ulaanbaatar 88 47.55 N 106.53 E
Ulanbel' 86 44.48 N 71.10 E
Ulan Buh Shamo ⬥ [2] 102 40.00 N 106.30 E
Ulan-Burgasy, chrebet ʌʌ 88 52.45 N 109.00 E
Ulan-Erge 80 46.19 N 44.53 E
Ulang ≃ 236 14.27 N 83.14 W
Ulanhot → Horqin Youyi Qianqi 89 46.05 N 122.05 E
Ulānia 126 22.12 N 90.29 E
Ulanov 78 49.42 N 28.08 E
Ulanovo 78 51.46 N 34.18 E
Ulanovskij 82 54.04 N 37.51 E
Ulanów 30 50.30 N 22.16 E
Ulansuhai Nur ⊜ 102 40.56 N 108.49 E
Ulan-Ude 88 51.50 N 107.37 E
Ulan Ul Hu ⊜ 120 34.45 N 90.25 E
Ulan-Ušotej 88 50.45 N 105.29 E
Ular, Pulau I 271c 1.14 N 103.45 E
Ulaş 130 39.27 N 37.03 E
Ul'ašovo 24 65.27 N 56.57 E
Ulatis Creek ≃ 226 38.18 N 121.00 W
Ul'atuj 88 51.09 N 116.14 E
Ulawa Island I 175e 9.46 S 161.57 E
Ulawun, Mount ʌ 164 5.03 S 151.20 E
Ulaya 154 7.04 S 36.54 E
Ułazów 30 50.17 N 23.00 E
Ul'ba 86 50.16 N 83.22 E
Ul'banskij zaliv c 89 53.45 N 137.50 E
Ulchin 98 36.59 N 129.23 E
Ul'chun-Partija 88 49.56 N 112.46 E
Ulcinj 38 41.55 N 19.11 E
Ulco 158 28.21 S 24.15 E
Ulcombe 260 51.12 N 0.39 E
Ulcumayo 248 11.01 S 75.55 W
Uldum 41 55.51 N 9.36 E
Uldz ≃ 88 49.56 N 115.31 E
Uleåborg → Oulu 26 65.01 N 25.28 E
Ulefoss 26 59.17 N 9.16 E
Ulen 198 47.04 N 96.15 W
Ulety 88 51.22 N 112.29 E
Ulfborg 26 56.16 N 8.20 E
Ulft 52 51.54 N 6.23 E
Ulgajsyn 86 49.38 N 60.17 E
Ulgueira 266c 38.47 N 9.28 W
Ulhās ≃ 272c 19.13 N 73.01 E
Ulhāsnagar 122 19.13 N 73.07 E
Uliast 86 48.57 N 91.17 E
Uliastaj (Džavchlant) 88 47.45 N 96.49 E
Úlice 60 49.45 N 13.09 E
Ulindi ≃ 154 1.40 S 25.52 E
Ulingan 164 4.30 S 145.25 E
Ulithi I [1] 108 9.58 N 139.40 E
Ulja 74 58.51 N 141.50 E
Uljanino 82 55.21 N 38.26 E
Uljanovka, Ross. 76 59.38 N 30.46 E
Uljanovka, Ukr. 78 48.20 N 30.13 E
Uljanovka, Ukr. 78 50.58 N 34.18 E
Uljanovo, Ross. 76 53.43 N 35.32 E
Uljanovo, Uzb. 85 40.07 N 68.30 E
Uljanovsk 80 54.20 N 48.24 E
Uljanovskoje, Kaz. 86 50.02 N 73.42 E
Uljanovskoje, Ross. 89 46.17 N 142.13 E
Uljuan tekojärvi ⊜ 26 64.19 N 25.57 E
Ul'kajak ≃ 86 48.54 N 62.00 E
Ul'kan 88 57.14 N 107.19 E
Ul'kan ≃ 88 55.53 N 107.45 E
Ul'ken-Karoj, ozero ⊜ 86 54.00 N 71.58 E
Ulla 76 55.14 N 29.15 E
Ulla ≃, Bela. 76 55.14 N 29.14 E
Ulla ≃, Esp. 34 42.39 N 8.44 W
Ulladulla 170 35.21 S 150.29 E
Ulladulla Head › 170 35.22 S 150.30 E
Ullāpāra 126 24.19 N 89.34 E
Ullapool 46 57.54 N 5.10 W
Ullastrell 266d 41.31 N 1.58 E
Üllendahl ⬥ [8] 263 51.19 N 7.18 E
Ullerslev 41 55.22 N 10.40 E
Ullervad 40 58.40 N 13.52 E
Ullin 194 37.17 N 89.11 W
Üllő 264c 47.23 N 19.21 E
Ullswater ⊜ 44 54.34 N 2.54 W
Ullučaj ≃ 84 42.18 N 48.08 E
Ullŭng-do I 92 37.29 N 130.52 E
Ullvettern ⊜ 40 59.27 N 14.16 E
Ullvi 40 59.42 N 16.37 E
Ulm, Dtsch. 58 48.24 N 10.00 E
Ulm, Mt., U.S. 202 47.25 N 111.30 W
Ulma 38 47.53 N 25.18 E
Ul'ma ≃ 89 51.54 N 129.18 E
Ulmarra 166 29.37 S 153.02 E
Ulmen 56 50.13 N 6.59 E
Ulmeni 38 45.04 N 26.39 E
Ulmer, Mount ʌ 9 77.35 S 86.09 W
Ulmeu-Meisereich 56 50.13 N 6.58 E
Ulongué 154 14.37 S 34.19 E
Ulpur 126 23.04 N 89.50 E
Ulricehamn 26 57.47 N 13.25 E
Ulrichskirchen 61 48.24 N 16.29 E
Ulrichstein 56 50.34 N 9.11 E
Ulrum 52 53.22 N 6.20 E
Ulsan 98 35.34 N 129.19 E
Ulsta 46a 60.30 N 1.09 W
Ulsteinvik 26 62.20 N 5.53 E
Ulster 210 41.51 N 76.30 W
Ulster □ [6] 210 41.56 N 74.00 W
Ulster □ [9] 48 54.35 N 7.00 W
Ulster ≃ 56 50.51 N 9.59 E
Ulster Canal ≊ 48 54.08 N 7.22 W
Ultimo, Val d' V 64 46.35 N 11.00 E
Ultraoriental, Cordillera (Serra do Divisor) ʌʌ 248 8.20 S 73.30 W
Ulu, Indon. 112 2.45 N 125.24 E
Ulu, Ross. 74 60.19 N 127.24 E
Ulu, Sūd. 140 10.43 N 33.29 E
Ulúa ≃ 236 15.53 N 87.44 W
Ulubāria 126 22.28 N 88.06 E
Ulubat Gölü ⊜ 130 40.10 N 28.35 E
Ulubey, Tür. 130 38.25 N 29.18 E
Ulubey, Tür. 130 40.53 N 37.43 E
Uluborlu 130 38.05 N 30.28 E
Uluçınar 130 36.27 N 35.51 E
Uludağ ʌ 130 40.04 N 29.13 E
Uludāngar 272b 22.51 N 88.31 E
Uludere 128 37.27 N 42.51 E
Ulugan Bay c 116 10.07 N 118.47 E
Ulugqat 85 39.48 N 74.21 E
Uluinggalau ʌ 175g 16.54 S 179.59 E
Ulujul ≃ 86 57.46 N 85.30 E
Ulukışla, Kıbrıs 130 35.13 N 33.37 E
Ulukışla, Tür. 130 37.33 N 34.30 E
Ulul I 14 8.35 N 149.40 E
Ulu Laho, Bukit ʌ 114 5.43 N 101.27 E
Ulunchan 88 54.51 N 111.02 E
Ulundi 158 28.17 S 31.26 E
Ulunga 89 46.31 N 136.56 E
Ulungur ≃ 86 46.59 N 87.27 E
Ulungur Hu ⊜ 86 47.15 N 87.20 E
Ulurijskij Golec, gora ʌ 88 50.12 N 111.45 E
Uluru National Park ♦ 162 25.20 S 131.00 E
Ulus 130 41.35 N 32.39 E
Ulusara 126 24.16 N 90.36 E
Ulut ≃ 116 12.00 N 125.27 E
Ulutau 86 48.39 N 67.01 E
Ulutau, gora ʌ 86 48.39 N 66.56 E
Ulutau, gory ʌʌ 86 49.00 N 67.00 E
Ulu Tiram 114 1.36 N 103.49 E
Ulu Yam 114 3.27 N 101.38 E
Ulva 272c 18.59 N 73.02 E
Ulva I 46 56.29 N 6.14 W
Ulvenhout 52 51.34 N 4.48 E
Ulverston 44 54.12 N 3.06 W
Ulverstone 166 41.09 S 146.10 E
Ulvöarna II 26 63.01 N 18.40 E
Ulvshale › [1] 41 55.02 N 12.16 E
Ulvshyttan 40 60.18 N 15.22 E
Ulvsund ᛘ 41 54.59 N 12.11 E
Ulyanovsk → Uljanovsk 80 54.20 N 48.24 E
Ulysses, Ks., U.S. 198 37.34 N 101.21 W
Ulysses, Ne., U.S. 198 41.04 N 97.12 W
Ulysses, Pa., U.S. 214 41.54 N 77.46 W
Uly-Žilanšik ≃ 86 48.51 N 63.47 E
Ulzë 38 41.41 N 19.54 E
Uma 89 52.36 N 120.37 E
Umag 64 45.25 N 13.32 E
Umaji 96 33.33 N 134.03 E
Umal'tinskij 89 51.56 N 133.36 E
Umán, Méx. 232 20.53 N 89.45 W
Uman', Ukr. 78 48.44 N 30.14 E
Uman I 175c 7.18 N 151.53 E
Umanak 176 70.40 N 52.07 W
Umanak Fjord c [2] 176 70.55 N 53.00 W
Umancevo 80 47.44 N 44.16 E
'Umān → Oman □ [1] 118 22.00 N 58.00 E
Umargãon 122 20.12 N 72.45 E
Umari 250 6.38 S 38.42 W
Umari ≃ 248 7.05 S 64.34 W
'Umarī, Qā' al- ⊜ 132 31.42 N 36.57 E
Umaria 124 23.32 N 80.50 E
Umarizal 250 5.59 S 37.49 W
Umarkot 120 25.22 N 69.44 E
Umatac 174p 13.18 N 144.39 E
Umatilla, Fl., U.S. 220 28.55 N 81.39 W
Umatilla, Or., U.S. 202 45.55 N 119.20 W
Umatilla ≃ 202 45.55 N 119.20 W
Umatilla, Lake ⊜ [1] 202 45.44 N 120.35 W
Umatilla Indian Reservation ⬥ [4] 202 45.41 N 118.31 W
Umayan ≃ 116 8.13 N 125.50 E
Umaze 270 34.57 N 135.03 E
Umba 24 66.41 N 34.15 E
Umbagog Lake ⊜ 188 44.45 N 71.05 W
Umbai 114 2.10 N 102.20 E
Umbaúba 250 11.22 S 37.39 W
Umbelasha ≃ 140 9.51 N 24.50 E
Umbertide 66 43.18 N 12.20 E
Umbogintwini 158 30.00 S 30.58 E
Umboi Island I 164 5.36 S 148.00 E
Umbrail, Pass (Giogo di Santa Maria))(64 46.34 N 10.25 E
Umbria □ [4] 66 43.00 N 12.30 E
Umbriatico 68 39.21 N 16.55 E
Umbroli 272c 19.11 N 73.06 E
Umbukul 164 2.30 S 150.00 E
Umbuzero, ozero ⊜ 24 67.43 N 34.25 E
Ume ≃ 154 16.40 S 28.26 E
Umeå 26 63.50 N 20.15 E
Umeälven ≃ 24 63.47 N 20.16 E
Umedani 270 34.44 N 135.51 E
Umedpur 126 22.31 N 89.59 E
Umfolozi Game Reserve ⬥ [4] 158 28.19 S 31.50 E
Umfors 24 65.56 N 15.00 E
Umfreville Lake ⊜ 184 50.18 N 94.45 W
Umfuli ≃ 154 17.30 S 29.23 E
Umgungundhlovu ⊥ 158 28.27 S 31.28 E
Umguza 154 19.25 S 27.51 E
Umhausen 64 47.08 N 10.56 E
Umhlanga Rocks 158 29.43 S 31.06 E
Umi 96 33.34 N 130.30 E
Umingan 116 15.56 N 120.50 E
Umkomaas 158 30.15 S 30.42 E
Umm ad-Daraj, Jabal ʌ 132 32.19 N 35.48 E
Umm 'Ajārim ⊥ [8] 142 30.50 N 32.49 E
Umm al-Abīd 146 27.31 N 15.02 E
Umm al-'Arā'is, Wādī V 146 26.26 N 13.55 E
Umm al-Arānib 146 26.08 N 14.45 E
Umm al-Birak 128 23.25 N 39.13 E
Umm al-Ḥawāyā, Jabal ʌ 142 28.41 N 31.06 E
Umm al-Jimāl, Khirbat ⊥ 132 32.20 N 36.22 E
Umm al-Khashab 144 17.21 N 42.32 E
Umm al-Qaywayn 128 25.35 N 55.34 E
Umm al-Qiṭṭayn 132 32.19 N 36.38 E
Umm al-Quṣūr 142 27.23 N 30.54 E
Ummanz 54 54.28 N 13.10 E
Umm Artah, Wādī V 142 28.41 N 32.37 E
Umm as-Sa'd ⊥ 132 33.16 N 36.47 E
Umm Badr 140 14.14 N 27.57 E
Umm Balad, Wādī V 142 27.40 N 32.39 E
Umm Bayyū'd 140 12.05 N 31.40 E
Umm Bel 140 13.32 N 28.04 E
Umm Boim 140 11.43 N 25.57 E
Umm Dabbī 140 14.37 N 30.23 E
Umm Dam 140 13.45 N 30.59 E
Umm Dhibbān, Sūd. 140 14.14 N 29.37 E
Umm Dhibbān, Sūd. 140 15.26 N 32.51 E
Umm Digulgulaya 140 10.29 N 24.57 E
Umm Dīnār 142 30.12 N 31.04 E
Umm Durmān (Omdurman) 140 15.38 N 32.30 E
Umm el Faḥm 132 32.31 N 35.09 E
Ummeln 52 51.58 N 8.27 E
Ummendorf 54 52.09 N 11.11 E
Umm Habwah, Jabal ʌ [2] 142 27.23 N 31.29 E
Umm Ḥamāṭ 132 31.02 N 35.46 E
Umm Jamālah 140 11.27 N 28.12 E
Umm Kaddādah 140 13.36 N 26.42 E
Umm Khunān 273c 29.55 N 31.15 E
Umm Khushayb, Wādī V 142 30.24 N 32.43 E
Umm Kuwaykah 140 13.00 N 32.17 E
Umm Lajj 128 25.04 N 37.13 E
Umm Marahik, Jabal ʌ [2] 140 13.40 N 26.53 E
Umm Mirdi 140 18.59 N 33.32 E
Umm Mitmān ⊥ [8] 142 30.41 N 32.30 E
Umm Qantur 140 14.17 N 31.22 E
Umm Qaṣr 128 30.02 N 47.56 E
Umm Qurayn 140 9.58 N 28.55 E
Umm Quṣayr 132 31.40 N 35.53 E
Umm Raqm, Jabal ʌ 142 30.14 N 31.52 E
Umm Rīshah, Birkat ⊜ 142 30.21 N 30.22 E
Umm Rumaylah ⊤ [4] 140 16.55 N 31.40 E
Umm Ruwābah 140 12.54 N 31.13 E
Umm Saggāt, Wādī V 140 15.15 N 23.12 E
Umm Saysabān, Jabal ʌ 132 29.45 N 35.10 E
Umm Sayyālah 140 14.25 N 31.10 E
Umm Shalīl 140 10.51 N 23.42 E
Umm Shanqah 140 13.14 N 27.14 E
Umm Shuṭūr 140 7.17 N 33.14 E
Umm Sidr, Wādī V 142 27.54 N 32.33 E
Umm Sughra ⊤ [4] 140 15.03 N 27.12 E
Umm 'Umayd, Ra's ʌ 142 27.50 N 32.19 E
Umm 'Umayyid, Bi'r ⊤ [4] 142 27.53 N 32.30 E
Umm 'Umayyid, Wādī V 142 27.37 N 32.41 E
Umm Urūmah I 128 25.46 N 36.32 E
Umm Walad 132 32.39 N 36.26 E
Umm Zaytah, Jabal ʌ [2] 142 29.49 N 32.16 E
Umnak 180 53.17 N 168.20 W
Umnak Island I 180 53.25 N 168.10 W
Umnak Pass ᛘ 180 53.20 N 167.45 W
Umnäs 24 65.24 N 16.10 E
Umniati 154 18.39 S 29.49 E
Umniati ≃ 154 17.30 S 29.23 E
Um'ot, Ross. 80 54.08 N 42.42 E
Um'ot, Ross. 80 52.31 N 42.58 E
Umpferstedt 54 50.59 N 11.25 E
Umpqua ≃ 202 43.42 N 124.03 W
Umpulo 152 12.38 S 17.42 E
'Umrān 144 15.50 N 43.56 E
'Umrānī, Wādī al- V 142 27.37 N 30.53 E
Umraniye 130 39.10 N 31.15 E
Umraniye ⬥ [8] 267b 41.01 N 29.05 E
Umred 122 20.51 N 79.20 E
Umreth 120 22.42 N 73.07 E
Umsini, Gunung ʌ 164 1.22 S 133.45 E
Ŭmsŏng 98 36.56 N 127.41 E
Umstead State Park ♦ 192 35.52 N 78.47 W
Umtanum Creek ≃ 224 46.52 N 120.35 W
Umtata 158 31.35 S 28.47 E
Umtentweni 158 30.42 S 30.28 E
Umuahia 150 5.33 N 7.29 E
Umuarama 255 23.45 S 53.20 W
Umurbey 130 40.14 N 26.36 E
Umurlu 130 37.50 N 27.58 E
Umzimkulu 158 30.16 S 29.56 E
Umzingwani ≃ 154 22.12 S 29.56 E
Umzinto 158 30.22 S 30.33 E
Una, Bra. 255 15.18 S 39.04 W
Una, India 120 20.49 N 71.02 E
Una, India 123 31.29 N 76.17 E
Una ≃ 36 45.16 N 16.55 E
Una, Mount ʌ 172 42.13 S 172.35 E
Una, Ribeirão ≃ 287b 23.31 S 46.18 W
Unac ≃ 36 44.30 N 16.09 E
Uña de Gato 196 25.58 N 99.41 W
Unadilla, Ga., U.S. 192 32.15 N 83.44 W
Unadilla, N.Y., U.S. 210 42.19 N 75.18 W
Unadilla ≃ 210 42.20 N 75.25 W
Unaí 255 16.23 S 46.53 W
Unakami 94 35.46 N 140.45 E
Unalakleet 180 63.53 N 160.47 W
Unalaska 180 53.52 N 166.32 W
Unalaska Island I 180 53.45 N 166.45 W
Unanderra 170 34.27 S 150.52 E
Unango 154 12.50 S 35.20 E
Únanov 61 48.54 N 16.04 E
Unao 124 25.35 N 78.36 E
Unare ≃ 246 10.03 N 65.14 W
Unauna, Pulau I 112 0.10 S 121.35 E
Unayyir, Ḥarrat al- ⊥ [9] 128 25.20 N 37.45 E
'Unayzah, Ar. Su. 128 26.06 N 43.56 E
'Unayzah, Urd. 132 30.29 N 35.48 E
'Unayzah, Jabal ʌ, Asia 128 32.12 N 39.18 E
'Unayzah, Jabal ʌ, Urd. 132 30.30 N 35.47 E
Unazuki 94 36.49 N 137.35 E
Uncasville 207 41.26 N 72.06 W
Unchahra 124 24.23 N 80.47 E
Ŭnch'ŏn 98 38.34 N 125.26 E
Uncia 248 18.27 S 66.37 W
Uncompahgre ≃ 200 38.45 N 108.06 W
Uncompahgre Peak ʌ 200 38.04 N 107.28 W
Uncompahgre Plateau ʌʌ [1] 200 38.30 N 108.25 W
Uncukul' 84 42.42 N 46.48 E
Uncular 130 40.28 N 41.28 E
Unda 88 51.42 N 116.56 E
Unda ≃ 88 51.25 N 116.05 E
Unden ⊜ 40 58.47 N 14.26 E
Undenäs 40 58.39 N 14.25 E
Underberg 158 29.50 S 29.22 E
Under River 260 51.15 N 0.14 E
Undersåker 26 63.20 N 13.23 E
Underwood, In., U.S. 218 38.36 N 85.46 W
Underwood, N.D., U.S. 198 47.27 N 101.08 W
Underwood, Wa., U.S. 224 45.43 N 121.31 W
Undløse 41 55.36 N 11.35 E
Undory 80 54.37 N 48.25 E
Undu, Tanjung › 115b 10.05 S 120.51 E
Undu Point › 175g 16.08 S 179.57 W
Undva nina › 76 58.32 N 21.55 E
Unea Island I 164 4.55 S 149.10 E
Uneča 76 52.50 N 32.40 E
Uneča ≃ 76 52.50 N 31.56 E
Uneiuxi ≃ 246 0.34 S 64.58 W
Úněšov 60 49.53 N 13.09 E
Unga Island I 180 55.15 N 160.45 W
Ungama Bay c 154 2.45 S 40.20 E
Ungaran 115a 7.07 S 110.24 E
Ungarie 166 33.38 S 146.58 E
Ungarn → Hungary □ [1] 30 47.00 N 20.00 E
Ungava, Péninsule d' › [1] 176 60.00 N 74.00 W
Ungava Bay c 176 59.30 N 67.30 W
Ungch'ŏn 98 35.07 N 128.44 E
Ungen' 78 47.12 N 27.48 E
Unggi 98 42.20 N 130.24 E
Ungurkuj 88 50.27 N 106.58 E
Ungvár → Užgorod 78 48.37 N 22.18 E
Unhos 266c 38.50 N 9.07 W
Unhošt' 54 50.04 N 14.08 E
Uni 80 57.46 N 51.30 E
União 250 4.35 S 42.52 W
União da Vitória 252 26.13 S 51.05 W
União dos Palmares 250 9.10 S 36.02 W
Unica 24 62.38 N 34.38 E
Unicoi 192 36.11 N 82.20 W
Unicorn Branch ≃ 208 39.15 N 75.52 W
Unidad Santa Fe ⬥ [8] 286a 19.23 N 99.15 W
Uniejów 30 51.58 N 18.49 E
Unieux 62 45.24 N 4.16 E
Unije, Otok I 36 44.38 N 14.15 E
Unimak Island I 180 54.50 N 164.00 W
Unimak Pass ᛘ 180 54.35 N 164.43 W
Unini ≃ 246 1.41 S 61.31 W
Unión, Arg. 252 35.09 S 65.57 W
Union, On., Can. 212 42.42 N 81.12 W
Unión, C.R. 236 8.36 N 83.03 W
Unión, Para. 252 24.48 S 56.33 W
Union, Il., U.S. 216 42.14 N 88.33 W
Union, Ia., U.S. 190 42.14 N 93.03 W
Union, Ky., U.S. 218 38.56 N 84.40 W
Union, La., U.S. 194 30.06 N 90.54 W
Union, Ms., U.S. 194 32.34 N 89.07 W
Union, Mo., U.S. 219 38.26 N 91.00 W
Union, N.J., U.S. 210 40.41 N 74.15 W
Union, Oh., U.S. 218 39.53 N 84.18 W
Union, Or., U.S. 202 45.12 N 117.51 W
Union, S.C., U.S. 192 34.42 N 81.37 W
Union, Wa., U.S. 224 47.21 N 123.06 W
Union, W.V., U.S. 192 37.35 N 80.32 W
Union □ [6], In., U.S. 218 39.38 N 84.56 W
Union □ [6], N.J., U.S. 208 40.40 N 74.11 W
Union □ [6], Oh., U.S. 214 40.18 N 83.19 W
Union □ [6], Pa., U.S. 210 40.58 N 76.54 W
Unión ⬥ [8] 258 34.53 S 56.08 W
Union Bay 182 49.35 N 124.53 W
Union Beach 208 40.26 N 74.10 W
Union Bridge 208 39.34 N 77.10 W
Union Center 210 42.09 N 76.04 W
Union City, Ca., U.S. 226 37.35 N 122.04 W
Union City, Ga., U.S. 192 33.35 N 84.32 W
Union City, In., U.S. 194 40.07 N 85.05 W
Union City, Mi., U.S. 216 42.04 N 85.09 W
Union City, N.J., U.S. 276 40.46 N 74.01 W
Union City, Oh., U.S. 216 40.11 N 84.48 W
Union City, Pa., U.S. 214 41.53 N 79.50 W
Union City, Tn., U.S. 194 36.25 N 89.03 W
Union City Dam ⬥ [6] 214 41.55 N 79.54 W
Uniondale, S. Afr. 158 33.40 S 23.08 E
Uniondale, In., U.S. 216 40.50 N 85.15 W
Uniondale, N.Y., U.S. 276 40.42 N 73.35 W
Union Dale, Pa., U.S. 210 41.43 N 75.30 W
Unión de Reyes 240p 22.48 N 81.32 W
Unión de San Antonio 234 21.06 N 101.58 W
Union des Émirats Arabes → United Arab Emirates □ [1] 128 24.00 N 54.00 E
Unión de Tula 234 19.58 N 104.16 W
Union Flat Creek ≃ 202 46.50 N 117.59 W
Union Gap 202 46.33 N 120.28 W
Union Grove, Tx., U.S. 222 32.34 N 94.55 W
Union Grove, Wi., U.S. 216 42.41 N 88.03 W
Unión Hidalgo 234 16.28 N 94.50 W
Union Hill 210 43.13 N 77.23 W
Union Lake 216 42.36 N 83.26 W
Union Lake ⊜, Mi., U.S. 216 42.03 N 85.11 W
Union Lake ⊜, Mi., U.S. 281 42.37 N 83.26 W
Union Lake ⊜, N.J., U.S. 208 39.25 N 75.03 W
Union Mills 216 41.29 N 86.46 W
Union Park 220 28.30 N 81.15 W
Union Pier 216 41.49 N 86.41 W
Union Point 192 33.36 N 83.04 W
Unionport, In., U.S. 218 40.07 N 85.06 W
Unionport, Oh., U.S. 214 40.21 N 80.51 W
Union Seamount ✧ [3] 16 49.35 N 132.45 W
Union Springs, Al., U.S. 194 32.08 N 85.42 W
Union Springs, N.Y., U.S. 210 42.50 N 76.41 W
Union Station ⬥ [5], On., Can. 275b 43.39 N 79.23 W
Union Station ⬥ [5], Ca., U.S. 280 34.04 N 118.14 W
Union Station ⬥ [5], D.C., U.S. 284c 38.54 N 77.00 W
Union Station ⬥ [5], Il., U.S. 278 41.53 N 87.38 W
Uniontown, Al., U.S. 194 32.26 N 87.30 W
Uniontown, Ky., U.S. 194 37.46 N 87.55 W
Uniontown, Md., U.S. 208 39.35 N 77.06 W
Uniontown, Oh., U.S. 214 40.58 N 81.24 W
Uniontown, Pa., U.S. 188 39.54 N 79.44 W
Union Valley Reservoir ⊜ [1] 226 38.50 N 120.26 W
Union Village 207 41.59 N 71.32 W
Unionville, On., Can. 275b 43.52 N 79.18 W
Unionville, Ct., U.S. 207 41.45 N 72.53 W
Unionville, In., U.S. 218 39.14 N 86.25 W
Unionville, Mi., U.S. 190 43.39 N 83.27 W
Unionville, Mo., U.S. 194 40.28 N 93.00 W
Unionville, N.J., U.S. 285 40.01 N 74.46 W
Unionville, N.Y., U.S. 210 41.18 N 74.34 W
Unionville, Oh., U.S. 214 41.47 N 81.00 W
Unionville, Pa., U.S. 285 39.54 N 75.44 W
Unionville Center 214 40.08 N 83.21 W
Uniopolis 216 40.36 N 84.05 W
Unipouheos Indian Reserve ⬥ [4] 184 53.52 N 110.21 W
Unisan 116 13.51 N 121.59 E
United 214 40.13 N 79.29 W
United Arab Emirates (Al-Imārāt al-'Arabīyah al-Muttaḥidah) □ [1], Asia 118 24.00 N 54.00 E
United Arab Emirates (Al-Imārāt al-'Arabīyah al-Muttaḥidah) □ [1], Asia 128 24.00 N 54.00 E
United Arab Republic → Egypt □ [1] 140 27.00 N 30.00 E
United Kingdom □ [1], Europe 22 54.00 N 2.00 W
United Kingdom □ [1], Europe 28 54.00 N 2.00 W
United Kingdom Sovereign Base Area ■ 130 35.00 N 33.45 E
United Nations Headquarters ⊎ 276 40.45 N 73.58 W
United States □ [1] 178 38.00 N 97.00 W
United States Air Force Academy ■ 200 39.00 N 104.55 W
United States Coast Guard Academy ■ 207 41.22 N 72.06 W
United States Merchant Marine Academy ⊎ [2] 276 40.48 N 73.46 W
United States Military Academy ■ 210 41.23 N 73.58 W
United States Naval Academy ■ 208 38.59 N 76.30 W
United States Steel Corporation (Lorain Plant) ⊎ [3], Oh., U.S. 279a 41.27 N 82.07 W
United States Steel Corporation ⊎ [3], Pa., U.S. 279b 40.20 N 79.54 W
United States Steel Corporation ⊎ [3], Pa., U.S. 279b 40.25 N 79.54 W
United States Steel Corporation Fairless Works ⊎ [3] 285 40.09 N 74.45 W
Unity 184 52.27 N 109.10 W
Unity Reservoir ⊜ [1] 279b 40.17 N 79.30 W
Universal City 196 29.32 N 98.17 W
Universal City ⊎ [3] 280 34.09 N 118.21 W
Universal Mall ⬥ [9] 281 42.30 N 83.05 W
Università Degli Studi ⊎ [2] 266b 45.28 N 9.14 E
Universitaria, Ciudad ⊎ [2] 266d 41.23 N 2.08 E
University 194 34.21 N 89.32 W
University City 219 38.39 N 90.19 W
University Gardens 276 40.46 N 73.43 W
University Heights, Ca., U.S. 226 37.26 N 122.12 W
University Heights, Oh., U.S. 279a 41.29 N 81.32 W
University Park, Il., U.S. 216 41.36 N 87.39 W
University Park, Md., U.S. 284c 38.58 N 76.57 W
University Park, N.M., U.S. 200 32.06 N 106.39 W
University Park, Tx., U.S. 222 32.52 N 96.47 W
University Place 224 47.14 N 122.32 W
University View 218 40.00 N 83.03 W
Unjha 120 23.48 N 72.24 E
Unkel 56 50.35 N 7.13 E
Unken 64 47.39 N 12.43 E
Unkurda 86 55.48 N 59.24 E
Unley 168b 34.57 S 138.35 E
Unna 52 51.32 N 7.41 E
'Unnāb, Jabal al- ʌ 132 29.57 N 36.55 E
'Unnāb, Wādī al- V 132 30.11 N 36.39 E
Unnão 124 26.32 N 80.30 E
Uno, Canal Numero ≊ 252 36.17 S 57.08 W
Uno, Ilha I 150 11.12 N 16.15 W
Unoke 94 36.43 N 136.42 E
Ŭnp'a 98 38.26 N 125.45 E
Unpenji-san ʌ 96 34.02 N 133.44 E
Unqua Point › 276 40.39 N 73.26 W
Unquillo 252 31.14 S 64.19 W
Ŭnsan 98 39.25 N 126.01 E
Unseburg 54 51.56 N 11.30 E

English	Deutsch	Español	Français	Português
≃ River	Fluß	Río	Rivière	Rio
≊ Canal	Kanal	Canal	Canal	Canal
ʟ Waterfall, Rapids	Wasserfall, Stromschnellen	Cascada, Rápidos	Chute d'eau, Rapides	Cascata, Rápidos
ᛘ Strait	Meeresstraße	Estrecho	Détroit	Estreito
c Bay, Gulf	Bucht, Golf	Bahía, Golfo	Baie, Golfe	Baía, Golfo
⊜ Lake, Lakes	See, Seen	Lago, Lagos	Lac, Lacs	Lago, Lagos
≋ Swamp	Sumpf	Pantano	Marais	Pântano
⌂ Ice Features, Glacier	Eis- und Gletscherformen	Accidentes Glaciales	Formes glaciaires	Acidentes glaciares
⊤ Other Hydrographic Features	Andere Hydrographische Objekte	Otros Elementos Hidrográficos	Autres données hydrographiques	Outros acidentes hidrográficos
✧ Submarine Features	Untermeerische Objekte	Accidentes Submarinos	Formes de relief sous-marin	Acidentes submarinos
□ Political Unit	Politische Einheit	Unidad Politica	Entité politique	Unidade política
⊎ Cultural Institution	Kulturelle Institution	Institución Cultural	Institution culturelle	Instituição cultural
⊥ Historical Site	Historische Stätte	Sitio Histórico	Site historique	Sitio histórico
♦ Recreational Site	Erholungs- und Ferienort	Sitio de Recreo	Centre de loisirs	Area de Lazer
⊠ Airport	Flughafen	Aeropuerto	Aéroport	Aeroporto
■ Military Installation	Militäranlage	Instalación Militar	Installation militaire	Instalação militar
⬥ Miscellaneous	Verschiedenes	Misceláneo	Divers	Diversos

Vaci-Vauf I · 183

ESPAÑOL — Nombre | Página | Lat.°′ | Long.°′ W = Oeste
FRANÇAIS — Nom | Page | Lat.°′ | Long.°′ W = Ouest
PORTUGUÊS — Nome | Página | Lat.°′ | Long.°′ W = Oeste

Vači 84 42.05 N 47.13 E
Vacía Talega, Punta ≻ 240m 18.27 N 65.54 W
Vacoas 157c 20.18 S 57.29 E
Vad, Ross. 80 55.32 N 44.12 E
Vad, Sve. 40 60.02 N 15.39 E
Vad ≃ 80 54.33 N 42.37 E
Väddö I 40 60.00 N 18.50 E
Vădeni 38 45.22 N 27.56 E
Vader 224 46.24 N 122.57 W
Vadheim 26 61.13 N 5.49 E
Vādi 272c 18.56 N 73.06 E
Vadino 76 55.16 N 33.16 E
Vadinsk 80 53.43 N 43.04 E
Vadnagar 120 23.47 N 72.38 E
Vadodara 122 22.18 N 73.12 E
Vado de Cedillos 200 31.05 N 105.50 W
Vado de Piedra 196 29.50 N 104.40 W
Vado Hondo 200 31.09 N 111.22 W
Vado Ligure 62 44.17 N 8.27 E
Vadret, Piz ʌ 58 46.41 N 9.57 E
Vadsbro 40 58.58 N 16.36 E
Vadsø 24 70.05 N 29.46 E
Vadstena 26 58.27 N 14.54 E
Vaduz 58 47.09 N 9.31 E
Vadvetjåkko Nationalpark ♠ 24 68.35 N 18.20 E
Væggerløse 41 54.42 N 11.56 E
Værøy I 24 67.40 N 12.39 E
Vaga ≃ 24 62.48 N 42.56 E
Vagaj 86 57.56 N 69.01 E
Vagaj ≃ 86 57.59 N 69.01 E
Vågåmo 26 61.53 N 9.06 E
Vaganski Vrh ʌ 36 44.22 N 15.31 E
Vaggeryd 26 57.30 N 14.07 E
Vaghena Island I 175e 7.26 S 157.46 E
Vaglia 66 43.54 N 11.17 E
Vaglio Basilicata 68 40.40 N 15.55 E
Vagney 58 48.01 N 6.43 E
Vagnhärad 40 58.55 N 17.30 E
Vagues 258 34.19 S 59.26 W
Váh ≃ 30 47.55 N 18.00 E
Vaiano 66 43.58 N 11.07 E
Vaich, Loch ⊜ 46 57.43 N 4.46 W
Vaiden 194 33.19 N 89.44 W
Vaigai ≃ 122 9.21 N 79.00 E
Vaigat Ʉ 176 70.11 N 53.00 W
Vaihingen an der Enz 56 48.56 N 8.58 E
Vaijāpur 122 19.55 N 74.44 E
Vaikam 122 9.46 N 76.24 E
Väike-Maarja 76 59.08 N 26.15 E
Väike Pakri I 76 59.20 N 24.00 E
Vail, Co., U.S. 200 39.38 N 106.22 W
Vail, Ia., U.S. 198 42.03 N 95.11 W
Vaila I 46a 60.12 N 1.37 W
Vailala ≃ 164 7.25 S 145.25 E
Vaileka 175g 17.23 S 178.09 E
Vail Lake ⊜[1] 228 33.29 N 116.58 W
Vailly-sur-Aisne 50 49.25 N 3.31 E
Vailly-sur-Sauldre 50 47.27 N 2.39 E
Vail Mills 210 43.03 N 74.13 W
Vailoatai 174u 14.22 S 170.47 W
Vail Point ≻ 212 44.43 N 80.45 W
Vails Gate 210 41.27 N 74.04 W
Vaimali 175f 16.34 S 168.11 E
Vaiņode 76 56.26 N 21.50 E
Vaiont, Lago di ⊜ 64 46.21 N 10.21 E
Vaippār ≃ 122 9.01 N 78.17 E
Vair ≃ 58 48.27 N 5.42 E
Vairano Scalo 68 41.20 N 14.08 E
Vairao 174s 17.47 S 149.17 W
Vaires-sur-Marne 261 48.52 N 2.39 E
Vaison-la-Romaine 62 44.14 N 5.04 E
Vaitahu 174x 9.56 S 139.06 W
Vaîte 58 47.35 N 5.44 E
Vaitogi 174u 14.21 S 170.44 W
Vaitown 150 6.52 N 10.52 W
Vaitupu I 14 7.28 S 178.41 E
Vaja ≃ 80 57.27 N 46.00 E
Vajgač 72 70.25 N 58.46 E
Vajgač, ostrov I 72 70.00 N 59.30 E
Vakaga □[5] 146 10.00 N 22.30 E
Vakaga ≃ 146 9.48 N 21.32 E
Vākhān ≃ 120 37.00 N 72.40 E
Vākhān ◆[1] 120 37.00 N 73.00 E
Vaklan 272c 19.07 N 73.06 E
Vaksdal 26 60.29 N 5.44 E
Vala ≃ 80 56.59 N 51.16 E
Valaam 24 61.23 N 30.57 E
Valaam, ostrov I 26 61.22 N 30.57 E
Vålådalen 26 63.10 N 12.57 E
Valadeces 196 26.14 N 98.40 W
Valadim 154 12.22 S 36.10 E
Valais (Wallis) □[3] 58 46.10 N 7.30 E
Valaisannes, Alpes ʌʌ 58 46.00 N 7.30 E
Val-Alain 206 46.24 N 71.45 W
Valamaz 80 57.32 N 52.05 E
Valandovo 38 41.19 N 22.34 E
Valangin 58 47.01 N 6.54 E
Valap 272c 19.03 N 73.08 E
Valare, Baie C 174s 17.31 S 149.46 W
Valašské Klobouky 30 49.08 N 18.01 E
Valašské Meziříčí 30 49.28 N 17.58 E
Valatie 210 42.24 N 73.40 W
Vala Ull 272c 19.02 N 73.07 E
Val-Bélair 206 46.51 N 71.26 W
Valbella 58 46.45 N 9.33 E
Vålberg 26 59.24 N 13.12 E
Valbert 56 51.07 N 7.44 E
Valbo 40 60.40 N 17.04 E
Valbondione 64 46.02 N 10.00 E
Valbonnais 62 44.54 N 5.54 E
Valcanuta ◆[8] 267a 41.53 N 12.25 E
Vâlcĕdrâm 38 43.42 N 23.27 E
Valcheta 254 40.42 S 66.09 W
Valchetta ≃ 267a 41.58 N 12.30 E
Valchiusella 62 45.32 N 7.42 E
Valcivières 62 45.35 N 3.48 E
Valcourt 206 45.29 N 72.18 W
Valdagno 64 45.39 N 11.18 E
Valdahon 58 47.09 N 6.21 E
Valdai Hills → Valdajskaja vozvyšennost' ʌʌ[2] 76 57.00 N 33.30 E
Valdaj, Ross. 24 63.26 N 35.30 E
Valdaj, Ross. 76 57.59 N 33.14 E
Valdajskaja vozvyšennost' ʌʌ[2] 24 57.00 N 33.30 E
Valdarno V 66 43.45 N 11.15 E
Valdavia ≃ 34 42.24 N 4.16 W
Val-David 206 46.01 N 74.12 W
Valdebeba, Arroyo de ≃ 266a 41.23 N 2.10 E
Valdeblore 62 44.04 N 7.12 E
Val-de-Cães 250 1.23 S 48.29 W
Valdecañas, Embalse de ⊜[1] 34 39.45 N 5.30 W
Valdelândia 255 15.11 S 50.02 W
Val-de-Marne □[5] 261 48.47 N 2.29 E
Valdemārpils 76 57.22 N 22.35 E
Valdemarsvik 26 58.12 N 16.36 E
Valdepeñas 34 38.46 N 3.23 W
Valderaduey ≃ 34 41.31 N 5.42 W
Valderas 34 42.05 N 5.27 W
Valderice 70 38.03 N 12.38 E
Valderrama 116 11.00 N 122.08 E
Valderrobres 34 40.53 N 0.09 E
Valders 190 44.03 N 87.53 W
Valdés, Península ≻[1] 254 42.30 S 64.00 W
Val-des-Bois 188 45.54 N 75.35 W
Valdese 192 35.44 N 81.33 W
Valdes Island I 224 49.04 N 123.38 W
Valdéz, Ec. 246 1.15 N 79.00 W
Valdez, Ak., U.S. 180 61.07 N 146.16 W
Valdieri 62 44.17 N 7.24 E
Val-d'Isère 62 45.27 N 6.59 E
Valdivia, Chile 254 39.48 S 73.14 W
Valdivia, Col. 246 7.11 N 75.27 W
Valdobbiadene 64 45.54 N 12.00 E
Valdoie 58 47.40 N 6.51 E
Val-d'Oise □[5] 50 49.10 N 2.10 E
Val-d'Or 190 48.07 N 77.47 W
Valdorf 52 52.09 N 8.51 E
Valdosta 192 30.49 N 83.16 W
Valdoviño 34 43.36 N 8.08 W
Valdres V 26 60.55 N 9.10 E
Valdurna (Durnholz) 64 46.44 N 11.26 E
Vale, Guernsey 43b 49.29 N 2.31 W
Vale, Or., U.S. 202 43.58 N 117.14 W
Valea lui Mihai 38 47.31 N 22.09 E
Vale de Lobos 266c 38.49 N 9.17 W
Valeene 218 38.26 N 86.24 W
Valeggio sul Mincio 64 45.21 N 10.44 E
Valehouse Reservoir ⊜[1] 262 53.29 N 1.57 W
Valemount 182 52.50 N 119.15 W
Valença, Bra. 255 13.22 S 39.05 W
Valença, Bra. 256 22.15 S 43.43 W
Valença, Port. 34 42.02 N 8.38 W
Valença do Piauí 250 6.24 S 41.45 W
Valençay 50 47.09 N 1.34 E
Valence 62 44.56 N 4.54 E
Valence → València 34 39.28 N 0.22 W
València, Esp. 34 39.28 N 0.22 W
Valencia, Hond. 236 14.47 N 85.18 W
Valencia, Pil. 116 7.57 N 125.03 E
Valencia, Ca., U.S. 228 34.26 N 118.36 W
Valencia, Pa., U.S. 214 40.40 N 79.59 W
Valencia, Ven. 246 10.11 N 68.00 W
València □[4] 34 39.30 N 0.45 W
València, Golf de C 34 39.50 N 0.30 E
Valencia, Lago de ⊜ 246 10.15 N 67.45 W
Valencia, Quebrada ≃ 286c 10.30 N 66.46 W
Valencia de Alcántata 34 39.25 N 7.14 W
Valencia de Don Juan 34 42.18 N 5.31 W
Valencia Island I 48 51.52 N 10.20 W
Valenciennes 50 50.21 N 3.32 E
Vălenii de Munte 38 45.12 N 26.03 E
Valensole 62 43.50 N 5.59 E
Valentano 66 42.34 N 11.49 E
Valente 250 11.34 S 39.27 W
Valentigney 58 47.28 N 6.50 E
Valentin 89 43.08 N 134.17 E
Valentín Alsina ◆[8] 288 34.40 S 58.25 W
Valentine, Ne., U.S. 198 42.52 N 100.33 W
Valentine, Tx., U.S. 196 30.34 N 104.29 W
Valentine Mountain ʌ 224 48.32 N 123.56 W
Valentinovka 265b 55.55 N 37.56 E
Valenton 261 48.45 N 2.28 E
Valenza 62 45.01 N 8.38 E
Valenzano 68 41.02 N 16.53 E
Valenzuela 269f 14.42 N 120.58 E
Våler 26 60.40 N 11.50 E
Valera 246 9.19 N 70.37 W
Valérien, Mont ʌ[2] 261 48.53 N 2.13 E
Vale Royal □[8] 262 53.17 N 2.37 W
Valets, Lac ⊜ 190 48.32 N 76.30 W
Valette, La → Valletta 36 35.54 N 14.31 E
Valfabbrica 66 43.09 N 12.36 E
Valflaunès 62 43.48 N 3.52 E
Valfurva 64 46.27 N 10.25 E
Valfurva V 64 46.26 N 10.26 E
Valga 76 57.47 N 26.02 E
Valge ≃ 76 59.35 N 25.42 E
Valgorge 62 44.35 N 4.07 E
Valgrisanche 62 45.38 N 7.04 E
Valguarnera Caropepe 70 37.30 N 14.23 E
Valhalla, S. Afr. 158 25.49 S 28.08 E
Valhalla, N.Y., U.S. 210 41.04 N 73.46 W
Valhalla, Lake ⊜ 276 40.56 N 74.22 W
Valiente, Península ≻[1] 236 9.05 N 81.51 W
Valiente, Punta ≻ 236 9.11 N 81.55 W
Valier, Il., U.S. 194 38.01 N 89.03 W
Valier, Mt., U.S. 202 48.18 N 112.14 W
Valier, Pa., U.S. 214 40.55 N 79.03 W
Valili ʌ 175g 16.39 S 179.10 E
Valinda 280 34.02 N 117.56 W
Valinhos 256 22.57 S 47.01 W
Valjevo 38 44.16 N 19.53 E
Valka 76 57.46 N 26.00 E
Valkeakoski 26 61.16 N 24.02 E
Valkenburg 56 50.52 N 5.50 E
Valkenswaard 52 51.21 N 5.28 E
V'alki, Ross. 82 55.39 N 38.05 E
Valki, Ukr. 78 49.50 N 35.37 E
Valkininkas 76 54.21 N 24.50 E
Valla 40 59.02 N 16.23 E
Valladares 196 26.53 N 100.37 W
Valladolid, Ec. 246 4.33 S 79.08 W
Valladolid, Esp. 34 41.39 N 4.43 W
Valladolid, Méx. 232 20.41 N 88.12 W
Valladolid □[4] 34 41.40 N 4.50 W
Vallage ◆[1] 58 48.24 N 5.00 E
Vallåkra 41 55.58 N 12.52 E
Vallarsa 64 45.47 N 11.07 E
Vallata 68 41.02 N 15.15 E
Vallauris 62 43.35 N 7.03 E
Vallco Fashion Park ◆[9] 282 37.19 N 122.01 W
Valldal 26 62.20 N 7.21 E
Valldoreix 266d 41.28 N 2.04 E
Valle, Esp. 34 43.14 N 4.18 W
Valle, It. 64 46.04 N 10.25 E
Valle, Lat. 76 56.30 N 24.44 E
Valle □[5] 236 13.30 N 87.35 W
Valle, Arroyo ≃ 226 37.39 N 121.54 W
Vallecas ◆[8] 266a 40.23 N 3.37 W
Valle Castellana 66 42.44 N 13.29 E
Vallecillo 196 26.40 N 99.58 W
Vallecito 226 38.07 N 120.27 W
Vallecitos 200 36.05 N 106.20 W
Vallecitos Creek ≃ 282 37.36 N 121.53 W
Vallecorsa 66 41.27 N 13.24 E
Valle Crucis Abbey ᵿ[1] 42 52.59 N 3.12 W
Valle d'Aosta □[4] 62 45.45 N 7.25 E
Valle de Bravo 234 19.11 N 100.08 W
Valle de Guadalupe 234 21.00 N 102.37 W
Valle de Guanape 246 9.54 N 65.41 W
Valle de Juárez 234 19.53 N 102.51 W
Valle de la Pascua 246 9.13 N 66.00 W
Valle del Cauca □[5] 246 3.45 N 76.30 W
Valle de Olivos 232 27.12 N 106.17 W
Valle de Santiago 234 20.23 N 101.12 W
Valle de Zaragoza 232 27.28 N 105.49 W
Valle di Cadore 64 46.24 N 12.20 E
Valle di Sotto 64 46.25 N 10.21 E
Valledolmo 70 37.45 N 13.49 E
Valledupar 246 10.29 N 73.15 W
Valle Edén 252 31.50 S 56.09 W
Vallefiorita 68 38.46 N 16.27 E
Vallegrande 248 18.29 S 64.06 W
Valle Hermoso, Arg. 252 31.07 S 64.29 W
Valle Hermoso, Méx. 196 25.39 N 97.52 W
Vallehermoso, Pil. 116 10.20 N 123.19 E
Vallejo 226 38.06 N 122.15 W
Valle Lomellina 62 45.09 N 8.40 E
Vallelunga Pratameno 70 37.41 N 13.50 E
Valle Mosso 62 45.38 N 8.09 E
Vällen ⊜ 40 60.03 N 18.20 E
Vallenar 252 28.35 S 70.46 W
Vallendar 56 50.24 N 7.37 E
Vallensbæk 41 55.38 N 12.22 E
Vallentuna 40 59.32 N 18.05 E
Vallepietra 66 41.55 N 13.14 E
Valleraugue 62 44.05 N 3.38 E
Valle Redondo 204 32.31 N 116.46 W
Vallermosa 71 39.22 N 8.48 E
Vallerotonda 66 41.33 N 13.55 E
Valleroy 56 49.12 N 5.55 E
Valles Caldera ⊥[6] 200 35.52 N 106.33 W
Valles → Ciudad de Valles 234 21.59 N 99.01 W
Vallet 32 47.10 N 1.16 W
Valletta 36 35.54 N 14.31 E
Valley, Al., U.S. 194 32.49 N 85.10 W
Valley, Ne., U.S. 198 41.18 N 96.20 W
Valley, Wa., U.S. 182 48.10 N 117.43 W
Valley ≃ 184 51.21 N 99.55 W
Valley Bend 188 38.46 N 79.56 W
Valley Center, Ca., U.S. 228 33.13 N 117.02 W
Valley Center, Ks., U.S. 198 37.50 N 97.22 W
Valley City, N.D., U.S. 198 46.55 N 97.59 W
Valley City, Oh., U.S. 214 41.14 N 81.56 W
Valley Cottage 210 41.07 N 73.57 W
Valley Creek ≃, Pa., U.S. 285 40.06 N 75.28 W
Valley Creek ≃, Pa., U.S. 285 39.58 N 75.40 W
Valley Creek ≃, Tx., U.S. 196 31.43 N 100.02 W
Valleydale 280 34.06 N 117.56 W
Valley Falls, Ks., U.S. 198 39.20 N 95.27 W
Valley Falls, N.Y., U.S. 210 42.54 N 73.34 W
Valley Falls, R.I., U.S. 207 41.54 N 71.23 W
Valley Farms 200 32.59 N 111.26 W
Valleyfield 186 49.08 N 53.37 W
Valley Forge 208 40.05 N 75.28 W
Valley Forge Estates 285 40.05 N 75.26 W
Valley Forge National Historical Park ♠ 208 40.06 N 75.27 W
Valley Grove 214 40.05 N 80.34 W
Valley Head, Al., U.S. 194 34.34 N 85.36 W
Valley Head, W.V., U.S. 188 38.32 N 80.02 W
Valley Home 226 37.50 N 120.55 W
Valley Mede 284b 39.17 N 76.50 W
Valley Mills 222 31.39 N 97.28 W
Valley of Desolation National Monument ♠ 158 32.17 S 24.30 E
Valley of Fire State Park ♠ 204 36.26 N 114.30 W
Valley of the Kings ⊥ 140 25.45 N 32.37 E
Valley Park 219 38.32 N 90.29 W
Valley Plaza ◆[9] 280 34.11 N 118.24 W
Valley Springs, Ca., U.S. 226 38.12 N 120.50 W
Valley Springs, S.D., U.S. 198 43.34 N 96.28 W
Valley Station 194 38.06 N 85.52 W
Valley Stream 210 40.39 N 73.42 W
Valley Stream ≃ 276 40.39 N 73.45 W
Valley Stream State Park ♠ 276 40.41 N 73.42 W
Valleyview, Ab., Can. 182 55.04 N 117.17 W
Valley View, Il., U.S. 216 41.50 N 88.03 W
Valley View, Oh., U.S. 279a 41.23 N 81.37 W
Valley View, Pa., U.S. 210 40.38 N 76.32 W
Valley View, Tx., U.S. 196 33.29 N 97.10 W
Valley View Park 228 34.13 N 117.20 W
Vallgrund I 26 63.12 N 21.14 E
Valliant 196 34.00 N 95.05 W
Valli del Pasubio 64 45.41 N 11.15 E
Vallières 58 45.54 N 5.56 E
Vallimanca, Arroyo ≃ 252 35.40 S 60.02 W
Vallio 64 45.38 N 10.23 E
Vallirana 266d 41.23 N 1.56 E
Vallø 41 55.24 N 12.15 E
Vallo della Lucania 68 40.14 N 15.17 E
Valloire 62 45.10 N 6.26 E
Vallombrosa 64 43.44 N 11.32 E
Vallonia 218 38.50 N 86.05 W
Vallon-Pont-d'Arc 62 44.24 N 4.24 E
Vallorbe 58 46.43 N 6.22 E
Vallorcine 58 46.02 N 6.56 E
Vallouise 62 44.51 N 6.29 E
Vallromanes 266d 41.32 N 2.18 E
Valls 34 41.17 N 1.15 E
Valluga ʌ 58 47.09 N 10.12 E
Vallvidrera ◆[8] 266d 41.25 N 2.07 E
Vallvidrera, Riera de ≃ 266d 41.25 N 2.01 E
Val-Marie 184 49.14 N 107.44 W
Valmaseda 34 43.12 N 3.12 W
Valmeyer 219 38.17 N 90.18 W
Valmiera 76 57.33 N 25.24 E
Valmondois 261 49.06 N 2.12 E
Valmont 50 49.44 N 0.31 E
Valmontone 66 41.46 N 12.57 E
Valmy 56 49.05 N 4.46 E
Valognes 32 49.31 N 1.28 W
Valois 210 42.32 N 76.53 W
Valois, Baie de C 275a 45.26 N 73.47 W
Valok 78 45.47 N 34.57 E
Valona → Vlorë 38 40.27 N 19.30 E
Valongo 34 41.11 N 8.30 W
Valoria la Buena 34 41.48 N 4.32 W
Vālpārai 122 10.22 N 76.58 E
Valparaíso, Bra. 255 21.13 S 50.51 W
Valparaíso, Chile 252 33.02 S 71.38 W
Valparaíso, Méx. 234 22.46 N 103.34 W
Valparaiso, Fl., U.S. 194 30.29 N 86.29 W
Valparaiso, In., U.S. 216 41.28 N 87.03 W
Valparaiso, Ne., U.S. 198 41.04 N 96.49 W
Valparaíso □[4] 252 32.45 S 71.20 W
Valparaíso ≃ 234 22.33 N 103.39 W
Valpelline V 62 45.50 N 7.25 E
Valpolicella ◆[1] 64 45.25 N 10.52 E
Valpovo 38 45.39 N 18.26 E
Valprato Soana 62 45.31 N 7.33 E
Valréas 62 44.23 N 4.59 E
Valrico 220 27.57 N 82.16 W
Val Roveto V 66 41.52 N 13.30 E
Vals ≃ 158 27.23 S 26.30 E
Vals, Tanjung ≻ 164 8.26 S 137.38 E
Val-Saint-Michel 206 46.52 N 71.27 W
Valsbaai C 158 34.12 S 18.40 E
Valserine ≃ 58 46.06 N 5.50 E
Valserrhein ≃ 58 46.42 N 9.10 E
Valsertal V 58 46.37 N 9.10 E
Valsetz 202 44.50 N 123.39 W
Valsinni 68 40.10 N 16.26 E
Valsjöbyn 26 64.04 N 14.08 E
Valskog 40 59.27 N 15.57 E
Vals-les-Bains 62 44.40 N 4.22 E
Vals Platz 58 46.37 N 9.11 E
Vals-Près-le-Puy 62 45.01 N 3.52 E
Valstagna 64 45.51 N 11.39 E
Val-Suzon 58 47.25 N 4.54 E
Valtellina V 64 46.11 N 9.55 E
Valthermond 52 52.53 N 6.59 E
Valtice 61 48.44 N 16.45 E
Valtierrilla 234 20.32 N 101.08 W
Valtimo 26 63.40 N 28.48 E
Valtorta 58 45.59 N 9.32 E
Valtournanche 62 45.53 N 7.37 E
Valujec 76 52.46 N 33.23 E
Valujevka 80 46.44 N 43.43 E
Valujevo 265b 55.35 N 37.21 E
Valujki 78 50.13 N 38.08 E
Valvasone 64 45.59 N 12.52 E
Valverde 148 27.48 N 17.55 W
Valverde del Camino 34 37.34 N 6.45 W
Val Verde Park 228 34.27 N 118.40 W
Valyermo 228 34.26 N 117.50 W
Vamba ≃ 152 7.27 S 14.17 E
Vamdrup 41 55.25 N 9.17 E
Våmhus 26 61.08 N 14.28 E
Vamizi, Ilha I 154 11.02 S 40.40 E
Vammala 26 61.20 N 22.54 E
Vamori Wash V 200 31.57 N 112.21 W
Van, Tür. 128 38.28 N 43.20 E
Van, Pa., U.S. 214 41.19 N 79.40 W
Van, Tx., U.S. 222 32.31 N 95.38 W
Van □[4] 128 39.00 N 43.45 E
Vanajavesi ⊜ 26 61.09 N 23.25 E
Vanak ◆[8] 267d 35.45 N 51.23 E
Van Alstyne 196 33.25 N 96.34 W
Vanån ≃ 40 60.31 N 14.14 E
Vananda 182 49.45 N 124.33 W
Vanapa ≃ 164 9.05 S 147.10 E
Vanault-les-Dames 56 48.51 N 4.46 E
Vanavana I[1] 14 20.47 S 139.09 W
Vanavara 74 60.22 N 102.16 E
Van Buren, Ar., U.S. 194 35.26 N 94.20 W
Van Buren, In., U.S. 216 40.37 N 85.30 W
Van Buren, Me., U.S. 186 47.09 N 67.56 W
Van Buren, Mo., U.S. 194 36.59 N 91.00 W
Van Buren, Oh., U.S. 216 41.08 N 83.38 W
Van Buren □[6] 216 42.14 N 86.04 W
Van Buren Point 214 42.27 N 79.25 W
Vanč 85 38.23 N 71.26 E
Vanč ≃ 85 38.18 N 71.19 E
Vance Air Force Base ■ 196 36.21 N 97.55 W
Vanceboro 188 45.33 N 67.25 W
Vanceburg 218 38.35 N 83.19 W
Vancleave 194 30.32 N 88.41 W
Van Cortlandt Park ♠ 276 40.54 N 73.53 W
Van Cortlandtville 210 41.19 N 73.54 W
Vancouver, B.C., Can. 224 49.16 N 123.07 W
Vancouver, Wa., U.S. 224 45.38 N 122.39 W
Vancouver, Cape ≻, Austl. 162 35.01 S 118.12 E
Vancouver, Cape ≻, Ak., U.S. 180 60.33 N 165.27 W
Vancouver, Mount ʌ 180 60.20 N 139.40 W
Vancouver International Airport ⊠ 224 48.39 N 123.26 W
Vancouver Island I 182 49.45 N 126.00 W
Vancouver Island Ranges ʌʌ 182 49.25 N 125.25 W
Vancouver Lake ⊜ 224 45.41 N 122.44 W
Van Daalen ≃ 164 3.05 S 138.09 E
Vandalia, Il., U.S. 219 38.57 N 89.05 W
Vandalia, Mi., U.S. 216 41.55 N 85.55 W
Vandalia, Mo., U.S. 219 39.18 N 91.29 W
Vandalia, Oh., U.S. 218 39.53 N 84.11 W
Vandalia Lake ⊜[1] 219 39.01 N 89.09 W
Vandam 84 40.57 N 47.57 E
Vandavāsi 122 12.30 N 79.37 E
Vandekerckhove Lake ⊜ 184 57.02 N 101.25 W
Vandel 41 55.42 N 9.13 E
Vandenberg Air Force Base ■ 204 34.43 N 120.33 W
Van den Bosch, Tanjung ≻ 164 4.06 S 132.55 E
Vandenesse 58 47.13 N 4.37 E
Vanderbijlpark 158 26.42 S 27.54 E
Vanderbilt, Mi., U.S. 190 45.08 N 84.39 W
Vanderbilt, Tx., U.S. 196 28.49 N 96.37 W
Vanderbilt Mansion National Historic Site ⊥ 210 41.47 N 73.56 W
Vanderbilt Museum ᵿ 276 40.54 N 73.22 W
Vandercook Lake 216 42.11 N 84.23 W
Vandergrift 214 40.36 N 79.33 W
Vanderhoof 182 54.01 N 124.01 W
Vanderlin Island I 164 15.44 S 137.02 E
Vandervoort 194 34.22 N 94.21 W
Van Diemen, Cape ≻, Austl. 164 11.10 S 130.23 E
Van Diemen, Cape ≻, Austl. 164 16.31 S 139.41 E
Van Diemen Gulf C 164 11.50 S 132.00 E
Vandling 210 41.38 N 75.29 W
Vandoeuvre-lès-Nancy 58 48.39 N 6.11 E
Vandoies (Vintl) 64 46.49 N 11.43 E
Vändra 76 58.39 N 25.02 E
Van Duzen ≃ 204 40.33 N 124.08 W
Vandúzi ≃ 154 18.56 S 34.01 E
Vandykpark 273d 26.16 S 28.19 E
Vandžiogala 76 55.07 N 23.58 E
Vanegas 234 23.51 N 100.52 W
Vänern ⊜ 26 58.55 N 13.30 E
Vänersborg 26 58.22 N 12.19 E
Van Etten 210 42.11 N 76.33 W
Vang, Mount ʌ 9 73.56 S 68.39 W
Vanga 154 4.39 S 39.13 E
Vangaindrano 157b 23.21 S 47.36 E
Vängelälven ≃ 26 63.41 N 16.25 E
Van Gölü ⊜ 128 38.33 N 42.46 E
Vangsnes 26 61.11 N 6.38 E
Vanguard 184 49.55 N 107.20 W
Vangunu, Mount ʌ 175e 8.42 S 158.00 E
Vangunu Island I 175e 8.38 S 158.00 E
Van Hook Arm C 198 47.50 N 102.25 W
Van Horn 196 31.02 N 104.49 W
Van Horne 190 42.00 N 92.05 W
Van Hornesville 210 42.54 N 74.50 W
Vani 84 42.06 N 42.30 E
Vanier 212 45.26 N 75.40 W
Vanikolo I 14 11.39 S 166.54 E
Vaniköy ◆[8] 267b 41.04 N 29.04 E
Vanimo 164 2.40 S 141.20 E
Vanino 89 49.05 N 140.15 E
Vānīvilāsa Sāgara ⊜[1] 122 13.52 N 76.26 E
Vāniyambādi 122 12.41 N 78.37 E
Vankarem 180 67.51 N 175.50 W
Vankarem ≃ 180 67.42 N 176.17 W
Vankarem, laguna C 180 67.40 N 176.00 W
Vankaremskaja nizmennost' ⩩ 180 67.30 N 176.00 W
Van Kleef Aquarium ♠ 271c 1.18 N 103.51 E
Vankleek Hill 206 45.31 N 74.39 W
Vanlay 50 48.02 N 4.01 E
Van Lear 192 37.46 N 82.45 W
Vanlue 216 40.58 N 83.28 W
Vanna I 24 70.09 N 19.51 E
Vännäs 26 63.55 N 19.45 E
Vanndale 194 35.18 N 90.46 W
Vanne ≃ 50 48.12 N 3.16 E
Vanne et du Loing, Aqueduc de ≊[1] 261 48.36 N 2.26 E
Vannes 32 47.39 N 2.46 W
Vannes-sur-Cosson 50 47.43 N 2.13 E
Van Ninh 110 12.42 N 109.14 E
Van Norman Lakes ⊜[1] 228 34.18 N 118.28 W
Vannovka 85 42.32 N 70.21 E
Van Nuys ◆[8] 228 34.11 N 118.26 W
Van Nuys Airport ⊠ 280 34.12 N 118.29 W
Van Nuys-Sherman Oaks War Memorial Park ♠ 280 34.10 N 118.27 W
Vanoi ≃ 64 46.06 N 11.45 E
Vanoise, Massif de la ʌʌ 62 45.20 N 6.40 E
Vanoise, Parc National de la ♠ 62 45.20 N 6.45 E
Van Ormer 214 40.41 N 78.30 W
Van Phong, Vung C 110 12.33 N 109.18 E
Vanport 214 40.41 N 80.20 W
Van Reenen 158 28.22 S 29.24 E
Van Reenen's Plaats 158 30.55 S 21.14 E
Van Rees, Pegunungan ʌʌ 164 2.35 S 138.15 E
Vanrhynsdorp 158 31.36 S 18.44 E
Vanrook 166 16.57 S 141.57 E
Vanryndam ⊜[1] 273d 26.09 S 28.21 E
Vansant 192 37.13 N 82.05 W
Van Saun Mill Brook ≃ 276 40.55 N 74.03 W
Vansbro 40 60.31 N 14.13 E
Van Sciver Lake ⊜ 285 40.09 N 74.48 W
Van Sickle Island I 282 38.04 N 121.53 W
Vansittart Island I 176 65.50 N 84.00 W
Vansjön ⊜ 40 59.59 N 16.57 E
Vanskoje 78 55.56 N 36.52 E
Vanstadensrus 158 29.59 S 27.02 E
Vantaa (Vanda) 26 60.16 N 25.03 E
Vantaa ≃ 26 60.13 N 24.59 E
Vanthali 120 21.29 N 70.20 E
Vanua Lava I 175f 13.48 S 167.28 E
Vanua Levu I 175g 16.33 S 179.15 E
Vanua Mbalavu Island I 175g 17.40 S 178.57 W
Vanuatu □[1], Oc. 14 16.00 S 167.00 E
Vanuatu □[1], Oc. 175f 16.00 S 167.00 E
Vanves 261 48.50 N 2.18 E
Van Vleck 222 29.01 N 95.53 W
Van Voorhis 279b 40.10 N 79.58 W
Van Wert 216 40.52 N 84.35 W
Van Wert □[6] 216 40.52 N 84.35 W
Vanwyksdorp 158 33.46 S 21.28 E
Vanwyksvlei 158 30.18 S 21.49 E
Vanzaghello 266b 45.35 N 8.47 E
Vanzago 266b 45.32 N 9.00 E
Van Zandt □[6] 222 32.35 N 95.50 W
Vanzylsrus 158 26.52 S 22.04 E
Vao 175f 22.39 S 167.32 E
Vapn'arka 78 48.32 N 28.44 E
Vaprio d'Adda 62 45.35 N 9.31 E
Vaqueros Creek ≃ 226 36.16 N 121.20 W
Var □[5] 62 43.30 N 6.20 E
Var ≃ 62 43.39 N 7.12 E
Vara 26 58.16 N 12.57 E
Vara ≃ 64 44.09 N 9.53 E
Varada ≃ 122 14.55 N 75.40 E
Varadero 240p 23.09 N 81.16 W
Varades 32 47.23 N 1.02 W
Varages 62 43.36 N 5.58 E
Varaita ≃ 62 44.49 N 7.36 E
Varaita, Valle V 62 44.35 N 7.10 E
Varaklāni 76 56.37 N 26.44 E
Varallo, It. 62 45.49 N 8.15 E
Varallo, It. 266b 45.40 N 8.38 E
Varāmīn 128 35.20 N 51.39 E
Vārānasi (Benares) 124 25.20 N 83.00 E
Varandej 24 68.48 N 58.00 E
Varangerfjorden C[2] 24 70.00 N 30.00 E
Varangerhalvøya ≻[1] 24 70.25 N 29.30 E
Varangéville 56 48.38 N 6.19 E
Varano, Lago Di C 68 41.53 N 15.45 E
Varano de'Melegari 64 44.41 N 10.01 E
Varapodio 68 38.19 N 15.59 E
Varaždin 36 46.19 N 16.20 E
Varazze 62 44.22 N 8.34 E
Varberg 26 57.06 N 12.15 E
Varces 62 45.05 N 5.41 E
Varciche 84 42.08 N 42.43 E
Vardak □[4] 120 34.15 N 68.00 E
Vardaman 194 33.52 N 89.10 W
Vardar (Axiós) ≃ 38 40.35 N 22.50 E
Varde 26 55.38 N 8.29 E
Vardenik 84 40.08 N 45.27 E
Vardenis 84 40.11 N 45.43 E
Vardenskij chrebet ʌʌ 84 39.58 N 45.25 E
Vardhoúsia Óri ʌʌ 38 38.44 N 22.07 E
Vardø 24 70.21 N 31.02 E
Vardūj ≃ 123 37.01 N 70.47 E
Varedo 62 45.36 N 9.09 E
Varegovo 80 57.47 N 39.17 E
Varel 52 53.22 N 8.10 E
Varela 252 34.07 S 66.27 W
Varėna 76 54.13 N 24.34 E
Varengeville-sur-Mer 50 49.55 N 0.59 E
Varenikovskaja 78 45.07 N 37.37 E
Varenna 58 46.01 N 9.17 E
Varenne ≃ 50 49.53 N 1.08 E
Varennes 206 45.41 N 73.26 W
Varennes, Îles de II 275a 45.40 N 73.27 W
Varennes-en-Argonne 56 49.14 N 5.02 E
Varennes-Jarcy 261 48.41 N 2.34 E
Varennes-Saint-Sauveur 58 46.29 N 5.15 E
Varennes-sur-Allier 32 46.19 N 3.24 E
Varennes-sur-Amance 58 47.54 N 5.37 E
Varenovka 83 47.18 N 39.02 E
Vareš 38 44.09 N 18.19 E
Varese 62 45.48 N 8.48 E
Varese □[4] 62 45.48 N 8.40 E
Varese, Lago di ⊜ 62 45.49 N 8.45 E
Varese Ligure 62 44.22 N 9.37 E
Varèze ≃ 62 45.25 N 4.45 E
Varfolomejevka 80 50.01 N 48.12 E
Vårgårda 26 58.02 N 12.48 E
Vargas □[5] 286c 10.34 N 66.52 W
Vargaši 86 55.23 N 65.48 E
Vargem 256 22.53 S 46.25 W
Vargem, Riacho da ≃ 250 8.42 S 39.09 W
Vargem Alegre 256 22.30 S 43.55 W
Vargem do Laje 256 22.08 S 44.49 W
Vargem Grande 250 3.33 S 43.56 W
Vargem Grande ◆[8] 287a 22.59 S 43.29 W
Vargem Grande, Ribeirão da ≃ 256 22.17 S 45.40 W
Vargem Grande do Sul 256 21.50 S 46.53 W
Vargem Grande Paulista 256 23.36 S 47.01 W
Varginha 256 21.33 S 45.26 W
Vargön 26 58.22 N 12.22 E
Varigotti 62 44.11 N 8.24 E
Väringen ⊜ 40 59.26 N 15.23 E
Varirata National Park ♠ 164 9.20 S 147.20 E
Varjão 255 17.03 S 49.37 W
Varkallai 122 8.40 N 76.50 E
Varkaus 26 62.19 N 27.55 E
Varkhān ≃ 128 32.55 N 65.30 E
Varlamovo 86 54.38 N 60.40 E
Värmdölandet I 40 59.20 N 18.33 E
Värmeln ⊜ 26 59.32 N 12.54 E
Värmland □[9] 26 59.48 N 13.03 E
Värmlands Län □[6] 26 59.45 N 13.15 E
Värmlandsnäs ≻[1] 26 59.00 N 13.10 E
Varna, Blg. 38 43.13 N 27.55 E
Varna (Vahrn), It. 64 46.44 N 11.38 E
Varna, Ross. 86 53.24 N 60.58 E
Varna, N.Y., U.S. 210 42.27 N 76.26 W
Värnamo 26 57.11 N 14.02 E
Varnavino 80 57.24 N 45.04 E
Varnenski zaliv C 38 43.11 N 27.56 E
Varner-Hogg Plantation State Historic Park ♠ 222 29.09 N 95.37 W
Varnhem 26 58.23 N 13.39 E
Varniai 76 55.45 N 22.22 E
Varnsdorf 54 50.52 N 14.40 E
Varnville 192 32.51 N 81.04 W
Värö 26 57.16 N 12.11 E
Városliget ♠ 264c 47.31 N 19.06 E
Varpaisjärvi 26 63.22 N 27.45 E
Várpalota 30 47.12 N 18.09 E
Varpan ⊜ 40 60.38 N 15.36 E
Varresbeck ◆[8] 263 51.15 N 7.06 E
Vars, On., Can. 212 45.21 N 75.21 W
Vars, Fr. 62 44.37 N 6.41 E
Vars, Col de)(62 44.32 N 6.42 E
Vârşec 38 43.12 N 23.17 E
Varsi 62 44.40 N 9.51 E
Varsinais-Suomi ◆[1] 26 60.40 N 22.30 E
Värska 76 57.58 N 27.38 E
Varsovie → Warszawa 30 52.15 N 21.00 E
Varsseveld 52 51.57 N 6.28 E
Vårsta 40 59.10 N 17.48 E
Vartašen 84 41.06 N 47.28 E
Varto 130 39.10 N 41.28 E
V'artsil'a 24 62.11 N 30.41 E
Varty Lake ⊜ 212 44.23 N 76.48 W
Varuna ≃ 124 25.21 N 83.03 E
Varva 78 50.31 N 32.41 E
Varvarin 38 43.43 N 21.19 E
Varvarovka, Ukr. 78 48.42 N 36.02 E
Varvarovka, Ukr. 78 49.33 N 35.12 E
Varvarovka, Ukr. 83 48.05 N 38.24 E
Varysburg 210 42.46 N 78.19 W
Várzea 256 22.33 S 44.46 W
Várzea, Rio da ≃ 252 27.13 S 53.19 W
Várzea Alegre 250 6.47 S 39.17 W
Várzea da Palma 255 17.36 S 44.44 W
Varzea de Sintra 266c 38.49 N 9.24 W
Várzea Grande 248 15.39 S 56.08 W
Varzeão 252 24.34 S 49.26 W
Várzea Paulista 256 23.12 S 46.50 W
Varzi, It. 62 44.49 N 9.12 E
Varzi, Ross. 80 56.03 N 52.50 E
Varzino 24 68.19 N 38.19 E
Varzo 36 46.12 N 8.15 E
Varzob 85 38.46 N 68.49 E
Varzob ≃ 85 38.30 N 68.45 E
Varzuga 24 67.24 N 36.32 E
Varzy 50 47.22 N 3.23 E
Varzyk 85 41.07 N 71.14 E
Vas 64 45.56 N 11.56 E
Vas □[6] 61 47.05 N 16.45 E
Vasai (Bassein) 122 19.21 N 72.48 E
Vasalemma 76 59.14 N 24.18 E
Vašana ≃ 82 54.36 N 37.10 E
Vasar 272c 19.11 N 73.09 E
Vasa → Vaasa 26 63.06 N 21.36 E
Vascão, Ribeirão do ≃ 34 37.31 N 7.31 W
Vaşcău 38 46.28 N 22.28 E
Väse 40 59.23 N 13.57 E
Vāshi 272c 19.04 N 72.59 E
Vashon 224 47.26 N 122.27 W
Vashon Heights 224 47.30 N 122.28 W
Vashon Island I 224 47.24 N 122.27 W
Vasilevići 78 52.14 N 29.49 E
Vasilija, mys ≻ 180 64.34 N 178.33 E
Vasiliká 38 40.28 N 23.08 E
Vasiliški 76 53.47 N 24.51 E
Vasiljevka, Bela. 78 52.15 N 31.31 E
Vasiljevka, Ross. 89 46.52 N 134.03 E
Vasiljevka, Ukr. 78 47.26 N 35.16 E
Vasiljevo, Ross. 24 60.46 N 38.59 E
Vasiljevo, Ross. 80 55.52 N 48.42 E
Vasiljevskij, ostrov I 265a 59.56 N 30.15 E
Vasiljevskij Moch 76 57.01 N 35.55 E
Vasiljevskoje, Ross. 80 56.56 N 41.40 E
Vasiljevskoje, Ross. 80 56.31 N 45.49 E
Vasiljevskoje, Ross. 82 55.00 N 37.25 E
Vasiljevskoje, Ross. 82 56.20 N 37.54 E
Vasil'kov 78 50.12 N 30.19 E
Vasil'kovka 78 48.13 N 36.02 E
Vasil'sursk 80 56.08 N 46.01 E
Vasis 86 57.22 N 74.44 E
Vaška ≃ 24 64.53 N 45.47 E
Vaskelovo 76 60.22 N 30.22 E
Vaskess Bay C 174o 1.51 N 157.31 W
Vaškovci 78 48.24 N 27.08 E
Vaškovcy 78 48.23 N 25.30 E
Vaslui 38 46.38 N 27.44 E
Vaslui □[6] 38 46.30 N 27.45 E
Väsman ⊜ 40 60.11 N 15.04 E
Vass 192 35.15 N 79.16 W
Vassako-Bolo, Réserve Naturelle Intégrale de la ◆[4] 146 8.10 N 19.45 E
Vassar 190 43.22 N 83.35 W
Vassdalseggi ʌ 26 59.46 N 7.10 E
Vassieux-en-Vercors 62 44.53 N 5.22 E
Vassouras 256 22.25 S 43.40 W
Vassy 50 47.34 N 4.10 E
Västanfors 40 59.59 N 15.49 E
Västerås 40 59.37 N 16.33 E
Västeråsfjärden C 40 59.34 N 16.34 E
Västerbotten □[9] 26 64.36 N 20.04 E
Västerbottens Län □[6] 24 64.00 N 17.30 E
Västerby 40 60.19 N 15.55 E
Västerdalälven ≃ 40 60.33 N 15.08 E
Västerfärnebo 40 59.57 N 16.17 E
Västergötland □[9] 26 58.01 N 13.03 E
Västerhaninge 40 59.07 N 18.06 E
Västernorrlands Län □[6] 26 63.00 N 17.30 E
Västervik 26 57.45 N 16.38 E
Västmanland □[9] 40 59.38 N 15.15 E
Västmanlands Län □[6] 40 59.45 N 16.20 E
Vasto 66 42.07 N 14.42 E
Västra Laxsjön ⊜ 40 58.54 N 14.38 E
Västra Ringsjön ⊜ 41 55.53 N 13.28 E
Västra Torup 41 56.09 N 13.29 E
Vastseliina 76 57.44 N 27.17 E
Vas'ugan ≃ 86 59.07 N 80.46 E
Vas'uganje ⩩ 86 58.00 N 77.00 E
Vas'unino 82 55.15 N 37.01 E
Vašutino 265b 55.56 N 37.26 E
Vašutkiny ozera ⊜ 24 68.06 N 61.18 E
Vasvár 61 47.03 N 16.49 E
Vát 61 47.17 N 16.47 E
Vaţa de Jos 38 46.10 N 22.35 E
Vatan 32 47.05 N 1.48 E
Vaternish Point ≻ 46 57.36 N 6.38 W
Vatersay I 46 56.55 N 7.32 W
Vaterstetten 60 48.07 N 11.47 E
Vathí 38 37.45 N 26.59 E
Vatican (Cité du) → Vatican City □[1] 267a 41.54 N 12.27 E
Vatican City (Città del Vaticano) □[1], Europe 66 41.54 N 12.27 E
Vatican City (Città del Vaticano) □[1], Europe 267a 41.54 N 12.27 E
Vaticano, Capo ≻ 68 38.38 N 15.50 E
Vatikanstadt → Vatican City □[1] 66 41.54 N 12.27 E
V'atka ≃ 80 55.36 N 51.30 E
V'atka → Kirov 80 58.38 N 49.42 E
Vatlirchvin, gora ʌ 180 68.08 N 179.52 W
Vatnajökull ⊼ 24a 64.25 N 16.50 W
Vatneyri 24a 65.38 N 23.57 W
Vätö I 40 59.49 N 18.57 E
Vatoa Island I 175g 19.50 S 178.13 W
Vatoloha ʌ 157b 17.52 S 47.48 E
Vatomandry 157b 19.20 S 48.59 E
Vatra Dornei 38 47.21 N 25.21 E
V'atskije Pol'any 80 56.14 N 51.04 E
V'atskij uval ʌʌ[2] 80 57.20 N 49.10 E
V'atskoje, Ross. 80 57.52 N 40.16 E
V'atskoje, Ross. 89 48.44 N 135.43 E
Vattalkundu 122 10.10 N 77.46 E
Vättern ⊜ 26 58.24 N 14.36 E
Vättersee → Vättern ⊜ 26 58.24 N 14.36 E
Vattholma 40 60.01 N 17.44 E
Vättis 58 46.55 N 9.27 E
Vatu Ira Channel Ʉ 175g 17.17 S 178.31 E
Vatukoula 175g 17.31 S 177.51 E
Vatulele I 175g 18.33 S 177.37 E
Vatulino 82 55.39 N 36.09 E
Vatutino 78 49.02 N 31.04 E
Vaubecourt 56 48.56 N 5.07 E
Vauclaix 50 47.14 N 3.49 E
Vauclin, Montagne du ʌ 240e 14.33 N 60.53 W
Vaucluse 274a 33.51 S 151.17 E
Vaucluse □[5] 62 44.00 N 5.10 E
Vaucluse, Fontaine de ⊥ 62 43.55 N 5.08 E
Vaucluse, Plateau de ʌʌ[1] 62 44.00 N 5.22 E
Vaucouleurs 58 48.36 N 5.40 E
Vaucouleurs ≃ 261 48.59 N 1.44 E
Vaucresson 261 48.50 N 2.09 E
Vaud □[3] 58 46.40 N 6.30 E
Vaudherland 261 49.00 N 2.29 E
Vaudoy-en-Brie 50 48.41 N 3.05 E
Vaudreuil (Saint-Michel-de-Vaudreuil) 206 45.24 N 74.01 W
Vaudreuil □[5] 206 45.26 N 74.15 W
Vaudreuil, Baie de C 275a 45.24 N 74.00 W
Vaufrey 58 47.21 N 6.55 E

Symbol	English	Deutsch	Español	Français	Português
≃	River	Fluß	Río	Rivière	Rio
≊	Canal	Kanal	Canal	Canal	Canal
ᒪ	Waterfall, Rapids	Wasserfall, Stromschnellen	Cascada, Rápidos	Chute d'eau, Rapides	Cascata, Rápidos
Ʉ	Strait	Meeresstraße	Estrecho	Détroit	Estreito
C	Bay, Gulf	Bucht, Golf	Bahía, Golfo	Baie, Golfe	Baía, Golfo
⊜	Lake, Lakes	See, Seen	Lago, Lagos	Lac, Lacs	Lago, Lagos
⩩	Swamp	Sumpf	Pantano	Marais	Pântano
⊼	Ice Features, Glacier	Eis- und Gletscherformen	Accidentes Glaciales	Formes glaciaires	Acidentes glaciares
⩱	Other Hydrographic Features	Andere Hydrographische Objekte	Otros Elementos Hidrográficos	Autres données hydrographiques	Outros acidentes hidrográficos

Symbol	English	Deutsch	Español	Français	Português
⊕	Submarine Features	Untermeerische Objekte	Accidentes Submarinos	Formes de relief sous-marin	Acidentes submarinos
□	Political Unit	Politische Einheit	Unidad Política	Entité politique	Unidade política
ᵿ	Cultural Institution	Kulturelle Institution	Institución Cultural	Institution culturelle	Instituição cultural
⊥	Historical Site	Historische Stätte	Sitio Histórico	Site historique	Sitio histórico
♠	Recreational Site	Erholungs- und Ferienort	Sitio de Recreo	Centre de loisirs	Area de Lazer
⊠	Airport	Flughafen	Aeropuerto	Aéroport	Aeroporto
■	Military Installation	Militäranlage	Instalación Militar	Installation militaire	Instalação militar
◆	Miscellaneous	Verschiedenes	Misceláneo	Divers	Diversos

Symbols in the index entries represent the broad categories identified in the key at the right. Symbols with superior numbers (⋏[1]) identify subcategories (see complete key on page I · 1).

Symbole im Register stellen die rechts im Schlüssel erklärten Kategorien dar. Symbole mit hochgestellten Ziffern (⋏[1]) bezeichnen Unterabteilungen einer Kategorie (vgl. vollständiger Schlüssel auf Seite I · 1).

Los símbolos incluídos en el texto del índice representan las grandes categorías identificadas con la clave a la derecha. Los símbolos con números en su parte superior (⋏[1]) identifican las subcategorías (véase la clave completa en la página I · 1).

Les symboles de l'index représentent les catégories indiquées dans la légende à droite. Les symboles suivis d'un indice (⋏[1]) représentent des sous-catégories (voir légende complète à la page I · 1).

Os símbolos incluídos no texto do índice representam as grandes categorias identificadas com a chave à direita. Os símbolos com números em sua parte superior (⋏[1]) identificam as subcategorias (veja-se a chave completa à página I · 1).

Symbol	English	Deutsch	Español	Français	Português
∧	Mountain	Berg	Montaña	Montagne	Montanha
⋏	Mountains	Gebirge	Montañas	Montagnes	Montanhas
)(	Pass	Paß	Paso	Col	Passo
V	Valley, Canyon	Tal, Cañon	Valle, Cañón	Vallée, Canyon	Vale, Canhão
≃	Plain	Ebene	Llano	Plaine	Planície
›	Cape	Kap	Cabo	Cap	Cabo
I	Island	Insel	Isla	Île	Ilha
II	Islands	Inseln	Islas	Îles	Ilhas
♦	Other Topographic Features	Andere Topographische Objekte	Otros Elementos Topográficos	Autres données topographiques	Outros acidentes topográficos

ESPAÑOL · FRANÇAIS · PORTUGUÊS

Nombre / Nom / Nome	Página / Page	Lat.°′	Long.°′ W = Oeste / Ouest
Vester Sottrup	41	54.57 N	9.43 E
Vestfjorden ⊂[2]	24	68.08 N	15.00 E
Vestfold □[6]	26	59.15 N	10.10 E
Vestmannaeyjar	24a	63.26 N	20.12 W
Vestone	64	45.42 N	10.24 E
Vestreno	58	46.06 N	9.18 E
Vestsjælland □[6]	41	55.35 N	11.30 E
Vestvågøya I	24	68.15 N	13.50 E
Vésubie ≃	62	43.52 N	7.12 E
Vesubio → Vesuvio ∧[1]	68	40.49 N	14.26 E
Vesuvio (Vesuvius) ∧[1]	68	40.49 N	14.26 E
Vesuvius Bay	224	48.53 N	123.35 W
Vesuvius → Vesuvio ∧[1]	68	40.49 N	14.26 E
Vesuv → Vesuvio ∧[1]	68	40.49 N	14.26 E
Veszprém	30	47.06 N	17.55 E
Veszprém □[6]	30	46.50 N	17.30 E
Vésztő	30	46.55 N	21.16 E
Vet ≃	158	27.40 S	25.40 E
Vetapālem	122	15.47 N	80.19 E
Vetčin	76	52.27 N	28.10 E
Veterans Stadium ♦	285	39.54 N	75.10 W
Vétheuil	50	49.04 N	1.42 E
Vetju	24	62.57 N	50.44 E
Vetka	76	52.33 N	31.10 E
Vetlanda	26	57.26 N	15.04 E
Vetl'anka	80	52.52 N	51.09 E
Vetluga	80	57.51 N	45.47 E
Vetluga ≃	80	56.18 N	46.24 E
Vetlužskij, Ross.	80	57.11 N	45.07 E
Vetlužskij, Ross.	80	58.23 N	45.26 E
Vetoškino	80	57.18 N	49.44 E
Vetovo	38	43.42 N	26.16 E
Vetralla	66	42.19 N	12.03 E
Vetren	38	42.16 N	24.03 E
Vetrino	76	55.25 N	28.28 E
Vetriolo	64	46.02 N	11.18 E
Vetrișoaia	38	46.26 N	28.13 E
Větřni	61	48.46 N	14.17 E
Vetschau	54	51.47 N	14.04 E
Vettisfossen ∟	26	61.22 N	7.55 E
Vetto	64	44.29 N	10.20 E
Vettore, Monte ∧	66	42.49 N	13.16 E
Vetulonia	66	42.51 N	10.58 E
Veules-les-Roses	50	49.52 N	0.48 E
Veulettes-sur-Mer	50	49.51 N	0.36 E
Veurne (Furnes)	50	51.04 N	2.40 E
Vevay	218	38.44 N	85.04 W
Vevelstad	24	65.43 N	12.30 E
Veveno, Khawr ∨	140	6.40 N	32.58 E
Vevey	58	46.28 N	6.51 E
Vex	58	46.13 N	7.24 E
Veyle ≃	58	46.18 N	4.50 E
Veynes	62	44.32 N	5.49 E
Veyrier	62	45.53 N	6.10 E
Vézelay	50	47.28 N	3.44 E
Vézelise	58	48.29 N	6.05 E
Vézénobres	62	44.03 N	4.09 E
Vézère ≃	32	44.53 N	0.53 E
Vezirköprü	130	41.09 N	35.28 E
Vezouze ≃	58	48.35 N	6.29 E
Vezza d'Oglio	64	46.14 N	10.24 E
Vezzana, Cima della ∧	64	46.17 N	11.50 E
Vezzano	64	46.05 N	11.00 E
Vezzano Ligure	64	44.09 N	9.52 E
Viacha	248	16.39 S	68.18 W
Viadana	64	44.56 N	10.31 E
Viadutos	252	27.34 S	52.01 W
Viale	252	31.53 S	60.01 W
Vialonga	266c	38.52 N	9.05 W
Via Mala ∨	58	46.40 N	9.26 E
Viamão	252	30.05 S	51.02 W
Viamonte	252	33.44 S	63.06 W
Vian	196	35.29 N	94.58 W
Viana	250	3.13 S	45.00 W
Viana, Ilha do I	287a	22.52 S	43.08 W
Viana del Bollo	34	42.11 N	7.06 W
Viana do Alentejo	34	38.20 N	8.00 W
Viana do Castelo	34	41.42 N	8.50 W
Vianden	56	49.57 N	6.11 E
Vianen	52	52.00 N	5.05 E
Viangchan (Vientiane)	110	17.58 N	102.36 E
Viangphoukha	110	20.41 N	101.04 E
Viar ≃	34	37.36 N	5.50 W
Viareggio	64	43.52 N	10.14 E
Viarmes	50	49.08 N	2.22 E
Viatka → Kirov	80	58.38 N	49.42 E
Viaur ≃	32	44.08 N	2.23 E
Vibank	184	50.20 N	103.55 W
Víboras, Arroyo de las ≃	258	33.57 S	58.21 W
Viborg, Dan.	26	56.26 N	9.24 E
Viborg, S.D., U.S.	198	43.10 N	97.04 W
Viborg □[6]	41	56.18 N	9.27 E
Viborg → Vyborg	76	60.42 N	28.45 E
Vibo Valentia	68	38.40 N	16.06 E
Vibraye	50	48.03 N	0.44 E
Viburnum	194	37.42 N	91.08 W
Viby	41	55.33 N	12.02 E
Viby ◆[8]	41	56.07 N	10.10 E
Vic (Vich)	34	41.56 N	2.15 E
Vic, Étang de ⊂	62	43.29 N	3.50 E
Vicálvaro ◆[8]	266a	40.24 N	3.36 W
Vícam	232	27.35 N	110.20 W
Vicarello	66	42.10 N	12.12 E
Vicari	70	37.49 N	13.34 E
Vicchio	66	43.56 N	11.28 E
Vicco	192	37.12 N	83.03 W
Vic-en-Bigorre	32	43.23 N	0.03 E
Vicente, Point ›	280	33.44 N	118.25 W
Vicente Casares	258	34.57 S	58.38 W
Vicente de Carvalho	256	23.56 S	46.19 W
Vicente Guerrero, Méx.	234	18.24 N	92.53 W
Vicente Guerrero, Méx.	234	19.08 N	98.10 W
Vicente Guerrero, Méx.	234	23.45 N	103.59 W
Vicente Guerrero, Presa ⊜[1]	234	24.00 N	98.45 W
Vicente López	258	34.32 S	58.28 W
Vicente López □[5]	288	34.32 S	58.30 W
Vicente Noble	238	18.23 N	71.11 W
Vicenza	64	45.33 N	11.33 E
Vicenza □[4]	64	45.40 N	11.27 E
Viceroy	184	49.27 N	105.22 W
Vichada □[5]	246	5.00 N	69.30 W
Vichada ≃	246	4.55 N	67.50 W
Vichadero	252	31.48 S	54.43 W
Vichigasta	252	29.29 S	67.31 W
Vichoreva ≃	88	56.47 N	101.22 E
Vichorevka	88	56.12 N	101.09 E
Vichra ≃	76	54.01 N	31.52 E
Vichuga → Vičuga	80	57.13 N	41.56 E
Vichuquén	252	34.53 S	72.00 W
Vichy	32	46.08 N	3.26 E
Vici	196	36.08 N	99.17 W
Vickery	214	41.23 N	82.56 W
Vicksburg, Mi., U.S.	216	42.07 N	85.31 W
Vicksburg, Ms., U.S.	194	32.21 N	90.52 W
Vicksburg, Pa., U.S.	210	40.56 N	76.59 W
Vicksburg National Military Park ♦	194	32.24 N	90.52 W
Vico	36	42.10 N	8.48 E
Vico, Lago di ⊜	66	42.19 N	12.10 E
Vico Canavese	62	45.30 N	7.47 E
Vico del Gargano	68	41.54 N	15.57 E
Vico Equense	68	40.40 N	14.25 E
Vicoforte	62	44.21 N	7.54 E
Vicopisano	66	43.42 N	10.35 E
Viçosa, Bra.	250	9.24 S	36.14 W
Viçosa, Bra.	255	20.45 S	42.53 W
Viçosa do Ceará	250	3.34 S	41.05 W
Vicosoprano	58	46.22 N	9.37 E
Vicovaro	66	42.01 N	12.54 E
Vicq	261	48.49 N	1.50 E
Vic-Sur-Aisne	50	49.24 N	3.07 E
Vic-sur-Cère	32	44.59 N	2.37 E
Vic-sur-Seille	56	48.47 N	6.32 E
Victor, Ca., U.S.	226	38.08 N	121.12 W
Victor, Id., U.S.	202	43.36 N	111.06 W
Victor, Ia., U.S.	190	41.43 N	92.17 W
Victor, Mt., U.S.	202	46.25 N	114.08 W
Victor, N.Y., U.S.	210	42.58 N	77.24 W
Victor, Lac ⊜	186	50.35 N	61.50 W
Victorbur	52	53.29 N	7.20 E
Victor Harbor	168b	35.34 S	138.37 E
Victoria, Arg.	252	32.37 S	60.10 W
Victoria, Cam.	152	4.01 N	9.12 E
Victoria, B.C., Can.	224	48.25 N	123.22 W
Victoria, P.E., Can.	186	46.13 N	63.29 W
Victoria, Chile	252	38.13 S	72.20 W
Victoria, Gren.	241k	12.12 N	61.42 W
Victoria, Guinée	150	10.50 N	14.33 W
Victoria (Xianggang), H.K.	271d	22.17 N	114.09 E
Victoria, Malay.	112	5.17 N	115.15 E
Victoria, Pil.	116	13.12 N	121.15 E
Victoria, Pil.	116	15.35 N	120.41 E
Victoria, Rom.	38	45.45 N	24.41 E
Victoria, Sey.	138	4.38 S	55.27 E
Victoria, Ks., U.S.	198	38.51 N	99.08 W
Victoria, Tx., U.S.	196	28.48 N	97.00 W
Victoria, Va., U.S.	192	36.59 N	78.13 W
Victoria □[3]	166	38.00 S	145.00 E
Victoria □[4]	154	20.54 S	31.21 E
Victoria □[6], On., Can.	212	44.35 N	78.50 W
Victoria □[6], Tx., U.S.	222	28.55 N	97.00 W
Victoria ◆[8]	288	34.28 S	58.31 W
Victoria ≃, Austl.	160	15.12 S	129.43 E
Victoria ≃, Nf., Can.	186	48.45 N	56.40 W
Victoria ≃, Méx.	234	21.02 N	99.50 W
Victoria, Isla I	254	45.18 S	73.58 W
Victoria, Lake ⊜, Afr.	154	1.00 S	33.00 E
Victoria, Lake ⊜, Austl.	166	34.00 S	141.16 E
Victoria, Mount ∧, Mya.	110	21.14 N	93.55 E
Victoria, Mount ∧, Pap. N. Gui.	164	8.55 S	147.35 E
Victoria, Pont ◆[5]	275a	45.29 N	73.32 W
Victoria and Albert Museum ʊ	272c	18.59 N	72.50 E
Victoria Beach	184	50.43 N	96.33 W
Victoria Beach ⊥[2]	273a	6.25 N	3.25 E
Victoria → Ciudad Victoria	234	23.44 N	99.08 W
Victoria de Durango → Durango	234	24.02 N	104.40 W
Victoria Falls	154	17.56 S	25.50 E
Victoria Falls ∟	154	17.55 S	25.51 E
Victoria Falls National Park ♦	154	17.55 S	25.40 E
Victoria Gardens ♦	272c	18.59 N	72.50 E
Victoria Harbour	212	44.45 N	79.46 W
Victoria International Airport ⊠	224	48.39 N	123.26 W
Victoria Island I, N.T., Can.	176	71.00 N	110.00 W
Victoria Island I, Nig.	273a	6.26 N	3.26 E
Victoria Lake ⊜	273d	26.14 S	28.09 E
Victoria Lake ⊜[1]	186	48.18 N	57.30 W
Victoria Land ◆[1]	9	75.00 S	163.00 E
Victoria Lawn Tennis Association Courts ♦	274b	37.51 S	145.02 E
Victoria Memorial Hall ʊ	271c	1.17 N	103.51 E
Victoria Memorial Museum ʊ	272b	22.33 N	88.21 E
Victoria Nile ≃	154	2.14 N	31.26 E
Victoria Park	168a	31.58 S	115.55 E
Victoria Park ♦, H.K.	271d	22.17 N	114.11 E
Victoria Park ♦, Eng., U.K.	262	53.23 N	2.34 W
Victoria Peak ∧, Belize	232	16.48 N	88.37 W
Victoria Peak ∧, B.C., Can.	182	50.03 N	126.06 W
Victoria Peak ∧, H.K.	271d	22.17 N	114.08 E
Victoria Peaks ∧∧	116	9.22 N	118.20 E
Victoria Point	171a	27.35 S	153.18 E
Victoria Range ∧∧, N.Z.	172	42.09 S	172.08 E
Victoria Range ∧∧, Pil.	116	9.32 N	118.23 E
Victoria River	164	15.37 S	131.08 E
Victoria River Downs	164	16.24 S	131.00 E
Victorias	116	10.54 N	123.05 E
Victoria State Car Club Race Circuit ♦	274b	37.45 S	145.11 E
Victoria Station ◆[5], Eng., U.K.	260	51.29 N	0.09 W
Victoria Station ◆[5], Eng., U.K.	262	53.29 N	2.15 W
Victoria Strait ⋓	176	69.15 N	100.30 W
Victoria Terminus ◆[5]	272c	18.57 N	72.50 E
Victoria University of Manchester ʊ[2]	262	53.28 N	2.14 W
Victoriaville	206	46.03 N	71.57 W
Victoria → Vitória	255	20.19 S	40.21 W
Victoria West	158	31.25 S	23.04 E
Victorica	252	36.13 S	65.27 W
Victorino	246	2.48 N	67.50 W
Victorino de la Plaza	252	36.36 S	62.40 W
Víctor Rosales	234	22.57 N	102.42 W
Victorville	228	34.32 N	117.17 W
Victory, Mount ∧	164	9.10 S	149.05 E
Victory Gardens	276	40.52 N	74.32 W
Victory Heights	214	41.22 N	79.46 W
Victory Hills	279b	40.11 N	79.53 W
Victory Mills	210	43.05 N	73.36 W
Victory Monument ⊥	269a	13.46 N	100.33 E
Vičuga	80	57.13 N	41.56 E
Vicuña	252	30.02 S	70.44 W
Vicuña Mackenna	252	33.54 S	64.23 W
Vidal, Kaap ›	158	28.09 S	32.33 E
Vidal Gormaz, Isla I	254	52.00 S	74.45 W
Vidalia, Ga., U.S.	192	32.13 N	82.24 W
Vidalia, La., U.S.	194	31.33 N	91.25 W
Vidal Ramos	252	27.23 S	49.22 W
Vidauban	62	43.26 N	6.26 E
Videbæk	26	56.05 N	8.38 E
Videira	252	27.00 S	51.08 W
Videle	38	44.16 N	25.31 E
Vidigueira	34	38.13 N	7.48 W
Vidim, Česko.	54	50.28 N	14.31 E
Vidim, Ross.	88	56.29 N	103.09 E
Vidin	38	43.59 N	22.52 E
Vidisha	124	23.32 N	77.49 E
Vidlica	24	61.10 N	32.21 E
Vidnoje	82	55.34 N	37.41 E
Vidogošči	82	56.42 N	36.23 E
Vidor	194	30.07 N	94.00 W
Vidos ≃	267b	40.58 N	28.53 E
Vidöstern ⊜	26	57.04 N	14.01 E
Vidourle ≃	62	43.32 N	4.08 E
Vidra, Rom.	38	44.16 N	26.11 E
Vidra, Rom.	38	45.55 N	26.54 E
Vidsel	24	65.51 N	20.24 E
Vidzeme □[9]	76	57.10 N	25.30 E
Vidzy	76	55.24 N	26.38 E
Vie ≃	50	49.05 N	0.04 E
Viecht	60	48.30 N	12.04 E
Viechtach	60	49.05 N	12.53 E
Viedma	254	40.48 S	63.00 W
Viedma, Lago ⊜	254	49.35 S	72.35 W
Viehberg ∧	61	48.33 N	14.37 E
Viehhausen	60	48.59 N	11.58 E
Vieil Armand ♦	58	47.52 N	7.10 E
Vieillard, Lac du ⊜	190	47.23 N	78.02 W
Vieille Case	240d	15.36 N	61.24 W
Vieira do Minho	34	41.39 N	8.09 W
Viejo, Cerro ∧	248	4.49 S	79.27 W
Viekšniai	76	56.16 N	22.31 E
Vielank	54	53.15 N	11.08 E
Viella	34	42.42 N	0.48 E
Vielle-Eglise-en-Yvelines	261	48.40 N	1.53 E
Vielsalm	56	50.17 N	5.55 E
Viels-Maisons	50	48.54 N	3.24 E
Viena → Vienne ≃	32	47.13 N	0.05 E
Vienenburg	54	51.57 N	10.34 E
Vienna, On., Can.	212	42.41 N	80.48 W
Vienna, Ga., U.S.	192	32.05 N	83.47 W
Vienna, Il., U.S.	194	37.25 N	88.54 W
Vienna, In., U.S.	218	38.39 N	85.46 W
Vienna, Md., U.S.	208	38.29 N	75.49 W
Vienna, Mo., U.S.	194	38.11 N	91.56 W
Vienna, N.J., U.S.	210	40.52 N	74.53 W
Vienna, Oh., U.S.	214	41.14 N	80.40 W
Vienna, S.D., U.S.	198	44.42 N	97.30 W
Vienna, Va., U.S.	208	38.29 N	75.49 W
Vienna, Va., U.S.	208	38.54 N	77.15 W
Vienna, W.V., U.S.	188	39.19 N	81.32 W
Vienna → Wien	61	48.13 N	16.20 E
Vienne	62	45.31 N	4.52 E
Vienne □[5]	32	46.35 N	0.30 E
Vienne ≃	32	47.13 N	0.05 E
Vienne-en-Arthies	261	49.04 N	1.44 E
Vienne-le-Château	56	49.11 N	4.53 E
Vienne → Wien	61	48.13 N	16.20 E
Vientiane → Viangchan	110	17.58 N	102.36 E
Vientos, Paso de los → Windward Passage ⋓	238	20.00 N	73.50 W
Vieques	240m	18.09 N	65.27 W
Vieques, Aeropuerto ⊠	240m	18.07 N	65.30 W
Vieques, Isla de I	240m	18.08 N	65.25 W
Vieques, Pasaje de ⋓	240m	18.11 N	65.37 W
Vieques, Sonda de ⋓	240m	18.15 N	65.23 W
Vière ≃	56	48.46 N	4.41 E
Viereck	54	53.32 N	14.02 E
Vieremä	26	63.45 N	27.01 E
Vierfontein	158	27.03 S	26.46 E
Vierhouten	52	52.20 N	5.50 E
Vieringhausen ◆[8]	263	51.11 N	7.10 E
Vierlande ◆[1]	52	53.26 N	10.14 E
Viernau	54	50.40 N	10.32 E
Viernheim	56	49.32 N	8.34 E
Vierraden	54	53.06 N	14.17 E
Viersen	56	51.15 N	6.23 E
Vierumäki	26	61.06 N	25.57 E
Vierwaldstättersee ⊜	58	47.00 N	8.28 E
Vierzehnheiligen ʊ[1]	56	50.08 N	11.02 E
Vierzon	50	47.13 N	2.05 E
Viesca	232	25.21 N	102.48 W
Viesecke	54	53.01 N	12.01 E
Vieselbach	54	51.00 N	11.08 E
Viesīte	76	56.21 N	25.33 E
Vieste	68	41.53 N	16.10 E
Vietgest	54	53.45 N	12.20 E
Vietnam □[1], Asia	108	16.00 N	108.00 E
Vietnam □[1], Asia	110	16.00 N	108.00 E
Vietnam Veterans Memorial ⊥	284c	38.53 N	77.03 W
Vietri di Potenza	68	40.36 N	15.30 E
Vietri sul Mare	68	40.40 N	14.44 E
Viet Tri	110	21.18 N	105.26 E
Vieux-Condé	50	50.27 N	3.34 E
Vieux-Ferette	58	47.30 N	7.18 E
Vieux-Fort, P.Q., Can.	186	51.26 N	57.49 W
Vieux-Fort, Guad.	241o	15.57 N	61.43 W
Vieux Fort, St. Luc.	241f	13.44 N	60.57 W
Vieux-Fort, Pointe du ›	241o	15.57 N	61.43 W
Vieux Fort Bay ⊂	241f	13.44 N	60.58 W
Vieux-Habitants	241o	16.04 N	61.46 W
Vieux-Thann	58	47.48 N	7.08 E
Vievis	76	54.46 N	24.48 E
View Park	280	34.00 N	118.20 W
Vieytes	258	35.16 S	57.35 W
Vif	62	45.03 N	5.40 E
Vig	41	55.51 N	11.36 E
Viga ≃	76	59.14 N	43.41 E
Vigala	76	58.43 N	24.22 E
Vigan	116	17.34 N	120.23 E
Vigarano Mainarda	64	44.50 N	11.30 E
Vigatto	64	44.43 N	10.20 E
Vigeland	26	58.05 N	7.18 E
Vigentino ◆[8]	266b	45.25 N	9.11 E
Vigersted	41	55.29 N	11.54 E
Vigese, Monte ∧	64	44.12 N	11.06 E
Vigésima Quinta de Abril, Ponte ◆[5]	266c	38.41 N	9.11 W
Vigevano	62	45.19 N	8.51 E
Viggianello	68	39.58 N	16.05 E
Viggiano	68	40.20 N	15.54 E
Viggiù	62	45.52 N	8.54 E
Vigia	250	0.48 S	48.08 W
Vigie Airport ⊠	241f	14.01 N	60.59 W
Vignacourt	50	50.01 N	2.12 E
Vignale	62	45.01 N	8.24 E
Vignanello	66	42.23 N	12.17 E
Vigneulles-lès-Hattonchâtel	56	48.59 N	5.43 E
Vigneux-sur-Seine	261	48.42 N	2.25 E
Vignola	64	44.29 N	11.00 E
Vignory	58	48.17 N	5.06 E
Vignot	56	48.46 N	5.36 E
Vigny	261	49.05 N	1.56 E
Vigo	34	42.14 N	8.43 W
Vigo, Ría de ⊂[1]	34	42.15 N	8.45 W
Vigodarzere	64	45.27 N	11.53 E
Vigo di Fassa	64	46.25 N	11.40 E
Vigolzone	62	44.55 N	9.40 E
Vigone	62	44.51 N	7.30 E
Vigonovo	64	45.23 N	12.00 E
Vigo-Rendena	64	46.05 N	10.43 E
Vigrestad	26	58.34 N	5.42 E
Viguzzolo	62	44.54 N	8.55 E
Vigy	56	49.12 N	6.18 E
Vihanti	26	64.29 N	25.00 E
Vihāri	123	30.02 N	72.21 E
Vihiers	32	47.09 N	0.32 W
Vihowa	123	31.08 N	70.30 E
Vihren ∧	38	41.46 N	23.24 E
Vihti	26	60.25 N	24.20 E
Viiala	26	61.13 N	23.47 E
Viinijärvi	26	62.39 N	29.14 E
Viinijärvi ⊜	26	62.44 N	29.17 E
Viipuri → Vyborg	76	60.42 N	28.45 E
Viitasaari	26	63.04 N	25.52 E
Viivikonna	76	59.19 N	27.42 E
Vijāpur	120	23.34 N	72.45 E
Vijayawāda	122	16.31 N	80.37 E
Vijosë (Aóös) ≃	38	40.37 N	19.20 E
Vik	40	59.44 N	17.28 E
Vik ⊥	40	59.44 N	17.27 E
Vika	40	60.31 N	15.42 E
Vikajärvi	24	66.37 N	26.12 E
Vikārābād	122	17.20 N	77.54 E
Vikbolandet ›[1]	40	58.32 N	16.40 E
Vikeke	112	8.52 S	126.22 E
Viken	41	56.09 N	12.34 E
Viken ⊜	26	58.39 N	14.20 E
Vikern ⊜	40	59.30 N	14.55 E
Vikersund	26	59.59 N	10.02 E
Vikhroli ◆[8]	272c	19.07 N	72.56 E
Viking	182	53.06 N	111.46 W
Viking Village	218	39.05 N	84.18 W
Vikmanshyttan	40	60.17 N	15.49 E
Vikna	24	64.57 N	10.58 E
Vikna I	24	64.57 N	10.58 E
Vikramasingapuram	122	8.43 N	77.24 E
Viksøyri	26	61.05 N	6.35 E
Viktor	24	66.09 N	58.07 E
Viktorovka	86	52.51 N	62.32 E
Viktring	61	46.35 N	14.16 E
Vikulovo	86	56.49 N	70.37 E
Vil'a	80	55.15 N	42.13 E
Vila Alferes Chamusca	156	24.29 S	33.00 E
Vila Augusta	287b	23.28 S	46.32 W
Vila Babi	287a	22.42 S	43.23 W
Vila Boacaya ◆[8]	287b	23.29 S	46.44 W
Vila Caldas Xavier	154	15.59 S	34.12 E
Vila da Maganja	154	17.18 S	37.30 E
Vila da Ribeira Brava	150a	16.37 N	24.18 W
Viladecans	266d	41.19 N	2.00 E
Viladecavalls del Vallès	266d	41.33 N	1.58 E
Vila de Manica	156	18.56 S	32.53 E
Vila de Rei	34	39.40 N	8.09 W
Vila Dirce	287b	23.35 S	46.48 W
Vila do Bispo	34	37.05 N	8.55 W
Vila do Conde	34	41.21 N	8.45 W
Vila do Porto	148a	36.56 N	25.09 W
Vila Embaú	256	22.37 S	45.02 W
Vila Flor	34	41.18 N	7.09 W
Vila Fontes	156	17.50 S	35.21 E
Vila Formosa ◆[8]	287b	23.34 S	46.33 W
Vilafranca del Penedès	34	41.21 N	1.42 E
Vila Franca de Xira	34	38.57 N	8.59 W
Vila Galvão	287b	23.27 S	46.33 W
Vila Gamito	154	14.12 S	33.00 E
Vila Gomes da Costa	156	24.19 S	33.38 E
Vila Gouveia	156	18.03 S	33.11 E
Vila Guilherme ◆[8]	287b	23.30 S	46.36 W
Vilaine ≃	32	47.30 N	2.27 W
Vila Isabel ◆[8]	287a	22.55 S	43.15 W
Vila Jaguára ◆[8]	287b	23.31 S	46.45 W
Viļaka	76	57.11 N	27.41 E
Vila Luísa	156	25.44 S	32.40 E
Vilama, Laguna de ⊜	252	22.36 S	66.55 W
Vila Machado	156	19.18 S	34.11 E
Vila Madalena ◆[8]	287b	23.33 S	46.42 W
Vila Maria ◆[8]	287b	23.31 S	46.34 W
Vila Mariana ◆[8]	287b	23.35 S	46.38 W
Vila Matilde ◆[8]	287b	23.32 S	46.31 W
Vilanculos	156	22.01 S	35.19 E
Viļāni	76	56.33 N	26.57 E
Vila Nova ≃	250	0.04 S	51.13 W
Vila Nova de Famalicão	34	41.25 N	8.32 W
Vila Nova de Foz Côa	34	41.05 N	7.12 W
Vila Nova de Gaia	34	41.08 N	8.37 W
Vilanova de la Roca	266d	41.33 N	2.17 E
Vilanova i la Geltrú	34	41.14 N	1.44 E
Vila Novo de Ourém	34	39.39 N	8.35 W
Vila Paiva de Andrada	156	18.44 S	34.03 E
Vila Progresso	287a	22.55 S	43.03 W
Vila Prudente ◆[8]	287b	23.35 S	46.33 W
Vila-real, Esp.	34	39.56 N	0.06 W
Vila Real, Port.	34	41.18 N	7.45 W
Vila Real de Santo António	34	37.12 N	7.25 W
Vilar Formoso	34	40.37 N	6.50 W
Vilarinho do Monte	250	1.37 S	52.01 W
Vilassar de Dalt	266d	41.31 N	2.22 E
Vilassar de Mar	266d	41.30 N	2.24 E
Vila Vasco da Gama	154	14.54 S	32.14 E
Vila Velha, Bra.	250	3.13 N	51.13 W
Vila Velha, Bra.	255	20.20 S	40.17 W
Vila Velha de Ródão	34	39.38 N	7.40 W
Vila Verde, Port.	34	41.39 N	8.26 W
Vila Verde, Port.	266c	38.50 N	9.22 W
Vila Viçosa	34	38.47 N	8.13 W
Vil'ča	78	51.22 N	29.24 E
Vilcabamba, Cordillera de ∧∧	248	12.45 S	73.20 W
Vîlcea □[6]	38	45.19 N	24.00 E
Vildbjerg	41	56.12 N	8.46 E
Vilejka	76	54.30 N	26.53 E
Vilelas	252	27.57 S	62.38 W
Vilenki	82	54.16 N	38.55 E
Vil'gort, Ross.	24	61.35 N	50.40 E
Vil'gort, Ross.	24	60.34 N	56.24 E
Vilhelmina	26	64.37 N	16.39 E
Vilhena	248	12.43 S	60.07 W
Vilija ≃	76	54.54 N	25.35 E
Viljandi	76	58.22 N	25.36 E
Viljoensdrif	158	26.44 S	27.55 E
Viljoenshof	158	34.40 S	19.42 E
Viljoenskroon	158	27.12 S	27.00 E
Viljoenspos	158	27.35 S	30.30 E
Vilkaviškis	76	54.39 N	23.02 E
Vil'kickogo, ostrov I, Ross.	72	73.29 N	75.50 E
Vil'kickogo, ostrov I, Ross.	74	75.44 N	152.20 E
Vil'kickogo, proliv ⋓	74	77.55 N	103.00 E
Vilkija	76	55.03 N	23.35 E
Vilkovo	78	45.25 N	29.35 E
Villa Abecia	248	21.00 S	65.23 W
Villa Aberastain	252	31.39 S	68.35 W
Villa Acuña → Ciudad Acuña	232	29.18 N	100.55 W
Villa Adelina ◆[8]	288	34.31 S	58.32 W
Villa Adriana ⊥	66	41.56 N	12.45 E
Villa Alejandrina	258	33.46 S	58.21 W
Villa Alemana	252	33.03 S	71.23 W
Villa Álvarez	234	19.14 N	103.43 W
Villa Ana	252	28.29 S	59.37 W
Villa Ángela	252	27.35 S	60.43 W
Villa Atamisqui	252	28.29 S	63.48 W
Villa Atuel	252	34.50 S	67.54 W
Villaba	116	11.13 N	124.23 E
Villa Ballester ◆[8]	258	34.32 S	58.33 W
Villabassa (Niederdorf)	64	46.44 N	12.10 E
Villabate	70	38.04 N	13.26 E
Villabé	261	48.35 N	2.27 E
Villa Bella	248	10.23 S	65.24 W
Villa Berthet	252	27.17 S	60.25 W
Villablino	34	42.56 N	6.19 W
Villa Borghese ʊ	267a	41.55 N	12.29 E
Villa Bosch ◆[8]	288	34.35 S	58.34 W
Villa Bruzual	246	9.20 N	69.06 W
Villa Cañás, Arg.	252	34.00 S	61.36 W
Villacañas, Esp.	34	39.38 N	3.20 W
Villa Carlos Paz	252	31.24 S	64.31 W
Villacarriedo	34	43.14 N	3.48 W
Villacarrillo	34	38.07 N	3.05 W
Villa Castelli, Arg.	252	29.00 S	68.11 W
Villa Castelli, It.	68	40.35 N	17.28 E
Villacastín	34	40.47 N	4.25 W
Villach	64	46.36 N	13.50 E
Villacidro	71	39.27 N	8.44 E
Villa Ciudadela ◆[8]	258	34.38 S	58.34 W
Villa Clara □[4]	240p	22.30 N	80.00 W
Villa Comaltitlan	236	15.13 N	92.35 W
Villa Concepción del Tío	252	31.19 S	62.50 W
Villa Constitución	252	33.14 S	60.20 W
Villa Cortese	266b	45.34 N	8.53 E
Villa Corzo	234	16.10 N	93.15 W
Villacoublay, Aérodrome de ⊠	261	48.45 N	2.10 E
Villa Creek ≃	226	35.27 N	120.58 W
Villa Cuauhtémoc, Méx.	234	19.24 N	99.34 W
Villa Cuauhtémoc, Méx.	234	22.11 N	97.50 W
Villada	34	42.15 N	4.58 W
Villa de Apaseo El Alto	234	20.27 N	100.37 W
Villa de Arista	234	22.39 N	100.50 W
Villa de Arriaga	234	21.54 N	101.23 W
Villadeati	62	45.04 N	8.10 E
Villa de Cos	234	23.17 N	102.21 W
Villa de Cura	246	10.02 N	67.29 W
Villa de Guadalupe	234	23.22 N	100.46 W
Villa del Carmen	252	32.57 S	65.03 W
Villa del Pueblito	234	20.32 N	100.27 W
Villa del Río	34	37.59 N	4.17 W
Villa del Rosario, Arg.	252	31.35 S	63.32 W
Villa del Rosario, Arg.	252	30.47 S	57.55 W
Villa de María	252	29.54 S	63.43 W
Villa de Mayo	258	34.30 S	58.41 W
Villa de Nova Sintra	150a	14.52 N	24.43 W
Villa de Reyes	234	21.48 N	100.56 W
Villa de San Antonio	236	14.16 N	87.36 W
Villa de San Francisco	236	14.10 N	86.58 W
Villa de Soto	252	30.51 S	64.59 W
Villa d'Este ⊥	267a	41.57 N	12.48 E
Villa Devoto ◆[8]	288	34.36 S	58.31 W
Villa Diamante ◆[8]	288	34.41 S	58.26 W
Villa di Chiavenna	58	46.20 N	9.29 E
Villadiego	34	42.31 N	4.00 W
Villa Dolores	252	31.56 S	65.12 W
Villa Domínico ◆[8]	258	34.41 S	58.19 W
Villadose	64	45.04 N	11.53 E
Villadossola	58	46.04 N	8.16 E
Villa Elisa	252	32.10 S	58.24 W
Villa Elisa ◆[8]	258	34.50 S	58.05 W
Villa Escalante	234	19.24 N	101.39 W
Villa Flores	234	16.14 N	93.14 W
Villa Florida	252	26.23 S	57.09 W
Villafranca d'Asti	62	44.55 N	8.02 E
Villafranca del Bierzo	34	42.36 N	6.48 W
Villafranca de los Barros	34	38.34 N	6.20 W
Villafranca di Verona	64	45.21 N	10.50 E
Villafranca in Lunigiana	64	44.17 N	9.57 E
Villafranca Piemonte	62	44.47 N	7.33 E
Villafranca Sicula	70	37.35 N	13.17 E
Villafranca Tirrena	70	38.14 N	15.26 E
Villafrati	70	37.54 N	13.29 E
Villagarcía, Esp.	34	42.36 N	8.45 W
Villa García, Méx.	234	22.10 N	101.57 W
Village	196	35.33 N	97.33 W
Village Creek ≃	194	35.28 N	91.19 W
Village Green	285	39.52 N	75.26 W
Villa General Roca	252	32.39 S	66.28 W
Village of Drummond Hill	285	39.43 N	75.42 W
Village of the Branch	276	40.51 N	73.11 W
Villa Gesell	252	37.15 S	56.55 W
Villa Giambruno	288	34.48 S	58.13 W
Villa González Ortega	234	22.30 N	101.55 W
Villagrán, Méx.	232	24.29 N	99.29 W
Villagrán, Méx.	234	20.31 N	100.59 W
Villagrande Strisaili	71	39.58 N	9.30 E
Villa Grazia	70	38.09 N	13.10 E
Villagrazia ◆[8]	70	38.05 N	13.20 E
Villa Grove	194	39.51 N	88.09 W
Villaguay	252	31.51 S	59.01 W
Villa Guerrero, Méx.	234	21.59 N	103.36 W
Villa Guerrero, Méx.	234	18.52 N	99.39 W
Villa Guillermina	252	28.14 S	59.28 W
Villa Hayes	252	25.06 S	57.34 W
Villahermosa	234	17.59 N	92.55 W
Villa Hernandarias	252	31.13 S	59.59 W
Villa Hidalgo, Méx.	204	30.59 N	116.10 W
Villa Hidalgo, Méx.	234	21.40 N	102.36 W
Villa Hidalgo, Méx.	234	21.44 N	105.15 W
Villa Hidalgo Yalalag	234	17.11 N	96.11 W
Villa Huidobro	252	34.50 S	64.35 W
Villaines-la-Juhel	32	48.21 N	0.17 W
Villa Insurgentes	232	25.12 N	111.44 W
Villa Iris	252	38.10 S	63.15 W
Villa Jiménez	234	19.55 N	101.35 W
Villa José L. Suárez ◆[8]	288	34.32 S	58.35 W
Villa Juanita	234	17.47 N	95.09 W
Villa Juárez, Méx.	232	27.10 N	109.50 W
Villa Juárez, Méx.	234	22.20 N	100.17 W
Villa Krause	252	31.34 S	68.32 W
Villa La Angostura	254	40.47 S	71.40 W
Villalago	66	41.56 N	13.50 E
Villa Larca	252	32.37 S	64.59 W
Villa La Venta	234	18.10 N	94.07 W
Villalba, Esp.	34	43.18 N	7.41 W
Villalba, It.	70	37.39 N	13.50 E
Villalba, P.R.	240m	18.08 N	66.30 W
Villaldama	232	26.30 N	100.26 W
Villa Lia	258	34.07 S	59.26 W
Villalon	116	11.31 N	124.22 E
Villalón de Campos	34	42.06 N	5.02 W
Villalonga	254	39.53 S	62.35 W
Villalpando	34	41.52 N	5.24 W
Villa Lugano ◆[8]	288	34.41 S	58.28 W
Villalvernia	62	44.49 N	8.51 E
Villa Lynch ◆[8]	288	34.36 S	58.31 W
Villa Madero, Arg.	288	34.42 S	58.30 W
Villa Madero, Méx.	234	19.24 N	101.16 W
Villa Mainero	232	24.32 N	99.38 W
Villamar	71	39.37 N	8.59 E
Villa María, Arg.	252	32.25 S	63.15 W
Villa Maria, Pa., U.S.	214	41.05 N	80.30 W
Villa Maria del Triunfo	286d	12.10 S	76.56 W
Villa María Grande	252	31.39 S	59.54 W
Villa Martín, Bol.	248	20.46 S	67.47 W
Villamartín, Esp.	34	36.52 N	5.38 W
Villamarzana	64	45.01 N	11.41 E
Villamassargia	71	39.16 N	8.38 E
Villa Matoque	252	25.49 S	63.49 W
Villa Mazán	252	28.40 S	66.34 W
Villa Media Agua	252	31.59 S	68.25 W
Villa Mercedes	252	30.07 S	68.42 W
Villa Minozzo	64	44.22 N	10.28 E
Villamontes	248	21.15 S	63.30 W
Villa Morelos	234	20.00 N	101.25 W
Villandraut	32	44.28 N	0.23 W
Villa Nova, Md., U.S.	284b	39.21 N	76.44 W
Villa Nova, Oh., U.S.	216	40.33 N	84.26 W
Villanova, Pa., U.S.	208	40.02 N	75.20 W
Villanova d'Asti	62	44.57 N	7.56 E
Villanova Mondovì	62	44.21 N	7.45 E
Villanova Monferrato	62	45.11 N	8.28 E
Villanova Monteleone	71	40.30 N	8.28 E
Villanova sull'Arda	64	45.01 N	10.00 E
Villanova Tulo	71	39.47 N	9.13 E
Villanova University ʊ[2]	285	40.02 N	75.21 W
Villa Nueva, Arg.	252	32.26 S	63.15 W
Villa Nueva, Arg.	252	32.54 S	68.47 W
Villanueva, Col.	246	10.37 N	72.59 W
Villa Nueva, Guat.	236	14.31 N	90.35 W
Villanueva, Hond.	236	15.17 N	88.00 W
Villanueva, Méx.	234	22.21 N	102.53 W
Villa Nueva, Nic.	236	12.58 N	86.49 W
Villanueva, N.M., U.S.	200	35.16 N	105.21 W
Villanueva de Córdoba	34	38.20 N	4.37 W
Villanueva de la Serana	34	38.58 N	5.48 W
Villanueva de la Sierra	34	40.12 N	6.24 W
Villanueva de los Infantes	34	38.44 N	2.59 W
Villanueva del Río y Minas	34	37.39 N	5.42 W
Villa Numancia	288	34.55 S	58.24 W
Villa Obregón	234	21.07 N	102.42 W
Villa Ocampo	252	28.28 S	59.22 W
Villa Ojo de Agua	252	29.31 S	63.42 W
Villa Oliva	252	26.01 S	57.53 W
Villa Opicina	64	45.40 N	13.49 E
Villa Oropeza	248	19.10 S	65.17 W
Villa Ottone (Uttenheim)	64	46.52 N	11.57 E
Villa Papale ʊ	267a	41.45 N	12.39 E
Villa Park, Ca., U.S.	228	33.48 N	117.48 W
Villa Park, Il., U.S.	278	41.53 N	87.59 W
Villa Park Dam ◆[6]	280	33.48 N	117.46 W
Villa Pérez	240m	18.12 N	66.47 W
Villapiana	68	39.51 N	16.28 E
Villapiana Lido	68	39.48 N	16.29 E
Villapinzón	246	5.13 N	73.36 W
Villa Potenza	66	43.19 N	13.25 E
Villaputzu	71	39.26 N	9.34 E
Villa Quinteros	252	27.14 S	65.33 W
Villa Quintilio Varo ⊥	267a	41.58 N	12.47 E
Villa Ramírez	252	32.11 S	60.12 W
Villarcayo	34	42.56 N	3.34 W
Villar-d'Arène	62	45.02 N	6.20 E
Villard-Bonnot	62	45.14 N	5.53 E
Villard-de-Lans	62	45.04 N	5.33 E
Villardefrades	34	41.43 N	5.15 W
Villar del Arzobispo	34	39.44 N	0.49 W
Villareal	116	11.34 N	124.56 E
Villa Real ◆[8]	288	34.37 S	58.31 W
Villa Regina	252	39.06 S	67.04 W
Villa Reynolds	252	33.43 S	65.23 W
Villa Rica	192	33.43 N	84.55 W
Villa Rivero	248	17.37 S	65.48 W
Villaroche	261	48.37 N	2.39 E
Villaroche ■	261	48.37 N	2.40 E
Villa Romana del Casale ⊥	70	37.22 N	14.20 E
Villa Rosa, Arg.	258	34.25 S	58.52 W
Villarosa, It.	70	37.35 N	14.10 E
Villar Pellice	62	44.48 N	7.09 E
Villar Perosa	62	44.56 N	7.15 E
Villarreales	196	26.07 N	100.20 W
Villarrica, Chile	254	39.16 S	72.13 W
Villarrica, Col.	246	3.58 N	74.37 W
Villarrica, Para.	252	25.45 S	56.26 W
Villarrica, Lago ⊜	254	39.15 S	72.06 W
Villarrobledo	34	39.16 N	2.36 W
Villarrubia de los Ojos	34	39.13 N	3.36 W
Villars, Arg.	258	34.50 S	58.56 W
Villars, Schw.	58	46.18 N	7.04 E
Villars-Colmars	62	44.10 N	6.36 E
Villars-en-Azois	58	48.04 N	4.45 E
Villars-les-Dombes	58	46.00 N	5.01 E
Villars-sur-Var	62	43.56 N	7.06 E
Villa Ruiz	258	34.25 S	59.15 W
Villas	208	39.01 N	74.56 W
Villa Sáenz Peña ◆[8]	288	34.36 S	58.31 W
Villa San Andrés ◆[8]	288	34.33 S	58.32 W
Villa Sandino	236	12.03 N	84.59 W
Villa San Giovanni	68	38.13 N	15.38 E
Villa San José	252	32.12 S	58.13 W
Villa San Martín	252	28.18 S	64.12 W
Villasanta	62	45.37 N	9.18 E
Villa Santa, Montaña ∧	236	14.12 N	86.27 W
Villa Santa Maria	66	41.57 N	14.21 E
Villa Santina	64	46.24 N	12.55 E
Villa Santo Domingo	234	23.20 N	101.44 W
Villa Santos Lugares ◆[8]	288	34.36 S	58.32 W
Villasayas	34	41.21 N	2.37 W
Villa Serrano	248	19.06 S	64.22 W
Villasimius	71	39.08 N	9.31 E
Villasis	116	15.54 N	120.35 E
Villasor	71	39.23 N	8.56 E
Villa Talavera	248	19.49 S	65.25 W
Villa Tunari	248	16.55 S	65.25 W
Villa Turdera ◆[8]	288	34.48 S	58.25 W
Villa Unión, Arg.	252	29.18 S	68.12 W
Villa Unión, Arg.	252	29.24 S	62.47 W
Villa Unión, Méx.	232	28.15 N	100.43 W
Villa Unión, Méx.	234	23.58 N	104.02 W
Villa Unión, Méx.	234	23.12 N	106.14 W
Villa Urquiza ◆[8]	288	34.34 S	58.29 W
Villa Valeria	252	34.20 S	64.55 W
Villa Vallelonga	66	41.52 N	13.37 E
Villaverde ◆[8]	266a	40.21 N	3.42 W
Villaverla	64	45.39 N	11.29 E
Villa Verona	226	39.28 N	121.33 W
Villavicencio	246	4.09 N	73.37 W
Villaviciosa	34	43.29 N	5.26 W
Villaviciosa de Córdoba	34	38.05 N	5.01 W
Villa Victoria	234	18.47 N	103.24 W
Villa Viscarra	248	17.59 S	65.36 W
Villa Vomano	66	42.37 N	13.46 E
Villazón	248	22.06 S	65.36 W
Villa Zorraquín	252	31.19 S	58.02 W
Villé	58	48.20 N	7.18 E
Villebon, Lac ⊜	190	47.58 N	77.17 W
Villebon-sur-Yvette	261	48.42 N	2.15 E
Villeconin	261	48.31 N	2.08 E
Villecresnes	261	48.43 N	2.32 E
Villecroze	62	43.35 N	6.16 E
Ville-d'Avray	261	48.50 N	2.11 E
Ville-de-Laval → Laval	206	45.35 N	73.45 W
Villedieu	32	48.50 N	1.13 W
Ville-en-Tardenois	50	49.11 N	3.48 E
Villefort	62	44.26 N	3.56 E
Villefranche	58	45.59 N	4.43 E
Villefranche-de-Rouergue	32	44.21 N	2.02 E
Villefranche-Sur-Cher	50	47.18 N	1.46 E
Villefranche-sur-Mer	62	43.42 N	7.19 E
Villejuif	50	48.48 N	2.22 E
Villejust	261	48.41 N	2.14 E
Ville-Marie	190	47.19 N	79.26 W
Villemaur-sur-Vanne	50	48.15 N	3.44 E
Villemeux-sur-Eure	50	48.40 N	1.28 E
Villemoisson-sur-Orge	261	48.40 N	2.19 E
Villemomble	261	48.53 N	2.31 E
Villena	34	38.38 N	0.51 W
Ville Nacíonal	234	17.50 N	96.14 W
Villenauxe-la-Grande	50	48.35 N	3.33 E
Villeneuve, It.	62	45.42 N	7.14 E
Villeneuve, Schw.	58	46.24 N	6.55 E
Villeneuve-d'Ascq	50	50.37 N	3.10 E
Villeneuve-d'Aveyron	32	44.26 N	2.02 E
Villeneuve-de-Berg	62	44.33 N	4.30 E
Villeneuve-la-Garenne	261	48.56 N	2.20 E
Villeneuve-la-Guyard	50	48.20 N	3.04 E
Villeneuve-l'Archevêque	50	48.14 N	3.33 E
Villeneuve-le-Comte	261	48.49 N	2.50 E
Villeneuve-le-Roi	50	48.44 N	2.25 E
Villeneuve-lès-Avignon	62	43.58 N	4.48 E
Villeneuve-lès-Maguelonne	62	43.32 N	3.52 E
Villeneuve-Saint-Denis	261	48.49 N	2.48 E
Villeneuve-Saint-Georges	50	48.44 N	2.27 E
Villeneuve-sous-Dammartin	261	49.02 N	2.39 E
Villeneuve-sur-Lot	32	44.25 N	0.42 E
Villeneuve-sur-Yonne	50	48.05 N	3.18 E
Villennes-sur-Seine	261	48.56 N	2.00 E
Villenoy	50	48.57 N	2.52 E
Villeny	50	47.37 N	1.45 E
Villeparisis	50	48.56 N	2.37 E
Villepinte	261	48.58 N	2.32 E
Ville Platte	194	30.41 N	92.16 W
Villepreux	261	48.50 N	2.01 E
Villequier	50	49.31 N	0.40 E
Villeron	261	49.03 N	2.33 E
Villeroy	50	48.59 N	2.47 E
Villers-Bocage, Fr.	32	49.05 N	0.39 W
Villers-Bocage, Fr.	50	49.59 N	2.20 E
Villers-Bretonneux	50	49.52 N	2.31 E
Villers-Carbonnel	50	49.52 N	2.54 E
Villers-Cotterêts	50	49.15 N	3.05 E
Villers-devant-Orval	56	49.37 N	5.19 E
Villers-en-Arthies	261	49.05 N	1.44 E
Villersexel	58	47.33 N	6.26 E
Villers-Farlay	58	47.00 N	5.45 E
Villers-la-Ville	50	50.35 N	4.32 E
Villers-le-Lac	58	47.04 N	6.40 E
Villers-lès-Nancy	58	48.40 N	6.09 E
Villers-lès-Pots	58	47.13 N	5.21 E
Villers-Outréaux	50	50.02 N	3.18 E
Villers-Saint-Paul	50	49.17 N	2.29 E
Villers-Semeuse	56	49.44 N	4.45 E
Villerupt	56	49.28 N	5.56 E

	English	Deutsch	Español	Français	Português
≃	River	Fluß	Río	Rivière	Rio
≍	Canal	Kanal	Canal	Canal	Canal
∟	Waterfall, Rapids	Wasserfall, Stromschnellen	Cascada, Rápidos	Chute d'eau, Rapides	Cascata, Rápidos
⋓	Strait	Meeresstraße	Estrecho	Détroit	Estreito
⊂	Bay, Gulf	Bucht, Golf	Bahía, Golfo	Baie, Golfe	Baía, Golfo
⊜	Lake, Lakes	See, Seen	Lago, Lagos	Lac, Lacs	Lago, Lagos
⋿	Swamp	Sumpf	Pantano	Marais	Pântano
⍓	Ice Features, Glacier	Eis- und Gletscherformen	Accidentes Glaciales	Formes glaciaires	Acidentes glaciares
⫪	Other Hydrographic Features	Andere Hydrographische Objekte	Otros Elementos Hidrográficos	Autres données hydrographiques	Outros acidentes hidrográficos

	English	Deutsch	Español	Français	Português
✦	Submarine Features	Untermeerische Objekte	Accidentes Submarinos	Formes de relief sous-marin	Acidentes submarinos
□	Political Unit	Politische Einheit	Unidad Politica	Entité politique	Unidade política
ʊ	Cultural Institution	Kulturelle Institution	Institución Cultural	Institution culturelle	Instituição cultural
⊥	Historical Site	Historische Stätte	Sitio Histórico	Site historique	Sitio histórico
♦	Recreational Site	Erholungs- und Ferienort	Sitio de Recreo	Centre de loisirs	Area de Lazer
⊠	Airport	Flughafen	Aeropuerto	Aéroport	Aeroporto
■	Military Installation	Militäranlage	Instalación Militar	Installation militaire	Instalação militar
◆	Miscellaneous	Verschiedenes	Misceláneo	Divers	Diversos

ENGLISH | DEUTSCH

Name / Name	Page / Seite	Lat.°′ / Breite°′	Long.°′ / Länge°′ E = Ost
Villerville	50	49.24 N	0.08 E
Ville-Saint-Georges → Saint-Georges	188	46.07 N	70.40 W
Villes-sur-Auzon	62	44.03 N	5.14 E
Ville-sur-Tourbe	56	49.11 N	4.47 E
Villeta	246	5.01 N	74.28 W
Villetta Barrea	66	41.47 N	13.56 E
Villeurbanne	62	45.46 N	4.53 E
Villevaudé	261	48.55 N	2.39 E
Villeziers	261	48.40 N	2.10 E
Villiers	158	27.03 S	28.35 E
Villiers-Adam	261	49.04 N	2.14 E
Villiersdorp	158	34.00 S	19.19 E
Villiers-le-Bâcle	261	48.44 N	2.08 E
Villiers-le-Bel	261	49.00 N	2.23 E
Villiers-le-Sec	261	49.04 N	2.23 E
Villiers-Saint-Frédéric	261	48.49 N	1.54 E
Villiers-Saint-Georges	50	48.39 N	3.25 E
Villiers-sur-Marne	261	48.50 N	2.33 E
Villiers-sur-Morin	261	48.52 N	2.53 E
Villigst	263	51.26 N	7.35 E
Villingen-Schwenningen	30	48.04 N	8.28 E
Villisca	198	40.55 N	94.58 W
Villmanstrand → Lappeenranta	26	61.04 N	28.11 E
Villmergen	58	47.21 N	8.15 E
Villorba	64	45.44 N	12.14 E
Villoresi, Canale ≍	62	45.33 N	9.31 E
Villotta	64	45.52 N	12.45 E
Vilm I	54	54.19 N	13.32 E
Vilmnitz	54	54.21 N	13.31 E
Vilna	182	54.07 N	111.55 W
Vilna → Vilnius	76	54.41 N	25.19 E
Vilnius	76	54.41 N	25.19 E
Vilosnes-sur-Meuse	56	49.20 N	5.14 E
Vilppula	26	62.01 N	24.31 E
Vils	58	47.33 N	10.38 E
Vils ≃, Dtsch.	60	49.09 N	11.58 E
Vils ≃, Dtsch.	60	48.37 N	13.11 E
Vils ≃, Europe	58	47.33 N	10.40 E
Vilsandi saar I	76	58.23 N	21.52 E
Vilsbiburg	60	48.27 N	12.12 E
Vilseck	60	49.37 N	11.48 E
Vilsheim	60	48.27 N	12.07 E
Vilshofen	60	48.39 N	13.12 E
Vil'uj ≃	74	64.24 N	126.26 E
Vil'ujsk	74	63.45 N	121.35 E
Vil'ujskoje vodochranilišče ⊜1	74	62.30 N	111.00 E
Viluppuram	122	11.56 N	79.29 E
Vil'va	86	58.37 N	56.52 E
Vilvoorde	50	50.56 N	4.26 E
Vimercate	62	45.37 N	9.22 E
Vimianzo	34	43.07 N	9.02 W
Vimmerby	26	57.40 N	15.51 E
Vimodrone	266b	45.31 N	9.17 E
Vimoutiers	50	48.55 N	0.12 E
Vimpeli	26	63.09 N	23.48 E
Vimperk	60	49.03 N	13.47 E
Vimy	50	50.22 N	2.49 E
Vina	204	39.55 N	122.03 W
Vina ≃	146	7.45 N	15.36 E
Viñac	248	12.56 S	75.47 W
Viña del Mar	252	33.02 S	71.34 W
Vinadi	58	46.55 N	10.29 E
Vinadio	62	44.18 N	7.10 E
Viñales	240p	22.37 N	83.43 W
Vinalhaven	188	44.02 N	68.49 W
Vinalhaven Island I	188	44.05 N	68.52 W
Vinantes	261	49.01 N	2.44 E
Vina Roni, Mount ∧	175e	8.10 S	157.28 E
Vinaròs	34	40.28 N	0.29 E
Vinay	62	45.13 N	5.24 E
Vinazco ≃	234	20.56 N	97.44 W
Vincennes, Fr.	50	48.51 N	2.26 E
Vincennes, In., U.S.	194	38.40 N	87.31 W
Vincennes, Bois de ♠	261	48.50 N	2.25 E
Vincennes, Château de ⊥	261	48.51 N	2.26 E
Vincennes, Étang de ⊜	261	48.47 N	2.45 E
Vincennes Bay C	9	66.30 S	109.30 E
Vincent	194	33.22 N	86.22 W
Vincent, Point ≻	174c	29.00 S	167.55 E
Vincentown	208	39.56 N	74.44 W
Vinces	246	1.32 S	79.45 W
Vinchiaturo	66	41.29 N	14.35 E
Vinchina	252	28.46 S	68.10 W
Vinchos	248	13.16 S	74.21 W
Vinci	66	43.47 N	10.55 E
Vinco	214	40.25 N	78.52 W
Vindeby	41	55.03 N	10.38 E
Vindelälven ≃	24	63.54 N	19.52 E
Vindeln	26	64.12 N	19.44 E
Vinden, Mount ∧	162	27.01 S	115.38 E
Vinderslev	41	56.15 N	9.26 E
Vinderup	26	56.29 N	8.47 E
Vindhya Range ⋀	120	23.00 N	77.00 E
Vinding	41	55.41 N	9.35 E
Vindinge	41	55.19 N	10.45 E
Vine Brook ≃	283	42.27 N	71.13 W
Vinegar Hill ∧	202	44.43 N	118.34 W
Vine Grove	194	37.48 N	85.58 W
Vine Hill	282	38.00 N	122.06 W
Vineland, Mi., U.S.	216	42.03 N	86.30 W
Vineland, N.J., U.S.	208	39.29 N	75.01 W
Vinemont	194	34.14 N	86.51 W
Vine Valley	210	42.43 N	77.20 W
Vineyard Canyon V	226	35.46 N	120.41 W
Vineyard Haven	207	41.27 N	70.36 W
Vineyard Lake ⊜	216	42.05 N	84.13 W
Vineyard Sound ʮ	207	41.25 N	70.46 W
Vingåker	40	59.02 N	15.52 E
Vingeanne ≃	58	47.21 N	5.29 E
Ving Ngün	110	22.37 N	99.16 E
Vinh	110	18.40 N	105.40 E
Vinhais	34	41.50 N	7.00 W
Vinhas, Ribeira das ≃	266c	38.42 N	9.25 W
Vinh Chau	110	9.19 N	105.59 E
Vinhedo	256	23.01 S	46.59 W
Vinh Loc	269c	10.49 N	106.34 E
Vinh Long	110	10.15 N	105.58 E
Vinh Tuy, Viet	110	9.37 N	105.22 E
Vinh Tuy, Viet	110	17.24 N	106.36 E
Vinica	36	45.28 N	15.15 E
Vinita	196	36.38 N	95.09 W
Vinju Mare	38	44.26 N	22.52 E
Vinkekuil	158	32.42 S	20.27 E
Vinkeveen	52	52.13 N	4.54 E
Vinkovci	38	45.17 N	18.49 E
Vin'kovcy	78	49.02 N	27.14 E
Vinnhorst	52	52.25 N	9.43 E
Vinnica	78	49.14 N	28.29 E
Vinnica □8	78	48.30 N	28.30 E
Vinniki	78	49.48 N	24.08 E
Vinnitsa → Vinnica	78	49.14 N	28.29 E
Vinnum	263	51.41 N	7.24 E
Vinogradov	78	48.09 N	23.02 E
Vinogradovo, Ross.	82	55.25 N	38.32 E
Vinogradovo, Ross.	82	55.57 N	37.32 E
Vinogrobol'	78	51.51 N	36.26 E
Vinön I	40	59.12 N	15.43 E
Vinon-sur-Verdon	62	43.43 N	5.48 E
Vinovo	62	44.57 N	7.38 E
Vinslöv	26	56.06 N	13.55 E
Vinson Massif ∧	9	78.35 S	85.25 W
Vinstra	26	61.36 N	9.45 E
Vintilă Vodă	38	45.28 N	26.44 E
Vinto	248	17.58 S	67.04 W
Vinton, Ia., U.S.	190	42.10 N	92.01 W
Vinton, La., U.S.	194	30.11 N	93.34 W
Vinton, Va., U.S.	192	37.16 N	79.53 W
Vintondale	214	40.28 N	78.55 W
Vintrosa	40	59.15 N	14.57 E
Viñuelas, Arroyo de ≃	266a	40.33 N	3.33 W
Viny	76	58.22 N	32.13 E
Vinzelberg	54	52.33 N	11.40 E
Vinzili	86	56.58 N	65.46 E
Viola, Il., U.S.	190	41.12 N	90.35 W
Viola, N.Y., U.S.	276	41.08 N	74.05 W
Viola, Wi., U.S.	190	43.30 N	90.40 W
Viola, Val V	64	46.27 N	10.15 E
Violín, Isla I	236	8.51 N	83.39 W
Viols-le-Fort	62	43.45 N	3.42 E
Viosne ≃	261	49.03 N	2.06 E
Vipava	36	45.51 N	13.58 E
Vipava ≃	64	45.54 N	13.33 E
Vipiteno (Sterzing)	64	46.54 N	11.26 E
Vipos	252	26.29 S	65.22 W
Vipperow	54	53.19 N	12.41 E
Vir, Otok I	36	44.18 N	15.04 E
Vira	58	46.08 N	8.51 E
Virac	116	13.35 N	124.15 E
Viracopos, Aeroporto de ⊠	256	23.00 S	47.08 W
Virac Point ≻	116	13.31 N	124.13 E
Viradouro	255	20.53 S	48.18 W
Virago Sound ʮ	182	54.00 N	132.36 W
Viramgām	120	23.07 N	72.02 E
Virandozero	24	64.05 N	35.58 E
Viranşehir	130	37.13 N	39.45 E
Vīrarājendrapet	122	12.12 N	75.48 E
Virbalis	76	54.38 N	22.49 E
Virden, Mb., Can.	184	49.51 N	100.55 W
Virden, Il., U.S.	219	39.30 N	89.46 W
Virden, N.M., U.S.	200	32.41 N	109.00 W
Vire	32	48.50 N	0.53 W
Vire ≃	32	49.20 N	1.07 W
Virelles	50	50.04 N	4.20 E
Virelles, Étang de ⊜	50	50.04 N	4.21 E
Vireux-Molhain	56	50.05 N	4.43 E
Vîrfurile	38	46.19 N	22.31 E
Virgem da Lapa	255	16.49 S	42.21 W
Virgen	64	47.00 N	12.27 E
Vírgen del San Cristóbal ᵾ1	286e	33.26 S	70.39 W
Vírgenes, Cabo ≻	254	52.22 S	68.20 W
Vírgenes, Islas → British Virgin Islands □2	240m	18.30 N	64.30 W
Vírgenes, Islas → Virgin Islands □2	240m	18.20 N	64.50 W
Virgen Tal V	64	47.00 N	12.25 E
Virgil, On., Can.	284a	43.13 N	79.08 W
Virgil, Ks., U.S.	198	37.58 N	96.00 W
Virgil, N.Y., U.S.	210	42.31 N	76.12 W
Virgilina	192	36.33 N	78.52 W
Virgilio	64	45.07 N	10.47 E
Virgin ≃	200	36.31 N	114.20 W
Virgin, North Fork ≃	200	37.10 N	113.01 W
Virginal-Samme	50	50.38 N	4.12 E
Virgin Gorda I	240m	18.30 N	64.24 W
Virgin Gorda Peak ∧	240m	18.30 N	64.24 W
Virginia, Austl.	168b	34.40 S	138.34 E
Virgínia, Bra.	256	22.20 S	45.06 W
Virginia, Ire.	48	53.49 N	7.04 W
Virginia, S. Afr.	158	28.12 S	26.49 E
Virginia, Il., U.S.	219	39.57 N	90.12 W
Virginia, Mn., U.S.	190	47.31 N	92.32 W
Virginia □3	178	37.30 N	78.45 W
Virginia Beach	208	36.51 N	75.58 W
Virginia City, Mt., U.S.	202	45.17 N	111.56 W
Virginia City, Nv., U.S.	226	39.18 N	119.38 W
Virginia Creek ≃	226	38.13 N	119.14 W
Virginia Falls ⌊	180	61.38 N	125.42 W
Virginia Gardens	220	25.49 N	80.17 W
Virginia Hills	208	38.47 N	77.06 W
Virginia Key I	220	25.44 N	80.09 W
Virginia Peak ∧	204	39.45 N	119.28 W
Virginia Ranch Reservoir ⊜1	226	39.20 N	121.19 W
Virginia Range ⋀	226	39.18 N	119.30 W
Virginiatown	190	48.08 N	79.35 W
Virginia Water	260	51.24 N	0.34 W
Virginie occidentale → West Virginia □3	188	38.45 N	80.30 W
Virgin Islands □2, N.A.	230	18.20 N	64.50 W
Virgin Islands □2, N.A.	240m	18.20 N	64.50 W
Virgin Islands II	240m	18.00 N	64.40 W
Virgin Islands National Park ♠	240m	18.20 N	64.45 W
Virginópolis	255	18.45 S	42.45 W
Virgin Passage C1	240m	18.20 N	65.10 W
Virginville	208	40.31 N	75.52 W
Virgolândia	255	18.27 S	42.18 W
Virieu	62	45.29 N	5.28 E
Virieu-le-Grand	62	45.51 N	5.39 E
Virihaure ⊜	24	67.20 N	16.35 E
Virje	36	46.04 N	16.59 E
Virkkala	26	60.12 N	24.01 E
Virklund	41	56.07 N	9.34 E
Virneburg	56	50.20 N	7.04 E
Virôchey	110	13.59 N	106.49 E
Viroflay	50	48.48 N	2.10 E
Viroin ≃	56	50.05 N	4.43 E
Virojoki	26	60.35 N	27.42 E
Víron	267c	37.57 N	23.45 E
Vironvay	50	49.12 N	1.13 E
Viroqua	190	43.33 N	90.53 W
Virovitica	36	45.50 N	17.23 E
Virpazar	38	42.15 N	19.05 E
Virrat	26	62.14 N	23.47 E
Virsbo	40	59.52 N	16.02 E
Virserum	26	57.19 N	15.35 E
Virtaniemi	24	68.53 N	28.27 E
Virton	56	49.34 N	5.32 E
Vîrtopu	38	44.12 N	23.21 E
Virtsu	76	58.34 N	23.31 E
Virú	248	8.25 S	78.45 W
Virudunagar	122	9.36 N	77.58 E
Viru-Jaagupi	76	59.15 N	26.28 E
Virulento	196	28.52 N	104.21 W
Virunga, Parc National de ♠	154	1.00 S	29.15 E
Virungu	154	7.04 S	29.46 E
Viru-Nigula	76	59.27 N	26.41 E
Virvyčia ≃	76	56.13 N	22.34 E
Viry-Châtillon	50	48.40 N	2.23 E
Vis	36	43.03 N	16.12 E
Vis ≃, Fr.	62	43.56 N	3.42 E
Vis (Fish) ≃, Namibia	156	28.07 S	17.45 E
Vis ≃, S. Afr.	158	30.53 S	20.23 E
Vis, Otok I	36	43.02 N	16.11 E
Visale	175e	9.15 S	159.42 E
Visalia	226	36.19 N	119.17 W
Visalia Airport ⊠	226	36.19 N	119.23 W
Visayan Islands II	116	11.00 N	123.30 E
Visayan Sea ≂2	116	11.35 N	123.51 E
Visbek	52	52.48 N	8.19 E
Visby	26	57.38 N	18.18 E
Viscaya, Bahía de → Biscay, Bay of C	32	44.00 N	4.00 W
Viscount	184	51.57 N	105.39 W
Viscount Melville Sound ʮ	176	74.10 N	108.00 W
Visé	56	50.44 N	5.42 E
Višegrad	38	43.47 N	19.17 E
Vis-en-Artois	50	50.15 N	2.56 E
Višera ≃	76	58.34 N	31.24 E
Viserba	66	44.05 N	12.44 E
Viseu, Bra.	250	1.12 S	46.07 W
Viseu, Port.	34	40.39 N	7.55 W
Vișeu ≃	38	47.55 N	24.09 E
Vișeu de Sus	38	47.44 N	24.22 E
Vishākhapatnam	122	17.42 N	83.18 E
Vishoek	158	34.08 S	18.26 E
Visim	86	57.39 N	59.30 E
Visingsö I	26	58.03 N	14.20 E
Visitation, Île de la I	275a	45.35 N	73.40 W
Viskafors	26	57.38 N	12.50 E
Viskan ≃	26	57.14 N	12.12 E
Višķil	80	58.05 N	48.19 E
Viskinge	41	55.40 N	11.16 E
Visl'ajevo	82	54.25 N	36.43 E
Vislanda	26	56.47 N	14.27 E
Vislinskij zaliv C	30	54.27 N	19.40 E
Vismen ⊜	40	59.17 N	14.17 E
Visnagar	120	23.42 N	72.33 E
Višn'aki	265b	55.47 N	37.54 E
Višn'akovo	82	55.45 N	38.10 E
Višnevčik	78	49.02 N	26.28 E
Visnevo	76	54.08 N	26.14 E
Višnevoje, Ross.	80	52.38 N	43.26 E
Višnevoje, Ukr.	78	48.27 N	33.56 E
Višňové	61	48.59 N	16.09 E
Višn'ovec	78	49.54 N	25.45 E
Višn'ovka, Kaz.	86	50.49 N	72.12 E
Višn'ovka, Mol.	78	46.20 N	28.26 E
Viso, Monte ∧	62	44.40 N	7.07 E
Visoki Dečani, Manastir ᵾ1	38	42.30 N	20.31 E
Visoko	38	43.59 N	18.11 E
Visokoi Island I	18	56.42 S	27.12 W
Visp	58	46.18 N	7.53 E
Vispa ≃	58	46.18 N	7.52 E
Visrivier	158	31.55 S	25.25 E
Vissefjärda	26	56.32 N	15.35 E
Visselhövede	52	52.59 N	9.35 E
Vissenbjerg	41	55.23 N	10.08 E
Visso	66	42.56 N	13.05 E
Vissoie	58	46.13 N	7.36 E
Vista, Ca., U.S.	228	33.12 N	117.14 W
Vista, N.Y., U.S.	210	41.12 N	73.31 W
Vista Alegre, Arg.	252	38.45 S	68.11 W
Vista Alegre, Bra.	256	21.27 S	42.35 W
Vista Alegre, Chile	286e	33.30 S	70.43 W
Vista Alegre, Perú	286d	12.09 S	77.00 W
Vista Flores	252	33.38 S	69.09 W
Vistahermosa de Negrete	234	20.16 N	102.29 W
Vista La Mesa	228	32.35 N	117.01 W
Vista Park	228	35.21 N	118.55 W
Vistina	76	59.47 N	28.29 E
Vistre ≃	62	43.40 N	4.15 E
Vistula → Wisła ≃	30	54.22 N	18.55 E
Visun' ≃	78	47.07 N	32.53 E
Vit ≃	38	43.41 N	24.45 E
Vita, Mb., Can.	184	49.08 N	96.34 W
Vita, It.	70	37.52 N	12.49 E
Vita ≃	246	6.11 N	67.31 W
Vitacura	286e	33.24 S	70.36 W
Vitali	116	7.22 N	122.18 E
Vitanje	36	46.23 N	15.18 E
Vitarte	248	12.02 S	76.56 W
Vit'azevka	78	48.01 N	31.53 E
Vite	122	17.17 N	74.33 E
Vitebsk	76	55.12 N	30.11 E
Vitebsk Station ✦5	265a	59.55 N	30.21 E
Vitel, Laguna ⊜	258	35.32 S	58.07 W
Viterbo	66	42.25 N	12.06 E
Viterbo □4	66	42.25 N	12.05 E
Vitiaz Strait ʮ	164	5.50 S	147.20 E
Vitichi	248	20.13 S	65.29 W
Vitigudino	34	41.01 N	6.26 W
Viti Levu I	175g	18.00 S	178.00 E
Vitim	74	59.28 N	112.34 E
Vitim ≃	74	59.26 N	112.34 E
Vitimskij	88	58.14 N	113.18 E
Vitimskoje ploskogorje ⋀1	88	54.00 N	113.30 E
Vitinia ✦8	267a	41.47 N	12.24 E
Vitis	61	48.45 N	15.10 E
Vítkov	30	49.46 N	17.45 E
Vito	175e	6.02 S	155.24 E
Vítor	248	16.26 S	71.49 W
Vitor ≃	248	16.37 S	72.19 W
Vitória, Bra.	250	2.54 S	52.01 W
Vitória, Bra.	255	20.19 S	40.21 W
Vitoria (Gasteiz), Esp.	34	42.51 N	2.40 W
Vitória, Ilha da I	256	23.45 S	45.01 W
Vitória da Conquista	255	14.51 S	40.51 W
Vitória de Santo Antão	250	8.07 S	35.18 W
Vitória do Mearim	250	3.28 S	44.53 W
Vitorino Freire	250	4.04 S	45.10 W
Vitravo ≃	68	39.11 N	17.05 E
Vitré	28	48.08 N	1.12 W
Vitrey-sur-Mance	58	47.49 N	5.45 E
Vitry-aux-Loges	50	47.56 N	2.16 E
Vitry-en-Artois	50	50.20 N	2.59 E
Vitry-la-Ville	50	48.50 N	4.28 E
Vitry-le-François	56	48.44 N	4.35 E
Vitry [-sur-Seine]	50	48.48 N	2.24 E
Vitshumbi	154	0.41 S	29.23 E
Vittangi	24	67.41 N	21.36 E
Vitte	54	54.34 N	13.06 E
Vitteaux	58	47.24 N	4.32 E
Vittel	58	48.12 N	5.57 E
Vittinge	40	59.54 N	17.04 E
Vittoria, On., Can.	212	42.46 N	80.19 W
Vittoria, It.	70	36.57 N	14.32 E
Vittorio Veneto	64	45.59 N	12.18 E
Vittsjö	26	56.20 N	13.40 E
Vitulano	68	41.10 N	14.38 E
Vitznau	58	47.01 N	8.29 E
Viù	62	45.14 N	7.22 E
Vivarais □9	62	44.40 N	4.30 E
Vivarais, Monts du ⋀	62	44.55 N	4.15 E
Viver	34	39.55 N	0.36 W
Vivero	34	43.40 N	7.35 W
Viverols	62	45.26 N	3.53 E
Viverone, Lago di ⊜	62	45.25 N	8.02 E
Vivi ≃	74	63.52 N	97.50 E
Vivian	194	32.52 N	93.59 W
Viviers	62	44.29 N	4.41 E
Viviers-du-Lac	62	45.39 N	5.54 E
Vivione, Passo del)(	64	46.02 N	10.12 E
Vivonne	32	46.26 N	0.16 E
Vivoratá	252	37.40 S	57.39 W
Vivorillo, Cayos II	236	15.50 N	83.18 W
Viwa I	175g	17.08 S	176.54 E
Vizagapatam → Vishākhapatnam	122	17.42 N	83.18 E
Vizcaíno, Desierto de ✦2	232	27.40 N	113.40 W
Vizcaíno, Isla I	258	33.47 S	59.15 W
Vize	130	41.34 N	27.45 E
Vize, ostrov I	72	79.30 N	77.00 E
Vizianagaram	122	18.07 N	83.25 E
Vizille	62	45.05 N	5.46 E
Vižinada	36	45.20 N	13.46 E
Vizinga	24	61.05 N	50.04 E
Vižnica	78	48.15 N	25.12 E
Vizzini	70	37.10 N	14.53 E
Vizzola	266b	45.38 N	8.42 E
Vjatka ≃	80	55.36 N	51.30 E
Vjunka ≃	265b	55.42 N	38.01 E
Vjuny	86	55.31 N	82.55 E
Vlaanderen → Flanders □9	50	51.00 N	3.00 E
Vlaardingen	52	51.54 N	4.21 E
Vlachovo Březí	30	49.05 N	13.57 E
Vladař ∧	54	50.05 N	13.14 E
Vlădeasa, Vîrful ∧	38	46.45 N	22.48 E
Vlădeni	38	47.25 N	27.20 E
Vladičin Han	38	42.42 N	22.04 E
Vladikavkaz	84	43.03 N	44.40 E
Vladimir	80	56.10 N	40.25 E
Vladimir □8	80	56.00 N	40.00 E
Vladimirec	78	51.25 N	26.08 E
Vladimirovka, Kaz.	86	50.51 N	51.08 E
Vladimirovka, Kaz.	86	53.28 N	64.02 E
Vladimirovka, Ukr.	83	47.32 N	32.55 E
Vladimirovka, Ukr.	83	47.44 N	37.23 E
Vladimirskij Tupik	76	55.42 N	33.18 E
Vladimirskoje	76	56.49 N	45.07 E
Vladimir-Volynskij	78	50.51 N	24.20 E
Vladivostok	89	43.10 N	131.56 E
Vladyčnoje	76	58.49 N	39.29 E
Vladykino ✦8	265b	55.52 N	37.36 E
Vlašim	30	49.42 N	14.54 E
Vlaskovo	82	56.11 N	36.31 E
Vlasotince	38	42.58 N	22.08 E
Vlasovo, Ross.	74	70.48 N	135.00 E
Vlasovo, Ross.	82	56.38 N	38.14 E
Vlazoviči	76	53.01 N	32.18 E
Vledder	52	52.52 N	6.12 E
Vleesbaai C	158	34.16 S	21.57 E
Vleikolk	158	29.43 S	20.50 E
Vleuten	52	52.05 N	5.02 E
Vlieland I	52	53.15 N	5.00 E
Vlijmen	52	51.42 N	5.15 E
Vlissingen (Flushing)	52	51.26 N	3.35 E
Vlodrop	52	51.08 N	6.05 E
Vloesberg → Flobecq	50	50.44 N	3.44 E
Vlonë → Vlorë	38	40.27 N	19.30 E
Vlorë	38	40.27 N	19.30 E
Vlorës, Gji i C	38	40.25 N	19.25 E
Vlotho	52	52.10 N	8.51 E
Vltava ≃	30	50.21 N	14.30 E
Vluyn	52	51.26 N	6.32 E
Vnukovo	82	55.38 N	37.16 E
Vnukovo Airport ⊠	265b	55.37 N	37.17 E
Voca	196	31.01 N	99.11 W
Vochrinka	82	55.24 N	38.18 E
Vochtoga	76	58.47 N	41.07 E
Vočin	36	45.37 N	17.32 E
Vöckla ≃	64	48.00 N	13.36 E
Vöcklabruck	60	48.01 N	13.39 E
Vöcklamarkt	60	48.00 N	13.29 E
Vodla ≃	24	61.49 N	36.00 E
Vodlozero, ozero ⊜	24	62.20 N	36.55 E
Vodňany	30	49.09 N	14.11 E
Vodnjan	64	44.57 N	13.51 E
Vodnyj	24	63.32 N	53.18 E
Vodo	64	46.25 N	12.14 E
Vodosalma	24	64.29 N	30.44 E
Vodovatovo	80	55.24 N	43.34 E
Vodzimonje	80	56.49 N	51.38 E
Voël ≃	158	33.07 S	25.07 E
Voerde, Dtsch.	52	51.35 N	6.41 E
Voerde, Dtsch.	263	51.18 N	7.24 E
Voesch	263	51.24 N	6.26 E
Vogelenzang	52	52.19 N	4.35 E
Vogelheim ✦8	263	51.29 N	6.59 E
Vogelkop → Doberai, Jazirah ≻1	164	1.30 S	132.30 E
Vogel Peak → Dimlang ∧	146	8.24 N	11.47 E
Vogelsang, Dtsch.	54	53.43 N	14.09 E
Vogelsang, Dtsch.	56	50.35 N	6.27 E
Vogelsberg ⋀	56	50.30 N	9.15 E
Vogesen → Vosges ⋀	58	48.30 N	7.10 E
Voghera	62	44.59 N	9.01 E
Vognema	76	59.59 N	38.10 E
Vogogna	58	46.01 N	8.17 E
Vogtland ✦1	54	50.30 N	12.05 E
Voh	175f	20.58 S	164.42 E
Vohburg an der Donau	60	48.46 N	11.37 E
Vohenstrauss	60	49.37 N	12.21 E
Vohibinany	157b	18.49 S	49.04 E
Vohilava	157b	21.04 S	48.00 E
Vohimarina	157b	13.21 S	50.02 E
Vohipeno	157b	22.22 S	47.51 E
Vohitsora	157b	23.54 S	44.17 E
Võhma	76	58.38 N	25.33 E
Vöhringen, Dtsch.	58	48.02 N	8.18 E
Vöhringen, Dtsch.	58	48.16 N	10.04 E
Vöhringen, Dtsch.	58	48.20 N	8.40 E
Vöhrum	52	52.20 N	10.10 E
Vohwinkel ✦8	263	51.14 N	7.09 E
Voi	154	3.23 S	38.34 E
Void	58	48.41 N	5.37 E
Voight Creek ≃	224	47.06 N	122.10 W
Voikkaa	26	60.56 N	26.37 E
Voinești	38	47.05 N	27.26 E
Voinjama	150	8.25 N	9.45 W
Voinka	78	45.52 N	33.59 E
Voire ≃	58	48.27 N	4.25 E
Voiron	62	45.22 N	5.35 E
Voise	50	48.24 N	1.43 E
Voise ≃	50	48.35 N	1.35 E
Voisenon	261	48.34 N	2.40 E
Voisins-le-Bretonneux	50	48.45 N	2.03 E
Voiteur	58	46.45 N	5.37 E
Voitsberg	61	47.03 N	15.10 E
Voja ≃	80	57.23 N	49.55 E
Vojens	41	55.15 N	9.19 E
Vojevodskoje	86	52.47 N	85.35 E
Vojkovice	54	50.15 N	13.02 E
Vojkovo, Ukr.	78	45.31 N	33.52 E
Vojkovo, Ukr.	83	48.00 N	38.02 E
Vojkovskij	83	47.46 N	38.20 E
Vojmsjön ⊜	26	64.55 N	16.40 E
Vojnić	36	45.19 N	15.42 E
Vojnica	24	65.12 N	30.15 E
Vojnilov	78	49.08 N	24.30 E
Vojtanov	54	50.06 N	12.19 E
Vojvodina □4	38	45.00 N	20.00 E
Voj-Vož, Ross.	24	64.20 N	55.03 E
Voj-Vož, Ross.	24	62.56 N	54.56 E
Vokeo Island I	164	3.10 S	144.05 E
Volano	66	45.55 N	11.03 E
Volant	214	41.07 N	80.16 W
Volary	60	48.55 N	13.54 E
Volcán, Arg.	252	23.54 S	65.27 W
Volcán, Pan.	236	8.46 N	82.38 W
Volcán Isluga, Parque Nacional ♠	248	19.30 S	68.30 W
Volčanka	80	52.33 N	49.59 E
Volcano, Ca., U.S.	226	38.26 N	120.37 W
Volcano, Hi., U.S.	229d	19.25 N	155.14 W
Volcano Island I	116	14.00 N	121.00 E
Volcano Islands → Kazan-rettō II	14	25.00 N	141.00 E
Volcán Poás, Parque Nacional ♠	236	10.10 N	84.15 W
Volčansk, Ross.	86	59.56 N	60.04 E
Volčansk, Ukr.	78	50.18 N	36.57 E
Volčejarovka	83	48.50 N	38.22 E
Volčenskij	78	48.14 N	40.07 E
Volchonka-Zil ✦8	265b	55.40 N	37.37 E
Volchov	76	59.55 N	32.20 E
Volchov ≃	76	60.08 N	32.20 E
Volčicha	86	52.02 N	80.23 E
Volčij Nos, mys ≻	76	60.31 N	32.35 E
Volčja ≃	78	48.00 N	36.08 E
Volčje	78	49.14 N	22.53 E
Volčki	80	52.29 N	40.42 E
Volda	26	62.09 N	6.06 E
Volders	64	47.17 N	11.34 E
Volendam	52	52.30 N	5.04 E
Volga, Ross.	76	57.57 N	38.24 E
Volga, Ia., U.S.	190	42.48 N	91.32 W
Volga, S.D., U.S.	198	44.19 N	96.55 W
Volga ≃, Ross.	72	45.55 N	47.52 E
Volga ≃, Ia., U.S.	190	42.45 N	91.17 W
Volga-Baltic Canal → Volgo-Baltijskij kanal ≍	24	59.00 N	38.00 E
Volgino	76	58.27 N	33.52 E
Volgo, ozero ⊜	76	56.55 N	33.10 E
Volgo-Baltijskij kanal ≍	24	59.00 N	38.00 E
Volgodonsk	80	47.33 N	42.08 E
Volgo-Donskoj sudochodnyj kanal imeni V.I. Lenina ≍	80	48.40 N	43.37 E
Volgograd (Stalingrad)	80	48.44 N	44.25 E
Volgogradskoje vodochranilišče ⊜1	80	49.20 N	45.00 E
Volgorečensk	76	57.30 N	41.02 E
Volissós	38	38.29 N	25.58 E
Vol'ka	76	52.47 N	25.39 E
Volkach	56	49.52 N	10.13 E
Volkel	52	51.38 N	5.40 E
Völkermarkt	61	46.39 N	14.38 E
Völkermarkter Stausee ⊜1	61	46.39 N	14.38 E
Völkerschlacht-Denkmal ⊥	54	51.18 N	12.24 E
Völklingen	56	49.15 N	6.50 E
Volkmarsen	56	51.24 N	9.07 E
Volkovincy	78	49.13 N	27.39 E
Volkovo, Ross.	76	59.15 N	41.27 E
Volkovo, Ross.	82	55.46 N	36.15 E
Volkovo Cemetery ✦	265a	59.54 N	30.22 E
Volkovskoje	82	54.49 N	37.13 E
Volkovysk	76	53.10 N	24.28 E
Volksdorf ✦8	52	53.39 N	10.10 E
Völksen	52	52.13 N	9.37 E
Volksrust	158	27.24 S	29.53 E
Vollenhove	52	52.41 N	5.58 E
Vollersode	52	53.18 N	8.56 E
Vollme	263	51.10 N	7.36 E
Vollore-Montagne	62	45.47 N	3.41 E
Vollore-Ville	62	45.47 N	3.36 E
Vollsjö	41	55.42 N	13.46 E
Volma ≃	76	53.35 N	28.19 E
Volmarstein	56	51.22 N	7.23 E
Volme ≃	263	51.24 N	7.27 E
Volmerange-les-Mines	56	49.27 N	6.05 E
Volmerswerth ✦8	263	51.11 N	6.46 E
Volmunster	56	49.07 N	7.21 E
Vol'naja Gorka	76	58.43 N	30.51 E
Volnay	58	47.00 N	4.47 E
Vol'nogorsk	78	48.29 N	34.01 E
Vol'noje, Ross.	80	47.09 N	47.38 E
Vol'noje, Ross.	86	54.17 N	71.21 E
Volnovacha	83	47.36 N	37.31 E
Vol'nyj	80	45.55 N	45.14 E
Vol'nyj, ostrov I	265a	59.58 N	30.14 E
Voločajevka Vtoraja	89	48.34 N	134.34 E
Voločanka	74	71.00 N	94.28 E
Voločisk	78	49.32 N	26.11 E
Volockaja	76	60.17 N	42.59 E
Volodarka, Ross.	86	52.43 N	83.38 E
Volodarka, Ukr.	78	49.31 N	29.55 E
Volodarsk, Ross.	76	56.13 N	43.10 E
Volodarsk, Ukr.	83	48.06 N	39.35 E
Volodarskij, Ross.	80	46.24 N	48.32 E
Volodarskij, Ross.	82	55.30 N	37.57 E
Volodarskij ✦8	265a	59.49 N	30.05 E
Volodarskoje, Kaz.	86	53.18 N	68.08 E
Volodarskoje, Ukr.	83	47.12 N	37.20 E
Volodarsk-Volynskij	78	50.37 N	28.25 E
Volodino	86	57.06 N	83.54 E
Vologda	76	59.12 N	39.55 E
Vologda ≃	76	59.17 N	40.13 E
Voloje	76	54.09 N	34.35 E
Volokolamsk	82	56.02 N	35.57 E
Volokonovka	78	50.29 N	37.51 E
Volokovaja	24	66.28 N	48.10 E
Volonga	24	67.07 N	47.41 E
Volonne	62	44.07 N	6.01 E
Volontirovka	78	46.26 N	29.37 E
Vólos	38	39.21 N	22.56 E
Vološino, Ross.	83	47.31 N	39.40 E
Vološino, Ross.	83	48.55 N	39.56 E
Vološka	24	61.20 N	40.06 E
Vološn'a ≃	82	55.51 N	35.54 E
Vološno	76	58.29 N	28.29 E
Volosoviči	76	54.46 N	28.50 E
Volosovo	76	59.26 N	29.29 E
Volosskaja Balaklejka	83	49.37 N	37.20 E
Volot	76	57.56 N	30.42 E
Volovec	78	48.43 N	23.11 E
Volovo, Ross.	76	53.35 N	38.02 E
Volovo, Ross.	78	52.03 N	37.53 E
Voložin	76	54.05 N	26.32 E
Volpago del Montello	64	45.47 N	12.07 E
Volpedo	62	44.53 N	8.59 E
Volpiano	62	45.12 N	7.46 E
Völpke	54	52.08 N	11.09 E
Völs → Fiè	64	46.31 N	11.30 E
Volsini, Monti ⋀	66	42.40 N	11.55 E
Vol'sk	80	52.02 N	47.23 E
Volstruisleegte	158	33.05 S	23.28 E
Volta □4	150	7.00 N	0.30 E
Volta ≃	150	5.46 N	0.41 E
Volta, Lake ⊜1	150	7.30 N	0.15 E
Volta Blanche (White Volta) ≃	150	9.10 N	1.15 W
Voltaggio	62	44.37 N	8.50 E
Voltago	64	46.16 N	12.00 E
Volta Grande	256	21.46 S	42.32 W
Voltaire, Cape ≻	164	14.16 S	125.35 E
Volta Mantovana	64	45.19 N	10.39 E
Volta Noire (Black Volta) ≃	150	8.41 N	1.33 W
Volta Redonda	256	22.32 S	44.07 W
Volta Rouge ≃	150	10.34 N	0.30 W
Volterra	66	43.24 N	10.51 E
Vol'teva	24	64.30 N	44.12 E
Voltri	62	44.26 N	8.45 E
Volturara Appula	68	41.30 N	15.03 E
Volturara Irpina	68	40.53 N	14.55 E
Volturino	68	41.28 N	15.07 E
Volturino, Monte ∧	68	40.25 N	15.49 E
Volturno ≃	68	41.01 N	13.55 E
Volubilis ⊥	148	34.00 N	5.30 W
Voluntown	207	41.34 N	71.52 W
Volusia □6	220	28.51 N	81.05 W
Vólvi, Límni ⊜	38	40.41 N	23.23 E
Volx	62	43.53 N	5.51 E
Volyncy, Bela.	76	55.42 N	28.11 E
Volyncy, Ross.	80	57.48 N	45.28 E
Volyně	60	49.10 N	13.53 E
Volynka	78	51.37 N	32.26 E
Volyňka ≃	60	49.16 N	13.54 E
Volynskaja Oblast' □8	78	51.00 N	25.00 E
Volynskaja vozvyšennost' ⋀1	78	50.30 N	25.30 E
Volzhskiy → Volžskij	80	48.50 N	44.44 E
Volžsk	80	55.53 N	48.21 E
Volžskij, Ross.	80	53.27 N	50.07 E
Volžskij, Ross.	80	48.50 N	44.44 E
Vom	150	9.41 N	8.42 E
Vomano ≃	66	42.39 N	14.02 E
Vombsjön ⊜	41	55.41 N	13.36 E
Vomp	64	47.20 N	11.41 E
Vonavona Island I	175e	8.15 S	157.05 E
Vonda	184	52.19 N	106.06 W
Vondanka	24	59.07 N	47.49 E
Vondrozo	157b	22.49 S	47.20 E
Von Frank Mountain ∧	180	63.33 N	154.20 W
Võnnu	76	58.17 N	27.05 E
Vonozero	76	60.22 N	34.26 E
Vonsild	41	55.31 N	9.29 E
Von Treuer Tableland ⋀1	162	26.38 S	122.53 E
Voorburg	52	52.05 N	4.23 E
Voordeelspan	158	29.05 S	21.32 E
Voorheesville	210	42.39 N	73.56 W
Voorne I	52	51.55 N	4.00 E
Voorschoten	52	52.07 N	4.27 E
Voorst	52	52.10 N	6.09 E
Voorthuizen	52	52.11 N	5.35 E
Vop' ≃	76	54.56 N	32.44 E
Vopnafjördur	24a	65.47 N	14.44 W
Vopnafjördur C	24a	65.52 N	14.40 W
Vörå (Vöyri)	26	63.09 N	22.15 E
Vor'a ≃, Ross.	76	54.54 N	35.01 E
Vor'a ≃, Ross.	82	55.52 N	38.13 E
Vorarlberg □3	64	47.15 N	9.55 E
Vorau	61	47.25 N	15.54 E
Vorbach	60	49.49 N	11.45 E
Vorbasse	41	55.38 N	9.05 E
Vorbjovo	88	57.23 N	102.18 E
Vorchdorf	60	48.00 N	13.55 E
Vörden, Dtsch.	52	52.28 N	8.05 E
Vorden, Ned.	52	52.07 N	6.18 E
Vorder-Grauspitz ∧	58	47.03 N	9.36 E
Vorderkrimmi	64	47.14 N	12.12 E
Vordernberg	61	47.28 N	15.00 E
Vorderrhein ≃	58	46.49 N	9.25 E
Vorderriss	64	47.33 N	11.26 E
Vordingborg	41	55.01 N	11.55 E
Voreifel ⋀	56	50.15 N	7.10 E
Voreppe	62	45.18 N	5.38 E
Vorey	62	45.11 N	3.54 E
Vorga	76	53.45 N	32.45 E
Vorhalle ✦8	263	51.23 N	7.28 E
Vorhelm	52	51.48 N	7.56 E
Voríai Sporádhes II	38	39.17 N	23.23 E
Vøringsfossen ⌊	26	60.26 N	7.15 E
Vórios Evvoïkós Kólpos C	38	38.40 N	23.15 E
Vorkuta	24	67.27 N	63.58 E
Vorlich, Ben ∧	46	56.20 N	4.14 W
Vorma ≃	26	60.09 N	11.27 E
Vormholz	263	51.24 N	7.18 E
Vormsi I	76	59.00 N	23.20 E
Vorn'any	76	54.44 N	26.01 E
Vorobjevo, Ross.	82	56.11 N	35.45 E
Vorobjevo, Ross.	86	56.08 N	76.32 E
Vorobji	82	55.09 N	36.48 E
Vorobjovka	80	50.38 N	40.56 E
Vorob'jovo, Ross.	76	59.38 N	40.55 E
Vorob'jovo, Ukr.	78	45.20 N	33.15 E
Vorochta	78	48.18 N	24.36 E
Voron'	76	55.00 N	28.39 E
Voron, porog ⌊	88	57.05 N	98.40 E
Vorona ≃	80	51.22 N	42.03 E
Voroncovka, Kaz.	86	48.49 N	81.32 E
Voroncovka, Ross.	78	50.37 N	40.21 E
Voroncovka, Ross.	86	59.39 N	60.14 E
Voroncovka, Ross.	88	58.51 N	112.56 E
Voroncovka, Ukr.	78	45.51 N	33.47 E
Voroncovo, Ross.	76	57.18 N	28.42 E
Voroncovo, Ross.	80	55.16 N	40.27 E
Voronej → Voronež	78	51.40 N	39.10 E
Voronež, Ross.	78	51.40 N	39.10 E
Voronež, Ukr.	78	51.46 N	33.28 E
Voronež □8, Ross.	76	51.55 N	40.00 E
Voronež □8, Ross.	83	49.40 N	40.00 E
Voronež ≃	76	51.56 N	39.25 E
Voronezh → Voronež	78	51.40 N	39.10 E
Voronežskij Zapovednik ✦4	76	51.56 N	39.37 E
Voronino	82	56.24 N	36.52 E
Voronja ≃	24	69.10 N	35.50 E
Voronjo, Ross.	24	68.27 N	35.21 E
Voronjo, Ross.	80	58.00 N	42.01 E
Voronki, Ross.	82	55.48 N	37.16 E
Voron'ki, Ukr.	78	50.14 N	33.02 E
Voronkovo	78	47.43 N	29.08 E
Voronok	76	52.23 N	32.40 E
Voronov, mys ≻	76	60.15 N	32.05 E
Voronovica	78	49.06 N	28.41 E
Voronovkova Niva	76	57.04 N	29.16 E
Voronovo, Bela.	76	54.09 N	25.19 E
Voronovo, Ross.	82	55.19 N	37.10 E
Voronovo, Ross.	86	56.01 N	83.52 E
Voropajevo	76	55.09 N	27.13 E
Voroshilovsk → Kommunarsk	83	48.30 N	38.47 E
Voroshilovsk → Stavropol'	72	45.02 N	41.59 E
Voroshilov → Ussurijsk	89	43.48 N	131.59 E
Vorošilovgrad → Lugansk	83	48.34 N	39.20 E
Vorotajevka	80	51.56 N	47.16 E
Vorotynec	80	56.04 N	45.52 E
Vorotynsk	82	54.25 N	36.05 E
Vorovskolesskaja	84	44.23 N	42.25 E
Vorožba	78	51.12 N	34.14 E
Vorožejka	86	58.12 N	90.02 E
Vorpommern □9	54	53.40 N	13.45 E
Vorra	60	49.33 N	11.30 E
Vorsfelde	54	52.26 N	10.49 E
Vorskla ≃	78	48.53 N	34.06 E
Vorsma	80	55.59 N	43.16 E
Vorst, Bel.	56	51.04 N	5.01 E
Vorst, Dtsch.	56	51.18 N	6.25 E
Vørterkaka Nunatak ∧	9	72.20 S	27.29 E
Võrtsjärv ⊜	76	58.16 N	26.03 E
Võru	76	57.50 N	27.01 E
Voruch	85	39.52 N	70.35 E
Vorzel'	78	50.33 N	30.09 E
Vosburg	158	30.33 S	22.52 E
Voschod	80	47.24 N	41.50 E
Vösendorf	61	48.07 N	16.20 E
Vosges □5	58	48.10 N	6.20 E
Vosges ⋀	58	48.30 N	7.10 E
Vosja	76	59.01 N	41.11 E
Voskresenka, Ross.	80	51.01 N	46.28 E
Voskresenka, Ross.	88	53.15 N	119.31 E
Voskresenki	82	54.57 N	38.04 E
Voskresenovskoje	265a	59.43 N	30.47 E
Voskresensk	82	55.19 N	38.42 E
Voskresenskoje, Ross.	76	53.12 N	38.43 E
Voskresenskoje, Ross.	76	58.54 N	38.36 E
Voskresenskoje, Ross.	76	59.26 N	37.56 E
Voskresenskoje, Ross.	76	57.49 N	37.40 E
Voskresenskoje, Ross.	80	56.51 N	45.26 E
Voskresenskoje, Ross.	80	51.51 N	46.56 E
Voskresenskoje, Ross.	82	54.07 N	37.07 E
Voskresenskoje, Ross.	82	56.20 N	38.29 E
Voskresenskoje, Ross.	86	53.08 N	56.10 E
Voskresenskoje, Ukr.	78	47.02 N	32.09 E
Voslapp	52	53.36 N	8.05 E
Voss	26	60.39 N	6.26 E
Vosselaar	56	51.19 N	4.53 E
Vossijatskoje	78	47.41 N	32.07 E
Vossman's Beacon	158	26.11 S	30.40 E
Vostočnaja Kambal'nica	24	68.18 N	46.00 E
Vostočno-Kazachstanskaja Oblast' □8	86	49.00 N	84.00 E
Vostočno-Kounradskij	86	47.02 N	75.07 E
Vostočno-Sibirskoje more (East Siberian Sea) ≂2	12	74.00 N	166.00 E
Vostočnyj, Ross.	82	55.47 N	37.52 E
Vostočnyj, Ross.	86	58.48 N	61.52 E
Vostočnyj, Ross.	89	53.29 N	143.03 E
Vostočnyj, Ross.	89	48.17 N	142.34 E
Vostočnyj Sajan ⋀	88	53.00 N	97.00 E
Vostok I	14	10.06 S	152.23 W
Vostok ✦3	9	78.30 S	106.50 E
Vostr'akovo	82	55.23 N	37.49 E
Vostrecovo	89	45.53 N	134.58 E
Vostrovo	86	52.09 N	80.38 E
Vosves	261	48.31 N	2.36 E
Votaw	222	30.26 N	94.41 W
Votice	30	49.38 N	14.39 E
Votkinsk	80	57.03 N	53.59 E
Votkinskoje vodochranilišče ⊜1	86	57.00 N	54.30 E
Vot'pa	86	60.13 N	62.57 E
Votuporanga	255	20.24 S	49.59 W
Voué	50	48.28 N	4.07 E
Vouga ≃	34	40.41 N	8.40 W
Vougba	152	5.10 N	23.06 E
Vougeot	58	47.10 N	4.58 E
Vouillé	32	46.39 N	0.10 E
Voujeaucourt	58	47.28 N	6.46 E
Voulangis	261	48.51 N	2.54 E
Voulou	146	8.33 N	22.36 E

Symbols in the index entries represent the broad categories identified in the key at the right. Symbols with superior numbers (⋀1) identify subcategories (see complete key on page I · 1).

Symbole im Register stellen die rechts im Schlüssel erklärten Kategorien dar. Symbole mit hochgestellten Ziffern (⋀1) bezeichnen Unterabteilungen einer Kategorie (vgl. vollständiger Schlüssel auf Seite I · 1).

Los símbolos incluidos en el texto del índice representan las grandes categorías identificadas con la clave a la derecha. Los símbolos con números en su parte superior (⋀1) identifican las subcategorías (véase la clave completa en la página I · 1).

Les symboles de l'index représentent les catégories indiquées dans la légende à droite. Les symboles suivis d'un indice (⋀1) représentent des sous-catégories (voir légende complète à la page I · 1).

Os símbolos incluídos no texto do índice representam as grandes categorias identificadas com a chave à direita. Os símbolos com números em sua parte superior (⋀1) identificam as subcategorias (veja-se a chave completa à página I · 1).

∧ Mountain	Berg	Montaña	Montagne	Montanha
⋀ Mountains	Gebirge	Montañas	Montagnes	Montanhas
)(Pass	Paß	Paso	Col	Passo
V Valley, Canyon	Tal, Cañon	Valle, Cañón	Vallée, Canyon	Vale, Canhão
≃ Plain	Ebene	Llano	Plaine	Planície
≻ Cape	Kap	Cabo	Cap	Cabo
I Island	Insel	Isla	Île	Ilha
II Islands	Inseln	Islas	Îles	Ilhas
⊥ Other Topographic Features	Andere Topographische Objekte	Otros Elementos Topográficos	Autres données topographiques	Outros acidentes topográficos

ESPAÑOL	FRANÇAIS	PORTUGUÊS
Nombre / Página / Lat.°' / Long.°' W=Oeste	Nom / Page / Lat.°' / Long.°' W=Ouest	Nome / Página / Lat.°' / Long.°' W=Oeste

Leyenda de símbolos

Símbolo	English	Deutsch	Español	Français	Português
≈	River	Fluß	Río	Rivière	Rio
↳	Canal	Kanal	Canal	Canal	Canal
ᴌ	Waterfall, Rapids	Wasserfall, Stromschnellen	Cascada, Rápidos	Chute d'eau, Rapides	Cascata, Rápidos
≍	Strait	Meeresstraße	Estrecho	Détroit	Estreito
ᴄ	Bay, Gulf	Bucht, Golf	Bahía, Golfo	Baie, Golfe	Baía, Golfo
⊘	Lake, Lakes	See, Seen	Lago, Lagos	Lac, Lacs	Lago, Lagos
⊤	Swamp	Sumpf	Pantano	Marais	Pântano
⊠	Ice Features, Glacier	Eis- und Gletscherformen	Accidentes Glaciales	Formes glaciaires	Formes glaciaires
◇	Other Hydrographic Features	Andere Hydrographische Objekte	Otros Elementos Hidrográficos	Autres données hydrographiques	Outros dados hidrográficos
✦	Submarine Features	Untermeerische Objekte	Accidentes Submarinos	Formes de relief sous-marin	Acidentes submarinos
□	Political Unit	Politische Einheit	Unidad Politica	Entité politique	Unidade política
♰	Cultural Institution	Kulturelle Institution	Institución Cultural	Institution culturelle	Instituição cultural
⌂	Historical Site	Historische Stätte	Sitio Histórico	Site historique	Sitio histórico
⛺	Recreational Site	Erholungs- und Ferienort	Sitio de Recreo	Centre de loisirs	Area de Lazer
✈	Airport	Flughafen	Aeropuerto	Aéroport	Aeroporto
⚔	Military Installation	Militäranlage	Instalación Militar	Installation militaire	Instalação militar
●	Miscellaneous	Verschiedenes	Misceláneo	Divers	Diversos

ESPAÑOL / FRANÇAIS / PORTUGUÊS

Nombre / Nom / Nome	Página / Page / Página	Lat.°′	Long.°′ W = Oeste / W = Ouest / W = Oeste
Waterlooville	42	50.53 N	1.02 W
Waterman, Il., U.S.	216	41.46 N	88.46 W
Waterman, Wa., U.S.	224	47.34 N	122.35 W
Waterman Mountain ∧	228	34.20 N	117.56 W
Waterman Wash ∨	200	33.21 N	112.31 W
Water Mill	207	40.55 N	72.21 W
Waterport	210	43.20 N	78.16 W
Waterport Pond ⊜[1]	212	43.19 N	78.16 W
Waterproof	194	31.48 N	91.23 W
Waterside	214	40.11 N	78.23 W
Waterside Park	276	40.56 N	73.20 W
Watersmeet	190	46.16 N	89.10 W
Waterton ≃	182	49.32 N	113.16 W
Waterton-Glacier International Peace Park ♠	202	48.47 N	113.45 W
Waterton Lakes National Park ♠	182	49.05 N	113.50 W
Watertown, Ct., U.S.	207	41.36 N	73.07 W
Watertown, Ma., U.S.	207	42.22 N	71.11 W
Watertown, N.Y., U.S.	212	43.58 N	75.54 W
Watertown, S.D., U.S.	198	44.53 N	97.06 W
Watertown, Wi., U.S.	216	43.11 N	88.43 W
Waterval-Boven	156	25.40 S	30.20 E
Watervale	168b	33.57 S	138.38 E
Water Valley, Ms., U.S.	194	34.09 N	89.37 W
Water Valley, N.Y., U.S.	284a	42.42 N	78.51 W
Water View	208	37.43 N	76.36 W
Waterville, N.S., Can.	186	45.03 N	64.41 W
Waterville, P.Q., Can.	206	45.16 N	71.54 W
Waterville, Ire.	48	51.49 N	10.13 W
Waterville, Ks., U.S.	198	39.41 N	96.44 W
Waterville, Me., U.S.	188	44.33 N	69.37 W
Waterville, Ma., U.S.	207	42.40 N	72.04 W
Waterville, Mn., U.S.	190	44.13 N	93.34 W
Waterville, N.Y., U.S.	210	42.55 N	75.22 W
Waterville, Oh., U.S.	216	41.30 N	83.43 W
Waterville, Pa., U.S.	210	41.19 N	77.22 W
Waterville, Wa., U.S.	202	47.38 N	120.04 W
Watervliet, Mi., U.S.	216	42.11 N	86.15 W
Watervliet, N.Y., U.S.	210	42.43 N	73.42 W
Watervliet Reservoir ⊜[1]	210	42.43 N	73.58 W
Wates, Indon.	114	1.00 N	100.16 E
Wates, Indon.	115a	7.55 S	112.07 E
Wates, Indon.	115a	7.51 S	110.10 E
Watford, On., Can.	214	42.57 N	81.53 W
Watford, Eng., U.K.	42	51.40 N	0.25 W
Watford □[8]	260	51.40 N	0.25 W
Watford City	198	47.48 N	103.16 W
Wa'th	140	8.10 N	32.07 E
Wathaman ≃	184	57.16 N	102.52 W
Wathaman Lake ⊜	184	56.55 N	103.43 W
Wathena	198	39.45 N	94.56 W
Watheroo	162	30.17 S	116.04 E
Watheroo National Park ♠	162	30.14 S	115.52 E
Wathlingen	52	52.32 N	10.09 E
Wath upon Dearne	44	53.29 N	1.20 W
Wati	120	28.02 N	96.59 E
Watino	182	55.43 N	117.37 W
Watkins Glen	210	42.22 N	76.52 W
Watkins Glen International Raceway ♠	210	42.20 N	76.55 W
Watkins Glen State Park ♠	210	42.22 N	76.55 W
Watkins Island I	284c	39.02 N	77.17 W
Watkins Lake ⊜	281	42.40 N	83.22 W
Watkinsville	192	33.51 N	83.24 W
Watlaar	164	5.28 S	133.07 E
Watling Island → San Salvador I	238	24.02 N	74.28 W
Watlington	42	51.37 N	1.00 W
Watoga State Park ♠	188	38.07 N	80.05 W
Watonga	196	35.50 N	98.24 W
Watonwan ≃	198	44.04 N	94.07 W
Watopeka ≃	206	45.34 N	72.00 W
Watou	50	50.51 N	2.37 E
Wat Phai Tan, Khlong ≊	269a	13.48 N	100.33 E
Watrous, Sk., Can.	184	51.40 N	105.28 W
Watrous, N.M., U.S.	200	35.47 N	104.58 W
Watsa	154	3.03 N	29.32 E
Watseka	216	40.46 N	87.44 W
Watsi Kengo	152	0.48 S	20.33 E
Watson, Austl.	162	30.29 S	131.31 E
Watson, Sk., Can.	184	52.07 N	104.31 W
Watson, In., U.S.	218	38.22 N	85.41 W
Watsonia	274b	37.43 S	145.05 E
Watson Lake	180	60.07 N	128.48 W
Watsons Bay	274a	33.51 S	151.17 E
Watsons Creek	274b	37.40 S	145.13 E
Watsons Creek ≃	274b	37.43 S	145.16 E
Watsontown	210	41.05 N	76.51 W
Watsonville	226	36.54 N	121.45 W
Watt	222	31.39 N	96.51 W
Watten	50	50.50 N	2.13 E
Watten, Loch ⊜	46	58.29 N	3.19 W
Wattens	64	47.17 N	11.36 E
Wattenscheid	56	51.29 N	7.08 E
Wattenwil	58	46.46 N	7.30 E
Wattignies	50	50.35 N	3.03 E
Wattiwarriganna ≃	162	28.57 S	136.10 E
Wattle Flat	170	33.08 S	149.41 E
Wattle Glen	274b	37.40 S	145.11 E
Wattle Park ♠	274b	37.50 S	145.07 E
Watt Mountain ∧	240d	15.19 N	61.19 W
Watton	42	52.35 N	0.48 E
Wattrelos	50	50.42 N	3.13 E
Watts ◆[8]	280	33.56 N	118.15 W
Watts Bar Lake ⊜[1]	192	35.48 N	84.39 W
Watts Branch ≃	284c	39.03 N	77.15 W
Wattsburg	214	42.00 N	79.49 W
Watts Island I	208	37.48 N	75.53 W
Watts Mills	192	34.31 N	82.02 W
Wattville	273d	26.13 S	28.18 E
Wattwil	58	47.18 N	9.06 E
Watu	152	3.18 S	20.03 E
Watubela, Kepulauan II	164	4.35 S	131.40 E
Wat Wat	164	4.29 S	152.21 E
Watzekopf ∧	58	46.59 N	10.48 E
Watzmann ∧	64	47.33 N	12.55 E
Wau	164	7.20 S	146.45 E
Waubach	56	50.55 N	6.03 E
Waubaushene	212	44.45 N	79.42 W
Waubaushene Channel ⋓	212	44.46 N	79.45 W
Waubay	198	45.19 N	97.18 W
Waubay Lake ⊜	198	45.25 N	97.25 W
Waubesa, Lake ⊜	216	43.01 N	89.20 W
Waubra	169	37.21 S	143.39 E
Waubuno Creek ≃	212	42.58 N	81.08 W
Wauchope, Austl.	162	20.36 S	134.15 E
Wauchope, Austl.	166	31.27 S	152.44 E
Wauchula	220	27.32 N	81.48 W
Wauconda, Il., U.S.	216	42.15 N	88.08 W
Wauconda, Wa., U.S.	182	48.43 N	119.00 W
Wauconda, Wa., U.S.	202	48.43 N	119.00 W
Waugh	184	49.40 N	95.13 W
Waugh Mountain ∧	202	45.29 N	114.47 W
Waukara, Bukit ∧	112	1.15 S	119.42 E
Waukaringa	166	32.18 S	139.26 E
Waukarlycarly, Lake ⊜	162	21.25 S	121.50 E
Waukegan	216	42.21 N	87.50 W
Waukena	226	36.08 N	119.31 W
Waukesha	216	43.00 N	88.13 W
Waukesha □[6]	216	43.02 N	88.20 W
Waukomis	196	36.16 N	97.53 W
Waukon	190	43.16 N	91.28 W
Waulsort	56	50.13 N	4.52 E
Wauna	224	47.22 N	122.38 W
Waunakee	216	43.11 N	89.27 W
Wauneta	198	40.25 N	101.22 W
Waupaca	190	44.21 N	89.05 W
Waupecan Creek ≃	216	41.20 N	88.28 W
Waupoos Island I	212	43.59 N	76.58 W
Waupun	190	43.38 N	88.43 W
Wauregan	207	41.44 N	71.54 W
Waurika	196	34.10 N	97.59 W
Waurika Lake ⊜[1]	196	34.15 N	98.05 W
Wausa	198	42.29 N	97.32 W
Wausau	190	44.57 N	89.37 W
Wausaukee	190	45.22 N	87.57 W
Wauseon	216	41.32 N	84.08 W
Waushakum Pond ⊜	283	42.16 N	71.26 W
Wautoma	190	44.04 N	89.17 W
Wauwa	154	3.27 N	27.21 E
Wauwatosa	216	43.02 N	88.00 W
Wauzeka	190	43.05 N	90.52 W
Wave Hill	162	17.29 S	130.57 E
Waveland, Ma., U.S.	283	42.17 N	70.53 W
Waveland, Ms., U.S.	194	30.17 N	89.22 W
Waveney ≃	42	52.28 N	1.45 E
Waver ≃	44	54.52 N	3.17 W
Waverley, Austl.	169	37.53 S	145.10 E
Waverley, Austl.	274a	33.54 S	151.16 E
Waverley, N.Z.	172	39.46 S	174.38 E
Waverley, S. Afr.	158	31.58 S	26.28 E
Waverley, Ma., U.S.	283	42.23 N	71.11 W
Waverley ◆[8]	273d	26.08 S	28.04 E
Waverly, Al., U.S.	194	32.44 N	85.35 W
Waverly, Fl., U.S.	220	27.59 N	81.37 W
Waverly, Il., U.S.	219	39.35 N	89.57 W
Waverly, Ia., U.S.	190	42.43 N	92.28 W
Waverly, Ks., U.S.	198	38.23 N	95.36 W
Waverly, Mi., U.S.	216	42.44 N	84.33 W
Waverly, Mn., U.S.	190	45.04 N	93.57 W
Waverly, Mo., U.S.	194	39.12 N	93.31 W
Waverly, Ne., U.S.	198	40.55 N	96.31 W
Waverly, N.Y., U.S.	210	42.00 N	76.31 W
Waverly, Oh., U.S.	218	39.07 N	82.59 W
Waverly, Pa., U.S.	210	41.32 N	75.42 W
Waverly, Tn., U.S.	194	36.05 N	87.47 W
Waverly, Va., U.S.	208	37.02 N	77.05 W
Waverly Hall	192	32.41 N	84.44 W
Wavre	56	50.43 N	4.37 E
Wavrin	50	50.34 N	2.55 E
Wāw	140	7.42 N	28.00 E
Wāw ≃	140	7.03 N	27.13 E
Wawa, On., Can.	190	47.59 N	84.47 W
Wawa, Nig.	150	9.55 N	4.25 E
Wawa, Sūd.	140	20.26 N	30.21 E
Wawa ≃	236	13.53 N	83.28 W
Wawaka	216	41.27 N	85.28 W
Wāw al-Kabīr	146	25.20 N	16.43 E
Wawanesa	184	49.36 N	99.41 W
Wawarsing	210	41.46 N	74.21 W
Wawasee, Lake ⊜	216	41.24 N	85.41 W
Wawayanda State Park ♠	276	41.11 N	74.26 W
Wawiag ≃	190	48.25 N	91.07 W
Wawoi ≃	164	8.01 S	143.33 E
Waworada, Teluk c	115b	8.44 S	118.51 E
Wawota	184	49.55 N	102.00 W
Waxahachie	222	32.23 N	96.50 W
Waxahachie, Lake ⊜[1]	222	32.20 N	96.49 W
Waxhaw	192	34.55 N	80.44 W
Waxuecun	106	31.07 N	121.38 E
Waxweiler	56	50.05 N	6.22 E
Way, Lake ⊜	162	26.48 S	120.18 E
Waya I	175g	17.18 S	177.08 E
Wayabula	108	2.17 N	128.12 E
Wayaopu	106	30.33 N	118.53 E
Waycross	192	31.12 N	82.21 W
Wayi	154	5.11 N	30.10 E
Wayland, Ia., U.S.	190	41.08 N	91.39 W
Wayland, Ky., U.S.	192	37.26 N	82.48 W
Wayland, Ma., U.S.	283	42.21 N	71.21 W
Wayland, Mi., U.S.	216	42.40 N	85.38 W
Wayland, N.Y., U.S.	210	42.34 N	77.35 W
Wayland, Oh., U.S.	214	41.10 N	81.04 W
Waylyn	192	32.51 N	79.59 W
Waymansville	218	39.04 N	86.03 W
Waymart	210	41.34 N	75.24 W
Wayne, Ab., Can.	182	51.23 N	112.39 W
Wayne, Mi., U.S.	216	42.16 N	83.23 W
Wayne, Ne., U.S.	198	42.13 N	97.01 W
Wayne, N.J., U.S.	210	40.55 N	74.16 W
Wayne, N.Y., U.S.	210	42.28 N	77.06 W
Wayne, Oh., U.S.	214	41.18 N	83.28 W
Wayne, Ok., U.S.	196	34.55 N	97.18 W
Wayne, Pa., U.S.	208	40.02 N	75.23 W
Wayne, W.V., U.S.	188	38.13 N	82.26 W
Wayne □[6], Il., U.S.	219	38.25 N	88.40 W
Wayne □[6], In., U.S.	218	39.50 N	84.54 W
Wayne □[6], Mi., U.S.	216	42.14 N	83.12 W
Wayne □[6], N.Y., U.S.	210	43.04 N	77.00 W
Wayne □[6], Oh., U.S.	214	40.48 N	81.56 W
Wayne □[6], Pa., U.S.	210	41.34 N	75.16 W
Wayne City	194	38.20 N	88.35 W
Wayne Lakes	218	40.01 N	84.39 W
Waynesboro, Ga., U.S.	192	33.05 N	82.00 W
Waynesboro, Ms., U.S.	194	31.40 N	88.38 W
Waynesboro, Pa., U.S.	208	39.45 N	77.34 W
Waynesboro, Tn., U.S.	194	35.19 N	87.45 W
Waynesboro, Va., U.S.	192	38.04 N	78.53 W
Waynesburg, Oh., U.S.	214	40.40 N	81.15 W
Waynesburg, Pa., U.S.	188	39.53 N	80.10 W
Waynesfield	216	40.36 N	83.59 W
Wayne State University ⊍[2]	281	42.21 N	83.04 W
Waynesville, Il., U.S.	194	40.15 N	89.08 W
Waynesville, Mo., U.S.	194	37.49 N	92.12 W
Waynesville, N.C., U.S.	192	35.29 N	82.59 W
Waynesville, Oh., U.S.	218	39.32 N	84.05 W
Waynoka	196	36.34 N	98.52 W
Waynoka, Lake ⊜[1]	218	38.55 N	83.47 W
Wayoh Reservoir ⊜[1]	262	53.39 N	2.24 W
Waza	146	11.25 N	14.34 E
Waza, Parc National de ♠	146	11.20 N	13.40 E
Wazah	120	33.22 N	69.26 E
Wāzah Khwāh	120	32.12 N	68.21 E
Waziers	50	50.23 N	3.07 E
Wāzin	146	31.57 N	10.40 E
Wazīrābād	123	32.27 N	74.07 E
Wazīrābād ◆[8]	272a	28.43 N	77.14 E
Wāzīrpur ◆[8]	272a	28.41 N	77.10 E
Wazuka	96	34.47 N	135.55 E
Wazuka ≃	270	34.45 N	135.53 E
Wda ≃	30	53.25 N	18.29 E
We, Pulau I	114	5.51 N	95.18 E
Wea Creek ≃	216	40.24 N	86.57 W
Weagamow Lake ⊜	184	52.53 N	91.22 W
Weald Park ♠	260	51.38 N	0.14 E
Wealdstone ◆[8]	260	51.36 N	0.20 W
Weam	164	8.40 S	141.08 E
Wear ≃	44	54.55 N	1.22 W
Wearhead	44	54.45 N	2.13 W
Wearyan ≃	164	15.57 S	136.51 E
Weatherford, Ok., U.S.	196	35.31 N	98.42 W
Weatherford, Tx., U.S.	222	32.45 N	97.47 W
Weatherford, Lake ⊜[1]	222	32.47 N	97.41 W
Weatherly	210	40.56 N	75.50 W
Weatogue	207	41.51 N	72.49 W
Weaubleau	194	37.53 N	93.32 W
Weaver, Austl.	168b	34.56 S	137.40 E
Weaver, Al., U.S.	194	33.45 N	85.48 W
Weaver, Tx., U.S.	222	33.10 N	95.25 W
Weaver ≃	44	53.19 N	2.44 W
Weaver ≊	262	53.19 N	2.45 W
Weaverham	44	53.16 N	2.35 W
Weaver Lake ⊜	184	52.45 N	96.35 W
Weavertown	279b	40.16 N	80.11 W
Weaverville, Ca., U.S.	204	40.43 N	122.56 W
Weaverville, N.C., U.S.	192	35.41 N	82.33 W
Webau	54	51.10 N	12.04 E
Webb, Sk., Can.	184	50.11 N	108.12 W
Webb, Ms., U.S.	194	33.56 N	90.20 W
Webb Brook ≃	283	42.32 N	71.14 W
Webb City	194	37.08 N	94.27 W
Webber Lake ⊜	184	54.28 N	94.00 W
Webberville	216	42.40 N	84.10 W
Webbwood	190	46.16 N	81.53 W
Weber ≃	200	41.13 N	112.16 W
Weber, Mount ∧	182	55.32 N	128.31 W
Weber City	192	36.37 N	82.33 W
Weber Creek ≃	226	38.46 N	121.00 W
Weber Hill	219	38.27 N	90.34 W
Weberi Bekera	144	9.39 N	39.03 E
Webster, Ab., Can.	182	55.26 N	118.42 W
Webster, Fl., U.S.	220	28.36 N	82.03 W
Webster, In., U.S.	218	39.54 N	84.57 W
Webster, Ma., U.S.	207	42.03 N	71.52 W
Webster, N.Y., U.S.	210	43.12 N	77.25 W
Webster, Pa., U.S.	214	40.11 N	79.50 W
Webster, S.D., U.S.	198	45.19 N	97.31 W
Webster, Wi., U.S.	190	45.52 N	92.22 W
Webster City	190	42.28 N	93.48 W
Webster Crossing	210	42.40 N	77.38 W
Webster Groves	219	38.35 N	90.21 W
Webster Lake ⊜	216	41.19 N	85.41 W
Websters Corners, B.C., Can.	224	49.13 N	122.30 W
Websters Corners, N.Y., U.S.	284a	41.47 N	78.45 W
Webster Springs	188	38.28 N	80.24 W
Weches	222	31.33 N	95.14 W
Wechmar	54	50.53 N	10.47 E
Wechselburg	54	51.00 N	12.47 E
Weda	108	0.21 N	127.52 E
Wedau ◆[8]	263	51.24 N	6.48 E
Wedau, Sportpark ♠	263	51.25 N	6.47 E
Weddell Island I	254	51.55 S	61.00 W
Weddell Sea ⊤[2]	9	72.00 S	45.00 W
Wedderburn	166	36.25 S	143.37 E
Wedding ◆[8]	264a	52.33 N	13.22 E
Weddinghofen	263	51.36 N	7.37 E
Wedel	52	53.35 N	9.41 E
Wedemark	52	52.33 N	9.44 E
Wedge, Central Mount ∧	162	22.51 S	131.50 E
Wedge Mountain ∧	182	50.10 N	122.50 W
Wedgeport	186	43.44 N	65.59 W
Wedgewood	219	38.47 N	90.17 W
Wedmore	42	51.14 N	2.49 W
Wedowee	194	33.18 N	85.29 W
Wedron	216	41.26 N	88.46 W
Weduar, Tanjung ›	164	6.00 S	132.50 E
Wedweil	140	9.00 N	27.12 E
Wedza	154	18.35 S	31.35 E
Weebo	162	28.01 S	121.03 E
Weed	204	41.25 N	122.23 W
Weed Heights	226	38.59 N	119.12 W
Weedon	206	45.42 N	71.28 W
Weedon Beck	42	52.14 N	1.05 W
Weedon Island I	220	27.51 N	82.36 W
Weed Patch	228	35.19 N	118.55 W
Weed Patch Hill ∧[2]	218	39.10 N	86.13 W
Weedsport	210	43.02 N	76.33 W
Weedville	214	41.17 N	78.30 W
Weehawken	276	40.46 N	74.01 W
Weeim, Pulau I	164	1.29 S	130.14 E
Wee Jasper	171b	35.09 S	148.41 E
Weekapauq	207	41.20 N	71.45 W
Weeki Wachee Spring ♠	220	28.32 N	82.35 W
Weeki Wachee Swamp ☷	220	28.31 N	82.37 W
Weeks Point ›	276	40.53 N	73.39 W
Weekstown	208	39.35 N	74.36 W
Weelde	56	51.25 N	5.00 E
Weeley	42	51.51 N	1.07 E
Weel Shimbirro	144	2.23 N	44.16 E
Weems	208	37.39 N	76.26 W
Weende	52	51.33 N	9.55 E
Weenen	158	28.57 S	30.03 E
Weener	52	53.10 N	7.21 E
Weeney Bay c	274a	34.01 S	151.10 E
Weeping Water	198	40.52 N	96.08 W
Weequahic Lake ⊜	276	40.42 N	74.12 W
Weert	52	51.15 N	5.43 E
Weesatche	222	28.51 N	97.27 W
Weesby	41	54.50 N	9.08 E
Weesow	264a	52.39 N	13.43 E
Weesp	52	52.17 N	5.02 E
Weetfeld ◆[8]	263	51.38 N	7.49 E
Weethalle	166	33.53 S	146.38 E
Weeting	42	52.27 N	0.37 E
Weeton	262	53.48 N	2.56 W
Weetulta	168b	34.15 S	137.38 E
Wee Waa	166	30.14 S	149.26 E
Weeze	52	51.37 N	6.12 E
Wefensleben	54	52.11 N	11.09 E
Weferlingen	54	52.19 N	11.02 E
Wegberg	56	51.08 N	6.16 E
Wegdraai	158	28.50 S	21.52 E
Wegeleben	54	51.53 N	11.10 E
Wegendorf	264a	52.36 N	13.45 E
Wegenstedt	54	52.23 N	11.11 E
Wegeringhausen	56	51.02 N	7.45 E
Weggis	58	47.02 N	8.26 E
Węgliniec	30	51.17 N	15.13 E
Węgorzewo	30	54.14 N	21.44 E
Węgorzyno	30	53.32 N	15.33 E
Węgrów	30	52.25 N	22.01 E
Wegscheid	60	48.36 N	13.48 E
Wehdel	52	53.30 N	8.48 E
Wehebach Stausee ⊜[1]	56	50.45 N	6.20 E
Wehingen	58	48.08 N	8.47 E
Wehofen ◆[8]	263	51.32 N	6.46 E
Wehr	58	47.37 N	7.54 E
Wehringhausen ◆[8]	263	51.21 N	7.27 E
Wehrsdorf	54	51.03 N	14.22 E
Wei ≃, Zhg.	98	37.05 N	119.28 E
Wei ≃, Zhg.	98	36.51 N	115.43 E
Wei ≃, Zhg.	102	34.30 N	110.20 E
Weichang (Zhuizishan)	98	42.00 N	117.32 E
Weichselboden	61	47.40 N	15.10 E
Weichsel → Wisła ≃	30	54.22 N	18.55 E
Weichuan	98	34.17 N	113.58 E
Weicun	106	31.59 N	119.55 E
Weida	54	50.45 N	12.04 E
Weida ≃	54	50.47 N	12.06 E
Weiden am See	61	47.55 N	16.52 E
Weidenberg	60	49.57 N	11.43 E
Weiden in der Oberpfalz	60	49.41 N	12.10 E
Weidenstetten	56	48.33 N	9.59 E
Weiding	60	49.16 N	12.46 E
Weidling	264b	48.17 N	16.19 E
Weidlingau ◆[8]	264b	48.13 N	16.13 E
Weidlingbach	264b	48.16 N	16.15 E
Weidlingerbach ≃	264b	48.18 N	16.20 E
Weifang	98	36.42 N	119.04 E
Weigelstown	208	39.59 N	76.49 W
Weihai	98	37.28 N	122.07 E
Weihaiwei → Weihai	98	37.28 N	122.07 E
Weihmichl	60	48.36 N	12.03 E
Weihnachtsinsel → Christmas Island □[2]	112	10.30 S	105.40 E
Wei Island I	164	3.20 S	144.25 E
Weijiagou	105	40.28 N	115.08 E
Weijiatang	106	31.25 N	118.55 E
Weijiazhuang	105	39.37 N	116.22 E
Weijiazui	100	30.29 N	117.20 E
Weijingtang	106	31.27 N	120.39 E
Weikersheim	56	49.29 N	9.54 E
Weil ≃	56	50.28 N	8.16 E
Weil am Rhein	58	47.37 N	7.38 E
Weilburg	56	50.29 N	8.15 E
Weil der Stadt	56	48.45 N	8.52 E
Weiler	58	47.36 N	9.55 E
Weilerbach	56	49.29 N	7.37 E
Weilerswist	56	50.45 N	6.50 E
Weilheim	64	47.50 N	11.08 E
Weilheim an der Teck	56	48.37 N	9.32 E
Weilmoringle	166	29.15 S	146.51 E
Weilmünster	56	50.26 N	8.22 E
Weimar, Dtsch.	54	50.59 N	11.19 E
Weimar, Dtsch.	56	51.22 N	9.23 E
Weimar, Ca., U.S.	226	39.02 N	120.58 W
Weimar, Tx., U.S.	222	29.42 N	96.46 W
Weinan	102	34.29 N	109.29 E
Weinböhla	54	51.10 N	13.34 E
Weinel Cross Roads	279b	40.37 N	79.37 W
Weiner	194	35.37 N	90.53 W
Weinfelden	58	47.34 N	9.06 E
Weingarten, Dtsch.	56	49.05 N	8.31 E
Weingarten, Dtsch.	58	47.48 N	9.38 E
Weinheim	56	49.33 N	8.39 E
Weining, Zhg.	102	26.43 N	104.18 E
Weining, Zhg.	104	41.21 N	123.49 E
Weinsberg	56	49.10 N	9.17 E
Weinsberger Wald ◆[3]	61	48.30 N	14.50 E
Weinviertel ◆[1]	61	48.38 N	16.25 E
Weipa	164	12.41 S	141.52 E
Weippe	202	46.22 N	115.56 W
Weir, India	124	27.01 N	77.11 E
Weir, Ks., U.S.	198	37.18 N	94.46 W
Weir, Ms., U.S.	194	33.16 N	89.17 W
Weir ≃, Austl.	166	28.50 S	149.06 E
Weir ≃, Mb., Can.	184	56.54 N	93.21 W
Weir ≃, Ma., U.S.	283	42.16 N	70.53 W
Weir, Lake ⊜	220	29.00 N	81.57 W
Weir River	184	56.49 N	94.04 W
Weirsdale	220	28.58 N	81.55 W
Weirton	214	40.25 N	80.35 W
Weisberg → Monguelfo	64	46.45 N	12.06 E
Weisburd	252	27.18 S	62.36 W
Weisburg	218	39.13 N	85.03 W
Weischlitz	54	50.26 N	12.02 E
Weisendorf	56	49.37 N	10.49 E
Weiser	202	44.15 N	116.58 W
Weiser ≃	202	44.15 N	116.59 W
Weishan (Xiazhen), Zhg.	98	34.52 N	117.09 E
Weishan, Zhg.	100	29.20 N	120.25 E
Weishan, Zhg.	100	29.41 N	120.48 E
Weishan, Zhg.	102	25.15 N	100.20 E
Weishancheng	100	32.34 N	113.24 E
Weishanhe	104	40.47 N	123.31 E
Weishan Hu ⊜	98	34.40 N	117.15 E
Weishanzhuang	105	39.40 N	116.25 E
Weishi	98	34.25 N	114.11 E
Weismain	54	50.05 N	11.14 E
Weisner Mountain ∧	194	34.02 N	85.40 W
Weissach	56	48.50 N	8.55 E
Weissbriach	64	46.41 N	13.15 E
Weisse Elster ≃	54	51.26 N	11.57 E
Weissenbach	264b	48.05 N	16.13 E
Weissenbach am Lech	58	47.26 N	10.39 E
Weissenberg	54	51.11 N	14.40 E
Weissenborn	54	50.52 N	13.25 E
Weissenbrunn	54	50.12 N	11.20 E
Weissenburg	58	46.39 N	7.28 E
Weissenburg in Bayern	56	49.01 N	10.58 E
Weissenfels	54	51.12 N	11.58 E
Weissenhorn	58	48.18 N	10.09 E
Weissensee	54	51.11 N	11.04 E
Weissensee ◆[8]	264a	52.33 N	13.27 E
Weissensee ⊜	64	46.42 N	13.22 E
Weissenstadt	54	50.06 N	11.53 E
Weissenstein, Dtsch.	56	48.42 N	9.53 E
Weissenstein, Öst.	64	46.41 N	13.44 E
Weissenstein ∧	58	47.15 N	7.31 E
Weissenstein Tunnel ◆[5]	58	47.12 N	7.23 E
Weissenthurm	56	50.24 N	7.27 E
Weisser Main ≃	54	50.04 N	11.24 E
Weisser Nil → White Nile ≃	140	15.38 N	32.31 E
Weisser See → Beloje, ozero ⊜	76	60.11 N	37.37 E
Weisser Stein ∧	56	50.23 N	6.20 E
Weisses Meer → Beloje more ⊤[2]	24	65.30 N	38.00 E
Weisse Spitze ∧	64	46.52 N	12.21 E
Weissfluh ∧	58	46.50 N	9.48 E
Weisshorn ∧	58	46.06 N	7.42 E
Weissig	54	51.05 N	13.52 E
Weisskugel (Palla Bianca) ∧	64	46.48 N	10.44 E
Weiss Lake ⊜[1]	192	34.15 N	85.35 W
Weissmeer-Ostsee Kanal → Belomorsko-Baltijskij kanal ≊	24	62.48 N	34.48 E
Weissport	210	40.50 N	75.42 W
Weisstannen	58	46.59 N	9.21 E
Weisswasser	54	51.30 N	14.38 E
Weisweiler	56	50.50 N	6.19 E
Weitang	105	40.24 N	117.24 E
Weitang ≃	104	42.19 N	122.18 E
Weitendorf	54	53.54 N	12.16 E
Weitensfeld	61	46.51 N	14.11 E
Weiterstadt	56	49.54 N	8.35 E
Weitian	100	27.43 N	118.46 E
Weitin	54	53.34 N	13.12 E
Weiting	106	31.22 N	120.47 E
Weitmar ◆[8]	263	51.27 N	7.12 E
Weitnau	58	47.38 N	10.07 E
Weitou	100	24.34 N	118.34 E
Weitra	61	48.42 N	14.54 E
Weituo	107	30.03 N	106.08 E
Weitzgrund	54	52.11 N	12.32 E
Weiwan	98	36.43 N	115.54 E
Weixdorf	54	51.09 N	13.48 E
Weixi, Zhg.	102	27.14 N	99.12 E
Weixi, Zhg.	107	30.12 N	106.39 E
Weixian, Zhg.	98	36.57 N	115.15 E
Weixian, Zhg.	98	36.22 N	114.56 E
Weixian (Hanting), Zhg.	98	36.52 N	119.07 E
Weixin	102	27.48 N	105.06 E
Weiyuan	107	29.33 N	104.39 E
Weiyuan ≃	102	22.50 N	100.20 E
Weiyuankou	100	30.09 N	115.15 E
Weiyuanpu	98	42.39 N	124.16 E
Weiz	61	47.13 N	15.37 E
Weizhen	98	37.17 N	114.44 E
Weizhou Dao I	102	21.03 N	109.04 E
Weizhou Wan c	100	24.34 N	118.30 E
Weizhuang	105	39.02 N	115.20 E
Weizi	98	40.04 N	123.10 E
Weizigou, Zhg.	104	42.25 N	122.47 E
Weizigou, Zhg.	104	41.05 N	120.38 E
Weizigou, Zhg.	104	42.05 N	120.34 E
Weizigoumen	98	41.58 N	116.49 E
Weiziyu	98	41.29 N	124.31 E
Wejherowo	30	54.37 N	18.15 E
Wekiva ≃	220	28.52 N	81.23 W
Wekiwa Springs State Park ♠	220	28.43 N	81.27 W
Wekoewa Punt ›	241s	12.14 N	68.24 W
Wekusko Lake ⊜	184	54.45 N	99.50 W
Welaka	192	29.28 N	81.40 W
Welbourn Hill	162	27.21 S	134.06 E
Welch, Ok., U.S.	196	36.52 N	95.05 W
Welch, Tx., U.S.	196	32.56 N	102.08 W
Welch, W.V., U.S.	192	37.25 N	81.35 W
Welch Creek ≃	282	37.32 N	121.51 W
Welches	224	45.19 N	121.57 W
Welch Peak ∧	224	49.10 N	121.36 W
Welcome, On., Can.	212	43.58 N	78.21 W
Welcome, Mn., U.S.	198	43.40 N	94.37 W
Welcome, S.C., U.S.	192	34.49 N	82.26 W
Welcome Lake ⊜	212	45.25 N	78.25 W
Welcome Monument ⊥	269e	6.11 S	106.49 E
Welden	58	48.27 N	10.40 E
Weldiya	144	11.50 N	39.41 E
Weldon, Sk., Can.	184	53.00 N	105.08 W
Weldon, Il., U.S.	219	40.07 N	88.45 W
Weldon, N.C., U.S.	192	36.25 N	77.35 W
Weldon, Tx., U.S.	222	31.01 N	95.34 W
Weldon ≃	194	40.06 N	93.38 W
Weldona	198	40.20 N	103.58 W
Weldon Brook ≃	276	40.58 N	74.35 W
Weleetka	196	35.20 N	96.08 W
Welega □[4]	144	9.40 N	35.50 E
Weleri	115a	6.58 S	110.04 E
Welfare Island I	276	40.45 N	73.57 W
Welgedag	273d	26.12 S	28.30 E
Welhamgreen	260	51.44 N	0.13 W
Welheim ◆[8]	263	51.32 N	6.59 E
Weligama	122	5.58 N	80.25 E
Welikaja → Velikaja ≃	76	57.48 N	28.20 E
Welkenraedt	56	50.40 N	5.59 E
Welker Seamount ✦[3]	16	55.07 N	140.20 W
Welkite	144	8.15 N	37.50 E
Welkom	158	27.59 S	26.45 E
Well	52	51.34 N	6.06 E
Welland	212	42.59 N	79.15 W
Welland ≃, On., Can.	212	43.04 N	79.03 W
Welland ≃, Eng., U.K.	42	52.53 N	0.02 E
Welland Canal ≊	212	43.03 N	79.13 W
Welland Junction	284a	42.57 N	79.14 W
Wellard	168a	32.19 S	115.50 E
Wellaune	54	51.34 N	12.33 E
Wellborn, Fl., U.S.	192	30.13 N	82.49 W
Wellborn, Tx., U.S.	222	30.32 N	96.18 W
Wellerode	56	51.14 N	9.34 E
Wellers Bay c	212	44.00 N	77.34 W
Wellers Creek ≃	278	42.03 N	87.53 W
Wellesbourne	42	52.12 N	1.35 W
Welles Harbor c	174g	28.12 N	177.26 W
Wellesley, On., Can.	212	43.28 N	80.45 W
Wellesley, Ma., U.S.	207	42.17 N	71.17 W
Wellesley ≃	168a	33.17 S	115.44 E
Wellesley College ⊍[2]	283	42.18 N	71.19 W
Wellesley Hills	283	42.19 N	71.17 W
Wellesley Island I	212	44.19 N	75.58 W
Wellesley Islands II	164	16.42 S	139.30 E
Wellesley Island State Park ♠	212	44.19 N	76.01 W
Wellesley Lake ⊜	180	62.30 N	139.50 W
Wellfleet	207	41.56 N	70.02 W
Well Hill	260	51.21 N	0.09 E
Wellin	56	50.05 N	5.07 E
Welling ◆[8]	260	51.28 N	0.07 E
Wellingborough	42	52.19 N	0.42 W
Wellinghofen ◆[8]	263	51.28 N	7.29 E
Wellington, Austl.	166	32.33 S	148.57 E
Wellington, B.C., Can.	224	49.13 N	124.01 W
Wellington, On., Can.	212	43.57 N	77.21 W
Wellington, N.Z.	172	41.18 S	174.47 E
Wellington, S. Afr.	158	33.38 S	18.57 E
Wellington, Eng., U.K.	42	52.43 N	2.31 W
Wellington, Eng., U.K.	42	50.59 N	3.14 W
Wellington, Co., U.S.	200	40.42 N	105.00 W
Wellington, Il., U.S.	216	40.32 N	87.41 W
Wellington, Ks., U.S.	198	37.15 N	97.22 W
Wellington, Mo., U.S.	194	39.08 N	93.58 W
Wellington, Nv., U.S.	226	38.45 N	119.22 W
Wellington, Oh., U.S.	214	41.10 N	82.13 W
Wellington, Tx., U.S.	196	34.51 N	100.12 W
Wellington, Ut,. U.S.	200	39.32 N	110.44 W
Wellington □[6]	212	43.50 N	80.30 W
Wellington, Isla I	254	49.20 S	74.40 W
Wellington Bay c, N.T., Can.	176	69.30 N	106.30 W
Wellington Bay c, On., Can.	212	43.56 N	77.21 W
Wellington Channel ⋓	176	75.00 N	93.00 W
Wellington Point	171a	27.29 S	153.15 E
Wellington Reservoir ⊜[1]	168a	33.24 S	116.01 E
Wellington Station	186	46.27 N	64.00 W
Wellman, Ia., U.S.	190	41.27 N	91.50 W
Wellman, Tx., U.S.	196	33.03 N	102.26 W
Wells, B.C., Can.	182	53.06 N	121.34 W
Wells, Eng., U.K.	42	51.13 N	2.39 W
Wells, Mi., U.S.	190	45.47 N	87.04 W
Wells, Mn., U.S.	190	43.44 N	93.43 W
Wells, Nv., U.S.	204	41.06 N	114.57 W
Wells, N.Y., U.S.	210	43.24 N	74.17 W
Wells, Tx., U.S.	222	31.29 N	94.56 W
Wells □[6]	216	40.44 N	85.11 W
Wells, Lake ⊜	162	26.43 S	123.10 E
Wells, Mount ∧	168a	32.42 S	116.20 E
Wells, Mount ∧[2]	162	17.26 S	127.14 E
Wellsboro	210	41.44 N	77.18 W
Wells Bridge	210	42.22 N	75.15 W
Wellsburg, Ia., U.S.	190	42.27 N	92.56 W
Wellsburg, N.Y., U.S.	210	42.00 N	76.43 W
Wellsburg, W.V., U.S.	214	40.16 N	80.36 W
Wells Cathedral ⊍[1]	42	51.13 N	2.39 W
Wellsford	172	36.17 S	174.31 E
Wells Gray Provincial Park ♠	182	52.20 N	120.00 W
Wells Lake ⊜	184	57.15 N	101.00 W
Wells-next-the-Sea	42	52.58 N	0.51 E
Wells Point ›	284b	39.17 N	76.23 W
Wells State Park ♠	207	42.09 N	72.05 W
Wells Tannery	214	40.05 N	78.10 W
Wellston, Oh., U.S.	188	39.07 N	82.31 W
Wellston, Ok., U.S.	196	35.41 N	97.03 W
Wellsville, Ks., U.S.	198	38.43 N	95.04 W
Wellsville, Mo., U.S.	219	39.04 N	91.34 W
Wellsville, N.Y., U.S.	210	42.07 N	77.56 W
Wellsville, Oh., U.S.	214	40.36 N	80.38 W
Wellsville, Pa., U.S.	208	40.03 N	76.56 W
Wellsville, Ut,. U.S.	200	41.38 N	111.55 W
Wellton	200	32.40 N	114.08 W
Welmel ≃	144	5.38 N	40.47 E
Welmen	263	51.39 N	6.41 E
Welney	42	52.31 N	0.15 E
Welo □[4]	144	11.50 N	40.20 E
Welper	263	51.25 N	7.12 E
Wels	61	48.10 N	14.02 E
Welschbillig	56	49.51 N	6.34 E
Welse ≃	54	53.10 N	14.18 E
Welsford	186	45.27 N	66.20 W
Welsh	194	30.14 N	92.49 W
Welshpool, Austl.	169	38.39 S	146.26 E
Welshpool, Wales, U.K.	42	52.40 N	3.09 W
Welsickendorf	54	51.54 N	13.08 E
Welsleben	54	52.00 N	11.38 E
Weltenburg	60	48.54 N	11.50 E
Welver	52	51.38 N	7.57 E
Welverdiend	158	26.23 S	27.16 E
Welwitschia	156	20.21 S	14.57 E
Welwyn Garden City	42	51.50 N	0.13 W
Welwyn Hatfield □[8]	260	51.47 N	0.12 W
Welzheim	56	48.53 N	9.38 E
Welzow	54	51.34 N	14.10 E
Wem	42	52.51 N	2.44 W
Wema	152	0.26 S	21.38 E
Wembere ≃	154	4.10 S	34.11 E
Wembley	182	55.09 N	119.08 W
Wembley ◆[8]	260	51.33 N	0.18 W
Wembley Stadium ♠, S. Afr.	273d	26.14 S	28.03 E
Wembley Stadium ♠, Eng., U.K.	260	51.33 N	0.17 W
Wembury	42	50.19 N	4.05 W
Wemding	56	48.52 N	10.43 E
Wemeldinge	52	51.31 N	4.00 E
Wemme	224	45.20 N	121.57 W
Wemperhardt	56	50.09 N	6.05 E
Wemyss Bay	46	55.53 N	4.54 W
Wen ≃, Zhg.	98	36.38 N	119.22 E
Wen ≃, Zhg.	98	35.28 N	118.32 E
Wen'an	105	38.52 N	116.28 E
Wen'an Wa ☷	105	38.54 N	116.37 E
Wenas Creek ≃	224	46.42 N	120.35 W
Wenatchee	202	47.25 N	120.18 W
Wenatchee ≃	202	47.27 N	120.19 W
Wenatchee, Lake ⊜	224	47.49 N	120.47 W
Wenatchee Mountains ⋏	202	47.20 N	120.45 W
Wenchang	110	19.41 N	110.48 E
Wencheng	100	27.50 N	120.05 E
Wenchi	150	7.42 N	2.07 W
Wenchow → Wenzhou	100	28.01 N	120.39 E
Wendaohezi	104	41.46 N	124.09 E
Wendel	279b	40.18 N	79.41 W
Wendell, Id., U.S.	202	42.46 N	114.42 W
Wendell, N.C., U.S.	192	35.46 N	78.22 W
Wendelsheim	56	49.46 N	7.59 E
Wendelstein	60	49.21 N	11.08 E
Wendelstein ∧	64	47.42 N	12.00 E
Wendelville	284a	43.04 N	78.47 W
Wenden, Dtsch.	52	52.19 N	10.30 E
Wenden, Dtsch.	56	50.57 N	7.51 E
Wenden, Az., U.S.	200	33.49 N	113.32 W
Wendeng	98	37.12 N	122.04 E
Wendesi	164	2.25 S	134.13 E
Wendilou	104	41.13 N	121.08 E
Wendisch Rietz	54	52.13 N	14.01 E
Wendish Baggendorf	54	54.04 N	12.56 E
Wendji	152	0.04 S	18.10 E
Wendland ◆[1]	54	53.00 N	11.10 E
Wendo	144	6.38 N	38.27 E
Wendover, Eng., U.K.	42	51.46 N	0.46 W
Wendover, Ut,. U.S.	200	40.44 N	114.02 W
Wenduine	50	51.18 N	3.05 E
Wenebegon ≃	190	46.53 N	83.12 W
Wenebegon Lake ⊜	190	47.24 N	83.08 W
Wenfang	100	28.02 N	117.19 E
Weng	60	48.40 N	12.23 E
Weng ≃	100	24.10 N	113.24 E
Weng'an	102	26.53 N	107.22 E
Wengbo	120	31.23 N	86.40 E
Wengcheng	100	24.23 N	113.51 E
Wengdang	124	28.50 N	90.03 E
Wenge	152	0.03 N	24.01 E
Wengen, Dtsch.	58	47.41 N	10.09 E
Wengen, Schw.	58	46.36 N	7.56 E
Wengern	263	51.24 N	7.21 E
Wengjiabu	106	30.23 N	120.21 E
Wengong	107	30.11 N	104.09 E
Wenguantun	104	41.53 N	123.30 E
Wengyang	100	28.03 N	120.58 E
Wengyuan	100	24.21 N	114.08 E
Wenham	207	42.36 N	70.53 W
Wenham Lake ⊜	283	42.35 N	70.53 W
Wenham Swamp ☷	283	42.37 N	70.55 W
Wenheng	100	25.42 N	116.45 E
Wenī	124	28.21 N	83.34 E
Wenigzell	61	47.26 N	15.47 E
Wenjiachang	107	30.41 N	103.55 E
Wenjiang	107	30.42 N	103.49 E
Wenjiangban	100	26.01 N	117.51 E
Wenjiazhen	100	28.20 N	116.05 E
Wenling	100	28.22 N	121.20 E
Wenlock	164	13.06 S	142.58 E
Wenlock ≃	164	12.02 S	141.55 E
Wenlock Edge ⊥[4]	42	52.30 N	2.40 W
Wenlong	100	24.48 N	114.54 E
Wenmingsi	100	25.33 N	113.20 E
Wennigsen	52	52.16 N	9.34 E
Wenning ≃	44	54.07 N	2.39 W
Wennington ◆[8]	260	51.30 N	0.13 E
Wenniu	102	24.18 N	104.31 E
Wenns	58	47.10 N	10.44 E
Wenona, Il., U.S.	216	41.03 N	89.03 W
Wenona, Md., U.S.	208	38.08 N	75.57 W
Wenonah	208	39.47 N	75.08 W
Wenquan, Zhg.	86	44.59 N	81.04 E
Wenquan, Zhg.	100	23.37 N	113.43 E
Wenquansi	104	41.20 N	124.04 E
Wenshan	102	23.30 N	104.20 E
Wenshang	98	35.44 N	116.29 E
Wenshui, Zhg.	102	28.28 N	106.30 E
Wenshui, Zhg.	102	37.28 N	112.01 E
Wensickendorf	264a	52.45 N	13.23 E
Wensleydale ∨	44	54.19 N	2.00 W
Wensum ≃	42	52.37 N	1.19 E
Went ≃	44	53.39 N	0.59 W
Wentorf	52	53.30 N	10.15 E
Wentworth, Austl.	166	34.07 S	141.55 E
Wentworth, N.C., U.S.	192	36.24 N	79.46 W
Wentworth, S.D., U.S.	198	43.59 N	96.57 W
Wentworth Falls	170	33.43 S	150.22 E
Wentworth Park	273d	26.07 S	27.48 E
Wentworthville	274a	33.48 S	150.58 E
Wentzville	219	38.48 N	90.51 W
Wenxi	102	35.26 N	111.11 E
Wenxian	102	32.58 N	104.46 E
Wenxingchang	107	29.52 N	106.29 E
Wenyu ≃	105	39.56 N	116.40 E
Wenzenbach	60	49.05 N	12.12 E
Wenzhou	100	28.01 N	120.39 E
Wenzhu	100	27.01 N	113.58 E
Wenzhuangzicun	104	42.16 N	123.51 E
Weobley	42	52.09 N	2.51 W
Weohyakapka, Lake ⊜	220	27.49 N	81.25 W
Wepener	158	29.46 S	27.00 E
Wépion	56	50.25 N	4.52 E
Weppersdorf	61	47.35 N	16.26 E
Wequetequock	207	41.21 N	71.52 W
Wera ≃	115b	8.20 S	120.43 E
Werbellin	54	52.53 N	13.41 E
Werbellinsee ⊜	54	52.54 N	13.40 E
Werben	54	52.52 N	11.58 E
Werbomont	56	50.23 N	5.41 E
Werchojansker Gebirge → Verchojanskij chrebet ⋏	74	67.00 N	129.00 E
Werda	156	25.15 S	23.16 E
Werdau	54	50.44 N	12.22 E
Werden ◆[8]	263	51.23 N	7.00 E
Werder, Dtsch.	54	52.23 N	12.56 E
Werder, Ityo.	144	6.58 N	45.20 E
Werder ◆[1]	54	53.40 N	13.25 E
Werdohl	56	51.15 N	7.45 E
Were Ilu	144	10.37 N	39.28 E
Werfen	64	47.28 N	13.11 E
Weri	164	3.12 S	132.38 E
Werkel	56	51.09 N	9.18 E
Werkendam	52	51.49 N	4.53 E
Werl	52	51.33 N	7.54 E
Werlaburgdorf	54	52.04 N	10.31 E
Werl-Aspe	52	52.04 N	8.43 E
Werleshausen	56	51.19 N	9.54 E
Werlte	52	52.51 N	7.41 E
Wermelskirchen	56	51.08 N	7.13 E
Wermsdorf	54	51.17 N	12.56 E
Wern ≃	56	50.02 N	9.44 E
Wernadinga	166	18.07 S	139.58 E
Wernberg, Dtsch.	60	49.32 N	12.10 E
Wernberg, Öst.	64	46.37 N	13.56 E
Werne	52	51.40 N	7.38 E
Werne ◆[8]	263	51.29 N	7.18 E

≃	River	Fluß	Río	Rivière	Rio	✦	Submarine Features	Untermeerische Objekte	Accidentes Submarinos	Formes de relief sous-marin	Acidentes submarinos
≊	Canal	Kanal	Canal	Canal	Canal	□	Political Unit	Politische Einheit	Unidad Politica	Entité politique	Unidade política
⌊	Waterfall, Rapids	Wasserfall, Stromschnellen	Cascada, Rápidos	Chute d'eau, Rapides	Cascata, Rápidos	⊍	Cultural Institution	Kulturelle Institution	Institución Cultural	Institution culturelle	Instituição cultural
⋓	Strait	Meeresstraße	Estrecho	Détroit	Estreito	⊥	Historical Site	Historische Stätte	Sitio Histórico	Site historique	Sitio histórico
c	Bay, Gulf	Bucht, Golf	Bahía, Golfo	Baie, Golfe	Baía, Golfo	♠	Recreational Site	Erholungs- und Ferienort	Sitio de Recreo	Centre de loisirs	Area de Lazer
⊜	Lake, Lakes	See, Seen	Lago, Lagos	Lac, Lacs	Lago, Lagos	⊠	Airport	Flughafen	Aeropuerto	Aéroport	Aeroporto
☷	Swamp	Sumpf	Pantano	Marais	Pântano	■	Military Installation	Militäranlage	Instalación Militar	Installation militaire	Instalação militar
⊟	Ice Features, Glacier	Eis- und Gletscherformen	Accidentes Glaciales	Formes glaciaires	Acidentes glaciares	◆	Miscellaneous	Verschiedenes	Misceláneo	Divers	Diversos
⊤	Other Hydrographic Features	Andere Hydrographische Objekte	Otros Elementos Hidrográficos	Autres données hydrographiques	Outros acidentes hidrográficos						

ENGLISH / DEUTSCH

Name	Page	Lat.°′	Long.°′
Werneck, Bra.	256	22.13 S	43.19 W
Werneck, Dtsch.	56	49.59 N	10.05 E
Werneuchen	54	52.38 N	13.44 E
Wernigerode	54	51.50 N	10.47 E
Wernitz	264a	52.34 N	12.55 E
Wernsdorf	264a	52.22 N	13.43 E
Wernsdorfer See ⊜	264a	52.23 N	13.42 E
Wernshausen	54	50.43 N	10.21 E
Wernstein	60	48.30 N	13.28 E
Werra ≃	30	51.26 N	9.39 E
Werribee	169	37.54 S	144.40 E
Werribee ≃	169	37.59 S	144.41 E
Werribee Gorge State Park ♦	169	37.40 S	144.21 E
Werribee South	169	37.56 S	144.42 E
Werries	52	51.41 N	7.53 E
Werrington	274a	33.45 S	150.46 E
Werris Creek	166	31.21 S	150.39 E
Werschweiler	56	49.27 N	7.13 E
Wersten ◆[8]	263	51.11 N	6.49 E
Wertach	58	47.36 N	10.25 E
Wertach ≃	58	48.24 N	10.53 E
Wertheim	56	49.46 N	9.31 E
Werther, Dtsch.	52	52.04 N	8.24 E
Werther, Dtsch.	54	51.29 N	10.46 E
Wertingen	56	48.34 N	10.41 E
Wervershoof	52	52.44 N	5.09 E
Wervik	50	50.47 N	3.02 E
Wervin	262	53.15 N	2.52 W
Werwaru	164	8.13 S	128.11 E
Weschnitz ≃	56	49.43 N	8.24 E
Weseke	52	51.54 N	6.51 E
Wesel	52	51.40 N	6.38 E
Wesel-Datteln-Kanal ≅	263	51.38 N	6.36 E
Wesenberg	54	53.17 N	12.58 E
Wesendahl	264a	52.36 N	13.49 E
Wesendorf	52	52.35 N	10.31 E
Weser ≃	52	53.32 N	8.34 E
Weser-Elbe-Kanal (Mittellandkanal) ≅	54	52.16 N	11.41 E
Weser-Ems □[6]	52	52.45 N	8.00 E
Wesergebirge ⋏	52	52.15 N	9.10 E
Wesham	262	53.48 N	2.53 W
Wesickaman Creek ≃	285	39.44 N	74.43 W
Wesī Śahar	124	28.15 N	84.23 E
Weskan	198	38.52 N	101.57 W
Weslaco	196	26.09 N	97.59 W
Weslemkoon Lake ⊜	212	45.02 N	77.25 W
Wesley, Dom.	240d	15.34 N	61.19 W
Wesley, Ia., U.S.	190	43.05 N	93.59 W
Wesleyville, Nf., Can.	186	49.09 N	53.34 W
Wesleyville, Pa., U.S.	214	42.08 N	80.00 W
Wessel, Cape ›	164	10.59 S	136.46 E
Wesseling	56	50.49 N	6.58 E
Wessel Islands II	164	11.30 S	136.25 E
Wesselsbron	158	27.50 S	25.23 E
Wesselsvlei	158	27.23 S	23.47 E
Wessington	198	44.27 N	98.41 W
Wessington Springs	198	44.04 N	98.34 W
Wessobrunn	64	47.52 N	11.01 E
Wesson	194	31.42 N	90.23 W
Wessum	52	52.05 N	6.58 E
West, Ms., U.S.	194	33.11 N	89.46 W
West, Tx., U.S.	222	31.48 N	97.05 W
West ≃, N.Y., U.S.	210	42.41 N	77.22 W
West ≃, Vt., U.S.	188	42.52 N	72.33 W
West Abington	207	42.05 N	70.58 W
Westacres	216	42.35 N	83.26 W
West Acton	207	42.28 N	71.28 W
West Alexander	214	40.06 N	80.31 W
West Alexandria	218	39.44 N	84.31 W
Westall, Point ›	162	32.55 S	134.04 E
West Allen ≃	44	54.55 N	2.19 W
West Allis	216	43.01 N	88.00 W
Westalton	219	38.51 N	90.13 W
West Amityville	276	40.41 N	73.26 W
West Andover	207	42.39 N	71.09 W
West Athens	280	33.55 N	118.18 W
West Atlantic City	208	39.23 N	74.28 W
West Babylon	210	40.43 N	73.21 W
Westbahnhof ◆[5]	264b	48.11 N	16.20 E
West Baines ≃	164	15.36 S	129.58 E
West Bangor	210	40.52 N	75.14 W
Westbank	182	49.50 N	119.38 W
West Bank □[9]	132	31.40 N	35.15 E
West Barnstable	207	41.42 N	70.22 W
West Barrington	207	41.44 N	71.20 W
West Bay, N.S., Can.	186	45.43 N	61.10 W
Westbay, Fl., U.S.	194	30.17 N	85.52 W
West Bay c, Fl., U.S.	194	30.16 N	85.47 W
West Bay c, Tx., U.S.	222	29.15 N	94.57 W
West Bay Shore	276	40.42 N	73.16 W
West Belmar	208	40.10 N	74.02 W
West Bend, Ia., U.S.	198	42.57 N	94.26 W
West Bend, Wi., U.S.	190	43.25 N	88.11 W
West Bengal □[3]	124	24.00 N	88.00 E
West Bergholt	42	51.55 N	0.51 E
West Berlin	208	39.48 N	74.56 W
West-Berlin □[3]	264a	52.30 N	13.15 E
West Bernard Creek ≃	222	29.23 N	95.58 W
Westbevern	52	52.01 N	7.47 E
West Bhāgīrath Plain ≚	126	23.30 N	88.00 E
West Bijou Creek ≃	198	39.51 N	104.08 W
West Billerica	283	42.33 N	71.19 W
West Blocton	194	33.07 N	87.07 W
West Bloomfield	210	42.54 N	77.32 W
West Bolivar	214	40.23 N	79.10 W
Westborough	207	42.16 N	71.37 W
Westbourne	184	50.09 N	98.35 W
West Bow Creek ≃	198	42.46 N	97.08 W
West Boxford	283	42.42 N	71.04 W
West Boylston	207	42.22 N	71.47 W
West Bradenton	220	27.30 N	82.37 W
West Branch, Ia., U.S.	190	41.40 N	91.20 W
West Branch, Mi., U.S.	190	44.16 N	84.14 W
West Branch Reservoir ⊜[1]	210	41.25 N	73.42 W
West Branch State Park ♦	214	41.07 N	81.05 W
Westbridge	182	49.10 N	118.59 W
West Bridgewater	207	42.01 N	71.00 W
West Bridgford	42	52.56 N	1.08 W
West Bristol	285	40.06 N	74.53 W
West Bromwich	42	52.31 N	1.56 W
Westbrook, Austl.	171a	27.36 S	151.52 E
Westbrook, On., Can.	212	44.16 N	76.38 W
Westbrook, Ct., U.S.	207	41.17 N	72.26 W
Westbrook, Me., U.S.	188	43.40 N	70.22 W
Westbrook, Mn., U.S.	198	44.02 N	95.26 W
Westbrook, Tx., U.S.	196	32.21 N	101.01 W
West Brook ≃	276	41.04 N	74.18 W
West Brookfield	207	42.14 N	72.08 W
Westbrookville	210	41.30 N	74.34 W
West Burlington, Ia., U.S.	190	40.49 N	91.09 W
West Burlington, N.Y., U.S.	210	42.42 N	75.11 W
West Burra I	46a	60.05 N	1.21 W
Westbury, Eng., U.K.	42	52.41 N	2.57 W
Westbury, Eng., U.K.	42	51.16 N	2.11 W
Westbury, N.Y., U.S.	276	40.45 N	73.35 W
Westbury-on-Severn	42	51.50 N	2.24 W
West Butte ∧	202	48.57 N	111.32 W
Westby, Austl.	171b	35.30 S	147.25 E
Westby, Mt., U.S.	198	48.52 N	104.03 W
Westby, Wi., U.S.	190	43.39 N	90.51 W
West Cache Creek ≃	196	34.13 N	98.23 W
West Caicos I	238	21.39 N	72.28 W
West Calder	46	55.52 N	3.35 W
West Caldwell	276	40.50 N	74.18 W
West Cameron	208	40.45 N	76.41 W
West Camp	210	42.07 N	73.56 W
West Canada Creek ≃	188	43.01 N	74.58 W
West Cape ›	172	45.54 S	166.26 E
West Cape Howe ›	162	35.08 S	117.36 E
West Cape May	208	38.56 N	74.56 W
West Carlisle	196	33.35 N	101.56 W
West Caroline Basin ⊹[1]	14	4.00 N	138.00 E
West Carrollton	218	39.40 N	84.15 W
West Carson	280	33.57 N	118.23 W
West Carthage	212	43.58 N	75.36 W
West Catfish Creek ≃	212	42.46 N	81.04 W
West Channel ≃[1]	180	68.51 N	136.10 W
West Chelmsford	283	42.37 N	71.23 W
Westchester, Il., U.S.	216	41.51 N	87.52 W
West Chester, Pa., U.S.	208	39.57 N	75.36 W
Westchester, Va., U.S.	284c	38.51 N	77.16 W
Westchester □[6]	210	41.02 N	73.46 W
Westchester ◆[8], Ca., U.S.	280	33.55 N	118.25 W
Westchester ◆[8], N.Y., U.S.	276	40.51 N	73.52 W
West Chester Airport ⊠	285	39.59 N	75.35 W
Westchester County Airport ⊠	207	41.04 N	73.43 W
Westchester Creek ≃	276	40.48 N	73.51 W
Westchester Estates	284c	38.47 N	76.55 W
Westchester Station	186	45.37 N	63.40 W
West Chester University of Pennsylvania ꝟ[2]	285	39.57 N	75.36 W
West Chicago	216	41.53 N	88.12 W
West Clandon	260	51.15 N	0.30 W
West Clarksville	210	42.08 N	78.15 W
West Clear Creek ≃	200	34.34 N	111.51 W
West Cleddau ≃	42	51.46 N	4.54 W
Westcliffe	200	38.08 N	105.27 W
Westcliffe ◆[8]	273d	26.11 S	28.02 E
Westcliff-on-Sea	260	51.32 N	0.41 E
West College Corner	218	39.34 N	84.48 W
West Collingswood Heights	285	39.59 N	75.07 W
West Columbia, S.C., U.S.	192	33.59 N	81.04 W
West Columbia, Tx., U.S.	222	29.08 N	95.38 W
West Concord, Ma., U.S.	207	42.27 N	71.23 W
West Concord, Mn., U.S.	190	44.09 N	92.53 W
West Conshohocken	285	40.04 N	75.19 W
West Cote Blanche Bay c	194	29.40 N	91.45 W
Westcott	260	51.13 N	0.22 W
Westcott Cove c	276	41.02 N	73.30 W
West Covina	228	34.04 N	117.56 W
West Creek	208	39.38 N	74.18 W
West Creek ≃, In., U.S.	216	41.12 N	87.30 W
West Creek ≃, Pa., U.S.	214	41.30 N	78.15 W
Westdale, Ma., U.S.	283	42.01 N	70.59 W
Westdale, N.Y., U.S.	210	43.23 N	75.49 W
West Danby	210	42.19 N	76.32 W
West Davenport	210	42.27 N	74.58 W
West Deane Park ♦	275b	43.40 N	79.34 W
West Decatur	214	40.56 N	78.17 W
West Delaware Aqueduct ≅[1]	210	41.52 N	74.31 W
Westdene ◆[8]	273d	26.11 S	27.59 E
West Dennis	207	41.39 N	70.10 W
West Derby ◆[8]	262	53.26 N	2.54 W
West Derry	214	40.20 N	79.20 W
West Des Moines	190	41.34 N	93.42 W
West Ditch ≅	276	40.56 N	74.19 W
West Dolores ≃	200	37.35 N	108.21 W
West Drayton ◆[8]	260	51.30 N	0.29 W
West Duffins Creek ≃	212	43.51 N	79.04 W
West Duxbury	283	42.03 N	70.47 W
West Easton	210	40.41 N	75.14 W
West Eaton	210	42.51 N	75.39 W
Westecunk Creek ≃	208	39.37 N	74.16 W
West Edmeston	210	42.46 N	75.17 W
West Edmondale	284b	39.18 N	76.43 W
West Elizabeth	279b	40.17 N	79.54 W
West Elk Mountains ⋏	200	38.40 N	107.15 W
West Elk Peak ∧	200	38.43 N	107.13 W
West Elkton	218	39.35 N	84.33 W
West Ellicott	214	42.05 N	79.16 W
West Elmira	210	42.04 N	76.50 W
West End, Ba.	238	26.41 N	78.58 W
West End, Eng., U.K.	260	51.44 N	0.04 W
West End, Eng., U.K.	260	51.20 N	0.38 W
West End, Ar., U.S.	194	34.13 N	92.03 W
West End, Il., U.S.	216	42.17 N	89.09 W
West End, N.Y., U.S.	210	42.28 N	75.05 W
West End, N.C., U.S.	192	35.14 N	79.34 W
West End ◆[8], Eng., U.K.	260	51.32 N	0.24 W
West End ◆[8], Pa., U.S.	279b	40.27 N	80.02 W
Westende, Bel.	50	51.10 N	2.46 E
Westende, Dtsch.	263	51.25 N	7.24 E
Westendorf	64	47.26 N	12.13 E
Westenfeld ◆[8]	263	51.28 N	7.09 E
Westenholz	52	51.45 N	8.28 E
Westenschouwen	52	51.41 N	3.42 E
Westerbauer ◆[8]	263	51.20 N	7.23 E
Westerblokker	52	52.39 N	5.08 E
Westerbönen	263	51.36 N	7.46 E
Westerbork	52	52.51 N	6.37 E
Westerburg	56	50.33 N	7.58 E
Westercelle	52	52.36 N	10.05 E
Westerdale	46	58.27 N	3.30 W
Westeregeln	54	51.57 N	11.23 E
Westerham	42	51.16 N	0.05 E
Westerhausen	54	51.48 N	11.03 E
Westerholt	52	51.36 N	7.05 E
Westerholz ◆[3]	263	51.32 N	7.28 E
Westerich □[9]	56	49.15 N	7.20 E
Westerkappeln	52	52.18 N	7.52 E
Westerland	30	54.54 N	8.18 E
Westerlo, Bel.	56	51.05 N	4.55 E
Westerlo, N.Y., U.S.	210	42.31 N	74.03 W
Westerly	207	41.22 N	71.49 W
Western	198	40.23 N	97.11 W
Western □[4], Ghana	150	5.30 N	2.30 W
Western □[4], Kenya	154	0.30 N	34.35 E
Western □[4], Sol.Is.	175e	8.00 S	157.00 E
Western □[4], Zam.	152	16.00 S	24.00 E
Western □[5], Pap. N. Gui.	164	7.00 S	142.00 E
Western □[5], Ug.	154	1.00 N	31.00 E
Western ≃	166	22.22 S	142.25 E
Western Area □[4]	150	8.20 N	13.00 W
Western Australia □[3]	160	25.00 S	122.00 E
Western Branch ≃	284c	38.55 N	76.48 W
Western Canal ≅	226	39.28 N	121.35 W
Western Channel ⊔	98	34.40 N	129.00 E
Western Cove c	168b	35.43 S	137.38 E
Western Desert → Gharbīyah, Aṣ-Ṣaḥrā' al- ◆[2]	140	27.00 N	27.00 E
Western Division □[5]	175g	18.00 S	177.30 E
Western Ghāts ⋏	122	14.00 N	75.00 E
Western Highlands □[5]	164	5.45 S	144.30 E
Western Isles □[4]	46	57.40 N	7.00 W
Westernport	188	39.29 N	79.02 W
Western Port c	169	38.22 S	145.20 E
Western Port Bay c	169	38.15 S	145.20 E
Western Sahara □[2], Afr.	134	24.30 N	13.00 W
Western Sahara □[2], Afr.	148	24.30 N	13.00 W
Western Samoa □[1], Oc.	14	13.55 S	172.00 W
Western Samoa □[1], Oc.	175a	13.55 S	172.00 W
Western Sayans → Zapadnyj Sajan ⋏	74	53.00 N	94.00 E
Western Shore	186	44.32 N	64.19 W
Western Springs	278	41.48 N	87.54 W
Westernville	210	43.18 N	75.23 W
Westerschelde c[1]	52	51.25 N	3.45 E
Westerstede	52	53.15 N	7.55 E
Westervelt	219	39.29 N	88.52 W
Westerville	214	40.07 N	82.55 W
Westerwald ⋏	56	50.40 N	7.55 E
West European Basin ⊹[1]	10	47.00 N	15.00 W
West Exeter	210	42.48 N	75.09 W
West Fairview	208	40.16 N	76.54 W
Westfalen □[9]	52	51.50 N	7.30 E
Westfalenhalle ꝟ	263	51.30 N	7.27 E
West Falkland I	254	51.50 S	60.00 W
West Falls	210	42.42 N	78.41 W
West Falmouth	207	41.36 N	70.38 W
West Fargo	198	46.52 N	96.54 W
West Farleigh	260	51.15 N	0.27 E
West Farmington	214	41.23 N	80.58 W
Westfield, Eng., U.K.	42	50.55 N	0.35 E
Westfield, Il., U.S.	194	39.27 N	88.01 W
Westfield, In., U.S.	218	40.02 N	86.07 W
Westfield, Ma., U.S.	207	42.07 N	72.45 W
Westfield, N.J., U.S.	210	40.39 N	74.20 W
Westfield, N.Y., U.S.	214	42.19 N	79.34 W
Westfield, Pa., U.S.	210	41.55 N	77.32 W
Westfield, Tx., U.S.	222	30.01 N	95.24 W
Westfield, Wi., U.S.	190	43.53 N	89.29 W
Westfield ≃	207	42.05 N	72.35 W
Westfield, Middle Branch ≃	207	42.16 N	72.52 W
Westfield, West Branch ≃	207	42.13 N	72.52 W
Westfield Center	214	41.01 N	81.55 W
West Fiord c[2]	176	76.02 N	90.00 W
Westford, Ma., U.S.	283	42.34 N	71.26 W
Westford, N.Y., U.S.	210	42.39 N	74.48 W
West Fork	194	35.55 N	94.11 W
West Foxboro	283	42.05 N	71.17 W
West Frankfort	194	37.53 N	88.55 W
West Friesland ◆[1]	52	52.45 N	4.50 E
West Frisian Islands → Waddeneilanden II	52	53.26 N	5.30 E
West Fulton	210	42.34 N	74.28 W
Westgate, Austl.	166	26.35 S	146.12 E
Westgate, Mi., U.S.	216	43.03 N	85.42 W
Westgate on Sea	42	51.23 N	1.21 E
West Genesee Terrace	210	43.03 N	76.16 W
West-Ghats → Western Ghāts ⋏	122	14.00 N	75.00 E
West Gilgo Beach	276	40.37 N	73.25 W
West Glacier	202	48.29 N	113.58 W
West Glamorgan □[6]	42	51.35 N	3.35 W
West Glens Falls	210	43.18 N	73.43 W
West Glenville	210	42.56 N	74.04 W
West Goshen	207	41.49 N	73.15 W
West Granby	207	41.57 N	72.50 W
West Grand Lake ⊜	188	45.15 N	67.50 W
West Groton	207	42.36 N	71.37 W
West Grove	208	39.49 N	75.49 W
Westham	208	37.35 N	77.32 W
West Ham ◆[8]	260	51.31 N	0.01 E
West Hamburg	208	40.33 N	76.00 W
West Ham Football Club ♦	260	51.32 N	0.02 E
Westham Island I	224	49.05 N	123.10 W
West Hamlin	188	38.17 N	82.11 W
Westhampton, N.Y., U.S.	207	40.49 N	72.39 W
Westhampton, Va., U.S.	284c	38.54 N	77.11 W
West Hanningfield	260	51.40 N	0.30 E
West Hanover	283	42.07 N	70.53 W
West Harbor c	276	40.54 N	73.32 W
West Harrison	218	39.15 N	84.49 W
West Hartford	207	41.45 N	72.44 W
West Hartland	207	42.00 N	72.58 W
Westhausen	56	48.53 N	10.11 E
Westhaven, Ca., U.S.	204	41.03 N	124.06 W
West Haven, Ct., U.S.	207	41.16 N	72.57 W
Westhaven, Il., U.S.	278	41.35 N	87.51 W
West Haverstraw	210	41.12 N	73.59 W
West Hazleton	210	40.57 N	75.59 W
Westhead	262	53.34 N	2.51 W
West Hebron	210	43.14 N	73.22 W
West Heidelberg	274b	37.45 S	145.02 E
Westheim	56	49.03 N	9.44 E
West Helena	194	34.33 N	90.38 W
Westhemmerde	263	51.33 N	7.47 E
West Hempstead	276	40.42 N	73.39 W
West Henrietta	210	43.02 N	77.40 W
West Hickory	214	41.34 N	79.25 W
Westhill	46	57.09 N	2.17 W
West Hill ◆[8]	275b	43.46 N	79.11 W
Westhofen	263	51.25 N	7.31 E
Westhoff	222	29.12 N	97.28 W
Westhoffen	58	48.36 N	7.26 E
West Hollywood, Ca., U.S.	228	34.05 N	118.21 W
West Hollywood, Fl., U.S.	220	26.01 N	80.10 W
Westholme	224	49.52 N	123.42 W
West Homestead	279b	40.24 N	79.55 W
Westhope, N.D., U.S.	198	48.54 N	101.01 W
Westhope, Oh., U.S.	216	41.18 N	83.57 W
West Horndon	260	51.34 N	0.21 E
West Horsley	260	51.16 N	0.27 W
Westhoughton	262	53.33 N	2.32 W
West Hoxton	274a	33.55 S	150.49 E
West Humber ≃	212	43.44 N	79.33 W
West Humble	260	51.15 N	0.20 W
West Huntington	276	40.42 N	73.18 W
West Hurley	210	42.00 N	74.06 W
Westhuyzen	158	27.30 S	25.27 E
West Hyde	260	51.37 N	0.30 W
West Ice Shelf ⊓	9	67.00 S	85.00 E
Westick	263	51.35 N	7.38 E
Westig	263	51.22 N	7.45 E
West Indies II	230	19.00 N	70.00 W
Westindische Inseln → West Indies II	230	19.00 N	70.00 W
West Irian → Irian Jaya □[4]	164	5.00 S	138.00 E
West Island I, Austl.	164	15.36 S	136.34 E
West Island I, Ma., U.S.	207	41.36 N	70.50 W
West Islip	210	40.42 N	73.18 W
West Jan Mayen Ridge ⊹[3]	10	71.00 N	13.00 W
West Jefferson, N.C., U.S.	192	36.24 N	81.29 W
West Jefferson, Oh., U.S.	218	39.56 N	83.16 W
West Jordan	200	40.36 N	111.56 W
Westkapelle, Bel.	50	51.19 N	3.18 E
Westkapelle, Ned.	52	51.32 N	3.27 E
West Keansburg	276	40.27 N	74.09 W
West Kettle ≃	182	49.07 N	119.00 W
West Kilbride	46	55.42 N	4.51 W
West Kill	210	42.13 N	74.31 W
West Kingsdown	42	51.21 N	0.17 E
West Kingston	207	41.28 N	71.33 W
West Kirby	44	53.22 N	3.10 W
Westkirchen	52	51.53 N	8.02 E
West Kittanning	214	40.49 N	79.32 W
West Lafayette, In., U.S.	216	40.25 N	86.54 W
West Lafayette, Oh., U.S.	214	40.16 N	81.45 W
Westlake, La., U.S.	194	30.15 N	93.15 W
Westlake, Oh., U.S.	214	41.27 N	81.55 W
Westlake, Tx., U.S.	222	32.59 N	97.12 W
West Lake ⊜, On., Can.	212	43.56 N	77.17 W
West Lake ⊜, Fl., U.S.	220	25.12 N	80.49 W
West Lake ⊜, N.J., U.S.	276	40.58 N	74.22 W
West Lamma Channel ⊔	271d	22.13 N	114.04 E
West Lancashire □[8]	262	53.35 N	2.50 W
Westland, Mi., U.S.	216	42.19 N	83.24 W
Westland, Pa., U.S.	214	40.17 N	80.16 W
Westland Center ◆[9]	281	42.20 N	83.23 W
Westland National Park ♦	172	43.30 S	170.10 E
Westlands	207	42.37 N	71.20 W
West Lanham Hills	284c	38.57 N	76.53 W
West Laramie	200	41.18 N	105.37 W
West Lawn	284c	38.52 N	77.11 W
West Lebanon, In., U.S.	216	40.16 N	87.23 W
West Lebanon, Pa., U.S.	214	40.35 N	79.22 W
West Leechburg	214	40.37 N	79.37 W
Westleigh, S. Afr.	158	27.31 S	27.21 E
Westleigh, Eng., U.K.	262	53.30 N	2.31 W
West Leipsic	216	41.07 N	84.00 W
Westley	226	37.33 N	121.12 W
West Leyden	212	43.28 N	75.28 W
West Liberty, Ia., U.S.	190	41.34 N	91.15 W
West Liberty, Ky., U.S.	192	37.55 N	83.15 W
West Liberty, Oh., U.S.	216	40.15 N	83.45 W
West Liberty, Pa., U.S.	214	41.00 N	80.03 W
West Liberty, W.V., U.S.	214	40.10 N	80.35 W
West Liberty ◆[8]	279b	40.24 N	80.01 W
Westliche Sahara → Western Sahara □[2]	148	24.30 N	13.00 W
Westliche Sierra Madre → Madre Occidental, Sierra ⋏	232	25.00 N	105.00 W
Westline	214	41.47 N	78.46 W
West Linn	224	45.21 N	122.36 W
West Linton	46	55.46 N	3.22 W
West Little Owyhee ≃	202	42.28 N	117.15 W
Westlock	182	54.09 N	113.52 W
West Lorne	214	42.36 N	81.36 W
West Los Angeles ◆[8]	280	34.03 N	118.28 W
West Lulworth	42	50.38 N	2.15 W
West Lunga ≃	154	13.06 S	24.39 E
West Lunga National Park ♦	154	12.55 S	25.10 E
West Malling	42	51.18 N	0.25 E
West Malling Aerodrome ⊠	260	51.16 N	0.24 E
West Manayunk	285	40.01 N	75.14 W
West Manchester	218	39.54 N	84.37 W
West Mansfield, Ma., U.S.	207	41.59 N	71.14 W
West Mansfield, Oh., U.S.	216	40.24 N	83.32 W
West Mariana Basin ⊹[1]	14	15.00 N	137.00 E
West Mayfield	214	40.47 N	80.20 W
West Meadowview	216	41.08 N	87.52 W
Westmeath □[6]	48	53.30 N	7.30 W
West Medway	207	42.08 N	71.25 W
West Melbourne	220	28.04 N	80.39 W
West Memphis	194	35.08 N	90.11 W
West Meon	42	51.01 N	1.05 W
Westmere	210	42.41 N	73.52 W
West Mersea	42	51.47 N	0.55 E
West Miami	220	25.45 N	80.17 W
West Middlesex	214	41.10 N	80.27 W
West Middletown	214	40.15 N	80.25 W
West Midlands □[6]	42	52.30 N	2.00 W
West Mifflin	214	40.22 N	79.52 W
West Milford	210	41.07 N	74.22 W
West Millbury	207	42.11 N	71.48 W
West Mill Creek ≃	222	29.55 N	96.17 W
West Milton, Oh., U.S.	218	39.57 N	84.19 W
West Milton, Pa., U.S.	210	41.01 N	76.52 W
West Milwaukee	216	43.00 N	87.58 W
West Mineola	222	32.41 N	95.31 W
Westminster, Ca., U.S.	228	33.45 N	118.02 W
Westminster, Co., U.S.	200	39.50 N	105.02 W
Westminster, Md., U.S.	208	39.34 N	76.59 W
Westminster, Ma., U.S.	207	42.32 N	71.54 W
Westminster, Oh., U.S.	216	40.42 N	83.58 W
Westminster, S.C., U.S.	192	34.39 N	83.05 W
Westminster Abbey ꝟ[1]	260	51.30 N	0.07 W
Westminster Mall ◆[9]	280	33.45 N	118.01 W
West Modesto	226	37.37 N	121.02 W
West Monroe	194	32.31 N	92.08 W
Westmont, Ca., U.S.	280	33.56 N	118.18 W
Westmont, Il., U.S.	278	41.47 N	87.58 W
Westmont, N.J., U.S.	285	39.54 N	75.02 W
Westmont, Pa., U.S.	214	40.18 N	78.57 W
West Monterey	214	41.03 N	79.39 W
West Montreal ≃	190	47.56 N	80.39 W
West Moors	42	50.49 N	1.55 W
Westmoreland, Ks., U.S.	198	39.23 N	96.24 W
Westmoreland, N.Y., U.S.	210	43.07 N	75.24 W
Westmoreland, Tn., U.S.	194	36.33 N	86.14 W
Westmoreland, Va., U.S.	208	38.04 N	76.34 W
Westmoreland □[6], Pa., U.S.	214	40.18 N	79.33 W
Westmoreland □[6], Va., U.S.	208	38.10 N	76.50 W
Westmoreland City	214	40.20 N	79.41 W
Westmoreland State Park ♦	208	38.09 N	76.50 W
Westmorland	204	33.02 N	115.37 W
Westmount	206	45.29 N	73.36 W
West Mountain ∧	188	43.51 N	74.43 W
West Mud Creek ≃	222	32.07 N	95.10 W
West Mustang Creek ≃	222	29.04 N	96.26 W
West Nab ∧	262	53.35 N	1.53 W
West Nanticoke	210	40.13 N	76.01 W
West New Britain □[5]	164	5.45 S	149.30 E
West Newbury	207	42.48 N	70.59 W
West Newton, Ma., U.S.	283	42.21 N	71.14 W
West Newton, Pa., U.S.	214	40.12 N	79.46 W
West New York	276	40.47 N	74.00 W
West Nicholson	154	21.06 S	29.25 E
West Nishnabotna ≃	198	40.39 N	95.37 W
West Nodaway ≃	194	40.38 N	95.01 W
West Norriton	208	40.08 N	75.22 W
West Norwood ◆[8]	260	51.26 N	0.06 W
West Novaya Zemlya Trough ⊹[1]	10	73.30 N	50.00 E
West Nueces ≃	196	29.16 N	99.56 W
West Nyack	210	41.06 N	73.58 W
West Okaw ≃	219	39.32 N	88.42 W
Weston, Austl.	170	32.49 S	151.28 E
Weston, Malay.	112	5.13 N	115.36 E
Weston, Eng., U.K.	262	53.19 N	2.44 W
Weston, Co., U.S.	200	37.07 N	104.50 W
Weston, Ct., U.S.	207	41.12 N	73.22 W
Weston, Id., U.S.	202	42.02 N	111.58 W
Weston, Ma., U.S.	207	42.22 N	71.18 W
Weston, Mi., U.S.	216	41.46 N	84.06 W
Weston, Mo., U.S.	194	39.24 N	94.54 W
Weston, Ne., U.S.	198	41.11 N	96.44 W
Weston, Oh., U.S.	216	41.20 N	83.47 W
Weston, Or., U.S.	202	45.48 N	118.25 W
Weston, Pa., U.S.	210	40.57 N	76.09 W
Weston, W.V., U.S.	188	39.02 N	80.28 W
Weston □[8]	275b	43.43 N	79.31 W
Westonaria	273d	26.19 S	27.39 E
West Oneonta	210	42.28 N	75.07 W
Westönnen	52	51.33 N	7.58 E
Weston Reservoir ⊜[1]	283	42.21 N	71.18 W
Westons Mill Pond ⊜	276	40.28 N	74.25 W
Westons Mills	210	42.04 N	78.23 W
Weston-super-Mare	42	51.21 N	2.59 W
Weston upon Trent	42	52.45 N	2.02 W
West Orange, N.J., U.S.	276	40.47 N	74.14 W
West Orange, Tx., U.S.	194	30.05 N	93.46 W
Westover, Md., U.S.	208	38.07 N	75.42 W
Westover, Pa., U.S.	214	40.45 N	78.40 W
Westover, Tn., U.S.	194	35.36 N	88.52 W
Westover, W.V., U.S.	188	39.38 N	79.58 W
Westover Air Force Base ■	207	42.12 N	72.33 W
Westoverledingen	52	53.10 N	7.28 E
Westowne	284b	39.17 N	76.43 W
West Palm Beach	220	26.42 N	80.03 W
West Palm Beach Canal ≅	220	26.38 N	80.03 W
West Paris	188	44.19 N	70.34 W
West Park	210	41.48 N	73.58 W
West Paterson	276	40.53 N	74.11 W
West Pawlet	210	43.21 N	73.15 W
West Peckham	260	51.15 N	0.22 E
West Pensacola	194	30.25 N	87.16 W
Westphalia, Ks., U.S.	198	38.10 N	95.29 W
Westphalia, Mi., U.S.	216	42.55 N	84.47 W
Westphalia, Mo., U.S.	219	38.26 N	91.59 W
West Pittsburg, Ca., U.S.	226	38.01 N	121.56 W
West Pittsburg, Pa., U.S.	214	40.55 N	80.21 W
West Pittston	210	41.19 N	75.47 W
West Plains	194	36.43 N	91.51 W
West Point, Ca., U.S.	226	38.23 N	120.31 W
West Point, Ga., U.S.	192	32.52 N	85.11 W
Westpoint, In., U.S.	216	40.21 N	87.03 W
West Point, Ia., U.S.	190	40.43 N	91.27 W
West Point, Ky., U.S.	194	37.59 N	85.56 W
West Point, Ms., U.S.	194	33.36 N	88.39 W
West Point, Ne., U.S.	198	41.50 N	96.42 W
West Point, N.Y., U.S.	210	41.23 N	73.57 W
West Point, Oh., U.S.	214	40.43 N	80.42 W
West Point, Pa., U.S.	285	40.12 N	75.18 W
West Point, Va., U.S.	208	37.31 N	76.47 W
West Point ∧	180	64.57 N	144.40 W
West Point ›, Austl.	166	35.01 S	135.57 E
West Point ›, P.E., Can.	186	46.37 N	64.25 W
West Point Lake ⊜[1]	192	33.00 N	85.10 W
West Pond ⊜	276	40.53 N	73.38 W
Westport, Nf., Can.	186	49.47 N	56.38 W
Westport, N.S., Can.	186	44.16 N	66.21 W
Westport, On., Can.	212	44.41 N	76.26 W
Westport, Ire.	48	53.48 N	9.32 W
Westport, N.Z.	172	41.45 S	171.36 E
Westport, Ct., U.S.	207	41.08 N	73.21 W
Westport, In., U.S.	218	39.10 N	85.34 W
Westport, Ky., U.S.	218	38.28 N	85.28 W
Westport, Ma., U.S.	207	41.37 N	71.04 W
Westport, Or., U.S.	224	46.07 N	123.22 W
Westport, Pa., U.S.	214	41.18 N	77.51 W
Westport, Wa., U.S.	224	46.53 N	124.06 W
West Portland	224	45.25 N	122.45 W
West Portland Park	224	45.21 N	122.37 W
Westport Point	207	41.31 N	71.04 W
West Portsmouth	218	38.45 N	83.01 W
West Prairie ≃	182	55.30 N	116.31 W
West Puente Valley	280	34.04 N	117.59 W
West Pullman ◆[8]	278	41.41 N	87.39 W
Westpunt ›	241s	12.37 N	70.03 W
West Pymble	274a	33.46 S	151.08 E
West Quoddy Head ›	188	44.49 N	66.57 W
West Rand	273d	26.07 S	27.45 E
Westray I	46	59.18 N	3.00 W
Westray Firth ⊔	46	59.12 N	2.55 W
West Redding	207	41.19 N	73.26 W
Westrem	50	50.58 N	3.52 E
West Richfield	214	41.14 N	81.39 W
West Richland	202	46.18 N	119.20 W
West River c	208	38.52 N	76.31 W
West Road ≃	182	53.19 N	122.52 W
West Rosebud Creek ≃	202	45.29 N	109.27 W
West Roxbury ◆[8]	283	42.17 N	71.09 W
West Rupert	210	43.14 N	73.14 W
West Rutland	188	43.35 N	73.02 W
West Ryde	274a	33.48 S	151.05 E
West Sacramento	226	38.34 N	121.31 W
West Saint Marys ≃	186	45.15 N	62.04 W
West Saint Modeste	186	51.36 N	56.42 W
West Salem, Il., U.S.	194	38.31 N	88.00 W
West Salem, Oh., U.S.	214	40.58 N	82.06 W
West Salem, Wi., U.S.	190	43.53 N	91.04 W
West Salt Creek ≃	200	39.13 N	108.54 W
Westsamoa → Western Samoa □[1]	175a	13.55 S	172.00 W
West Sand Lake	210	42.39 N	73.37 W
West Saugerties	210	42.07 N	74.03 W
West Sayville	276	40.43 N	73.05 W
West Sayville County Park ♦	276	40.43 N	73.06 W
West Scenic Park	220	27.55 N	81.39 W
West Scotia Basin ⊹[1]	18	57.00 S	53.00 W
West Seneca	210	42.50 N	78.45 W
West Sepik □[5]	164	4.00 S	141.30 E
West Shoal Lake ⊜	184	50.20 N	97.41 W
West Siberian Plain → Zapadno-Sibirskaja ravnina ≚	72	60.00 N	75.00 E
Westsibirisches Flachland → Zapadno-Sibirskaja ravnina ≚	72	60.00 N	75.00 E
West Side Canal ≅	226	35.19 N	119.23 W
West Side Tennis Club ♦	276	40.43 N	73.51 W
West Simsbury	207	41.52 N	72.51 W
West Slope	224	45.29 N	122.45 W
West Spanish Peak ∧	200	37.23 N	104.59 W
West Springfield, Ma., U.S.	207	42.06 N	72.37 W
West Springfield, Pa., U.S.	214	41.57 N	80.29 W
West Springfield, Va., U.S.	208	38.46 N	77.13 W
West Stewartstown	206	44.59 N	71.31 W
West Stockbridge	207	42.20 N	73.22 W
West Stony Creek ≃	210	43.15 N	74.13 W
West Suffield	207	41.59 N	72.41 W
West Sunbury	214	41.00 N	79.54 W
West Sussex □[6]	42	50.55 N	0.35 W
West Swanzey	207	42.52 N	72.20 W
West Terre Haute	194	39.27 N	87.27 W
West-Terschelling	52	53.21 N	5.13 E
West Thompson Lake ⊜[1]	207	41.57 N	71.54 W
West Thurrock	260	51.29 N	0.16 E
West Tiana	207	40.52 N	72.33 W
West Tilbury	260	51.29 N	0.24 E
West Tisbury	207	41.22 N	70.40 W
West Toodyay	168a	31.33 S	116.27 E
West Torrens	168b	34.56 S	138.32 E
Westtown, N.Y., U.S.	210	41.20 N	74.32 W
Westtown, Pa., U.S.	285	39.56 N	75.33 W
West Townsend	207	42.40 N	71.44 W
West Turffontein ◆[8]	273d	26.16 S	28.02 E
West Union, Ia., U.S.	190	42.57 N	91.48 W
West Union, Oh., U.S.	218	38.47 N	83.32 W
West Union, W.V., U.S.	188	39.17 N	80.46 W
West Union Creek ≃	282	37.25 N	122.16 W
West Unity	216	41.35 N	84.26 W
West University Place	222	29.43 N	95.26 W
West Upton	207	42.10 N	71.37 W
Westvale	210	43.02 N	76.13 W
West Valley, Mt., U.S.	202	46.08 N	113.01 W
West Valley, N.Y., U.S.	210	42.24 N	78.37 W
West Valley City	200	40.42 N	111.57 W
West Vancouver	182	49.22 N	123.12 W
West View	214	40.31 N	80.02 W
West View Amusement Park ♦	279b	40.31 N	80.02 W
Westview Heights	207	41.33 N	73.05 W
Westville, N.S., Can.	186	45.34 N	62.43 W
Westville, In., U.S.	216	41.32 N	86.54 W
Westville, N.H., U.S.	207	42.49 N	71.07 W
Westville, N.J., U.S.	285	39.52 N	75.07 W
Westville, Oh., U.S.	218	40.07 N	83.51 W
Westville, Ok., U.S.	194	35.59 N	94.34 W
Westville, Pa., U.S.	214	41.13 N	78.50 W
Westville Center	206	44.57 N	74.24 W
Westville Grove	285	39.51 N	75.07 W
Westville Lake ⊜[1]	207	42.05 N	72.05 W
Westville Oaks	285	39.51 N	75.08 W
West Virginia □[3], U.S.	178	38.45 N	80.30 W
West Virginia □[3], U.S.	188	38.45 N	80.30 W
West-Vlaanderen □[4]	50	51.00 N	3.00 E
West Walker ≃	226	38.53 N	119.10 W
West Wallsend	170	32.54 S	151.35 E
Westward Ho90	42	51.02 N	4.15 W
West Wareham	207	41.47 N	70.45 W
West Warren	207	42.12 N	72.14 W
West Warwick	207	41.42 N	71.31 W
West Water ≃	46	56.47 N	2.38 W
West Webster	210	43.12 N	77.29 W
Westwego	194	29.54 N	90.08 W
West Wellow	42	50.58 N	1.35 W
West Whittier	280	33.59 N	118.03 W
West Wickham ◆[8]	260	51.22 N	0.01 W
West Willington	207	41.52 N	72.18 W
West Willow	216	42.14 N	83.34 W
West Windsor	210	42.06 N	74.46 W
West Winfield, N.Y., U.S.	210	42.53 N	75.11 W
West Winfield, Pa., U.S.	214	40.48 N	79.42 W
Westwold	182	50.28 N	119.45 W
Westwood, Ca., U.S.	204	40.18 N	121.00 W
Westwood, In., U.S.	218	39.55 N	85.25 W
Westwood, Ma., U.S.	207	42.12 N	71.14 W
Westwood, Mi., U.S.	216	42.18 N	85.38 W
Westwood, N.J., U.S.	210	40.59 N	74.01 W
Westwood, Pa., U.S.	214	40.18 N	78.56 W
Westwood ◆[8]	280	34.04 N	118.27 W
Westwood Lakes	220	25.44 N	80.22 W
Westworth Village	222	32.45 N	97.25 W
West Wyalong	166	33.55 S	147.13 E
West Wycombe	42	51.39 N	0.49 W
West Yarmouth	207	41.39 N	70.14 W
West Yegua Creek ≃	222	30.20 N	96.52 W
West Yellow Creek ≃	194	39.38 N	93.04 W
West Yellowstone	202	44.39 N	111.06 W
West York	208	39.57 N	76.45 W
West Yorkshire □[6]	44	53.45 N	1.40 W
Wetan, Pulau I	164	7.54 S	129.32 E
Wetar, Pulau I	112	7.48 S	126.18 E
Wetar, Selat ⊔	112	8.20 S	126.30 E
Wetaskiwin	182	52.58 N	113.22 W
Wete	154	5.04 S	39.43 E
Wethau	54	51.08 N	11.52 E
Wetherby	44	53.56 N	1.23 W
Wetherill Park	274a	33.51 S	150.54 E
Wethersfield	207	41.43 N	72.40 W
Wethmar	263	51.37 N	7.33 E
Wetiko Hills ⋏[2]	184	54.30 N	92.20 W
Wetluga → Vetluga ≃	80	56.18 N	46.24 E
Wetmore	198	39.38 N	95.48 W
Wet Mountains ⋏	200	38.00 N	105.10 W
Weto	152	7.57 N	7.50 E
Wetten	52	51.34 N	6.17 E
Wetter, Dtsch.	56	50.54 N	8.43 E
Wetter, Dtsch.	56	51.23 N	7.23 E
Wetter ≃	56	50.18 N	8.49 E
Wetterau □[9]	56	50.15 N	8.50 E
Wetteren	50	51.00 N	3.53 E
Wetterhorn ∧	58	46.39 N	8.08 E
Wetterstein Gebirge ⋏	64	47.25 N	11.05 E
Wettigan	110	18.57 N	95.21 E
Wettin	54	51.35 N	11.48 E
Wettingen	58	47.28 N	8.19 E
Wettringen	52	52.12 N	7.19 E
Wetumka	196	35.14 N	96.14 W
Wetumpka	194	32.32 N	86.12 W
Wetwang	44	54.01 N	0.34 W
Wetzikon	58	47.19 N	8.47 E
Wetzlar	56	50.33 N	8.29 E
Wetzstein ∧[2]	54	50.27 N	11.27 E
Wevelgem	50	50.48 N	3.10 E
Wevelinghoven	56	51.06 N	6.37 E
Wewahitchka	192	30.06 N	85.12 W
Wewak	164	3.35 S	143.40 E
Wewelsfleth	52	53.50 N	9.24 E
Wewer	52	51.41 N	8.42 E
Wewoka	196	35.09 N	96.29 W
Wexford, Ire.	48	52.20 N	6.27 W
Wexford, Pa., U.S.	214	40.38 N	80.03 W
Wexford □[6]	48	52.20 N	6.40 W
Wexford ◆[8]	275b	43.45 N	79.18 W
Wexford Harbour c	48	52.20 N	6.24 W
Wey ≃	42	51.23 N	0.28 W
Weyakwin Lake ⊜	184	54.30 N	106.00 W
Weyanoke	284c	38.48 N	77.09 W
Weyarn	64	47.51 N	11.48 E
Weyauwega	190	44.19 N	88.56 W
Weybridge	42	51.23 N	0.28 W
Weyburn	184	49.41 N	103.52 W
Weyer ◆[8]	263	51.10 N	7.01 E
Weyer Markt	61	47.52 N	14.41 E
Weyersheim	56	48.43 N	7.48 E
Weyhausen	52	52.47 N	10.23 E
Weyhe	52	52.59 N	8.52 E
Weymouth, N.S., Can.	186	44.25 N	66.00 W
Weymouth, Eng., U.K.	42	50.36 N	2.28 W
Weymouth, Ma., U.S.	207	42.13 N	70.56 W
Weymouth, N.J., U.S.	208	39.30 N	74.46 W
Weymouth, Cape ›	164	12.37 S	143.27 E
Weymouth Back ≃	283	42.15 N	70.55 W
Weymouth Fore ≃	283	42.16 N	70.56 W
Weymouth Great Pond ⊜	283	42.12 N	71.02 W
Wezemaal	56	50.57 N	4.46 E
Wezep	52	52.27 N	6.00 E
Whakatane	172	37.58 S	177.00 E
Whakatane ≃	172	37.57 S	177.00 E
Whalan	274a	33.45 S	150.49 E
Whale Creek ≃	276	40.27 N	74.13 W

Symbols in the index entries represent the broad categories identified in the key at the right. Symbols with superior numbers (⋏[1]) identify subcategories (see complete key on page *I · 1).*

Symbole im Register stellen die rechts im Schlüssel erklärten Kategorien dar. Symbole mit hochgestellten Ziffern (⋏[1]) bezeichnen Unterabteilungen einer Kategorie (vgl. vollständiger Schlüssel auf Seite *I · 1).*

Los símbolos incluídos en el texto del índice representan las grandes categorias identificadas con la clave a la derecha. Los símbolos con numeros en su parte superior (⋏[1]) identifican las subcategorías (véase la clave completa en la página *I · 1).*

Les symboles de l'index représentent les catégories indiquées dans la légende à droite. Les symboles suivis d'un indice (⋏[1]) représentent des sous-catégories (voir légende complète à la page *I · 1).*

Os símbolos incluídos no texto do índice representam as grandes categorias identificadas com a chave à direita. Os símbolos com números em sua parte superior (⋏[1]) identificam as subcategorias (veja-se a chave completa à página *I · 1).*

∧ Mountain	Berg	Montaña	Montagne	Montanha
⋏ Mountains	Gebirge	Montañas	Montagnes	Montanhas
)(Pass	Paß	Paso	Col	Passo
V Valley, Canyon	Tal, Cañon	Valle, Cañón	Vallée, Canyon	Vale, Canhão
≚ Plain	Ebene	Llano	Plaine	Planície
› Cape	Kap	Cabo	Cap	Cabo
I Island	Insel	Isla	Île	Ilha
II Islands	Inseln	Islas	Îles	Ilhas
⩦ Other Topographic Features	Andere Topographische Objekte	Otros Elementos Topográficos	Autres données topographiques	Outros acidentes topográficos

ESPAÑOL — Nombre / Página / Lat.°′ / Long.°′ W = Oeste
FRANÇAIS — Nom / Page / Lat.°′ / Long.°′ W = Ouest
PORTUGUÊS — Nome / Página / Lat.°′ / Long.°′ W = Oeste

Whaley Bridge 44 53.20 N 1.59 W
Whaley Lake 210 41.33 N 73.40 W
Whaleysville 208 38.23 N 75.18 W
Whaleyville 208 36.37 N 76.41 W
Whalley 44 53.50 N 2.24 W
Whalom 207 42.34 N 71.44 W
Whalsay I 46a 60.20 N 0.59 W
Whangaehu ≏ 172 40.03 S 175.06 E
Whangamata 172 37.12 S 175.52 E
Whangamomona 172 39.09 S 174.44 E
Whanganui National Park ♦ 172 39.20 S 175.00 E
Whangara 172 38.34 S 178.13 E
Whangarei 172 35.43 S 174.19 E
Whangaruru Harbour c 172 35.22 S 174.21 E
Whaplode 42 52.48 N 0.02 W
Wharfe ≏ 44 53.51 N 1.07 W
Wharfedale V 44 54.01 N 1.56 W
Wharles 262 53.49 N 2.50 W
Wharton, N.J., U.S. 210 40.53 N 74.34 W
Wharton, Oh., U.S. 214 40.52 N 83.21 W
Wharton, Tx., U.S. 222 29.18 N 96.06 W
Wharton, W.V., U.S. 188 37.54 N 81.40 W
Wharton □[6] 222 29.17 N 96.13 W
Wharton Basin ✦[1] 12 21.00 S 100.00 E
Wharton Lake ◎ 176 64.00 N 99.55 W
Wharton State Forest ♦ 285 39.45 N 74.40 W
Whataroa 172 43.17 S 170.25 E
Whatatutu 172 38.23 S 177.50 E
What Cheer 190 41.24 N 92.21 W
Whatcom □[6] 224 48.48 N 121.59 W
Whatcom, Lake ◎ 224 48.43 N 122.20 W
Whately 207 42.26 N 72.38 W
Whatley 194 31.39 N 87.42 W
Whatshan Lake ◎ 182 50.00 N 118.03 W
Whauphill 44 54.49 N 4.29 W
Wheao ≏ 172 38.34 S 176.39 E
Wheatfield 216 40.33 N 87.06 W
Wheathampstead 42 51.49 N 0.17 W
Wheatland, Ca., U.S. 226 39.00 N 121.25 W
Wheatland, Ia., U.S. 190 41.49 N 90.50 W
Wheatland, Pa., U.S. 214 41.12 N 80.28 W
Wheatland, Wy., U.S. 200 42.03 N 104.57 W
Wheatland Hills 208 40.02 N 76.21 W
Wheatland Reservoir ◎[1] 200 41.52 N 105.36 W
Wheatley, On., Can. 214 42.06 N 82.27 W
Wheatley, Eng., U.K. 42 51.44 N 1.08 W
Wheatley, Ar., U.S. 194 34.54 N 91.06 W
Wheatley Hill 44 54.45 N 1.23 W
Wheaton, Il., U.S. 216 41.51 N 88.06 W
Wheaton, Md., U.S. 208 39.02 N 77.03 W
Wheaton, Mn., U.S. 198 45.48 N 96.29 W
Wheaton Plaza ➔[9] 284c 39.02 N 77.03 W
Wheaton Regional Park ♦ 284c 39.03 N 77.02 W
Wheat Ridge 200 39.45 N 105.04 W
Wheelbarrow Peak ∧ 204 37.27 N 116.05 W
Wheeler, In., U.S. 216 41.30 N 87.10 W
Wheeler, Ms., U.S. 194 34.34 N 88.36 W
Wheeler, Tx., U.S. 196 35.26 N 100.16 W
Wheeler ≏, P.Q., Can. 176 57.02 N 67.13 W
Wheeler ≏, Sk., Can. 184 57.20 N 105.30 W
Wheeler Air Force Base ■ 229c 21.29 N 158.03 W
Wheeler Dam ➔[6] 283 42.48 N 71.12 W
Wheeler Island I 282 38.05 N 121.56 W
Wheeler Lake ◎[1] 194 34.40 N 87.05 W
Wheeler Peak ∧, Ca., U.S. 226 38.25 N 119.17 W
Wheeler Peak ∧, Nv., U.S. 204 38.59 N 114.19 W
Wheeler Peak ∧, N.M., U.S. 200 36.34 N 105.25 W
Wheeler Ridge 228 35.06 N 119.01 W
Wheelersburg 218 38.43 N 82.51 W
Wheelers Hill 274b 37.55 S 145.11 E
Wheeling, Il., U.S. 216 42.08 N 87.55 W
Wheeling, W.V., U.S. 214 40.03 N 80.43 W
Wheeling Creek ≏ 214 40.03 N 80.41 W
Wheelock 222 30.54 N 96.24 W
Wheelock ≏ 44 53.12 N 2.26 W
Wheelton 262 53.41 N 2.36 W
Wheelwright, Arg. 252 33.47 S 61.13 W
Wheelwright, Ky., U.S. 192 37.19 N 82.43 W
Wheelwright Park ♦ 283 42.15 N 70.49 W
Wheeny Creek ≏ 170 33.26 S 150.50 E
Whela Creek ≏ 162 26.17 S 116.50 E
Whelan, Mount ∧[2] 166 23.25 S 138.54 E
Whelpleyhill 260 51.44 N 0.33 W
Whernside ∧ 44 54.14 N 2.23 W
Whetstone Creek ≏ 214 40.23 N 83.03 W
Whetstone Gulf State Park ♦ 212 43.44 N 75.27 W
Whickham 44 54.56 N 1.41 W
Whidbey Island I 224 48.15 N 122.40 W
Whidbey Island Naval Air Station ■ 224 48.17 N 122.37 W
Whiddon Down 42 50.43 N 3.51 W
Whigham 192 30.52 N 84.19 W
Whigville 207 41.43 N 72.56 W
Whim Creek 162 20.50 S 117.50 E
Whinham, Mount ∧ 162 26.04 S 130.15 E
Whippany 210 40.49 N 74.25 W
Whippany ≏ 276 40.51 N 74.21 W
Whirl Creek ≏ 212 43.28 N 81.12 W
Whirlwind Reefs ✦[2] 164 4.42 S 148.16 E
Whiskey Peak ∧ 200 42.18 N 107.35 W
Whiskeytown-Shasta-Trinity National Recreation Area ♦ 204 40.45 N 122.15 W
Whisky Chitto Creek ≏ 194 30.31 N 92.55 W
Whiston 262 53.25 N 2.50 W
Whitacres 207 41.48 N 72.39 W
Whitaker 279b 40.24 N 79.53 W
Whitakers 192 36.06 N 77.42 W
Whitbourne 186 47.25 N 53.32 W
Whitburn, Eng., U.K. 44 54.57 N 1.22 W
Whitburn, Scot., U.K. 46 55.52 N 3.42 W
Whitby, On., Can. 212 43.52 N 78.56 W
Whitby, Eng., U.K. 44 54.29 N 0.37 W
Whitby, Eng., U.K. 262 53.17 N 2.54 W
Whitby Abbey v[1] 44 54.28 N 0.38 W
Whitchurch, Eng., U.K. 42 51.53 N 0.51 W
Whitchurch, Eng., U.K. 42 51.14 N 1.20 W
Whitchurch, Eng., U.K. 42 51.52 N 2.39 W
Whitchurch, Eng., U.K. 42 52.58 N 2.41 W
Whitchurch-Stouffville 212 43.58 N 79.15 W
Whitcombe, Mount ∧ 172 43.13 S 170.55 E
White, Ga., U.S. 192 34.16 N 84.44 W
White, S.D., U.S. 198 44.26 N 96.38 W
White □[6] 216 40.45 N 86.46 W
White ≏, B.C., Can. 182 50.23 N 115.35 W
White ≏, On., Can. 190 48.33 N 86.16 W
White ≏, N.A. 180 63.11 N 139.36 W
White ≏, U.S. 194 33.53 N 91.03 W
White ≏, U.S. 198 43.45 N 99.30 W
White ≏, U.S. 200 40.04 N 109.41 W
White ≏, Az., U.S. 200 33.44 N 110.13 W
White ≏, In., U.S. 194 38.25 N 87.44 W
White ≏, Mi., U.S. 190 43.25 N 86.21 W
White ≏, Nv., U.S. 204 37.42 N 115.10 W
White ≏, Or., U.S. 224 45.14 N 121.04 W
White ≏, Tx., U.S. 196 33.14 N 100.56 W
White ≏, Vt., U.S. 188 43.37 N 72.20 W
White ≏, Wa., U.S. 224 47.12 N 122.15 W
White ≏, Wa., U.S. 224 47.50 N 120.49 W
White ≏, Wi., U.S. 190 46.36 N 90.42 W
White ≏, Wi., U.S. 216 42.41 N 88.17 W
White, East Fork ≏, Az., U.S. 200 33.47 N 110.00 W
White, East Fork ≏, In., U.S. 194 38.33 N 87.14 W
White, Lake ◎ 162 21.05 S 129.00 E
White, Lake ◎[1] 218 39.07 N 83.02 W
White, North Fork ≏, Az., U.S. 200 33.47 N 110.00 W
White, North Fork ≏, Co., U.S. 200 39.58 N 107.38 W
White, South Fork ≏ 200 39.58 N 107.38 W
White, West Fork ≏ 224 47.07 N 121.37 W
White Bay c 186 50.00 N 56.30 W
White Bear Indian Reserve ➔[4] 184 49.45 N 102.15 W
White Bear Lake 190 45.03 N 93.00 W
Whitebear Lake ◎ 184 51.05 N 108.05 W
White Bluff 194 36.06 N 87.13 W
White Breast Creek ≏ 190 41.24 N 93.02 W
White Butte ∧ 198 46.23 N 103.19 W
Whitecap Lake ◎ 184 56.54 N 95.14 W
White Cap Mountain ∧ 188 45.35 N 69.13 W
White Castle 194 30.10 N 91.08 W
White Center 224 47.31 N 122.21 W
White Chuck ≏ 224 48.11 N 121.27 W
White City, Fl., U.S. 220 29.53 N 85.13 W
White City, Ks., U.S. 198 38.47 N 96.44 W
White City Stadium ♦ 260 51.31 N 0.14 W
White Clay Creek ≏, U.S. 198 43.12 N 102.48 W
White Clay Creek ≏, U.S. 285 39.42 N 75.37 W
White Cliffs, Austl. 162 28.26 S 122.57 E
White Cliffs, Austl. 166 30.51 S 143.05 E
White Cloud 190 43.33 N 85.46 W
White Cloud Island I 212 44.50 N 80.58 W
Whitecoomb ∧, N.Z. 172 45.36 S 169.05 E
White Coomb ∧, Scot., U.K. 44 55.26 N 3.20 W
Whitecourt 182 54.09 N 115.41 W
White Creek 210 42.58 N 73.18 W
White Creek ≏, In., U.S. 218 38.58 N 86.01 W
White Creek ≏, Wa., U.S. 224 46.01 N 121.08 W
White Deer, Pa., U.S. 210 41.05 N 76.52 W
White Deer, Tx., U.S. 196 35.26 N 101.10 W
White Deer Creek ≏ 210 41.05 N 76.53 W
White Earth ≏ 198 48.09 N 102.42 W
White Earth Indian Reservation ➔[4] 198 47.18 N 95.50 W
White Esk ≏ 44 55.12 N 3.10 W
Whiteface 196 33.36 N 102.37 W
Whiteface ≏ 190 46.58 N 92.48 W
Whiteface Mountain ∧ 188 44.22 N 73.54 W
Whitefield, Eng., U.K. 44 53.33 N 2.18 W
Whitefield, Eng., U.K. 262 53.33 N 2.18 W
Whitefield, N.H., U.S. 188 44.22 N 71.36 W
Whitefish 202 48.24 N 114.20 W
Whitefish ≏ 190 45.55 N 86.57 W
Whitefish Bay 216 43.06 N 87.54 W
Whitefish Bay c, On., Can. 184 49.26 N 94.14 W
Whitefish Bay c, N.A. 190 46.40 N 84.50 W
Whitefish Lake ◎, Ab., Can. 182 54.22 N 111.55 W
Whitefish Lake ◎, Mb., Can. 184 55.34 N 93.13 W
Whitefish Lake ◎, N.T., Can. 176 62.41 N 106.48 W
Whitefish Lake ◎, On., Can. 190 48.03 N 84.29 W
Whitefish Lake ◎, On., Can. 212 45.18 N 79.47 W
Whitefish Lake ◎, On., Can. 212 44.31 N 76.14 W
Whitefish Lake ◎, Ak., U.S. 180 61.21 N 160.00 W
Whitefish Lake ◎, Mt., U.S. 202 48.27 N 114.22 W
White Fish Lake Indian Reserve ➔[4] 182 54.20 N 111.45 W
Whitefish Point 190 46.45 N 84.59 W
Whitefish Point › 190 46.45 N 85.00 W
Whitefish Range ⛰ 202 48.40 N 114.26 W
Whiteford 208 39.42 N 76.20 W
Whiteford Point › 42 51.38 N 4.14 W
White Fox 184 53.27 N 104.05 W
White Fox ≏ 184 53.32 N 104.00 W
Whitegate 48 51.50 N 8.14 W
White Gull Creek ≏ 184 53.44 N 104.20 W
Whitehall (Paulstown), Ire. 48 52.41 N 7.01 W
Whitehall, Scot., U.K. 46 59.07 N 2.37 W
White Hall, Ar., U.S. 194 34.16 N 92.05 W
White Hall, Il., U.S. 219 39.26 N 90.24 W
White Hall, Md., U.S. 208 39.37 N 76.37 W
Whitehall, Mi., U.S. 190 43.24 N 86.20 W
Whitehall, Mt., U.S. 202 45.52 N 112.05 W
Whitehall, N.Y., U.S. 188 43.33 N 73.24 W
Whitehall, Oh., U.S. 218 39.58 N 82.53 W
Whitehall, Pa., U.S. 214 40.21 N 79.59 W
Whitehall, Wi., U.S. 190 44.22 N 91.18 W
Whitehaven, Eng., U.K. 44 54.33 N 3.35 W
White Haven, Pa., U.S. 210 41.03 N 75.46 W
Whitehead 48 54.46 N 5.43 W
White Holme Reservoir ◎[1] 262 53.41 N 2.02 W
Whitehorse, Yk., Can. 180 60.43 N 135.03 W
White Horse, N.J., U.S. 208 40.11 N 74.42 W
White Horse, Vale of V 42 51.37 N 1.37 W
Whitehorse Hill ∧[2] 42 51.34 N 1.34 W
Whitehouse, Scot., U.K. 46 57.13 N 2.37 W
Whitehouse, N.J., U.S. 210 40.37 N 74.46 W
Whitehouse, Oh., U.S. 216 41.31 N 83.48 W
White House, Tn., U.S. 194 36.35 N 86.49 W
Whitehouse, Tx., U.S. 222 32.13 N 95.14 W
White House v 284c 38.54 N 77.02 W
White House Station 210 40.36 N 74.46 W
White Island I, Ant. 9 66.44 S 48.35 E
White Island I, N.T., Can. 176 65.50 N 84.50 W
White Island I, N.Z. 172 37.31 S 177.11 E
White Lake, Mi., U.S. 281 42.41 N 83.33 W
White Lake, N.Y., U.S. 210 41.40 N 74.50 W
White Lake, S.D., U.S. 198 43.43 N 98.42 W
White Lake, Wi., U.S. 190 45.09 N 88.45 W
White Lake ◎, On., Can. 190 48.48 N 85.36 W
White Lake ◎, On., Can. 212 44.47 N 76.45 W
White Lake ◎, On., Can. 212 44.27 N 77.03 W
White Lake ◎, On., Can. 212 45.18 N 76.31 W
White Lake ◎, La., U.S. 194 29.45 N 92.30 W
White Lake ◎, Mi., U.S. 281 42.40 N 83.34 W
Whiteland 218 39.33 N 86.05 W
Whitelaw 182 56.07 N 118.04 W
Whiteley Village 260 51.21 N 0.26 W
White Lick Creek ≏ 218 39.30 N 86.23 W
White Lick Creek, East Fork ≏ 218 39.35 N 86.22 W
White Lick Creek, West Fork ≏ 218 39.38 N 86.23 W
Whiteman Air Force Base ■ 194 38.44 N 93.34 W
Whiteman Airpark ⊠ 280 34.15 N 118.25 W
Whiteman Range ⛰ 164 5.50 S 149.55 E
Whitemans Creek ≏ 212 43.10 N 80.21 W
Whitemark 166 40.07 S 148.01 E
White Marsh 284b 39.23 N 76.26 W
Whitemarsh Run ≏ 284b 39.22 N 76.25 W
White Meadow Lake 210 40.55 N 74.31 W
White Meadow Lake ◎ 276 40.55 N 74.31 W
White Mills 210 41.32 N 75.12 W
White Mountain 180 64.41 N 163.24 W
White Mountain Peak ∧ 204 37.38 N 118.15 W
White Mountains ⛰, U.S. 204 37.30 N 118.15 W
White Mountains ⛰, Az., U.S. 200 33.45 N 109.40 W
White Mountains ⛰, N.H., U.S. 188 44.10 N 71.35 W
Whitemouth 184 49.57 N 95.59 W
Whitemouth ≏ 184 50.07 N 96.02 W
Whitemouth Lake ◎ 184 49.14 N 95.40 W
Whitemud ≏ 184 50.15 N 98.37 W
Whiten Head › 46 58.34 N 4.36 W
White Nile (Al-Baḥr al-Abyaḍ) ≏ 140 15.38 N 32.31 E
White Nile Dam → Jabal al-Awliyā', Khazzān ➔[6] 140 15.14 N 32.29 E
White Oak, Md., U.S. 284c 39.02 N 77.00 W
White Oak, Pa., U.S. 279b 40.20 N 79.48 W
White Oak, Tx., U.S. 222 32.32 N 94.52 W
White Oak ≏ 192 34.40 N 77.07 W
White Oak Creek ≏, Oh., U.S. 218 38.47 N 83.57 W
White Oak Creek ≏, Tx., U.S. 194 33.16 N 94.39 W
White Oak Creek, East Fork ≏ 218 39.00 N 83.53 W
White Oak Creek, North Fork ≏ 218 39.00 N 83.53 W
White Oak Lake ◎[1] 194 33.40 N 93.10 W
White Oak Regional Park ♦ 279a 40.21 N 79.47 W
White Pass)(, N.A. 180 59.38 N 135.05 W
White Pass)(, Wa., U.S. 224 46.38 N 121.24 W
White Pigeon 216 41.47 N 85.38 W
White Pine, Mi., U.S. 190 46.45 N 89.35 W
Whitepine, Mt., U.S. 182 47.45 N 115.29 W
White Pine, Tn., U.S. 192 36.06 N 83.17 W
White Pines, Ca., U.S. 226 38.18 N 120.21 W
White Pines, Il., U.S. 278 41.57 N 87.57 W
White Plains, Md., U.S. 208 38.35 N 76.56 W
White Plains, N.Y., U.S. 210 41.02 N 73.45 W
White Plains, N.C., U.S. 192 36.26 N 80.38 W
White Pond ◎ 283 42.26 N 71.23 W
White River, On., Can. 190 48.35 N 85.15 W
Whiteriver, Az., U.S. 200 33.50 N 109.57 W
White River, S.D., U.S. 198 43.34 N 100.44 W
White River Junction 188 43.38 N 72.19 W
White Rock 224 49.02 N 122.49 W
White Rock Creek ≏, Ks., U.S. 198 39.55 N 97.51 W
White Rock Creek ≏, Tx., U.S. 222 30.54 N 95.16 W
White Rock Creek ≏, Tx., U.S. 222 32.43 N 96.44 W
White Rock Lake ◎[1] 222 32.50 N 96.44 W
White Rocks ∧ 192 36.40 N 83.27 W
Whiterocks ≏ 200 40.26 N 109.55 W
White Roding 260 51.48 N 0.16 E
White Russia → Belarus □[1] 22 53.50 N 28.00 E
Whitesail Lake ◎ 182 53.30 N 127.00 W
White Salmon 224 45.43 N 121.29 W
White Salmon ≏ 224 45.43 N 121.31 W
Whitesand ≏ 184 51.34 N 101.55 W
White Sands Beach 207 41.18 N 72.09 W
White Sands Missile Range ■ 200 32.23 N 106.28 W
White Sands National Monument ♦ 200 32.46 N 106.20 W
Whitesboro, N.J., U.S. 208 39.02 N 74.51 W
Whitesboro, N.Y., U.S. 210 43.07 N 75.17 W
Whitesboro, Tx., U.S. 196 33.39 N 96.54 W
Whitesburg 192 37.07 N 82.49 W
White Sea → Beloje more ⚲[2] 24 65.30 N 38.00 E
White Settlement 222 32.45 N 97.27 W
Whiteshell Provincial Park ♦ 184 50.00 N 95.25 W
Whiteside 219 39.11 N 91.01 W
Whiteside, Canal ȣ 254 53.55 S 70.15 W
White's Landing 214 41.25 N 82.54 W
White Springs 192 30.19 N 82.45 W
White Stone 208 37.38 N 76.23 W
Whitestone ➔[8] 276 40.47 N 73.49 W
White Stone Lake ◎ 184 56.25 N 97.31 W
Whitestown 218 39.59 N 86.20 W
White Sulphur Springs, Mt., U.S. 202 46.32 N 110.54 W
White Sulphur Springs, N.Y., U.S. 210 41.48 N 74.50 W
White Sulphur Springs, W.V., U.S. 192 37.47 N 80.17 W
Whites Valley 210 41.42 N 75.22 W
Whitesville, Ky., U.S. 194 37.40 N 86.52 W
Whitesville, N.Y., U.S. 210 42.02 N 77.45 W
Whitesville, W.V., U.S. 188 37.58 N 81.31 W
White Swan 224 46.22 N 120.43 W
Whiteswan Lakes ◎ 184 54.05 N 105.10 W
Whitevale 212 43.53 N 79.09 W
White Valley 214 40.25 N 79.36 W
Whiteville, N.C., U.S. 192 34.20 N 78.42 W
Whiteville, Tn., U.S. 194 35.19 N 89.08 W
White Volta (Volta Blanche) ≏ 150 9.10 N 1.15 W
Whitewater, Ks., U.S. 198 37.57 N 97.08 W
Whitewater, Mt., U.S. 202 48.45 N 107.37 W
Whitewater, Wi., U.S. 216 42.50 N 88.43 W
Whitewater ≏, U.S. 218 39.10 N 84.47 W
Whitewater ≏, Ca., U.S. 204 33.30 N 116.03 W
Whitewater ≏, Mo., U.S. 194 37.01 N 89.43 W
Whitewater, Dry Fork ≏ 218 39.11 N 84.47 W
Whitewater, East Fork ≏ 218 39.24 N 85.01 W
Whitewater, Greens Fork ≏ 218 39.45 N 85.07 W
Whitewater, Nolands Fork ≏ 218 39.41 N 85.07 W
Whitewater Baldy ∧ 200 33.20 N 108.39 W
Whitewater Bay c 220 25.16 N 81.00 W
Whitewater Creek ≏, N.A. 202 48.30 N 107.11 W
Whitewater Creek ≏, Ga., U.S. 192 32.21 N 84.03 W
Whitewater Creek ≏, Wi., U.S. 216 42.52 N 88.45 W
Whitewater Lake ◎, Mb., Can. 184 49.15 N 100.20 W
Whitewater Lake ◎, Wi., U.S. 216 42.47 N 88.42 W
Whitewater State Park ♦ 218 39.36 N 84.58 W
White Woman Creek ≏ 198 38.25 N 100.54 W
Whitewood, Austl. 166 21.28 S 143.36 E
Whitewood, Sk., Can. 184 50.20 N 102.15 W
Whitewood, S.D., U.S. 198 44.27 N 103.38 W
Whitewood, Lake ◎ 198 44.20 N 97.18 W
Whitewright 196 33.30 N 96.23 W
Whitfield 42 51.09 N 1.18 E
Whithorn, Jam. 241q 18.15 N 78.02 W
Whithorn, Scot., U.K. 44 54.44 N 4.25 W
Whitianga 172 36.50 S 175.42 E
Whiting, In., U.S. 216 41.40 N 87.29 W
Whiting, Ia., U.S. 198 42.07 N 96.08 W
Whiting, Ks., U.S. 198 39.35 N 95.36 W
Whiting, N.J., U.S. 208 39.57 N 74.22 W
Whiting, Wi., U.S. 190 44.29 N 89.33 W
Whiting Bay 44 55.29 N 5.06 W
Whiting Field Naval Air Station ■ 194 30.43 N 87.02 W
Whitingham 207 42.47 N 72.53 W
Whitinsville 207 42.06 N 71.40 W
Whitland 42 51.50 N 4.37 W
Whitley □[6] 216 41.10 N 85.29 W
Whitley Bay 44 55.03 N 1.25 W
Whitley City 192 36.43 N 84.28 W
Whitley Row 260 51.15 N 0.09 E
Whitman 207 42.04 N 70.56 W
Whitman Mission National Historic Site ⊥ 202 46.01 N 118.30 W
Whitmans Pond ◎ 283 42.12 N 70.57 W
Whitman Square 208 39.45 N 75.03 W
Whitmire 192 34.30 N 81.36 W
Whitmore Lake 216 42.25 N 83.46 W
Whitmore Lake ◎ 281 42.26 N 83.45 W
Whitmore Mountains ⛰ 9 82.35 S 104.30 W
Whitmore Village 229c 21.30 N 158.01 W
Whitner Heights 226 36.37 N 119.32 W
Whitney, On., Can. 212 45.30 N 78.14 W
Whitney, Pa., U.S. 214 40.15 N 79.24 W
Whitney, Tx., U.S. 222 31.57 N 97.19 W
Whitney, Lake ◎[1] 222 31.55 N 97.23 W
Whitney, Mount ∧ 204 36.35 N 118.18 W
Whitney Point 210 42.19 N 75.58 W
Whitney Point Lake ◎[1] 210 42.25 N 75.55 W
Whitney Woods Reservation ♦ 283 42.13 N 70.51 W
Whitstable 42 51.22 N 1.02 E
Whitsunday Island I 166 20.17 S 148.59 E
Whittaker 216 42.08 N 83.36 W
Whittemore, Ia., U.S. 198 43.03 N 94.25 W
Whittemore, Mi., U.S. 190 44.14 N 83.48 W
Whittier, Ak., U.S. 180 60.47 N 148.42 W
Whittier, Ca., U.S. 228 33.58 N 118.01 W
Whittier, N.C., U.S. 192 35.26 N 83.22 W
Whittier Narrows Dam ➔[6] 280 34.01 N 118.04 W
Whittier Narrows Flood Control Basin ◎[1] 280 34.02 N 118.04 W
Whittingham 44 55.24 N 1.54 W
Whittington 42 52.52 N 3.00 W
Whittle, Cap › 186 50.11 N 60.08 W
Whittle Hill ∧[2] 262 53.40 N 2.16 W
Whittle-le-Woods 262 53.41 N 2.38 W
Whittlesea, Austl. 169 37.31 S 145.07 E
Whittlesea, Ciskei 158 32.10 S 26.50 E
Whittlesey 42 52.34 N 0.08 W
Whittlesey, Mount ∧[2] 190 46.18 N 90.37 W
Whitwell 194 35.12 N 85.31 W
Whitwick 42 52.44 N 1.21 W
Whitworth 44 53.40 N 2.10 W
Whitworth Peak ∧ 224 49.05 N 121.13 W
Wholdaia Lake ◎ 176 60.43 N 104.10 W
Whonock 224 49.11 N 122.28 W
W. Howard Frankland Bridge ➔[5] 220 27.56 N 82.35 W
Whyalla 166 33.02 S 137.35 E
Whycocomagh 186 45.59 N 61.07 W
Whymper, Mount ∧ 224 48.57 N 124.10 W
Wiang Pa Pao 110 19.22 N 99.30 E
Wiang Phan 110 20.26 N 99.53 E
Wiarton 212 44.45 N 81.09 W
Wiasi 150 10.21 N 1.20 W
Wiau Lake ◎ 182 55.23 N 111.18 W
Wiawso 150 6.12 N 2.29 W
Wiay I 46 57.23 N 7.13 W
Wiązów 30 50.49 N 17.11 E
Wibaux 198 46.59 N 104.11 W
Wiblingen ➔[8] 58 48.21 N 9.58 E
Wichian Buri 110 15.39 N 101.07 E
Wichita 198 37.41 N 97.20 W
Wichita ≏ 196 34.07 N 98.10 W
Wichita Falls 196 33.54 N 98.29 W
Wichita Mountains ⛰ 196 34.45 N 98.40 W
Wichlinghofen ➔[8] 263 51.27 N 7.30 E
Wick 46 58.26 N 3.06 W
Wick ≏ 46 58.27 N 3.05 W
Wickatunk 276 40.21 N 74.14 W
Wickede 52 51.29 N 7.52 E
Wickede ➔[8] 263 51.32 N 7.37 E
Wickenburg 200 33.58 N 112.43 W
Wickepin 162 32.46 S 117.30 E
Wicker Memorial Park ♦ 278 41.34 N 87.28 W
Wickett 196 31.34 N 102.59 W
Wickford 42 51.38 N 0.31 E
Wickham, Austl. 162 20.31 S 117.08 E
Wickham, P.Q., Can. 206 45.45 N 72.30 W
Wickham, Eng., U.K. 42 50.54 N 1.10 W
Wickham ≏ 164 16.22 S 131.06 E
Wickham, Cape › 166 39.36 S 143.57 E
Wickham Bishops 260 51.47 N 0.40 E
Wickham Market 42 52.09 N 1.22 E
Wickiup Reservoir ◎[1] 202 43.40 N 121.43 W
Wickliffe, Ky., U.S. 194 36.58 N 89.05 W
Wickliffe, Oh., U.S. 214 41.06 N 80.43 W
Wickliffe, Oh., U.S. 214 41.36 N 81.27 W
Wicklow 48 52.59 N 6.03 W
Wicklow □[6] 48 53.00 N 6.30 W
Wicklow Head › 48 52.58 N 6.00 W
Wicklow Mountains ⛰ 48 53.02 N 6.24 W
Wickrath 56 51.07 N 6.24 E
Wicksteed Lake ◎ 190 46.46 N 79.40 W
Wicomico 208 37.17 N 76.31 W
Wicomico □[6] 208 38.22 N 75.36 W
Wicomico ≏ 208 38.13 N 75.55 W
Wicomico Church 208 37.49 N 76.23 W
Wiconisco 208 40.34 N 76.41 W
Wiconisco Creek ≏ 208 40.32 N 76.58 W
Wid ≏ 262 51.45 N 0.27 E
Widas ≏ 115a 7.30 S 112.08 E
Widden Brook ≏ 170 32.32 S 150.22 E
Widdern 56 49.19 N 9.25 E
Widdert ➔[8] 263 51.08 N 7.04 E
Widdop Reservoir ◎[1] 262 53.48 N 2.06 W
Widdrington Station 44 55.15 N 1.36 W
Wide Bay c, Pap. N. Gui. 164 5.05 S 152.05 E
Wide Bay c, Ak., U.S. 180 57.20 N 156.25 W
Widecombe in the Moor 42 50.35 N 3.48 W
Widemouth Bay 42 50.47 N 4.32 W
Widen 188 38.27 N 80.51 W
Widener College v[2] 285 39.52 N 75.21 W
Wide Open 44 55.03 N 1.38 W
Widerøe, Mount ∧ 9 72.08 S 23.30 E
Wide Ruin Wash V 200 35.13 N 109.52 W
Widford 260 51.43 N 0.27 E
Widgeegoara Creek ≏ 166 27.30 S 145.55 E
Widgiemooltha 162 31.30 S 121.34 E
Widnes 44 53.22 N 2.44 W
Wi-do I 98 35.36 N 126.17 E
Widodaren 115a 7.25 S 111.14 E
Widuchowa 54 53.10 N 14.25 E
Widur 124 27.55 N 85.10 E
Wiebelskirchen 56 49.22 N 7.11 E
Więcbork 30 53.22 N 17.30 E
Wieck 54 54.06 N 13.26 E
Wied ≏ 56 50.26 N 7.27 E
Wieda 54 51.38 N 10.34 E
Wiederitzsch 54 51.24 N 12.22 E
Wiedlisbach 58 47.15 N 7.39 E
Wiefelstede 52 53.15 N 8.07 E
Wiehe 54 51.16 N 11.25 E
Wiehengebirge ⛰ 52 52.20 N 8.40 E
Wiehengebirge, Naturpark ♦ 52 52.20 N 8.20 E
Wiehl 56 50.57 N 7.31 E
Wiek 54 54.37 N 13.17 E
Wieleń 30 52.54 N 16.10 E
Wielichowo 30 52.08 N 16.21 E
Wieliczka 30 49.59 N 20.04 E
Wielkopolska ➔[1] 30 51.50 N 17.20 E
Wielkopolski Park Narodowy ♦ 30 52.15 N 16.50 E
Wieluń 30 51.14 N 18.34 E
Wiemelhausen ➔[8] 263 51.28 N 7.13 E
Wien (Vienna), Öst. 61 48.13 N 16.20 E
Wien (Vienna), Öst. 264b 48.13 N 16.20 E
Wien □[3] 264b 48.12 N 16.22 E
Wien ≏ 264b 48.13 N 16.23 E
Wien, Universität v[2] 264b 48.13 N 16.22 E
Wiener Berg ⛰[2] 264b 48.10 N 16.22 E
Wienerherberg 264b 48.03 N 16.33 E
Wiener Neudorf 61 48.05 N 16.19 E
Wiener Neustadt 61 47.49 N 16.15 E
Wiener Neustädter Kanal ≋ 61 48.05 N 16.22 E
Wienerwald ⛰ 61 48.10 N 16.00 E
Wienhagen ∧[2] 263 51.08 N 7.33 E
Wienhausen 52 52.35 N 10.11 E
Wien-Schwechat, Flughafen ⊠ 264b 48.07 N 16.33 E
Wiepke 54 52.36 N 11.20 E
Wieprz ≏ 30 51.34 N 21.49 E
Wieprza ≏ 30 54.26 N 16.22 E
Wieprz-Krzna, Kanał ≋ 30 51.56 N 22.56 E
Wiera ≏ 56 50.55 N 9.10 E
Wierden 52 52.22 N 6.35 E
Wieren 54 52.53 N 10.39 E
Wiergate 194 31.00 N 93.42 W
Wieringermeer ➔[1] 52 52.45 N 5.00 E
Wieringerwerf 52 52.51 N 5.02 E
Wieruszów 30 51.18 N 18.08 E
Wierzyca ≏ 30 53.51 N 18.50 E
Wies 61 46.43 N 15.16 E
Wies v[1] 58 47.40 N 10.53 E
Wiesa 54 50.36 N 13.01 E
Wiesau 60 49.55 N 12.11 E
Wiesbaden 56 50.05 N 8.14 E
Wiesbaden □[5] 56 50.20 N 8.20 E
Wiescheid ➔[8] 263 51.08 N 6.59 E
Wiescherhöfen ➔[8] 263 51.39 N 7.46 E
Wiese ≏ 58 47.35 N 7.35 E
Wiesede 52 53.27 N 7.46 E
Wieselburg 61 48.08 N 15.09 E
Wiesen 58 46.43 N 9.43 E
Wiesenburg 54 52.07 N 12.26 E
Wiesenfeld 56 51.16 N 10.06 E
Wiesensteig 56 48.34 N 9.37 E
Wiesent ≏ 60 49.42 N 11.05 E
Wiesentheid 56 49.47 N 10.20 E
Wieseth ≏ 56 49.10 N 10.39 E
Wiesloch 56 49.17 N 8.42 E
Wiesmoor 52 53.25 N 7.43 E
Wieting 61 46.52 N 14.32 E
Wietmarschen 52 52.31 N 7.07 E
Wietze 52 52.39 N 9.50 E
Wietzen 52 52.43 N 9.04 E
Wigan 44 53.33 N 2.38 W
Wigan □[8] 262 53.32 N 2.35 W
Wiggensbach 58 47.44 N 10.14 E
Wigger ≏ 58 47.18 N 7.53 E
Wiggington 260 51.47 N 0.38 W
Wiggins, Co., U.S. 198 40.13 N 104.04 W
Wiggins, Ms., U.S. 194 30.51 N 89.08 W
Wiggins Fork ≏ 202 43.27 N 109.28 W
Wigglesworth 44 54.01 N 2.17 W
Wight, Isle of I 42 50.40 N 1.20 W
Wigmore, Eng., U.K. 42 52.19 N 2.51 W
Wigmore, Eng., U.K. 260 51.21 N 0.35 E
Wignehies 50 50.01 N 4.00 E
Wigston 42 52.36 N 1.05 W
Wigton 44 54.49 N 3.09 W
Wigtown 44 54.52 N 4.26 W
Wigtown Bay c 44 54.46 N 4.15 W
Wijalpurā 124 26.55 N 85.51 E
Wijchen 52 51.48 N 5.43 E
Wijhe 52 52.24 N 6.07 E
Wijk aan Zee 52 52.29 N 4.35 E
Wijk bij Duurstede 52 51.58 N 5.20 E
Wil 58 47.27 N 9.03 E
Wilbarger Creek ≏ 222 30.11 N 97.23 W
Wilber 198 40.28 N 96.57 W
Wilberforce, Austl. 170 33.33 S 150.50 E
Wilberforce, Oh., U.S. 218 39.42 N 83.52 W
Wilberforce Falls ⌊ 176 67.07 N 108.47 W
Wilbraham 207 42.07 N 72.25 W
Wilbur 202 47.45 N 118.42 W
Wilburton 196 34.55 N 95.18 W
Wilcannia 166 31.34 S 143.23 E
Wilcock, Península ›[1] 254 50.40 S 74.00 W
Wilcox, Sk., Can. 184 50.07 N 104.44 W
Wilcox, Ne., U.S. 198 40.21 N 99.10 W
Wilcox, Pa., U.S. 214 41.34 N 78.41 W
Wilcox, Tx., U.S. 222 30.27 N 96.22 W
Wilcox, Mount ∧ 207 42.13 N 73.16 W
Wildalpen 61 47.39 N 14.59 E
Wildau 54 52.19 N 13.38 E
Wildbad im Schwarzwald 56 48.45 N 8.32 E
Wildberg, Dtsch. 54 52.52 N 12.37 E
Wildberg, Dtsch. 56 48.37 N 8.44 E
Wildboarclough 262 53.13 N 2.02 W
Wildcat Canyon Regional Park ♦ 282 37.56 N 122.17 W
Wildcat Creek ≏, Ca., U.S. 282 37.57 N 122.23 W
Wildcat Creek ≏, In., U.S. 216 40.28 N 86.52 W
Wildcat Creek, Middle Fork ≏ 216 40.25 N 86.46 W
Wildcat Creek, South Fork ≏ 216 40.26 N 86.48 W
Wildcat Hill ∧[2] 184 53.17 N 102.30 W
Wild Coast ♦[2] 158 32.30 S 28.45 E
Wilde ➔[8] 288 34.42 S 58.20 W
Wildegg 58 47.25 N 8.11 E
Wildeman ≏ 164 5.33 S 139.13 E
Wildemann 52 51.49 N 10.17 E
Wildenbruch 264a 52.17 N 13.04 E
Wildenfels 54 50.40 N 12.35 E
Wildenstein 58 47.59 N 6.58 E
Wildenthal 54 50.27 N 12.37 E
Wilder 202 43.40 N 116.54 W
Wilderness 158 34.00 S 22.36 E
Wilderness of Judaea (Midbar Yehuda) ➔[2] 132 31.30 N 35.18 E
Wilderness State Park ♦ 190 45.42 N 84.57 W
Wildersville 194 35.46 N 88.21 W
Wildervank 52 53.04 N 6.51 E
Wildeshausen 52 52.54 N 8.26 E
Wildfield 212 43.49 N 79.44 W
Wildflecken 56 50.23 N 9.54 E
Wildfontein 158 31.04 S 24.50 E
Wildhaus 58 47.12 N 9.22 E
Wildhay ≏ 182 54.02 N 117.20 W
Wildhorn ∧ 58 46.21 N 7.22 E
Wildhorse Creek ≏, U.S. 198 40.36 N 102.00 W
Wildhorse Creek ≏, Ok., U.S. 196 34.32 N 97.10 W
Wild Horse Creek ≏, Wy., U.S. 198 44.39 N 106.08 W
Wild Horse Draw V 196 31.11 N 104.50 W
Wild Horse Hill ∧[2] 168a 33.12 S 116.40 E
Wild Horse Lake ◎ 202 48.58 N 110.00 W
Wild Horse Plains 168b 34.22 S 138.17 E
Wildnest Lake ◎ 184 55.00 N 102.20 W
Wildon 61 46.53 N 15.31 E
Wild Rice ≏, Mn., U.S. 198 47.20 N 96.50 W
Wild Rice ≏, N.D., U.S. 198 46.45 N 96.47 W
Wild Rice, South Branch ≏ 198 47.12 N 96.38 W
Wildrose, N.D., U.S. 198 48.37 N 103.11 W
Wild Rose, Wi., U.S. 190 44.10 N 89.14 W
Wildseeloder ∧ 64 47.26 N 12.32 E
Wildspitze ∧ 58 46.53 N 10.52 E
Wildstrubel ∧ 58 46.24 N 7.32 E
Wildwood, Ab., Can. 182 53.37 N 115.14 W
Wildwood, Fl., U.S. 220 28.51 N 82.02 W
Wildwood, Il., U.S. 216 42.21 N 88.00 W
Wildwood, N.J., U.S. 208 38.59 N 74.48 W
Wildwood, Pa., U.S. 214 40.36 N 79.58 W
Wildwood, Lake ◎ 276 41.09 N 74.32 W
Wild Wood Beach 284b 39.15 N 76.25 W
Wildwood Canyon Park ♦ 280 34.13 N 118.17 W
Wildwood Crest 208 38.58 N 74.50 W
Wiley 224 46.33 N 120.39 W
Wilfersdorf 61 48.35 N 16.38 E
Wilge ≏, S. Afr. 158 27.03 S 28.20 E
Wilge ≏, S. Afr. 158 25.34 S 29.10 E
Wilgena 162 30.46 S 134.44 E
Wilgespruit ≏ 273d 26.07 S 27.52 E
Wilhelm, Lake ◎[1] 214 41.23 N 80.08 W
Wilhelm, Mount ∧ 164 5.45 S 145.05 E
Wilhelmina Gebergte ⛰ 250 3.45 N 56.30 W
Wilhelminakanaal ≋ 52 51.47 N 4.51 E
Wilhelminaoord 52 52.53 N 6.10 E
Wilhelmina Peak → Trikora, Puncak ∧ 164 4.15 S 138.45 E
Wilhelmsburg 61 48.06 N 15.36 E
Wilhelmsburg ➔[8] 52 53.30 N 10.00 E
Wilhelmshaven 52 53.31 N 8.08 E
Wilhelmshöhe, Schloss ⊥ 56 51.21 N 9.22 E
Wilhelmshorst 54 52.19 N 13.03 E
Wilhelmstadt ➔[8] 264a 52.31 N 13.11 E
Wilhelmstal 156 21.54 S 16.19 E
Wilhelmstein, Schloss ⊥ 52 52.28 N 9.18 E
Wilis, Gunung ∧ 115a 7.52 S 111.48 E
Wilkau-Hasslau 54 50.40 N 12.31 E
Wilkerson Pass)(200 39.02 N 105.32 W
Wilkes-Barre 210 41.14 N 75.52 W
Wilkes-Barre Scranton Airport ⊠ 210 41.20 N 75.45 W
Wilkesboro 192 36.08 N 81.09 W
Wilkes Island I 174a 19.18 N 166.34 E
Wilkes Land ➔[1] 9 69.00 S 120.00 E
Wilkeson 224 47.06 N 122.02 W
Wilket Creek ≏ 275b 43.43 N 79.21 W
Wilket Creek Park ♦ 275b 43.43 N 79.21 W
Wilkhaven 46 57.52 N 3.45 W
Wilkie 184 52.25 N 108.43 W
Wilkinsburg 214 40.26 N 79.51 W
Wilkinson 218 39.53 N 85.36 W
Wilkinson Lakes ◎ 162 29.40 S 132.39 E
Wilkins Sound ȣ 9 70.15 S 73.00 W
Wilkins Township 279b 40.25 N 79.50 W
Will □[6] 216 41.32 N 88.05 W
Will, Mount ∧ 180 57.31 N 128.46 W
Willacoochee 192 31.20 N 83.02 W
Willamette ≏ 202 45.39 N 122.46 W
Willamette, Middle Fork ≏ 202 44.01 N 123.01 W
Willamette, North Fork ≏ 202 43.46 N 122.32 W
Willamina 224 45.04 N 123.29 W
Willamina Creek ≏ 224 45.05 N 123.28 W
Willandra Billabong Creek ≏ 166 33.08 S 144.06 E
Willapa 224 46.40 N 123.39 W
Willapa ≏ 224 46.42 N 123.50 W
Willapa Bay c 224 46.37 N 124.00 W
Willard, Mo., U.S. 194 37.18 N 93.25 W
Willard, N.M., U.S. 200 34.35 N 106.01 W
Willard, N.Y., U.S. 210 42.40 N 76.52 W
Willard, Oh., U.S. 214 41.03 N 82.44 W
Willard, Ut,. U.S. 200 41.24 N 112.02 W
Willard, Wa., U.S. 224 45.48 N 121.38 W
Willard, Punta › 232 28.50 N 113.15 W
Willards 208 38.23 N 75.20 W
Willaston, Austl. 168b 34.36 S 138.45 E
Willaston, Eng., U.K. 262 53.18 N 3.00 W
Willaumez Peninsula ›[1] 164 5.05 S 150.05 E
Willcox 200 32.15 N 109.49 W
Willcox Playa ◎ 200 32.08 N 109.51 W
Willebadessen 52 51.37 N 9.02 E
Willebroek 50 51.04 N 4.22 E
Willem Pretorius Game Reserve ➔[4] 158 28.16 S 27.13 E
Willemsoord 52 52.49 N 6.05 E
Willemstad, Ned. 52 51.42 N 4.26 E
Willemstad, Ned. Ant. 241s 12.06 N 68.56 W
Willenhall 42 52.36 N 2.02 W
Willerburn Acres 284c 39.03 N 77.10 W
Willeroo 164 15.17 S 131.35 E
Willer-sur-Thur 58 47.51 N 7.05 E
Willerswalde 54 54.07 N 13.08 E
Willesden ➔[8] 260 51.33 N 0.14 W
Willet 210 42.28 N 75.55 W
Willett Pond ◎ 283 42.11 N 71.14 W
Willey Creek ≏ 279a 41.25 N 81.25 W
William, Lac ◎ 206 46.07 N 71.34 W
William, Mount ∧, Austl. 166 37.17 S 142.36 E
William, Mount ∧, Austl. 169 37.13 S 144.47 E
William, Mount ∧[2] 168a 32.57 S 116.07 E
William "Bill" Dannelly Reservoir ◎[1] 194 32.10 N 87.10 W
William Boyce Regional Park ♦ 279b 40.28 N 79.45 W
William Girling Reservoir ◎[1] 260 51.37 N 0.02 W
William H. Harsha Lake ◎[1] 218 39.02 N 84.07 W
William Lake ◎ 184 53.50 N 99.25 W
Williamnagar 124 25.30 N 90.35 E
William Patterson College v[2] 276 40.56 N 74.12 W
William P. Gleason Park ♦ 278 41.33 N 87.21 W
William Preston Lane Jr. Memorial Bridge ➔[5] 208 39.00 N 76.28 W
Williams, Austl. 168a 33.01 S 116.52 E
Williams, Az., U.S. 200 35.14 N 112.11 W
Williams, Ca., U.S. 226 39.09 N 122.08 W
Williams, Ia., U.S. 190 42.29 N 93.32 W
Williams, Mn., U.S. 198 48.46 N 94.57 W
Williams □[6] 216 41.35 N 84.33 W
Williams ≏, Austl. 166 20.04 S 141.08 E
Williams ≏, Austl. 168a 32.59 S 116.24 E
Williams ≏, Austl. 170 32.45 S 151.45 E
Williams, Cape › 9 70.29 S 164.05 E
Williams Air Force Base ■ 200 33.18 N 111.40 W
Williams Bay 216 42.34 N 88.32 W
Williamsburg, On., Can. 212 44.58 N 75.15 W

Symbol	English	Deutsch	Español	Français	Português
≏	River	Fluß	Río	Rivière	Rio
≋	Canal	Kanal	Canal	Canal	Canal
⌊	Waterfall, Rapids	Wasserfall, Stromschnellen	Cascada, Rápidos	Chute d'eau, Rapides	Cascata, Rápidos
ȣ	Strait	Meeresstraße	Estrecho	Détroit	Estreito
c	Bay, Gulf	Bucht, Golf	Bahía, Golfo	Baie, Golfe	Baía, Golfo
◎	Lake, Lakes	See, Seen	Lago, Lagos	Lac, Lacs	Lago, Lagos
≡	Swamp	Sumpf	Pantano	Marais	Pântano
⌂	Ice Features, Glacier	Eis- und Gletscherformen	Accidentes Glaciales	Formes glaciaires	Acidentes glaciares
⚲	Other Hydrographic Features	Andere Hydrographische Objekte	Otros Elementos Hidrográficos	Autres données hydrographiques	Outros acidentes hidrográficos
✦	Submarine Features	Untermeerische Objekte	Accidentes Submarinos	Formes de relief sous-marin	Acidentes submarinos
□	Political Unit	Politische Einheit	Unidad Politica	Entité politique	Unidade política
v	Cultural Institution	Kulturelle Institution	Institución Cultural	Institution culturelle	Institução cultural
⊥	Historical Site	Historische Stätte	Sitio Histórico	Site historique	Sitio histórico
♦	Recreational Site	Erholungs- und Ferienort	Sitio de Recreo	Centre de loisirs	Area de Lazer
⊠	Airport	Flughafen	Aeropuerto	Aéroport	Aeroporto
■	Military Installation	Militäranlage	Instalación Militar	Installation militaire	Instalação militar
➔	Miscellaneous	Verschiedenes	Misceláneo	Divers	Diversos

ENGLISH Name / DEUTSCH Name	Page / Seite	Lat.°′ / Breite°′	Long.°′ / Länge°′ E = Ost
Williamsburg, In., U.S.	218	39.57 N	84.59 W
Williamsburg, Ia., U.S.	190	41.39 N	92.00 W
Williamsburg, Ky., U.S.	192	36.44 N	84.09 W
Williamsburg, Ma., U.S.	207	42.23 N	72.43 W
Williamsburg, Mo., U.S.	219	38.55 N	91.42 W
Williamsburg, Oh., U.S.	218	39.03 N	84.03 W
Williamsburg, Pa., U.S.	214	40.27 N	78.12 W
Williamsburg, Va., U.S.	208	37.16 N	76.42 W
Williamsburg ◆[8]	276	40.42 N	73.57 W
Williamsburg Bridge ◆[5]	276	40.43 N	73.58 W
Williams Center	216	41.26 N	84.36 W
Williams Creek ≃, Austl.	274a	33.57 S	150.58 E
Williams Creek ≃, In., U.S.	218	39.36 N	85.09 W
Williamsdale	171b	35.35 S	149.09 E
Williamsfield	214	41.32 N	80.32 W
Williams Fork ≃	200	40.26 N	107.39 W
Williams Lake	182	52.08 N	122.09 W
Williams Lake Indian Reserve ◆[4]	182	52.07 N	122.00 W
Williams Mountain ∧[2]	194	34.15 N	94.33 W
Williamson, N.Y., U.S.	210	43.13 N	77.11 W
Williamson, W.V., U.S.	192	37.40 N	82.16 W
Williamson □[6]	222	30.40 N	97.32 W
Williamson ≃	202	42.28 N	121.57 W
Williamson Head ≻	9	69.09 S	157.49 E
Williamsport, Nf., Can.	186	50.32 N	56.19 W
Williamsport, In., U.S.	216	40.17 N	87.17 W
Williamsport, Oh., U.S.	214	39.35 N	83.07 W
Williamsport, Pa., U.S.	210	41.14 N	77.00 W
Williamston, Mi., U.S.	216	42.41 N	84.16 W
Williamston, N.C., U.S.	192	35.51 N	77.03 W
Williamston, S.C., U.S.	192	34.37 N	82.28 W
Williamstown, Austl.	168b	34.40 S	138.53 E
Williamstown, Austl.	169	37.52 S	144.54 E
Williamstown, On., Can.	206	45.08 N	74.35 W
Williamstown, Ky., U.S.	218	38.38 N	84.33 W
Williamstown, Ma., U.S.	207	42.42 N	73.12 W
Williamstown, N.J., U.S.	208	39.41 N	74.59 W
Williamstown, N.Y., U.S.	212	43.26 N	75.54 W
Williamstown, Pa., U.S.	208	40.34 N	76.37 W
Williamstown, Vt., U.S.	188	44.07 N	72.32 W
Williamstown, W.V., U.S.	188	39.24 N	81.27 W
Williamstown Junction	285	39.45 N	74.56 W
Williamstown Lake ⊜[1]	218	38.41 N	84.32 W
Williamsville, Il., U.S.	219	39.57 N	89.32 W
Williamsville, N.Y., U.S.	210	42.57 N	78.44 W
Williamtown	170	32.49 S	151.50 E
Willich	56	51.16 N	6.33 E
Willikies	240c	17.05 N	61.42 W
Willimantic	207	41.42 N	72.12 W
Willimantic ≃	207	41.43 N	72.12 W
Willingale	260	51.44 N	0.19 E
Willingboro	208	40.01 N	74.52 W
Willingdon, Ab., Can.	182	53.50 N	112.08 W
Willingdon, Eng., U.K.	42	50.47 N	0.15 E
Willingdon, Mount ∧	182	51.45 N	116.15 W
Willingen	56	51.17 N	8.37 E
Willingham	42	52.19 N	0.04 E
Willington, Eng., U.K.	42	52.50 N	1.33 W
Willington, Eng., U.K.	44	54.43 N	1.41 W
Willis, Mi., U.S.	216	42.09 N	83.33 W
Willis, Tx., U.S.	222	30.25 N	95.28 W
Willis ≃	192	37.41 N	78.07 W
Willisau	58	47.07 N	8.00 E
Willis Group II	164	16.18 S	150.00 E
Willis Island I	186	48.48 N	53.42 W
Williston, S. Afr.	158	31.20 S	20.53 E
Williston, Fl., U.S.	192	29.23 N	82.26 W
Williston, N.D., U.S.	198	48.08 N	103.38 W
Williston, Oh., U.S.	214	41.36 N	83.20 W
Williston, S.C., U.S.	192	33.24 N	81.25 W
Williston Lake ⊜[1]	176	55.40 N	123.40 W
Williston Park	276	40.45 N	73.38 W
Willisville	194	37.59 N	89.35 W
Willis Wharf	208	37.30 N	75.48 W
Williton	42	51.10 N	3.20 W
Willits	204	39.24 N	123.21 W
Willmar	198	45.07 N	95.02 W
Willmersdorf	264a	52.40 N	13.41 E
Willmore Wilderness Provincial Park ♦	182	53.45 N	119.00 W
Willoughby, Austl.	170	33.48 S	151.12 E
Willoughby, Oh., U.S.	214	41.38 N	81.25 W
Willoughby, Cape ≻	166	35.51 S	138.07 E
Willoughby Bay ⊂	240c	17.02 N	61.44 W
Willoughby Hills	214	41.35 N	81.25 W
Willow, Ak., U.S.	180	61.45 N	150.03 W
Willow, Mi., U.S.	216	42.07 N	83.24 W
Willow, N.Y., U.S.	210	42.05 N	74.14 W
Willow ≃, Ab., Can.	182	55.58 N	113.55 W
Willow ≃, B.C., Can.	182	54.03 N	122.21 W
Willow ≃, Mn., U.S.	190	46.40 N	93.35 W
Willow ≃, Wi., U.S.	190	44.59 N	92.46 W
Willowbrook, Sk., Can.	184	51.13 N	102.47 W
Willow Brook, Ca., U.S.	280	33.54 N	118.13 W
Willowbrook, Il., U.S.	278	41.46 N	87.56 W
Willowbrook, Md., U.S.	284c	39.02 N	77.11 W
Willow Brook ≃, On., Can.	212	43.53 N	80.16 W
Willow Brook ≃, Eng., U.K.	42	52.32 N	0.24 W
Willow Brook ≃, N.J., U.S.	276	40.20 N	74.10 W
Willowbrook Mall ◆[9]	276	40.53 N	74.15 W
Willowbrook Park ♦	276	40.36 N	74.09 W
Willow Bunch	184	49.24 N	105.37 W
Willow Bunch Lake ⊜	184	49.27 N	105.28 W
Willow City	198	48.36 N	100.17 W
Willow Creek, Ca., U.S.	204	40.56 N	123.38 W
Willow Creek, Mt., U.S.	202	45.49 N	111.38 W
Willow Creek ≃, Ab., Can.	182	49.46 N	113.21 W
Willow Creek ≃, On., Can.	212	44.25 N	79.53 W
Willow Creek ≃, Ca., U.S.	226	37.09 N	119.27 W
Willow Creek ≃, Ca., U.S.	226	39.22 N	122.05 W
Willow Creek ≃, Il., U.S.	216	41.42 N	89.10 W
Willow Creek ≃, In., U.S.	216	41.15 N	85.08 W
Willow Creek ≃, Mi., U.S.	281	42.20 N	83.25 W
Willow Creek ≃, Mt., U.S.	202	48.10 N	111.11 W
Willow Creek ≃, Mt., U.S.	202	48.09 N	106.38 W
Willow Creek ≃, Mt., U.S.	202	46.28 N	108.28 W
Willow Creek ≃, Nv., U.S.	204	38.10 N	116.35 W
Willow Creek ≃, N.D., U.S.	198	48.34 N	100.27 W
Willow Creek ≃, Oh., U.S.	279a	41.20 N	82.03 W
Willow Creek ≃, Or., U.S.	202	44.00 N	117.13 W
Willow Creek ≃, Or., U.S.	202	45.48 N	120.01 W
Willow Creek ≃, Ut., U.S.	200	40.02 N	109.45 W
Willow Creek, North Fork ≃	226	37.13 N	119.30 W
Willow Creek, South Fork ≃	226	39.32 N	122.10 W
Willowdale ◆[8]	275b	43.47 N	79.26 W
Willowdale State Forest ♦	283	42.40 N	70.54 W
Willowdene	273d	26.18 S	29.57 E
Willowemac	210	41.55 N	74.41 W
Willowemoc Creek ≃	210	41.53 N	74.48 W
Willow Glen ◆[8]	282	37.18 N	121.53 W
Willow Grove	208	40.08 N	75.06 W
Willow Grove Naval Air Station ■	208	40.12 N	75.08 W
Willow Grove Park ♦	285	40.08 N	75.08 W
Willow Hill	214	40.06 N	77.48 W
Willowick	214	41.37 N	81.28 W
Willow Lake	198	44.37 N	97.38 W
Willow Lake ⊜, N.T., Can.	176	62.11 N	119.10 W
Willow Lake ⊜, N.Y., U.S.	276	40.43 N	73.50 W
Willowlake ≃	176	62.52 N	123.08 W
Willow Metropolitan Park ♦	281	42.08 N	83.22 W
Willowmore	158	33.17 S	23.29 E
Willow Park	222	32.45 N	97.39 W
Willowra	162	21.15 S	132.35 E
Willowra Aboriginal Reserve ◆[4]	162	21.15 S	132.35 E
Willow Reservoir ⊜[1]	190	45.45 N	89.50 W
Willow Ridge Estates	284a	43.01 N	78.49 W
Willow River	182	54.04 N	122.28 W
Willow Run, De., U.S.	285	39.44 N	75.37 W
Willow Run, Mi., U.S.	216	42.14 N	83.35 W
Willow Run, Va., U.S.	284c	38.49 N	77.10 W
Willow Run Airport ⊠	281	42.14 N	83.32 W
Willows	226	39.31 N	122.11 W
Willow Springs, Ca., U.S.	228	34.53 N	118.18 W
Willow Springs, Il., U.S.	278	41.44 N	87.51 W
Willow Springs, Mo., U.S.	194	36.59 N	91.58 W
Willow Springs, Pa., U.S.	279b	40.19 N	79.44 W
Willow Street	208	39.59 N	76.17 W
Willowvale	158	32.16 S	28.30 E
Willow Woods	284c	38.50 N	77.16 W
Will Rogers Beach State Park ♦	280	34.01 N	118.30 W
Will Rogers State Park ♦	280	34.03 N	118.31 W
Willroth	56	50.34 N	7.31 E
Wills, Lake ⊜	162	21.25 S	128.51 E
Wills Creek ≃, Austl.	166	22.43 S	140.02 E
Wills Creek ≃, Oh., U.S.	188	40.09 N	81.55 W
Wills Creek Lake ⊜[1]	214	40.08 N	81.45 W
Willseyville	210	42.17 N	76.23 W
Willshire	216	40.45 N	84.48 W
Wills Point	222	32.43 N	96.01 W
Willston	284c	38.52 N	77.09 W
Willunga	168b	35.17 S	138.33 E
Wilmar	194	33.37 N	91.55 W
Wilmer, Al., U.S.	194	30.49 N	88.21 W
Wilmer, Pa., U.S.	285	40.07 N	75.32 W
Wilmer, Tx., U.S.	222	32.35 N	96.41 W
Wilmerding	279b	40.23 N	79.48 W
Wilmersdorf ◆[8]	264a	52.30 N	13.19 E
Wilmette	216	42.04 N	87.43 W
Wilmington, Austl.	166	32.39 S	138.07 E
Wilmington, Eng., U.K.	260	51.26 N	0.12 E
Wilmington, De., U.S.	208	39.44 N	75.32 W
Wilmington, Il., U.S.	216	41.18 N	88.08 W
Wilmington, Ma., U.S.	207	42.32 N	71.10 W
Wilmington, N.C., U.S.	192	34.13 N	77.56 W
Wilmington, Oh., U.S.	218	39.26 N	83.49 W
Wilmington, Vt., U.S.	188	42.52 N	72.52 W
Wilmington ◆[8]	280	33.47 N	118.16 W
Wilmington Manor	285	39.41 N	75.35 W
Wilmington Manor Gardens	285	39.40 N	75.34 W
Wilmore, Ky., U.S.	192	37.51 N	84.39 W
Wilmore, Pa., U.S.	214	40.23 N	78.43 W
Wilmot, Ar., U.S.	194	33.03 N	91.34 W
Wilmot, Oh., U.S.	214	40.39 N	81.38 W
Wilmot, S.D., U.S.	198	45.24 N	96.51 W
Wilmot, Wi., U.S.	216	42.31 N	88.11 W
Wilmot Woods ♦	278	42.18 N	87.56 W
Wilmslow	44	53.20 N	2.15 W
Wilna → Vilnius	76	54.41 N	25.19 E
Wilnecote	42	52.36 N	1.40 W
Wilnsdorf	56	50.49 N	8.09 E
Wilpattu National Park ♦	122	8.20 N	80.00 E
Wilpen	214	40.17 N	79.12 W
Wilpshire	262	53.47 N	2.28 W
Wilsall	202	45.59 N	110.39 W
Wilsdruff	54	51.05 N	13.32 E
Wilseder Berg ∧[2]	52	53.10 N	9.56 E
Wilseyville	226	38.23 N	120.31 W
Wilshamstead	42	52.05 N	0.27 W
Wilson, Austl.	166	32.00 S	138.22 E
Wilson, Ar., U.S.	194	35.34 N	90.02 W
Wilson, Ct., U.S.	207	41.48 N	72.38 W
Wilson, Il., U.S.	278	42.21 N	87.54 W
Wilson, Ks., U.S.	198	38.49 N	98.28 W
Wilson, La., U.S.	194	30.55 N	91.06 W
Wilson, N.Y., U.S.	210	43.18 N	78.49 W
Wilson, N.C., U.S.	192	35.43 N	77.54 W
Wilson, Ok., U.S.	196	34.09 N	97.25 W
Wilson, Pa., U.S.	208	40.41 N	75.14 W
Wilson, Tx., U.S.	196	33.19 N	101.44 W
Wilson ≃, Austl.	164	16.47 S	128.17 E
Wilson ≃, Austl.	166	27.38 S	141.24 E
Wilson ≃, Or., U.S.	224	45.28 N	123.53 W
Wilson, Cape ≻	176	66.59 N	81.28 W
Wilson, Mount ∧, Az., U.S.	200	35.59 N	114.37 W
Wilson, Mount ∧, Ca., U.S.	280	34.13 N	118.04 W
Wilson, Mount ∧, Co., U.S.	200	37.51 N	107.59 W
Wilson, Mount ∧, Nv., U.S.	204	38.15 N	114.23 W
Wilson, Mount ∧, Or., U.S.	224	45.04 N	121.39 W
Wilson, Mount ∧[2], Austl.	162	20.14 S	127.39 E
Wilson, Mount ∧[2], Austl.	168b	35.13 S	138.38 E
Wilson, Point ≻, Austl.	169	38.05 S	144.30 E
Wilson, Point ≻, Wa., U.S.	224	48.08 N	122.45 W
Wilson Cliffs ≛[4]	162	22.03 S	127.09 E
Wilson Creek ≃, Tx., U.S.	222	33.07 N	96.35 W
Wilson Creek ≃, Wa., U.S.	202	47.25 N	119.07 W
Wilson Lake ⊜[1], Al., U.S.	194	34.49 N	87.30 W
Wilson Lake ⊜[1], Ks., U.S.	198	38.57 N	98.40 W
Wilson Range ⋏	162	28.50 S	124.25 E
Wilson Run ≃, De., U.S.	285	39.48 N	75.35 W
Wilson Run ≃, Pa., U.S.	279b	40.13 N	79.37 W
Wilsons Beach	186	44.56 N	66.56 W
Wilson's Creek National Battlefield ♦	194	37.06 N	93.27 W
Wilsons Promontory ≻	166	38.55 S	146.20 E
Wilsons Promontory National Park ♦	166	39.00 S	146.25 E
Wilsonville, Il., U.S.	219	39.04 N	89.51 W
Wilsonville, Ne., U.S.	198	40.06 N	100.06 W
Wilsonville, Or., U.S.	224	45.18 N	122.46 W
Wilster	52	53.55 N	9.22 E
Wilthen	54	51.06 N	14.24 E
Wilton, Eng., U.K.	42	51.05 N	1.52 W
Wilton, Ct., U.S.	207	41.11 N	73.26 W
Wilton, Me., U.S.	188	44.35 N	70.13 W
Wilton, N.H., U.S.	207	42.50 N	71.44 W
Wilton, N.Y., U.S.	210	43.11 N	73.45 W
Wilton, N.D., U.S.	198	47.09 N	100.46 W
Wilton, Wi., U.S.	190	43.48 N	90.31 W
Wilton ≃	164	14.45 S	134.33 E
Wilton Creek ≃	212	44.12 N	76.56 W
Wilton Farm Acres	284b	39.18 N	76.50 W
Wilton Manors	220	26.09 N	80.08 W
Wiltshire □[6]	42	51.15 N	1.50 W
Wiltz	56	49.48 N	5.55 E
Wiluna	162	26.36 S	120.13 E
Wimapedi ≃	184	55.27 N	99.07 W
Wimauma	220	27.42 N	82.17 W
Wimberley	196	30.00 N	98.06 W
Wimbleball Reservoir ⊜[1]	42	51.04 N	3.28 W
Wimbledon	198	47.10 N	98.27 W
Wimbledon ◆[8]	260	51.25 N	0.12 W
Wimbledon Common ♦	260	51.26 N	0.14 W
Wimborne Minster	42	50.48 N	1.59 W
Wimereux	50	50.46 N	1.37 E
Wimmelburg	54	51.31 N	11.30 E
Wimmenau	56	48.55 N	7.25 E
Wimmera ≃	169	36.55 S	142.56 E
Wimmis	58	46.41 N	7.38 E
Winagami Lake ⊜	182	55.38 N	116.45 W
Winam ⊂	154	0.15 S	34.35 E
Winamac	216	41.03 N	86.36 W
Winburg	158	28.37 S	27.00 E
Winburne	214	40.57 N	78.08 W
Wincanton	42	51.04 N	2.25 W
Wincham	262	53.16 N	2.29 W
Winchcombe	42	51.57 N	1.58 W
Winchelsea, Austl.	169	38.15 S	143.59 E
Winchelsea, Eng., U.K.	42	50.55 N	0.42 E
Winchendon	207	42.41 N	72.02 W
Winchester, On., Can.	212	45.06 N	75.21 W
Winchester, N.Z.	172	44.12 S	171.17 E
Winchester, Eng., U.K.	42	51.04 N	1.19 W
Winchester, Ca., U.S.	228	33.42 N	117.05 W
Winchester, Id., U.S.	202	46.14 N	116.37 W
Winchester, Il., U.S.	219	39.37 N	90.27 W
Winchester, In., U.S.	218	40.10 N	84.58 W
Winchester, Ky., U.S.	192	37.59 N	84.10 W
Winchester, Ma., U.S.	283	42.27 N	71.08 W
Winchester, N.H., U.S.	207	42.46 N	72.23 W
Winchester, Oh., U.S.	218	38.56 N	83.39 W
Winchester, Tn., U.S.	194	35.11 N	86.06 W
Winchester, Tx., U.S.	222	30.01 N	97.01 W
Winchester, Va., U.S.	188	39.11 N	78.10 W
Winchester Cathedral ♥[1]	42	51.04 N	1.19 W
Winchmore Hill	260	51.39 N	0.39 W
Winchmore Hill ◆[8]	260	51.38 N	0.06 W
Wind ≃, Yk., Can.	180	65.49 N	135.18 W
Wind ≃, Wa., U.S.	224	45.43 N	121.47 W
Wind ≃, Wy., U.S.	202	43.35 N	108.13 W
Windang	170	34.32 S	150.53 E
Windau → Ventspils	76	57.24 N	21.36 E
Windber	214	40.14 N	78.50 W
Wind Cave National Park ♦	198	43.32 N	103.25 W
Windeck	56	50.48 N	7.37 E
Winder	192	33.59 N	83.43 W
Winder, Lake ⊜	220	28.15 N	80.51 W
Windera	166	26.03 S	151.50 E
Windermere, B.C., Can.	182	50.30 N	115.58 W
Windermere, Eng., U.K.	44	54.23 N	2.54 W
Windermere, Fl., U.S.	220	28.30 N	81.32 W
Windermere ⊜	44	54.22 N	2.56 W
Windermere Lake ⊜	190	47.56 N	83.47 W
Winder Village	285	40.06 N	74.52 W
Windfall, Ab., Can.	182	54.11 N	116.15 W
Windfall, In., U.S.	216	40.21 N	85.57 W
Windgap	210	40.51 N	75.18 W
Windham, Ct., U.S.	207	41.41 N	72.09 W
Windham, N.H., U.S.	283	42.48 N	71.18 W
Windham, N.Y., U.S.	210	42.19 N	74.15 W
Windham, Oh., U.S.	214	41.14 N	81.02 W
Windham □[6], Ct., U.S.	207	41.55 N	71.55 W
Windham □[6], Vt., U.S.	207	42.50 N	72.43 W
Windham Manor	284c	39.04 N	77.00 W
Windhoek	156	22.34 S	17.06 E
Windhoek □[5]	156	22.30 S	17.00 E
Windigo ≃	184	53.22 N	91.48 W
Windigo Lake ⊜	184	52.35 N	91.32 W
Windisch	58	47.29 N	8.13 E
Windischeschenbach	60	49.48 N	12.09 E
Windischgarsten	61	47.44 N	14.20 E
Wind Lake	216	42.49 N	88.09 W
Wind Lake ⊜	216	42.50 N	88.09 W
Windlass Run ≃	284b	39.24 N	76.24 W
Windleite ∧	54	51.22 N	10.56 E
Windlesham	260	51.22 N	0.40 W
Windley Key I	220	24.57 N	80.35 W
Windmill Point ≻, On., Can.	284a	42.52 N	79.01 W
Windmill Point ≻, Mi., U.S.	281	42.22 N	82.55 W
Windmill Point ≻, Va., U.S.	208	37.37 N	76.17 W
Windom, Mn., U.S.	198	43.51 N	95.07 W
Windom, N.Y., U.S.	210	42.47 N	78.48 W
Windom Peak ∧	200	37.37 N	107.35 W
Windorah	166	25.26 S	142.39 E
Windorf, Dtsch.	60	48.37 N	13.13 E
Windorf, Öst.	61	48.27 N	14.02 E
Window Rock	200	35.40 N	109.03 W
Wind Point	216	42.47 N	87.45 W
Wind River Indian Reservation ◆[4]	202	43.26 N	109.00 W
Wind River Peak ∧	200	42.42 N	109.07 W
Wind River Range ⋏	200	43.05 N	109.25 W
Windrush ≃	42	51.42 N	1.25 W
Windsbach	56	49.14 N	10.50 E
Windsor, Austl.	168b	34.25 S	138.20 E
Windsor, Austl.	170	33.37 S	150.49 E
Windsor, Nf., Can.	186	48.57 N	55.40 W
Windsor, N.S., Can.	186	44.59 N	64.08 W
Windsor, On., Can.	214	42.18 N	83.01 W
Windsor, On., Can.	281	42.18 N	83.01 W
Windsor, P.Q., Can.	206	45.34 N	72.00 W
Windsor, Eng., U.K.	42	51.29 N	0.38 W
Windsor, Ca., U.S.	204	38.33 N	122.49 W
Windsor, Co., U.S.	200	40.28 N	104.54 W
Windsor, Ct., U.S.	207	41.51 N	72.38 W
Windsor, Il., U.S.	194	39.26 N	88.35 W
Windsor, In., U.S.	218	40.09 N	85.12 W
Windsor, Mo., U.S.	194	38.31 N	93.31 W
Windsor, N.J., U.S.	208	40.15 N	74.35 W
Windsor, N.Y., U.S.	210	42.05 N	75.39 W
Windsor, N.C., U.S.	192	35.59 N	76.56 W
Windsor, Oh., U.S.	214	41.32 N	80.56 W
Windsor, Pa., U.S.	208	39.54 N	76.35 W
Windsor, Vt., U.S.	188	43.29 N	72.23 W
Windsor, Va., U.S.	208	36.48 N	76.44 W
Windsor, Wi., U.S.	216	43.13 N	89.20 W
Windsor, Gare ◆[5]	275a	45.30 N	73.34 W
Windsor, University of ♥[2]	281	42.18 N	83.04 W
Windsor Airport ⊠	214	42.17 N	82.58 W
Windsor and Maidenhead □[8]	260	51.28 N	0.37 W
Windsor Castle ⊥	42	51.29 N	0.36 W
Windsor Forest	192	31.58 N	81.07 W
Windsor Forest ◆[3]	42	51.27 N	0.43 W
Windsor Great Park ♦	260	51.27 N	0.37 W
Windsor Heights	214	40.12 N	80.40 W
Windsor Hills	280	33.59 N	118.21 W
Windsor Locks	207	41.55 N	72.37 W
Windsor Race Course ♦	260	51.29 N	0.39 W
Windsor Raceway ♦	281	42.15 N	83.05 W
Windsor Terrace	284b	39.19 N	76.43 W
Windsorton	158	28.16 S	24.44 E
Windsorville	207	41.53 N	72.32 W
Windthorst	196	33.34 N	98.26 W
Windward Islands II	238	13.00 N	61.00 W
Windward Passage)(	238	20.00 N	73.50 W
Windy Hills	285	39.48 N	75.35 W
Windy Lake ⊜	184	54.22 N	102.35 W
Windy Peak ∧, Co., U.S.	200	38.21 N	106.16 W
Windy Peak ∧, Wa., U.S.	202	48.56 N	119.58 W
Windy Run ≃	284c	38.54 N	77.05 W
Winefred ≃	184	56.02 N	110.36 W
Winefred Lake ⊜	182	55.30 N	110.35 W
Winejok	140	9.01 N	27.34 E
Winesburg	214	40.37 N	81.42 W
Winfield, Ab., Can.	182	52.58 N	114.26 W
Winfield, Al., U.S.	194	33.55 N	87.49 W
Winfield, Il., U.S.	216	41.52 N	88.10 W
Winfield, Ia., U.S.	190	41.07 N	91.26 W
Winfield, Ks., U.S.	198	37.14 N	96.59 W
Winfield, Mo., U.S.	219	38.59 N	90.44 W
Winfield, N.J., U.S.	276	40.38 N	74.17 W
Winfield, Tx., U.S.	222	33.10 N	95.07 W
Winfield, W.V., U.S.	188	38.31 N	81.53 W
Wing	198	47.08 N	100.16 W
Wing ≃	198	46.29 N	94.58 W
Wingate, Eng., U.K.	44	55.44 N	1.23 W
Wingate, Md., U.S.	208	38.16 N	76.04 W
Wingate, N.C., U.S.	192	34.59 N	80.26 W
Wingate Mountains ⋏	164	14.29 S	130.42 E
Wingates	262	53.34 N	2.32 W
Wingdale	210	41.39 N	73.34 W
Wingecarribee ≃	170	34.23 S	150.07 E
Wingecarribee Reservoir ⊜[1]	170	34.34 S	150.30 E
Wingello	170	34.42 S	150.09 E
Wingene	50	51.04 N	3.16 E
Wingen-sur-Moder	56	48.55 N	7.22 E
Wingerworth	44	53.12 N	1.26 W
Wingham, Austl.	166	31.52 S	152.22 E
Wingham, On., Can.	212	43.53 N	81.19 W
Wingham, Eng., U.K.	42	51.17 N	1.13 E
Wing Lake Shores	281	42.33 N	83.17 W
Wingles	50	50.29 N	2.51 E
Wingo	194	36.38 N	88.44 W
Wings Field ⊠	285	40.08 N	75.16 W
Wingst	52	53.43 N	9.03 E
Winhole Channel)(	276	43.37 N	73.48 W
Winhöring	60	48.16 N	12.39 E
Winifred	202	47.33 N	109.22 W
Winifreda	252	36.15 S	64.14 W
Winisk	176	55.15 N	85.12 W
Winisk ≃	176	55.17 N	85.05 W
Winisk Lake ⊜	176	52.55 N	87.22 W
Wink	196	31.45 N	103.06 W
Winkana	110	15.44 N	98.01 E
Winkelman	200	32.59 N	110.46 W
Winkelpos	158	27.35 S	26.49 E
Winkler, Mb., Can.	184	49.11 N	97.56 W
Winkler, Tx., U.S.	222	31.56 N	96.13 W
Winklern	64	46.52 N	12.52 E
Winlaw	182	49.37 N	117.34 W
Winlock	224	46.29 N	122.56 W
Winneba	150	5.25 N	0.36 W
Winnebago, Il., U.S.	190	42.15 N	89.14 W
Winnebago, Mn., U.S.	190	43.46 N	94.09 W
Winnebago, Ne., U.S.	198	42.14 N	96.28 W
Winnebago □[6]	216	42.17 N	89.06 W
Winnebago ≃	190	43.03 N	92.57 W
Winnebago, Lake ⊜	190	44.00 N	88.25 W
Winnebago Indian Reservation ◆[4], Ne., U.S.	198	42.15 N	96.31 W
Winnebago Indian Reservation ◆[4], Wi., U.S.	190	44.15 N	90.38 W
Winnecke, Mount ∧[2]	162	18.47 S	130.20 E
Winnecke Creek ≃	162	18.35 S	131.34 E
Winneconne	190	44.06 N	88.42 W
Winneconnet	283	41.59 N	71.08 W
Winneconnet Pond ⊜	283	41.58 N	71.08 W
Winnekendonk	52	51.36 N	6.17 E
Winnekenni Park ♦	283	42.47 N	71.04 W
Winnemucca	204	40.58 N	117.44 W
Winnemucca Lake ⊜	204	40.09 N	119.20 W
Winnenden	56	48.53 N	9.24 E
Winner	198	43.22 N	99.51 W
Winnetka	216	42.06 N	87.44 W
Winnetka ◆[8]	280	34.13 N	118.35 W
Winnett	202	47.00 N	108.21 W
Winnfield	194	31.55 N	92.38 W
Winnibigoshish, Lake ⊜	190	47.27 N	94.12 W
Winnie	194	29.49 N	94.23 W
Winning	162	23.09 S	114.32 E
Winningen, Dtsch.	54	51.49 N	11.26 E
Winningen, Dtsch.	56	50.18 N	7.31 E
Winnipeg	184	49.53 N	97.09 W
Winnipeg ≃	184	50.38 N	96.19 W
Winnipeg, Lake ⊜	184	52.00 N	97.00 W
Winnipeg Beach	184	50.31 N	96.58 W
Winnipegosis	184	51.39 N	99.56 W
Winnipegosis, Lake ⊜	184	52.30 N	100.00 W
Winnipesaukee, Lake ⊜	188	43.35 N	71.20 W
Winnsboro, La., U.S.	194	32.09 N	91.43 W
Winnsboro, S.C., U.S.	192	34.22 N	81.05 W
Winnsboro, Tx., U.S.	222	32.57 N	95.17 W
Winnsboro, Lake ⊜[1]	222	32.55 N	95.21 W
Winnsboro Mills	192	34.21 N	81.05 W
Winnweiler	56	49.34 N	7.51 E
Winona, Ks., U.S.	198	39.03 N	101.14 W
Winona, Mi., U.S.	190	46.52 N	88.55 W
Winona, Mn., U.S.	190	44.03 N	91.38 W
Winona, Ms., U.S.	194	33.28 N	89.43 W
Winona, Mo., U.S.	194	37.00 N	91.19 W
Winona, Oh., U.S.	214	40.50 N	80.54 W
Winona, Tx., U.S.	222	32.29 N	95.10 W
Winona Lake, In., U.S.	216	41.13 N	85.49 W
Winona Lake, N.Y., U.S.	210	41.31 N	74.03 W
Winona Lake ⊜	216	41.13 N	85.50 W
Winooski	188	44.29 N	73.11 W
Winooski ≃	188	44.30 N	73.15 W
Winooski, North Branch ≃	188	44.15 N	72.35 W
Winschoten	52	53.08 N	7.02 E
Winscombe	42	51.18 N	2.50 W
Winsen, Dtsch.	52	52.41 N	9.54 E
Winsen, Dtsch.	52	53.22 N	10.12 E
Winsford, Eng., U.K.	42	51.06 N	3.33 W
Winsford, Eng., U.K.	44	53.12 N	2.32 W
Winshill	42	52.48 N	1.36 W
Winside	198	42.10 N	97.10 W
Winslow, Eng., U.K.	42	51.57 N	0.54 W
Winslow, Az., U.S.	200	35.01 N	110.41 W
Winslow, Me., U.S.	188	44.32 N	69.37 W
Winslow, N.J., U.S.	285	39.39 N	74.52 W
Winslow Reef ≛[2]	14	1.36 S	174.57 W
Winsted, Ct., U.S.	207	41.55 N	73.03 W
Winsted, Mn., U.S.	190	44.57 N	94.02 W
Winston, Fl., U.S.	220	28.01 N	82.00 W
Winston, Or., U.S.	202	43.07 N	123.24 W
Winston Churchill Memorial ♥	219	38.52 N	91.58 W
Winston Creek ≃	224	46.30 N	122.40 W
Winston-Salem	192	36.05 N	80.14 W
Winsum	52	53.19 N	6.31 E
Wintego Lake ⊜	184	55.33 N	102.52 W
Winter	190	45.49 N	91.00 W
Winter Beach	220	27.43 N	80.25 W
Winterberg, Dtsch.	56	51.11 N	8.32 E
Winterberg, Dtsch.	263	51.17 N	7.18 E
Winterberg ∧[2]	263	51.20 N	7.13 E
Winterberge ⋏	158	32.28 S	26.15 E
Winterbourne Abbas	42	50.43 N	2.34 W
Winter Creek ≃	280	34.12 N	118.02 W
Winterfeld	54	52.44 N	11.14 E
Winter Garden	220	28.33 N	81.35 W
Winter Gardens	228	32.50 N	116.56 W
Winter Harbor	188	44.23 N	68.05 W
Winter Harbour	182	50.31 N	128.02 W
Winterhaven, Ca., U.S.	204	32.44 N	114.38 W
Winter Haven, Fl., U.S.	220	28.01 N	81.43 W
Winter Hill ∧[2]	262	53.38 N	2.31 W
Wintering ≃	198	48.12 N	100.34 W
Wintering Lake ⊜	184	55.24 N	97.42 W
Winter Island I, N.T., Can.	176	66.14 N	83.04 W
Winter Island I, Ca., U.S.	282	38.03 N	121.51 W
Winter Island I, Ma., U.S.	283	42.32 N	70.52 W
Winterlingen	58	48.11 N	9.07 E
Winter Park, Fl., U.S.	220	28.35 N	81.20 W
Winter Park, N.C., U.S.	192	34.12 N	77.53 W
Winterport	188	44.38 N	68.51 W
Winters, Ca., U.S.	226	38.31 N	121.58 W
Winters, Tx., U.S.	196	31.57 N	99.57 W
Winters Bayou ≃	222	30.22 N	95.06 W
Winters Canal ≅	226	38.32 N	121.58 W
Wintersdorf	54	51.03 N	12.21 E
Winterset, Ia., U.S.	190	41.19 N	94.00 W
Winterset, Oh., U.S.	214	40.06 N	81.25 W
Winter Springs	220	28.41 N	81.18 W
Winters Run ≃	208	39.26 N	76.18 W
Winterstown	208	39.50 N	76.37 W
Wintersville	214	40.22 N	80.42 W
Winterswijk	52	51.58 N	6.44 E
Winterthur, Schw.	58	47.30 N	8.43 E
Winterthur, De., U.S.	285	39.48 N	75.35 W
Winterthur Museum ♥	285	39.48 N	75.36 W
Winterton, Nf., Can.	186	47.58 N	53.20 W
Winterton, S. Afr.	158	28.46 S	29.35 E
Winterton, Eng., U.K.	44	53.39 N	0.36 W
Winterton-on-Sea	42	52.43 N	1.42 E
Winterville, Ga., U.S.	192	33.58 N	83.16 W
Winterville, Ms., U.S.	194	33.30 N	91.03 W
Winterville, N.C., U.S.	192	35.31 N	77.24 W
Winthrop, Ct., U.S.	207	41.21 N	72.29 W
Winthrop, Ia., U.S.	190	42.28 N	91.44 W
Winthrop, Me., U.S.	188	44.18 N	69.58 W
Winthrop, Ma., U.S.	283	42.22 N	70.59 W
Winthrop, Mn., U.S.	190	44.32 N	94.21 W
Winthrop, Wa., U.S.	182	48.28 N	120.11 W
Winthrop, Lake ⊜	283	42.11 N	71.25 W
Winthrop Harbor	216	42.28 N	87.49 W
Wintinna	162	27.44 S	134.07 E
Wintinna Creek ≃	162	27.47 S	134.14 E
Winton, Austl.	166	22.23 S	143.02 E
Winton, N.Z.	172	46.09 S	168.20 E
Winton, S. Afr.	158	27.29 S	22.34 E
Winton, Ca., U.S.	226	37.23 N	120.37 W
Winton, N.C., U.S.	192	36.23 N	76.55 W
Winton, Wa., U.S.	224	47.44 N	120.44 W
Wintzenheim	58	48.04 N	7.17 E
Winwick	262	53.26 N	2.36 W
Winz	263	51.23 N	7.09 E
Winzenberg	263	51.06 N	7.38 E
Winzer	60	48.44 N	13.04 E
Winzermark	263	51.23 N	7.08 E
Wipper ≃, Dtsch.	54	51.47 N	11.42 E
Wipper ≃, Dtsch.	54	51.17 N	11.10 E
Wipper ≃, Dtsch.	263	51.07 N	7.24 E
Wipperdorf	54	51.28 N	10.42 E
Wipperfeld	263	51.05 N	7.19 E
Wipperfürth	56	51.07 N	7.23 E
Wippra	54	51.34 N	11.16 E
Wirāṭnagar	124	26.29 N	87.17 E
Wīrendranagar	124	28.35 N	81.38 E
Wireton, Il., U.S.	278	41.40 N	87.42 W
Wireton, Pa., U.S.	279b	40.34 N	80.14 W
Wīrgañj	124	27.00 N	84.52 E
Wiriagar ≃	164	2.17 S	132.52 E
Wirksworth	44	53.05 N	1.34 W
Wirosari	115a	7.05 S	111.05 E
Wirral □[8]	262	53.22 N	3.05 W
Wirral ≻[1]	44	53.20 N	3.03 W
Wirraminna	166	31.12 S	136.15 E
Wirrulla	162	32.24 S	134.31 E
Wisbech	42	52.40 N	0.10 E
Wisby → Visby	26	57.38 N	18.18 E
Wiscasset	188	44.00 N	69.39 W
Wische ◆[1]	54	52.50 N	11.55 E
Wischhafen	52	53.46 N	9.19 E
Wisconsin □[3], U.S.	178	44.45 N	89.30 W
Wisconsin □[3], U.S.	190	44.45 N	89.30 W
Wisconsin ≃	190	43.00 N	91.10 W
Wisconsin, Lake ⊜[1]	190	43.24 N	89.43 W
Wisconsin Dells	190	43.37 N	89.46 W
Wisconsin Dells V	190	43.41 N	89.49 W
Wisconsin Rapids	190	44.23 N	89.49 W
Wiscoy	210	42.30 N	78.05 W
Wisdom	202	45.37 N	113.27 W
Wisdom, Lake ⊜	164	5.20 S	147.05 E
Wise	192	36.58 N	82.34 W
Wise □[6]	222	33.07 N	97.40 W
Wise ≃	202	45.48 N	112.57 W
Wiseman	180	67.25 N	150.06 W
Wisemans Ferry	170	33.24 S	150.59 E
Wises Landing	218	38.35 N	85.25 W
Wishart	184	51.34 N	104.00 W
Wishaw	46	55.47 N	3.56 W
Wishek	198	46.16 N	99.33 W
Wishkah ≃	224	46.58 N	123.45 W
Wishram	224	45.39 N	120.57 W
Wisła	30	49.40 N	18.52 E
Wisła ≃	30	54.22 N	18.55 E
Wisley Aerodrome ⊠	260	51.18 N	0.28 W
Wisley Gardens ♦	260	51.19 N	0.29 W
Wisłok ≃	30	50.13 N	22.32 E
Wisłoka ≃	30	50.27 N	21.23 E
Wismar, Dtsch.	54	53.53 N	11.28 E
Wismar, Guy.	246	6.00 N	58.18 W
Wismarbucht ⊂	54	53.57 N	11.25 E
Wisner, La., U.S.	194	31.58 N	91.39 W
Wisner, Ne., U.S.	198	41.59 N	96.54 W
Wissahickon Creek ≃	285	40.01 N	75.12 W
Wissant	50	50.53 N	1.40 E
Wissembourg	56	49.02 N	7.57 E
Wissen	56	50.47 N	7.43 E
Wissenkerke	52	51.35 N	3.45 E
Wissey ≃	42	52.33 N	0.21 E
Wissinoming ◆[8]	285	40.01 N	75.04 W
Wissmar	56	50.38 N	8.41 E
Wissous	261	48.44 N	2.20 E
Wister	194	34.58 N	94.43 W
Wisznice	30	51.48 N	23.12 E
Witbank	158	25.56 S	29.07 E
Witberge ⋏	158	30.45 S	27.32 E
Witbooisvlei	156	25.04 S	18.27 E
Witchekan Lake ⊜	184	53.25 N	107.35 W
Witches Falls National Park ♦	171a	27.56 S	153.10 E
Witch Hazel	224	45.30 N	122.46 W
Witdraai	158	26.58 S	20.45 E
Witfield	273d	26.11 S	28.12 E
Witham	42	51.48 N	0.38 E
Witham ≃	44	53.06 N	0.13 W
Withamsville	218	39.03 N	84.16 W
Withens Clough Reservoir ⊜[1]	262	53.42 N	2.02 W
Witheridge	42	50.55 N	3.42 W
Withernsea	44	53.44 N	0.02 E
Witherspoon, Mount ∧	180	61.23 N	147.12 W
Withington ◆[8]	262	53.26 N	2.14 W
Withington Green	262	53.14 N	2.18 W
Withlacoochee ≃, U.S.	192	30.24 N	83.10 W
Withlacoochee ≃, Fl., U.S.	192	29.00 N	82.45 W
Withnell	262	53.42 N	2.34 W
Withokspruit ≃	273d	26.19 S	28.21 E
Witjira National Park ♦	162	26.25 S	135.40 E
Wit-Kei ≃	158	32.09 S	27.24 E
Witkoppies ∧	158	27.44 S	29.20 E
Witkowo	30	52.27 N	17.47 E
Witless Bay	186	47.16 N	52.50 W
Witley	42	51.09 N	0.38 W
Wit-Mfolozi ≃	158	28.22 S	31.58 E
Witney	42	51.48 N	1.29 W
Witnica	30	52.40 N	14.55 E
Wit Nossob ≃	156	23.05 S	18.45 E
Witpoort	158	27.10 S	26.08 E
Witrivier	156	24.40 S	31.00 E
Witry-lès-Reims	50	49.18 N	4.07 E
Witsand	158	34.24 S	20.50 E
Witt	219	39.15 N	89.20 W
Wittabrenna Creek ≃	166	29.20 S	142.43 E
Witteberg ⋏	158	28.40 S	28.02 E
Witteberge ⋏	158	33.18 S	20.36 E
Wittelsheim	58	47.49 N	7.15 E
Witten	56	51.26 N	7.20 E
Wittenau ◆[8]	264a	52.35 N	13.20 E
Wittenberg, Dtsch.	54	51.52 N	12.39 E
Wittenberg, Wi., U.S.	190	44.49 N	89.10 W
Wittenberge	54	53.00 N	11.44 E
Wittenburg	54	53.31 N	11.04 E
Wittenheim	58	47.49 N	7.20 E
Wittenoom	162	22.17 S	118.19 E
Wittensee ⊜	41	54.23 N	9.45 E
Wittering	42	52.37 N	0.27 W
Wittgensdorf	54	50.53 N	12.52 E
Wittichenau	54	51.23 N	14.14 E
Wittingen	54	52.43 N	10.44 E
Wittislingen	56	48.37 N	10.25 E
Wittlaer	56	51.19 N	6.44 E
Wittlich	56	49.59 N	6.53 E
Wittman	208	38.47 N	76.17 W
Wittmar	54	52.07 N	10.38 E
Wittmund	52	53.34 N	7.47 E
Witton Park ♦	262	53.45 N	2.31 W
Wittow ≻[1]	54	54.38 N	13.19 E
Wittstock	54	53.10 N	12.29 E
Witu	154	2.23 S	40.26 E
Witu Islands II	164	4.40 S	149.25 E
Witvlai	156	22.23 S	18.32 E
Witwatersrand, University of the ♥[2]	273d	26.12 S	28.02 E
Witwatersrand Gold Mine ◆[7]	273d	26.12 S	28.11 E
Witwatersrant ◆[1]	158	26.00 S	27.00 E
Witzenhausen	56	51.20 N	9.51 E
Witzhelden	263	51.07 N	7.06 E
Witzputz	156	27.25 S	17.43 E
Wiveliscombe	42	51.03 N	3.19 W
Wivenhoe	42	51.52 N	0.58 E
Wivenhoe Reservoir ⊜[1]	171a	27.20 S	152.35 E
Wiwa Creek ≃	184	50.02 N	106.31 W
Wixom	216	42.31 N	83.32 W
Wiżajny	30	54.23 N	22.51 E
Wizernes	50	50.43 N	2.14 E
Wjatka → V'atka ≃	80	55.36 N	51.30 E
W. Kerr Scott Reservoir ⊜[1]	192	36.07 N	81.15 W
Wkra ≃	30	52.27 N	20.44 E
Wladiwostok → Vladivostok	89	43.10 N	131.56 E
Władysławowo	30	54.49 N	18.25 E
Wleń	30	51.01 N	15.40 E
Wlingi	115a	8.05 S	112.19 E
Włocławek	30	52.39 N	19.02 E
Włocławek □[4]	30	52.30 N	19.05 E
Włodawa	30	51.34 N	23.32 E
Włoszczowa	30	50.52 N	19.59 E
Wnion ≃	42	52.45 N	3.54 W
Woady Yaloak ≃	169	38.06 S	143.33 E
Wobaer	85	39.19 N	75.32 E
Wöbbelin	54	53.24 N	11.30 E
Woburn	207	42.28 N	71.09 W
Woburn ◆[8]	275b	43.46 N	79.13 W
Woburn Sands	42	52.01 N	0.39 W
Woden, Austl.	171b	35.22 S	149.08 E
Woden, Tx., U.S.	222	31.30 N	94.32 W
Wodgina	162	21.11 S	118.40 E
Wodonga	166	36.07 S	146.54 E
Wodzisław Śląski	30	50.00 N	18.28 E
Woensdrecht	52	51.26 N	4.18 E
Woerdeke	85	39.41 N	77.53 E
Woerden	52	52.05 N	4.54 E
Woerth	56	48.56 N	7.45 E
Woëvre ◆[1]	56	49.05 N	5.40 E
Wofosi	105	40.09 N	115.18 E
Wo Fo Si (Temple of the Sleeping Buddha) ♥[1]	105	40.01 N	116.12 E
Wognum	52	52.41 N	5.01 E
Wohlde	41	54.24 N	9.17 E
Wohlen	58	47.21 N	8.17 E
Wohlensee ⊜	58	46.58 N	7.20 E
Wohlford, Lake ⊜[1]	228	33.10 N	116.59 W
Wohlthat Mountains ⋏	9	71.35 S	12.20 E
Wohra ≃	56	50.49 N	8.55 E
Woi	140	7.53 N	31.10 E
Woincourt	50	50.04 N	1.32 E
Woippy	56	49.09 N	6.09 E
Wojcieszów	30	50.58 N	15.56 E
Wokalup	168a	33.06 S	115.53 E
Wokam, Pulau I	164	5.37 S	134.30 E
Wokha	120	26.06 N	94.16 E
Woking, Ab., Can.	182	55.35 N	118.46 W
Woking, Eng., U.K.	42	51.20 N	0.34 W
Woking □[8]	260	51.19 N	0.32 W
Wokingham	42	51.25 N	0.51 W
Wokingham Creek ≃	166	22.19 S	142.30 E
Wolbach	198	41.24 N	98.24 W
Wolbeck	52	51.55 N	7.43 E
Wolbrom	30	50.24 N	19.46 E
Wolcott, Ct., U.S.	207	41.36 N	72.59 W
Wolcott, In., U.S.	216	40.45 N	87.02 W
Wolcott, N.Y., U.S.	210	43.13 N	76.48 W
Wolcott Creek ≃	210	43.17 N	76.50 W
Wolcottsburg	210	43.04 N	78.38 W
Wolcottsville	210	43.07 N	78.31 W
Wolcottville	216	41.32 N	85.22 W
Wołcza ≃	54	53.58 N	14.53 E
Wołczenica ≃	54	53.52 N	14.44 E
Wołczyn	30	51.01 N	18.03 E
Woldberg ⋏[1]	52	52.25 N	5.55 E
Woldegk	54	53.27 N	13.35 E
Woldingham	260	51.17 N	0.02 W

Symbols in the index entries represent the broad categories identified in the key at the right. Symbols with superior numbers (⋏[1]) identify subcategories (see complete key on page *I* · *1)*.

Symbole im Register stellen die rechts im Schlüssel erklärten Kategorien dar. Symbole mit hochgestellten Ziffern (⋏[1]) bezeichnen Unterabteilungen einer Kategorie (vgl. vollständiger Schlüssel auf Seite *I* · *1)*.

Los símbolos incluidos en el texto del índice representan las grandes categorías identificadas con la clave a la derecha. Los símbolos con numeros en su parte superior (⋏[1]) identifican las subcategorías (véase la clave completa en la página *I* · *1)*.

Les symboles de l'index représentent les catégories indiquées dans la légende à droite. Les symboles suivis d'un indice (⋏[1]) représentent des sous-catégories (voir légende complète à la page *I* · *1)*.

Os símbolos incluídos no texto do índice representam as grandes categorias identificadas com a chave à direita. Os símbolos com números em sua parte superior (⋏[1]) identificam as subcategorias (veja-se a chave completa à página *I* · *1)*.

∧ Mountain	Berg	Montaña	Montagne	Montanha
⋏ Mountains	Gebirge	Montañas	Montagnes	Montanhas
)(Pass	Paß	Paso	Col	Passo
V Valley, Canyon	Tal, Cañon	Valle, Cañón	Vallée, Canyon	Vale, Canhão
≚ Plain	Ebene	Llano	Plaine	Planície
≻ Cape	Kap	Cabo	Cap	Cabo
I Island	Insel	Isla	Île	Ilha
II Islands	Inseln	Islas	Îles	Ilhas
≛ Other Topographic Features	Andere Topographische Objekte	Otros Elementos Topográficos	Autres données topographiques	Outros acidentes topográficos

ESPAÑOL — Nombre | Página | Lat.°′ | Long.°′ W = Oeste
FRANÇAIS — Nom | Page | Lat.°′ | Long.°′ W = Ouest
PORTUGUÊS — Nome | Página | Lat.°′ | Long.°′ W = Oeste

Nombre	Página	Lat.°′	Long.°′ W = Oeste
Wolds, The ⋀[2]	44	53.20 N	0.10 W
Woleai I[1]	108	7.21 N	143.52 E
Woleu-Ntem □[4]	152	1.30 N	12.00 E
Wolf ≃, On., Can.	190	48.49 N	88.30 W
Wolf ≃, U.S.	194	35.09 N	90.04 W
Wolf ≃, Ks., U.S.	198	39.54 N	95.11 W
Wolf ≃, Ms., U.S.	194	30.21 N	89.18 W
Wolf ≃, Wi., U.S.	190	44.11 N	88.48 W
Wolf, Isla I	246a	1.23 N	91.49 W
Wolf, Volcán ∧[1]	246a	0.02 N	91.20 W
Wolfach	58	48.17 N	8.13 E
Wolf-Bay	186	50.16 N	60.08 W
Wolf Creek, Mt., U.S.	202	47.00 N	112.04 W
Wolf Creek, Or., U.S.	202	42.41 N	123.23 W
Wolf Creek ≃, U.S.	196	36.35 N	99.30 W
Wolf Creek ≃, Ca., U.S.	226	39.02 N	121.08 W
Wolf Creek ≃, Co., U.S.	200	40.12 N	108.29 W
Wolf Creek ≃, In., U.S.	216	41.15 N	87.07 W
Wolf Creek ≃, Ia., U.S.	190	42.20 N	92.09 W
Wolf Creek ≃, Mt., U.S.	198	48.05 N	105.40 W
Wolf Creek ≃, Mt., U.S.	202	47.37 N	109.38 W
Wolf Creek ≃, Oh., U.S.	214	41.16 N	83.11 W
Wolf Creek ≃, Pa., U.S.	214	41.03 N	80.07 W
Wolf Creek ≃, S.D., U.S.	198	43.21 N	97.37 W
Wolf Creek ≃, S.D., U.S.	198	44.42 N	98.40 W
Wolf Creek Lake ⊜[1]	198	38.14 N	95.41 W
Wolf Creek Pass)(	200	37.29 N	106.48 W
Wolf Creek State Park ♦	219	39.30 N	88.41 W
Wolfdale	214	40.12 N	80.17 W
Wolfe □[6]	206	45.45 N	71.30 W
Wolfeboro	188	43.35 N	71.12 W
Wolfe City	196	33.22 N	96.04 W
Wolfegg	58	47.49 N	9.47 E
Wolfe Island	212	44.12 N	76.26 W
Wolfe Island I	212	44.12 N	76.20 W
Wolfe Lake ⊜	212	44.40 N	76.30 W
Wolfen	54	51.40 N	12.16 E
Wolfenbüttel	52	52.10 N	10.32 E
Wolfenden, Mount ∧	182	50.26 N	127.33 W
Wolfenschiessen	58	46.55 N	8.24 E
Wolfertschwenden	58	47.53 N	10.16 E
Wolfforth	196	33.30 N	102.01 W
Wolfgangsee ⊜	64	47.44 N	13.26 E
Wolfhagen	56	51.19 N	9.10 E
Wölfis	54	50.48 N	10.46 E
Wolf Island I	212	44.33 N	78.15 W
Wolflake, In., U.S.	216	41.20 N	85.30 W
Wolf Lake, Mi., U.S.	216	43.15 N	86.06 W
Wolf Lake ⊜, Ab., Can.	182	54.42 N	110.59 W
Wolf Lake ⊜, On., Can.	212	44.44 N	78.11 W
Wolf Lake ⊜, Yk., Can.	180	60.40 N	131.40 W
Wolf Lake ⊜, U.S.	278	41.40 N	87.31 W
Wolf Lake ⊜, N.J., U.S.	276	40.57 N	74.42 W
Wolf Mountain ∧	180	65.17 N	154.02 W
Wolfpassing	264b	48.19 N	16.11 E
Wolf Point	202	48.05 N	105.38 W
Wolframs-Eschenbach	56	49.14 N	10.43 E
Wolfratshausen	64	47.54 N	11.25 E
Wolf Rock I[2]	28	49.57 N	5.49 W
Wolf Run	214	40.30 N	80.54 W
Wolfsberg	61	46.51 N	14.51 E
Wolfsberg ∧[2]	263	51.38 N	6.27 E
Wolfsburg	54	52.25 N	10.47 E
Wolf's Castle	42	51.54 N	4.58 W
Wolfsegg am Hausruck	60	48.06 N	13.40 E
Wolfstein	56	49.35 N	7.36 E
Wolftrap Creek ≃	284c	38.58 N	77.17 W
Wolf Trap Farms for the Performing Arts ♦	284c	38.56 N	77.16 W
Wolfurt	58	47.28 N	9.45 E
Wolfville	186	45.05 N	64.22 W
Wolgan ≃	170	33.12 S	150.28 E
Wolgast	54	54.03 N	13.46 E
Wolga → Volga ≃	72	45.55 N	47.52 E
Wolgograder Stausee → Volgogradskoje vodochranilišče ⊜[1]	80	49.20 N	45.00 E
Wolgograd → Volgograd	80	48.44 N	44.25 E
Wolhusen	58	47.04 N	8.04 E
Wolin	30	53.50 N	14.35 E
Wolin I	54	53.55 N	14.31 E
Woliński Park Narodowy ♦	30	53.55 N	14.30 E
Wolkenstein	54	50.39 N	13.04 E
Wolkersdorf	61	48.23 N	16.31 E
Wölkisch	54	51.13 N	13.21 E
Wolkramshausen	54	51.25 N	10.44 E
Wollangambe ≃	170	33.21 S	150.35 E
Wollaston	42	52.15 N	0.40 W
Wollaston, Islas II	254	55.40 S	67.30 W
Wollaston Beach ⊥[2]	283	42.17 N	71.01 W
Wollaston Lake ⊜, On., Can.	212	44.50 N	77.50 W
Wollaston Lake ⊜, Sk., Can.	176	58.15 N	103.20 W
Wollaston Peninsula ≻[1]	176	70.00 N	115.00 W
Wollemi Creek ≃	170	33.13 S	150.31 E
Wollemi National Park ♦	166	32.50 S	150.30 E
Wollogorang	166	17.13 S	137.57 E
Wollombi	170	32.56 S	151.09 E
Wollombi Brook ≃	170	32.33 S	151.04 E
Wollondilly ≃	170	33.57 S	150.26 E
Wollongong	170	34.25 S	150.54 E
Wöllstein	56	49.49 N	7.58 E
Wolmaransstad	158	27.12 S	26.13 E
Wolmirsleben	54	51.57 N	11.29 E
Wolmirstedt	54	52.15 N	11.37 E
Wolnzach	60	48.36 N	11.37 E
Wołomin	30	52.21 N	21.14 E
Wołów	30	51.21 N	16.39 E
Wolowaru	115b	8.46 S	121.54 E
Wolseley, Sk., Can.	184	50.25 N	103.19 W
Wolseley, S. Afr.	158	33.26 S	19.12 E
Wolsey	198	44.24 N	98.28 W
Wolsingham	44	54.44 N	1.52 W
Wolsztyn	30	52.08 N	16.06 E
Wolterdingen	52	53.02 N	9.50 E
Woltersdorf, Dtsch.	54	52.24 N	12.22 E
Woltersdorf, Dtsch.	54	52.26 N	13.45 E
Woluogu	105	39.40 N	117.46 E
Wolvega	52	52.53 N	6.00 E
Wolverhampton	42	52.36 N	2.08 W
Wolverine	190	45.16 N	84.36 W
Wolverine Lake	281	42.33 N	83.29 W
Wolverine Loon Lake ⊜	281	42.33 N	83.30 W
Wolverine Mountain ∧	180	65.20 N	149.51 W
Wolvertem	50	50.57 N	4.18 E
Wolverton	42	52.04 N	0.50 W
Wolwehoek	158	26.55 S	27.48 E
Wölzerbach ≃	61	47.08 N	14.23 E
Wolziger See ⊜	54	52.16 N	13.50 E
Woman ≃	190	47.57 N	82.19 W
Wombarra	170	34.16 S	150.58 E
Wombat, Mount ∧	169	36.51 S	145.40 E
Wombeyan Caves ⊥[5]	170	34.18 S	149.56 E
Wombourne	42	52.32 N	2.11 W
Wombwell	44	53.31 N	1.24 W
Womelsdorf	208	40.22 N	76.11 W
Women's Rights National Historical Park ♦	210	42.54 N	76.47 W
Wommels	52	53.06 N	5.36 E
Wompatuck State Park ♦	283	42.13 N	70.51 W
Wonarah	162	19.55 S	136.20 E
Wondai	166	26.19 S	151.52 E
Wondelgem	50	51.05 N	3.43 E
Wonderfonteinspruit ≃	273d	26.16 S	27.42 E
Wonderkop	158	27.50 S	27.26 E
Wonder Lake	216	42.25 N	88.21 W
Wonderland	204	40.24 N	121.19 W
Wonderland Center ◆[9]	281	42.22 N	83.20 W
Wonderland Dog Track ♦	283	42.25 N	71.00 W
Wondinong	162	27.52 S	118.25 E
Wŏndong-ni	98	34.23 N	126.40 E
Wonersh	260	51.12 N	0.33 W
Wonewoc	190	43.39 N	90.13 W
Wong ≃	124	27.10 N	89.30 E
Wongan Hills	162	30.53 S	116.42 E
Wonga Park	274b	37.44 S	145.16 E
Wonga-Wongué, Parc National de ♦	152	0.30 S	9.30 E
Wonggarasi	112	0.33 N	121.36 E
Wong Ka Wai	271d	22.24 N	113.58 E
Woniushi	104	42.31 N	123.03 E
Wŏnjang-ni	98	39.05 N	125.32 E
Wŏnju	98	37.22 N	127.58 E
Wonogiri	115a	7.49 S	110.55 E
Wonokromo	115a	7.18 S	112.44 E
Wonosari	115a	7.58 S	110.35 E
Wonosegoro	115a	7.18 S	110.39 E
Wonosobo	115a	7.22 S	109.54 E
Wonotobo Vallen ∟	250	4.22 N	57.58 W
Wonreli	112	8.05 S	127.09 E
Wŏnsan	98	39.09 N	127.25 E
Wonthaggi	169	38.36 S	145.35 E
Woocalla	166	31.42 S	137.13 E
Wood, Pa., U.S.	214	40.10 N	78.08 W
Wood, S.D., U.S.	198	43.29 N	100.28 W
Wood □[6], Oh., U.S.	216	41.22 N	83.39 W
Wood □[6], Tx., U.S.	222	32.48 N	95.20 W
Wood ≃, B.C., Can.	182	52.10 N	118.30 W
Wood ≃, Sk., Can.	184	50.08 N	106.10 W
Wood ≃, U.S.	207	41.26 N	71.43 W
Wood ≃, Ak., U.S.	180	64.35 N	148.41 W
Wood ≃, Ne., U.S.	198	41.02 N	98.05 W
Wood ≃, Wy., U.S.	202	44.07 N	108.58 W
Wood, Mount ∧, Yk., Can.	180	61.14 N	140.31 W
Wood, Mount ∧, Mt., U.S.	202	45.17 N	109.49 W
Woodacre	226	38.05 N	122.36 W
Woodall Mountain ∧[2]	194	34.45 N	88.11 W
Wood Bay ⊂	180	69.45 N	129.00 W
Woodberry Forest	284c	38.48 N	76.56 W
Woodbine, Ga., U.S.	192	30.57 N	81.43 W
Woodbine, Ia., U.S.	198	41.44 N	95.42 W
Woodbine, Md., U.S.	208	39.21 N	77.03 W
Woodbine, N.J., U.S.	208	39.14 N	74.48 W
Woodbourne, N.Y., U.S.	210	41.45 N	74.35 W
Woodbourne, Oh., U.S.	218	39.38 N	84.10 W
Woodbourne, Pa., U.S.	285	40.12 N	74.53 W
Woodbridge, Eng., U.K.	42	52.06 N	1.19 E
Woodbridge, Ca., U.S.	226	38.09 N	121.18 W
Woodbridge, Ct., U.S.	207	41.21 N	73.00 W
Woodbridge, N.J., U.S.	210	40.33 N	74.17 W
Woodbridge, Va., U.S.	208	38.39 N	77.15 W
Woodbridge Center ◆[9]	276	40.33 N	74.18 W
Woodbridge Creek ≃	276	40.32 N	74.15 W
Woodbridge Island I	283	42.48 N	70.50 W
Woodburn, Il., U.S.	219	39.03 N	90.00 W
Woodburn, In., U.S.	216	41.07 N	84.51 W
Woodburn, Or., U.S.	224	45.08 N	122.51 W
Woodbury, Eng., U.K.	42	50.41 N	3.24 W
Woodbury, Ct., U.S.	207	41.32 N	73.12 W
Woodbury, Ga., U.S.	192	32.59 N	84.34 W
Woodbury, Mi., U.S.	216	42.46 N	85.05 W
Woodbury, N.J., U.S.	208	39.50 N	75.09 W
Woodbury, N.Y., U.S.	276	40.49 N	73.28 W
Woodbury, Pa., U.S.	214	40.14 N	78.22 W
Woodbury, Tn., U.S.	194	35.49 N	86.04 W
Woodbury Creek ≃	285	39.52 N	75.11 W
Woodbury Heights	285	39.49 N	75.09 W
Woodchester	168b	35.13 S	138.57 E
Woodchopper	180	65.18 N	143.25 W
Woodchurch	42	51.05 N	0.46 E
Woodcliff Lake	276	41.01 N	74.04 W
Woodcliff Lake ⊜	276	41.01 N	74.03 W
Woodcock	214	41.45 N	80.05 W
Woodcock, Mount ∧	162	19.16 S	134.02 E
Woodcrest, Ca., U.S.	228	33.52 N	117.21 W
Woodcrest, Pa., U.S.	285	39.59 N	75.35 W
Wood Dale	278	41.57 N	87.58 W
Woodenbong	166	28.23 S	152.37 E
Woodend	169	37.22 S	144.32 E
Woodfibre	182	49.40 N	123.15 W
Woodfield ◆[9]	278	42.03 N	88.03 W
Woodford, Austl.	171a	26.57 S	152.47 E
Woodford, Ire.	48	53.03 N	8.23 W
Woodford, Eng., U.K.	262	53.21 N	2.10 W
Woodford □[6], Il., U.S.	216	40.43 N	89.16 W
Woodford □[6], Ky., U.S.	218	38.06 N	84.15 W
Woodford ◆[8]	260	51.36 N	0.02 E
Woodford Aerodrome ⊠	262	53.20 N	2.09 W
Woodford Bridge ◆[8]	260	51.36 N	0.04 E
Woodford Halse	42	52.10 N	1.12 W
Wood Green ◆[8]	260	51.36 N	0.07 W
Woodhall Spa	44	53.09 N	0.13 W
Woodham	260	51.21 N	0.30 W
Woodham Ferrers	260	51.40 N	0.36 E
Woodham Mortimer	260	51.43 N	0.37 E
Woodham Walter	260	51.44 N	0.37 E
Woodhaven	216	42.08 N	83.14 W
Woodhaven ◆[8]	276	40.41 N	73.51 W
Woodhead Reservoir ⊜[1]	262	53.30 N	1.52 W
Woodhill	275b	43.45 N	79.41 W
Wood Hill ∧[2]	283	42.39 N	71.13 W
Woodhull, Il., U.S.	190	41.10 N	90.18 W
Woodhull, N.Y., U.S.	210	42.05 N	77.25 W
Woodinville	224	47.45 N	122.09 W
Wood Islands	186	45.58 N	62.45 W
Woodlake, Ca., U.S.	204	36.25 N	119.06 W
Wood Lake, Ne., U.S.	198	42.38 N	100.14 W
Woodlake, Tx., U.S.	222	31.01 N	95.02 W
Wood Lake ⊜, On., Can.	212	45.01 N	79.05 W
Wood Lake ⊜, Sk., Can.	184	55.17 N	103.17 W
Woodland, Ca., U.S.	226	38.40 N	121.46 W
Woodland, Ga., U.S.	192	32.47 N	84.33 W
Woodland, Il., U.S.	216	40.43 N	87.44 W
Woodland, Me., U.S.	188	45.09 N	67.24 W
Woodland, Mi., U.S.	216	42.43 N	85.08 W
Woodland, N.C., U.S.	192	36.19 N	77.12 W
Woodland, Pa., U.S.	214	40.59 N	78.20 W
Woodland, Wa., U.S.	224	45.54 N	122.44 W
Woodland Beach	216	41.57 N	83.19 W
Woodland Heights	214	41.25 N	79.43 W
Woodland Hills ◆[8]	280	34.11 N	118.35 W
Woodland Hills Park ♦	279a	41.28 N	81.36 W
Woodland Park, Co., U.S.	200	38.59 N	105.03 W
Woodland Park, Pa., U.S.	210	41.18 N	77.03 W
Woodlands, N.Z.	172	46.22 S	168.33 E
Woodlands, Sing.	271c	1.27 N	103.46 E
Woodlands, N.Y., U.S.	276	41.01 N	73.50 W
Woodlawn, Il., U.S.	219	38.20 N	89.02 W
Woodlawn, Ky., U.S.	194	37.02 N	88.34 W
Woodlawn, Md., U.S.	284b	39.19 N	76.43 W
Woodlawn, Md., U.S.	284c	38.57 N	76.53 W
Woodlawn, Wa., U.S.	224	47.01 N	123.48 W
Woodlawn ◆[8]	278	41.47 N	87.36 W
Woodlawn Beach	210	42.48 N	78.51 W
Woodlawn Heights	284b	39.11 N	76.39 W
Woodley	42	51.28 N	0.54 W
Woodlyn	285	39.52 N	75.20 W
Woodlynne	285	39.55 N	75.05 W
Woodmansey	44	53.50 N	0.29 W
Woodmansterne	260	51.19 N	0.10 W
Woodmere, N.Y., U.S.	210	40.37 N	73.42 W
Woodmere, Oh., U.S.	279a	41.28 N	81.29 W
Woodmoor	284b	39.20 N	76.44 W
Wood Mountain ∧	184	49.14 N	106.20 W
Wood Mountain Indian Reserve ◆[4]	184	49.21 N	106.24 W
Woodplumpton	262	53.48 N	2.47 W
Woodport	276	40.59 N	74.36 W
Woodrarung Range ⋀	162	27.10 S	115.30 E
Woodridge, Austl.	171a	27.38 S	153.06 E
Woodridge, Mb., Can.	184	49.17 N	96.09 W
Woodridge, Il., U.S.	216	41.44 N	88.03 W
Wood-Ridge, N.J., U.S.	276	40.50 N	74.05 W
Woodridge, N.Y., U.S.	210	41.43 N	74.34 W
Wood River, Ak., U.S.	180	59.04 N	158.26 W
Wood River, Il., U.S.	219	38.51 N	90.05 W
Wood River, Ne., U.S.	198	40.49 N	98.35 W
Wood River Lakes ⊜	180	59.30 N	158.45 W
Wood River Mountains ⋀	180	59.32 N	159.30 W
Woodroffe ≃	166	21.28 S	137.58 E
Woodroffe, Mount ∧	162	26.20 S	131.45 E
Woodrow	192	35.08 N	77.05 W
Woodrow Wilson Memorial Bridge ◆[5]	284c	38.48 N	77.02 W
Woodruff, Az., U.S.	200	34.46 N	110.02 W
Woodruff, S.C., U.S.	192	34.44 N	82.02 W
Woodruff, Wi., U.S.	190	45.53 N	89.41 W
Woodruff Creek ≃	281	42.21 N	83.43 W
Woods	168b	34.15 S	138.31 E
Woods, Lake ⊜	162	17.50 S	133.30 E
Woods, Lake of the ⊜	184	49.15 N	94.45 W
Woods Bay ⊂	212	45.08 N	80.00 W
Woodsboro, Md., U.S.	208	39.31 N	77.18 W
Woodsboro, Tx., U.S.	196	28.14 N	97.19 W
Woodsburgh	276	40.37 N	73.42 W
Woods Creek ≃, N.Y., U.S.	276	40.39 N	73.24 W
Woods Creek ≃, N.Y., U.S.	284a	43.04 N	78.58 W
Woodsfield	188	39.45 N	81.06 W
Woods Hole	207	41.31 N	70.40 W
Woodside, Austl.	166	38.31 S	146.52 E
Woodside, Austl.	168b	34.57 S	138.52 E
Woodside, Eng., U.K.	260	51.45 N	0.11 W
Woodside, Ca., U.S.	226	37.25 N	122.15 W
Woodside, De., U.S.	208	39.04 N	75.34 W
Woodside, Pa., U.S.	285	40.13 N	74.53 W
Woodside ◆[8]	276	40.45 N	73.55 W
Woodside National Historic Park ♦	212	43.26 N	80.08 W
Woodson, Il., U.S.	219	39.38 N	90.13 W
Woodson, Tx., U.S.	196	33.01 N	99.03 W
Woods Point	169	37.35 S	146.15 E
Woods Reservoir ⊜[1]	194	35.20 N	86.00 W
Woodstock, Austl.	166	22.15 S	141.57 E
Woodstock, N.B., Can.	186	46.09 N	67.34 W
Woodstock, On., Can.	212	43.08 N	80.45 W
Woodstock, Eng., U.K.	42	51.52 N	1.21 W
Woodstock, Ct., U.S.	207	41.56 N	71.58 W
Woodstock, Il., U.S.	216	42.18 N	88.26 W
Woodstock, Md., U.S.	284b	39.19 N	76.52 W
Woodstock, N.Y., U.S.	210	42.02 N	74.07 W
Woodstock, Oh., U.S.	218	40.10 N	83.32 W
Woodstock, Vt., U.S.	188	43.37 N	72.31 W
Woodstock, Va., U.S.	188	38.52 N	78.30 W
Woodstown	208	39.39 N	75.19 W
Wood Street	260	51.15 N	0.38 W
Woodsville	188	44.09 N	72.02 W
Woodvale Airfield ⊠	262	53.35 N	3.03 W
Woodview Manor	278	42.06 N	87.53 W
Wood Village	224	45.32 N	122.19 W
Woodville, Austl.	168b	34.53 S	138.32 E
Woodville, On., Can.	212	44.24 N	78.59 W
Woodville, N.Z.	172	40.20 S	175.52 E
Woodville, Al., U.S.	194	34.38 N	86.16 W
Woodville, Ca., U.S.	226	36.06 N	119.12 W
Woodville, Fl., U.S.	192	30.20 N	84.15 W
Woodville, Ga., U.S.	192	33.40 N	83.06 W
Woodville, Ma., U.S.	207	42.14 N	71.33 W
Woodville, Mi., U.S.	216	43.39 N	85.40 W
Woodville, Ms., U.S.	194	31.06 N	91.17 W
Woodville, N.Y., U.S.	210	42.40 N	77.22 W
Woodville, Oh., U.S.	214	41.27 N	83.21 W
Woodville, Tx., U.S.	194	30.46 N	94.24 W
Woodward, Ia., U.S.	190	41.51 N	93.55 W
Woodward, Ok., U.S.	196	36.26 N	99.23 W
Woodward, Pa., U.S.	210	40.54 N	77.21 W
Woodward Reservoir ⊜[1]	226	37.51 N	120.52 W
Woodway, Tx., U.S.	222	31.30 N	97.12 W
Woodway, Wa., U.S.	224	47.47 N	122.23 W
Woodworth, Oh., U.S.	214	40.59 N	80.40 W
Woodworth, Wi., U.S.	216	42.34 N	88.00 W
Woody ≃	184	52.30 N	100.51 W
Woody Creek ≃	202	47.27 N	106.21 W
Woody Head ≻	166	29.22 S	153.22 E
Woody Island	180	57.47 N	152.22 W
Wool	42	50.41 N	2.14 W
Woolacombe	42	51.10 N	4.13 W
Woolamai, Cape ≻	169	38.34 S	145.21 E
Wool Bay	168b	35.00 S	137.45 E
Wooldridge	158	33.13 S	27.15 E
Wooler	44	55.33 N	2.01 W
Woolford	208	38.30 N	76.11 W
Woolgangie	162	31.10 S	120.32 E
Woolgoolga	166	30.07 S	153.12 E
Woollahra	274a	33.53 S	151.15 E
Woolmarket	194	30.28 N	88.59 W
Woolooware Bay ⊂	274a	34.02 S	151.09 E
Woolpit	42	52.13 N	0.54 E
Woolrich	210	41.12 N	77.23 W
Woolsey Peak ∧	200	33.10 N	112.53 W
Woolston	262	53.24 N	2.32 W
Woolton ◆[8]	262	53.23 N	2.52 W
Woolwich ◆[8]	260	51.29 N	0.04 E
Woomargama	171b	35.50 S	147.15 E
Woomera	166	31.31 S	137.10 E
Woomera Prohibited Area ◆[4]	162	29.45 S	134.30 E
Woonona	170	34.21 S	150.55 E
Woonsocket, R.I., U.S.	207	42.00 N	71.30 W
Woonsocket, S.D., U.S.	198	44.03 N	98.16 W
Woorabinda	166	24.08 S	149.28 E
Wooramel	162	25.44 S	114.17 E
Wooramel ≃	162	25.47 S	114.10 E
Woorim	171a	27.08 S	153.12 E
Wooroloo	168a	31.48 S	116.19 E
Wooster	214	40.48 N	81.56 W
Wootton	42	52.11 N	0.53 W
Wootton Bassett	42	51.33 N	1.54 W
Wootton Wawen	42	52.16 N	1.47 W
Woqooyi Gelbeed □[4]	144	10.00 N	44.00 E
Worb	58	46.56 N	7.34 E
Worbis	54	51.25 N	10.21 E
Worcester, S. Afr.	158	33.39 S	19.27 E
Worcester, Eng., U.K.	42	52.11 N	2.13 W
Worcester, Ma., U.S.	207	42.15 N	71.48 W
Worcester, N.Y., U.S.	210	42.35 N	74.45 W
Worcester, Pa., U.S.	285	40.12 N	75.21 W
Worcester □[6], Md., U.S.	208	38.11 N	75.24 W
Worcester □[6], Ma., U.S.	207	42.16 N	71.48 W
Worcester Municipal Airport ⊠	207	42.16 N	71.52 W
Worden, Il., U.S.	219	38.55 N	89.50 W
Worden, Mt., U.S.	202	45.57 N	108.09 W
Worden Pond ⊜	207	41.26 N	71.35 W
Wördern	61	48.20 N	16.13 E
Wörgl	64	47.29 N	12.04 E
Workai, Pulau I	164	6.40 S	134.40 E
Work Channel ⋓	182	54.30 N	130.15 W
Workers' Stadium ♦	271a	39.55 N	116.27 E
Workington	44	54.39 N	3.35 W
Worksop	44	53.18 N	1.07 W
Workum	52	52.57 N	5.26 E
Worland	202	44.01 N	107.57 W
World End Pond ⊜	283	42.45 N	71.12 W
Worli ◆[8]	272c	19.01 N	72.50 E
Wörlitz	54	51.50 N	12.25 E
Wormerveer	52	52.28 N	4.46 E
Wormhoudt	50	50.53 N	2.28 E
Wormit	46	56.25 N	2.59 W
Wormley	260	51.44 N	0.01 W
Worms	56	49.38 N	8.22 E
Worms Head ≻	42	51.34 N	4.20 W
Wormshill	260	51.17 N	0.42 E
Wörnitz ≃	56	48.42 N	10.45 E
Woronesch → Voronež	78	51.40 N	39.10 E
Woronoco	207	42.09 N	72.49 W
Woronora	274a	34.01 S	151.03 E
Woronora ≃	274a	34.00 S	151.04 E
Woronora Reservoir ⊜[1]	170	34.08 S	150.56 E
Worplesdon	260	51.16 N	0.37 W
Worpswede	52	53.13 N	8.56 E
Wörrstadt	56	49.50 N	8.07 E
Wörsbach ≃	56	50.22 N	8.09 E
Worsbrough	44	53.31 N	1.29 W
Worsley	262	53.30 N	2.23 W
Worsthorne	262	53.47 N	2.11 W
Wörth, Dtsch.	56	49.48 N	9.09 E
Worth, Dtsch.	263	51.13 N	7.39 E
Worth, Il., U.S.	216	41.41 N	87.47 W
Worth, Lake ⊜[1]	222	32.48 N	97.28 W
Wortham	222	31.47 N	96.27 W
Wörth am Rhein	56	49.03 N	8.16 E
Wörth an der Donau	60	49.00 N	12.25 E
Wörth an der Isar	60	48.37 N	12.24 E
Worthen	42	52.38 N	3.00 W
Wörther See ⊜	61	46.37 N	14.10 E
Worthing	42	50.48 N	0.23 W
Worthington, In., U.S.	194	39.07 N	86.58 W
Worthington, Md., U.S.	284b	39.14 N	76.47 W
Worthington, Mn., U.S.	198	43.37 N	95.35 W
Worthington, N.Y., U.S.	276	41.02 N	73.50 W
Worthington, Oh., U.S.	214	40.05 N	83.01 W
Worthington, Pa., U.S.	214	40.50 N	79.37 W
Worthington Peak ∧	204	37.55 N	115.37 W
Wörthsee ⊜	60	48.03 N	11.10 E
Worthville, Ky., U.S.	218	38.36 N	85.04 W
Worthville, Pa., U.S.	214	41.02 N	79.08 W
Worton	208	39.16 N	76.05 W
Wŏrun-dong	98	39.36 N	125.20 E
Wosimi	164	2.54 S	134.31 E
Wostok → Vostok ᵿ[3]	9	78.30 S	106.50 E
Wosu	112	2.21 S	121.50 E
Wotap, Pulau I	164	7.21 S	131.16 E
Wotho I[1]	14	10.06 N	165.59 E
Wotje I[1]	14	9.27 N	170.02 E
Wotton, P.Q., Can.	206	45.44 N	71.48 W
Wotton, Eng., U.K.	260	51.13 N	0.23 W
Wotton-under-Edge	42	51.39 N	2.21 W
Wotu	112	2.35 S	120.48 E
Woudenberg	52	52.05 N	5.25 E
Woudrichem	52	51.49 N	5.00 E
Woudsend	52	52.56 N	5.36 E
Wouldham	260	51.21 N	0.28 E
Wounded Knee	198	43.08 N	102.21 W
Wounded Knee Creek ≃	198	43.26 N	102.32 W
Wounta	236	13.33 N	83.32 W
Wounta, Laguna de ⊂	236	13.38 N	83.34 W
Wour	146	21.21 N	15.57 E
Wouri ≃	152	4.06 N	9.43 E
Woutchaba	152	5.13 N	13.05 E
Wouw	52	51.32 N	4.24 E
Wowan	166	23.55 S	150.12 E
Wowoni, Pulau I	112	4.08 S	123.06 E
Woyla ≃	114	4.18 N	95.56 E
Woy Woy	170	33.30 S	151.20 E
Woźniki	30	50.36 N	19.03 E
Wragby	44	53.18 N	0.19 W
Wrangel Island → Vrangel'a, ostrov I	74	71.00 N	179.30 W
Wrangell	180	56.28 N	132.23 W
Wrangell, Cape ≻	181a	52.50 N	172.26 E
Wrangell, Mount ∧	180	62.00 N	144.06 W
Wrangell Island I	180	56.15 N	132.10 W
Wrangell Mountains ⋀	180	62.00 N	143.00 W
Wrangell-Saint Elias National Park ♦	180	61.00 N	142.00 W
Wrath, Cape ≻	46	58.37 N	5.01 W
Wray	198	40.04 N	102.13 W
Wraysbury	260	51.27 N	0.33 W
Wrea Green	262	53.46 N	2.55 W
Wreck Bay ⊂	170	35.11 S	150.40 E
Wreck Island I	208	37.16 N	75.48 W
Wreck Reef ⊹[2]	166	22.13 S	155.17 E
Wrecks, Bay of ⊂	174o	1.52 N	157.17 W
Wredenhagen	54	53.17 N	12.31 E
Wremen	52	53.39 N	8.30 E
Wren	216	40.48 N	84.46 W
Wrens	192	33.12 N	82.23 W
Wrentham, Ab., Can.	182	49.32 N	112.10 W
Wrentham, Eng., U.K.	42	52.23 N	1.40 E
Wrentham, Ma., U.S.	207	42.04 N	71.19 W
Wrentham State Forest ♦	283	42.02 N	71.20 W
Wrexham	44	53.03 N	3.00 W
Wriezen	54	52.43 N	14.08 E
Wright	278	41.31 N	87.21 W
Wright, Mount ∧, Austl.	166	31.12 S	142.26 E
Wright, Mount ∧, Mt., U.S.	202	47.58 N	112.49 W
Wright Brothers National Memorial ⊥	192	35.55 N	75.50 W
Wright City, Mo., U.S.	219	38.49 N	91.01 W
Wright City, Ok., U.S.	194	34.03 N	95.00 W
Wright City, Tx., U.S.	222	32.12 N	94.59 W
Wrightington Bar	262	53.37 N	2.42 W
Wright Patman Lake ⊜[1]	194	33.16 N	94.14 W
Wright-Patterson Air Force Base ■	218	39.49 N	84.03 W
Wright Peak ∧	204	38.59 N	122.46 W
Wrights	219	39.23 N	90.18 W
Wrightsboro	222	29.22 N	97.34 W
Wrights Corners	210	43.13 N	78.46 W
Wrightson, Mount ∧	200	31.42 N	110.50 W
Wrightstown, N.J., U.S.	208	40.02 N	74.37 W
Wrightstown, Pa., U.S.	208	40.17 N	74.58 W
Wrightstown, Wi., U.S.	190	44.19 N	88.09 W
Wrightsville, Ga., U.S.	192	32.43 N	82.43 W
Wrightsville, Pa., U.S.	214	40.01 N	76.31 W
Wrightsville Beach	192	34.12 N	77.47 W
Wrightwood	228	34.21 N	117.37 W
Wrigley, N.T., Can.	180	63.16 N	123.37 W
Wrigley, Tn., U.S.	194	35.54 N	87.20 W
Wrigley Field ♦	278	41.57 N	87.39 W
Wrigley Gulf ⊂	9	74.00 S	129.00 W
Writtle	42	51.44 N	0.26 E
Wrocław (Breslau)	30	51.06 N	17.00 E
Wrocław □[4]	30	51.15 N	17.00 E
Wrong Lake ⊜	184	52.38 N	96.10 W
Wronki	30	52.43 N	16.23 E
Wrotham	42	51.19 N	0.19 E
Wrotham Heath	260	51.18 N	0.21 E
Wrottesley, Cape ≻	176	74.33 N	121.32 W
Wroughton	42	51.31 N	1.46 W
Wroxham	42	52.42 N	1.24 E
Wroxton	184	51.14 N	101.53 W
Września	30	52.20 N	17.34 E
Wschowa	30	51.48 N	16.19 E
Wu ≃, Zhg.	98	34.25 N	117.55 E
Wu ≃, Zhg.	100	28.57 N	116.39 E
Wu ≃, Zhg.	100	24.48 N	113.35 E
Wu ≃, Zhg.	102	29.43 N	107.24 E
Wu ≃, Zhg.	102	27.12 N	109.48 E
Wu ≃, Zhg.	102	27.03 N	109.53 E
Wu'an	98	36.40 N	114.12 E
Wubaozhen	107	29.14 N	104.29 E
Wubin	162	30.06 S	116.38 E
Wubu	102	37.33 N	110.39 E
Wuchagou	89	46.46 N	120.16 E
Wuchang	89	44.54 N	127.08 E
Wuchang Hu ⊜	100	30.17 N	116.47 E
Wuchang → Wuhan	100	30.36 N	114.17 E
Wucheng, Zhg.	98	37.09 N	115.53 E
Wucheng (Jiucheng), Zhg.	98	37.13 N	116.02 E
Wucheng, Zhg.	100	29.36 N	118.10 E
Wucheng, Zhg.	100	33.28 N	113.44 E
Wucheng, Zhg.	100	29.10 N	115.59 E
Wuch'i	100	24.16 N	120.31 E
Wuchin → Changzhou	106	31.47 N	119.57 E
Wuch'iu Yü I	100	25.00 N	119.27 E
Wuchow → Wuzhou	102	23.30 N	111.27 E
Wuchuan, Zhg.	102	21.25 N	110.40 E
Wuchuan, Zhg.	102	28.25 N	107.56 E
Wuchuan, Zhg.	102	41.05 N	111.23 E
Wuchung → Wuzhong	102	37.57 N	106.10 E
Wucun	105	38.57 N	115.19 E
Wuda	102	39.30 N	106.40 E
Wudao	98	39.28 N	121.28 E
Wudaogou, Zhg.	98	41.43 N	127.05 E
Wudaogou, Zhg.	98	42.08 N	125.51 E
Wudaoliang	120	35.11 N	93.35 E
Wudaolianggou	104	40.59 N	120.35 E
Wudi	98	37.44 N	117.35 E
Wudian, Zhg.	100	32.42 N	117.18 E
Wudian, Zhg.	100	31.57 N	112.46 E
Wuding	102	25.32 N	102.23 E
Wuding ≃	102	37.05 N	110.20 E
Wudinna	166	33.03 S	135.28 E
Wudu, Zhg.	100	27.37 N	119.00 E
Wudu, Zhg.	100	28.23 N	118.14 E
Wudu, Zhg.	102	33.24 N	104.50 E
Wuduhe	102	31.03 N	111.03 E
Wuerqihan	89	49.37 N	121.45 E
Wufeng	102	30.11 N	110.33 E
Wufeng Shan I	106	31.07 N	120.16 E
Wufengxi	107	30.37 N	104.29 E
Wufu	100	30.06 N	120.58 E
Wugang	102	26.44 N	110.38 E
Wugong	102	34.20 N	108.04 E
Wugong Shan ∧	100	27.35 N	114.18 E
Wugong Shan ⋀	100	27.21 N	113.50 E
Wugouying	100	33.28 N	114.08 E
Wugunuoer	89	49.10 N	119.19 E
Wuhai	102	39.39 N	106.41 E
Wuhan	100	30.36 N	114.17 E
Wuhe, Zhg.	100	33.10 N	117.54 E
Wuhe, Zhg.	100	24.26 N	115.25 E
Wuhle ≃	264a	52.29 N	13.34 E
Wuhsing → Huzhou	106	30.52 N	120.06 E
Wuhsi → Wuxi	106	31.35 N	120.18 E
Wuhu, Zhg.	100	31.21 N	118.22 E
Wuhu, Zhg.	100	31.11 N	118.35 E
Wuhua	100	23.57 N	115.48 E
Wuhuanchi	104	42.20 N	121.51 E
Wuhuang	107	29.58 N	104.46 E
Wuhudongmiao	102	38.19 N	107.20 E
Wüjang	120	33.38 N	79.50 E
Wuji, Zhg.	98	38.13 N	114.57 E
Wuji, Zhg.	98	34.12 N	119.02 E
Wujia ≃	102	41.10 N	108.45 E
Wujiabeigou	104	40.57 N	123.50 E
Wujiang, Zhg.	100	31.52 N	118.28 E
Wujiang, Zhg.	100	27.14 N	115.15 E
Wujiang, Zhg.	106	31.10 N	120.38 E
Wujiangdu	102	27.16 N	106.48 E
Wujianpu	107	29.10 N	105.50 E
Wujiapai	105	39.32 N	117.18 E
Wujiapu	105	38.52 N	117.07 E
Wujiazhen	107	29.38 N	105.24 E
Wujiazhuang, Zhg.	105	40.35 N	115.20 E
Wujiazhuang, Zhg.	106	32.18 N	120.10 E
Wujiazi, Zhg.	89	46.27 N	123.34 E
Wujiazi, Zhg.	104	42.13 N	122.08 E
Wujiazi, Zhg.	104	42.30 N	121.10 E
Wujing	100	25.16 N	114.36 E
Wukang	106	30.33 N	119.58 E
Wukari	150	7.51 N	9.47 E
Wukeshu, Zhg.	89	46.02 N	123.45 E
Wukeshu, Zhg.	89	44.48 N	126.08 E
Wulai	100	24.52 N	121.33 E
Wulajia	89	48.23 N	129.58 E
Wulanheduojia	102	42.40 N	113.20 E
Wulanhutong	98	41.44 N	114.49 E
Wulanmutou	104	42.23 N	121.21 E
Wulanwusu, Zhg.	86	44.20 N	85.50 E
Wulanwusu, Zhg.	102	41.39 N	107.48 E
Wular Lake ⊜	123	34.20 N	74.33 E
Wulasitai, Zhg.	89	43.15 N	121.27 E
Wulasitai, Zhg.	89	43.28 N	122.44 E
Wulateqianqi	102	40.39 N	109.05 E
Wulaxi	102	28.38 N	101.40 E
Wuleidao Wan ⊂	98	36.55 N	122.00 E
Wulfen	52	51.43 N	7.00 E
Wülfrath	56	51.17 N	7.02 E
Wulfsen	52	53.18 N	10.08 E
Wulfsode	52	53.04 N	10.13 E
Wulften	52	51.40 N	10.10 E
Wulian (Hongning)	98	35.47 N	119.15 E
Wulian Feng ⋀	102	28.03 N	103.57 E
Wuliangdian	104	41.52 N	122.16 E
Wuliang Shan ⋀	102	24.30 N	100.45 E
Wuliaru, Pulau I	164	7.27 S	131.04 E
Wulichuan	102	33.49 N	111.08 E
Wulie ≃	105	40.54 N	117.55 E
Wuling	98	35.53 N	114.36 E
Wuling Shan ∧	105	40.36 N	117.29 E
Wulitaizi	104	41.28 N	123.21 E
Wulizhuang	100	33.49 N	118.57 E
Wulka ≃	61	47.52 N	16.40 E
Wüllen	52	52.04 N	6.58 E
Wullwye Creek ≃	171b	36.30 S	148.49 E
Wulong, Zhg.	102	29.20 N	107.43 E
Wulong, Zhg.	104	41.39 N	124.13 E
Wulong ≃	98	36.35 N	120.56 E
Wulongbei	98	40.21 N	124.16 E
Wulsdorf ◆[8]	52	53.30 N	8.35 E
Wultschau	61	48.42 N	14.50 E
Wulu ≃	85	39.38 N	74.38 E
Wuluhan	115a	8.21 S	113.33 E
Wuluhayingzi	104	42.20 N	121.34 E
Wulumuch'i → Ürümqi	90	43.48 N	87.35 E
Wulumuqi → Ürümqi	90	43.48 N	87.35 E
Wuluo	102	26.09 N	108.15 E
Wulur	164	7.09 S	128.39 E
Wulu Station ◆[5]	271a	39.56 N	116.16 E
Wum	152	6.23 N	10.04 E
Wumang Dao I	98	39.14 N	123.03 E
Wumiaoxiang	107	30.23 N	104.17 E
Wuming	102	23.10 N	108.18 E
Wümme ≃	52	53.10 N	8.44 E
Wunamu	86	46.06 N	85.44 E
Wundowie	168a	31.46 S	116.22 E
Wundwin	110	21.05 N	96.02 E
Wuneba	154	4.50 N	30.20 E
Wungong Brook ≃	168a	32.06 S	115.59 E
Wuning	100	29.17 N	115.06 E
Wünnenberg	52	51.31 N	8.42 E
Wunnummin Lake ⊜	176	52.55 N	89.10 W
Wun Rog	140	9.00 N	28.21 E
Wünschendorf	54	50.48 N	12.05 E
Wünsdorf	54	52.10 N	13.28 E
Wunsiedel	60	50.02 N	12.01 E
Wunstorf	52	52.25 N	9.26 E
Wuntho	110	23.54 N	95.41 E
Wunuer	89	48.53 N	121.15 E
Wupaowan	107	29.50 N	103.59 E
Wupatki National Monument ♦	200	35.24 N	111.14 W
Wuping	100	25.08 N	116.06 E
Wupper ≃	263	51.05 N	7.00 E
Wuppertal, Dtsch.	56	51.16 N	7.11 E
Wuppertal, Dtsch.	263	51.16 N	7.11 E
Wuppertal, S. Afr.	158	32.15 S	19.15 E
Wuqi, Zhg.	100	27.10 N	120.23 E
Wuqi, Zhg.	102	37.08 N	108.10 E
Wuqia	85	39.42 N	75.13 E
Wuqiang (Xiaofan)	98	38.03 N	115.58 E
Wuqing (Yangcun)	105	39.23 N	117.04 E
Wuraming	168a	32.48 S	116.16 E
Wurarga	162	28.25 S	116.17 E
Würenlingen	58	47.32 N	8.16 E
Wurgwitz	54	51.01 N	13.37 E
Wurm ≃, Dtsch.	56	51.08 N	6.10 E
Würm ≃, Dtsch.	56	48.53 N	8.42 E
Würm ≃, Dtsch.	60	48.10 N	11.28 E
Wurmannsquick	60	48.21 N	12.47 E
Wurmberg ∧	54	51.45 N	10.37 E
Wurno	150	13.17 N	5.24 E
Wurong	164	6.07 S	140.47 E
Würselen	56	50.49 N	6.08 E
Wurtsboro	210	41.35 N	74.29 W
Wurtsboro Hills	210	41.36 N	74.30 W
Wurtsmith Air Force Base ■	190	44.27 N	83.23 W
Wuruf	164	6.43 S	146.25 E
Wuryantoro	115a	7.54 S	110.51 E
Wurzbach	54	50.28 N	11.32 E
Würzburg	56	49.48 N	9.56 E
Wurzen	54	51.22 N	12.44 E
Wusanga	152	3.22 S	22.50 E
Wusha	100	30.39 N	117.18 E
Wushan, Zhg.	100	32.04 N	117.03 E
Wushan, Zhg.	102	34.38 N	105.04 E
Wushan, Zhg.	102	31.05 N	109.48 E
Wushan, Zhg.	106	31.44 N	118.58 E
Wusheng, Zhg.	100	29.56 N	119.25 E
Wusheng, Zhg.	107	30.21 N	106.17 E
Wushengchang	107	29.00 N	103.43 E
Wushenqi	102	38.58 N	109.01 E
Wushi, Zhg.	102	22.11 N	110.11 E
Wushi, Zhg.	106	31.44 N	120.59 E
Wushishi	150	9.46 N	6.07 E
Wushu	100	26.20 N	114.56 E
Wusi	175f	15.22 S	166.36 E
Wusih → Wuxi	106	31.35 N	120.18 E
Wuskwatim Lake ⊜	184	55.32 N	98.32 W
Wusong	106	31.23 N	121.29 E
Wusong ≃	106	31.15 N	121.29 E
Wust	54	52.33 N	12.07 E
Wüsten	52	52.06 N	8.47 E
Wüstensachsen	56	50.30 N	10.00 E
Wusterhausen	54	52.54 N	12.28 E
Wusterhusen	54	54.07 N	13.37 E
Wustermark	54	52.33 N	12.56 E
Wüstermarke	54	51.49 N	13.36 E
Wusterwitz	54	52.22 N	12.18 E
Wüsting	52	53.07 N	8.20 E
Wustrow, Dtsch.	54	52.55 N	11.07 E
Wustrow, Dtsch.	54	54.05 N	11.34 E
Wustrow ≻[1]	54	54.05 N	11.34 E
Wusuli (Ussuri) ≃	89	48.27 N	135.04 E
Wusuo	100	25.02 N	116.02 E
Wuta	106	31.31 N	120.39 E
Wutach ≃	58	47.37 N	8.15 E
Wutai, Zhg.	85	39.28 N	78.09 E
Wutai, Zhg.	86	44.36 N	82.06 E
Wutai, Zhg.	98	41.18 N	113.59 E
Wutai, Zhg.	102	38.44 N	113.17 E
Wutai Shan ∧	98	39.04 N	113.35 E
Wutai Shan ⋀	98	39.13 N	113.45 E
Wutaizi	104	42.27 N	123.17 E
Wutan	102	28.29 N	111.40 E
Wutanchang	107	29.15 N	106.04 E
Wutang	106	31.31 N	119.10 E
Wutangdun	106	30.38 N	120.08 E
Wutangjie	100	29.59 N	122.22 E
Wuteve, Mount ∧	150	8.09 N	9.56 W
Wutianzhen	100	30.23 N	117.12 E
Wutong	102	25.18 N	110.01 E
Wutonghaolai	89	42.55 N	120.15 E
Wutongqiao	107	29.26 N	103.51 E
Wutongwozi	102	42.27 N	95.17 E
Wutsin → Changzhou	106	31.47 N	119.57 E
Wutun	100	27.51 N	118.04 E
Wut'ungch'iao → Wutongqiao	107	29.26 N	103.51 E
Wutungkiao → Wutongqiao	107	29.26 N	103.51 E
Wutuohuo	102	40.51 N	101.48 E
Wuustwezel	50	51.23 N	4.36 E
Wuvulu Island I	164	1.45 S	142.50 E
Wuwei, Zhg.	100	31.18 N	117.54 E
Wuwei (Liangzhou), Zhg.	102	37.58 N	102.49 E
Wuxi, Zhg.	102	31.25 N	109.34 E
Wuxi (Wuhsi), Zhg.	106	31.35 N	120.18 E
Wuxi, Zhg.	106	31.20 N	118.39 E
Wuxi ≃	100	29.00 N	118.56 E
Wuxiang	102	36.51 N	113.00 E
Wuxingchang	106	31.13 N	119.23 E
Wuxuan	102	23.36 N	109.42 E
Wuyang, Zhg.	100	33.26 N	113.34 E

Symbol	English	Deutsch	Español	Français	Português
≃	River	Fluß	Río	Rivière	Rio
≊	Canal	Kanal	Canal	Canal	Canal
∟	Waterfall, Rapids	Wasserfall, Stromschnellen	Cascada, Rápidos	Chute d'eau, Rapides	Cascata, Rápidos
⋓	Strait	Meeresstraße	Estrecho	Détroit	Estreito
⊂	Bay, Gulf	Bucht, Golf	Bahía, Golfo	Baie, Golfe	Baía, Golfo
⊜	Lake, Lakes	See, Seen	Lago, Lagos	Lac, Lacs	Lago, Lagos
≡	Swamp	Sumpf	Pantano	Marais	Pântano
⊓	Ice Features, Glacier	Eis- und Gletscherformen	Accidentes Glaciales	Formes glaciaires	Acidentes glaciares
⊤	Other Hydrographic Features	Andere Hydrographische Objekte	Otros Elementos Hidrográficos	Autres données hydrographiques	Outros acidentes hidrográficos
⊹	Submarine Features	Untermeerische Objekte	Accidentes Submarinos	Formes de relief sous-marin	Acidentes submarinos
□	Political Unit	Politische Einheit	Unidad Politica	Entité politique	Unidade política
ᵿ	Cultural Institution	Kulturelle Institution	Institución Cultural	Institution culturelle	Institução cultural
⊥	Historical Site	Historische Stätte	Sitio Histórico	Site historique	Sitio histórico
♦	Recreational Site	Erholungs- und Ferienort	Sitio de Recreo	Centre de loisirs	Area de Lazer
⊠	Airport	Flughafen	Aeropuerto	Aéroport	Aeroporto
■	Military Installation	Militäranlage	Instalación Militar	Installation militaire	Instalação militar
◆	Miscellaneous	Verschiedenes	Misceláneo	Divers	Diversos

Symbols in the index entries represent the broad categories identified in the key at the right. Symbols with superior numbers (⩘[1]) identify subcategories (see complete key on page *I · 1*).

Symbole im Register stellen die rechts im Schlüssel erklärten Kategorien dar. Symbole mit hochgestellten Ziffern (⩘[1]) bezeichnen Unterabteilungen einer Kategorie (vgl. vollständiger Schlüssel auf Seite *I · 1*).

Los símbolos incluídos en el texto del índice representan las grandes categorías identificadas con la clave a la derecha. Los símbolos con numeros en su parte superior (⩘[1]) identifican las subcategorías (véase la clave completa en la página *I · 1*).

Les symboles de l'index représentent les catégories indiquées dans la légende à droite. Les symboles suivis d'un indice (⩘[1]) représentent des sous-catégories (voir légende complète à la page *I · 1*).

Os símbolos incluídos no texto do índice representam as grandes categorias identificadas com a chave à direita. Os símbolos com números em sua parte superior (⩘[1]) identificam as subcategorias (veja-se a chave completa à página *I · 1*).

∧ Mountain	Berg	Montaña	Montagne	Montanha
⩘ Mountains	Gebirge	Montañas	Montagnes	Montanhas
)(Pass	Paß	Paso	Col	Passo
∨ Valley, Canyon	Tal, Cañon	Valle, Cañón	Vallée, Canyon	Vale, Canhão
≚ Plain	Ebene	Llano	Plaine	Planície
› Cape	Kap	Cabo	Cap	Cabo
ı Island	Insel	Isla	Île	Ilha
ıı Islands	Inseln	Islas	Îles	Ilhas
≐ Other Topographic Features	Andere Topographische Objekte	Otros Elementos Topográficos	Autres données topographiques	Outros acidentes topográficos

ESPAÑOL **FRANÇAIS** **PORTUGUÊS**

Nombre | Página | Lat.°' | Long.°' W = Oeste
Nom | Page | Lat.°' | Long.°' W = Ouest
Nome | Página | Lat.°' | Long.°' W = Oeste

Xuan-Yela I · 195

Symbols in the index entries represent the broad categories identified in the key at the right. Symbols with superior numbers (⩘[1]) identify subcategories (see complete key on page I · 1).

Symbole im Register stellen die rechts im Schlüssel erklärten Kategorien dar. Symbole mit hochgestellten Ziffern (⩘[1]) bezeichnen Unterabteilungen einer Kategorie (vgl. vollständiger Schlüssel auf Seite I · 1).

Los símbolos incluídos en el texto del índice representan las grandes categorías identificadas con la clave a la derecha. Los símbolos con numeros en su parte superior (⩘[1]) identifican las subcategorías (véase la clave completa en la página I · 1).

Les symboles de l'index représentent les catégories indiquées dans la légende à droite. Les symboles suivis d'un indice (⩘[1]) représentent des sous-catégories (voir légende complète à la page I · 1).

Os símbolos incluídos no texto do índice representam as grandes categorias identificadas com a chave à direita. Os símbolos com números em sua parte superior (⩘[1]) identificam as subcategorias (veja-se a chave completa à página I · 1).

	English	Deutsch	Español	Français	Português
∧	Mountain	Berg	Montaña	Montagne	Montanha
⩘	Mountains	Gebirge	Montañas	Montagnes	Montanhas
)(	Pass	Paß	Paso	Col	Passo
V	Valley, Canyon	Tal, Cañon	Valle, Cañón	Vallée, Canyon	Vale, Canhão
≚	Plain	Ebene	Llano	Plaine	Planície
>	Cape	Kap	Cabo	Cap	Cabo
I	Island	Insel	Isla	Île	Ilha
II	Islands	Inseln	Islas	Îles	Ilhas
◆	Other Topographic Features	Andere Topographische Objekte	Otros Elementos Topográficos	Autres données topographiques	Outros acidentes topográficos

ESPAÑOL			FRANÇAIS			PORTUGUÊS		
Nombre	Página	Lat.°′ / Long.°′ W = Oeste	Nom	Page	Lat.°′ / Long.°′ W = Ouest	Nome	Página	Lat.°′ / Long.°′ W = Oeste

(The body of this page is a multi-column geographical index containing several thousand place-name entries in Spanish, French, and Portuguese, each with page number and latitude/longitude coordinates. The entries run in the order Yukon through Yutz in the Spanish column, Yütz'u through Zagare in the French column, and Zagnanado through Žel'va, Bela. in the Portuguese/main column.)

Legend (bottom of page):

Symbol	English	Deutsch	Español	Français	Português
≈	River	Fluß	Río	Rivière	Rio
☰	Canal	Kanal	Canal	Canal	Canal
∟	Waterfall, Rapids	Wasserfall, Stromschnellen	Cascada, Rápidos	Chute d'eau, Rapides	Cascata, Rápidos
⊃	Strait	Meeresstraße	Estrecho	Détroit	Estreito
⊂	Bay, Gulf	Bucht, Golf	Bahía, Golfo	Baie, Golfe	Baía, Golfo
≋	Lake, Lakes	See, Seen	Lago, Lagos	Lac, Lacs	Lago, Lagos
≈	Swamp	Sumpf	Pantano	Marais	Pântano
⊞	Ice Features, Glacier	Eis- und Gletscherformen	Accidentes Glaciares	Formes glaciaires	Acidentes glaciares
✦	Other Hydrographic Features	Andere Hydrographische Objekte	Otros Elementos Hidrográficos	Autres données hydrographiques	Outros acidentes hidrográficos
⬚	Submarine Features	Untermeerische Objekte	Accidentes Submarinos	Formes de relief sous-marin	Acidentes submarinos
◻	Political Unit	Politische Einheit	Unidad Política	Entité politique	Unidade política
⚑	Cultural Institution	Kulturelle Institution	Institución Cultural	Institution culturelle	Instituição cultural
⌂	Historical Site	Historische Stätte	Sitio Histórico	Site historique	Sitio histórico
⚲	Recreational Site	Erholungs- und Ferienort	Sitio de Recreo	Centre de loisirs	Área de Lazer
✈	Airport	Flughafen	Aeropuerto	Aéroport	Aeroporto
⚔	Military Installation	Militäranlage	Instalación Militar	Installation militaire	Instalação militar
⊡	Miscellaneous	Verschiedenes	Misceláneo	Divers	Diversos

ENGLISH

Name	Page	Lat.°′	Long.°′
Želva, Liet.	76	55.13 N	25.06 E
Zel'v'anka ≃	76	53.24 N	24.32 E
Zelzate	50	51.12 N	3.49 E
Žemaičių Naumiestis	76	55.22 N	21.42 E
Žemaitija □[9]	76	55.45 N	23.00 E
Žembejtinskij	80	50.30 N	52.39 E
Zembin	76	54.22 N	28.13 E
Zembla Septentrional → Severnaja Zeml'a II	74	79.30 N	98.00 E
Zembra, Île I	36	37.08 N	10.48 E
Žemčug	88	51.41 N	102.24 E
Zemcy	76	56.15 N	32.23 E
Zemetčino	80	53.30 N	42.38 E
Zemgale □[9]	76	56.30 N	25.00 E
Zémio	154	5.02 N	25.08 E
Zeml'ansk	78	51.54 N	38.44 E
Zemmer	56	49.53 N	6.41 E
Zemmora	34	35.44 N	0.45 E
Zemmour ◆[1]	148	24.50 N	12.15 W
Zemo-Kedi	84	41.26 N	46.24 E
Zémongo, Réserve de Faune de ◆[4]	140	6.45 N	25.15 E
Zemoul, Oued V	148	29.12 N	7.52 W
Žemovo	82	54.45 N	38.49 E
Zempin	54	54.04 N	13.57 E
Zempoala	234	19.24 N	96.24 W
Zempoala ≃	234	20.16 N	97.27 W
Zempoala ⊥	234	19.27 N	96.23 W
Zempoala, Punta ›	234	19.28 N	96.19 W
Zemst	50	50.59 N	4.28 E
Zemun	38	44.50 N	20.24 E
Zenas	218	39.07 N	85.29 W
Zendeh Jān	128	34.21 N	61.45 E
Zeneta	184	50.44 N	102.02 W
Zeng ≃	100	23.09 N	113.46 E
Zengcheng	100	23.19 N	113.49 E
Zengjiawan	105	39.22 N	118.24 E
Zengkou ≃	105	39.19 N	117.37 E
Zenica	38	44.12 N	17.55 E
Zenifim, Har ∧[2]	132	30.06 N	34.51 E
Zenith	224	47.23 N	122.19 W
Zen'kov	78	50.13 N	34.22 E
Zenn ≃	56	49.31 N	10.58 E
Zenna	58	46.06 N	8.45 E
Zenne (Senne) ≃	50	51.04 N	4.26 E
Zenon Park	184	53.04 N	103.45 W
Zenon Videla Dorna	258	35.33 S	58.53 W
Zenson di Piave	64	45.41 N	12.29 E
Zentralafrikanische Republik → Central African Republic □[1]	136	7.00 N	21.00 E
Zentral-Friedhof ◆	264b	48.09 N	16.27 E
Zentral-Massiv → Central, Massif ⋏	32	45.00 N	3.10 E
Zentsūji	96	34.14 N	133.47 E
Zenza do Itombe	152	9.16 S	14.13 E
Zenzeli	80	45.56 N	47.03 E
Zepernick	54	52.39 N	13.32 E
Zephyr	196	31.41 N	98.48 W
Zephyr Cove	226	39.00 N	119.57 W
Zephyrhills	220	28.14 N	82.10 W
Zepu	120	38.13 N	77.16 E
Zérab, Ouadi V	146	11.03 N	19.47 E
Zeralda	34	36.41 N	2.53 E
Zeravšan	85	39.11 N	68.40 E
Zeravšan ≃	72	39.22 N	63.45 E
Zeravšanskij chrebet ⋏	85	39.15 N	68.30 E
Zerbst	54	51.58 N	12.04 E
Žerdevka	80	51.51 N	41.28 E
Žerebec ≃	83	48.57 N	38.03 E
Zereh, Gowd-e ±[7]	128	29.45 N	61.50 E
Zerenda	86	52.55 N	69.10 E
Žerev ≃	78	51.12 N	29.04 E
Zerf	56	49.36 N	6.41 E
Zerga, Merja c	34	34.51 N	6.17 W
Zergenta	80	47.42 N	45.12 E
Zeri	62	44.21 N	9.46 E
Zerind	38	46.37 N	21.31 E
Żerków	30	52.05 N	17.34 E
Zermatt	58	46.02 N	7.45 E
Zernez	58	46.43 N	10.05 E
Zernograd	78	46.50 N	40.19 E
Žernovka	82	54.49 N	37.46 E
Zernsdorf	54	52.18 N	13.41 E
Zero ≃	64	45.32 N	12.22 E
Zeroud, Oued V	36	35.50 N	10.13 E
Zerqan	38	41.30 N	20.21 E
Žešart	24	62.05 N	49.34 E
Zestafoni	84	42.07 N	43.02 E
Žest'anka	80	51.36 N	49.24 E
Žestoki	82	56.19 N	36.22 E
Žestylevo	82	56.24 N	37.39 E
Zetel	52	53.25 N	7.58 E
Žetybaj	80	48.51 N	48.04 E
Žetykol', ozero ⊜	86	51.02 N	60.54 E
Zeulenroda	54	50.39 N	11.58 E
Zeuthen	54	52.20 N	13.37 E
Zeuthener See ⊜	264a	52.21 N	13.39 E
Zeven	52	53.18 N	9.16 E
Zevenaar	52	51.56 N	6.05 E
Zevenbergen	52	51.38 N	4.36 E
Zevenbergschen Hoek	52	51.41 N	4.40 E
Zevenwouden ◆[1]	52	52.57 N	6.00 E
Zevio	64	45.22 N	11.08 E
Zeyādah Kot	272b	22.27 N	88.20 E
Zeyawadi	110	18.33 N	96.26 E
Zeytinbağı	130	40.23 N	28.47 E
Zeytinburnu ◆[8]	267b	40.59 N	28.54 E
Zeytindağ	130	38.58 N	27.04 E
Zeyveh	84	39.07 N	47.42 E
Zeze	270	35.00 N	135.54 E
Zêzere ≃	34	39.28 N	8.20 W
Zghartā	130	34.24 N	35.54 E
Zgierz	30	51.52 N	19.25 E
Zgornje Hoče	61	46.29 N	15.38 E
Zgorzelec	30	51.12 N	15.01 E
Zgurovka	78	50.31 N	31.46 E
Zhabuchaka Hu ⊜	120	31.30 N	84.00 E
Zhage	102	26.20 N	103.51 E
Zhagenasongduo	102	33.12 N	94.33 E
Zhag'yab	102	30.32 N	98.00 E
Zhahasutai	86	42.58 N	85.20 E
Zhai ≃	100	32.19 N	115.02 E
Zhaihe	100	32.08 N	114.54 E
Zhaili	100	27.42 N	117.22 E
Zhailing	98	41.00 N	116.53 E
Zhaiqiao	106	31.35 N	119.55 E
Zhaitang	105	39.57 N	115.42 E
Zhaitun	104	41.46 N	122.06 E
Zhakou, Zhg.	102	29.59 N	112.10 E
Zhakou, Zhg.	106	30.23 N	120.47 E
Zhakou, Zhg.	106	30.13 N	120.08 E
Zhalantun → Butha Qi	89	48.02 N	122.43 E
Zhalanyingzi	104	41.29 N	120.37 E
Zhalun	120	32.25 N	81.35 E
Zhaluomude	89	49.13 N	120.22 E
Zhancheng	98	37.41 N	117.46 E
Zhang ≃, Zhg.	100	31.05 N	113.11 E
Zhang ≃, Zhg.	100	25.51 N	114.46 E
Zhang ≃, Zhg.	102	36.10 N	115.05 E
Zhangbei	98	41.04 N	114.48 E
Zhangcang	98	35.54 N	119.57 E
Zhangcun, Zhg.	100	33.20 N	115.59 E
Zhangcun, Zhg.	100	28.50 N	117.57 E
Zhangcun, Zhg.	106	30.28 N	119.22 E
Zhangcun, Zhg.	106	30.40 N	119.57 E
Zhangdang	104	41.54 N	124.05 E
Zhangde	100	34.07 N	113.27 E
Zhangdiyingzi	89	50.30 N	127.16 E
Zhangdu	100	30.38 N	118.13 E
Zhangdu Hu ⊜	100	30.40 N	114.42 E
Zhangfang	105	39.35 N	115.41 E
Zhangfengji	98	35.14 N	116.01 E
Zhanggang	100	30.34 N	112.51 E
Zhanggezhuang, Zhg.	98	36.47 N	119.47 E
Zhanggezhuang, Zhg.	105	40.08 N	116.56 E
Zhanggou	104	42.07 N	124.06 E
Zhangguangcai Ling ⋏	89	45.25 N	129.20 E
Zhangguizhuang	105	39.07 N	117.18 E
Zhanggutai	98	42.40 N	122.28 E
Zhanghezhuang	105	38.56 N	114.56 E
Zhanghuang	102	22.01 N	109.27 E
Zhanghuanggang	106	32.07 N	120.30 E
Zhanghuban	100	26.23 N	118.29 E
Zhangji	98	34.08 N	117.24 E
Zhangjiachang, Zhg.	107	29.26 N	104.34 E
Zhangjiachang, Zhg.	107	29.33 N	104.54 E
Zhangjiachang, Zhg.	107	29.57 N	103.48 E
Zhangjiadian	105	39.44 N	114.54 E
Zhangjiagou	100	30.18 N	113.22 E
Zhangjiaji	100	32.09 N	112.23 E
Zhangjiajie	104	41.28 N	124.08 E
Zhangjiakou (Kalgan)	105	40.50 N	114.53 E
Zhangjiapang	100	30.25 N	115.47 E
Zhangjiapu	104	41.18 N	122.02 E
Zhangjiaqiao, Zhg.	106	31.36 N	120.36 E
Zhangjiaqiao, Zhg.	107	30.02 N	104.15 E
Zhangjiatou	106	31.38 N	119.05 E
Zhangjiatun, Zhg.	104	41.05 N	121.44 E
Zhangjiatun, Zhg.	105	40.37 N	114.57 E
Zhangjiawa	105	40.10 N	117.52 E
Zhangjiawan	105	39.51 N	116.41 E
Zhangjiawopu	104	41.10 N	122.17 E
Zhangjiayingzi	104	42.04 N	120.57 E
Zhangjingqiao	106	31.39 N	120.27 E
Zhangjinhe	100	30.14 N	112.35 E
Zhangliangdian	100	33.42 N	113.02 E
Zhangliantang	106	31.01 N	121.02 E
Zhangling	98	36.32 N	119.29 E
Zhanglu	98	36.16 N	115.33 E
Zhangmang	100	32.03 N	114.32 E
Zhangming	102	31.49 N	104.51 E
Zhangmuqiao	100	31.26 N	116.44 E
Zhangmushi	100	27.01 N	112.38 E
Zhangmutou	100	22.55 N	114.05 E
Zhangping	100	25.19 N	117.25 E
Zhangpu, Zhg.	100	24.09 N	117.36 E
Zhangpu, Zhg.	106	31.17 N	120.57 E
Zhangqiangzhen	98	42.39 N	122.59 E
Zhangqiao	100	32.21 N	117.38 E
Zhangqiu (Mingshui)	98	36.43 N	117.30 E
Zhangsanta	102	39.37 N	110.14 E
Zhangsanying	98	41.34 N	117.39 E
Zhangshitai	104	41.50 N	122.51 E
Zhangshuping	102	31.20 N	111.02 E
Zhangshuxia	100	25.54 N	112.45 E
Zhangtaitai	104	40.59 N	121.05 E
Zhangtaizi	104	41.22 N	123.16 E
Zhangting	100	30.02 N	121.19 E
Zhangwan	100	26.43 N	119.36 E
Zhangwenpu	105	40.26 N	116.04 E
Zhangwu, Zhg.	104	42.22 N	122.31 E
Zhangwu, Zhg.	106	30.47 N	119.33 E
Zhangwutaimen	104	42.16 N	122.42 E
Zhangxinliuji	100	33.43 N	115.48 E
Zhangyan, Zhg.	106	31.48 N	119.44 E
Zhangyan, Zhg.	106	30.48 N	121.16 E
Zhangyangongtun	104	40.58 N	120.46 E
Zhangye	102	38.56 N	100.27 E
Zhangze	106	30.55 N	121.15 E
Zhangzhishan	106	31.56 N	121.01 E
Zhangzhou (Longxi)	100	24.33 N	117.39 E
Zhangzhu	106	31.16 N	119.37 E
Zhangzhuang, Zhg.	98	37.03 N	116.32 E
Zhangzhuang, Zhg.	98	36.02 N	118.01 E
Zhangzhuang, Zhg.	106	31.57 N	119.52 E
Zhangzi Dao I	98	39.00 N	122.44 E
Zhanhua (Fuguo)	98	37.42 N	118.08 E
Zhanji	98	34.14 N	115.52 E
Zhanjiajing	107	29.15 N	104.55 E
Zhanjiang	102	21.16 N	110.28 E
Zhanjiaqiao, Zhg.	100	29.19 N	113.34 E
Zhanjiaqiao, Zhg.	106	30.25 N	120.08 E
Zhanyang	100	25.30 N	119.28 E
Zhanyi	102	25.38 N	103.43 E
Zhanyu	89	44.31 N	122.37 E
Zhao'an	100	23.47 N	117.12 E
Zhao'an Wan c	100	23.38 N	117.19 E
Zhaobeikou	105	38.55 N	116.06 E
Zhaochuan	105	40.41 N	115.18 E
Zhaocun	105	39.35 N	116.14 E
Zhaodong	89	46.05 N	125.59 E
Zhaogezhuang, Zhg.	98	37.27 N	120.37 E
Zhaogezhuang, Zhg.	105	39.45 N	118.24 E
Zhaoguang	89	48.07 N	126.43 E
Zhaohe	100	33.12 N	112.49 E
Zhaohuazhen	107	29.02 N	105.08 E
Zhaojiagou	104	40.47 N	123.27 E
Zhaojiapuzi	104	40.51 N	123.49 E
Zhaojiaqiao	106	30.44 N	121.12 E
Zhaojiatangfang	104	42.07 N	122.57 E
Zhaojiatun	104	41.24 N	121.53 E
Zhaojiawopeng	104	42.30 N	123.06 E
Zhaojiaying	105	38.58 N	116.42 E
Zhaojue	102	28.15 N	102.50 E
Zhaomaozhuang	105	39.28 N	117.59 E
Zhaomutun	104	41.10 N	121.38 E
Zhaoping	102	24.03 N	110.52 E
Zhaoqiao	100	28.42 N	114.45 E
Zhaoqing (Gaoyao)	102	23.03 N	112.27 E
Zhaosu	86	43.06 N	81.08 E
Zhaotan	100	29.42 N	116.48 E
Zhaotong	102	27.19 N	103.48 E
Zhaotun	104	41.54 N	121.59 E
Zhaoxian, Zhg.	98	37.45 N	114.46 E
Zhaoxian, Zhg.	98	35.44 N	118.55 E
Zhaoxing	89	47.43 N	131.19 E
Zhaoya	107	29.00 N	105.35 E
Zhaoyi	105	39.55 N	116.43 E
Zhaoyuan, Zhg.	89	45.31 N	125.09 E
Zhaoyuan, Zhg.	98	37.22 N	120.24 E
Zhaozhou	89	45.41 N	125.21 E
Zhaozhuang, Zhg.	98	34.45 N	116.27 E
Zhaozhuang, Zhg.	98	34.14 N	116.38 E
Zhaozhuangzi	105	39.10 N	117.20 E
Zhapu	106	30.36 N	121.05 E
Zhari Namco ⊜	120	31.05 N	85.35 E
Zhashui	102	33.40 N	109.01 E
Zhaxi Co ⊜	120	32.10 N	85.05 E
Zhaxigang	120	32.32 N	79.41 E
Zhayi	102	28.34 N	99.09 E
Zhaze	106	32.09 N	119.29 E
Zhdanov → Mariupol'	83	47.06 N	37.33 E
Zhecheng	98	34.06 N	115.19 E
Zhegao	100	31.46 N	117.45 E
Zhegu	120	28.43 N	91.43 E
Zhêhor	102	31.41 N	100.24 E
Zhejiang (Chekiang) □[4]	100	29.00 N	120.00 E
Zhelang	100	22.43 N	115.32 E
Zhelin, Zhg.	100	29.14 N	115.30 E
Zhelin, Zhg.	100	23.36 N	117.06 E
Zhelin, Zhg.	106	30.50 N	121.29 E
Zhen ≃	100	24.55 N	113.44 E
Zhen'an	102	33.27 N	109.01 E
Zhenbeikou	102	39.15 N	106.17 E
Zhenbiancheng	105	40.10 N	115.49 E
Zhenchang, Zhg.	105	39.47 N	115.24 E
Zhenchang, Zhg.	106	32.04 N	121.02 E
Zhenfeng	102	25.23 N	105.41 E
Zheng'an	102	28.31 N	107.29 E
Zheng'anpu	104	41.43 N	121.56 E
Zhengcun	105	39.13 N	115.40 E
Zhengding	98	38.10 N	114.34 E
Zhengdongyu	106	31.59 N	120.10 E
Zhengfang	100	28.42 N	117.53 E
Zhengguanchang	107	29.54 N	106.35 E
Zhengguo	100	23.25 N	113.53 E
Zhenghe	100	27.22 N	118.50 E
Zhengji	98	34.26 N	117.01 E
Zhengjiadiancun	104	41.05 N	122.20 E
Zhengjiawu	100	29.29 N	120.05 E
Zhenglan Qi (Dund Hot)	98	42.16 N	115.49 E
Zhengning	102	35.22 N	108.24 E
Zhengping	100	25.22 N	114.46 E
Zhen'guosi	271a	39.51 N	116.21 E
Zhengxiangbai Qi (Qagan Nur)	98	42.16 N	114.52 E
Zhengyang	100	32.37 N	114.23 E
Zhengyangguan	100	32.28 N	116.32 E
Zhengyi	106	31.23 N	120.52 E
Zhengzhou (Chengchow)	102	34.48 N	113.39 E
Zhengzhuang	100	28.11 N	119.01 E
Zhengzi	107	29.22 N	104.16 E
Zhengzichang	107	29.08 N	106.38 E
Zhenhai, Zhg.	100	29.57 N	121.42 E
Zhenhai, Zhg.	100	24.16 N	118.06 E
Zhenhai, Zhg.	102	21.53 N	112.25 E
Zhenjiang, Zhg.	98	40.44 N	125.28 E
Zhenjiang, Zhg.	106	32.13 N	119.26 E
Zhenjiangguan	102	32.25 N	103.35 E
Zhenjiaqiao	106	32.08 N	120.49 E
Zhenjinqiao	107	30.12 N	104.22 E
Zhenkang	102	24.06 N	99.16 E
Zhenlai	89	45.52 N	123.14 E
Zhenning	102	26.05 N	105.46 E
Zhenping	102	33.08 N	112.19 E
Zhenru	106	31.15 N	121.24 E
Zhentou	100	27.04 N	114.56 E
Zhentou ≃	100	32.58 N	114.24 E
Zhentoudian	100	29.10 N	117.29 E
Zhentoushi	100	28.01 N	113.20 E
Zhenxi	107	29.29 N	104.33 E
Zhenxiaguan	100	27.12 N	120.28 E
Zhenxing	98	42.38 N	124.53 E
Zhenxiong	102	27.27 N	104.50 E
Zhenyu	100	27.08 N	120.18 E
Zhenyuan, Zhg.	102	35.46 N	107.18 E
Zhenyuan, Zhg.	102	26.53 N	108.19 E
Zhenze	106	30.55 N	120.30 E
Zhenzhumen	98	41.53 N	126.45 E
Zhenzichang, Zhg.	107	29.59 N	105.11 E
Zhenzichang, Zhg.	107	29.52 N	104.12 E
Zhenzichang, Zhg.	107	30.38 N	104.20 E
Zhenzijie	107	28.48 N	106.40 E
Zhenziling	104	42.10 N	124.12 E
Zhenzizhen	105	39.50 N	118.20 E
Zheqiao	100	26.27 N	112.48 E
Zherong	100	27.16 N	119.54 E
Zheshan	106	30.15 N	120.24 E
Zhetang	106	31.45 N	118.55 E
Zhidan	102	37.00 N	108.40 E
Zhidoi	102	33.08 N	94.50 E
Zhierling	98	40.26 N	114.16 E
Zhigou	98	35.55 N	119.13 E
Zhijiang	102	27.27 N	109.41 E
Zhijin	102	26.41 N	105.37 E
Zhili	106	30.52 N	120.16 E
Zhitan	100	29.35 N	117.16 E
Zhitang, Zhg.	106	31.33 N	121.01 E
Zhitang, Zhg.	106	31.36 N	120.58 E
Zhitomir → Žitomir	78	50.16 N	28.40 E
Zhitouji	100	33.28 N	118.18 E
Zhiwucun	106	30.38 N	119.47 E
Zhixi	100	23.57 N	114.33 E
Zhixia	100	29.42 N	119.36 E
Zhixiqiao	106	31.49 N	119.29 E
Zhiyang	100	33.47 N	113.07 E
Zhizushan	104	41.50 N	121.24 E
Zhob	120	31.20 N	69.27 E
Zhob ≃	120	32.04 N	69.50 E
Zhonganpu	104	41.37 N	121.58 E
Zhong'aozhen	107	29.46 N	105.41 E
Zhongba, Zhg.	100	23.43 N	115.22 E
Zhongba, Zhg.	120	29.38 N	84.13 E
Zhongbu, Zhg.	100	31.25 N	117.45 E
Zhongbu, Zhg.	100	31.40 N	117.45 E
Zhongbu, Zhg.	100	28.50 N	117.16 E
Zhongchuan	100	26.58 N	119.27 E
Zhongcun	102	33.27 N	110.05 E
Zhongdai	106	30.46 N	120.59 E
Zhongdian	102	27.50 N	99.40 E
Zhongdu, Zhg.	100	24.56 N	116.26 E
Zhongdu, Zhg.	100	33.04 N	118.46 E
Zhongdu, Zhg.	107	28.46 N	103.58 E
Zhongduan	100	25.17 N	116.41 E
Zhongerchong	104	41.58 N	123.58 E
Zhonggang	100	32.38 N	115.45 E
Zhonggong	98	36.30 N	117.01 E
Zhonggoumen	98	41.00 N	116.26 E
Zhonggu	104	42.27 N	124.00 E
Zhongguan	106	30.39 N	120.11 E
Zhongguo → China □[1]	90	35.00 N	105.00 E
Zhonghe	102	27.11 N	103.52 E
Zhonghechang	107	30.12 N	104.49 E
Zhongheying	102	23.48 N	103.36 E
Zhonghezhen	107	30.34 N	104.06 E
Zhonghuamen	106	32.01 N	118.46 E
Zhonghuopu	100	29.44 N	113.59 E
Zhongjianchang	107	28.46 N	106.13 E
Zhongjiang	102	31.00 N	104.18 E
Zhongjiatai	104	40.48 N	122.46 E
Zhonglou	98	35.24 N	119.02 E
Zhongluotan	100	23.23 N	113.23 E
Zhongluyantai	104	41.32 N	123.17 E
Zhongmeihe	100	31.19 N	116.45 E
Zhongmou	98	34.46 N	114.01 E
Zhongning	102	37.27 N	105.38 E
Zhongpingchang	102	31.15 N	110.10 E
Zhongqiao	106	31.11 N	119.11 E
Zhongsha	100	26.24 N	116.36 E
Zhongshan, Zhg.	100	26.12 N	117.26 E
Zhongshan (Shiqizhen), Zhg.	100	22.31 N	113.22 E
Zhongshan ʊ[3]	9	69.22 S	76.23 E
Zhongshan Park ♠	269b	31.13 N	121.25 E
Zhongtiao Shan ⋏	102	35.12 N	111.35 E
Zhongting ≃	105	39.03 N	116.46 E
Zhongtou	100	34.00 N	113.21 E
Zhongwei	102	37.33 N	105.10 E
Zhongwopu	102	38.30 N	102.59 E
Zhongxian, Zhg.	100	27.17 N	116.47 E
Zhongxian, Zhg.	102	30.29 N	108.05 E
Zhongxiang	100	31.11 N	112.33 E
Zhongxiangzhen	107	29.50 N	104.08 E
Zhongxin, Zhg.	100	23.16 N	113.38 E
Zhongxin, Zhg.	100	24.14 N	114.44 E
Zhongxin, Zhg.	104	40.47 N	124.08 E
Zhongxing, Zhg.	106	32.17 N	119.34 E
Zhongxing, Zhg.	107	30.12 N	103.32 E
Zhongxingchang	107	29.07 N	105.18 E
Zhongxinzhen, Zhg.	107	30.16 N	106.15 E
Zhongxinzhen, Zhg.	107	30.30 N	104.03 E
Zhongyangqu	104	40.47 N	122.05 E
Zhongyaozhan	89	50.46 N	125.54 E
Zhongyi	100	31.08 N	114.52 E
Zhongying	105	39.38 N	117.06 E
Zhongzangcun	105	38.52 N	115.38 E
Zhongzhan	100	25.16 N	114.24 E
Zhongzhuang	105	39.25 N	114.47 E
Zhou ≃	105	39.47 N	117.23 E
Zhouba	107	29.06 N	103.43 E
Zhoubachang	107	28.59 N	103.52 E
Zhoucun	98	36.47 N	117.48 E
Zhoudangfan	100	31.54 N	114.31 E
Zhoujiachang	107	30.33 N	104.25 E
Zhoujiadai	106	32.12 N	120.26 E
Zhoujiadu	106	31.11 N	121.29 E
Zhoujiagou	107	30.08 N	104.30 E
Zhoujiatun, Zhg.	104	41.34 N	121.05 E
Zhoujiatun, Zhg.	104	41.29 N	121.50 E
Zhoujiatun, Zhg.	104	41.04 N	120.47 E
Zhoujiatun, Zhg.	104	41.16 N	120.58 E
Zhoujiawopu	104	42.31 N	122.45 E
Zhoujiayao	104	41.19 N	122.48 E
Zhoujingxiang	106	31.32 N	120.23 E
Zhoukoudianzhen	105	39.41 N	115.56 E
Zhoulichang	107	29.55 N	105.09 E
Zhouning	100	27.16 N	119.12 E
Zhoupo	107	29.48 N	104.01 E
Zhoupu	106	31.07 N	121.34 E
Zhouqu	102	33.43 N	104.10 E
Zhouquan	106	30.35 N	120.21 E
Zhoushan Dao I	100	30.05 N	122.10 E
Zhoushan Qundao II	100	30.00 N	122.00 E
Zhoushu	106	31.28 N	120.59 E
Zhoushuizi	98	38.57 N	121.34 E
Zhoutieqiao	106	31.26 N	120.00 E
Zhouwangmiao	106	30.28 N	120.29 E
Zhouxi	100	29.13 N	116.20 E
Zhouxiang	100	30.10 N	121.08 E
Zhouxinzhen	106	31.30 N	120.18 E
Zhouzhai	106	32.02 N	121.31 E
Zhouzhi	102	34.12 N	108.10 E
Zhouzhuang, Zhg.	105	39.09 N	115.18 E
Zhouzhuang, Zhg.	106	31.06 N	120.51 E
Zhouzhuang, Zhg.	106	32.15 N	120.08 E
Zhuanghang	106	30.54 N	121.23 E
Zhuanghe	98	39.43 N	123.01 E
Zhuangji	98	34.20 N	115.15 E
Zhuanglang	102	34.58 N	106.07 E
Zhuangtou	105	40.55 N	117.57 E
Zhuangtouyingzi, Zhg.	104	41.43 N	120.32 E
Zhuangtouyingzi, Zhg.	104	41.50 N	120.43 E
Zhuangxi	107	30.33 N	104.31 E
Zhuangyuanqiao	100	27.54 N	120.48 E
Zhuanping Shan ∧	107	29.07 N	103.37 E
Zhuanqiao	106	31.04 N	121.23 E
Zhuantouwan	100	31.29 N	112.24 E
Zhuanwantai	104	41.20 N	122.22 E
Zhuao	100	29.05 N	121.16 E
Zhucang	102	27.18 N	107.26 E
Zhucheng	98	36.00 N	119.24 E
Zhudi	269b	31.12 N	121.18 E
Zhudian	100	30.33 N	115.12 E
Zhuergan	89	52.04 N	120.48 E
Zhufengzhen	106	30.35 N	118.56 E
Zhufuo	107	29.02 N	105.51 E
Zhugan ≃	100	32.18 N	114.42 E
Zhuganpu	100	32.13 N	114.39 E
Zhugao	107	30.37 N	104.40 E
Zhuge, Zhg.	98	36.00 N	118.32 E
Zhuge, Zhg.	100	29.15 N	119.18 E
Zhugentan	107	29.25 N	103.50 E
Zhugou	98	36.52 N	120.15 E
Zhugouzhen	100	32.47 N	113.42 E
Zhugusi	102	37.01 N	102.27 E
Zhuhe	100	29.44 N	113.06 E
Zhuhongyu	104	40.48 N	123.00 E
Zhuji	100	29.43 N	120.14 E
Zhujiabeng	106	31.21 N	120.41 E
Zhujiabian	106	31.38 N	119.11 E
Zhujiachang, Zhg.	107	29.48 N	104.20 E
Zhujiachang, Zhg.	107	30.03 N	104.13 E
Zhujiafang	104	41.20 N	122.40 E
Zhujiahang	106	30.51 N	121.19 E
Zhujiahe	106	31.08 N	120.53 E
Zhujia Jian I	100	29.54 N	122.24 E
Zhujiajiao	106	31.06 N	121.02 E
Zhujiajiaotou	106	31.24 N	121.11 E
Zhujiang Kou c[1]	100	22.36 N	113.44 E
Zhujiangqing	100	27.18 N	114.44 E
Zhujiaqiao	106	30.26 N	119.03 E
Zhujiawan, Zhg.	100	32.28 N	117.29 E
Zhujiawan, Zhg.	100	30.56 N	114.10 E
Zhujiawan, Zhg.	105	40.08 N	114.56 E
Zhujiawopeng	104	42.27 N	122.13 E
Zhujiesi	102	33.34 N	97.21 E
Zhukeng	100	23.49 N	112.55 E
Zhukou, Zhg.	98	34.07 N	115.04 E
Zhukou, Zhg.	100	27.41 N	118.53 E
Zhukou, Zhg.	100	26.58 N	117.16 E
Zhukovskiy → Žukovskij	82	55.35 N	38.08 E
Zhulanbu	100	25.36 N	115.46 E
Zhulin, Zhg.	100	32.20 N	113.38 E
Zhulin, Zhg.	106	31.45 N	119.27 E
Zhulong ≃	98	38.47 N	115.59 E
Zhulongqiao	100	32.21 N	118.09 E
Zhuluke	98	41.36 N	119.54 E
Zhumadian	100	32.58 N	114.03 E
Zhuolu	105	40.22 N	115.12 E
Zhuoni	102	34.32 N	103.24 E
Zhuotian	100	25.38 N	116.13 E
Zhuoxian	105	39.30 N	115.58 E
Zhuozi	102	40.52 N	112.33 E
Zhuqianzongpuzi	104	42.17 N	123.18 E
Zhuqiao, Zhg.	98	37.22 N	120.05 E
Zhuqiao, Zhg.	106	31.07 N	121.44 E
Zhuqiao, Zhg.	106	30.26 N	120.36 E
Zhurushan	100	30.26 N	113.48 E
Zhushan	102	32.10 N	110.19 E
Zhusigang	100	31.14 N	118.23 E
Zhutan	100	28.04 N	114.10 E
Zhutang, Zhg.	106	31.06 N	118.39 E
Zhutang, Zhg.	106	31.47 N	120.24 E
Zhutian	100	28.43 N	117.01 E
Zhuting, Zhg.	100	27.24 N	113.04 E
Zhuting, Zhg.	100	27.48 N	114.02 E
Zhuwo	105	40.02 N	115.48 E
Zhuwotuo	107	30.31 N	104.34 E
Zhuwumiao	100	30.54 N	116.19 E
Zhuxi, Zhg.	100	28.10 N	118.53 E
Zhuxi, Zhg.	102	32.09 N	109.42 E
Zhuxi, Zhg.	107	29.32 N	105.40 E
Zhuxianzhen	98	34.37 N	114.16 E
Zhuxichang	100	28.58 N	114.06 E
Zhuya	98	36.38 N	118.12 E
Zhuyang	98	36.16 N	117.22 E
Zhuyangxi	107	29.03 N	105.57 E
Zhuyangzhen	102	34.20 N	110.44 E
Zhuyuan	107	29.34 N	104.08 E
Zhuzeqiao	106	31.34 N	119.20 E
Zhuzhenji	100	32.31 N	118.42 E
Zhuzhou (Chuchow)	100	27.50 N	113.09 E
Zhuzikou	100	29.17 N	112.41 E
Zi ≃, Zhg.	98	37.12 N	118.34 E
Zi ≃, Zhg.	102	28.41 N	112.43 E
Zi ≃, Zhg.	102	31.59 N	96.53 E
Zia Indian Reservation ◆[4]	200	35.30 N	106.43 W
Zia International Airport ⊠	126	23.46 N	90.23 E
Ziama Mansouria	34	36.40 N	5.29 E
Ziano	64	46.17 N	11.34 E
Ziārat	120	30.23 N	67.43 E
Ziārat-e Shāh Maqṣūd	120	31.59 N	65.30 E
Ziārat Gali Chāh ⫪[4]	128	28.20 N	63.38 E
Žiar nad Hronom	30	48.36 N	18.52 E
Zibdīn	132	33.22 N	35.28 E
Zibo (Zhangdian)	98	36.47 N	118.01 E
Zicapa	234	17.57 N	99.02 W
Zicavo	36	41.54 N	9.08 E
Zichang	102	37.19 N	109.33 E
Žichovice	60	49.16 N	13.37 E
Zichuan	98	36.38 N	117.55 E
Žičicy	76	55.07 N	31.17 E
Zickhusen	54	53.45 N	11.25 E
Židačov	78	49.23 N	24.08 E
Ziddi	85	39.03 N	68.48 E
Žideli	86	48.40 N	70.29 E
Zid'ki	78	49.42 N	36.21 E
Židlochovice	61	49.02 N	16.37 E
Ziębice	30	50.37 N	17.00 E
Ziegelroda	54	51.20 N	11.28 E
Ziegendorf	54	53.18 N	11.49 E
Ziegenhain	56	50.55 N	9.15 E
Ziegenhals	264a	52.21 N	13.40 E
Ziegenrück	54	50.37 N	11.38 E
Zielona Góra (Grünberg)	30	51.56 N	15.31 E
Zielona Góra □[4]	30	52.00 N	15.20 E
Ziemetshausen	58	48.18 N	10.31 E
Zierenberg	56	51.22 N	9.18 E
Zierikzee	52	51.38 N	3.55 E
Ziersdorf	61	48.31 N	15.55 E
Ziesar	54	52.16 N	12.17 E
Ziesendorf	54	54.00 N	12.02 E
Ziethen	54	53.53 N	13.40 E
Žiežmariai	76	54.48 N	24.27 E
Ziftā	142	30.43 N	31.15 E
Žigajlovka	78	50.38 N	35.07 E
Žigalgan	84	44.36 N	50.46 E
Žigalovo	88	54.48 N	105.08 E
Žigansk	74	66.45 N	123.20 E
Zigazinskij	86	53.50 N	57.20 E
Zigong (Tzukung)	107	29.24 N	104.47 E
Ziguéy	146	14.43 N	15.47 E
Zigui	102	31.00 N	110.31 E
Ziguinchor	150	12.35 N	16.16 W
Ziguinchor □[4]	150	12.45 N	16.20 W
Žigulevsk	80	53.25 N	49.27 E
Žiguli	80	53.22 N	49.19 E
Žiguli ⋏	80	53.20 N	49.40 E
Zigutaicun	104	42.01 N	121.16 E
Zig Zag, Cerro ∧[2]	286d	12.12 S	76.59 W
Zihedian	98	36.48 N	118.22 E
Zihuatanejo	234	17.38 N	101.33 W
Zihukou, Zhg.	100	28.44 N	112.33 E
Zihukou, Zhg.	100	28.55 N	118.08 E
Ziiyang	102	32.31 N	108.48 E
Zijančurino	86	51.33 N	56.55 E
Žijenkum	85	42.50 N	69.00 E
Zijiao	98	37.21 N	117.25 E
Zijin	100	23.40 N	115.11 E
Zijingguan	105	39.23 N	115.12 E
Zijin Shan ∧[2]	106	32.04 N	118.51 E
Zikejevo	76	53.44 N	34.52 E
Zikhron Ya'aqov	132	32.34 N	34.57 E
Zikoufang	100	26.22 N	117.24 E
Zilair	86	52.14 N	57.30 E
Žilaja Kosa	80	46.49 N	53.12 E
Žilaja Tambica	24	62.32 N	36.09 E
Zile	130	40.18 N	35.54 E
Zili	102	26.50 N	100.27 E
Žilina	30	49.14 N	18.46 E
Žilino	76	54.54 N	21.56 E
Zillah, Lībiyā	146	28.33 N	17.35 E
Zillah, Wa., U.S.	202	46.24 N	120.15 W
Ziller ≃	64	47.24 N	11.50 E
Zillertal V	64	47.20 N	11.50 E
Zillertaler Alpen (Alpi Aurine) ⋏	64	47.00 N	11.55 E
Zillis	58	46.38 N	9.27 E
Zillisheim	58	47.41 N	7.16 E
Zilly	54	51.56 N	10.49 E
Zilme	144	16.25 N	43.49 E
Žiloj, ostrov I	84	40.19 N	50.36 E
Žiloj Bor	76	59.06 N	34.37 E
Žil'ovo	82	54.59 N	38.02 E
Ziltendorf	54	52.12 N	14.37 E
Zilupe	76	56.23 N	28.07 E
Zilwaukee	190	43.28 N	83.55 W
Zima	88	53.55 N	102.04 E
Zima ≃	88	53.52 N	102.02 E
Žima, gora ∧	88	53.18 N	107.38 E
Zimapán	234	20.45 N	99.21 W
Zimatlán	234	16.52 N	96.47 W
Zimba	154	17.19 S	26.13 E
Zimbabwe □[1], Afr.	138	20.00 S	30.00 E
Zimbabwe □[1], Afr.	154	20.00 S	30.00 E
Zimbor	38	47.00 N	23.16 E
Zimella	64	45.20 N	11.22 E
Zimi	150	7.19 N	11.18 W
Zimljansker-Stausee → Ciml'anskoje vodochranilišče ⊜[1]	80	48.00 N	43.00 E
Zimmara, Monte ∧	70	37.45 N	14.16 E
Zimn'ackij	80	49.44 N	42.53 E
Zimnicea	38	43.39 N	25.21 E
Zimogorje	83	48.35 N	38.56 E
Zimonino	76	53.47 N	31.52 E
Zimovniki	80	47.08 N	42.28 E
Zimovskoje	86	57.31 N	86.52 E
Zin, Naḥal V	132	30.57 N	35.19 E
Zinal	58	46.08 N	7.38 E
Zinapécuaro [de Figueroa]	234	19.52 N	100.49 W
Zinave, Parque Nacional de ♠	156	21.35 S	33.35 E
Zinder	150	13.48 N	8.59 E
Zinder □[5]	146	15.00 N	10.30 E
Zinga	152	3.43 N	18.35 E
Zinga Mulike	154	9.09 S	38.44 E
Zingaro, Passo dello)(	70	37.43 N	14.50 E
Zingst	54	54.26 N	12.41 E
Zingst ›[1]	54	54.25 N	12.50 E
Zingwanda	140	7.10 N	27.56 E
Ziniaré	150	12.35 N	1.18 W
Žiniške ≃	85	43.14 N	78.30 E
Zinkgruvan	40	58.49 N	15.05 E
Zin'kov	78	49.04 N	27.04 E
Zinnik → Soignies	50	50.35 N	4.04 E
Zinnowitz	54	54.04 N	13.55 E
Zinswiller	56	48.55 N	7.35 E
Zion, Il., U.S.	216	42.26 N	87.49 W
Zion, Md., U.S.	208	39.40 N	75.57 W
Zionhill	208	40.29 N	75.24 W
Zion National Park ♠	200	37.10 N	113.00 W
Zionsville	218	39.57 N	86.15 W
Zionz Lake ⊜	184	51.25 N	91.52 W
Zipaquirá	246	5.02 N	74.00 W
Žipkovšino	88	51.52 N	112.59 E
Zippori	132	32.45 N	35.17 E
Zipsendorf	54	51.02 N	12.16 E
Ziqlāb, Wādī V	132	32.30 N	35.34 E
Zir	130	39.59 N	32.31 E
Zīra	123	30.58 N	74.59 E
Žir'akovo	86	57.53 N	65.37 E
Zirándaro	234	18.27 N	100.59 W
Zirāpur	124	24.01 N	76.22 E
Žir'atino	76	53.15 N	33.44 E
Zirbitzkogel ∧	61	47.04 N	14.34 E
Zirchow	54	53.53 N	14.08 E
Zirgan	86	53.14 N	55.55 E
Žirje, Otok I	36	43.40 N	15.39 E
Zirl	64	47.17 N	11.14 E
Zirndorf	56	49.26 N	10.58 E
Žirnov	80	48.13 N	41.06 E
Žirnovsk	80	51.00 N	44.46 E
Ziro	120	27.38 N	93.42 E
Žiroškino	82	55.22 N	38.03 E
Žirovnice	30	49.15 N	15.11 E
Zishan	100	25.57 N	115.35 E
Zistersdorf	61	48.32 N	16.45 E
Zisterzienserabtei ʊ[1]	56	49.01 N	8.47 E
Zisuntang	106	30.38 N	118.42 E
Zitadelle ⊥	264a	52.33 N	13.13 E
Žiteli	24	65.04 N	47.26 E
Žitenice	54	50.35 N	14.08 E
Žitjevo	76	59.54 N	41.06 E
Žitkoviči	78	52.14 N	27.54 E
Žitkovo	76	60.42 N	29.20 E
Žitkur	80	48.57 N	46.17 E
Zitlala	234	17.38 N	99.05 W
Zitlaltepec	234	19.12 N	97.54 W
Žitnoje	80	45.49 N	47.41 E
Žitomir	78	50.16 N	28.40 E
Zitong	102	31.43 N	105.10 E
Zittau	54	50.54 N	14.47 E
Zitundo	156	26.45 S	32.50 E
Ziwa Magharibi □[4]	154	2.00 S	31.30 E
Ziway, Lake ⊜	144	8.00 N	38.50 E
Ziwuji	100	32.55 N	115.58 E
Zixi, Zhg.	100	27.42 N	117.02 E
Zixi, Zhg.	100	28.01 N	117.46 E
Zixing	100	25.58 N	113.24 E
Ziya ≃	105	39.09 N	117.10 E
Ziyamet	130	35.28 N	34.08 E
Ziyang	107	30.07 N	104.39 E
Ziyuan	102	26.01 N	110.31 E
Ziyun	102	25.43 N	106.05 E
Ziz, Oued V	148	30.39 N	4.26 W
Žizdra	76	53.45 N	34.44 E
Žizdra ≃	82	54.14 N	36.12 E

DEUTSCH

Name	Seite	Breite°′	Länge°′ E = Ost
Zizers	58	46.56 N	9.34 E
Zizhong	107	29.48 N	104.50 E
Zizhou	102	37.37 N	109.41 E
Žižica	76	56.17 N	31.21 E
Žižickoje, ozero ⊜	76	56.14 N	31.15 E
Žižma ≃	76	53.54 N	25.36 E
Zlarin	36	43.42 N	15.50 E
Zlatá Koruna ʊ[1]	61	48.52 N	14.22 E
Zlatar	36	46.06 N	16.05 E
Zlaté Moravce	30	48.25 N	18.24 E
Zlatica	38	42.43 N	24.08 E
Zlatograd	38	41.23 N	25.06 E
Zlatoust	86	55.10 N	59.40 E
Zlatoustovsk	89	52.58 N	133.38 E
Zlín	30	49.13 N	17.41 E
Zlīṭan	146	32.28 N	14.34 E
Žlobin	76	52.54 N	30.03 E
Złocieniec	30	53.33 N	16.01 E
Złoczew	30	51.25 N	18.36 E
Zlonice	54	50.15 N	14.07 E
Złotoryja	30	51.08 N	15.55 E
Złotów	30	53.22 N	17.02 E
Žlutice	54	50.03 N	13.10 E
Zlydnev	80	48.46 N	45.48 E
Zlynka, Ross.	76	52.25 N	31.44 E
Zlynka, Ukr.	78	48.28 N	31.32 E
Zmeinogorsk	86	51.10 N	82.13 E
Zmeinyj, ostrov I	78	45.15 N	30.12 E
Žmerinka	78	49.02 N	28.06 E
Żmigród	30	51.29 N	16.55 E
Zmijev	78	49.40 N	36.19 E
Žminj	36	45.09 N	13.55 E
Zmi'ovka	76	52.40 N	36.23 E
Zna → Cna ≃	80	54.32 N	42.05 E
Znaim → Znojmo	61	48.52 N	16.02 E
Znamenka, Kaz.	86	50.05 N	79.32 E
Znamenka, Ross.	76	54.54 N	34.34 E
Znamenka, Ross.	80	52.24 N	41.26 E
Znamenka, Ross.	86	53.10 N	79.30 E
Znamenka, Ross.	86	53.32 N	91.54 E
Znamenka, Ross.	88	54.42 N	104.50 E
Znamenka, Ukr.	78	48.43 N	32.40 E
Znamenka, Ukr.	83	48.51 N	37.22 E
Znamenka Vtoraja	78	48.43 N	32.35 E
Znamensk	76	54.37 N	21.13 E
Znamenskoje, Ross.	76	53.17 N	35.41 E
Znamenskoje, Ross.	80	53.19 N	42.57 E
Znamenskoje, Ross.	86	57.08 N	73.55 E
Znamenskoje, Ross.	265b	55.45 N	37.09 E
Żnin	30	52.52 N	17.43 E
Znob'-Novgorodskoje	78	52.16 N	33.36 E
Znojmo	61	48.52 N	16.02 E
Zoagli	62	44.20 N	9.16 E
Zoar	158	33.30 S	21.28 E
Zoar Village State Memorial ⊥	214	40.36 N	81.27 W
Zoarville	214	40.35 N	81.24 W
Zobia	154	2.58 N	25.56 E
Zöblitz	54	50.39 N	13.14 E
Zóbuè	154	15.38 S	34.26 E
Zocca	64	44.21 N	10.59 E
Žochova, ostrov I	74	76.04 N	152.40 E
Zod	84	40.12 N	45.52 E
Žodino	76	54.06 N	28.21 E
Žodiški	76	54.38 N	26.26 E
Zoétélé	152	3.15 N	11.53 E
Zoetermeer	52	52.03 N	4.30 E
Zofingen	58	47.18 N	7.57 E
Zogang	102	29.55 N	97.44 E
Zogno	62	45.48 N	9.40 E
Zográfos	267c	37.59 N	23.46 E
Zohar	132	31.36 N	34.42 E
Zohar, Miẓpé ∧[2]	132	31.13 N	35.14 E
Zohreh ≃	128	30.04 N	49.31 E
Zola Predosa	64	44.29 N	11.12 E
Zolder	56	51.01 N	5.18 E
Zoldo Alto	64	46.22 N	12.06 E
Zolfo Springs	220	27.29 N	81.47 W
Zolka ≃	84	44.17 N	43.51 E
Żółkiewka	30	50.55 N	22.51 E
Zollhaus	56	50.17 N	8.04 E
Zollikofen	58	47.00 N	7.28 E
Zollikon	58	47.20 N	8.35 E
Zolling	60	48.27 N	11.46 E
Zol'noje	80	53.27 N	49.48 E
Zoločov, Ukr.	78	50.17 N	35.59 E
Zoločov, Ukr.	78	49.47 N	24.52 E
Zolotaja Gora	89	54.16 N	126.36 E
Zolotaja Lipa ≃	78	48.59 N	25.04 E
Zolotari	80	49.46 N	46.21 E
Zolotar'ovka	80	53.04 N	45.20 E
Zolotkovo	80	55.32 N	41.06 E
Zolotniki	78	49.17 N	25.23 E
Zolotoje, Ross.	80	50.51 N	45.53 E
Zolotoje, Ukr.	83	48.41 N	38.31 E
Zolotoj Kolodec	83	48.32 N	37.15 E
Zolotoj Potok	78	48.54 N	25.20 E
Zolotonoša	78	49.40 N	32.02 E
Zolotucha	80	47.49 N	46.44 E
Zolotuchino	78	52.05 N	36.23 E
Žoltoje, Ukr.	78	48.30 N	33.31 E
Žoltoje, Ukr.	78	47.47 N	33.50 E
Ž'oltoje, Ukr.	83	48.39 N	39.07 E
Žoltyje Vody	78	48.21 N	33.31 E
Žolymbet	86	51.45 N	71.44 E
Zomba	154	15.23 S	35.18 E
Zomergem	50	51.07 N	3.33 E
Zone Point ›	42	50.08 N	5.00 W
Zongchang	107	28.52 N	104.36 E
Zongjiaxiang	269b	31.12 N	121.22 E
Zongo	152	4.21 N	18.36 E
Zonguldak	130	41.27 N	31.49 E
Zonguldak □[4]	130	41.30 N	32.15 E
Zongwe	154	5.05 S	27.55 E
Zongyang	100	30.42 N	117.12 E
Zonhoven	56	50.59 N	5.21 E
Zonnebeke	50	50.52 N	2.59 E
Zons	56	51.07 N	6.50 E
Zonza	36	41.45 N	9.10 E
Zoo, Bahnhof ◆[5]	264a	52.30 N	13.20 E
Zooafskolk	158	29.56 S	20.24 E
Zoom ≃	52	51.30 N	4.14 E
Zoppot → Sopot	30	54.28 N	18.34 E
Zopui	120	23.39 N	92.14 E
Zörbig	54	51.37 N	12.07 E
Zorge	54	51.38 N	10.38 E
Zorge ≃	54	51.27 N	10.54 E
Zorgo	150	12.15 N	0.36 W
Zorgongo	150	12.16 N	0.48 W
Zorinsk	83	48.25 N	38.34 E
Zorita	34	39.17 N	5.42 W
Zorkul', ozero ⊜	120	37.27 N	73.40 E
Zorn ≃	56	48.45 N	7.55 E
Zorneding	60	48.05 N	11.49 E
Zornica	38	42.23 N	26.56 E
Zorra, Arroyo de la ≃	196	29.31 N	101.13 W
Zorritos	246	3.40 S	80.40 W
Zorzor	150	7.46 N	9.28 W
Zöschen	54	51.21 N	12.07 E
Zossen	54	52.13 N	13.27 E
Zoti	84	41.53 N	42.28 E
Zottegem	50	50.52 N	3.48 E
Zou □[5]	150	8.00 N	2.15 E
Zou ≃	150	6.28 N	2.25 E
Zouan-Hounien	150	6.55 N	8.13 W
Zouar	146	20.27 N	16.32 E
Zouérat	148	22.42 N	12.30 W
Zoug → Zug	58	47.10 N	8.31 E
Zoulabot	152	3.17 N	14.02 E
Zoumagang	107	29.28 N	106.18 E
Zoumayi	98	39.07 N	114.34 E
Zouping	98	36.53 N	117.42 E
Zourma	150	11.22 N	0.49 W
Zousfana, Oued V	148	30.29 N	2.17 W
Zoutelande	52	51.30 N	3.30 E
Zoutkamp	52	53.20 N	6.18 E
Zouxian	98	35.24 N	117.00 E

Symbols in the index entries represent the broad categories identified in the key at the right. Symbols with superior numbers (⋏[1]) identify subcategories (see complete key on page *I · 1).*

Symbole im Register stellen die rechts im Schlüssel erklärten Kategorien dar. Symbole mit hochgestellten Ziffern (⋏[1]) bezeichnen Unterabteilungen einer Kategorie (vgl. vollständiger Schlüssel auf Seite *I · 1).*

Los símbolos incluídos en el texto del índice representan las grandes categorias identificadas con la clave a la derecha. Los símbolos con numeros en su parte superior (⋏[1]) identifican las subcategorías (véase la clave completa en la página *I · 1).*

Les symboles de l'index représentent les catégories indiquées dans la légende à droite. Les symboles suivis d'un indice (⋏[1]) représentent des sous-catégories (voir légende complète à la page *I · 1).*

Os símbolos incluídos no texto do índice representam as grandes categorias identificadas com a chave à direita. Os símbolos com números em sua parte superior (⋏[1]) identificam as subcategorias (veja-se a chave completa à página *I · 1).*

∧ Mountain	Berg	Montaña	Montagne	Montanha
⋏ Mountains	Gebirge	Montañas	Montagnes	Montanhas
)(Pass	Paß	Paso	Col	Passo
V Valley, Canyon	Tal, Cañon	Valle, Cañón	Vallée, Canyon	Vale, Canhão
≃ Plain	Ebene	Llano	Plaine	Planície
› Cape	Kap	Cabo	Cap	Cabo
I Island	Insel	Isla	Île	Ilha
II Islands	Inseln	Islas	Îles	Ilhas
± Other Topographic Features	Andere Topographische Objekte	Otros Elementos Topográficos	Autres données topographiques	Outros acidentes topográficos

ESPAÑOL

Nombre	Página	Lat.°'	Long.°' W = Oeste
Zova	132	31.48 N	35.06 E
Zovka	76	58.26 N	28.52 E
Zovnino	78	49.23 N	32.41 E
Žovten', Ukr.	78	49.03 N	24.45 E
Žovten', Ukr.	78	47.14 N	30.20 E
Žovtnevoje, Ukr.	78	46.52 N	32.02 E
Žovtnevoje, Ukr.	78	49.39 N	34.09 E
Žovtnevoje, Ukr.	78	50.57 N	34.22 E
Žovtnevoje, Ukr.	78	51.15 N	28.07 E
Zozov	78	49.19 N	29.01 E
Zrenjanin	38	45.23 N	20.24 E
Zriba	36	36.20 N	10.16 E
Zrmanja ≃	36	44.15 N	15.32 E
Zruč nad Sázavou	30	49.45 N	15.07 E
Zscherndorf	54	51.36 N	12.15 E
Zschieren ◄⁸	54	51.00 N	13.52 E
Zschopau	54	50.44 N	13.04 E
Zschopau ≃	54	51.08 N	13.03 E
Zschorlau	54	50.34 N	12.38 E
Zschornewitz	54	51.43 N	12.25 E
Zschortau	54	51.28 N	12.21 E
Žuanbalyk	86	45.04 N	61.51 E
Žuantobe	86	44.45 N	68.54 E
Zuarungu	150	10.47 N	0.48 W
Zuata ≃	246	7.52 N	65.22 W
Zubaydīyah, Jabal az- ⌃	132	33.48 N	37.02 E
Zubayr, Jazā'ir az- II	144	15.05 N	42.08 E
Zubayr, Wādī V	142	27.27 N	32.41 E
Zubcov	76	56.10 N	34.34 E
Zubkoviči	78	51.02 N	27.41 E
Zubova Pol'ana	80	54.04 N	42.51 E
Zubovka	80	54.16 N	51.06 E
Zubovo, Ross.	76	54.33 N	35.29 E
Zubovo, Ross.	76	60.19 N	36.57 E
Zubovo, Ross.	80	56.52 N	44.08 E
Zuccarello	62	44.07 N	8.07 E
Zuccone, Monte ⌃	62	44.26 N	9.37 E
Zuchwil	58	47.12 N	7.33 E
Zuckerhütl ⌃	64	46.58 N	11.09 E
Zudar	54	54.15 N	13.20 E
Z'udev, ostrov I	80	45.35 N	47.58 E
Zuel	64	46.31 N	12.08 E
Zuénoula	150	7.26 N	6.03 W

FRANÇAIS

Nom	Page	Lat.°'	Long.°' W = Ouest
Zuera	34	41.52 N	0.47 W
Zufār ◄¹	118	17.00 N	54.10 E
Zufaytat Mashtūl	142	30.20 N	31.21 E
Zug	58	47.10 N	8.31 E
Zug □³	58	47.00 N	8.30 E
Zugdeli	88	55.03 N	111.10 E
Zugdidi	84	42.30 N	41.53 E
Zugersee @	58	47.08 N	8.30 E
Zug Island I	281	42.17 N	83.07 W
Zugló ◄⁸	264c	47.31 N	19.08 E
Zugres	83	48.01 N	38.15 E
Zugspitze ⌃	64	47.25 N	10.59 E
Zugurma Game Reserve ◄⁴	150	9.55 N	5.00 E
Zühlsdorf	54	52.44 N	13.24 E
Zui	76	57.06 N	31.37 E
Zuid-Beijerland	52	51.45 N	4.22 E
Zuid-Beveland I	52	51.25 N	3.45 E
Zuidbroek	52	53.10 N	6.52 E
Zuidelijk Flevoland ◄¹	52	52.22 N	5.20 E
Zuiderzee — IJsselmeer ▽²	52	52.45 N	5.25 E
Zuid-Holland □⁴	52	52.00 N	4.30 E
Zuidhorn	52	53.14 N	6.24 E
Zuidlaren	52	53.05 N	6.41 E
Zuid-Willemsvaart ☰	52	51.12 N	5.52 E
Zuidwolde	52	53.15 N	6.35 E
Zuja	78	45.03 N	34.20 E
Žuja ≃	88	58.45 N	118.11 E
Zújar, Embalse del @¹	34	38.50 N	5.20 W
Zujevka, Ross.	80	58.25 N	51.10 E
Zujevka, Ukr.	83	48.04 N	38.15 E
Ž'ukajka	80	58.12 N	54.43 E
Žukopa ≃	76	56.33 N	32.42 E
Žukopa ≃	76	56.54 N	32.46 E
Žukovka, Ross.	76	53.32 N	33.44 E
Žukovka, Ross.	86	56.05 N	91.42 E
Žukovka, Ross.	265b	55.44 N	37.15 E
Žukovskaja	80	47.37 N	42.28 E
Žukovskij	82	55.35 N	38.08 E

PORTUGUÊS

Nome	Página	Lat.°'	Long.°' W = Oeste
Žukovskoje	80	46.05 N	41.21 E
Žukowo	30	54.21 N	18.22 E
Zula	144	15.11 N	39.41 E
Zula ≃	234	20.21 N	102.46 W
Žulanka	86	54.22 N	80.36 E
Žulayl, Wādī az- V	132	32.09 N	36.03 E
Žuldyz	80	49.16 N	49.30 E
Žulebino	265b	55.42 N	37.51 E
Zuli ≃	102	36.35 N	104.35 E
Zulia □³	246	10.00 N	72.10 W
Zulia ⌃	154	4.07 N	33.58 E
Zulia ≃	246	9.04 N	72.18 W
Zülpich	56	50.41 N	6.39 E
Zulueta	240p	22.22 N	79.34 W
Zululand □⁹	158	28.10 S	32.00 E
Z'ul'z'a	88	52.33 N	116.13 E
Žumala	80	50.29 N	49.47 E
Zumar, Tur'at az- ☰	273c	29.58 N	31.15 E
Zumarraga	116	11.38 N	124.50 E
Zumba	246	4.52 S	79.09 W
Zumbo ≃	154	15.36 S	30.25 E
Zumbro ≃	190	44.18 N	91.56 W
Zumbro, North Fork ≃	190	44.15 N	92.29 W
Zumbro, South Fork ≃	190	44.15 N	92.29 W
Zumbrota	190	44.17 N	92.40 W
Zumpango del Río	234	17.39 N	99.30 W
Zumpango de Ocampo	234	19.48 N	99.06 W
Zundert	52	51.28 N	4.40 E
Zundi	152	10.28 S	16.48 E
Zune	156	18.59 S	35.18 E
Zungeru	150	9.48 N	6.09 E
Zungri	68	38.39 N	15.59 E
Zungur	150	9.58 N	9.47 E
Zungwini	158	27.34 S	30.53 E
Zunhua	105	40.12 N	117.58 E
Zuni, N.M., U.S.	200	35.04 N	108.51 W
Zuni, Va., U.S.	208	36.51 N	76.49 W
Zuni ≃	200	34.39 N	109.40 W
Zuni Indian Reservation ◄⁴	200	35.15 N	108.20 W

Zunsuzhi	102	44.40 N	112.50 E
Zunyi	102	27.39 N	106.57 E
Zuo ≃	102	22.50 N	108.06 E
Zuo'an	100	26.10 N	114.16 E
Zuodeng	102	23.27 N	106.57 E
Zuogezhuang	105	39.01 N	116.37 E
Zuomaozigou	104	42.12 N	120.41 E
Zuomuchedong Hu @	120	28.25 N	88.15 E
Zuoquan	102	37.03 N	113.30 E
Zuosuo	102	27.45 N	100.54 E
Zuotema	120	35.50 N	80.45 E
Zuowei	105	40.41 N	114.43 E
Zuoxiunulemiao	88	48.08 N	115.38 E
Zuoyun	102	40.02 N	112.54 E
Zuoz	58	46.36 N	9.58 E
Zūq Musbīh	132	33.58 N	35.37 E
Žura, Mol.	78	47.31 N	29.04 E
Zura, Ross.	80	57.37 N	53.26 E
Zūrābād	128	38.49 N	44.35 E
Žuraviči, Bela.	76	53.15 N	30.33 E
Žuraviči, Ukr.	78	50.59 N	25.43 E
Žuravl'ovka, Kaz.	86	51.57 N	69.56 E
Žuravl'ovka, Ukr.	83	48.13 N	38.58 E
Zurayghit	128	26.29 N	40.33 E
Žurban	89	54.12 N	127.56 E
Zurich, On., Can.	190	43.26 N	81.37 W
Zürich, Ned.	52	53.06 N	5.23 E
Zürich, Schw.	58	47.23 N	8.32 E
Zürich □³	58	47.25 N	8.40 E
Zürich, Flughafen ☒	58	47.27 N	8.33 E
Zurich, Lake @	278	42.12 N	88.06 W
Zürichsee @	58	47.13 N	8.45 E
— Zürich	58	47.23 N	8.32 E
Zurmi	150	12.46 N	6.48 E
Zuromin	30	53.04 N	19.55 E
Zurq, Al-Qārāt az- ⌃²	142	29.00 N	29.55 E
Zürs	58	47.10 N	10.10 E
Zuru	150	11.27 N	5.12 E
Zurzach	58	47.35 N	8.18 E
Zuša ≃	76	53.27 N	36.23 E

Zusam ≃	56	48.42 N	10.45 E
Žusandala ◄²	86	44.20 N	75.00 E
Zushi	94	35.18 N	139.35 E
Zusmarshausen	58	48.24 N	10.35 E
Züssow	54	53.59 N	13.32 E
Žut, Otok I	36	43.52 N	15.19 E
Zutiua ≃	250	3.43 S	45.29 W
Žutovo Vtoroje	80	47.49 N	43.51 E
Zutphen	52	52.08 N	6.12 E
Zützen	54	51.57 N	13.38 E
Zuwārah	146	32.56 N	12.06 E
Zuwayzā	132	31.42 N	35.55 E
Z'uzel'skij	86	56.29 N	60.07 E
Žužemberk	36	45.50 N	14.56 E
Z'uzino	265b	55.40 N	38.07 E
Z'uzino ◄⁸	265b	55.39 N	37.35 E
Žuzymdyk	85	43.05 N	69.08 E
Zv'agino	265b	55.59 N	37.48 E
Zvannoje	78	51.23 N	34.33 E
Zvenigorod	82	55.44 N	36.51 E
Zvenigorodka	78	49.04 N	30.57 E
Zvenigovo	80	55.58 N	48.02 E
Zverevo	83	48.01 N	40.07 E
Zverinogolovskoje	86	54.28 N	64.50 E
Zvezdec	38	42.07 N	27.25 E
Zvezdnyj	88	56.49 N	106.27 E
Zvikovec	60	49.56 N	13.42 E
Zvishavane	154	20.20 S	30.02 E
Zvolen	30	48.35 N	19.08 E
Zvon ⌃	60	49.33 N	12.39 E
Zvornik	38	44.23 N	19.06 E
Zwaag	52	52.40 N	5.05 E
Zwaagwesteinde	52	53.15 N	6.04 E
Zwadiba	152	3.04 N	14.02 E
Zwanenburg	52	52.23 N	4.45 E
Zwartemeer	52	52.43 N	7.03 E
Zwarte Meer ◄	52	52.37 N	5.57 E
Zwartsluis	52	52.37 N	6.04 E
Zweckel ◄⁸	263	51.36 N	6.59 E
Zwedru	150	6.04 N	8.08 W
Zweibrücken	56	49.15 N	7.21 E
Zweifall	56	50.43 N	6.15 E

Zweisimmen	58	46.33 N	7.22 E
Zweite Wiener Hochquellenleitung ☰¹	61	48.10 N	16.14 E
Zwenkau	54	51.13 N	12.19 E
Zwentendorf	61	48.21 N	15.55 E
Zwesten	56	51.03 N	9.10 E
Zwettl	61	48.37 N	15.10 E
Zwevegem	50	50.48 N	3.20 E
Zwevezele	50	51.02 N	3.12 E
Zwickau	54	50.44 N	12.29 E
Zwickauer Mulde ≃	54	51.10 N	12.48 E
Zwiefalten	58	48.14 N	9.28 E
Zwiefaltendorf	58	48.13 N	9.31 E
Zwierzyniec	30	50.37 N	22.58 E
Zwiesel	60	49.01 N	13.14 E
Zwieselstein	64	46.56 N	11.02 E
Zwijndrecht	52	51.49 N	4.39 E
Zwillbrock	52	52.04 N	6.42 E
Zwingenberg, Dtsch.	56	49.25 N	9.02 E
Zwingenberg, Dtsch.	56	49.43 N	8.37 E
Zwischenahner Meer @	52	53.12 N	8.01 E
Zwochau	54	51.28 N	12.16 E
Zwoleń	30	51.22 N	21.35 E
Zwölfaxing	264b	48.06 N	16.28 E
Zwolle, Ned.	52	52.30 N	6.05 E
Zwolle, La., U.S.	194	31.37 N	93.38 W
Zwönitz	54	50.38 N	12.49 E
Zwota	54	50.21 N	12.25 E
Žychlin	30	52.15 N	19.39 E
Zymoetz ≃	182	54.33 N	128.26 W
Zyr'anka	74	65.45 N	150.51 E
Zyr'anovsk	86	49.43 N	84.20 E
Zyr'anovskij	86	57.46 N	61.42 E
Zyr'anskoje	86	56.50 N	86.38 E
Žyrardów	30	52.04 N	20.25 E
Zyryanovsk — Zyr'anovsk	86	49.43 N	84.20 E
Žyrzyn	30	51.30 N	22.07 E
Žywiec	30	49.41 N	19.12 E

	English	Deutsch	Español	Français	Português
≈	River	Fluß	Río	Rivière	Río
☰	Canal	Kanal	Canal	Canal	Canal
∟	Waterfall, Rapids	Wasserfall, Stromschnellen	Cascada, Rápidos	Chute d'eau, Rapides	Cascata, Rápidos
Ա	Strait	Meeresstraße	Estrecho	Détroit	Estreito
⊂	Bay, Gulf	Bucht, Golf	Bahía, Golfo	Baie, Golfe	Baía, Golfo
@	Lake, Lakes	See, Seen	Lago, Lagos	Lac, Lacs	Lago, Lagos
⊞	Swamp	Sumpf	Pantano	Marais	Pântano
⋒	Ice Features, Glacier	Eis- und Gletscherformen	Accidentes Glaciales	Formes glaciaires	Acidentes glaciares
▽	Other Hydrographic Features	Andere Hydrographische Objekte	Otros Elementos Hidrográficos	Autres données hydrographiques	Outros acidentes hidrográficos

	English	Deutsch	Español	Français	Português
◄	Submarine Features	Untermeerische Objekte	Accidentes Submarinos	Formes de relief sous-marin	Acidentes submarinos
□	Political Unit	Politische Einheit	Unidad Política	Entité politique	Unidade política
⊥	Cultural Institution	Kulturelle Institution	Institución Cultural	Institution culturelle	Instituição cultural
⊥	Historical Site	Historische Stätte	Sitio Histórico	Site historique	Sítio histórico
※	Recreational Site	Erholungs- und Ferienort	Sitio de Recreo	Centre de loisirs	Área de Lazer
☒	Airport	Flughafen	Aeropuerto	Aéroport	Aeroporto
◆	Military Installation	Militäranlage	Instalación Militar	Installation militaire	Instalação militar
♦	Miscellaneous	Verschiedenes	Misceláneo	Divers	Diversos